A Complete Guide to the

TAX REFORM ACT of 1986

Explanation • Code Sections as amended •
Committee Reports • Index

Date of Enactment: October 22, 1986
Public Law 99-514

This publication is designed to provide accurate and authoritative information in regard to the subject matter covered. It is sold with the understanding that the publisher is not engaged in rendering legal, accounting, or other professional service. If legal advice or other expert assistance is required, the services of a competent professional person should be sought.—*From a Declaration of Principles jointly adopted by a Committee of the American Bar Association and a Committee of Publishers and Associations.*

A Complete Guide to the Tax Reform Act of 1986

Prepared by Prentice-Hall Information Services

Harold A. Grossman, J.D., Editor-in-Chief
Donald E. Mindrebo, J.D., Managing Editor

Coordinating Editors

Alan S. Robinson, J.D.
Aziz S. Sahwell, LL.M.
Howard W. Wolosky, J.D., LL.M.

Contributing Editors

Norman Arkawy, J.D.
Christopher E. Bergin, J.D.
Julian Block, J.D., LL.M. (Taxation)
James Boylan, J.D.
Caroline C. Bristol, J.D.
Fred Clark, LL.B.
John Clark, J.D., LL.M. (Taxation)
Peter F. Daly, B.A.
Alan G. DeNee, J.D.
Stephen A. Friedman, J.D.,
    LL.M. (Taxation)
Nancy S. Goodman, J.D.
John Kent Graham, J.D.
Richard D. Grant, J.D.
Craig M. Heller, J.D.
Marvin Hillman, J.D.
Kurt D. Horning, J.D.
Susan C. Hughes, J.D.
Jessica Indig-Brown, J.D.
William B. Katz, J.D.
Gerald M. Levinson, J.D.
Lawrence H. MacKirdy, J.D.
Gina A. Makoujy, J.D.
Janet Mazefsky, M.L.S.
Robert W. McGee, J.D., Ph.D., C.P.A.
Fidel C. Mendoza, LL.B.

Robert J. Murdich, J.D.
Frederick L. Nakarai, J.D.
Richard Niles, J.D.
Lillian V. O'Brien, B.S.
Melvin Orenstein, J.D., LL.M. (Taxation)
Carlos F. Ortiz, J.D.
Rose Papaccioli
Aaron I. Reichel, J.D.
Alan Rubin, J.D.
Emma H. Rubinsky, J.D.
Rosemary Saldan, J.D.
Gustav J. Schlaier, J.D.
Yogi M. Solanki, J.D., LL.M. (Taxation)
Alfred Tamburro, J.D.
Edward V. Titano, J.D.
Susan K. Toleno, B.S.
Robert Trinz, M.S. (Taxation)
Mary Jeanne Vellardito, J.D.
Anne Waldron, J.D.
Peter Wang, J.D.
Robert C. Wilkie, J.D.
Sylvia Woods, J.D.
Denis L. Yurkovic, J.D.

Washington Bureau

William Fant
James Fattibene
Luan Hogue

Reuben Lattimore
Ian K. Louden

Editorial Assistants

Patricia Alex
Marjorie Anderson
Stephanie Anderson
Carolyn Arevalo
Eileen Burger
Mary Jo Cortellino
Marilyn Darlington

Julie D'Guerra
Theresa Fajen
Mildred Genser
Donald Hardie
Carolyn Hawkins
Virginia Hudecek
Jose Jalandra

Denise Marshall
Sherri L. Nickles
Anne Nicoletti
Patricia O'Reilly
Marla Rabin
Marcia Sam
Linda Schnee

Deborah Schutte
Doris Smith
Angela Sweikart
Ann Tusa
Barbara A. Vetrano
Michael Wulff

Production Staff

Carl Giaimo
Gail Gneiding

Lucille Matthews
Ken Pawson

Kerry Reardon
Marie Rivera

Arthur Sabatini
Sue Ellen Sobel

HOW TO USE THIS GUIDE

This COMPLETE GUIDE includes all the information needed for in-depth research of the law enacted by the Tax Reform Act of 1986.

- Editorial Explanation.
- Act sections not amending the Internal Revenue Code.
- Amended Code sections with new and deleted matter clearly shown.
- Congressional Committee Reports—an official explanation of the new law as finally enacted.

Arrangement

Editorial Explanation arranged according to subject matter. Detailed Table of Contents and Index provide entry points. *Begins at ¶101.*

Glossary of Abbreviations used in the Explanation is at *¶1905.*

Table of effective dates is arranged in Act section number order and lists main Code sections affected. *¶1911.*

Act sections that do not amend the Code are arranged in Act section number order. *Begin at ¶2001.*

Code as Amended is arranged in Code section number order. Just turn to the Code section you want. *Begins at ¶2851.*

Committee Reports are arranged in Act section number order. Thus, the key to the official explanation is the number of the Act section that makes the change. Act section numbers appear at the end of each Explanation paragraph. *Begin at ¶3851.*

Research Aids

Subject matter approach is generally the most useful in a new law. Find your subject through the detailed Table of Contents or the Index. These refer you to paragraphs in the Explanation. Each editorial paragraph refers to amended Code sections and to Act sections. You can turn to the statutory language (in *Act or Code* section number order), or to the Committee Reports (in *Act* section number order). *Index leads you to the Explanation paragraphs. ¶4901.*

Code section number approach takes you directly to the statutory language of amended or added sections. New matter in *italics* and deleted matter in footnotes help you to pinpoint the precise nature of each change. Effective dates are carefully spelled out. At the end of each Code section there is a reference to the place in the Committee Reports which explains the change.

Act section number approach takes you to Congressional Committee Reports. This official explanation is arranged and edited to reflect the final version of the law as it was enacted. It draws upon Senate, House, and Conference Reports and statements on the floor of the Senate.

List of Code sections affected itemizes sections of the Code amended, added, or repealed. Opposite each item the table lists the section of the '86 Act that made the change. This list is useful for checking whether a particular Code section is affected by the new law. It also offers another means of entry to the Code as amended and the Committee Reports. *List of Code sections is at ¶4851.*

SUMMARY OF TABLE OF CONTENTS

[Detailed Table of Contents begins on the following page]

SUMMARY OF TABLE OF CONTENTS

[Detailed Table of Contents begins on the following page]

DETAILED TABLE OF CONTENTS

Table of Contents

Table of Contents

[The page following this is 11.]

THE TAX REFORM ACT OF 1986

A Brief Overview

It's the most drastic overhaul of taxes in the last 40 years. The new law has something for every taxpayer. It's so all-encompassing that, from now on, the tax law will be called The Internal Revenue Code of 1986. This book will take you through and explain each provision of the new law—in detail. But first, here's a rundown of the key provisions of the new law to set the scene.

Individual Tax Rate Reductions. The centerpiece of the TRA is a cut in individual tax rates. The top tax bracket will be reduced from 50% to 28% over two years.

The TRA scraps the current fifteen brackets with a top rate of 50% and substitutes two brackets: 15% and 28%. There is a blended rate for 1987—a mix of the old and new rates with a five-bracket rate schedule featuring a 38.5% top rate. Beginning in 1988, the new rate system is fully in place (with annual adjustments to offset inflation). Starting 1-1-88, the first $29,750 of taxable income is subject to the 15% rate (first $17,850 for singles). Income in excess of $29,750 ($17,850 for singles) is taxed at the 28% rate. But there is a catch.

> **5% SURTAX:** Starting in 1988, the TRA imposes a 5% surtax on income between $71,900 and $149,250 ($43,150 and $89,560 for singles). This is designed to phase out the benefit high-income taxpayers get from the 15% bracket.

Net result: Each additional dollar you earn between the two income levels is taxed at an effective rate of 33%. If your taxable income exceeds the higher level, there is an additional phaseout for the personal exemption. [See ¶101.]

Personal Exemptions. The TRA increases the personal exemptions you claim for yourself, your spouse and your dependents. The current exemption figure of $1,080 goes to $1,900 in 1987, $1,950 in 1988 and $2,000 in 1989. The personal exemption amount will be adjusted for inflation starting in 1990. However, older taxpayers can no longer claim extra exemptions for being age 65 or over. Nor can blind taxpayers (but see below).

Another crackdown. Under the TRA, starting in 1987, a dependent who can be claimed on someone else's return can no longer take a personal exemption on his own return.

New requirement. You may have to get a Social Security number for your child next year. Starting with returns filed after 1987, a taxpayer claiming a dependent who is at least five years old, must include the dependent's Social Security number on his return.

Standard Deduction. The TRA gives a big boost to the flat standard deduction for nonitemizers. The deduction is increased to $5,000 for joint filers and surviving spouses. ($3,000 for singles, $4,400 for heads of households, and $2,500 for marrieds filing separately). This takes effect in 1988 (for 1987, the amounts are $3,760 for joint filers and $2,540 for singles and heads of households, and $1,880 for marrieds filing separately). There is an extra standard deduction of $600 for each married person age 65 and over and each blind taxpayer, starting in 1987. The extra deduction is $750 if the blind or elderly person is single and not a surviving spouse. This is in addition to the full standard deduction. Another break: Taxpayers age 65 or over or blind may claim the higher 1988 standard deductions for 1987. The standard deductions are adjusted for inflation starting in 1989.

Children. In 1986, your child can use his $1,080 personal exemption to shelter his unearned income from tax. In 1987, if he can be claimed as a dependent on your return, your child has no personal exemption. The TRA, however, does provide some relief. Starting in 1987, unlike earlier years, your child can use $500 of his standard deduction to offset unearned income. That, of course, leaves only $2,040 to shelter his earned income ($2,540 full standard deduction less $500). [See ¶102.]

Itemized Deductions. You can still get deductions for charitable contributions, real estate taxes, and state and local income and property taxes.

The rules for deducting charitable contributions are relatively unchanged. For example, the charitable deduction for nonitemizers goes off the books at the end of 1986, as scheduled.

If you donate appreciated property (e.g., stock) in 1986 that would have produced long-term capital gain if sold, you will not only get a deduction for the property's full fair market value in 1986, you also pay no tax on the paper gain. Under the TRA, after 1986, the untaxed portion of a donation of appreciated property is considered a tax preference item for purposes of the alternative minimum tax. [See ¶132; 712].

Moving expenses. Before 1987, the deduction for job-related moving expenses can be claimed by taxpayers whether or not they itemize. Starting in 1987, it can be taken only by employees and self-employed persons who itemize their deductions. [See ¶116.]

Sales tax. State and local sales taxes are no longer deductible, starting in 1987. So if you're buying a big ticket item (e.g., a car) in the near future, do it before the end of 1986.

Interest. Starting in 1987, interest paid on consumer debt (for instance, car loans and credit card charges) is not deductible regardless of when the debt is incurred. That includes interest on tax underpayments (except deferred estate taxes). Interest on debt incurred for investment reasons can be written off only up to the amount of your investment income. The cutback for both kinds of interest is phased in over five years.

> **KEY EXCEPTION:** You can continue to deduct mortgage interest on your principal residence and a second home. However, mortgage interest on the part of a loan that exceeds the cost of a home (plus any improvements) is subject to the interest deduction crackdown, unless the loan proceeds are used for medical or educational purposes. But even if the proceeds are used for medical or educational purposes, the loan can't exceed the fair market value of the home—less any other outstanding mortgage. *Special grandfather rule:* Interest on debt incurred before 8-16-86 will be deductible even though it exceeds the cost basis of the residence.

Medical expenses. Starting in 1987, the TRA increases the deduction floor for unreimbursed medical costs from 5% to 7½% of adjusted gross income.

Miscellaneous deductions. The TRA changes the rules for deducting miscellaneous expenses. This category includes investment-connected expenses (e.g., stock market publications), fees paid to tax return preparers and all business expenses (including business travel and entertainment) incurred by an employee and not reimbursed by an employer.

Starting in 1987, a taxpayer's total miscellaneous expenses, with a few minor exceptions (e.g., gambling losses to the extent of gambling winnings), are deductible only to the extent the total exceeds 2% of the taxpayer's adjusted gross income. [See ¶126.]

Withholding and Estimated Taxes. The TRA requires changes in the income tax withholding tables in 1987 and 1988. It also affects the estimated taxes of many individual taxpayers.

Key change. Before 1987, individuals could avoid underpayment penalties if their quarterly estimated tax payments equaled the lesser of 80% of their current year's tax bill or 100% of their prior year's liability. Amounts withheld from wages are considered estimated tax payments. The TRA lifts the 80% figure to 90%, starting in 1987. It leaves the 100% figure unchanged.

Capital Gains. One of the biggest changes introduced by the TRA is the elimination of the tax-favored treatment of net long-term capital gains. The TRA does away with the 60% net long-term capital gain exclusion. Individual taxpayers must treat net long-term gain (profit on property held more than six months) like ordinary income. Effective date: Tax years beginning after 12-31-86.

NOTE: Even though ordinary income is taxed in 1987 at blended rates higher than 15% and 28%, the top tax rate is 28% on net long-term capital gains in 1987. [See ¶302]

Short-term gains. In 1987, the top tax on net short-term capital gains is taxed at the blended rate applicable to ordinary income. Top rate: 38.5%. The maximum is 50% before 1987. The 15% and 28% brackets will take full effect starting in 1988.

The TRA does not do away with the distinction between capital gains and losses and ordinary income and deductions. For example, as under current law, you still net your capital gains and losses. Capital losses fully offset capital gains. However, to the extent your capital losses exceed your capital gains, the net loss can only be deducted against $3,000 of ordinary income in any one year. One difference from prior law: Starting in 1987, both long- and short-term capital losses offset ordinary income, dollar-for-dollar. Capital losses that cannot be deducted against the current year's ordinary income can still be carried forward to later years.

Selling publicly-traded securities. This is the last year you get a tax choice when you sell publicly-traded securities during the last five trading days of the year. Starting in 1987, you pay tax the year you make the sale. In 1986, however, you can treat the transaction as an installment sale and pay tax in 1987 (i.e., when the cash settlement is made). Or you can elect out of installment tax treatment and pay tax in 1986, the year you make the sale).

Capital Gain for Corporations. The TRA eliminates the preferential capital gains treatment for corporations. Corporate net long-term gain is taxed at the same rates as corporate ordinary income. Effective 1-1-87, despite a higher tax rate on ordinary income, the top rate on corporate capital gain is 34%.

IRA Contributions. The TRA makes major changes in the tax rules for Individual Retirement Accounts. Many taxpayers who belong to a company-funded retirement plan can no longer deduct their IRA contributions. That includes members of corporate pension and profit-sharing plans, Keogh plans, and those with 403(b) annuities. Effective date: Tax years starting after 1986.

• *Full deduction:* You can continue to make deductible IRA contributions of up to $2,000 annually ($2,250 for a spousal IRA) if (1) neither you nor your spouse belong to a company-funded retirement plan or (2) either you or your spouse do belong and your adjusted gross income is less than $40,000 ($25,000 if single). For this purpose, adjusted gross income does not take into account the IRA contribution.

• *Partial deduction:* Your deductible IRA contribution is reduced proportionately if you or your spouse belong to a company retirement plan and your adjusted gross income is between

$40,000 and $50,000 ($25,000 and $35,000 for single taxpayers). For example, a married plan member with an adjusted gross income of $45,000 can make a $1,000 deductible IRA contribution ($1,125 to a spousal IRA). *Reason:* His adjusted gross income is half-way between the $40,000 and $50,000 phaseout levels.

• *No deduction:* Plan members with adjusted gross incomes in excess of $50,000 ($35,000 for singles) cannot claim a deduction for an IRA contribution. [See ¶1101]

Cash or Deferred SEP. In tax years starting after 1986, employers can give employees a choice: continue to take all your compensation in cash or have up to $7,000 of it contributed to a simplified employee pension. To the extent the employee goes the SEP route, he owes no tax on the amount contributed.

Retirement Plan Rules. The changes in the retirement plan rules may be the most sweeping in the entire TRA. In general, they take effect in plan years starting after 1988.

More plan coverage. A qualified retirement plan cannot discriminate in favor of employees who are officers, shareholders or highly paid. Under prior law, a plan did not discriminate against the rank and file if it covered as few as 56% of all employees. The new TRA minimum percentage test is 70%.

Quicker vesting of benefits. A qualified retirement plan must provide for accrued benefits to vest within a certain period of time. The TRA shortens the vesting period, so employees are entitled to benefits sooner.

Minimum benefits for integrated plan members. Under prior law, it was possible for an employer to avoid making any retirement plan contributions for lower-paid employees, if the plan was integrated with Social Security. The TRA, however, ensures that all employees will receive at least some employer-provided retirement plan benefits in addition to Social Security benefits. [See ¶1110.]

Employee contributions. Starting after 1986, the TRA imposes special nondiscrimination rules for employee contributions. In general, the new rules are violated if highly-paid employees make disproportionately large contributions to the plan.

Loans to plan members. For loans made after 1986, the TRA reduces the $50,000 borrowing limit by the member's highest outstanding loan balance during the preceding 12 months. Also starting after 1986, the more-than-5-year repayment period applies only to the purchase of a principal residence by a plan member.

Pensions for early retirees. Starting in 1987, the TRA ties the normal retirement age for pensions to the Social Security retirement age (currently 65, but scheduled to increase from 65 to 67 between years 2000 and 2022.) Early pension benefits are also tied into the reduction in Social Security benefits for early retirement (e.g., at age 62, you get 80% of the benefit you would receive at age 65). Anyone retiring at age 62, for example, can receive 80% of the top-dollar pension benefit at age 65. The 80% dollar limit is reduced for early retirees before age 62. The $75,000 safe harbor for pension benefits starting on or after age 55 is repealed.

> **NOTE:** Pension benefits that accrued before 1987 will not be reduced to TRA levels.

New Plan Withdrawal Rules. The TRA completely revamps the rules on retirement plan withdrawals.

Early withdrawals. Under prior law, retirement plan withdrawals before age 59½, death, or disability were taxable. But there was no tax penalty if the ordinary employee wanted to tap his retirement plan for personal purposes (e.g., to buy a car or pay college tuition). Only early withdrawals from an IRA or from a retirement plan by 5% owners, were subject to a 10% penalty.

> **NEW LAW CHANGE:** The TRA imposes a 10% penalty on early withdrawals from all retirement plans by all taxpayers, starting in 1987. *Exceptions:* IRA and plan rollovers, life annuities, early retirement and certain hardships.

Another change. Before 1987, a withdrawal was considered to be first a withdrawal of nontaxable employee contributions. Only withdrawals in excess of employee contributions were taxable. Starting in 1987, the TRA treats a withdrawal on a pro rata basis—only part of the withdrawal is tax-free as a return of the employee's contribution. Exception: withdrawals from plans that permitted employee withdrawals on May 5, 1986.

Withdrawals at retirement. The special tax breaks for lump-sum payouts are curbed, starting with distributions after 1986. Ten-year averaging is replaced by five-year averaging. However, you are entitled to elect five-year averaging only once—and then only after you reach age 59½. The lump-sum capital gains break is phased out over six years.

> **SPECIAL RELIEF:** An employee who was at least age 50 on 1-1-86, is entitled to special treatment: He can choose between ten-year averaging using 1986 tax rates and five-year averaging using the new tax rates. He can also disregard the six-year phaseout for capital gain treatment and tax his capital gain at a flat 20%. If he elects this special relief, he cannot elect lump-sum treatment again after reaching 59½.

Mandatory withdrawals. In years starting after 1988, all members of a company retirement plan, Keogh plan, or tax-sheltered annuity must start making plan withdrawals no later than April 1 of the year after the year they become age 70½.

Three-year rule. Before the TRA, all retirement plan annuity payouts were first treated as a tax-free recovery of the employee's contributions if the payments in the first three years equaled or exceeded the employee contributions. This special rule is repealed for annuities starting after July 1, 1986.

Cash or Deferred (Sec. 401k) Plans. The TRA limits the amount that can be deferred. The maximum deferral drops from $30,000 to $7,000, in years starting after 1986.

Also starting in 1987, the TRA applies new 401(k) rules to prohibit discrimination in favor of highly compensated employees. These same rules also apply to employer matching contributions, in years starting after 1986.

Tough New Rules for T&E Deductions. Starting in 1987:

• The deduction for business entertainment expenses (including meals) is limited to 80% of cost.

• The deduction for business meals on overnight travel is also reduced by 20%.

• The deductible portion of employee unreimbursed travel and transportation expenses and entertainment expenses is lumped in with other miscellaneous expenses. Most miscellaneous deductions are deductible only to the extent the total exceeds 2% of the employee's annual adjusted gross income.

> **EMPLOYER REIMBURSEMENT:** An employer reimbursement for employee travel and entertainment is not subject to the 2% floor. The reimbursement is tax-free to the employee and deductible by the employer. Reimbursement deductions attributable to meals and business entertainment are reduced by 20%, however.

• The TRA completely eliminates the deduction for the so-called quiet business meal. You get a business entertainment deduction for a meal only if business is discussed before, during, or after the meal.

Investment Real Estate Hit Hard. The TRA is tough on real estate investments.

Depreciation. For properties placed in service after 1986, the TRA both lengthens the depreciation period and changes the rate at which the properties can be written off. The TRA increases the depreciation period from 19 years to 27½ years for residential rental property and 31½ years for commercial property. And both types must be written off using straight-line depreciation. This produces equal deductions over the whole writeoff period. [See ¶201 et seq.]

At-risk Rules. The TRA brings real estate under the restrictions of the so-called at-risk rules. The at-risk rules limit the loss writeoff on an investment to the cash invested plus borrowed amounts on which the investor is personally liable (i.e., recourse debt). Up to now, the at-risk rules have applied to all investments except real estate. The TRA extends the at-risk rules to real estate put in service after 1986.

> **BIG EXCEPTION:** Real estate bought with nonrecourse (i.e., no personal liability) debt is exempt from the at-risk rules if the financing comes from a bank, the Government, or is insured by the Government.

Tax shelters. Beginning in 1987, loss writeoffs from tax shelters can generally shelter only income from other properties or other tax-sheltered investments. But here again there is an exception for real estate. [See ¶501 et seq.]

Rehabilitation credit. The TRA reduces, but does not eliminate, the big tax credit for rehabilitating certain types of buildings. The credit is equal to a percentage of the cost of rehabilitating older commercial and industrial properties and certified historic structures (including residential properties). There are only two credits: a 20% credit for historic structures and a 10% credit for industrial and commercial properties originally placed in service before 1936. The new credits generally apply to property placed in service after 1986. [See ¶217.]

Low-income housing credit. Before the TRA, investors were allowed special fast writeoffs for the cost of rehabilitating low-income housing. This break will go off the books at the end of 1986, and the TRA does not extend it. The TRA does provide a new tax credit for owners of low-income housing put in service after 1986 and before 1990. There are three separate credits for: (1) new construction and rehabilitation of existing housing; (2) certain federally subsidized new construction and rehabilitation; and (3) acquisition cost of existing housing [see ¶218].

Investors in cooperative apartments. Owners of stock in cooperative apartments are entitled to a special pass-through income tax break. They can deduct their share of real estate taxes and mortgage interest paid by the cooperative. However, before the TRA, this break was available only to individual stockholders. Starting in 1987, the TRA allows corporations, trusts, estates and partnerships to become stockholders in a cooperative apartment. This change facilitates the investment in cooperative apartment stock. [See ¶623.]

Homeowner's breaks untouched. The TRA did not change four tax breaks for homeowners: (1) property taxes remain fully deductible; (2) interest remains fully deductible on a mortgage taken out to buy a principal or second home; (3) a homeowner can continue to avoid current tax on a sale by spending the proceeds on the purchase of a new home; (4) homeowners age 55 or over still have a one-time exclusion that allows them to escape tax on the first $125,000 of sale profit, whether they replace the home or not.

Municipal Bonds. The TRA continues favorable tax treatment for most municipal bonds. You can still buy municipal bonds that pay tax-free interest. And the bonds you now own continue to pay tax-free interest.

TRA change. The interest on some municipal bonds will not be tax exempt. (These are bonds that finance certain private activities) But even this crackdown generally applies only to bonds issued after 9-1-86. [See ¶1301 et seq.]

> NOTE: Tax-free interest on private activity bonds issued on or after 8-8-86 is subject to the toughened alternative minimum tax. [See ¶711.]

Tax Shelter Crackdown. The TRA rules prevent you from using a loss from a "passive activity" to shelter your "active income" (e.g., salary) or "portfolio income" (e.g., dividends, interest, and capital gains). You are allowed to write off tax shelter loss only against other tax shelter income. If you have no other current tax shelter income, your loss is carried over to offset tax shelter income in future years. If you haven't used up the loss by the time you sell the investment, it is offset against your otherwise taxable gain on the sale.

The crackdown takes effect gradually over a five-year period. In 1987, investors can write off 65% of tax shelter losses against non-tax shelter income. In 1988, only 40% can be written off. In 1989 and 1990, writeoffs are limited to 20% and 10% respectively. The crackdown is fully in place starting in 1991. The phase-in applies only to tax shelter investments made prior to the date of enactment of the '86 Act. In 1987, losses from investments made after the enactment date are fully subject to the passive loss rule. There are exceptions for the first $25,000 loss or credit from rental realty, low-income housing credits, and working interests in oil and gas drilling. [See ¶503.]

Some Corporations Helped, Others Hurt. The TRA slashes some corporate tax bills dramatically. Other corporations face tax hikes. Why the difference? It's mainly because of the repeal of the investment tax credit. [See ¶208.] Corporations that invest heavily in equipment and machinery may pay bigger post-TRA tax bills. All corporations, however, benefit from new lower tax rates. [See ¶601.]

New Tax Rate Cut. The new tax rates become fully effective for tax years starting on or after 7-1-87.

Taxable income	New rates
Less than $50,000	15% of taxable income
Over $50,000 but not over $75,000	$7,500 plus 25% of the excess over $50,000
Over $75,000 but not over $100,000	$13,750 plus 34% of the excess over $75,000
Over $100,000 to $335,000	$22,250 plus 39% of the excess over $100,00C
Above $335,000	Flat 34% on all income

A corporation benefits from the rate reduction in the tax year that includes 7-1-87. Income received at any time during that year is taxed under blended rates, combining the old and the new. The rates that apply to your corporation depend on how much of its tax year falls after 7-1-87.

Installment Sales. Taxpayers selling under a revolving credit plan may no longer use the installment method for sales made after 12-31-86. They must report their profits in the year the sale is made. And the use of the installment method is limited if the tax-payer has outstanding debt—the smaller the debt, the more profit qualifies for installment reporting. This change is effective 1-1-87 for sales made on or after 3-1-86. [See ¶803.]

Bad debts. Effective for tax years starting after 12-31-86, all taxpayers will use the specific charge-off method to deduct bad debts; the reserve method will no longer be available (except for certain commercial b nks). [See ¶807.]

Equipment Purchases. The TRA repeals the investment tax credit for property placed in service after 1985. Nevertheless, it retains much of the simplicity and fast writeoffs of the accelerated cost recovery system (ACRS). You can continue to write off some equipment purchases over five years. There are special rules on business cars. Most other equipment is now written off over seven years. [See ¶201 et seq.]

Starting with equipment placed in service in 1987, you may be in line for bigger deductions in the early years after purchase, because of two TRA changes: (1) depreciation deductions are computed using a faster rate, and (2) you can expense (i.e., deduct currently) a larger amount the year you purchase equipment and place it in service.

For property placed in service before 1987, ACRS is computed using the 150% declining balance method. That means your first year deduction is one-and-a-half times as large as it would be using straight-line depreciation. In general, depreciation on most personal property placed in service after 1986 is figured on the 200% declining balance method. So for property with the same writeoff period, you get first year deductions that are twice as large as straight-line depreciation—or one-third more than under pre-1987 law.

Even if the property must now be written off over seven years, instead of five, your total deductions for the first two years are still larger than those figured under pre-1987 law—despite the new, longer writeoff period.

What's more, you can elect to use the new depreciation rules on property placed in service after 7-31-86. For example, suppose you purchase a $5,000 piece of business equipment that qualifies for five-year writeoffs under both the old and new systems. You place the equipment in service on 8-1-86. Under the old rules, you get a $750 depreciation deduction for 1986. But if you elect to use the new double declining balance system, your 1986 deduction is $1,000.

Larger expensing deduction. Before 1987, you can elect to expense each year up to $5,000 of the cost of property used in your business. The TRA raises to $10,000 the amount of equipment that you can expense in a year, starting with 1987.

The expensing deduction cannot, however, be used by large purchasers. If a company buys more than $200,000 of eligible property during a year, the expensing deduction ceiling is reduced on a dollar-for-dollar basis for purchases in excess of $200,000. [See ¶206.]

NOTE: You cannot claim depreciation deductions on the portion of equipment purchases that you expense. And since the investment tax credit is eliminated as of 1-1-86, you no longer forfeit a tax credit when you elect to expense equipment purchases.

Timing purchases. One TRA provision cuts back on the first year depreciation deductions that you would otherwise be entitled to take. Before 1987, you get the same first-year depreciation deduction on property, regardless of when during the year it is actually placed in service. So equipment placed in service in January is treated the same as equipment placed in service in December. In general, this remains true under the TRA. Equipment placed in service after 1986 is treated as if you started using it on July 1, no matter when during the year you actually start using it. (This also means that it will take six years to write off five-year property.) However, there is an exception for year-end purchases.

Business Car Writeoffs. The TRA changes the writeoffs for cars placed in service after 1986. Cars are now five-year writeoff property. And it actually takes six years to write off the cost of a car. Reason: Under the TRA, your depreciation deductions start on July 1 of the year you place the car in service. So the five-year writeoff period runs over into a sixth calendar year.

TAX SURPRISE: Despite the longer depreciation periods, there will only be a small cut in your annual writeoffs—at least in the early years. Reason: The TRA accelerates the rate at which you writeoff your cost. For example, under the old rules you can deduct 63% of your cost in the first two years; under the TRA, it's 52%.

Under prior law, you could use the accelerated method of computing deductions only if you used your car more than 50% for business. Otherwise, the car had to be written off through straight-line depreciation. There was also a cap on depreciation deductions for cars costing over $12,800. Your depreciation deductions for a business car could not exceed $3,200 for the first year and $4,800 for subsequent years. (These figures were reduced proportionately for cars used only partially for business.) The TRA leaves the 50% business use rule intact. And depreciation deductions for cars costing more than $12,800 continue to be subject to deduction caps. However, the yearly amount of the caps is reduced to reflect the new, slightly less favorable depreciation schedule. [See ¶202.]

Fringe Benefits. The TRA reinstates the tax-free treatment of several widely used fringe benefits. For instance, the tax-free status of educational assistance and group legal services plans expired at the end of 1985. The new law extends these tax breaks for two years, through 1987.

The exclusion from tax for educational assistance benefits had been subject to an annual cap of $5,000 per employee. Benefits in excess of this amount were treated as taxable compensation. The TRA increases the maximum exclusion for educational assistance payments to $5,250, starting in 1986.

Untouched Tax Breaks. Under the TRA, employers can continue to provide their employees tax-free fringe benefits, such as:

- Up to $50,000 of group-term life insurance;
- $5,000 of death benefits;
- Dependent care assistance (but subject to an annual $5,000 ceiling starting in 1986).
- Health insurance (but see below).

Most fringe benefits that are tax-free must be provided to employees on a nondiscriminatory basis. That means the employer must provide the benefits to rank-and-file workers as well as to key employees. Starting in 1987, health plans funded through an insurance carrier are covered by nondiscrimination rules, the same rules that apply to self-insured health plans. So employers can no longer provide tax-free health plan benefits on a key employee-only basis. [See ¶1151 et seq.]

New Tax Deduction for Self-Employed Taxpayers. Starting in 1987, a self-employed individual is allowed to deduct 25% of what he pays himself under a medical reimbursement plan. The plan can also cover his dependents if it covers his employees' dependents. The remaining 75% of the payments are deductible medical expenses. [See ¶1161.]

Stock Option Plans. There are two basic kinds of executive option plans—statutory (incentive stock options) and nonstatutory (nonqualified).

Sequence of exercise. Starting with options issued after 1986, an executive no longer must exercise incentive stock options in the order they are granted to him. This is the same rule that has applied to nonqualified options. What this means: If the price of the stock falls well below the option price, the executive can be issued a second incentive option with a lower exercise price.

No capital gain. Under prior law, with an incentive stock option, the bargain element (the spread between the option's exercise price and the price of the stock) was taxed as long-term capital gain when the stock was sold (as long as the stock was held for more than one year before sale). With the loss of the capital gain exclusion the bargain element in both options is taxed at the same rates as ordinary income.

Family Tax-Saving Strategies. Perhaps the simplest way for a parent to shift taxable income to a child is to give the child a gift of income-producing property. The TRA puts an end to this basic income-shifting technique for many families. Investment income received by a child under age 14 is generally taxed to the child at the parent's top rate. And, it makes no difference if the source of the income came from someone other than the parent—it's still taxed to the child at the parent's highest marginal rate. Effective date: Income received after 1986, even if cash or property was transferred to the child before 1987.

What's more, starting in 1987, your child cannot use his or her personal exemption to shelter income if the child can be claimed as a dependent on your return. However, a minor can use up to $500 of his or her standard deduction to offset unearned income from any source. [See ¶102.] The child is allowed to use his or her own tax rate on another $500 of investment income. Result: If the child is under age 14, only income in excess of $1,000 must be taxed at the parent's top tax rate. [See ¶1405.]

Clifford Trust Repealed. How the trust works: The parent transfers income-producing property to a trust that lasts more than ten years. The trust income is distributed and taxed to the low-bracket child. The property reverts to the parent when the trust terminates.

After the TRA, the trust income is taxed to the person who funds the trust if the property reverts to him (or to his spouse) — even if the reversion takes place more than ten years after the transfer to the trust. In other words, the income-splitting benefit of the short-term trust is eliminated, regardless of the age of the child. Effective date: Income from property transferred to a trust after March 1, 1986. [See ¶1402.]

> **IMPORTANT:** The income-splitting benefit of a Clifford trust set up on or before March 1, 1986 may also be undercut. Reason: After 1986, trust payouts to a child under age 14 can be taxed at the parent's top rate.

Minimum Tax. *Individuals.* The basic structure of the alternative minimum tax for individual taxpayers stays the same under the TRA. However, the rate goes to 21% (from 20%) starting in 1987. And the special exemptions that apply to the tax ($40,000 for joint filers, $30,000 for singles) are phased out for taxpayers with alternative minimum taxable income in excess of $150,000, if married or $112,500, if single. The exemptions are cut by 25% of the amount of alternative minimum taxable income that exceeds these levels. Result: More taxpayers will be subject to the alternative minimum tax.

Two items are no longer subject to minimum tax because they are no longer tax-preferred under the regular tax: the dividend exclusion and the long-term capital gain exclusion. The bargain element of incentive stock options continues to be a tax preference subject to minimum tax. Individual taxpayers cannot use losses from passive investments to offset minimum taxable income. Unlike the phase-in rule for loss writeoffs of regular tax, this takes full effect in 1987. [See ¶701 et seq.]

Corporations. The TRA substantially changes the corporate minimum tax. Starting in 1987, the corporate minimum tax is like the individual minimum tax: it's paid only if it exceeds the regular income tax. (Before the TRA, it was an add-on to the regular corporate tax.) The tax rate is 20%. The exemption is the first $40,000 of minimum taxable income. The exemption amount is reduced by 25% of a corporation's minimum taxable income above $150,000. [See ¶701 et seq.]

> **SPECIAL CORPORATE PREFERENCES:** One half the difference between a corporation's book income and its regular taxable income is a taxable preference in 1987, 1988, and 1989. After 1989, earnings and profits will be used to determine the preference. Corporations also treat as a tax preference a portion of intangible drilling costs.

All taxpayers. The TRA also makes other changes in the minimum tax rules. Here are some key changes that affect both individuals and corporations:

- *Municipal bond interest.* Interest on some tax-exempt bonds issued after August 7, 1986 for a nongovernment purpose will be a preference item.

- *Charitable contribution of appreciated property.* To the extent that untaxed appreciation is allowed as a regular tax deduction, the appreciation on charitable contributions is a preference item, starting in 1987.

- *Net operating losses.* NOLs are deductible against minimum taxable income only to the extent of 90% of that income, *starting in 1987.*

- *Intangible drilling costs.* Intangible drilling costs are a preference item to the extent of the difference between (1) the IDC deduction and (2) the excess of what could have been deducted using 10-year amortization over 65% of net oil and gas income.

- *Depreciation.* Accelerated depreciation for both real and personal property placed in service after 1986 is still a tax preference. However, in later years, when straight-line depreciation exceeds accelerated, the excess can offset other tax preferences.

- *Installment sales.* Taxpayers in the business of selling goods or real estate cannot use the installment method to defer minimum taxable income for tax years beginning after 1986.

- *Completed contract.* Income for the minimum tax cannot be deferred by using the completed contract method of accounting in years starting after 1986.

Life Insurance. The basic tax-favored treatment of life insurance stays in place under the TRA. However, the TRA does add some changes that affect life insurance policyholders. [See ¶1001 et seq.]

Lump-sum payout to spouse-beneficiary. Previously, a spouse who chose to take an installment payout of life insurance proceeds got an income tax break. The spouse could receive up to $1,000 of tax-free interest annually on the unpaid amount. The TRA repeals the $1,000 interest exclusion.

Interest on policyholder loans. The TRA restates the rule that interest on debt incurred to buy or carry single-premium life insurance is not deductible (the IRS has already stated that this rule includes loans against the cash value of single-premium policies).

The new law also places a cap on the amount of interest an employer can deduct when borrowing against a life insurance policy purchased on the life of an employee. Interest may be deducted only on the first $50,000 of borrowing. Effective date: Insurance contracts purchased after June 20, 1986.

IRS enforcement procedures. At the same time it lowers rates and eliminates deductions, the TRA toughens tax penalties. It also provides for more information reporting and increases the IRS budget for agents, audits and the expansion of compliance systems.

Steeper penalties. The penalty for failure to pay taxes goes from ½% to 1% per month for amounts assessed after 1986, regardless of when the failure to pay occurred. The penalty for substantial underpayment of taxes is also doubled—from 10% to 20% for returns due after 1986. In addition, the negligence and fraud penalties are expanded after 1986.

More reporting. Taxpayers will have to provide the Government with more information on real estate transactions, Federal contracts, and royalty payments.

For example, the person responsible for closing a real estate transaction must report the transaction for contracts closing after 1986. The penalty for not filing information returns stays at $50 for each failure. However, the yearly limit increases from $50,000 to $100,000 for returns due after 1986. [See ¶1521.]

The TRA also adds a new penalty of up to $5 for each inaccurate or incomplete information return (up to an annual maximum of $20,000). Effective date: returns due after 1986. [See ¶1501.]

Estate and Gift Tax. The big news in estate and gift taxes is what didn't happen. The TRA made relatively few changes.

Generation skipping transfer tax. Under prior law, this special tax was imposed on transfers in trust set up to benefit two or more generations younger than the generation of the grantor. The tax was paid when the child died and was roughly equivalent to the estate tax that would have been owed if the property had been directly transferred from the grandparent to child and then again from parent to child. Any unused portion of the decedent's unified credit could be used to shelter generation-skipping transfers and an additional $250,000 exemption is available for transfers to grandchildren.

Under the TRA, the credit and exemption are replaced with a single $1 million dollar exemption per transferor ($2 million for joint transfers by married couples). However, for the first time, the TRA subjects direct transfers from grandparents to grandchildren to the generation-skipping tax, subject to a $2 million per grandchild exclusion for transfers made prior to 1-1-90. The tax itself is a flat rate equal to the maximum estate and gift tax rate (now 55% but scheduled to decline to 50% in 1988). Effective date: In general, transfers after the date of enactment. [See ¶1413.]

New Income Tax Rates for Trusts and Estates. Trusts and estates use a special tax rate schedule starting in 1988. (There's a special rate schedule for 1987). The first $5,000 of trust income is taxed at 15%; anything over that is taxed at 28%. The benefit of the 15% bracket is phased out where taxable trust income is between $13,000 and $26,000.

Neither trusts nor estates paid estimated income taxes under prior law. And estates could pay income tax in four equal installments starting with the due date of the return and every three months thereafter. In tax years starting after 1986, trusts and estates must follow the same estimated income tax rules as individuals. And the special installment payment rule for estates is repealed in tax years starting after 1986.

Miscellaneous TRA Changes.

- *Dividend exclusion.* The $100/$200 dividend exclusion for individuals is repealed after 1986. [See ¶604]

- *Two-earner married couples.* The deduction for working married couples is repealed for tax years after 1986. [See ¶106]

- *Income averaging.* After 1986, general income averaging is repealed. [See ¶107]

- *Earned income credit.* Starting in 1987, a tax credit for low-income working individuals with children is increased from 11% of the first $5,000 to 14% of the first $5,714 of earned income (maximum credit: $800). The credit is phased out at a rate of 10% for income levels over $6,500. Thus in 1987, there is no credit if adjusted gross income exceeds $14,500. The phaseout level and the maximum are between $9,000 and $17,000 respectively, after 1987. The maximum amount and the phaseout levels will be adjusted annually for inflation starting 1987. [See ¶108]

- *Office at home deductions.* Most miscellaneous itemized deductions, including those for the business use of an employee's home, are limited by a 2%-of-adjusted gross income-floor after 1986. Also starting in 1987, no home office deduction (other than deductions for mortgage interest and property taxes) are allowed because an employee leases his home office to his employer. Allowable home office deductions are limited to a taxpayer's gross income less his business expenses, other than expenses allocable to the home office itself. The amount of other home office deductions is limited to gross income from the business activity. [See ¶129]

- *Political contributions tax credit.* The TRA knocks out the credit for contributions made to political candidates and organizations after 1986. The maximum credit in 1986 is one-half the dollar amount of the contributions (up to $100 for joint filers, $50 for singles). [¶131.]

• *Casualty loss deduction.* Under the TRA, casualty losses to nonbusiness property cannot be deducted unless (1) an insurance claim is filed, and (2) the losses are not covered by insurance. Effective date: Losses sustained after 1986. [See ¶1005.]

• *Hobby expenses.* Before 1987, hobby expenses are deductible up to the amount of hobby income. Additionally, starting in 1987, your otherwise deductible hobby expenses are aggregated with your other miscellaneous itemized expenses. The total is deductible only to the extent it exceeds 2% of adjusted gross income. The test of whether an activity is considered a business or a hobby is based upon its profitability. Starting in 1987, in order to be presumed a business, the activity must be profitable in three out of five consecutive years. Before 1987, the presumption was two out of five years. A special exception continues to apply to horse breeding or racing. [See ¶130.]

• *Prizes and awards.* All prizes and awards made after 1986 are taxable to the recipient, with two exceptions: (1) Awards for charitable, scientific, artistic or similar achievements are tax-free if the recipient assigns the prize or award to a tax-exempt charity or a governmental unit. (2) Employee awards of personal property (e.g., a watch or crystal bowl) for length of service or safety achievements are tax-free to the extent they are deductible by the employer. The per-employee deduction limit is generally $400. However, it is possible to deduct $1,600 if the employer has a qualified award plan. [See ¶111]

• *Corporate dividend received deduction.* The 85% dividend received deduction for corporations is lowered to 80% for dividends received or accrued after 1986 in tax years ending after 1986. [See ¶602.]

• *Tax on liquidating distributions.* Generally speaking, starting with liquidations completed after 1986, property distributed in a complete liquidation is deemed to have been sold by the corporation at its fair market value. Thus, the corporation is taxed on any appreciation. This repeals the *General Utilities* rule. It permitted a corporation to escape paying income tax on appreciated property by undergoing a complete liquidation and distributing the property to its shareholders. [See ¶615 et seq.]

• *Research credit.* The tax credit for research expenses expired at the end of 1985. The TRA extends the credit beyond 1985 and applies it to expenses incurred before 1989. The amount is lowered to 20% (it was 25%) of the increase in current research expenses over the average in the three preceding years. The TRA targets the credit to technological research that leads to new business. [See ¶211 et seq.]

• *Targeted job credit.* The tax credit for hiring people from one or more of nine targeted groups (e.g., economically disadvantaged

Vietnam veterans) expired at the end of 1985. Although the TRA limits the credit in some respects, it extends the credit for three years—to wages paid by employers who start work before 1989. [See ¶1701.]

- *Tax Accounting.* Manufacturers cannot currently deduct their direct costs of production (e.g., wages and raw material costs). They must be inventoried and offset against proceeds from sales. Up to now, a variety of rules applied to a manufacturer's indirect costs of production: some had to be inventoried (e.g., rent); others were included in inventory for tax purposes only if they were inventoried on financial reports (e.g., retirement plan contributions); still others were currently deductible (e.g., advertising expenses).

Under prior law, both retailers and wholesalers had to include in inventory the direct costs of acquiring goods for resale. But none of their indirect costs had to be inventoried. The treatment of indirect expenses when constructing your own property was less certain.

Beginning in 1987, the TRA sets up uniform rules that apply to all costs incurred in manufacturing or constructing property or in purchasing and holding property for resale (producing farms are exempt from the new rules). Interest costs will generally be capitalized where the interest is allocable to real property construction or the construction of personal property but is long-lived and to be used by the taxpayer. Comprehensive capitalization rules will also apply to long-term contracts. [See ¶805 et seq.]

- *Tax years for S corporations and personal service corporations.* The TRA requires that all partnerships, S corporations, and personal service corporations conform their tax years to the tax years of their owners, starting after 1986. Exception: The years can be different if you can establish a business purpose for the difference. [See ¶808.]

- *Unemployment compensation.* Unemployment benefits received after 1986 are fully taxable. The TRA repeals the limited exclusion for unemployment benefits. [See ¶109.]

- *Interest rate on tax overpayments and underpayments.* Starting in 1987, the interest rate paid to taxpayers on tax overpayments will be the Federal short-term rate plus 2%. Taxpayers will pay the Federal short-term rate plus 3% on underpayments. The rates will be adjusted quarterly based on the rate during the first month of the preceding calendar quarter. [See ¶1511.]

- *Foreign earned income exclusion.* Starting in 1987, the TRA puts a $70,000 cap on the income exclusion available to American taxpayers who have their tax home in a foreign country. [See ¶1201 et seq.]

Impact on State Taxes. Many states start their tax computations with federal adjusted gross income or, in the case of corporations, federal taxable income with certain adjustments. This means that, unless their legislators act fast, items which affect federal adjusted gross income or taxable income in the new tax law are going to affect state taxes. Remember to bear these points in mind when you are assessing how the new tax law's rules will affect your tax liability. And make sure you consult the *P-H State and Local Tax Service* to keep on top of changes in your area.

[The page following this is 101.]

INDIVIDUALS

〔¶101〕 Rate Reductions for Individuals. The new law introduces new and deceptively simple tax rate schedules. Prior law taxed individuals in as many as 15 brackets at rates that began at 11% and went as high as 50%. This structure is replaced with what appears to be a two-bracket rate setup—15% and 28%. However, the top tax rate is actually 33%. Reason: Beginning with the 1988 tax year, there are two separate 5% surtaxes for high-income taxpayers.

• The first 5% surtax phases out the tax benefit a taxpayer gains from having part of his income taxed at the 15% rate. The surtax commences at prescribed income levels and ends at the point where the 13% differential between the 15% and 28% brackets is recouped.

Example: For marrieds filing jointly for 1988, the first $29,750 of income is taxed at 15%, and the excess above $29,750 is taxed at 28%. The 5% surtax begins at taxable income in excess of $71,900 and ends at $149,250. Thus, if taxable income is $149,250, the surtax reaches a maximum of $3,867.50. That figure represents an extra 13% tax on the first $29,750 of taxable income.

• The second 5% surtax phases out the tax benefit gained from personal and dependency exemptions. This surtax kicks in at the point where the first 5% surtax is levied in full—that is, at the point where the tax benefit from the 15% rate disappears.

Example: For marrieds filing jointly for 1988, the second surtax begins at taxable income in excess of $149,250.

The second surtax disappears once the tax benefit gained from exemptions is recouped. Each personal and dependency exemption is equal to $1,900 for 1987, $1,950 for 1988, and $2,000 for 1989. Thus, for 1988, the maximum personal exemption surtax for a high-bracket taxpayer is $546 per exemption claimed. That figure is 28% of $1,950.

Special rates for 1987. To reconcile the new schedules with prior law's schedules, Congress came up with "blended" rate schedules for 1987 only.

WATCH THIS: The special rate schedules for 1987 have five conventional tax brackets. That is, there are no surtaxes levied on high-income taxpayers.

Another fundamental change. Beginning with tax year 1987, tax brackets start at taxable income of zero. Taxable income is adjusted gross income less personal exemptions less (1) the standard deduc-

¶101

tion (which replaces the zero bracket amount) or (2) total itemized deductions, whichever is greater. Under prior law, the zero bracket amount was built into the tax rate schedules. Thus, the lowest bracket began at the point where taxable income exceeded the applicable zero bracket amount. The nonitemizer found taxable income by subtracting personal exemptions (and the special charitable deduction) from AGI. The itemizer arrived at taxable income by subtracting from AGI the total of personal exemptions and the excess of itemized deductions over the zero bracket amount.

Following are the new tax rates for 1987 and 1988. The tax rates for 1988 reflect the first 5% surtax. The second 5% surtax depends on the number of personal and dependency exemptions claimed by the taxpayer.

MARRIEDS FILING JOINTLY OR SURVIVING SPOUSES

Tax Year 1987		Tax Year 1988	
Taxable Income (TI)	Tax Payable	Taxable Income (TI)	Tax Payable
$0—$3,000	11% of TI	$0—$29,750	15% of TI
$3,000—$28,000	$330 + 15% of (TI − $3,000)	$29,750—$71,900	$4,462.50 + 28% of (TI − $29,750)
$28,000—$45,000	$4,080 + 28% of (TI − $28,000)	$71,900—$149,250	$16,264.50 + 33% of (TI − $71,900)*
$45,000—$90,000	$8,840 + 35% of (TI − $45,000)	$149,250 +	28% of TI**
$90,000 +	$24,590 + 38.5% of (TI − $90,000)		

*Reflects first 5% surtax.
**PLUS lesser of (1) 28% of the sum of personal and dependency exemptions or (2) 5% of (TI − $149,250).

HEADS OF HOUSEHOLD

Tax Year 1987		Tax Year 1988	
Taxable Income (TI)	Tax Payable	Taxable Income (TI)	Tax Payable
$0—$2,500	11% of TI	$0—$23,900	15% of TI
$2,500—$23,000	$275 + 15% of (TI − $2,500)	$23,900—$61,650	$3,585 + 28% of (TI − $23,900)
$23,000—$38,000	$3,350 + 28% of (TI − $23,000)	$61,650—$123,790	$14,155 + 33% of (TI − $61,650)*
$38,000—$80,000	$7,550 + 35% of (TI − $38,000)	$123,790 +	28% of TI**
$80,000 +	$22,250 + 38.5% of (TI − $80,000)		

*Reflects first 5% surtax.
**PLUS lesser of (1) 28% of the sum of personal and dependency exemptions or (2) 5% of (TI − $123,790).

SINGLE TAXPAYERS

Tax Year 1987		Tax Year 1988	
Taxable Income (TI)	Tax Payable	Taxable Income (TI)	Tax Payable
$0—$1,800	11% of TI	$0—$17,850	15% of TI
$1,800—$16,800	$198 + 15% of (TI − $1,800)	$17,850—$43,150	$2,677.50 + 28% of (TI − $17,850)
$16,800—$27,000	$2,448 + 28% of (TI − $16,800)	$43,150—$89,560	$9,761.50 + 33%* of (TI − $43,150)
$27,000—$54,000	$5,304 + 35% of (TI − $27,000)	$89,560 +	28% of TI**
$54,000 +	$14,754 + 38.5% of (TI − $54,000)		

*Reflects first 5% surtax.
**PLUS lesser of (1) 28% of the sum of personal and dependency exemptions or (2) 5% of (TI − $89,560).

MARRIEDS FILING SEPARATELY

Tax Year 1987		Tax Year 1988	
Taxable Income (TI)	Tax Payable	Taxable Income (TI)	Tax Payable
$0—$1,500	11% of TI	$0—$14,875	15% of TI
$1,500—$14,000	$165 + 15% of (TI − $1,500)	$14,875—$35,950	$2,231.25 + 28% of (TI − $14,875)
$14,000—$22,500	$2,040 + 28% of (TI − $14,000)	$35,950—$113,300	$8,132.25 + 33% of (TI − $35,950)*
$22,500—$45,000	$4,420 + 35% of (TI − $22,500)	$113,300 +	28% of TI**
$45,000 +	$12,295 + 38.5% of (TI − $45,000)		

*Reflects first 5% surtax. The maximum surtax, or rate adjustment, equals 13% of the maximum amount of taxable income within the 15% bracket applicable for marrieds filing jointly.
**PLUS lesser of (1) 28% of the sum of personal and dependency exemptions or (2) 5% of (TI − $113,300).

Following are three examples that illustrate the operation of the new rates.

Example (1): Joint return filers Mr. and Mrs. Anderson have $60,000 of taxable income in 1987 and 1988. Their tax bill for 1987 is $14,090. That's $8,840 plus 35% of ($60,000 − $45,000). Their tax bill for 1988 is $12,932.50. That's $4,462.50 plus 28% of ($60,000 − $29,750).

Example (2): Joint return filers Mr. and Mrs. Jones have taxable income of $85,000 in 1987 and 1988. Their tax bill in 1987 is $22,840. That's the sum of $8,840 plus 35% of ($85,000 − $45,000). Their tax bill in 1988 is $20,587.50. That's the sum of $16,264.50 plus 33% of ($85,000 − $71,900). The tax reflects a 5% surtax on the $13,100 of taxable income in excess of $71,900.

Example (3): For tax years 1987 and 1988, joint return filers Mr. and Mrs. Smith have three dependent children and $160,000 of taxable income. Their tax bill for 1987 is $51,540. That's the sum of $24,590 and 38.5% of ($160,000 − $90,000). Their tax bill for 1988 is the sum of two figures:

(1) Flat tax of 28% on all income [income exceeds point at which first 5% surtax is levied in full] ... $44,800.00

(2) Lesser of:
    (a) 28% of ($1,950 exemption × 5) $2,730.00
    (b) 5% of ($160,000 − $149,250) 537.50   537.50

Total $45,337.50

Estates and trusts. The tax rate schedules for estates and trusts are as follows:

Tax Year 1987		Tax Year 1988	
Taxable Income (TI)	Tax Payable	Taxable Income (TI)	Tax Payable
$0—$500	11% of TI	$0—$5,000	15% of TI
$500—$4,700	$55 + 15% of (TI − $500)	$5,000—$13,000	$750 + 28% of (TI − $5,000)
$4,700—$7,550	$685 + 28% of (TI − $4,700)	$13,000—$26,000	$2,990 + 33% of (TI − $13,000)
$7,550—$15,150	$1,483 + 35% of (TI − $7,550)	$26,000 +	28% of TI
$15,150 +	$4,143 + 38.5% of (TI − $15,150)		

NOTE: The taxable income amounts at which the 28% rate starts will be adjusted for inflation, beginning with the 1989 tax year. See ¶105.

Act Sec. 101(a) amends Sec. 1, relating to tax imposed on individuals, effective for tax years beginning after 12-31-86. Act. Sec. 101(b) amends Sec. 15(d), relating to inflation adjustments.

[¶102] Standard Deduction Reactivated and Increased. Beginning with tax year 1987, the new law replaces the zero bracket amount with the standard deduction. The basic standard deduction amounts for taxpayers other than the elderly and the blind are as follows:

	1987	1988
Marrieds filing jointly and surviving spouses	$3,760	$5,000
Heads of household	$2,540	$4,400
Single taxpayers	$2,540	$3,000
Married filing separate returns	$1,880	$2,500

Boost for the elderly and the blind. For the 1987 tax year, taxpayers who are age 65 or over or are blind (defined as under prior law) may claim the higher standard deduction shown in the 1988 column. Also, beginning with the 1987 tax year, the standard deduction for an unmarried taxpayer who is not a surviving spouse and is age 65 or over or blind is increased by an additional standard deduction of $750. For a married taxpayer who is age 65 or over or blind, the additional standard deduction is $600. Thus, the additional standard deduction is $1,200 if both spouses are blind or 65 or over, or one is age 65 or over and the other is blind.

> **Example:** Ted and Andrea Smith are both age 66 and file jointly. They may claim a $6,200 standard deduction for tax year 1987 ($5,000 plus $1,200 for age 65 or over status).

> **Example:** Arthur Smith, a blind taxpayer, may claim a $3,750 standard deduction for tax year 1987 ($3,000 plus $750 increase). If Arthur were 65 or over, his standard deduction would be $4,500 ($3,000 plus $1,500 increase).

Dependent child's unearned income. Effective for the 1987 tax year, the standard deduction of a taxpayer (such as a child) who may be claimed as a dependent on another's return cannot exceed the greater of $500 or his earned income. Result: For 1987, if a child has no earned income, his or her unearned income in excess of $500 is subject to tax at a minimum rate of 11% (15% in 1988). The tax rate may be higher if the child is under age 14 and has "net unearned income" [see ¶1405 *et seq.*]. Another change: Effective for 1987, a taxpayer who may be claimed as a dependent by another taxpayer cannot claim a personal exemption [¶103].

By contrast, for tax year 1986, a dependent child with no earned income does not pay tax on the first $1,080 of unearned income (it's sheltered by the personal exemption).

Taxpayers ineligible for standard deduction. The standard deduction is zero for the following five categories:

- Married taxpayers filing separately if either spouse itemizes deductions.

- Individuals who are nonresident aliens.

- U.S. citizens with excludable income from U.S. possessions.

- Individuals who file returns for periods of less than 12 months because of accounting period changes.

- Estates or trusts, common trust funds, or partnerships.

Definition of taxable income. The new law simplifies the calculation of an individual's tax liability. Here's a comparison of the old and new definitions of taxable income for computing tax liability.

Under prior law, nonitemizers arrived at taxable income by subtracting the charitable deduction for a nonitemizer and all personal exemptions from AGI. The nonitemizer went directly to a tax table or tax rate schedule to figure tax liability. The zero bracket amount was incorporated in both the tax rate schedules and tax tables.

¶102

Thus, the tax tables and schedules indicated a zero tax liability if taxable income did not exceed the applicable ZBA.

Taxpayers who itemized reduced their itemized deductions by the applicable ZBA (to avoid getting twice the allowable ZBA) and subtracted the remaining (so-called excess) itemized deductions and personal exemptions from AGI to arrive at taxable income. Then, like a nonitemizer, the itemizer went to a tax table or tax rate schedules.

Under the new law, a nonitemizer offsets AGI with the standard deduction and personal exemptions to arrive at taxable income (the charitable deduction for nonitemizers is eliminated). An itemizer offsets AGI with personal exemptions and *all* itemized deductions to arrive at taxable income. Since the standard deduction has already been taken into account in arriving at taxable income, the new tax rate schedules and tax tables begin at the first dollar of taxable income.

Tax tables. The IRS is authorized to prepare tax tables reflecting the tax liability of itemizers and nonitemizers. Since the prior tables that incorporated the ZBA are replaced by tables that do not incorporate the standard deduction, the Committee Reports authorize the IRS to adjust the size of the intervals between taxable income amounts in the new tables to reflect meaningful differences in tax liability.

The standard deduction, the additional standard deduction, and the special $500 standard deduction for a taxpayer who can be claimed as a dependent by another, will be indexed for inflation beginning in 1989.

Act Sec. 102(a), relating to definition of taxable income, the basic standard deduction and additional standard deduction, amends Sec. 63. Act Sec. 102(b), relating to tax tables, amends Sec. 3(a). Act Secs. 102(a) and (b) are effective for tax years beginning after 12-31-86.

[¶103] **Personal Exemptions Increased.** The new law raises the personal exemption for an individual, the individual's spouse, and each dependent to $1,900 for 1987, $1,950 for 1988, and $2,000 for 1989. By contrast, each personal exemption was $1,080 for tax year 1986.

Personal exemptions will be indexed for inflation beginning with the 1990 tax year. See ¶105.

Phase-out of personal exemption for high-income taxpayers. Beginning with the 1988 tax year, the new law phases out the tax benefit that a high income taxpayer gains from personal exemptions. The phase-out affects *all* exemptions that may be claimed on a return including exemptions for a spouse and dependents. The purpose: to limit the windfall that wealthy taxpayers may reap from lower tax rates. The mechanism for the phase-out is a 5% surtax that begins at the point where the tax benefit from the 15% rate disappears [¶101], and ends where the tax benefit from personal exemptions is recouped in full.

The phase-out of personal exemptions by way of a surtax begins at the following levels of taxable income:

Filing Status	Taxable Income*
Marrieds filing jointly or surviving spouses	$149,250
Heads of household	$123,790
Single taxpayers	$ 89,560
Marrieds filing separately	$113,300

*Beginning with tax year 1989, these figures will be indexed for inflation.

For tax year 1988, the surtax is equal to the lesser of

• # of personal exemptions × $1,950 × 28% [nominal top tax bracket], or

• 5% of the excess of taxable income over the appropriate dollar figure from our table.

For 1988, the exemption is totally phased out at $10,920 of income per exemption above the figures shown in our table.

> **Example:** Mr. and Mrs. Sample have four dependent children and file a joint return for tax year 1988. If they have $180,000 of taxable income, the surtax is equal to $1,537.50. That's 5% of $30,750 ($180,000 − $149,250). Put another way, the Sample family's personal exemptions are effectively reduced to $6,209, as follows:

> Gross exemptions ($1,950 × 6 exemptions) $11,700
> Amount lost by way of surtax ($1,537.50 × 1/.28) (5,491)
> Net effective deduction for exemptions .... $ 6,209

> **Example:** John Cable is a single taxpayer with no dependents. His taxable income for 1988 is $120,000. Result: Cable's surtax is $546 ($1,950 × 28%). In other words, Cable's personal exemption is completely phased out.

Elderly and the blind. Under prior law, a taxpayer could claim an additional personal exemption if he was age 65 or over or blind. The new law repeals this additional personal exemption, beginning with the 1987 tax year. However, the loss of this extra exemption is recouped in part by way of an additional standard deduction for the elderly or blind ($750 extra for an unmarried taxpayer other than a surviving spouse, $600 for a married taxpayer). See ¶102.

Dependent child loses personal exemption. Under the new law, no exemption is allowed a taxpayer (such as a child) who can be claimed as a dependent by another taxpayer (e.g., a parent). This restriction eliminates the double benefit allowed under prior law when a dependent child was also allowed to claim a personal exemption on his or her own return.

NOTE: It doesn't matter that the parent doesn't claim the dependency deduction. The key factor is that the parent *could have* done so.

Act Sec. 103(a), relating to increase in personal exemptions, amends Sec. 151(f). Act Sec. 103(b), relating to repeal of additional exemptions for taxpayers age 65 or over or blind, amends Sec. 151 by striking out (c) and (d) and redesignating (e) and (f) as (c) and (d), respectively. Act Sec. 103 is effective for tax years beginning after 12-31-86.

[¶104] Tax Return Filing Levels. The new law makes conforming changes to Sec. 6012 (which defines those taxpayers required to file a return) to accommodate the personal exemptions, new standard deductions, and additional standard deduction that may be claimed by the elderly. In general, a taxpayer must file a return only if his gross income equals or exceeds the following levels:

Taxpayer Class	*1987 Gross Income Level	*1988 Gross Income Level
Marrieds filing jointly, both under age 65	$ 7,560	$ 8,900
Marrieds filing jointly, one spouse age 65 or over	$ 9,400	$ 9,500
Marrieds filing jointly, both age 65 or over	$10,000	$10,100
Surviving spouse under age 65	$ 5,660	$ 6,950
Surviving spouse age 65 or over	$ 7,500	$ 7,550
Head of household under age 65	$ 4,440	$ 6,350
Head of household age 65 or over	$ 7,050	$ 7,100
Single person under age 65	$ 4,440	$ 4,950
Single person age 65 or over	$ 5,650	$ 5,700
Married filing separate return	$ 1,900	$ 1,950
Married whose spouse may be claimed as a dependent by another taxpayer	$ 1,900	$ 1,950

---

*The figures shown represent the sum of the personal exemption, the regular standard deduction, and the additional standard deduction for taxpayers age 65 or over.

Other rules. In general, a taxpayer must file an income tax return if his or her gross income equals or exceeds the exemption amount [see ¶103] if:

(1) The taxpayer may be claimed as a dependent by another taxpayer and has unearned income in excess of $500 or has total gross income in excess of the standard deduction.

(2) The taxpayer cannot claim any standard deduction [see ¶102].

The new law says that, for tax-filing purposes, an individual who may be claimed as a dependent by another has an exemption equal to zero [Sec. 6012(a)(1)(D)(ii), as amended by Act Sec. 104]. But the Conference Report is kindlier. It indicates that if a child has no earned income, he must file only if his unearned income exceeds $500. An estate of an individual under chapter 7 or 11 of the United States Code (relating to bankruptcy) must file a return if its gross income for tax year 1987 is not less than $3,780 ($4,450 for 1988). The new law makes other housekeeping changes (e.g., the personal holding company tax is 38.5% for tax years beginning in 1987 and 28% for later years).

Act Sec. 104 amends the following Code Sections: Secs. 21, 32, 108, 129, 152, 172, 402, 441, 443, 541, 613A, 667, 861, 862, 904, 1398, 2032A, 3402, 6012, 6013, 6014, 6212, and 6504. Act Sec. 104 is effective for tax years beginning after 12-31-86.

[¶105] Inflation Indexing of Rate Structures, Standard Deductions, and Exemptions. The new rate structures will be adjusted for inflation annually beginning with tax year 1989. Any inflation adjustments will apply to the breakpoint between the 15% and 28% brackets and to the income levels at which the two 5% surtaxes are applied. The standard deduction amounts also will be adjusted for inflation beginning with tax year 1989. The inflation adjustment for 1989 is equal to the percentage increase in the Consumer Price Index (CPI) for 1988 over the CPI for 1987. The personal exemption will be indexed beginning with tax year 1990. The adjustment for 1990 is equal to the percentage increase in the CPI for 1989 over the CPI for 1988. The 12-month period for measuring the CPI will end August 31 of each calendar year. In general, inflation adjustments that are not a multiple of $50 will be rounded down to the next lowest multiple of $50. For marrieds filing separately, inflation adjustments (to the rate structure and personal exemption) that are not a multiple of $25 will be rounded down to the next lowest multiple of $25.

Act Sec. 101(a), amends Sec. 1(f) (indexing of rate structure), Act Sec. 102(a) amends Sec. 63(c)(4) (indexing of standard deductions), and Act Sec. 103(a) amends Sec. 151(d)(3) (indexing of exemptions). Effective dates are shown above.

[¶106] Repeal of Two-Earner Deduction. Effective for tax years beginning on or after 1987, the new law repeals the special deduction granted to families when both spouses work. Under prior law, this deduction was equal to 10% of the lesser of (1) $30,000, or (2) the qualified earned income of the lower-earning spouse.

Act Sec. 131(a) repeals Sec. 221 relating to two-earner deduction. Act Sec. 131(b) makes conforming amendments to Sec. 62 and Sec. 86(b)(2) and to the table of sections for part VII of subchapter B of chapter 1. Act Sec. 131 is effective for tax years beginning after 12-31-86.

[¶107] Repeal of Income Averaging. The new law repeals the general income averaging break for all taxpayers, effective for tax years beginning on or after 1-1-87.

Act Sec. 141 repeals Part I of Subchapter Q of the Internal Revenue Code, and makes technical amendments to Secs. 3, 5, and 6511, effective as shown above.

[¶108] Earned Income Credit Increased. The new law grants extra relief to taxpayers eligible for the earned income credit. Effective for the 1987 tax year, the earned income credit is equal to 14% of the first $5,714 of earned income for a maximum credit of $800. In addition, there's an increase in the income level at which the credit is phased down. For tax year 1987, the credit is phased down by 10% of AGI (or earned income, if greater) in excess of $6,500. There is no credit once AGI or earned income hits $14,500. For tax year 1988, the 10% phase-down begins when AGI or earned income exceeds $9,000 and ends when AGI or earned income equals $17,000.

Under prior law, the earned income credit was equal to 11% of the first $5,000 of earned income. The credit was reduced by 12 ⅑ % of AGI or earned income in excess of $6,500, and there was no credit once income exceeded $11,000.

Another change. The new law provides for automatic, CPI-based inflation adjustments to the earned-income dollar levels. For 1987, the basic $5,714 earned-income figure and the $6,500 phase-down level will be indexed for inflation between 8-31-84 and 8-31-86. The $9,000 phase-down level will be indexed beginning with the 1988 tax year. The adjustments will be rounded as follows: an adjustment that is not a multiple of $10 will be rounded to the nearest multiple of $10; or if the increase is a multiple of $5, it will be increased to the next highest multiple of $10.

Taxpayers eligible for the credit. As under prior law, the following taxpayers are eligible for the earned income credit:

• Marrieds filing jointly who are entitled to a dependency exemption for a child or stepchild.

• Surviving spouses or unmarried individuals who maintain a household for a dependent child or stepchild.

• A custodial parent, even if that parent agrees to let the noncustodial parent claim a dependency exemption for the child.

NOTE: Employers must notify employees whose wages are not subject to income tax withholding that they may be eligible for the refundable earned income credit. This rule does not apply if the employee is exempt from withholding under IRC Sec. 3402(h).

Act Sec. 111 amends Sec. 32(a), (b) and (f) and adds Sec. 32(i). It also makes technical and conforming changes to Sec. 3507, relating to advance payment of the earned income credit. Act Sec. 111(e), relating to employer notification, does not amend the Code. Act Sec. 111 is effective for tax years beginning after 12-31-86.

[¶109] Unemployment Compensation Fully Taxed. The new law repeals the partial exclusion for unemployment benefits. All benefits received after 12-31-86 are included in taxable income.

Act Sec. 121 amends Sec. 85, relating to unemployment compensation, effective for amounts received after 12-31-86, in tax years ending after such date.

[¶110] Limitations on Tax-Free Scholarships. The new law overhauls the rules authorizing tax-free treatment for individuals who receive scholarships and fellowship grants from colleges, universities, and other educational institutions.

Scholarships and grants. Prior law excluded from taxable income scholarships and fellowship grants received by degree candidates from schools for their tuition, matriculation, and other fees and regular living expenses, like room and board. The exclusion also applied to allowances received to cover their expenses for travel, research, clerical help, or equipment.

Under the new law, the exclusion is limited to amounts used by degree candidates for "qualified tuition and related expenses" in accordance with the conditions of the grant or scholarship. Qualified expenses are limited to (1) tuition and fees for enrollment or attendance by a student enrolled in a school described in Sec. 170(b)(1)(A)-(ii), and (2) fees, books, supplies and equipment required for the course of study. There is no exclusion for grant or scholarship dollars used for room and board. The Committee Reports say that the exclusion applies only if the terms of the grant or scholarship do not earmark or designate its use for nonqualified expenses (e.g. room and board) and do not specify that the funds cannot be used for tuition or course-related expenses.

The Committee Reports clarify that the exclusion applies to individuals other than students attending a primary or secondary school or pursuing a degree at a university or college. These individuals are deemed "degree candidates," and thus are eligible for the exclusion, if they are granted a scholarship for full-or part-time study at an educational institution described in Sec. 170(b)(1)(a)(ii) that (1) provides an educational program acceptable for full credit toward a bachelor's or higher degree, or offers a training program leading to gainful employment in a recognized occupation, (2) is authorized by Federal or State Law to provide such a program, and (3) is accredited by a nationally recognized accreditation agency.

Payments for teaching or research. As a general rule, compensation for teaching or research is fully taxable. But prior law excluded that part of scholarship or fellowship grants received as payment for teaching, research, or other part-time services, as long as all degree candidates were required to perform such duties.

The new law ends this special exclusion. Amounts received for teaching or research are taxable in full whether the compensation takes the form of a paycheck or a tuition reduction.

Special rule: The new law excludes from gross income amounts received as a "qualified tuition reduction." This is the amount of a tuition reduction received by an employee of an educational institution described in Sec. 170(b)(1)(A)(ii). The reduction in tuition must be for education (below the graduate level) at the employer's or other eligible institution. The tuition reduction can be for the employee or for a person treated as an employee under Sec. 132(f) (e.g., the employee's child). The exclusion applies to an employee who is an officer, owner, or highly compensated owner of the institution only if the tuition reduction is available to employees on a nondiscriminatory basis.

Other escape hatches remain open. The new rules for scholarships and fellowships do not affect the exclusion under Sec. 127 for employer-provided educational assistance to an employee [¶1162]. And taxpayers can continue to claim deductions for qualified work-related education expenses.

> **NOTE:** Under the new law, unreimbursed work-related educational expenses are deductible as miscellaneous itemized expenses subject to a new 2% floor. See ¶128.

Effective date and transition rule: The new law changes apply to tax years beginning after 12-31-86, but only for scholarships and fellowships granted after 8-16-86. The Committee Reports indicate that for scholarships and fellowships granted after 8-16-86 and before 1-1-87, prior law's Sec. 117 exclusion applies to amounts that are received prior to 1-1-87, and are attributable to expenses incurred prior to 1-1-87.

The Committee Reports also indicate that noncompensatory scholarships or grants newly includable in gross income are considered earned income for purposes of the special standard deduction rule that applies to a taxpayer who may be claimed as a dependent by another taxpayer [see ¶102].

Act Sec. 123(a) amends Sec. 117, relating to scholarships. Act Sec. 123(b) amends Sec. 74(a), relating to prizes and awards, Sec. 1441(b), relating to withholding of tax on nonresident aliens, Sec. 7871(a)(6), relating to Indian tribal governments treated as States for certain purposes, and the table of sections for part III of subchapter B of chapter 1. Act Sec. 123 is effective as shown above.

〔¶111〕 Charitable and Employee Achievement Award Exclusions Cut Back. The new law modifies the exclusion for awards in recognition of charitable and like achievements. The exclusion applies only if the recipient designates that the prize is to be transferred by the payor to a governmental unit or to certain charitable, educational, religious, etc., organizations. Also, the new law authorizes an exclusion for "employee achievement awards." These are awards for length of service or safety achievement. There is an exclusion, subject to certain limitations, of up to $400 of cost ($1,600 if made under a qualified plan where the average cost does not exceed $400). Let's take a closer look at these provisions, which take effect starting with the 1987 tax year.

Limitation on exclusion for prizes and awards. The new law limits the exclusion from taxable income for prizes and awards made primarily in recognition of religious, charitable, scientific, educational, artistic, literary, or civic achievements. Prior law allowed the exclusion only if the winner satisfied two requirements. First, the recipient was selected without action on his part—that is, he did not apply for the prize or award by, say, entering a contest. Second, he is not required, as a condition of receipt, to render substantial future services.

The new law retains the two requirements and adds a third one that allows the exclusion only if the winner assigns the award to charity. Specifically, the recipient must "designate" that the prize or award is to be transferred by the payor to a governmental unit or tax-exempt charitable, educational, religious, etc., organization, contributions to which are deductible under Sec. 170(c)(1) or (2), respectively.

> **HOW TO DO IT:** The Committee Reports set an exclusion-qualification deadline that bars the winner's use of the award proceeds before they are assigned to charity. To pass muster, the winner's designation and the award-paying organization's fulfillment of that designation must occur before any impermissible use by the winner of the money or other property awarded. Otherwise, no exclusion and the award is taxable.

For a cash award, the designation/fulfillment has to occur before the winner spends, deposits, or otherwise invests the funds. Other impermissible uses include use of the property with the winner's permission or by someone associated with the winner, such as a family member.

Employee achievement awards. The new law provides an exclusion for employees who receive achievement awards that satisfy certain requirements. These employees can exclude such awards from their gross income, within separate limits of $400 and $1,600. Besides limits on amounts that employees can exclude, there are limits on amounts that employers can deduct.

Employee achievement award defined. It is an item of tangible personal property that an employer transfers to an employee for length-of-service achievement or for safety achievement. The property must be awarded as part of a meaningful presentation and under conditions and circumstances that do not create a significant likelihood of the payment of disguised compensation.

The Committee Reports provide examples of disguised compensation situations. They include employee awards made at the time of annual salary adjustments, as a substitute for a prior program of awarding cash bonuses or in a way that discriminates in favor of highly paid employees.

> **NOTE:** Only tangible personal property qualifies. There is no exclusion for awards of cash, gift certificates, or equivalent items.

Length-of-service awards. An employee may not exclude an award when it is received during his or her first five years of employment for the employer making the award or when he or she has previously received an award during that year or any of the preceeding four years, unless the previous award qualifies under the Sec. 132(e) exclusion for de minimis fringe benefits.

Safety-achievement awards. There is no exclusion for an award made to an employee not in the category of eligible employees or if, during the year, the employer previously made safety awards to more than 10% of the eligible employees.

Which employees are eligible and which ones ineligible? All are eligible, except for managers, administrators, clerical workers, and other professional employees.

Qualified plan award. It is defined as an employee achievement award provided under a qualified award plan—that is, an established written plan or program of the taxpayer that does not discriminate in favor of highly compensated employees, within the meaning of Sec. 414(q), as to eligibility or benefits.

Deduction limitations on employers. The new law bars a deduction for an employee-achievement award except to the extent its cost does not exceed the limitation imposed by Sec. 274(j). As a general rule, there is a $400 limit on the deduction by an employer for all safety and length-of-service awards (other than qualified plan awards) provided to the same employee during the tax year. There is, however, a ceiling of $1,600 on the deduction for all qualified plan awards, whether for safety or length of service, when an employer makes one or more QPAs to the same employee during the tax year.

NOTE: There is no parlaying of the separate $400/$1,600 limits. In addition to these separate limits, the $1,600 limit applies in the aggregate when an employee receives one or more QPAs during the year and also one or more awards that are not QPAs. That means no adding together of the $400 and $1,600 limits to allow deductions exceeding an aggregate of $1,600 for awards to the same employee in a tax year. For a partnership, the $400 and $1,600 limits apply to the partnership, as well as to each partner.

There is an average cost ceiling on awards. QPA treatment is unavailable if the average cost per recipient of all achievement awards made under all qualified award plans of the employer during the tax year exceeds $400. For purposes of the average cost calculation, QPAs of nominal value are not included.

When the cost of a QPA exceeds $1,600, its entire cost is added into the total of award costs under the plan. It is immaterial that the allowable deduction for the cost is only $1,600 or less.

Limitations on amounts excludable by employees. The fair market value of an achievement award is fully excludable from gross income by the employee when the cost of the award is fully deductible by the employer under the $400/$1,600 limits.

NOTE: The deduction limit amount for a tax-exempt employer is the amount that would be deductible if the employer were not tax exempt.

Example: International Widgets awards a crystal bowl as a length-of-service award (other than a QPA) to Jane Brown. For the year in question, International makes no other safety or length-of-service award to Jane; nor did it make a length-of-service award to her during the previous four years. The bowl cost International $375; its FMV is $415. The $415 is excludable from Brown's income.

Excess deduction awards. An employee cannot exclude the entire FMV of an achievement award when its cost exceeds the amount allowable as a deduction by an employer because of the $400/$1,600 limits. There is, however, a cap on how much an employee has to include in income.

The includable amount is the *greater* of (1) the portion of the cost to the employer that is not allowable as an employer deduction, but not an amount in excess of the award's FMV, *or* (2) the excess of the award's FMV over the maximum allowable employer deduction. An employee can exclude the remaining portion of the award's FMV.

Example: Consolidated Enterprises pays $500 for a watch (not a QPA) that goes as a safety award to John Green, an eligible employee. For the year in question, Consolidated made no achievement awards to Green and did not previously make safety awards to more than 10% of the eligible employees. Consolidated's deduction is limited to $400. Green must include as income the greater of (1) $100,

¶1111

which is the difference between the watch's cost ($500) and Consolidated's $400 deduction limit, or (2) the excess of the watch's FMV over Consolidated's $400 deduction. With an assumed FMV of $475, Green includes $100. With a FMV of $600, he includes $200.

An employee award's FMV, whether or not it comes under the definition of an achievement award, is includable in an employee's income under Sec. 61 and is not shielded from taxes by the exclusions under Sec. 74 for prizes and awards or under Sec. 102 for gifts, except to the extent the exclusions under Sec. 74(c) for achievement awards or under Sec. 132(e) for de minimis fringes apply. Consequently, the FMV of an employee award (or any part of it) not excludable from income must be included by an employer on the employee's W-2.

> **NOTE:** Any excludable award is excludable from wages for employment tax purposes and from the Social Security benefit base.

De minimis fringe benefits. The new law does not modify the Sec. 132(e) exclusion for de minimis fringes. Consequently, there is an income exclusion for an employee award when its FMV, after considering the frequency with which the employer provides similar benefits to its employees, is so small it is unreasonable or administratively impractical to require the employer to account for the award.

The Committee Reports explain when it is appropriate to disregard employee awards excludable under Sec. 132(e) in determining how frequently an employee receives a length-of-service award or how many employees receive safety awards in the same tax year. Ordinarily, they are disregarded. But they may need to be considered when an employer's practice of giving its employees length-of-service or safety awards that qualify under Secs. 74 and 274 affects the question whether other items given to these employees, particularly if given as length-of-service or safety awards, qualify as Sec. 132(e) de minimis fringes.

When is it unreasonable or administratively impractical to account for a particular item? An employer may have to account when a program exists under which it regularly accounts for other like items and complies with the statutory reporting requirements.

> **NOTE:** The IRS may refuse to treat fringes as de minimis when an employee receives items that have the maximum FMV, consistent with the exclusions for achievement awards and de minimis fringes. The Committee Reports say the IRS should question an exclusion when an employer provides several employee awards and other items, supposedly shielded by Sec. 132(e), to the same employees in the same year.

Traditional retirement gifts ordinarily treated as de minimis fringes. The Committee Reports clarify the applicability of the Sec. 132(e) exclusion for de minimis fringes to traditional retirement gifts received by an employee who retires after long service when the Sec. 74 exclusion for length-of-service award is inapplicable because the employee received such an award within the previous four years. In determining whether such a retirement gift passes muster as a de minimis fringe, the IRS should consider how long the employee worked for the employer.

Example: Susan White receives a gold watch on retirement after 25 years of employment. Her watch can qualify as a de minimis fringe. It doesn't matter that other watches she previously received did not so qualify.

Act Sec. 122(a)(1) amends Sec. 74, relating to prizes and awards. Act Sec. 122(a)(2) makes conforming amendments to Secs. 4941 and 4945. Act. Sec. 122(b) adds new subsection (c) to Sec. 102, relating to gifts and inheritances. Act Secs. 122(c) and (d) amend Sec. 274, relating to certain entertainment, etc., expenses, and adds new Sec. 274(j). Act. Sec. 122(e), relating to treatment for purposes of employment taxes, amends Secs. 3121(a)(20), 3231(e)(5), 3306(b)(16), 3401(a)(20) and Sec. 209(s) of the Social Security Act. Act Sec. 122 is effective for prizes and awards granted after 12-31-86.

[¶112] State and Local Sales Taxes Aren't Deductible. Effective for tax years beginning on or after 1-1-87, the deduction for state and local sales taxes is repealed. Such taxes incurred in connection with the acquisition or disposition of business or investment property are added to basis or reduce the amount realized.

Act Sec. 134 amends Sec. 164, relating to deduction of taxes, effective as shown above.

[¶113] Nondeductible Medical Expense Floor Increased. The new law increases the nondeductible floor beneath medical expenses from 5% to 7.5% of adjusted gross income, starting with the 1987 tax year.

Accommodating personal residence in needs of handicapped. The Committee Reports say the full cost of certain home-related capital expenditures incurred by a physically handicapped individual qualifies as a medical expense (subject to the 7.5% floor). Qualifying costs include expenditures for: (1) constructing entrance or exit ramps to the residence; (2) widening doorways at entrances or exits to the residence; (3) widening or otherwise modifying hallways and interior doorways to accommodate wheelchairs; (4) railings, support bars, or other modifications to bathrooms to accommodate handicapped individuals; (5) lowering of or other modifications to kitchen cabinets and equipment to accommodate access by handicapped individuals; and (6) adjustment of electrical outlets and fixtures.

NOTE: As a general rule, the cost of a medically related home improvement counts as a medical deduction only to the extent the cost exceeds the increase in the home's value as a result of the improvement. Under the new law, the increase in the home's value as a result of qualifying improvements is deemed to be zero.

Act Sec. 133 amends Sec. 213(a), relating to medical expenses, effective for tax years beginning after 12-31-86.

[¶114] Deduction for Adoption Expenses Repealed. The new law repeals the itemized deduction of up to $1,500 for adoption expenses for children with special needs and replaces it with an expansion of the Adoption Assistance Program under Title IV-E of the Social Security Act [see ¶1711].

Act Sec. 135(a) repeals Sec. 222, relating to adoption expenses. Act Sec. 135(b) redesignates Sec. 223 as Sec. 220 and amends the table of sections for part VII of subchapter B of chapter 1. Act Sec. 135 is effective for tax years beginning on or after 1-1-87.

[¶115] Housing Allowances for Ministers and Military Personnel. The new law provides that the receipt of a tax-free parsonage housing allowance or an off-base military housing allowance does not cause the loss of deductions for home-mortgage interest and property taxes.

Act Sec. 144 adds new Sec. 265(6) effective for tax years before, on, or after 12-31-86.

[¶116] Major Changes for Moving Expense Deduction. Effective for the 1987 tax year, reimbursed and unreimbursed moving expenses migrate "below the line"—that is, they are deductible from AGI to arrive at taxable income. The changes apply to self-employeds as well as employees. Under current law, all eligible moving expenses—reimbursed and unreimbursed—are deducted above the line.

The new itemized deduction for moving expenses is *not* subject to a 2%-of-AGI floor [¶128]. A taxpayer who claims the standard deduction and does not itemize forfeits the deduction for moving expenses.

Act Sec. 132(c) amends Sec. 62 effective for tax years beginning after 12-31-86.

[¶117] Major Crackdown on T&E Expenses. The new law makes sweeping changes in the tax rules for business travel and entertainment expenses, effective for the 1987 tax year.

• A business meal is deductible only if it is "directly related" or "associated with" the active conduct of a taxpayer's trade or business. In other words, you must talk business at the table or have the meal before or after a substantial and bona fide business discussion. Under prior law, a "quiet business meal"—one held in an atmosphere conducive to business—was deductible even though business was not actually discussed [¶118].

• As a general rule, the deduction for business meals and business entertainment is limited to 80% of cost. The new rule also applies to meals consumed while away from home overnight on business [¶119].

• There are new limits on business-entertainment deductions for "skyboxes" at sports events [¶120].

• Deductions for tickets to entertainment events are generally limited to 80% of face value [¶121].

• Deductions for each day of business travel by luxury water transport are limited to twice the highest domestic federal per-diem reimbursement rate [¶122].

• Unreimbursed employee expenses for business travel, transportation, and entertainment become miscellaneous itemized deductions subject to a 2%-of-AGI "floor" [¶128].

Other travel crackdowns. Expenses for travel as a form of education [¶123] and certain types of charitable travel [¶124] are nondeductible. Finally, the new law eliminates deductions for attending investment-related seminars and conventions [¶125].

[¶118] No More Deductions for Quiet Business Meals. Under prior law, a taxpayer could deduct the cost of a meal with a business associate or client as long as the meal took place in an atmosphere conducive to business discussions. There was no requirement that business be discussed at the table. Effective for tax years beginning after 12-31-86, the new law eliminates the deduction for such "quiet business meals." Under the new law, a business meal, like business entertainment, is deductible (subject to the new 80% rule) only if it is "directly related to" or "associated with" the active conduct of a taxpayer's trade or business.

Directly related. In general, a business meal or business entertainment is "directly related" if four conditions are met:

• The taxpayer has more than a general expectation of deriving income, or a specific business benefit, from the meal or entertainment. However, the taxpayer is not required to show that income or a specific business benefit actually resulted.

• The taxpayer did in fact engage in business discussions during the meal or entertainment (or if he didn't, it was for reasons beyond his control).

• The principal nature of the expense was the active conduct of the taxpayer's trade or business.

- The meal or entertainment expense was for the taxpayer, his business guest or guests, and their spouses.

Example (1): Jack Arnold's company supplies computer products to Big Manufacturing Company. In 1987, Arnold has lunch with Big's head of purchasing as a way of keeping in touch with an important source of business. Result: The cost of the meal is not deductible (it would have been under the "quiet business meal" rule).

Example (2): Same facts as before, except that Arnold makes the lunch appointment to make a sales pitch about a new line of computer equipment. Result: The cost of the meal is deductible, subject to the new 80% rule [¶119].

Food and beverages consumed by a taxpayer while on travel status is considered a business meal that is directly related to the taxpayer's trade or business [see ¶119].

Associated with. A meal or entertainment is deductible if it directly precedes or follows a substantial and bona fide business (or practice) related discussion. The business discussion (or negotiation, transaction, conference, etc.) must be substantial in relation to the meal or entertainment. If the taxpayer's business guest is from out of town, the meal or entertainment can take place the day before or after the business discussion.

Additional requirements. The cost of a business meal, like the cost of business entertainment, is not deductible to the extent it is "lavish and extravagant" under the circumstances. And the cost of beverages and food is deductible as a business meal only if the taxpayer (or his representative) is present at the meal. The representative can be the taxpayer's employee, or an independent contractor acting on his behalf.

For example, the cost of food and beverages is not deductible as a business meal if one of the parties to a contract negotiation buys dinner for the other parties but doesn't attend the meal. It makes no difference that the other parties discuss business while they break bread.

The Committee Reports say the presence requirement is met if the taxpayer's independent contractor, such as an attorney or accountant, is present at the meal. The independent contractor must be someone who renders significant services on behalf of the taxpayer (other than attending meals on the taxpayer's behalf or providing services relating to the meal) and attends the meal to perform those services.

Example: Recreational Co. retains Attorney Adams to represent it in acquiring Accessories, Ltd. Adams and representatives of Accessories attend a dinner to discuss the acquisition and Recreational foots the bill. Result: Recreational can deduct the cost of the bill (subject to the 80% rule, see ¶119).

Suppose neither the taxpayer nor his representative attends the meal. Is the entire cost nondeductible? No. The taxpayer can claim the expense as a business gift. However, the deduction is limited to $25 per recipient per year. There's no requirement that a taxpayer be present at the time a business gift is made.

Act Sec. 142(a) amends Sec. 274(e), adds new Sec. 274(k), and makes other technical and conforming amendments to Sec. 274, effective for tax years beginning after 12-31-86.

[¶119] New 80% Rule for Business Meals and Entertainment. Effective for the 1987 tax year, the deduction for otherwise allowable business meals and business entertainment is limited to 80% of cost. The new rule applies also to (1) meals while away from home overnight on business, and (2) meals provided by employers to employees (but see exceptions, below). Meals consumed during a job-related move are affected as well.

Besides meals and entertainment, expenses subject to the 80% rule include taxes and tips related to the meal or entertainment and other related expenses (e.g., nightclub cover charges, room rental for cocktail party, and parking at the theater or sports arena). Transportation to and from the business meal or entertainment is not subject to the 80% rule.

Example: Tom Burke pays a $10 cab fare to meet his client for dinner at Sam's Place. The bill comes to $100 plus $6 tax and a $15 tip. Burke's deduction is $106.80. That's 80% of $121, plus the $10 cab fare.

Meals while on travel status. A taxpayer may deduct 80% of the cost of meals consumed while he is away from home overnight on business. Being on travel status automatically qualifies meals as being directly related to the taxpayer's trade or business, *but only if the taxpayer eats alone,* or eats with non-business-connected persons and claims a deduction for his meal only. Apparently, if a taxpayer on travel status has a meal with a business client or associate, he can deduct 80% of the cost only if the meal is directly related to or associated with his trade or business.

Example: Ted Smith, a Washington-based lawyer, flies to Los Angeles on business. If he eats lunch alone, 80% of the cost is deductible. But suppose he invites a client or business associate to lunch as a goodwill gesture and picks up the tab. Apparent result: A zero deduction for the cost of Smith's meal and his client's meal. Reason: The meal was not directly related to or associated with his trade or business.

OBSERVATION: From the tax viewpoint, it's preferable to eat alone while you're on travel status. This way, you don't have to cope with the new, tough deduction standards that apply to business meals.

Reimbursed expenses. If a taxpayer is reimbursed for the cost of business meals or entertainment (and makes an adequate accounting), the 80% rule applies to the one who makes the reimbursement, not the taxpayer.

> **Example:** During tax year 1987, Bill Pace, an executive with ABC Corp., spends $2,000 on business-related meals and entertainment. Bill makes a complete accounting of his expenses to ABC and is reimbursed in full. Result: ABC may deduct $1,600 of the reimbursement. Bill does not have to report the expense or the reimbursement on his tax return [see ¶128].

Per-diem arrangements. An employer may reimburse employees for away-from-home travel at a fixed per-diem rate. If the reimbursement does not exceed the government-approved maximum, the expenses are deemed accounted for if the employee (1) keeps a record of the time, place, and business purpose of his expenses, and (2) gives the same information to the employer. The employee is not required to keep track of actual expenses for travel, lodging, or meals. (Note: More than 10% owners must keep complete records, including the amount of each expense.)

In general, an employer may deduct only 80% of its reimbursement for away-from-home meals. But if the employee isn't required to keep track of meal expenses, how will the employer know what part of the per diem is subject to the 80% rule?

Probable result: As long as the per diem doesn't exceed the government maximum (currently $75), the employer will continue to deduct 100% of its reimbursement. An analogy can be made to the new rules for business travel by luxury water transport [¶122]. The 80% rule is not applied if the cost of on-board meals is not separately stated or clearly identifiable. The same rule should hold true for per-diem reimbursement arrangements.

Interplay of 80% rule and other limitations. In general, the 80% rule is imposed *after* application of limits imposed by Secs. 162 and 274 (e.g., disallowance of lavish and extravagant expenses), but *before* application of the new 2% floor for "second tier" miscellaneous itemized deductions [¶128].

> **Example:** During tax year 1987, Bob Smith, an employee, incurs $1,000 of business entertainment expenses for which he is not reimbursed. Of the total $1,000 expense, $200 is deemed lavish and extravagant. Smith's AGI is $50,000 and he has $500 of other "second tier" miscellaneous itemized deductions. Here's how he figures his deduction:

> Total business entertainment expense.................$1,000
> Less amount deemed lavish and extravagant..........(200)
> _____
> 800
> Less 20% reduction ....(160)
> _____
> 640

Plus other "second tier" miscellaneous
itemized deductions 500
                                                    ─────
                                                    1,140
Less 2% of adjusted gross income .... (1,000)
                                                    ─────
Deductible amount .... $ 140

A special rule applies for business travel by luxury water transport [see ¶122]. If the cost of meals and entertainment is separately stated, then the 80% rule is applied *before* computation of the new deduction limit on luxury water transport expenses.

Exceptions to 80% rule. Expenses that fall in the following categories are not subject to the 80% rule and are deductible in full:

• Amounts treated as compensation: The full value of the benefit must be treated as compensation to the recipients, whether or not they are employees.

• De minimis fringe benefits: These include items excludable under Sec. 132 as a subsidized eating facility or a de minimis fringe (e.g., holiday gifts of turkeys, hams, etc.).

• Employer-provided recreation: This consists of amounts paid for recreational, social, or similar activities or employee events (e.g., holiday parties or summer outings).

• Items made available to the public as samples or promotional material.

• Meals and entertainment sold to customers: The taxpayer must sell the item in a bona fide transaction for adequate and full consideration. For example, a restaurant can deduct the full cost of the meals it supplies to patrons.

• Sports tickets: Expenses to a sports event, to the extent otherwise allowable as a business deduction, are deductible in full if three conditions are met: (1) the event's primary purpose is to benefit a Sec. 501(c)(3) charity, (2) the entire net proceeds must go to the charity, and (3) the event uses volunteers to perform substantially all the event's work.

This exception covers the entire cost of a ticket package that includes seating at the event and related services, such as parking, use of entertainment areas, contestant positions, and meals furnished at and as part of the event. What's more, the special break applies to a charity golf outing even if the tournament offers prizes to participating golfers or uses paid concessionaires or security personnel.

SCHOOL GAMES HIT: Tickets to high school or college football or basketball games or other similar scholastic events are *not* covered by the exception. According to the Committee Reports, these games generally flunk the volunteers test—when the institutions (or parties

¶119

acting on their behalf) pay individuals to perform such services as coaching or recruiting.

- Qualifying banquet meetings during 1987 and 1988. There is a full deduction during 1987 and 1988 for the cost of a meal that is provided as an integral part of a qualified banquet meeting, provided charges for the meal are not separately stated.

The two-year reprieve ends at the close of 1988. Starting 1-1-89, qualified banquet meeting meals are subject to the 20% disallowance rule in the same way as other meals.

A qualified banquet meeting is a convention, seminar, annual meeting, or similar business program that includes the meal. For the exception to apply, the banquet meeting must pass a three-step test: First, more than 50% of the participants at the meeting are away from home—that is, their travel expenses are deductible under the "overnight" rule; second, at least 40 persons attend the banquet meeting; and third, the meal is part of the banquet meeting and includes a speaker.

Act Sec. 142(b), adds new Sec. 274(n), relating to additional restrictions on expenses for meals, travel, and entertainment, effective for tax years beginning after 12-31-86.

[¶120] Skybox Rentals. A business may entertain its clients and customers by letting them use its leased skybox at a sports arena. Under prior law, the cost of the skybox was deductible if the entertainment was "directly related to" or "associated with" the taxpayer's business. Reason: Rented skyboxes were not considered to be nondeductible entertainment facilities.

The new law disallows part of the deduction for skyboxes that are rented for more than one event. The disallowance is phased in over a period of three years.

What is a skybox? A skybox is defined in the Committee Reports as a private luxury box or other facility at a sports arena that is separate from other seating and is available at a higher price (counting rental costs and charges for food and beverages) than other seating. The new rules come into play only if a skybox is rented at a sports arena for more than one event. For example, a skybox rental for two football games in the same stadium is covered by the new rules. Also covered: rentals by a taxpayer (or a related party) of different skyboxes in the same stadium, or reciprocal arrangements by two or more taxpayers to share skyboxes.

How the disallowance rule works. As under prior law, the taxpayer must use the skybox for "directly related" or "associated with" entertainment. If this condition is satisfied, the taxpayer's deduction is limited to the sum of the face value of the nonluxury box seat tickets for the seats in the leased skybox. All the seats in the skybox are counted, even though the box is not fully occupied during the event. However, the taxpayer may not deduct the excess cost of the skybox. The rule is phased in as follows: one-third of the excess cost is disallowed in 1987, and two-thirds is disallowed in 1988. The entire excess cost is disallowed for 1989 and later years.

The taxpayer may also deduct stated charges for food and beverages under the general rules for business entertainment.

REMINDER: The deduction for skybox seats, food, and beverages is limited to 80% of cost [¶119].

Example: In 1987, XYZ Corp. pays $6,000 to rent a 10-seat skybox at City Stadium for three football games. Nonluxury box seats at each event range in cost from $25 to $35 a seat. In March, an XYZ representative and five clients of XYZ use the skybox for the first game. The entertainment follows a bona-fide business discussion (e.g., merger talks), and XYZ incurs an $85 expense for food and beverages during the game. Although the method of allocation is yet to be determined, XYZ Corp. will likely compute its deduction for the first sports event as follows:

(1)	Food and beverages	$ 85
(2)	Deduction for seats ($35 × 10 seats)	350
(3)	Excess cost of skybox	

$6,000/3 events	$2,000	
Cost of seats	(350)	
Excess cost	1,650	
33.33% disallowance for 1987	(550)	
	$1,100	1,100
		$1,535
		×.80
Deduction for first event		$1,228

WATCH THIS: The Committee Reports say that the face-value limitation can't be circumvented through an inflated price for nonluxury box seats.

Suppose City Stadium in our example tries to boost the deduction for box rentals by reserving and charging $50 a seat for a small group of seats not significantly better than the $35 seats. Since the $50 cost is inflated, it is disregarded.

Act Sec. 142(b) adds Sec. 274(l)(2), relating to skybox rentals, generally effective for tax years beginning after 12-31-86. There is a phase-in for tax years beginning in 1987 and 1988.

〔¶121〕 Ticket Deductions Limited to Face Value. The new law limits deductions for tickets to entertainment events to 80% of their face value, which includes tax.

The face-value limitation bars payments to

- a scalper for a ticket, even if not otherwise disallowed under Sec. 162(a)(2) as an illegal payment; and
- a legitimate ticket agency for the part of the cost in excess of the ticket's face value.

Charitable fund raisers' exception. The full deduction remains available for tickets for sporting events that are considered charitable fund raisers. A qualifying event must turn over the entire net proceeds to a charity and use volunteers for substantially all the work performed in carrying out the event. [See ¶119].

> **Example:** Delphic Information Systems pays a scalper $200 for two $40 tickets to a Broadway play. The tickets are used for entertainment "associated with" the active conduct of Delphic's business [¶118]. The deduction for the tickets is limited to $64. That's the $80 face value of the tickets times 80%.

> **COMMENT:** Local law allows legitimate ticket agencies to include their fees in the price they charge for tickets to plays, ball games, and other events. Mandating like-treatment for scalpers and agencies may adversely affect the ability of agencies to sell tickets to businesses.

Act Sec. 142(b) adds new Sec. 274(l)(1), relating to entertainment tickets, effective for tax years beginning after 12-31-86.

〔¶122〕 New Deduction Limit for Luxury Water Travel. The new law generally limits deductions for business travelers who use ocean liners, cruise ships, or other forms of "luxury water transportation." There is no exemption for someone who uses luxury water transportation because of an illness or disability that rules out travel on an airplane.

The deduction per day on the boat cannot exceed twice the highest per-diem amount paid by the U.S. government to traveling employees in the coterminous U.S., disregarding any limited special exception, such as a higher limit authorized only for high-ranking executive personnel.

> **Example:** Al Lang has to make a New York-to-London business trip. To ease the strain of travel across the Atlantic, he undertakes a six-day voyage on the S.S. Luxurious. The applicable per-diem amount is $75. Therefore, the per-diem-limitation allows Lang to deduct no more than $900 ($150 a day × 6 days).

The cost of on-board meals and entertainment is subject to the new 80% rule if these charges are separately stated. And the 80% rule is applied before the new per-diem limit. However, if the cost of on-board meals and entertainment is *not* separately stated and is not clearly identifiable, then the 80% rule does not apply. The taxpayer may claim a deduction equal to twice the applicable Federal per-diem limit.

Exceptions. The new law expressly bars application of the per-diem rules to expenses that are allocable to business-related conventions, seminars, or other meetings on cruise ships. Therefore, the new law leaves unchanged the Sec. 274(h)(2) rules that allow deductions of up to $2,000 for certain cruise-ship conventions, provided the ship is a U.S. flagship and all ports of call are in the U.S. or its possessions.

In addition, the exceptions from the water-travel per-diem-limitation are the same as the exceptions from the 20% disallowance rule [¶119].

Act Sec. 142(b) adds new Sec. 274(m)(1), relating to luxury water transportation, effective for tax years beginning after 12-31-86.

[¶123]   Travel as a Form of Education Is Nondeductible. Beginning with the 1987 tax year, the new law bars any deductions for travel expenses by teachers and others when their travel is a form of education. But the law retains deductions for travel that is necessary to engage in activities that give rise to deductible education.

> **Example (1):** Jack Peters is a French teacher who uses a sabbatical leave from his school for a journey to France to improve his understanding of its language and culture. His travel outlays are nondeductible.

> **Example (2):** Alexander Verne, who is employed by a school to teach courses on French literature, goes to Paris to do library research that cannot be done elsewhere, or to take courses available only at the Sorbonne. Assuming his nontravel research or courses are deductible, his travel costs are also deductible.

> **NOTE:** Just because Verne steers clear of the educational-travel prohibition does not mean he gets to fully deduct his travel. The travel deduction is trimmed by these new limitations:

• Meals must be reduced by 20% [see ¶119]; and
• Remaining unreimbursed away-from-home travel expenses are allowable only to the extent they exceed 2% of his adjusted gross income [see ¶128].

Act Sec. 142(b) adds new Sec. 274(m)(2), relating to travel as a form of education, effective for tax years beginning after 12-31-86.

[¶124]   Charitable Deduction Denied for Certain Travel. The new law ends deductions for "charitable" trips that are disguised vacations. Charitable deductions will now be limited for travel expenses (including meals and lodging) incurred by volunteer workers who perform services away from their homes on behalf of charities. The deductions are allowable only if there is "no significant element of personal pleasure, recreation, or vacation" in the away-from-home travel.

The travel-expense disallowance rules apply to payments made directly by the taxpayer of his or her own expenses or of an associated person, such as a member of the taxpayer's family, as well as indirectly through reimbursement by the charity. A reimbursement includes any arrangement for the taxpayer to make a payment to the charity and its payment of the taxpayer's travel outlays. To stop an end run around the disallowance rules, the new law also bars reciprocal arrangements, where two unrelated taxpayers pay each other's expenses or members of a group contribute to a fund that pays for all of their expenses.

Exception. The Committee Reports say the deduction remains available for payment by the taxpayer of expenses for third parties who are participants in the charitable activity.

> **Example:** Virginia Hickey, a Girl Scout leader, takes her scouts on a camping trip. She gets a deduction for her payment of expenses for girls who belong to the group and are unrelated to her, but not for expenses for her own children.

You don't lose a deduction for your own expenses merely because you enjoy taking care of chores for a charity.

For example, what about Hickey's own expenses? They are deductible, provided she is on duty in a genuine and substantial sense throughout the trip, even if she enjoys the trip or supervising children. But her expenses are nondeductible if she (1) only has nominal duties relating to the performance of services for the group or (2) for significant portions of the trip is not required to perform services.

No effect on other deductions. The disallowance rules do not apply to deductions for travel (other than for charitable travel) on behalf of a charitable organization. These rules, for example, don't affect the deductibility of a Sec. 162 business expense incurred by an employee of a charity.

Act Sec. 142(d) adds new Sec. 170(k), relating to charitable contributions for certain travel expenses, and makes technical and conforming amendments to Sec. 170, effective for tax years beginning after 12-31-86.

[¶125] Investment Seminars Lose Tax Luster. The new law disallows deductions for costs of attending conventions, seminars, or similar meetings for investment purposes unrelated to carrying on a trade or business. The disallowance is aimed solely at expenses that serve a Sec. 212 purpose, such as production of income, not those that serve a Sec. 162 trade-or-business purpose.

Example: International Investors holds a convention at which stock market investors pay to discuss strategies with representatives of brokerage firms and listen to presentations from executives about their companies. Result: The Sec. 212 restriction bars deductions by the investors for their expenses, but doesn't affect the deductibility under Sec. 162 of expenses by stock brokers and others at the convention for business reasons. Among the expenses disallowed are travel to the convention site, attendance fees, and meals, lodging, and local travel while attending.

Act Sec. 142(c) adds new Sec. 274(h)(7), relating to deductions for seminars, and makes technical and conforming amendments to Sec. 274(h), effective for tax years beginning after 12-31-86.

〖¶126〗 Major Changes for Miscellaneous Itemized Deductions and Employee Business Expenses. Effective for the 1987 tax year, the rules for miscellaneous itemized deductions and employee business expenses are changed in two fundamental ways:

• The new law creates two tiers of miscellaneous itemized deductions. Those deductions placed in the first tier are not subject to a percent-of-AGI floor. Deductions in the second tier are deductible only to the extent they cumulatively exceed 2% of adjusted gross income.

• Unreimbursed employee business expenses become "second tier" itemized deductions. In other words, they are subject to the new 2%-of-AGI "floor" and are not deductible at all if the taxpayer does not itemize deductions.

Under prior law, all miscellaneous expenses were treated alike and were not subject to a percent-of-AGI floor. And employee business expenses such as unreimbursed travel and transportation costs were deducted "above the line." In other words, they were adjustments to arrive at AGI and were available whether or not the taxpayer itemized other deductions.

〖¶127〗 'First Tier' Miscellaneous Itemized Deductions. The following expenses are deductible in full by taxpayers who itemize:

• Impairment-related work expenses of handicapped individuals [new Sec. 67(d)].

• Federal estate tax on income in respect of a decedent [Sec. 691(c)].

• Certain adjustments when a taxpayer restores amounts held under a claim of right [Sec. 1341].

• Amortizable bond premium [Sec. 171].

• Gambling losses to the extent of gambling winnings [Sec. 165(d)].

• Deductions allowable in connection with personal property used in a short sale.

Impairment-related work expenses are expenses of a handicapped individual [as defined in Sec. 190(b)(3)] for attendant care services at the individual's place of employment, or other expenses necessary for the individual to work, which are deductible under Sec. 162.

Other expenses that are deductible without regard to a percent-of-AGI floor include certain terminated annuity payments [new Sec. 72(b)(3)] and certain costs of cooperative housing corporations [Sec. 216].

[¶128] **'Second Tier' Miscellaneous Itemized Deductions.** Expenses in this category are deductible only to the extent they cumulatively exceed 2% of adjusted gross income. There are two groups of expenses subject to the new floor:

(1) *Miscellaneous expenses allowed under prior law.* This group consists of old-law miscellaneous expenses *other than* those expenses placed in the first-tier class of miscellaneous itemized deductions. Beginning with tax year 1987, all of the following expenses are affected by the new rule:

Employee Expenses

- Dues to professional societies
- Employment-related education
- Malpractice insurance premiums
- Expenses of looking for a job, including employment agency fee
- Cost of having resume prepared
- Office-at-home expenses
- Subscriptions to professional journals and magazines
- Work clothes and uniforms
- Union dues and fees
- 80% of unreimbursed business-entertainment expenses

Expenses for Production of Income

- Legal and accounting fees
- Custodial fees related to income-producing property
- Fees paid to an IRA custodian
- Fees paid to collect interest or dividends
- Hobby expenses up to hobby income
- Investment counsel fees
- Rental cost of safe deposit box used to store non-tax-exempt securities

- Fees paid for investment counsel
- Tax counsel and assistance
- Cost of tax services, periodicals, return preparation manuals, and similar expenses related to the determination, collection, or refund of a tax
- Appraisal fees establishing a casualty loss or charitable contribution

YEAR-END ACTION: Taxpayers should consider accelerating second-tier miscellaneous expenses. For example, if an individual is seeking investment counsel or tax-oriented estate planning advice, he or she would be wise to incur the expense in 1986 rather than 1987.

(2) *Employee business expenses.* Under prior law, employee travel and transportation expenses were "above the line" deductions *whether or not* the employee was reimbursed for the expenses by his employer. Since they were adjustments to arrive at AGI, the deduction was available even if the employee did not itemize deductions. An employee's expenses for business entertainment were claimed above the line to the extent of the employer's reimbursement. Excess entertainment expenses were deducted below the line (on Schedule A, as miscellaneous itemized deductions).

Under the new law, travel and transportation expenses up to the amount of the reimbursement continue to be claimed above the line. However, expenses in excess of any reimbursement become below-the-line miscellaneous deductions and are subject to the new 2% floor. The same holds true for an employee's business-entertainment expenses. Expenses up to the amount of any reimbursement are claimed above the line; excess expenses are claimed below the line and are subject to the 2% floor.

The following chart sorts things out. It shows how an employee handles his business-connected travel, transportation, and entertainment expenses under the old law and the new law:

EMPLOYEE BUSINESS EXPENSES

TYPE OF EXPENSE	PRIOR LAW	NEW LAW
Travel & Transportation		
(1) Employee is fully reimbursed and makes an adequate accounting.*	Neither expenses nor reimbursements are reported on the return.	Same as under prior law.
(2) Employee is fully reimbursed but does not make an adequate accounting.*	Reimbursement reported as income; expenses reported above the line.	Same as under prior law, but meal expenses while on travel status subject to new 80% rule [¶119].**

¶128

TYPE OF EXPENSE	PRIOR LAW	NEW LAW
(3) Expenses exceed reimbursements.	Reimbursement reported as income; all expenses claimed above the line.	Reimbursement reported as income. Expenses up to reimbursement claimed above the line; excess expenses claimed below the line, subject to 2% floor. 80% rule applies to unreimbursed meals.
(4) No employer reimbursement.	Expenses claimed above the line.	Expenses claimed below the line, subject to 2% floor. Meal expense subject to 80% rule.

Business Entertainment

(5) Reimbursement equals expenses and employee accounts for expenses.	Same as Item (1), above.	Same as Item (1), above.
(6) Reimbursement equals expense, but no accounting by employee	Same as Item (2), above.	Same as Item (2), above. 80% rule applies to expenses.**
(7) Expenses exceed reimbursement.	Reimb. reported as income. Expenses up to reimb. reported above the line; expenses in excess of reimb. reported below the line.	Same as under prior law, except ded'n for unreimbursed expenses limited to 80% of cost [¶119]; and expenses reported below the line are subject to the 2% floor.
(8) No employer reimbursement.	Expenses claimed below the line.	Expenses claimed below the line, but subject to 80% rule and 2% floor.

---

*An adequate accounting to the employer generally consists of the time, date, place, business purpose and amount of expense (or mileage, in the case of car travel). For travel and transportation expenses, accounting is simplified if reimbursement does not exceed Government-approved per-diem or per-mile rate. Expenses for business travel, transportation, and entertainment are deductible by the employee only if he or she has kept the proper records.

**If the employee does not account for expenses, employer deducts 100% of reimbursement as compensation, and employee is subject to 80% rule.

What about outside salespersons? Under current law, an outside salesperson claims all business expenses above the line—entertainment as well as travel and transportation. Outside salespersons lose this preferential treatment under the new law. In other words, starting in 1987, they are in the same boat as regular employees.

Application of the 2% floor. The 2% floor comes into play after all other deduction limitations are taken into account.

Example: During tax year 1987, Ted Smith, an employee of XYZ Corp., incurs $2,000 of unreimbursed business-entertainment expenses. Smith's adjusted gross income for 1987 is $60,000. For simplicity, we'll assume Smith does not have other second-tier miscellaneous itemized deductions. *Result:* Smith's deduction for business entertainment is computed as follows:

Total entertainment expenses	$2,000
Less statutory 20% reduction	(400)
	$1,600
Less 2% of AGI................................	(1,200)
Net second-tier miscellaneous itemized deduction	$ 400

Entities subject to the 2% rule. The new law gives the Treasury authority to issue regs that will apply the 2% floor to pass-through entities, including mutual funds, grantor trusts, partnerships and S corporations. Estates, nongrantor trusts, cooperatives, and REITS will not be affected, however. The Treasury is also given authority to issue reporting requirements necessary to carry out this new provision.

Estates and trusts. In general, estates or trusts compute their AGI in the same way as individuals. However, expenses paid or incurred in connection with trust or estate administration that would not have been incurred had the property not been held in a trust or estate, are deductible in arriving at adjusted gross income.

Special break for performers. Effective for tax years beginning after 1986, qualifying performing artists can report their income and expenses as if they were independent contractors. Such artists will be entitled to a new above-the-line deduction for business expenses if they meet all of these conditions:

• they are employed as performing artists by two or more employers during the tax year;
• expenses relating to the profession of being a performing artist exceeded 10% of gross income attributable to services as a performing artist; and
• adjusted gross income (before deducting expenses relating to performing) does not exceed $16,000.

Act Sec. 132(a) adds new Sec. 67(a) and (b), relating to miscellaneous itemized deductions subject to 2% floor, new Sec. 67(c), relating to disallowance of indirect deduction through pass-through entity, new Sec. 67(d), relating to impairment-related work expenses of handicapped individuals, and new Sec. 67(e), relating to determination of adjusted gross income in the case of estates and trusts. Act Sec. 132(b) amends Sec. 62(2), relating to trade or business deductions of employees and certain expenses of performing artists, and adds new subsection (b) to Sec. 62, relating to definition of qualified performing artists. Act Sec. 132(d) makes a clerical amendment to the table of sections for part I of subchapter B of chapter 1. Act Sec. 132 is effective for tax years beginning after 12-31-86.

〔¶129〕 Home-Office Deduction Rules Tightened. The new law overrides two Tax Court decisions that liberalized the rules for office-at-home deductions:

The Feldman decision. As a general rule, office-at-home expenses may be deducted only if the office is used regularly and exclusively as a principal place of business or as a place to meet or deal with customers and clients. An employee who uses an office-at-home in connection with his employment qualifies for deductions only if the use of the office is for the convenience of the employer. In *Feldman* (84 TC 1), the Tax Court held that the general rule for office-at-home expenses does not apply where the office was leased by the employee to the employer.

The new law denies home-office deductions where an employee leases a portion of his or her home to the employer. Independent contractors are treated as employees and the taxpayer for whom the services are performed is treated as the employer. The new rule does not apply to deductions that would be allowed in any event (i.e., home mortgage interest [¶509] or real property taxes).

The Scott decision. Otherwise allowable office-at-home expenses are limited to the gross income derived from the business activity conducted at the home office. In Prop. Reg. Sec. 1.280A-2(i)(2)(iii), the IRS defines gross income for this purpose as gross income from the business less expenses that are not related to use of the unit itself. Such expenses consists of office supplies, postage, payments made to others, etc. In *Scott* (84 TC 683), the Tax Court rejected the IRS definition of gross income. It held that gross income is not reduced by outside expenses required for the activity.

Result: The *Scott* decision meant a taxpayer could use net losses from his home-office-business to offset other income. If a taxpayer had $2,000 of gross income from his home-office business and $2,500 of expenses related to the business (postage, office supplies, business travel), he could deduct $2,000 of his home office costs even though he had zero net income from the activity.

In essence, the new law codifies the IRS approach. Home-office deductions (other than expenses deductible in any event, such as mortgage interest and property tax) are limited to gross income reduced by all deductible expenses that are not allocable to the use of the unit itself.

> **SILVER LINING:** The new law allows taxpayers to carry forward any deductions disallowed by the gross-income limit, subject to the continuing application of the limit. Under prior law, such carryforwards were not allowed.

Act Secs. 143(b) and (c) amend Sec. 280A(c), relating to office-at-home deductions, effective for tax years beginning after 12-31-86.

〖¶130〗 Hobby Losses Rule Tightened. The new law changes the hobby losses rule so that an activity is presumed to be operated for profit, rather than as a hobby, if it is profitable in *three* out of five consecutive years (it was two out of five years under prior law). There's no change, though, in the exception for horse breeding, training, showing, or racing. These activities are presumed to be operated for profit, rather than a hobby, if profitable in two out of seven consecutive years.

Act Sec. 143(a) amends Sec. 183(d), relating to hobby losses, effective for tax years beginning after 12-31-86.

〖¶131〗 No Credit for Political Contributions. The new law repeals the credit of up to $50 ($100 on a joint return) allowed individuals for half of their contributions to political candidates and certain political campaign organizations, starting with the 1987 tax year.

Act Sec. 112(a) repeals Sec. 24, relating to contributions to candidates for public office. Act Sec. 112(b)(1) amends Sec. 527(g), relating to treatment of newsletter funds. Act Sec. 112(b)(2) amends Sec. 642(a), relating to credits against tax estates and trusts. Act Sec. 112(b)(3) amends Sec. 901(i)(3), relating to cross references. Act Sec. 112(b)(4) amends Sec. 7871(a)(6), relating to Indian tribal governments treated as States for certain purposes. Act Sec. 112(b)(5) amends the table of sections for subpart A of part IV of subchapter A of chapter 1. Act Sec. 112 is effective for tax years beginning after 12-31-86.

〖¶132〗 Charitable Gifts of Appreciated Property. In conforming the repeal of the capital gains exclusion for individuals [¶301], the new law in certain situations limits the deductible amount of contributions of appreciated capital gains property by individuals and corporations to the donor's basis in the property.

Reduction rule. A donor may elect to apply the charitable reduction rule to all contributions of capital gain property made during a tax year to which the reduction rule doesn't otherwise apply, in exchange for being able to claim a charitable deduction for up to 50% (instead of 30%) of his or her adjusted gross income. Under the new law, a donor who contributes appreciated long-term capital gain property and elects to apply the reduction rule will be able to deduct only his or her cost or basis in the property.

There's no change to the reduction rule in Sec. 170(e)(1)(A) for contributions of ordinary income property or to the exception to the reduction rule in Sec. 170(e)(5) for contributions of "qualified appreciated stock" to private nonoperating foundations.

The new law also includes a conforming amendment to Sec. 170(e)(1)(B) on certain corporate charitable contributions of appreciated property. Under present law, the deduction for corporate contributions of unrelated-use tangible personal property, or of any ap-

¶132

preciated property donated to private nonoperating foundations, is generally limited to the corporation's basis in the property plus the excludable amount of any long-term capital gain that would have been realized if the property had been sold. In conforming the repeal of the capital gains exclusion for corporations, the new law essentially limits the deductible amount of these corporate contributions to the corporation's basis in the property. No change is made to the reduction rule in Sec. 170(e)(1)(A) for contributions of ordinary income property.

Act Secs. 301 and 302, amending Secs. 170 and 1202, effective for tax years beginning after 12-31-86. Act Secs. 311 and 601 amending Secs. 11 and 1201, effective for tax years beginning on or after 7-1-87. The graduated income tax rates and the rate schedule for tax years including 7-1-87 will reflect blended rates.

[The page following this is 201.]

ACCELERATED COST RECOVERY SYSTEM AND INVESTMENT TAX CREDIT

[¶201] Overview. The new law revamps the ACRS system of depreciation that had been introduced as the key to economic expansion by the 1981 Tax Reform Act. In a word, the depreciation setup is being overhauled—and the investment tax credit is being repealed—to help pay for the dramatic reduction in personal income tax rates.

> **SOMETHING OLD, SOMETHING NEW:** The new system, which is generally effective for property placed in service after 12-31-86, retains many of the original ACRS rules. The 3, 5, 10, and 15-year classes are kept and two new classes are introduced (7 and 20-year property). There's no distinction made between new and used property and salvage value continues to be disregarded. Cars and light trucks are shifted from the 3-year to the 5-year class. Office equipment moves from the 5-year class to the 7-year class. Depreciation for property in the 3, 5, and 10-year classes is speeded up from 150% to 200% declining balance. The regular investment credit is repealed for property placed in service after 1985, but the expensing deduction is boosted from $5,000 to $10,000, effective for the 1987 tax year.

The big loser under the new ACRS setup is real estate. Both residential and nonresidential real property must be depreciated using the straight line method. The recovery period is extended to 27½ years for residential property and to 31½ years for nonresidential property.

The new law continues the old ACRS system's prohibition against component depreciation. The recovery period for an addition or improvement begins on the later of the date it is placed in service or the date the original property is placed in service. The recovery method for an addition or improvement is identical to the method used for the underlying property. For example, assume residential rental property is placed in service during 1987. In 1990, an improvement is made to the property. The cost of the improvement is recovered over a 27½-year period beginning in 1990.

There's a new alternative depreciation system that's used to compute corporate earnings and profits and the depreciation preference subject to the alternative minimum tax. The new system is also used to depreciate property used outside of the U.S., property financed with tax-exempts or leased to tax-exempt entities, and property imported from foreign countries that maintain discriminatory trade practices.

New complications. Many taxpayers will have three sets of depreciation rules to contend with: (1) the old "useful life" system of depreciation that applies to property placed in service before 1981 (and to property covered by antichurning transactions); (2) the original ACRS setup, which applies to assets placed in service after 1980 and before 1987 (and to property covered by transition rules and a new set of antichurning rules); and (3) the new ACRS setup.

Finally, businesses will have to watch the clock when they buy depreciable assets. Reason: If more than 40% of the year's depreciable acquisitions are placed in service in the final quarter, then all non-realty assets must be depreciated using a new "mid-quarter" convention instead of the normal mid-year convention.

The new ACRS rules apply to any new or used tangible depreciable property, other than (1) property depreciated with the unit-of-production method, or any other method not expressed in a term of years (other than the retirement replacement betterment method or similar method); (2) public utility property, if a normalization method of accounting is not used; (3) any motion picture or video tape; (4) a sound recording as described in Sec. 48(r)(5); or (5) any property subject to the original ACRS rules (e.g., because of a transition or antichurning rule).

[¶202] **Asset Classes, Recovery Periods, and Depreciation Methods for Personal Property.** The cost of property (other than residential rental property and nonresidential real property) is recovered over a 3, 5, 7, 10, 15, or 20-year period, depending on the type of property. The depreciation method for property in the 3, 5, 7, and 10-year classes is 200% declining balance, with a switch to straight line to maximize the deduction. The depreciation method for 15-and 20-year property is 150% declining balance, with a switch to straight line to maximize the deduction.

3-year property. This class includes property with a 4-year-or-less midpoint life under the ADR (Asset Depreciation Range) system, *other than* cars and light-duty trucks (they are shifted to the 5-year class).

Under the ADR system, property with a midpoint life of 4 years or less includes: special handling devices for the manufacture of food and beverages; special tools and devices for the manufacture of rubber products; special tools for the manufacture of finished plastic products, fabricated metal products, or motor vehicles; and breeding hogs. Racehorses more than 2-years old when placed in service, and other horses more than 12-years old when placed in service, are included in the 3-year class.

5-year property. This class consists of property with an ADR midpoint of more than 4 years and less than 10 years. This includes assets such as computers, typewriters, copiers, duplicating equipment, heavy general purpose trucks, trailers, cargo containers and trailer-mounted containers. The new law specifically includes the following items in the 5-year class: cars, light-duty trucks, computer-based telephone central office switching equipment (assigned a new ADR midpoint of 9.5 years), semiconductor manufacturing equipment (assigned a new ADR midpoint of 5 years), renewable energy and biomass properties that are small power plant production facilities, qualified technological equipment [¶205], and equipment used with research and experimentation.

7-year property. This new class includes (1) any property with an ADR midpoint of 10 years or more and less than 16 years, and (2) property with no ADR midpoint that is not assigned to another class. Included in this class: office furniture, fixtures and equipment (was in the 5-year class), railroad track (assigned a new 10-year midpoint) and single-purpose agricultural and horticultural structures (assigned a new 15-year midpoint).

10-year property. This class includes property with an ADR midpoint of 16 years or more and less than 20 years (e.g., assets used in petroleum refining, or in the manufacture of tobacco products and certain food products).

15-year property. This class consists of property with an ADR midpoint of 20 years or more and less than 25 years. Specifically included in this class are municipal sewage treatment plants, telephone distribution plants, and comparable equipment used by non-telephone companies for the two-way exchange of voice and data communications (assigned a new 24-year ADR midpoint). "Comparable equipment" does not include cable television equipment used primarily for one-way communication.

20-year property. This new class consists of property with an ADR midpoint of 25 years and more, other than Sec. 1250 real property with an ADR midpoint of 27.5 years and more. Municipal sewers, which are assigned a 50-year midpoint, are in this class.

In the case of a short tax year, the Conference Agreement says the ACRS deduction for property in the 3, 5, 7, 10, 15, and 20 year classes is computed as if the property had been in service for half the number of months in the short tax year.

Asset reclassification. The new law gives the Treasury authority to reclassify assets to reflect their anticipated useful life and anticipated decline in value over time. Initially, the Treasury is expected to focus on assets that have no ADR midpoint, clothing held for rental, and scientific equipment.

Five-year freeze: The new law prevents the Treasury from assigning certain assets a longer recovery period than the 1986 TRA specifies. The Treasury may, however, assign a shorter recovery period to these assets. The freeze applies to the following assets, as long as they are placed in service prior to 1-1-92: horses, cars, light general purpose trucks, semiconductor manufacturing equipment, com-

¶202

puter-based telephone central office switching equipment, research and experimentation property, qualified technological equipment, renewable energy and biomass properties, railroad track, single-purpose agricultural and horticultural structures, telephone distribution plants and comparable equipment, municipal wastewater treatment plants, and municipal sewers.

The Committee Reports say that the Treasury may reclassify property affected by the freeze if the property is placed in service after 12-31-91 and before 7-1-92. However, the Treasury must notify the House Ways and Means Committee and the Senate Finance Committee of the proposed change at least six months before the change is to go into effect.

Averaging conventions and depreciation percentages. The half-year convention applies to all property assigned to the 3, 5, 7, 10, 15 or 20-year classes. All property is treated as placed in service (or disposed of) in the middle of the year. Thus, a taxpayer gets a half-year of depreciation when he places an asset in service and a half-year of depreciation when the property is disposed of or retired from service. Salvage value is ignored. The original ACRS system had statutory depreciation percentages. The new system prescribes the depreciation methods we've listed and does not provide recovery tables.

SPECIAL HELP: The following table was prepared by the Prentice-Hall Editorial Staff. It lists recovery percentages for property in the 3, 5, 7, 10, 15, and 20-year classes. Percentages are based on the mathematical application of the prescribed depreciation methods. (There are no official recovery percentages at this time.)

Annual Recovery (Percent of Original Depreciable Basis)

Recov-ery Year	3-Year Class (200% d.b.)	5-Year Class (200% d.b.)	7-Year Class (200% d.b.)	10-Year Class (200% d.b.)	15-Year Class (150% d.b.)	20-Year Class (150% d.b.)
1	33.00	20.00	14.28	10.00	5.00	3.75
2	45.00	32.00	24.49	18.00	9.50	7.22
3	15.00*	19.20	17.49	14.40	8.55	6.68
4	7.00	11.52*	12.49	11.52	7.69	6.18
5		11.52	8.93*	9.22	6.93	5.71
6		5.76	8.93	7.37	6.23	5.28
7			8.93	6.55*	5.90*	4.89
8			4.46	6.55	5.90	4.52
9				6.55	5.90	4.46*
10				6.55	5.90	4.46
11				3.29	5.90	4.46
12					5.90	4.46
13					5.90	4.46
14					5.90	4.46
15					5.90	4.46
16					3.00	4.46
17						4.46

Recovery Year	3-Year Class (200% d.b.)	5-Year Class (200% d.b.)	7-Year Class (200% d.b.)	10-Year Class (200% d.b.)	15-Year Class (150% d.b.)	20-Year Class (150% d.b.)
18						4.46
19						4.46
20						4.46
21						2.25

*Year of switch to straight line to maximize depreciation deduction.

OBSERVATION: The original ACRS system gave the taxpayer a half-year of depreciation for the tax year he placed an asset in service, but allowed him to recover the balance of depreciable basis over the years remaining in the property's recovery period. There was no recovery allowance for the year of disposition or retirement. Thus, conceptually, the taxpayer was considered to have placed property in service at the beginning of the recovery period, but was allowed only a half-year's worth of depreciation for the placed-in-service year. By contrast, the new system views property as placed in service in the middle of the first year. For example, the statutory recovery period for 3-year property begins in the middle of the year an asset is placed in service and ends three years later.

In practical terms, the new rule means taxpayers must wait an extra year to recover the cost of depreciable assets—the actual writeoff periods are 4, 6, 8, 11, 16, and 21 years.

Another difference. Under the original ACRS system, there was no recovery deduction in the year of an asset's disposition or sale. The new system gives the taxpayer a half year of depreciation for the year of disposition or sale.

Special election. Taxpayers may elect to recover the cost of assets placed in service after 7-31-86 and before 1-1-87, using the modified ACRS rules. The election may not be used for property covered under the transition rules [¶209]. The Committee Reports indicate that the election may be made on an asset-by-asset basis. The election makes sense for assets that stay in the 3-, 5-, or 10-year recovery class under the modified ACRS setup. Reason: The modified ACRS rules produce a larger recovery deduction in the early years than the original ACRS rules did. However, the election shouldn't be used for assets that are shifted into a longer recovery class under the modified ACRS setup.

Example (1): In October 1986, Ace Corp. buys and places into service $300,000 of assets that qualify as 3-year property under the original and the modified ACRS rules. Without the special election, Ace's ACRS deductions are $75,000 for the first year (25%), $114,000 for the second (38%), and $111,000 (37%) for the third. With the special election (unless a transitional rule applies, see ¶209), depreciation deductions are $99,000 for the first year (33%), $135,000 for the second (45%), $45,000 for the third year (15%) and $21,000 for the fourth year (7%).

¶202

Example (2): Barry Stanford buys a car in November, 1986. Lori Mack buys a car in February, 1987. Both cars cost $10,000 and are used 100% for business.

Result: Under the original ACRS rules, Stanford's car is 3-year recovery property. His depreciation is figured from statutory tables. His writeoffs are $2,500, for 1986; $3,800, for 1987; and $3,700, for 1988.

Mack's depreciation is figured using a five-year recovery period and 200% declining-balance with a switch to straight-line. Her writeoffs are $2,000 for 1987; $3,200 for 1988; $1,920 for 1989; $1,152 for 1990; $1,152 for 1991; and $576 for 1992.

> **NOTE:** If Stanford used the special election for post-7-31-86 assets, his ACRS deductions would be the same as Mack's.

Example (3): Widget Corp. buys a new machine in January 1986 and January 1987. Each costs $100,000 and each machine is 5-year property under the old and new law.

Result: Widget's depreciable basis is $100,000. Widget's depreciation deductions for the 1986 acquisition, figured from statutory tables, are $15,000, for 1986; $22,000, for 1987; and $21,000, for 1988, 1989, and 1990.

Widget's depreciation for the 1987 acquisition is figured using 200% declining-balance with a switch to straight-line. A half-year convention is used. Depreciation writeoffs are $20,000 for 1987; $32,000 for 1988; $19,200 for 1989; $11,520 for 1990; $11,520 for 1991; and $5,760 for 1992.

New dollar caps for 'luxury' autos. Sec. 280F places dollar limits on the amount of annual depreciation that may be claimed for "luxury" business autos. For autos placed in service after 4-2-85, first-year depreciation was capped at $3,200 and depreciation in each succeeding year was capped at $4,800. Under prior law's three-year ACRS setup, the caps came into play when a car's cost exceeded $12,800 [$3,200 + ($4,800 × 2)]. The new law adjusts the dollar caps on depreciation so that the price range of cars affected by the caps remains roughly the same. Thus, effective for autos placed in service after 12-31-86, the dollar caps are $2,560 for the first year, $4,100 for the second year, $2,450 for the third year, and $1,475 for each succeeding year. Result: Depreciation deductions that may be claimed on business autos are as follows (percentages are applied to original depreciable basis):

First year	Lesser of $2,560 or 20%
Second year	Lesser of $4,100 or 32%
Third year	Lesser of $2,450 or 19.20%
Fourth year	Lesser of $1,475 or 11.52%
Fifth year	Lesser of $1,475 or 11.52%

Sixth year .... Lesser of $1,475 or 5.76%

Any depreciable basis remaining after six years is recovered at a rate that cannot exceed $1,475 a year.

Example (1): In January 1987, ABC Corp. places in service a $12,900 car and a $15,000 car. The business/investment use percentage of each car is 100%. Results:

	Car (1) Depreciation	Car (2) Depreciation
1987	$2,560	$2,560
1988	4,100	4,100
1989	2,450	2,450
1990	1,475	1,475
1991	1,475	1,475
1992	743	864
1993	97	1,475
1994	-0-	601
Total	*$12,900*	*$15,000*

The dollar caps must be reduced if business/investment use is less than 100%.

Example (2): A self-employed taxpayer buys a $20,000 car in April 1987. He uses the car 70% for business, 30% for personal driving. Result: His depreciation deduction for 1987 is $1,792 (lesser of $2,560 × 70% business use, or 20% of $14,000).

If qualified business use in the placed-in-service year does not exceed 50%, then the car's basis must be recovered over five years using the straight-line method and the half-year convention. What's more, depreciation is limited to the dollar caps adjusted for business/investment use percentage). If qualified business use falls to 50% or less of total use during the recovery period, part of depreciation claimed in prior years is recaptured and the taxpayer must switch to straight line depreciation.

New rules for leased cars? Lessees of luxury business cars must cope with an annual income inclusion that, in effect, reduces the deduction for lease payments. This income inclusion is the leasing equivalent of the investment credit and depreciation caps that applied to buyers of luxury business cars and is figured with the aid of special tables in the Sec. 280F regulations. Since the investment credit is repealed for post-1985 buyers, the income inclusion tables may well be revised for cars leased after 12-31-85. The new depreciation dollar caps may result in yet another set of leasing tables for post-1986 leases. The Treasury may also revise the one-time-only income inclusion that applies for the year that a leased car (or other "listed property") is used 50% or less for business.

Special rule for final-quarter purchases. Under ACRS, there's a natural temptation to accelerate purchases of personal property planned, for say, the first quarter of the next tax year into the last months of this tax year. *Reason:* You get a half-year of recovery deductions in the first year regardless of when the asset is placed in service.

This strategy continues to work under the new ACRS setup, if you avoid a new snare. If the aggregate bases of property placed in service during the last three months of the tax year exceed 40% of the aggregate bases of all the property placed in service during the year, then the taxpayer cannot use the mid-year convention. Instead, he must use the mid-quarter convention for *all property* (other than nonresidential real property and residential rental property) placed in service during the year. For purposes of the 40% rule, residential rental property and nonresidential realty is ignored. The Committee Reports indicate that members of an affiliated group [within the meaning of Sec. 1504, without regard to Sec. 1504(b)] are treated as one taxpayer for purposes of the 40% determination.

Under the mid-quarter convention, the first-year depreciation allowance is based on the number of quarters that the asset was in service. Property placed in service at any time during a quarter is treated as having been placed in service in the middle of the quarter.

> **AVOID THE PITFALL:** Businesses must carefully time their equipment purchases and placed-in-service dates. The mid-quarter convention is avoided as long as the aggregate bases of property placed in service during the last three months of the tax year do not exceed 66% of the aggregate bases of property placed in service during the first nine months of the tax year.

> **Example:** During the first nine months of its tax year, XYZ Corp. places in service $124,000 of depreciable nonrealty assets. XYZ can place in service another $81,840 of non-realty assets during the last three months (66% of $124,000) without running afoul of the new rule.

For tax years in which some placed-in-service property is covered by prior law ACRS, and other placed-in-service property is covered by the new ACRS rules, the 40% determination is made with respect to all the property. However, the mid-quarter convention applies only to property depreciated under the new ACRS rules.

Optional recovery methods. A taxpayer may elect to recover the cost of assets using the straight-line method over the applicable ACRS recovery period. The taxpayer also may elect to use the alternative depreciation system [¶205]. In either case, the mid-year convention applies (unless the taxpayer fails the new year-end rule and must use the mid-quarter rule) and salvage value is ignored. An election to use an optional recovery method for a particular class of property is binding for all property in that class placed in service during the year. The election is irrevocable.

Recapture provisions. The recapture rules for tangible property (other than residential rental or nonresidential real property) remain the same: All gain on a disposition is treated as ordinary income to the extent of ACRS deductions claimed by the taxpayer. For purposes of recapture, deductions allowed under Sec. 179 (expensing), Sec. 190 (removal or architectural and transportation barriers) or Sec. 193 (tertiary injectant expenses) are treated as depreciation deductions.

Other rules. You may continue to set up mass asset accounts for any property in the same ACRS class and placed in service in the same year. As under prior law (unless otherwise provided by regulations), the full amount of proceeds realized on a disposition of property from a mass asset account is treated as ordinary income (with no reduction for basis). But no reduction is made in the depreciable basis remaining in the account. For technical reasons, the repeal of the investment tax credit [¶208] will result in an expanded definition of assets eligible for inclusion in mass asset accounts.

The new law continues to condition eligibility of public utility property for ACRS recovery on the normalization of ACRS tax benefits in setting rates charged to customers and in reflecting results in regulated books of account. The new law also provides for the normalization of excess deferred tax reserves resulting from a reduction in corporate income tax rates. If such reserves are not normalized, the taxpayer must use the depreciation method, useful life determination, averaging convention, and salvage value limits used to set rates and reflecting operating results in regulated books of account.

[¶203] **Real Estate Depreciation.** Taxpayers have been on a rollercoaster ride when it comes to depreciating real estate. Property placed in service before 1981 was depreciable over its useful life (e.g., 35 to 40 years for new property). The recovery period dropped all the way down to 15 years for property placed in service after 1980, edged up to 18 years for property placed in service after 3-15-84, and went to 19 years if placed in service after 5-8-85.

Effective for property placed in service after 12-31-86, the new law boosts the recovery period to 27.5 years for residential rental property and to 31.5 years for nonresidential real property. What's more, the recovery method is slowed down to the straight-line rate using the mid-month convention. Residential rental property is defined the same way it was under prior law. A property qualifies if at least 80% of the gross rental income is rental income from dwelling units.

Residential rental property includes manufactured homes which are residential rental property. Residential rental property does not include hotels, motels, and other establishments rented to transients. Nonresidential real property is any Sec. 1250 property that is not residential rental property and that either has no ADR midpoint or has an ADR midpoint that's not less than 27½ years. Because the mid-month convention applies, there is no adjustment made for short tax years.

SPECIAL HELP: The following tables were prepared by the Prentice-Hall Editorial Staff. They list recovery percentages for residential rental and nonresidential real property. They are based on a mathematical application of the prescribed depreciation methods. (There are no official tables at this time.)

Recovery Percentages for Residential Rental Property

Recovery Year	Month Placed in Service											
	1	2	3	4	5	6	7	8	9	10	11	12
1	3.48	3.18	2.88	2.58	2.27	1.97	1.67	1.36	1.06	.76	.45	.15
2—27	3.64	3.64	3.64	3.64	3.64	3.64	3.64	3.64	3.64	3.64	3.64	3.64
28	1.88	2.18	2.48	2.78	3.09	3.39	3.64	3.64	3.64	3.64	3.64	3.64
29	-0-	-0-	-0-	-0-	-0-	-0-	.05	.36	.66	.96	1.27	1.57

Recovery Percentages for Nonresidential Real Property

Recovery Year	Month Placed in Service											
	1	2	3	4	5	6	7	8	9	10	11	12
1	3.04	2.78	2.51	2.25	1.98	1.72	1.46	1.19	.93	.66	.40	.13
2—31	3.17	3.17	3.17	3.17	3.17	3.17	3.17	3.17	3.17	3.17	3.17	3.17
32	1.86	2.12	2.39	2.65	2.92	3.17	3.17	3.17	3.17	3.17	3.17	3.17
33	-0-	-0-	-0-	-0-	-0-	.01	.27	.54	.80	1.07	1.33	1.60

Example: Realty Corp. bought an apartment building in January 1986. It buys an apartment building and a department store building in January 1987. Each costs $300,000.

The 1986 apartment building has a 19-year ACRS recovery period. Realty's depreciation is figured from statutory tables. Its writeoff is $26,400 for 1986, and $25,200 for 1987.

The 1987 apartment building is assigned a 27½ -year useful life, and the department store building is given a 31½ -year life. Realty's depreciation for the apartment building is $10,440, for 1987, and $10,920, for 1988. Its writeoffs for the department store building are $9,120 for 1987, and $9,510 for 1988.

A taxpayer may elect to recover the cost of residental property and nonresidential realty using the straight-line method (and the mid-month convention) over a 40-year period. A table for 40-year recovery is shown at ¶205.

New rule for leasehold improvements. If a building is erected on leased property, its cost must be recovered over the 27½ or 31½ year period, regardless of the term of the lease. The cost of other improvements to leased property is recovered using the applicable ACRS recovery period. When the lease is terminated, the lessee figures gain or loss by reference to the improvement's basis at that time. As a result of the new rule, Sec. 178 is amended to cover only the amortization of lease-acquisition costs. Such costs may be amortized over the lease term. However, under the new law, any lease renewals (including renewal options and any other period for which the parties reasonably expect the lease to be renewed) must be included in figuring the amortization period, but only if less than 75% of the lease-acquisition cost is for the lease's remaining term (excluding any renewal period remaining on the lease acquisition date).

Depreciation recapture. Gain on a disposition of residential rental or nonresidential realty is not recaptured as ordinary income to the extent of depreciation deductions claimed by the taxpayer.

Act Sec. 201(a) amends Sec. 168(a) and (b), relating to applicable depreciation methods under ACRS, Sec. 168(c), relating to recovery periods, Sec. 168(d), relating to applicable conventions and special mid-quarter convention, Sec. 168(e), relating to classification of property, Sec. 168(f), relating to property not covered by ACRS, 168(g)(7), relating to election to use alternative depreciation method, Sec. 168(i)(1), relating to authority of the Treasury Secretary to reclassify assets, Sec. 168(i)(3), relating to lease term, Sec. 168(i)(4) relating to general asset accounts, Sec. 168(i)(5), relating to changes in use. Sec. 168(i)(6), relating to additions or improvements to property, Sec. 168(i)(8), relating to treatment of leasehold improvements, and Sec. 168(i)(9), relating to normalization rules. Act Sec. 201(d)(4) makes technical and conforming amendments to Sec. 280F, relating to luxury automobiles and other listed property. Act Sec. 201(d)(5) makes technical and conforming changes to Secs. 291(a)(1), 291(c)(1), and 291(e)(2). Act Sec. 201(d)(6) makes technical and conforming changes to Secs. 312(k)(4). Act Sec. 201(d)(7) makes technical and conforming changes to Sec. 465(b)(3)(C), Sec. 46(c)(8)(D)(v), and Sec. 4162(c)(3). Act Sec. 201(d)(8) amends Sec. 467, relating to certain payments for the use of property. Act. Sec. 201(d)(9) through (d)(14) makes technical and conforming changes to Secs. 514(c)(9)(B)(vi)(II), 751(c), 1245(a)(1), 1245(a)(2), 1245(a)(3), 1245(a)(5), 1245(a)(6), 4162(c)(3), 6111(c)(3)(B), 7701(e)(4)(A), and 7701(e)(5). The above provisions generally apply to property placed in service after 12-31-86 in tax years ending after that date. Transition rules are covered at ¶209. Act Sec. 203(a)(1)(B) allows taxpayers to elect the new ACRS system for assets placed in service after 7-31-86 and before 1-1-87.

[¶204] Antichurning Provisions and Nonrecognition Transactions. There's a new set of antichurning provisions for personal property. The modified ACRS setup does not apply if (1) the property was owned or used at any time during 1986 by the taxpayer or a related person; (2) the property is acquired from a person who owned it at any time during 1986 and, as part of the transaction, the user of the property did not change; or (3) the taxpayer leased the property to a person (or someone related to the person) who owned or used the property during 1986. (A special rule prevents multiple churning transactions.) In such churning transactions, the taxpayer must use the original ACRS system. Note: The modified ACRS may be elected for assets placed in service after 7-31-86. [See ¶203.]

A special rule applies to property used for personal purposes before 1987 and converted to business use after 1986. In this case, the property is treated as having been placed in service when it is first used for business. In other words, the antichurning rules don't apply to converted property.

> **IMPORTANT:** The antichurning rules do not apply if their application would result in a more generous writeoff for the placed-in-service year than the new ACRS system allows.

> **Example:** A business auto used by John Smith during 1986 is transferred to Donald Smith, a related taxpayer, in 1987. The transaction is *not* covered by the antichurning rules. Reason: If the antichurning rules applied, then Donald Smith would be able to depreciate the car over three years (prior law's ACRS recovery) instead of over five years using the half-year convention (new law's recovery rule).

Real estate. There are no 1986/1987 antichurning rules for real estate. *Reason:* The new ACRS setup results in a much slower writeoff than under the original ACRS system. If there were antichurning provisions, taxpayers would deliberately disqualify transactions in order to use the more liberal old law provisions.

> **COMMENT:** The original antichurning provisions remain in place. These provisions prevent taxpayers from converting pre-ACRS property (e.g., placed in service prior to 1981) into ACRS property. Thus, a taxpayer who owned real estate before 1981 could not qualify for the modified ACRS rules by engaging in a 1987 churning transaction.

Nonrecognition transactions. A special rule applies to transactions covered by Secs. 332, 351, 361, 371(a), 374(a), 721 or 731 [other than termination of a partnership under Sec. 708(b)(1)(B)]. Here, the transferee is treated as the transferor for purposes of computing the depreciation deduction. This treatment is limited to that part of the transferee's basis that does not exceed the adjusted basis in the hands of the transferor. If the transferee's basis is more than the transferor's basis, then the excess is depreciated under the new law's ACRS rules.

Another special rule applies if a taxpayer disposes of property and then reacquires it. In such cases, the depreciation deduction is computed as if the property had not been disposed of.

NOTE: The special rules for nonrecognition transactions and for dispositions and reacquisitions do not apply to any transaction covered by the antichurning rules.

Act Sec. 201(a) amends Sec. 168(f)(5), relating to property placed in service in churning transactions, and Sec. 168(i)(7), relating to treatment of certain transferees and property reacquired by the taxpayer. Act. Sec. 201(a) is generally effective for assets placed in service after 12-31-86 in tax years ending after that date.

[¶205] **Alternative Depreciation System.** Effective for property placed in service after 12-31-86, the new law creates an alternative depreciation system that must be used to:

(1) Compute the portion of depreciation treated as a tax preference for purposes of the corporate and individual alternative minimum tax [¶701 *et seq.*].

(2) Figure the earnings and profits of a domestic corporation or an "80/20" company.

(3) Compute depreciation allowances for property that is:

- Tangible property used predominantly outside the U.S.
- Leased or otherwise used by a tax-exempt entity.
- Financed with the proceeds of tax-exempt bonds.
- Imported from foreign countries that maintain discriminatory trade practices or otherwise engage in discriminatory acts.

How the new system works. In general, depreciation is computed using straight-line recovery without regard to salvage value. Exception: For purposes of the minimum tax, depreciation of personal property is computed using the 150% declining-balance method. In general, the mid-year convention applies, but the taxpayer must use the mid-month convention for residential rental property and nonresidential real property. *Note:* The mid-quarter convention must be used for all personal property placed in service during the year if the new year-end 40% rule is failed [¶203].

The recovery periods under the alternative depreciation system are:

- 5 years for cars, light general purpose trucks, qualified technological equipment, and semiconductor manufacturing equipment.
- 9.5 years for computer-based telephone central office switching equipment.
- 10 years for railroad track.
- 12 years for personal property with no class life.

- 15 years for single-purpose agricultural or horticultural structures.

- 24 years for municipal waste water treatment plants and telephone distribution plans and comparable equipment used for 2-way exchange of voice and data communications.

- 27.5 years for low-income housing financed by tax-exempts.

- 40 years for nonresidential real and residential rental property, and 1245 property which is real property with no useful life.

- 50 years for municipal sewers.

Other property has a recovery period equal to its class life.

PLANNING AID: The tables below show straight-line depreciation percentages under the alternative recovery system for property in the 5, 9.5, 12, and 40-year classes.

Important. These tables are not official material, but were prepared by the Prentice-Hall Editorial Staff. However, the table for the 5, 9.5, and 12-year classes is identical to the IRS table used under prior law to compute optional recovery allowances for property used outside the United States. These optional recovery allowances are computed using the straight-line method and the mid-year convention [IRC Sec. 168(b)(3)(A) and (B)(iii), prior to amendment by the new law]. Straight-line recovery tables for other class lives may be found at Prop. Reg. Sec. 1.168-2(g)(3) [¶15,602.66 P-H Federal Taxes].

The table for property in the 40-year class is identical to the 40-year table prescribed by the IRS for property subject to prior law's tax-exempt entity leasing provisions [Temp. Reg. 1.168(j)-1T ¶15,602.95 P-H Federal Taxes] and for real property not used predominantly for business under Sec. 280F [IRS Pub. 534]. The IRS 40-year table uses straight-line and the mid-month convention.

Recovery Percentages Under
Alternative Depreciation System

Recovery Year	5-Year Class	9.5-Year Class	12-Year Class
1	10	5	4
2	20	11	9
3	20	11	9
4	20	11	9
5	20	11	9
6	10	11	8
7		10	8
8		10	8
9		10	8
10		10	8
11			8
12			8
13			4

Recovery Percentages for 40-Year Class

Recovery Year	Month Placed in Service											
	1	2	3	4	5	6	7	8	9	10	11	12
1	2.4	2.2	2.0	1.8	1.6	1.4	1.1	0.9	0.7	0.5	0.3	0.1
2—40	2.5	2.5	2.5	2.5	2.5	2.5	2.5	2.5	2.5	2.5	2.5	2.5
41	0.1	0.3	0.5	0.7	0.9	1.1	1.4	1.6	1.8	2.0	2.2	2.4

Qualified technological equipment: This is any computer or related peripheral equipment, any high technology telephone station equipment installed on the customer's premises, and any high technology medical equipment. A computer is any programmable electronic device that accepts information, processes it, and supplies the results with or without human intervention and consists of a central processing unit (CPU) containing extensive storage, logic, arithmetic, and control capabilities. Related peripheral equipment is an off- or on-line device designed to be controlled by a computer's CPU. Computer or related peripheral equipment does not include: any equipment that is an integral part of other property that is not a computer; typewriters, or calculators; adding or accounting machines; copiers, duplicating, or similar equipment; and any equipment used primarily for entertainment or amusement.

High technology medical equipment is any electronic, electromechanical, or computer-based high-technology equipment used in the screening, monitoring, observation, diagnosis, or treatment of patients in a laboratory, medical, or hospital environment.

Property used predominantly outside the United States. As under prior law, property falls in this classification if it is used outside the United States for more than half of a tax year. There's a special exception for a satellite or other spacecraft (or any interest therein) launched within the United States and held by a U.S. person.

Property leased or otherwise used by a tax-exempt entity. In general, the new law retains prior law's definition of tax-exempt use property, including the special rule that defines the recovery period as the greater of (1) 125% of the lease term or (2) the depreciation period that otherwise applies to the property. However, qualified technological equipment (as defined above) leased to a tax-exempt entity for five years or less is not treated as tax-exempt use property. A corporation that is 50% or more owned by one or more tax-

¶205

exempt entities (other than foreign persons or entities) is treated as a tax-exempt entity. The holdings of tax-exempt entities owning less than 5% of the stock are disregarded if the corporation is publicly traded.

Property financed with the proceeds of tax-exempt bonds. The new law modifies the definition of tax-exempt bond financed property to include any property that is financed directly or indirectly by an obligation that pays out tax-exempt interest under Sec. 103(a). The proceeds of an obligation are treated as being used to finance property acquired in connection with the obligation's issuance in the order in which the property was acquired. Tax-exempt bond financed property does not include qualified residential rental projects [as defined by Sec. 142(a)(7)].

Certain imported property. The President may by Executive Order mandate use of the alternative depreciation system for property imported from foreign countries that maintain trade restrictions or engage in discriminatory action or policies that unjustifiably restrict U.S. commerce. Property is imported if it was completed outside of the United States or less than 50% of its basis is attributable to value added in the United States. For this purpose, the United States includes its possessions and Puerto Rico.

Act Sec. 201(a) amends Sec. 168(g)(1)-(7), relating to alternative depreciation system for certain property, Sec. 168(h)(1)-(8), relating to tax-exempt use property, and Sec. 168(i)(2), relating to qualified technological equipment. Act. Sec. 201(b) amends Sec. 312(k)(3), relating to depreciation used for purposes of earnings and profits. Act. Sec. 201 is generally effective for property placed in service after 12-31-86 in tax years ending after that date.

[¶206] Increased Expensing Deduction. Instead of depreciating qualifying property under the modified ACRS system, a taxpayer may elect under Sec. 179 to treat all or part of its cost as a currently deductible expense in the placed-in-service year. Effective for qualifying property placed in service after 1986, the expensing deduction is equal to $10,000. The expensing deduction had been limited to $5,000 for tax years 1982-87. Qualifying property is recovery property that is bought for use in the active conduct of a trade or business.

The new law modifies prior law's expensing rules in four other ways:

• If the aggregate cost of qualifying property placed in service during the tax year exceeds $200,000, then the credit is reduced dollar-for-dollar by the cost of qualifying property in excess of $200,000.

• Marrieds filing separate returns are treated as one taxpayer for purposes of the $10,000 expensing limit (and the reduction that applies if qualifying property placed in service exceeds $200,000). Unless the taxpayers elect otherwise, 50% of the cost of qualifying property is allocated to each spouse.

• The amount expensed cannot exceed the taxable income derived from the trade or business in which the property is used. Taxable income of each trade or business is computed separately and without regard to the amount expensed. Any expensed amount in excess of taxable income is carried forward to future tax years and added to other amounts eligible for expensing.

• Conversion of the expensed property to personal use *at any time* before the end of the property's recovery period results in recapture income (excess of expensed amount over ACRS deduction that would have been allowed). A property is converted to personal use if it is not used predominantly for trade or business use. Under prior law, there was no recapture if the property was converted to personal use after the end of the second tax year following the tax year in which the property was placed in service.

NOTE: For purposes of computing a corporation's earnings and profits, any amount expensed under Sec. 179 is treated as a deduction ratably over five tax years, beginning with the tax year in which the expensing deduction is claimed.

Act Sec. 201(b) amends Sec. 312(k)(3)(B), relating to treatment for E&P purposes of amounts expensed under Sec. 179. Act. Sec. 202 amends Sec. 179(b), Sec. 179(d)(1) and Sec. 179(d)(10), relating to expensing of depreciable assets. Act. Secs. 201 and 202 are generally effective for property placed in service after 12-31-86 in tax years ending after that date.

[¶207] **Repeal of Finance Leases.** The new law repeals the finance lease provisions, effective for agreements entered into after 12-31-86.

Act Sec. 201 repeals Sec. 168(f)(8), relating to finance leases, generally effective for property placed in service after 12-31-86.

[¶208] **Investment Tax Credit Repeal.** The regular investment tax credit is repealed for property placed in service after 12-31-85. However, the investment tax credit continues to be available for (1) property covered by transition rules [¶209]; (2) certain qualified progress expenditures for periods before 1-1-86; and (3) the portion of adjusted basis of qualified timber property treated as Sec. 38 property under Sec. 48(a)(1)(F). A tax credit is available for qualified rehabilitation expenses [¶217]. In addition, effective for tax years beginning on or after 7-1-87, regular investment credits (other than the ITC available for timber property) carried forward or claimed under a transitional rule are reduced by 35%. In the case of a tax year beginning before and ending after 7-1-87, the 35% reduction is prorated based on the ratio that post-6-30-87 months in the tax year bears to total months in the tax year. For example, in the case of a tax year that is based on the calendar year, the reduction for 1987 is 17.5%. The reduction in the ITC compensates for the new, lower tax rates. The amount by which the credit is reduced can't be claimed as a credit in a future tax year.

Another change: The depreciable basis of transition property placed in service after 12-31-85 and eligible for the ITC under the transition rules must be reduced by the full amount of the ITC. The full basis reduction can't be escaped by claiming a reduced ITC percentage under Sec. 48(q)(4). However, the full-basis reduction is computed after taking into account the 35% reduction.

Special relief for possible estimated tax problems. The repeal of the ITC for assets placed in service after 12-31-85 may cause estimated tax problems (e.g., an estimated tax payment may have been based on the availability of the ITC). According to the Committee Reports, the conferees intend that no estimated tax penalties be imposed in such situations. However, relief is available only to the extent that (1) an underpayment results from taking into account the ITC on property placed in service after 12-31-85 and before the Reform Act's enactment date, and (2) the taxpayer pays the underpayment within 30 days after the enactment date.

NOTE: A taxpayer may be entitled to much broader estimated-tax relief under Act Sec. 1543 [see ¶1544].

Carrybacks. Qualifying farmers are allowed a 15-year carryback of existing ITC carryforwards. This carryback, which may be elected for the first tax year beginning after 12-31-86, is limited to the lesser of three amounts:

- 50% of existing carryforwards;
- The net tax liability for the carryback period; or
- $750.

Qualified farmers are those taxpayers who derived 50% or more of their gross income from farming in the three tax years before the tax year in which the carryback election is made.

Another special 15-year ITC carryback applies to domestic corporations engaged in the manufacture and production of steel. The new law also includes a new recapture penalty if the tax benefits of previously allowed ITCs on public utility property are not normalized, and special recapture rules for qualified progress expenditures.

Act Sec. 211(a) adds new Sec. 49(a), generally repealing the ITC for property placed in service after 12-31-85. Act Sec. 211(a) also adds new Secs. 48(b) through (e), relating to exceptions to the ITC repeal, 35% reduction in the ITC for tax years beginning on or after 7-1-87, the full basis adjustment requirement, and (continued) transition property [see ¶209]. Act. Sec. 211(b) provides special normalization rules, Act Sec. 211(c) makes conforming amendments to the table of sections for subpart E of part IV of subchapter A of chapter 1, and Act Sec. 211(d) provides a transition rule of limited application. Act Sec. 212 provides a 15-year carryback of existing carryforwards of steel companies, which may be elected by a qualifying corporation for its first tax year beginning after 12-31-86. Act Sec. 213 provides a 15-year carryback of existing carryforwards of qualifying farmers, elective as shown above.

[¶209] **Effective Dates and Transition Rules.** The new ACRS system, the new alternative depreciation system, and the increased expensing deduction are generally effective for property placed in service after 12-31-86, in tax years ending after that date. The investment tax credit is repealed for property placed in service after 12-31-85 in tax years ending after that date.

Transition rules for ACRS. Prior law's ACRS rules continue to apply for property constructed, reconstructed, or acquired under a written contract binding as of 3-1-86, and placed in service by the following dates:

Type of Property	Placed-in-Service Date
ADR midpoint of at least 7 years but less than 20 years	January 1, 1989
Property with no ADR midpoint	January 1, 1989
ADR midpoint of 20 years or more	January 1, 1991
Residential rental property and nonresidential realty	January 1, 1991

Real property covered by the rehabilitation tax credit transition rules [¶217] may be depreciated under prior law's ACRS rules.

There is no transitional relief for property with an ADR midpoint of less than seven years. For purposes of the transition rules, computer-based telephone switching equipment is considered to have an ADR midpoint of six years.

NOTE: Property covered by the antichurning rules [¶204] may be subject to prior law's ACRS system as well.

Transition rules for ITC. The investment tax credit is allowed for property constructed, reconstructed, or acquired under a written contract binding on 12-31-85, and placed in service by the following dates:

Type of Property	Placed in Service Date
ADR midpoint of less than 5 years	July 1, 1986
ADR midpoint of at least 5 years but less than 7 years	January 1, 1987
Computer-based telephone central office switching equipment	January 1, 1987

ADR midpoint of at least 7 but
  less than 20 years   January 1, 1989
Property with no ADR midpoint   January 1, 1989
ADR midpoint of 20 years or more   January 1, 1991

Some taxpayers may have difficulty identifying the binding contract and placed in service dates of specific assets. Where the taxpayer's accounting system does not identify such dates, the Committee Reports indicate that the taxpayer is to assume that the first items placed in service after 12-31-86 (ACRS) or 12-31-85 (ITC) were those they had under a binding contract on that date. A similar rule is to apply to self-constructed property.

Corporate takeovers. A special rule applies if at least 80% of a target corporation's stock is acquired on or before 12-31-86 (ACRS) or 12-31-85 (ITC). Here, the acquiring corporation is treated as having purchased the assets before the general effective date, if it makes a Sec. 338 election to treat the stock purchase as an asset purchase after the binding contract dates.

Binding-contract rule. The transitional rules apply only to written contracts:

- In which the construction, reconstruction, erection, or acquisition is itself the subject matter of the contract.
- That are enforceable under state law against the taxpayer and do not limit damages to a specified amount (e.g., by use of liquidated damages provisions). A contract that limits damages to an amount equal to at least 5% of the total contract price is treated as not limiting damages.
- That are binding on the taxpayer. The grant of an unconditional put (i.e., an option to sell) to another taxpayer is a binding contract. However, an option to buy is not a binding contract.
- That are not substantially modified after 3-1-86 (ACRS) or 12-31-85 (ITC).

The binding-contract rule will not apply to supply agreements with manufacturers where the contract does not specify the amount or design specifications of the property to be purchased. Such agreements are not treated as binding contracts until purchase orders are actually placed. A purchase order for a specific number of items, based on the pricing provisions of the supply ageement, will be treated as a binding contract.

Special rules apply to films (TV or motion-picture) for purposes of the ITC transition dates: production on a film is treated as construction; written contemporary evidence of a binding contract in accordance with industry practice is treated as a written binding contract; and a license agreement between a TV network and a producer is treated as a binding contract. Finally, the ITC may be claimed on motion-picture films if financing was arranged by a public offering before 9-26-85, 40% of the funds was spent on films that began production before that date, and all the films financed by the public offering are required to be distributed under distribution agreements entered into before that date.

A taxpayer that enters into a binding contract for a component (e.g., an aircraft engine) is not considered to have entered into a binding contract for the entire property (e.g., the aircraft as a whole). If a taxpayer holds a binding contract and transfers his rights, the modified ACRS rules do not apply to the transferee, as long as the property wasn't placed in service before the transfer by the transferor. If a partnership that holds a binding contract undergoes a deemed termination and reconstitution under Sec. 708(b)(1)(B), then the old partnership is considered to have transferred its rights to the property under the contract to the new partnership.

There's special transition relief for written binding contracts that are not between the person who will own the property and the person who will build or supply the property. The relief applies to a written supply or service contract, or a lease agreement, that was binding on 3-1-86 (for ACRS recovery) or 12-31-85 (for ITC allowances). The exception applies only when the specifications and amount of the property are readily ascertainable from the terms of the contract or related documents.

Sale-leasebacks. Property that is sold and leased back is treated as having met the ACRS or ITC general or transitional effective dates if:

- The property qualified in the seller's hands under a transitional rule *or* was placed in service by the seller prior to 1-1-87 (for ACRS recovery) or 1-1-86 (for ITC allowances).
- The property was leased back by the buyer to the seller by the earlier of (1) the applicable placed-in-service date that applies under the transitional rules, or (2) three months after the property was originally placed in service.

Self-constructed property. The transitional rules apply to self-constructed property if a minimum amount was incurred or committed as of 3-1-86 (for ACRS recovery) or 12-31-85 (for ITC allowances) and construction or reconstruction began by the appropriate date. The minimum amount is the lesser of $1 million or 5% of the property's cost. The engineer or general contractor is treated as constructing the property. Construction is considered to have commenced when physical work of a significant nature starts. It does not include construction of minor parts or components, or preliminary work such as planning and designing, securing financing, etc.

¶209

222   Tax Reform Act of 1986

Equipped buildings. A liberal transition rule applies to buildings, equipment and machinery to be used in the structure, and appurtenances (e.g., structures such as railroad sidings, and peripheral machinery and equipment). Prior law's ACRS rules, and prior law's investment credit allowances will continue to apply to the entire equipped building and its appurtenances if on or before 3-1-86 (for ACRS recovery) or 12-31-85 (for ITC allowances):

• A specific written plan existed for the work or acquisition (and the plan is not substantially modified after the appropriate date or dates),

• More than half the cost of the building and its equipment and machinery (but not appurtenances) was incurred or committed, and

• Construction or reconstruction of the property commenced.

If the more-than-50% rule is not met, then each item of machinery and equipment is treated separately for purposes of the transition rules.

IMPORTANT: The equipped building must be placed in service before the appropriate ACRS/ITC dates (shown in the chart) in order to qualify for the transitional rule.

A comparable transitional rule applies to plant facilities which are not housed in a building.

Property financed with tax-exempt bonds. In general, depreciable property placed in service after 12-31-86 must be recovered with the new alternative depreciation system to the extent it is financed with tax-exempt bonds issued after 3-1-86. However, this rule does not apply if

• The original use of the property commences with the taxpayer and the construction, reconstruction, or rehabilitation started before 3-2-86 and was completed after that date;

• A binding contract to incur significant expenses was entered into before 3-2-86 and some or all of the expenses were incurred after 3-1-86; or

• The property was acquired on or after 3-2-86 under a binding contract entered into before that date, and is described in an inducement resolution or other comparable preliminary approval adopted by the issuing authority (or voter referendum) before 3-2-86.

A post-3-1-86 refunding issue is treated as a new issue and the unrecovered cost of property financed with its proceeds must be depreciated using the alternative system. If significant costs (more than 10% of those reasonably anticipated) were made before 1-1-87, the alternative depreciation system does not apply to the extent the facilities are financed with an obligation issued solely to refinance a pre-3-2-86 issue.

Other transitional rules. The new law has special transitional rules for qualified urban renewal projects, projects licensed or certified by the Federal Energy Regulatory Commission, and qualified solid waste disposal facilities. There are other transition rules that benefit specific projects.

Act Sec. 203 provides effective dates and general transition rules for the revised ACRS system. Act Sec. 204 provides special transition rules for specific projects. Act Sec. 211(a) adds new Sec. 49(e), relating to transition rules for the ITC. Act Sec. 211(b) provides special normalization rules for public utility property. Act Sec. 211(c) makes a conforming amendment to the table of sections for subpart E of part IV of subchapter A of chapter 1. Act Sec. 211(d) provides a special ITC transition rule. Act Sec. 211(e) provides general effective date for ITC repeal (property placed in service after 12-31-85 in tax years ending after that date), and provides transition relief for certain films, effective date for normalization rules, and additional exceptions from the ITC repeal.

[¶210] General Business Credit Offset Reduced. The limitation on the income tax liability in excess of $25,000 of an individual or corporation that may be offset by the general business credit is reduced to 75% from 85%, effective for tax years beginning after 12-31-85.

Act Sec. 221, reducing the general business credit offset amount, amends Sec. 38(c)(1), effective for tax years beginning after 12-31-85.

Research and Development

[¶211] Research Tax Credit Revived in Modified Form. The new law grants a three-year lease on life to the research tax credit, which was scheduled to expire at the end of 1985. The credit will be available for eligible expenses paid or incurred through 12-31-88. Under prior law, the credit was 25% of the excess of qualified research expenses over average research expenses in the base period (generally, the three preceding tax years). Sixty-five percent of contract research expenses (for work done by others, including basic research by universities and tax exempt research organizations) counted as research expenses.

The new law reduces the R&E credit to 20% and keeps the base-period rule only for qualified research expenses, which are defined more narrowly than under prior law. Effective for tax years beginning after 1986, the new law introduces a new 20%

credit and a special set of operating rules for "basic research expenses," a new category that replaces prior law's contract research expenses.

Qualified research expenses. To be eligible for the regular credit, research expenses must qualify for expensing or amortization under Sec. 174, be conducted in the United States, and be paid by the taxpayer (e.g., not funded by government grant). In addition, the research must be research and development in the experimental or laboratory sense and must pass a new three-part test.

  • It must be undertaken to discover information that is technological in nature. The research must fundamentally rely on the principles of the physical, biological, engineering, or computer sciences.

  • Substantially all of the research activities must constitute elements of a process of experimentation relating to a new or improved function, performance, or reliability or quality. Research involves a process of experimentation only if the design of the item as a whole is uncertain at the outset. Examples: Developing and testing a new drug or designing a new computer system.

  • The application of the research is intended to be useful in the development of a new or improved business component. This is a product, process, software, technique, formula or invention to be sold, leased or licensed or used by the taxpayer in a trade or business. Research is conducted for a qualified purpose if it relates to (1) a new or improved function; (2) performance; (3) reliability or quality; or (4) reduced cost.

The three requirements are first applied at the product level. If the product as a whole does not qualify for the credit, then subsets of the product are examined to see whether a portion of the total cost qualifies. For example, even if research on a new computer system as a whole does not satisfy all the tests, the development of a specific component (e.g., a new integrated chip or circuit) may qualify.

Special rules for internal use computer software. Software developed primarily for the taxpayer's internal use qualifies for the credit only if it is used in qualified research (other than the development of the software itself) or in a production process that involves a credit-eligible component. The development of internal use software for general or administrative functions (such as payroll or accounting) is ineligible for the credit.

Treasury regulations are to prescribe three more tests for internal use software. It must (1) be innovative; (2) involve significant economic risk; and (3) not be commercially available elsewhere.

Ineligible expenses. Research expenses related to the following items do not qualify for the credit:

- Style, taste, cosmetic, or seasonal design factors.
- The social sciences, arts, or humanities.
- Efficiency surveys, management studies, market research (including advertising and promotion), routine data collection, and routine quality-control testing or inspection.
- Expenses incurred after commercial production has begun.
- The costs of ascertaining the existence, location, extent, or quality of any ore or mineral deposit (including oil and gas). *Note:* Expenses of developing new or innovative methods of extracting minerals qualify.
- Development of any plant process, machinery, or technique for the commercial production of a business component, unless the process is technologically new or improved.
- Adaptation of a business component to suit a particular customer's needs.
- Partial or complete reproduction of an existing business component from plans, specifications, a physical examination, or publicly available information.

OBSERVATION: Although an expense is not eligible for the credit, it may qualify for expensing or 60-month amortization under Sec. 174.

Rental costs. Rental payments made for personal property are not eligible for the research credit. However, payments for computer time are eligible if made to further qualified research.

Basic research expenses. Effective for tax years beginning after 1986, there's a new tax credit equal to 20% of all basic research expenses in excess of a special base amount. The credit is available to any corporation other than an S corporation, a personal holding company, or a service organization as defined by Sec. 414(m)(3). Basic research consists of any original investigation for the advancement of scientific knowledge not having a specific commercial objective. The research does not have to be conducted in the same field as the taxpayer's trade or business. The expenses are not deductible until actually paid in cash under a written agreement between the taxpayer and the qualifying organization. The term qualified organizations includes most colleges, universities, tax-exempt scientific research organizations, and certain tax-exempt conduit or grant organizations (other than private foundations).

¶1211

How to figure the 20% tax credit for basic research expenses. The credit is equal to 20% of the excess of qualifying basic research expenses over a special floor that consists of

- the minimum basic research amount, plus
- the maintenance-of-effort amount.

The minimum basic research amount is the greater of

- the average of contract research expenses during the base period [contract research expenses were the old-law equivalent of basic research expenses], or
- 1% of the average of in-house research expenses, contract research expenses, and credit-eligible basic research expenses during the base period.

In general, the base period is the three-tax-year period ending with the tax year immediately preceding the first tax year of the taxpayer beginning after 12-31-83.

The maintenance-of-effort amount is the average of all nondesignated university contributions made during the base period (as defined above), adjusted by the Sec. 1 cost-of-living factor for the calendar year in which the tax years begins, less the nondesignated university contributions made during the current tax year. Nondesignated university contributions are contributions to colleges, universities, tax-exempt research foundations, etc., for which a Sec. 170 charitable deduction was allowable and which weren't taken into account in computing the research credit.

Interplay of regular 20% credit and basic-research 20% credit. Basic-research expenses eligible for the new 20% credit are not eligible for and are not figured into the computation of the regular 20% credit (i.e., they are not included in base-period research expenses). However, basic-research expenses that are ineligible for the new 20% credit because of the special floor do count as expenses eligible for the regular 20% credit.

> **Example:** ABC Corp.'s qualified research expenses exceed base-period research expenses by $80,000. It has a total of $60,000 in basic research expenses. Assume the basic research floor amount is $20,000. Result: ABC may claim an $8,000 credit for basic research ($60,000 less $20,000 times 20%). It may also claim a $20,000 credit for qualified research expenses ($80,000 of qualified research expenses, plus $20,000 of basic research expenses for which the new credit was not claimed, times 20%). Total research credit: $28,000.

Other limitations. The research credit is now subject to the overall limitation that applies to general business tax credits (e.g., credits can offset only 75% of tax liability over $25,000) [¶210]. And a tough rule applies to sole proprietors, partners, beneficiaries of an estate or trust, and shareholders of S corporations: the research credit may offset only the tax attributable to the taxpayer's interest in the trade or business that generated the credit. That's the total tax bill less the tax that would be owed on income exclusive of the credit-producing trade or business.

> **OBSERVATION:** This credit limitation is much harsher than the general credit limit imposed by the new passive-loss rules [¶502]. The general limit restricts passive-source credits to tax owed on "passive activity" income only if the taxpayer does not materially participate in the activity. The limit on research credits applies whether or not the taxpayer materially participates in the trade or business that gives rise to the credits.

Act Sec. 231(a) adds new Sec. 30(h)(1), relating to termination of the research credit for amounts paid or incurred after 12-31-88, and new Sec. 30(h)(2), relating to computation of base-period expenses for tax years beginning before 1-1-89 and ending after 12-31-88. Act Sec. 231(b) amends Sec. 30(d), relating to definition of qualified research. Act Sec. 231(c)(1) amends Sec. 30(a), relating to reduction of research credit. Act Sec. 231(c)(2) amends Sec. 30(e), relating to expenses eligible for basic research expenses. Act Sec. 231(d) amends Sec. 38(b), relating to research credit treated as other business credits, redesignates Sec. 30 as Sec. 41, and makes technical and conforming amendments to Secs. 28, 41(g), 108(b)(2), 280C(b)(3), 381(c), 936(h)(5)(C)(i)(I)(a), 6411, and 6511(d)(6). Act Sec. 231(d) also adds new Sec. 39(d) and makes technical and conforming amendments to the table of sections for part IV of subchapter A of chapter 1. Act Sec. 231(e) amends Sec. 41(b)(2)(A) [as redesignated], relating to denial of credit with respect to payments for certain leased personal property. The modifications to the research credit are generally effective for tax years ending after 12-31-85, except that the modifications to the basic research tax credit are effective for tax years beginning after 12-31-86.

[¶212] Augmented Deduction for Certain Contributions of Scientific Research Property. The general rule is that the charitable contribution deduction must be reduced by the amount of ordinary gain the taxpayer would have realized had the property been sold at fair market value instead of being donated. A special rule permits corporations to take an augmented charitable deduction for donations of newly manufactured scientific equipment or apparatus to a college or university for research use in the physical or biological sciences. The new law extends the category of eligible donees to include tax-exempt organizations that (1) are organized and operated primarily to conduct scientific research; (2) are described in Sec. 501(c)(3); and (3) are not private foundations.

Act Sec. 231(f), amends Code Sec. 170(e)(4), effective for tax years beginning after 12-31-85.

[¶213] Orphan Drug Credit Extended. The new law extends the 50% credit for clinical testing of orphan drugs for three years through 12-31-90.

Act Sec. 232, relating to the credit for clinical testing expenses for certain drugs, amends Code Sec. 28, effective upon enactment.

[¶214] Repeal of Rapid Writeoff of Trademark and Trade Name Expenditures and 50-year Amortization of Certain Railroad Property. The election to amortize over at least a 60-month period expenditures for acquiring, protecting, expanding, registering, or defending a trademark or trade name is repealed. Therefore, trademark and trade name expenditures will be capitalized and generally recovered on disposition of the asset. The repeal is effective for amounts paid or incurred after 12-31-86. However, prior law will continue to apply to expenditures incurred (1) pursuant to a written contract that was binding as of 3-1-86; or (2) as to developing, protecting, expanding, registering, or defending trademarks or trade names begun as of 3-1-86, if the lesser of $1 million or 5% of the cost has been incurred or committed by that date, provided in each case the trademark or trade name is placed in service before 1-1-88.

Repeal of 50-year amortization: Effective for expenses after 12-31-86, the new law repeals special 50-year amortization of railroad grading and tunnel-bore expenditures. Such expenses will be capitalized and recovered on disposition of the asset.

Act Sec. 241, repealing five-year amortization of trademark and trade name expenditures, repeals Sec. 177, effective generally for expenditures paid or incurred after 12-31-86. Act Sec. 242 repeals Sec. 185 (relating to 50-year amortization), effective for expenses paid or incurred after 12-31-86. Expenses covered by special transition rules may continue to be amortized over 50 years.

[¶215] Deduction for Loss in Value of Certain Bus Operating Authorities and Freight Forwarder Authority. An ordinary deduction is allowed ratably over a 60-month period for taxpayers who held one or more intercity bus operating authorities on 11-19-82. The deduction's amount is the aggregate adjusted bases of all bus operating authorities that were held by the taxpayer on 11-19-82, or acquired after that date under a contract binding on that date.

The 60-month period begins with the later of 11-1-82, or, at the taxpayer's election, the first month of the taxpayer's first tax year beginning after that date. Adjustments must be made to the bases of authorities to reflect amounts allowable as deductions.

Under regulations to be prescribed, corporate or noncorporate taxpayers holding an eligible bus operating authority can elect to allocate to the authority a portion of the cost to the taxpayer of stock in an acquired corporation (unless an election under IRC Sec. 338 is in effect). The election is available if the bus operating authority was held (directly or indirectly) by the taxpayer when its stock was acquired. Here, part of the stock basis is allocated to the authority only if the corporate or noncorporate taxpayer would have been able to make such an allocation had the authority been distributed in a liquidation to which prior law Sec. 334(b)(2) applied. The election is available only if the stock was acquired on or before 11-19-82 (or pursuant to a binding contract in effect on that date).

The provision is effective retroactively for tax years ending after 11-18-82. The period of limitations is extended for filing claims for refund or credit of any overpayment of tax resulting from this rule, if that claim is prevented on or before the date that is one year after date of enactment. In that case, a refund or credit claim may be made or allowed if filed on or before the date that is six months after that date. In addition, the new amortization provision also includes freight forwarders, contingent on deregulation.

Act Sec. 243, creating a deduction for loss in value of certain bus operating authorities, effective generally retroactively for tax years ending after 11-18-82, and for freight forwarder operating authority effective to tax years ending after the month preceding the deregulation month.

[¶216] Expensing of Costs for Removal of Architectural Barriers. The new law makes permanent the provision allowing expensing of up to $35,000 of costs incurred for removing architectural and transportation barriers to the handicapped and elderly. Under prior law, the expensing provision was not available for expenses incurred in tax years beginning after 12-31-85.

Act Sec. 244 extending the expensing deduction, amends Sec. 190(d)(2), effective for amounts incurred in taxable years beginning after 1985.

[¶217] Tax Credit for Rehabilitation Expenses. The new law replaces the three-tier rehabilitation credit with a two-tier credit for qualified rehabilitation expenses. The new credit percentage is 20% for the rehabilitation of certified historic structures and 10% for the rehabilitation of buildings, other than historic structures, originally placed in service before 1936.

Under prior law the rehabilitation tax credit was 15% for nonresidential buildings at least 30 years old, 20% for nonresidential buildings at least 40 years old, and 25% for certified historic structures.

As under prior law, the new credit for the rehabilitation of historic structures applies to both residential and nonresidential buildings, while the new credit for the rehabilitation of buildings (other than historic structures) only applies to nonresidential buildings.

Prior law provisions that determine whether rehabilitation expenditures qualify for the credit generally have been retained. An expenditure is not eligible for the credit unless the taxpayer elects to recover the rehabilitation costs using the straight-line method of depreciation. A lessee's expenditures don't qualify for the credit unless the remaining lease term, on the date the rehabilitation is completed, is at least as long as the applicable recovery period (31½ years for nonresidential property, 27½ years for residential property).

External-walls requirement. The new law significantly modifies the external walls requirement. The prior provision that required 75% of the existing external walls to be retained in place as external walls has been deleted, and replaced by the prior law alternate test. This test requires the retention in place of (1) at least 75% of the existing external walls, including at least 50% as external walls, as well as (2) at least 75% of the building's internal structural framework. So a completely gutted building cannot qualify for the rehabilitation credit. A building's internal structural framework generally includes all load-bearing internal walls and any other internal structural supports, including the columns, girders, beams, trusses, spandrels, and all other members that are essential to the building's stability. Although the external-walls requirement is waived for historic structures, the Secretary of the Interior is expected to continue generally to deny certification to rehabilitation where less than 75% of external walls are not retained in place.

Basis reduction. The new law deleted the prior law provision that required a basis reduction for only 50% of the credit for certified historic structures. So a full adjustment is required for both the 10% and 20% rehabilitation credits.

Effective date and transition rules: In general, the new rules are effective for property placed in service after 12-31-86. Special transition rules apply to:

• Property placed in service as rehabilitation property before 1-1-94, if the rehabilitation was completed under a written contract binding on 3-1-86.

• Rehabilitation of property (including any leasehold interest) acquired before 3-2-86 or acquired on or after that date, if (1) the rehabilitation was completed under a written contract binding on 3-1-86, and a historic certification application was submitted to the Department of the Interior (or its designee) before 3-2-86, or (2) the lesser of $1,000,000 or 5% of the rehabilitation cost was incurred before 3-2-86, or is required to be incurred under a written contract binding on 3-1-86.

There are additional transition rules for specific projects.

Property covered by the transition rules is eligible for a 25% credit (historic rehab), 13% credit (nonresidential buildings at least 40 years old), or 10% credit (for nonresidential buildings at least 30 years old). However, a full basis adjustment is required even if the

1-1-89, and the property is placed in service before 1-1-91. Special transitional rules apply under Sec. 252(f).

⟦¶219⟧ Merchant Marine Capital Construction Funds. The new law recodifies the tax provisions of the Merchant Marine Act of 1936, and adopts the same definitions of terms as those included in the Merchant Marine Act, as added.

Tax treatment of nonqualified withdrawals. Nonqualified withdrawals made after 12-31-85 are to be taxed at the maximum individual or corporate rate. Interest is payable from the date the withdrawn amount is reported. The rule is modified in cases where the taxpayer derived no tax benefit from depositing the funds.

Fund reports. The Transportation and Commerce Secretaries must certify to the Treasury Secretary that the monies in a fund are appropriate for vessel construction requirements. If fund balances exceed what is appropriate to meet vessel construction program objectives, the fundholder must develop appropriate program objectives within three years or treat the excess as a nonqualified withdrawal.

25-year deposit limitation. Monies must be withdrawn from the fund for a qualified purpose within 25 years. Monies that are not either withdrawn or committed by the end of the 25-year period are classified as nonqualified withdrawals, using a 5-year phase-in rule.

Act Sec. 261, relating to Merchant Marine Capital Construction Funds, adds new Code Sec. 7518, effective for tax years beginning after 12-31-86.

[The page following this is 301.]

CAPITAL GAINS AND LOSSES

[¶301] Long-Term Capital Gain Break Repealed. The new law repeals the capital gain deduction for individuals. Under prior law, individuals and other noncorporate taxpayers could deduct 60% of net capital gain from gross income. The $3,000 annual loss limitation for noncorporate taxpayers is retained, but long-term losses (like short-term losses) offset ordinary income on a one-for-one basis. Under prior law, long-term losses offset ordinary income on a two-for-one basis. Sec. 1231 gain will continue to be computed separately from long-term gain. Although individual and corporate capital gain will lose its special tax status, the Code's capital-gains statutory structure is retained to make it easier to reinstate a capital gains rate differential if there is a future increase in the tax rates.

For details on how the capital gains changes affect charitable gifts of appreciated property, see ¶132.

Act Sec. 301 repeals the Sec. 1202 capital gains deduction, and amends Code Sec. 170 effective for tax years beginning after 12-31-86.

[¶302] Capital Gains Rate for 1987 and 1988. For tax year 1987, a noncorporate taxpayer's long-term capital gains and short-term capital gains will be taxed as ordinary income. However, long-term capital gains will be taxed at a maximum rate of 28%. But short-term gains will be taxed at ordinary rates. For tax year 1988, there will no longer be a distinction between short-and long-term capital gains. Gains will be taxed at a maximum rate of 28% (unless the taxpayer must pay a 5% surcharge, see ¶101).

Effective for the 1987 tax year, corporate long-term capital gains will be taxed as ordinary income but will be subject to a maximum tax rate of 34%. Prior law's special corporate capital gains rate of 28% is repealed.

In general, the 34% alternative tax rate applies to taxable years beginning after 12-31-86. For tax years that straddle 1-1-87, the 28% alternative rate applies to gain recognized before 1-1-87. Note: The alternative tax rate for corporate net capital gains doesn't apply for gain included in income in tax years when the new corporate rates are fully effective (years starting on or after 7-1-87). Reason: The maximum corporate rate will be 34%.

> **Example (1):** Bob and Jane are married and have taxable income, other than from capital transactions, of $50,000. They also sold stock they had held 15 months at a $10,000 gain. If these figures applied to 1986, their total tax liability would be $12,577, figured as follows:
>
> | | |
> |---|---:|
> | Taxable ordinary income .... | $50,000 |
> | Taxable income from long-term capital gain (40% of $10,000) .... | 4,000 |
> | Total taxable income .... | $54,000 |
> | Tax (38% marginal rate) .... | $12,577 |

If these figures applied to 1987, their total tax liability would be $13,390.

(2) Set up a "short sale against the box" in 1986, but don't close the sale until 1987. A short sale happens when you have your broker borrow stock and sell it on your behalf. At this point, your profit is locked in. Gain from a short sale is automatically short term. However, you don't have to pay tax on the gain until the sale is closed at a later date. You close a short sale against the box by repaying the broker with the stock you own. Tax result: You nail down your 1986 profit, and you defer the tax on the short-term gain until 1987.

Strategy # 3: This is the last year you get a tax choice when you sell publicly traded securities during the last five trading days of the year. Starting in 1987, you pay tax the year you make the sale. In 1986, however, you can treat the transaction as an installment sale and pay tax in 1987 (i.e., when the cash settlement is made). Or you can elect out of installment tax treatment and pay tax in 1986 (i.e., the year you made the sale).

The tax flexibility you have by selling listed stocks or bonds during the last five trading days is especially important in 1986. You can have net short-term gain taxed in 1987 under the installment sale rules. And you can have net long-term gain taxed in 1986 by electing out of installment sale treatment.

> **NOTE:** Taxpayers who are at least 55 years' old can still exclude the first $125,000 of gain on the sale of a principal residence. The rule does not change under the new law.

Act Secs. 302 and 311, limiting the maximum tax rate on net capital gains to 28% and repealing the corporate alternative capital gain tax rate, amend Secs. 1 and 1211, effective for tax years beginning after 12-31-86.

[¶303] Changes for ISOs. Executive stock option plans may be either qualified (incentive stock options) or nonqualified. An advantage of an incentive stock option is that the taxpayer doesn't owe a tax until the stock acquired with the option is sold. Exercising a nonqualified option triggers a tax. However, the employer can deduct the nonqualified option when it is exercised, whereas there is no deduction when the incentive stock option is exercised.

These attributes do not change under tax reform. But the tax reform does create some new similarities.

Sequence of exercise. For options issued before 1987, executives had to use the first in first out method. They had to exercise options in the order they were granted, whether the options were qualified or nonqualified. The FIFO method won't be required for options exercised after 1986. So if the stock price falls below the option price, the company can issue the executive a second incentive option with a lower exercise price.

Capital gain. Since capital gains will be taxed at the same rate as ordinary income, there will no longer be a tax break when the stock is sold. Before the new law, the spread betweem the option's exercise price and the stock price (the bargain element) was taxed as long-term capital gain if the stock was held for more than a year before sale.

Special break for 1987. For 1987 only, the top capital gain rate will be 28%, compared to a top ordinary rate of 38½%. So incentive stock sold in 1987 will still get a tax break, provided it was held more than one year before sale.

Modified dollar caps. Starting in 1987, there is a $100,000 per employee limit on the value of stock covered by options that are exercisable in any one calendar year. Before 1987, the limit applied to the value of options granted in any one year.

Act Sec. 321 repeals the requirement that incentive stock options be exercisable in chronological order, and modifies the $100,000 limitation, amending Sec. 422A(b)(7) for options granted after 1986.

【¶304】 Covered Call Options—Year-End Rule Expanded. The qualified covered call exception to the loss deferral rule is denied to taxpayers who don't hold a covered call option for 30 days after the related stock is disposed of at a loss, when gain on the option is included in the next year.

Act Sec. 331 expands the year-end rule for straddles by amending Sec. 1092(c)(4)(E), effective for positions established after 1986.

【¶311】 Capital Gains for Timber and Dairy Cattle. The end of special treatment for long-term capital gains means that under the new law, taxpayers won't get that treatment for gain from timber dispositions treated as sales. However, the new law will let taxpayers revoke a past election (under Sec. 631(a)) to treat the cutting of timber as a sale or exchange.

Act Sec. 406 states that the capital gains amendments will not apply to any gain from the sale of dairy cattle under a valid contract with the U.S. Department of Agriculture under the milk production termination program for gains made after 1-1-87 and before 9-1-87.

Act Sec. 311, allowing the revocation of elections to treat the cutting of timber as a sale or exchange, amends Sec. 631(a), effective for elections made before 8-17-86.

[The page following this is 401.]

AGRICULTURE, ENERGY, AND NATURAL RESOURCES

Farming

〔¶401〕 Limitation on Expensing of Soil and Water Conservation Expenditures. The new law limits the expensing deduction for soil and water conservation expenditures to amounts incurred that are consistent with a conservation plan approved by the Department of Agriculture's Soil Conservation Service. If no SCS plan exists for the location, improvement costs that are consistent with a state conservation agency plan will satisfy the federal standards. The following costs may not be expensed:

- Draining or filling of wetlands.
- Preparing land for installing and operating a center pivot irrigation system.

The Conference Report clarifies that while prior approval of the taxpayer's project by the SCS or comparable state agency isn't necessary to qualify the expenditures under this provision, there must be an overall plan for the taxpayer's area that has been approved by an agency in effect at any time during the tax year.

Act Sec. 401, relating to the limitation on expensing soil and water conservation expenditures, adds new Sec. 175(c)(3), effective for amounts paid or incurred after 12-31-86, in tax years ending after that date.

〔¶402〕 Expenditures for Clearing Land. Land clearing costs to prepare for farming that were formerly deductible must now be added to the land's basis. The Committee Reports clarify, however, that routine brush clearing and other ordinary maintenance activities related to property already used in farming continue to be currently deductible. These expenditures must be ordinary and necessary business expenses under Section 162. According to the Committee Reports, the special election to expense fertilizer and soil conditioning expenditures is retained.

Act Sec. 402, relating to repeal of special expenditures for clearing land, repeals Sec. 182, and amends Secs. 263(a) and 1252(a)(1)(A), effective for amounts paid or incurred after 12-31-85, in tax years ending after that date.

〔¶403〕 Dispositions of 'Converted Wetlands' or 'Highly Erodible Croplands.' A gain on the disposition of "converted wetland" or "highly erodible cropland" that's converted to agricultural use (other than livestock grazing) is treated as ordinary income. The Treasury is to apply rules similar to those under Sec. 1245. A loss is treated as a long-term capital loss.

"Converted wetland" means land that is

• converted wetland within the meaning of Section 1201(4) of the 1985 Food Security Act (16 U.S.C. 3801(4)); and

• held by the person who originally converted the wetland, by a person who at any time used the land for farming, or by a person whose adjusted basis in the property is determined by reference to the basis of the person in whose hands the property was converted. According to the House Committee Report, land that had been converted could become eligible for Section 1231 treatment in the hands of a later buyer or legatee, provided the buyer or legatee used the land only for nonfarming purposes.

Generally, the Food Security Act defines converted wetland as land that has been drained or filled to make possible the production of agricultural goods, if it wouldn't have been possible but for this action.

"Highly erodible cropland" means any land as defined in Section 1201(6) of the Food Security Act (16 U.S.C. 3801(6)) that the taxpayer uses for farming other than animal grazing.

According to the House Committee Report, generally highly erodible cropland is land that

• the Department of Agriculture classifies as class IV, VI, VII, or VIII land under its land capability classification system, or

• would have an excess average annual rate of erosion in relation to the soil loss tolerance level, as determined by the Department of Agriculture.

Act Sec. 403, treatment of dispositions of converted wetlands or highly erodible croplands, adds new Sec. 1257, effective for dispositions first used for farming after 3-1-86 in tax years ending after that date.

[¶404] **Prepayments of Farming Expenses.** Under the new law, cash-basis taxpayers who are in the trade or business of farming aren't allowed a deduction for specified amounts paid for feed, seed, fertilizer, and other similar farm supplies earlier than the time when these items are actually used or consumed (that is, until the tax year in which economic performance occurs). The limitation applies to prepaid expenses to the extent they exceed 50% of the deductible farming expenses for the tax year (other than prepaid farm supplies) for which economic performance has occurred.

Farming is defined in Sec. 464(c)—generally, the cultivation of land or the raising of any agricultural or horticultural commodity, including animals.

These provisions generally apply to any farmer to the extent that more than 50% of the person's farming expenses paid during the tax year (other than prepaid farm supplies) are prepaid expenses. The new law doesn't, however, treat the taxpayers as farm syndicates. Under the Committee Reports, for purposes of the 50% test, expenses include the farm operating expenses such as

- ordinary and necessary farming expenses under Sec. 162,
- interest and taxes paid,
- depreciation allowances on farm equipment, and
- other expenses generally reported on Schedule F of Form 1040.

The new law provides two exceptions to the 50% test. If either exception is met, prepaid expenses will continue to be deducted as under current law, even though the prepaid expenses are more than 50% of farming expenses for that year.

Exception (1): If a qualified farm-related taxpayer fails to satisfy the 50% test because of a change in business operations directly attributable to extraordinary circumstances. This includes government crop diversion programs and circumstances under Sec. 464(d).

Exception (2): If a qualified farm-related taxpayer satisfies the 50% test on the basis of the three preceding tax years. For this purpose, the farming expenses (other than prepaid farm supplies) for the three-year period are aggregated.

Farm-related taxpayer includes:
(1) any person whose principal residence is on the farm;
(2) any person with a principal occupation of farming; or
(3) any family member of persons described in (1) or (2).

The exception applies only to an eligible farmer's farming activities attributable to the farm on which the residence is located, or to farms included in the "principal occupation" of farming activities.

The House and Senate Committee Reports make clear that the new law doesn't amend the farming syndicate rules of Sec. 464, and that this provision will operate independently of that provision. Also, farmers won't have to generally take year-end inventories of prepaid items as a result of the new law.

For explanation of the treatment of preproductive period expenses of farmers, and of the treatment of expenses for replanting groves, orchards, or vineyards destroyed in natural disasters, see ¶805.

Act Sec. 404, on prepayments of farming expenses, adds Sec. 464(f), effective for amounts paid or incurred after 3-1-86, in tax years beginning after that date.

[¶405] Treatment of Discharge of Debt Income. The new law provides that discharge of debt income arising from an agreement between a solvent individual engaged in farming and an unrelated qualified person to discharge qualified farming debt is treated as income realized by an insolvent individual.

Generally, if an insolvent taxpayer has income from the discharge of trade or business debt, the taxpayer can exclude that income if the taxpayer's "tax attributes" are reduced by the amount of income. Tax attributes include otherwise unused net operating loss deductions, investment tax credits, foreign tax credits, capital loss carryovers, and basis of the taxpayer's depreciable property. If the amount of discharge of debt income exceeds the taxpayer's available tax attributes, tax on the excess income is forgiven to the extent of the taxpayer's insolvency.

According to the Senate Report, qualified farm debt is one incurred to finance producing agricultural products (including timber) or livestock in the United States, or farm business debt secured by farmland or farm machinery and equipment used in agricultural production.

Individuals are treated as engaged in farming if at least 50% of the average annual gross receipts during the three tax years preceding the year in which the discharge of debt occurs were derived from farming.

Further, the new law includes basis in farmland in the list of tax attributes that may be reduced by the discharge of debt income. However, all tax attributes other than basis in farmland, including property other than farmland, must be reduced before the discharge of debt income is applied against that attribute.

Act Sec. 405, on treatment of discharge of indebtedness income for farmers, adding Sec. 108(g), and amending Sec. 1017(b), effective for discharges of indebtedness occurring after 4-9-86, in tax years ending after that date.

[¶406] **Retaining Capital Gains Treatment for Sales of Dairy Cattle Under Milk Production Termination Programs.** The amendments made by Title III (Capital Gains and Losses), Subtitle A (Individual Capital Gains) and Subtitle B (Corporate Capital Gains) don't apply to any gain from the sale of dairy cattle under a valid contract with the U.S. Department of Agriculture covering the milk production termination program to the extent the gain is properly taken into account under the taxpayer's accounting method on or after 1-1-87 and before 9-1-87.

Timber

[¶408] **Capital Gains for Timber.** The end of special treatment for long-term capital gains means that under the new law, taxpayers won't get that treatment for gain from timber dispositions treated as sales. However, the new law will let taxpayers revoke a past election (under Sec. 631(a)) to treat the cutting of timber as a sale or exchange.

The option will allow elections made for tax years beginning before January 1, 1987, to be revoked without IRS consent. The revocation can cover any tax year ending after December 31, 1986. Such a revocation won't prevent a taxpayer from making another election in a later year, but any future revocations will require IRS consent. See also ¶311.

> **NOTE:** The new law keeps the existing breaks for reforestation, including the investment credit for qualified reforestation expenses. See also ¶208.

Act Sec. 311(d)(2) allows the revocation of elections to treat the cutting of timber as a sale or exchange, effective for tax years beginning after 12-31-86. Act. Sec. 211(a), allowing a credit for qualified reforestation expenses, adds Sec. 49(b)(3) effective for expenses incurred after 12-31-85 in tax years ending after that date.

Oil, Gas & Geothermal Properties

[¶409] **Intangible Drilling Costs.** The new law increases, from 20% to 30%, the amount of otherwise deductible intangible drilling costs [IDCs] that integrated producer corporations must capitalize and amortize. Moreover, the amortization period has been increased from 36 months to 60 months, beginning with the month in which the costs are paid or incurred. The new law continues the rule that amortization deductions of capitalized IDCs must be included in any recapture calculations under Section 1254.

The new law adds the provision that the portion of the property's adjusted basis that's attributable to intangible costs capitalized under these rules can't be included in the property's depletable basis.

Foreign IDCs. Under the new law, the option to deduct IDCs no longer applies to IDCs incurred outside of the United States. Such costs can now be recovered either (1) in equal installments over the 10-year period starting with the year in which the costs were paid or incurred, or (2) if the taxpayer elects, by adding them to the basis for cost depletion. Both the House and Senate committee reports stated that for these purposes, the United States includes the 50 states and the District of Columbia, plus those continental shelf areas that are adjacent to U.S. territorial waters and over which the United States has exclusive rights regarding exploring for and exploiting natural resources.

> **NOTE:** 60-month amortization for integrated producer corporations doesn't apply to these foreign costs.

Dry holes. The new law provides that the new foreign IDC rules don't apply to costs paid or incurred regarding a nonproductive well. The Conference Committee report states that the new general rule on IDC capitalization doesn't affect the option to expense dry hole costs in the year the dry hole is completed.

Act Sec. 411(a), increasing the required capitalization of IDCs for integrated producer corporations, amends Section 291(b), and Act Sec. 411(b)(1) requiring the amortization of foreign IDC, adds new Sec. 263(i) and makes a clerical amendment to Sec. 263(a), all effective for costs paid or incurred after 12-31-86, in tax years ending after that date. There is also a special transition rule for IDCs of U.S. companies with certain interests in North Sea development.

[¶410] Bonuses and Advance Royalties. The new law reverses *Commissioner v. Engle* [(1984), 464 U.S. 206, 53 AFTR2d 84-415], in which the Supreme Court held that taxpayers could treat lease bonuses and advance royalties as part of gross income from the property in computing percentage depletion under the post-1974 rules. The new law limits percentage depletion on oil, gas, and geothermal wells to amounts received for actual production, specifically excluding lease bonuses, advance royalties, and other amounts payable without regard to production.

Act Sec. 412(a)(1), which prohibits percentage depletion on oil and gas payments not related to production, adds Sec. 613A(d)(5), and Act Sec. 412(a)(2), which prohibits percentage depletion on geothermal payments not related to production, adds Section 613(e)(4), both effective for amounts received or accrued after 8-16-86, in tax years ending after that date.

[¶411] Gain From Disposition of Interest in Oil, Gas, or Geothermal Property. The new law has greatly expanded the scope of Sec. 1254, which previously required recapture only of IDCs. It now not only requires recapture of depletion on oil, gas, and geothermal property, but also depletion, mine exploration costs, and mine development costs on hard mineral property [See ¶414].

Thus, on disposition of Sec. 1254 property that involves only oil, gas, or geothermal production, the taxpayer must recapture the lesser of (1) amounts that were deducted under Section 263 rather than added to basis, plus depletion deductions that reduced the basis of the property (that is, none after the adjusted basis of the property reaches zero), or (2) the amount realized (for a sale, exchange, or involuntary conversion) or fair market value (for anything else), minus the property's adjusted basis.

The new law keeps most of the other existing rules of Section 1254, dropping only the provision that allows the amount of recapturable IDCs to be reduced by the amount by which depletion would have increased if the expensed IDCs had been capitalized.

Act Sec. 413, relating to gain from disposition of an interest in Section 1254 property, amends Code Sec. 1254, effective for property placed in service after 12-31-86, except property acquired under a written contract entered into before 9-26-85 and binding at all times thereafter.

[¶412] Mine Exploration and Development Costs. The new law increases, from 20% to 30%, the amount of otherwise deductible mine exploration and development costs that corporations must capitalize. Moreover, those costs must now be amortized over 60 months, beginning with the month in which the costs are paid or incurred, instead of being written off under the schedule that was in the Code.

The new law requires that amortization deductions of mine exploration and development costs be included in any recapture calculations under the new rules of Sec. 1254 [see ¶414]. It also provides that the portion of the property's adjusted basis that's attributable to costs capitalized under these rules can't be included in the property's depletable basis.

Foreign costs. Under the new law, the option to deduct mine exploration and development costs no longer applies to costs incurred outside of the United States. Such costs can now be recovered either (1) in equal installments over the 10-year period starting with the year in which the costs were paid or incurred, or (2) if the taxpayer elects, by adding them to the basis for cost depletion. Both the House and Senate committee reports stated that for these purposes, the United States includes the 50 states and the District of Columbia, plus those continental shelf areas that are adjacent to U.S. territorial waters and over which the United States has exclusive rights regarding exploring for and exploiting natural resources.

> **NOTE:** Sixty-month amortization for corporations doesn't apply to these foreign costs.

Act Sec. 411(a), increasing the required capitalization of mine exploration and development costs for corporations, amends Section 291(b), Act Sec. 411(b)(2)(A), requiring the amortization of foreign mine development costs, renumbers Section 616(d) as Section 616(e) and adds new Sec. 616(d), Act Sec. 411(b)(2)(B), requiring the amortization of foreign mine exploration costs, amends Sec. 617(h), and Act Sec. 411(b)(2)(C) makes certain clerical amendments, all effective for costs paid or incurred after 12-31-86, in tax years ending after that date.

[¶413] Percentage Depletion. The new law raises, from 15% to 20%, the amount of "excess" percentage depletion on iron ore and coal (including lignite) that a corporation can't deduct. "Excess" percentage depletion is the amount by which the otherwise allowable percentage depletion deduction for the tax year exceeds the basis of the property, as adjusted through the end of the previous tax year.

Disposals. With the end of special treatment for long-term capital gains [See also ¶301], disposals of coal (including lignite) or domestic iron ore with a retained economic interest will no longer qualify for such treatment, although they'll still be considered as sales. The new law provides, however, that in a tax year for which the top rate on net capital gain is the same as the top rate on ordinary income, royalties on such disposals will nevertheless be eligible for percentage depletion.

Act Sec. 412(b), increasing the amount of percentage depletion on iron ore and coal disallowed for corporations, amends Sec. 291(a)(2), effective for tax years beginning after 12-31-86. Act Sec. 311(b)(3), allowing percentage depletion on certain coal and iron ore disposals treated as sales, amends Sec. 631(c), effective, except for a special transition rule, for tax years beginning after 12-31-86.

[¶414] Gain on Disposition of Mining Property. Under the new law, mine exploration and development costs and percentage depletion on hard mineral property are recaptured under the same set of rules—Sec. 1254—that apply to IDCs and, now, percentage depletion, on oil, gas, and geothermal property. These new rules take precedence over the old rules requiring recapture of mine exploration costs on disposition of the property (Sec. 617(d)), but leave in force the rules requiring recapture of mine exploration costs when a mine reaches the producing stage (Sec. 617(b)).

On a disposition of Sec. 1254 property that involves only solid mineral production, the taxpayer must recapture the lesser of (1) amounts that were deducted under Section 616 or Section 617 rather than added to basis, plus depletion deductions that reduced the basis of the property (that is, none after the adjusted basis reaches zero), or (2) the amount realized (for a sale, exchange, or involuntary conversion) or fair market value (for anything else) minus the property's adjusted basis.

The remaining rules are essentially those that already applied to IDC recapture. If the disposition is of part or all of an undivided interest, only a proportionate part of the deductions and expenditures have to be recaptured. However, if the taxpayer disposes of any other portion of the property (such as a full interest in part of the acreage) all of the deductions and expenditures have to be recaptured to the extent of the gain. The exception to the partial recapture rule is that if the taxpayer can establish—to the IRS's satisfaction—that the deductions and expenditures don't apply to the interest disposed of, there's no recapture on that disposition.

There's generally no recapture on any disposition, complete or partial, if the disposition is a gift, a transfer on death, or one of a group of certain tax-free transactions. Special rules apply to partnership property, and to sales or exchanges of S corporation stock if part of the gain is attributable to recapturable costs under Section 1254.

Act Sec. 413(a), relating to gain from disposition of an interest in mineral property, amends Sec. 1254, and Act Sec. 413(b), making a conforming amendment, adds Sec. 617(d)(5), both effective for property placed in service after 12-31-86, except property acquired under a written contract entered into before 9-26-85 and binding at all times thereafter.

Energy-Related Tax Credits and Other Incentives

[¶415] **Business Energy Tax Credits.** Although the regular investment credit has been repealed, the new law still allows businesses to take an investment credit on certain energy expenditures, as shown in the following table.

Property	Credit Percentage	From	To
Solar energy	15%	1-1-86	12-31-86
	12%	1-1-87	12-31-87
	10%	1-1-88	12-31-88
Geothermal	15%	1-1-86	12-31-86
	10%	1-1-87	12-31-88
Ocean Thermal	15%	1-1-86	12-31-88
Biomass	15%	1-1-86	12-31-86
	10%	1-1-87	12-31-87

Under prior Code rules, all of these credits were to have expired at the end of 1985. The prior law percentage was 10% for biomass property. The credits for wind energy property, intercity buses, alternative energy property, and small hydroelectric projects were allowed to expire as of the end of 1985, as was the residential energy credit.

The new law adds no new rules regarding dual-purpose solar or geothermal energy property. The Conference Committee, however, states that this is an area regarding which the Treasury should issue regs under existing law.

Long-term projects. A credit will still be available for certain long-term projects, involving alternative energy sources and small-scale hydroelectric facilities, if an "affirmative commitment" was made. Such a commitment exists only when engineering studies, permit applications, and binding contracts are made by the dates set out in Sec. 46(b)(2)(C) and (D). If a credit is otherwise available for projects that qualify under the affirmative commitment rules, the new law will allow it, but subject to some of the limitations that now apply to the investment credit on transition property [See also ¶209]. Thus, there will be a 35% reduction in the regular amount of such credits (10% on alternative energy projects, 11% for the hydroelectric facilities) for tax years beginning on or after 7-1-87 (with a proration for tax years that straddle 7-1-87 [¶2087], and the adjusted basis of the property will have to be reduced by the full amount of the credit taken.

Act Sec. 421(a), which extends certain business energy investment credits, amends Sec. 46(b)(2)(A), and Act Sec. 421(b), regarding certain long-term projects, adds Sec. 46(b)(2)(E), both effective in periods after 12-31-85, under the standing investment credit transitional rules of Sec. 48(m).

[¶416] **Alcohol Import Duty.** The new law adds new requirements to exemptions from tariff duties on ethyl alcohol for fuel use from certain areas. The exemptions apply to imports from U.S. insular possessions and countries of the Caribbean Basin Initiative (beneficiary countries). The new law generally requires that to come within the duty exemption, the alcohol must either be (1) dehydrated in and the product of a full-scale fermentation process in the insular possession or beneficiary country, or (2) must be dehydrated in an insular possession or beneficiary country from hydrous ethyl alcohol of a certain value (from 30% to 75% of the value of the final product, depending on the year involved) from another insular possession or beneficiary country.

Act Sec. 423, restricting certain exemptions from import duties on ethyl alcohol, amends Item 901.50 of the Appendix to the Tariff Schedules of the United States, implicitly amends general headnote 3(a) of the Tariff Schedules of the United States, Sec. 213 of the Caribbean Basin Economic Recovery Act, and Secs. 313(b) and (j)(2) of the Tariff Act of 1930, and makes conforming amendments to general headnote 3(a)(i) of the Tariff Schedules of the United States, the headnotes to part 1, subpart A, of the appendix to the Tariff Schedules of the United States, and Sec. 213(a)(1) of the Caribbean Basin Economic Recovery Act, all generally effective for articles entered after 12-31-86 and before the expiration date of item 901.50 of the Appendix to the Tariff Schedules of the United States. Special transition rules apply to articles from certain facilities.

[¶417] **Alcohol Fuels and Excise Taxes.** Under the prior law, "neat" alcohol fuels (consisting of at least 85% alcohol not derived from petroleum or natural gas) were completely exempted from the 9-cents-a-gallon excise tax on special motor fuels. The new law repeals that exemption, and substitutes a reduction of 6 cents a gallon, for a special motor fuels excise tax of 3 cents a gallon on neat alcohol fuels.

The new law also extends the exemption for taxicabs from the excise taxes on motor fuels through 9-30-88.

Act Sec. 422(a), which repeals the special fuels excise tax exemption for neat alcohol fuels, amends Sec. 4041(b)(2)(A), effective for sales or use after 12-31-86. Act Sec. 422(b), extending the taxicab rules, amends Sec. 6427(e)(3), effective 10-1-85.

[The page following this is 501.]

TAX SHELTERS

[¶501] **Extension of At-Risk Rules to Real Estate.** Under the at-risk rules, individuals and certain closely held corporations cannot deduct losses in excess of their actual economic investment in an activity. Under the new law, these at-risk rules have been extended to include the activity of holding real estate. Real estate was exempted under prior law.

Losses attributable to real property placed in service after 1986 will be deductible only up to the amount the taxpayer has placed at risk—that is, the amount the taxpayer could actually lose by engaging in the activity. This amount includes cash contributions to the activity, the adjusted basis of other property contributed to the activity, and borrowed amounts used in the activity for which the taxpayer is personally liable, or has pledged property not used in the activity as security for repayment of the borrowed amounts. A person is generally not considered at risk if he or she isn't personally liable for repayment of the debt (nonrecourse loans) or the lender has an interest other than as a creditor in the activity.

Exception for qualified nonrecourse financing. Taxpayers are not subject to the at-risk rules to the extent they use arm's-length third party commercial financing secured solely by real property. This exception will apply only if the third party lender is not (1) "related" to the taxpayer; (2) the seller of the property or someone "related" to the seller; or (3) a person who is paid a fee with respect to the taxpayer's investment in the property.

Certain qualified nonrecourse financing will be treated as an amount at risk when borrowing from a related person if the terms of the loan are commercially reasonable and on substantially the same terms as loans involving unrelated persons.

Commercially reasonable defined. A loan is commercially reasonable if there is a written unconditional promise to pay on demand, or at a specified time, a definite sum of money and the interest rate being charged is a reasonable market rate. If the interest rate is below the reasonable market rate a portion of the principal may be considered interest. In that case, the principal may exceed the fair market value of the property. An interest rate would not be commercially reasonable if it were significantly below the market rate of comparable loans made by qualified persons not related to the borrowers.

If the interest rate exceeds a reasonable market rate, or is contingent on profits or gross receipts, a portion of the principal amount may represent a disguised equity interest (and a portion of the interest in fact is a return on equity) with the result that the stated principal amount may exceed the fair market value of the financed property. Thus, generally, an interest rate would not be considered commercially reasonable if it significantly exceeds the market rate on comparable loans by unrelated qualified persons. Nor would an interest rate be considered commercially reasonable if it were contingent. However, interest rates that are not fixed may be commercially reasonable. Those rates, however, must be calculated with respect to a market interest index such as the prime rate charged by a major commercial bank, LIBOR, the rate on government securities (such as Treasury bills or notes), or the applicable Federal rate.

The terms of the financing would also not be considered commercially reasonable if, for example, the term of the loan exceeds the useful life of the property, or if the right to foreclosure or collection with respect to the debt is limited, except to the extent provided under state law.

Convertible debt is not treated as qualified nonrecourse financing. The conferees felt that it was not appropriate to treat investors as at risk with respect to nonrecourse debt that is convertible and that consequently represents a right to an equity interest, because taxpayers are not intended to be treated as at risk for amounts representing others' rights to equity investments.

Special rule for partnerships. The Senate Finance Committee Report stated that a partnership's nonrecourse financing may increase a partner's (including a limited partner's) amount at risk provided the financing is qualified nonrecourse for both the partner and the partnership. The amount the partners are treated at risk cannot be more than the total amount of the qualified nonrecourse financing at the partnership level. The special rule for partnerships is in Sec. 465(b)(6)(C).

Act Sec. 503, extending the at-risk rules to the holding of real property, amends Sec. 465. It applies to losses incurred after 12-31-86 with respect to property placed in service after 12-31-86. For an interest in an S corporation, a partnership, or other pass-through entity acquired after 12-31-86, the amendments apply to losses incurred after 12-31-86 that are attributable to property placed in service by the S corporation, partnership, or pass-through entity on, before, or after January 1, 1986. A special rule applies to an athletic stadium in Pennsylvania.

[¶502] **Losses and Credits From Passive Activities.** Congress seems determined to put tax shelters out of business. The crackdown started 10 years ago with the requirement that an investor's deductions not exceed his amount at risk. Almost every major tax law since 1976 has expanded the at-risk rule. And as we've seen, the new law isn't an exception. Having gone as far as it could with the at-risk rule, Congress decided to attack shelters with a new weapon called the passive-loss rule.

How it works. All income is placed into one of three baskets: (1) income from passive activities—such as limited partners' interests in a business; (2) active income (e.g., salary, bonuses, etc.); and (3) portfolio income (e.g., dividends and interest). Losses generated by "passive activities" can offset only passive income. They cannot be applied against income in the other two baskets—but they can be carried over to future years and applied against passive income. Similarly, tax credits from passive activities (other than foreign tax credits) can offset only the tax payable on passive income.

Practical result: A taxpayer's passive losses can still shelter every dollar of passive income. But if he doesn't have sufficient passive income, the deductions and credits generated by a passive activity don't do the taxpayer any good in the current year. He's got the tax equivalent of an umbrella on a sunny day.

> **Example:** Ellen Jones is an investor in two passive activities (she has an investment in two partnerships in whose businesses she doesn't materially participate). One activity generates $3,000 of income; the other $10,000 of deductions (net loss). The $3,000 of passive income is sheltered by $3,000 of passive losses. Jones cannot use the remaining $7,000 of excess deductions to shelter her active income or portfolio income.

Annual passive losses in excess of annual passive income (e.g., the $7,000 of net loss in the example above), and excess credits, may be carried forward and used to offset future years' passive income or (for credits) the tax on that income. *Exception:* Losses are allowed in full when a taxpayer disposes of his entire interest in the passive activity.

Taxpayers affected. The passive-loss rule applies to individuals, estates, trusts, closely held C corporations (generally, if five or fewer individuals own directly or indirectly more than 50% of the stock), and personal service corporations (other than corporations where the owner-employees together own less than 10% of the stock). It's a wide-ranging measure that affects passive interests in any trade or business as well as tax shelters. There's a blanket exception for working interests in oil and gas properties and a limited exception for real estate investors.

The rules in general apply for tax years beginning after 1986, and are phased in during 1987—1991. Also, there is a transitional exception for certain investors in low income housing. See ¶507.

Act Sec. 501 dealing with limitations on losses and credits from passive activities adds Sec. 469 generally effective for tax years beginning after 12-31-86, and as indicated in ¶507. Act Sec. 502 providing a transitional rule exception for investors in low income housing doesn't amend the Code.

[¶503] **Passive Activities.** There are two categories of passive activities:

- Any trade or business or, to the extent provided in regs any activity conducted for profit, in which the taxpayer does not materially participate; and

- Any rental activity, whether or not the taxpayer materially participates.

Passive trade-or-business activities. Any trade or business is a passive activity for a taxpayer who does not materially participate in the enterprise. Material participation is defined as a year-round active involvement in the operations of the activity on a regular, continuous, and substantial basis.

> **Example:** Father supplies Son with capital to start a business and becomes a general partner in the venture. Although Father approves major capital outlays, he does not participate in the business on a regular basis. Result: Father cannot shelter portfolio or salary income with his share of start-up losses from the business.

> **NOTE:** The term "trade or business" includes any activity involving research and experimentation under Sec. 174.

Signposts of material participation. According to the Committee Reports, there are three main factors to be considered, but none of them is conclusive of the presence or absence of material participation.

- Is the activity the taxpayer's principal trade or business? Examples: A person whose main business is farming is more likely to materially participate in a farm than an executive who invests in a farming operation. On the other hand, a taxpayer whose sideline business is producing documentaries is not engaged in a passive activity merely because his principal business is being a film executive.

- How close is the taxpayer to the activity? Although a taxpayer is more likely to be actively involved in a business that is located in his vicinity, proximity is not enough. He still must actively participate in the business. But distance from the enterprise is not always a bar. For example, a software developer who lives in New York may be actively involved in his company even if it's located in Silicon Valley.

- Does the taxpayer have knowledge and experience in the enterprise? For example, a doctor who knows little about cattle is unlikely to be materially involved in a cattle-feeding operation. However, even if the doctor had experience with cattle feeding, he still must be involved in day-to-day operations to avoid the passive-loss rule. In other words, rubber-stamping decisions made by others won't do.

Special exception: A farmer who materially participates in his farm holds on to that status after retirement; and so does the spouse of a deceased farmer.

The material-participation standard is applied to a taxpayer (or his or her spouse) who owns an interest in the business as a proprietor, general partner, or S corporation shareholder. A personal service corporation or closely held C corporation meets the standard if there is material participation by one or more shareholders owning more than 50% of the stock. A closely held C corporation may use an alternative test. The material participation standard is met if

- at least one full-time employee works full time and year-round in the active management of the activity,
- at least three nonowner employees work full time in the activity for the entire year, and
- business deductions of the activity exceed 15% of its gross income.

A taxpayer that directly or indirectly owns an interest in any activity as a limited partner automatically fails the material participation test. However, the Treasury is given authority to prescribe regulations that will prevent taxpayers from manipulating this rule to circumvent the passive-loss limitation. Example: A taxpayer would not be able to sop up large passive losses by converting his ownership of income-generating activities into limited partnership form. What's more, income from personal services to the passive activity isn't "passive activity income" that can sop up the losses from passive activities.

Rental activities. Rental activities, which are presumed to be passive, include all activities that generate income from payments for the use of tangible property, rather than for the performance of substantial services. Signposts of a rental activity: a lease term that is long in relation to the property's useful life; day-to-day expenses are insignificant in relation to rents or in relation to depreciation and carrying costs; and no significant services are supplied to each new lessee.

Examples of rental activities: long-term rentals of apartments, office equipment, and automobiles, or the rental of a vessel under a bare-boat charter or a plane under a dry lease (no pilot or captain and no fuel provided), and net-leased property. A property is net-leased if the lessor's deductions (other than rents and reimbursed amounts) are less than 15% of rental income, or when the lessor is guaranteed a specific return or is guaranteed against loss of income.

Examples of businesses that are not rental activities: short-term car rentals, and rentals of hotel rooms or similar space to transients.

¶503

In general, real estate rentals—short- or long-term—are presumed to be rental activities and thus are automatically passive in nature. There are three exceptions:

• Real estate dealers are generally not treated as engaging in a passive activity.

• Taxpayers may use up to $25,000 of real estate losses and credit equivalents to shelter nonpassive income if they are "active participants" [see ¶505].

• Mortgage interest on a principal residence or second residence is not subject to the passive-loss rule even if the taxpayer rents out the residence.

> **OBSERVATION:** Although residence interest is excluded, other residence-related deductions are subject to the passive rule if the taxpayer rents out the home and is not actively involved in his "rental business." This can happen if a management agent handles all aspects of the business, including approval of tenants (as is the case with some "rent-pooled" vacation homes).

[¶504] **How the Passive-Loss Rule Works.** To begin with, a taxpayer must pass the expanded at-risk rule [¶501]. Deductions disallowed because the taxpayer's at-risk amount is insufficient are suspended by Sec. 465. Such deductions become subject to the passive-loss rule only if the taxpayer's at-risk amount increases in future years.

> **SALT IN THE WOUND:** A taxpayer's at-risk amount is reduced by losses allowed under Sec. 465 even if the losses are suspended by the passive-loss rule. Similarly, a taxpayer's basis is reduced by deductions (e.g., depreciation) even if the deductions are not usable currently because of the passive loss rule.

Losses from passive activities can offset only passive activity income and cannot shelter "active" income such as salary. "Portfolio income" generated by the activity or earned by the taxpayer is not passive income and can't be offset by passive losses. "Portfolio income" consists of (1) interest, dividends, and royalties (unless earned in the ordinary course of a trade or business); and (2) gain or loss on the sale of property that generates portfolio income or is held for investment. Income (e.g., interest) earned on working capital is treated as portfolio income.

Exceptions. A closely held C corporation (other than a personal-service corporation) may use passive losses and credits to offset its "net active income." This is taxable income of the company figured without regard to passive income or loss or portfolio income. And if a taxpayer becomes materially involved in what had been a passive activity, he may use suspended losses to offset the activity's income even though his interest is no longer passive.

Any tax credit generated by a passive activity (other than foreign tax credits) may offset only the tax attributable to passive income. That's the excess of the tax owed on all income less the tax that would be owed on non-passive-source income (passive-source credits are disregarded in both cases).

ALLOCATIONS REQUIRED: A taxpayer must allocate income, deductions, and credits among passive and active elements. And if he owns several passive activities, he must prorate suspended losses and credits among the activities.

Example: During 1987, AB General Partnership operates an investment counseling business out of one floor of a three-story building that it owns. The other two floors are net-leased to a commercial tenant. AB also has portfolio income (e.g., dividends and interest) and a passive interest in an income-producing farm.

Results: The partners can use two-thirds of the building's deductions to offset rental income and income from the farm. Any excess deductions from the rented portion of the building cannot be used to shelter portfolio income or income from the counseling business. Since the remaining one-third of the building's deductions are allocable to a business in which the partners materially participate, it is not subject to the passive-loss rule.

NOTE: If AB were organized as a closely held C corporation, it could use excess deductions from the rented portion of the building to shelter its net active income.

Example: John Smith is a passive investor in three ventures. He has $15,000 of deductions in excess of income from Venture A, and $10,000 of excess deductions from Venture B. Venture C produces $15,000 of passive income. *Result:* Smith can offset $15,000 of passive income with $15,000 of passive loss. His net passive loss of $10,000, suspended under new Sec. 469, is allocated as follows: Activity A, $6,000 ($10,000 net passive loss × $15,000/$25,000); Activity B, $4,000 ($10,000 net passive loss × $10,000/$25,000).

Suspended losses and credits may be carried forward (but not back) and used to offset future years' passive-source income. A suspended loss is allowed in full when the entire interest is sold to an unrelated third party in a taxable transaction. Suspended losses (and any loss on the sale) are deductible against income in the following order: any gain recognized on the transaction; net income or gain for the tax year from all passive activities; and any other income or gain. Losses from the sale or exchange of a capital asset are limited to the amount of gains from the sale or exchange of capital assets, plus $3,000 (in the case of individuals). The capital-loss limit is applied *before* the determination of the amount of losses upon a disposition. In an installment sale, passive losses become available as the buyer makes payments. Losses are freed up in the same ratio that gain recognized each year bears to the total gain on the sale.

CREDITS VANISH: Since the passive-loss rule is designed to limit writeoffs to real economic losses, any unused suspended credits are not allowed when a passive activity is sold. In other words, the credits vanish into thin air.

A special rule applies if the taxpayer made a basis adjustment at purchase as a result of claiming a tax credit (e.g., a rehabilitation tax credit). When that property is disposed of, the taxpayer may elect to increase the property's basis by the amount of credit suspended by the passive-loss rules. However, the basis adjustment can't exceed the amount of the original basis adjustment.

Suspended losses are not freed up by

- a change in the form of ownership (e.g., transfer of proprietorship interest to an S corporation),
- a like-kind exchange (except to the extent of taxable "boot"), or
- a partial disposition of a passive activity.

Other transfers. Any suspended losses remaining at a taxpayer's death are allowed as deductions on his final return to the extent the basis of the property in the hands of the transferee exceeds the property's adjusted basis immediately prior to the decedent's death.

Example: When John Smith dies, his basis in a limited partnership interest is $10,000 and its value is $20,000. If he holds $15,000 of suspended losses, $5,000 may be deducted on his final return (suspended losses minus the $10,000 excess of the transferee's basis over Smith's basis. If suspended losses are $10,000 or less, nothing is deductible.

Finally, if a taxpayer makes a gift of his entire interest in a passive activity, the donee's basis is increased by any suspended losses. If the interest is later sold at a loss, however, the donee's basis is limited to the fair market value on the date the gift was made.

[¶505] Limited Relief for Active Participants in Real Estate. The new law gives some relief to a natural person who actively participates in a rental real estate activity. He can offset nonpassive income with up to $25,000 of losses and credits (in deduction equivalents) from his "active" real estate interests. The limit is $12,500 for marrieds filing separate returns. The deduction equivalent of credits is the amount that, if allowed as a deduction, would reduce tax by an amount equal to the credit.

IMPORTANT: The deduction equivalent of a low-income housing credit or rehabilitation credit counts toward the $25,000 allowance *whether or not* the taxpayer actively participates in the activity that gave rise to the credit. In the case of a low-income housing credit, this rule applies only to property placed in service before 1990, and only with respect to the original compliance period for the property, except if the property was placed in service before 1991, and 10% or more of total project costs are incurred before 1989.

Example: A taxpayer is an active participant in a real estate venture that produces $20,000 of credits in 1988, but no deductions or income. If he is a joint filer with taxable income of, say, $70,000 he may claim a $7,000 credit for 1988. Reason: In his 28% tax bracket, $25,000 of deductions would create a tax saving of $7,000. The $13,000 balance of his credit is suspended by the passive-loss rule.

Phase-out of $25,000 allowance. For deductions, the $25,000 allowance is reduced by one-half of the taxpayer's AGI in excess of $100,000 ($50,000 for marrieds filing separately). Thus, there is no allowance for deductions once AGI exceeds $150,000 ($75,000 for marrieds filing separately). For credits from qualifying rehabilitation projects [¶217] and low-income housing projects [¶218], the $25,000 allowance (in deduction equivalents) is reduced by one-half of the taxpayer's AGI in excess of $200,000 ($100,000 for marrieds filing separately). Thus there's no credit if AGI exceeds $250,000 ($125,000 for marrieds filing separately). For purposes of the credit phase-out, AGI is figured without regard to: (1) any net passive losses, (2) IRA contributions and (3) taxable social security benefits.

What if a taxpayer has both credits and losses from a real estate activity in which he actively participates? In this case, the Senate Finance Committee Report indicates that the credit that may be claimed (before application of the phase-out) equals (1) tax owed on income other than any net passive losses, but reduced by real estate deductions allowed under the relief measure, less (2) the tax he would owe if allowable real estate deductions equaled $25,000 (or a lesser limit, if his AGI exceeds the $100,000 or $200,000 limit). Credits are disregarded in both calculations.

Example: In January 1988, Warren Able becomes a general partner and active participant in a real estate venture that produces a rehabilitation tax credit. He is not involved in any passive activities. For tax year 1988, Able is allocated $10,000 of deductions and $10,000 of rehabilitation credits. The project does not throw off any income for the year. For 1988, Able's adjusted gross income without regard to the real estate deal is $90,000. His taxable income, counting $10,000 of real estate deductions, equals $70,000. The $25,000 allowance less $10,000 of deductions leaves a balance of $15,000.

Result: Able may claim $4,200 of rehabilitation tax credits for 1988. That's the equivalent of $15,000 of deductions in Able's 28% bracket. That $4,200 also represents the difference (disregarding credits) between (1) the tax Able would have paid counting $10,000 of real estate deductions, and (2) the tax payable counting $25,000 of real estate deductions. The $5,800 balance of his credit is suspended by the passive-loss rule.

The active-participation standard for rental real estate is more liberal than the material participation standard that applies to other activities. All that's required is that the taxpayer or his or her spouse participate in a bona fide sense. For example, making management decisions, such as approving tenants, lease terms, and repairs, is sufficient even if an agent handles the day-to-day affairs of the real estate rental activity. However, a taxpayer cannot be an active participant if he is a limited partner or holds a less than 10% interest in the real estate rental enterprise. The estate of a decedent who had actively participated in a real estate venture is deemed to actively participate in the venture for a two-year period following the decedent's death.

[¶506] **Working Interests in Oil and Gas Properties Excepted From Passive-Loss Rule.** A taxpayer who holds a working interest in an oil and gas property is exempted entirely from the passive loss rule, whether or not he materially participates in the activity. A working interest is one that is burdened with the cost of developing and operating the property. Typical characteristics: responsibility for authorizing expenses; receiving periodic reports about drilling, completion, and expected production; the possession of voting rights and rights to continue operations if the present operator steps out; a share in tort liability (e.g., uninsured losses from a fire); and some responsibility to share in additional costs.

A taxpayer whose liability is limited (e.g., he holds a limited partnership interest or S corporation shares) is not treated as owning a working interest. Also specifically excepted from the definition of a working interest: rights to overriding royalties or production payments; and contract rights to extract or share in oil and gas profits without liability for a share of production costs.

[¶507] **Effective Date and Phase-In of Passive-Loss Rule.** In general, the passive-loss rule applies to tax years beginning after 12-31-86. But there's a five-year phase-in for losses or credits from passive activities held on the new law's enactment date (these are called credits and losses from "pre-1987 interests"). The phase-in also applies if the taxpayer holds a contract to purchase a passive activity and the contract is binding on the date of enactment. For tax years beginning in 1987, 35% of passive losses and credits from pre-1987 interests is subject to the new rules. For tax years 1988, 1989, and 1990, the portion of the loss or credit from pre-1987 interests subject to the rules is 60%, 80%, and 90% respectively. For 1991 and later years, 100% of these passive losses and credits is subject to the passive loss rule.

Example: In June 1986, Dan Smith buys a limited partnership interest in a cattle deal. In January 1987, he buys a limited partnership interest in a farm. For tax year 1987, the ventures produce $70,000 of deductions but no income ($56,000 from the cattle deal and $14,000 from the farm). Here's how things work out for 1987:

Loss subject to phase-in [from activity held on enactment date]....................................	$56,000
Loss not subject to phase-in [from activity acquired after law's enactment date]........................	14,000
	$70,000

Amount subject to passive loss rule		
(1) $56,000 × .35	$19,600	
(2) $14,000 × 100%	14,000	
Total suspended losses	$33,600	(33,600)
Allowable losses		$36,400

NOTE: Any passive loss disallowed for a tax year during the phase-in period and carried forward may be allowed in a later year only to the extent there is net passive income in the later year (or the activity is disposed of).

Transitional exception for investors in low-income housing. Losses of certain investors of cash or property in specially defined "qualified low income housing projects" placed in service before 1989, which are sustained during a "relief period" aren't treated as losses from a passive activity for the passive activity loss rules. This applies to investors who are natural persons (and their estates for the first and second tax years ending after their death), who made their initial investments after 12-31-83 and who are required to make payments after 12-31-86 of 50% or more of the total original obligated investment. For projects placed in service on or before 8-16-86, the taxpayer must hold an interest in the project on 8-16-86. For property placed in service after 8-16-86, the taxpayer must hold an interest in the project on 12-31-86. (An interest is treated as held on 8-16-86 or 12-31-86 if there's a binding contract to acquire it on such date). The "relief period" starts with the tax year of the investor's initial investment, and ends with the *earliest* of (1) the sixth tax year after the tax year of initial investment; or (2) the first tax year after the year the investor is obligated to make his last investment; or (3) the tax year that precedes the first year when the project ceases to qualify. A special transition rule applies to partnerships which placed low-income housing in service on or after 12-31-85 and before 8-17-86. The benefit of the above relief is obtained at the price of loss of any Sec. 42 low-income housing credit for the project.

[¶508] **New Limits on Investment Interest Deductions.** Taxpayers other than corporations have been limited by Sec. 163(d) in the amount they can deduct for interest on debt incurred to buy or carry property held for investment. The limit has been $10,000 a year, plus the taxpayer's net investment income. Beginning in 1987, investment interest will be deductible only to the extent of net investment income each year (with an indefinite carryforward of disallowed investment interest). Moreover, the scope of the investment interest limitation will be expanded. There's a five-year phase-in of the new rule.

Investment interest. Interest subject to the limitation includes all interest (except consumer interest and qualified residence interest) on debt not incurred in a person's active trade or business.

So if you borrow to purchase or carry investment property, the interest you pay is investment interest. Also, if you have a trade or business in which you do not materially participate, any interest expense allocable to the business activity is investment interest provided the activity is not a "passive activity" under the passive loss rule. If you borrow money to purchase or carry an interest in a passive activity, your interest expense will be investment interest to the extent the interest is attributable to portfolio income.

> **ALERT:** Any interest that is taken into account in determining your income or loss from a passive activity is not investment interest. In addition, it doesn't include interest allocable to a rental real estate activity in which the taxpayer actively participates.

Net investment income. This is defined as the excess of investment income over investment expenses.

Under the new law, investment income includes:

- Gross income from interest, dividends, rents, and royalties.
- Gain from the disposition of investment property.
- Portfolio income under the passive loss rules.
- Income from a trade or business in which the taxpayer does not materially participate if the activity is not a "passive activity" under the passive loss rule.

Investment expenses include deductions (other than interest) that are directly connected with the production of net investment income (including actual depreciation or depletion deductions allowable).

> Any income or expenses from activities subject to the passive-loss rules (explained at ¶502) is not treated as investment income or investment expenses.

2% floor on miscellaneous expenses. In determining deductible investment expenses, investment expenses are considered as those allowed after the application of the rule limiting deductions for miscellaneous expenses to those exceeding 2% of adjusted gross income. In computing the amount of expenses that exceed the 2% floor, expenses that are not investment expenses are intended to be disallowed before any investment expenses are disallowed.

Net lease property. Property subject to a net lease is not treated as investment property because it is treated as a passive activity under the passive loss rule. Income from rental real estate in which the taxpayer actively participates is not included in investment income.

Effective Date: The new investment interest rules are generally effective for tax years beginning after 12-31-86. There is a phase-in of the disallowance over a five-year period. During this phase-in period (1987 through 1990), the amount of investment interest disallowed is generally equal to:

(1) the excess of investment interest over prior law's $10,000 allowance ($5,000 for marrieds filing a separate return, and zero in the case of trusts), plus

(2) the applicable percentage of investment interest *up to* the $10,000 (or $5,000) allowance.

The applicable percentage is 35% for 1987, 60% for 1988, 80% for 1989, and 90% for 1990.

> **Example:** For tax year 1987, Arnold Smith, an individual taxpayer, has $20,000 of investment interest in excess of investment income. Mr. Smith has no investments covered by the passive loss rule. The amount of investment interest expense disallowed for 1987 is computed as follows:
>
> (1) Excess of $20,000 investment interest over prior
>   law's $10,000 allowance.................................. $10,000
> (2) 35% of the investment interest that does
>   not exceed $10,000   3,500
>
> Total disallowed interest $13,500

Mr. Smith may deduct the $6,500 balance of his investment interest expense in excess of investment income.

> **NOTE:** For taxable years beginning on or after 1-1-87 and before 1-1-91, the amount of net investment income is reduced by the amount of losses from passive activities that is allowed as a deduction by virtue of the phase-in of the passive loss rule (other than net losses from rental real estate in which the taxpayer actively participates). For example, if a taxpayer has a passive loss which would be disallowed were the passive loss rule fully phased in (as in taxable years beginning after 12-31-90), but a percentage of which is allowed under the passive loss phase-in rule, the amount of loss so allowed reduces the amount of the taxpayer's net investment income under the investment interest limitation for that year. Interest that is disallowed for a year during the phase-in period and carried forward may be allowed in a later year only to the extent the investment income in the later year exceeds the net investment interest paid or incurred in the later year.

Act Sec. 511, expanding the scope of the interest limitation deduction, amends Sec. 163(d), effective for interest paid or incurred in tax years beginning on or after 1-1-87 with a phase-in over a 5-year period. [See phase-in rules above.]

[¶509] **Qualified Residence Interest.** Under the new law, qualified residence interest is deductible in full. It is neither investment interest nor consumer interest [¶510]. It is interest on debt secured by a security interest perfected under local law on the taxpayer's principal residence or second residence. A principal residence is one that qualifies for nontaxable exchange treatment under Sec. 1034. To qualify as a second residence, the taxpayer must use the dwelling as his or her residence for part of the year if he or she rents the home to others.

The amount deductible as qualified residence interest consists of interest on debt that does not exceed

- the taxpayer's cost for the residence, plus
- the cost of any improvements.

ALERT: Taxpayers whose homes have declined in value must be careful. Interest on the portion of a loan that exceeds the fair market value of the home at the time the loan is made will not be deductible.

If the debt exceeds the taxpayer's cost plus improvements, the excess is deductible as qualified residence interest only to the extent the borrowed amounts incurred after 8-16-86 are used for educational or medical purposes. If the amount of any debt incurred on or before 8-16-86, and secured by the residence on 8-16-86 (reduced by any principal payments) is more than the cost basis of the residence, then such amount is treated as the taxpayer's basis. Any increase in the amount of the taxpayer's debt that takes place after 8-16-86, but which is secured by the residence on 8-16-86 is treated as incurred after 8-16-86. Interest on outstanding debt secured by the taxpayer's principal or second residence is fully deductible to the extent the debt does not exceed the fair market value of the residence.

Suppose the loan exceeds the sum of cost basis plus improvements, and the loan proceeds are used for personal purposes (e.g. purchase of a car). Unless the taxpayer qualifies for the 8-16-86 exception (see above), interest on the excess loan amount is treated as nondeductible consumer interest. There is a phase-in of the consumer interest rule [See ¶510].

Consider these examples:

Example (1): Mr. and Mrs. Smith bought a home for $80,000 ten years ago. In September 1986 the balance on their first mortgage is $50,000 and the market value of their home is $150,000.

Result: The Smiths can continue to deduct the interest on their first mortgage. They can also borrow another $30,000 using their home as collateral (e.g., refinance the first mortgage, obtain a second mortgage, or a "home equity credit line") and deduct the interest, regardless of how they use the $30,000.

Example (2): Same facts, except the Smiths refinanced their first mortgage in September 1986 and got a new mortgage for $90,000.

Result: The mortgage interest on $80,000 of the mortgage principal is deductible regardless of how the funds are used. The interest on $10,000 of the mortgage principal is deductible only if the $10,000 is used for educational purposes (e.g., to finance child's education) or medical purposes (e.g., to pay a large hospital bill).

If taxpayers borrow against the equity in their home to make an investment, the interest that's not deductible as qualified residence interest may be deducted as investment interest, subject to the new investment interest rules (and the phase-in of these rules).

Example (3): Mr. and Mrs. Jones bought a home for $125,000 ten years ago and have a balance on their first mortgage of $50,000. The fair market value of their home has increased to $200,000. In September 1986 they borrow another $100,000 against increased equity in their home and use the money to buy rental property.

Result: The interest on their original mortgage and $75,000 of the $100,000 loan is deductible as qualified residence interest. The interest on the remaining $25,000 of the $100,000 loan is deductible as investment interest [¶508] to the extent of the investment income.

NOTE: If the proceeds of the $100,000 loan are used to finance a business, then interest on $25,000 of the loan could be deducted as a trade or business expense.

Taxpayer's "cost" of the residence. In determining the cost basis of your residence, do not take into account any of the adjustments made under Sec. 1034(e), relating to the postponing of gain on the sale and purchase of a residence, or Sec. 1033(b), relating to involuntary conversions. Although you add the cost of improvements to your basis, do not make any adjustments for depreciation. If the residence is acquired from a decedent, the basis of the residence is determined under Sec. 1014, which would generally require the basis to be the fair market value of the residence at the date of the decedent's death or at an alternative valuation date. Generally, under this rule, the amount of debt on which the taxpayer may deduct interest will not be less than the purchase price of the residence.

Medical and educational expenses defined. Medical payments do not include amounts paid for insurance. Educational expenses include tuition at a primary or secondary school, college or graduate school. It also includes amounts paid for living expenses while at those schools. The educational expenses must be for the taxpayer, his or her spouse, or dependent as defined in Sec. 152. And the qualified educational or medical expenses must be incurred within a reasonable period of time before or after the debt is incurred.

Special rules. The Senate Finance Committee reported that if a taxpayer owns more than two residences, he may designate each year which residence (other than his principal residence) he wants to have treated as his second residence. If a joint return is filed, a second residence includes a residence owned by the taxpayer or his spouse and which is owned by either or both spouses. For marrieds filing separate returns, each spouse can deduct qualified residence interest secured by one residence. In the alternative, one spouse can consent in writing to allow the other spouse to claim qualified residence interest on two residences (as long as one is a principal residence).

Housing cooperatives, state homestead laws. Interest on debt secured by the taxpayer's stock in a housing cooperative unit that is the taxpayer's residence won't be treated as nondeductible consumer interest to the extent the debt doesn't exceed the fair market value of the cooperative unit. The taxpayer's share of interest expense of the housing cooperative which is allocable to his unit and his share of the co-op's common residential areas also will not be treated as nondeductible consumer interest.

The taxpayer's debt secured by the stock in the cooperative is treated as debt secured by the residence of the taxpayer. However, there are situations where the taxpayer can not use the stock as security. For example, there may be state or local restrictions or the cooperative agreement may prevent it. In such cases the stock may be treated as securing such debt, if the taxpayer can establish to the satisfaction of the IRS that the debt was incurred to acquire the stock. The fact that state homestead laws may restrict the rights of secured parties with regard to certain residential mortgages will not necessarily make the interest nondeductible. The taxpayer's payment of interest will be qualified residence interest if the lenders security interest is perfected and the debt otherwise qualifies.

Act Sec. 511, adds Sec. 163(h), effective for tax years beginning after 12-31-86.

[¶510] Personal Interest Is Nondeductible. Starting with tax years beginning after 12-31-86, personal interest is no longer deductible. Personal interest is defined as interest on any debt, *other than* (1) interest on debt incurred or carried in connection with the taxpayer's trade or business or a Sec. 212-type investment activity, (2) qualified residence interest [explained at ¶509], (3) interest taken into account in computing the taxpayer's income or loss from passive activities for the year, or (4) interest payable on certain estate tax deficiencies. Interest on debt incurred in connection with a taxpayer's trade or business of performing services as an employee is *not* trade or business interest. For example, an employee who must supply his own car for work cannot deduct interest on a loan obtained to buy his business car. Interest on a tax deficiency is personal interest.

The disallowance of deductions for personal interest is phased in over a five-year period: 35% of personal interest is nondeductible in 1987, 60% in 1988, 80% in 1989, 90% in 1990, and 100% in 1991 and later.

Act Sec. 511 adds Sec. 163(h), effective as shown above.

[The page following this is 601.]

CORPORATE TAX

〔¶601〕 Corporate Tax Rate Lowered. Corporate tax rates are generally reduced. A three-step graduated rate structure is substituted for the five-step rate structure. The top corporate tax rate is reduced from 46% to 34%.

Income tax rate schedule. The corporate tax rates are as follows:

Taxable Income	Tax Rate (%)
Not over $50,000	15
Over $50,000 but not over $75,000	25
Over $75,000	34

For corporate taxable income in excess of $100,000, there's an additional 5% tax but that tax can't be greater than $11,750.

> **IMPACT:** The benefit of graduated rates for corporations with taxable income between $100,000 and $335,000 is phased out. Corporations with income in excess of $335,000, in effect, pay a flat tax at a 34% rate.

Effective Dates: The revised income tax rates are effective for tax years beginning on or after 7-1-87. For tax years that include 7-1-87, the old rates and the new rates will be blended.

Capital gains and charitable deductions. The new law also changes capital gains treatment [see ¶301 and 302]. For details on how capital gains changes affect charitable gifts of appreciated property, see ¶132.

Act Sec. 601, relating to corporate rate reductions, amends Sec. 11(b), applying to tax years starting on or after 7-1-87.

〔¶602〕 Dividends-Received Deduction Decreased. The corporate dividends-received deduction is lowered to 80% from 85% for regular dividends received by corporations, dividends received on certain preferred stock, and dividends on debt-financed portfolio stock. The limit on the aggregate amount of the deduction is also lowered to 80% from 85% for corporations and insurance companies.

The decrease was necessary to prevent the reduction in corporate rates from resulting in a significant reduction in the tax rate on dividends eligible for this deduction.

Act Sec. 611, reducing the dividends received deduction, amends Secs. 243, 244, 246-246A, 805(a)(4)(B), applicable to dividends received or accrued after 12-31-86, in tax years ending after such date. The changes to Sec. 246(b) as to limitation on aggregate amount of deductions applies for tax years starting after 12-31-86.

〔¶603〕 Extraordinary Dividends—Holding Period Lengthened for Basis Reduction. A corporation that disposes of a share of stock must reduce its basis (but not below zero) by the nontaxable portion of any extraordinary dividend paid on the share if the stock has not been held for more than two years before the date of announcement or declaration about the dividend. If there is no formal or informal agreement to pay the particular dividend before the declaration date, the date of this agreement is treated as the dividend announcement date for applying the two-year holding period requirement. A distribution that would otherwise be an extraordinary dividend under the two-year rule will not be considered extraordinary if the distributee has held the stock for the entire period the distributing corporation (and any predecessor corporation) has been in existence. The basis reduction is required only to figure gain or loss on the share's disposition. If the aggregate nontaxed portions of extraordinary dividends exceed the shareholder's basis, the excess is treated as gain from a sale or exchange at the time of disposition. Under prior law, this basis reduction was required only if the stock was sold or disposed of before it had been held for one year.

Different treatment of dividends on certain qualifying preferred stock applies. Absent the special rule under the basic definition of an extraordinary dividend (below), a preferred stock that pays a greater-than-5% dividend within any period of 85 days or less is paying an extraordinary dividend. This exception is intended to provide relief for certain transactions to the extent there is no potential for effectively purchasing a dividend that accrued prior to the date of purchase (dividend-stripping). Preferred stock is treated as qualifying if it meets certain dividend requirements. Also, dividends on qualifying preferred stock are treated as **extra**ordinary dividends only to the extent the dividends received by the taxpayer during the period it owned the stock exceed the dividends it earned.

Taxpayers have the option of determining the distribution's status as an extraordinary dividend by reference to the share's fair market value on the day before the ex-dividend date, in lieu of its adjusted basis. The alternative fair market value test applies for Sec. 1059(c)(3)(B) (which treats certain dividends having ex-dividend dates within a 365-day period as extraordinary).

> **COMMENT:** Taxpayers may want to do this if the stock has significantly appreciated since its original purchase.

Fair market value must be established to the IRS. No part of a distribution may reduce basis twice, as for members of an affiliated group filing consolidated returns.

Extraordinary dividends are those that exceed 10% (5% for shares of stock preferred as to dividends) of the shareholder's basis in the share.

Also, the term "extraordinary dividend" is expanded to include any distribution (without regard to the holding period for the stock or the distribution's relative magnitude) to a corporate shareholder in partial liquidation of the distributing corporation. A distribution here is treated as in partial liquidation if it satisfies the proper requirements. Also, the term extraordinary dividend includes any stock redemption that is non-pro rata (again, irrespective of holding period or the distribution's relative size).

The rules don't apply to distributions between an affiliated group's members filing consolidated returns, except as provided in regs.

Act Sec. 614, amending the holding period for basis reduction by the non-taxable portion of extraordinary dividends, amends Sec. 1059, applicable to dividends declared after 7-18-86, in tax years ending after that date. For purposes of Sec. 1059(c)(3), dividends declared after 7-18-86 are not aggregated with dividends declared on or before 7-18-86. Sec. 1059(e)(1) concerning redemptions, applies to dividends declared after the date of enactment, in tax years ending after such date.

[¶604] **Dividend Exclusion for Individuals Repealed.** There is no longer a dividend exclusion for individuals. The limited exclusion of the first $100 of qualified dividends received by an individual shareholder and $200 by a married couple filing a joint return is repealed.

Act Sec. 612, relating to the repeal of the partial exclusion of dividends received by individuals repeals Sec. 116, and makes clerical changes affecting Secs. 301(g)(4), 584(c), 642(j), 643(a)(7), 702(a)(5), 854(a), (b), 857(c), applicable to tax years beginning after 12-31-86.

[¶605] **Stock Redemption Expenses.** A corporation gets no deduction for any amount it pays or incurs in connection with its stock's redemption.

NOTE: This rule isn't limited to hostile takeovers but applies to any corporate redemption.

Expenses in hostile takeovers. This provision is intended to clarify the rule that all expenses a corporation incurs in buying back its own stock are nonamortizable capital expenses. The new rule is designed to emphasize this point. To prevent the corporation's hostile takeover, some corporate taxpayers, under prior law, have considered so-called greenmail payments as deductible business expenses.

Amounts subject to rule. Amounts subject to this rule include (1) amounts paid to repurchase stock; (2) premiums paid for the stock; (3) legal, accounting, brokerage, transfer agent, appraisal, and similar fees incurred in the repurchase; (4) any other expense that's necessary or incident to the repurchase whether representing costs incurred by the purchasing corporation or by the selling shareholder (and paid or reimbursed by the purchasing corporation), or incurred by persons or entities related to either; and (5) amounts paid to a selling shareholder (or any related person) under an agreement entered into as part of or in connection with a repurchase of stock, in which the seller agrees not to buy, finance a purchase, acquire, or in any way be a party or agent to acquiring the corporation's stock for a specified or indefinite period of time.

Exceptions. This rule doesn't apply to the dividends-paid deduction (within the meaning of Sec. 561), relating to payments (or deemed payments) for accumulated earnings. (Note: These amounts continue to qualify for the dividends-paid deduction the same way as under prior law.)

The rule also does not apply to

- personal holding company, and foreign personal holding company taxes, and for the regular income tax for regulated investment companies and real estate investment trusts;
- deductible interest; and
- otherwise deductible expenses incurred by a regulated investment company that is an open-end mutual fund as to redeeming its stock on a shareholder's demand.

Example: Costs incurred by a regulated investment company in processing redemption applications and issuing checks to pay for redeemed shares are deductible the same way as under prior law.

COMMENT: In denying a deduction for payments as to stock redemptions, no inference is intended regarding these payments' deductibility under prior law. Also, no inference is intended as to the character of these payments in the payee's hands.

Act Sec. 613, relating to the treatment of stock redemption expenses adds new Sec. 162(k) and redesignates old Sec. 162(l) as Sec. 162(m), effective for amounts paid or incurred after 2-28-86 in tax years ending after that date.

Net Operating Loss Carryovers

[¶606] **Limitations on Net Operating Loss and Other Carryovers.** The new law significantly curtails trafficking in net operating losses. Under prior law, corporations were frequently acquired and disposed of for the net operating loss deductions the target corporation could provide the acquiring corporation.

A new cap on NOLs. Briefly, after an ownership change, the taxable income available for offset by prechange NOLs is limited annually to a prescribed rate times the loss corporation's value immediately before the change. This is the general approach. To see how the new rules work, you need to understand a host of never-before-defined statutory terms (e.g., "Sec. 382 limitation" and such) as well as certain special rules, as we'll explain later.

NOTE: After a substantial ownership change, rather than reducing the NOL carryforward itself, the earnings against which an NOL carryforward can be deducted are limited under the new law. This limitation-on-earnings approach is intended to allow NOL carryforwards to survive after an acquisition, and, at the same time, limit a corporation's ability to utilize the carryforwards against another taxpayer's income.

Is there an ownership change? Before applying the special limitations explained below, find out first if there is an ownership change. An ownership change occurs generally if the percentage of stock of the new loss corporation owned by any one or more 5% shareholders has increased by more than 50 percentage points relative to the lowest percentage of stock of the old loss corporation owned by those 5% shareholders at any time during the testing period. It can also happen after an equity structure shift. The testing period is normally the three-year period ending on the day of an owner shift involving a 5% shareholder or any equity structure shift. (But the period can be shortened, for example, if there was an earlier ownership change.) In any case, no testing period will start before 5-6-86.

Whether an ownership change has occurred is figured by aggregating the increases in percentage ownership for each 5% shareholder whose percentage ownership has increased during the testing period. For this rule, all stock owned by persons who own less than 5% of a loss corporation's stock is generally treated as stock owned by a single 5% shareholder or any equity structure shift. Generally, all "stock" is taken into account except stock that (1) is not entitled to vote; (2) is limited and preferred as to dividends and does not significantly participate in corporate growth; (3) has redemption and liquidation rights that do not generally exceed the stock's issue price on issuance; and (4) is not convertible to any other class of stock.

An owner shift involving a 5% shareholder is any change in the respective ownership of a corporation stock that affects the stock percentage held by a 5% shareholder (any person who holds 5% or more of the corporation stock during the testing period) before or after the change. For this rule, all less-than-5% shareholders are aggregated and treated as one 5% shareholder. Thus, an owner shift involving a 5% shareholder includes (but is not limited to) these transactions—

- A taxable purchase of loss corporation stock by a person who holds at least 5% of the stock before the purchase.

- A disposition of stock by a person who holds at least 5% of the loss corporation stock either before or after the disposition.

- A taxable purchase of loss corporation stock by a person who becomes a 5% shareholder as a result of the purchase.

- A Sec. 351 exchange (involving nonrecognition of gain or loss on transfers to controlled corporations) that affects the percentage of stock ownership of a loss corporation by one or more 5% share-holders.

• A decrease in the loss corporation outstanding stock (e.g., by virtue of a redemption) that affects the stock ownership percentage of the loss corporation by one or more 5% shareholders.

• A debt conversion (or pure preferred stock that is excluded from the definition of stock) to stock if the loss corporation's stock ownership percentage by one or more 5% shareholders is affected.

• A loss corporation's stock issuance that affects the percentage of stock ownership by one or more 5% shareholders.

Equity structure shift. An equity structure shift is any tax-free reorganization (within the meaning of Sec. 368) other than a divisive reorganization or an "F" reorganization. To the extent provided in regs, this term may include other transactions, such as public offerings not involving a 5% shareholder or taxable reorganization-type transactions (e.g., mergers or other reorganization-type transactions that do not qualify for tax-free treatment due to the nature of the consideration or the failure to satisfy any of the other requirements for a tax-free transaction). For determining whether an ownership change has occurred following an equity structure shift, the less - than-5% shareholders of each corporation that was a party of a reorganization will be segregated and treated as a single, separate 5% shareholder.

Multiple transactions. Whether there's an ownership change is figured by comparing the relevant shareholder's stock ownership immediately after either an owner shift involving a 5% shareholder or an equity structure shift with the lowest percentage of such shareholders' ownership at any time during the testing period preceding either the owner shift involving a 5% shareholder or the equity structure shift. Thus, changes in ownership that happen because of a series of transactions involving both owner shifts involving a 5% shareholder and equity structure shifts may be treated as an ownership change.

> **IMPORTANT:** The percentage of stock held by any person is determined on the basis of value. Changes in the holdings of certain preferred stock are disregarded. So would be changes in proportionate ownership attributable solely to fluctuations in the relative values of different classes or amounts of stock, under regs to be prescribed.

[¶607] Attribution of Stock Ownership. You apply the constructive ownership rules of Sec. 318 to find out who owns what stock for determining whether an ownership change has occurred. However, the rules for attributing ownership from corporations to their shareholders are applied without regard to the extent of the shareholders' ownership in the corporation. Thus, any stock owned by a corporation is treated as being owned proportionately by its shareholders. Similarly, stock attributed from a partnership, estate, or trust is not treated as being held by the entity. The family attribution rules of Sec. 318(a)(1) and 318(a)(5)(B) do not apply. But an individual, his spouse, his parents, his children, and his grandparents are treated as a single shareholder. "Back" attribution to partnerships, trusts, estates, and corporations from partners, beneficiaries, and shareholders will not apply except as provided in regs. Except as provided in regs., an option's holder is treated as owning the underlying stock if that presumption results in an ownership change.

No ownership change in certain stock transfers. In determining whether an ownership change has taken place, do not count any stock received or acquired in the following transactions:

- Stock acquired by reason of death.
- Stock acquired by gift or transfers in trust.
- Stock received in satisfaction of a pecuniary bequest.
- Property transferred between spouses or incident to divorce.
- Stock acquired by reason of divorce or separation.
- Employer securities acquired by a tax credit employee stock ownership plan or an employee stock ownership plan (but only if the ESOP holds at least 50% of the stock immediately after the transfer and certain other requirements are met) or by a plan participant.

[¶608] **Continuity-of-Business-Enterprise Test.** This is the next crucial issue after an ownership change (and before applying the special limitations). Reason: Unless the continuity-of-business-enterprise test is met during the two-year period starting on the change date, a loss corporation's NOL carryforwards (including any recognized "built-in" losses explained later) are disallowed completely (except to the extent of any recognized built-in gains or Sec. 338 gain explained later). Generally, the doctrine of business continuity requires the loss corporation (or the surviving corporation) to continue the loss corporation's historic business or use a significant portion of the loss corporation's assets in a business. This is the same test applicable to a tax-free reorganization under Sec. 368. The test applies regardless of the type of transaction that results in the change of control.

> **TAX TIP:** Changes in the loss corporation's key employees or its business location won't flunk the continuity-of-business test. The test may be met, even if the loss corporation discontinues more than a minor portion of its historic business.

[¶609] **How to Figure the Annual Limitation.** Assuming that the business-continuity test is met, for any tax year ending after the change date, the amount of a loss corporation's taxable income that can be offset by a prechange loss cannot exceed the "Sec. 382 limitation" for that year. The *Sec. 382 limitation* for any tax year is the key figure. It is an amount equal to the loss corporation's value immediately before the ownership change, multiplied by the federal long-term tax-exempt rate published by the IRS (more about the federal prescribed rate later).

If the limitation for a tax year exceeds the taxable income for the year, the amount of the limitation for the next tax year is increased by the amount of the excess. The limitation is also increased by certain built-in gains. A *prechange loss* includes (1) for the tax year in which a change occurs, the portion of the loss corporation's NOL that is allocable (figured, except as provided in regs, on a daily pro rata basis without regard to recognized built-in gains or losses) to the period in such year before the change date, (2) NOL carryforwards that arose in a tax year preceding the tax year of the change, and (3) certain recognized built-in losses and deductions (explained later).

The change date is the date on which an owner shift resulting in an ownership change occurs, or the date of the reorganization for an equity structure shift resulting in an ownership change.

> **NOTE:** For any tax year in which a corporation has income that may be offset by both a prechange loss (i.e., an NOL subject to limitation) and an NOL not subject to limitation, taxable income is treated as having been first offset by the prechange loss. This rule minimizes the NOLs that are subject to special limitations.

Loss corporation's value. Generally, a loss corporation's value is the fair market value of its stock, including preferred stock, immediately before the ownership change. If there is a redemption connected with an ownership change—either before or after the change—the loss corporation's value is calculated after taking the redemption into account. Future regulations may treat other corporate contractions the same as redemptions. Also, regs may treat warrants, options, contracts to acquire stock, convertible debt, and similar interests as stock for determining the loss corporation's value. Stock value is usually (though not conclusively) proven by the price at which stock changes hands in an arms-length transaction. A loss corporation's value may be reduced by capital contributions.

The long-term tax-exempt rate is the highest of the federal long-term rates found under Sec. 1274(d) (relating to the Applicable Federal Rate imputed for OID, etc.), as adjusted to reflect differences between rates on long-term taxable and tax-exempt obligations, in effect for the month in which the change date occurs or the two prior months. The long-term tax-exempt rate will be computed as the yield on diversified pool of prime, general obligation tax-exempt bonds with remaining periods to maturity of more than 9 years. The IRS will publish the long-term tax-exempt rate within 30 days after the new law is signed by the President and monthly after that.

> **COMMENT:** The prescribed rate has been chosen as the measure of a loss corporation's expected return on its assets. Using a rate lower than the long-term federal rate is necessary to ensure that the NOL carryover value to the buying corporation is not more than its value to the loss corporation. Otherwise, there would be a tax incentive for acquiring loss corporations. If the loss corporation were to sell its assets and invest in long-term Treasury obligations, it could absorb its NOL carryovers at a rate equal to the yield on long-term government obligations.

Special rule for postchange year that includes change date. Since taxable income *before* the ownership change isn't subject to special limitations, a different limitation applies for the postchange year that includes the change date. For the tax year in which a change occurs, the annual limit doesn't apply to the portion of a loss corporation's taxable income allocable to the period of the year before the change date, figured (except as provided in regs) on a daily pro rata basis. The limitation here is equal to an amount that bears the same ratio to the Sec. 382 limitation (figured without regard to this rule) as the number of days in the year on or after the change date bears to the total number of days in the year. A similar allocation rule applies for short tax years. A postchange year is any tax year ending after the change date. Taxable income, for this rule, is computed without regard to recognized built-in gains and losses.

Capital contributions that are received by a loss corporation, the principal purpose of which is to avoid or increase the special limitations, will reduce the loss corporation's value. Except as provided by regs, a capital contribution made during the two-year period ending on the change date is presumed to be part of a tax avoidance plan.

> **NOTE:** This part of the new law's antiabuse rules is designed to prevent taxpayers from circumventing the special limitations. Taxpayers are discouraged from making preacquisition infusions of assets to inflate artificially a loss corporation's value (thereby accelerating the use of NOL carryovers).

Cash and other 'nonbusiness assets.' If at least one-third of the value of a corporation's assets consists of "nonbusiness assets," then the loss corporation's value is reduced by the excess of the value of these assets over the portion of the corporation's debts attributable to these assets. Nonbusiness assets include cash, marketable stock or securities, and any asset held for investment. The amount of a corporation's debt attributable to nonbusiness assets is the amount that bears the same ratio to the debts as the nonbusiness asset value bears to the corporation's total asset value. Stock or securities in a subsidiary are not nonbusiness assets. Instead, the parent is deemed to own its ratable share of the subsidiary's assets. A corporation is treated as holding stock in a subsidiary if it owns 50% or more of the combined voting power of all classes of stock entitled to vote, and 50% or more of the total value of all classes of stock. Exceptions are provided for RICs, REITs, and real estate mortgage investment conduits.

> **NOTE:** Like the special rule on capital contributions, this anti-abuse rule is similarly designed to prevent taxpayers from trafficking in loss corporations by reducing a loss corporation's assets to cash or other passive assets and then selling off a corporate shell consisting primarily of NOLs and cash or other passive assets.

[¶610] Built-In Gains and Losses. Built-in losses are subject to special limitations because they are economically equivalent to preacquisition NOL carryovers. Built-in gains (e.g., accelerated depreciation or installment sales reporting) are often the product of special tax provisions that accelerate deductions or defer income. So relief is available for these gains.

If a loss corporation has a net unrealized built-in gain, the amount of the limitation for any tax year ending within the five-year recognition period is increased by the recognized built-in gain for the tax year. The recognition period starts on the change date and ends at the close of the fifth postchange year. If a loss corporation has a net unrealized built-in loss, the recognized built-in loss for any tax year ending within the five-year period ending at the end of the fifth postchange year (the recognition period) is treated as a prechange loss subject to limitation. A net unrealized built-in loss is the amount by which the aggregate adjusted bases of a corporation's assets exceed its asset value immediately before the ownership change. If the value exceeds the bases, there's a net unrealized built-in gain. If 80% or more in value of the stock of a corporation is acquired in one transaction (or in a series of related transactions in a 12-month period), for determining the net unrealized built-in loss, the asset value may not exceed the grossed up amount paid for the stock properly adjusted for indebtedness for the corporation and other relevant items.

De minimis exception. The special rule for built-in gains (or losses) doesn't apply if the amount of a net unrealized built-in gain (or loss) does not exceed 25% of the value of the corporation's assets. For this rule, the total basis or value is computed by excluding any cash, cash item or marketable security that has a value that does not substantially differ from adjusted basis.

Limits on recognized built-in gains and losses. The recognized built-in gain (or loss) for a tax year cannot exceed the net unrealized built-in gain (or loss), reduced by the recognized built-in gains (or losses) for prior years ending in the recognition period. Recognized built-in gain is any gain recognized on an asset's disposition during the recognition period, if the taxpayer establishes that (1) the asset was held by the loss corporation immediately before the change date, and (2) the gain does not exceed the excess of the asset value on the change date over its adjusted basis on that date. Recognized built-in loss is any loss that is recognized on an asset's disposition during the recognition period, except to the extent the taxpayer establishes that (1) the asset was not held by the loss corporation immediately before the change date, or (2) the loss (or a portion of the loss) is greater than the excess of the asset's adjusted basis on the change date over its value on that date.

The amount of any recognized built-in loss that exceeds the Sec. 382 limitation for any post-change year must be carried forward (not carried back) under rules similar to the rules that apply to NOL carryovers and will be subject to the special limitations in the same manner as a pre-change loss.

The Sec. 382 limitation for any tax year in which gain is recognized by reason of Sec. 338 election (treating stock purchases as asset purchase) is increased by the excess of the amount of the gain over the portion of the gain taken into account in computing recognized built-in gains for the tax year.

Accrued deductions. Future regs may treat as built-in losses amounts that accrue before the ownership change date but are allowable as a deduction on or after that date (e.g., deductions deferred by Sec. 267 in related-party transactions). But depreciation allowances can't be treated as accrued deductions or built-in losses.

NOTE: The Treasury Department is directed to study built-in deductions and report to the tax writing committees by 1-1-89.

[¶611] **The Bankruptcy Exception.** The special limitations do not apply after an ownership change if

• the loss corporation was under a bankruptcy court's jurisdiction immediately before the ownership change, and

• its shareholders and creditors (determined immediately before the change) own 50% of its stock immediately after the change.

For this rule, a creditor's stock that was converted from debt is taken into account only if the debt was held by the creditor for at least 18 months before the bankruptcy case was filed or arose in the ordinary course of the loss corporation's business.

If the bankruptcy exception applies, the loss corporation's pre-change NOL carryovers are reduced by 50% of the excess of the discharged debt over the value of the stock transferred to the creditors.

Second ownership change. After an ownership change that qualifies for the bankruptcy exception, a *second* ownership change during the following two-year period will result in the elimination of NOL carryovers that arose before the first ownership change.

> **NOTE:** This limitation reflects the view that any value created during the two-year period is likely attributable to capital contributions. As explained earlier [¶609], these contributions are presumptively removed from a loss corporation's value.

Special rule for thrifts. A modified version of the bankruptcy exception applies to certain ownership changes of a thrift institution involved in a G reorganization or similar transaction. The bankruptcy exception is applied to qualified thrift reorganizations by requiring shareholders and creditors (including depositors) to retain a 20% (rather than 50%) interest. For this rule, the troubled thrift's deposits that become deposits in the acquiring corporation are treated as stock. The general bankruptcy rule that eliminates from the NOL carryovers interest deductions on debt that was converted doesn't apply to interest paid on deposits by thrifts qualifying under this rule.

> **NOTE:** Transactions involving solvent thrifts, including a purchase of a thrift's stock, or merger of a thrift into another corporation, are subject to the general rules relating to ownership changes.

[¶612] New Guidelines for Other Carryovers. In addition to the NOLs discussed earlier [see ¶606 et seq.], the new law also revises special limitations on unused business credits and research credits, excess foreign tax credits, and capital loss carryovers. In general, the new limitations applying to these carryovers (under Sec. 383) are similar to the new rules on NOL carryovers (under Sec. 382). Capital loss carryforwards will (under future regs) be limited to an amount determined on the basis of the tax liability that is attributable to so much of the taxable income as does not exceed the Sec. 382 limitation for the tax year, with the same ordering rules that apply under present law.

> **NOTE:** The new law expands the scope of Sec. 383, on carryovers other than NOLs to include passive activity losses and credits and minimum tax credits.

[¶613] Tax-Motivated Transactions. Acquisitions made to evade or avoid taxes remain under the strict sanctions of Sec. 269, usually resulting in the disallowance of deductions and credits. Similarly, the regulations governing the filing of consolidated returns (referred to as SRLY and CRCO rules) continue to apply.

Future regs may be prescribed to prevent the avoidance of the special limitations through the use of related persons, pass-through entities, or other intermediaries.

[¶614] **Effective Dates; Repeal of Old Rules.** The new law generally applies to an owner shift involving a 5% shareholder occurring after 12-31-86. As for equity structure shifts, it takes effect for reorganizations under plans adopted after that date. A reorganization plan is considered adopted on the earlier of the date when (1) the boards of directors of all parties to the reorganization adopt the plan or recommend its adoption, or (2) the shareholders approve.

The new law generally repeals the 1976 Tax Reform Act amendments that would generally limit the use of NOL carryovers and focus on changes of ownership alone. The repeal is retroactively effective as of 1-1-86.

Under special transitional rules, preexisting laws still apply to ownership changes on or after 1-1-87 in special situations. A transition rule applies if a petition was filed in a bankruptcy court before 8-14-86. Also, new law changes do not apply to (1) stock-for-debt exchanges and stock sales made pursuant to a plan of reorganization as to a petition for reorganization filed under Chapter 11 on 8-26-82, and which filed with a U.S. district court a first amended and related plan of reorganization before 3-1-86, and (2) ownership change of a Delaware corporation incorporated in August 1983, which may result from the exercise of a put or call option under an agreement entered into on 9-14-83, but only as to tax years beginning after 1991 regardless of whether an ownership change takes place. Similar special rules have been provided in other special situations.

Act Sec. 621, relating to limitation on net operating loss and excess credit carryforwards, amends Secs. 382 and 383, is effective generally after 12-31-86 and as shown above. It also makes a conforming amendment to Sec. 318(b)(5), and repeals 1976 Tax Reform Act amendments retroactively that would have extensively revised Secs. 382 and 383, relating to special limitations on NOL and credit carryovers.

General Utilities Doctrine Repealed

[¶615] **Gain and Loss Recognized on Liquidating Distributions (General Utilities Doctrine).** As a general rule, corporate earnings from sales of appreciated property are taxed twice:

- First, to the corporation when the sale occurs, and then
- To the shareholders when the net proceeds are distributed as dividends.

What happened at the corporate level? The income was taxed at ordinary rates if it resulted from selling inventory or other ordinary income assets. Of course, if capital assets held long-term were involved, capital gain rates applied. With some exceptions, shareholders were taxed at ordinary income rates to the extent of their pro rata share of the distributing corporation's current and accumulated earnings and profits.

Under prior law, an important exception (commonly known as the General Utilities doctrine) would permit the corporation to escape tax at the corporate level by distributing appreciated property to its shareholders and on certain liquidating sales of property. At the same time, the shareholder or third-party buyer would get a stepped-up, fair market value basis, with associated additional depreciation, depletion or amortization deductions. *Result:* The "price" of a step up in the basis of property subject to the *General Utilities* rule was typically that the shareholder paid a single capital gains tax on a liquidating distribution from the corporation. Broadly speaking, the new law repeals the *General Utilities* doctrine.

> **COMMENT:** The repeal of the *General Utilities* doctrine is designed to require the corporate level recognition of gain on a corporation's sale or distribution of appreciated property, irrespective of whether it occurs in a liquidating or nonliquidating context. Future regs will ensure that the purpose of the new rules is not circumvented by using any other provision, including the consolidated return regulations or the tax-free reorganization provisions.

Distributions in liquidation. What happens now? Gain or loss is generally recognized by a corporation on a liquidating sale of its assets. Gain or loss is also generally recognized to a corporation on a distribution of its property in complete liquidation. The distributing corporation is treated as if the corporation had sold the property to the distributee-shareholders at its fair market value. However, gain or loss is not recognized for any distribution of property by a corporation to the extent there is nonrecognition of gain or loss to the recipient under the tax-free reorganization provisions.

If the distributed property is subject to a liability, or the shareholders assume a liability connected with the distribution, the property value is treated as not less than the amount of the liability. Thus, in this case, gain is generally recognized to the extent the liability exceeds the distributor's basis.

Converting from C corporation to S corporation. A corporate-level tax is imposed on any gain that arose before the conversion (built-in gain) and is recognized by the S corporation in any tax year, through sale or distribution, within 10 years of the date the S election took effect. The total amount of gain to be recognized is limited to the corporation's aggregate net built-in gain when the S corporation was converted. Gains on sales or distributions of assets by the S corporation are presumed to be built-in gains, except to the extent the taxpayer can establish the appreciation accrued after conversion.

The amount of tax is computed by applying the highest rate on ordinary income (or, if applicable, the alternative rate on capital gain income) to the lesser of (1) the recognized built-in gains of the S corporation for the tax year; or (2) the amount which would be the taxable income of the corporation for this tax year, if it were not an S corporation.

Any NOL carryforward arising in a tax year for which the corporation was a C corporation is allowed as a deduction against the lesser of the amounts above. The general business credit carryforward is allowed, as are certain other credits.

The tax does not apply to corporations that have always been S corporations.

> **COMMENT:** The rules generally apply to elections made after 12-31-86. The rules don't apply to S elections made before 1-1-87. Thus, the prior-law version of IRS Sec. 1374 applies.

The amount of built-in gains taken into account for any tax year cannot exceed the excess, if any, of the net unrealized built-in gain over the recognized built-in gains for prior tax years beginning in the 10-year period.

[¶616] Nonrecognition on Distributions in Complete Liquidation of Subsidiaries. There is an exception to the recognition rule for property distributed in a 100% liquidation involving a subsidiary—that is, when a subsidiary is completely liquidated into its parent.

> **COMMENT:** Since this kind of intercorporate transfer within the group is a nonrecognition event, a carryover basis follows. *Result:* The corporate level tax is paid if the corporation receiving this distributed property disposes of it to an outsider.

What happens when there's a liquidation of a subsidiary and an 80% corporate shareholder receives property with a carryover basis? The nonrecognition rule applies as to any property actually distributed to the controlling corporate shareholder (rather than pro rata share of each gain or loss). What about a minority shareholder receiving the property in this kind of liquidation? The distribution is treated the same way as a distribution in a nonliquidating redemption.

> **COMMENT:** Gain (but not loss) is recognized to the distributing corporation.

Suppose an 80% shareholder is a tax-exempt organization. Non-recognition doesn't apply under the exception for 80% corporate shareholders unless the property received in the distribution is used by the organization in an unrelated trade or business right after the distribution. However, if the property later stops being used in the acquiring organization's trade or business, the organization is then taxed (along with any other tax imposed, like Sec. 1245 depreciation recapture). The tax is the lesser of: (a) the built-in gain in the property when the distribution is made; or (b) the difference between the property's adjusted basis and its fair market value at the time of the cessation.

Nonrecognition is also denied in subsidiary's liquidation when the controlling shareholder is a foreign corporation. The regs might provide some exceptions to this.

> **COMMENT:** It's expected that nonrecognition may be allowed if the appreciation on the distributed property is not being removed from the U.S. before recognition.

[¶617] **Limiting Recognition of Losses.** Two rules are provided to prevent the recognition of losses at the corporate level.

Some background. There is a concern that taxpayers might try various means to avoid the repeal of the *General Utilities* doctrine, or otherwise take advantage of the new rules, to recognize losses in inappropriate situations or inflate the amount of losses actually sustained. How? Under the general rule allowing loss recognition on liquidating distributions, taxpayers might be able to create artificial losses at the corporate level or to duplicate shareholder losses by contributing built-in loss property to the corporation. The two rules are as follows:

1. Generally, no loss is recognized by a liquidating corporation as to any property distribution to a related person (within the meaning of Sec. 267), unless it's distributed to all shareholders on a pro rata basis *and* the property is not acquired by the liquidating corporation in a Sec. 351 transaction (transfer to corporation controlled by transferor) or as a capital contribution five years before the distribution.

> **OBSERVATION:** A liquidating corporation wouldn't be allowed to recognize loss on a distribution of recently acquired property to a shareholder who, directly or indirectly, owns more than 50% in value of the corporation's stock. Also, a liquidating corporation can't recognize loss on any property (regardless of when or how acquired) that's distributed to this shareholder on non-pro rata basis.

2. Suppose a property's contribution to a corporation in advance of its liquidation is primarily to recognize loss on the property's sale or distribution and thus eliminate or limit corporate level gain. What happens? The basis (for loss) of any property acquired by corporation in a Sec. 351 transaction or a capital contribution is re-

duced (not below zero) by the excess of the property's basis on the contribution date over its fair market value then.

> **COMMENT:** It's assumed (except when the regs indicate otherwise) that any Sec. 351 transaction or capital contribution within a two-year period before the complete liquidation plan's adoption has this main purpose. It's possible that a contribution more than two years before the adoption might have a prohibited purpose. However, this is considered unusual.

Recapture in lieu of disallowance. If a plan of complete liquidation is adopted in a tax year following the date on which the tax return, including the loss disallowed by the above rule is filed, in appropriate cases, the liquidating corporation may recapture the disallowed loss on the tax return for the tax year in which the plan of liquidation is adopted. Alternatively, the corporation could file an amended return for the tax year in which the loss was reported.

> **Example:** Blake owns a 10% interest in Acme Corp., a calendar year corporation. On 1-1-87, he contributes to Acme nondepreciable property with a $1,000 basis and a $100 fair market value in exchange for additional stock. On 9-30-87, Acme sells the property to Green, an unrelated third party, for $200. Acme includes the $800 loss on its 1987 tax return. Then, on 12-31-88, Acme adopts a liquidation plan. Acme has two choices: (1) It could file an amended return reflecting that the $800 loss was disallowed, because the property's basis would be reduced to $200. (2) It could recapture the loss on its 1988 return. The recapture here is limited to the lesser of the built-in loss of $900 ($1,000, transferred basis less $100, property's value), or loss recognized on the property's disposition, $800 ($1,000 less $200 amount realized. Thus, unless Acme files an amended return, it must recapture $800 on its return for its tax year ending 12-31-88.

> **NOTE:** Future regs might provide that the presumed prohibited purpose for contributions of property two years in advance of the liquidation plan's adoption will be disregarded *unless* there is no clear and substantial relationship between the contributed property and the conduct of the corporation's current or future business enterprises.

[¶618] Nonliquidating Distributions of Appreciated Property. Generally, a corporation's tax treatment of nonliquidating distributions of appreciated property has, in the past, been the same as liquidating distributions. However, recently, nonliquidating distributions have been made subject to stricter rules than liquidating distributions. Corporations have usually been required to recognize gains as a result of nonliquidating distributions of appreciated property.

Under the new rules, nonliquidating distributions are treated the same as liquidating distributions. This means that gain must generally be recognized to a distributing corporation if appreciated property (other than the corporation's obligation) is distributed to shareholders outside of complete liquidation.

Repeal of exceptions to recognition. The new law repeals exceptions to recognition that were provided for nonliquidating distributions to 10%, long-term noncorporate shareholders, and for certain distributions of property relating to the payment of estate taxes or certain redemptions of private foundation stock.

[¶619] Election to Treat Sales or Distributions of Subsidiary Stock as Asset Transfers. The treatment of liquidating sales and distributions of subsidiary stock is, under the new law, conformed to the present law treatment of nonliquidating sales or distributions of such stock; thus, such liquidating sales or distributions are generally taxable at the corporate level.

> **NOTE:** According to the Conference Committee Report, it's appropriate to conform the treatment of liquidating and nonliquidating sales or distributions and to require recognition when appreciated property, including stock of a subsidiary, is transferred to a corporate or an individual recipient outside the economic unit of the selling or distributing affiliated group.

In certain cases, a corporate buyer and a seller of an 80%-controlled subsidiary can elect to treat the sale of the subsidiary stock as if it had been the sale of the underlying assets [Sec. 338(h)(10)]. Among the election filing requirements are that the selling corporation and its target subsidiary are members of an affiliated group filing a consolidated return for the tax year that include the acquisition date. If an election is made, the underlying assets of the company that was sold receive a stepped-up, fair market value basis. The selling consolidated group recognizes the gain or loss attributable to the assets. There is no separate tax on the seller's gain attributable to the stock.

> **COMMENT:** This rule offers taxpayers relief from a potential multiple taxation at the corporate level of the same economic gain, which might result when a transfer of appreciated corporate stock is taxed without providing corresponding step-up in basis of the corporation's assets.

The new rule expands the so-called "Sec. 338(h)(10) concept," to the extent provided in the regs, to situations in which the selling corporation owns 80% of the value of the subsidiary's voting power, but doesn't file a consolidated return. Similar principles may also be applied to taxable sales or distributions of controlled corporation stock.

> **NOTE:** Regulations under this elective procedure should flesh out the principles that support the liquidation-reincorporation doctrine.

For example, to the extent that regs make available an election to treat a stock transfer of controlled corporation stock to persons related to the corporation, there may be special rules for that corporation's Sec. 381(c) tax attributes so that net operating losses may not be used to offset liquidation gains, earnings and profits may not be manipulated, or accounting methods may not be changed. This election is expected to affect the way in which a corporation's distribution to its shareholders will be characterized for figuring shareholder level income tax consequences.

Report on corporation income taxation. The Treasury will consider whether changes in subchapter C (relating to income taxation of corporations and their shareholders) and related provisions are desirable. Report of its study will be made to the tax-writing committees no later than 1-1-88.

Effective Dates: The new law applies generally to (1) any distribution in complete liquidation, and any sale or exchange, made by a corporation after 7-31-86, unless the corporation is completely liquidated before 1987; (2) any Sec. 338 transaction for which the acquisition date occurs after 1986; and (3) any distribution (not in complete liquidation) made after 1986. Under a transitional rule, the new law does not apply to distributions or sales made under a liquidation plan adopted before 11-20-85. Transactions are treated as made under a pre-11-20-85 liquidation plan, if before 11-20-85:

• The liquidating corporation's board of directors adopted a resolution to solicit shareholder approval for a Sec. 336 or 337 transaction, or the transaction was approved by the shareholders or directors; or

• There was an offer to buy a majority of the liquidating corporation's voting stock, or the board of directors adopted a resolution recommending or approving an acquisition; or

• A ruling request was submitted to the IRS with respect to a Sec. 336 or 337 transaction (including a Sec. 338 election).

IMPORTANT: In any of these cases, all of the sales or distributions must be completed before 1-1-88.

Other grandfathered transactions include:

• Liquidations completed before 1-1-87.

• Liquidations under a liquidation plan adopted before 8-1-86 and completed before 1-1-88.

• Deemed liquidations under Sec. 338 as to stock purchases constituting control before 1-1-87.

• A liquidation of a corporation if a majority of the voting stock is acquired on or after 8-1-86 under a written binding contract in effect before 8-1-86, and if the liquidation is completed before 1988.

• Deemed liquidations under Sec. 338, or actual liquidations, of companies that are acquired under a binding contract entered into before 8-1-86, if the deemed or actual liquidation occurs before 1-1-88.

Also, complete relief (except for ordinary income and short-term gain property) is provided for small, closely held companies on liquidating sales or distributions occurring before 1-1-89, if the liquidation is completed by that date. Relief phases out for these companies with value between $5 and $10 million.

Act Secs. 631-634, relating to recognition of gain and loss on liquidating distributions of property in liquidation amend Secs. 311, 336, 337, 367(e), 453(h)(1)(A), (B), (E), 453B(d), 1363(c), 1367(f)(2), 1374, repealing Secs. 332(c), 333, 334(c), 338(h)(12), with conforming and clerical changes made to Secs. 26(b)(2), 312(n)(4), 334(a), 341(e), 346(b), 453(h), 467(c)(5), 897(d), 1056(a), 1255(b)(2), 1276(c)(3), 1375(b)(1)(B), effective as to (1) any distribution in complete liquidation, and any sale or exchange made by a corporation after 7-31-86, unless such corporation is completely liquidated before 1-1-87, (2) any transaction under Sec. 338 for which acquisition date occurs after 12-31-86, and (3) any distribution (not in complete liquidation) made after 12-31-86; for built-in gains of S corporations, the rules apply to tax years starting after 12-31-86, but only in cases where the first tax year for which the corporation is an S corporation is by an election made after 12-31-86. Special exceptions apply for certain plans of liquidation and as to binding contracts.

Other Corporate Rules

[¶620] Allocating Purchase Price in Asset Sales. The new law requires both the buyer and the seller in certain asset acquisitions to divide the purchase price among the transferred assets using a prescribed formula. Under prior law, without a special rule, a seller would generally prefer to assign a larger portion of the purchase price to capital assets such as goodwill. A buyer, on the other hand, would favor a higher basis for inventory or other ordinary-income assets.

Effect on sales of going concerns. The new law's allocation rules apply only to "applicable asset acquisitions." An applicable asset acquisition is any transfer of assets that amounts to a business in which the buyer's basis is determined wholly by reference to the consideration paid for the assets. For this rule, a group of assets will be considered a business, if their character is such that goodwill or going concern value could under any circumstances attach to the assets. For example, a group of assets that would be treated as an active trade or business within the meaning of Sec. 355 (involving the distribution of a controlled corporation's stock) will in all events be considered a business. In addition, businesses that are not active businesses under Sec. 355 will also be subject to this rule. A transfer will not be treated as not meeting the applicable-asset-acquisition test merely because a portion of the assets transferred qualifies for nonrecognition of gain or loss for like-kind exchange of property held for productive use or investment.

IMPORTANT: The new law covers both direct and indirect transfers of a business. So you must apply the special allocation rules to a sale of a business by an individual or a partnership, or a sale of a partnership interest in which the basis of the purchasing partner's proportionate share of the partnership's assets is adjusted to reflect the purchase price.

Who must allocate and how. Both the buyer and the seller must use the residual method to allocate the consideration received for the assets among the assets acquired in the transaction. The purchase price is a key factor in figuring the buyer's basis in the assets and the seller's gain or loss on the sale. Briefly, under the residual method, the goodwill and going concern value is the excess of the business's purchase price over the aggregate fair market values of the tangible assets and the identifiable intangible assets other than goodwill and going concern value. The method used here is the same as the one prescribed in Temporary Reg. Sec. 1.338(b)-2T for allocating purchase price to assets following a stock purchase.

Under that reg, the price of the assets acquired must be reduced by cash and cash-like items, then the balance is allocated first to certain tangible assets, followed by certain intangibles (neither allocation can be more than the assets' FMV). The remaining cost must then be allocated to goodwill and going concern value. Under prior rules, the price could be spread across these assets in proportion to their FMVs even though the purchase price was in excess of FMV.

NOTE: The mandatory use of the residual method doesn't restrict the IRS's ability to challenge the taxpayer's determination of any asset's fair market value by any appropriate method. For example, in certain cases, the IRS may reasonably make an independent showing of the value of goodwill or going concern value as a means of questioning the validity of the taxpayer's valuation of other assets.

Information required. Future regulations may require the seller and buyer to file information returns disclosing amounts allocated to goodwill or going concern value, and to any other categories of assets or specific assets.

Effective Date: The new law applies to transactions after 5-6-86, unless a contract was binding on and after 5-6-86.

OBSERVATION: Buyers of assets still negotiating without a binding contract since 5-6-86 should take a second look at their after-tax purchase costs. Since the new law is retroactively effective to 5-6-86, any price premium paid above the physical asset values must be assigned to goodwill rather than depreciable assets.

Act Sec. 641, providing special allocation rules for certain asset acquisitions, adds a new Sec. 1060 and redesignates former Sec. 1060 as Sec. 1061, effective as shown above.

[¶621] **Related Party Sales.** The rules limiting installment sales and ordinary income treatment on certain sales between related parties are modified. The definition of related parties is expanded so that persons and entities with certain more than 50% relationships are covered (rather than the 80% relationships under prior law) and certain other cases are covered. In some cases, ratable basis recovery by seller and conformity between buyer and seller regarding recognition of income and basis are required, instead of denying deferred income treatment to the seller.

Act Sec. 642, related to definition of related party, amends paragraph (2) of Sec. 707(b), paragraph (1) of Sec. 1239(b), paragraph (c)(1) of Sec. 1239, paragraph (2) of Sec. 1239(c) and amending paragraph (1) of Sec. 453(f), and adds a subsection (8) to Sec. 453(f), and amends Sec. 453(g), effective for sales after date of enactment in tax years ending after that date, unless made under a binding contract in effect before 8-14-86.

[¶622] **Amortizable Bond Premium.** The amortizable bond premium deduction is treated as interest, except as otherwise provided by regulations. Thus, for example, bond premium is treated as interest for applying the investment interest limitations.

NOTE: Suppose, before the new law's enactment, a taxpayer made an election under IRC Sec. 171(c) (election as to taxable bonds). This election applies to obligations acquired after enactment only if the taxpayer chooses to have that election apply (under regulations to be issued by the IRS).

Act Sec. 643, relating to amortizable bond premium, amends Sec. 171 by redesignating subsection (e) as (f) and inserting new subsection (e), effective for obligations acquired after date of enactment, in tax years ending after that date. Elections in effect on that date may apply at taxpayer's option.

[¶623] **Allocation of Housing Co-op Taxes and Interest.** A tenant-shareholder in a housing cooperative can deduct his or her proportionate share of amounts paid for (1) real estate taxes allowable as a deduction to the cooperative that are paid on the cooperative's land or building and (2) interest allowable as a deduction to the cooperative paid on debt incurred to acquire the cooperative's land (and or building). Under prior law, the tenant-shareholder's proportionate share of the deduction was based only on the percentage of cooperative stock that he or she owned.

The problem. Some cooperatives distribute equal shares to all tenant-shareholders, others allow prepayment of a tenant-shareholder's share of the cooperative's debt, and others operate in jurisdictions where the local government separately assesses taxes regardless of the percentage of stock owned. The proportionate-share definition doesn't work in all situations.

Cooperative housing corporations that charge tenant-shareholders with a portion of the cooperative's interest or taxes in a way that reasonably reflects the cost to the cooperative of the interest or taxes allocable to each tenant-shareholder's dwelling unit may elect to have these tenant-shareholders deduct the separately allocated amounts for income tax purposes (rather than amounts based on proportionate ownership of shares of the cooperative).

In addition, the tax treatment of persons owning stock in cooperative housing corporations is extended to corporations, trusts, and other entities that are shareholders. Also, maintenance and lease deductions by tenant-shareholders are disallowed in situations where the amount paid by such tenant-shareholders is properly chargeable to the capital account of the cooperative.

What about depreciation? Tenant-shareholders using depreciable property in a trade or business or for the production of income can take depreciation to the extent of that portion of their stock's adjusted basis that's allocable to the depreciable property. Deductions that exceed this basis can be carried over to the next tax years. No deduction is allowed to the tenant-shareholders for any amount paid or accrued to the cooperative (in excess of proportionate interest and real estate taxes) to the extent that these amounts are properly allocable to amount chargeable to the cooperative's capital account. Any deduction disallowed is applied to increase the adjusted basis of the tenant-shareholder's stock.

> **COMMENT:** This rule generally prevents tenant-shareholder's (including a corporation) from obtaining deductions for the co-op's capital costs more quickly than if they had owned the unit.

Act Sec. 644, changing cooperative ownership requirements, amends Sec. 216(b) and (c) and adds new subsection (d) effective for taxable years beginning after 12-31-86.

[¶624] Co-op Refinancing Rules. The new law provides special rules for two specified limited-profit housing cooperatives that refinanced their debt. The rules apply to income earned on the reserve funds in tax years beginning before 1986 and payments made from the respective reserve funds in tax years beginning after 1985.

Act Sec. 644, sets up special rules for two housing cooperatives, generally effective for tax years starting before 1-1-86. However, the treatment of certain amounts paid from a qualified refinancing-related reserve shall apply to amounts paid or incurred, and property acquired in tax years starting after 12-31-85.

¶624

Real Estate Investment Trusts (REITs)

[¶625] **Qualification Requirements.** The new law eases some of the qualification requirements for REITs. REITs have been relieved of certain shareholder and income and asset requirements for the first year that an entity otherwise qualifies as a REIT. Relief is also granted from certain income and asset requirements for the first year after a REIT receives new equity capital and certain new debt capital. In addition to these breaks REITs will be permitted to hold assets in wholly owned subsidiaries.

The new law also made some important changes in the definition of rents from real property. By modifying the definition, the new law enables REITs to perform those services that would not result in the receipt of unrelated business income if performed by certain tax-exempt entities, without using an independent contractor. The new law also includes in the definition of rents from real property (and the definition of interest) rent or interest that is based on the net income of the tenant or debtor, but only if such net income is based on amounts that would be treated as rents from real property if received directly by the REIT.

The new law also permits income from certain shared appreciation mortgages to be treated as qualifying income for a REIT.

Distribution requirements. The new law grants some relief from the distribution requirement when the REIT has certain types of income that are not accompanied by the receipt of cash. However, in that case the REIT must pay tax on the amounts not distributed. Also under the new law the minimum distribution requirement of regulated investment companies will apply to REITs.

Other changes. There is an expansion of the safe harbor granted REITs under which sales by a REIT may not be treated as prohibited transactions. There is also a modification in the computation of the amount of capital gains dividends that a REIT must pay. And one of the penalties relating to the distribution of dividends has been eliminated.

Act Sec. 661, providing that an entity may elect REIT status even though it meets the stock ownership test under Sec. 542(a)(2) or has fewer than 100 shareholders, amends Sec. 856(a)(6) and Sec. 857 and adds 856(h), effective for tax years beginning after 12-31-86.

[¶626] **Asset and Income Requirements.** If a REIT owns a "qualified REIT subsidiary," all the assets, liabilities, and items of income, deduction, and credit of the subsidiary are to be treated as if they were those of the REIT. To be a qualified REIT subsidiary, 100% of the stock must be owned by the REIT during the entire period the subsidiary is in existence.

To qualify as a real estate investment trust, 75% or more of the trust's income must come from real property. Under the new law, if a REIT receives equity capital and invests it in stock or bonds, any interest, dividends, or gains from the sale of the investments qualifies as income for purposes of the 75% test. *Limitations:* Only income received for the one-year period beginning on the date that the REIT received such capital will qualify. In addition, during that period, stock or bonds bought with the new equity capital will be treated as "real estate assets" for purposes of the "75% asset test," which requires that 75% or more of the value of the trust's total assets must be in real estate assets, cash, cash items, and government securities. The new law defines equity capital as any amount received by the REIT in exchange for the REIT's stock (other than pursuant to a dividend reinvestment plan), or in the public offerings of the debt obligations of such trust which have maturities of at least 5 years.

For the income requirements any income derived from a "shared appreciation provision" is treated as gain recognized on the sale of the "secured property." A shared appreciation provision is any provision that is in connection with an obligation that is held by the REIT and secured by an interest in real property, which provision entitles the REIT to receive a specified portion of any gain realized on the sale or exchange of such real property (or of any gain that would be realized if the property were sold on a specified date). Secured property for these purposes means the real property that secures the obligation that has the shared appreciation provision.

Also, for the income requirements, the REIT is treated as holding the secured property for the period during which it held the shared appreciation provision (or, if shorter, the period during which the secured property was held by the person holding such property), and the secured property is treated as property described in Sec. 1221(1) if it is such property in the hands of the obligor on the obligation to which the shared appreciation provision relates (or if it would be such property if held by the REIT).

Act Sec. 662, providing that all assets, liabilities, and items of income, deduction, and credit of a "qualified REIT subsidiary" are treated as those same items of the REIT and providing that any income from a "shared appreciation provision" shall be treated as gain on the sale of secured property, adds Sec. 856(i) and (j) and amends Sec. 856(c) for tax years beginning after 12-31-86.

[¶627] **Rents and Interest.** The new law modifies the definition of rents from real property. The new definition permits REITs to perform those services that would not result in the receipt of "unrelated business income" if performed by certain tax-exempt entities, without using an independent contractor.

Under the new law rents or interest that are based on the net income of a tenant or debtor are treated as rent from real property or as interest, respectively, if certain conditions are met. To qualify, the rent (or interest) must be received from a tenant (or debtor) that receives substantially all of its income from the leased property (or the property that secures the loan) from the subleasing (or leasing) of substantially all of such property, and the rent received by the tenant (or debtor) consists entirely of amounts that would be treated as rents from real property (or interest) if received directly by the REIT.

Act Sec. 663, providing that amounts received by a REIT in connection with rental property qualify as rents from real property even though the REIT performs services, amends Sec. 856(d), (f) effective for tax years beginning after 12-31-86.

[¶628] Distribution Requirements. REITs must distribute 95% of their taxable income. The new law provides certain relief from this requirement when a REIT has certain types of income that are not accompanied by a receipt of cash. However, the REIT must pay tax on the amounts not distributed.

Act Sec. 664, providing relief from the requirement of having to distribute 95% of the REIT's taxable income, amends Sec. 857(a) and adds (e), effective for tax years beginning after 12-31-86.

[¶629] Treatment of Capital Gains. Under the new law, a REIT in determining the maximum amount of capital gain dividends that it may pay for a tax year cannot offset its net capital gain with the amount of any net operating loss, whether current or carried over from a previous tax year. If the REIT elects to pay capital gains dividends in excess of its net taxable income, the REIT would increase the amount of its net operating loss carryover by such amount.

Act Sec. 665, providing that a REIT's net operating loss would not be offset against its net capital gain for purposes of determining the maximum amount of capital gains dividends, amends Sec. 857(b) effective for tax years beginning after 12-31-86.

[¶630] Prohibited Transactions. A REIT may be hit with a 100% tax on net income from "prohibited transactions," excluding foreclosures. However, there are a number of safe harbors that permit the REIT to avoid the tax. Under the new law, the number of property sales that a REIT may make within the safe harbor is increased from five to seven or the adjusted bases of all sales is not more than 10% of the adjusted bases of all of the REITS assets as of the beginning of the year.

Under the new law, losses from prohibited transactions may not be taken into account in determining the amount of net income from prohibited transactions. However, any net loss from prohibited transactions may be taken into account in computing REIT taxable income.

Act Sec. 666, modifies the rules relating to prohibited transactions of REITs, amends Sec. 857(b)(6), effective for tax years beginning after 12-31-86.

⟦¶631⟧ No Penalty on Deficiency Dividends. The penalty tax under Sec. 6697 relating to deficiency dividends is repealed by the new law. The penalty is now limited to regulated investment companies.

Act Sec. 667, repealing the penalty tax on deficiency dividends of REITs, amends Sec. 6697, effective for tax years beginning after 12-31-86.

⟦¶632⟧ Excise Tax on Undistributed Income. The excise tax on undistributed income has been increased to 4% of the amount by which the required distribution exceeds the amount distributed in the taxable year. The required distribution is the sum of 85% of ordinary income, plus 95% of capital gain net income, increased by any prior shortfall in meeting the required distribution.

Act Sec. 668, amends Sec. 4981 increasing the excise tax on undistributed income, effective for calendar years beginning after 12-31-86.

REAL ESTATE MORTGAGE INVESTMENT CONDUITS (REMICs)

⟦¶633⟧ REMICs—A Brand New Tax Entity. The new law creates a special tax vehicle for entities which issue multiple classes of investor interests backed by a pool of mortgages. The new vehicle is called the Real Estate Mortgage Investment Conduit (REMIC), which, as its name implies, is generally a conduit entity for tax purposes. There are complex rules covering qualification as a REMIC, and transfers to and liquidations of the entity. There are two tiers of ownership interests in REMICs and each is taxed differently.

The REMIC is intended to be the exclusive vehicle for issuing multiple-class mortgage-backed securities. Result: If the qualification requirements are met, any corporate, partnership, trust, or similar entity is granted pass-through REMIC status. For example, a REMIC organized as a partnership would be governed by the new REMIC Code Sections (860A through G) covering its transactions and the holders of its interests, not by the partnership provisions of Subchapter K.

Qualifying as a REMIC. The entity must be a calendar year taxpayer that elects REMIC status for the tax year, and, if applicable, for all prior tax years. The entity qualifies as a REMIC only if it meets two tests:

(1) Asset test. Substantially all assets at the close of the fourth month ending after the "startup day" and each quarter ending thereafter must consist of qualified mortgages and permitted investments. The "startup day" is any day selected by the REMIC that is on or before the first day on which REMIC interests are issued. A qualified mortgage is any obligation (including any participation or certificate of beneficial ownership interest) that is (1) principally secured by an interest in real property; (2) transferred to the REMIC on or before the startup day or is purchased by the REMIC within the three-month period beginning on the startup day. Stripped coupons and stripped bonds are treated as qualifying mortgages if the bonds from which the coupons or bonds were stripped would have been qualified mortgages. Regular interests in other REMICs transferred to the REMIC on or before the startup day and qualified replacement mortgages are treated as qualified mortgages. A qualified replacement mortgage is one that would have been treated as a qualified mortgage and is received either (1) in exchange for a defective mortgage within two years of the startup day; or (2) in exchange for another qualified mortgage within a three-month period beginning on the startup day.

Permitted investments are cash flow investments, qualified reserve assets, and foreclosure property. Cash flow investments are investments of amounts received under qualified mortgages for a temporary period before distribution to holders of REMIC interests. Such cash flow investments are limited to those that pay out passive income in the nature of interest. Qualified reserve assets are any intangible property held for investment as part of a qualified reserve fund. This is a fund maintained by the REMIC to provide for payment of expenses and to provide for additional security for payments due to holders of regular interests. Amounts in the reserve fund must be reduced as regular REMIC interests are retired. Foreclosure property is property that would be treated as foreclosure property under Sec. 856(e) if acquired by a REIT and is acquired by the REMIC in connection with the default or imminent default of a qualified mortgage. Foreclosure property ceases to be a permitted investment if it is held by the REMIC for more than one year after acquisition.

(2) Investors' interests. All interests in the REMIC must consist of one or more classes of regular interests and a single class of residual interests.

A regular interest is one with terms that are fixed on the startup day and unconditionally entitles the holder to receive a specified principal amount and provides that interest payments (or similar payments) are payable based on a fixed rate. Payments may be based on a variable rate, to the extent provided in regs. The payments on a regular interest can be contingent on the extent of prepayments from qualifying mortgages and the amount of income from qualifying investments. However, the regular interest cannot carry interest payments that are disproportionate to the specified principal amount. A residual interest is any REMIC interest which is not a regular interest and which is designated as a residual interest by the REMIC. There can be only class of residual interests, and distributions (if any) must be made pro rata to all holders.

The Treasury is to issue regulations that offer relief in the event of an inadvertent REMIC termination. But the relief is to be accompanied by appropriate sanctions (e.g., imposition of corporate tax for period of time in which qualification requirements are not met).

Although the REMIC is a conduit entity, it is subject to a penalty tax equal to 100% of its net income from prohibited transactions (computed without taking into account losses from or deductions connected with the prohibited transactions). Prohibited transactions include dispositions of qualified mortgages other than dispositions related to: a substitution of a qualified replacement mortgage for a defective mortgage; REMIC bankruptcy or insolvency; foreclosure, default or imminent default of a mortgage; or a qualified liquidation. Other prohibited transactions: income from assets a REMIC is not permitted to hold, income receive as compensation for services, and the disposition of a cash flow investment other than a disposition related to a qualified liquidation.

Other REMIC rules. The basis of any property received by a REMIC in exchange for regular or residual interests is generally equal to the fair market value of the property at the time of the transfer. Gain or loss is not recognized when a REMIC liquidates and sells its assets. However, all assets must be sold and the proceeds (other than amounts retained to meet claims) distributed to holders of REMIC interests within a 90-day period beginning on the day the liquidation plan is adopted.

Taxation of regular interests. Holders of regular interests are taxed as if they held a debt instrument and must report REMIC income on the accrual basis. The taxable original issue discount (OID) for an accrual period is based on the increase in the present value of the remaining payments on the instrument, taking into account payments includible in the stated redemption price but received on the regular interest during the period. The present value calculation is made at the beginning of each accrual period, using the yield to maturity of the instrument at the time of its issuance (compounded at the end of each quarter, adjusted for the length of the accrual period, and calculated based on certain prepayment assumptions to be specified in regs). The present value calculation takes into account any prepayments that have occurred before the close of the accrual period.

Gain on the disposition of a regular interest is treated as ordinary income to the extent of any unaccrued OID. This is the excess of:

(1) the amount that would have been includible in gross income if the regular interest yielded a return equal to 110% of the applicable federal rate [as defined in Sec. 1274(d), without regard to Sec. 1274(d)(2)], determined as of the time the taxpayer acquired his interest, over

(2) the total amount of ordinary income derived from the regular interest and included in the taxpayer's income prior to disposition.

Taxation of residual interests. At the end of each calendar quarter, the holder of a residual interest has ordinary income or loss equal to his daily portion of the REMIC's taxable income or loss. Distributions up to the holder's adjusted basis are taxed as ordinary income and excess distributions are treated as gain from the sale or exchange of the interest. The holder's adjusted basis is increased by the amount of REMIC taxable income that he takes into account and is decreased (but not below zero) by (1) distributions actually received; and (2) any net loss of the REMIC that the holder takes into account.

The amount of REMIC net loss that the holder may take into account is limited to the adjusted basis of his interest as of the close of the quarter (or time of disposition, if earlier), determined without regard to the net loss for the quarter. Any loss that is disallowed may be carried over indefinitely and may be used only to offset income generated by the same REMIC.

For determining the tax implications of holding a residual REMIC interest, REMIC taxable income or net loss is figured as if the entity were a calendar year individual using the accrual method of accounting, with four modifications. First, a deduction is allowed for those amounts that would be deductible as interest if regular interests were treated as debt of the REMIC. Second, market discount on any market discount bond held by the REMIC is includable for the year in which the discount accrues. Third, income, gain, loss or deductions from prohibited transactions are not taken into account. Fourth, deductions under Sec. 703(a)(2), other than deductions allowable under Sec. 212, are not allowed.

Special rules: A portion of net REMIC income taken into account by a holder may not be offset by any net operating losses (a special exception applies to thrift institutions). This same portion of income is treated as unrelated business income under Sec. 511, and is ineligible for a reduction in the rate of withholding tax in the case of a holder who is a nonresident alien.

The portion of income subject to the special rule is any excess of net REMIC income taken into account by the residual interest holder for any calendar quarter, over the sum of the daily accruals for the residual interest. The daily accrual is found by allocating to each day in the calendar quarter a ratable portion of the product of the adjusted issue price of the interest at the beginning of the accrual period, and 120% of the long-term federal rate. The initial issue price is the price paid for the interest at issuance. The adjusted issue price is the initial issue price plus the amount of daily accruals for the prior calendar quarters, less the amount of any distributions prior to the end of the calendar quarter.

Dispositions of residual interests. In general, the wash sale provisions of Sec. 1091 apply if the seller of a residual interest buys (or enters into another transaction that triggers Sec. 1091) any REMIC or comparable interest in a "taxable mortgage pool" (see below) within a prohibited period of time. The prohibited period commences six months before the disposition of the regular interest and ends six months after the date of the disposition.

Exchange of property for REMIC interests. The contribution of qualified mortgages or other property to a REMIC in exchange for regular or residual interests results in neither gain nor loss to the transferor. The adjusted bases of the interests received are equal to the adjusted bases of the property contributed.

If the issue price of a regular interest exceeds its adjusted basis (as determined above), the excess is included in gross income under rules similar to the accrual of market discount required by Sec. 1276(b). If the issue price of a residual interest exceeds its adjusted basis (as determined above), then the excess is amortized and included in the holder's income on a straight line basis over the expected life of the REMIC.

If the adjusted basis of a regular interest exceeds its issue price, the excess is treated as if it were amortizable bond premium (Sec. 171). If the adjusted basis of a residual interest exceeds its issue price, the excess is deductible ratably over the expected life of the REMIC.

Taxable mortgage pools. REMICs are intended to be the exclusive vehicle for issuing multiple class mortgage backed securities without the imposition of a double tax. To accomplish this goal, the new law treats any taxable mortgage pool (TMP) as a taxable corporation that is not an includible corporation for purposes of filing consolidated returns. This rule is generally effective beginning in 1992. A TMP is any non-REMIC entity (other than a domestic building and loan association) if (1) substantially all its assets consist of debt obligations and more than 50% of the obligations consist of real estate mortgages; (2) it is the obligor under debt obligations with two or more maturities; and (3) payments on the debt obligations bear a relationship to the payments on the debt obligations held by the entity (e.g., the underlying mortgages).

Other rules: The new REMIC provisions carry special rules that relate to REITs, certain financial institutions, and foreign holders.

Regulatory authority and Treasury study. The Treasury is granted broad authority to issue regs clarifying the application of the new REMIC rules. The conferees also request the Treasury to conduct a study of the REMIC provisions' effectiveness and their impact on thrift institutions.

Information reporting. Amounts includible in the income of a regular holder are subject to the information reporting requirements of Sec. 6049. What's more, the REMIC must report interest (and OID accrual) to a broad group of holders, including corporations, dealers in securities or commodities, REITs, common trusts funds, and certain other trusts. The REMIC also is required to report sufficient information to allow holders to figure the accrual of any market discount or amortization of any premium.

Act Sec. 671(a), providing new rules for real estate mortgage investment conduits, adds Secs. 860A through 860G. Act Sec. 671(b) makes technical amendments to Sec. 856(c)(6), relating to REITs. Act Sec. 672 amends Sec. 1272(a), relating to OID accruals. Act Sec. 673 adds Sec. 7701(i), relating to taxable mortgage pools. Act Sec. 674 adds Sec. 6049(d)(7), relating to compliance provisions. Act Secs. 671-674 are generally effective for tax years beginning after 12-31-86. The amendments made by Act Sec. 672, relating to OID, apply to debt instruments issued after 12-31-86 in tax years ending after that date. The amendments made by Act Sec. 673, relating to taxable mortgage pools take effect on 1-1-92, and do not apply to any entity in existence on 12-31-91. The exception for entities in existence on 12-31-91 will cease to apply as of the first day after 12-31-91 on which there is a substantial transfer of cash or other property to the entity. The wash-sale rules contained in Act Sec. 673 apply to tax years beginning after 12-31-86.

Miscellaneous Provisions

[¶634] Regulated Investment Companies—Excise Tax Imposed. For any calendar year, a nondeductible excise tax applies on every RIC, equal to 4% of the excess, if any, of the required distribution for the calendar year, over the distributed amount for the calendar year. The excise tax is to be paid not later than March 15 of the succeeding calendar year. "Required distribution" for any calendar year means the sum of 97% of the RIC's ordinary income for the calendar year, plus 90% of the RIC's capital gain net income for the 1-year period ending on Oct. 31 of the calendar year; increased by the excess, if any, of the grossed up required distribution for the preceding calendar year, over the distributed amount for the preceding calendar year.

Special rules apply for RICs with tax years ending on Nov. 30 or Dec. 31, for dividends declared in December, earnings and profits, and treatment of certain capital losses.

Business development companies. A business development company registered under the Investment Company Act of 1940, as amended (15 U.S.C. 80a-1 to 80b-2) may qualify as a RIC.

Hedging exception. The computation of gross income of a RIC for the Sec. 851(b)(3) requirement that less than 30% of the gross income of the RIC be derived from the sale or exchange of stock or securities held for less than three months is modified. For applying this test, any increase in value on a position that is part of a designated hedge is offset by any decrease in value (whether or not realized) or any other position that is part of such hedge. This rule applies for calculating both gains from the sale or other disposition of stock or securities held for less than three months, and also the gross income of the RIC for Sec. 851(b)(3) purposes.

Treatment of series funds as separate corporations. For RICs having more than one fund, each fund is treated as a separate corporation, under Sec. 851. "Fund" means a segregated portfolio of assets, the beneficial interests in which are owned by the holders of a class or series of stock of the RIC that is preferred over all other classes or series in respect of such portfolio of assets.

Extension of period for mailing notices to shareholders. Generally, the notice requirements for shareholders are lengthened to 60 days from 45 days.

Act Secs. 651-657, imposing an excise tax on RICs and other technical requirements, enacts Sec. 4982, effective for calendar years beginning after 12-31-86; amends paragraph (1) of Sec. 851(a) (business development companies), effective for tax years beginning after 12-31-86; adds new subsection (g) to Sec. 851 (hedging transactions), effective for tax years beginning after date of enactment; adds new subsection (q) to Sec. 851 (series funds as separate corporations), effective for tax years beginning after date of enactment (with special rule for existing series funds); and amends Secs. 852(b)(3), 852(b)(5)(A), 853(c), 854(b)(2) and 855(c) (notice period), effective for tax years beginning after the date of enactment.

[¶635] Personal Holding Company Income Exception for Certain Computer Software Royalties and Securities Brokers. An exception to the definition and inclusion in personal holding company income is provided for computer software royalties received by certain corporations that: (1) are actively engaged in the business of developing computer software; (2) derive at least 50% of their gross income from such computer software; (3) incur substantial trade or business expenses; and (4) distribute most of their passive income other than computer software royalties. The exception is also extended to foreign PHCs.

AFFILIATED GROUPS: If the royalty recipient is a member of an affiliated group and another group member meets the first three requirements, then the recipient is treated as meeting the requirements.

Interest income received from specified sources by a particular broker-dealer in securities is not included in PHC income, for interest received after the enactment date.

In addition, excluded from the definition of passive investment income for subchapter S, is computer software royalties derived by a specified taxpayer, which royalties would not be treated as PHC income, effective for tax years beginning after 12-31-84. An exception from the definiton of PHC income also applies for certain royalties derived by a toy manufacturer from the licensing of toys, under rules similar to those provided for computer software royalties, effective for royalties received or accrued in tax years beginning after 12-31-81.

Act Sec. 645, amending the definition of PHC income, amends Secs. 543, 553, effective for royalties received before, on, and after 12-31-86.

[¶636] Certain Entity Not Taxed as Corporation. A special rule under which a certain trust will not be taxed as a corporation if, among other things, it makes an election and agrees not to exercise business powers contained in its trust instrument.

Act Sec. 646, relating to the treatment of certain entities as trusts for tax purposes. Election shall be in effect during the period (1) starting on the first day of the first tax year starting after the enactment date and following the tax year in which the election is made, and (2) ending as of the end of the tax year before the tax year in which the entity ceases to satisfy all conditions provided.

[¶637] Special Rule for Disposing of a Subsidiary's Stock. If for a tax year of an affiliated group filing a consolidated return ending on or before 12-31-87, there is a disposition of a subsidiary's stock, the amount that must be included in income will be included ratably over a 15-year period starting with the tax year in which the disposition occurs. This special rule applies only if the sub was incorporated on 12-24-69, and participates in a mineral joint venture with a corporation organized under the laws of the foreign country in which the venture is located.

Act Sec. 645, relating to the special rule for disposition of stock of subsidiary is effective as shown above.

[The page following this is 701.]

ALTERNATIVE MINIMUM TAX

[¶701] **Overview.** The new law repeals the corporate add-on minimum tax after 1986 and replaces it with an alternative minimum tax (AMT). It also expands the alternative minimum tax for individuals. The intent: to insure that no taxpayer with substantial economic income can avoid significant tax liability by using tax exclusions, deductions, and credits. The new law requires corporations to make estimated tax payments to cover their minimum tax.

Corporations. The alternative minimum tax base is equal to (1) regular taxable income, plus (2) tax preferences, less (3) certain deductions. Corporate preferences and adjustments include accelerated depreciation, capital gains, mining exploration and development costs, amortization of certified pollution control facilities, circulation expenditures, research and experimentation costs, tax-exempt interest, use of the completed contract method, percentage depletion, intangible drilling costs, charitable contributions of appreciated property, installment sales of dealer property, reserves for losses on financial institution bad debts, shipping company capital construction funds, and business untaxed reported profits. The resulting amount, called alternative minimum taxable income, is reduced by an exemption amount, then multiplied by 20%, the alternative minimum tax rate. This tax may then be offset by the minimum foreign tax credit to figure a tentative minimum tax. The new rules ensure that corporate taxpayers pay tax equal to at least 20% of their economic income above the exemption amount. Individual taxpayers must pay at least 21% of income above the exemption amount. The corporate exemption amount is $40,000, less 25% of the excess of alternative minimum taxable income over $150,000.

The amount of minimum tax owed is the amount by which the tentative minimum tax exceeds the regular tax.

Individuals. The new law retains much of the prior law's treatment of the AMT but increases the rate to 21%. It now, however, permits adjustments to deferral preferences. Reason: The minimum tax deduction may sometimes exceed the regular tax deduction, especially in the last few years of an asset's life. The amount of minimum tax liability relating to deferral preferences is allowed as a carryforward credit against regular tax liability.

In addition to some of the preferences that apply to corporations, individual tax preferences also include a limitation on itemized deductions, incentive stock options, passive farm losses, and passive activity losses. The exemption amount is reduced by 25% of the alternative minimum taxable income in excess of (1) $150,000 for joint returns; (2) $75,000 for trusts and married filing separately; and $112,500 for single taxpayers. Under prior law, dividends that were excludable from gross income (up to $100 per person, $200 for a joint return) were treated as a minimum tax preference. Since this exclusion has been repealed, there is no longer a preference for dividends.

The only itemized deductions allowed for minimum tax purposes are those for casualty and theft losses, gambling losses to the extent of gambling gains, charitable deductions, medical deductions (to the extent in excess of 10% of adjusted gross income), interest expenses (restricted to housing interest plus net investment income), and certain estate taxes. Disallowed investment deductions may be carried over. Miscellaneous itemized deductions and itemized deductions for state and local taxes aren't allowed, and the investment interest rule is not phased in. For minimum tax, for a loan refinancing that gives rise to qualified housing interest, interest paid on the new loan is treated as qualified housing interest to the extent that it is so qualified under the prior loan, and the loan amount wasn't increased. A residence isn't a qualified residence for minimum tax unless it meets the requirements for a qualified residence applying for regular tax. A refund of state and local taxes paid, for which no minimum tax deduction was allowed, isn't included in alternative minimum taxable income.

The AMT paid is allowed as a credit against the regular tax liability in later years. But the minimum tax credit can't reduce taxes below the later year tentative minimum tax. The minimum tax credit applies only to minimum tax liability incurred because of deferral preferences, such as depreciation, where the tax preference results from the timing rather than the amount of the deduction.

Taxpayers may elect to have minimum tax treatment apply for regular tax purposes. If an election is made, no preference is added or treated as an adjustment for minimum tax purposes. Nonrefundable regular tax credits (e.g., the general business credit) whose benefit is lost because of the minimum tax can be carried over for regular tax under the general carryover rules.

Incentive tax credits aren't allowed against the minimum tax. Credits that can't be used for regular tax because of the minimum tax can be used as credit carryovers against the regular tax.

Act Sec. 701, relating to the alternative minimum tax, amends Secs. 55-58 and adds new Secs. 53 and 59, effective generally for tax years beginning after 12-31-86.

Minimum Tax Adjustments and Preferences

	Corporate	Noncorporate
Depreciation	X	X
Pollution control facilities	X	X
Completed contract method	X	X
Percentage depletion	X	X
Intangible drilling costs	X	X
Installment sales of dealer property	X	X

	Corporate	Noncorporate
Mining exploration & development costs	X	X
Circulation expenditures	X	X
Research and experimentation expenditures	X	X
Tax exempt interest on private activity bonds	X	X
Charitable contributions of appreciated property	X	X
Incentive stock options		X
Passive farm losses		X
Passive activity losses		X
Bad debt reserves of financial institutions	X	
Shipping company capital construction funds	X	
Business untaxed reported profits	X	

Adjustments and Preferences for All Taxpayers

[¶702] **Depreciation.** For property placed in service after 1986, the excess of ACRS depreciation over alternative depreciation (Sec. 168(g)) is a preference for the year. Alternative depreciation is the straight-line allowance over the ADR midpoint life (40 years for realty other than low-income housing). This is an adjustment made similarly to the depreciation adjustment for computing earnings and profits. It's made by using a *total* alternative depreciation allowance *for all items*, instead of the year's total ACRS allowance in regular taxable income, to arrive at AMT income. It results in a reduction of the preference, since "negative adjustments" in the year's allowances for older assets (total deduction increased by alternative less lower ACRS allowance) offset "positive adjustments" (total deduction decreases) because of higher ACRS depreciation of newer items. Accelerated depreciation on personal property is computed using the 150% declining balance method with a switch to straight-line at the optimum point.

>   **Example:** Baker Corp. fully deducts for regular tax the cost of a $6,000 asset the year it's placed in service, but writes it off evenly over three years for minimum tax. Result: Regular taxable income becomes $4,000 less than minimum taxable income in the first year, and $2,000 more than minimum taxable income in the second and third years. Suppose a $3,000 item is placed in service in year two. Then the $2,000 difference between the regular and minimum tax deduction for that item would offset the $2,000 minimum tax positive adjustment for the older asset.

For property placed in service before 1987, the old rules continue to apply. So the preference, composed of the excess of ACRS depreciation over straight-line is computed on an item-by-item basis.

No minimum tax adjustment is made for property depreciated under the income forecast or alternative recovery methods (Sec.

168(f)(1)-(4)). The general minimum tax rules (using a 15-year life) apply to rehabilitation expenditures of low-income housing (Sec. 167(k)) that is placed in service after 1986.

Adjusted basis. For computing the minimum tax, the adjusted basis of depreciable property subject to the adjustment is equal to the asset's cost less accumulated minimum tax depreciation. *Result:* Since allowances for regular tax purposes and for minimum tax differ, the adjusted basis of each asset, e.g., for gain or loss on disposition may also be different. Thus, a sale could result in gain for regular tax and in a loss for minimum tax.

Act Sec. 701, relating to depreciation, amends Secs. 56(a)(1) and 57(a)(7), generally effective for tangible property placed in service after 12-31-86.

[¶703] **Pollution Control Facilities.** Rapid amortization of a certified pollution control facility is a tax preference (as under prior law). Taxpayers must use the alternative recovery system for minimum tax purposes for facilities placed in service after 1986. The preference applies without regard to the applicability of Sec. 291 for regular tax purposes.

Act Sec. 701, relating to amortization of certified pollution control facilities, adds Sec. 56(a)(5), effective for tax years ending after 12-31-86.

[¶704] **Completed Contract Method.** Taxpayers using the completed contract or certain other methods of accounting for long-term contracts entered into after 2-28-86 for regular tax must use the percentage of completion method (as modified by Sec. 460(b)) on these contracts for minimum tax purposes. The tax preference is calculated by substituting the minimum tax for the regular tax treatment as an adjustment toward alternative minimum taxable income.

Act Sec. 701, relating to long-term contracts, amends Sec. 56(a)(3), effective for any long-term contract entered into after 2-28-86.

[¶705] **Percentage Depletion.** As under prior law, this tax preference is measured by the excess of the regular tax percentage depletion allowance over the property's adjusted basis at year-end (before the current year's deduction).

> **Example:** Oilman takes percentage depletion of $40,000 on a mineral property with a prededuction adjusted basis of $10,000. The tax preference is $30,000 ($40,000 − $10,000).

Act Sec. 701, redesignates old Sec. 57(a)(8) relating to depletion as new Sec. 57(a)(1), effective for tax years beginning after 1986.

[¶706] **Intangible Drilling Costs.** The new law on IDC tax preference items is basically the same as the prior law for individuals. But under the new law, the amount of intangible drilling costs treated as a tax preference is composed of the excess of the "excess intangible drilling costs" over 65% (rather than 100% as under prior law) of net income from oil, gas, and geothermal properties. Net oil and gas income is determined for this formula without subtracting excess intangible drilling costs.

Example: Taxpayer has $10,000 net oil and gas income (before subtracting excess intangible drilling costs) and $8,200 of excess intangible drilling costs. The tax preference is $1,700 or $8,200 minus 65% of $6,500).

Excess IDC is the regular IDC deduction minus the normative deduction (i.e, the amount that would have been deducted under 120-month straight-line amortization, or (at taxpayer's election) under a cost depletion method). There's no preference for costs of nonproductive wells. The IDC preference is computed separately for (1) geothermal deposit properties defined under Sec. 613(e)(3), and (2) other properties for which IDCs are incurred.

Example: Driller has oil wells with net oil and gas income of $10,000 and excess IDCs of $8,200, and geothermal deposit properties with net income of $10,000 and excess IDCs of $4,200. There's a $1,700 preference for the oil wells, and none for the geothermal properties.

Taxpayers can elect to amortize the year's IDCs ratably over a 10-year period for all tax purposes.

Act Sec. 701, relating to intangible drilling costs, amend Secs. 57(a)(2), and (b), and 59(e), generally effective for tax years beginning after 12-31-86.

[¶707] Installment Sales of Dealer Property. The installment method does not apply to the disposition of dealer property after 3-1-86 for minimum tax purposes. So taxpayers must recognize all gains on disposition in the year of disposition. The rule applies to inventory.

NOTE: For calendar year taxpayers electing the installment method for regular tax purposes, gain on dispositions made between 3-1-86 and 12-31-86 is treated as recognized in 1986 for minimum tax purposes. The effect is that amounts included in regular taxable income after 1986 under the installment method aren't included in alternative minimum taxable income for those years. The preference applies to the same transactions subject to proportionate disallowance of the installment method (i.e., dealer sales and sales of trade, business or rental property when the purchase price is more than $150,000).

Act Sec. 701 relating to installment sales of dealer property adds new Sec. 56(a)(6), effective for tax years beginning after 12-31-86.

[¶708] Mining Exploration and Development Costs. Costs paid or incurred after 1986 that are expensed (or amortized under

Sec. 291) for regular tax purposes are written off through straight-line amortization over 10 years for the alternative minimum tax. For personal holding companies, only the excess over 10-year amortization is a preference. The 10-year amortization rule applies for minimum tax without regard to the applicability of Sec. 291 for regular tax. Their minimum tax treatment is similar to that of depreciation.

> **Example:** Miner, who incurs a one-time expense of $1,000 for mining exploration and development, deducts $1,000 the year the expense was incurred in computing regular tax, but gets only a $100 deduction in each of 10 years for minimum tax purposes. Since these deductions differ, the basis of the property for gain or loss will also differ for regular and minimum tax purposes.

On a loss to the mining property (e.g., if a mine is abandoned), any remaining mining exploration and development costs that weren't amortized under the above rules are written off for minimum tax purposes.

Election. The new law allows an election to write off all or part of Sec. 616(a) mining exploration and development expenditures over 10 years from the year made for both regular and minimum tax purposes, to even out the regular and minimum annual deduction from them.

Act Sec. 701 relating to mining exploration and development costs amends Secs. 56(a)(2) and 59(e), effective for costs paid or incurred after 12-31-86.

[¶709] Circulation and Research & Experimental Expenditures. For individuals and personal holding companies, the excess of expensing circulation expenditures over three-year amortization (10-year amortization for R&E expenditures) is a preference. Amounts paid or incurred by noncorporate taxpayers after 1986 that are deductible against regular tax under Secs. 173 or 174(a) must be capitalized and ratably deducted over 3 years (circulation expenditures) or over 10 years (R&E expenditures) in computing alternative minimum taxable income. However, if the taxpayer's property generating the circulation expenditure or a specific project generating an R&E expenditure incurs a loss, then all hitherto unamortized expenditures relating to it, which could be taken as a Sec. 165(a) loss, are taken as a minimum tax deduction for the loss year. The rules also apply to Sec. 173 circulation expenditures of a personal holding company.

> **Example:** In 1987, John Smith incurs $30,000 of deductible circulation expenditures and $10,000 R&E expenditures, and deducts $40,000 in computing regular tax. He claims a minimum tax deduction for them of $10,000 (⅓ of $30,000) and $1,000 (¹⁄₁₀ of $10,000) respectively in 1987 and also in 1988. If in 1989 the newspaper that generated the circulation expenditure folds and the project giving rise to the R&E expenditures is abandoned, the remaining $10,000 circu-

lation expenditures and $8,000 of R&E expenditures are a minimum tax deduction for 1989.

Election. All or part of circulation or R&E expenditures can at the taxpayer's election be written off over a 3-year period (circulation expenditures) or a 10-year period (R&E expenditures) for all tax purposes to even out annual regular and minimum tax.

Act Sec. 701 relating to circulation and R&E expenditures amends Secs. 56(b)(2) and 59(e), effective for amounts paid or incurred after 12-31-86.

【¶710】 **Capital Gains.** For individuals, the capital gains deduction has been repealed for regular tax purposes. Thus, for regular tax computation, the full amount of gain is taxed (but not more than 28% for 1987). Apparently, the difference between the 28% maximum capital gains rate and a higher regular rate is not considered a preference item. For individuals and corporations, capital gains are fully included in minimum taxable income.

【¶711】 **Tax-Exempt Interest on Private Activity Bonds.** Interest on private activity bonds defined in new Sec. 142 [See 1301 et seq.] that are issued after 8-7-86 (except for bonds covered under the joint statement on effective dates of 3-14-86, bonds issued after 9-1-86) is a tax preference item. Examples include bonds financing mass commuting facilities, facilities to furnish water (other than irrigation), sewage disposal facilities, solid waste disposal facilities, and qualified multifamily residential rental projects. But interest on bonds refunding pre-1986 issues and interest on qualified Sec. 501(c)(3) bonds aren't preferences. The exception for certain refundings of bonds issued before 8-8-86 (or 9-1-86) also applies to a series of current refundings of an issue originally issued before those dates. This exception doesn't apply to refundings of pre-8-8-86 (or 9-1-86) bonds.

The Ways & Means Committee Report indicates that interest on the following types of bonds issued after 8-7-86 isn't intended to be a tax preference:

- Bonds exempt from the new, unified volume limitation because of transitional exceptions in the new law.
- Bonds subject to the limitation as advance refundings that are allowed under a transitional exception.
- Bonds only partly subject to the new volume limit (e.g., the over-$1 million part of nonessential function bonds).
- Bonds issued on behalf of Section 501(c)(3) organizations.

SILVER LINING: Expenses and interest incurred on tax-exempt bonds whose income is a preference reduce the preference for minimum tax, even though they're not deductible against the regular tax because of Sec. 265.

Act Sec. 701 relating to tax-exempt interest on private activity bonds amends Sec. 57(a)(5), effective for bonds issued after 8-7-86 and as shown above.

[¶712] Charitable Contributions of Appreciated Property.
A part of the contribution of appreciated long-term capital gain property (including Sec. 1231 trade or business property) is an item of tax preference. In general, the preference is composed of the amount of reduction in the regular tax charitable deduction that would result if all contributed long-term capital gain property were accounted for at its adjusted basis. In its computation: (1) Unrealized losses on contributed loss property reduce unrealized gains on contributed appreciated items. (2) Carryforwards of the charitable deduction because of the 30% limit are ignored—amounts carried forward are a preference only when deducted against regular tax. The preference doesn't apply to deduction carryovers on charitable contributions made before 8-16-86.

Act Sec. 701 relating to charitable contributions of appreciated property amends Sec. 57(a)(6), generally effective for tax years beginning after 12-31-86.

Additional Individual Preferences

[¶713] Incentive Stock Options. The new law retains as a preference item the excess of fair market value of the stock over the exercise price. However, for minimum tax purposes, the basis of stock acquired through the exercise of an incentive stock option after 1986 equals the fair market value taken into account in determining the preference amount.

> **Example:** Frank Canavan pays an exercise price of $10 to purchase stock having a fair market value of $15. The preference in the year of exercise is $5, and the stock has a $10 basis for regular tax purposes and $15 for minimum tax purposes. If, in a subsequent year, he sells the stock for $20, the gain recognized is $10 for regular tax purposes and $5 for minimum tax purposes.

[¶714] Passive Farm Losses. A passive farm loss is the loss incurred from a tax shelter farming activity. Individual passive farm losses are generally preferences. A taxpayer's insolvency reduces the preference amount. (Insolvency is the excess of liabilities over the fair market value of the assets—Sec. 108(d)(3)).
A tax shelter farm activity may be a farming syndicate (Secs. 464(c) and 461(i)(4)(A)) or any other farming activity where the taxpayer does not participate materially. A taxpayer materially participates if: (1) he meets the terms of the material participation standard for regular tax purposes (Sec. 469); (2) a family member (Sec.

2032A(e)(2)) participates; or (3) he meets the Sec. 2032A(b)(4) or (5) retired, disabled, or surviving spouse requirement.

Deductions in excess of the gross income allocable to the passive farm loss activity are disallowed for minimum tax purposes. Each farm is generally treated as a separate activity. The preference applies to personal service corporations.

> **NOTE:** Income from one passive farming activity cannot be netted against other passive farming activity losses. A disallowed farming loss must be carried forward and netted against future income from the same activity, or until there is a disposition.

Act Sec. 701 relating to passive farm losses amends Sec. 58(a), effective for tax years beginning after 12-31-86.

[¶715] **Passive Activity Losses.** The passive activity loss limitation for minimum tax purposes is identical to that for regular tax purposes, with the following exceptions:

- The minimum tax rule is effective in 1987, whereas the regular tax rule is phased in over five years;

- For minimum tax purposes, the disallowed loss amount is reduced by the excess of the taxpayer's liabilities over the market value of assets (applies only to insolvent taxpayers); and

- The minimum tax rules, including the passive farm loss rule, apply to the measurement and allowability of all relevant income, deduction, and credit items for limitation purposes. The passive loss disallowance is determined after all preferences and adjustments have been computed. So the suspended loss amount may be different for minimum and regular tax purposes.

Act Sec. 701 relating to passive activity losses amends Sec. 58(b), effective for tax years beginning after 12-31-86.

[¶716] **Dividends Excluded From Gross Income.** Prior law treated dividends excluded from gross income ($100 a person, $200 for joint returns) as a tax preference. The new law repeals the dividend exclusion, so it is no longer a tax preference.

Additional Corporation Preferences

[¶717] **Bad Debt Reserves of Financial Institutions.** As under prior law, bad debt reserve addition allowances above those based on an actual experience reserve are a tax preference for commercial banks and thrift institutions.

Act Sec. 701, relating to financial institution's bad debt reserves, in effect redesignates old Sec. 57(a)(7) as new Sec. 57(a)(4).

[¶718] Shipping Company Capital Construction Funds.
Shipping company capital construction funds, established under Sec.
607 of the Merchant Marine Act of 1936, are minimum tax preferences. Deposits to the fund after 1986 aren't deductible, and fund
earnings after 1986 aren't excludable in computing minimum taxable income. Pre-1987 fund deposits or earnings are treated as withdrawn before post-1986 deposits or earnings.

*Act Sec. 701 relating to shipping company capital construction funds
amends Sec. 56(c)(2), effective for tax years beginning after 12-31-86.*

[¶719] Effect of Section 291. Corporate minimum tax preferences are determined after applying Sec. 291 (which reduces the
benefit of specified corporate preference items). So, for example, if
Sec. 291 reduces a corporation's bad debt reserve for regular tax
purposes, the amount of the reduction isn't double-counted by also
being treated as a tax preference.

*Act Sec. 701 relating to the effect of Sec. 291, adds new Sec. 59(f), effective
for tax years beginning after 12-31-86.*

[¶720] Business Untaxed Reported Profits. This rule states
that a corporation's minimum taxable income (for 1987, 1988, and
1989) includes one-half of the excess of adjusted book net income
over alternative minimum taxable income (before additions arising
from the preference). Corporate book income is the net income or
loss reflected in the taxpayer's applicable financial statement. Conforming adjustments are made to net income to reflect consolidated
tax returns, to remove federal and foreign income taxes, and for
other purposes. Alaska native corporations can adjust for cost recovery and depletion in their adjusted gross income computations.

Applicable financial statement. Book income is taken from the
applicable financial statement. For corporations having more than
one financial statement, the "applicable" statement for determining
net book income is chosen based on a priority system.

• If financial statements are filed with the Securities and Exchange Commission, those statements are used.

• If no statements are filed with the SEC, then certified audited
statements used for credit purposes, reporting to shareholders, or for
any other substantial nontax purpose are used.

• Next are financial statements that must be filed with the federal government or with a federal agency other than the SEC, or a
state or local government or agency.

• If none of these statements exists, a financial statement or report used for credit purposes, for reporting to owners or for any
other substantial nontax purpose becomes the applicable financial
statement. Within this last category, a financial statement used for

credit purposes has priority over one provided to owners. A financial statement used for any other substantial nontax purpose has the lowest priority.

If no financial statements exist, the financial net income or loss is equal to earnings and profits for the year. Taxpayers that don't file a financial statement with the SEC or other governmental agency and don't have a certified audited financial statement may elect to use earnings and profits. If the earnings and profits election is made, earnings and profits must be used as long as the taxpayer is eligible for the election.

Adjustments to income made after the financial statements have been issued won't be considered unless the financial statements are restated. If there are both unadjusted high priority and adjusted low priority financial statements, the high priority statements are to be used.

> **Example:** Acme Corporation provides its shareholders with certified audited financial statements. After issuance, the company determines that the results of operations would be better reflected if other generally accepted accounting principles were applied to certain items. So it prepares a second, unaudited set of financial statements for credit purposes, and does not recall the earlier statements.

The earlier certified statements will have priority over the later uncertified statements. But if the earlier statements weren't certified, the later statements would apply because statements used for credit purposes have priority over statements issued to shareholders if both or neither are certified. If both statements had equal priority, the later statement would be the applicable financial statement.

If supplementary documents are issued instead of restating previously issued financial statements, issuing the supplementary documents is considered the same as issuing restated financial statements.

Adjustments. The companies included in the consolidated tax return may not be the same as those included in the financial statements (i.e., foreign companies and Sec. 936 corporations cannot be consolidated for tax purposes). So the financial statements must be adjusted to include only those companies that are included in the consolidated tax return. Book income is adjusted to include actual or deemed distributions (as measured for tax purposes) from corporations not in the tax consolidated group. If an ownership interest in the other corporation is accounted for by the equity or consolidation method, an adjustment to reverse inclusion is required. Book income must be adjusted to eliminate dividends from corporations that are included in the consolidated tax return but included in the measure of financial statement net income only when dividends are paid.

Companies that have different year-ends for financial and tax purposes must take the prorata share of financial income from each applicable financial statement that falls within the tax year. Companies with a 52-53 week year will have a year-end that coincides with the same week as the 52-53 week year-end.

If the prorata share of financial statement income cannot be determined because the statement is not available by the time the tax return is filed, an estimate can be made. The tax return can be amended when the income figures become available. The Treasury may prescribe rules that will allow taxpayers to use adjusted net book income for the accounting year that ends within the taxpayer's tax year instead of amending the return.

Extraordinary items stated net of tax must be adjusted to remove any federal or foreign tax expense or benefits before the item is included in adjusted net book income.

Computation. A corporation's alternative minimum taxable income equals half of the excess of adjusted net book income over the alternative minimum taxable income figured before the preference is added.

Example (1): Able's adjusted net book income and alternative minimum taxable income (before including the preference amount) are $1,000 and $200, respectively. Half the excess of adjusted net book income over alternative minimum taxable income ($400) is added to alternative minimum taxable income ($200), which makes alternative minimum taxable income $600 [$200 + ½ ($1,000 − $200)].

Example (2): Baker has adjusted net book income of $200 and alternative minimum taxable income (before adjustment) of negative $100. Since adjusted net book income exceeds alternative minimum taxable income, half the $300 difference is added to alternative minimum taxable income, making alternative minimum taxable income $50 [− $100 + ½ ($300)].

Example (3): Charlie's adjusted net book loss is $300. The alternative minimum tax loss (before adjustment) is $700. Alternative tax loss, after adjustment, is $500 [− $700 + ½ ($400)].

NOTE: This provision has been criticized because it is viewed as giving the Financial Accounting Standards Board (the standard-setting organization for financial statement reporting) influence over tax policy, which is beyond the scope of its authority. Another criticism is that some companies might change their financial accounting policies to reduce their tax liability, thereby making their financial statements less meaningful.

Book income will be used to determine minimum income only for 1987, 1988, and 1989. After 1989, earnings and profits will be used instead. The earnings and profits definition is modified for pre-effective date transactions so as to more closely achieve the goals of the use of book income. A Treasury study is mandated.

Act Secs. 701 and 702 relating to business untaxed reported profits amends Sec. 56(f) and (g) effective for tax years beginning after 12-31-86.

[¶721] Alternative Minimum Tax Itemized Deductions.
Most individual alternative minimum tax itemized deductions are unchanged. Thus, the only itemized deductions allowable are those for (1) casualty, theft, and gambling losses; (2) charitable contributions; (3) medical expenses; (4) qualified interest; (5) the Sec. 691(c) estate tax deduction; and (6) certain estate and trust distributions to beneficiaries. The law on qualified interest is changed as follows: limited business interests are included in the calculation to limit investment interest deductions under the regular tax, and consumer interest may not be deducted as a minimum tax itemized deduction, even if it would be deductible if treated as investment interest. There is an investment interest carryover.

Act Sec. 701, relating to alternative minimum tax itemized deductions amend Sec. 56(b)(1), effective for tax years beginning after 12-31-86.

[¶722] Minimum Tax Credit. Taxpayers can now use the amount of the minimum tax they pay as a credit that reduces the following year's regular tax, net of other nonrefundable credits (or the excess of this regular tax over the tentative minimum tax, if that's less). Unused credits can be carried over indefinitely, but can't be carried back. They can be carried over as tax attributes in corporate acquisitions covered by Sec. 381(a).

The year's minimum tax credit is in general composed of the aggregate post-1986 liability for alternative minimum tax reduced by regular tax, to the extent it wasn't previously used as a credit. However, taxpayers take into account in the alternative minimum tax computation only those liabilities that result from deferral preferences—but not from preferences that result from permanent exclusions for regular tax purposes. So the minimum tax for this credit is reduced by the amount of minimum tax liability that would have been incurred if the only preferences were the exclusion preferences, which are percentage depletion and regular tax itemized deductions that are denied for minimum tax purposes.

> **Example:** Al and Carol Smith file a joint return with zero regular taxable income, $400,000 in deferral preferences, and $100,000 in exclusion preferences (including itemized deductions disallowed for minimum tax). With the 21% alternative minimum tax rate and the phase-out of the exemption, the minimum tax would be $105,000 [21% ($400,000 + $100,000 − $0)]. But if they had only exclusion preferences, the minimum tax liability would have been $12,600 [21% ($100,000 − $40,000 exemption)]. So the minimum tax credit that can be used next year is $92,400 ($105,000 − $12,600).

¶722

Act Sec. 701, relating to the minimum tax credit, adds new Sec. 53, effective for tax years beginning after 12-31-86.

[¶723] Foreign Tax Credit. Under the new law, the foreign tax credit is generally allowable for purposes of the alternative minimum tax under rules similar to those for individuals under prior law. In the alternative minimum tax formula, the credit against the "tentative" minimum tax is generally figured on the tax base against which the minimum 20% or 21% rate is applied, while the regular tax reducing it is figured by using the regular foreign tax credit. The Sec. 904 limitation on the amount of the credit must be applied separately for minimum tax and regular tax purposes, because of the differences between regular taxable income and alternative minimum taxable income, in foreign tax applicable to them, and in the ratios of foreign taxable income to worldwide income. Taxpayers must also keep track of the foreign tax credit carryforwards allowable for both regular and minimum tax purposes.

When Sec. 904(credit limitation) is applied to the minimum tax rules and alternative minimum taxable income is increased by a percentage of the excess of book income over alternative minimum taxable income, the percentage of that income from sources within the United States will be treated the same as other U.S. source alternative minimum taxable income. So the book income preferences won't change the percentage that applies to the alternative minimum tax Sec. 904 limitation.

Up to 90% of tentative minimum tax liability, before foreign tax credits, can be offset by foreign tax credits, even if, under Sec. 904, more than 90% of the liability could be offset by the foreign tax credit. Foreign tax credits disallowed under this rule are treated, for carryover purposes, like credits disallowed under Sec. 904. This rule is applied before comparing the minimum and regular tax liability amounts.

Example. In 1987, a taxpayer has alternative taxable income of $10 million. In the absence of NOLs or foreign tax credits, tentative minimum tax liability (liability determined without regard to the amount of regular tax liability) would be $2.1 million. Foreign tax credits can't be used to reduce liability to less than $210,000, whether or not the taxpayer has any minimum tax net operating losses.

Act Sec. 701, relating to the foreign tax credit adds new Sec. 59(a), effective for tax years beginning after 12-31-86.

[¶724] Incentive Tax Credits. Under prior law, taxpayers claimed nonrefundable credits against the regular tax even if they provided no benefit (that is, they reduced tax liability to less than the minimum tax liability). The portion of the credit that didn't provide a benefit because of the minimum tax was allowed as a carryover to other tax years.

The new law doesn't generally allow taxpayers to claim such credits for the current year to the extent they reduce the regular tax liability to less than the tentative minimum tax liability, but unused credits are allowed as carryovers to other tax years. Corporate taxpayers may use incentive tax credits to offset 25% of the tentative minimum tax liability. Income eligible for the Sec. 936 credit is not included in minimum taxable income of the Sec. 936 corporation.

Incentive tax credits aren't allowed against the minimum tax. Credits that can't be used for regular tax due to the minimum tax can be used as credit carryovers against the regular tax.

> **NOTE:** Taxpayers don't have to file a form showing the minimum tax computation on account of this rule, if they don't owe a minimum tax and if the minimum tax doesn't limit the use of incentive credits.

> **Example:** Al King has a $100 regular tax liability (disregarding incentive credits), and a $10 targeted jobs tax credit. If his tentative minimum tax was less than $90, he wouldn't have to file a minimum tax form.

Act Sec. 701, relating to incentive tax credits, amends Sec. 26(a)-(c), 28(d)(2), 29(b)(5), and 38(c), effective for tax years beginning after 12-31-86.

[¶725] **Special Rules Apply for Net Operating Losses.** Generally, they are the same as the prior law rules for the individual alternative minimum tax. The alternative minimum tax net operating loss and carryovers are computed separately. The computation takes the differences between the regular tax base and the alternative minimum tax base into account.

The net operating loss for alternative minimum tax purposes is computed the same way as the net operating loss for regular purposes, with the following two exceptions:

• Current year tax preference items are added back to taxable income; and

• Individuals may use only those itemized deductions (as modified under Sec. 172(d)) allowable in computing alternative minimum taxable income.

For computing the loss in years other than the loss year, the recomputed loss is deducted from the alternative minimum taxable income, as modified by Sec. 172(b)(2)(A), in the carryover year, whether or not the taxpayer is subject to the minimum tax in that year.

> **Example (1):** In year one, Sherry Penn has income of $20,000. Her losses are $35,000, of which $10,000 are preference items. The alternative minimum tax net operating loss for the year is $5,000 [$20,000 − ($35,000 − $10,000)]. She can carry the $5,000 loss forward or back to reduce income that is subject to the alternative minimum tax.

Example (2): The following year, Penn has alternative minimum taxable income, without regard to the net operating loss deduction, of $20,000. She reduces her alternative minimum taxable income to $15,000 because of last year's $5,000 carryforward. Her net operating loss deduction for the regular tax isn't affected by this computation. She has a $15,000 loss carryover from last year, which she can use with the regular tax.

Transition rule. A transition rule for corporations allows, for alternative minimum tax purposes, all preeffective date regular tax net operating losses to be carried forward as minimum tax net operating losses. They can be carried forward to the first tax year for which the tax, as amended under the new law, applies. They can also be carried forward until used up. Prior law is retained for individuals with respect to the calculation of alternative minimum tax net operating losses.

Corporations that had a deferral of add-on minimum tax liability before 1987 because of certain net operating losses have to make an adjustment. For these corporations, the add-on minimum tax won't be imposed after 1986. But the alternative minimum tax net operating loss carried to the first year beginning after 1986 must be reduced by the amount of the preferences that gave rise to the liability. Net operating losses cannot offset more than 90% of minimum taxable income. Amounts disallowed because of the 90% limitation may be carried over to other taxable years.

Example: A taxpayer has $10 million of alternative minimum taxable income in 1987, and minimum tax NOLs of $11 million. The NOLs reduce alternative minimum taxable income to $1 million. So tentative minimum tax liability is $210,000. The taxpayer can carry forward $2 million of minimum tax NOLs to 1988. Since the allowability of net operating losses is determined before the allowability of foreign tax credits, this taxpayer wouldn't be allowed to use any minimum tax foreign tax credits before 1987.

An election under Sec. 172(b)(3)(C) to relinquish the carryback applies both for regular tax and minimum tax purposes.

Act Sec. 701, relating to net operating losses, amends Sec. 56(d), effective for tax years beginning after 12-31-86.

[¶726] Regular Tax Elections. For certain expenditures that would result in a tax preference if treated under the regular tax rules, taxpayers can elect to have the minimum tax rule for deducting the expenditure apply for regular tax purposes (a normative election). This rule applies to the following expenditures:

- Circulation expenditures.
- Research and experimental expenditures.
- Intangible drilling costs.
- Mining development and exploration expenditures.

Taxpayers can make these elections on a dollar-for-dollar basis. So a taxpayer who incurs intangible drilling costs of $100,000 on a well may elect normative treatment for any portion of the $100,000. To the extent the election applies, no deduction is allowed either for regular or minimum tax purposes. And the election may be revoked only with the Treasury Secretary's consent. Partners of S corporation shareholders can make the election separately for their allocable share of the expenditure.

Act Sec. 701, relating to regular tax elections, adds new Sec. 53, effective for tax years beginning after 12-31-86.

[¶727] Other Rules. The new law has several miscellaneous rules that affect the application of the alternative minimum tax. Corporations must make estimated tax payments for both minimum tax and regular tax purposes. Estates and trusts are allowed to take certain alternative minimum tax itemized deductions. The Treasury will issue regulations that prescribe how items treated for regular and minimum tax purposes are to be apportioned between the estate or trust and the beneficiaries.

The new law prescribes rules for allocating items that are treated differently for regular and minimum tax purposes for common trust funds, regulated investment companies, and real estate investment trusts. There are also rules on certain technical issues such as short tax years and exemption amounts for consolidated returns. As under prior law, the Treasury has been instructed to prescribe regulations for the application of the tax benefit rule to items that are treated differently for regular and minimum tax purposes.

Code sections suspending losses, such as Secs. 465, 704(d), 1366(d), and other sections specified in regulations are recomputed for minimum tax purposes to apply to amounts otherwise deductible for minimum tax purposes. The amount of the deductions suspended or recaptured may differ for regular and minimum tax purposes, respectively. This rule applies to all taxpayers subject to the at-risk rules.

For an estate or trust, instead of allocating tax preference items between the estate or trust and its beneficiaries (as under prior law), minimum tax will apply by determining distributable net income on a minimum tax basis (except to the extent inconsistent with the modifications under Sec. 643(a) with the minimum tax exemption amount being treated the same way as the deduction for personal exemptions under Sec. 643(a)(2).

[The page following this is 801.]

ACCOUNTING PROVISIONS

[¶801] Limits on Use of Cash Method and Easing of Accrual Method. Starting in 1987, the new law forbids C corporations, partnerships with any C corporation partners, tax shelters, and Sec. 511(b) tax-exempt trusts with unrelated business taxable income to use the cash method or a hybrid method reporting partly on a cash basis. *Exceptions:* Business (but not tax shelters) with average annual gross receipts (less returns and allowances) of $5 million or less for the preceding three tax years or the shorter period they conducted business, employee-owned service businesses in the field of health, law, accounting, engineering, architecture, actuarial science, performing arts or consulting (qualified personal service corporations), and farming and timber businesses can continue on the cash method.

Starting in 1987, the new law: (1) allows accrual taxpayers to report income from personal services (other than those typical of public utilities, banks, or financial institutions) no earlier than they are billed; (2) treats economic performance of services provided by nonemployees as occurring when they are performed or when they are billed, whichever is later (for employees it's when they're performed) for the "economic performance" deduction test; and (3) allows nonaccrual of billings for services that on the basis of experience the taxpayer won't collect, unless interest or a late penalty is charged.

Businesses that can continue using the cash method. Eligibility to use the cash method remains controlled by prior law rules, but is now in general limited to S corporations, sole proprietorships, and partnerships that have no C corporation partners. Qualified personal service corporations that can use it under the exception to the limitation must be substantially involved in performing services in fields listed above (function test). Also, all of their stock must be substantially owned (95% in value) by employees or former employees performing services in these fields, their estates, or anyone acquiring an ownership interest because of that person's death within the prior 24 months.

Employees may also own the stock indirectly through a holding company with subsidiaries in the same field of service. Stock owned by an ESOP or pension plan is considered owned by the plan beneficiaries. This ownership test operates without regard to community property laws, and stock owned by a partnership, S corporation or personal service corporation is considered owned by its partners or shareholders. Farming businesses (defined in new Sec. 263(d)(4)) that can use the cash method are generally those engaged in growing, raising, managing, or training crops or livestock; or raising or harvesting trees that bear fruit, nuts, or other crops, or Christmas or other ornamental trees. The $5 million or below three-year average gross receipts of other businesses that can use it is computed using the gross receipts (less returns or allowances) for the preceding three years (or shorter period when business was conducted). Gross receipts for short tax years are annualized. Affiliates or entities under common control treated as a "single employer" (Sec. 52(a), (b) or 414(m), (o)) are a single entity for the exceptions from the cash method prohibition.

> **NOTE:** The new law doesn't specifically state that gross receipts for the three-year test can be reduced by sales discounts.

Uncollectible billings. Accrual taxpayers now won't accrue income for personal services they don't expect to collect, if they don't charge interest or penalties for untimely payment. Those offering discounts for early payment accrue the gross amount billed, and reduce income by the discount when they're actually paid. According to the Ways and Means Committee Report, estimated uncollectible billings are computed as follows:

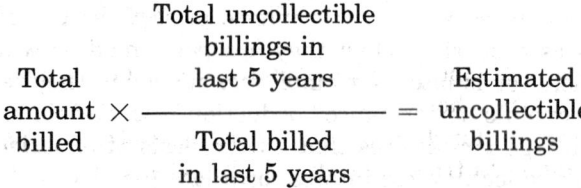

$$\text{Total amount billed} \times \frac{\text{Total uncollectible billings in last 5 years}}{\text{Total billed in last 5 years}} = \text{Estimated uncollectible billings}$$

According to the Committee Reports, the year's expected uncollectibles are computed by multiplying year-end outstanding receivables by the percentage of receivables created in the last five years that were determined to be uncollectible.

Taxpayers that have not been in existence for five years will use the shorter period of their existence in the formula. Partial or total worthlessness of unreported billings doesn't create a deduction; and their actual collection gives rise to reportable income. A change from the cash method required by the new law rules is considered a change in accounting method initiated by the taxpayer with IRS consent. To prevent duplication or omission of income and expense items, a Sec. 481 adjustment (spread generally over four years or less) must be made. It's expected that the concepts of Rev. Proc. 84-74, 1984-2 CB 736, will generally determine the actual timing of the adjustment items. For operating hospitals—in general JCAH-or-comparably-accredited hospital institutions, but not rest or nursing homes, day care centers, research labs, or ambulatory care facilities—the adjustments can be spread over up to 10 (rather than 4) years.

Transitional rule election. Taxpayers can elect to retain the cash method for any loan, lease, or a related party transaction entered into before 9-25-85.

Act Sec. 801, amends Sec. 461(i) and adds Sec. 448, effective for tax years beginning after 12-31-86, and as shown above.

〔¶802〕 Simplified Dollar-Value LIFO for Small Business. Starting in 1987, the new law replaces the prior law LIFO election to use a single inventory pool by businesses with average gross receipts of $2 million or less, with a simplified dollar-value LIFO election for businesses with average gross receipts of $5 million or less. This new simplified LIFO method calls for inventory pools grouped by Bureau of Labor Statistics Producer and Consumer general price index categories, for indexing annual cost changes by use of BLS monthly published indexes, and use of cumulative indexes developed by the link-chain method. It's designed to allow small businesses to use LIFO without undue complexities or excessive compliance costs. Businesses that elected the single pool method can continue using it under prior law rules. But they can't use the new simplified method at the same time, and can revoke the old election without IRS consent.

Electing simplified dollar-value LIFO. The new method can be used only by businesses that had average annual gross receipts (less returns and allowances) of $5 million or less for the preceding three tax years or the shorter period they were in business, determined under rules similar to those of new Sec. 448(c)(3)—See ¶801. All members of a controlled group (determined under Sec. 52(b) regs used for determining a "single employer") are considered a single taxpayer for measuring the gross receipts ceiling. The election (initially made for a tax year without IRS consent under regs to come) applies also to later years and covers all of the taxpayer's LIFO inventories. The taxpayer must change from the simplified dollar-value LIFO method to another method the first year it fails to meet the $5 million average annual gross receipts test. It may change to another method at any time, and needs to get the IRS's permission only if permission to change would have been required before adoption of simplified dollar-value LIFO. *Reason:* not to place taxpayers under any more of a burden than they would have been had they not adopted simplified dollar-value LIFO.

Operation of method. Inventory values using simplified dollar-value LIFO are generally computed under Reg. Sec. 1.472-8 but with these main differences:

- More than one inventory pool is used to avoid construction of an index specific to the taxpayer. Retailers using the retail method group their pools by the 11 general categories in the BLS consumer price index for all urban consumers (currently Table 3 for food expenditure categories and Table 5 for nonfood expenditure categories, monthly CPI detailed reports) noted in Reg. Sec. 1.472-8(e)(3)(iv). *Examples:* Food and beverages; apparel commodities.) All other taxpayers use the 15 general two-digit categories in the monthly BLS producers prices and price indexes for commodity groupings and individual items (currently Table 6). *Examples:* Farm products; furniture and household durables. The annual change in costs for each general category pool as a whole is measured by the percentage change for the year in the published index for the category.

- Present dollar inventory values are discounted back to equivalent values in the base year through the link-chain approach (a current cumulative index is constructed from year-by-year index components), rather than by comparing the dollar amount of inventory items measured in present year prices against the dollar amount of the same inventory items in base year prices (double-extension method).

The taxpayer selects a month of the year whose index he will use to measure annual changes in his pool; he must use the same month in later years unless the IRS consents to a change. Originally released BLS index figures are used, unless corrected figures are published *before* the taxpayer files his return—the index figure that's *actually* used for the year must be adhered to next year (any over or undervaluation will adjust itself automatically at the end of next year).

The first year when the simplified dollar-value LIFO method is used is the base year. Converting to the method may involve adjustments. On a change from FIFO, the taxpayer assigns inventory items to the new pools, combines their values, and the total is his base year layer. A change from a method that allows inventories to be stated at less than cost (e.g., FIFO) requires restoration of any previous writedowns from cost to income. (The base year dollar values will include these amounts.) Conversion from another LIFO method is done similarly, but preexisting LIFO layers must be preserved and prior year layers restated in base year dollars by comparing the prices paid to the item's present value.

Example: ABC changes from FIFO to simplified dollar-value LIFO. Inventories consist of a chemical in the BLS "Chemicals and Allied Products" general category, and a high school chemistry text book in the BLS "Pulp, Paper, and Allied Products" general category. Published index numbers for the "Chemicals and Allied Products" general category are 200 for the prior year and 220 for the current year (the "first LIFO year"). The prior year's index number for "Pulp, Paper, and Allied Products" is 142 and for the current year it's 150. In the prior year, the present dollar value of the ending inventory was $30,000 for the chemical and $30,000 for the textbooks. In the current year, the present dollar value of the taxpayer's ending inventory is $35,000 for the chemical and $30,000 for the textbooks. Items in the two general categories are included in separate dollar-value LIFO pools. The annual index for each pool is equal to one plus the percentage change in the index for the general category, as follows:

Pool	Current year index	Prior year index	Change	Percent change	Index
#1	220	200	20	0.1000	1.1000
#2	150	142	8	.0563	1.0563

In later years, the annual index would be multiplied by the cumulative index for the preceding year to compute the current cumulative index (in the first year the annual and cumulative index are the same). The present dollar value of the ending inventory for the current year is divided by the cumulative index to restate it in its equivalent value in base year dollars. This amount is assigned to the LIFO layers and multiplied by the cumulative index for the year to which the layer relates to find an indexed dollar value for that layer. The sum of the indexed dollar values for the layers is the ending LIFO inventory value for the pool. Here are the figures for the first year:

Pool #1

Current year dollar value of inventory	$35,000
Divided by index	1.100
Inventory in base-year dollars	$31,818

LIFO layers	Base-year dollar value	Dollar index	Indexed dollar value
Base-year	$30,000	1.0000	$30,000
First LIFO year	1,818	1.1000	2,000
Ending inventory	$31,818		$32,000

Pool #2

Current year dollar value of inventory	$30,000
Divided by index	1.0563
Inventory in base-year dollars	$28,401

	Base-year dollar value	Index	Indexed dollar value
Base year	$28,401	1.0000	$28,401
First LIFO year	0	0	0
Ending inventory	$28,401		$28,401

Total ending inventory:

Pool #1	$32,000
Pool #2	28,401
	$60,401

Act Sec. 802, relating to simplified dollar-value LIFO, amends Sec. 474, effective for tax years beginning after 12-31-86 and as shown above.

[¶803] Installment Sales—Allocating Debt. Under the old law, a taxpayer who sells property on the installment basis is taxed as payments are received, the rationale being that it would be unfair to require a tax on the entire gain in the year of sale when only a small portion of total sale proceeds may have been received in the year of sale. But a taxpayer that pledges the installment obligation is in a much better cash flow position than one that doesn't, so it was felt that there is often no need to defer taxing the gain when the installment receivables are turned into cash by pledging them.

The new law limits use of the installment method in three cases. The installment method is not available for:

• Certain installment receivables, based on the taxpayer's outstanding debt. Taxpayers who sell timeshares and residential lots may elect to pay interest on the deferred tax liability instead of being subject to the general installment sales rules. There's an exception for certain sales by a manufacturer to a dealer when the term of the installment obligation is based on the time the property is resold by the dealer;

• Revolving credit plan sales; and

• Sales of certain publicly traded property.

Proportionate disallowance rule in general. Use of the installment method is limited for sales of (real or personal) inventory, business, or rental property. The limit depends on the taxpayer's "allocable installment indebtedness." (AII). When applying the proportionate disallowance rule, installment debt from the sale of personal-use property by an individual, and property produced or used in farming aren't treated as applicable installment obligations. So installment debt from the sale of crops or livestock held for slaughter aren't AII. The calculation is annual rather than quarterly for taxpayers that don't have applicable installment debt that arose from an installment sale of either personal property by a person that regularly sells property of the same type on the installment method, or real property that was held for sale to customers in the ordinary course of trade or business. Otherwise, the calculation is quarterly. The Treasury is authorized to issue regs to prevent avoiding the proportionate disallowance rule when the calculation is made annually.

Allocable installment indebtedness. The allocable installment indebtedness is computed using this formula:

$$AII = \frac{a}{b + c} \ (d) - AII \ (p)$$

a = the face amount of "applicable installment obligations" outstanding at year-end

b = the face amount of all installment obligations (applicable and nonapplicable)

c = the adjusted basis of all other taxpayer assets (straight-line depreciation may be elected for determining adjusted basis)

d = average quarterly debt

AII(p) = AII from prior years' applicable installment obligations

Individuals exclude certain farm or personal use property, related secured debt, or related installment obligations from the computation.

"Applicable installment obligations" arise from the post-February 1986 installment sale of

- personal inventory property;

- real property held for sale in the ordinary course of trade or business; or

- real property (other than certain farm property) used in the trade or business or held for the production of rental income, provided (1) the selling price is more than $150,000, and (2) the seller or other affiliated group member holds the obligation.

In later years, taxpayers don't have to recognize gain from prior year applicable installment obligations for payments that aren't higher than the amount of AII attributable to the obligations. AII is reduced as payments are received. Payments on an applicable installment obligation that are in excess of the AII allocable to the obligation are accounted for under the ordinary installment method rules. Adjustments to individual allocable installment obligations generally aren't made except to reflect payments that don't result in gain recognition. But additional AII may be allocated to installment obligations that arose in prior years if the AII for a particular year is more than the applicable installment obligation amount arising in that year and outstanding at year-end. Any excess is first allocated to outstanding applicable installment obligations from the previous year (to the extent the face value exceeds the AII), and then allocated to each preceding tax year until the entire excess is allocated.

Indebtedness calculation. Average indebtedness is computed quarterly (annually for the two exceptions explained above). All debt included in the provision that is outstanding at the end of the quarter is included in the quarterly computation. Accounts payable, accrued debt, bank loans, bond debt, and other payables should be in-

¶1803

cluded in the computation. Debt payments made to avoid the limitation are to be ignored.

> **COMMENT:** This rule opens up a potential Pandora's box because of the "intent" requirement.

Affiliated groups. All persons treated as a single taxpayer under Sec. 52(a) or (b) are treated as one taxpayer for the proportionate disallowance rule. In applying the rule to the controlled group, the installment percentage is computed by combining the controlled group's assets and multiplying it by the aggregate average quarterly (or annual) controlled group's debt to find the total AII. The total AII is then allocated pro rata to the applicable installment obligations held by individual members of the group, regardless of the amount of debt held by any particular member. The regular provisions of the proportionate disallowance rule are then applied. The Treasury may issue regs that forbid using the installment method in whole or in part for transactions if the effect of the proportionate disallowance rule would be avoided by using related parties, pass-through entities, or intermediaries. So a corporation, partnership, or trust may be treated as related to its shareholders, partners, or beneficiaries if the proportionate disallowance rule otherwise might be avoided.

The regs may aggregate related party assets when applying the proportionate disallowance rule. For example, the assets and debt of a partnership and each partner may be combined to calculate the extent to which each partner may report gain from an installment sale of partnership assets.

> **Example:** Acme Company, a calendar year dealer in real property, started business in 1987. In that year, it sold one property, at a profit, for $250,000, but did not receive any payments in 1987. Acme's assets, excluding the installment obligation, had an aggregate adjusted basis of $1 million at the end of 1987. Acme's debt amounted to $200,000 on March 31, $250,000 on June 30, $400,000 on September 30, and $350,000 on December 31, for an average quarterly debt of $300,000. Acme's AII for 1987 is $60,000, computed as follows:

$$\text{AII} = \frac{a}{b + c} \ (d) - \text{AII (p)}$$

$$\frac{\$250,000}{\$250,000 + \$1,000,000} \ (\$300,000) - 0 = \$60,000$$

Acme is considered to have received $60,000 as of the end of 1987, even though nothing was actually received.

In 1988, Acme sold another property at a profit, for $400,000. No payments on either sale were received in 1988. The aggregate adjusted asset basis at the end of 1988 was $1,300,000, and average quarterly debt was $420,000. AII for 1988 is $80,000, computed as follows:

$$\frac{\$650,000}{\$650,000 + \$1,300,000} (\$420,000) - \$60,000 = \$80,000$$

So Acme is deemed to have received $80,000 in 1988, even though nothing is actually received.

In 1989, Acme sold a third property at a profit for $500,000, and the 1987 installment obligation was paid in full. No other payments were received. At year-end, aggregate adjusted asset bases, other than installment obligations, totaled $1,100,000, and average quarterly debt was $600,000. The first $60,000 of the $250,000 payment from the 1987 installment obligation won't result in gain recognition, and reduces the amount of AII that is treated as allocated to that obligation. The next $190,000 is treated as an additional payment on the obligation that results in the recognition of additional gain under the installment method.

The AII allocated to taxable income before 1989, for purposes of computing 1989 AII, is $80,000 ($60,000 from 1987 plus $80,000 from 1988, minus $60,000 from 1987). Acme's 1989 AII is $190,000, computed as follows:

$$\frac{\$900,000}{\$900,000 + \$1,100,000} (\$600,000) - \$80,000 = \$190,000$$

The entire $190,000 AII is allocated to the 1989 installment obligation. If the 1989 AII had been more than the amount of applicable installment obligations arising in 1989 and outstanding at year-end ($500,000), the first $500,000 is allocated to the 1989 installment obligation, and the remainder to the 1988 obligation.

Timeshares and residential lots. There is a special election for timeshares and residential lots. Under the election, the proportionate disallowance rule doesn't apply to installment obligations that arise when a dealer sells certain types of property to an individual. The election applies only if the individual's obligation isn't guaranteed or insured by any third person other than an individual. The obligation must arise from the sale of a timeshare or of unimproved land, the development of which will not be done by the land's seller, or any seller's affiliate.

For election purposes, a timeshare is a right to use a specified parcel of residential real property (including campground sites) for up to six weeks a year. All individual and related party timeshares are combined for determining whether the six-week test is met.

Sellers meeting these conditions can elect not to have the general installment sales rules apply, if the seller pays interest on the deferred tax liability attributable to use of the installment method. To make the election, the interest rate must be 100% of the applicable federal rate applicable to the maturity of the note, without regard to the three-month lookback rule of Sec. 1274(d)(2).

Exception for manufacturer/dealer sales. There is an exception for installment sales of tangible personal property by the manufacturer (or manufacturer's affiliate) to a dealer. The exception applies only if (1) the dealer must make principal payments only when the dealer resells or rents the property, (2) the manufacturer has the right to repurchase the property at a fixed or ascertainable price within nine months of the sale to the dealer, and (3) certain other conditions are met.

50% test. To meet the other conditions, the aggregate face amount of the installment obligations that otherwise qualify for the exception must equal at least 50% of total credit sales to dealers. This test must be met both in the current and preceding tax year. But if the taxpayer met all exception requirements in the previous year, then the taxpayer wouldn't fail to meet the 50% test before the second consecutive year in which the test was not actually met. The 50% test computes the receivables' aggregate face amount using the monthly receivable weighted average. The requirement must be met in the first tax year after enactment. Obligations issued before enactment meet the requirement if they are conformed to the law's requirement within 60 days of enactment. Receivables qualifying for the exception aren't subject to the law's installment method limitation provision.

Revolving credit plans. Taxpayers who sell property on a revolving credit plan aren't allowed to account for the sales using the installment method. Payments are treated as received entirely in the year of sale. The Treasury has regulatory authority to disallow use of the installment method when the tax rules would otherwise be avoided through related parties, pass-through entities, or intermediaries. Revolving credit plans are discussed in Reg. Sec. 1.453-2(d).

Phase-in. Taxpayers who sell property under revolving credit plans and who may no longer use the installment method may include income from the adjustment over four years or less. While the proportionate disallowance rule is generally effective for tax years ending after 1986 (for sales of property after February 1986), any property sales after February 1986 but before the taxpayer's first tax year ending after 1986 (i.e., if the taxpayer has a calendar tax year, or has a short tax period ending between 2-28-86 and 12-31-86) are treated as arising in the taxpayer's first tax year ending after 1986.

For installment debt arising from the sale of real property in the ordinary course of business, any gain attributable to allocable installment debt allocated to any of those installment obligations that arise (or are deemed to arise) in the first tax year ending after 1986, is taken into account ratably over the three tax years beginning with the first tax year. For installment debt arising in the second tax year ending after 1986, any gain is taken into account ratably over two tax years beginning with the second tax year.

For installment debt from the sale of personal property in the normal course of business, any increase in the taxpayer's tax liability for the first tax year ending after 1986 caused by applying the proportionate disallowance rule is treated as imposed ratably over three tax years, beginning with the first tax year. Any increase in tax liability in the taxpayer's second tax year ending after 1986 because of the proportionate disallowance rule (disregarding the ratable share of the prior year tax increase) is treated as imposed ratably over the two tax years beginning with the second tax year.

For applicable installment obligations other than those from the sale of real or personal property in the normal course of business, the proportionate disallowance rule is effective for tax years ending after 1986, for sales after 8-16-86. Sales after 8-16-86 and before the taxpayer's first tax year ending after 1986 are to be treated as arising in the first tax year ending after 1986.

The revolving credit plan sales rules are effective for tax years beginning after 1986. Adjustments resulting from a change in accounting method are taken into account over four years or less. Where four years are used, 15% is taken into account the first year, 25% the second year, and 30% in each of the next two years.

The rules for sales of publicly traded property take effect for sales after 1986.

Act Sec. 811, relating to allocation of indebtedness as payment on installments, adds Sec. 453C. The elimination of the installment method for sales on a revolving credit plan is effective for sales of property after 12-31-86. The proportionate disallowance rule is effective as of 1-1-87 for sales made on or after 3-1-86.

[¶804] **No Installment Method for Publicly Traded Property.** Sales of publicly traded property, including stocks and bonds, don't qualify for the installment method. The fair market value of an installment obligation received in exchange for property is equal to the fair market value of the property at time of sale. Gains or losses from sales made on an established market are recognized the day the trade is executed, not the settlement date, which may be a few days later. This rule applies both to accrual and cash basis taxpayers. Payments are treated as being received entirely in the year of sale. The Treasury has regulatory authority to disallow use of the installment method when the tax rules would otherwise be avoided through related parties, pass-through entities, or intermediaries.

¶804

Example: John Jones sells his interest in a wholly owned corporation. The corporation's only assets are stock or securities that are traded on an established securities market. The Treasury may deny use of the installment method to record gain because the transaction involves related parties.

Example: Jane Smith, a retiring partner in a large investment partnership, makes an installment sale of her interest. A substantial portion of the interest's value is attributable to stocks and securities held by the partnership. If she could not have sold or caused the sale of the partnership's assets directly, the gain on sale may be reported on the installment method.

Act Sec. 812, relating to publicly traded property, amends Secs. 453 and 453A, effective for sales after 12-31-86.

[¶805]   Capitalization of Inventory Costs. Prior law required all direct material and labor costs to be included in inventory cost and deducted as cost of goods sold as the inventory is sold. Prior law also required certain indirect manufacturing costs to be included in inventory cost (thereby treating them as product costs rather than period costs). The new law requires that certain other indirect costs, previously classified as period costs and deducted at the end of the accounting period, be treated as product costs, included in the cost of the product, and deducted as the product is sold. Similar indirect costs, incurred for noninventory items, must also be capitalized.

NOTE: The new inventory accounting rules will result in major changes in the way companies account for inventory. The changes will defer deductions, increase taxable income, and may create an administrative nightmare for the accounting department.

Summary of changes. Certain (period) costs that are now deducted at the end of the accounting period will have to be capitalized, built into product cost, and deducted as part of cost of goods sold as each product is sold.

Example: Acme Publishing Company incurs costs of $900,000 in 1987 that would have been expensed under the old rules, but must now be built into inventory cost. If the inventory item is sold 20% in 1987, 50% in 1988, and 30% in 1989, the amounts that can be deducted as cost of goods sold will be $180,000, $450,000, and $270,000 in 1987, 1988, and 1989, respectively. Under the old rule, all $900,000 could have been deducted in 1987. The new rule permits a deduction of only $180,000 in 1987, which will increase 1987 taxes by $244,800 for a company in the 34% bracket [34% ($900,000 − $180,000)]. However, taxes in 1988 and 1989 will be reduced by a total of $244,800 because portions of the deferred costs can be deducted in those years. *Result:* Total deductions will be identical over three years, but cash flow will be pinched in the first year.

Items affected. Several items now being expensed will have to be capitalized and built into cost of goods sold. Among these are:

- costs incident to purchasing inventory (e.g., wages or salaries of employees responsible for purchasing);

- repackaging, assembly, and other costs incurred in processing goods while in the taxpayer's possession;

- storage costs (e.g., rent or depreciation, insurance premiums, and taxes attributable to a warehouse and wages of warehouse personnel);

- a portion of general and administrative costs allocable to these functions;

- a portion of pension and profit-sharing costs; and

- certain interest costs, including imputed interest.

The uniform capitalization rules only affect inventories valued at cost. So the rules won't affect inventories valued at market by a taxpayer using the lower of cost or market method, or by a dealer in securities using the market method. But the rules will apply to inventories valued at cost by a taxpayer using the lower of cost or market method.

NOTE: The new law does not address the case where a taxpayer using the lower of cost or market method uses cost one year and market the next. When cost is used, the uniform capitalization rules apply. When market is used, the rules don't apply.

Other adverse effects. Implementing the change may be an administrative nightmare. Items to include or exclude will be difficult to determine in many cases. Allocation of general and administrative expenses must be arbitrary, and subject to challenge on audit.

If the Financial Accounting Standards Board rules on inventory accounting and imputed interest differ from the tax rules (which they do), it will necessitate establishing two new deferred tax accounts, which the accounting department will have to track.

Change in accounting method. The inventory change is regarded as a change in accounting method. The Sec. 481 adjustment resulting from the change is to be included in income over four years or less, using the provisions of Rev. Proc. 84-74, 1984-2 C.B. 736. Net operating loss and tax credit carryforwards may offset a positive Sec. 481 adjustment. For purposes of determining estimated tax payments, the Sec. 481 adjustment will be recognized ratably throughout the tax year of adjustment.

In computing the Sec. 481 adjustment, taxpayers using the simplified method for property acquired for resale must apply this method in restating beginning inventory. Taxpayers using LIFO that lack sufficient data to compute the adjustment precisely may use the methods of approximation available to manufacturers (based on the data for the three prior years for which there were increments in the inventory).

The new rules apply to all real or personal property produced by the taxpayer as well as property acquired for resale. But inventory acquired for resale that is personal (not real) property is excluded from the new rule for taxpayers having average annual gross receipts of $10 million or less for the three prior tax years. Gross receipts include those generated from all trades or businesses under common control, including partnerships, and corporations. A controlled group of corporations includes those corporations owned, directly or indirectly, more than 50% by the taxpayer.

Exceptions. The new capitalization rules don't apply to (1) property produced by taxpayers for their personal (not business) use; (2) deductible Sec. 174 research and experimental expenditures; (3) Sec. 616(a) deductible mine development costs and Sec. 263(c) deductible oil and gas or geothermal well intangible drilling costs; (4) property produced under contracts required to be reported under a long-term contract method; and (5) plants or animals produced in a farming business, (see below). The uniform capitalization rules apply to all depreciation deductions for federal income tax purposes. The Senate provision, which was not adopted, would have exempted existing assets from the capitalization of all tax depreciation. The Statement of Managers will provide that cushion gas (and emergency reserve gas to the extent provided by regulations) is not inventory under the capitalization rules. Taxpayers aren't required to allocate to this gas any portion of their overhead or other indirect costs under the new uniform capitalization rules. The Treasury will be directed to provide simplified methods of applying rules to retailers and wholesalers in appropriate circumstances, with examples to be provided in the Statement of Managers.

Self-constructed property and noninventory property produced for sale. The uniform capitalization rules for production activities is limited to tangible property. The rule for property acquired for resale includes both tangible and intangible property. For this purpose, tangible property includes films, sound recordings, video tapes, books, and other similar property embodying words, ideas, concepts, images, or sounds by the creator thereof. So the uniform capitalization rules apply to the costs of producing a motion picture or researching and writing a book.

Interest capitalization. Interest is capitalized and allocated only to real or personal property produced by the taxpayer that has (1) a long useful life; (2) an estimated production period of more than two years; or (3) an estimated production period of more than one year and a cost of more than $1 million. A property has a long useful life if it is real property that has a class life of at least 20 years. The production period begins when production begins and ends when the property is ready to be placed in service or sold.

Amount allocated. Interest on debt that is directly attributable to production expenditures is allocated to the asset's cost. Interest that could have been avoided had the production costs not been incurred is also allocated to the asset's cost. In other words, interest incurred on money borrowed to finance production of the item is capitalized, and interest that could have been avoided had the taxpayer used funds to pay off existing debt instead of to produce the item in question is also capitalized.

The avoided cost method of determining interest allocable to production applies irrespective of whether application of the method, or a similar method, is required, authorized or considered appropriate under financial or regulatory accounting principles. So a regulated utility must apply the avoided cost method even though a different method is authorized or required by FASB Statement No. 34 or the regulatory authority having jurisdiction over the utility.

Qualified residence interest is not capitalized. For flow-through entities, such as partnerships and S corporations, the interest capitalization rule is applied first at the entity level, then at the beneficiary level. Interest on debt incurred or continued for property used to produce capitalizable property shall also be capitalized.

Simplified method for taxpayers acquiring property for resale. The Treasury plans to provide a simplified method for applying the uniform capitalization rules for taxpayers who acquire property for resale. Those not electing the simplified method must apply the procedures and rules used by manufacturers. Once a method is chosen, it must be used consistently. IRS permission is needed to change.

Taxpayers using the simplified method will initially compute their inventory balances without regard to the new uniform capitalization rules. Costs to be capitalized under the new rules are then added, along with other costs, to determine the ending balance. So taxpayers using the LIFO method, for example, will calculate the particular year's LIFO index without regard to the new capitalization rules. Costs capitalized under the new rules will be added to the LIFO layers applicable to the various years for which the costs were accumulated. For taxpayers using the FIFO method who do not sell their entire beginning inventory during the year, a proportionate part of the additional costs capitalized in the beginning inventory will be included in the ending inventory.

The simplified method will be applied separately to each trade or business.

Four categories of indirect cost are allocable to inventory under the simplified method:

- Off-site storage and warehousing costs, including, but not limited to warehouse rent or depreciation, property taxes, insurance premiums, security costs, and other costs directly identifiable with the storage facility;

- Purchasing costs such as buyers' wages or salaries;

- Handling, processing, assembly, repackaging, and similar costs, including labor costs attributable to unloading goods, but not including labor costs attributable to loading of goods for final shipment, or labor at a retail facility, and

- The portion of general and administrative costs allocable to these functions.

Storage costs. Storage costs are included based on the ratio of total annual storage costs to the sum of the beginning inventory balance and gross purchases during the year.

> **Example:** Gannon, who uses FIFO, had $1 million in annual storage costs, beginning inventory (without simplified method adjustments) of $2 million, gross purchases of $8 million, and an ending inventory (without adjustment) of $3 million. The ratio of storage costs to beginning inventory and purchases is 10% ($1 million divided by $2 million + $8 million). So for each inventory dollar, 10 cents of storage costs must be capitalized. The ending inventory will be increased by $300,000. The $700,000 storage cost balance would be included in cost of goods sold.

For LIFO taxpayers, where ending inventory exceeds beginning inventory, the additional capitalized storage costs are calculated by multiplying the inventory increase for the year by the applicable ratio. If the taxpayer in the above example used LIFO instead of FIFO, an additional $100,000 (10% of $1 million) of storage costs would be included in ending inventory. But unlike FIFO, storage costs included in a LIFO beginning inventory remain in inventory until the LIFO layer is depleted (which only happens when the ending inventory is less than the beginning inventory), and aren't deducted as cost of goods sold.

Purchasing costs. Purchasing costs are allocated between inventory and cost of goods sold based on the ratio of purchasing costs to gross purchases during the year. So if the taxpayer in the above example had purchase costs of $500,000 during the year, the ratio of purchasing costs to gross purchases would be 6.25% ($500,000 divided by $8 million). So 6.25 cents of purchasing costs would be capitalized for each dollar's worth of items in ending inventory that were purchased during the year. If the FIFO method were used, $187,500 (6.25% of $3 million) of purchasing costs would be capitalized.

For taxpayers using LIFO, ending inventory consists of newly acquired items only to the extent that ending inventory exceeds beginning inventory. Capitalized purchasing costs would be computed by multiplying the increase in inventory that took place during the year (ending inventory less beginning inventory) by the applicable ratio. The taxpayer in the above example would capitalize $62,500 (6.25% of $1 million) of purchasing costs. In contrast to a FIFO taxpayer, the purchasing costs attributable to a LIFO taxpayer's beginning inventory would be retained in ending inventory.

Processing and repackaging costs. Processing, repackaging and similar costs are allocated based on the ratio of total processing, repackaging and similar costs to the sum of the beginning inventory balance and gross purchases during the year.

General and administrative expenses. General and administrative expenses that are allocable in part to storage, purchasing, and processing activities and in part to activities for which capitalization isn't required are allocated based on the ratio of direct labor costs incurred in a particular function to gross payroll costs.

Example: Baumgarth Company's accounting department has operating costs of $75,000 for the year. Its direct labor purchasing costs were $500,000 and gross payroll was $1.5 million. The portion of the accounting department cost subject to capitalization allocated to the purchase function would be $25,000 ($500,000 divided by $1.5 million × $75,000). If direct labor warehousing costs were $250,000, the accounting department cost allocated to the capitalizable storage and warehousing functions would be $12,500 ($250,000 divided by $1.5 million × $75,000).

Preproductive period expenses of farmers. The new law provides general, uniform rules for determining costs that must be capitalized by all producers of real or tangible personal property, including inventory, property held for sale, and assets constructed by the taxpayer for business use. Special rules apply to the capitalization of interest and farm costs. "Production" means construction, manufacture, development, improvement, and raising or growing, and also covers costs paid or incurred by the taxpayer on property produced for him under a contract. Prior law special rules dealing with capital expenditures of citrus and almond growers and certain farming syndicate expenditures (Sec. 278) and of amortization of real property construction period interest and taxes (Sec. 189) are repealed. Generally, the new rules cover costs and interest that are paid or incurred after 1986.

Production costs in general. Producers will generally capitalize direct production costs and an allocable portion of indirect production costs including taxes. Indirect production costs will be allocated among items produced, or between inventory and current expense costs, under rules similar to those of Reg. Sec. 1.471-11(d) and 1.451-3(d)(9). The new capitalization rules don't cover (1) property pro-

¶1805

duced by taxpayers for their personal (not business) use; (2) Sec. 616(a) deductible mine development costs and Sec. 263(c) deductible oil and gas or geothermal well intangible drilling costs, (3) property produced under contracts required to be reported under a long-term contract method, (4) deductible Sec. 174 research and experimental costs, and (5) timber and certain ornamental trees such as evergreens that are more than six years old when severed from their roots. Deductible contributions to qualified retirement plans must be allocated (under regs to come) between production (for example, inventory) and other costs. This allocation is independent of (that is, made after) any allocation required by Sec. 412 minimum standard funding rules.

Timber. The rules for capitalizing and expensing timber costs haven't changed. So costs that would be capitalized under prior law will continue to be capitalized, and costs that were deductible before will continue to be deductible. The definition of timber under the new law is intended to be coextensive with the definition of timber, including ornamental trees, under prior law. Nothing in the definition of timber shall be construed to narrow the types of activities that constitute the growing of timber for purposes of the exclusion of timber from the uniform capitalization rules.

Special rules for interest. Interest costs allocable to production must be capitalized only if they're allocable to producing property that has (1) a production period of more than two years, or (2) a production period of more than one year and a cost over $1 million, or (3) a long useful life (this generally includes real property, including buildings and other real property classified as 15-year, 18-or 19-year property under prior law, and certain other long-lived assets).

The production period for this rule begins when construction or production begins and ends when the property is ready to be placed in service or held for sale. For plants or animals, the "production period" means the preproductive period. Planning and design activities generally don't cause the production period to begin. Interest on debt that can be directly traced to production or construction costs is first allocated to production or construction. These costs include the cumulative production costs, including previously capitalized interest that must be capitalized. If production or construction expenditures exceed debt directly traceable to them, interest on other debt will be allocated to this excess to the extent that interest costs would have been reduced if production costs hadn't been incurred, using the average of interest rates on the taxpayer's outstanding debt (other than debt that is directly traceable to production or construction).

Regulations are expected to prevent avoidance of these rules through use of related parties. If the production or construction is for a customer who makes progress or advance payments, the customer is treated as constructing the property to the extent of the payments. Thus, interest costs attributable to the payments are capitalizable by the customer, and the contractor capitalizes only interest attributable to the excess of accumulated contract costs over accumulated payments he receives during the year.

> **NOTE:** The new rule may make it necessary for companies to set up a deferred tax account. A deferred tax account is necessary if a company uses different accounting methods for financial reporting and tax reporting, provided the difference in revenue or expense that results from using different methods is of a temporary rather than permanent nature.

Capitalization by farmers and ranchers. For taxpayers in the business of farming, the new capitalization rules generally apply to plants and animals only if they have a preproductive period of over two years, and livestock held for slaughter is completely excluded from them. "Farming" includes operating nurseries or sod farms, and raising trees bearing fruits or nuts or other crops. It doesn't include the raising, harvesting, or growing of timber or ornamental evergreen trees that are more than six years old at the time they are severed from their roots. *Special rules:* Corporations and partnerships with corporate partners that must use the accrual method under Sec. 447 must capitalize costs and taxes regardless of the length of the preproductive period and must also capitalize preproductive period interest to the extent the period exceeds two years. Taxpayers using the Sec. 447(g) accrual period should be able to continue using it.

The "preproductive period" for plants begins when the plant or seed is first planted or acquired by taxpayer. It ends when the plant becomes productive or is sold. Using supplies produced on a farm is treated as their disposition. If there's more than one crop or yield, the first marketable crop or yield controls the end of the period. The "preproductive period" of a plant commercially grown in the United States is the average nationwide preproductive period for the particular crop. The Treasury is expected to publish periodically a list of various plant preproductive periods. The animal "preproductive period" begins at the time of acquisition, breeding, or embryo implantation, and ends when the animal is ready to perform its intended function. For example, the preproductive period for a cow used for breeding ends when the first calf is dropped. It's expected that capitalizable costs may be determined under regs using a reasonable valuation method (for example, a simplified method such as farm-price or unit-livestock-price).

Election to expense farmers' preproductive period costs. Farmers (including producers of livestock, nursery stock, Christmas, and other ornamental trees and agricultural crops) can elect to deduct all preproductive costs of tangible personal property produced in the farm business (for example, plant and animal costs) that were deductible under prior law. But if they make the election, any gain on disposition of the product is recaptured (in general treated as Section 1245 depreciation) and taxed as ordinary income to the extent of expensed deductions that otherwise would have been capitalized. Also, they have to use the alternative cost recovery system for all farm assets used predominantly in farming and placed in service in any tax years covered by the election. The election can't be made by (1) tax shelters as defined in Sec. 6161(b)(2)(C)(ii), (2) taxpayers required to use the accrual method under Sec. 447, and (3) farming syndicates, as defined in Sec. 464(c). And it can't cover pistachio nut planting, maintenance, or development costs.

The election also doesn't apply to the cost of planting, cultivating, maintaining, or developing any citrus or almond grove, incurred before the end of the fourth tax year after the trees were planted. If a grove is planted over more than one tax year, the part of the grove planted in each tax year is treated as a separate grove for determining the year of planting.

Partnerships and S corporations make the election at the partner or shareholder level. The election must be made in the first tax year that begins after 1986 during which the taxpayer is a farmer. Taxpayers making the election may (according to the House Committee Report) estimate the amount of preproductive period expenses that are subject to recapture using methods similar to one of the simplified inventory methods permitted to accrual method taxpayers under current law. The election can be revoked or changed only with IRS consent. It's binding on the taxpayer's spouse and minor children ("family members"), and on any corporations and their controlled groups and partnerships in which the taxpayer or his "family members" own at least a 50% direct or indirect (Sec. 318) interest by value. Minor children are defined as those who haven't attained age 18 before the close of the tax year.

The new uniform capitalization rules are generally effective for costs and interest paid or incurred after 12-31-86 in tax years ending after 1986. Assets constructed by the taxpayer for his or her own use that had substantial construction before 1987 are exempt from the new rules. There are special rules for urban renovation projects.

The new rules apply to inventories for the taxpayer's first tax year beginning after 1986. Adjustments resulting from the change in inventory accounting (under Sec. 481) must be spread over a period of no more than four years under rules for changes initiated by taxpayer and approved by the IRS (Rev.Proc. 84-74, 1984-2 C.B. 736). The law contemplates that (1) all changes in the rules for absorption of costs into inventory will be treated as accounting method changes; (2) inventory on hand as of the effective date be revalued to reflect the new, greater absorption of costs and; (3) Regs and rulings will allow taxpayers who can't revalue a part of the inventory because necessary information isn't available to revalue by estimates using available date (for example, FIFO inventories, and particularly the LIFO dollar value method). The House Ways & Means Report contains suggested rules for LIFO layer revaluations.

Expenses for Replanting Groves, Orchards, or Vineyards Destroyed in Natural Disasters. The new law provides that if a farmer experiences loss or damage because of freezing temperatures, disease, drought, pests, or casualty, the capitalization requirements of Secs. 278(a) and (b) don't apply to otherwise deductible costs. Deductible costs include replanting, cultivating, maintaining, or developing the grove, orchard or vineyard even though the costs aren't incurred solely by the farmer suffering the loss and even though replanting doesn't take place on the same property. However two conditions must be met:

- The taxpayer who owned the property at the time of the loss or damage must have an equity interest of more than 50% in the property.

- The additional persons incurring the loss must hold part of the remaining equity interest in the property and must materially participate in the planting, cultivation, maintenance, or development. Whether an individual materially participates in an activity is determined similarly to the method under Sec. 2032A (current use valuation of farm property).

Also, replanting costs can qualify even though the grove is replanted in a different location, provided the costs don't relate to acreage exceeding the acreage of the property on which the loss or damage occurred.

The special rule for preproductive period expenses following loss or damage due to freezing temperatures, and so forth, applies only to crops that are normally eaten or drunk by humans. So jojoba bean production, for example, doesn't qualify under this special exception.

Act Sec. 803(a), relating to capitalization of inventory costs, adds new Sec. 263A, generally effective for costs incurred after 12-31-86. The new rules for inventory take effect for tax years beginning after 12-31-86. If a change in accounting method is involved, an adjustment is required over four years or less. The new rules do not apply for internally used self-constructed property where substantial construction occurred before 3-1-86. Act Sec. 803, relating to capitalization where taxpayer produces property, adds new Sec. 471(b), amends Secs. 447(a) and (b) and 471(a), and repeals Secs. 189 and 278. Act Sec. 803, on deductions for expenses incurred in replanting citrus and almond groves, amends Sec. 278(c), effective for amounts expended or incurred after the enactment date in tax years ending after that date.

〔¶806〕 Accounting For Long-Term Contracts. All direct costs, including research and experimental costs, that are incurred in a long-term contract, are allocated to that contract in a way similar to that outlined in Sec. 451. Certain other period (general and administrative) costs are also allocated in the case of cost-plus and federal long-term contracts. Interest costs are also allocated to the contract, using the same approach as that of Financial Accounting Standards Board Statement No. 34 (which includes avoided interest).

Interest accrues during the production period. The production period starts at the later of (1) the contract commencement date, or (2) for accrual method taxpayers, as soon as at least 5% of total estimated costs, including design and planning costs, have been incurred. The contract commencement date is the first date any costs (other than bidding or negotiation expenses) are incurred on the contract. The production period ends on the contract completion date.

The following costs are expensed as incurred, and are not capitalized as long-term contract costs: (1) expenses for unsuccessful bids and proposals; (2) research and development expenses that are not related to a particular contract; and (3) marketing, selling, and advertising expenses. Taxpayers using the completed contract method must capitalize an additional amount of costs equal to the fully reimbursed portion of independent research and development costs and unsuccessful bid and proposal costs attributable to federal government contracts that require certification of such costs.

The direct allocation, cost-plus, and federal contract rules do not apply for real property construction contracts that are initially estimated to be completed within two years of the commencement date, for taxpayers having average annual gross receipts of $10 million or less for the three years before the year the contract is entered into. Gross receipts include those generated from all trades or businesses under common control, including partnerships, joint ventures, and corporations. A controlled group of corporations includes those corporations owned, directly or indirectly, more than 50% by the taxpayer.

Construction contracts include any contract to build, rehabilitate, construct, reconstruct, or install an integral component to, or improvements to, real property.

A long-term contract is a contract for the production, manufacture, building, installation, or construction of property that is not started and completed in the same tax year. Manufacturing contracts are not treated as long-term contracts unless the manufactured item (1) is not included in the taxpayer's finished goods inventory, and (2) the item normally takes more than 12 months to complete (regardless of the completion period stated in the contract).

Aggregation. Two or more interdependent contracts may be treated as a single contract.

Accounting methods. The completed contract method can no longer be used, except by taxpayers that expect to complete the construction contract within two years, and have average annual gross receipts of $10 million or less. For taxpayers that cannot use the completed contract method, two other methods are available. The percentage of completion method may still be used, although the capitalization rules have changed, as explained at ¶805.

The other method, called the percentage of completion—capitalized cost method, is new. This method requires 40% of the contract to be accounted for using the percentage of completion method and 60% accounted for using the taxpayer's regular method. If the taxpayer's normal method is the completed contract method, 60% of the costs and revenues would be recognized upon contract completion. If an accrual method such as an accrual shipment method is used, the items in question would be accounted for at shipment date. The look-back method must be applied to the 40% portion of the contract that uses the percentage of completion method. So interest is paid to or by the taxpayer on the difference between the amount actually taken into account each year and the amount that would have been taken into account recomputing the 40% portion under the look-back method.

> **NOTE:** Taxpayers that use one accounting method on the tax return and another method on the financial statements must set up a deferred tax account to keep track of timing differences. So anyone that uses the percentage of completion—capitalized cost method must set up a deferred tax account, since the method is unacceptable for financial statement reporting.

Act Sec. 804, relating to long-term contracts, adds new Code Sec. 460, effective for contracts entered into after 2-28-86.

〖¶807〗 Bad Debt Reserves. For tax years beginning after 1986, the new law eliminates the bad debt reserve method of deducting bad debts for taxpayers other than financial institutions. Taxpayers need not charge off wholly worthless debts on their books to deduct them. The reserve method is also repealed for dealers that guarantee, endorse, or provide indemnity agreements for debt arising out of the sale by a dealer of real or tangible personal property in the ordinary course of business.

> **NOTE:** The Committee Reports note that a delay in the charge-off of a debt on the books isn't intended to shift the deduction from the year when it's clear that the taxpayer actually became aware that the debt was wholly worthless.

ANOTHER POINT: The direct chargeoff method varies from generally accepted financial accounting principles, so companies that used the reserve method for both financial accounting and tax purposes and that must now change methods for tax purposes must set up a deferred tax account where none was required previously.

Transition rule. The change from the reserve method to the specific chargeoff method is a change in accounting method initiated by the taxpayer with IRS consent. To prevent duplication of deductions, the balance in any reserve account on the effective date must be taken into income ratably over four years. For guarantee bad debt reserves, the reserve balance is first reduced by the suspense account balance. The remaining balance is taken into income ratably over four years. (Sec. 481 adjustment).

Act Sec. 805, relating to bad debt reserves, repeals Code Sec. 166(c) and redesignates subsection (g) as subsection (f), effective for tax years beginning after 12-31-86.

[¶808] Conforming Tax Years for Partnerships, S Corporations, and Personal Service Corporations. The new law requires all partnerships, S corporations, and personal service corporations to conform their tax years to that of the owners. A partnership must have the same tax year as that of its majority interest partners, unless it establishes, to the Treasury's satisfaction, a good business reason for having a different tax year. If the majority owners don't have the same tax year, the partnership must adopt the same tax year as its principal partners. If the principal partners don't have the same tax year, and no majority of partners have the same tax year, the partnership must adopt a calendar year as its tax year.

Example: Alpha Partnership's principal partner is Beta, Inc., a fiscal year corporation. Beta owns a 10% interest in Alpha's partnership profits and capital. The other partners are individual calendar year taxpayers who each have partnership interests of less than 5%. Prior law would require Alpha to adopt Beta's tax year, since Beta is Alpha's principal partner. The new law requires Alpha to adopt a calendar tax year, since that is the tax year of the majority of Alpha's partners.

An S corporation must adopt a permitted year, regardless of when the corporation elected to be taxed as an S corporation. A personal service corporation must adopt a calendar year.

Exception. When the Treasury is satisfied there is a business purpose for having a different tax year, that year will be permitted provided deferral is three months or less. So a partnership that can establish a good business purpose can have a September 30, October 31, or November 30 year-end, even if all the partners are calendar year taxpayers. But taxpayers will not receive an automatic three-month deferral. A business purpose must exist, and wanting to defer the tax is not considered a business purpose. Taxpayers that have already obtained the Treasury's permission for a different year-end don't have to request permission again because of the law change.

A partnership doesn't have to adopt the tax year of its majority interest partners unless partners having the same tax year have owned a majority interest in partnership profits and capital for the partnership's preceding three tax years. Tax years beginning before the new law's effective date are taken into account for determining whether the three-year test has been met.

> **Example:** John and Jane each have owned 50% of Delta Partnership since its inception in July 1984. Delta's fiscal year ends June 30. John and Jane are both calendar year taxpayers. Delta must conform its tax year to that of its principal partners for the tax year beginning July 1, 1987. So Delta will have two tax years ending in 1987. The first one spans July 1, 1986 to June 30, 1987. The second is from July 1 to December 31, 1987. So John and Jane will have 18 months' worth of partnership income dumped into their 1987 calendar year.

A partnership, S corporation, or personal service corporation that is required to change its tax year is treated as doing so with the IRS's consent. For a partnership or S corporation, each partner or owner may elect to take any resulting excess of income over expense into income ratably over the first four tax years (including the owner's year that would otherwise include the income or loss of the entity's short tax year) beginning after 12-31-86. Without an election, net income or loss for the short year is included currently in its entirety. The short tax year of a personal service corporation is annualized.

A partnership or S corporation that received permission to use a fiscal year-end under the provisions of Rev. Proc. 74-33, 1974-2 C.B. 489 (other than a year-end that resulted in a deferral of three months or less) can continue to use such taxable year. A partnership, S corporation, or personal service corporation may adopt, retain, or change to a tax year established by IRS if the use of such tax year meets the requirements of the 25% test as described in Rev. Proc. 83-25, 1983-1, C.B. 689 (25% or more of gross receipts for the 12-month period in question are recognized in the last two months of the period and the requirement has been met for the specified three consecutive 12-month periods).

To be classified as a personal service corporation for tax year determination purposes,

- the corporation cannot be an S corporation,
- the principal activity must be performance of personal services, if the services are substantially performed by employee-owners, and

- employee-owners are employees who own outstanding stock at least one day during the tax year.

NOTE: Personal service corporations may not deduct payments to owner-employees before the year paid.

The Sec. 318 attribution rules apply to determine constructive ownership, except that the attribution of stock owned by a corporation to the employee is applied without regard to any requirement that the employee own a certain percentage of corporation stock.

The new law ends (or at least curtails) a popular tax deferral strategy.

Example: Dr. Jones reports income on a calendar year basis and is the employee-owner of a professional corporation with a January 31 year-end. He earns $200,000 a year but receives a monthly salary of $10,000, or $120,000 for the year. Then, in January of the next year, the remaining $80,000 goes to him as a bonus. *Result:* the entire $200,000 is deductible by the fiscal year corporation in one tax year. But Jones reports the $200,000 over two tax years, $120,000 the first year and $80,000 the following year.

Under the new law, there would be no deferral because the corporation would have to change it's year-end to December 31. However, the corporation could have a September 30, October 31, or November 30 year-end if it could establish a business purpose to the satisfaction of the IRS. But tax deferral is not a business purpose.

Act Sec. 806, relating to tax years, amends Code Secs. 267, 441, 706, and 1378, effective for tax years beginning after 12-31-86.

[¶809]   Qualified Discount Coupons.   The new law repeals the provision that allows taxpayers to deduct the cost of redeeming qualified discount coupons in the current year, even though some coupons may actually be redeemed the following year. Only redemption costs actually incurred currently may be deducted currently.

Transition rule. Any change in accounting method required by the law change is regarded as a taxpayer-initiated change, with the IRS's consent. Any adjustment must first reduce any suspense account balance. The net amount is then taken into income ratably over four years or less. Net operating loss and tax credit carryforwards will be allowed to offset any positive Sec. 481 adjustment. For computing estimated tax payments, the Sec. 481 adjustment will be recognized in taxable income ratably throughout the year in question.

Act Sec. 823, relating to qualified discount coupons, repeals Sec. 466, and amends Sec. 481(h), effective for tax years beginning after 12-31-86.

[¶810]   Utilities Using Accrual Accounting.   The cycle meter reading accounting method used by utilities does not recognize income as earned. Accrual method utility companies must now recognize utility service income the year it is earned. The time earned is the time the customer uses the service, not the time the meter is read or the time the invoice is mailed.

> **Example:** Apple and Stoneland Utility Company, a calendar year company, reads Smith's meter the 12th of each month. The reading for January 12, 1987 indicates that $310 of utility services have been rendered since the December 12 reading. On its 1986 tax return, A&S will include income of $190, or $10 a day for the last 19 days of December. Its 1987 tax return will include the $120 earned the first 12 days of January, 1987.

The following utility services are subject to this pro rata allocation formula: electrical energy, water or sewage disposal, gas or steam furnished through a local distribution system, telephone and other communications services, and the pipeline transportation of gas or steam. Similar rules should apply to other utility services that come into existence in the future. This allocation method applies to regulated and nonregulated utilities.

An accounting change resulting from this rule change is considered to be a taxpayer initiated change in accounting method with the IRS's consent. A Sec. 481 adjustment is required. The difference between the old and new accounting methods must be taken into income or expense ratably over no more than four years. Net operating loss and tax credit carryforwards will be allowed to offset any positive Sec. 481 adjustment. Taxpayers required to accrue income at the time utility services are furnished may accrue any deductions for related costs if economic performance has occurred. Any change in accounting method includes any related change in accounting method for the related items of expense or deduction. The Sec. 481 adjustment is to be computed on the net amount of the two changes and taken into income ratably over a four-year period.

Act Sec. 821, relating to utility accrual accounting, adds Code Sec. 451(f), effective for tax years beginning after 12-31-86.

[¶811] **Contributions to Corporation's Capital as a Customer or in Aid of Construction.** For tax years beginning after 1986, the new law repeals the special rule that treats contributions to regulated public utilities in aid of construction as excludable contributions to a corporation's capital. Instead, it expressly bars contributions to a corporation's capital in aid of construction or as a customer or a potential customer, from treatment as contributions to capital that are excludable from the corporation's income under Sec. 118.

The law change is intended to have a utility report as gross income the value of property or money that it receives to provide or encourage the provision of services to or for the benefit of the contributor (e.g., if the contribution results in the utility's providing services earlier or favoring the contributor in any way, regardless of whether it's the utility's general policy to require or encourage types of potential customers such as developers of multiple tracts to transfer property or money to the utility). It's intended that if all members of a particular group transfer property to a utility the value be included in the utility's income unless it's clearly shown that the benefit of the public as a whole was the primary motivating factor.

SILVER LINING: The prior law's rules disallowing deductions and credits for expenditures made with contributions in aid of construction, and making the basis of property acquired with them zero, are gone too.

Act Sec. 824, amends Secs. 118 and 362(c), effective for contributions received after 12-31-86.

[¶812] **Discharge of Debt.** Prior law allowed deferral of gain recognition on the discharge of certain business debt. The new law requires taxpayers to recognize debt charges in income immediately, unless the taxpayer is insolvent or unless the discharge is under Title 11 (Bankruptcy).

Act Sec. 822, relating to discharge of debt, amends Code Sec. 108(a), effective for debt discharges occurring after 12-31-86.

[The page following this is 901.]

FINANCIAL INSTITUTIONS

[¶900] **Overview.** Generally, commercial banks and thrift institutions have the same income and deductions as ordinary business corporations and are subject to the same income taxes as ordinary business corporations. There are special rules, however, that only apply to these institutions. They include the deduction for bad debts, the deduction on interest used to purchase or carry tax-exempt bonds, gain or loss from the sale of securities, carrying net operating losses backward or forward, tax-free reorganizations, and immunity from taxation to protect financial institution depositors.

Bank. The term "bank" includes commercial banks, trust companies, and thrift institutions that are subject to federal or state bank supervisory authorities and a substantial part of whose business consists of receiving deposits and making loans and discounts or of exercising fiduciary powers similar to those permitted national banks.

Thrift institutions. For purposes of the Internal Revenue Code, thrift institutions are domestic building and loan associations, savings and loan associations, mutual savings banks, or cooperative nonprofit mutual banks. The Code further defines "domestic building and loan association" as building and loan or savings and loan institutions which are federally insured or subject to federal or state regulation, the business of which consists principally of acquiring public savings and investing in loans. Also, at least 60% of these institutions' assets must consist of certain "qualifying assets" (Sec. 7701(a)(19)(C); Reg. §301.7701-13A).

> **WARNING:** Although thrift institutions are included in the definition of bank, there are special Code provisions that apply only to commercial banks or thrift institutions (e.g., reserve for bad debt deduction). Therefore, in some instances, grouping all financial institutions under the heading "bank" would be misleading and incorrect.

[¶901] **Reserve for Bad Debts.** The new law eliminates some of the special rules that applied to commercial banks and thrift institutions in computing their deduction for bad debts.

Large banks. Large commercial banks must now use a method to figure their bad debt reserve deduction that is different from all other commercial banks. Banks that aren't large commercial banks can continue to use prior law. The provision was added because Congress felt that some banks, especially the larger ones, were using the reserve method for figuring losses from bad debts to substantially lower their income tax liabilities. Because an across-the-board elimination of the bad debt reserve deduction could result in some potential adverse effects on smaller banks, prior law was retained to balance these concerns.

A commercial bank is considered a "large bank" if for any tax year after 12-31-86, the sum of the averaged adjusted basis of all assets of that bank exceeds $500 million, or, if the bank is part of a bank holding company (i.e., parent-subsidiary controlled group), the sum of the adjusted bases of all the assets of that group exceeds $500 million.

Commercial banks different from thrifts. For purposes of the bad debt reserve deduction, a commercial bank is defined as a domestic or foreign corporation whose business substantially consists of receiving deposits or making loans and discounts, or of exercising fiduciary powers like those permitted national banks, and who are subject to federal or state bank regulatory authorities. It doesn't include thrift institutions—domestic building and loan associations, savings and loan associations, mutual savings banks, or cooperative nonprofit mutual banks.

There are two methods to figure bad debts. For large banks, the new law provides for bad debt deductions only when the loans become wholly or partially worthless for tax years after 1986. This eliminates concern that the prior reserve methods of accounting resulted in deductions being taken for tax purposes for losses that substantially occurred in the future and were inconsistent with the treatment of other deductions under the all-events test.

Under the prior law, all banks could deduct bad debts by using a specific charge-off method or by using a reserve method. The charge-off method allows banks to deduct bad debts that have become worthless during the tax year. The reserve method allows banks to take a deduction equal to the amount necessary to increase the year-end bad debt reserve allowance to an amount computed under the experience method or the percentage of eligible loans method.

The experience method for banks generally is based on the average loan loss over the most recent six-year period. Under the percentage of eligible loans method, banks are allowed a deduction for additions to reserves sufficient to maintain a tax reserve up to 0.6% of eligible loans outstanding. After the 1987 tax year, the percentage method will be unavailable, leaving commercial banks with only the experience method of accounting to compute the bad debt deduction.

Computing bad debt deduction of large banks. Unless large banks elect the cut-off method, they will have to recapture the amount of their bad debt reserves into income.

Four-year adjustment spread. Under the adjustment spread method, a bank is treated as having initiated a change in its accounting method for its calculation of losses on bad debts in its disqualification year—the first year the bank can no longer use the reserve method, but no earlier than 12-31-86. The new law prevents large banks from getting a double deduction for bad debts. This accounting method change is treated as having been made with IRS consent.

By changing its method of accounting, a large bank must take into income the balance of any bad debt reserve accounts that exist on the last day of the year before the disqualification year—the first taxable year beginning after 12-31-86. Income for 1987 will be 10% of the reserves on the last day of the year before the disqualification year.

The income amount to be recaptured over the next four tax years after the disqualification year will be 20% in 1988, 30% in 1989, and 40% in 1990.

Banks may also elect to include more than 10% of their reserve balance in income in the first taxable year. If that election is made, $2/9$ of the remainder of the reserve balance (after reduction for the amount included in income in the first taxable year) must be included in income in the second taxable year, $1/3$ of the remainder in the third taxable year, and $4/9$ of the remainder in the fourth taxable year.

Financially troubled bank. Under the new law, if a bank's average of its nonperforming loans exceeds 75% of the average of its equity capital for the year, it's a financially troubled bank, and it doesn't elect the cut-off method, the bank doesn't have to recapture existing bad debt reserves. For each year that the bank is financially troubled, the recapture of the bad debt reserve is suspended.

If the bank is part of a bank holding company, then the determination of whether the bank is financially troubled is made with respect to all the banks in the holding company.

Nonperforming loans include loans that are "past due 90 days or more and still accruing," nonaccrual loans, and "renegotiated 'troubled debt'" under the Federal Financial Institutions Examination Council. Equity capital is assets less liabilities, but doesn't include the balance in any reserve for bad debts. Nonperforming loan and equity capital averages are based on the average of those amounts at each time during the taxable year that the bank is required to report for regulatory purposes.

> **IMPORTANT:** Allowing financially troubled banks to suspend the inclusion of their bad debt reserve in income doesn't affect the requirements that a large bank account for its bad debts using the specific charge-off method.

Cut-off election. Large banks may elect to account for existing loans using a cut-off method. For large banks electing the cut-off method, no change in the accounting method is presumed, and the bank continues to use the reserve method to account for bad debts on loans outstanding on the last day of the tax year before the disqualification year. By electing the cut-off method, all charge-offs and recoveries of the bank's loan are adjustments to the reserve accounts and not separate income and expense items.

No additional deductions in the disqualification year or thereafter are permitted for additions to the reserve for bad debts under the cut-off method.

Reductions in bad debt reserve for thrift institutions. Under the new law, thrift institutions that use the percentage of taxable income method may deduct 8% from taxable income as an addition to the reserve for bad debts. The prior law allowed thrift institutions using this method to deduct 40% as an addition to reserve for bad debts if 82% of the thrifts assets were qualified (72% for mutual savings banks without stock). That deduction phased down to zero when less than 60% of the thrifts assets were qualified.

Methods of treating bad debt. Thrift institutions can elect to treat bad debts by deducting for specific debts as they become wholly or partially worthless or by deducting an addition to the reserve for bad debts. For thrift institutions, the reasonable addition to the reserve for bad debts is equal to the reserve for losses computed under the "experience" method, the "percentage of eligible loans" method, or the "percentage of taxable income" method. While commercial banks and thrift institutions can elect to use either the experience or percentage of eligible loans methods, only thrift institutions can compute their bad debt reserve deduction using the percentage of taxable income method.

For thrift institutions electing the percentage of taxable income method, an annual deduction is allowed for a statutory percentage of taxable income. The addition to the reserve for bad debts under this method is an amount equal to the applicable percentage of taxable income for the taxable year involved, subject to special rules which are dependent on the percentage of qualifying assets held by the thrift institution.

Although these methods shouldn't be mixed, thrift institutions may switch between them from year to year. At a minimum, 60% of a thrift institution's assets must be "qualified" to be eligible for deductions under the percentage of taxable income method. For mutual banks without stock, however, 50% of their assets must be "qualified" to be eligible for the deduction under that method.

Qualified assets include cash, U.S. bonds, taxable bonds of states or municipalities, CDs in corporations issuing deposit accounts, residential real property loans, church loans, urban renewal loans, institutional loans, foreclosed property, and educational loans.

Calculating the bad debt deduction. The new law eliminates the rules reducing the amount of the percentage of taxable income deduction available to thrifts that hold 60% of their assets in qualifying assets, but fail to hold a sufficient percentage of qualifying assets to use the maximum percentage of taxable income deduction. It doesn't stop thrift institutions from continuing to use the experience method to calculate the addition to the reserve for bad debts.

The percentage of eligible loans method is unavailable to thrift institutions under the new law.

> **THRIFT 60% TEST:** Only thrift institutions that hold at least 60% of their assets as qualifying assets are eligible for the full 8%-of-taxable-income deduction. And the 60% test applies to all thrift institutions.

No Sec. 291 tax preference. Thrifts that claim the 8% taxable income deduction won't have a tax preference for purposes of the 20% reduction of Sec. 291 under the new law. The excess of the percentage of taxable income deduction over the deduction that would have been allowable on the basis of actual experience will be treated as a tax preference item for computing the corporate minimum tax under Sec. 57.

Special recognition provision. The new law also provides for a special recognition provision that applies to reserve balances in excess of the balance computed under the experience method. Deductions claimed using the 8% taxable income method in excess of deductions computed under the experience method are still subject to recognition as income if distributed to shareholders.

Reserves for losses on loans of SBICs. The new law eliminates the special rules for computing the amount of bad debt reserves and bad debt reserve additions for losses on loans of small business investment companies (operating under the Small Business Investment Act of 1958) and state-created business development corporations.

> *Act Sec. 901, changes the method for determining reserves for bad debts for commercial banks, amends Sec. 585(a) and 585(b)(1), and adds Sec. 585(c), effective for tax years beginning after 12-31-86, and as shown. Act Sec. 901, changes the method for determining reserves for bad debts for thrifts, amends Sec. 291(e)(1)(A) and Sec. 291(e)(1)(B), amends Sec. 582(c)(1), adds Sec. 582(c)(5), amends Sec. 593(a), 593(b)(1), Sec. 593(b)(1)(B), Sec. 593(b)(2), removes Sec. 593(b)(3) and Sec. 593(b)(5), redesignates Sec. 593(b)(4) as Sec. 593(b)(3), and amends 593(e)(1)(B) effective for tax years beginning after 12-31-86. Act Sec. 901, eliminates reserves for losses on loans of SBICs and business development corporations, repeals Sec. 586, effective for tax years beginning after 12-31-86. Clerical amendments to Act Sec. 901.*

[¶902] **Interest Incurred to Carry Tax-Exempt Bonds.** The new law denies banks, thrift institutions, and other financial institutions a deduction for 100% of their interest expense allocable to buying or carrying of tax-exempt obligations acquired after 8-7-86 for interest incurred after 12-31-86. It attempts to place financial institutions on an equal plane with all other taxpayers.

Bonds that are acquired after 8-7-86, in taxable years ending in 1986, are subject to the prior law's 20% disallowance rule for the taxable year ending in 1986. The bonds, however, are subject to the new law's 100% disallowance rule for subsequent taxable years.

Individuals and other corporations can't deduct interest payments on debt incurred or continued to buy or carry tax-exempt obligations. Legislative, judicial, and IRS interpretations, however, have generally permitted banks, thrifts, and other financial institutions to invest their depository funds in tax-exempt obligations without losing their deduction for interest paid on their deposits or their short-term obligations. And under the corporate tax-preference rules, financial institutions have had to reduce by 20% their interest deduction allocable to tax-exempt obligations acquired after 1982.

Tax-exempt obligations are defined as any obligations whose interest is wholly tax exempt and includes shares in regulated investment companies that distribute exempt-interest dividends during the recipient's tax year.

Computing pro-rata allocation of interest expense. The amount of interest allocable to tax-exempt obligations under the new law is figured in the same way as the 20% reduction in financial institution preference items that exist under the prior law (after taking into account any interest disallowed to all taxpayers under the general rules of Sec. 265). And this allocation rule is mandatory. Therefore, there is no deduction for that portion of a financial institution's otherwise allowable interest expense that is equivalent to the ratio of the average adjusted basis of tax-exempt obligations held by the financial institution and acquired after 8-7-86 to the average adjusted basis of the financial institution's total assets.

The term "interest expense" under the new law means the aggregate amount allowable to the financial institution as a deduction for interest for the tax year. The term "interest" includes amounts paid in respect of deposits, investment certificates, or withdrawable or repurchaseable shares, whether or not designated as interest.

20% disallowance rule continued. The 20% disallowance rule under prior law continues to apply to tax-exempt obligations acquired by financial institutions from 1-1-83 to 8-7-86. Financial institutions that have acquired tax-exempt obligations after 8-7-86 will reduce their otherwise allowable interest expense by the sum of 100% of interest allocable to tax-exempt obligations acquired after 8-7-86 and 20% of interest allocable to tax-exempt obligations acquired on or before 8-7-86.

> **Example:** 25% of First State Bank's assets consist of tax-exempt obligations acquired after 8-7-86 and an additional 25% consists of tax-exempt obligations acquired between 1-1-83 and 8-7-86. First State Bank would be denied 30% of its otherwise allowable interest deduction—25% is attributable to obligations acquired after 8-7-86

and 5% (.20 × 25%) is attributable to obligations acquired between 1-1-83 and 8-7-86.

Under the disallowance rule of the new law, the acquisition date of an obligation is the date on which the holding period begins with respect to the obligations belonging to the acquiring financial institution. As such, bond acquisitions that are part of a tax-free reorganization aren't treated as a new acquisition under the new law.

Coordination with new Sec. 263A. Under the new law, the interest-disallowance rule must be applied to that portion of the financial institution's interest expense before new law provision Sec. 263A [¶805], relating to capitalization of certain preproductive expenses, can be applied.

Special face-amount certificate-company rule repealed. The new law subjects face-amount certificate companies that have registered under the Investment Company Act of 1940 and subject to state banking laws, to the same disallowance rules as other financial institutions. Previously, deductions on the interest paid or accrued on the certificates and on amounts received for the purchase of the certificates to be issued weren't disallowed.

Financial institutions defined. Financial institutions subject to the new disallowance rule include entities that accept deposits from the public in the ordinary course of their trade or business and that are subject to federal or state bank supervisory authorities. This includes commercial banks, thrift institutions, and foreign banks doing business in the U.S.

Exception for qualified tax-exempt obligations. The new law provides for an exception for qualified tax-exempt obligations acquired by financial institutions which applies whether the obligation is acquired at the original issuance or by a secondary purchaser. Qualified tax-exempt obligations are treated as acquired by the financial institution before 8-8-86 and interest allocable to these obligations remain subject to the prior law's 20% disallowance rule.

Qualified tax-exempt obligations include obligations that aren't private activity bonds and that are issued by an issuer which reasonably anticipates to issue, together with subordinate governmental entities, no more than $10 million of tax-exempt obligations—other than private activity bonds—during the calendar year. The bonds must be designated as qualified tax-exempt obligations by the issuer, and the issuer (including subordinate governmental entities) cannot designate more than $10 million of obligations for any calendar year. Also, refundings of outstanding bonds may qualify for this exception and count toward the $10 million limitation under the same terms as new issuers.

¶1902

Qualified Sec. 501(c)(3) organization bonds [see ¶1301 et seq.] are not treated as private activity bonds for purposes of this exception. Also, for purposes of this exception, qualified Sec. 501(c)(3) bonds that are issued before 8-15-86 are treated as private activity bonds if they are IDB's, mortgage subsidiary bonds, student loan bonds, or other private loan bonds for which tax exemption is allowed under the prior law.

The new law defines subordinate governmental entities as entities deriving their issuing authority from another entity or as entities subject to substantial control by another entity. Entities shouldn't be considered subordinate solely because of geographical inclusion in a larger entity.

Transitional exceptions. There are transitional exceptions under the new law.

- *Tax exempt obligations acquired:* All tax-exempt obligations acquired under written commitments to purchase or repurchase the obligation before 9-25-85 are treated as obligations acquired before 8-8-86, and are subject to the 20% disallowance rule.

- *Specified identified projects:* Specified identified projects are treated as tax-exempt obligations acquired before 8-8-86 belonging to the first and all subsequent financial institutions acquiring the obligations.

There is an additional transitional rule that treats obligations issued under an allocation of a particular state's volume limitations for private activity bonds as acquired on or before 8-7-86 in the hands of the first and all subsequent financial institutions acquiring the obligations.

Act Sec. 902, denying financial institutions 100% of interest deduction allocable to tax-exempt obligations, amends Sec. 265 by striking out the second sentence from Sec. 265(2), by designating Sec. 265(1)-(4) as Sec. 265(a), and by adding Sec. 265(b), amends 291(e)(1)(B), Sec. 291(e)(1)(B)(i), and Sec. 291(e)(1)(B)(ii), and is effective for obligations acquired after 8-7-86 for interest incurred after 12-31-86 and as shown above according to the transitional exceptions. Clerical amendments to Act Sec. 902.

[¶903] Net Operating Losses for Financial Institutions. The new law repeals the special rules for commercial banks and thrift institutions which allow them to carry net operating losses back to the preceding 10 tax years and forward to the succeeding 5 tax years. Now these financial institutions are subject to the same general rule as all other taxpayers, who are allowed to carry back net operating losses 3 tax years and forward 15 tax years.

Effective Date: Generally the new law is effective for bank and thrift NOLs incurred in tax years after 12-31-86; however, it has special carryover rules for banks and thrift institutions.

Special commercial bank rule retained. The new law retains the special 10-year carryback for commercial banks (not including thrift institutions) for that portion of NOLs attributable to bad debts for losses incurred in tax years beginning before 1994. Under this special rule, the portion of a commercial bank's NOLs attributable to deductions for losses on bad debts is the excess of the NOL for the taxable year over the net operating loss for that taxable year computed without regard to any deduction for losses or bad debts.

Special thrift rule. The new law allows thrift institutions that have incurred losses in tax years after 12-31-81 and before 1-1-86 to carry forward net operating losses to eight years. Under the prior law, they could only carry them forward five years. Also, for losses incurred by thrift institutions after 12-31-81 and before 1-1-86, the new law retains the prior law's special 10-year carryback rule.

The 18-year total carryover period is equal to the total carryover period available to taxpayers generally (3-year carryback and 15-year carryforward).

Act Sec. 903, repealing the special rules for net operating losses of financial institutions generally, amends Sec. 172(b)(1)(F), 172(b)(1)(G), and 172(b)(1)(H), effective for NOLs incurred after 12-31-86, and as shown above; special commercial bank rule on carryover period of NOLs incurred after 12-31-86 and before 1-1-94, amending Sec. 172(b)(1)(A), Sec. 172(b)(1)(B), redesignating Sec. 172(l) as 172(m) and adding new Sec. 172(l), adding new Sec. 172(b)(1)(L); adding special thrift rule on carryover period of NOLs incurred after 12-31-81 and before 1-1-86, adding Sec. 172(b)(1)(M).

[¶1904] Special Rules for Financially Troubled Thrifts. The new law repeals the special rules relating to tax-free reorganizations, net operating loss carryovers, and FSLIC contributions which provide tax relief to financially troubled thrift institutions. Thrifts no longer will receive preferential tax treatment in these areas to the detriment of other taxpayers.

IMPORTANT: New acquisitions and reorganizations involving financially troubled thrifts are subject to the same rules as any other reorganized corporation.

Tax-free reorganization status. The new law repeals the special provisions that provide a tax-free reorganization for the merger of a financially troubled thrift into another corporation. Under prior law, as long as certain conditions were met, a merger of a financially troubled thrift into another corporation qualified as a tax-free reorganization without complying with the continuity of interest requirement of Sec. 368.

Net operating loss carryovers. Under the new law, the special treatment of net operating losses in a financially troubled thrift are repealed. Prior law provided that when a financially troubled thrift was involved in a tax-free reorganization, the requirements to avoid limitations on net operating loss carryovers under Sec. 382 were considered met.

IMPORTANT: The new law substantially changes the special limitations on the use of NOL carryforwards under Sec. 382 and Sec. 383 [see ¶606 et seq.].

Special exception. The conversion of a mutual savings and loan association holding a federal charter dated 3-22-85, to a stock savings and loan association under the rules and regulations of the Federal Home Loan Bank Board, is specially excepted from the application of Sec. 383 under the new law.

FSLIC contributions. Under the new law, payments by the Federal Savings and Loan Insurance Corporation to financially troubled thrifts in connection with a merger are no longer excluded from the recipient thrift's income and no longer exempt from the general requirement that a taxpayer's basis in its assets be reduced by non-shareholder contributions to capital.

Expenses allocable to tax-exempt income. The new law provides that the FSLIC payments to financially troubled thrifts that were exempt under the prior law exclusion aren't subject to the provision disallowing a deduction for expenses attributable to such payments.

Effective Date: The repeal of the special rules are effective for acquisitions or mergers occurring after 12-31-88. The repeal of the special treatment for FSLIC payments is effective for payments made after 12-31-88, unless the payments are made under an acquisition or merger occurring on or before 12-31-88.

Act Sec. 904, repealing special rules for financially troubled thrifts involving tax-free reorganizations, net operating loss carryovers, and FSLIC contributions, repeals Sec. 597 and amends Sec. 265(a)(1) and Sec. 368(a)(3)(D), and is effective for acquisitions after 12-31-88 and for FSLIC contributions after 12-31-88, except as shown above.

[¶905] **Losses on Deposits in Insolvent Financial Institutions.** Because circumstances surrounding deposits in financial institutions are different from debts owed to taxpayers, the new law allows qualified individuals to elect to deduct losses on deposits arising from the insolvency or bankruptcy of a qualified financial institution as a casualty loss in the year in which the amount of the loss is reasonably estimated. The election must be made on the tax return for the taxable year and once made, cannot be changed without the IRS's consent.

Under prior law, a loss realized by a taxpayer from a deposit or account in a financial institution was deductible in the year it was determined that there was no prospect of recovery in the same manner as any other type of bad debt loss. Also, unless the deposit was created or acquired in connection with the taxpayer's trade or business, the loss on the deposit was treated as a short-term capital loss (the deduction of which is limited under the IRC).

Definitions. A qualified individual is any individual other than a 1% stock owner in the institution in which the loss was sustained, an officer of that institution, or certain relatives or "related persons" (as defined in Sec. 267(b)) of those owners or officers.

A qualified financial institution is a commercial bank (as defined in Sec. 581), a thrift institution (as defined in Sec. 591), a federally insured or state-insured or guaranteed credit union, or any other similar institution supervised or chartered under federal or state law.

Deposit means any deposit, withdrawable certificate, or withdrawable or repurchasable share of or in a qualified financial institution under the new law.

Under the new law, qualified individuals that elect to treat the loss on a deposit in a qualified financial institution as a casualty loss can't deduct the loss as a bad debt under Sec. 166.

IMPORTANT: The election applies only when the loss is caused by the insolvency or bankruptcy of the financial institution.

Qualified individuals don't have to claim the loss in the year in which the loss is first reasonably estimated. They can claim the loss in a later year either as a casualty loss deduction or as a bad debt deduction.

Method of accounting. Once the election is made, it's an election of an accounting method for the taxpayer with regard to all deposits in that qualified financial institution and requires that all the taxpayer's other losses on other deposits in the institution be treated in the same manner.

Amount of loss recognized. The amount of loss recognized under the election is the difference between the taxpayer's basis in the deposit and the amount which is a reasonable estimate of the deposit amount that will eventually be received.

Recovery of loss. If a loss that has been claimed as a casualty deduction is later recovered, then the lesser of the recovery amount or the tax benefit received from the election is included in income in the year of the recovery.

Interest treatment on frozen deposits. The new law specially provides for the treatment of interest on frozen deposits in certain financial institutions. Frozen deposits are deposits which, as of the close of the calendar year, may not be withdrawn because the qualified financial institution is threatened with bankruptcy or insolvency or is actually bankrupt or insolvent.

¶1905

Under the new law, accrued, but unpaid interest on a deposit in a qualified financial institution for taxable years beginning after 12-31-82 and before 1-1-87, isn't includible in the depositor's taxable income for the taxable year when such interest isn't subject to withdrawal at the end of the taxable year. The interest income is includible in gross income in the taxable year in which the interest is withdrawable. Interest not included in gross income is treated as credited in the next calendar year.

Qualified individuals making this election must have it apply to the taxable year period beginning after 12-31-82 and before 1-1-87.

Qualified financial institutions can't take deductions for interest not includible in gross income until the interest is includible in gross income. For interest attributable to the period beginning 1-1-83 and ending on 12-31-87, the interest deduction of financial institutions is determined without regard to the qualified institution's interest deduction deferral.

Act Sec. 905, treatment of losses on deposits in insolvent financial institutions, adding new Sec. 165(l); prior Sec. 165(l) redesignated as Sec. 165(m), adding new sec. 451(f), effective for all tax years beginning after 12-31-82, and as shown above.

[The page following this is 1001.]

INSURANCE PRODUCTS AND COMPANIES

Life Insurance Products

[¶1001] **Survivor-Spouse's $1,000 Annual Exclusion.** Under the new law, all amounts paid to any beneficiary of a life insurance policy at a date later than the death of the insured (i.e., paid in installments or as an annuity) are included in gross income to the extent the amount paid exceeds the amount payable as a death benefit. The exclusion of the first $1,000 in excess of the pro rata portion of the death benefit from the annual gross income of the surviving spouse is repealed.

If an insurer pays insurance death proceeds to a beneficiary in installments or as an annuity, old law treated a prorated amount of each installment as a nontaxable payment of the death benefit, with the remainder generally includible in gross income. However, the first $1,000 received by a surviving spouse in any year in excess of the amount treated as a payment of the death benefit was excludable from gross income. The new law requires insurers to compute the nontaxable annuity income based on sex-neutral mortality tables.

Act Sec. 1001 amends Sec. 101(d), relating to repeal of exclusion, and Sec. 101(d)(2)(B), relating to computation of annuity, effective for amounts received with respect to deaths occurring after the date of enactment in tax years ending after the date of enactment.

[¶1002] **Structured Settlements.** Old law excluded from income any amount received because of personal injury or sickness, whether as a lump-sum or periodically and whether by suit or agreement. The person liable to pay periodic amounts may assign the liability to a life insurance company. The amount paid to the insurer for agreeing to fund the liability isn't included in the insurer's income.

The new law repeals the insurer's tax break for all structured settlements except "qualified assignments"; i.e., settlements resulting from personal injury or sickness. Damages awarded for any other torts don't qualify. So the full amount paid to the insurance company in these latter cases is included in its gross income.

However, the *annuitant's* structured settlement tax break is unaffected by the new law.

Rev. Rul. 79-220 [CB 1979-2 p. 74] shows how to structure tax-free annuity payments under Sec. 104(a)(2) in settlement of a suit for personal injuries.

> **Example:** Brown sues Aker for personal injury damages. Before the trial, Brown accepts Aker's casualty insurance company's offer to settle for (1) a lump-sum payment of $80,000 and (2) $30,000 a year in monthly payments of $2,500 for the longer of Brown's lifetime or

20 years. To provide the $2,500 monthly payments, the casualty company buys a single-premium 20-years-certain immediate annuity from a life insurance company. Payments are made directly to Brown, but the casualty company owns the annuity contract.

Rev. Rul. 79-220 says the full amount of the monthly payments is excludable from Brown's income under Sec. 104(a)(2). Purchase of the annuity from the life insurance company was merely an investment by the casualty company to guarantee the funds to satisfy its continuing obligation to Brown.

Act Sec. 1002 amends Sec. 130. The provision is effective for assignments entered into after 12-31-86 in tax years ending after that date.

[¶1003] Policyholder Loans. The new law retains the present rule that amounts paid or accrued on debt to buy or maintain a single premium life insurance policy, including a contract in which an amount is deposited to pay a substantial number of premiums, are not deductible. Moreoover, the deduction for interest on a policyholder loan is denied for loans to officers, employees, or owners of an interest in a trade or business of the taxpayer if such loans are, in the aggregate, more than $50,000 per officer, employee, or owner.

Act Sec. 1003 amends Code Sec. 264(a)(1) effective for interest on loans under policies purchased after 6-20-86.

[¶1004] Personal Casualty Losses. Under the new law, to the extent that a personal casualty loss of an individual is covered by insurance, it will be taken into account in figuring the personal casualty loss deduction only if the individual files a timely insurance claim for that loss.

Act Sec. 1004 adds new Sec. 165(h)(4)(E), effective for losses sustained in tax years beginning after 12-31-86.

[¶1005] Funeral Expense Policies. The new law provides that small burial policies may qualify as life insurance policies even though the policy provides for future increases in death benefits. To qualify, the initial death benefit under the policy must be $5,000 or less, and the contract must provide for fixed annual increases in the death benefit of no more than 10% of the initial death benefit, or 8% of the death benefit at the end of the immediately preceding year, provided the aggregate amount doesn't exceed $25,000.

Ed. note: The first printing of the conference bill contained no statutory language on this provision. This may be subject to a technical correction. As passed by the Conference Committee, the provision is effective for contracts issued after 12-31-84.

[¶1011] **Special Life Insurance Company Deduction Repealed.** The 20% special life insurance company deduction was enacted as part of the 1984 Tax Reform Act to ease the sudden, substantial increase in life insurance company tax liability. With the new law's overall reduction of corporate tax rates, this special relief is no longer necessary. Thus, the new law repeals the 20% special life insurance company deduction for tax years beginning after 12-31-86.

Certain debt-financed stock acquisitions. The new law also amends the special rule that applies when a life insurance company owns the stock of another corporation through a partnership, and acquired that stock through debt financing on 1-14-81. In determining the small life insurance company deduction under amended Sec. 806(a), tentative life insurance company taxable income is computed without taking into account any income, gain, loss, or deduction that's attributable to the ownership of that stock. Further, $^{46}/_{36.8}$ of any income, gain, loss, or deduction that's attributable to the ownership of that stock is taken into account in determining the company's taxable income.

Special rate on certain bonds. Despite the new law's repeal of corporate capital gains treatment, any gain recognized by any of 15 specified life insurance companies on redemption at maturity of any bond issued before 7-19-84 and acquired by the company before 9-25-85 is subject to tax at a 28% rate.

Act Sec. 1011(a) repeals Sec. 806(a) and redesignates Secs. 806(b), (c), and (d) as Secs. 806(a), (b), and (c), respectively. Act Sec. 1011(b) makes technical and conforming amendments to Secs. 453B(e)(2)(B), 465(c)(7)(D)(v), 801(a)(2)(C), 804, 805, 806, 813(a)(4)(A), 815(c)(2)(A)(ii), and the table of sections for subpart C of part I of subchapter L. Act Sec. 1011(c)(2) amends Sec. 217(k) of the 1984 TRA, relating to the special rule for certain debt-financed stock acquisitions. Act Sec. 1011(d), relating to the special rate on certain bonds, doesn't amend the Code. The provisions of Act Sec. 1011 are generally effective for tax years beginning after 12-31-86.

[¶1012] **Operations Loss Deduction of Insolvent Life Insurance Companies.** Before 1984, stock life insurance companies were allowed certain special deductions and had to add the amount of those deductions to a deferred tax account known as the policyholders surplus account (PSA). The tax deferral on these amounts ended when they were distributed to shareholders and in certain other situations. Amounts included in the company's income as a result of the ending of deferral couldn't be offset by the company's loss from operations or operations loss carryovers.

The 1984 Tax Reform Act repealed the deductions that gave rise to additions to the PSA. But while a stock life insurance company can no longer add amounts to its PSA, it must maintain its existing account and include in income amounts distributed directly or indirectly to shareholders from that account.

The new law creates an exception to the rule that includable income from PSA distributions can't be offset by current operations losses or unused loss carryovers. Under the new law, a stock life insurance company can apply such losses and loss carryovers against taxable income attributable to PSA distributions if

- the company was insolvent (its liabilities exceeded the fair market value of its assets) on 11-15-85;
- the company is liquidated under court order in a title 11 or similar case; and
- PSA distributions resulting from the liquidation would increase the company's tax liability for the liquidation year.

No carryover of any operations loss of the company that arises during or before the liquidation year can be used in any tax year following the liquidation year.

Act Sec. 1013, which does not amend the Code, is effective for liquidations on or after 11-15-85, in tax years ending after that date.

[¶1013] Tax Exempts Engaged in Insurance Activities. Under the new law, a charity or social welfare organization is tax exempt only if no substantial part of its activities consists of providing commercial-type insurance. "No substantial part" has the same meaning as under prior law applying to these organizations.

UBI. If the organization is tax exempt, the providing of commercial-type insurance is treated as unrelated business income. However, the insurance activities are taxed under the rules relating to insurance companies (Subchapter L of the Code) and not taxed under the UBI rules.

Commercial-type insurance generally is any insurance of a type provided by insurance companies. The issuance of annuity contracts is treated as providing insurance. Providing insurance or annuities under a qualified pension plan isn't considered providing commercial-type insurance.

Exceptions. Commercial-type insurance doesn't include

- insurance provided at substantially below cost to a class of charitable recipients;
- health insurance provided by a health maintenance organization of a kind customarily provided by these organizations and is incidental to the organization's principal activity of providing

health care. Organizations providing supplemental HMO-type services (such as dental services) also aren't affected by the new law if they operate in the same way as an HMO;

• property and casualty insurance provided directly or through a wholly owned corporation by a church or convention or association of churches for the organization. Property or casualty insurance doesn't include life, accident, and health insurance (whether or not cancelable). This exception doesn't apply if the insurance is provided not only to the church, but also to other persons;

• retirement and welfare benefits provided by a church, etc., directly or indirectly for the organization's employees and their beneficiaries. This exception doesn't apply if the insurance is provided to others.

Blue Cross/Blue Shield organizations. The new law provides special treatment for existing Blue Cross/Blue Shield organizations and other organizations that meet certain requirements and substantially all of whose activities are providing health insurance. Health insurance includes insurance that provides coverage of medical expenses.

Special treatment. The special treatment applies to Blue Cross/Blue Shield organizations that

• were in existence on 8-16-86;

• are determined at that time to be tax exempt and the exemption hasn't been revoked; and

• were tax exempt for the last tax year beginning before 1-1-87, provided that no material change occurs in the structure or operations of the organization after 8-16-86, and before the close of 1986 or any later tax year.

Material change in operations. According to the Conference Report, the Treasury must apply the following principles in determining whether a material change in operations or structure occurred.

• The merger or split up of one or more existing Blue Cross/Blue Shield organizations won't be a material change in operation or structure.

• If an existing Blue Cross/Blue Shield organization acquires a new line of business or is acquired by another business (other than a health business), the acquisition isn't a material change in operations or structure of the organization if (1) the assets of the other business are a de minimis percentage (that is, less than 10%) of the assets of the existing Blue Cross/Blue Shield organization at the time of the acquisition, or (2) the taxpayer can demonstrate to the Treasury that, based on all the facts and circumstances, the acquisition isn't a material change in operations or structure of the existing Blue Cross/Blue Shield organization.

• A material change in operations occurs if an existing Blue Cross/Blue Shield organization drops its high-risk coverage or substantially changes the terms and conditions under which high-risk coverage is offered by the organization from the terms and conditions in effect as of 8-16-86. A change in high-risk coverage is considered substantial if the effect of the change is to defeat the purpose of high-risk coverage. High-risk coverage for this purpose generally means the coverage of individuals and small groups to the extent the organization (1) provides coverage under specified terms and conditions as of 8-16-86, or (2) meets the statutory minimum definition of high-risk coverage for new organizations. A material change in operations doesn't occur if an existing organization alters its operations to provide high-risk coverage that meets the minimum standards under the new law for new Blue Cross/Blue Shield organizations.

The Conference Report states that, to the extent such determinations of tax exemption for any tax year beginning before 1987 weren't under audit or in litigation before 8-16-86, the IRS won't seek to revoke the determinations.

Existing organizations. Existing Blue Cross/Blue Shield organizations and other organizations eligible for this treatment are subject to tax as stock property and casualty insurance companies.

A special deduction is provided to these organizations as to their health business equal to 25% of the claims and expenses incurred during the tax year less the adjusted surplus at the beginning of the tax year. This deduction is calculated by computing surplus, taxable income, claims incurred, expenses incurred, tax-exempt income, and NOL carryovers, attributable to health business. Thus, the deduction isn't allowable as to items attributable to life insurance business. The expenses attributable to health business are those incurred during the tax year in connection with the administration, adjustment, or settlement of claims under health business. The deduction can't exceed taxable income attributable to health business for the year (calculated without regard to this deduction).

For organizations eligible for this deduction in the first tax year beginning after 12-31-86, the amount of the adjusted surplus to be applied in the first year for which the deduction is allowable is the surplus reported on the organization's annual statement (that is the annual statement approved by the National Association of Insurance Commissioners) at the close of the preceding year, adjusted by not taking into account distributions (such as distributions to shareholders, or contributions or loans to affiliates that reduce surplus, but not including ordinary and necessary expenses or deductible policyholder dividends) after 8-16-86. For orgniazations that first become eligible for the provision in a later tax year, the amount of the adjusted surplus for the first year of the deduction is the surplus reported on the annual statement at the close of the preceding year.

The initial surplus amount is adjusted under the provision at the close of each tax year by adding the taxable income or loss of the organization for the year (determined without regard to NOL carryovers and without regard to the deduction under this provision), plus net tax-exempt income for the year. Net tax-exempt income means dividends for which the dividends received deduction was allowed, and interest that is tax exempt, less the expenses of earning the tax-exempt interest that were disallowed under Sec. 265, and less the adjustment that was made for proration of tax-exempt income under Sec. 805(a) or 832(b)(5). If an organization eligible for the deduction doesn't take the deduction in any year, adjusted surplus must be calculated for the intervening years between the last year the organization took the deduction and the next year in which it takes the deduction, so as to take account properly of the calculation of the deduction in the later year.

The deduction applies only for regular tax purposes. Thus, the deduction is treated as a preference item for purposes of the corporate minimum tax.

In addition to this special deduction, these organizations are given a fresh start as to changes in accounting methods resulting from the change from tax exempt to taxable status. No adjustment is made under Section 481 on account of an accounting method change.

These organizations aren't subject to the treatment of unearned premium reserves generally applicable to property and casualty insurance companies. To ease the transition from tax exempt to taxable status, Blue Cross/Blue Shield organizations were given relief from the requirement that 20% of the increase in unearned premium reserves be included in income.

Finally, the basis of assets of these organizations is equal, for purposes of determining gain or loss, to the amount of the assets' FMV on the first day of the organizations's tax year beginning after 12-31-86. Thus, for formerly tax-exempt organizations using a calendar year and whose first tax year begins 1-1-87, the basis of each asset of the organization is equal to the amount of its FMV value on 1-1-87. The basis step-up is provided solely for purposes of determining gain or loss on sale or exchange of the assets, not for purposes of determining amounts of depreciation or for other purposes.

New organizations. The above special provisions apply to existing tax-exempt Blue Cross/Blue Shield organizations and to those other organizations that satisfy the additional criteria described below.

¶10 13

Other organizations, to receive the special treatment described above, must meet these requirements.

- At least 10% of the health insurance (determined as a percentage of the total number of individuals covered annually) provided by the organization must be provided to individuals and small groups (disregarding Medicare supplemental coverage). A "small group" is the lesser of 15 individuals or the number of individuals required for a small group under the state law where the covered groups are located.

- The organization must provide continuous full-year open enrollment for individuals and small groups. Open enrollment includes conversions from group to individual coverage, without a lapse in coverage, provided the individual seeking to convert from group to individual coverage notifies the organization providing group coverage of his conversion request by the date of his separation from service. Conversion includes any change in the type of coverage.

- Any individual seeking health insurance must be offered coverage that includes coverage of pre-existing conditions of high-risk individuals without a price differential and the coverage becomes effective within a reasonable waiting period after the time coverage is sought. According to the Conference Report a reasonable waiting period is intended to be not more than three months. Further, health insurance coverage must be provided regardless of age, income, or employment status of persons under 65.

- At least 35% of the organization's health insurance premiums are determined on a community-rated basis. This is determined as a percentage of the total number of persons covered on an annual basis. Community rating means that premiums are determined on the basis of the average annual cost of health insurance over the population in the community.

- The organization must be organized and operated in a manner so that no part of the net earnings inures to any private shareholder's or individual's benefit.

- Substantially all of the organizations activities involve providing health insurance.

Fraternal societies.   As to tax-exempt fraternal beneficiary societies that are engaged in insurance activities, the new law reemphasizes the requirement of prior law that they must keep an active lodge system. Also, the Treasury must audit and study tax-exempt fraternal beneficiary organizations that received gross annual insurance premiums exceeding $25 million in tax year 1984. The organization's use of revenue from insurance activities will also be studied. The results of the study and recommendations must be submitted to the House Ways and Means Committee, the Senate Finance Committee, and the Joint Committee on Taxation by 1-1-88.

Special rules. There are special transitional provisions for the following: Mutual of America; Teachers Insurance Annuity Association-College Retirement Equities Fund; YMCA; Missouri Hospital Association and Delta Dental Plans Association.

Act Sec. 1012 redesignates Sec. 501(m) as Sec. 501(n) and adds new Sec. 501(m), relating to tax exemption of organizations engaged in insurance activities, and adds new Sec. 833, relating to treatment of Blue Cross/Blue Shield organizations effective as shown above.

〖¶1014〗 Discounting Unpaid Losses. Under the new law, unpaid losses of life insurance companies—other than losses on life insurance contracts, which are discounted under life insurance rules— are subject to the new discounting rules applicable to unpaid losses of property and casualty companies. But unlike property and casualty companies, loss adjustment expenses of life insurance companies aren't subject to discounting. *Reason:* They're not deductible. This new rule applies for purposes of Secs. 805(a)(1) and 807(c)(2).

Act Sec. 1023 amends Secs. 807(c), 832(b)(5)(A)(ii) (as amended by Act Sec. 1022), and 832(b)(6), and adds new Sec. 846, effective for tax years beginning after 12-31-86.

〖¶1015〗 Mutual Treatment of Stock Life Affiliates. [Ed. Note: This provision appeared in the House version of the bill, but not the Senate version. It wasn't included in the Conference bill but was included in House-passed Concurrent Resolution No. 395. It is likely to appear in technical corrections legislation.] This provision temporarily repeals the requirement that stock life insurance subsidiaries of a mutual life common parent be taxed as *mutual* life companies when the parent has elected to treat all its individual noncancellable (or guaranteed renewable) accident and health insurance contracts as *cancellable* contracts. Under the '84 TRA, a mutual company can treat these contracts as cancellable (for determining its status as a life company under Section 816) if it made an election to do so on the return for its first tax year beginning after 12-31-83, with the election being effective for that year and later years.

Act Sec. 1014 amends Sec. 217(i) of the 1984 TRA, effective for tax years beginning after 12-31-86 and before 1-1-92.

Property and Casualty Insurance Companies

〖¶1021〗 Unearned Premiums of P&C Companies. Under the new law, property and casualty companies (stock and mutual) can generally deduct only 80% of any *increase* in unearned premiums—or, conversely, must generally include only 80% of any *decrease* in unearned premiums —in figuring "premiums earned." Premiums earned, less losses incurred and expenses incurred, make up a P&C company's underwriting income.

> **Example:** At the end of 1986, PC Insurance Company, a calendar-year taxpayer, had $1,000 of unearned premiums on outstanding business. At the end of 1987, PC's unearned premiums totalled $1,100. In figuring premiums earned for 1987, PC's net deduction for the $100 increase in unearned premiums is $80 ($100 × 80%). (Under prior law, 100% of the increase would have been deductible.) At the end of 1988, PC's unearned premiums declined to $900. PC must include $160 ($200 × 80%) of the $200 decrease in figuring premiums earned for 1988.

Life insurance reserves that are included in unearned premiums aren't subject to this reduced 80% deduction/inclusion rule. Thus, increases and decreases in these reserves are still taken into account 100% in figuring premiums earned.

Also, the new law provides a special rule for insurance against default in payment of principal or interest on certain securities (including bonds, debentures, and notes) that have a maturity of more than five years. For such insurance, P&C companies can deduct 90% of the increase in unearned premiums and must include in income 90% of any decrease. Insurance on securities with a maturity of five years or less is subject to the general 80% rule.

Treatment of outstanding balances. The new law also provides that P&C companies must include in income 20% of the amount of unearned premiums outstanding at the end of the most recent tax year beginning before 1-1-87. This 20% is includable ratably over a six-year period, starting with the first tax year beginning after 12-31-86. Thus, 3⅓% of the amount outstanding is includable in each year of the period. This amount is included in income by adding it into the computation of premiums earned. Amounts attributable to life insurance reserves aren't taken into account in applying this ratable inclusion rule.

> **Example:** At the end of 1986, PC Insurance Company, a calendar-year taxpayer, had $1,000 of unearned premiums (no part of which is attributable to life insurance reserves) on outstanding business. PC must include in income $33.33 a year ($1,000 × 3⅓%) for 1987 through 1992. Thus, over the six tax years beginning after 1986, PC will have included in income 20% (6 × 3⅓%) of its 1986 year-end unearned premiums.

For unearned premiums that are attributable to insurance against default on securities with a maturity of more than five years, 10% of the amount outstanding at the end of the most recent tax year beginning before 1-1-87 must be included in income. This 10% is includable ratably over a six-year period, starting with the first tax year beginning after 12-31-86. Thus, 1⅔% of the amount outstanding is includable in each of the six years of the period.

If a company ceases to be taxable as a P&C company during the ratable-inclusion period, the inclusion schedule is accelerated. Thus, the remaining amount that's subject to the ratable-inclusion rule is included in the company's income for the tax year *preceding* the year in which the company ceases to be taxed as a P&C company. This rule applies only if a company ceases to be a P&C company for a tax year beginning before 1-1-93.

> **Example:** At the end of 1986, PC Insurance Company, a calendar-year taxpayer, had $1,000 of unearned premiums on outstanding business. No part of that $1,000 is attributable to life insurance reserves or insurance against default on securities. Thus, $200 (20% of $1,000) is subject to the ratable-inclusion rule. For 1987, PC includes $33.33 (3⅓% of $1,000) in income. For 1988, it includes the same amount. If PC ceases to be a property and casualty insurance company for tax year 1990, the amount it must include in income for 1989 is $133.34—that is, $200 minus the total amount it included in 1987 and 1988 ($66.66).

This acceleration of the inclusion schedule doesn't apply to the extent that a successor insurance company is subject to the requirements of Sec. 381(c)(22) (relating to carryovers of a transferor's corporate attributes in certain corporate readjustments).

Title insurers exempt. Title insurers are exempt from the reduced 80% deduction/inclusion rule. Instead, the new law applies discounting to title insurance state law unearned premium reserves. In applying the discounting rule, "undiscounted unearned premiums" at the end of the tax year is the amount of unearned premiums shown on the yearly statement filed for the year ending with or within that tax year. The discounting period is the period over which the unearned premium reserves are deferred under state law. Premiums received during any calendar year are treated as received in the middle of that year. The discount rate is the rate generally applicable to property and casualty insurance companies (see ¶1022). Title insurance case reserves are subject to discounting under the same method as property and casualty insurance loss reserves (see ¶1022).

Under a transitional rule for the first tax year beginning after 12-31-86, the amount of title insurance unearned premiums at the end of the preceding tax year (as defined in Sec. 832(b)(4)) is determined as if the discounting provisions had applied to the unearned premiums in that preceding tax year. In applying the discounting methodology for that preceding tax year, the interest rate and premium recognition pattern applicable to years ending in 1987 are used.

Under a fresh-start rule, any difference between the undiscounted and discounted unearned premiums for that preceding tax year generally isn't taken into account in determining a company's taxable income—but it will increase the company's E&P for its first tax year beginning after 12-31-86.

Act Sec. 1021 amends Sec. 832(b)(4)(B) (relating to the computation of premiums earned) and adds new Secs. 832(b)(4)(C) and 832(b)(7) effective generally for tax years beginning after 12-31-86. New Secs. 832(b)(4)(C) and 832(b)(7)(B)(ii) (relating to the inclusion in income of a percentage of unearned premiums outstanding at the end of the most recent tax year beginning before 1-1-87) are effective ratably over the six tax years beginning after 12-31-86 and before 1-1-93.

[¶1022] **Discounting Unpaid Losses.** To take into account the time value of money, the new law imposes a pretax discounting rule on a P&C company's unpaid losses (reported losses that haven't been paid, estimates of losses incurred but not reported, resisted claims, and unpaid loss adjustment expenses).

A P&C company's underwriting income equals its premiums earned during the tax year, less expenses incurred and losses incurred. Under the new law, losses incurred in the tax year equals (1) losses paid, increased by (2) salvage and reinsurance recoverable outstanding at the end of the preceding tax year, and decreased by (3) salvage and reinsurance recoverable outstanding at the end of the current tax year; and the result of steps (1) through (3) is further increased by (4) unpaid losses on life insurance contracts plus *discounted* unpaid losses outstanding at the end of the current tax year, and then decreased by (5) unpaid losses on life insurance contracts, and *discounted* unpaid losses outstanding at the end of the preceding tax year. (Losses incurred may be further reduced by the new law's proration provision for certain dividends and tax-exempt income. See ¶1032.)

Discounted unpaid losses at the end of a particular tax year is the sum of the discounted unpaid losses (as of the end of that tax year) attributable to—and separately computed for—each accident year for each line of business. The amount of discounted unpaid losses attributable to a particular accident year is the present value of those losses as of the end of the tax year, figured by using (1) the undiscounted unpaid losses as of the end of the tax year, (2) the applicable interest rate, and (3) the applicable loss payment pattern for each line of business.

> **LIMIT:** The amount of *discounted* unpaid losses attributable to any accident year for any line of business can't exceed the aggregate amount of unpaid losses for that accident year and line of business as reported on the company's annual statement for the year ending with or within the tax year.

Definitions. "Accident year" means the calendar year in which the incident occurs that gives rise to the related unpaid loss.

"Line of business" means a category for the reporting of claims and claim payments on the NAIC-approved annual statement (Schedules O and P) for fire and casualty companies. Multiple peril lines, however, are treated as a single line of business.

"Undiscounted unpaid losses" are generally equal to the unpaid losses shown on the P&C company's annual statement for the fiscal year ending with or within the company's tax year, and include unpaid loss adjustment expenses shown on the statement. (Unpaid loss adjustment expenses won't be included in "expenses unpaid" in computing expenses incurred.) If any unpaid losses are discounted on the annual statement, they can be grossed up to their undiscounted amount, provided that the extent of the discounting can be determined from information disclosed on or with the annual statement.

The "applicable interest rate" is the rate for the calendar year with which the accident year ends. The rate will be determined by the Treasury, and will be phased in to 100% of a 60-month rolling average of applicable federal midterm rates (based on annual compounding). No month beginning before 8-1-86 will be included in the 60-month period.

The "applicable loss payment pattern" is the pattern for the calendar year with which the accident year ends. The loss payment pattern will be determined by the Treasury for each line of business once every five years starting with 1987. Thus, the loss payment pattern determined for 1987 will be the pattern for calendar years 1987 through 1991. The Treasury will determine the pattern based on the historical loss payment pattern for each line of business. The Treasury's determination must be made (1) by using the aggregate experience reported on relevant insurance company annual statements, (2) on the basis of the most recent published aggregate loss payment pattern data available on the first day of the determination year, (3) by assuming that all losses paid during a year are paid in the middle of that year, and (4) by applying a series of computational rules and assumptions provided under the new law.

The computational rules assume that losses on Schedule O lines are paid over a 4-year period, and that losses on Schedule P lines are paid over an 11-year period, starting with the accident year. For Schedule O lines, losses unpaid at the end of year 2 are treated as paid equally in years 3 and 4. For Schedule P lines, losses paid after the end of the 11-year period are generally treated as paid in year 11. But under a special limitation rule, the amount treated as paid in year 11 can't exceed the amount treated as paid in year 10. If the amount treated as paid in year 10 is zero or a negative amount, then the limitation rule is applied by using the average of the amounts treated as paid in years 8, 9, and 10, instead of the amount treated as paid in year 10. The Conference Report indicates that if the three-year average results in a negative amount, additional preceding years should be averaged in successively until the average is positive. The 11-year period can be extended by up to 5 years to take into account any excess. However, the amount that can be treated as paid in each year of the extension period is subject to the same limitation that applies to year 11—that is, it can't exceed the amount treated as paid in year 10. Any balance that remains at the end of the fifth year of the extension period is treated as paid in that fifth year.

A company can elect to apply the discounting rules for all its lines of business by using its *own* loss payment pattern for the most recent calendar year for which it filed an annual statement before the beginning of the accident year. The company must use the same series of computational rules and assumptions as the Treasury must use, including the assumption that all losses paid during a year are paid in the middle of that year. The election is available for each determination year, which is calendar year 1987 and every fifth year thereafter. Once the taxpayer makes a determination, it can't later redetermine its loss payment pattern to adjust for more recent information. The election isn't available for international or reinsurance lines. The Treasury is authorized to issue whatever regulations are necessary to carry out the purposes of this provision.

International and reinsurance lines. Under the new law, the discounting of unpaid losses for international and reinsurance lines of business is generally to be implemented by using a loss payment pattern determined by the Treasury based on a composite of all Schedule P lines (auto liability, other liability, medical malpractice, workers' compensation, and multiple peril). However, the Treasury is authorized to issue regulations requiring a company to follow a different loss payment pattern for international and reinsurance lines.

The Conference Report indicates that international and reinsurance business that is allocated to a particular line of business is discounted under the rules applicable to that line, and not under the general rule for international and reinsurance business.

Certain accident and health lines. Active life reserves for life insurance and noncancellable accident and health benefits that are subject to the life company reserve rules aren't subject to the new discounted unpaid loss rules. Also, unpaid losses relating to disability insurance (other than credit disability insurance) are to be determined under the general rules applicable to noncancellable accident and health contracts of life companies (Sec. 807(d)), with several adjustments.

For both life and P&C companies, accident and health coverage (other than disability) that isn't subject to the life company reserve requirements (for example, cancellable accident and health coverage) is subject to the discounting rules. However, instead of using a loss payment pattern, the rules will be applied on the assumption that unpaid losses are paid in the year following the accident year. (See also ¶1014.)

Title insurance. For title insurance companies, discounting applies to title insurance state law unearned premium reserves (see ¶1021). The discounting period is the period over which the reserves are deferred under state law. The discount rate is the rate generally applicable to P&C companies. Title insurance case reserves are discounted under the same method as P&C insurance loss reserves.

Effective Date: The new provisions for unpaid losses are effective for tax years beginning after 12-31-86. Under a transitional rule for the first tax year beginning after 12-31-86, the unpaid losses and expenses (as defined in Sec. 832(b)(5)(B), (6)) at the end of the preceding tax year as well as the unpaid losses (as defined in Secs. 807(c)(2) and 805(a)(1)) at the end of the preceding tax year are determined *as if* the discounting provisions had applied to the unpaid losses in that preceding tax year. In applying the discounting methodology for that preceding tax year, the interest rate and loss payment patterns for accident years ending with calendar year 1987 are used.

Under a fresh-start rule, any difference between the undiscounted and discounted unpaid losses for that preceding tax year generally aren't taken into account in determining a company's taxable income—but it will increase the company's E&P for its first tax year beginning after 12-31-86.

Further, the fresh-start rule won't apply to any reserve strengthening in a tax year beginning in 1986. Any such reserve strengthening will be treated as made in the company's first tax year beginning after 12-31-86.

Act Sec. 1023 amends Secs. 832(b)(5)(A)(ii) (as amended by Act Sec. 1022), 832(b)(6), and 807(c), and adds new Sec. 846, effective for tax years beginning after 12-31-86. It also makes a clerical amendment to the table of sections for part III of subchapter L (as redesignated by Act Sec. 1024).

[¶1023] Deduction for PAL Contributions Repealed. The new law repeals the mutual property and casualty company deduction for contributions to a protection against loss account for tax years beginning after 12-31-86. Also, mutual P&C companies must include in income the balance in their existing PAL accounts.

The amount of the PAL account balance that a mutual P&C company must include in income for any tax year beginning after 12-31-86 is the amount the company would have had to include if the PAL provision hadn't been repealed. For this purpose, no additions to the PAL account can be made for any tax year beginning after 12-31-86.

Act Sec. 1024(a) repeals part II of subchapter L (other than Secs. 822 and 826); redesignates parts III and IV as parts II and III, respectively; redesignates Secs. 822 and 826 as Secs. 834 and 835, respectively, and transfers them to the end of part II (as redesignated); and amends Sec. 831, relating to tax on nonlife insurance companies. Act Sec. 1024(b) amends Sec. 501(c)(15), relating to insurance companies as exempt organizations. Act Sec. 1024(c) makes conforming amendments to Secs. 832, 834(a) and (d) (as redesignated by Act Sec. 1024(a)), 835 (as redesignated by Act Sec. 1024(a)), 841, 842, 844, 891, 1201(a), 1504(b), 1563(b)(2), and the table of sections for part II of subchapter L (as redesignated by Act Sec. 1024(a)). Act Sec. 1024(d), which contains transitional rules for PAL account balances and unused loss carryovers under former Sec. 825, does not amend the Code. All provision of Act Sec. 1024 are effective for tax years beginning after 12-31-86.

[¶1024]   Revised Treatment for Small Mutual P&C Companies. The new law changes the requirements for a property and casualty company to qualify for tax-exempt status. Under the new law, a mutual *or stock* P&C company or association qualifies as a tax-exempt organization if its net written premiums or its direct written premiums (whichever are greater) for the tax year don't exceed $350,000. Under prior law, only mutual companies could qualify for tax exemption, and then only if certain gross receipts didn't exceed $150,000. Life companies still can't qualify under the new law.

If a company is a member of a controlled group, the net or direct written premiums of *all* members of the group are treated as received by that company in applying the $350,000 limit. "Controlled group" for this purpose has the same meaning as in Sec. 1563(a), except that Sec. 1563(a)(4) (relating to life company controlled groups) and Sec. 1563(b)(2)(D) (relating to life companies as excluded members) don't apply, and a 50% (rather than an 80%) ownership test applies.

Special rates, deductions, and exemptions repealed. The new law repeals the special rates, deductions, and exemptions for small mutual P&C companies—namely, the cap on tax when income is less than $12,000, the alternative tax for small companies, and the special deduction for small companies having gross amount of less than $1,100,000. It also consolidates parts II and III of Subchapter L into part II.

New alternative tax. The new law replaces these provisions with a new alternative tax that, at the taxpayer's election, will apply instead of any tax imposed on P&C companies under new Sec. 831(a). Thus, both mutual and stock P&C companies can elect the new alternative tax. The alternative tax is computed by applying the regular corporate rates to the company's taxable investment income.

To be eligible for the alternative tax, the P&C company's net written premiums or direct written premiums (whichever are greater) for the tax year must exceed $350,000 and must not exceed $1,200,000. If a company is a member of a controlled group, the net or direct written premiums of all members of the group are treated as received by that company in applying the dollar limitations. "Controlled group" for this purpose has the same meaning as in Sec. 1563(a), except that Sec. 1563(a)(4) (relating to life company controlled groups) and Sec. 1563(b)(2)(D) (relating to life companies as excluded members) don't apply, and a 50% (rather than 80%) ownership test applies.

Transitional rule. Under a transitional rule, any unused loss carryover under Sec. 825 (as in effect before the 1986 TRA) that is from a tax year beginning before 1-1-87, and that could have been used in a tax year beginning after 12-31-86 but for that section's repeal, will be included in the NOL deduction under Sec. 832(c)(10) of the 1954 Code without regard to the limitations of Sec. 844(b) of the 1954 Code.

Act Sec. 1024(a) repeals part II of subchapter L (other than Secs. 822 and 826); redesignates parts III and IV as parts II and III, respectively; redesignates Secs. 822 and 826 as Secs. 834 and 835, respectively, and transfers them to the end of part II (as redesignated); and amends Sec. 831, relating to tax on nonlife insurance companies. Act Sec. 1024(b) amends Sec. 501(c)(15), relating to insurance companies as exempt organizations. Act Sec. 1024(c) makes conforming amendments to Secs. 832, 834(a) and (d) (as redesignated by Act Sec. 1024(a)), 835 (as redesignated by Act Sec. 1024(a)), 841, 842, 844, 891, 1201(a), 1504(b), 1563(b)(2), and the table of sections for part II of subchapter L (as redesignated by Act Sec. 1024(a)). Act Sec. 1024(d), which contains transitional rules for PAL account balances and unused loss carryovers under former Sec. 825, does not amend the Code. All provision of Act Sec. 1024 are effective for tax years beginning after 12-31-86.

[¶1031] Self-Insured Medical Malpractice Insurance Pools. The new law adds a provision designed to encourage membership in self-insured medical malpractice insurance pools.

Exclusion for association. Under the new provision, an "eligible physicians' and surgeons' mutual protection and interindemnity arrangement or association" generally can exclude from income any initial payment it receives during the tax year from a new member—provided the payment (1) doesn't release the new member from current or future dues, assessments, or premiums, and (2) is required before membership benefits can be received. However, this exclusion won't apply to the initial payment if it's reasonable to expect that the payment will be deductible by any member under the rule described below.

If an association refunds to a member any amount that it previously excluded from income, the amount refunded isn't treated as a policyholder dividend; nor is it deductible by the association. Except for the termination of a member's membership, any amount distributed to a member is treated as paid out of surplus in excess of amounts excluded.

An "eligible physicians' and surgeons' mutual protection and interindemnity arrangement or association" is one that provides (1) only medical malpractice liability protection for its members, or (2) medical malpractice liability protection in conjunction with other liability coverage against claims related to a physician's or surgeon's professional practice. In addition, the association must

- have been providing medical malpractice protection (or have received a permit to offer and sell memberships) under the laws of any state before 1-1-84;
- not be subject to regulation by any state insurance department;
- be able to make unlimited assessments against all members to cover current claims and losses; and
- not be a member of, nor protected by, any state insurance guarantee plan or association.

Deduction for members. To the extent not otherwise allowable, the new provision allows a new member to treat his or her initial payment to an eligible association as a deductible Sec. 162 business expense for the tax year in which the payment is made. The deduction is limited, however, to the amount the member would have had to pay to an independent insurance company for similar annual coverage. That amount is further reduced by any annual dues, assessments, or premiums paid during the tax year. Excess payments not allowed as a deduction in the year paid can be carried forward for five years, subject to the same limitation. The deduction isn't available for any initial payment made by a person who is a member of more than one eligible association on or after the effective date of the new law.

If a member receives a refund of all or part of his or her initial payment, the member must include the refund in income to the extent he or she took a deduction for the initial payment. Amounts refunded in excess of the initial payment are also included in the member's income unless they're excludable under another provision of the Code.

Act Sec. 1031 does not amend the Code. It is effective for payments made to and receipts of eligible associations, and refunds of payments by eligible associations, after the date of enactment in tax years ending after that date.

[¶1032] **Proration for Tax-Exempt Interest and Dividends Received.** Under prior law, property and casualty insurance companies calculated underwriting income by deducting losses incurred (as well as expenses incurred) from premiums earned. "Losses incurred" generally consisted of losses paid during the year and increases in reserves for losses incurred but not paid.

The new law takes into account that all or part of an addition to loss reserves may come out of income that isn't taxable, giving rise to a double tax benefit. Thus, the new law introduces a proration provision that reduces a P&C company's deduction for losses incurred by 15% of (1) its tax-exempt interest and (2) the deductible portion of dividends received (with special rules for dividends from affiliates).

Dividends from affiliates. For dividends from affiliates that are 100% deductible under Sec. 243, 244, or 245(b) (100% dividends), the amount that is subject to the percentage reduction by the recipient P&C company is that portion that is attributable to "prorated amounts"—that is, the portion attributable to tax-exempt interest and non-100% dividends received by the affiliate paying the dividend.

> **Example:** In 1987, PC Insurance Company, a property and casualty insurer, has tax-exempt interest of $1,000 and receives a $100 dividend from a nonaffiliate (80% deductible). PC also receives a $400 dividend from Affiliate Corp. (100% deductible by PC). Of that $400, $200 is attributable to tax-exempt interest and nonaffiliate dividends (prorated amounts) received by Affiliate Corp. Under the new law, PC's deduction for losses incurred must be reduced by $192 ([$1,000 × 15%]+ [$80 × 15%]+ [$200 × 15%]).

Special rules apply when a P&C company receives a 100% dividend from any *insurance* affiliate (including a life company). The decrease in the deductions of the recipient P&C company resulting from a portion of the dividend being attributable to prorated amounts is reduced (but not below zero) by the amount of any increase in the affiliate's taxable income or decrease in its deductions resulting from applying the new law's proration provisions (Sec. 832(b)(5)(B) for P&C companies, and Sec. 805(a)(4)(A) for life companies) to those amounts on the affiliate's level.

In figuring what portion of a 100% dividend is attributable to prorated amounts when the recipient is a P&C company and the paying corporation is an insurance affiliate, the dividend is treated as paid first out of earnings and profits attributable to prorated amounts. The portion of E&P attributable to prorated amounts is figured without any reduction for federal income taxes.

Exception. Generally, the proration provisions for P&C companies don't apply to interest or dividends received or accrued on obligations or stock acquired on or before 8-7-86. For 100% dividends from affiliates, the P&C company will be treated as having acquired the affiliate's stock on the later of (1) the date the affiliate acquired the obligation giving rise to tax-exempt interest or the stock on which the affiliate received a nonaffiliate dividend; or (2) the first day on which the P&C company and the affiliate were members of the same affiliated group. For example, a recipient P&C company will be subject to the proration provisions on the portion of a 100% dividend that is attributable to tax-exempt interest of the affiliate if the affiliate acquired the tax-exempt obligation after August 7, 1986—even though the P&C company acquired the affiliate's stock before 8-8-86.

Act Sec. 1022, relating to the reduction of deductions for losses incurred, amends Sec. 832(b)(5), effective for tax years beginning after 12-31-86.

[¶1033] Study of P&C Companies.—The Treasury must conduct a study of the tax treatment of policyholder dividends by mutual property and casualty insurance companies, the treatment of property and casualty insurance companies under the minimum tax, and the effect of the 1986 TRA on revenue targets for the property and casualty insurance industry. The results of the study, together with recommendations, must be submitted to the House Ways and Means Committee, the Senate Finance Committee, and the Joint Committee on Taxation by 1-1-89.

Act Sec. 1025.

[The page following this is 1101.]

EMPLOYEE BENEFITS

Individual Retirement Arrangements

[¶1101] IRA Deduction Restricted. The new law restricts the deduction for contributions to individual retirement arrangements. Reason: The new law's lower tax rates are expected to stimulate additional savings and reduce the need for IRA deductions for those who participate in other tax-favored retirement plans. The new law continues to permit deductions for contributions, but the deduction is reduced proportionately for adjusted gross income between $40,000 and $50,000 (between $25,000 and $35,000 for unmarried taxpayers) if the taxpayer and his or her spouse file a joint return and either is an active participant in an employer-maintained retirement plan for any part of the plan year ending with or within the taxable year. Employer-maintained retirement plan means, for this purpose, a plan that is qualified under Sec. 401(a), an annuity plan qualified under Sec. 403(a), a simplified employee pension plan, a plan established for employees of the United States, a State, or a political subdivision, or by a government agency or instrumentality, a Sec. 501(c)(18) plan funded only by contributions of employees, or a tax-sheltered 403(b) annuity. For married taxpayers who file separate returns, deductible contributions for each spouse are phased out between $0 and $10,000 if the spouse participates in an employer-sponsored plan. The phase-out is based on adjusted gross income, determined *before* the reduction for deductible IRA contributions.

The new law provides for a minimum contribution of $200 for any taxpayer whose AGI is not above the phase out range even if the phase out rules would provide for a lesser contribution.

Active participation. The determination whether an individual is an active participant depends on the type of plan in which the individual participates or is eligible to participate. Generally, an individual is an active participant in a defined contribution plan if any employer contribution or forfeiture is added to such individual's account during the tax year. In a defined benefit plan, an individual is an active participant if not excluded under the plan's eligibility requirements during any part of the plan year ending with or within the individual's tax year. Thus, individuals may be active participants in defined benefit plans for a year even though they accrue *no* benefits during the year. For example, an individual may meet the plan's eligibility requirements, but decline to make mandatory contributions to the plan. An individual is also treated as an active participant in a plan for any tax year during which that individual makes a voluntary or mandatory employee contribution, whether the employer contributes or not. The determination of whether an individual is an active participant is made without regard to whether the individual's rights under a plan are vested.

Certain members of reserve components of the Armed Forces and volunteer fire-fighters are not treated as active participants solely because of such service.

Qualified voluntary deductible contributions repealed. The new law repeals the deduction for "qualified voluntary employee contributions." Therefore, for taxable years beginning after December 31, 1986, individuals will not be permitted to make deductible voluntary employee contributions to qualified plans.

Act Sec. 1101, amends Sec. 219 to restrict deduction for certain contributions to IRAs, and repeals deduction for certain employee contributions to qualified plans, effective for tax years beginning after 12-31-86.

[¶1102]   Nondeductible IRA Contributions OK.   The new law permits active participants in employer-sponsored plans to make *nondeductible* contributions to IRAs if they are not eligible to make deductible contributions, thus providing a limited tax incentive for discretionary retirement savings. Although these contributions may not be deducted, taxes on their earnings are deferred. An individual making a nondeductible contribution to an IRA must designate the contribution as such. The designation is made on the individual's tax return. Nondeductible contributions may be made up to the due date (without extensions) for filing the tax return for the year to which the designation relates. The new law permits an individual to treat contributions as nondeductible even though he or she is eligible to make deductible contributions.

Limits on nondeductible contributions. The maximum amount that may be contributed as a nondeductible contribution is the same as is permitted as a deductible contribution by an individual who is not an active participant in an employer-sponsored plan. Thus, the maximum permissible nondeductible contribution is $2,000 ($2,250 for a spousal IRA). These limits are reduced by the amount of any deductible contributions made by the taxpayer.

Contributions that exceed either the deductible limit or the nondeductible limit, whichever applies, are subject to an annual 6% excise tax on "excess contributions" under Sec. 4973. However, excess contributions made in one year may be applied against the contribution limits in a later year if the contributions in the later year are less than the limit. So if an employee who was an active participant in an employer-sponsored plan in a prior year made excess nondeductible contributions for the prior year, the excess may be recharacterized as a deductible contribution in the current year if the individual is no longer an active participant. Similarly, an excess deductible contribution could be recharacterized as a nondeductible contribution in a later year.

Distributions of nondeductible contributions. Distributions from IRAs are taxed under Sec. 72. Under special rules for IRAs, under Sec. 72 (1) all IRAs of an individual are treated as one IRA; (2) all distributions during the same taxable year are treated as one distribution; and (3) the value of the contract (determined after adding back any distributions during the year), income on the contract and investment in the contract is determined as of the close of the calendar year with or within which the individual's tax year ends. An individual who makes a nondeductible contribution to an IRA, or receives a distribution from an IRA during a taxable year, must provide information on the individual's tax return for the year which will enable the IRS to determine the proportion of the IRA balance, as of the end of the calendar year with or within which the taxable year ends, which represents nondeductible contributions. If the required information is provided, the portion of the amount withdrawn which bears the same ratio to the total amount withdrawn as the individual's aggregate nondeductible contributions bear to the aggregate balance of all of the individual's IRAs (including rollover IRAs and SEPs) is excludible from income for the taxable year of withdrawal. If the required information is *not* provided, distributions from an IRA to which both deductible and nondeductible contributions have been made are presumed to be distributed out of deductible contributions and earnings. This presumption may be rebutted by satisfactory evidence that all or part of the contributions were nondeductible.

Distributions that are treated as a return of nondeductible contributions are a nontaxable return of basis. The Committee Report accompanying the Senate's version of the Act, from which the provisions are derived, indicates that if an individual rolls over all or any part of the amount paid or distributed, the portion of the amount rolled over that represents nondeductible contributions retains its character as such in computing the tax on a later distribution.

If an individual overstates the amount of nondeductible contributions for any year, the new law imposes a $100 penalty.

The trustee of an IRA must report certain information to the Secretary of the Treasury and to the individuals for whom an IRA is maintained for each calendar year. This information includes (1) contributions to the IRA during the calendar year; (2) distributions from the IRA during the calendar year; and (3) the aggregate account balance as of the end of the calendar year. This information must be reported by the January 31 following the end of the calendar year. The penalty for failure to report the required information is $25 per day, to the maximum of $15,000.

Act Sec. 1102 amends Sec. 408 of the Code to add subsection (o) permitting nondeductible contributions to IRAs, amends Sec. 4973(b)(1) to include non-

deductible contributions in the definition of excess contribution, amends Sec. 408(d) to apply the Sec. 72 rules to distributions from IRAs, and amends Sec. 6693 to provide for penalty for overstating nondeductible contributions, effective for tax years beginning after 12-31-86.

[¶1103] Spousal Deduction Allowed When Spouse Has Small Amount of Earned Income. Prior law conditioned the full $2,250 spousal IRA deduction on one of the spouses having no earned income or earned income of at least $250. This requirement created an anomalous result when a spouse had minimal earned income. For example, a taxpayer earning $20,000 a year whose spouse had no earned income for the same period could deduct the full $2,250 spousal IRA contribution. On the other hand, a taxpayer earning $20,000 whose spouse earned, say, $50 for the year could deduct only $2,050.

The new law eliminates the "no-compensation" requirement for spousal IRAs. The spousal IRA is now available either if (1) a spouse has no compensation for the tax year or (2) elects to be treated as having no compensation for the year. And if a spousal IRA deduction is claimed on a joint return for a tax year, the spouse is deemed to have elected to be treated as having no compensation.

Whether a spousal IRA contribution is deductible or nondeductible depends on whether either spouse is an active participant in an employer-sponsored plan for the year, and whether the AGI of the couple is above the phase-out level [¶1101]. For example, if the AGI on a joint return is above $50,000 and *either* spouse is an active participant in an employer-sponsored plan, the entire IRA contribution is nondeductible. If AGI is less than $40,000, *or* if neither spouse participates in an employer-sponsored plan, the IRA contribution is deductible. If either spouse participates in an employer-sponsored plan, and AGI is between $40,000 and $50,000, a portion of the IRA contribution will be deductible. [¶1101].

Act Sec. 1103, amends Sec. 219(c)(1)(B) to permit full deduction for spousal IRA where spouse has minimal income, effective for tax years beginning before, on, or after 12-31-85.

[¶1104] Limits on Elective Deferrals to 403(b) Annuities. Under prior law, contributions on behalf of employees under tax-sheltered annuities, were subject to a special "exclusion allowance," which was the excess of (1) 20% of the participant's includable compensation, multiplied by the number of his years of service, over (2) amounts previously contributed to such annuity contracts in his behalf. Alternatively, the employee could elect to have the same overall limitations as were applied to annual additions to defined contribution plans under Sec. 415(c)—the lesser of $30,000 or 25% of a participant's compensation—apply. However, employees who worked for a tax-exempt organization that didn't offer a salary reduction agreement were limited to a $2,000 IRA contribution.

To alleviate this disparity, the new law clamps a lid on the amount that an employee can elect to defer for a tax year under all 403(b) annuities. For tax years beginning after 12-31-86, the maximum amount of such deferrals cannot exceed the greater of $9,500 or the maximum permissible elective deferral for CODAs (as indexed). This limit is determined without regard to any community property laws and is coordinated with elective deferrals under a CODA.

Limitation on aggregate deferrals. Unlike the limit on annual additions to defined contribution plans under Sec. 415(c), the limit on elective deferrals to 403(b) annuities applies to total deferrals made on an employee's behalf under *all* qualified CODAs and 403(b) annuities which the employee participates in during his or her *tax year* (rather than a plan's limitation year). This limit, however, applies only to elective *employee* deferrals to a CODA or 403(b) annuity, and does not apply to employer contributions. As a result, total 403(b) and CODA contributions are subject to the Sec. 403(b)(2) exclusion allowance or, if the employee so elects, the new law's overall Sec. 415(c) limitations [¶1106].

Excess deferrals. Amounts of elective employee deferrals that exceed the limit for a tax year are included in the employee's income for the year and must be allocated among the CODA or 403(b) annuities the employee participates in by the following March 1. The plan or plans must distribute the excess allocations (plus earnings) to the employee by the following April 15. Such distributions (and earnings) are includable in an employee's income for the year to which the excess deferral relates, but are not subject to the additional 10% tax on early distributions under Sec. 72(t). Such excess deferrals will be taken into account in applying special nondiscrimination tests [¶1112] even though they are distributed, except to the extent that regulations to be issued by the Secretary of the Treasury provide otherwise. On the other hand, if an excess deferral is *not* distributed by April 15 following the year of deferral, the excess remains in the CODA (or 403(b) annuity) and will (1) be hit by the Sec. 72(t) penalty; (2) again be taxed when actually distributed notwithstanding that the excess was included in income for the year of deferral, and (3) be taken into account in applying the special nondiscrimination tests.

Example: For 1987, Taxpayer elects to defer $5,000 under a 403(b) annuity, and $5,000 under a CODA maintained by employer Y. Under the new law, however, Taxpayer may exclude only $9,500 from the $10,000 of elective deferrals. Consequently, the $500 excess, plus a proportionate share of earnings, must be withdrawn from the 403(b) annuity by April 15, 1988. Taxpayer must include the excess in his income for 1987 only, and is not subject to the additional 10% tax under Sec. 72(t) for early withdrawals. The excess deferral is taken into account when testing the annuities under the special nondiscrimination test [¶1112] for the year of deferral (subject to regulations to be issued). However, if the excess deferral were not made by 4-15-88, it would remain in the 403(b) annuity and be subject to the withdrawal restrictions. Moreover, Taxpayer would have no basis in the excess despite the inclusion of it in his 1987 income, and the full amount of the excess would again be included in his income when actually distributed. Finally, the undistributed excess deferral would be taken into account in applying the special nondiscrimination tests for the year of deferral.

Catch-up election for certain 'qualified' employees. The new law provides an exception to the annual limit on contributions (including elective deferrals) to tax-sheltered 403(b) annuities. Any "qualified" employee who has completed 15 years of service with an educational organization, hospital, home health service or agency, health or welfare service agency, or church, convention, or association of churches (so-called qualified organizations) can make additional salary reduction contributions. However, the additional contribution in any one year cannot exceed $3,000, and an aggregate limit of $15,000 applies to total additional contributions. In addition, the exception to the deferral limit is unavailable if a taxpayer's lifetime elective deferrals top his or her lifetime limit ($5,000 × years of service performed by the individual with the employer).

Effective Date: The annual deferral limit applies to deferrals that relate to employees' tax years beginning after 12-31-86. However, for a qualified CODA or 403(b) annuity maintained under one or more collective bargaining agreements ratified before 3-1-86, the deferral limit does not apply to contributions for years beginning before the earlier of the termination date of the last CBA (without regard to the extension of such CBA), or 1-1-89.

Act Sec. 1105, relating to the annual limit on elective deferrals to 403(b) plans, amends Sec. 402, effective as shown above.

Cash or Deferred Arrangements

[¶1105] **$7,000 Limitation on Elective Deferrals to CODAs.** Under prior law, amounts employees could elect to defer to a qualified cash or deferred arrangement or to receive in cash were subject to the same overall limitations as were contributions to defined contribution plans under Sec. 415(c)—the lesser of $30,000 or 25% of a participant's compensation. However, employees whose employer did not maintain a qualified CODA, were limited to a $2,000 IRA contribution.

The new law reduces the aggregate amount that an employee can elect to defer for a tax year under all qualified CODAs. Generally, for tax years beginning after 12-31-86, such deferrals cannot exceed $7,000 in any tax year of the individual. This limit is determined without regard to any community property laws and is reduced by elective deferrals under Sec. 403(b) tax deferred annuities. The $7,000 cap is indexed for inflation at the same time and in the same way as the dollar limitation on benefits from defined benefit plans under Sec. 415.

Limit on elective deferrals. Like the limitations on elective deferrals under 403(b) annuities, the $7,000 limit applies to all elective deferrals by an individual, under all cash or deferred arrangements in the individual's tax year (rather than the plan's limitation year). Moreover, the limits are coordinated with the benefits under a Sec. 457 unfunded deferred compensation plan of a state or local government, a Sec. 501(c)(18) plan, or a SEP.

The limit on elective deferrals to a CODA is reduced by the amount of the individual's contributions to a 403(b) annuity contract to the extent that the contributions are made through a salary reduction agreement. However, the $7,000 limit is *increased* (but not to more than $9500) by the amount of employer contributions to a 403(b) annuity made through salary reduction. Thus, if an individual maintains a 403(b) annuity in addition to a CODA, total elective deferrals may be as high as $9500.

The limit on elective deferrals applies only to elective *employee* deferrals to a CODA and not to employer contributions (other than employer contributions through salary reduction agreements). As a result, total employee and employer CODA contributions are subject to the new law's overall Sec. 415(c) limitations of the lesser of (1) $30,000 (or 25% of the defined benefit plan dollar limit, if greater); or (2) 25% of compensation.

Treatment of excess deferrals. Elective employee deferrals that, together with contributions to SEPs in which the employee participates and any contributions to a Sec. 501(c)(18) plan on the employee's behalf, exceed the $7,000 limit for a tax year are included in the employee's income for the year. The excess may be allocated among the CODAs the employee participates in by the following March 1. The plan or plans to which the excess deferrals are allocated may then distribute the excess allocations (plus earnings) to the employee by the following April 15.

Such distributions (and earnings) are includable in an employee's income for the year to which the excess deferral relates, but are not subject to the additional tax on early distributions. Earnings of the plan are allocated to excess contributions on a pro-rata basis. Excess deferrals are taken into account in applying special nondiscrimination tests if not distributed during the taxable year of deferral. Moreover, if an excess deferral is not distributed by April 15 following the year of deferral, the excess remains in the CODA and (1) may be subject to a penalty for early withdrawals if distributed later; (2) will again be taxed when actually distributed notwithstanding that the excess was included in income for the year of deferral; and (3) will be taken into account in applying the special nondiscrimination tests. Moreover, the undistributed excess deferral will *not* be treated as an investment in the contract by the employee.

> **Example:** For 1987, Taxpayer defers $5,000 under employer X's qualified CODA and $3,000 under employer Y's CODA. Under the new law, Taxpayer may only exclude $7,000 of the $8,000 of elective deferrals. Consequently, the $1,000 excess may be withdrawn from X's plan or Y's plan, or partially from both plans. If Taxpayer documents the $1,000 excess by 3-1-88, he can request that $750 (plus earnings) be distributed from X's plan, and that $250 (plus earnings) be distributed from Y's plan. If the $1,000 excess (plus earnings) is distributed from the CODAs by 4-15-88, Taxpayer is required to include the excess (plus income) in his income for 1987 only, and will not be subject to the 10% additional tax for pre-age 59½ withdrawals under Sec. 72(t). Employers X and Y will be required, except as may be otherwise provided by regulations, to take the excess deferrals into account when testing their CODAs under the special nondiscrimination tests for the year of deferral. However, if either CODA fails to distribute the excess by 4-15-88, the excess will remain in the plan and will be subject to the withdrawal restrictions. Moreover, Taxpayers will have no basis in the excess despite the inclusion of it in his 1987 income, and the full amount of the excess will again be included in his income when actually distributed. Finally, the undistributed excess deferral will be taken into account as elective deferrals in applying the special nondiscrimination tests for the year of deferral.

Effective dates. The new law's limitation on elective deferrals is generally effective for tax years beginning after 12-31-86. For partnerships having fiscal years ending in 1987, the $7,000 limit applies on a pro-rata basis. However, for plans maintained under collective bargaining agreements ratified before 3-1-86, the new law will not apply to contributions made for tax years beginning before the earlier of (1) the date the last such collective bargaining agreement ends (without regard for any extension of the agreement after 2-28-86) or (2) 1-1-89. Such contributions *will be* taken into account in applying the new limits to other plans in which an individual participates. The provisions of the new law do not apply to elective deferrals of an employer which are attributable to services performed before 1-1-87 even if the deferral is actually made during 1987, provided (1) the employee makes the deferral election before 1-1-87 and (2) the employer identifies the amount of the deferral before that date.

Act Sec. 1105, amending Code Sec. 402 and imposing new limits on maximum elective deferrals under cash or deferred arrangements, effective for plan years beginning after 12-31-86, and effective for plan years beginning after 12-31-88 for plans maintained by state or local governments. Effective as indicated for collectively bargained plans.

〔¶1106〕 Limits on Contributions and Benefits. The early and deferred retirement adjustments to the $90,000 maximum limit for benefits under a defined benefit plan are now tied to the Social Security retirement age. Under prior law, the maximum was reduced for benefits beginning before age 62 and increased for benefits beginning after age 65. Now, the maximum permissible benefit will be reduced if payments begin before the Social Security retirement age, and will be increased if they begin after that age. (The Social Security retirement age, as defined in new Code Sec. 415(b)(8), is the retirement age in Sec. 216(l) of the Social Security Act, determined without regard to the age increase factor, and assuming early retirement age to be 62.) There is no longer a $75,000 maximum for benefits beginning at or after age 55—the dollar limit will be determined by regulations that are consistent with the reduction for benefits under the Social Security Act. However, if benefits begin before the Social Security early retirement age, the maximum dollar limit will be actuarially reduced. (In 1986, the Social Security retirement age is 65.)

Exceptions. Tax-exempt and governmental employers and organizations are exempt from the actuarial reduction provision and the change in normal retirement age. In addition, new provisions have been added to Sec. 415(b)(2) that allow a qualified plan for police or firefighters to continue to apply the under-age-62 and over-age-65 adjustments (and the $75,000 limit for benefits beginning at or after age 55), and to pay a cost-of-living indexed equivalent of a $50,000-a-year pension after 20 years of service even if the actuarial equivalent of the $90,000 or $75,000 limit would be less than the cost-of-living adjusted $50,000.

New Sec. 415(b)(9) provides that for commercial airline pilots, the normal retirement dollar limit applies at age 60 instead of the Social Security retirement age. *Reason:* the FAA requires airline pilots to retire at age 60.

The 100%-of-compensation limit of Sec. 415(b)(1)(B) has not been changed. Similarly, the 25%-of-compensation limit for annual additions to a defined contribution plan has not been changed, with one exception: contributions made by retired nonkey employees for retiree medical coverage are not subject to the 25% limit. However, the dollar limit for annual additions has been linked to the defined benefit plan dollar limit. It is now the greater of $30,000 or one-quarter of the dollar limit for defined benefit plans. Thus, the defined contribution dollar limit will exceed $30,000 when cost-of-living increases raise the defined benefit limit beyond $120,000.

Cost-of-living adjustments. The $90,000 limit for defined benefit plans will be adjusted for increases in the cost of living beginning in 1988. There will be no cost-of-living adjustment to the defined contribution limit until the defined benefit limit reaches $120,000. So for the immediate future (even after 1988), the dollar limit on annual additions will remain $30,000. If inflation causes the defined benefit limit to exceed $120,000, the defined contribution dollar limit will be one-quarter of the defined benefit limit each year.

Cost-of-living arrangements. The law now permits a defined benefit plan to maintain a "qualified cost-of-living arrangement" under which employer and employee contributions may be applied to provide cost-of-living increases to the primary benefit (Sec. 415(k)(2)). To qualify, the arrangement must not discriminate in favor of highly paid employees and must comply with all applicable qualification requirements of Sec. 401(a). For example, the right to the employer-provided portion of a cost-of-living benefit will accrue and vest along with the normal retirement benefit. However, a plan may provide that a participant will not be entitled to receive cost-of-living adjustments derived from employer contributions if the participant doesn't contribute the amount required under the plan or if the participant receives a lump-sum distribution of his or her accrued benefit derived from employer contributions. (Note, also, that a plan is *permitted* to include a qualified cost-of-living arrangement; it is *not* required.)

Participation in the arrangement must be voluntary. An employee may make an election in the year he or she attains the earliest retirement age under the plan or separates from service (or in both years). Adjustments must be limited to increases in the cost-of-living after annuity starting date. The increases must be based on cost-of-living indexes prescribed by the Treasury, but a qualified arrangement may provide that an increase for any year will not be less than 3% of the primary retirement benefit.

Key employees generally may not participate in a qualified cost-of-living arrangement. However, if a plan is not top heavy, officers may participate if they are key employees solely because they are officers (i.e., they are not 5% owners or in one of the other categories included in Sec. 416(i)(1) except Sec. 416(i)(1)(A)(i)).

Employee contributions to a qualified cost-of-living arrangement won't be treated as annual additions to the employer's defined contribution plan under Sec. 415(c), but will be treated as additions in applying the limit for a combination of plans under Sec. 415(e). Transfers from a defined contribution plan will be treated as employee contributions to the cost-of-living arrangement (Sec. 415(k)(2)(A)(ii)) and will not be treated as distributions from the defined contribution plan (Sec. 402(e)(4)(N)). Moreover, the "balance to the credit of the employee" in the defined contribution plan will not include any amount transferred to a qualified cost of living arrangement.

Limit on compensation taken into account. Under prior law, a top-heavy plan could take only $200,000 of an employee's annual compensation into account in determining benefits. There was no limit on plans that were not top-heavy. New Sec. 401(a)(17) limits the amount for *all* qualified plans to $200,000 for plan years beginning after 12-31-88. The limit, which applies for all purposes in testing for discrimination, will be increased at the same time and in the same way as the dollar limit for defined benefit plans.

Annual additions. Instead of including only half of an employee's contributions or the amount in excess of 6% of compensation in annual additions, as under prior law, Sec. 415(c)(2) now defines the annual addition to include *all* employee contributions along with employer contributions and forfeitures.

For purposes of calculating the defined contribution plan fraction in applying the combined plan limit of Sec. 415(e), the prior law will still apply in calculating the fraction for years beginning before 1-1-87. Thus, recomputation is not necessary.

Reduction of benefit limit. Under prior law, the defined benefit plan limit for an employee with less than 10 years of *service with the sponsoring employer* was reduced by 10% for each year less than 10. Under present law, the 10% per year reduction in the dollar limit applies to years of *participation in the plan* rather than years of service with the employer; years of service will still be used in computing the reduction in the percentage of compensation limit.

> **Example:** Jack Wilks, whose salary was $70,000, retires after 8 years of service with 6 years of participation. His maximum benefit would be the lesser of 80% of $70,000 or 60% of $90,000 = $54,000. Bob Keyes, whose salary was $70,000, retires after 8 years of service with 7 years of participation. His maximum benefit would be $56,000 (70% of $90,000 = $63,000).

Effective Dates: The new provisions generally apply to years beginning after 12-31-86. However, a plan will not be disqualified for any year beginning before 1-1-89 if it complies with the new law in operation and is amended no later than the end of the first plan year beginning after that date, and the amendment is retroactive to the first plan year beginning after 1986. [See ¶1141.]

For collectively bargained plans under agreements ratified before 3-1-86, the new provisions won't apply until the agreement ends or 1-1-89, whichever is earlier.

Compensation limit. As noted, the $200,000 limit on compensation to be taken into account in determining benefits will apply to benefits accruing in years beginning after 12-31-88. However, for collectively bargained plans, the limit will not apply until the later of the date described in the preceding paragraph or 1-1-91.

Tax on excess distributions. In addition to the Sec. 415 limits on benefits from defined benefit plans, new Sec. 4981 imposes a 15% excise tax on any "excess distributions" an individual receives in any calendar year from any combination of qualified retirement plans, tax-sheltered annuities, and IRAs. With certain exceptions, an "excess distribution" is the aggregate amount of retirement distributions an individual gets in a calendar year from all tax-favored retirement arrangements that exceeds $112,500 or 125% of the defined benefit plan dollar limit under Sec. 415(b)(1)(A), whichever is greater.

> **Example:** Retiree receives, in 1986, $77,000 from her defined benefit plan, $16,000 from a profit-sharing plan, and $27,000 from an IRA. Her total distributions ($120,000) exceed the Sec. 4981 limit ($112,500) by $7,500. She will have to pay an excise tax of $1,125 (15% of $7,500) in addition to her income tax.

The limiting amount will remain $112,500 until the Sec. 415(b)(1)(A) limit exceeds $90,000 (125% of $90,000 is $112,500).

Exceptions. The tax on excess distributions will be reduced by the amount, if any, of the tax imposed on early distributions attributable to the excess distribution (see ¶1123). Excess distributions do not include retirement distributions made after a retiree's death (these may be subject to an additional estate tax). Nor do they include retirement distributions paid to another person under a qualified domestic relations order if includable in the income of the recipient (these payments are treated as distributions to the person who receives them and will be subject to an excess distribution tax imposed on that person if the aggregate of distributions that person receives exceeds $112,500). Also excepted from the excise tax are amounts attributable to after-tax employee contributions and distributions which are not includible in income because of a rollover contribution.

Lump-sum distributions. If retirement distributions include a lump-sum distribution that is eligible for favorable tax treatment under Sec. 402(e)(4)(B), the limitation will be applied separately to the lump-sum distribution, and will be increased to 5 times the normal limit. In 1986, this will be $562,500 (5 × $112,500).

Postdeath distributions. Instead of an annual excess distribution tax, there is an additional estate tax equal to 15% of the individual's excess retirement *accumulation* when benefits are payable to an individual's beneficiaries after the individual dies.

Excess retirement accumulation is the excess of the value of the decedent's interests in all tax favored plans over the present value of annual payments of $112,500 (as indexed) for a period equal to the life expectancy of the decedent immediately before death. This tax may not be offset by any credits against the estate tax.

Effective Date: Distributions made after 12-31-86 except that for distributions made on account of a plan termination prior to 1-1-87, the provisions will not apply to distributions made before 1-1-88.

Accrued benefits. A transitional rule insures that a participant's previously accrued benefit under a defined benefit plan won't be reduced by the new limits or affected by the actuarial reduction for benefits beginning before the Social Security retirement age. The rule applies to a participant who was a participant as of 1-1-87 in a plan in existence on 5-6-86. If such an individual's accrued benefit as of the end of the last plan year beginning before 1-1-87 is greater than the new dollar limit, the accrued benefit is the dollar limit for that individual, provided that any change in the terms of the plan or any cost-of-living adjustment after 5-5-86 will not be taken into account. Moreover, an individual who is subject to the excise tax on excess may be able to elect instead to be covered by (1) a "grandfather" rule, which exempts from the tax benefits accrued as of 8-1-86; or (2) an alternate rule which increases the $112,500 limit. Under the grandfather rule, the part of the benefit accrued before 8-1-86 will be taken into account in determining whether there is an excess distribution, but the excise tax will be imposed only on the benefits accrued after 8-1-86. The grandfather rule is only available if accrued benefits as of 8-1-86 are equal to at least $562,500, and must be elected on a return for a year ending before 1-1-89.

If an individual does not elect the grandfather rule, then the amount of the distribution subject to the tax under the general rule will be applied to benefits accrued as of 8-1-86 by substituting for $112,500 the greater of $150,000, or $112,500, as indexed.

Act Sec. 1106 adds Secs. 401(a)(17); 402(e)(4)(N); 415(b)(2)(F), (G), and (H); 415(b)(8); 415(b)(9); 415(k)(2); amends Secs. 415(b)(2) and (5); 415(c)(1) and (4); 415(d); and 416(a); (c); and repeals Sec. 416(d); and Act Sec. 1133 adds Sec. 4981A, effective for distributions made after 12-31-86, except for distributions made on account of plan terminations before 1-1-87.

[¶1107] **Unfunded Deferred Compensation Arrangements of State and Local Governments and Tax-Exempt Employers.** Under Sec. 457, state and local governments may establish unfunded deferred compensation plans, under which employees may elect to defer receipt of current compensation. Provided the plan meets certain requirements, deferred amounts are not included in the employee's gross income until they are paid or made available. The new law extends the Sec. 457 rules applicable to unfunded deferred compensation plans maintained by state and local governments to such plans maintained by private tax-exempt organizations, and modifies pre- and post-death distribution rules for all such plans.

The maximum amount that can be deferred annually is the lesser of $7,500 or 33⅓ % of the employee's compensation (net of the deferred amount). However, the maximum deferral may increase to as much as $15,000 a year for the three years before the tax year in which the participant reaches the normal retirement age under the plan. The deferral limit is reduced by amounts contributed to a tax-deferred Sec. 403(b) annuity on behalf of the employee.

Offset for deferrals under qualified cash or deferred arrangements. The new law provides that the amount a participant may defer under an eligible deferred compensation plan must be reduced, dollar for dollar, by elective deferrals under a qualified cash or deferred arrangement (except a qualified cash or deferred arrangement maintained by a rural electric cooperative). An employee's elective deferrals under a SEP [¶1108], or deductible employee contributions to a 501(c)(18) [¶1109] plan, also reduce the amount the employee may defer under an eligible deferred compensation plan. As under prior law, amounts contributed to a tax-deferred 403(b) annuity are taken into account in figuring whether the employee's deferrals under an eligible deferred compensation plan exceed the limits on such deferrals.

Minimum distribution requirements. Under prior law, payments from an eligible deferred compensation plan that began before the employee's death were required to satisfy a payout schedule under which the benefits projected to be paid to the employee would be greater than 50% of the total benefits payable with respect to the employee. If the employee died before the entire amount deferred was paid out, any unpaid amount had to be paid to the employee's beneficiary over a period not greater than 15 years, unless the beneficiary was the employee's spouse, in which case payments could be made over the life of the spouse.

The prior law's distribution provisions for Sec. 457 plans permitted deferrals to accumulate on a tax-favored basis for a longer period than is permitted under a qualified plan. The new law modifies the distribution requirements for such plans to resolve this perceived anomaly. Under the new law, payments starting before the employee's death must be under a payout schedule providing for projected payments to the employee that are equal to at least 66⅔ % of the total benefits payable. Payments must begin no later than the "required beginning date," as defined in Sec. 401(a)(9).

If the employee dies after beginning to receive payments, but before the total deferred amount has been distributed, the remaining amount must be distributed at least as rapidly as under the original payout schedule. If the employee dies before beginning to receive benefits, the requirements of Sec. 401(a)(9) apply. Moreover, the entire deferred amount must be distributed to the employee's beneficiary over a period not greater than 15 years, except that if the beneficiary is the employee's spouse, benefits may be paid over the life expectancy of the spouse.

If distributions (pre-or post-death) are to be made over a period greater than one year, the distribution must be made in substantially nonincreasing periodic payments, paid not less frequently than annually.

Constructive receipt. Amounts deferred under an eligible deferred compensation plan of a state or local government are generally includable in the employee's taxable income in the year paid or *made available.* The new law provides that benefits under such a plan won't be considered as made available merely because the employee is permitted to elect to receive a lump-sum payable within 60 days of the election. This rule applies, however, only if the total amount payable to the employee is not greater than $3,500, and no additional amounts may be deferred under the plan with respect to the employee. Thus, if the total benefits payable to an employee exceed $3,500, and the employee has the option to elect to receive a lump-sum benefit, the entire amount of the benefit would be immediately includable in the employee's taxable income even though the employee declined to exercise the option.

Transfers between eligible plans. Under the new law, a participant in an eligible governmental deferred compensation plan may elect to have any portion of the amount payable to the participant transferred to another eligible deferred compensation plan of a state or local government or tax-exempt organization. The amount transferred will not be included in the participant's income solely as a result of the transfer.

State judicial plans. Qualified state judicial plans and certain other plans of tax-exempt organizations are exempted from the new requirements for eligible deferred compensation plans.

Certain existing deferrals and arrangements. Under a grandfather rule, Sec. 457 does not apply to amounts deferred under a plan of a tax-exempt organization which (1) were deferred from tax years beginning before 1-1-87, or (2) are deferred later pursuant to an agreement which was in writing on 8-16-86, and which provided for annual deferrals of a fixed amount or amounts determined under a fixed formula on that date.

Act Sec. 1107, amends Code Sec. 457, permitting tax-exempt employers to maintain eligible deferred compensation plans and permitting certain cash-outs and transfers, effective for tax years after 12-31-86; coordinating deferrals under eligible deferred compensation plans of state and local governments with deferrals under other plans, and modifying the distribution requirements for eligible governmental deferred compensation plans, effective for tax years beginning after 12-31-88.

Simplified Employee Pensions

[¶1108] Special Rules for SEPs. Under prior law the administrative costs and burdens of qualified pension plans provided a disincentive for small employers to establish such plans, in spite of the generous tax breaks accorded qualified plans. The new law changes the rules for simplified employee pensions (SEPs) to encourage the use of this low-cost retirement savings option. The changes further simplify the administration of SEPs, and add a special elective deferral feature for small employers.

Deferral elections under SEPs. Under the new law, employees who participate in a SEP (other than a SEP maintained by a state or local goverment) may elect to have contributions made to the SEP or paid to the employee in cash. Contributions to the SEP pursuant to such election are not currently taxable to the employee, and are not treated as employee contributions. Elective deferrals under a SEP are treated like elective deferrals under a qualified CODA, and are therefore subject to the same $7,000 cap on elective deferrals. Also, like elective deferrals under a CODA, elective deferrals under a SEP are exclusions from income, but are includable in the definition of wages for employment tax (FICA and FUTA) purposes.

The elective deferral option is available under a SEP only if certain conditions are met. First, at least 50% of the employees of the employer must elect to have amounts contributed to the SEP. Second, the employer must have no more than 25 employees at any time during the year preceding the year for which elective deferrals may be made. In addition, the amount deferred each year by *each* highly compensated employee, as a percentage of pay (the "deferral percentage") can be no more than 125% of the *average* deferral percentage of all other employees. Integration with Social Security contributions is not permitted for this test, nor can any nonelective SEP contributions be combined with the elective deferrals. Employer matching contributions conditioned on elective SEP deferrals are not allowed.

The definition of a highly compensated employee is the same as is applied for the special nondiscrimination test applicable to qualified cash or deferred arrangements under Sec. 401(k) [¶1116].

If the 125% test is not satisfied for a given year, rules similar to the rules regarding excess contributions to a qualified CODA apply.

When contributions deemed made. Under the new law, SEPs may be maintained on a calendar year basis, or on the basis of the employer's tax year. If the SEP is maintained on the basis of the calendar year, contributions made in a calendar year are deductible by the employer in the tax year with or within which the calendar year ends, and contributions are treated as made on the last day of the calendar year if made by the due date (plus extensions) for filing the employer's tax return. If the SEP is maintained on a tax-year basis, contributions are deductible for the tax year in which they are made. They are deemed made on the last day of a tax year if they are made on or before the due date (with extensions) for filing the employer's tax return for the tax year.

Participation requirements. Prior law participation requirements mandated that an employer maintaining a SEP make contributions to the SEP on behalf of each employee who had attained age 25, and performed services for the employer during at least three of the immediately preceding five years. The new law continues the service requirement, but reduces the age requirement to age 21 and adds a *de minimis* exception which permits the employer to decline to contribute on behalf of employees who do not receive at least $300 in compensation from the employer during the year.

Under the new law, the 100% participation requirement applies separately to elective deferral arrangements, and for the purposes of such arrangements all employees who are eligible to elect to have contributions made on their behalf instead of receiving cash are treated as receiving an employer contribution. Thus, an employer can establish a SEP funded entirely by elective deferrals and get 100% participation at no cost to itself (other than the nominal cost of administering to plan). Of course, at least 50% of the employer's employees must actually elect a deferral, and deferrals by highly compensated employees are limited by the actual deferrals of other employees.

Integration rules. Prior law permitted an employer to combine nonelective SEP contributions with employer OASDI contributions in testing the SEP for discrimination, provided the employer did not maintain another integrated plan. This permitted small employers to maintain plans which provided little or no benefit to rank-and-file employees, while contributing greater amounts on behalf of highly compensated employees than such employees could contribute to a personal IRA. The new law eliminates the prior integration rules, and requires nonelective SEP contributions to be tested for nondiscrimination under the new rules for qualified defined contribution plans [¶1110]. These rules permit a limited disparity between the contribution percentages applicable to compensation below and above the Social Security taxable wage base.

¶1108

Indexing of compensation limitation and de minimis threshold. The $200,000 limit on compensation taken into account in determining SEP contributions, and the $300 threshold for participation is indexed for inflation at the same time and in the same manner as the dollar limitation for defined benefit plans.

Act Sec. 1108, amends Code Secs. 219, 402, 404(h) and 408(k) to permit elective deferrals under SEPs, and makes conforming amendments to Secs. 3121(a)(5) and 3306(b)(5), effective for years beginning after 12-31-86.

501(c)(18) Plans

[¶1109] **Contributions to Sec. 501(c)(18) Plans are Deductible.** Sec. 501(c)(18) exempts from federal taxation any trust which is part of a pension plan funded only by the contributions of employees, provided the plan meets certain nondiscrimination requirements. Under prior law, employee contributions to such plans were deductible, through a fiction created by the IRS in *Rev. Rul. 54-190,* that the contributions were union dues. In 1982 the IRS declared *Rev. Rul. 54-190* obsolete, thus disrupting the historical treatment of contributions to Sec. 501(c)(18) plans. The new law provides a mechanism to allow deductions for such contributions, but subjects the deductible contributions to requirements similar to the rules for qualified cash or deferred arrangements, including the limits on annual elective deferrals and the special nondiscrimination rules. Thus, if an employee elects to make contributions to such a plan, the contribution is deductible up to the lesser of $7,000 or 25% of the compensation of the employee includible in income for the tax year. The amounts contributed to the plan reduce the $7,000 annual cap on elective deferrals under qualified cash or deferred arrangements and SEPs.

The election to make deductible contributions to a Sec. 501(c)(18) plan is available only if the plan satisfies a special nondiscrimination test similar to the test applicable to a qualified cash or deferred arrangement. If the test is not satisfied, rules similar to the rules applicable to excess contributions under a qualified cash or deferred arrangement apply.

Act Sec. 1109 amends Sec. 501(c)(18), providing for deductible contributions by employees under Sec. 501(c)(18) plans, effective for tax years beginning after 12-31-86.

Nondiscrimination Rules

[¶1110] **Nondiscrimination Rules for Integrated Plans.** Prior law rules against discrimination in favor of highly compensated employees were intended to prevent management groups from using pension plans as a tax-avoidance device to shelter their own income, without providing for coverage of rank-and-file employees under such plans. The requirements of nondiscriminatory coverage were intended to assure that such employees were not omitted from the plans, while nondiscriminatory benefit requirements were meant to assure that the lower-paid employees received meaningful benefits under the plans. Because it was felt that a plan designed in good faith to supplement Social Security should be permitted to qualify for favorable tax treatment, the prior law's nondiscrimination rules permitted plans which provided benefits which, when aggregated with Social Security, were nondiscriminatory to qualify even though plan benefits by themselves did not meet the nondiscrimination standards.

However, it has been found that Social Security benefits don't adequately replace the preretirement earnings of low or middle-income workers. Because these individuals are frequently financially unable to save sufficiently for retirement, tax incentives are provided to encourage employers to provide workers with additional retirement benefits under qualified plans. The prior law's rules on integrating qualified plan benefits with Social Security benefits permitted employers to eliminate plan benefits for lower-paid employees, thus undermining the original policy—to provide tax incentives for the establishment of qualified plans. The new law revises and simplifies the rules governing the integration of qualified plans and ensures that *all* employees covered by these plans receive some minimum benefit.

Permitted disparity in defined contribution plans. Defined contribution plans are plans under which no specified *benefit* is provided, but rather contributions are allocated to individual accounts established for each plan participant. Under prior law, employer contributions could be allocated first to the accounts of participants having compensation in excess of a specified amount (generally the Social Security taxable wage base) until a percentage of excess compensation equal to the OASDI tax rate was allocated. Only if any employer contributions were left after this allocation was completed would employees who had no excess compensation receive a share. Thus, for example, in 1986 a profit-sharing plan could provide contributions of 5.7% of 1986 compensation in excess of $42,000 (the 1986 taxable wage base) and no contributions with respect to compensation up to $42,000. Therefore, employees earning less than $42,000 would receive no contribution for the year.

The integration rules for defined contribution plans are changed under the new law. Now these plans are qualified only if the excess contribution percentage—the percentage of compensation contributed with respect to excess compensation—does not exceed the lesser of 200% of the base contribution percentage, or the sum of (1) the base contribution percentage and (2) the greater of the rate of tax imposed on employers under FICA (5.7% for 1986) as of the beginning of the year, or 5.7%. The base contribution percentage is the percentage of compensation contributed to the plan with respect to that portion of compensation which is not excess compensation. The amount specified in the plan as the integration break point is called the "integration level."

For example, if a profit-sharing plan provides for contributions for each employee equal to 10% of the employee's compensation which is in excess of the Social Security taxable wage base, the plan need provide only a 5% contribution on compensation up to the taxable wage base. On the other hand, if the plan provides for a contribution of 12% of excess compensation in 1986, it must provide a base contribution of at least 6.3%. Why? Because the permitted disparity cannot exceed the OASDI tax rate of 5.7%.

A defined contribution plan may specify an integration break point which is less than the taxable wage base, but not one which is greater. Moreover, such a lower compensation level will not be permitted if it results in discrimination in favor of highly compensated employees.

Permitted disparity in defined benefit plans. To satisfy the new law's requirements for integrated defined benefit plans, a plan must be within the disparity limits prescribed for excess plans or offset plans.

Excess plans. An excess plan is one that is designed to provide benefits (or additional benefits) based on the portion of an employee's earnings in excess of the earnings on which Social Security benefits are based (covered compensation). A defined benefit pension plan meets the disparity limits for excess plans if (1) the excess benefit percentage does not exceed a "maximum excess allowance", (2) any optional form of benefit, preretirement benefit, actuarial factor, or other benefit or feature provided by the plan with respect to compensation in excess of an amount specified in the plan for the year (the integration level) is provided with respect to compensation below the integration level, and (3) benefits are based on average annual compensation.

The excess and base benefit percentages are computed in the same manner as the excess and base contribution percentages are computed for defined contribution plans, except that the computation is based on benefits rather than contributions. Thus, the term "excess benefit percentage" refers to the benefits provided under the plan (expressed as a percentage of compensation) with respect to that portion of compensation in excess of the integration level specified in the plan. The base benefit percentage refers to the benefits provided under the plan (expressed as a percentage of compensation) with respect to compensation not in excess of the integration level. The maximum excess allowance is, for benefits attributable to any year of service with the employer taken into account under the plan, ¾ of one percentage point. For total benefits under the plan, the maximum excess allowance is ¾ of one percentage point multiplied by all the participant's years of service with the employer (to a maximum of 35 years) taken into account under the plan. The maximum excess allowance will in no event exceed the basic benefit percentage.

Average annual compensation is the average of a participant's compensation over the three consecutive years of his service with the employer which produces the highest such average.

Offset plans. Offset plans are defined benefit plans under which each employee is provided with a benefit which, as a percentage of pay, is nondiscriminatory. This benefit is then reduced, or offset, for each employee by the employer-provided portion of the employee's Social Security benefit. A defined plan is within the disparity limits for integrated offset plans if it provides that a participant's accrued benefit derived from employer contributions (Sec. 411(c)(1)) may not be reduced by more than the "maximum offset allowance". For benefits attributable to any year of service with the employer taken into account under the plan, the maximum offset allowance is equal to ¾ of 1% of the participant's final average compensation. The maximum offset allowance for total benefits is ¾ of 1% of the participant's final average compensation multiplied by the participant's years of service with the employer (to a maximum of 35 years) taken into account under the plan. The maximum offset allowance may not be, however, greater than 50% of the benefit that would have accrued without regard to the offset.

Final average compensation is the participant's average annual compensation for the three consecutive years ending with the current year or, if the participant does not have three years of service, the full period of the participant's service. Final average compensation is determined without taking into account compensation in any year which is in excess of the Social Security taxable wage base.

The new law directs the Secretary of the Treasury to prescribe regulations under which a defined benefit plan may use two or more integration levels. According to the Conference Committee Report accompanying the new law, the regulations will require that the permitted disparity with respect to each such integration level be based on the percentage of compensation up to each level replaced by the employer-provided Social Security PIA.

Reduction of maximum excess or offset allowance. If an excess plan has an integration level in excess of covered compensation, the ¾ of one percentage point factor in the maximum excess allowance will be reduced under rules to be prescribed by the Secretary of the Treasury. The factor will also be reduced with respect to any participant in an offset plan who has final average compensation in excess of covered compensation. These reductions will be based on percentages of compensation replaced by the portion of Social Security primary insurance amounts attributable to employer contributions.

The maximum excess or offset allowance will also be reduced, under regulations to be prescribed by the Secretary of the Treasury, for defined benefit plans which provide for unreduced benefits commencing before the Social Security retirement age.

Covered compensation. Covered compensation means, as under prior law, the average of the Social Security taxable wage base for each year in the 35-year period ending with the year in which the employee attains age 65. In calculating covered compensation for any year, it must be assumed that no increases in the taxable wage base will occur after the year of determination and before the year in which the employee attains age 65.

Railroad plans. The new law provides a special rule for plans which include employees of a railroad who are entitled to benefits under Railroad Retirement Act of 1974. These plans may be integrated, under rules similar to the integration rules for Social Security benefits, with the employer-derived tier 2 railroad retirement benefits and any supplemental annuity under the Railroad Retirement Act of 1974.

Multiple plans. Regulations are to be prescribed by the Secretary of the Treasury to prevent the multiple use of the permitted disparities with respect to any employee covered by two or more plans.

Benefits based on final pay. A defined benefit pension plan (including an offset or excess plan) is not considered discriminatory merely because it provides that the employer-provided benefit for any participant is limited to the excess (if any) of (1) the participant's final pay with the employer, over (2) the employer-provided social security benefit attributable to the participant's service with the employer. The Secretary of the Treasury is directed to prescribe rules for "normalizing" accrued benefits for purposes of this rule. This limit may not, however, be applied to reduce minimum benefits under the top-heavy rules (Sec. 416).

For purposes of determining the final-pay limit that may be imposed by an integrated defined benefit plan, a participant's final pay is the total compensation paid to the participant by the employer during the participant's highest year of compensation ending with or within the five-year period ending with the year in which the participant separated from service with the employer.

Act Sec. 1111, amends Sec. 401(l) of the Code to provide new rules for the nondiscriminatory coordination of qualified plans with OASDI and makes conforming amendments to Sec. 401(a) effective generally for benefits attributable to plan years beginning after 12-31-88. For plans maintained pursuant to collective bargaining agreements ratified before 3-1-86, the effective date is the first day of the first plan year beginning after the earlier of the termination of the CBA (or 1-1-89, if later) or 1-1-91.

[¶1111] Minimum Coverage Requirements. Prior law required that qualified plans be for the benefit of employees generally, rather than for the benefit of only officers, shareholders, and highly compensated employees. To assure that plans did not disproportionately benefit members of the prohibited group, minimum coverage requirements were imposed. To meet these requirements, plans had to either cover at least 56% of all the sponsoring employer's employees, or to cover a classification of employees the Secretary of Treasury found to be nondiscriminatory. The determination of whether a classification was nondiscriminatory was made on the basis of all the facts and circumstances surrounding each case.

New percentage test. Under the new law, at least 70% of the sponsoring employer's nonhighly compensated employees must be covered by the plan, or the percentage of covered nonhighly compensated employees must be at least 70% of the percentage of highly compensated employees who are covered. However, for a cash or deferred arrangement or for the portion of a defined contribution plan consisting of employee and matching employer contributions, an employee will be deemed to be covered under the plan as long as the employee is *eligible* to contribute under the plan. Thus, for example, if all nonhighly compensated employees of an employer are eligible to make elective deferrals under a CODA, but only 65% do, the plan may still satisfy the percentage test.

Average benefit percentage test. Plans which do not satisfy either of the new percentage tests will still be deemed to be in compliance with the test if they satisfy an "average benefit percentage test." A plan will, in turn, pass this alternative test if it satisfies the prior Sec. 410(b)(1)(B) classification test, and the average benefit percentage for nonhighly compensated employees (as a percentage of compensation) is at least 70% of the average benefit percentage for highly compensated employees.

The term "average benefit percentage" means, as to a group of employees, the average of each employee's "benefit percentage." The "benefit percentage" is the employer-provided contributions (including forfeitures) or benefits of an employee under a plan, expressed as a percentage of that employee's compensation (as defined under Sec. 414(s)).

> **Example:** Assume that an employer has 100 employees, 40 of whom are covered by a plan which satisfies the prior law's classification test. Of the 40, 10 are highly compensated. The average benefit percentage of the highly compensated employees is 75%; the average benefit percentage of the remaining 30 employees is 55%. Because the average benefit percentage of the nonhighly compensated

¶1111

employees (55%) is greater than 70% of the average benefit percentage of the highly compensated employees (75%) the plan meets the new fair cross-section test.

In determining the average benefit percentage of a group of employees, elective deferrals under a cash or deferred arrangement are considered to be employer-provided contributions.

Excludable employees. Under the new law, as under prior law, certain employees can be excluded for purposes of the coverage tests. Generally, excludable employees are those who are included in a unit covered by a collective bargaining agreement, and nonresident aliens with no income from sources within the U.S. If a plan is maintained under a collective bargaining agreement between air pilots and one or more employers, persons not covered by the CBA may be excludable.

Minimum age and service requirements. If a plan has minimum age and service requirements for participation, as permitted under Sec. 410(a)(1), and all such employees are excluded from participation in the plan, such employees may be excluded from consideration in testing whether the plan meets the new percentage tests and, for the purposes of the average benefit percentage test, whether the plan covers a nondiscriminatory classification of employees. For the purpose of determining the average benefit percentages, the plan can exclude only those employees who fail to meet the *lowest* age and service requirements of *any* plan maintained by the employer.

If a group of employees who do not meet a plan's age 21 and one year of service requirement is covered by a separate plan, the employer may elect to test that group separately. If the separate plan meets either of the new percentage tests with respect to that group, the group can be excluded from consideration in determining whether any plan of the employer meets the new percentage tests, even though other employees not meeting the age and service requirements are not excluded. The Conference Committee Report accompanying the new law indicates that a group of employees not meeting the age 21 and one year of service requirement may be tested separately even if *not* covered by a separate plan, provided the group is defined in a nondiscriminatory manner, solely by reference to the age and service requirements.

Aggregation of plans. As under prior law, an employer may designate more than one plan as a unit to satisfy the coverage tests, provided the designated plans provide benefits which do not discriminate in favor of the prohibited group. For purposes of applying the average benefit percentage test, two or more comparable plans may be aggregated to determine whether the classification test under the prior law is satisfied. The general principles set out in Rev. Rul. 81-202 to determine comparability are still used, but must be modified to reflect the new integration rules [¶1110].

Separate lines of business. Generally, the rule under prior law, that all employees of a controlled group of corporations, members of an affiliated service group, or trades or businesses under common control, are aggregated and treated as employees of a single employer for purposes of the qualification requirements is preserved. However, if an employer establishes to the satisfaction of the Secretary of the Treasury that the employer operates separate lines of business or operating units for valid business reasons, a plan maintained for employees in one line of business or operating unit may satisfy the coverage requirements separately with respect to those employees, provided certain requirements are met [¶1115].

Dispositions and acquisitions. Under special transition rules for certain dispositions or acquisitions of businesses, if an employer becomes or ceases to be a member of a controlled group or affiliated service group, the coverage rules will be deemed satisfied with respect to any plan covering employees of such employer during the transition period (as defined in the bill), provided that (1) the coverage rules were satisfied immediately before the acquisition or disposition; and (2) the coverage under the plan does not change significantly during the transition period (other than by reason of the acquisition or disposition). The transition period is defined under the bill as beginning on the date of the acquisition or disposition and ending on the last day of the first plan year beginning after the acquisition or disposition.

Sanctions. The new law changes the penalty for a plan's failure to meet the new qualification requirements. Such plans will remain qualified with respect to nonhighly-compensated employees, but highly-compensated employees will be taxed on the present value of their employer-derived vested accrued benefits and income on any contributions to the extent such amounts have not been previously taxed.

Minimum participation rule. The general rule permitting several comparable plans to be designated as a single unit for the purpose of the nondiscrimination and coverage tests might in some cases permit arrangements which discriminate in favor of the prohibited group. The new law resolves this perceived problem by modifying the general rule. Now a plan will in no event be qualified unless it benefits the lesser of 50 employees or 40% of all the employer's employees. Comparable plans *may not* be designated as a single unit for the purpose of satisfying this requirement, nor can the test be applied on a line of business or operating unit basis. However, for a cash or deferred arrangement, or for the portion of a defined contribution plan calling for employee and matching employer contributions, all employees who are eligible to contribute are considered to benefit under the plan whether they actually contribute or not. Employees who may be excluded under the general coverage rules (i.e., employees who have not satisfied age and service requirements, collective bargaining employees, etc.) may be excluded for the purposes of this requirement. However, if any highly compensated employee who is excludable is covered for more than one year, all employees must be counted.

The new law provides a transition rule, under which plans which do not satisfy this minimum participation rule may be merged or terminated. If a plan which fails to meet the minimum participation rule was in existence on 8-16-86, and there is no transfer of assets or liabilities, merger, or spinoff involving the plan after 8-16-86, the plan may be merged or terminated before the end of the first plan year for which the rule applies, and the excise tax on asset reversions will not apply. The present values of accrued benefits under the plans must be determined using the highest interest rate which may be used for calculating present values under Sec. 411(a)(11)(B). The minimum participation rule does not apply to multiemployer plans, unless they are plans established by unions for professionals (e.g., doctors or lawyers).

Act Sec. 1112 amends Secs. 401 and 410 of the Code to change coverage requirements for qualified plans. The cha~~~~~ ~~~~~~~~ ~~~~~~~~~~~ ~~~~~~~~~ years beginning after 12-31-88. ... tive bargaining agreements that were ratified before 3-1-86, the new law will not apply to plan years beginning before the earlier of (1) the date the last such collective bargaining agreement terminates (determined without regard for extensions of the agreement after 2-28-86) or (2) 1-1-91.

[¶1112] Tax-Sheltered Annuities Subject to Coverage and Nondiscrimination Rules. Under prior law, tax-sheltered Sec. 403(b) annuities—purchased for employees by tax-exempt charitable, educational or religious organizations, public schools, or state or local educational institutions—generally received significant tax advantages even though they were exempt from all of the coverage and nondiscrimination rules that applied to qualified plans. Because of this exemption, tax-exempt organizations could provide 403(b) annuities for any employees they chose, and thus could provide disproportionately large benefits to highly paid workers. To end this type of *carte blanche* for TEOs with respect to 403(b) annuities, the new law extends certain nondiscrimination rules to 403(b) annuity programs (other than those maintained by churches).

Nondiscriminatory coverage of nonelective 403(b) annuities. The new law provides that the Sec. 401(a)(4) nondiscrimination rules and Sec. 410(b) coverage rules for qualified plans also apply to any tax-sheltered annuity that an employer contributes to (so-called "nonelective contributions"). Thus, such 403(b) annuity programs must cover employees in general, rather than merely the employer's highly paid workers, and must satisfy either a percentage or fair cross-section test under Sec. 410. A tax-sheltered annuity meets the percentage test if either 70% of all nonhighly compensated employees benefit under the plan, or the percentage of nonhighly compensated employees who benefit under the plan is at least 70% of the percentage of highly compensated employees who benefit. On the other hand, a 403(b) plan that doesn't satisfy either of the preceding percentage tests still satisfies Sec. 410 if it benefits employees on the basis of a classification deemed by the IRS not to discriminate in favor of officers, shareholders, and highly paid workers, and the average benefit percentage for nonhighly compensated employees is at least 70% of the average benefit percentage for highly compensated employees.

The average benefit percentage for a group of employees is, for applying the fair cross-section test, the average of the employer-provided benefit of each employee within the group. For the classification test, the prior-law rule that the IRS must consider all of the facts and circumstances still holds true.

In addition to the percentage and classification coverage tests, 403(b) annuities (other than those maintained for church employees) must provide contributions or benefits that do not discriminate in favor of highly paid workers under Sec. 401(a)(4). An annuity program satisfies this requirement if either benefits or contributions for highly paid workers, when expressed as a percentage of their compensation, doesn't exceed a similar percentage for other employees. And contributions or benefits under 403(b) annuities may be integrated with the employer-provided portion of Social Security benefits as could qualified plan benefits and contributions under prior law. The rules governing Social Security integration are the same as the new rules for qualified plans [¶1110].

Qualified plans and 403(b) aggregation. A tax-sheltered annuity that, by itself, doesn't satisfy the preceding coverage and nondiscrimination tests, may be aggregated with a qualified plan maintained by the same employer to satisfy the tests provided both the plan and annuity provide comparable benefits and don't discriminate in favor of the highly paid. In applying the average benefit percentage component of the average benefit percentage test to a tax sheltered annuity, an employer may include all qualified plans in determining the average benefit percentages. Note, however, that this aggregation rule applies only for purposes of determining whether a *tax-sheltered annuity* satisfies the Sec. 401(a)(4) and 410(b) coverage and nondiscrimination tests; it is not applicable in determining whether the qualified plan satisfies these requirements. The categories of employees which may be excluded in applying the cov-

¶1112

erage rules to qualified plans may also be excluded in the case of tax-sheltered annuities. In addition, student employees of an educational institution who normally work less than 20 hours per week can be excluded.

Special rule for 403(b) annuities permitting elective deferrals. The new law provides special coverage and nondiscrimination rules for annuities permitting only elective (i.e., employee) deferrals, and for elective deferrals under 403(b) programs to which an employer also makes nonelective contributions. The general nondiscrimination rules continue to apply to nonelective contributions under the latter programs. Under the new law, a tax-sheltered annuity allowing elective deferrals will be discriminatory as to those deferrals unless *all* employees of the annuity sponsor have the option to make deferrals to the program. To insure all employees have the option of making elective deferrals, employers can't require minimum dollar or percentage contributions as a condition of participation other than reasonable *de minimis* contribution thresholds (i.e., a minimum yearly contribution of $300, 1% of compensation, or $25 monthly would be OK). Elective 403(b) deferrals include employer contributions under a salary reduction agreement (whether or not in writing) that are excludable from a worker's income.

> **NOTE:** Generally, for the special coverage and nondiscrimination rules that apply to elective deferrals, all employees (other than nonresident aliens with no U.S.-source income) must be included. This includes employees who haven't satisfied a program's minimum age or service requirements, or who are covered under collective bargaining agreements; such employees must be considered for purposes of the special elective deferral test. However, employees who participate in "eligible deferred compensation plans" (as defined in Sec. 457) may be excluded, and in applying the nondiscrimination tests to educational institutions, students who customarily work less than 20 hours per week may be excluded.

In addition, the Sec. 414(n) leased employee rules continue to apply for the special coverage and nondiscrimination tests. But the elective deferral rules apply only to the entity of the employer sponsoring the 403(b) annuity. For example, when determining whether all employees of an employer have a chance to make elective deferrals, the relevant workforce of a state university offering an annuity includes only university employees, not all employees of the state.

Exclusions. Tax-sheltered annuities for church employees are exempt from the new law's nondiscrimination rules. This includes a convention or association of churches, an elementary or secondary school controlled by such a convention or association, and certain "qualified church-controlled organizations." However, the Committee Reports that accompany the new law specifically provide that the new coverage and nondiscrimination rules apply to church-run universities and hospitals that sell goods or services to the public for profit and receive more than 25% of their support from certain specific sources.

Act Sec. 1120, relating to nondiscrimination requirements for tax-sheltered annuities, amends Sec. 403, effective for years beginning after 12-31-88.

[¶1113] **Minimum Vesting Standards.** Under the various alternative vesting schedules provided for in the prior law (i.e., 10-year cliff, 5-15 year graded, Rule of 45), the more mobile, shorter service employees were likely to terminate employment before vesting in any accrued benefits. Thus, the prior law did not meet the needs of women, minorities, and lower-paid employees. Accordingly, the new law provides for more rapid vesting than was required under prior law.

Vesting schedules. The three standard vesting schedules under prior law are replaced by two new schedules. A plan satisfies the first schedule if participants have a nonforfeitable right to 100% of their accrued benefits derived from employer contributions on completion of five years of service. The second schedule requires that participants be vested in 20% of their employer derived after three years of service, with an additional 20% vesting each year thereafter until the participant is 100% vested in the employer-derived accrued benefit after seven years of service.

Top-heavy plans. The prior law's vesting requirements for top-heavy plans are not changed under the new law. Thus, a top-heavy plan must still meet one of the two special vesting schedules applicable to top-heavy plans.

Class year plans. Class year plans, under prior law, were profit sharing, stock bonus, or money purchase plans which provided for separate vesting on a year-to-year basis. The new law repeals the class year vesting provisions.

Changes in vesting schedule. Under the new law, if a plan's vesting schedule is modified by plan amendment, the plan will not be qualified unless each participant with at least three years of service is permitted to elect, within a reasonable period after the adoption of the amendment, to have the nonforfeitable percentage of the participant's accrued benefit computed without regard to the amendment.

Multiple employer plans. The new law makes an exception for participants in multiemployer plans (within the meaning of Sec. 414(f)) who are covered by collective bargaining agreements. Under such plans a participant's benefit derived from employer contributions must be 100% vested no later than on the participant's completion of 10 years of service.

The new law also provides that a plan may require two years of service (down from three years) as a condition of eligibility to participate if the plan provides for 100% vesting on participation. The vesting provisions of the new law are also applicable to ESOPs [¶1172, et. seq.].

Act Sec. 1113 amends Secs. 410(a) and 411(a) of the Code, and Sec. 1012 of ERISA, to require more rapid vesting in accrued benefits, effective for plan years beginning after 12-31-88. However, for plans maintained pursuant to collective bargaining agreements which were ratified before 3-1-86, the new provision will not be effective for years beginning before the earlier of (1) the later of 1-1-89 or the termination of the collective bargaining agreement, or (2) 1-1-91.

[¶1114] Highly-Compensated Employee. Generally, qualified plans are prohibited from discriminating in favor of highly-compensated employees. Under prior law, it was not clear which employees were considered to be highly-compensated (except for the purpose of the special nondiscrimination rules for CODAs [¶1116]).

The new law redefines the group of highly compensated employees. Now, an employee is treated as highly compensated for a year if, at any time during the year or the preceding year, the employee (1) was a 5% owner of the employer; (2) received more than $75,000 in annual compensation from the employer; (3) received more than $50,000 in annual compensation from the employer and was a member of the top-paid group of the employer during the same year (i.e., one of the top 20% of employees by pay during the year); or (4) was an officer of the employer and earned more than 150% of the dollar limit on annual additions. If for any year no officer receives compensation in excess of this amount, the highest paid officer is treated as a highly compensated employee. The $50,000 and $75,000 thresholds are indexed at the same time and in the same manner as the adjustments to the dollar limits on benefits for defined benefit pension plans.

To identify which employees are highly compensated, all members of a controlled group of employers are treated as one employer.

The top-paid group of employees includes all employees whose compensation paid during the year is in the top 20% of the employer's workforce. Under a special rule, an employer may exclude certain employees in computing the size of the employer's workforce for purposes of calculating the number of employees who are in the top-paid group.

The following employees may be excluded in determining the size of the top-paid group (but not for identifying the particular employees in the top-paid group): (1) employees who have not completed 6 months of service; (2) employees who work less than 37½ hours per week; (3) employees who normally work fewer than six months a year; (4) except to the extent provided in regulations, employees who are included in a unit of employees covered by a bona fide collective bargaining agreement; (5) employees who have not attained age 21; and (6) employees who are nonresident aliens and who receive no U.S. source earned income.

Under this special rule, an employer may elect to apply numbers (1), (2), (3), and (5) above by substituting any shorter period of service or lower age than is specified in (1), (2), (3), or (5), as long as the employer applies the test uniformly for determining its top-paid group with respect to all its qualified plans and employee benefit plans.

> **Example:** An employer's total workforce is 100 employees, 20 of whom have not completed 6 months of service. None of the 100 employees is within any of the other excluded categories under this rule. Under the above rules for determining the top-paid group, 16 employees may be treated as included in the top-paid group. This is because the 20 employees who have not completed the minimum requirements for eligibility may be disregarded in determining the size of the top-paid group. The top-paid group cannot be larger than 20% of 80 employees (the number of employees who are not disregarded). Thus, the 16 employees of the employer that earn the highest compensation (including any employees who have not completed 180 days but who are among the 16 highest paid employees of the employer) are to be treated as in the top-paid group. Each of the employees in the top-paid group who earns more than $50,000 a year is treated as a highly compensated employee. Other employees (and any of the 16 employees earning less than $50,000) may also be a highly compensated employee under one of the other tests (e.g., officer or 5% owner).

The new law provides a special rule for determining which employees are highly compensated in any given year. Under this special rule, an employee who in the preceding year did not receive compensation in excess of $75,000, or was not a member of the top-paid group and receiving compensation in excess of $50,000, or was not an officer of the employer, is not treated as a highly compensated employee for the current year unless the employee is a 5% owner of the employer. This special rule doesn't apply to any employee who is among the highest-paid 100 employees in the current year.

An individual who was a highly compensated employee for the preceding year (without regard to one-year lookback or to the application of this special rule) remains highly compensated for the current year. The 100-employee rule is intended as a rule of convenience to employers with respect to new employees hired during the current year, increases in compensation, and certain other factors. If any employee is not within the top-100 employees by pay for the current year (and was not a highly compensated employee in the preceding year), then that employee is not treated as highly compensated for the year, but will be treated as highly compensated for the following year if the employee otherwise falls within the definition of highly compensated employee.

> **Example:** A calendar year employer has 12,000 total employees in 1990 and in 1991, and for each year 4,000 employees may be disregarded in determining the number of employees to be treated as the number in the top-paid group. Thus, 1,600 (20% of 8,000) employees are in the top-paid group. The employer's highly compensated employees for 1991 will include the following:
>
> (1) Any employee who at any time during 1990 or 1991 owned more than 5% of the employer;
>
> (2) Any employee who, in 1990, (i) earned more than $75,000 in annual compensation, (ii) was an officer and earned more than 150% of the dollar limit on annual additions to a defined contribution plan; or (iii) earned more than $50,000 in annual compensation and was among the 1,600 most highly compensated employees; and
>
> (3) Any employee who, in 1991, (i) was an officer and earned more than 150% of the dollar limit on annual additions to a defined contribution plan; or earned more than $50,000 in annual compensation, and (ii) was among the 100 most highly compensated employees.
>
> Thus, an employee who is not a highly compensated employee in 1990 (without regard to this special 100-employee rule) will not be treated as highly compensated for 1991 unless such employee either (i) acquires ownership of more than 5% of the employer in 1991 or (ii) both becomes an officer earning more than 150% of the defined contribution dollar limit or earns more than $50,000 in 1991 and becomes one of the 100 most highly compensated employees in 1991.

> **NOTE:** To figure who are highly compensated employees, "officer" and "5% owner" have the meaning set forth in Sec. 416(i) (relating to top-heavy plans).

The new law provides a special rule for determining the highly compensated employees in the case of employers who were incorporated on 12-15-24. Under this special rule, if more than one half of the employees in the top 20% of employees by pay earn less than $25,000 (indexed), then members of the top-paid group are determined without regard to whether they earn more than $50,000.

Under the new law, any family member (i.e., an employee's spouse, parent, and lineal descendants) of either a 5% owner or one of an employer's top-ten paid workers is treated with the employee as a single highly compensated employee in applying the special CODA nondiscrimination tests if the family member benefits under the CODA. For example, if the most highly compensated employee and his or her spouse both participate in an employer's CODA, then the deferrals made, and compensation earned, by each are aggregated for purposes of applying the special nondiscrimination test to the highly compensated employee's elective deferrals.

An employee who has separated from service continues to be treated as a highly compensated employee if the individual was a highly compensated employee when the separation from service occurred, or at any time after the employee attained age 55. Under this rule, an employee is treated as highly compensated if the employee was highly compensated at any time during the current or the preceding year. In addition, the Secretary is to prescribe rules to treat other former employees as highly compensated employees, if appropriate.

The Senate Finance Committee Report indicates that the Secretary of the Treasury will prescribe rules to treat an individual as separated from service if the employee performs only de minimis services for the employer during the year. Thus, an individual will not be able to avoid the rules regarding former employees by continuing to perform minimal services, and arguing that a separation from service has not occurred.

Act Sec. 1114, adds Code Sec. 414(q), defining highly compensated employee, and makes conforming amendments to Secs. 106(b), 117(d), 120(c), 120(d), 127(b), 129(d), 132(h), 274(e), 401(a), 404A, 406(b), 407(b), 411(d), 414(m), 415(c), 423(b), 501(c), 505(b), and 4975(d) and to ERISA Sec. 408(b) effective for plan years beginning after 12-31-86, except that certain of the conforming amendments are effective for plan years beginning after 12-31-87.

[¶1115]   **Separate Lines of Business: Compensation.** Generally, the rule under prior law, that all employees of a controlled group of corporations, members of an affiliated service group, or trades or businesses under common control, are aggregated and treated as employees of a single employer for purposes of plan qualification requirements is preserved. However, the new law provides an important exception to this rule. If an employer establishes to the satisfaction of the Secretary of the Treasury that the employer operates separate lines of business for valid business reasons, a plan maintained for employees in one line of business may satisfy the nondiscrimination requirements if such plan satisfies the requirements as to those employees. This exception is not available, however, unless the plan also satisfies the prior law's classification test, taking into account all those employees who must be considered under the general rule.

Safe harbor for separate line of business. A line of business will be treated as a separate line of business if it is a separate, self-sustaining unit, and (1) the line of business has at least 50 employees who do not perform services for any other line of business; (2) the employer notifies the Secretary of the Treasury that the line of business is to be treated as a separate line of business; and (3) the employer receives a determination that the line of business may be treated as a separate line of business. However, (3) is not required if the "highly-compensated employee percentage" of the line of business or operating unit is not less than one-half, nor more than twice the percentage of all employees of the employer who are highly compensated. The "highly compensated employee percentage" is the percentage of all employees performing services for a line of business who are highly-compensated employees [¶1114]. The highly compensated employee percentage of a line of business will be treated as not less than one-half of the percentage of all employees of the employer who are highly compensated if at least 10% of all highly-compensated employees of the employer are employed by the line of business or operating unit. An operating unit in a separate geographic area operated separately for a bona fide business reason will be considered to be a separate line of business.

The net effect of these requirements is to require that any separate line of business or operating unit include a meaningful proportion of highly-compensated employees and other employees. Thus, an employer may not circumvent the nondiscrimination rules by attempting to claim, for example, that substantially all highly-compensated employees are in a separate line of business or operating units from other employees, and then providing discriminatory benefits to the highly compensated employees. The separate line of business exception will, however, permit separate businesses, which are under common control (or even separate divisions of a single corporation) but whose operations are essentially unrelated, to plan retirement benefit programs on the basis of the needs of the employees involved in their operations without being required to coordinate with other businesses whose employees have different needs and expectations.

The separate line of business exception will not apply in the case of an affiliated service group.

Compensation. The new law adopts a uniform definition of compensation for purposes of the new nondiscrimination requirements. Generally, compensation is compensation for service performed for an employer which is currently includible in income. An employer may elect to include salary reduction contributions to CODAs, tax sheltered annuities, or SEPs as compensation, provided that these contributions are treated as compensation on a consistent basis. The Secretary of the Treasury is directed to prescribe regulations providing for alternate definitions of compensation. However, such alternate definitions will only be available to employers if they do not discriminate in favor of highly-compensated employees.

Act Sec. 1115 adds Secs. 414(r) and 414(s), to the Code to provide exception to general coverage rules for separate lines of business, and to provide a uniform definition of compensation effective for plan years beginning after 12-31-86.

[¶1116]   Cash or Deferred Arrangements. Under the nondiscrimination rules and contribution levels of the prior law, significant contributions by highly compensated employees were permitted without comparable participation by rank-and-file employees. Because a basic purpose of extending tax incentives to establish qualified plans is to provide for benefits to rank-and-file employees who might not otherwise save for retirement, the new law revises the nondiscrimination rules to better achieve this goal. At the same time, the new law tightens up the withdrawal provisions under the prior law to increase the likelihood that savings which receive favorable tax treatment are in fact used to provide retirement income.

Nondiscrimination requirements. The new law modifies the existing special nondiscrimination tests applicable to cash or deferred arrangements (CODAs) in several ways. First, the new law provides that the actual deferral percentage (ADP—the percentage of compensation deferred under a CODA) for an employer's highly compensated employees cannot exceed 125% of the ADP of the employer's eligible nonhighly compensated workers. Alternatively, the ADP of highly compensated employees cannot top 200% of the ADP of nonhighly paid workers, or the ADP of all nonhighly paid workers plus two percentage points, whichever is less. If a highly compensated employee participates in more than one CODA maintained by the employer, his or her elective deferrals under all the CODAs must be aggregated for purposes of the ADP computation. And the Treasury is authorized under the new law to prescribe regulations for the aggregation of elective CODA deferrals with employer matching contributions and qualified nonelective contributions. Qualified nonelective contributions are, for this purpose, employer contributions (other than matching contributions) which are not elective, and which are subject the same vesting and distribution restrictions as are applicable to elective contributions.

Aggregation for highly compensated. Under prior law, if any employee participated in more than one cash or deferred arrangement of the employer, elective deferrals under all the plans were required to be aggregated for purposes of the special nondiscrimination tests. The new law amends this requirement, and provides that only the elective deferrals of highly compensated employees must be aggregated. The Committee Report accompanying the new law indicates, however, that employers can elect to aggregate all employees under all CODAs and treat all such plans as one plan for purposes of applying the nondiscrimination test.

Highly compensated employees. The special nondiscrimination test for CODAs compares the average deferral, as a percentage of compensation, of the highly compensated employees with the average deferral of all other employees. Under prior law, highly compensated employees were simply the highest paid one-third of all employees. The new law redefines the group of highly compensated employees [¶1114].

Excess contributions. The new law allows CODAs which don't satisfy the special nondiscrimination tests to distribute excess contributions, plus earnings thereon. If the excess contributions (plus earnings) are distributed within two-and-one-half months after the year of deferral, the plan can avoid the ten-percent excise tax which is otherwise payable. A CODA will not be disqualified because of a failure to satisfy the special nondiscrimination rules, provided the excess contributions, plus any earnings allocable thereto, are distributed by the end of the plan year following the year for which the contributions are made. Such excess contributions may be distributed without regard to the provisions of the plan until the date the plan is required to be amended to comply with the new limits (Sec. 1141), and may be made without the consent of the participant or the participant and spouse. These excess contributions may be distributed notwithstanding any other provision of law, and will not be subject to the penalty tax on early distributions [¶1123].

"Excess contributions" means, for any plan year, the aggregate of elective deferrals by highly compensated employees over the maximum elective deferrals that would be made by such employees without violating the special nondiscrimination rules applicable to cash or deferred arrangements. To figure the amount of excess contributions and the employees to whom the excess contributions are to be distributed, the elective deferrals of highly compensated employees are reduced in the order of their actual deferral percentages beginning with those highly compensated employees with the highest actual deferral percentages. The excess contributions must be distributed to those highly compensated employees for whom the reduction is made in order to satisfy the special nondiscrimination tests.

> **Example:** Elective deferrals by the three highly compensated employees—Adams, Brown, and Carter—are 10%, 8%, and 6% of compensation, respectively. Assume that the actual deferral percentage limit on elective deferrals for the highly compensated employees under the qualified cash or deferred arrangement for the 1987 plan year is 7%. To reduce the actual deferral percentage for Adams, Brown, and Carter to 7%, it is necessary first to reduce the elective deferrals of Adam's percentage, which is the highest, to 8% (the same as Brown, who has the next highest percentage). Since the actual deferral percentage for highly compensated employees still exceeds 7%, it is necessary to next reduce Adam's and Brown's deferrals to 7.5%. This reduces this actual deferral percentage for the group to 7%. Thus, excess contributions of 2.5% of compensation (plus income) must be distributed to Adams; while .5% of compensation (plus income) must be distributed to Brown.

Other restrictions. Restrictions on withdrawals from CODAs are substantially modified. First, the new law provides that distributions may be made to a participant in a qualified cash or deferred arrangement on account of the sale of a subsidiary or the assets used in a trade or business of the employer, or termination of the plan of which the arrangement is a part. Distributions on the sale of a subsidiary may be made to a participant even though the participant has not separated from service with the subsidiary. However, distributions on account of a plan termination, or because of a sale of a subsidiary or assets, must be a distribution of the participant's entire interest in the plan. Moreover, distribution on account of a sale of assets may be made only if substantially all of the assets used in a trade or business of the employer are sold.

The Committee Report accompanying the new law indicates that hardship withdrawals under a qualified cash or deferred arrangement are limited to the amount of an employee's elective deferrals. Hardship withdrawals are not permitted from income on any contributions or from employer matching or nonelective employer contributions taken into account for purposes of the special nondiscrimination test and, as under prior law, are not permitted from a pre-ERISA money purchase pension plan. Prior law standards relating to the definition of a hardship continue to apply. In addition, the new law imposes further restrictions to prohibit discrimination. Under Sec. 401(k)(4), as amended, a qualified cash or deferred arrangement cannot require, as a condition of participation in the arrangement, that an employee complete a period of service with the employer (or employers) maintaining the plan in excess of one year of service.

Also, an employer generally may not condition, either directly or indirectly, contributions and benefits (other than matching contributions) on an employee's election to defer compensation under a cash or deferred arrangement.

Effective Dates: The CODA nondiscrimination rules are generally effective for plan years beginning after 12-31-86. The provisions permitting withdrawals on plan termination or sale of assets apply to distributions after 12-31-84. (The new rules relating to aggregation of deferrals under multiple plans and distributions of excess contributions are effective for plan years beginning after 12-31-86.)

For a plan maintained under a collective bargaining agreement between employee representatives and one or more employers ratified before 3-1-86, the amendments are not effective for plan years beginning the earlier of (1) the later of (i) 1-1-89, or (ii) the date on which the last of the collective bargaining agreements terminates, or (2) 1-1-91. Extensions or renegotiations of the collective bargaining agreement, if ratified after 2-28-86, are disregarded.

Generally, under the new law tax-exempt organizations and state and local governments are not permitted to maintain CODAs. However, under a transitional rule, the provision is not immediately applicable to any cash or deferred arrangement maintained by a tax-exempt organization adopted before 7-1-86, or a CODA maintained by a state or local government that was adopted by the employer before 5-6-86. The provision is effective for years beginning after 12-31-88 for such plans.

The prohibition against conditioning receipt of other benefits on an employee's election to defer compensation under a CODA is also subject to a special transition rule, under which a CODA will not be considered to be nonqualified because it is part of a "qualified offset arrangement" with a defined benefit plan if the arrangement was maintained by the employer on 4-16-86 and at all times thereafter certain conditions are met. For this purpose, a federally funded research center engaged in cancer research is deemed to be an employer. For such an arrangement, benefit accruals under the defined benefit plan are treated as matching employer contributions.

Act Sec. 1116, amending Code Sec. 401(k) effective as shown above.

[¶1117] Matching Contributions and Employee Contributions. To assure that employers do not shift too much of the retirement savings burden to employees, and that plans providing tax-favored savings benefits to highly paid employees provide comparable benefits to rank-and-file employees, the new law applies special nondiscrimination rules to employer matching contributions and employee contributions under qualified defined contribution plans, and to qualified defined benefit plans to the extent contributions are allocated to separate accounts on behalf of individual employees. These new rules apply in lieu of the usual nondiscrimination tests.

Special nondiscrimination tests. Two alternative tests are applied to matching employer and employee contributions to a qualified plan, one of which must be met for the plan to remain qualified. Under the first test, the contribution percentage for highly compensated employees must be no greater than 125% of the contribution percentage for all other eligible employees. Alternatively, the plan may satisfy the nondiscrimination test if the contribution percentage for highly compensated employees does not exceed the lesser of 200% of the contribution percentage for all other eligible employees, or such percentage plus two percentage points.

Example: Corporation M maintains a money purchase pension plan which provides for mandatory employee contributions of up to 10% of pay. Employee contributions are "matched" by the employer, on a dollar for dollar basis. No other contributions by employees or the employer are permitted. It is determined that for the 1987 plan year, the average contribution by rank-and-file employees was 3% of pay. Thus, the average total contribution for such employees (i.e., the contribution percentage) was 6%. During the same year, the contribution percentage for highly compensated emloyees was 8% (four percent employee contributions plus four percent matching employer contributions). Because the contribution percentage for the highly-compensated employees (8%) exceeds 125% of the contribution percentage of all other employees, (6%) the first nondiscrimination test is not satisfied. However, the second test is satisfied. 8% is less than 200% of 6%, and does not exceed 6% plus two percentage points.

Contribution percentages. The contribution percentage for a specified group of employees is the average of the ratios (calculated separately for each employee) of the sum of matching contributions and employee contributions to the employees' compensation for the plan year. Under regulations to be issued, an employer may also include elective contributions to a CODA in determining the contribution percentage. Nonelective contributions may also be included, provided they are nonforfeitable when made, and are subject to the same withdrawal restrictions as elective contributions under a CODA. However, if when these CODA contributions and nonelective contributions are disregarded, other employer contributions favor highly compensated employees in a way that violates the general nondiscrimination rules, the nonelective contributions cannot be used in calculating the contribution percentage. Thus, contributions used to satisfy one nondiscrimination test cannot again be used to satisfy the special nondiscrimination test. The new law requires the Secretary of the Treasury to prescribe regulations to prevent the multiple use of the alternative nondiscrimination test for any highly compensated employee.

Highly compensated employees are defined the same as for purposes of the general nondiscrimination rules [¶1114]. In plans which require employee contributions as a condition of participation, otherwise eligible employees who do not make contributions are treated as participants on whose behalf no contributions are made for purposes of the special nondiscrimination tests.

Aggregation rules. If a highly compensated employee participates in more than one plan maintained by the employer, all employer matching contributions, employee contributions, elective contributions, and if the employer so elects, qualified nonelective contributions made by or on behalf of such employee are aggregated for the purpose of determining the contribution percentage for such employee. Of course, the employer could decide to aggregate plans with respect to *all* participating employees, rather than just the highly-compensated employee, to test whether the special nondiscrimination test is satisfied.

If a plan subject to the special nondiscrimination rules is combined with another plan, also subject to the special test, for the purposes of satisfying the coverage requirements of Sec. 410(b), or the general nondiscrimination requirements of Sec. 401(a)(4), such plans must be treated as one plan for the purposes of applying the nondiscrimination test for employer matching and employee contributions.

¶1117

Excess contributions. Excess contributions are contributions by or on behalf of highly compensated employees which are in excess of the contributions which could be made for such individuals without violating the special nondiscrimination rules. If it is determined that the special nondiscrimination rules for employer matching contributions and employee contributions are not satisfied, the plan will be disqualified unless the excess contributions are distributed (or if forfeitable, forfeited) before the close of the following plan year. The rules for such distributions are generally the same as those applied to excess contributions to CODAs [¶1116]. Contributions which are forfeited may be used to reduce employer contributions or may be reallocated among other participants. However, no highly compensated employee who has been determined to have excess contributions may share in such reallocation.

The new law provides that excess contributions (other than those which are forfeited) may be distributed notwithstanding any other provision of law, and will not be subject to the additional tax on early withdrawals from qualified plans [¶1123].

Excise tax. The new law imposes an excise tax on the employer equal to 10% of the excess contributions (including excess contributions to a SEP or a 501(c)(18) plan). However, for this purpose excess contributions do not include excess contributions which are distributed or forfeited within two and one-half months after the close of the plan year in which the excess contributions arose.

Effective Dates: The provisions of the new law relating to matching employer and employee contributions are generally effective for plan years beginning after 12-31-86 or, in the case of tax-sheltered annuities, 12-31-88. However, a special effective date applies to plans maintained pursuant to a collective bargaining agreement. Under this special rule, for a plan maintained pursuant to a collective bargaining agreement between employee representatives and one or more employers ratified before 3-1-86, the amendments are not effective for plan years beginning before the earlier of (1) the later of (i) 1-1-89, or (ii) the date on which the last of the collective bargaining agreements terminates; or (2) 1-1-91. Extensions or renegotiations of the collective bargaining agreement, if ratified after 2-28-86, are disregarded.

Act Sec. 1117, amends Sec. 401 and Sec. 4979 of the Code to provide special nondiscrimination rules for employee contributions and matching employer contributions, and to provide for an excise tax on excess contributions, and makes technical amendments to Secs. 414 and 415, effective as stated above.

[¶1118]   Uniform Benefit Accrual Rule for Top-Heavy Determinations. Plans which primarily benefit an employer's key employees, and which are top-heavy under Sec. 416, must satisfy additional, tough qualification requirements. To prevent employers from avoiding the Sec. 416 rules by artificially accelerating benefit accruals for non-key employees, so that plan benefits for key employees never exceed 60% of all benefits and the plan never becomes top-heavy, the new law sets a uniform accrual rule for all plans for top-heavy (or super top-heavy) determination purposes. Solely for the purpose of testing whether the present value of cumulative accrued benefits for key employees exceeds 60% of similar benefits for all employees (90% in the case of determining whether a plan is super top-heavy), cumulative accrued benefits are measured by applying the "fractional rule" method of testing minimum benefit accruals.

Fractional rule accrual method. The fractional rule method of testing minimum benefit accruals is satisfied if the benefit accrued under a defined benefit plan is no less than the normal retirement benefit (with compensation projected to normal retirement age at present levels) multiplied by a fraction, the numerator of which is actual years of participation and the denominator of which is years of participation if the participant separated from service at a plan's normal retirement age. In essence, a normal retirement benefit is projected using current compensation; then, the minimum benefit accrual is the portion that represents years of participation to the total number of years from plan entry date to normal retirement age (ignoring service breaks). For example, if the projected normal retirement benefit is $1,000 and an employee has ten years of participation against a maximum 40 years to normal retirement age, his or her benefit accrual is $2,500 [$1,000 × (10 years/40 years)].

> **Example:** A defined benefit plan provides a normal retirement benefit at age 65 of 30% of average compensation for the high three consecutive years. Participant, age 40, with average compensation for the high three consecutive years of $20,000, has completed 15 years of participation by the close of the current plan year. A minimum benefit accrual of $2,250 [30% × $20,000 × $15/40$] will satisfy the fractional rule test. (The fraction numerator is years of participation; the denominator is the difference between 65 and entry age 25.)

Note that use of the fractional rule for purposes of testing benefit accruals applies *only* for purposes of determining whether a plan is top-heavy or super top-heavy. The new law does not require the use of the fractional rule for purposes of accruing plan benefits. Under an exception to this general rule, cumulative accrued benefits may be determined under any of the accrual methods described in Sec. 411(a) if the employer-sponsor uses that method for *all* plans which it maintains.

Act Sec. 1118, requiring that plan benefits be treated as accruing ratably for purposes of determining whether it is top-heavy, amends Sec. 416, effective for plan years beginning after 12-31-86.

[¶1119] Money Purchase Plans Can Now Allocate Forfeitures to Participants' Accounts. Even though money purchase pension plans are defined contribution plans providing individual accounts for participants, they must provide definitely determinable benefits as must defined benefit plans and thus must contain a definite contribution formula. Prior law also treated money purchase plans as defined benefit plans for forfeiture purposes, and so required that forfeitures under money purchase plans could not be used to increase participants' benefits, but instead had to be applied to reduce future employer contributions or to pay administrative costs under Sec. 401(a)(8). The new law limits the requirement that forfeitures not be used to increase benefits to defined benefit plans, and thus allows money purchase pension plans to reallocate forfeitures to other participants under a nondiscriminatory formula. These plans, however, are not *required* to allocate forfeitures and can still opt to use forfeitures to reduce future employer contributions or administrative costs.

Act Sec. 1119, creating uniform rules for forfeitures under all defined contribution plans, amends Sec. 401(a)(8), effective for years beginning after 12-31-85.

Treatment of Distributions.

[¶1121] Uniform Minimum Distribution Rules. Distributions from a qualified retirement plan, an IRA or a tax-sheltered annuity must begin no later than April 1 following the calendar year in which the employee reaches age $70\frac{1}{2}$. The distinction, under prior law, between a participant who is a 5% owner and an "ordinary" employee has been removed from IRC Sec. 401(a)(9). Under prior law, a participant who was not a 5% owner could postpone the beginning of his distribution until he retired after age $70\frac{1}{2}$. Now, distribution to any participant generally must begin at age $70\frac{1}{2}$.

Exception. The prior law applies to an individual who reaches age $70\frac{1}{2}$ before 1-1-88 if the individual is not a 5% owner in the plan year ending in the year the individual attains age $66\frac{1}{2}$ or any succeeding plan year. Moreover, an employee will not be subject to the excise tax for failure to satisfy the minimum distribution requirement because distributions are made in accordance with an election made before January 1, 1984 in accordance with Sec. 242(b)(2) of TEFRA.

Penalty. The 50% excise tax formerly imposed on underpayments of benefits from an IRA is now imposed on distributions from any qualified retirement plan. As under prior law, the IRS may waive the penalty if the underpayment was due to a reasonable error and steps are being taken to correct the underpayment.

Act Sec. 1121, setting uniform minimum distribution requirements, amends Secs. 401(a)(9), 402(a)(5), 408(d)(3), and 4974, effective for distributions made after 12-31-88, except as noted above.

[¶1122] Taxation of Distributions. The tax treatment of lump-sum distributions has been changed drastically. Capital gains treatment is phased out, except for certain distributions made to individuals who were at least 50 years old on 1-1-86 under a "grandfather rule." Capital gains treatment will not be available at all (except under the grandfather rule) for distributions after 1992. For distributions made during 1987-1991, treatment of amounts attributable to pre-1974 participation as long-term capital gain will be phased out. In 1987, they will all be treated as capital gain taxable at a 20% rate. In the following years, decreasing percentages will qualify for the 20% capital gain tax:

1988	95%
1989	75%
1990	50%
1991	25%

The 10-year forward averaging provision for LSDs has been changed to a 5-year averaging provision, with one exception: An individual who was 50 years old before 1-1-86, may use 10-year averaging, computing his tax using the tax rate in effect in 1986.

Check this out. An individual who gets a large LSD may owe less tax using the 5-year averaging computation rather than 10-year averaging. For example, on $550,000 taxable as an LSD, the tax would be $142,400 with 5-year averaging; $164,682 with 10-year averaging. Averaging is no longer available for a distribution received before age 59½, except for an individual who was at least 50 years old on 12-31-85.

Annuities. Benefits under qualified (Sec. 403(a)) annuity plans and (Sec. 403(b)) annuities will be taxable only when they are actually distributed. Under prior law, a beneficiary was taxable on amounts actually paid *or made available.*

The basis recovery rules for distributions from plans to which employees contributed have been changed.

• *Amounts not received as annuities:* Amounts received prior to the annuity starting date are now treated partially as taxable employer contributions and income, and partially as nontaxable employee contributions. Under prior law, the amounts received were not taxable as income until they exceeded the employee's total contributions. Generally, the nontaxable portion of a distribution under the new provision (IRC Sec. 72(e)(8)) is the same percentage as the percentage of the employee's nonforfeitable account balance that represents employee contributions. So, for example, under prior law if an individual had contributed $20,000 to his plan, he could withdraw up to $20,000 without tax liability. Now, such withdrawal would be taxable. If the employee's nonforfeitable account balance were $50,000 at the time of the distribution, $8,000 of the $20,000 distribution (⅖) would be treated as nontaxable return of investment and $12,000 would be treated as taxable income. Employee contributions to a defined contribution plan or to a separate account of a defined benefit plan are treated as a separate contract, and a withdrawal is not treated as partially attributable to employer contributions. However, it may be partially taxable as earnings on the contributions.

• *Three-year rule:* Under prior law, if a retiree receiving annuity payments would recover his entire contribution within 3 years, there was no tax liability until the full recovery was received. This provision has been repealed, except for employees whose annuity starting date is before 7-1-86.

• *Exclusion ratio:* In computing the exclusion ratio for annuity payments, the expected total return is determined as of the date of the payment. An employee's total exclusion is limited to the amount the employee contributed. If an annuitant dies before his entire basis is recovered, the unrecovered amount may be claimed as a deduction in the annuitant's final taxable year. Under prior law, if an employee outlived his life expectancy, determined at the annuity starting date, he could exclude from taxation an amount greater than he had actually contributed.

Effective Date: In general, the new pre-annuity starting date rules apply to distributions after 7-1-86 in tax years ending after that date. But this provision applies only to the extent that amounts received before the annuity starting date, when increased by amounts previously received under the contract after 12-31-86, exceed the investment in the contract as of 12-31-86 for a plan which on 5-5-86 permitted the withdrawal of employee contributions before separation from service. The post-annuity starting date basis recovery rules are generally effective with respect to individuals whose annuity starting date is after 7-1-86. The change in the constructive receipt rule for annuity payments is effective for taxable years beginning after 12-31-85.

Act Sec. 1122, relating to the taxation of distributions, amended Secs. 72(b) and (e); 402(e); 403(a), (b), and (c); and repealed Secs. 72(d); 402(a)(2) and 403(a)(2), effective for distributions after 12-31-86, except as indicated above.

〔¶1123〕 Additional Tax on Early Distributions. The new law establishes an additional tax on early distributions from any qualified retirement plan, qualified annuity, IRA, or tax-sheltered annuity before the recipient reaches age 59½. The tax is 10% of the taxable portion of the distribution that is attributable to employer contributions and the amount allocable to after-tax employee contributions and "matching" contributions.

Exceptions. The additional tax doesn't apply to any distributions prior to 3-15-87 and taxable in 1986 to individuals whose employment terminated in 1986, or to payments to an alternate payee pursuant to a qualified domestic relations order. Also excepted are distributions (1) that are part of a scheduled series of substantially equal periodic payments for the life of the participant (or the joint lives of the participant and the participant's beneficiary) or the life expectancy of the participant (or the joint life expectancies of the participant and the participant's beneficiary); (2) a distribution to an employee who has attained age 55, separated from service, and met the requirements for early retirement under the plan; (3) a distribution which is used to pay medical expenses to the extent the expenses are deductible under Sec. 213 (determined without regard to whether the taxpayer itemizes deductions); (4) distributions after the death of the employee; (5) certain distributions of excess contributions to and excess deferrals under a qualified cash or deferred arrangement; (6) dividend distributions under Sec. 404(k); and (7) distributions from ESOPs if received before 1-1-90.

Change in periodic payments penalized. If life annuity payments are changed before age 59½, the 10% tax will be imposed on the payments, plus interest for the period of tax deferral.

Conforming change. The 10% penalty for premature distribution from an annuity contract will now apply to 60-month payments (only life annuities will be excluded). And a change in annuity payments before age 59½, will subject the payments to the penalty tax that would have been imposed if the contract had not been exempt, plus interest for the deferral period.

Effective Date: Generally tax years beginning after 12-31-86; for Sec. 403(b) annuities, tax years beginning after 12-31-88.

Act Secs. 1123 and 1124, creating additional tax on early distributions, amends Sec. 72(m) and (q), changes Sec. 72(t) to 72(u), adds new Secs. 72(t) and 403(b) and repeals Sec. 408(f). The new rules will not apply with respect to benefits under a designation made by an employee before 1-1-84 under Sec. 242(b)(2) of TEFRA.

〔¶1131〕 New Limits on Employer Deductions. The carryforward provision of Sec. 404(a)(3)(A) has been repealed. In the past, if an employer's contribution to a profit-sharing or stock bonus plan was less than the allowable 15% of compensation limit, the unused deductible amount could be carried over to the following year, allowing a deduction of up to 25% in that year. No more. The maximum amount that an employer may deduct in any one year is 15% of compensation. The only exception is for limitation carryforwards accumulated for tax years beginning before 1-1-87.

Combination of plans. Two or more profit-sharing or stock-bonus plans are treated as one plan for purposes of limiting employer deductions (Sec. 404(a)(3)(A)(iv)). The prior limitation on deduction for contributions to a pension and a profit-sharing plan has been extended to any combination of defined benefit and defined contribution plans if any employee is covered under both plans (Sec. 404(a)(7)). Thus, the limitation—the greater of 25% of compensation or the amount contributed to the defined benefit plans up to the funding standard of Sec. 412—applies to combinations of defined benefit pension plans and money purchase pension plans. A money purchase plan that limits employer contributions to amounts deductible under Sec. 404(a)(7) will not be treated as failing to provide definitely determinable benefits. A Sec. 412(i) plan funded exclusively with individual insurance contracts will be treated as a defined benefit plan.

Excess contributions taxed. New Code section 4972 imposes a 10% excise tax on "nondeductible contributions" by an employer to a qualified plan. The tax, which is on the employer, is determined as of the close of the employer's tax year.

Nondeductible contributions are defined as the sum of (1) the amount of the employer's contribution that exceeds the amount deductible under Section 404; and (2) any excess amount contributed in the preceding tax year that has not been returned to the employer or applied as a deductible contribution in the current year.

> **Example:** Employer made an excess contribution of $100,000 in 1986. Employer pays nondeductible tax of $10,000. In 1987, employer makes the maximum deductible contribution. Employer pays a tax of $10,000 on the unreturned excess of 1986. In 1988, employer's contribution is reduced so that the $100,000 is deductible as a carryover. There is no tax for 1988.

Effective Date: Tax years of the employer beginning after 12-31-86, with the exception that unused pre-1987 limitation carryforwards will be allowed.

Note: The tax on excess distributions is explained at ¶1106.

Act Sec. 1131, relating to adjustments to IRC Sec. 404 limitations, amends Secs. 404(a)(3)(A) and 404(a)(7) for taxable years beginning after 12-31-86.

[¶1132] Excise Tax on Reversions. Although assets of a qualified plan may not be diverted to uses other than for the exclusive benefit of employees and their beneficiaries, amounts remaining after the plan is terminated and all benefits have been distributed, as a result of actuarial error, may revert to the employer. A new provision of the law (Sec. 4980) imposes a 10% excise tax on any such reversions (except from a plan maintained by a tax-exempt Sec. 501(a) employer).

Who pays the tax. The tax is imposed on the employer.

ESOP exception. There is no taxable reversion if assets of a plan are transferred to an employee stock ownership plan and invested in employer securities within 90 days of the transfer or used to repay loans used to buy these securities, and at least half of the participants in the terminated plan are participants in the ESOP. Any amount transferred and not allocated to the accounts of participants in the ESOP in the year of the transfer must be held in a suspense account and allocated in later years. The amount allocated in the year of the transfer must be equal to at least the lesser of the amount which may be allocated under Sec. 415 [¶1106], or ⅛ of the total amount transferred. This exception expires for terminations after 12-31-88.

Act Sec. 1132, relating to an excise tax on reversions of qualified plan assets, adds IRC Sec. 4980, effective for reversions occurring after 12-31-85, unless plan termination date is before 1-1-86.

[¶1133] Treatment of Loans. The new law makes it impossible for a plan participant to maintain a constant outstanding loan balance of $50,000 without income tax liability. In the past, a loan that bore reasonable interest and was repayable within five years would not be treated as a taxable distribution if the amount loaned and the balance of all outstanding loans to the participant from the plan did not exceed one-half of the present value of the participant's nonforfeitable accrued benefit or $50,000, whichever was less.

Present law. The $50,000 limit has been changed to $50,000 reduced by the excess (if any) of highest outstanding balance of loans from the plan during the one-year period ending on the day before the date on which such loan was made over the outstanding balance of loans from the plan on the date the loan was made. The effect is to reduce the $50,000 limit by the amount paid on any outstanding loan during the one-year period immediately preceding the making of a new loan.

Amortization. The law now requires level amortization over the period of the loan, with payments made not less frequently than four times a year. Under prior law, a loan could be repayable in a single balloon payment at the end of five years.

The difference. Under prior law, a participant could borrow $50,000 (assuming his vested accrued benefit was large enough), pay periodic interest but make no payment of principal for five years. Then, after repaying the loan, he could immediately borrow another $50,000. The outstanding balance would always be $50,000. Now, the participant would have to repay his original loan at the rate of $10,000 a year (for a 5-year loan). And since the $50,000 limit at any time is reduced by the amount paid on the outstanding loan during the immediately preceding one-year period, he would not be able to borrow more until after more than one year's payments had been made on the first loan.

> **Example:** Employee Adams borrows $50,000 from his profit sharing plan on 1-1-87. Under the terms of the loan agreement, Adams must pay $2,500 back to the plan every 4-1, 7-1, 9-1, and 1-1, beginning 4-1-87. As of 4-2-88, Adams has made 5 payments, totalling $12,500, leaving him with a balance of $37,500. The highest outstanding balance during the one-year period ending on 4-1-88 was $47,500, on 4-1-87. Therefore, the $50,000 limit must be reduced by $10,000 ($47,500–$37,500 = $10,000). This means that the total balance of all outstanding loans Adams may have cannot exceed $40,000. Since his outstanding balance on 4-1-88 is $37,500, he can only borrow another $2,500. If Adams waits until 9-2-89, he will be able to borrow another $17,500. Why? Because he will have paid $10,000 on the outstanding loan during the one-year period from 9-2-88 to 9-2-89, so that the $50,000 limit is reduced to $40,000. However, on 9-2-89, his outstanding balance is only $22,000; therefore he can borrow an additional $17,500.

Residence loan. The repayment period may be longer than five years only if the loan is used to acquire a principal residence *of the participant.* Prior law allowed an extended period loan for acquisition, construction, or rehabilitation of a principal residence for the participant or a member of the participant's family.

Nondeductible interest. Certain participants cannot claim tax deductions for interest they pay on loans from qualified plans. Interest paid by a key employee (as defined in Code Section 416) or any loan or interest paid by any employee if the loan is secured by elective deferral amounts in a cash-or-deferred plan or a Section 403(b) plan will be treated as nondeductible employee contributions to the plan.

Act Sec. 1133, changing the treatment of loans, amends Sec. 72(p), effective for loans made, extended, or revised after 12-31-86.

Other Pension Rules

[¶1134] **Deferred Annuity Contracts and Qualified Plans Put on More Equal Footing.** Prior law placed fewer restrictions on deferred annuity contracts than on qualified employee benefit plans, and gave employers the chance to fund substantial amounts of deferred compensation for employees while enjoying many of the same types of tax breaks available to qualified plans. In addition, because deferred annuities could be provided to a limited class of employees (e.g., the highly paid) rather than employees generally, prior law could be used to skirt the nondiscrimination rules that apply to qualified plans. The new law eliminates the bias in favor of deferred annuities and against qualified plans by providing that nonindividual owners of deferred annuity contracts (e.g., a corporation or trust) will be currently taxed on any increase in the cash surrender value of the deferred annuity over the contract's basis during the tax year. For these purposes, the "basis" of a deferred annuity equals the investment in the deferred annuity contract, i.e., the total amount of contract premiums paid minus policyholder dividends or other amounts that haven't been included in income. The owner of a deferred variable annuity contract—an annuity which battles the effects of inflation by combining the appreciation prospect (and depreciation risk) of a portfolio of common stocks with the guarantee against loss from longevity available through an annuity—is treated under the new law as owning a pro rate share of the assets and income of any separate account underlying the variable contract. Thus, the owner is now taxed on the unrealized appreciation of assets underlying a variable contract.

When an annuity is not an annuity. The new law achieves these results by providing that any annuity contract held by a person who is not a natural person (i.e., a corporation) will not be treated as an annuity contract under Sec. 72. However, a deferred annuity contract nominally owned by a nonindividual, but beneficially owned by a natural person, will be treated as being held by the natural person. Consequently, if a corporation holds a group annuity contract as agent for a group of persons who are the beneficial owners of the contract, the contract is treated as an annuity contract under Sec. 72. To prevent the IRS from running into problems in monitoring compliance with the rule that a deferred annuity cannot be used to fund nonqualified deferred compensation on a tax-favored basis, an employer will be treated as the holder of a contract that it nominally owns for the beneficial interest of employees.

Increase in annuity's cash surrender value over basis. The increase the cash surrender value of a deferred annuity contract over its basis equals the "income on the contract." This means a deferred annuity's net surrender value at the end of the tax year plus aggregate distributions under the contract for all years, over the investment in the contract (total contract premiums less dividends). The IRS is authorized to substitute fair market value for net surrender value if necessary to accurately reflect the income on a particular deferred annuity contract.

Exempt annuities. The new rules do not apply to deferred annuities acquired for purposes of estate administration, held as qualified funding assets by a structured settlement company, held by an employer with respect to a terminated pension plan, held by a qualified pension plan, an IRA or a 403(b) annuity, or immediate annuities.

¶1134

An immediate annuity is an annuity purchased with a single premium, which has a starting date no later than one year after the date of purchase.

Early withdrawal tax. The new law modifies the rules relating to the additional income tax on early withdrawals from deferred annuity contracts. Now, if a withdrawal is made from a deferred annuity contract before the owner dies, becomes disabled, or attains age 59½ a 10% additional income tax [see ¶1123] applies unless the withdrawal is part of a series of substantially equal periodic payments over the life of the owner, or the lives of the owner and a beneficiary.

If an individual commences receiving distributions before attaining age 59½ in a form that is exempt from the additional income tax, and the payment of the individual's benefits is later changed (before the individual attains age 59½) to a form that does not satisfy the conditions for the exemption, the Secretary of the Treasury is authorized to impose the 10% excise tax on all distributions under the contract received by the individual before age 59½, including amounts previously received in the exempt form. Moreover, the recapture tax will apply if the individual does not receive benefits in the exempt form for at least five years even if the individual is over age 59½ when the form is changed. The recapture will only apply to benefits received before age 59½.

If an annuity contract is owned by a nonnatural person (other than a qualified plan), there will be no additional tax imposed on an early withdrawal because there has been no tax benefit attributable to deferral of tax on the income on the contract.

As under present law, distributions under an annuity contract that constitutes a tax-sheltered annuity are not subject to a tax on premature withdrawals. Distributions under an annuity contract that is held by a qualified plan are subject to the additional income tax on premature withdrawals from a qualified plan.

Act Sec. 1135, relating to the tax treatment of deferred annuities owned by nonindividuals, amends Sec. 72, effective for contributions to annuity contracts made after 2-28-86, and applies to the early withdrawal tax effective for taxable years beginning after 12-31-86.

[¶1135] Profits Not Required for Profit Sharing Plans. In a major break with past law, the new law changes the rule requiring that employer contributions to a profit sharing plan be made out of profits. Now such contributions are not limited to the employer's current or accumulated profits. The new law applies without regard to whether the employer is tax-exempt.

Act Sec. 1136 adds Sec. 401(a)(27), effective for years beginning after 12-31-85.

[¶1136] **Collective Bargaining Must Be Bona Fide.** To prevent arrangements between employers and promoters of certain tax avoidance arrangements, whereby employers and their employees are superficially represented by agents in collective bargaining, but under which there's no good faith bargaining on retirement benefits, the new law clarifies that no agreement will be treated as a collective bargaining agreement unless it is a bona fide agreement between bona fide employee representatives and one or more employers.

Act Sec. 1137 amends Sec. 7701(a)(46), effective on enactment.

[¶1137] **Penalty for Overstatement of Pension Liabilities.** The law provides a new penalty for overstating income tax deductions for pension liabilities. Under prior law, if the IRS determined that pension liabilities had been overstated, the limit on employer deductions was recalculated using reasonable actuarial assumptions and the excess deduction was disallowed. Under the new provision (IRC Section 6659A), in addition to losing the deduction, the employer will be hit with a tax penalty.

If the amount of the deduction for pension liabilities claimed on an employer's tax return is 150% or more of the amount determined to be the correct deduction, a penalty is added to the employer's tax liability. The amount of the penalty is a percentage of the underpayment of tax, determined as follows:

10% if the claimed deduction is between 150 and 200% of the correct amount.

20% if between 201 and 250% of the correct amount.

30% if more than 250% of the correct amount.

> **Example:** Corporation (46% tax rate) claims $160,000 pension liability; correct valuation is $100,000. The $60,000 overvaluation results in an underpayment of $27,600 (46% of $60,000). The penalty of $2,760 (10% of the underpayment) is added to Corporation's tax in addition to the $27,600 it must pay to cure the underpayment.

De minimis exception. There is no penalty if the underpayment of tax is less than $1,000.

Waiver. The IRS may waive the penalty if the taxpayer shows that there was a reasonable basis for the deduction claimed and that the claim was made in good faith.

Act Sec. 1138, providing a penalty for overstating pension liabilities, adds IRC Sec. 6659A, effective for overstatements made after the date of enactment.

[¶1138] **Treatment of Certain Fisherman as Self-Employed.** Under prior law, certain fisherman were treated as self-employed individuals for employment tax purposes, but as common law employees for the purposes of determining whether a pension, profit sharing, or stock bonus plan maintained by the owner or operator of the boats on which they work was a qualified plan. Thus, such individuals were prevented from establishing Keogh plans. The new law provides that fisherman who are treated as self-employeds for employment tax purposes are treated as such for the rules on qualified pension, profit sharing, or stock bonus plans.

Act Sec. 1143, amends Sec. 401(c) effective for tax years beginning after 12-31-86.

[¶1139] Interest Rate Assumptions for Mandatory Cash-Outs. Prior law required that the interest rate assumption used to determine the present value of accrued benefits be no greater than the interest rate that would be used (as of the date of distribution) by the PBGC to determine the present value of a lump sum distribution on plan termination. This favorable interest rate requirement provided an inducement for employees to elect lump sum distributions rather than periodic payments of retirement benefits. Thus, the pre-retirement savings policy underlying tax incentives for qualified plans was subverted. Accordingly, the new law increases the interest rate assumption to be used in calculating lump sum payouts (and thus decreases the amount of such payouts). Under the new law, the PBGC rate must be used to determine whether the participant can be cashed-out involuntarily, and whether the value of the vested accrued benefit is less than $25,000. If the value of the benefit is less than $25,000, the amount to be distributed is calculated using PBGC rates. If the value is greater than $25,000, the amount to be distributed is required to be determined using an interest rate no greater than 120% of the interest rate (deferred or immediate, whichever is appropriate) that would be used by the PBGC (as of the date of distribution) on the plan's termination. In no event, will the amount to be distributed be reduced to *less* than $25,000 when 120% of the PBGC interest rate is used. As under prior law, for determining the PBGC interest rate as of the date of distribution, the PBGC rate in effect at the beginning of plan year can be used throughout the plan year if the plan so provides.

NOTE: The new law clarifies that a plan amendment adopting the new provisions will *not* be deemed to be a reduction in accrued benefits.

Act Sec. 1139 amends Secs. 411(a)(11) and 417 of the Code, and Sec. 203(e) of ERISA, changing the maximum interest rate assumptions to determine the amount of lump sum payouts. The amendment is applicable to distributions made after 12-31-84, and distributions required under Sec. 303 of ERISA but does not apply to distributions made between 12-31-84 and 12-31-85 if made in accordance with regulations issued under REA.

[¶1140] **Time Limit for 401(k) Opinion Letters.** No later than 5-1-87, the Secretary of the Treasury is required to begin issuing opinion letters with respect to Sec. 401(k) master and prototype plans.

Act Sec. 1142, effective on enactment date.

[¶1141] **Required Plan Amendments.** A plan must be amended to comply with all applicable provisions of the new law, but there is a long remedial amendment period—plan amendments must be made no later than the last day of the first plan year beginning on or after 1-1-89. To remain qualified, a plan must comply in operation with the new provisions as of the effective date of each provision (generally, years beginning after 12-31-86), and the amendments must apply retroactively to the effective date.

Treasury is directed to prescribe a model amendment which will allow plans to meet the requirements of the new law.

Collectively bargained plans. For a plan maintained pursuant to an agreement ratified before 3-1-86, the date for compliance with the new law provisions is the first plan year beginning after 1-1-91 or, if earlier, the first plan year beginning after the later of (1) 1-1-89 or (2) the termination of the bargaining agreement.

Act Sec. 1140, relating to plan amendments is effective on enactment.

[¶1142] **Regulations to be Issued.** Under the new law the Secretary of the Treasury is required to issue, not later than 2-1-88, regulations regarding:

- the application of nondiscrimination rules to integrated plans (Act Sec. 1111),
- coverage requirements for qualified plans (Act Sec. 1112),
- minimum vesting rules (Act Sec. 1113),
- definition of highly compensated employee (Act Sec. 1114),
- separate lines of business and definition of compensation (Act Sec. 1115),
- 401(k) plans (Act Sec. 1116),
- nondiscrimination requirements for employer matching and employee contributions (Act Sec. 1117),
- nondiscrimination requirements for tax-sheltered annuities (Act Sec. 1120), and
- tax on excess distributions (Act Sec. 1133).

Act Sec. 1141 Requiring Secretary of the Treasury to issue regulations before 2-1-88, effective on enactment date.

[¶1143] **Investment in Collectibles.** Sec. 408(m) of the Code generally prohibits investment of IRAs in collectibles, because it is considered too difficult to verify the existence of collectibles. The new law creates a limited exception to this rule and permits IRA investment in legal tender gold and silver coins minted by the United States. Such coins must, of course, be held by a disinterested third party, and cannot be held by the individual investor. The exception applies to acquisitions after 12-31-86.

Act Sec. 1144, amends Code Sec. 408 to permit IRA investment in certain gold and silver coins, effective for acquisitions after 12-31-86.

[¶1144] **Exemption from REA Survivor Benefit Requirements.** The new law amends the joint and survivor annuity requirements of the Retirement Equity Act of 1984 [¶1898]. These requirements are not applicable to plans:

- Established before 1-1-54, by agreement between employee representatives and the federal government during a period in which the government operated a major part of the productive facilities of the industry under its seizure powers; and
- Which substantially limit participation to individuals who ceased to be employed in employment covered by the plan before 1-1-76.

Act Sec. 1145, amending survivor benefit requirements of REA effective on date of enactment.

[¶1145] **Leased Employee.** Generally, a leased employee must be treated, for pension coverage, as an employee of the recipient of his or her services unless he or she is covered by a "safe harbor" plan maintained by the leasing organization. The new law changes the requirements of a safe harbor plan in two ways. The required contribution rate has been raised from 7½% to 10%. And the plan must cover all employees of the leasing organization other than those who are not leased to recipients and those whose compensation from the leasing organization is less then $1,000 a year during the plan year and each of the 3 prior plan years.

Employees covered under the safe harbor plan must receive the 10% of compensation allocation irrespective of the number of hours of service credited to the employee during the year, whether the employee is employed on any specified date during the year, and the participant's age. Compensation means the compensation used for Sec. 415 purposes, *plus* elective deferrals under a CODA or 403(b) annuity, and elective contributions under a cafeteria plan.

The provision determining when an individual becomes a leased employee protected by Sec. 414(n) has been modified. For purposes of the requirements, service is to include any period during which the employee would have been a leased employee but for the requirement that substantially full-time services be performed for at least one year.

If leased employees constitute more than 20% of the nonhighly-compensated workforce of a recipient, the law now requires that such employees be covered by the recipient's pension plan regardless of whether the leasing organization maintains a safe harbor plan. The Conference Committee Report indicates that under this 20% rule, "leased employees" includes all persons who perform services for the recipient both as an employee or a nonemployee (i.e., a leased employee) if such person would be a leased employee protected by Sec. 414(n) if all services had been performed as a nonemployee. "Recipient" includes, in addition to the employer or employers for which services are performed, other employers aggregated as affiliated or under common control.

The new law directs the Treasury to issue regulations that will minimize the recordkeeping requirements for an employer which has no top-heavy plans and which uses leased employees "for an insignificant percentage of the employer's total work load."

Effective Date: Services performed after 12-31-86. Modification of years of service applies to taxable years beginning after 12-31-83.

Act Sec. 1146, relating to treatment of leased employees, amends Sec. 414(n) and (0), effective as shown above.

[¶1146] Tax Treatment of Federal Thrift Savings Fund. Beginning in 1987, a government employee is allowed to contribute up to 10% of the employee's rate of basic pay to the Thrift Savings Plan maintained by the Federal government. These employee contributions to the Thrift Savings Plan are not includible in the employee's income for the year of deferral, but rather are includible in income when distributed from the Plan.

Act Sec. 1147, adding new Sec. 7701(j), effective on date of enactment.

Fringe Benefit Plans

[¶1151] Nondiscrimination Rules. Under prior law, virtually every type of fringe benefit plan was governed by its own set of nondiscrimination rules as to eligibility and benefits. The new law sets up a comprehensive set of nondiscrimination rules for certain statutory fringe benefit plans and cafeteria plans. These tests aren't exclusive. A plan must satisfy prior law concentration tests in addition to the new nondiscrimination tests.

Statutory fringe benefit plans. Plans specifically covered by the new rules include employer group-term life insurance plans (under

Section 79) and accident and health plans (under Section 105(e)), whether insured or self insured. Employers can elect to apply the new rules to qualified group legal services plans (under Section 120(b)), educational assistance programs (under Section 127(b)), and dependent care assistance programs (under Section 129(d)). Once the election is made, the plan will be considered as meeting the nondiscrimination contained in that section, if the plan meets the new comprehensive rules. Note that the group legal services and educational assistance exclusions are scheduled to expire before the effective date of the new rules.

Income inclusion. Under the new law, except as provided in regs, all employees must include in income an amount equal to the employee's employer-provided benefit under a statutory fringe benefit plan unless the plan is in writing, the employees' rights under the plan are legally enforceable, employees are given reasonable notification of benefits available under the plan, the plan is maintained for the exclusive benefit of employees, and the plan was established with the intention of being maintained indefinitely. In addition to applying to the previously mentioned statutory fringe benefits, these requirements apply to qualified tuition reduction programs (under Section 117(d)), cafeteria plans (under Section 125), fringe benefit programs providing no additional cost services, employee discounts, or employer provided operating facilities (under Section 132), and welfare benefit plans (under Section 505). The employer-provided benefit, for these purposes, is the value of benefits provided to the employee. If the plan doesn't meet these requirements, the income inclusion precludes a separate inclusion under the nondiscrimination rules.

A highly compensated employee who participates in a discriminatory statutory fringe benefit plan which meets the requirements of the previous paragraph must include in gross income, according to the statute, only the discriminatory portion of the coverage provided (if a group-term life insurance or accident and health plan), or the discriminatory portion of the benefits provided (if another type of plan), provided such value is timely reported. (According to the Conference report, it's the discriminatory portion of benefits actually provided for both groups.) Otherwise, it's the entire benefit. A plan will be considered discriminatory unless it passes both the nondiscriminatory eligibility test and the nondiscriminatory benefits test.

AMOUNT INCLUDABLE: The amount includable is the "excess benefit," which is the excess of the employer-provided benefit over the "highest permitted benefit." The highest permitted benefit is determined by reducing the nontaxable benefits of highly compensated employees (beginning with the employee with the greatest nontaxable benefits) until such plan would not be treated as a discriminatory benefit plan. For these purposes, plans of the same type are to be aggregated. In addition, for group-term life insurance, the value of the discriminatory excess is the greater of the cost of coverage (under Section 79(c)) or the actual cost of coverage for an employee age 40. The excess benefit amount is includable in the employee's tax year with or within which the plan year ends. Note that the employer-provided benefit generally includes benefits provided under salary reduction (except for the 90%/50% arm of the eligibility test).

Highly compensated. A highly compensated employee, for purposes of all employee benefit nondiscrimination rules, is the same as under the new uniform rules (new Sec. 414(q)) [¶1114]. Generally, this includes employees who (1) are 5% owners (under Sec. 416(i)); (2) earn more than $75,000 in annual compensation, (3) earn more than $50,000 in annual compensation and whose compensation is in the top 20% of all of the employer's employees, and (4) are officers of the employer (under Sec. 416(i)) and receive more than 150% of the dollar limit on annual additions to a defined contribution plan. It also includes former employees who were highly compensated at the time of separation from service or after age 55. Employees who are excluded from coverage under the plan [see ¶1155] are also excluded from determining who is highly compensated. Unlike the general rules, a family member of a highly compensated employee covered by a separate accident or health plan isn't treated as the employee.

Effective Date: The new nondiscrimination provisions are effective for plan years beginning after 12-31-87. However, if regs aren't issued by that time, the rules are effective for the earlier of plan years beginning at least three months after the regs are issued or plan years beginning after 12-31-88. For collective bargaining agreements ratified before 3-1-86, the new rules won't apply before the earlier of the termination of such agreements (without regard to extensions after that date) or 1-1-91. For church plans (under Section 414(e)(3)) maintaining insured accident and health plans, the new rules apply to years beginning after 12-31-88.

Act Sec. 1151(a), establishing the new nondiscrimination rules, adds new Secs. 89(a)-(c), and (k) generally effective for plan years beginning after 12-31-87 and as shown above.

[¶1152] Group-Term Life Insurance and Accident and Health Plans. Group term life insurance plans and accident and health plans (whether or not self-insured) and, if the employer elects, dependent care assistants, educational, assistance, and group legal service plans, won't be considered discriminatory if both a nondiscrimination eligibility test and a nondiscrimination benefits test are met.

Eligibility test. A statutory fringe benefit plan must meet a three-part eligibility test. First, at least 50% of all eligible employees must not be highly compensated. However, if the percentage of highly compensated employees who are eligible isn't greater than the percentage of nonhighly compensated employees who are eligible, the 50% requirement would be considered met.

Second, at least 90% of the nonhighly compensateds must be eligible and would receive a benefit that's at least 50% of the value of the largest benefit available under all such plans to any highly compensated employee. Special rules define when such plans are aggregated. In addition, coverage of employees may be tested separately from dependents.

Third, a plan can't contain any provision relating to eligibility which (by its terms or otherwise) discriminates in favor of highly compensated employees.

Benefits test. A statutory fringe benefit plan meets the benefit test if the average employer-provided benefit received over the plan year by nonhighly compensated employees under all plans is at least 75% of the average such benefit received by highly compensated employees. The average employer-provided benefit for highly compensated is equal to the aggregate of employer-provided benefits received by such employees divided by the number of such employees. The figure for nonhighly compensated employees is determined in a similar way.

In applying the test to health plans, an employer may elect to disregard any employee if the employee and his or her spouse or dependents are covered by a health plan maintained by another employer that provides core benefits (defined in ¶1155). In addition, the employer can elect to apply the benefits test separately to employees and dependents not covered by plans of other employees as opposed to those that are covered by such plans.

If the employer makes either election, the employer must get a sworn statement attesting to the existence of a spouse and dependents, and core benefits under another plan. In the absence of a statement, a nonhighly compensated employee and his or her dependents will be treated as not covered by another plan while a highly compensated employee will be treated as not having dependents and as being covered by another employer's plan.

For purposes of the election to disregard employees, an employer can't elect to disregard a highly compensated employer (or his or her spouse or dependents) who receives health plan benefits that are more than 133 1/3% of the average employer-provided benefit of nonhighly compensated employees.

NOTE: The new law contains the prior law rule that group-term life insurance benefits won't be treated as discriminatory if the amount of coverage bears a uniform relationship to compensation. The nondiscrimination rules can be applied to the value of such coverage expressed as a percentage of compensation, with the same cap on includable compensation that's applicable to qualified plans.

Alternative test. A group-term life insurance or an accident or health plan will be considered to meet both the eligibility test and the benefits test if at least 80% of the nonhighly compensated employees are covered by the plan and the plan doesn't discriminate (by its terms or otherwise) in favor of the highly compensated employees.

Aggregation rules. For health plans, an employer may treat a group of comparable plans as a single plan for purposes of the eligibility and alternative tests. Such plans are comparable if the smallest benefit available is at least 95% of the largest benefit available to any participant under any plan.

For other plans, the employer can elect to aggregate different types of statutory employee benefit plans, as long as all plans of the same type are included in the aggregation.

Accident or health plans. For purposes of the 50% arm of the eligibility test and the 80% alternative test, if the employer's health plan provides family coverage, the employer can apply the tests separately to the coverage for employees and the coverage for spouses and dependents as if two different plans.

A health plan's benefits may be integrated with benefits provided under Medicare, or any other law, or under any other health plans covering the employee or the employee's family as long as it does so in a manner that doesn't discriminate in favor of the highly compensated.

An exception is provided to the equal coverage requirement for employees who normally work less than 30 hours a week. A plan won't be considered discriminatory merely because an employer provided benefit is proportionately reduced for employees who normally work less than 30 hours a week. The exception applies only if the average workweek of nonhighly compensated employees is 30 hours or more. The Conference Committee report provides safe harbors for adjustments to such benefits.

The Conference Committee authorizes Treasury to disregard certain state-mandated benefits when applying the nondiscrimination tests to accident and health plans.

Disability benefits. A disability benefit plan providing an excludable benefit won't fail the nondiscrimination rules merely because benefits bear a uniform relationship to total or regular compensation or benefits are integrated (but not so as to discriminate in favor of the highly compensated) with benefits provided under any law or any other accident plan covering the employee.

Act Sec. 1151(a) , relating to nondiscrimination benefits and eligibility tests adds Secs. 89(d)(g), effective generally for plan years beginning after 12-31-87, and as shown at ¶1151.

[¶1153] **Cafeteria Plans and Other Plans.** The new law makes a number of changes to the cafeteria plan rules. The new rules make it clear that any qualified benefit (as defined in the new law) provided to a highly compensated under a discriminatory plan (as to eligibility) is included in the gross income of such employee. The prior law nondiscrimination benefits test is gone. However, the prior law concentration tests of benefits for key employees is retained. The end result is that in addition to meeting the cafeteria plan rules, each benefit must meet any separate nondiscrimination or concentration tests applicable to it.

The new law also makes it clear that the rules apply to plans that don't offer cash or taxable benefits.

The new law also does the following:

- Permits full-time life insurance sales representatives to be treated as employees for certain cafeteria or plan purposes;

- Allows employees of educational organizations to elect post-retirement life insurance in cafeteria plans;

- Clarifies that salary reduction under cafeteria plans is excluded from FICA and FUTA wage basis; and

- Applies the new uniform definitions of highly compensated employee, excludable employee, and employer to cafeteria plans.

Other plans. A dependent care assistance program, for which the employer didn't elect statutory fringe benefit treatment, is subject to a special benefits test. A plan will meet the requirements if the average benefit provided under all such plans of the employer to non-highly compensated employees is at least 55% of the benefits provided to highly compensated employees. For purposes of providing benefits under a salary reduction agreement, employees with compensation (under Section 415(q)(7)) below $25,000 are disregarded. For these purposes, the average benefit for nonhighly compensated employees is equal to the value of benefits provided on their behalf divided by the number of nonhighly compensated. The average benefit for the highly compensated is computed separately.

In addition, dependent care assistance programs must meet the prior law Section 129(d)(4) concentration test limiting the benefits available to 5% owners.

Act Sec. 1151(d), relating to cafeteria plans, amends Sec. 125, generally effective for plan years beginning after 12-31-87 and as shown in ¶1151. Act Sec. 1166, relating to certain full-time insurance salespeople, amends Sec. 7701(a)(20), effective for years beginning after 12-31-85. Act Sec. 1151(d)(2), relating to FICA and FUTA rules amend Secs. 3121(a)(5), 3306(b)(5), and 209(e) of the Social Security Act, effective for taxable years beginning after 12-31-83. Act Sec. 1151(f), dealing with dependent care assistance programs amends Sec. 129, effective as shown in ¶1151.

[¶1154] Line of Business Exception. If an employer establishes to the Treasury's satisfaction that separate lines of business or operating units are operated for bona fide business reasons, the employer may apply the eligibility, benefit, and alternative tests separately to each line or unit. However, the plan must still satisfy a "reasonable classification test" requirements, on an employer-wide basis. The new law contains a rule (new Sec. 414(r)) under which a separate line of business will be treated as operated for bona fide business purposes.

A separate line of business or operating unit will be considered operated for bona fide business reasons if

- the line or unit has at least 50 employees,
- the employer notifies Treasury that such line is being treated as separate, and
- such line gets Treasury approval or meets Treasury guidelines.

A special safe harbor exempts a line of business from the last requirement if the percentage of highly compensated employees (compared to total employees) in the line of business is not less than 50% nor more than 200% of the percentage which highly compensated employees are of all employees. The 50% requirement will be met if at least 10% of all highly compensated employees of the employer perform services solely for such line of business.

Special rules apply to allocating headquarters personnel, affiliated service groups, and units in separate geographical areas.

Act Sec. 1151(a), dealing with nondiscrimination rules, adds new Sec. 89(g)(5), containing the line of business exception generally effective for plan years ending after 12-31-87 and as shown at ¶1151.

[¶1155] Excludable Employees. Under the new law, certain classes of employees may be disregarded in applying the nondiscrimination rules to any employee benefit plan if neither the plan, nor any other plan of the same type, provides eligibility for any employee in the class. If one employee is covered, then all such employees are included for purposes of the nondiscrimination rules. For purposes of cafeteria plans, all benefits under the plan will be treated as provided under plans of the same type. These classes are considered "excludable employees" for purposes of all employee benefit nondiscrimination rules. Those classes include:

- Employees who haven't completed one year of service (6 months of service for core benefits under health plans), or shorter if specified in the plan. An employee can be excluded until the first day of the first month beginning after the completion of the initial service requirement. Note that noncore benefits include dental, vision, psychological, and orthodontia expenses and elective cosmetic surgery.

• Employees working less than 17½ hours a week (or shorter if specified in the plan).

• Employees working not more than six months during any year (or shorter if specified in the plan).

• Employees who haven't attained age 21 (or lower, if specified in the plan).

• Employees covered by a collective bargaining agreement and the benefit in question was the subject of good faith bargaining, and

• Nonresident aliens with no U.S. earned income. For this class, the fact that some members may benefit won't make the plan discriminatory.

Line of business. If the employer elects to apply the rules on a line of business basis, the excluded employees are determined on such line of business basis.

Separate testing. Employees excludable on the basis of the age and service requirements may be tested separately even if some or all of the excludable employees are covered by a plan that also covers nonexcludable employees. Alternatively an employer may elect to test one group of excludable employees separately without testing all excludable employees separately if such group is defined in a nondiscriminatory manner solely by reference to the age and service requirements.

Aggregation. If an employer aggregates plans of different types for the benefits test, the excludable employee rules apply as if the same type. As a result, the lowest age and service requirement apply. The same is true for all other requirements.

Other plans. The definition of excludable employee also applies to tuition reduction plans, educational assistance programs, and *de minimis* fringe benefits.

Act Sec. 1151(a), relating to the nondiscrimination rules, adds new Sec. 89(h), defining excludable employees, generally effective for plan years beginning after 12-31-87 and as shown at ¶1151.

[¶1156] **Special Rules.** *Aggregation.* If an accident or health plan, alone, would fail the 50% arm of the benefit test or the alternative 80% test, the plan may be aggregated with one or more plans providing the same type of benefit, provided the average value of employer-provided coverage per employee in each such other plan is at least 95% of that in the failing plan.

Options. Each option or different benefit offered under an accident or health plan or group life insurance plan is treated as a separate plan. However, group-term life insurance that varies in proportion to salary isn't treated as a different option.

Former employees. Under regs to be issued, rules similar to the nondiscriminatory coverage rules are to apply separately to former employees. The Senate Committee Report sets forth reasonable restrictions (retirement, disability) on which to base such rules.

Self-employeds. For purposes of the rules governing group legal services plans, educational assistance programs, and dependent care assistance programs, a self-employed is treated as an employee. A self-employed's compensation is his or her earned income as defined in section 401(c)(2). Also for these purposes, a sole proprietor is treated as his own employer and a partnership is treated as the employer of its working partners.

Controlled groups. Employees treated as employed by a single employer under Sec. 414(b), (c), and (m) are treated likewise for purposes of Sections 79, 89, 106, 117(d), 120, 125, 127, 129, 132, 162(i)(2), 162(k), 274(j), and 505 (with some exceptions, fringe benefit plans). Special transitional rules apply when an organization becomes or ceases to be part of a controlled group as defined in Sec. 414(b), (c), (m) or (o). Also, leased employees are treated as employees of the organization for whom the employees perform services (that is, the lessee).

New definitions. Just as it does for cafeteria plans, the new law substitutes the new definitions of highly compensated employees [¶1114], employer, and excludable employees [¶1155] for welfare benefit plans.

Regulatory authority. Also the new law gives Treasury the authority to issue regs to carry out the new rules.

Effective Date: The new nondiscrimination provisions are effective for plan years beginning after 12-31-87. However, if regs aren't issued by that time, the rules are effective for the earlier of plan years beginning at least three months after the regs are issued or plan years beginning after 12-31-88. For collective bargaining agreements ratified before 3-1-86, the new rules won't apply before the earlier of the termination of such agreements (without regard to extensions after that date) or 1-1-91. For church plans (under Section 414(e)(3)) maintaining insured accident and health plans, the new rules apply to years beginning after 12-31-88.

Act Sec. 1151(a), relating to nondiscrimination rules, adds new Secs. 89(i)-(1); Act Secs. 1151(b)-(i), repealing and modifying the old rules, amend Secs. 79(d), 105(h), 117(d)(3), 120(b), 125(b)(1), 125(g), 127(b)(1), 129(d), 132(g), 414(n), 414(t), and 505(b)(2), generally effective for plan years beginning after 12-31-87 and as shown above.

[¶1157] **Reporting and Penalty.** If an employee is required to include any amount in income under the new requirements, the employer must report the amount to the employee and the IRS on Forms W-2 by the appropriate due date. Failure to provide the forms will result in an additional tax to the employer equal to the highest individual tax rate for the year in question multiplied by the amount of the total employer provided benefit of the affected employee for the same type of benefit. Only one such addition will be paid for any amount. Note that reasonable cause is a defense to the penalty.

In addition, employers who maintain group-term life insurance plans, accident and health plans, group legal services plans, educational assistance programs, dependent care assistance programs, or cafeteria plans must file informational returns showing, in addition to the previously required information, the number of highly compensated employees of the employer, the number eligible to participate and the number that participates. However, Treasury has the power to waive the requirement that all employers file, in favor of a filing by a representative group of employers.

Act Sec. 1151(a) and (b) relating to reporting and penalties adds new Secs. 89(l) and 6652(l), effective as shown in ¶1151. Act Sec. 1151(h), relating to information returns, amends Sec. 6039D, effective as shown in ¶1151.

Other Fringe Benefit Provisions

[¶1161] **Health Insurance Costs for Self-Employeds.** The new law allows self-employeds (under Sec. 401(c)(1)) to deduct 25% of the amounts paid for health insurance for the self-employed and the individual's spouse and dependents. The amount is allowable as a deduction in calculating adjusted gross income. However, it isn't to be taken into account for purposes of determining the itemized medical expense deduction. Of course, the other 75% of the expense is taken into account for purposes of the medical expense deduction.

Limitations. There are a number of limitations on the deduction. The taxpayer won't get the deduction to the extent the amount exceeds earned income (under section 401(c)(1)). The deduction is allowed only if the coverage is provided under one or more plans meeting the new fringe benefit nondiscrimination rules. As a result, other employees will have to be covered. In addition, there's no deduction if the self-employed is eligible to participate in a subsidized accident and health plan maintained by an employer of the self-employed or the self-employed's spouse.

Guidance. The new law directs Treasury to provide guidance to self-employeds to help them comply with the new nondiscrimination rules.

NOTE: Special rules apply for nondiscrimination purposes, if the year in question occurs before the effective date of the nondiscrimination rules.

Act Sec. 1161, adding the health insurance deduction for self-employeds, adds new Sec. 162(m), effective for tax years beginning after 12-31-86 and before 1-1-90.

⟦¶1162⟧ Educational Assistance and Legal Services Programs Extended. The new law extends the exclusions for educational assistance programs and group legal services plans for two more years. So the educational assistance exclusion will expire for tax years beginning after 12-31-87 and the group legal services exclusion will expire for tax years ending after 12-31-87. It also increases the cap on annual excludable educational assistance to $5,250 (from $5,000).

For cafeteria plans providing group legal services benefits, the new law is treated in the same manner as a change in family status. *Result:* Participants have 60 days after enactment (according to the Senate Committee Report) to revoke the old election and make a new one that will apply to all legal services provided in 1986. However, if the plan provided that benefit on 8-16-86, the election can't be made.

Act Sec. 1162(a), relating to the educational assistance exclusion, amends Secs. 127(a)(2) and (d), effective for tax years beginning after 12-31-85; Act Sec. 1162(b), dealing with group legal services plans, amends Sec. 120(e), effective for years ending after 12-31-85.

⟦¶1163⟧ Qualified Campus Lodging. The new law sets up rules for including in income qualified campus lodging provided by a school to an employee. Generally, gross income won't include the value of qualified campus lodging. However, it will be included to the extent the rent paid is less than the lesser of (1) 5% of the appraised value of the lodging or (2) the average of rentals paid (other than by employees or students) to the institution for comparable housing. So, if the rent is equal to or exceeds the lesser of those figures, no amount is includable in income.

Qualified campus lodging is lodging furnished to an employee (his or her spouse, or any dependents) of an educational institution (defined in Sec. 170(b)(1)(A)(ii). The lodging must be located on, or in proximity to, the campus of the institution and must be provided for use as a residence.

It's expected that regs will determine how an appraisal should be made for purposes of the exclusion.

Act Sec. 1164, relating to qualified campus lodging, adds new Sec. 119(d), effective for tax years beginning after 12-31-85.

[¶1164] **Vacation Pay Accrual Tightened.** For tax years beginning after 1986, the new law limits the deduction for additions to the earned vacation pay accrual account to amounts paid during the employer's current tax year or within 8½ months (rather than 12 months) after the close of the tax year in which the vacation pay was earned.

Act Sec. 1165, dealing with vacation pay accruals amends Sec. 463(a)(1), effective for tax years beginning after 12-31-86.

[¶1165] **New $5,000 Limit on Dependent Care Assistance Exclusion.** The new law limits the exclusion for employer-provided dependent care assistance to $5,000 a year ($2,500 for marrieds filing separately). Previously, the exclusion was limited to the amount of earned income—so, for most taxpayers, the new law represents a cut in the amount of the exclusion.

The new law also explains how to value child care when it's provided at a facility located on the employer's premises. Except to the extent provided in regs, the amount excludable is the value of services provided to employees who actually use the facility.

Act Secs. 1163(a) and (b), limiting the dependent care exclusion, amend Secs. 129(a) and (e) effective for tax years beginning after 12-31-86.

[¶1166] **Welfare Benefit Study Due Date.** The new law extends the due date of the study (mandated by the '84 TRA) on the possible means of providing minimum standards for welfare benefit plans for current and retired employees. The new due date is one year after the date of enactment of the new law.

Act Sec. 1167, relating to a welfare benefit study, amends '84 TRA Sec. 560(b).

[¶1167] **Military Benefit Exclusion.** The new law consolidates the tax treatment of military benefits. Generally, it excludes from income benefits that were authorized by law on 9-9-86 and that were excludable on that date. The Conference Committee report contains an exhaustive list, which the committee believes contains the only excludable benefits under non-Code provisions. Other benefits are excluded from income by the Code.

The Committee Report gives the Treasury the power to expand the list should it determine that any benefit was inadvertently omitted.

The new law prohibits any modification or adjustment to a benefit after 9-9-86 unless the adjustment is under a law or regulation in effect that day, and is determined by reference to a fluctuation in cost, price, currency or similar index.

Act Sec. 1168, relating to military benefits, adds new Sec. 134, effective for taxable years beginning after 12-31-86.

Employee Stock Ownership Plans

[¶1172]   Termination of ESOP Credit. The new law moves up by one year the sunset of the payroll-based tax credit ESOP. As a result, the ESOP credit won't apply to compensation paid or accrued after 12-31-86. Unused credits can still be carried over under the rules of Section 404(i) and Section 6699. The new law also creates an exception to the repeal for one particular plan.

Act Sec. 1171, repealing the ESOP credit, repeals Secs. 41, 404(i), and 6699m and amends Secs. 38, 56, 108(b) and 401(a) for compensation paid or accrued after 12-31-86 in taxable years ending after that date. Act Sec. 1177(a) creates an exemption from the PAYSOP repeal.

[¶1173]   Estate Tax Exclusion for Sales to ESOPs or EWOCs. To encourage the transfer of employer securities to ESOPs or eligible worker owned cooperatives (EWOCs), the new law establishes an estate tax exclusion of 50% of the qualified proceeds of a qualified sale of employer securities. A qualified sale of employer securities is a sale by the executor to an ESOP (under Sec. 4975(e)(7)) or an EWOC (under Sec. 1042(c)).

Qualified proceeds are the amounts received by the estate from the sale of employer securities before the due date (including extensions) for the estate tax return. Qualified proceeds don't include proceeds from the sale of employer securities if the securities were received from a qualified plan (under Sec. 401(a)) or a transfer pursuant to an option to acquire stock under Secs. 83, 422, 422A, 423, or 424.

Prohibited allocation rules. A statement must be filed by the executor with the IRS, in which the employer or the EWOC consents to the application of the new Sec. 4979A prohibited allocation penalty. These rules basically require the ESOP to inure to the exclusive benefit of the employees. Generally, the rules provide for an excise tax for violation of the prohibited allocation rules under new Sec. 409(n), equal to 50% of the prohibited allocation [see ¶1854]. Briefly, a prohibited allocation is one in which securities are allocated, within 10 years after the later of the sale or the allocation attributable to final payment of the acquisition loan, to the benefit of (1) a decedent whose estate makes the sale, (2) any person related to the decedent under Sec. 267(b), or (3) any other person who owns (under Sec. 318(a)) more than 25% of any class of outstanding stock of the corporation or 25% of the total value of any class of outstanding stock. In addition, the plan will be treated as having distributed to such person (or his or her estate), the amount so allocated.

Act Sec. 1172, relating to the new 50% exclusion, adds new Sec. 2057 and amends Sec. 409(n), effective for sales after the enactment date and before 1-1-92 by an estate required to file a return (including extensions of time) after the enactment date.

【¶1174】 **Securities Acquisitions Loans.** The new law extends some of the breaks for loans used to acquire employer securities.

Dividends used to repay loans. The new law allows an employer to deduct dividends paid on employer securities, which are used to make payments on an employer securities acquisition loan (defined in Sec. 404(a)(9)). Such deduction would be allowable in the corporation's tax year during which the loan was repaid. Previously, the deduction was limited to dividends paid out to the employees or other beneficiaries.

Loans by regulated investment company. The new law provides that regulated investment companies (RICs) are eligible lenders for purposes of the 50% exclusion for interest paid on securities acquisition rules. Such treatment will flow through to the RIC's shareholders under rules similar to those in Sec. 103(a) for government obligations. One-half of the interest received on such loans will be treated as interest excludable under Sec. 103 for purposes of determining the amount of exempt-interest dividends the RIC may pay.

Loans to employer corporation. The 50% interest exclusion is also available to eligible lenders for interest received on a loan to a corporation to the extent that, within 30 days, employer securities are transferred to the plan in an amount equal to such proceeds and such contributions are allocated to participants' accounts within one year of the loan. In addition, the original commitment period of such loan isn't to exceed seven years. If the period is longer, the exclusion applies only to the first seven years.

The new law also provides that the exclusion is now available for interest on loans incurred after the date of enactment to an employer corporation to the extent the proceeds are used to refinance such loans. Previously, the exclusion was limited to loans to corporations or ESOPs, the proceeds of which were used to acquire such securities.

Effective Date: According to the Conference Committee report, the interest exclusion is extended to refinancing of loans used to acquire employer securities after May 23, 1984. According to the statute, that date only applies to the exclusion for RICs.

Act Sec. 1173(a), relating to the dividends paid deductions, amends Sec. 404(k), effective for tax years beginning after the date of enactment; Act Sec. 1173(b)(1), extending the interest exclusion to RICs amends Secs. 133(a) and 852(b)(5), effective for loans after the date of enactment including loans used to refinance loans used to acquire employer securities before the date of enactment if such loans were used to acquire the securities after 5-23-84; Act

Sec. 1173(b)(2), extending the 50% interest exclusion for corporations, amends Sec. 133(b)(1), effective (1) for refinancing loans made after the date of enactment and (2) for securities transferred after the date of enactment for loans incurred after 7-18-84.

[¶1175] Termination Distributions. Under prior law, employer securities allocated to an employee's account under a tax credit ESOP couldn't be distributed within 84 months of allocation. There were a few exceptions. The new law adds plan terminations to the list of exceptions. Thus, the 84-month rule won't apply to distributions from terminated tax credit ESOPs [see ¶1172].

Act Sec. 1174(a), relating to termination distributions from certain ESOPs amends Sec. 409(d)(1), effective for termination distributions after 12-31-84.

[¶1176] ESOP Distribution Rules. The new law makes a number of changes to the ESOP distribution rules. An ESOP is to permit distributions to employees who separate from service before normal retirement age. Unless an employee elects otherwise, the distribution of the entire account balance will begin no later than one year after the later of the plan year (1) in which the participant ceases employment due to retirement, disability, or death or (2) which is the fifth plan year following separation from service (provided the participant doesn't return to the employer).

If any part of the employee's account balance includes securities attributable to a securities acquisition loan that hasn't been fully repaid, those securities subject to the loan won't be considered part of the account balance until the close of the plan year when the loan is repaid.

> **NOTE:** These rules are intended to accelerate the beginning of payment. If the general rules (Sec. 401(a)(14)) provide an earlier payment date, the participant should elect that schedule.

Distribution period. Unless the plan provides that a participant may elect a longer period, the plan is to provide distributions over a period not longer than five years. If the participant has an account balance greater than $500,000, the period may be five years plus one additional year (up to five additional years) for each $100,000 (or fraction thereof) of the excess. Those dollar figures are to be indexed under the rules of Section 415(d).

Act Sec. 1174(b), relating to the distribution requirements, adds new Sec. 409(o), and amends Sec. 409(a)(3), effective for distributions attributable to stock acquired after 12-31-86.

[¶1177] Put Option Requirements. The new law keeps the prior law requirement of the right to demand that benefits be distributed in the form of employer securities and the requirement that a participant receiving distributions of employer securities from a

¶1177

tax credit on leveraged ESOP be given a put option for securities that aren't readily tradable. However, the periods for payment of the option price are modified.

For put options exercised for stock that is part of a total distribution, the new law treats the distribution requirements as met if the amount is paid in substantially equal periodic payments (not less frequently than annually) over a period not greater than five years beginning not later than 30 days after the exercise of the options. In addition, there must be adequate security and reasonable interest paid on the unpaid amounts. Note that a total distribution is that distribution within one tax year to the receipient of his or her account balance.

For put options exercised as part of an installment distribution, the employer must pay the option price not later than 30 days after the options exercise.

Stock bonus plans. The new law extends the put option requirement for employer securities that aren't readily tradable to stock bonus plans. In so doing, stock bonus plans are also subject to the new ESOP distribution rules.

Act Sec. 1174(c)(1), relating to put option payouts, adds new Secs. 409(h)(5) and (6), effective for distributions attributable to stock acquired after December 31, 1986, but a plan may elect to have the amendment apply to all distributions after the date of enactment; Act Sec. 1174(c)(2), dealing with stock bonus plans, amends Sec. 401(a)(23), effective for distributions attributable to stock acquired after 12-31-86.

[¶1178] **Limitation on Annual Additions.** Annual additions for participants in an ESOP are generally subject to the defined contribution limits under Sec. 415(c)(1), the lesser of 25% of compensation or $30,000. For ESOPs described in Sec. 4975(e)(7) or a tax credit ESOP, the amount is raised to the lesser of $60,000 or the amount of employer securities contributed to, or acquired by the plan. Under prior law, the increased limits applied only if no more than one-third of the employer contributions for the year were allocated to officers, 10% shareholders, and highly compensated employees (those making $60,000 or more).

The new law keeps the increased limits. However, it limits the prohibited group to highly compensated employees as defined in new Sec. 414(q) (explained at ¶1114).

Act Sec. 1174(d), relating to increased annual additions for ESOPs, amends Sec. 415(c)(6), effective for tax years beginning after 12-31-86.

[¶1179] **Voting Rights Passthrough.** The new law allows certain closely held newspapers to establish ESOPs to be established with nonvoting stock, notwithstanding the voting rights passthrough requirements. However, those nonvoting shares would be treated as qualified employer securities only if the employer has that class of nonvoting stock outstanding *and* the specific shares acquired were outstanding for at least 24 months.

Act Sec. 1176(a), dealing with voting rights, amends Sec. 401(a)(22), effective 12-31-86. Act Sec. 1176(b), relating to qualified securities amends Sec. 409(l)(4), effective for securities acquisitions after 12-31-86. Act 1177(b) exempts a certain newspaper from the new diversification and independent appraisal rules of Act Sec. 1175.

[¶1180] Investment Diversification. In an effort to avoid forcing employees near retirement age to have all their eggs in one basket, employees who have attained age 55 and completed at least 10 years of service must now be given an opportunity to diversify the investments in their own accounts.

The employee must be able to make the election within 90 days of the end of the plan year in the qualified election period. The qualified election period is the period consisting of the plan year in which the employer attains age 55 (or completes 10 years of service, if later) and ending with the fifth succeeding plan year.

The amount eligible for diversification must be at least 25% of the participant's account balance at the end of the year less amounts previously diversified. For the last year of the election period, the amount must be at least 50% of the account balance less amounts previously diversified.

To the extent that a participant elects to diversify, the new law requires an ESOP to offer at least three investment options that aren't inconsistent with the regs to be issued. Alternatively, the plan can meet the requirement by distributing to the participant, within 90 days after the close of the annual election period, the amount the employee elects to diversify.

> **ROLLOVER INTO IRA:** According to the House Committee Report, a participant receiving a distribution in satisfaction of the election, can roll the distribution into an IRA.

Act Sec. 1175(a), allowing investment diversification, adds Sec. 401(a)(28) (A) and (B), effective for stock acquired after 12-31-86.

[¶1181] Independent Appraiser. Under the new law, the valuation of employer securities that aren't readily tradable on an established securities market, for all activities carried on by the ESOP, must be made by an independent appraiser (as defined in Section 170(a)(1)).

Act Sec. 1175(a), requiring an independent appraiser, adds Sec. 401(a)(28)(C), effective for stock acquired after 12-31-86, effective on enactment.

[The page following this is 1201.]

FOREIGN TAX

Foreign Tax Credit

[¶1201] Separate Credit Limitations. To restrict the taxpayer's ability to average high and low foreign taxes in calculating the foreign tax credit, the new law creates separate credit limitations for passive income, "high withholding tax interest," financial services income, shipping income, and dividends from noncontrolled Section 902 corporations. These separate limitations are generally in addition to those of prior Section 904(d), which prevented taxpayers from averaging foreign tax rates on other income classes that may be easily resourced or are generally subject to abnormally high or low foreign tax.

The separate passive income category replaces the category for passive interest income, and generally is any income that would be foreign personal holding company income under Subpart F. The new category includes foreign personal holding company inclusions and passive foreign investment company inclusions. It excludes high withholding tax interest, financial services income, shipping income, dividends from noncontrolled Section 902 corporations, export financing interest, high-taxed income, and foreign oil and gas extraction income. The term "export financing interest" means interest derived from financing the sale or other disposition for use or consumption outside the United States of property manufactured, produced, grown, or extracted in the United States by the taxpayer or a related person, when not more than 50% of the property's fair market value is attributable to products imported into the United States. The term "high-taxed income" means income that would be passive income if the sum of the foreign income taxes paid or accrued by the taxpayer as to the income and the foreign income taxes deemed paid by the taxpayer as to the income exceeds the highest U.S. tax rate multiplied by the amount of the income.

High withholding tax interest. This category covers interest subject to a foreign country's or U.S. possession's withholding or other gross-basis tax of at least 5%. It excludes export financing interest.

Financial services income. This category covers income derived in the active conduct of a banking, financing, or similar business, or derived from the investment by an insurance company of its unearned premiums or reserves ordinary and necessary for the proper conduct of its insurance business, and is of a kind that would be insurance income as defined in Section 953(a). It excludes export financing interest and high withholding tax interest.

Shipping income. This category covers income received or accrued by a person that is of a kind that would be foreign base company shipping income.

Dividends. This category covers dividends from a noncontrolled Section 902 corporation—that is, a foreign corporation in which the recipient owns between 10% and 50% of the voting power of its stock.

> **DE MINIMIS EXCEPTION:** A CFC has no separate category income in a tax year in which it has no Subpart F income due to the applicability of the Subpart F de minimis rule. The rule applies if the sum of foreign base company income and tax haven insurance income for the year is less than the lesser of 5% of gross income or $1 million. [See ¶1219.]

Transitional rules. Taxes paid or accrued in a tax year beginning before 1-1-87, as to interest income will be treated as taxes paid or accrued as to passive income. Taxes paid or accrued in a tax year beginning before 1-1-86, as to overall limitation income will be treated as such, except to the extent the taxpayer establishes the taxes were paid or accrued as to shipping income or financial services income. Taxes paid or accrued in a tax year beginning before 1-1-87, as to any other separate category of income described before that date will be treated as taxes paid or accrued as to a corresponding category of income described after the date.

Look-through rules. Interest, rents, and royalties received or accrued from a CFC in which the taxpayer is a U.S. shareholder will be treated as income in a separate category to the extent it is properly allocable. Dividends paid out of E&P of a CFC in which the taxpayer is a U.S. shareholder will be treated as income in a separate category in proportion to the ratio of the part of E&P attributable to income in that category to total E&P. Subpart F inclusions will be treated as income in a separate category to the extent the amount included is attributable.

Source rule. Except to the extent provided in regulations, interest paid or accrued by a CFC to a U.S. shareholder (or CFC related to the shareholder) will first be allocated to foreign personal holding company income in the passive income category.

Act Sec. 1201, relating to separate foreign tax credit limitations, adds new Secs. 904(d)(1)(A), (B), (C), (D), and (E) by striking out old (A) and redesignating old (B), (C), (D), and (E) as (F), (G), (H), and (I), and amends Secs. 864(d)(5)(A)(i), 904(d) subsection heading, 904(d)(1), 904(d)(2), 904(d)(3) and 954(b)(5), effective generally for tax years beginning after 12-31-86. A transitional rule, which applies for foreign taxes on interest paid by borrowers in 33 less developed countries, is phased out over the five-tax year period beginning with the taxpayer's first tax year beginning after 1989. A special rule applies to one U.S. corporation.

[¶1202] **Subsidies.** The new law codifies Reg. Sec. 1.901-2(e)(3), providing that income, war profits, and excess profits taxes won't be creditable to the extent that the foreign country uses the amount of tax to provide a subsidy to the taxpayer, a related person, or any party to the transaction or a related transaction, and the subsidy is determined by reference to the tax's amount or computation base.

Act Sec. 1204, relating to the treatment of certain subsidies, adds new Sec. 901(i) by redesignating old (i) as (j), effective for foreign taxes paid or accrued in tax years beginning after 12-31-86.

[¶1203] **Separate Limitation Losses.** The new law provides that losses for a tax year in a separate foreign tax credit limitation category offset U.S.-source income only to the extent that the aggregate of those losses exceeds the aggregate of foreign income earned in other categories. These losses will be allocated proportionately among the foreign income categories in which the taxpayer earns income in the loss year. U.S.-source losses are allocated proportionately among the foreign income categories, but only after the allocation of foreign-source losses.

Recharacterization rule. If foreign losses in one category are allocated to foreign income in a second category in this way and the first (loss) category has income in a later tax year, the income is recharacterized as income in the second category, previously offset by the loss, in proportion to the earlier loss allocation.

Act Sec. 1203, relating to separate limitation losses, adds new Sec. 904(f)(5), effective for losses incurred in tax years beginning after 12-31-86.

[¶1204] **Deemed-Paid Credit.** Under the new law, the deemed-paid foreign tax credit of a U.S. corporation owning at least 10% of the voting stock of a foreign corporation is computed with reference to the pool of the distributing corporation's post-1986 accumulated E&P and accumulated foreign taxes. The change is intended to prevent taxpayers from losing deemed-paid credits because the foreign corporation had a deficit in E&P in some years that the IRS considered to reduce accumulated profits (for prior years in which foreign taxes were paid), reducing the amount of creditable taxes. The new law is also intended to limit the taxpayer's ability to average high-tax and low-tax years, resulting in a deemed-paid credit that reflects a higher than average foreign tax rate over a period of years.

Pool of accumulated E&P. A U.S. corporation that owns at least 10% of the voting stock of a foreign corporation from which it receives dividends will be deemed to have paid the same proportion of the foreign corporation's post-1986 foreign income taxes as the amount of the dividends bears to its post-1986 undistributed earnings. Post-1986 undistributed earnings are the accumulated E&P for tax years beginning after 1986.

> **PROSPECTIVE ONLY:** The pooling will be prospective only—future dividends and Subpart F inclusions will be treated as made first out of the accumulated profits derived after the effective date, and then out of pre-effective date accumulated profits under the ordering principles of prior law.

Second-and third-tier corporations. Similar rules apply if the foreign corporation (first-tier corporation) owns at least 10% of a second foreign corporation (second-tier corporation), or if the first-tier corporation owns at least 10% of a second-tier corporation that owns at least 10% of a third corporation (third-tier corporation)—though there is a 5% stock ownership requirement calculated by multiplying the percentage owned by each corporation in the next lower-tier corporation.

Act Sec. 1202, relating to the deemed-paid credit, amends Sec. 902, 960(a)(1), 6038(a)(1)(B), 6038(c)(4)(C), and the table of sections for subpart A of part III of subchapter N of chapter 1, effective for distributions by foreign corporations out of, and inclusions under Sec. 951(a) attributable to, E&P for tax years beginning after 12-31-86.

[¶1205] **Limitation on Carryback.** Under the new law, taxes paid or accrued in a tax year beginning after 1986 may be treated as paid or accrued in a tax year beginning before 1987 only to the extent the post-1986 taxes could be carried back if the tax was determined by applying the tax rate in effect on the day before the Act enactment date. Such taxes will be treated as imposed on overall limitation income. No taxes paid or accrued in a tax year beginning after 1986 as to high withholding tax interest may be carried back.

Act Sec. 1205 does not amend the Code.

Source Rules

[¶1211] **Personal Property.** To more clearly reflect the situs of economic activity, the new law modifies rules for sourcing income from sales of tangible and intangible personal property. General rule: income from a sale of personal property by a U.S. resident is U.S.-source, and by a nonresident is foreign-source. Separate rules apply for inventory property, depreciable personal property, intangibles, sales through offices, and stock of affiliates.

Under prior law, income from the purchase and resale of tangible and intangible personal property generally was sourced at the place of the sale, which was deemed to be where title passes. Income from manufacture in one country and sale in another country was sourced half at the place of manufacture and half at the place of sale. Royalty income was sourced in the country of use.

U.S. resident. Under the new law, an individual is a U.S. resident if he or she has a tax home in the United States under Sec. 911(d)(3). A corporation, partnership, trust, or estate is a U.S. resident if it is a U.S. person under Sec. 7701(a)(30).

> **NOTE:** A U.S. citizen or resident alien won't be considered a resident of another country for a sale of personal property unless a 10% income tax on the gain is paid to the country.

Inventory property. Income from the sale of inventory property will be sourced by the old personal property rules under Secs. 861(a)(6), 862(a)(6), and 863(b).

Depreciable property. If depreciation deductions have been allocated against U.S. or foreign-source income, then gain from the sale of depreciable property must be similarly sourced. Gain in excess of these deductions will be sourced as if the property were inventory property. If certain depreciable property is used predominantly within or outside the United States in a tax year, the allowable depreciation deductions are allocated entirely against U.S. or foreign-source income, respectively.

Intangible property. Payments from the sale of intangibles will be sourced as if they were royalties only to the extent the payments are contingent on the intangible's productivity, use, or disposition. Payments from the sale of goodwill will be sourced where it was generated.

Sales through offices. If a U.S. resident maintains a foreign office or other fixed place of business, income from sales of personal property attributable to that office is foreign-sourced—provided a 10% income tax is paid to the foreign country. This rule doesn't apply for income sourced under the rules for inventory property, depreciable personal property, intangibles, or stock of affiliates.

If a nonresident has a U.S. office or other fixed place of business, income from the sale of personal property (including inventory property) attributable to the office is U.S. sourced, except for inventory sold for use, disposition, or consumption outside the United States if the taxpayer's office materially participated in the sale, and amounts included in gross income under Sec. 951(a)(1)(A).

Stock of affiliates. Income from the sale of stock in a foreign corporate affiliate by a U.S. resident is foreign-source income if the affiliate is engaged in the active conduct of a trade or business, and the sale takes place in the foreign country in which the affiliate derived more than 50% of its gross income during a three-year period.

The new law also repeals the Sec. 871(e) rule that, on a sale of intangible property in which more than 50% of the gain is from contingent payments, all the gain is considered so contingent.

Act Sec. 1211, relating to the source rules for personal property sales, adds new Sec. 865, repeals Sec. 871(e), and amends Secs. 861(a)(6), 862(a)(6), 863(b)(2), 863(b)(3), 864(c)(4)(B), 871(a)(1)(D), 881(a)(4), and 904(b)(3), effective generally for tax years beginning after 12-31-86. For a foreign person other than a CFC, the amendments are effective for transactions entered into after 3-18-86. The Treasury must conduct a study of the source rules for sales of inventory property and submit a report to the House Ways and Means Committee and Senate Finance Committee by 9-30-87.

【¶1212】 80-20 Corporations. Previously, dividends and interest paid by a U.S. corporation deriving more than 80% of its income from foreign sources were treated as foreign-source income. Also, interest paid by a resident alien deriving more than 80% of his or her income from foreign sources was treated as foreign-source income.

Interest. Under the new law, interest received from a resident alien or U.S. corporation is treated as U.S.-source income, unless the resident alien or U.S. corporation meets an 80% foreign business requirement. The requirement is met and the interest is foreign source if at least 80% of the resident alien's or U.S. corporation's worldwide gross income is derived from foreign sources and is attributable to the active conduct of a trade or business in a foreign country or U.S. possession by the resident alien or U.S. corporation (or by a subsidiary or chain of subs) for a three-year period.

However, a related person that receives interest from a resident alien or U.S. corporation meeting the 80% foreign business requirement can only treat as foreign-source income the percentage of interest equal to the ratio of the resident alien's or U.S. corporation's foreign gross income to its worldwide gross income (for the three-year period).

Dividends. Under the new law, dividends received from a U.S. corporation other than a Sec. 936 possessions corporation are U.S.-source income.

However, nonresident aliens and foreign corporations receiving dividends from a U.S. corporation that meets the 80% foreign business requirement aren't subject to U.S. withholding tax on the percentage of the dividends paid that the U.S. corporation's foreign-source income bears to its worldwide gross income over the three-year period.

U.S. sourced but tax exempt. Under the new law, interest on deposits not effectively connected with the conduct of a U.S. trade or business and income derived by a foreign central bank of issue from bankers' acceptances are U.S. source income, but are exempt from U.S. withholding tax. Deposits are deposits with banks, deposits or withdrawable accounts with federal or state chartered savings insti-

tutions, and amounts held by an insurance company under an
agreement to pay interest.

*Act Sec. 1214, relating to the treatment of 80-20 corporations, adds new
Secs. 871(i) by redesignating old (i) as (j), 881(d) by redesignating old (d) as
(e), 1441(c)(10), and 6049(b)(5)(iv), and amends Secs. 861(a)(1), 861(a)(2)(A),
861(c), 861(d), and 6049(b)(5), (B), effective for payments after 12-31-86. A special rule applies for the treatment of certain interest. A transitional rule applies. A special rule applies for a particular U.S. corporation.*

[¶1213] **Transportation Income.** The new law treats 50% of
all income from transporation that begins or ends in the United
States but not both as U.S.-source income. The rule doesn't apply to
personal service income unless it is attributable to transportation
between the United States and a U.S. possession. Previously, transportation income was allocated between U.S. and foreign sources in
proportion to the expenses incurred.

The new law also repeals the special sourcing rules for the lease
or disposition of vessels, aircraft, or spacecraft constructed in the
United States, and the lease of aircraft to a regularly scheduled U.S.
air carrier.

Tax on transportation income. The new law imposes a 4% tax on
the U.S.-source gross transportation income of NRAs and foreign
corporations. As under prior law, transportation income is gross income derived from, or in connection with, the use (or hiring or leasing for use) of a vessel or aircraft, or the performance of directly related services.

Exceptions. Transportation income received or accrued by an
NRA or foreign corporation that is effectively connected with the
foreign person's U.S. trade or business is instead taxed on a net basis. The income is effectively connected if the foreign person has a
U.S. fixed place of business involved in earning transportation income, and substantially all the U.S.-source gross transportation income is attributable to regularly scheduled transportation.

Reciprocal exemption by residence. The new law provides that
gross income derived by a foreign resident or a corporation organized in a foreign country from operating a ship or aircraft (including rental on a full or bareboat basis) is exempt from U.S. tax if the
foreign country grants an equivalent exemption to U.S. citizens and
U.S. corporations. Under prior law, the ship or aircraft had to be
documented or registered under the law of a foreign country.

A foreign corporation may not claim the reciprocol exemption if
50% or more of the value of its stock is owned (or considered owned)
by persons who aren't residents of a foreign country that grants U.S.
persons an equivalent exemption. The 50% test won't apply to a foreign corporation if its stock is primarily and regularly traded on an

established securities market in the foreign country in which it is organized, or if it is wholly owned by such a corporation.

Act Sec. 1212, relating to transportation income, adds new Secs. 872(b)(5), 872(b)(6), 883(a)(4), 883(c), and 887, repeals Sec. 861(e) by redesignating old (f) as (e), and amends Sec. 863(b)(1), 863(c)(2), 872(b)(1), 872(b)(2), 883(a)(1), 883(a)(2), and the table of subparts for part II of subchapter N, effective generally for tax years beginning after 12-31-86. A special rule applies for certain leased property. A special rule applies for four ships to be leased by the U.S. Navy.

[¶1214] Allocating Interest Expense. Under the new law, corporate members of an affiliated group must allocate and apportion interest expense against U.S. or foreign-source income on a consolidated group basis. Exception: Financial institutions may allocate interest expense separately, as one taxpayer, if their business is predominantly with unrelated persons and they are required by state or federal law to be operated separately from nonfinancial institutions.

Other expenses. Expenses other than interest not directly allocable to a class of income will be allocated and apportioned on a consolidated basis.

Asset method. Eliminating the use of the gross income method for allocating and apportioning interest expense, the new law provides that only the asset method can be used. Not taken into account under the asset method are tax-exempt assets and certain dividends (and stock on which the dividends are paid) for which a deduction is allowed. The adjusted basis of an asset that is stock in a foreign corporation in which affiliated group members own at least 10% of its voting stock will be increased by the foreign corporation's E&P attributable to the stock and accumulated while the taxpayer held it, and will be reduced by an E&P deficit.

The new law gives the Treasury the authority to prescribe regulations providing for
• resourcing income of any affiliated group member or modifying the consolidated return regulations,
• direct allocation of interest expense incurred to carry out an integrated financial transaction, and
• apportionment of the expense allocable to foreign source income subject to separate foreign tax credit limitations.

Act Sec. 1215, relating to rules for allocating interest, adds new Sec. 864(e) and amends the Sec. 864 section heading and the table of sections for part I of subchapter N of chapter 1, effective generally for tax years beginning after 12-31-86. Under transitional rules, for the first three years beginning after 12-31-86, the amendment generally will apply only to an applicable percentage (25%, 50%, 75%) of interest expenses paid or accrued by the taxpayer during the tax year as to an indebtedness not exceeding the outstanding indebtedness on 11-16-85. Special rules apply for two U.S. corporations.

〔¶1215〕 Research and Experimental Expenditures. The new law modifies the rules for allocating research and experimental expenditures against U.S. and foreign-source income for one year while Congress analyzes the need for a permanent tax incentive. It doesn't renew the moratorium on the Reg. Sec. 1.861-8 rules.

The new law generally provides that 50% of all amounts allowable as a research and experimental expenditure deduction will be apportioned to U.S.-source income and deducted in determining U.S. taxable income. The remaining amount will be apportioned on the basis of gross sales or gross income. Exception: If research expenditures are incurred to meet legal requirements as to improvements or marketing of specific products or processes and the results aren't likely to generate much gross income outside a single source, they will be allocated entirely to that source.

Act Sec. 1216, relating to the modification of research expenditure allocation rules, does not amend the Code and applies to Secs. 861(b), 862(b), and 863(b) effective for tax years beginning after 8-1-86 and on or before 8-1-87.

〔¶1216〕 Space and Ocean Income. Under the new law, except as provided in regulations, income derived from an activity conducted in space and from an activity conducted on or under water that isn't within the jurisdiction of the United States, a U.S. possession, or a foreign country (including Antarctica) by a U.S. person will be sourced in the United States, and by a non-U.S. person will be sourced outside the United States.

Exceptions. Space and ocean activities don't include those creating transportation income under Sec. 863(c), having to do with mines, oil and gas wells, or other deposits within the jurisdiction of a country, or creating "international communications income." International communications income is income derived from transmitting any communications or data between the United States and a foreign country, and is sourced 50% in the United States and 50% in the foreign country.

Bill Sec. 1213, relating to space and ocean income, adds new Secs. 863(d) and 863(e), effective for tax years beginning after 12-31-86.

Income Earned Through Foreign Corporations

〔¶1217〕 Subpart F Income. Generally, the United States currently taxes a controlled foreign corporation's 10% or more U.S. shareholders on their pro rata share of the CFC's Subpart F income. The new law narrows exceptions to taxation under Subpart F and treats certain other types of easily manipulated income as Subpart F income.

Sale of nonincome producing property. Under the new law, the definition of foreign personal holding company income (FPHCI) for Subpart F purposes includes the excess of gain over losses from the sale or exchange of property that (1) gives rise to dividends and interest (other than those excluded under the active business exceptions for banks and insurance companies), royalties and rents (other than active business, unrelated party), and annuities, or (2) doesn't give rise to any income. The rule doesn't apply to gain from the sale or exchange of property that is inventory property in the hands of the seller or of property by a regular dealer in that property.

Commodities transactions. The new law provides that the definition of FPHCI includes the excess of gain over loss from any transaction (including a futures, forward, or similar transaction) in any commodity. As under prior law, the rule doesn't apply to gains from bona fide hedging transactions reasonably necessary to the conduct of a business by a producer, processor, merchant, or handler of a commodity in the way the business is customarily and usually conducted by others. A new exception covers active business gains if substantially all the CFC's business is as an active producer, processor, merchant, or handler of commodities.

Foreign currency gains. Under the new law, the definition of FPHCI includes the excess of foreign currency gains over foreign currency losses attributable to Sec. 988 transactions. Exception: This doesn't apply to transactions directly related to the business needs of the CFC.

Income equivalent to interest. The new law provides that the definition of FPHCI includes income equivalent to interest, including commitment fees for loans made.

Banking and insurance income. The new law repeals the rules excluding from FPHCI dividends, interest, and gains from the sale or exchange of stocks or securities received from unrelated persons in the active conduct of a banking, financing, or similar business, or from an insurance company's investment of unearned premiums, reserves, and certain other funds. The new law also repeals the rule excluding from FPHCI interest paid by a related person to a CFC if both are engaged in a banking, financing, or similar business. However, interest earned by U.S.-controlled foreign banks in connection with export financing for related U.S. persons would be eligible for deferral to the same extent that it was eligible under previous law.

Income from related persons. Excluded from FPHCI under the new law are (1) dividends and interest received from a related person that is created or organized under the laws of the same foreign country under whose laws the CFC is created or organized and has a substantial part of its assets used in its trade or business there, and (2) rents and royalties received from a related person for the use of, or the privilege of using, property within the country under whose laws the CFC is created or organized. The exclusion doesn't apply to the extent the interest, rent, or royalty reduces the payor's Subpart F income.

Definition of related person. Whether CFC income is foreign base company income may depend on whether it is received from a related person. Under the new law, the definition of "related person" includes an individual, corporation, partnership, trust, or estate that controls or is controlled by the CFC as well as a corporation, partnership, trust, or estate controlled by the same persons that control the CFC. For a corporation, control meant the direct or indirect ownership of 50% or more of the total combined voting power of all classes of voting stock or the total value of stock. For a partnership, trust, or estate, control is the direct or indirect ownership of 50% or more of the total value of beneficial interests in the entity.

Previously, a related person included an individual, partnership, trust, or estate that controlled the CFC, a corporation that controlled or was controlled by the CFC, or a corporation controlled by the same person or persons that controlled the CFC. For this purpose, control meant the direct or indirect ownership of stock possessing more than 50% of the total combined voting power of all classes of voting stock.

Shipping income. The new law repeals the rule excluding from foreign base company income the foreign base company shipping income reinvested in foreign base company shipping operations. The new law provides that foreign base company shipping income includes income derived from a space or ocean activity as defined in Section 863(d)(2).

Insurance income. The new law provides that the definition of insurance income subject to Subpart F taxation includes any income attributable to the issuing (or reinsuring) of any insurance or annuity contract in connection with risks in a country other than the CFC's country of incorporation, or in connection with same-country risks in an arrangement in which another CFC receives a substantially equal amount of premiums for insuring other-country risks, and would be taxed as if it were the income of a U.S. insurance company.

The new law subjects the related person insurance income of offshore captive insurance companies to current U.S. taxation. For the purpose of taking into account related person insurance income, the U.S. ownership threshold for CFC status is reduced to 25% or more. Related person insurance income means insurance income attributable to a policy of insurance or reinsurance as to which the primary insured is a U.S. shareholder in the foreign corporation receiving the income or a related person to the shareholder. The rule won't apply if:

- the corporation's gross related person insurance income for the tax year is less than 20% of its gross insurance income for the year,

- less than 20% of the total combined voting power of all classes of the corporation's voting stock and less than 20% of the total value of its stock and policies during the tax year are owned by persons who are the primary insured under any insurance or reinsurance policies issued by the corporation, or by persons related to those persons,

- the foreign corporation elects to treat the related person insurance income as income effectively connected with the conduct of a U.S. trade or business.

The new law repeals the 5% de minimis exception for income from insurance of U.S. risks and repeals the exceptions for investment income from unearned premiums and reserves.

Not used to reduce taxes. The new law provides that foreign base company income and insurance income doesn't include any income item received by a CFC if the taxpayer satisfies the Treasury that the income was subject to an effective rate of foreign income tax greater than 90% of the maximum rate of U.S. corporate tax. The rule doesn't apply to foreign base company oil-related income. Under prior law, a significant purpose test was used.

Deficits. The new law repeals the Sec. 952(d) chain deficit rule, and limits the Sec. 952(c) accumulated deficit rule allowing a CFC to reduce Subpart F income by the sum of its prior year E&P deficits.

To coordinate the Subpart F rules and the separate foreign tax credit limitation for passive income rules, the new law provides that prior year deficits in E&P and other companies' deficits in E&P don't reduce Subpart F income. Income recaptured as passive income under the foreign loss recharacterization rule is Subpart F income in accordance with the character of the original income requiring recapture.

Act Sec. 1221, relating to Subpart F income, adds new Sec. 953(c), repeals Secs. 954(b)(2) and 954(g) by redesignating old (h) as (g), and amends Secs. 864(d)(5)(A)(iii), 864(d)(5)(A)(iv), 952(a)(1), 952(c), 952(d), 953 section heading, 953(a), 954(a)(5), 954(b)(4), 954(c), 954(d)(3), 954(e), 954(f), 955(a)(1)(A), 955(a)(2)(A), 957(b), and table of sections for Subpart F of part III of subchapter N of chapter 1, effective generally for tax years of foreign corporations beginning after 12-31-86. A special rule applies for repeal of the exclusion for reinvestment shipping income. An exception applies for certain reinsurance contracts.

[¶1218] Definition of CFC and FPHC. To prevent U.S. shareholders from avoiding tax on the earnings of U.S.-controlled foreign corporations, the new law amends the definitions of CFC and FPHC to consider stock value as well as voting power. Under the new law, the term "controlled foreign corporation" means a foreign corporation for which more than 50% of its total combined voting power of all classes of voting stock or the total value of its stock is owned by 10%-or-more U.S. shareholders on any day during its tax year. This rule applies in determining whether an insurance company is a CFC under the more than 25% U.S. ownership test. The stock requirement for FPHC status is met when more than 50% of its total combined voting power of all classes of voting stock or the total value of its stock is owned by or for no more than five U.S. citizens or residents.

Act Sec. 1222, relating to the definitions of CFC and FPHC, amends Secs. 552(a)(2), 957(a), and 957(b), effective generally for tax years of foreign corporations beginning after 12-31-86, except that for applying Secs. 951(a)(1)(B) and 956 the amendments will take effect on 8-16-86. A transitional rule applies for corporations treated as CFCs due to the amendments. A special rule applies to a particular individual beneficiary of a trust.

[¶1219] Subpart F De Minimis and Full Inclusion Rules. Under the new law, none of a CFC's gross income for the tax year will be treated as foreign base company income (FBCI) or insurance income, if the sum of its FBCI and gross insurance income for the tax year is less than the lesser of 5% of gross income, or $1 million. All of a CFC's gross income for the tax year will be treated as FBCI or insurance income, if the sum of its FBCI and gross insurance income for the tax year exceeds 70% of gross income. Previously, the thresholds were 10% and 70% of FBCI.

Act Sec. 1223, relating to the Subpart F de minimis and full inclusion rules, amends Secs. 864(d)(5)(A)(ii), 881(c)(4)(A)(i), and 954(b)(3), effective for tax years beginning after 12-31-86.

[¶1220] CFC Status of Possessions Corporations. The new law repeals the exemption of corporations organized in U.S. possessions from CFC status. As a result, 10% or more U.S. shareholders will be currently taxed under Subpart F. Under prior law, a corporation created or organized in, or under the laws of, Puerto Rico or a U.S. possession wasn't a CFC if at least 80% of its gross income was from possession sources for the three-year period immediately preceding the end of the tax year and at least 50% of its gross income was from the active conduct of certain trades or businesses within a possession.

Act Sec. 1224, repealing the CFC exemption of possessions corporations, repeals Sec. 957 by redesignating (d) as new (c), effective generally for tax years of foreign corporations beginning after 12-31-86, except that for applying Secs. 951(a)(1)(B) and 956 the amendments will take effect on 8-16-86. A transitional rule applies to corporations treated as CFCs due to the amendment.

【¶1221】 **Passive Foreign Investment Companies.** The new law provides that generally a U.S. person must pay U.S. tax and an interest charge based on the value of tax deferral when the shareholder disposes of his or her PFIC stock or receives an excess distribution. The rule doesn't apply to U.S. shareholders in PFICs that are qualified electing funds.

PFIC definition. A PFIC is a foreign corporation if 75% or more of its gross income for the tax year is passive income, or at least 50% of the average value of its assets during the tax year produce, or are held for producing, passive income. "Passive income" is income includible in the foreign tax credit limitation for passive income under Sec. 904(d)(2)(A). Passive income excludes income derived by bona fide banks and insurance companies. In determining whether the corporate shareholder is a PFIC under the asset test or income test, a proportionate part of the assets and income of a 25%-owned subsidiary is attributed to the corporate shareholder. A PFIC doesn't include a foreign investment company described in Sec. 1247 (one electing before 1963 to distribute income currently). It also doesn't include a corporation in a start-up phase of an active business or a corporation in transition from one active business to another active business.

Under the new law, the gain recognized on disposition of PFIC stock or on receipt of an excess distribution from a PFIC is considered as earned pro rata over the shareholder's holding period and is treated as ordinary income. The portion of distribution not characterized as excess distributions are taxable in the current year. An excess distribution is a current year distribution as to stock to the extent it represents a ratable portion of the total distributions as to the stock during the year that are in excess of 125% of the average amount of distributions as to the stock during the three preceding years.

A taxpayer who uses PFIC stock as security for a loan is treated as having disposed of the stock.

A U.S. person is considered to own his or her proportionate share of the stock of a PFIC owned by a (1) partnership, estate, or trust of which the U.S. person is a partner or beneficiary, or (2) foreign corporation for which the U.S. person owns 50% or more of the value of its stock.

Qualified electing funds. A U.S. person who owns (or is treated as owning) stock of a qualified electing fund must include in gross income his or her share of the PFIC's E&P, with basis adjustments for undistributed amounts and for distributions previously included in income. A qualified electing fund is a PFIC that properly elects qualified electing fund status and complies with Treasury requirements for determining E&P and ascertaining stock ownership. The election must be made before the 15th day of the third month of the tax year following the tax year for which the election is being made.

Subject to an interest charge, a U.S. shareholder in a qualified electing fund can elect to defer U.S. tax on amounts included in income for which no current distributions are received.

Act Sec. 1235, relating to passive foreign investment companies, adds new Secs. 542(c)(10), 551(g) by redesignating old (g) as (h), 904(g)(1)(A)(iii), 951(f), 1246(f), by redesignating old (f) as (g), 1291, 1293, 1294, 1295, 1296, 1297, and 6503(j) by redesignating old (j) as (k), and amends Secs. 532(b), 542(c), 851(b), 904(g)(1)(A), 904(g)(2) paragraph heading, and the table of parts for subchapter P of chapter 1, effective for tax years beginning after 12-31-86.

〔¶1222〕 Accumulated Earnings and PHC. The new law provides that, for a foreign corporation, the accumulated earnings tax and personal holding company tax will be calculated by taking into account only capital gains and losses that are effectively connected with the conduct of a U.S. trade or business and aren't tax exempt under a treaty.

Act Sec. 1225, relating to a foreign corporation's accumulated earnings tax and PHC tax, adds new Secs. 535(b)(9) and 545(b)(7), effective for gains and losses realized on or after 3-1-86.

Special Provisions for U.S. Persons

〔¶1223〕 Possession Tax Credit. The new law modifies the possession tax credit.

Active trade or business test. A U.S. corporation must meet an active trade or business test and a possession-source income test to qualify for the possession tax credit. Under the new law, the percentage of the corporation's gross income that must be derived from the active conduct of a trade or business in the possession increases from 65% or more to 75% or more for tax years beginning after 1986. As before, the corporation must derive 80% or more of its gross income from sources within a possession.

Received in U.S. The new law modifies the prior law rule that denied the possession tax credit for otherwise eligible income received by the U.S. corporation within the United States. The credit is available for active business income received from an unrelated person.

Qualified investment income. To allow the Puerto Rico government to implement its twin-plant program to encourage companies with Puerto Rico operations to develop or expand manufacturing in qualified Caribbean Basin countries, the new law modifies the definition of qualified possession-source investment income (QPSII). Prior law limited QPSII to income derived from investments within a possession in which the taxpayer conducted an active trade or business.

Under the new law, subject to conditions under regulations, an investment in a financial institution will be treated as for use in Puerto Rico—to the extent used by the financial institution (or the Government Development Bank for Puerto Rico or the Puerto Rico Economic Development Bank) for investment in active business assets or development projects in a qualified Caribbean Basin country consistent with Caribbean Basin Economic Recovery Act goals, and under a specific authorization granted by the GDBPR under Puerto Rico Treasury regulations. A similar rule applies for direct investment in the GDBPR or the PREDB. For this purpose, a qualified Caribbean Basin country is any beneficiary country (under Sec. 212(a)(1)(A) of the CBERA) that satisfies Sec. 274(h)(6)(A)(i) and (ii). The rule doesn't apply unless the person in whose trade or business the investment is made (or other recipient) and the financial institution (or the GDBPR or PREDB) certify to the Treasury and the Puerto Rico Treasury that the loan will be promptly used to acquire active business assets or to make other authorized expenditures, and the financial institution (or the GDBPR or PREDB) and the recipient agree to allow the Treasury and the Puerto Rico Treasury to examine their books and records to ensure that the requirements are met.

Treatment of intangibles. A possession corporation may derive some intangible income tax free if it elects either a cost-sharing rule or a 50/50 profit split method of computing taxable income. For companies that elect the cost-sharing rule, the new law sets the required cost-sharing payment at the greater of 110% of the payment required under present law, or the royalty payment that would be required (under Secs. 482 and 367 as amended by the law) if the possessions corporation were considered a foreign corporation as to manufacturing intangibles it is treated as owning. For companies that elect the 50/50 profit split, the new law increases the amount of product area research expenditures to 120% for computing combined taxable income.

Treatment of royalty payments. The new law requires that royalty payments relating to intangibles that a U.S. person transfers to a related foreign corporation or possessions corporation must be commensurate with the income attributable to the intangible. The standard applies in determining the amounts imputed under Sec. 367(d) and the appropriate Sec. 482 allocation in other situations.

Act Sec. 1231, relating to the possession tax credit, adds new Sec. 936(d)(4), repeals Sec. 936(a)(2)(C), and amends Secs. 367(d)(2)(A), 482, 936(a)(2)(B), 936(b), 936(h)(5)(C)(i)(I), and 936(h)(5)(C)(ii)(II), effective generally for tax years beginning after 12-31-86. A special rule applies for transfer of intangibles. Act Sec. 1231(f), also amends Sec. 936(h)(5)(C)(ii)(II), effective for tax years beginning after 12-31-82. A special transitional rule applies to a particular corporation.

〔¶1224〕 Panama Canal Commission Employees. The new law clarifies that nothing in the Panama Canal Treaty or any implementing agreement is to be construed as exempting any U.S. citizen or resident from any U.S. tax under the 1954 or 1986 Code. The new law also provides that Panama Canal Commission employees and Defense Department civilian employees stationed in Panama may exclude from gross income allowances comparable to those excludable under Sec. 912(1) by the State Department employees stationed there.

Act Sec. 1232(a), relating to the treatment of individuals in Panama, is effective generally for all tax years, whether beginning before, on, or after the enactment date (or for a tax not imposed as to a tax year, to taxable events after the enactment date). Act Sec. 1232(b), relating to employees' allowances, is effective for tax years beginning after 12-31-86.

〔¶1225〕 Foreign Earned Income Exclusion. The new law limits a qualifying individual's total foreign earned income exclusion for a tax year to $70,000. Previously, the maximum exclusion was $80,000, increasing to $85,000 in 1988, $90,000 in 1989, and $95,000 in 1990 and thereafter.

The new law also denies the Sec. 911 exclusion to individuals who violate federal travel restrictions. When an individual's activities in a foreign country violate regulations under the Trading With the Enemy Act or the International Emergency Economic Powers Act that include provisions generally prohibiting U.S. citizens and residents from engaging in travel-related transactions in that country

• the individual's foreign earned income won't include income attributable to services performed in that country during that period, and his or her housing expenses won't include expenses allocable to the period for housing there or for housing of his or her spouse or dependents in another country while present there, and

• the individual won't be treated as a bona fide resident of, or as present in, a foreign country for any day in which he or she was present in that country during that period.

NOTE: Currently, Treasury regulations generally prohibit travel-related transactions of U.S. citizens and residents in Cuba, Kampuchea, Libya, North Korea, and Vietnam.

Act Sec. 1233, relating to the foreign earned income exclusion, adds new Sec. 911(d)(8) by redesignating old (8) as (9), and amends Sec. 911(b)(2)(A), effective for tax years beginning after 12-31-86.

Foreign Taxpayers

[¶1251] **Branch Profits Tax.** The new law imposes a 30% branch profits tax on the E&P of a U.S. branch of a foreign corporation attributable to its income effectively connected (or treated as such) with a U.S. trade or business. It retains the 30% second-level withholding taxes on dividends and interest paid by a foreign corporation to a foreign person, but reduces the U.S. business thresholds that trigger the taxes and modifies the determination of U.S. source interest subject to U.S. tax.

New branch profits tax. The base for the branch profits tax (the dividend equivalent amount) is the foreign corporation's effectively connected E&P for the tax year—reduced for an increase in U.S. net equity and increased for a decrease in U.S. net equity. "U.S. net equity" means U.S. assets (money and adjusted bases of assets) reduced by U.S. liabilities.

Treaty coordination. An income tax treaty between the United States and a foreign country will reduce or eliminate the branch profits tax only if the foreign corporation is a qualified resident of the foreign country, or the treaty allows a withholding tax on dividends paid by the foreign corporation. A "qualified resident" is a foreign corporation that is a resident of a foreign country unless more than 50% by value of its stock is owned by individuals who are neither residents of the foreign country nor U.S. citizens or resident aliens, or at least 50% of its income is used to meet liabilities to nonresidents of the foreign country or the United States. A foreign corporation will be treated as a qualified resident if its stock is primarily and regularly traded on an established securities market in the foreign country, or is wholly owned by another foreign corporation organized in that country and its stock is so traded. The Treasury may treat a foreign corporation as a qualified resident if it meets requirements that the Treasury establishes.

In general, if an income tax treaty between the United States and the country in which the corporation is a qualified resident specifically provides a branch profits tax, the treaty rate applies. If no branch profits rate is specified, the treaty rate on dividends paid by a U.S. corporation to its treaty country parent corporation applies. Any other treaty limitation on the branch profits tax applies.

If a foreign corporation is subject to the branch profits tax for a tax year, it is exempt from the second-level withholding taxes on dividends paid during that tax year. A foreign corporation that isn't a qualified resident cannot claim treaty benefits as to dividends paid by the foreign corporation that are subject to the second-level withholding tax, or received by the foreign corporation.

The Treasury may prescribe regulations to carry out the purposes of the provision.

Second-level withholding taxes. The new law provides that a portion of interest and dividends paid by a foreign corporation are U.S.-

source income if at least 25% of the corporation's worldwide gross income is effectively connected with the conduct of a U.S. trade or business for a three-year period. When the threshold is reached, the second-level withholding tax applies to a foreign corporation's payment of interest or dividends to a foreign person. Previously, the threshold was 50%.

Act Sec. 1241, relating to the branch profits tax, adds new Secs. 884 and 906(b)(6), and amends Secs. 861(a)(1), 861(a)(2)(B), and the table of sections for subpart B of part II of subchapter N of chapter 1, effective for tax years beginning after 12-31-86.

[¶1252] Deferred Payments and Appreciation. To prevent a foreign taxpayer from avoiding U.S. tax by receiving income after its U.S. trade or business has ceased to exist, the new law provides that an NRA or foreign corporation's income or gain for a tax year attributable to a transaction in another tax year will be treated as effectively connected with the conduct of a U.S. trade or business as long as it would have been so treated if it were taken into account in the other tax year.

If property is sold or exchanged within 10 years after being used or held for use in connection with a U.S. trade or business, income or gain attributable to the sale or exchange is treated as effectively connected.

Act Sec. 1242, relating to deferred payments and appreciation, adds new Secs. 864(c)(6) and (7), and amends Sec. 864(c)(1), effective for tax years beginning after 12-31-86.

[¶1253] Tax-Free Exchanges by Expatriates. Individuals who give up their U.S. citizenship for a principal purpose of avoiding U.S. tax may still make tax-free exchanges of U.S. property for foreign property. However, gain on the sale or exchange of property whose basis is determined in whole or in part by reference to the basis of property located in the United States, stock of a U.S. corporation, or a debt obligation of a U.S. person will be treated as gain from the sale of U.S. property. So a later recognized gain on the foreign property will be subject to U.S. tax.

Act Sec. 1243, relating to tax-free exchanges by expatriates, amends Sec. 877(c), effective for sales or exchanges of property received in exchanges after 9-25-85.

[¶1254] Reinsurance Study. The new law requires the Treasury to make a study of whether existing U.S. income tax treaties place U.S. reinsurance corporations at a significant disadvantage with their foreign competitors, and to report the results to the Senate Finance Committee and the House Ways and Means Committee before 1-1-88.

Act Sec. 1244, relating to foreign insurers, makes no changes in the Code.

Foreign Currency Transactions

[¶1261]　**Foreign Currency Transactions.**　There's a comprehensive new set of rules for the U.S. taxation of foreign exchange transactions.

Functional currency.　Under the new law, all determinations must be made in the taxpayer's functional currency—that is, the U.S. dollar or the currency of the economic environment in which a significant part of the business activities of any qualified business unit of the taxpayer are conducted and that is used by the unit to keep its books and records. If the unit's activities are primarily conducted in U.S. dollars, its functional currency will be the U.S. dollar. "Qualified business unit" refers to any separate and clearly identified unit of a trade or business of a taxpayer that keeps separate books and records.

A taxpayer may elect to use the U.S. dollar as the functional currency for any qualified business unit that keeps its books and records in U.S. dollars or uses an accounting method approximating a separate transactions method, to the extent that regulations provide. The election will be effective for the tax year for which it is made and all later tax years unless revoked with Treasury consent.

A change in the functional currency is treated as a change in the taxpayer's accounting method for Sec. 481 purposes.

E&P and foreign taxes.　For determining the tax of a shareholder of a foreign corporation, the corporation's E&P is determined in its functional currency. For a U.S. person, the E&P distributed (or deemed distributed or otherwise taken into account) must, if necessary, be translated into U.S. dollars at the appropriate exchange rate.

For computing the amount of foreign taxes deemed paid under Secs. 902 and 960, a foreign income tax paid by a foreign corporation is translated into U.S. dollars using the exchange rate as of the time of payment. An adjustment to the tax paid by a foreign corporation is translated into U.S. dollars using the exchange rate as of when the adjustment was made.

Foreign currency gain or loss on distributions of previously taxed E&P attributable to exchange rate movements between the times of deemed and actual distribution is treated as ordinary income or loss from the same source as the associated income inclusion. The Treasury may prescribe regulations for treating distributions of previously taxed E&P through tiers of foreign corporations.

Translation of branch income. The new law provides that taxpayers with branches whose functional currency isn't the U.S. dollar must use the profit and loss method to compute branch income. The taxpayer must compute the income or loss separately for each qualified business unit in the unit's functional currency, translating the amount to U.S. dollars using the weighed average exchange rate for the tax period over which the income or loss accrued. The taxpayer will recognize exchange gain or loss on remittances to the extent the currency's value at the time of the remittance differs from the value when earned. Remittances after 1986 are treated as paid on a pro rata basis out of post-1986 accumulated earnings. Exchange gain or loss on the remittances will be deemed ordinary income or loss, sourced by reference to the source of income.

Foreign currency transactions. Foreign currency gain or loss attributable to a Sec. 988 transaction must be computed separately and treated as ordinary income or loss. Forward contracts, futures contracts, and options that aren't marked to market are accorded capital gain or loss treatment if they are capital assets and certain identification requirements are met. To the extent that regulations provide, foreign currency gain or loss will be treated as interest income or expense.

Foreign currency gain or loss refers to gain or loss realized due to a change in the exchange rate on or after the booking date (the date that an asset or liability is taken into account for tax purposes) and before the date it is paid.

"Sec. 988 transaction" refers to transactions in which the amount that the taxpayer is entitled to receive or is required to pay is denominated in a nonfunctional currency, or is determined by reference to the value of one or more nonfunctional currencies. Sec. 988 transactions are: (1) the acquisition of, or becoming the obligor under, a debt instrument; (2) accruing or otherwise taking into account an item of expense or gross income or receipt to be paid or received on a later date; (3) entering into or acquiring a forward contract, futures contract, option, or similar financial instrument if it isn't marked to market at the end of the tax year; and (4) the disposition of a nonfunctional currency.

If a Sec. 988 transaction is part of a hedging transaction, all transactions that are part of the transaction will be integrated and treated as one transaction or otherwise treated consistently, to the extent that regulations provide. Neither the Sec. 1092 loss deferral rule nor the Sec. 1256 marked-to-market rules will apply.

Under the loss deferral rule, an obligor's interest in a foreign currency denominated obligation is a position, and a foreign currency for which there is an interbank market is presumed to be "actively traded" property. The new law repeals the special treatment that allowed banks to qualify for the hedging exception to the straddle provisions.

Generally the source of an amount treated as ordinary gain or loss is determined by reference to the residence of the taxpayer or the qualified business unit whose books properly reflect the asset, liability, or income or expense item. An individual's residence is the country of his or her tax base. A U.S. entity's residence is the United States, and a foreign entity's residence is a foreign country. A qualified business unit's residence is the country in which its principal place of business is located. A special rule governs certain related party loans.

The new law applies to Sec. 988 transactions entered into by an individual only to the extent that expenses allocable to the transaction would have been deductible under Sec. 162 or 212 (other than the part concerning tax-related expenses).

The new law authorizes the Treasury to prescribe regulations necessary to carry out the purpose of the new rules, including (1) procedures for taxpayers with qualified business units using a net worth accounting method before the new provisions were enacted, (2) the limitation of the recognition of foreign currency loss on certain remittances from qualified business units, (3) the recharacterization of interest and principal payments as to obligations denominated in certain hyperinflationary currencies, (4) alternative adjustments to the application of Sec. 905(c), and (5) the appropriate treatment of related party transactions (including transactions between the taxpayer's qualified business units).

Act Sec. 1261, relating to the treatment of foreign currency transactions, adds new Secs. 985, 986, 987, 988, 989, and 1092(d)(7), repeals Sec. 1256(e)(4) by redesignating old (5) as (4), and amends the table of subjects for part III of subchapter N of chapter 1, effective generally for tax years beginning after 12-31-86. For applying Sec. 902 and 960, the amendments are effective for E&P of the foreign corporation for tax years beginning after 12-31-86, and foreign taxes paid or accrued by the foreign corporation as to such E&P.

Tax Treatment of Possessions

[¶1271] **The U.S. Possessions.** The U.S. Virgin Islands, Guam, the Northern Mariana Islands, and American Samoa currently use the mirror system of taxation. Each possession transforms the 1954 Internal Revenue Code, as amended, into a local tax code by substituting its name for the name "United States" when appropriate. The new law eliminates the prior law requirement that Guam and the Northern Mariana Islands use a mirror system, coordinates these tax systems and that of American Samoa with the U.S. tax system, and reforms the mirror system in the Virgin Islands.

[¶1272] **The Virgin Islands.** The V.I. Revised Organic Act will be treated as if enacted before the Code, so that the Code will control in cases of conflict. The V.I. Act also will have no effect on any person's U.S. tax liability. The U.S. Treasury will have the authority to specify parts of the Code that won't be mirrored.

The Virgin Islands will be allowed to enact nondiscriminatory local taxes in addition to those of the mirror system, and to rebate or reduce the V.I. tax liabilities of

- non-U.S. individuals attributable to V.I. source income and income effectively connected with the conduct of a V.I. trade or business, and

- V.I. corporations with less than 10% U.S. stock ownership attributable to non-U.S. source income and income not effectively connected with the conduct of a U.S. trade or business.

Individuals. The United States will be treated as including the Virgin Islands for purposes of determining U.S. tax liability of U.S. or V.I. citizens or residents and, under the V.I. mirror Code, the Virgin Islands will be treated as including the United States for purposes of determining V.I. tax liability.

An individual qualifying as a bona fide V.I. resident on the last day of the tax year will pay tax to the Virgin Islands on worldwide income and have no U.S. tax liability.

For a U.S. citizen or resident (other than a bona fide V.I. resident) deriving V.I. income, V.I. tax liability will be a fraction of the individual's U.S. tax liability, based on the ratio of adjusted gross income derived from V.I. sources to worldwide adjusted gross income. That individual will file identical returns with the United States and the Virgin Islands and the individual's V.I. tax payment will be credited against his or her U.S. tax liability.

If spouses file a joint return and only one spouse is a V.I. resident, the resident status of the spouse with the greater adjusted gross income will control.

Corporations. The new law modifies the Sec. 881(b) rule for the exemption from 30% withholding to require that 65% of the corporation's income (formerly 20%) be effectively connected with a U.S. or U.S. possession trade or business and that no substantial part of the income can be used to satisfy obligations to persons other than U.S. or U.S. possession residents.

V.I. corporations qualify for the Sec. 936 credit.

[¶1273] **The Other Possessions.** *Taxing authority.* The new law grants Guam, American Samoa, and the Northern Mariana Islands full authority over their local tax systems for income from sources within, or effectively connected with a trade or business in, the possession and for income received or accrued by a resident of

¶1273

the possession. American Samoa already has this authority. However, each of these grants of authority is effective only if an implementing agreement is in effect between the possession and the United States, providing for elimination of double taxation, prevention of U.S. tax evasion or avoidance, exchange of information, and resolution of other problems.

The possession's tax law must not discriminate against U.S. persons or U.S. possession residents, and for the implementation year and the four following tax years, the possession's revenue must not decrease. The Northern Mariana Islands may retain the mirror system regardless of whether Guam enacts its own law.

Exclusion of possession income. For an individual resident of Guam, American Samoa, or the Northern Mariana Islands, gross income won't include income derived from sources within the possession, and income effectively connected with the individual's conduct of a trade or business within the possession. The individual won't be allowed any deductions (except the Sec. 151 deduction) or credits allocable or chargeable against excluded amounts. Amounts paid to a possession resident for services as a U.S. or U.S. agency employee are taxable. The new law gives the Treasury the authority to prescribe regulations for determining possession residency, source of income, and whether income is effectively connected.

The Sec. 876 exclusion from withholding for alien residents of Puerto Rico is extended to residents of Guam, American Samoa, and the Northern Mariana Islands.

Remuneration paid for services for the U.S. or a U.S. agency performed by a U.S. citizen within a possession is eliminated from the definition of wages subject to withholding to the extent the U.S. or U.S. agency withholds taxes under an agreement with the possession.

Corporations. The new law modifies the Sec. 881(b) rule for the exemption from 30% withholding to include American Samoa (as well as Guam, the Northern Mariana Islands, and the Virgin Islands), and to require that 65% of the corporation's income (instead of 20%) be effectively connected with a U.S. or U.S. possession trade or business for the three-year period ending at the end of its tax year. No substantial part of the income can be used to satisfy obligations to persons other than U.S. or U.S. possession residents. As under prior law, less than 25% in value of the corporations stock can be beneficially owned by foreign persons.

For Subpart F purposes, a corporation organized in Guam, the Northern Mariana Islands, or American Samoa won't be considered a U.S. person if at least 80% of the corporation's income for the three-year period ending at the end of its tax year was from sources in the possession or effectively connected with a trade or business there, and at least 50% of gross income for the period was from the active conduct of a trade or business in that possession.

[¶1274] **Cover Over.** Guam, American Samoa, the Northern Mariana Islands, and the Virgin Islands will receive the net collection of income tax as to individuals who are bona fide residents of the possession, the taxes withheld on compensation of U.S. government personnel stationed in the possession, and taxes paid to the United States by civilian employees resident in the possession.

[¶1275] **Guamanian Banks.** The new law repeals the rule that treated interest income on U.S. government obligations held by banks organized in Guam as effectively connected income.

Act Sec. 1236, relating to interest received by Guam banks, amends Sec. 882(e), effective for tax years beginning after 11-16-85.

Act Sec. 1271, relating to the authority of Guam, American Samoa, and the Northern Mariana Islands to enact revenue laws, makes no changes to the Code. Act Sec. 1272, relating to the exclusion of possession source income by individuals, adds new Sec. 3401(a)(8)(D), and 7655(b)(1) by redesignating old (1) and (2) as (2) and (3), repeals Secs. 153(4) by redesignating old (5) as (4), 932 and 935, and amends Secs. 32(c)(1)(C), 48(a)(2)(B)(vii), 63(c)(6), 876, 931, 933(1), 933(2), 1402(a)(8), 1402(a)(9), 6091(b)(1)(B)(iii), the table of sections for subpart A of part II of subchapter N of chapter 1, and the table of sections for subpart D of part III of subchapter N of chapter 1. Act Sec. 1273, relating to the treatment of corporations organized in Guam, American Samoa, or the Northern Mariana Islands, amends Secs. 881(b), 957(c), and 1442(c). Act Sec. 1274, relating to the coordination of U.S. and V.I. income taxes, adds new Sec. 932 and amends the table of sections for subpart D. Act Sec. 1275, relating to the eligibility of V.I. corporations to use the possession tax credit, adds new Sec. 934(b), repeals Sec. 934A, and amends Secs. 28(d)(3)(B), 48(a)(2)(B)(vii), 246(e), 338(h)(6)(B)(i), 864(d)(5)(B), 934, 936(d)(1), 7651(5)(B), and the table of sections for subpart D of part III of subchapter N of chapter 1. Act Sec. 1276, relating to the cover over of income taxes, amends Sec. 7654 and the table of sections for subchapter D of chapter 78. The amendments are generally effective for tax years beginning after 12-31-86. Under a special rule, the amendments apply as to Guam, American Samoa, or the Northern Mariana Islands (and residents and corporations) only if an implementing agreement is in effect between the United States and the possession. Special rules for the Virgin Islands provide that the Sec. 1275(c) amendments apply as to Virgin Islands (and residents and corporations) only if an implementing agreement is in effect between the United States and the Virgin Islands, and also cover the application of the Sec. 1275(b) amendment for pre-1987 open years. A rule provides that if an implementing agreement isn't executed within the first year of the Act, the Treasury must report to the Senate Finance Committee, the House Ways and Means Committee, and the House Interior and Insular Affairs Committee. A rule provides that if a U.S. person becomes a resident of Guam, American Samoa, or the Northern Mariana Islands, the Sec. 877(c) rules will apply during the 10-year period beginning when he or she became a resident, effective for dispositions after 12-31-86 in tax years ending after that date.

[¶1281] **Transfer Prices for Imported Property.** Under the new law, if property is imported into the United States in a transaction between related persons within the meaning of Sec. 482, the costs taken into account in computing the buyer's basis or inventory cost of the property cannot be greater than the costs taken into account in computing the property's customs value.

"Customs value" is the value taken into account for determining the amount of any duties that may be imposed on importing property. "Import" means the entering, or withdrawal from warehouse, for consumption—unless regulations provide otherwise.

Act Sec. 1248, relating to the transfer prices for imported property, adds new Sec. 1059A, and amends the table of sections for part IV of subchapter O of chapter 1, effective for transactions entered into after 3-18-86.

[¶1282] **Income of Foreign Governments.** The new law codifies the rule under Reg. Sec. 1.892-1(a)(3) that the tax exemption for foreign governments is limited to investment income.

The exemption applies to a foreign government's income received from (1) U.S. investments in stocks, bonds, or other domestic securities owned by the government, or financial instruments held to execute its financial or monetary policy, or (2) interest on deposits in U.S. banks of moneys belonging to the government.

Commercial activities. The exemption won't apply to a foreign government's income derived from the conduct of U.S. or foreign commercial activity, or received from or by a controlled commercial entity. A "controlled commercial entity" is an entity engaged in commercial activities if the government (1) directly or indirectly holds a 50% or more value or voting interest in the entity, or directly or indirectly holds any other interest that provides the foreign government with effective control of the entity.

International organizations. Also exempt from U.S. taxation is the income of an international organization received from U.S. investments in stocks, bonds, or other domestic securities owned by it, or from interest on deposits in U.S. banks of moneys belonging to it, or from any other U.S. source.

Act Sec. 1247, relating to income of foreign governments and international organizations, amends Sec. 892, effective for amounts received on or after 7-1-86, except that no amount will be required to be deducted and withheld due to the amendment from any payment made before the enactment date.

[¶1283] **Dual Residence Companies.** The new law limits double dipping by dual resident companies—that is, the use of a deduction by a corporation that is a U.S. resident and a resident of another country to reduce the U.S. tax of commonly owned corporations in both countries.

Under the new law, a corporation's "dual consolidated loss" for a tax year cannot reduce the taxable income of another member of its affiliated group for that or any other tax year. A "dual consolidated loss" is the net operating loss of a U.S. corporation subject to a foreign income tax on worldwide income or on a residence basis. To the extent provided in regulations, a dual consolidated loss won't include a loss that doesn't offset the income of a foreign corporation under foreign income tax law.

Act Sec. 1249, relating to the treatment of dual residence corporations, adds new Sec. 1503(d), effective for net operating losses for tax years beginning after 12-31-86.

[¶1284] **Withholding Tax on Foreign Partners.** The new law generally provides that if a partnership has any income, gain, or loss effectively connected (or treated as such) with the conduct of a U.S. trade or business, the withholding agent must withhold a 20% tax on any amount distributed to a foreign partner.

Limitation. If the partnership's gross income effectively connected with a U.S. trade or business over a three-tax year period is less than 80% of the partnership's total gross income over that period, then withholding is required only on the proportion of current distributions that the partnership's gross income effectively connected with its U.S. trade or business bears to its total gross income over its previous three tax years.

Exceptions. Withholding isn't required

• on the portion of any distribution for which a 30% (or lower treaty rate) tax must be withheld under Sec. 1441 or 1442, or

• if substantially all the U.S.-source income and effectively connected income of a U.S. partnership is properly allocated to U.S. persons—unless regulations provide otherwise.

Act Sec. 1246, relating to the withholding tax on amounts paid by partnerships to foreign partners, adds new Sec. 1446, and amends Sec. 6401(b)(2) and the table of sections for subchapter A of chapter 3, effective for distributions after 12-31-87 (or, if earlier, the effective date of Sec. 1446 regulations, but no earlier than 1-1-87).

[¶1285] **Compliance Provisions for U.S. Individuals and Foreign-Owned Corporations.** The new law provides that a U.S. citizen applying for a passport and a resident alien applying for a permanent resident visa (green card) will have to file an IRS information return. The return must include the individual's taxpayer identification number, a passport applicant's foreign country of residence, information as to whether a green card applicant must file a tax return, and other information required. A new $500 penalty will apply for each failure to provide a statement through willful neglect. Any U.S. agency that collects the return must provide it to the Treasury.

Collection of tax. Under the new law, pensions and similar payments delivered outside the United States are subject to withholding, unless the recipient certifies to the payor that the recipient isn't a U.S. citizen who resides abroad or a tax-avoidance expatriate. Previously, the recipient could elect not to have withholding apply.

Foreign-owned corporations. Under the new law, a foreign-controlled U.S. corporation, and a foreign-controlled foreign corporation engaged in a U.S. trade or business must furnish certain information as to its transactions with any related party (under Secs. 482, 267(b), or 707(b)(1)).

Foreign-controlled corporations and U.S.-controlled foreign corporations must furnish information that Treasury requires for carrying out the installment sales rules.

Act Sec. 1234(a), relating to information returns for U.S. individuals, adds new Sec. 6039E, and amends the table of sections for subpart A of part III of subchapter A of chapter 61, effective for applications submitted after 12-31-87 (or, if earlier, the effective date of Sec. 6039E regulations, but no earlier than 1-1-87). Act Sec. 1234(b), relating to withholding on deferred payments abroad, adds new Sec. 3405(d)(13), effective for payments after 12-31-86.

Act Sec. 1245, relating to information as to foreign-owned corporations, adds new Secs. 6038(a)(1)(F) and 6038A(b)(4), and amends Secs. 6038(a)(1), 6038A(b)(1), 6038A(b)(2), 6038A(b)(3), and 6038A(c)(2), effective for tax years beginning after 12-31-86.

[¶1286]   Dividends-Received Deduction.   Under the new law, a deduction is allowed for dividends received by a U.S. corporation from a foreign corporation (other than an FPHC or a passive foreign investment company) if the taxpayer owns at least 10% of its stock by vote and value. The allowable deduction is based on the proportion of the foreign corporation's post-1986 earnings that have been subject to U.S. corporate income tax and that have not been distributed. Amounts of Subpart F income previously taxed that are distributed to U.S. shareholders reduce E&P in arriving at the proportion.

NOTE: The new law elsewhere reduces the 85% dividends-received deduction to 80% [See ¶602.].

Act Sec. 1226(a), relating to the dividends-received deduction, amends Sec. 245(a), effective generally for distributions out of E&P for tax years beginning after 12-31-86. Act Sec. 1226(b), relating to the reduction of E&P, amends Secs. 246A(a) and 959(d), effective for distributions after the enactment date.

[¶1287]   Special Transitional Rules.   The new law provides special rules for one U.S. corporation concerning the application of Sec. 954 to certain dividends and for one U.S. corporation concerning the application of Sec. 897.

Act Sec. 1227, relating to Sec. 954, applies for Sec. 954(c)(3)(A), effective for dividends received after 12-31-86.

Act Sec. 1228, relating to Sec. 897, is effective on the enactment date.

[The page following this is 1301.]

TAX-EXEMPT BONDS

[¶1301] Overview. The tax exemption for interest on bonds issued by state and local governments (i.e., obligations of a state, the District of Columbia, U.S. possessions, or their political subdivisions) continues under the new law, with some significantly changed rules. The rules for tax-exempt "private activity" obligations, issued to provide conduit financing for activities other than general governmental operations or governmentally owned-and-operated facilities, have been significantly tightened and the "private activity" category is more broadly defined. Also, restrictions on all tax-exempts (i.e., both governmental issues and private activity issues) have been expanded or added. The Conference Report says that prior law principles continue to control the tax exemption except to the extent of amendments made.

> **NEW CODE SETUP:** The statutory rules for tax-exempt bonds (as changed by the new law) have been technically reordered. They are now included in Sec. 103 and new Secs. 141—150. Sec. 103A has been deleted, and the provision governing determination of marital status (old Sec. 143) has been redesignated as Sec. 7703. Sec. 103 grants the tax exemption to interest on state and local obligations. But it denies the exemption to (1) private activity bonds that aren't "qualified bonds" (the definition of private activity bonds and statutory rules for "qualified" bonds are in new Secs. 141—147); (2) arbitrage bonds (new Sec. 148 contains the arbitrage restrictions to be complied with for exemption); and (3) bonds that don't meet the requirement of Sec. 149. New Sec. 150 contains definitions and special rules.

Bonds now become "private activity bonds" (taxable unless they fit under a specifically exempt category—i.e., unless they are "qualified bonds") in either of these two cases: (1) more than 10% of the proceeds of the issue (or $15 million per facility, if that's less, for output facilities) is for direct or indirect use in a trade or business of anyone except a governmental unit, *and* direct or indirect payments of more than 10% of the debt service on the bonds (or $15 million per facility, if that's less, for output facilities) are made with respect to such trade or business; and (2) more than 5% of the proceeds of the issue, or $5 million if that's less, is used to make or finance loans to entities other than state or local governments. And for qualified private activity bonds, at least 95% of the proceeds must be spent for the exempt purpose of the borrowing [¶1302]. The new law repeals the prior-law tax exemption for several categories of exempt facility private activity bonds (formerly exempt activity IDBs) and adds a new exempt category for hazardous waste disposal facilities [¶1303]. It retains the general 12-31-86 sunset date for qualified small issue bonds (formerly small issue IDBs); but postpones the sunset date for small issue manufacturing facilities until 12-31-89 and treats small issue bonds for first time farmers same as manufacturing bonds. A new category of qualified redevelopment bonds is designed to finance redevelopment of blighted areas [¶1304].

Qualified nonhospital bonds for Sec. 501(c)(3) organizations will now have to fit under a $150 million limit, ¶1305. Qualified mortgage bonds and mortgage credit certificates (MCCs) can now be issued through 12-31-88 under changed rules, and the trade-in-value of MCCs issued for exchanged qualified mortgage authority has been upped to 25%. And limited equity housing cooperatives can elect multifamily residential rental project rules for bonds providing the housing [¶1306.]

A single volume cap now covers other private activity bonds and qualified mortgage bonds; qualified veterans' mortgage bonds remain subject to their prior law volume cap [¶1307]. And all private activity bonds have to meet public approval requirements and comply with prohibited facilities and change in use restrictions [¶1308].

Major rule changes for all tax-exempts involve arbitrage and advance refunding. Arbitrage restrictions that apply to all tax-exempt bonds prevent investment of their proceeds in materially higher yielding obligations. The minor portion of bond proceeds not covered by arbitrage rules has been whittled down to 5% of the bond proceeds. The arbitrage restrictions have been expanded to cover acquisitions of taxable investment property such as deferred payment contracts to fund pension plans. The new law eliminates the prior law election under regs to forgo the temporary period exception and be allowed to earn higher arbitrage. Restrictions on nonpurpose investments have been expanded. And the new law extends to all tax-exempts a requirement of rebating to the U.S. of arbitrage earned on the gross proceeds of an issue invested in nonpurpose obligations [¶1309]. Also, only qualified 501(c)(3) bonds and governmental bonds can now be advance refunded, and advance refundings, where permitted, are subject to severe restrictions [¶1310].

Among other rules: Information reporting has been extended to all tax-exempts. And rules for GSOCs (state-established corporations for the benefit of state citizens with power to borrow and invest in business enterprises) have been repealed as deadwood [¶1311; 1312].

Tax exempt interest on private activity bonds (but not qualified 501(c)(3) bonds) is now a tax preference for the individual and corporate minimum tax [see ¶711]. And depreciation on property financed with tax exempts is subject to an alternative depreciation system [see ¶205].

Effective Dates: The rules generally apply to bonds issued after 8-15-86. However, provisions and bonds covered by the Joint Statements on Effective Dates of 3-14-86 and 7-17-86 apply to bonds issued on or after 9-1-86. The Joint Statements cover the amendments to the definition of a private activity bond, including refunding bonds, (i.e., they cover the 10% trade or business use test (10% or

$15 million for output facilities), the 5% unrelated use limitation, and the $5 million limitation contained in the amended private loan restriction). The Joint Statement's 9-1-86 effective date *doesn't* cover bonds that under prior law are (1) industrial development bonds; (2) bonds that would be IDBs, treating Sec. 501(c)(3) organizations as private persons engaged in trades and businesses; (3) student loan bonds; (4) mortgage revenue bonds; or (5) other private ("consumer") loan bonds for which tax exemption is permitted. Major exceptions to these dates are noted as part of the coverage of the law changes [or at ¶1313].

> **CAUTION:** The rules are subject to various effective date transitional rules and exceptions, often targeted to specific situations.

Act Sec. 1301(a) dealing with tax exempt bonds amends Sec. 103. Act Sec. 1301(b) dealing with tax exemption requirements adds Code Secs. 141—150. Act Sec. 1301(c) dealing with a direction to amend arbitrage regs. to eliminate the election to forgo the temporary period exception and Act Sec. 1301(d) dealing with modifications in the SLGS program, and Act Sec. 1301(e) dealing with IRS advance ruling policy on management contracts don't amend the Code. Act Sec. 1301(f) increasing the MCC trade-in rate amends Sec. 25(b)—(f). Act Sec. 1301(g) dealing with failures to report on compliance with residential rental project rules adds new Sec. 6652(j). Act Sec. 1302(h) dealing with deleting the report on mortgage revenue bonds repeals '84 TRA Sec. 611(d)(7). Act Sec. 1301(i) dealing with the direction to amend output regulations doesn't amend the Code. Act Sec. 1301(j) repeals Sec. 103A and redesignates old Sec. 143 as new Sec. 7703. Act Sec. 1302 providing that treatment of Sec. 501(c)(3) bonds as private activity bonds doesn't indicate their treatment in future legislation, doesn't amend the Code. Act Sec. 1303 deals with repeal of GSOC provisions (see ¶1312 for Sections amended). Subtitle B of Title XIII (Act Sec. 1311 et. seq.) deal with effective dates and transitional rules. These law changes are generally effective as indicated above and at ¶1302—1313.

[¶1302] General Restrictions on Tax-Exempts. The requirements of tax-exempt obligations issued to finance activities other than general governmental obligations or governmentally-owned-and-operated facilities (i.e., of private activity bonds) have been significantly tightened.

Prior law provided limited exemptions for private activity state and local bonds. These bonds have been in general treated as follows:

• If all or a major part (more than 25% according to regs) of the gross proceeds of a bond issue was for direct or indirect use in a trade or business of a nonexempt (i.e., private) person, and if the payment of a major part (as defined in the regs) of the issue's principal and interest was derived from or secured by the business, the bonds (known as industrial development bonds—IDBs) became taxable. However, IDBs that finance specified exempt activities, bonds issued for development of industrial parks, and exempt "small issues" of IDBs (up to $1 million issues, or issues whose amount when added to capital expenditures wasn't more than $10 million) remained tax-exempt.

• If a significant portion of a bond issue was to be used for mortgages on owner-occupied-residences, the bonds (known as Mortgage Subsidy bonds—MSBs) became taxable. However, qualified mortgage bonds financing the purchase or qualified rehabilitation or improvement of single-family owner-occupied homes, and qualified veterans' mortgage bonds financing mortgage loans to veterans remained tax-exempt.

• Sec. 501(c)(3) bonds financing activities of charitable, educational, etc., organizations (e.g., private nonprofit hospitals or colleges), and bonds issued by qualified governmental units to finance student loans were also tax exempt. IDBs and student loan bonds, qualified veterans' mortgage bonds, and qualified mortgage bonds had to meet separately designed state bond volume limits.

Use and security interests tests. Under the new law, bonds become private activity bonds (taxable unless they fit into a specifically exempt category) if (1) more than 10% of the gross proceeds of the issue (or $15 million per facility, if that's less, in case of financing for construction, rehabilitation or operation of output facilities) is for direct or indirect use in a trade or business of anyone except a governmental unit (*use test*); and (2) more than 10% of the principal of or interest on the bonds (or $15 million per facility, if that's less, in case of output facilities) is secured by or to be derived from property to be used in such a trade or business (*security interest test*). Bonds transitioned under Reg. Sec. 1.103-7(b)(iii) are under the new law treated consistent with the transition rule of the regs.

For a private activity bond to enjoy exemption, it must be a "qualified bond." Such a bond issue must fit in one of these exempt categories: (1) exempt facility bonds; (2) qualified mortgage bonds; (3) qualified veterans' mortgage bonds; (4) qualified small issue bonds; (5) qualified student loan bonds; (6) qualified redevelopment bonds; or (7) qualified 501(c)(3) bonds. It must also be within the applicable bond volume cap [¶1307], and meet certain other requirements (now in new Sec. 147). Law changes covering exempt categories of private activity bonds are explained later.

NOTE: The IRS is directed to modify the present rules for determining private use of output facilities (Reg. Sec. 1.103-7(b)(5)) to reflect the reduced limits on private use of governmental bonds and to delete the de minimis 3% rule. The Conference Report notes that the presence of a nongovernmental person acting solely as a conduit for the exchange of power output among governmentally-owned and operated facilities is to be disregarded in deciding whether the use and security interest tests are satisfied. And "swapping" of power between governmentally owned and operated utilities and investor-owned utilities under certain conditions does not give rise to trade or business use. It also notes that spot sales (under single agreement for 30 days or less) of excess power capacity other than under an output contract with specific buyers aren't treated as trade or business use.

The House Ways & Means Committee Report notes that for the percentage and dollar limit *use tests* that classify a bond issue as a "private activity bond" issue, nongovernmental use in a trade or business includes the use of the bond proceeds in all activities (1) of a nongovernmental person other than a natural person, (2) of the federal government, or (3) of Sec. 501(c)(3) charitable organizations. As under prior law, nongovernmental use can involve use of the bond proceeds; or use of bond-financed property through its ownership or its actual or beneficial use via a lease or a management, incentive payment or output contract. The use of bond proceeds or a facility as a member of the general public doesn't count—but such use must be on the same basis as is available to other members of the general public. What is nongovernmental use is determined by the facts and circumstances.

Example: A school building can be incidentally available for scout meetings or community recreation on an equal basis; and municipal parks are generally available. But operation of bond-financed mass commuting facilities by private persons under a longer-term management contract, use of a ball park mostly for a team's at-home games, use of a government-owned-and-operated convention center by an organization under an extended contract, use of a typical airport by airlines, or use of bond proceeds to provide a nonexempt business with electricity (rather than merely offering volume discounts) are uses in a nongovernmental trade or business for the test.

The new law clarifies that both direct and indirect payments to a bond issuer by a private user of bond financed facilities are considered for the security interest test. The Senate Finance Committee Report notes that these payments can be either formally pledged as security or directly used to pay debt service, but that they don't include revenues from generally applicable taxes (as opposed to special charges imposed on those satisfying the "use test" rather than on the public generally). *Example:* If land is sold to private persons for redevelopment, lump-sum or installment payments for the land to the government whose tax revenues secure the bonds, or to an agency acting for it, are considered for the security interest test. The same applies if lease payments by a private lessor of a facility, or receipts from a special user tax (e.g., a ticket tax at a stadium) are the formally pledged bond security.

MANAGEMENT CONTRACTS: Effective on the date of enactment, the new law directs the IRS to liberalize its current advance ruling guidelines (Rev Proc. 82-14, 1982-1 CB on private use under management contract as a trade or business use, and Rev Proc 82-15, 1982-1 CB 460 on qualified 501(c)(3) bonds) to allow up-to-5-year management contracts to provide for prescribed flat-amount or share-of-gross-revenue fees under certain conditions. One such condition is that at least 50% of the payments must be on a fixed-fee basis.

Private loan bonds. If at least 5% of the gross proceeds of the issue (or $5 million if that's less) is to be used to make or finance direct or indirect loans to others than governmental units, the bond is a private activity "private loan" bond (consumer loan bond under prior law), taxable unless it's in a specifically exempt category (e.g., exempt facility bonds, mortgage revenue (formerly mortgage subsidy) bonds or student loan bonds). Excluded from the private loan bond category are (1) loans to anticipate government tax receipts of a general nature and for an essential government function (e.g., short-term tax and revenue anticipation notes (TANs and RANs)), and (2) bonds to finance schools, highways, and government buildings and government owned and operated facilities. Also excluded are these exempt private activity issues: bonds issued as part of the Texas Veterans' Land Bond program (with their prior law sunset date of March 15, 1987 deleted by the new law), bonds issued as part of the Oregon Renewable Source Small Energy Conservation Program and the Iowa Industrial New Jobs Training Programs—but they must comply with the "related-use" requirement.

Related-use requirement. The new law generally requires an exempt private activity bond issue to devote at least 95% (90% under prior law) of the bond proceeds for the exempt purpose of the borrowing. [For federally guaranteed student loan bonds, however, see ¶1305]. Costs of issuance (including attorney fees and underwriter's spread) don't count towards the satisfaction of the 95% requirement. Private trade or business use of govermental bond proceeds in excess of 5% of the bond proceeds must be related to government facilities also being financed with the bonds. Private use satisfies this requirement only if the financing provided for the private use is proportional to the total financing provided by the issue for the related governmental facility.

> **CAUTION:** Aggregate costs of the issuance of exempt private activity bonds that are paid from bond proceeds can't exceed 2% of the amount of the bonds.

Other rules. Current law is retained on the treatment of certain volunteer fire departments as qualified issuers of tax-exempt bonds, with a clarification that the 95% "related use" requirement, above, must be adhered to.

The law framers intend that generally for bonds (including refunding bonds) issued after 8-15-86, the use of bond-financed property by a university to perform general (but not product development) research supported or sponsored by private persons under a *cooperative research agreement* shouldn't be treated as private business use (and the research support shouldn't be treated as a repayment of the bonds), if the resulting technology is available to sponsors and to unrelated nonsponsors on the same terms. For example, an agreement with a right of first refusal at a competitive price determined when the technology is available for use wouldn't be business use. [For qualified 501(c)(3) bonds generally, see ¶1305.]

Effective Dates: In general, these changes apply to bonds issued after 9-1-86. However, (1) the rule that indirect payments satisfy the security interest test, (2) the private loan bond rule and the exceptions from it, (3) the volunteer department bond rule, and (4) the rules on cooperative research agreements apply to bonds issued after 8-15-86.

[¶1303] **Exempt Facility Private Activity Bonds.** The new law repeals the prior law tax exemption for IDB financing of convention and trade show facilities, parking facilities, (but note that parking, such as airport parking, may be exempt as functionally related and subordinate to an exempt facility), sports facilities, air and water pollution control facilities, and industrial park IDBs, for bonds issued after 8-15-86 with transitional exceptions. A transitional exemption for certain hydroelectric generating facilities whose FERC approval was pending and whose application for license (and not just for a preliminary permit) was docketed when the exemption for such facilities expired (generally 12-31-85) is retained by the new law.

Categories of exempt facility private activity bonds, which remain exempt under the new law, and the new category for hazardous waste treatment facilities are enumerated below. As explained previously [¶1302], at least 95% of the proceeds of a bond issue must be devoted to provide the exempt facilities that qualify it. And while the bonds can continue to finance property functionally related and subordinate to the exempt facilities, office space financed with exempt-facility bonds is limited to office space located at the exempt facility and of a size necessary for the facility's day-to-day operations (as opposed to administrative office buildings). Exempt facility categories, (covered by new Sec. 142), generally for bonds issued after 8-15-86, include:

• *Multifamily qualified residential rental projects.* The new law removes the prior-law special rules for multifamily residential rental projects located in targeted areas that are financed by these IDBs. [For election by limited equity housing cooperatives of residential rental housing rules, see ¶1306. For "qualified redevelopment bonds" see ¶1304].

The new law allows the bond issuer to qualify for tax-exempt financing if the issue elects to meet either of the following: (1) at least 40% of the units must be occupied by tenants whose income is no more than 60% of the area median income, or (2) at least 20% of the units must be occupied by tenants whose income is no more than 50% of area median income. The election must be made on or before the date of issuance. The low-or-moderate income occupancy requirement and, under the new law a tenant's low or moderate income status, must be satisfied continuously during a qualified project period (generally redefined as starting when 10% of the project's residential units are first occupied (or at bond issuance, if later), and ending the earliest of (1) 15 years after 50% of the units are occupied, (2) when no tax exempts on the project remain outstanding, or (3) when Sec. 8 of the '37 U.S. Housing Act assistance terminates. However, if a tenant's income qualifies when he initially occupies a unit or on a later determination date, only an increase to above 140% of the qualifying income level (after adjustment for family size) will disqualify the tenant from being counted for the project's income occupancy requirement. The new law clarifies that family size adjustments (same as under Sec. 8 of the '37 U.S. Housing Act) are required for determining the area median incomes used to qualify tenants as having low or moderate income.

> **Example:** If a project qualifies under the test requiring 60% or less of area median income, *a family of four* with such income will count towards qualifying it, but a single person will count only if his income is 42% or less (i.e., there's a 10% reduction of the 60% benchmark for each family member under four).

Projects that (1) charge significantly lower-than-market rents to low-income tenants and (2) elect (when they make the occupancy percentage election) to have at least 15% of the low income units occupied by tenants with 40% or less of the area median income, can have tenants counted for the income occupancy requirement as long as the tenant's family income doesn't increase up to more than 170% of the otherwise applicable maximum.

Operators of exempt bond-financed projects must certify annually to the IRS that they have complied with the low-and-moderate-income occupancy requirements, and the IRS can request certification of other data to monitor compliance.

> **PENALTY:** Each failure to certify (unless due to reasonable cause and not wilfull disregard) is penalized $100 per failure, but doesn't in itself affect the tax-exempt status of the bonds.

As under prior law, noncompliance with the income occupancy rules must be corrected within a reasonable period after discovery. However, the violation of these rules in general occurs only on a (other than temporary) rental to a nonqualified person at a time when the income occupancy requirements rules aren't met. As under present law, interest on bonds financing the project becomes taxable retroactively to the date of their issuance if the occupancy requirements aren't complied with. Further, interest accrued on bond-financed loans from the first day of the tax year when the project ceases to qualify as "qualified residential rental property" until the project complies with the income occupancy requirements will now be nondeductible [¶1308]. The new law also calls for an at-least annual report by the IRS to Congressional Committees on the compliance with qualified residential rental project rules.

- *Airports* are generally defined as under prior law. They include related storage and training facilities. Tax exempt airport bonds can't now be used to finance hotels, retail shops (including food and beverage facilities) that are larger in size than needed to serve passengers and employees at the airport, retail facilities for passengers (e.g., rental car lots) located outside the terminal, office buildings for nongovernmental persons other than airport authorities, and industrial parks or manufacturing facilities.

- *Docks and wharves* are generally defined as under prior law. They include related storage and training facilities. Tax-exempt bonds financing them now can't be used to finance hotels, retail shops (including food and beverage facilities) that are larger in size than needed to serve passengers and employees at the port, office buildings for nongovernmental persons other than port authorities, and industrial parks or manufacturing facilities.

- *Mass commuting facilities* are in general defined as under prior law. But bonds financing them can't finance hotels, retail shops inside a terminal that are larger than needed to serve passengers and facility employees, retail facilities (other than public parking) outside the mass commuting terminal, office buildings for nongovernmental persons other than employees of the operating authority, or industrial parks or manufacturing facilities.

> **NOTE:** Airports, docks and wharves, and mass commuting facilities must be governmentally owned—this requirement is measured by a safe harbor rule.

- *Local furnishing of electricity and gas* (with a retained requirement for furnishing electricity and gas within two contiguous counties or a city and one contiguous county and retained exceptions provided by Secs. 644 and 645 of the '84 TRA).

- *Hazardous waste disposal facilities.* This new category of tax-exempts that can be issued after the date of enactment is limited to financing disposal facilities to incinerate and entomb hazardous waste as defined under Sec. 1004 of the Solid Waste Disposal Act. Facilities subject to permit requirements under the Resource Conservation and Recovery Act generally qualify. Eligible facilities must be owned and operated by persons not related to the producers of the hazardous waste, and must receive and dispose of hazardous waste from the general public rather than serve only a single or limited

¶1303

group of persons. There's an exception for facilities owned or operated by the waste producer that permits exempt bond financing only of the part of the facility used by the general public. The conferees intend that hazardous waste doesn't include radioactive waste, and that prior law rules regarding solid waste disposal IDBs also continue to apply here.

• *Sewage and solid waste disposal facilities,* in general are defined as under prior law, but with the exemption for certain alcohol producing and steam generating facilities repealed.

Other exempt categories include

• *Local district heating or cooling facilities,* and

• *Facilities for furnishing of water* (including irrigation systems).

[¶1304] **Small Issue Private Activity Bonds and New Qualified Redevelopment Bonds.** The new law retains the 12-31-86 sunset date for small issue IDBs (now qualified small issue bonds covered in new Sec. 144(a)) other than for manufacturing facilities, but postpones the prior law sunset date for small issue IDBs financing manufacturing facilities for another year (i.e., through 12-31-89). "Small issue" bond issues must now devote at least 95% of the bond proceeds to the exempt purpose of the borrowing. The new law also (1) treats small issue bonds for first-time farmers the same as manufacturing bonds for small-issue IDB sunset dates—i.e., they can be issued through 12-31-89; (2) expands the definition of "first-time farmer" to include previously insolvent farmers (by disregarding previous ownership of land disposed of in a Sec. 108 transaction); and (3) allows first-time farmers to use up to $62,500 to acquire used agricultural equipment. However, the new law also restricts the aggregate small-issue IDB financing for all depreciable property used in farming to a lifetime limit of $250,000 per principal user (including persons "related" to him). Bonds that were issued under prior law are counted towards the new $250,000 limit, as is depreciable property financed under the first-time farmer exceptions. The law changes are generally effective for bonds issued after 8-15-86.

Qualified redevelopment bonds. A new category of state-law authorized tax-exempt private activity bonds can be issued after 8-15-86 by qualified governmental units for preplanned redevelopment in a locally designated "blighted area." Qualified redevelopment bonds are covered in new Sec. 144(c). Real property tax revenue increases that result from the redevelopment must be first devoted to debt service on the bonds. But owners or users of the property in the "blighted areas" can't be subjected to higher charges or fees, or assessed under a rate or method higher than that of property outside this area. The bonds can be secured by pledges of generally applicable taxes if the taxes are the principal security for the bonds. At least 95% or more of the proceeds of the bonds must finance the exempt purposes. These purposes are (1) the acquisition under condemnation of real property to be transferred to nongovernmental persons; (2) clearing and preparing land for redevelopment and its transfer to nongovernmental persons for fair market value; (3) rehabilitating or redeveloping the real property; and (4) relocating occupants of the acquired real property.

A blighted area," designated by the general purpose local government unit in which it's located (e.g., cities or counties) under state-established criteria before the bonds are issued, must generally subtend at least 100 contiguous acres. However, the area can be less, if (1) it's at least 10 contiguous acres and (2) generally no more than 25% of bond financed land is provided to one person (or a group of related persons) under a pre-approved plan. Criteria for designation should consider excessive, previously improved vacant land; vacant, old or substandard buildings; excessive vacancies and real property tax delinquencies. A finding of a substantial number of statutory factors is needed for the designation as "blighted."

Aggregate blighted areas designated, as such, by a government unit can contain only up-to-20% of the government unit's real property measured by assessed value. For areas designated in different years, the percentages determined at time of designation are aggregated for this test. Also, special rules apply if there are areas designated before 1-1-86 for which qualifying activities were in progress on that date.

Qualified redevelopment bonds must meet requirements that apply to private activity bonds generally. No more than 25% of the proceeds may be used for certain recreational and commercial activities. No proceeds can be used to finance private or commercial golf courses, country clubs, massage parlors, hot tub or suntan facilities, liquor stores, or race track or other primarily gambling facilities. However, the restriction on acquisition of land doesn't apply.

NOTE: Bonds financing governmental facilities such as street paving, sidewalks, street lighting, etc., don't have to meet the qualification requirements of qualified redevelopment bonds. Rules for financing of qualified redevelopment and the governmental facilities through a single issue are expected to be developed by the Treasury Department.

[¶1305] Qualified 501(c)(3) Bonds and Student Loan Bonds. Generally for bonds issued after 8-15-86, the proceed of which will be for the use of Sec. 501(c)(3) organizations, the new law continues the exemption if they're "qualifed 501(c)(3) bonds" (new Code Sec. 145). To qualify under this category, at least 95% of the net bond proceeds must be used for qualified activities. Rules similar to the 95% "related use" test covered at ¶1302 (the private business use and security interest tests using a 5% rather than 10% benchmark), apply. As under prior law, use of bond proceeds in an unrelated trade or business (determined under Sec. 513(a)) is a nonexempt use. Also, facilities financed with qualified 501(c)(3) bonds must be owned by a Sec. 501(c)(3) organization or by or on behalf of a governmental unit—ownership by others would presumably result in a violation of the above 95% use limitations.

The Senate Finance Committee intends that: (1) bonds for state and local government-owned universities or hospitals should be treated as governmental bonds rather than qualified 501(c)(3) bonds, to the extent that such entities are government agencies or instrumentalities (determined similarly as under prior law); and (2) the IRS should adopt rules for allocating costs of mixed-use facilities, (e.g., where eligible facilities of a Sec. 501(c)(3) organization are part of a larger facility, or where portions of a Sec. 501(c)(3) organization facility may be used by nonexempt persons), according to a reasonable method that reflects the proportionate benefit derived by their users. Only the parts of such facilities (including common elements) owned and used by Sec. 501(c)(3) organizations are eligible for 501(c)(3) bond financing. [For cooperative research agreements see ¶1302.]

Similarly to IDBs, the term of qualified 501(c)(3) bonds can't be longer than 120% of the economic life of property financed by them. Exceptions relate to pooled financings for two or more Sec. 501(c)(3) organizations, and to certain FHA insurance programs that require longer loan terms.

NOTE ON 501(c)(3) BONDS: The new law (Act Sec. 1302) provides that the treatment of Sec. 501(c)(3) bonds as private activity bonds isn't an indication of their treatment in future legislation. Any future law change that applies to private activity bonds will apply to Sec. 501(c)(3) bonds only if the future legislation so expressly provides.

$150 million limit for non-hospital 501(c)(3) bonds. A qualified 501(c)(3) bond issue must either be a "qualified hospital bond" issue, or must fit within a $150 million limit on outstanding non-hospital qualified section 501(c)(3) bonds other than qualified hospital bonds). For qualified hospital bonds, at least 95% of the net proceeds must be used to finance an accredited hospital facility (rest or nursing homes, day care centers, medical school facilities, research laboratories or ambulatory care facilities aren't "hospitals"). The hospital must be either governmentally owned or owned by a Sec. 501(c)(3) organization, and operated by a Sec. 501(c)(3) organization.

Any non-hospital qualified Sec. 501(c)(3) bond issue qualifies under the dollar limit if its authorized face amount (when added to the face amount of outstanding tax-exempt qualified 501(c)(3) non-hospital bonds that benefit the organization during a 3-year "test period") makes the total face amount go over $150 million. The $150 million limit takes into account only qualified section 501(c)(3) bonds. The Conferees intend that if an issue is partly used for hospitals, only the portion actually used for hospitals is exempt from the $150 million limit as hospital bonds. They also permit Sec. 501(c)(3) organizations to elect not to treat bonds as qualified 501(c)(3) bonds (e.g., to participate in a multifamily residential rental project and benefit from bonds qualifying as qualified residential rental bonds). Bonds issued before 8-16-86 for Sec. 501(c)(3) organizations count toward the limit only if more than 25% of the proceeds were to be used directly or indirectly by such an organization or organizations and the new law security interest test is satisfied.

Student loan bonds. The new law continues the exemption of qualified student loan bonds (new Sec. 144(b)), defined as under prior law (including bonds issued by qualified government units or qualified scholarship funding corporations in connection with the GSL and PLUS programs of the U.S. Department of Education). It also expands this exempt category to cover certain state supplemental loan programs, including any state approved program of general application not covered by Part B of Title IV of the 1965 Higher Education Act (relating to guaranteed student loans), if loans under it are limited to the difference between (1) total cost of attendance and (2) other student assistance with certain exceptions. However, at least 90% of the proceeds (under rules similar to the "related use requirements" covered at ¶1302) of bonds connected with the GSL and PLUS programs must be used for the purpose of the borrowing; and that percentage rises to "at least" 95% in the case of supplemental student loan bonds. Also, student loan bonds can't be issued to finance loans to students who are enrolled in schools outside the issuing state unless they are legal residents of the issuing state. The law changes are effective generally for bonds issued after 8-15-86.

[¶1306] **Mortgage Subsidy Bonds, MCCs, and Limited Equity Housing Bonds.** Under the new law, mortgage subsidy bonds are renamed mortgage revenue bonds (new Sec 143). The prior law sunset dates have been postponed for a year—mortgage revenue bonds and mortgage credit certificates (MCCs) can be issued through 12-31-88 under changed rules. The alternative to issue mortgage credit certificates instead of qualified mortgage bonds has been retained. However, the maximum aggregate principal amount of MCCs that can be distributed by an electing issuer is increased to 25% (up from prior law's 20%) of qualified mortgage bond authority that is exchanged for authority to issue MCCs. Here are some other law changes.

At least 95% of bond proceeds other than issuance costs and amounts deposited in a reasonably required reserve fund must be used for loans to first-time home buyers. But as under prior law, there's no requirement that a minimum percentage of financing in targeted areas be provided to first-time homebuyers. Bond issuance costs paid from bond proceeds of mortgage revenue bonds generally can't exceed 2% of the amount of the bonds (3½% if the bond issue doesn't exceed $20 million). Except in targeted areas, all bond-financed loans must be made to persons having incomes of 115% or less of the median income in the state or in the area, whichever is higher. In targeted areas, a third of the financing can be made to borrowers without regard to the income limit, and the balance must be provided to mortgagors with income not exceeding 140% of the higher area or statewide median income. The purchase price of bond-financed residences can't be greater than 90% (110% in targeted areas) of the average area purchase price applicable to the residence. The new law repeals the prior law requirement that issuers of qualified mortgage bonds and MCCs annually publish and file with the Treasury Department statements on their policies for issuance of these bonds and MCCs.

> **CAUTION:** Qualified mortgage bonds must now fit within unified state volume limits for private activity bonds [see ¶1307]. Qualified veterans' mortgage bonds remain subject to their separate prior law volume cap.

Under the new law, at least 95% of the proceeds of *qualified veterans' mortgage bonds* must be used to finance veteran's mortgage loans. Bond issuance costs aren't counted towards this requirement, and generally can't exceed 2% of the amount of the bonds.

Limited equity housing cooperatives can elect multifamily residential rental project rules. Limited equity housing cooperatives can now irrevocably elect to treat any limited cooperative equity housing as residential rental property rather than as owner-occupied housing. Under the election, bonds issued to provide the housing will be governed by targeting and compliance rules that apply to multifamily residential rental projects. The cooperative's tenant shareholders won't get a Sec. 216 deduction for their ratable share of interest and taxes paid by the cooperative. And bonds issued to finance units in the cooperative will be counted towards the state's volume limitation for qualified mortgage bonds, but will be treated as IDBs for multifamily residential rental property for all other purposes. A failure to elect will make the financing subject to all limitations that cover qualified mortgage bonds, including first-time purchaser and purchase price limitations.

To make the election, (1) the cooperative must be a cooperative housing corporation (Sec. 216(b)(1)), (2) the cost of its stock can't exceed the amount paid by the original shareholders (as adjusted for cost of living increases) plus cost of improvements and certain other payments, (3) the cooperative's net asset value in excess of combined transfer values of outstanding stock must be used only for public or charitable purposes and not directly benefit any shareholder, and (4) the cooperative must continue to qualify as a limited equity cooperative during the period when the tax-exempts are outstanding. [For new rules affecting multifamily residential rental project bonds, see ¶1302—1303].

Effective Date: These rules generally apply to bonds issues after 8-15-86, and MCCs issued under bond authority exchanged after 8-15-86.

[¶1307] Single Volume Cap Now Covers Private Activity Bonds and Qualified Mortgage Bonds. Instead of the separate volume limits for most private activity bonds and for qualified mortgage bonds, a single annual volume cap, effective for bonds issued after 8-15-86, covers exempt facility bonds, small issue bonds, qualified redevelopment bonds, student loan bonds, qualified mortgage bonds, and private loan bonds for which an exemption is provided (new Sec. 146).

> **CAUTION:** Private use of proceeds of governmental bonds (which aren't classified as private activity bonds) in excess of 15 million dollars and up to the permitted 10% of private use is also subject to the new volume cap. Note that this rule only covers governmental bond issues in excess of $150 million.

Qualified veterans' mortgage bonds remain subject to their separate prior law volume cap. Bonds not covered by a volume cap include (1) qualified 501(c)(3) bonds; (2) exempt facility bonds for governmentally owned airports and docks and wharves; and (3) exempt facility bonds for solid waste disposal facilities if all property financed with the bonds is governmentally owned.

The new unified annual volume cap for each state until 12-31-87, is equal to the greater of $75 per resident of the state or $250 million. After 1987 the cap it reduced to the greater of $50 per resident or $150 million. The District of Columbia is treated as a state for the volume limit. U.S. possessions with populations more than the least populous state are limited to the $75/$50 per capita amounts. U.S. possessions with populations less than the least populous state have a volume limit equal to the per capita amount *actually received* by the least populous state (i.e., the $250/$150 million safe harbor divided by the least populous state's population). In general, the new volume limit is administered similarly to the prior law limits on IDBs, student loan bonds and qualified mortgage bonds. A federal allocation formula is provided, subject to an override by the Governor (during an interim period), or by state legislation.

> **NOTE:** There are no set-asides for particular types of bonds from the new volume cap.

Carryforward of volume cap. An issuer can irrevocably elect to carry forward for up to three succeeding years a part of the new volume cap, but only for specific carryforward projects that are irrevocably designated in advance. The election can't cover projects financed with small issue bonds, and carryforward authority to issue qualified mortgage bonds or MCCs is limited to those issued by their new sunset date. The name of the user of an exempt facility and the proposed address of the facility needn't be specified when a carryforward election is made as long as the facility can be otherwise identified with reasonable certainty.

[¶1308] Prohibited Facilities, Public Approval, and Changes in Use. Private activity bonds issued after 8-15-86 (with transitional exceptions) can't be used to provide airplanes, skyboxes or private luxury boxes, health club or gambling facilities, or alcohol stores. (Exception: A health club can be financed by qualified Sec. 501(c)(3) bonds if the health club is directly used for the organization's exempt purpose). And all private activity bonds issued after 12-31-86 must meet public approval requirements. This usually involves approval of the bond issue or the financing of a facility by a voter referendum, or by the legislature or elected executive officer of the issuing government unit (and government units where financed facilities are located) after a public hearing. Issues refunding previously approved bonds, whose maturity is no later than that of the original bonds, are excepted from the public approval rule.

Loss of deductions when qualified use or ownership of facilities changes. Effective for changes in use occuring after 8-15-86, in addition to any loss of tax exemption that may result under other rules, the new law generally denies for property financed with private activity and private loan bonds the tax deduction for interest (including the interest element of user fees) that accrues during the period that starts from the first day of the year in which property financed by these bonds is used in a way not qualifying for its exempt financing and ends when the property is again used for the bonds' qualified purpose (or until the bonds are redeemed, if that's earlier). In general, the nondeductible amount is equal to the interest (or its equivalent) paid on the bond-financed loans.

Special rules. First, in case of qualified mortgage and qualified veterans' mortgage bonds, interest on a bond-financed mortgage loan becomes nondeductible if the financed residence ceases to be a principal residence of a mortgagor for a continuous period of at least a year. IRS can waive the disallowance in case of hardship (e.g., if residence is occupied by minor children of deceased mortgagor). Second, for exempt facility bonds financing a qualified residential rental project, interest on the financed loan accruing from the first day of the tax year when the project ceases to qualify until the date it starts qualifying is nondeductible. Finally, if any part of a facility financed with proceeds of qualified 501(c)(3) bonds is no longer used by a qualifying organization, the Sec. 501(c)(3) organization that continues to own the part of the facility and benefits from the bonds has income from an unrelated trade or business. The amount of that income is at least equal to the fair rental value of that part of the facility for the period of unqualified use. According to the Senate Finance Committee Report, interest on the bond-financed loans isn't deductible against income from the business from the first day of the year when the change in use occurs.

In addition, if all or part of a facility financed by tax-exempt bonds is required to be owned as a condition of the exemption by (or on behalf of) a government unit or Sec. 501(c)(3) organization, and stops being so owned, then amounts paid or accrued for that part of the facility's use become nondeductible to the extent of interest accrued on the exempt financing from the date such ownership ceases. Regs can prescribe rules for allocating interest when only a part of a facility has a change in use or ownership.

[¶1309] **Arbitrage Restrictions Tightened.** Generally for bonds issued after 8-15-86, the arbitrage rules now cover 95% of the bond proceeds. Under prior law any tax exempt obligation became taxable if it was an arbitrage bond—in general if more than 15% of the proceeds of the issue were reasonably expected to be used (directly or indirectly) either to acquire taxable obligations that produce a materially higher yield or replace funds used for such arbitrage. The new law reduces the 15% (minor portion) leeway down to the lesser of: (a) 5% of the proceeds, or (b) $100,000. However, reasonably required reserve or replacement funds (limited by the new law to no more than 10% of bond proceeds unless the Treasury specifically approves a larger amount for an issue) are no longer treated as part of the "minor portion" amounts. *Note:* Amounts deposited in the reserve are subject to the rebate requirement (see below) up to the allowed 10% amount. The new law also spells out that deliberate or intentional acts to produce arbitrage render the bonds "arbitrage bonds" whose interest is taxable retroactively from the date the bonds are issued. These rules generally apply to bonds issued after 8-15-86 (but for bonds covered by the Joint Statements of Effective Dates of 3-14-86 and 7- 17-86, they apply to bonds issued on or after 9-1-86).

Determination of materially higher yield. The Senate Finance Committee Report notes that prior law reg determinations of what's a "materially higher yield" are in general retained under the new law. Generally, the maximum permitted spread between the acquired taxable obligations and the tax exempt issue has been 0.125 percentage points (plus costs, that varied depending on whether the acquired taxable investments were "purpose obligations" acquired to carry out the purpose of the issue or "nonpurpose obligations"). The maximum permitted spread for "acquired program obligations" (purpose obligations acquired under student loan and other programs that contemplated their acquisition) is the greater of (1) 1.5 percentage points plus reasonable administrative costs, or (2) reasonable and direct costs of the loan program.

The rule treating bond insurance premiums as interest on the bonds if the insurance reduces their interest rate is retained, and it's intended that similar treatment be extended under regs to costs of other credit enhancement devices (e.g., letters of credit obtained through arms'-length transactions such as competitive bidding). However, credit enhancement fees are to be treated as interest only to the extent they represent a reasonable charge for the transfer of credit risk (i.e., indirect payments of issuance costs through credit enhancers aren't interest expenses). The rules apply generally to bonds issued after 8-15-86 (but for bonds covered by the Joint Statements of 3-14-86 and 7-17-86 they apply to bonds issued on or after 9-1-86).

CAUTION: The Senate Finance Committee Report states that the new law's requirement to determine yield consistently with original discount rules [Secs. 1273 and 1274] overrules the result in *State of Washington v. Comm.* (CA-DC, 1982) 50 AFTR2d 82-5914, 692 F2d 128. For bonds issued after 12-31-85, bond yield means the discount rate at which all anticipated payments of principal and interest on the bonds equals the net proceeds of the issue *after deducting the costs of issuance.* The deduction of issuance costs in effect allows payment of issuance costs out of arbitrage.

'Arbitrage investment' definition broadened and temporary period exception tightened. The arbitrage restrictions have been expanded to cover the acquisition of any taxable investment property with proceeds of tax-exempts. According to the Senate Finance Report, this can cover a materially higher yield investment regardless of its purpose (i.e., even if it's acquired as an acquired purpose or acquired program obligation). For instance, a purchase of a deferred payment contract, or of an annuity contract to fund a pension plan of a qualified government unit is subject to the same arbitrage restrictions as direct funding of the pension plan with bond proceeds (for bonds issued to fund deferred compensation arrangements the rules apply to bonds issued after 9-25-85). However, the arbitrage restrictions don't apply to real or tangible property acquired with bond proceeds for reasons other than investment. The rules apply generally to bonds issued after 8-15-86 (they apply to bonds issued on or after 9-1-86 for bonds covered by the Joint Statements of 3-14-86 and 7-17-86).

The new law eliminates the prior law election under the regs to forgo the temporary periods exception to the arbitrage rules and be allowed to earn arbitrage on purpose obligations of 0.5 percentage points over the yield of tax exempts. And a new statutory rule covering the initial temporary period applies to pooled financings (other than of mortgage revenue bonds). Initial temporary periods for pooled financings are limited to six months (other than for certain GSL and PLUS student loan bonds during a two-year transition period which doesn't apply to bonds issued after 12-31-88). And temporary periods for repayments that will be relent are limited to three months. The rules generally apply to bonds issued after 8-15-86 (or to bonds issued on or after 9-1-86 for bonds covered by the Joint Statements).

Restrictions on nonpurpose investments expanded. The new law extends to all tax exempts (including refunding issues), a prior law restriction on most IDBs and qualified mortgage bonds that limits the amount of bonds proceeds that can be invested in nonpurpose obligations. Under the new law, no more than the amount of 150% of the debt service on the issue for the bond year can be invested in nonpurpose obligations at any time during the year, and that investment must be reduced promptly when the outstanding issue is reduced or repaid. The Senate Finance Committee Report notes that this restriction doesn't apply to investments during temporary periods during which unlimited arbitrage can be earned (however, the rebate, see below, can apply to such amounts), and it doesn't require the sale of investments at a loss that would exceed the amount otherwise rebatable to the U.S. at that time or credited to mortgagors under qualified veterans' mortgage bond rules (see below).

Rebate. The new law extends to all tax exempts a requirement (previously applicable to most IDBs) of rebating to the United States, the arbitrage earned on the gross proceeds of an issue invested in nonpurpose obligations. The term "gross proceeds" is intended to be broadly interpreted, and include the original proceeds, the investment return and repayment of principal received from investing the original proceeds and amounts used or available to pay debt service. Nonpurpose obligations, for these purposes, include amounts invested in a debt service reserve fund or an escrow established with proceeds of a refunding issue.

Arbitrage profits to be rebated are equal to (1) the excess of (a) the total earned on the nonpurpose obligations (but not on the arbitrage itself) *over* (b) the amount that would have been earned if they were invested at yield equal to the yield of the tax exempts, *plus* (2) all income earned on the arbitrage itself.

The Senate Finance Committee Report notes that this requires a separate accounting of bond proceeds from tax and other revenues, but that the IRS can prescribe simplified accounting for limited bond issues.

For late payments of the arbitrage rebate, the Treasury can waive loss of tax exemption on the bonds where the error or late payment is not due to willful neglect, and to condition the relief on a payment of a penalty of up to 50% of the amount not properly paid. Interest accrues on the amount not properly paid in the same way as on late payments of tax. The Treasury can waive the penalty and interest.

The rebate rule doesn't apply to a bond issue all of whose gross proceeds are spent for their governmental purpose within six months from the issue date (only one six-month period is allowed even for an issue in series, or for more than one draw-down of proceeds).

Special rules and exceptions to the arbitrage and rebate rules relate to:

- *Bonds financing operations of small government units* with general taxing powers that reasonably expect to issue, at most, $5 million of tax-exempts in the calendar year.

- Governmental bonds (but not tax and revenue anticipation notes) and qualified 501(c)(3) bonds, if all but a minor portion of the gross proceeds of an issue are spent for the exempt purpose of the borrowing within six months. If the gross proceeds of an issue, other than the lesser of 5% or $100,000 of the proceeds are so spent, there's an additional six months to spend the remainder before rebate payments are required. And for this exception, redemption of the allowable de-minimis portion before the added six months expires is treated as an expenditure for the purpose of the borrowing.

- The new law retains a prior law alternative of either a credit on qualified mortgage revenue bonds to mortgagors or the rebate to the U.S., and extends such a choice to *qualified veterans' mortgage bonds.*

- *Arbitrage earned on GSL and PLUS student loan bonds* during an initial 18-month temporary period isn't subject to the rebate requirement to the extent that (1) the bond proceeds are used by the end of the 18-month period to finance student loans, (2) the arbitrage profits are used to pay the costs of issuance and reasonable administration costs financed with the proceeds of the issue, and (3) the costs are not reimbursed. The transition rule doesn't apply to bonds issued after 12-31-88.

- *Proceeds of tax and revenue anticipation notes.* Under a safe harbor rule, if at the end of six months (or a lesser period after issuance, the cumulative deficit of the governmental unit has exceeded 90% of the issue size, proceeds and earnings on them are treated as having been spent for purposes of the arbitrage rebate requirement. Cumulative cash flow deficit is here defined as the excess of the amount the governmental unit spends during the six months period (or the shorter term of the bonds) over the sum of all amounts (other than the bond proceeds) that are available for payment of expenses during the period. Redemption of bonds isn't treated as an expenditure for a governmental purpose under the rebate rules. This safe harbor rule doesn't affect the amounts of tax anticipation notes that may be issued or that qualify for temporary periods.

• *Student loan bonds.* The new law repeals the prior law's direction for special regs to the extent inconsistent with the new arbitrage restrictions.

• Effective on date of enactment, the Treasury is directed to modify the SLGS program to provide investments similar to those offered by money market funds paying yields that would eliminate arbitrage profits and operate the program at no net cost to the government. The new rules would permit demand deposits under the SLGS program by deleting advance notice requirements related to the purchase of SLGS and minimum maturity requirements.

The rebate rules and the special rules in general apply to bonds issued after 12-31-85, but for bonds and provisions covered by the Joint Statements of 3-14-86 and 7-17-86 they apply as to bonds issued on or after 9-1-86, and for arbitrage rebate requirements for certain pooled financing, they apply to bonds issued after 3:00 p.m. EDT, 7-17-86.

[¶1310] **New Restrictions on Advance Refundings.** Under prior law, bonds other than IDBs and mortgage subsidy bonds could be advance refunded. Mortgage subsidy bonds and IDBs couldn't be refunded more than 180 days before the refunded bonds were redeemed unless the refunded bonds had a maturity of less than three years.

Under the new law, advance refunding bonds are those issued more than 90 days before the refunded bonds are redeemed (e.g., called so no further interest accrues) and refundings before 1-1-86 are treated as advance refundings only if the refunded bonds weren't redeemed within 180 days of the issuance of the refunding bonds. And, *only qualified 501(c)(3) bonds and governmental bonds* can be advance refunded.

Restrictions that apply in instances where advance refundings are permitted (if they aren't met, the refunding bonds become taxable) are

• Bonds originally issued before 1-1-86 can be advance refunded 2 times, with a transitional rule permitting one additional advance refunding after 3-14-86 if the bonds were advance refunded 2 or

¶1310

more times before 3-15-86. Bonds originally issued after 12-31-85 can be advance refunded only once.

• In the case of advance refundings of bonds originally issued after 12-31-85, that produce debt service savings (determined without regard to issuance costs), the refunded bonds must be redeemed no later than the first date on which their call isn't prohibited.

• In the case of bonds originally issued before 1-1-86 and advance refundings that may produce debt service savings, the refunded bonds must be redeemed no later than the first date on which the issue may be called at a premium of 3% or less.

• The temporary period during which unlimited arbitrage profits may be earned on the refunding bonds expires 30 days after the date of their issuance, and for the refunded bonds no later than the date of issuance of the advance refunding bonds.

• The 150% of annual debt service limitation on nonpurpose investments [see ¶1309] doesn't apply to advance refunding proceeds invested in an escrow for the redemption of the refunded bonds.

• Advance refundings are generally prohibited if they involve a device to obtain a material financial advantage other than savings arising from lower interest rates (e.g., so called flip-flop devices, proceeds of prior issue invested in higher escrow to pay future debt service and advance refunding bonds used to pay project costs, advance refundings enabling the issuer to get a rebate of prior issue's insurance, etc.).

• Reserve funds and minor portions for advance refunding bonds [see ¶1309] can't exceed the lesser of the amount so dedicated for the refunded bonds, or the amounts permitted under the new law.

• In the case of advance refundings of governmental bonds, advance refunding bonds are subject to the new unified volume cap on private activity and qualified mortgage bonds to the extent of permitted private use of the refunded bonds in excess of $15 million [see ¶1307].

Effective Dates: The new advance refunding rules generally apply to advance refunding bonds issued after 8-15-86 in case of advance refundings of 501(c)(3) organization bonds, other private activity bonds for which advance refunding was permitted under prior law, and governmental bonds originally issued after 8-15-86. They generally apply to bonds issued on or after 9-1-86 for bonds and provisions covered by the Joint Statements of 3-14-86 and 7-17-86.

[¶1311] **Information Reporting Extended to All Tax-Exempts.** Information reporting rules, similar to those previously applicable to IDBs and certain other qualified bonds have been extended by the new law to cover *all* tax-exempts issued after 12-31-86. In general, the information required is the same as under prior law, but the new law authorizes the IRS to vary the type of specific information required of facility and nonfacility bonds respectively. And it's intended that IRS allow issuers of small amounts of bonds to file a simplified consolidated report.

〔¶1312〕 General Stock Ownership Corporation (GSOC) Provisions and Determination of Marital Status. Effective 1-1-84, (in the Committee Report—the date of enactment in the statute), the new law repeals as deadwood, provisions relating to General Stock Ownership Corporations, (state-established corporations for the benefit of state citizens with power to borrow and invest in business enterprises). No GSOC has been organized, and GSOCs could be organized only before 1984.

Redetermination of marital status. To make place for Code provisions dealing with tax-exempt bonds (new Secs. 141-147), the new law has redesignated the provision dealing with determination of marital status (old sec. 143) as Sec. 7703.

Act Sec. 1303 dealing with repeal of GSOC rules repeals Code Secs. 1391-1397, Sec. 172(b)(1)(j), 1016(a)(21), 3402(r) and 6039B, and amends Sec. 172(k)(2) and (4), and redesignates Sec. 172(b)(1)(k) as 172(b)(1)(j), and Secs. 1016(a)(23)-(27) as Secs. 1016(a)(21)-(26), effective as shown above. Act. Sec. 1301(j) redesignates old Sec. 143 (determination of marital status) as new Sec. 7703 effective on date of enactment.

〔¶1313〕 Other Rules and Effective Dates. The new law permits one current refunding of certain FSLIC and FDIC guaranteed bonds that were used to finance multifamily rental housing, provided no additional volume of outstanding bonds results and certain other requirements rendering the refunding in substance a renegotiation of interest rates are satisfied. The refundings are subject to all the new arbitrage provisions of the new law. The rules apply to bonds issued after enactment.

The rules in the Exempt Bond Title of the new law are generally effective for obligations issued after 8-15-86. However, for provisions and bonds covered by the Joint Statements on Effective Dates of 3-14-86 and 7-17-86 the new rules generally apply to bonds issued on or after 9-1-86. Major exceptions to this rule are usually noted as part of the coverage of the law changes involved.

General transitional rules. (1) *Binding contract and started construction exceptions.* This rule in general excepts from the new law changes, bonds financing facilities covered by pre-9-26-85 approval in an inducement resolution or comparable approval, and either whose construction, reconstruction, or rehabilitation began before 9-26-85, or which are covered by a pre-9-26-85 binding contract to incur more than 10% of reasonably anticipated costs of construction, or which are acquired under a pre-9-26-85 binding contract. However, for bonds actually issued after the enactment date, specified

¶1313

new law rules are engrafted into Sec. 103 for purposes of this exception.

(2) Refunding issues. In case of non-advance refundings, the new law changes (other than those dealing with arbitrage and information reporting) don't apply to bonds whose proceeds are used exclusively to refund tax exempt bonds that were issued on or before 1-1-86, and whose amount isn't greater than the amount of refunded bonds, and which have a maturity no later than 17 years after issue or comply with the rule requiring maturity to be no more than 120% of economic life of financed facilities. In case of advance refundings, certain tax exempt governmental bonds and 501(c)(3) organization bonds are excepted from the new law rules subject to certain conditions. Another transitional rule permits one additional advance refunding of bonds issued on or before 1-1-86 which may be advance refunded under the new law.

(3) Additional transitional rules cover many situations or projects. Also, a transitional rule covers pre-1988 obligations that were covered by specified transitional rules of the '84 TRA.

[The page following this is 1401.]

TRUSTS AND ESTATES; MINOR CHILDREN

Trusts and Estates

[¶1401] **Income Taxation of Trusts and Estates.** The new law revises the tax rate schedules for nongrantor trusts and estates. Under the revised rates the first $5000 of taxable income of trusts is taxed at 15%. Any taxable trust income over $5000 is taxed at 28%. Additionally, the benefit of the 15% bracket is phased-out when the taxable income of the trust is between $13,000 and $26,000.

The tax rates for estates under the new law are the same as for nongrantor trusts. [For more details and a tax rate schedule, see ¶101.]

Act Sec. 101, revising rate schedules applicable to trusts and estates, amends Sec. 1. There are blended rates for 1987.

[¶1402] **Revision of Grantor Trust Rules.** The new law abolishes income-shifting breaks for Clifford Trusts. As a general rule, income from 10-year and other grantor trusts is taxed to the grantor, not the beneficiary, if the property put into the trust will revert to the grantor or the grantor's spouse. It is immaterial how long the trust lasts. These new rules will not apply when the trust may revert only after the death of the income beneficiary who is the grantor's lineal descendent.

The 10-year rule was replaced with a rule that treats a trust as a grantor trust when the grantor has a reversionary interest whose value, at the time of the transfer of the property into the trust, amounts to more than 5% of the value of the transferred property.

Also, if a grantor's spouse is living with the grantor at the time of the creation of any power or interest held by the spouse, the grantor is treated as holding that power or interest—a restriction that kills spousal remainder trusts.

What the old rules allowed. By way of background, the grantor trust rules treat the grantor of a trust as its owner when there is a transfer of property to a trust by a grantor who retains certain powers or interests over the trust. As a result, income attributable to the trust is taxed to its grantor—that is, the person who sets up the trust, rather than to its beneficiary.

But a prior-law exception to the grantor trust rules allowed a grantor-to-beneficiary shift of the taxes on trust income used to pay for, say, college costs. The exception became applicable when at least ten years had to elapse before certain powers and interests that were retained by the grantor could revert to the grantor.

Consequently, a long-favored way for many high-bracket individuals to shift income from themselves to children, grandchildren and other lower-taxed family members is to transfer money, stocks, real estate or other income-generating assets for a period of at least ten years into reversionary trust arrangements known as "Clifford" or "short-term" trusts. During the period that the trust is in existence, the income is taxed to the child or other person named to receive the trust income. At the end of the trust period, the grantor regains the assets used to fund the Clifford Trust.

A spousal remainder trust provides another way for a parent-to-child shift of the taxes on income earmarked for educational expenses. One parent funds the trust. It can be set up for less than ten years and the specified period can end upon the child's completion of college, with the trust asset then becoming the property of the grantor's spouse.

Effective Date: Generally, the revised rules apply to trust transfers made after 3-1-86. That translates into no income shifting for income from Clifford Trusts started after that date.

There is, however, an exception from the new rules for Clifford trusts that were created under a binding property settlement entered into on or before 3-1-86. These trusts are unaffected by the new rules and can continue to shift income to the beneficiary.

Remember, though, that the income shifted through pre-March-2 trusts is subject to the new rules for taxing unearned income received by children under the age of 14. [See ¶1405—1407.]

> **Example:** Assume that a parent set up and funded a pre-March-2 trust. The trust named an under-14 child as beneficiary. *Result* : The trust income is taxed at the parent's tax rate, not the child's.

Act Secs. 1401 and 1402, relating to the taxation of grantor trusts, amends Secs. 672, 673, 674, 676 and 677, effective as shown above.

[¶1403] **Taxable Years of Trusts.** Under the new law, all trusts, both existing and newly created, must use a calendar taxable year. However, tax exempt trusts under Sec. 501(a) and wholly charitable trusts under Sec. 4947(a)(1) may use a fiscal year.

If a trust has a taxable year different than the taxable year of its beneficiaries, prior law allowed the deferral of taxation by one month for each month that the taxable year of the trust ended sooner than the taxable year of its beneficiaries. So, for a trust with a taxable year ending on January 31, and with the trust beneficiary on a calendar year, the taxation of trust income distributed to the beneficiary was deferred 11 months.

Act Sec. 1403, relating to taxable years of trusts, adds new Sec. 645, effective for taxable years beginning after 12-31-86.

[¶1404] **Trusts and Estates To Make Estimated Income Tax Payments.** The new law requires that both new and existing trusts and estates pay estimated tax in the same manner as individuals. An estate, however, need not pay estimated tax in its first two years. The law also repeals the rules that allowed estates to pay their income tax over four equal installments after the year it is earned.

Under prior law trusts and estates were not required to make estimated tax payments and estates could elect to pay income tax in four equal installments beginning with the due date of the return and for each three-month period thereafter.

Trustees are allowed to assign any amounts of a trust's quarterly payments to the beneficiaries. The election is made on the tax return of the trust. Since the return is to be filed within 65 days after the end of the trust's taxable year, the amount of the credits assigned to the beneficiaries is considered a distribution under the 65-day rule of Sec. 663. Thus, the beneficiaries are deemed to have received the distribution on the last day of the trust's year. According to the Conference Committee's statutory language, the amount deemed distributed won't be treated as a payment of the trust's estimated tax, but will be treated as a payment of the beneficiary's estimated tax on the January 15 following the tax year. This election is available only to the extent the trust's total estimated tax payments for the year exceeds its own tax liability. However, the Committee Report indicates the beneficiaries will still treat the credit as received at the time the election is made for their estimated taxes.

Act Sec. 1404, requiring trusts and estates to make estimated income tax payments and repealing estate's election to pay income tax in four equal installments, amends Secs. 643 and 6654 and repeals Sec. 6152, effective for taxable years beginning after 12-31-86.

Minor's Income

[¶1405] **New Tax Rules for Child's Unearned Income.** The new law cracks down on family income splitting, a device used by higher-bracket parents to cut overall family taxes by shifting income-producing assets to lower-bracket children. The mechanism for the crackdown is new Sec. 1(j), which is effective for tax years beginning after the date of enactment.

The new law taxes "net unearned income" for a child under 14 at the parent's tax rate, even if the money or other property was given to the child before 1987.

If the child is age 14 or older, his or her net unearned income is taxed at the child's rates, not the parent's. [See ¶1406 for the calculation of the tax on net unearned income for a child under 14.]

¶1405

What the old rules allow. Under prior law, a family was able to reduce its aggregate tax liability by shifting income-producing property among family members. Consider, for example, parents who wanted to minimize taxes paid on income from funds set aside for the college education of their child. A common maneuver for these parents, whose dividend income would otherwise be taxed at their high tax bracket, was to transfer shares of stock into a custodian account for their child. By doing so, they deflected part of the family's income to a child taxed at a lower rate.

What the new rules allow. There are two sets of rules for taxing unearned income received by children. The first set is for children under 14 years of age, while the second is for children over 14 years of age and older.

Children under the age of 14. For an under-14 child, net unearned income, including income derived from gifts made *before* 1987, is taxed at the parent's rate—that is, as if the parent had received the income, rather than at the child's lower rate. The under-14 rules remain applicable until the child reaches age 14.

Exemption from the under-14 rules. Certain kinds of income are exempt from the new rules and continue to be taxed at the child's rate. The exemption is for all wages earned by the child, whether the wages come from babysitting, delivering newspapers, or even from a job with a business owned by a parent.

Child age 14 or over. The under-age-14 rules no longer apply when a child reaches the age of 14 before the close of the tax year in question. Instead, a more advantageous set of rules applies. In general, all unearned income is taxed at the child's rate (as is earned income).

Other changes. The new law does more than just put a crimp in income splitting by upper-bracket families. It also exposes more of a family's income to tax and will require many more parents to file income tax returns for their children. Reason: Beginning with the 1987 tax year, a taxpayer cannot claim a personal exemption if he or she is eligible to be claimed as a dependent by another taxpayer [see ¶103].

> **NOTE:** Starting in 1987, the parent must include the child's social security number on the parent's return and the child must include the parent's number on the child's return.

[¶1406] Computing Unearned Income of Child Under 14. The child's net unearned income is taxed to the child at the parent's top marginal rate—that is, the peak tax bracket of the parent. Thus, income received from the child's bank accounts, CDs, money market funds, stocks, and the like regardless of who set up or bought the property is taxed to the child at the parent's top rate. The new provision applies if (1) the child has not attained age 14 before the close of the tax year, and (2) either parent of the child is alive at the close of the tax year.

How to calculate tax. The tax imposed on the child equals the *greater of*:

(1) The tax that would be imposed on the child's income without the special rules on the child's unearned income; or

(2) The sum of the tax that would be payable had the child not received unearned income, and the child's share of the parental-source tax.

The child will pay tax at the parent's rates on his or her *net unearned income*. The child's *net unearned income* is the child's unearned income less the sum of $500 and the greater of: (1) $500 of the standard deduction or $500 of itemized deductions, or (2) the deductions allowed the child that are directly connected with the production of the child's unearned income. The net unearned income cannot exceed the child's total taxable income for the year in question. These rules can best be explained with examples.

Example (1): Johnny Jones, age 13, has $300 of unearned income and no earned income. His standard deduction is $300 which is allocated against his unearned income. Johnny pays no tax.

Example (2): Tommy Green, age 13, has $1,400 of unearned income and no earned income. The $1,400 is first reduced by his standard deduction of $500. Of the remaining $900, $500 is taxed at Tommy's rates, and the remaining $400 is net unearned income and taxed at the top rate of his parents.

Example (3): Debbie Smith, age 12, has $700 of earned income and $300 of unearned income. Her standard deduction is $700. The standard deduction is first applied against Debbie's unearned income. The $400 balance of the standard deduction is allocated against the $400 of earned income. She does not have any net unearned income. The remaining $300 is taxed at Debbie's rates.

PARENT'S LOOKBACK: A parent must do an "as if" calculation of his own return before he completes his child's. He must figure the difference between (1) the tax he would have paid had his income included each under-age-14 child's unearned income, and (2) the tax he actually pays.

For purposes of computing the child's tax, net unearned income is taken into account in determining the parent's low-bracket phase-out and the phase-out of the personal exemptions the parent may be eligible to claim. However, net unearned income is *not* taken into account by a parent in computing his or her tax liability.

More complications. A further calculation is required if there is more than one under-age-14 child with unearned income. Each child's share of the parent's tax is prorated based on the ratio of each child's unearned income to total unearned income of the parent's children.

What if the child's parents are divorced? In this situation, the custodial parent is the one whose tax income is taken into account when computing the tax on a child's unearned income. And if the parents are married but file separate returns, the income of the parent with the greater taxable income is taken into account.

[Ed note: The Conference Committee Report indicates that the provisions on a child's unearned income are effective for tax years beginning after the date of enactment. However, the Conference Bill states that the effective date is as shown below.]

Act Sec. 1411, relating to unearned income of minor children under age 14, amends Sec. 1, effective for taxable years beginning after 12-31-86.

【¶1407】 Trust Income. Special rules apply to income received by children from property put into arrangements known as Clifford or ten-year trusts. These trusts are discussed at ¶1402. Presumably, income received by an under-14 child if from property put into a trust before 3-2-86, is subject to the new rules on net unearned income. This income continues to be taxed at the *child's* rate when the child is over 14. For trust transfers after 3-1-86, all of the trust income received by the child is taxed to the grantor.

【¶1408】 Coping With the New Rules on Child's Income. Taxpayers can use these strategies to minimize or avoid the new rules on unearned income:

Gift of assets that defer income: The new rule taxing income at the parental rate does not apply once a child reaches age 14. So the idea is to give younger children assets that defer taxable income until a child reaches that age. Some examples:

- U.S. Government Savings (EE) bonds: income may be deferred until the bond is cashed in. Note that this won't work if a child already owns EE bonds and has elected to report each year's interest accrual as income (to take advantage of his personal exemption and low rates). Reason: The child can't change his mind—he must continue to report each year's Savings Bond accrual as income.

- Growth stock: Typically, growth stock pays little in the way of dividends. However, the profit on an astute investment may more than offset the lack of dividends. The child can hold the stock until he reaches age 14. If he sells it at a profit, he'll be taxed at his low rates.

- Deep discount municipal bonds: Such bonds produce tax-free income during ownership. If the bond matures on or after the date when the child reaches age 14, the discount (face value less cost basis) is taxed in the child's low tax bracket.

Employment of child: Taxpayers in a position to do so should employ their children in their business and pay them a reasonable wage for the work they actually perform (e.g., light office help, such as filing). Result: The child's earned income will be sheltered by the new standard deduction (and the parent's business gains a deduction for the wages). The new under-age-14 rules have no effect on earned income, even if derived from a parent's business.

Estate and Gift Taxes

[¶1421] **Information Necessary for Valid Current Use Valuation Election.** An executor may elect to value certain real property used in farming or other closely held business operations for estate tax purposes based on its current use rather than its full fair market value. There was concern that, in certain cases, the federal estate tax return (Form 706) did not sufficiently inform taxpayers of what information must be provided to elect current use valuation and that an agreement to the election by all persons with an interest in the property is required to be attached to Form 706. So the new law provides limited relief permitting additional time to supply information necessary for a valid election.

For decedents dying *before* January 1, 1986, if the estate made a timely current use valuation election and provided substantially all the information elicited by Form 706, the election is valid. However, if the estate fails to provide the Treasury with additional information with respect to the election within 90 days after the information is requested, the election will be disallowed as invalid.

This relief does not apply to the estate of any decedent if the statute of limitations for assessment of tax has expired before the date of enactment of the new law.

Act Sec. 1421, relating to information necessary for valid special use valuation election, is effective on the date of enactment with a special targeted transitional exception.

[¶1422] **Estate and Gift Tax Break for Qualified Conservation Contributions.** The new law liberalizes the estate and gift tax deduction rules for contributions of certain property interests to charitable organizations, the U.S., or state or local governments.

Until now, the estate, gift, *and income* tax deductions for a "qualified conservation contribution" of a partial interest in real property (including a gift in which the mineral interest was retained by the donor) were conditioned on the requirement that the gift be made for, and limited by its terms to, certain defined conservation purposes [Code Sec. 170(h)(4)(A)].

The new law keeps this requirement for the income tax deduction. Now, however, gifts that don't satisfy the conservation purpose requirement will still qualify for estate and gift tax deductions. There's also a targeted amendment for certain gifts to Acadia National Park in Maine.

Act Sec. 1422(a), liberalizing the estate tax rules for contributions of real property, redesignates Sec. 2055(f) as Sec. 2055(g) and adds new Sec. 2055(f), and Act Sec. 1422(b), liberalizing the gift tax rules for contributions of real property, redesignates Sec. 2522(d) as Sec. 2522(e) and adds new Sec. 2522(d), all effective for transfers and contributions made after 12-31-86.

[¶1423] Indirect Transfer to Qualified Organization. The new law allows an estate tax charitable deduction to a particular estate that transferred property indirectly to charity, according to the decedent's wishes.

[¶1431] Generation-Skipping Transfer Tax. As part of the Tax Reform Act of 1976, the generation-skipping transfer (GST) tax was imposed, naturally, to tax generation-skipping transfers. What is a generation-skipping transfer? It's one that allows a beneficiary in a generation below the transferor to enjoy benefits of ownership in the property without having the property included in his or her estate (or pay gift tax) when it is transferred to (or for the benefit of) beneficiaries in an even lower generation.

> **Example:** A transfers property in trust in which his child, B receives the income for life and the remainder passes to A's grandchildren, C, on the child's death.

Since B, the grantor's child, had only a life estate in the trust corpus (other nontaxable ownership interests include the right to be trustee, a limited power of appointment, powers subject to ascertainable standards relating to health, education and support, and power to invade under "5 or 5" powers under Sec. 2014) it would not be included in the child's gross estate for estate tax purposes. So the GST tax was invented to impose an equivalent estate (or gift tax) on the transfer of the beneficial enjoyment of the trust corpus or income from A's child to A's grandchild in the above example. "Generation-skipping" is involved because the original transfer is taxed in A's generation and again in C's generation but it "skips" taxation in B's generation. In other words, the loophole was the use of long-term trusts that split the beneficial enjoyment of property between individuals in more than one generation without the imposition of an estate or gift tax on the shift of interest between the different generations. Under prior law, the estate or gift tax rate bracket of the skipped generation, B, above, formerly called the "deemed transferor"—was used as a measuring rod to tax the transfer as if the property was actually transferred outright to C from B.

Enter another taxable event—the direct skip. Under prior law and the new law, GST tax is imposed on a "taxable termination" and a "taxable distribution." The former is illustrated in the example above when B's death terminates B's life income interest in the trust and the trust property passes to C, the generation-skipping beneficiary. A "taxable distribution" results whenever there is a distribution of trust property to the generation-skipping beneficiary.

> **NOTE:** Prior law generation-skipping distributions of trust income were not subject to the GST tax. Under the new law, the distributions are subject to the tax whether from trust income or trust corpus but the recipient can take an income tax deduction for the GST tax imposed on the distribution.

The direct skip loophole closed: Since the GST tax replaced the estate tax in B's generation (see our example above) estate planners had to get around both the estate tax and the GST tax. The way to do it was to avoid B's generation altogether (if B could afford it) and have A make the transfer *directly* to the grandchild, C—the so-called "layering" technique. This loophole is now closed by the new law. Now a generation-skipping transfer includes *any* transfer of property to (or for the benefit of) persons two or more generations below that of the transferor without the payment of estate or gift tax in the "skipped" generation even when the "skipped" person in that generation (B above) had no ownership interest in the property. So the new GST definition now includes "direct" generation-skipping transfers, i.e., (A to C above. C is called the "skip person") as well as transfers in which a member of the skipped generation has an interest in or power over the property.

Generation assignment changes. The new classification are the same as under prior law except that lineal descendants of the transferor's spouse also are assigned to generations like those for similar descendants of the transferor. Also, there's a special rule on generation assignment for the grantor's grandchildren: When the grandchild's parent who is a lineal descendant of the grantor is deceased, the grandchild is "moved up" a generation, so transfers to that grandchild would not be GSTs.

Now for the good news. (1) For each grantor there is a special $2,000,000 GST exemption per grandchild for direct skips in trust or otherwise. This can be doubled to $4,000,000 for married individuals who elect to treat the transfers as made one-half by each. This exemption expires on January 1, 1990.

(2) Also, every person is permitted to make GSTs aggregating as much as $1,000,000 during his or her lifetime and at death, that will be completely exempt from the GST tax. By electing to treat the GSTs as made one-half by each, a married couple has as much as

$2,000,000 of GSTs they can make without GST tax. Transfers above that amount are subject to tax at a rate equal to the maximum gift and estate tax rate. The former $250,000 exclusion for GSTs to grandchildren was repealed.

> **WATCH THIS:** When a person allocates all or a part of the $1,000,000 exemption to a GST, all future appreciation on the designated exempt property is also exempt. So if a grantor transfers $1,000,000 in trust for his children and grandchildren and allocates the entire $1,000,000 exemption to the trust, none of the trust will ever be subject to GST tax even if the trust property increases to $10,000,000. But if only $500,000 of the exemption is allocated, one-half of the value of all distributions to the grandchildren will be subject to the GST tax and one-half the value of the trust property will be subject to that tax when the children's interest terminates.

QTIP property. Part of the $1,000,000 exemption can be allocated to offset a GST on the death of the transferor's surviving spouse when the property qualified as terminable interest property for estate and gift tax purposes under Secs. 2056(b)(7) and 2523(f).

Other exemptions. As under prior law, GST amounts subject to estate and gift taxes are exempt. Also, the GST doesn't apply to any amount exempt from gift tax because of the gift tax $10,000 exclusion (Sec. 2503(b)) or the exclusion for tuition and medical expense payments under Sec. 2503(e).

Flat rate. Under the new law, all GSTs not covered by the exemptions or exclusions are taxed at a flat 55% rate which is equal to the present maximum estate and gift tax rate scheduled to go down to 50% in 1988.

Tax base and liability for payment. Under the new law, generation-skipping transfers are taxed as follows:

(1) Taxable distributions. Distributions are subject to tax on the amount received by the transferee. The transferee pays the tax.

(2) Taxable terminations. The value of the property in which the interest terminates is the amount subject to tax. The trustee pays the tax.

(3) Direct skips. The value of the property received by the transferee is the amount subject to tax. The person making the transfer pays the tax.

Effective Date: The GST tax changes apply to transfers made after enactment with (1)-(3) below. The $2 million per grandchild exclusion sunsets January 1, 1990.

(1) Lifetime transfers made after September 25, 1985 are subject to the amended tax; (2) transfers from trusts that were irrevocable on September 25, 1985 are exempt to the extent the transfers were not made out of corpus added after that date; (3) if the decedent was incompetent on October 22, 1986 and at all times until his death, transfers by will in existence on that date are exempt.

WATCH REFUND TIMING: The former GST tax is repealed retroactive to June 11, 1976, its effective date. Any tax paid will be refunded. Taxpayers who would otherwise be barred by the statute of limitations have one year from the date of enactment to file for refunds.

Delayed effective dates. Election may be made to treat *inter vivos* and testamentary contingent transfers in trust for the benefit of a grandchild as direct skips if the transfers occur before the date of enactment, and the transfers would be direct skips except that the trust instrument provides that, if the grandchild dies before vesting of the interest transferred, the interest is transferred to the grandchild's heirs (rather than the grandchild's estate). Transfers treated as direct skips as a result of this election are subject to federal gift and estate tax on the grandchild's death in the same way as if the contingent gift over had been to the grandchild's estate.

There is an exemption from the revised generation-skipping transfer tax testamentary direct skips occurring under wills executed before the date of enactment if the testator dies before 1-1-87.

Act Secs. 1431-1433, relating to the generation-skipping transfer tax, repeals Secs. 2601—2603, 2611—2614, 2621—2622, retroactive to June 11, 1976 and adds Secs. 2601—2604, 2611—2613, 2621—2624, 2631—2632, 2641—2642, 2651—2654 and 2661—2663, effective as shown above.

[The page following this is 1501.]

COMPLIANCE AND TAX ADMINISTRATION

Penalties

[¶1501] **Information Reports.** The accuracy of information reporting is of vital importance to the federal taxation system. Under the new law, several penalties for inaccurate or incomplete returns have been increased.

Consolidated penalties for information reporting failures. To promote fairness in their application and to simplify their administration, the penalties for failure to file an information return with the IRS and for failure to supply a taxpayer with a copy of the information return have been consolidated. And the maximum penalty for each category of failure has been raised from $50,000 to $100,000. Also, a new $5 penalty (maximum $20,000 in a calendar year) has been added for a failure to include correct information on an information return which is due after December 31, 1986 (the penalty applies to both omissions of information and inclusions of incorrect information on both returns filed with the IRS and copies supplied to the taxpayer). But the maximum $20,000 cap doesn't apply when the rules have been intentionally disregarded. The new penalty doesn't apply at all if the penalty for failure to supply a correct taxpayer I.D. number has been imposed.

Interest and dividend returns. Special, stricter rules apply to interest and dividend returns or statements. While the information reporting penalties don't apply to failures that are due to reasonable cause and not willful neglect, interest and dividend reporting failures will be excused only if the taxpayer exercised due diligence. And the maximum amount limitations applicable to the other penalties don't apply.

Failure to supply TIN. The maximum penalty for failing to supply taxpayer identification numbers is increased from $50,000 to $100,000.

Effective Date: These changes apply to returns which have a due date (determined without regard to extensions) that is after December 31, 1986.

Act Sec. 1501, revising penalties for failure to file information returns and statements, adds new Sec. 6721 through 6724, and amends Secs. 6041(d), 6042(c), 6044(e), 6045(b), 6049(c), 6050A(b), 6050B(b), 6050E(b), 6050F(b), 6050G(b), 6050H(d), 6050I(e), 6050K(b), 6052(b), and 6676(a), effective for returns due (without regard to extensions) after 12-31-86. Secs. 6652(a) and 6678 are repealed.

Act Sec. 1501(c)(2) amends Sec. 6042(c), relating to information reports for payments of dividends and corporate earnings and profits. Act Sec. 1501(c)(3) amends Sec. 6044(e), relating to information reports for patronage dividends. Act Sec. 1501(c)(5) amends Sec. 6049(c), relating to information returns for payments of interest. Act Secs. 1501(c)(2), (3), and (5) are effective for information returns due (without regard to extensions) after enactment date.

[¶1502] **Increased Penalty for Failure to Pay.** The new law increases in specified situations the amount of delinquency penalty imposed for a failure to either pay the tax shown or required to be shown on a taxpayer's return from .5% to 1% per month. The increased rate applies on the earlier of the IRS's notice and demand for immediate payment where collection of the tax is in jeopardy, or 10 days after a notice before levy is given.

Relief for penalty overlap eliminated. The penalty imposed for a failure to pay the tax required to be shown on a taxpayer's return will also no longer be reduced by the penalty imposed for a failure to file a return.

Effective Date: The new provisions apply to amounts assessed after December 31, 1986, whether the failure to pay began before or after that date.

Act Sec. 1502, increasing the penalty for failure to pay tax, adds new Sec. 6651(d), and deletes Sec. 6651(c)(1)(B), effective for assessments after 12-31-86.

[¶1503] **Penalties for Negligence and Fraud.** Under the new law, the negligence penalty now applies to an underpayment of *any* tax in the Code. The new law continues the application of the penalty to the *entire* amount of the underpayment, not just the portion attributable to negligence.

> **WATCH THIS:** In redefining negligence under the new law, *any* failure to report on a return an amount that has been reported on an information return (not just for interest and dividend payments) will now automatically be treated as negligence for purpose of the penalty, unless there's clear and convincing evidence to the contrary.

Fraud penalty rate increased. The rate at which the penalty for fraud is imposed is increased from 50% to 75%. However, the fraud penalty now applies only to the part of an underpayment that is actually attributable to fraud. Before, if there was a million dollar underpayment and even a dollar of it was attributable to fraud, the *entire* underpayment was subject to the penalty. Under the new law, if any fraud is found, the taxpayer has the burden of showing what part of an underpayment isn't attributable to fraud. The limitation period rules aren't affected—if a return is fraudulent in some respects, the limitation period on the entire return never expires.

Act Sec. 1503, relating to the fraud and negligence penalty provisions, amends Sec. 6653, effective for returns due after 12-31-86.

[¶1504] **Penalty for Substantial Understatement.** The new law increases the penalty for substantial understatement of tax liability from 10% to 20% of the amount of the underpayment attributable to the understatement.

Act Sec. 1504, relating to penalties for substantial understatement, amends Sec. 6661(a), effective for returns due after 12-31-86.

Interest Provisions

[¶1511] **Differential Interest Rate.** Prior law required taxpayers to pay interest on tax underpayments and required Treasury to pay interest on overpayments. The underpayment and overpayment rates were identical —the prime rate.

The new law pegs the overpayment rate to the Federal short-term rate plus two percentage points, and the underpayment rate to the Federal short-term rate plus three percentage points, both rounded to the nearest full percentage. The rate is adjusted quarterly, is determined during the first month of each quarter, and takes effect the following quarter. For example, the January federal short-term rate is the rate used to determine the interest to be charged on underpayments and overpayments for April, May, and June. The Secretary determines the interest rate based on average market yield on outstanding U.S. marketable obligations with remaining maturity periods of three years or less.

Treasury may prescribe regulations for netting overpayments and underpayments covering the first three years after enactment.

Act Sec. 1511, relating to interest on tax underpayments and overpayments, amends Code Sec. 6621, effective for interest for periods after 12-31-86.

[¶1512] **Interest on Accumulated Earnings Tax Underpayments.** The new law imposes interest on accumulated earnings tax underpayments from the return due date. Prior law imposed interest from the date IRS demands payment of the tax.

Act Sec. 1512, relating to interest on the accumulated earnings tax, amends Code Sec. 6601(b), effective for returns due (without regard to extension) after 12-31-85.

Information Reporting Provisions

[¶1521] **Reporting of Real Estate Transactions.** The new law expands the obligation to report the gross proceeds of sales of stock, commodities, etc., to the IRS. Starting in 1987, one of the participants in a real estate transfer also must report the sale of that real estate, including single-family homes.

Who is responsible for reporting. The responsibility for reporting sales on Forms 1099 falls on a number of participants in a descending order of responsibility. This means that the first person responsible for reporting is the real estate broker. Under this rule, "broker" is defined as the person responsible for the closing (including an attorney or a title company). In the absence of that person, the responsibility then passes to the mortgage lender, then to the seller's broker, then to the buyer's broker, and finally, any other person designated in IRS regs to be prescribed.

Sales of single-family homes. In the past, if you sold your principal residence, the only "notice" to the IRS would be your new address on Form 1040, if you failed to submit Schedule D, used when there is a taxable gain, or Form 2119, used when a home seller: (1) postpones tax on all or part of the gain by buying a replacement residence, (2) elects the over-age-55 exclusion of up to $125,000, or (3) suffers a loss, which is nondeductible.

Co-op apartments. The expanded reporting requirements apply to "real estate transactions." An apparently yet-to-be-resolved question is whether a literal reading of the law exempts sales of co-op apartments. The reason for the uncertainty is that the usual interest in a co-op is personal property; ownership is evidenced by a stock certificate that entitles the owner to occupy a certain apartment within a building and to use the common grounds.

No uncertainty, though, for condo owners. They own real estate, in the same way as owners of single-family homes.

Backup withholding. Real estate transactions are subject to the backup withholding requirements under Sec. 3406 only to the extent required by IRS regs. The Finance Committee indicated that it expects Treasury to provide guidance on how the backup withholding will work.

Act Sec. 1521(a) amends Sec. 6045, relating to returns of brokers. Act Sec. 1521(b), amends Sec. 3406(h)(5), relating to backup withholding. Act Sec. 1521 is effective, without regard to whether the IRS has issued implementing regulations, for real estate transactions closing after 12-31-86.

[¶1522] **Reporting of Persons Receiving Federal Contracts.** The new law requires Federal executive agencies to file information returns with the IRS on persons who receive Federal contracts, subcontracts, and licenses. A return must state the name, address and identification number of each person and whatever other information Regs may prescribe.

Act Sec. 1522(a), dealing with information reporting on persons receiving Federal contracts, adds Sec. 6050M; Act Sec. 1522(b) amends the table of sections for subpart B of part III of subchapter A of chapter 61, effective for all contracts and subcontracts entered into (and licenses granted) before, on, or after 1-1-87.

[¶1523] **Reporting of Royalties.** The new law requires payers of royalties to file Forms 1099 on payments aggregating $10 or more in a calendar year.

Royalties required to be reported. They include payments with respect to the right to exploit natural resources, such as oil, gas, coal, timber, sand, gravel, and other mineral interests, as well as payments for the right to exploit intangible property, such as copyrights, trade names, trademarks, books and other literary compositions, musical compositions, artistic works, secret processes or formulas, and patents.

Act Sec. 1523(a) adds Sec. 6050N, relating to returns regarding payment of royalties. Act Sec. 1523(b)(1) amends Sec. 3406(b), relating to backup withholding. Act Sec. 1523(b)(2), amends Sec. 6041(a), relating to information at source. Act Sec. 1523(b)(3), amends Sec. 6676(a) and (b), relating to failure to supply identifying numbers. Act Sec. 1523(c), amends the table of sections for subpart B of part III of subchapter A of chapter 61. Act Sec. 1523 is effective for payments made after 12-31-86.

[¶1524] **Reporting Dependent's Taxpayer I.D.s.** Beginning with all returns due on or after January 1, 1988 (without regard to extensions), any individual who claims a dependency deduction for a dependent who is 5 years old or older, must report the dependent's taxpayer I.D. number (social security number) on the individual's tax return. The penalty for failure to do so is $5 a TIN per return.

RELIGIOUS EXEMPTION: There is a special rule for religious groups that are exempt from the social security laws.

Act Sec. 1524 adds Sec. 6109(e), relating to identifying numbers, and Sec. 6676(e), relating to failure to supply identifying numbers, effective for returns due (without regard to extensions) after 12-31-87.

[¶1525] **Reporting Tax Exempt Interest.** Beginning with returns for tax years starting after 12-31-86, taxpayers who must file a return will have to report how much tax-exempt interest they have received or accrued during the tax year.

Act Sec. 1525 adds new Sec. 6012(d), effective for tax years starting after 12-31-86.

[¶1526] **Separate Mailing Requirement for Certain Information Reports Eased.** The new law reduces mailing costs for payors of interest, dividends, and patronage dividends who must provide copies of information returns to the recipient of the payment. The payors can do so either in person (as under prior law) or in a statement mailing by first-class mail.

Other enclosures that can accompany statement mailing. Only three kinds of enclosures, says the Senate Committee Report, can be made with a statement mailing: (1) a check, (2) a letter explaining why no check is enclosed (such as, for example, because a dividend has not been declared payable), or (3) a statement of the taxpayer's specific account with the payor (such as a year-end summary of the taxpayer's transactions with the payor).

> **NOTE:** These three kinds are in addition to the other enclosures, such as other information reports or tax forms, that the IRS previously permitted to be enclosed.

Statements on envelopes and enclosures. The statement "Important Tax Return Document Enclosed" must appear on both the outside of the envelope and each enclosure (the check, letter, or account statement).

> **WARNING:** A mailing is not considered a statement mailing if the payor encloses any other material, such as advertising, promotional material, or a quarterly or annual report. Such enclosures are impermissible because they may make it less likely that some taxpayers will recognize the importance of the information report and use it in completing their returns.

Act Sec. 1501(c)(2) amends Sec. 6042(c), relating to information reports for payments of dividends and corporate earnings and profits. Act Sec. 1501(c)(3) amends Sec. 6044(e), relating to information reports for patronage dividends. Act Sec. 1501(c)(5) amends Sec. 6049(c), relating to information returns for payments of interest. Act Secs. 1501(c)(2), (3), and (5) are effective for information returns due (without regard to extensions) after enactment date.

Tax Shelter Fees and Penalties

[¶1531] Tax Shelter Ratio Test Tightened for Shelter Registrations. Tax shelter organizers must register certain shelters with the IRS. Prior law required registration when, among other things, the shelter ratio (the ratio of deductions and 200% of the credits to cash actually invested) was greater than 2 to 1. The new law substitutes 350% for 200% in determining the above ratio.

Act Sec. 1531 amends Sec. 6111(c)(2), relating to tax shelter ratios, effective for tax shelters in which interests are first offered for sale after 12-31-86.

[¶1532] Increased Penalty for Not Registering Shelter. As of the enactment date, the minimum penalty for failure to register is higher. The increased penalty is the greater of 1% of the aggregate amount invested in the shelter or $500 (up from the greater of $500 or 1% (up to $10,000) of the aggregate amount invested). The prior law $10,000 cap on the penalty has been eliminated.

Act Sec. 1532 amends Sec. 6707(a)(2), relating to penalty for failure to register tax shelters, effective for tax shelters in which interests are first offered for sale after enactment date.

[¶1533] **Higher Penalty for Not Reporting Tax Shelter Registration Number.** The new law increases the penalty for a tax shelter investor who fails to include the shelter registration number on a return, unless due to reasonable cause. The increased penalty is $250 (up from $50) in the case of returns filed after enactment date.

Act Sec. 1533 amends Sec. 6707(b)(2), relating to penalty for failure to furnish tax shelter identification number, effective for returns filed after enactment date.

[¶1534] **Bigger Penalty for Not Keeping Shelter Investor List.** As of the enactment date, there is a greater maximum penalty for a shelter organizer or seller who fails to maintain a list of investors in a potentially abusive tax shelter, unless the failure is due to reasonable cause. The penalty is still $50 for each name missing from the list, but the maximum is raised to $100,000 (from $50,000) in any calendar year.

Act Sec. 1534 amends Sec. 6708(a), relating to failure to maintain list of investors in potentially abusive tax shelters, effective for failures occurring or continuing after enactment date.

[¶1535] **Interest on Substantial Underpayments Attributable to Shelters.** Under the new law, the rate of interest imposed on underpayments of tax of more than $1,000 that are attributable to sham or fraudulent transactions (and tax-motivated transactions, as already provided by prior law) is 120% of the generally applicable interest rate.

Act Sec. 1535 amends Sec. 6621(c), relating to interest on substantial underpayments attributable to tax-motivated transactions, effective for interest accruing after 12-31-84 (but not on underpayments with respect to which there was a final court decision before enactment date).

Estimated Taxes

[¶1541] **Individual Estimated Tax Payments.** The new law increases from 80% to 90% the proportion of the current year's tax liability that an individual taxpayer must make as estimated tax payments to avoid the penalty for underpayment of estimated tax. Under this rule, quarterly estimated tax installments must be 22.5%, 45%, 67.5%, and 90% of the year's tax liability (up from 20%, 40%, 60%, and 80%). Under the new law, estimated tax payments based on 90% of actual tax liability for the current year, or on 100% of last year's tax, *whichever is less,* avoid the penalty for underpayment of estimated tax.

Act Sec. 1541, relating to estimated tax payments by individuals, amends Secs. 6654(d)(1)(B)(i), 6654(d)(2)(C)(ii), 6654(i)(1)(C); 6654(j)(3)(B), effective for taxable years beginning after 12-31-86.

[¶1542] **Private Foundation's Investment Income Excise Tax.** The new law requires private foundations to make quarterly estimated payments of the excise tax on investment income. These payments are to be made in the same manner as regular corporate estimated income taxes.

Act Sec. 1542 adds Sec. 6154(h), effective for taxable years beginning after 12-31-86.

[¶1543] **Unrelated Business Income Tax.** Tax-exempt organizations must make quarterly payments of estimated tax for the unrelated business income tax. Payments are to be made in the same manner as regular corporate estimated income taxes.

Act Sec. 1542 adds Sec. 6154(h), effective for taxable years beginning after 12-31-86.

[¶1544] **Waiver of 1986 Estimated Tax Penalties.** To cover the many changes that increase tax liabilities from the beginning of 1986, the new law allows individual taxpayers until 4-15-87, and corporations until 3-15-87 (the final filing dates for calendar year returns) to pay their full 1986 income tax liabilities without a penalty of underpayments of estimated tax to the extent that the underpayments are attributable to changes made by the new law.

Act Sec. 1543, relating to waiver of estimated tax penalties, effective as noted above.

Tax Court and Tax Cases

[¶1551] **Attorney Fees.** The new law extends permanently the provisions authorizing awards of reasonable attorney's fees in tax cases. Also, it eliminates the previous $25,000 cap on such awards, and substitutes a $75 an hour limitation, unless the court determines that a higher rate is justified and expert witnesses are to be compensated under prevailing market rates, but no higher than the highest rate of compensation for expert witnesses paid by the U.S. In addition, the new law authorizes funding of attorneys' fee awards from the same source as non-tax cases. The present-law burden of proof is unchanged.

Effective Date. The new law applies to amounts paid after September 30, 1986, in civil actions or proceedings commenced after December 31, 1985. The provision relating to funding of fees applies to actions begun after February 28, 1983.

Act Sec. 1551, relating to attorney fees, amends Sec. 7430, effective as shown above.

[¶1552] Exhaustion of Administrative Remedies. The new law provides that failure to exhaust administrative remedies is an additional basis for the imposition of the discretionary penalty by the Tax Court.

Act Sec. 1552, dealing with administrative remedies, amends Sec. 6673, effective for proceedings commenced after enactment date.

[¶1553] Tax Court Inventory. The Tax Court and the IRS are now required to report to Congress, every two years beginning with 1987, on Tax Court case inventory and measures taken to close cases more efficiently.

Act Sec. 1552(c), relating to the Tax Court inventory report, is effective for 1987 and each 2-calendar year period thereafter.

[¶1554] Tax Court Periodic Practice Fees. The new law authorizes the Tax Court to impose a periodic registration fee on practitioners admitted to practice before it. The Tax Court is to establish the amount of the fee and the frequency of its collection, but the fee may not exceed $30 per year.

Act Sec. 1553, relating to practice fees, adds Sec. 7475 and is effective 1-1-87.

[¶1555] Jurisdiction Over Late Payment Penalty. The new law provides that the Tax Court has jurisdiction over the penalty for failure to pay an amount shown on the return if the Tax Court already has jurisdiction to redetermine a deficiency on that return.
Effective Date. The new law is effective for any action or proceeding before the Tax Court which has not become final before the date of enactment.

Act Sec. 1554, relating to determinations by the Tax Court, amends Sec. 6214, effective as shown above.

[¶1556] Attendance by United States Marshals. The new law provides that the U.S. Marshal for any district in which the Tax Court sits must attend any session of the Tax Court when requested to do so by the Chief Judge.

Act Sec. 1555, relating to attendance by U.S. Marshals, amends Sec. 7456, and is effective on the date of enactment.

[¶1557] Provisions Relating to Special Trial Judges. The new law consolidates into new Sec. 7443A of the Code a number of provisions relating to Special Trial Judges. It specifies that Special

¶**1557**

Trial Judges are to be paid 90% of the salary paid to Tax Court Judges, and that Special Trial Judges are to be reimbursed for travel and subsistence expenses to the same extent as are Tax Court Judges.

Effective Date: Generally the new law will be effective on the date of enactment. The provision relating to the salary of Special Trial Judges is effective on the first day of the first month beginning after the date of enactment.

Act Sec. 1556, relating to Special Trial Judges, adds new Sec. 7443A, and is effective as shown above.

[¶1558] **Retirement Pay of Tax Court Judges.** The new law permits Tax Court judges meeting specified age and tenure requirements to elect to retire, practice law after retirement, and receive retirement pay.

Act Sec. 1557, relating to retirement pay of Tax Court Judges, amends Secs. 7447 and 7448, generally effective on the date of enactment.

[¶1559] **Interlocutory Appeals and Survivor's Annuities.** Under the new law, an appeal from an interlocutory order of the Tax Court is authorized if a Tax Court judge includes in an interlocutory order a statement that a controlling question of law is involved, that there is substantial ground for difference of opinion regarding it, and that an immediate appeal from the order might materially advance the ultimate termination of the litigation.

The Court of Appeals is given discretion as to whether to permit the appeal. Neither the application for nor the granting of an appeal stays proceedings in the Tax Court, unless a stay is ordered by either the Tax Court or the Court of Appeals.

Also under the new law, the survivors annuity provisions covering Tax Court Judges are conformed to those applicable to other Federal judges. This provision is generally effective on November 1, 1986.

Act Sec. 1558, relating to appeals from interlocutory orders of the Tax Court, adds Sec. 7842(a)(2), effective for Tax Court orders entered after enactment date.

Act Sec. 1559, relating to annuities for surviving spouses and dependent children of Tax Court Judges, amends Sec. 7448, generally effective 11-1-86.

IRS Administrative Provisions

[¶1561] **Third Party Recordkeeping Disputes—Limitations.** For disputes between a third-party recordkeeper and the IRS that are not resolved within six months after the IRS issues an administrative summons, the statute of limitations on assessments and collection is suspended until the issue is resolved. The issue isn't resolved while an action to compel the production of documents is pending. The third party recordkeeper must notify a John Doe taxpayer (unidentified in the summons) whose records are the subject of the dispute that the statute of limitations has been suspended. The statute is suspended whether or not the third party gives notice.

As under prior law, the statute is suspended from the date a taxpayer intervenes in a dispute between the IRS and a third-party recordkeeper until the dispute is resolved.

Act Sec. 1561 amends Sec. 7609(e) and (i), relating to suspension of the statute of limitations for third-party recordkeepers, effective on enactment date.

[¶1562] Authority to Rescind Notice of Deficiency With Taxpayer's Consent. Under prior law, an IRS 90-day letter could not be withdrawn once this statutory notice of deficiency had been issued. Under the new law, it can be withdrawn if the IRS and taxpayer both agree to have it withdrawn.

Act Sec. 1562, relating to the authority to rescind a deficiency notice, adds new Sec. 6212(d), effective for deficiency notices issued on or after 1-1-86.

[¶1563] IRS Can Abate Interest Due to Its Own Errors or Delays. The new law gives the IRS the authority to abate interest that is generated because an IRS official either fails to perform a ministerial act in a timely fashion or errs in performing a ministerial act, provided the taxpayer is not at least significantly responsible for the delay. Although the IRS is authorized to abate interest, it is not required to do so, except in cases of erroneous refunds of up to $50,000.

This provision is not intended to be used routinely, but is to be used in cases where failure to abate would be perceived as grossly unfair. Interest is to be abated only for the time attributable to the failure to perform the ministerial act that occurs after the IRS contacts the taxpayer. Only those acts occurring after preliminary prerequisites, such as conferencing and supervisory review, would be considered ministerial acts for this purpose.

> **Example:** If there's an unreasonable delay in issuing a 90-day letter (deficiency notice) after the IRS and the taxpayer have completed efforts to resolve the matter, there would be grounds for interest abatement. The IRS can issue regulations that provide guidance as to what will be considered timely performance of ministerial acts, and define ministerial acts.

Generally, the IRS cannot charge interest on refunds made because of IRS error, until the date it demands repayment. For instance, a taxpayer who gets a $1,000 refund, rather than the $100 refund he rightfully claimed, because of an IRS error will not be charged interest on the excess $900 until the date repayment is claimed. But there are two exceptions to the no-interest-on-refund-rule. A taxpayer will be charged interest on an erroneous refund, if:

- the taxpayer (or a related party) has in any way caused the overstated refund to occur, or
- the erroneous refund exceeds $50,000.

Act Sec. 1563, relating to IRS abatement of interest, adds new Sec. 6404(e), effective for interest accruing in tax years beginning after 12-31-78.

[¶1564] Interest and Compounding Halted on Suspended Deficiency. The new law suspends both the interest on a tax (income, estate, gift, and certain excise taxes) deficiency and the compounding of interest on previously accrued interest. The suspension starts 31 days after the taxpayer has filed a waiver of restrictions on assessment of the underlying taxes and ends when a notice and demand is issued to the taxpayer.

Act Sec. 1564, relating to the suspension of compounding where interest on the deficiency is suspended, amends Code Sec. 6601(c), effective for interest accruing after 12-31-82.

[¶1565] No Levy on Certain Military Disability Payments. Under prior law, various payments, including unemployment benefits, workmen's compensation, a portion of ordinary wages, and certain pensions and annuities, are exempt from levy (the IRS cannot seize these assets in payment of delinquent taxes). The new law adds various military service-connected disability payments to this list of exempt items. Direct compensation payments are included, as well as other support payments for education and housing.

Act Sec. 1565, relating to certain service-connected disability payments exempt from levy, amends Code Sec. 6334(a), effective for payments made after 12-31-86.

[¶1566] IRS Seizure and Administrative Sale Increased to $100,000. Prior law allowed the IRS to seize property used in violating the tax law, and to sell personal property valued at $2,500 or less using administrative rather than judicial action, after having the property appraised and after giving notice to potential claimants. A claimant could post a $250 bond and require the government to proceed to sell the property by judicial action.

The new law allows the Treasury to administratively sell up to $100,000 of personal property. An appraisal would be necessary. Notice to potential claimants would have to be published in a newspaper. Potential claimants can require a judicial forfeiture action by posting a $2,500 bond.

Act Sec. 1566, relating to an increase in value of personal property subject to certain listing and notice procedures, amends Code Sec. 7325, effective on date of enactment.

[¶1567] IRS Special Agent's T&E Recordkeeping. Law enforcement officers generally are not subject to the Sec. 274(d) substantiation rules and the Sec. 132 income and wage inclusion rules for specified use of a law enforcement vehicle. Under prior law, IRS special agents were not classified as "law enforcement officers" for this purpose. Under the new law, they are considered law enforcement officers.

Act Sec. 1567, relating to automobile recordkeeping requirements for federal law enforcement officers, clarifies the applicability of Secs. 132 and 274, effective 1-1-85.

[¶1568] Disclosure of Returns and Return Information To Certain Cities. Cities having populations of over 2 million (determined on the basis of the most recent available decennial U.S. census data) that impose an income or wage tax may, at the Treasury Secretary's option, get returns and return information for the same purposes for which states get it. Cities must reimburse the IRS for this information. The disclosure and safeguard rules that apply to states also apply to cities, as do the state requirements for maintaining a system of standardized information requests, the reasons for the request, and the strict security against information release. The law permits disclosure only for the local jurisdiction's tax administration. Disclosure of returns or return information to an elected official or to the chief official of the local jurisdiction is forbidden. Unauthorized disclosure by an employee of an agency receiving this information will subject the employee to fine and imprisonment as provided by Sec. 7213 and to the civil action provided by Sec. 7431.

Act Sec. 1568, relating to disclosure of returns and return information to certain cities, amends Sec. 6103(b), effective on enactment date.

[¶1569] Priority of Local Law in Certain Forfeitures. The new law provides that a forfeiture under local law of property seized by a law enforcement agency of either a State or a political subdivision of a State relates back to the time of seizure. The provision does not apply to the extent that local law provides that someone other than the governmental unit has priority over the governmental unit in the property. For purposes of this provision, a State or local tax agency is not considered to be a law enforcement agency.

Act Sec. 1569, relating to the treatment of certain forfeitures, adds new Sec. 6323(i)(3), effective on enactment date.

[¶1570] **Release of Certain Seized Property to Owner.** Under the new law, before the sale of the seized property of a delinquent taxpayer, the IRS must determine (based upon criteria prescribed by the Treasury) whether the purchase of the property at the minimum price is in the best interests of the federal government. Property would continue to be sold to the highest bidder who meets or exceeds the minimum price.

If no bid meets or exceeds the minimum price, the government would buy the property at the minimum price only if in its best interests. If not in the best interests of the government, the property would be released back to the owner. The property would still be subject to a government lien. Also, any expense of the levy and sale would be added to the amount of delinquent taxes due.

Act Sec. 1570, relating to manner and conditions of sale of seized property, amends Sec. 6335(e)(1), effective for property seized after enactment date and for property seized on or before enactment date, if held by U.S. on such date.

[¶1571] **Allocation of Employee Tips.** Prior law required employers to provide an information report of an allocation of tips in large food or beverage establishments. The regs provide two ways to make this allocation. One is to allocate based on the portion of gross receipts of the establishment attributable to the employee during a payroll period. The second is to allocate based on the portion of the total number of hours worked in the establishment attributable to the employee during a payroll period.

Under the new law, the method of allocation based on the number of hours worked may be used only by an establishment that employs less than the equivalent of 25 full-time employees during a payroll period. Establishments employing the equivalent of 25 or more full-time employees would have to use the portion-of-gross-receipts-method to allocate tips during the payroll period (without an agreement between the employer and employees).

Act Sec. 1571, relating to modification of tips allocation method under Reg. §31.6053-3(f)(1)(iv), is effective for payroll periods beginning after 12-31-86.

[¶1572] **Treatment of Forfeitures of Land Sales Contracts.** Generally, before Federal tax liens can be extinguished, notice must be given to the Government. The new law provides that forfeitures of land sales contracts are subject to these notification requirements, effective for forfeitures after the thirtieth day after the day of enactment. The effect of this provision is to provide the Government with both notice and the opportunity to redeem the property, which it currently has with respect to most other transfers of real estate.

Act Sec. 1572, relating to treatment of forfeitures of land sales contracts, adds new Sec. 7425(c)(4), effective as noted above.

〔¶1581〕 Withholding Schedules To Mesh With Actual Liability. The new law also requires the IRS to make changes in Form W-4 and the withholding tables used by employers. Reason for the changes: To have the amount withheld from an employee's wages more closely match the employee's actual tax liability under the amendments made by the new law.

All employees must file revised W-4 Forms by 9-30-87. If an employee fails to do so, an employer must withhold income taxes as if the employee claimed one allowance (if the employee checked the "Single" box on the most recent Form W-4 that the employee filed) or two allowances (if the employee checked the "Married" box).

The new law also repeals the prior authority of the IRS to issue regs that permit employees to request decreases in withholding.

Act Sec. 1581(a) requires modification of withholding schedules, as stated above. Act Sec. 1581(b) amends Sec. 3402(i), relating to certain decreases in withholding not permitted, effective on enactment date. Act Sec. 1581(c), relating to employees filing new Forms W-4, effective for wages paid after 9-30-87.

〔¶1582〕 Report on Return-Free System. The new law directs the IRS to report to Congress on the possibility of a return-free system for individuals. The IRS must report its findings within six months after the date of enactment of the new law.

Act Sec. 1582 effective as indicated above.

[The page following this is 1601.]

EXEMPT AND NONPROFIT ORGANIZATIONS

[¶1601] **Exchange of Membership Lists.** The new law adds another item to the list of activities that won't be considered an unrelated trade or business of an organization otherwise tax exempt under Section 501. Any trade or business of such an organization that consists of exchanging or renting lists of donors to or members of the organization won't be considered "unrelated." This overrules *Disabled American Veterans v. U.S.* [(Ct. Cl., 1981), 650 F. 2d 1128, 48 AFTR 2d 81-5047], which held otherwise.

Act Sec. 1601, adding a UBI exemption, adds new Sec. 513(h)(1), effective for exchanges and rental of membership lists after the date of enactment.

[¶1602] **Distribution of Low Cost Items.** The term "unrelated trade or business" of a tax-exempt organization won't include activities relating to the distribution of low cost items incidental to soliciting contributions. An article is considered low cost if all items distributed to a single taxpayer cost, in the aggregate, not more than $5. Note that the $5 will be indexed after 1987.

A distribution will be considered incidental to soliciting charitable contributions if (1) the recipient didn't request the distribution, (2) the distribution is made without the express consent of the recipient, and (3) the article is accompanied by a request for a donation and a statement that the recipient can keep the low cost item regardless of whether a donation is made.

Act Sec. 1601, adding a UBI exemption, adds new Secs. 513(h)(2) and (3), effective for distributions of low cost articles after the date of enactment.

[¶1603] **Trade Show UBI Exemption Expanded.** The new law excludes from the definition of an "unrelated trade or business," trade show activities of Section 501(c)(3) organizations (charitable organizations such as churches and schools) and Section 501(c)(4) organizations (civic leagues, social welfare organizations). Previously, the exclusion was limited to Section 501(c)(5) organizations (labor or agricultural organizations) and Section 501(c)(6) organizations (business leagues and chambers of commerce). The exclusion applies to trade shows or conventions at which suppliers of the organization educate attendees on new developments or products related to the organization's exempt activities.

Act Sec. 1602, relating to the UBI exemption, amends Sec. 513(d)(3), effective for activities in taxable years beginning after the enactment date.

[¶1604] **Tax Exemption for Certain Title Holding Companies.** The new law creates a new type of tax-exempt organization— a corporation or trust that is organized for the exclusive purpose of acquiring, holding title to, and collecting income from real property and remitting it to certain tax-exempt organizations that are shareholders or beneficiaries. The organization can have no more than 35 shareholders or beneficiaries and only one class of stock or beneficial interest.

The new law limits participation in the trust or corporation to certain qualified plans, government entities, and Section 501(c)(3) organizations. In addition, the shareholders or beneficiaries have certain powers to dismiss the investment adviser and to terminate their interests.

> **NOTE:** The new law also allows the organization to use the exception to the tax on unrelated business income under the Section 514 debt-financing rules for real property.

Act Sec. 1603, relating to tax-exempt title holding companies, adds new Sec. 501(c)(25) and amends Sec. 514(c)(9), effective for taxable years beginning after 12-31-86.

[¶1605] Membership Organization Deduction Rules. The new law creates an exception to the general rule that a membership organization can deduct expenses for furnishing goods and services to members only from income derived from transactions with members. The exception applies to membership organizations engaged primarily in the gathering and distribution of news to their members for publication. According to the Senate report, the exception applies to the Associated Press.

Act Sec. 1604, relating to membership organizations, amends Sec. 277(b), effective on the date of enactment.

[¶1606] Technological Transfer Organization Tax Exemption. The new law creates a tax exemption for a certain organization that transfers technology from universities and scientific research organizations to the private sector. Among the requirements is that the organization was incorporated on July 20, 1981. The only organization this seems to apply to is the Washington Research Foundation. This provision overrules the Tax Court decision in *Washington Research Foundation* [P-H Memo TC ¶85,570].

Act Sec. 1605, creating a tax exemption is effective on the date of enactment.

[¶1607] Definition of Government Official. The new law raises the compensation limit for determining who is a government official in the definition "disqualified person" under the self-dealing rules. That term now includes officials in the executive, legislative, or judicial branch of a state, possession, local government, or District of Columbia with compensation of $20,000 or more. The limit had been $15,000.

Act Sec. 1606, defining government officials amends Sec. 4946(c), for compensation received after 12-31-85.

【¶1608】 Acquisition Debt Exception. Under the new law, the Section 514(c) acquisition indebtedness rule doesn't apply to certain debts incurred with bonds to acquire land for a community college in 1984 and which will be sold in 1986 or 1987.

Act Sec. 1607, relating to acquisition indebtedness, creates an exception for a sale by a certain community college.

【¶1609】 Amounts Paid for Special Seating. The new law allows taxpayers a charitable deduction for contributions incurred for renovating a certain college football stadium merely because the taxpayer receives the right to buy special seating in the stadium.

Act Sec. 1608 creates an exception for football fans of a certain university for amounts paid in taxable years beginning after 12-31-83.

[The page following this is 1701.]

OTHER PROVISIONS

[¶1701] Jobs Credit Modified and Extended. The new law extends the targeted jobs credit for three years so that it applies to wages paid individuals who begin work before January 1, 1989.

Now the bad news. The credit for first-year wages paid is reduced to 40% (from 50%) of the first $6,000 of qualified wages. The 25% credit for the first $6,000 of wages paid in an individuals second year of employment is repealed. Also, no wages paid to a targeted group member will be taken into account if the individual (1) is employed by the employer less than 90 days (14 days for economically disadvantaged summer youth employees) or (2) has completed less than 120 hours of work (20 hours for summer employees).

The new law also extends the authorization for appropriations through fiscal year 1988.

Act Sec. 1701, modifying the targeted jobs credit, amends Secs. 51(a), (b), (c), (d) and (i) and ERTA Sec. 261(f)(2), for individuals beginning work after 12-31-85 and before 1-1-89.

[¶1702] Collection of Diesel Fuel Excise Tax. The new law authorizes certain qualified retailers to elect imposition of the 15¢ a gallon excise tax on the sale of diesel fuel used in highway vehicles on the wholesaler (rather than the retailer) of the fuel. It will be imposed on the manufacturer when the sale is directly to the retailer.

The retailer is required to notify the seller in writing of the election. Failure to notify will result in the retailer being liable for the tax and will result in the imposition of a penalty of 5% of the tax involved.

Act Sec. 1702(a) amends Sec. 4041(n), relating to imposition of tax on special fuels; Act Sec. 1702(b) amends Sec. 6652, relating to failure to file certain information returns, registration statements, etc., effective for sales after the first calendar quarter beginning more than 60 days after the date of enactment.

[¶1703] Social Security Coverage for Clergy. The new law makes two changes for clergy with respect to Social Security coverage. First, the rules under which Treasury can grant an exemption from coverage have been clarified.

Second, the new law establishes a window under which a previous exemption can be revoked. The application for revocation must be filed no later than the due date of the first income tax return for the first taxable year beginning after the date of enactment but before the applicant becomes entitled to benefits. However, once revoked, the clergyman can't again seek an exemption.

Act Sec. 1704(a), granting exemptions, amends Sec. 1402(e), effective for applications filed 12-31-86. Act Sec. 1704(b), permitting revocations, is effective, generally, for service performed in taxable years ending on or after the enactment date.

【¶1704】 Indian Tribe FUTA Liability Cleared. The new law relieves two Indian tribes of Federal Unemployment Tax owed by each for services performed before 1988 and during a period they weren't covered by a state unemployment compensation program, if they weren't covered by state unemployment coverage on June 11, 1986.

Act Sec. 1705 relieves two Indian tribes of FUTA liability for work performed before 1-1-88.

【¶1705】 Technical Service Personnel. Under the new law, individuals retained to provide services as engineers, designers, drafters, computer programmers, systems analysts, and other similarly skilled personnel for a technical services firm to its clients are to be considered employees of the firm for purposes of withholding income and employment taxes if that is their common law status. Such status can't be avoided if the employee later incorporates and claims to be an employee of the corporation.

Act Sec. 1706, relating to technical service employees, amends Sec. 530 of the '78 Revenue Act, effective for services rendered after 12-31-86.

【¶1706】 Gasoline Excise Tax. The new law applies the 9¢ a gallon gasoline excise tax on the earlier of removal or sale of the gasoline by the refiner or importer, or the terminal operator (if a bulk transfer). The 9¢ a gallon tax will also apply to gasoline removed or sold by a blender or compounder, subject to a credit for tax paid and collected by the refiner or importer. The tax will be reduced to 3¢ a gallon for registered-gasohol producers who blend at the terminal (defining gasohol as gasoline that's at least 10% alcohol). Gasoline later separated from gasohol is taxable at $5\frac{2}{3}$¢ a gallon.

> **NOTE:** Every person subject to the excise tax must register with the Treasury before incurring any liability.

Blenders can claim a credit for tax paid on purchases of gasoline to the extent the blended gasoline isn't used as fuel. The buyer may get a refund on establishing that the ultimate use isn't as a taxable fuel. A special accelerated refund procedure is provided for gasohol blenders who buy tax-paid.

The new law also establishes a floor stock tax for gasoline subject to the tax held by a dealer for sale on 1-1-88, but which was not previously taxed, of 9¢ a gallon. Special rules apply for obtaining a refund of such taxes if the dealer is entitled to such refund under Section 6416.

Finally, Treasury is given fairly broad regulatory authority and is directed to study gasoline tax evasion (and report by 12-31-86).

Effective Date: The gasoline excise tax applies to gasoline removed after 12-31-87. The sales taxes on gasoline are scheduled to expire after 9-30-88; however, according to the statute, the 3¢ tax on gasohol producers will continue to apply to sales until 12-31-92.

Act Sec. 1703 relating to the gasoline excise tax amends Secs. 4081-4083, 4101, 6421 and 6427, effective 1-1-88 and as shown above.

[¶1707] Exclusion for Certain Foster Care Payments. Under prior law, a foster parent could exclude from income amounts paid as reimbursements from an appropriate governmental authority for the cost of caring for a qualified foster child in the taxpayer's home. To get the exclusion, the taxpayer had to account for the expenses. Any excess reimbursement would have to be included in income.

The new law makes two changes to the rules. First, the exclusion will apply to certain payments made for the cost of care for a qualifying foster adult. A qualifying individual is a person placed by appropriate state agencies. However, no exclusion can be claimed for more the five individuals over the age of 18 (as opposed to 10 children). Second, the new law gets rid of the accounting requirement by extending the exclusion to all amounts received by the foster parent, for care of the foster child, not just reimbursements.

Act Sec. 1707(a), extending the foster care exclusion, and Act Sec. 1707(b), dealing with payments, amend Sec. 131 effective for taxable years beginning after 12-31-85.

[¶1708] Extension of Rules for Spouses of Vietnam MIAs. The new law reinstates retroactively four tax relief provisions that apply to families of members of the U.S. Armed Forces missing in Vietnam. The provisions, which expired on December 31, 1982, will apply to all taxable years beginning after that date. The four provisions do the following:

(1) For defining a surviving spouse (for filing status purposes), the date of death of an MIA is the date on which the determination of death is made.

(2) The income of an MIA who died in MIA status is exempt from income tax for the year in which the determination of death is made and any prior year that ends after the first day the MIA served in a combat zone.

(3) The spouse of a person in MIA status can elect to file a joint return.

(4) The rules under Section 7508(a) postponing the performing if certain acts by reason of service in a combat zone, apply to spouses of MIAs. Those acts include filing returns and paying taxes.

Act Sec. 1708(a), extending the rules for MIAs, amends Secs. 2(a)(3)(B), 692(b), 6013(f)(1), and 7508(b), effective for taxable years beginning after 12-31-82.

[¶1709] Native Alaskan Income from Reindeer Tax Exempt. The new law exempts from tax, income from the sale of reindeer held in trust by the government for native Alaskans under the 1937 Reindeer Industry Act.

Act Sec. 1709, relating to the reindeer industry, amends Sec. 8 of the 1937 Reindeer Industry Act as if included in that law.

[¶1710] AFDC/Medicaid Quality Control Study. Under the new law, the study by Health and Human Services and the National Academy of Sciences on the federal quality control system, originally due within 18 months after the enactment of the 1985 Consolidated Omnibus Budget Reconciliation Acts is now due one year after a contract is entered into for the studies.

Act Sec. 1710, relating to quality control studies, amends Sec. 12301 of the '85 Consolidated Omnibus Budget Reconciliation Act.

[¶1711] Adoption Assistance Program Expanded. The new law repeals the itemized deduction for adoption expenses for children with special needs. In its place, is an expanded Adoption Assistance Program of Title IV-E of the Social Security Act.

The program will provide 50% federal matching funds to states to pay "nonrecurring adoption expenses" for the adoption of a special needs child. Such expenses include adoption fees, court costs, attorneys fees, and other expenses directly related to legal adoption of a special needs child which aren't incurred in violation of state or federal law.

Act Sec. 1711, relating to adoption assistance, amends Social Security Act Secs. 471(a), 473(a), and 475(3), effective for expenditures after 12-31-86.

[The page following this is 1801.]

TECHNICAL CORRECTIONS

⟦¶1800⟧ Overview. The Technical Corrections Title (Title XVIII) of the new law mostly contains technical, clarifying, conforming, and clerical amendments to the rules enacted by the 1984 Tax Reform Act ('84 TRA), the 1984 Retirement Equity Act (REA), and other recent legislation. Many of these amendments have a far-reaching substantive effect, and are in the nature of significant new law changes. They are generally effective as if included in the original provisions of the legislation to which they relate, and are thus often retroactive. These law changes also include transitional and special rules that cover specific taxpayers.

The Technical Corrections provisions are treated as enacted immediately before the provisions of other Titles of the new law. They would be, therefore, normally treated as supplanted or varied by any conflicting or varying law changes made by the other Titles (as of the effective date of these law changes), under the general rules for interpreting legislation.

Amendments to the Tax Reform Act of 1984

⟦¶1801⟧ Finance Lease Rules. In 1982, TEFRA liberalized the determination of whether a transaction is a lease for limited-use property and fixed price purchase options. The effective date of these "finance lease" rules (originally scheduled to generally cover agreements made after 1983) was postponed by the '84 TRA to cover agreements made after 1987. The new law allows an election, under regs to be issued, to have this postponement apply to pre-3-7-84 acquisitions, construction starts, or binding contracts, even though a transitional rule excepts such property from the postponement.

The new law also allows the postponement for specified farm finance lease agreements, which relate to property allocable to persons other than C corporations that became partners or beneficiaries of partnership-or-grantor-trust-lessors before 9-26-85.

Act Sec. 1801(a)(1) relating to the election to postpone finance lease rules amends Sec. 12(c)(1) of the '84 TRA effective as if included in that provision. Act Sec. 1801(a)(2) relating to farm finance leases doesn't amend the Code.

⟦¶1802⟧ Telephone Excise Extension Clerical Omission Corrected. The 3% telephone excise tax now applies by statute to bills first rendered in 1983-87. The new law restores "1985" to the text of the law.

Act Sec. 1801(b) amends Sec. 4251(b)(2), effective as if included in the '84 Tax Reform Act.

[¶1803] Alcohol and Tobacco Taxes, Electronic Fund Transfers. The new law clarifies that all members of a controlled group of corporations (defined the same as in Sec. 1563 but with a 50% (rather than 80%) common ownership test) are treated as one person for the electronic transfer requirements. The Treasury can apply this to a common-controlled group, including its noncorporate members. It's understood that these rules will be administratively applied only to taxes due after 3-28-85.

Distilled spirits in foreign trade zone on 10-1-85. The new law clarifies that distilled spirits held in a foreign trade zone on 10-1-85 and entered into U.S. customs territory after that date are subject to the $2 per proof gallon floor stocks tax imposed under the '84 TRA, despite provisions of 19 USC Sec. 81a, et seq. or other laws.

Act Sec. 1801(c)(1) and (2) relating to electronic fund transfers adds Secs. 5061(e)(3) and 5703(b)(3), effective generally for taxes paid after 9-30-84. Act Sec. 1801(c)(3) relating to foreign trade zones adds Sec. 27(b)(7)(F) of the '84 Tax Reform Act.

[¶1804] **Tax-Exempt Entity Leasing Rules Clarified.** Generally for property placed in service after 5-23-83, the '84 TRA sharply curtailed the exploitation of the benefits of ACRS depreciation and the investment credit for "tax-exempt use property" by "tax-exempt entities." The new law clarifies and amends these rules, as well as the special rules connected with them that are engrafted into the investment credit rules, and the treatment of transactions structured as service contracts.

19-year realty used in an unrelated trade or business. For 19-year realty, only the part used under a "disqualifying lease" is tax-exempt use property, and only if over 35% of the property is so leased. The new law clarifies that the part of 19-year realty that's used under an over-20-year lease (treated as a disqualifying lease) in an unrelated trade or business of the tax exempt entity isn't considered as used under a disqualifying lease (including for the 35% threshold).

Scope of tax-exempt entity rules expanded. The term "tax-exempt entity" can include certain previously tax-exempt organizations (Sec. 168(j)(4)(E)). The new law clarifies that the rules for these organizations cover any property (other than property owned by the former tax-exempt or its successor), rather than only property leased to the organization. The organization must have been tax-exempt at any time during the five-year period ending when the property was first used by the former tax-exempt (i.e., when it was first placed in service under a lease to it, or is treated under the new law as used by it by virtue of membership in a pass-through entity that leases or owns it).

For property owned by partnerships and other pass-through entities (Sec. 168(j)(9)), the new law treats a "tax-exempt controlled entity" (generally defined as a taxable corporation "owned" at least 50% by value by tax exempt entities) as a tax-exempt entity or its successor. Alternatively, such a subsidiary organization can make an irrevocable election binding its tax-exempt entity owners to have them treat gain recognized on a disposition of an interest in it, and dividends allocable to its nontaxable income and interest that is received or accrued from it, as unrelated business taxable income. Unless earlier application is elected, these rules generally apply to property placed in service after 9-27-85 except for property acquired under a binding written contract in effect on 9-27-85. The new law also clarifies that the Federal Home Loan Mortgage Corporation isn't a tax-exempt entity.

Other tax-exempt lease rules. The new law repeals IRS authority to determine if high technology telephone station or medical equipment is subject to rapid obsolescence. And it clarifies that the determination whether a tax-exempt partner's share of partnership items is treated as derived from an unrelated trade or business is made without regard to the unrelated debt-financed income rules of Sec. 514.

Investment credit and tax-exempt leasing rules. The new law clarifies that any part of property that's treated as "tax-exempt use property" under rules governing property leased to or owned by partnerships (Sec. 168(j)(8) or (9)), is ineligible for the investment credit under rules governing property used by certain tax exempts or by government units or foreign persons or entities (Sec. 48(a)(4), (5)). It applies rules similar to the tax-exempt use property partnership rules to investment credits on property leased to thrift institutions (Sec. 46(e)(4)), and clarifies that the credit for rehabilitation expenditures on buildings leased to thrifts is to be governed by rules for buildings leased to tax exempt entities. And it clarifies that (1) the Sec. 47(a)(7) short-term lease exception from investment credit recapture rules for aircraft under specified pre-1990 leases of up to three years for use predominantly outside the U.S. doesn't cause the aircraft to cease being Sec. 38 property until total use under such a lease exceeds three years, and (2) such use extends the general recapture period.

Service contracts treated as leases of property. The tax-exempt leasing definition of "related entity" is added through a reference to the Sec. 7701(e) rules dealing with arrangements structured as service contracts.

Effective Dates: The new law makes the following clarifications to the tax exempt leasing rules of the 1984 law. The new law (1)

¶1804

Clarifies that the exception for property acquired (or covered by a binding contract) before 10-22-83 relates only to treatment of property owned by partnerships (Sec. 168(j)(9)). (2) Clarifies that the exception for certain aircraft used by a foreign person or entity applies only to aircraft originally placed in service after 5-23-83 (and before 1-1-86). (3) Amends the exception relating to pre-5-23-84 government action by making a special rule for certain credit unions and for other specific situations. (4) Broadens the "substantial improvement" exception to the rule that improvements qualify for transitional relief, to clarify that it applies to real property, and to personal property not covered by pre-3-29-85 binding contracts or started construction. (5) Among provisions affecting specific situations, clarifies the exception relating to Clemson University, and Pennsylvania Railroad Station in Newark, New Jersey.

Act Sec. 1802(a)(1) relating to 19-year realty amends Sec. 168(j)(3)(D). Act Sec. 1802(a)(2) relating to the definition of tax exempt entity rules amends Sec. 168(j)(4)(E) and(j)(9). Act Sec. 1802(a)(3) relating to high technology items amends Sec. 168(j)(5)(C). Act Secs. 1802(a)(4)—(8) relating to tax-exempt partners' shares and investment credit rules amends Sec. 168(j)(8) and (9), Sec. 46(e)(4) and Sec. 48(a)(5), and adds Sec. 47(a)(9). Act Sec. 1802(a)(9) relating to service contracts amends Sec. 7701(e)(4). Act Sec. 1802(a)(10) relating to effective date rules amends 1984 Tax Reform Act Sec. 31(g)(3), (15)(D), (4), (17)(H), (20)(B). These changes and certain clerical amendments made are effective as if included in the 1984 Tax Reform Act and as noted above.

[¶1805] Changes in Treatment of Debt Instruments. The new law changes in this area involve original issue discount, market discount, imputed interest, and amortization of bond premium.

Short-term nongovernmental and government obligations. Based on longstanding judicial authority and regs, the new law expressly treats gain realized on post-1984 dispositions of short-term nongovernment obligations as ordinary income to the extent of the holder's ratable share of OID, based on the number of days he held it. The holder can irrevocably elect to compute the accrued OID under an economic accrual formula. The rules cover obligations (whether or not tax-exempt) with a fixed maturity of a year or less, other than those of the U.S., a U.S. Possession, a state or its political subdivision, or the District of Columbia. Generally for obligations acquired after 7-18-84, the new law also no longer defines short-term government taxable obligations for ordinary income treatment of acquisition discount on their disposition as those payable without interest and issued on a discount basis. And it allows an irrevocable election to compute the holder's acquisition discount under an economic accrual formula.

   CLARIFICATION: OID on a short-term debt instrument is deductible only in the year of payment by cash method obligors. A new law provision stating this is designed to clarify that a similar proposed provision was deleted during enactment of the 1984 Act only because it was thought to be an unneeded declaration of preexisting law.

Accrual taxpayers, dealers, banks, mutual funds, and certain others must include in income on a current basis the OID or acquisition discount on short-term obligations. Effective for obligations acquired after 9-27-85, this mandatory accrual covers interest on the obligation, OID and acquisition discount, or any combination of them, that is allocable to the tax year.

Market discount rules. Generally for obligations issued after 7-18-84, under the new law, the transferor of a market discount bond in a Sec. 351 nontaxable corporate organization exchange is taxed on any accrued market discount whether or not he receives stock or securities in the exchange. The Committee Reports note that the corporate transferee of the bond gets a Sec. 362(a) carryover basis for it that reflects the transferor's gain, and has a market discount bond if the bond's stated redemption price exceeds this basis.

The new law also clarifies that a bond acquired by a taxpayer at original issue (or a bond with a transferred basis determined by reference to the basis of the person who acquired it at original issue) isn't a market discount bond. *Exceptions.* Bonds whose holder has a cost basis for them that's less than their issue price (e.g., bonds acquired by large investors at "wholesale" prices lower than those available to "retail" customers), and bonds issued under a Sec. 368(a)(1) reorganization plan in exchange for bonds having market discount, can be market discount bonds. For the rules treating accrued market discount as ordinary income on disposition (Sec. 1276), the above exception for bonds issued in a reorganization covers only bonds issued after 7-18-84 if they have the same term and interest rate as the bonds they're exchanged for.

The new law also provides rules for treatment of market discount on debt instruments whose principal is paid in more than one installment. These rules apply to debt instruments acquired after enactment date.

Until the Treasury issues regs for computing market discount, the conferees intend that the holder can elect to accrue market discount either at a constant interest rate; or in proportion to accrual of OID; or for non-OID obligations in proportion to stated interest paid during the accrual period.

Other imputed interest and OID rules. The new law:

• Clarifies that the discount rate for determining unstated interest, for pre-7-1-85 "related party" sales or exchanges covered by former Sec. 483(f) as in effect before enactment of the "Simplification of Imputed Interest Rules" (P.L. 99-121) is 6% compounded semiannually;

- Gives the Treasury authority to designate in regs other publicly traded property that's treated, for purposes of the OID rules, like property that's regularly traded on an established market;

- Requires the current inclusion in income of acquisition discount on stripped bonds and coupons by the "stripper" or anyone with a transferred basis from him, and provides that stripped bonds and coupons are subject to the general rules of Sec. 1286 with certain modifications;

- Makes a technical change in Sec. 483(d)(1) to clarify what OID debt instruments are excluded from the Sec. 483 rules;

- Clarifies that P.L. 98-612, effective 10-31-84, (the stop-gap legislation which extended pre-'84 TRA rules for debt instruments received for property with certain limitations and special rules), covers only sales *after 12-31-84* —but it didn't accelerate the 12-31-84 effective date of the 1984 Act; and

- Clarifies that interest on debt instruments issued in post-1984 transactions for property (whether or not with adequate stated interest) can't be computed under a method other than economic accrual (as described in Rev. Rul. 83-84, according to the Committee Reports). The new law also changes the date of the binding contract exception to this rule for transactions involving adequate stated interest—it will apply to contracts binding on 6-8-84 (rather than 3-1-84).

- The new law clarifies that current inclusion of OID covers capital asset obligations issued after 1984 (and not on 12-31-84 and later).

Amortizable bond premium. The new law extends amortization of bond premium (elective for taxable obligations) to obligations issued by individuals. It requires amortizable bond premium to be computed under a constant yield method, using the basis of the bond, and compounding at the end of each "accrual period" (defined in Sec. 1271(a)(5)). These rules cover obligations issued after 9-27-85. *Special rule.* A Sec. 171(c) election effective on the enactment date of the new law won't cover post-9-27-85 obligations unless the taxpayer elects otherwise under regs to come. And for determining the amortizable bond premium of bonds received in post-5-6-86 exchanges for property in which the bond acquires an exchanged (substituted) basis, the basis of the bond can't be more than its fair market value immediately after the exchange. This rule also applies to such bonds if they're later transferred and retain a substituted basis (e.g., if given as a gift). However, bonds received in a bond-for-bond reorganization exchange are generally not covered by this rule.

Act Sec. 1803(a)(1)—(4) and (8) relating to short-term obligations amends Sec. 1271(a)(3), 1281(a), 1282(a), 163(e)(2), and 1283(d)(3), and adds Sec. 1271(a)(4). Act Sec. 1803(a)(5)—(6) and (13) relating to market discount rules amends Sec. 1276(d)(1) and 1278(a)(1). Act Secs. 1803(a)(7) and (10) and 1803(b) relating to other OID and imputed interest rules amend Sec. 483(d)(1), 1273(b)(3) and 1281(b)(1), and 1984 Tax Reform Act Sec. 44(b)(3), and 44(b)(4) as added by Sec. 2 of P.L. 86-12 and 44(g). Act Sec. 1803(a)(9) dealing with "related party sales" doesn't amend the Code. Act Sec. 1803(a)(11) and (12) dealing with amortizable bond premium amends Sec. 171(b)(3) and (d) and adds Sec. 171(b)(4). These and certain changes are effective as if included in the 1984 Tax Reform Act and as indicated above.

[¶1806] Law Changes for Corporations and Shareholders. Law changes in this area include the dividends received and dividends-paid deductions, complete liquidations of subsidiaries and reorganization provisions, earnings and profits computations on distributions of appreciated property, and golden parachute payments.

Corporate dividends-received deduction for debt financed stock of foreign corporations. The new law clarifies how the limitation percentage for the dividends received deduction in case of debt-portfolio stock (Sec. 246A(a)) is applied to dividends from Sec. 245(a) foreign corporations. *Example:* Assume 60% of a Sec. 245(a) foreign corporation's gross income is effectively connected with the conduct of a U.S. trade or business. In addition, 70% of the foreign corporation's purchase price for portfolio stock of the foreign corporation is debt-financed. Under Sec. 246A, the domestic corporation generally deducts 15.3% (30% *times* 85% *times* 60%) of the dividend from the foreign corporation.

45 (or 90)-day holding period. The dividends-received deduction is denied if the dividend stock isn't held for 45 days (90 days for certain preference dividends), without counting more than 45 (or 90) days after the ex-dividend date or days when the corporation's risk of loss is diminished. The new law deletes a prior law condition for this denial. Dividend stock acquired after 3-1-86 doesn't have to be disposed of for this denial to occur. Denial, for example, occurs automatically if the stock hasn't been held for the required period by the 45th (or 90th) day after the ex-dividend date. Both Committee Reports also note that an out-of-the-money call option that doesn't protect against loss if the stock price falls doesn't cause a denial of the deduction (citing Rev.Rul. 80-238).

Interest incurred to buy or carry tax-exempts. The '84 TRA authorized regs that would prevent tax avoidance through linking of borrowings to investments, or diminishing risks through use of related persons, pass-through entities, or other intermediaries (Sec. 7701(f)). The new law provides that these rules (generally effective 7-18-84), will apply to law restrictions that disallow interest incurred by corporations and individuals to buy or carry tax-exempts (Sec. 265(2)) as to term loans made after 7-18-84, demand loans outstanding after 7-18-84 (other than those outstanding on 7-18-84 and repaid before

9-18-84) and it clarifies that post-7-18-84 loan renegotiations, extensions, or revisions will be considered post-7-18-84 loans. It also defines term and demand loans similarly to their definition in the rules for below-market-interest loans.

Loss on sale of mutual fund stock after exempt-interest dividend. A law change prevents the purchase of regulated investment company stock just before the ex-dividend date, the receipt of an exempt-interest dividend, and the stock's disposition at a recognized loss after waiting 31 days. If stock (whose holding period begins after 3-28-85) isn't held for more than six months, loss on its sale or exchange is denied to the extent of exempt-interest dividends received on it. Regs can make exceptions for periodic liquidation plans. They can also shorten the six-month period to no less than 31 days or to the interval between regular tax-exempt interest dividends, (whichever is longer), if the mutual fund regularly distributes at least 90% of its net tax-exempt interest.

Dividends-paid deduction of a holding or investment company. To prevent a holding or investment company that isn't a regulated investment company (RIC) from effecting a capital-gains taxed redemption and then being free of accumulated earnings tax under Sec. 562(b)(1), the new law denies (except to the extent permitted by regs) the dividends-paid deduction against the accumulated earnings tax in cases of liquidation and redemption distributions by such companies after 9-27-85.

Affiliated groups. Under the new law, for tax years beginning after 1984, the term "stock" for determining an affiliated group doesn't generally include preferred stock with redemption and liquidation rights that don't exceed the *issue price* of the stock (rather than "the paid-in capital or par value" represented by it, as under prior law). This redefinition makes irrelevant the stock's accounting treatment when it's issued. Also, under the new law, a DISC or a corporation with post-1984 accumulations of DISC income (rather than a DISC or "former DISC") won't be an includable corporation. The Committee Report notes that under current law there's less reason to keep a former DISC and its parent from filing consolidated returns, and this law change isn't intended to affect the status of certain S corporations with DISC subsidiaries "grandfathered" by the 1982 Subchapter S Revision Act.

Effective Dates: The new law:

- Sunsets the '84 TRA grandfather rule for 6-22-84 members of an affiliated group, which deals with the determination whether they continue to be such members for pre-1988 years. The grandfather rule stops applying as of the first day after 6-22-84 on which the corporation won't qualify as a group member under pre-'84 TRA law;

• Clarifies the exception to the grandfather rule that covers post-6-22-84 "selldowns", by making it inapplicable for transactions that don't reduce the percentage (by value) of the "solddown" corporation's stock that's held by the other group members;

• Applies the sell-down exception in certain cases when there's a pre-6-22-84 letter of intent between the corporation and a securities underwriter;

• Allows a common parent to irrevocably elect to have the '84 TRA amendments apply to tax years beginning after 1983; and

• Allows an Alaska Native corporation to offset the income of its profitable nonnative subsidiary with its own NOLs.

Complete liquidation of subsidiaries. Several law changes are designed to coordinate the rules for nontaxable complete liquidations of subsidiaries, with '84 TRA changes in the definition of affiliated groups.

First, Sec. 332 now won't apply unless the corporation receiving a liquidating distribution is the owner of the liquidating corporation's stock under the 80% voting and value tests of Sec. 1504(a)(2). According to both Committee Reports, other rules governing the definition of affiliated groups (except that disregarding intergroup stock transfers—(Sec. 1504(a)(5)(E)) also apply. And the new rule will apply even if the corporations involved in the liquidating distribution aren't "includible corporations" under Sec. 1504(b). These rules generally cover distributions under post-3-28-85 complete liquidation plans. They also generally cover distributions under *earlier* complete liquidation plans if: (1) any distribution is made in a tax year beginning after 1984 (or after 1983, if the common parent elects earlier application of 1984 Act rules), and (2) the liquidating corporation and any corporation receiving complete liquidation distributions are members of a group filing consolidated returns for the year that includes the distribution date. However, these rules don't apply if the liquidating corporation is an affiliated group member under affiliated group transitional rules of '84 TRA Sec. 60(b)(2), (5) (6) or (8).

Second, the Sec. 337(c)(3) definition of "distributee corporation" is amended to define it as any corporation that receives a Sec. 332 complete liquidation distribution from the selling corporation, as well as any corporation "up the line" that receives a Sec. 332 distribution in complete liquidation of a distributee that had received a Sec. 332 distribution. These rules apply to complete liquidation plans involving any distribution in tax years beginning after 1984 (or after 1983, if the common parent irrevocably elects earlier application of '84 TRA rules).

Third, the Sec. 338 definition of "qualified stock purchase" is conformed to the Sec. 1504(a)(2) definition for purchases begun after 12-31-85.

NOTE: These rules are designed to prevent certain occurrences. For a parent and a subsidiary that wouldn't have met Sec. 332 ownership but would have met those of Sec. 1504, the rules would prevent a complete liquidation by the subsidiary with a Sec. 337 nontaxable sale of assets (see Sec. 337(c)(2)), and the subsidiary's liquidation also being nontaxable to the parent under Reg. §1.1502-14(b) consolidated return rules. For a parent and a subsidiary that would have met Sec. 332 ownership rules but not those of Sec. 1504, the rules would prevent a nontaxable Sec. 332 liquidation of the subsidiary with the parent also liquidating tax free under Sec. 337.

E&P adjustment on appreciated property distributions. Under the new law, for distributions or redemptions in tax years beginning after 9-30-84, a corporation's distribution of appreciated property increases its earnings and profits by the excess of the property's fair market value (FMV) over the property's adjusted basis. The distribution then results in a decrease to earnings and profits under the rules of Sec. 312(a), using fair market value instead of adjusted basis to measure the decrease. This change isn't intended to affect earnings and profits determinations as to one-month (Sec. 333) liquidating distributions. Other E&P law changes: The current law rule covering redemptions (old law Sec. 312(n)(8) now redesignated as (n)(7)) applies to redemption distributions in tax years beginning after 9-30-84, and as a result of the special rule for certain foreign corporations (old law Sec. 312(n)(9) now redesignated (n)(8)) the rule covering installment sales (old (n)(6) redesignated as (n)(5)) now applies to tax years beginning after 12-31-87 (rather than 12-31-85).

Reorganizations. Under the new law, the transferor corporation doesn't recognize gain or loss on any exchange of property under the reorganization plan, regardless of whether properties received are distributed under the plan. The liquidation provisions of Secs. 336 and 337 don't apply to any liquidation of a transferor corporation under the reorganization plan. And the basis of property that it receives under the plan will be the same as it would be in the hands of the transferor of the property, adjusted by gain or loss recognized to such transferor on such transfer. No gain or loss is recognized by the acquired corporation on the disposition under the plan of stock or securities it receives in a party to the reorganization. Gain is recognized on distribution of boot. Special rules govern transfers to creditors of the acquired corporation. In "C" type (stock for assets) reorganizations, no gain or loss is recognized to the transferor on any disposition of stock or securities of another party to the reorganization, which it receives under the plan. But the transferor can have taxable gain (under Sec. 311(d)) on distributions of other property that it receives. And the new law clarifies that distributions to creditors satisfy the distribution requirements of Sec. 368(a)(2)(G). The new rules apply to reorganization plans adopted after the enactment date.

The new law provides that as to plans adopted after 7-18-84, for a "D" reorganization, the term "control" is defined by Sec. 304(c), if the transaction meets the requirements of Sec. 354(b)(1)(A) and (B)—i.e., if the transferee acquires substantially all the transferor's assets; and the stock, securities, and other properties received by the transferor, as well as its own properties, are distributed under the reorganization plan. It also clarifies that for plans adopted after 7-18-84, a C reorganization involving a drop-down of assets to a subsidiary will continue to qualify as a C reorganization despite the rules of Sec. 368(a)(2)(A).

Collapsible corporation income can relate to short-term period stock. For sales and exchanges after 9-27-85, gain from the sale or exchange of a collapsible corporation can be ordinary income even if the stock was held for 6 months or less.

Golden parachute provisions. For agreements after 6-14-84, the new law excludes from treatment as "parachute payments," those payments relating to small business corporations (defined similarly to S corporations) whose stock wasn't readily tradeable on an established securities market or otherwise, provided there was shareholder approval for the payment. It also excludes any part of a payment that the taxpayer establishes by clear and convincing evidence to be reasonable compensation for services to be rendered on or after the change of control, from treatment as "excess parachute payments". And it reduces "excess parachute payments" by amounts that the taxpayer proves to be reasonable compensation for services actually rendered before the change in control (for this rule, reasonable compensation for services before the change is first offset against the base amount). Further, it excludes from treatment as "parachute payments" payments to or from qualified retirement plan trusts or annuities or SEPs. Such payments aren't considered in determining if the threshold for excess parachute payments is exceeded.

In addition, it treats all members of an affiliated group (specially defined) as a single corporation for the golden parachute rules, and treats an officer or "highly compensated individual" of any member of the group as that of the single corporation. The new law also limits the number of persons treated as "highly compensated individuals," to employees (or former employees) who are among the *lesser* of (1) the highest-paid 1% performing personal services for the corporation, or (2) the highest-paid 250 individuals who perform services for the corporation or for each member of an affiliated group that's treated as a single corporation for the golden parachute rules. Finally, payments under agreements that violate securities laws or regulations can be parachute payments only if these laws or regs are generally enforced (the burden of proving such a violation is on the IRS).

NOTE: The Senate Committee Report notes that these changes are retroactive as if included at the inception of the golden parachute rules, and that shareholder approval for a payment could be obtained for earlier transactions after the enactment date of the new law. The Conference Report notes that the amendments intend no inference as to the definition of a change in control.

Corporate tax preferences. Among technical and clerical changes in this area is an amendment to Sec. 291(a)(4) as in effect before enactment of the '84 TRA, clarifying that the cutback of preferences relating to DISC income doesn't apply to S corporations for years beginning after 1982.

Other law changes. The new law also delays the effective date of '84 TRA amendments relating to distributions of appreciated property (Sec. 311(d)) for a specified parent-subsidiary group (extends a transitional exception to cover pre-1988 distributions).

Act Sec. 1804(a) and (b)(1) dealing with the dividends received deduction amends Secs. 246A(a) and 246(c). Act Secs. 1804(b)(2) and (3) dealing with related party rules and interest incurred to carry tax-exempts amends 1984 TRA Secs. 53(e)(3) and 54. Act Sec. 1804(c) dealing with mutual fund stock amends Sec. 852(b)(4). Act Sec. 1804(d) dealing with the dividends paid deduction amends Sec. 562(b)(1). Act Sec. 1804(e) dealing with affiliated groups amends Sec. 1504(a)(4) and 1984 TRA Sec. 60(b)(4). Act Sec. 1804(e)(6)—(8) dealing with complete liquidation of subsidiaries amends Secs. 332(b)(1), 337(c)(3)(B) and 338(d)(3). Act Sec. 1804(f) dealing with appreciated property distributions amends Sec. 312(b), repeals Secs. 312(c)(3) and (n)(4), redesignates Sec. 312(n)(5)—(9) as (n)(4)—(8). Act Secs. 1804(g) and (h) dealing with reorganizations amend Secs. 358(a), 361 and 368(a)(2) and (c). Act Sec. 1804(i) relating to collapsible corporations amends Sec. 341(a). Act Sec. 1804(j) dealing with golden parachute payments adds Secs. 280G(b)(2), (5), (6), (d)(5) and amends Secs. 280G(b)(2) and (4), (c) and (d). Act Sec. 1804(k) dealing with corporate tax preferences amends pre-1984 Act version of Sec. 291(a)(4), 1984 Act Secs. 68(e)(2) and (3) and (c)(2), and Sec. 57(b)(1) and (2). The law changes are effective as if included in the 1984 TRA and as shown above.

[¶1807] Partnership and Trust Rules. The new law clarifies that the partnership rules for allocating cash basis items to periods to which the items are attributable, under economic accrual principles, apply, for periods after 3-31-84, if the allocation is needed, even though no change in partnership interests occurs during the current tax year. It also makes clear, that the rules for treating as a disguised sale a partner's post-3-31-84 transfer of money or other property to a partnership, accompanied by a related transfer by the partnership to the transferor or another partner, can also apply to treat a transaction as an exchange of property. And it limits the application of the Sec. 761(e) rule that distributions not otherwise treated as exchanges are treated as exchanges for purposes of specified Code provisions to distributions of partnership interests (subject to regs exceptions to the rule).

Transfers of partnership or trust interest by corporations. The new law specifically limits the gain recognized by a corporation on post-3-31-84 distributions of partnership or trust interests to which Sec. 311 applies, to gain that would have been recognized if the distributed interest were sold (that is, a sale at its FMV). To prevent avoidance of the Sec. 311 nonrecognition of losses rule, Regs can provide that gain on a distributed partnership interest is computed independently of any loss on property contributed to the partnership for the principal purpose of recognizing that loss. Also, both Committee Reports note that treatment of "unrealized receivables" such as depreciation recapture under Sec. 751(a) remains applicable to the distribution of partnership interests.

Like-kind exchanges. Under the new law, to get like-kind exchange nonrecognition for post-3-31-84 transfers, property received by the taxpayer must be identified *on or before* the 45th day after his transfer of relinquished property (rather than "before" that day).

Estate or trust distributions in kind. The new law clarifies that an estate or trust's election to recognize gain or loss on post-6-1-84 distributions of property (formerly Sec. 643(d)(3) now redesignated as 643(e)(3)) applies to all distributions during the tax year that it covers, unless it's revoked with IRS consent.

Effective Date: The new law creates an exception from the '84 TRA rules that treat multiple trusts for tax years beginning after 3-1-84 as a single trust under some circumstances, for trusts that were irrevocable on 3-1-84 except for the parts of the trusts that are allocable to later transfers.

Act Sec. 1805(a) (b) and (c)(2) dealing with allocation of cash method items, disguised sales, and certain distributions amends Secs. 706(d)(2), 707(a)(2), and 761(e). Act Sec. 1805(c)(1) dealing with transfers of partnership or trust interests adds new Sec. 386(d). Act Sec. 1805(d) relating to like-kind exchanges amends Sec. 1031(a)(3). Act Sec. 1806 dealing with trusts amends Code Sec. 643(e) (formerly (d)), and 1984 Act Sec. 82(b). These and clerical changes are effective as if included in the 1984 TRA and as indicated above.

[¶1808] **Accounting Changes.** In the area of the "economic performance" requirement for taking deductions, the new law requires cash basis tax shelters to satisfy the "economic performance" requirement for deducting a payment made, if economic performance occurs *before the close* of the 90th day after year-end (rather than *within* 90 days after year-end). This is intended to cover, for instance, deductions as to wells spudded just before year-end. Also, pre-11-23-85 nonrefundable payments to an insurer to insure against tort liability relating to asbestos are declared to satisfy the economic performance test for Sec. 461(h).

Designated tort settlement funds. Irrevocable "qualified payments" to a "designated settlement fund" established under a court order principally for satisfying present and future personal injury or property damage claims against the taxpayer (or related persons) can (at taxpayer's election revocable only with IRS consent) be treated as satisfying "economic performance" for purposes of Sec. 461(h). Among the requirements: (1) The fund can't receive payment other than "qualified payments" (court ordered payments in money or property that can't be retransferred to the taxpayer, and can't include stock or debt of the taxpayer or a related person). (2) A majority of those administering the fund must be parties independent to taxpayer. (3) The fund's terms can't allow the taxpayer to hold any beneficial interest in it (this can occur if taxpayer's future liability is contingent on the fund's income).

The rules don't apply to worker's compensation payments or Sec. 461(f) contested liability. Related persons are defined in Sec. 267(b). The fund is, under special rules, taxed as a separate entity at maximum trust rates on income from its investments, reduced only by administrative costs (including state and local taxes) and by incidental expenses (including legal, accounting, and actuarial expenses that would have been deductible by a corporation) but not on the qualified payments. For tax procedural purposes it's treated as a corporation. The taxpayer's property contributions to the fund are treated as sales of the property at fair market value—they can result in gain or loss, and his deduction is limited to fair market value. No deduction is allowed the taxpayer for a contribution of insurance settlements that are excluded by the taxpayer. The fund can't deduct its distributions. The new law makes clear that trust or escrow payments made to other types of funds to satisfy tort liability won't (except as permitted by regs.) satisfy "economic performance." Transitional rules relate to a corporation that filed a Chapter 11 reorganization petition on 8-26-82 and a restated plan of reorganization before 3-1-86.

The Conference Report notes that: (1) The settlement fund rules don't affect the treatment of Sec. 130 personal injury liability assignments, (2) Payments by a designated settlement fund to a claimant are treated as made by the taxpayer for determining the claimant's taxable income, (3) Taxpayers cannot both exclude an amount recovered and deduct an amount paid to the fund on the same liability. It also notes that, except as provided in Regs, escrow accounts, settlement funds, or similar funds are subject to current tax, and that if the contribution to it isn't deductible, the account or fund is taxable as a grantor trust (this reverses a finding in Rev.Rul. 71-119, 1971-1 CB 163).

Limitations on farming businesses. The new law clarifies that any tax shelter (as defined in Sec. 6661(b)) will be generally treated as a farming syndicate for the Sec. 464 deduction limits on farming syndicates, but interests of persons whose "holdings are attributable to active management" won't be subject to Sec. 464.

Mining and solid waste reclamation and closing costs. The new law clarifies that the reserve established under the elective uniform method for deducting these costs before economic performance must be increased annually by accrued deductions allocable to the reserve. It also clarifies that the '84 TRA rules become effective on 7-18-84, for tax years ending after that date.

Decommissioning nuclear power plants. The new law clarifies the operating rules for "qualified nuclear decommissioning reserve funds," which allow electing taxpayers to deduct contributions made to them. Among them: (1) A contribution is considered made during a tax year if made within 2½ months after year-end (this can be relaxed by regs for payments as to pre-1987 tax years); (2) the Sec. 486A tax on fund income is instead of any other federal income tax—this tax isn't deductible and procedurally it's treated like a corporate income tax; and (3) the fund can invest only in assets similar to those allowed to Black Lung Trust Funds. It also clarifies that the '84 TRA rules are effective for tax years ending after 7-18-84.

Deferred payments for services. The new law clarifies that contributions to qualified retirement plans or annuities and deferred compensation plans covered by Sec. 404 and 404A, won't be subject to Sec. 467(g) Regs on deferred payments for services. The new law also allows a specified taxpayer formerly providing architectural reserves to use the cash method.

Effective Dates: The new law also clarifies the effective date for 1984 Act rules on loss carrybacks for deferred statutory or tort liability deductions (they apply to losses for tax years beginning after 1983). And it allows an election under regs to come to have Sec. 461(h) apply to the taxpayer's entire tax year in which 7-19-84 occurs.

Act Sec. 1807(a) amends Secs. 461(i)(2), (4), 468(a)(1) and (2), 468A(a), (c), (d), (e) and (f), and 1984 TRA Sec. 91(g)(2)(A), and adds Sec. 468A(g), and 1984 TRA Sec. 91(g)(5)—(6). Act Sec. 1807(a)(7) dealing with designated tort settlement funds adds Code Sec. 468B. Act Sec. 1807(b) relating to deferred payments for services amends Sec. 467(g). These and clerical changes made are effective as if included in the 1984 Act (generally for tax years ending after 7-18-84, and as to tax shelter rules for deductions allowable after 3-31-84) and as indicated above.

[¶1809] **Tax Straddle Rules.** Generally as to positions established after 7-18-84, the new law (1) allows payments that compensate a lender of securities used in a short sale (e.g., for dividends and interest payments), to reduce interest and carrying charges incurred on personal property that's part of a straddle which is required to be capitalized; (2) clarifies that the tax straddle rules don't apply to direct positions in stock, but can apply to positions in "interests in stock" such as exchange-traded stock options (other than qualified covered calls that offset stock); and (3) allows regs to ensure that elections by S corporations connected with the introduction of the mark-to-market and other straddle rules by the '84 TRA are properly coordinated with S corporation tax year limitations.

The new law also clarifies the treatment of losses from pre-1982 straddles. It expressly treats losses that are incurred on any positions by a commodities dealer in commodities trading, as incurred in a trade or business, thus confining this profit-motive presumption to such dealers (e.g., investment bankers regularly trading in commodities). The new law defines dealers to whom it applies. The House Committee Report notes that the new law restates the general rule that losses from a position in a straddle are deductible only if the position is part of a transaction entered into for profit (c.f. *Miller v. Comm.*, 84 TC 55). The Conference Report notes that an individual who owns a seat on the Commodities Exchange is a "commodities dealer", and that losses indirectly incurred by a commodity dealer (i.e., as a partner, S corporation shareholder, or beneficiary of a trust on transactions by these entities) are also treated as commodity dealer losses for this provision.

Act Sec. 1808 amends Secs. 263(g)(2)(B), 1092(d)(3) and 1984 TRA Secs. 102 and 108.

[¶1810] **Depreciation and Investment Credit.** Generally for property placed in service after 3-15-84, the new law:

• Clarifies that elective straight-line recovery of low income housing is over a 15- 35- or 45-year period (and not a 19-year or 18-year period).

• Requires the mid-month convention to be used for 19-year (or 18-year) real property when computing ACRS allowances, the accelerated cost recovery tax preference item, and earnings and profits adjustments for depreciation. It similarly requires the monthly convention to be used for low-income housing, and makes other technical clarifications.

• In effect, generally limits films, videotapes, and sound recordings placed in service after 3-28-85 to depreciation through the income forecast or similar methods by excluding them from accelerated methods. and

• For property placed in service after 4-11-84, reinstates an inadvertently omitted provision in the definition of new investment credit property, to include in it the basis attributable to taxpayer's reconstruction of Sec. 38 property; and clarifies that the three-month sale-lease back rule doesn't apply to such property. It clarifies that, for example, if an owner places property in service by leasing it to L, and within three months sells it to P and leases it back from P subject to L's lease, the property can be new Sec. 38 property in P's hands. The Senate Committee Report notes that this would be the result under prior statutory language. The new law also allows the lessee and lessor to elect out of the three-month rule.

Real property financed with tax-exempt bonds. The new law clarifies that IDB-financed 19-year (or 18-year real property (with exceptions that include low-income housing) is recoverable no faster than under the straight line (without salvage) using a 19-year (or 18-year) period. It also clarifies that the '84 TRA rules covering realty financed with tax exempts don't apply to property excepted from the bond rules added by TEFRA in 1982 (described in TEFRA Sec. 216(b)(3)).

Transferees of recovery property. Under the new law, for Sec. 168(f)(10)(B)(i) basis carryover transfers (involving certain nontaxable corporate liquidations, reorganization exchanges, and partnership contributions and distributions—but now excluding terminations of partnerships because of at least 50% sales or exchanges of capital or profit interests within 12 months), the transferee "steps into the transferor's shoes" as to cost recovery deductions to the extent the transferee's basis doesn't increase. However, for transfers described in Secs. 168(f)(10)(B)(ii) (i.e., transfers between related persons) and 168(f)(10)(B)(iii) (i.e., sale-leasebacks), the transferee generally depreciates the property as a new owner, but remains bound by the transferor's Sec. 168(b)(3) or (f)(2)(C) elections of the straight-line method recovery and period to the extent his basis didn't increase. The new rules apply to property placed in service by the transferee after 12-31-85. The House Committee Report notes that the law changes don't intend to affect intergroup transactions of consolidated return filers.

Installment sales. The new law clarifies that the rule that denied installment sales treatment to depreciation recapture generally after 6-6-84 applies to sales of partnership interests.

Act Sec. 1809 amends Secs. 168(b)(2), (3) and (4), (f)(2), (10) and (12), 167(c), 48(b), (q), 57(a)(12), 312(k)(3) and 453(i)(2). The law changes are effective as if included in the 1984 TRA and as indicated above.

[¶1811] Foreign Tax Credit. The new law generally tightens the '84 TRA rules recharacterizing foreign income as U.S. income for the credit, and those recharacterizing dividends as interest income for the separate interest limitation on the credit.

Recharacterizing foreign income as U.S. income. For the special source rules of Sec. 904(g) (generally effective 3-28-85), the new law treats an 80/20 company (a domestic corporation that earns less than 20% of its gross income from U.S. sources over a 3-year period) as a U.S.-owned foreign corporation as to its interest and dividend payments which are treated as foreign source income under Sec. 861(a)(1)(B) and (2)(A). The new rule is designed to prevent conversion by U.S. taxpayers of U.S. source to foreign source income for the credit, by routing it through an 80/20 company. It's generally effective on 3-28-85.

Special effective date rule. For an 80/20 company's tax year ending after 3-28-85, *only* its post-3-28-85 income generally falls under the special source rules; but its income for the entire tax year is considered in determining whether it qualifies for nonapplication of the special source rules under the 10% threshold of Sec. 904(g)(5).

The new law also clarifies that the special source rules (Sec. 904(g)) apply despite any U.S. Treaty obligation to the contrary. *Exception:* A treaty entered into after 7-18-84 (the enactment date of the '84 TRA) can specifically override these rules by referring to Sec. 904(g)). The Committee Report notes that the '84 TRA generally takes precedence over preexisting treaty provisions (e.g., the Act's accumulated earnings tax provisions override a conflicting U.S.-Jamaica Treaty provision). And, the transitional rule that covers "applicable CFCs" is clarified and modified by the new law as to interest paid on obligations of affiliated foreign corporations that were issued before 6-22-84.

Recharacterizing dividends as separate limitation interest. The new law changes the definition of "designated payor corporations" that can give rise to dividends recharacterized as separate limitation interest income (Sec. 904(d)(3)). First, generally as of 12-31-85, it expressly makes any corporation formed or availed of for avoiding the recharacterization (look-through) rules (e.g., a foreign banking subsidiary majority- owned by foreigners and without 10% U.S. shareholders) a "designated payor corporation". Second, it engrafts rules dealing with 80/20 companies to the "designated payor" definition, to subject such companies to the separate credit limit for interest income generally as of 3-28-85 (and subject to the special effective date rule noted earlier).

The new law also (1) removes the de-minimis separate limitation interest (10%) exception to the recharacterization (Sec. 904(d)(3)(C)) in case of foreign personal holding company and Subpart F inclusions of income; (2) clarifies that if a "designated payor corporation" receives dividends and interest from another member of the same affiliated group (specially defined), they can be treated as separate limitation interest only if they're directly or indirectly attributable to separate limitation interest of any other member of the group;

and (3) makes a law change designed to ensure that dividends and interest received from a regulated investment company by portfolio (less than 10% voting stock) shareholders aren't treated as separate limitation interest.

Act Sec. 1810(a) dealing with recharacterizing foreign income as U.S. income adds new Sec. 904(g)(9), and amends 1984 TRA Sec. 121(b)(2)(D)(ii) and (b)(2)(E). Act Sec. 1810(a)(4) dealing with Treaty obligations doesn't amend the Code. Act Sec. 1810(b) dealing with recharacterization as separate limitation interest amends Secs. 904(d)(2), (d)(3)(C) and (E) and adds new Sec. 904(d)(3)(I). The law changes are effective as if included in the 1984 TRA (generally for distributions after 7-18-84) and as indicated above.

[¶1812] **Withholding on Sales of U.S. Real Property by Foreigners.** The new law makes the following modifications in the withholding system set up by the '84 TRA that replaced the information reporting system initially required by the 1980 Foreign Investment in Real Property Tax Act.

Dispositions or distributions by U.S. partnerships, trusts, or estates. On dispositions of U.S. real property interests by a domestic partnership, trust or estate, the partnership, trustee or executor will now withhold 28% of the gain realized on the disposition, to the extent it's allocable to a foreign partner or beneficiary or to a foreign "owner" of the trust under grantor trust rules (under prior law it was 10% of the total amount received). The new law covers dispositions that occur following 31 days after its enactment. Both Committee Reports note that regs are intended to provide exceptions to the withholding when the disposition is currently taxable at the entity (e.g., trust or estate) level; and that a partnership, trustee, or executor without sufficient sale proceeds to satisfy withholding (e.g., in case of installment sales) can request a qualifying statement from the IRS that allows it to withhold a lesser amount.

The new law also clarifies that distributions of U.S. real property interests to foreign persons are subject to withholding when they're taxable under any of the substantive FIRPTA rules (i.e., Sec. 897), and not just for sales of partnership, trust, or estate interests by foreigners (Sec. 897(g)). And it clarifies that the IRS can issue regs to require withholding on gains realized through tiers of entities.

Corporations. A foreign corporation's election to be treated as a domestic corporation for purposes of FIRPTA substantive and reporting provisions (Secs. 897 and 6039C) has been extended to cover the withholding provisions (Sec. 1445) as well. The temporary regs which require the electing foreign corporation to attach to a "non-foreign affidavit" a copy of the acknowledgement of the election provided it by the IRS, offer to U.S. buyers a reasonable assurance of the validity of the affidavit.

The new law also (1) clarifies that no withholding is required on liquidating or redemption distributions by domestic current or former "U.S. real property holding corporations" (U.S. RPHCs) to foreign shareholders of interests that are excluded from treatment as "U.S. real property interests" under Sec. 897(c)(1)(B); and (2) for dispositions of interests in nonpublicly traded domestic corporations, the corporation's affidavits for withholding exemption will now have to state both that the corporation isn't and hasn't been a U.S. RPHC and that as of disposition, interests in it aren't "U.S. real property interests" by reason of Sec. 897(c)(1)(B)—i.e., the affidavit now covers a "non-U.S. real property interest" exemption.

Other rules. The new law clarifies that no notice-giving or withholding duty is imposed on an agent of a foreign corporate transferor who doesn't have *actual knowledge* that a "non-U.S. real property interest" affidavit of a domestic corporation whose stock he transfers is false. The Committee Report notes, however, that such an agent is charged with knowledge of falsity of a false "non-foreign" affadavit furnished by his own principal. It also conforms the FIRPTA penalty provisions (Sec. 6652(g)) to '84 TRA rules, and it clarifies the filing and tax payment requirements for real property interests located in the Virgin Islands.

Act Sec. 1810(f) amends Secs. 897(i), 1445(b)(3), (d)(1), (e)(1), (3), (4) and (6), 6039C(d), and 6652(g). The law changes are effective as if included in the 1984 Tax Reform Act (generally for post-1984 dispositions) and as indicated above.

[¶1813] **Transfers to Foreign Persons in Divisive Reorganizations and Distributions.** The new law makes Sec. 355 (and 356) stock (or related "boot") transfers by domestic corporations to foreign persons (whether or not corporate) give rise to recognized gain under Sec. 367(e) to the extent that regs provide.

Act Sec. 1810(g) amends Secs. 367(a)(1) and (e), 6501(c)(8), 7482(b), and repeals Sec. 367(f) providing a transitional rule, effective as if included in the 1984 Tax Reform Act (generally for post-1984 transfers or exchanges).

[¶1814] **Other Foreign Provisions.** The new law also makes changes in the following areas affected by the foreign provisions of the '84 TRA.

Related person factoring income. Under the '84 TRA, income from factoring receivables of a U.S. obligor acquired directly or indirectly from a "related" U.S. person is generally currently taxable under controlled foreign corporation or foreign personal holding company rules. Receivables transferred after 3-1-84 are treated as "U.S. property." The income is treated as interest on a loan to the obligor. The new law does the following: First, it provides that the exclusion from "U.S. property" of post-1962 earnings and profits

(Sec. 956(b)(2)(H)) applies in case of acquisitions of related person factoring receivables. In addition, the new law exempts from current inclusion, income from factoring receivables whose acquirer and related-person-transferor are organized under the laws of the same foreign country and the related transferor has a substantial part of its assets used in its trade or business there. *Exception:* This rule doesn't apply if the transferor would have derived from a collection on the receivable any foreign base company income (without regard of the 10% exception) or income that's effectively connected with a U.S. trade or business. According to both Committee Reports, this treatment of factoring income also extends to income from analogous transaction-financing loans by CFCs to related parties. Finally, the new law provides that the factoring income treated as interest is subject to the foreign tax credit separate limitation *without regard* to the exception that applies to certain interest received from members of the same affiliated group.

Repeal of 30% withholding on interest paid to foreigners. Generally for portfolio interest on obligations issued after 7-18-84, the new law expressly narrows the definition of "portfolio interest" covered by the repeal to interest that would've been covered by the 30% tax but for the repeal. This is designed to confine the correlative denial to CFCs of the benefit of otherwise applicable Subpart F exceptions to such portfolio interest only. In addition, the exception from the repeal of the 30% tax that covers interest received by "10% shareholders" is broadened to include shareholdings derived constructively through attribution of stock owned by a foreign shareholder in the U.S. payor to a less-than-50%-owned foreign subsidiary. The new law also clarifies that the beneficial owner of a registered obligation can claim a refund of tax withheld on interest covered by the repeal (within the general limitation period for refund claims) if he files a statement after (and not necessarily before) interest payments are made.

Original issue discount. Effective for payments after 9-16-84 on obligations issued after 3-31-72, the rule that delays until time of payment the deduction for interest on an OID obligation held by a related foreign person, doesn't apply to the extent the OID is effectively connected with the lender's U.S. trade or business *unless* the OID income is either exempt from U.S. tax or subject to a lower treaty rate. The new law also provides that a payment of principal or interest on an OID obligation to a foreign investor is taxable income to the extent of previously untaxed OID accrued on the obligation, whether or not the OID accrued since the last interest payment. And it provides that on a sale, exchange, or retirement of an OID obligation, the foreign investor is taxed on hitherto untaxed

¶1814

OID that accrued while he held it, even if that OID exceeds his gain on the obligation's disposition.

Foreign personal holding company rules. Generally for tax years that begin after 1983, the new law supplies a definition of "related person" for the "same country dividend and interest" exclusion from gross income and foreign personal holding company income in FPHC calculations. It imports the definition from the provision dealing with CFC foreign base company sales income (Sec. 954(d)(3)). The new law also clarifies that the "tracing" rule covering stock held through foreign entities applies to all foreign trusts and estates interposed between U.S. taxpayers and FPHCs.

Gain on indirect transfers of stock in a foreign corporation. Under the 1984 Tax Reform Act, a post-7-18-84 exchange by a U.S. corporation of its stock for stock of its 10%-or-more-owned (by voting stock) foreign corporation is generally recast as a distribution of the foreign corporation's stock by the U.S. corporation to its shareholder for purposes of Sec. 1248(a). That provision treats as ordinary income, gains by certain U.S. persons on dispositions of stock in a foreign corporation to the extent of the foreign corporation's allocable earnings and profits. The new law:

• Clarifies that such an indirect transfer is recast as either a stock redemption or liquidation distribution, whichever is appropriate. A liquidating distribution could be then treated as a nonrecognition distribution in complete liquidation of a subsidiary by a corporate shareholder (Sec. 332), and the U.S. corporation could qualify for the Sec. 1248(f)(1) exception from Sec. 1248(f)(2).

• Extends the period for electing retroactive application (to post-10-9-75 transactions) of the '84 TRA amendments, which provide that a CFC's accumulated earnings and profits that previously characterized a U.S. person's gain as ordinary income won't do so another time (i.e., prevented "double counting"). The election can now be made until one year from enactment of the new law (rather than within 180 days after enactment of the '84 TRA).

• As noted at ¶1875, amends Sec. 1248(g)(2) to limit this exception to a shareholder's gain characterized as dividend income under Sec. 356.

Stapled entities. Generally effective 7-18-84, the '84 TRA in effect treats as a U.S. corporation taxable on its worldwide income, a foreign corporation whose interests are "stapled" to the stock interests of a U.S. corporation. The new law excludes from the "stapled entity" rules a foreign corporation if it has established to the IRS that both it and the U.S. corporation to which it's stapled are foreign-owned (i.e., each of them is less-than 50% owned, by total stock vote or value either directly or indirectly by U.S. persons). The new law also authorizes regs to provide that any tax not paid by the foreign corporation will be collected from the U.S. corporation to which it's stapled or from the shareholders of the foreign corporation.

Insurance of related parties by CFCs. Generally effective for tax years of the CFC that begin after 7-18-84, the new law clarifies that the broader Sec. 864(d)(4) definition of "related person" is used for determining the amount of insurance or reinsurance service income that is foreign base company service income. It clarifies that a primary insured is a "related" person if it's a 10% U.S. shareholder or a person related to him.

Definition of resident alien. Generally for tax years that begin after 1984, the new law allows foreign teachers or trainees in the U.S. whose entire compensation was nontaxable under Sec. 872(b)(3) to qualify as "exempt individuals" for purposes of the "substantial presence" test to avoid becoming resident aliens, even if they were "exempt" as a teacher, trainee, or student for any part of four out of seven calendar years. They can't be treated as "exempt" for a calendar year, if they were exempt for any part of four (under prior law two) out of the six years that preceded it. And under the substantial presence test, days in which a professional athlete is present in the U.S. competing in certain charitable sports events aren't counted.

The new law also allows a "qualifying alien individual" who doesn't meet the "permanent residence" and "substantial presence" tests for resident alien treatment for the current year but who satisfies the "substantial presence" test for the following year, to elect tax treatment as a U.S. resident for part of the current calendar year. Under this first-year election, the individual (1) can't be a U.S. resident for the preceding calendar year; (2) must be present in the U.S. for at least 31 consecutive days in the current year; and (3) the individual must be present in the U.S. for at least 75% of the number of days in a "testing period" that starts with the first day of such a 31-day presence and ends with the last day of the current year.

For the 75% test, a total of up to 5 days of actual absence from the U.S. is disregarded, and days on which the individual is an "exempt individual" are not days of presence in the U.S. for both the 31-day and 75% test. The election results in the alien's treatment as a U.S. resident for the part of the current year that starts with the first day of the earliest presence period that meets both the 31-day and 75% tests. The election (revocable only with IRS consent) is made on the return for the current year, but not before the substantial presence test for the following year has been met.

Example: Alien (not a U.S. resident for the preceding year) vacations in the U.S. January 1—31 of the current year, then leaves and returns on October 15. He is considered absent for only 10 days from the U.S. during the remainder of current year, and satisfies the substantial presence test for next year. Result: He can elect to be treated as U.S. resident (e.g., to get joint filing, personal exemptions and itemized deduction) starting on October 15 of the current year (both the 31-day and 75% tests are satisfied for the period October 15—December 31 of the current year).

Act Sec. 1810(c) dealing with related person factoring income amends Secs. 864(d)(5)(A) and 956(b)(3)(A) and adds new Sec. 864(d)(7). Act Sec. 1810(d) dealing with the repeal of the 30% withholding tax amends Secs. 871(a)(1), (h)(2), (3)(C), 881(c)(2), 1441(c)(9) and 1442(a). Act Sec. 1810(e) dealing with OID deductions and income amends Secs. 163(e)(3), 871(a)(1)(C) and 881(a)(3). Act Sec. 1810(h) dealing with FPHC rules amends Secs. 551(f) and 552(c). Act Sec. 1810(i) dealing with gain on indirect transfers of a foreign corporation's stock amend Sec. 1248(i)(1)(B), and also Sec. 133(d)(3)(B) of the 1984 Tax Reform Act. Act Sec. 1810(j) dealing with stapled entities amends Sec. 269B(b) and adds new Sec. 269B(e). Act Sec. 1810(k) dealing with insurance of related parties by CFCs amends Sec. 954(e). Act Sec. 1810(l) dealing with the definition of resident aliens amends Sec. 7701(b). The law changes are effective as if included in the 1984 TRA and as indicated above.

[¶1815] Reporting, Deposits, and Penalties. There are a number of changes to the '84 TRA's compliance provisions. First, effective for mortgage interest payments received after 1984, cooperative housing corporations must report to tenant shareholders and the IRS the tenant's proportionate part of interest paid to the co-op. Second, the failure to supply a taxpayer identification number for obligations in existence on 12-31-84 won't be penalized under Sec. 6676 (rather than 6652) if it relates to mortgage interest reporting rules of amounts received before 1986. Third, a partnership need not make a return under Sec. 6050K (rather than under Sec. 6050K(c)) for post-1984 exchanges of partnership interests until it's notified of the exchange. Fourth, for payments received after 1984, failures to furnish substitute payment statements by brokers (Sec. 6045(d)) are included among penalized failures to file statements (Sec. 6678), and the penalty for intentional disregard to report them is 10% of the aggregate reportable amount. Finally, for tax years that begin after the enactment date, nominees who hold partnership interests for others must furnish the partnership with IRS-prescribed information (e.g., name, address) about the actual owners of the interests, and must be supplied with partnership return information that they will furnish to the actual interest owners as prescribed by regs to come. Similar rules govern trust and estate interests held by nominees.

The new law also supplies by cross reference a definition of "underpayment" in the provision penalizing valuation understatements of estate and gift taxes effective for returns filed after 1984. And it clarifies that the '84 TRA rules for post-7-31-84 deposits of $20,000 or more apply to any taxpayer required to deposit any tax under Sec. 6302(c) more than once a month.

Act Sec. 1811 amends Secs. 6031, 6050K(c), 6652(a)(3), 6678(a)(3) and 7502(e)(3), and amends 1984 Act Sec. 145(d), and adds Secs. 6050H(g) and 6660(f). The law changes are effective as if included in the 1984 Act and as indicated above.

[¶1816] **Miscellaneous 1984 Reform Law Provisions.** *The "tax benefit" rule.* For amounts recovered after 1983, the new law provides that the exclusion from gross income under the tax benefit rule is limited to amounts that didn't reduce income tax under Chapter 1 of the Code (Secs. 1—1399). This applies, e.g., if an individual who receives a state income tax refund, either had no taxable income in the prior year or was subject to the alternative minimum tax, or if credits reduced the tax to zero. In other cases, the exclusion is determined by comparing the refund with the amount by which itemized deductions exceeded the zero bracket amount (standard deduction), and including the lesser amount in current year's income.

Below-market loans. Generally for term loans made after, and demand loans outstanding after, 6-6-84, the new law grants authority for regs to treat a loan with an indefinite maturity as a demand loan (because of the impracticality of determining the present value of the payments due under it). "Demand loans" for determining the timing of deemed interest and compensation payments also include loans whose interest arrangement isn't transferable and which is contingent on the performance of future services. The new law provides for semiannual compounding in calculating interest on demand loans under Sec. 7872 and excepts from withholding deemed payments of compensation arising from below-market term loans. It clarifies that enactment of Sec. 7872 doesn't affect the definition of self-dealing with private foundations. Finally, the new law provides an exception from Sec. 7872 for obligations of the State of Israel if the obligation is payable in U.S. dollars and bears an annual interest rate of not less than 4%.

Transactions with 'related' persons. Generally for deductions and transactions in tax years beginning after 1983, the new law requires regs to apply the principles that match the timing of a payor's deduction and a payee's inclusion in income (Sec. 267(a)(2)) for payments made to payors who aren't U.S. persons. This could apply, for instance, to require a U.S. subsidiary to use the cash method for payments to its foreign parent that's not engaged in a U.S. trade or business; or to match a "related" payor's accounting methods for amounts accrued to a controlled foreign corporation, to that corporation's method for U.S. tax purposes; or to match accounting methods for accruals of payments to foreign persons in whose hands the payments aren't "effectively connected" income. The new law also extends the exception from the loss deferral rules for inventory transfers to or from a foreign corporation (Sec. 267(f)(3)(B)) to sales between a partnership and a foreign corporation "related" by a more-than-50% common ownership.

For sales or exchanges after 9-27-85 that involve a controlled partnership, the new law extends the loss disallowance rules and the treatment of gains as ordinary income (Sec. 707(b)(1)(A), (2)(A)) to transactions with a *constructive more-than-50% owner* of a partnership interest who isn't an actual partner. The rule is intended to replace the rule in Temp. Reg. Sec. 1.267(a)-2T(c), Questions 2 and 3.

The new law also provides that the deduction-and-income matching rules of Sec. 267(a)(2) apply between partnerships commonly owned through more-than-50% interests.

Distributions related to repeal of exemption of Freddie Mac. The new law expressly denies the dividends-received deduction for dividends paid by the Federal Home Loan Mortgage Corporation (Freddie Mac) out of E&P accumulated before 1-1-85, and repeals the prior law rule that treats Freddie Mac as having no accumulated profits as of 1-1-85. It clarifies that dividends paid by Freddie Mac can't produce more than one dividends-received deduction as to income (routed via and) received from a Federal Home Loan Bank. And it provides that a dividends received deduction for dividends paid by a Home Loan Bank is determined by reference to its retained earnings for financial purposes. It also allows a dividends received deduction for dividends received after 1984 directly from Freddie Mac by taxable corporate shareholders. The new law also provides that for all Code purposes the late-1984 preferred stock distribution by Freddie Mac to Federal Home Loan Banks, and the January 1985 distributions of that stock by these banks to their member institutions, are treated as money distributions equal to the stock's value when distributed by the Home Loan Banks followed by the institutions' payment of this money to Freddie Mac in return for its stock.

Listed property and luxury automobiles. The new law clarifies that the maximum weight of vehicles defined as "passenger automobile" (but not of trucks and vans within that definition)for the limitations on the investment credit and depreciation (Sec. 280F), as well as for the gas guzzler excise tax (Sec. 4064) is indicated in terms of their gross *unloaded* weight (i.e., without passengers or cargo). For the gas guzzler tax, the rule applies as of 1-1-80 with special rules for 1985 and 1986 station wagons. And for the gas guzzler tax, the term "manufacturer" doesn't include a "small manufacturer" who merely lengthens existing cars. The Treasury is to prescribe alternative rate schedules for small manufacturers.

The new law clarifies that both deductions for *rentals and other lease payments* (as well as other deductions or credits) by employees on listed property are conditioned on its use for the employer's convenience and as a condition of employment. It also provides that to be excepted from treatment as listed property, a computer must be owned or leased by the person operating the business establishment and used exclusively in the establishment. (This is designed to prevent credits or deductions for employee-owned computers used mostly in the office.)

The new law excludes from treatment as "listed property" property almost entirely used in transporting persons or goods for compensation or under hire.

The changes for listed property and luxury cars in general apply to property placed in service and leases entered into after 6-18-84.

Act Sec. 1812(a) dealing with the tax benefit rule amends Sec. 111(a) and (c), 381(c)(12), 1351(d)(2) and 1398(g)(3). Act Sec. 1812(b) dealing with below market loans amends Sec. 7872(f)(2), (5) and (9) and Sec. 4941(d)(2). Act Sec. 1812(b)(5) dealing with Israel Bonds doesn't amend the Code. Act Sec. 1812(c) amends Secs. 267(f)(3)(B), 707(b)(1)(A) and (2)(A) and adds Sec. 267(a)(3). It also provides a transitional rule for a specified situation (Act Sec. 1812(c)(5)). Act Sec. 1812(d) dealing with Freddie Mac distributions amends Sec. 246(a)(2) and 1984 Tax Reform Act Sec. 177(d)(4). Act Sec. 1812(e) amends Sec. 280F(d)(2)—(5) and 4064(b). The law changes are effective as if included in the 1984 Tax Reform Act and as indicated above.

Life Insurance

[¶1821] Corrections to Life Insurance Company Code Provisions. The new law contains several corrections to the life insurance company Code provisions, as amended by the '84 TRA.

Reserves. The new law provides that, in computing the increases or decreases of amounts discounted at interest under insurance and annuity contracts (Sec. 807(c)(3)), the amount taken into account for any such contract can't be less than the net surrender value of that contract.

The new law also provides that when a Treasury mortality and morbidity table is used for a type of contract (because there is no commissioner's standard table for such a contract) and the Treasury *changes* that table by regulation, the new table will be treated as if it were a new prevailing commissioner's standard table adopted by the 26th state as of a date specified by the Treasury. That date can be no earlier than the date the regulation is issued.

Excess interest. The new law amends the definition of "excess interest" under Sec. 808(d)(1) to make it clear that excess interest refers only to the *excess amounts* , and not to the *entire* amount in the nature of interest (including the amount determined at the prevailing state assumed interest rate).

Fresh-start adjustment and policyholder dividends. The '84 TRA changed the method by which life insurance companies figure their deduction for policyholder dividends—that is, such deductions are now figured on an accrual, rather than a reserve, basis. This change wasn't treated as an accounting method change. Thus, no income or loss was recognized as to existing policyholder dividend reserves, and life companies were given a "fresh start" in figuring policyholder dividend deductions.

The fresh start was intended to mitigate the detriment caused by the statutory accounting change. However, by changing its business practice (e.g., by guaranteeing policy dividends on termination, or by changing the payment date by making policy dividends available on declaration), a company can accelerate into the current year deductions that under its former business practice would have been deductible in the following year. This would, in part, put the company in the position it enjoyed under prior law.

To correct this problem, the new law reduces a company's policyholders dividend deduction by the amount that was accelerated because of a change in business practice. This reduction (which is made before any reduction for the ownership differential provision for mutual companies) is limited, on a cumulative basis, to the amount of the company's 1984 fresh-start adjustment. Both the amount of the accelerated deduction and the amount of the 1984 fresh-start adjustment are figured separately for each line of business. The 1984 fresh-start adjustment is the company's amount of policyholder dividend reserves as of 12-31-83, reduced by (1) dividends accrued before 1-1-84; and (2) previously nondeductible dividends under pre-1984 TRA Sec. 809(f).

The reduction for accelerated deductions doesn't apply to a mere change in the amount of policyholder dividends. Nor does it apply to dividends paid or accrued on policies issued after 12-31-83 unless the policy was issued in exchange for a substantially similar policy that was issued on or before 12-31-81. Further, it doesn't apply to policyholder dividends paid or accrued as to a group policy bought by an employer under an employee welfare benefit plan.

Equity base. The new law clarifies the term "equity base," which is a factor in determining a mutual life company's differential earnings amount. The new law specifically provides that no item will be taken into account more than once in determining the equity base. This ensures that items that are *specifically* included in the equity base aren't included a second time because they're *indirectly* included under another specifically included item.

50 largest stock companies. The new law modifies the statutory authority given to the Treasury to issue regulations that would exclude companies from the group of 50 largest stock companies. (The numerical average of the earnings rates of the 50 largest stock companies is a factor taken into account in figuring a mutual life company's differential earnings amount.) Under the new law, the Treasury must exclude from the group for any calendar year any company that has a negative equity base. It can also exclude by regulations any other company whose equity base is so small that its inclusion in the group would seriously distort the stock earnings rate; however, such companies can be excluded only to the extent their exclusion doesn't cause the *total* number of excluded companies to exceed two. Thus, if two or more companies must be excluded because they have negative equity bases, then no "distorting companies" can be excluded. The new law also provides that, in determining the base period stock earnings rate, the Treasury must exclude from the group any company that had a negative equity base at any time during 1981, 1982, or 1983.

The new law also makes it clear that only the 50 largest *domestic* stock life insurance companies are taken into account. Similarly, only *domestic* mutual life insurance companies are taken into account in determining the average mutual earnings rate.

Statement gain or loss from operations. The new law modifies the definition of "statement gain or loss from operations" under Sec. 809(g)(1). The term refers to net gain or loss from operations as set out in the annual statement, determined without regard to federal income taxes, with further adjustment for certain items. The new law makes it clear that statement gain or loss from operations must be adjusted by substituting (1) the amount of the *deduction* for policyholder dividends, unreduced by the differential earnings amount, for (2) the amount shown on the annual statement for policyholder dividends. Using the unreduced tax amount eliminates a circularity in the computation of the differential earnings amount.

Differential earnings rate and estimated tax. The new law provides that if, as to any estimated tax installment, the differential earnings rate for the second tax year preceding the year for which the installment is paid is *less* than the rate applicable to the tax year for which the installment is paid (see Sec. 809(c)(1)), then in applying estimated tax underpayment penalties to that installment, the amount of tax will be determined by using that lesser rate.

Also, the recomputation of a mutual life company's differential earnings amount for any tax year won't affect the company's liability for estimated tax payments for the tax year in which the recomputed amount is included in, or deducted from, income under Sec. 809(f).

Proration formulas. The new law makes several clarifying amendments to the computation of "company share" and "policyholder's share."

- In arriving at the company's share of net investment income, net investment income is reduced by *all* interest on amounts left on deposit with the company.

- "Required interest," an item taken into account in computing policy interest, includes not only interest on reserves determined at the prevailing state assumed rate, but also interest determined at another appropriate rate if the prevailing state assumed rate isn't used.

- The denominator of the "minifraction" used for computing gross investment income's proportionate share of policyholder dividends is redefined as (1) life insurance gross income, reduced by (2) the excess of the closing balance of Sec. 807(c) reserve items over the opening balance for the tax year. Also, in computing the denominator, life insurance gross income is determined by *including* tax-exempt interest, and by computing decreases in reserves without reducing the closing balance of the reserve items by the company's share of tax-exempt interest.

- "Net investment income" is redefined as (1) 90% of gross investment income *or* (2) for gross investment income attributable to assets held in segregated asset accounts under variable contracts, 95% of gross investment income.

- In computing net increases or decreases in reserves (Sec. 807(a) and (b)) as well as the company's share and policyholder's share, gross investment income and tax-exempt income do *not* include interest received as to a Section 133(b) ESOP loan. ESOP loan interest is also excluded from life insurance gross income in determining gross investment income's proportionate share of policyholder dividends.

Foreign life insurance companies. If additional income has been imputed to a foreign life insurance company doing business in the United States (because the surplus held in the United States is less than the required surplus), the imputed income is added to life insurance gross income *before* computing the special and small life insurance company deductions. The imputed income is treated as gross investment income.

PSA distributions. As a result of the '84 TRA, life insurance companies can no longer make additions to their pre-1984 policyholders surplus accounts. They must, however, maintain those PSAs and include in income any direct or indirect distributions to shareholders from their PSAs. The new law provides that a bona fide loan with arm's-length terms and conditions won't be considered a direct or indirect PSA distribution.

For loans made before 3-1-86 that don't contain arm's-length terms and conditions, the amount that will be treated as an indirect PSA distribution is limited to the foregone interest on the loan. This limitation applies unless the loan was renegotiated, extended, renewed, or revised after 2-28-86.

The new law also reinstates a pre-1984 TRA provision (Sec. 819(b)) that provides instructions for PSA distributions of foreign life companies doing business in the United States.

Deficiency reserves. The new law excludes deficiency reserves from the definition of "life insurance reserves" and "total reserves" for purposes of Sec. 816 (which defines "life insurance company") and Sec. 813(a)(4)(B) (which defines "surplus held in the United States" for foreign life companies doing business in the United States).

Nondiversified contracts. The new law clarifies the special rule for variable life insurance contracts based on investments in Treasury securities. To the extent that any segregated asset account with respect to a variable life insurance contract is invested in U.S. Treasury securities, the investments made by the account will be considered adequately diversified under Sec. 818(h)(1). (Under that Section, variable contracts based on segregated asset accounts aren't treated as annuity, endowment, or life insurance contracts when investments made by the account aren't adequately diversified.)

The new law also provides that if all the beneficial interests in a regulated investment company (RIC) or a trust are held by one or more (1) insurance companies (or affiliated companies) in their general account or in segregated asset accounts, or (2) fund managers (or affiliated companies) in the creation or management of the RIC or trust, then the assets of the RIC or trust will be taken into account in applying the diversification requirements. This change broadens the prior-law "look through" rules to allow the use of seed money, or the ownership of fund shares by an insurance company or fund manager, in operating the underlying investment fund.

Deferred compensation plans. Diversification requirements for segregated asset accounts underlying variable contracts don't apply to pension plan contracts— that include government plans. The new law makes it clear that government plans include eligible state deferred compensation plans under Section 457(b), as well as government plans under Section 414(d).

Dividends within affiliated group. The new law reinstates a special rule for life insurance companies filing or required to file consolidated returns. The rule was eliminated by the '84 TRA, and is reinstated with modifications reflecting the structural changes made by the life company provisions of the '84 TRA. Under the new special rule, for life companies filing or required to file consolidated returns, any determination under the life company provisions of Subchapter L as to dividends paid by one member of the affiliated group to another member will be made as if the group weren't filing a consolidated return.

Dividends from subsidiaries. A life company's deduction for dividends received from a subsidiary is generally determined by prorating the dividends between the company and the policyholders. Under prior law, 100% dividends (those that would be 100% deductible by the recipient under Sec. 243, 244, or 245(b)) weren't subject to proration between the company and policyholders, except to the extent they were paid out of tax-exempt interest or dividends that would not qualify as 100% dividends in the taxpayer's hands. This rule applied whether the payer was a life company or any other corporation.

The new law generally retains the prior law proration rules for 100% dividends paid by a corporation other than an insurance company— but it adds a special rule for 100% dividends paid to a life company by another life company out of E&P for tax years beginning after 12-31-83. If the payer company's share under Sec. 812 for that tax year exceeds the recipient's share for its tax year in which it receives or accrues the dividend, then the recipient's deduction for the 100% dividend is reduced. The amount of the reduction is computed by multiplying (1) the part of the dividend that is attributable to prorated amounts (tax-exempt interest and non-100% dividends) by (2) the percentage obtained by subtracting the recipient's share from the payer company's share. The part of the dividend that is attributable to prorated amounts is determined by treating any dividend by the payer company as coming first out of E&P for tax years beginning after 12-31-83, attributable to prorated amounts; and by determining the portion of E&P attributable to prorated amounts without any reduction for federal income taxes. The new law also states that similar rules will apply to 100% dividends paid by an insurance company that isn't a life insurance company.

High-surplus mutual rules. The new law contains a provision that doesn't amend the Code, but affects the five-year transitional rule for high-surplus mutual life companies under Sec. 809(i). Under the provision, for a mutual life company that was incorporated on 2-23-1888, and acquired a stock subsidiary during 1982, the amount of the company's equity base for purposes of the transitional rule is $175 million. This provision applies without regard to any other provision that would otherwise limit the company's equity base.

Variable contracts. The new law adds a provision that allows certain variable contracts with guarantees to be treated as variable contracts under Sec. 817(d). Obligations under the guarantee that exceed obligations under the contract without regard to the guarantee will be accounted for as part of the company's general account. Under a special effective date, this provision applies to contracts issued after 12-31-86, and to contracts issued before 1-1-87 if the contract was treated as a variable contract on the taxpayer's return.

Act Sec. 1821(a) amends Sec. 807(c), relating to reserves; Act Sec. 1821(b) amends Sec. 808(d)(1)(B), relating to excess interest; Act Sec. 1821(c) adds new Sec. 808(f), relating to fresh-start adjustment and policyholder dividends; Act Sec. 1821(d) amends Sec. 809(b)(2), relating to equity base; Act Sec. 1821(e) amends Sec. 809(d)(4)(C), relating to 50 largest stock companies; Act Sec. 1821(f) amends Sec. 809(g)(1), relating to statement gain or loss from operations; Act Sec. 1821(g) amends Sec. 809(c), relating to estimated tax payments; Act Sec. 1821(h) amends Sec. 809(f), relating to recomputation of differential earnings amount; Act Sec. 1821(i) amends Secs. 812(b), (c), and adds new Sec. 812(g), relating to proration formulas; Act Sec. 1821(j) amends Sec. 813(a)(1), relating to foreign life companies; Act Sec. 1821(k) amends Secs. 815(a), (f), relating to distributions from policyholders surplus account; Act Sec. 1821(l) adds new Sec. 816(h), relating to deficiency reserves; Act Sec. 1821(m) amends Sec. 817(h), relating to nondiversified contracts; Act Sec. 1821(n) amends Sec. 818(a)(6)(A), relating to deferred compensation plans; Act Sec. 1821(o) amends Sec. 818(e), relating to consolidated returns; Act Sec. 1821(p) amends Sec. 805(a)(4), relating to dividends from subsidiaries; Act Sec. 1821(q), relating to high-surplus mutuals, doesn't amend the Code; Act Sec. 1821(r) makes a clerical amendment to Sec. 809(f)(3); Act Sec. 1821(s) amends Sec. 807(d)(5)(C), relating to changes in Treasury tables; Act Sec. 1821(t), relating to variable contracts, amends Sec. 817(d); all effective as if included in the 1984 TRA and as shown above.

【¶1822】 **Life Company 'Fresh-Start' Rule.** The new law provides several clarifications on the effect of the '84 TRA's "fresh-start" rule for life insurance reserves. The '84 TRA required life insurance companies to recompute their life insurance reserves. Under a provision of the '84 TRA that didn't amend the Code—the fresh-start rule—any change in accounting method or in the method of computing reserves that was required solely because of the provisions of the Act generally did not give rise to income or loss. However, the benefit of the fresh start was denied to (1) reserves transferred under a reinsurance agreement entered into after 9-27-83 and before 1-1-84, and (2) reserve strengthening reported for federal income tax purposes after 9-27-83 for a tax year ending before 1-1-84.

The new law makes the following clarifications:

- The change in a life company's reserves attributable to the fresh start will be taken into account in computing the company's E&P. The adjustment to E&P must be made for the company's first tax year beginning in 1984 (1985 in the case of two particular life insurance companies).

- As to reserves for which the fresh start is denied, the new law clarifies that the rule that allows a company to spread a change in the basis of computing reserves over 10 years will apply to the extent a 10-year spread would have been required under pre-'84 TRA law.

¶1822

- To prevent abuse of the fresh-start provisions by use of reinsurance transactions *after* 1983 when the reinsurer is on a fiscal rather than a calendar year, the new law conforms the closing date (1-1-84 under the '84 TRA) to the date for revaluation of reserves. Thus, if a reinsurer's tax year is a fiscal year, "the first day of the first taxable year beginning after 1983" is substituted for "January 1, 1984."

- Under the '84 TRA, an election after 9-27-83, to revalue preliminary term reserves to net level reserves (former Section 818(c)) was generally not given effect. There was an exception to this rule that gave effect to a Section 818(c) election if more than 95% of the reserves computed under the election were attributable to risks under life insurance contracts issued by the taxpayer under an insurance plan first filed after 3-1-82 and before 9-28-83. However, the legislative history to the '84 TRA indicated that a post-9-27-83 Sec. 818(c) election would be treated as reserve strengthening for purposes of denying the benefits of the fresh-start rule. The new law clarifies that a Sec. 818(c) election made under the exception described above won't be treated as reserve strengthening for purposes of denying the fresh start. Also, if a corporation made a Sec. 818(c) election before 9-28-83, and was acquired in a Sec. 338 qualified stock purchase before 12-31-83, the fact that the corporation is treated as a *new* corporation won't render the Sec. 818(c) election nonapplicable to it. For such a corporation, the new law extends the time for making a Sec. 818(c) election as to its first tax year beginning in 1983 and ending after 9-28-83, and for making a Sec. 338 election as to the qualified stock purchase, to 60 days after the enactment date of the 1986 TRA. It also extends the statute of limitations as to either election if the election would not have been timely but for the extension.

- Under the '84 TRA, qualified life companies can elect not to recompute reserves for contracts issued before the first day of the first tax year beginning after 12-31-83. And if a company makes that election, and had tentative life insurance company taxable income (LICTI) of $3 million or less for its first tax year beginning after 12-31-83, it could make a second election to treat the reserve for any contract issued on or after the first day of that tax year (and before 1-1-89) as being equal to the statutory reserve for that contract (with an adjustment similar to the Menge formula under TEFRA). The new law makes the following changes: (1) When testing whether a company can make the second election, it must compute the $3 million tentative LICTI limitation by determining reserves as if the second election were in effect; (2) for a company making the second election, the reserve will be the *greater* of the adjusted statutory reserve or the net surrender value of the contract; and (3) the Menge adjustment is to be applied to the opening and closing reserves in computing net increases or decreases in life insurance reserves.

Act Sec. 1822 amends 1984 TRA Secs. 216(b)(1); (b)(3)(A), (c); (b)(4)(B); and (c)(2)(A), (B); and adds new Sec. 216(b)(4)(C) to the 1984 TRA; all effective as if included in the 1984 TRA and as shown above.

[¶1823] **Life Company Net Level Reserve Election.** Recognizing that, for practical reasons, *no company* would elect to use the special rule for companies using the net level reserve method for noncancellable accident and health insurance contracts ('84 TRA, Sec. 217(n)), the new law expands the coverage of the rule. Under the new law, a company can use the net level reserve method for tax purposes on any directly written noncancellable accident and health insurance contract—whether under existing or *new* plans of insurance. To qualify for treatment under this rule for any tax year, the company must have (1) used the net level reserve method to compute at least 99% of its statutory reserves for such contracts as of 12-31-82, and (2) received more than half of its total direct premiums for calendar year 1982 from directly written noncancellable accident and health insurance. In addition, after 12-31-83, the company will be treated as using the proper reserve method for directly written noncancellable accident and health contracts for a tax year if, through that tax year, the company has continuously used the net level reserve method for computing at least 99% of its tax and statutory reserves on such contracts. As to any contracts for which the company *doesn't* use the net level reserve method, the company must use the same method for tax reserves as it uses for statutory reserves.

Act Sec. 1823(a) amends 1984 TRA Sec. 217(n), relating to the net level reserve election, effective as if included in the 1984 TRA and as shown above.

[¶1824] **Insurance Company Estimated Tax Underpayments.** The '84 TRA contained a special rule providing relief from penalties for estimated tax underpayments caused by the insurance company provisions. The new law repeals that special rule in favor of a broader general relief provision of the new law. For corporations, the new provision (contained in Act Sec. 1879) provides generally that no penalties will be imposed for estimated tax underpayments for any period before March 16, 1985, to the extent that the underpayment was caused by the 1984 TRA.

Act Sec. 1824 repeals 1984 TRA Sec. 218.

[¶1825] **Tax Treatment of Universal Life and Other Investment-Oriented Policies.** Since 1982 (TEFRA), to qualify as life insurance, a policy had to meet requirements of applicable state and foreign law, plus either of two alternative tests: (1) the cash value accumulation test or (2) the guideline premium and cash corridor test.

In addition, since 1982, prior law further provided three general computational rules that restrict the actual provisions and benefits that can be offered in a life insurance contract. First, the net single premium (under the cash value accumulation test) or the guideline premium limitation for any contract assumes the death benefit never increases (it treats qualified additional benefits the same way). Second, the maturity date is no earlier than the insured's 95th birthday, and no later than the insured's 100th birthday. Third, the amount of any endowment benefit may not exceed the smallest death benefit payable at any time.

The new law clarifies the second computational rule: The maturity date may not be before age 95 or later than age 100. This conforms the second computational rule to the first and third.

The new law also adds an additional computational rule to apply the second computational rule and to determine the cash value on the maturity date under the third computational rule. The death benefits are deemed to be provided until the maturity date in the second computational rule. This, coupled with the second computational rule generally will disqualify contracts endowing at face value before age 95, but will allow pre age 95 endowment amounts of less than face value.

The additional computational rule doesn't apply to qualification determinations under the cash value corridor test.

Tax effect. Assuming earnings in excess of premiums at the end of 20 years on a $100,000 policy issued at age 35 amount to $53,260 and cash values are $80,000, the policyholder's income taxes—from the year his policy fails the tests until the end of year 20—will total $13,315 in the 25% bracket, $17,576 in the 33% bracket, $22,369 in the 42% bracket, and $26,630 in the 50% bracket.

Death benefits taxable, too. Only the $20,000 insurance at risk at age 55 ($100,000 minus $80,000) will qualify for the Sec. 101(a)(1) exclusion. Result: If the insured dies at age 55, a steep tax will hit the $80,000 included in the beneficiary's income.

Universal life withdrawals. Sec. 7702(f)(7)(B) states: "In the case of any change which reduces the future benefits under the contract, such change shall be treated as an exchange of the contract for another contract."

And Sec. 1035(a)-(1) states: "No gain or loss shall be recognized on the exchange of a contract of life insurance for another contract of life insurance. . ."

But Sec. 1031(b) says: "If an exchange would be within the provisions of section 1035(a). . .if it were not for the fact that the property received in exchange consists. . . also of. . .money, then the gain. . .shall be. . .the sum of such money and the fair market value of such. . .property."

Question. Do partial withdrawals from universal life policies trigger current income taxes to the extent the withdrawal plus the cash value of the new policy exceed the policyholder's investment in the original contract?

The '84 TRA authorized regulations in this withdrawal area, revising some of the adjustment rules prospectively, if necessary.

But the new law replaces Treasury's authority to prescribe regulations affecting withdrawals with these specific new rules:

Any withdrawals from a life insurance contract will be treated as "first paid out of income" only if the reduction in benefits occurs during 15 years after the issue date.

For the first five years, the maximum amount paid first out of income will depend on whether the contract meets (1) the cash value accumulation test or (2) the guideline premium/cash value corridor test.

Under (1), the required distribution is the excess of the cash value over the net single premium determined after the reduction.

Under (2), the required distribution is the greater of the excess of total premiums paid over the redetermined guideline premium limit or the excess of the cash value over the redetermined cash value corridor.

From the end of year 5 to the end of year 15, the maximum amount paid first out of income is the excess of the cash value before the distribution over the maximum cash value that wouldn't violate the cash value corridor after the reduction in benefits.

No interest deduction on policy loans. Many life underwriters characterize universal life insurance policies as annual premium contracts that qualify for interest deductions under the four-out-of-seven rule [Sec. 264(c)(1)].

But single premium policies include contracts where an amount is deposited with the insurer to pay a substantial number of future premiums [Sec. 264(a)(2) and Reg. §264-2]. The Committee Report—restating these Code and Reg. sections—points out that Sec. 264 never has allowed interest deductions on loans against universal life and other single premium policies. Such contracts are not eligible for the four-out-of-seven rule.

Contracts that don't qualify as life insurance contracts. Under the '84 TRA, a policyholder must include in income the excess of the contract's cash value increase and cost of insurance during the year over the year's net premium (premium minus dividend).

The new law uses the gross premium in computing income; it doesn't use the dividend to reduce the premium.

Contracts issued during 1984 that meet new requirements. Under the new law, any policy issued in 1984 that qualified under Sec. 7702 also will qualify under prior law Sec. 101(f) as extended through 1984.

Certain contracts issued after 9-30-84. The new law clarifies the '84 TRA's Sec. 7702 transition rule. The new law allows 3% rather than 4% as the minimum interest rate under the cash value accumulation test, without regard to any higher rate guaranteed initially.

Act Sec. 1825(a) amends the Sec. 7702(e)(1) computational rules that restrict the benefits under a life insurance contract; Act Sec. 1825(b) amends Sec. 7702(f)(7), that determines how universal life withdrawals are taxed; Act Sec. 1825(c) amends Sec. 7702(g) on treatment of contracts that don't qualify as life insurance contracts; Act Sec. 1825(d) and (e) and Sec. 221(d)(1) and (2)(C) clarify Sec. 7702.

[¶1826] **Deferred Annuity Withdrawals.** The '84 law imposed a 5% penalty on any distribution from a deferred annuity before age 59½, unless the policyholder was disabled, died, or received an annuity for life or a minimum period of at least five years. Premature withdrawals were taxed to the extent the cash value exceeded the investment in the contract.

Distribution at annuity holder's death. Under the '84 law, when an annuity holder died before the annuity starting date, the cash value had to (1) be distributed within five years after the date of death, or (2) used within one year of death to provide a life annuity or installments payable over a period not longer than the beneficiary's life expectancy. In addition, a spousal beneficiary could continue the contract under the same terms as the decedent.

If the annuity holder died on or after the annuity starting date, any remaining proceeds had to be distributed to the beneficiary at least as rapidly as the rate of distribution to the decedent.

The new law makes clear that these rules need not be met by annuity contracts provided under a qualified pension plan or an IRA. These annuities must satisfy the qualified plan or IRA distribution rules.

In addition, the new law clarifies the application of the required distribution rules when the contract holder is not an individual. Here, the primary annuitant is the holder of the contract. The "primary annuitant" is the person whose life primarily affects the payout's timing or amount; e.g., that person whose life measures the annuity starting date or the annuity benefits. The new law also clarifies the penalty exception for death benefits. The penalty doesn't apply to any benefit on or after an individual's death or, where the contract holder isn't an individual, on or after the primary annuitant's death.

If an individual owner transfers an annuity contract by gift or, if the holder is not an individual or if there is any change in the primary annuitant, the transfer or change is treated as the death of the holder. This implements the forced distribution rules adopted under the '84 TRA law (intended to terminate tax deferral allowed when annuity contracts no longer were required as a retirement vehicle for the contractholder who was enjoying the tax deferral on the income). Without the correction covering transfers of annuity contracts by gift, the required distribution rules adopted in the '84 law could be avoided easily by a transfer to a person much younger.

Otherwise, the rules would allow taxpayers to continue tax deferral beyond the life of an individual taxpayer. As with the required distribution rules, a distribution of the entire interest in the contract will not be required with respect to any Sec. 1041(a) transfer (relating to transfers of property between spouses or incident to divorce).

Premature withdrawal penalty. For further explanation on post-12-31-86 early distributions, see ¶1123.

The new law (1) shows how to treat joint contractholders when one dies and (2) clarifies that the forced distribution requirements adopted in the '84 Act apply on the death of any contract holder. These provisions apply only to contracts issued six months after the new law's date of enactment.

Act Sec. 1826 amends Secs. 72(q), that levies the 5% penalty, and also amends Secs. 72(e) and (s), effective as if included in the '84 TRA and as shown above.

【¶1827】 Group-Term Insurance. The '84 law provided that a retired employee's group-term life insurance may continue only on the same terms as an active employee. In effect, an employer no longer could pay the full cost of as much insurance as desired without any cost included in the retired employee's income. The law exempted employees retired on disability.

In addition, employer-paid premiums for any key employee under a discriminatory group-term plan—including the first $50,000—were included in the employee's income. And the amount couldn't be determined under Table I. Instead, the key employee's taxable income included the actual cost.

Effective Date: The rules applied to taxable years beginning after 12-31-83, but not to any plan in existence on 1-1-84. However, the exception applied only to individuals age 55 or more and either (1) retired on or before 1-1-84, or (2) employed during 1983 and —if the plan was discriminatory—retired before 1-1-87.

Under the new law, in a discriminatory plan, any key employee's cost is the greater of the actual group-term cost or the Table I cost. The '84 law's intent was to discourage the further use of discriminatory group-term plans. But this requirement would work only if the actual cost exceeded the Table I cost. The new law gives full effect to prior Congressional intent not to encourage discrimination (when actual cost may be less than Table I cost). Key employee is redefined to include any retired employee if he or she was a key employee at retirement. For applying the nondiscrimination requirements of the group-term life insurance provisions, the new law also clarifies that, to the extent provided in regulations, coverage and benefit tests may be applied separately to active and former employees.

The new law also makes a clerical correction to coordinate Sec. 83(e)(5), with Sec. 79. Sec. 83(e)(5) currently excepts the cost of group-term life insurance to which Sec. 79 applies from the application of Sec. 83 (governing the taxation of property transferred in connection with performance of services). The new law provides: Sec. 83 doesn't apply to group-term life insurance covered by Sec. 79. When an employee retires, the present value of any future group-term life insurance coverage that may become nonforfeitable on retirement will be taxed immediately to the employee upon retirement if the employee receives a permanent guarantee of life insurance coverage from the insurance company. But if the coverage is group-term life insurance within the meaning of Sec. 79, the cost of the coverage will be taxable annually to the retired employee.

Act Sec. 1827 amends Sec. 79, relating to separate treatment of former employees, cost to a key employee under a discriminatory plan, and Sec. 83(e), covering the immediate inclusion in a retiree's income of the present value of the lifetime coverage, effective for taxable years ending after the date of enactment.

[¶1828] **Amendment Related to Certain Changes of Insurance Policies.** The new law extends the tax-free policy-exchange rules to endowment contracts issued by nontaxable insurance companies.

Act Sec. 1828 amends Sec. 1035(b).

[¶1829] **Waiver of Interest.** The new law provides that no interest will be payable for any period before 7-19-84, on any underpayment of tax to the extent the underpayment was caused by the life insurance company provisions in Subtitle A of Title 11 of the '84 TRA.

Act Sec. 1829, effective as shown above.

[¶1830] Modco **Grandfather Provision Reaffirmed.** The 1982 Tax Equity and Fiscal Responsibility Act repealed Section 820, under which life insurance companies could elect to treat modified coinsurance as conventional coinsurance. TEFRA also grandfathered the federal income tax treatment of existing agreements for tax years before 1982. Thus, unless the IRS could prove fraud, the tax savings attributable to Modco agreements would be free from an IRS challenge for pre-1982 years.

In 1986, however, the IRS issued audit guidelines on when agents should raise pre-1982 Modco issues *even in the absence of fraud.* Under the guidelines, the IRS would take a close look at Modco agreements that were antedated to take effect before they were signed, and the rate at which investment income was transferred under Modco agreements.

The new law reaffirms TEFRA's grandfather rule. Thus, the IRS won't be able to challenge pre-1982 Modco agreements except for fraud.

Act Sec. 1830, relating to the scope of Sec. 255 of 1982 TEFRA, does not amend the Code.

Private Foundations

[¶1831] **Reduction in Section 4940 Excise Tax.** The new law modifies the rules under which the excise tax on a private foundation's net investment income is reduced from 2% to 1%. The reduction is permitted if qualified distributions during the year equaled or exceeded the sum of the foundations assets for the year multiplied by the average percentage payout for the previous five years plus 1% of the foundation's net investment income for the year. In addition, the average percentage payout had to be at least 5% ($3\frac{1}{3}$% if a private operating foundation).

The new law replaces the average percentage payout requirement by providing that the rate reduction is available only if the foundation wasn't liable for tax for failure to make minimum expenditures for charitable purposes (under Sec. 4942) for any year during the base period.

Clerical amendments. The new law makes a clerical amendment expanding the application of the definition of "capital gain property." It also makes it clear that a game-of-chance exception to the definition of unrelated trade or business applies only to North Dakota.

Act Sec. 1831, defining capital gain property, amends Sec. 170(b)(1)(C)(iv); Act Sec. 1832, modifying the excise tax reduction, amends Sec. 4940(e)(2)(B); both effective as if included in the 1984 TRA (effective for taxable years beginning after 12-31-84). Act Sec. 1833, corrects a reference to second tier taxes, by amending Sec. 6214(c), effective as if included in the 1984 TRA. Act

Sec. 1834, dealing with games of chance, amends 1984 TRA Sec. 311(a)(3)(A), effective for games of chance conducted after 6-30-81.

Tax Simplification Provisions

〔¶1841〕 Estimated Tax of Nonresident Aliens. The new law restores the pre-1984 TRA estimated tax provisions applying to nonresident aliens. These payments must be made in three (not four) installments, due June 15, September 15, and January 15. And 50% of the amount will be due with the first payment.

Act Sec. 1841, reinstating the nonresident alien estimated tax, redesignates Secs. 6654(j), (i), and (l), as (k), (l), and (m) and adds new (j), effective as if included in the 1984 TRA (tax years beginning after 12-31-84).

〔¶1842〕 Property Transfers in Divorce. The new law makes the following changes to clear up some provisions from the '84 TRA. First, the Section 267 loss disallowance rules won't apply to any transfer incident to a divorce under Sec. 1041(a).

Second, a transferor must recognize gain under a transfer in trust, incident to divorce, to the extent that liabilities assumed by the trust exceed the transferor's basis, notwithstanding Sec. 1041.

Third, the transferor must recognize gain on the transfer of installment obligations to the trust.

Fourth, the Sec. 2516 property settlement gift tax exclusion applies to transfers of "ex-husbands" and "ex-wives" as well as "husbands" and "wives."

Act Sec. 1842(a), relating to loss transactions, adds new Sec. 267(g); Act Sec. 1842(b), relating to transfers in trust adds new Sec. 1041(e); Act Sec. 1842(c), relating to installment obligations, amends Sec. 453B; Act Sec. 1842(d), relating to property settlements, amends Sec. 7701(a)(17); all effective as if included in the 1984 TRA, for transfers after 7-18-84.

〔¶1843〕 Alimony and Support. The new law makes it clear that payments under any decree won't be disqualified from treatment as alimony or separate maintenance solely because the decree doesn't specifically state that the payments will terminate at the payee's death.

The new law also makes it clear what events are considered a contingency for child support purposes by correcting a cross reference.

Six-year rule reduced to three. The new law revises the frontloading alimony rules by generally reducing the six-year rule to three years. If alimony payments in the first year exceed the average of annual payments in the second year (reduced by excess payments for that year) and the third year, by more than $15,000 the excess amounts are recaptured in the third year by requiring the payor to include the excess in income and allowing the payee a deduction for such excess payments. A similar rule operates the extent payments in the second year exceed payments in the third year by more than $15,000.

As under prior law, recapture isn't required (1) if either party dies; (2) if the payee remarries within certain time limits; (3) for certain temporary support payments; or (4) for certain fluctuations that aren't within the control of the payor.

Effective Date: The new three-year rule is effective for divorce or separation instruments executed after 12-31-86. A special rule allows pre-1987 instruments that are modified after 1986 to come within the new rules. The new law also reduces the recapture period to three years for instruments not covered by the changes (pre-1987 instruments).

Act Secs. 1843(a) and (d), correcting cross references, amends Sec. 71; Act Sec. 1843(b), relating to alimony contingencies, amends Sec. 71(b)(1)(D); Act Sec. 1843(c), reducing the six-year rules to three years, amends Sec. 71(f); all effective as included in the '84 TRA (for decrees and agreements executed after 12-31-84) and as shown above.

[¶1844] **At-Risk Rules.** The new law clarifies how the investment credit at-risk rules are affected by nonqualified nonrecourse financing. The new rules provide that any net increase in nonqualified financing will be treated as reducing the property's credit base (and thus the qualified investment) in the year the property was first placed in service. The same is true of any increase in the credit base.

A number of corrections clarify that the appropriate term, for investment credit at-risk purposes, is "credit base" and not "qualified investment." Another correction applies the Sec. 168(e)(4) definition of related person for at-risk purposes.

Act Sec. 1844, relating to the investment credit at-risk rules, amends Secs. 46(c)(8)(D)(v), (c)(9)(A), (c)(9)(C)(i), and 47(d)(1) and (d)(3)(e) and repeals Sec. 47(d)(3)(F), effective as if included in the 1984 TRA (property placed in service after 7-18-84).

[¶1845] **Distilled Spirits.** The '84 TRA provision allowing manufacturers of distilled spirits to "draw back" all but $1 of the distilled spirit tax if used for non-beverage products is effective for products manufactured or produced after October 31, 1984.

Act Sec. 1845 adds new TRA Sec. 456(d), as if included in the 1984 TRA.

[¶1846] **Carryover and Carrybacks.** A number of corrections are made in Sec. 39, which reflect the new numbering system that applies to credits.

Act Sec. 1847, correcting cross references, amend Sec. 39, effective as if included in the 1984 TRA (tax years beginning after 12-31-83).

[¶1847] Minimum Tax. The new law restores the pre-'84 law principles relating to credit carryovers by taxpayers subject to the alternative minimum tax. So for purposes of determining credit carryovers and carrybacks to other years for the residential energy credit, certified mortgage interest credit, research credit, and general business credit, the amount of the limitations under Secs. 26, 30(g), or 38(c) will be the amount of *credit allowable* reduced but not below zero by the alternative minimum tax and certain other credits. The '84 TRA language had the three limitations reduced, rather than the allowable credit.

In addition, a conforming amendment provides that, for alternative minimum tax purposes, in determining foreign taxes paid in one year that may be treated as paid or accrued in another taxable year under Sec. 904(c), the Sec. 904(c) limitation will be equal to the credit allowable under Sec. 27(a) (the foreign tax credit) increased by the amount determined by the ratio under Section 55(c)(2)(C).

Clerical amendments. The new law also provides that the period for assessing a deficiency attributable to elections to have the alcohol fuels credit or targeted jobs credit not apply (or any revocation) is one year after the date of notification.

Act Sec. 1847(a), relating to minimum tax carrybacks and carryovers, amends Sec. 55(c)(3) and Sec. 55(c)(2)(E), effective for taxable years beginning after 12-31-83 (general credits) and 12-31-82 (foreign tax credits). Act Sec. 1847(b)(13), setting up a deficiency assessment period adds new Sec. 6501(n), effective as if included in the 1984 TRA. Act Sec. 1847(b) makes technical amendments to Secs. 30(b)(2)(D), 48(l), 86(f), 108(b)(2), 146(b)(2), 151(e)(5), 280(b), 415(c)(3)(C), 422(A)(c), 655(d), 6411, 6501, 6511 and 6999 and Sec. 1631(b) of the 1984 TRA.

[¶1848] Conforming Corrections. The new law makes a number of corrections reflecting the repeal of the extra investment credit and individual retirement bonds.

Act Sec. 1848, getting rid of certain deadwood, repeals Sec. 46(f)(9) and amends Secs. 404(a)(8), 2039(e), 4973(b), and 6047 (which in some places is misdesignated 6704).

Employee Benefit Provisions

[¶1851] Funded Welfare Benefit Plans. Under the '84 TRA, amounts otherwise allowable as a deduction for a contribution to a welfare benefit fund for any year can't exceed the qualified cost of the fund for the year. That cost is the sum of the fund's qualified direct cost and any addition to reserves for the year (qualified asset account), less the fund's after-tax income. Generally, a welfare benefit is any benefit, other than one under a qualified retirement plan, for which the employer deductions are usually postponed until taken into income by employees (or independent contractors) or vacation pay subject to certain elections. A "fund" is any tax-exempt social club, VEBA, supplemental unemployment benefit compensation trust (SUB), or group legal service plan; any trust, corporation or other organization not exempt from tax; and any such account held for any employer by a qualified third party.

The new law makes a number of changes and clarifications to the funded welfare benefit plans.

Definition of fund. The new law amends the definition of fund to exclude amounts held under an insurance contract described in Sec. 264(a)(1), certain qualified nonguaranteed contracts, and, according to the committee report, certain guaranteed renewal contracts.

An insurance policy described in Sec. 264(a)(1) is one on the life of an officer, employee, or person financially interested in the employer's trade or business and the employer is the direct or indirect beneficiary of the policy.

Also excluded are amounts held under certain "qualified nonguaranteed insurance contracts." That's a contract under which (1) there is no guarantee of renewal and, (2) other than insurance protection, the only payments to which the employees or employer are entitled are experience rated refunds or policy dividends that aren't guaranteed and that are determined by factors other than the amount of welfare benefits paid to (or on behalf of) the employees or their beneficiaries. As a result, if the amounts are subject to a significant current risk of economic loss that may be determined by factors other than employee payouts, the amount held by the insurance company won't be considered a fund.

An arrangement that satisfies these requirements, however, will qualify for treatment as a fund unless the amount of any experience-rated refund or policy dividend payable to an employer for a policy year is treated by the employer as received or accrued in the tax year in which the policy year ends.

According to the Senate Committee report, amounts held by an insurance company for a reasonable premium stabilization reserve for an employer are treated as a fund. Amounts released from such a reserve to buy current insurance coverage are to be treated as experience-related refunds or policy dividends.

Finally, the new law provides that any account defined as a fund under regs issued under Sec. 419(e)(3)(c) will be considered a fund no earlier than six months after the final regs are published. This rule doesn't apply to certain reserves for post-retirement benefits or arrangements with certain refund features.

One further exclusion. According to the House Committee report, a "fund" doesn't include amounts held by an insurance company subject to certain "guaranteed renewal contracts." Those are contracts under which the employer's right to renew is guaranteed, but the level of premiums is not.

Postretirement medical benefits and qualified plans. Under the '84 TRA, any amount allocated to a separate account for a key employee for postretirement medical benefits is treated as an annual addition to a defined contribution plan. The new law makes it clear that the amount so treated is not subject to the 25% of compensation limit applicable to annual additions for defined contribution limit.

   WATCH THIS: The amount so contributed would be subject to the Sec. 415(c)(1)(A) dollar limits for annual additions.

Separate accounting for key employees. The '84 TRA, to provide an overall limit for preretirement deductions for post-retirement medical and life insurance benefits of key employees, required a separate accounting for contributions to provide certain postretirement benefits to an employee who is or ever was (after the '84 TRA) a key employee. The new law clarifies that the separate accounting doesn't apply until the first taxable year for which a reserve is computed under Sec. 419A(c)(2).

Discriminatory postretirement reserves. Under the new law, no reserve may be taken into account in determining an account limit, under Sec. 419(c)(2), for postretirement medical or life insurance benefits for covered employees, unless the plan meets the nondiscrimination requirements under Sec. 505(b) for those benefits. Those requirements must be met even if they don't apply in determining the tax-exempt status of the fund. A special exception to the ban against taking the reserve into account applies to collective bargaining agreements that Treasury finds were the subject of good faith bargaining.

The new law also provides that life insurance benefit won't be taken into account to the extent the aggregate amount of such benefits provided for an employee exceeds $50,000.

   GRANDFATHER CLAUSES: Certain postretirement group insurance plans that failed the Sec. 505(b) nondiscrimination plans or the benefits of which exceed $50,000, that were grandfathered by the '84 TRA, continue to be taken into account for determining the reserve account limit.

Actuarial certification. As a general rule, unless there is an actuarial certification for benefits, the account limit for certain welfare benefit funds can't exceed special safe-harbor limits. The actuarial certification requirement now applies to post-retirement medical and life insurance benefits as well, unless a safe-harbor computation is used.

Aggregation rules. Under the new law, in computing the limits applicable to the reserves for disability benefits, SUBs, and severance pay benefits, and postretirement medical and life insurance benefits, all welfare benefit funds of a single employer are treated as a single fund. For all other purposes, the employer may elect to treat two or more welfare benefit plans as a single plan.

Adjustment to existing reserves. The '84 TRA provided that the account limit for any of the first four years to which the welfare benefit rules apply will be increased by an applicable percentage of the existing excess reserve. The '84 TRA didn't make it clear what "existing excess reserves" meant. The new law defines it as the excess (if any) of the amount of assets set aside at the close of the first taxable year ending after 7-18-84 to provide disability benefits, medical benefits, SUB or severance pay benefits, or life insurance benefits over the account limit (disregarding the adjustment) determined for the taxable year for which the increase is computed. This rule increasing the account limit applies only to a welfare benefit fund that, as of 7-18-84, had assets set aside to provide the previously mentioned benefits.

Unrelated business income. The '84 TRA set up a tax on unrelated business income of a social club, VEBA, SUB, or group legal services plan on the lesser of the fund's income or the amount by which assets in the fund exceed a specific limit on amounts set aside for exempt purposes. An employer must include in income an amount similar (deemed unrelated income) to that includable by a welfare benefit fund that's not tax exempt (subject to regs to limit double taxation).

The new law does the following:

- Clarifies that the tax on unrelated business income applies to 10-or-more employer plans.

- Clarifies that the account limit is determined as if the rules limiting deductions for employer contributions applied.

- Points out that the '84 TRA rule, which states that the amount that may be set aside for purposes of the unrelated business income tax won't apply to income from pre-existing reserve for post-retirement medical or life insurance benefits, applies only to assets set aside as of 7-18-84.

- Deletes the provision barring a "set aside" for assets used in providing certain benefits (generally facilities).

- Provides that if any amount included in the gross income of an employer as deemed unrelated income from a welfare benefit fund then the amount of the income tax imposed on that income is to be treated as an employer contribution as of the last day of

¶1851

the taxable year. As a result, the tax is deductible, subject to the deduction limits for fund contributions. Also, the tax on such income is to be treated as if it were imposed on the fund for purposes of determining the fund's after-tax income.

Disqualified benefit. The '84 TRA imposed a nondeductible excise tax on a welfare benefit fund that provides a disqualified benefit. The tax is 100% of the benefit.

The new law changes the definition of disqualified benefits. These benefits now include: (1) any post-retirement medical or life insurance benefit provided for a key employee for whom the employer was required to establish a separate account and the payment is not from the account; (2) any post-retirement medical or life insurance benefit provided to an individual in whose favor discrimination is prohibited unless the plan meets the nondiscrimination requirements under Sec. 505(b) with respect to the benefit, even if those requirements don't apply to such plans; and (3) any portion of the welfare benefit fund reverting to the employer.

As to the first definition, preretirement benefits that were disqualified under the '84 TRA won't be considered disqualified merely because they're not paid to a key employee from a separate account.

A benefit that comes within the second definition won't be disqualified if it is maintained under a recognized collective bargaining agreement and the benefit was the subject of good faith bargaining.

A payment that reverts to the benefit of an employer under the third definition won't be disqualified if attributable to a contribution for which no deduction is allowable in the current or proceeding taxable year. A reduction must be made to the amount treated as a carryover to the extent nondeducted contributions revert to the employer's benefit.

The first two definitions of disqualified benefit won't apply to post-retirement benefits charged against a pre-TRA of 1984 existing reserve for post-retirement medical or life insurance benefits.

Exemption for collectively bargained and pay-all welfare benefit fund. The new law permanently exempts collectively bargained welfare benefit funds from the account limits. That includes limits set up by any regs. So contributions are deductible and assets held by such funds are tax exempt.

Also exempted are certain VEBAs funded solely with employee contributions. The exemption is available if the plan has at least 50 employees and no employee is entitled to refund other than a refund based on the experience of the entire fund. As a result, there is an element of risk. However, according to the Conference report, a pay-all VEBA also won't lose the exemption merely because the refund may vary depending on the number of years the employee contributed to the fund.

Fully vested vacation benefits. The new law provides a transitional rule in the case of a fully vested vacation pay plan in which payments are required within one year after the accrual of vacation. If the taxpayer makes the Section 463 election for the first taxable year ending after the '84 TRA enactment date (7-18-84), then instead of establishing a suspense account, the election is treated as a change in accounting method and the adjustments required by the change will be taken into account under Sec. 481.

The time for making that election for the first taxable year ending after 7-18-84 is extended to six months after the new law's enactment date. However, the rule applies only if vacation pay is expected to be paid (or is in fact paid) within 12 months after the close of employer's year.

Other changes and corrections. The new law also does the following:

- Clarifies that the Sec. 404(a) deduction rules would disallow deductions for deferred compensation plans under any other provisions except Sec. 404(a)(5), not just Sections 162 and 212. These rules also apply to foreign deferred compensation under Sec. 404A and the welfare benefit fund provisions.

- Clarifies that the rules apply to plans for independent contractors.

- Extends the application of the higher account limits to all welfare benefit funds maintained under collective bargaining agreements, not just those established by such agreements.

- Clarifies that the Sec. 404(b) contribution rules apply not only to unfunded deferred benefits.

- Makes certain that all of Section 505(b) is used to determine discrimination.

- Gives a clearer definition of "collective bargaining agreement" for purposes of the discrimination requirements.

Effective Dates: The new law clarifies certain 1984 TRA effective dates. First, the tax on disqualified benefits applies to benefits provided after December 31, 1985. That tax doesn't apply to benefits charged against existing reserves for certain post-retirement benefits.

The '84 TRA changes relating to the unrelated business income tax apply to taxable years ending after December 31, 1985. Such changes are to be treated as a change in income tax rate for purposes of Section 15.

Act Sec. 1851(a)(8), clarifying the definition of fund, adds new Sec. 419(e)(4); Act Sec. 1851(a)(2)(A), dealing with annual additions, amends Sec. 419(d)(2); Act Sec. 1851(a)(2)(B), relating to separate accounts, amends Sec.

¶**1851**

419A(d)(1); Act Sec. 1851(a)(3)(A), relating to post retirement reserves, amends Sec. 419A(e); Act Sec. 1851(a)(5), dealing with actuarial certification, amends Sec. 419(c)(5)(A); Act Sec. 1851(a)(6), dealing with the aggregation rules, amends Sec. 419(h)(1); Act Sec. 1851(a)(7), clarifying adjustments of existing reserves, amends Secs. 419A(f)(7)(C) and (D); Act Secs. 1851(a)(9) and (10), relating to the tax on unrelated business income, amends Secs. 419A(g) and 512(a)(3)(E); Act Sec. 1851(a)(11), relating to the tax on disqualified benefits, amends Sec. 4976(b); Act Secs. 1851(a)(12) and (14), amending the TRA effective dates, amends Sec. 511(e) of the 1984 TRA; Act Sec. 1851(a)(13), exempting certain VEBAs from the account limits, amends Sec. 419A(f)(5); Act Sec. 1851(b), relates to vacation pay plansand amends Sec. 404; Act Secs. 1851(a)(1), (a)(4), (b)(2), and (c) making technical corrections amend Sec. 419(g)(1), 419A(f)(5), 404(b) and 505(a) and (b); all effective as if included in the 1984 TRA and as shown above.

[¶1852] **Pension Plan Provisions.** Retirement plans don't escape correction. Here are the changes.

Distributions. The new law clarifies that distributions from individual retirement accounts and annuities must start no later than April 1 of the calendar year following the year in which the owner reaches 70½. Such distributions are also subject to the incidental death benefit rule (present value of payments projected to be made to the owner must be more than 50% of the present value of total payments to be made). In addition, distributions from a Sec. 403(b) annuity must begin no later than when the employee reaches age 70½, under rules that are similar to those that apply to IRAs.

The new law also defines a 5% owner for purposes of the required beginning date (that is, no later than April 1 following the year the 5% owner reaches age 70½). Such individual is a 5% owner if the individual was a 5% owner at any time during the plan year ending in the calendar year in which the individual attains age 70½ or the four preceding years. If the individual becomes a 5% owner in a year after attaining age 70½, the required beginning date is the April 1 following that year. [Ed. note: House-passed Concurrent Resolution No. 395 provides that if such individual's required beginning date would, before this change, occur after 12-31-86, but after the change would occur before 1-1-87, then the individual will be treated as if he or she became a 5% owner in the plan year ending in 1986. This provision is not part of the new law. It is included here for informational purposes only.]

The new law repeals the exception to the required distribution rules for amounts held by an ESOP (subject to the 84-month rule). In its place is an exception to the 84-month rule for required distributions.

The new law also makes it clear that a distribution required under the incidental death benefit rules is a required distribution for purposes of the required distribution rules.

Rollovers and required distributions. Amounts that must be distributed under the required distribution rules aren't eligible for rollover treatment. This rule applies only to the amount required to be distributed (not to any excess).

Distributions before age 59½. The additional income tax on distributions to 5% owners before age 59½ will apply to all distributions except those on account of death or disability. The tax won't apply to amounts attributable to contributions paid before 1-1-85. The new law defines a 5% owner, for purposes of the tax, as any individual who at any time during the five plan years before the plan year in which the distribution is made is a 5% owner.

Thus, the status at the time of distributions determines if the extra tax applies—not the status at the time of contribution.

Qualifying rollover distributions. In the rollover area, the following clarifications are made:

- Distributions of the entire balance to an employee's credit in a qualified plan may be eligible for rollover under the partial distribution rollover rules as long as the distribution isn't a qualified total distribution. If the total distribution is on account of plan termination or is eligible for lump-sum distribution treatment, the partial distribution rules don't apply.

- Accumulated deductible employee contributions aren't taken into account for purposes of calculating the balance to the credit of an employee under the partial distribution rules.

- A self-employed individual is treated as an employee for purposes of the taxation of distribution and the rollover rules.

- An employee's spouse who receives a distribution after the employee's death can make a rollover to an IRA but not another qualified plan.

Plans substantially made up of employee contributions. If substantially all contributions under a plan are employee contributions, then distributions will be considered to be from income until all income is distributed. Such a plan is defined by the new law as one in which 85% or more during a representative period are employee contributions. For the 85% test, deductible employee contributions are not taken into account.

The new law also provides that the Sec. 72(q) additional income tax on premature distribution from an annuity doesn't apply to distributions from a plan substantially all of the contributions of which are employee contributions.

Whether a contribution is an employee or employer contribution under such a plan will be computed under the rules of Sec. 72(f) and Section 72(m)(2). The same rules apply for determining an investment in an annuity contract for an annuitant under Section 72(e)(6).

The new law makes it clear that distribution of income from a nonexempt trust before the annuity starting date will be determined without regard to Sec. 72(e)(5) (relating to investments in pre-8-14-82 contracts) rather than Sec. 72(e)(1) (the general annuity exclusion rules).

Top-heavy plans. The new law amends the definition of key employee to exclude any officer or employee of an entity referred to in Sec. 414(d) (relating to government plans). As a result, certain accounting and nondiscrimination rules won't apply to such individuals. Also, government plans stay exempt fron the top-heavy rules.

The new law also makes it clear that cumulative accrued benefits of any employee who has not performed any services for an employer maintaining a plan during a period of five plan years ending on the determination date may be disregarded for purposes of determining whether the plan is top heavy. Previously, the "performing services" requirement had been "receiving compensation."

Employee death benefit exclusion. After repealing the employee death benefit exclusion, the '84 TRA created an estate tax exclusion under which the estate of a spouse of a plan participant doesn't have to include any community property interest in the surviving spouse-participant's interest in plan benefits. A similar rule applied for certain transfers for the gift tax. The new law repeals the exclusions for estates of decedents dying after the new law date of enactment (for estate tax purposes) and transfers after that date (for gift tax purposes). However, if the transfer is made in a community property state, it qualifies for the marital deduction.

The new law also repeals the gift tax exemption for the employee's exercise or nonexercise of an election under which an annuity would be paid to a beneficiary after the employee's death from a qualified plan, tax-deferred annuity, IRA, or military pension.

The new law modifies the grandfather rules for the repeal of the estate tax exclusion. There are two ways to qualify. First, the individual must have irrevocably elected a form of benefits and been in pay status on the effective date of the repeal. Second, under the new law, if an individual separated from service before 1-1-85 (for purposes of '84 TRA Section 525(b)(2)) or 1-1-83 (for purposes of TEFRA Section 245(c)), and otherwise meets the requirements of those sections, the individual's estate may qualify for the exclusion provided the individual elected a form of benefit before the effective date and didn't change the form of benefit before his or her death.

Affiliated service groups and leasing arrangements. The new law repeals the special authority to issue regulations to prevent abuses through the use of affiliated service groups and employee leasing arrangements (for avoiding employee benefit requirements) in favor of the general regulatory authority. The new law also reinstates certain definitions relating to affiliated service groups that were inadvertently repealed by the '84 TRA.

Sec. 401(k) deferral tests. The new law makes it clear that as long as a Sec. 401(k) cash-or-deferred arrangements meets either of the Sec. 401(k)(3) deferral percentage tests, it will be considered to pass the Sect. 401(a)(4) test (i.e., doesn't discriminate in favor of officers, shareholders, or the highly compensated).

The new law also provides for the aggregation of all contributions to Sec. 401(k) arrangements of a single employer. If an employee participates in more than one arrangement of an employer, all such arrangements are treated as one arrangement for purposes of the Sec. 401(k)(3) deferral tests.

Postretirement medical benefits. The new law conforms the treatment of postretirement medical benefits provided by a pension or annuity plan to those for welfare benefit plans. Any pension or annuity (previously "defined benefit") plan providing that benefit must maintain a separate account for each key employee (previously 5% owner) under Sec. 416(i). In addition, as with the postretirement medical benefit plan, the amount treated as an annual addition under the rules coordinating the benefit with the overall limit on qualified plan isn't subject to the 25% of compensation limit in Sec. 415(c)(1)(B). It will be subject to the dollar limit in Sec. 415(c)(1)(A).

Multiemployer employer plan withdrawal liability. The new law modifies the 9-26-80 effective date of the withdrawal liability of the Multi-Employer Pension Plan Amendments Act of 1980 for two employers who meet certain conditions. For one, the magic date is 1-16-82 while for the other it's 6-30-81.

Act Sec. 1852(a)(1), relating to IRA distributions, amends Secs. 408(a)(6) and (b)(3); Act Sec. 1852(a)(3), relating to Sec. 403(b) annuities, amends Sec. 403(b); Act Sec. 1852(a)(4)(A), clarifying the required beginning date, amends Sec. 401(a)(9)(C); Act Sec. 1852(a)(4)(B), relating to ESOPs, amends Sec. 409(d); Act Sec. 1852(a)(6), dealing with the incidental death benefit rules, adds new Sec. 401(a)(9)(G); Act Sec. 1852(a)(5), relating to required distributions and rollovers, amends Secs. 402(a)(5) and 403(a)(4)(B), (b)(8), and 4(d)(3); Act Sec. 1852(a)(2), relating to the tax on early distributions, amends Sec. 72(m)(5)(A); Act Secs. 1852(b)(1) and (2), relating to partial rollovers, amends Secs. 402(a)(5)(E) and (D); Act Sec. 1852(b)(3), relating to self-employees, adds new Sec. 402(g) and amends Sec. 402(e)(4); Act Sec. 402(a)(7), dealing with employees' spouses, amends Sec. 402(a)(7); Act Sec. 1852(c), relating to contributions to plans substantially made by employees, amends Secs. 72(e)(7)(B), (f), (m)(2) and (q)(2) and 402(b); Act Sec. 1852(d), relating to top heavy rules, amends Secs. 416(g)(4) and (i)(1)(A); Act Sec. 1852(e), relating to the estate and gift tax exclusion, repeals Sec. 406(e)(5), 407(e)(5), 2039(c) and 2517, and amends Sec. 525(b) of the 1984 TRA for estates of decedents dying after and transfers made after the date of enactment; Act Sec. 1852(f), relating to affiliated service groups, amends Sec. 526(d)(2) of the 1984 TRA; Act Sec. 1852(g), dealing with Sec. 401(k) plans, amends Sec. 401(k)(3); Act Sec. 1852(h), relating to post retirement medical benefits, amends Secs. 401(h) and 416(l); Secs. 1852(a)(7) and (b)(5)—(10), making clerical corrections amend Sec. 408(c)(1), 4974(a) and (b), 402(a)(5) and (6), 401(a), and 403(b)(8)(C) and 1984 TRA Sec. 522(e); Act Sec. 1852(i), modifying the withdrawal liability effective date, amends 1984 TRA Sec. 558; all effective as if included in the 1984 TRA and as shown above.

[¶1853] **Fringe Benefits.** Having added the fringe benefits provisions to the Code in 1984, Congress now makes a number of technical corrections.

Dependent child. The exclusions for no additional cost services and qualified employee discounts apply to the employee, his or her spouse, and dependent children (all collectively referred to as the employee). The new law defines dependent child to be a child (1) who is the dependent of the employee or (2) both of whose parents are dead and who hasn't attained age 25.

Employee discount. The new law conforms the definition of employee discount with that of no additional cost service by applying the exclusions where the price paid by the employee for goods or services provided by the employer for the use of the employee (plus spouse or dependent child) is less than the price for nonemployee customers.

Customer. The definition of customers generally includes only nonemployee customers. However, for purposes of determining gross profit percentages for the qualified employee discount exclusion, "customers" will also include employee customers.

Cafeteria plans. The new law changes the definition of permissible cafeteria plan benefits by calling them "qualified benefits" rather than "statutory nontaxable benefits." This makes it clear, according to the House Committee Report, that certain taxable benefits can be provided in the plan and don't lose their taxable status.

The new law contains two transitional rules for cafeteria plans. One applies to cafeteria plans in existence on 7-18-84 maintained under collective bargaining agreements. Those plans will be granted relief until the expiration of the last collective bargaining agreement under the plan. The second rule grants transition relief to a plan that suspended a type or amount of benefit after 2-10-84 and later reinstates the benefit.

Excise tax on fringe benefits. The '84 TRA created a 30% excise tax on certain excess benefits provided by companies with a number of lines of business, which elected to continue its pre-1984 policy. The new law makes it clear that at all times on and after 1-1-84 and before the close of the year in question, substantially all employees have to be entitled to employee discounts or services provided by the employee in one line of business for the election to remain in effect. Previously, the requirement only had to be met on 1-1-84.

Also, the new law provides that the tax only applies to employment within the U.S. In addition, there's an exception to the tax for an agricultural cooperative that's a member of a certain controlled group.

Predivestiture retired employees. The new law provides a transitional rule under which the fair market value of free telephone service provided to employees of the Bell system who retired before 1-1-84 is excluded from income.

Leased section of department store. For purposes of qualified employee discounts, a leased section of a department store is treated as part of the line of business of the store and employees of the leased section are treated as employees of the store if the leased section makes over-the-counter sales of property. The new law makes it clear that the exclusion applies to beautician services, provided there are substantial sales of beauty aids by such service in the ordinary course of business.

Working condition fringes. According to the House Committee Report, the rules for the product testing provision covering automobile testing (which were mentioned in the '84 TRA Committee Report, but not the act itself) are clarified. There must be limitations on the employee's personal use of the car. This requirement is met if there's a reasonable charge for that use.

The exception to the working condition fringe for auto salespeople also applies to auto sales managers and others who regularly perform either function. This clarification is contained in the Committee Reports.

De minimis fringe benefits. The *de minimis* fringe benefit exclusion applies to public transit passes and reimbursements, as long as the value of the total of such benefits is not more than $15 a month. This provision is contained only in the committee reports—not in the statute.

Qualified tuition reduction. A tuition reduction plan will be treated as meeting the nondiscriminatory fringe benefit requirements if it met the current requirements on the day eligibility closed and at all times thereafter, and such plan closed on 6-30-72, 6-30-74, or 12-31-75. Such plans can exclude employees covered by collectively bargained plans if the plan was a subject of good faith bargaining. Another exception applies for a particular student.

Act Sec. 1853(a)(1), defining dependent child amends Sec. 132(f)(2)(b)(ii); Act Sec. 1853(a)(2), defining employee discount, amends Sec. 132(c)(3)(A); Act Sec. 1853(a)(3), defining customer, amends Sec. 132(i); Act Sec. 1853(b)(1), converting statutory nontaxable benefits into qualified benefits, amends Secs. 125(c), (d), and (f); Act Sec. 1853(b)(2), creating a cafeteria plan transitional rule, amends Sec. 531(b)(D) of the 1984 TRA; Act Sec. 1853(b)(3), relating to suspend benefits, amends Sec. 531(b)(E), Act Sec. 1853(c), relating to the excess benefits excise tax, amends Secs. 4977(c) and adds new Sec. 4977(f); Act Sec. 1853(d), relating to retired A T &T employees, amends Sec. 559 of the 1984 TRA; Act Sec. 1853(e), relating to the definition of leased section of a department store; Act Sec. 1853(f), relates to tuition reductions, effective as if included in the 1984 TRA and as shown above.

[¶1854] **ESOPs and EWOCs.** A taxpayer may elect to defer the recognition of gain on the sale of certain qualified securities to an employee stock ownership plan or to an eligible worker-owned cooperative to the extent the corporation reinvests in qualified replacement property within a certain period of time. The new law clarifies the requirements for the sale.

Qualified securities. The new law provides that the nonrecognition provision applies only if the gain on the sale would have been long-term capital gain (i.e., held more than 6 months). Previously, the requirement had been that the stock be held more than one year.

Also, the new law clarifies that the executor of the individual who makes the sale can invest the proceeds in qualified replacement property if the individual dies before making or designating the investment.

30% test. Effective for sales after 7-18-84, the employee organization (ESOP or EWOC) must own, immediately after the sale, 30% of each class of stock (other than preferred stock described in Sec. 1504(a)(4)) or 30% of the total value of all stock (other than preferred stock described in Sec. 1504(a)(4)) of the corporation that issued the qualified securities. Ownership will be determined under the Sec. 318(a)(4) attribution rules (but only for sales after 5-6-86).

Prohibited allocations. The new law clarifies that for sales of securities after the date of enactment, the requirement that the ESOP or EWOC be maintained for the exclusive benefit of employees. Generally, no portion of the qualified securities (or assets attributable to the securities) for which a Sec. 1042 election has been made may be allocated, during the "non-allocation period" to (1) a taxpayer (i.e., seller) seeking nonrecognition treatment, (2) persons related to that taxpayer under Sec. 267(b) with certain exceptions for de minimis amounts, or (3) any person who owns (after applying the Sec. 318(a) attribution rules) more than 25% of any class of stock of the issuing corporation or any class of stock of certain related corporations. The "nonallocation period" is the 10-year period beginning with the later of the date of the sale of qualified securities or the date of the plan allocation attributable to final payment of acquisition indebtedness attributable to the sale.

If the plan doesn't meet the exclusive benefit requirement, the plan will be disqualified for those participants receiving prohibited allocations. Thus, the allocation will be included in that person's income. In addition, if there is a prohibited allocation, a 50% excise tax will be imposed on the amount involved in the prohibited allocation. The tax is to be paid by the employer maintaining an ESOP or by the EWOC involved. A special three-year statute of limitations applies to the excise tax.

NOTE: The same rules apply to allocations after a sale by an estate claiming the new 50% estate tax exclusion for qualified sales of employer securities (see ¶1173). The new rules don't apply to amounts provided to prohibited class members outside of the plan.

Qualified replacement property. Qualified replacement property is any security issued by a domestic corporation, other than the corporation that issued the securities involved in the nonrecognition transaction, that had no passive income exceeding 25% of gross receipts for the year preceding the year of the transaction. An operating corporation is one in which more than 50% of the assets are used in the active conduct of a trade or business. Financial institutions described in Secs. 581 or 593 and insurance companies described in subchapter L are operating corporations.

Special rules apply to controlling and controlled corporations to treat them as a single corporation. Also, securities will be treated as replacement property if it is a security within Sec. 165(g)(2) (other than securities issued by a governmental or political subdivision).

TRANSITIONAL RULE: An extended replacement period applies to sellers who acquired replacement property that's no longer qualified. Provided the acquisition was before 1-1-87, replacement can be made until then.

Eligible taxpayers. Generally, C corporations may not elect nonrecognition treatment for sales after March 28, 1985. However, such treatment is made available for sales made before July 1, 1985 if a binding contract was in effect on March 28, 1985 and at all times afterward.

Basis reduction. Generally, the basis of the replacement property is reduced by the nonrecognized gain. That reduction won't be taken into account for purposes of determining market discount under Sec. 1278(a)(2)(A)(ii).

Recapture on disposition. Effective for disposition of replacement property after the date of enactment, gain must be recognized on the property "disposed of" at the time of such disposition. The amount of gain that must be recognized will be the amount not recognized because of the election.

NOTE: If the taxpayer making the election owns stock representing control of the corporation that issued the replacement property and the corporation disposes of a substantial portion of its assets out of the ordinary course of business, the taxpayer will be treated as having disposed of the qualified replacement property.

Recapture won't apply: (1) to Sec. 368 reorganizations (unless the person making the election owns stock representing control on the acquiring or acquired corporation), (2) by reason of the electing person's death, (3) by gift, or (4) to any transaction subject to Sec. 1042(a).

Deductions for dividends on employer stock. The new law clarifies the general rule that permits an employer to deduct the dividends paid during the year for employer stock held by an ESOP but only to the extent they're actually paid out currently to participants or beneficiaries. Other changes are as follows:

- Although the deductible dividends are treated as distributions under the plan, they are fully taxable. They are not treated as distributions of net employee contributions. This rule doesn't apply to dividends paid before 1-1-86 if the taxpayer treated the distribution as a nontaxable return of capital in a return filed before the enactment date.

- The employer deduction for dividends paid on employer stock held by an ESOP is permitted only in the year in which the dividend is paid in cash to the participant or in the year in which the dividend is distributed by the plan to the beneficiary, effective only for dividends paid after the date of enactment. However, according to the conference report, a deduction is allowed for certain dividends, even if the stock isn't yet allocated to an account.

- Current distributions of dividends paid on employer stock allocated to a participant's account won't be treated as a disqualifying distribution under Sec. 401, 409, or 4975(e)(7).

- Treasury can disallow the dividend-paid deduction if the dividend constitutes, in substance, an avoidance of taxation.

- The corporation will be allowed the deduction whether the dividends are passed through to plan participants or to their beneficiaries.

- Dividends paid on employer stock held by an ESOP are treated as paid under a contract separate from the contract under which the stock is held. This rule doesn't apply to dividends paid before 1-1-86 if the employer deducted the dividends for the year they were paid to the ESOP and filed a return for that year before the date of enactment.

Interest earned on ESOP loans. Certain financial institutions may, under Sec. 133, exclude from gross income 50% of the interest received on loans to a corporation or ESOP to the extent the proceeds are used to acquire employer securities (within the definition of Sec. 409(l)). The new law makes it clear that for purposes of Sec. 291(e), which defines a financial institution preference item, the interest exclusion won't be treated as exempt from tax.

For purposes of the exclusion, in testing the adequacy of the stated interest rate for purposes of Section 483 (installment payments) and Sec. 1271 through 1275 (original issue discount), appropriate adjustments will be made to the applicable federal rate to take into account the partial interest exclusion.

Loans between a corporation and an ESOP won't be subject to the below- market interest rules if the interest rate is equal to the rate paid on a related securities acquisition loan to such corporation. Also, although a securities acquisition loan can't originate with a member of the controlled group, it can be held by such member. However, during the time it is held, the member won't qualify for the interest exclusion.

In addition, a loan to a corporation will be treated as a securities acquisition loan, even though the proceeds of such loans are lent to the corporate-sponsored ESOP, provided repayment is on terms substantially similar to the terms of the loan to the corporation. Repayment by the ESOP to the corporation can be on more rapid terms if plan allocations don't discriminate in favor of the highly compensated and the repayment period for the loan to the corporation doesn't exceed seven years.

ESOP's payment of estate tax. An executor of a decedent's estate will generally be relieved of estate tax liability to the extent the ESOP or EWOC is required to pay the liability on the employer securities transferred. To qualify, qualified employer securities must be acquired by the ESOP "from or on behalf of the decedent." The ESOP plan administrator or EWOC authorized officer must consent to the payment and the employer whose employees participate must guarantee payment. In addition, if the estate qualifies for the deferred payments of taxes under the installment method of Section 6166 for the interest in such securities and the executor elects to make such payments, the ESOP or EWOC may also so elect.

> **RELIEF LIMITED:** The new law makes it clear that, for estates of decedents dying after 9-27-85, only executors of those estates that qualify for the Section 6166 deferral may be relieved of the estate tax liability by the ESOP under this provision.

The new law also provides that the transfer of employer securities to an ESOP or EWOC won't be treated as a disposition or withdrawal that triggers acceleration of the remaining unpaid tax. After the transfer, the issue of whether the estate and the ESOP (or EWOC) remains eligible to make installment payments, will be treated separately. In addition, required distributions of securities (because of retirement after age 59½, death, disability, or separations from service of more than a year) won't be treated as a disposition or withdrawal requiring acceleration and won't be taken into account in determining if a later disposition will cause acceleration.

The new law also makes it clear that agreement by an EWOC can be made by an authorized officer. And whereas the employer must guarantee payment of estate tax for transfers to an ESOP, the EWOC must make the guarantee for transfers to it.

For purposes of these provisions, estate tax liability includes interest, penalty, additions to tax or any other amount relating to any tax imposed by Section 2001, as well as the tax itself.

Excise tax. There's a 10% excise tax on premature distributions of qualified securities acquired by an ESOP or EWOC under Sec. 1042. The employer (for an ESOP) or the EWOC is liable for the tax. The new law corrects a number of cross references to this effect. Also, any exchange of qualified securities because of a liquidation by the issuer into the EWOC is a transaction that meets the requirements of Section 332 (complete liquidation of subsidiaries), using a 100% rather than 80% ownership test, won't be treated as a disposition for purposes of the 10% excise tax.

Voting rights. The new law allows an ESOP or EWOC trustee, which by its by-laws require the interests of the plan to be governed by a one- vote per participant basis, to so vote the ESOPs interests in the corporation, effective on enactment. It also requires that the voting rights be passed through to participants on certain issues like merger, liquidation, dissolution and similar transactions. The pass-through provision applies to votes after 12-31-86 for stock acquired after 12-31-87.

Distributions. The new law also provides that an ESOP of a closely held business may distribute employer securities instead of cash, subject to the requirement that such securities may be resold to the employer. This permits a plan sponsored by a corporation whose stock is subject to ownership restrictions (only employees or qualified trusts) to distribute employer securities. Previously, the distribution could only be in cash.

Net unrealized appreciation. Under the new law, appreciation on ESOP held employer stock isn't realized until the stock is sold after a distribution. If there's a corporate acquisition, and employer securities are exchanged for cash or corporate securities, the basis of the securities received is stepped up to reflect the fair market value of the securities used to acquire the new ones.

Under the new law, if there's a straight stock-for-stock exchange, the ESOP carries over the basis of the old stock to the new. If there's a sale, and the proceeds are reinvested in new employer securities within 90 days (plus extensions), the plan will have the same basis as it had in the old stock. The new rule applies to transactions after 12-31-84, but for transactions before the enactment date, the reinvestment period ends the earlier of one year after the transaction or 180 days after enactment.

Act Secs. 1854(a)(1) and (4), redefining qualified securities, amends Secs. 1042(a) and (c)(1); Act Sec. 1854(a)(2), relating to the 30% test, amends Sec.

1042(b)(2) effective for sales after 7-18-84, with a 5-6-86 effective date for the Sec. 318(a) attribution rule; Act Sec. 1854(a)(3), (10), and (11)(A), relating to the exclusive benefit rules, amend Sec. 1042(b)(3) and 1042(e) and adds new Secs. 4979A, effective for sales after the date of enactment; Act Sec. 1854(a)(5), defining qualified replacement property, amends Sec. 1042(c)(4); Act Sec. 1854(a)(6), excluding C corporations, adds new Sec. 1042(c)(7) effective for sales after 3-28-85 with a binding contract exception; Act Sec. 1854(a)(7), relating to the basis reduction, amends Sec. 1042(e); Act Sec. 1854(a)(8), dealing with recapture, inserts a new Sec. 1042(e), by redesignating (e) as (f), effective for dispositions after the date of enactment; Act Sec. 1854(a)(9)(B) and (C), (10), (11), and (12) technically correct Secs. 1042(b)(4) and 1042(c)(5); Act Secs. 1854(b)(1) and (2), relating to the dividends paid deductions, amends Secs. 72(e)(5) and 404(k) for dividends paid after enactment; Act Sec. 1854(b)(3), relating to required distributions, amends Sec. 404(k)(3), Act Sec. 1854(b)(4), dealing with unreasonable compensation, amends Sec. 404(k); Act Sec. 1854(b)(5), defining recipient, amends Sec. 404(k)(2), Act Sec. 1854(c), relating to the partial interest exclusion, adds new Secs. 133(d), 291(e)(1)(iv) and 7872(f)(11) and amends Sec. 133(b); Act Sec. 1854(d), relating to estate tax liability, amends Sec. 2210(a), (c), (d) and (g); Act Sec. 1854(e), relating to the excise tax on premature distributions, amends Secs. 4978(a)(1), (b)(1), (c), (d)(1)(C), and (e)(2) and (3), and adds new Sec. 4978(d)(3); Act Sec. 1854(f)(1) relating to voting rights amends Sec. 409(e); Act Sec. 1854(f)(2), relating to net unrealized appreciation adds new Sec. 402(g) and amends Secs. 4975(e)(7) and 1042(b)(3)(B); Act Sec. 1854(f)(3), relating to stock distributions amends Sec. 409(h)(2); effective as if included in the 1984 TRA and as shown above.

[¶1855] **Miscellaneous Employee Benefit Provisions.** *Incentive stock options.* The new law clarifies that the fair market value of stock for ISOP purposes, will be determined without regard to lapse restrictions, effective as in the '84 TRA. However, the same rule, for purposes of the minimum tax, won't apply to options exercised before 1-1-85 if the option was granted under the plan adopted or corporate action taken before 5-15-84. A problem occurred because the effective date relating to ISOPs were cross-referenced incorrectly. The new law corrects the mistake.

Restricted stock. ERTA treated stock subject to Sec. 16(b) of the 1934 Securities Exchange Act as being subject to a substantial risk of forfeiture for six months after receipt. Unless the recipient elected to be taxed on receipt, the taxpayer had to treat as income the value of the stock at the expiration of the Sec. 16(b) period, less any amount paid. The new law permits certain particular individuals to elect to have those provisions apply retroactively to 1973 but limits any individual reduction in tax to $100,000.

Sec. 83(b) elections. The new law expands the group of employees who can make a Section 83(b) election to include in income the bargain element in a sale of restricted stock to an employee when the employee pays fair market value (i.e., there's no bargain element). Such employees can now make such election to include $-0- for all transfers relating to the performance of services on or before 11-18-82, not just those after 6-30-76. The election must be made on a return for any taxable year ending after 7-18-84 and beginning before the enactment date of the new law.

Act Sec. 1855(a), correcting the ISOP effective dates, amends Sec. 555(c) of the 1984 TRA effective as if included in that act. Act Sec. 1879(p), relates to restricted stock and ERTA Sec. 252, applying that section retroactively to 1973; Act Sec. 1854(c), relating to Sec. 83(b) elections, amends 1984 TRA Sec. 556(b), for transfers before 6-30-76.

Tax Exempt Bonds

[¶1861] **Mortgage Subsidy Bonds.** The new law makes a number of changes to the mortgage subsidy bond provisions of 1984 TRA. First, Treasury may grant extension of time for publishing or submitting annual policy statements that issuers of mortgage subsidy bonds are required to make. Those statements explain measures taken to comply with the objective of providing low income housing.

The new law also clarifies that veterans eligible for loans financed by qualified veterans' mortgage bonds must apply for financing by the later of 30 years leaving active service or January 31, 1985 (moved from January 1, 1985).

Finally, the new law provides that the annual policy statement requirement along with the information reporting the state certification requirements will be treated as met if the issuers in good faith tried to meet the requirements and the failure to so meet them is due to inadvertent error.

Act Sec. 1861(a), relating to policy statements, adds new Sec. 103A(o)(4); Act Sec. 1861(b), relating to veterans loans amends Sec. 103A(o)(4)(B); Act Sec. 1861(c), dealing with good faith efforts, amends Sec. 103A(c)(2); all effective as if included in the 1984 TRA.

[¶1862] **Mortgage Credit Certificates.** The new law provides that the requirements that apply to qualified mortgage subsidy bonds dealing with information reporting, state certification, and annual policy statements will also apply to mortgage credit certificate issuers. In addition the good faith effort rules that apply to mortgage subsidy bonds under Secs. 103A(c)(2)(B) and (C) will also apply to mortgage credit certificates. The new law also clarifies how the mortgage credit can be carried forward for three years. Finally, for purposes of figuring the credit, the credit is based on interest paid or accrued (as opposed to incurred).

Act Sec. 1862, relating to qualified mortgage credit certificates, amends Secs. 25(a)(1)(B), (c)(2)(A), and (e)(1)(B) and redesignates Sec. 6708 as 6709; effective as if included in the 1984 TRA.

[¶1863] **Advance Refunding of Certain Veterans' Bonds.**
The new law provides that certain issuers may advance refund up to
$300 million of qualified veterans' mortgage funds. The refunding
replaces the 1984 TRA provision allowing that agency to receive
cash flow loans not exceeding $300 million from the Federal Financ-
ing Bank. There's also a special carryforward of the amounts under
the unused "volume" cap. According to both Committee Reports, Oregon is the only state affected.

Act Sec. 1863, relating to advance refunding, amends Sec. 613 of the 1984
TRA, effective on the date of enactment with an exception.

[¶1864] **Private Activity Bonds Volume Limitations.** Generally, a state's annual private activity bond volume limitation may
only be used to finance facilities within the state. There are exceptions provided the state's share of the facility's use exceeds the
state's share of bonds issued to finance the facilities. Those exceptions are (1) eligible sewage and waste disposed facilities or facilities
for the local furnishing of electricity and gas; (2) certain water furnishing facilities, and (3) qualified hydroelectric generating facilities.

This provision is effective for bonds issued after the new law's
date of enactment. However, states may elect to apply the provision
to bonds issued on or before that date.

Allocation to nongovernmental units. Under the new law, a state
may allocate its private activity bond volume limitations to issuing
authorities that aren't governmental units as well as those that are.

Exempt activities. The determination of whether facilities forming a part of an airport, dock, wharf, mass commuting facility, or
trade or convention center may be financed outside a state's volume
limitations is to be made on a property-by-property basis rather
than by reference to the entire facility. However, all property to be
financed under this exception must be owned by or on behalf of the
governmental unit.

Information reporting. The new law allows Treasury to require
reports on allocation of volume limitations.

Carryforward of unused bond authority. Under the new law, the
election to carryforward any unused volume limitation must be
made for specific projects. Identification of specific projects must be
more specific than the '84 TRA seemed to indicate (including the address of the project); in fact, the conference report considers identification to be of primary importance.

Act Sec. 1864(a), relating to out-of-state facilities, adds new Sec. 103(n)(13),
for bonds issued after the new law's date of enactment with an election to
include previous issues; Act Sec. 1864(b), relating to in-state allocations,
amends Sec. 103(n)(6); Act Sec. 1864(c), relating to publicly owned facilities,

amends Sec. 103(n)(7)(c)(i); Act Sec. 1864(d), dealing with information report-
ing, adds new Sec. 103(l)(2)(f); Act Sec. 1864(c), related to the unused bond
cap carryforward, amends Sec. 103(n)(1); all effective as if included in the
1984 TRA and as shown above.

【¶1865】 Federal Guarantees. The new law conforms the rules
for obligations issued to finance certain energy projects under federal programs to the general rules denying tax-exempt status if
there's a federal guarantee present. There's transitional relief for a
convention center in Carbondale, Illinois, financed under a guarantee issued by the Farmer's Home Administration before July 1,
1984. There's also a transitional exception for four solid waste facilities for which it's anticipated that the federal government will purchase a more than insignificant amount of the output and expenditures were made before October 19, 1983. Those facilities are located
in Annapolis and Aberdeen, Maryland, Portsmouth, Virginia and
Charleston, South Carolina. Another exemption is created for a thermal transfer facility near Tullahoma, Tennessee.

Act Sec. 1865, relating to federal guarantees, amends Sec. 103(h)(5), effec-
tive as if included in the '84 TRA.

【¶1866】 Limit on Small Issue Exception. Under the new
law, small issue industrial development bonds can (in some cases) be
refunded (through other bonds) to reduce the interest rate on the
borrowing, even though a beneficiary benefits from more than $40
million in total tax-exempt financing. Such IDBs can be refunded if
(1) the maturity date of the refunding bond isn't later than that of
the refunded bond; (2) the amount of the refunding bonds doesn't
exceed the refunded bonds; (3) the interest rate on the refunding
bond is less than the interest rate on the refunded bond; and (4) the
proceeds of the refunding bonds are used to redeem the refunded
bonds not later than 30 days after the date the refunding bonds are
issued.

Act Sec. 1866, creates exceptions to the refunding prohibition of Section
623 of the 1984 TRA.

【¶1867】 Exception to Arbitrage Limitation. The new law
corrects a reference to a resource recovery project of Essex County,
New Jersey contained in an exception to the arbitrage restrictions
(i.e., limiting the investment of bond proceeds in bonds that aren't
related to the purpose of the borrowing). It also expands a rule that
applies to Muskogee, Oklahoma to include a limited exception from
the IDB arbitrage rebate rules.

Act Sec. 1867 amends Sec. 624(c)(2) of the 1984 TRA, and extends an ex-
ception to the arbitrage restrictions, as if included in that act.

[¶1868] **Arbitrage Restrictions for Student Loan Bonds.** The new law makes it clear that a series of refundings of student loan bonds are included in the exception from coverage of the regs treating student loan bonds as arbitrage bonds for purposes of the arbitrage restrictions.

Act Sec. 1868, relating to student loan bonds, amends Sec. 625(a)(3)(C) of the 1984 TRA as if included in that act.

[¶1869] **Consumer Loan Bonds.** The new law renames consumer loan bonds as private loan bonds. This makes it clear that all bonds for which 5% or more of the proceeds are used to finance loans to nonexempt persons, are subject to the consumer loan bond restrictions, which, in turn, are subject to exceptions for certain types of bonds.

The new law creates transitional exceptions for (1) Baltimore, Maryland; (2) an Illinois student loan program; (3) St. Johns River Power Park, Florida; (4) the White Pine Power Project, Nevada; and (5) the Eastern Maine Electric Cooperative, and according to both committee reports; (6) Mead-Phoenix Power Project.

The private loan bond restriction won't apply to tax-increment financing bonds issued before August 16, 1986, substantially all of the proceeds of which are used to finance (1) certain governmental improvements to real property; (2) acquisition of such property under eminent domain, preparing the property for new use, or transfer to a private developer; or (3) payments of reasonable relocation costs to the property's previous users. The activities must be under a redevelopment plan adopted before the bonds are issued. In addition, repayment of the issued must be secured by increases in property tax revenue from the property. The provision applies to bonds issued before 8-16-86.

Act Sec. 1869, relating to consumer loan bonds, amends Code Secs. 103(o) and Sec. 626(b)(2)(A) of the 1984 TRA effective as if included in that act and as shown above.

[¶1870] **Limitation of Use for Land Acquisition.** The 1984 TRA limited the issuance of bonds for use in acquiring land. The new law makes it clear, that an issue won't be tax exempt if 50% or more of the proceeds will be used to acquire land for an industrial park.

Act Sec. 1870, relating to land acquisiton amends Sec. 103(b)(16)(A), as if included in the 1984 TRA.

[¶1871] **Non-Code Bonds.** The new law makes it clear that tax-exempt bonds issued under provisions of the law other than the

Tax Reform Act of 1986

Code, must be issued in registered form. Also, the consumer loan bond rules apply to those non-Code bonds.

The new law also conforms a limited exception permitting advance refunding of certain bonds for facilities issued before the 1984 TRA.

Act Sec. 1871(a), relating to non-Code bonds, amends Sec. 103(m)(1), effective for bonds issued after 3-28-85. Act Sec. 1871(b), making a conforming amendment, amends Sec. 103(b), effective as if included in the 1984 TRA.

[¶1872] Effective Date Clarification. The new law clarifies the provisions to which the effective dates of '84 TRA Sec. 631(c) applies (i.e., bonds issued after 12-31-83 with a 10-19-83 binding contract exception). They include, among others, the prohibition on federal guarantees, aggregate small issue IDBs, restrictions of financing certain facilities and aggregation of related facilities. Only those provisions are subject to the binding contract exception, which itself is clarified. The binding contract exception applies only to (1) activities for which construction began before 10-19-83 and was finished on or after that date or (2) property acquired on or after 10-19-83. The clarification to the binding contract exception applies to bonds issued after 3-28-85.

Health club facilities. The prohibition on financing health clubs applies to bonds issued after 4-12-84, subject to transitional rules.

Special exception. The new law creates an exception to the '84 TRA rules (especially the ban on federal guarantees) for a solid waste disposal facility in Huntsville, Alabama.

Act Sec. 1872, relating to effective dates amends Sec. 631 and repeals Sec. 632(a)(1) of the 1984 TRA, effective as shown above.

[¶1873] Exceptions. The new law makes it clear that items exempted from the rules under Section 632(a) of the '84 TRA are excepted from the arbitrage rules and the items exempted under Sec. 632(d) are exempt from the consumer (private) loan bond rules.

The new law excepts five hydroelectric generating facilities (Hastings, Minnesota, Warren County, New York, and Richmond, Placerville, and Los Banos, California) from the small-issue IDB rules.

Act Sec. 1873, creating exceptions to the private activity bond rules, amends Sec. 632 of the 1984 TRA, effective as if included in the act.

Miscellaneous Provisions

[¶1875] Corrections to the Technical Corrections. *Tax preferences of trusts and estates.* For purposes of the alternative minimum tax, itemized deductions as well as the preferences, themselves, must be apportioned between the estate or trust, on the one hand, and the beneficiaries on the other, according to regs.

Corporate provision. Under prior law, if a shareholder of a 50% owned corporation transfers stock of that corporation to another 50% owned corporation in exchange for property, the transaction was treated as a redemption of the shareholder's stock in the acquiring corporation. The transferred stock was considered to be transferred as a contribution to capital of the acquiring corporation. Its basis would be the transferor's basis plus any gain recognized.

The new law provides that the contribution to capital rule won't apply if the shareholder is treated as having exchanged its stock under Sec. 302(a). The corporation will be treated as buying the stock for purposes of Sec. 338. However, the tax treatment for the shareholder remains the same.

Pension provisions. The new law conforms the rules relating to qualified rollover distributions to the 10% additional income tax on early withdrawals from qualified plans by key-employees and 5% owners. Generally, distributions from a qualified trust or annuity made after the date of enactment to a 5% owner may not be rolled over into another qualified plan. Distributions after July 18, 1984, but on or before the date of enactment of the new law may not be rolled over if any part of the distribution is a benefit attributable to contributions made while the employee is a key employee in a top heavy plan.

5% owner defined. A 5% owner is any individual who is a 5% owner (under Section 416(i)) at any time during the five plan years preceding the year of distribution. If there's a qualified total distribution, a 5% owner must wait five years from the time of distribution to make a tax-free rollover from the IRA, to which the distribution was rolled over, to another qualified plan.

The new law also makes it clear that the '84 TRA's repeal of the rule relating to the return of excess contributions made on behalf of a self- employed, applies to contributions made in tax years after 12-13-83.

SEPs. In the area of simplified employee pensions, the new law conforms the limits on certain distributions of excess IRA contributions and the limits on employer contributions on behalf of certain officers, shareholders or owner employees to the Sec. 415(c)(1)(A) dollar limits on annual additions to qualified defined contribution plans ($30,000), effective as if included in TEFRA.

Keoghs. In the area of Keogh plans, the new law makes it clear the earned income of a self-employed is determined without regard to the deductions allowable for Keogh contributions, solely for the purpose of determining to the extent the contributions are ordinary and necessary.

The new law takes into account the fact that a self-employed individual's deductions for contributions aren't necessarily limited to the cost of his or her own benefits. As a result effective as if included in TEFRA, a self-employed can deduct his or her allocable share of Keogh contributions (for example, his or her partnership share if the business is a partnership).

Other pension provisions. The new law also takes into account that there may be a double deduction in determining compensation under Sec. 219(f)(1). Previously, the term "compensation" was earned income under Sec. 401(c)(2) reduced by the amount allowable as a deduction under Sec. 62(7). Since Sec. 401(c)(2) already took into account the deduction rules under Section 404, a double deduction may have been possible. The reference to Sec. 62(7) has been removed, effective as if included in TEFRA.

Under the new law, the rule precluding anticipated cost-of-living adjustments to the overall benefit limits applies to limit benefits payable as a single life annuity beginning at age 62—not just those paid in alternative forms, those beginning before age 62, and those beginning after age 65.

In the withholding area, the new law exempts from the pension withholding rules, amounts subject to withholding of tax on income paid to nonresident aliens by the person paying the amount on which would be so subject but for a tax treaty.

Finally, the new law points out that a disabled's compensation is determined under Sec. 415(c)(3)(C) for all defined contribution plans.

Partnerships. The new law extends the special three-year period of limitations for assessing income tax against partnerships to include assessments of any addition to tax or additional amount arising under subchapter A of Chapter 68.

In addition, under prior law, the general deficiency procedures generally don't apply to certain computational adjustments for any partnerships (which are subject to their own special rules). The new law creates exceptions for: (1) affected items that require partner level determinations or (2) items that are "nonpartnership" items (under Sec. 6231(e)(1)(B). The general procedure will be applied separately to each deficiency attributable to each item. Also, any notice or proceeding under the general rules won't preclude or be precluded by any other notice, proceeding, or determination dealing with the partner's tax liabilities. This coordinates the Tax Court deficiency rules for partner level determinations arising from a partnership proceeding with the deficiency procedures applying to the taxpayer from items unrelated to the partnership proceeding. As a result, a second deficiency notice is possible in certain instances.

Interest on carrybacks and refunds. For purposes of computing interest on refunds arising from net operating loss carrybacks when a tentative adjustment claim is filed, the refund is treated as filed on the date that the tentative adjustment claim is filed. The effective date of this '84 TRA provision is for applications filed after 7-18-84.

Nominee reporting. The new law requires a nominee holding an interest in a trust or an estate for another person to supply to the trust or estate, the name and address of such person along with any other information Treasury requires. The nominee in turn, must forward the information given to him or her by the estate or trust fiduciary to the person for whom the interest is held. *Result:* Information should be passed through more easily. Note that Treasury will provide the rules for transmitting the information.

Gain from dispositions of foreign corporate stock. Under Section 1248, gain on the sale or exchange of stock of foreign corporations will be treated as a dividend to the extent of earnings and profits if, among other things, the United States taxpayer owns 10% or more of the stock. The new law removes, from coverage of these rules, gain realized on exchanges to which Section 356 (receipt of additional consideration in an otherwise tax-free exchange) applies.

Act Sec. 1875(a), dealing with the minimum tax, amends Sec. 58(c); Act Sec. 1875(b), dealing with the capital contribution rule, amends Sec. 304(a)(1); Act Secs. 1875(c)(1), (2), and (8), amends Code Secs. 402(a)(5)(F)(ii) and 408(d)(3), and 1984 TRA Sec. 713(c), effective as shown above; Act Sec. 1875(c)(5), relating to returns of excess contributions, amends 1984 TRA Sec. 713(d)(1); Act Sec. 1875(c)(6), raising the SEP limit, amends Secs. 219(b)(2)(c) and 408(d)(5) for years beginning after 12-31-83; Act Sec. 1875(c)(7), dealing with the definition of earned income for Keogh plans, amends Secs. 404(a)(8)(C) and (D); Act Secs. 1875(c)(3) and (4), relating to the definitions of AGI and compensation, amend Secs. 62(7) and 219(f)(1), for years beginning after 12-31-83; Act Sec. 1875(c)(9), relating to annuity adjustments, amends Sec. 415(b)(2)(E)(iii); Act Sec. 1875(c)(10), relating to withholding, amends Sec. 3405(d)(1)(B), Act Sec. 1875(c)(11), relating to disability income, amends Sec. 415(c)(3); Act Sec. 1875(d)(1), relating to a statute of limitations adds Sec. 6229(g), effective for partnership years beginning after 9-3-82; Act Sec. 1875(d)(2), dealing with deficiency procedures, amends Secs. 6230, 6213 and 6503, for partnership years beginning after 9-3-82 (TEFRA's effective date); Act Sec. 1875(d)(3), dealing with carrybacks under Sec. 6611(f), effective for applications filed after 7-18-84; Act Sec. 1875(d)(4), misnumbered (3), relating to trust and estate passthroughs, amends Sec. 6034A, effective for taxable years of trusts and estates beginning after the enactment date. Act Sec. 1875(e), correcting a cross reference, amends Sec. 201(a) of the 1965 Land and Water Conservation Fund Act; Act Sec. 1875(f) corrects spelling; Act Sec. 1875(g), relating to exemptions to the foreign stock sales rules, amends Sec. 1248(g), effective for exchanges after 3-1-86.

[¶1876] **Foreign Sales Corporations.** The new law makes a number of changes to the FSC rules.

FSC income without administrative pricing rules. The new law provides that "effectively connected foreign trade income" that a FSC earns without using administrative pricing rules (Sec. 923(a)(2) nonexempt income), will be treated like other effectively connected foreign trade income. Taxes on that income won't be creditable, but distributions out of earnings and profits will qualify for a 100% dividends-received deduction (i.e., they will be subject to tax only at the FSC level).

FSC income under Sec. 1248. The new law changes the prior treatment under which FSC earnings and profits attributable to certain foreign trade income were excluded from ordinary income treatment under Sec. 1248 on disposition of foreign corporate stock. Under the new law, Sec. 923(a)(2) non-exempt income and certain foreign trade income, which would be taxable on a distribution, are subject to ordinary income treatment under Section 1248.

Preference cutbacks. The new law makes it clear that the Sec. 291 preference cutback for FSCs applies to the FSC and *not* the corporate shareholder. The exempt portion of foreign trade income is reduced from 32% to 30% for income determined without administrative pricing rules and from $16/23$ to $15/23$ for income determined with them. The portion of foreign trade income will be adjusted for shareholders for whom there are no preference cutbacks.

Also, the deemed distribution of $1/17$ of a DISC's excess taxable income applies, as with the preference cutback factor, only to C corporations. And a special rule is provided to determine the method for computing such distribution attributable to boycott income.

Foreign trade income under Subpart F. The new law clarifies that there will be no taxation under Subpart F's anti-avoidance rules of income already taxed at the FSC level.

Dividends-received deduction. In addition to the old 100% dividends-received deduction for distributions from earnings and profits attributable to foreign trade income of a FSC, the new law adds an 85% deduction for dividends from earnings and profits attributable to qualified interest and carrying charges derived from a transaction resulting in foreign trade income. Gross income giving rise to earnings and profits from both foreign trade income and qualified interest and carrying charges won't be taken into account to calculate a dividends-received deduction under the general rules for the other income of the FSC.

Foreign tax credit limitation. The new law provides that distributions from a FSC (or former FSC) out of earnings and profits attributable to qualified interest and carrying charges, as well as foreign trade income, are subject to a separate foreign tax credit limitation from the other items listed in Section 904(d)(1).

The new law also provides that taxes paid or accrued by a foreign corporation to a foreign country or United States possession on income effectively connected with the conduct of a trade or business within the United States won't be taken into account for purposes of the deemed paid credit under Section 902. In addition, no accumulated profits attributable to such income will be taken into account for purposes of the credit. This provision prevents certain corporate U.S. shareholders from taking a double credit.

Exchange of information. Under the new law, a corporation can't continue to be an FSC if its country of incorporation ceases to qualify as a host country for FSCs. The new law also would grant host country status to certain countries entering information exchange agreements and tax treaties with the United States.

Finally, effective for periods after 1985, the principal bank account of an FSC (other than a small FSC), must be maintained in a U.S. possession or a country that qualifies as a host country for that entire taxable year.

Possessions taxation. Under the new law a U.S. possession can impose a tax on any FSC income attributable to the sale of property or the performance of services for ultimate use, consumption, or disposition within the possession. Also, a U.S. possession can exempt from tax any foreign trade income or interest, dividends, or carrying charge of a FSC. In addition, no provision of law may be construed as requiring any tax imposed by the U.S. on a FSC to be covered over (or otherwise transferred) to any U.S. possession. Finally, the rule exempting FSCs from the Sec. 934 limitation of reduction in income tax liability incurred to the Virgin Islands has been repealed.

Interest on DISC-related deferred liability. The new law makes it clear that an interest charge is imposed on the deferred income tax liability of a former DISC in the same way it's imposed on a DISC.

Exemption of accumulated DISC income. Generally, pre-1985 accumulated DISC income is exempt from tax by treating post-1984 distributions as previously taxed income for which there had been a deemed distribution. The new law provides that distributions in liquidation will be treated as "an actual distribution" of previously taxed income. Also, the earnings and profits of any corporation receiving a distribution that's treated as previously taxed income will be increased by the amount of the tax-free distribution.

Taxable year. The '84 TRA's provision requiring conformity of tax years between FSCs (and DISCs) and their shareholders is effective for taxable years beginning after 12-31-84.

Qualified DISC distributions. The new law, in the case of a distribution to a C corporation, would treat $16/17$ of a DISC distribution that's designed to meet the 95%-qualified-export-receipts test as coming from accumulated DISC income. The balance is treated as previously taxed income. That's because post-1984 law treats only $1/17$ of income as a deemed distribution and currently taxable.

Receipts from another FSC. An FSC will now be able to treat receipts received from another FSC that's a member of the same controlled group as foreign trading gross receipts if no FSC in the group uses the pricing rules of Sec. 925(a)(1) (the gross receipts methods of calculating income).

Former export trading corporation. Under the new law, corporations that had been export trade corporations but were not such for their most recent taxable year ending before 7-18-84, may qualify for the 1984 law's treatment of active export trade corporation. This treatment includes exempting certain income from U.S. tax.

To qualify, the former export trade corporation must be precluded by Sec. 971(a)(3)(B) from again electing such status or must elect, within six months after the new law's date of enactment, never to qualify for such status.

Accumulated DISC income of cooperatives. Amounts distributed from accumulated DISC income to a cooperative described in Sec. 1381 that are excluded from income won't be included in the gross income of the cooperative's members when distributed to them. In addition, the cooperative isn't allowed a deduction when distribution to the members occur.

Contracts and effective dates. The foreign management, foreign economic process, and administrative pricing prerequisites will be treated as met for (1) any lease of longer than three years that was entered before 1-1-85, (2) any contract under which the completed contract method of accounting, which was entered into before 1-1-85, and (3) any other type of contract that was entered into before 1-1-85, but only for the first three taxable years of the FSC ending after that date or as regs will prescribe.

Act Sec. 1876(a), relating to FSC non-exempt income, amends Secs. 927(d)(6) and 1248(d)(6); Act Sec. 1876(b), dealing with preference cutbacks, amends Sec. 212(a)(4); Act Sec. 1876(c), dealing with Subpart F, amends Secs. 951(e) and 952(b); Act Secs. 1876(d)(1) and (j), refining the dividends-received deduction, amend Sec. 245(c); Act Secs. 1876(d)(2) and (3), relating to the foreign tax credit, amend Secs. 904(d)(1)(D) and 906(b); Act Sec. 1876(e), dealing with exchange of information, amends Sec. 927(e)(3) and for periods after 3-28-85, Sec. 924(c)(2); Act Sec. 1876(f), coordinating FSCs with possessions taxation, amends Sec. 927(e)(5) and repeals 934(F), as added by 1984 TRA Sec. 801(d)(7)(F); Act Sec. 1876(g), clarifying the interest rules for deferred liability, adds Sec. 995(F)(7); Act Sec. 1876(h), dealing with the exemption for accumulated DISC income, amends Sec. 805(b)(2)(A) of the 1984 TRA; Act Sec. 1876(i), relating to taxable years, amends Sec. 805(a)(4), effective for taxable years beginning after 12-31-84; Act Sec. 1876(k), concerning DISC distribution to C corporations, amends Sec. 996(a)(2); Act Sec. 1876(l), dealing with controlled groups amends Sec. 924(F)(1); Act Sec. 1876(m) relates to certain former export trade corporations; Act Sec. 1876(n), dealing with distributions to cooperatives, amends 1984 TRA Sec. 805(b)(2); Act Sec. 1876(o), clarifying the binding contract exception, amends '84 TRA Sec. 805(a)(2); Act Sec. 1876(p), making clerical amendments, amends Secs. 995(f) and 901, and 1984 TRA

Secs. 802(c) and 805(a)(2)(A); all effective as if included in the 1984 TRA and as shown above.

〔¶1877〕 Highway Revenue Provisions. The new law makes technical corrections to three areas of the highway revenue provisions. First, the new law makes it clear that the credit for gasoline and special fuels applies to, among others, amounts payable to the taxpayer under Sec. 6427 for any qualified diesel-powered highway vehicle bought, as well as for fuels used for nontaxable purposes or resold, during the taxable year, regardless of the noncommercial aviation special rules.

Second, the new law allows a full 15¢ a gallon refund (instead of 12¢) of excise tax on diesel fuel used in a school bus engaged in transporting students and school employees.

Third, the additional 6% excise tax on a later sale of a piggyback trailer originally sold after 7-17-84 and before 7-18-85, won't apply to any sale occurring more than six years after the original sale.

Act Sec. 1877(a), relating to the special fuels credit, amends Sec. 34(a)(3); Act Sec. 1877(b), dealing with the diesel tax refund, amends Sec. 6427(b)(2); Act Sec. 1877(c) phasing out the tax on piggyback trailers, amends Sec. 4051(d)(3); all effective as if included in the 1984 TRA.

〔¶1878〕 Miscellaneous Revenue Provisions. *Capital gain holding period.* To conform the market discount bond rules to the capital gain holding period, these bonds don't include those with a maturity of six months or less.

Sport fishing tax. The new law adds fishing hook disgorgers to the list of items subject to the 10% sport fishing equipment tax.

Excise tax exemption for certain helicopter uses. The exemption from aviation excise taxes for helicopters engaged in qualified timber and hard mineral activities where no FAA facilities are used, has been expanded to fully cover such use for oil and gas activities.

The language of the '84 TRA had inadvertently extended the rules to only some oil and gas activities.

Estate tax credit. The new law clarifies an estate tax credit for two specific contributions of land to the Toiyabe National Forest.

Debt-financed realty of tax-exempt organizations. The 1984 TRA exempted certain debt-financed realty held by qualified exempt organizations from the unrelated business income tax. An organization will qualify for the exemption if the organization is in a partnership (with taxable entities) as long as each allocation to a qualified organization is a qualified allocation under Sec. 168(j)(6). The exemption also applies if each partner is a qualified organization.

The new law makes it clear that, for purposes of the all-qualified organization exemption, an organization won't be considered qualified if any of its income is unrelated business income. For purposes of the other exemption, Treasury may treat the allocation rule as met if it is convinced that there's no tax avoidance potential.

The new law also makes it clear that a qualified organization includes a Sec. 170(b)(1)(A)(ii) educational organization and its affiliated support organizations under Sec. 509(c)(3), as well as certain pension trusts.

Targeted jobs credit. The new law sorts out the problem of two Sec. 51(j)s by designating the successor employer section as Sec. 51(k) and the election out as Sec. 51(j).

Military housing rollover. The new law corrects a provision to the '84 TRA to conform to the committee report for that act. As a result, the extended nonrecognition period for rollover of gain of a personal residence by certain military personnel won't expire before the day that's one year after the last day the taxpayer is stationed outside the United States or is required to reside in government quarters at a remote base site in the United States. This period can't exceed eight years after the old residence's date of sale. The '84 TRA didn't contain the "one-year" period.

Deduction for demolition costs. The new law provides that the prohibition on deducting costs incurred in demolition applies only to demolitions beginning after 7-18-84 (other than to demolitions of certified historic structure). If a demolition is delayed until the completion of a replacement structure on the same site, the demolition will be treated as beginning when the construction began. There's a transitional rule for one bank headquarters building and one company's petroleum storage facilities.

Tribal governments treated as states. The new law corrects a cross reference in the section expanding the treatment of tribal governments as states.

Regulated investment companies. The new law provides that adequate records of shareholders need no longer be kept by a regulated investment company. These records were originally intended to assure that the company was not a personal holding company. Under pre-'84 TRA law, keeping adequate records was a requirement for RIC status.

However, the new law provides that the investment company taxable income of an RIC that doesn't keep these records will be taxed at the highest corporate tax rate under Section 11(b).

KEEP RECORDS: Unless an RIC is also a PHC, the RIC will have to keep shareholder records to take advantage of the graduated rates in the lower tax brackets.

Act Sec. 1878(a), dealing with market discount, amends TRA Sec. 1001(b); Act Sec. 1878(b), relating to sport fishing, amends Sec. 4162(a)(6); Act Sec. 1878(c), dealing with helicopters, amends Secs. 4041(l)(1) and 4261(e)(1); Act

Sec. 1878(d), relating to gifts of land, amends 1984 TRA Section 1028(b); Act Sec. 1878(e), relating to UBI, amends Sec. 514(c)(9); Act Sec. 1878(f), dealing with the targeted jobs credit, amends Sec. 51(j); Act Sec. 1878(g), dealing with housing rollovers, amends Sec. 1034(h)(2); Act Sec. 1878(h), creating a transitional rule for demolition costs, amends 1984 TRA Sec. 1063(c), effective for demolition beginning after July 18, 1984, Act Sec. 1878(i), dealing with tribal governments, amends the 1984 TRA Sec. 1065(b); Act Sec. 1878(j), relating to RICs, amends Secs. 852(a) and (b)(1); all effective as if included in the 1984 TRA and as shown above.

[¶1879] Miscellaneous Provisions. *Estimated tax penalty waiver.* The '84 TRA tightened the estimated tax rules. The rules were designed to increase liability from the beginning of 1984. The new law grants relief by allowing individuals until 4-15-85 and corporations until 3-15-85 to pay the full 1984 income tax liabilities without incurring any additions to tax because of underpayments to estimated tax, to the extent the underpayments were due to the changes.

Orphan drug credit. The term "clinical testing" for purposes of the orphan drug credit is, under the '84 TRA, defined with reference to the date an application is approved under the Federal Food, Drug, and Cosmetic Act. The new law expands the term by also defining it with reference, for drugs that are biological products, to the date on which a license for such drug is issued under Sec. 351 of the Public Health Services Act.

The new law redefines "rare disease or condition" as one that (1) affects less than 200,000 people in the United States or (2) affects more than 200,000 in the United States but for which there's no reasonable expectation that the cost of developing and making available in the United States a drug for such disease or condition will be recovered from sales of the drug in the United States.

The changes to the credit apply to amounts paid or incurred after December 31, 1982, in taxable years ending after that date.

Nonconventional source fuel credit. Under the new law, the sale of qualifying fuel to an unrelated person, by a corporation that files a consolidated return with the corporation producing the fuel, can qualify for the nonconventional source fuel credit. This provision is effective as if included in Sec. 231 of the 1980 Crude Oil Windfall Profit Tax Act—that is, taxable years ending after 1979.

Fringe benefit reports. The new law clarifies that the return filing and recordkeeping requirements of Sec. 6039D apply to qualified group legal services plans, cafeteria plans, and educational assistance plans.

Joint Committee report requirements. The new law repeals the requirement that the Joint Committee on Taxation submit an annual report to Congress on proposed refunds or credits in excess of $200,000, including names of the taxpayers and amounts involved.

Recovery period for real property. The new law makes it clear that the statutory recovery period with reference to Sec. 467(a) rental agreements is 19 years. The change is effective as if included in the Imputed Interest Act, generally for property placed in service after May 8, 1985, with binding contract exceptions.

Rural electric cooperatives. The new law clarifies that any organization that's tax exempt and that provides electric service on a cooperative basis can maintain a Sec. 401(k) cash-or-deferred arrangement. The same is true of a national association of such rural cooperatives. This provision is effective for plan years beginning after 12-31-84.

Newly discovered oil. Under the new law, newly discovered oil includes for windfall profit purposes, production from a property that didn't produce commercial quantities during 1978. For those purposes only, a property won't be treated as producing oil in commercial quantities during 1978, if during 1978, (1) the aggregate amount of oil produced didn't exceed 2,200 barrels (whether or not the oil was sold), and (2) no well on the property was in production for a total of more than 72 hours. According to the Conference report, a dual well is treated as two wells. This provision applies to oil removed after February 29, 1980.

Investment credit for Sec. 501(d) organizations. The new law provides that any business of Sec. 501(d) religious or apostolic associations, conducted for the common benefit of its members and the income of which is included in gross income, is to be treated as a Sec. 511 unrelated trade or business for purposes of the investment credit. As a result, provided certain requirements are met, the credit is passed through to its members pro rata, in the same manner as income is apportioned.

The used property and recapture provisions will apply at the organizational level (but the increase in tax from recapture will be passed through). In addition, no individual can claim a credit under this section if that person can claim a credit in his or her own right. The new provisions are effective for periods after 1978. A special rule extends the period for claiming refunds or credits by use of the section, for closed years, to one-year after the date of enactment.

Mutual savings bank. A stock association that's treated as a mutual savings bank for purposes of computing a bad debt deduction will now be treated as a mutual savings bank for purposes of the tax-exemption for mutual organizations insuring these banks. This provision is effective for taxable years ending after August 13, 1981 (as if included in ERTA).

Reorganization of investment companies. For purposes of determining if certain investment companies qualify for tax-free reorganization, the stock of a regulated investment company, real estate investment trust, or diversified investment company won't be treated as stock of a single issuer under the diversification requirements of Sec. 368(a)(2)(F)(ii). This provision is effective as if included in Sec. 2131 of the 1976 Tax Reform Act.

S corporation changes. For purposes of the qualified trust requirements, shares of a trust treated as separate trusts under Sec. 663(c) (the DNI rules) will be treated as separate trusts under the S corporation rules. Also, the S corporation's accumulated adjustments account (amounts available for distribution) won't be reduced because of federal taxes that arose while the corporation was a C corporation. Both provisions apply to taxable years beginning after 1982.

QTIP gift tax. The new law provides that effective for gifts after 1985, the QTIP gift tax election made under Sec. 2523(f) must be made under the gift tax return rules of Sec. 6075(b). Previously it had to be made by April 15 after the calendar year of transfer. In addition, a special rule allows a certain donor to file a late return.

Windfall profit tax exemption. Oil interests held by the Episcopal Royalty Company will be treated as "qualified charitable interests," for oil recovered after 2-29-80.

Refunds for medicinal alcohol. Medicinal alcohol produced in Puerto Rico and the Virgin Islands will qualify for refunds of the tax on distilled spirits paid when the alcohol is brought into the United States. The producers will be treated as U.S. persons. The refund is determined as if tax is paid at the rate prescribed in Section 7652(f). The new law applies to articles brought into the United States after the date of enactment, with a clarification for allowable payments to Puerto Rico and the Virgin Islands.

Self-insured workers compensation funds. The new law creates a moratorium on IRS collection activities beginning on the date of enactment and ending on 8-16-87 for certain self-insured workers compensation funds. The provision does the following:

- The time to file a Tax Court petition won't expire before 8-16-87 (if the time to file hadn't expired before 8-16-86).
- All pending and continuing audits are suspended until 8-16-87.
- The running of interest is suspended from 8-16-86 to 8-16-87.
- The collection of penalties is suspended until 8-16-87.

Alcohol, tobacco, and firearms tax returns. The new law provides that Treasury regs will set out the place for filing returns and other documents for alcohol, tobacco, and firearms. As a result, the Secretary has authority to assign all such returns to a particular IRS service center. This applies to all documents due on or after the first day of the first calendar month beginning more than 90 days after the date of enactment.

Stripped tax-exempt bonds. The new law applies the stripped bond rules to stripped tax-exempt bonds. For stripped bonds and coupons, the original issue discount (OID) under Section 1286(a) is equal to the amount of OID that produces a yield to maturity (based on the purchase price of the coupon or bond on the purchase date equal to the lower of the (10 coupon rate before separation of coupons or (2) the actual yield to maturity of the stripped bond or coupon.

The amount of OID is tax exempt, but it must be taken into account in determining adjusted basis. This provision applies to any purchase or sale of any stripped tax-exempt bond or stripped coupon after the date of enactment.

Disposition of subsidiary. One specific corporation is given permission to report the sale of stock in its subsidiary over a 15-year period.

Single Employer Pension Plan Amendments Act of 1986. The new law makes a number of technical corrections to the recently enacted Single Employee Pension Plan Act. The new law

- Clarifies the notice requirement for significant reduction in benefit accruals by defining the plans to which it applies (in ERISA Sec. 204(h)(2)) [misnumbered Sec. 206(h)(2)].

- Applies the ERISA Sec. 4049 trust rules to certain terminated plans.

- Corrects the definition of "multiemployer plan."

The notice requirement applies only for plan amendments adopted on or after the date of enactment. The Sec. 4049 trust rules are effective 1-1-86. The correction of the multiemployer plan definition is effective on 4-7-86.

Act Sec. 1879(a) waives estimated tax penalties; Act Sec. 1879(b), dealing with the orphan drug credit, amends Secs. 28(b)(2)(A) and 28(d)(1), effective for amounts paid or incurred after 12-31-82; Act Sec. 1879(c), dealing with the nonconventional fuels credit, amends Sec. 29(d)(8), effective for taxable years ending after 12-31-79; Act Sec. 1879(d), relating to fringe benefits, amends Sec. 6039D(d); Act Sec. 1879(e), relating to the Joint Committee report, amends Sec. 6405; Act Sec. 1879(f), dealing with rental property agreements, amends Sec. 467(e)(3)(A), effective for property placed in service after 5-8-85, with binding contract exceptions; Act Sec. 1879(g), relating to rural electric cooperatives, amends Secs. 401(k)(1) and (2) and adds Sec. 401(k)(6), effective for plan years beginning after 12-31-84; Act Sec. 1879(h), defining newly discovered oil, amends Sec. 4991(e)(2), effective for oil removed after 2-29-80; Act Sec. 1879(j), extending the investment credit to Sec. 501(d) organizations, amends Sec. 48(r), effective for periods after 12-31-78; Act Sec.

1879(k), relating to mutual savings banks, amends Sec. 501(c)(14)(B), effective to taxable years ending after 8-13-81; Act Sec. 1879(l), dealing with investment company reorganizations, amends Sec. 368(a)(2)(F)(ii), effective for transfers after 2-17-76; Act Sec. 1879(m), relating to S corporations, amends Secs. 1361(d)(3) and 1368(e)(1), effective for taxable years beginning after 12-31-82; Act Sec. 1879(n), changing the QTIP gift tax filing requirements, amends Sec. 2523(f)(4)(A), effective for transfers made after 12-31-85; Act Sec. 1879(o) treats a windfall profit tax exemption, effective for oil recovered after 2-29-80; Act Sec. 1579(i), relating to medicinal alcohol, adds new Sec. 7652(g), effective for articles brought to the United States after the date of enactment; Act Sec. 1879(q) suspends the operation of collection activities, effective 8-16-86 to 8-17-86; Act Sec. 1879(r) relating to alcohol, firearms, and tobacco returns, amends Sec. 6091(b); Act Sec. 1879(s), dealing with stripped tax-exempt bonds, amends Sec. 1286(d); Act Sec. 1879(f) permits a tax deferral on the sale of a subsidiary; Act Sec. 1879(u), relating to the Single Employer Pension Plan Amendments Act, amends ERISA Secs. 204(h) (misnumbered 206(h)) and 4049(a), and repeals SEPPAA Sec. 11016(c)(1), effective as if included in the act to which each section relates and as shown above.

[¶1881] Effective Date. The new law provides that except as otherwise stated in the technical corrections section, any provision is treated as included in the provision of the '84 TRA (or other law) to which it relates and, as such, is effective on the '84 TRA (or other law) provision's effective date.

[¶1882] Social Security Treatment for Church Employees and Clergy. *Application to members of religious faiths.* The Social Security Act allows a church or qualifying church-controlled organization to make a one-time election to exclude from the definition of "employment," for purposes of FICA taxes, services performed in the employ of the church or organization. If an election is made to exclude services for FICA purposes, the employee is treated similarly to a self-employed person as to those services. Thus, the employee is liable for self-employment (SECA) taxes on remuneration for these services. The amount of remuneration on which an employee of an electing organization is liable for SECA tax is generally the same as the amount that would have been subject to FICA tax absent an election.

Also, under Sec. 1402(g), an exemption from SECA taxes is provided for self-employed members of a religious sect who are conscientiously opposed to public or private death, retirement, or medical insurance (including social security). This exemption isn't available to employees. It is granted only on application by the individual, which must include evidence of the sect's tenants or teachings and of the individual's adherence to them. To get an exemption, the individual must waive all social security benefits.

The new law makes clear that the exemption from SECA taxes for members of certain religious faiths (Sec. 1402(g)) isn't available for services as to which SECA tax is due as a result of an election under the Social Security Act. Thus, if a member of a religious faith covered by that exception is an employee of a church, and that church elects to treat the employee as self-employed for FICA tax purposes, the employee can't also claim a Sec. 1402(g) exception from SECA taxes as to those services. This provision prevents the combination of an election under the Social Security Act, and a Sec. 1402(g) exception, from resulting in avoiding any employment taxes on the services performed for the electing organization. The provision doesn't affect the individual's ability to claim a Sec. 1402(g) exception as to other services not covered by an election.

Computing income subject to SECA tax. Under the Social Security Act, the remuneration on which the employee of an electing church or organization is liable for SECA tax generally is the same as the amount that would have been subject to FICA tax if that individual had continued to be treated as an employee. So trade or business expenses aren't subtracted in computing self-employment income (reimbursed business expenses aren't included in self-employment income, however), and the $400 threshold generally applicable to self-employment income doesn't apply. Similarly, a $100 (per employer) threshold for a tax year applies in determining whether remuneration for services covered by an election is subject to SECA tax. However, after 1989, these employees will be eligible for a deduction in computing SECA taxes for the product of net earnings from self-employment and one-half of the SECA rate.

The new law provides several changes to insure that church employee income will be determined, as far as possible, using FICA principles, and that the taxation of other self-employment income won't be affected by an election. Specifically, the bill specifies that the SECA tax base for services covered by an election is to be computed in a separate "basket" from the tax base for other self-employment income. Thus, church employee income isn't reduced by any deduction, while other income and deductions aren't affected by items attributable to church employee income. (This rule doesn't apply to the deduction for the product of all net self-employment earnings and one-half the SECA tax rate, beginning after 1989.) Also, the $100 threshold for taxing church employee income, and the $400 threshold applicable to other self-employment income, are separately applied under the bill (that is, church employee income doesn't count toward the general $400 threshold).

Effective Date: This provision is effective only for a remuneration paid or derived in tax years beginning on or after 1-1-86.

Voluntary revocation of election. Under the Social Security Act, a church must make an election to treat services performed for the church as subject to SECA (rather than FICA) taxes before its first quarterly employment tax return is due, or if later, 90 days after 7-18-84. Once made, the church can't revoke the election. However, the Treasury can permanently revoke an election if the electing church doesn't provide required information regarding its employees for a period of two years or more and, on the Treasury's request, fails to give previously unfurnished information for the period covered by the election. This rule could allow an electing church effectively to revoke its election by failing to provide the required information.

The new law allows a church to revoke an election under regulations the Treasury will prescribe. Treasury could still revoke an election for failure to provide required information. A church that revokes an election (or for which the election is revoked) can't make another election because the time for making such an election would have lapsed.

The regulations allowing a church or qualified church-controlled organization to revoke a Sec. 3121(w)(2) election will provide that any such revocation isn't to be effective before January 1, 1987, unless such electing church or organization had withheld and paid over all employment taxes due, as if such election had never been in effect, during the period from the stated effective date of the election being revoked through 12-31-86.

Act Sec. 1882, amending Sec. 211 of the Social Security Act, and Secs. 1402(g) and 3121(w)(2), takes effect on enactment, except that the provisions affecting computation of income subject to SECA taxes is effective after 1985.

[¶1883] AFDC and Child Support Programs. *Disregarding income of stepparent.* The AFDC (aid to families with dependent children) plan requirement for treatment of a stepparent's earned income allows a monthly disregard of $75 (in recognition of work expenses). Currently, the Secretary can prescribe the disregard or a lesser amount for individuals not in full-time employment or not employed throughout the month.

The new law deletes the Secretary's authority for the disregard of a lesser amount in the case of earnings of a stepfather, since the Deficit Reduction Act deleted the comparable authority for the general income disregard provision of Sec. 402(a)(8) of the Act.

Family unit rule. The Social Security Act requires the inclusion in the AFDC family unit of all parents of the dependent child, and all siblings who are themselves dependent children.

The new law clarifies that the sibling who is deprived of parental support or care by reason of the employment of a parent (and meets the other criteria of a dependent child), as well as one who is deprived by reason of the death, absence, or incapacity of a parent, is to be included in the AFDC. No such distinction between these two categories was intended, and this provision will clarify that, in a state that provides AFDC on the basis of the unemployment of a parent, siblings who are dependent children for that reason must be included in the AFDC unit.

Income of a minor AFDC parent. The Social Security Act requires, that in determining the income of a minor parent (of an AFDC child) who is living with her own parents or legal guardian, the state agency must include the income of the parents or legal guardian. In deciding what age defines "minor" for this purpose, the Act refers to the upper age limit chosen by the state for establishing eligibility as an AFDC child.

The new law clarifies that for purposes of defining the age limit of a "minor" parent, the age is that selected by the state for purposes of defining a dependent child, without regard to whether the minor parent is attending school. It clarifies that only the age limit, and not the school attendance element, was intended to be relevant to the income computation. (This is meant to reduce any incentive on the part of the minor parent to drop out of school.) This provision applies to minor parents up to age 18.

Federal incentive payments in interstate support collections. To encourage states to enforce complicated interstate child support obligations which arise when the custodial parent and child(ren) live in one state and the noncustodial parent lives in another state, Congress provided that in interstate cases "support which is collected by one state on behalf of individuals residing in another state shall be treated as having been collected in full by each such state." As a result, in interstate collection efforts, both states are to be credited with the collection for the purposes of calculating the incentive payment.

The new law clarifies the intent of Congress that the incentive be credited to both the state *initiating* the collection and the state *making* the collection. It describes the initiating state as the state requesting the collection, rather than the state of residence of the individuals on whose behalf the collection is made. The change is necessary because the state of residence isn't always the same as the state initiating the collection request.

Exclusion from AFDC unit of siblings receiving foster care maintenance payments. Before the 1984 Deficit Reduction Act added the family unit rule in AFDC, a sibling of an AFDC child, residing in the AFDC household but receiving foster care maintenance payments, was excluded from the AFDC family.

The new law adds a new section to make clear that the sibling of an AFDC child receiving foster care maintenance payments isn't a member of the AFDC unit.

Act Sec. 1883(b)(1)(A), amending Sec. 402(a)(8) of the 1984 Deficit Reduction Act, is effective 10-1-84; Act Sec. 1883(b)(2)(A), amending Sec. 402(a)(38) of the Social Security Act, is effective 10-1-84; Act Sec. 1883(b)(2)(B), amending Sec. 402(a)(38) of the Social Security Act, is effective 10-1-84; Act Sec.

1883(b)(3), amending Sec. 402(a)(39) of the Social Security Act, is effective 10-1-84; Act Sec. 1883(b)(7), amending Sec. 458(d) of the Social Security Act, takes effect on the date of enactment; Act Sec. 1883(b)(9), is effective 10-1-84; Act Sec. 1883(a), making technical corrections to Secs. 202 and 210 of the Social Security Act, is effective, generally, on the date of enactment.

For those amendments with an effective date of 10-1-84 (Act Secs. 1883(1), (2), (3), (9)), no state is considered to have failed to comply with the Social Security Act or to have made overpayments or underpayments by reason of its compliance with these amendments for the period beginning 10-1-84 and ending on the day preceding the date of enactment.

[¶1884] **Federal Unemployment Tax Act.** *Partial limitation on the reduction of credit against unemployment tax.* States can borrow funds from the Federal Unemployment accounts to pay unemployment benefits. Depending on the month in which such a loan is advanced, a state has between 22 and 34 months to repay the loan. If the loan is not repaid in time, the FUTA tax credit for employers in the state is reduced by .3% for each year the loan is in arrears.

For states that take legislative steps to improve the solvency of their unemployment insurance systems, the FUTA credit reduction is limited to 0.1% a year for each year a state has a loan in arrears. This limitation on the FUTA credit reduction is effective for 1983, 1984, and 1985.

The new law clarifies that the limitation on the FUTA credit reduction in states meeting the solvency test expires at the end of calendar year 1985, not 1986 as the Code presently indicates.

Definition of 'agricultural worker.' Section 3306(O)(1)(A)(i) provides, that for purposes of the Federal Unemployment Tax Act, an individual who is a member of a crew furnished by a crew leader to perform agricultural labor for any other person shall be treated as an employee of such crew leader if such crew leader holds a valid certificate of registration under the 1963 Farm Labor Contractor Act. This act has been repealed and replaced with the 1983 Migrant and Seasonal Agricultural Workers Protection Act.

Thus, the new law strikes the reference to the 1963 Farm Labor Contractor Act and replaces it with a reference to the 1983 Migrant and Seasonal Agricultural Workers Protection Act.

Act Sec. 1884, amending Sec. 3302(f)(8) (relating to a partial limitation on the reduction of the credit against the unemployment tax), and Sec. 3306(o)(1-)(A) (relating to crew leaders who are registered or provide specialized agricultural labor), is effective on the date of enactment.

[¶1885] **Tariff Schedule Amendments.** *Telecommunications product classification corrections.* The 1984 Trade and Tariff Act revised the provisions of part 5 of schedule 6 of the Tariff Schedules applicable to telecommunications products to better reflect the state of current technology in such products.

The new law makes conforming changes to several headnotes in the Tariff Schedules which refer to the items in part 5 of schedule 6, which were changed by the 1984 Trade and Tariff Act. It also adds the appropriate column 2 rate of duty for new items 685.34, which was inadvertently omitted.

Other corrections. The new law makes corrections in the article descriptions of Tariff Schedule items 906.38, 907.38, 912.13, and in headnote 1 of part 4D of schedule 1 and headnote 1 of part 4C of schedule 3 (as amended by the 1984 Trade and Tariff Act), to correct spelling, utilize proper chemical nomenclature, correct Tariff Schedule references, and eliminate duplication.

Act Sec. 1885, amending Secs. 111, 112, 123, 124, 146, 182 of the 1984 Trade and Tariff Act and various provisions of the Tariff Schedules of the United States, is effective, generally, for articles entered, or withdrawn from, a warehouse for consumption on or after the date that is 15 days after the date of the new law's enactment.

[¶1886] **Countervailing and Antidumping Duty Provisions.** *Definition of "interested party."* Section 612(a)(3) of the 1984 Trade and Tariff Act amended section 711(9) of the 1930 Tariff Act to include industry-labor coalitions within the definition of "interested party" for purposes of countervailing duty or antidumping investigations.

The new law makes similar conforming changes in Secs. 702(b)(1) and 732(b)(1) of the 1930 Tariff Act to ensure that industry-labor coalitions will be considered proper petitioners under the countervailing duty and antidumping laws.

Imports under suspension agreements. Sec. 704(b) of the 1930 Tariff Act authorized suspending countervailing duty investigations if the foreign government or exporters accounting for substantially all imports of merchandise agreed to eliminate or offset the subsidy or to cease exports of subsidized merchandise within six months after the suspension.

The new law restores Sec. 704(d)(2) of the 1930 Tariff Act, which was inadvertently deleted. Sec. 704(d)(2) requires that a suspension agreement provide a means of ensuring that exports shall not surge during the six-month period of phase-in of measures to eliminate or offset subsidies.

Waiver of deposit of estimated antidumping duties. The 1930 Tariff Act authorizes the administering authority, for 90 days after publication of an antidumping order, to continue to permit entry of merchandise subject to the order under bond, instead of the deposit of estimated duties for individual importers, if it has reason to believe these importers have taken steps to eliminate or substantially reduce dumping margins. This provision covers all merchandise entered as of the date of the first affirmative antidumping determination, whether or not sold to an unrelated buyer that is necessary to compute price.

The new law amends the 1930 Tariff Act to change its scope to cover only entries entered and resold to unrelated buyers during the period between the first affirmative antidumping determination and the International Trade Commission's final affirmative determination. This amendment was inadvertently omitted from the 1984 Trade and Tariff Act.

Revocation of orders. A party seeking revocation of an antidumping order has the burden of persuasion as to whether there are changed circumstances sufficient to warrant revocation. The new law applies the same standard to revocations of countervailing duty orders as applies to antidumping orders. The amendment corrects an inadvertent omission from the 1984 Trade and Tariff Act, since there's no reason to distinguish between the two types of revocations.

Upstream subsidies. Sec. 771A(a) of the 1930 Tariff Act, as added by Sec. 613 of the 1984 Trade and Tariff Act, defines upstream subsidies in part in terms of the types of practices described under Sec. 771(5)(B)(i)(ii), or (iii) of the Tariff Act as domestic subsidies. The new law amends the 1930 Tariff Act to correct the unintended omission of Sec. 771(5)(B)(iv) from the list of domestic subsidy practices which may constitute an upstream subsidy.

Release of confidential information. The 1930 Tariff Act contains various provisions relating to the release of confidential information. As amended by Sec. 619 of the 1984 Trade and Tariff Act, it provides that the administering authority may release such information under an administrative protective order if it's accompanied by a statement of permission.

The new law amends the 1930 Tariff Act to substitute the terms "proprietary" for "confidential" throughout Sec. 777, a change that was omitted inadvertently from the 1984 Trade and Tariff Act. The provision also amends subsection (b)(1)(B)(i) to correct the inadvertent omission of the International Trade Commission as being permitted to release information, as well as the administering authority, consistent with the rest of the section.

Effective Dates: Sec. 626(b) of the 1984 Trade and Tariff Act made amendments in Secs. 602, 609, 611, 612, and 620 of that Act to Title VII of the 1930 Tariff Act applicable to investigations initiated on or after the date of enactment and the amendments made by section 623 were made applicable to civil actions pending or filed on or after the date of enactment.

The new law amends Sec. 626(b) so that the amendments in Secs. 602, 609, 611, 612, and 620 of the 1984 Trade and Tariff Act will apply to reviews of oustanding antidumping and countervailing duty orders, as well as to new investigations. These orders would involve merchandise entered, or withdrawn from warehouse, for consumption many years after the date of enactment. This amendment is consistent with the Congressional intent of these amendments to reduce the cost and increase of efficiency of proceedings.

The new law authorizes the administering authority to delay implementation of any of the amendments to Title VII as to investigations in progress on the date of enactment of the 1984 Trade and Tariff Act if it determines that immediate implementation would prevent compliance with an applicable statutory deadline. New questionnaires would have to be issued to seek information required by certain amendments that may not be obtainable on cases in progress within the statutory deadlines.

The law also clarifies that the amendments made by the 1984 Trade and Tariff Act to the 1930 Tariff Act concerning the rate of interest payable on overpayments and underpayments of antidumping and countervailing duties apply to merchandise unliquidated as of five days after date of enactment, that is, on or after 11-4-84, consistent with U.S. Customs Service practice.

Act Sec. 1886, amending Secs. 702(b)(1), 704, 732(b)(1), 751(b)(1), 771A(a), 777, 7369(c)(1) of Title IV of the 1930 Tariff Act and Secs. 611(a)(2)(B)(iii), 613, 619, 626(b) of the 1984 Trade and Tariff Act, is effective, generally, on that Act's enactment date (10/29/84); Act Secs. 1886(a)(1), (3), (5), (6), (9), (11), (12) making technical corrections to Title VII of the 1930 Tariff Act, is effective, generally, on the date of enactment.

[¶1887] **Amendments to the 1974 Trade Act.** *Waiver authority under generalized system of preferences (GSP).* The 1974 Trade Act limits Presidential authority to waive more restrictive GSP competitive need limits as to products from advanced beneficiary developing countries to no more than 15% of the total value of GSP duty-free imports during the preceding calendar year.

The new law clarifies that the 15% limit on the President's waiver authority applies to the aggregate value of all waivers granted in a given year on GSP imports from advanced beneficiary countries taken as a group, not to each country individually.

Transistors. To fully implement an agreement to reduce U.S. duties on transistors, the bill corrects a numbering error of a TSUS line item.

Act Sec. 1887, amending Sec. 504(c)(3)(D)(ii) of the 1974 Trade and Tariff Act, is effective, generally, on the date of enactment; Act Secs. 1887(a)(1)—(4), making technical corrections to various sections of the 1974 Trade Act, is effective on the date of enactment.

[¶1888] **Amendments to the 1930 Tariff Act.** *Marking of pipes, tubes, and fittings.* The 1984 Trade and Tariff Act added a new subsection (c) to Sec. 403 of the 1930 Traiff Act, providing that no exceptions may be made to the marking requirements of section 304 for certain pipes and pipe fittings, and required these products to be marked with the country of origin by means of die stamping, cast-in-mold lettering, etching, or engraving.

The new law provides a limited exception to the marking requirement for articles which, due to their nature, may not be marked by one of the four prescribed methods because it's technically or commercially infeasable to do so. These articles may be marked by an equally permanent method of marking, such as paint stenciling, or in the case of a small diameter pipe, tube, or fitting, by tagging the containers or bundles. Those articles that Customs decides can be marked by die stamping, cast-in-mold lettering, etching or engraving without adversely affecting their structural integrity or significantly reducing their commercial utility would continue to be marked in this manner.

Tagging of containers or bundles may only be used for small diameter pipes, tubes, and fittings for which individual marking would be impractical or inconspicuous. If Customs determines that tagging is the only feasible method of marking imported goods so that the ultimate consumer will know the country of origin of the goods, such products must be bundled and tagged in accordance with applicable industry standards. The U.S. Customs Service must report back to the Ways and Means Committee within one year after enactment on how the provision is working.

Drawback to incidental operations. The 1984 Trade and Tariff Act amends the 1930 Tariff Act to permit substituting domestic fungible merchandise for imported merchandise under prescribed circumstances and still get the benefits of drawback when these products are exported. However, incidental operations which may be performed on imported merchandise under section 313(j)(4) without depriving them of drawback privileges may not be performed on such substituted domestic merchandise.

The new law changes this so that incidental operations may be performed on both domestic and imported merchandise so that the intent of the original provision (that is, allowing fungible domestic and imported merchandise to be mixed together and still be entitled to drawback) is accomplished.

Interested parties. Sec. 771(9) of the 1930 Tariff Act, as amended by section 612(a) of the 1984 Trade and Tariff Act, defines the term "interested party" for purposes of countervailing duty or antidumping proceedings to incude industry-labor coalitions. The term is also used in the provisions for judicial review of such proceedings under Title V of the 1930 Tariff Act.

The law amends the 1930 Tariff Act to conform the definition of the term interested party to the inclusion of industry-labor coalitions under Sec. 771(9) of the 1930 Tariff Act.

Customs provision. The bill deletes duplicative language created by the 1985 Continuing Resolution.

Act Sec. 1888, amending Secs. 304(c), 313(j), 514(a), 516(a)(2) of the 1930 Tariff Act and Secs. 202, 207 of the 1984 Trade and Tariff Act, is effective on the Act's enactment date; Act Secs. 1888(3), (6), making technical corrections to Secs. 339(c)(2)(A), 516A(a)(3) of the 1930 Tariff Act, is effective on the Act's enactment date.

[¶1889] Amendments to the 1984 Trade and Tariff Act.

Chipper knife steel. The new law deletes unnecessary language added by the 1984 Trade and Tariff Act.

Watch glasses. The 1984 Trade and Tariff Act reduced the level of duty on watch glasses other than round to the same level as the duty applicable to round watch glasses. However, the Act doesn't provide for the third-year staged reduction on 1-1-87, for watch glasses other than round. The new law amends the Act to provide for the third-year reduction to 4.9% ad valorem tax for such watch glasses.

Act Sec. 1889, amending Secs. 126, 174(b) of the 1984 Trade and Tariff Act, is effective on the Act's enactment date; Act Secs. 1889(3)—(7), correcting various paragraphs in the 1984 Trade and Tariff Act, is effective on the Act's enactment date.

[¶1890] Amendments to the Caribbean Basin Economic Recovery Act.
The Caribbean Basin Economic Recovery Act (CBI) allows products of a beneficiary country to be processed in a bonded warehouse in Puerto Rico after being imported directly from such country and be eligible for duty-free treatment under the CBI on withdrawal from the warehouse if they meet the rule-of-origin requirements set out in Sec. 213(a)(1)(B).

The new law corrects a reference to a wrong Tariff Schedules item in Sec. 213(f)(5)(B) of the CBI and clarifies that products entering Puerto Rico directly from *any* CBI beneficiary country, not merely the country of manufacture, should qualify for entry under bond.

Act Sec. 1890, amending Sec. 213 of the Caribbean Basin Economic Recovery Act, is effective on the Act's enactment date.

[¶1891] Customs Brokers.
The new law makes corrections to conforming amendments made by the 1984 Trade and Tariff Act in Title 28 of the U.S. Code to cross-references in the 1930 Tariff Act relating to customs brokers. It also deletes an incorrect reference in Sec. 1581(g)(1) of Title 28.

Act Sec. 1891, amending Sec. 212 of the 1984 Trade and Tariff Act, is effective on the Act's enactment date.

[¶1892] **Articles Given Duty-Free Treatment Under the 1984 Trade and Tariff Act.** Sections 112, 115, 118, 167, and 179 of the 1984 Trade and Tariff Act were made effective 15 days after enactment because the provisions providing for retroactive application of such provisions were inadvertently omitted from the Act.

The new law provides for the retroactive application of sections 112, 115, 118, 167, and 179 of the 1984 Trade and Tariff Act.

Act Sec. 1892, amending Secs. 112, 115, 118, 167, 179 of the 1984 Trade and Tariff Act, is retroactively effective to the date of enactment of such sections (10/29/84).

[¶1893] **Customs Users Fees.**

Transit passenger fees. The new law clarifies that the exemption from the $5 fee applicable to passengers arriving on commercial aircraft and vessels also exempts passengers originating in the United States who transit only those locations to which the exemption applies before reentering the United States.

Foreign pre-clearance services. The new law precludes Customs from assessing overtime charges against airlines for pre-clearance of passengers in foreign locations when U.S. Customs officers undertake such pre-clearance.

Remittance fee regulations. The new law directs that regulations issued by the IRS to collect such fees should be consistent with the current regulations on collecting the airport departure tax.

Reinstating limit on charges for inspection services. The new law provides that overtime charges for inspectional or quarantine services (other than customs services) on Sundays or holidays be reimbursed as if they had been performed during a weekday. This is intended to reinstate the limit on weekend and holiday overtime charges for private aircraft and others not benefitting from the inspectional overtime account funded through the customs user fees.

Vessels, barges, bulk carriers, and ferries. A cap of $5,955 is placed on the fees charged for the arrival of any commercial vessel of more than 100 net tons in the United States. This cap on vessel fees is computed on the basis of 15 arrivals per year. The fee on commercial vessels applies to each arrival at a U.S. port regardless of whether these arrivals occur as a series of calls at U.S. ports on the same trip or on several trips.

A lower user fee of $100 on barges and bulk carriers arriving from Canada and Mexico is provided, as such vessels compete with trucks and rail cars arriving by land from Canada and Mexico, which are subject to much lower user fees. A cap of $1,500, also representing

15 arrivals, is placed on the annual total of the user fees that such barges and bulk carriers arriving from contiguous countries must pay.

Regardless of which fee may be applicable during the calendar year, no barge or bulk carrier is liable for more than the $5,955 annual cap applicable to vessels.

The new law exempts tugboats from the application of any vessel fees. This exemption is intended to prevent the Customs Service from applying the vessel user fee to a tugboat that provides propulsion to barges or merely accompanies vessels that are themselves subject to a user fee. This exception does not apply to tugboats that are not being used as tugboats at the time of arrival.

The new law contains a definition of "ferry" for the purposes of the exemption from the user fee applicable to commercial vessels of over 100 net tons. For purposes of this exemption, a ferry includes a vessel that transports passengers, vehicles, or railroad cars, or any combination thereof, for distances of 300 miles or less. While such a ferry is exempted from the fee, trucks or railroad cars carried by such a ferry would be subject to the applicable fee. For commercial vessels subject to the user fee that transport vehicles or rail cars, there is no fee assessed on the vehicles or rail cars.

Railroad cars. The fee would be changed to $7.50 for cars carrying merchandise, and no fee would be assessed on empty cars.

Customs broker fees. The new law clarifies that the annual fee for the issuance of a broker permit is to be prorated so that the applicable fee in 1986 would be one-half the annual fee, based on the 7-1-86 effective date of the fee. The Customs Service is required to provide 60 days notice of the due date for the fee, and is barred from revoking a delinquent broker's permit absent such notice.

Customs broker's freight forwarding. The new law clarifies Congressional intent as to the compensation of customs brokers for certain services. It provides licensed customs brokers, when performing ocean freight forwarder services on export shipments from the United States, with the benefits of the right of independent action as to the level of forwarder compensation in a shipping conference's freight tariff. Under current law, a conference may prohibit its members from taking independent action on forwarder compensation. The new law clarifies that a conference must allow its members to take independent action on compensation to the extent that compensation is or will be paid to a forwarder who is also a licensed customs broker under the 1930 Tariff Act.

The new law also benefits customs brokers when they act in the capacity of a licensed freight forwarder on shipments exported from the United States. Despite the requirement of current law that conferences not deny forwarders a reasonable percentage of the carrier's freight charges as compensation for the forwarder's service, some conferences are limiting forwarder's compensation to a percentage of some, but not all, of the rates and charges assessed against the cargo in their tariffs. The new law clarifies that when compensation is paid to a forwarder who is also a licensed customs broker, the compensation must be based on all the freight charges, including, but not limited to, surcharges, handling charges, service charges, terminal charges, supplements, currency adjustment factors, and any and all other charges required to be paid by the shipper or consignee under the tariff.

> **NOTE:** The new law does not in any way modify or diminish the existing scope or protections of the 1984 Shipping Act as applied to ocean freight forwarders in general. Its purpose is to impose additional requirements on conferences or carrier groups in their concerted dealings with forwarders who are also licensed customs brokers.

Act Sec. 1893, amending Secs. 13031 (a), (b), (d), (e), (f) of the 1985 Consolidated Omnibus Budget Reconciliation Act and Sec. 53 of the 1970 Airport and Airway Development Act, is effective, generally, for services rendered after the date that is 15 days after the date of enactment. On written request, Act Sec. 1893(g)(2) permits the Secretary of the Treasury to refund excess fees paid due to this enactment for customs services provided after 7-6-86 and on or before the date that is 15 days after the date of enactment. If a customs broker's permit fee exceeds $62.50 for 1986, Act Sec. 1893(g)(3) permits the Secretary of the Treasury to refund the excess or, if requested by the customs broker, credit the excess to 1987. Act Sec. 1888(8), amending Sec. 641 of the 1930 Tariff Act (regarding compensation of ocean freight forwarders), is effective on enactment.

[¶1894] Foreign Trade Zones. The new law clarifies that the fifth provision in the Foreign Trade Zone Act allows domestic denatured alcohol to be used in the manufacture of other articles.

[¶1895] Technical Corrections to the 1985 Consolidated Omnibus Budget Reconciliation Act.

Medicare. The new law corrects the termination of the ACCESS demonstration program, currently 9-30-86, to 7-31-87. It also clarifies that the Director of OTA should initially provide for such terms for members of the Prospective Payment Assessment Commission so that no more than eight members' terms would expire in the same year.

It also makes the following clarifications: (1) clarifies that all hospitals that have a medicare provider agreement would have to abide by the emergency care requirements of COBRA and the requirements regarding participation in the CHAMPUS program; (2) allows skilled nursing facilities to make an election to be paid on a prospective payment basis on their costs reporting periods rather than on a federal fiscal-year basis; (3) clarifies that the medicare HI tax on state and local governments does not apply to certain campaign workers; (4) clarifies that a one-year transition period is provided for foreign medical graduates who have not passed the FMGEMS; (5) allows the Secretary to announce HMO/CMP rates by September 7 of each year rather than publish them; (6) clarifies the effective date of the provision regarding penalties for billing for assistants at surgery for certain cataract procedures; (7) allows temporary use of carrier prepayment screens as a substitute for preprocedure review; (8) clarifies that the termination date of the ACCESS demonstration project is 7-31-87; (9) corrects and clarifies the section regarding payments under the indirect medical education provision; (10) corrects and clarifies the section regarding payment under the disproportionate share provision; and (11) corrects citation, indentation, and other technical errors.

Continuing health care. The new law makes the following technical corrections to the continuing health care provisions of COBRA.

Notification requirement. The new law establishes a 60-day notification period for divorced or legally separated spouses of covered employees, or dependent children ceasing to be dependent children under the generally applicable requirements of the plan, to notify the plan administrator of a qualifying event entitling the spouse or dependent children to continuation health coverage.

Maximum period of continuation coverage. The new law clarifies that a qualfied beneficiary may have more than one qualifying event that entitles the beneficiary to continuation coverage, but in no event may the coverage period as to such events generally exceed a 36-month period. The second qualifying event must take place during the period of coverage of the first qualifying event to be eligible for a total of 36 months continuation coverage beginning from the first qualifying event.

Election of coverage. The new law clarifies that each qualified beneficiary is entitled to a separate election of continuation coverage. For example, if a covered employee does not elect continuation coverage, the spouse or dependent children are entitled to elect such coverage. Moreover, even if the employee elects certain coverage, the spouse or dependents may elect different coverage.

Failure to pay premiums. The new law provides that the grace period for failure to pay premiums is the longest of (1) 30 days; (2) the period the plan allows employees for failure to pay premiums; or (3) the period the insurance company allows the plan or the employer for failure to pay premiums.

Type of coverage. The new law provides that, for all purposes, qualified beneficiaries are to be treated under the plan in the same manner as similarly situated beneficiaries for whom a qualifying event has not taken place. For example, if the plan provides for an open enrollment period, then qualified beneficiaries are to be permitted to make elections during the open enrollment period in the same manner as active employees. Thus, an individual who is a qualified beneficiary by reason of being a spouse of a covered employee would have the same rights as active employees during an open enrollment period and would not be limited to the rights of spouses of covered employees.

"Health benefits" mean health benefit plans, including dental and vision care (within the meaning of Sec. 213). It is not intended that an employer could compel a qualified beneficiary to pay for non core benefits (such as dental and vision care) even if active employees are required to buy coverage for such benefits under the plan.

Act Sec. 1895, amending Secs. 9122(b), 9202(j), 9517(c)(2), and 9528(a) of the 1985 Consolidated Omnibus Budget Reconciliation Act, Secs. 602(2), 602(3), 605(2), 606(3), and 607 of ERISA, Secs. 2202(2) and 2206(3) of the Public Health Service Act, Secs. 1164(b)(4), 1837(i)(1), 1842(b)(4), 1842(h), 1842(k), 1866(a), 1867(e)(3), 1876(a)(1), 1886(d), 1886(g), 1886(h), 1888(d)(1), 1902(a)(10), 1902(a)(13), 1903(m)(2), 1905(a), and 1920(a) of the Social Security Act, and Code Secs. 162(k)(2), (6), (7), 3121(u)(2)(B)(i), is effective, generally, as if included in the 1985 Consolidated Omnibus Budget Reconciliation Act.

[¶1896] **Extension of Time for Investment Farmers to File for Refunds.** The new law provides that claims arising from the minimum tax amendment made by the 1985 Consolidated Omnibus Budget Reconciliation Act (relating to certain insolvent farmers allowed to reduce capital gains preference items for purposes of the individual minimum tax) may be made within one year after the enactment of the new law.

Act Sec. 1896, amending Sec. 13208 of the 1985 Consolidated Omnibus Budget Reconciliation Act, is effective on the Act's enactment.

[¶1897] **Technical Corrections to the REA.** The new law includes provisions which make technical corrections in the Retirement Equity Act of 1984, and clarify certain provisions of that act.

Break-in-service rules. Class year plans. A class-year plan is a profit-sharing, stock bonus, or money purchase plan which provides for separate vesting of benefits attributable to employer contributions for each plan year. Such benefits generally must be 100% vested as of the close of the fifth plan year of service following the plan year for which the contribution is made. Under the new law, such benefits cannot be forfeited unless, before becoming vested, the employee incurs five consecutive one-year break-in-service. A plan year of service is a plan year, on the last day of which the participant is performing services for the employer; break-in-service years are all other plan years.

Lump-sum distributions. To receive the favorable tax treatment accorded lump-sum distributions, a participant must receive a distribution of the entire balance to his credit in the plan within one taxable year. If a participant, who is partially vested in his accrued benefit, separates from service and receives a distribution of his or her vested interest before incurring five consecutive one-year breaks in service, the potential increase in vesting that might occur if he or she returned to employment might make the distribution ineligible for lump-sum treatment. The new law provides that the determination of whether a distribution made on account of separation from service qualifies as a lump-sum distribution, is made without regard to any increase in vesting that could occur if the participant is reemployed by the employer. If, however, the employee is reemployed and, as a result, his or her vested interest in benefits accrued before the break-in-service increases, the tax savings from treating the distribution as a lump-sum distribution are recaptured. If the tax savings are recaptured, the previous lump-sum distribution will not prevent the participant from treating a subsequent distribution as a lump-sum distribution.

Rollovers. The new law also provides that, for the purpose of determining whether a distribution on account of a separation from service is eligible for rollover treatment, the balance to the credit of the employee is determined without regard to any potential increase in vesting. If, however, the employee is reemployed and the vested percentage of benefits accrued before the separation from service increases, subsequent distributions generally will not be eligible for favorable tax treatment. Favorable tax treatment of subsequent distributions may be available if the rolled over distribution is made without the consent of the participant (e.g., a distribution of $3,500 or less).

Repayment of mandatory employee contributions. Under prior law, if a plan participant who was less than 50% vested in the accrued benefit derived from employer contributions withdrew any portion of mandatory employee contributions from the plan, the accrued benefit derived from employee contributions could be forfeited. However, the plan had to provide that the forfeited amounts would be restored if the employee repaid the amount of mandatory contributions withdrawn. Defined contribution plans could require that repayment be made before the employee incurred a one-year break-in-service.

The new law conforms the repayment period for mandatory contributions to the repayment period for accrued benefits after a separation from service, and eliminates the distinction between defined contribution and defined benefit plans. Now either type of plan may provide that repayment of mandatory contributions which have been withdrawn, or of accrued benefits which have been distributed, must be made no later than (1) in the case of a withdrawal or distribution on account of separation from service, the earlier of five years after the date of subsequent reemployment by the employer or the close of the fifth consecutive one-year break-in-service, and (2) in the case of any other withdrawal, five years after the date of withdrawal.

Maximum age requirements—SEPs. The new law conforms the maximum age which may be required as a condition of participation in a Simplified Employee Pension Plan to the REA requirements for other qualified plans. The maximum age is reduced from 25 to 21. This change is effective for plan years beginning after the date of enactment.

Joint and survivor annuities and preretirement survivor annuities. Under REA, it is unclear whether the qualified joint and survivor annuity (QJSA) provisions or the qualified preretirement survivor annuity (QPSA) provisions apply when (1) a participant retires, or attains the normal retirement age under the plan, but dies before the annuity starting date, and (2) a participant receives a disability benefit under a plan. The new law provides that the QJSA is payable if the participant does not die before the annuity starting date unless it has been waived. The QPSA is payable (unless waived) if the participant dies before the annuity starting date.

The annuity starting date is the first day of the first period for which an amount is payable as an annuity. If the benefit isn't payable as an annuity, the annuity starting date is the first day on which all events have occurred which entitle the participant to a benefit.

If a disability benefit is an auxiliary benefit, the commencement of disability benefits would not be an annuity starting date. If a participant who is receiving a disability benefit will, upon reaching the normal retirement age, receive a retirement benefit which satisfies the benefit accrual and vesting rules of Sec. 411, without taking the disability benefit into account, the disability benefit is auxiliary. In such a case, if the employee died before reaching the plan's normal retirement date, the employee's spouse would be entitled to the QPSA. If the employee dies after reaching the normal retirement age, the spouse would be entitled to the survivor portion of a QJSA.

The new law also clarifies that a plan which is exempt from the QJSA and QPSA requirements is not required to pay the participant's vested accrued benefit to the participant's spouse on the death of the participant unless the participant and spouse were married for at least one year on the date of the participant's death.

Transferee plan rules. Under REA, a plan not otherwise subject to the QJSA or QPSA rules will be subjected to those rules if it receives a direct transfer of assets in connection with a merger, spin-off, or conversion of a plan which is subject to the rules, or receives a direct transfer of assets from such a plan solely with respect to a participant. The new law clarifies that a transfer completed before 1-1-85 will not cause a plan not otherwise subject to the survivor annuity rules to be made subject to them. Further, under the new law, the survivor annuity rules, if applicable, will be limited to benefits attributable to the transferred assets, provided the plan accounts for the transferred assets and the allocable investment yield from those assets separately.

Amount of QPSA. REA provides that the amount of a QPSA must be no less than the amount which would be payable to the surviving spouse under a QJSA if (1) in the case of a participant who dies after attaining the earliest retirement age under the plan, the participant had retired on the day before his death with an immediate QJSA, and (2) in the case of a participant who dies on or before the earliest retirement age, the participant had separated from service on the date of death, survived until the earliest retirement age, and then retired with an immediate QJSA.

The new law clarifies that the QPSA payable to the spouse of a participant who separates from service prior to death, will be calculated by reference to the date of separation. Thus, no benefits accrue after the participant's separation from service.

If a participant's accrued benefit is attributable to both employee and employer contributions, the QPSA must be treated as attributable to employee contributions in the same ratio as the portion of the accrued benefit which is derived from employee contributions bears to the participant's total accrued benefit. The plan is not permitted to allocate the survivor annuity only to employee contributions. For the purposes of determining the amount of QPSA under a defined contribution plan subject to the survivor annuity requirements, the participant's vested account balance includes any portion attributable to employee contributions.

The earliest retirement age should be determined counting only the participant's actual years of service at separation from service or death. Therefore, if a participant dies or leaves employment before satisfying a service requirement for early retirement, the "earliest retirement age" will be the date the participant would have reached the normal retirement age under the plan.

Spousal consent requirements. Under the new law, a spouse's consent to the waiver of the QJSA or QPSA, must either name a non-spouse beneficiary to receive any death benefits which become payable, and the form of the death benefit, or acknowledge that the spouse voluntarily relinquishes the right to name the beneficiary and/or specify the form of payment. If the spouse's consent specifies the beneficiary or form of payment, a subsequent change in either will require a new spousal consent.

NOTE: This position varies from that of the IRS regs [Reg. Sec. 1.401(a)-11T, Q-A 25], which would require that *all* spousal consents specify the nonspouse beneficiary.

If a waiver of a survivor benefit is required, the consenting spouse must be given an opportunity to consent to the waiver only in favor of a specific beneficiary or form of payment. The plan may not restrict the spouse's ability to waive the survivor benefit by providing only a general consent under which the spouse relinquishes the right to designate a beneficiary or form of payment.

The new law clarifies that a spousal consent to a waiver of a survivor benefit is not a transfer for gift tax purposes.

Spousal consent is required for the accrued benefit of a participant to be used as security for loans from plans which are subject to the survivor annuity requirements. Unlike Reg. Sec. 1.417(e)-IT(d), which requires spousal consent to all loans from qualified plans, the new law does not require consent to a loan from a profit-sharing plan which is not a transferee plan with respect to the participant.

If a participant's accrued benefit is used as security for a loan and the participant's spouse consents, then upon default the plan may realize its security interest, even if at the time of default the participant is married to a different spouse. Similar rules apply if the participant is unmarried when the security agreement is made, and a default occurs later when the participant is married.

For the purpose of determining the amount of any survivor benefit, any security interest held by the plan because of an outstanding loan is taken into account, as is the value of amounts payable under any outstanding Qualified Domestic Relations Order (QDRO).

The notice requirements and election periods pertaining to spousal consent to waivers of survivor annuity benefits also apply to spousal consents to (1) waive survivor benefits under plans exempt from the QPSA and QJSA requirements; (2) pledge the participant's accrued benefits as security for a loan; (3) permit distributions after the annuity starting date; and (4) permit immediate distribution of amounts in excess of $3,500.

The provisions relating to spousal consents to changes in beneficiary designations and changes in benefit form apply to plan years beginning after the date of enactment.

The provision relating to notice and election periods for plans that are exempt from the survivors benefit requirements is effective on the date of enactment.

The provisions relating to spousal consents to pledge accrued benefits as security for loans apply to loans made after 8-18-85. However, any loan that is revised, extended, renewed, or renegotiated after 8-18-85, is treated as a new loan (and a new security pledge).

Notice requirement for persons hired after age 35. REA requires that plan participants be notified of their rights to decline the QPSA during the period beginning with the first day of the plan year in which the participant attains age 32 and ending with the last day of the plan year in which he or she attains age 35. Under the new law the notice period will not in any event end before the latest of (1) a reasonable time after the individual becomes a plan participant; (2) a reasonable time after survivor benefits cease to be subsidized; or (3) a reasonable time after the survivor benefit requirements become applicable with respect to a participant. If a participant separates from service prior to age 35, the plan must notify the participant, within a reasonable time after separation from service, of the participant's right to decline the QPSA.

Subsidized benefits. Under REA, a plan is not required to notify a participant of his or her right to waive the QJSA or QPSA if the plan fully subsidizes the cost of the benefits. Under the new law, the exception would not apply if a participant were permitted to waive the benefit or to designate a nonspouse beneficiary. Moreover, a benefit will not be considered to be fully subsidized if the costs are spread among all plan participants, or a group of plan participants, even if benefits of those to whom the costs are allocated are not affected by a waiver or failure to waive survivor benefits.

QDROs. Under REA, payments to an alternate payee, pursuant to a Qualified Domestic Relations Order, do not violate the prohibitions in ERISA and the Code against the assignment or alienation of benefits under the pension plan. The alternate payee is treated as a distributee of benefits for tax purposes. Moreover, net employee contributions are apportioned between the participant and the alternate payee. Under the new law the special tax treatment of payments under QDRO is applicable only if the alternate payee is the spouse or former spouse of the participant. Effective for payments after the date of enactment, if the alternate payee is other than a spouse or former spouse (e.g., a child), the payments are included in the participant's income, and all employee contributions (and other investment in the contract) recoverable by the participant under general basis-recovery rules.

When a plan administrator receives a domestic relations order, it must determine within an 18-month period whether the order is a "qualified" domestic relations order. The new law clarifies that the 18-month period begins on the date payments are due to commence under the order.

During the 18-month period, the plan administrator is to defer payment of the amounts subject to the domestic relations order until it determines whether the domestic relations order is qualified. The new law eliminates the prior law's requirement that the deferred amounts be held in an escrow account, and requires only that the deferred amounts be separately accounted for.

If a domestic relations order is determined not to be qualified, the plan administrator must pay the deferred amounts to the person entitled thereto as if there were no order. However, if the administrator is notified that the parties are attempting to cure the defects in the order, it is required to continue to defer the amounts until the end of the 18-month period.

Generally, a domestic relations order will not be qualified if it requires benefits to be paid in a form not permitted under the plan. However, if the form of benefit ceases to be permitted under the plan, as a result of a plan amendment or a change in the law, a QDRO will not lose its qualified status. If the plan is amended in a way which makes the form of benefit no longer permissible, the alternate payee will be entitled to continue receiving benefits in the form specified in the order, or to elect another form of benefit which will not affect the amount or form of benefit payable to the participant. If the form of benefit specified in the order becomes impermissible because of a change in the law, the plan must permit the alternate payee to select a form of payment permitted under the plan, which does not affect, in any way, the amount or form of benefit payable to the participant.

A QDRO can also require that benefits be paid to the alternate payee prior to the participants separation from service, provided the participant has attained the earliest retirement age. Earliest retirement age means, for this purpose, the earlier of: (1) the earliest date benefits are payable under the plan or (2) the later of the date the participant attains age 50 or the date on which the participant could obtain a distribution from the plan if the participant separated from service.

The present value of the benefits payable to an alternate payee is determined without regard to the value of the benefit payable to the participant. Likewise, the present value of the benefit payable to the participant is determined without regard to the present value of the benefit payable to the alternate payee.

The new law permits a spouse will be treated as a nonspouse to the extent provided in a QDRO. If a QDRO provides, for example, for the division of a participant's accrued benefits under a plan as part of a separation agreement, and also provides that the nonparticipant spouse is entitled to no other part of the accrued benefits, the usual survivor benefit provisions will not apply. A QDRO may also provide that a former spouse is to be treated as a surviving spouse for purposes of the survivor annuity provisions, in which case the participant's present spouse would not be treated as a surviving spouse.

The new law also clarifies that a plan which offers a joint and survivor annuity option cannot be required by a QDRO to make payments, prior or subsequent to the participant's separation from service, in the form of a QISA to the alternate payee and his or her subsequent spouse.

Death benefit—transitional rules. REA imposes certain survivor benefit provisions on plans with respect to participants who die before the plans are required to be amended to comply with the Act. During the transition period, the plan is required to pay survivor benefits to a surviving spouse notwithstanding possible contractual claims of other designated beneficiaries. The new law protects the plan against having to pay double death benefits by providing that the death benefit otherwise payable to such designated beneficiaries may be reduced by the present value of benefits required under REA to be paid to the survivor spouse. Moreover, the plan will be treated as satisfying the QJSA requirements if the survivor benefit was paid to the spouse in a nonannuity form.

Plan loans to owner-employees. The new law amends ERISA to remove the absolute ban on plan loans to owner-employees. However, it gives Treasury almost absolute discretion in setting up procedures for granting exemptions from the prohibition. For these purposes only, the term owner-employee includes the owner-employee (defined in Sec. 401(c)(3)), a member of his or her family (under Sec. 267(c)(4)), and certain 50% controlled corporations. Also included are S corporation shareholder-employees and IRA participants and beneficiaries.

The new law also permits Treasury to establish procedures to allow plans to (1) pay owner-employees compensation for personal services rendered to the plan and (2) buy or sell any property to the owner-employee.

The fact that the prohibition was repealed doesn't mean that loans will be permitted in the near future. That's because Treasury need not establish such procedures for granting exemptions if it finds that permitting such transactions

- isn't administratively feasible;
- isn't in the interests of the plan or its participants; and
- isn't protective of the rights of the participants and beneficiaries.

This provision applies only for transactions occurring after the date of enactment.

Special rules for distributions from ESOPs. The new law provides that distribution options under an ESOP may be modified in a nondiscriminatory manner without violating the Sec. 411(d)(6) prohibition against removing options. Moreover, the restrictions on mandatory distributions in excess of $3,500 are not applicable to deductible dividend distributions from ESOPs to participants or beneficiaries.

Additional technical corrections. The new law makes further technical amendments to REA, to clarify that the annuity starting date for nonannuity benefits is the date all events have occurred to entitle the participant to the benefits, to coordinate with federal garnishment restrictions, to clarify that QDRO provisions do not apply to plans not subject to assignment and alienation restrictions, to define when an accrued benefit worth more than $3,500 isn't considered forfeitable for minimum vesting purposes, and clarify when a plan administrator must provide notices of rollover treatment.

Act Sec. 1898(a) amends Code Secs. 402, 408, 411; ERISA Secs. 203(c), (d) clarifying class year vesting rules, lump sum payments to partially vested employees, rules relating to withdrawal of mandatory contributions, effective for plan years beginning after 12-31-84, except that class year vesting rules and the SEP maximum age requirement apply to plan years beginning after enactment date. Provisions do not apply to collectively bargained plans before expiration of latest collective bargaining agreement or 7-1-88, if earlier. Act Sec. 1898(b) amends Code Secs. 401(a), 417; ERISA Sec. 205, relating to joint and survivor annuities, spousal consents, notice requirements, generally effective for plan years beginning after 12-31-84. Requirement that spouse must consent to change in form of benefits is effective for plan years beginning after date of enactment. Provisions relating to spousal consent to loans apply to loans made, revised renewed, renegotiated, or extended after 8-18-85. Act Sec. 1898(c) amends Code Secs. 72, 401(m), 402(a), 414(p); ERISA Sec. 206(d) to clarify rules relating to Qualified Domestic Relations Orders, effective for plan years beginning after 12-31-84, except that provision taxing participants on payments received by a non-spouse alternate payee is applicable to payments made after date of enactment. Act. Sec. 1898(h) amends transitional rules under REA Section 303(c), to preclude double death benefits, effective 8-23-84, and amends Sec. 2503 to preclude a gift tax on certain waivers. Act Secs. 1898(d)-(g) amends Code Secs. 402(f), 411(a)(11), 411(d)(6); ERISA Secs. 203(e), 204(g); REA Sec. 302(b), relating to distributions from ESOPs, notice of rollover treatment, REA effective date for collectively bargained plans. Act Sec. 1898(i) amends ERISA Sec. 408(d), for plan loans, effective for transactions after the date of enactment. This section is generally effective for years beginning after 12-31-84. Provision permitting changes in ESOP distribution option applies to plan amendments after 7-30-84, with special rule for collectively bargained plans.

[¶1898] **Distribution of Child Support Collections.**

The Social Security Act provides that when child support is collected on behalf of an AFDC child, amounts for current support exceeding the current AFDC payment (for which the State and Federal governments may reimburse themselves), are paid to the family up to the amount of monthly support required by the court order.

The new law changes the amount required by "court order" to "court or administrative order," to conform it with a parallel provision added by the 1984 Child Support Enforcement Amendments to use administrative processes for establishing support obligations.

Act Sec. 1899, amending Sec. 457(b)(3) of the Social Security Act, takes effect on the date of the '84 Child Support Enforcement Amendments enactment.

[The page following this is 1905.]

GLOSSARY

ACRS	Accelerated Cost Recovery System	**FERC**	Federal Energy Regulatory Commission
ADR	Asset Depreciation Range	**FICA**	Federal Insurance Contribution Act (Social Security)
AFR	Applicable Federal Rate		
AGI	Adjusted Gross Income	**FIFO**	First-In, First-Out
AII	Allocable Installment Indebtedness	**FMV**	Fair Market Value
		FPHC	Foreign Personal Holding Company
AMT	Alternative Minimum Tax	**FPHCI**	Foreign Personal Holding Company Income
CBA	Collective Bargaining Agreement	**FSC**	Foreign Sales Corporation
CBERA	Caribbean Basin Economic Recovery Act	**FTI**	Foreign Trade Income
		FUTA	Federal Unemployment Tax Act
CBI	Caribbean Basin Initiative		
CFC	Controlled Foreign Corporation	**GDBPR**	Government Development Bank for Puerto Rico
CODA	Cash or Deferred Arrangement		
COLA	Cost of Living Adjustment	**GSL**	Guaranteed Student Loan Bonds
CPI	Consumer Price Index	**GSOC**	General Stock Ownership Corporation
CRCO	Consolidated Return Change of Ownership		
		IDB	Industrial Development Bonds
CSRS	Civil Service Retirement System	**IDC**	Intangible Drilling Cost
DB	Defined Benefit		
DC	Defined Contribution	**IRA**	Individual Retirement Arrangement
DISC	Domestic International Sales Corporation	**ITC**	Investment Tax Credit
E&P	Earnings and Profits	**LIBOR**	London Interbank Offered Rates
ERISA	Employee Retirement Income Security Act of 1974	**LIFO**	Last-In, First-Out
		LSD	Lump Sum Distribution
ESOP	Employee Stock Ownership Plan	**MCC**	Mortgage Credit Certificate
EWOC	Eligible Worker Owned Cooperatives	**MRB**	Mortgage Revenue Bonds
		NAIC	National Association of Insurance Commissioners
FBCI	Foreign Base Company Income		

NOL	Net Operating Loss	**REIT**	Real Estate Investment Trust
NRA	Nonresident Alien		
OASDI	Old Age, Survivor and Disability Insurance	**REMIC**	Real Estate Mortgage Investment Conduit
OID	Original Issue Discount		
		RFC	Regulated Futures Contract
PAL	Protection Against Loss		
PBGC	Pension Benefit Guaranty Corporation	**RIC**	Regulated Investment Companies
		SEC	Securities and Exchange Commission
P&C	Property and Casualty		
PFIC	Passive Foreign Investment Company	**SEP**	Simplified Employee Pension
		SLGS	State and Local Goverment Series
PHC	Personal Holding Company		
PLUS	Parent Loans for Undergraduate Students	**SRLY**	Separate Return Limitation Year
		TCA	Technical Corrections Act
PRDB	Puerto Rico Development Bank		
		T&E	Travel and Entertainment
PSA	Policyholders Surplus Account		
		TEFRA	Tax Equity and Fiscal Responsibility Act of 1982
PSC	Personal Service Corporation		
QDC	Qualified Direct Costs		
QPA	Qualified Plan Awards	**TIN**	Taxpayer Identification Number
QPSII	Qualified Possession-Source Investment Income	**UBI**	Unrelated Business Income
		VDEC	Voluntary Deductible Employee Contributions
QSA	Qualified Segregated Asset		
QTIP	Qualified Terminal Interest Property	**VEBA**	Voluntary Employee Beneficiary Association
R&D	Research & Development		
		WB	Welfare Benefit Plan
R&E	Research and Experimentation	**ZBA**	Zero Bracket Amount

TABLE OF EFFECTIVE DATES

[¶1911]   This table contains the effective dates of the provisions of the Tax Reform Act of 1986 arranged by Act section number. It lists the subject matter of the Act provision and lists in brackets the main sections of the Internal Revenue Code (or other law) being amended. If a provision has more than one effective date, or if there are exceptions or transitional rules, the table usually lists the general effective date and refers you to the paragraph in the Explanation that gives the transitional and special rules.

Abbreviations-The table uses the following abbreviations: TYBA means tax years beginning after. TYEA means tax years ending after.

Act Sec.	Topic	Effective Date
2	Internal Revenue Code of 1954 ('54 Code) redesignated as Internal Revenue Code of 1986 ('86 Code).	Enactment date.
3	Act section references are to '86 Code unless otherwise provided; proration of rate changes limited to corporate rate reductions. [pertains to Sec. 15]	Enactment date.

TITLE I—INDIVIDUAL INCOME TAX PROVISIONS

Subtitle A—Rate Reductions; Increase in Standard Deduction and Personal Exemptions

Act Sec.	Topic	Effective Date
101	Basic tax rate structure revised in two stages for individuals and estates and trusts. [Sec. 1; 15]	TYBA 12-31-86; inflation indexing of tax tables for calendar years after 1988.
102	Standard deduction replaces zero bracket amount; taxable income redefined. [Secs. 3; 63]	TYBA 12-31-86; inflation indexing of standard deduction for TYBA 12-31-89.
103	Deductions for personal exemptions revised. [Sec. 151]	TYBA 12-31-86; inflation adjustment for TYBA 12-31-89.
104	Technical amendments made to conform filing requirements and other provisions. [Secs. 21; 32; 108; 129; 152; 172; 402; 441; 443; 541; 613A; 667; 861; 862; 904; 1398; 2032A; 3402; 6012; 6013; 6014; 6212; 6504]	TYBA 12-31-86.

Subtitle B—Provisions Related to Tax Credits

Act Sec.	Topic	Effective Date
111	Earned income credit increased; provision made for inflation indexing. [Sec. 32]	TYBA 12-31-86.
112	Political contributions credit repealed. [Sec. 24]	TYBA 12-31-86.

Subtitle C—Provisions Related to Exclusions

Act Sec.	Topic	Effective Date
121	Limited exclusion for unemployment compensation benefits repealed. [Sec. 85]	Amounts received after 12-31-86 in TYEA such date.
122	Exclusion for charitable and employee achievement awards reduced. [Secs. 74; 102; 274]	Prizes and awards granted after 12-31-86.
123	Limits imposed on income exclusions for scholarships, fellowships, and tuition reductions. [Sec. 117]	TYBA 12-31-86, but applies only for scholarships and fellowships granted after 8-16-86, see ¶110.

Act Sec.	Topic	Effective Date
	Subtitle D—Provision Related to Deductions	
131	Two-earner married couple deduction repealed. [Sec. 221]	TYBA 12-31-86.
132	Nondeductible floor imposed on certain misc. itemized deductions; moving expenses allowed only as itemized deduction; treatment of employee business expenses revised. [Secs. 62; 67]	TYBA 12-31-86.
133	Nondeductible floor for medical expenses increased from 5 to 7.5% [Sec. 213]	TYBA 12-31-86.
134	State and local sales tax deduction repealed. [Sec. 164]	TYBA 12-31-86.
135	Adoption expense deduction repealed. [Sec. 222]	TYBA 12-31-86.
	Subtitle E—Miscellaneous Provisions	
141	Income averaging repealed. [Secs. 1301; 1302; 1303; 1304; 1305]	TYBA 12-31-86.
142	Limitations on deductions for meals, travel and entertainment expenses. [Secs. 162; 170; 274]	TYBA 12-31-86.
143	Presumption that activity is for profit for hobby loss rules made tougher; home office deduction rules tightened. [Secs. 183; 280A]	TYBA 12-31-86.
144	Housing allowances for ministers and military personnel cause no loss of deduction for home-mortgage interest and property taxes. [Sec. 265]	All taxable years beginning before, on, or after 12-31-86.
	TITLE II—PROVISIONS RELATING TO CAPITAL COST	
	Subtitle A—Depreciation Provisions	
201	Rules relating to Accelerated Cost Recovery System (ACRS) modified; alternative depreciation system added. [Secs. 168; 312(k); 7701]	Generally provisions apply to property placed in service after 12-31-86 for TYEA that date, unless subject to transitional rules. For property placed in service after 7-31-86 and before 1-1-87, election may be made to have rules apply. For special rules, see ¶209.
202	Limits on election to expense certain depreciable business assets increased. [Sec. 179]	Property placed in service after 12-31-86 in TYEA that date.
	Subtitle B—Repeal of Regular Investment Tax Credit	
211	Repeal of regular investment tax credit; rules for reduction in carried credits provided. [Sec. 49]	Generally applies to property placed in service after 12-31-85. For transitional rules and special effective dates, see ¶209.
212	Elective 15-year carryback of existing carryforwards of qualified steel companies. [Pertains to Secs. 38; 46]	Corporation's first TYBA 12-31-86.
213	Elective 15-year carryback of existing carryforwards of qualified farmers. [Pertains to Secs. 38; 46]	Farmer's first TYBA 12-31-86.
	Subtitle C—General Business Credit Reduction	
221	Reduction of general business credit to offset tax liability. [Sec. 38(c)(1)]	TYBA 12-31-85.

Act Sec.	Topic	Effective Date
	Subtitle D—Research and Development Provisions	
231	Qualified research tax credit provisions modified; credit for basic research expenses added. [Secs. 30; 38; 41]	TYBA 12-31-85 generally; basic research credit applies to costs TYBA 12-31-86.
232	Credit for orphan drug testing extended. [Sec. 28(e)]	Enactment date; credit extended to 12-31-90.
	Subtitle E—Changes in Certain Amortization Provisions	
241	Rapid writeoff of trademark and trade name expenditures repealed. [Sec. 177]	Expenditures paid or incurred after 12-31-86 generally.
242	Amortization of railroad grading and tunnel bores repealed. [Sec. 185]	Expenditures paid or incurred after 12-31-86 generally.
243	Deduction allowed for certain bus or freight forwarding authorities. ['81 ERTA Sec. 266]	For bus authorities applies to TYEA 11-18-82; for freight forwarding authorities applies to TYEA month preceding deregulation month. See ¶215.
244	Expensing of costs for removing architectural barriers for the elderly and handicapped made permanent. [Sec. 190(d)]	Effective for TYBA 12-31-85.
	Subtitle F—Provisions Relating to Real Estate	
251	Investment credit for certain rehabilitation expenditures modified. [Secs. 46(b); 48(g), (q)]	Generally applies for property placed in service after 12-31-86. For special transitional rules on certain property placed in service by 1-1-94, see ¶217.
252	New credits for providing low-income housing added. [Secs. 38(b); 42]	Generally applies to property placed in service after 12-31-86 in TYEA that date, see ¶218.
	Subtitle G—Merchant Marine Capital Construction Funds	
261	Tax treatment of deposits to Merchant Marine capital construction fund coordinated with Merchant Marine Act provisions. [Sec. 26(b); 7518]	TYBA 12-31-86.
	TITLE III—CAPITAL GAINS	
	Subtitle A—Individual Capital Gains	
301	Exclusion for long-term capital gains of individuals repealed. [Sec. 1202]	TYBA 12-31-86.
302	Maximum 28-percent capital gains rate for taxpayers other than corporations. [Sec. 1(j)]	TYBA 12-31-86.
	Subtitle B—Repeal of Corporate Capital Gains Treatment	
311	Corporate capital gains treatment repealed. [Sec. 1201]	Generally TYBA 12-31-86. Transitional rules provided for years beginning in 1986 and ending in 1987. See ¶302 and 311.
	Subtitle C—Incentive Stock Options	
321	Requirement that incentive stock options are exercisable only in chronological order repealed. [Sec. 422A(b)(7)]	Options granted after 12-31-86.

Act Sec.	Topic	Effective Date
331	Year-end qualified covered call exception rule expanded. [Sec. 1092(c)(4)(E)]	Positions established after 12-31-86.

Subtitle D—Straddles

331	Year-end qualified covered call exception rule expanded [Sec. 1092(c)(4)(E)]	Positions established after 12-31-86.

TITLE IV—AGRICULTURE, ENERGY, AND NATURAL RESOURCES

Subtitle A—Agriculture

401	Expensing of soil and conservation expenditures limited. [Sec. 175(c)]	For amounts paid or incurred after 12-31-86 in TYEA that date.
402	Expenditures for clearing land are added to the land's basis. [Sec. 182]	For amounts paid or incurred after 12-31-85 for TYEA that date.
403	Gain on disposition of "converted wet lands" or "highly erodible cropland" is treated as ordinary income; loss is long-term capital loss. [Sec. 1257]	For dispositions first used for farming after 3-1-86 in TYEA that date.
404	Deductibility of certain prepaid farming expenses for cash-basis taxpayers limited. [Sec. 464]	For amounts paid or incurred after 3-1-86 in TYBA that date.
405	Rules created for treatment of discharge of qualified indebtedness of solvent farmers. [Secs. 108; 1017(b)]	Discharge of indebtedness occurring after 4-9-86 in TYEA that date.
406	Pre-'86 TRA capital gains treatment retained for dairy cattle under Milk Production Termination Program.	Gains on sale of cattle taken into account after 1-1-87 and before 9-1-87.

Subtitle B—Treatment of Oil, Gas, Geothermal, and Hard Minerals

411	Changes made in treatment of IDCs and mining exploration and development costs; special rules for IDC and mining exploration and development costs for foreign ventures. [Secs. 263(i); 291(b); 617(h)]	Generally apply for costs paid or incurred after 12-31-86 in TYEA that date; transitional rules for certain North Sea interests acquired on or before 12-31-85.
412	Repeal of percentage depletion deduction on oil, gas, and geothermal payments not based on production; reduction in percentage depletion deduction on coal and iron ore. [Secs. 291(a)(2); 613A(d)(5)]	Repeal provisions apply for payments received or accrued after 8-16-86 in TYEA that date; reduction applies to TYBA 12-31-86.
413	IDC recapture rules extended to mine exploration and development costs and percentage depletion. [Sec. 1254]	For dispositions of property placed in service after 12-31-86, unless acquired under a written contract entered into before 9-26-85 and binding at all times thereafter.

Subtitle C—Other Provisions

421(a)	Extension of business energy investment credit for solar, geothermal, ocean thermal and biomass property. [Sec. 46(b)(2)(A)]	For periods beginning after 12-31-85, within transition rules of Code Sec. 48(m). Biomass credit ends after 12-31-87; others end after 12-31-88.
421(b)	Application of certain '86 TRA investment credit transition rules to long-term alternative energy and hydroelectric projects. [Sec. 46(b)(2)(E)]	For periods beginning after 12-31-85, within transition rules of Code Sec. 48(m).

Act Sec.	Topic	Effective Date
422(a)	Exemption from excise tax on special fuels for "neat" alcohol fuels reduced. [Sec. 4041(b)(2)(A)]	For sales and use after 12-31-86.
422(b)	Extension of taxis' partial exemption from excise taxes on motor fuels. [Sec. 6427(e)]	From 10-1-85 through 9-30-88.
423	Restrictions on exemption from import duty for alcohol and mixtures used as fuel.	Generally for articles entered after 12-31-86, see ¶416.

TITLE V—TAX SHELTER LIMITATIONS; INTEREST LIMITATIONS

Subtitle A—Limitations on Tax Shelters

Act Sec.	Topic	Effective Date
501	New rules limiting use of losses and credits from passive sources; special rules for taxpayers who are active participants in real estate activities and exemption for working interest in oil and gas. [Sec. 469]	TYBA 12-31-86, except as to carryovers from a tax year beginning before 1-1-87, see ¶507.
502	Losses from investment in qualified low-income housing not treated as loss from passive activity; transitional rules. [pertains to Sec. 469]	Generally property placed in service before 1-1-89, see ¶507.
503	At-risk limitations extended to real property; special rules for partnerships. [Sec. 465(b), (c)]	Losses incurred after 12-31-86 with respect to property placed in service after 12-31-86 and partnership, S corp., and pass-through entity property placed in service on, before, or after 1-1-86. See ¶501.

Subtitle B—Interest Expense

Act Sec.	Topic	Effective Date
511	Limitations on deduction for nonbusiness investment and personal interest. [Sec. 163(d), (h)]	TYBA 12-31-86.

TITLE VI—CORPORATE PROVISIONS

Subtitle A—Corporate Rate Reductions

Act Sec.	Topic	Effective Date
601	Corporate tax rates reduced. [Sec. 11]	For tax years beginning on or after 7-1-87.

Subtitle B—Treatment of Stock and Stock Dividends

Act Sec.	Topic	Effective Date
611	Reduction in dividends received deduction. [Sec. 243; 244; 246A; 805]	Dividends received or accrued after 12-31-86 in TYEA such date; amended limit on aggregate deduction applies to TYBA 12-31-86.
612	Partial dividend exclusion for individuals repealed. [Sec. 116]	TYBA 12-31-86.
613	Corp.'s stock redemption expenses made nondeductible. [Sec. 162(l)]	Amounts paid or incurred after 2-28-86 in TYEA that date.
614	Stock basis reduced for nontaxed portion of extraordinary dividends. [Sec. 1059]	Dividends declared after 7-18-86 in TYEA that date; dividends aren't aggregated with those declared before 7-18-86; rules on redemptions apply to dividends declared after enactment date in TYEA such date.

Subtitle C—Limitation on Net Operating Loss Carryforwards and Excess Credit Carryforwards

Act Sec.	Topic	Effective Date
621	Limitations on net operating loss and other carryforwards; '76 TRA amendments repealed. [Secs. 382; 383; and '76 TRA Sec. 806(e), (f); and '84 TRA Sec. 59(b)]	Generally effective after 12-31-86; repeal of '76 TRA amendments take effect 1-1-86, see ¶614.

Act Sec.	Topic	Effective Date
	Subtitle D—Recognition of Gain and Loss on Distributions of Property in Liquidation	
631	Recognition of gain or loss on liquidating sale or distribution rules amended. [Secs. 311; 312(n); 332; 333; 334; 336; 337; 338(h); 367; 453(h)]	Distributions and sales made after 7-31-86 unless complete liquidation before 1-1-87. For grandfathered liquidations and other transitional rules, see ¶619.
632	Rules on treatment of C corps. electing S corp. status amended. [Secs. 1363; 1374]	TYBA 12-31-86, but only in cases where 1st taxable year for which corp. is an S corp. is under an election made after 12-31-86. For special effective dates and transitional rules, see ¶619.
634	Treasury study of corporate provisions authorized.	Study due 1-1-88.
	Subtitle E—Other Corporate Provisions	
641	Allocating purchase price in certain asset sales. [Sec. 1060]	Acquisitions after 5-6-86 unless entered under a binding contract in effect on that date and at all times thereafter.
642	Definition of related party for certain sales amended. [Sec. 1239(b)(1)]	Generally sales after enactment date in TYEA that date, unless made after 8-14-86 under a contract in effect on that date and binding at all times thereafter.
643	Amortizable bond premium treated as interest. [Sec. 171]	Obligations acquired after enactment date in TYEA that date, but Sec. 171(c) election applies to bonds issued after enactment date only if taxpayer chooses.
644	Cooperative housing corp. provisions amended. [Sec. 216]	Generally TYBA 12-31-86. Treatment of amounts received to refinance indebtedness apply to taxable years beginning before 1-1-86; qualified refinancing related reserve applies to amounts paid or incurred, and property acquired, in TYBA 12-31-85.
645	Rules relating to personal holding company and foreign personal holding company income amended. [Sec. 543; 553]	Generally apply to royalties received before, on, and after 12-31-86. For special rules for certain specified taxpayers, see ¶635.
646	Election for certain entities to be treated as trusts rather than corporations.	Generally enactment date, see ¶636.
647	Special income inclusion rule for disposition of subsidiary stock.	Dispositions included on consolidated returns for taxable year ending on or before 12-31-87.
	Subtitle F—Regulated Investment Companies	
651	Excise tax imposed on undistributed income of regulated investment companies. [Sec. 852; 4902]	Calendar years beginning after 12-31-86.
652	Treatment of business development companies revised. [Sec. 851]	TYBA 12-31-86.
653	Regulated investment company's treatment of hedging transactions revised. [Sec. 851]	TYBA enactment date.
654	Series funds treated as separate corps. [Sec. 851]	Generally TYBA enactment date; special rules applied for certain existing series funds. See ¶634.
655	Period for mailing notices to shareholders extended. [Secs. 852-855]	TYBA enactment date.

Act Sec.	Topic	Effective Date
656	Rules on protection of mutual funds receiving third-party summonses amended. [Sec. 7609(a)]	Summonses served after enactment date.
657	Certain distributions by regulated investment company to shareholder not treated as preferential dividends. [Sec. 562]	Distributions made after enactment date.

Subtitle G—Real Estate Investment Trusts

661	REIT qualification requirements modified; closely held and E&P rules amended; accounting changes. [Sec. 856(a); 857(a); 859]	TYBA 12-31-86.
662	REIT asset and income requirements modified; treatment of certain wholly-owned subsidiaries, temporary investment of new equity capital, and Shared Appreciation Mortgages revised. [Sec. 856]	TYBA 12-31-86.
663	Amendments made to definitions of rents and interest; requirements for independent contractor modified. [Sec. 856(d), (f)]	Generally TYBA 12-31-86. Amendment for interest income won't apply to loans made pursuant to a binding commitment entered into before 5-28-76.
664	Exclusion of certain noncash income from REIT distribution requirements. [Sec. 857(a)(1), (e)]	TYBA 12-31-86.
665	REIT treatment of capital gains modified; coordination of NOL deduction with capital gains dividend payment; rules mailing of annual dividend reports clarified [Sec. 857(b)(3), (C); 858(c)]	TYBA 12-31-86.
666	Rules on prohibited transactions of REITs modified. [Sec. 857(b)(6)(B), (C)]	TYBA 12-31-86.
667	REIT deficiency dividends exempted from Sec. 6697 penalty. [Sec. 860; 6697]	TYBA 12-31-86.
668	Excise tax imposed on undistributed income of REITs. [Sec. 4981]	Calendar years beginning after 12-31-86.

Subtitle H—Taxation of Interests in Entities Holding Real Estate Mortgages

671	Creation of Real Estate Mortgage Investment Conduits, (REMICs); taxation of entity, interest holders and residual interests; definitions and other rules provided. [Secs. 860A—G]	TYBA 12-31-86.
672	OID rules applied to interests in REMICs. [Sec. 1272]	Debt instruments issued after 12-31-86 in TYEA such date.
673	Definition of taxable mortgage pool modified to reflect creation of REMICs; special rule for coordination with wash-sale provisions made. [Sec. 7701(i)]	Generally 1-1-92; Provision won't apply to entities existing on 12-31-91 unless there is a substantial transfer to such entity. Wash-sale coordination applies to TYBA 12-31-86.
674	Compliance provisions amended to reflect creation of REMICs. [Sec. 6049]	TYBA 12-31-86.

Act Sec.	Topic	Effective Date

TITLE VII—ALTERNATIVE MINIMUM TAX

Act Sec.	Topic	Effective Date
701	Rules relating to the imposition of the alternative minimum tax on individuals and corporations, including adjustments to computations; corporate add-on minimum tax repealed. [Secs. 26; 28; 29; 38; 53; 55—59; 6154; 6425; 6655]	Generally provisions apply to TYBA 12-31-86. For other dates relating to adjustments and preference items, see ¶702—715.
702	Treasury directed to study E&P adjustments on alternative minimum tax on corporations.	Enactment date.

TITLE VIII—ACCOUNTING PROVISIONS

Subtitle A—General Provisions

Act Sec.	Topic	Effective Date
801	Use of cash method limited. [Sec. 448]	Generally TYBA 12-31-86. Election not to have provisions apply may be made for certain related party transactions entered into before 9-25-85; see ¶801.
802	Election provided for simplified dollar-value LIFO method for certain small businesses. [Sec. 474]	TYBA 12-31-86 except amendment doesn't apply to elections made prior to enactment date as long as they remain in effect.
803	Certain expenses must be included in inventory costs and capitalized. [Secs. 189; 263A; 280]	Costs incurred after 12-31-86 in TYBA that date; rule for casualty losses applies to expenses incurred on or after enactment. For other transitional rules and special effective dates, see ¶805.
804	Method of accounting for long-term contracts modified. [Sec. 460]	Long-term contracts entered into after 2-28-86, see ¶806.
805	Reserve for bad debts of taxpayers other than financial institutions repealed. [Sec. 166(c), (f)]	TYBA 12-31-86, see ¶807.
806	Determinations of tax years of partnerships, S corps. and personal service corps. [Secs. 441; 706; 1378]	TYBA 12-31-86, see ¶808.

Subtitle B—Treatment of Installment Obligations

Act Sec.	Topic	Effective Date
811	Use of installment method limited by amount of allocable installment indebtedness. [Sec. 453C]	Generally applies to TYEA 12-31-86, for property dispositions after 2-28-86. For exceptions and special rules, see ¶803.
812	Installment method disallowed for revolving credit plans and certain sales of publicly traded property. [Sec. 453(j)]	Generally TYBA 12-31-86, see ¶803 & 804.

Subtitle C—Other Provisions

Act Sec.	Topic	Effective Date
821	Income of accrual taxpayer attributable to utility services must be included in year services are provided. [Sec. 451(f)]	TYBA 12-31-86.
822	Application of discharge of indebtedness rules to qualified business indebtedness repealed. [Sec. 108(a)]	Debt discharges after 12-31-86.
823	Qualified discount coupons deduction repealed. [Sec. 466]	TYBA 12-31-86.
824	Income exclusion for contributions received by regulated public utility in aid of construction repealed. [Sec. 118]	Amounts received after 12-31-86 in TYEA such date.

Act Sec.	Topic	Effective Date

Act Sec.	Topic	Effective Date
	Subtitle C—Property and Casualty Insurance Companies	
1021	Reduction of deduction for unearned premiums; 6-year ratable inclusion of 20% of unearned premiums as of end of most recent tax year beginning before 1-1-87. [Sec. 832(b)]	Generally TYBA 12-31-86. See ¶1021 for special rule.
1022	Deduction for losses incurred by property and casualty companies reduced by percentage of tax-exempt interest and deductible portion of dividends received. [Sec. 832(b)(5)]	Generally TYBA 12-31-86. For percentages and exceptions, see ¶1032.
1023	Unpaid losses and certain unpaid expenses relating to insurance contracts discounted. [Secs. 807(c); 832(b)(5), (b)(6); 846]	TYBA 12-31-86. For transitional and special rules, see ¶1022.
1024	Protection against loss account repealed; special treatment for small companies revised; provisions combined. [Secs. 501(c)(15); 821-826; 831; 834; 835]	TYBA 12-31-86 for transitional see ¶1023 & 1024.
1025	Treasury study of tax treatment of mutual property and casualty companies authorized.	Due date of 1-1-89.
	Subtitle D—Miscellaneous Provisions	
1031	Treatment of contributions to physician's mutual protection and interindemnity associations.	Payments made to and receipts of, and refunds by, eligible associations after enactment date in TYEA that date.

TITLE XI—PENSIONS AND DEFERRED COMPENSATION; EMPLOYEE BENEFITS; EMPLOYEE STOCK OWNERSHIP PLANS

Subtitle A—Pensions and Deferred Compensation

Part I—Limitations on Tax-Deferred Savings

Subpart A—Rules Applicable to IRAS

1101	Limitation on eligibility to make IRA contributions. [Sec. 219]	Contributions for TYBA 12-31-86.
1102	Rules for nondeductible contributions to IRAs. [Secs. 408(d), (o); 3405(d)(1)(b), 4973(b); 6693(c)]	Contributions and distributions for TYBA 12-31-86.
1103	Spousal deduction when spouse has minimal income. [Sec. 219(c)(1)]	TYB before, on, or after 12-31-85.

Subpart B—Other Provisions

1105	Limits imposed on income exclusion for elective deferrals. [Secs. 402(g); 6051(a)]	Generally TYBA 12-31-86. For special rules see ¶1104 & 1105.
1106	Adjustments made for limits to contributions and benefits under qualified plans. [Secs. 401(a)(17); 402(e)(4)(N); 404(1); 415(b), (c), (d), (k); 416(d)]	Generally for years beginning after 12-31-86. For special rules, see ¶1106.
1107	Modification of rules on deferred compensation plans for State and local governments and tax-exempt organizations. [Sec. 457]	Generally TYBA 12-31-88. Provisions on transfer between plans and cash-outs apply to TYBA 12-31-86, see ¶1107.

Act Sec.	Topic	Effective Date
1108	Rules for simplified employee plans (SEPs) modified. [Secs. 219(b); 402(h); 404(h); 408(k); 3121(a)(5); 3306(b)(5)]	TYBA 12-31-86.
1109	Deduction permitted for Section 501(c)(18) plans. [Secs. 219(b); 501(c)(18)]	TYBA 12-31-86.

Part II—Nondiscrimination Requirements

Subpart A—General Requirements

1111	Nondiscrimination rules for integrated plans revised. [Sec. 401(a)(5), (L)]	Generally for benefits attributable to plan years beginning after 12-31-88, see ¶1110.
1112	Minimum coverage requirements for qualified employee plans modified. [Secs. 401(a)(26; 410(b)]	Generally for plan years beginning after 12-31-88, see ¶1111.
1113	Minimum vesting standards for certain plans revised. [Sec. 411(a)]	Generally for plan years beginning after 12-31-88. For effective dates for collectively bargained plans, see ¶1113.
1114	Highly compensated employee redefined. [Sec. 414(q)]	Generally for TYBA 12-31-86; conforming amendments for employee benefits sections apply for TYBA 12-31-87; conforming sections for pension sections apply for TYBA 12-31-88.
1115	Special rules added for employers operating separate lines of business provided. [Sec. 414(r)]	Years beginning after 12-31-86.

Subpart B—Other Provisions

1116	Rules relating to requirements for CODAs amended; transitional rule provided for certain governmental and tax-exempt pans; special rules on qualified offset arrangements and on sale of assets. [Sec. 401(k)]	Generally apply to year beginning after 12-31-88. Non-discrimination rules generally apply to years beginning after 12-31-86. For special rules, see ¶1116.
1117	Nondiscrimination requirements test provided for employer matching contributions and employee contributions; excise tax imposed on certain excess contributions. [Secs. 401(m); 4979]	Plan years after 12-31-86. For dates on annuity contracts and collectively bargained plans, see ¶1117.
1118	Benefits treated as accruing ratably when determining top-heaviness. [Sec. 416]	Plan years beginning after 12-31-86.
1119	Money purchase plans allowed to reallocate forfeitures under nondiscriminatory plans. [Sec. 401(a)(8)]	Plan years beginning after 12-31-85.
1120	Nondiscrimination requirements for tax-sheltered annuities provided. [Sec. 403(b)]	Years beginning after 12-31-88.

Part III—Treatment of Distributions

1121	Uniform minimum distribution rules added; excise tax added for failure to distribute. [Secs. [Secs. 401(a)(9); 402(a)(5); 408(d)(3); 4974]	Generally applies to TYBA 12-31-88. Rule for transfers treated as rollover contributions applies to TYBA 12-31-86.

Act Sec.	Topic	Effective Date
1122	Rules on tax treatment of lump sum distributions revised; specific provisions include repeal of capital gains, employees' annuities, and frozen deposits. [Secs. 72(b), (d), (e); 402(e); 403(a)(2), (b), (c)]	Generally amounts distributed after 12-31-86 in TYBA that date. For special rules, see ¶1122.
1123	Additional tax imposed on early distributions from qualified retirement plans. [Secs. 72(m), (q), (t); 408(f)]	Generally applies to TYBA 12-31-86. For Sec. 403(b) annuities, applies to TYBA 12-31-88. See also ¶1123.
1124	Election added to treat certain lump sum distribution in 1987 as received in 1986.	Applies to separation from service in 1986 with distribution after 12-31-86 and before 3-16-87.

Part IV—Miscellaneous Provisions

Act Sec.	Topic	Effective Date
1131	Adjustments made to limitations on deductible contributions to certain plans; excise tax imposed on nondeductible contributions. [Secs. 404(a)(3)(A), (a)(7); 4972]	TYBA 12-31-86.
1132	Excise tax imposed for reversion of plan assets to employer. [Sec. 4980]	Generally reversions occurring after 12-31-85, except for plans terminating before 1-1-86. ESOP exception expires for plan terminations after 12-31-88.
1133	Excise tax added for excess distributions from qualified retirement plans. [Sec. 4981A]	Distributions made, and decedents dying (for purposes of estate tax), after 12-31-86. Provision does not apply to distributions before 1-1-88 under terminations before 1-1-87.
1134	Tax treatment of loans to plan participants. [Sec. 72(p)]	Loans made, renewed, renegotiated, modified, or extended after 12-31-86.
1135	Deferred annuity contracts limited to natural persons. [Sec. 72(u)]	Contributions to annuity contracts after 2-28-86.
1136	Contributions to profit-sharing plans allowed when there are no profits. [Sec. 401(a)(26)]	Plan years beginning after 12-31-85.
1137	Requirement added that collective bargaining agreement be bona fide. [Sec. 7701(a)(46)]	Enactment date.
1138	Penalty added for overstatements of pension liabilities. [Sec. 6659A]	Overstatements made after enactment date.
1139	Increase in interest rate assumption used to calculate lump sum benefits. [Secs. 411(a); 417(e)(3)]	Distributions made after 12-31-84, except distributions made after that date and before 1-1-87 under regs issued under '84 REA. See ¶1139.
1140	Amendments to conform to new law; Treasury to issue model amendment; special rule for collectively bargained plans.	Generally plan years beginning after 1-1-89, see §1141.
1141	Issuance of final regs on nondiscrimination requirements, coverage and vesting, 401(k) plans, and excess distributions.	Before 2-1-88.
1142	Treasury to accept opinion letters with respect to master and prototype of 401(k) plans.	Not later than 5-1-87.
1143	Certain fishermen treated as self-employed individuals. [Sec. 401(c)]	TYBA 12-31-86.
1144	IRAs can acquire gold and silver coins; acquisition not treated as distribution. [Sec. 408(m)]	Acquisitions after 12-31-86.

Act Sec.	Topic	Effective Date
1145	Exemptions created from joint and survivor, and preretirement survivor, annuity requirements imposed under '84 REA.	Amendments apply with same effective dates as '84 REA provisions.
1146	Leased employee provisions modified. [Sec. 414(n), (o)]	Generally TYBA 12-31-83. Safe-harbor provision applies for services performed after 12-31-86.
1147	Federal Thrift Savings Fund treated as exempt trust. [Sec. 7701(j)]	Enactment date.

Subtitle B—Employee Benefit Provisions

Part I—Nondiscrimination Rules for Certain Statutory Employee Benefit Plans

1151	New nondiscrimination requirements for employee benefit plans and uniform definitions; amended rules applying to cafeteria plans. [Secs. 89; 125(b); 6039D; 6652]	Generally provisions apply to later of (a) 12-31-87 or (b) earlier of 3 months after issuance of regs or 12-31-88. For effective dates on church plans and cafeteria plan provisions, see ¶1151—1157.

Part II—Other Provisions

1161	Deduction of 25% of health insurance costs allowed self-employeds; Treasury to provide guidance in meeting requirements. [Sec. 162(m)]	TYBA 12-31-86, see also ¶1161.
1162	Extends income exclusion and cap for educational assistance programs; extends group legal services exclusion and adds transitional rule for legal services under cafeteria plans. [Secs. 120(e); 127(d)]	Educational assistance-provisions apply to TYBA 12-31-85; legal services to TYEA 12-31-85.
1163	Dependent care assistance exclusion limited to $5,000; clarification where child care facilities on the employer's premises. [Sec. 129]	TYBA 12-31-86.
1164	Exclusion created for qualified campus lodging for school employees. [Sec. 119(d)]	TYBA 12-31-85.
1165	Special accrued vacation pay provision limited. [Sec. 463(a)(1)]	TYBA 12-31-86.
1166	Full-time life insurance salespeople may be treated as employees for cafeteria plan purposes. [Sec. 7701(a)(20)]	TYBA 12-31-85.
1167	Due date for previously authorized Treasury study on standards for welfare benefit plans extended. ['84 TRA Sec. 560]	One year after enactment date of '86 TRA.
1168	Qualified military benefits excluded from income. [Sec. 134]	TYBA 12-31-86.

Subtitle C—Changes Relating to Employee Stock Ownership Plans

1171	Repeal of payroll based ESOP credit. [Sec. 41]	Compensation paid or accrued after 12-31-86 in TYEA that date, see ¶1172.
1172	Estate tax deduction for proceeds from sale of qualified securities to ESOPs or EWOCs. [Sec. 2057]	Sales after enactment date and before 1-1-92, for returns required to be filed after enactment date.

Act Sec.	Topic	Effective Date
1173	Tax treatment of dividends to ESOPs to repay securities acquisitions loans; interest exclusion provisions. [Secs. 404(k); 852(b)(5)]	Dividends paid in TYBA enactment date; loans used for acquisitions after enactment date, see ¶1174.
1174(a)	Distributions permitted on ESOP terminations. [Sec. 409(d)]	Plan terminations after 12-31-84.
1174(b),—(c)	Distribution and payment requirements modified; put option provision added. [Sec. 409(h), (o)]	Distributions attributable to stock acquired after 12-31-86, see also ¶1177.
1174(d)	Nondiscrimination requirements for ESOP modified. [Sec. 415]	Years beginning after 12-31-86.
1175	Investment diversification requirement for ESOPs. [Sec. 401(a)(28)]	Stock acquired after 12-31-86.
1176	Special requirement provisions added relating to voting rights of newspapers with stock not publicly traded. [Sec. 401(a)(22)]	Effective 12-31-86; acquisitions of securities after 12-31-86.

TITLE XII—FOREIGN TAX PROVISIONS

Subtitle A—Foreign Tax Credit Modifications

Act Sec.	Topic	Effective Date
1201	Separate foreign tax credit limitations for certain types of income; special rules provided for treatment of "qualified loan" interest. [Sec. 904(d)]	TYBA 12-31-86. For special rules, see ¶1201.
1202	Deemed-paid credit determined on accumulated basis. [Secs. 902; 960(a)]	Distributions by foreign corporations from and inclusions attributable to E&P for TYBA 12-31-86.
1203	Treatment of separate limitation losses clarified. [Sec. 904(f)]	Losses incurred in TYBA 12-31-86.
1204	Taxes used to provide subsidies not allowed for foreign tax credit purpose. [Sec. 901(i)]	Foreign taxes paid or accrued in TYBA 12-31-86.
1205	Limitation on carryback of excess tax credit. [pertains to sec. 904]	Applies to carrybacks to years before 1987, see ¶1205.

Subtitle B—Source Rules

Act Sec.	Topic	Effective Date
1211	Determination of source for sales of personal property; Authorization of Treasury study of source rules. [Secs. 865]	Generally TYBA 12-31-86. For foreign persons other than CFCs, source rules apply to transactions entered into after 3-18-86. Study is due 9-30-87.
1212	Tax imposed on transportation income of NRAs and foreign corps.; special rules provided for certain leased property. [Secs. 861(e); 863; 872; 883; 887]	Generally applies to TYBA 12-31-86. Rules for leased property apply for property held on and leased before 1-1-86; U.S. Navy property held on and leased before 1-1-87, see ¶1213.
1213	Source rules created for space and certain ocean activities. [Sec. 863]	TYBA 12-31-86.
1214	Limitations on special treatment of 80-20 corps.; exceptions to provisions for certain interest. [Secs. 861; 871; 881; 1441]	Generally apply for payments made after 12-31-86. Grandfather rule applies to interest on obligations outstanding on 12-31-85, see ¶1212.
1215	Allocation of interest and other expenses to foreign source income. [Sec. 864]	Generally TYBA 12-31-86. For transitional rules for certain outstanding indebtedness and certain qualified corporations, see ¶1214.

Act Sec.	Topic	Effective Date
1216	Allocation of research and experimental expenditures. [Secs. 861(b); 862(b); 863(b)]	TYBA 8-1-86 and on or before 8-1-87.

Subtitle C—Taxation of Income Earned Through Foreign Corporations

1221	Defines Subpart F income subject to current taxation. [Secs. 952; 953; 954]	Generally foreign corp. TYBA 12-31-86, see ¶1217.
1222	CFCs and FPHCs redefined to reflect stock value as well as voting power. [Secs. 552(a)(2); 957(a)]	Generally foreign corp. TYBA 12-31-86, see ¶1218.
1223	Subpart F de minimis rule amended. [Sec. 954(b)(3)]	Foreign corp. TYBA 12-31-86.
1224	Possessions corp. exemption from CFC status repealed. [Sec. 957(c)]	Generally foreign corp. TYBA 12-31-86. Transitional rule applies for corps. treated as CFCs under this provision, see ¶1220.
1225	Accumulated earnings tax and personal holding company tax calculations amended for effectively connected gains and losses. [Secs. 535(b)(9); 545(b)(7)]	Gains and losses realized on or after 3-1-86.
1226	Dividends received deduction provisions for dividends received from foreign corp. revised. [Sec. 245(a)]	Generally applies to distributions out of E&P for TYBA 12-31-86. E&P reduction applies after enactment date.
1227	Special rule for qualified Brazilian corp. as to certain dividends.	Dividends received after 12-31-86.
1228	Special rule for qualified corp. as to gain on disposition of investment in U.S. real property. [Sec. 897]	Enactment date.

Subtitle D—Special Tax Provisions for United States Persons

1231	Modifications made to possessions tax credit. [Sec. 936]	Generally TYBA 12-31-86. For special rules, see ¶1223.
1232	Panama Canal Treaty doesn't exempt anyone from U.S. taxation; partial exclusion provided for certain employee allowances.	Generally to all taxable years beginning before, on, or after date of enactment; exclusion applies to TYBA 12-31-86. See also ¶1224.
1233	Foreign earned income exclusion reduced; exclusion eliminated for individuals violating federal travel restrictions. [Sec. 911(b), (d)]	TYBA 12-31-86.
1234	Information required on application for resident status. Withholding election not available for certain foreign deferred payments. [Secs. 3405; 6039E]	Information provision applies to applications submitted after 12-31-87, or, if earlier, to those after effective date of regs (however not earlier than 1-1-87). Withholding provision applies to payments after 12-31-86.
1235	Treatment of certain passive foreign investment companies. [Secs. 1291; 1293—1297]	Foreign corp. TYBA 12-31-86.
1236	Interest on U.S. obligations received by certain Guam banks not taxed as effectively connected. [Sec. 882(e)]	TYBA 11-16-85.

Subtitle E—Treatment of Foreign Taxpayers

1241	Branch profits tax added. [Sec. 884]	TYBA 12-31-86.

Act Sec.	Topic	Effective Date
1242	Certain deferred payments and income from property transactions treated as effectively connected. [Sec. 864(c)]	TYBA 12-31-86.
1243	Property received in tax-free exchanges by expatriates treated as U.S. income. [Sec. 877(c)]	To sales or exchanges of property received in exchanges after 9-25-85.
1244	Treasury study of competitiveness of U.S. reinsurance companies authorized.	Study due 1-1-88.
1245	Information required with respect to certain foreign-owned corporations. [Sec. 6038A].	TYBA 12-31-86.
1246	Withholding tax imposed on amounts paid by U.S. and foreign partnerships to foreign partners. [Sec. 1446]	Distributions after 12-31-87, or, if earlier, the later of the effective date of regs (however not before 1-1-87).
1247	Exemption provision revised for certain income of foreign governments and international organizations. [Sec. 892]	Amounts accrued or received on or after 7-1-86; no withholding obligation is imposed for amounts paid before enactment date.
1248	Limitation on cost of property imported from related persons. [Sec. 1059A]	Transactions entered into after 3-18-86.
1249	Limits imposed on reduction to income for certain losses of dual resident corps. [Sec. 1503(d)]	NOLs for TYBA 12-31-86.

Subtitle F—Foreign Currency Transactions

Act Sec.	Topic	Effective Date
1261	Rules on treatment of foreign currency transactions added. [Secs. 985—989; 1092(d)(7); 1256(e)]	TYBA 12-31-86. For special rules relating to E&P of foreign corps., see ¶1261.

Subtitle G—Tax Treatment of Possessions

Part I—Treatment of Guam, American Samoa, and the Northern Mariana Islands

Act Sec.	Topic	Effective Date
1271—1273	Tax treatment of Guam, American Samoa, and Northern Marianas amended. [Secs. 876; 881(b); 931; 957(c); 3401(a)(8)(D)]	TYBA 12-31-86, as long as specific agreements with possessions remain in effect.

Part II—Treatment of the Virgin Islands

Act Sec.	Topic	Effective Date
1274	Coordination of U.S. and Virgin Islands tax systems. [Sec. 932]	TYBA 12-31-86, as long as agreement remains in effect.
1275	Possessions tax credit allowed Virgin Islands corps. [Secs. 28(d)(3)(B); 48(a)(2)(B); 338(h)(6)(B); 864(d)(5)(B); 936(d); 7651]	Generally TYBA 12-31-86, see ¶1275.

Part III—Cover Over of Income Taxes

Act Sec.	Topic	Effective Date
1276	Coordination of U.S. and certain possession individual income taxes. [Sec. 7654]	TYBA 12-31-86.

TITLE XIII—TAX-EXEMPT BONDS

Subtitle A—Amendments of Internal Revenue Code of 1954

Act Sec.	Topic	Effective Date
1301	Rules on tax exemption of interest on state and local bonds reorganized and amended; arbitrage and output regulations, mortgage credit certificate program, and penalty for failure to file report on compliance with qualified residential rental project rules; state and local government series and guidelines on business use of property under management contracts	Generally bonds issued after 8-15-86 except mortgage credit certificate program provisions—increase in trade-in rate applies to nonissued bond amounts elected after 8-15-86, and conforming amendments apply to certificates issued after 8-15-86. For transitional rules see ¶1301.

Act Sec.	Topic	Effective Date
	modified; mortgage review bond program report repealed. [Secs. 25; 103; 141—150; 6652; and '84 TRA Sec. 611(d)(7)]	
1302	Treatment of qualified 501(c)(3) bonds clarified. [Sec. 103(c)]	Generally bonds issued after 8-15-86. For transitional rules, see ¶1305.
1303	General stock ownership corp. [GSOC] provisions repealed. [Sec. 1391—1397]	Enactment date

Subtitle B—Effective Dates and Transitional Rules

Act Sec.	Topic	Effective Date
1312—1318	Transitional rules on construction or binding agreements and certain government bonds issued after 8-15-86; refundings; volume caps and specific facilities; special rules overriding other provisions; provisions relating to certain established state programs; definitions relating to effective dates and transitional rules.	For transitional and special rule effective dates, see ¶1301—1303.

Subtitle A—Income Taxation of Trusts and Estates

TITLE XIV—TRUST AND ESTATES; UNEARNED INCOME OF CERTAIN MINOR CHILDREN; GIFT AND ESTATE TAXES; GENERATION-SKIPPING TRANSFER TAX

Act Sec.	Topic	Effective Date
1401	Grantor treated as holding spouse's power or interest. [Sec. 672]	Transfers in trust made after 3-1-86.
1402	Limits to reversionary interest rule exceptions. [Sec. 673]	Transfers in trust made after 3-1-86, except when made pursuant to certain property settlement agreements entered into on or before 3-1-86, see ¶1402.
1403	Taxable year of trusts to be calendar year, except for exempt and charitable trusts. [Sec. 645]	TYBA 12-31-86 but transition rule applies to trust beneficiaries required to include amounts in income under '86 TRA. See ¶1403.
1404	Trusts and certain estates to make estimated payments of income taxes. [Secs. 643(g); 6654(k)]	TYBA 12-31-86.

Subtitle B—Unearned Income of Certain Minor Children

Act Sec.	Topic	Effective Date
1411	Certain unearned income of minor children taxed as if parent's income. [Secs. 1; 6103(e)(1)(A)]	TYBA 12-31-86.

Subtitle C—Gift and Estate Taxes

Act Sec.	Topic	Effective Date
1421	Information necessary for valid special use valuation election. [pertains to Sec. 2032(A)]	Any decedent dying before 1-1-86, but not if, before enactment date, specified statute of limitations for returns has expired.
1422	Gift and estate tax deductions for certain conservation easement donations; special rules for irrevocable transfers of easements. [Secs. 2055; 2522]	Transfers and contributions made after 12-31-86.
1423	Special relief; decedent's property conveyance to charitable foundation treated as charitable contribution. [pertains to Sec. 2055]	Enactment date.

Act Sec.	Topic	Effective Date
	Subtitle D—Generation-Skipping Transfers	
1431; 1432	New tax on generation-skipping transfers GSTs; former law repealed. [Secs. 164(a), (b); 303(d); 691(c)(3); 2032(c); 2515; 2601—2663; 6166]	Generally GSTs made after enactment date. Former GST rules repealed retroactive to 6-11-76; taxpayers otherwise barred by statute of limitations have 1 year from enactment date to file for refunds. For additional special rules and election for certain transfers benefiting grandchild, see ¶1431.

TITLE XV—COMPLIANCE AND TAX ADMINISTRATION

Subtitle A—Revision of Certain Penalties, Etc.

Act Sec.	Topic	Effective Date
1501	Penalties for failure to file information returns and to supply a taxpayer with copy of return consolidated; new penalty for failure to include correct information on information return. [Secs. 6031(b); 6034A(a); 6041(d); 6042(c); 6044(e); 6045(b); 6049(c); 6050A(b); 6050B(b); 6050E-6050I; 6050K(b); 6052(b); 6676(b); 6721—6724]	Returns with a due date (without regard to extensions) after 12-31-86, see ¶1501.
1502	Increased penalty for failure to pay tax due. [Sec. 6651]	Generally for periods after 12-31-86, see ¶1502.
1503	Negligence penalty expanded for underpayments of any tax in Code; fraud penalty increased, but only on amount of employment attributable to fraud. [Sec. 6653]	Returns due (without regard to extensions) after 12-31-86.
1504	Penalty for substantial understatement of tax liability is increased. [Sec. 6661]	Returns due (without regard to extensions) after 12-31-86.

Subtitle B—Interest Provisions

Act Sec.	Topic	Effective Date
1511	Determination of interest rates for overpayments and underpayments revised; differential interest rate adopted. [Sec. 6621]	Interest determined after 12-31-86.
1512	Interest on accumulated earnings tax underpayment accrues from return due date. [Sec. 6601(b)]	Returns due (without regard to extensions) after 12-31-85.

Subtitle C—Information Reporting Provisions

Act Sec.	Topic	Effective Date
1521	Information reports for certain real estate transactions required. [Secs. 6045; 3406]	Real estate transactions closing after 12-31-86.
1522	Information reports required for persons receiving certain Federal contracts. [Sec. 6050M]	Contracts (and subcontracts) entered into, and licenses granted before, on, or after 1-1-87.
1523	Information returns required on payment of royalties. [Sec. 6050N]	Payments made after 12-31-86.
1524	Taxpayer IDs (TINs) required for claimed dependents. [Sec. 6109(a); 6676(a)]	Returns due (without regard to extensions) after 12-31-87.
1525	Tax-exempt interest must be shown on return. [Sec. 6012(d)]	TYBA 12-31-86.

Subtitle D—Provisions Relating to Tax Shelters

Act Sec.	Topic	Effective Date
1531	Tax shelter ratio test for shelter registration modified. [Sec. 6111]	Tax shelters in which interests are first offered for sale after 12-31-86.

Act Sec.	Topic	Effective Date
1532	Penalty for failure to register tax shelter increased. [Sec. 6707]	Shelters in which interests are first offered for sale after enactment date.
1533	Penalty for failure to report tax shelter identification number increased to $250. [Sec. 6707]	Returns filed after enactment date.
1534	Penalty for failure to maintain list of shelter investors increased. [Sec. 6708]	Failures occurring or continuing after enactment date.
1535	Treatment of sham or fraudulent transactions clarified. [Sec. 6621]	Interest accruing after 12-31-84 (but not on underpayments relating to final court decision before enactment date).

Subtitle E—Estimated Tax Provisions

Act Sec.	Topic	Effective Date
1541	Individual estimated tax payments test increased. [Sec. 6654]	TYBA 12-31-86.
1542	Estimated tax payments required for TEO's UBI tax and private foundation's investment income excise tax. [Sec. 6154].	TYBA 12-31-86.
1543	Waiver of 1986 estimated tax penalties. [pertains to Secs. 6654; 6655]	For individuals, periods before 4-15-87; for corporations, periods before 3-15-87.

Subtitle F—Provisions Regarding Judicial Proceedings

Act Sec.	Topic	Effective Date
1551	Awards of reasonable costs and attorney's fees in tax cases modified and extended permanently. [Sec. 7430]	Generally amounts paid after 9-30-86 in proceedings commenced after 12-31-85, see ¶1551.
1552	Failure to exhaust administrative remedies is additional basis for imposition of discretionary penalty by Tax Court. Treasury and Tax Court will report to Congress every two years on Tax Court inventory. [Sec. 6673]	Proceedings started after enactment date; reports to begin for 1987.
1553	Registration fee is imposed on practitioners admitted to practice before Tax Court. [Sec. 7475]	1-1-87.
1554	Clarification that Tax Court has jurisdiction over penalty for failure to pay amount of tax shown on return. [Sec. 6214]	Actions or proceedings before Tax Court not final before enactment date.
1555	Tax Court has authority to require attendance of U.S. Marshals at any Tax Court session. [Sec. 7456]	Enactment date.
1556	Appointments, authority, and clarification of pay and travel rules for Special Trial Judges. [Sec. 7443A]	Enactment date (salary provision effective first day of first month beginning after enactment date).
1557	Tax Court judges permitted to practice law after retirement continue to receive retirement pay. [Secs. 7447; 7448]	Generally enactment date.
1558	Appeals from interlocutory orders of Tax Court. [Sec. 7842(a)(2)]	Tax Court orders entered after enactment date.
1559	Provisions on annuities for surviving spouses and dependent children of Tax Court judges amended. [Sec. 7448]	Generally amounts paid, services performed, and annuity starting dates after 11-1-86, see ¶1559.

Act Sec.	Topic	Effective Date
	Subtitle G—Tax Administration Provisions	
1561	Statute of limitations suspended third-party records not timely produced after service of summons.	Enactment date.
1562	Authority given to rescind notice of deficiency. [Sec. 6212(d)]	Deficiency notices issued on or after 1-1-86.
1563	Authority given IRS to abate interest on deficiencies or payments due to IRS error or delay. [Sec. 6404(e)]	Generally interest accruing on deficiencies or payment for TYBA 12-31-78; one-year extension to seek refund for certain otherwise barred claims.
1564	Interest compounding suspended when interest on deficiency suspended. [Sec. 6601(c)]	Interest accruing after 12-31-82; one-year extension to seek refund for certain otherwise barred claims.
1565	Exemption from levy provided for certain service-connected disability payments. [Sec. 6334(a)]	Amounts payable after 12-31-86.
1566	Value of personal property that may be seized and sold by IRS increased. [Sec. 7325]	Enactment date.
1567	Recordkeeping requirements imposed for automobile use by IRS special agents. [pertains to Secs. 132; 274]	1-1-85.
1568	Disclosure of returns and return information made to certain cities. [Sec. 6103(b)]	Enactment date.
1569	Application of relation-back rule to certain forfeitures under local authorities. [Sec. 6323(i)(3)]	Enactment date.
1570	Certain seized property released to owner if not declared sold at auction. [Sec. 6335(e)(1)]	Property seized after enactment date and property held by the U.S. that is seized on or before that date.
1571	Method of allocation of employee tips modified.	Payroll periods starting after 12-31-86.
1572	For discharge of lien provisions, sales include forfeitures of land sales contracts. [Sec. 7425(c)(4)]	Forfeitures after 30th day after enactment date.
	Subtitle H—Miscellaneous Provisions	
1581	Modification of withholding schedules; filing of new W-4 Forms; repeal of authority to permit employees to request decreases in withholding. [Sec. 3402]	Generally enactment date; special rule if employee doesn't furnish W-4 before 10-1-87.
1582	Treasury directed to prepare report on return-free system.	Six months after enactment date.
	TITLE XVI—EXEMPT AND NONPROFIT ORGANIZATIONS	
1601	Exemption from UBI tax for certain low cost article distributions and exchange and rentals of membership or donor lists. [Sec. 513(h)]	Distributions and exchanges after enactment date.
1602	Trade show activities' exclusion from UBI expanded. [Sec. 513(d)]	Activities in TYBA enactment date.

Act Sec.	Topic	Effective Date
1603	Exemption extended to certain companies holding title for tax-exempt organizations. [Sec. 501(c)(25)]	TYBA 12-31-86.
1604	Additional exception to Sec. 277 deduction limitation rule for organizations who gather and distribute news to members for publication. [Sec. 277]	TYBA enactment date.
1605	Tax-exempt status for organization transfering technology from qualified organizations to public.	Enactment date.
1606	Annual compensation rate used in defining certain governmental officials increased. [4946(c)(5)]	Compensation received after 12-31-85.
1607	Transitional rule for acquisition of indebtedness of a community college regarding certain land.	Enactment date.
1608	Right to stadium seating won't disqualify charitable contributions to certain school.	Amounts paid in taxable years beginning on or after 1-1-84.

TITLE XVII—MISCELLANEOUS PROVISIONS

Act Sec.	Topic	Effective Date
1701	Targeted jobs credit modified and extended for three years. [Sec. 51]	Individuals who begin work for employer after 12-31-85 but before 1-1-89.
1702	Election to collect tax on sales of diesel fuel at wholesale level rather than retail level. [Sec. 4041; 6652]	Effective for sales of fuel for use in highway vehicles after first calendar quarter beginning more than 60 days after enactment date.
1703	Gasoline excise tax shifted from producer to refiner, importer, or terminal operator; bond may be required; exempt purposes; special rule for filing gasohol credit; floor stock taxes imposed. [Sec. 4081—4083; 4101; 6421]	Gasoline removed after 12-31-87.
1704	Rules granting exemption from Social Security coverage clarified; application for revocation of election. [Sec. 1402]	Applications filed after 12-31-86; revocation provisions generally apply to service performed in taxable years ending on or after enactment date.
1705	Exception to FUTA taxes for employees of certain Indian tribes.	For services performed before, on, or after enactment date, but before 1-1-88.
1706	Certain technical service personnel treated as employees for withholding purposes. [Sec. 530 of '78 Revenue Act]	Remuneration paid and services rendered after 12-31-86.
1707	Exclusion for certain foster care payments. [Sec. 131]	TYBA 12-31-85.
1708	Reinstatement of tax breaks for spouses of Vietnam MIAs. [Secs. 2(a)(3)(B); 692(b); 6013(f)(1); 7508(b)]	TYBA 12-31-82.
1709	Native Alaskans exempted from tax for sale of reindeer and reindeer products during period of trust. [Sec. 8 of '37 Reindeer Industry Act.]	As if included in Sec. 8 of 9-1-37 Act.
1711	Adoption assistance program modified. [Sec. 473(a) of Social Security Act]	Expenditures made after 12-31-86.

Act Sec.	Topic	Effective Date
	TITLE XVIII—TECHNICAL CORRECTIONS	
1800	Coordination of technical corrections to earlier Acts with law changes made by other Titles of '86 TRA.	Technical corrections are treated as enacted *immediately before* other provisions of '86 TRA.
	Subtitle A—Amendments Related to the Tax Reform Act of 1984	
	Chapter 1—Amendments Related to Title 1 of the Act	
1801(a)	Election out of lease finance rules that never went into effect for most taxpayers. [Sec. 12(c)(1) of '84 TRA]	Pre-3-7-84 acquisitions, started construction or binding contracts.
1801(b)	Telephone excise tax extension omission corrected. [Sec. 4251]	Bills first rendered during 1985.
1801(c)	Electronic transfer of alcohol and tobacco taxes by controlled groups; floor stock tax on distilled spirits. [Secs. 5061; 5703; and '84 TRA Sec. 27(b)]	Electronic transfer provisions apply to taxes required to be paid on or after 9-30-84; floor stock tax applies to distilled spirits in foreign trade zone on 10-1-85.
1802	Clarification of tax-exempt entity leasing rules and of special effective date provisions. [Secs. 46(e)(4); 47(a)(9); 48(a)(5); 168(j); 7701(e)(4); and '84 TRA Sec. 31(g)]	Generally property placed in service after 5-23-83 in TYEA such date, subject to special effective date rules explained at ¶1804.
1803	Changes in treatment of debt instruments made; amendments include OID, market discount, imputed interest, and amortization of bond premium. [Secs. 163; 171; 483; 1271; 1273; 1276; 1278; 1281; 1282; 1283; and '84 TRA Sec. 44(b)]	Short-term nongovernment and government provisions apply generally for sales and exchanges after 1984. Specific rules apply to obligations acquired after 7-18-84 or 9-27-85, and post-5-6-86 exchanges. For additional special effective dates, see ¶1805.
1804(a)	Limitation on dividends received deduction clarified as to debt-financed portfolio stock of foreign corporations. [Sec. 246A(a)]	Generally applies to portfolio stock with holding periods starting after 7-18-84 in TYEA such date.
1804(b)	Holding period rule for dividends received deduction. Application of related party provisions to interest incurred to buy or carry tax-exempt obligations clarified. [Sec. 246(c) and '84 TRA Sec. 53(a)(3)]	Holding period provision applies to stock acquired after 3-1-86. Related person provisions apply as of 7-18-84; interest provisions apply generally to term loans made and demand loans outstanding after 7-18-84.
1804(c)	Loss on regulated investment stock held less than 6 months disallowed if exempt interest dividends received. [Sec. 852(b)]	Stock with holding periods starting after 3-28-85.
1804(d)	Dividends paid disallowance for liquidation distributions of holding or investment companies other than RICs. [Sec. 562(b)(1)]	Distributions after 9-27-85.
1804(e)	Affiliated group definitions revised. [Secs. 1504(a), (b); 332(b)(1); 337(c)(3); 338(d)]	Generally TYBA 12-31-84. Sec. 332(b)(1) change applies to complete liquidation plans adopted after 3-28-55. For other special rules, qualified stock purchases, corps. affiliated on 6-22-84, certain sell-downs and native corps, see ¶1806.
1804(f)	E&P adjustments on appreciated property distributions. [Sec. 312(b), (c), (n)]	Generally distributions or redemptions in TYBA 9-30-84. See also ¶1806.
1804(g)	Amendments to treatment of transferor corporations in reorganizations. [Secs. 361; 368(a)(2)(G)(i)]	Reorganization plans adopted after enactment date of this Act.
1804(h)	Definition of control for "D" reorganizations clarified. [Sec. 368(a), (c)]	Generally applies to plans adopted after 7-18-84.

Act Sec.	Topic	Effective Date
1804(i)	Collapsible corporation ordinary income provision extends to short-term stock. [Sec. 341]	Sales, exchanges, and distributions after 9-27-85.
1804(j)	Revision of golden parachute provisions. [Sec. 280G]	Generally agreements made or amended after 6-14-84 in TYEA such date.
1804(k)	Reduction of preference benefits doesn't apply to S corporations. [pre-1984 version of Sec. 291(a)(4)]	TYBA 12-31-82.
1805(a)	Clarification on prorated cash method items. [Sec. 706(d)]	Periods after 3-31-84.
1805(b)	Certain transfers treated as disguised sales. [Sec. 707(a)]	Transfers after 3-31-84.
1805(c)	Limitation on gain recognized on distribution of partnership interest by corporation; limitation of sale or exchange treatment to distributions of partnership interests. [Secs. 386(d); 761(e)]	Distributions and sales after 3-31-84.
1805(d)	Property identification for like-kind exchanges allowed on day of exchange. [Sec. 1031(a)]	Generally applies to transfers after 3-31-84.
1806(a)	Estate, or trust's election to recognize gain applies to all distributions-in-kind during taxable year. [Sec. 643(e)(3)]	Distributions after 6-1-84 in TYEA such date.
1806(b)	Treatment of multiple trusts as one trust limited for pre-existing irrevocable trusts. ['84 TRA Sec. 82(b)]	Generally TYBA 3-1-84; for pre-existing irrevocable trusts, applies only to portions attributable to post-3-1-84 contributions to corpus.
1807	Various accounting changes and clarifications to rule for taxable year of deduction. [Secs. 461; 467; 468; 468A; 468B; and '84 TRA Sec. 91(g)]	Generally, amounts deductible after 7-18-84 as to TYEA such date, without regard to economic performance requirements. For special rules, see ¶1808.
1808	Tax straddle rules clarified. [Secs. 263; 1092; and '84 TRA Sec. 102]	Generally positions established after 7-18-84 in TYEA such date, subject to various exceptions and elections.
1809(a)	Clarification of depreciation rules for real property and low-income housing. [Secs. 57(a)(12); 168(b), (f); 312(k); and '84 TRA Sec. 111]	Generally applies to property placed in service after 3-15-84.
1809(b)	Rules on treatment of transferees of recovery property clarified. [Sec. 168(f)(10)]	Property placed in service after 12-31-85 in TYEA that date.
1809(c)	Applicability of Section 751 (unrealized receivables) to recapture provisions for installment sales. [Sec. 453(i)]	Generally dispositions made after 6-6-84.
1809(d)	Limitation on depreciation methods for films, videotapes, and sound recordings. [Sec. 167(c)]	Property placed in service after 3-28-85.
1809(e)	Definition of "new Sec. 38 property" clarified. [Sec. 48(b)]	Property placed in service after 4-11-84.
1810(a)	Recharacterizing foreign income as U.S. income; source rules; coordination with Treaty obligations. [Sec. 904(g)(9); '84 TRA Secs. 121(b); 125(b)(5)]	Recharacterizing foreign income: generally 3-28-85, see ¶1811. Effect of Treaty obligations: Treaties entered after enactment date. Transitional rule relates to separate application of Sec. 904.

Act Sec.	Topic	Effective Date
1810(b)	Rules relating to separate limitation interest amended. [Sec. 904(d)]	Generally for distributions after 7-18-84. For changes regarding designated payor corporations that can give rise to dividends recharacterized as separate limitation interest income, see ¶1811.
1810(c)	Exception to related persons factoring income for persons doing business in same foreign country. [Secs. 864(d); 956(b)]	Receivables transferred after 3-1-84.
1810(d)	Portfolio interest definition amended for non-withholding provisions. [Secs. 871(a), (h); 881(c); 1441(c); 1442(a)]	Portfolio interest on obligations issued after 7-18-84.
1810(e)	Effectively connected OID of foreign related persons. [Secs. 163(e); 871(a); 881(a)]	Obligations issued after 6-9-84.
1810(f)	Rules provided for withholding on sales of U.S. real property by foreigners under FIRPTA. [Sec. 897(i); 1445(b), (d), (e); 6039C(d); 6652(g)].	Generally provisions apply to post-1984 dispositions. Provision on dispositions by partnerships, estates and trusts applies to disposition after 30 days after enactment date of '86 TRA.
1810(g)	Extent of gain recognition on transfers to foreign persons in divisive reorganizations. [Secs. 367(a), (e), (f); 6501(c); 7482(b)]	Generally, post-12-31-84 transfers or exchanges in TYEA that date.
1810(h)	Related party defined for foreign personal holding co.; tracing rule extended to foreign estates and trusts. [Secs. 551(f); 552(c)]	Regarded related party, taxable years of foreign corps. beginning after 3-15-84. Tracing rule extension applies to taxable years of foreign corps. beginning after 12-31-83, with 1-year extension in specified instances.
1810(i)	Gain on indirect transfers of stock of foreign corporations; retroactive election for certain transfers extended. [Sec. 1248(i) and '84 TRA Sec. 133(d)]	Generally transfers after 7-18-84. Retroactive one year after enactment of '86 TRA.
1810(j)	Collection of tax from stapled entities; limitation on application of stapled entity rules. [Sec. 269B(b), (e)]	Generally 7-18-84.
1810(k)	Amended definition of related parties for CFC insurance income provisions. [Sec. 954(e)]	Taxable years of CFCs beginning after 7-18-84.
1810(l)	Changes made in substantial presence test for resident alien status. [Sec. 7701]	Generally TYBA 12-31-84.
1811(a)	Special rule created for cooperative housing corporation's reporting of interest to shareholders. [Sec. 6050H(g)]	Mortgage interest payments received after 12-31-84.
1811(b)	Improvements made to nominee reporting of partnership interests; corrections made to provisions on exchange of partnership interests. [Secs. 6031; 6050K(c)]	Reporting provisions: TYBA enactment date. Exchange provisions: 12-31-84.
1811(c)	Conforming amendment made for brokers' substitute payments statement and failure to file provisions. [Sec. 6678(a)]	Payments after 12-31-84.
1811(d)	Cross-reference made to estate and gift tax underpayment provisions for valuation understatements. [Sec. 6660]	Returns filed after 12-31-84.
1811(e)	Clarification of rule relating to federal tax deposits of $20,000 or more. [Sec. 7502(e)]	Deposits that must be made after 12-31-84.

Act Sec.	Topic	Effective Date
1812(a)	Application of tax benefit rule amended. [Sec. 111(a),(c); 381(c); 1315(d); 1398(g)]	Amounts recovered after 12-31-83 in TYEA that date.
1812(b)	Rules governing below-market loans modified. [Sec. 4941(d)(2); 7872(f)]	Generally term loans made and demand loans outstanding after 6-6-84.
1812(c)	Rules relating to transactions with certain related parties revised. [Sec. 178(b); 267(a); 707(b)]	Foreign persons provision applies generally to TYBA 12-31-83; partnership provision applies to sales or exchanges after 3-1-86.
1812(d)	Rules on Federal Home Loan Bank dividends "Freddie Macs" amended. [Sec. 246(a) and '84 TRA Sec. 177(d)]	Generally applies on or after 1-1-85.
1812(e)	Definitions in personal use property provisions clarified. [Sec. 280F(d)]	Generally apply to property placed in service and leases entered after 6-18-84 in TYEA that date.

Chapter 2—Amendments Related to Title II of the Act

Act Sec.	Topic	Effective Date
1821(a)—(s)	Amendments to rules for taxation of life insurance companies. [Secs. 805; 807—809; 812; 813; 815—818]	TYBA 12-31-83.
1821(t)	Variable contracts with guarantees. [Sec. 817(d)]	Contracts issued after 12-31-86, and contracts issued before 1-1-87 if treated as variable contract on taxpayer's return.
1822	Technical corrections to transitional rules for reserves of life insurance companies. ['84 TRA Sec. 216]	See explanation at ¶1822.
1823	Clarifications to special rule under the Act for companies using the net level reserve method for noncancellable accident and health insurance contracts. ['84 TRA Sec. 217(n)]	See explanation at ¶1823.
1824	Repeal of estimated tax underpayment relief provision. ['84 TRA Sec. 218]	Interest on underpayments of installments required to be paid before 7-18-84.
Sec. 1825(a)	Computational rules related to definition of life insurance contract amended. [Sec. 7702(b)(2), (e)(1), (e)(2)]	Generally contracts issued after 12-31-84 in TYEA such date.
1825(b)	Adjustments to future benefits clarified. [Sec. 7702(f)(7)]	Generally contracts issued after 12-31-84 in TYEA such date.
1825(c)	Tax treatment of contracts that don't qualify clarified. [Sec. 7702(g)(1)(B)]	Generally contracts issued after 12-31-84 in TYEA such date.
1825(d)	Contracts issued during 1984 can qualify as flexible premium contracts by satisfying post-1984 requirements. ['84 TRA Sec. 221(b)]	Generally effective 1-1-84 for flexible premium contracts entered into before 1-1-85.
1825(e)	Initial excess interest guarantees disregarded in determining guaranteed rates for qualification as life insurance contract. ['84 TRA Sec. 221(d)(2)(C)]	Effective 1-1-84 for certain contracts issued before 10-1-84.
1826(a)	Qualified retirement plans exempted from distribution requirements as to deceased annuitants. [Sec. 72(s)]	Contracts issued after 1-18-85 in TYEA such date.
1826(b)	Special rules for transfers of annuity contracts or where holder isn't an individual. [Sec. 72(e), (s)]	Contracts issued after date which is 6 months after '86 TRA enactment date in TYEA such date.

Act Sec.	Topic	Effective Date
1826(c)	Exception for distribution after death clarified. [Sec. 72(q)(2)(B)]	Distributions made after date 6 months after '86 TRA enactment date.
1826(d)	Exception for annuities which are qualified funding assets amended. [Sec. 72(q)(2)(G)]	Contracts issued after 1-18-85 in TYEA such date.
1827(a)	Determination of cost in discriminatory group-term insurance plans. [Sec. 79(d)]	TYEA enactment date of '86 TRA.
1827(b)—(e)	Provisions on treatment of former employees clarified. [Secs. 79; 83; and '84 TRA Sec. 223(d)(2)]	See ¶1827.
1828	Amendment related to certain policy exchanges. [Sec. 1035(b)(1)]	Effective for taxable years ending before, on, or after '86 TRA enactment date.
1829	Waiver of interest on tax underpayments of life insurance companies caused by '84 TRA provisions. [Pertains to Secs. 801—845]	Periods before 7-19-84.
1830	Reaffirmation of Modco grandfather rule. ['82 TEFRA Sec. 255(c)(2)]	Tax years beginning before 1-1-82.

Chapter 3—Amendments Related to Title III of the Act

Act Sec.	Topic	Effective Date
1831	Scope of definition of contributed capital gain property clarified. [Sec. 170(b)(1)(C)]	TYEA 7-18-84.
1832	Rule disqualifying certain foundations from excise tax rate reduction. [Sec. 4940(e)]	TYBA 12-31-84.
1833	Technical correction. [Sec. 6214(c)]	Taxable events occurring after 12-31-84.
1834	Certain games of chance exempted from UBI rules. ['84 TRA Sec. 311(a)(3)]	Games of chance conducted after 6-30-81 in TYEA that date.

Chapter 4—Amendments Related to Title IV of the Act

Act Sec.	Topic	Effective Date
1841	Special rules for estimated tax for NRAs. [Sec. 6654(j)]	TYBA 12-31-84.
1842	Transfers between spouses or incident to divorce. [Secs. 267(g); 453B(g); 1041(e)]	Generally transfers after 7-18-84 in TYEA that date.
1843	Recomputation regarding excess front-loading of alimony payments; 6-year rule reduced to 3. [Sec. 71]	New 3-year rule is effective for divorce or separation instruments executed after 12-31-86. For instruments executed before that time, see ¶1843.
1844	Recapture rule for investment credit at-risk rules clarified. [Secs. 46(c); 47(d)]	Generally property placed in service after 7-18-84 in TYEA that date.
1845	Effective date of distilled spirit drawback rule revised. ['84 TRA Sec. 452]	Products manufactured or produced after 10-31-84.
1846	Transitional rule as to carryforward clarified; as to carryback, amended. [Sec. 39(d)]	TYBA 12-31-83 and to carrybacks from such years.
1847	Provisions relating to minimum tax carryovers and to foreign tax credit clarified; clerical amendments added to reflect renumbering of credits. [Sec. 55(c)]	TYBA 12-31-83 and to carrybacks from such years.
1848	Deadwood eliminated as to retirement bonds and extra investment credit. [Secs. 46(f)(9); 401(c)(2); 2039(e); 4973(b); 6047]	Obligations issued after 12-31-83; and credit amounts after 12-31-83.

Act Sec.	Topic	Effective Date

Chapter 5—Amendments Related to Section 216 of the Act

Act Sec.	Topic	Effective Date
1851(a)	Rules for contributions to welfare benefit plans clarified; UBI tax amended; new definition of disqualified benefit for excise tax purposes; special rules for collective bargaining agreements. [Secs. 419; 419A(f)(5); 512(a)(3); 4976(b)]	Generally contributions paid or incurred, benefits provided, and UBI after 12-31-85 in TYEA that date.
1851(b)	Transitional rule for certain taxpayers with fully vested vacation plans. [Secs. 404(a); 463]	Election must be made within six months after '86 TRA enactment date.
1851(c)	Qualifications for VEBAs, SUBs, and group legal services plans. [Sec. 505]	Years beginning after 12-31-84.
1852(a)(1), (4)-(6)	Required distribution rules for pensions amended; required beginning date defined; no rollovers for required distribution rules. [Secs. 401; 402(a); 403; 4974]	Generally years beginning after 12-31-84.
1852(a)(2)	10% additional tax on distributions before age 59 1/2 extended to 5% owner. [Sec. 72(m)(5)]	Amounts attributable to contributions paid or benefits accrued after 12-31-84.
1852(a)(3)	Required distribution rules applied to Sec. 403(b) annuities. [Sec. 403(b)(10)]	Benefits accrued after 12-31-86 in TYEA that date.
1852(b)	Partial distribution rollover rules apply to some distributions of entire balance; rollover by surviving spouse of decedent's spouse's account limited to IRA. [Sec. 401(a); 402(a), (e), (g); 403(b); 405; and '84 TRA Sec. 522]	Distributions made after 7-18-84 in TYEA such date.
1852(c)	Distributions from plans where substantially all benefits are derived from employee contributions. [Secs. 72; 402]	Amounts received or loan made after 90 days after 7-18-84.
1852(d)(1)	Top heavy plan provisions disregard government plans. [Sec. 416(i)]	Plan years beginning after 12-31-83.
1852(d)(2)	Top heavy provisions disregard benefits of certain retired employees. [Sec. 416(g)]	Plan years beginning after 12-31-84.
1852(e)(1), (2)	Repeal of community property interest exception to estate and gift tax rules; repeals gift tax exclusion for election of beneficiary. [Secs. 406; 407; 2039; 2517]	Estates of decedents dying after and transfers after enactment date of '86 TRA.
1852(e)(3)	Estate tax exclusion grandfathered for certain benefit elections. [84 'TRA Sec. 525(b)]	For decedents dying after 12-31-84 who separated from service before 1-1-85 or before 1-1-83 with respect to '82 TEFRA Sec. 245(c).
1852(f)	Affiliated service group regulation authority. ['84 TRA Sec. 526(d)]	TYBA 12-31-83.
1852(g)	Sec. 401(k) of single employer to be aggregated; special nondiscrimination rules. [Sec. 401(k)(3)]	Plan years beginning after 12-31-84 generally.
1852(h)	Treatment of post-retirement medical benefits for key employees conformed to welfare benefit fund rules. [Sec. 401(h); 415(l); 416(l)]	Years beginning after 3-31-84.
1852(i)	Liability of 2 specific employers for withdrawals from multiemployer plans voided. ['74 ERISA Sec. 4402]	See ¶1852.

Act Sec.	Topic	Effective Date
1853(a)-(e)	Fringe benefit exclusion clarified; cafeteria plans clarified with transitional and special rules; additional excise tax clarified; special rules for telephone service organization and department store leased operations. [Secs. 125; 132; 4977; and '84 TRA Secs. 531; 559]	Generally 1-1-85, see ¶1853
1853(f)	Tuition reduction transitional rules. [pertains to Sec. 117(d) (3)]	Education furnished after 6-30-85 in TYEA such date.
1854	Rules on treatment of ESOPs amended; specific provisions relate to gains on sales of qualified securities, prohibited allocations, dividends on stock, employer deductions, treatment of loans, and estate and excise tax treatment. [Sec. 72(e); 133; 291; 402(g); 404(k); 409; 1042; 2210; 4975; 4978; 4979A; 6166]	Generally provisions apply to TYBA, or transactions entered into after, 7-18-84. For special effective dates for certain provisions, see ¶1854.
1855(a)	ISOP minimum tax transitional rule clarified. ['84 TRA Sec. 555]	Generally applies to modifications of options after 3-20-84.
1855(b)	Permits taxpayers receiving stock in exchange for performance of services to elect Sec. 83(b). [Sec. '84 TRA 556]	TYEA 7-18-84 and beginning before '86 TRA enactment date.

Chapter 6—Amendments Related to Title VI of the Act

Act Sec.	Topic	Effective Date
1861	Mortgage subsidy bond good faith requirements for annual policy statement clarified; veteran mortgage bond rules liberalized. [Secs. 25; 103A]	Reporting requirement applies to obligations issued after 12-31-84. Veterans must apply for mortgage loans by the later of 30 years after service or 1-31-85, effective after 7-18-84.
1862	Mortgage subsidy bond procedural rules apply to mortgage credit certificates (MCCs). [Secs. 25; 6708]	For interest paid or accrued after 12-31-84 on indebtedness incurred after that date.
1863	Advance refunding of certain veterans bonds allowed. [Sec. 613 of '84 TRA]	'86 TRA enactment date; exception for loan made to Oregon under credit agreement entered 4-16-85.
1864(a)	Out-of-state exception to private activity limitation created for bonds in which state shares benefit.	Obligations issued after '85 TRA enactment date in TYEA that date. Issuers can elect to have the exception apply to any issue on or before '86 TRA enactment date.
1864(b)-(e)	Private activity bond information reporting, exempt activities, carryforwards. [Sec. 103(n)]	Obligations issued after 12-31-83, with an exception for certain action before 6-19-84.
1865	Exception against federally guaranteed loan treatment made for certain projects. ['84 TRA Sec. 622]	For requirements of individual projects, see ¶1865.
1866	Transitional rule provided for aggregate limit on small issue bond exception. ['84 TRA Sec. 623]	Obligations issued after 12-31-83.
1867	Amends reference to exceptions to arbitrage bond provisions for Essex County, New Jersey project and adds exception for Muskogee, Oklahoma project. ['84 TRA Sec. 624(c)]	Exception for N.J. applies to bond authorized on 11-10-83 and approved on 7-7-81 and 12-31-81. For Okla., grant approved on 5-5-81 and obligation issued before 1-1-86.
1868	Series of refundings of student loan bonds are exceptions to the arbitrage rules. ['84 TRA Sec. 625(a)]	Obligations issued after the earlier of the date the '65 Higher Education Act expires or the date such act is reauthorized after 7-18-84.

Act Sec.	Topic	Effective Date
1869	Renames consumer loan bonds as private loan bonds and creates exceptions. [Sec. 103(o) and '84 TRA Sec. 626(b)(2)(A)]	Obligations issued after 7-18-84. The denial of tax exemption won't apply to tax increment financing bonds issued before 8-16-86. Transitional rules apply to exceptions. See¶1869.
1870	Limitations on use of industrial development bonds (IDB) for land acquisitions. [Sec. 103(b)(16)]	Obligations issued after 12-31-83.
1871	Registered form and consumer loan bond rules apply to non-Code bonds. [Sec. 103(m)]	Obligations issued after 3-28-85 in TYEA such date.
1872	10-19-83 binding contract exception is extended to certain bonds issued after 3-28-85. ['84 TRA Sec. 631(c)]	7-18-84.
1873	Exception to private loan bond rules for certain electric generating facilities. ['84 TRA Sec. 632]	7-18-84.

Chapter 7—Miscellaneous Provisions

Act Sec.	Topic	Effective Date
1875(a)	Clarification of minimum tax apportionment between trust or estate beneficiary. [Sec. 58(c)]	Transfers occurring after 8-31-82 in TYEA that date.
1875(b)	Redemption of a controlling shareholder's interest. [Sec. 304(a)(1)]	Transfers occurring after 8-31-82 in TYEA that date.
1875(c)(1)-(2), (8)	10% additional income tax applied to withdrawals by 5% owner. [Secs. 402(a)(5)(F)(ii); 408(d)(3)]	Distributions after the enactment date; for those who aren't 5% owners, the provision applies to distributions after 12-31-83 and on or before the enactment date. The tax applies to key employees after 7-18-84 and on or before '86 TRA enactment date.
1875(c)(3)-(4)	Definitions of compensation and gross income clarified. [Secs. 62(7); 219]	Years beginning after 12-31-83.
1875(c)(5)	Repeal of rule relating to return of excess contributions to self-employed. ['84 TRA Sec. 713(d)(1)]	Contributions made in TYBA 12-31-83.
1875(c)(6)	SEP dollar limits conformed to defined contribution dollar limits. [Secs. 219(b)(2); 408(d)(5)]	Years beginning after 12-31-83.
1875(c)(7)	Defines earned income for Keogh plans. [Sec. 404(a)(8)]	TYBA 12-31-84.
1875(c)(9)	Rules prohibiting anticipated cost-of-living adjustments to benefits conformed. [Sec. 415(b)(2)(E)]	Years beginning after 1983.
1875(c)(10)	Exemption from pension withholding rules for certain nonresident aliens. [Sec. 3405(d)(1)(B)]	Distributions after 12-31-82.
1875(c)(11)	Definition of compensation for disabled. [Sec. 415(c)(3)]	Years beginning after 1983.
1875(d)	Time for computing interest on tentative carrybacks revised. Application of deficiency proceedings to computational adjustment. Reporting by nominees holding estate and trust interests. [Secs. 6629(g); 6230(o); 6034A]	Applications filed after 7-18-84. Partnership years ending after 9-3-82. Taxable years of estates and trusts beginning after enactment date of '86 TRA.
1875(e), (f)	Technical corrections.	7-18-84.

Act Sec.	Topic	Effective Date
1875(g)	Exception from the Section 1248 dividend rules. [Sec. 1248(g)]	Exchanges after 3-1-86. Transitional rule for treatment of certain exchanges. See ¶1875.
1876(a)-(e)(1), (f)-(h), (j)-(l), (n), (o)	Corrections and clarifications for FSCs and DISCs. [Secs. 245, 291; 901; 904; 906; 923; 924; 927; 934; 951; 952; 995-996; 1248; and '84 TRA Secs. 802 and 805]	Generally transactions after 12-31-84 in TYEA such date. Special rules for certain contracts, see ¶1876.
1876(e)(2)	New principal bank account requirement for FSCs. [Sec. 924(c)(2)]	Periods after 3-28-85.
1876(i)	Taxable year of FSC and DISC must conform to that of majority shareholder. ['84 TRA Sec. 805(a)(4)]	TYBA 12-31-84.
1876(m)	Election of former export trade corporations to qualify for special treatment. ['84 TRA Sec. 805(b)]	Elections within six months after '86 TRA enactment date.
1876(o)	Treatment of existing contracts taken over by a FSC. ['84 TRA Sec. 805(a)(2)]	Certain leases and contracts entered into before 1-1-85, see ¶1876.
1876(p)	Clerical amendments.	See ¶1876.
1877(a)	Clarification and extension of gasoline and special fuels credit. [Sec. 34(a)(3)]	8-1-84.
1877(b)	Refund of excise tax on diesel fuel increased for school buses. [Sec. 6427(b)(2)]	8-1-84.
1877(c)	No tax on certain resales of piggyback trailers. [Sec. 4051(d)(3)]	Use or resale occurring more than 6 years after original sale.
1878(a)	Capital gain holding period conformed. ['84 TRA Sec. 1001(b)]	Property acquired after 6-22-84 and before 1-1-88.
1878(b)	Sport fishing tax extended. [Sec. 4162(a)(6)]	Generally articles sold by the manufacturer, producer or importer after 9-30-84.
1878(c)	Exemption from aviation excise tax on helicopters extended to oil and gas activities. [Sec. 4041(l)(1)]	4-1-84 for fuel tax exemption; transportation beginning after 3-31-84 for amounts paid after that date.
1878(d)	Estate tax credit for gifts to the Toiyabe National Forest. ['84 TRA Sec. 1028]	Special rule for two estates.
1878(e)	Rules for debt-financed realty of tax-exempt organization extended and clarified. [Sec. 514(c)]	Indebtedness incurred after 7-18-84 with a transitional rule for partnerships.
1878(f)	Targeted jobs credit corrected. [Sec. 51(j) and '84 TRA Sec. 1041(k)(5)(B)]	Individuals beginning work after 7-18-84. Special rule for certain employer.
1878(g)	Rollover period for homes of military personnel extended by one year. [Sec. 1034(h)(2)]	Sales of old residences after 7-18-84.
1878(h)	Change of effective date for disallowance of demolition costs. ['84 TRA Sec. 1063(c)]	Demolitions (of other than a certified historic structure) beginning after 7-19-84 in TYEA 12-31-83. Special rules for demolitions beginning after replacement structure on same site is finished. For special rules for bank and petroleum company, see ¶1878.
1878(i)	Indian tribal government cross-reference corrected. ['84 TRA Sec. 1065(b)]	TYBA 12-31-84.

Act Sec.	Topic	Effective Date
1878(j)	Eliminates requirement that RICs keep adequate shareholder records; higher tax imposed on RICs that don't keep such records. [Sec. 852]	TYBA 12-31-82 generally.
1879(a)	Relief from 1984 estimated tax underpayments caused by '84 TRA changes. [Secs. 6654; 6655]	1984 estimated tax underpayments; before 4-16-85 for individuals, 3-16-85 for corporations.
1879(b)	Orphan drug credit definitions of "clinical testing" and "rare disease or condition" modified. [Sec. 28]	Amounts paid or incurred after 12-31-82 in TYEA that date.
1879(c)	Nonconventional source fuel credit includes sales within affiliated group. [Sec. 29(d)]	Sales in TYEA 12-31-79.
1879(d)	Fringe benefit reporting requirements clarified. [Sec. 6039D(d)]	1-1-85.
1879(e)	Joint Committee Report to Congress on credits and refunds provision repealed. [Sec. 6405]	Effective as if originally part of '84 TRA.
1879(f)	Conform the 19-year real property recovery period to rental agreements. [Sec. 467(e)]	Property placed in service after 5-8-85, with binding contract exception.
1879(g)	Rural electric cooperatives qualify for Sec. 401(k) plans. [Sec. 401(k)]	Plan years beginning after 12-31-84.
1879(h)	New definition of newly discovered oil for WPT. [Sec. 4991(e)(2)]	Oil removed after 2-29-80.
1879(i)	Refunds extended to medicinal alcohol imported from Puerto Rico and the Virgin Islands. [Sec. 7652(g)]	Articles brought into the U.S. after enactment date. Clarification for payments to Puerto Rico or the Virgin Islands.
1879(j)	Investment credit allowed to certain Section 501(d) organization members. [Sec. 48(r)]	Periods after 12-31-78 in TYEA that date. Claim for refunds must be made within one year of enactment date.
1879(k)	Stock association treated as mutual savings bank for insurance purposes. [Sec. 501(c)(14)(B)]	TYEA 8-13-81.
1879(l)	Stock of REITs, RICs, or diversified investment companies isn't stock of single issuer for reorganization purposes. [Sec. 368(a)(2)(F)]	Exchanges after 2-17-76.
1879(m)(1)(A)	Shares are treated as separate qualified subch. S trusts. [Sec. 1361(d)(3)]	TYBA 12-31-82.
1879(m)(1)(B)	No adjustment to accumulated adjustments accounts for federal taxes paid while a C corporation. [Sec. 1368(e)(1)]	TYBA 12-31-82.
1879(n)	QTIP election filing requirements for gifts conformed to general gift tax return rules. [Sec. 2523(f)]	Transfers after 12-31-85. Special rate for October '84 transfers.
1879(o)	An exemption from the Windfall Profit Tax for a certain charitable interest. [pertains to Secs. 4991(b); 4994]	Oil recovered after 2-29-80.
1879(p)	Amendments to transfers of stock under '81 ERTA. ['81 ERTA Sec. 252].	Refunds, credits, and deficiencies barred by statute of limitations may be made within 6 months of '86 TRA enactment date.

Act Sec.	Topic	Effective Date
1879(q)(1),(3),(4)-	Moratorium on collection activities against self-insured workers' compensation fund. Additional time to file Tax Court proceedings.	Period beginning on '86 TRA enactment date and ending on 8-16-87.
1879(q)(2)	Suspension of running of interest on underpayments of self-insured workers' compensation fund.	Period beginning on 8-16-86 and ending 8-16-87.
1879(r)	Separate treatment for filing of returns for alcohol, tobacco, and firearms taxes. [Sec. 6091 (b)(6)]	1st day of 1st calendar month beginning more than 90 days after '86 TRA enactment date.
1879(s)	Amendment made to rules on stripped tax-exempt bonds. [Sec. 1286(d)]	Purchases and sales of stripped obligations or coupons after '86 TRA enactment date.
1879(t)	Ratable income inclusion on disposition of certain specified subsidiary.	'86 TRA enactment date.
1879(u)	Amendments made with relation to Single-Employer Pension Plan Amendments Act. ['74 ERISA Secs. 206(h); 4049(a)]	Generally apply as if included in '86 Single-Employer Pension Plan Amendments Act; ERISA Sec. 206(h)(2) rule applies to plan amendments after '86 TRA enactment date.

Subtitle B—Related to Other Programs Affected by the Deficit Reduction Act of 1984

Chapter 1—Amendments Related to Social Security Act Programs

1882(a)	Exception from social security taxes for members of certain religious faiths clarified. [Sec. 1402(g)]	'86 TRA enactment date.
1882(b)	Special rules for determining church employee income. [Sec. 1402(j)]	Remuneration paid or derived in TYBA 12-31-85.
1882(c)	Revocation of church election to treat services performed for the church as subject to SECA allowed. [Sec. 3121(w)]	'86 TRA enactment date.

Chapter 2—Amendments Related to Unemployment Compensation Program

1883	Technical corrections regarding AFDC and child support programs.	See ¶1883.
1884	Limitation on FUTA credit reduction in states meeting solvency test clarified; agricultural worker defined. [Secs. 3302(c), (f); 3306]	'86 TRA enactment date.

Chapter 3—Amendments Related to Trade and Tariff Programs

1885—1894	Various amendments related to trade and tariff provisions.	See ¶1885—1894.

Subtitle C—Miscellaneous

Chapter 1—Amendments Related to the Consolidated Omnibus Budget Reconciliation Act of 1985

1895(b)(18)(A)	Definition of medicare Federal employment amended. [Sec. 3121(u)(2)(B)(ii) and '85 COBRA Sec. 13205(a)(1)]	Services performed after 3-31-86.
1895(d)(1)-(5), (7), (8)	Amendments relating to continuation of employer-based health insurance coverage. [Sec. 162(k)(2), (7) and '74 ERISA Sec. 602; 605; 607]	Effective as if included in enactment of '85 COBRA.
Sec. 1895(d)(6)	Notice requirement provisions amended. [Sec. 162(k)(6) and '74 ERISA Sec. 606]	Applies only to qualifying events occurring after '86 TRA enactment date.

Act Sec.	Topic	Effective Date
Sec. 1895(d)(9)	Aggregation rules for employer for '74 ERISA amended. ['74 ERISA Sec. 607 and pertaining to IRC Sec. 414]	Take effect same as '86 TRA Sec. 1151(e) and (i). See ¶1895.
1896	Gives insolvent farmers who are allowed to reduce capital gains preference items for individual minimum tax purposes one year from enactment to file claim for credit or refund. ['85 COBRA Sec. 13208]	Enactment date.
Sec. 1897	Clerical errors in amendments to coal tax corrected. [Sec. 4121(b)]	Sales after 3-31-86.

Chapter 2—Amendments Related to the Retirement Equity Act of 1984

Act Sec.	Topic	Effective Date
1898(a)(1)	Treatment of class-year plans under 5-year break and service rules clarified. [Sec. 411(d); '74 ERISA Sec. 203(c)]	Contributions made for plan years beginning after '86 TRA enactment date except for plan years not affected under '84 REA Sec. 302(b).
1898(a)(2)-(4)	Amendments to lump-sum treatment rules, rollovers, and withdrawal of mandatory contributions. [Secs. 402(a),(e); 411; and '74 ERISA Sec. 203(d)]	Effective as if originally included in '84 REA.
1898(a)(5)	Minimum age requirement for SEPs reduced to age 21. [Sec. 408(k)]	Plan years beginning after '86 TRA enactment date.
Sec. 1898(b)(1)-(3), (5), (7)-(14)	Clarification of qualified preretirement survivor annuity and transferee plan rules; coordination with qualified joint and survivor annuity, notice requirements, nonforfeitable accrued benefit definition of vested participant, subsidized plan rules, annuity starting date, and plan and survivor benefit application. [Secs. 401; 417; and '74 ERISA Sec. 205]	Effective as if originally included in '84 REA.
1898(b)(4)	Spousal consent required for plan assets to be used as security for a loan. [Sec. 417; '74 ERISA Sec. 205(c)]	Loans made after 8-18-85. Loans revised, extended, renewed, or renegotiated after 8-18-85 are treated as made after that date.
1898(b)(6)	Spouse must consent to certain changes in beneficiary designations. [Sec. 417(a)(2); '74 ERISA Sec. 205(c)(2)]	Plan years beginning after '86 TRA enactment date.
1898(c)	Clarification of rules relating to Qualified Domestic Relations Orders. [Secs. 72(m)(10); 401(m); 402(a); 414(p); '74 ERISA Sec. 206(d)]	Effective as if originally included in '84 REA except amendment relating to individuals other than spouses or former spouse applies to payments made after enactment date.
1898(d)-(h)	ESOP dividend distributions not subject to mandatory cash-out restrictions; rollover notice requirements clarified; ESOPs permitted to modify distribution options; effective date for certain collectively bargained plans extended; transitional rules double death benefits eliminated. [Secs. 402(f); 411(a), (d)(6) and '74 ERISA Secs. 203; 204(g) and '84 REA Secs. 302(b)(2); 303(c)]	Effective as if originally included in '84 REA.
1898(i)	Technical amendments to '74 ERISA. ['74 ERISA Sec. 408(d)]	Transactions after '86 TRA enactment date.

Chapter 3—Amendment Related to the Child Support Enforcement Amendments of 1984

Act Sec.	Topic	Effective Date
1899	Distribution of child support collections. [Sec. 457(b)(3) of the Social Security Act]	'86 TRA enactment date.

Act Sec.	Topic	Effective Date

Chapter 4—Miscellaneous Amendments Correcting Errors of Spelling, Punctuation, Etc.

1899A	Miscellaneous amendments correcting errors of spelling, punctuation, etc. [Various IRC secs.]	'86 TRA enactment date.

NEW LAW

[¶2001] This division reproduces new law enacted by the Tax Reform Act of 1986 (H.R. 3838).

● Act sections that do not amend or directly affect Code sections start at ¶2002.

● Code sections appear as amended, added or repealed starting at ¶2851. They are in Code section order. New matter is shown in *italics*. Deleted matter and effective dates are shown in footnotes.

● Cross references at the end of each Act or Code section refer to the exact place in the Committee Reports division of the Guide where you will find the official explanation of the change.

● If you prefer, you can read the P-H explanation of the changes before consulting these amended Code sections. The Explanation begins at ¶101. References in the explanation to the Code sections will lead you to the statutory language of this division.

ACT SECTIONS NOT AMENDING THE CODE

Act sections or portions thereof that *do not amend* specific Code sections are at ¶2002—2158. Sections of the Code as amended by other Act sections begin at ¶2851.

TABLE OF CONTENTS

Subtitle C—Limitation on Net Operating Loss Carryforwards and Excess Credit Carryforwards

TITLE XIII—FOREIGN TAX PROVISIONS

Subtitle B—Effective Dates and Transitional Rules

* * * * * * * * * * * *

* * * * * * * * * * * *

TITLE XIV—TRUSTS AND ESTATES; UNEARNED INCOME OF CERTAIN MINOR CHILDREN; GIFT AND ESTATE TAXES; GENERATION-SKIPPING TRANSFER TAX

* * * * * * * * * * * *

Subtitle C—Gift and Estate Taxes

Subtitle D—Generation Skipping Transfers

* * * * * * * * * * * *

TITLE XV—COMPLIANCE AND TAX ADMINISTRATION

* * * * * * * * * * * *

Subtitle B—Interest Provisions

* * * * * * * * * * * *

Subtitle E—Estimated Tax Provisions

* * * * * * * * * * * *

Subtitle F—Provisions Regarding Judicial Proceedings

* * * * * * * * * * * *

* * * * * * * * * * * *

Subtitle G—Tax Administration Provisions

* * * * * * * * * * * *

* * * * * * * * * * * *

Subtitle H—Miscellaneous Provisions

* * * * * * * * * * * *

* * * * * * * * * * * *

TAX REFORM ACT OF 1986

[¶2002] SECTION 1. SHORT TITLE; TABLE OF CONTENTS.

(a) **Short Title.**—This Act may be cited as the "Tax Reform Act of 1986".

(b) **Table of Contents.**—[The provisions of the Tax Reform Act of 1986 amending the Code are reflected in Code order. ¶2851 et seq.]

[¶2003] SEC. 2. INTERNAL REVENUE CODE OF 1986.

(a) **Redesignation of 1954 Code.**—The Internal Revenue Title enacted August 16, 1954, as heretofore, hereby, or hereafter amended, may be cited as the "Internal Revenue Code of 1986".

(b) **References in Laws, Etc.**—Except when inappropriate, any reference in any law, Executive order, or other document—

(1) to the Internal Revenue Code of 1954 shall include a reference to the Internal Revenue Code of 1986, and

(2) to the Internal Revenue Code of 1986 shall include a reference to the provisions of law formerly known as the Internal Revenue Code of 1954.

[¶2004] SEC. 3. AMENDMENT OF 1986 CODE; COORDINATION WITH SECTION 15.

(a) **Amendment of 1986 Code.**—Except as otherwise expressly provided, whenever in this Act an amendment or repeal is expressed in terms of an amendment to, or repeal of, a section or other provision, the reference shall be considered to be made to a section or other provision of the Internal Revenue Code of 1986.

(b) **Coordination With Section 15.**—

(1) **In general.**—Except as provided in paragraph (2), for purposes of section 15 of the Internal Revenue Code of 1986, no amendment or repeal made by this Act shall be treated as a change in the rate of a tax imposed by chapter 1 of such Code.

(2) **Exception.**—Paragraph (1) shall not apply to the amendment made by section 601 (relating to corporate rate reductions).

[¶2005] SEC. 111. INCREASE IN EARNED INCOME CREDIT.

* * * * * * * * * * * *

(e) **Employee Notification.**—The Secretary of the Treasury is directed to require, under regulations, employers to notify any employee who has not had any tax withheld from wages (other than an employee whose wages are exempt from withholding pursuant to section 3402(n) of the Internal Revenue Code of 1986) that such employee may be eligible for a refund because of the earned income credit.

[For official explanation, see Committee Reports, ¶3855]

[¶2006] SEC. 122. PRIZES AND AWARDS.

* * * * * * * * * * * *

(e) **Treatment for Purposes of Employment Taxes.**—Each of the following provisions are amended by striking out "117 or" and inserting in lieu thereof "74(c), 117, or":

* * * * * * * * * * * *

(5) Section 209(s) of the Social Security Act.

[For official explanation, see Committee Reports, ¶3858]

[¶2007] SEC. 203. EFFECTIVE DATES; GENERAL TRANSITIONAL RULES.

* * * * * * * * * * * *

(b) **General Transitional Rule.**—

(1) **In General.**—The amendments made by section 201 shall not apply to—

(A) any property which is constructed, reconstructed, or acquired by the taxpayer pursuant to a written contract which was binding on March 1, 1986,

(B) property which is constructed or reconstructed by the taxpayer if—

(i) the lesser of (I) $1,000,000 or (II) 5 percent of the cost of such property has been incurred or committed by March 1, 1986, and

(ii) the construction or reconstruction of such property began by such date, or

(C) an equipped building or plant facility if construction has commenced as of March 1, 1986, pursuant to a written specific plan and more than one-half of the cost of such equipped building or facility has been incurred or committed by such date.

(2) Requirement that certain property be placed in service before certain date.—

(A) In General.—Paragraph (1) and section 204(a) (other than paragraph (8) or (12) thereof) shall not apply to any property unless such property has a class life of at least 7 years and is placed in service before the applicable date determined under the following table:

In the case of property with a class life of:	The applicable date is:
At least 7 but less than 20 years	January 1, 1989
20 years or more	January 1, 1991.

(B) Residential rental and nonresidential real property.—In the case of residential rental property and nonresidential real property, the applicable date is January 1, 1991.

(C) Class lives.—For purposes of subparagraph (A)—

(i) the class life of property to which section 168(g)(3)(B) of the Internal Revenue Code of 1986 (as added by section 201) shall be the class life in effect on January 1, 1986, except that computer-based telephone central office switching equipment described in section 168(e)(3)(B)(iii) of such Code shall be treated as having a class life of 6 years.

(ii) property described in section 204(a) shall be treated as having a class life of 20 years, and

(iii) property with no class life shall be treated as having a class life of 12 years.

(D) Substitution of applicable dates.—If any provision of this Act substitutes a date for an applicable date, this paragraph shall be applied by using such date.

(3) Property qualifies if sold and leased back in 3 months.—Property shall be treated as meeting the requirements of paragraphs (1) and (2) or section 204(a) with respect to any taxpayer if such property is acquired by the taxpayer from a person—

(A) in whose hands such property met the requirements of paragraphs (1) and (2) or section 204(a), or

(B) who placed the property in service before January 1, 1987,

and such property is leased back by the taxpayer to such person not later than the earlier of the applicable date under paragraph (2) or the day which is 3 months after such property was placed in service.

(4) Plant facility.—For purposes of paragraph (1), the term "plant facility" means a facility which does not include any building (or with respect to which buildings constitute an insignificant portion) and which is—

(A) a self-contained single operating unit or processing operation,

(B) located on a single site, and

(C) identified as a single unitary project as of March 1, 1986.

(c) Property Financed With Tax-Exempt Bonds.—

(1) In general.—Subparagraph (C) of section 168(g)(1) of the Internal Revenue Code of 1986 (as added by this Act) shall apply to property placed in service after December 31, 1986, in taxable years ending after such date, to the extent such property is financed by the proceeds of an obligation (including a refunding obligation) issued after March 1, 1986.

(2) Exceptions.—

(A) Construction or binding agreements.—Subparagraph (C) of section 168(g)(1) of such Code (as so added) shall not apply to obligations with respect to a facility—

(i)(I) the original use of which commences with the taxpayer, and the construction, reconstruction, or rehabilitation of which began before March 2, 1986, and was completed on or after such date,

(II) with respect to which a binding contract to incur significant expenditures for construction, reconstruction, or rehabilitation was entered into before March 2, 1986, and some of such expenditures are incurred on or after such date, or

　　(III)　acquired on or after March 2, 1986, pursuant to a binding contract entered into before such date, and

　(ii)　described in an inducement resolution or other comparable preliminary approval adopted by the issuing authority (or by a voter referendum) before March 2. 1986.

(B)　Refunding.—

　(i)　In general.—Except as provided in clause (ii), in the case of property placed in service after December 31, 1986, which is financed by the proceeds of an obligation which is issued solely to refund another obligation which was issued before March 2, 1986, subparagraph (C) of section 168(g)(1) of such Code (as so added) shall apply only with respect to an amount equal to the basis in such property which has not been recovered before the date such refunded obligation is issued.

　(ii)　Significant expenditures.—In the case of facilities the original use of which commences with the taxpayer and with respect to which significant expenditures are made before January 1, 1987, subparagraph (C) of section 168(g)(1) of such Code (as so added) shall not apply with respect to such facilities to the extent such facilities are financed by the proceeds of an obligation issued solely to refund another obligation which was issued before March 2, 1986.

(C)　Facilities.—In the case of an inducement resolution or other comparable preliminary approval adopted by an issuing authority before March 2, 1986, for purposes of subparagraphs (A) and (B)(ii) with respect to obligations described in such resolution, the term "facilities" means the facilities described in such resolution.

(D)　Significant expenditures.—For purposes of this paragraph, the term "significant expenditures" means expenditures greater than 10 percent of the reasonably anticipated cost of the construction, reconstruction, or rehabilitation of the facility involved.

(d)　Mid-Quarter Convention.—In the case of any taxable year in which property to which the amendments made by section 201 do not apply is placed in service, such property shall be taken into account in determining whether section 168(d)(3) of the Internal Revenue Code of 1986 (as added by section 201) applies for such taxable year to property to which such amendments apply.

(e)　Normalization Requirements.—

　(1)　In general.—A normalization method of accounting shall not be treated as being used with respect to any public utility property for purposes of section 167 or 168 of the Internal Revenue Code of 1986 if the taxpayer, in computing its cost of service for ratemaking purposes and reflecting operating results in its regulated books of account, reduces the excess tax reserve more rapidly or to a greater extent than such reserve would be reduced under the average rate assumption method.

　(2)　Definitions.—For purposes of this subsection—

　(A)　Excess tax reserve.—The term "excess tax reserve" means the excess of—

　(i)　the reserve for deferred taxes (as described in section 167(l)(3)(G)(ii) or 168(e)(3)(B)(ii) of the Internal Revenue Code of 1954 as in effect on the day before the date of the enactment of this Act), over

　(ii)　the amount which would be the balance in such reserve if the amount of such reserve were determined by assuming that the corporate rate reductions provided in this Act were in effect for all prior periods.

　(B)　Average rate assumption method.—The average rate assumption method is the method under which the excess in the reserve for deferred taxes is reduced over the remaining lives of the property as used in its regulated books of account which gave rise to the reserve for deferred taxes. Under such method, if timing differences for the property reverse, the amount of the adjustment to the reserve for the deferred taxes is calculated by multiplying—

　(i)　the ratio of the aggregate deferred taxes for the property to the aggregate timing differences for the property as of the beginning of the period in question, by

　(ii)　the amount of the timing differences which reverse during such period.

[For official explanation, see Committee Reports, ¶3870]

〖¶2008〗   SEC. 204.   ADDITIONAL TRANSITIONAL RULES.

(a) **Other Transitional Rules.—**

  (1) **Urban renovation projects.—**

    (A) **In General.**—The amendments made by section 201 shall not apply to any property which is an integral part of any qualified urban renovation project.

    (B) **Qualified urban renovation project.**—For purposes of subparagraph (A), the term "qualified urban renovation project" means any project—

      (i)   described in subparagraph (C), (D), (E), or (G) which before March 1, 1986, was publicly announced by a political subdivision of a State for a renovation of an urban area within its jurisdiction,

      (ii)   described in subparagraph (C), (D) or (G) which before March 1, 1986, was identified as a single unitary project in the internal financing plans of the primary developer of the project, and

      (iii)   described in subparagraph (C) or (D), which is not substantially modified on or after March 1, 1986.

    (C) **Project where agreement on December 19, 1984.**—A project is described in this subparagraph if—

      (i)   a political subdivision granted on July 11, 1985, development rights to the primary developer-purchaser of such project, and

      (ii)   such project was the subject of a development agreement between a political subdivision and a bridge authority on December 19, 1984.

For purposes of this subparagraph, subsection (b)(2) shall be applied by substituting "January 1, 1994" for "January 1, 1991".

    (D) **Certain additional projects.**—A project is described in this subparagraph if it is described in any of the following clauses of this subparagraph and the primary developer of all such projects is the same person:

      (i)   A project is described in this clause if the development agreement with respect thereto was entered into during April 1984 and the estimated cost of the project is approximately $194,000,000.

      (ii)   A project is described in this clause if the development agreement with respect thereto was entered into during May 1984 and the estimated cost of the project is approximately $190,000,000.

      (iii)   A project is described in this clause if the project has an estimated cost of approximately $92,000,000 and at least $7,000,000 was spent before September 26, 1985, with respect to such project.

      (iv)   A project is described in this clause if the estimated project cost is approximately $39,000,000 and at least $2,000,000 of construction cost for such project were incurred before September 26, 1985.

      (v)   A project is described in this clause if the development agreement with respect thereto was entered into before September 26, 1985, and the estimated cost of the project is approximately $150,000,000.

      (vi)   A project is described in this clause if the board of directors of the primary developer approved such project in December 1982, and the estimated cost of such project is approximately $107,000,000.

      (vii)   A project is described in this clause if the board of directors of the primary developer approved such project in December 1982, and the estimated cost of such project is approximately $59,000,000.

      (viii)   A project is described in this clause if the Board of Directors of the primary developer approved such project in December 1983, following selection of the developer by a city council on September 26, 1983, and the estimated cost of such project is approximately $107,000,000."

    (E) **Project where plan confirmed on October 4, 1984.**—A project is described in this subparagraph if—

      (i)   a State or an agency, instrumentality, or political subdivision thereof approved the filing of a general project plan on June 18, 1981, and on October 4, 1984, a State or an agency, instrumentality, or political subdivision thereof confirmed such plan,

      (ii)   the project plan as confirmed on October 4, 1984, included construction or renovation of office buildings, a hotel, a trade mart, theaters, and a subway complex, and

(iii) significant segments of such project were the subject of one or more conditional designations granted by a State or an agency, instrumentality, or political subdivision thereof to one or more developers before January 1, 1985.

The preceding sentence shall apply with respect to a property only to the extent that a building on such property site was identified as part of the project plan before September 26, 1985, and only to the extent that the size of the building on such property site was not substantially increased by reason of a modification to the project plan with respect to such property on or after such date. For purposes of this subparagraph, subsection (b)(2) shall be applied by substituting "January 1, 1998" for "January 1, 1991."

(F) A project is described in this paragraph if it is a sports and entertainment facility which—

(i) is to be used by both a National Hockey League team and a National Basketball Association team;

(ii) is to be constructed on a platform utilizating air rights over land acquired by a state authority and identified as Site B in a report dated May 30, 1984, prepared for a state urban development corporation; and

(iii) is eligible for real property tax, and power and energy benefits pursuant to the provisions of state legislation approved and effective July 7, 1982, or

(iv) the mixed-use development is—

(I) to be constructed above a public railroad station utilized by the national railroad passenger corporation and commuter railroads serving two States; and

(II) will include the reconstruction of such station so as to make it a more efficient transportation center and to better integrate the station with the development above, such reconstruction plans to be prepared in cooperation with a State transportation authority.

For purposes of this subparagraph, subsection (b)(2) shall be applied by substituting "January 1, 1993" for the applicable date that would otherwise apply.

(G) A project is described in this subparagraph if—

(i) an inducement resolution was passed on March 9, 1984, for the issuance of obligations with respect to such project,

(ii) such resolution was extended by resolutions passed on August 14, 1984, April 2, 1985, August 13, 1985, and July 8, 1986,

(iii) an application was submitted on January 31, 1984, for an Urban Development Action Grant with respect to such project, and

(iv) an Urban Development Action Grant was preliminarily approved for all or part of such project on July 3, 1986.

(H) A project is described in this subparagraph if it is a redevelopment project, with respect to which $10 million in industrial revenue bonds were approved by a State Development Finance Authority on January 15, 1986, a village transferred approximately $4 million of bond volume authority to the State in June 1986, and a binding Redevelopment Agreement was executed between a city and the development team on July 1, 1986.

(2) **Certain projects granted FERC licenses, etc.**—The amendments made by section 201 shall not apply to any property which is part of a project—

(A) which is certified by the Federal Energy Regulatory Commission before March 2, 1986, as a qualifying facility for purposes of the Public Utility Regulatory Policies Act of 1978,

(B) which was granted before March 2, 1986, a hydroelectric license for such project by the Federal Energy Regulatory Commission, or

(C) which is a hydroelectric project of less than 80 megawatts that field [should read filed] an application for a permit exemption, or license with the Federal Energy Regulatory Commission before March 2, 1986.

(3) **Supply or service contracts.**—The amendments made by section 201 shall not apply to any property which is readily identifiable with and necessary to carry out a written supply or service contract, or agreement to lease, which was binding on March 1, 1986.

(4) **Property treated under prior tax acts.**—The amendments made by section 201 shall not apply to property described in section 12(c)(2) or 31(g)(5) and 31(g)(17)(j) of the Tax Reform Act of 1984, to property described in section 209(d)(1)(B) of the Tax Equity and Fiscal Responsibility Act of 1982, as amended by the Tax Reform Act of

1984 and to property described in section 216(b)(3) of the Tax Equity and Fiscal Responsibility Act of 1982.

(5) **Special rules for property included in master plans of integrated projects.—** The amendments made by section 201 shall not apply to any property placed in service pursuant to a master plan which is clearly identifiable as of March 1, 1986, for any project described in any of the following subparagraphs of this paragraph:

(A) A project is described in this subparagraph if—

(i) the project involves production platforms for offshore drilling, oil and gas pipeline to shore, process and storage facilities, and a marine terminal, and

(ii) at least $900,000,000 of the costs of such project were incurred before September 26, 1985.

(B) A project is described in this subparagraph if—

(i) such project involves a fiber optic network of at least 20,000 miles, and

(ii) before September 26, 1985, construction commenced pursuant to the master plan and at least $85,000,000 was spent on construction.

(C) A project is described in this subparagraph if—

(i) such project passes through at least 10 States and involves intercity communication links (including one or more repeater sites, terminals and junction stations for microwave transmissions, regenerators or fiber optics and other related equipment),

(ii) the lesser of $150,000,000 or 5 percent of the total project cost has been expended, incurred, or committed before March 2, 1986, by one or more taxpayers each of which is a member of the same affiliated group (as defined in section 1504(a)), and

(iii) such project consists of a comprehensive plan for meeting network capacity requirements as encompassed within either:

(I) a November 5, 1985, presentation made to and accepted by the Chairman of the Board and the president of the taxpayer, or

(II) the approvals by the Board of Directors of the parent company of the taxpayer on May 3, 1985, and September 22, 1985, and of the executive committee of said board on December 23, 1985.

(D) A project is described in this subparagraph if—

(i) such project is part of a flat rolled product modernization plan which was initially presented to the Board of Directors of the taxpayer on July 8, 1983,

(ii) such program will be carried out at 3 locations, and

(iii) such project will involve a total estimated minimum capital cost of at least $250,000,000.

(E) A project is described in this subparagraph if the project is being carried out by a corporation engaged in the production of paint, chemicals, fiberglass, and glass, and if—

(i) the project includes a production line which applies a thin coating to glass in the manufacture of energy efficient residential products, if approved by the management committee of the corporation on January 29, 1986,

(ii) the project is a turbogenerator which was approved by the president of such corporation and at least $1,000,000 of the cost of which was incurred or committed before such date.

(iii) the project is a waste-to-energy disposal system which was initially approved by the management committee of the corporation on March 29, 1982, and at least $5,000,000 of the cost of which was incurred before September 26, 1985,

(iv) the project, which involves the expansion of an existing service facility and the addition of new lab facilities needed to accommodate topcoat and undercoat production needs of a nearby automotive assembly plant, was approved by the corporation's management committee on March 5, 1986, or

(v) the project is part of a facility to consolidate and modernize the silica production of such corporation and the project was approved by the president of such corporation on August 19, 1985.

(F) A project is described in this subparagraph if—

(i) such project involves a port terminal and oil pipeline extending generally from the area of Los Angeles, California, to the area of Midland, Texas, and

(ii) before September 26, 1985, there is a binding contract for dredging and channeling with respect thereto and a management contract with a construction manager for such project.

(G) A project is described in this subparagraph if—

(i) the project is a newspaper printing and distribution plant project with respect to which a contract for the purchase of 8 printing press units and related equipment to be installed in a single press line was entered into on January 8, 1985, and

(ii) the contract price for such units and equipment represents at least 50 percent of the total cost of such project.

(H) A project is described in this subparagraph if it is the second phase of a project involving direct current transmission lines spanning approximately 190 miles from the United States-Canadian border to Ayer, Massachusetts, alternating current transmission lines in Massachusetts from Ayers to Millbury to West Medway, DC-AC converted terminals to Monroe, New Hampshire, and Ayer, Massachusetts, and other related equipment and facilities.

(I) A project is described in this subparagraph if it involves not more than two natural gas-fired combined cycle electric generating units each having a net electrical capability of approximately 233 megawatts, and a sales contract for approximately ½ of the output of the 1st unit was entered into in December 1985.

(J) A project is described in this subparagraph if—

(i) the project involves an automobile manufacturing facility (including equipment and incidental appurtenances) to be located in the United States, and

(ii) either—

(I) the project was the subject of a memorandum of understanding between 2 automobile manufacturers that was signed before September 25, 1985, the automobile manufacturing facility (including equipment and incidental appurtenances) will involve a total estimated cost of approximately $750,000,000, and will have an annual production capacity of approximately 240,000 vehicles or

(II) the Board of Directors of an automobile manufacturer approved a written plan for the conversion of an existing facility to produce a new model of a vehicle currently not produced in the United States, such facility will be placed in service by July 1, 1987, and such Board action occurred in July 1985, with respect to a $523 million expenditure, in June 1983, with respect to a $475 million expenditure, or in July 1984, with respect to a $312 million expenditure.

(K) A project is described in this subparagraph if either—

(i) the project involves a joint venture between a utility company and a paper company for a super calendar paper mill, and at least $50,000,000 were incurred or committed with respect to such project before March 1, 1986, or

(ii) the project involves a paper mill for the manufacture of newsprint (including a cogeneration facility) is generally based on a written design and feasibility study that was completed on December 15, 1981, and will be placed in service before January 1, 1991, or

(iii) the project is undertaken by a Maine corporation and involves the modernization of pulp and paper mills in Millinocket and/or East Millinocket, Maine, or

(iv) the project involves the installation of a paper machine for production of coated publication papers, the modernization of a pulp mill, and the installation of machinery and equipment with respect to related processes, as of December 31, 1985, in excess of $50 million was incurred for the project, as of July 1986, in excess of $150 million was incurred for the project, and the project is located in Pine Bluff, Arkansas, or

(v) involves property of a type described in ADR classes 26.1, 26.2, 25, 00.3 and 00.4 included in a paper plant which will manufacture and distribute tissue, towel or napkin products; is located in Effingham County, Georgia; and is generally based upon a written General Description which was submitted to the Georgia Department of Revenue on or about June 13, 1985.

(L) A project is described in this subparagraph if—

(i) a letter of intent with respect to such project was executed on June 4, 1985, and

(ii) a 5-percent downpayment was made in connection with such project for 2 10-unit press lines and related equipment.

(M) A project is described in this subparagraph if—
(i) the project involves the retrofit of ammonia plants,
(ii) as of March 1, 1986, more than $390,000 had been expended for engineering and equipment, and
(iii) more than $170,000 was expensed in 1985 as a portion of preliminary engineering expense.

(N) A project is described in this subparagraph if the project involves bulkhead intermodal flat cars which are placed in service before January 1, 1987, and either—
(i) more than $2,290,000 of expenditures were made before March 1, 1986, with respect to a project involving up to 300 platforms, or
(ii) more than $95,000 of expenditures were made before March 1, 1986, with respect to a project involving up to 850 platforms.

(O) A project is described in this subparagraph if—
(i) the project involves the production and transportation of oil and gas from a well located north of the Arctic Circle, and
(ii) more than $200,000,000 of cost had been incurred or committed before September 26, 1985.

(P) A project is described in this subparagarph if—
(i) a commitment letter was entered into with a financial institution on January 23, 1986, for the financing of the project,
(ii) the project involves intercity communication links (including microwave and fiber optics communications systems and related property),
(iii) the project consists of communications links between—
(I) Omaha, Nebraska, and Council Bluffs, Iowa,
(II) Waterloo, Iowa and Sioux City, Iowa,
(III) Davenport, Iowa and Springfield, Illinois, and
(iv) the estimated cost of such project is approximately $13,000,000.

(Q) A project is described in this subparagraph if—
(i) such project is a mining modernization project involving mining, transport, and milling operations,
(ii) before September 26, 1985, at least $20,000,000 was expended for engineering studies which were approved by the Board of Directors of the taxpayer on January 27, 1983, and
(iii) such project will involve a total estimated minimum cost of $350,000,000.

(R) A project is described in this subparagraph if—
(i) such project is a dragline acquired in connection with a 3-stage program which began in 1980 to increase production from a coal mine,
(ii) at least $35,000,000 was spent before September 26, 1985, on the 1st 2 stages of the program, and
(iii) at least $4,000,000 was spent to prepare the mine site for the dragline.

(S) A project is described in this subparagraph if it is a project consisting of a mineral processing facility using a heap leaching system (including waste dumps, low-grade dumps, a leaching area, and mine roads) and if—
(i) convertible subordinated debentures were issued in August 1985, to finance the project,
(ii) construction of the project was authorized by the Board of Directors of the taxpayer on or before December 31, 1985,
(iii) at least $750,000 was paid or incurred with respect to the project on or before December 31, 1985, and
(iv) the project is placed in service on or before December 31, 1986.

(T) A project is described in this subparagraph if it is a plant facility on Alaska's North Slope and—
(i) the approximate cost is $575 million, of which approximately $100 million was spent on off-site construction or
(ii) the approximate cost of which is $450 million, of which approximately $100 [sic] was spent on off-site construction, more than 50 percent of the project cost was spent prior to December 31, 1985, and which will be placed in service in 1987.

(U)   A project is described in this subparagraph if it involves the connecting of existing retail stores in the downtown area of a city to a new covered area, the total project will be 250,000 square feet, a formal Memorandum of Understanding relating to development of the project was executed with the city on July 2, 1986, and the estimated cost of the project is $18,186,424.

(V)   A project is described in this subparagraph if it includes a 200,000 square foot office tower, a 200-room hotel, a 300,000 square foot retail center, an 800-space parking facility, the total cost is projected to be $60 million, and $1,250,000 was expended with respect to the site before August 25, 1986.

(W)   A project is described in this subparagraph if it is a joint use and development project, including an integrated hotel, convention center, office, related retail facilities and public mass transportation terminal, and vehicle parking facilities which satisfies the following conditions:

(i)   is developed within certain air space rights and upon real property exchanged for such joint use and development project which is owned or acquired by a state department of transportation, a regional mass transit district in a county with a population of at least 5,000,000 and a community redevelopment agency;

(ii)   such project affects an existing, approximately forty (40) acre public mass transportation bus-way terminal facility located adjacent to an interstate highway;

(iii)   a memorandum of understanding with respect to such joint use and development project is executed by a state department of transportation, such a county regional mass transit district and a community redevelopment agency on or before December 1, 1986, and

(iv)   a major portion of such joint use and development project is placed in service by December 31, 1990.

(X)   A project is described in this subparagraph if—

(i)   it is an $8 million project to provide advanced control technology for adipic acid at a plant, which was authorized by the company's Board of Directors in October 1985, at December 31, 1985, $1.4 million was committed and $.4 million expended with respect to such project, or

(ii)   it is an $8.3 million project to achieve compliance with state and federal regulations for particulates emissions, which was authorized by the company's Board of Directors in December 1985, by March 31, 1986, $250,000 was committed and $250,000 was expended with respect to such project, or

(iii)   it is a $22 million project for the retrofit of a plant that makes a raw material for aspartame, which was approved in the company's December 1985 capital budget, if approximately $3 million of the $22 million was spent before August 1, 1986.

(Y)   A project is described in this subparagraph if such project passes through at least 9 states and involves an intercity communication link (including multiple repeater sites and junction stations for microwave transmissions and amplifiers for fiber optics); thelink from Buffalo to New York/Elizabeth was completed in 1984; the link from Buffalo to Chicago was completed in 1985; and the link from New York to Washington is completed in 1986.

(6)   **Natural gas pipeline.**—The amendments made by section 201 shall not apply to any interstate natural gas pipeline (and related equipment) if—

(A)   3 applications for the construction of such pipeline were filed with the Federal Energy Regulatory Commission before November 22, 1985 (and 2 of which were filed before September 26, 1985), and

(B)   such pipeline has 1 of its terminal points near Bakersfield, California.

(7)   **Certain leasehold improvements.**—The amendments made by section 201 shall not apply to any reasonable leasehold improvements, equipment and furnishings placed in service by a lessee or its affiliates if—

(A)   the lessee or an affiliate is the original lessee of each building in which such property is to be used,

(B)   such lessee is obligated to lease the building under an agreement to lease entered into before September 26, 1985, and such property is provided for such building, and

(C)   such buildings are to serve as world headquarters of the lessee and its affiliates.

Act §204(a)(7) ¶2008

For purposes of this paragraph, a corporation is an affiliate of another corporation if both corporations are members of a controlled group of corporations within the meaning of section 1563(a) of the Internal Revenue Code of 1954 without regard to section 1563(b)(2) of such Code. Such lessee shall include a securities firm that meets the requirements of subparagraph (A), except the lessee is obligated to lease the building under a lessee entered into on June 18, 1986.

(8) **Solid waste disposal facilities.**—The amendments made by section 201, and section 203(c), shall not apply to the taxpayer who originally places in service any qualified solid waste disposal facility (as defined in section 7701(e)(3)(B) of the Internal Revenue Code of 1986) if before March 2, 1986—

(A) there is a binding written contract between a service recipient and a service provider with respect to the operation of such facility to pay for the services to be provided by such facility, or

(B) a service recipient or governmental unit (or any entity related to such recipient or unit) made a financial commitment of at least $200,000 for the financing or construction of such facility,

(C) such facility is the Tri-Cities Solid Waste Recovery Project involving Fremont, Newark, and Union City, California, and has received an authority to construct from the Environmental Protection Agency or from a State or local agency authorized by the Environmental Protection Agency to issue air quality permits under the Clean Air Act.

(9) **Certain submersible drilling units.**—In the case of a binding contract entered into on October 30, 1984, for the purchase of 6 semi-submersible drilling units at a cost of $425,000,000, such units shall be treated as having an applicable date under subsection 203(b)(2) of January 1, 1991.

(10) **Wastewater or sewage treatment facility.**—The amendments made by section 201 shall not apply to any property which is part of a wastewater or sewage treatment facility if either—

(A) site preparation for such facility commenced before September 1985, and a parish council approved a service agreement with respect to such facility on December 4, 1985,

(B) a city-parish advertised in September 1985, for bids for construction of secondary treatment improvements for such facility, in May 1985, the city-parish received statements from 16 firms interested in privatizing the wastewater treatment facilities, and the metropolitan council selected a privatizer at its meeting on November 20, 1985, and adopted a resolution authorizing the Mayor to enter into contractual negotiation with the selected privatizer;

(C) the property is part of a wastewater treatment facility with respect to which a binding service agreement between a privatizer and the Western Carolina Regional Sewer Authority with respect to such facility was signed before January 1, 1986;

(D) such property is part of a wastewater treatment facility (located in Cameron County, Texas, within one mile of the City of Harlingen), an application for a wastewater discharge permit was filed with respect to such facility on December 4, 1985, and a City Commission approved a letter of intent relating to a service agreement with respect to such facility on August 7, 1986; or a wastewater facility (located in Harlingen, Texas) which is a subject of the letter of intent and service agreement described in subparagraph (A)(2) of this paragraph and the design of which was contracted for in a letter of intent dated January 23, 1986."

(11) **Certain aircraft.**—The amendments made by section 201 shall not apply to any new aircraft with 19 or fewer passenger seats if—

(A) The aircraft is manufactured in Kansas, Florida, Georgia, or Texas. For purposes of this subparagraph, an aircraft is "manufactured" at the point of its final assembly;

(B) The aircraft was in inventory or in the planned production schedule of the final assembly manufacturer, with orders placed for the engine(s) on or before August 16, 1986, and

(C) The aircraft is purchased or subject to a binding contract on or before December 31, 1986, and is delivered and placed in service by the purchaser, before July 1, 1987.

Section 211(d)(2)(B) shall not apply to aircraft which meet the requirements of this subparagraph.

(12) Certain satellites.—The amendments made by section 201 shall not apply to any satellite with respect to which—

(A) on or before January 28, 1986, there was a binding contract to construct or acquire a satellite, and

(i) an agreement to launch was in existence on that date, or

(ii) on or before August 5, 1983, the Federal Communications Commission had authorized the construction and for which the authorized party has a specific although undesignated agreement to launch in existence on January 28, 1986;

(B) by order adopted on July 25, 1985, the Federal Communications Commission granted the taxpayer an orbital slot and authorized the taxpayer to launch and operate 2 satellites with a cost of approximately $300,000,000; or

(C) the International Telecommunications Satellite Organization or the International Maritime Satellite Organization entered into written binding contracts before May 1, 1985.

(13) Certain nonwire line cellular telephone systems.—The amendments made by section 201 shall not apply to property that is part of a nonwire line system in the Domestic Public Cellular Radio Telecommunications Service for which the Federal Communications Commission has issued a construction permit before September 26, 1985, but only if such property is placed in service before January 1, 1987.

(14) Certain cogeneration facilities.—The amendments made by section 201 shall not apply to projects consisting of 1 or more facilities for the cogeneration and distribution of electricity and steam or other forms of thermal energy if—

(A) at least $100,000 was paid or incurred with respect to the project before March 1, 1986, a memorandum of understanding was executed on September 13, 1985, and the project is placed in service before January 1, 1989,

(B) at least $500,000 was paid or incurred with respect to the projects before May 6, 1986, the projects involve a 22-megawatt combined cycle gas turbine plant and a 45-megawatt coal waste plant, and applications for qualifying facility status were filed with the Federal Energy Regulatory Commission on March 5, 1986,

(C) the project cost approximates $125,000,000 to $140,000,000 and an application was made to the Federal Energy Regulatory Commission in July 1985,

(D) an inducement resolution for such facility was adopted on September 10, 1985, a development authority was given an inducement date of September 10, 1985, for a loan not to exceed $80,000,000 with respect to such facility, and such facility is expected to have a capacity of approximately 30 megawatts of electric power and 70,000 pounds of steam per hour.

(E) at least $1,000,000 was incurred with respect to the project before May 6, 1986, the project involves a 52-megawatt combined cycle gas turbine plant and a petition was filed with the Connecticut Department of Public Utility Control to approve a power sales agreement with respect to the project on March 27, 1986.

(15) Certain electric generating stations.—The amendments made by section 201 shall not apply to a project consisting of a coal-fired electric generating station (including multiple generating units, coal mine equipment, and transmission facilities) if—

(A) a tax-exempt entity will own an equity interest in all property included in the project (except the coal mine equipment), and

(B) at least $72,000 was expended in the acquisition of coal leases, land and water rights, engineering studies, and other development costs before May 6, 1986.

For purposes of this subparagraph, subsection (b)(2) shall be applied by substituting "January 1, 1986" for "January 1, 1991."

(16) Sports arenas.—

(A) Indoor sports facility.—The amendments made by section 201 shall not apply to up to $20,000,000 of improvements made by a lessee of any indoor sports facility pursuant to a lease from a State commission granting the right to make limited and specified improvements (including planned seat explanations), if architectural renderings of the project were commissioned and received before December 22, 1985.

(B) Metropolitan sports arena.—The amendments made by section 201 shall not apply to any property which is part of an arena constructed for professional sports activities in a metropolitan area, provided that such arena is capable of seat-

Act §204(a)(16) ¶2008

ing no less than 18,000 spectators and a binding contract to incur significant expenditures for its construction was entered into before June 1, 1986.

(17) **Certain waste-to-energy facilities.**—The amendments made by section 201 shall not apply to 2 agricultural waste-to-energy powerplants (and required transmission facilities), in connection with which a contract to sell 100 megawatts of electricity to a city was executed in October 1984.

(18) **Certain coal-fired plants.**—The amendments made by section 201 shall not apply to one of three 540 megawatt coal-fired plants that are placed in service after a sale leaseback occurring after January 1, 1986, if—

    (A) the Board of Directors of an electric power cooperation authorized the investigation of a sale leaseback of a nuclear generation facility by resolution dated January 22, 1985, and

    (B) a loan was extended by the Rural Electrification Administration on February 20, 1986, which contained a covenant with respect to used property leasing from unit II.

(19) **Certain rail systems.**—

    (A) The amendments made by section 201 shall not apply to a light rail transit system, the approximate cost of which is $235,000,000, if, with respect to which, the board of directors of a corporation (formed in September 1984 for the purpose of developing, financing, and operating the system) authorized a $300,000 expenditure for a feasibility study in April 1985.

    (B) The amendments made by section 201 shall not apply to any project for rehabilitation of regional railroad rights of way and properties including grade crossings which was authorized by the Board of Directors of such company prior to October 1985; and/or was modified, altered or enlarged as a result of termination of company contracts, but approved by said Board of Directors no later than January 30, 1986, and which is in the public interest, and which is subject to binding contracts or substantive commitments by December 31, 1987.

(20) **Certain detergent manufacturing facility.**—The amendments made by section 201 shall not apply to a laundry detergent manufacturing facility, the approximate cost of which is $13,200,000, with respect to which a project agreement was fully executed on March 17, 1986.

(21) **Certain resource recovery facility.**—The amendments made by section 201 shall not apply to any of 3 resource recovery plants, the aggregate cost of which approximates $300,000,000, if an industrial development authority adopted a bond resolution with respect to such facilities on December 17, 1984, and the projects were approved by the department of commerce of a Commonwealth on December 27, 1984.

(22) The amendments made by section 201 shall not apply to a computer and office support center building in Minneapolis, with respect to which the first contract, with an architecture firm, was signed on April 30, 1985, and a construction contract was signed on March 12, 1986.

(23) **Certain district heating and cooling facilities.**—The amendment made by section 201 shall not apply to pipes, mains, and related equipment included in district heating and cooling facilities, with respect to which the development authority of a State approved the project through an inducement resolution adopted on October 8, 1985, and in connection with which approximately $11,000,000 of tax-exempt bonds are to be issued.

(24) **Certain vessels.**—

    (A) Certain offshore vessels.—The amendments made by section 201 shall not apply to any offshore vessel the construction contract for which was signed on February 28, 1986, and the approximate cost of which is $9,000,000.

    (B) Certain inland river vessel.—The amendments made by section 201 shall not apply to a project involving the reconstruction of an inland river vessel docked on the Mississippi River at St. Louis, Missouri, on July 14, 1986, and with respect to which:

        (i) the estimated cost of reconstruction is approximately $39,000,000;

        (ii) reconstruction was commenced prior to December 1, 1985;

        (iii) at least $17,000,000 was expended before December 31, 1985; and

    (C) Special automobile carrier vessels.—The amendments made by section 201 shall not apply to two new automobile carrier vessels which will cost approximately $47,000,000 and will be constructed by a U.S.-flag carrier to operate, under the U.S.-flag with an American crew, to transport foreign automobiles to the

United States, in a case where negotiations for such transportation arrangements commenced in April 1985, formal contract bids were submitted prior to the end of 1985, and definitive transportation contracts were awarded in May 1986.

(D) The amendments made by section 201 shall not apply to a 562-foot passenger cruise ship, which was purchased in 1980 for the purpose of returning the vessel to U.S. service, the approximate cost of refurbishment of which is approximately $47 million.

(25) Certain wood energy projects.—The amendments made by section 201 shall not apply to two wood energy products [should read projects] for which applications with the Federal Energy Regulatory Commission were filed before January 1, 1986, which are described as follows:

(A) a 26.5 megawatt plant in Fresno, California, and
(B) a 26.5 megawatt plant in Rocklin, California.

(26) The amendments made by section 201 shall not apply to property which is a geothermal project of less than 20 megawatts that was certified by the Federal Energy Regulatory Commission on July 14, 1986, as a qualifying small power production facility for purposes of the Public Utility Regulatory Policies Act of 1978 pursuant to an application filed with the Federal Energy Regulatory Commission on April 17, 1986."

(27) Certain economic development projects—The amendments made by section 201 shall not apply to any of the following projects:

(A) A mixed use development on the East River the total cost of which is approximately $400,000,000, with respect to which a letter of intent was executed on January 24, 1984, and with respect to which approximately $2.5 million had been spent by March 1, 1986.

(B) A 356-room hotel, banquet, and conference facility (including 525,000 square feet of office space) the approximate cost of which is $158,000,000, with respect to which a letter of intent was executed on June 1, 1984 and with respect to which an inducement resolution and bond resolution was adopted on August 20, 1985.

(C) Phase 1 of a 4-phase project involving the construction of laboratory space and ground-floor retail space the estimated cost of which is $32,000,000 and with respect to which a memorandum of understanding was made before August 29, 1983.

(D) A project involving the development of a 490,000 square foot mixed-use building at 152 W. 57th Street and 7th Avenue, New York, New York, the estimated cost of which is $100,000,000, and with respect to which a building permit application was filed in May 1986.

(E) A mixed-use project containing a 300 unit, 12-story hotel, garage, two multi-rise office buildings, and also included a park, renovated riverboat, and barge with festival marketplace, the capital outlays for which approximate $68 million.

(F) The construction of a three-story office building that will serve as the home office for an insurance group and its affiliated companies, with respect to which a city agreed to transfer its ownership of the land for the project in a Redevelopment Agreement executed on September 18, 1985, once certain .conditions are met.

(G) A commercial bank formed under the laws of the State of New York which entered into an agreement on September 5, 1985, to construct its headquarters at 60 Wall Street, New York, New York, with respect to such headquarters.

(H) Any property which is part of a commercial and residential project, the first phase of which is currently under construction, to be developed on land which is the subject of an ordinance passed on July 20, 1981, by the city council of the city in which such land is located, designating such land and the improvements to be placed thereon as a residential-business planned development, which development is being financed in part by the proceeds of industrial development bonds in the amount of $62,000 issued on December 4, 1985.

(28) The amendment made by section 201 shall not apply to an $80 million capital project steel seamless tubular casings minimill and melting facility located in Youngstown, Ohio, which was purchased by the taxpayer in April 1985, and—

(A) the purchase and renovation of which was approved by a committee of the Board of Directors on February 22, 1985, and
(B) as of December 31, 1985, more than $20,000,000 was incurred or committed with respect to the renovation.

(29) The amendments made by section 201 shall not apply to any project for residential rental property if—

    (A) an inducement resolution with respect to such project was adopted by the State housing development authority on January 18, 1985, and

    (B) such project was the subject of law suits filed on June 22, 1984, and November 21, 1985.

(30) The amendments made by section 201 shall not apply to a 30 megawatt electric generating facility fueled by geothermal and wood waste, the approximate cost of which is $55 million, and with respect to which a 30-year power sales contract was executed on March 22, 1985.

(31) The amendments made by section 201 shall not apply to railroad maintenance-of-way equipment, with respect to which a Boston bank entered into a firm binding contract with a major northeastern railroad before March 2, 1986, to finance $10.2 million of such equipment, if all of the equipment was placed in service before August 1, 1986.

(32) The amendment made by section 201 shall not apply to—

    (A) a facility constructed on approximately seven acres of land located on Ogle's Poso Creek Oil field, the primary fuel of which will be bituminous coal from Utah or Wyoming, with respect to which an application for an authority to construct was filed on July 30, 1984, an authority to construct was issued on February 28, 1985, and a prevention of significant deterioration permit application was submitted on June 17, 1985,

    (B) a facility constructed on approximately seven acres of land located on Teorco's Jasmin oil field, the primary fuel of which will be bituminous coal from Utah or Wyoming, with respect to which an authority to construct was filed on August 30, 1984, an authority to construct was issued on May 4, 1985, and a prevention of significant deterioration permit application was submitted on July 3, 1985,

    (C) the Mountain View Apartments, in Hadley, Massachusetts,

    (D) a facility expected to have a capacity of not less than 65 megawatts of electricity, the steam from which is to be sold to a pulp and paper mill, with respect to which application was made to the Federal Regulatory Commission for certification as a qualified facility on November 1, 1985, and received such certification on January 24, 1986,

    (E) $2.2 million of equipment ordered on January 27, 1986, in connection with a 60,000 square foot plant that was completed in 1983,

    (F) a magnetic resonance imaging machine, with respect to which a binding contract to purchase was entered into in April 1986, in connection with the construction of a magnetic resonance imaging clinic with respect to which a Determination of Need certification was obtained from a State Department of Public Health on October 22, 1985, if such property is placed in service before December 31, 1986,

    (G) to a company located in Salina, Kansas, which has been engaged in the construction of highways and city streets since 1946, but only to the extent of $1,410,000 of investment in new section 38 property,

    (H) a $300,000 project undertaken by a small metal finishing company located in Minneapolis, Minnesota, the first parts of which were received and paid for in January 1986, with respect to which the company received Board approval to purchase the largest piece of machinery it has ever ordered in 1985,

    (I) A $1.2 million finishing machine that was purchased on April 2, 1986 and placed into service in September 1986 by a company located in Davenport, Iowa,

    (J) A 25 megawatt small power production facility, with respect to which Qualifying Facility status no. QF86-593-000 was granted on March 5, 1986,

    (K) A $600 million 250 megawatt plant placed in service by the Sierra Pacific Power Company,

    (L) 128 units of rental housing the Point Gloria Limited Partnership.

    (M) Kenosha Harbor, in Kenosha, Wisconsin,

    (N) Lakeland Park Phase II, in Baton Rouge, Louisiana,

    (O) the Santa Rosa Hotel, in New Orleans, Louisiana,

    (P) the Sheraton Baton Rouge, in Baton Rouge, Louisiana,

    (Q) $300,000 of equipment placed in service in 1986, in connection with the renovation of the Best Western Townhouse Convention Center in Cedar Rapids, Iowa,

    (R) the segment of a nationwide fiber optics telecommunications network placed in service by SouthernNet, the total estimated cost of which is $37 million,

(S) two cogeneration facilities, placed in service by the Reading Anthracite Company, costing approximately $110 million each, with respect to which filings were made with the Federal Energy Regulatory Commission on December 31, 1985 and which are located in Pennsylvania,

(T) a fiber optics network placed in service by Kansas City Southern Industries, the total estimated cost of which is $25 million,

(U) 3 newly constructed fishing vessels, and one vessel that is overhauled, placed in service by Mid Coast Marine, but only to the extent of $6.7 million of investment,

(V) $350,000 of equipment acquired in connection with the reopening of a plant in Bristol, Rhode Island, which plant was purchased by Buttonwoods, Ltd., Associates on February 7, 1986,

(W) $4.046 million of equipment placed in service by Brendle's Inc., acquired in connection with a Distribution Center,

(X) a multi-family mixed-use housing project located in a home rule city, the zoning for which was changed to residential business planned development on November 26, 1985, and with respect to which both the home rule city and the State housing finance agency adopted inducement resolutions on December 20, 1985,

(Y) the Myrtle Beach Convention Center, in South Carolina, to the extent of $25 million of investment, and

(Z) railroad cars placed in service by the Pullman Leasing Company, pursuant to an April 3, 1986 purchase order, costing approximately $10 million

(33) The amendments made by section 201 shall not apply to—

(A) $400,000 of equipment placed in service by Super Key Market, if such equipment is placed in service before January 1, 1987,

(B) the Trolley Square project, the total project cost of which is $24.5 million, and the amount of depreciable real property of which is $14.7 million.

(C) a waste-to-energy project in Derry, New Hampshire, costing approximately $60 million,

(D) the City of Los Angeles Co-composting project, the estimated cost of which is $62 million, with respect to which, on July 17, 1985, the California Pollution Control Financing Authority issued an initial resolution in the maximum amount of $75 million to finance this project,

(E) the St. Charles, Missouri Mixed-Use Center,

(F) Oxford Place in Tulsa, Oklahoma,

(G) an amount of investment generating $20 million of investment tax credits attributable to property used on the Illinois Diversatch Campus,

(H) $25 million of equipment used in the Melrose Park Engine Plant that is sold and leased back by Navistar,

(I) 80 thousand vending machines, for a cost approximating $3.4 million placed into service by Folz Vending Co.

(J) a 24 megawatt alternative energy facility placed in service by Peat Products, with respect to which certification by the Federal Energy Regulatory Commission on April 3, 1986, and

(K) Burbank Manors, in Illinois.

(b) Special Rule for Certain Property. The provisions of section 168(f)(8) of the Internal Revenue Code of 1954 (as amended by section 209 of the Tax Equity and Fiscal Responsibility Act of 1982) shall continue to apply to any transaction permitted by reason of section 12(c)(2) of the Tax Reform Act of 1984 or section 209(d)(1)(B) of the Tax Equity and Fiscal Responsibility Act of 1982.

(c) Applicable Date in Certain Cases.—

(1) Section 203(b)(2) shall be applied by substituting "January 1, 1992" for January 1, 1991" in the following cases.

(A) in the case of a 2-unit nuclear powered electric generating plant (and equipment and incidental appurtenances), constructed pursuant to contracts entered into by the owner operator of the facility before December 31, 1975, including contracts with the engineer/constructor and the nuclear steam system supplier, such contracts shall be treated as contracts described in section 203(b)(1)(A),

(B) a cogeneration facility with respect to which an application with the Federal Energy Regulatory Commission was filed on August 2, 1985, and approved October 15, 1985,

(C) in the case of a 1,300 megawatt coal-fired steam powered electric generating plant (and related equipment and incidental appurtenances), which the three owners determined in 1984 to convert from nuclear power to coal power and for which more than $600 million had been incurred or committed for construction before September 25, 1985, except that no investment tax credit will be allowable under section 49(d)(3) added by section 211(a) of this Act for any qualified progress expenditures made after December 31, 1990.

(2) Section 203(b)(2) shall be applied by substituting "April 1, 1992" for the applicable date that would otherwise apply, in the case of the second unit of a twin steam electric generating facility and related equipment which was granted a certificate of public convenience and necessity by a public service commission prior to January 1, 1982, if the first unit of the facility was placed in service prior to January 1, 1985, and before September 26, 1985, more than $100,000,000 had been expended toward the construction of the second unit.

(3) Section 203(b)(2) shall be applied by substituting "January 1, 1990," for the applicable date that would otherwise apply in the case of—

(A) new commercial passenger aircraft used by a domestic airline, if a binding contract with respect to such aircraft was entered into before April 1, 1986, and such aircraft has a present class life of 12 years,

(B) a pumped storage hydroelectric project with respect to which an application was made to the Federal Energy Regulatory Commission for a license on February 4, 1974, and license was issued August 1, 1977, the project number of which is 2740,

(C) a facility for the manufacture of an improved particleboard, if—a binding contract to purchase such equipment was executed March 3, 1986, such equipment will be placed in service by January 1, 1988, and such facility is located in or near Moncure, North Carolina, and

(D) a newsprint mill in Pend Oreille county, Washington, costing about $290 million.

(7) [Should read (4)] The amendements made by section 201 shall not apply to a limited amount of the following property or a limited amount of property set forth in submission before September 16, 1986, by the following taxpayers—

(A) Arena project, Michigan,
(B) Campbell Soup Company, Pennsylvania and California,
(C) Overton, Florida,
(D) Legett and Platt,
(E) East Bank Housing Project,
(F) Standard Telephone Company,
(G) Presidential Air,
(H) Ann Arbor Railroad,
(I) Ada, Michigan Cogeneration,
(J) Anchor Store Project, Michigan,
(K) Biogen Power,
(L) $14 million of television transmitting towers placed in service by Media General, Inc., which were subject to binding contracts as of January 21, 1986, and will be placed in service before January 1, 1988,
(M) Hardage Company,
(N) Mesa Airlines,
(O) Yarn-spinning equipment used at Spring Cotton Mills, and
(P) 328 units of low-income housing at Angelus Plaza.

(d) Railroad Grading and Tunnel Bores.—

(1) **In general.**—In the case of expenditures for railroad grading and tunnel bores which were incurred by a common carrier by railroad to replace property destroyed in a disaster occurring on or about April 17, 1983, near Thistle, Utah, such expenditures, to the extent not in excess of $15,000,000, shall be treated as recovery property which is 5-year property under section 168 of the Internal Revenue Code of 1954 (as in effect before the amendments made by this Act) and which is placed in service at the time such expenditures were incurred.

(2) **Business interruption proceeds.**—Business interruption proceeds received for loss of use, revenues, or profits in connection with the disaster described in paragraph (1) and devoted by the taxpayer described in paragraph (1) to the construction of replacement track and related grading and tunnel bore expenditures shall be treated as

constituting an amount received from the involuntary conversion of property under section 1033(a)(2) of such Code.

(3) **Effective date.**—This subsection shall apply to taxable years ending after April 17, 1983.

(e) **Treatment of Certain Disaster Losses.**—

(1) **In general.**—In the case of a disaster described in paragraph (2), at the election of the taxpayer, the amendments made by section 201 of this Act—

(A) shall not apply to any property placed in service during 1987 or 1988, or

(B) shall apply to any property placed in service during 1985 or 1986,

which is property to replace property lost, damaged, or destroyed in such disaster.

(2) **Disaster to which section applies.**—This section shall apply to a flood which occurred on November 3 through 7, 1985, and which was declared a natural disaster area by the President of the United States.

[For official explanation, see Committee Reports, ¶3870]

[¶2009] SEC. 211. REPEAL OF REGULAR INVESTMENT TAX CREDIT.

* * * * * * * * * * *

(b) **Normalization Rules.**—If, for any taxable year beginning after December 31, 1985, the requirements of paragraph (1) or (2) of section 46(f) of the Internal Revenue Code of 1986 are not met with respect to public utility property to which the regular percentage applied for purposes of determining the amount of the investment tax credit—

(1) all credits for open taxable years as of the time of the final determination referred to in section 46(f)(4)(A) of such Code shall be recaptured, and

(2) if the amount of the taxpayer's unamortized credits (or the credits not previously restored to rate base) with respect to such property (whether or not for open years) exceeds the amount referred to in paragraph (1), the taxpayer's tax for the taxable year shall be increased by the amount of such excess.

If any portion of the excess described in paragraph (2) is attributable to a credit which is allowable as a carryover to a taxable year beginning after December 31, 1985, in lieu of applying paragraph (2) with respect to such portion, the amount of such carryover shall be reduced by the amount of such portion. Rules similar to the rules of this subsection shall apply in the case of any property with respect to which the requirements of section 46(f)(9) of such Code are met.

* * * * * * * * * * *

(d) **Exception for Certain Aircraft Used in Alaska.**—

(1) The amendments made by subsection (a) shall not apply to property originally placed in service after December 29, 1982, and before August 1, 1985, by a corporation incorporated in Alaska on May 21, 1953, and used by it—

(A) in part, for the transportation of mail for the United States Postal Service in the State of Alaska, and

(B) in part, to provide air service in the State of Alaska on routes which had previously been served by an air carrier that received compensation from the Civil Aeronautics Board for providing service.

(2) In the case of property described in subparagraph (A)—

(A) such property shall be treated as recovery property described in section 208(d)(5) of the Tax Equity and Fiscal Responsibility Act of 1982 ("TEFRA");

(B) "48 months" shall be substituted for "3 months" each place it appears in applying—

(i) section 48(b)(2)(B) of the Code, and

(ii) section 168(f)(8)(D) of the Code (as in effect after the amendments made by the Technical Corrections Act of 1982 but before the amendments made by TEFRA); and

(C) the limitation of section 168(f)(8)(D)(ii)(III) (as then in effect) shall be read by substituting "the lessee's original cost basis.", for "the adjusted basis of the lessee at the time of the lease.".

(3) The aggregate amount of property to which this paragraph shall apply shall not exceed $60,000,000.

(e) **Effective Date.—**

* * * * * * * * * * * *

(3) **Normalization rules.—**The provisions of subsection (b) shall apply to any violation of the normalization requirements under paragraph (1) or (2) of section 46(f) of the Internal Revenue Code of 1986 occurring in taxable years ending after December 31, 1985.

* * * * * * * * * * * *

[For official explanation, see Committee Reports, ¶3870]

[¶2010]   **SEC. 212.   EFFECTIVE 15-YEAR CARRYBACK OF EXISTING CARRY-FORWARDS OF STEEL COMPANIES.**

(a)   **General Rule.—**If a qualified corporation makes an election under this section for its 1st taxable year beginning after December 31, 1986, with respect to any portion of its existing carryforwards, the amount determined under subsection (b) shall be treated as a payment against the tax imposed by chapter 1 of the Internal Revenue Code of 1986 made by such corporation on the last day prescribed by law (without regard to extensions) for filing its return of tax under chapter 1 of such Code for such 1st taxable year.

(b)   **Amount.—**For purposes of subsection (a), the amount determined under this subsection shall be the lesser of—

(1)   50 percent of the portion of the corporation's existing carryforwards to which the election under subsection (a) applies, or

(2)   the corporation's net tax liability for the carryback period.

(c)   **Corporation Making Election May Not Use Same Amounts Under Section 38.—**In the case of a qualified corporation which makes an election under subsection (a), the portion of such corporation's existing carryforwards to which such an election applies shall not be taken into account under section 38 of the Internal Revenue Code of 1986 for any taxable year beginning after December 31, 1986.

(d)   **Net Tax Liability for Carryback Period.—**For purposes of this section—

(1)   **In general.—**A corporation's net tax liability for the carryback period is the aggregate of such corporation's net tax liability for taxable years in the carryback period.

(2)   **Net tax liability.—**The term "net tax liability" means, with respect to any taxable year, the amount of the tax imposed by chapter 1 of the Internal Revenue Code of 1954 for such taxable year, reduced by the sum of the credits allowable under part IV of subchapter A of such chapter 1 (other than section 34 thereof). For purposes of the preceding sentence, any tax treated as not imposed by chapter 1 of such Code under section 26(b)(2) of such Code shall not be treated as tax imposed by such chapter 1.

(3)   **Carryback period.—**The term "carryback period" means the period—

(A)   which begins with the corporation's 15th taxable year preceding the 1st taxable year from which there is an unused credit included in such corporation's existing carryforwards (but in no event shall such period begin before the corporation's 1st taxable year ending after December 31, 1961), and

(B)   which ends with the corporation's last taxable year beginning before January 1, 1986.

(e)   **No Recomputation of Minimum Tax, Etc.—**Nothing in this section shall be construed to affect—

(1)   the amount of the tax imposed by section 56 of the Internal Revenue Code of 1986, or

(2)   the amount of any credit allowable under such Code,

for any taxable year in the carryback period.

(f)   **Reinvestment Requirement.—**

(1)   **In general.—**Any amount determined under this section must be committed to reinvestment in, and modernization of the steel industry through investment in modern plant and equipment, research and development, and other appropriate projects, such as working capital for steel operations and programs for the retraining of steel workers.

(2)   **General rule.—**In this section applies to LTV Corporation, then, in lieu of the requirements of paragraph (1),

(A)   such corporation shall place such refund in a separate account; and

(B)   amounts in such separate account—

(i) shall only be used by the corporation—

(I) to purchase an insurance policy which provides that, in the event the corporation becomes involved in a title 11 or similar case (as defined in section 368(a)(3)(A) of the Internal Revenue Code of 1954), the insurer will provide life and health insurance coverage during the 1-year period beginning on the date such involvement begins to any individual with respect to whom the corporation would (but for such involvement) have been obligated to provide such coverage, the coverage provided by the insurer will be identical to the coverage which the corporation would (but for such involvement) have been obligated to provide, and provides that the payment of insurance premiums will not be required during such 1-year period to keep such policy in force, or

(II) directly in connection with the trade or business of the corporation in the manufacturer or production of steel; and

(ii) shall be used (or obligated) for purposes described in clause (i) not later than 3 months after the corporation receives the refund.

(g) Definitions.—For purposes of this section—

(1) Qualified corporation.—

(A) In general.—The term "qualified corporation" means any corporation which is described in section 806(b) of the Steel Import Stabilization Act and a company which was incorporated on February 11, 1983, in Michigan.

(B) Certain predecessors included.—In the case of any qualified corporation which has carryforward attributable to a predecessor corporation described in such section 806(b), the qualified corporation and the predecessor corporation shall be treated as 1 corporation for purposes of subsections (d) and (e).

(2) Existing carryforwards.—The term "existing carryforward" means the aggregate of the amounts which—

(A) are unused business credit carryforwards to the taxpayer's 1st taxable year beginning after December 31, 1986 (determined without regard to the limitations of section 38(c) and any reduction under section 49 of the Internal Revenue Code of 1986), and

(B) are attributable to the amount of the regular investment credit determined under section 46(a)(1) of such Code (relating to regular percentage), or any corresponding provision of prior law, determined on the basis that the regular investment credit was used first.

[For official explanation, see Committee Reports, ¶3870]

[¶2011] SEC. 213. EFFECTIVE 15-YEAR CARRYBACK OF EXISTING CARRYFORWARDS OF QUALIFIED FARMERS.

(a) General Rule.—If a taxpayer who is a qualified farmer makes an election under this section for its 1st taxable year beginning after December 31, 1986, with respect to any portion of its existing carryforwards, the amount determined under subsection (b) shall be treated as a payment against the tax imposed by chapter 1 of the Internal Revenue Code of 1986 made by such taxpayer on the last day prescribed by law (without regard to extensions) for filing its return of tax under chapter 1 of such Code for such 1st taxable year.

(b) Amount.—For purposes of subsection (a), the amount determined under this subsection shall be equal to the smallest of—

(1) 50 percent of the portion of the taxpayer's existing carryforwards to which the election under subsection (a) applies,

(2) the taxpayer's net tax liability for the carryback period (within the meaning of section 212(d) of this Act), or

(3) $750.

(c) Taxpayer Making Election May Not Use Same Amounts Under Section 38.—In the case of a qualified farmer who makes an election under subsection (a), the portion of such farmer's existing carryforwards to which such an election applies shall not be taken into account under section 38 of the Internal Revenue Code of 1986 for any taxable year beginning after December 31, 1986.

(d) No Recomputation of Minimum Tax, Etc.—Nothing in this section shall be construed to affect—

(1) the amount of the tax imposed by section 56 of the Internal Revenue Code of 1954, or

(2) the amount of any credit allowable under such Code, for any taxable year in the carryback period (within the meaning of section 212(d)(3) of this Act).

(e) **Definitions and Special Rules.**—For purposes of this section—

(1) **Qualified farmer.**—The term "qualified farmer" means any taxpayer who, during the 3-taxable year period preceding the taxable year for which an election is made under subsection (a), derived 50 percent or more of the taxpayer's gross income from the trade or business of farming.

(2) **Existing carryforward.**—The term "existing carryforward" means the aggregate of the amounts which—

(A) are unused business credit carryforwards to the taxpayer's 1st taxable year beginning after December 31, 1986 (determined without regard to the limitations of section 38(c) of the Internal Revenue Code of 1986), and

(B) are attributable to the amount of the investment credit determined under section 46(a) of such Code (or any corresponding provision of prior law) with respect to section 38 property which was used by the taxpayer in the trade or business of farming, determined on the basis that such credit was used first.

(3) **Farming.**—The term "farming" has the meaning given such term by section 2032A(e)(4) and (5) of such Code.

[For official explanation, see Committee Reports, ¶3870]

〔¶2012〕 SEC. 231. AMENDMENTS RELATING TO CREDIT FOR INCREASING RESEARCH ACTIVITIES.

(a) **3-Year Extension of the Research Credit.—**

* * * * * * * * * * *

(2) **Conforming amendment.**—Subsection (d) of section 221 of the Economic Recovery Tax Act of 1981 is amended—

(A) by striking out ", and before January 1, 1986" in paragraph (1), and

(B) by striking out the last sentence of paragraph (2)(A).

* * * * * * * * * * *

[For official explanation, see Committee Reports, ¶3872]

〔¶2013〕 SEC. 243. DEDUCTION FOR BUS AND FREIGHT FORWARDER OPERATING AUTHORITY.

(a) **Bus Operating Authority.—**

(1) **In general.**—Subject to the modifications contained in paragraph (2), section 266 of the Economic Recovery Tax Act of 1981 shall be applied as if the term "motor carrier operating authority" included a bus operating authority.

(2) **Modifications.**—For purposes of paragraph (1), section 266 of such Act shall be applied—

(A) by substituting "November 19, 1982" for "July 1, 1980" each place it appears, and

(B) by substituting "November 1982" for "July 1980" in subsection (a) thereof.

(3) **Bus operating authority defined.**—For purposes of this subsection and section 266 of such Act, the term "bus operating authority" means—

(A) a certificate or permit held by a motor common or contract carrier of passengers which was issued pursuant to subchapter II of chapter 109 of title 49, United States Code, and

(B) a certificate or permit held by a motor carrier authorizing the transportation of passengers, as a common carrier, over regular routes in intrastate commerce which was issued by the appropriate State agency.

(b) **Freight Forwarder Operating Authority.—**

(1) **In general.**—Subject to the modifications contained in paragraph (2), section 266 of the Economic Recovery Tax Act of 1981 shall be applied as if subsection (b) thereof contained "or a freight forwarder" after "contract carrier of property".

(2) **Modifications.**—The modifications referred to in this paragraph are:

(A) **60-month period to begin in 1987.**—The 60-month period referred to in section 266(a) of such Act shall begin with the later of—

(i) the deregulation month, or

(ii) at the election of the taxpayer, the 1st month of the taxpayer's 1st taxable year beginning after the deregulation month.

(B) Authority must be held as of beginning of 60-month period.—A motor carrier operating authority shall not be taken into account unless such authority is held by the taxpayer at the beginning of the 60-month period applicable to the taxpayer under subparagraph (A).

(C) Adjusted basis not to exceed adjusted basis at beginning of 60-month period.—The adjusted basis taken into account with respect to any motor carrier operating authority shall not exceed the adjusted basis of such authority as of the beginning of the 60-month period applicable to the taxpayer under subparagraph (A).

(3) **Deregulation month.**—For purposes of this section, the term "deregulation month" means the month in which the Secretary of the Treasury or his delegate determines that a Federal law has been enacted which deregulates the freight forwarding industry.

(c) **Special Rule for Motor Carrier Operating Authority.**—In the case of a corporation which was incorporated on December 29, 1969, in the State of Delaware, notwithstanding any other provision of law, there shall be allowed as a deduction for the taxable year of the taxpayer beginning in 1980 an amount equal to $2,705,188 for its entire loss due to a decline in value of its motor carrier operating authority by reason of deregulation.

(d) **Effective Dates.—**

(1) **Bus operating authority.—**

(A) In general.—Subsection (a) shall apply to taxable years ending after November 18, 1982.

(B) Statute of limitations.—If refund or credit of any overpayment of tax resulting from subsection (a) is prevented at any time on or before the date which is 1 year after the date of the enactment of this Act by the operation of any law or rule of law (including res judicata), refund or credit of such overpayment (to the extent attributable to the application of such subsection) may, notwithstanding such law or rule of law, be made or allowed if claim therefore is filed on or before the date which is 18 months after such date of enactment.

(2) **Freight forwarder operating authority.**—Subsection (b) shall apply to taxable years ending after the month preceding the deregulation month.

[For official explanation, see Committee Reports, ¶3876]

[¶2013-A] **SEC. 251 MODIFICATION OF INVESTMENT TAX CREDIT FOR REHABILITATION EXPENDITURES.**

* * * * * * * * * * * *

(d) **Effective Date.—**

* * * * * * * * * * * *

(3) **Certain additional rehabilitations.**—The amendments made by this section and section 201 shall not apply to—

(A) the rehabilitation of 8 bathhouses within the Hot Springs National Park or of buildings in the Central Avenue Historic District at such Park,

(B) the rehabilitation of the Upper Pontabla Building in New Orleans, Louisiana,

(C) the rehabilitation of at least 60 buildings listed on the National Register at the Frankford Arsenal,

(D) the rehabilitation of De Baliveriere Arcade, St. Louis Centre, and Drake Apartments in Missouri,

(E) the rehabilitation of The Tides in Bristol, Rhode Island,

(F) the rehabilitation and renovation of the Outlet Company building and garage in Providence, Rhode Island,

(G) the rehabilitation of 10 structures in Harrisburg, Pennsylvania, with respect to which the Harristown Development Corporation was designated redeveloper and received an option to acquire title to the entire project site for $1 on June 27, 1984,

(H) the rehabilitation of a project involving the renovation of 3 historic structures on the Minneapolis riverfront, with respect to which the developer of the project entered into a redevelopment agreement with a municipality dated January 4, 1985, and industrial development bonds were sold in 3 separate issues in May, July, and October 1985,

(I) the rehabilitation of a bank's main office facilities of approximately 120,000 square feet, in connection with which the bank's board of directors authorized a $3,300,000 expenditure for the renovation and retrofit on March 20, 1984,

(J) the rehabilitation of 10 warehouse buildings built between 1906 and 1910 and purchased under a contract dated February 17, 1986,

(K) the rehabilitation of a facility which is customarily used for conventions and sporting events if an analysis of operations and recommendations of utilization of such facility was prepared by a certified public accounting firm pursuant to an engagement authorized on March 6, 1984, and presented on June 11, 1984, to officials of the city in which such facility is located,

(L) Mount Vernon Mills in Columbia, South Carolina,

(M) the Barbara Jordan II Apartments,

(N) the rehabilitation of the Federal Building and Post Office, 120 Hanover Street, Manchester, New Hampshire,

(O) the rehabilitation of the Charleston Waterfront project in South Carolina,

(P) the Hayes Mansion in San Francisco,

(Q) the renovation of a facility owned by the National Railroad Passenger Corporation ("Amtrak") for which project Amtrak engaged a development team by letter agreement dated August 23, 1985, as modified by letter agreement dated September 9, 1985,

(R) the rehabilitation of a structure or its components which is listed in the National Register of Historic Places, is located in Allegheny County, Pennsylvania, will be substantially rehabilitated (as defined in section 48(g)(1)(C) prior to amendment by this Act), prior to December 31, 1989; and was previously utilized as a market and an auto dealership,

(S) The Bellevue Stratford Hotel in Philadelphia, Pennsylvania,

(T) The Dixon Mill Housing project in Jersey City, New Jersey,

(U) Motor Square Garden,

(V) the Blackstone Apartments, and the Shriver-Johnson building, in Sioux Falls, South Dakota,

(W) the Holy Name Academy in Spokane, Washington,

(X) the Nike/Clemson Mill in Exeter, New Hampshire,

(Y) the Central Bank Building in Grand Rapids, Michigan, and

(Z) the Heritage Hotel, in the City of Marquette, Michigan.

(4) **Additional rehabilitations.**—The amendments made by this section and section 201 shall not apply to—

(A) the Fort Worth Town Square Project in Texas,

(B) the American Youth Hostel in New York, New York,

(C) The Riverwest Loft Development (including all three phases, two of which do not involve rehabilitations),

(D) the Gaslamp Quarter Historic District in California,

(E) the Eberhardt & Ober Brewery, in Pennsylvania,

(F) the Captain's Walk Limited Partnership-Harris Place Development, in Connecticut,

(G) the Velvet Mills in Connecticut,

(H) the Roycroft Inn, in New York,

(I) Old Main Village, in Mankato, Minnesota,

(J) the Washburn-Crosby A Mill, in Minneapolis, Minnesota,

(K) the Lakeland marbel Arcade in Lakeland, Florida,

(L) the Willard Hotel, in Washington, D.C.,

(M) the H. P. Lau Building in Lincoln, Nebraska,

(N) the Starks Building, in Louisville, Kentucky,

(O) the Bellevue High School, in Bellevue, Kentucky,

(P) the Major Hampden Smith House, in Owensboro, Kentucky,

(Q) the Doe Run Inn, in Brandenburg, Kentucky,

(R) the State National Bank, in Frankfort, Kentucky,

(S) the Captain Jack House, in Fleming, Kentucky,

(T) the Elizabeth Arlinghaus House, in Louisville, Kentucky,

(U) Limerick Shamrock, in Louisville, Kentucky,

(V) the Robert Mills Project, in South Carolina,

(W) the 620 Project, consisting of 3 buildings, in Kentucky,

(X)   the Warrior Hotel, Ltd., the first two floors of the Martin Hotel, and the 105,000 square foot warehouse constructed in 1910, all in Sioux City, Iowa,

(Y)   the waterpark condominium residential project, to the extent of $2 million of expenditures, and

(Z)   the Apollo and Bishop Building Complex on 125th Street, the Bigelow-Hartford Carpet Mill in New York, New York,

(5)   **Reduction in credit for property under transitional rules.**—In the case of property placed in service after December 31, 1986, and to which the amendments made by this section do not apply, subparagraph (A) of section 46(b)(4) of the Internal Revenue Code of 1954 (as in effect before the enactment of this Act) shall be applied—

(A)   by substituting "10 percent" for "15 percent", and

(B)   by substituting "13 percent" for "20 percent".

(6)   **Expensing of rehabilitation expenditures for the Frankford Arsenal.**—In the case of any expenditures paid or incurred in connection with the rehabilitation of the Frankford Arsenal during the 8-year period beginning on January 1, 1987, such expenditures (including expenditures for repair and maintenance of the building and property) shall be allowable as a deduction in the taxable year in which paid or incurred in an amount not in excess of the submissions made by the taxpayer before September 16, 1986.

[For official explanation, see Committee Reports, ¶3878]

[¶2014]   SEC. 252.   LOW-INCOME HOUSING CREDIT.

* * * * * * * * * * * *

(f)   **Transitional Rules.**—

(1)   **Limitation to non-ACRS buildings not to apply to certain buildings, etc.**—

(A)   In general.—In the case of a building which is part of a project described in subparagraph (B)—

(i)   section 42(c)(2)(B) of the Internal Revenue Code of 1986 (as added by this section) shall not apply, and

(ii)   such building shall be treated as not federally subsidized for purposes of section 42(b)(1)(A) of such Code.

(B)   Project described.—A project is described in this subparagraph if—

(i)   an urban development action grant application with respect to such project was submitted on September 13, 1984,

(ii)   a zoning commission map amendment related to such project was granted on July 17, 1985, and

(iii)   the number assigned to such project by the Federal Housing Administration is 023-36602.

(C)   Additional units eligible for credit.—In the case of a building to which subparagraph (A) applies and which is part of a project which meets the requirements of subparagraph (D), for each low-income unit in such building which is occupied by individuals whose income is 30 percent or less of area median gross income, one additional unit (not otherwise a low-income unit) in such building shall be treated as a low-income unit for purposes of such section 42.

(D)   Project described.—A project is described in this subparagraph if—

(i)   rents charged for units in such project are restricted by State regulations,

(ii)   the annual cash flow of such project is restricted by State law,

(iii)   the project is located on land owned by or ground leased from a public housing authority,

(iv)   construction of such project begins on or before December 31, 1986, and units within such project are placed in service on or before June 1, 1990, and

(v)   for a 20-year period, 20 percent or more of the residential units in such project are occupied by individuals whose income is 50 percent or less of area median gross income.

(E)   Maximum additional credit.—The maximum annual additional credit allowable under section 42 of such Code by reason of subparagraph (C) shall not exceed 25 percent of the eligible basis of the building.

(2) Additional allocation of housing credit ceiling.—

(A) In general.—There is hereby allocated to each housing credit agency described in subparagraph (B) in additional housing credit dollar amount determined in accordance with the following table:

For calendar year:	The additional allocation is:
1987	$3,900,000
1988	$7,600,000
1989	$1,300,000

(B) Housing credit agencies described.—The housing credit agencies described in this subparagraph are:

(i) A corporate governmental agency constituted as a public benefit corporation and established in 1971 under the provisions of Article XII of the Private Housing Finance Law of the State.

(ii) A city department established on December 20, 1979, pursuant to chapter XVIII of a municipal code of such city for the purpose of supervising and coordinating the formation and execution of projects and programs affecting housing within such city.

(iii) The State housing finance agency referred to in subparagraph (C), but only with respect to projects described in subparagraph (C).

(C) Project described.—A project is described in this subparagraph if such project is a qualified low-income housing project which—

(i) receives financing from a State housing finance agency from the proceeds of bonds issued pursuant to chapter 708 of the Acts of 1966 of such State pursuant to loan commitments from such agency made between May 8, 1984, and July 8, 1986, and

(ii) is subject to subsidy commitments issued pursuant to a program established under chapter 574 of the Acts of 1983 of such State having award dates from such agency between May 31, 1984, and June 11, 1985.

(D) Special rules.—

(i) Any building—

(I) which is allocated any housing credit dollar amount by a housing credit agency described in clause (iii) of subparagraph (B), and

(II) which is placed in service after June 30, 1986, and before January 1, 1987,

shall be treated for purposes of the amendments made by this section as placed in service on January 1, 1987.

(ii) Section 42(c)(2)(B) of the Internal Revenue Code of 1986 shall not apply to any building which is allocated any housing credit dollar amount by any agency described in subparagraph (B).

(E) All units treated as low income units in certain cases.—In the case of any building—

(i) which is allocated any housing credit dollar amount by any agency described in subparagraph (B), and

(ii) which after the application of subparagraph (D)(ii) is a qualified low-income building at all times during any taxable year,

such building shall be treated as described in section 42(b)(1)(B) of such Code and having an applicable fraction for such year of 1.

(3) Certain projects placed in service before 1987.—

(A) In general.—In the case of a building which is part of a project described in subparagraph (B)—

(i) section 42(c)(2)(B) of such Code shall not apply,

(ii) such building shall be treated as placed in service during the first calendar year after 1986 and before 1990 in which such building is a qualified low-income building (determined after the application of clause (i)), and

(iii) for purposes of section 42(h) of such Code, such building shall be treated as having allocated to it a housing credit dollar amount equal to the dollar amount appearing in the clause of subparagraph (B) in which such building is described.

(B) Project described.—A project is described in this subparagraph if the Code number assigned to such project by the Farmers' Home Administration appears in the following table:

The code number is:	The housing credit dollar amount is:
(i) 49284553664	$16,000
(ii) 4927742022446	$22,000
(iii) 492707422769087	$64,000
(iv) 490270742387293	$48,000
(v) 4927074218234	$32,000
(vi) 49270742274019	$36,000
(vii) 51460742345074	$53,000.

(C) **Determination of adjusted basis.**—The adjusted basis of any building to which this paragraph applies for purposes of section 42 of such Code shall be its adjusted basis as of the close of the taxable year ending before the first taxable year of the credit period for such building.

(D) **Certain rules to apply.**—Rules similar to the rules of subparagraph (E) of paragraph (2) shall apply for purposes of this paragraph.

(4) Definitions.—For purposes of this subsection, terms used in such subsection which are also used in section 42 of the Internal Revenue Code of 1986 (as added by this section) shall have the meanings given such terms by such section 42.

[For official explanation, see Committee Reports, ¶3879]

[¶2015] SEC. 261. PROVISIONS RELATING TO MERCHANT MARINE CAPITAL CONSTRUCTION FUNDS.

(a) **Purpose.**—The purpose of this section is to coordinate the application of the Internal Revenue Code of 1986 with the capital construction program under the Merchant Marine Act, 1936.

* * * * * * * * * * * *

(d) **Departmental Reports and Certification.**—Section 607 of the Merchant Marine Act, 1936, is amended by adding at the end thereof the following new subsection:

"(m) **Departmental Reports and Certification.**—

"(1) **In general.**—For each calendar year, the Secretaries shall each provide the Secretary of the Treasury, within 120 days after the close of such calendar year, a written report with respect to those capital construction funds that are under their jurisdiction.

"(2) **Contents of reports.**—Each report shall set forth the name and taxpayer identification number of each person—

"(A) establishing a capital construction fund during such calendar year;

"(B) maintaining a capital construction fund as of the last day of such calendar year;

"(C) terminating a capital construction fund during such calendar year;

"(D) making any withdrawal from or deposit into (and the amounts thereof) a capital construction fund during such calendar year; or

"(E) with respect to which a determination has been made during such calendar year that such person has failed to fulfill a substantial obligation under any capital construction fund agreement to which such person is a party."

(e) **Conforming Amendments.**—

(1) Subparagraph (A) of section 607(d)(1) of the Merchant Marine Act, 1936 is amended by inserting "and section 7518 of such Code" after "this section".

(2) Subparagraph (D) of section 607(d)(1) of such Act is amended by inserting "and section 7518 of such Code" after "this section".

(3) Subparagraph (C) of section 607(e)(2) of such Act is amended by striking out "85 percent" and inserting in lieu thereof "the percentage applicable under section 243(a)(1) of the Internal Revenue Code of 1986".

(4) Subparagraph (E) of section 607(e)(4) of such Act is amended to read as follows:

"(E) the portion of any dividend referred to in paragraph (2)(C) not taken into account under such paragraph."

(5) Paragraph (3) of section 607(g) of such Act is amended to read as follows:

"(3) If any portion of a qualified withdrawal for a vessel, barge, or container is made out of the capital gain account, the basis of such vessel, barge, or container shall be reduced by an amount equal to such portion."

(6) Subsection (h) of section 607 of such Act is amended by adding at the end thereof the following new paragraphs:

"(5) **Amount not withdrawn from fund after 25 years from deposit taxed as nonqualified withdrawal.—**

"(A) In general.—The applicable percentage of any amount which remains in a capital construction fund at the close of the 26th, 27th, 28th, 29th, or 30th taxable year following the taxable year for which such amount was deposited shall be treated as a nonqualified withdrawal in accordance with the following table:

"If the amount remains in the fund at the close of the—	The applicable percentage is—
26th taxable year	20 percent
27th taxable year	40 percent
28th taxable year	60 percent
29th taxable year	80 percent
30th taxable year	100 percent

"(B) Earnings treated as deposits.—The earnings of any capital construction fund for any taxable year (other than net gains) shall be treated for purposes of this paragraph as an amount deposited for such taxable year.

"(C) Amounts committed treated as withdrawn.—For purposes of subparagraph (A), an amount shall not be treated as remaining in a capital construction fund at the close of any taxable year to the extent there is a binding contract at the close of such year for a qualified withdrawal of such amount with respect to an identified item for which such withdrawal may be made.

"(D) Authority to treat excess funds as withdrawn.—If the Secretary determines that the balance in any capital construction exceeds the amount which is appropriate to meet the vessel construction program objectives of the person who established such fund, the amount of such excess shall be treated as a nonqualified withdrawal under subparagraph (A) unless such person develops appropriate program objectives within 3 years to dissipate such excess.

"(E) Amounts in fund on January 1, 1987.—For purposes of this paragraph, all amounts in a capital construction fund on January 1, 1987, shall be treated as deposited in such fund on such date.

"(6) **Nonqualified withdrawals taxed at highest marginal rate.—**

"(A) In general.—In the case of any taxable year for which there is a nonqualified withdrawal (including any amount so treated under paragraph (5)), the tax imposed by chapter 1 of the Internal Revenue Code of 1986 shall be determined—

"(i) by excluding such withdrawal from gross income, and

"(ii) by increasing the tax imposed by chapter 1 of such Code by the product of the amount of such withdrawal and the highest rate of tax specified in section 1 (section 11 in the case of a corporation) of such Code.

With respect to the portion of any nonqualified withdrawal made out of the capital gain account during a taxable year to which section 1(j) or 1201(a) of such Code applies, the rate of tax taken into account under the preceding sentence shall not exceed 28 percent (34 percent in the case of a corporation).

"(B) Tax benefit rule.—If any portion of a nonqualified withdrawal is properly attributable to deposits (other than earnings on deposits) made by the taxpayer in any taxable year which did not reduce the taxpayer's liability for tax under chapter 1 for any taxable year preceding the taxable year in which such withdrawal occurs—

"(i) such portion shall not be taken into account under subparagraph (A), and

"(ii) an amount equal to such portion shall be treated as allowed as a deduction under section 172 of such Code for the taxable year in which such withdrawal occurs.

"(C) Coordination with deduction for net operating losses.—Any nonqualified withdrawal excluded from gross income under subparagraph (A) shall be excluded in determining taxable income under section 172(b)(2) of the Internal Revenue Code of 1986."

* * * * * * * * * * * *

(g) **Effective Date.**—The amendment made by this section shall apply to taxable years beginning after December 31, 1986.

[For official explanation, see Committee Reports, ¶3880]

[¶2016] SEC. 302. 28 PERCENT CAPITAL GAINS RATE FOR TAXPAYERS OTHER THAN CORPORATIONS.

* * * * * * * * * * * *

(c) **Transitional Rule.**—The tax under section 1 of the Internal Revenue Code of 1986 on the long-term capital gain on rights to royalties paid under leases and assignments binding on September 25, 1985, by a limited partnership formed on March 1, 1977, which on October 30, 1979, assigned leases and which assignment was amended on April 27, 1981, shall not exceed 20 percent.

[For official explanation, see Committee Reports, ¶3886]

[¶2017] SEC. 311. REPEAL OF CORPORATE CAPITAL GAINS TREATMENT.

* * * * * * * * * * * *

(d) **Transitional Rules.**—
(1) **Taxable years which begin in 1986 and end in 1987.**—In the case of any taxable year which begins before January 1, 1987, and ends on or after such date, paragraph (2) of section 1201(a) of the Internal Revenue Code of 1954, as in effect on the date before the date of enactment of this Act, shall be applied as if it read as follows:
"(2) the sum of—
"(A) 28 percent of the lesser of—
"(i) the net capital gain determined by taking into account only gain or loss which is properly taken into account for the portion of the taxable year before January 1, 1987, or
"(ii) the net capital gain for the taxable year, and
"(B) 34 percent of the excess (if any) of—
"(i) the net capital gain for the taxable year, over
"(ii) the amount of the net capital gain taken into account under subparagraph (A)."

(2) **Revocation of elections under section 631(a).**—Any election under section 631(a) of the Internal Revenue Code of 1954 made (whether by a corporation or a person other than a corporation) for a taxable year beginning before January 1, 1987, may be revoked by the taxpayer for any taxable year ending after December 31, 1986. For purposes of determining whether the taxpayer may make a further election under such section, such election (and any revocation under this paragraph) shall not be taken into account.

[For official explanation, see Committee Reports, ¶3887]

[¶2018] SEC. 406. RETENTION OF CAPITAL GAINS TREATMENT FOR SALES OF DAIRY CATTLE UNDER MILK PRODUCTION TERMINATION PROGRAM.

The amendments made by subtitles A and B of title III shall not apply to any gain from the sale of dairy cattle under a valid contract with the United States Department of Agriculture under the milk production termination program to the extent such gain is properly taken into account under the taxpayer's method of accounting after January 1, 1987, and before September 1, 1987.

[¶2019] SEC. 423. ETHYL ALCOHOL AND MIXTURES THEREOF FOR FUEL USE.

(a) **In General.**—Except as provided in subsection (b), no ethyl alcohol or a mixture thereof may be considered—
(1) for purposes of general headnote 3(a) of the Tariff Schedules of the United States, to be—

Act §423(a) ¶2019

(A) the growth or product of an insular possession of the United States,

(B) manufactured or produced in an insular possession from materials which are the growth, product, or manufacture of any such possession, or

(C) otherwise eligible for exemption from duty under such headnote as the growth or product of an insular possession; or

(2) for purposes of section 213 of the Caribbean Basin Economic Recovery Act, to be—

(A) an article that is wholly the growth, product, or manufacture of a beneficiary country,

(B) a new or different article of commerce which has been grown, produced, or manufactured in a beneficiary country,

(C) a material produced in a beneficiary country, or

(D) otherwise eligible for duty-free treatment under such Act as the growth, product, or manufacture of a beneficiary country;

unless the ethyl alcohol or mixture thereof is an indigenous product of that insular possession or beneficiary country.

(b) Exception.—

(1) Subject to the limitation in paragraph (2), subsection (a) shall not apply to ethyl alcohol that is imported into the United States during calendar years 1987 and 1988 and produced in—

(A) an azeotropic distillation facility located in an insular possession of the United States or a beneficiary country, if that facility was established before, and in operation on, January 1, 1986, or

(B) an azeotropic distillation facility—

(i) at least 50 percent of the total value of the equipment and components of which were—

(I) produced in the United States, and

(II) owned by a corporation at least 50 percent of the total value of the outstanding shares of stock of which were owned by a United States person (or persons) on or before January 1, 1986, and

(ii) substantially all of the equipment and components of which were, on or before January 1, 1986—

(I) located in the United States under the possession or control of such corporation,

(II) ready for shipment to, and installation in, a beneficiary country, and

(iii) which—

(I) has on the date of enactment of this Act, or

(II) will have at the time such facility is placed in service (based on estimates made before the date of enactment of this Act),

a stated capacity to produce not more than 42,000,000 gallons of such product per year.

(2) The exception provided under paragraph (1) shall cease to apply during each of calendar years 1987 and 1988 to ethyl alcohol produced in a facility described in subparagraph (A) or (B) of paragraph (1) after 20,000,000 gallons of ethyl alcohol produced in that facility are entered into the United States during that year.

(c) Definitions.—For purposes of this section—

(1) The term "ethyl alcohol or a mixture thereof" means (except for purposes of subsection (e)) ethyl alcohol or any mixture thereof described in item 901.50 of the Appendix to the Tariff Schedules of the United States.

(2) Ethyl alcohol or a mixture thereof may be treated as being an indigenous product of an insular possession or beneficiary country only if the ethyl alcohol or a mixture thereof—

(A) has been both dehydrated and produced by a process of full-scale fermentation within that insular possession or beneficiary country; or

(B) has been dehydrated within that insular possession or beneficiary country from hydrous ethyl alcohol that includes hydrous ethyl alcohol which is wholly the product or manufacture of any insular possession or beneficiary country and which has a value not less than—

(i) 30 percent of the value of the ethyl alcohol or mixture, if entered during calendar year 1987, except that this clause shall not apply to any ethyl alcohol or mixture which has been dehydrated in the United States Virgin Islands by a facility with respect to which—

(I) the owner has entered into a binding contract for the engineering and design of full-scale fermentation capacity, and

(II) authorization for operation of a full-scale fermentation facility has been granted by the Island authorities before May 1, 1986,

(ii) 60 percent of the value of the ethyl alcohol or mixture, if entered during calendar year 1988, and

(iii) 75 percent of the value of the ethyl alcohol or mixture, if entered after December 31, 1988.

(3) The term "beneficiary country" has the meaning given to such term under section 212 of the Caribbean Basin Economic Recovery Act (19 U.S.C. 2702).

(4) The term "United States person" has the meaning given to such term by section 7701(a)(3) of the Internal Revenue Code of 1986.

(5) The term "entered" means entered, or withdrawn from warehouse for consumption in the customs territory of the United States.

(d) **Amendment to Appendix to Schedules.**—The item designation for item 901.50 of the Appendix to the Tariff Schedules of the United States is amended to read as follows: "Ethyl alcohol (provided for in item 427.88, part 2D, schedule 4) or any mixture containing such ethyl alcohol (provided for in part 1, 2 or 10, schedule 4) if such ethyl alcohol or mixture is to be used as fuel or in producing a mixture of gasoline and alcohol, a mixture of a special fuel and alcohol, or any other mixture to be used as fuel (including motor fuel provided for an item 475.25), or is suitable for any such uses."

(e) **Drawbacks.**—

(1) For purposes of subsections (b) and (j)(2) of section 313 of the Tariff Act of 1930 (19 U.S.C. 1313), as amended by section 1888(2) of this Act, any ethyl alcohol (provided for in item 427.88 of the Tariff Schedules of the United States) or mixture containing such ethyl alcohol (provided for in part 1, 2, or 10 of schedule 4 of such Schedules) which is subject to the additional duty imposed by item 901.50 of the Appendix to such Schedules may be treated as being fungible with, or of being of the same kind and quality as, any other imported ethyl alcohol (provided for in item 427.88 of such Schedules) or mixture containing such ethyl alcohol (provided for in part 1, 2, or 10 of schedule 4 of such Schedules) only if such other imported ethyl alcohol or mixture thereof is also subject to such additional duty.

(2) Paragraph (1) shall not apply with respect to ethyl alcohol (provided for in item 427.88 of the Tariff Schedules of the United States) or mixture containing such ethyl alcohol (provided for in part 1, 2, or 10 of schedule 4 of such Schedules) that is exempt from the additional duty imposed by item 901.50 of the Appendix to such Schedules by reason of—

(A) subsection (b), or

(B) any agreement entered into under section 102(b) of the Trade Act of 1974.

(f) **Conforming Amendments.**—

(1) General headnote 3(a)(i) of the Tariff Schedules of the United States is amended by inserting "and except as provided in schedule 423 of the Tax Reform Act of 1986," after "part 7 of schedule 7,".

(2) Section 213(a)(1) of the Caribbean Basin Economic Recovery Act (19 U.S.C. 2703(a)(1)) is amended by inserting "and subject to section 423 of the Tax Reform Act of 1986," after "Unless otherwise excluded from eligibility by this title,".

(3) The headnotes to subpart A of part 1 of the Appendix to the Tariff Schedules of the United States are amended by adding at the end thereof the following:

"2. For purposes of item 901.50, the phrase 'is suitable for any such uses' does not include ethyl alcohol (provided for in item 427.88, part 2D, schedule 4) that is certified by the importer of record to the satisfaction of the Commissioner of Customs (hereinafter in this headnote referred to as the 'Commissioner') to be ethyl alcohol or a mixture containing such ethyl alcohol imported for uses other than liquid motor fuel use or use in producing liquid motor fuel related mixtures. If the importer of record certifies nonliquid motor fuel use for purposes of establishing actual use or suitability under item 901.50, the Commissioner shall not liquidate the entry of ethyl alcohol until he is satisfied that the ethyl alcohol has in fact not been used for liquid motor fuel use or use in producing liquid motor fuel related mixtures. If he is not satisfied within a reasonable period of time not less than 18 months from the date of entry, then the duties provided for in item 901.50 shall be payable retroactive to the date of entry. Such duties shall also become payable, retroactive to the date of entry, immediately upon the diversion to liquid motor fuel use of any ethyl alcohol or ethyl alcohol mixture certified upon entry as having been imported for non-liquid motor fuel use."

Act §423(f) ¶2019

(g) Effective Period.—

(1) The provisions of, and the amendments made by, this section (other than subsection (e)) shall apply to articles entered—

(A) after December 31, 1986, and

(B) before the expiration of the effective period of item 901.50 of the Appendix to the Tariff Schedules of the United States.

(2) The provisions of subsection (e) shall take effect on the date of the enactment of this Act.

[For official explanation, see Committee Reports, ¶3901]

〔¶2020〕 SEC. 502. TRANSITIONAL RULE FOR LOW-INCOME HOUSING.

(a) General Rule.—Any loss sustained by a qualified investor with respect to an interest in a qualified low-income housing project for any taxable year in the relief period shall not be treated as a loss from a passive activity for purposes of section 469 of the Internal Revenue Code of 1986.

(b) Relief Period.—For purposes of subsection (a), the term "relief period" means the period beginning with the taxable year in which the investor made his initial investment in the qualified low-income housing project and ending with whatever of the following is the earliest—

(1) the 6th taxable year after the taxable year in which the investor made his initial investment,

(2) the 1st taxable year after the taxable year in which the investor is obligated to make his last investment, or

(3) the taxable year preceding the 1st taxable year for which such project ceased to be a qualified low-income housing project.

(c) Qualified Low-Income Housing Project.—For purposes of this section, the term "qualified low-income housing project" means any project if—

(1) such project meets the requirements of clause (i), (ii), (iii), or (iv) of section 1250(a)(1)(B) as of the date placed in service and for each taxable year thereafter which begins after 1986 and for which a passive loss may be allowable with respect to such project,

(2) the operator certifies to the Secretary of the Treasury or his delegate that such project met the requirements of paragraph (1) on the date of the enactment of this Act (or, if later, when placed in service) and annually thereafter,

(3) such project is constructed or acquired pursuant to a binding written contract entered into on or before August 16, 1986, and

(4) such project is placed in service before January 1, 1989.

(d) Qualified Investor.—For purposes of this section—

(1) In general.—The term "qualified investor" means any natural person who holds (directly or through 1 or more entities) an interest in a qualified low-income housing project—

(A) if—

(i) in the case of a project placed in service before August 16, 1986, such person held an interest in such project on August 16, 1986, and the taxpayer made his initial investment after December 31, 1983, or

(ii) in the case of a project not described in paragraph (A), such investor held an interest in such project on December 31, 1986, and

(B) if such investor is required to make payments after December 31, 1986, of 50 percent or more of the total original obligated investment for such interest.

For purposes of subparagraph (A), a person shall be treated as holding an interest on August 16, 1986, or December 31, 1986, if on such date such person had a binding contract to acquire such interest.

(2) Treatment of estates.—The estate of a decedent shall succeed to the treatment under this section of the decedent but only with respect to the 1st 2 taxable years of such estate ending after the date of the decedent's death.

(d) [should read (e)] Special rules.—

(1) Where more than 1 building in project.—If there is more than 1 building in any project, the determination of when such project is placed in service shall be based on when the 1st building in such project is placed in service.

(2) Only cash and other property taken into account.—In determining the amount any person invests in (or is obligated to invest in) any interest, only cash and other property shall be taken into account.

(3) **Coordination with credit.**—No low-income housing credit shall be determined under section 42 of the Internal Revenue Code of 1986 with respect to any project with respect to which any person has been allowed any benefit under this section.

[For official explanation, see Committee Reports, ¶3903]

[¶2021] **SEC. 612. REPEAL OF PARTIAL EXCLUSION OF DIVIDENDS RE-CEIVED BY INDIVIDUALS.**

* * * * * * * * * * *

(b) **Technical amendments.**—

* * * * * * * * * * *

(2)(A) * * *

(B) If the amendments made by section 1001 of the Tax Reform Act of 1984 cease to apply, effective with respect to property to which such amendments do not apply, subsection (c) of section 584 is amended by striking out "6 months" each place it appears and inserting in lieu thereof "1 year".

* * * * * * * * * * *

[For official explanation, see Committee Reports, ¶3913]

[¶2022] **SEC. 621. LIMITATION OF NET OPERATING LOSS CARRYFOR-WARDS.**

* * * * * * * * * * *

(d) **Report on Depreciation and Built-In Deductions; Report on Bankruptcy Work-outs.**—The Secretary of the Treasury or his delegate—

(1) shall, not later than January 1, 1989, conduct a study and report to the Committee on Ways and Means of the House of Representatives and the Committee on Finance of the Senate with respect to the treatment of depreciation, amortization, depletion, and other built-in deductions for purposes of sections 382 and 383 of the Internal Revenue Code of 1986 (as amended by this section), and

(2) shall, not later than January 1, 1988, conduct a study and report to the committees referred to in paragraph (1) with respect to the treatment of informal bankruptcy workouts for purposes of sections 108 and 382 of such Code.

(e) **Repeal of Changes Made by Tax Reform Act of 1976.**—

(1) Subsections (e) and (f) of section 806 of the Tax Reform Act of 1976 (including the amendment treated as part of such subsections under section 59(b) of the Tax Reform Act of 1984) are hereby repealed.

(2) Subsection (g) of such section 806 is amended by striking out paragraphs (2) and (3).

(f) **Effective Dates.**—

* * * * * * * * * * *

(2) **For Amendments to Tax Reform Act of 1976.**—

(A) *In general.*—The repeals made by subsection (e)(1) and the amendment made by subsection (e)(2) shall take effect on January 1, 1986.

(B) *Election to have amendments apply.*—

(i) If a taxpayer described in clause (ii) elects to have the provisions of this subparagraph apply, the amendments made by subsections (e) and (f) of section 806 of the Tax Reform Act of 1976 shall apply to the reorganization described in clause (ii).

(ii) A taxpayer is described in this clause if the taxpayer filed a title 11 or similar case on December 8, 1981, filed a plan of reorganization on February 5, 1986, filed an amended plan on March 14, 1986, and received court approval for the amended plan and disclosure statement on April 16, 1986.

(C) *Application of old rules to certain debt.*—In the case of debt of a corporation incorporated in Colorado on November 8, 1924, with headquarters in Denver, Colorado—

(i) the amendments made by subsections (a), (b), and (c) shall not apply to any debt restructuring of such debt which was approved by the debtor's Board of Directors and the lenders in 1986, and

(ii) the amendments made by subsections (e) and (f) of section 806 of the Tax Reform Act of 1976 (including the amendment treated as part of such subsections under section 59(b) of the Tax Reform Act of 1984) shall apply to such debt restructuring.

(D) Special rule for oil and gas well drilling business.—In the case of a Texas corporation incorporated on July 23, 1935, in applying section 382 of the Internal Revenue Code of 1986 (as in effect before and after the amendments made by subsections (a), (b), and (c)) to a loan restructuring agreement during 1985, section 382(a)(5)(C) of the Internal Revenue Code of 1954 (as added by the amendments made by subsections (e) and (f) of section 806 of the Tax Reform Act of 1976) shall be applied as if it were in effect with respect to such restructuring or reorganization.

* * * * * * * * * * * *

(9) **Definitions.**—Except as otherwise provided, terms used in this subsection shall have the same meaning as when used in section 382 of the Internal Revenue Code of 1986 (as amended by this section).

[For official explanation, see Committee Reports, ¶3916]

[¶2023] SEC. 633. EFFECTIVE DATES.

* * * * * * * * * * * *

(c) **Exception for Certain Plans of Liquidation and Binding Contracts.—**

(1) **In general.**—The amendments made by this subtitle shall not apply to—

(A) any distribution or sale or exchange made pursuant to a plan of liquidation adopted before August 1, 1986, if the liquidating corporation is completely liquidated before January 1, 1988,

(B) any distribution or sale or exchange made by any corporation if 50 percent or more of the voting stock by value of such corporation is acquired on or after August 1, 1986, pursuant to a written binding contract in effect before such date and if such corporation is completely liquidated before January 1, 1988,

(C) any distribution or sale or exchange made by any corporation if substantially all of the assets of such corporation are sold on or after August 1, 1986, pursuant to 1 or more written binding contracts in effect before such date and if such corporation is completely liquidated before January 1, 1988, or

(D) any transaction described in section 338 of the Internal Revenue Code of 1986 with respect to any target corporation if a qualified stock purchase of such target corporation is made on or after August 1, 1986, pursuant to a written binding contract in effect before such date and the acquisition date (within the meaning of such section 338) is before January 1, 1988.

(2) **Special rule for certain actions taken before November 20, 1985.**—For purposes of paragraph (1), transactions shall be treated as pursuant to a plan of liquidation adopted before August 1, 1986, if—

(A) before November 20, 1985—

(i) the board of directors of the liquidating corporation adopted a resolution to solicit shareholder approval for a transaction of a kind described in section 336 or 337, or

(ii) the shareholders or board of directors have approved such a transaction,

(B) before November 20, 1985—

(i) there has been an offer to purchase a majority of the voting stock of the liquidating corporation, or

(ii) the board of directors of the liquidating corporation has adopted a resolution approving an acquisition or recommending the approval of an acquisition to the shareholders, or

(C) before November 20, 1985, a ruling request was submitted to the Secretary of the Treasury or his delegate with respect to a transaction of a kind described in section 336 or 337 of the Internal Revenue Code of 1954 (as in effect before the amendments made by this subtitle).

For purposes of the preceding sentence, any action taken by the board of directors or shareholders of a corporation with respect to any subsidiary of such corporation shall be treated as taken by the board of directors or shareholders of such subsidiary.

(d) **Transitional Rule for Certain Small Corporations.—**

(1) **In general.**—In the case of the complete liquidation before January 1, 1989, of a qualified corporation, the amendments made by this section shall not apply to the

applicable percentage of each gain or loss which (but for this paragraph) would be recognized by reason of the amendments made by this subtitle.

(2) **Paragraph (1) not to apply to certain items.**—Paragraph (1) shall not apply to—

(A) any gain or loss which is an ordinary gain or loss (determined without regard to section 1239 of the Internal Revenue Code of 1986),

(B) any gain or loss on a capital asset held for not more than 6 months, and

(C) any gain to the extent section 453B of such Code applies.

(3) **Applicable percentage.**—For purposes of this subsection, the term "applicable percentage" means—

(A) 100 percent if the applicable value of the qualified corporation is less than $5,000,000, or

(B) 100 percent reduced by an amount which bears the same ratio to 100 percent as—

(i) the excess of the applicable value of the corporation over $5,000,000, bears to

(ii) $5,000,000.

(4) **Applicable value.**—For purposes of this subsection, the applicable value is the fair market value of all of the stock of the corporation on the date of the adoption of the plan of complete liquidation (or if greater, on August 1, 1986).

(5) **Qualified corporation.**—For purposes of this subsection, the term "qualified corporation" means any corporation if—

(A) on August 1, 1986, and at all times thereafter before the corporation is completely liquidated, more than 50 percent (by value) of the stock in such corporation is held by 10 or fewer qualified persons, and

(B) the applicable value of such corporation does not exceed $10,000,000.

(6) **Definitions and special rules.**—For purposes of this subsection—

(A) Qualified person.—The term "qualified person" means—

(i) an individual,

(ii) an estate, or

(iii) any trust described in clause (ii) or (iii) of section 1361(c)(2)(A) of the Internal Revenue Code of 1986.

(B) Attribution rules.—

(i) Entities.—Any stock held by a corporation, trust, or partnership shall be treated as owned proportionally by its shareholders, beneficiaries, or partners. Stock considered to be owned by a person by reason of the application of the preceding sentence shall, for purposes of applying such sentence, be treated as actually owned by such person.

(ii) Family members.—Stock owned (or treated as owned under clause (i)) by members of the same family (within the meaning of section 318(a)(1) of the Internal Revenue Code of 1986) shall be treated as owned by 1 person.

(C) Controlled group of corporations.—All members of the same controlled group (as defined in section 267(f)(1) of such Code) shall be treated as 1 corporation for purposes of this subsection.

(7) **Section 338 Transactions.**—The provisions of this subsection shall also apply in the case of a transaction described in section 338 of the Internal Revenue Code of 1986 where the acquisition date (within the meaning of such section 338) is before January 1, 1989.

(8) **Application of section 1374.**—Rules similar to the rules of this subsection shall apply for purposes of applying section 1374 of the Internal Revenue Code of 1986 (as amended by section 632) in the case of a qualified corporation which becomes an S corporation for a taxable year beginning before January 1, 1989.

(d) [should read (e)] **Complete Liquidation Defined.**—For purposes of this section, a corporation shall be treated as completely liquidated if all of the assets of such corporation are distributed in complete liquidation, less assets retained to meet claims.

(e) [should read (f)] **Other Transitional Rules.**—

(1) The amendments made by this subtitle shall not apply to any liquidation of a corporation incorporated under the laws of Pennsylvania on August 3, 1970, if—

(A) the board of directors of such corporation approved a plan of liquidation before January 1, 1986,

Act §633(e) ¶2023

(B) an agreement for the sale of a material portion of assets of such corporation was signed on May 9, 1986 (whether or not the assets are sold in accordance with such agreement), and

(C) the corporation is completely liquidated on or before December 31, 1988.

(2) The amendments made by this subtitle shall not apply to any liquidation (or deemed liquidation under section 338 of the Internal Revenue Code of 1986) of a diversified financial services corporation incorporated under the laws of Delaware on May 9, 1929, pursuant to a binding written contract entered into on or before December 31, 1986; but only if the liquidation is completed (or in the case of a section 338 election, the acquisition date occurs) before January 1, 1988.

(3) The amendments made by this subtitle shall not apply to any distribution, or sale, or exchange—

(A) of the assets owned (directly or indirectly) by a testamentary trust established under the will of a decedent dying on June 15, 1956, to its beneficiaries,

(B) made pursuant to a court order in an action filed on January 18, 1984, if such order—

(i) is issued after July 31, 1986, and

(ii) directs the disposition of the assets of such trust and the division of the trust corpus into 3 separate subtrusts.

For purposes of the preceding sentence, an election under section 338(g) of the Internal Revenue Code of 1986 (or an election under section 338(h)(10) of such Code,) qualifying as a section 337 liquidation pursuant to regulations prescribed by the Secretary under section 1.338(h)(10)-1T(j) made in connection with a sale or exchange pursuant to a court order described in subparagraph (B) shall be treated as a sale of exchange.

(4)(A) The amendments made by this subtitle shall not apply to any distribution, or sale, or exchange—

(i) if—

(I) an option agreement binding on the selling corporation to sell substantially all its assets is executed before August 1, 1986, the corporation adopts (by approval of its shareholders) a conditional plan of liquidation before August 1, 1986 to become effective upon the exercise of such option agreement (or modification thereto), and the assets are sold pursuant to the exercise of the option (as originally executed or subsequently modified provided that the purchase is not thereby increased), or

(II) in the event that the optionee does not acquire substantially all the assets of the corporation, the optionor corporation sells substantially all its assets to another purchaser at a purchase price not greater than that contemplated by such option agreement pursuant to an effective plan of liquidation, and

(ii) the complete liquidation of the corporation occurs within 12 months of the time the plan of liquidation becomes effective, but in no event later than December 31, 1989.

(B) For purposes of subparagraph (A), a distribution, or sale, or exchange, of a distributee corporation (within the meaning of section 337(c)(3) of the Internal Revenue Code of 1986) shall be treated as satisfying the requirements of subparagraph (A) if its subsidiary satisfies the requirements of subparagraph (A).

(C) For purposes of section 56 of the Internal Revenue Code of 1986 (as amended by this Act), any gain or loss not recognized by reason of this paragraph shall not be taken into account in determining the adjusted net book income of the corporation.

(5) In the case of a corporation incorporated under the laws of Wisconsin on April 3, 1948—

(A) a voting trust established not later than December 31, 1987, for purposes of holding employees' shares of stock in such corporation, shall qualify as a trust permitted as a shareholder of an S corporation, and

(B) the amendment made by section 632 (other than subsection (b) thereof) shall not apply to such corporation if it elects to be an S corporation before January 1, 1989.

(6) The amendments made by this subtitle shall not apply to the liquidation of a corporation incorporated on January 26, 1982, under the laws of the State of Alabama with a principal place of business in Colbert County, Alabama, but only if such corporation is completely liquidated on or before December 31, 1987.

(7) The amendments made by this subtitle shall not apply to the acquisition by a Delaware bank holding company of all of the assets of an Iowa Bank holding company pursuant to a written contract dated December 9, 1981.

(8) The amendments made by this subtitle shall not apply to the liquidation of a corporation incorporated under the laws of Delaware on January 20, 1984, if more than 40 percent of the stock of such corporation was acquired by purchase on June 11, 1986, and there was a tender offer with respect to all additional outstanding shares of such corporation on July 29, 1986, but only if the corporation is completely liquidated on or before December 31, 1987.

(f) [should read (g)] Treatment of Certain Distributions in Response To Hostile Tender Offer.—

(1) In general.—No gain or loss shall be recognized under the Internal Revenue Code of 1986 to a corporation (hereinafter in this subsection referred to as "parent") on a qualified distribution.

(2) Qualified Distribution Defined.—For purposes of paragraph (1)—

(A) In general.—The term "qualified distribution" means a distribution—

(i) by parent of all of the stock of a qualified subsidiary in exchange for stock of parent which was acquired for purposes of such exchange pursuant to a tender offer dated February 16, 1982, and

(ii) pursuant to a contract dated February 13, 1982, and

(iii) which was made not more than 60 days after the board of directors of parent recommended rejection of an unsolicited tender offer to obtain control of parent.

(B) Qualified subsidiary.—The term "qualified subsidiary " means a corporation created or organized under the laws of Delaware on September 7, 1976, all of the stock of which was owned by parent immediately before the qualified distribution.

[¶2024] SEC. 634. STUDY OF CORPORATE PROVISIONS.

The Secretary of the Treasury or his delegate shall conduct a study of proposals to reform the provisions of subchapter C of chapter 1 of the Internal Revenue Code of 1986. Not later than January 1, 1988, the Secretary shall submit to the Committee on Ways and Means of the House of Representatives and the Committee on Finance of the Senate a report on the study conducted under this section (together with such recommendations as he may deem advisable).

[For official explanation, see Committee Reports, ¶3920]

[¶2025] SEC. 644. PROVISIONS RELATING TO COOPERATIVE HOUSING CORPORATIONS.

* * * * * * * * * * * *

(e) Treatment of Amounts Received in Connection With the Refinancing of Indebtedness of Certain Cooperative Housing Corporations; Treatment of Amounts Paid From Qualified Refinancing-Related Reserve.—

(1) Payment of closing costs and creation of reserve excluded from gross income—For purposes of the Internal Revenue Code of 1954, no amount shall be included in the gross income of a qualified cooperative housing corporation by reason of the payment or reimbursement by a city housing development agency or corporation of amounts for—

(A) closing costs, or

(B) the creation of reserves for the qualified cooperative housing corporation,

in connection with a qualified refinancing.

(2) Income from reserve fund treated as member income.—

(A) In general.—Income from a qualified refinancing-related reserve shall be treated as derived from its members for purposes of—

(i) section 216 of the Internal Revenue Code of 1954 (relating to deduction of taxes, interest, and business depreciation by cooperative housing corporation tenant-stockholder), and

Act §644(e)(2) ¶2025

(ii) section 277 of such Code (relating to deductions incurred by certain membership organizations in transactions with members).

(B) No inference.—Nothing in the provisions of this paragraph shall be constured to infer that change in law is intended with respect to the treatment of deductions under section 277 of the Internal Revenue Code of 1954 with respect to cooperative housing corporations, and any determination of such issue shall be made as if such provisions had not been enacted.

(3) **Treatment of certain interest claimed as deductions.**—Any amount—

(A) claimed (on a return of tax imposed by chapter 1 of the Internal Revenue Code of 1954) as a deduction by a qualified cooperative housing corporation for interest for any taxable year beginning before January 1, 1986, on a second mortgage loan made by a city housing development agency or corporation in connection with a qualified refinancing, and

(B) reported (before April 16, 1986) by the qualified cooperative housing corporation to its tenant-stockholders as interest described in section 216(a)(2) of such Code, shall be treated for purposes of such Code as if such amount were paid by such qualified cooperative housing corporation during such taxable year.

(4) **Qualified cooperative housing corporation.**—

(A) In general.—For purposes of this subsection, the term "qualified cooperative housing corporation" means any corporation if—

(i) such corporation is, after the application of paragraphs (1) and (2), a cooperative housing corporation (as defined in section 216(b) of the Internal Revenue Code of 1954),

(ii) such corporation is subject to a qualified limited-profit housing companies law, and

(iii) such corporation either—

(I) filed for incorporation on July 22, 1965, or

(II) filed for incorporation on March 5, 1964.

(B) Qualified limited-profit housing companies law.—For purposes of subparagraph (A), the term "qualified limited-profit housing companies law" means any limited-profit housing companies law which limits the resale price for a tenant-stockholder's stock in a cooperative housing corporation to the sum of his basis for such stock plus his proportionate share of part or all of the amortization of any mortgage on the building owned by such corporation.

(5) **Qualified refinancing.**—For purposes of this subsection, the term "qualified refinancing" means any refinancing—

(A) which occurred—

(i) with respect to a qualified cooperative housing corporation described in paragraph (4)(A)(iii)(I) on September 20, 1978, or

(ii) with respect to a qualified cooperative housing corporation described in paragraph (4)(A)(iii)(II) on November 21, 1978, and

(B) in which a qualified cooperative housing corporation refinanced a first mortgage loan made to such corporation by a city housing development agency with a first mortgage loan made by a city housing development corporation and insured by an agency of the Federal Government and a second mortgage loan made by such city housing development agency, in the process of which a reserve was created (as required by such Federal agency) and closing costs were paid or reimbursed by such city housing development agency or corporation.

(6) **Qualified refinancing-related reserve.**—For purposes of this subsection, the term "qualified refinancing-related reserve" means any reserve of a qualified cooperative housing corporation with respect to the creation of which no amount was included in the gross income of such corporation by reason of paragraph (a).

(7) **Treatment of amounts paid from qualified refinancing-related reserve.**—

(A) In general.—With respect to any payment from a qualified refinancing-related reserve out of amounts excluded from gross income by reason of paragraph (1)—

(i) no deduction shall be allowed under chapter 1 of such Code, and

(ii) the basis of any property acquired with such payment (determined without regard to this subparagraph) shall be reduced by the amount of such payment.

(B) Ordering rules.—For purposes of subparagraph (A), payments from a reserve shall be treated as being made—

    (i)   first from amountss excluded from gross income by reason of paragraph (1) to the extent thereof, and

    (ii)   then from other amounts in the reserve.

(f) Effective Date.—

* * * * * * * * * * * *

    (2) Subsection (e).—

        (A)   Except as provided in subparagraph (B), subsection (e) shall apply to taxable years beginning before January 1, 1986.

        (B)   Subsection (e)(7) shall apply to amounts paid or incurred, and property acquired, in taxable years beginning, after December 31, 1985.

[For official explanation, see Committee Reports, ¶3924]

[¶2026]   SEC. 645. SPECIAL RULES RELATING TO PERSONAL HOLDING COMPANY TAX.

* * * * * * * * * * * *

    (b) Special Rules for Broker-Dealers.—In the case of a broker-dealer which is part of an affiliated group which files a consolidated Federal income tax return, the common parent of which was incorporated in Nevada on January 27, 1972, the personal holding company income (within the meaning of section 543 of the Internal Revenue Code of 1986) of such broker-dealer, shall not include any interest received after the date of the enactment of this Act with respect to—

    (1)   any securities or money market instruments held as inventory,

    (2)   margin accounts, or

    (3)   any financing for a customer secured by securities or money market instruments.

    (c) Special Rule for Royalties Received by Qualified Taxpayer.—

    (1) In general.—Any qualifed royalty received or accrued in taxable years beginning after December 31, 1981, by a qualified taxpayer shall be treated in the same manner as a royalty with respect to software is treated under the amendments made by this section.

    (2) Qualified taxpayer.—For purposes of this subsection, a qualified taxpayer is any taxpayer incorporated on September 7, 1978, which is engaged in the trade or business of manufacturing dolls and accessories.

    (3) Qualified royalty.—For purposes of this subsection, the term "qualified royalty" means any royalty arising from an agreement entered into in 1982 which permits the licensee to manufacture and sell dolls and accessories.

    (d) Special Rule for Treatment of Active Business Computer Royalties for S Corporation Purposes.—In the case of a taxpayer which was incorporated on May 3, 1977, in California and which elected to be taxed as an S corporation for its taxable year ending on December 31, 1985, any active business computer royalties (within the meaning of section 543(d) of the Internal Revenue Code of 1986 as added by this Act) which are received by the taxpayer in taxable years beginning after December 31, 1984, shall not be treated as passive investment income (within the meaning of section 1362(d)(3)(D)) for purposes of subchapter S of chapter 1 of such Code.

* * * * * * * * * * * *

[For official explanation, see Committee Reports, ¶3925]

[¶2027]   SEC. 646. CERTAIN ENTITIES NOT TREATED AS CORPORATIONS.

    (a) General Rule.—For purposes of the Internal Revenue Code of 1986, if the entity described in subsection (b) makes an election under subsection (c), such entity shall be treated as a trust to which subpart E of part 1 of subchapter J of chapter 1 of such Code applies.

    (b) Entity.—An entity is described in this subsection if—

    (1)   such entity was created in 1906 as a common law trust and is governed by the trust laws of the State of Minnesota,

    (2)   Such entity receives royalties from iron ore leases and

    (3)   income interest in such entity are publicly traded on a national stock exchange.

Act §646(b) ¶2027

(c) Election.—

   (1) In general.—An election under this subsection to have the provisions of this section apply—

      (A) shall be made by the board of trustees of the entity, and

      (B) shall not be valid unless accompanied by an agreement described in paragraph (2).

   (2) Agreement.—The agreement described in this paragrpah is a written agreement signed by the board of trustess of the entity which provides that the entity will not—

      (A) sell any trust property,

      (B) purchase any additional trust properties, or

      (C) receive any income other than—

         (i) income from long-term mineral leases, or

         (ii) interest or other income attributable to ordinary and necessary reserves of the entity.

   (3) Period for which election is in effect.—An election under this subsection shall be in effect during the period—

      (A) beginning on the first day of the first taxable year beginning after the date of the enactment of this Act and following the taxable year in which the election is made, and

      (B) ending as of the close of the taxable year preceding the taxable year in which the entity ceases to be described in subsection (b) or violates any term of the agreement under paragraph (2).

   (4) Manner of election.—Any election under this subsection shall be made in such manner as the Secretary of the Treasury or his delegate may prescribe.

(d) Special Rules for Taxation of Trust.—

   (1) Election treated as a liquidation.—If an election is made under subsection (c) with respect to any entity—

      (A) such entity shall be treated as having been liquidated into a trust immediately before the period described in subsection (c)(3) in a liquidation to which section 333 of the Internal Revenue Code of 1954 (as in effect before the amendments made by this Act) applies, and

      (B) any person holding an interest in the property held by such entity as of such time shall be treated as a qualified electing shareholder for purposes of section 333 of such Code (as so in effect).

   (2) Termination of election.—If an entity ceases to be described in subsection (b) or violates any term of the agreement described in subsection (c)(2), then the tax imposed on such entity for the taxable year in which such cessation or violation occurs shall be increased by the sum of—

      (A) the amount of taxes which would have been imposed on such entity during any taxable year with respect to which an election under subsection (c) was in effect if such election had not been in effect, plus

      (B) interest determined for the period—

         (i) beginning on the due date for any such taxable year, and

         (ii) ending on the due date for the taxable year in which such cessation or violation occurs,

by using the rates and method applicable under section 6621 for underpayments of tax for such period.

   (3) Trust ceasing to exist.—Paragraph (2) shall not apply if the trust ceases to be described in subsection (b) or violates the agreement in subsection (c)(2) because the trust ceases to exist or by reason of subsection (e).

(e) Termination of Election.—Any election under subsection (c) shall not apply to any taxable year beginning more than 5 years after the date of the enactment of this Act unless the trust petitions a court of competent jurisdiction and the court acts to remove from the trust instrument any powers deemed by the court to be inconsistent with the operation of the entity as a trust for tax purposes (as described in an Internal Revenue Service ruling dated November 1, 1983).

[For official explanation, see Committee Reports, ¶3926]

⟦¶2028⟧ SEC. 647. SPECIAL RULE FOR DISPOSITION OF STOCK OF SUBSIDIARY.

If for a taxable year of an affiliated group filing a consolidated return ending on or before December 31, 1987, there is a disposition of stock of a subsidiary (within the meaning of Treasury Regulation section 1.1502-19), the amount required to be included in income with respect to such disposition under Treasury Regulation section 1.1502-19(a) shall, notwithstanding such section, be included in income ratably over the 15-year period beginning with the taxable year in which the disposition occurs. The preceding sentence shall apply only if such subsidiary was incorporated on December 24, 1969, and is a participant in a mineral joint venture with a corporation organized under the laws of the foreign country in which the joint venture mineral project is located.

⟦¶2028-A⟧ SEC. 701. ALTERNATIVE MINIMUM TAX FOR INDIVIDUALS AND CORPORATIONS.

* * * * * * * * * * *

(f) **Effective Dates.—**

* * * * * * * * * * *

(2) **Adjustment of net operating loss.—**

(A) Individuals.—In the case of a net operating loss of an individual for a taxable year beginning after December 31, 1982, and before January 1, 1987, for purposes of determining the amount of such loss which may be carried to a taxable year beginning after December 31, 1986, for purposes of the minimum tax, such loss shall be adjusted in the manner provided in section 55(d)(2) of the Internal Revenue Code of 1954 as in effect on the day before the date of the enactment of this Act.

(B) Corporations.—If the minimum tax of a corporation was deferred under section 56(b) of the Internal Revenue Code of 1954 (as in effect on the day before the date of the enactment of this Act) for any taxable year beginning before January 1, 1987, and the amount of such tax has not been paid for any taxable year beginning before January 1, 1987, the amount of the net operating loss carryovers of such corporation which may be carried to taxable years beginning after December 31, 1986, for purposes of the minimum tax shall be reduced by the amount of tax preferences a tax on which was so deferred.

(3) **Installment sales.—**Section 56(a)(6) of the Internal Revenue Code of 1986 (as amended by this section) shall not apply to any disposition to which the amendments made by section 811 of this Act (relating to allocation of dealer's indebtedness to installment obligations) do not apply by reason of section 811(c)(2) of this Act.

(4) **Exception for charitable contributions before August 16, 1986.—**Section 57(a)(6) of the Internal Revenue Code of 1986 (as amended by this section) shall not apply to any deduction attributable to contributions made before August 16, 1986.

(5) **Book income.—**

(A) In general.—In the case of a corporation to which this paragraph applies, the amount of any increase for any taxable year under section 56(c)(1)(A) of the Internal Revenue Code of 1986 (as added by this section) shall be reduced (but not below zero) by the excess (if any) of—

(i) 50 percent of the excess of taxable income for the 5-taxable year period ending with the taxable year preceding the 1st taxable year to which such section applies over the adjusted net book income for such period, over

(ii) the aggregate amounts taken into account under this paragraph for preceding taxable years.

(B) Taxpayer to whom paragraph applies.—This paragraph applies to a taxpayer which was incorporated in Delaware on May 31, 1912.

(C) Terms.—Any term used in this paragraph which is used in section 56 of such Code (as so added) shall have the same meaning as when used in such section.

(6) **Certain public utility.—**

(A) In the case of investment tax credits described in subparagraph (B) or (C), subsection 38(c)(3)(A)(ii) of the Internal Revenue Code of 1986 shall be applied by substituting "25 percent" for "75 percent", and section 38(c)(3)(B) of the Internal Revenue Code of 1986 shall be applied by substituting "75 percent" for "25 percent".

(B) If, on September 26, 1985, a regulated electric utility owned an individed interest, within the range of 1,111 and 1,149, in the "maximum dependable capacity, net, megawatts electric" of an electric generating unit located in Illinois or Mississippi for which a binding written contract was in efect on December 31, 1980, then any investment tax credit with respect to such unit shall be described in this subparagraph. The aggregate amount of investment tax credits with respect to such unit shall be described in this subparagraph.

(C) If, on September 25, 1985, a regulated electric utility owned an undivided interest, within the range of 1,104 and 1,111, in the "maximum dependable capacity, net, megawatts electric" of an electric generating unit located in Louisiana for which a binding written contract was in effect on December 31, 1980, then any investment tax credit of such electric utility shall be described in this subparagraph. The aggregate amount of investment tax credits allowed solely by reason of being described by this subparagraph shall not exceed $20,000,000.

[For official explanation, see Committee Reports, ¶3931]

[¶2029] SEC. 702. STUDY OF BOOK AND EARNINGS AND PROFITS ADJUSTMENTS.

The Secretary of the Treasury or his delegate shall conduct a study of the operation and effect of the provisions of sections 56(f) and 56(g) of the Internal Revenue Code of 1986.

[For official explanation, see Committee Reports, ¶3932]

[¶2030] SEC. 804. MODIFICATIONS OF METHOD OF ACCOUNTING FOR LONG-TERM CONTRACT.

* * * * * * * * * * * *

(b) **Change In Regulations.**—The Secretary of the Treasury or his delegate shall modify the income tax regulations relating to accounting for long-term contracts to carry out the provisions of section 460 of the Internal Revenue Code of 1986 (as added by subsection (a)).

* * * * * * * * * * * *

[For official explanation, see Committee Reports, ¶3937]

[¶2030-A] SEC. 824. INCLUSION IN GROSS INCOME OF CONTRIBUTIONS IN AID OF CONSTRUCTION.

* * * * * * * * * * * *

(c) **Effective Date.—**

* * * * * * * * * * * *

(2) **Treatment of certain water supply projects.**—The amendments made by this section shall not apply to amounts which are paid by the New Jersey Department of

Environmental Protection for construction of alternative water supply projects in zones of drinking water contamination and which are designated by such department as being taken into account under this paragraph. Not more than $4,631,000 of such amounts may be designated under the preceding sentence.

(3) **Treatment of certain contributions by transportation authority.**—The amendments made by this section shall not apply to contributions in aid of construction by a qualified transportation authority which were clearly identified in a master plan in existence on September 13, 1984, and which are designated by such authority as being taken into account under this paragraph. Not more than $68,000,000 of such contributions may be designated under the preceding sentence. For purposes of this paragraph, a qualified transportation authority is an entity which was created on February 20, 1967, and which was established by an interstate compact and consented to by Congress in Public Law 89-774, 80 Stat. 1324 (1966).

(4) **Treatment of certain partnerships.**—In the case of a partnership with a taxable year beginning May 1, 1986, if such partnership realized net capital gain during the period beginning on the 1st day of such taxable year and ending on May 29, 1986, pursuant to an indemnity agreement dated May 6, 1986, then such partnership may elect to treat each asset to which such net capital gain relates as having been distributed to the partners of such partnership in proportion to their distributive share of the capital gain or loss realized by the partnership with respect to such asset and to treat each such asset as having been sold by each partner on the date of the sale of the asset by the partnership. If such an election is made, the consideration received by the partnership in connection with the sale of such assets shall be treated as having been received by the partners in connection with the deemed sale of such assets. In the case of a tiered partnership, for purposes of this paragraph each partnership shall be treated as having realized net capital gain equal to its proportionate share of the net capital gain of each partnership in which it is a partner, and the election provided by this paragraph shall apply to each tier.

[For official explanation, see Committee Reports, ¶3946]

[¶2031]   SEC. 1011.   REPEAL OF SPECIAL LIFE INSURANCE COMPANY DEDUCTION.

*   *   *   *   *   *   *   *   *   *   *   *   *

(c) **Effective Date.—**

*   *   *   *   *   *   *   *   *   *   *   *   *

(2) **Special rule.**—Section 217(k) of the Tax Reform Act of 1984 is amended—
  (A) by striking out "the special deductions under section 806" and inserting in lieu thereof "the small life insurance company deduction under section 806(a)", and
  (B) by adding at the end thereof the following: "For purposes of determining taxable income, the amount of any income, gain, loss, or deduction attributable to the ownership of such stock shall be an amount equal to 46 times the amount of such income, gain, loss, or deduction, divided by 36.8."

(d) **Treatment of Certain Market Discount Bonds.—**

(1) **In general.**—Notwithstanding the amendments made by subtitle B of title III, any gain recognized by a qualified life insurance company on the redemption at maturity of any bond which was issued before July 19, 1984, and acquired by such company on or before September 25, 1985, shall be subject to tax at the rate of 28 percent.

(2) **Qualified life insurance company.**—For purposes of paragraph (1), the term 'qualified life insurance company' means any of the following companies: Aetna, Provident Life and Accident, Massachusetts Mutual, Mutual Benefit, Connecticut Mutual, Phoenix Mutual, John Hancock, New England Life, Pennsylvania Mutual, Transamerica, Northwestern, Provident Mutual, Prudential, Mutual of Omaha, and Metropolitan.

[For official explanation, see Committee Reports, ¶3958]

[¶2033]   SEC. 1012.   REPEAL OF TAX-EXEMPT STATUS FOR CERTAIN OR-GANIZATIONS PROVIDING COMMERCIAL-TYPE INSURANCE.

* * * * * * * * * * * *

(c)   Effective Date.—

* * * * * * * * * * * *

(2)   Study of fraternal beneficiary associations.—The Secretary of the Treasury or his delegate shall conduct a study of organizations described in section 501(c)(8) of the Internal Revenue Code of 1986 and which received gross annual insurance premiums in excess of $25,000,000 for the taxable years of such organizations which ended during 1984. Not later than January 1, 1988, the Secretary of the Treasury shall submit to the Committee on Ways and Means of the House of Representatives, the Committee on Finance of the Senate, and the Joint Committee on Taxation the results of such study, together with such recommendations as he determines to be appropriate. The Secretary of the Treasury shall have authority to require the furnishing of such information as may be necessary to carry out the purposes of this paragraph.

* * * * * * * * * * * *

[For official explanation, see Committee Reports, ¶3959]

[¶2034]   SEC. 1013.   OPERATIONS LOSS DEDUCTION OF INSOLVENT COM-PANIES MAY OFFSET DISTRIBUTIONS FROM POLICYHOLDERS SURPLUS ACCOUNT.

(a)   In General.—If—

(1)   on November 15, 1985, a life insurance company was insolvent,

(2)   pursuant to the order of any court of competent jurisdiction in a title 11 or similar case (as defined in section 368(a)(3) of the Internal Revenue code of 1954), such company is liquidated, and

(3)   as a result of such liquidation, the tax imposed by section 801 of such Code for any taxable year (hereinafter in this subsection referred to as the "liquidation year") would (but for this subsection) be increased under section 815(a) of such Code,

then the amount described in section 815(a)(2) of such Code shall be reduced by the loss from operations (if any) for the liquidation year, and by the unused operations loss carry-overs (if any) to the liquidation year (determined after the application of section 810 of such Code for such year). No carryover of any loss from operations of such company arising during the liquidation year (or any prior taxable year) shall be allowable for any taxable year succeeding the liquidation year.

(b)   Definitions.—For purposes of subsection (a)—

(1)   Insolvent.—The term "insolvent" means the excess of liabilities over the fair market value of assets.

(2)   Loss from operations.—The term "loss from operations" has the meaning given such term by section 810(c) of such Code.

(c)   Effective Date.—This section shall apply to liquidations on or after November 15, 1985, in taxable years ending after such date.

[For official explanation, see Committee Reports, ¶3960]

[¶2035]   SEC. 1023.   DISCOUNTING OF UNPAID LOSSES AND CERTAIN UN-PAID EXPENSES.

* * * * * * * * * * * *

(e)   Effective Date.—

* * * * * * * * * * * *

(3)   Fresh start.—

(A)   In general.—Except as otherwise provided in this paragraph, any difference between—

(i)   the amount determined to be the unpaid losses and expenses unpaid for the year preceding the 1st taxable year of an insurance company beginning after December 31, 1986, determined without regard to paragraph (2), and

(ii)   such amount determined with regard to paragraph (2),

shall not be taken into account for purposes of the Internal Revenue Code of 1986.

(B)   Reserve strengthening in years after 1985.—Subparagraph (A) shall not apply to any reserve strengthening in a taxable year beginning in 1986, and such strengthening shall be treated as occurring in the taxpayer's 1st taxable year beginning after December 31, 1986.

(C)   Effect on earnings and profits.—The earnings and profits of any insurance company for its 1st taxable year beginning after December 31, 1986, shall be increased by the amount of the difference determined under subparagraph (A) with respect to such company.

[For official explanation, see Committee Reports, ¶3963]

[¶2036] SEC. 1024. REPEAL OF PROTECTION AGAINST LOSS ACCOUNT; REVISION OF SPECIAL TREATMENT FOR SMALL COMPANIES; COMBINATION OF PARTS II AND III.

* * * * * * * * * * * *

(d) Transitional Rules.—

(1) **Treatment of amounts in protection against loss account.**—In the case of any insurance company which had a protection against loss account for its last taxable year beginning before January 1, 1987, there shall be included in the gross income of such company for any taxable year beginning after December 31, 1986, the amount which would have been included in gross income for such taxable year under section 824 of the Internal Revenue Code of 1954 (as in effect on the day before the date of the enactment of this Act). For purposes of the preceding sentence, no addition to such account shall be made for any taxable year beginning after December 31, 1986.

(2) **Transitional rule for unused loss carryover under section 825.**—Any unused loss carryover under section 825 of the Internal Revenue Code of 1954 (as in effect on the day before the date of the enactment of this Act) which—

    (A) is from a taxable year beginning before January 1, 1987, and

    (B) could have been carried under such section to a taxable year beginning after December 31, 1986, but for the repeal made by subsection (a)(1),

shall be included in the net operating loss deduction under section 832(c)(10) of such Code without regard to the limitations of section 844(b) of such Code.

(e) Effective Date.—The amendments made by this section (and the provisions of subsection (d)) shall apply to taxable years beginning after December 31, 1986.

[For official explanation, see Committee Reports, ¶3964]

[¶2037] SEC. 1025. STUDY OF TREATMENT OF PROPERTY AND CASUALTY INSURANCE COMPANIES.

The Secretary of the Treasury or his delegate shall conduct a study of—

    (1) the treatment of policyholder dividends by mutual property and casualty insurance companies,

    (2) the treatment of property and casualty insurance companies under the minimum tax, and

    (3) the operation and effect of, and revenue raised by, the amendments made by this subtitle.

Not later than January 1, 1989, such Secretary shall submit to the Committee on Ways and Means of the House of Representatives, the Committee on Finance of the Senate, and the Joint Committee on Taxation, the results of such study, together with such recommendations as he determines to be appropriate. The Secretary of the Treasury shall have authority to require the furnishing of such information as may be necessary to carry out the purposes of this section.

[For official explanation, see Committee Reports, ¶3965]

[¶2038] SEC. 1031. PHYSICIANS' AND SURGEONS' MUTUAL PROTECTION AND INTERINDEMNITY ARRANGEMENTS OR ASSOCIATIONS.

(a) Certain Physicians' and Surgeons' Mutual Protection and Interindemnity Arrangements or Associations.—

(1) **Treatment of arrangements or associations.—**

    (A) **Capital contributions.**—There shall not be included in the gross income of any eligible physicians' and surgeons' mutual protection and interindemnity arrangement or association any initial payment made during any taxable year to such arrangement or association by a member joining such arrangement or association which—

        (i) does not release such member from obligations to pay current or future dues, assessments, or premiums; and

        (ii) is a condition precedent to receiving benefits of membership.

Act §1031(a)(1) ¶2038

Such initial payment shall be included in the gross income of such arrangement or association for such taxable year if it is reasonable to expect that such payment will be deductible pursuant to paragraph (2) by any member of such arrangement or association.

    (B)   Return of contributions.—

        (i)   In general.—The repayment to any member of any amount of any payment excluded under subparagraph (A) shall not be treated as policyholder dividend, and is not deductible by the arrangement or association.

        (ii)   Source of returns.—Except in the case of the termination of a member's interest in the arrangement or association, any amount distributed to any member shall be treated as paid out of surplus in excess of amounts excluded under subparagraph (A).

    (2)   Deduction for members of eligible arrangements or associations.—

        (A)   Payment as trade or business expenses.—To the extent not otherwise allowable under this title, any member of any eligible arrangement or association may treat any initial payment made during a taxable year to such arrangement or association as an ordinary and necessary expense incurred in connection with a trade or business for purposes of the deduction allowable under section 162, to the extent such payment does not exceed the amunt which would be payable to an independent insurance company for similar annual insurance coverge (as determined by the Secretary), and further reduced by any annual dues, assessments, or premiums paid during such taxable year. Such deduction shall not be allowable as to any initial payment made to an eligible arrangement or association by any person who is a member of any other eligible arrangement or association on or after the effective date of the Tax Reform Act of 1986. Any excess amount not allowed as a deduction for the taxable year in which such payment was made pursuant to the limitation contained in the 1st sentence of this subparagraph shall, subject to such limitation, be allowable as a deduction in any of the 5 succeeding taxable years, in order of time, to the extent not previously allowed as a deduction under this sentence.

        (B)   Refunds of initial payments.—Any amount attributable to any initial payment to such arrangement or association described in paragraph (1) which is later refunded for any reason shall be included in the gross income of the recipient in the taxable year received, to the extent a deduction for such payment was allowed. Any amount refunded in excess of such payment shall be included in gross income except to the extent otherwise excluded from income by this title.

    (3)   Eligible arrangements or associations.—The terms "eligible physicians' and surgeons' mutual protection and interindemnity arrangement or association" and "eligible arrangement or association" mean and are limited to any mutual protection and interindemnity arrangement or association that provides only medical malpractice liability protection for its members or medical malpractice liability protection in conjunction with protection against other liability claims incurred in the course of, or related to, the professional practice of a physician or surgeon and which—

        (A)   was operative and was providing such protection, or had received a permit for the offer and sale of memberships, under the laws of any State before January 1, 1984,

        (B)   is not subject to regulation by any State insurance department,

        (C)   has a right to make unlimited assessments against all members to cover current claims and losses, and

        (D)   is not a member of, nor subject to protection by, any insurance guaranty plan or association of any State.

(b)   Effective Date.—The provisions of subsection (a) shall apply to payments made to and receipts of physicians' and surgeons' mutual protection and interindemnity arrangements or associations, and refunds of payments by such arrangements or associations, after the date of the enactment of this Act, in taxable years ending after such date.

[For official explanation, see Committee Reports, ¶3966]

[¶2039] SEC. 1106. ADJUSTMENTS TO LIMITATIONS ON CONTRIBUTIONS AND BENEFITS UNDER QUALIFIED PLANS.

        *   *   *   *   *   *   *   *   *   *

    (h) Plans May Incorporate Section 415 Limitations by Reference.—Notwithstanding any other provision of law, except as provided in regulations prescribed by the Secretary of the Treasury or his delegate, a plan may incorporate by reference the limitations under section 415 of the Internal Revenue Code of 1986.

* * * * * * * * * * * *

[For official explanation, see Committee Reports, ¶3972]

〔¶2040〕 SEC. 1113. MINIMUM VESTING STANDARDS.

* * * * * * * * * * * *

(e) Amendments to ERISA.—

  (1) In General.—Paragraph (2) of section 203(a) of the Employee Retirement Income Security Act of 1974 (29 U.S.C. 1053(a)(2)) is amended to read as follows:

  "(2) A plan satisfies the requirements of this paragraph if it satisfies the following requirements of subparagraph (A), (B), or (C).

    "(A) A plan satisfies the requirements of this subparagraph if an employee who has completed at least 5 years of service has a nonforfeitable right to 100 percent of the employee's accrued benefit derived from employer contributions.

    "(B) A plan satisfies the requirements of this subparagraph if an employee has a nonforfeitable right to a percentage of the employee's accrued benefit derived from employer contributions determined under the following table:

"Years of service:	The nonforfeitable percentage is:
3	20
4	40
5	60
6	80
7 or more	100.

    "(C) A plan satisfies the requirements of this subparagraph if—

      "(i) the plan is a multiemployer plan (within the meaning of section 3(37)), and

      "(ii) under the plan—

        "(I) an employee who is covered pursuant to a collective bargaining agreement described in section 414(f)(1)(B) and who has completed at least 10 years of service has a nonforfeitable right to 100 percent of the employee's accrued benefit derived from employer contributions, and

        "(II) the requirements of subparagraph (A) or (B) are met with respect to employees not described in subclause (I)."

  (2) Repeal of class year vesting.—Subsection (c) of section 203 of such Act is amended by striking out paragraph (3).

  (3) Minimum participation standards.—Section 202(B)(i) of such Act is amended by striking out "3 years" each place it appears and inserting in lieu thereof "2 years".

  (4) Conforming amendments.—

    (A) Minimum vesting standards.—Section 203(c)(1)(B) of such Act is amended by striking out "5 years" and inserting in lieu thereof "3 years".

    (B) Benefit accrual requirements.—Subsection (i) of section 204 of such Act (29 U.S.C. 1054(i)) is amended to read as follows:

    "(i) Cross Reference.—

        "For special rules relating to plan provisions adopted to preclude discrimination, see section 203(c)(2).".

(e) [Should read (f).] Effective Dates.—

  (1) In general.—Except as provided in paragraph (2), the amendments made by this section shall apply to plan years beginning after December 31, 1988.

  (2) Special rule for collective bargaining agreements.—In the case of a plan maintained pursuant to 1 or more collective bargaining agreements between employee representatives and 1 or more employers ratified before March 1, 1986, the amendments made by this section shall not apply to employees covered by any such agreement in plan years beginning before the earlier of—

    (A) the later of—

      (i) January 1, 1989, or

(ii) the date on which the the last of such collective bargaining agreements terminates (determined without regard to any extension thereof after February 28, 1986), or

(B) January 1, 1991.

(3) Participation required.—The amendments made by this section shall not apply to any employee who does not have 1 hour of service in any plan year to which the amendments made by this section apply.

[For official explanation, see Committee Reports, ¶3978]

[¶2042] **SEC. 1114. DEFINITION OF HIGHLY COMPENSATED EMPLOYEE.**

* * * * * * * * * * * * *

(b) Conforming Amendments.—

* * * * * * * * * * * * *

(15)(A) * * *

(B) Section 408(b)(1)(B) of the Employee Retirement Income Security Act of 1974 (29 U.S.C. 1108(b)(1)) is amended by striking out "highly compensated employees, officers, or shareholders" and inserting in lieu thereof "highly compensated employees (within the meaning of section 414(q) of the Internal Revenue Code of 1986)".

* * * * * * * * * * * * *

(c) Effective Date.—

* * * * * * * * * * * * *

(3) Conforming amendments to pension provisions.—The amendments made by paragraphs (7), (8), (9), (10), (11), (12), and (15) of subsection (b) shall apply to years beginning after December 31, 1988.

* * * * * * * * * * * * *

[For official explanation, see Committee Reports, ¶3979]

[¶2043] **SEC. 1122. TAXATION OF DISTRIBUTIONS.**

* * * * * * * * * * * * *

(h) Effective Dates.—

* * * * * * * * * * * * *

(3) Special rule for individuals who attained age 50 before January 1, 1986.—

(A) In general.—In the case of a lump sum distribution to which this paragraph applies—

(i) the existing capital gains provisions shall continue to apply, and

(ii) the requirement of subparagraph (B) of section 402(e)(4) of the Internal Revenue Code of 1986 (as amended by subsection (a)) that the distribution be received after attaining age $59\frac{1}{2}$ shall not apply.

(B) Computation of tax.—If subparagraph (A) applies to any lump sum distribution of any taxpayer for any taxable year, the tax imposed by section 1 of the Internal Revenue Code of 1986 on such taxpayer for such taxable year shall be equal to the sum of—

(i) the tax imposed by such section 1 on the taxable income of the taxpayer (reduced by the portion of such lump sum distribution to which clause (ii) applies), plus

(ii) 20 percent of the portion of such lump sum distribution to which the existing capital gains provisions continue to apply by reason of this paragraph.

(C) Lump sum distributions to which paragraph applies.—This paragraph shall apply to any lump sum distribution if—

(i) such lump sum distribution is received by an individual who has attained age 50 before January 1, 1986, and

(ii) the taxpayer makes an election under this paragraph.

Not more than 1 election may be made under this paragraph with respect to an employee. An election under this subparagraph shall be treated as an election under section 402(e)(4)(B) of such Code with respect to any other lump sum distribution.

(4) 5-year phase-out of capital gains treatment.—

(A) Notwithstanding the amendment made by subsection (b), if the taxpayer elects the application of this paragraph with respect to any distribution after December 31, 1986, and before January 1, 1992, the phase-out percentage of the amount which would have been treated, without regard to this subparagraph, as long-term capital gain under the existing capital gains provisions shall be treated as long-term capital gain.

(B) For purposes of this paragraph—

In the case of distributions during calendar year:	The phase-out percentage is:
1987	100
1988	95
1989	75
1990	50
1991	25.

(C) No more than 1 election may be made under this paragraph with respect to an employee. An election under this paragraph shall be treated as an election under section 402(e)(4)(B) of the Internal Revenue Code of 1986 with respect to any other lump sum distribution.

(5) **Election of 10-year averaging.**—An individual who has attained age 50 before January 1, 1986, and elects the application of paragraph (3) or section 402(e)(1) of the Internal Revenue Code of 1986 (as amended by this Act) may elect to have such section applied by substituting "10 times" and for "5 times" and "$\frac{1}{10}$" for "$\frac{1}{5}$" in subparagraph (B) thereof. For purposes of the preceding sentence, section 402(e)(1) of such Code shall be applied by using the rate of tax in effect under section 1 of the Internal Revenue Code of 1954 for taxable years beginning during 1986.

(6) **Existing capital gain provisions.**—For purposes of paragraphs (3) and (4), the term 'existing capital gains provisions' means the provisions of paragraph (2) of section 402(a) of the Internal Revenue Code of 1954 (as in effect on the day before the date of the enactment of this Act) and paragraph (2) of section 403(a) of such Code (as so in effect).

* * * * * * * * * * *

[For official explanation, see Committee Reports, ¶3987]

[¶2044] SEC. 1124. ELECTION TO TREAT CERTAIN LUMP SUM DISTRIBUTIONS RECEIVED DURING 1987 AS RECEIVED DURING 1986.

(a) **In General.**—If an employee separates from service during 1986 and receives a lump sum distribution (within the meaning of section 402(e)(4)(A) of such Code) after December 31, 1986, and before March 16, 1987, on account of such separation from service, then, for purposes of the Internal Revenue Code of 1986, such employee may elect to treat such lump sum distribution as if it were received when such employee separated from service.

(b) **Special Rule for Terminated Plan.**—In the case of an employee who receives a distribution from a terminated plan which was maintained by a corporation organized under the laws of the State of Nevada, the principal place of business of which is Denver, Colorado, and which filed for relief from creditors under the United States Bankruptcy Code on August 28, 1986, the employee may treat a lump sum distribution received from such plan before June 30, 1987, as if it were received in 1986.

[For official explanation, see Committee Reports, ¶3989]

[¶2045] SEC. 1139. INTEREST RATE ASSUMPTIONS.

* * * * * * * * * * *

(c) **Amendments to ERISA.**—

(1) **In general.**—Paragraph (2) of section 203(e) of the Employee Retirement Income Security Act of 1974 (29 U.S.C. 1053(e)(2)) is amended to read as follows:

"(2)(A) For purposes of paragraph (1), the present value shall be calculated—

"(i) by using an interest rate no greater than the applicable interest rate if the vested accrued benefit (using such rate) is not in excess of $25,000, and "(ii) by using an interest rate no greater than 120 percent of the applicable interest rate if the vested accrued benefit exceeds $25,000 (as determined under clause (i)).

In no event shall the present value determined under subclause (II) be less than $25,000.

"(B) Applicable interest rate.—For purposes of subparagraph (A), the term 'applicable interest rate' means the interest rate which would be used (as of the date of the distribution) by the Pension Benefit Guaranty Corportion for purposes of determining the present value of a lump sum distribution on plan termination."

(2) **Conforming amendment.**—Paragraph (3) of section 205(g) of such Act (29 U.S.C. 1055(g)(3)) is amended to read as follows:

"(3)(A) For purposes of paragraphs (1) and (2), the present value shall be calculated—

"(i) by using an interest rate no greater than the applicable interest rate if the vested accrued benefit (using such rate) is not in excess of $25,000, and

"(ii) by using an interest rate no greater than 120 percent of the applicable interest rate if the vested accrued benefit exceeds $25,000 (as determined under clause (i)).

In no event shall the present value determined under subclause (II) be less than $25,000.

"(B) For purposes of subparagraph (A), the term 'applicable interest rate' means the interest rate which would be used (as of the date of the distribution) by the Pension Benefit Guaranty Corporation for purposes of determining the present value of a lump sum distribution on plan termination.".

(d) Effective Date.—

(1) **In general.**—The amendments made by this section shall apply to distributions in plan years beginning after December 31, 1984, except that such amendments shall not apply to any distributions in plan years beginning after December 31, 1984, and before January 1, 1987, if such distributions were made in accordance with the requirements of the regulations issued under the Retirement Equity Act of 1984.

(2) **Reduction in accrued benefits.—**

(A) In general.—If a plan—

(i) adopts a plan amendment before the close of the first plan year beginning on or before January 1, 1989, which provides for the calculation of the present value of the accrued benefits in the manner provided by the amendments made by this section, and

(ii) the plan reduces the accrued benefits for any plan year to which such plan amendment applies in accordance with such plan amendment,

such reduction shall not be treated as a violation of section 411(d)(6) of the Internal Revenue Code of 1986 or section 204(g) of the Employee Retirement Income Security Act of 1974 (29 U.S.C. 1054(g)).

(B) Special rule.—In the case of a plan maintained by a corporation incorporated on April 11, 1934, which is headquartered in Tarrant County, Texas—

(i) such plan may be amended to remove the option of an employee to receive a lump sum distribution (within the meaning of section 402(e)(5) of such Code) if such amendment—

(I) is adopted within 1 year of the date of the enactment of this Act, and

(II) is not effective until 2 years after the employees are notified of such amendment, and

(ii) the present value of any vested accrued benefit of such plan determined during the 3-year period beginning on the date of the enactment of this Act shall be determined under the applicable interest rate (within the meaning of section 411(a)(11)(B)(ii) of such Code, except that if such value (as so determined) exceeds $50,000, then the value of any excess over $50,000 shall be determined by using the interest rate specified in the plan as of August 16, 1986.

[For official explanation, see Committee Reports, ¶3998]

[¶2046] SEC. 1140. PLAN AMENDMENTS NOT REQUIRED UNTIL JANUARY 1, 1989.

(a) In General.—If any amendment made by this subtitle or subtitle C requires an amendment to any plan, such plan amendment shall not be required to be made before the first plan year beginning on or after January 1, 1989, if—

(1) during the period after such amendment takes effect and before such first plan year, the plan is operated in accordance with the requirements of such amendment or in accordance with an amendment prescribed by the Secretary and adopted by the plan, and

(2) such plan amendment applies retroactively to the period after such amendment takes effect and such first plan year.

A pension plan shall not be treated as failing to provide definitely determinable benefits or contributions, or to be operated in accordance with the provisions of the plan, merely because it operates in accordance with this provision.

(b) Model Amendment.—

(1) Secretary to prescribe amendment.—The Secretary of the Treasury or his delegate shall prescribe an amendment or amendments which allow a plan to meet the requirements of any amendment made by this subtitle or subtitle C—

(A) which requires an amendment to such plan, and

(B) is effective before the first plan year beginning after December 31, 1988.

(2) Adoption by plan.—If a plan adopts the amendment or amendments prescribed under paragraph (1) and operates in accordance with such amendment or amendments, such plan shall not be treated as failing to provide definitely determinable benefits or contributions or to be operated in accordance with the provisions of the plan.

(c) Special Rule for Collectively Bargained Plans.—In the case of a plan maintained pursuant to 1 or more collective bargaining agreements between employee representatives and 1 or more employers ratified before March 1, 1986, subsection (a) shall be applied by substituting for the first plan year beginning on or after January 1, 1989, the first plan year beginning after the earlier of—

(1) the later of—

(A) January 1, 1989, or

(B) the date on which the last of such collective bargaining agreements terminate (determined without regard to any extension thereof after February 28, 1986), or

(2) January 1, 1991.

[For official explanation, see Committee Reports, ¶3999]

⟦¶2047⟧ SEC. 1141. ISSUANCE OF FINAL REGULATIONS.

The Secretary of the Treasury or his delegate shall issue before February 1, 1988, such final regulations as may be necessary to carry out the amendments made by—

(1) section 1111, relating to application of nondiscrimination rules to integrated plans,

(2) section 1112, relating to coverage requirements for qualified plans,

(3) section 1113, relating to mininum vesting standards,

(4) section 1114, relating to the definition of highly compensated employee,

(5) section 1115, relating to separate lines of business and the definition of compensation,

(6) section 1116, relating to rules for section 401(k) plans,

(7) section 1117, relating to nondiscrimination requirements for employer matching and employer contribution,

(8) section 1120, relating to nondiscrimination requirements for tax sheltered annuities, and

(9) section 1133, relating to tax on excess distributions.

[For official explanation, see Committee Reports, ¶4000]

⟦¶2048⟧ SEC. 1142. SECRETARY TO ACCEPT APPLICATIONS WITH RESPECT TO SECTION 401(k) PLANS.

The Secretary of the Treasury or his delegate shall, not later than May 1, 1987, begin accepting applications for opinion letters with respect to master and prototype plans for qualified cash or deferred arrangements under section 401(k) of the Internal Revenue Code of 1986.

[For official explanation, see Committee Reports, ¶4001]

Act §1142 ¶2048

〔¶2049〕 SEC. 1145. REQUIREMENT OF JOINT AND SURVIVOR ANNUITIES AND PRERETIREMENT SURVIVOR ANNUITIES NOT TO APPLY TO CERTAIN PLAN.

* * * * * * * * * * * *

(b) **Amendments to the Employee Retirement Income Security Act of 1974.**—Section 205(b) of the Employee Retirement Income Security Act of 1974 (29 U.S.C. 1082(b)) is amended by adding at the end thereof the following new paragraph:

"(3) This section shall not apply to a plan which the Secretary of the Treasury or his delegate has determined is a plan described in section 404(c) of the Internal Revenue Code of 1986 (or a continuation thereof) in which participation is substantially limited to individuals who, before January 1, 1976, ceased employment covered by the plan."

(c) **Amendments to Retirement Equity Act.**—Section 303 of the Retirement Equity Act of 1984 is amended by adding at the end thereof the following new subsection:

"(f) The amendments made by section 301 of this Act shall not apply to the termination of a defined benefit plan if such termination—

"(1) is pursuant to a resolution directing the determination of such plan which was adopted by the Board of Directors of a corporation on July 24, 1984, and

"(2) occurred on November 30, 1984."

(d) **Effective Date.**—The amendments made by this section shall apply as if included in the amendments made by the Retirement Equity Act of 1984.

[For official explanation, see Committee Reports, ¶4004]

〔¶2050〕 SEC. 1151. NONDISCRIMINATION RULES FOR COVERAGE AND BENEFITS UNDER CERTAIN STATUTORY EMPLOYEE BENEFIT PLANS.

* * * * * * * * * * * *

(d) **Coordination With Cafeteria Plans.**—

* * * * * * * * * * * *

(2) **Application with employment taxes.**—

* * * * * * * * * * * *

(C) Section 209(e) of the Social Security Act is amended by inserting before the semicolon at the end thereof the following: ", or (9) under a cafeteria plan (within the meaning of section 125 of the Internal Revenue Code of 1986)".

* * * * * * * * * * * *

(k) **Effective Dates.**—

* * * * * * * * * * * *

(5) **Cafeteria plans.**—The amendments made by subsection (d)(2) shall apply to taxable years beginning after December 31, 1983.

[For official explanation, see Committee Reports, ¶4007]

〔¶2051〕 SEC. 1161. DEDUCTIBILITY OF HEALTH INSURANCE COSTS OF SELF-EMPLOYED INDIVIDUALS.

* * * * * * * * * * * *

(b) **Effective Date.**—

* * * * * * * * * * * *

(3) **Assistance.**—The Secretary of the Treasury or his delegate shall provide guidance to self-employed individuals to assist them in meeting the requirements of section 89 of the Internal Revenue Code of 1986 with respect to coverage required by the amendments made by this section.

[For official explanation, see Committee Reports, ¶4008]

〔¶2052〕 SEC. 1162. 2-YEAR EXTENSION OF EXCLUSIONS FOR EDUCATIONAL ASSISTANCE PROGRAMS AND GROUP LEGAL PLANS.

* * * * * * * * * * * *

(c) **Effective Dates.**—

* * * * * * * * * * * *

(3) **Cafeteria plan with group legal benefits.**—If, within 60 days after the date of the enactment of this Act, an employee elects under a cafeteria plan under section 125 of the Internal Revenue Code of 1986 coverage for group legal benefits to which section 120 of such Code applies, such election may, at the election of the taxpayer, apply to all legal services provided during 1986. The preceding sentence shall not apply to any plan which on August 16, 1986, offered such group legal benefits under such plan.

[For official explanation, see Committee Reports, ¶4009]

[¶2053] SEC. 1167. EXTENSION OF DUE DATE FOR STUDY OF WELFARE BENEFIT PLANS.

Section 560(b) of the Tax Reform Act of 1984 is amended by striking out "February 1, 1985" and inserting in lieu thereof "the date which is 1 year after the date of the enactment of the Tax Reform Act of 1986".

[For official explanation, see Committee Reports, ¶4014]

[¶2054] SEC. 1177. TRANSITION RULES.

(a) **Section 1171.**—The amendments made by section 1171 shall not apply in the case of a tax credit employee stock ownership plan if—
   (1) such plan was favorably approved on September 23, 1983, by employees, and
   (2) not later than January 11, 1984, the employer of such employees was 100 percent owned by such plan.

(b) **Subtitle Not To Apply to Certain Newspaper.**—The amendments made by this subtitle shall not apply to any daily newspaper—
   (1) which was first published on December 17, 1855, and which began publication under its current name in 1954, and
   (2) which is published in a constitutional home rule city (within the meaning of section 143(d)(3)(C) of the Internal Revenue Code of 1986) which has a population of less than 2,500,000.

[¶2055] SEC. 1201. SEPARATE APPLICATION OF SECTION 904 WITH RESPECT TO CERTAIN CATEGORIES OF INCOME.

* * * * * * * * * * * *

(e) **Effective Dates.—**

* * * * * * * * * * * *

(2) **Qualified loans.—**
   (A) In general.—The following shall not be treated as high withholding tax interest for purposes of applying section 904(d) of the Internal Revenue Code of 1986 (as amended by this section):
      (i) Any interest received or accrued by any taxpayer during any taxable year beginning after December 31, 1986, and before January 1, 1990, on any pre-1990 qualified loan, and
      (ii) The phase-out percentage of any interest received or accrued by any taxpayer during any taxable year beginning after December 31, 1989 on any post-1989 qualified loan.

   (B) Phase-out percentage.—For purposes of subparagraph (A) the phase-out percentage is—

In the case of the following taxable years beginning after 12/31/89:	The phase out percentage is:
1st	80
2nd	60
3rd	40
4th	20
5th or succeeding	0

   (C) Pre-1990 qualified loan.—For purposes of subparagraph (A), the term "pre-1990 qualified loan" means, with respect to any taxable year beginning before January 1, 1990, any qualified loan outstanding at any time during such taxable year to the extent that the total amount of foreign taxes which would be creditable

Act §1201(e)(2) ¶2055

(without regard to the limitation of section 904 of the Internal Revenue Code of 1986) with respect to all qualified loans outstanding at any time during such taxable year does not exceed the applicable credit limit for such taxable year.

(D) Post-1989 qualified loans.—For purposes of subparagraph (A), the term "post-1989 qualified loan" means any qualified loan outstanding as of the close of the 1st taxable year of the taxpayer beginning after December 31, 1988, to the extent that the total amount of foreign taxes which would be creditable (without regard to the limitation of section 904 of the Internal Revenue Code of 1986) with respect to all qualified loans outstanding as of the close of such taxable year does not exceed the applicable credit limit for post-1989 qualified loans.

(E) Classification of qualified loans.—For purposes of this paragraph, if the foreign taxes creditable for any taxable year beginning before January 1, 1990, with respect to any qualified loan, when added to the aggregate amount of foreign taxes creditable for such taxable year with respect to qualified loans entered into by the taxpayer before the date on which such qualified loan was entered into, exceed the applicable credit limit, then that portion of a qualified loan which causes the taxpayer to exceed the applicable credit limit shall not be treated as a pre-1990 or post-1989 qualified loan, as the case may be.

(F) Applicable credit limit.—

(i) In general.—The applicable credit limit shall be equal to—

(I) except as provided in subclause (II), 110 percent of the base credit amount multiplied by the applicable interest rate adjustment for the taxable year, and

(II) in the case of post-1989 qualified loans, the amount determined under subclause (I) (without regard to the interest rate adjustment) multiplied by the interest rate adjustment for post-1989 qualified loans.

(ii) Base credit amount.—The base credit amount of a taxpayer shall be an amount equal to the principal amount of qualified loans held by such taxpayer on November 16, 1985, multiplied by the product of—

(I) the interest rate applicable to such loan on November 16, 1985, and

(II) the foreign withholding tax rate applicable to interest payable with respect to such loan on November 16, 1985.

(G) Interest rate adjustment.—

(i) In general.—Except as provided in clause (ii), the applicable interest rate adjustment shall equal the ratio of the weighted average 6-month London Interbank Offered Rate (LIBOR) for the taxable year in question to LIBOR on November 15, 1985.

(ii) Post-1989 qualified loans.—The applicable interest rate adjustment for post-1989 qualified loans shall be equal to the ratio of LIBOR on the last day of the taxpayer's 1st taxable year beginning after December 31, 1988 to LIBOR on November 15, 1985.

(H) Qualified loan.—For purposes of this subsection, the term "qualified loan" means any loan made by the taxpayer to any of the following countries or any resident thereof for use in such country:

(i)	Argentina.	(xvii)	Morocco.
(ii)	Bolivia.	(xviii)	Mozambique.
(iii)	Brazil.	(xix)	Niger.
(iv)	Chile.	(xx)	Nigeria.
(v)	Columbia.	(xxi)	Panama.
(vi)	Costa Rica.	(xxii)	Peru.
(vii)	The Dominican Republic.	(xxiii)	The Philippines.
		(xxiv)	Romania.
(viii)	Ecuador.	(xxv)	Senegal.
(ix)	Guyana.	(xxvi)	Sierra Leone.
(x)	Honduras.	(xxvii)	The Sudan.
(xi)	The Ivory Coast.	(xviii)	Togo.
(xii)	Jamaica.	(xxix)	Uruguay.
(xiii)	Liberia.	(xxx)	Venezuela.
(xiv)	Madagascar.	(xxxi)	Yugoslavia.
(xv)	Malawi.	(xxxii)	Zaire.
(xvi)	Mexico.	(xxxiii)	Zambia.

(I) No benefit for increased withholding taxes.—No benefit shall be allowable by reason of this paragraph for any foreign withholding tax imposed on interest payable with respect to any qualified loan to the extent the rate of such tax exceeds the foreign withholding tax rate applicable to interest payable with respect to such loan on November 16, 1985.

(3) **Special rule for taxpayer with overall foreign loss.—**

(A) In general.—If a taxpayer incorporated on June 20, 1928, the principal headquarters of which is in Minneapolis, Minnesota, sustained an overall foreign loss (as defined in section 904(f)(2) of the Internal Revenue Code of 1954) in taxable years beginning before January 1, 1986, in connection with 2 separate trades or businesses which the taxpayer had, during 1985, substantially disposed of in tax-free transactions pursuant to section 355 of such Code, then an amount, not to exceed $40,000,000 of foreign source income, which, but for this paragraph, would not be treated as overall limitation income, shall be so treated.

(B) Substantial disposition.—For purposes of this paragraph, a taxpayer shall be treated as having substantially disposed of a trade or business if the retained portion of such business had sales of less than 10 percent of the annual sales of such business for taxable years ending in 1985.

[For official explanation, see Committee Reports, ¶4027]

[¶2056] SEC. 1205. LIMITATION ON CARRYBACK OF FOREIGN TAX CREDITS TO TAXABLE YEARS BEGINNING BEFORE 1987.

(a) **Determination of Excess Credits.—**

(1) **In general.—**Any taxes paid or accrued in a taxable year beginning after 1986 may be treated under section 904(c) of the Internal Revenue Code of 1954 as paid or accrued in a taxable year beginning before 1987 only to the extent such taxes would be so treated if the tax imposed by chapter 1 of such Code for the taxable year beginning after 1986 were determined by applying section 1 or 11 of such Code (as the case may be) as in effect on the day before the date of the enactment of this Act.

(2) **Adjustments.—**Under regulations prescribed by the Secretary of the Treasury or his delegate proper adjustments shall be made in the application of paragraph (1) to take into account—

(A) the repeal of the zero bracket amount, and

(B) the changes in the treatment of capital gains.

(b) **Coordination With Separate Baskets.—**Any taxes paid or accured in a taxable year beginning after 1986 which (after the application of subsection (a)) are treated as paid or accrued in a taxable year beginning before 1987 shall be treated as imposed on income described in section 904(d)(1)(E) of the Internal Revenue Code of 1954 (as in effect on the day before the date of the enactment of this Act). No taxes paid or accrued in a taxable year beginning after 1986 with respect to high withholding tax interest (as defined in section 904(d)(2)(B) of the Internal Revenue Code of 1986 as amended by this Act) may be treated as paid or accrued in a taxable year beginning before 1987.

[For official explanation, see Committee Reports, ¶4027]

[¶2057] SEC. 1211. DETERMINATION OF SOURCE IN CASE OF SALES OF PERSONAL PROPERTY.

* * * * * * * * * * *

(d) Study.—The Secretary of the Treasury or his delegate shall conduct a study of the source rules for sales of inventory property. Not later than September 30, 1987, the Secretary of the Treasury or his delegate shall submit to the Committee on Ways and Means of the House of Representatives and the Committee on Finance of the Senate a report of such study (together with such recommendatios as he may deem advisable).

[For official explanation, see Committee Reports, ¶4028]

[¶2058] SEC. 1215. RULES FOR ALLOCATING INTEREST, ETC., TO FOREIGN SOURCE INCOME.

* * * * * * * * * * *

(c) **Effective Dates.—**

* * * * * * * * * * * *

(2) **Transitional rules.—**

(A) **General phase-in.**—Except as provided in subparagraph (B), in the case of the 1st 3 taxable years of the taxpayer beginning after December 31, 1986, the amendments made by this section shall apply only to the applicable percentage (determined under the following table) of the interest expenses paid or accrued by the taxpayer during the taxable year with respect to an aggregate amount of indebtedness which does not exceed the aggregate amount of indebtedness outstanding on November 16, 1985:

In the case of the:	The applicable percentage is:
1st taxable year	25
2nd taxable year	40
3rd taxable year	75.

(B) **Consolidation rule not to apply to certain interest.—**

(i) Interest attributable to increase in indebtedness from January 1, 1984, through May 28, 1985.—In the case of the first 5 taxable years of the taxpayer beginning after December 31, 1986, with respect to interest expenses attributable to the excess of—

(I) the amount of the outstanding debt of the taxpayer on May 29, 1985, over

(II) the amount of the outstanding debt of the taxpayer on December 31, 1983,

paragraph (1) of section 864(e) of the Internal Revenue Code of 1986 (as added by this section) shall apply only to the applicable percentage (determined under the following table) of such interest expenses paid or accrued by the taxpayer during the taxable year:

In the case of the:	The applicable percentage is:
1st taxable year	16⅔
2nd taxable year	33⅓
3rd taxable year	50
4th taxable year	66⅔
5th taxable year	83⅓

(ii) Interest attributable to increase in indebtedness from January 1, 1983, through December 31, 1983.—In the case of the first 4 taxable years of the taxpayer beginning after December 31, 1986, with respect to interest expenses attributable to the excess of—

(I) the amount of the outstanding debt of the taxpayer on January 1, 1984, over

(II) the amount of the outstanding debt of the taxpayer on December 31, 1982,

paragraph (1) of section 864(e) of the Internal Revenue Code of 1986 (as added by this section) shall apply only to the applicable percentage (determined under the following table) of such interest expenses paid or accrued by the taxpayer during the taxable year:

In the case of the:	The applicable percentage is:
1st taxable year	20
2nd taxable year	40
3rd taxable year	60
4th taxable year	80.

(iii) Ordering rule.—For purposes of this subparagraph, indebtedness outstanding on November 16, 1985, shall be treated as attributable first to any excess described in clause (i), then to any excess described in clause (ii), and then to other indebtedness.

(iv) Treatment of affiliated group.—For purposes of this subparagraph, all members of the same affiliated group of corporations (as defined in section 864(e)(5)(A) of the Internal Revenue Code of 1986, as added by this section) shall be treated as one taxpayer whether or not such members filed a consolidated return.

(C) Special rule.—In the case of the first 9 taxable years beginning after December 31, 1986, the following applicable percentages shall be applied (in lieu of those set forth in subparagraph (A)) to interest expenses paid or accrued with respect to the amount of indebtedness described in subparagraph (D) or (E):

In the case of the:	The applicable percentage is:
1st taxable year	10
2nd taxable year	20
3rd taxable year	30
4th taxable year	40
5th taxable year	50
6th taxable year	60
7th taxable year	70
8th taxable year	80
9th taxable year	90

(D) Indebtedness outstanding on May 29, 1985.—Indebtedness is described in this subparagraph if it is indebtedness (which was outstanding on May 29, 1985) of a corporation incorporated on June 13, 1917, which has its principal place of business in Bartlesville, Oklahoma.

(E) Indebtedness outstanding on May 29, 1985.—Indebtedness is described in this subparagraph if it is indebtedness (which was outstanding on May 29, 1985) of a member of an affiliated group (as defined in section 1504(a)), the common parent of which was incorporated on August 26, 1926, and has its principal place of business in Harrison, New York.

(3) **Special rule.—**

(A) In general.—In the case of a qualified corporation, in lieu of applying paragraph (2), the amendments made by this section shall not apply to interest expenses allocable to any indebtedness to the extent such indebtedness does not exceed $500,000,000 if—

(i) the indebtedness was incurred to develop or improve existing property that is owned by the taxpayer on November 16, 1985, and was acquired with the intent to develop or improve the property,

(ii) the loan agreement with respect to the indebtedness provides that the funds are to be utilized for purposes of developing or improving the above property, and

(iii) the debt to equity ratio of the companies that join in the filing of the consolidated return is less than 15 percent.

(B) Qualified corporation.—For purposes of subparagraph (A), the term "qualified corporation" means a corporation—

(i) which was incorporated in Delaware on June 29, 1964,

(ii) the principal subsidiary of which is a resident of Arkansas, and

(iii) which is a member of an affiliated group the average daily United States production of oil of which is less than 50,000 barrels and the average daily United States refining of which is less than 150,000 barrels.

(4) **Special rules for subsidiary.—**The amendments made by this section shall not apply to interest on up to the applicable dollar amount of indebtedness of a subsidiary incorporated on February 11, 1975, the indebtedness of which on May 6, 1986, included—

(A) $100,000,000 face amount of 11¾ percent notes due in 1990,

(B) $100,000,000 of 8¾ percent notes due in 1989,

(C) 6¾ percent Japanese yen notes due in 1991, and

(D) 5⅜ percent Swiss franc bonds due in 1994.

For purposes of this paragraph, the term "applicable dollar amount" means $600,000,000 in the case of taxable years beginning in 1987 through 1991,

Act §1215(c)(4) ¶2058

$500,000,000 in the case of the taxable year beginning in 1992, $400,000,000 in the case of the taxable year beginning in 1993, $300,000,000 in the case of the taxable year beginning in 1994, $200,000,000 in the case of the taxable year beginning in 1995, $100,000,000 in the case of the taxable year beginning in 1996, and zero in the case of the taxable year beginning after 1996.

(5) **Special rule for financial corporation.**—For purposes of section 864(e)(5) of the Internal Revenue Code of 1986 (as added by this section), a corporation shall be treated as described in subparagraph (C) of such section for any taxable year if—

(A) such corporation is a Delaware corporation incorporated on August 20, 1959, and

(B) such corporation was primarily engaged in the financing of dealer inventory or consumer purchases on May 29, 1985, and at all times thereafter before the close of the taxable year.

(6) **Special rules for allocating general and administrative expenses.**—

(A) In general.—In the case of an affiliated group of domestic corporations the common parent of which has its principal office in New Brunswick, New Jersey, and has a certificate of organization which was filed with the Secretary of State of New Jersey on November 10, 1887, the amendments made by this section shall not apply to the phase-in percentage of general and administrative expenses paid or incurred in its 1st 3 taxable years beginning after December 31, 1986.

(B) Phase-in percentage.—For purposes of subparagraph (A):

In the case of taxable years beginning in:	The phase-in percentage is:
1987	75
1988	50
1989	25

[For official explanation, see Committee Reports, ¶4032]

[¶2059] SEC. 1216. 1-YEAR MODIFICATION IN REGULATIONS PROVIDING FOR ALLOCATION OF RESEARCH AND EXPERIMENTAL EXPENDITURES.

(a) **General Rule.**—For purposes of section 861(b), section 862(b), and section 863(b) of the Internal Revenue Code of 1954, notwithstanding section 864(e) of such Code—

(1) 50 percent of all amounts allowable as a deduction for qualified research and experimental expenditures shall be apportioned to income from sources within the United States and deducted from such income in determining the amount of taxable income from sources within the United States, and

(2) the remaining portion of such amounts shall be apportioned on the basis of gross sales or gross income.

The preceding sentence shall not apply to any expenditures described in section 1.861-8(e)(3)(i)(B) of the Income Tax Regulations.

(b) **Qualified Research and Experimental Expenditures.**—For purposes of this section—

(1) **In general.**—The term "qualified research and experimental expenditures" means amounts—

(A) which are research and experimental expenditures within the meaning of section 174 of such Code, and

(B) which are attributable to activities conducted in the United States.

(2) **Treatment of depreciation, etc.**—Rules similar to the rules of section 174(c) of such Code shall apply.

(c) **Effective Date.**—This section shall apply to taxable years beginning after August 1, 1986, and on or before August 1, 1987.

[For official explanation, see Committee Reports, ¶4033]

[¶2060] SEC. 1221. INCOME SUBJECT TO CURRENT TAXATION.

* * * * * * * * * * * *

(g) **Effective Dates.**—

* * * * * * * * * * * *

(2) **Special rule for repeal of exclusion for reinvestment shipping income.**—

(A) In general.—In case of any qualified controlled foreign corporation—

 (i) the amendments made by subsection (c) shall apply to taxable years ending on or after January 1, 1992, and

 (ii) sections 955(a)(1)(A) and 955(a)(2)(A) of the Internal Revenue Code of 1986 (as amended by subsection (c)(3) shall be applied by substituting "ending before 1992" for "beginning before 1987".

(B) Qualified controlled foreign corporation.—For purposes of subparagraph (A), the term "qualified controlled foreign corporation" means any controlled foreign corporation (as defined in section 957 of such Code)—

 (i) if the United States agent of such corporation is a domestic corporation incorporated on March 13, 1951, and

 (ii) if—

  (I) the certificate of incorporation of such corporation is dated July 23, 1963, and

  (II) such corporation has a wholly owned subsidiary and its certificate of incorporation is dated November 2, 1965.

(3) Exception for certain reinsurance contracts.—

(A) In general.—In the case of the 1st 3 taxable years of a qualified controlled foreign insurer beginning after December 31, 1986, the amendments made by this section shall not apply to the phase-in percentage of any qualified reinsurance income.

(B) Phase-in percentage.—For purposes of subparagraph (A):

In the case of taxable years beginning in:	The phase-in percentage is:
1987	75
1988	50
1989	25

(C) Qualified controlled foreign insurer.—For purposes of this paragraph, the term "qualified controlled foreign insurer" means—

 (i) any controlled foreign corporation which on August 16, 1986, was a member of an affiliated group (as defined in section 1504(a) of the Internal Revenue Code of 1986 without regard to subsection (b)(3) thereof) which had as its common parent a corporation incorporated in Delaware on July 9, 1967, with executive offices in New York, New York, or

 (ii) any controlled foreign corporation which on August 16, 1986, was a member of an affiliated group (as so defined) which had as its common parent a corporation incorporated in Delaware on March 31, 1982, with executive offices in Philadelphia, Pennsylvania.

(D) Qualified reinsurance income.—For purposes of this paragraph, the term 'qualified reinsurance income' means any insurance income attributable to risks (other than risk described in section 953(a) or 954(e) of such Code as in effect on the day before the date of the enactment of this Act) assumed as of August 16, 1986, under a reinsurance contract in effect on such date. For purposes of the preceding sentence, insurance income shall mean the underwriting income (as defined in section 832(b)(3) of such Code) and investment income derived from an amount of assets (to be segregated and separately identified) equivalent to the ordinary and necessary insurance reserves and necessary surplus equal to $1/3$ of earned premium attributable to such contracts.

[For official explanation, see Committee Reports, ¶4034]

⟦¶2061⟧ SEC. 1227. SPECIAL RULE FOR APPLICATION OF SECTION 954 TO CERTAIN DIVIDENDS.

(a) In General.—For purposes of section 954(c)(3)(A) of the Internal Revenue Code of 1986, any dividends received by a qualified controlled foreign corporation (within the meaning of section 951 of such Code) during any of its last 5 taxable years beginning after December 31, 1986, with respect to its 32.7 percent interest in a Brazilian corporation shall be treated as if such Brazilian corporation were a related person to the qualified controlled foreign corporation to the extent the Brazilian corporation's income is attributable to its interest in the trade or business of mining in Brazil.

(b) Quality [should read Qualified] Controlled Foreign Corporation.—For purposes of this section, a qualified controlled foreign corporation is a corporation the greater than 99 percent shareholder of which is a company originally incorporated in Montana on July 9, 1951 (the name of which was changed on August 10, 1966).

(c) Effective Date.—The amendment made by this section shall apply to dividends received after December 31, 1986.

[¶2062] **SEC. 1228.   SPECIAL RULE FOR APPLYING SECTION 897.**

(a) In General.—For purposes of section 897 of the Internal Revenue Code of 1986, gain shall not be recognized on the transfer, sale, exchange, or other disposition, of shares of stock of a United States real property holding company, if—

(1)   such United States real property holding company is a Delaware corporation incorporated on January 17, 1984,

(2)   the transfer, sale, exchange, or other disposition is to any member of a qualified ownership group,

(3)   the recipient of the share of stock elects, for purposes of such section 897, a carryover basis in the transferred shares, and

(4)   an election under this section applies to such transfer, sale, exchange, or other disposition.

(b) Member of a Qualified Ownership Group.—For purposes of this section, the term "member of a qualified ownership group" means a corporation incorporated on June 16, 1890, under the laws of the Netherlands or a corporation incorporated on October 18, 1897, under the laws of the United Kingdom or any corporation owned directly or indirectly by either or both such corporations.

(c) Election.—An election under this section shall be made at such time and in such manner as the Secretary of the Treasury or his delegate may prescribe, and an election under this section may only be made with respect to 1 transfer, sale, exchange, or other disposition.

(d) Effective Date.—The provisions of this section shall take effect on the date of the enactment of this section.

[¶2063] **SEC. 1231.   MODIFICATIONS TO SECTION 936.**

* * * * * * * * * * * *

(g) Effective Dates.—

* * * * * * * * * * * *

(4)   **Transitional Rule.**—In the case of a corporation—

(A)   with respect to which an election under section 936 of the Internal Revenue Code of 1986 (relating to possessions tax credit) is in effect,

(B)   which produced an end-product form in Puerto Rico on or before September 3, 1982,

(C)   which began manufacturing a component of such product in Puerto Rico in its taxable year beginning in 1983, and

(D)   with respect to which Puerto Rican tax exemption was granted on June 27, 1983,

such corporation shall treat such component as a separate product for such taxable year for purposes of determining whether such corporation had a significant business presence in Puerto Rico with respect to such product and its income with respect to such product.

[For official explanation, see Committee Reports, ¶4041]

[¶2064] **SEC. 1232.   TREATMENT OF CERTAIN PERSONS IN PANAMA.**

(a) General Rule.—Nothing in the Panama Canal Treaty (or in any agreement implementing such Treaty) shall be construed as exempting (in whole or in part) any citizen or resident of the United States from any tax under the Internal Revenue Code of 1954 or 1986. The preceding sentence shall apply to all taxable years whether beginning before, on, or after the date of the enactment of this Act (or in the case of any tax not imposed with respect to a taxable year, to taxable events after the date of enactment of this Act.)

(b) **Treatment of Employees of Panama Canal Commission and Department of Defense for Purposes of Section 912.**—Employees of the Panama Canal Commission and civilian employees of the Defense Department of the United States stationed in Panama may exclude from gross income allowances which are comparable to the allowances excludable under section 912(1) of the Internal Revenue Code of 1986 by employees of the State Department of the United States stationed in Panama. The preceding sentence shall apply to taxable years beginning after December 31, 1986.

[For official explanation, see Committee Reports, ¶4042]

〔¶2065〕 SEC. 1244. STUDY OF UNITED STATES REINSURANCE INDUSTRY.
The Secretary of the Treasury or his delegate shall conduct a study to determine whether United States reinsurance corporations are placed at a significant competitive disadvantage with foreign reinsurance corporations by existing treaties between the United States and foreign countries. The Secretary shall report before January 1, 1988, the results of such study to the Committee on Finance of the United States Senate and the Committee on Ways and Means of the House of Representatives.

[For official explanation, see Committee Reports, ¶4050]

〔¶2066〕 SEC. 1271. AUTHORITY OF GUAM, AMERICAN SAMOA, AND THE NORTHERN MARIANA ISLANDS TO ENACT REVENUE LAWS.

(a) **In General.**—Except as provided in subsection (b), nothing in the laws of the United States shall prevent Guam, American Samoa, or the Northern Mariana Islands from enacting tax laws (which shall apply in lieu of the mirror system) with respect to income—

(1) from sources within, or effectively connected with the conduct of a trade or business within, any such possession, or

(2) received or accrued by any resident of such possession.

(b) **Agreements To Alleviate Certain Problems Relating to Tax Administration.**—Subsection (a) shall apply to Guam, American Samoa, or the Northern Mariana Islands only if (and so long as) an implementing agreement is in effect between the United States and such possession with respect to—

(1) the elimination of double taxation involving taxation by such possession and taxation by the United States,

(2) the establishment of rules under which the evasion or avoidance of United States income tax shall not be permitted or facilitated by such possession,

(3) the exchange of information between such possession and the United States for purposes of tax administration, and

(4) the resolution of other problems arising in connection with the administration of the tax laws of such possession or the United States.

Any such implementing agreement shall be executed on behalf of the United States by the Secretary of the Treasury after consultation with the Secretary of the Interior.

(c) **Revenues Not To Decrease.**—The total amount of the revenue received by any possession referred to in subsection (a) pursuant to its tax laws during the implementation year and each of the 4 fiscal years thereafter shall not be less than the revenue (adjusted for inflation) which was received by such possession pursuant to tax laws for its last fiscal year before the implementation year.

(d) **Nondiscriminatory Treatment Required.**—Nothing in any tax law of a possession referred to in subsection (a) may discriminate against any United States person or any resident (corporate or otherwise) of any other possession.

(e) **Enforcement.**—

(1) **In general.**—If the Secretary of the Treasury (after consultation with the Secretary of the Interior) determines that any possession has failed to comply with subsection (c) or (d), the Secretary of the Treasury shall so notify the Governor of such possession in writing. If such possession does not comply with subsection (c) or (d) (as the case may be) within 90 days of such notification, the Secretary of the Treasury shall notify the Congress of such noncompliance. Unless the Congress by law provides otherwise, the mirror system of taxation shall be reinstated in such possession and shall be in full force and effect for taxable years beginning after such notification to the Congress.

(2) **Special rule for revenue requirements.**—If the failure to comply with subsection (c) is for good cause and does not jeopardize the fiscal integrity of the possession, the Secretary may waive the requirements of subsection (c) for such period as he determines appropriate.

(f) **Definitions and Special Rules.**—

(1) **Implementation year.**—For purposes of this section, the term "implementation year" means the 1st fiscal year of the possession in which the tax laws authorized by subsection (a) take effect.

(2) **Mirror system.**—For purposes of this section, the mirror system of taxation consists of the provisions of law (in effect on the day before the date of the enactment of this Act) which make the provisions of the income tax laws of the United States (as in effect from time to time) in effect in a possession of the United States.

(3) **Special rule for Northern Mariana Islands.**—Notwithstanding the provisions of the last clause of section 601(a) of Public Law 94-241, the Commonwealth of the Northern Mariana Islands may elect to continue its mirror system of taxation without regard to whether Guam enacts tax laws under the authority provided in subsection (a).

[For official explanation, see Committee Reports, ¶4057]

【¶2067】 SEC. 1274.   COORDINATION OF UNITED STATES AND VIRGIN ISLANDS INCOME TAXES.

* * * * * * * * * * * *

(b) **Authority To Impose Nondiscriminatory Local Income Taxes.**—Nothing in any provision of Federal law shall prevent the Virgin Islands from imposing on any person nondiscriminatory local income taxes. Any taxes so imposed shall be treated in the same manner as State and local income taxes under section 164 of the Internal Revenue Code of 1954 and shall not be treated as taxes to which section 901 of such Code applies.

(c) **Regulations on Application of Mirror System.**—The Secretary of the Treasury or his delegate shall prescribe such regulations as may be necessary or appropriate for applying this title for purposes of determining tax liability incurred to the Virgin Islands.

* * * * * * * * * * * *

[For official explanation, see Committee Reports, ¶4057]

【¶2068】 SEC. 1277.   EFFECTIVE DATE.

* * * * * * * * * * * *

(b) **Special Rule for Guam, American Samoa, and the Northern Mariana Islands.**—The amendments made by this subtitle shall apply with respect to Guam, American Samoa, or the Northern Mariana Islands (and to residents thereof and corporations created or organized therein) only if (and so long as) an implementing agreement under section 1271 is in effect between the United States and such possession.

(c) **Special Rules for the Virgin Islands.**—

(1) **In general.**—The amendments made by section 1275(c) shall apply with respect to the Virgin Islands (and residents thereof and corporations created or organized therein) only if (and so long as) an implementing agreement is in effect between the United States and the Virgin Islands with respect to the establishment of rules under which the evasion or avoidance of United States income tax shall not be permitted or facilitated by such possession. Any such implementing agreement shall be executed on behalf of the United States by the Secretary of the Treasury, after consultation with the Secretary of the Interior.

(2) **Section 1275(b).**—

(A) **In general.**—The amendment made by section 1275(b) shall apply with respect to—

(i) any taxable year beginning after December 31, 1986, and
(ii) any pre-1987 open year.

(B) **Special rules.**—In the case of any pre-1987 open year—

(i) the amendment made by section 1275(b) shall not apply to income from sources in the Virgin Islands or income effectively connected with the conduct of a trade or business in the Virgin Islands, and
(ii) the taxpayer shall be allowed a credit—

(I)   against any additional tax imposed by subtitle A of the Internal Revenue Code of 1954 (by reason of the amendment made by section 1275(b)) on income not described in clause (i) and

(II)   for any tax paid to the Virgin Islands before the date of the enactment of this Act and attributable to such income.

For purposes of clause (ii)(II), any tax paid before January 1, 1987, pursuant to a process in effect before August 16, 1986, shall be treated as paid before the date of the enactment of this Act.

(C)   Pre-1987 open year.—For purposes of this paragraph, the term "pre-1987 open year" means any taxable year beginning before January 1, 1987, if on the date of the enactment of this Act the assessment of a deficiency of income tax for such taxable year is not barred by any law or rule of law.

(D)   Exception.—In the case of any pre-1987 open year, the amendment made by section 1275(b) shall not apply to any domestic corporation if—

(i)   during the fiscal year which ended May 31, 1986, such corporation was actively engaged directly or through a subsidiary in the conduct of a trade or business in the Virgin Islands and such trade or business consists of business related to marine activities, and

(ii)   such corporation was incorporated on March 31, 1983, in Delaware.

(E)   Exception for certain transactions.—

(i)   In general.—In the case of any pre-1987 open year, the amendment made by section 1275(b) shall not apply to any income derived from transactions described in clause (ii) by 1 or more corporations which were formed in Delaware on or about March 6, 1981, and which have owned 1 or more office buildings in St. Thomas, United States Virgin Islands, for at least 5 years before the date of the enactment of this Act.

(ii)   Description of transactions.—The transactions described in this clause are—

(I)   the redemptions of limited partnership interests for cash and property described in an agreement (as amended) dated March 12, 1981,

(II)   the subsequent disposition of the properties distributed in such redemptions, and

(III)   interest earned before January 1, 1987, on bank deposits of proceeds received from such redemptions to the extent such deposits are located in the United States Virgin Islands.

(iii)   Limitation.—The aggregate reduction in tax by reason of this subparagraph shall not exceed $8,312,000. If the taxes which would be payable as the result of the application of the amendment made by section 1275(b) to pre-1987 open years exceeds the limitation of the preceding sentence, such excess shall be treated as attributable to income received in taxable years in reverse chronological order.

(d)   **Report on Implementing Agreements.**—If, during the 1-year period beginning on the date of the enactment of this Act, any implementing agreement described in subsection (b) or (c) is not executed, the Secretary of the Treasury or his delegate shall report to the Committee on Finance of the United States Senate, the Committee on Ways and Means, and the Committee on Interior and Insular Affairs of the House of Representatives with respect to—

(1)   the status of such negotiations, and

(2)   the reason why such agreement has not been executed.

(e)   **Treatment of Certain United States Persons.**—Except as otherwise provided in regulations prescribed by the Secretary of the Treasury or his delegate, if a United States person becomes a resident of Guam, American Samoa, or the Northern Mariana Islands, the rules of section 877(c) of the Internal Revenue Code of 1954 shall apply to such person during the 10-year period beginning when such person became such a resident. The preceding sentence shall apply to dispositions after December 31, 1985, in taxable years ending after such date.

[For official explanation, see Committee Reports, ¶4057]

[¶2069]   SEC. 1301.   STATE AND LOCAL BONDS.

* * * * * * * * * * * * *

(c) **Amendment to Arbitrage Regulations.**—The provision in the Federal income tax regulations relating to the arbitrage requirements which permits a higher yield on acquired obligations if the issuer elects to waive the benefits of the temporary period provisions shall not apply to bonds issued after August 31, 1986.

(d) **State and Local Government Series Modifications.**—Notwithstanding any other provision of law or any regulations promulgated thereunder (including the provisions of 31 CFR part 344) the Secretary of the Treasury shall extend by January 1, 1987, the State and Local Government Series program to provide—

(1) instruments allowing flexible investment of bond proceeds in a manner eliminating the earning of rebatable arbitrage,

(2) demand deposits under such program by eliminating advance notice and minimum maturity requirements related to the purchase of bonds,

(3) operation of such program at no net cost to the Federal Government, and

(4) deposits for a stated maturity under reasonable advance notice requirements.

(e) **Management Contracts.**—The Secretary of the Treasury or his delegate shall modify the Secretary's advance ruling guidelines relating to when use of property pursuant to a management contract is not considered a trade or business use by a private person for purposes of section 141(a) of the Internal Revenue Code of 1986 to provide that use pursuant to a management contract generally shall not be treated as trade or business use as long as—

(1) the term of such contract (including renewal options) does not exceed 5 years,

(2) the exempt owner has the option to cancel such contract at the end of any 3-year period,

(3) the manager under the contract is not compensated (in whole or in part) on the basis of a share of net profits, and

(4) at least 50 percent of the annual compensation of the manager under such contract is based on a periodic fixed fee.

* * * * * * * * * * *

(h) **Repeal of Report on Mortgage Revenue Bond Program.**—Paragraph (7) of section 611(d) of the Tax Reform Act of 1984 is hereby repealed.

(i) **Amendment to Output Regulations.**—The Secretary of the Treasury or his delegate shall amend the provision in the Federal income tax regulations relating to when use pursuant to certain output contracts is considered to satisfy the private business tests of paragraphs (1) and (2) of section 141(b) of the Internal Revenue Code of 1986 to eliminate the requirement of a 3 percent guaranteed minimum payment.

* * * * * * * * * * *

[For official explanation, see Committee Reports, ¶4058]

[¶2070]   SEC. 1302. TREATMENT OF SECTION 501(c)(3) BONDS.

Nothing in the treatment of section 501(c)(3) bonds as private activity bonds under the amendments made by this title shall be construed as indicating how section 501(c)(3) bonds will be treated in future legislation, and any change in future legislation applicable to private activity bonds shall apply to section 501(c)(3) bonds only if expressly provided in such legislation.

[For official explanation, see Committee Reports, ¶4058]

[¶2071]   SEC. 1312. TRANSITIONAL RULES FOR CONSTRUCTION OR BINDING AGREEMENTS AND CERTAIN GOVERNMENT BONDS ISSUED AFTER AUGUST 15, 1986.

(a) **Exception for Construction or Binding Agreements.**—

(1) **In general.**—The amendments made by section 1301 shall not apply to bonds (other than a refunding bond) with respect to a facility—

(A)(i) the original use of which commences with the taxpayer, and the construction, reconstruction, or rehabilitation of which began before September 26, 1985, and was completed on or after such date,

(ii) the original use of which begins with the taxpayer and with respect to which a binding contract to incur significant expenditures for construction, reconstruction, or rehabilitation was entered into before September 26, 1985, and some of such expenditures are incurred on or after such date, or

(iii) acquired on or after September 26, 1985, pursuant to a binding contract entered into before such date, and

(B) described in an inducement resolution or other comparable preliminary approval adopted by an issuing authority (or by a voter referendum) before September 26, 1985.

(2) Significant expenditures.—For purposes of paragraph (1)(A), the term "significant expenditures" means expenditures greater than 10 percent of the reasonably anticipated cost of the construction, reconstruction, or rehabilitation of the facility involved.

(b) Certain Amendments To Apply to Bonds Under Subsection (a) Transitional Rule.—

(1) In general.—In the case of a bond issued after August 15, 1986, and to which subsection (a) of this section applies, the requirements of the following provisions shall be treated as included in section 103 and section 103A (as appropriate) of the 1954 Code:

(A) The requirement that 95 percent or more of the net proceeds of an issue are to be used for a purpose described in section 103(b)(4) or (5) of such Code in order for section 103(b)(4) or (5) of such Code in order for section 103(b)(4) or (5) of such code to apply, including the application of section 142(b)(2) of the 1986 Code (relating to limitation on office space).

(B) The requirement that 95 percent or more of the net proceeds of an issue are to be used for a purpose described in section 103(b)(6)(A) of the 1954 Code in order for section 103(b)(6)(A) of such Code to apply.

(C) The requirements of section 143 of the 1986 Code (relating to qualified mortgage bonds and qualified veterans' mortgage bonds) in order for section 103A(b)(2) of the 1954 Code to apply.

(D) The requirements of section 144(a)(11) of the 1986 Code (relating to limitation on acquisition of depreciable farm property) in order for section 103(b)(6)(A) of the 1954 Code to apply.

(E) The requirements of section 147(b) of the 1986 Code (relating to maturity may not exceed 120 percent of economic life).

(F) The requirements of section 147(f) of the 1986 Code (relating to public approval required for private activity bonds).

(G) The requirements of section 147(g) of the 1986 Code (relating to restriction on issuance costs financed by issue).

(H) The requirements of section 148 of the 1986 Code (relating to arbitrage).

(I) The requirements of section 149(e) of the 1986 Code (relating to information reporting).

(J) The provisions of section 150(b) of the 1986 Code (relating to changes in use).

(2) Certain requirements apply only to bonds issued after December 31, 1986.—In the case of subparagraphs (F) and (I) of paragraphs (1), paragraph (1) shall be applied by substituting "December 31, 1986" for "August 15, 1986".

(3) Application of volume cap.—Except as provided in section 1315, any bond to which this subsection applies shall be treated as a private activity bond for purposes of section 146 of the 1986 Code if such bond would have been taken into account under section 103(n) or 103A(g) of the 1954 Code (determined without regard to any carryforward election) were such bond issued before August 16, 1986.

(4) Application of provisions.—For purposes of applying the requirements referred to in any subparagraph of paragraph (1) or of subsection (a)(3) or (b)(3) of section 1313 to any bond, such bond shall be treated as described in the subparagraph of section 141(d)(1) of the 1986 Code to which the use of the proceeds of such bond most closely relates.

(c) Special Rules for Certain Government Bonds Issued After August 15, 1986.—

(1) In general.—In the case of any bond described in paragraph (2)—

(A) section 1311(a) and (c) and subsection (b) of this section shall be applied by substituting "August 31, 1986" for "August 15, 1986" each place it appears,

(B) subsection (b)(1) shall be applied without regard to subparagraphs (F), (G), and (J), and

(C) such bond shall not be treated as a private activity bond for purposes of applying the requirements referred to in subparagraphs (H) and (I) of subsection (b)(1).

(2) **Bond described.**—A bond is described in this paragraph if such bond is not—

(A) an industrial development bond, as defined in section 103(b)(2) of the 1954 Code but determined—

(i) by inserting "directly or indirectly" after "is" in the material preceding clause (i) of subparagraph (B) thereof, and

(ii) without regard to subparagraph (B) of section 103(b)(3) of such Code,

(B) a mortgage subsidy bond (as defined in section 103(A)(b)(1) of such Code, without regard to any exception from such definition), or

(C) a private loan bond (as defined in section 103(o)(2)(A) of such Code, without regard to any exception from such definition other than section 103(o)(2)(C) of such Code).

(d) **Election Out.**—This section shall not apply to any issue with respect to which the issuer elects not to have this section apply.

[For official explanation, see Committee Reports, ¶4058]

[¶2072] SEC. 1313. TRANSITIONAL RULES RELATING TO REFUNDINGS.

(a) **Certain Current Refundings.—**

(1) **In general.**—Except as provided in paragraph (3), the amendments made by section 1301 shall not apply to any bond the proceeds of which are used exclusively to refund (other than to advance refund) a qualified bond (or a bond which is part of a series of refundings of a qualified bond) if—

(A) the amount of the refunding bond does not exceed the outstanding amount of the refunded bond, and

(B)(i) the average maturity of the issue of which the refunding bond is a part does not exceed 120 percent of the average reasonably expected economic life of the facilities being financed with the proceeds of such issue (determined under section 147(b) of the 1986 Code), or

(ii) the refunding bond has a maturity date not later than the date which is 17 years after the date on which the qualified bond was issued.

In the case of a qualified bond which was (when issued) a qualified mortgage bond or a qualified veterans' mortgage bond, subparagraph (B)(i) shall not apply and subparagraph (B)(ii) shall be applied by substituting "32 years" for "17 years".

(2) **Qualified bond.**—For purposes of paragraph (1), the term "qualified bond" means any bond (other than a refunding bond)—

(A) issued before August 16, 1986, or

(B) issued after August 15, 1986, if section 1312(a) applies to such bond.

(3) **Certain amendments to apply.**—The following provisions of the 1986 Code shall be treated as included in section 103 and section 103A (as appropriate) of the 1954 Code and shall apply to refunding bonds described in paragraph (1):

(A) The requirements of section 147(f) (relating to public approval required for private activity bonds) but only if the maturity date of the refunding bond is later than the maturity date of the refunded bond.

(B) The requirements of section 147(g) (relating to restriction on issuance costs financed by issue).

(C) The requirements of section 148 (relating to arbitrage).

(D) The requirements of section 149(e) (relating to information reporting).

(E) The provisions of section 150(b) of such Code (relating to changes in use).

Subparagraphs (A) and (D) shall apply only if the refunding bond is issued after December 31, 1986.

(4) **Special rules for certain government bonds issued after August 15, 1986.**—In the case of any bond described in section 1312(c)(2)—

(A) paragraph (2) of this subsection shall be applied by substituting "August 31, 1986" for "August 15, 1986",

(B) paragraph (3) shall be applied without regard to subparagraphs (A), (B), and (E), and

(C) such bond shall not be treated as a private activity bond for purposes of applying the requirements referred to in subparagraphs (C) and (D) of paragraph (3).

(b) **Certain Advance Refundings.—**

(1) In general.—Except as provided in paragraph (3), the amendments made by section 1301 shall not apply to any bond the proceeds of which are used exclusively to advance refund a bond if—

    (A) the refunded bond is described in paragraph (2), and

    (B) the requirements of subsection (a)(1)(B) are met.

(2) Non-IDB's, etc.—A bond is described in this paragraph if such bond is not described in subsection (b)(2) or (o)(2)(A) of section 103 of the 1954 Code and was issued (or was issued to refund a bond issued) before August 16, 1986.

(3) Certain amendments to apply.—The following provisions of the 1986 Code shall be treated as included in section 103 and 103A (as appropriate) of the 1954 Code and shall apply to refunding bonds described in paragraph (1):

    (A) The requirements of section 147(f) (relating to public approval required for private activity bonds).

    (B) The requirements of section 147(g) (relating to restriction on issuance costs financed by issue).

    (C) The requirements of section 148 (relating to arbitrage), except that section 148(d)(3) shall not apply to proceeds of such bonds to be used to discharge the refunded bonds.

    (D) The requirements of paragraphs (3) and (4) of section 149(d) (relating to advance refundings).

    (E) The requirements of section 149(e) (relating to information reporting).

    (F) The provisions of section 150(b) of such Code (relating to changes in use).

Subparagraphs (A) and (E) shall apply only if the refunding bond is issued after December 31, 1986.

(4) Special rule for certain government bonds issued after August 15, 1986.—In the case of any bond described in section 1312(c)(2)—

    (A) paragraph (2) of this subsection shall be applied by substituting "September 1, 1986" for "August 16, 1986",

    (B) paragraph (3) shall be applied without regard to subparagraphs (A), (B), and (F), and

    (C) such bond shall not be treated as a private activity bond for purposes of applying the requirements referred to in subparagraphs (C) and (E).

(5) Certain refunding bonds subject to volume cap.—Any refunding bond described in paragraph (1) the proceeds of which are used to refund a bond issued as part of an issue 5 percent or more of the net proceeds of which are to be used to provide an output facility (within the meaning of section 141(b)(4) of the 1986 Code) shall be treated as a private activity bond for purposes of section 146 of the 1986 Code (to the extent of the nongovernmental use of such issue, under rules similar to the rules of section 146(m)(2) of such Code). For purposes of the preceding sentence, use by a 501(c)(3) organization with respect to its activities which do not constitute unrelated trades or businesses (determined by applying section 513(a) of the 1986 Code) shall not be taken into account.

(c) Treatment of Current Refundings of Certain IDB's and 501(c)(3) Bonds.—

    (1) $40,000,000 limit for certain small issue bonds.—Paragraph (10) of section 144(a) of the 1986 Code shall not apply to any bond the proceeds of which are used exclusively to refund a tax-exempt bond to which such paragraph and the corresponding provision of prior law do not apply if—

        (A) the refunding bond has a maturity date not later than the maturity date of the refunded bond,

        (B) the amount of the refunding bond does not exceed the outstanding amount of the refunded bond,

        (C) the interest rate on the refunding bond is lower than the interest rate on the refunded bond, and

        (D) the net proceeds of the refunding bond are used to redeem the refunded bond not later than 90 days after the date of the issuance of the refunding bond.

    (2) $150,000,000 limitation for certain 501(c)(3) bonds.—Subsection (b) of section 145 of the 1986 Code (relating to $150,000,000 limitation for nonhospital bonds) shall not apply to any bond the proceeds of which are used exclusively to refund a tax-exempt bond to which such subsection does not apply if—

        (A)(i) the average maturity of the issue of which the refunding bond is a part does not exceed 120 percent of the average reasonably expected economic life of the facilities being financed with the proceeds of such issue (determined under section 147(b) of the 1986 Code), or

(ii) the refunding bond has a maturity date not later than the later of the date which is 17 years after the date on which the qualified bond (as defined in subsection (a)(2)) was issued, and

(B) the requirements of subparagraphs (B) and (D) of paragraph (1) are met with respect to the refunding bond.

Subsection (b) of section 145 of the 1986 Code shall not apply to the 1st advance refunding after March 14, 1986, of a bond issued before January 1, 1986.

(3) **Application to later issues.**—Any bond to which section 144(a)(10) or 145(b) of the 1986 Code does not apply by reason of this section shall be taken into account in determining whether such section applies to any later issue.

[For official explanation, see Committee Reports, ¶4058]

〚¶2073〛 SEC. 1314. SPECIAL RULES WHICH OVERRIDE OTHER RULES IN THIS SUBTITLE.

(a) **Arbitrage Restriction on Investments in Annuities.**—In the case of a bond issued after September 25, 1985, section 103(c) of the 1954 Code shall be applied by treating the reference to securities in paragraph (2) thereof as including a reference to an annuity contract.

(b) **Temporary Period for Advance Refundings.**—In the case of a bond issued after December 31, 1985, to advance refund a bond, the initial temporary period under section 103(c) of the 1954 Code with respect to the proceeds of the refunding bond shall end not later than 30 days after the date of issue of the refunding bond.

(c) **Determination of Yield.**—In the case of a bond issued after December 31, 1985, for purposes of section 103(c) of the 1954 Code, the yield on an issue shall be determined on the basis of the issue price (within the meaning of sections 1273 and 1274 of the 1986 Code).

(d) **Arbitrage Rebate Requirement.**—

(1) **In general.**—Except as otherwise provided in this subsection, in the case of a bond issued after December 31, 1985, section 103 of the 1954 Code shall be treated as including the requirements of section 148(f) of the 1986 Code in order for section 103(a) of the 1954 Code to apply.

(2) **Government bonds.**—In the case of a bond described in section 1312(c)(2) (and not described in paragraph (3) of this subsection), paragraph (1) shall be applied by substituting "August 31, 1986" for "December 31, 1985".

(3) **Certain pools.**—

(A) **In general.**—In the case of a bond described in section 1312(c)(2) and issued as part of an issue described in subparagraph (B), (C), (D), or (E), paragraph (1) shall be applied by substituting "3 p.m. E.D.T., July 17, 1986" for "December 31, 1985". Such a bond shall not be treated as a private activity bond for purposes of applying section 148(f) of the 1986 Code.

(B) **Loans to unrelated governmental units.**—An issue is described in this subparagraph if any portion of the proceeds of the issue is to be used to make or finance loans to any governmental unit other than any governmental unit which is subordinate to the issuer and the jurisdiction of which is within—

(i) the jurisdiction of the issuer, or

(ii) the jurisdiction of the governmental unit on behalf of which such issuer issued the issue.

(C) **Less than 75 percent of projects identified.**—An issue is described in this subparagraph if less than 75 percent of the proceeds of the issue is to be used to make or finance loans to initial borrowers to finance projects identified (with specificity) by the issuer, on or before the date of issuance of the issue, as projects to be financed with the proceeds of the issue.

(D) **Less than 25 percent of funds committed to be borrowed.**—An issue is described in this subparagraph if, on or before the date of issuance of the issue, commitments have not been entered into initial borrowers to borrow at least 25 percent of the proceeds of the issue.

(E) **Certain long maturity issues.**—An issue is described in this subparagraph if—

(i) the maturity date of any bond issued as part of such issue exceeds 30 years, and

(ii) any principal payment on any loan made or financed by the proceeds of the issue is to be used to make of finance additional loans.

(F) Special rules.—

(i) Exception from subparagraphs (C) and (D) where similar pools issued by issuer.—An issue shall not be treated as described in subparagraph (C) or (D) with respect to any issue to make or finance loans to governmental units if—

(I) the issuer, before 1986, issued 1 or more similar issues to make or finance loans to governmental units, and

(II) the aggregate face amount of such issues issued during 1986 does not exceed 250 percent of the average of the annual aggregate face amounts of such similar issues issued during 1983, 1984, or 1985.

(ii) Determination of issuance.—For purposes of subparagraph (A), an issue shall not be treated as issued until—

(I) the bonds issued as part of such issue are offered to the public (pursuant to final offering materials), and

(II) at least 25 percent of such bonds is sold to the public.

For purposes of the preceding sentence, the sale of a bond to a securities firm, broker, or other person acting in the capacity of an underwriter or wholesaler shall not be treated as a sale to the public.

(e) **Information Reporting.**—In the case of a bond issued after December 31, 1986, nothing in section 103(a) of the 1986 Code or any other provision of law shall be construed to provide an exemption from Federal income tax for interest on any bond unless such bond satisfies the requirements of section 149(e) of the 1986 Code. A bond described in section 1312(c)(2) shall not be treated as a private activity bond for purposes of applying such requirements.

(f) **Abusive Transaction Limitation on Advance Refundings To Apply.**—In the case of a bond issued after December 31, 1986, nothing in section 103(a) of the 1986 Code or any other provision of law shall be construed to provide an exemption from Federal income tax for interest on any bond if the issue of which such bond is a part is described in paragraph (4) of section 149(d) of the 1986 Code (relating to abusive transactions).

(g) **Section To Override Other Rules.**—Except as otherwise expressly provided by reference to a provision to which a subsection of this section applies, nothing in any other section of this subtitle shall be construed as exempting any bond from the application of such provision.

[For official explanation, see Committee Reports, ¶4058]

[¶2074]   SEC. 1315.   TRANSITIONAL RULES RELATING TO VOLUME CAP.

(a) **In General.**—Except as otherwise provided in this section, section 146(f) of the 1986 Code shall not apply with respect to an issuing authority's volume cap under section 103(n) of the 1954 Code, and no carryforward under such section 103(n) shall be recognized for bonds issued after August 15, 1986.

(b) **Certain Bonds for Carryforward Projects Outside of Volume Cap.**—Bonds issued pursuant to an election under section 103(n)(10) of the 1954 Code (relating to elective carryforward of unused limitation for specified project) made before November 1, 1985, shall not be taken into account under section 146 of the 1986 Code if the carryforward project is a facility to which the amendments made by section 1301 do not apply by reason of section 1312(a) of the Act.

(c) **Volume Cap Not To Apply With Respect to Certain Facilities and Purposes.**—Section 146 of the 1986 Code shall not apply to any bond issued with respect to any facility or purpose described in a paragraph of subsection (d) if—

(1) such bond would not have been taken into account under section 103(n) of the 1954 Code (determined without regard to any carryforward election) were such bond issued before August 16, 1986, or

(2) such bond would not have been taken into account under section 103(n) of the 1954 Code (determined with regard to any carryforward election made before January 1, 1986) were such bond issued before August 16, 1986.

(d) **Facilities and Purposes Described.**—

(1) A facility is described in this paragraph if the amendments made by section 201 of this Act (relating to depreciation) do not apply to such facility by reason of section 204(a)(8) of this Act (or, in the case of a facility which is governmentally owned, would not apply to such facility were it owned by a non-governmental person).

(2) A facility or purpose is described in this paragraph if the facility or purpose is described in a paragraph of section 1317.

(3) A facility is described in this paragraph if the facility—

    (A) serves Los Osos, California, and

    (B) would be described in paragraph (1) were it a solid waste disposal facility.

The aggreate face amount of bonds to which this paragraph applies shall not exceed $35,000,000.

(4) A facility is described in this paragraph if it is a sewage disposal facility with respect to which—

    (A) on September 13, 1985, the State public facilities authority took official action authorizing the issuance of bonds for such facility, and

    (B) on December 30, 1985, there was an executive order of the State Governor granting allocation of the State ceiling under section 103(n) of the 1954 Code in the amount of $250,000,000 to the Industrial Development Board of the Parish of East Baton Rouge, Louisiana.

The aggregate face amount of bonds to which this paragraph applies shall not exceed $98,500,000.

(5) A facility is described in this paragraph if—

    (A) such facility is a solid waste disposal facility in Charleston, South Carolina, and

    (B) a State political subdivision took formal action on April 1, 1980, to commit development funds for such facility.

For purposes of determining whether a bond issued as part of an issue for a facility described in the preceding sentence is an exempt facility bond for purposes of part IV of subchapter B of chapter 1 of the 1986 Code, "90 percent" shall be substituted for "95 percent" in section 142(a) of the 1986 Code.

The aggregate face amount of bonds to which this paragraph applies shall not exceed $75,000,000.

(6) A facility is described in this paragraph if—

    (A) such facility is a wastewater treatment facility for which site preparation commenced before September 1985, and

    (B) a parish council approved a service agreement with respect to such facility on December 4, 1985.

The aggregate face amount of bonds to which this paragraph applies shall not exceed $120,000,000.

(e) Treatment of Redevelopment Bonds.—Any bond to which section 1317(6) of this Act applies shall be treated for purposes of this section as described in subsection (c)(1).

[For official explanation, see Committee Reports, ¶4058]

[¶2075] SEC. 1316. PROVISIONS RELATING TO CERTAIN ESTABLISHED STATE PROGRAMS.

(a) Certain Loans to Veterans for the Purchase of Land.—

    (1) In general.—A bond described in paragraph (2) shall be treated as described in section 141(d)(1) of the 1986 Code, but subsections (a), (b), (c), and (d) of section 147 of such Code shall not apply to such bond.

    (2) Bond described.—A bond is described in this paragraph if—

      (A) such bond is a private activity bond solely by reason of section 141(c) of such Code, and

      (B) such bond is issued as part of an issue 95 percent or more of the net proceeds of which are to be used to carry out a program established under State law to provide loans to veterans for the purchase of land and which has been in effect in substantially the same form during the 30-year period ending on July 18, 1984, but only if such proceeds are used to make loans or to fund similar obligations—

        (i) in the same manner in which,

        (ii) in the same (or lesser) amount or multiple of acres per participant, and

        (iii) for the same purposes for which,

    such program was operated on March 15, 1984.

(b) Renewable Energy Property.—

(1) In general.—A bond described in paragraph (2) shall be treated as described in section 141(d)(1) of the 1986 Code.

(2) Bond described.—A bond is described in this paragraph if paragraph (1) of section 103(b) of the 1954 Code would not (without regard to the amendments made by this title) have applied to such bond by reason of section 243 of the Crude Oil Windfall Profit Tax Act of 1980 if—

    (A) such section 243 were applied by substituting "95 percent or more of the net proceeds" for "substantially all of the proceeds" in subsection (a)(1) thereof, and

    (B) subparagraph (E) of subsection (a)(1) thereof referred to section 149(b) of the 1986 Code.

(c) Certain State Programs.—

(1) In general.—A bond described in paragraph (2) shall be treated as described in section 141(d)(1) of the 1986 Code.

(2) Bond described.—A bond is described in this paragraph if such bond is issued as part of an issue 95 percent or more of the net proceeds of which are to be used to carry out a program established under sections 280A, 280B, and 280C of the Iowa Code, but only if—

    (A) such program has been in effect in substantially the same form since July 1, 1983, and

    (B) such proceeds are to be used to make loans or fund similar obligations for the same purposes as permitted under such program on July 1, 1986.

(3) $100,000,000 limitation.—The aggregate face amount of outstanding bonds to which this subsection applies shall not exceed $100,000,000.

(d) Use by Certain Federal Instrumentalities Treated as Use by Governmental Units.—Use by an instrumentality of the United States shall be treated as use by a State or local governmental unit for purposes of section 103, and part IV of subchapter B of chapter 1, of the 1986 Code with respect to a program approved by Congress before August 3, 1972, but only if—

(1) a portion of such program has been financed by bonds issued before such date, to which section 103(a) of the 1954 Code applied pursuant to a ruling issued by the Commissioner of the Internal Revenue Service, and

(2) construction of 1 or more facilities comprising a part of such program commenced before such date.

(e) 1 Refunding Permitted of Certain Bonds Invested in Federally Insured Deposits.—

(1) In general.—Section 149(b)(2)(B)(ii) of the 1986 Code shall not apply to any bond issued to refund a bond—

    (A) which, when issued, would have been treated as federally guaranteed by reason of being described in clause (ii) of section 103(h)(2)(B) of the 1954 Code if such section had applied to such bond, and

    (B)(i) which was issued before April 15, 1983, or

        (ii) to which such clause did not apply by reason of the except clause in section 631(c)(2) of the Tax Reform Act of 1984.

Section 147(c) of the 1986 Code shall not apply to any refunding bond permitted under the preceding sentence if section 103(b)(16) of the 1954 Code did not apply to the refunded bond when issued.

(2) Requirements.—A refunding bond meets the requirements of this paragraph if—

    (A) the refunding bond has a maturity date not later than the maturity date of the refunded bond,

    (B) the amount of the refunding bond does not exceed the outstanding amount of the refunded bond,

    (C) the weighted average interest rate on the refunding bond is lower than the weighted average interest rate on the refunded bond, and

    (D) the net proceeds of the refunding bond are used to redeem the refunded bond not later than 90 days after the date of the issuance of the refunding bond.

(f) Certain Hydroelectric Generating Property.—

(1) **In general.**—A bond described in paragraph (2) shall be treated as described in section 141(d)(1) of the 1986 Code.

(2) **Description.**—A bond is described in this paragraph if such bond is issued as part of an issue 95 percent or more of the net proceeds of which are to be used to provide a facility described in section 103(b)(4)(H) of the 1954 Code determined—

(A) by substituting "an application for a license" for "an application" in section 103(b)(8)(E)(ii) of the 1954 Code, and

(B) by applying the requirements of section 142(b)(2) of the 1986 Code.

(g) Treatment of Bonds Subject to Transitional Rules Under Tax Reform Act of 1984.—

(1) Subsections (d)(3) and (f) of section 148 of the 1986 Code shall not apply to any bond described in section 624(c)(2) of the Tax Reform Act of 1984.

(2)(A) There shall not be taken into account under section 146 of the 1986 Code any bond described in the paragraph (3) of section 631(a) of the Tax Reform Act of 1984 relating to exception for certain bonds for a convention center and resource recovery project.

(B) If a bond issued as part of an issue substantially all of the proceeds of which are used to provide the convention center to which such paragraph (3) applies, such bond shall be treated as an exempt facility bond as defined in section 142(a) of the 1986 Code.

(C) If a bond which is issued as part of an issue substantially all of the proceeds of which are used to provide the resource recovery project to which paragraph (3) applies, such bond shall be treated as an exempt facility bond as defined in section 142(a) of the 1986 Code and section 149(b) of such Code shall not apply.

(3) The amendments made by section 1301 shall not apply to bonds issued to finance any property described in section 631(d)(4) of the Tax Reform Act of 1984.

(4) The amendments made by section 1301 shall not apply to—

(A) any bond issued to finance property described in section 631(d)(5) of the Tax Reform Act of 1984.

(B) any bond described in paragraph (2), (3), (4), (5), (6), or (7) of section 632(a), or section 632(b), of such Act, and

(C) any bond to which section 632(g)(2) of such Act applies.

In the case of bonds to which this paragraph applies, the requirements of sections 148 and 149(d) shall be treated as included in section 103 of the 1954 Code and shall apply to such bonds.

(5) The preceding provisions of this subsection shall not apply to any bond issued after December 31, 1988.

(6) The amendments made by section 1301 shall not apply to any bond issued to finance property described in section 216(b)(3) of the Tax Equity and Fiscal Responsibility Act of 1982.

(7) In the case of a bond described in section 632(d) of the Tax Reform Act of 1984—

(A) section 141 of the 1986 Code shall be applied without regard to subsection (a)(2) and subsection (b)(5) and paragraphs (1) and (2) of subsection (b) thereof shall be applied by substituting "25 percent" for "10 percent" each place it appears, and

(B) section 149(b) of the 1986 Code shall not apply.

(8)(A) The amendments made by section 1301 shall not apply to any bond to which section 629(a)(1) of the Tax Reform Act of 1984 applies, but such bond shall be treated as a private activity bond for purposes of section 146 of the 1986 Code.

(B) Section 629 of the Tax Reform Act of 1984 is amended—

(i) in subsection (c)(2), by striking out "$625,000,000" and inserting in lieu thereof "$911,000,000",

(ii) in subsection (c)(3), by adding at the end thereof the following new subparagraphs:

"(D) Improvements to existing generating facilities.

"(E) Transmission lines.

"(F) Electric generating facilities.", and

"(iii) in subsection (a), by adding at the end thereof the following new sentence: "The preceding sentence shall be applied by inserting 'and a rural electric cooperative utility' after 'regulated public utility' but only if not more than 1 percent of the load of the public power authority is sold to such rural electric cooperative utility."

(h) Certain Pollution Bonds.—Any bond which is treated as described in section 103(b)(4)(F) of the 1954 Code by reason of section 13209 of the Consolidated Omnibus Budget Reconciliation Act of 1985 shall be treated as a exempt facility bond for purposes of part IV of subchapter B of chapter 1 of the 1986 Code, and section 147(d) of the 1986 Code shall not apply to such bond.

(i) Transition Rule for Aggregate Limit per Taxpayer.—For purposes of section 144(a)(10) of the 1986 Code, tax increment bonds described in section 1869(c)(3) of this Act which are issued before August 16, 1986, shall not be taken into account under subparagraph (B)(ii) thereof.

(j) Extension of Advance Refunding Exception for Qualified Public Facility.—Paragraph (4) of section 631(c) of the Tax Reform Act of 1984 is amended—

   (1) by striking out "or the Dade County, Florida, airport" in the last sentence, and

   (2) by adding at the end thereof the following new sentence:

"In the case of refunding obligations not to exceed $40,000,000 with respect too the Dade County, Florida, airport, the first sentence of this paragraph shall be applied by substituting 'December 31, 1987' for 'December 31, 1984' and the amendments made by section 1301 of the Tax Reform Act of 1986 shall not apply."

(k) Expansion of Exception for River Place Project.—Section 1104 of the Mortgage Subsidy Bond Tax Act of 1980, as added by the Tax Reform Act of 1984, is amended—

   (1) by striking out "December 31, 1984," in subsection (p) and inserting in lieu thereof "December 31, 1984 (other than obligations described in subsection (r)(1))," and

   (2) by striking out "$55,000,000," in subsection (r)(1)(B) and inserting in lieu thereof "$110,000,000 of which $55,000,000 must be redeemed no later than November 1, 1987".

(l) Certain Refundings.—Section 628(g) of the Tax Reform Act of 1984 (and the amendments made by section 1301 of this Act) shall not apply to any refunding obligation if the refunded issue was approved by a city building commission on April 29, 1982, and was issued on May 11, 1982, and the refunding obligations were issued before January 1, 1987.

[For official explanation, see Committee Reports, ¶4058]

[¶2076] SEC. 1317. TRANSITIONAL RULES FOR SPECIFIC FACILITIES.

(1) Docks and wharves.—A bond issued as part of an issue 95 percent or more of the net proceeds of which are to be used to provide any dock or wharf (within the meaning of section 103(b)(4)(D) of the 1954 Code) shall be treated as an exempt facility bond (for a facility described in section 142(a)(2) of the 1986 Code) for purposes of part IV of subchapter B of chapter 1 of the 1986 Code if such dock or wharf is described in any of the following subparagraphs:

   (A) A dock or wharf is described in this subparagraph if—

      (i) the issue to finance such dock or wharf was approved by official city action on September 3, 1985, and by voters on November 5, 1985, and

      (ii) such dock or wharf is for a slack water harbor with respect to which a Corps of Engineers grant of approximately $2,000,000 has been made under section 107 of the Rivers and Harbors Act.

The aggregate face amount of bonds to which this subparagraph applies shall not exceed $2,500,000.

   (B) A dock or wharf is described in this subparagraph if—

      (i) inducement resolutions were adopted on May 23, 1985, September 18, 1985, and September 24, 1985, for the issuance of the bonds to finance such dock or wharf.

      (ii) a harbor dredging contract with respect thereto was entered into on August 2, 1985, and

      (iii) a construction management and joint venture agreement with respect thereto was entered into on October 1, 1984.

The aggregate face amount of bonds to which this subparagraph applies shall not exceed $625,000,000.

   (C) A facility is described in this subparagraph if—

      (i) the legislature first authorized on June 29, 1981, the State agency issuing the bond to issue at least $30,000,000 of bonds,

(ii)   the developer of the facility was selected on April 26, 1985, and

(iii)   an inducement resolution for the issuance of such issue was adopted on October 9, 1985.

The aggregate face amount of bonds to which this subparagraph applies shall not exceed $200,000,000.

(D)   A facility is described in this subparagraph if—

(i) an inducement resolution was adopted on October 17, 1985, for such issue, and

(ii)   the city council for the city in which the facility is to be located approved on July 30, 1985, an application for an urban development action grant with respect to such facility.

The aggregate face amount of bonds to which this subparagraph applies shall not exceed $36,500,000. A facility shall be treated as described in this subparagraph if it would be so described if "90 percent" were substituted for "95 percent" in the material preceding subparagraph (A) of this paragraph.

(2)   **Pollution control facilities.**—A bond issued as part of an issue 95 percent or more of the net proceeds of which are to be used to provide air or water pollution control facilities (within the meaning of section 103(b)(4)(C) of the 1954 Code) shall be treated as an exempt facility bond for purposes of part IV of subchapter B of chapter 1 of the 1986 Code if such facility is described in any of the following subparagraphs:

(A)   A facility is described in this subparagraph if—

(i)   inducement resolutions with respect to such facility were adopted on September 23, 1974, and on April 5, 1985,

(ii)   a bond resolution for such facility was adopted on September 6, 1985, and

(iii)   the issuance of the bonds to finance such facility was delayed by action of the Securities and Exchange Commission (file number 70-7127).

The aggregate face amount of bonds to which this subparagraph applies shall not exceed $120,000,000.

(B)   A facility is described in this subparagraph if—

(i)   there was an inducement resolution for such facility on November 19, 1985, and

(ii)   design and engineering studies for such facility were completed in March of 1985.

The aggregate face amount of bonds to which this subparagraph applies shall not exceed $25,000,000.

(C)   A facility is described in this subparagraph if—

(i)   a resolution was adopted by the county board of supervisors pertaining to an issuance of bonds with respect to such facility on April 10, 1974, and

(ii)   such facility was placed in service on June 12, 1985.

The aggregate face amount of bonds to which this subparagraph applies shall not exceed $90,000,000. For purposes of this subparagraph, a pollution control facility includes a sewage or solid waste disposal facility (within the meaning of section 103(b)(4)(E) of the 1954 Code).

(D)   A facility is described in this subparagraph if—

(i)   the issuance of the bonds for such facility was approved by a State agency on August 22, 1979, and

(ii)   the authority to issue such bonds was scheduled to expire (under terms of the State approval) on August 22, 1989.

The aggregate face amount of bonds to which this subparagraph applies shall not exceed $198,000,000.

(E)   A facility is described in this subparagraph if—

(i)   such facility is 1 of 4 such facilities in 4 States with respect to which the Ball Corporation transmitted a letter of intent to purchase such facilities on February 26, 1986, and

(ii)   inducement resolutions were issued on December 30, 1985, January 15, 1986, January 22, 1986, and March 17, 1986 with respect to bond issuance in the 4 respective States.

The aggregate face amount of bonds to which this subparagraph applies shall not exceed $6,000,000.

(F)   A facility is described in this subparagraph if—

(i) inducement resolutions for bonds with respect to such facility were adopted on September 27, 1977, May 27, 1980, and October 8, 1981, and

(ii) such facility is located at a geothermal power complex owned and operated by a single investor-owned utility.

For purposes of this subparagraph and section 103 of the 1986 Code, all hydrogen sulfide air and water pollution control equipment, together with functionally related and subordinate equipment and structures, located or to be located at such power complex shall be treated as a single pollution control facility. The aggregate face amount of bonds to which this subparagraph applies shall not exceed $600,000,000.

(G) A facility is described in this subparagraph if—

(i) such facility is an air pollution control facility approved by a State bureau of pollution control on July 10, 1986, and by a State board of economic development on July 17, 1986, and

(ii) on August 15, 1986, the State bond attorney gave notice to the clerk to initiate validation proceedings with respect to such issue and on August 28, 1986, the validation decree was entered.

The aggregate face amount of bonds to which this subparagraph applies shall not exceed $900,000.

(I) A facility is described in this subparagraph if—

(i) a private company met with a State air control board on November 14, 1985, to propose construction of a sulften unit, and

(ii) the sulften unit is being constructed under a letter of intent to construct which was signed on April 8, 1986.

The aggregate face amount of bonds to which this subparagraph applies shall not exceed $11,000,000.

(J) A facility is described in this subparagraph if it is part of a 250 megawatt coal-fired electric plant in northeastern Nevada on which the Sierra Pacific Power Company began construction in 1980. The aggregate face amount of bonds to which this subparagraph applies shall not exceed $200,000,000.

(K) A facility is described in this subparagraph if—

(i) there was an inducement resolution adopted by a State industrial development authority on January 14, 1976, and

(ii) such facility is named in a resolution of such authority relating to carryforward of the State's unused 1985 private activity bond limit passed by such industrial development authority on December 18, 1985.

This subparagraph shall apply only to obligations issued at the request of the party pursuant to whose request the January 14, 1976, inducement was given. The aggregate face amount of bonds to which this subparagraph applies shall not exceed $75,000,000.

(L) A facility is described in this subparagraph if a city council passed an ordinance (ordinance number 4626) agreeing to issue bonds for such project, December 16, 1985. The aggregate face amount of obligations to which this subparagraph applies shall not exceed $45,000,000.

(3) **Sports facilities.**—A bond issued as part of an issue 95 percent or more of the net proceeds of which are to be used to provide sports facilities (within the meaning of section 103(b)(4)(B) of the 1954 Code) shall be treated as an exempt facility bond for purposes of part IV of subchapter B of chapter 1 of the 1986 Code if such facilities are described in any of the following subparagraphs:

(A) A facility is described in this subparagraph if it is a domed stadium—

(i) which was the subject of a city ordinance passed on September 23, 1985,

(ii) for which a loan of approximately $4,000,000 for land acquisition was approved on October 28, 1985, by the State Controlling Board, and

(iii) a stadium operating corporation with respect to which was incorporated on March 20, 1985.

The aggregate face amount of bonds to which this subparagraph applies shall not exceed $200,000,000.

(B) A facility is described in this subparagraph if—

(i) it is a stadium with respect to which a lease agreement for the ground on which the stadium is to be built was entered into between a county and the stadium corporation for such stadium on July 3, 1984,

(ii)   there was a resolution approved on November 14, 1984, by an industrial development authority setting forth the terms under which the bonds to be issued to finance such stadium would be issued, and

(iii)   there was an agreement for consultant and engineering services for such stadium entered into on September 28, 1984.

The aggregate fact amount of bonds to which this subparagraph applies shall not exceed $90,000,000.

(C)   A facility is described in this subparagraph if—

(i)   it is a stadium to be used by an American League baseball team currently using a stadium in a city having a population in excess of 2,500,000 and described in section 146(d)(3) of the 1936 Code, or by one or more professional sports teams currently using stadiums in such city (or professional sports teams which locate in such city following the relocation from such city of one or more professional sports teams currently using one or more of such stadiums), and

(ii)   the obligations to be used to provide financing for such stadium are issued pursuant to an inducement resolution adopted by a State agency on November 20, 1985 (whether or not the beneficiary of such issue is the beneficiary (if any) specified in such resolution).

The aggregate face amount of bonds to which this subparagraph applies shall not exceed $250,000,000. In the case of a carryforward of volume cap for a stadium described in the first sentence of this subparagraph, such carryforward shall be permitted whether or not there is a change in the beneficiary of the project.

(D)   A facility is described in this subparagraph if—

(i)   such facility is a stadium or sports arena for Memphis, Tennessee,

(ii)   there was an inducement resolution adopted on November 12, 1985, for the issuance of bonds to expand or renovate an existing stadium and sports arena and/or to construct a new arena, and

(iii)   the city counsel for such city adopted a resolution on April 19, 1983, to include funds in the capital budget of the city for such facility or facilities.

The aggregate face amount of bonds to which this subparagraph applies shall not exceed $35,000,000.

(E)   A facility is described in this subparagraph if such facility is a baseball stadium located in Bergen, Essex, Union, Middlesex, or Hudson County, New Jersey with respect to which governmental action occurred on November 7, 1985. The aggregate face amount of bonds to which this subparagraph applies shall not exceed $150,000,000.

(F)   A facility is desribed in this subparagraph if—

(i)   it is a facility with respect to which—

(I)   an inducement resolution dated December 24, 1985, was adopted by the county industrial development authority,

(II)   a public hearing of the county industrial development authority was held on February 6, 1986, regarding such facility, and

(III)   a contract was entered into by the county, dated February 19, 1986, for engineering services for a highway improvement in connection with such project, or

(ii)   it is a domed football stadium adjacent to Cervantes Convention Center in St. Louis, Missouri, with respect to which a proposal to evaluate market demand, financial operations, and economic impact was dated May 9, 1986.

The aggregate face amount of bonds to which this subparagraph applies shall not exceed $175,000,000.

(G)   A project to provide a roof or dome for an existing sports facility is described in this subparagraph if—

(i)   in December 1984 the county sports complex authority filed a carryforward election under section 103(n) of the 1954 Code with respect to such project,

(ii)   in January 1985, the State authorized issuance of $30,000,000 in bonds in the next 3 years for such project, and

(iii)   an 11-member task force was appointed by the county executive in June 1985, to further study the feasibility of the project.

The aggregate face amount of bonds to which this subparagraph applies shall not exceed $30,000,000.

(H)   A sports facility renovation or expansion project is described in this subparagraph if—

(i)   an amendment to the sports team's lease agreement for such facility was entered into on May 23, 1985, and

(ii)   the lease agreement had previously been amended in January 1976, on July 6, 1984, on April 1, 1985, and on May 7, 1985.

The aggregate face amount of bonds to which this subparagraph applies shall not exceed $20,000,000.

(I)   A facility is described in this subparagraph if—

(i)   an appraisal for such facility was completed on March 6, 1985,

(ii)   an inducement resolution was adopted with respect to such facility on June 7, 1985, and

(iii)   a State bond commission granted preliminary approval for such project on September 3, 1985.

The aggregate face amount of bonds to which this subparagraph applies shall not exceed $3,200,000.

(J)   A sports facility renovation or expansion project is described in this subparagraph if—

(i)   such facility is a domed stadium which commenced operations in 1965,

(ii)   such facility has been the subject of an ongoing construction, expansion, or renovation program of planned improvements,

(iii)   part 1 of such improvements began in 1982 with a preliminary renovation program financed by tax-exempt bonds,

(iv)   part 2 of such program was previously scheduled for a bond election on February 25, 1986 pursuant to a Commissioners Court Order of October 29, 1985, and

(v)   the bond election for improvements to such facility was subsequently postponed on December 10, 1985, in order to provide for more comprehensive construction planning.

The aggregate face amount of bonds to which this subparagraph applies shall not exceed $60,000,000.

(K)   A facility is described in this subparagraph if—

(i)   the 1985 State legislature appropriated a maximum sum of $22,500,000 to the State urban development corporation to be made available for such project, and

(ii)   a development and operation agreement was entered into among such corporation, the city, the State budget director, and the county industrial development agency, as of March 1, 1986.

The aggregate face amount of bonds to which this subparagraph applies shall not exceed $28,000,000.

(L)   A facility is described in this subparagraph if—

(i)   it is to consist of 1 or 2 stadiums appropriate for football games and baseball games with related structures and facilities,

(ii)   governmental action was taken on August 7, 1985, by the county commissions, and on December 19, 1985, by the city council, concerning such facility, and

(iii)   such facility is located in a city having a National League baseball team.

The aggregate face amount of bonds to which this subparagraph applies shall not exceed $200,000,000.

(M)   A facility is described in this subparagraph if—

(i)   such facility consists of 1 or 2 stadium projects (1 of which may be a stadium renovation or expansion project) with related structures and facilities,

(ii)   a special advisory commission commissioned a study by a national accounting firm with respect to a project for such facility, which study was released in September 1985, and recommended construction of either a new multipurpose or a new baseball-only stadium,

(iii)   a nationally recognized design and architectural firm released a feasibility study with respect to such project in April 1985, and

(iv)   the metropolitan area in which the facility is located is presently the home of an American League baseball team.

The aggregate face amount of bonds to which this subparagraph applies shall not exceed $200,000,000.

(N)   A facility is described in this subparagraph if—

Act §1317(3)(N) ¶2076

(i) it is to consist of 1 or 2 stadiums appropriate for football games and baseball games with related structures and facilities,

(ii) the site for such facility was approved by the council of the city in which such facility is to be located on July 9, 1985, and

(iii) the request for proposals process was authorized by the council of the city in which such facility is to be located on November 5, 1985, and such requests were distributed to potential developers on November 15, 1985, with responses due by February 14, 1986.

The aggregate face amount of bonds to which this subparagraph applies shall not exceed $200,000,000.

(O) A facility is described in this subparagraph if—

(i) such facility is described in a feasibility study dated September 1985, and

(ii) resolutions were adopted or other actions taken on February 21, 1985, July 18, 1985, August 8, 1985, October 17, 1985, and November 7, 1985, by the Board of Supervisors of the county in which such facility will be located with respect to such feasibility study, appropriations to obtain land for such facility, and approving the location of such facility in the county.

The aggregate face amount of bonds to which this subparagraph applies shall not exceed $20,000,000.

(P) A facility is described in this subparagraph if such facility constructed on a site acquired with the sale of revenue bonds approved by a city council on December 9, 1985, (Ordinances No. 669 and 670, series 1985). The aggregate face amount of bonds to which this subparagraph applies shall not exceed $90,000,000.

(Q) A facility is described in this subparagraph if—

(i) resolutions were adopted approving a ground lease dated June 27, 1983, by a sports authority (created by a State legislature) with respect to the land on which the facility will be erected,

(ii) such facility is described in a market study dated June 13, 1983, and

(iii) such facility was the subject of an Act of the State legislature which was signed on July 1, 1983.

The aggregate face amount of bonds to which this subparagraph applies shall not exceed $81,000,000.

(R) A facility is described in this subparagraph if such facility is a baseball stadium and adjacent parking facilities with respect to which a city made a carryforward election of $52,514,000 on February 25, 1985. The aggregate face amount of bonds to which this subparagraph applies shall not exceed $50,000,000.

(S) A facility is described in this subparagraph if—

(i) such facility is to be used by both a National Hockey League team and a National Basketball Association team,

(ii) such facility is to be constructed on a platform using air rights over land acquired by a State authority and identified as site B in a report dated May 30, 1984, prepared for a State urban development corporation, and

(iii) such facility is eligible for real property tax (and power and energy) benefits pursuant to State legislation approved and effective as of July 7, 1982.

The aggregate face amount of bonds to which this subparagraph applies shall not exceed $225,000,000.

(T) A facility is described in this subparagraph if—

(i) a resolution authorizing the financing of the facility through an issuance of revenue bonds was adopted by the City Commission on August 5, 1986, and

(ii) the metropolitan area in which the facility is to be located is currently the spring training home of an American league baseball team located during the regular season in a city described in subparagraph (C).

The aggregate face amount of bonds to which this subparagraph applies shall not exceed $10,000,000.

(U) A facility is described in this subparagraph if it is a football stadium located in Oakland, California, with respect to which a design was completed by a nationally recognized architectural firm for a stadium seating approximately 72,000, to be located on property adjacent to an existing coliseum complex. The aggregate face amount of bonds to which this subparagraph applies shall not exceed $100,000,000.

(V) A facility is described in this subparagraph if it is a sports arena (and related parking facility) for Grand Rapids, Michigan. The aggregate face amount of bonds to which this subparagraph applies shall not exceed $80,000,000.

(W) A facility is described in this subparagraph if such facility is located adjacent to the Anacostia River in the District of Columbia. The aggregate face amount of bonds to which this subparagraph applies shall not exceed $225,000,000.

(X) A facility is described in this subparagraph if it is a spectator sports facility for the City of San Antonio, Texas. The aggregate face amount of bonds to which this subparagraph applies shall not exceed $125,000,000.

(Y) A facility is described in this subparagraph if it will be part of, or adjacent to, an existing stadium which has been owned and operated by a State university and if—

(i) the stadium was the subject of a feasibility report by a certified public accounting firm which is dated December 28, 1984, and

(ii) a report by an independent research organization was prepared in December 1985 demonstrating support among donors and season ticket holders for the addition of a dome to the stadium.

The aggregate face amount of bonds to which this subparagraph applies shall not exceed $50,000,000.

(4) Residential rental property.—A bond issued as part of an issue 95 percent or more of the net proceeds of which are to be used to finance a residential rental project within the meaning of section 103(b)(4) of the 1954 Code shall be treated as an exempt facility bond within the meaning of section 142(a)(7) of the 1986 Code if the facility with respect to the bond is issued satisfies all low-income occupancy requirements applicable to such bonds before August 15, 1986. The bonds are issued pursuant to—

(A) a contract to purchase such property dated August 12, 1985; and

(B) the county housing authority approved the property and the financing thereof on September 24, 1985,

(C) there was an inducement resolution adopted on October 10, 1985, by the county industrial development authority.

The aggregate face amount of bonds to which this paragraph applies shall not exceed $25,400,000.

(5) Airports.—A bond issued as a part of an issue 95 percent or more of the net proceeds of which are to be used to provide an airport (within the meaning of section 103(b)(4)(D) of the 1954 Code) shall be treated as an exempt facility bond (for facilities described in section 142(a)(1) of the 1986 Code) for purposes of part IV of subchapter B of chapter 1 of the 1986 Code if the facility is described in any of the following subparagraphs:

(A) A facility is described in this subparagraph if such facility is a hotel at an airport facility serving a city described in section 631(a)(3) of the Tax Reform Act of 1984 (relating to certain bonds for a convention center and resource recovery project). The aggregate face amount of bonds to which this subparagraph applies shall not exceed $40,000,000.

(B) A facility is described in this subparagraph if such facility is the primary airport for a city described in paragraph (3)(C). The aggregate face amount of bonds to which this subparagraph applies shall not exceed $500,000,000. Section 148(d)(2) of the 1986 Code shall not apply to any issue to which this subparagraph applies. A facility shall be described in this subparagraph if it would be so described if "90 percent" were substituted for "95 percent" in the material preceding subparagraph (A).

(C) A facility is described in this subparagraph if such facility is a hotel at Logan airport and such hotel is located on land leased from a State authority under a lease contemplating development of such hotel dated May 1, 1983, or under an amendment, renewal, or extension of such a lease. The aggregate face amount of bonds to which this subparagraph applies shall not exceed $40,000,000.

(D) A facility is described in this subparagraph if such facility is the airport for the County of Sacramento, California. The aggregate face amount of bonds to which this subparagraph applies shall not exceed $150,000,000.

(6) Redevelopment projects.—A bond issued as part of an issue 95 percent or more of the net proceeds of which are to be used to finance redevelopment activities as part of a project within a specific designated area shall be treated as a qualified redevelopment bond for purposes of part IV of subchapter B of chapter 1 of the 1986 Code if such project is described in any of the following subparagraphs:

Act §1317(6) ¶2076

(A) A project is described in this subparagraph if it was the subject of a city ordinance numbered 82-115 and adopted on December 2, 1982, or numbered 9590 and adopted on April 6, 1983. The aggregate face amount of bonds to which this subparagraph applies shall not exceed $9,000,000.

(B) A project is described in this subparagraph if it is a redevelopment project for an area in a city described in paragraph (3)(C) which was designated as commercially blighted on November 14, 1975, by the city council and the redevelopment plan for which will be approved by the city council before January 31, 1987. The aggregate face amount of bonds to which this subparagraph applies shall not exceed $20,000,000.

(C) A project is described in this subparagraph if it is a redevelopment project for an area in a city described in paragraph (3)(C) which was designated as commercially blighted on March 28, 1979, by the city council and the redevelopment plan for which was approved by the city council on June 20, 1984. The aggregate face amount of bonds to which this subparagraph applies shall not exceed $100,000,000.

(D) A project is described in this subparagraph if it is any one of three redevelopment projects in areas in a city described in paragraph (3)(C) designated as blighted by a city council before January 31, 1987 and with respect to which the redevelopment plan is approved by the city council before January 31, 1987. The aggregate face amount of bonds to which this subparagraph applies shall not exceed $20,000,000.

(E) A project is described in this subparagraph if such project is for public improvements (including street reconstruction and improvement of underground utilities) for Great Falls, Montana, with respect to which engineering estimates are due on October 1, 1986. The aggregate face amount of bonds to which this subparagraph applies shall not exceed $3,000,000.

(F) A project is described in this subparagraph if—

(i) such project is located in an area designated as blighted by the governing body of the city on February 15, 1983 (Resolution No. 4573), and

(ii) such project is developed pursuant to a redevelopment plan adopted by the governing body of the city on March 1, 1983 (Ordinance No. 15073).

The aggregate face amount of bonds to which this subparagraph applies shall not exceed $5,000,000.

(G) A project is described in this subparagraph if—

(i) such project is located in an area designated by the governing body of the city in 1983,

(ii) such project is described in a letter dated August 8, 1985, from the developer's legal counsel to the development agency of the city, and

(iii) such project consists primarily of retail facilities to be built by the developer named in a resolution of the governing body of the city on August 30, 1985.

The aggregate face amount of bonds to which this subparagraph applies shall not exceed $75,000,000.

(H) A project is described in this subparagraph if—

(i) such project is a project for research and development facilities to be used primarily to benefit a State university and related hospital, with respect to which an urban renewal district was created by the city council effective October 11, 1985, and

(ii) such project was announced by the university and the city in March 1985.

The aggregate face amount of bonds to which this subparagraph applies shall not exceed $40,000,000.

(I) A project is described in this subparagraph if such project is a downtown redevelopment project with respect to which—

(i) an urban development action grant was made, but only if such grant was preliminarily approved on November 3, 1983, and received final approval before June 1, 1984, and

(ii) the issuer of bonds with respect to such facility adopted a resolution indicating the issuer's intent to adopt such redevelopment project on October 6, 1981, and the issuer adopted an ordinance adopting such redevelopment project on December 13, 1983.

The aggregate face amount of bonds to which this subparagraph applies shall not exceed $10,000,000.

(J)   A project is described in this subparagraph if—

(i)   with respect to such project the city council adopted on December 16, 1985, an ordinance directing the urban renewal authority to study blight and produce an urban renewal plan,

(ii)   the blight survey was accepted and approved by the urban renewal authority on March 20, 1986, and

(iii)   the city planning board approved the urban renewal plan on May 7, 1986.

The aggregate face amount of bonds to which this subparagraph applies shall not exceed $60,000,000.

(K)   A project is described in this subparagraph if—

(i)   the city redevelopment agency approved resolutions authorizing issuance of land acquisition and public improvements bonds with respect to such project on August 8, 1978,

(ii)   such resolutions were later amended in June 1979, and

(iii)   the State Supreme Court upheld a lower court decree validating the bonds on December 11, 1980.

The aggregate face amount of bonds to which this subparagraph applies shall not exceed $380,000,000.

(L)   A project is described in this subparagraph if it is a mixed use redevelopment project either—

(i)   in an area (known as the Near South Development Area) with respect to which the planning department of a city described in paragraph 3(C) promulgated a draft development plan dated March 1986, and which was the subject of public hearings held by a subcommittee of the plan commission of such city on May 28, 1986, and June 10, 1986, or

(ii)   in an area located within the boundaries of any one or more census tracts which are directly adjacent to a river whose course runs through such city.

The aggregate face amount of bonds to which this subparagraph applies shall not exceed $75,000,000.

(M)   A project is described in this subparagraph if it is a redevelopment project for an area in a city described in paragraph 3(C) and such area—

(i)   was the subject of a report released in May 1986, prepared by the National Park Service, and

(ii)   was the subject of a report released January 1986, prepared by a task force appointed by the Mayor of such city.

The aggregate face amount of bonds to which this subparagraph applies shall not exceed $75,000,000.

(N)   A project is described in this subparagraph if it is a city-university redevelopment project approved by a city ordinance No. 152-0-84 and the development plan for which was adopted on January 28, 1985. The aggregate face amount of bonds to which this subparagraph applies shall not exceed $23,760,000.

(O)   A project is described in this subparagraph if—

(i)   an inducement resolution was passed on March 9, 1984, for issuance of bonds with respect to such project,

(ii)   such resolution was extended by resolutions passed on August 14, 1984, April 2, 1985, August 13, 1985, and July 8, 1986,

(iii)   an urban development action grant was preliminarily approved for part or all of such project on July 3, 1986, and

(iv)   the project is located in a district designated as the Peabody-Gayoso District.

The aggregate face amount of bonds to which this subparagraph applies shall not exceed $140,000,000.

(P)   A project is described in this subparagraph if the project is a 1-block area of a central business district containing a YMCA building with respect to which—

(i)   the city council adopted a resolution expressing an intent to issue bonds for the project on September 27, 1985,

(ii)   the city council approved project guidelines for the project on December 20, 1985, and

(iii)   the city council by resolution (adopted on July 30, 1986) directed completion of a development agreement.

Act §1317(6)(P) ¶2076

The aggregate face amount of bonds to which this subparagraph applies shall not exceed $26,000,000.

(Q) A project is described in this subparagraph if the project is a 2-block area of a central business district designated as blocks E and F with respect to which—

(i) the city council adopted guidelines and criteria and authorized a request for development proposals on July 22, 1985,

(ii) the city council adopted a resolution expressing an intent to issue bonds for the project on September 27, 1985, and

(iii) the city issued requests for development proposals on March 28, 1986.

The aggregate face amount of bonds to which this subparagraph applies shall not exceed $47,000,000.

(R) A project is described in this subparagraph if the project is an urban renewal project covering approximately 5.9 acres of land in the Shaw area of the northwest section of the District of Columbia and the 1st portion of such project was the subject of a District of Columbia public hearing on June 2, 1986. The aggregate face amount of bonds to which this subparagraph applies shall not exceed $10,000,000.

(S) A project is described in this subparagraph if such project is a hotel, commercial, and residential project on the east bank of the Grand River in Grand Rapids, Michigan, with respect to which a developer was selected by the city in June 1985 and a planning agreement was executed in August 1985. The aggregate face amount of bonds to which this subparagraph applies shall not exceed $39,000,000.

(T) A project is described in this subparagraph if such project is the Wurzburg Block Redevelopment Project in Grand Rapids, Michigan. The aggregate face amount of bonds to which this subparagraph applies shall not exceed $60,000,000.

(U) A project is described in this subparagraph if such project is consistent with an urban renewal plan adopted or ordered prepared before August 28, 1986, by the city council of the most populous city in a state which entered the Union on February 14, 1859. The aggregate face amount of bonds to which this subparagraph applies shall not exceed $83,000,000.

(V) A project is described in this subparagraph if such project is consistent with an urban renewal plan which was adopted (or ordered prepared) before August 13, 1985, by an appropriate jurisdiction of a state which entered the Union on February 14, 1859. The aggregate face amount of bonds to which this subparagraph applies shall not exceed $135,000,000 and the limitation on the period during which bonds under this section may be issued shall not apply to such bonds.

(W) A project is described in this paragraph if such project—

(i) is located on lands submerged under the waters of a Great Lake or on adjacent lands which formerly were submerged under the waters of such lake;

(ii) project lands were improved with a stadium which was demolished prior to December 31, 1983, and

(iii) legislation for the project was included in a biennium budget for such the [sic] State in which it is to be located prior to December 31, 1983.

The aggregate face amount of bonds to which this subparagraph applies shall not exceed $105,000,000.

(X) Any designated area with respect to which a project is described in any subparagraph of this paragraph shall be taken into account in applying section 144(c)(4)(C) of the 1986 Code in determining whether other areas (not so described) may be designated.

(7) **Convention centers.**—A bond issued as part of an issue 95 percent or more of the net proceeds of which are to be used to provide any convention or trade show facility (within the meaning of section 103(b)(4)(C) of the 1954 Code) shall be treated as an exempt facility bond for purposes of part IV of subchapter B of chapter 1 of the 1986 Code if such facility is described in any of the following subparagraphs:

(A) A facility is described in this subparagraph if—

(i) a feasibility consultant and a design consultant were hired on April 3, 1985, with respect to such facility, and

(ii) a draft feasibility report with respect to such facility was presented on November 3, 1985, to the Mayor of the city in which such facility is to be located.

The aggregate face amount of bonds to which this subparagraph applies shall not exceed $190,000,000. For purposes of this subparagraph, not more than

$20,000,000 of bonds issued to advance refund existing convention facility bonds sold on May 12, 1978, shall be treated as bonds described in this subparagraph.

(B) A facility is described in this subparagraph if—

   (i) an application for a State loan for such facility was approved by the city council on March 4, 1985, and

   (ii) the city council of the city in which such facility is to be located approved on March 25, 1985, an application for an urban development action grant.

The aggregate face amount of bonds which this subparagraph applies shall not exceed $10,000,000.

(C) A facility is described in this subparagraph if—

   (i) on November 1, 1983, a convention development tax took effect and was dedicated to financing such facility,

   (ii) the State supreme court of the State in which the facility is to be located validated such tax on February 8, 1985, and

   (iii) an agreement was entered into on November 14, 1985, between the city and county in which such facility is to be located on the terms of the bonds to be issued with respect to such facility.

The aggregate face amount of bonds to which this subparagraph applies shall not exceed $66,000,000.

(D) A facility is described in this subparagraph if such facility was initially approved in 1983 and is for San Jose, California. The aggregate face amount of bonds to which this subparagraph applies shall not exceed $100,000,000.

(E) A facility is described in this subparagraph if—

   (i) such facility is meeting rooms for a convention center, and

   (ii) resolutions and ordinances were adopted with respect to such meeting rooms on January 17, 1983, July 11, 1983, December 17, 1984, and September 23, 1985.

The aggregate face amount of bonds to which this subparagraph applies shall not exceed $75,000,000.

(F) A facility is described in this subparagraph if it is an international trade center which is part of the 125th Street redevelopment project in New York, New York. The aggregate face amount of obligations to which this subparagraph applies shall not exceed $165,000,000.

(G) A facility is described in this subparagraph if—

   (i) such facility is located in a city which was the subject of a convention center market analysis or study dated March 1983, and prepared by a nationally recognized accounting firm,

   (ii) such facility's location was approved by a task force created jointly, in December 1985, by the Governor or the State within which such facility will be located and the mayor of the capital city of such State, and

   (iii) the size of such facility is not more than 200,000 square feet.

The aggregate face amount of bonds to which this subparagraph applies shall not exceed $70,000,000.

(H) A facility is described in this paragraph if an analysis of operations and recommendations of utilizaton of such facility was prepared by a certified public accounting firm pursuant to an engagement authorized on March 6, 1984, and presented on June 11, 1984, to officials of the city in which such facility is located. The aggregate face amount of bonds to which this subparagraph applies shall not exceed $75,000,000.

(I) A facility is described in this subparagraph if—

   (i) voters approved a bond issue to finance the acquisition of the site for such facility on May 4, 1985,

   (ii) title of the property was transferred from the Illinois Center Gulf Railroad to the city on September 30, 1985, and

   (iii) a United States judge rendered a decision regarding the fair market value of the site of such facility on December 30, 1985.

The aggregate face amount of bonds to which this subparagraph applies shall not exceed $131,000,000.

(J) A facility is described in this subparagraph if—

   (i) such facility is to be used for an annual civic festival, and

(ii) a referendum was held in the spring of 1985 in which voters permitted the city council to lease 130 acres of dedicated parkland to such festival, and

(iii) the city council passed an inducement resolution on June 19, 1986.

The aggregate face amount of bonds to which this subparagraph applies shall not exceed $5,000,000.

(K) A facility is described in this subparagraph if—

(i) voters approved a bond issued to finance a portion of the cost of such facility on December 1, 1984, and

(ii) such facility was the subject of a market study and financial projections dated March 21, 1986, prepared by a nationally recognized accounting firm.

The aggregate face amount of bonds to which this subparagraph applies shall not exceed $5,000,000.

(L) A facility is described in this subparagraph if—

(i) on July 12, 1984, the city council passed a resolution increasing the local hotel and motel tax to 7 percent to assist in paying for such facility,

(ii) on October 25, 1984, the city council selected a consulting firm for such facility, and

(iii) with respect to such facility, the city council appropriated funds for additional work on February 7, 1985, October 3, 1985, and June 26, 1986.

The aggregate face amount of bonds to which this subparagraph applies shall not exceed $120,000,000.

(M) A facility is described in this subparagraph if—

(i) a board of county commissioners, in an action dated January 21, 1986, supported an application for official approval of the facility, and

(ii) the State economic development commission adopted a resolution dated February 25, 1986, determining the facility to be an eligible facility pursuant to State law and the rules adopted by the commission.

The aggregate face amount of bonds to which this subparagraph applies shall not exceed $7,500,000.

(8) **Sports or convention facilities.**—A bond issued as a part of an issue 95 percent or more of the net proceeds of which are to be used to provide either a sports facility (within the meaning of section 103(b)(4)(B) of the 1954 Code) or a convention facility (within the meaning of section 103(b)(4)(C) of the 1954 Code) shall be treated as an exempt facility bond for purposes of part IV of subchapter B of chapter 1 of the 1986 Code if such facility is described in any of the following subparagraphs:

(A) A combined convention and arena facility, or any part thereof (whether on the same or different sites), is described in this subparagraph if—

(i) bonds for the expansion, acquisition, or construction of such combined facility are payable from a tax and are issued under a plan initially approved by the voters of the taxing authority on April 25, 1978, and

(ii) such bonds were authorized for expanding a convention center, for acquiring an arena site, and for building an arena or any of the foregoing pursuant to a resolution adopted by the governing body of the bond issuer on March 17, 1986, and superseded by a resolution adopted by such governing body on May 27, 1986.

The aggregate face amount of bonds to which this subparagraph applies shall not exceed $160,000,000.

(B) A sports or convention facility is described in this subparagraph if—

(i) on March 4, 1986, county commissioners held public hearings on creation of a county convention facilities authority, and

(ii) on March 7, 1986, the county commissioners voted to create a county convention facilities authority and to submit to county voters a ½ cent sales and use tax to finance such facility.

The aggregate face amount of bonds to which this subparagraph applies shall not exceed $150,000,000.

(C) A sports or convention facility is described in this subparagraph if—

(i) a feasibility consultant and a design consultant were hired prior to October 1980 with respect to such facility,

(ii) a feasibility report dated October 1980 with respect to such facility was presented to a city or county in which such facility is to be located, and

(iii) on September 7, 1982, a joint city/county resolution appointed a committee which was charged with the task of independently reviewing the studies and present need for the facility.

The aggregate face amount of bonds to which this subparagraph applies shall not exceed $60,000,000.

(D) A sports or convention facility is described in this subparagraph if—

(i) such facility is a multipurpose coliseum facility for which, before January 1, 1985, a city, an auditorium district created by the State legislature within which such facility will be located, and a limited partnership executed an enforceable contract,

(ii) significant governmental action regarding such facility was taken before May 23, 1983, and

(iii) inducement resolutions were passed for issuance of bonds with respect to such facility on May 26, 1986.

The aggregate face amount of bonds to which this subparagraph applies shall not exceed $25,000,000.

(9) Parking facilities.—A bond issued as part of an issue 95 percent or more of the net proceeds of which are to be used to provide a parking facility (within the meaning of section 103(b)(4)(D) of the 1954 Code) shall be treated as an exempt facility bond for purposes of part IV of subchapter B of chapter 1 of the 1986 Code if such facility is described in any of the following subparagraphs:

(A) A facility is described in this subparagraph if—

(i) there was an inducement resolution on March 9, 1984, for the issuance of bonds with respect to such facility, and

(ii) such resolution was extended by resolutions passed on August 14, 1984, April 2, 1985, August 13, 1985, and July 8, 1986.

The aggregate face amount of bonds to which this subparagraph applies shall not exceed $30,000,000.

(B) A facility is described in this subparagraph if—

(i) such facility is for a university medical school,

(ii) the last parcel of land necessary for such facility was purchased on February 4, 1985, and

(iii) the amount of bonds to be issued with respect to such facility was increased by the State legislature of the State in which the facility is to be located as part of its 1983-1984 general appropriations act.

The aggregate face amount of bonds to which this subparagraph applies shall not exceed $9,000,000.

(C) A facility is described in this subparagraph if—

(i) the development agreement with respect to the project of which such facility is a part was entered into during May 1984, and

(ii) an inducement resolution was passed on October 9, 1985, for the issuance of bonds with respect to the facility.

The aggregate face amount of bonds to which this subparagraph applies shall not exceed $35,000,000.

(D) A facility is described in this subparagraph if the city council approved a resolution of intent to issue tax-exempt bonds (Resolution 34083) for such facility on April 30, 1986. The aggregate face amount of bonds to which this subparagraph applies shall not exceed $8,000,000. Solely for purposes of this subparagraph, a heliport constructed as part of such facility shall be deemed to be functionally related and subordinate to such facility.

(E) A facility is described in this subparagraph if—

(i) resolutions were adopted by a public joint powers authority relating to such facility on March 5, 1985, May 1, 1985, October 2, 1985, December 4, 1985, and February 5, 1986; and

(ii) such facility is to be located at an exposition park which includes a coliseum and sports arena.

The aggregate face amount of bonds to which this subparagraph applies shall not exceed $150,000,000.

(F) A facility is described in this subparagraph if—

(i) it is to be constructed as part of an overall development that is the subject of a development agreement dated October 1, 1983, between a developer and an organization described in section 501(c)(3) of the 1986 Code, and

(ii) an environmental notification form with respect to the overall development was filed with a State environmental agency on February 28, 1985.

Act §1317(9) (F) ¶2076

The aggregate face amount of bonds to which this subparagraph applies shall not exceed $60,000,000.

(G) A facility is described in this subparagraph if—

(i) an inducement resolution was passed by the city redevelopment agency on December 3, 1984, and a resolution to carryforward the private activity bond limit was passed by such agency on December 21, 1984, with respect to such facility, and

(ii) the owner participation agreement with respect to such facility was entered into on July 30, 1986.

The aggregate face amount of bonds to which this subparagraph applies shall not exceed $18,000,000.

(H) A facility is described in this subparagraph if—

(i) an application (dated August 28, 1986) for financial assistance was submitted to the county industrial development agency with respect to such facility, and

(ii) the inducement resolution for such facility was passed by the industrial development agency on September 10, 1986.

The aggregate face amount of bonds to which this subparagraph applies shall not exceed $8,000,000.

(I) A facility is described in this subparagraph if—

(i) it is located in a city the parking needs of which were comprehensively described in a "Downtown Parking Plan" dated January 1983, and approved by the city's City Plan Commission on June 1, 1983, and

(ii) obligations with respect to the construction of which are issued on behalf of a State or local governmental unit by a corporation empowered to issue the same which was created by the legislative body of a State by an Act introduced on May 21, 1985, and thereafter passed, which Act became effective without the governor's signature on June 26, 1985.

The aggregate face amount of bonds to which this subparagraph applies shall not exceed $50,000,000.

(J) A facility is described in this subparagraph if—

(i) such facility is located in a city which was the subject of a convention center market analysis or study dated March 1983 and prepared by a nationally recognized accounting firm,

(ii) such facility is intended for use by, among others, persons attending a convention center located within the same town or city, and

(iii) such facility's location was approved by a task force created jointly, in December 1985, by the governor of the State within which such facility will be located and the mayor of the capital city of such State.

The aggregate face amount of bonds to which this subparagraph applies shall not exceed $30,000,000.

(K) A facility is described in this subparagraph if—

(i) scale and components for the facility were determined by a city downtown plan adopted October 31, 1984 (resolution number 3882), and

(ii) the site area for the facility is appoximately 51,200 square feet.

The aggregate face amount of bonds to which this subparagraph applies shall not exceed $5,000,000.

(L) A facility is described in this subparagraph if—

(i) the property for such facility was offered for development by a city renewal agency on March 19, 1986 (resolution number 920), and

(ii) the site area for the facility is approximately 25,600 square feet.

The aggregate face amount of bonds to which this subparagraph applies shall not exceed $5,000,000.

(M) A facility is described in this subparagraph if such facility was approved by official action of the city council on July 26, 1984 (resolution number 33718), and is for the Moyer Theatre. The aggregate face amount of bonds to which this subparagraph applies shall not exceed $8,000,000.

(N) A facility is described in this subparagraph if it is part of a renovation project involving the Outlet Company building in Providence, Rhode Island. The aggregate face amount of obligations to which this subparagraph applies shall not exceed $6,000,000.

(10) Certain advance refundings.—

(A) Section 149(d)(3) of the 1986 Code shall not apply to a bond issued by a State admitted to the Union on November 16, 1907, for the advance refunding of not more than $186,000,000 State turnpike obligations.

(B) A refunding of the Charleston, West Virginia Town Center Garage Bonds shall not be treated for purposes of part IV of subchapter A of chapter 1 of the 1986 Code as an advance refunding if it would not be so treated if "100" were substituted for "90" in section 149(d)(5) of such Code.

(11) Principal user provisions.—

(A) In the case of a bond issued as part of an issue the proceeds of which are to be used to provide a facility described in subparagraph (B) or (C), the determination of whether such bond is an exempt facility bond shall be made by substituting "90 percent" for "95 percent" and [should read in] section 142(a) of the 1986 Code.

(B) A facility is described in this subparagraph if—

(i) it is a waste-to-energy project for which a contract for the sale of electricity was executed in September 1984, and

(ii) the design, construction, and operation contract for such project was signed in March 1985 and the order to begin construction was issued on March 31, 1986.

The aggregate face amount of bonds to which this subparagraph applies shall not exceed $29,100,000.

(C) A facility is described in this subparagraph if it is a solid waste disposal facility for Charleston, South Carolina, and a State political subdivision took formal action on April 1, 1980, to commit development funds for such facility.

(12) Qualified scholarship funding bonds.—Subsections (d)(3) and (f) of section 148 of the 1986 Code shall not apply to any bond or series of bonds the proceeds of which are used exclusively to refund qualified scholarship funding bonds (as defined in section 150 of the 1986 Code) issued before January 1, 1986, if—

(A) the amount of the refunding bonds does not exceed the aggregate face amount of the refunded bonds,

(B) the maturity date of such refunding bond is not later than later of—

(i) the maturity date of the bond to be refunded, or

(ii) the date which is 15 years after the date on which the refunded bond was issued (or, in the case of a series of refundings, the date on which the original bond was issued),

(C) the bonds to be refunded were issued by the California Student Loan Finance Corporation, and

(D) the face amount of the refunding bonds does not exceed $175,000,000.

(13) Residential rental property projects.—A bond issued as part of an issue 95 percent or more of the net proceeds of which are to be used to provide a project for residential rental property which satisfies the requirements of section 103(b)(4)(A) of the 1954 Code shall be treated as an exempt facility bond (for projects described in section 142(a)(7) of the 1986 Code) for purposes of part IV of subchapter B of chapter 1 of the 1986 Code if the project is described in any of the following subparagraphs:

(A) A residential rental property project is described in this subparagraph if—

(i) a public building development corporation was formed on June 6, 1984, with respect to such project,

(ii) a partnership of which the corporation is a general partner was formed on June 8, 1984, and

(iii) the partnership entered into a preliminary agreement with the State public facilities authority effective as of May 4, 1984, with respect to the issuance of the bonds for such project.

The aggregate face amount of bonds to which this subparagraph applies shall not exceed $6,200,000.

(B) A residential rental property project is described in this subparagraph if—

(i) the Board of Commissioners of the city housing authority officially selected such project's developer on December 19, 1985,

(ii) the Board of the City Redevelopment Commission agreed on February 13, 1986, to conduct a public hearing with respect to the project on March 6, 1986,

(iii)   an official action resolution for such project was adopted on March 6, 1986, and

(iv)   an allocation of a portion of the State ceiling was made with respect to such project on July 29, 1986.

The aggregate face amount of bonds to which this subparagraph applies shall not exceed $10,000,000.

(C)   A residential rental property project is described in this subparagraph if—

(i)   the issuance of $1,289,882 of bonds for such project was approved by a State agency on September 11, 1985, and

(ii)   the authority to issue such bonds was scheduled to expire (under the terms of the State approval) on September 9, 1986.

The aggregate face amount of bonds to which this subparagraph applies shall not exceed $1,300,000.

(D)   A residential rental property project is described in this subparagraph if—

(i)   the issuance of $7,020,000 of bonds for such project was approved by a State agency on October 10, 1985, and

(ii)   the authority to issue such bonds was scheduled to expire (under the terms of the State approval) on October 9, 1986.

The aggregate face amount of bonds to which this subparagraph applies shall not exceed $7,020,000.

(E)   A residential rental property project is described in this subparagraph if—

(i)   it is to be located in a city urban renewal project area which was established pursuant to an urban renewal plan adopted by the city council on May 17, 1960,

(ii)   the urban renewal plan was revised in 1972 to permit multifamily dwellings in areas of the urban renewal project designated as a central business district,

(iii)   an inducement resolution was adopted for such project on December 14, 1984, and

(iv)   the city council approved on November 6, 1985, an agreement which provides for conveyance to the city of fee title to such project site.

The aggregate face amount of bonds to which this subparagraph applies shall not exceed $60,000,000.

(F)   A residential rental property project is described in this subparagraph if—

(i)   such project is to be located in a city urban renewal project area which was established pursuant to an urban renewal plan adopted by the city council on May 17, 1960,

(ii)   the urban renewal plan was revised in 1972 to permit multifamily dwellings in areas of the urban renewal project designated as a central business district,

(iii)   the amended urban renewal plan adopted by the city council on May 19, 1972, also provides for the conversion of any public area site in Block J of the urban renewal project area for the development of residential facilities, and

(iv)   acquisition of all of the parcels comprising the Block J project site was completed by the city on December 28, 1984.

The aggregate face amount of bonds to which this subparagraph applies shall not exceed $60,000,000.

(G)   A residential rental property project is described in this subparagraph if—

(i)   such project is to be located on a city-owned site which is to become available for residential development upon the relocation of a bus maintenance facility,

(ii)   preliminary design studies for such project site were completed in December 1985, and

(iii)   such project is located in the same State as the projects described in subparagraphs (E) and (F).

The aggregate face amount of bonds to which this subparagraph applies shall not exceed $100,000,000.

(H)   A residential rental property project is described in this subparagraph if—

(i)   at least 20 percent of the residential units in such project are to be utilized to fulfill the requirements of a unilateral agreement date July 21, 1983, relating to the provision of low- and moderate-income housing,

(ii)   the unilateral agreement was incorporated into ordinance numbers 83-49 and 83-50, adopted by the city council and approved by the mayor on August 24, 1983, and

(iii) an inducement resolution was adopted for such project on September 25, 1985.

The aggregate face amount of bonds to which this subparagraph applies shall not exceed $8,000,000.

(I) A residential rental property project is described in this subparagraph if—

(i) a letter of understanding was entered into on December 11, 1985, between the city and county housing and community development office and the project developer regarding the conveyance of land for such project, and

(ii) such project is located in the same State as the projects described in subparagraphs (E), (F), (G), and (H).

The aggregate face amount of bonds to which this subparagraph applies shall not exceed an amount which, together with the amounts allowed under subparagraphs (E), (F), (G), and (H), does not exceed $250,000,000.

(J) A residential rental property project is described in this subparagraph if it is a multifamily residential development located in Arrowhead Springs, within the county of San Bernardino, California, and a portion of the site of which currently is owned by the Campus Crusade for Christ. The aggregate face amount of bonds to which this subparagraph applies shall not exceed $350,000,000.

(K) A residential rental property project is described in this subparagraph if—

(i) it is a new residential development with approximately 309 dwelling units located in census tract No. 3202, and

(ii) there was an inducement ordinance for such project adopted by a city council on November 20, 1985.

The aggregate face amount of bonds to which this subparagraph applies shall not exceed $32,000,000.

(L) A residential rental property project is described in this subparagraph if—

(i) it is a new residential development with approximately 70 dwelling units located in census tract No. 3901, and

(ii) there was an inducement ordinance for such project adopted by a city council on August 14, 1984.

The aggregate face amount of bonds to which this subparagraph applies shall not exceed $4,000,000.

(M) A residential rental property project is described in this subparagraph if—

(i) it is a new residential development with approximately 98 dwelling units located in census tract No. 4701, and

(ii) there was an inducement ordinance for such project adopted by a city council on August 14, 1984.

The aggregate face amount of bonds to which this subparagraph applies shall not exceed $7,000,000.

(N) A project or projects are described in this subparagraph if they are part of the Willow Road residential improvement plan in Menlo Park, California. The aggregate face amount of obligations to which this subparagraph applies shall not exceed $9,000,000.

(O) A residential rental property project is described in this subparagraph if—

(i) an inducement resolution for such project was approved on July 18, 1985, by the city council,

(ii) such project was approved by such council on August 11, 1986, and

(iii) such project consists of approximately 22 duplexes to be used for housing qualified low and moderate income tenants.

The aggregate face amount of bonds to which this subparagraph applies shall not exceed $1,500,000.

(P) A residential rental property project is described in this subparagraph if—

(i) an inducement resolution for such project was approved on April 22, 1986, by the city council,

(ii) such project was approved by such council on August 11, 1986, and

(iii) such project consists of a unit apartment complex (having approximately 60 units) to be used for housing qualified low and moderate income tenants.

The aggregate face amount of bonds to which this subparagraph applies shall not exceed $1,625,000.

(Q) A residential rental property project is described in this subparagraph if—

(i) a State housing authority granted a notice of official action for the project on May 24, 1985, and

(ii) a binding agreement was executed for such project with the State housing finance authority on May 14, 1986, and such agreement was accepted by the State housing authority on June 5, 1986.

The aggregate face amount of bonds to which this subparagraph applies shall not exceed $7,800,000.

(R) A residential rental property project is described in this subparagraph if such project is either of 2 projects (located in St. Louis, Missouri) which received commitments to provide construction and permanent financing through the issuance of bonds in principal amounts of up to $242,130 and $654,045, on July 16, 1986. The aggregate face amount of bonds to which this subparagraph applies shall not exceed $1,000,000.

(S) A residential rental property project is described in this subparagraph if—

(i) a local housing authority approved an inducement resolution for such project on January 28, 1985, and

(ii) a suit relating to such project was dismissed without right of further appeal on April 4, 1986.

The aggregate face amount of bonds to which this subparagraph applies shall not exceed $13,200,000.

(T) A residential rental property project is described in this subparagraph if—

(i) such project is the renovation of a hotel for residents for senior citizens,

(ii) an inducement resolution for such project was adopted on November 20, 1985, by the State Development Finance Authority, and

(iii) such project is to be located in the metropolitan area of the city described in paragraph (3)(C).

The aggregate face amount of bonds to which this subparagraph applies shall not exceed $9,500,000.

(U) A residential rental property project is described in this subparagraph if—

(i) such project is the renovation of apartment housing,

(ii) an inducement resolution for such project was adopted on December 20, 1985, by the State Housing Development Authority, and

(iii) such project is to be located in the metropolitan area of the city described in paragraph (3)(C).

The aggregate face amount of bonds to which this subparagraph applies shall not exceed $12,000,000.

(V) A residential rental project is described in this subparagraph if it is a renovation and construction project for low-income housing in central Louisville, Kentucky, and local board approval for such project was granted April 22, 1986. The aggregate face amount of bonds to which this subparagraph applies shall not exceed $500,000.

(W) A residential rental project is described in this subparagraph if—

(i) such project is 1 of 6 residential rental projects having in the aggregate approximately 1,010 units,

(ii) inducement resolutions for such projects were adopted by the county residential finance authority on November 21, 1985, and

(iii) a public hearing of the county residential finance authority was held by such authority on December 19, 1985, regarding such projects to be constructed by an in-commonwealth developer.

The aggregate face amount of bonds to which this subparagraph applies shall not exceed $62,000,000.

(X) A residential rental project is described in this subparagraph if—

(i) an inducement resolution with respect to such project was adopted by the State housing development authority on January 25, 1985, and

(ii) the issuance of bonds for such project was the subject of a law suit filed on October 25, 1985.

The aggregate face amount of bonds to which this subparagraph applies shall not exceed $64,000,000. In the case of bonds to which this subparagraph applies, the requirements of sections 148 and 149(d) of the 1986 Code shall not be treated as included in section 103 of the 1954 Code and shall apply to such bonds.

(Y) A project or projects are described in this subparagraph if they are financed with bonds issued by the Tulare, California, County Housing Authority. The aggregate face amount of obligations to which this subparagraph applies shall not exceed $8,000,000.

(Z)   A residential rental project is described in this subparagraph if such project is a multifamily mixed-use housing project located in a city described in paragraph (3)(C), the zoning for which was changed to residential-business planned development on November 26, 1985, and with respect to which both the city on December 4, 1985, and the state housing finance agency on December 20, 1985, adopted inducement resolutions. The aggregate face amount of obligations to which this subparagraph applies shall not exceed $90,000,000.

(14)   Qualified student loans.—The amendments made by section 1301 shall not apply to any qualified student loan bonds (as defined in section 144 of the 1986 Code) issued by the Volunteer State Student Assistance Corporation. The aggregate face amount of bonds to which this paragraph applies shall not exceed $90,000,000. In the case of bonds to which this paragraph applies, the requirements of sections 148 and 149(d) of the 1986 Code shall be treated as included in section 103 of the 1954 Code and shall apply to such bonds.

(15)   Annuity contracts.—The treatment of annuity contracts as investment property under section 148(b)(2) of the 1986 Code shall not apply to any bond described in any of the following subparagraphs:

(A)   A bond is described in this subparagraph if such bond is issued by a city located in a noncontiguous State if—
(i)   the authority to acquire such a contract was approved on September 24, 1985, by city ordinance A085-176, and
(ii)   formal bid requests for such contracts were mailed to insurance companies on September 6, 1985.

The aggregate face amount of bonds to which this subparagraph applies shall not exceed $57,000,000.

(B)   A bond is described in this subparagraph if—
(i)   on or before May 12, 1985, the governing board of the city pension fund authorized an agreement with an underwriter for possible execution and delivery of tax-exempt certificates of participation by a nonprofit corporation, and
(ii)   the proceeds of the sale of such certificates are to be used to purchase an annuity to fund the unfunded liability of the City of Berkeley, California's Safety Members Pension Fund.

The aggregate face amount of bonds to which this subparagraph applies shall not exceed $40,000,000.

(C)   A bond is described in this subparagraph if such bond is issued by the South Dakota Building Authority if on September 18, 1985, representatives of such authority and its underwriters met with bond counsel and approved financing the purchase of an annuity contract through the sale and leaseback of State properties. The aggregate face amount of bonds to which this subparagraph applies shall not exceed $175,000,000.

(D)   A bond is described in this subparagraph if—
(i)   such bond is issued by Los Angeles County, and
(ii)   such county, before September 25, 1985, paid or incurred at least $50,000 of costs related to the issuance of such bonds.

The aggregate face amount of bonds to which this subparagraph applies shall not exceed $500,000,000.

(16)   Solid waste disposal facility.—The amendments made by section 1301 shall not apply to any solid waste disposal facility if—
(A)   construction of such facility was approved by State law I.C. 36-9-31,
(B)   there was an inducement resolution on November 19, 1984, for the bonds with respect to such facility, and
(C)   a carryforward election of unused 1984 volume cap was made for such project on February 25, 1985.

The aggregate face amount of bonds to which this paragraph applies shall not exceed $120,000,000. In the case of bonds to which this paragraph applies, the requirements of section 148, 149(d), and 149(g) of the 1986 Code shall be treated as included in section 103 of the 1954 Code and shall apply to such bonds.

(17)   Refunding of bond anticipation notes.—There shall not be taken into account under section 146 of the 1986 Code any refunding of bond anticipation notes—
(A)   issued in December of 1984 by the Rhode Island Housing and Mortgage Finance Corporation,

(B) which mature in December of 1986,

(C) which is not an advance refunding within the meaning of section of 149(d)(5) of the 1986 Code (determined by substituting "180 days" for "90 days" therein), and

(D) the aggregate face amount of the refunding bonds does not exceed $25,500,000.

(18) **Certain airports.**—The amendments made by section 1301 shall not apply to a bond issued as part of an issue 95 percent or more of the net proceeds of which are to be used to provide any airport (within the meaning of section 103(b)(4)(D) of the 1954 Code) if such airport is a mid-field airport terminal and accompanying facilities at a major air carrier airport which during April 1980 opened a new precision instrument approach runway 10R28L. The aggregate face amount of bonds to which this subparagraph applies shall not exceed $425,000,000.

(19) **Mass commuting facilities.**—A bond issued as a part of an issue 95 percent or more of the net proceeds of which are to be used to provide a mass commuting facility (within the meaning of section 103(b)(4)(D) of the 1954 Code) shall be treated as an exempt facility bond (for facilities described in section 142(a)(3) of the 1986 Code) for purposes of part IV of subchapter B of chapter 1 of the 1986 Code if such facility is described in 1 of the following subparagraphs:

(A) A facility is described in this subparagraph if—

(i) such facility provides access to an international airport,

(ii) a corporation was formed in connection with such project in September 1984,

(iii) the Board of Directors of such corporation authorized the hiring of various firms to conduct a feasibility study with respect to such project in April 1985, and

(iv) such feasibility study was completed in November 1985.

The aggregate face amount of bonds to which this subparagraph applies shall not exceed $150,000,000.

(B) A facility is described in this subparagraph if—

(i) enabling legislation with respect to such project was approved by the State legislature in 1979,

(ii) a 1-percent local sales tax assessment to be dedicated to the financing of such project was approved by the voters on August 13, 1983, and

(iii) a capital fund with respect to such project was established upon the issuance of $90,000,000 of notes on October 22, 1985.

The aggregate face amount of bonds to which this subparagraph applies shall not exceed $200,000,000 and such bonds must be issued before January 1, 1996.

(C) A facility is described in this subparagraph if—

(i) bonds issued therefor are issued by or on behalf of an authority organized in 1979 pursuant to enabling legislation originally enacted by the State legislature in 1973, and

(ii) such facility is part of a system connector described in a resolution adopted by the board of directors of the authority on March 27, 1986.

The aggregate face amount of bonds to which this subparagraph applies shall not exceed $400,000,000. Notwithstanding the last paragraph of this subsection, this subparagaph shall apply to bonds issued before January 1, 1996.

(D) A facility is described in this subparagraph if—

(i) the facility is a light rail transitway project,

(ii) enabling legislation with respect to the issuing authority was approved by the State legislature in May 1973,

(iii) on October 28, 1985, a board issued a request for consultants to conduct a feasibility study on mass transit corridor analysis in connection with the facility, and

(iv) on May 12, 1986, a board approved a further binding contract for expenditures of approximately $1,494,963, to be expended on a facility study.

The aggregate face amount of bonds to which this subparagraph applies shall not exceed $250,000,000. Notwithstanding the last paragraph of this subsection, this subparagraph shall apply to bonds issued before January 1, 1996.

(20) **Private colleges.**—Section 148(f) of the 1986 Code shall not apply to any bond which is issued as part of an issue if such bond—

(A) is issued by a political subdivision pursuant to home rule and interlocal cooperation powers conferred by the constitution and laws of a State to provide funds to finance the costs of the purchase and construction of educational facilities for private colleges and universities, and

(B) was the subject of a resolution of official action by such political subdivision (Resolution No. 86-1039) adopted by the governing body of such political subdivision on March 18, 1986.

The aggregate face amount of bonds to which this paragraph applies shall not exceed $100,000,000.

(21) Pooled financing programs.—

(A) Section 147(b) of the 1986 Code shall not apply to any hospital pooled financing program with respect to which—

(i) a formal presentation was made to a city hospital facilities authority on January 14, 1986, and

(ii) such authority passed a resolution approving the bond issue in principle on February 5, 1986.

The aggregate face amount of bonds to which this subparagraph applies shall not exceed $95,000,000.

(B) Subsection (c) and (f) of section 148 of the 1986 Code shall not apply to bonds for which closing occurred on July 16, 1986, and for which a State municipal league served as administrator for use in a State described in section 103A(g)(5)(C) of the Internal Revenue of 1954. The aggregate face amount of obligations to which this subparagraph applies shall not exceed $585,000,000.

(22) Downtown redevelopment project.—

(A) In the case of a bond described in subparagraph (B), section 141 of the 1986 Code shall be applied without regard to subsection (a)(2), subsection (b)(3), and subsection (b)(5); and paragraphs (1) and (2) of subsection (b) shall be applied by substituting "25 percent" for "10 percent" each place it appears.

(B) A bond is described in this subparagaph if such bond is issued as part of an issue 95 percent or more of the net proceeds of which are to be used to provide a project to acquire and redevelop a downtown area if—

(i) on August 15, 1985, a downtown redevelopment authority adopted a resolution to issue bonds for such project,

(ii) before September 26, 1985, the city expended (or entered into binding contracts to expend) more than $10,000,000 in connection with such project, and

(iii) the state supreme court issued a ruling regarding the proposed finance structure for such project on December 11, 1985.

The aggregate face amount of bonds to which this paragraph applies shall not exceed $85,000,000 and such bonds must be issued before January 1, 1992.

(23) Mass commuting and parking facilities.—A bond issued as part of an issue 95 percent or more of the net proceeds of which are to be used to provide any mass commuting facility or parking facility (within the meaning of section 103(b)(4)(D) of the 1954 Code) shall be treated as an exempt facility bond for purposes of part IV of subchapter IV of subchapter B of chapter 1 of the 1986 Code if such facility is provided in connection with the rehabilitation, renovation, or other improvement to an existing railroad station owned on the date of the enactment of this Act by the National Railroad Passenger Corporation in the Northeast Corridor and which was placed in partial service in 1934 and was placed in the National Register of Historic Places in 1978. The aggregate face amount of bonds to which this paragraph applies shall not exceed $30,000,000.

(24) Tax-exempt status of bonds of certain educational organizations.—

(A) In general.—For purposes of section 103 and part IV of subchapter B of chapter 1 of the 1986 Code, a qualified educational organization shall be treated as a governmental unit, but only with respect to a trade or business carried on by such organization which is not an unrelated trade or business (determined by applying section 513(a) of such Code to such organization).

(B) Qualified educational organization.—For purposes of subparagraph (A), the term "qualified educational organization" means a college or university—

(i) which was reincorporated and renewed with perpetual existence as a corporation by specific act of the legislature of the State within which such college or university is located on March 19, 1913, or

(ii) which—

(I) was initially incorporated or created on February 28, 1787, on April 29, 1854, or on May 14, 1888, and

(II) as an instrumentality of the State, serves as a "State-related" university by a specific act of the legislature of the State within which such college or university is located.

(25) **Tax-exempt status of bonds of certain public utilities.—**

(A) In general.—Except as provided in subparagraph (B), a bond shall be treated as a qualified bond for purposes of section 103 of the 1986 Code if such bond is issued after the date of the enactment of this Act with respect to a public utility facility if such facility is—

(i) located at any non-federally owned dam (or on project waters or adjacent lands) located wholly or partially in 3 counties, 2 of which are contiguous to the third, where the rated capacity of the hydroelectric generating facilities at 5 of such dams on October 18, 1979, was more than 650 megawatts each,

(ii) located at a dam (or on the project waters or adjacent lands) at which hydroelectric generating facilities were financed with the proceeds of tax-exempt obligations before December 31, 1968,

(iii) owned and operated by a State, political subdivision of a State, or any agency or instrumentality of any of the foregoing, and

(iv) located at a dam (or on project waters or adjacent lands) where the general public has access for recreational purposes to such dam or to such project waters or adjacent lands.

(B) Special rules for subparagraph (a).—

(i) Bonds subject to cap.—Section 146 of the 1986 Code shall apply to any bond described in subparagraph (A) which (without regard to subparagraph (A)) is a private activity bond.

(ii) Limitation on amount of bonds to which subparagraph (a) applies.—The aggregate face amount of bonds to which subparagraph (A) applies shall not exceed $750,000,000, not more than $350,000,000 of which may be issued before January 1, 1992.

(iii) Limitation on purposes.—Subparagraph (A) shall only apply to bonds issued as part of an issue 95 percent or more of the net proceeds of which are used to provide 1 or more of the following:

(I) A fish by-pass facility or fisheries enhancement facility.

(II) A recreational facility or other improvement which is required by Federal licensing terms and conditions or other Federal, State, or local law requirements.

(III) A project of repair, maintenance, renewal, or replacement, and safety improvement.

(IV) Any reconstruction, replacement, or improvement, including any safety improvement, which increases, or allows an increase in, the capacity, efficiency, or productivity of the existing generating equipment.

(26) **Convention and parking facilities.—**A bond shall not be treated as a private activity bond for purposes of section 103 and part IV of subchapter B of chapter 1 of the 1986 Code if—

(A) such bond is issued to provide a sports or convention facility described in section 103(b)(4)(B) or (C) of the 1954 Code,

(B) such bond is not described in section 103(b)(2) or (o)(2)(A) of such Code,

(C) legislation by a State legislature in connection with such facility was enacted on July 19, 1985, and was designated Chapter 375 of the Laws of 1985, and

(D) legislation by a State legislature in connection with the appropriation of funds to a State public benefit corporation for loans in connection with the construction of such facility was enacted on April 17, 1985, and was designated Chapter 41 of the Laws of 1985.

The aggregate face amount of bonds to which this subparagraph applies shall not exceed $35,000,000.

(27) **Small issue termination.—**Section 144(a)(12) of the 1986 Code shall not apply to any bond issued as part of an issue 95 percent or more of the net proceeds of which are to be used to provide a facility described in any of the following subparagraphs:

(A) A facility is described in this subparagraph if—

(i) the facility is a hotel and office facility located in a State capital,

(ii)   the economic development corporation of the city in which the facility is located adopted an initial inducement resolution on October 30, 1985, and

(iii)   a feasibility consultant was retained on February 21, 1986, with respect to such facility.

The aggregate face amount of bonds to which this subparagraph applies shall not exceed $10,000,000.

(B)   A facility is described in this subparagraph if such facility is financed by bonds issued by a State finance authority which was created in April 1985 by Act 1062 of the State General Assembly, and the Bond Guarantee Act (Act 505 of 1985) allowed such authority to pledge the interest from investment of the State's general fund as a guarantee for bonds issued by such authority. The aggregate face amount of bonds to which this subparagraph applies shall not exceed $75,000,000.

(C)   A facility is described in this subparagraph if such facility is a downtown mall and parking project for Holland, Michigan, with respect to which an initial agreement was formulated with the city in May 1985 and a formal memorandum of understanding was executed on July 2, 1986. The aggregate face amount of bonds to which this subparagraph applies shall not exceed $18,200,000.

(D)   A facility is described in this subparagraph if such facility is a downtown mall and parking ramp project for Traverse City, Michigan, with respect to which a final development agreement was signed in June 1986. The aggregate face amount of bonds to which this subparagraph applies shall not exceed $21,500,000.

(E)   A facility is described in this subparagraph if such facility is the rehabilitation of the Heritage Hotel in Marquette, Michigan. The aggregate face amount of bonds to which this subparagraph applies shall not exceed $5,000,000.

(F)   A facility is described in this subparagraph if it is the Lakeland Center Hotel in Lakeland, Florida. The aggregate face amount of obligations to which this subparagraph applies shall not exceed $10,000,000.

(G)   A facility is described in this subparagraph if it is the Marble Arcade office building renovation project in Lakeland, Florida. The aggregate face amount of obligations to which this subparagraph applies shall not exceed $5,900,000.

(H)   A facility is described in this subparagraph if it is a medical office building in Bradenton, Florida, with respect to which—

(i)   a memorandum of agreement was entered into on October 17, 1985, and

(ii)   the city council held a public hearing and approved issuance of the bonds on November 14, 1985.

The aggregate face amount of obligations to which this subparagraph applies shall not exceed $8,500,000.

(I)   A facility is described in this subparagraph if it consists of the rehabilitation of the Andover Town Hall in Andover, Massachusetts. The provisions of section 149(b) of the 1986 Code (relating to federally guaranteed obligations) shall not apply to obligations to finance such project solely as a result of the occupation of a portion of such building by a United States Post Office.

(J)   A facility is described in this subparagraph if it is the Central Bank Building renovation project in Grand Rapids, Michigan. The aggregate face amount of obligations to which this subparagraph applies shall not exceed $1,000,000.

(28)   Certain private loans not taken into account.—For purposes of determining whether any bond is a private activity bond, an amount of loans (but not in excess of $75,000,000) provided from the proceeds of 1 or more issues shall not be taken into account if such loans are provided in furtherance of—

(A)   a city Emergency Conservation Plan as set forth in an ordinance adopted by the city council of such city on February 17, 1983, or

(B)   a resolution adopted by the city council of such city on March 10, 1983, committing such city to a goal of reducing the peak load of such city's electric generation and distribution system by 553 megawatts in 15 years.

(29)   Certain private business use not taken into account.—

(A)   The nonqualified amount of the proceeds of an issue shall not be taken into account under section 141(b)(5) of the 1986 Code or in determining whether a bond described in subparagraph (B) (which is part of such issue) is a private activity bond for purposes of section 103 and part IV of subchapter B of chapter 1 of the 1986 Code.

(B)   A bond is described in this subparagraph if—

(i) such bond is issued before January 1, 1993, by a State admitted to the Union on June 14 1776, and

(ii) such bond is issued pursuant to a resolution of the State Bond Commission adopted before September 26, 1985.

(C) The nonqualified amount to which this paragraph applies shall not exceed $150,000,000.

(D) For purposes of this paragraph, the term "nonqualified amount" has the meaning given such term by section 141(b)(8) of the 1986 Code, except that such term shall include the amount of the net proceeds of an issue which is to be used (directly or indirectly) to make or finance loans (other than loans described in section 141(c)(2) of the 1986 Code) to persons other than governmental units.

(30) **Volume cap not to apply to certain facilities.**—For purposes of section 146 of the 1986 Code, any exempt facility bond for the following facility shall not be taken into account: The facility is a facility for the furnishing of water which was authorized under Public Law 90-537 of the United States if—

(A) construction of such facility began on May 6, 1973, and

(B) forward funding will be provided for the remainder of the project pursuant to a negotiated agreement between State and local water users and the Secretary of the Interior signed April 15, 1986.

The aggregate face amount of bonds to which this subparagraph applies shall not exceed $391,000,000.

(31) **Certain hydroelectric generating property.**—A bond shall be treated as described in paragraph (2) of section 1316(f) of this Act if—

(A) such bond would be so described but for the substitution specified in such paragraph,

(B) on January 7, 1983, an application for a preliminary permit was filed for the project for which such bond is issued and received docket no. 6986, and

(C) on September 20, 1983, the Federal Energy Regulatory Commission issued an order granting the preliminary permit for the project.

The aggregate face amount of bonds to which this paragraph applies shall not exceed $12,000,000.

(32) **Volume cap.**—The State ceiling applicable under section 146 of the 1986 Code for calendar year 1987 for the State which ratified the United States Constitution on May 29, 1790, shall be $150,000,000 higher than the State ceiling otherwise applicable under such section for such year.

(33) **Application of $150,000,000 limitation for certain qualified 501(c)(3) bonds.**—Proceeds of an issue described in any of the following subparagraphs shall not be taken into account under section 145(b) of the 1986 Code.

(A) Proceeds of an issue are described in this subparagraph if—

(i) such proceeds are used to provide medical school facilities or medical research and clinical facilities for a university medical center,

(ii) such proceeds are of—

(I) a $21,550,000 issue on August 1, 1980,

(II) a $84,400,000 issue on September 1, 1984, and

(III) a $48,500,000 issue (Series 1985 A and 1985 B), and

(iii) the issuer of all such issues is the same.

(B) Proceeds of an issue are described in this subparagraph if such proceeds are for use by Yale University and—

(i) the bonds are issued after August 8, 1986, and before August 7, 1988, by the State of Connecticut Health and Educational Facilities Authority, or

(ii) the bonds are the 1st or 2nd refundings (including advance refundings) of the bonds described in clause (i) or of original bonds issued before August 7, 1986, by such Authority.

(C) Proceeds of an issue are described in this subparagraph if—

(i) such issue is issued on behalf of a university established by Charter granted by King George II of England on October 31, 1754, to accomplish a refunding (including an advance refunding) of bonds issued to finance 1 or more projects, and

(ii) the application or other request for the issuance of the issue to the appropriate State issuer was made by or on behalf of such university before February 26, 1986.

The aggregate face amount of bonds to which this subparagraph applies shall not exceed $250,000,000.

(D) Proceeds of an issue are described in this subparagraph if—

(i) such proceeds are to be used for finance construction of a new student recreation center,

(ii) a contract for the development phase of the project was signed by the university on May 21, 1986, with a private company for 5 percent of the costs of the project, and

(iii) a committee of the university board of administrators approved the major program elements for the center on August 11, 1986.

The aggregate face amount of bonds to which this subparagraph applies shall not exceed $25,000,000.

(E) Proceeds of an issue are described in this subparagraph if—

(i) such proceeds are to be used in the construction of new life sciences facilities for a university for medical research and education,

(ii) the president of the university authorized a faculty/administration planning committee for such facilities on September 17, 1982,

(iii) the trustees of such university authorized site and architect selection on October 30, 1984, and

(iv) the university negotiated a $2,600,000 contract with the architect on August 9, 1985.

The aggregate face amount of bonds to which this subparagraph applies shall not exceed $47,500,000.

(F) Proceeds of an issue are described in this subparagraph if such proceeds are to be used to renovate undergraduate chemistry and engineering laboratories, and to rehabilitate other basic science facilities, for an institution of higher education in Philadelphia, Pennsylvania, chartered by legislative Acts of the Commonwealth of Pennsylvania, including an Act dated September 30, 1791. The aggregate face amount of bonds to which this subparagraph applies shall not exceed $6,500,000.

(G) Proceeds of an issue are described in this subparagraph if such proceeds are of bonds which are the first advance refunding of bonds issued during 1985 for the development of a computer network, and construction and renovation or rehabilitation of other facilities, for an institution of higher education described in subparagraph (H). The aggregate face amount of bonds to which this subparagraph applies shall not exceed $80,000,000.

(H) Proceeds of an issue are described in this subparagraph if—

(i) the issue is issued on behalf of a university founded in 1789, and

(ii) the request to issue bonds for items to be determined by the issuer was transmitted to Congress on November 7, 1985.

The aggregate face amount of bonds to which this subparagraph applies shall not exceed $200,000,000.

(I) Proceeds of an issue are described in this subparagraph if the issue is issued on behalf of a university established on August 6, 1872, for a project approved by the trustees thereof on November 11, 1985. The aggregate face amount of bonds to which this subparagraph applies shall not exceed $100,000,000.

(J) Proceeds of an issue are described in this subparagraph if—

(i) the issue is issued on behalf of a university for which the founding grant was signed on November 11, 1885, and

(ii) such bond is issued for the purpose of providing a Near West Campus Redevelopment Project and a Student Housing Project.

The aggregate face amount of bonds to which this subparagraph applies shall not exceed $105,000,000.

(J) Proceeds of an issue are described in this subparagraph if—

(i) they are the proceeds of advance refunding obligations issued on behalf of a university established on April 21, 1831, and

(ii) the application or other request for the issuance of such obligations was made to the appropriate State issuer before July 12, 1986.

The aggregate face amount of obligations to which this subparagraph applies shall not exceed $175,000,000.

(K) Proceeds of an issue are described in this subparagraph if—

(i) the issue is for the purpose of financing or refinancing costs associated with university facilities including 900 units of housing for students, faculty, and

Tax Reform Act of 1986

staff in up to two buildings and an office building containing up to 2,000 square feet of space, and

  (ii) a bond act authorizing the issuance of such bonds for such project was adopted on July 8, 1986, and such act under Federal law was required to be transmitted to Congress.

The aggregate face amount of obligations to which this subparagraph applies shall not exceed $150,000,000.

  (L) Proceeds of an issue are described in this subparagraph if such issue is for Cornell University in an aggregate face amount of not more than $150,000,000.

  (M) Proceeds of an issue are described in this subparagraph if—

  (i) such issue would not (if issued before August 16, 1986) be an industrial development bond (as defined in section 103(b)(2) of the 1954 Code), and

  (ii) such bonds were approved by city voters on January 19, 1985, for an art museum and 2 theaters.

The aggregate face amount of obligations to which this subparagraph applies shall not exceed $2,300,000.

  (N) Proceeds of an issue are described in this subparagraph if—

  (i) such issue is issued by a State dormitory authority on behalf of one or more universities described in section 501(c)(3) of the 1986 Code or a foundling hospital, and

  (ii) the application by the university for the issuance of such bond was made before October 27, 1985.

The aggregate face amount of bonds to which this subparagraph applies shall not exceed $150,000,000. In the case of bonds to which this paragraph applies, the requirements of section 148 and 149(d) of the 1986 Code shall be treated as included in section 103 of the 1954 Code and shall apply to such bonds.

  (O) Any bond to which section 145(b) of the 1986 Code does not apply by reason of this section shall be taken into account in determining whether such section applies to any later issue.

  (34) Arbitrage rebate.—Section 148(f) of the 1986 Code shall not apply to any period before October 1, 1990, with respect to any bond the proceeds of which are to be used to provide a high-speed rail system for the State of Ohio. The aggregate face amount of bonds to which this paragraph applies shall not exceed $2,000,000,000.

  (35) Extension of carryforward period.—

  (A) In the case of a carryforward under section 103(n)(10) of the 1954 Code of $170,000,000 of bond limit for calendar year 1984 for a project described in subparagraph (B), clause (i) of section 103(n)(10)(C) of the 1954 Code shall be applied by substituting "6 calendar years" for "3 calendar years", and such carryforward may be used by any authority designated by the State in which the facility is located.

  (B) A project is described in this subparagraph if—

  (i) such project is a facility for local furnishing of electricity described in section 645 of the Tax Reform Act of 1984, and

  (ii) construction of such facility commenced within the 3-year period following the calendar year in which the carryforward arose.

  (36) Power purchase bonds.—A bond issued to finance purchase of power from a power facility at a dam being renovated pursuant to P.L. 98-381 shall not be treated as a private activity bond if it would not be such under section 141(b)(1) and (2) of the 1986 Code if 25 percent were substituted for 10 percent and the provisions of section 141(b)(3), (4), and (5) of the 1986 Code did not apply. The aggregate face amount of bonds to which this paragraph applies shall not exceed $80,000,000.

  (37) Qualified mortgage bonds.—A bond issued as part of either of 2 issues no later than September 8, 1986, shall be treated as a qualified mortgage bond within the meaning of section 141(d)(1)(B) of the 1986 Code if it satisfies the requirements of section 103A of the 1954 Code and if the issues are issued by the two most populous cities in the Tar Heel State. The aggregate face amount of bonds to which this paragraph applies shall not exceed $4,000,000.

  (38) Exempt Facility Bonds.—A bond shall be treated as an exempt facility bond within the meaning of section 142(a) of the 1986 Code if it is issued to fund residential, office, retail, light industrial, recreational and parking development known as Tobacco Row. Such bond shall be subject to section 146 and sections 148 and 149 of the 1986 Code. The aggregate face amount of bonds to which this paragraph applies shall not exceed $100,000,000.

(39) **Certain wastewater treatment facility.**—A bond shall not be subject to the provisions of section 146 of the 1986 Code if it is issued to acquire and complete a wastewater treatment facility—

(A) which was organized by an inter-local agreement dated October 17, 1978,

(B) for which $78,143,557 has been spent as of July 31, 1986, and

(C) for which the first construction contract was let on February 27, 1981.

The aggregate face amount of bonds to which this paragraph applies shall not exceed $100,000,000.

(40) **Refunding of certain taxable debt.**—A bond issued to refinance taxable debt shall not be treated as a qualified 501(c)(3) bond within the meaning of section 141(d)(1)(G) of the 1986 Code if an authorizing resolution as adopted by the issuer on August 14, 1986 for St. Mary's Hospital. The aggregate face amount of bonds to which this paragraph applies shall not exceed $22,314,000.

(41) **Time to maturity for certain obligations.**—The requirement of section 147(b) of the 1986 Code shall apply to current refunding bonds issued with respect to two power facilities on which construction has been suspended by measuring the economic life of the facilities from the date of the refunding bonds if the facilities have not been placed in service as of the date of issuance of the refunding bonds. The aggregate face amount of bonds to which this paragraph applies shall not exceed $2,000,000,000.

(42) **Residential rental property.**—A bond issued to finance a residential rental project within the meaning of 103(b)(4) of the 1954 Code shall be treated as an exempt facility bond within the meaning of section 142(a)(7) of the 1986 Code if the county housing finance authority adopted an inducement resolution with respect to the project on May 8, 1985, and the project is located in Polk County, Florida. The aggregate face amount of bonds to which this paragraph applies shall not exceed $4,100,000.

(43) **Extension of advance refunding for certain facilities.**—Paragraph (4) of section 631(c) of the Tax Reform Act of 1984 is amended—

(A) by striking out the second sentence thereof,

(B) by adding at the end thereof the following new sentence: "In the case of refunding obligations not exceeding $100,000,000 issued by the Alabama State Docks Department, the first sentence of this paragraph shall be applied by substituting "December 31, 1987" for "December 31, 1984."

(44) **Pool bonds.**—The following amounts of pool bonds are exempt from the arbitrage rebate requirement of section 148(f) of the 1986 Code:

Pool	Maximum Bond Amount
Tennessee Utility Districts Pool	$80,000,000
New Mexico Hospitals Bond Pool	$35,000,000
Pennsylvania Local Government Investment Trust Pool	$375,000,000
Indiana Bond Bank Pool	$240,000,000
Hernando County, Florida Bond Pool	$300,000,000
Utah Municipal Finance Cooperative Pool	$262,000,000
North Carolina League of Municipalities Pool	$200,000,000
Kentucky Municipal League Bond Pool	$170,000,000
Kentucky Association of Counties Bond Pool	$100,000,000
Homewood Municipal Bond Pool	$50,000,000
Colorado Association of School Boards Pool	$300,000,000
Tennessee Municipal League Pooled Bonds	$75,000,000
Georgia Municipal Association Pool	$130,000,000

(45) **Certain carryforward elections.**—Notwithstanding any other provision of this title—

(A) In the case of a metropolitan service district created pursuant to State revised statutes, chapter 268, up to $100,000,000 unused 1985 bond authority may be carried forward to any year until 1989 (regardless of the date on which such carryforward election is made).

(B) If—

    (i) official action was taken by an industrial development board on September 16, 1985, with respect to the issuance of not more than $98,500,000, of waste water treatment revenue bonds, and

    (ii) an executive order of the governor granted a carryforward of State bond authority for such project on December 30, 1985,

such carryforward election shall be valid for any year through 1988. The aggregate face amount of obligations to which this subparagraph applies shall not exceed $98,500,000.

(46) Treatment of certain obligations to finance hydroelectric generating facility.—If

    (A) obligations are issued in an amount not exceeding $5,000,000 to finance the construction of a hydroelectric generating facility located on the North Fork of Cache Creek in Lake County, California, which was the subject of a preliminary resolution of the issuer of the obligations on June 29, 1982, or are issued to refund any of such obligations,

    (B) substantially all of the electrical power generated by such facility is to be sold to a nongovernmental person pursuant to a long-term power sales agreement in accordance with the Public Utility Regulatory Policies Act of 1978, and

    (C) the initially issued obligations are issued on or before December 31, 1986, and any of such refunding obligations are issued on or before December 31, 1996,

then the person referred to in subparagraph (B) shall not be treated as a principal user of such facilities by reason of such sales for purposes of subparagraphs (D) and (E) of section 103(b)(6) of the 1954 Code.

(47) Treatment of certain obligations to finance steam and electric cogeneration facility.—If—

    (A) obligations are issued on or before December 31, 1986, in an amount not exceeding $4,400,000 to finance a facility for the generation and transmission of steam and electricity having a maximum electrical capacity of approximately 5.3 megawatts and located within the City of San Jose, California, or are issued to refund any of such obligations,

    (B) substantially all of the electrical power generated by such facility that is not sold to an institution of higher education created by statute of the State of California is to be sold to a nongovernmental person pursuant to a long-term power sales agreement in accordance with the Public Utility Regulatory Policies Act of 1978, and

    (C) the initially issued obligations are issued on or before December 31, 1986, and any of such refunding obligations are issued on or before December 31, 1996,

then the nongovernmental person referred to in subparagraph (B) shall not be treated as a principal user of such facilities by reason of such sales for purposes of subparagraphs (D) and (E) of section 103(b)(6) of the Internal Revenue Code of 1954.

(48) Treatment of certain obligations.—A bond which is not an industrial development bond under section 103(b)(2) of the Internal Revenue Code of 1954 shall not be treated as a private activity bond for purposes of part IV of subchapter B of chapter 1 of the 1986 Code if 95 percent or more of the net proceeds of the issue of which such bond is a part are used to provide facilities described in either of the following subparagraphs:

    (A) A facility is described in this subparagraph if it is a governmentally-owned and operated State fair and exposition center with respect to which—

        (i) the 1985 session of the State legislature authorized revenue bonds to be issued in a maximum amount of $10,000,000, and

        (ii) a market feasibility study dated June 30, 1986, relating to a major capital improvemental program at the facility was prepared for the advisory board of the State fair and exposition center by a certified public accounting firm.

The aggregate face amount of obligations to which this subparagraph applies shall not exceed $10,000,000.

    (B) A facility is described in this subparagraph if it is a convention, trade, or spectator facility which is to be located in the State with respect to which subparagraph (O) applies and with respect to which feasibility and preliminary design consultants were hired on May 1, 1985 and October 31, 1985. The aggregate face amount of obligations to which this subparagraph applies shall not exceed $175,000,000.

(49) Transition rule for refunding certain housing bonds.—Sections 146 and 149(d) for the 1986 Code shall not apply to the refunding of any bond issued under section 11(b) of the Housing Act of 1937 before December 31, 1983, if—

(A) the bond has an original term to maturity of at least 40 years,

(B) the maturity date of the refunding bonds does not exceed the maturity date of the refunded bonds,

(C) the amount of the refunding bonds does not exceed the outstanding amount of the refunded bonds,

(D) the interest rate on the refunding bonds is lower than the interest rate of the refunded bonds, and

(E) the refunded bond is required to be redeemed not later than the earliest date on which such bond could be redeemed at par.

(50) Transition bonds subject to certain rules.—In the case of any bond to which any provision of this subsection applies—

(A) **Minimum Tax treatment.**—Any bond which, without regard to this section, would be a private activity bond (as defined in section 141(a) of the 1986 Code) shall be so treated for purposes of section 55 of such Code unless such bond would not be described in section 103(b)(2) or (o)(2) of the 1954 Code were such bond issued before August 16, 1986.

(B) **Certain restrictions apply.**—Except as otherwise expressly provided, sections 103 and 103A of the 1954 Code shall be applied as if the requirements of section 148 and subsection (d) and (g) of section 149 of the 1986 Code were included in each such section.

(51) Certain additional projects.—Section 141(a) of the 1986 Code shall be applied by substituting "25" for "10" each place it appears and by not applying sections 141(a)(3) and 141(c)(1)(B) to bonds substantially all of the proceeds are used for—

(A) A project is described in this subparagraph if it consists of a capital improvements program for a metropolitan sewer district, with respect to which a proposition was submitted to voters on August 7, 1984. The aggregate face amount of obligations to which this subparagraph applies shall not exceed $60,000,000.

(B) Facilities described in this subparagraph if it consists of additions, extensions, and improvements to the wastewater system for Lakeland, Florida. The aggregate face amount of obligations to which this subparagraph applies shall not exceed $20,000,000.

(C) A project is described in this subparagraph if it is the Central Valley Water Reclamation Project in Utah. The aggregate face amount of obligations to which this subparagraph applies shall not exceed $100,000,000.

(D) A project is described in this subparagraph if it is a project to construct approximately 26 miles of toll expressways, with respect to which any appeal to validation was filed July 11, 1986. The aggregate face amount of obligations to which this subparagraph applies shall not exceed $450,000,000.

(52) Termination.—This section shall not apply to any bond issued after December 31, 1990.

[For official explanation, see Committee Reports, ¶4058]

[¶2077]   SEC. 1318. DEFINITIONS, ETC., RELATING TO EFFECTIVE DATES AND TRANSITIONAL RULES.

For purposes of this subtitle—

(1) **1954 code.**—The term "1954 Code" means the Internal Revenue Code of 1954 as in effect on the day before the date of the enactment of this Act.

(2) **1986 code.**—The term "1986 Code" means the Internal Revenue Code of 1986 as amended by this Act.

(3) **Bond.**—The term "bond" includes any obligation.

(4) **Advance refund.**—A bond shall be treated as issued to advance refund another bond if it is issued more than 90 days before the redemption of the refunded bond.

(5) **Net proceeds.**—The term "net proceeds" has the meaning given such term by section 150(a) of the 1986 Code.

(6) **Continued application of the 1954 code.**—Nothing in this subtitle shall be construed to exempt any bond from any provision of the 1954 Code by reason of a delay in (or exemption from) the application of any amendment made by subtitle A.

(7) **Treatment as exempt facility.**—Any bond which is treated as an exempt facility bond by section 1316 or 1317 shall not fail to be so treated by reason of subsection (b) of section 142 of the 1986 Code.

[For official explanation, see Committee Reports, ¶4058]

[¶2078] SEC. 1421. INFORMATION NECESSARY FOR VALID SPECIAL USE VALUATION ELECTION.

(a) **In General.**—In the case of any decedent dying before January 1, 1986, if the executor—

(1) made an election under section 2032A of the Internal Revenue Code of 1954 on the return of tax imposed by section 2001 of such Code within the time prescribed for filing such return (including extensions thereof), and

(2) provided substantially all the information with respect to such election required on such return of tax,

such election shall be a valid election for purposes of section 2032A of such Code.

(b) **Executor Must Provide Information.**—An election described in subsection (a) shall not be valid if the Secretary of the Treasury or his delegate after the date of the enactment of this Act requests information from the executor with respect to such election and the executor does not provide such information within 90 days of receipt of such request.

(c) **Effective Date.**—The provisions of this section shall not apply to the estate of any decedent if before the date of the enactment of this Act the statute of limitations has expired with respect to—

(1) the return of tax imposed by section 2001 of the Internal Revenue Code of 1954, and

(2) the period during which a claim for credit or refund may be timely filed.

(d) **Special Rule for Certain Estate.**—Notwithstanding subsection (a)(2), the provisions of this section shall apply to the estate of an individual who died on January 30, 1984, and with respect to which—

(1) a Federal estate tax return was filed on October 30, 1984, electing current use valuation, and

(2) the agreement required under section 2032A was filed on November 9, 1984.

[For official explanation, see Committee Reports, ¶4065]

[¶2079] SEC. 1422. GIFT AND ESTATE TAX DEDUCTIONS FOR CERTAIN CONSERVATION EASEMENT DONATIONS.

* * * * * * * * * * *

(d) **Special Donations.**—If the Secretary of the Interior acquires by donation after December 31, 1986, a conservation easement (within the meaning of section 2(h) of S. 720, 99th Congress, 1st Session, as in effect on August 16, 1986), such donation shall qualify for treatment under section 2055(f) or 2522(d) of the Internal Revenue Code of 1954, as added by this section.

* * * * * * * * * * *

[For official explanation, see Committee Reports, ¶4066]

[¶2080] SEC. 1423. CONVEYANCE OF CERTAIN REAL AND PERSONAL PROPERTY OF DECEDENT TO CHARITABLE FOUNDATION TREATED AS CHARITABLE CONTRIBUTION.

Notwithstanding any other law or any rule of law (including res judicata, laches, or lapse of time), in the case of any real property or personal property located in Bangkok, Thailand, which—

(1) was owned by James H. W. Thompson at the time of his death, and

(2) has been transferred to the Jim Thompson Foundation (also known as the J.H.W. Thompson Foundation), a charitable foundation established in Thailand for the purpose of operating a museum consisting of such real and personal property,

such property shall be treated, for purposes of section 2055 of the Internal Revenue Code of 1954 (relating to deductions for transfers for public, charitable, and religious uses), as having been transferred as a bequest or a devise directly from the estate of James H. W. Thompson to the Jim Thompson Foundation and the value of such property included in the gross estate shall be deducted from the gross estate of James H. W. Thompson for purposes of the tax imposed by section 2001 of such Code.

[For official explanation, see Committee Reports, ¶4067]

[¶2081] SEC. 1433. EFFECTIVE DATES.

* * * * * * * * * * * *

(c) Repeal of Existing Tax on Generation-Skipping Transfers.—

(1) In general.—In the case of any tax imposed by chapter 13 of the Internal Revenue Code of 1954 (as in effect on the day before the date of the enactment of this Act), such tax (including interest, additions to tax, and additional amounts) shall not be assessed and if assessed, the assessment shall be abated, and if collected, shall be credited or refunded (with interest) as an overpayment.

(2) Waiver of statute of limitations.—If on the date of the enactment of this Act (or at any time within 1 year after such date of enactment) refund or credit of any overpayment of tax resulting from the application of paragraph (1) is barred by any law or rule of law, refund or credit of such overpayment shall, nevertheless, be made or allowed if claim therefore is filed before the date 1 year after the date of the enactment of this Act.

(d) Election for Certain Transfers Benefiting Grandchild.—

(1) In general.—For purposes of chapter 13 of the Internal Revenue Code of 1986 (as amended by this Act) and subsection (b) of this section, any transfer in trust for the benefit of a grandchild of a transferor shall be treated as a direct skip if—

    (A) the transfer occurs before the date of enactment of this Act,

    (B) the transfer would be a direct skip except for the fact that the trust instrument provides that, if the grandchild dies before vesting of the interest transferred, the interest is transferred to the grandchild's heir (rather than the grandchild's estate), and

    (C) an election under this subsection applies to such transfer.

Any transfer treated as a direct skip by reason of the preceding sentence shall be subject to Federal estate tax on the grandchild's death in the same manner as if the contingent gift over had been to the grandchild's estate.

(2) Election.—An election under paragraph (1) shall be made at such time and in such manner as the Secretary of the Treasury or his delegate may prescribe.

[For official explanation, see Committee Reports, ¶4068]

[¶2082] SEC. 1511. DIFFERENTIAL INTEREST RATE.

* * * * * * * * * * * *

(b) Coordination by Regulation.—The Secretary of the Treasury or his delegate may issue regulations to coordinate section 6621 of the Internal Revenue Code of 1954 (as amended by this section) with section 6601(f) of such Code. Such regulations shall not apply to any period after the date 3 years after the date of the enactment of this Act.

(c) Technical Amendments.—

* * * * * * * * * * * *

    (17) Section 1961(c)(1) of title 28, United States Code, is amended by striking out "a rate established under section 6621" and inserting in lieu thereof "the underpayment rate or overpayment rate (whichever is appropriate) established under section 6621".

    (18) Section 2411 of title 28, United States Code, is amended by striking out "an annual rate established under section 6621" and inserting in lieu thereof "the overpayment rate established under section 6621".

* * * * * * * * * * * *

[For official explanation, see Committee Reports, ¶4075]

[¶2083] SEC. 1543. WAIVER OF ESTIMATED PENALTIES FOR 1986 UNDERPAYMENTS ATTRIBUTABLE TO THIS ACT.

No addition to tax shall be made under section 6654 or 6655 of the Internal Revenue Code of 1986 (relating to failure to pay estimated tax) for any period before April 16, 1987 (March 16, 1987, in the case of a taxpayer subject to section 6655 of such Code), with respect to any underpayment, to the extent such underpayment was created or increased by any provision of this Act.

[For official explanation, see Committee Reports, ¶4089]

[¶2084] SEC. 1552. FAILURE TO PURSUE ADMINISTRATIVE REMEDIES.

* * * * * * * * * * * *

(c) Report.—The Secretary of the Treasury or his delegate and the Tax Court shall each prepare a report for 1987 and for each 2-calendar year period thereafter on the inventory of cases in the Tax Court and the measures to close cases more efficiently. Such reports shall be submitted to the Committee on Ways and Means of the House of Representatives and the Committee on Finance of the Senate.

[For official explanation, see Committee Reports, ¶4091]

[¶2085] SEC. 1567. CERTAIN RECORDKEEPING REQUIREMENTS.

(a) In General.—For purposes of section 132 and 274 of the Internal Revenue Code of 1954, use of an automobile by a special agent of the Internal Revenue Service shall be treated in the same manner as use of an automobile by an officer of any other law enforcement agency.

(b) Effective Date.—The provisions of this section shall take effect on January 1, 1985.

[For official explanation, see Committee Reports, ¶4105]

[¶2086] SEC. 1571. MODIFICATION OF TIPS ALLOCATION METHOD.

Effective for any payroll period beginning after December 31, 1986, an establishment may utilize the optional method of tips allocation described in the last sentence of section 31.6053-3(f)(1)(iv) of the Internal Revenue Regulations only if such establishment employs less than the equivalent of 25 full-time employees during each payroll period.

[For official explanation, see Committee Reports, ¶4109]

[¶2087] SEC. 1581. WITHHOLDING ALLOWANCES TO REFLECT NEW RATE SCHEDULES.

(a) In General.—The Secretary of the Treasury or his delegate shall modify the withholding schedules and withholding exemption certificates under section 3402 of the Internal Revenue Code of 1954 to better approximate actual tax liability under the amendments made by this Act.

* * * * * * * * * * * *

(c) Employer's Responsibility.—If an employee has not filed a revised withholding allowance certificate before October 1, 1987, the employer shall withhold income taxes from the employee's wages—
> (1) as if the employee claimed 1 withholding allowance, if the employee checked the "single" box in the employee's previous withholding allowance certificate, or
> (2) as if the employee claimed 2 withholding allowances, if the employee checked the "married" box on the employee's previous withholding allowance certificate.

[For official explanation, see Committee Reports, ¶4111]

[¶2088] SEC. 1582. REPORT ON RETURN-FREE SYSTEM.

(a) Report.—The Secretary of the Treasury or his delegate shall prepare a report on a return-free system for the Federal income tax of individuals. Such report shall include—
> (1) the identification of classes of individuals who would be permitted to use a return-free system,
> (2) how such a system would be phased in,
> (3) what additional resources the Internal Revenue Service would need to carry out such a system, and
> (4) the types of changes to the Internal Revenue Code of 1954 which would inhibit or enhance the use of such a system.

(b) **Due Date.**—The report under subsection (a) shall be submitted, not later than 6 months after the date of the enactment of this Act, to the Committee on Ways and Means of the House of Representatives and the Committee on Finance of the Senate.

[For official explanation, see Committee Reports, ¶4112]

[¶2089] SEC. 1605. TAX-EXEMPT STATUS FOR AN ORGANIZATION IN-TRODUCING INTO PUBLIC USE TECHNOLOGY DEVELOPED BY QUALIFIED ORGANIZATIONS.

(a) **In General.**—For purposes of the Internal Revenue Code of 1986, an organization shall be treated as an organization organized and operated exclusively for charitable purposes if such organization—

    (1) is organized and operated exclusively—

        (A) to provide for (directly or by arranging for and supervising the performance by independent contractors)—

            (i) reviewing technology disclosures from qualified organizations,

            (ii) obtaining protection for such technology through patents, copyrights, or other means, and

            (iii) licensing, sale, or other exploitation of such technology,

        (B) to distribute the income therefrom, to such qualified organizations after paying expenses and other amounts as agreed with the originating qualified organizations, and

        (C) to make research grants to such qualified organizations,

    (2) regularly provides the services and research grants described in paragraph (1) exclusively to 1 or more qualified organizations, except that research grants may be made to such qualified organizations through an organization which is controlled by 1 or more organizations each of which—

        (A) is an organization described in section 501(c)(3) of the Internal Revenue Code of 1986 or the income of which is excluded from taxation under section 115 of such Code, and

        (B) may be a recipient of the services or research grants described in paragraph (1),

    (3) derives at least 80 percent of its gross revenues from providing services to qualified organizations located in the same State as the State in which such organization has its principal office, and

    (4) was incorporated on July 20, 1981.

(b) **Qualified Organizations.**—For purposes of this section, the term "qualified organization" has the same meaning given to such term by subparagraphs (A) and (B) of section 41(e)(6) (as redesignated by section 231(d)(2)) of the Internal Revenue Code of 1986.

(c) **Treatment of Investment in a Technology Transfer Service Organization.**—

    (1) **In general.**—A qualified investment made by a private foundation in an organization described in subparagraph (C) shall be treated as an investment described in section 4944(c) of the Internal Revenue Code of 1986 and shall not result in imposition of taxes under section 4941, 4943, 4944, 4945, or 507(c) of such Code.

    (2) **Definitions.**—For purposes of this subsection—

        (A) Qualified investment.—The term "qualified investment" means a transfer by a private foundation of—

            (i) all of the patents, copyrights, know-how, and other technology or rights thereto of the private foundation, and

            (ii) investment assets, net receivables and cash not exceeding $35,000,000,

to such organization in exchange for debt.

        (B) Private foundation.—The term "private foundation" means—

            (i) a nonprofit corporation which was incorporated before 1913 which is described in sections 501(c)(3) and 509(a) of such Code, and which is exempt from taxation under section 501(a) of such Code, and

            (ii) the principal purposes of which are to support research by and to provide technology transfer services to organizations described in section 170(b)(1)(A) of such Code—

                (I) which are exempt from taxation under section 501(a) of such Code, or

                (II) the income of which is excluded from taxation under section 115 of such Code.

(C) Technology transfer organization.—The term "technology transfer organization" means a corporation established after the date of the enactment of this Act—

(i) which is organized and operated to advance the public welfare through the provision of technology transfer services to research organizations,

(ii) no part of the net earnings of which inures to the benefit of, or is distributable to, any private shareholder, individual, or entity, other than a private foundation or research organization,

(iii) which does not participate in, or intervene in (including the publishing or distributing of statements) any political campaign on behalf of any candidate for public office,

(iv) no substantial part of the activities of which is carrying on propaganda, or otherwise attempting, to influence legislation, and

(v) upon liquidation or dissolution of which all of its net assets can be distributed only to research organizations.

(d) **Effective Date.**—This section shall take effect on the date of the enactment of this Act.

[For official explanation, see Committee Reports, ¶4118]

[¶2090] SEC. 1607. TRANSITION RULE FOR ACQUISITION INDEBTEDNESS WITH RESPECT TO CERTAIN LAND.

For purposes of applying section 514(c) of the Internal Revenue Code of 1986, with respect to a disposition during calendar year 1986 or calendar year 1987 of land acquired during calendar year 1984, the term "acquisition indebtedness" does not include indebtedness incurred in connection with bonds issued after January 1, 1984, and before July 19, 1984, on behalf of an organization which is a community college and which is described in section 511(a)(2)(B) of such Code.

[¶2091] SEC. 1608. TREATMENT OF CERTAIN AMOUNTS PAID TO OR FOR THE BENEFIT OF CERTAIN INSTITUTIONS OF HIGHER EDUCATION.

(a) **In General.**—Amounts paid by a taxpayer to or for the benefit of an institution of higher education described in paragraph (1) or (2) of subsection (b) (other than amounts separately paid for tickets) which would otherwise qualify as a charitable contribution within the meaning of section 170 of the Internal Revenue Code of 1986 shall not be disqualified because such taxpayer receives the right to seating or the right to purchase seating in an athletic stadium of such institution.

(b) **Described Insitutions.**—

(1) An institution is described in this paragraph if—

(A) such institution was mandated by a State constitution in 1876,

(B) such institution was established by a State legislature in March 1881, and is located in a State capital pursuant to a statewide election in September 1981,

(C) the campus of such institution formally opened on September 15, 1883, and

(D) such institution is operated under the authority of a 9-member board of regents appointed by the governor.

(2) An institution is described in this paragraph if such institution has an athletic stadium—

(A) the plans for renovation of which were approved by a board of supervisors in December 1984, and reaffirmed by such board in December 1985 and January 1986, and

(B) the plans for renovation of which were approved by a State board of ethics for public employees in February 1986.

(c) **Effective Date.**—The provisions of this section shall apply to amounts paid in taxable years beginning on or after January 1, 1984.

[¶2092] SEC. 1701. EXTENSION AND MODIFICATION OF TARGETED JOBS CREDIT.

* * * * * * * * * * * *

(d) **Extension of Authorization.**—Paragraph (2) of section 261(f) of the Economic Recovery Tax Act of 1981 is amended by striking out "fiscal years 1983, 1984, and 1985" and inserting in lieu thereof "fiscal years 1983, 1984, 1985, 1986, 1987, and 1988".

(e) **Effective Date.**—The amendments made by this section shall apply with respect to individuals who begin work for the employer after December 31, 1985.

[For official explanation, see Committee Reports, ¶4123]

〖¶2093〗 SEC. 1703. GASOLINE TAX GENERALLY COLLECTED AT TERMINAL LEVEL.

* * * * * * * * * * * *

(f) Floor Stock Taxes.—

(1) In general.—On gasoline subject to tax under section 4081 of the Internal Revenue Code of 1986 which, on January 1, 1988, is held by a dealer for sale, and with respect to which no tax has been imposed under such section, there is hereby imposed a floor stocks tax at the rate of 9 cents a gallon.

(2) Overpayment of floor stocks taxes.—Section 6416 of such Code shall apply in respect of the floor stocks taxes imposed by this section, so as to entitle, subject to all provisions of such section, any person paying such floor stocks taxes to a credit or refund thereof for any reasons specified in such section.

(3) Due date of taxes.—The taxes imposed by this subsection shall be paid before February 16, 1988.

(4) Transfer of floor stocks taxes to Highway Trust Fund.—For purposes of determining the amount transferred to the Highway Trust Fund for any period, the taxes imposed by this subsection shall be treated as if they were imposed by section 4081 of the Internal Revenue Code of 1986.

(5) Definitions and special rule.—For purposes of this subsection—
    (A) Dealer.—The term "dealer" includes a wholesaler, jobber, distributor, or retailer.
    (B) Held by a dealer.—Gasoline shall be considered as "held by a dealer" if title thereto has passed to such dealer (whether or not delivery to him has been made) and if for purposes of consumption title to such gasoline or possession thereof has not at any time been transferred to any person other than a dealer.
    (C) Gasoline.—The term "gasoline" has the same meaning given to such term by section 4082(a) of the Internal Revenue Code of 1986.

(g) Study of Evasion of Gasoline Tax.—

(1) In general.—The Secretary of the Treasury or his delegate shall conduct a study of the incidence of the evasion of the gasoline tax.

(2) Report.—The report of the study under paragraph (1) shall be submitted, not later than December 31, 1986, to the Committee on Ways and Means of the House of Representatives and the Committee on Finance of the Senate.

* * * * * * * * * * * *

[For official explanation, see Committee Reports, ¶4125]

〖¶2094〗 SEC. 1704. EXEMPTION FROM SOCIAL SECURITY COVERAGE FOR CERTAIN CLERGY.

* * * * * * * * * * * *

(b) Revocation of Exemption.—

(1) In general.—Notwithstanding section 1402(e)(3) of the Internal Revenue Code of 1986, as redesignated by subsection (a)(2)(B) of this section, any exemption which has been received under section 1402(e)(1) of such Code by a duly ordained, commissioned, or licensed minister of a church, a member of a religious order, or a Christian Science practitioner, and which is effective for the taxable year in which this Act is enacted, may be revoked by filing an application therefor (in such form and manner, and with such official, as may be prescribed in regulations made under chapter 2 of subtitle A of such Code), if such application is filed—
    (A) before the applicant becomes entitled to benefits under section 202(a) or 223 of the Social Security Act (without regard to section 202(j)(1) or 223(b) of such Act), and
    (B) no later than the due date of the Federal income tax return (including any extension thereof) for the applicant's first taxable year beginning after the date of the enactment of this Act.
Any such revocation shall be effective (for purposes of chapter 2 of subtitle A of the Internal Revenue Code of 1986 and title II of the Social Security Act), as specified in

Act §1704(b)(1) ¶2094

the application, either with respect to the applicant's first taxable year ending on or after the date of the enactment of this Act or with respect to the applicant's first taxable year beginning after such date, and for all succeeding taxable years; and the applicant for any such revocation may not thereafter again file application for an exemption under such section 1402(e)(1). If the application is filed on or after the due date of the Federal income tax return for the applicant's first taxable year ending on or after the date of the enactment of this Act and is effective with respect to that taxable year, it shall include or be accompanied by payment in full of an amount equal to the total of the taxes that would have been imposed by section 1401 of the Internal Revenue Code of 1986 with respect to all of the applicant's income derived in that taxable year which would have constituted net earnings from self-employment for purposes of chapter 2 of subtitle A of such Code (notwithstanding paragraph (4) or (5) of section 1402(c) of such Code) but for the exemption under section 1402(e)(1) of such Code.

(2) **Effective date.**—Paragraph (1) of this subsection shall apply with respect to service performed (to the extent specified in such paragraph) in taxable years ending on or after the date of the enactment of this Act and with respect to monthly insurance benefits payable under title II of the Social Security Act on the basis of the wages and self-employment income of any individual for months in or after the calendar year in which such individual's application for revocation (as described in such paragraph) is effective (and lump-sum death payments payable under such title on the basis of such wages and self-employment income in the case of deaths occurring in or after such calendar year).

[For official explanation, see Committee Reports, ¶4126]

[¶2095] SEC. 1705. APPLICABILITY OF UNEMPLOYMENT COMPENSATION TAX TO CERTAIN SERVICES PERFORMED FOR CERTAIN INDIAN TRIBAL GOVERNMENTS.

(a) **In General.**—For purposes of the Federal Unemployment Tax Act, service performed in the employ of a qualified Indian tribal government shall not be treated as employment (within the meaning of section 3306 of such Act) if it is service—

(1) which is performed—

(A) before, on, or after the date of the enactment of this Act, but before January 1, 1988, and

(B) during a period in which the Indian tribal government is not covered by a State unemployment compensation program, and

(2) with respect to which the tax imposed under the Federal Unemployment Tax Act has not been paid.

(b) **Definition.**—For purposes of this section, the term "qualified Indian tribal government" means an Indian tribal government the service for which is not covered by a State unemployment compensation program on June 11, 1986.

[For official explanation, see Committee Reports, ¶4127]

[¶2096] SEC. 1706. TREATMENT OF CERTAIN TECHNICAL PERSONNEL.

(a) **In General.**—Section 530 of the Revenue Act of 1978 is amended by adding at the end thereof the following new subsection:

"(d) **Exception.**—This section shall not apply in the case of an individual who, pursuant to an arrangement between the taxpayer and another person, provides services for such other person as an engineer, designer, drafter, computer programmer, systems analyst, or other similarly skilled worker engaged in a similar line of work."

(b) **Effective Date.**—The amendment made by this section shall apply to remuneration paid and services rendered after December 31, 1986.

[For official explanation, see Committee Reports, ¶4128]

[¶2097] SEC. 1709. AMENDMENT TO THE REINDEER INDUSTRY ACT OF 1937.

(a) **Tax Exemption for Reindeer-Related Income.**—Before the period at the end of the first sentence of section 8 of the Act of September 1, 1937 (50 Stat. 900, chapter 897), insert the following: ": Provided, That during the period of the trust, income derived directly from the sale of reindeer and reindeer products as provided in this Act shall be exempt from Federal income taxation".

(b) **Effective Date.**—The amendment made by this section shall take effect as if originally included in the provision of the Act of September 1, 1937, to which such amendment relates.

[For official explanation, see Committee Reports, ¶4131]

[¶2098] SEC. 1710. QUALITY CONTROL STUDIES.

Section 12301 of the Consolidated Omnibus Reconciliation Act of 1985 is amended—

(1) by striking out "of the enactment of this Act" in subsection (a)(3) and inserting in lieu thereof "the Secretary and the National Academy of Sciences enter into the contract required under paragraph (2)";

(2) by striking out "18 months after the date of the enactment of this Act" in subsection (c)(1) and inserting in lieu thereof "6 months after the date on which the results of both studies required under subsection (a)(3) have been reported".

[For official explanation, see Committee Reports, ¶4132]

[¶2099] SEC. 1711. ADOPTION ASSISTANCE AGREEMENTS UNDER ADOPTION ASSISTANCE PROGRAM: PAYMENT OF NONRECURRING EXPENSES RELATED TO ADOPTIONS OF CHILDREN WITH SPECIAL NEEDS.

(a) **In General.**—Section 473(a) of the Social Security Act is amended—

(1) by redesignating paragraphs (2), (3), and (4) as paragraphs (3), (4), and (5), respectively, and

(2) by striking out all of paragraph (1) through "adopt a child who—" and inserting in lieu thereof the following:

"(1)(A) Each State having a plan approved under this part shall enter into adoption assistance agreements (as defined in section 475(3)) with the adoptive parents of children with special needs.

(B) Under any adoption assistance agreement entered into by a State with parents who adopt a child with special needs, the State—

"(i) shall make payments of nonrecurring adoption expenses incurred by or on behalf of such parents in connection with the adoption of such child, directly through the State agency or through another public or nonprofit private agency, in amounts determined under paragraph (3), and

"(ii) in any case where the child meets the requirements of paragraph (2), may make adoption assistance payments to such parents, directly through the State agency or through another public or nonprofit private agency, in amounts so determined.

"(2) For purposes of paragraph (1)(B)(ii), a child meets the requirements of this paragraph if such child—

(b) **Definition and Payment of Nonrecurring Adoption Expenses.**—Section 473(a) of the Social Security Act, as amended by subsection (a) of this section, is further amended by adding at the end thereof the following new paragraph:

"(6)(A) For purposes of paragraph (1)(B)(i), the term 'nonrecurring adoption expenses' means reasonable and necessary adoption fees, court costs, attorney fees, and other expenses which are directly related to the legal adoption of a child with special needs and which are not incurred in violation of State or Federal law.

"(B) A State's payment of nonrecurring adoption expenses under an adoption assistance agreement shall be treated as an expenditure made for the proper and efficient administration of the State plan for purposes of section 474(a)(3)(B)."

(c) **Technical and Conforming Amendments.—**

(1) The first sentence of section 470 of the Social Security Act is amended by striking out "foster care" and all that follows down through "title XVI)" and inserting in lieu thereof the following: "foster care and transitional independent living programs for children who otherwise would be eligible for assistance under the State's plan approved under part A and adoption assistance for children with special needs".

(2) Paragraphs (1) and (11) of section 471(a) of such Act are each amended by striking out "adoption assistance payments" and inserting in lieu thereof "adoption assistance".

(3) Section 473(a)(3) of such Act, as redesignated by subsection (a)(1) of this section, is amended—

(A) by striking out "adoption assistance payments" in the first sentence and inserting in lieu thereof "payments to be made in any case under clauses (i) and (ii) of paragraph (1)(B)", and

(B) by inserting after "the adoption assistance payment" the first place it appears in the second sentence the following: "made under clause (ii) of paragraph (1)(B)".

(4) Section 473(a)(5) of such Act, as so redesignated, is amended by striking out ", pursuant to an interlocutory decree, shall be eligible for adoption assistance payments under this subsection," and inserting in lieu thereof "in accordance with applicable State and local law shall be eligible for such payments,".

(5) Section 473(b)(1)(A) of such Act is amended by striking out "subsection (a)(1)" and inserting in lieu thereof "subsection(a)(2)".

(6) Section 475(3) of such Act is amended by striking out clause (A) and inserting in lieu thereof the following: "(A) specifies the nature and amount of any payments, services, and assistance to be provided under such agreement, and".

(d) **Effective Date.**—The amendments made by this section shall apply only with respect to expenditures made after December 31, 1986.

[For official explanation, see Committee Reports, ¶4133]

[¶2100] SEC. 1800. COORDINATION WITH OTHER TITLES.

For purposes of applying the amendments made by any title of this Act other than this title, the provisions of this title shall be treated as having been enacted immediately before the provisions of such other titles.

[¶2101] SEC. 1801. AMENDMENTS RELATED TO DEFERRAL OF CERTAIN TAX REDUCTIONS.

(a) **Amendments Related to Section 12 of the Act.—**

(1) **Election out of transitional rules.**—Paragraph (1) of section 12(c) of the Tax Reform Act of 1984 (relating to finance lease provisions) is amended by adding at the end thereof the following new sentence:

"The preceding sentence shall not apply to any property with respect to which an election is made under this sentence at such time after the date of the enactment of the Tax Reform Act of 1986 as the Secretary of the Treasury or his delegate may prescribe."

(2) **Treatment of certain farm finance leases.—**

(A) In general.—If—

(i) any partnership or grantor trust is the lessor under a specified agreement,

(ii) such partnership or grantor trust met the requirements of section 168(f)(8)(C)(i) of the Internal Revenue Code of 1954 (relating to special rules for finance leases) when the agreement was entered into, and

(iii) a person other than a C corporation became a partner in such partnership (or a beneficiary in such trust) before September 26, 1985,

then, for purposes of applying the revenue laws of the United States in respect to such agreement, the portion of the property allocable to partners (or beneficiaries) not described in clause (iii) shall be treated as if it were subject to a separate agreement and the portion of such property allocable to the partner or beneficiary described in clause (iii) shall be treated as if it were subject to a separate agreement.

(B) Specified agreement.—For purposes of subparagraph (A), the term "specified agreement" means an agreement to which subparagraph (B) of section 209(d) of the Tax Equity and Fiscal Responsibility Act of 1982 applies which is—

(i) an agreement dated as of December 20, 1982, as amended and restated as of February 1, 1983, involving approximately $8,734,000 of property at December 31, 1983,

(ii) an agreement dated as of December 15, 1983, as amended and restated as of January 3, 1984, involving approximately $13,199,000 of property at December 31, 1984, or

(iii) an agreement dated as of October 25, 1984, as amended and restated as of December 1, 1984, involving approximately $966,000 of property at December 31, 1984.

* * * * * * * * * * * *

(c) **Amendments Related to Section 27 of the Act.—**

* * * * * * * * * * * *

(3) Paragraph (7) of section 27(b) of the Tax Reform Act of 1984 (relating to floor stocks tax on distilled spirits) is amended by adding at the end thereof the following new subparagraph:

"(F) Treatment of distilled spirits in foreign trade zones.—Notwithstanding the Act of June 18, 1934 (48 Stat. 998, 19 U.S.C. 81a) or any other provision of law, distilled spirits which are located in a foreign trade zone on October 1, 1985, shall be subject to the tax imposed by paragraph (1) and shall be treated for purposes of this subsection as held on such date for sale if—

"(i) internal revenue taxes have been determined, or customs duties liquidated, with respect to such distilled spirits before such date pursuant to a request made under the first proviso of section 3(a) of such Act, or

"(ii) such distilled spirits are held on such date under the supervision of customs pursuant to the second proviso of such section 3(a).

Under regulations prescribed by the Secretary, provisions similar to sections 5062 and 5064 of such Code shall apply to distilled spirits with respect to which tax is imposed by paragraph (1) by reason of this subparagraph."

[For official explanation, see Committee Reports, ¶4135]

[¶2102] SEC. 1802. AMENDMENTS RELATED TO TAX-EXEMPT ENTITY LEASING PROVISIONS.

(a) **Amendments Relating to Section 31 of the Act.—**

*　*　*　*　*　*　*　*　*　*　*　*

(2) **Treatment of certain previously tax-exempt organizations.—**

*　*　*　*　*　*　*　*　*　*　*　*

(F) Clause (i)(I) of section 31(g)(16)(C) of the Tax Reform Act of 1984 (defining exempt arbitrage profits) is amended by striking out "section 168(j)(4)(E)(i)(I)" and inserting in lieu thereof "section 168(j)(4)(E)(i)".

*　*　*　*　*　*　*　*　*　*　*　*

(10) **Effective date provisions.—**

(A) Subparagraph (B) of section 31(g)(3) of the Tax Reform Act of 1984 is amended by striking out "The amendments made by this section" and inserting in lieu thereof "Paragraph (9) of section 168(j) of the Internal Revenue Code of 1954 (as added by this section)".

(B) Effective with respect to property placed in service by the taxpayer after July 18, 1984, clause (ii) of section 31(g)(15)(D) of the Tax Reform Act of 1984 (relating to certain aircraft) is amended to read as follows:

"(ii) such aircraft is originally placed in service by such foreign person or entity (or its successor in interest under the contract) after May 23, 1983, and before January 1, 1986."

(C) Paragraph (4) of section 31(g) of the Tax Reform Act of 1984 is amended by adding at the end thereof the following new subparagraph:

"(C) Special rule for credit unions.—In the case of any property leased to a credit union pursuant to a written binding contract with an expiration date of December 31, 1984, which was entered into by such organization on August 23, 1984—

"(i) such credit union shall not be treated as an agency or instrumentality of the United States; and

"(ii) clause (ii) of subparagraph (A) shall be applied by substituting 'January 1, 1987' for 'January 1, 1985'."

(D)(i) Clause (ii) of section 31(g)(20)(B) of the Tax Reform Act of 1984 (defining substantial improvement) is amended by striking out subclauses (I) and (II) and inserting in lieu thereof the following:

"(I) by substituting 'property' for 'building' each place it appears therein,

"(II) by substituting '20 percent' for '25 percent' in clause (ii) thereof, and

"(III) without regard to clause (iii) thereof."

(ii) The amendment made by clause (i) shall not apply to any property if—

(I) on or before March 28, 1985, the taxpayer (or a predecessor in interest under the contract) or the tax-exempt entity entered into a written binding contract to acquire, construct, or rehabilitate the property, or

(II)   the taxpayer or the tax-exempt entity began the construction, reconstruction, or rehabilitation of the property on or before March 28, 1985.

(E)   Paragraph (4) of section 31(g) of the Tax Reform Act of 1984 is amended by adding at the end thereof the following new subparagraphs:

"(D)   Special rule for Greenville Auditorium Board.—For purposes of this paragraph, significant official governmental action taken by the Greenville County Auditorium Board of Greenville, South Carolina, before May 23, 1983, shall be treated as significant official governmental action with respect to the coliseum facility subject to a binding contract to lease which was in effect on January 1, 1985.

"(E)   Treatment of certain historic structures.—If—

"(i)   On June 16, 1982, the legislative body of the local governmental unit adopted a bond ordinance to provide funds to renovate elevators in a deteriorating building owned by the local governmental unit and listed in the National Register, and

"(ii)   the chief executive officer of the local governmental unit, in connection with the renovation of such building, made an application on June 1, 1983, to a State agency for a Federal historic preservation grant and made an application on June 17, 1983, to the Economic Development Administration of the United States Department of Commerce for a grant,

the requirements of clauses (i) and (ii) of subparagraph (A) shall be treated as met."

(F)   Subparagraph (H) of section 31(g)(17) of the Tax Reform Act of 1984 is amended by adding at the end thereof the following new sentence: "In the case of Clemson University, the preceding sentence applies only to the Continuing Education Center and the component housing project."

(G)   Subparagraph (L) of section 31(g)(17) of the Tax Reform Act of 1984 is amended by adding at the end thereof the following:

"Property is described in this subparagraph if such property was leased to a tax-exempt entity pursuant to a lease recorded in the Registry of Deeds of Essex County, New Jersey, on May 7, 1984, and a deed of such property was recorded in the Registry of Deeds of Essex County, New Jersey, on May 7, 1985."

(b)   Amendments Related to Section 32 of the Act.—

* * * * * * * * * * *

(2)   Subsection (c) of section 32 of the Tax Reform Act of 1984 is amended by striking out "section 168(f)(13)" and inserting in lieu thereof "section 168(f)(14)".

[For official explanation, see Committee Reports, ¶4136]

[¶2103]   SEC. 1803.   AMENDMENTS RELATED TO TREATMENT OF BONDS AND OTHER DEBT INSTRUMENTS.

(a)   Amendments Related to Section 41 of the Act.—

* * * * * * * * * * *

(9)   **Treatment of transfers of land between related parties.**—In the case of any sale or exchange before July 1, 1985, to which section 483(f) of the Internal Revenue Code of 1954 (as in effect on the day before the date of the enactment of Public Law 99-121) applies, such section shall be treated as providing that the discount rate to be used for purposes of section 483(c)(1) of such Code shall be 6 percent, compounded semiannually.

* * * * * * * * * * *

(b)   Amendments Related to Section 44 of the Act.—

(1)   **Clarification of transitional rule for purposes of imputed interest rules.**—Paragraph (4) of section 44(b) of the Tax Reform Act of 1984 (relating to special rules for sales before July 1, 1985), as added by section 2 of Public Law 98-612, is amended—

(A)   by striking out "before July 1, 1985" in subparagraph (A) and inserting in lieu thereof "after December 31, 1984, and before July 1, 1985",

(B)   by striking out "before July 1, 1985" in the paragraph heading and inserting in lieu thereof "after December 31, 1984, and before July 1, 1985", and

(C)   by adding at the end thereof the following new subparagraph:

"(G)   Clarification of application of this paragraph, etc.—This paragraph and paragraphs (5), (6), and (7) shall apply only in the case of sales or exchanges to which section 1274 or 483 of the Internal Revenue Code of 1954 (as amended by section 41) applies."

(2) **Clarification of interest accrual, etc.**—Subparagraph (A) of section 44(b)(3) of the Tax Reform Act of 1984 is amended by striking out "and before January 1, 1985," each place it appears.

(3) **Exception for binding contracts.**—Subparagraph (B) of section 44(b)(3) of the Tax Reform Act of 1984 is amended to read as follows:

"(B) Exception for binding contracts.—

"(i) Subparagraph (A)(i)(I) shall not apply to any sale or exchange pursuant to a written contract which was binding on March 1, 1984, and at all times thereafter before the sale or exchange.

"(ii) Subparagraph (A)(i)(II) shall not apply to any sale or exchange pursuant to a written contract which was binding on June 8, 1984, and at all times thereafter before the sale or exchange."

(4) **Clerical amendment.**—Clause (ii) of section 44(b)(6)(B) of the Tax Reform Act of 1984 (as added by section 2 of Public Law 98-612) is amended by striking out "greater than" and inserting in lieu thereof "not greater than".

(5) **Clarification of effective date for repeal of capital asset requirement.**—Subsection (g) of section 44 of the Tax Reform Act of 1984 is amended by striking out "before December 31, 1984" and inserting in lieu thereof "on or before December 31, 1984".

[For official explanation, see Committee Reports, ¶4137]

〔¶2104〕 SEC. 1804. AMENDMENTS RELATED TO CORPORATE PROVISIONS.

* * * * * * * * * * * *

(b) **Amendments Related to Section 53 and Section 54 of the Act.**—

* * * * * * * * * * * *

(2) **Effective date for related person provisions.**—Paragraph (3) of section 53(e) of the Tax Reform Act of 1984 (relating to effective date for related person provisions) is amended to read as follows:

"(3) **Related person provisions.**—

"(A) In General.—Except as otherwise provided in subparagraph (B), the amendment made by subsection (c) shall take effect on July 18, 1984.

"(B) Special rule for purposes of section 265(2).—The amendment made by subsection (c) insofar as it relates to section 265(2) of the Internal Revenue Code of 1954 shall apply to—

"(i) term loans made after July 18, 1984, and

"(ii) demand loans outstanding after July 18, 1984 (other than any loan outstanding on July 18, 1984, and repaid before September 18, 1984).

"(C) Treatment of renegotiations, etc.—For purposes of this paragraph, any loan renegotiated, extended, or revised after July 18, 1984, shall be treated as a loan made after such date.

"(D) Definition of term and demand loans.—For purposes of this paragraph, the term 'demand loan' and 'term loan' have the respective meanings given such terms by paragraphs (5) and (6) of section 7872(f) of the Internal Revenue Code of 1954, except that the second sentence of such paragraph (5) shall not apply."

(3) **Special rule for certain distributions before January 1, 1988.**—Paragraph (3) of section 54 of the Tax Reform Act of 1984 (relating to exceptions for distributions before January 1, 1985, to 80-percent corporate shareholders) is amended by adding at the end thereof the following new subparagraph:

"(D) Special rule for certain distributions before January 1, 1988.—

"(i) In general.—In the case of a transaction to which this subparagraph applies, subparagraph (A) shall be applied by substituting '1988' for '1985' and the amendments made by subtitle D of title VI shall not apply.

"(ii) Transaction to which subparagraph applies.—This subparagraph applies to a transaction in which a Delaware corporation which was incorporated on May 31, 1927, and which was acquired by the transferee on December 9, 1968, transfers to the transferee stock in a corporation—

"(I) with respect to which such Delaware corporation is a 100-percent corporate shareholder, and

"(II) which is a Tennessee corporation which was incorporated on October 5, 1981, and which is a successor to an Indiana corporation which was incorporated on June 28, 1946, and acquired by the transferee on December 9, 1968."

(e) Amendments Related to Section 60 of the Act.—

* * * * * * * * * * * *

(2) **Treatment of certain corporations affiliated on June 22, 1984.**—Paragraph (2) of section 60(b) of the Tax Reform Act of 1984 (relating to special rule for corporations affiliated on June 22, 1984) is amended by adding at the end thereof the following new sentence: "The preceding sentence shall cease to apply as of the first day after June 22, 1984, on which such corporation does not qualify as a member of such group under section 1504(a) of the Internal Revenue Code of 1954 (as in effect on the day before the date of the enactment of this Act)."

(3) **Treatment of certain sell-downs after June 22, 1984.**—Paragraph (3) of section 60(b) of the Tax Reform Act of 1984 (relating to special rule not to apply to certain sell-downs after June 22, 1984) is amended to read as follows:

"(3) **Special rule not to apply to certain sell-downs after June 22, 1984.**—If—

"(A) the requirements of paragraph (2) are satisfied with respect to a corporation,

"(B) more than a de minimis amount of the stock of such corporation—

"(i) is sold or exchanged (including in a redemption), or

"(ii) is issued,

after June 22, 1984 (other than in the ordinary course of business), and

"(C) the requirements of the amendment made by subsection (a) are not satisfied after such sale, exchange, or issuance,

then the amendment made by subsection (a) shall apply for purposes of determining whether such corporation continues to be a member of the group. The preceding sentence shall not apply to any transaction if such transaction does not reduce the percentage of the fair market value of the stock of the corporation referred to in the preceding sentence held by members of the group determined without regard to this paragraph."

(4) **Treatment of certain corporations affiliated on June 22, 1984, etc.**—Subsection (b) of section 60 of the Tax Reform Act of 1984 is amended by striking out paragraph (5) and inserting in lieu thereof the following new paragraphs:

"(5) **Native corporations.—**

"(A) In the case of a Native Corporation established under the Alaska Native Claims Settlement Act (43 U.S.C. 1601 et seq.), or a corporation all of whose stock is owned directly by such a corporation, during any taxable year (beginning after the effective date of these amendments and before 1992), or any part thereof, in which the Native Corporation is subject to the provisions of section 7(h)(1) of such Act (43 U.S.C. 1606(h)(1))—

"(i) the amendment made by subsection (a) shall not apply, and

"(ii) the requirements for affiliation under section 1504(a) of the Internal Revenue Code of 1986 before the amendment made by subsection (a) shall be applied solely according to the provisions expressly contained therein, without regard to escrow arrangements, redemption right, or similar provisions.

"(B) Except as provided in subparagraph (C), during the period described in subparagraph (A), no provision of the Internal Revenue Code of 1986 (including sections 269 and 482) or principle of law shall apply to deny the benefit or use of losses incurred or credits earned by a corporation described in subparagraph (A) to the affiliated group of which the Native Corporation is the common parent.

"(C) Losses incurred or credits earned by a corporation described in subparagraph (A) shall be subject to the general consolidated return regulations, including the provisions relating to separate return limitation years, and to sections 382 and 383 of the Internal Revenue Code of 1986.

"(D) Losses incurred and credits earned by a corporation which is affiliated with a corporation described in subparagraph (A) shall be treated as having been incurred or earned in a separate return limitation year, unless the corporation incurring the losses or earning the credits satisfies the affiliation requirements of section 1504(a) without application of subparagraph (A).

"(6) **Treatment of certain corporations affiliated on June 22, 1984.**—In the case of an affiliated group which—

"(A)   has as its common parent a Minnesota corporation incorporated on April 23, 1940, and

"(B)   has a member which is a New York corporation incorporated on November 13, 1969,

for purposes of determining whether such New York corporation continues to be member of such group, paragraph (2) shall be applied by substituting for 'January 1, 1988,' the earlier of January 1, 1994, or the date on which the voting power of the preferred stock in such New York corporation terminates.

"(7)   **Election to have amendments apply for years beginning after 1983.**—If the common parent of any group makes an election under this paragraph, notwithstanding any other provision of this subsection, the amendments made by subsection (a) shall apply to such group for taxable years beginning after December 31, 1983. Any such election, once made, shall be irrevocable.

"(8)   **Treatment of certain affiliated groups.**—If—

"(A)   a corporation (hereinafter in this paragraph referred to as the 'parent') was incorporated in 1968 and filed consolidated returns as the parent of an affiliated group for each of its taxable years ending after 1969 and before 1985,

"(B)   another corporation (hereinafter in this paragraph referred to as the 'subsidiary') became a member of the parent's affiliated group in 1978 by reason of a recapitalization pursuant to which the parent increased its voting interest in the subsidiary from not less than 56 percent to not less than 85 percent, and

"(C)   such subsidiary is engaged (or was on September 27, 1985, engaged) in manufacturing and distributing a broad line of business systems and related supplies for binding, laminating, shredding, graphics, and providing secure identification,

then, for purposes of determining whether such subsidiary corporation is a member of the parent's affiliated group under section 1504(a) of the Internal Revenue Code of 1954 (as amended by subsection (a)), paragraph (2)(B) of such section 1504(a) shall be applied by substituting '55 percent' for '80 percent'.

"(9)   **Treatment of certain corporations affiliated during 1971.**—In the case of a group of corporations which filed a consolidated Federal income tax return for the taxable year beginning during 1971 and which—

"(A)   included as a common parent on December 31, 1971, a Delaware corporation incorporated on August 26, 1969, and

"(B)   included as a member thereof a Delaware corporation incorporated on November 8, 1971,

for taxable years beginning after December 31, 1970, and ending before January 1, 1988, the requirements for affiliation for each member of such group under section 1504(a) of the Internal Revenue Code of 1954 (before the amendment made by subsection (a)) shall be limited solely to the provisions expressly contained therein and by reference to stock issued under State law as common or preferred stock. During the period described in the preceding sentence, no provision of the Internal Revenue Code of 1986 (including sections 269 and 482) or principal of law, except the general consolidated return regulations (including the provisions relating to separate return limitation years) and sections 382 and 383 of such Code, shall apply to deny the benefit or use of losses incurred or credits earned by members of such group."

(5)   **Treatment of certain sell-downs.**—Paragraph (4) of section 60(b) of the Tax Reform Act of 1984 (relating to exception for certain sell-downs) is amended by adding at the end thereof the following new sentence: "For purposes of the preceding sentence, if there is a letter of intent between a corporation and a securities underwriter entered into on or before June 22, 1984, and the subsequent issuance or sale is effected pursuant to a registration statement filed with the Securities and Exchange Commission, such stock shall be treated as issued or sold pursuant to a registration statement filed with the Securities and Exchange Commission on or before June 22, 1984."

* * * * * * * * * * * *

(9)   **Treatment of certain corporation organized on February 22, 1983.**—In the case of a Rhode Island corporation which was organized on February 11, 1983, and which on February 25, 1983—

(A)   purchased the stock of another corporation,

(B) filed an election under section 338(g) of the Internal Revenue Code of 1986 with respect to such purchase, and

(C) merged into the acquired corporation, such purchase of stock shall be considered as made by the acquiring corporation, such election shall be valid, and the acquiring corporation shall be considered a purchasing corporation for purposes of section 338 of such Code without regard to the duration of the existence of the acquiring corporation.

(f) **Amendments Related to Section 61 of the Act.—**

     (1) **Treatment of distributions of appreciated property.—**

* * * * * * * * * * * *

(F) Any reference in subsection (e) of section 61 of the Tax Reform Act of 1984 to a paragraph of section 312(n) of the Internal Revenue Code of 1954 shall be treated as a reference to such paragraph as in effect before its redesignation by subparagraph (D).

* * * * * * * * * * * *

(3) **Effective date for treatment of redemptions.—**Paragraph (7) of section 312(n) of the Internal Revenue Code of 1954 (as redesignated by paragraph (1)(D) of this subsection), and the amendments made by section 61(a)(2) of the Tax Reform Act of 1984, shall apply to distributions in taxable years beginning after September 30, 1984.

* * * * * * * * * * * *

(k) **Amendments Relating to Section 68 of the Act.—**

* * * * * * * * * * * *

(2) **Clarification of effective dates.—**

(A) Paragraph (2) of section 68(e) of the Tax Reform Act of 1984 (relating to section 1250 gain) is amended by striking out "of the Internal Revenue Code of 1954" and inserting in lieu thereof "of the Internal Revenue Code of 1954, and the amendment made by subsection (c)(2) of this section,".

(B) Paragraph (3) of section 68(e) of the a Tax Reform Act of 1984 (relating to pollution control facilities) is amended by striking out "of such Code" and inserting in lieu thereof "of such Code, and so much of the amendment made by subsection (c)(1) of this section as relates to pollution control facilities,".

(3) **Clerical amendments.—**

* * * * * * * * * * * *

(B) Paragraph (2) of section 68(c) of the Tax Reform Act of 1984 is amended by striking out "section 57(h)" and inserting in lieu thereof "section 57(b)".

* * * * * * * * * * * *

[For official explanation, see Committee Reports, ¶4138]

【¶2105】 SEC. 1806. AMENDMENTS RELATED TO TRUST PROVISIONS.

* * * * * * * * * * * *

(b) **Treatment of Multiple Trusts.—**Subsection (b) of section 82 of the Tax Reform Act of 1984 (relating to treatment of multiple trusts) is amended by inserting before the period at the end thereof the following: "; except that, in the case of a trust which was irrevocable on March 1, 1984, such amendment shall so apply only to that portion of the trust which is attributable to contributions to corpus after March 1, 1984".

* * * * * * * * * * * *

[For official explanation, see Committee Reports, ¶4140]

【¶2106】 SEC. 1807. AMENDMENTS RELATED TO ACCOUNTING CHANGES.

(a) **Amendments Related to Section 91 of the Act.—**

* * * * * * * * * * * *

(3) **Treatment of mining and solid waste reclamation and closing costs.—**

* * * * * * * * * * * *

(B) **Effective date.—**Subsection (g) of section 91 of the Tax Reform Act of 1984 (relating to effective dates) is amended by adding at the end thereof the following new paragraph:

(4) Effective date for treatment of mining and solid waste reclamation and closing costs.—Except as otherwise provided in subsection (h), the amendments made by subsection (b) shall take effect on the date of the enactment of this Act with respect to taxable years ending after such date."

* * * * * * * * * * * *

(4) Treatment of decommissioning of nuclear powerplant.—
    (A) Time when payments deemed made.—

* * * * * * * * * * * *

        (ii) Transitional rule.—To the extent provided in regulations prescribed by the Secretary of the Treasury or his delegate, subsection (g) of section 468A of the Internal Revenue Code of 1954 (as added by clause (i)) shall be applied with respect to any payment on account of a taxable year beginning before January 1, 1987, as if it did not contain the requirement that the payment be made within 2½ months after the close of the taxable year. Such regulations may provide that, to the extent such payment to the Fund is made more than 2½ months after the close of the taxable year, any adjustment to the tax attributable to such payment shall not affect the amount of interest payable with respect to periods before the payment is made. Such regulations may provide appropriate adjustments to the deduction allowed under such section 468A for any such taxable year to take into account the fact that the payment to the Fund is made more than 2½ months after the close of the taxable year.

* * * * * * * * * * * *

    (F) Effective date.—Subsection (g) of section 91 of the Tax Reform Act of 1984 is amended by adding at the end thereof the following new paragraph:
    "(5) Rules for nuclear decommissioning costs.—The amendments made by subsections (c) and (f) shall take effect on the date of the enactment of this Act with respect to taxable years ending after such date."

(5) Effective date for net operating loss provisions.—Subsection (g) of section 91 of the Tax Reform Act of 1984 is amended by adding at the end thereof the following new paragraph:
    "(6) Modification of net operating loss carryback period.—The amendments made by subsection (d) shall apply to losses for taxable years beginning after December 31, 1983."

(6) Clarification of election for earlier effective date.—Subparagraph (A) of section 91(g)(2) of the Tax Reform Act of 1984 (relating to taxpayer may elect earlier application) is amended—
    (A) by striking out "incurred before" and inserting in lieu thereof "incurred on or before",
    (B) by striking out "incurred on or after" and inserting in lieu thereof "incurred after", and
    (C) by adding at the end thereof the following new sentence:
"The Secretary of the Treasury or his delegate may by regulations provide that (in lieu of an election under the preceding sentence) a taxpayer may (subject to such conditions as such regulations may provide) elect to have subsection (h) of section 461 of such Code apply to the taxpayer's entire taxable year in which occurs July 19, 1984."

(7) Special rules for designated settlement funds.—

* * * * * * * * * * * *

    (C) Special rule for taxpayer in bankruptcy reorganization.—In the case of any settlement fund which is established for claimants against a corporation which filed a petition for reorganization under chapter 11 of title 11, United States Code, on August 26, 1982, and which filed with a United States district court a first amended and restated plan of reorganization before March 1, 1986—
        (i) any portion of such fund which meets the requirements of subparagraphs (A), (C), (D), and (F) of section 468B(d)(2) of the Internal Revenue Code of 1954 (as added by this paragraph) shall be treated as a designated settlement fund for purposes of section 468B of such Code,
        (ii) such corporation (or any successor thereof) shall be liable for the tax imposed by section 468B of such Code on such portion of the fund (and the fund shall not be liable for such tax), such tax shall be deductible by the corpo-

ration, and the rate of tax under section 468B of such Code for any taxable year shall be equal to 15 percent, and

(iii) any transaction by any portion of the fund not described in clause (i) shall be treated as a transaction made by the corporation.

(D) Clarification of law with respect to certain funds.—

(i) In general.—Nothing in any provision of law shall be construed as providing that an escrow account, settlement fund, or similar fund is not subject to current income tax. If contributions to such an account or fund are not deductible, then the account or fund shall be taxed as a grantor trust.

(ii) Effective date.—The provisions of clause (i) shall apply to accounts or funds established after August 16, 1986.

(8) **Transitional rule for certain amounts.**—For purposes of section 461(h) of the Internal Revenue Code of 1954, economic performance shall be treated as occurring on the date of a payment to an insurance company if—

(A) such payment was made before November 23, 1985, for indemnification against a tort liability relating to personal injury or death caused by inhalation or ingestion of dust from asbestos-containing insulation products,

(B) such insurance company is unrelated to taxpayer,

(C) such payment is not refundable, and

(D) the taxpayer is not engaged in the mining of asbestos nor is any member of any affiliated group which includes the taxpayer so engaged.

* * * * * * * * * * *

(c) **Transition Rule.**—A taxpayer shall be allowed to use the cash receipts and disbursements method of accounting for taxable years ending after January 1, 1982, if such taxpayer—

(1) is a partnership which was founded in 1936,

(2) has over 1,000 professional employees,

(3) used a long-term contract method of accounting for a substantial part of its income from the performance of architectural and engineering services, and

(4) is headquartered in Chicago, Illinois.

[For official explanation, see Committee Reports, ¶4141]

[¶2107] SEC. 1808. AMENDMENTS RELATED TO TAX STRADDLE PROVISIONS.

(a) **Treatment of Subchapter S Corporations.**—

(1) Section 102 of the Tax Reform Act of 1984 (relating to section 1256 extended to certain options) is amended by adding at the end thereof the following new subsection:

"(j) **Coordination of Election Under Subsection (d)(3) With Elections Under Subsections (g) and (h).**—The Secretary of the Treasury or his delegate shall prescribe such regulations as may be necessary to coordinate the election provided by subsection (d)(3) with the elections provided by subsections (g) and (h)."

(2) Paragraph (3) of section 102(d) of the Tax Reform Act of 1984 (relating to subchapter S election) is amended by striking out "(as so defined)" and inserting in lieu thereof "(as so defined) or such other day as may be permitted under regulations".

* * * * * * * * * * *

(d) **Section 108.**—Section 108 of the Tax Reform Act of 1984 is amended—

(1) by striking out "if such position is part of a transaction entered into for profit" and inserting in lieu thereof "if such loss is incurred in a trade or business, or if such loss is incurred in a transaction entered into for profit though not connected with a trade or business",

(2) by striking out subsection (b) and inserting in lieu thereof the following:

"(b) **Loss Incurred in a Trade or Business.**—For purposes of subsection (a), any loss incurred by a commodities dealer in the trading of commodities shall be treated as a loss incurred in a trade or business",

(3) by striking out the heading for subsection (c) and inserting in lieu thereof the following:

"(c) **Net Loss Allowed.**—",

(4) by striking out subsection (f) and inserting in lieu thereof the following:

"**(f) Commodities Dealer.**—For purposes of this section, the term 'commodities dealer' means any taxpayer who—

"(1) at any time before January 1, 1982, was an individual described in section 1402(i)(2)(B) of the Internal Revenue Code of 1954 (as added by this subtitle), or

"(2) was a member of the family (within the meaning of section 704(e)(3) of such Code) of an individual described in paragraph (1) to the extent such member engaged in commodities trading through an organization the members of which consisted solely of—

"(A) 1 or more individuals described in paragraph (1), and

"(B) 1 or more members of the families (as so defined) of such individuals.", and

(4) [should be (5)] by striking out subsection (h) and inserting in lieu thereof the following:

"**(h) Syndicates.**—For purposes of this section, any loss incurred by a person (other than a commodities dealer) with respect to an interest in a syndicate (within the meaning of section 1256(e)(3)(B) of the Internal Revenue Code of 1954) shall not be considered to be a loss incurred in a trade or business."

[For official explanation, see Committee Reports, ¶4142]

〖¶2108〗 SEC. 1809. AMENDMENTS RELATED TO DEPRECIATION PROVISIONS.

(a) Amendments Related to Section 111 of the Act.—

* * * * * * * * * * * *

(4) Treatment of property financed with tax-exempt bonds.—

* * * * * * * * * * * *

(C) Any property described in paragraph (3) of section 631(d) of the Tax Reform Act of 1984 shall be treated as property described in clause (ii) of section 168(f)(12)(C) of the Internal Revenue Code of 1954 as amended by subparagraph (B).

(5) Coordination with imputed interest changes.—In the case of any property placed in service before May 9, 1985 (or treated as placed in service before such date by section 105(b)(3) of Public Law 99-121)—

(A) any reference in any amendment made by this subsection to 19-year real property shall be treated as a reference to 18-year real property, and

(B) section 168(f)(12)(B)(ii) of the Internal Revenue Code of 1954 (as amended by paragraph (4)(A)) shall be applied by substituting "18 years" for "19 years".

* * * * * * * * * * * *

[For official explanation, see Committee Reports, ¶4143]

〖¶2109〗 SEC. 1810. AMENDMENTS RELATED TO FOREIGN PROVISIONS.

(a) Amendments Related to Section 121 of the Act.—

* * * * * * * * * * * *

(2) Treatment of certain foreign corporations engaged in trade or businesses within the United States.—Subparagraph (E) of section 121(b)(2) of the Tax Reform Act of 1984 (relating to special rules for applicable CFC) is amended by adding at the end thereof the following new clause:

"(iii) Treatment of certain foreign corporations engaged in business in United States.—For purposes of clause (ii), a foreign corporation shall be treated as a United States person with respect to any interest payment made by such corporation if—

"(I) at least 50 percent of the gross income from all sources of such corporation for the 3-year period ending with the close of its last taxable year ending on or before March 31, 1984, was effectively connected with the conduct of a trade or business within the United States, and

"(II) at least 50 percent of the gross income from all sources of such corporation for the 3-year period ending with the close of its taxable year preceding the payment of such interest was effectively connected with the conduct of a trade or business within the United States."

(3) **Treatment of certain short-term borrowing.**—Clause (ii) of section 121(b)(2)(D) of the Tax Reform Act of 1984 (defining applicable CFC) is amended by striking out "or the holding of short-term obligations" and all that follows and inserting in lieu thereof "(or short-term borrowing from nonaffiliated persons) and lending the proceeds of such obligations (or such borrowing) to affiliates."

(4) **Coordination with treaty obligations.**—Section 904(g) of the Internal Revenue Code of 1954 shall apply notwithstanding any treaty obligation of the United States to the contrary (whether entered into on, before, or after the date of the enactment of this Act) unless (in the case of a treaty entered into after the date of the enactment of this Act) such treaty by specific reference to such section 904(g) clearly expresses the intent to override the provisions of such section.

(5) **Transitional rule related to section 125(b)(5) of the act.**—For purposes of section 125(b)(5) of the Tax Reform Act of 1984 (relating to separate application of section 904 in case of income covered by transitional rules), any carryover under section 904(c) of the Internal Revenue Code of 1954 allowed to a taxpayer which was incorporated on August 31, 1962, attributable to taxes paid or accrued in taxable years beginning in 1981, 1982, 1983, or 1984, with respect to amounts included in gross income under section 951 of such Code in respect of a controlled foreign corporation which was incorporated on May 27, 1977, shall be treated as taxes paid or accrued on income separately treated under such section 125(b)(5).

* * * * * * * * * * * *

(i) **Amendments Related to Section 133 of the Act.**—

* * * * * * * * * * * *

(2) Clause (iii) of section 133(d)(3)(B) of the Tax Reform Act of 1984 (relating to amendments related to section 1248) is amended by striking out "180 days after the date of the enactment of this Act" and inserting in lieu thereof "the date which is 1 year after the date of the enactment of the Tax Reform Act of 1985".

* * * * * * * * * * * *

[For official explanation, see Committee Reports, ¶4144]

[¶2110] SEC. 1811. AMENDMENTS RELATED TO REPORTING, PENALTY, AND OTHER PROVISIONS.

(a) **Amendments Related to Section 145 of the Act.**—

* * * * * * * * * * * *

(2) Paragraph (2) of section 145(d) of the Tax Reform Act of 1984 is amended by striking out "section 6652" and inserting in lieu thereof "section 6676".

* * * * * * * * * * * *

[For official explanation, see Committee Reports, ¶4145]

[¶2111] SEC. 1812. AMENDMENTS RELATED TO MISCELLANEOUS PROVISIONS.

* * * * * * * * * * * *

(b) **Amendments Related to Section 172 of the Act.**—

* * * * * * * * * * * *

(5) **Certain Israel bonds not subject to rules relating to below-market loans.**—Section 7872 of the Internal Revenue Code of 1954 (relating to treatment of loans with below-market interest rates) shall not apply to any obligation issued by Israel if—

(A) the obligation is payable in United States dollars, and

(B) the obligation bears interest at an annual rate of not less than 4 percent.

(c) **Amendments Related to Section 174 of the Act.**—

* * * * * * * * * * * *

(5) **Exception for certain indebtedness.**—Clause (i) of section 174(c)(3)(A) of the Tax Reform Act of 1984 shall be applied by substituting "December 31, 1983" for "September 29, 1983" in the case of indebtedness which matures on January 1, 1999, the payments on which from January 1989 through November 1993 equal U/L plus $77,600, the payments on which from December 1993 to maturity equal U/L plus $50,100, and which accrued interest at 13.75 percent through December 31, 1989.

(d) **Amendments Related to Section 177 of the Act.—**

* * * * * * * * * * * *

(2) **Clarification of effective date.—**Paragraph (4) of section 177(d) of the Tax Reform Act of 1984 (relating to effective dates) is amended to read as follows:

"**(4) Clarification of earnings and profits of Federal Home Loan Mortgage Corporation.—**

"(A) Treatment of distribution of preferred stock, etc.—For purposes of the Internal Revenue Code of 1954, the distribution of preferred stock by the Federal Home Loan Mortgage Corporation during December of 1984, and the other distributions of such stock by Federal Home Loan Banks during January of 1985, shall be treated as if they were distributions of money equal to the fair market value of the stock on the date of the distribution by the Federal Home Loan Banks (and such stock shall be treated as if it were purchased with the money treated as so distributed). No deduction shall be allowed under section 243 of the Internal Revenue Code of 1954 with respect to any dividend paid by the Federal Home Loan Mortgage Corporation out of earnings and profits accumulated before January 1, 1985.

"(B) Section 246(a) not to apply to distributions out of earnings and profits accumulated during 1985.—Subsection (a) of section 246 of the Internal Revenue Code of 1954 shall not apply to any dividend paid by the Federal Home Loan Mortgage Corporation during 1985 out of earnings and profits accumulated after December 31, 1984."

* * * * * * * * * * * *

[For official explanation, see Committee Reports, ¶4146]

【¶2112】 SEC. 1821. AMENDMENTS RELATED TO SECTION 211 OF THE ACT.

* * * * * * * * * * * *

(k) **Treatment of Certain Distributions to Shareholders From Pre-1984 Policyholders Surplus Account.—**

* * * * * * * * * * * *

(3) In the case of any loan made before March 1, 1986 (other than a loan which is renegotiated, extended, renewed, or revised after February 28, 1986), which does not meet the requirements of the last sentence of section 815(a) of the Internal Revenue Code of 1954 (as added by paragraph (2)), the amount of the indirect distribution for purposes of such section 815(a) shall be the foregone interest on the loan (determined by using the lowest rate which would have met the arms-length requirements of such sentence for such a loan).

* * * * * * * * * * * *

(q) **Special Rule for Application of High Surplus Mutual Rules.—**In the case of any mutual life insurance company—

(1) which was incorporated on February 23, 1888, and
(2) which acquired a stock subsidiary during 1982,

the amount of such company's excess equity base for purposes of section 809(i) of such Code shall, notwithstanding the last sentence of section 809(i)(2)(D), equal $175,000,000.

* * * * * * * * * * * *

[For official explanation, see Committee Reports, ¶4147]

【¶2113】 SEC. 1822. AMENDMENTS RELATED TO SECTION 216 OF THE ACT.

(a) **Clarification of Application of 10-Year Spread.—**Subparagraph (C) of section 216(b)(3) of the Tax Reform Act of 1984 (relating to 10-year spread inapplicable where no 10-year spread under prior law) is amended by striking out "was required to have been taken into account" and inserting in lieu thereof "would have been required to be taken into account".

(b) **Treatment of Certain Elections Under Section 818(c).—**Subparagraph (B) of section 216(b)(4) of the Tax Reform Act of 1984 (relating to the elections under section 818(c) after September 27, 1983, not taken into account) is amended by striking out

"Subparagraph (A)" and inserting in lieu thereof "Paragraph (3) and subparagraph (A) of this paragraph".

(c)   Election Not To Have Reserves Recomputed.—
(1)   Clause (ii) of section 216(c)(2)(A) of the Tax Reform Act of 1984 (relating to election with respect to contracts issued after 1983 and before 1989) is amended by striking out "$3,000,000" and inserting in lieu thereof "$3,000,000 (determined with regard to this paragraph)".
(2)   Subparagraph (A) of section 216(c)(2) of the Tax Reform Act of 1984 is amended by striking out "be equal to" and all that follows down through the period at the end thereof and inserting in lieu thereof the following: "be equal to the greater of the statutory reserve for such contract (adjusted as provided in subparagraph (B)) or the net surrender value of such contract (as defined in section 807(e)(1) of the Internal Revenue Code of 1954)."
(3)   Subparagraph (B) of section 216(c)(2) of the Tax Reform Act of 1984 is amended—
(A)   by striking out "statutory reserves" and inserting in lieu thereof "opening and closing statutory reserves", and
(B)   by striking out "under section 805(c)(1) of such Code" and inserting in lieu thereof "under the principles of section 805(c)(1) of such Code".

(d)   Special Rule Where Reinsurer Not Using Calendar Year as Taxable Year.—Subparagraph (A) of section 216(b)(3) of the Tax Reform Act of 1984 is amended by adding at the end thereof the following: "For purposes of this subparagraph, if the reinsurer's taxable year is not a calendar year, the first day of the reinsurer's first taxable year beginning after December 31, 1983, shall be substituted for 'January 1, 1984' each place it appears."

(e)   Clarification of Effect of Fresh Start on Earnings and Profits.—Paragraph (1) of section 216(b) of the Tax Reform Act of 1984 is amended by adding at the end thereof the following new sentences: "The preceding sentence shall apply for purposes of computing the earnings and profits of any insurance company for its 1st taxable year beginning in 1984. The preceding sentence shall be applied by substituting '1985' for '1984' in the case of an insurance company which is a member of a controlled group (as defined in section 806(d)(3)), the common parent of which is
"(A)   a company having its principal place of business in Alabama and incorporated in Delaware on November 29, 1979, or
"(B)   a company having its principal place of business in Houston, Texas, and incorporated in Delaware on June 9, 1947."

(f)   Treatment of Section 818(c) Elections Made by Certain Acquired Companies.—Paragraph (4) of section 216(b) of the Tax Reform Act of 1984 is amended by adding at the end thereof the following new subparagraph:
"(C)   Section 818(c) elections made by certain acquired companies.—
"(i)   In general.—If the case of any corporation—
"(I)   which made an election under such section 818(c) before September 28, 1983, and
"(II)   which was acquired in a qualified stock purchase (as defined in section 338(c) of the Internal Revenue Code of 1954) before December 31, 1983,
the fact that such corporation is treated as a new corporation under section 338 of such Code shall not result in the election described in clause (i) not applying to such new corporation.
"(ii)   Time for making section 818(c) or 338 election.—In the case of any corporation described in clause (i), the time for making an election under section 818(c) of such Code (with respect to the first taxable year of the corporation beginning in 1983 and ending after September 28, 1983), or making an election under section 338 of such Code with respect to the qualified stock purchase described in clause (i)(II), shall not expire before the close of the 60th day after the date of the enactment of the Tax Reform Act of 1986.
"(iii)   Statute of limitations.—In the case of any such election under section 818(c) or 338 of such Code which would not have been timely made but for clause (ii), the period for assessing any deficiency attributable to such election (or for filing claim for credit or refund of any overpayment attributable to such election) shall not expire before the date 2 years after the date of the enactment of this Act.

[For official explanation, see Committee Reports, ¶4148]

〔¶2114〕 SEC. 1823. AMENDMENT RELATED TO SECTION 217 OF THE ACT.

Subsection (n) of section 217 of the Tax Reform Act of 1984 (relating to special rule for companies using net level reserve method for noncancellable accident and health insurance contracts) is amended to read as follows:

"**(n) Special Rule for Companies Using Net Level Reserve Method for Noncancellable Accident and Health Insurance Contracts.**—A company shall be treated as meeting the requirements of section 807(d)(3)(A)(iii) of the Internal Revenue Code of 1954, as amended by this Act, with respect to any directly-written noncancellable accident and health insurance contract (whether under existing or new plans of insurance) for any taxable year if—

"(1) such company—

"(A) was using the net level reserve method to compute at least 99 percent of its statutory reserves on such contracts as of December 31, 1982, and

"(B) received more than half its total direct premiums in 1982 from directly-written noncancellable accident and health insurance,

"(2) after December 31, 1983, and through such taxable year, such company has continuously used the net level reserve method for computing at least 99 percent of its tax and statutory reserves on such contracts, and

"(3) for any such contract for which the company does not use the net level reserve method, such company uses the same method for computing tax reserves as such company uses for computing its statutory reserves."

[For official explanation, see Committee Reports, ¶4149]

〔¶2115〕 SEC. 1824. AMENDMENT RELATED TO SECTION 218 OF THE ACT.

Section 218 of the Tax Reform Act of 1984 is hereby repealed.

[For official explanation, see Committee Reports, ¶4150]

〔¶2116〕 SEC. 1825. AMENDMENTS RELATED TO SECTION 221 OF THE ACT.

* * * * * * * * * * * *

(d) Treatment of Flexible Premium Contracts Issued During 1984 Which Meet New Requirements.—Subsection (b) of section 221 of the Tax Reform Act of 1984 (relating to 1-year extension of flexible premium contract provisions) is amended by adding at the end thereof the following new paragraph:

"**(3) Transitional rule.**—Any flexible premium contract issued during 1984 which meets the requirements of section 7702 of the Internal Revenue Code of 1954 (as added by this section) shall be treated as meeting the requirements of section 101(f) of such Code."

(e) Treatment of Certain Contracts Issued Before October 1, 1984.—Clause (i) of section 221(d)(2)(C) of the Tax Reform Act of 1984 (relating to certain contracts issued before October 1, 1984) is amended—

(1) by striking out "in clause (i) thereof" in the material preceding subclause (I), and

(2) by striking out "any mortality charges" in subclause (I) and inserting in lieu thereof "any mortality charges and any initial excess interest guarantees".

[For official explanation, see Committee Reports, ¶4151]

〔¶2117〕 SEC. 1827. AMENDMENTS RELATED TO SECTION 223 OF THE ACT.

* * * * * * * * * * * *

(b) Clarification of Effective Date.—

(1) Subparagraph (A) of section 223(d)(2) of the Tax Reform Act of 1984 (relating to treatment of former employees in case of existing group-term insurance plans) is amended by striking out the material following clause (ii) and inserting in lieu thereof the following:

"but only with respect to an individual who attained age 55 on or before January 1, 1984, and was employed by such employer (or a predecessor employer) at any time during 1983. Such amendments also shall not apply to any employee who retired from employment on or before January 1, 1984, and who, when he retired, was covered by the plan (or a predecessor plan)."

(2) Subparagraph (C) of section 223(d)(2) of the Tax Reform Act of 1984 is amended by striking out "after December 31, 1986," and by striking out "shall not be taken into account" and inserting in lieu thereof "may, at the employer's election, be disregarded".

(3) **Comparable successor plans.**—Paragraph (2) of section 223(d) of the Tax Reform Act of 1984 is amended by adding at the end thereof the following new subparagraph:

"(D) Comparable successor plans.—For purposes of subparagraph (A), a plan shall not fail to be treated as a comparable successor to a plan described in subparagraph (A)(i) with respect to any employee whose benefits do not increase under the successor plan."

* * * * * * * * * * *

[For official explanation, see Committee Reports, ¶4153]

[¶2118] SEC. 1829. WAIVER OF INTEREST ON CERTAIN UNDERPAYMENTS OF TAX.

No interest shall be payable for any period before July 19, 1984, on any underpayment of a tax imposed by the Internal Revenue Code of 1954, to the extent such underpayment was created or increased by any provision of subtitle A of title II of the Tax Reform Act of 1984 (relating to taxation of life insurance companies).

[For official explanation, see Committee Reports, ¶4155]

[¶2119] SEC. 1830. SCOPE OF SECTION 255 OF THE TAX EQUITY AND FISCAL RESPONSIBILITY ACT OF 1982.

In the case of any taxable year beginning before January 1, 1982, in applying the provisions of section 255(c)(2) of the Tax Equity and Fiscal Responsibility Act of 1982, the Internal Revenue Service shall give full and complete effect to the terms of any modified coinsurance contract. The terms to be given effect within the meaning of this provision shall include, but are not limited to, the effective date and investment income rate as stated in such contract.

[For official explanation, see Committee Reports, ¶4156]

[¶2120] SEC. 1834. AMENDMENT RELATED TO SECTION 311 OF THE ACT.

Subparagraph (A) of section 311(a)(3) of the Tax Reform Act of 1984 is amended by striking out "a State law" and inserting in lieu thereof "a State law (originally enacted on April 22, 1977)".

[For official explanation, see Committee Reports, ¶4160]

[¶2121] SEC. 1843. AMENDMENTS RELATED TO SECTION 422 OF THE ACT.

* * * * * * * * * * *

(c) **Recomputation Where Excess Front-Loading of Alimony Payments.—**

* * * * * * * * * * *

(3) **Transitional rule.**—In the case of any instrument to which the amendment made by paragraph (1) does not apply, paragraph (2) of section 71(f) of the Internal Revenue Code of 1954 (as in effect on the day before the date of the enactment of this Act) shall apply only with respect to the first 3 post-separation years.

* * * * * * * * * * *

[For official explanation, see Committee Reports, ¶4161]

[¶2122] SEC. 1845. AMENDMENT RELATED TO SECTION 452 OF THE ACT.

Section 456 of the Tax Reform Act of 1984 is amended by adding at the end thereof the following new subsection:

"(d) **Section 452.**—The amendment made by section 452 shall apply to products manufactured or produced after October 31, 1984."

[For official explanation, see Committee Reports, ¶4161]

〔¶2123〕 SEC. 1847. AMENDMENTS RELATED TO SECTION 474 OF THE ACT.

* * * * * * * * * * * *

(b)   Clerical Amendments.—

* * * * * * * * * * * *

(12)   Paragraph (1) of section 163(b) of the Tax Reform Act of 1984 is amended by inserting "(as amended by sections 211, 314, and 474 of this Act)" after "Section 6501".

* * * * * * * * * * * *

[For official explanation, see Committee Reports, ¶4161]

〔¶2124〕 SEC. 1851. AMENDMENTS RELATED TO WELFARE BENEFIT PLAN PROVISIONS.

(a)   Amendments Related to Section 511 of the Act.—

* * * * * * * * * * * *

(3)   Clarification of section 419A(e).—

* * * * * * * * * * * *

(B) Subsection (e) of section 419A of the Internal Revenue Code of 1954 (as amended by subparagraph (A)) shall not apply to any group-term life insurance to the extent that the amendments made by section 223(a) of the Tax Reform Act of 1984 do not apply to such insurance by reason of paragraph (2) of section 223(d) of such Act.

* * * * * * * * * * * *

(8)(A) * * *

(B)   Effective date of regulations.—Except in the case of a reserve for post-retirement medical or life insurance benefits and any other arrangement between an insurance company and an employer under which the employer has a contractual right to a refund or dividend based solely on the experience of such employer, any account held for an employer by any person and defined as a fund in regulations issued pursuant to section 419(e)(3)(C) of the Internal Revenue Code of 1954 shall be considered a "fund" no earlier than 6 months following the date such regulations are published in final form.

* * * * * * * * * * * *

(12)   Clarification of effective date.—Subsection (e) of section 511 of the Tax Reform Act of 1984 is amended by adding at the end thereof the following new paragraphs:

"(6)   Amendments related to tax on unrelated business income.—The amendments made by subsection (b) shall apply with respect to taxable years ending after December 31, 1985. For purposes of section 15 of the Internal Revenue Code of 1954, such amendments shall be treated as a change in the rate of a tax imposed by chapter 1 of such Code.

"(7)   Amendments related to excise taxes on certain welfare benefit plans.—The amendments made by subsection (c) shall apply to benefits provided after December 31, 1985.

* * * * * * * * * * * *

(14)   Clerical amendment.—Paragraph (2) of section 511(e) of the Tax Reform Act of 1984 is amended by striking out "and section 514".

(b)   Amendments Related to Section 512 of the Act.—

(1)   Transitional rule for certain taxpayers with fully vested vacation pay plans.—
(A)   In general.—In the case of any taxpayer—
(i)   who maintained a fully vested vacation pay plan where payments are expected to be paid (or are in fact paid) within 1 year after the accrual of the vacation pay, and

(ii) who makes an election under section 463 of the Internal Revenue Code of 1954 for such taxpayer's 1st taxable year ending after the date of the enactment of the Tax Reform Act of 1984,

in lieu of establishing a suspense account under such section 463, such election shall be treated as a change in the taxpayer's method of accounting and the adjustments required as a result of such change shall be taken into account under section 481 of such Code.

(B) Extension of time for making election.—In the case of any taxpayer who meets the requirements of subparagraph (A)(i), the time for making an election under section 463 of such Code for such taxpayer's 1st taxable year ending after the date of the enactment of the Tax Reform Act of 1984 shall not expire before the date 6 months after the date of the enactment of this Act.

* * * * * * * * * * * *

[For official explanation, see Committee Reports, ¶4171]

[¶2125] SEC. 1852. AMENDMENTS RELATED TO PENSION PLAN PROVISIONS.

* * * * * * * * * * * *

(b) Amendments Related to Section 522 of the Act.—

* * * * * * * * * * * *

(9) Subsection (e) of section 522 of the Tax Reform Act of 1984 is amended by striking out "the date of the amendment" and inserting in lieu thereof "the date of the enactment".

* * * * * * * * * * * *

(e) Amendments Related to Section 525 of the Act.—

* * * * * * * * * * * *

(3) Section 525(b) of the Tax Reform Act of 1984 is amended by adding at the end thereof the following new paragraph:

"(4) Irrevocable election.—For purposes of paragraph (2) and section 245(c) of the Tax Equity and Fiscal Responsibility Act of 1982, an individual who—

"(A) separated from service before January 1, 1985, with respect to paragraph (2), or January 1, 1983, with respect to section 245(c) of the Tax Equity and Fiscal Responsibility Act of 1982, and

"(B) meets the requirements of such paragraph or such section other than the requirement that there be an irrevocable election, and that the individual be in pay status,

shall be treated as having made an irrevocable election and as being in pay status within the time prescribed with respect to a form of benefit if such individual does not change such form of benefit before death."

(f) Amendment Related to Section 526 of the Act.—Paragraph (2) of section 526(d) of the Tax Reform Act of 1984 is amended by striking out "paragraph (6)" and inserting in lieu thereof "paragraph (7)".

* * * * * * * * * * * *

(i) Amendment Related to Section 4402 of ERISA.—Section 4402 of the Employee Retirement Income Security Act of 1974 (29 U.S.C. 1461) is amended by adding at the end thereof the following new subsection:

"(h)(1) In the case of an employer who entered into a collective bargaining agreement—

"(A) which was effective on January 12, 1979, and which remained in effect through May 15, 1982, and

"(B) under which contributions to a multiemployer plan were to cease on January 12, 1982,

any withdrawal liability incurred by the employer pursuant to part 1 of subtitle E as a result of the complete or partial withdrawal of the employer from the multiemployer plan before January 12, 1982, shall be void.

"(2) In any case in which—

"(A) an employer engaged in the grocery wholesaling business—

"(i) had ceased all covered operations under a multiemployer plan before June 30, 1981, and had relocated its operations to a new facility in another State, and

"(ii) had notified a local union representative on May 14, 1980, that the employer had tentatively decided to discontinue operations and relocate to a new facility in another State, and

"(B) all State and local approvals with respect to construction of and commencement of operations at the new facility had been obtained, a contract for construction had been entered into, and construction of the new facility had begun before September 26, 1980,

any withdrawal liability incurred by the employer pursuant to part 1 of subtitle E as a result of the complete or partial withdrawal of the employer from the multiemployer plan before June 30, 1981, shall be void."

[For official explanation, see Committee Reports, ¶4172]

〖¶2126〗 **SEC. 1853. AMENDMENTS RELATED TO FRINGE BENEFIT PROVISIONS.**

* * * * * * * * * * * *

(b) Amendments to Section 125.—

(2) Transitional rule.—Paragraph (5) of section 531(b) of the Tax Reform Act of 1984 (relating to exception for certain cafeteria plans and benefits) is amended by adding at the end thereof the following new subparagraph:

"(D) Collective bargaining agreements.—In the case of any cafeteria plan in existence on February 10, 1984, and maintained pursuant to 1 or more collective bargaining agreements between employee representatives and 1 or more employers, the date on which the last of such collective bargaining agreements terminates (determined without regard to any extension thereof agreed to after July 18, 1984) shall be substituted for 'January 1, 1985' in subparagraph (A) and for 'July 1, 1985' in subparagraph (B). For purposes of the preceding sentence, any plan amendment made pursuant to a collective bargaining agreement relating to the plan which amends the plan solely to conform to any requirement added by this section (or any requirement in the regulations under section 125 of the Internal Revenue Code of 1954 proposed on May 6, 1984) shall not be treated as a termination of such collective bargaining agreement."

(3) Special rule where contributions or reimbursements suspended.—Paragraph (5) of section 531(b) of the Tax Reform Act of 1984 is amended by adding at the end thereof the following new subparagraph:

"(E) Special rule where contributions or reimbursements suspended.—For purposes of subparagraphs (A) and (B), a plan shall not be treated as not continuing to fail to satisfy the rules referred to in such subparagraphs with respect to any benefit provided in the form of a flexible spending arrangement merely because contributions or reimbursements (or both) with respect to such plan were suspended before January 1, 1985."

(c) Amendments to Section 4977.—

* * * * * * * * * * * *

(3) For purposes of determining whether the requirements of section 4977(c) of the Internal Revenue Code of 1954 are met in the case of an agricultural cooperative incorporated in 1964, there shall not be taken into account employees of a member of the same controlled group as such cooperative which became a member during July 1980.

(d) Treatment of Telephone Concession Service for Certain Retirees.—Section 559 of the Tax Reform Act of 1984 is amended by adding at the end thereof the following subsection:

"(e) Telephone Service for Pre-Divestiture Retirees.—In the case of an employee who, by reason of retirement or disability, separated before January 1, 1984, from the service of an entity subject to the modified final judgment—

"(1) all entities subject to the modified final judgment shall be treated as a single employer in the same line of business for purposes of determining whether telephone service provided to the employee is a no-additional-cost service as defined in section 132 of the Internal Revenue Code of 1954; and

"(2) payment by an entity subject to the modified final judgment of all or part of the cost of local telephone service provided to the employee by a person other than an entity subject to the modified final judgment (including rebate of the amount paid by the employee for the service and payment to the person providing the service) shall be treated as telephone service provided to the employee by such single employer for purposes of determining whether the telephone service is a no-additional-cost service as defined in section 132 of the Internal Revenue Code of 1954.

For purposes of this subsection, the term 'employee' has the meaning given to such term by section 132(f) of the Internal Revenue Code of 1954."

(e) Treatment of Certain Leased Operations of Department Stores.—For purposes of section 132(h)(2)(B) of the Internal Revenue Code of 1954, a leased section of a department store which, in connection with the offering of beautician services, customarily makes sales of beauty aids in the ordinary course of business shall be treated as engaged in over-the-counter sales of property.

(f) Transitional Rules for Treatment of Certain Reductions in Tuition.—

(1) A tuition reduction plan shall be treated as meeting the requirements of section 117(d)(3) of the Internal Revenue Code of 1954 if—

(A) such plan would have met the requirements of such section (as amended by this section but without regard to the lack of evidence that benefits under such plan were the subject of good faith bargaining) on the day on which eligibility to participate in the plan was closed,

(B) at all times thereafter, the tuition reductions available under such plan are available on substantially the same terms to all employees eligible to participate in such plan, and

(C) the eligibility to participate in such plan closed on June 30, 1972, June 30, 1974, or December 31, 1975.

(2) For purposes of applying section 117(d)(3) of the Internal Revenue Code of 1954 to all tuition reduction plans of an employer with at least 1 such plan described in paragraph (1) of this subsection, there shall be excluded from consideration employees not included in the plan who are included in a unit of employees covered by an agreement that the Secretary of the Treasury or his delegate finds to be a collective bargaining agreement between employee representatives and 1 or more employers, if, with respect to plans other than plans described in paragraph (1), there is evidence that such benefits were the subject of good faith bargaining.

(3) Any reduction in tuition provided with respect to a fulltime course of education furnished at the graduate level before July 1, 1988, shall not be included in gross income if—

(A) such reduction would not be included in gross income under the Internal Revenue Service regulations in effect on the date of the enactment of the Tax Reform Act of 1984, and

(B) such reduction is provided with respect to a student who was accepted for admission to such course of education before July 1, 1984, and began such course of education before June 30, 1985.

[For official explanation, see Committee Reports, ¶4173]

[¶2127] SEC. 1854. AMENDMENTS RELATED TO EMPLOYEE STOCK OWNERSHIP PLANS.

(a) Amendments Related to Section 541.—

* * * * * * * * * * *

(2)(A) * * *

(B)(i) The requirement that section 1042(b) of the Internal Revenue Code of 1954 shall be applied with regard to section 318(a)(4) of such Code shall apply to sales after May 6, 1986.

(ii) In the case of sales after July 18, 1984, and before the date of the enactment of this Act, paragraph (2) of section 1042(b) of such Code shall apply as if it read as follows:

"(2) Employees must own 30 percent of stock after sale.—The plan or cooperative referred to in paragraph (1) owns, immediately after the sale, at least 30 percent of the employer securities or 30 percent of the value of employer securities (within the meaning of section 409(1) outstanding at the time of sale."

* * * * * * * * * * *

(5)(A) * * *

(B) If—

(i) before January 1, 1987, the taxpayer acquired any security (as defined in section 165(g)(2) of the Internal Revenue Code of 1954) issued by a domestic corporation or by any State or political subdivision thereof,

(ii) the taxpayer treated such security as qualified replacement property for purposes of section 1042 of such Code, and

(iii) such property does not meet the requirements of section 1042(c)(4) of such Code (as amended by subparagraph (A)),

then, with respect to so much of any gain which the taxpayer treated as not recognized under section 1042(a) by reason of the acquisition of such property, the replacement period for purposes of such section shall not expire before January 1, 1987.

* * * * * * * * * * *

[For official explanation, see Committee Reports, ¶4174]

[¶2128] SEC. 1855. AMENDMENTS RELATED TO MISCELLANEOUS EMPLOYEE BENEFIT PROVISIONS.

(a) **Amendment Related to Section 555 of the Act.**—Subsection (c) of section 555 of the Tax Reform Act of 1984 (relating to technical amendments to the incentive stock option provisions) is amended—

(1) by striking out "subsection (a)" in paragraph (1) and inserting in lieu thereof "subsection (a)(1)",

(2) by striking out "subsection (b)" in paragraph (2) and inserting in lieu thereof "subsection (a)(2)",

(3) by striking out "after March 20, 1984," in paragraph (2), and

(4) by striking out "subsection (c)" in paragraph (3) and inserting in lieu thereof "subsection (b)".

(b) **Amendment Related to Section 556 of the Act.**—Section 556 of the Tax Reform Act of 1984 is amended by striking out so much of such section as precedes paragraph (1) thereof and inserting in lieu thereof the following:

"SEC. 556. TIME FOR MAKING CERTAIN SECTION 83(b) ELECTIONS.

"In the case of any transfer of property in connection with the performance of services on or before November 18, 1982, the election permitted by section 83(b) of the Internal Revenue Code of 1954 may be made, notwithstanding paragraph (2) of such section 83(b), with the income tax return for any taxable year ending after July 18, 1984, and beginning before the date of the enactment of the Tax Reform Act of 1986 if—".

[For official explanation, see Committee Reports, ¶4175]

[¶2129] SEC. 1863. AMENDMENT RELATED TO SECTION 613 OF THE ACT.

(a) **General Rule.**—Section 613 of the Tax Reform Act of 1984 (relating to authority to borrow from Federal Financing Bank) is amended to read as follows:

"SEC. 613. ADVANCE REFUNDING OF CERTAIN VETERANS' MORTGAGE BONDS PERMITTED.

"(a) **In General.**—Notwithstanding section 103A(n) of the Internal Revenue Code of 1954, an issuer of applicable mortgage bonds may issue advance refunding bonds with respect to such applicable mortgage bonds.

"(b) **Limitation on Amount of Advanced Refunding.**—

"(1) **In general.**—The amount of advanced refunding bonds which may be issued under subsection (a) shall not exceed the lesser of—

"(A) $300,000,000, or

"(B) the excess of—

"(i) the projected aggregate payments of principal on the applicable mortgage bonds during the 15-fiscal year period beginning with fiscal year 1984, over

"(ii) the projected aggregate payments during such period of principal on mortgages financed by the applicable mortgage bonds.

Act §1863(a) ¶2129

(2) Assumptions used in making projection.—The computation under paragraph (1)(B) shall be made by using the following percentages of the prepayment experience of the Federal Housing Administration in the State or region in which the issuer of the advance refunding bonds is located:

"Fiscal Year:	Percentage:
1984	15
1985	20
1986	25
1987 and thereafter	30.

"(c) Definitions.—For purposes of this section.—

"(1) Applicable mortgage bonds.—The term 'applicable mortgage bonds' means any qualified veterans' mortgage bonds issued as part of an issue—

"(A)   which was outstanding on December 31, 1981,

"(B)   with respect to which the excess determined under subsection (b)(1)(B) exceeds 12 percent of the aggregate principal amount of such bonds outstanding on July 1, 1983,

"(C)   with respect to which the amount of the average annual prepayments during fiscal years 1981, 1982, and 1983 was less than 2 percent of the average of the loan balances as of the beginning of each of such fiscal years, and

"(D)   which, for fiscal year 1983, had a prepayment experience rate that did not exceed 20 percent of the prepayment experience rate of the Federal Housing Administration in the State or region in which the issuer is located.

"(2) Qualified veterans' mortgage bonds.—The term 'qualified veterans' mortgage bonds' has the meaning given to such term by section 103A(c)(3) of the Internal Revenue Code of 1954.

"(3) Fiscal year.—The term 'fiscal year' means the fiscal year of the State."

(b) Effective Date.—The amendment made by subsection (a) shall take effect on the date of the enactment of this Act; except that such amendment shall not apply with respect to any loan made by the Federal Financing Bank to the State of Oregon pursuant to a credit agreement entered into on April, 16, 1985 (as such agreement was in effect on such date). The Secretary of the Treasury shall guarantee any loan made by the Federal Financing Bank to the State of Oregon pursuant to such agreement.

[For official explanation, see Committee Reports, ¶4178]

〔¶2130〕 SEC. 1865. AMENDMENT RELATED TO SECTION 622 OF THE ACT.
*   *   *   *   *   *   *   *   *   *   *   *   *

(b) Treatment of Certain Guarantees by Farmers Home Administration.—An obligation shall not be treated as federally guaranteed for purposes of section 103(h) of the Internal Revenue Code of 1954 by reason of a guarantee by the Farmers Home Administration if—

(1)   such guarantee is pursuant to a commitment made by the Farmers Home Administration before July 1, 1984, and

(2)   such obligation is issued to finance a convention center project in Carbondale, Illinois.

(c) Treatment of Certain Obligations Used to Finance Solid Waste Disposal Facility.—

(1)   **In general.**—Any obligation which is part of an issue a substantial portion of the proceeds of which is to be used to finance a solid waste disposal facility described in paragraph (2) shall not, for purposes of section 103(h) of the Internal Revenue Code of 1954, be treated as an obligation which is federally guaranteed by reason of the sale of fuel, steam, electricity, or other forms of usable energy to the Federal Government or any agency or instrumentality thereof.

(2)   **Solid waste disposal facility.**—A solid waste disposal facility is described in this paragraph if such facility is described in section 103(b)(4)(E) of such Code and—

(A)   if—

(i)   a public State authority created pursuant to State legislation which took effect on July 1, 1980, took formal action before October 19, 1983, to commit development funds for such facility,

(ii) such authority issues obligations for such facility before January 1, 1988, and

(iii) expenditures have been made for the development of such facility before October 19, 1983,

(B) if—

(i) such facility is operated by the South Eastern Public Service Authority of Virginia, and

(ii) on December 20, 1984, the Internal Revenue Service issued a ruling concluding that a portion of the obligations with respect to such facility would not be treated as federally guaranteed under section 103(h) of such Code by reason of the transitional rule contained in section 631(c)(3)(A)(i) of the Tax Reform Act of 1984,

(C) if—

(i) a political subdivision of a State took formal action on April 1, 1980, to commit development funds for such facility,

(ii) such facility has a contract to sell steam to a naval base,

(iii) such political subdivision issues obligations for such facility before January 1, 1988, and

(iv) expenditures have been made for the development of such facility before October 19, 1983, or

(D) if—

(i) such facility is a thermal transfer facility,

(ii) is to be built and operated by the Elk Regional Resource Authority, and

(iii) is to be on land leased from the United States Air Force at Arnold Engineering Development Center near Tullahoma, Tennessee.

(3) Limitations.—

(A) In the case of a solid waste disposal facility described in paragraph (2)(A), the aggregate face amount of obligations to which paragraph (1) applies shall not exceed $65,000,000.

(B) In the case of a solid waste disposal facility described in paragraph (2)(B), the aggregate face amount of obligations to which paragraph (1) applies shall not exceed $20,000,000. Such amount shall be in addition to the amount permitted under the Internal Revenue Service ruling referred to in paragraph (2)(B)(ii).

(C) In the case of a solid waste disposal facility described in paragraph (2)(C), the aggregate face amount of obligations to which paragraph (1) applies shall not exceed $75,000,000.

(D) In the case of a solid waste disposal facility described in paragraph (2)(D), the aggregate face amount of obligations to which paragraph (1) applies shall not exceed $25,000,000.

[For official explanation, see Committee Reports, ¶4180]

⟦¶2131⟧ SEC. 1866. TRANSITIONAL RULE FOR LIMIT ON SMALL ISSUE EXCEPTION.

The amendment made by section 623 of the Tax Reform Act of 1984 shall not apply to any obligation issued to refund another tax-exempt IDB to which the amendment made by such section 623 did not apply if—

(1) the refunding obligation has a maturity date not later than the maturity date of the refunded obligation,

(2) the amount of the refunding obligation does not exceed the amount of the refunded obligation,

(3) the interest rate on the refunding obligation is lower than the interest rate on the refunded issue, and

(4) the proceeds of the refunding obligation are used to redeem the refunded obligation not later than 30 days after the date of the issuance of the refunding obligations.

For purposes of the preceding sentence, the term "tax-exempt IDB" means any industrial development bond (as defined in section 103(b) of the Internal Revenue Code of 1954) the interest on which is exempt from tax under section 103(a) of such Code.

[For official explanation, see Committee Reports, ¶4181]

【¶2132】 SEC. 1867. AMENDMENTS RELATED TO SECTION 624 OF THE ACT.

(a) Paragraph (2) of section 624(c) of the Tax Reform Act of 1984 (relating to effective date for limitations on arbitrage on nonpurpose obligations) is amended by striking out "by the Essex County Port Authority of New York and New Jersey as part of an issue approved" and inserting in lieu thereof "for the Essex County New Jersey Resource Recovery Project authorized by the Port Authority of New York and New Jersey on November 10, 1983, as part of an agreement approved".

(b) The amendment made by section 624 of the Tax Reform Act of 1984 shall not apply to obligations issued with respect to the Downtown Muskogee Revitalization Project for which a UDAG grant was preliminarily approved on May 5, 1981, if—

    (1) such obligation is issued before January 1, 1986, or

    (2) such obligation is issued after such date to provide additional financing for such project except that the aggregate amount of obligations to which this subsection applies shall not exceed $10,000,000.

[For official explanation, see Committee Reports, ¶4182]

【¶2133】 SEC. 1868. AMENDMENT RELATED TO SECTION 625 OF THE ACT.

Subparagraph (C) of section 625(a)(3) of the Tax Reform Act of 1984 (relating to arbitrage regulations) is amended by striking out "obligation issued exclusively" and inserting in lieu thereof "obligation (or series of refunding obligations) issued exclusively".

[For official explanation, see Committee Reports, ¶4183.]

【¶2134】 SEC. 1869. AMENDMENTS RELATED TO SECTION 626 OF THE ACT.

* * * * * * * * * * * *

(c) **Transitional Rules.—**

    (1) **Treatment of certain obligations issued by the city of Baltimore.—**Obligations issued by the city of Baltimore, Maryland, after June 30, 1985, shall not be treated as private loan bonds for purposes of section 103(o) of the Internal Revenue Code of 1954 (or as private activity bonds for purposes of section 103 and part IV of subchapter A of chapter 1 of the Internal Revenue Code of 1986, as amended by title XIII of this Act) by reason of the use of a portion of the proceeds of such obligations to finance or refinance temporary advances made by the city of Baltimore in connection with loans to persons who are not exempt persons (within the meaning of section 103(b)(3) of such Code) if—

        (A) such obligations are not industrial development bonds (within the meaning of section 103(b)(2) of the Internal Revenue Code of 1954),

        (B) the portion of the proceeds of such obligations so used is attributable to debt approved by voter referendum on or before November 2, 1982,

        (C) the loans to such nonexempt persons were approved by the Board of Estimates of the city of Baltimore on or before October 19, 1983, and

        (D) the aggregate amount of such temporary advances financed or refinanced by such obligations does not exceed $27,000,000.

    (2) **White Pine Power Project.—**The amendment made by section 626(a) of the Tax Reform Act of 1984 shall not apply to any obligation issued during 1984 to provide financing for the White Pine Power Project in Nevada.

    (3) **Tax increment bonds.—**The amendment made by section 626(a) of the Tax Reform Act of 1984 shall not apply to any tax increment financing obligation issued before August 16, 1986, if—

        (A) substantially all of the proceeds of the issue are to be used to finance—

            (i) sewer, street, lighting, or other governmental improvements to real property,

            (ii) the acquisition of any interest in real property pursuant to the exercise of eminent domain, the preparation of such property for new use, or the transfer of such interest to a private developer, or

            (iii) payments of reasonable relocation costs of prior users of such real property,

        (B) all of the activities described in subparagraph (A) are pursuant to a redevelopment plan adopted by the issuing authority before the issuance of such issue.

        (C) repayment of such issue is secured exclusively by pledges of that portion of any increase in real property tax revenues (or their equivalent) attributable to the redevelopment resulting from the issue, and

(D) none of the property described in subparagraph (A) is subject to a real property or other tax based on a rate or valuation method which differs from the rate and valuation method applicable to any other similar property located within the jurisdiction of the issuing authority.

(4) **Eastern Maine electric cooperative.**—The amendment made by section 626(a) of the Tax Reform Act of 1984 shall not apply to obligations issued by Massachusetts Municipal Wholesale Electric Company Project No. 6 if—

(A) such obligation is issued before January 1, 1986,

(B) such obligation is issued after such date to refund a prior obligation for such project, except that the aggregate amount of obligations to which this subparagraph applies shall not exceed $100,000,000, or

(C) such obligation is issued after such date to provide additional financing for such project except that the aggregate amount of obligations to which this subparagraph applies shall not exceed $45,000,000.

Subparagraph (B) shall not apply to any obligations issued for the advance refunding of any obligation.

(5) **Clarification of transitional rule for certain strudent loan programs.**—Subparagraph (A) of section 626(b)(2) of the Tax Reform Act of 1984 is amended by striking out "$11 million" in the table contained in such subparagraph and inserting in lieu thereof "$70 million".

(6) **Treatment of obligations to finance St. Johns River Power Park.**—

(A) In general.—The amendment made by section 626(a) of the Tax Reform Act of 1984 shall not apply to any obligation issued to finance the project described in subparagraph (B) if—

(i) such obligation is issued before September 27, 1985,

(ii) such obligation is issued after such date to refund a prior tax exemption obligation for such project, the amount of such obligation does not exceed the oustanding amount of the refunded obligation, and such prior tax exempt obligation is retired not later than the date 30 days after the issuance of the refunding obligation, or

(iii) such obligation is issued after such date to provide additional financing for such project except that the aggregate amount of obligations to which this clause applies shall not exceed $150,000,000.

Clause (ii) shall not apply to any obligation issued for the advance refunding of any obligation.

(B) Description of project.—The project described in this subparagraph in the St. Johns River Power Park system in Florida which was authorized by legislation enacted by the Florida Legislature in February of 1982.

[For official explanation, see Committee Reports, ¶4183]

[¶2135] SEC. 1872. AMENDMENTS RELATED TO SECTION 631 OF THE ACT.

(a) **Clarification of General Effective Date.**—

(1) Paragraph (1) of section 631(c) of the Tax Reform Act of 1984 (relating to effective date for other provisions relating to tax-exempt bonds) is amended by striking out "made by this subtitle" and inserting in lieu thereof "made by sections 622, 623, 627, and 628(c), (d), and (e) (and the provisions of sections 625(c), 628(f), and 629(b))".

(2)(A) Subparagraph (A) of section 631(c)(3) of the Tax Reform Act of 1984 is amended by striking out "amendments made by this subtitle (other than section 621)" and inserting in lieu thereof "amendments (and provisions) referred to in paragraph (1)."

(B) Effective with respect to obligations issued after March 28, 1985, subparagraph (A) of section 631(c)(3) of the Tax Reform Act of 1984 is amended by striking out clauses (i) and (ii) and inserting in lieu thereof the following:

"(i) the original use of which commences with the taxpayer and the construction, reconstruction, or rehabilitation of which began before October 19, 1983, and was completed on or after such date,

"(ii) the original use of which commences with the taxpayer and with respect to which a binding contract to incur significant expenditures for construction, reconstruction, or rehabilitation was entered into before October 19, 1983, and some of such expenditures are incurred on or after such date, or

"(iii) acquired after October 19, 1983, pursuant to a binding contract entered into on or before such date."

(3) Paragraph (3) of section 631(c) of the Tax Reform Act of 1984 is amended by adding at the end thereof the following new subparagraph:

"(C) Exception.—Subparagraph (A) shall not apply with respect to the amendment made by section 628(e) and the provisions of sections 628(f) and 629(b)."

(4) Subparagraph (B) of section 631(c)(3) of the Tax Reform Act of 1984 is amended by striking out "subsection (b)(2)(A)" and inserting in lieu thereof "subsection (b)(2)".

(b) **Special Rule for Health Club Facilities.**—Subsection (c) of section 631 of the Tax Reform Act of 1984 is amended by adding at the end thereof the following new paragraph:

"(5) **Special rule for health club facilities.**—In the case of any health club facility, with respect to the amendment made by section 627(c)—

"(A) paragraph (1) shall be applied by substituting 'April 12, 1984' for 'December 31, 1983', and

"(B) paragraph (3) shall be applied by substituting 'April 13, 1984' for 'October 19, 1983' each place it appears."

(c) **Treatment of Certain Solid Waste Disposal Facilities.**—

(1) **In general.**—Subsection (d) of section 631 of the Tax Reform Act of 1984 (relating to provisions of subtitle not to apply to certain property) is amended by adding at the end thereof the following:

"(5) Any solid waste disposal facility described in section 103(b)(4)(E) of the Internal Revenue Code of 1954 if—

"(A) a city government, by resolutions adopted on April 10, 1980, and December 27, 1982, took formal action to authorize the submission of a proposal for a feasibility study for such facility and to authorize the presentation to the Department of the Army (U.S. Army Missle Command) of a proposed agreement to jointly pursue construction and operation of such facility,

"(B) such city government (or a public authority on its behalf) issues obligations for such facility before January 1, 1988, and

"(C) expenditures have been made for the development of such facility before October 19, 1983. Notwithstanding the foregoing provisions of this subsection, the amendments made by section 624 (relating to arbitrage) shall apply to obligations issued to finance property described in paragraph (5)."

(2) **Conforming amendment.**—Paragraph (1) of section 632(a) of the Tax Reform Act of 1984 is hereby repealed.

[For official explanation, see Committee Reports, ¶4187]

[¶2136] SEC. 1873. AMENDMENTS RELATED TO SECTION 632 OF THE ACT.

(a) **Clerical Amendment.**—Subsection (a) of section 632 of the Tax Reform Act of 1984 is amended by striking out "section 623" in the matter preceding paragraph (1) thereof and inserting in lieu thereof "section 624".

(b) **Certain Obligations Not Treated as Private Loan Bonds.**—Subsection (d) of section 632 of the Tax Reform Act of 1984 is amended by adding at the end thereof the following new sentence: "The amendment made by section 626 shall not apply to any obligation described in the preceding sentence."

(c) **Treatment of Certain Obligations to Finance Hydroelectric Generating Facility.**—If—

(1) obligations are to be issued in an amount not to exceed $9,500,000 to finance the construction of an approximately 4 megawatt hydroelectric generating facility owned and operated by the city of Hastings, Minnesota, and located on United States Army Corps of Engineers lock and dam No. 2 or are isued to refund any of such obligations,

(2) substantially all of the electrical power generated by such facility is to be sold to a nongovernmental person pursuant to a long-term power sales agreement in accordance with the Public Utilities Regulatory Policies Act of 1978, and

(3)   the initially issued obligations are issued on or before December 31, 1986, and any of such refunding obligations are issued on or before December 31, 1996,

then the person referred to in paragraph (2) shall not be treated as the principal user of such facilities by reason of such sales for purposes of subparagraphs (D) and (E) of section 103(b)(6) of the Internal Revenue Code of 1954.

(d) Treatment of Certain Obligations To Finance Hydroelectric Generating Facility.—If—

(1)   obligations are to be issued in an amount not to exceed $6,500,000 to finance the construction of an approximately 2.6 megawatt hydroelectric generating facility located on the Schroon River in Warren County, New York, near Warrensburg, New York,

(2)   such facility has a Federal Energy Regulatory Commission project number 8719-0000 under a preliminary permit issued on November 8, 1985, and

(3)   substantially all of the electrical power generated by such facility is to be sold to a nongovernmental person pursuant to a long-term power sales agreement in accordance with the Public Utilities Regulatory Policies Act of 1978,

then the person referred to in paragraph (3) shall not be treated as the principal user of such facilities by reason of such sales for purposes of subparagraphs (D) and (E) of section 103(b)(6) of the Internal Revenue Code of 1954.

(e) Treatment of Certain Obligations To Finance Hydroelectric Generating Facilities.—If—

(1)   obligations in the amount of $6,000,000 issued on November 30, 1984, to finance the construction of an approximately 1.0 megawatt hydroelectric generating facility and an approximately .6 megawatt hydroelectric generating facility, both of which are located near Los Banos, California,

(2)   such facilities have Federal Energy Regulatory Commission project numbers 5129-001 and 5128-001, respectively, under license exemptions issued on December 6, 1983, and

(3)   substantially all of the electrical power generated by such facility is to be sold to a nongovernmental person pursuant to a long-term power sales agreement in accordance with the Public Utilities Regulatory Policies Act of 1978.

then the person referred to in paragraph (3) shall not be treated as the principal user of such facilities by reason of such sales for purposes of subparagraphs (D) and (E) of section 103(b)(6) of the Internal Revenue Code of 1954.

(f) Treatment of Certain Obligations to Finance Methane Recovery Electric Generating Facilities.—If—

(1)   obligations are to be issued in an amount not to exceed $3,000,000 to finance the construction of a methane recovery electric generating facility located on a sanitary landfill near Richmond, California, and

(2)   substantially all of the electrical power generated by such facility is to be sold to a nongovernmental person pursuant to a long-term power sales agreement entered into on April 16, 1985, in accordance with the Public Utilities Regulatory Policies Act of 1978,

then the person referred to in paragraph (2) shall not be treated as the principal user of such facilities by reason of such sales for purposes of subparagraphs (D) and (E) of section 103(b)(6) of the Internal Revenue Code of 1954.

(g) Treatment of Certain Obligations to Finance Hydroelectric Generating Facilities.—If—

(1)   obligations are to be issued in an amount not to exceed $6,000,000 to finance the construction of a hydroelectric generating facility having a Federal Energy Regulatory Commission license number 3189, and located near Placerville, California,

(2)   an inducement resolution for such project was adopted in March 1985, and

(3)   substantially all of the electrical power generated by such facility is to be sold to a nongovernmental person pursuant to a long-term power sales agreement in accordance with the Public Utilities Regulatory Policies Act of 1978,

then the person referred to in paragraph (3) shall not be treated as the principal user of such facilities by reason of such sales for purposes of subparagraphs (D) and (E) of section 103(b)(6) of the Internal Revenue Code of 1954.

[For official explanation, see Committee Reports, ¶4188]

Act §1873(g) ¶2136

[¶2137]   SEC. 1875.   AMENDMENTS RELATED TO TITLE VII OF THE ACT.

* * * * * * * * * * * *

(c)   **Amendments Related to Section 713.—**

* * * * * * * * * * *

(2)   Section 713(c) of the Tax Reform Act of 1984 is amended by adding at the end thereof the following new paragraph:

"(4)   Effective date for paragraph (3).—The amendment made by paragraph (3) shall apply to distributions after July 18, 1984."

* * * * * * * * * * *

(5)   Section 713(d)(1) of the Tax Reform Act of 1984 is amended by striking out "Paragraph" and inserting in lieu thereof "Effective with respect to contributions made in taxable years beginning after December 31, 1983, paragraph".

* * * * * * * * * * *

(d)   **Amendments Relating to Section 714 of the Act.—**

* * * * * * * * * * *

(3)   **Effective date provision.—**Notwithstanding section 715 of the Tax Reform Act of 1984, the amendments made by section 714(n)(2) of such Act shall apply only to applications filed after July 18, 1984.

* * * * * * * * * * *

(e)   **Amendment Related to Section 734 of the Act.—**Subsection (a) of section 201 of the Land and Water Conservation Fund Act of 1965 (16 U.S.C. 4601-11) is amended by striking out "section 209(f)(5) of the Highway Revenue Act of 1956" and inserting in lieu thereof "section 9503(c)(4)(B) of the Internal Revenue Code of 1954".

* * * * * * * * * * *

(g)   **Amendment of Section 1248.—**

* * * * * * * * * * *

(3)   **Transitional rule.—**An exchange shall be treated as occurring on or before March 1, 1986, if—

(A)   on or before such date, the taxpayer adopts a plan of reorganization to which section 356 applies, and

(B)   such plan or reorganization is implemented and distributions pursuant to such plan are completed on or before the date of enactment of this Act.

[For official explanation, see Committee Reports, ¶4189]

[¶2138]   SEC. 1876.   AMENDMENTS RELATED TO TITLE VIII OF THE ACT.

* * * * * * * * * * *

(h)   **Clarification of Exemption of Accumulated DISC Income.—**Subparagraph (A) of section 805(b)(2) of the Tax Reform Act of 1984 (relating to exemption of accumulated DISC income from tax) is amended by adding at the end thereof the following new sentence: "For purposes of the preceding sentence, the term 'actual distribution' includes a distribution in liquidation, and the earnings and profits of any corporation receiving a distribution not included in gross income by reason of the preceding sentence shall be increased by the amount of such distribution."

(i)   **Clarification of Effective Date for Requirement That Taxable Year of DISC and FSC Conform to Taxable Year of Majority Shareholder.—**Paragraph (4) of section 805(a) of the Tax Reform Act of 1984 is amended to read as follows:

"(4)   Section 803.—The amendments made by section 803 shall apply to taxable years beginning after December 31, 1984."

* * * * * * * * * * *

(m)   **Treatment of Certain Former Export Trade Corporation.—**If—

(1)   a corporation which is not an export trading corporation for its most recent taxable year ending before the date of the enactment of the Tax Reform Act of 1984 but was an export trading corporation for any prior taxable year, and

(2)(A)   such corporation may not qualify as an export trade corporation for any taxable year beginning after December 31, 1984, by reason of section 971(a)(3) of the Internal Revenue Code of 1954, or (B) such corporation makes an election, before the date 6 months after the date of the enactment of this Act, not to be traded as an export trade corporation with respect to taxable years beginning after December 31, 1984,

rules similar to the rules of paragraph (2) and (4) of section 805(b) of the Tax Reform Act of 1984 shall apply to such corporation. For purposes of the preceding sentence, the term "export trade corporation" has the meaning given such term by section 971 of such Code.

(n) Treatment of Distribution of Accumulated DISC Income Received by Cooperatives.—Paragraph (2) of section 805(b) of the Tax Reform Act of 1984 (relating to transition rules for DISC's) is amended by adding at the end thereof the following new subparagraph:

"(C) Treatment of distribution of accumulated disc income received by cooperatives.—In the case of any actual distribution received by an organization described in section 1381 of such Code and excluded from the gross income of such corporation by reason of subparagraph (A)—

"(i) such amount shall not be included in the gross income of any member of such organization when distributed in the form of a patronage dividend or otherwise, and

"(ii) no deduction shall be allowed to such organization by reason of any such distribution."

(o) Treatment of Certain Contracts.—Paragraph (2) of section 805(a) of the Tax Reform Act of 1984 (relating to transitional rule for certain contracts) is amended to read as follows:

"(2) **Special rule for certain contracts.**—To the extent provided in regulations prescribed by the Secretary of the Treasury or his delegate, any event or activity required to occur or required to be performed, before January 1, 1985, by section 924(c) or (d) or 925(c) of the Internal Revenue Code of 1954 shall be treated as meeting the requirements of such section if such event or activity is with respect to—

"(A) any lease of more than 3 years duration which was entered into before January 1, 1985,

"(B) any contract with respect to which the taxpayer uses the completed contract method of accounting which was entered into before January 1, 1985, or

"(C) in the case of any contact other than a lease or contract described in subparagraph (A) or (B), any contract which was entered into before January 1, 1985; except that this subparagraph shall only apply to the first 3 taxable years of the FSC ending after January 1, 1985, or such later taxable years as the Secretary of the Treasury or his delegate may prescribe."

(p) Clerical Amendments.—

* * * * * * * * * * * *

(3) Paragraph (3) of section 802(c) of the Tax Reform Act of 1984 is hereby repealed.

(4) Subparagraph (A) of section 805(a)(2) of the Tax Reform Act of 1984 is amended by striking out "the taxpayer" and inserting in lieu thereof "the DISC or a related party".

* * * * * * * * * * * *

[For official explanation, see Committee Reports, ¶4190]

⟦¶2139⟧ SEC. 1878. AMENDMENTS RELATED TO TITLE X OF THE ACT.

(a) **Amendment Related to Section 1001 of the Act.**—Subsection (b) of section 1001 of the Tax Reform Act of 1984 is amended by adding at the end thereof the following new paragraph:

"(24) Clause (i) of section 1278(a)(1)(B) (relating to short-term obligations)."

* * * * * * * * * * * *

(d) **Amendments Related to Section 1028 of the Act.**—Subsection (b) of section 1028 of the Tax Reform Act of 1984 (relating to credit against estate tax for transfers to Toiyabe National Forest) is amended to read as follows:

"(b) **Amount of credit.**—

"(1) **In general.**—The amount allowed as a credit under subsection (a) shall be equal to the lesser of—

"(A) the fair market value of the real property transferred by each estate as of the valuation date used for purposes of the tax imposed by chapter 11 of such Code, or

"(B) the Federal estate tax liability (and interest thereon) of each estate.

"(2) **Special rule for Rabe estate.**—In the case of the estate described in paragraph (2) of subsection (a), the amount allowed as a credit under subsection (a) shall be equal to the Federal estate tax liability (and interest accruing thereon through the date of a transfer described in paragraph (1) of subsection (c)) of such estate."

* * * * * * * * * * *

(f) **Amendments Related to Section 1041 of the Act.—**

* * * * * * * * * * *

(2) Subparagraph (B) of section 1041(c)(5) of the Tax Reform Act of 1984 is amended by striking out "section 51(j)" and inserting in lieu thereof "section 51(k)".

* * * * * * * * * * *

(h) **Amendment Related to Section 1063 of the Act.**—Subsection (c) of section 1063 of the Tax Reform Act of 1984 (relating to permanent disallowance of deduction for expenses of demolition of certain structures) is amended to read as follows:

"(c) **Effective Dates.—**

"(1) The amendments made by this section shall apply to taxable years ending after December 31, 1983, but shall not apply to any demolition (other than of a certified historic structure) commencing before July 19, 1984.

"(2) For purposes of paragraph (1), if a demolition is delayed until the completion of the replacement structure on the same site, the demolition shall be treated as commencing when construction of the replacement structure commences.

"(3) The amendments made by this section shall not apply to any demolition commencing before September 1, 1984, pursuant to a bank headquarters building project if—

"(A) on April 1, 1984, a corporation was retained to advise the bank on the final completion of the project, and

"(B) on June 12, 1984, the Comptroller of the Currency approved the project.

"(4) The amendments made by this section shall not apply to the remaining adjusted basis at the time of demolition of any structure if—

"(A) such structure was used in the manufacture, storage, or distribution of lead alkyl antiknock products and intermediate and related products at facilities located in or near Baton Rouge, Louisiana, and Houston, Texas, owned by the same corporation, and

"(B) demolition of at least one such structure at the Baton Rouge facility commenced before January 1, 1984."

(i) **Amendment Related to Section 1065 of the Act.**—Subsection (b) of section 1065 of the Tax Reform Act of 1984 (relating to rules treating Indian tribal governments as States) is amended by striking out "section 7871" and inserting in lieu thereof "section 7871(a)".

* * * * * * * * * * *

[For official explanation, see Committee Reports, ¶4192]

[¶2140] SEC. 1879. MISCELLANEOUS PROVISIONS.

(a) **Waiver of Estimated Tax Penalties.**—No addition to tax shall be made under section 6654 or 6655 of the Internal Revenue Code of 1954 (relating to failure to pay estimated income tax) for any period before April 16, 1985 (March 16, 1985 in the case of a taxpayer subject to section 6655 of such Code), with respect to any underpayment, to the extent that such underpayment was created or increased by any provision of the Tax Reform Act of 1984.

* * * * * * * * * * * *

(i) **Medicinal Alcohol, Etc. Brought Into the United States From Puerto Rico or the Virgin Islands Eligible for Drawback.—**

* * * * * * * * * * *

(3)(A) Section 7652 of the Internal Revenue Code of 1954 (other than subsection (f) thereof) shall not prevent the payment to Puerto Rico or the Virgin Islands of amounts with respect to medicines, medicinal preparations, food products, flavors, or flavoring extracts containing distilled spirits, which are unfit for beverage purposes and which are brought into the United States from Puerto Rico or the Virgin Islands on or before the date of the enactment of this Act.

(B) With respect to articles brought into the United States after September 27, 1985, subparagraph (A) shall apply only if the Secretary of the Treasury or his delegate is satisfied that the amounts paid to Puerto Rico or the Virgin Islands under subparagraph (A) are being repaid to the proper persons who used the distilled spirits in such articles.

(j) **Allowance of Investment Credit to Eligible Section 501(d) Organizations.—**

* * * * * * * * * * * *

(3) **Special rule.—**If refund or credit of any overpayment of tax resulting from the application of this subsection is prevented at any time before the close of the date which is 1 year after the date of the enactment of this Act by operation of any law or rule of law (including res judicata), refund or credit of such overpayment (to the extent attributable to the application of the amendments made by this subsection) may, nevertheless, be made or allowed if claim therefor is filed before the close of such 1-year period.

* * * * * * * * * * * *

(n) **Amendment Relating to Section 2523.—**

* * * * * * * * * * * *

(3) **Special rule for certain transfers in October 1984.—**An election under section 2523(f) of the Internal Revenue Code of 1954 with respect to an interest in property which—

(A) was transferred during October 1984, and

(B) was transferred pursuant to a trust instrument stating that the grantor's intention was that the property of the trust would constitute qualified terminable interest property as to which a Federal gift tax marital deduction would be allowed upon the grantor's election,

shall be made on the return of tax imposed by section 2501 of such Code for the calendar year 1984 which is filed on or before the due date of such return or, if a timely return is not filed, on the first such return filed after the due date of such return and before December 31, 1986.

(o) **Amendments Relating to Section 4994.—**

(1) For purposes of section 4991(b), a "qualified charitable interest" shall include on economic interest in crude oil held by the Episcopal Royalty Company, an entity created in 1961 as a subsidiary of the Protestant Episcopal Church Foundation of the Diocese of Oklahoma.

(2) The amendment made by this subsection shall apply to oil removed after February 29, 1980.

(p) **Amendment Related to Section 252 of the Economic Recovery Tax Act of 1981.—**

(1) Notwithstanding subsection (c) of section 252 of the Economic Recovery Tax Act of 1981, the amendment made by subsection (a) of such section 252 (and the provisions of subsection (b) of such section 252) shall apply to any transfer of stock to any person if—

(A) such transfer occurred in November or December of 1973 and was pursuant to the exercise of an option granted in November or December of 1971,

(B) in December 1973 the corporation granting the option was acquired by another corporation in a transaction qualifying as a reorganization under section 368 of the Internal Revenue Code of 1954,

(C) the fair market value (as of July 1, 1974) of the stock received by such person in the reorganization in exchange for the stock transferred to him pursuant to the exercise of such option was less than 50 percent of the fair market value of the stock so received (as of December 4, 1973),

(D) in 1975 or 1976 such person sold substantially all of the stock received in such reorganization, and

(E)   such person makes an election under this section at such time and in such manner as the Secretary of the Treasury or his delegate shall prescribe.

(2)   Limitation on amount of benefit.—Subsection (a) shall not apply to transfers with respect to any employee to the extent that the application of subsection (a) with respect to such employee would (but for this paragraph) result in a reduction in liability for income tax with respect to such employee for all taxable years in excess of $100,000 (determined without regard to any interest).

(3)   Statute of limitations.—

(A)   Overpayments.—If refund or credit of any overpayment of tax resulting from the application of subsection (a) is prevented on the date of the enactment of this Act (or at any time within 6 months after such date of enactment) by the operation of any law or rule of law, refund or credit of such overpayment (to the extent attributable to the application of subsection (a)) may, nevertheless, be made or allowed if claim therefor is filed before the close of such 6-month period.

(B)   Deficiencies.—If the assessment of any deficiency of tax resulting from the application of subsection (a) is prevented on the date of the enactment of this Act (or at any time within 6 months after such date of enactment) by the operation of any law or rule of law, assessment of such deficiency (to the extent attributable to the application of subsection (a)) may, nevertheless, be made within such 6-month period.

(q)   Treatment of Certain Self-Insured Workers' Compensation Funds.—

(1)   Moratorium on collection activities.—During the period beginning on the date of the enactment of this Act and ending on August 16, 1987, the Secretary of the Treasury or his delegate—

(A)   shall suspend any pending audit of any self-insured workers' compensation fund where the audit involves the issue of whether such fund is a mutual insurance company,

(B)   shall not initiate any audit of any such fund involving such issue, and

(C)   shall take no steps to collect from such fund any underpayment, interest, or penalty involving such issue.

(2)   Suspension of running of interest.—No interest shall be payable under chapter 67 of the Internal Revenue Code of 1986 on any underpayment by a self-insured workers' compensation fund involving such issue for the period beginning on August 16, 1986, and ending on August 16, 1987.

(3)   Additional time to file tax court proceeding.—If the period during which a petition involving such issue could have been filed with the Tax Court by any self-insured workers' compensation fund had not expired before August 16, 1986, such period shall not expire before August 16, 1987.

(4)   Self-insured workers' compensation fund.—For purposes of this subsection, the term "self-insured workers' compensation fund" means any self-insured workers' compensation fund established pursuant to applicable State law regulating self-insured workers' compensation funds.

*   *   *   *   *   *   *   *   *   *   *   *

(t)   Disposition of Certain Subsidiary.—If for a taxable year of an affiliated group filing a consolidated return ending on or before December 31, 1987, there is 1 disposition of stock of a subsidiary incorporated in Delaware on December 24, 1969, and whose principal place of business is in New Orleans, Louisiana (within the meaning of Treasury Regulation section 1.1502-19), the amount required to be included in income with respect to such disposition under Treasury Regulation section 1.1502-19(a) shall, notwithstanding such section, be included in income ratably over the 15-year period beginning with the taxable year in which the disposition occurs and ending with the 14th succeeding taxable year.

(u)   Amendments Related to Single Employer Pension Plan Amendments Act of 1986.—

(1)   Clarification of applicability of notice requirement for significant reductions in benefit accruals.—Section 206(h) of the Employee Retirement Income Security Act of 1974 (29 U.S.C. 1054(h); 100 Stat. 243) is amended—

(A)   by striking out "single-employer plan" and inserting in lieu thereof "plan described in paragraph (2)";

(B)   by redesignating paragraphs (1), (2), and (3) as subparagraphs (A), (B), and (C), respectively;

(C) by striking out "paragraph (1), (2), or (3)" and inserting in lieu thereof "subparagraph (A), (B), or (C)";

(D) by inserting "(1)" after "(h)"; and

(E) by adding at the end of the following new paragraph:

(2) A plan is described in this paragraph if such plan is—

(A) a defined benefit plan, or

"(B) an individual account plan which is subject to the funding standards of section 302."

(2) Treatment of section 4049 trusts established pursuant to section 4042(i).—Section 4049(a) of the Employee Retirement Income Security Act of 1974 (29 U.S.C. 1349(a); 100 Stat. 258) is amended by inserting "or 4042(i)" after "section 4041(c)(3)(B)(ii) or (iii)".

(3) Correction of definition of multiemployer plan for purposes of title I.—Section 11016(c)(1) of the Single-Employer Pension Plan Amendments Act of 1986 (100 Stat. 273) and the amendment made thereby are repealed.

(4) Effective date.—

(A) General rule.—Except as provided in subparagraph (B), the preceding provisions of this subsection shall be effective as if such provisions were included in the enactment of the Single-Employer Pension Plan Amendments Act of 1986.

(B) Special rule.—Subparagraph (B) of section 206(h)(2) of the Employee Retirement Income Security Act of 1974 (as amended by paragraph (1)) shall apply only with respect to plan amendments adopted on or after the date of the enactment of this Act.

[For official explanation, see Committee Reports, ¶4193]

[¶2141]   SEC. 1881.   EFFECTIVE DATE.

Except as otherwise provided in this subtitle, any amendment made by this subtitle shall take effect as if included in the provision of the Tax Reform Act of 1984 to which such amendment relates.

[¶2142]   SEC. 1882.   AMENDMENTS RELATED TO COVERAGE OF CHURCH EMPLOYEES (SECTION 2603 OF THE DEFICIT REDUCTION ACT).

* * * * * * * * * * * *

(b)   Treatment of Income of Certain Church, Etc., Employees.—

* * * * * * * * * * * *

(2)   Amendments of social security act.—

(A) In general.—Section 211 of the Social Security Act is amended by adding at the end thereof the following new subsection:

"(i)(1) In applying subsection (a)—

"(A) church employee income shall not be reduced by any deduction;

"(B) church employee income and deductions attributable to such income shall not be taken into account in determining the amount of other net earnings from self-employment.

"(2)(A) Subsection (b)(2) shall be applied separately—

"(i) to church employee income, and

"(ii) to other net earnings from self-employment.

"(B) In applying subsection (b)(2) to church employee income, ' $100' shall be substituted for ' $400'.

"(3) Paragraph (1) shall not apply to any amount allowable as a deduction under subsection (a)(11), and paragraph (1) shall be applied before determining the amount so allowable.

"(4) For purposes of this section, the term 'church employee income' means gross income for services which are described in section 210(a)(8)(B) (and are not described in section 210(a)(8)(A))."

(B) Technical and conforming amendments.—

(i) Net earnings.—Section 211(a)(13) of such Act is amended to read as follows:

"(13) In the case of church employee income, the special rules of subsection (i)(1) shall apply."

Act §1882(b)(2) ¶2142

(ii)   Self-employment income.—Section 211(b) of such Act is amended by adding at the end thereof the following new sentence: "In the case of church employee income, the special rules of subsection (i)(2) shall apply for purposes of paragraph (2)."

(3)   **Effective date.**—The amendments made by this subsection shall apply to remuneration paid or derived in taxable years beginning after December 31, 1985.

[For official explanation, see Committee Reports, ¶4195]

[¶2143] SEC. 1883. TECHNICAL CORRECTIONS IN OTHER PROVISIONS RELATED TO SOCIAL SECURITY ACT PROGRAMS.

(a)   **Amendments Relating to OASDI Program.—**

(1)   Section 202(c)(5)(B) of the Social Security Act is amended by striking out "or (I)" and inserting in lieu thereof "or (J)".

(2)   Section 202(q)(5)(A)(i) of such Act is amended by striking out "prescribed by him" and inserting in lieu thereof "prescribed by the Secretary".

(3)   Section 202(q)(5)(C) of such Act is amended by striking out "she shall be deemed" and inserting in lieu thereof "he or she shall be deemed".

(4)   Section 210(a)(5)(G) of such Act is amended by striking out "Any other service" and inserting in lieu thereof "any other service".

(5)   Effective on the date of the enactment of the Deficit Reduction Act of 1984—

(A)   section 2601(d)(1)(B)(ii) of that Act is amended by striking out "210(a)(5)(g)(iii)" and inserting in lieu thereof "210(a)(5)(G)(iii)"; and

(B)   section 2663(c)(1) of that Act is amended by striking out subparagraph (B).

(6)   Section 211(c)(2) of the Social Security Act is amended by indenting subparagraph (G) two additional ems (for a total indentation of four ems) so as to align its left margin with the margins of the other subparagraphs in such section.

(7)   Section 215(i)(5)(B) of such Act is amended—

(A)   by striking out "subdivision (I)" in clause (ii) and inserting in lieu thereof "clause (i)(I)"; and

(B)   by striking out "subdivisions (I) and (II)" in the matter between clauses (iii) and (iv) and inserting in lieu thereof "clause (i)".

(8)   The heading of section 218(m) of such Act is amended to read as follows:

"Wisconsin Retirement Fund".

(9)   Section 221(e) of such Act is amended by striking out "under this section" in the first sentence.

(10)   Section 223(g)(1) of such Act is amended by striking out the second comma after the term "benefits" where such term first appears in the matter following subparagraph (C).

*   *   *   *   *   *   *   *   *   *   *   *

(b)   **Amendments Relating to AFDC and Child Support Programs.—**

(1)(A)   Section 402(a)(31)(A) of the Social Security Act is amended by striking out "(or such lesser amount as the Secretary may prescribe in the case of an individual not engaged in fulltime employment or not employed throughout the month)".

(B)   The amendment made by this paragraph shall be effective beginning October 1, 1984.

(2)(A)   Section 402(a)(38)(B) of such Act is amended by striking out "section 406(a)," and inserting in lieu thereof "section 406(a) or in section 407(a) (if such section is applicable to the State),".

(B)   Section 402(a)(38) of such Act (as amended by subparagraph (A) of this paragraph) is further amended by relocating so much of subparagraph (B) as follows "section 407(a) (if such section is applicable to the State)," and placing it after and below subparagraph (B), beginning flush, and indenting it two ems so that its left margin is aligned with the left margin of that portion of section 402(a)(38) that precedes subparagraph (A) thereof.

(C)   The amendments made by this paragraph shall be effective beginning October 1, 1984.

(3)(A)   Section 402(a)(39) of such Act is amended by striking out "under the age selected by the State pursuant to section 406(a)(2)" and inserting in lieu thereof "under the age of 18".

(B)   The amendment made by subparagraph (A) shall be effective beginning October 1, 1984.

(4)(A)   Section 402(a) of such Act is amended by striking out "and" after the semicolon at the end of paragraph (37), and by making any additional changes which may be necessary to assure that paragraphs (34) through (37) each end with a semicolon, paragraph (38) ends with "; and", and paragraph (39) ends with a period.

(B)   Effective on the date of the enactment of the Deficit Reduction Act of 1984, section 2639(a) of that Act is amended by striking out the period immediately following "utility providing home energy" (in the quoted matter) and inserting in lieu thereof a semicolon.

(5)   The placement of the last sentence of section 402(a) of the Social Security Act is modified to the extent necessary to assure that it begins flush to the full left margin without any indentation, immediately after and below the last of the numbered paragraphs.

(6)   Section 457(c) of such Act is amended by striking out "subsection (b)(3)(A) and (B)" in the matter following paragraph (2) and inserting in lieu thereof "subsection (b)(4)(A) and (B)".

(7)   Section 458(d) of such Act is amended by striking out "on behalf of individuals residing in another State" and inserting in lieu thereof "at the request of another State".

(8)   Section 464(b)(2)(A) of such Act is amended by striking out "threshhold" and inserting in lieu thereof "threshold".

(9)   Section 474(a) of such Act is amended by moving paragraph (4) two ems to the left, so that its left margin is in flush alignment with the margins of the preceding paragraphs.

(10)(A)   Part E of title IV of such Act is amended by adding at the end thereof the following new section:

"EXCLUSION FROM AFDC UNIT OF CHILD FOR WHOM FOSTER CARE MAINTENANCE PAYMENTS ARE MADE

"Sec. 478.   Notwithstanding any other provision of this title, a child with respect to whom foster care maintenance payments are made under this part shall not, for the period for which such payments are made, be regarded as a member of a family for purposes of determining the amount of the benefits of the family under part A, and the income and resources of such child shall not be counted as the income and resources of a family under such part.".

(B)   The amendment made by subparagraph (A) shall become effective October 1, 1984.

(11)(A)   The failure by a State to comply with the provisions of any amendment made by paragraph (1), (2), (3), or (10) or the imposition by a State of any requirement inconsistent with such provisions, in the administration of its plan approved under section 402(a) of the Social Security Act during the period beginning October 1, 1984, and ending on the day preceding the date of the enactment of this Act, shall not be considered to be failure to comply substantially with a provision required to be included in the State's plan, or to constitute (solely by reason of such inconsistency) the imposition of a prohibited requirement in the administration of the plan, for purposes of section 404(a) of such Act.

(B)   No State shall be considered to have made any overpayment or underpayment of aid, under its plan approved under section 402(a) of the Social Security Act, by reason of its compliance or noncompliance with the provisions of any amendment made by paragraph (1), (2), (3), or (10) (or solely because of the extent to which its requirements are consistent or inconsistent with such provisions) in the administration of the plan during the period specified in subparagraph (A).

(c)   **Amendments to General Provisions.—**
(1)   Section 1101(a) of such Act is amended by shifting paragraphs (3), (4), and (5) to the right to the extent necessary to assure that their left margins are aligned with the left margins of the other numbered paragraphs.

(2)   Section 1136(b)(7) of such Act is amended by striking out "nongovermental" and inserting in lieu thereof "nongovernmental".

(d)   **Amendments Relating to SSI Program.—**
(1)   The heading of section 1631(g) of such Act is amended to read as follows:

"Reimbursement to States for Interim Assistance Payments".

(2)   Section 1612(a)(1)(C) of such Act is amended by striking out "section 43" and inserting in lieu thereof "section 32".

Act §1883(d) ¶2143

(3) Section 1612(b) of such Act is amended—
(A) by striking out the semicolon at the end of paragraph (2)(A) and inserting in lieu thereof ", and";
(B) by striking out the period at the end of paragraph (2)(B) and inserting in lieu thereof a semicolon; and
(C) by making any changes which may be necessary to assure that paragraph (11) ends with a semicolon, paragraph (12) ends with "; and", and paragraph (13) ends with a period.

(e) **Amendments Relating to Social Services Program.—**
(1)(A) Section 2003(d) of such Act is repealed.
(B) Section 2003(b) of such Act is amended by striking out "(subject to subsection (d))".
(2) Section 2007 of such Act is repealed.

(f) **Effective Date.—**Except as otherwise provided in this section, the amendments made by this section shall take effect on the date of the enactment of this Act.

[For official explanation, see Committee Reports, ¶4196]

[¶2144] SEC. 1885. AMENDMENTS TO THE TARIFF SCHEDULES.

(a) **In General.—**The Tariff Schedules of the United States are amended as follows:
(1) **Telecommunications product classification corrections.—**
(A) Schedule 6 is amended as follows:
(i) Headnote 1 to subpart C of part 4 is amended by striking out "688.43" and inserting in lieu thereof "688.42".
(ii) Headnote 3 of part 5 of schedule 6 is amended by striking out "items 685.11 through 685.19, inclusive," and inserting in lieu thereof "items 684.92, 684.98, 685.00, and 685.08".
(iii) Item 685.34 is amended by inserting "35% ad val." in Column No. 2.
(iv) Item 685.55 is amended by striking out "685.11 to 685.50" and inserting in lieu thereof "684.92 to 685.49".
(B) Headnote 2(ii) to part 7 of schedule 8 is amended by striking out "688.43" and inserting in lieu thereof "688.42".
(C) Subpart B of part 2 of schedule 6 is amended by inserting before the superior heading to items 608.26 and 608.29, and at the same indention level as that heading, the following new item:

| "608.25 | Silicon electrical steel .... | 5.6% ad. val. + additional duties (see headnote 4) | 5.1% ad. val. + additional duties (see headnote 4) (D) Free (E,I) | 33% ad. val. additional duties (see headnote 4)" |

(2) **Corrections to the Appendix.—**Subpart B of part 1 to the Appendix is amended as follows:
(A) The article description for item 906.38 is amended to read as follows: "N-Acetylsulfanilyl chloride (provided for in item 405.31, part 1B, schedule 4)".
(B) Item 907.38 is amended by striking out "411.87" and inserting in lieu thereof "411.82".
(C) Item 912.13 is amended by striking out "670.20" and inserting in lieu thereof "670.21".
(D) Item 907.63 is amended by striking out "(provided for in item 437.13" and inserting in lieu thereof "put up in measured doses in chewing gum form (provided for in item 438.02".

(3) **Miscellaneous corrections.—**The Schedules are further amended as follows:
(A) Headnote 1 of subpart D of part 4 of schedule 1 is amended by striking out "(casein plus albumin)" and inserting in lieu thereof "(casein plus lactalbumin)".
(B) Headnote 1 of subpart C of part 4 of schedule 3 is amended—
(i) by inserting "or" after the semicolon at the end of clause (v); and
(ii) by striking out "; or" at the end of clause (vi) and inserting in lieu thereof a period.

(b) Effective Date.—
(1)   The amendments made by this section shall apply with respect to articles entered, or withdrawn from warehouse, for consumption on or after the date that is 15 days after the date of enactment of this Act.
(2)   Notwithstanding section 514 of the Tariff Act of 1930 or any other provision of law, upon proper request filed with the customs officer concerned on or before the date that is 90 days after the date of enactment of this Act, the entry of any article—
(A)   which was made on or after November 14, 1984, and before the date that is 15 days after the date of enactment of this Act; and
(B)   with respect to which there would have been no duty, or a lesser duty, by reason of any amendment made by subsection (a) if such entry were made on or after the date that is 15 days after the date of enactment of this Act,
shall be liquidated or reliquidated as though such entry had been made on the date that is 15 days after the date of enactment of this Act.
(3)   The rate of duty in column number 1 for item 608.25 of the Tariff Schedules of the United States shall be subject to all staged rate reductions for item 608.38 of such Schedules that—
(A)   take effect after the date of enactment of this Act, and
(B)   were proclaimed by the President before the date of enactment of this Act.

[For official explanation, see Committee Reports, ¶4198]

[¶2145] SEC. 1886. TECHNICAL CORRECTIONS TO COUNTERVAILING AND ANTIDUMPING DUTY PROVISIONS.

(a)   In General.—Title VII of the Tariff Act of 1930 is amended as follows:
(1)(A)   Subsection (c) of section 701 (19 U.S.C. 1671(c)) is redesignated as subsection (d).
(B)   Subsection (g) of such section 701 (as added by section 613(b) of the Trade and Tariff Act of 1984) is—
(i)   amended by striking out "(g) Whenever" and inserting in lieu thereof "(c) Upstream Subsidy.—Whenever"; and
(ii)   inserted immediately after subsection (b) of that section.
(2)   Sections 702(b)(1), 732(b)(1), and 733(b)(2) (19 U.S.C. 1671a(b)(1); 1673a(b)(1); 1673(b)(2)) are each amended by striking out "(C), (D), or (E)" each place it appears and inserting in lieu thereof "(C), (D), (E), or (F)"
(3)   Subsection (h) of section 703 (19 U.S.C. 1671b(h)) is redesignated as subsection (g), and—
(A)   paragraph (2)(A) of that subsection (as redesignated) is amended by striking out "days under section 705(a)(1) or 225 days under section 705(a)(2), as appropriate" and inserting in lieu thereof "or 225 days, as appropriate, under section 705(a)(1)"; and
(B)   paragraph (2)(B)(ii) of that subsection (as so redesignated) is amended by striking out "days under section 705(a)(2)" and inserting in lieu thereof "or 225 days, as appropriate, under section 705(a)(1)".
(4)   Section 704 is amended—
(A)   by amending subsection (d)—
(i)   by redesignating paragraph (2) as paragraph (3); and
(ii)   by inserting after paragraph (1) the following new paragraph:
"(2)   Exports of merchandise to United States not to increase during interim period.—The administering authority may not accept any agreement under subsection (b) unless that agreement provides a means of ensuring that the quantity of the merchandise covered by that agreement exported to the United States during the period provided for elimination or offset of the subsidy or cessation of exports does not exceed the quantity of such merchandise exported to the United States during the most recent representative period determined by the administering authority."; and
(B)   by amending subsection (i)(1)(D) by striking out "international" and inserting in lieu thereof "intentional".
(5)   Paragraph (2) of section 706(a) is amended by aligning the margin of the matter appearing after subparagraph (B) with the margin of the matter appearing before subparagraph (A).
(6)(A)   Section 708 is amended by striking out "Sec. 708." and inserting in lieu thereof the following flush section heading:

"SEC. 708. EFFECT OF DEROGATION OF EXPORT-IMPORT BANK FINANC-
ING.".

(B) The table of contents for such title VII is amended by inserting in numerical sequence the following:

"Sec. 708. Effect of derogation of Export-Import Bank financing."

(7) Paragraph (1) of section 736(c) (19 U.S.C. 1673e(c)(1)) is amended by inserting
", and was sold to any person that is not related to such manufacturer, producer, or
exporter," immediately before "on or after the date of publication of—".

(8) The last sentence of section 751(b)(1) (19 U.S.C. 1675(b)(1)) is amended by
inserting "or countervailing duty" after "antidumping" each place it appears.

(9) Clause (i) of section 771(7)(F) (19 U.S.C. 1677(7)(F)(i)) is amended—

(A) by striking "any merchandise" in that part which precedes subclause (I)
and inserting in lieu thereof "the merchandise"; and

(B) by striking out "find orders" in subclause (VIII) and inserting in lieu
thereof "final orders".

(10) Subsection (a) of section 771A (19 U.S.C. 1677-1(a)) is amended by striking
out "(ii), or (iii)" and inserting in lieu thereof "(ii), (iii), or (iv)".

(11) Subsection (g) of section 773 (19 U.S.C. 1677b(g)) is redesignated as subsection (f).

(12) Section 775 (19 U.S.C. 1677d) is amended by striking out "an proceeding"
each place it appears in the text and in the heading and inserting in lieu thereof "a
proceeding".

(13) Section 777 (19 U.S.C. 1677f) is amended—

(A) by striking out "confidential", "nonconfidential", and "confidentiality"
each place they appear in the text and in the side headings and inserting in lieu
thereof "proprietary", "non-proprietary", and "proprietary status", respectively;
and

(B) by inserting "or the Commission" after "administering authority" in subsection (b)(1)(B)(i).

(b) Amendments to Effective Date Provisions.—Section 626(b) of the Trade and Tariff Act of 1984 (relating to the effective dates of the amendments made therein to title
VII of the Tariff Act of 1930) is amended—

(1) by amending paragraph (1) by inserting ", and to reviews begun under section
751 of that Act," after "1930"; and

(2) by adding at the end thereof the following new paragraphs:

"(3) The administering authority may delay implementation of any of the amendments referred to in subsections (a) and (b)(1) with respect to any investigation in
progress on the date of enactment of this Act if the administering authority determines that immediate implementation would prevent compliance with a statutory
deadline in title VII of the Tariff Act of 1930 that is applicable to that investigation.

"(4) The amendment made by section 621 shall apply with respect to merchandise
that is unliquidated on or after November 4, 1984."

[For official explanation, see Committee Reports, ¶4199]

[¶2146] **SEC. 1887. AMENDMENTS TO THE TRADE ACT OF 1974.**

(a) In General.—The Trade Act of 1974 is amended as follows:

(1) Subclause (II) of section 102(b)(4)(B)(ii) of the Trade Act of 1974 (19 U.S.C.
2112(b)(4)(B)(ii)(II)) is amended by striking out "subsection (A)(ii)(I)" and inserting in
lieu thereof "subparagraph (A)(ii)(I)".

(2) Subsection (n) of section 135 (as added by section 306(c)(2)(B)(v) of the Trade
and Tariff Act of 1984) is redesignated as subsection (m).

(3) Section 141(d)(6) is amended by striking out "3679(b) of the Revised Statutes
(31 U.S.C. 665(b))" and inserting in lieu thereof "1342 of title 31, United States
Code".

(4) Subsection (d) of section 141 (19 U.S.C. 2171(d)) is amended—

(A) by striking out "and" at the end of paragraph (9),

(B) by striking out the period at the end of paragraph (10) and inserting in lieu
thereof "; and", and

(C) redesignating the paragraph added by section 304(d)(2)(A)(iii) of the Trade
and Tariff Act of 1984 as paragraph (11).

(5) Subparagraphs (A), (B), and (C) of section 502(b)(4) (19 U.S.C. 2462(b)(4)) are
amended to read as follows:

"(A)   has nationalized, expropriated, or otherwise seized ownership or control of property, including patents, trademarks, or copyrights, owned by a United States citizen or by a corporation, partnership, or association which is 50 percent or more beneficially owned by United States citizens,

"(B)   has taken steps to repudiate or nullify an existing contract or agreement with a United States citizen or a corporation, partnership, or association which is 50 percent or more beneficially owned by United States citizens, the effect of which is to nationalize, expropriate, or otherwise seize ownership or control of property, including patents, trademarks, or copyrights, so owned, or

"(C)   has imposed or enforced taxes or other exactions, restrictive maintenance or operational conditions, or other measures with respect to property, including patents, trademarks, or copyrights, so owned, the effect of which is to nationalize, expropriate, or otherwise seize ownership or control of such property,".

(6)   That part of section 504(c)(3)(D)(ii) (19 U.S.C. 2464(c)(3)(D)(ii) that precedes subclause (I) is amended—

(A)   by striking out "from any beneficiary developing country";

(B)   by striking out "1984 which exceeds 15" and inserting in lieu thereof "1986 the aggregate value of which exceeds 15"; and

(C)   by striking out "if for the preceding calendar year such beneficiary developing country—" and inserting in lieu thereof "from those beneficiary developing countries which for the preceding calendar year—".

(b)   Transistors.—

(1)   Section 128(b) of the Trade Act of 1974 (19 U.S.C. 2138) is amended by striking out "587.70" in paragraph (1) and inserting in lieu thereof "687.70".

(2)(A)   Item 687.70 of the Tariff Schedules of the United States is amended by striking out "4.2% ad val." and inserting in lieu thereof "Free".

(B)   The amendment made by subparagraph (A) shall apply with respect to articles entered, or withdrawn from warehouse, for consumption on or after the date that is 15 days after the date of enactment of this Act.

(C)   Notwithstanding section 514 of the Tariff Act of 1930 or any other provision of law, upon proper request filed with the customs officer concerned on or before the date that is 90 days after the date of enactment of this Act, the entry of any article described in item 687.70 of the Tariff Schedules of the United States which was made on or after March 1, 1985, and before the date that is 15 days after the date of enactment of this Act shall be liquidated or reliquidated as though such entry had been made on the date that is 15 days after the date of enactment of this Act.

[For official explanation, see Committee Reports, ¶4200]

[¶2147]   **SEC. 1888.   AMENDMENTS TO THE TARIFF ACT OF 1930.**
The Tariff Act of 1930 is amended as follows:

(1)   Subsection (c) of section 304 (19 U.S.C. 1304(c)) is amended—

(A)   by striking out "No" and inserting in lieu thereof the following: "(1) Except as provided in paragraph (2), no"; and

(B)   by adding at the end thereof the following new paragraph:

"(2)   If, because of the nature of an article, it is technically or commercially infeasible to mark it by one of the four methods specified in paragraph (1), the article may be marked by an equally permanent method of marking such as paint stenciling or, in the case of small diameter pipe, tube, and fittings, by tagging the containers or bundles."

(2)   Subsection (j) of section 313 (19 U.S.C. 1313(j)) is amended—

(A)   by redesignating the paragraphs (3) and (4) inserted by section 202(1)(B) of the Trade and Tariff Act of 1984 as paragraphs (2) and (3), respectively; and

(B)   by amending the paragraph redesignated as paragraph (4) by section 202(1)(A) of the Trade and Tariff Act of 1984 to read as follows:

"(4)   The performing of incidental operations (including, but not limited to, testing, cleaning, repacking, and inspecting) on—

"(A)   the imported merchandise itself in cases to which paragraph (1) applies, or

"(B)   the merchandise of the same kind and quality in cases to which paragraph (2) applies, that does not amount to manufacture or production for drawback purposes under the preceding provisions of this section shall not be treated as a use of that merchandise for purposes of applying paragraph (1)(B) or (2)(C).".

(3) Section 339(c)(2)(A) (19 U.S.C. 1339) is amended by striking out "relief" and inserting in lieu thereof "injury".

(4) Section 514(a) (19 U.S.C. 1514(a)) is amended by striking out "as defined in section 771(9)(C), (D), (E), and (F) of this Act".

(5) Section 516(a)(2) (19 U.S.C. 1516(a)(2)) is amended by adding at the end thereof the following new sentence:

Such term includes an association, a majority of whose members is composed of persons described in subparagraph (A), (B), or (C).

(6) Section 516A(a)(3) (19 U.S.C. 1516a(a)(3)) is amended by striking out "(2)(A)-(ii)" and inserting in lieu thereof "(2)(A)(i)(II)".

(7) Section 613a of the Tariff Act of 1930 (19 U.S.C. 1613a), as added by section 317 of the Joint Resolution entitled "A Joint Resolution making appropriations for fiscal year 1985, and for other purposes.", approved October 12, 1984 (98 Stat. 2054, Public Law 98-473), is repealed.

(8) Section 641 (19 U.S.C. 1641) is amended by adding at the end thereof the following new subsection:

(i) Compensation of Ocean Freight Forwarders.—

"**(1) In general.—**Notwithstanding any other provision of law, no conference or group of two or more ocean common carriers in the foreign commerce of the United States that is authorized to agree upon the level of compensation paid to ocean freight forwarders may—

"(A) deny to any member of such conference or group the right, upon notice of not more than 10 calendar days, to take independent action on any level of compensation paid to a ocean freight forwarder who is also a customs broker, and

"(B) agree to limit the payment of compensation to an ocean freight forwarder who is also a customs broker to less than 1.25 percent of the aggregate of all rates and charges applicable under the tariff assessed against the cargo on which the forwarding services are provided.

"**(2) Administration.—**The provisions of this subsection shall be enforced by the agency responsible for administration of the Shipping Act of 1984 (46 U.S.C. 1701, et seq.).

"**(3) Remedies.—**Any person injured by reason of a violation of paragraph (1) may, in addition to any other remedy, file a complaint for reparation as provided in section 11 of the Shipping Act of 1984 (46 U.S.C. 1710), which may be enforced pursuant to section 14 of such Act (46 U.S.C. 1713).

"**(4) Definitions.—**For purposes of this subsection, the terms 'conference', 'ocean common carrier', and 'ocean freight forwarder' have the respective meaning given to such terms by section 3 of the Shipping Act of 1984 (46 U.S.C. 1702)."

[For official explanation, see Committee Reports, ¶4201]

[¶2148] SEC. 1889. AMENDMENTS TO THE TRADE AND TARIFF ACT OF 1984.

The Trade and Tariff Act of 1984 (Public Law 98-573) is amended as follows:

(1) Section 126 is amended by striking out the following:

"(3) Paragraphs (1) and (2) of section 126 of the bifll are amended to read as follows:".

(2) Section 174(b) is amended by adding at the end of the table appearing therein the following:

"January 1, 1987 .... 4.9% ad val.".

(3) Paragraph (7) of subsection (b) of section 212 is redesignated as subsection (c) of that section.

(4) The table in section 234(a) is amended by striking out "711.49" and inserting in lieu thereof "712.49".

(5) Paragraph (3) of section 307(b) is amended by striking out "or paragraph (3)".

(6) Paragraph (4) of section 404(e) is amended by striking out "147.44" and inserting in lieu thereof "147.33".

(7) Section 504 is amended by striking out "Tariff Act of 1930" and inserting in lieu thereof "Trade Act of 1974".

(8) Paragraph (3) of section 619 is amended by striking out "subsection (b)" and inserting in lieu thereof "subsection (b)(1)".

[For official explanation, see Committee Reports, ¶4202]

〔¶2149〕 SEC. 1890. AMENDMENTS TO THE CARIBBEAN BASIN ECONOMIC RECOVERY ACT.

Section 213 of the Caribbean Basin Economic Recovery Act (19 U.S.C. 2703) is amended—

(1) by amending paragraph (3) of subsection (a) (as added by section 235 of the Trade and Tariff Act of 1984)—

(A) by redesignating that paragraph as paragraph (4), and aligning its margin with that of paragraph (3), and

(B) by striking out "such" the first time it appears therein and inserting in lieu thereof "any beneficiary"; and

(2) by striking out "138.42" in subsection (f)(5)(B) and inserting in lieu thereof "138.46".

[For official explanation, see Committee Reports, ¶4203]

〔¶2150〕 SEC. 1891. CONFORMING AMENDMENTS REGARDING CUSTOMS BROKERS.

Title 28 of the United States Code is amended—

(1) by striking out "(3) or (c)" in section 1581(g)(1) and inserting in lieu thereof "(3)"; and

(2) by striking out "641(a)(1)(C)" in section 1582(1) and inserting in lieu thereof "641(b)(6)".

[For official explanation, see Committee Reports, ¶4204]

〔¶2151〕 SEC. 1892. SPECIAL EFFECTIVE DATE PROVISIONS FOR CERTAIN ARTICLES GIVEN DUTY-FREE TREATMENT UNDER THE TRADE AND TARIFF ACT OF 1984.

(a) **In General.**—Notwithstanding section 514 of the Tariff Act of 1930 or any other provision of law, upon proper request filed with the appropriate customs officer on or before the date that is 90 days after the date of enactment of this Act, any entry—

(1) which was made after the applicable date and before November 14, 1984, and

(2) with respect to which there would have been no duty or a lesser duty by reason of any amendment made by section 112, 115, 118, 167, or 179 of the Trade and Tariff Act of 1984 if such entry were made on November 14, 1984,

shall be liquidated or reliquidated as though such entry had been made on November 14, 1984.

(b) **Applicable Date.**—For purposes of this section—

(1) The term "applicable date" means—

(A) with respect to any entry for which the amendment described in subsection (a)(2) is any amendment made by section 118 of the Trade and Tariff Act of 1984, June 1, 1982;

(B) with respect to any entry for which the amendment described in subsection (a)(2) is any amendment made by section 112, 115, or 179 of the Trade and Tariff Act of 1984, June 30, 1983; and

(C) with respect to any entry for which the amendment described in subsection (a)(2) is the amendment made by section 167 of the Trade and Tariff Act of 1984, October 30, 1983.

(2) The term "entry" includes any withdrawal from warehouse.

[For official explanation, see Committee Reports, ¶4205]

〔¶2152〕 SEC. 1893. TECHNICAL AMENDMENTS RELATING TO CUSTOMS USER FEES.

(a) **Schedule of Fees.**—

(1) Subsection (a) of section 13031 of the Consolidated Omnibus Budget Reconciliation Act of 1985 (19 U.S.C. 58c(a)) is amended—

(A) by striking out "Subject to the limitation in subsection (b)(2), for" in paragraph (2) and inserting in lieu thereof "For",

(B) by adding at the end thereof the following new paragraph:

"(8) For the arrival of a barge or other bulk carrier from Canada or Mexico, $100."

(2) Paragraph (3) of section 13031(a) of the Consolidated Omnibus Budget Reconciliation Act of 1985 (19 U.S.C. 58c(a)(3)) is amended to read as follows:

"(3) For the arrival of each railroad car carrying passengers or commercial freight, $7.50."

(b) Limitations on Fees.—

(1) Subsection (b) of section 13031 of the Consolidated Omnibus Budget Reconciliation Act of 1985 (19 U.S.C. 58c(b)) is amended by adding at the end thereof the following new paragraphs:

"(4) No fee may be charged under subsection (a)(5) with respect to the arrival of any passenger—

"(A) who is in transit to a destination outside the customs territory of the United States, and

"(B) for whom customs inspectional services are not provided.

"(5) No fee may be charged under subsection (a)(1) for the arrival of—

"(A) a vessel during a calendar year after a total of $5,955 in fees charged under paragraph (1) or (8) of subsection (a) has been paid to the Secretary of the Treasury for the provision of customs services for all arrivals of such vessel during such calendar year,

"(B) any vessel which, at the time of the arrival, is being used solely as a tugboat, or

"(C) any barge or other bulk carrier from Canada or Mexico.

"(6) No fee may be charged under subsection (a)(8) for the arrival of a barge or other bulk carrier during a calendar year after a total of $1,500 in fees charged under paragraph (1) or (8) of subsection (a) has been paid to the Secretary of the Treasury for the provision of customs services for all arrivals of such barge or other bulk carrier during such calendar year.

"(7) No fee may be charged under paragraphs (2), (3), or (4) of subsection (a) for the arrival of any—

"(A) commercial truck,

"(B) railroad car, or

"(C) private vessel,

that is being transported, at the time of the arrival, by any vessel that is not a ferry."

(2) Subparagraph (A) of section 13031(b)(1) of the Consolidated Omnibus Budget Reconciliation Act of 1985 (19 U.S.C. 58c(b)(1)(A)) is amended to read as follows:

"(A) the arrival of any passenger whose journey—

"(i) originated in—

"(I) Canada,

"(II) Mexico,

"(III) a territory or possession of the United States, or

"(IV) any adjacent island (within the meaning of section 101(b)(5) of the Immigration and Nationality Act (8 U.S.C. 1101(b)(5)), or

"(ii) originated in the United States and was limited to—

"(I) Canada,

"(II) Mexico,

"(III) territories and possessions of the United States, and

"(IV) such adjacent islands;".

(3) Paragraph (1) of section 13031(b) of the Consolidated Omnibus Budget Reconciliation Act of 1985 (19 U.S.C. 58c(b)(1)) is amended—

(A) by striking out the period at the end of subparagraph

(B) and inserting in lieu thereof "; or", and

(B) by adding at the end thereof the following new subparagraph:

"(C) the arrival of any ferry."

(4) Subsection (c) of section 13031 of the Consolidated Omnibus Budget Reconciliation Act of 1985 (19 U.S.C. 58c(c)) is amended—

(A) by amending paragraph (1) to read as follows:

"(1) The term 'ferry' means any vessel which is being used—

"(A) to provide transportation only between places that are no more than 300 miles apart, and

"(B) to transport only—

"(i) passengers, or

"(ii)   vehicles, or railroad cars, which are being used, or have been used, in transporting passengers or goods.", and

(B)   by adding at the end thereof the following new paragraph:

"(5)   The term 'barge or other bulk carrier' means any vessel which—
"(A)   is not self-propelled, or
"(B)   transports fungible goods that are not packaged in any form."

(c)   Special Provisions Relating to Customs Broker Permits—

(1)   Subsection (d) of section 13031 of the Consolidated Omnibus Budget Reconciliation Act of 1985 (19 U.S.C. 58c(d)) is amended by adding at the end thereof the following new paragraph:

"(4)(A)   Notice of the date on which payment of the fee imposed by subsection (a)(7) is due shall be published by the Secretary of the Treasury in the Federal Register by no later the date that is 60 days before such due date.

"(B)   A customs broker permit may be revoked or suspended for nonpayment of the fee imposed by subsection (a)(7) only if notice of the date on which payment of such fee is due was published in the Federal Register at least 60 days before such due date.

"(C)   The customs broker's license issued under section 641(b) of the Tariff Act of 1930 (19 U.S.C. 1641(b)) may not be revoked or suspended merely by reason of nonpayment of the fee imposed under subsection (a)(7)."

(2)   Notwithstanding section 13031(a)(7) of the Consolidated Omnibus Budget Reconciliation Act of 1985 (19 U.S.C. 58c(a)(7)), the fee imposed by section 13031(a) of such Act with respect to each customs broker permit held by an individual, partnership, association, or corporate customs broker for calendar year 1986 is $62.50.

(3)(A)   The Secretary of the Treasury shall reinstate any customs broker's license or customs broker permit issued under subsection (b) or (c) of section 641 of the Tariff Act of 1930 (19 U.S.C. 1641) that was suspended or revoked on or before the date of enactment of this Act solely by reason of nonpayment of the fee imposed by section 13031(a)(7) of the Consolidated Omnibus Budget Reconciliation Act of 1985.

(B)   Notwithstanding any other provision of law, the Secretary of the Treasury may not suspend or revoke any customs broker permit issued under section 641(c) of the Tariff Act of 1930 (19 U.S.C. 1641(c)) solely by reason of nonpayment of the fee imposed by section 13031(a)(7) of the Consolidated Omnibus Budget Reconciliation Act of 1985 before the date that is 60 days after the date of enactment of this Act.

(d)   Provision of Foreign Pre-Clearance Services.—

(1)   Paragraph (1) of section 13031(e) of the Consolidated Omnibus Budget Reconciliation Act of 1985 (19 U.S.C. 58c(e)(1)) is amended to read as follows:

"(1)   Notwithstanding section 451 of the Tariff Act of 1930 (19 U.S.C. 1451) or any other provision of law (other than paragraph (2)), the customs services required to be provided to passengers upon arrival in the United States shall be adequately provided in connection with scheduled airline flights at customs serviced airports when needed and at no cost (other than the fees imposed under subsection (a)) to airlines and airline passengers."

(2)   Subsection (e) of section 13031 of such Act is amended by—

(A)   striking out "This subsection" in paragraph (2) and inserting in lieu thereof "Paragraph (1)", and

(B)   by adding at the end thereof the following new paragraph:

(3)   Notwithstanding section 451 of the Tariff Act of 1930 (19 U.S.C. 1451) or any other provision of law—

"(A)   the customs services required to be provided to passengers upon arrival in the United States shall be adequately provided in connection with scheduled airline flights when needed at places located outside the customs territory of the United States at which a customs officer is stationed for the purpose of providing such customs services, and

"(B)   other than the fees imposed under subsection (a), the airlines and airline passengers shall not be required to reimburse the Secretary of the Treasury for the costs of providing overtime customs inspectional services at such places."

(e)   Regulations on Remittance of Fees.—Subsection (g) of section 13031 of the Consolidated Omnibus Budget Reconciliation Act of 1985 (19 U.S.C. 58c(g)) is amended by

Act §1893(e)   ¶2152

adding at the end thereof the following new sentence: "Regulations issued by the Secretary of the Treasury under this subsection with respect to the collection of the fees charged under subsection (a)(5) and the remittance of such fees to the Treasury of the United States shall be consistent with the regulations issued by the Secretary of the Treasury for the collection and remittance of the taxes imposed by subchapter C of chapter 33 of the Internal Revenue Code of 1954, but only to the extent the regulations issued with respect to such taxes do not conflict with the provisions of this section."

(f) Reinstating Limit on Charges for Other Inspection Services.—Section 53 of the Airport and Airway Development Act of 1970 (49 U.S.C. 1741), as amended by section 13031(h)(2) of the Consolidated Omnibus Budget Reconciliation Act of 1985, is further amended by adding at the end thereof the following new subsection:

"(e)(1) The cost of any inspection or quarantine service which is required to be performed by the Federal Government or any agency thereof at airports of entry or other places of inspection as a consequence of the operation of aircraft, and which is performed during regularly established hours of service on Sundays or holidays shall be reimbursed by the owners or operators of such aircraft only to the same extent as if such service had been performed during regularly established hours of service on weekdays. Notwithstanding any other provision of law, administrative overhead costs associated with any inspection or quarantine service required to be performed by the United States Government, or any agency thereof, at airports of entry as a result of the operation of aircraft, shall not be assessed against the owners or operators thereof.

"(2) Nothing in this subsection may be construed as requiring reimbursement for costs incurred by the Secretary of the Treasury in providing customs services described in section 13031(e)(1) of the Consolidated Omnibus Budget Reconciliation Act of 1985."

(g) Effective Date; Refunds.—

(1) The amendments made by this section shall apply with respect to services rendered after the date that is 15 days after the date of enactment of this Act.

(2) Upon written request filed by any person with the Secretary of the Treasury (hereafter in this subsection referred to as the "Secretary") before the date that is 90 days after the date of enactment of this Act which is accompanied by such documentation establishing proof of payment as the Secretary may require, the Secretary shall refund (out of funds in the Treasury of the United States not otherwise appropriated) to such person an amount equal to the excess of—

(A) the amount of fees imposed by section 13031 of the Consolidated Omnibus Budget Reconciliation Act of 1985 that were paid by such person to the Secretary with respect to customs services provided—

(i) after July 6, 1986, and

(ii) on or before the date that is 15 days after the date of enactment of this Act, over

(B) the amount of fees such person would have been required to pay to the Secretary by reason of such section with respect to such services if the amendments made by subsections (a)(1) and (b) applied with respect to such services.

(3) If the customs broker permit fee paid by any person for calendar year 1986 under section 13031(a)(7) of the Consolidated Omnibus Budget Reconciliation Act of 1985 exceeds $62.50, the Secretary shall either—

(A) refund (out of funds in the Treasury of the United States not otherwise appropriated) to such person the amount of the excess, or

(B) if requested by such person, credit the amount of the excess to the fee due under such section 13031(a)(7) with respect to such permit for calendar year 1987.

[For official explanation, see Committee Reports, ¶4206]

[¶2153] SEC. 1894. FOREIGN TRADE ZONES.

Section 3 of the Act of June 18, 1934 (48 Stat. 999, chapter 590; 19 U.S.C. 81c) is amended by adding at the end thereof the following new subsection:

"(c) Notwithstanding the provisions of the fifth proviso of subsection (a), any article (within the meaning of section 5002(a)(14) of the Internal Revenue Code of 1986) may be manufactured or produced from domestic denatured distilled spirits, and articles thereof, in a zone."

[For official explanation, see Committee Reports, ¶4207]

〔¶2154〕 SEC. 1895. COBRA TECHNICAL CORRECTIONS RELATING TO SO-CIAL SECURITY ACT PROGRAMS.

(a) **Amendment Relating to the OASDI Program.**—Section 12108(b) of the Consolidated Omnibus Budget Reconciliation Act of 1985 is amended by striking out "1985" and inserting in lieu thereof "1986".

(b) **Amendments Relating to the Medicare Program—**

(1) **Indirect medical education.**—(A) Paragraph (2)(C)(i) of subsection (d) of section 1886 of the Social Security Act (42 U.S.C. 1395ww) is amended by striking out "(taking into account, for discharges occurring after September 30, 1986, the amendments made by section 9104(a) of the Medicare and Medicaid Budget Reconciliation Amendments of 1985)".

(B) Paragraph (3)(A) of such subsection is amended by adding at the end the following: "If the formula under paragraph (5)(B) for determining payments for the indirect costs of medical education is changed for any fiscal year, the Secretary shall readjust the standardized amounts previously determined for each hospital to take into account the changes in that formula".

(C) Clause (ii) of paragraph (3)(C) of such subsection is amended to read as follows:

"(ii) Reducing for savings from amendment to indirect teaching adjustment for discharges after September 30, 1986.—The Secretary shall further reduce each of the average standardized amounts by a proportion equal to the proportion (estimated by the Secretary) of the amount of payments under this subsection based on DRG prospective payment amounts which is the difference between—

"(I) the sum of the additional payment amounts under paragraph (5)(B) (relating to indirect costs of medical education) if the indirect teaching adjustment factor were equal to 1.159r (as 'r' is defined in paragraph (5)(B)(ii)), and

"(II) that sum using the factor specified in paragraph (5)(B)(ii)(II)".

(D)(i) Except as provided in clause (ii), the amendments made by this paragraph apply to discharges occurring on or after October 1, 1986.

(ii) The amendments made by this paragraph shall not be first applied to discharges occurring as of a date unless, for discharges occurring on that date, the amendments made by section 9105(a) of the Consolidated Omnibus Budget Reconciliation Act of 1985 (incorporating the amendments made by paragraph (2) of this subsection) are also being applied.

(2) **Disproportionate share.**—(A) Paragraph (2)(C) of subsection (d) of section 1886 of the Social Security Act (42 U.S.C. 1395ww), as amended by section 9105(b) of the Consolidated Omnibus Budget Reconciliation Act of 1985 (in this section referred to as "COBRA" is amended—

(i) by adding "and" at the end of clause (ii),

(ii) by striking out ", and" at the end of clause (iii) and inserting in lieu thereof a period, and

(iii) by striking out clause (iv).

(B) Paragraph (3)(C) of such subsection is amended by adding at the end the following:

(iii) Reducing for disproportionate share payments.—The Secretary shall further reduce each of the average standardized amounts by reducing the standardized amount for each hospital (as previously determined without regard to this clause) by a proportion equal to the proportion (established by the Secretary) of the amount of payments under this subsection based on DRG prospective payment amounts which are additional payments described in paragraph (5)(F) (relating to disproportionate share payments) for subsection (d) hospitals.".

(C) Paragraph (5)(F)(vi)(I) of such subsection is amended—

(i) by striking out "supplementary" and inserting in lieu thereof "supplemental", and

(ii) by striking out "fiscal year" and inserting in lieu thereof "period".

(D) The amendments made by subparagraph (C) apply to discharges occurring on or after May 1, 1986, and the amendments made by subparagraphs (A) and (B) apply to discharges occurring on or after October 1, 1986.

(3) **Alignment correction.**—Subparagraph (B) of section 1886(g)(2) of the Social Security Act (as added by section 9107(a)(1)(C) of the Consolidated Omnibus Budget

Reconciliation Act of 1985) is amended by moving its alignment (and the alignment of each of its clauses) two additional ems to the left.

(4) **Emergency care requirement.**—Section 1867(e)(3) of the Social Security Act (42 U.S.C. 1395dd(e)(3)), as inserted by section 9121(b) of COBRA, is amended by striking out "and has, under the agreement, obligated itself to comply with the requirements of this section".

(5) **Redesignating overlapping provisions.**—Paragraph (1) of section 1866(a) of the Social Security Act (42 U.S.C. 1395cc(a)) is amended—

(A) by striking out "and" inserted at the end of subparagraph (I) by section 9122(a)(2) of COBRA,

(B) by striking out the period at the end of subparagraph (J) and inserting in lieu thereof ", and", and

(C) by redesignating the subparagraph (I) inserted by section 9403(b) of COBRA as subparagraph (K) and transferring and inserting such subparagraph after subparagraph (J).

(6) **CHAMPUS.**—Section 9122(b) of COBRA is amended by striking out "to agreements entered into or renewed on or after the date of the enactment of this Act, but shall apply only".

(7) **Skilled nursing facility payments.**—(A) Section 1888(d)(1) of the Social Security Act (42 U.S.C. 1395yy(d)(1)), as added by section 9126(a) of COBRA, is amended by striking out "fiscal year" each place it appears and inserting in lieu thereof "cost reporting period".

(B) Section 1888(d)(4) of the Social Security Act is amended—

(i) in the first sentence, by striking out "each fiscal year" and inserting in lieu thereof "cost reporting periods beginning in a fiscal year", and

(ii) in the second sentence, by striking out "fiscal year" and all that follows up to the period and inserting in lieu thereof "cost reporting period no later than 30 days before the beginning of that period".

(C) Section 9126(d)(1) of COBRA is amended by striking out "fiscal years" and inserting in lieu thereof "cost reporting periods".

(D) The amendments made by subparagraphs (A) and (B) apply to cost reporting periods beginning on or after Ocotber 1, 1986.

(8) **ProPAC.**—Section 9127(b) of COBRA is amended by inserting ", except that the Director may provide initially for such terms as will insure that (on a continuing basis) the terms of no more than eight members will expire in any one year" after "years".

(9) **Direct medical education.**—Section 1886(h) of the Social Security Act (42 U.S.C. 1395ww(h)), added by 9202(a) of COBRA, is amended—

(A) is paragraph (2)(C), by striking out "paragraph (B)" and inserting in lieu thereof "subparagraph (B)",

(B) in the matter preceding subclause (I) of paragraph (4)(E)(ii), by inserting "but before July 1, 1987," after "1986,",

(C) by redesignating subparagraph (E) of paragraph (4) as subparagraph (D), and

(D) in paragraph (5)(B), by striking out "As used in this paragraph, the" and inserting in lieu thereof "The".

(10) **Citation correction.**—Section 9202(j) of COBRA is amended by inserting "or section 402 of the Social Security Amendments of 1967" after "section 1886(c) of the Social Security Act.".

(11) **HMO/CMP rates.**—(A) The matter in section 1876(a)(1)(A) of the Social Security Act (42 U.S.C. 1395mm(a)(1)(A)) preceding clause (i), as amended by section 9211(d) of COBRA, is amended by striking out "publish" and inserting in lieu thereof "announce (in a manner intended to provide notice to interested parties)".

(B) The amendment made by subparagraph (A) shall apply to determinations of per capita payment rates for 1987 and subsequent years.

(12) **Indentation.**—Section 1837(i)(1) of the Social Security Act (42 U.S.C. 1395p(i)(1)), as amended by section 9219(a)(2)(A) of COBRA, is amended by moving the alignment of subparagraph (A) two additional ems to the left so as to align its left margin with the left margins of subparagraphs (B) and (C) of such section.

(13) **Access demonstration project.**—Section 9221(a) of COBRA is amended by striking out "September 30, 1986" and inserting in lieu thereof "July 31, 1987".

(14) Physician payment.—(A) Section 1842(b)(4)(C) of the Social Security Act (42 U.S.C. 1395u(b)(4)(C)), as amended by section 9301(b)(1)(C) of COBRA, is amended—

    (i) by striking out clause (ii), and

    (ii) by striking out "(i)" in clause (i).

  (B) Section 9301(c)(5) of COBRA is amended by striking out "1842(b)(7)" and inserting in lieu thereof "1842(h)(7)".

(15) Redundant words.—Section 1842(h) of the Social Security Act (42 U.S.C. 1395u(h)), as amended by section 9301(c) of COBRA, is amended—

  (A) in paragraph (5), as redesignated by section 9301(c)(3)(D) of COBRA, by striking out "such" each place it appears, and

  (B) in paragraph (6), as so redesignated by striking out "the the" and inserting in lieu thereof "the".

(16) Assistants at surgery.—(A) Section 1842(k) of the Social Security Act (42 U.S.C. 1395u(k)), added by section 9307(c) of COBRA, is amended by inserting "presents or causes to be presented a claim or" after "willfully" each place it appears.

  (B) The amendment made by subparagraph (A) shall apply to claims presented after the date of the enactment of this Act.

  (C) For purposes of section 1862(a)(15) of the Social Security Act (42 U.S.C. 1395y(a)(15)), added by section 9307(a)(3) of COBRA, and for surgical procedures performed during the period beginning on April 1, 1986, and ending on December 15, 1986, a carrier is deemed to have approved the use of an assistant in a surgical procedure, before the surgery is performed, based on the existence of a complicating medical condition if the carrier determines after the surgery is performed that the use of the assistant in the procedure was appropriate based on the existence of a complicating medical condition before or during the surgery.

(17) Citation.—Section 1164(b)(4)(B) of the Social Security Act (42 U.S.C. 1320c-13(b)(4)(B)), as added by section 9401(b) of COBRA, is amended by striking out "paragraphs" and inserting in lieu thereof "subparagraphs".

(18) Medicare tax on state and local employees.—

     *   *   *   *   *   *   *   *   *   *   *   *   *

  (B) Section 210(p)(2) of the Social Security Act (42 U.S.C. 410(p)(2)), as added by section 13205(b)(1) of COBRA, is amended—

    (i) by striking out "or" at the end of subparagraph (C),

    (ii) by striking out the period at the end of subparagraph (D) and inserting in lieu thereof ", or", and

    (iii) by adding at the end the following:

"(E) by an election official or election worker if the remuneration paid in a calendar year for such service is less than $100."

  (C) The amendments made by this paragraph shall apply to services performed after March 31, 1986.

(19) Punctuation.—Section 210(p)(4)(B) of the Social Security Act (42 U.S.C. 410(p)(4)(B)), as amended by section 13205(b)(1) of COBRA, is amended by striking out any quotation marks that appear before "(A)".

(c) Amendments Relating to the Medicaid Program.—

(1) Extra word.—Section 1902(a)(13)(D) of the Social Security Act (42 U.S.C. 1396a(a)(13)(D)), as inserted by section 9505(c)(1)(C) of COBRA and as amended and redesignated by paragraphs (2) and (3) of section 9509(a) of COBRA, is amended by adding "and" at the end.

(2) Capitalization.—Section 1903b(m)(2)(F)) of the Social Security Act (42 U.S.C. 1396(m)(2)(F), as amended by section 9517(a)(2)(A) of COBRA, is amended by striking out "in the case" and inserting in lieu thereof "In the case".

(3) Case-management services.—(A) Section 1905(a) of the Social Security Act (42 U.S.C. 1395d(a)) is amended—

    (i) by striking out "and" at the end of paragraph (18),

    (ii) by redesignating paragraph (19) as paragraph (20), and

    (iii) by inserting after paragraph (18) the following new paragraph:

"(19) case-management services (as defined in section 1915(g)(2)); and".

(B) Section 1902(j) of the Social Security Act (42 U.S.C. 1396a(j)), as amended by section 9505(d)(1) of COBRA, is amended by striking out "(19)" and inserting in lieu thereof "(20)".

(C) Section 1902(a)(10)(C)(iv) of the Social Security Act (42 U.S.C. 1396a(a)(10)(C)(iv)), as amended by section 9505(d)(2) of COBRA, is amended by striking out "through (18)" and inserting in lieu thereof "through (19)".

(4) Health insuring organizations.—Section 9517(c)(2) of COBRA is amended—

(A) in subparagraph (A), by adding at the end the following "For purposes of this paragraph, a health insuring organization is not considered to be operational until the date on which it first enrolls patients.";

(B) in subparagraph (B), by striking out "(iv)" and inserting in lieu thereof "(vi)"; and

(C) by adding at the end the following new subparagraph:

"(C) In the case of the Hartford Health Network, Inc., clauses (ii) and (vi) of section 1903(m)(2)(A) of the Social Security Act shall not apply during the period for which a waiver by the Secretary of Health and Human Services, under section 1915(b) of such Act, of certain requirements of section 1902 of such Act is in effect (pursuant to a request for a waiver under section 1915(b) of such Act submitted before January 1, 1986)."

(5) References to other provisions.—Section 1920(a) of the Social Security Act (42 U.S.C. 1396s(a)), as added by section 9526 of COBRA, is amended—

(A) in paragraph (1)—

(i) by redesignating subparagraphs (B) and (C) as subparagraphs (C) and (D), respectively, and

(ii) by inserting after "—(A)" the following: "Section 402(a)(32) of this Act (relating to individuals who are deemed recipients of aid but for whom a payment is not made).

(B) in paragraph (2)—

(i) by inserting "(A)" after the dash, and

(ii) by adding at the end the following new subparagraph:

"(B) Section 1634(b) of this Act (relating to preservation of benefit status for disabled widows and widowers who lost SSI benefits because of 1983 changes in actuarial reduction formula)."; and

(C) in paragraph (3), by striking out "Section 473(b)" and inserting in lieu thereof "Sections 472(h) and 473(b)".

(6) Reference correction.—Section 9528(a) of COBRA is amended by striking out "1101(a)(8)(P)" and inserting in lieu thereof "1101(a)(8)(B)".

(7) Indentation.—Section 1902(a)(10)(A)(ii)), of the Social Security Act (42 U.S.C. 1396a(a)(10)(A)(ii)), as amended by sections 9505(b)(2) and 9519(b)(1) of COBRA, is amended—

(A) by indenting subclause (VII) two additional ems so as to align its left margin with the left margins of subclauses (I) through (VI) of such section, and

(B) by indenting subclause (VIII) (and each of its subdivisions) four additional ems so as to align its left margin with the left margins of subclauses (I) through (VI) of such section.

(d) Amendments Relating to Continuation of Employer-Based Health Insurance Coverage.—

(1) Effect of modifications to plan coverage provisions.—

* * * * * * * * * * * *

(B) **ERISA amendment.**—Paragraph (1) of section 602 of the Employee Retirement Income Security Act of 1974 (29 U.S.C. 1162(1); 100 Stat. 228) is amended by adding at the end the following: "If coverage is modified under the plan for any group of similarly situated beneficiaries, such coverage shall also be modified in the same manner for all individuals who are qualified beneficiaries under the plan pursuant to this part in connection with such group."

(C) **PHSA amendment.**—Paragraph (1) of section 2202 of the Public Health Service Act is amended by adding at the end the following: "If coverage is modified under the plan for any group of similarly situated beneficiaries, such coverage shall also be modified in the same manner for all individuals who are qualified beneficiaries under the plan pursuant to this part in connection with such group."

(2) Maximum required period of continuation coverage.—

* * * * * * * * * * * * *

(B) ERISA amendment.—Subparagraph (A) of section 602(2) of the Employee Retirement Income Security Act of 1974 (29 U.S.C. 1162(2); 100 Stat. 228) is amended to read as follows:

"(A) Maximum required period.—

"(i) General rule for terminations and reduced hours.—In the case of a qualifying event described in section 603(2), except as provided in clause (ii), the date which is 18 months after the date of the qualifying event.

"(ii) Special rule for multiple qualifying events.—If a qualifying event occurs during the 18 months after the date of a qualifying event described in section 603(2), the date which is 36 months after the date of the qualifying event described in section 603(2).

"(iii) General rule for other qualifying events.—In the case of a qualifying event not described in section 603(2), the date which is 36 months after the date of the qualifying event."

(C) PHSA amendment.—Subparagraph (A) of section 2202(2) of the Public Health Service Act is amended to read as follows:

"(A) Maximum required period.—

"(i) General rule for terminations and reduced hours.—In the case of a qualifying event described in section 2203(2), except as provided in caluse (ii), the date which is 18 months after the date of the qualifying event.

"(ii) Special rule for multiple qualifying events.—If a qualifying event occurs during the 18 months after the date of a qualifying event described in section 2203(2), the date which is 36 months after the date of the qualifying event described in section 2203(2).

"(iii) General rule for other qualifying events.—In the case of a qualifying event not described in section 2203(2), the date which is 36 months after the date of the qualifying event."

(3) Grace period for payment of premiums.—

* * * * * * * * * * * * *

(B) ERISA amendment.—Subparagraph (C) of section 602(2) of the Employee Retirement Income Security Act of 1974 (29 U.S.C. 1162(2)(C); 100 Stat. 228) is amended by adding at the end the following: "The payment of any premium (other than any payment referred to in the last sentence of paragraph (3)) shall be considered to be timely if made within 30 days after the date due or within such longer period as applies to or under the plan."

(C) PHSA amendment.—Subparagraph (C) of section 2202(2) of the Public Health Service Act is amended by adding at the end the following: "The payment of any premium (other than any payment referred to in the last sentence of paragraph (3)) shall be considered to be timely if made within 30 days after the date due or within such longer period as applies to or under the plan."

(4) Termination of continuation coverage upon coverage by other group health plan rather than upon reemployment or remarriage.—

* * * * * * * * * * * *

(B) ERISA amendment.—Section 602(2) of the Employee Retirement Income Security Act of 1974 (29 U.S.C. 1162(2); 100 Stat. 228) is amended—

(i) by striking out subparagraph (E);

(ii) by striking out clause (i) of subparagraph (D) and inserting in lieu thereof the following:

"(i) covered under any other group health plan (as an employee or otherwise), or"; and

(iii) by striking out the heading for subparagraph (D) and inserting in lieu thereof the following: "Group health plan coverage or medicare eligibility.—".

(C) PHSA amendment.—Section 2202(2) of the Public Health Service Act is amended—

(i) by striking out subparagraph (E);

(ii) by striking out clause (i) of subparagraph (D) and inserting in lieu thereof the following:

"(i) covered under any other group health plan (as an employee or otherwise), or"; and

    (iii) by striking out the heading for subparagraph (D) and inserting in lieu thereof the following: "Group health plan coverage or medicare eligibility.—".

(5) Clarification relating to election by beneficiaries.—

* * * * * * * * * * * * *

    (B) ERISA amendment.—Section 605(2) of the Employee Retirement Income Security Act of 1974 (29 U.S.C. 1162(2); 100 Stat. 230) is amended—
    (i) by inserting "of continuation coverage" after "any election"; and
    (ii) by adding at the end the following: "If there is a choice among types of coverage under the plan, each qualified beneficiary is entitled to make a separate selection among such types of coverage.".

    (C) PHSA amendment.—Section 2205(2) of the Public Health Service Act is amended—
    (i) by inserting "of continuation coverage" after "any election"; and
    (ii) by adding at the end the following: "If there is a choice among types of coverage under the plan, each qualified beneficiary is entitled to make a separate selection among such types of coverage".

(6) Notice requirement.—

* * * * * * * * * * * * *

    (B) ERISA amendment.—Paragraph (3) of section 606 of the Employees Retirement Income Security Act of 1974 (29 U.S.C. 1166(3); 100 Stat. 230) is amended by inserting "within 60 days after the date of the qualifying event"; after "section 603".

    (C) PHSA amendment.—Paragraph (3) of section 2206 of the Public Health Service Act is amended by inserting "within 60 days after the date of the qualifying event" after "section 603".

    (D) Effective date.—The amendments made by this paragraph shall only apply with respect to qualifying events occurring after the date of the enactment of this Act.

* * * * * * * * * * * * *

(8) Definition of group health plan for ERISA.—Paragraph (1) of section 607 of the Employee Retirement Income Security Act of 1974 (29 U.S.C. 1167(1); 100 Stat. 231) is amended to read as follows:

"(1) Group health plan.—The term 'group health plan' means an employee welfare benefit plan providing medical care (as defined in section 213(d) of the Internal Revenue Code of 1954) to participants or beneficiaries directly or through insurance, reimbursement, or otherwise.".

(9) Aggregation rules for employer for ERISA.—
    (A) In general.—Section 607 of the Employee Retirement Income Security Act of 1974 (29 U.S.C. 1167; 100 Stat. 231) is amended by adding at the end of the following new paragraph:

"(4) Employer.—Subsection (n) (relating to leased employees) and subsection (t) (relating to application of controlled group rules to certain employee benefits) of section 414 of the Internal Revenue Code of 1986 shall apply for purposes of this part in the same manner and to the same extent as such subsections apply for purposes of section 106 of such Code. Any regulations prescribed by the Secretary pursuant to the preceding sentence shall be consistent and coextensive with any regulations prescribed for similar purposes by the Secretary of the Treasury (or such Secretary's delegate) under such subsections.".

    (B) Effective date.—The amendment made by subparagraph (A) shall take effect in the same manner and to the same extent as the amendments made by subsections (e) and (i) of section 1151 of this Act.

(e) Effective Date.—Except as otherwise provided in this section, the amendments made by this section shall be effective as if included in the enactment of the Consolidated Omnibus Budget Reconciliation Act of 1985.

[For official explanation, see Committee Reports, ¶4208]

⟦¶2155⟧ SEC. 1896. EXTENSION OF TIME FOR FILING FOR CREDIT OR REFUND WITH RESPECT TO CERTAIN CHANGES INVOLVING INSOLVENT FARMERS.

Section 13208 of the Consolidated Omnibus Budget Reconciliation Act of 1985 (relating to certain insolvent taxpayers allowed to reduce capital gains preference item for purposes of the individual minimum tax) is amended by adding at the end thereof the following new subsection:

"**(c) Statute of Limitations.**—If refund or credit of any overpayment of tax resulting from the application of the amendment made by subsection (a) is prevented at any time before the close of the date which is 1 year after the date of the enactment of this Act, by the operation of any law or rule of law (including res judicata), refund or credit of such overpayment (to the extent attributable to the application of such amendment) may, nevertheless, be made or allowed if claim therefor is filed on or before the close of such 1-year period."

[For official explanation, see Committee Reports, ¶4209]

[¶2156] SEC. 1898. TECHNICAL CORRECTIONS TO THE RETIREMENT EQUITY ACT OF 1984.

(a) Amendments Related to Sections 102 and 202 of the Act.—

  (1) Treatment of class-year plans.—

* * * * * * * * * * * *

    (B) Amendment of ERISA.—Paragraph (3) of section 203(c) of the Employee Retirement Income Security Act of 1974 is amended to read as follows:

"(3)(A) The requirements of subsection (a)(2) shall be treated as satisfied in the case of a class-year plan if such plan provides that 100 percent of each employee's right to or derived from the contributions of the employer on the employee's behalf with respect to any plan year is nonforfeitable not later than when such participant was performing services for the employer as of the close of each of 5 plan years (whether or not consecutive) after the plan year for which the contributions were made.

"(B) For purposes of subparagraph (A) if—

"(i) any contributions are made on behalf of a participant with respect to any plan year, and

"(ii) before such participant meets the requirements of subparagraph (A), such participant was not performing services for the employer as of the close of each of any 5 consecutive plan years after such plan year,

then the plan may provide that the participant forfeits any right to or derived from the contributions made with respect to such plan year.

"(C) For purposes of this part, the term 'class year plan' means a profit-sharing, stock bonus, or money purchase plan which provides for the separate nonforfeitability of employees' rights to or derived from the contributions for each plan year."

    (C) Effective date.—The amendments made by this paragraph shall apply to contributions made for plan years beginning after the date of the enactment of this Act; except that, in the case of a plan described in section 302(b) of the Retirement Equity Act of 1984, such amendments shall not apply to any plan year to which the amendments made by such Act do not apply by reason of such section 302(b).

* * * * * * * * * * * *

  (4) Treatment of withdrawal of mandatory contributions.—

* * * * * * * * * * * *

    (B) Amendments of ERISA.—

    (i) Clause (ii) of section 203(a)(3)(D) of the Employee Retirement Income Security Act of 1974 is amended by striking out the last sentence and inserting in lieu thereof the following: "The plan provision required under this clause may provide that such repayment must be made (I) in the case of a withdrawal on account of separation from service, before the earlier of 5 years after the first date on which the participant is subsequently re-employed by the employer, or the close of the first period of 5 consecutive 1-year breaks in service commencing after the withdrawal; or (II) in the case of any other withdrawal, 5 years after the date of the withdrawal."

     (ii) Subsection (e) of section 204 of the Employee Retirement Income Security Act of 1974 is amended by striking out the last sentence and inserting in lieu thereof the following:

"The plan provision required under this subsection may provide that such repayment must be made (A) in the case of a withdrawal on account of separation from service, before the earlier of 5 years after the first date on which the participant is subsequently reemployed by the employer, or the close of the first period of 5 consecutive 1-year breaks in service commencing after the withdrawal; or (B) in the case of any other withdrawal, 5 years after the date of the withdrawal."

* * * * * * * * * * *

(b) Amendments Related to Sections 103 and 203 of the Act.—

    (1) Clarification of qualified preretirement survivor annuity in case of terminated vested participant.—

* * * * * * * * * * *

    (B) Amendment of ERISA.—Paragraph (1) of section 205(e) of the Employee Retirement Income Security Act of 1974 (defining qualified preretirement survivor annuity) is amended by adding at the end thereof the following new sentence:

"In the case of an individual who separated from service before the date of such individual's death, subparagraph (A)(ii)(I) shall not apply."

    (2) Clarification of transferee plan rules.—

* * * * * * * * * * * *

    (B) Amendments of ERISA.—
     (i) Clause (iii) of section 205(b)(1)(C) of the Employee Retirement Income Security Act of 1974 is amended by striking out "a transferee" and inserting in lieu thereof "a direct or indirect transferee (in a transfer after December 31, 1984)".
     (ii) Paragraph (1) of section 205(b) of such Act is amended by adding at the end thereof the following new sentence:

"Clause (iii) of subparagraph (C) shall apply only with respect to the transferred assets (and income therefrom) if the plan separately accounts for such assets and any income therefrom."

    (3) Clarification of coordination between qualified joint and survivor annuity and qualified preretirement survivor annuity.—

* * * * * * * * * * *

    (B) Amendment of ERISA.—Paragraph (1) of section 205(a) of the Employee Retirement Income Security Act of 1974 is amended by striking out "who retires under the plan" and inserting in lieu thereof "who does not die before the annuity starting date".

    (4) Requirement of spousal consent for using plan assets as security for loans.—

* * * * * * * * * * *

    (B) Amendment of ERISA.—
     (i) subparagraph (B) of section 205(c)(1) of the Employee Retirement Income Security Act of 1974 is amended by striking out "paragraphs (2) and (3)" and inserting in lieu thereof "paragraphs (2), (3), and (4)".
     (ii) Subsection (c) of section 205 of such Act is amended by redesignating paragraphs (4), (5), and (6) as paragraphs (5), (6), and (7), respectively, and by inserting after paragraph (3) the following new paragraph:

"(4) Each plan shall provide that, if this section applies to a participant when part or all of the participant's accrued benefit is to be used as security for a loan, no portion of the participant's accrued benefit may be used as security for such loan unless—
  "(A) the spouse of the participant (if any) consents in writing to such use during the 90-day period ending on the date on which the loan is to be so secured, and
  "(B) requirements comparable to the requirements of paragraph (2) are met with respect to such consent."
     (iii) Section 205 of such Act is amended by redesignating subsection (j) as subsection (k) and by inserting after subsection (i) the following new subsection:

"(j) If the use of any participants accrued benefit (or any portion thereof) as security for a loan meets the requirements of subsection (c)(4), nothing in this section shall prevent any distribution required by reason of a failure to comply with the terms of such loan."

(C)   Effective dates.—

(i)   the amendments made by this paragraph shall apply with respect to loans made after August 18, 1985.

(ii)   In the case of any loan which was made on or before August 18, 1985, and which is secured by a portion of the participant's accrued benefit, nothing in the amendments made by sections 103 and 203 of the Retirement Equity Act of 1984 shall prevent any distribution required by reason of a failure to comply with the terms of such loan.

(iii)   For purposes of this subparagraph, any loan which is revised, extended, renewed, or renegotiated after August 18, 1985, shall be treated as made after August 18, 1985.

(5)   Clarification of notice requirement for individuals who become participants after age 35, etc.—

* * * * * * * * * * * *

(B)   Amendment of ERISA.—Subparagraph (B) of section 205(c)(3) of the Employee Retirement Income Security Act of 1974 is amended to read as follows:

"(B)(i)   Each plan shall provide to each participant, within the applicable period with respect to such participant (and consistent with such regulations as the Secretary may prescribe), a written explanation with respect to the qualified preretirement survivor annuity comparable to that required under subparagraph (A).

"(ii)   For purposes of clause (i), the term 'applicable period' means, with respect to a participant, whichever of the following periods ends last:

"(I)   The period beginning with the first day of the plan year in which the participant attains age 32 and ending with the close of the plan year preceding the plan year in which the participant attains age 35.

"(II)   A reasonable period after the individual becomes a participant.

"(III)   A reasonable period ending after paragraph (5) ceases to apply to the participant.

"(IV)   A reasonable period ending after section 401(a)(11) applies to the participant.

"(V)   A reasonable period after separation from service in case of a participant who separates before attaining age 35."

(6)   Spousal consent for changes in designations.—

* * * * * * * * * * * *

(B)   Amendment of ERISA.—Subparagraph (A) of section 205(c)(2) of the Employee Retirement Income Security Act of 1974 is amended to read as follows:

"(A)(i)   the spouse of the participant consents in writing to such election, (ii) such election designates a beneficiary (or a form of benefits) which may not be changed without spousal consent (or the consent of the spouse expressly permits designations by the participant without any requirement of further consent by the spouse), and (iii) the spouse's consent acknowledges the effect of such election and is witnessed by a plan representative or a notary public, or".

(C)   Effective date.—The amendments made by this paragraph shall apply to plan years beginning after the date of the enactment of this Act.

(7)   Clarification of nonforfeitable accrued benefit.—

* * * * * * * * * * * *

(B)   Amendment of ERISA.—Subparagraph (C) of section 205(b)(1) of the Employee Retirement Income Security Act of 1974 is amended by striking out "the participant's nonforfeitable accrued benefit" and inserting in lieu thereof "the participant's nonforfeitable accrued benefit (reduced by any security interest held by the plan by reason of a loan outstanding to such participant)".

(8)   Clarification of definition of vested participant.—

* * * * * * * * * * * *

(B)   Amendment of ERISA.—Paragraph (1) of section 205(h) of the Employee Retirement Income Security Act of 1974 is amended by striking out "the accrued benefit derived from employer contributions" and inserting in lieu thereof "such participant's accrued benefit".

Act §1898(b)(8)   ¶2156

(9) **Clarification of qualified preretirement survivor annuity.—**

* * * * * * * * * * *

(B) Amendments of ERISA.—

(i) Paragraph (2) of section 205(e) of the Employee Retirement Income Security Act of 1974 is amended by striking out "the account balance of the participant as of the date of death" and inserting in lieu thereof "the portion of the account balance of the participant (as of the date of death) to which the participant had a nonforfeitable accrued benefit".

(ii) Subsection (e) of section 205 of the Employee Retirement Income Security Act of 1974 is amended by adding at the end thereof the following new paragraph:

"(3) For purposes of paragraphs (1) and (2), any security interest held by the plan by reason of a loan outstanding to the participant shall be taken into account in determining the amount of the qualified preretirement survivor annuity."

(10) **Clarification of requirements for spousal consent.—**

* * * * * * * * * * *

(B) Amendment to ERISA.—Section 205 of the Employee Retirement Income Security Act of 1974 (as amended by paragraph (4)) is amended by redesignating subsection (k) as subsection (l) and by inserting after subsection (j) the following new subsection:

"(k) No consent of a spouse shall be effective for purposes of subsection (g)(1) or (g)(2) (as the case may be) unless requirements comparable to the requirements for spousal consent to an election under subsection (c)(1)(A) are met."

(11) **Clarification of rule for subsidized plans.—**

* * * * * * * * * * *

(B) Amendment to ERISA.—Subparagraph (A) of section 205(c)(5) of the Employee Retirement Income Security Act of 1974 (as redesignated by paragraph (4)(B)) is amended by striking out "if the plan" and inserting in lieu thereof "if such benefit may not be waived (or another beneficiary selected) and if the plan".

(12) **Clarification of annuity starting date.—**

* * * * * * * * * * *

(B) Amendment to ERISA.—Paragraph (2) of section 205(h) of the Employee Retirement Income Security Act of 1974 is amended to read as follows:

"(2)(A) The term 'annuity starting date' means—

"(i) the first day of the first period for which an amount is payable as an annuity, or

"(ii) in the case of a benefit not payable in the form of an annuity, the first day on which all events have occurred which entitle the participant to such benefit.

"(B) for purposes of subparagraph (A), the first day of the first period for which a benefit is to be received by reason of disability shall be treated as the annuity starting date only if such benefit is not an auxiliary benefit."

(13) **Clarification of plans to which requirements apply.—**

* * * * * * * * * * *

(B) Amendment to ERISA.—Clause (i) of section 205(b)(1)(C) of the Employee Retirement Income Security Act of 1974 is amended by striking out "subsection (c)(2)(A)" and inserting in lieu thereof "subsection (c)(2)".

(14) **Certain plans do not need to provide certain survivor benefits.—**

* * * * * * * * * * *

(B) Amendment to ERISA.—Section 205(b) of the Employee Retirement Income Security Act of 1974 is amended by adding at the end thereof the following new paragraph:

"(3) A plan shall not be treated as failing to meet the requirements of paragraph (1)(C) or (2) merely because the plan provides that benefits will not be payable to the surviving spouse of the participant unless the participant and such spouse had been married throughout the 1-year period ending on the earlier of the participant's annuity starting date or the date of the participant's death."

* * * * * * * * * * *

(c)   **Amendments Related to Sections 104 and 204 of the Act.**

* * * * * * * * * * * * *

(2)   **Procedures for period during which determination is being made.—**

* * * * * * * * * * * *

(B)   Amendments of ERISA.—

(i)   Clause (i) of section 206(d)(3)(H) of the Employee Retirement Income Security Act of 1974 is amended by striking out "shall segregate in a separate account in the plan or in an escrow account the amounts" and inserting in lieu thereof "shall separately account for the amounts (hereinafter in this subparagraph referred to as the 'segregated amounts')".

(ii)   Clause (ii) of section 206(d)(3)(H) of such Act is amended—

(I)   by striking out "18 months" and inserting in lieu thereof "the 18-month period described in clause (v)", and

(II)   by striking out "plus any interest" and inserting in lieu thereof "including any interest".

(iii)   Clause (iii) of section 206(d)(3)(H) of such Act is amended—

(I)   by striking out "18 months" and inserting in lieu thereof "the 18-month period described in clause (v)", and

(II)   by striking out "plus any interest" and inserting in lieu thereof "including any interest".

(iv)   Clause (iv) of section 206(d)(3)(H) of such Act is amended by striking out "the 18-month period" and inserting in lieu thereof "the 18-month period described in clause (v)".

(v)   Subparagraph (H) of section 206(d)(3) of such Act is amended by adding at the end thereof the following new clause:

"(v)   For purposes of this subparagraph, the 18-month period described in this clause is the 18-month period beginning with the date on which the first payment would be required to be made under the domestic relations order."

* * * * * * * * * * * * *

(4)   **Clarification of application of domestic relation provisions.—**

* * * * * * * * * * * *

(B)   Amendment of ERISA.—Paragraph (3) of section 206(d) of the Employee Retirement Income Security Act of 1974 is amended by redesignating subparagraph (L) of subparagraph (N) and by inserting after subparagraph (K) the following new subparagraph:

"(L)   This paragraph shall not apply to any plan to which paragraph (1) does not apply."

(5)   **Benefit payments made in accordance with qualified domestic relations orders not treated as garnishments for purposes of Consumer Credit Protection Act.—**Paragraph (3) of section 206(d) of the Employee Retirement Income Security Act of 1974 (as amended by paragraph (4)(B)) is further amended by inserting after subparagraph (L) the following new subparagraph:

"(M)   Payment of benefits by a pension plan in accordance with the applicable requirements of a qualified domestic relations order shall not be treated as garnishment for purposes of section 303(a) of the Consumer Credit Protection Act.".

(6)   **Treatment of certain spouses.—**

* * * * * * * * * * * *

(B)   Amendment of ERISA.—Clause (i) of section 206(d)(3)(F) of the Employee Retirement Income Security Act of 1974 is amended by striking out "section 205" and inserting in lieu thereof "section 205 (and any spouse of the participant shall not be treated as a spouse of the participant for such purposes)".

(7)   **Clerical amendments.—**

* * * * * * * * * * * *

(B)   Amendments of ERISA.—

(i)   Clause (ii) of section 206(d)(3)(F) of the Employee Retirement Income Security Act of 1974 is amended by striking out "the former spouse" and inserting in lieu thereof "the surviving former spouse".

Act §1898(c)(7) ¶2156

(ii)   Subclause (I) of section 206(d)(3)(G)(i) of such Act is amended by striking out "any other alternate payee" and inserting in lieu thereof "each alternate payee".

(iii)   Subparagraph (E) of section 206(d)(3) of such Act is amended—

(I)   by striking out "In the case of any payment before a participant has separated from service, a" in clause (i) and inserting in lieu thereof "A", and

(II)   by inserting "in the case of any payment before a participant has separated from service," before "on or" in subclause (I).

(iv)   Clause (ii) of section 206(d)(3)(E) of such Act is amended to read as follows:

"(ii)   For purposes of this subparagraph, the term 'earliest retirement age' means the earlier of—

"(I)   the date on which the participant is entitled to a distribution under the plan, or

"(II)   the later of the date of the participant attains age 50 or the earliest date on which the participant could begin receiving under the plan if the participant separated from service."

(d)   Amendments Related to Sections 105 and 205 of the Act.—

(1)   Vested accrued benefit.—

* * * * * * * * * * * *

(B)   Amendments to ERISA.—Paragraph (1) of section 203 of the Employee Retirement Income Security Act of 1974 is amended to read as follows:

"(1)   If the present value of any vested accrued benefit exceeds $3,500, a pension plan shall provide that such benefit may not be immediately distributed without the consent of the participant."

(2)   Distributions under section 404(k).—

* * * * * * * * * * * *

(B)   Amendment to ERISA.—Section 203(e) of the Employee Retirement Income Security Act of 1974 is amended by adding at the end thereof the following new paragraph:

"(3)   This subsection shall not apply to any distribution of dividends to which section 404(k) of the Internal Revenue Code of 1954 applies."

* * * * * * * * * * * *

(f)   Amendment Related to Section 301 of the Act.—

(1)   Special rule for ESOPs.—

* * * * * * * * * * * *

(B)   Amendment to ERISA.—Section 204(g) of the Employee Retirement Income Security Act of 1974 is amended by adding at the end thereof the following new paragraph:

"(3)   For purposes of this subsection, any—

"(A)   tax credit employee stock ownership plan (as defined in section 409(a) of the Internal Revenue Code of 1954), or

"(B)   employee stock ownership plan (as defined in section 4975(e)(7) of such Code),

shall not be treated as failing to meet the requirements of this subsection merely because it modifies distribution options in a nondiscriminatory manner.

(2)   Clerical amendment.—Paragraph (1) of section 204(g) of the Employee Retirement Income Security Act of 1974 is amended by striking out "section 302(c)(8)" and inserting in lieu thereof "section 302(c)(8) or 4281".

(g)   Amendment Related to Section 302 of the Act.—Paragraph (2) of section 302(b) of the Retirement Equity Act of 1984 is amended by striking out "January 1, 1987" and inserting in lieu thereof "July 1, 1988".

(h)   Amendments Related to Section 303 of the Act.—

(1)(A)   Subsection (c) of section 303 of the Retirement Equity Act of 1984 (relating to transitional rule for requirement of joint and survivor annuity and preretirement survivor annuity) is amended by adding at the end thereof the following new paragraph:

"(4) Elimination of double death benefits.—

"(A) In general.—In the case of a participant described in paragraph (2), death benefits (other than a qualified joint and survivor annuity or a qualified preretirement survivor annuity) payable to any beneficiary shall be reduced by the amount payable to the surviving spouse of such participant by reason of paragraph (2). The reduction under the preceding sentence shall be made on the basis of the respective present values (as of the date of the participant's death) of such death benefits and the amount so payable to the surviving spouse.

"(B) Spouse may waive provisions of paragraph (2).—In the case of any participant described in paragraph (2), the surviving spouse of such participant may waive the provisions of paragraph (2). Such waiver shall be made on or before the close of the second plan year to which the amendments made by section 103 of this Act apply. Such a waiver shall not be treated as a transfer of property for purposes of chapter 12 of the Internal Revenue Code of 1954 and shall not be treated as an assignment or alienation for purposes of section 401(a)(13) of the Internal Revenue Code of 1954 or section 206(d) of the Employee Retirement Income Security Act of 1974."

* * * * * * * * * * * *

(2) Subparagraph (A) of section 303(e)(2) of the Retirement Equity Act of 1984 (relating to treatment of certain participants who perform services on or after January 1, 1976) is amended by striking out "in the first plan year" and inserting in lieu thereof "in any plan year".

(3) Paragraph (2) of section 303(c) of the Retirement Equity Act is amended by adding at the end thereof the following new sentence: "In the case of a profit-sharing or stock bonus plan to which this paragraph applies, the plan shall be treated as meeting the requirements of the amendments made by sections 103 and 203 with respect to any participant if the plan made a distribution in a form other than a life annuity to the surviving spouse of the participant of such participant's nonforfeitable benefit."

(i) **Technical Amendment to Section 408(d) of ERISA.—**

(1) Subsection (d) of section 408 of the Employee Retirement Income Security Act of 1974 is amended by striking out "(a),".

(2) The amendment made by paragraph (1) shall apply to transactions after the date of the enactment of this Act.

(j) **Effective Date.—**Except as otherwise provided in this section, any amendment made by this section shall take effect as if included in the provision of the Retirement Equity Act of 1984 to which such amendment relates.

[For official explanation, see Committee Reports, ¶4211]

⟦¶2157⟧ SEC. 1899. AMENDMENT RELATED TO THE CHILD SUPPORT ENFORCEMENT AMENDMENTS OF 1984.

(a) **In General.—**Section 457(b)(3) of the Social Security Act is amended by inserting "or administrative" after "court".

(b) **Effective Date.—**The amendment made by this section shall become effective on the date of the enactment of this Act.

⟦¶2158⟧ SEC. 1899A. MISCELLANEOUS AMENDMENTS CORRECTING ERRORS OF SPELLING, PUNCTUATION, ETC.

* * * * * * * * * * * *

(66) Paragraph (2) of section 101(b) of the Tax Reform Act of 1984 is amended by inserting "(as such paragraphs (4) and (5) are amended by this section and section 102)" after "(4), and (5)".

(67) Subparagraph (C) of section 102(e)(3) of the Tax Reform Act of 1984 is amended by striking out "paragraph (7)(A) (including the heading)" and inserting in lieu thereof "paragraphs (6)(B) and (7)(A) (including any headings)".

(68) Paragraph (1) of section 127(b) of the Tax Reform Act of 1984 is amended by inserting "(as amended by section 128)" under "subsection (c)".

(69) Subparagraph (A) of section 221(d)(2) of the Tax Reform Act of 1984 is amended by striking out "rapid that" and inserting in lieu thereof "rapid than".

* * * * * * * * * * * *

CODE SECTIONS AS AMENDED

[¶2851] CODE SEC. 1. TAX IMPOSED.

(a) Married Individuals Filing Joint Returns and Surviving Spouses.—There is hereby imposed on the taxable income of [1]—

(1) every married individual (as defined in section 7703) who makes a single return jointly with his spouse under section 6013, and
(2) every surviving spouse (as defined in section 2(a)), a tax determined in accordance with the following table:

If taxable income is:	The tax is:
Not over $29,750	*15% of taxable income.*
Over $29,750	*$4,462.50, plus 28% of the excess over $29,750.*

(b) Heads of Households.—*There is hereby imposed on the taxable income of every head of a household (as defined in section 2(b)) a tax determined in accordance with the following table:*

If taxable income is:	The tax is:
Not over $23,900	*15% of taxable income.*
Over $23,900	*$3,585, plus 28% of the excess over $23,900.*

[Footnote ¶2851] Matter in *italics* in Sec. 1(a)—(h) added by section 101(a), '86 TRA, which struck out:
(1) "every married individual (as defined in section 143) who makes a single return jointly with his spouse under section 6013, and every surviving spouse (as defined in section 2(a)), a tax determined in accordance with the following tables:

(1) **For taxable years beginning in 1982.**—[Not reproduced]
(2) **For taxable years beginning in 1983.**—[Not reproduced]
(3) **For taxable years beginning after 1983.**—

If taxable income is:	The tax is:
Not over $3,400	No tax.
Over $3,400 but not over $5,500	11% of the excess over $3,400.
Over $5,500 but not over $7,600	$231, plus 12% of the excess over $5,500.
Over $7,600 but not over $11,900	$483, plus 14% of the excess over $7,600.
Over $11,900 but not over $16,000	$1,085, plus 16% of the excess over $11,900.
Over $16,000 but not over $20,200	$1,741, plus 18% of the excess over $16,000.
Over $20,200 but not over $24,600	$2,497, plus 22% of the excess over $20,200.
Over $24,600 but not over $29,900	$3,465, plus 25% of the excess over $24,600.
Over $29,900 but not over $35,200	$4,790, plus 28% of the excess over $29,900.
Over $35,200 but not over $45,800	$6,274, plus 33% of the excess over $35,200.
Over $45,800 but not over $60,000	$9,772, plus 38% of the excess over $45,800.
Over $60,000 but not over $85,600	$15,168, plus 42% of the excess over $60,000.
Over $85,600 but not over $109,400	$25,920, plus 45% of the excess over $85,600.
Over $109,400 but not over $162,400	$36,630, plus 49% of the excess over $109,400.
Over $162,400	$62,600, plus 50% of the excess over $162,400.

(b) **Heads of Households.**—There is hereby imposed on the taxable income of every individual who is the head of a household (as defined in section 2(b)) a tax determined in accordance with the following tables:
(1) **For taxable years beginning in 1982.**—[Not reproduced]
(2) **For taxable years beginning in 1983.**—[Not reproduced]
(3) **For taxable years beginning after 1983.**—

(c) *Unmarried Individuals (Other Than Surviving Spouses and Heads of Households).*—There is hereby imposed on the taxable income of every individual (other than a surviving spouse as defined in section 2(a) or the head of a household as defined in section 2(b)) who is not a married individual (as defined in section 7703) a tax determined in accordance with the following table:

If taxable income is:	The tax is:
Not over $17,850	15% of taxable income.
Over $17,850	$2,677.50, plus 28% of the excess over $17,850.

(d) *Married Individuals Filing Separate Returns.*—There is hereby imposed on the taxable income of every married individual (as defined in section 7703) who does not make a single return jointly with his spouse under section 6013, a tax determined in accordance with the following table:

If taxable income is:	The tax is:
Not over $14,875	15% of taxable income.
Over $14,875	$2,231.25, plus 28% of the excess over $14,875.

(e) *Estates and Trusts.*—There is hereby imposed on the taxable income of—

    (1) every estate, and

    (2) every trust,

taxable under this subsection a tax determined in accordance with the following table:

[Footnote ¶2851 continued]

If taxable income is:	The tax is:
Not over $2,300	No tax.
Over $2,300 but not over $4,400	11% of the excess over $2,300.
Over $4,400 but not over $6,500	$231, plus 12% of the excess over $4,400.
Over $6,500 but not over $8,700	$483, plus 14% of the excess over $6,500.
Over $8,700 but not over $11,800	$791, plus 17% of the excess over $8,700.
Over $11,800 but not over $15,000	$1,318, plus 18% of the excess over $11,800.
Over $15,000 but not over $18,200	$1,894, plus 20% of the excess over $15,000.
Over $18,200 but not over $23,500	$2,534, plus 24% of the excess over $18,200.
Over $23,500 but not over $28,800	$3,806, plus 28% of the excess over $23,500.
Over $28,800 but not over $34,100	$5,290, plus 32% of the excess over $28,800.
Over $34,100 but not over $44,700	$6,986, plus 35% of the excess over $34,100.
Over $44,700 but not over $60,600	$10,696, plus 42% of the excess over $44,700.
Over $60,600 but not over $81,800	$17,374, plus 45% of the excess over $60,600.
Over $81,800 but not over $108,300	$26,914, plus 48% of the excess over $81,800.
Over $108,300	$39,634, plus 50% of the excess over $108,300.

(c) **Unmarried Individuals (Other Than Surviving Spouses and Heads of Households).**—There is hereby imposed on the taxable income of every individual (other than a surviving spouse as defined in section 2(a) or the head of a household as defined in section 2(b)) who is not a married individual (as defined in section 143) a tax determined in accordance with the following tables:

    (1) **For taxable years beginning in 1982.**—[Not reproduced]

    (2) **For taxable years beginning in 1983.**—[Not reproduced]

    (3) **For taxable years beginning after 1983.**—

If taxable income is:	The tax is:
Not over $2,300	No tax.
Over $2,300 but not over $3,400	11% of the excess over $2,300.
Over $3,400 but not over $4,400	$121, plus 12% of the excess over $3,400.
Over $4,400 but not over $6,500	$241, plus 14% of the excess over $4,400.
Over $6,500 but not over $8,500	$535, plus 15% of the excess over $6,500.

If taxable income is:	The tax is:
Not over $5,000	15% of taxable income.
Over $5,000	$750, plus 28% of the excess over $5,000.

(f) Adjustments in Tax Tables so That Inflation Will Not Result in Tax Increases.—

(1) In general.—Not later than December 15 of 1988, and each subsequent calendar year, the Secretary shall prescribe tables which shall apply in lieu of the tables contained in subsections (a), (b), (c), (d), and (e) with respect to taxable years beginning in the succeeding calendar year.

(2) Method of prescribing tables.—The table which under paragraph (1) is to apply in lieu of the table contained in subsection (a), (b), (c), (d), or (e), as the case may be, with respect to taxable years beginning in any calendar year shall be prescribed—

(A) by increasing the minimum and maximum dollar amounts for each rate bracket for which a tax is imposed under such table by the cost-of-living adjustment for such calendar year,

(B) by not changing the rate applicable to any rate bracket as adjusted under subparagraph (A), and

(C) by adjusting the amounts setting forth the tax to the extent necessary to reflect the adjustments in the rate brackets.

(3) Cost-of-living adjustment.—For purposes of paragraph (2), the cost-of-living adjustment for any calendar year is the percentage (if any) by which—

(A) the CPI for the preceding calendar year, exceeds

(B) the CPI for the calendar year 1987.

[Footnote ¶2851 continued]

Over $8,500 but not over $10,800	$835, plus 16% of the excess over $8,500.
Over $10,800 but not over $12,900	$1,203, plus 18% of the excess over $10,800.
Over $12,900 but not over $15,000	$1,581, plus 20% of the excess over $12,900.
Over $15,000 but not over $18,200	$2,001, plus 23% of the excess over $15,000.
Over $18,200 but not over $23,500	$2,737, plus 26% of the excess over $18,200.
Over $23,500 but not over $28,800	$4,115, plus 30% of the excess over $23,500.
Over $28,800 but not over $34,100	$5,705, plus 34% of the excess over $28,800.
Over $34,100 but not over $41,500	$7,507, plus 38% of the excess over $34,100.
Over $41,500 but not over $55,300	$10,319, plus 42% of the excess over $41,500.
Over $55,300 but not over $81,800	$16,115, plus 48% of the excess over $55,300.
Over $81,800	$28,835, plus 50% of the excess over $81,800.

(d) Married Individuals Filing Separate Returns.—There is hereby imposed on the taxable income of every married individual (as defined in section 143) who does not make a single return jointly with his spouse under section 6013 a tax determined in accordance with the following tables:

(1) **For taxable years beginning in 1982.**—[Not reproduced]
(2) **For taxable years beginning in 1983.**—[Not reproduced]
(3) **For taxable years beginning after 1983.**—

If taxable income is:	The tax is:
Not over $1,700	No tax.
Over $1,700 but not over $2,750	11% of the excess over $1,700.
Over $2,750 but not over $3,800	$115.50, plus 12% of the excess over $2,750.
Over $3,800 but not over $5,950	$241.50, plus 14% of the excess over $3,800.
Over $5,950 but not over $8,000	$542.50, plus 16% of the excess over $5,950.
Over $8,000 but not over $10,100	$870.50, plus 18% of the excess over $8,000.
Over $10,100 but not over $12,300	$1,248.50, plus 22% of the excess over $10,100.

Code §1(f)(3) ¶2851

(4) CPI for any calendar year.—For purposes of paragraph (3), the CPI for the calendar year is the average of the Consumer Price Index as of the close of the 12-month period ending on August 31 of such calendar year.

(5) Consumer price index.—For purposes of paragraph (4), the term "Consumer Price Index" means the last Consumer Price Index for all-urban consumers published by the Department of Labor. For purposes of the preceding sentence, the revision of the Consumer Price Index which is most consistent with the Consumer Price Index for calendar year 1986 shall be used.

(6) Rounding.—

    (A) In general.—If any increase determined under paragraph (2)(A), subsection (g)(4), section 63(c)(4), or section 151(d)(3) is not a multiple of $50, such increase shall be rounded to the next lowest multiple of $50.

    (B) Table for married individuals filing separately.—In the case of a married individual filing a separate return, subparagraph (A) (other than with respect to section 63(c)(4)) shall be applied by substituting "$25" for "$50" each place it appears.

(g) Phaseout of 15-Percent Rate and Personal Exemptions.—

    (1) In general.—The amount of tax imposed by this section (determined without regard to this subsection) shall be increased by 5 percent of the excess (if any) of—

        (A) taxable income, over

        (B) the applicable dollar amount.

    (2) Limitation.—The increase determined under paragraph (1) with respect to any taxpayer for any taxable year shall not exceed the sum of—

        (A) 13 percent of the maximum amount of taxable income to which the 15-percent rate applies under the table contained in subsection (a), (b), (c), or (e) (whichever applies), and

---

[Footnote ¶2851 continued]

Over $12,300 but not over $14,950	$1,732.50, plus 25% of the excess over $12,300.
Over $14,950 but not over $17,600	$2,395, plus 28% of the excess over $14,950.
Over $17,600 but not over $22,900	$3,137, plus 33% of the excess over $17,600.
Over $22,900 but not over $30,000	$4,886, plus 38% of the excess over $22,900.
Over $30,000 but not over $42,800	$7,584, plus 42% of the excess over $30,000.
Over $42,800 but not over $54,700	$12,960, plus 45% of the excess over $42,800.
Over $54,700 but not over $81,200	$18,315, plus 49% of the excess over $54,700.
Over $81,200	$31,300, plus 50% of the excess over $81,200.

(e) Estates and Trusts.—There is hereby imposed on the taxable income of every estate and trust taxable under this subsection a tax determined in accordance with the following tables:

    (1) For taxable years beginning in 1982.—[Not reproduced]

    (2) For taxable years beginning in 1983.—[Not reproduced]

    (3) For taxable years beginning after 1983.—

If taxable income is:	The tax is:
Not over $1,050	11% of taxable income.
Over $1,050 but not over $2,100	$115.50, plus 12% of the excess over $1,050.
Over $2,100 but not over $4,250	$241.50, plus 14% of the excess over $2,100.
Over $4,250 but not over $6,300	$542.50, plus 16% of the excess over $4,250.
Over $6,300 but not over $8,400	$870.50, plus 18% of the excess over $6,300.
Over $8,400 but not over $10,600	$1,248.50, plus 22% of the excess over $8,400.
Over $10,600 but not over $13,250	$1,732.50, plus 25% of the excess over $10,600.
Over $13,250 but not over $15,900	$2,395, plus 28% of the excess over $13,250.
Over $15,900 but not over $21,200	$3,137, plus 33% of the excess over $15,900.
Over $21,200 but not over $28,300	$4,886, plus 38% of the excess over $21,200.
Over $28,300 but not over $41,100	$7,584, plus 42% of the excess over $28,300.
Over $41,100 but not over $53,000	$12,960, plus 45% of the excess over $41,100.

(B) 28 percent of the deductions for personal exemptions allowable to the taxpayer for the taxable year under section 151.

In the case of any individual taxable under subsection (d), subparagraph (A) shall apply as if such individual were taxable under subsection (a).

(3) Applicable dollar amount.—For purposes of paragraph (1), the applicable dollar amount shall be determined under the following table:

In the case of a taxpayer to which the following subsection of this section applies:	The applicable dollar amount is:
Subsection (a)	$71,900
Subsection (b)	61,650
Subsection (c)	43,150
Subsection (d)	35,950
Subsection (e)	13,000

(4) Adjustment for inflation.—In the case of any taxable year beginning in a calendar year after 1988, each dollar amount contained in paragraph (3) shall be increased by an amount equal to—

  (A) such dollar amount, multiplied by

  (B) the cost-of-living adjustment determined under subsection (f)(3) for the calendar year in which the taxable year begins.

(h) Tax Schedules for Taxable Years Beginning in 1987.—In the case of any taxable year beginning in 1987—

  (1) subsection (g) shall not apply, and

  (2) the following tables shall apply in lieu of the tables set forth in subsections (a), (b), (c), (d), and (e):

  (A) Married individuals filing joint returns and surviving spouses.—The table to apply for purposes of subsection (a) is as follows:

If taxable income is:	The tax is:
Not over $3,000	11% of taxable income.
Over $3,000 but not over $28,000	$330, plus 15% of the excess over $3,000.

[Footnote ¶2851 continued]

Over $53,000 but not over $79,500	$18,315, plus 49% of the excess over $53,000.
Over $79,500	$31,300, plus 50% of the excess over $79,500.

(f) Adjustments in Tax Tables so That Inflation Will Not Result in Tax Increases.—

(1) In general.—Not later than December 15 of 1984 and each subsequent calendar year, the Secretary shall prescribe tables which shall apply in lieu of the tables contained in paragraph (3) of subsections (a), (b), (c), (d), and (e) with respect to taxable years beginning in the succeeding calendar year.

(2) Method of prescribing tables.—The table which under paragraph (1) is to apply in lieu of the table contained in paragraph (3) of subsection (a), (b), (c), (d), or (e), as the case may be, with respect to taxable years beginning in any calendar year shall be prescribed—

  (A) by increasing—

    (i) the maximum dollar amount on which no tax is imposed under such table, and

    (ii) the minimum and maximum dollar amounts for each rate bracket for which a tax is imposed under such table, by the cost-of-living adjustment for such calendar year,

  (B) by not changing the rate applicable to any rate bracket as adjusted under subparagraph (A)(ii), and

  (C) by adjusting the amounts setting forth the tax to the extent necessary to reflect the adjustments in the rate brackets.

If any increase determined under subparagraph (A) is not a multiple of $10, such increase shall be rounded to the nearest multiple of $10 (or if such increase is a multiple of $5, such increase shall be increased to the next highest multiple of $10).

(3) Cost-of-living adjustment.—For purposes of paragraph (2), the cost-of-living adjustment for any calendar year is the percentage (if any) by which—

  (A) the CPI for the preceding calendar year, exceeds

  (B) the CPI for the calendar year 1983.

(4) CPI for any calendar year.—For purposes of paragraph (3), the CPI for any calendar year is the average of the Consumer Price Index as of the close of the 12-month period ending on September 30 of such calendar year.

(5) Consumer price index.—For purposes of paragraph (4), the term "Consumer Price Index" means the last Consumer Price Index for all-urban consumers published by the Department of Labor.

Effective date (Sec. 151(a), '86 TRA).—Applies to taxable years beginning after 12-31-86.

Over $28,000 but not over $45,000 ..	$4,080, plus 28% of the excess over $28,000.
Over $45,000 but not over $90,000 ..	$8,840, plus 35% of the excess over $45,000.
Over $90,000	$24,590, plus 38.5% of the excess over $90,000.

(B) *Heads of households.*—*The table to apply for purposes of subsection (b) is as follows:*

If taxable income is:	The tax is:
Not over $2,500	11% of taxable income.
Over $2,500 but not over $23,000 ...	$275, plus 15% of the excess over $2,500.
Over $23,000 but not over $38,000 ..	$3,350, plus 28% of the excess over $23,000.
Over $38,000 but not over $80,000 ..	$7,550, plus 35% of the excess over $38,000.
Over $80,000	$22,250, plus 38.5% of the excess over $80,000.

(C) *Unmarried individuals other than surviving spouses and heads of households.*—*The table to apply for purposes of subsection (c) is as follows:*

If taxable income is:	The tax is:
Not over $1,800	11% of taxable income.
Over $1,800 but not over $16,800 ...	$198, plus 15% of the excess over $1,800.
Over $16,800 but not over $27,000 ..	$2,448, plus 28% of the excess over $16,800.
Over $27,000 but not over $54,000 ..	$5,304, plus 35% of the excess over $27,000.
Over $54,000	$14,754, plus 38.5% of the excess over $54,000.

(D) *Married individuals filing separate returns.*—*The table to apply for purposes of subsection (d) is as follows:*

If taxable income is:	The tax is:
Not over $1,500	11% of taxable income.
Over $1,500 but not over $14,000 ...	$165, plus 15% of the excess over $1,500.
Over $14,000 but not over $22,500 ..	$2,040, plus 28% of the excess over $14,000.
Over $22,500 but not over $45,000 ..	$4,420, plus 35% of the excess over $22,500.
Over $45,000	$12,295, plus 38.5% of the excess over $45,000.

(E) *Estates and trusts.*—*The table to apply for purposes of subsection (e) is as follows:*

If taxable income is:	The tax is:
Not over $500	11% of taxable income.
Over $500 but not over $4,700	$55, plus 15% of the excess over $500.
Over $4,700 but not over $7,550	$685, plus 28% of the excess over $4,700.
Over $7,550 but not over $15,150 ...	$1,483, plus 35% of the excess over $7,500.
Over $15,150	$4,143, plus 38.5% of the excess over $15,150.

(i) *Certain Unearned Income of Minor Children Taxed as if Parent's Income.*—

(1) *In general.*—*In the case of any child to whom this subsection applies, the tax*

【Footnote ¶2851 continued】

Sec. 1(i) in *italics* added by section 1411(a), '86 TRA.
Effective date (Sec. 1411(c), '86 TRA).—Applies to taxable years beginning after 12-31-86.

imposed by this section shall be equal to the greater of—
  (A) the tax imposed by this section without regard to this subsection, or
  (B) the sum of—
    (i) the tax which would be imposed by this section if the taxable income of such child for the taxable year were reduced by the net unearned income of such child, plus
    (ii) such child's share of the allocable parental tax.

  (2) Child to whom subsection applies.—This subsection shall apply to any child for any taxable year if—
    (A) such child has not attained age 14 before the close of the taxable year, and
    (B) either parent of such child is alive at the close of the taxable year.

  (3) Allocable parental tax.—For purposes of this subsection—
    (A) In general.—The term "allocable parental tax" means the excess of—
      (i) the tax which would be imposed by this section on the parent's taxable income if such income included the net unearned income of all children of the parent to whom this subsection applies, over
      (ii) the tax imposed by this section on the parent without regard to this subsection.
  For purposes of clause (i), net unearned income of all children of the parent shall not be taken into account in computing any deduction or credit of the parent.
    (B) Child's share.—A child's share of any allocable parental tax of a parent shall be equal to an amount which bears the same ratio to the total allocable parental tax as the child's net unearned income bears to the aggregate net unearned income of all children of such parent to whom this subsection applies.

  (4) Net unearned income.—For purposes of this subsection—
    (A) In general.—The term "net unearned income" means the excess of—
      (i) the portion of the gross income for the taxable year which is not earned income (as defined in section 911(d)(2)), over
      (ii) the sum of—
        (I) the amount in effect for the taxable year under section 63(c)(5)(A) (relating to limitation on standard deduction in the case of certain dependents), plus
        (II) the greater of the amount described in subclause (I) or, if the child itemizes his deduction for the taxable year, the amount of the deductions allowed by this chapter for the taxable year which are directly connected with the production of the portion of gross income referred to in clause (i).
    (B) Limitation based on taxable income.—The amount of the net unearned income for any taxable year shall not exceed the individual's taxable income for such taxable year.

  (5) Special rules for determining parent to whom subsection applies.—For purposes of this subsection, the parent whose taxable income shall be taken into account shall be—
    (A) in the case of parents who are not married (within the meaning of section 7703), the custodial parent of the child, and
    (B) in the case of married individuals filing separately, the individual with the greater taxable income.

  (6) Providing of parent's TIN.—The parent of any child to whom this subsection applies for any taxable year shall provide the TIN of such parent to such child and such child shall include such TIN on the child's return of tax imposed by this section for such taxable year.

(j) Maximum Capital Gains Rate.—
  (1) In general.—If a taxpayer has a net capital gain for any taxable year to which this subsection applies, then the tax imposed by this section shall not exceed the sum of—
    (A) a tax computed at the rates and in the same manner as if this subsection had not been enacted on the greater of—

[Footnote ¶2851 continued]

Sec. 1(j) in *italics* added by section 302(a), '86 TRA.
Effective date (Sec. 302(b) and (c), '86 TRA.)—(b) Generally applies to taxable years beginning after 12-31-86.
(c) Transitional Rule.—The tax under section 1 of the '86 Code on the long-term capital gain on rights to royalties paid under leases and assignments binding on 9-25-85, by a limited partnership formed on 3-1-77, which on 10-30-79, assigned leases and which assignment was amended on 4-27-81, shall not exceed 20 percent.

Code §1(j)(1) ¶2851

    (i)   *the taxable income reduced by the amount of net capital gain, or*

    (ii)   *the amount of taxable income taxed at a rate below 28 percent, plus*

  (B) *a tax of 28 percent of the amount of taxable income in excess of the amount determined under subparagraph (A), plus*

  (C) *the amount of increase determined under subsection (g).*

  (2) *Years to which subsection applies.*—*This subsection shall apply to*—

  (A) *any taxable year beginning in 1987, and*

  (B) *any taxable year beginning after 1987 if the highest rate of tax set forth in subsection (a), (b), (c), (d), or (e) (whichever applies) for such taxable year exceeds 28 percent.*

[For official explanation, see Committee Reports, ¶3852; 3886; 4064]

[¶2852] CODE SEC. 2. DEFINITIONS AND SPECIAL RULES.

  (a) Definition of Surviving Spouse.—

* * * * * * * * * * * *

  (3) Special rule where deceased spouse was in missing status.—If an individual was in a missing status (within the meaning of section 6013(f)(3)) as a result of service in a combat zone (as determined for purposes of section 112) and if such individual remains in such status until the date referred to in subparagraph (A) or (B), then, for purposes of paragraph (1)(A), the date on which such individual died shall be treated as the earlier of the date determined under subparagraph (A) or the date determined under subparagraph (B):

  (A) the date on which the determination is made under section 556 of title 37 of the United States Code or under section 5566 of title 5 of such Code (whichever is applicable) that such individual died while in such missing status, or

  [1](B) *except in the case of the combat zone designated for purposes of the Vietnam conflict, the date which is 2 years after the date designated under section 112 as the date of termination of combatant activities in that zone.*

* * * * * * * * * * * *

  (c) Certain Married Individuals Living Apart.—For purposes of this part, an individual shall be treated as not married at the close of the taxable year if such individual is so treated under the provisions of [2]*section 7703(b).*

* * * * * * * * * * * *

[For official explanation, see Committee Reports, ¶4058; 4130]

[¶2853] CODE SEC. 3. TAX TABLES FOR INDIVIDUALS.

  [1]*(a) Imposition of Tax Table Tax.—*

[Footnote ¶2852] Matter in *italics* in Sec. 2(a)(3)(B) added by section 1708(a)(1), '86 TRA, which struck out:

(1) "(B) the date which is—

(i) December 31, 1982, in the case of service in the combat zone designated for purposes of the Vietnam conflict, or

(ii) 2 years after the date designated under section 112 as the date of termination of combatant activities in that zone, in the case of any combat zone other than that referred to in clause (i)."

Effective date (Sec. 1708(b), '86 TRA).—Applies to taxable years beginning after 12-31-82.

Matter in *italics* in Sec. 2(c) added by section 1301(j)(10), '86 TRA, which struck out:

(2) "section 143(b)"

Effective date (Sec. 1311(a), '86 TRA).—Generally applies to bonds issued after 8-15-86. For transitional rules see footnote ¶2071—2077.

[Footnote ¶2853] Matter in *italics* in Sec. 3(a) added by section 102(b), '86 TRA, which struck out:

(1) "**(1) In general.**—In lieu of the tax imposed by section 1, there is hereby imposed for each taxable year on the tax table income of every individual whose tax table income for such year does not exceed the ceiling amount, a tax determined under tables, applicable to such taxable year, which shall be prescribed by the Secretary and which shall be in such form as he determines appropriate. In the tables so prescribed, the amounts of tax shall be computed on the basis of the rates prescribed by section 1.

(2) Ceiling amount defined.—For purposes of paragraph (1), the term "ceiling amount" means, with respect to any taxpayer, the amount (not less than $20,000) determined by the Secretary for the tax rate category in which such taxpayer falls.

(3) Certain taxpayers with large number of exemptions.—The Secretary may exclude from the application of this section taxpayers in any tax rate category having more than the number of exemptions for that category determined by the Secretary.

(4) Tax table income defined.—For purposes of this section, the term "tax table income" means adjusted gross income—

(A) reduced by the sum of—

(1) In general.—In lieu of the tax imposed by section 1, there is hereby imposed for each taxable year on the taxable income of every individual—

    (A) who does not itemize his deductions for the taxable year, and

    (B) whose taxable income for such taxable year does not exceed the ceiling amount,

a tax determined under tables, applicable to such taxable year, which shall be prescribed by the Secretary and which shall be in such form as he determines appropriate. In the table so prescribed, the amounts of the tax shall be computed on the basis of the rates prescribed by section 1.

(2) Ceiling amount defined.—For purposes of paragraph (1), the term "ceiling amount" means, with respect to any taxpayer, the amount (not less than $20,000) determined by the Secretary for the tax rate category in which such taxpayer falls.

(3) Authority to prescribe tables for taxpayers who itemize deductions.—The Secretary may provide that this section shall apply also for any taxable year to individuals who itemize their deductions. Any tables prescribed under the preceding sentence shall be on the basis of taxable income.

(b) Section Inapplicable to Certain Individuals.—This section shall not apply to—[2]

   [3](1) an individual making a return under section 443(a)(1) for a period of less than 12 months on account of a change in annual accounting period, and

   [4](2) an estate or trust.

* * * * * * * * * * *

[For official explanation, see Committee Reports, ¶3853; 3865]

[¶2854] CODE SEC. 5. CROSS REFERENCES RELATING TO TAX ON INDIVIDUALS.

(a) Other Rates of Tax on Individuals, etc.—

* * * * * * * * * * *

   (4) For *alternative* minimum tax, [1] see section 55.

(b) Special Limitations on Tax.—

   (1) For limitation on tax in case of income of members of Armed Forces on death, see section 692.[2]

   [3]**(2)** For computation of tax where taxpayer restores substantial amount held under claim of right, see section 1341.

[For official explanation, see Committee Reports, ¶3865; 3931]

[¶2855] CODE SEC. 11. TAX IMPOSED.

(a) Corporations in General.—A tax is hereby imposed for each taxable year on the taxable income of every corporation.

[Footnote ¶2853 continued]
   (i) the excess itemized deductions, and
   (ii) the direct charitable deduction, and
   (B) increased (in the case of an individual to whom section 63(e) applies) by the unused zero bracket amount.
   (5) Section may be applied on the basis of taxable income.—The Secretary may provide that this section shall be applied for any taxable year on the basis of taxable income in lieu of tax table income."
Effective date (Sec. 151(a), '86 TRA).—Applies to taxable years beginning after 12-31-86.

Matter in *italics* in Sec. 3(b) added by section 141(b)(1), '86 TRA, which struck out:
   (2) "(1) an individual to whom section 1301 (relating to income averaging) applies for the taxable year,"
   (3) "(2)"
   (4) "(3)"
Effective date (Sec. 151(a), '86 TRA).—Applies to taxable years beginning after 12-31-86.
[Footnote ¶2854] Matter in *italics* in Sec. 5(a)(4) added by section 701(e)(4)(A), '86 TRA, which struck out:
   (1) "for taxpayers other than corporations"
Effective date (Sec. 701(f), '86 TRA).—Generally applies to taxable years beginning after 12-31-86. For special rules, see footnote ¶2879.

Matter in *italics* in Sec. 5(b) added by section 141(b)(2), '86 TRA, which struck out:
   (2) "(2) For limitation of tax where an individual chooses the benefits of income averaging, see section 1301."
   (3) "(3)"
Effective date (Sec. 151(a), 86 TRA).—Applies to taxable years beginning after 12-31-86.

Tax Reform Act of 1986

¹(b) *Amount of tax.*—*The amount of the tax imposed by subsection (a) shall be the sum of*—

  (1)   15 percent of so much of the taxable income as does not exceed $50,000,

  (2)   25 percent of so much of the taxable income as exceeds $50,000 but does not exceed $75,000, and

  (3)   34 percent of so much of the taxable income as exceeds $75,000.

In the case of a corporation which has taxable income in excess of $100,000 for any taxable year, the amount of tax determined under the preceding sentence for such taxable year shall be increased by the lesser of (A) 5 percent of such excess, or (B) $11,750.

* * * * * * * * * * * *

[For official explanation, see Committee Reports, ¶3911]

〔¶2856〕 CODE SEC. 12.   CROSS REFERENCES RELATING TO TAX ON COR-PORATIONS.

* * * * * * * * * * * *

¹*(7)   For alternative minimum tax, see section 55.*

[For official explanation, see Committee Reports, ¶3931]

〔¶2857〕 CODE SEC. 15.   EFFECT OF CHANGES.

  (a)   General rule.—If any rate of tax imposed by this chapter changes, and if the taxable year includes the effective date of the change (unless that date is the first day of the taxable year), then—

  (1)   tentative taxes shall be computed by applying the rate for the period before the effective date of the change, and the rate for the period on and after such date, to the taxable income for the entire taxable year; and

  (2)   the tax for such taxable year shall be the sum of that proportion of each tentative tax which the number of days in each period bears to the number of days in the entire taxable year.

* * * * * * * * * * * *

¹*(d)   Section not to apply to inflation adjustments.*—*This section shall not apply to any change in rates under subsection (f) of section 1 (relating to adjustments in tax tables so that inflation will not result in tax increases).*

[For official explanation, see Committee Reports, ¶3852]

〔¶2858〕 CODE SEC. 21.   EXPENSES FOR HOUSEHOLD AND DEPENDENT CARE SERVICES NECESSARY FOR GAINFUL EMPLOYMENT.

  (a)   Allowance of Credit.—

  (1)   In general.—In the case of an individual who maintains a household which includes as a member one or more qualifying individuals (as defined in subsection (b)(1)), there shall be allowed as a credit against the tax imposed by this chapter for

---

〔Footnote ¶2855〕   Matter in *italics* in Sec. 11(b) added by section 601(a), '86 TRA, which struck out:

  (1)   "(b)   Amount of Tax.—The amount of the tax imposed by subsection (a) shall be the sum of—

  (1)   15 percent (16 percent for taxable years beginning in 1982) of so much of the taxable income as does not exceed $25,000;

  (2)   18 percent (19 percent for taxable years beginning in 1982) of so much of the taxable income as exceeds $25,000 but does not exceed $50,000;

  (3)   30 percent of so much of the taxable income as exceeds $50,000 but does not exceed $75,000;

  (4)   40 percent of so much of the taxable income as exceeds $75,000 but does not exceed $100,000; plus

  (5)   46 percent of so much of the taxable income as exceeds $100,000.

In the case of a corporation with taxable income in excess of $1,000,000 for any taxable year, the amount of tax determined under the preceding sentence for such taxable year shall be increased by the lesser of (A) 5 percent of such excess, or (B) $20,250."

Effective date (Sec. 601(b), '86 TRA).—(1) Generally applies to taxable years beginning on or after 7-1-87.

(2)   Cross reference.—

For treatment of taxable years which include 7-1-87, see section 15 of the '86 Code.

〔Footnote ¶2856〕   Matter in *italics* in Sec. 12(7) added by section 701(e)(4)(B), '86 TRA, which struck out:

  (1)   "(7)   For minimum tax for tax preferences, see section 56."

Effective date (Sec. 701(f), '86 TRA).—(1)   Generally applies to taxable years beginning after 12-31-86. For transitional and special rules, see footnote ¶2879.

〔Footnote ¶2857〕   Matter in *italics* in Sec. 15(d) added by section 101(b), '86 TRA, which struck out:

  (1)   "(d)   Section Not to Apply to Section 1 Rate Changes Made by Economic Recovery Tax Act of 1981.—This section shall not apply to any change in rates under section 1 attributable to the amendments made by section 101 of the Economic Recovery Tax Act of 1981 or subsection (f) of section 1 (relating to adjustments in tax tables so that inflation will not result in tax increases.)"

Effective date (Sec. 151(a), '86 TRA).—Applies to taxable years beginning after 12-31-86.

the taxable year an amount equal to the applicable percentage of the employment-related expenses (as defined in subsection (b)(2)) paid by such individual during the taxable year.

(2) **Applicable percentage defined.**—For purposes of paragraph (1), the term "applicable percentage" means 30 percent reduced (but not below 20 percent) by 1 percentage point for each $2,000 (or fraction thereof) by which the taxpayer's adjusted gross income for the taxable year exceeds $10,000.

(b) **Definitions of Qualifying Individual and Employment-Related Expenses.**—For purposes of this section—

(1) **Qualifying individual.**—The term "qualifying individual" means—

(A) a dependent of the taxpayer who is under the age of 15 and with respect to whom the taxpayer is entitled to a deduction under [1]*section 151(c),*
(B) a dependent of the taxpayer who is physically or mentally incapable of caring for himself, or
(C) the spouse of the taxpayer, if he is physically or mentally incapable of caring for himself.

* * * * * * * * * * * *

(e) **Special Rules.**—For purposes of this section—

* * * * * * * * * * * *

(6) **Payments to related individuals.**—

No credit shall be allowed under subsection (a) for any amount paid by the taxpayer to an individual—
(A) with respect to whom, for the taxable year, a deduction under [1]*section 151(c)* (relating to deduction for personal exemptions for dependents) is allowable either to the taxpayer or his spouse, or
(B) who is a child of the taxpayer (within the meaning of [2]*section 151(c)(3))* who has not attained the age of 19 at the close of the taxable year.
For purposes of this paragraph, the term "taxable year" means the taxable year of the taxpayer in which the service is performed.

* * * * * * * * * * * *

〖¶2859〗 CODE SEC. 22. CREDIT FOR THE ELDERLY AND THE PERMANENTLY AND TOTALLY DISABLED.

* * * * * * * * * * * *

(e) **Definitions and Special Rules.**—For purposes of this section—

* * * * * * * * * * * *

(2) **Marital status.**—Marital status shall be determined under [1]*section 7703.*

* * * * * * * * * * * *

[For official explanation, see Committee Reports, ¶4058.]

〖¶2860〗 CODE SEC. 24. CONTRIBUTIONS TO CANDIDATES FOR PUBLIC OFFICE.
[Repealed by section 112(a), '86 TRA].[1]

[For official explanation, see Committee Reports, ¶3856.]

〖Footnote ¶2858〗 Matter in *italics* in Sec. 21(b)(1)(A), (e)(6)(A) and (B) added by section 104(b)(1)(A) and (B), '86 TRA, which struck out:
(1) "section 151(e)"
(2) "section 151(e)(3)"
Effective date (Sec. 151(a), '86 TRA).—Applies to taxable years beginning after 12-31-86.
〖Footnote ¶2859〗 Matter in *italics* in Sec. 22(e)(2) added by section 1301(j)(8), '86 TRA, which struck out:
(1) "section 143"
Effective date (Sec. 1311(a), '86 TRA).—Applies to bonds issued after 8-15-86. For transitional and special rules, see ¶2071—2077.
〖Footnote ¶2860〗 (1) **Effective date** (Sec. 151(a), '86 TRA).—Applies to taxable years beginning after 12-31-86.

〔¶2861〕 CODE SEC. 25.   INTEREST ON CERTAIN HOME MORTGAGES.

(a) Allowance of Credit.—

(1) In general.—There shall be allowed as a credit against the tax imposed by this chapter for the taxable year an amount equal to the product of—

(A) the certificate credit rate, and

(B) the interest paid or [1]*accrued* by the taxpayer during the taxable year on the remaining principal of the certificated indebtedness amount.

* * * * * * * * * * * *

(b) Certificate Credit Rate; Certified Indebtedness Amount.—For purposes of this section—

* * * * * * * * * * * *

(2) Certified indebtedness amount.—The term "certified indebtedness amount" means the amount of indebtedness which is—

(A) incurred by the taxpayer—

(i) to acquire the principal residence of the taxpayer,

(ii) as a qualified home improvement loan (as defined in [2]*section 143(k)(4)*) with respect to such residence, or

(iii) as a qualified rehabilitation loan (as defined in [3]*section 143(k)(5))* with respect to such residence, and

(B) specified in the mortgage credit certificate.

(c) Mortgage Credit Certificate; Qualified Mortgage Credit Certificate Program.— For purposes of this section—

* * * * * * * * * * * *

≫P-H CAUTION→ There are two versions of Sec. 25(c)(2)(A). Sec. 25(c)(2)(A), generally effective for certificates issued after 8-15-86, follows. For Sec. 25(c)(2)(A), generally effective for certificates issued before 8-16-86, see below.

▲ (2) Qualified mortgage credit certificate program.—

(A) In general.—The term "qualified mortgage credit certificate program" means any program—

(i) which is established by a State or political subdivision thereof for any calender year for which it is authorized to issue qualified mortgage bonds,

(ii) under which the issuing authority elects (in such manner and form as the Secretary may prescribe) not to issue an amount of qualified mortgage bonds which it may otherwise issue during such calendar year under [4]*section 103,*

(iii) under which the indebtedness certified by mortgage credit certificates meets the requirements of the following subsections of [4]*section 143* (as modified by subparagraph (B) of this paragraph):

[5]*(I)   subsection (c) (relating to residence requirements),*

〔Footnote ¶2861〕 Matter in *italics* in Sec. 25(a)(1)(B) added by section 1862(d)(1), '86 TRA, which struck out:

(1) "incurred"

Effective date (Sec. 1881, '86 TRA, and section 612(g), '84 TRA).—(1) Generally applies to interest paid or accrued after 12-31-84, on indebtedness incurred after 12-31-84.

(2) Elections.—Applies to elections under Sec. 25(c)(2)(A)(ii) of the Code (as added by this section) for calendar years after 1983.

Matter in *italics* in Sec. 25(b)(2)(A)(ii), (iii) and (e)(8)(B) added by section 1301(f)(2)(A), (B), and (K), '86 TRA, which struck out:

(2) "section 103A(l)(6)"

(3) "section 103A(l)(7)"

Effective date (Sec. 1311(b)(2), '86 TRA).—Generally applies to certificates issued after 8-15-86. For special and transitional rules, see ¶2071—2077.

▲ Matter in *italics* in Sec. 25(c)(2)(A)(ii) and (iii), preceded by a triangle, added by section 1301(f)(2)(c)(ii)(D) and (E), '86 TRA, which struck out:

(4) "section 103A"

(5) (I)   subsection (d) (relating to residence requirements),

(II)   subsection (e) (relating to 3-year requirement),

(III)   subsection (f) (relating to purchase price requirement),

(IV)   subsection (h) (relating to portion of loans required to be placed in targeted areas), and

(V)   subsection (j), other than paragraph (2) thereof (relating to other requirements),

Effective date (Sec. 1311(b)(2), '86 TRA).—Generally applies to certificates issued after 8-15-86. For special and

　　(II)　subsection (d) (relating to 3-year requirement),
　　(III)　subsection (e) (relating to purchase price requirement),
　　(IV)　subsection (f) (relating to income requirements),
　　(V)　subsection (h) (relating to portion of loans required to be placed in targeted areas), and
　　(VI)　paragraph (1) of subsection (i) (relating to other requirements),

　　(iv)　under which no mortgage credit certificate may be issued with respect to any residence any of the financing of which is provided from the proceeds of a qualified mortgage bond or a qualified veterans' mortgage bond,

　　(v)　except to the extent provided in regulations, which is not limited to indebtedness incurred from particular lenders,

　　(vi)　except to the extent provided in regulations, which provides that a mortgage credit certificate is not transferrable, and

　　(vii)　if the issuing authority allocates a block of mortgage credit certificates for use in connection with a particular development, which requires the developer to furnish to the issuing authority and the homebuyer a certificate that the price for the residence is no higher than it would be without the use of a mortgage credit certificate.

Under regulations, rules similar to the rules of subparagraphs (B) and (C) of ⁶*section 143(a)(2) shall apply to the requirements of this subparagraph.*

≫**P-H CAUTION→** There are two versions of Sec. 25(c)(2)(A). Sec. 25(c)(2)(A), generally effective for certificates issued before 8-16-86, follows. Sec. 25(c)(2)(A), generally effective for certificates issued after 8-15-86, see above.

▲▲ **(2)　Qualified mortgage credit certificate program.—**
　　(A)　In general.—The term "qualified mortgage credit certificate program" means any program—
　　　(i)　which is established by a State or political subdivision thereof for any calender year for which it is authorized to issue qualified mortgage bonds,
　　　(ii)　under which the issuing authority elects (in such manner and form as the Secretary may prescribe) not to issue an amount of qualified mortgage bonds which it may otherwise issue during such calendar year under section 103A,
　　　(iii)　under which the indebtedness certified by mortgage credit certificates meets the requirements of the following subsections of section 103A (as modified by subparagraph (B) of this paragraph):
　　　　(I)　subsection (d) (relating to residence requirements),
　　　　(II)　subsection (e) (relating to 3-year requirement),
　　　　(III)　subsection (f) (relating to purchase price requirement),
　　　　(IV)　subsection (h) (relating to portion of loans required to be placed in targeted areas), and
　　　　(V)　⁷subsection (j), *other than paragraph (2) thereof* (relating to other

---

⟦Footnote ¶2861 continued⟧
transitional rules, see ¶2071—2077.

Matter in *italics* in the last sentence of Sec. 25(c)(2)(A) [except for the phrase "section 143(a)(2)"] added by section 1862(b), '86 TRA.
Effective date (Sec. 1881, '86 TRA and section 612(g), '84 TRA).—See above.

"section 143(a)(2)" in *italics* in the last sentence of Sec. 25(c)(2)(A) added by section 1301(f)(2)(E), '86 TRA, which struck out:
　(6)　"section 103A(c)(2)"
Effective date (Sec. 1311(b)(2), '86 TRA).—Generally applies to certificates issued after 8-15-86. For special and transitional rules see ¶2071—2077.

▲▲ Matter in *italics* in Sec. 25(c)(2)(A)(iii)(V), preceded by two triangles added by section 1862(a), '86 TRA, which struck out:
　(7)　"paragraph (I) of"
Effective date (Sec. 1881, '86 TRA and section 612(g), '84 TRA).—(1) Generally applies to interest paid or accrued after 12-31-84, on indebtedness incurred after 12-31-84.
　(2)　Elections.—Applies to elections under Sec. 25(c)(2)(A)(ii) of the Code (as added by this section for calendar years after 1983.

3014 Tax Reform Act of 1986

requirements),

(iv) under which no mortgage credit certificate may be issued with respect to any residence any of the financing of which is provided from the proceeds of a qualified mortgage bond or a qualified veterans' mortgage bond,

(v) except to the extent provided in regulations, which is not limited to indebtedness incurred from particular lenders,

(vi) except to the extent provided in regulations, which provides that a mortgage credit certificate is not transferrable, and

(vii) if the issuing authority allocates a block of mortgage credit certificates for use in connection with a particular development, which requires the developer to furnish to the issuing authority and the homebuyer a certificate that the price for the residence is no higher than it would be without the use of a mortgage credit certificate.

Under regulations, rules similar to the rules of subparagraphs (B) and (C) of [6]section 143(a)(2) shall apply to the requirements of this subparagraph.

(B) Modifications of [8]*section 143.*—Under regulations prescribed by the Secretary, in applying for purposes of [9]*subclauses (II), (IV), and (V)* of subparagraph (A)(iii)—

(i) each qualified mortgage certificate credit program shall be treated as a separate issue.

(ii) the product determined by multiplying—

(I) the certified indebtedness amount of each mortgage credit certificate issued under such program, by

(II) the certificate credit rate specified in such certificate,

shall be treated as proceeds of such issue and the sum of such products shall be treated as the total proceeds of such issue, and

[10]*(iii) paragraph (1) of section 143(d) shall be applied by substituting "100 percent" for "95 percent or more".*

Clause (iii) shall not apply if the issuing authority submits a plan to the Secretary for administering the 95-percent requirement of section 143(d)(1) and the Secretary is satisfied that such requirement will be met under such plan.

(d) **Determination of Certificate Credit Rate.**—For purposes of this section—

* * * * * * * * * * * * *

(2) **Aggregate limit on certificate credit rates.**—

(A) In general.—In the case of each qualified mortgage credit certificate program, the sum of the products determined by multiplying—

(i) the certified indebtedness amount of each mortgage credit certificate issued under such program, by

(ii) the certificate credit rate with respect to such certificate,

shall not exceed [11]*25 percent* of the nonissued bond amount.

(B) Nonissued bond amount.—For purposes of subparagraph (A), the term "nonissued bond amount" means, with respect to any qualified mortgage credit certificate program, the amount of qualified mortgage bonds which the issuing authority is otherwise authorized to issue and elects not to issue under subsection (c)(2)(A)(ii).[12]

[Footnote ¶2861 continued]

Matter in *italics* in Sec. 25(c)(2)(B) and (e)(10) added by section 1301(f)(2)(C)(i), (F) and (M), '86 TRA, which struck out:

(8) "section 103A"

(9) "subclauses (II) and (IV)"

(10) "(iii) paragraph (1) of section 103A(e) shall be applied by substituting '100 percent' for '90 percent or more'.

Clause (iii) shall not apply if the issuing authority submits a plan to the Secretary for administering the 90-percent requirement of section 103A(e)(1) and the Secretary is satisfied that such requirement will be met under such plan."

Effective date (Sec. 1311(b)(2), '86 TRA).—Applies to certificates issued after 8-15-86. For special and transitional rules see ¶2071—2077.

Matter in *italics* in Sec. 25(d)(2)(A) added by section 1301(f)(1)(A), '86 TRA, which struck out:

(11) "20 percent"

Effective date (Sec. 1311(b)(1), '86 TRA).—Generally applies to nonissued bond amounts issued after 8-15-86. For special and transitional rules see ¶2071—2077.

Section 1301(f)(2)(G), '86 TRA, struck out Sec. 25(d)(3):

(12) "(3) **Additional limit in certain cases.**—In the case of a qualified mortgage credit certificate program in a State which—

(e) **Special Rules and Definitions.**—For purposes of this section—
  (1) **Carryforward of unused credit.**—
    (A) In general.—If the credit allowable under subsection (a) for any taxable year exceeds the applicable tax limit for such taxable year, such excess shall be a carryover to each of the 3 succeeding taxable years and, subject to the limitations of subparagraph (B), shall be added to the credit allowable by subsection (a) for such succeeding taxable year.
    [13]*(B) Limitation.—The amount of the unused credit which may be taken into account under subparagraph (A) for any taxable year shall not exceed the amount (if any) by which the applicable tax limit for such taxable year exceeds the sum of—*
      (i) the credit allowable under subsection (a) for such taxable year determined without regard to this paragraph, and
      (ii) the amounts which, by reason of this paragraph, are carried to such taxable year and are attributable to taxable years before the unused credit year.

* * * * * * * * * * * * *

  (2) **Indebtedness not treated as certified where certain requirements not in fact met.**—Subsection (a) shall not apply to any indebtedness if all the requirements of [14]*subsections (c)(1), (d), (e), (f), and (i) of section 143* and clauses (iv), (v), and (vii) of subsection (c)(2)(A) were not in fact met with respect to such indebtedness. Except to the extent provided in regulations, the requirements described in the preceding sentence shall be treated as met if there is a certification, under penalty of perjury, that such requirements are met.

* * * * * * * * * * * *

  (6) **Interest paid or accrued to related persons.**—No credit shall be allowed under subsection (a) for any interest paid or accrued to a person who is a related person to the taxpayer (within the meaning of [15]*section 144(a)(3)(A)*).

* * * * * * * * * * * *

  (8) **Qualified rehabilitation and home improvement.**—
    (A) Qualified rehabilitation.—The term "qualified rehabilitation" has the meaning given such term by [16]*section 143(k)(5)(B).*
    (B) Qualified home improvement.—The term "qualified home improvement" means an alteration, repair, or improvement described in [2]*section 143(k)(4).*

  (9) **Qualified mortgage bond.**—The term "qualified mortgage bond" has the meaning given such term by [17]*section 143(a)(1).*

  (10) **Manufactured housing.**—For purposes of this section, the term "single family residence" includes any manufactured home which has a minimum of 400 square feet of living space and a minimum width in excess of 102 inches and which is of a kind customarily used at a fixed location. Nothing in the preceding sentence shall be con-

[**Footnote ¶2861 continued**]

  (A) has a State ceiling (as defined in section 103A(g)(4)) for the year an election is made that exceeds 20 percent of the average annual aggregate principal amount of mortgages executed during the immediately preceding 3 calendar years for single family owner-occupied residences located within the jurisdiction of such State, or
  (B) issued qualifies mortgage bonds in an aggregate amount less than $150,000,000 for calendar year 1983,
the certificate credit rate for any mortgage credit certificate shall not exceed 20 percent unless the issuing authority submits a plan to the Secretary to ensure that the weighted average of the certificate credit rates in such mortgage credit certificate program does not exceed 20 percent and the Secretary approves such plan."
  Effective date (Sec. 1311(b)(2), '86 TRA).—Generally applies to certificates issued after 8-15-86. For special and transitional rules see ¶2071—2077.

Matter in *italics* in 25(e)(1)(B) added by 1862(c), '86 TRA, which struck out:
  (13) "(B) Limitation.—The amount of the unused credit which may be taken into account under subparagraph (A) for any taxable year shall not exceed the amount by which the applicable tax limit for such taxable year exceeds the sum of the amounts which, by reason of this paragraph, are carried to such taxable years and are attributable to taxable years before the unused credit year."
  Effective date (Sec. 1881, '86 TRA and section 612(g), '84 TRA).—See above.

Matter in italics in Sec. 25(e)(2), (6), (8)(A), (9) and (f)(1) added by section 1301(f)(2)(H)—(J), (L) and (N), 86 TRA, which struck out:
  (14) "subsection (d)(1), (e), (f), and (j) of section 103A"
  (15) "section 103(b)(6)(C)(i)"
  (16) "section 103A(l)(7)(B)"
  (17) "section 103A(c)(1)"

strued as providing that such a home will be taken into account in making determinations under [8]*section 143.*

(f) Reduction in Aggregate Amount of Qualified Mortgage Bonds Which May Be Issued Where Certain Requirements Not Met.—

(1) **In general.**—If for any calendar year any mortgage credit certificate program which satisfies procedural requirements with respect to volume limitations prescribed by the Secretary fails to meet the requirements of paragraph (2) of subsection (d), such requirements shall be treated as satisfied with respect to any certified indebtedness of such program, but the applicable State ceiling under [18]*subsection (d) of section 146* for the State in which such program operates shall be reduced by 1.25 times the correction amount with respect to such failure.

(2) **Correction amount.—**
  (A) In general.—For purposes of paragraph (1), the term "correction amount" means an amount equal to the excess credit amount divided by [19]*0.25.*
  (B) Excess credit amount.—
    (i) In general.—For purposes of subparagraph (A)(ii), the term "excess credit amount" means the excess of—
      (I) the credit amount for any mortgage credit certificate program, over
      (II) the amount which would have been the credit amount for such program had such program met the requirements of paragraph (2) of subsection (d).
    (ii) Credit amount.—For purposes of clause (i), the term "credit amount" means the sum of the products determined under clauses (i) and (ii) of subsection (d)(2)(A).

(3) **Special rule for states having constitutional home rule cities.**—In the case of a State having one or more constitutional home rule cities (within the meaning of [20] *section 146(d)(3)(C),* the reduction in the State ceiling by reason of paragraph (1) shall be allocated to the constitutional home rule city, or to the portion of the State not within such city, whichever caused the reduction.

(4) **Exception where certification program.**—The provisions of this subsection shall not apply in any case in which there is a certification program which is designed to [21] *ensure* that the requirements of this section are met and which meets such requirements as the Secretary may by regulations prescribe.

* * * * * * * * * * * *

[For official explanation, see Committee Reports, ¶4058; 4177.]

〔¶2862〕 CODE SEC. 26. LIMITATION BASED ON TAX LIABILITY; DEFINITION OF TAX LIABILITY.

(a) **Limitation Based on Amount of Tax.**—The aggregate amount of credits allowed by this subpart for the taxable year shall not exceed the [1] *excess (if any) of—*
  (1) *the taxpayer's regular tax liability for the taxable year, over*
  (2) *the tentative minimum tax for the taxable year (determined without regard to the alternative minimum tax foreign tax credit).*

(b) *Regular* **Tax Liability.**—For purposes of this [2] *part—*

〔Footnote ¶2861 continued〕

(18) "paragraph (4) of section 103A(g)"
Effective date (Sec. 1311(b)(2), '86 TRA).—Generally applies to certificates issued after 8-15-86. For special and transitional rules see ¶2071—2077.

Matter in italics in Sec. 25(f)(2)(A) added by section 1301(f)(1)(B), '86 TRA, which struck out:
(19) "0.20"
Effective date (Sec. 1311(b)(1), '86 TRA—Generally applies to nonissued bond amounts elected after 8-15-86. For special and transitional rules see ¶2071—2077.

Matter in *italics* in Sec. 25(f)(3) added by section 1301(f)(2)(O), '86 TRA, which struck out:
(20) "section 103A(g)(5)(C)"
Effective date (Sec. 1311(b)(2), '86 TRA).—Generally applies to certificates issued after 8-15-86. For special and transitional rules see ¶2071—2077.

Matter in *italics* in Sec. 25(f)(4) added by section 1899A(1), '86 TRA, which struck out:
(21) "insure"
〔Footnote ¶2862〕 Matter in *italics* in Sec. 26(a), and (b), added by section 701(c)(1)(A), (B)(i)—(iii), and (v), '86 TRA, which struck out:
(1) "taxpayer's tax liability for such taxable year."
(2) "section"

(1) **In general.**—The term "*regular* tax liability" means the tax imposed by this chapter for the taxable year.

(2) **Exception for certain taxes.**—For purposes of paragraph (1), any tax imposed by any of the following provisions shall not be treated as tax imposed by this chapter:

(A) [3] *section 55 (relating to minimum tax),*

(B) subsection (m)(5)(B), (o)(2), or (q) of section 72 (relating to additional tax on certain distributions),

(C) section 408(f) (relating to additional tax on income from certain retirement accounts),

(D) section 531 (relating to accumulated earnings tax),

(E) section 541 (relating to personal holding company tax),

(F) section 1351(d)(1) relating to recoveries of foreign expropriation losses),

(G) section 1374 (relating to tax on certain [4] *built-in* gains of S corporations), [5]

(H) section 1375 (relating to tax imposed when passive investment income of corporation having subchapter C earnings and profits exceeds 25 percent of gross receipts)[6],

(I) *subparagraph (A) of section 7518(g)(6) (relating to nonqualified withdrawals from capital construction funds taxed at highest marginal rate)* [7] *, and*

(J) *sections 871(a) and 881 (relating to certain income of nonresident aliens and foreign corporations,*

[8](c) *Tentative Minimum Tax.*—*For purposes of this part, the term 'tentative minimum tax' means the amount determined under section 55(b)(1).*"

[For official explanation, see Committee Reports, ¶3880; 3918; 3931.]

[¶2863] CODE SEC. 28. CLINICAL TESTING EXPENSES FOR CERTAIN DRUGS FOR RARE DISEASES OR CONDITIONS.

(a) **General Rule.**—There shall be allowed as a credit against the tax imposed by this chapter for the taxable year an amount equal to 50 percent of the qualified clinical testing expenses for the taxable year.

(b) **Qualified Clinical Testing Expenses.**—For purposes of this section—

(1) **Qualified clinical testing expenses.**—

(A) **In general.**—Except as otherwise provided in this paragraph, the term "qualified clinical testing expenses" means the amounts which are paid or incurred by the taxpayer during the taxable year which would be described in subsection (b) of [1]*section 41* if such subsection were applied with the modifications set forth in subparagraph (B).

(B) **Modifications.**—For purposes of subparagraph (A), subsection (b) of [1]*section 41* shall be applied—

(i) by substituting "clinical testing" for "qualified research" each place it appears in paragraphs (2) and (3) of such subsection, and

---

[Footnote ¶2862 continued]

(3) "section 56 (relating to corporate minimum tax),"
Effective date (Sec. 701(f)(1), '86 TRA).—Generally applies to taxable years beginning after 12-31-86. For special and transitional rules, see footnote ¶2879.

Matter in *italics* in Sec. 26(b)(2)(G) added by section 632(c)(1), '86 TRA, which struck out:
(4) "capital"
Effective date (Sec. 633(b), '86 TRA).—Applies to taxable years beginning after 12-31-86, but only in cases where the 1st taxable year for which the corporation is an S corporation is pursuant to an election made after 12-31-86. For special and transitional rules, see ¶2023.

Matter in *italics* in Sec. 26(b)(2)(I) added by section 261(c), '86 TRA, which struck out:
(5) "and"
(6) "."
Effective date (Sec. 261(g), '86 TRA).—Applies to taxable years beginning after 12-31-86.

Matter in *italics* in Sec. 26(b)(2)(J), and (c), added by section 701(c)(1)(B)(iv) and (C), '86 TRA, which struck out:
(7) "."
(8) (c) **Similar Rule for Alternative Minimum Tax for Taxpayers Other than Corporations.**—
    For treatment of tax imposed by section 55 as not imposed by this chapter, see section 55(c)."
Effective date (Sec. 701(f)(1), '86 TRA).—Generally applies to taxable years beginning after 12-31-86. For special and transitional rules see footnote ¶2879.
[Footnote ¶2863] Matter in *italics* in Sec. 28(b)(1) and (c) added by section 231(d)(3)(A)(i), (ii) and (iv), '86 TRA, which struck out:
(1) "section 30"

(ii) by substituting "100 percent" for "65 percent" in paragraph (3)(A) of such subsection.

(C) Exclusion for amounts funded by grants, etc.—The term "qualified clinical testing expenses" shall not include any amount to the extent such amount is funded by any grant, contract, or otherwise by another person (or any governmental entity).

(D) Special rule.—For purposes of this paragraph [1] *section 41* shall be deemed to remain in effect for periods after [2] *December 31, 1988.*

(2) **Clinical testing.—**

(A) In general.—The term "clinical testing" means any human clinical testing—

(i) which is carried out under an exemption for a drug being tested for a rare disease or condition under section 505(i) of the Federal Food, Drug, and Cosmetic Act (or regulations issued under such section),

(ii) which occurs—

(I) after the date [3] such drug is designated under section 526 of such Act, and

(II) before the date on which an application with respect to such drug is approved under section 505(b) of such Act *or, if the drug is a biological product, before the date on which a license for such drug is issued under section 351 of the Public Health Services Act,* and

(iii) which is conducted by or on behalf of the taxpayer to whom the designation under such section 526 applies.

(B) Testing must be related to use for rare disease or condition.—Human clinical testing shall be taken into account under subparagraph (A) only to the extent such testing is related to the use of a drug for the rare disease or condition for which it was designated under section 526 of the Federal Food, Drug, and Cosmetic Act.

(c) **Coordination With Credit For Increasing Research Expenditures.—**

(1) **In general.—**Except as provided in paragraph 82), any qualified clinical testing expenses for a taxable year to which an election under this section applies shall not be taken into account for purposes of determining the credit allowable under [1] *section 41* for such taxable year.

(2) **Expenses included in determining base period research expenses.—**Any qualified clincial testing expenses for any taxable year which are qualified research expenses (within the meaning of [1] *section 41(b)* shall be taken into account in determining base period research expenses for purposes of applying [1] *section 41* to subsequent taxable years.

(d) **Definition and Special Rules.—**

(1) **Rare disease or condition.—**For purposes of this section, the term "rare disease or condition" means any disease or condition which[4]—

(A) affects less than 200,000 persons in the United States, or

(B) affects more than 200,000 persons in the United States but for which there is no reasonable expectation that the cost of developing and making available in the United States a drug for such disease or condition will be recovered from sales in the United States for such drug.

[Footnote ¶2863 continued]

(2) "December 31, 1985"
Effective date (Sec. 231(g), '86 TRA).—Applies to taxable years beginning after 12-31-85.

Matter in *italics* in Sec. 28(b)(2) added by section 1879(b)(1), '86 TRA, which struck out:
(3) "of"
Effective date (Sec. 1879(b)(3), '86 TRA).—Applies to amounts paid or incurred after 12-31-82, in taxable years ending after such date.

Matter in *italics* in Sec. 28(d)(1) added by Sec. 1879(b)(2), '86 TRA, which struck out:
(4) "occurs so infrequently in the United States that there is no reasonable expectation that the cost of developing and making available in the United States a drug for such disease or condition will be recovered from sales in the United States of such drug. Determinations under the preceding sentence with respect to any drug shall be made on the basis of the facts and circumstances as of the date such drug is designated under section 526 of the Federal Food, Drug, and Costmetic Act."
Effective date (Sec. 1879(b)(3), '86 TRA).—Applies to amounts paid or incurred after 12-31-82, in taxable years ending after such date.

Determinations under the preceding sentence with respect to any drug shall be made on the basis of the facts and circumstances as of the date such drug is designated under section 526 of the Federal Food, Drug, and Cosmetic Act.

(2) Limitation based on amount of tax.—The credit allowed by this section for any taxable year shall not exceed the [5]*excess (if any) of—*

(A) the regular tax (reduced by the sum of the credits allowable under subpart A and section 27), over

(B) the tentative minimum tax for the taxable year.

(3) Special limitations on foreign testing.—

* * * * * * * * * * * *

(B) Special limitation for corporations to which section [6] **936 applies.**—No credit shall be allowed under this section with respect to any clinical testing conducted by a corporation to which [7] an election under section 936 applies.

(4) Certain rules made applicable.—Rules similar to the rules of paragraphs (1) and (2) of [8]*section 41(f)* shall apply for purposes of this section.

* * * * * * * * * * * *

(e) Termination.—This section shall not apply to any amount paid or incurred after December 31, [9]*1990.*

[For official explanation, see Committee Reports, ¶3872; 3873; 3931; 4057; 4193.]

【¶2864】 CODE SEC. 29. CREDIT FOR PRODUCING FUEL FROM A NON-CONVENTIONAL SOURCE.

* * * * * * * * * * * *

(b) Limitations and Adjustments.—

* * * * * * * * * * * *

(5) Application with other credits.—The credit allowed by subsection (a) for [1] *any taxable year shall not exceed the excess (if any) of—*

(A) the regular tax for the taxable year reduced by the sum of the credits allowable under subpart A and sections 27 and 28, over

(B) the tentative minimum tax for the taxable year.

* * * * * * * * * * * *

(d) Other Definitions and Special Rules.—For purposes of this section—

* * * * * * * * * * * *

【Footnote ¶2863 continued】

Matter in *italics* in Sec. 28(d)(2) added by section 701(c)(2), '86 TRA, which struck out:

(5) "taxpayer's tax liability for the taxable year (as defined in section 26(b)), reduced by the sum of the credits allowable under subpart A and section 27.

Effective date (Sec. 701(f), '86 TRA).—Generally applies to taxable years beginning after 12-31-86. For special rules, see footnote ¶2879.

Section 1275(c)(4), '86 TRA, struck out from Sec. 28(d)(3)(B):

(6) "934(b) or"

(7) "section 934(b) applies or to which"

Effective date (Sec. 1277, '86 TRA).—Generally applies to taxable years beginning after 12-31-86. For special rules, see ¶2068.

Matter in *italics* in Sec. 28(d)(4) added by section 231(d)(3)(A)(iii), '86 TRA, which struck out:

(8) "section 30(f)"

Effective date (Sec. 231(g)(1), '86 TRA).—Applies to taxable years beginning after 12-31-85.

Matter in *italics* in Sec. 28(e) added by section 232, '86 TRA, which struck out:

(9) "1987"

【Footnote ¶2864】 **(1)** Matter in *italics* in Sec. 29(b)(5) added by section 701(c)(3), '86 TRA, which struck out:

(1) "a taxable year shall not exceed the taxpayer's tax liability for the taxable year (as defined in section 26(b)), reduced by the sum of the credits allowable under subpart A and sections 27 and 28."

Effective date (Sec. 701(f), '86 TRA).—Generally applies to taxable years beginning after 12-31-86. For special rules, see footnote ¶2879.

The last sentence in *italics* in Sec. 29(d)(8) added by section 1879(c)(1), '86 TRA.

Effective date (Sec. 1879(c)(2), '86 TRA and section 231(c), P.L. 96-223, 4-2-80).—Applies to taxable years ending after 12-31-79.

(8) **Related persons.**—Persons shall be treated as related to each other if such persons would be treated as a single employer under the regulations prescribed under section 52(b). *In the case of a corporation which is a member of an affiliated group of corporations filing a consolidated return, such corporation shall be treated as selling qualified fuels to an unrelated person if such fuels are sold to such a person by another member of such group.*

* * * * * * * * * * * *

[For official explanation, see Committee Reports, ¶3931; 4193.]

⟦¶2866⟧   CODE SEC. 32.   EARNED INCOME.

(a) **Allowance of Credit.**—In the case of an eligible individual, there is allowed as a credit against the tax imposed by this subtitle for the taxable year an amount equal to [1]*14 percent* of so much of the earned income for the taxable year as does not exceed [2]*$5,714* .

(b) **Limitation.**—The amount of the credit allowable to a taxpayer under subsection (a) for any taxable year shall not exceed the excess (if any) of—

[3]*(1)   the maximum credit allowable under subsection (a) to any taxpayer, over*
   (2)   10 percent of so much of the adjusted gross income (or, if greater, the earned income) of the taxpayer for the taxable year as exceeds $9,000.

In the case of any taxable year beginning in 1987, paragraph (2) shall be applied by substituting "$6,500" for "$9,000".

(c) **Definition.**—For purposes of this section—
   (1) **Eligible individual.**—
      (A) **In general.**—The term "eligible individual" means an individual who, for the taxable year—
         (i) is married (within the meaning of [4]*section 7703*) and is entitled to a deduction under section 151 for a child (within the meaning of [5]*section 151(c)(3)* or would be so entitled but for paragraph (2) or (4) of section 152(e),
         (ii) is surviving spouse (as determined under section 2(a)), or
         (iii) is a head of a household (as determined under subsection (b) of section 2 without regard to subparagraphs (A)(ii) and (B) of paragraph (1) of such subsection).
      (B) **Child must reside with taxpayer in the United States.**—An individual shall be treated as satisfying clause (i) of subparagraph (A) only if the child has the same principal place of abode as the individual for more than one-half of the taxable year and such abode is in the United States. An individual shall be treated as satisfying clause (ii) or (iii) of subparagraph (A) only if the household in question is in the United States.
      [6]*(C)   Individual who claims benefits of section 911 not eligible individual.—The term "eligible individual" does not include an individual who, for the taxable year,*

⟦**Footnote ¶2866**⟧   Matter in *italics* in Sec. 32(a) and (b) added by section 111(a) and (b), '86 TRA, which struck out:
(1) "11 percent"
(2) "$5,000"
(3) "(1)   550, over
(2) 12²/₉ percent of so much of the adjusted gross income (or, if greater, the earned income) of the taxpayer for the taxable year as exceeds $6,500."
Effective date (Sec. 151(a), '86 TRA).—Applies to taxable years beginning after 12-31-86.

Matter in *italics* in Sec. 32(c)(1)(A)(i) and (d) added by section 1301(j)(8), '86 TRA, which struck out:
(4) "section 143"
Effective date (Sec. 1311(a), '86 TRA).—Generally applies to bonds issued after 8-15-86. For special rules, see footnote ¶2071—2077.
Matter in *italics* in Sec. 32(c)(1)(A)(i) added by section 104(b)(1)(B), '86 TRA, which struck out:
(5) "section 151(e)(3)"
Effective date (Sec. 151(a), '86 TRA).—Applies to taxable years beginning after 12-31-86.
Matter in italics in Sec. 32(c)(1)(C) added by section 1272(d)(4), '86 TRA, which struck out:
(6) "(C) Individual who claims benefits of section 911, or 931 not eligible individual.—The term "eligible individual" does not include an individual who, for the taxable year, claims the benefits of—
(i) section 911 (relating to citizens or resident of the United States living abroad),
(ii) section 931 (relating to income from sources within possession of the United States).
Effective date (Sec. 1277(a), '86 TRA).—Applies to taxable years beginning after 12-31-86. For special rules, see footnote ¶2068.

claims the benefits of section 911 (relating to citizens or residents of the United States living abroad).

* * * * * * * * * * * *

(d) Married Individuals.—In the case of an individual who is married (within the meaning of section ⁴*section 7703*), this section shall apply only if a joint return is filed for taxable year under section 6013.

* * * * * * * * * * * *

(f) Amount of Credit To Be Determined Under Tables.—

   (1) In general.—The amount of the credit allowed by this section shall be determined under tables prescribed by the Secretary.

   (2) Requirements for tables.—The tables prescribed under paragraph (1) shall reflect the provisions of subsections (a) and (b) and shall have income brackets of not greater than $50 each—

    ⁷*(A) for earned income between $0 and the amount of earned income at which the credit is phased out under subsection (b), and*

    (B) for adjusted gross income between the dollar amount at which the phaseout begins under subsection (b) and the amount of adjusted gross income at which the credit is phased out under subsection (b).

* * * * * * * * * * * *

(i) Inflation Adjustments.—

   (1) In general.—In the case of any taxable year beginning after the applicable calendar year, each dollar amount referred to in paragraph (2)(B) shall be increased by an amount equal to—

    (A) such dollar amount, multiplied by

    (B) the cost-of-living adjustment determined under section 1(f)(3), for the calendar year in which the taxable year begins, by substituting "calendar year 1984"for "calendar year 1987" in subparagraph (B) thereof.

   (2) Definitions, etc.—For purposes of paragraph (1)—

    (A) Applicable calendar year.—The term "applicable calendar year" means—

      (i) 1986 in the case of the dollar amounts referred to in clause (i) or (ii) of subparagraph (B), and

      (ii) 1987 in the case of the dollar amount referred to in clause (iii) of subparagraph (B).

    (B) Dollar amounts.—The dollar amounts referred to in this subparagraph are—

      (i) the $5,714 amount contained in subsection (a),

      (ii) the $6,500 amount contained in the last sentence of subsection (b), and

      (iii) the $9,000 amount contained in subsection (b)(2).

   (3) Rounding.—If any increase determined under paragraph (1) is not a multiple of $10, such increase shall be rounded to the nearest mulltiple of $10 (or, if such increase is a multiple of $5, such increase shall be increased to the next higher multiple of $10).

[For official explanation, see Committee Reports, ¶3855; 4057; 4058.]

【¶2867】 CODE SEC. 34. CERTAIN USES OF GASOLINE AND SPECIAL FUELS.

(a) General Rule.—There shall be allowed as a credit against the tax imposed by this subtitle for the taxable year an amount equal to the sum of the amounts payable to the taxpayer—

   (1) under section 6420 with respect to gasoline used during the taxable year on a farm for farming purposes (determined without regard to section 6420(g)),

   (2) under section 6421 with respect to gasoline used during the taxable year (A) otherwise than as a fuel in a highway vehicle or (B) in vehicles while engaged in furnishing certain public passenger land transportation service (determined without regard to section 6421(i)), and

   (3) under section 6427—

【Footnote ¶2866 continued】

Matter in *italics* if Sec. 32(f)(2) and (i) added by section 111(c) and (d)(1), '86 TRA, which struck out:

(7) "(A) for earned income between $0 and $11,000, and

(B) for adjusted gross income between $6,500 and $11,000."

Effective date (Sec. 151(a), '86 TRA).—Applies to taxable years beginning after 12-31-86.

[1](A) with respect to fuels used for nontaxable purposes or resold, or

(B) with respect to any qualified diesel-powered highway vehicle purchased (or deemed purchased under section 6427(g)(6)),

during the taxable year (determined without regard to [2]section 6427(k)).

* * * * * * * * * * * * *

[For official explanation, see Committee Reports, ¶4125; 4191.]

[¶2868] CODE SEC. 38. GENERAL BUSINESS CREDIT.

(a) **Allowance of Credit.**—There shall be allowed as a credit against the tax imposed by this chapter for the taxable year an amount equal to the sum of —

(1) the business credit carryforwards carried to such taxable year.

(2) the amount of the current year business credit, plus

(3) the business credit carrybacks carried to such taxable year.

(b) **Current Year Business Credit.**—For purposes of this subpart, the amount of the current year business credit is the sum of the following credits determined for the taxable year:

(1) the investment credit determined under section 46(a),

(2) the targeted jobs credit determined under section 51(a),

(3) the alcohol fuels credit determined under section 40(a), [1]

(4) [2]the research credit determined under section 41(a), plus

(5) the low-income housing credit determined under section 42(a).

≫**P-H CAUTION**→ There are two versions of Sec. 38(c). Sec. 38(c), as amended by section 701(c)(4), '86 TRA, generally effective after 12-31-86 follows. For Sec. 38(c)(1), as amended by section 221(a), '86 TRA, generally effective after 12-31-85, see below.

▲ (c) **Limitation Based on Amount of Tax.**—

[3](1) In general.—The credit allowed under subsection (a) for any taxable year shall not exceed the lesser of—

(A) the allowable portion of the taxpayer's net regular tax liability for the taxable year, or

(B) the excess (if any) of the taxpayer's net regular tax liability for the taxable year over the tentative minimum tax for the taxable year.

(2) Allowable portion of net regular tax liability.—For purposes of this subsection, the allowable portion of the taxpayer's net regular tax liability for the taxable year is the sum of—

(A) so much of the taxpayer's net regular tax liability for the taxable year as does not exceed $25,000, plus

(B) 75 percent of so much of the taxpayer's net regular tax liability for the taxable year as exceeds $25,000.

[**Footnote ¶2867**] Matter in *italics* in Sec. 34(a)(3), (other than *"section 6427(k)"* in the last phrase) , added by section 1877(a), '86 TRA, which struck out:

(1) "with respect to fuels used for nontaxable purposes or resold during the taxable year (determined without regard to section 6427(j)."

Effective date (Sec. 1881, '86 TRA and section 911(e), '86 TRA).—Takes effect on 8-1-84.

"section 6427(k)" in *italics* in the last phrase of Sec. 34(a)(3), added by section 1703(e)(2)(F), '86 TRA, which struck out:

(2) "section 6427(j)"

Effective date (Sec. 1703(h), '86 TRA).—Applies to gasoline removed (as defined in section 4082 of the '86 Code) after 12-31-87.

[**Footnote ¶2868**] Section 252(b)(1), '86 TRA, struck out from Sec. 38(b)(3):

(1) "plus"

Effective date (Sec. 252(e)(1), '86 TRA).—See below.

Matter in *italics* in Sec. 38(b)(4), added by section 231(d)(1), '86 TRA, which struck out:

(2) "the employee stock ownership credit determined under section 41(a)."

Effective date (Sec. 231(g)(1), '86 TRA).—Applies to taxable years beginning after 12-31-85.

Matter in *italics* in Sec. 38(b)(5) added by section 252(b)(1), '86 TRA.

Effective date (Sec. 252(e)(1), '86 TRA).—Applies to buildings placed in service after 12-31-86, in taxable years ending after such date. For special rules for rehabilitation expenditures, see footnote ¶2871.

▲ Matter in *italics* in Sec. 38(c), preceeded by a triangle added by section 701(c)(4), '86 TRA, which struck out:

(3) "**In General.**—The credit allowed under subsection (a) for any taxable year shall not exceed the sum of—

(A) so much of the taxpayer's net tax liability for the taxable year as does not exceed $25,000, plus

(B) 85 percent of so much of the taxpayer's net tax liability for the taxable year as exceeds $25,000.

(2) **Net tax liability.**—For purposes of paragraph (1), the term "net tax liability" means the tax liability (as defined in section 26(b)), reduced by the sum of the credits allowable under subparts A and B of this part."

For purposes of the preceding sentence, there term "net regular tax liability" means the regular tax liability reduced by the sum of the credits allowable under subparts A and B of this part.

(3) Regular investment tax credit may offset 25 percent of minimum tax.—In the case of any C corporation, to the extent the credit under subsection (a) is attributable to the application of the regular percentage under section 46, the limitation of paragraph (1) shall be the greater of—

(A) the lesser of—

(i) the allowable portion of the taxpayer's net regular tax liability for the taxable year, or

(ii) the excess (if any) of the taxpayer's net regular tax liability for the taxable year over 75 percent of the tentative minimum tax for the taxable year, or

(B) 25 percent of the taxpayer's tentative minimum tax for the year.

In no event shall this paragraph permit the allowance of a credit which (in combination with the alternative tax net operating loss deduction and the alternative minimum tax foreign tax credit) would reduce the tax payable under section 55 below an amount equal to 10 percent of the amount which would be determined under section 55(b) without regard to the alternative tax net operating loss deduction and the alternative minimum tax foreign tax credit.

[4]**(4) Special rules.—**

* * * * * * * * * * * * *

≫P-H CAUTION→ There are two versions of Sec. 38(c)(1). Sec. 38(c)(1), as amended by section 221(a), '86 TRA, generally effective after 12-31-85, follows. For Sec. 38(c), as amended by section 701(c)(4), '86 TRA, generally effective after 12-31-86, see above.

▲▲ **(c) Limitation Based on Amount of Tax.—**

(1) In General.—The credit allowed under subsection (a) for any taxable year shall not exceed the sum of—

(A) so much of the taxpayer's net tax liability for the taxable year as does not exceed $25,000, plus

(B) [5]*75 percent* of so much of the taxpayer's net tax liability for the taxable year as exceeds $25,000.

* * * * * * * * * * * * *

[Footnote ¶2868 continued]

(4) "(3)"

Effective date (Sec. 701(f)(1) and (6), '86 TRA).—(1) Generally applies to taxable years beginning after 12-31-86.

* * * * * * * * * * * * *

(6) Certain public utility.—

(A) In the case of investment tax credits described in subparagraph (B) or (C), subsection 38(c)(3)(A)(ii) of the '86 Code shall be applied by substituting "25 percent" for "75 percent", and section 38(c)(3)(B) of the '86 Code shall be applied by substituting "75 percent" for "25 percent".

(B) If, on 9-25-85, a regulated electric utility owned an undivided interest, within the range of 1,111 and 1,149, in the maximum dependable capacity, net, megawatts electric of an electic generating unit located in Illinois or Mississippi for which a binding written contract was in effect on 12-31-80, then any investment tax credit with respect to such unit shall be described in this subparagraph. The aggregate amount of investment tax credits with respect to the unit in Mississippi allowed solely by reason of being described in this subparagraph shall not exceed $141,000,000.

(C) If, on 9-25-85, a regulated electric utility owned an undivided interest, within the range of 1,104 and 1,111, in the "maximum dependable capacity", net "megawatts electric" of an electric generating unit located in Louisiana for which a binding written contract was in effect on 12-31-80, then any investment tax credit of such electric utility shall be described in this subparagraph. The aggregate amount of investment tax credits allowed solely by reason of being described by this subparagraph shall not exceed $20,000,000.

For other special and transitional rules, see footnote ¶2879.

▲▲ Matter in *italics* in Sec. 38(c)(1)(B), preceded by two triangles, added by section 221(a), '86 TRA, which struck out:

(5) "85 percent"

Effective date (Sec. 221(b), '86 TRA).—Applies to taxable years beginning after 12-31-85.

(d) Special Rules for Certain Regulated Companies.—In the case of any taxpayer to which section 46(f) applies, for purposes of sections 46(f), 47(a), *and 196(a)* and any other provision of this title where it is necessary to ascertain the extent to which the credits determined under section 40(a), [7]*41(a), 42(a),* 46(a), or 51(a) are used in a taxable year or as a carryback or carryforward, the order in which such credits are used shall be determined on the basis of the order in which they are listed in subsection (b).

[For official explanation, see Committee Reports, ¶3871; 3872; 3879; 3931; 4016.]

【¶2869】 CODE SEC. 39. CARRYBACK AND CARRYFORWARD OF UN-USED CREDITS.

* * * * * * * * * * * *

(d) Transitional Rules.—

    (1) Carryforwards.—

        (A) In general.—Any carryforward from an unused credit year under section 46, 50A, 53, 44E, or 44G *as in effect before the enactment of the Tax Reform Act of 1984)* which has not expired before the beginning of the first taxable year beginning after December 31, 1983, shall be aggregated with other such carryforwards from such unused credit year and shall be a business credit carryforward to each taxable year beginning after December 31, 1983, which is 1 of the first taxable years after such unused credit year.

        (B) Amount carried forward.—The amount carried forward under subparagraph (A) to any taxable year shall be properly reduced for any amount allowable as a credit with respect to such carryforward for any taxable year before the year to which it is being carried.

    (2) Carrybacks.—In determining the amount allowable as a credit for any taxable year beginning before January 1, 1984, as the result of the carryback of a general business tax credit from a taxable year beginning after December 31, 1983—

        (A) paragraph (1) of subsection (b) shall be applied as if it read as follows:

"**(1)** the sum of the credits allowable for such taxable year under sections 38, 40, 44B, 44E, and 44G (as in effect before enactment of the Tax Reform Act of 1984), plus, and

        (B) for purposes of section 38(c) the net tax liability for such taxable year shall be the tax liability (as [1]defined in [2]*section 26(b))* reduced by the sum of the credits allowable for such taxable year under sections 33, 37, 41, 44A, 44C, 44D, 44F, and 44H (as so in effect).

    (3) *Similar rules for research credit.*—*Rules similar to the rules of paragraphs (1) and (2) shall apply to the credit allowable under section 30 (as in effect before the date of enactment of the Tax Reform Act of 1986) except that—*

        (A) "December 31, 1985" shall be substituted for "December 31, 1983" each place it appears, and

        (B) "January 1, 1986" shall be substituted for "January 1, 1984".

[For official explanation, see Committee Reports, ¶3872; 4161.]

【Footnote ¶2868 continued】

"and 196(a)" in *italics* in Sec. 38(d) added by section 1171(b)(2), '86 TRA, which struck out:
(6) ", and 404(i)"
(7) "41(a)"
Effective date (Sec. 1171(c), '86 TRA).—(1) Generally applies to compensation paid or accrued after 12-31-86, in taxable years ending after such date.
(2) Sections 404(i) and 6699 to continue to apply to pre-1987 credits.—The provisions of sections 404(i) and 6699 of the '86 Code shall continue to apply with respect to credits under section 41 of such Code attributable to compensation paid or accrued before 1-1-87 (or under section 38 of such Code with respect to qualified investment before 1-1-83).

"41(a)" in *italics* in Sec. 38(d), added by section 231(d)(3)(B), '86 TRA.
Effective date (Sec. 231(g)(1), '86 TRA).—Applies to taxable years beginning after 12-31-85.
"42(a)" in *italics* in Sec. 38(d), added by section 252(b)(2), '86 TRA.
Effective date (Sec. 252(e), '86 TRA).—Generally applies to buildings placed in service after 12-31-86, in taxable years ending after such date. For special rule for rehabilitation expenditures, see footnote ¶2871.
【Footnote ¶2869】 Matter in *italics* in Sec. 39(d)(1)(A) and (2)(B) added by section 1846, '86 TRA, which struck out:
(1) "so"
(2) "section 25(b)"
Effective date (Sec. 1881, '86 TRA, and section 475(a), '84 TRA).—Applies to taxable years beginning after 12-31-83, and to carrybacks from such years.

Sec. 39(d)(3) in *italics* added by section 231(d)(3)(C)(i), '86 TRA.
Effective date (Sec. 231(g) '86 TRA).—Applies to taxable years beginning after 12-31-85.

≫**P-H CAUTION→** There are two versions of Sec. 41. Sec. 41, re-pealed generally effective after 12-31-86, follows. For Sec. 41 (formerly 30) renumbered, generally effective after 12-31-85, see ¶2870-A, below.

〔¶2870〕 CODE SEC. 41. EMPLOYEE STOCK OWNERSHIP CREDIT. [Repealed by section 1171(a), '86 TRA].[1]

[For official explanation, see Committee Reports, ¶4016.]

≫**P-H CAUTION→** There are two versions of Sec. 41. See 41 (for-merly 30) renumbered generally effective after 12-31-85, follows. For Sec. 41, repealed generally effective after 12-31-86, see ¶2870, above.

〔¶2870-A〕 CODE SEC. [1]41. CREDIT FOR INCREASING RESEARCH ACTIVI-TIES.

[2]*(a) General Rule.—For purposes of section 38, the research credit determined under this section for the taxable year shall be an amount equal to the sum of—*
  (1) 20 percent of the excess (if any) of—
    (A) the qualifed research expenses of the taxable year, over
    (B) the base period research expenses, and
  (2) 20 percent of the basic research payments determined under subsection (e)(1)(A).

(b) Qualified Research Expenses.—For purposes of this section—

* * * * * * * * * * * *

  (2) In-house research expenses.—
    (A) In general.—The term "in-house research expenses" means—
      (i) any wages paid or incurred to an employee for qualified services per-formed by such employee,
      (ii) any amount paid or incurred for supplies used in the conduct of quali-fied research, and
      [3]*(iii) under regulations prescribed by the Secretary, any amount paid or in-curred to another person for the right to use computers in the conduct of qualified research."*
    Clause (iii) shall not apply to any amount to the extent that the taxpayer (or any person with whom the taxpayer must aggregate expenditures under subsection (f)(1)) receives or accrues any amount from any other person for the right to use substantially identical personal property.
    (B) Qualified services.—The term "qualified services" means services consisting of—
      (i) engaging in qualified research, or
      (ii) engaging in the direct supervision or direct support of research activities which constitute qualified research.

If substantially all of the services performed by an individual for the taxpayer during the taxable year consists of services meeting the requirements of clause (i) or (ii), the term "qualified services" means all of the services performed by such individual for the taxpayer during the taxable year.

    (C) Supplies.—The term "supplies" means any tangible property other than—
      (i) land or improvements to land, and
      (ii) property of a character subject to the allowance for depreciation.

    (D) Wages.—
      (i) In general.—The term "wages" has the meaning given such term by section 3401(a).
      (ii) Self-employed individuals and owner-employees.—In the case of an employee (within the meaning of section 401(c)(1)), the term "wages" includes the earned income (as defined in section 401(c)(2)) of such employee.
      (iii) Exclusion for wages to which [4]*target jobs credit* applies.—The term "wages" shall not include any amount taken into account in determining the targeted jobs credit under section 51(a).

[5]*(d) Qualified Research Defined.—For purposes of this section—*
    (1) In general.—The term "qualified research" means research—
    (A) with respect to which expenditures may be treated as expenses under section 174,
    (B) which is undertaken for the purpose of discovering information—
      (i) which is technological in nature, and
      (ii) the application of which is intended to be useful in the development of a new or improved business component of the taxpayer, and
    (C) substantially all of the activities of which constitute elements of a process of experimentation for a purpose described in paragraph (3).
Such term does not include any activity described in paragraph (4).

    (2) Tests to be applied separately to each business component.—For purposes of this subsection—
    (A) In general.—Paragraph (1) shall be applied separately with respect to each business component of the taxpayer.
    (B) Business component defined.—The term "business component" means any product, process, computer software, technique, formula, or invention which is to be—
      (i) held for sale, lease, or license, or
      (ii) used by the taxpayer in a trade or business of the taxpayer.
    (C) Special rule for production processes.—Any plant process, machinery, or technique for commercial production of a business component shall be treated as a separate business component (and not as part of the business component being produced).

    (3) Purposes for which research may qualify for credit.—For purposes of paragraph (1)(C)—
    (A) In general.—Research shall be treated as conducted for a purpose described in this paragraph if it relates to—
      (i) a new or improved function,
      (ii) performance, or
      (iii) reliability or quality.
    (B) Certain purposes not qualified.—Research shall in no event be treated as conducted for a purpose described in this paragraph if it relates to style, taste, cosmetic, or seasonal design factors.

    (4) Activities for which credit not allowed.—The term "qualified reseach" shall not include any of the following:
    (A) Research after commercial production.—Any research conducted after the beginning of commercial production of the business component.

[Footnote ¶2870-A continued]

Matter in *italics* in Sec. 41(b)(2)(D)(iii) added by section 1847(b)(1), '86 TRA, which struck out:
(4) "new jobs or WIN credit"
Effective date (Sec. 1881, '86 TRA and section 475(a), '84 TRA).—Generally applies to taxable years beginning after 12-31-83, and to carrybacks from such years.
Matter in *italics* in Sec. 41(d) added by section 231(b), '86 TRA, which struck out:
(5) "(d) Qualified Research.—For purposes of this section the term "qualified research" has the same meaning as the term research of experimental has under section 174, except that such term shall not include—
(1) qualified research conduct outside the United States,
(2) qualified research in the social sciences or humanities, and
(3) qualified research to the extent funded by any grant, contract, or otherwise by another person (or any governmental entity)."
Effective date (Sec. 231(g)(1), '86 TRA).—Applies to taxable years beginning after 12-31-85.

    (B) Adaptation of existing business components.—Any research related to the adaptation of an existing business component to a particular customer's requirement or need.

    (C) Duplication of existing business component.—Any research related to the reproduction of an existing business component (in whole or in part) from a physical examination of the business component itself or from plans, blueprints, detailed specifications, or publicly available information with respect to such business component.

    (D) Surveys, studies, etc.—Any—

       (i) efficiency survey,

       (ii) activity relating to management function or technique,

       (iii) market research, testing, or development (including advertising or promotions),

       (iv) routine data collection, or

       (v) routine or ordinary testing or inspection for quality control.

    (E) Computer software.—Except to the extent provided in regulations, any research with respect to computer software which is developed by (or for the benefit of) the taxpayer primarily for internal use by the taxpayer, other than for use in—

       (i) an activity which constitutes qualified research (determined with regard to this subparagraph), or

       (ii) a production process with respect to which the requirements of paragraph (1) are met.

    (F) Foreign research.—Any research conducted outside the United States.

    (G) Social sciences, etc.—Any research in the social sciences, arts, or humanities.

    (H) Funded research.—Any research to the extent funded by any grant, contract, or otherwise by another person (or government entity).

[6] *(e) Credit Allowable With Respect to Certain Payments to Qualified Organizations for Basic Research.—For purposes of this section—*

    (1) In general.—In the case of any taxpayer who makes basic research payments for any taxable year—

[**Footnote ¶2870-A continued**]

Matter in *italics* in Sec. 41(e) added by section 231(c)(2), '86 TRA, which struck out:

(6) "(e) Credit Available With Respect to Certain Basic Research by Colleges, Universities, and Certain Research Organizations.—

(1) **In general.—**65 percent of any amount paid or incurred by a corporation (as such term is defined in section 170(e)(4)(D)) to any qualified organization for basic research to be performed by such organization shall be treated as contract research expenses. The preceding sentence shall apply only if the amount is paid or incurred pursuant to a written research agreement between the corporation and the qualified organization.

(2) **Qualified organization.—**For purposes of this subsection, the term 'qualified organization' means—

(A) any educational organization which is described in section 170(b)(1)(A)(ii) and which is an institution of higher education (as defined in section 3304(f)), and

(B) any other organization which—

(i) is described in section 501(c)(3) and exempt from tax under section 501(a),

(ii) is organized and operated primarily to conduct scientific research, and

(iii) is not a private foundation.

(3) **Basic research.—**The term 'basic research' means any original investigation for the advancement of scientific knowledge not having a specific commercial objective, except that such term shall not include—

(A) basic research conducted outside the United States, and

(B) basic research in the social sciences or humanities.

(4) **Special rules for grants to certain funds.—**

(A) In general.—For purposes of this subsection, a qualified fund shall be treated as a qualified organization and the requirements of paragraph (1) that the basic research be performed by the qualified organization shall not apply.

(B) Qualified fund.—For purposes of subparagraph (A), the term 'qualified fund' means any organization which—

(i) is described in section 501(c)(3) and exempt from tax under section 501(a) and is not a private foundation.

(ii) is established and maintained by an organization established before July 10, 1981, which meets the requirements of clause (i),

(iii) is organized and operated exclusively for purposes of making grants pursuant to written research agreements to organizations described in paragraph (2)(A) for purposes of basic research, and

(iv) makes an election under this paragraph.

(C) Effect of election.—

(i) In general.—Any organization which makes an election under this paragraph shall be treated as a private foundation for purposes of this title (other than section 4940, relating to excise tax based on investment income).

(ii) Election revocable only with consent.—An election under this paragraph, once made, may be revoked only with the consent of the Secretary."

Effective date (Sec. 231(g)(3), '86 TRA).—Applies to taxable years beginning after 12-31-86.

Code §41(d)(4) ¶2870-A

(A) the amount of basic research payments taken into account under subsection (a)(2) shall be equal to the excess of—

(i) such basic research payments, over

(ii) the qualfied organization base period amount, and

(B) that portion of such basic research payments which does not exceed the qualified organization base period amount shall be treated as contract research expenses for purposes of subsection (a)(1).

(2) *Basic research payments defined.*—For purposes of this subsection—

(A) *In general.*—The term "basic research payment" means, with respect to any taxable year, any amount paid in cash during such taxable year by a corporation to any qualified organization for basic research but only if—

(i) such payment is pursuant to a written agreement between such corporation and such qualified organization, and

(ii) such basic research is to be performed by such qualified organization.

(B) *Exception to requirement that research be performed by the organization.*—In the case of a qualified organization described in subparagraph (C) or (D) of paragraph (6), clause (ii) of subparagraph (A) shall not apply.

(3) *Qualified organization base period amount.*—For purposes of this subsection, the term "qualified organization base period amount" means an amount equal to the sum of—

(A) the minimum basic research amount, plus

(B) the maintenance-of-effort amount.

(4) *Minimum basic research amount.*—For purposes of this subsection—

(A) *In general.*—The term "minimum basic research amount" means an amount equal to the greater of—

(i) 1 percent of the average of the sum of amounts paid or incurred during the base period for—

(I) any in-house research expenses, and

(II) any contract research expenses, or

(ii) the amounts treated as contract research expenses during the base period by reason of this subsection (as in effect during the base period).

(B) *Floor amount.*—Except in the case of a taxpayer which was in existence during a taxable year (other than a short taxable year) in the base period, the minimum basic research amount for any base period shall not be less than 50 percent of the basic research payments for the taxable year for which a determination is being made under this subsection.

(5) *Maintenance-of-effort amount.*—For purposes of this subsection—

(A) *In general.*—The term "maintenance-of-effort amount" means, with respect to any taxable year, an amount equal to the excess (if any) of—

(i) an amount equal to—

(I) the average of the nondesignated university contributions paid by the taxpayer during the base period, multiplied by

(II) the cost-of-living adjustment for the calendar year in which such taxable year begins, over

(ii) the amount of nondesignated university contributions paid by the taxpayer during such taxable year.

(B) *Nondesignated university contributions.*—For purposes of this paragraph, the term "nondesignated university contribution" means any amount paid by a taxpayer to any qualified organization described in paragraph (6)(A)—

(i) for which a deduction was allowable under section 170, and

(ii) which was not taken into account—

(I) in computing the amount of the credit under this section (as in effect during the base period) during any taxable year in the base period, or

(II) as a basic research payment for purposes of this section.

(C) *Cost-of-living adjustment defined.*—

(i) *In general.*—The cost-of-living adjustment for any calendar year is the cost-of-living adjustment for such calendar year determined under section 1(f)(3).

(ii) *Special rule where base period ends in a calendar year other than 1983 or 1984.*—If the base period of any taxpayer does not end in 1983 or 1984, section 1(f)(3)(B) shall, for purposes of this paragraph, be applied by substituting the calendar year in which such base period ends for 1987.

(6) *Qualified organization.*—For purposes of this subsection, the term "qualified organization" means any of the following organizations:

(A) *Educational institutions.—Any educational organization which—*
  (i) *is an institution of higher education (within the meaning of section 3304(f)), and*
  (ii) *is described in section 170(b)(1)(A)(ii).*

(B) *Certain scientific research organizations.—Any organization not described in subparagraph (A) which—*
  (i) *is described in section 501(c)(3) and is exempt from tax under section 501(a),*
  (ii) *is organized and operated primarily to conduct scientific research, and*
  (iii) *is not a private foundation.*

(C) *Scientific tax-exempt organizations.—Any organization which—*
  (i) *is described in—*
    (I) *section 501(c)(3) (other than a private foundation), or*
    (II) *section 501(c)(6),*
  (ii) *is exempt from tax under section 501(a),*
  (iii) *is organized and operated primarily to promote scientific research by qualified organizations described in subparagraph (A) pursuant to written research agreements, and*
  (iv) *currently expends—*
    (I) *substantially all of its funds, or*
    (II) *substantially all of the basic research payments received by it,*
  for grants to, or contracts for basic research with, an organization described in subparagraph (A).

(D) *Certain grant organizations.—Any organization not described in subparagraph (B) or (C) which—*
  (i) *is described in section 501(c)(3) and is exempt from tax under section 501(a) (other than a private foundation),*
  (ii) *is established and maintained by an organization established before July 10, 1981, which meets the requirements of clause (i),*
  (iii) *is organized and operated exclusively for the purpose of making grants to organizations described in subparagraph (A) pursuant to written research agreements for purposes of basic research, and*
  (iv) *makes an election, revocable only with the consent of the Secretary, to be treated as a private foundation for purposes of this title (other than section 4940, relating to excise tax based on investment income).*

(7) *Definitions and special rules.—For purposes of this subsection—*
  (A) Basic research.—The term "basic research" means any original investigation for the advancement of scientific knowledge not having a specific commercial objective, except that such term shall not include—
    (i) basic research conducted outside of the United States, and
    (ii) basic research in the social sciences, arts, or humanities.

  (B) Base period.—The term "base period" means the 3-taxable-year period ending with the taxable year immediately preceding the 1st taxable year of the taxpayer beginning after December 31, 1983.

  (C) Exclusion from incremental credit calculation.—For purposes of determining the amount of credit allowable under subsection (a)(1) for any taxable year, the amount of the basic research payments taken into account under subsection (a)(2)—
    (i) shall not be treated as qualified research expenses under subsection (a)(1)(A), and
    (ii) shall not be included in the computation of base period research expenses under subsection (a)(1)(B).

  (D) Trade or business qualification.—For purposes of applying subsection (b)(1) to this subsection, any basic research payments shall be treated as an amount paid in carrying on a trade or business of the taxpayer in the taxable year in which it is paid (without regard to the provisions of subsection (b)(3)(B)).

  (E) Certain corporations not eligible.—The term "corporation" shall not include—
    (i) an S corporation,
    (ii) a personal holding company (as defined in section 542), or
    (iii) a service organization (as defined in section 414(m)(3)).

* * * * * * * * * * * * *

[7](g) *Special Rule for Pass-Thru of Credit.—In the case of an individual who—*
  (1) owns an interest in an unincorporated trade or business.
  (2) is a partner in a partnership.
  (3) is a beneficiary of an estate or trust, or
  (4) is a shareholder in an S corporation,

the amount determined under subsection (a) for any taxable year shall not exceed an amount (separately computed with respect to such person's interest in such trade or business or entity) equal to the amount of tax attributable to that portion of a person's taxable income which is allocable or apportionable to the person's interest in such trade or business or entity.

  (h) Termination—

  (1) In general.—This section shall not apply to any amount paid or incurred after December 31, 1988.

  (2) Computation of base period expenses.—In the case of any taxable year which begins before January 1, 1989, and ends after December 31, 1988, any amount for any base period with respect to such taxable year shall be the amount which bears the same ratio to such amount for such base period as the number of days in such taxable year before January 1, 1989, bears to the total number of days in such taxable year.

[For official explanation, see Committee Reports, ¶3872; 4161.]

[¶2871] CODE SEC. 42. LOW INCOME HOUSING CREDIT.

  (a) In General.—For purposes of section 38, the amount of the low-income housing credit determined under this section for any taxable year in the credit period shall be an amount equal to—

[Footnote ¶2870-A continued]

Matter in *italics* in Sec. 41(g) added by section 231(d)(3)(C)(ii), '86 TRA, which struck out:

(7) "(g) Limitation Based on Amount of Tax.—
(1) Liability for tax.—
(A) In general.—Except as provided in subparagraph (B), the credit allowed by subsection (a) for any taxable year shall not exceed the taxpayer's tax liability for the taxable year (as defined in section 26(b)), reduced by the sum of the credit allowable under subpart A and sections 27, 28 and 29.
(B) Special rule for passthrough of credit.—In the case of an individual who—
(i) owns an interest in an unincorporated trade or business,
(ii) is a partner in a partnership,
(iii) is a beneficiary of an estate or trust, or
(iv) is a shareholder in an S corporation,
the credit allowed by subsection (a) for any taxable year shall not exceed the lesser of the amount determined under subparagraph (A) for the taxable year or an amount (separately computed with respect to such person's interest in such trade or business or entity) equal to the amount of tax attributable to that portion of a person's taxable income which is allocable or apportionable to the person's interest in such trade or business or entity.
(2) Carryback and carryover of unused credit.—
(A) Allowance of credit—If the amount of the credit determined under this section for any taxable year exceeds the limitation provided by paragraph (1) for such taxable year (hereinafter in this paragraph referred to as the "unused credit year"), such excess shall be—
(i) a research credit carryback to each of the 3 taxable years preceding the unused credit year, and
(ii) a research credit carryover to each of the 15 taxable years following the unused credit year,
and shall be added to the amount allowable as a credit by this section for such years. If any portion of such excess is a carryback to a taxable year beginning before July 1, 1981, this section shall be deemed to have been in effect for such taxable year for purposes of allowing such carryback as a credit under this section. The entire amount of the unused credit for an unused credit year shall be carried to the earliest of the 18 taxable years to which (by reason of clauses (i) and (ii)) such credit may be carried, and then to each of the other 17 taxable years to the extent that, because of the limitation contained in subparagraph (b), such unused credit may not be added for a prior taxable year to which such unused credit may be carried.
(B) Limitation.—The amount of the unused credit which may be added under subparagraph (A) for any preceding or succeeding taxable year shall not exceed the amount by which the limitation provided by paragraph (1) for such taxable year exceeds the sum of—
(i) the credit allowable under this section for such taxable year, and
(ii) the amounts which, by reason of this paragraph, are added to the amount allowable for such taxable year and which are attributable to taxable years preceding 6th unused credit year."
Effective date (Sec. 231(g)(1), '86 TRA).—Applies to taxable years beginning after 12-31-85.
Sec. 41(h) in *italics* added by section 231(a)(1), '86 TRA.
Effective date (Sec. 231(g)(2), '86 TRA).—Applies to taxable years ending after 12-31-85.
[Footnote ¶2871] Sec. 42 added by section 252(a), '86 TRA.
Effective date. (Sec. 252(e) and (f), '86 TRA).—(1) Generally applies to buildings placed in service after 12-31-86, in taxable years ending after such date.
(2) Special rule for rehabilitation expenditures.—Subsection (e) of section 42 of the '86 Code (as added by this section) shall apply for purposes of paragraph (1).
For transitional rules, see ¶2014.

(1) the applicable percentage of

(2) The qualified basis of each qualified low-income building.

(b) Applicable Percentage: 70 Percent Present Value Credit for Certain New Buildings; 30 Percent Present Value Credit for Certain Other Buildings.—For purposes of this section—

(1) Building placed in service during 1987.—In the case of any qualified low-income building placed in service by the taxpayer during 1987, the term "applicable percentage" means—

(A) 9 percent for new buildings which are not federally subsidized for the taxable year, or

(B) 4 percent for—

(i) new buildings which are federally subsidized for the taxable year, and

(ii) existing buildings.

(2) Buildings placed in service after 1987.—

(A) In General.—In the case of any qualified low-income building placed in service by the taxpayer after 1987, the term applicable percentage means the appropriate percentage prescribed by the Secretary for the month in which such building is placed in service.

(B) Method of prescribing percentages.—The percentages prescribed by the Secretary for any month shall be percentages which will yield over a 10-year period amount of credit under subsection (a) which have present value equal to—

(i) 70 percent of the qualified basis of a building described in paragraph (1)(A), and

(ii) 30 percent of the qualified basis of a building described in paragraph (1)(B).

(C) Method of discounting.—The present value under subparagraph (B) shall be determined—

(i) as of the last day of the 1st year of the 10-year period referred to in subparagraph (B),

(ii) by using a discount rate equal to 72 percent of the average of the annual Federal mid-term rate and the annual Federal long-term rate applicable under section 1274(d)(1) to the month in which the building was placed in service and compounded annually, and

(iii) by assuming that the credit allowable under this section for any year is received on the last day of such year.

(3) Cross reference.—For treatment of certain rehabilitation expenditures as separate new buildings, see subsection (e).

(c) Qualified Basis; Qualified Low-Income Building.—For purposes of this section—

(1) Qualified basis.—

(A) Determination.—The qualified basis of any qualified low-income building for any taxable year is an amount equal to—

(i) the applicable fraction (determined as of the close of such taxable year) of

(ii) the eligible basis of such building (determined under subsection (d)(5)).

(B) Applicable Fraction.—For purposes of subparagraph (A), the term "applicable fraction" means the smaller of the unit fraction or the floor space fraction.

(C) Unit fraction.—For purposes of subparagraph (B), the term "unit fraction" means the fraction—

(i) the numerator of which is the number of low-income units in the building, and

(ii) the denominator of which is the number of residential rental units (whether or not occupied) in such building.

(D) Floor space fraction.—For purposes of subparagraph (B), the term "floor space fraction" means the fraction—

(i) the numerator of which is the total floor space of the low-income units in such building, and

(ii) the denominator of which is the total floor space of the residential rental units (whether or not occupied) in such building.

(2) Qualified low-income building.—The term "qualified low-income building" means any building—

Code §42(c)(2) ¶2871

(A) which at all times during the compliance period with respect to such building is part of a qualified low-income housing project, and

(B) to which the amendments made by section 201(a) of the Tax Reform Act of 1986 apply.

(d) Eligible Basis.—For purposes of this section—

(1) New Buildings.—The eligible basis of a new building is its adjusted basis.

(2) Existing buildings.—

(A) In general.—The eligible basis of an existing building is—

(i) in the case of a building which meets the requirements of subparagraph (B), the sum of—

(I) the portion of its adjusted basis attributable to its acquisition cost, plus

(II) amounts chargeable to capital account and incurred by the taxpayer (before the close of the 1st taxable year of the credit period for such building) for property (or additions or improvements to property) of a character subject to the allowance for depreciation, and

(ii) zero in any other case.

(B) Requirements.—A building meets the requirements of this subparagraph if—

(i) the building is acquired by purchase (as defined in section 179(d)(2)),

(ii) there is a period of at least 10 years between the date of its acquisition by the taxpayer and the later of—

(I) the date the building was last placed in service, or

(II) the date of the most recent nonqualified substantial improvement of the building, and

(iii) the building was not previously placed in service by the taxpayer or by any person who was a related person with respect to the taxpayer as of the time previously placed in service.

(C) Acquisition cost.—For purposes of subparagraph (A), the cost of any building shall not include so much of the basis of such building as is determined by reference to the basis of other property held at any time by the person acquiring the building.

(D) Special rules for subparagraph (b).—

(i) Nonqualified, substantial, improvement.—For purposes of subparagraph (B)(ii)—

(I) In general.—The term "nonqualified substantial improvement" means any substantial improvement if section 167(k) was elected with respect to such improvement or section 168 (as in effect on the day before the date of the enactment of the Tax Reform Act of 1986) applied to such improvement.

(II) Date of substantial improvement.—The date of a substantial improvement is the last day of the 24-month period referred to in subclause (III).

(III) Substantial improvement.—The term "substantial improvement" means the improvements added to capital account with respect to the building during any 24-month period, but only if the sum of the amounts added to such account during such period equals or exceeds 25 percent of the adjusted basis of the building (determined without regard to paragraphs (2) and (3) of section 1016(a)) as of the 1st day of such period.

(ii) Special rule for nontaxable exchanges.—For purposes of determining under subparagraph (B)(ii) when a building was last placed in service, there shall not be taken into account any placement in service in connection with the acquisition of the building in a transaction in which the basis of the building in the hands of the person acquiring it is determined in whole or in part by reference to the adjusted basis of such building in the hands of the person from whom acquired.

(iii) Related person etc.—

(I) Application of section 179.—For purposes of subparagraph (B)(i), section 179(d) shall be applied by substituting "10 percent" for "50 percent" in section 267(b) and 707(b) and in section 179(b)(7).

(II) Related person.—For purposes of subparagraph (B)(iii), a person (hereinafter in this subclause referred to as the "related person") is related to any person if the related person bears a relationship to such person specified in section 267(b) or 707(b)(1), or the related person and such person are engaged in trades or businesses under common control (within the meaning of subsections (a) and (b) of section 52). For purposes of the preceding sentence, in applying section 267(b) or 707(b)(1), "10 percent" shall be substituted for "50 percent".

(3) Eligible basis reduced where disproportionate standard for units.—The eligible basis of any building shall be reduced by an amount equal to the portion of the adjusted basis of the building which is attributable to residential rental units in the building which are not low-income units and which are above the average quality standard of the low-income units in the building.

(4) Special rules relating to determination of adjusted basis.—For purposes of this subsection—

(A) In general.—Except as provided in subparagraph (B), the adjusted basis of any building shall be determined without regard to the adjusted basis of any property which is not residential rental property.

(B) Basis of property in common areas, etc., included.—The adjusted basis of any building shall be determined by taking into account the adjusted basis of property (of a character subject to the allowance for depreciation) used in common areas or provided as comparable amenities to all residential rental units in such building.

(C) No reduction for depreciation.—The adjusted basis of any building shall be determined without regard to paragraphs (2) and (3) of section 1016(a).

(5) Eligible basis determined when building placed in service.—

(A) In general.—Except as provided in subparagraph (B), the eligible basis of any building for the entire compliance period for such building shall be its eligible basis on the date such building is placed in service.

(B) Eligible basis reduced by federal grants.—If, during any taxable year of the compliance period, a grant is made with respect to any building or the operation thereof and any portion of such grant is funded with Federal funds (whether or not includible in gross income), the eligible basis of such building for such taxable year and all succeeding taxable years shall be reduced by the portion of such grant which is so funded.

(6) Credit allowable for certain federally assisted buildings acquired during 10-year period described in paragraph (2)(b)(II).—

(A) In general.—On application by the taxpayer, the Secretary (after consultation with the appropriate Federal official) may waive paragraph (2)(B)(ii) with respect to any federally-assisted building if the Secretary determines that such waiver is necessary—

(i) to avert an assignment of the mortgage secured by property in the project (of which such building is a part) to the Department of Housing and Urban Development or the Farmers' Home Administration,

(ii) to avert a claim against a Federal mortgage insurance fund (or such Department or Administration) with respect to a mortgage which is so secured, or

(iii) to the extent provided in regulations, by reason of other circumstances of financial distress.

The preceding sentence shall not apply to any building described in paragraph (7)(B).

(B) Federally-assisted building.—For purposes of subparagraph (A), the term "federally assisted building" means any building which is substantially assisted, financed, or operated under—

(i) section 8 of the United States Housing Act of 1937,

(ii) section 221(d)(3) or 236 of the National Housing Act of 1934, or

(iii) section 515 of the Housing Act of 1949,

as such Acts are in effect on the date of the enactment of the Tax Reform Act of 1986.

(C) Appropriate federal official.—For purposes of subparagraph (A), the term "appropriate Federal official" means—

(i) the Secretary of Housing and Urban Development in the case of any building described in subparagraph (B) by reason of clause (i) or (ii) thereof, and

(ii) the Secretary of Agriculture in the case of any building described in subparagraph (B) by reason of clause (iii) thereof.

Code §42(d)(6) ¶2871

(7) Acquisition of building before end of prior compliance period.—

(A) In general.—Under regulations prescribed by the Secretary, in the case of a building described in subparagraph (B) which is acquired by the taxpayer—

(i) paragraph (2)(B) shall not apply, but

(ii) the credit allowable by reason of subsection (a) to the taxpayer for any period after such acquisition shall be equal to the amount of credit which would have been allowable under subsection (a) for such period to the prior owner referred to in subparagraph (B) has such owner not disposed of the building.

(B) Description of building.—A building is described in this subparagraph if—

(i) a credit was allowed by reason of subsection (a) to any prior owner of such building, and

(ii) the taxpayer acquired such building before the end of the compliance period for such building with respect to such prior owner (determined without regard to any disposition by such prior owner.)

(e) Rehabilitation Expenditures Treated as Separate New Building.—

(1) In general.—Rehabilitation expenditures paid or incurred by the taxpayer with respect to any building shall be treated for purposes of this section as a separate new building.

(2) Rehabilitation expenditures—For purposes of paragraph (1)—

(A) In general.—The term "rehabilitation expenditures" means amounts chargeable to captial account and incurred for property (or additions or improvements to property) of a character subject to the allowance for depreciation in connection with the rehabilitation of a building.

(B) Cost of acquisition, etc, not included.—Such term does not include the cost of acquiring any building (or interest therein) or any amount not permitted to be taken into account under paragraph (3) or (4) of subsection (d).

(3) Average of rehabilitation expenditures must be $2,000 or more.—

(A) In general.—Paragraph (1) shall apply to rehabilitation expenditures with respect to any building only if the qualified basis attributable to such expenditures incurred during any 24-month period, when divided by the low-income units in the building, is $2,000 or more.

(B) Date of determination.—The determination under subparagraph (A) shall be made as of the close of the 1st taxable year in the credit period with respect to such expenditures.

(4) Special Rules.—For purposes of applying this section with respect to expenditures which are treated as a separate building by reason of this subsection—

(A) such expenditures shall be treated as placed in service at the close of the 24-month period referred to in paragraph (3)(A), and

(B) the applicable fraction under subsection (c)(1) shall be the applicable fraction for the building (without regard to paragraph (1)) with respect to which the expenditures were incurred.

Nothing in subsection (d)(2) shall prevent a credit from being allowed by reason of this subsection.

(5) No double counting.—Rehabilitation expenditures may, at the election of the taxpayer, be taken into account under this subsection or subsection (d)(2)(A)(i)(II) but not under both such subsections.

(6) Regulations to apply subsection with respect to group of units in building.—The Secretary may prescribe regulations, consistent with the purposes of this subsection, treating a group of units with respect to which rehabilitation expenditures are incurred as a separate new building.

(f) Definition and Special Rules Relating to Credit Period.—

(1) Credit period defined.—For purposes of this section, the term "credit period" means, with respect to any building, the period of 10 taxable years beginning with the taxable year in which the building is placed in service or, at the election of the taxpayer, the succeeding taxable year. Such an election, once made, shall be irrevocable.

(2) Special rule for 1st year of credit period.—

(A) In general.—The credit allowable under subsection (a) with respect to any building for the 1st taxable year of the credit period shall be determined by substituting for the applicable fraction under subsection (c)(1) the fraction—

(i) the numerator of which is the sum of the applicable fractions determined under subsection (c)(1) as of the close of each full month of such year during which such building was in service, and

(ii) the denominator of which is 12.

(B) Disallowed 1st year credit allowed in 11th year.—Any reduction by reason of subparagraph (A) in the credit allowable (without regard to subparagraph (A)) for the 1st taxable year of the credit period shall be allowable under subsection (a) for the 1st taxable year following the credit period.

(3) Special rule where increase in qualified basis after 1st year of credit period.—

(A) Credit increased.—If—

(i) as of the close of any taxable year in the compliance period (after the 1st year of the credit period) the qualified basis of any building exceeds

(ii) the qualified basis of such building as of the close of the 1st year of the credit period,

the credit allowable under subsection (a) for the taxable year (determined without regard to this paragraph) shall be increased by an amount equal to the product of such excess and the percentage equal to ⅔ of the applicable percentage for such building.

(B) 1st year computation applies.—A rule similar to the rule of paragraph (2)(A) shall apply to the additional credit allowable by reason of this paragraph for the 1st year in which such additional credit is allowable.

(g) Qualified Low-Income Housing Project.—For purposes of this section—

(1) In general.—The term "qualified low-income housing project" means any project for residential rental property if the project meets the requirements of subparagraph (A) or (B) whichever is elected by the taxpayer:

(A) 20-50 test.—The project meets the requirements of this subparagraph if 20 percent or more of the residential units in such project are both rent-restricted and occupied by individuals whose income is 50 percent or less of area median gross income.

(B) 40-60 test.—The project meets the requirements of this subparagraph if 40 percent or more of the residential units in such project are both rent-restricted and occupied by individuals whose income is 60 percent or less of area median gross income.

Any election under this paragraph, once made, shall be irrevocable. For purposes of this paragraph, any property shall not be treated as failing to be residential rental property merely because part of the building in which such property is located is used for purposes other than residential rental purposes.

(2) Rent-restricted units.—

(A) In general.—For purposes of paragraph (1), a residential unit is rent-restricted if the gross rent with respect to such unit does not exceed 30 percent of the income limitation under paragraph (1) applicable to individuals occupying such unit.

(B) Gross rent.—For purposes of subparagraph (A), gross rent—

(i) does not include any payment under section 8 of the United States Housing Act of 1937 or any comparable Federal rental assistance program (with respect to such unit or occupants thereof), and

(ii) includes any utility allowance determined by the Secretary after taking into account such determinations under section 8 of the United States Housing Act of 1937.

(3) Date for meeting requirements.—

(A) Projects consisting of 1 building.—In the case of a project which does not have any other building in service, such project shall not be treated as meeting the requirements of paragraph (1) unless it meets such requirements not later than the date which is 12 months after the date such project is placed in service.

(B) Projects consisting of more than 1 building.—In the case of a project which has a building in service when a later building is placed in service as part of such project, such project shall not be treated as meeting the requirements of paragraph (1) with respect to such later building unless—

(i) such project meets such requirements without regard to such later building on the date such later building is placed in service, and

Code §42(g)(3) ¶2871

(ii) such project meets such requirements with regard to such later building not later than the date which is 12 months after the date such later building is placed in service.

(4) Certain rules made applicable.—Paragraphs (2) (other than subparagraph (A) thereof), (3), (4), (5), (6), and (7) of section 142(d), and section 6652(j), shall apply for purposes of determining whether any project is a qualified low-income housing project and whether any unit is a low-income unit.

(5) Election to treat building after compliance period as not part of a project.— For purposes of this section, the taxpayer may elect to treat any building as not part of a qualified low-income housing project for any period beginning after the compliance period for such building.

(h) Limitation on Aggregate Credit Allowable With Respect to Projects Located in a State.—

(1) Credit may not exceed credit amount allocated to building.—No credit shall be allowed by reason of this section for any taxable year with respect to any building in excess of the housing credit dollar amount allocated to such building under this subsection. An allocation shall be taken into account under the preceding sentence only if it occurs not later than the earlier of—

(A) the 60th day after the close of the taxable year, or

(B) the close of the calendar year in which such taxable year ends.

(2) Allocated credit amount to apply to all taxable years ending during or after credit allocation year.—Any housing credit dollar amount allocated to any building for any calendar year—

(A) shall apply to such building for all taxable years in the compliance period ending during or after such calendar year, and

(B) shall reduce the aggregate housing credit dollar amount of the allocating agency only for such calendar year.

(3) Housing credit dollar amount for agencies.—

(A) In general.—The aggregate housing credit dollar amount which a housing credit agency may allocate for any calendar year is the portion of the State housing credit ceiling allocated under this paragraph for such calendar year to such agency.

(B) State ceiling initially allocated to state housing credit agencies.—Except as provided in subparagraphs (D) and (E), the State housing credit ceiling for each calendar year shall be allocated to the housing credit agency of such State. If there is more than 1 housing credit agency of a State, all such agencies shall be treated as a single agency.

(C) State housing credit ceiling.—the State housing credit ceiling applicable to any State for any calendar year shall be an amount equal to $1.25 multiplied by the State population.

(D) Special rule for states with constitutional home rule cities.—For purposes of this subsection—

(i) In general.—The aggregate housing credit dollar amount for any constitutional home rule city for any calendar year shall be an amount which bears the same ratio to the State housing credit ceiling for such calendar year as—

(I) the population of such city, bears to

(II) the population of the entire State.

(ii) Coordination with other allocations.—In the case of any State which contains 1 or more constitutional home rule cities, for purposes of applying this paragraph with respect to housing credit agencies in such State other than constitutional home rule cities, the State housing credit ceiling for any calendar year shall be reduced by the aggregate housing credit dollar amounts determined for such year for all constitutional home rule cities in such State.

(iii) Constitutional home rule city.—For purposes of this paragraph, the term "constitutional home rule city" has the meaning given such term by section 146(d)(3)(C).

(E) State may provide for different allocation.—Rules similar to the rules of section 146(e) (other than paragraph (2)(B) thereof) shall apply for purposes of this paragraph.

(F) Population.—For purposes of this paragraph, population shall be determined in accordance with section 146(j).

(4) Credit for buildings financed by tax-exempt bonds subject to volume cap not taken into account.—

(A) In general.—Paragraph (1) shall not apply to the portion of any credit allowable under subsection (a) which is attributable to eligible basis financed by any obligation the interest on which is exempt from tax under section 103 and which is taken into account under section 146.

(B) Special rule where 70 percent or more of building is financed with tax-exempt bonds subject to volume cap.—For purposes of subparagraph (A), if 70 percent or more of the aggregate basis of any building and the land on which the building is located is financed by any obligation described in subparagraph (A), paragraph (1) shall not apply to any portion of the credit allowable under subsection (a) with respect to such building.

(5) Portion of state ceiling set-aside for certain projects involving qualified nonprofit organizations.—

(A) In general.—Not more than 90 percent of the State housing credit ceiling for any State for any calendar year shall be allocated to projects other than qualified low-income housing projects described in subparagraphs (B).

(B) Projects involving qualified nonprofit organizations.—For purposes of subparagraph (A), a qualified low-income housing project is described in this subparagraph if a qualified nonprofit organization is to materially participate (within the meaning of section 469(h) in the development and operation of the project throughout the compliance period.

(C) Qualified nonprofit organization.—For purposes of this paragraph, the term "qualified nonprofit organization" means any organization if—

(i) such organization is described in paragraph (3) or (4) of section 501(c) and is exempt from tax under section 501(a), and

(ii) 1 of the exempt purposes of such organization includes the fostering of low-income housing.

(D) State may not override set-aside.—Nothing in subparagraph (E) of paragraph (3) shall be construed to permit a State not to comply with subparagraph (A) of this paragraph.

(6) Special rules.—

(A) Building must be located within jurisdiction of credit agency.—A housing credit agency may allocate its aggregate housing credit dollar amount only to buildings located in the jurisdiction of the governmental unit of which such agency is a part.

(B) Housing credit dollar amount may not be carried over, etc.—

(i) No carryover.—The portion of the aggregate housing credit dollar amount of any housing credit agency which is not allocated for any calendar year may not be carried over to any other calendar year.

(ii) Allocation may not be earlier than year in which building placed in service.—A housing credit agency may allocate its housing credit dollar amount for any calendar year only to buildings placed in service before the close of such calendar year.

(C) Agency allocations in excess of limit.—If the aggregate housing credit dollar amounts allocated by a housing credit agency for any calendar year exceed the portion of the State housing credit ceiling allocated to such agency for such calendar year, the housing credit dollar amounts so allocated shall be reduced (to the extent of such excess) for buildings in the reverse of the order in which the allocations of such amounts were made.

(D) Credit allowable determined without regard to averaging convention, etc.—For purposes of this subsection, the credit allowable under subsection (a) with respect to any building shall be determined—

(i) without regard to paragraphs (2)(A) and (3)(B) of subsection (f), and

(ii) by applying subsection (f)(3)(A) without regard to "the percentage equal to ⅔ of."

(7) Other definitions.—For purposes of this subsection—

(A) Housing credit agency.—The term "housing credit agency" means any agency authorized to carry out this subsection.

(B) Possessions treated as states.—The term "State" includes a possession of the United States.

(i) Definitions and Special Rules.—For purposes of this section—

(1) **Compliance period.**—The term "compliance period" means, with respect to any building, the period of 15 taxable years beginning with the 1st taxable year of the credit period with respect thereto.

(2) **Determination of whether building is federally subsidized.—**

(A) In general.—Except as otherwise provided in this paragraph, for purposes of subsection (b)(1), a new building shall be treated as federally subsidized for any taxable year if, at any time during such taxable year, there is outstanding any obligation the interest on which is exempt from tax under section 103, or any below market Federal loan, the proceeds of which are used (directly or indirectly) with respect to such building or the operation thereof.

(B) Election to reduce eligible basis by outstanding balance of loan.—A loan shall not be taken into account under subparagraph (A) if the taxpayer elects to exclude an amount equal to the outstanding balance of such loan from the eligible basis of the building for purposes of subsection (d).

(C) Below market federal loan.—For purposes of subparagraph (A), the term "below market Federal loan" means any loan funded in whole or in part with Federal funds if the interest rate payable on such loan is less than the applicable Federal rate in effect under section 1274(d)(1) (as of the date on which the loan was made).

(3) **Low-income unit.—**

(A) In general.—The term "low-income unit" means any unit in a building if—

(i) such unit is rent-restricted (as defined in subsection (g)(2)), and

(ii) the individuals occupying such unit meet the income limitation applicable under subsection (g)(1) to the project of which such building is a part.

(B) Exceptions.—A unit shall not be treated as a low-income unit unless the unit is suitable for occupancy and used other than on a transient basis.

(C) Special rule for buildings having 4 or fewer units.—In the case of any building which has 4 or fewer residential rental units, no unit in such building shall be treated as a low-income unit if the units in such building are owned by—

(i) any individual who occupies a residential unit in such building, or

(ii) any person who is related (as defined in subsection (d)(2)(D)(iii)) to such individual.

(4) **New building.**—The term "new building" means a building the original use of which begins with the taxpayer.

(5) **Existing building.**—The term "existing building" means any building which is not a new building.

(j) **Recapture of Credit.—**

(1) **In general.—If—**

(A) as of the close of any taxable year in the compliance period, the amount of the qualified basis of any building with respect to the taxpayer is less than

(B) the amount of such basis as of the close of the preceding taxable year,

then the taxpayer's tax under this chapter for the taxable year shall be increased by the credit recapture amount.

(2) **Credit recapture amount.**—For purposes of paragraph (1), the credit recapture amount is an amount equal to the sum of—

(A) the aggregate decrease in the credit allowed to the taxpayer under section 38 for all prior taxable years which would have resulted if the accelerated portion of the credit allowable by reason of this section were not allowed for all prior taxable years with respect to the excess of the amount described in paragraph (1)(B) over the amount described in paragraph (1)(A), plus

(B) interest at the overpayment rate established under section 6621 on the amount determined under subparagraph (A) for each prior taxable year for the period beginning on the due date for filing the return for the prior taxable year involved.

No deduction shall be allowed under this chapter for interest described in subparagraph (B).

(3) **Accelerated portion of credit.**—For purposes of paragraph (2), the accelerated portion of the credit for the prior taxable years with respect to any amount of basis is the excess of—

(A) the aggregate credit allowed by reason of this section (without regard to this subsection) for such years with respect to such basis, over

(B) the aggregate credit which would be allowable by reason of this section for such years with respect to such basis if the aggregate credit which would (but for this subsection) have been allowable for the entire compliance period were allowable ratably over 15 years.

(4) Special rules.—

(A) Tax benefit rule.—The tax for the taxable year shall be increased under paragraph (1) only with respect to credits allowed by reason of this section which were used to reduce tax liability. In the case of credits not so used to reduce tax liability, the carryforwards and carrybacks under section 39 shall be appropriately adjusted.

(B) Only basis for which credit allowed taken into account.—Qualified basis shall be taken into account under paragraph (1)(B) only to the extent such basis was taken into account in determining the credit under subsection (1) for the preceding taxable year referred to in such paragraph.

(C) No recapture of additional credit allowable by reason of subsection (f)(3).— Paragraph (1) shall apply to a decrease in qualified basis only to the extent such decrease exceeds the amount of qualified basis with respect to which a credit was allowable for the taxable year referred to in paragraph (1)(B) by reason of subsection (f)(3).

(D) No credits against tax.—Any increase in tax under this subsection shall not be treated as a tax imposed by this chapter for purposes of determining the amount of any credit under subpart A, B; or D of this part.

(E) No recapture by reason of casualty loss.—The increase in tax under this subsection shall not apply to a reduction in qualified basis by reason of a casualty loss to the extent such loss is restored by reconstruction or replacement within a reasonable period established by the Secretary.

(5) Certain partnerships treated as the taxpayer.—

(A) In general.—For purposes of applying this subsection to a partnership to which this paragraph applies—

(i) such partnership shall be treated as the taxpayer to which the credit allowable under subsection (a) was allowed,

(ii) the amount of such credit allowed shall be treated as the amount which would have been allowed to the partnerhship were such credit allowable to such partnership,

(iii) paragraph (4)(A) shall not apply, and

(iv) the amount of the increase in tax under this subsection for any taxable year shall be allocated among the partners of such partnership in the same manner as such partnerships's taxable income for such year is allocated among such partners.

(B) Partnerships to which paragraph applies.—This paragraph shall apply to any partnership—

(i) which has 35 or more partners each of whom is a natural person or an estate, and

(ii) which elects the application of this paragraph.

(C) Special rules.—

(i) Husband and wife treated as 1 partner.—For purposes of subparagraph (B)(i), a husband and wife (and their estates) shall be treated as 1 partner.

(ii) Election irrevocable.—Any election under subparagraph (B), once made, shall be irrevocable.

(6) No recapture on disposition of building where bond posted.—In the case of a disposition of a building, the taxpayer shall be discharged from liability for any additional tax under this subsection by reason of such disposition if—

(A) the taxpayer furnishes to the Secretary a bond in an amount satisfactory to the Secretary and for the period required by the Secretary, and

(B) it is reasonably expected that such building will continue to be operated as a qualified low-income building for the remaining compliance period with respect to such building.

(k) Application of At-Risk Rules.—For purposes of this section—

(1) In general.—Except as otherwise provided in this subsection, rules similar to the rules of section 46(c)(8) (other than subparagraph (D)(iv)(I) thereof), section 46(c)(9), and section 47(d)(1) shall apply in determining the qualified basis of any building in the same manner as such sections apply in determining the credit base of property.

(2) Special rules for determining qualified person.—For purposes of paragraph (1)—

(A) In general.—If the requirements of subparagraphs (B), (C), and (D) are met with respect to any financing borrowed from a qualified nonprofit organization (as defined in subsection (h)(5)), the determination of whether such financing is qualified commercial financing with respect to any qualified low-income building shall be made without regard to whether such organization—

(i) is actively and regularly engaged in the business of lending money, or

(ii) is a person described in section 46(c)(8)(D)(iv)(II).

(B) Financing secured by property.—The requirements of this subparagraph are met with respect to any financing if such financing is secured by the qualified low-income building.

(C) Portion of building attributable to financing.—The requirements of this subparagraph are met with respect to any financing for any taxable year in the compliance period if, as of the close of such taxable year, not more than 60 percent of the eligible basis of the qualified low-income building is attributable to such financing (reduced by the principal and interest of any governmental financing which is part of a wrap-around mortgage involving such financing).

(D) Repayment of principal and interest.—The requirements of this subparagraph are met with respect to any financing if such financing is fully repaid on or before the earliest of—

(i) the date on which such financing matures,

(ii) the 90th day after the close of the compliance period with respect to the qualified low-income building, or

(iii) the date of its refinancing or the sale of the building to which such financing relates.

(3) Present value of financing.—If the rate of interest on any financing described in paragraph (2)(A) is less than the rate which is 1 percentage point below the applicable Federal rate as of the time such financing is incurred, then the qualified basis (to which such financing relates) of the qualified low-income building shall be the present value of the amount of such financing, using as the discount rate such applicable Federal rate. For purposes of the preceding sentence, the rate of interest on any financing shall be determined by treating interest to the extent of government subsidies as not payable.

(4) Failure to fully repay.—

(A) In general.—To the extent that the requirements of paragraph (2)(D) are not met, then the taxpayer's tax under this chapter for the taxable year in which such failure occurs shall be increased by an amount equal to the applicable portion of the credit under this section with respect to such building, increased by an amount of interest for the period—

(i) beginning with the due date for the filing of the return of tax imposed by chapter 1 for the 1st taxable year for which such credit was allowable, and

(ii) ending with the due date for the taxable year in which such failure occurs,

determined by using the underpayment rate and method under section 6621.

(B) Applicable portion.—For purposes of subparagraph (A), the term "applicable portion" means the aggregate decrease in the credits allowed to a taxpayer under section 38 for all prior taxable years which would have resulted if the eligible basis of the building were reduced by the amount of financing which does not meet requirements of paragraph (2)(D).

(C) Certain rules to apply.—Rules similar to the rules of subparagraphs (A) and (D) of subsection (j)(4) shall apply for purposes of this subsection.

(l) Certifications to Secretary.—

(1) Certification with respect to 1st year of credit period.—Not later than the 90th day following the close of the 1st taxable year in the credit period with respect to any qualified low-income building, the taxpayer shall certify to the Secretary (in such form and in such manner as the Secretary prescribes)—

(A) the taxable year, and calendar year, in which such building was placed in service,

(B) the adjusted basis and eligible basis of such building as of the close of the 1st year of the credit period,

(C) the maximum applicable percentage and qualified basis permitted to be taken into account by the appropriate housing credit agency under subsection (h),

(D) the election made under subsection (g) with respect to the qualified low-income housing project of which such building is a part, and

(E) such other information as the Secretary may require.

In the case of a failure to make the certification required by the preceding sentence on the date prescribed therefor, unless it is shown that such failure is due to reasonable cause and not to willful neglect, no credit shall be allowable by reason of subsection (a) with respect to such building for any taxable year ending before such certification is made.

(2) **Annual reports from housing credit agencies.**—Each agency which allocates any housing credit amount to any building for any calendar year shall submit to the Secretary (at such time and in such manner as the Secretary shall prescribe) an annual report specifying—

(A) the amount of housing credit amount allocated to each building for such year, and

(B) sufficient information to identify each such building and the taxpayer with respect thereto, and

(C) such other information as the Secretary may require.

The penalty under section 6652(j) shall apply to any failure to submit the report required by the preceding sentence on the date prescribed therefor.

(m) **Regulations.**—The Secretary shall prescribe such regulations as may be necessary or appropriate to carry out the purposes of this section, including regulations—

(1) dealing with—

(A) projects which include more than 1 building or only a portion of a building,

(B) buildings which are placed in service in portions,

(2) providing for the application of this section to short taxable years, and

(3) preventing the avoidance of the rules of this section.

(n) **Termination—**

(1) **In general.**—Except as provided in paragraph (2), the State housing credit ceiling under subsection (h) shall be zero for any calendar year after 1989.

(2) **Carryover of 1989 limit for certain projects in progress.—**

(A) **In general.**—The aggregate housing credit amount of any agency for 1989 which is not allocated for 1989 shall be treated for purposes of applying this section to any building described in subparagraph (B) as the housing credit amount of such agency for 1990.

(B) **Description.**—A building is described in this subparagraph if—

(i) such building is constructed, reconstructed, or rehabilitated by the taxpayer,

(ii) more than 10 percent of the reasonably anticipated cost of such construction, reconstruction, or rehabilitation has been incurred as of January 1, 1989, and

(iii) such building is placed in service before January 1, 1991.

(C) **Certain rule not to apply.**—Subsection (h)(6)(B)(i) shall not apply for purposes of this paragraph.

[For official explanation, see Committee Reports, ¶3879.]

[¶2872] **CODE SEC. 46. AMOUNT OF CREDIT.**

(a) **Amount of Investment Credit.**—For purposes of section 38, the amount of the investment credit determined under this section for any taxable year shall be an amount equal to the sum of the following percentages of the qualified investment (as determined under subsections (c) and (d)):

(1) the regular percentage,

(2) in the case of energy property, the energy percentage, and

(3) in the case of that portion of the basis of any property which is attributable to qualified rehabilitation expenditures, the rehabilitation percentage.

(b) **Determination of Percentages.**—For purposes of subsection (a)—

(1) **Regular percentage.**—The regular percentage is 10 percent.

(2) Energy percentage.—

   (A) In general.—The energy percentage shall be determined in accordance with the following table:

Column A—Description	Column B—Percentage	Column C—Period	
In the case of:	The energy percentage is:	For the period: Beginning on:	And ending on:
(i) General Rule.—Property not described in any of the following provisions of this column.	10 percent.	Oct. 1, 1978.	Dec. 31, 1982.
(ii) Solar Wind, or Geothermal Property.—Property described in section 48(l)(2)(A)(ii) or ¹48(l)(3)(A)(viii).	A. 10 percent.	Oct. 1, 1978.	Dec. 31, 1979.
	B. 15 percent.	Jan. 1, 1980.	Dec. 31, 1985
(iii) Ocean Thermal Property.—Property described in section 48(l)(3)(A)(ix).	15 percent.	Jan. 1, 1980.	Dec. 31, 1985.
(iv) Qualified Hydroelectric Generating Property.—Property described in section 48(l)(2)(A)(vii).	11 percent.	Jan. 1, 1980.	Dec. 31, 1985.
(v) Qualified Intercity Buses.—Property described in section 48(l)(2)(A)-(ix).	10 percent.	Jan. 1, 1980.	Dec. 31, 1985.
(vi) Biomass Property.—Property described in section 48(l)(15).	10 percent.	Oct. 1, 1978.	Dec. 31, 1985.
(vii) Chlor-Alkali Electrolytic Cells.—Property described in section 48(l)(5)(M).	10 percent.	Jan. 1, 1980.	Dec. 31, 1982.
(viii) Solar Energy Property.—Property described in section 48(l)(4) (other than wind energy property).	*A. 15 percent*	*Jan 1, 1986*	*Dec. 31, 1986.*
	B. 12 percent	*Jan. 1, 1987*	*Dec. 31, 1987.*
	C. 10 percent	*Jan. 1, 1988*	*Dec. 31, 1988.*
(ix) Geothermal Property.—Property described in section 48(l)(3)(A)(viii).	*A. 15 percent*	*Jan. 1, 1986*	*Dec. 31, 1986.*
	B. 10 percent	*Jan. 1, 1987*	*Dec. 31, 1988.*
(x) Ocean Thermal Property.—Property described in section 48(l)(3)(A)(ix).	*15 percent*	*Jan. 1, 1986*	*Dec. 31, 1988.*
(xi) Biomass Property.—Property described in section 48(l)(15).	*A.15 percent*	*Jan. 1, 1986*	*Dec. 31, 1986.*
	B. 10 percent	*Jan. 1, 1987*	*Dec. 31, 1987.*

* * * * * * * * * * * * *

〔Footnote ¶2872〕 Matter in *italics* in Sec. 46(b)(2)(A)(ii) added by section 1847(b)(11), '86 TRA, which struck out:

  (1) "48(*l*)(3)(A)(vii)"

  Effective date (Sec. 1881, '86 TRA and section 475(a) and (c), '84 TRA).—(a) Generally applies to taxable years beginning after 12-31-83, and to carrybacks from such years.

  (c) Clarification of effect of amendments on investment tax credit.—Nothing in the amendments made by section 474(o) of '84 TRA shall be construed as reducing the amount of any credit allowable for qualified investment in taxable years beginning before 1-1-84.

  Matter in *italics* in Sec. 46(b)(2)(A)(viii)—(xi) and (E) added by section 421(a) and (b), '86 TRA.

  Effective date (Sec. 421(c), '86 TRA).—Applies to periods beginning after 12-31-85, under rules similar to rules under section 48(m) of the '86 Code.

(E) Certain rules made applicable.—Rules similar to the rules of subsections (c) and (d) of section 49 shall apply to any credit allowable by reason of subparagraph (C) or (D).

* * * * * * * * * * * *

(4) Rehabilitation percentage.—

    (A) In general.—[2]*The term "rehabilitation percentage" means—*

〔Footnote ¶2872 continued〕

Matter in *italics* in Sec. 46(b)(4) added by section 251(a), '86 TRA which struck out:

(2)   "In the case of qualified rehabilitation expenditures with respect to a:

	The rehabilitation percentage is:
30-year building	15
40-year building	20
Certified historic structure	25.

(B) Regular and energy percentages not to apply.—The regular percentages and the energy percentages shall not apply to that portion of the basis of any property which is attributable to qualified rehabilitation expenditures.

(C) Definitions.—For purposes of this paragraph—

(i) 30-year building.—The term '30-year building' means a qualified rehabilitated building other than a 40-year building and other than a certified historic structure.

(ii) 40-year building.—The term '40-year building' means a qualified rehabilitated building (other than a certified historic structure) which would meet the requirements of section 48(g)(1)(B) if '40' were substituted for '30' each place it appears in subparagraph (B) thereof.

(iii) Certified historic structure.—The term 'certified historic structure' means a qualified rehabilitation building which meets the requirements of section 48(g)(3)."

Effective date (Sec. 251(d), '86 TRA).—(1) Generally applies to property placed in service after 12-31-86, in taxable years ending after such date.

(2) General transitional rule.—The amendments made by this section and section 201 shall not apply to any property placed in service before 1-1-94, if such property is placed in service as part of—

(A) a rehabilitation which was completed pursuant to a written contract which was binding on 3-1-86, or

(B) a rehabilitation incurred in connection with property (including any leasehold interest) acquired before 3-2-86, or acquired on or after such date pursuant to a written contract that was binding on 3-1-86, if—

(i) the rehabilitation was completed pursuant to a written contract that was binding on 3-1-86,

(ii) parts 1 and 2 of the Historic Preservation Certification Application were filed with the Department of the Interior (or its designee) before 3-2-86, or

(iii) the lesser of $1,000,000 or 5 percent of the cost of the rehabilitation is incurred before 3-2-86, or is required to be incurred pursuant to a written contract which was binding on 3-1-86.

(3) Certain additional rehabilitations.—The amendments made by this section and section 201 shall not apply to—

(A) the rehabilitation of 8 bathhouses within the Hot Springs National Park or of buildings in the Central Avenue Historic District at such Park,

(B) the rehabilitation of the Upper Pontabla Building in New Orleans, Louisiana,

(C) the rehabilitation of at least 60 buildings listed on the National Register at the Frankford Arsenal,

(D) the rehabilitation of De Baliveriere Arcade, St. Louis Centre, and Drake Apartments in Missouri,

(E) the rehabilitation of The Tides in Bristol, Rhode Island,

(F) the rehabilitation and renovation of the Outlet Company building and garage in Providence, Rhode Island,

(G) the rehabilitation of 10 structures in Harrisburg, Pennsylvania, with respect to which the Harristown Development Corporation was designated developer and received an option to acquire title to the entire project site for $1 on 6-27-84,

(H) the rehabilitation of a project involving the renovation of 3 historic structures on the Minneapolis riverfront, with respect to which the developer of the project entered into a redevelopment agreement with a municipality dated 1-4-85, and industrial deveopment bonds were sold in 3 separate issues in May, July, and October 1985,

(I) the rehabilitation of a bank's main office facilities of approximately 120,000 square feet in connection with which the bank's board of directors authorized a $3,300,000 expenditure for the renovation and retrofit on March 20, 1984,

(J) the rehabilitation of 10 warehouse buildings between 1906 and 1910 and purchased under a contract dated 2-17-86,

(K) the rehabilitation of a facility which is customarily used for conventions and sporting events if an analysis of operations and recommendations of utilization of such facility was prepared by a certified public accounting firm pursuant to an engagement authorized on 3-6-84, and presented on 6-11-84, to officials of the city in which such facility is located,

(L) Mount Vernon Mills in Columbia, South Carolina,

(M) the Barbara Jordan II Apartments,

(N) the rehabilitation of the Federal Building and Post Office, 120 Hanover Street, Manchester, New Hampshire,

(O) the rehabilitation of the Charleston Waterfront project in South Carolina,

(P) the Hayes Mansion in San Francisco,

(Q) the renovation of a facility owned by the National Railroad Passenger Corporation ("Amtrak") for which

    (i) 10 percent in the case of qualified rehabilitation expenditures with respect to a qualified rehabilitated building other than a certified historic structure, and

    (ii) 20 percent in the case of such expenditure with respect to a certified historic structure.

    (B) Regular and energy percentages not to apply.—The regular percentage and the energy percentages shall not apply to that portion of the basis of any property which is attributable to qualified rehabilitation expenditures.

(c) Qualified Investment.—

    (1) In general.—For purposes of this subpart, the term "qualified investment" means, with respect to any taxable year, the aggregate of—

    (A) the applicable percentage of the basis of each new section 38 property (as defined in section 48(b)) placed in service by the taxpayer during such taxable year, plus

---

〔Footnote ¶2872 continued〕

project Amtrak engaged a development team by letter agreement dated 8-23-85, as modified by letter agreement dated 9-9-85,

  (R) the rehabilitation of a structure or its components which is listed in the National Register of Historic Places, is located in Allegheny County, Pennsylvania, will be substantially rehabilitated (as defined in section 48(g)(1)(C) prior to amendment by this Act), prior to 12-31-89, and was previously utilized as a market and an auto dealership,

  (S) The Bellevue Stratford Hotel in Philadelphia, Pennsylvania,

  (T) the Dixon Mill Housing project in Jersey City, New Jersey,

  (U) Motor Square Garden,

  (V) the Blackstone Apartments, and the Shriver-Johnson building, in Sioux Falls, South Dakota,

  (W) the Holy Name Academy in Spokane, Washington,

  (X) the Nike/Clemson Mill in Exeter, New Hampshire,

  (Y) the Central Bank Building in Grand Rapids, Michigan, and

  (Z) the Heritage Hotel, in the City of Marquette, Michigan.

  (4) Additional rehabilitations.—The amendments made by this section and section 201 shall not apply to—

  (A) the Fort Worth Town Square Project in Texas,

  (B) the American Youth Hostel in New York, New York,

  (C) The Riverwest Loft Development (including all three phases, two of which do not involve rehabilitations),

  (D) the Gaslamp Quarter Historic District in California,

  (E) the Eberhardt & Ober Brewery, in Pennsylvania,

  (F) the Captain's Walk Limited Partnership-Harris Place Development, in Connecticut,

  (G) the Velvet Mills in Connecticut,

  (H) the Roycroft Inn, in New York,

  (I) Old Main Village, in Mankatto, Minnesota,

  (J) the Washburn-Crosby A Mill, in Minnespolis, Minnesota,

  (K) the Lakeland marbel Arcade in Lakeland, Florida,

  (L) the Willard Hotel, in Washington, D.C.,

  (M) the H.P. Lau Building in Lincoln, Nebraska,

  (N) the Starks Building, in Louisville, Kentucky,

  (O) the Bellevue High School, in Bellevue, Kentucky,

  (P) the Major Hampden Smith House, in Owensboro, Kentucky,

  (Q) the Doe Run Inn, in Brandenburg, Kentucky,

  (R) the State National Bank, in Frankfort, Kentucky,

  (S) the Captain Jack House, in Fleming, Kentucky,

  (T) the Elizabeth Arlinghaus House, in Louisville, Kentucky,

  (U) Limerick Shamrock, in Louisville, Kentucky,

  (V) the Robert Mills Project, in South Carolina,

  (W) the 620 Project, consisting of 3 buildings, in Kentucky,

  (X) the Warrior Hotel, Ltd., the first two floors of the Martin Hotel, and the 105,000 square foot warehouse constructed in 1910, all in Sioux City, Iowa,

  (Y) the waterpark condominium residential project, to the extent of $2 million of expenditures, and

  (Z) the Apollo and Bishop Building Complex on 125th Street, the Bigelow-Hartford Carpet Mill in New York, New York.

  (5) Reduction in credit for property under transitional rules.—In the case of property placed in service after 12-31-86, and to which the amendments made by this section do not apply, subparagraph (A) of section 46(b)(4) of the '54 Code (as in effect before the enactment of this Act) shall be applied—

  (A) by substituting "10 percent" for "15 percent", and

  (B) by substituting "13 percent" for "20 percent".

  (6) Expensing of rehabilitation expenditures for the Frankford Arsenal.—In the case of any expenditures paid or incurred in connection with the rehabilitation of the Frankford Arsenal during the 8-year period beginning on 1-1-87, such expenditures (including expenditures for repair and maintenance of the building and property) shall be allowable as a deduction in the taxable year in which paid or incurred in an amount not in excess of the submissions made by the taxpayer before 9-16-86.

(B) the applicable percentage of the cost of each used section 38 property (as defined in section 48(c)(1)) placed in service by the taxpayer during such taxable year.

* * * * * * * * * * * *

(8) Certain nonrecourse financing excluded from credit base.—

(D) Nonqualified nonrecourse financing.—

(i) In general.—For purposes of this paragraph and paragraph (9), the term "nonqualified nonrecourse financing" means any nonrecourse financing which is not qualified commercial financing.

(ii) Qualified commercial financing.—For purposes of this paragraph, the term "qualified commercial financing" means any financing with respect to any property if—

(I) such property is acquired by the taxpayer from a person who is not a related person,

(II) the amount of the nonrecourse financing with respect to such property does not exceed 80 percent of the credit base of such property, and

(III) such financing is borrowed from a qualified person or represents a loan from any Federal, State, or local government or instrumentality thereof, or is guaranteed by any Federal, State, or local government.

Such term shall not include any convertible debt.

(iii) Nonrecourse financing.—For purposes of this subparagraph, the term "nonrecourse financing" includes—

(I) any amount with respect to which the taxpayer is protected against loss through guarantees, stop-loss agreements, or other similar arrangements, and

(II) except to the extent provided in regulations, any amount borrowed from a person who has an interest (other than as a creditor) in the activity in which the property is used or from a related person to a person (other than the taxpayer) having such an interest.

In the case of amounts borrowed by a corporation from a shareholder, subclause (II) shall not apply to an interest as a shareholder.

(iv) Qualified person.—For purposes of this paragraph, the term "qualified person" means any person which is actively and regularly engaged in the business of lending money and which is not—

(I) a related person with respect to the taxpayer,

(II) a person from which the taxpayer acquired the property (or a related person to such person), or

(III) a person who receives a fee with respect to the taxpayer's investment in the property (or a related person to such person).

(v) Related person.—For purposes of [3] *this subparagraph,* the term "related person" has the meaning given such term by [4] *section 465(b)(3)(C).* Except as otherwise provided in regulations prescribed by the Secretary, the determination

---

[Footnote ¶2872 continued]

"This subparagraph" in *italics* in Sec. 46(c)(8)(D)(v) added by section 1844(a), '86 TRA, which struck out:
(3) "clause (i)"

Effective date (Sec. 1881, '86 TRA and section 431(e), '84 TRA).—(1) Generally applies to property placed in service after 7-18-84 in taxable years ending after such date; except that such amendments shall not apply to any property to which the amendments made by section 211(f) of '81 ERTA do not apply.

(2) Amendments may be elected retroactively.—At the election of the taxpayer, the amendments made by this section shall apply as if included in the amendments made by section 211(f) of '81 ERTA. Any election made under the preceding sentence shall apply to all property of the taxpayer to which the amendments made by such section 211(f) apply and shall be made at such time and in such manner as the Secretary of the Treasury or his delegate may by regulations prescribe.

"section 465(b)(3)(C)" in *italics* in Sec. 46(c)(8)(D)(v) added by section 201(d)(7)(B), '86 TRA, which struck out:
(4) "section 168(e)(4)"

Effective date (Sec. 203(a)(1) and (b), '86 TRA).—(A) Generally applies to property placed in service after 12-31-86, in taxable years ending after such date.

(B) Election to have amendments made by section 201 apply.—A taxpayer may elect (at such time and in such manner as the Secretary of the Treasury or his delegate may prescribe) to have the amendments made by section 201 apply to any property placed in service after and before 1-1-87.

For transitional and special rules, see ¶2007—2008 and Sec. 251(d), '86 TRA, above.

---

of whether a person is a related person shall be made as of the close of the taxable year in which the property is placed in service.

* * * * * * * * * * * *

(9) Subsequent decreases in nonqualified nonrecourse financing with respect to the property.—

(A) In general.—If, at the close of a taxable year following the taxable year in which the property was placed in service, there is a net decrease in the amount of nonqualified nonrecourse financing with respect to such property, such net decrease shall be taken into account as [5]*an increase in the credit base for* such property in accordance with subparagraph (C).

(B) Certain transactions not taken into account.—For purposes of this paragraph, nonqualified nonrecourse financing shall not be treated as decreased through the surrender or other use of property financed by nonqualified nonrecourse financing.

(C) Manner in which taken into account.—

(i) Credit determined by reference to taxable year property placed in service.—For purposes of determining the amount of credit allowable under section 38 and the amount of credit subject to the early disposition or cessation rules under section 47, any increase in a taxpayer's [6]*credit base for any property by reason of this paragraph shall be taken into account as if it were property placed in service by the taxpayer in the taxable year in which the property referred to in subparagraph (A) was first placed in service.*

(ii) Credit allowed for year of decrease in nonqualified nonrecourse financing.—Any credit allowable under this subpart for any increase in qualified investment by reason of this paragraph shall be treated as earned during the taxable year of the decrease in the amount of nonqualified nonrecourse financing.

* * * * * * * * * * * *

(e) Limitations with Respect to Certain Persons.—

(1) In general.—In the case of—

(A) an organization to which section 593 applies, and

(B) a regulated investment company or a real estate investment trust subject to taxation under subchapter M (sec. 851 and following),

the qualified investment shall equal such person's ratable share of such qualified investment.

* * * * * * * * * * * *

(4) Special rules where section 593 organization is lessee.—

* * * * * * * * * * * *

(D) Special rules for partnerships, etc.—For purposes of paragraph (1)(A), rules similar to the rules of paragraphs (8) and (9) of section 168(j) shall apply.

(E) Exception for qualified rehabilitation buildings leased to section 593 organizations.—Subparagraph (A) shall not apply to qualified investment attributable to qualified rehabilitation expenditures for any portion of a building if such portion of the building would not be tax-exempt use property (as defined in section 168(j)) if the section 593 organization were a tax-exempt entity (as defined in section 168(j)(4)).

(f) Limitation in Case of Certain Regulated Companies.—

* * * * * * * * * * * *

[Footnote ¶2872 continued]

Matter in *italics* in Sec. 46(c)(9)(A) and (C)(i) added by section 1844(b)(3) and (5), '86 TRA, which struck out:
(5) "additional qualified investment in"
(6) "qualfied investment in property by reason of this paragraph shall be deemed to be additional qualified investment made by the taxpayer in the year in which the property referred to in subparagraph (A) was first placed in service."
Effective date (Sec. 1881, '86 TRA, and section 431(e), '84 TRA).—See above.

Sec. 46(e)(4)(D) and (E) in *italics* added by section 1802(a)(6) and (8), '86 TRA.
Effective date (Sec. 1881, '86 TRA, and section 31(g), '84 TRA, as amended by section 1802(a)(2)(F) and (10), '86 TRA).—(1) Generally applies—
(A) to property placed in service by the taxpayer after 5-23-83, in taxable years ending after such date, and
(B) to property placed in service by the taxpayer on or before 5-23-83, if the lease to the tax-exempt entity is entered into after 5-23-83.
For transitional and special rules, see footnote ¶2935-A, below.

Sec. 46(f)(9) repealed by Section 1848(a), '86 TRA:

(9)   [Repealed]⁷

* * * * * * * * * * * *

[For official explanation, see Committee Reports, ¶3870; 3878; 3899; 4136; 4161.]

[¶2873]   CODE SEC. 47.   CERTAIN DISPOSITIONS, ETC., OF SECTION 38 PROPERTY.

(a)   **General Rule.**—Under regulations prescribed by the Secretary—

* * * * * * * * * * * *

(9)   *Aircraft leased to foreign persons or entities.—*

(A)   *In general.—Any aircraft which was new section 38 property for the taxable year in which it was placed in service and which is used by any foreign person or entity (as defind in section 168(i)(4)(C)) under a qualified lease (as defined in paragraph (7)(C)) entered into before January 1, 1990, shall not be treated as ceasing to be section 38 property by reason of such use until such aircraft has been so used for a period or periods exceeding 3 years in total.*

(B)   *Recapture period extended.—For purposes of paragraphs (1) and (5)(B) of this subsection, any period during which there was use described in subparagraph (A) of an aircraft shall be disregarded.*

* * * * * * * * * * * *

(d)   **Increases in Nonqualified Nonrecourse Financing—**

(1)   **In general.**—If, as of the close of the taxable year, there is a net increase with respect to the taxpayer in the amount of nonqualified nonrecourse financing (within the meaning of section 46(c)(8)) with respect to any property to which section 46(c)(8) applied, then the tax under this chapter for such taxable year shall be increased by an amount equal to the aggregate decrease in credits allowed under section 38 for all prior taxable years which would have resulted from reducing the ¹*credit base (as defined in section 48(c)(8)(C)) taken into account with respect to such property by the amount of such net increase. For purposes of determining the amount of credit subject to the early disposition or cessation rules of subsection (a) the net increase in the amount of the nonqualified nonrecourse financing with respect to the property shall be treated as reducing the propety's credit base (and correspondingly reducing the qualified investment in the property) in the year in which the property was first placed in service.*

[Footnote ¶2872 continued]

(7)   "**(9)   Special rule for additional credit.**—If the taxpayer makes an election under subparagraph (E) of subsection (a)(2), for a taxable year beginning after December 31, 1975, then, notwithstanding the prior paragraphs of this subsection, no credit shall be allowed by section 38 in excess of the amount which would be allowed without regard to the provisions of subparagraph (E) of subsection (a)(2) if—

(A)   the taxpayer's cost of service for ratemaking purposes or in its regulated books of account is reduced by reason of any portion of such credit which results from the transfer of employer securities or cash to a tax credit employee stock ownership plan which meets the requirements of section 409A;

(B)   the base to which the taxpayer's rate of return for ratemaking purposes is applied is reduced by reason of any portion of such credit which results from a transfer described in subparagraph (A) to such employee stock ownership plan; or

(C)   any portion of the amount of such credit which results from a transfer described in subparagraph (A) to such employee stock ownership plan is treated for ratemaking purposes in any way other than as though it had been contributed by the taxpayer's common shareholders."

Effective date   (Sec. 1881, '86 TRA, and section 491(f)(1), '84 TRA).—Applies to obligations issued after 12-31-83.

[Footnote ¶2873]   Sec. 47(a)(9) in *italics* added by section 1802(a)(5)(A), '86 TRA.

Effective date   (Sec. 1881, '86 TRA, and section 31(g), '84 TRA, as amended by section 1802(a)(2)(F) and (10), '86 TRA).—Generally applies—

(A)   to property placed in service by the taxpayer after 5-23-83, in taxable years ending after such date, and

(B)   to property placed in service by the taxpayer on or before 5-23-83, if the lease to the tax-exempt entity is entered into after 5-23-83.

For special and transitional rules, see footnote ¶2935-A.

Matter in *italics* in Sec. 47(d)(1) and (3)(E)(i) added by section 1844(b)(1) and (4), '86 TRA, which struck out:
(1)   "qualified investment"
Effective date   (Sec. 1881, '86 TRA, and section 431(e), '84 TRA).—(1)   Generally applies to property placed in service after 7-18-84 in taxable years ending after such date; except that such amendments shall not apply to any property to which the amendments made by section 211(f) of the '81 ERTA do not apply.

(2)   Amendments may be elected retroactively.—At the election of the taxpayer, applies as if included in the amendments made by section 211(f) of '81 ERTA. Any election made under the preceding sentence shall apply to all property of taxpayer to which the amendments made by such section 211(f) apply and shall be made at such time and in such manner as the Secretary of the Treasury or his delegate may by regulations prescribe.

Code §47(d)(1) ¶2873

* * * * * * * * * * * *

(3) Special rules for certain energy property.—

* * * * * * * * * * * *

(E) Special rule for certain dispositions.—
(i) In general.—If any property which is held by the taxpayer and to which this paragraph applies is disposed of by the taxpayer, then for purposes of paragraph (1) and notwithstanding subparagraph (B), the credit recapture amount for the taxpayer shall be an amount equal to the unpaid principal on the loan described in subparagraph (B)(i) as of the date of disposition; *reduced by the sum of the credit recapture amounts with respect to such property for all preceding taxable years;*
(ii) Assumption, etc.—Any amount of the loan described in subparagraph (B)(i) which is assumed or taken subject to by any person shall be treated for purposes of clause (i) as not reducing unpaid principal with respect to such loan.
(F) **[Repealed]**[2]
(G) Additional interest.—In the case of any increase in tax under paragraph (1) by reason of the application of this paragraph, there shall be added to such tax interest on such tax (determined *at the underpayment rate established* under section 6621) as if the increase in tax under paragraph (1) was for the taxable year in which the property was placed in service.

* * * * * * * * * * * *

[For official explanation, see Committee Reports, ¶4075; 4136; 4161.]

[¶2874] CODE SEC. 48. DEFINITIONS; SPECIAL RULES.

(a) **Section 38 Property.—**

* * * * * * * * * * * *

(2) **Property used outside the United States.—**
(A) In general.—Except as provided in subparagraph (B), the term "section 38 property" does not include property which is used predominantly outside the United States.
(B) Exceptions.—Subparagraph (A) shall not apply to—
(i) any aircraft which is registered by the Administrator of the Federal Aviation Agency and which is operated to and from the United States or is operated under contract with the United States;
(ii) rolling stock which is used within and without the United States and which is—
(I) of a domestic railroad corporation providing transportation subject to subchapter I of chapter 105 of title 49, or
(II) of a United States person (other than a corporation described in subclause (I)) but only if the rolling stock is not leased to one or more foreign persons for periods aggregating more than 12 months in any 24-month period;
(iii) any vessel documented under the laws of the United States which is operated in the foreign or domestic commerce of the United States;
(iv) any motor vehicle of a United States person (as defined in section 7701(a)(30)) which is operated to and from the United States;
(v) any container of a United States person which is used in the transportation of property to and from the United States;

[Footnote ¶2873 continued]

Sec. 47(d)(3)(F) repealed by section 1844(b)(2), '86 TRA.
(2) "(F) Application with subsection (a).—The amount of any increase in tax under subsection (a) with respect to any property to which this paragraph applies shall be determined by reducing the qualified investment with respect to such property by the aggregate credit recapture amounts for all taxable years under this paragraph."
Effective date (Sec. 1881, '86 TRA, and section 431(e), '84 TRA).—See above.

Matter in *italics* in Sec. 47(d)(3)(G) added by section 1511(c)(2), '86 TRA.
Effective date (Sec. 1511(d), '86 TRA).—Applies for purposes of determining interest for periods after 12-31-86.

(vi) any property (other than a vessel or an aircraft) of a United States person which is used for the purpose of exploring for, developing, removing, or transporting resources from the outer Continental Shelf (within the meaning of section 2 of the Outer Continental Shelf Lands Act, as amended and supplemented; (43 U.S.C. 1331);

(vii) any property which is owned by a domestic corporation (other than a corporation which has an election in effect under section 936[1]) or by a United States citizen (other than a citizen entitled to the benefits of section 931, [2]*or* 933[3]) and which is used predominantly in a possession of the United States by such a corporation or such a citizen, or by a corporation created or organized in, or under the law of, a possession of the United States;

(vii) any communications satellite (as defined in section 103(3) of the Communications Satellite Act of 1962, 47 U.S.C. 702(3)), or any interest therein, of a United States person;

(ix) any cable, or any interest therein, of a domestic corporation engaged in furnishing telephone service to which section 46(c)(3)(B)(iii) applies (or of a wholly owned domestic subsidiary of such a corporation), if such cable is part of a submarine cable system which constitutes part of a communication link exclusively between the United States and one or more foreign countries;

(x) any property (other than a vessel or an aircraft) of a United States person which is used in international or territorial waters within the northern portion of the Western Hemisphere for the purpose of exploring for, developing, removing, or transporting resources from ocean waters or deposits under such waters, and

(xi) any property described in subsection (1)(3)(A)(ix) which is owned by a United States person and which is used in international or territorial waters to generate energy for use in the United States.

For purposes of clause (x), the term "northern portion of the Western Hemisphere" means the area lying west of the 30th meridian west of Greenwich, east of the international dateline, and north of the Equator, but not including any foreign country which is a country of South America.

* * * * * * * * * * * *

(4) Property used by certain tax-exempt organizations.—Property used by an organization (other than a cooperative described in section 521) which is exempt from the tax imposed by this chapter shall be treated as section 38 property only if such property is used predominantly in an unrelated trade or business the income of which is subject to tax under section 511. If the property is debt-financed property (as defined in [4]*section 514(b)*, the basis or cost of such property for purposes of computing qualified investment under section 46(c) shall include only that percentage of the basis or cost which is the same percentage as is used under [5]*section 514(a)*, for the year the property is placed in service, in computing the amount of gross income to be taken into account during such taxable year with respect to such property. If any qualified rehabilitated building is used by the tax-exempt organization pursuant to a lease, this paragraph shall not apply to that portion of the basis of such building which is attributable to qualified rehabilitation expenditures.

(5) Property used by governmental units or foreign persons or entities.—

(A) In general.—Property used—

(i) by the United States, any State or political subdivision thereof, any possession of the United States, or any agency or instrumentality of any of the foregoing, or

---

⟦Footnote ¶2874⟧ Section 1275(c)(5), '86 TRA, struck out from Sec. 48(a)(2)(B)(vii):
(1) "or which is entitled to the benefits of section 934(b)"
Effective date (Sec. 1277(a), '86 TRA).—Generally applies to taxable years beginning after 12-31-86. For special rules, see ¶2068.

Section 1272(d)(5), '86 TRA, struck out from Sec. 48(a)(2)(B)(vii):
(2) "932,"
Effective date (Sec. 1277(a), '86 TRA).—Generally applies to taxable years beginning after 12-31-86. For special rules, see ¶2068.

Section 1275(c)(5), '86 TRA, struck out from Sec. 48(a)(2)(B)(vii):
(3) ", or 934(c),"
Effective date (Sec. 1277(a), '86 TRA).—Generally applies to taxable years beginning after 12-31-86. For special rules, see ¶2068.

Matter in *italics* in Sec. 48(a)(4), (5)(B)(iii), (D), and (E) added by section 1802(a)(4)(C), (5)(B), and (9)(A), '86 TRA, which struck out:
(4) "section 514(c)"
(5) "section 514(b)"

Code §48(a)(5) ¶2874

(ii) by any foreign person or entity (as defined in section 168(j)(4)(C)), but only with respect to property to which section 168(j)(4)(A)(iii) applies (determined after the application of section 168(j)(4)(B)),

shall not be treated as section 38 property.

(B) Exception for short-term leases.—

(i) In general.—This paragraph and paragraph (4) shall not apply to any property by reason of use under a lease with a term of less than 6 months (determined under section 168(j)(6)).

(ii) Exceptions for certain oil drilling property and certain containers.—For purposes of this paragraph and paragraph (4), clause (i) shall be applied by substituting the lease term limitation in section 168(j)(3)(C)(ii) for the lease term limitation in clause (i) in the case of property which is leased to a foreign person or entity or—

(I) which is used in offshore drilling for oil and gas (including drilling vessels, barges, platforms, and drilling equipment) and support vessels with respect to such property, or

(II) which is a container described in section 48(a)(2)(B)(v) (without regard to whether such container is used outside the United States) or container, chassis or trailer but only if such container, chassis, or trailer has a present class life of not more than 6 years.[6]

(C) Exception for qualified rehabilitated buildings leased to governments, etc.— If any qualified rehabilitated building is leased to a governmental unit (or a foreign person or entity), this paragraph shall not apply to that portion of the basis of such building which is attributable to qualified rehabilitation expenditures.

(D) *Special rules for partnerships, etc.—For purposes of this paragraph and paragraph (4), rules similar to the rules of paragraphs (8) and (9) of section 168(j) shall apply.*

[7](E) Cross reference.—

* * * * * * * * * * * * *

(b) New Section 38 Property.—For purposes of this subpart

(1) In general.—The term "new section 38 property" means section 38 property the original use of which commences with the taxpayer. *Such term includes any section 38 property the reconstruction of which is completed by the taxpayer, but only with respect to that portion of the basis which is properly attributable to such reconstruction.*

(2) Special rule for sale-leasebacks.—For purposes of *the first sentence of* paragraph (1), in the case of any section 38 property which—

(A) is originally placed in service by a person, and

(B) is sold and leased back by such person, or is leased to such person, within 3 months [8]*after* the date such property was originally placed in service,

such property shall be treated as originally placed in service not earlier than the date on which such property is used under the [9]*leaseback (or lease) referred to in subparagraph (B). The preceding sentence shall not apply to any property if the lessee and lessor of such property make an election under this sentence. Such an election, once made, may be revoked only with the consent of the Secretary.*

(d) Certain Leased Property.—

[**Footnote ¶2874 continued**]

(6) "(iii) Exception for certain aircraft.—

(I) In general.—In the case of any aircraft used under a qualifying lease (as defined in section 47(a)(7)(C)) and which is leased to a foreign person or entity before January 1, 1990, clause (i) shall be applied to substituting "3 years" for "6 months".

(II) Recapture period extended.—For purposes of applying subparagraph (B) of section 47(a)(5) and paragraph (1) of section 47(a), there shall not be taken into account any period of a lease to which subclause (I) applies."

(7) "(D)"

Effective date (Sec. 1881, '86 TRA and section 31(g), '84 TRA, as amended by section 1802(a)(2)(F) and (10), '86 TRA).—Generally applies—(A) to property placed in service by the taxpayer after 5-23-83, in taxable years ending after such date, and

(B) to property placed in service by the taxpayer on or before 5-23-83, if the lease to the tax-exempt entity is entered into after 5-23-83.

For special and transitional rules, see footnote ¶2935-A.

Matter in *italics* in Sec. 48(b)(1) and (2) added by section 1809(e)(1) and (2), '86 TRA, which struck out:

(8) "of"

(9) "lease"

Effective date (Sec. 1881, '86 TRA and section 114(b), '86 TRA).—Applies to property originally placed in service after 4-11-84 (determined without regard to amendment).

---

* * * * * * * * * * * *

(4) Property to which paragraph (2) applies.—Paragraph (2) shall apply only to property which—

   (A) is new section 38 property,

   (B) has a class life (determined under section 167(m)) in excess of 14 years,

   (C) is leased for a period which is less than 80 percent of its class life, and

   (D) is not leased subject to a net lease (within the meaning of [10]*section 57(c)(1)(B) (as in effect on the day before the date of the enactment of the Tax Reform Act of 1986.*

* * * * * * * * * * * *

(6) Coordination with at-risk rules.—

* * * * * * * * * * * *

   (C) Lessee subject to at-risk limitations.—

     (i) In general.—In the case of any lease where—

      (I) the lessee is an at-risk lessee,

      (II) the property is at-risk property, and

      (III) the at-risk percentage is less than the required percentage,

any credit allowable under section 38 to the lessee by reason of an election under this subsection (hereinafter in this paragraph referred to as the "total credit") shall be allowable only as provided in subparagraph (D).

     (ii) At-risk percentage.—For purposes of this paragraph, the term "at-risk percentage" means the percentage obtained by dividing—

      (I) the present value (as of the time the lease is entered into) of the aggregate lease at-risk payments, by

      (II) the lessee acquisition amount.

For purposes of subclause (I), the present value shall be determined by using a discount rate equal to the *underpayment* rate in effect under section 6621 as of the time the lease is entered into.

[Footnote ¶2874 continued]

Matter in *italics* in Sec. 48(d)(4)(D) added by section 701(e)(4)(C), '86 TRA, which struck out:
(10) "section 57(c)(1)(B)"
Effective date (Sec. 701(f), '86 TRA).—Generally applies to taxable years beginning after 12-31-86. For special and transitional rule, see footnote ¶2879.

Matter in *italics* in Sec. 48(d)(6)(C)(ii) added by section 1511(c)(3), '86 TRA.
Effective date (Sec. 1511(d), '86 TRA).—Applies for purposes of determining interest for periods after 12-31-86.

Matter in *italics* in Sec. 48(g) added by section 251(b), '86 TRA, which struck out:
(11) "(1) Qualified rehabilitated building defined.—
(A) In general.—The term "qualified rehabilitated building" means any building (and its structural components)—
(i) which has been substantially rehabilitated,
(ii) which was placed in service before the beginning of the rehabilitation, and
(iii) 75 percent or more of the existing external walls of which are retained in place as external walls in the rehabilitation process.
(B) 30 years must have elapsed since construction.—In the case of a builing other than a certified historic structure, a building shall not be qualified rehabilitated building unless there is a period of at least 30 years between the date the physical work on the rehabilitation began and the date the building was first placed in service.
(C) Substantially rehabilitated defined.—
(i) In general.—For purposes of subparagraph (A)(i), a building shall be treated as having been substantially rehabilitated only if the qualified rehabilitation expenditures during the 24-month period selected by the taxpayer (at the time and in the manner prescribed by regulations) and ending with or within the taxable year exceed the greater of—
(I) the adjusted basis of such property, or
(II) $5,000.
The adjusted basis of the building (and its structural components), shall be determined as of the beginning of the first day of such 24-month period, or of the holding period of the building (and its structural components), (within the meaning of section 1250(e)), whichever is later. For purposes of the preceding sentence, the determination of the beginning of the holding period shall be made without regard to any reconstruction by the taxpayer in connection with the rehabilitation.
(ii) Special rule for phased rehabilitation.—In the case of any rehabilitation which may reasonably be expected to be completed in phases set forth in architectural plans and specifications completed before the rehabilitation begins, clause (i) shall be applied by substituting "60-month period" for "24-month period."
(iii) Lessees.—The Secretary shall prescribe by regulation rules for applying this provision to lessees.
(D) Reconstruction.—Rehabilitation includes reconstruction.

Code §48(a)(6) ¶2874

(iii) Required percentage.—For purposes of clause (i)(III), the term "required percentage" means the sum of—

(I) 2 times the sum of the percentages applicable to the property under section 46(a), plus

(II) 10 percent.

In the case of 3-year property, such term means 60 percent of the required percentage determined under the preceding sentence.

(iv) Lessee acquisition amount.—For purposes of this paragraph, the term "lessee acquisition amount" means the amount for which the lessee is treated as having acquired the property by reason of an election under this subsection.

(v) Lease at-risk payment.—For purposes of this paragraph, the term "lease at-risk payment" means any rental payment—

(I) which the lessee is required to make under the lease in all events, and

(II) with respect to which the lessee is not protected against loss through nonrecourse financing, guarantees, stop-loss agreements, or other similar arrangements.

* * * * * * * * * * * *

(g) **Special Rules for Qualified Rehabilitated Buildings.**—For purposes of this subpart—

[11](1)   *Qualified rehabilitation building.—For purposes of this subsection—*

(A)   In general.—The term "qualified rehabilitated building" means any building (and its structural components) if—

(i)   such building has been substantially rehabilitated,

(ii)   such building was placed in service before the beginning of the rehabilitation, and

(iii)   in the case of any building other than a certified historic structure, in the rehabilitation process—

(I)   50 percent or more of the existing external walls of such building are retained in place as external walls,

(II)   75 percent or more of the existing external walls of such building are retained in place as internal or external walls, and

(III)   75 percent or more of the existing internal structural framework of such building is retained in place.

【Footnote ¶2874 continued】

(E) Alternative test for definition of qualified rehabilitated building.—The requirement in clause (iii) of subparagraph (A) shall be deemed to be satisfied if in the rehabilitation process—

(i) 50 percent or more of the existing external walls of the buildings are retained in place as external walls,

(ii) 75 percent or more of the existing external walls of such buildings are retained in place as internal or external walls, and

(iii) 75 percent or more of the existing internal structural framework of such building is retained in place.

(2) Qualified rehabilitation expenditure defined.—

(A) In general.—The term "qualified rehabilitation expenditure" means any amount properly chargeable to capital account which is incurred after December 31, 1981—

(i) for real property (or additions or improvements to real property) which have a recovery period (within the meaning of section 168) of 19 (15 years years in the case of low-income housing) years, and

(ii) in connection with the rehabilitation of a qualified rehabilitation building,

(B) Certain expenditures not included.—The term "qualified rehabilitation expenditure" does not include—

(i) Accelerated methods of depreciation may not be used.—Any expenditures with respect to which an election has not been made under section 168(b)(3) (to use the straight-line method of depreciation). The preceding sentence shall not apply to any expenditure to the extent subsection (f)(12) or (j) of section 168 applies to such expenditure.

(ii) Cost of aquisition.—The cost of acquiring any building or interest therein.

(iii) Enlargements.—Any expenditure attributable to the enlargement of an existing building.

(iv) Certified historic structure, etc.—Any expenditure attributable to the rehabilitation of a certified historic structure or a building in a registered historic district, unless the rehabilitation is a certified rehabilitation (within the meaning of the subparagraph (C)). The preceding sentence shall not apply to a building in a registered historic district if—

(I) such building was not a certified historic structure,

(II) the Secretary of the Interior certified to the Secretary that such building is not of historic significance to the district, and

(III) if the certification referred to in subclause (II) occurs after the beginning of the rehabilitation of such building, the taxpayer certifies to the Secretary that, at the beginning of such rehabilitation, he in good faith was not aware of the requirements of subclause (II).

(v) Expenditure of lessee.—Any expenditure of a lessee of a building if, on the date of the rehabilitation is completed, the remaining term of the lease (determined without regard to any renewal periods) is less that 19 year (15 years in the case of low-income housing).

    (B) Building must be first placed in service before 1936.—In the case of a building other than a certified historic structure, a building shall not be a qualified rehabilitation building unless the building was first placed in service before 1936.

    (C) Substantially rehabilitated defined.—

      (i) In general.—For purposes of subparagraph (A)(i), a building shall be treated as having been substantially rehabilitated only if the qualified rehabilitation expenditures during the 24-month period selected by the taxpayer (at the time and in the manner prescribed by regulations) and ending with or within the taxable year exceed the greater of—

        (I) the adjusted basis of such building (and its structural components), or

        (II) $5,000.

    The adjusted basis of the building (and its structural component) shall be determined as of the beginning of the 1st day of such 24-month period, or of the holding period of the building, whichever is later. For purposes of the preceding sentence, the determination of the beginning of the holding period shall be made without regard to any reconstruction by the taxpayer in connection with the rehabilitation.

      (ii) Special rule for phased rehabilitation.—In the case of any rehabilitation which may reasonably be expected to be completed in phases set forth in architectural plans and specifications completed before the rehabilitation begins, clause (i) shall be applied by substituting "60-month period" for "24-month period".

      (iii) Lessees.—The Secretary shall prescribe by regulation rules for applying this subparagraph to lessees.

    (D) Reconstruction.—Rehabilitation includes reconstruction.

  (2) Qualified rehabilitation expenditure defined.—For purposes of this section—

    (A) In general.—The term "quaified rehabilitation expenditure" means any amount properly chargeable to capital account—

      (i) for property for which depreciation is allowable under section 168 and which is—

        (I) nonresidential real property,

        (II) residential rental property,

        (III) real property which has a class life of more than 12.5 years, or

        (IV) an addition or improvement to property or housing described in subclause (I), (II), or (III), and

      (ii) in connection with the rehabilitation of a qualified rehabilitated building.

⟦Footnote ¶2874 continued⟧

  (vi) Tax exempt use property.—

  (I) In general.—Any expenditure in connection with the rehabilitation of a building which is allocable to that portion of such building which is (or may reasonably by expected to be) tax-exempt use property (within the meaning of section 168(j)).

  (II) Clause not to apply for purposes of paragraph (1)(c).—This clause shall not apply for purposes of determining under paragraph (1)(C) whether a building has been substantially rehabilitated.

  (C) Certified rehabilitation.—For purposes of subparagraph (B), the term "certified rehabilitation" means any rehabilitation of a certified historic structure which the Secretary of the Interior has certified to the Secretary as being consistent with the historic character of such property or the district in which such property is located.

  (D) Low-income housing.—For purposes of subparagraph (B), the term "low-income housing" has the meaning given such term by section 168(c)(2)(F).

  (3) Certified historic structure defined.—

  (A) In general.—The term "certified historic structure" means any building (and its structural components) which—

  (i) is listed in the National Register, or

  (ii) is located in a registered historic district and is certified by the Secretary of the Interior to the Secretary as being of historic signficance to the district.

  (B) Registered historic district.—The term "registered historic district" means—

  (i) any district listed in the National Register, and

  (ii) any district—

  (I) which is designated under a statute of the appropriate State or local government, if such statute is certified by the Secretary of the Interior to the Secretary as containing criteria which will substantially achieve the purpose of preserving and rehabilitating buildings of historic significance to the district, and

  (II) which is certified by the Secretary of the Interior to the Secretary as meeting substantially all of the requirements for the listing of districts in the National Register.

  (4) Property treated as new section 38 property.—Property which is treated as section 38 property by reason of subsection (a)(1)(E) shall be treated as new section 38 property."

  Effective date (Sec 251(d), '86 TRA).—Generally applies to property placed in service after 12-31-86, in taxable years ending after such date. For special and transitional rules, see footnote ¶2872.

Code §48(g)(2) ¶2874

(B)   *Certain expenditures not included.—The term "qualified rehabilitation expenditure" does not include—*

(i)   *Straight line depreciation must be used.—Any expenditure with respect to which the taxpayer does not use the straight line method over a recovery period determined under subsection (c) or (g) of section 168. The preceding sentence shall not apply to any expenditure to the extent the alternative depreciation system of section 168(g) applies to such expenditure by reason of subparagraph (B) or (C) of section 168(g)(1).*

(ii)   *Cost of acquisition.—The cost of acquiring any building or interest therein.*

(iii)   *Enlargements.—Any expenditure attributable to the enlargement of an existing building.*

(iv)   *Certified historic structure, etc.—Any expenditure attributable to the rehabilitation of a certified historic structure or a building in a registered historic district, unless the rehabilitation is a certified rehabilitation (within the meaning of subparagraph (C)). The preceding sentence shall not apply to a building in a registered historic district if—*

(I)   *such building was not a certified historic structure,*

(II)   *the Secretary of the Interior certified to the Secretary that such building is not of historic significance to the district, and*

(III)   *if the certification referred to in subclause (II) occurs after the beginning of the rehabilitation of such building, the taxpayer certifies to the Secretary that, at the beginning of such rehabilitation, he in good faith was not aware of the requirement of subclause (II).*

(v)   *Tax-exempt use property.—*

(I)   *In general.—Any expenditure in connection with the rehabilitation of a building which is allocable to that portion of such building which is (or may reasonably be expected to be) tax-exempt use property (within the meaning of section 168(h)).*

(II)   *Clause not to apply for purposes of paragraph (1)(c).—This clause shall not apply for purposes of determining under paragraph (1)(C) whether a building has been substantially rehabilitated.*

*(vi)   *Expenditures of lessee.—Any expenditure of a lessee of a building if, on the date the rehabilitation is completed, the remaining term of the lease (determined without regard to any renewal periods) is less than the recovery period determined under section 168(c).*

(C)   *Certified rehabilitation.—For purposes of subparagraph (B), the term "certified rehabilitation" means any rehabilitation of a certified historic structure which the Secretary of the Interior has certified to the Secretary as being consistent with the historic character of such property or the district in which such property is located.*

(D)   *Nonresidential real property; residential property; class life.—For purposes of subparagraph (A), the terms "nonresidential real property", "residential rental property", and "class life" have the respective meansing given such terms by section 168.*

(3)   *Certified historic structure defined.—For purposes of this subsection—*

(A)   *In general.—The term "certified historic structure" means any building (and its structural components) which—*

(i)   *is listed in the National Register, or*

(ii)   *is located in a registered historic district and is certified by the Secretary of the Interior to the Secretary as being of historic significance to the district.*

(B)   *Registered historic district.—The term "registered historic district" means—*

(i)   *any district listed in the National Register, and*

(ii)   *any district—*

(I)   *which is designated under a statute of the appropriate State or local government, if such statute is certified by the Secretary of the Interior to the Secretary as containing criteria which will substantially achieve the purpose of preserving and rehabilitating buildings of historic significance to the district, and*

(II)   *which is certified by the Secretary of the Interior of the Secretary as meeting substantially all of the requirements for the listing of districts in the National Register.*

[Footnote ¶2874 continued]

*Sec. 48(g)(2)(B)(vi)(I), before its amendment by Sec. 251(b), '86 TRA was amended by Sec. 1802(a)(9)(B), '86 TRA, which struck out the number "(3)" from "section 168(j)(3)".

Effective date (Sec. 1881, '86 TRA and section 31(g), '84 TRA, as amended by section 1802(a)(2)(F) and (10), '86 TRA.—See above.

   (4)   Property treated as new section 38 property.—Property which is treated as section 38 property by reason of subsection (a)(1)(E) shall be treated as new section 38 property.

* * * * * * * * * * * *

   (5)   Specially defined energy property.—The term "specially defined energy property" means—

      (A) a recuperator,
      (B) a heat wheel,
      (C) a regenerator,
      (D) a heat exchanger,
      (E) a waste heat boiler,
      (F) a heat pipe,
      (G) an automatic energy control system,
      (H) a turbulator,
      (I)   a preheater,
      (J)   a combustible gas recovery system,
      (K) an economizer,
      (L)   modifications to alumina electrolytic cells,
      (M) modifications to chlor-alkali electrolytic cells, or
      (N) any other property of a kind specified by the Secretary by regulations,

the principal purpose of which is reducing the amount of energy consumed in any existing industrial or commercial process and which is installed in connection with an existing industrial or commercial facility. The Secretary shall not specify any property under subparagraph (N) unless he determines that such specification meets the requirements of paragraph (9) of [12]*section 23(c)* for specification of items under [13]*section 23(c)(4)(A)(viii)*

* * * * * * * * * * * *

(q)   Basis Adjustment to Section 38 Property.—

* * * * * * * * * * * *

   (3)   Special rule for qualified rehabilitated buildings.—In the case of any credit determined under section 46(a) for any qualified rehabilitation expenditure in connection with a qualified rehabilitated building[14] paragraphs (1) and (2) of this subsection and paragraph (5) of subsection (d) shall be applied without regard to the phrase "50 percent of".

* * * * * * * * * * * *

  [15]**(7)   Special rule for qualified films.—**

* * * * * * * * * * * *

(r)   *Certain Section 501(d) Organizations.—*

   (1)   In general.—In the case of eligible section 501(d) organizations—
     (A)   any business engaged in by such organization for the common benefit of its members and the taxable income from which is included in the gross income of its members shall be treated as an unrelated business for purposes of paragraph (4) of subsection (a),
     (B)   the qualified investment for each taxable year with respect to such business shall be apportioned pro rata among such members in the same manner as the taxable income of such organization, and

---

【Footnote ¶2874 continued】

Matter in *italics* in Sec. 48(l)(5) added by section 1847(b)(6), '86 TRA, which struck out:
(12)   "section 44C(c)"
(13)   "section 23(c)(4)(A)(viii)"
Effective date   (Sec. 1881, '86 TRA and section 475(a), '84 TRA).—Applies to taxable years beginning after 12-31-83, and to carrybacks from such years.

Section 251(c), '86 TRA, struck out from Sec. 48(q)(3):
(14)   "other than a certified historic structure"
Effective date   (Sec. 251(d), '86 TRA).—Generally applies to property placed in service after 12-31-86, in taxable years ending after such date. For transitional and special rules, see footnote ¶2872.

Matter in *italics* in Sec. 48(q)(7) added by section 1809(d)(2), '86 TRA, which struck out:
(15)   "(6)"
Effective date   (Sec. 1881, '86 TRA and section 113(c)(2)(C), '84 TRA, and section 205(c)(1), '82 TEFRA).—Generally applies to periods after 12-31-82.

Code §48(r)(1)   ¶2874

(C)   any individual to whom any investment has been apportioned under subparagraph (B) shall be treated for purposes of this subpart (other than section 47) as the taxpayer with respect to such investment, and such investment shall not (by reason of such apportionment) lose its character as an investment in new section 38 property or used section 38 property, as the case may be.

(2)   Limitation on used section 38 property applied at organization level.—The limitation under subparagraph (A) of subsection (c)(2) shall apply with respect to the section 501(d) organization.

(3)   Recapture.—For purposes of applying section 47 to any property for which credit was allowed under section 38 by reason of this subsection—

(A)   the section 501(d) organization shall be treated as the taxpayer to which the credit under section 38 was allowed,

(B)   the amount of such credit allowed with respect to the property shall be treated as the amount which would have been allowed to the section 501(d) organization were such credit allowable to such organization,

(C)   subparagraph (D) of section 47(a)(5) shall not apply, and

(D)   the amount of the increase in tax under section 47 for any taxable year with respect to property to which this subsection applies shall be allocated pro rata among the members of such organization in the same manner as such organization's taxable income for such year is allocated among such members.

(4)   No investment credit allowed to member if member claims other investment credit.—No credit shall be allowed to an individual by reason of this subsection if such individual claims a credit under section 38 without regard to this subsection. The amount of the credit not allowed by reason of the preceding sentence shall not be allowed to any other person.

(5)   Eligible section 501(d) organization.—For purposes of this subsection, the term "eligible section 501(d) organization" means any organization—

(A)   which elects to be treated as an organization described in section 501(d) and which is exempt from tax under section 501(a), and

(B)   which does not provide a substantially higher standard of living for any person or persons than it does for the majority of the members of the community.

[16]*(s)*   **Special Rules Relating to Sound Recordings. —**

* * * * * * * * * * *

(5)   Sound Recording.—[17]*For purposes of this subsection, the term "sound recording" means works which result from the fixation of a series of musical, spoken, or other sounds, regardless of the nature of the material objects (such as discs, tapes, or other phonorecordings) in which sounds are embodied.*

* * * * * * * * * * * *

(s)   [should read (t)] Cross Reference.—
For application of this subpart to certain acquiring corporations, see section 381(c)(26).

[For official explanation, see Committee Reports, ¶4057; 4136; 4194; 4143; 3931; 4075; 3878; 4161; 4193.]

【Footnote ¶2874 continued】

Matter in *italics* in Sec. 48(r) and (s) added by section 1879(j)(1), '86 TRA, which struck out:
(16)   "(r)"
Effective date (Sec. 1879(j)(2) and (3), '86 TRA).—Generally applies to periods after 12-31-78 (under rules similar to the rules of section 48(m) of the '54 Code), in taxable years ending after such date.

* * * * * * * * * * *

(3)   Special rule.—If refund or credit of any overpayment of tax resulting from the application of this subsection is prevented at any time before the close of the date which is 1 year after the date of the enactment of this Act by operation of any law or rule of law (including res judicata), refund or credit of such overpayment (to the extent attributable to the application of the amendments made by this subsection) may, nevertheless, be made or allowed if claim therefor is filed before the close of such 1-year period.

Matter in *italics* in Sec. 48(s)(5), [former (r)(5)] added by section 803(b)(2)(B), '86 TRA, which struck out:
(17)   "For purposes of this subsection, the term 'sound recording' means any sound recording described in section 280(c)(2)."
Effective date (Sec. 803(d)(1), '86 TRA).—Generally applies to costs incurred after 12-31-86, in taxable years ending after such date. For transitional and special rules, see footnote ¶2961-A.

〔¶2875〕 CODE SEC. 49. TERMINATION OF REGULAR PERCENTAGE.

(a) General Rule.—For purposes of determining the amount of the investment tax credit determined under section 46, the regular percentage shall not apply to any property placed in service after December 31, 1985.

(b) Exceptions.—Subject to the provisions of subsections (c) and (d), subsection (a) shall not apply to the following:

(1) Transition property.—Property which is transition property (within the meaning of subsection (e)).

(2) Qualified progress expenditure for periods before January 1, 1986.—In the case of any taxpayer who had made an election under section 46(d)(6), the portion of the adjusted basis of any progress expenditure property attributable to qualified progress expenditures for periods before January 1, 1986.

(3) Qualified timber property.—The portion of the adjusted basis of qualified timber property which is treated as section 38 property under section 48(a)(1)(F).

(c) 35-Percent reduction in credit for taxable years after 1986.—

(1) Reduction in current year investment credit.—Any portion of the current year business credit under section 38(b) for any taxable year beginning after June 30, 1987, which is attributable to the regular investment credit shall be reduced by 35 percent.

(2) Unexpired carryforwards to 1st taxable year beginning after June 30, 1987.—Any portion of the business credit carryforward under section 38(a)(1) attributable to the regular investment credit which has not expired as of the close of the taxable year preceding the 1st taxable year of the taxpayer beginning after June 30, 1987, shall be reduced by 35 percent.

(3) Special rule for taxable years beginning before and ending after July 1, 1987.—In the case of any taxable year beginning before and ending after July 1, 1987—

(A) any portion of the current year business credit under section 38(b) for such taxable year, or

(B) any portion of the business credit carryforward under section 38(a)(1) to such year,

which is attributable to the regular investment credit shall be reduced by the applicable percentage.

(4) Treatment of disallowed credit.—

(A) **In general.**—The amount of the reduction of the regular investment credit under paragraphs (1) and (2) shall not be allowed as a credit for any taxable year.

〔Footnote ¶2875〕 Sec. 49. added by section 211(a), '86 TRA.

Effective date (Sec. 211(e)(1), (2) and (4), '86 TRA).—(1) Generally applies to property placed in service after 12-31-85, in taxable years ending after such date.

(2) Exceptions for certain films.—For purposes of determining whether any property is transition property within the meaning of section 49(e) of the '86 Code—

(A) in the case of any motion picture or television fim, construction shall be treated as including production for purposes of section 203(b)(1) of this Act, and written contemporary evidence of an agreement (in accordance with industry practice) shall be treated as a written binding contract for such purposes,

(B) in the case of any television film, a license agreement or agreement for production services between a television network and a producer shall be treated as a binding contract for purposes of section 203(b)(1)(A) of this Act, and

(C) a motion picture film shall be treated as a described in section 203(b)(1)(A) of this Act if—

(i) funds were raised pursuant to a public offering before 9-26-85, for the production of such film,

(ii) 40 percent of the funds raised pursuant to such public offering are being spent on films the production of which commenced before such date, and

(iii) all of the films funded by such public offering are required to be distributed pursuant to distribution agreements entered into before 9-26-85.

＊ ＊ ＊ ＊ ＊ ＊ ＊ ＊ ＊ ＊ ＊

(4) Additional exceptions.—

(A) Paragraphs (c) and (d) of section 49 of the '54 Code shall not apply to any continuous caster facility for slabs and blooms which is subject to a lease and which is part of a project the second phase of which is a continuous slab caster which was placed is service before 12-31-35.

(B) For purposes of determining whether an automobile manufacturing facility (including equipment and incidental appurtenances) is transition property within the meaning of section 49(e), property with respect to which the Board of Directors of an automobile manufacturer formally approved the plan for the project on 1-7-85 shall be treated as transition property, but only with respect to $70 million of regular investment tax credits.

(B) **No carryback for year straddling July 1, 1987; gross up of carryforwards.**—The amount of the reduction of the regular investment credit under paragraph (3)—

    (i)   may not be carried back to any taxable year, but

    (ii)   shall be added to the carryforwards from the taxable year before applying paragraph (2).

(5) **Definitions and special rules.**—For purposes of this subsection—

    (A) **Applicable percentage.**—The term "applicable percentage" means, with respect to a taxable year beginning before and ending after July 1, 1987, the percentage which bears the same ratio to 35 percent as—

        (i)   the number of months in such taxable year after June 30, 1987, bears to

        (ii)   the number of months in such taxable year.

    (B) **Regular investment credit.**—

        (i) **In general.**—The term "regular investment credit" has the meaning given such term by section 48(o).

        (ii) **Exception for timber property.**—The term "regular investment credit" shall not include any portion of the regular investment credit which is attributable to section 38 property described in section 48(a)(1)(F).

    (C) **Portion of credits attributable to regular investment credit.**—The portion of any current year business credit or business credit carryforward which is attributable to the regular investment credit shall be determined on the basis that the regular investment credit is used first.

(d) **Full basis adjustment.**—

    (1) **In general.**—In the case of periods after December 31, 1985, section 48(q) (relating to basis adjustment to section 38 property) shall be applied with respect to transaction property—

        (A)   by substituting "100 percent" for "50 percent" in paragraph (1), and

        (B)   without regard to paragraph (4) thereof (relating to election of reduced credit in lieu of basis adjustment).

    (2) **Special rule for qualified progress expenditures.**—If the taxpayer made an election under section 48(q)(4) with respect to any qualified progress expenditures for periods before January 1, 1986—

        (A)   paragraph (1) shall not apply to the portion of the adjusted basis attributable to such expenditures, and

        (B)   such election shall not apply to such expenditures for periods after December 31, 1985.

(e) **Transition Property.**—For purposes of this section—

    (1) **Transition property.**—The term "transition property" means any property placed in service after December 31, 1985, and to which the amendments made by section 201 of the Tax Reform Act of 1986 do not apply, except that in making such determination—

        (A)   section 203(a)(1)(A) of such Act shall be applied by substituting "1985" for "1986",

        (B)   sections 203(b)(1) and 204(a)(3) of such Act shall be applied by substituting "December 31, 1985" for "March 1, 1986",

        (C)   in the case of transition property with a class life of less than 7 years—

            (i)   section 203(b)(2) of such Act shall apply, and

            (ii)   in the case of property with a class life—

                (I)   of less than 5 years, the applicable date shall be July 1, 1986, and

                (II)   at least 5 years, but less than 7 years, the applicable date shall be January 1, 1987, and

        (D)   section 203(b)(3) shall be applied by substituting "1986" for "1987".

    (2) **Treatment of progress expenditures.**—No progress expenditures for periods after December 31, 1985, with respect to any property shall be taken into account for purposes of applying the regular percentage unless it is reasonable to except that such property will be transition property when placed in service. If any progress expenditures are taken into account by reason of the preceding sentence and subsequently there is not a reasonable expectation that such property would be transition property when placed in service, the credits attributable to progress expenditures with respect to such property shall be recaptured under section 47.

[For official explanation, see Committee Reports, ¶3870.]

〔¶2876〕 CODE SEC. 51. AMOUNT OF CREDIT.

(a) Determination of Amount.—For purposes of section 38, the amount of the target jobs credit determined under this section for the taxable year shall be [1] *equal to 40 percent of the qualified first-year wages for such year.*

(b) Qualified Wages Defined.—For purposes of this subpart—

(1) **In general.**—The term "qualified wages" means the wages paid or incurred by the employer during the taxable year to individuals who are member of a targeted group.

(2) **Qualified first-year wages.**—The term "qualified first-year wages" means, with respect to any individual, qualified wages attributable to service rendered during the 1-year period beginning with the day the individual begins work for the employer.[2]

[3](3) **Only first $6,000 of wages per year taken into account.**—The amount of the qualified first-year wages[4] which may be taken into account with respect to any individual shall not exceed $6,000 per year.

(c) Wages Defined.—For purposes of this subpart—

* * * * * * * * * * * * *

(3) **Termination.**—The term "wages" shall not include any amount paid or incurred to an individual who begins work for the employer after [5]*December 31, 1988.*

(d) Members of Targeted Groups.—For purposes of this subpart—

* * * * * * * * * * * * *

(12) **Qualified summer youth employee.**—

(A) **In general.**—The term "qualified summer youth employee" means an individual—

(i) who performs services for the employer between May 1 and September 15,

(ii) who is certified by the designated local agency a having attained age 16 but not 18 on the hiring date (or if later, on May 1 of the calendar year involved).

(iii) who has not been an employee of the employer during the period prior to the 90-day period described in subparagraph (B)(iii), and

(iv) who is certified by the designated local agency as being a member of an economically disadvantaged family (as determined under paragraph (11)).

(B) **Special rules for determining amount of credit.**—For purposes of applying this subpart to wages paid or incurred to any qualified summer youth employee—

(i) subsection (a)(1) shall be applied by substituting "85 percent" for [6]"40 percent",[7]

[8]*(ii)* subsections (b)(2) shall be applied by substituting "any 90-day period between May 1 and September 15" for the "1-year period beginning with the day the individual begins work for the employer," and

[9]*(iii)* subsection [10]*(b)(3)* shall be applied by substituting $3,000" for $6,000".

* * * * * * * * * * * *

〔Footnote ¶2876〕 Matter in *italics* in Sec. 51(a)—(c) and (i) added by section 1701(a)—(c), '86 TRA, which struck out:

(1) "the sum of—
(1) 50 percent of the qualified first-year wages for such year, and
(2) 25 percent of the qualified second-year wages for such year."
(2) "(3) **Qualified second-year wages.**—The term 'qualified second-year wages' means, with respect to any individual, the qualified wages attributable to service rendered during the 1-year period beginning on the day after the last day of the 1-year period with respect to such individual determined under paragraph (2)."
(3) "(4)"
(4) ", and the amount of the qualified second-year wages,"
(5) "December 31, 1985"
(6) "50 percent"
(7) "(ii) subsections (a)(2) and (b)(3) shall not apply,"
(8) "(iii)"
(9) "(iv)"
(10) "(b)(4)"

Effective date (Sec. 1701(e), '86 TRA).—Applies with respect to individuals who begin work for the employer after 12-31-85.

Matter in *italics* in Sec. 51(k) added by section 1878(f)(1), '86 TRA, which sruck out:

(i)   **Certain Individuals Ineligible.—**

* * * * * * * * * * * * *

(3)   Individuals not meeting minimum employment period.—No wages shall be taken into account under subsection (a) with respect to any individual unless such individual either—

(A)   is employed by the employer at least 90 days (14 days in the case of an individual described in subsection (d)(12)), or

(B)   has completed at least 120 hours (20 hours in the case of an individual described in subsection (d)(12)) of services performed for the employer.

* * * * * * * * * * * * *

[11] *(k)*   **Election to Have Targeted Jobs Credit Not Apply.—**

* * * * * * * * * * * * *

[For official explanation, see Committee Reports, ¶4123; 4192.]

[¶2877]   CODE SEC. 53. CREDIT FOR PRIOR YEAR MINIMUM TAX LIABILITY.

(a)   **Allowance of Credit**—There shall be allowed as a credit against the tax imposed by this chapter for any taxable year an amount equal to the minimum tax credit for such taxable year.

(b)   **Minimum Tax Credit.—**For purposes of subsection (a), the minimum tax credit for any taxable year is the excess (if any) of—

(1)   the adjusted net minimum tax imposed for all prior taxable years beginning after 1986, over

(2)   the amount allowable as a credit under subsection (a) for such prior taxable years.

(c)   **Limitation.—**The credit allowable under subsection (a) for any taxable year shall not exceed the excess (if any) of—

(1)   the regular tax liability of the taxpayer for such taxable year reduced by the sum of the credits allowable under subparts A, B, D, E, and F of this part, over

(2)   the tentative minimum tax for the taxable year.

(d)   **Definitions.—**For purposes of this section—

(1)   **Net minimum tax.—**

(A)   In general.—The term "net minimum tax" means the tax imposed by section 55.

(B)   Credit not allowed for exclusion preferences.—

(i)   Adjusted net minimum tax.—The adjusted net minimum tax for any taxable year is—

(I)   the amount of the net minimum tax for such taxable year, reduced by

(II)   the amount which would be the net minimum tax for such taxable year if the only adjustments and items of tax preference taken into account were those specified in clause (ii).

(ii)   Specified items.—The following are specified in this clause—

(I)   the adjustments provided for in subsections (b)(1) and (c)(3) of section 56, and

(II)   the items of tax preference described in paragraphs (1), (5), and (6) of section 57(a).

In the case of taxable years beginning after 1989, the adjustments provided in section 56(g) shall be treated as specified in this clause to the extent attributable to items which are excluded from gross income for any taxable year for purposes of the regular tax, or are not deductible for any taxable year under the adjusted earnings and profits method of section 56(g).

(2)   **Tentative minimum tax.—**The term "tentative minimum tax" has the meaning given to such term by section 55(b).

[For official explanation, see Committee Reports, ¶3931.]

[Footnote ¶2876 continued]

(11)   "(j)"

Effective date (Sec. 1881, '86 TRA and 1041(c)(5), '84 TRA).—Generally applies to individuals who begin work for the employer after 7-18-84. Under a special rule for employees performing services for other persons, Sec. 51(k)(2) applies to individuals who begin work for the employer after 12-31-84.

[Footnote ¶2877]   Sec. 53 added by section 701(b), '86 TRA.

Effective date (Sec. 701(f)(1), '86 TRA).—Generally applies to taxable years beginning after 12-31-86. For special rules see footnote ¶2879.

≫**P-H CAUTION**→ There are two versions of Sec. 55. Sec. 55, generally effective after 12-31-86, follows. For Sec. 55, generally effective before 1-1-87, see ¶2878-A, below.

〖¶2878〗 CODE SEC. 55. ALTERNATIVE MINIMUM TAX IMPOSED.

(a) General rule.—There is hereby imposed (in addition to any other tax imposed by this subtitle) a tax equal to the excess (if any) of—

    (1) the tentative minimum tax for the taxable year, over

    (2) the regular tax for the taxable year.

(b) Tentative Minimum Tax.—For purposes of this part—

    (1) In general.—The tentative minimum tax for the taxable year is—

      (A) 20 percent (21 percent in the case of a taxpayer other than a corporation) of so much of the alternative minimum taxable income for the taxable year as exceeds the exemption amount, reduced by

      (B) the alternative minimum tax foreign tax credit for the taxable year.

    (2) Alternative minimum taxable income.—The term "alternative minimum taxable income" means the taxable income of the taxpayer for the taxable year—

      (A) determined with the adjustments provided in section 56 and section 58, and

      (B) increased by the amount of the items of tax preference described in section 57.

(c) Regular tax.—

    (1) In general.—For purposes of this section, the term "regular tax" means the regular tax liability for the taxable year (as defined in section 26(b)) reduced by the foreign tax credit allowable under section 27(a). Such term shall not include any tax imposed by section 402(e) and shall not include any increase in tax under section 47 *or section 42(j).*

    (2) Cross references.—For provisions providing that certain credits are not allowable against the tax imposed by this section, see sections 26(a), 28(d)(2), 29(b)(5), and 38(c).

(d) Exemption amount.—For purposes of this section—

    (1) Exemption amount for taxpayers other than corporations.—In the case of a taxpayer other than a corporation, the term "exemption amount" means—

      (A) $40,000 in the case of—

        (i) a joint return, or

        (ii) a surviving spouse,

      (B) $30,000 in a case of an individual who—

        (i) is not a married individual, and

        (ii) is not a surviving spouse, and

      (C) $20,000 in the case of—

        (i) a married individual who files a separate return, or

        (ii) an estate or trust.

For purposes of this paragraph, the term "surviving spouse" has the meaning given to such term by section 2(a), and marital statuts shall be determined under section 7703.

    (2) Corporations.—In the case of a corporation, the term "exemption amount" means $40,000.

〖Footnote ¶2878〗   Sec. 55 added by section 701(a), '86 TRA.

Effective date (Sec. 701(f)(1) and (2)(A), '86 TRA).—(1) Generally applies to taxable years beginning after 12-31-86.

(2) **Adjustment of net operating loss.**—

(A) **Individuals.**—In the case of a net operating loss of an individual for a taxable year beginning after 12-31-82 and before 1-1-87, for purposes of determining the amount of such loss which may be carried to a taxable year beginning after 12-31-86, for purposes of the minimum tax, such loss shall be adjusted in the manner provided in section 55(d)(2) of the '54 Code as in effect on the day before the date of the enactment of this Act.

For special rules, see ¶2879.

Matter in *italics* in Sec. 55(c)(1) added by section 252(c), '86 TRA.

Effective date (Sec. 252(e), '86 TRA).—Applies to buildings placed in service after 12-31-86, in taxable years ending after such date. For special and transitional rules see footnote ¶2871.

(3) **Phase-out of exemption amount.**—The exemption amount of any taxpayer shall be reduced (but not below zero) by an amount equal to 25 percent of the amount by which the alternative minimum taxable income of the taxpayer exceeds—

(A) $150,000 in the case of a taxpayer described in paragraph (1)(A) or (2),

(B) $112,500 in the case of a taxpayer described in paragraph (1)(B), and

(C) $75,000 in the case of a taxpayer described in paragraph (1)(C).

≫**P-H CAUTION**→ There are two versions of Sec. 55. Sec. 55 generally effective before 1-1-87, follows. For Sec. 55, generally effective after 12-31-86, see ¶2878, above.

【¶2878-A】 CODE SEC. 55. ALTERNATIVE MINIMUM TAX FOR TAXPAYERS OTHER THAN CORPORATIONS.

* * * * * * * * * * * *

(c) **Credits.**—

* * * * * * * * * * * *

(2) **Foreign tax credit allowed against alternative minimum tax.**—

* * * * * * * * * * * *

(E) Special rule for applying section 904(c).—In determining the amount of foreign taxes paid or accrued during the taxable year which may be deemed to be paid or accrued in a preceding or succeeding taxable year under section 904(c)—

(i) the limitation of section 904(a) shall be [1]*deemed to be the amount of foreign tax credit tax credit allowable under section 27(a) in computing the regular tax for the taxable year increased by the amount of the limitation determined under subparagraph (C), and*

(ii) any increase under subparagraph (B) shall be taken into account.

(3) **Carryover and carryback of certain credits.**—In the case of any taxable year for which a tax is imposed by this section, for purposes of determining the amount of any carryover or carryback to any other taxable year of any credit allowable under section 23, 25, 30 or 38, the amount of the limitation under section 26, 30(g), or 38(c) (as the case may be) shall be deemed to be—

(A) the amount of such [2]*credit allowable* for such taxable year (determined without regard to this paragraph), reduced (but not below zero) by

(B) the amount of the tax imposed by this section for the taxable year, reduced by—

(i) the amount of the credit allowable under section 27(a),

(ii) in the case of the limitation under section 30(g), the amount of such tax taken into account under this subparagraph with respect to the limitation under section 26, and

(iii) in the case of the limitation under section 38(c), the amount of such tax taken into account under this subparagraph with respect to limitations under sections 26 and 30(g).

* * * * * * * * * * * *

[For official explanation, see Committee Reports, ¶4161.]

≫**P-H CAUTION**→There are two versions of Sec. 56. Sec. 56, generally effective after 12-31-86, follows. For Sec. 56, generally effective before 1-1-87, see ¶2879-A, below.

【¶2879】 CODE SEC. 56. ADJUSTMENTS IN COMPUTING ALTERNATIVE MINIMUM TAXABLE INCOME.

(a) **Adjustments Applicable To All Taxpayers.**—In determining the amount of the

【Footnote ¶2878-A】 Matter in *italics* in Sec. 55(c)(2)(E)(i) added by section 1847(a)(2), '86 TRA, which struck out:

(1) "increased by the amount of the limitation determined under subparagraph (C), and"

Effective date (Sec. 1847(a)(2), '86 TRA).—Effective with respect to taxable years beginning after 12-31-82.

Matter in *italics* in Sec. 55(c)(3)(A) added by section 1847(a)(1), '86 TRA, which struck out:

(2) "limitation"

Effective date (Sec. 1881, '86 TRA, and section 475(a), '84 TRA).—Applies to taxable years beginning after 12-31-83, and to carrybacks from such years.

【Footnote ¶2879】 Sec. 56 added by section 701(a), '86 TRA.

Effective Date (Sec. 701(f), '86 TRA).—(1) Generally applies to taxable years beginning after 12-31-86.

(2) Adjustment of net operating loss.—

(A) Individuals.—In the case of a net operating loss of an individual for a taxable year beginning after 12-31-82, for purposes of determining the amount of such loss which may be carried to a taxable year beginning after 12-31-86, purposes of the minimum tax, such loss shall be adjusted in the manner provided in section 55(d)(2) of the '54 Code as in effect on the day before the date of the enactment of this Act.

alternative minimum taxable income for any taxable year the following treatment shall apply (in lieu of the treatment applicable for purposes of computing the regular tax):

(1) Depreciation.—

    (A) In General.—

        (i) Property other than certain real property.—Except as provided in clause (ii), the depreciation deduction allowable under section 167 with respect to any tangible property placed in service after December 31, 1986, shall be determined under the alternative system of section 168(g).

        (ii) 150-percent declining balance method for certain property.—The method of depreciation used shall be—

            (I) the 150 percent declining balance method,

            (II) switching to the straight line method for the 1st taxable year for which using the straight line method with respect to the adjusted basis as of the beginning of the year will yield a higher allowance.

[Footnote ¶2879 continued]

    (B) Corporations.—If the minimum tax of a corporation was deferred under section 56(b) of the '54 Code (as in effect on the day before the date of the enactment of this Act) for any taxable year beginning before 1-1-87, and the amount of such tax has not been paid for any taxable year beginning before 1-1-87, the amount of the net operating loss carryovers of such coporation which may be carried to taxable years beginning after 12-31-86, for purposes of the minimum tax shall be reduced by the amount of tax preferences a tax on which was so deferred.

    (3) Installment sales.—Section 56(a)(6) of the '86 Code (as amended by this section) shall not apply to any disposition to which the amendments made by section 811 of thi Act (relating to allocation of dealer's indebtedness to installment obligations) do not apply by reason of section 811(c)(2) of this Act..

    (4) Exception for charitable contributions before August 16, 1986.—Section 57(a)(6) of the '86 Code (as amended by this section) shall not apply to any deduction attributable to contributions made before 8-16-86.

    (5) Book income.—

    (A) In general.—In the case of a corporation to which this paragraph applies, the amount of any increase for any taxable year under section 56(c)(1)(A) of the '86 Code (as added by this section) shall be reduced (but not below zero) by the excess (if any) of—

    (i) 50 percent of the excess of taxable income for the 5-taxable year period ending with the taxable year preceding the 1st taxable year to which such section applies over the adjusted net book income for such period, over

    (ii) the aggregate amounts taken into account under this paragraph for preceding taxable years.

    (B) Taxpayer to whom paragraph applies.—This paragraph applies to a taxpayer which was incorporated in Delaware on 5-31-12.

    (C) Terms.—Any term used in this paragraph which is used in section 56 of such Code (as so added) shall have the same meaning as when used in such section.

    (6) Certain public utility.—

    (A) In the case of investment tax credits described in subparagraph (B) or (C), subsection 38(c)(3)(A)(ii) of the '86 Code shall be applied by substituting "25 percent" for "75 percent", and section 38(c)(3)(B) of the '86 Code shall be applied by substituting "75 percent" for "25 percent".

    (B) If, on 9-25-85, a regulated electric utility owned an undivided interest, within the range of 1,111 and 1,149, in the "maximum dependable capacity, net, megawatts electric" of an electric generating unit located in Illinois or Mississippi for which a binding written contract was in effect on 12-31-80, then any investment tax credit with respect to such unit shall be described in this subparagraph. The aggregate amount of investment tax credits with respect to such unit should be described in this subparagraph.

    (C) If, on 9-25-85, a regulated electric utility owned an undivided interest, within the range of 1,104 and 1,111 in the "maximum dependable capacity, net, megawatts electric" of an electric generating unit located in Louisiana for which a binding written contract was in effect on 12-31-80, then any investment tax credit of such electric utility shall be described in this subparagraph. The aggregate amount of investment tax credits allowed solely by reason of being described by thi subparagraph shall not exceed $20,000,000.

The preceding sentence shall not apply to any section 1250 property (as defined in section 1250(c)) or to any other property if the depreciation deduction determined under section 168 with respect to such other property for purposes of the regular tax is determined by using the straight line method.

(B) Exception for certain property.—This paragraph shall not apply to property described in paragraph (1), (2), (3), or (4) of section 168(f).

(C) Coordination with transitional rules.—

(i) In general.—This paragraph shall not apply to property placed in service after December 31, 1986, to which the amendments made by section 201 of the Tax Reform Act of 1986 do not apply.

(ii) Treatment of certain property placed in service before 1987.—This paragraph shall apply to any property to which the amendments made by section 201 of the Tax Reform Act of 1986 apply by reason of an election under section 203(a)(1)(B) of such Act without regard to the requirement of subparagraph (A) that the property be placed in service after December 31, 1986.

(D) Normalization rules.—With respect to public utility property described in section 167(1)(3)(A), the Secretary shall prescribe the requirements of a normalization method of accounting for this section.

(2) **Mining exploraion and development costs.—**

(A) In general.—With respect to each mine or other natural deposit (other than an oil, gas, or geothermal well) of the taxpayer, the amount allowable as a deduction under section 616(a) or 617(a) (determined without regard to section 291(b)) in computing the regular tax for costs paid or incurred after December 31, 1986, shall be capitalized and amortized ratably over the 10-year period beginning with the taxable year in which the expenditures were made.

(B) Loss allowed.—If a loss is sustained with respect to any property described for the expenditures described in subparagraph (A) for the taxable year in which such loss is sustained in an amount equal to the lesser of—

(i) the amount allowable under section 165(a) for the expenditures if they had remained capitalized, or

(ii) the amount of such expenditures which have not previously been amortized under subparagraph (A).

(3) **Treatment of certain long-term contracts.—**In the case of any long-term contract entered into by the taxpayer on or after March 1, 1986, the taxable income from such contract shall be determined under the percentage of completion method of accounting (as modified by section 460(b)).

(4) **Alternative tax net operating loss deduction.—**The alternative tax net operating loss deduction shall be allowed in lieu of the net operating loss deduction allowed under section 172.

(5) **Pollution control facilities.—**In the case of any certified pollution control facility placed in service after December 31, 1986, the deduction allowable under section 169 (without regard to section 291) shall be determined under the alternative system of section 168(g).

(6) **Installment sales of certain property.—**In the case of any—

(A) disposition after March 1, 1986, of property described in section 1221(1), or

(B) other disposition if an obligation arising from such disposition would be an applicable installment obligation (as defined in section 453C(e)) to which section 453C applies,

income from such disposition shall be determined without regard to the installment method under section 453 or 453A and all payments to be received for the disposition shall be deemed received in the taxable year of the disposition. This paragraph shall not apply to any disposition with respect to which an election is in effect under section 453C(e)(4).

(7) **Adjusted basis.—**The adjusted basis of any property to which paragraph (1) or (5) applies (or with respect to which there are any expenditures to which paragraph (2) or subsection (b)(2) applies) shall be determined on the basis of the treatment prescribed in paragraph (1), (2), or (5), or subsection (b)(2), whichever applies.

(b) **Adjustments Applicable to Individuals.—**In determining the amount of the alternative minimum taxable income of any taxpayer (other than a corporation), the following treatment shall apply (in lieu of the treatment applicable for purposes of computing the regular tax):

(1) Limitation on itemized deductions.—

(A) In general.—No deduction shall be allowed—

(i) for any miscellaneous itemized deduction (as defined in section 67(b)), or

(ii) for any taxes described in paragraph (1), (2), or (3) of section 164(a).

Clause (ii) shall not apply to any amount allowable in computing adjusted gross income.

(B) Medical expenses.—In determining the amount allowable as a deduction under section 213, subsection (a) of section 213 shall be applied by substituting "10 percent" for "7.5 percent".

(C) Interest.—In determining the amount allowable as a deduction for interest, subsections (d) and (h) of section 163 shall apply, except that—

(i) in lieu of the exception under section 163(h)(2)(D), the term "personal interest" shall not include any qualified housing interest (as defined in subsection (e)),

(ii) sections 163(d)(6) and 163(h)(6) (relating to phase-ins) shall not apply, and

(iii) interest on any specified private activity bond (and any amount treated as interest on a specified activity bond under section 56(a)(5)(B)), and any deduction referred to in section 57(a)(5)(A), shall be treated as includible in gross income (or as deductible) for purposes of applying section 163(d).

(D) Treatment of certain recoveries.—No recovery of any tax to which subparagraph (A)(ii) applied shall be included in gross income for purposes of determining alternative minimum taxable income.

(E) Standard deduction not allowed.—The standard deduction provided in section 63(c) shall not be allowed.

(2) Circulation and research and experimental expenditures.—

(A) In general.—The amount allowable as a deduction under section 173 or 174(a) in computing the regular tax for amounts paid or incurred after December 31, 1986, shall be capitalized and—

(i) in the case of circulation expenditures described in section 173, shall be amortized ratably over the 3-year period beginning with the taxable year in which the expenditures were made, or

(ii) in the case of research and experimental expenditures described in section 174(a), shall be amortized ratably over the 10-year period beginning with the taxable year in which the expenditures were made.

(B) Loss allowed.—If a loss is sustained with respect to any property described in subparagraph (A), a deduction shall be allowed for the expenditures described in subparagraph (A) for the taxable year in which such loss is sustained in an amount equal to the lesser of—

(i) the amount allowable under section 165(a) for the expenditures if they had remained capitalized, or

(ii) the amount of such expenditures which have not previously been amortized under subparagraph (A).

(C) Special rule for personal holding companies.—In the case of circulation expenditures described in section 173, the adjustments provided in this paragraph shall apply also to a personal holding company (as defined in section 542).

(c) Adjustments Applicable to Corporations.—In determining the amount of the alternative minimum taxable income of a corporation, the following treatment shall apply:

(1) Adjustment for book income or adjusted earnings and profits.—

(A) Book income adjustments.—For taxable years beginning in 1987, 1988, and 1989, alternative minimum taxable income shall be adjusted as provided under subsection (f).

(B) Adjusted earnings and profits.—For taxable years beginning after 1989, alternative minimum taxable income shall be adjusted as provided under subsection (g).

(2) Merchant marine capital construction funds.—In the case of a capital construction fund established under section 607 of the Merchant Marine Act, 1936 (46 U.S.C. 1177)—

(A) subparagraphs (A), (B), and (C) of section 7518(c)(1) (and the corresponding provisions of such section 607) shall not apply to—

(i) any amount deposited in such fund after December 31, 1986, or

Code §56(c)(2) ¶2879

(ii) any earnings (including gains and losses) after December 31, 1986, on amounts in such fund, and

(B) no reduction in basis shall be made under section 7518(f) (or the corresponding provisions of such section 607) with respect to the withdrawal from the fund of any amount to which subparagraph (A) applies.

For purposes of this paragraph, any withdrawal of deposits or earnings from the fund shall be treated as allocable first to deposits made before (and earnings received or accrued before) January 1, 1987.

(3) Special Deduction for certain organizations not allowed.—The deduction determined under section 833(b) shall not be allowed.

(d) Alternative tax net operating loss deduction defined.—

(1) In general.—For purposes of subsection (a)(4), the term "alternative tax net operating loss deduction" means the net operating loss deduction allowable for the taxable year under section 172, except that—

(A) the amount of such deduction shall not exceed 90 percent of alternative minimum taxable income determined without regard to such deduction, and

(B) in determining the amount of such deduction—

(i) the net operating loss (within the meaning of section 172(c)) for any loss year shall be adjusted as provided in paragraph (2), and

(ii) in the case of taxable years beginning after December 31, 1986, section 172(b)(2) shall be applied by substituting "90 percent of alternative minimum taxable income determined without regard to the alternative tax net operating loss deduction" for "taxable income" each place it appears.

(2) Adjustments to net operating loss computation.—

(A) Post-1986 loss years.—In the case of a loss year beginning after December 31, 1986, the net operating loss for such year under section 172(c) shall—

(i) be determined with the adjustments provided in this section and section 58, and

(ii) be reduced by the items of tax preference determined under section 57 for such year (other than subsection (a)(6) thereof).

(B) Pre-1987 years.—In the case of loss years beginning before January 1, 1987, the amount of the net operating loss which may be carried over to taxable years beginning after December 31, 1986, for purposes of paragraph (2), shall be equal to the amount which may be carried from the loss year to the first taxable year of the taxpayer beginning after December 31, 1986.

(e) Qualified housing interest.—For purposes of this part—

(1) In general.—The term "qualified housing interest" means interest which is paid or accrued during the taxable year on indebtedness which is incurred in acquiring, constructing, or substantially rehabilitating any property which—

(A) is the principal residence (within the meaning of section 1034) of the taxpayer at the time such interest accrues or is paid, or

(B) is a qualified dwelling which is a qualified residence (within the meaning of section 163(h)(3)).

Such term also includes interest on any indebtedness resulting from the refinancing of indebtedness meeting the requirements of the preceding sentence; but only to the extent that the amount of the indebtedness resulting from such refinancing does not exceed the amount of the refinanced indebtedness immediately before the refinancing.

(2) Qualified dwelling.—The term "qualified dwelling" means any—

(A) house,

(B) apartment,

(C) condominium, or

(D) mobile home not used on a transient basis (within the meaning of section 7701(a)(19)(C)(v)),

including all structures or other property appurtenant thereto.

(3) Special rule for indebtedness incurred before July 1, 1982.—The term "qualified housing interest" includes interest paid or accrued on indebtedness which—

(A) was incurred by the taxpayer before July 1, 1982, and

(B) is secured by property which, at the time such indebtedness was incurred, was—

(i) the principal residence (within the meaning of section 1034) of the taxpayer, or

(ii) a qualified dwelling used by the taxpayer (or any member of his family (within the meaning of section 267(c)(4))).

(f) Adjustments for book income of corporations.—

(1) In general.—The alternative minimum taxable income of any corporation for any taxable year beginning in 1987, 1988, or 1989 shall be increased by 50 percent of the amount (if any) by which—

(A) the adjusted net book income of the corporation, exceeds

(B) the alternative minimum taxable income for the taxable year (determined without regard to this subsection and the alternative tax net operating loss deduction).

(2) Adjusted net book income.—For purposes of this subsection—

(A) In general.—The term "adjusted net book income" means the net income or loss of the taxpayer set forth on the taxpayer's applicable financial statement, adjusted as provided in this paragraph.

(B) Adjustments for certain taxes.—The amount determined under subparagraph (A) shall be appropriately adjusted to disregard any Federal income taxes, or income, war profits, or excess profits taxes imposed by any foreign country or possession of the United States, which are directly or indirectly taken into account on the taxpayer's applicable financial statement. The preceding sentence shall not apply to any such taxes imposed by a foreign country or possession of the United States if the taxpayer does not choose to take, to any extent, the benefits of section 901.

(C) Special rules for related corporations.—

(i) Consolidated returns.—If the taxpayer files a consolidated return for any taxable year, adjusted net book income for such taxable year shall take into account items on the taxpayer's applicable financial statement which are properly allocable to members of such group included on such return.

(ii) Treatment of dividends.—In the case of any corporation which is not included on a consolidated return with the taxpayer, adjusted net book income shall take into account the earnings of such other corporation only to the extent of the sum of the dividends received from such other corporation and other amounts required to be included in gross income under this chapter in respect of the earnings of such other corporation.

(D) Statements covering different periods.—Appropriate adjustments shall be made in adjusted net book income in any case in which an applicable financial statement covers a period other than the taxable year.

(E) Special rule for cooperatives.—In the case of a cooperative to which section 1381 applies, the amount determined under subparagraph (A) shall be reduced by the amounts referred to in section 1382(b) (relating to patronage dividends and per-unit retain allocations) to the extent such amounts were not otherwise taken into account in determining adjusted net book income.

(F) Treatment of dividends from 936 corporations.—

(i) In general.—In determining the amount of adjusted net book income, any dividend received from a corporation eligible for the credit provided by section 936 shall be increased by the amount of any withholding tax paid to a possession of the United States with respect to such dividend.

(ii) Treatment as foreign taxes.—

(I) In general.—50 percent of any withholding tax paid to a possession of the United States with respect to dividends referred to in clause (i) (to the extent such dividends do not exceed the excess referred to in paragraph (1), determined without regard to clause (i)) shall, for purposes of this part, be treated as a tax paid by the corporation receiving the dividend to a foreign country.

(II) Treatment of taxes imposed on 936 corporation.—For purposes of this subparagraph, taxes paid by any corporation eligible for the credit provided by section 936 to a possession of the United States, shall be treated as a withholding tax paid with respect to any dividend paid by such corporation to the extent such taxes would be treated as paid by the corporation receiving the dividend under rules similar to the rules of section 902.

(G) Rules for Alaska Native Corporations.—The amount determined under subparagraph (A) shall be appropriately adjusted to allow:

(i) cost recovery and depletion attributable to property the basis of which is determined under section 21(c) of the Alaska Native Claims Settlement Act (43 U.S.C. 1620(c)), and

(ii) deductions for amounts payable made pursuant to section 7(i) or section 7(j) of such Act (43 U.S.C. 1606(i) and 1606(j)) only at such time as the deductions are allowed for tax purposes.

(H) Secretarial authority to adjust items.—Under regulations, adjusted net book income shall be properly adjusted to prevent the omission or duplication of any item.

(3) **Applicable financial statement.**—For purposes of this subsection—

(A) In general.—The term "applicable financial statement" means, with respect to any taxable year, any statement covering such taxable year—

(i) which is required to be filed with the Securities and Exchange Commission,

(ii) which is a certified audited income statement to be used for the purposes of a statement or report—

(I) for credit purposes,

(II) to shareholders, or

(III) for any other substantial nontax purpose,

(iii) which is an income statement required to be provided to—

(I) the Federal Government or any agency thereof,

(II) a State government or any agency thereof, or

(III) a political subdivision of a State or any agency thereof, or

(iv) which is an income statement to be used for the purposes of a statement or report—

(I) for credit purposes,

(II) to shareholders, or

(III) for any other substantial nontax purpose.

(B) Earnings and profits used in certain cases.—

If—

(i) a taxpayer has no applicable financial statement, or

(ii) a taxpayer has only a statement described in subparagraph (A)(iv) and the taxpayer elects the application of this subparagraph,

the net income or loss set forth on the taxpayer's applicable financial statement shall, for purposes of paragraph (3)(A), be treated as being equal to the taxpayer's earnings and profits for the taxable year (without diminution by reason of distributions during the tax year). Such election, once made, shall remain in effect for any taxable year for which the taxpayer is described in this subparagraph unless revoked with the consent of the Secretary.

(C) Special rule where more than 1 statement.—For purposes of subparagraph (A), if a taxpayer has a statement described in more than 1 clause or subclause, the applicable financial statement shall be the statement described in the clause or subclause with the lowest number designation.

(4) **Exception for certain corporations.**—This subsection shall not apply to any S corporation, regulated investment company, real estate investment trust, or REMIC.

(g) **Adjustments based on adjusted current earnings.—**

(1) **In general.**—The alternative minimum taxable income of any corporation for any taxable year beginning after 1989 shall be increased by 75 percent of the excess (if any) of—

(A) the adjusted current earning of the corporation, over

(B) the alternative minimum taxable income (determined without regard to this subsection and the alternative tax net operating loss deduction).

(2) **Allowance of negative adjustments.—**

(A) In general.—The alternative minimum taxable income for any corporation of any taxable year beginning after 1989, shall be reduced by 75 percent of the excess (if any) of—

(i) the amount referred to in subparagraph (B) of paragraph (1), over

(ii) the amount referred to in subparagraph (A) of paragraph (1).

(B) Limitation.—The reduction under subparagrph (A) for any taxable year shall not exceed the excess (if any) of—

(i) the aggregate increases in alternative minimum taxable income under paragraph (1) for prior taxable years, over

(ii) the aggregate reductions under subparagraph (A) of this paragraph for prior taxable years.

(3) Adjusted current earnings.—For purposes of this subsection, the term "adjusted current earnings" means the alternative minimum taxable income for the taxable year—

(A) determined with the adjustments provided in paragraph (4), and

(B) determined without regard to this subsection and the alternative tax net operating loss deduction.

(4) Adjustments.—In determining adjusted current earnings, the following adjustments shall apply:

(A) Depreciation.—

(i) Property placed in service after 1989.—The depreciation deduction with respect to any property place in service in a taxable year beginning after 1989 shall be determined under whichever of the following methods yields deductions with a smaller present value:

(I) The alternative system of section 168(g), or

(II) The method used for book purposes.

(iii) Property to which new ACRS system applies.—In the case of any property to which the amendments made by section 201 of the Tax Reform Act of 1986 apply and which is placed in service in a taxable year beginning before 1990, the depreciation deduction shall be determined—

(I) by taking into account the adjusted basis of such property (as determined for purposes of computing alternative minimum taxable income) as of the close of the last taxable year beginning before January 1, 1990, and

(II) by using the straight-line method over the remainder of the recovery period applicable to such property under the alternative system of section 168(g).

(iii) Property to which original ACRS system applies.—In the case of any property to which section 168 (as in effect on the day before the date of the enactment of the Tax Reform Act of 1986 and without regard to subsection (d)(1)(A)(ii) thereof) applies, the depreciation deduction shall be determined—

(I) by taking into account the adjusted basis of such property (as determined for purposes of computing the regular tax) as of the close of the last taxable year beginning before January 1, 1990, and

(II) by using the straight line method over the remainder of the recovery period which would apply to such property under the alternative system of section 168(g).

(iv) Property placed in service before 1981.—In the case of any property not described in clause (i), (ii), or (iii), the amount allowable as depreciation or amortization with respect to such property shall be determined in the same manner as for purposes of computing taxable income.

(v) Slower method used if used for book purposes.—In the case of any property to which clause (ii), (iii), or (iv) applies, if the depreciation method used for book purposes yields deductions for taxable years beginning after 1989 with a smaller present value than the method which would otherwise be used under such clause, the method used for book purposes shall be used in lieu of the method which would otherwise be used under such clause.

(B) Inclusion of items included for purposes of computing earnings and profits.—

(i) In general.—In the case of any amount which is excluded from gross income for purposes of computing alternative minimum taxable income but is taken into account in determining the amount of earnings and profits—

(I) such amount shall be included in income in the same manner as if such amount were includible in gross income for purposes of computing alternative minimum taxable income, and

(II) the amount of such income shall be reduced by any deduction which would have been allowable in computing alternative minimum taxable income if such amount were includible in gross income.

(ii) Inclusion of buildup in life insurance contracts.—In the case of any life insurance contract—

Code §56(g)(4) ¶2879

(I) the income on such contract (as determined under section 7702(g)) for any taxable year shall be treated as includible in gross income for such year, and

(II) there shall be allowed as a deduction that portion of any premium which is attributable to insurance coverage.

(iii) Inclusion of income on annuity contract.—In the case of any annuity contract, the income on such contract (as determined under section 72(u)(2)) shall be treated as includible in gross income for such year.

(C) Disallowance of items not deductible in computing earnings and profits.—

(i) In general.—A deduction shall not be allowed for any item if such item would not be deductible for any taxable year for purposes of computing earnings and profits.

(ii) Special rule for 100-percent dividends.—Clause (i) shall not apply to any deduction allowable under section 243 or 245 for a 100-percent dividend—

(I) if the corporation receiving such dividend and the corporation paying such dividend could not be members of the same affiliated group under section 1504 by reason of section 1504(b),

(II) but only to the extent such dividend is attributable to income of the paying corporation which is subject to tax under this chapter (determined after the application of sections 936 and 921).

For purposes of the preceding sentence, the term "100 percent dividend" means any dividend if the percentage used for purposes of determining the amount allowable as a deduction under section 243 or 245 with respect to such dividend is 100 percent.

(iii) Special rule for dividends from section 936 companies.—In the case of any dividend received from a corporation eligible for the credit provided by section 936, rules similar to the rules of subparagraph (F) of subsection (f)(1) shall apply, except that "75 percent" shall be substituted for "50 percent" in clause (ii)(I) thereof.

(D) Certain other earnings and profits adjustments.—

(i) In general.—The adjustments provided in section 312(n) shall apply; except that—

(I) paragraphs (1), (2), and (3) shall apply only to amounts paid or incurred in taxable years beginning after December 31, 1989,

(II) paragraph (4) shall apply only to taxable years beginning after December 31, 1989,

(III) paragraph (5) shall apply only to installment sales in taxable years beginning after December 31, 1989,

(IV) paragraph (6) shall apply only to contracts entered into on or after March 1, 1986, and

(V) paragraphs (7) and (8) shall not apply.

(ii) Special rule for intangible drilling costs and mineral exploration and development costs.—If—

(I) the present value of the deductions provided under subparagraph (A)-(ii) or (B)(ii) of section 312(n)(2) with respect to amounts paid or incurred in taxable years beginning after December 31, 1989, exceeds

(II) the present value of the deductions for such amounts under the method used for book purposes,

such amounts shall be deductible under the method used for book purposes in lieu of that provided in such subparagraph.

(E) Disallowance of loss on exchange of debt pools.—No loss shall be recognized on the exchange of any pool of debt obligations for another pool of debt obligations having substantially the same effective interest rates and maturities.

(F) Acquisition expenses of life insurance companies.—Acquisition expenses of life insurance companies shall be capitalized and amortized in accordance with the treatment generally required under generally accepted accounting principles as if this subparagraph applied to all taxable years.

(G) Depletion.—The allowances for depletion with respect to any property placed in service in a taxable year beginning after 1989, shall be determined under whichever of the following methods yields deductions with a smaller present value:

(i) cost depletion determined under section 611, or

(ii) the method used for book purposes.

(H) Treatment of certain ownership changes.—If—

(i) there is an ownership change (within the meaning of section 382) after the date of the enactment of the Tax Reform Act of 1986 with respect to any corporation, and,

(ii)(I) the aggregate adjusted bases of the assets of such corporation (immediately after the change), exceed

(II) the value of the stock of such corporation (as determined for purposes of section 382), properly adjusted for liabilities and other relevant items,

then the adjusted basis of each asset of such corporation (as of such time) shall be its proportionate share (determined on the basis of respective fair market values) of the amount referred to in clause (ii)(II).

(5) Other definitions.—For purposes of paragraph (4)—

(A) **Book purposes.**—The term "book purposes" means the treatment for purposes of preparing the applicable financial statement referred to in subsection (f).

(B) **Earnings and profits.**—The term "earnings and profits" means earnings and profits computed for purposes of subchapter C.

(C) **Present value.**—Present value shall be determined as of the time the property is placed in service (or, if later, as of the beginning of the first taxable year beginning after 1989) and under regulations prescribed by the Secretary.

(D) **Treatment of alternative minimum taxable income.**—The treatment of any item for purposes of computing alternative minimum taxable income shall be determined without regard to this subsection.

(6) Exception for certain corporations.—This subsection shall not apply to any S corporation, regulated investment company, real estate investment trust, or REMIC.

[For official explanation, see Committee Reports, ¶3931.]

≫**P-H CAUTION→** There are two versions of Sec. 56. Sec. 56, generally effective before 1-1-87, follows. For Sec. 56, generally effective after 12-31-86, see ¶2879, above.

[¶2879-A]   CODE SEC. 56.   CORPORATE MINIMUM TAX.

* * * * * * * * * * * *

(c) Regular Tax Deduction Defined.—For the purposes of this section, the term "regular tax deduction" means an amount equal to the taxes imposed by this chapter for the taxable year (computed without regard to this part and without regard to the taxes imposed by sections 531 and 541) reduced by the sum of the credits allowable under subparts A, B and D of part IV.[1]

* * * * * * * * * * *

[For official explanation, see Committee Reports, ¶4016.]

[Footnote ¶2879-A]   Section 1171(b)(3), '86 TRA, struck out from Sec. 56(c):

(1) "For purposes of the preceding sentence, the amount of credit determined under section 38 for any taxable year shall be determined without regard to the employee stock ownership credit determined under section 41."

Effective date (Sec. 1171(c), '86 TRA).—(1) Applies to compensation paid or accrued after 12-31-86, in taxable years ending after such date.

(2) Sections 404(i) and 6699 to continue to apply to pre-1987 credits.—The provisions of sections 404(i) and 6699 of the '86 Code shall continue to apply with respect to credits under section 41 of such Code attributable to compensation paid or accrued before 1-1-87 (or under section 38 of such Code with respect to qualified investment before 1-1-83).

≫**P-H CAUTION**→ There are two versions of Sec. 57. Sec. 57, generally effective after 12-31-86, follows. For Sec. 57, generally effective before 1-1-87, see ¶2880-A, below.

〔¶2880〕   CODE SEC. 57.   ITEMS OF TAX PREFERENCE.

(a)   General Rule.—For purposes of this part, the items of tax preference determined under this section are—

(1) Depletion.—With respect to each property (as defined in section 614), the excess of the deduction for depletion allowable under section 611 for the taxable year over the adjusted basis of the property at the end of the taxable year (determined without regard to the depletion deduction for the taxable year).

(2) Intangible drilling costs.—

(A) In general.—With respect to all oil, gas, and geothermal properties of the taxpayer, the amount (if any) by which the amount of the excess intangible drilling costs arising in the taxable year is greater than 65 percent of the net income of the taxpayer from oil, gas, and geothermal properties for the taxable year.

(B) Excess intangible drilling costs.—For purposes of subparagraph (A), the amount of the excess intangible drilling costs arising in the taxable year is the excess of—

(i) the intangible drilling and development costs paid or incurred in connection with oil, gas, and geothermal wells (other than costs incurred in drilling a nonproductive well) allowable under section 263(c) or 291(b) for the taxable year, over

(ii) The amount which would have been allowable for the taxable year if such costs had been capitalized and straight line recovery of intangibles (as defined in subsection (b)) had been used with respect to such costs

(C) Net income from oil, gas, and geothermal properties.—For purposes of subparagraph (A), the amount of the net income of the taxpayer from oil, gas, and geothermal properties for the taxable year is the excess of—

(i) the aggregate amount of gross income (within the meaning of section 613(a)) from all oil, gas, and geothermal properties of the taxpayer received or accrued by the taxpayer during the taxable year, over

(ii) the amount of any deductions allocable to such properties reduced by the excess described in subparagraph (B) for such taxable year.

(D) Paragraph applied separately with respect to geothermal properties and oil and gas properties.—This paragraph shall be applied separately with respect to—

(i) all oil and gas properties which are not described in clause (ii), and

(ii) all properties which are geothermal deposits (as defined in section 613(e)(3)).

(3) Incentive stock options.—

(A) In general.—With respect to the transfer of a share of stock pursuant to the exercise of an incentive stock option (as defined in section 422A), the amount by which the fair market value of the share at the time of exercise exceeds the option price. For purposes of this paragraph, the fair market value of a share of stock shall be determined without regard to any restriction other than a restriction which, by its terms, will never lapse.

(B) Basis adjustment.—In determining the amount of gain or loss recognized for purposes of this part on any disposition of a share of stock acquired pursuant to an exercise (in a taxable year beginning after December 31, 1986) of an incentive stock option, the basis of such stock shall be increased by the amount of the excess referred to in subparagraph (A).

(4) Reserves for losses on bad debts of financial institutions.—In the case of a financial institution to which section 585 or 593 applies, the amount by which the deduction allowable for the taxable year for a reasonable addition to a reserve for bad debts exceeds the amount that would have been allowable had the institution maintained its bad debt reserve for all taxable years on the basis of actual experience.

Code §57(a)(4) ¶2880

(5) **Tax-exempt interest.—**

(A) In general.—Interest on specified private activity bonds reduced by any deduction (not allowable in computing the regular tax) which would have been allowable if such interest were includible in gross income.

(B) Treatment of exempt-interest dividends.—Under regulations prescribed by the Secretary, any exempt-interest dividend (as defined in section 852(b)(5)(A)) shall be treated as interest on a specified private activity bond to the extent of its proportionate share of the interest on such bonds received by the company paying such dividend.

(C) Specified private activity bonds.—

(i) In general.—For purposes of this part, the term "specified private activity bonds" means any private activity bond (as defined in section 141) issued after August 7, 1986.

(ii) Exception for qualified 501(c)(3) Bonds.—For purposes of clause (i), the term "private activity bond" shall not include any qualified 501(c)(3) bond (as defined in section 145).

(iii) Exception for refundings.—For purposes of clause (i), the term "private activity bond" shall not include any refunding bond if the refunded bond (or in the case of a series of refundings, the original bond) was issued before August 8, 1986.

(iv) Certain bonds issued before September 1, 1986.—For purposes of this subparagraph, a bond issued before September 1, 1986, shall be treated as issued before August 8, 1986, unless such bond would be a private activity bond if—

(I) paragraphs (1) and (2) of section 141(b) were applied by substituting "25 percent" for "10 percent" each place it appears,

(II) paragraphs (3), (4), and (5) of section 141(b) did not apply, and

(III) subparagraph (B) of section 141(c)(1) did not apply.

(6) **Appreciated Property charitable deduction.—**

(A) In general.—The amount by which the deduction allowable under section 170 would be reduced if all capital gain property were taken into account at its adjusted basis.

(B) Capital gain property.—For purposes of subparagraph (A), the term "capital gain property" has the meaning given to such term by section 170(b)(1)(C)(iv). Such term shall not include any property to which an election under section 170(b)(1)(C)(iii) applies.

(7) **Accelerated depreciation or amortization on certain property placed in service before January 1, 1987.—**The amounts which would be treated as items of tax preference with respect to the taxpayer under paragraphs (2), (3), (4), and (12) of this subsection (as in effect on the day before the date of the enactment of the Tax Reform Act of 1986). The preceding sentence shall not apply to any property to which section 56(a)(1) or (5) applies.

(b) **Straight line recovery of intangibles defined.—**For purposes of paragraph (2) of subsection (a)—

(1) **In general.—**The term "straight line recovery of intangibles", when used with respect to intangible drilling and development costs for any well, means (except in the case of an election under paragraph (2)) ratable amortization of such costs over the 120-month period beginning with the month in which production from such well begins.

(2) **Election.—**If the taxpayer elects with respect to the intangible drilling and development costs for any well, the term "straight line recovery of intangibles" means any method which would be permitted for purposes of determining cost depletion with respect to such well and which is selected by the taxpayer for purposes of subsection (a)(2).

[For official explanation, see Committee Reports, ¶3931]

≫**P-H CAUTION**→ There are two versions of Sec. 57. Sec. 57, generally effective before 1-1-87, follows. For Sec. 57, generally effective after 12-31-86, see ¶2880, above.

〔¶2880-A〕 CODE SEC. 57. ITEMS OF TAX PREFERENCE.

  (a) In General.—For purposes of this part, the items of tax preference are—

* * * * * * * * * * * *

    (12) Accelerated cost recovery deduction.—

* * * * * * * * * * * *

      (B) 19-year real property and low-income housing.—With respect to each recovery property which is 19-year real property or low-income housing, the amount (if any) by which the deduction allowed under section 168(a) [1]*(or, in the case of property described in section 167(k), under section 167) for the taxable year exceeds the deduction which would have been allowable for the taxable year had the property been depreciated using a straight-line method (without regard to salvage value) over a recovery period of—*

        (i) 19 years in the case of 19-year real property, and

        (ii) 15 years in the case of low-income housing property.

* * * * * * * * * * * *

  (b) Application With Section 291.—

    (1) In general.—

* * * * * * * * * * *

      (B) Iron ore and coal.—In the case of any item of tax preference of a corporation described in paragraph (8) of subsection (a) (but only to the extent such item is allocable to a deduction for depletion for iron ore and coal, [2] *including lignite*), only 71.6 percent of the amount of such item of tax preference (determined without regard to this subsection) shall be taken into account as an item of tax preference.

    (2) Certain capital gains.—In determining the net capital gain of any corporation for purposes of paragraph (9)(B) of subsection (a), there shall be taken into account only 59⅚ percent of any gain from the sale or exchange of section 1250 property which is equal to [3]*80 percent* of the excess determined under section 291(a)(1) with respect to such property.

* * * * * * * * * * * *

≫**P-H CAUTION**→ There are two versions of Sec. 58. Sec. 58, generally effective after 12-31-86, follows. For Sec. 58, generally effective before 1-1-87, see ¶2881-A, below.

[For official explanation, see Committee Reports, ¶4138; 4143.]

〔¶2881〕 CODE SEC. 58. DENIAL OF CERTAIN LOSSES

  (a) Denial of Farm Loss.—

    (1) In general.—For purposes of computing the amount of the alternative minimum taxable income for any taxable year of a taxpayer other than a corporation—

      (A) Disallowance of farm loss.—No loss of the taxpayer for such taxable year from any tax shelter farm activity shall be allowed.

      (B) Deduction in succeeding taxable year.—Any loss from a tax shelter farm activity disallowed under subparagraph (A) shall be treated as a deduction allocable to such activity in the 1st succeeding taxable year.

    (2) Tax shelter farm activity.—For purposes of this subsection, the term "tax shelter farm activity" means—

〔Footnote ¶2880-A〕 Matter in *italics* in Sec. 57(a)(12)(B) added by section 1809(a)(3), '86 TRA, which struck out:

(1) "for the taxable year exceeds the deduction which would have been allowable for a taxable year had the property been depreciated using the straight-line method (without regard to salvage value) over a recovery period of—"

Effective date (Sec. 1881, '86 TRA and section 111(g), '84 TRA).—Generally applies with respect to property placed in service by the taxpayer after 3-15-84. For transitional and special rules, see footnote ¶2935-A.

Matter in *italics* in Sec. 57(b)(1)(B) and (2) added by section 1804(k)(3)(C), '86 TRA, which struck out:

(2) "(including lignite)"

(3) "85 percent"

Effective date (Sec. 1881, '86 TRA and section 68(e)(1), '84 TRA).—Applies to taxable beginning after 12-31-84.

〔Footnote ¶2881〕 Sec. 58 added by section 701(a), '86 TRA.

Effective date (Sec. 701(f)(1), '86 TRA).—Generally applies to taxable years beginning after 12-31-86. For transitional and special rules, see footnote ¶2879.

(A) any farming syndicate as defined in section 464(c) (as modified by section 461(i)(4)(A)), and

(B) any other activity consisting of farming which is a passive activity (within the meaning of section 469(d), without regard to paragraph (1)(B) thereof).

(3) **Application to personal service corporations.**—For purposes of paragraph (1), a personal service corporation (within the meaning of section 469(g)(1)(C)) shall be treated as a taxpayer other than a corporation.

(b) **Disallowance of Passive Activity Loss.**—In computing the alternative minimum taxable income of the taxpayer for any taxable year, section 469 shall apply, except that in applying section 469—

(1) the adjustments of section 56 shall apply.

(2) any deduction to the extent such deduction is an item of tax preference under section 57(a) shall not be taken into account, and

(3) the provisions of section 469(l) (relating to phase-in of disallowance) shall not apply.

(c) **Special Rules.**—For purposes of this section—

(1) **Special rule for insolvent taxpayers.**—

(A) In general.—The amount of losses to which subsection (a) or (b) applies shall be reduced by the amount (if any) by which the taxpayer is insolvent as of the close of the taxable year.

(B) Insolvent.—For purposes of this paragraph, the term "insolvent" means the excess of liabilities over the fair market value of assets.

(2) **Loss allowed for year of disposition of farm shelter activity.**—If the taxpayer disposes of his entire interest in any tax shelter farm activity during any taxable year, the amount of the loss attributable to such activity (determined after carryovers under subsection (a)(1)(B)) shall (to the extent otherwise allowable) be allowed for such taxable year in computing alternative minimum taxable income and not treated as a loss from a tax shelter farm activity.

[For official explanation, see Committee Reports, ¶3931.]

≫P-H CAUTION→ There are two versions of Sec. 58. Sec. 58, generally effective before 1-1-87, follows. For Sec. 58, generally effective after 1-1-86, see ¶2881, above.

【¶2881-A】 CODE SEC. 58. RULES FOR APPLICATION OF THIS PART.

* * * * * * * * * * * *

(c) **Estates and Trusts.**—In the case of an estate or trust the items of tax preference [1] *(and any itemized deductions)* for any taxable year shall be apportioned between the estate or trust and the beneficiaries in accordance with regulations prescribed by the Secretary.

* * * * * * * * * * * *

[For official explanation, see Committee Reports, ¶4189.]

【¶2882】 CODE SEC. 59. OTHER DEFINITIONS AND SPECIAL RULES.

(a) **Alternative Minimum Tax Foreign Tax Credit.**—For purposes of this part—

(1) **In general.**—The alternative minimum tax foreign tax credit for any taxable year shall be the credit which would be determined under section 27(a) for such taxable year if—

(A) the amount determined under section 55(b)(1)(A) were the tax against which such credit was taken for purposes of section 904 for the taxable year and all prior taxable years beginning after December 31, 1986,

(B) section 904 were applied on the basis of alternative minimum taxable income instead of taxable income, and

(C) for purposes of section 904, any increase in alternative minimum taxable income by reason of section 56(c)(1)(A) (relating to adjustment for book income) shall have the same proportionate source (and character) as alternative minimum taxable income determined without regard to such increase.

【Footnote ¶2881-A】 Matter in *italics* in Sec. 58(c) added by section 1875(a), '86 TRA.

Effective date (Sec. 1881, '86 TRA, and section 715, '84 TRA, and section 201(e)(1), '82 TEFRA).—Applies to taxable years beginning after 12-31-82.

【Footnote ¶2882】 Sec. 59 added by section 701(a), '86 TRA.

Effective date (Sec. 701(f)(1), '86 TRA).—Applies to taxable years beginning after 12-31-86. For transitional and special rules, see footnote ¶2879.

(2) Limitation to 90 percent of tax.—

(A) In general.—The alternative minimum tax foreign tax credit for any taxable year shall not exceed the excess (if any) of—

(i) the amount determined under section 55(b)(1)(A) for the taxable year, over

(ii) 10 percent of the amount which would be determined under section 55(b)(1)(A) without regard to the alternative tax net operating loss deduction.

(B) Carryback and carryforward.—If the alternative minimum tax foreign tax credit exceeds the amount determined under subparagraph (A), such excess shall, for purposes of this part, be treated as anamount to which section 904(c) applies.

(b) Minimum Tax Not To Apply to Income Eligible for Section 936 Credit.—In the case of any sorporation for which a credit is allowable for the taxale year under section 936, alternative minimum taxable income shall not include any amount with respect to which the requirements of subparagraph (A) or (B) of section 936(a)(1) are met.

(c) Treatment of Estates and Trusts.—In the case of any estate or trust, the alternative minimum taxable income of such estate or trust and any beneficiary thereof shall be determined by applying part I of subchapter J with the adjustments provided in this part.

(d) Apportionment of Differently Treated Items in Case of Certain Entities.—

(1) In general.—The differently treated items for the taxable year shall be apportioned (in accordance with regulations prescribed by the Secretary)—

(A) Regulated investment companies and real estate investment trusts.—In the case of a regulated investment company to which part I of subchapter M applies or a real estate investment company to which part II of subchapter M applies, between such company or trust and shareholders and holders of beneficial interest in such company or trust.

(B) Common trust funds.—In the case of a common trust fund (as defined in section 584(a)), pro rata among the participants of such fund.

(2) Differently treated items.—For purposes of this section, the term 'differently treated item' means any item of tax preference or any other item which is treated differently for purposes of this part than for purposes of computing the regular tax.

(e) Optional 10-Year Writeoff of Certain Tax Preferences.—

(1) In general.—For purposes of this title, any qualified expenditure to which an election under this paragraph applies shall be allowed as a deduction ratably over the 10-year period (3-year period in the case of circulation expenditures described in section 173) beginning with the taxable year in which such expenditure was made.

(2) Qualified expenditure.—For purposes of this subsection, the term 'qualified expenditure' menas any amount which, but for an election under this subsection, would have been allowable as a deduction for the taxable year in which paid or incurred under—

(A) section 173 (relating to circulation expenditures),

(B) section 174(a) (relating to research and experimental expenditures),

(C) section 263(c) (relating to intangible drilling and development expenditures),

(D) section 616(a) (relating to development expenditures), or

(E) section 617(a) (relating to mining exploration expenditures).

(3) Other sections not applicable.—Except as provided in this subsection, no deduction shall be allowed under any other section for any qualified expenditure to which an election under this subsection applies.

(4) Election.—

(A) In general.—An election may be made under paragraph (1) with respect to any portion of any qualified expenditure.

(B) Revocable only with consent.—Any election under this subsection may be revoked only with the consent of the Secretary.

(C) Partners and shareholders of S corporations.—In the case of a partnership, any election under paragraph (1) shall be made separatily by each partner with respect to the partner's allocable share of any qualified expenditure. A similar rule shall apply in the case of an S corporation and its shareholders.

(5) Dispositions.—

(A) Application of section 1254.—In the case of any disposition of property to which section 1254 applies (determined without regard to this section), any deduction under paragraph (1) with respect to amounts which are allocable to such property shall, for purposes of section 1254, be treated as a deduction allowable under section 263(c), 616(a), or 617(a), whichever is appropriate.

(B) Application of section 617(d).—In the case of any disposition of mining property to which section 617(d) applies (determined without regard to this subsection), any deduction under paragraph (1) with respect to amounts which are allocable to such property shall, for purposes of section 617(d), be treated as a deduction allowable under section 617(a).

(6) Amounts to which election apply not treated as tax preference.—Any portion of any qualified expenditure to which an election under paragraph (1) applies shall not be treated as an item of tax preference under section 57(a) and section 56 shall not apply to such expenditure.

(f) Coordination With Section 291.—Except as otherwise provided in this part, section 291 (relating to cutback of corporate preferences) shall apply before the application of this part.

(g) Tax Benefit Rule.—The Secretary may prescribe regulations under which differently treated items shall be properly adjusted where the tax treatment giving rise to such items will not result in the reduction of the taxpayer's regular tax for any taxable year.

(h) Coordination With Certain Limitations.—The limitations of sections 704(d), 465, and 1366(d) (and such other provisions as may be specified in regulations) shall be applied for purposes of computing the alternative minimum taxable income of the taxpayer for the taxable year—

(1) with the adjustments of section 56, and

(2) by not taking into account any deduction to the extent such deduction is an item of tax preference under section 57(a).

(i) Special Rule for Interest Treated as Tax Preference.—For purposes of this subtitle, interest shall not fail to be treated as wholly exempt from tax imposed by this title solely by reason of being included in alternative minimim taxable income.

[For official explanation, see Committee Reports, ¶3931.]

[¶2883] CODE SEC. 62. ADJUSTED GROSS INCOME DEFINED.

(a) General Rule.—For purposes of this subtitle, the term "adjusted gross income" means, in the case of an individual, gross income minus the following deductions:

(1) Trade and business deductions.—The deductions allowed by this chapter (other than by part VII of this subchapter) which are attributable to a trade or business carried on by the taxpayer, if such trade or business does not consist of the performance of services by the taxpayer as an employee.

[1]*(2) Certain trade and business deductions of employees.—*

(A) Reimbursed expenses of employees.—The deductions allowed by part VI (section 161 and following) which consist of expenses paid or incurred by the taxpayer, in connection with the performance by him of services as an employee, under a reimbursement or other expense allowance arrangement with his employer.

(B) Certain expenses of performing artists.—The deductions allowed by section 162 which consist of expenses paid or incurrred by a qualified performing artist in

connection with the performances by him of services in the performing arts as an employee.[2]

[3](3) **Losses from sale or exchange of property.**—The deductions allowed by part VI (sec. 161 and following) as losses from the sale or exchange of property.

[4](4) **Deductions attributable to rents and royalties.**—The deductions allowed by part VI (sec. 161 and following), by section 212 (relating to expenses for production of income), and by section 611 (relating to depletion) which are attributable to property held for the production of rents and royalties.

[5](5) **Certain deductions of life tenants and income beneficiaries of property.**—In the case of a life tenant of property, or an income beneficiary of property held in trust, or an heir, legatee, or devisee of an estate, the deduction for depreciation allowed by section 167 and the deduction allowed by section 611.

[6](6) **Pension, profit sharing and annuity plans of self-employed individuals.**—In the case of an individual who is an employee within the meaning of section 401(c)(1) the deduction allowed by section 404[7].[8]

[9](7) **Retirement savings.**—The deduction allowed by section 219 (relating to deduction of certain retirement savings).

[10](8) **Certain portion of lump-sum distributions from pension plans taxed under section 402(e).**—The deduction allowed by section 402(e)(3).

[11](9) **Penalties forfeited because of premature withdrawal of funds from time savings accounts or deposits.**—The deductions allowed by section 165 for losses incurred in any transaction entered into for profit, though not connected with a trade or business, to the extent that such losses include amounts forfeited to a bank, mutual savings bank, savings and loan association, building and loan association, cooperative bank or homestead association as a penalty for premature withdrawal of funds from a time savings account, certificate of deposit, or similar class of deposit.

[12](10) **Alimony.**—The deduction allowed by section 215.

[13](11) **Reforestation expenses.**—The deduction allowed by section 194.

[14](12) **Certain required repayments of supplemental unemployment compensation benefits.**—The deduction allowed by section 165 for the repayment to a trust described in paragraph (9) or (17) of section 501(c) of supplemental unemployment compensation benefits received from such trust if such repayment is required because of the receipt of trade readjustment allowances under section 231 or 232 of the Trade Act of 1974 (19 U.S.C. 2291 and 2292).[15]

【Footnote ¶2883 continued】

Matter in *italics* in Sec. 62(a)(3)—(6) added by section 301(b)(1), '86 TRA, which struck out:
(2) "(3) **Long-term capital gains.**—The deduction allowed by section 1202."
(3) "(4)"
(4) "(5)"
(5) "(6) "
(6) "(7)"
Effective date (Sec. 301(c), '86 TRA).—Applies to taxable years beginning after 12-31-86.

Section 1875(c)(3), '86 TRA, struck out from Sec. 62(a)(6) (former (7)):
(7) "to the extent attributable to contributions made on behalf of such individual"
Effective date (Sec. 1875(c)(12), '86 TRA, and section 241, '82 TEFRA).—Applies to years beginning after 12-31-83.

Section 132(c), '86 TRA, struck out Sec. 62(a)(8):
(8) "(8) **Moving expense deduction.**—The deduction allowed by section 217."
Effective date (Sec. 151(a), '86 TRA).—Applies to taxable years beginning after 12-31-86.

Matter in *italics* in Sec. 62(a)(7)—(12) added by section 301(b)(1), '86 TRA, which struck out:
(9) "(10)"
(10) "(11)"
(11) "(12)"
(12) "(13)"
(13) "(14)"
(14) "(15)"
Effective date (Sec. 301(c), '86 TRA).—Applies to taxable years beginning after 12-31-86.

Section 131(b)(1), '86 TRA, struck out Sec. 62(16):
(15) "(16) **Deduction for two-earner married couples.**—The deduction allowed by section 221."
Effective date (Sec. 151(a), '86 TRA).—Applies to taxable years after 12-31-86.

Code §62(a)(12) ¶2883

Nothing in this section shall permit the same item to be deducted more than once.

(b)   Qualified Performing Artist.—

(1)   In general.—For purposes of subsection (a)(2)(B), the term "qualified performing artist" means, with respect to any taxable year, any individual if—

> *(A)   such individual performed services in the performing arts as an employee during the taxable year for at least 2 employers,*
>
> *(B)   the aggregate amount allowable as a deduction under section 162 in connection with the performance of such services exceeds 10 percent of such individual's gross income attributable to the performance of such services, and*
>
> *(C)   the adjusted gross income of such individual for the taxable year (determined without regard to subsection (a)(2)(B)) does not exceed $16,000.*

(2)   Nominal employer not taken into account.—An individual shall not be treated as performing services in the performing arts as an employee for any employer during any taxable year unless the amount received by such individual from such employer for the performance of such services during the taxable year equals or exceeds $200.

(3)   Special rules for married couples.—

> *(A)   In general.—Except in the case of a husband and wife who lived apart at all times during the taxable year, if the taxpayer is married at the close of the taxable year, subsection (a)(2)(B) shall apply only if the taxpayer and his spouse file a joint return for the taxable year.*
>
> *(B)   Application of paragraph (1).—In the case of a joint return—*
>
> > *(i)   paragraph (1) (other than subparagraph (C) thereof) shall be applied separately with respect to each spouse, but*
> >
> > *(ii)   paragraph (1)(C) shall be applied with respect to their combined adjusted gross income.*
>
> *(C)   Determination of martial status.—For purposes of this subsection, marital status shall be determined under section 7703(a).*
>
> *(D)   Joint return.—For purposes of this subsection, the term "joint return" means the joint return of a husband and wife made under section 6013.*

[For official explanation, see Committee Reports, ¶3860; 3861; 3885; 4189.]

[¶2884]   CODE SEC. 63.   TAXABLE INCOME DEFINED.

[1]*(a)   In general.—Except as provided in subsection (b), for purposes of this subtitle, the*

[Footnote ¶2883 continued]

Sec. 62(b) in *italics* added by section 132(b)(2)(B), '86 TRA.

Effective date (Sec. 151(a), '86 TRA).—Applies to taxable years beginning after 12-31-86.

[Footnote ¶2884]   Matter in *italics* in Sec. 63 added by section 102(a), '86 TRA, which struck out:

(1)   "(a)   **Corporations.**—For purposes of this subtitle, in the case of a corporation, the term 'taxable income' means gross income minus the deductions allowed by this chapter.

(b)   **Individuals.**—For purposes of this subtitle, in the case of an individual, the term 'taxable income' means adjusted gross income—

(1)   reduced by the sum of—

(A)   the excess itemized deductions,

(B)   the deductions for personal exemptions provided by section 151, and

(C)   the direct charitable deduction, and

(2)   increased (in case of an individual for whom an unused zero bracket amount computation is provided by subsection (e)) by the unused zero bracket amount (if any).

(c)   **Excess Itemized Deductions.**—For purposes of this subtitle, the term 'excess itemized deductions' means the excess (if any) of—

(1)   the itemized deductions, over

(2)   the zero bracket amount

(d)   **Zero Bracket Amount.**—For purposes of this subtitle, the term 'zero bracket amount' means—

(1)   in the case of an individual to whom subsection (a), (b), (c), or (d) of section 1 applies, the maximum amount of taxable income on which no tax is imposed by the applicable subsection of section 1, or

(2)   zero in any other case.

(e)   **Unused Zero Bracket Amount.**—

(1)   **Individuals for whom computation must be made.**—A computation for the taxable year shall be made under this subsection for the following individuals:

(A)   a married individual filing a separate return where either spouse itemizes deductions,

(B)   a nonresident alien individual,

(C)   a citizen of the United States entitled to the benefits of section 931 (relating to income from sources within possessions of the United States), and

(D)   an individual with respect to whom a deduction under section 151(e) is allowable to another taxpayer for a taxable ear beginning in the calendar year in which the individual's taxable year begins.

(2)   **Computation.**—For purposes of this subtitle, an individual's unused zero bracket amount for the taxable year is an amount equal to the excess (if any) of—

term *"taxable income" means gross income minus the deductions allowed by this chapter (other than the standard deduction).*

(b) *Individuals Who Do Not Itemize Their Deductions.—In the case of an individual who does not elect to itemize his deductions for the taxable year, for purposes of this subtitle, the term "taxable income" means adjusted gross income, minus—*

    (1) *the standard deduction, and*

    (2) *the deduction for personal exemptions provided in section 151.*

(c) *Standard Deduction.—For purposes of this subtitle—*

    (1) *In general.—Except as otherwise provided in this subsection, the term "standard deduction" means the sum of—*

        (A) *the basic standard deduction, and*

        (B) *the additional standard deduction.*

    (2) *Basic standard deduction.—For purposes of paragraph (1), the basic standard deduction is—*

        (A) *$5,000 in the case of—*

            (i) *a joint return, or*

            (ii) *a surviving spouse (as defined in section 2(a)),*

        (B) *$4,400 in the case of a head of household (as defined in section 2(b)),*

        (C) *$3,000 in the case of an individual who is not married and who is not a surviving spouse or head of household, or*

        (D) *$2,500 in the case of a married individual filing a separate return.*

    (3) *Additional standard deduction for aged and blind.—For purposes of paragraph (1), the additional standard deduction is the sum of each additional amount to which the taxpayer is entitled under subsection (f).*

〔Footnote ¶2884 continued〕

  (A) the zero bracket amount, over

  (B) the itemized deductions.

In the case of an individual referred to in paragraph (1)(D), if such individual's earned income (as defined in section 911(d)(2)) exceeds the itemized deductions, such earned income shall be substituted for the itemized deductions in subparagraph (B).

  (f) Itemized Deductions.—For purposes of this subtitle, the term 'itemized deductions' means the deductions allowable by this chapter other than—

  (1) the deductions allowable in arriving at adjusted gross income,

  (2) the deductions for personal exemptions provided by section 151, and

  (3) the direct charitable deduction.

  (g) Election to Itemize.—

  (1) In general.—Unless an individual makes an election under this subsection for the taxable year, no itemized deduction shall be allowed for the taxable year. For purposes of this subtitle, the determination of whether a deduction is allowable under this chapter shall be made without regard to the preceding sentence.

  (2) Who may elect.—Except as provided in paragraph (3), an individual may make an election under this subsection for the taxable year only if such individual's itemized deductions exceed the zero bracket amount.

  (3) Certain individuals treated as electing to itemize.—An individual who has an unused zero bracket amount (as determined under subsection (e)(2)) shall be treated as having made an election under this subsection for the taxable year.

  (4) Time and manner of election.—Any election under this subsection shall be made on the taxpayer's return, and the Secretary shall prescribe the manner of signifying such election on the return.

  (5) Change of treatment.—Under regulations prescribed by the Secretary, a change of treatment with respect to the zero bracket amount and itemized deductions for any taxable year may be made after the filing of the return for such year. If the spouse of the taxpayer filed a separate return for any taxable year corresponding to the taxable year of the taxpayer, the change shall not be allowed unless, in accordance with such regulations—

  (A) the spouse makes a change of treatment with respect to the zero bracket amount and itemized deductions, for the taxable year covered in such separate return, consistent with the change of treatment sought by the taxpayer, and

  (B) the taxpayer and his spouse consent in writing to the assessment, within such period as may be agreed on with the Secretary, of any deficiency, to the extent attributable to such change of treatment, even though at the time of the filing of such consent the assessment of such deficiency would otherwise be prevented by the operation of any law or rule of law.

This paragraph shall not apply if the tax liability of the taxpayer's spouse, for the taxable year corresponding to the taxable year of the taxpayer, has been compromised under section 7122.

  (h) Marital Status.—For purposes of this section, marital status shall be determined under section 143.

  (i) Direct Charitable Deduction.—For purposes of this section, the term 'direct charitable deduction' means that portion of the amount allowable under section 170(a) which is taken as a direct charitable deduction for the taxable year under section 170(i)."

  Effective Date (Sec. 151(a), '86 TRA).—Applies to taxable years beginning after 12-31-86.

---

(4) Adjustments for inflation.—*In the case of any taxable year beginning in a calendar year after 1988, each dollar amount contained in paragraph (2) or (5)(A) or subsection (f) shall be increased by an amount equal to—*

(A)   such dollar amount, multiplied by

(B)   the cost-of-living adjustment determined under section 1(f)(3) for the calendar year in which the taxable year begins.

(5)   Limitation on standard deduction in the case of certain dependents.—*In the case of an individual with respect to whom a deduction under section 151 is allowable to another taxpayer for a taxable year beginning in the calendar year in which the individual's taxable year begins, the standard deduction applicable to such individual for such individual's taxable year shall not exceed the greater of—*

(A) $500, or

(B)   such individual's earned income.

(6)   Certain individuals, etc., not eligible for standard deduction.—*In the case of—*

(A)   a married individual filing a separate return where either spouse itemizes deductions,

(B)   a nonresident alien individual,[2]

[3](C)   an individual making a return under section 443(a)(1) for a period of less than 12 months on account of a change in his annual accounting period, or

[4](D)   an estate or trust, common trust fund, or partnership,

the standard deduction shall be zero.

(d)   Itemized Deductions.—*For purposes of this subtitle, the term "itemized deductions" means the deductions allowable under this chapter other than—*

(1)   the deductions allowable in arriving at adjusted gross income, and

(2)   the deduction for personal exemptions provided by section 151.

(e)   Election to Itemize.—

(1)   In general.—*Unless an individual makes an election under this subsection for the taxable year, no itemized deduction shall be allowed for the taxable year, For purposes of this subtitle, the determination of whether a deduction is allowable under this chapter shall be made without regard to the preceding sentence.*

(2)   Time and manner of election.—*Any election under this subsection shall be made on the taxpayer's return, and the Secretary shall prescribe the manner of signifying such election on the return.*

(3)   Change of election.—*Under regulations prescribed by the Secretary, a change of election with respect to itemized deductions for any taxable year may be made after the filing of the return for such year. If the spouse of the taxpayer filed a separate return for any taxable year corresponding to the taxable year of the taxpayer, the change shall not be allowed unless, in accordance with such regulations—*

(A)   the spouse makes a change of election with respect to itemized deductions for the taxable year covered in such separate returns, consistent with the change of treatment sought by the taxpayer, and

(B)   the taxpayer and his spouse consent in writing to the assessment (within such period as may be agreed on with the Secretary) of any deficiency, to the extent attributable to such change of election, even though at the time of the filing of such consent the assessment of such deficiency would otherwise be prevented by the operation of any law or rule of law.

This paragraph shall not apply if the tax liability of the taxpayer's spouse for the taxable year corresponding to the taxable year of the taxpayer has been compromised under section 7122.

(f)   Aged or Blind Additional Amounts.—

(1)   Additional amounts for the aged.—*The taxpayer shall be entitled to an additional amount of $600—*

(A)   for himself if he has attained age 65 before the close of his taxable year, and

---

[**Footnote ¶2884 continued**]

Matter in *italics* in Sec. 63(c)(6)(C) and (D) added by section 1272(d)(6), '86 TRA, which struck out:

(2)   "(C)   a citizen of the United States entitled to the benefits of section 931 (relating to income from sources within possessions of the United States),"

(3)   "(D)"

(4)   "(E)"

Effective date (Sec. 1277(a), '86 TRA).—Generally applies to taxable years beginning after 12-31-86. For transitional and special rules, see ¶2068.

   (B) for the spouse of the taxpayer if the spouse has attained age 65 before the close of the taxable year and an additional exemption is allowable to the taxpayer for such spouse under section 151(b).

   (2) Additional amount for blind.—The taxpayer shall be entitled to an additional amount of $600—

     (A) for himself if he is blind at the close of the taxable year, and

     (B) for the spouse of the taxpayer if the spouse is blind as of the close of the taxable year and an additional exemption is allowable to the taxpayer for such spouse under section 151(b).

For purposes of subparagraph (B), if the spouse dies during the taxable year the determination of whether such spouse is blind shall be made as of the time of such death.

   (3) Higher amount for certain unmarried individuals.—In the case of an individual who is not married and is not a surviving spouse, subparagraphs (1) and (2) shall be applied by substituting "$750" for "$600".

   (4) Blindness defined.—For purposes of this subsection, an individual is blind only if his central visual acuity does not exceed 20/200 in the better eye with correcting lenses, or if his visual acuity is greater than 20/200 but is accompanied by a limitation in the fields of vision such that the widest diameter of the visual field subtends an angle no greater than 20 degrees.

   (g) Marital Status.—For purposes of this section, marital status shall be determined under section 7703.

   (h) Transitional Rule for Taxable Years Beginning in 1987.—In the case of any taxable year beginning in 1987, paragraph (2) of subsection (c) shall be applied—

     (1) by substituting "$3,760" for "$5,000",

     (2) by substituting "$2,540" for "$4,400",

     (3) by substituting "$2,540" for "$3,000", and

     (4) by substituting "$1,880" for "$2,500".

The preceding sentence shall not apply if the taxpayer is entitled to an additional amount determined under subsection (f) (relating to additional amount for aged and blind) for the taxable year.

[For official explanation, see Committee Reports, ¶3853; 4057.]

〔¶2885〕 CODE SEC. 67. 2-PERCENT FLOOR ON MISCELLANEOUS ITEMIZED DEDUCTIONS.

   (a) General Rule.—In the case of an individual, the miscellaneous itemized deductions for any taxable year shall be allowed only to the extent that the aggregate of such deductions exceeds 2 percent of adjusted gross income.

   (b) Miscellaneous Itemized Deductions.—For purposes of this section, the term "miscellaneous itemized deductions" means the itemized deductions other than—

     (1) the deduction under section 163 (relating to interest),

     (2) the deduction under section 164 (relating to taxes),

     (3) the deduction under section 165(a) for losses described in subsection (c)(3) or (d) of section 165,

     (4) the deduction under section 170 (relating to charitable, etc., contributions and gifts),

     (5) the deduction under section 213 (relating to medical, dental, etc., expenses),

     (6) the deduction under section 217 (relating to moving expenses),

     (7) any deduction allowable for impairment-related work expenses,

     (8) the deduction under section 691(c) (relating to deduction for estate tax in case of income in respect of the decedent),

     (9) any deduction allowable in connection with personal property used in a short sale,

     (10) the deduction under section 1341 (relating to computation of tax where taxpayer restores substantial amount held under claim of right),

     (11) the deduction under section 72(b)(3) (relating to deduction where annuity payments cease before investment recovered),

     (12) the deduction under section 171 (relating to deduction for amortizable bond premium), and

〔Footnote ¶2885〕 Sec. 67 added by section 132(a), '86 TRA.
Effective date (Sec. 151(a), '86 TRA).—Applies to taxable years beginning after 12-31-86.

(13) the deduction under section 216 (relating to deductions in connection with cooperative housing corporations).

(c) Disallowance of Indirect Deduction Through Pass-Thru Entity.—The Secretary shall prescribe regulations which prohibit the indirect deduction through pass-thru entities of amounts which are not allowable as a deduction if paid or incurred directly by an individual and which contain such reporting requirements as may be necessary to carry out the purposes of this subsection. The preceding sentence shall not apply with respect to estates, trusts, cooperatives, and real estate investment trusts.

(d) Impairment-Related Work Expenses.—For purposes of this section, the term "impairment-related work expenses" means expenses—

(1) of a handicapped individual (as defined in section 190(b)(3)) for attendant care services at the individual's place of employment and other expenses in connection with such place of employment which are necessary for such individual to be able to work, and

(2) with respect to which a deduction is allowable under section 162 (determined without regard to this section).

(e) Determination of Adjusted Gross Income in Case of Estates and Trusts.—For purposes of this section, the adjusted gross income of an estate or trust shall be computed in the same manner as in the case of an individual, except that the deductions for costs which are paid or incurred in connection with the administration of the estate or trust and would not have been incurred if the property were not held in such trust or estate shall be treated as allowable in arriving at adjusted gross income.

[For official explanation, see Committee Reports, ¶3861.]

⟦¶2886⟧ CODE SEC. 71. ALIMONY AND SEPARATE MAINTENANCE PAYMENTS.

* * * * * * * * * * * *

(b) Alimony or Separate Maintenance Payments Defined.—For purposes of this section—

(1) **In general.**—The term "alimony or separate maintenance payment" means any payment in cash if—

(A) such payment is received by (or on behalf of) a spouse under a divorce or separation instrument,

(B) the divorce or separation instrument does not designate such payment as payment which is not includible in gross income under this section and not allowable as a deduction under section 215,

(C) in the case of any individual legally separated from his spouse under a decree of divorce or of separate maintenance, the payee spouse and the payor spouse are not members of the same household at the time such payment is made, and

(D) there is no liability to make such payment for any period after the death of the payee spouse and there is no liability to make any payment (in cash or property) as a substitute for such payments after the death of the payee spouse.[1]

* * * * * * * * * * * *

(c) Payments To Support Children.—

* * * * * * * * * * * *

(2) **Treatment of certain reductions related to contingencies involving child.**—For purposes of paragraph (1), if any amount specified in the instrument will be reduced—

(A) on the happening of a contingency specified in the instrument relating to a child (such as attaining a specified age, marrying, dying, leaving school, or a similar contingency), or

---

⟦Footnote ¶2886⟧   Section 1843(b), '86 TRA, struck out from Sec. 71(b)(1)(D):

(1) "(and the divorce or separation instrument states that there is no such liability)"

Effective date (Sec. 1881, '86 TRA, and section 422(e)(1) and (2), '84 TRA.—(1) In general.—Except as otherwise provided in this subsection, the amendments made by this section shall apply with respect to divorce or separation instruments (as defined in section 71(b)(2) of the '54 Code, as amended by this section) executed after 12-31-84.

(2) Modifications of instruments executed before January 1, 1985.—The amendments made by this section shall also apply to any divorce or separation instrument (as so defined) executed before 1-1-85, but modified on or after such date if the modification expressly provides that the amendments made by this secion shall apply to such modification.

Matter in *italics* in Sec. 71(c)(2)(B) and (g) added by section 1843(a) and (d), '86 TRA, which struck out:

(B) at a time which can clearly be associated with a contingency of a kind specified in [2]*subparagraph (A)*,

* * * * * * * * * * *

[3]*(f) Recomputation Where Excess Front-Loading of Alimony Payments—*
    (1) In general.—If there are excesss alimony payments—
        (A) the payor spouse shall include the amount of such excess payments in gross income for the payor spouse's taxable year beginning in the 3rd post-separation year, and
        (B) the payee spouse shall be allowed a deduction in computing adjusted gross income for the amount of such excess payments for the payee's taxable year beginning in the 3rd post-separation year.
    (2) Excess alimony payments.—For purposes of this subsection, the term "excess alimony payments" mean the sum of—
        (A) the excess payments for the 1st post-separation, and
        (B) the excess payments for the 2nd post-separation year.

〖Footnote ¶2886 continued〗

(2) "paragraph (1)"
Effective date (Sec. 1881, '86 TRA, and section 422(e)(1) and (2), '84 TRA).—See above.
Matter in *italics* in Sec. 71(f) added by section 1843(c)(1), '86 TRA, which struck out:
(3) "**(f) Special Rules To Prevent Excess Front-Loading Of Alimony Payments.—**
(1) **Requirement that payments be for more than 6 years.**—Alimony or separate maintenance payments (in excess of $10,000 during any calendar year) paid by the payor spouse to the payee spouse shall not be treated as alimony or separate maintenance payments unless such payments are to be made by the payor spouse to the payee spouse in each of the 6 post-separation years (not taking into account any termination contingent on the death of either spouse or the remarriage of the payee spouse).
(2) **Recomputation where payments decrease by more than $10,000**—If there is an excess amount determined under paragraph (3) for any computation year—
(A) the payor spouse shall include such excess amount in gross income for the payor spouses's taxable year beginning in the computation year, and
(B) the payee spouse shall be allowed a deduction in computing adjusted gross income for such excess amouunt for the payee spouse's taxable year beginning in the computation year.
(3) **Determination excess amount.**—The excess amount determined under this paragraph for any computation year is the sum of—
(A) the excess (if any) of—
(i) the amount of alimony or separate maintenance payments paid by the payor spouse during the immediately preceding post-separation year, over
(ii) the amount of the alimony or separate maintenance payments paid by the payor spouse during the computation year increased by $10,000, plus
(B) a like excess for each of the other preceding post-separation years.
In determining the amount of the alimony or separate maintenance payments paid by the payor spouse during any preceding post-separation year, the amount paid during such year shall be reduced by any excess previously determined in respect of such year under this paragraph.
(4) **Definitions.**—For purposes of this subsection—
(A) **Post-separation year.**—The term 'post-separation year' means any calendar year in the 6 calendar year period beginning with the first calendar year in which the payor spouse paid to the payee spouse alimony or separate maintenance payments to which this section applies.
(B) **Computation year.**—The term 'computation year' means the post-separation year for which the excess under paragraph (3) is being determined.
(5) **Exceptions.—**
(A) **Where payments cease by reason of death or remarriage.**—Paragraph (2) shall not apply to any post-separation year (and subsequent post-separation years) if—
(i) either spouse dies before the close of such post-separation year or the payee spouse remarries before the close of such post-separation year, and
(ii) the alimony or separate maintenance payments cease by reason of such death or remarriage.
(B) **Support payments.**—For purposes of this subsection, the term 'alimony or separate maintenance payment' shall not include any payment received under a decree described in subsection (b)(2)(C).
(C) **Fluctuating payments not within control payor spouse.**—For purposes of this subsection, the term 'alimony or separate maintenance payment' shall not include any payment to the extent it is made pursuant to a continuing liability (over a period of not less than 6 years) to pay a fixed portion of the income from a business or property or from compensation for employment or self-employment."
Effective date (Sec. 1843(c)(2) and (3), '86 TRA).—(A) Generally applies with respect to divorce or separation instruments (as defined in section 71(b)(2) of the '86 Code executed after 12-31-86.
(B) **Modifications of instruments executed before January 1, 1987.**—The amendments made by paragraph (1) shall also apply to any divorce or separation instrument (as so defined) executed before 1-1-87, but modified on or after such date if the modification expressly provides that the amendments made by paragraph (1) shall apply to such modification.
(3) **Transitional rule.**—In the case of any instrument to which the amendment made by paragraph (1) does not apply, paragraph (2) of section 71(f) of the '54 Code (as in effect on the day before date of the enactment of this Act) shall apply only with respect to the first 3 post-separation years.

Code §71(f)(2) ¶2886

(3)   *Excess payments for 1st post-separation year.*—For purposes of this subsection, the amount of the excess payments for the 1st post-separation year is the excess (if any) of—

     (A)   the amount of the alimony or separate maintenance payments paid by the payor spouse during the 1st post-separation year, over

     (B)   the sum of—

         (i)   the average of—

            (I)   the alimony or separate maintenance payments paid by the payor spouse during the 2nd post-separation year, reduced by the excess payments for the 2nd post-separation year, and

            (II)   the alimony or separate maintenance payments paid by the payor spouse during the 3rd post-separation year, plus

         (ii) $15,000.

(4)   *Excess payments for 2nd post-separation year.*—For purposes of this subsection, the amount of the excess payments for the 2nd post-separation year is the excess (if any) of—

     (A)   the amount of the alimony or separation maintenance payments paid by the payor spouse during the 2nd post-separation year, over

     (B)   the sum of—

         (i)   the amount of the alimony or separate maintenance payments paid by the payor spouse during the 3rd post-separation year, plus

         (ii) $15,000.

(5)   *Exceptions.*—

     (A)   *Where payment ceases by reason of death or remarriage.*—Paragraph (1) shall not apply if—

         (i)   either spouse dies before the close of the 3rd post-separation year, or the payee spouse remarries before the close of the 3rd post-separation year, and

         (ii)   the alimony or separate maintenance payments cease by reason of such death or remarriage.

     (B)   *Support payments.*—For purposes of this subsectiion, the term "alimony or separate maintenance payment" shall not include any payment received under a decree described in subsection (b)(2)(C).

     (C)   *Fluctuating payments not within control of payor spouse.*—For purposes of this subsection, the term "alimony or separate maintenance payment" shall not include any payment to the extent it is made pursuant to a continuing liability (over a period of not less than 3 years) to pay a fixed portion or portions of the income from a business or property or from compensation for employment or self-employment.

(6)   *Post-separation years.*—For purposes of this subsection, the term "1st post-separation years" means the 1st calendar year in which the payor spouse paid to the payee spouse alimony or separate maintenance payments to which this section applies. The 2nd and 3rd post-separation years shall be the 1st and 2nd succeeding calendar years, respectively.

(g)   *Cross References.*—

     (1)   For deduction of alimony or separate maintenance payments, see section 215.

     (2)   For taxable status of income of an estate or trust in the case of divorce, etc., see section 682.

[For official explanation, see Committee Reports, ¶4161.]

【¶2887】 CODE SEC. 72. ANNUITIES; CERTAIN PROCEEDS OF ENDOW-MENT AND LIFE INSURANCE CONTRACTS.

(a)   **General rule for Annuities.**—Except as otherwise provided in this chapter, gross income includes any amount received as an annuity (whether for a period certain or during one or more lives) under an annuity, endowment, or life insurance contract.

(b)   **Exclusion Ratio.**—

     (1)   *In general.*—Gross income does not include that part of any amount received as an annuity under an annuity, endowment, or life insurance contract which bears the same ratio to such amount as the investment in the contract (as of the annuity starting date) bears to the expected return under the contract (as of such date).[1]

【Footnote ¶2887】   Matter in *italics* in Sec. 72(b) added by 1122(c)(2), '86 TRA, which struck out:

(1) "This subsection shall not apply to any amount to which subsection (d)(1) (relating to certain employee annuities) applies."

Effective date (Sec. 1122(h)(2)(B) and (3)—(6), '86 TRA).—Generally applies to individuals whose annuity starting date is after 12-31-86.

(2) *Exclusion limited to investment.—The portion of any amount received as an annuity which is excluded from gross income under paragraph (1) shall not exceed the unrecovered investment in the contract immediately before the receipt of such amount.*

(3) *Deduction where annuity payments cease before entire investment recovered.—*
(A) *In general.—If—*
(i) *after the annuity starting date, payments as an annuity under the contract cease by reason of the death of an annuitant, and*
(ii) *as of the date of such cessation, there is unrecovered investment in the contract,*

the amount of such unrecovered investment (in excess of any amount specified in subsection (e)(5) which was not included in gross income) shall be allowed as a deduction to the annuitant for his last taxable year.
(B) *Payments to other persons.—In the case of any contract which provides for payments meeting the requirements of subparagraphs (B) and (C) of subsection (c)(2), the deduction under subparagraph (A) shall be allowed to the person entitled to such payments for the taxable year in which such payments are received.*

⟦Footnote ¶2887 continued⟧

* * * * * * * * * * * *

(3) Special rule for individuals who attained age 50 before January 1, 1986.—
(A) In general.—In the case of a lump sum distribution to which this paragraph applies—
(i) the existing capital gains provisions shall continue to apply, and
(ii) the requirement of subparagraph (B) of section 402(e)(4) '86 Code (as amended by subsection (a)) that the distribution be received after attaining age 59 1/2 shall not apply.
(B) Computation of tax.—If subparagraph (A) applies to any lump sum distribution of any taxpayer for any taxable year, the tax imposed by section 1 '86 Code on such taxpayer for such taxable year shall be equal to the sum of—
(i) the tax imposed by such section 1 on the taxable income of the taxpayer (reduced by the portion of such lump sum distribution to which clause (ii) applies), plus
(ii) 20 percent of the portion of such lump sum distribution to which the existing capital gains provisions continue to apply by reason of this paragraph.
(C) Lump sum distributions to which paragraph applies.—This paragraph shall apply to any lump sum distribution if—
(i) such lump sum distribution is received by an individual who has attained age 50 before 1-1-86, and
(ii) the taxpayer makes an election under this paragraph.
Not more than 1 election may be made under this paragraph with respect to an employee. An election under this subparagraph shall be treated as an election under section 402(e)(4)(B) '86 Code with respect to any other lump sum distribution.
(4) 5-year phase-out of capital gains treatment.—
(A) Notwithstanding the amendment made by subsection (b), if the taxpayer elects the application of this paragraph with respect to any distribution after 12-31-86 and before 1-1-92, the phase-out percentage of the amount which would have been treated, without regard to this subparagraph, as long-term capital gain under the existing capital gains provisions shall be treated as long-term capital gain.
(B) For purposes of this paragraph—

In the case of distributions during calendar year:	The phase-out percentage is:
1987	100
1988	95
1989	75
1990	50
1991	25

(C) No more than 1 election may be made under this paragraph with respect to an employee. An election under this paragraph shall be treated as an election under section 402(e)(4)(B) '86 Code with respect to any other lump sum distribution.
(5) Election of 10-year averaging.—An individual who has attained age 50 before 1-1-86, and elects the application of paragraph (3) or section 402(e)(1) '86 Code (as amended by this Act) may elect to have such section applied by substituting "10 times" for "5 times" and "1/10" for "1/5" in subparagraph (B) thereof. For purposes of the preceding sentence, section 402(e)(1) '86 Code shall be applied by using the rate of tax in effect under section 1 '54 Code for taxable years beginning during 1986.
(6) Existing capital gain provisions.—For purposes of paragraphs (3) and (4), the term 'existing capital gains provisions' means the provisions of paragraph (2) of section 402(a) of the '54 Code (as in effect on 10-21-86) and paragraph (2) of section 403(a) of such Code (as so in effect).

Code §72(b)(3) ¶2887

(C) Net operating loss deductions provided.—For purposes of section 172, a deduction allowed under this paragraph shall be treated as if it were attributable to a trade or business of the taxpayer.

(4) Unrecovered investment.—For purposes of this subsection, the unrecovered investment in the contract as of any date is—

(A) the investment in the contract as of the annuity starting date, reduced by

(B) the aggregate amount received under the contract on or after such annuity starting date and before the date as of which the determination is being made, to the extent such amount was excludable from gross income under this subtitle.

* * * * * * * * * * * * *

(d)   **[Repealed]**[2]

(e)   **Amounts Not Received as Annuities.—**

* * * * * * * * * * * * *

(4)   **Special rules for application of paragraph (2)(B).—**For purposes of paragraph (2)(B)—

* * * * * * * * * * * * *

(C) Treatment of transfers without adequate consideration.—

(i) In general.—If an individual who holds an annuity contract transfers it without full and adequate consideration, such individual shall be treated as receiving an amount equal to the excess of—

(I) the cash surrender value of such contract at the time of transfer, over

(II) the investment in such contract at such time,

under the contract as an amount not received as an annuity.

(ii) Exception for certain transfers between spouses or former spouses.—Clause (i) shall not apply to any transfer to which section 1041(a) (relating to transfers of property between spouses or incident to divorce) applies.

(iii) Adjustment to investment in contract of transferee.—If under clause (i) an amount is included in the gross income of the transferor of an annuity contract, the investment in the contract of the transferee in such contract shall be increased by the amount so included.

(5)   **Retention of existing rules in certain cases.—**

* * * * * * * * * * * * *

(D)   Contracts under qualified plans.—Except as provded in [3]*paragraphs (7) and*

[**Footnote ¶2887 continued**]

Section 1122(c)(1), '86 TRA, P.L. 99-514, 10-22-86, repealed Sec. 72(d):

(2) "(d) Employees' Annuities.—

(1) Employee's contributions recoverable in 3 years.—Where—

(A) part of the consideration for an annuity endowment, or life insurance contract is contributed by the employer, and

(B) during the 3-year period beginning on the date on which an amount is first received under the contract as an annuity, the aggregate amount receivable by the employee under the terms of the contract is equal to or greater than the consideration for the contract contributed by the employee,

then all amounts received as an annuity under the contract shall be excluded from gross income until there has been so excluded an amount equal to the consideration for the contract contributed by the employee. Thereafter all amounts so received under the contract shall be included in gross income.

(2) Special rules for application of paragraph (1).—For purposes of paragraph (1)—

(A) if the employee died before any amount was received as an annuity under the contract, the words 'receivable by the employee' shall be read as 'receivable by a beneficiary of the employee'; and

(B) any contribution made with respect to the contract while the employee is an employee within the meaning of section 401(c)(1) which is not allowed as a deduction under section 404 shall be treated as consideration for the contract contributed by the employee.

(3) Cross reference.—

For certain rules for determining whether amounts contributed by employer are includible in the gross income of the employee, see part I of subchapter D (sec. 401 and following, relating to pension, profit-sharing, and stock bonus plans, etc.)."

Effective date (Sec. 1122(h)(2)(A) and (3)—(6), '86 TRA, P.L. 99-514, 10-22-86).—Generally applies to individuals whose annuity starting date is after 7-1-86. For special rules see above.

Sec. 72(e)(4)(C) in *italics* added by section 1826(b)(3), '86 TRA, P.L. 99-514, 10-22-86.

Effective date (Sec. 1826(b)(4), '86 TRA, P.L. 99-514, 10-22-86).—Applies to contracts issued after 4-22-87, in taxable years ending after such date.

Matter in *italics* in Sec. 72(e)(5)(D) [other than the last flush sentence] added by section 1122(c)(3)(B), '86 TRA, P.L. 99-514, 10-22-86, which struck out:

(3) "paragraph (7)"

Effective date (Sec. 1122(h)(2)(C), (3)—(6), '86 TRA, P.L 99-514, 10-22-86).—In the case of any plan not de-

(8) this paragraph shall apply to any amount received—

(i) from a trust described in section 401(a) which is exempt from tax under section 501(a),

(ii) from a contract—

(I) purchased by a trust described in clause (i),

(II) purchased as part of a plan described in section 403(a),

(III) described in section 403(b), or

(IV) provided for employees of a life insurance company under a plan described in section 818(a)(3), or

(iii) from an individual retirement account or an individual retirement annuity.

Any dividend described in section 404(k) which is received by a participant or beneficiary shall, for purposes of this subparagraph, be treated as paid under a separate contract to which clause (ii)(I) applies.

* * * * * * * * * * * *

(7) **Special rules for plans where substantially all contributions are employee contributions.—**

(A) In general.—In the case of any plan or contract to which this paragraph applies, subparagraph (D) of paragraph (5) shall not apply to any amount received from such plan or contract.

(B) Plans or contracts to which this paragraph applies.—This paragraph shall apply to [4]*any plan* or contract—

(i) which is described in clause (i) or subclause (I), (II), or (III) of clause (ii) of paragraph (5)(D), and

(ii) with respect to which 85 percent *or more* of the total contributions during a representative period are derived from employee contributions.

For purposes of clause (ii), deductible employee contributions (as defined in subsection (o)(5)(A)) shall not be taken into account.

* * * * * * * * * * *

(8) Extension of paragraph (2)(B) to qualified plans.—

(A) In general.—Notwithstanding any other provision of this subsection (other than paragraph (7)), in the case of any amount received before the annuity starting date from a trust or contract described in paragraph (5)(D), paragraph (2)(B) shall apply to such amounts.

(B) Allocation of amount received.—For purposes of paragraph (2)(B), the amount allocated to the investment in the contract shall be the portion of the amount described in subparagraph (A) which bears the same ratio to such amount as the investment in the contract bears to the account balance. The determination under the preceding sentence shall be made as of the time of the distribution or at such other time as the Secretary may prescribe.

⌈Footnote ¶2887 continued⌋

scribed in section 72(e)(8)(D) of the '86 Code (as added by subsection (c)(3)), the amendments shall apply to amounts received after 7-1-86. For special rule, see above.

The flush sentence in *italics* in Sec. 72(e)(5) added by section 1854(b)(1), '86 TRA, P.L. 99-514, 10-22-86.

Effective date (Sec. 1881, '86 TRA, P.L. 99-514, 10-22-86, and section 542(d), '84 TRA, P.L. 98-369, 7-18-84).—Applies to taxable years beginning after 7-18-84, but under section 1854(b)(6), '86 TRA, shall not apply to dividends paid before 1-1-86, if the taxpayer treated such dividends in a manner inconsistent with such amendments on a return filed with the secretary before the enactment date.

Matter in *italics* in Sec. 72(e)(7)(B) added by section 1852(c)(1), '86 TRA, P.L. 99-514, 10-22-86, which struck out:

(4) "any trust"

Effective date (Sec. 1881, '86 TRA, P.L. 99-514, 10-22-86, and section 523(c), '84 TRA, P.L. 98-369, 7-18-84).—Applies to any amount received or loan made after 10-16-84.

Sec. 72(e)(8) and (9) in *italics* added by section 1122(c)(3)(A), '86 TRA, P.L. 99-514, 10-22-86.

Effective date (Sec. 1122(h)(2)(C) and (3)—(6), '86 TRA, P.L. 99-514, 10-22-86).—In the case of any plan not described in Sec. 72(e)(8)(D) (as added by subsection (c)(3)), the amendments shall apply to amounts received after 7-1-86. For special rules, see above.

    (C) Treatment of forfeitable rights.—If an employee does not have a nonforfeitable right to any amount under any trust or contract to which subparagraph (A) applies, such amount shall not be treated as part of the account balance.

    (D) Investment in the contract before 1987.—In the case of a plan which on May 5, 1986, permitted withdrawal of any employee contributions before separation from service, subparagraph (A) shall apply only to the extent that amounts received before the annuity starting date (when increased by amounts previously received under the contract after December 31, 1986) exceed the investment in the contract as of December 31, 1986.

    (9) **Treatment of employee contributions as separate contract.**—Any employee contributions (and any income allocable thereto) under a defined contribution plan shall be treated as a separate contract for purposes of this subsection.

(f) Special Rules for Computing Employees' Contributions.—In computing, for purposes of subsection (c)(1)(A), the aggregate amount of premiums or other consideration paid for the contract, for purposes of [5]*subsections (d)(1) and (e)(7)*, the consideration for the contract contributed by the employee, and for purposes of [6]*subsection (e)(6)*, the aggregate premiums or other consideration paid, amounts contributed by the employer shall be included, but only to the extent that—

    (1) such amounts were includible in the gross income of the employee under this subtitle or prior income tax laws; or

    (2) if such amounts had been paid directly to the employee at the time they were contributed, they would not have been includible in the gross income of the employee under the law applicable at the time of such contribution.

Paragraph (2) shall not apply to amounts which were contributed by the employer after December 31, 1962, and which would have not been includible in the gross income of the employee by reason of the application of section 911 if such amounts had been paid directly to the employee at the time of contribution. The preceding sentence shall not apply to amounts which were contributed by the employer, as determined under regulations prescribed by the Secretary, to provide pension or annuity credits, to the extent such credits are attributable to services performed before January 1, 1963, and are provided pursuant to pension or annuity plan provisions in existence on March 12, 1962, and on that date applicable to such services.

    *   *   *   *   *   *   *   *   *   *   *   *

(m) Special Rules Applicable to Employee Annuities and Distributions Under Employee Plans.—

    *   *   *   *   *   *   *   *   *   *   *   *

    (2) **Computation of consideration paid by the employee.**—In computing—

      (A) the aggregate amount of premiums or other consideration paid for the contract for purposes of subsection (c)(1)(A) (relating to the investment in the contract),

      (B) the consideration for the contract contributed by the employee for purposes of subsection (d)(1) (relating to employee's contributions recoverable in 3 years), *and subsection (e)(7) (relating to plans where substantially all contributions are employee contributions),* and

      (C) the aggregate premiums or other consideration paid for purposes of [6]*subsection (e)(6)* (relating to certain amounts not received as an annuity),

any amount allowed as a deduction with respect to the contract under section 404 which was paid while the employee was an employee within the meaning of section 401(c)(1) shall be treated as consideration contributed by the employer, and there shall not be taken into account any portion of the premiums or other consideration for the contract paid while the employee was an owner-employee which is properly allocable (as determined under regulations prescribed by the Secretary) to the cost of life, accident, health, or other insurance.

    *   *   *   *   *   *   *   *   *   *   *   *

    (5) **Penalties applicable to certain amounts received by** [7]*5-Percent Owners*

⌈Footnote ¶2887 continued⌋

  Matter in *italics* in Sec. 72(f), (m)(2)(B) and (C) added by section 1852(c)(3) and (4), '86 TRA, P.L. 99-514, 10-22-86, which struck out:

  (5) "subsection (d)(1)"

  (6) "subsection (e)(1)(B)"

  Effective date (Sec. 1881, '86 TRA, P.L. 99-514, 10-22-86, and section 523(c), '84 TRA, P.L. 98-369, 7-18-84).— Applies to any amount received or loan made after 10-16-84.

  Matter in *italics* in Sec. 72(m)(5) heading added by section 1852(a)(2)(C), '86 TRA, P.L. 99-514, 10-22-86, which struck out:

  (7) "Owner-Employers"

≫**P-H CAUTION→** There are two versions of Sec. 72(m)(5)(A). Sec. 72(m)(5)(A), generally effective after 12-31-86, follows. For Sec. 72(m)(5)(A), generally effective before 1-1-87, see below.

⁸▲ *(A) This paragraph applies to amounts which are received from a qualified trust described in section 401(a) or under a plan described in section 403(a) at any time by an individual who is, or has been, a 5-percent owner, or by a successor of such an individual, but only to the extent such amounts are determined, under regulations prescribed by the Secretary, to exceed the benefits provided for such individual under the plan formula.*

≫**P-H CAUTION→** There are two versions of Sec. 72(m)(5)(A). Sec. 72(m)(5)(A), generally effective before 1-1-87, follows. Sec. 72(m)(5)(A), generally effective after 12-31-86, see above.

⁹▲▲ *(A) This subparagraph shall apply—*

[Footnote ¶2887 continued]

Effective date (Sec. 1881, '86 TRA, P.L. 99-514, 10-22-86, and section 521(e)(1), (3)—(5), '84 TRA, P.L. 98-369, 7-18-84).—(1) Generally applies to taxable years beginning after 12-31-84.

* * * * * * * * * *

(3) Transition rule.—A trust forming part of a plan shall not be disqualified under paragraph (9) of Sec. 401(a) '54 Code, as amended by subsection (a)(1), by reason of distributions under a designation (before 1-1-84) by any employee in accordance with a designation described in section 242(b)(2) '82 TEFRA, P.L. 97-248, 9-3-82 (as in effect before the amendments made by this Act.)

(4) Special rule for governmental plans.—In the case of a governmental plan (within the meaning of section 414(d) '54 Code, paragraph (1) shall be applied by substituting "1986" for "1984".

(5) Special rule for collective bargaining agreements.—In the case of a plan maintained pursuant to one or more collective bargaining agreements ratified on or before 7-18-84 between employee representatives and one or more employers, the amendments made by this section shall not apply to years beginning before the earlier of—

(A) the date on which the last of the collective bargaining agreements relating to the plan terminates (determined without regard to any extension thereof agreed to after 10-22-86), or

(B) 1-1-88.

For purposes of subparagraph (A), any plan amendment made pursuant to a collective bargaining agreement relating to the plan which amends the plan solely to conform to any requirement added by this section shall not be treated as a termination of such collective bargaining agreement.

▲ Matter in *italics* in Sec. 72(m)(5)(A), preceded by a triangle, added by section 1123(d)(1), '86 TRA, P.L. 99-514, 10-22-86, which struck out:

(8) "(A) This subparagraph shall apply—

(i) to amounts which—

(I) are received from a qualified trust described in section 401(a) or under a plan described in section 403(a), and

(II) are received by a 5-percent owner before such owner attains the age of 59½ years, for any reason other than such owner becoming disabled (within the meaning of paragraph (7) of this section), and

(ii) to amounts which are received from a qualified trust described in section 401(a) or under a plan described in section 403(a) at any time by a 5-percent owner, or by the successor of such owner, but only to the extent that such amounts are determined (under regulations prescribed by the Secretary) to exceed the benefits provided for such individual under the plan formula.

Clause (i) shall not apply to any amount received by an individual in his capacity as a policyholder of an annuity, endowment, or life insurance contract which is in the nature of a dividend or similar distribution and clause (i) shall not apply to amounts attributable to benefits accrued before January 1, 1985."

Effective date (Sec. 1123(e)(1), (3) and (4), '86 TRA, P.L. 99-514, 10-22-86).—(1) Generally applies to taxable years beginning after 12-31-86.

* * * * * * * * * * * *

(3) Exception where distribution commences.—The amendments made by this section shall not apply to distributions to any employee from a plan maintained by any employer if—

(A) as of 3-1-86, the employee separated from service with the employer,

(B) as of 3-1-86, the accrued benefit of the employee was in pay status pursuant to a written election providing a specific schedule for the distribution of the entire accrued benefit of the employee, and

(C) such distribution is made pursuant to such written election.

(4) Transition rule.—The amendments made by this section shall not apply with respect to any benefits with respect to which a designation is in effect under section 242(b)(2), '82 TEFRA, P.L. 97-248, 9-3-82.

▲▲ Matter in *italics* in Sec. 72(m)(5)(A), preceded by two triangles, added by section 1852(a)(2)(A) and (C), '86 TRA, P.L. 99-514, 10-22-86, which struck out:

(9) "(A) This paragraph shall apply—

(i) to amounts (other than any amount received by an individual in his capacity as a policyholder of an annu-

(i) to amounts which—

    (I) are received from a qualified trust ^escribed in section 401(a) or under a plan described in section 403(a), and

    (II) are received by a 5-percent owner before such owner attains the age of 59½ years, for any reason other than such owner becoming disabled (within the meaning of paragraph (7) of this section), and

    (ii) to amounts which are received from a qualified trust described in section 401(a) or under a plan described in section 403(a) at any time by a 5-percent owner, or by the successor of such owner, but only to the extent that such amounts are determined (under regulations prescribed by the Secretary) to exceed the benefits provided for such individual under the plan formula.

Clause (i) shall not apply to any amount received by an individual in his capacity as a policyholder of an annuity, endowment, or life insurance contract which is in the nature of a dividend or similar distribution and clause (i) shall not apply to amounts attributable to benefits accrued before January 1, 1985.

* * * * * * * * * * * *

[10](C) *For purposes of this paragraph, the term "5-percent owner" means any individual who, at any time during the 5 plan years preceding the plan year ending in the taxable year in which the amount is received, is a 5-percent owner (as defined in section 416(i)(1)(B)).*

* * * * * * * * * * * *

(10) Determination of investment in the contract in the case of qualified domestic relations orders.—Under regulations prescribed by the Secretary, in the case of a distribution or payment made to an alternate payee *who is the spouse or former spouse of the participant* pursuant to a qualified domestic relations order (as defined in section 414(p)), the investment in the contract as of the date prescribed in such regulations shall be allocated on a pro rata basis between the present value of such distribution or payment and the present value of all other benefits payable with respect to the participant to which such order relates.

* * * * * * * * * * * *

(o) Special Rules for Distributions From Qualified Plans to Which Employee Made Deductible Contributions.—

* * * * * * * * * * * *

    (5) Definitions and special rules.—For purposes of this subsection—

    (A) Deductible employee contributions.—The term "deductible employee contributions," means any qualified voluntary employee contribution (as defined in section 219(e)(2)) made after December 31, 1981, in a taxable year beginning after such date *and made for a taxable year beginning before January 1, 1987,* and allowable as a deduction under section 219(a) for such taxable year.

* * * * * * * * * * * *

    (C) Qualified employer plan.—The term "qualified employer plan" has the meaning given to such term by [11]*subsection (p)(3)(A)(i).*

⌈Footnote ¶2887 continued⌋

ity, endowment, or life insurance contract which is in the nature of a dividend or similar distribution) which are received from a qualified trust described in section 401(a) or under a plan described in section 403(a) and which are received by an individual, who is, or has been, a 5-percent owner, before such individual attains the age of 59½ years, for any reason other than the individual's becoming disabled (within the meaning of paragraph (7) of this subsection), but only to the extent that such amounts are attributable to contributions paid on behalf of such individual (other than contributions made him as a 5-percent owner, while he was a 5-percent owner) and

(ii) to amounts which are received from a qualified trust described in section 401(a) or under a plan described in section 403(a) at any time by an individual who is, or has been, a 5-percent owner, or by the successor of such individual, but only to the extent that such amounts are determined, under regulations prescribed by the Secretary, to exceed the benefits provided for such individual under the plan formula."

Effective date (Sec. 1881, '86 TRA, P.L. 99-514, 10-22-86, and section 521(e)(1) and (3)—(5), '84 TRA, P.L. 98-369, 7-18-84).—(1) Generally applies to taxable years beginning after 12-31-84. For transitional rules, see above.

Matter in *italics* in Sec. 72(m)(5)(C) added by section 1852(a)(2)(B), '86 TRA, P.L. 99-514, 10-22-86, which struck out:

(10) "(C) For purposes of this paragraph, the term '*5-percent owner*' have the same meanings as when used in section 416."

Effective date (Sec. 1881, '86 TRA, P.L. 99-514, 10-22-86, and section 521(e)(1) and (3)—(5), '84 TRA, P.L. 98-369, 7-18-84).—(1) Generally applies to taxable years beginning after 12-31-84. For special and transitional rules, see above.

Matter in *italics* in Sec. 72(m)(10) added by section 1898(c)(1)(B), '86 TRA, P.L. 99-514, 10-22-86.

Effective date (Sec. 1898(c)(1)(C), '86 TRA, P.L. 99-514, 10-22-86).—Applies to payments made after 10-22-86.

Matter in *italics* in Sec. 72(o)(5)(A), (C) and (D) added by section 1101(b)(2)(C), '86 TRA, P.L. 99-514, 10-22-86, which struck out:

(11) "section 219(e)(3)"

(D) Government plan.—The term "government plan" has the meaning given such term by [12]*subsection (p)(3)(B).*

* * * * * * * * * * *

(p) Loans Treated as Distributions.—For purposes of this section—

* * * * * * * * * * *

(2) Exception for certain loans.—

(A) General rule.—Paragraph (1) shall not apply to any loan to the extent that such loan (when added to the outstanding balance of all other loans from such plan whether made on, before, or after August 13, 1982), does not exceed the lesser of—

[13]*(i) $50,000, reduced by the excess (if any) of—*

(I) the highest outstanding balance of loans from the plan during the 1-year period ending on the day before the date on which such loan was made, over

(II) the outstanding balance of loans from the plan on the date on which such loan was made, or

(ii) the greater of (I) one-half of the present value of the nonforfeitable accrued benefit of the employee under the plan, or (II) $10,000.

For purposes of clause (ii), the present value of the nonforfeitable accrued benefit shall be determined without regard to any accumulated deductible employee contributions (as defined in subsection (o)(5)(B)).

(B) Requirement that loan be repayable within 5 years.—

(i) In general.—Subparagraph (A) shall not apply to any loan unless such loan, by its terms, is required to be repaid within 5 years.

[14]*(ii) Exception for home loans.—Clause (i) shall not apply to any loan used to acquire any dwelling unit which within a reasonable time is to be used (determined at the time the loan is made) as the principal residence of the participant.*

(C) Requirement of level amortization.—Except as provided in regulations, this paragraph shall not apply to any loan unless substantially level amortization of such loan (with payments not less frequently than quarterly) is required over the term of the loan.

[15]*(D)* Related employers and related plans.—For purposes of this paragraph—

(i) the rules of subsection (b), (c), and (m) of section 414 shall apply, and

(ii) all plans of an employer (determined after the application of such subsections) shall be treated as 1 plan.

(3) Denial of interest deductions in certain cases.—

(A) In general.—No deduction otherwise allowable under this chapter shall be allowed under this chapter for any interest paid or accrued on any loan described in subparagraph (B).

(B) Loans to which subparagraph (A) applies.—For purposes of subparagraph (A), a loan is described in this subparagraph—

(i) if paragraph (1) does not apply to such loan by reason of paragraph (2), and

(ii) if—

(I) such loan is made to a key employee (as defined in section 416(i)), or

(II) such loan is secured by amounts attributable to elective 401(k) or 403(b) deferrals (as defined in section 402(g)(3)).

⟦Footnote ¶2887 continued⟧

(12) "section 219(e)(4)"

Effective date (Sec. 1101(c), '86 TRA, P.L. 99-514, 10-22-86).—Applies to contributions for taxable years beginning after 12-31-86.

Matter in *italics* in Sec. 72(p)(2)(A)—(D) amended by 1134(a), (b) and (d), '86 TRA, P.L. 99-514, 10-22-86, which struck out:

(13) "(i) $50,000, or"

(14) "(ii) Exception for home loans.—Clause (i) shall not apply to any loan used to acquire, construct, reconstruct, or substantially rehabilitate any dwelling unit which within a reasonable time is to be used (determined at the time the loan is made) as a principal residence of the participant or a member of the family (within the meaning of section 267(c)(4)) of the participant."

(15) "(C)"

Effective date (Sec. 1134(e), '86 TRA, P.L. 99-514, 10-22-86).—Applies to loans made, renewed, renegotiated, modified, or extended after 12-31-86.

Sec. 72(p)(3) in *italics* added by section 1134(c), '86 TRA, P.L. 99-514, 10-22-86.

Effective date (Sec. 1134(e), '86 TRA, P.L. 99-514, 10-22-86).—Applies to loans made, renewed, renegotiated, modified, or extended after 12-31-86.

[16](4)   **Qualified employer plan, etc.—**[17]*For purposes of this subsection—*

    (A)   *Qualified employer plan.—*

        (i)   *In general.—The term "qualified employer plan" means—*

           (I)   *a plan described in section 401(a) which includes a trust exempt from tax under section 501(a),*

           (II)   *an annuity plan described in section 403(a), and*

           (III)   *a plan under which amounts are contributed by an individual's employer for an annuity contract described in section 403(b).*

        (ii)   *Special rules.—The term "qualified employer plan"—*

           (I)   *shall include any plan which was (or was determined to be) a qualified employer plan or a government plan, but*

           (II)   *shall not include a plan described in subsection (e)(7).*

    (B)   *Government plan.—The term "government plan" means any plan, whether or not qualified, established and maintained for its employees by the United States, by a State or political subdivision thereof, or by an agency or instrumentality of any of the foregoing.*

[18](5)   **Special rules for loans, etc., from certain contracts.—**For purposes of this subsection, any amount received as a loan under a contract purchased under a qualified employer plan (and any assignment or pledge with respect to such a contract) shall be treated as a loan under such employer plan.

(q)   [19]**10-Percent Penalty for Premature Distributions From Annuity Contracts.—**

    (1)   Imposition of penalty.   If any taxpayer receives any amount under an annuity contract, the taxpayer's tax under this chapter for the taxable year in which such amount is received shall be increased by an amount equal to [20]*10-percent* of the portion of such amount which is includible in gross income.

    (2)   Subsection not apply to certain distributions.—

[21]*Paragraph (1) shall not apply to any distribution—*

    (A)   made on or after the date on which the taxpayer attains age $59\frac{1}{2}$.

    [22]*(B)   made on or after the death of the holder (or, where the holder is not an individual, the death of the primary annuitant (as defined in subsection (s)(6)(B))),*

    (C)   attributable to the taxpayer's becoming disabled within the meaning of subsection (m)(7),

    [23]*(D)   which is a part of a series of substantially equal periodic payments (not less frequently than annually) made for the life (or life expectancy) of the taxpayer or the joint lives (or joint life expectancies) of such taxpayer and his beneficiary.*

⎡Footnote ¶2887 continued⎤

Matter in *italics* in Sec. 72(p)(4) [former (3)] added by 1101(b)(2)(B), '86 TRA, P.L. 99-514, 10-22-86, which struck out:

(16)   "(3)"

(17)   "For purposes of this subsection, the term 'qualified employer plan' means any plan which was (or was determined to be) a qualified employer plan (as defined in section 219(e)(3) other than a plan described in subsection (e)(7)). For purposes of this subsection, such term includes any government plan (as defined in section 219(e)(4))."

Effective date   (Sec. 1101(c), '86 TRA, P.L. 99-514, 10-22-86).—Applies to contributions for taxable years beginning after 12-31-86.

Matter in *italics* in Sec. 72(p)(5) added by section 1134(c), '86 TRA, P.L. 99-514, 10-22-86, which struck out:

(18)   "(4)"

Effective date   (Sec. 1134(e), '86 TRA, P.L. 99-514, 10-22-86).—Applies to loans made, renewed, renegotiated, modified, or extended after 12-31-86.

Matter in *italics* in 72(q)(1) and (2) added by section 1123(b)(1) and (3) [should read (4)], '86 TRA, P.L. 99-514, 10-22-86, which struck out:

(19)   "5-percent"

(20)   "5-percent"

(21)   "This subsection"

Effective date   (Sec. 1123(e)(1), (3) and (4), '86 TRA, P.L. 99-514, 10-22-86).—Generally applies to taxable years beginning after 12-31-86. For exceptions and transitional rule, see above.

Matter in *italics* in Sec. 72(q)(2)(B) added by section 1826(c), '86 TRA, P.L. 99-514, 10-22-86, which struck out:

(22)   "(B)   made to a beneficiary (or to the estate of an annuitant) on or after the death of an annuitant,"

Effective date   (Sec. 1826(c), '86 TRA, P.L. 99-514, 10-22-86).—Applies to distributions made after the date 6 months after 10-22-86.

Matter in *italics* in Sec. 72(q)(2)(D) added by section 1123(b)(2), '86 TRA, P.L. 99-514, 10-22-86, which struck out:

(23)   "(D)   which is one of a series of substantially equal periodic payments made for the life of a taxpayer or over a period extending for at least 60 months after the annuity starting date."

Effective date   (Sec. 1123(e)(1), (3) and (4), '86 TRA, P.L. 99-514, 10-22-86).—(1) Generally applies to taxable years beginning after 12-31-86. For exceptions and transitional rule, see above.

    (E) from a plan, contract, account, trust, or annuity described in subsection (e)(5)(D), [24]*(determined without regard to subsection (e)(7),*

    (F) allocable to investment in the contract before August 14, 1982[25], *or*

    (G) under a qualified funding asset (within the meaning of section 130(d), but without regard to whether there is a qualified assignment),

    (I) [should read (H)] under an immediate annuity contract (within the meaning of section 72(u)(4)), or

    (J) [should read (I)] which is purchased by an employer upon the termination of a plan described in section 401(a) or 403(a) and which is held by the employer until such time as the employee separates from service.

    (3) Change in substantially equal payments.—If—

    (A) paragraph (1) does not apply to a distribution by reason of paragraph (2)(D), and

    (B) the series of payments under such paragraph are subsequently modified (other than by reason of death or disability)—

        (i) before the close of the 5-year period beginning on the date of the first payment and after the employee attains age 59½, or

        (ii) before the employee attains age 59½,

the taxpayer's tax for the 1st taxable year in which such modification occurs shall be increased by an amount determined under regulations, equal to the tax which (but for paragraph (2)(D)) would have been imposed, plus interest for the deferral period (within the meaning of subsection (t)(4)(B)).

*   *   *   *   *   *   *   *   *   *   *   *

    (s) Required Distributions Where Holder Dies Before Entire Interest is Distributed.—

    (1) In general.—A contract shall not be treated as an annuity contract for purposes of this title unless it provides that—

    (A) if [26]*any* holder of such contract dies on or after the annuity starting date

---

【Footnote ¶2887 continued】

  Matter in *italics* in Sec. 72(q)(2)(E) added by section 1852(c)(2), '86 TRA, P.L. 99-514, 10-22-86.

  Effective date (Sec. 1881, '86 TRA, P.L. 99-514, 10-22-86, and section 523(c), '84 TRA, P.L. 98-369, 7-18-84).—Applies to any amount received or loan made after 10-16-84.

  Matter in *italics* in Sec. 72(q)(2)(G) added by section 1826(d), '86 TRA, P.L. 99-514, 10-22-86, which struck out:

  (24) "or"

  (25) "."

  Effective date (Sec. 1881, '86 TRA, P.L. 99-514, 10-22-86, and section 222(c), '84 TRA, P.L. 98-369, 7-18-84).—(1) Generally applies to contracts issued after 1-18-85, which is 6 months after 7-18-84, in taxable years ending after such date.

  (2) Transitional Rules for Contracts Issued Before Effective Date.—In the case of any contract (other than a single premium contract) which is issued on or before the day which is 6 months after the date of the enactment of this Act, for purposes of section 72(q)(1)(A) of the '54 Code (as in effect on the day before the date of the enactment of this Act), any investment in such contract which is made during any calendar year shall be treated as having been made on January 1 of such calendar year.

  Sec. 72(q)(2)(I) and (J) [should read (H) and (I)] added by section 1123(b)(3) [should read (4)], '86 TRA, P.L. 99-514, 10-22-86.

  Effective date (Sec. 1123(e)(1), (3) and (4), '86 TRA, P.L. 99-514, 10-22-86).—Generally applies to taxable years beginning after 12-31-86. For exceptions and transitional rule, see above.

  Sec. 72(q)(3) in *italics* added by section 1123(b)(3), '86 TRA, P.L. 99-514, 10-22-86.

  Effective date (Sec. 1123(e)(1), (3) and (4), '86 TRA, P.L. 99-514, 10-22-86).—Generally applies to taxable years beginning after 12-31-86. For exceptions and transitional rule, see above.

  Matter in *italics* in Sec. 72(s)(1), (6) and (7) added by section 1826(b)(1), (2), '86 TRA, P.L. 99-514, 10-22-86, which struck out:

  (26) "the"

  Effective date (Sec. 1826(b)(4), '86 TRA, P.L. 99-514, 10-22-86).—Applies to contracts issued after the date which is 6 months after 10-22-86 in taxable years ending after such date.

  Sec. 72(s)(5) in *italics* added by section 1826(a), '86 TRA, P.L. 99-514, 10-22-86.

Code §72(s)(1) ¶2887

and before the entire interest in such contract has been distributed the remaining portion of such interest will be distributed at least as rapidly as under the method of distributions being used as of the date of his death, and

  (B) if [26]*any* holder of such contract dies before the annuity starting date, the entire interest in such contract will be distributed within 5 years after the death of such holder.

                    * * * * * * * * * * * *

  (5) Exceptions for annuity contracts which are part of qualified plans.—This subsection shall not apply to any annuity contract—
    (A) which is provided—
      (i) under a plan described in section 401(a) which includes a trust exempt from tax under section 501, or
      (ii) under a plan described in section 403(a),
    (B) which is described in section 403(b), or
    (C) which is an individual retirement annuity or provided under an individual retirement account or annuity.
  (6) Special rule where holder is corporation or other non-individual.—
    (A) In general.—For purposes of this subsection, if the holder of the contract is not an individual, the primary annuitant shall be treated as the holder of the contract.
    (B) Primary annuitant.—For purposes of subparagraph (A), the term "primary annuitant" means the individual, the events in the life of whom are of primary importance in affecting the timing or amount of the payout under the contract.
  (7) Treatment of changes in primary annuitant where holder of contract is not an individual.—For purposes of this subsection, in the case of a holder of an annuity contract which is not an individual, if there is a change in a primary annuity (as defined in paragraph (6)(B)), such change shall be treated as the death of the holder.

  (t) 10-Percent Additional Tax on Early Distributions From Qualified Retirement Plans.—

  (1) Imposition of additional tax.—If any taxpayer receives any amount from a qualified retirement plan (as defined in section 4974(c)), the taxpayer's tax under this chapter for the taxable year in which such amount is received shall be increased by an amount equal to 10 percent of the portion of such amount which is includible in gross income.

  (2) Subsection not to apply to certain distributions.—Except as provided in paragraphs (3) and (4), paragraph (1) shall not apply to any of the following distributions:
    (A) In general.—Distributions which are—
      (i) made on or after the date on which the employee attains age 59½,
      (ii) made to a beneficiary (or to the estate of the employee) on or after the death of the employee,
      (iii) attributable to the employee's being disabled within the meaning of subsection (m)(7),
      (iv) part of a series of substantially equal periodic payments (not less frequently than annually) made for the life (or life expectancy) of the employee or the joint lives (or joint life expectancies) of such employee and his beneficiary, or
      (v) made to an employee after separation from service on account of early retirement under the plan after attainment of age 55, or
      (vi) dividends paid with respect to stock of a corporation which are described in section 404(k).
    (B) Medical expenses.—Distributions made to the employee (other than distributions described in subparagraph (A) or (C)) to the extent such distributions do not

---

⎡Footnote ¶2887 continued⎤
  Effective date (Sec. 1881, '86 TRA and section 222(c), '84 TRA).—Generally applies to contracts isued after 1-18-85, which is 6 months after 7-18-84, in taxable years ending after such date. For transitional rules, see above.

Sec. 72(t) in *italics* added by section 1123(a), '86 TRA.
  Effective date (Sec. 1123(e)(1), (3) and (4), '86 TRA).—Generally applies to taxable years beginning after 12-31-86. For exceptions and transitional rules, see above.

Sec. 72(u) in *italics* added by section 1135(a), '86 TRA.
  Effective date (Sec. 1135(b), '86 TRA).—Applies to contributions to annuity contracts after 2-28-86.

exceed the amount allowable as a deduction under section 213 to the employee for amounts paid during the taxable year for medical care (determined without regard to whether the employee itemizes deductions for such taxable year).

(C) *Certain plans.*—

(i) *In general.*—Except as provided in clause (ii), any distribution made before January 1, 1990, to an employee from an employee stock ownership plan defined in section 4975(e)(7) to the extent that, on average a majority of assets in the plan have been invested in employer securities (as defined in section 409(l)) for the 5-year-plan period preceding the plan year in which the distribution is made.

(ii) *Benefits distributed must be invested in employer securities for 5 years.*— Clause (i) shall not apply to any distribution which is attributable to assets which have not been invested in employer securities at all times during the period referred to in clause (i).

(D) *Payments to alternate payees pursuant to qualified domestic relations orders.*—Any distribution to an alternate payee pursuant to a qualified domestic relations order (within the meaning of section 414(p)(1)).

(3) *Limitations.*—

(A) *Certain exceptions not to apply to individual retirement plans.*—Subparagraphs (A)(v), (B), and (C) of paragraph (2) shall not apply to distributions from an individual retirement plan.

(B) *Periodic payments under qualified plans must begin after separation.*—Paragraph (2)(A)(iv) shall not apply to any amount paid from a trust described in section 401(a) which is exempt from tax under section 501(a) or from a contract described in section 72(e)(5)(D)(ii) unless the series of payments begins after the employee separates from service.

(4) *Change in substantially equal payments.*—

(A) *In general.*—If—

(i) paragraph (1) does not apply to a distribution by reason of paragraph (2)(A)(iv), and

(ii) the series of payments under such paragraph are subsequently modified (other than by reason of death or disability)—

(I) before the close of the 5-year period beginning with the date of the first payment and after the employee attains age $59\frac{1}{2}$, or

(II) before the employee attains age $59\frac{1}{2}$,

the taxpayer's tax for the 1st taxable year in which such modification occurs shall be increased by an amount, determined under regulations, equal to the tax which (but for paragraph (2)(A)(iv)) would have been imposed, plus interest for the deferral period.

(B) *Deferral period.*—For purposes of this paragraph, the term "deferral period" means the period beginning with the taxable year in which (without regard to paragraph (2)(A)(iv)) the distribution would have been includible in gross income and ending with the taxable year in which the modification described in subparagraph (A) occurs.

(5) *Employee.*—For purposes of this subsection, the term "employee" includes any participant, and in the case of an individual retirement plan, the individual for whose benefit such plan was established.

(u) *Treatment of Annuity Contracts Not Held by Natural Persons.*—

(1) *In general.*—If any annuity contract is held by a person who is not a natural person—

(A) such contract shall not be treated as an annuity contract for purposes of this subtitle, and

(B) the income on the contract for any taxable year of the policyholder shall be treated as ordinary income received or accrued by the owner during such taxable year.

For purposes of this paragraph, holding by a trust or other entity as an agent for a natural person shall not be taken into account.

(2) *Income on the contract.*—

(A) *In general.*—For purposes of paragraph (1), the term "income on the contract" means, with respect to any taxable year of the policyholder, the excess of—

(i)   the sum of the net surrender value of the contract as of the close of the taxable year plus all distributions under the contract received during the taxable year or any prior taxable year, reduced by

(ii)   the sum of the amount of net premiums under the contract for the taxable year and prior taxable years and amounts includible in gross income for prior taxable years with respect to such contract under this subsection.

Where necessary to prevent the avoidance of this subsection, the Secretary may substitute "fair market value of the contract" for "net surrender value of the contract" each place it appears in the preceding sentence.

(B)   Net premiums.—For purposes of this paragraph, the term "net premiums" means the amount of premiums paid under the contract reduced by any policyholder dividends.

(3)   Exceptions.—This subsection shall not apply to any annuity contract which—

(A)   is acquired by the estate of a decedent by reason of the death of the decedent,

(B)   is held under a plan described in section 401(a) or 403(a), under a program described in section 403(b), or under an individual retirement plan,

(C)   is a qualified funding asset (as defined in section 130(d), but without regard to whether there is a qualified assignment),

(D)   which is purchased by an employer upon the termination of a plan described in section 401(a) or 403(a) and which is held by the employer until such time as the employee separates from service, or

(E)   which is an immediate annuity.

(4)   Immediate annuity.—For purposes of this subsection, the term "immediate annuity" means an annuity—

(A)   which is purchased with a single premium or annuity consideration, and

(B)   the annuity starting date (as defined in subsection (c)(4)) of which commences no later than 1 year from the date of the purchase of the annuity.

* (v)   Cross Reference.—

For limitation on adjustments to basis of annuity sold, see section 1021.

[For official explanation, see Committee Reports, ¶3968; 3987; 3988; 3993; 3994; 4152; 4172; 4174; 4211.]

[¶2888]   CODE SEC. 74.   PRIZES AND AWARDS.

(a)   **General Rule.**—Except as [1]otherwise provided in this section or in section 117 (relating to [2]qualified scholarships), gross income includes amounts received as prizes and awards.

(b)   **Exception** for Certain Prizes and Awards Transferred to Charities.—Gross income does not include amounts received as prizes and awards made primarily in recognition of religious, charitable, scientific, educational, artistic, literary, or civic achievement, but only if—

(1)   the recipient was selected without any action on his part to enter the contest or proceeding;[3]

(2)   the recipient is not required to render substantial future services as a condition to receiving the prize or award[4]; and

(3)   the prize or award is transferred by the payor to a governmental unit or organization described in paragraph (1) or (2) of section 170(c) pursuant to a designation made by the recipient.

(c)   *Exception for Certain Employee Achievement Awards.—*

(1)   *In general.—Gross income shall not include the value of an employee achievement award (as defined in section 274(j)) received by the taxpayer if the cost to the employer of the employee achievement award does not exceed the amount allowable as a deduction to the employer for the cost of the employee achievement award.*

(2)   *Excess deduction award.—If the cost to the employer of the employee achievement award received by the taxpayer exceeds the amount allowable as a deduction to the employer, then gross income includes the greater of—*

(A)   *an amount equal to the portion of the cost to the employer of the award that is not allowable as a deduction to the employer (but not in excess of the value of the award), or*

(B)   *the amount by which the value of the award exceeds the amount allowable as a deduction to the employer.*

The remaining portion of the value of such award shall not be included in the gross income of the recipient.

(3)   *Treatment of tax-exempt employers.—In the case of an employer exempt from taxation under this subtitle, any reference in this subsection to the amount allowable as a deduction to the employer shall be treated as a reference to the amount which would be allowable as a deduction to the employer if the employer were not exempt from taxation under this subtitle.*

(4)   *Cross reference.—*

For provisions excluding certain de minimis fringes from gross income, see section 132(e).

[For official explanation, see Committee Reports, ¶3858; 3859.]

〖¶2889〗   CODE SEC. 79.   GROUP-TERM LIFE INSURANCE PURCHASED FOR EMPLOYEES.

*   *   *   *   *   *   *   *   *   *   *   *

≫P-H CAUTION→   There are two versions of Sec. 79(d). Sec. 79(d), generally effective after 12-31-87, follows. For Sec. 79(d), generally effective before 1-1-88, see below.

▲   **(d)**   **Nondiscrimination Requirements.—**[1] *In the case of a group-term life insurance*

〖**Footnote ¶2889**〗   ▲ Matter in *italics* in Sec. 79(d) preceded by a triangle added by section 1151(c)(1), '86 TRA, which struck out:

"**(1)**   **In general.—**In the case of a discriminatory group-term life insurance plan

(A)   subsection (a)(1) shall not apply with respect to any key employee, and

(B)   the cost of group-term life insurance on the life of any key employee shall be the greater of—

(i)   such cost determined without regard to subsection (c), or

(ii)   such cost determined with regard to subsection (c).

(2)   **Discriminatory group-term life insurance plan.—**For purposes of this subsection, the term "discriminatory group-term life insurance plan" means any plan of an employer for providing group-term life insurance unless—

(A)   the plan does not discriminate in favor of key employees as to eligibility to participate, and

(B)   the type and amount of benefits available under the plan do not discriminate in favor of participants who are key employees.

(3)   **Nondiscriminatory eligibility classification.—**

(A)   In general.—A plan does not meet requirements of subparagraph (A) of paragraph (2) unless—

(i)   such plan benefits 70 percent or more of all employees of the employer,

(ii)   at least 85 percent of all employees who are participants under the plan are not key employees.

(iii)   such plan benefits such employees as qualify under a classification set up by the employer and found by the Secretary not to be discriminatory in favor of key employees, or

(iv)   in the case of a plan which is part of a cafeteria plan, the requirements of section 125 are met

(B)   Exclusion of certain employees.—For purposes of subparagraph (A), there may be excluded from consideration—

(i)   employees who have not completed 3 years of service;

(ii)   part-time or seasonal employees;

(iii)   employees not included in the plan who are included in a unit of employees covered by an agreement between employee representatives and one or more employers which the Secretary finds to be a collective bargaining agreement, if the benefits provided under the plan were the subject of good faith bargaining between such employee representatives and such employer or employers; and

(iv)   employees who are nonresident aliens and who receive no earned income within the meaning of section 911(d)(2)) from the employer which constitutes income from sources within the United States (within the meaning of section 861(a)(3)).

(4)   **Nondiscriminatory benefits.—**A plan does not meet the requirements of paragraph (2)(B) unless all benefits available to participants who are key employees are available to all other participants.

Code §79(d) ¶2889

plan which is a discriminatory employee benefit plan, subsection (a)(1) shall apply only to the extent provided in section 89.

≫**P-H CAUTION**→ There are two versions of Sec. 79(d). Sec. 79(d), generally effective before 1-1-88, follows. For Sec. 79(d), generally effective after 12-31-87, see above.

▲ ▲   (d)   **Nondiscrimination Requirements.—**

    (1) **In general.—**In the case of a discriminatory group-term life insurance plan—

      (A)   subsection (a)(1) shall not apply with respect to any key employee, and

      (B)   the cost of group-term life insurance on the life of any key employee [2]*shall be the greater of—*

         (i)   such cost determined without regard to subsection (c), or

         (ii)   such cost determined with regard to subsection (c).

* * * * * * * * * * * *

    (6) **Key employee defined.—**For purposes of this subsection, the term "key employee" has the meaning given to such term by paragraph (1) of section 416(i). [3]*Such term also includes any retired employee if such employee when he retired or separated from service was a key employee.*

* * * * * * * * * * * *

    (8)   Treatment of former employees.—To the extent provided in regulations, this subsection shall be applied separately with respect to former employees.

* * * * * * * * * * * *

[For official explanation, see Committee Reports, ¶4007; 4153.]

⟦Footnote ¶2889 continued⟧

  (5) **Special rule.—**A plan shall not fail to meet the requirements of paragraph (2)(B) merely because the amount of life insurance on behalf of the employees under the plan bears a uniform relationship to the total compensation or the basic or regular rate of compensation of such employees.

  (6) **Key employee defined.—**for purposes of this subsection, the term 'key employee' has the meaning given to such term by paragraph (1) of section 416(i). Such term also includes any retired employee if such employee when he retired or separated from service was a key employee.

  (7) **Certain controlled groups, etc.—**All employees who are treated as employed by a single employer under subsection (b), (c), or (m) of section 414 shall be treated as employed by a single employer for purposes of this section.

  (8) **Treatment of former employees.—**To the extent provided in regulations, this subsection shall be applied separately with respect to former employees. "

  Effective date (Sec. 1151(k)(1) and (2), '86 TRA).—(1) Generally applies to years beginning after the later of—

  (A) 12-31-87, or

  (B) the earlier of—

  (i) the date which is 3 months after the date on which the Secretay of the Treasury or his delegate issues such regulations as are necessary to carry out the provisions of section 89 of the '86 Code (as added by this section), or

  (ii) 12-31-88

  (2) Special rule for collective bargaining plan.—In the case of a plan maintained pursuant to 1 or more collective bargaining agreements between employee representatives and 1 or more employers ratified before 3-1-86, the amendments made by this section shall not apply to employees covered by such an agreement in years beginning before the earlier of—

  (A) the date on which the last of such collective bargaining agreements terminates (determined without regard to any extension thereof after 3-28-86, or

  (B) 1-1-91.

A plan shall not be required to take into account employees to which the preceding sentence applies for purposes of applying section 89 of the '86 Code (as added by this section) to employees to which the preceding sentence does not apply for any year preceding the year described in the preceding sentence.

  For exception for certain group-term insurance plans, see footnote ¶2895.

  ▲ ▲   Matter in *italics* in Sec. 79(d)(1)(B), preceded by two triangles, added by section 1827(a)(1), '86 TRA, which struck out:

  (2) "shall be determined without regard to subsection (c)."

  Effective date (Sec. 1827(a)(2), '86 TRA).—Applies to taxable years ending after the date of the enactment of this Act.

  ▲ ▲   Matter in *italics* in Sec. 79(d)(6) and (8) preceded by two triangles added by section 1827(c) and (d), '86 TRA, which struck out:

  (3) ", except that subparagraph (A)(iv) of such paragraph shall be applied by not taking into account employees described in paragraph (3)(B) who are not participants in the plan."

  Effective date (Sec. 1881, '86 TRA, and section 223(d), '84 TRA (as amended by Sec. 1827(b), '86 TRA)).—

  (1) Generally applies to taxable years beginning after 12-31-83. For transitional and special rules, see footnote ¶2891.

【¶2890】 CODE SEC. 81. [1]*INCREASE IN VACATION PAY SUSPENSE ACCOUNT.*
There shall be included in gross income for the taxable year the amount of any increase in any suspense account for such taxable year required by paragraph (2)(B) of section 463(c) (relating to accrual of vacation pay).

[For official explanation, see Committee Reports, ¶3939.]

【¶2891】 SEC. 83. PROPERTY TRANSFERRED IN CONNECTION WITH PERFORMANCE OF SERVICES.

*   *   *   *   *   *   *   *   *   *   *

(e) **Applicability of Section.**—This section shall not apply to—

*   *   *   *   *   *   *   *   *   *   *

(5) [1]group-term life insurance to which section 79 applies.

*   *   *   *   *   *   *   *   *   *   *

[For official explanation, see Committee Reports, ¶4153.]

【¶2892】 CODE SEC. 85. UNEMPLOYMENT COMPENSATION.

(a) [1]*General Rule.—In the case of an individual, gross income includes unemployment*

【Footnote ¶2890】 Matter in *italics* in Sec. 81 added by section 805(c)(1)(A), '86 TRA, which struck out:
(1) "CERTAIN INCREASES IN SUSPENSE ACCOUNTS.
There shall be included in gross income for the taxable year for which an increase is required—
(1) Certain dealers' reserves.—The amount of any increase in the suspense account required by paragraph (4)(B)(ii) of section 166(f) (relating to certain debt obligations guaranteed by dealers).
(2) Vacation pay.—The amount of any increase in the suspense account required by paragraph (2)(B) of section 463(c) (relating to accrual of vacation pay)."
Effective date (Sec. 805(d), '86 TRA).—(1) Generally applies to taxable years beginning after 12-31-86.
(2) Change in method of accounting.—In the case of any taxpayer who maintained a reserve for bad debts for such taxpayer's last taxable year beginning before 1-1-87, and who is required by the amendments made by this section to change its method of accounting for any taxable year—
(A) such change shall be treated as initiated by the taxpayer,
(B) such change shall be treated as made with the consent of the Secretary, and
(C) the net amount of adjustments required by section 481 of the '86 Code to be taken into account by the taxpayer shall—
(i) in the case of a taxpayer maintaining a reserve under section 166(f), be reduced by the balance in the suspense account under section 166(f)(4) of such Code as of the close of such last taxable year, and
(ii) be taken into account ratably in each of the first 4 taxable years beginning after 12-31-86.
【Footnote ¶2891】 Section 1827(e), '86 TRA, struck out from Sec. 83(e)(5):
(1) "the cost of"
Effective date (Sec. 1881, '86 TRA and section 223(d), '84 TRA, as amended by section 1827(b), '86 TRA).—
(1) Generally applies to taxable years beginning after 12-31-83.
(2) Inclusion of Former Employees In The Case of Existing Group-Term Insurance Plans.—
(A) In general.—The amendments made by subsection (a) shall not apply—
(i) to any group-term life insurance plan of the employer in existence on 1-1-84, or
(ii) to any group-term life insurance plan of the employer (or a successor employer) which is a comparable successor to a plan described in clause (i),
but only with respect to an individual who attained age 55 on or before 1-1-84 and was employed by such employer (or a predecessor employer) at any time during 1983. Such amendments also shall not apply to any employee who retired from employment on or before 1-1-84, and who, when he retired, was covered by the plan (or a predecessor plan).
(B) Special rule in the case of discrimination group-term life insurance plan.—In the case of any plan which, after 12-31-86, is a discriminatory group-term life insurance plan (as defined in section 79(d) of the '54 Code), subparagraph (A) shall not apply in the case of any individual retiring under such plan after 12-31-86.
(C) Benefits to certain retired individuals not taken into account for purposes of determining whether plan is discriminatory.—For purposes of determining whether a plan described in subparagraph (A) meets the requirements of section 79(d) of the '54 Code with respect to group-term life insurance for former employees, coverage provided to employees who retired on or before 12-31-86, may, at the employer's election, be disregarded.
(D) Comparable successor plans.—For purposes of subparagraph (A), a plan shall not fail to be treated as a comparable successor to a plan described in subparagraph (A)(i) with respect to any employee whose benefits do not increase under the successor plan.

【Footnote ¶2892】 Matter in *italics* in Sec. 85 added by section 121, '86 TRA, which struck out:
(1) "In General.—If the sum for the taxable year of the adjusted gross income of the taxpayer (determined without regard to this section, section 86, and section 221) and the unemployment compensation exceeds the base amount, gross income for the taxable year includes unemployment compensation in an amount equal to the lesser of—
(1) one-half of the amount of the excess of such sum over the base amount, or
(2) the amount of the unemployment compensation.

compensation.

[2]*(b)* **Unemployment Compensation Defined.**—For purposes of this section, the term "unemployment compensation" means any amount received under a law of the United States or of a State which is in the nature of unemployment compensation.

[For official explanation, see Committee Reports, ¶3857.]

[¶2893] CODE SEC. 86. SOCIAL SECURITY AND TIER 1 RAILROAD RE-TIREMENT BENEFITS.

(a) In General.—Gross income for the taxable year of any taxpayer described in sub-section (b) (not withstanding section 207 of the Social Security Act) includes social security benefits in an amount equal to the lesser of—

(1) one-half of the social security benefits received during the taxable year, or

(2) one-half of the excess described in subsection (b)(1).

(b) Taxpayers to Whom Subsection (a) Applies.—

* * * * * * * * * * * *

(2) **Modified adjusted gross income.**—For purposes of this subsection, the term "modified adjusted gross income" means adjusted gross income—

(A) determined without regard to this section and [1]*sections* 911, 931, and 933, and

(B) increased by the amount of interest received or accrued by the taxpayer during the taxable year which is exempt from tax.

(c) Base Amount.—For purposes of this section, the term "base amount" means—

(1) except as otherwise provided in this subsection, $25,000,

(2) $32,000, in the case of a joint return, and

(3) zero, in the case of a taxpayer who—

(A) is married at the close of the taxable year (within the meaning of [2]*section 7703*) but does not file a joint return for such year, and

(B) does not live apart from his spouse at all times during the taxable year.

* * * * * * * * * * * *

(f) Treatment as Pension or Annuity for Certain Purposes.—For purposes of—

(1) [3]*section 22(c)(3)(A)* (relating to reduction for amounts received as pension or annuity),

(2) section 32(c)(2) (defining earned income),

(3) section 219(f)(1) (defining compensation),

(4) section 221(b)(2) (defining earned income), and

(5) section 911(b)(1) (defining foreign earned income),

any social security benefit shall be treated as an amount received as a pension or annuity.

[For official explanation, see Committee Reports, ¶3860; 4058; 4161.]

[¶2894] CODE SEC. 88. CERTAIN AMOUNTS WITH RESPECT TO NU-CLEAR DECOMMISSIONING COSTS.

[Footnote ¶2892 continued]

(b) **Base Amount Defined.**—For purposes of this section, the term 'base amount' means—

(1) except as provided in paragraphs (2) and (3) $12,000,

(2) $18,000 in the case of a joint return under section 6013, or

(3) zero, in the case of taxpayer who—

(A) is married at the close of the taxable year (within the meaning of section 143) but does not file a joint return for such year, and

(B) does not live apart from his spouse at all times during the taxable year."

(2) "(c)"

Effective date (Sec. 151(b), '86 TRA).—Applies to amounts received after 12-31-86, in taxable years ending after such date.

[Footnote ¶2893] Matter in *italics* in Sec. 86(b)(2)(A) added by section 131(b)(2), which struck out:

(1) "sections 221,"

Effective date (Sec. 151(a), '86 TRA).—Applies to taxable years beginning after 12-31-86.

Matter in *italics* in Sec. 86(c)(3) added by section 1301(j)(8), '86 TRA, which struck out:

(2) "section 143"

Effective date (Sec. 1311(a), 86 TRA).—Applies to bonds issued after 8-15-86.

Matter in *italics* in Sec. 86(f)(1) added by section 1847(b)(2), '86 TRA, which struck out:

(3) "section 37(c)(3)(A)"

Effective date (Sec. 1881, '86 TRA, and section 475(a), '84 TRA).—Applies to taxable years beginning after 12-31-83, and to carrybacks from such years.

In the case of any taxpayer who is required to include the amount of any nuclear decommissioning costs in the taxpayer's cost of service ¹*for* ratemaking purposes, there shall be includible in the gross income of such taxpayer the amount so included for any taxable year.

[For official explanation, see Committee Reports, ¶4141.]

[¶2895] CODE SEC. 89. BENEFITS PROVIDED UNDER CERTAIN EMPLOYEE BENEFIT PLANS.

(a) Benefits Under Discriminatory Plans.—

(1) In general.—Notwithstanding any provision of part III of this subchapter, gross income of a highly compensated employee who is a participant in a discriminatory employee benefit plan during any plan year shall include an amount equal to such employee's excess benefit under such plan for such plan year.

(2) Year of inclusion.—Any amount included in gross income under paragraph (1) shall be taken into account for the taxable year of the employee with or within which the plan year ends.

(b) Excess Benefit.—For purposes of this section—

(1) In general.—The excess benefit of any highly compensated employee is the excess of such employee's employer-provided benefit under the plan over the highest permitted benefit.

(2) Highest permitted benefit.—For purposes of paragraph (1), the highest permitted benefit under any plan shall be determined by reducing the nontaxable benefits of highly compensated employees (beginning with the employees with the greatest nontaxable benefits) until such plan would not be treated as a discriminatory employee benefit plan if such reduced benefits were taken into account.

(3) Plans of same type.—In computing the excess benefit with respect to any benefit, there shall be taken into account all plans of the employer of the same type.

(4) Nontaxable benefits.—For purposes of this subsection, the term "nontaxable benefit" means any benefit provided under a plan to which this section applies which (without regard to subsection (a)(1)) is excludable from gross income under this chapter.

(c) Discriminatory Employee Benefit Plan.—For purposes of this section, the term "discriminatory employee benefit plan" means any statutory employee benefit plan unless such plan meets the—

    (1) eligibility requirements of subsection (d), and

    (2) benefit requirements of subsection (e).

[Footnote ¶2894] Matter in *italics* in Sec. 88 added by section 1807(a)(4)(E)(vii), '86 TRA, which struck out:
(1) "of"

Effective date (Sec. 1881, '86 TRA, and section 91(g)(5), '84 TRA, as added by section 1807(a)(4)(F), '86 TRA).—Takes effect on 7-18-84 with respect to taxable years ending after such date.

[Footnote ¶2895] Sec. 89 added by section 1151(a), '86 TRA.

Effective date (Sec. 1151(k), '86 TRA).—(1) Generally applies to years beginning after the later of—

(A) 12-31-87, or

(B) the earlier of—

(i) the date which is 3 months after the date on which the Secretary of the Treasury or his delegate issues such regulations as are necessary to carry out the provisions of section 89 of the '86 Code (as added by this section), or

(ii) 12-31-88.

(2) Special rule for collective bargaining plan.—In the case of a plan maintained pursuant to 1 or more collective bargaining agreements between employee representatives and 1 or more employers ratified before 3-1-86, the amendments made by this section shall not apply to employees covered by such an agreement in years beginning before the earlier of—

(A) the date on which the last of such collective bargaining agreements terminates (determined without regard to any extension thereof after 2-28-86), or

(B) 1-1-91.

A plan shall not be required to take into account employees to which the preceding sentence applies for purposes of applying section 89 of the '86 Code (as added by this section) to employees to which the preceding sentence does not apply for any year preceding the year described in the preceding sentence.

(3) Exception for certain group-term insurance plans.—In the case of a plan described in section 223(d)(2) of '84 TRA, such plan shall be treated as meeting the requirements of section 89 of the '86 Code (as added by this section) with respect to individuals described in section 223(d)(2) of such Act. An employer may elect to disregard such individuals in applying section 89 of such Code (as so added) to other employees of the employer.

(4) Special rule for church plans.—In the case of a church plan (within the meaning of section 414(e)(3) of the '86 Code) maintaining an insured accident and health plan, the amendments made by this section shall apply to years beginning after 12-31-88.

(d) **Eligibility Requirements.—**

(1) **In general.—**A plan meets the eligibility requirements of this subsection for any plan year if—

(A) at least 90 percent of all employees who are not highly compensated employees—

(i) are eligible to participate in such plan (or in any other plan of the employer of the same type), and

(ii) would (if they participated) have available under such plans an employer-provided benefit which is at least 50 percent of the largest employer-provided benefit available under all such plans of the employer to any highly compensated employee,

(B) at least 50 percent of the employees eligible to participate in such plan are not highly compensated employees, and

(C) such plan does not contain any provision relating to eligibility to participate which (by its terms or otherwise) discriminates in favor of highly compensated employees.

(2) **Alternative eligibility percentage test.—**A plan shall be treated as meeting the requirements of paragraph (1)(B) if—

(A) the percentage determined by dividing the number of highly compensated employees eligible to participate in the plan by the total number of highly compensated employees, does not exceed

(B) the percentage similarly determined with respect to employees who are not highly compensated employees.

(e) **Benefit Requirements.—**

(1) **In general.—**A plan meets the benefit requirements of this subsection for any plan year if the average employer-provided benefit received by employees other than highly compensated employees under all plans of the employer of the same type is at least 75 percent of the average employer-provided benefit received by highly compensated employees under all plans of the employer of the same type.

(2) **Average employer-provided benefit.—**For purposes of this subsection, the term "average employer-provided benefit" means, with respect to highly compensated employees, an amount equal to—

(A) the aggregate employer-provided benefits received by highly compensated employees under all plans of the type being tested, divided by

(B) the number of highly compensated employees (whether or not covered under such plans).

The average employer-provided benefit with respect to employees other than highly compensated employees shall be determined in the same manner as the average employer-provided benefit for highly compensated employees.

(f) **Special Rule Where Health or Group-Term Plan Meets 80-Percent Coverage Test.—**If at least 80 percent of the employees who are not highly compensated employees are covered under a health plan or group-term life insurance plan during the plan year, such plan shall be treated as meeting the requirements of subsections (d) and (e) for such year. The preceding sentence shall not apply if the plan does not meet the requirements of subsection (d)(1)(C) (relating to nondiscriminatory provisions).

(g) **Operating Rules.—**

(1) **Aggregation of comparable health plans.—**In the case of health plans maintained by an employer—

(A) **In general.—**An employer may treat a group of comparable plans as 1 plan for purposes of applying subsections (d)(1)(B), (d)(2) and (f).

(B) **Comparable plans.—**For purposes of subparagraph (A), a group of comparable plans is any group (selected by the employer) of plans of the same type if the smallest employer-provided benefit available to any participant in any such plan is at least 95 percent of the largest employer-provided benefit available to any participant in any such plan.

(2) **Special rules for applying benefit requirements to health plans.—**

(A) **Election.—**For purposes of determining whether the requirements of subsection (e) are met with respect to health plans, the employer may elect—

(i) to disregard any employee if such employee and his spouse and dependents (if any) are covered by a health plan providing core benefits maintained by another employer, and

(ii)   to apply subsection (e) separately with respect to coverage of spouses or dependents by such plans and to take into account with respect to such coverage only employees with a spouse or dependents who are not covered by a health plan providing core benefits maintained by another employer.

(B)   Sworn statements.—Any employer who elects the application of subparagraph (A) shall obtain and maintain, in such manner as the Secretary may prescribe, adequate sworn statements to demonstrate whether individuals have—
(i)   a spouse or dependents, and
(ii)   core health benefits under a plan of another employer.
The Secretary shall provide a method for meeting the requirements of this subparagraph through the use of valid sampling techniques.

(C)   Presumption where no statement.—In the absence of a statement described in subparagraph (B)—
(i)   an employee who is not a highly compensated employee shall be treated—
(I)   as not covered by another plan of another employer providing core benefits, and
(II)   as having a spouse and dependents not covered by another plan of another employer providing core benefits, and

(ii)   a highly compensated employee shall be treated—
(I)   as covered by another plan of another employer providing core benefits, and
(II)   as not having a spouse or dependents.

(D)   Certain individuals may not be disregarded.—In the case of a highly compensated employee who receive employer-provided benefits under all health plans of the employer which are more than 133⅓ percent of the average employer-provided benefit under such plan for employees other than highly compensated employees, the employer may not disregard such employee, or his spouse or dependents for purposes of clause (i) or (ii) of subparagraph (A).

(3)   **Employer-provided benefit.**—For purposes of this section—
(A)   In general.—Except as provided in subsection (k), an employee's employer-provided benefit under any statutory employee benefit plan is—
(i)   in the case of any health or group-term life insurance plan, the value of the coverage, or
(ii)   in the case of any other plan, the value of the benefits,
provided during the plan year to or on behalf of such employee to the extent attributable to contributions made by the employer.

(B)   Special rule for health plans.—The value of the coverage provided by any health plan shall be determined under procedures prescribed by the Secretary which shall—
(i)   set forth the values of various standard types of coverage involving a representative group, and
(ii)   provide for adjustments to take into account the specific coverage and group involved.

(C)   Special rule for group-term life plans.—
(i)   In general.—Except as provided in clause (ii), in determining the value of coverage under a group-term life insurance plan, the amount taken into account for any employee shall be based on the cost of the insurance determined under section 79(c) for an employee who is age 40.
(ii)   Excess benefit.—For purposes of subsection (b), the excess benefit with respect to coverage under a group-term life insurance plan shall be equal to the greater of—
(I)   the cost of such excess benefit (expressed as dollars of coverage) determined without regard to section 79(c), or
(II)   such cost determined with regard to section 79(c).

Code §89(g)(3) ¶2895

(D) Salary reductions.—Except for purposes of subsections (d)(1)(A)(ii) and (j)(5), any salary reduction shall be treated as an employer-provided benefit.

(4) Election to test plans of different types together.—

(A) In general.—Except as provided in subparagraph (B), the employer may elect to treat all plans of the types specified in such election as plans of the same type for purposes of applying subsection (e).

(B) Exception for health plans.—Subparagraph (A) shall not apply for purposes of determining whether any health plan meets the requirements of subsection (e); except that benefits provided under health plans which meet such requirements may be taken into account in determining whether plans of other types meet the requirements of subsection (e).

(5) Separate line or business exception.—If, under section 414(r), an employer is treated as operating separate lines of business for a year, the employer may apply the preceding provisions of this section separately with respect to employees in each such separate line of business. The preceding sentence shall not apply to any plan unless such plan is available to a group of employees as qualify under a classification set up by the employer and found by the Secretary not to be discriminatory in favor of highly compensated employees.

(6) Special rule for applying eligibility requirements and 80-percent test to health plans.—For purposes of determining whether the requirements of subsection (d)(1)(A)-(ii) or of subsection (f) are met with respect to health plans, the employer may elect—

(A) to apply this section separately with respect to coverage of spouses and dependents by such plans, and

(B) to take into account with respect to such coverage only those employees with a spouse or dependent (determined under rules similar to the rules of paragraphs (2)(B) and (C)).

(h) Excluded Employees.—

(1) In general.—The following employees shall be excluded from consideration under this section:

(A) Employees who have not completed 1 year of service (or in the case of core benefits under a health plan, 6 months of service). An employee shall be excluded from consideration until the 1st day of the 1st month beginning after completion of the period of service required under the preceding sentence.

(B) Employees who normally work less than 17½ hours per week.

(C) Employees who normally work during not more than 6 months during any year.

(D) Employees who have not attained age 21.

(E) Employees who are included in a unit of employees covered by an agreement which the Secretary finds to be a collective bargaining agreement between employee representatives and 1 or more employers if there is evidence that the type of benefits provided under the plan was the subject of good faith bargaining between the employee representatives and such employer or employers.

(F) Employees who are nonresident aliens and who receive no earned income (within the meaning of section 911(d)(2)) from the employer which constitutes income from sources within the United States (within the meaning of section 861(a)(3)).

Subparagraphs (A), (B), (C), and (D) shall be applied by substituting a shorter period of service, smaller number of hours or months, or lower age specified in the plan for the period of service, number of hours or months, or age (as the case may be) specified in such subparagraph.

(2) Certain exclusions not to apply if excluded employees covered.—Except to the extent provided in regulations, employees shall not be excluded from consideration under any subparagraph of paragraph (1) (other than subparagraph (F)) unless no employee described in such subparagraph (determined with regard to the last sentence of paragraph (1)) is eligible under the plan.

(3) Exclusion must apply to all plans.—

(A) In general.—An exclusion shall apply under any subparagraph of paragraph (1) (other than subparagraph (F) thereof) only if the exclusion applies to all statutory employee benefit plans of the employer of the same type. In the case of a cafeteria plan, all benefits under the cafeteria plan shall be treated as provided under plans of the same type.

(B) Exception.—Subparagraph (A) shall not apply to any difference in waiting periods for core and noncore benefits provided by health plans.

(4) Exception for separate line of business.—If any line of business is treated separately under subsection (h)(5), then paragraphs (2) and (3) shall be applied separately to such line of business.

(5) Requirements may be met separately with respect to excluded group.—Notwithstanding paragraphs (2) and (3), if employees do not meet minimum age or service requirements described in paragraph (1) (without regard to the last sentence thereof) and are covered under a plan of the employer which meets the requirements of this section separately with respect to such employees, such employees may be excluded from consideration in determining whether any plan of the employer meets the requirements of this section.

(i) Statutory Employee Benefit Plan.—For purposes of this section—

(1) In general.—The term "statutory employee benefit plan" means—
(A) an accident or health plan (within the meaning of section 105(e)), and
(B) any plan of an employer for providing group-term life insurance (within the meaning of section 79).

(2) Employer may elect to treat other plans as statutory employee benefit plan.—An employer may elect to treat any of the following plans as statutory employee benefit plans:
(A) A qualified group legal services plan (within the meaning of section 120(b)).
(B) An educational assistance program (within the meaning of section 127(b)).
(C) A dependent care assistance program (within the meaning of section 129(d)).

An election under this paragraph with respect to any plan shall apply with respect to all plans of the same type as such plan.

(3) Plans of the same type.—2 or more plans shall be treated as of the same type if such plans are described in the same subparagraph of paragraph (1) or (2).

(j) Other Definitions and Special Rules.—For purposes of this section—

(1) Highly compensated employee.—The term "highly compensated employee" has the meaning given such term by section 414(q).

(2) Health plan.—The term "health plan" means any plan described in paragraph (1)(A) of subsection (i).

(3) Treatment of former employees.—Except to the extent provided in regulations, this section shall be applied separately to former employees under requirements similar to the requirements that apply to employees.

(4) Group-term life insurance plans.—
(A) In general.—Any group-term life insurance plan shall not be treated as 2 or more separate plans merely because the amount of life insurance under the plan on behalf of employees bears a uniform relationship to the compensation (within the meaning of section 414(s)) of such employees.
(B) Limitation on compensation.—For purposes of subparagraph (A), compensation in excess of the amount applicable under section 401(a)(17) shall not be taken into account.
(C) Limitation.—This paragraph shall not apply to any plan if such plan is combined with plans of other types pursuant to an election under subsection (g)(4).

(5) Special rule for employees working less than 30 hours per week.—Any health plan shall not fail to meet the requirements of this section merely because the employer-provided benefit is proportionally reduced for employees who normally work less than 30 hours per week. The preceding sentence shall apply only where the average work week of employees who are not highly compensated employees is 30 hours or more.

Code §89(j)(5) ¶2895

(6) **Treatment of self-employed individuals.**—In the case of a statutory employee benefit plan described in subparagraph (A), (B), or (C) of subsection (i)(2)—

    (A) Treatment as employee, etc.—The term "employee" includes any self-employed individual (as defined in section 401(c)(1)), and the term "compensation" includes such individual's earned income (as defined in section 401(c)(2)).

    (B) Employer.—An individual who owns the entire interest in an unincorporated trade or business shall be treated as his own employer. A partnership shall be treated as the employer of each partner who is treated as an employee under subparagraph (A).

(7) **Certain plans treated as meeting other nondiscrimination requirements.**—If an employer makes an election under subsection (i)(2) to have this section apply to any plan and such plan meets the requirements of this section, such plan shall be treated as meeting any other nondiscrimination requirement imposed on such plan (other than any requirement under section 120(c)(3), 127(b)(3), or 129(d)(4)).

(8) **Special rules for certain dispositions or acquisitions.**—

    (A) In general.—If a person becomes, or ceases to be, a member of a group described in subsection (b), (c), (m), or (o) of section 414, then the requirements of this section shall be treated as having been met during the transition period with respect to any plan covering employees of such person or any other member of such group if—

        (i) such requirements were met immediately before each such change, and

        (ii) the coverage under such plan is not significantly changed during the transition period (other than by reason of the change in members of a group).

    (B) Transition period.—For purposes of subparagraph (A), the term "transition period" means the period—

        (i) beginning on the date of the change in members of a group, and

        (ii) ending on the last day of the 1st plan year beginning after the date of such change.

(9) **Coordination with Medicare, etc.**—If a plan may be coordinated with health benefits provided under any Federal, State, or foreign law or under any other health plan covering the employee or family member of the employee, such plan shall not fail to meet the requirements of this section with respect to health benefits merely because the amount of such benefits provided to any employee or family member of any employee are coordinated in a manner which does not discriminate in favor of highly compensated employees.

(10) **Disability benefits.**—

    (A) In general.—If a plan may be coordinated with disability benefits provided under any Federal, State, or foreign law or under any other plan covering the employee, such plan shall not fail to meet the requirements of this section with respect to disability benefits merely because the amount of such benefits provided to an employee are coordinated in a manner which does not discriminate in favor of highly compensated employees.

    (B) Certain disability plans exempt from nondiscrimination rules.—Subsection (a) shall not apply to any disability coverage other than disability coverage the benefits of which are excludable from gross income under section 105(b) or (c).

(11) **Separate application in the case of options.**—Each option or different benefit shall be treated as a separate plan.

(k) **Requirement That Plan Be in Writing, Etc.—**

(1) **In general.**—Notwithstanding any provision of part III of this subchapter, gross income of an employee shall include an amount equal to such employee's employer-provided benefit for the taxable year under an employee benefit plan to which this subsection applies unless, except to the extent provided in regulations—

    (A) such plan is in writing,

    (B) the employees' rights under such plan are legally enforceable,

    (C) employees are provided reasonable notification of benefits available in the plan,

    (D) such plan is maintained for the exclusive benefit of employees, and

    (E) such plan was established with the intention of being maintained for an indefinite period of time.

Such inclusion shall be in lieu of any inclusion under subsection (a) with respect to such plan.

(2) Plans to which subsection applies.—This subsection shall apply to—
(A) any statutory employee benefit plan,
(B) a qualified tuition reduction program (within the meaning of section 117(d)),
(C) a cafeteria plan (within the meaning of section 125),
(D) a fringe benefit program providing no-additional-cost services, qualified employee discounts, or employer-operated eating facilities which are excludable from gross income under section 132, and
(E) a plan to which section 505 applies.

(3) Special rule for determining inclusion.—For purposes of paragraph (1), an employee's employer-provided benefit shall be the value of the benefits provided to the employee.

(4) Plans to which contributions are made by more than 1 employer.—For purposes of paragraph (1)(D), in the case of a plan to which contributions are made by more than 1 employer, each employer shall be treated as employing employees of all other employers.

(l) Reporting Requirements.—

(1) In general.—If an employee of an employer maintaining a plan is required to include any amount in gross income under this section for any plan year ending with or within a calendar year, the employer shall separately include such amount on the statement which the employer is required to provide the employee under section 6051(a) (and any statement required to be furnished under section 6051(d)).

(2) Penalty.—
For penalty for failing to report, see section 6652(l).

(m) Regulations.—The Secretary shall prescribe such regulations as may be necessary or appropriate to carry out the purposes of this section, including regulations providing for appropriate adjustments in case of individuals not employees of the employer throughout the plan year.

[For official explanation, see Committee Reports, ¶4007.]

【¶2896】 **CODE SEC. 101.   CERTAIN DEATH BENEFITS.**

* * * * * * * * * * * *

(d) Payment of Life Insurance Proceeds at a Date Later Than Death.—

(1) General rule.—The amounts held by an insurer with respect to any beneficiary shall be prorated (in accordance with such regulations as may be prescribed by the Secretary) over the period or periods with respect to which such payments are to be made.[1] *There shall be excluded from the gross income of such beneficiary in the taxable year received any amount by such proration.*

Gross income includes, to the extent not excluded by the preceding sentence, amounts received under agreements to which this subsection applies.

(2) Amount held by an insurer.—An amount held by an insurer with respect to any beneficiary shall mean an amount to which subsection (a) applies which is—
(A) held by any insurer under an agreement provided for in the life insurance contract, whether as an option or otherwise, to pay such amount on a date or dates later than the death of the insured, and
(B) [2] equal to the value of such agreement to such beneficiary
(i) as of the date of death of the insured (as if any option exercised under the life insurance contract were exercised at such time), and
(ii) as discounted on the basis of the interest rate [3] used by the insurer in

【Footnote ¶2896】 Matter in *italics* in Sec. 101(d) added by section 1001(a)—(c), '86 TRA, which struck out:
(1) "There shall be excluded from the gross income of such beneficiary in the taxable year received—
(A) any amount determined by such proration, and
(B) in the case of the surviving spouse of the insured, that portion of the excess of the amounts received under one or more agreements specified in paragraph (2)(A) (whether or not payment of any part of such amounts is quaranteed by the insurer) over the amount determined in subparagraph (A) of this paragraph which is not greater than $1,000 with respect to any insured."
(2) "is"
(3) "and mortality tables"

calculating payments under the agreement *and mortality tables prescribed by the Secretary.*[4]

[5] *(3)* **Application of subsection.**—This subsection shall not apply to any amount to which subsection (c) is applicable.

* * * * * * * * * * * *

[For official explanation, see Committee Reports, ¶3954.]

[¶2897] CODE SEC. 102. GIFTS AND INHERITANCES.

(a) General rule.—Gross income does not include the value of property acquired by gift, bequest, devise, or inheritance.

* * * * * * * * * * * *

(c) Employee Gifts.—

(1) In general.—*Subsection (a) shall not exclude from gross income any amount transferred by or for an employer to, or for the beneift of, an employee.*

(2) Cross references.—
For provisions excluding certain employee achievement awards from gross income, see section 74(c).
For provisions excluding certain de minimis fringes from gross income, see section 132(e).

[For official explanation, see Committee Reports, ¶3858.]

≫P-H CAUTION→ There are two versions of Sec. 103. Sec. 103, generally applicable to bonds issued after 8-15-86, follows. For Sec. 103, generally applicable to bonds issued before 8-16-86, see ¶2898-A, below.

[¶2898] CODE SEC. 103. INTEREST ON [1]*STATE AND LOCAL BONDS.*

(a) Exclusion.—*Except as provided in subsection (b), gross income does not include interest on any State or local bond.*

(b) Exceptions.—*Subsection (a) shall not apply to*—

(1) Private activity bond which is not a qualified bond.—*Any private activity bond which is not a qualified bond (within the meaning of section 141).*

(2) Arbitrage bond.—*Any arbitrage bond (within the meaning of section 148).*

(3) Bond not in registered form, etc.—*Any bond unless such bond meets the applicable requirements of section 149.*

(c) Definitions.—*For purposes of this section and part IV*—

(1) State or local bond.—*The term "State or local bond" means an obligation of a State or political subdivision thereof.*

(2) State.—*The term "State" includes the District of Columbia and any possession of the United States.*

[Footnote ¶2896 continued]

(4) "(3) **Surviving spouse.**—For purposes of this section, the term 'surviving spouse' means the spouse of the insured as of the date of death including a spouse legally separated but not under a decree of absolute divorce."
(5) "(4)"
Effective Date (Sec. 1001(d), '86 TRA).—Applies to amounts received with respect to deaths occurring after the date of enactment of this Act, in taxable years ending after such date.
[Footnote ¶2897] Sec. 102(c) in *italics* added by section 122(b), '86 TRA.
Effective date (Sec. 151(c), '86 TRA).—Applies to prizes and awards granted after 12-31-86.
[Footnote ¶2898] Matter in *italics* in Sec. 103 added by section 1301(a), '86 TRA, which struck out:
(1) "CERTAIN GOVERNMENTAL OBLIGATIONS.
(a) **General rule.**—Gross income does not include interest on—
(1) the obligations of a State, a Territory, or a possession of the United States, or any political subdivision of any of the foregoing, or of the District of Columbia; and
(2) qualified scholarship funding bonds.
(b) **Industrial Development Bonds.**—
(1) **Subsection (a)(1) or (2) not to apply.**—Except as otherwise provided in this subsection, any industrial development bond shall be treated as an obligation not described in subsection (a)(1) or (2).
(2) **Industrial development bond.**—For purposes of this section the term 'industrial development bond' means any obligation—
(A) which is issued as part of an issue all or a major portion of the proceeds of which are to be used directly or indirectly in any trade or business carried on by any person who is not an exempt person (within the meaning of paragraph (3)), and
(B) the payment of the principal or interest on which (under the terms of such obligation or any underlying arrangement) is, in whole or in major part—
(i) secured by any interest in property used or to be used in a trade or business or in payments in respect of such property, or

【**Footnote ¶2898 continued**】

(ii) to be derived from payments in respect of property, or borrowed money, used or to be used in a trade or business.

(3) **Exempt person.**—For purposes of paragraph (2)(A), the term "exempt person" means

(A) a governmental unit, or

(B) an organization described in section 501(c)(3) and exempt from tax under section 501(a) (but only with respect to a trade or business, carried on by such organization which is not an unrelated trade or business, determined by applying section 513(a) to such organization).

(4) **Certain exempt activities.**—Paragraph (1) shall not apply to any obligation which is issued as part of an issue substantially all of the proceeds of which are to be used to provide—

(A) projects for residential rental property if at all times during the qualified project period—

(i) 15 percent or more in the case of targeted area projects, or

(ii) 20 percent or more in the case of any other project,

of the units in each project are to be occupied by individuals of low or moderate income,

(B) sports facilities,

(C) convention or trade show facilities,

(D) airports, docks, wharves, mass commuting facilities, parking facilities, or storage or training facilities directly related to any of the foregoing,

(E) sewage or solid waste disposal facilities or facilities for the local furnishing of electric energy or gas,

(F) air or water pollution control facilities,

(G) facilities for the furnishing of water for any purpose if—

(i) the water is or will be made available to members of the general public (including electric utility, industrial, agricultural, or commercial users), and

(ii) either the facilities are operated by a governmental unit or the rates for the furnishing or sale of the water have been established or approved by a state or political subdivision thereof, by an agency or instrumentality of the United States or by a public service or public utility commission or other similar body of any State or political subdivision thereof,

(H) qualified hydroelectric generating facilities,

(I) qualified mass commuting vehicles, or

(J) local district heating or cooling facilities.

For purposes of subparagraph (E), the local furnishing of electric energy or gas from a facility shall include furnishing solely within the area consisting of a city and 1 contiguous county. For purposes of subparagraph (A), any property shall not be treated as failing to be residential rental property merely because part of the building in which such property is located is used for purposes other than residential rental purposes.

(5) **Industrial parks.**—Paragraph (1) shall not apply to any obligation issued as part of an issue substantially all of the proceeds of which are to be used for the acquisition or development of land as the site for an industrial park. For purposes of the preceding sentence, the term 'development of land' includes the provision of water, sewage, drainage, or similar facilities or of transportation, power, or communication facilities, which are incidental to use of the site as an industrial park, but, except with respect to such facilities, does not include the provision of structures or buildings.

(6) **Exemption for certain small issues.**—

(A) In general.—Paragraph (1) shall not apply to any obligation issued as part of an issue the aggregate authorized face amount of which is $1,000,000 or less and substantially all of the proceeds of which are to be used (i) for the acquisition, construction, reconstruction, or improvement of land or property of a character subject to the allowance for depreciation, or (ii) to redeem part or all of a prior issue which was issued for purposes described in clause (i) or this clause.

(B) Certain prior issues taken into account.—If—

(i) the proceeds of two or more issues of obligations (whether or not the issuer of each issue is the same) are or will be used primarily with respect to facilities located in the same incorporated municipality or located in the same county (but not in any incorporated municipality),

(ii) the principal user of such facilities is or will be the same person or two or more related persons, and

(iii) but for this subparagraph, subparagraph (A) would apply to each such issue,

then, for purposes of subparagraph (A), in determining the aggregate face amount of any later issue there shall be taken into account the face amount of obligations issued under all prior such issues and outstanding at the time of such later issue (not including as outstanding any obligation which is to be redeemed from the proceeds of the later issue).

(C) Related persons.—For purposes of this paragraph and paragraph (13) a person is a related person if—

(i) the relationship between such persons would result in a disallowance of losses under section 267 or 707(b), or

(ii) such persons are members of the same controlled group of corporations (as defined in section 1563(a), except that 'more than 50 percent' shall be substituted for 'at least 80 percent' each place it appears therein).

(D) $10,000,000 limit in certain cases.—At the election of the issuer, made at such time and in such manner as the Secretary shall by regulations prescribe, with respect to any issue this paragraph shall be applied—

(i) by substituting '10,000,000' for '$1,000,000' in subparagraph (A), and

(ii) in determining the aggregate face amount of such issue, by taking into account not only the amount described in subparagraph (B), but also the aggregate amount of capital expenditures with respect to facilities described in subparagraph (E) paid or incurred during the 6-year period beginning 3 years before the date of such issue and ending 3 years after such date (and financed otherwise than out of the proceeds of outstanding issues to which subparagraph (A) applied), as if the aggregate amount of such capital expenditures constituted the face amount of a prior outstanding issue described in subparagraph (B).

[Footnote ¶2898 continued]

(E) Facilities taken into account.—For purposes of subparagraph (D)(ii), the facilities described in this subparagraph are facilities—

(i) located in the same incorporate municipality or located in the same county (but not in any incorporated municipality), and

(ii) the principal user of which is or will be the same person or two or more related persons.

For purposes of clause (i), the determination of whether or not facilities are located in the same governmental unit shall be made as of the date of issue of the issue in question.

(F) Certain capital expenditures not taken into account.—For purposes of subparagraph (D)(ii), any capital expenditure—

(i) to replace property destroyed or damaged by fire, storm, or other casualty, to the extent of the fair market value of the property replaced,

(ii) required by a change made after the date of issue of the issue in question in a Federal or State law or local ordinance of general application or required by a change made after such date in rules and regulations of general application issued under such a law or ordinance,

(iii) required by circumstances which could not be reasonably foreseen on such date of issue or arising out of a mistake of law or fact (but the aggregate amount of expenditures not taken into account under this clause with respect to any issue shall not exceed $1,000,000), or

(iv) described in clause (i) or (ii) of section 30(b)(2)(A) for which a deduction was allowed under section 174(a), shall not be taken into account.

(G) Limitation on loss of tax exemption.—In applying subparagraph (D)(ii) with respect to capital expenditures made after the date of any issue, no obligation issued as a part of such issue shall be treated as an obligation not described in subsection (a)(1) by reason of any such expenditure for any period before the date on which such expenditure is paid or incurred.

(H) Certain refinancing issues.—In the case of any issue described in subparagraph (A)(ii), an election may be made under subparagraph (D) only if all of the prior issues being redeemed are issues to which subparagraph (A) applies. In applying subparagraph (D)(ii) with respect to such a refinancing issue, capital expenditures shall be taken into account only for purposes of determining whether the prior issues being redeemed qualified (and would have continued to qualify) under subparagraph (A).

(I) Aggregate amount of capital expenditures where there is urban development action grant.—In the case of any issue substantially all of the proceeds of which are to be used to provide facilities with respect to which an urban development action grant has been made under section 119 of the Housing and Community Development Act of 1974, capital expenditures not to exceed $10,000,000 shall not be taken into account for purposes of applying subparagraph (D)(ii).

(J) Issues for residential purposes.—This paragraph shall not apply to any obligation which is issued as a part of an issue a significant portion of the proceeds of which are to be used directly or indirectly to provide residential real property for family units.

(K) Limitations on treatment of obligations as part of the same issue.—For purposes of this paragraph, separate lots of obligations which (but for this subparagraph) would be treated as part of the same issue shall be treated as separate issues unless the proceeds of such lots are to be used with respect to facilities—

(i) which are located in more than 1 State, or

(ii) which have, or will have, as the same principal user the same person or related persons.

(L) Franchises.—For purposes of subparagraph (K), a person (other than a governmental unit) shall be considered a principal user of a facility if such person (or a group of related persons which includes such person)—

(i) guarantees, arranges, participates in, or assists with the issuance (or pays any portion of the cost of issuance) of any obligation the proceeds of which are to be used to finance or refinance such facility, and

(ii) provides any property, or any franchise, trademark, or trade name (within the meaning of section 1253), which is to be used in connection with such facility.

(M) Paragraph not to apply if obligations issued with certain other tax-exempt obligations.—This paragraph shall not only apply to any obligation which is issued as part of an issue (other than an issue to which subparagraph (D) applies) if the interest on any other obligation which is part of such issue is excluded from gross income under any provision of law other than this paragraph.

(N) Termination dates.—

(i) In general.—This paragraph shall not apply to any obligation issued after December 31, 1986 (including any obligations issued to refund an obligation issued on or before such date).

(ii) Obligations used to finance manufacturing facilities.—In the case of an obligation which is part of an issue substantially all of the proceeds of which are to be used to provide a manufacturing facility, clause (i) shall be applied by substituting '1988' for '1986'.

(iii) Manufacturing facility.—For purposes of this subparagraph, the term 'manufacturing facility' means any facility which is used in the manufacturing or production of tangible personal property (including the processing resulting in a change in the condition of such property).

(O) Restrictions on financing certain facilities.—This paragraph shall not apply to an issue if—

(i) more than 25 percent of the proceeds of the issue are used to provide a facility the primary purpose of which is one of the following: retail food and beverage services, automobile sales or service, or the provision of recreation or entertainment; or

(ii) any portion of the proceeds of the issue is to be used to provide the following: any private or commercial golf course, country club, massage parlor, tennis club, skating facility (including roller skating, skateboard, and ice skating), racquet sports facility (including any handball or racquetball court), hot tub facility, suntan facility, or racetrack.

(P) Aggregation of issues with respect to single project.—For purposes of this paragraph, 2 or more issues part or all of which are to be used with respect to a single building, an enclosed shopping mall, or a strip of offices, stores, or warehouses using substantial common facilities shall be treated as 1 issue (and any person who is a prin-

[Footnote ¶2898 continued]

cipal user with respect to any of such issues shall be treated as a principal user with respect to the aggregated issue).

(7) [Repealed]

(8) **Qualified hydroelectric generating facilities.**—For purposes of this section—

(A) Qualified hydroelectric generating facility.—The term 'qualified hydroelectric generating facility' means any qualified hydroelectric generating property which is owned by a State, political subdivision thereof, or agency or instrumentality of any of the foregoing.

(B) Qualified hydroelectric generating property.—

(i) In general.—Except as provided in clause (ii), the term 'qualified hydroelectric generating property' has the meaning given to such term by section 48(l)(13).

(ii) Dam must be owned by governmental body.—The term 'qualified hydroelectric generating property' does not include any property installed at the site of any dam described in section 48(l)(13)(B)(i)(I) unless such dam was owned by one or more governmental bodies described in subparagraph (A) on October 18, 1979, and at all times thereafter until the obligations are no longer outstanding.

(C) Limitation.—Paragraph (4)(H) of this subsection shall not apply to any issue of obligations (otherwise qualifying under paragraph (4)(H) if the portion of the proceeds of such issue which is used to provide qualified hydroelectric generating facilities exceeds (by more than an insubstantial amount) the product of—

(i) the eligible cost of the facilities being provided in whole or in part from the proceeds of the issue, and

(ii) the installed capacity fraction.

(D) Installed capacity fraction.—The term 'installed capacity fraction' means the fraction—

(i) the numerator of which is 25, reduced by 1 for each megawatt by which the installed capacity exceeds 100 megawatts, and

(ii) the denominator of which is the number of megawatts of the installed capacity (but not in excess of 100).

For purposes of the preceding sentence, the term 'installed capacity' has the meaning given to such term by section 48(l)(13)(E).

(E) Eligible cost.—

(i) In general.—The eligible cost of any facilities is that portion of the total cost of such facilities which is reasonably expected—

(I) to be the cost to the governmental body described in subparagraph (A), and

(II) to be attributable to periods after October 18, 1979, and before 1986 (determined under rules similar to the rules of section 48(m)).

(ii) Longer period for certain hydroelectric generating property.—If an application has been docketed by the Federal Energy Regulatory Commission before January 1, 1986, with respect to the installation of any qualified hydroelectric generating property, clause (i)(II) shall be applied with respect to such property by substituting '1989' for '1986'.

(F) Certain prior issues taken into account.—If the proceeds of 2 or more issues (whether or not the issuer of each issue is the same) are or will be used to finance the same facilities, then, for purposes of subparagraph (C), in determining the amount of the proceeds of any later issue used to finance such facilities, there shall be taken into account the proceeds used to finance such facilities of all prior such issues which are outstanding at the time of such later issue (not including as outstanding any obligation which is to be redeemed from the proceeds of the later issue).

(9) **Qualified mass commuting vehicles.**—

(A) In general.—For purposes of paragraph (4)(I), the term 'qualified mass commuting vehicle' means any bus or subway car, rail car, ferry, or similar equipment—

(i) which is leased to a mass transit system wholly owned by 1 or more governmental units (or agencies or instrumentalities thereof), and

(ii) which is used by such system in providing mass commuting services (or, in the case of a ferry, mass transportation services).

(B) Termination.—Paragraph (4)(I) shall not apply to any obligation issued after December 31, 1984.

(10) **Local district heating or cooling facility.**—For purposes of this section—

(A) In general.—The term 'local district heating or cooling facility' means property used as an integral part of a local district heating or cooling system.

(B) Local district heating or cooling system.—

(i) In general.—The term 'local district heating or cooling system' means any local system consisting of a pipeline or network (which may be connected to a heating or cooling source) providing hot water, chilled water, or steam to 2 or more users for—

(I) residential, commercial, or industrial heating or cooling, or

(II) process steam.

(ii) Local system.—For purposes of this subparagraph, a local system includes facilities furnishing heating and cooling to an area consisting of a city and one contiguous county.

(11) [Repealed]

(12) **Projects for residential rental property.**—For purposes of paragraph (4)(A)—

(A) Targeted area project.—The term 'targeted area project' means—

(i) a project located in a qualified census tract (within the meaning of section 103A(k)(2)), or

(ii) an area of chronic economic distress (within the meaning of section 103A(k)(3)).

(B) Qualified project period.—The term 'qualified project period' means the period beginning on the first day on which 10 percent of the units in the project are occupied and ending on the later of—

(i) the date which is 10 years after the date on which 50 percent of the units in the project are occupied,

(ii) the date which is a qualified number of days after the date on which any of the units in the project are occupied, or

Code §103 ¶2898

[Footnote ¶2898 continued]

(iii) the date on which any assistance provided with respect to the project under section 8 of the United States Housing Act of 1937 terminates.

For purposes of clause (ii), the term 'qualified number' means, with respect to an obligation described in paragraph (4)(A), 50 percent of the number of days which comprise the term of the obligation with the longest maturity.

(C) Individuals of low and moderate income.—Individuals of low and moderate income shall be determined by the Secretary in a manner consistent with determinations of lower income families under section 8 of the United States Housing Act of 1937 (or if such program is terminated, under such program as in effect immediately before such termination), except that the percentage of median gross income which qualifies as low or moderate income shall be 80 percent.

(13) **Exception.**—Paragraphs (4), (5), and (6) shall not apply with respect to any obligation for any period during which it is held by a person who is a substantial user of the facilities or a related person. For purposes of this paragraph—

(A) a partnership and each of its partners (and their spouses and minor children) shall be treated as related persons, and

(B) an S corporation and each of its shareholders (and their spouses and minor children) shall be treated as related persons.

(14) **Maturity may not exceed 120 percent of economic life.—**

(A) General rule.—Paragraphs (4), (5), and (6) shall not apply to any obligation issued as part of an issue if—

(i) the average maturity of the obligations which are part of such issue, exceeds

(ii) 120 percent of the average reasonably expected economic life of the facilities being financed with the proceeds of such issue.

(B) Determination of averages.—For purposes of subparagraph (A)—

(i) the average maturity of any issue shall be determined by taking into account the respective issue prices of the obligations which are issued as part of such issue, and

(ii) the average reasonably expected economic life of the facilities being financed with any issue shall be determined by taking into account the respective cost of such facilities.

(C) Special rules.—

(i) Determination of economic life.—For purposes of this paragraph, the reasonably expected economic life of any facility shall be determined as of the later of—

(I) the date on which the obligations are issued, or

(II) the date on which the facility is placed in service (or expected to be placed in service).

(ii) Treatment of land.—

(I) Land not taken into account.—Except as provided in subclause (II), land shall not be taken into account under subparagraph (A)(ii).

(II) Issues where 25 percent or more of proceeds used to finance land.—If 25 percent or more of the proceeds of any issue is used to finance land, such land shall be taken into account under subparagraph (A)(ii) and shall be treated as having an economic life of 50 years.

(15) **Aggregate limit per taxpayer for small issue exception.—**

(A) In general.—Paragraph (6) of this subsection shall not apply to any issue if the aggregate authorized face amount of such issue allocated to any test-period beneficiary (when increased by the outstanding tax-exempt IDB's of such beneficiary) exceeds $40,000,000.

(B) Outstanding tax-exempt IDB's of any person.—For purposes of applying subparagraph (A) with respect to any issue, the outstanding tax-exempt IDB's of any person who is a test-period beneficiary with respect to such issue is the aggregate face amount of all industrial development bonds the interest on which is exempt from tax under subsection (a)—

(i) which are allocated to such beneficiary and

(ii) which are outstanding at the time of such later issue (not including as outstanding any obligation which is to be redeemed from the proceeds of the later issue).

(C) Allocation of face amount of an issue.—

(i) In general.—Except as otherwise provided in regulations, the portion of the face amount of an issue allocated to any test-period beneficiary of a facility financed by the proceeds of such issue (other than an owner of such facility) is an amount which bears the same relationship to the entire face amount of such issue as the portion of such facility used by such beneficiary bears to the entire facility.

(ii) Owners.—Except as other wise provided in regulations, the portion of the face amount of an issue allocated to any test-period beneficiary who is an owner of a facility financed by the proceeds of such issue is an amount which bears the same relationship to the entire face amount of such issue as the portion of such facility owned by such beneficiary bears to the entire facility.

(D) Test-period beneficiary.—For purposes of this paragraph, except as provided in regulations, the term 'test-period beneficiary' means any person who was an owner or a principal user of facilities being financed by the issue at any time during the 3-year period beginning on the later of—

(i) the date such facilities were placed in service, or

(ii) the date of the issue.

(E) Treatment of related persons.—For purposes of this paragraph, all persons who are related (within the meaning of paragraph (6)(C)) to each other shall be treated as one person.

(16) **Limitation on use for land acquisition.—**

(A) In general.—Paragraphs (4), (5), and (6) shall not apply with respect to any obligation issued as part of an issue if—

(i) any portion of the proceeds of such issue are to be used (directly or indirectly) for the acquisition of land (or an interest therein) to be used for farming purposes, or

(ii) 25 percent or more of the proceeds of such issue are to be used (directly or indirectly) for the acquisition of

[Footnote ¶2898 continued]

land not described in clause (i) (or an interest therein).

In the case of an obligation described in paragraph (5) (relating to industrial parks), clause (ii) shall be applied by substituting '50 percent' for '25 percent'.

(B) Exception for first-time farmers.—

(i) In general.—If the requirements of clause (ii) are met with respect to any land, subparagraph (A) shall not apply to such land, and paragraph (17) shall not apply to property located thereon or to property to be acquired within 1 year to be used in farming, but only to the extent of expenditures (financed with the proceeds of the issue) not in excess of $250,000.

(ii) Acquisition by first-time farmers.—The requirements of this clause are met with respect to any land if—

(I) such land is to be used for farming purposes, and

(II) such land is to be acquired by an individual who is a first time farmer, who will be the principal user of such land, and who will materially and substantially participate on the farm of which such land is a part in the operation of such farm.

(iii) First-time farmer.—For purposes of this subparagraph, the term 'first-time farmer' means any individual if such individual has not at any time had any direct or indirect ownership interest in substantial farmland in the operation of which such individual materially participated. For purposes of this subparagraph, any ownership or material participation by an individual's spouse or minor child shall be treated as ownership and material participation by the individual.

(iv) Farm.—For purposes of this subparagraph, the term 'farm' has the meaning given such term by section 6420(c)(2).

(v) Substantial farmland.—The term 'substantial farmland' means any parcel of land unless—

(I) such parcel is smaller than 15 percent of the median size of a farm in the county in which such parcel is located, and

(II) the fair market value of the land does not at any time while held by the individual exceed $125,000.

(C) Exception for certain land acquired for environmental purposes.—Any land acquired by a public agency in connection with an airport, mass transit, or port development project which consists of facilities described in paragraph (4)(D) shall not be taken into account under subparagraph (A) if—

(i) such land is acquired for a noise abatement, wetland preservation, future use, or other public purpose, and

(ii) there is not other significant use of such land.

(17) Acquisition of existing property not permitted.—

(A) In general.—Paragraphs (4), (5), and (6) shall not apply to any obligation issued as part of an issue if any portion of the proceeds of such issue is to be used for the acquisition of any property (or an interest therein) unless the first use of such property is pursuant to such acquisition.

(B) Exception for certain rehabilitations.—Subparagraph (A) shall not apply with respect to any building (and the equipment therefor) if—

(i) the rehabilitation expenditures with respect to such building equals or exceeds

(ii) 15 percent of the portion of the cost of acquiring such building (and equipment) financed with the proceeds of the issue.

A rule to the rule of the preceding sentence shall apply in the case of facilities other than a building except that clause (ii) shall be applied by substituting '100 percent' for '15 percent'.

(C) Rehabilitation expenditures.—

For purposes of this paragraph—

(i) In general.—Except as provided in this subparagraph, the term 'rehabilitation expenditures' means any amount properly chargeable to capital account which is incurred by the person acquiring the building for property (or additions or improvements to property) in connection with the rehabilitation of a building. In the case of an integrated operation contained in a building before its acquisition, such term included rehabilitating existing equipment in such building or replacing it with equipment having substantially the same function. For purposes of this clause, any amount incurred by a successor to the person acquiring the building or by the seller under a sales contract with such person shall be treated as incurred by such person.

(ii) Certain expenditures not included.—The term 'rehabilitation expenditures' does not include any expenditure described in section 48(g)(2)(B) (other than clause (i) thereof).

(iii) Period during which expenditures must be incurred.—The term 'rehabilitation expenditures' shall not include any amount which is incurred after the date 2 years after the later of—

(I) the date on which the building was acquired, or

(II) the date on which the obligation was issued.

(D) Special rule for certain projects—In the case of a project involving 2 or more buildings, this paragraph shall be applied on a project basis.

(18) No portion of bonds may be issued for skyboxes, airplanes, gambling establishments, etc.—Paragraphs (4), (5), and (6) shall not apply to any obligation issued as part of an issue if any portion of the proceeds of such issue is to be used to provide any airplane, skybox, or other private luxury box, any health club facility, and facility primarily used for gambling, or any store the principal business of which is the sale of alcoholic beverages for consumption off premises.

(c) Arbitrage.—

(1) Subsection (a)(1) or (2) not to apply to arbitrage bonds.—Except as otherwise provided in this subsection, any arbitrage bond shall be treated as an obligation not described in subsection (a)(1) or (2).

(2) Arbitrage Bond.—For purposes of this subsection, the term 'arbitrage bond' means any obligation which is issued as part of an issue all or a major portion of the proceeds of which are reasonably expected to be used directly or indirectly—

(A) to acquire securities (within the meaning of section 165(g)(2)(A) or (B)) or obligations (other than obliga-

⟦Footnote ¶2898 continued⟧

tions described in subsection (a)(1) or (2)) which may be reasonably expected at the time of issuance of such issue, to produce a yield over the term of the issue which is materially higher (taking into account any discount or premium) than the yield on obligations of such issue, or

(B) to replace funds which were used directly or indirectly to acquire securities or obligations described in subparagraph (A).

(3) **Exception.**—Paragraph (1) shall not apply to any obligation—

(A) which is issued as part of an issue substantially all of the proceeds of which are reasonably expected to be used to provide permanent financing for real property used or to be used for residential purposes for the personnel of an educational organization described in section 170(b)(1)(A)(ii) which grants baccalaureate or higher degrees, or to replace funds which were so used, and

(B) the yield on which over the term of the issue is not reasonably expected, at the time of issuance of such issue, to be substantially lower than the yield on obligations acquired or to be acquired in providing such financing.

This paragraph shall not apply with respect to any obligation for any period during which it is held by a person who is a substantial user of property financed by the proceeds of the issue of which such obligation is a part, or by a member of the family (within the meaning of section 318(a)(1)) of any such person.

(4) **Special rules.**—For purposes of paragraph (1), an obligation shall not be treated as an arbitrage bond solely by reason of the fact that—

(A) the proceeds of the issue of which such obligation is a part may be invested for a temporary period in securities or other obligations until such proceeds are needed for the purpose for which such issue was issued, or

(B) an amount of the proceeds of the issue of which such obligation is a part may be invested in securities or other obligations which are part of a reasonably required reserve or replacement fund.

The amount referred to in subparagraph (B) shall not exceed 15 percent of the proceeds of the issue of which such obligation is a part unless the issuer establishes that a higher amount is necessary.

(5) **Student loan incentive payments.**—Payments made by the Commissioner of Education pursuant to section 438 of the Higher Education Act of 1965 are not to be taken into account, for purposes of paragraph (2)(A), in determining yields on student loan notes.

(6) **Investments in nonpurpose obligations.**—

(A) In general.—For purposes of this title, any obligation which is part of an issue of industrial development bonds which does not meet the requirements of subparagraphs (C) and (D) shall be treated as an obligation which is not described in subsection (a).

(B) Exceptions.—Subparagraph (A) shall not apply to any obligation described in subsection (b)(4)(A) or to any housing program obligation under section 11(b) of the Housing Act of 1937.

(C) Limitation on investment in nonpurpose obligations.—

(i) In general.—An issue meets the requirements of this subparagraph only if—

(I) at no time during any bond year, the amount invested in nonpurpose obligations with a yield higher than the yield on the issue exceeds 150 percent of the debt service on the issue for the bond year, and

(II) the aggregate amount invested as provided in subclause (I) is promptly and appropriately reduced as the amount of outstanding obligations of the issue is reduced.

(ii) Exception for temporary periods.—Clause (i) shall not apply to—

(I) proceeds of the issue invested for an initial temporary period until such proceeds are needed for the governmental purpose of the issue, and

(II) temporary investment periods related to debt service.

(iii) Debt service defined.—For purposes of this subparagraph, the debt service on the issue for any bond year is the scheduled amount of interest and amortization of principal payable for such year with respect to such issue. For purposes of the preceding sentence, there shall not be taken into account amounts scheduled with respect to any bond which has been retired before the beginning of the bond year.

(iv) No disposition in case of loss.—This subparagraph shall not require the sale or disposition of any investment if such sale or disposition would result in a loss which exceeds the amount which would be paid to the United States (but for such sale or disposition) at the time of such sale or disposition.

(D) Rebate to United States.—An issue shall be treated as meeting the requirements of this subparagraph only if an amount equal to the sum of—

(i) the excess of—

(I) the aggregate amount earned on all nonpurpose obligations (other than investments attributable to an excess described in this clause), over

(II) the amount which would have been earned if all nonpurpose obligations were invested at a rate equal to the yield on the issue, plus

(ii) any income attributable to the excess described in clause (i),

is paid to the United States by the issuer in accordance with the requirements of subparagraph (E).

(E) Due date of payments under subparagraph (D).—The amount which is required to be paid to the United States by the issuer shall be paid in installments which are made at least once every 5 years. Each installment shall be in an amount which insures that 90 percent of the amount described in subparagraph (D) with respect to the issue at the time payment of such installment is required will have been paid to the United States. The last installment shall be made no later than 30 days after the day on which the last obligation of the issue is redeemed and shall be in an amount sufficient to pay the remaining balance of the amount described in subparagraph (D) with respect to such issue.

(F) Special rules for applying subparagraph (D).—

(i) In general.—In determining the aggregate amount earned on nonpurpose obligations for purposes of subparagraph (D)—

(I) any gain or loss on the disposition of a nonpurpose obligation shall be taken into account, and

(II) unless the issuer otherwise elects, any amount earned on a bona fide debt service fund shall not be taken

[Footnote ¶2898 continued]

into account if the gross earnings on such fund for the bond year is less than $100,000.

(ii) Temporary investments.—Under regulations prescribed by the Secretary, an issue shall, for purposes of this paragraph, be treated as meeting the requirements of subparagraph (D) if the gross proceeds of such issue are expended for the governmental purpose for which the bond was issued by no later than the day which is 6 months after the date of issuance of such issue. Gross proceeds which are held in a bona fide debt service fund shall not be considered gross proceeds for purposes of this clause only.

(G) Exemption from gross income of sum rebated.—Gross income does not include the sum described in subparagraph (D). Notwithstanding any other provision of this title, no deduction shall be allowed for any amount paid to the United States under subparagraph (D).

(H) Definitions.—For purposes of this paragraph—

(i) Nonpurpose obligations.—The term 'nonpurpose obligation' means any security (within the meaning of subparagraph (A) or (B) of section 165(g)(2)) or any obligation not described in subsection (a) which—

(I) is acquired with the gross proceeds of an issue, and

(II) is not acquired in order to carry out the governmental purpose of the issue.

(ii) Gross proceeds.—The gross proceeds of an issue include—

(I) amounts received (including repayments of principal) as a result of investing the original proceeds of the issue, and

(II) amounts used to pay debt service on the issue.

(iii) Yield.—The yield on the issue shall be determined on the basis of the issue price (within the meaning of section 1273 or 1274).

(7) Regulations.—The Secretary shall prescribe such regulations as may be necessary to carry out the purposes of this subsection.

(d) Certain Irrigation Dams.—A dam for the furnishing of water for irrigation purposes which has a subordinate use in connection with the generation of electric energy by water shall be treated as meeting the requirements of subsection (b)(4)(G) if—

(1) substantially all of the stored water is contractually available for release from such dam for irrigation purposes, and

(2) the water so released is available on reasonable demand to members of the general public.

(e) Qualified Scholarship Funding Bonds.—For purposes of subsection (a), the term 'qualified scholarship funding bonds' means obligations issued by a corporation which—

(1) is a corporation not for profit established and operated exclusively for the purpose of acquiring student loan notes incurred under the Higher Education Act of 1965, and

(2) is organized at the request of a State or one or more political subdivisions thereof or is requested to exercise such power by one or more political subdivisions and required by its corporate charter and bylaws, or required by State law, to devote any income (after payment of expenses, debt service, and the creation of reserves for the same) to the purchase of additional student loan notes or to pay over any income to the State or a political subdivision thereof.

(f) Certain Federally Guaranteed Obligations.—Any obligation the payment of interest or principal (or both) of which is guaranteed in whole or in part under title I of the New York City Loan Guarantee Act of 1978 shall, with respect to interest accrued during the period for which such guarantee is in effect, be treated as an obligation not described in subsection (a).

(g) Qualified Steam-Generating or Alcohol-Producing Facilities.—

(1) In general.—For purposes of subsection (b)(4)(E), the term 'solid waste disposal facility' includes—

(A) a qualified steam-generating facility, and

(B) a qualified alcohol-producing facility.

(2) Qualified steam-generating facility defined.—For purposes of paragraph (1), the term 'qualified steam-generating facility' means a steam-generating facility for which—

(A) more than half of the fuel (determined on a Btu basis) is solid waste or fuel derived from solid waste, and

(B) substantially all of the solid waste derived fuel is produced at a facility which is—

(i) located at or adjacent to the site for such steam-generating facility, and

(ii) owned and operated by the person who owns and operates the steam-generating facility.

(3) Qualified alcohol-producing facility.—For purposes of paragraph (1), the term 'qualified alcohol-producing facility' means a facility—

(A) the primary product of which is alcohol,

(B) more than half of the feedstock for which is solid waste or a feedstock derived from solid waste, and

(C) substantially all of the solid waste derived feedstock for which is produced at a facility which is—

(i) located at or adjacent to the site for such alcohol-producing facility, and

(ii) owned and operated by the person who owns and operates the alcohol-producing facility.

(4) Special location rule in case of steam-generating facility.—A facility for producing solid waste derived fuel shall be treated as a facility which meets the requirements of clauses (i) and (ii) of paragraph (2)(B) if—

(A) such facility and the steam-generating facility are owned and operated by or for a State or the same political subdivision or subdivisions of a State, and

(B) substantially all of the solid waste used in producing the solid waste derived fuel at the facility producing such fuel is collected from the area in which the steam-generating facility is located.

(h) Obligation Must Not Be Guaranteed, Etc.—

(1) In general.—An obligation shall not be treated as an obligation described in subsection (a) if such obligation is federally guaranteed.

(2) Federally guaranteed defined.—For purposes of paragraph (1), an obligation is federally guaranteed if—

(A) the payment of principal or interest with respect to such obligation is guaranteed (in whole or in part) by

[Footnote ¶2898 continued]

the United States (or any agency or instrumentality thereof),

(B) such obligation is issued as part of an issue and a significant portion of the proceeds of such issue are to be—

(i) used in making loans the payment of principal or interest with respect to which are to be guaranteed (in whole or in part) by the United States (or any agency or instrumentality thereof), or

(ii) invested (directly or indirectly) in federally insured deposits or accounts, or

(C) the payment of principal or interest on such obligation is otherwise indirectly guaranteed (in whole or in part) by the United States (or an agency or instrumentality thereof).

(3) **Exceptions.—**

(A) Certain insurance programs.—An obligation shall not be treated as federally guaranteed by reason of—

(i) any guarantee by the Federal Housing Administration, the Veterans' Administration, the Federal National Mortgage Association, the Federal Home Loan Mortgage Corporation, or the Government National Mortgage Association,

(ii) any guarantee of student loans and any guarantee by the Student Loan Marketing Association to finance student loans,

(iii) any guarantee by the Small Business Administration with respect to qualified contracts for pollution control facilities (within the meaning of section 404(a) of the Small Business Investment Act of 1958, as in effect on the date of the enactment of the Tax Reform Act of 1984) if—

(I) the Administrator of the Small Business Administration charges a fee for making such guarantee, and

(II) the amount of such fee equals or exceeds 1 percent of the amount guaranteed, or

(iv) any guarantee by the Bonneville Power Authority pursuant to the Northwest Power Act (16 U.S.C. 839d) as in effect on the date of the enactment of the Tax Reform Act of 1984 with respect to any obligation issued before July 1, 1989.

(B) Debt service, etc.—Paragraph (1) shall not apply to—

(i) proceeds of the issue invested for an initial temporary period until such proceeds are needed for the purpose for which such issue was issued,

(ii) investments of a bona fide debt service fund,

(iii) investments of a reserve which meet the requirements of subsection (c)(4)(B),

(iv) investments in obligations issued by the United States Treasury, or

(v) other investments permitted under regulations.

(C) Exception for housing programs.—

(i) In general.—Except as provided in clause (ii), paragraph (1) shall not apply to—

(I) an obligation described in subsection (b)(4)(A) or a housing program obligation under section 11(b) of the United States Housing Act of 1937,

(II) a qualified mortgage bond (as defined in section 103A(c)(1)), or

(III) a qualified veterans' mortgage bond (as defined in section 103A(c)(3)).

(ii) Exception not to apply where obligation invested in federally insured deposits or accounts.—Clause (i) shall not apply to any obligation which is federally guaranteed within the meaning of paragraph (2)(B)(ii).

(D) Loans to, or guarantees by, financial institutions.—Except as provided in paragraph (2)(B)(ii), an obligation which is issued as part of an issue shall not be treated as federally guaranteed merely by reason of the fact that the proceeds of such issue are used in making loans to a financial institution or there is a guarantee by a financial institution.

(4) **Definitions.—**For purposes of this subsection—

(A) Treatment of certain entities with authority to borrow from United States.—To the extent provided in regulations prescribed by the Secretary, any entity with statutory authority to borrow from the United States shall be treated as an instrumentality of the United States. Except in the case of a private activity bond (as defined in subsection (n)(7)), nothing in the preceding sentence shall be construed as treating the District of Columbia or any possession of the United States as an instrumentality of the United States.

(B) Federally insured deposit or account.—The term 'federally insured deposit or account' means any deposit or account in a financial institution to the extent such deposit or account is insured under Federal law by the Federal Deposit Insurance Corporation, the Federal Savings and Loan Insurance Corporation, the National Credit Union Administration, or any similar federally chartered corporation.

(5) **Certain obligations subsidized under energy program.—**

(A) In general.—An obligation to which this paragraph applies shall be treated as an obligation not described in subsection (a) if the payment of the principal or interest with respect to such obligation is to be made (in whole or in part) under a program of a State, or a political subdivision of a State the principal purpose of which is to encourage the production or conservation of energy.

(B) Obligations to which paragraph applies.—This paragraph shall apply to any obligations to which paragraph (1) of subsection (b) does not apply by reason of—

(i) subsection (b)(4)(H) (relating to qualified hydroelectric generating facilities), or

(ii) subsection (g) (relating to qualified steam-generating or alcohol-producing facilities).

(i) **Obligations of Certain Volunteer Fire Departments.—**

(1) In general.—An obligation of a volunteer fire department shall be treated as an obligation of a political subdivision of a State if—

(A) such department is a qualified volunteer fire department with respect to an area within the jurisdiction of such political subdivison, and

(B) such obligation is issued as part of an issue substantially all of the proceeds of which are to be used for the acquisition, construction, reconstruction, or improvement of a firehouse or firetruck used or to be used by such department.

(2) **Qualified volunteer fire department.—**For purposes of this subsection, the term 'qualified volunteer fire department' means, with respect to a political subdivison of a State, any organization—

[Footnote ¶2898 continued]

(A)   which is organized and operated to provide firefighting or emergency medical services for persons in an area (within the jurisdiction of such political (subdivision) which is not provided with any other firefighting services,

(B)   which is required (by written agreement) by the political subdivision to furnish firefighting services in such area.

(j)   **Obligations Must Be in Registered Form to Be Tax Exempt.—**

(1)   **In general.—**Nothing in subsection (a) or in any other provision of law shall be construed to provide an exemption from Federal income tax for interest on any registration-required obligation unless the obligation is in registered form.

(2)   **Registration-required obligation.—**The term 'registration-required obligation' means any obligation other than an obligation which—

(A)   is not of a type offered to the public,

(B)   has a maturity (at issue) of not more than 1 year, or

(C)   is described in section 163(f)(2)(B).

(3)   **Special rules.—**

(A)   Book entries permitted.—For purposes of paragraph (1), a book entry obligation shall be treated as in registered form if the right to the principal of, and stated interest on, such obligation may be transferred only through a book entry consistent with regulations prescribed by the Secretary.

(B)   Nominees.—The Secretary shall prescribe such regulations as may be necessary to carry out the purpose of paragraph (1) where there is a nominee or chain of nominees.

(k)   **Public Approval for Industrial Development Bonds.—**

(1)   **In general.—**Notwithstanding subsection (b), an industrial development bond shall be treated as an obligation not described in subsection (a) unless the requirements of paragraph (2) of this subsection are satisifed.

(2)   **Public approval requirement.—**

(A)   In general.—An obligation shall satisfy the requirements of this paragraph if such obligation is issued as a part of an issue which has been approved by—

(i)   the governmental unit—

(I)   which issued such obligation, or

(II)   on behalf of which such obligation was issued, and

(ii)   each governmental unit having jurisdiction over the area in which any facility, with respect to which financing is to be provided from the proceeds of such issue, is located (except that if more than I governmental unit within a State has jurisdiction over the entire area within such State in which such facility is located, only 1 such unit need approve such issue.

(B)   Approval by a governmental unit.—For purposes of subparagraph (A), an issue shall be treated as having been approved by any governmental unit if such issue is approved—

(i)   by the applicable elected representative of such governmental unit after a public hearing following reasonable public notice, or

(ii)   by voter referendum of such governmental unit.

(C)   Special rules for approval of facility.—If there has been public approval under subparagraph (A) of the plan of financing a facility, such approval shall constitute approval under subparagraph (A) for any issue—

(i)   which is issued pursuant to such plan within 3 years after the date of the first issue pursuant to the approval, and

(ii)   all or substantially all of the proceeds of which are to be used to finance such facility or to refund previous financing under such plan.

(D)   Refunding obligations.—No approval under subparagraph (A) shall be necessary with respect to any obligation which is issued to refund an obligation approved under subparagraph (A) (or treated as approved under subparagraph (C) unless the maturity date of such obligation is later than the maturity date of the obligation to be refunded.

(E)   Applicable elected representative.—For purposes of this paragraph—

(i)   In general.—The term 'applicable elected representative' means with respect to any govermental unit—

(I)   an elected legislative body of such unit, or

(II)   the chief elected executive officer, the chief elected State legal officer of the executive branch, or any other elected official of such unit designated for purposes of this paragraph by such chief elected officer or by State law.

(ii)   No applicable elected representative.—If (but for this clause) a governmental unit has no applicable elected representative, the applicable elected representative for purposes of clause (i) shall be the applicable elected representative of the governmental unit—

(I)   which is the next higher governmental unit with such a representative, and

(II)   from which the authority of the governmental unit with no such representative is derived.

(l)   **Information Reporting Requirements for Certain Bonds.—**

(1)   **In general.—**Notwithstanding subsection (b), any industrial development bond or any other obligation which is issued as part of an issue all or a major portion of the proceeds of which are to be used directly or indirectly—

(A)   to finance loans to individuals for educational expenses, or

(B)   by an organization described in section 501(c)(3) which is exempt from taxation by reason of section 501(a).

shall be treated as an obligation not described in paragraph (1) or (2) of subsection (a) unless such bond satisfies the requirements of paragraph (2).

(2)   **Information reporting requirement.—**An obligation satisfies the requirement of this paragraph if the issuer submits to the Secretary, not later than the 15th day of the 2nd calendar month after the close of the calender

[Footnote ¶2898 continued]

quarter in which the obligation is issued, a statement concerning the issue of which the obligation is a part which contains—

(A) the name and address of the issuer,

(B) the date of issue, the amount of lendable proceeds of the issue, and the stated interest rate, term and face amount of each obligation which is part of the issue,

(C) where required, the name of the applicable elected representative who approved the issue, or a description of the voter referendum by which the issue was approved,

(D) the name, address, and employer identification number of—

(i) each initial principal user of any facilities provided with the proceeds of the issue,

(ii) the common parent of any affiliated group of corporations (within the meaning of section 1504(a)) of which such initial principal user is a member, and

(iii) if the issue is treated as a separate issue under subsection (b)(6)(K), any person treated as a principal user under subsection (b)(6)(L),

(E) a description of any person to be financed from the proceeds of the issue, and (F) if such obligation is a private activity bond (as defined in subsection (n)(7)), such information as the Secretary may require for purposes of determining whether the requirements of subsection (n) are met with respect to such obligation.

(3) **Extension of time.**—The Secretary may grant an extension of time for the filing of any statement required under paragraph (2) if there is reasonable cause for the failure to file such statement in a timely fashion.

(m) **Obligations Exempt Other Than Under This Title.**—

(1) **Prior exemptions.**—For purposes of this title, notwithstanding any provisions of this section or section 103A any obligation the interest on which is exempt from taxation under this title under any provision of law which is in effect on the date of the enactment of this subsection (other than a provision of this title) shall be treated as an obligation described in subsection (a). In the case of an obligation issued after December 31, 1983, such obligation shall not be treated as described in this paragraph unless the appropriate requirements of subsections (b), (c), (h), (j), (k), (l), (n), and (o) of this section and section 103A are met with respect to such obligation. For purposes of applying such requirements, a possession of the United States shall be treated as a State; except that clause (ii) of subsection (n)(4)(A) shall not apply.

(2) **No other interest to be exempt except as provided by this title.**—Notwithstanding any other provision of law, no interest on any obligation shall be exempt from taxation under this title unless such interest—

(A) is on an obligation described in paragraph (l), or

(B) is exempt from tax under this title without regard to any provision of law which is not contained in this title and which is not contained in a revenue Act.

(3) **Exceptions.**—The following obligations shall be treated as obligations described in paragraph (1) (without regard to the second sentence thereof):

(A) Any obligation issued pursuant to the Northwest Power Act (16 U.S.C. 839d) as in effect on the date of the enactment of the Tax Reform Act of 1984.

(B) Any obligation issued pursuant to section 608(a)(b)(A) of Public Law 97-468.

(C) Any obligation issued before June 19, 1984, under section 11(b) of the United States Housing Act of 1937.

(n) **Limitation on Aggregate Amount of Private Activity Bonds Issued During Any Calendar Year.**—

(1) **In general.**—A private activity bond issued as part of an issue shall be treated as an obligation not described in subsection (a) if the aggregate amount of private activity bonds issued pursuant to such issue, when added to the aggregate amount of private activity bonds previously issued by the issuing authority during the calendar year, exceeds such authority's private activity bond limit for such calendar year.

(2) **Private activity bond limit for state agencies.**—For purposes of this subsection—

(A) **In general.**—The private activity bond limit for any agency of the State authorized to issue private activity bonds for any calendar year shall be 50 percent of the State ceiling for such calendar year.

(B) **Special rule where state has more than 1 agency.**—If more than 1 agency of the State is authorized to issue private activity bonds, all such agencies shall be treated as a single agency.

(3) **Private activity bond limit for other issuers.**—For purposes of this subsection—

(A) **In general.**—The private activity bond limit for any issuing authority (other than a State agency) for any calendar year shall be an amount which bears the same ratio to 50 percent of the State ceiling for such calendar year as—

(i) the population of the jurisdiction of such issuing authority, bears to

(ii) the population for the entire State.

(B) **Overlapping jurisdictions.**—For purposes of subparagraph (A)(i), the rules of section 103A(g)(3)(B) shall apply.

(4) **State ceiling.**—For purposes of this subsection—

(A) **In general.**—The State ceiling applicable to any State for any calendar year shall be the greater of

(i) an amount to $150 multiplied by the State's population, or

(ii) $200,000,000.

(B) **Phasein of limitation where amount of 1983 private activity bonds exceeds the ceiling.**—

(i) **In general.**—In the case of any State which has an excess bond amount for 1983, the State ceiling for calendar year 1984 shall be the sum of the State ceiling determined under subparagraph (A) plus 50 percent of the excess bond amount for 1983.

(ii) **Excess bond amount for 1983.**—For purposes of clause (i), the excess bond amount for 1983 in any State is the excess (if any) of—

(I) the aggregate amount of private activity bonds issued by issuing authorities in such State during the first 9 months of calendar year 1983 multiplied by $4/3$, over

(II) the State ceiling determined under subparagraph (A) for calendar year 1984.

(C) **Adjustment of ceiling to reflect partial termination of small issue exemption.**—In the case of calendar years after 1986, subparagraph (A) shall be applied by substituting '$100' for '$150'.

[Footnote ¶2898 continued]

(5) **Special rule for states with constitutional home rule cities.**—In the case of any State with 1 or more constitutional home rule cities (as defined in section 103A(g)(5)(C)), the rules of paragraph (5) of section 103A(g) shall apply for purposes of this subsection.

(6) **State may provide for different allocation.**—

(A) In general.—A State may, by law provide a different formula for allocating the State ceiling among the governmental units or other authorities in such State having authority to issue private activity bonds.

(B) Interim authority for governor.—

(i) In general.—The Governor of any State may proclaim a different formula for allocating the State ceiling among the governmental units or other authorities in such State having authority to issue private activity bonds.

(ii) Termination of authority.—The authority provided in clause (i) shall not apply after the earlier of—

(I) the first day of the first calendar year beginning after the legislature has met in regular session for more than 60 days after the date of the enactment of this paragraph, or

(II) the effective date of any State legislation with respect to the allocation of the State ceiling.

(C) State may not alter allocation to constitutional home rule cities.—The rules of paragraph (6)(C) of section 103A(g) shall apply for purposes of this paragraph.

(7) **Private activity bond.**—For purposes of this subsection—

(A) In general.—Except as otherwise provided in the paragraph, the term 'private activity bond' means any obligation the interest on which is exempt from tax under subsection (a) and which is—

(i) an industrial development bond, or

(ii) a student loan bond.

(B) Exception for multifamily housing.—The term 'private activity bond' shall not include any obligation described in subsection (b)(4)(A) nor any housing program obligation under section 11(b) of the United States Housing Act of 1937.

(C) Exception for certain facilities described in section 103(b)(4)(C) or (D).—

(i) In general.—The term 'private activity bond' shall not include any obligation described in subparagraph (C) or (D) of subsection 103(b)(4), but only if all of the property to be financed by the obligation is owned by or on behalf of a governmental unit.

(ii) Exception not to apply to certain parking facilities.—For purposes of clause (i), subparagraph (D) of subsection (b)(4) shall be applied as if it did not contain the phrase 'parking facilities.'

(iii) Determination of whether property owned by governmental unit.—For purposes of clause (i), property shall not be treated as not owned by a governmental unit solely by reason of the length of the lease to which it is subject if the lessee makes an irrevocable election (binding on the lessee and all successors in interest under the lease) not to claim depreciation or an investment credit with respect to such property.

(iv) Restriction where significant front end loading.—Under regulations prescribed by the Secretary, clause (i) shall not apply in any case where the property is leased under a lease which has significant front end loading of rental accruals or payments.

(D) Refunding issues.—The term 'private activity bond' shall not include any obligation which is issued to refund another obligation to the extent that the amount of such obligation does not exceed the amount of the refunded obligation. In the case of any student loan bond, the preceding sentence shall apply only if the maturity date of the refunding obligation is not later than the later of—

(i) the maturity of the obligation to be refunded, or

(ii) the date 17 years after the date on which the refunded obligation was issued (or in the case of a series of refundings, the date on which the original obligation was issued).

(8) **Student loan bonds.**—For purposes of this subsection, the term 'student loan bond' means an obligation which is issued as part of an issue all or a major portion of the proceeds of which are to be used directly or indirectly to finance loans to individuals for educational expenses.

(9) **Population.**—For purposes of this subsection, determinations of the population of any State (or issuing authority) shall be made with respect to any calendar year on the basis of the most recent census estimate of the resident population of such State (or issuing authority) published by the Bureau of the Census before the beginning of such calendar year.

(10) **Elective carryforward of unused limitation for specified project.**—

(A) In general.—If—

(i) an issuing authority's private activity bond limit for any calendar year after 1983, exceeds

(ii) the aggregate amount of private activity bonds issued during such calendar year by such authority,

such authority may elect to treat all (or any portion) of such excess as a carryforward for 1 or more carryforward projects.

(B) Election must identify project.—In any election under subparagraph (A), the issuing authority shall—

(i) identify (with reasonable specificity) the project (or projects) for which the carryforward is elected, and

(ii) specify the portion of the excess described in subparagraph (A) which is to be a carryforward for each such project.

(C) Use of carryforward.—

(i) In general.—If any issuing authority elects a carryforward under subparagraph (A) with respect to any carryforward project, any private activity bonds issued by such authority with respect to such project during the 3 calendar years (or, in the case of a project described in subsection (b)(4)(F), 6 calendar years) following the calendar year in which the carryforward arose shall not be taken into account under paragraph (1) to the extent the amount of such bonds do not exceed the amount of the carryforward elected for such project.

(ii) Order in which carryforward used.—Carryforwards elected with respect to any project shall be used in the order of the calendar years in which they arose.

(D) Election.—Any election made under this paragraph shall be made at such time and in such identification

Code §103 ¶2898

[For official explanation, see Committee Reports, ¶4058.]

➤➤**P-H CAUTION→** There are two versions of Sec. 103. Sec. 103, generally applicable for bonds issued before 8-16-86, follows. For Sec. 103, generally effective for bonds issued after 8-15-86, see ¶2898, above.

⟦Footnote ¶2898 continued⟧

or manner as the Secretary shall by regulations prescribe. Any such election (and any specification contained therein), once made, shall be irrevocable.

(E) Carryforward project.—For purposes of this paragraph, the term 'carryforward project' means—

(i) any project described in paragraph (4) or (5) of subsection (b), and

(ii) the purpose of issuing student loan bonds.

(11) **Treatment of qualified scholarship funding bonds.**—In the case of a qualified scholarship funding bond (as defined in subsection (e)), such bond shall be treated for purposes of this subsection as issued by a State or local issuing authority (whichever is appropriate).

(12) **Certification of no consideration for allocation.**

(A) In general.—Any private activity bond allocated any portion of the State limit shall not be exempt from tax under subsection (a) unless the public official if any responsible for such allocation certifies under penalty of perjury that the allocation was not made in consideration of any bribe, gift, gratuity, or direct or indirect contribution to any political campaign.

(B) Any criminal penalty made applicable.—Any person willfully making an allocation described in subparagraph (A) in consideration of any bribe, gift, gratuity, or direct or indirect contribution to any political campaign shall be subject to criminal penalty to the same extent as if such allocation were a willful attempt to evade tax imposed by this title.

(13) **Facility must be located within state.—**

(A) In general.—Except as provided in subparagraph (B), no portion of the State ceiling applicable to any State for any calendar year may be used with respect to financing for a facility located outside such State.

(B) Exception for certain facilities where state will get proportionate share of benefits.—Subparagraph (A) shall not apply to any issue described in subparagraph (E), (G), or (H) of subsection (b)(4) if the issuer establishes that the State's share of the use of the facility (or its output) will equal or exceed the State's share of the private activity bonds issued to finance the facility.

(o) **Private Loan Bonds.—**

(1) **Denial of tax exemption.**—For purposes of this title, any private loan bond shall be treated as an obligation which is not described in subsection (a).

(2) **Private loan bonds.**—For purposes of this subsection—

(A) In general.—The term 'private loan bond' means any obligation which is issued as part of an issue all or a significant portion of the proceeds of which are reasonably expected to be used directly or indirectly to make or finance loans (other than loans described in subparagraph (C)) to persons who are not exempt persons (within the meaning of subsection (b)(3)).

(B) Excluded obligations.—The term 'private loan bond' shall not include any—

(i) qualified student loan bond,

(ii) industrial development bond, or

(iii) qualified mortgage bond or qualified veterans' mortgage bond.

(C) Excluded loans.—A loan is described in this subparagraph if the loan—

(i) enables the borrower to finance any governmental tax or assessment of general application for an essential governmental function, or

(ii) is used to acquire or carry nonpurpose obligations (within the meaning of subsection (c)(6)(H)(i)).

(3) **Qualified student loans bonds.**—For purposes of this subsection, the term 'qualified student loan bond' means any obligation which is issued as part of an issue all or a major portion of the proceeds of which are reasonably expected to be used directly or indirectly to make or finance student loans under a program of general application to which the Higher Education Act of 1965 applies if—

(A) limitations are imposed under the program on—

(i) the maximum amount of loans outstanding to any student, and

(ii) the maximum rate of interest payable on any loan,

(B) the loans are directly or indirectly guaranteed by the Federal Government,

(C) the financing of loans under the program is not limited by Federal law to the proceeds of obligations the interest on which is exempt from taxation under this title, and

(D) special allowance payments under section 438 of the Higher Education Act of 1965—

(i) are authorized to be paid with respect to loans made under the program, or

(ii) would be authorized to be made with respect to loans under the program if such loans were not financed with the proceeds of obligations the interest on which is exempt from taxation under this title.

Such term shall not include any obligation issued under a State program which discriminates on the basis of the location (in the United States) at which the educational institution is located.

(p) **Cross References.**—For provisions relating to the taxable status of—

(1) **Certain obligations issued by Indian tribal governments (or their subdivisions), see section 7871.**

(2) **Exempt interest dividends of regulated investment companies, see section 852(b)(5)(B).**

(3) **Puerto Rican bonds, see section 3 of the Act of March 2, 1917, as amended (48 U.S.C. 745).**

(4) **Virgin Islands insular and municipal bonds, see section 1 of the Act of October 27, 1949 (48 U.S.C. 1403).**

(5) **Certain obligations issued under title I of the Housing Act of 1949, see section 102(g) of title I of such Act (42 U.S.C. 1452(g))."**

Effective date (Sec. 1311(a), '86 TRA).—Generally applies to bonds issued after 8-15-86. For transitional and special rules, see ¶2071—2077.

〖¶2898-A〗 CODE SEC. 103. INTEREST ON CERTAIN GOVERNMENTAL OB-LIGATIONS.

(a) General rule.—Gross income does not include interest on—

(1) the obligations of a State, a Territory, or a possession of the United States, or any political subdivision of any of the foregoing, or of the District of Columbia; and

(2) qualified scholarship funding bonds.

(b) Industrial Development Bonds.—

(1) Subsection (a)(1) or (2) not to apply.—Except as otherwise provided in this subsection, any industrial development bond shall be treated as an obligation not described in subsection (a)(1) or (2).

* * * * * * * * * * *

(13) Exception.—Paragraphs (4), (5), *and* (6)[1] shall not apply with respect to any

----

〖Footnote ¶2898-A〗 Matter in *italics* in Sec. 103(b)(13), (14)(A), and 17(A) added by section 1871(b), '86 TRA, which struck out:

(1) ", and 7"

Effective date (Sec. 1881, '86 TRA and section 631(c)—(f) and 632, '84 TRA, as amended by section 1872, '86 TRA).—

(c) Other Provisions Relating to Tax-Exempt Bonds.—

(1) In general.—Except as otherwise provided in this subtitle, the amendments made by sections 622, 623, 627, and 628(c), (d), and (e) (and the provisions of sections 625(c), 628(f), and 629(b)) shall apply to obligations issued after 12-31-83.

(2) Obligations invested in federally insured deposits.—Notwithstanding any other provision of this section, clause (ii) of section 103(h)(2)(B) of the '54 Code (as amended by this subtitle) shall apply to obligations issued after 4-14-83; except that such clause shall not apply to any obligation issued pursuant to a binding contract in effect on 3-4-83.

(3) Exceptions.—

(A) Construction or binding agreement.—The amendments (and provisions) referred to in paragraph (1) shall not apply to obligations with respect to facilities—

*(i) the original use of which commences with the taxpayer and the construction, reconstruction, or rehabilitation of which began before 10-19-83, and was completed on or after such date,

(ii) the original use of which commences with the taxpayer and with respect to which a binding contract to incur significant expenditures for construction, reconstruction, or rehabilitation was entered into before 10-19-86, and some of such expenditures are incurred on or after such date, or

(iii) acquired after 10-19-86, pursuant to a binding contract entered into on or before such date.

(B) Facilities.—Subparagraph (C) of subsection (b)(2) shall apply for purposes of subparagraph (A) of this paragraph.

(C) Exception.—Subparagraph (A) shall not apply with repect to the amendment made by section 628(e) and the provisions of sections 628(f) and 629(b).

(4) Repeal of advance refunding of qualified public facilities.—The amendment made by section 628(g) shall apply to refunding obligations issued after 7-18-84; except that if substantially all the proceeds of the refunded issue were used to provide airports or docks, such amendment shall only apply to refunding obligations issued after 12-31-84. In the case of any refunding obligation with respect to the Alabama State Docks Department or the Dade County Florida Airport, the preceding sentence shall be applied by substituting "December 31, 1985" for "December 31, 1984".

(5) Special rule for health club facilities.—In the case of any health club facility, with respect to the amendment made by section 627(c)—

(A) paragraph (1) shall be applied by substituting "April 12, 1984" for "December 31, 1983", and

(B) paragraph (3) shall be applied by substituting "April 13, 1984" for "October 19, 1983" each place it appears.

(d) Provisions of This Subtitle Not To Apply to Certain Property.—The amendments made by this subtitle shall not apply to any property (and shall not apply to obligations issued to finance such property) if such property is described in any of the following paragraphs:

(1) Any property described in paragraph (5)(6), or (7) of section 31(g) of '84 TRA.

(2) Any property described in paragraph (4), (8), or (17) of section 31(g) of '84 TRA, but only if the obligation is issued before 1-1-85, and only if before 6-19-84, the issuer had evidenced an intent to issue obligations exempt from taxation under the '54 Code in connection with such property.

(3) Any property described in paragraph (3) of section 216(b) of the '82 TEFRA.

(4) Any solid waste disposal facility described in section 103(b)(4)(E) of the '54 Code if—

(A) a State public authority created pursuant to State legislation which took effect on 6-18-73 took formal action before 10-19-83, to commit development funds for such facility,

(B) such authority issues obligations for any such facility before 1-1-87, and

(C) expenditures have been made for the development of any such facility before 10-19-83.

(5) Any solid waste disposal facility described in section 103(b)(4)(E) of the '54 Code if—

(A) a city government, by resolutions adopted on 4-10-80, and 12-27-82, took formal action to authorize the submission of a proposal for a feasibility study for such facility and to authorize the presentation to the Department of the Army (U.S. Army Missile Command) of a proposed agreement to jointly pursue construction and operation of such facility,

(B) such city government (or a public authority on its behalf) issues obligations for such facility before 1-1-88,

Code §103(b)(13) ¶2898-A

[Footnote ¶2898-A continued]

and

(C) expenditures have been made for the development of such facility before 10-19-83. Notwithstanding the foregoing provisions of this subsection, the amendments made by section 624 (relating to arbitrage) shall apply to obligations issued to finance property described in paragraph (5).

(e) Determination of Significant Expenditure.—

(1) In general.—For purposes of this section, the term "significant expenditures" means expenditures which equal or exceed the lesser of—

(A) $15,000,000, or

(B) 20 percent of the estimated cost of the facilities.

(2) Certain grants treated as expenditures.—For purposes of paragraph (1), the amount of any UDAG grant preliminarily approved on 5-5-81, or 4-4-83, shall be treated as an expenditure with respect to the facility for which such grant was so approved.

(f) Exceptions for Certain Other Amendments.—If —

(1) there was an inducement resolution (or other comparable preliminary approval) for an issue before 6-19-84, by any issuing authority, and

(2) such issue is issued before 1-1-85, the following amendments shall not apply:

(A) the amendments made by section 623,

(B) the amendments made by subsections (a) and (b) of section 627 (except to the extent such amendments relate to farm land),

(C) in the case of a race track, the amendment made by section 627(c), and

(D) the amendments made by section 628(c).

SEC. 632. MISCELLANEOUS EXCEPTIONS AND SPECIAL RULES.

(a) Exception From Provisions Other Than Arbitrage and Federal Guarantees.—Notwithstanding any other provision of this subtitle, the amendments made by this subtitle (other than by section 622 (relating to Federal guarantees) and section 624 (relating to arbitrage)) shall not apply to the following obligations:

(1) [Repealed]

(2) Obligations issued to finance a redevelopment program on 9 city blocks adjacent to a transit station but only if such program was approved on 10-25-83.

(3) Obligations issued pursuant to an inducement resolution adopted on 8-8-78, for a redevelopment plan for which a redevelopment trust fund was established on 9-7-77.

(4) Obligations issued to finance a UDAG project which was preliminarily approved on 12-29-82, and which received final approval on 5-3-84.

(5) Obligations issued to finance a parking garage pursuant to an inducement resolution adopted on 3-9-84, in connection with a project for which a UDAG grant application was made on 1-31-84.

(6) Obligations which—

(A) are issued to finance a downtown development project with respect to which an urban development action grant is made but only if such grant—

(i) was preliminarily appoved on 11-3-83, and

(ii) received final approval before 6-1-84, and

(B) are issued in connection with inducement resolutions that were adopted on 12-21-82, 7-5-83, and 3-1-83, but only to the extent the aggregate face amount of such obligations does not exceed $34,000,000.

(7) Obligations with respect to which an inducement resolution was adopted on 3-5-84, for the purpose of acquiring existing airport facilities at more than 12 locations in 1 State but—

(A) only if the Civil Aeronautics Board certifies that such transaction would reduce the amount of Federal subsidies provided under section 419 of the Airline Deregulation Act of 1978, and

(B) only to the extent the aggregate face amount of such obligations does not exceed $25,000,000.

(8) Obligations described in subsection (b).

(b) Certain Parking Facility Bonds.—For purposes of the '54 Code, any obligation issued with respect to a parking facility approved by an agency of a county government on 12-1-82, as part of an urban revitalization plan shall be treated as an obligation described in section 103(b)(4)(D) of such Code.

(c) Exception to Certain Bond Limitations.—The amendments made by section 621 (relating to the limitations on amount of private activity bonds) and section 626(a) (relating to the prohibition on acquiring existing facilities) shall not apply to obligations issued before 1-1-87, in connection with the Claymont, Delaware, regeneration plant of the Delaware Economic Development Authority, but only to the extent the aggregate face amount of such obligation does not exceed $30,000,000.

(d) Certain Obligations Treated as Not Federally Guaranteed.—For purposes of section 103(h) of the '54 Code, obligations (including refunding obligations) shall not be treated as federally guaranteed if—

(A) such obligations are issued with respect to any facility, and

(B) any obligation was issued on 6-3-82 in the principal amount of $11,312,125 for the purpose of financing the development, study, or related costs incurred with respect to such facility.

The amendment made by section 626 shall not apply to any obligations described in the preceding sentence.

(e) Certain Expenditures Treated as Significant Expenditures.—For purposes of this title, expenditures of $850,000 incurred with respect to any project involving $15,000,000 shall be treated as significant expenditures if such expenditures were incurred pursuant to an agreement entered into on 7-13-82, relating to the discharge of industrial waste after 1-1-86.

(f) Certain Ordinances Treated as Inducement Resolutions.—For purposes of this title, any ordinance passed on 5-3-82, with respect to a planned development district shall be treated as an inducement resolution with respect to obligations issued in 1984 in connection with a mall project for such district.

(g) Delayed Effective Date With Respect to Certain IDBS.—

(1) FERC projects.—Notwithstanding any other provision of this title, any amendments made by this title (other than the amendments to section 103(c) of the '54 Code) which, but for this paragraph, would apply to in-

obligation for any period during which it is held by a person who is a substantial user of the facilities or a related person.

(A) a partnership and each of its partners (and their spouses and minor children) shall be treated as related persons, and

(B) an S corporation and each of its shareholders (and their spouses and minor children) shall be treated as related persons.

(14) Maturity may not exceed 120 percent of economic life.—

(A) General rule.—Paragraph (4), (5), *and* (6) [1] shall not apply to any obligation issued as part of an issue if—

(i) the average maturity of the obligations which are part of such issue, exceeds

(ii) 120 percent of the average reasonably expected economic life of the facilities being financed with the proceeds of such issue.

* * * * * * * * * * *

(16) Limitation on use for land acquisition.—

(A) In general.—Paragraphs (4), (5), and (6) shall not apply with respect to any obligation issued as part of an issue if—

(i) any portion of the proceeds of such issue are to be used (directly or indirectly) for the acquisition of land (or an interest therein) to be used for farming purposes, or

(ii) 25 percent or more of the proceeds of such issue are to be used (directly or indirectly) for the acquisition of land not described in[2] *clause (ii)* (or an interest therein).

In the case of an obligation described in paragraph (5) (relating to industrial parks), clause (i) shall be applied by substituting "50 percent" for "25 percent".

* * * * * * * * * * *

(17) Acquisition of exisiting property not permitted.—

(A) In general.—Paragraphs (4), (5), *and* (6)[1]shall not apply to any obligation issued as part of an issue if any portion of the proceeds of such issue is to be used for the acquisition of any property (or an interest therein) unless the first use of such property is pursuant to such acquisition.

(h) Obligation Must Not Be Guaranteed, Etc.—

(1) In general.—An obligation shall not be treated as an obligation described in subsection (a) if such obligation is federally guaranteed.

⟦Footnote ¶2898-A continued⟧

dustrial development bonds issued after 12-31-84, shall not apply to any of the following obligations issued before 1-1-86:

(A) obligations issued with respect to Federal Energy Regulatory Commission project 4657, but to the extent the aggregate face amount of such obligations does not exceed $12,900,000;

(B) obligations issued with respect to Federal Energy Regulatory Commission project 2853, but only to the extent the aggregate face amount of such obligations does not exceed $28,600,000; or

(C) obligations issued with respect to Federal Energy Regulatory Commission project 4700, but only to the extent the aggregate face amount of such obligations does not exceed $3,850,000.

(2) Park Central New Town In Town Project.—Notwithstanding any other provision of this title, any amendments made by this title (other than the amendments to section 103(c) of the '54 Code) which, but for this paragraph, would apply to industrial development bonds issued after 12-31-84, shall not apply to any obligation issued before 1-1-88, with respect to Park Central New Town In Town Project located in Port Arthur, Texas, but only to the extent the aggregate face amount of such obligations does not exceed $80,000,000.

---

* Sec. 631(c)(3)(A)(i)—(iii), '84 TRA, added by Sec. 1872(a)(1)(B), '86 TRA, which struck out:

"(i) the original use of which commences with the taxpayer and the construction, reconstruction, or rehabilitation of which began before 10-19-83, or

(ii) with respect to which a binding contract to incur significant expenditures was entered into before 10-19-83."

Effective date (Sec. 1872(a)(1)(B), '86 TRA).—Effective with respect to obligations issued after 3-28-85.

Matter in *italics* in Sec. 103(b)(16)(A) added by section 1870, '86 TRA, which struck out:

(2) "clause (i)"

Effective date (Sec. 1881, '86 TRA and section 631(c)—(f) and 632, '84 TRA, amended by section 1872, '86 TRA).—See above.

---

   (2) Federally guaranteed defined.—For purposes of paragraph (1), an obligation is federally guaranteed if—

     (A) *the payment of principal or interest with respect to such obligation is[3] guaranteed* (in whole or in part) by the United States (or any agency or instrumentality thereof).

     (B) such obligation is issued as part of an issue and a significant portion of the proceeds of such issue are to be—

        (i) used in making loans the payment of princpial or interest with respect to which are to be guaranteed (in whole or in part) by the United States (or any agency or instrumentality thereof), or

        (ii) invested (directly or indirectly) in federally insured deposits or accounts, or

     (C) the payment of principal or interest on such obligation is otherwise indirectly guaranteed (in whole or in part) by the United States (or an agency or instrumentality thereof).

      * * * * * * * * * * *

(5) Certain obligations subsidized under energy program.—

     (A) **In general.**—An obligation to which this paragraph applies shall be treated as an obligation not described in subsection (a) if the payment of the principal or interest with respect to such obligation is to be made (in whole or in part) under a program of [4]*a State, or a political subdivision of a State* the principal purpose of which is to encourage the production or conservation of energy.

     (B) **Obligations to which paragraph applies.**—This paragraph shall apply to any obligations to which paragraph (1) of subsection (b) does not apply by reason of—

        (i) subsection (b)(4)(H) (relating to qualified hydroelectric generating facilities), or

        (ii) subsection (g) (relating to qualified steam-generating or alcohol-producing facilities).

      * * * * * * * * * * *

(l) Information Reporting Requirements for Certain Bonds.—

      * * * * * * * * * * *

   (2) Information reporting requirement.—An obligation satisfies the requirement of this paragraph if the issuer submits to the Secretary, not later than the 15th day of the 2nd calendar month after the close of the calendar quarter in which the obligation is issued, a statement of which the obligation is a part which contains—

     (A) the name and address of the issuer,

     (B) the date of issue, the amount of lendable proceeds of the issue, and the stated interest rate, term and face amount of each obligation which is part of the issue,

     (C) where required, the name of the applicable elected representative who approved the issue, or a description of the voter referendum by which the issue was approved,

     (D) the name, address, and employer identification number of—

        (i) each initial principal user of any facilities provided with the proceeds of the issue,

        (ii) the common parent of any affiliated group of corporations (within the meaning of section 1504(a)) of which such initial principal user is a member, and

        (iii) if the issue is treated as a separate issue under subsection (b)(6)(K), any person treated as a principal user under subsection (b)(6)(L),[5]

     (E) a description of any person to be financed from the proceeds of the issue,[6]

【Footnote ¶2898-A continued】

Matter in *italics* in Sec. 103(h)(2)(A) added by section 1899A(2), '86 TRA, which struck out:
(3) "guaranted"

Section 1865(a), '86 TRA, struck out from Sec. 103(h)(5)(A):
(4) **"the United States,"**
   Effective date (Sec. 1881, '86 TRA, and section 631(c)(1), '84 TRA, amended by section 1872, '86 TRA).—Generally applies to obligations issued after 12-31-83. For exceptions and special rules, see above.

Matter in *italics* in Sec. 103(b)(2)(D)—(F) added by section 1864(d), '86 TRA, which struck out:
(5) "and"
(6) "."
   Effective date (Sec. 1881, '86 TRA, and section 631(a), '84 TRA).—(a)(1) Generally applies to obligations issued after 12-31-83.

and

(F)   if such obligation is a private activity bond (as defined in subsection (n)(7)), such information as the Secretary may require for purposes of determining whether the requirements of subsection (n) are met with respect to such obligation.

* * * * * * * * * * *

(m)   Obligations Exempt Other Than Under This Title.—

(1)   Prior exemptions.—For purposes of this title, notwithstanding any provisions of this section 103A any obligation the interest on which is exempt from taxation under this title under any provision of law which is in effect on the date of the enactment of this subsection (other than a provision of this title) shall be treated as an obligation described in subsection (a). In the case of an obligation issued after December 31, 1983, such obligation shall not be treated as described in this paragraph unless the appropriate requirements of subsections (b), (c), (h), *(j)*, (k), (l), [7] *(n), and (o)* of this section and section 103A are met with respect to such obligation. For purposes of applying such requirements, a possession of the United States shall be treated as a State; except that clause (ii) of subsection (n)(4)(A) shall not apply.

* * * * * * * * * * *

(3)   Exceptions.—The following obligations shall be treated as obligations described in paragraph (1) (without regard to the second sentence thereof):

(A)   Any obligation issued pursuant to the Northwest Power Act (16 U.S.C. 839d) as in effect on the date of the enactment of the Tax Reform Act of 1984.

(B)   Any obligation issued pursuant to [8]*section 608(a)(6)(A)* of Public Law 97-468.

(C)   Any obligation issued before June 19, 1984, under section 11(b) of the United States Housing Act of 1937.

[Footnote ¶2898-A continued]

(2)   Inducement resolution before June 19, 1984.—The amendment made by section 621 shall not apply to any issue of obligations if—

(A)   there was an inducement resolution (or other comparable preliminary approval) for the issue before 6-19-84, and

(B)   the issue is issued before 1-1-85.

(3)   Certain projects preliminarily approved before October 19, 1983, given approval.—If—

(A)   there was an inducement resolution (or other comparable preliminary approval) for a project before 10-19-83, by any issuing authority,

(B)   a substantial user of such project notifies the issuing authority within 30 days after 7-18-84 that it intends to claim its rights under this paragraph, and

(C)   construction of such projects began 10-19-83, or the substantial user was under a binding contract on such date to incur significant expenditures with respect to such project,

such issuing authority shall allocate its share of the limitation under section 103(n) of such Code for the calendar year during which the obligations were to be issued pursuant to such resolution (or other approval) first to such project. If the amount of obligations required by all projects which meet the requirements of the preceding sentence exceeds the issuing authority's share of the limitation under section 103(n) of such Code, priority under the preceding sentence shall be provided first to those projects for which substantial expenditures were incurred before 10-19-83. If any issuing authority fails to meet the requirements of this paragraph, the limitation under section 103(n) of such Code for the issuing authority for the calendar year following such failure shall be reduced by the amount of obligations with respect to which such failure occurred.

(3)   [should read (4)]   Exception for certain bonds for a convention center and resource recovery project.—In the case of any city, if—

(A)   the city council of such city authorized a feasibility study for a convention center on 6-10-82, and

(B)   on 11-4-83, a municipal authority acting for such city accepted a proposal for the construction of a facility that is capable of generating steam and electricity through the combustion of municipal waste,

the amendment made by section 621 shall not apply to any issue, issued during 1984, 1985, 1986, or 1987 and substantially all of the proceeds of which are to be used to finance the convention center (or access ramps and parking facilities therefor) described in subparagraph (A) or the facility described in subparagraph (B).

For other exceptions and special rules, see above.

Matter in *italics* in Sec. 103(m)(1) added by section 1871(a)(1), '86 TRA, which struck out:

(7)   "and"

Effective date (Sec. 1871(a)(2), '86 TRA).—Applies to obligations issued after 3-28-85, in taxable years ending after such date.

Matter in *italics* in Sec. 103(m)(3)(B) added by section 1899A(3), '86 TRA, which struck out:

(8)   "section 608(6)(A)"

(n) **Limitation on Aggregate Amount of Private Activity Bonds Issued During Any Calendar Year.—**

(6) **State may provide for different allocation.—**

(A) In general.—A State may, by law provide a different formula for allocating the State ceiling among the governmental units *or other authorities* in such State having authority to issue private activity bonds.

(B) Interim authority for governor.—

(i) In general.—The Governor of any State may proclaim a different formula for allocating the State ceiling among the governmental units *or other authorities* in such State having authority to issue private activity bonds.

(ii) Termination of authority.—The authority provided in clause (i) shall not apply after the earlier of—

(I) the first day of the first calendar year beginning after the legislature has met in regular session for more than 60 days after the date of the enactment of this paragraph, or

(II) the effective date of any State legislation with respect to the allocation of the State ceiling.

(C) State may not alter allocation to constitutional home rule cities.—The rules of paragraph (6)(C) of section 103A(g) shall apply for purposes of this paragraph.

(7) **Private activity bond.—**For purposes of this subsection—

(A) In general.—Except as otherwise provided in the paragraph, the term "private activity bond" means any obligation the interest on which is exempt from tax under subsection (a) and which is—

(i) an industrial development bond, or

(ii) a student loan bond,

(B) Exception for multifamily housing.—The term "private activity bond" shall not include any obligation described in subsection (b)(4)(A) nor any housing program obligation under section 11(b) of the United States Housing Act of 1937.

(C) Exception for certain facilities described in section 103(b)(4)(C) or (D).—

(i) In general.—The term "private activity bond" shall not include any obligation described in subparagraph (C) or (D) of subsection 103(b)(4), but only if *all of* the property [9]*to be financed by the obligation* is owned by or on behalf of a governmental unit.

(ii) Exception not to apply to certain parking facilities.—For purposes of clause (i), subparagraph (D) of subsection (b)(4) shall be applied as if it did not contain the phrase "parking facilities."

(iii) Determination of whether property owned by governmental unit.—For purposes of clause (i), property shall not be treated as not owned by a governmental unit solely by reason of the length of the lease to which it is subject if the lessee makes an irrevocable election (binding on the lessee and all successors in interest under the lease) not to claim depreciation or an investment credit with respect to such property.

(iv) Restriction where significant front end loading.—Under regulations prescribed by the Secretary, clause (i) shall not apply in any case where the property is leased under a lease which has significant front end loading of rental accruals or payments.

* * * * * * * * * * * *

(10) **Elective carryforward of unused limitation for specified project.—**

(A) In general.—If—

(i) an issuing authority's private activity bond limit for any calendar year after 1983, exceeds

(ii) the aggregate amount of private activity bonds issued during such calendar year by such authority,

such authority may elect to treat all (or any portion) of such excess as a carryforward for 1 or more carryforward projects.

(B) Election must [10]*identify* project.—In any election under subparagraph (A),

---

【Footnote ¶2898-A continued】

Matter in *italics* in Sec. 103(n)(6)(A), (B)(i), (7)(C)(i), (10)(B), (i), and (D) added by section 1864(b), (c), and (e)(1) and (2), '86 TRA, which struck out:

(9) "described in such subparagraph"

(10) "specify"

Effective date (Sec. 1881, '86 TRA and section 631(a), '84 TRA).—(a)(1) Generally applies to obligations issued after 12-31-83. For special rules, see above.

Sec. 103(n)(13) in *italics* added by section 1864(a)(1), '86 TRA.

the issuing authority shall—

(i) [10]*identify (with reasonable specificity)* the project (or projects) for which the carryforward is elected, and

(ii) specify the portion of the excess described in subparagraph (A) which is to be a carryforward for each such project.

(C) Use of carryforward.—

(i) In general.—If any issuing authority elects a carryforward under subparagraph (A) with respect to any carryforward project, any private activity bonds issued by such authority with respect to such project during the 3 calendar years (or, in the case of a project described in subsection (b)(4)(F), 6 calendar years) following the calendar year in which the carryforward arose shall not be taken into account under paragraph (1) to the extent the amount of such bonds do not exceed the amount of the carryforward elected for such project.

(ii) Order in which carryforward used.—Carryforwards elected with respect to any project shall be used in the order of the calendar years in which they arose.

(D) Election.—Any election made under this paragraph shall be made at such time and in such manner as the Secretary shall by regulations prescribe. Any such election (and any *identification or* specification contained therein), once made, shall be irrevocable.

(E) Carryforward project.—For purposes of this paragraph, the term "carryforward project" means—

(i) any project described in paragraph (4) or (5) of subsection (b), and

(ii) the purpose of issuing student loan bonds.

* * * * * * * * * * *

(13) Facility must be located within state.—

(A) In general.—Except as provided in subparagraph (B), no portion of the State ceiling applicable to any State for any calendar year may be used with respect to financing for a facility located outside such State.

(B) Exception for certain facilities where state will get proportionate share of benefits.—Subparagraph (A) shall not apply to any issue described in subparagraph (E), (G), or (H) of subsection (b)(4) if the issuer establishes that the State's share of the use of the facility (or its output) will equal or exceed the State's share of the private activity bonds issued to finance the facility.

(o) [11]*Private* **Loan Bonds.—**

(1) Denial of tax exemption.—For purposes of this title, any [11]*private* loan bond shall be treated as an obligation which is not described in subsection (a).

(2) [11]*Private* **loan bonds.**—For purposes of this subsection—

(A) In general.—The term [11]*"private* loan bond" means any obligation which is issued as part of an issue all or a significant portion of the proceeds of which are reasonably expected to be used directly or indirectly to make or finance loans (other than loans described in subparagraph (C)) to persons who are not exempt persons (within the meaning of subsection (b)(3)).

(B) Excluded obligations.—The term [11]*"private* loan bond" shall not include any—

(i) qualified student loan bond,

(ii) industrial development bond, or

(iii) qualified mortgage bond or qualified veterans' mortgage bond.

(C) Excluded loans.—A loan is described in this subparagraph if the loan—

(i) enables the borrower to finance any governmental tax or assessment of general application or an essential governmental function, or

---

[**Footnote ¶2898-A continued**]

Effective date (Sec. 1864(a)(2), '86 TRA).—(A) Generally applies to obligations issued after the date of enactment of this Act, in taxable years ending after such date.

(B) At the election of the issuer (made at such time and in such manner as the Secretary of the Treasury or his delegate shall prescribe), the amendment made by paragraph (1) shall apply to any obligation issued on or before the date of the enactment of this Act.

Matter in *italics* in Sec. 103(o) and (p) (except for "*October 27, 1949*" in (p)(4)) added by section 1869(a) and (b), '86 TRA, which struck out:

(11) "private"

(ii) is used to acquire or carry nonpurpose obligations (within the meaning of [12]*subsection (c)(6)(H)(i).*

* * * * * * * * * * * *

[13]*(p)*   Cross References.—For provisions relating to the taxable status of—

(1)   Certain obligations issued by Indian tribal governments (or their subdivisions), see section 7871.

(2)   Exempt interest dividends of regulated investment companies, see section 852(b)(5)(B).

(3)   Puerto Rican bonds, see section 3 of the Act of March 2, 1917, as amended (48 U.S.C. 745).

(4)   Virgin Islands insular and municipal bonds, see section 1 of the Act of [14]*October 27, 1949* (48 U.S.C. 1403).

[Footnote ¶2898-A continued]

(12)   "subsection (c)(6)(G)(i)"

(13)   "(o)"

Effective date (Sec. 1881, '86 TRA, and section 626(b) and (c), '84 TRA, P.L. 98-369, 7-18-84, as amended by section 1869(c), '86 TRA, P.L. 99-514, 10-22-86).—(1) Generally applies to obligations issued after 7-18-84.

(2) Exceptions for certain loan programs.—

(A) In general.—The amendments made by this section shall not apply to obligations issued by a program described in the following table to the extent the aggregate face amount of such obligations does not exceed the amount of allowable obligations specified in the following table with respect to such program:

Program	Amount of Allowable Obligations
Colorado Student Obligation Bond Authority	$60 million
Connecticut Higher Education Supplementary Loan Authority	$15.5 million
District of Columbia	$50 million
Illinois Higher Education Authority	$11 million
State of Iowa	$16 million
Louisiana Public Facilities Authority	$75 million
Maine Health and Higher Education Facilities Authority	$5 million
Maryland Higher Education Supplemental Loan Program	$24 million
Massachusetts College Student Loan Authority	$90 million
Minnesota Higher Education Coordinating Board	$60 million
New Hampshire Higher Education and Health Facilities Authority	$39 million
New York Dormitory Authority	$120 million
Pennsylvania Higher Education Assistance Agency	$300 million
Georgia Private Colleges and University Authority	$31 million
Wisconsin State Building Commission	$60 million
South Dakota Health and Educational Facilities Authority	$6 million

(B) Pennsylvania higher education assistance agency.—Subparagraph (A) shall apply to obligations issued by the Pennsylvania Higher Education Assistance Agency only if such obligations are issued solely for the purpose of refunding student loan bonds outstanding on 3-15-84.

(3) Certain tax-exempt mortgage subsidy bonds.—For purposes of applying section 103(o) of the '54 Code, the term "consumer loan bond" shall not include any mortgage subsidy bond (within the meaning of section 103A(b) of such Code) to which the amendments made by section 1102 of the Mortgage Subsidy Bond Tax Act of 1980 do not apply.

(4) Refunding exception.—The amendments made by this section shall not apply to any obligation or series of obligations the proceeds of which are used exclusively to refund obligations issued before 3-15-84, except that—

(A) the amount of the refunding obligations may not exceed 101 percent of the aggregate face amount of the refunded obligations, and

(B) the maturity date of any refunding obligation may not be later than the date which is 17 years after the date on which the refunded obligation was issued (or, in the case of a series of refundings, the date on which the original obligation was issued).

(5) Exception for certain established programs.—The amendments made by this section shall not apply to any obligation substantially all of the proceeds of which are used to carry out a program established under State law which has been in effect in substantially the same form during the 30-year period ending on 7-18-84, but only if such proceeds are used to make loans or to fund similar obligations—

(A) in the same manner in which,

(B) in the same (or lesser) amount per participant, and

(C) for the same purposes for which,

such program was operated on 3-15-84. This subparagraph shall not apply to obligations issued on or after 3-15-87.

(6) Certain bonds for renewable energy property.—The amendments made by this section shall not apply to any obligations described in section 243 of the Crude Oil Windfall Profit Tax Act of 1980.

For other transitional rules, see ¶2134.

"*October 27, 1949*" in *italics* in Sec. 103(p)(4) added by section 1899A(4), '86 TRA, which struck out:

(14)   "October 27, 1919"

(5) Certain obligations issued under title I of the Housing Act of 1949, see section 102(g) of title I of such Act (42 U.S.C. 1452(g)).

[For official explanation, see Committee Reports, ¶4186; 4213; 4180; 4179; 4184.]

≫**P-H CAUTION**→ There are two versions of Sec. 103A. Sec. 103A, repealed generally effective for bonds issued after 8-15-86, follows. Sec. 103A, generally effective for bonds issued before 8-16-86, see ¶2898-C, below.

[¶2898-B] CODE SEC. 103A. MORTGAGE SUBSIDY BONDS.

[Repealed by section 1301(j)(1), '86 TRA].[1]

[For official explanation, see Committee Reports, ¶4058.]

≫**P-H CAUTION**→ There are two versions of Sec. 103A. Sec. 103A, generally effective for bonds issued before 8-16-86, follows. Sec. 103A, generally effective for bonds issued after 8-15-86, see ¶2898-B, above.

[¶2898-C] CODE SEC. 103A. MORTGAGE SUBSIDY BONDS.

* * * * * * * * * * * *

(c) **Qualified Mortgage Bond; Qualified Mortgage Issue, Qualified Veterans' Mortgage Bond.—**

(1) **Qualified Mortgage Bond Defined.—**
(A) In general.—For purposes of this title, the term "qualified mortgage bond" means an obligation which is issued as part of a qualified mortgage issue,
(B) Termination December 31, 1987.—No obligation issued after December 31, 1987, may be treated as a qualified mortgage bond.

(2) **Qualified mortgage issue defined.—**
(A) Definition.—For purposes of this title, the term "qualified mortgage issue" means an issue by a State or political subdivision thereof of 1 or more obligations, but only if—
(i) all proceeds of such issue (exclusive of issuance costs and a reasonably required reserve) are to be used to finance owner-occupied residences, and
(ii) such issue meets the requirements of subsection (d), (e), (f), (g), (h), (i), and (j).
(B) Good faith effort to comply with mortgage eligibility requirements.—An issue which fails to meet 1 or more of the requirements of subsections (d), (e), (f), and [1] *(j)(1) and (2)* shall be treated as meeting such requirements if—
(i) the issuer in good faith attempted to meet all such requirements before the mortgages were executed,
(ii) 95 percent or more of the proceeds devoted to owner-financing was devoted to residences with respect to which (at the time the mortgages were executed) all such requirements were met, and
(iii) any failure to meet the requirements of such subsections and paragraphs is corrected within a reasonable period after such failure is first discovered.
(C) Good faith effort to comply with other requirements.—An issue, which fails to meet 1 or more of the requirements of subsections (g), (h), [2] *(i)(j)(3), (4), and (5)* shall be treated as meeting such requirements if—
(i) the issuer in good faith attempted to meet all such requirements, and
(ii) any failure to meet such requirements is due to inadvertent error after taking reasonable steps to comply with requirements.

* * * * * * * * * * * *

(j) **Other Requirements.—**

* * * * * * * * * * * *

(5) **Policy statement.—**

* * * * * * * * * * * *

[Footnote ¶2898-B] **(1) Effective date** (Sec. 1311-1319, '86 TRA).—Generally applies to bonds issued after 8-15-86. For special and transitional rules, see ¶2071—2077.
[Footnote ¶2898-C] Matter in *italics* in Sec. 103A(c)(2)(B) and (C), (j)(5)(C), and (o)(4) added by section 1861, '86 TRA, which struck out:
(1) "(j)"
(2) "and (i)"

3132 Tax Reform Act of 1986 [2]

(C) Extension of time.—The Secretary may grant an extension of time for the publishing of a report described in subparagraph (B) or the submittal of such report to the Secretary if there is reasonable cause for the failure to publish or submit such report in a timely fashion.

* * * * * * * * * * *

(o) Additional Requirements for Qualified Veterans' Mortgage Bonds.—

(4) Qualified veteran.—For purposes of this subsection, the term "qualified veteran" means any veteran—

    (A) who served on active duty at some time before January 1, 1977, and

    (B) who applied for the financing before the later of—

        (i) the date 30 years after the last date on which such veteran left active service, or

        (ii) [3] *January 31, 1985.*

* * * * * * * * * * *

[For official explanation, see Committee Reports, ¶4176.]

[¶2899] CODE SEC. 105. AMOUNTS RECEIVED UNDER ACCIDENT AND HEALTH PLANS.

* * * * * * * * * * *

[1] *(h)* [2] **Sick Pay Under Railroad Unemployment Insurance Act.—**

[Footnote ¶2898-C continued]

(3) "January 1, 1985"

Effective date (Sec. 1881, '86 TRA, and section 611(d), '84 TRA).—(A) Generally applies to obligations issued after 7-18-84.

(B) Volume limitation.—The requirements of paragraph (3) of section 103A of the '54 Code (as added by this section) shall apply to obligations issued after 6-22-84. In applying such requirements to obligations issued after such date, obligations issued on or before such date shall not be taken into account under such paragraph (3).

(C) Qualified veterans' mortgage bonds authorized before 10-18-83, not taken into account.—The requirements of section 103A(o)(3) of the '54 Code shall not apply to any qualified veterans' mortgage bond if—

(i) the issuance of such bond was authorized by a State referendum before 10-18-83, or

(ii) the issuance of such bond was authorized pursuant to a State referendum before 12-1-83, where such referendum was authorized by action of the State legislature before 10-18-83.

(4) Transitional rule where state formula for allocating state ceiling expires.—

(A) In general.—If a State law which provided a formula for allocating the State ceiling under section 103A(g) of the '54 Code for calendar year 1983 expires as of the close of calendar year 1983, for purposes of section 103A(g) of such Code, such State law shall be treated as remaining in effect after 1983. In any case to which the preceding sentence applies, where the State's expiring allocation formula requires action by a State official to allocate the State ceiling among issuers, actions of such State official in allocating such ceiling shall be effective.

(B) Termination.—Subparagraph (A) shall not apply on or after the effective date of any State legislation enacted after the date of the enactment of this Act with respect to the allocation of the State ceiling.

(C) Special rule for Texas.—In the case of Texas, the Governor of such State may take the actions described in subparagraph (A) pursuant to procedures established by the Governor consistent with the State laws of Texas.

(5) Special rule for determination of statistical area.—For purposes of applying section 103A of the '54 Code and any other provision of Federal law—

(A) Rescission.—The Director of the Office of Management and Budget shall rescind the designation of the Kansas City, Missouri primary metropolitan statistical area (KCMO PMSA) and the designation of the Kansas City, Kansas primary metropolitan statistical area (Kansas City, KS PMSA), and shall not take any action to designate such two primary metropolitan statistical areas as a consolidated metropolitan statistical area.

(B) Designation.—The Director of the Office of Management and Budget shall designate a single metropolitan statistical area which includes the following:

(i) Kansas City, Kansas.

(ii) Kansas City, Missouri.

(iii) The counties of Johnson, Wyandotte, Leavenworth, and Miami in Kansas.

(iv) The counties of Cass, Clay, Jackson, Platte, Ray, and Lafayette in Missouri.

The metropolitan statistical area designation pursuant to this subsection shall be known as the "Kansas City Missouri-Kansas Metropolitan Statistical Area."

(6) Transitional rule for Kentucky and Nevada.—For purposes of section 103A(g) of the '54 Code, in the case of Kentucky and Nevada, subclause (I) of section 103A(g)(6)(B)(ii) of such Code shall be applied as if the first day referred to in such subclause were 1-1-87.

(7) Report to Congress.—The Secretary of the Treasury, in consultation with the Secretary of Housing and Urban Development, shall, not later than 1-1-87, submit a report to the Committee on Finance of the Senate and the Committee on Ways and Means of the House of Representatives regarding the performance of issuers of qualified mortgage bonds and mortgage credit certificates relative to the intent of Congress described in section 103A(j) of the '54 Code.

[Footnote ¶2899] Matter in *italics* in Sec. 105(h) added by section 1151(c)(2), '86 TRA, which struck out:

[Footnote ¶2899 continued]

(1) "(h) **Amount Paid to Highly Compensated Individuals Under a Discriminatory Self-Insured Medical Expense Reimbursement Plan.**—

(1) **In general.**—In the case of amounts paid to a highly compensated individual under a self-insured medical reimbursement plan which does not satisfy the requirements of paragraph (2) for a plan year, subsection (b) shall not apply to such amounts to the extent they constitute an excess reimbursement to such highly compensated individual.

(2) **Prohibition of discrimination.**—A self-insured medical reimbursement plan satisfies the requirements of this paragraph only if—

(A) the plan does not discriminate in favor of highly compensated individuals as to eligibility to participate; and

(B) the benefits provided under the plan do not discriminate in favor of participants who are highly compensated individuals.

(3) **Nondiscriminatory eligibility classifications.**—

(A) In general.—A self-insured medical reimbursement plan does not satisfy the requirements of subparagraph (A) of paragraph (2) unless such plan benefits—

(i) 70 percent or more of all employees, or 80 percent or more of all the employees who are eligible to benefit under the plan if 70 percent or more of all employees are eligible to benefit under the plan; or

(ii) such employees as qualify under a classification set up by the employer and found by the Secretary not to be discriminatory in favor of highly compensated individuals.

(B) Exclusion of certain employees.—For purposes of subparagraph (A) there may be excluded from consideration—

(i) employees who have not completed 3 years of service;

(ii) employees who have not attained age 25;

(iii) part-time or seasonal employees;

(iv) employees not included in the plan who are included in a unit of employees covered by an agreement between employee representatives and one or more employers which the Secretary finds to be a collective bargaining agreement, if accident and health benefits were the subject of good faith bargaining between such employee representatives and such employer or employers; and

(v) employees who are nonresident aliens and who receive no earned income (within the meaning of section 911(d)(2)) from the employer which constitutes income from source within the United States (within the meaning of section 861(a)(3)).

(4) **Nondiscriminatory benefits.**—A self-insured medical reimbursement plan does not meet the requirements of subparagraph (B) of paragraph (2) unless all benefits provided for participants who are highly compensated individuals are provided for all other participants.

(5) **Highly compensated individual defined.**—For purposes of this subsection, the term 'highly compensated individual' means an individual who is—

(A) one of the 5 highest paid officers,

(B) a shareholder who owns (with the application of section 318) more than 10 percent in value of the stock of the employer, or

(C) among the highest paid 25 percent of all employees (other than employees described in paragraph (3)(B) who are not participants).

(6) **Self-insured medical reimbursement plan.**—The term 'self-insured medical reimbursement plan' means a plan of an employer to reimburse employees for expenses referred to in subsection (b) for which reimbursement is not provided under a policy of accident and health insurance.

(7) **Excess reimbursement of highly compensated individual.**—For purposes of this section, the excess reimbursement of a highly compensated individual which is attributable to a self-insured medical reimbursement plan is—

(A) in the case of a benefit available to highly compensated individuals but not to all other participants (or which otherwise fails to satisfy the requirements of paragraph (2)(B)), the amount reimbursed under the plan to the employee with respect to such benefit, and

(B) in the case of benefits (other than benefits described in subparagraph (A) paid to a highly compensated individual by a plan which fails to satisfy the requirements of paragraph (2), the total amount reimbursed to the highly compensated individual for the plan year multiplied by a fraction—

(i) the numerator of which is the total amount reimbursed to all participants who are highly compensated individuals under the plan for the plan year, and

(ii) the denominator of which is the total amount reimbursed to all employees under the plan for such plan year.

In determining the fraction under subparagraph (B), there shall not be taken into account any reimbursement which is attributable to a benefit described in subparagraph (A).

(8) **Certain controlled groups, etc.**—All employees who are treated as employed by a single employer under subsection (b), (c), or (m) of section 414 shall be treated as employed by a single employer for purposes of this section.

(9) **Regulations.**—The Secretary shall prescribe such regulations as may be necessary to carry out the provisions of this section.

(10) **Time of inclusion.**—Any amount paid for a plan year that is included in income by reason of this subsection shall be treated as received or accrued in the taxable year of the participant in which the plan year ends."

(2) "(i)"

Effective date (Sec. 1151(k), '86 TRA).—

(1) **In general.**—The amendments made by this section shall apply to years beginning after the later of—

* * * * * * * * * * *

[For official explanation, see Committee Reports, ¶4007.]

〖¶2900〗 CODE SEC. 106. CONTRIBUTIONS BY EMPLOYER TO ACCIDENT AND HEALTH PLANS.

(a) **In general**—Gross income [1] *of an employee does not include employer-provided coverage under an accident or health plan.*

(b) **Exception for Highly Compensated Individuals Where Plan Fails To Provide Certain Continuation Coverage.**—

(1) **In general.**—Subsection (a) shall not apply to any amount contributed by an employer on behalf of a highly compensated [2]*employee* (within the meaning of [3]*section 414(q)* to a group health plan maintained by such employer unless all such plans maintained by such employer meet the continuing coverage requirements of section 162(k).

* * * * * * * * * * *

[For official explanation, see Committee Reports, ¶3979; 4007.]

〖¶2901〗 CODE SEC. 108. INCOME FROM DISCHARGE OF INDEBETEDNESS.

(a) **Exclusion From Gross Income.**—

(1) **In general.**—Gross income does not include any amount which (but for this subsection) would be includible in gross income by reason of the discharge (in whole or in part) of indebtedness of the taxpayer if—

〖Footnote ¶2899 continued〗

(ii) 12-31-88.

(2) Special rule for collective bargaining plan.—In the case of a plan maintained pursuant to 1 or more collective bargaining agreements between employee representatives and 1 or more employers ratified before 3-1-86, the amendments made by this section shall not apply to employees covered by such an agreement in years beginning before the earlier of—

(A) the date on which the last of such collective bargaining agreements terminates (determined without regard to any extension thereof after 2-28-86), or

(B) 1-1-91.

A plan shall not be required to take into account employees to which the preceding sentence applies for purposes of applying section 89 of the '86 Code (as added by this section) to employees to which the preceding sentence does not apply for any year preceding the year described in the preceding sentence.

(3) Exception for certain group-term insurance plans.—In the case of a plan described in section 223(d)(2) of the '84 TRA, such plan shall be treated as meeting the requirements of section 89 of the '86 Code (as added by this section) with respect to individuals described in section 223(d)(2) of such Act. An employer may elect to disregard such individuals in applying section 89 of such Code (as so added) to other employees of the employer.

(4) Special rule for church plans.—In the case of a church plan (within the meaning of section 414(e)(3) of the '86 Code) maintaining an insured accident and health plan, the amendments made by this section shall apply to years beginning after 12-31-88.

〖Footnote ¶2900〗 Matter in *italics* in Sec. 106(a) added by section 1151(j)(2), '86 TRA, which struck out:

(1) "does not include contributions by the employer to accident or health plans for compensation (through insurance or otherwise) to his employees for personal injuries or sickness."

Effective date (Section 1151(k), '86 TRA).—Generally applies to years beginning after the later of—

(A) 12-31-87, or

(B) the earlier of—

(i) the date which is 3 months after the date on which the Secretary of the Treasury or his delegate issues such regulations as are necessary to carry out the provisions of section 89 of the '86 Code (as added by this section), or

(ii) 12-31-88.

For special rules and exceptions, see footnote ¶2899.

Matter in *italics* in Sec. 106(b)(1) added by section 1114(b)(1), '86 TRA, which struck out:

(2) "individual"

(3) "section 105(h)(5)"

Effective date (Sec. 1114(c)(1) and (4), '86 TRA).—Generally applies to years beginning 12-31-86.

* * * * * * * * * * *

(4) Special rule for determining highly compensated employees.—For purposes of sections 401(k) and 401(m) of the '86 Code, in the case of an employer incorporated 12-15-24, if more than 50 percent of its employees in the top-paid group (within the meaning of section 414(q)(4) of such Code) earn less than $25,000 (indexed at the same time and in the same manner as under section 415(d) of such Code), then the highly compensated employees shall include employees described in section 414(q)(1)(C) of such Code determined without regard to the level of compensation of such employees.

    (A)   the discharge occurs in a title 11 case, *or*
    (B)   the discharge occurs when the taxpayer is insolvent[1]. [2]

    (2) Coordination of exclusions.—[3]*Subparagraph (B) of paragraph (1) shall not apply to a discharge which occurs in a title 11 case.*

*   *   *   *   *   *   *   *   *   *   *

(b) Reduction of Tax Attributes in Title 11 Case or Insolvency.—

    (1) In general.—The amount excluded from gross income under subparagraph (A) or (B) of subsection (a)(1) shall be applied to reduce the tax attributes of the taxpayer as provided in paragraph (2).

    (2) Tax attributes affected; order of reduction.—Except as provided in paragraph (5), the reduction referred to in paragraph (1) shall be made in the following tax attributes in the following order:

        (A) NOL.—Any net operating loss for the taxable year of the discharge, and any net operating loss carryover to such taxable year.

        [4]*(B) General business credit.—Any carryover to or from the taxable year of a discharge of an amount for purposes for determining the amount allowable as a credit under section 38 (relating to general business credit).*[5]

*   *   *   *   *   *   *   *   *   *   *

        (E) Foreign tax credit carryovers.—Any carryover to or from the taxable year of the discharge for purposes of determining the amount of the credit allowable under [6]*section 27.*

    (3) Amount of reduction.—

*   *   *   *   *   *   *   *   *   *   *

        (B) Credit carryover reduction.—The reductions described in subparagraphs (B) and (E) of paragraph (2) shall be [7]*33⅓* cents for each dollar excluded by subsection (a).

*   *   *   *   *   *   *   *   *   *   *

⟦Footnote ¶2901⟧   Matter in *italics* in Sec. 108(a)(1) and (2) added by section 822(a) and (b)(1), '86 TRA, which struck out:

  (1) ", or"
  (2) "(C) the indebtedness discharged is qualified business indebtedness."
  (3) "(A) Title 11 exclusion takes precedence.—Subparagraphs (B) and (C) of paragraph (1) shall not apply to a discharge which occurs in a title 11 case.

  (B) Insolvency exclusion takes precedence over qualified business exclusion.—Subparagraph (C) of paragraph (1) shall not apply to a discharge to the extent that the taxpayer is insolvent."
  Effective date (Sec. 822(c), '86 TRA).—Applies to discharges after 12-31-86.

Matter in *italics* in Sec. 108(b)(2)(B) added by section 231(d)(3)(D), '86 TRA, which struck out:
  (4) "(B) Research credit and general business credit.—Any carryover to or from the taxable year of a discharge of an amount for purposes for determining the amount allowable as a credit under—
  (i) section 30 (relating to credit for increasing research activities), or
  (ii) section 38 (relating to general business credit)."
  Effective date (Sec. 231(g), '86 TRA).—Applies to taxable years beginning after 12-31-85.

Section 1171(b)(4), '86 TRA, struck out from Sec. 108(b)(2)(B):
  (5) "For purposes of this subparagraph, there shall not be taken into account any portion of a carryover which is attributable to the employee stock ownership credit determined under section 41."
  Effective date (Sec. 1171(c)(1), '86 TRA).—Applies to compensation paid or accrued after 12-31-86, in taxable years ending after such date.

Matter in *italics* in Sec. 108(b)(2)(E) added by section 1847(b)(7), '86 TRA, which struck out:
  (6) "section 33"
  Effective date (Sec. 1881, '86 TRA, and section 475(a), '84 TRA).—Applies to taxable years beginning after 12-31-83, and carrybacks from such years.

Matter in *italics* in Sec. 108(b)(3)(B) added by section 104(b)(2), '86 TRA, which struck out:
  (7) "50"
  Effective date (Sec. 151(a), '86 TRA).—Applies to taxable years beginning after 12-31-86.

(c)   [struck out][8]

(d)   Meaning of Terms; Special Rules Relating to Subsections (a)[9] *and (b)*.

* * * * * * * * * * * *

(4)   [struck out][10]

* * * * * * * * * * * *

(6)   **Subsections (a)**[9] *and (b)* **to be applied at partner level.**—In the case of a partnership, subsections (a)[11] *and (b)* shall be applied at partner level.

(7)   **Special rules for S corporation.**—

(A)   Subsections (a)[11] *and (b)* to be applied at corporate level.—In the case of an S corporation, subsections (a)[11] *and (b)* shall be applied at the corporate level.

(B)   Reduction in carryover of disallowed losses and deductions.—In the case of an S corporation, for purposes of subparagraph (A) of subsection (b)(2), any loss or deduction which is disallowed for the taxable year of the discharge under section 1366(d)(1) shall be treated as a net operating loss for such taxable year.[12]

* * * * * * * * * * * *

(9)   **Time for making election, etc.**—

(A)   Time.—An election[13] under paragraph (5) of subsection (b) shall be made on the taxpayer's return for the taxable year in which the discharge occurs or at such other time as may be permitted in regulations prescribed by the Secretary.

* * * * * * * * * * * *

(e)   **General Rules for Discharge of Indebtedness (Including Discharges not in Title Cases or Insolvency).**—For purposes of this title—

* * * * * * * * * * * *

(7)   **Recapture of gain on subsequent sale of stock.**—

(A)   In general.—If a creditor acquires stock of a debtor corporation in satisfaction of such corporation's indebtedness, for purposes of section 1245—

(i)   such stock (and any other property the basis of which is determined in whole or in part by reference to the adjusted basis of such stock) shall be treated as section 1245 proprty,

(ii)   the aggregate amount allowed to the creditor—

(I)   as deductions under subsection (a)[14] *or (b)* of section 166 (by reason of the worthlessness or partial worthlessness of the indebtedness), or

(II)   as an ordinary loss on the exchange,

shall be treated as an amount allowed as a deduction for depreciation and

---

[Footnote ¶2901 continued]

Section 822(b)(2), '86 TRA, struck out Sec. 108(c).

(8) **"(c)   Tax Treatment of Discharge of Qualified Business Indebtedness.**—In the case of a discharge of qualified business indebtedness—

(1) Basis reduction.—

(A) In general.—The amount excluded from gross income under subparagraph (C) of subsection (a)(1) shall be applied to reduce the basis of the depreciable property of the taxpayer.

(B) Cross reference.—

For provisions for making the reduction described in subparagraph (A), see section 1017.

(2) Limitation.—The amount excluded under subparagraph (C) of subsection (a)(1) shall not exceed the aggregate adjusted bases of the depreciable property held by the taxpayer as of the beginning of the taxable year following the taxable year in which the discharge occurs (determined after any reductions under subsection (b))."

Effective date   (Sec. 822(c), '86 TRA).—Applies to discharges after 12-31-86.

Matter in *italics* in Sec. 108(d)(4), (6), (7) and (9) added by section 822(b)(3), '86 TRA, which struck out:

(9)   "(b), and (c)"

(10)   "**(4)   Qualified business indebtedness.**—Indebtedness of the taxpayer shall be treated as qualified business indebtedness if (and only if)—

(A)   the indebtedness was incurred or assumed—

(i)   by a corporation, or

(ii)   by an individual in connection with property used in his trade or business, and

(B)   such taxpayer makes an election under this paragraph with respect to such indebtedness."

(11)   ", (b), and (c)"

(12)   "The preceding sentence shall not apply to any discharge to the extent that subsection (a)(1)(C) applies to such discharge."

(13)   "under paragraph (4) of this subsection or"

Effective date   (Sec. 822(c), '86 TRA).—Applies to discharges after 12-31-86.

Matter in *italics* in Sec. 108(e)(7)(A)(ii), (B)—(E) added by section 805(c)(2), (3) and (4), '86 TRA, which struck out:

(14)   ", (b), or (c)"

(iii)   an exchange of such stock qualifying under section 354(a), 355(a), or 356(a) shall be treated as an exchange to which section 1245(b)(3) applies.

The amount determined under clause (ii) shall be reduced by the amount (if any) included in the creditor's gross income on the exchange.[15]

[16]*(B)   Special rule for cash basis taxpayers.*—In the case of any creditor who computes his taxable income under the cash receipts and disbursements method, proper adjustment shall be made in the amount taken into account under clause (ii) of subparagraph (A) for any amount which was not included in the creditor's gross income but which would have been included in such gross income if such indebtedness has been satisfied in full.

[17]*(C)   Stock of parent corporation.*—For purposes of this paragraph, stock of a corporation in control (within the meaning of section 368(c)) of the debtor corporation shall be treated as stock of the debtor corporation.

[18]*(D)   Treatment of successor corporation.*—For purposes of this paragraph, the term "debtor corporation" includes a successor corporation.

[19]*(E)   Partnership rule.*—Under regulations prescribed by the Secretary, rules similar to the rules of [20]*the foregoing subparagraphs* of this paragraph shall apply with respect to the indebtedness of a partnership.

* * * * * * * * * * *

(g)   Special Rules for Discharge of Qualified Farm Indebtedness of Solvent Farms.—

(1)   In general.—For purposes of this section and section 1017, the discharge by a qualified person of qualified farm indebtedness of a taxpayer who is not insolvent at the time of the discharge shall be treated in the same manner as if the discharge had occurred when the taxpayer was insolvent.

(2)   Qualified farm indebtedness.—For purposes of this subsection, indebtedness of a taxpayer shall be treated as qualified farm indebtedness if—

(A)   such indebtedness was incurred directly in connection with the operation by the taxpayer of the trade or business of farming, and

(B)   50 percent or more of the average annual gross receipts of the taxpayer for the 3 taxable years preceding the taxable year in which the discharge of such indebtedness occurs is attributable to the trade or business of farming.

(3)   Qualified person.—For purposes of this subsection, the term "qualified person" means a person described in section 46(c)(8)(D)(iv).

[For official explanation, see Committee Reports, ¶3872; 3894; 3939; 3944; 4016; 4161.]

【¶2902】   CODE SEC. 111. RECOVERY OF TAX BENEFIT ITEMS.
   (a)   Deductions.—Gross income does not include income attributable to the recovery during the taxable year of any amount deducted in any prior taxable year to the extent such amount did not reduce [1]*the amount of tax imposed by this chapter.*

【Footnote ¶2901 continued】

   (15)   "(B)   Taxpayers on reserve method.—In the case of a taxpayer to whom subsection (c) of section 166 (relating to reserve to bad debts) applies, the amount determined under clause (ii) of subparagraph (A) shall be the aggregate charges to the reserve resulting from the worthlessness or partial worthlessness of the indebtedness."
   (16)   "(C)"
   (17)   "(D)"
   (18)   "(E)"
   (19)   "(F)"
   (20)   "subparagraphs (A), (B), (C), (D), and (E)"
   Effective date   (Sec. 805(d), '86 TRA).—(1)   Generally applies to taxable years beginning after 12-31-86.
   (2)   Change in method of accounting.—In the case of any taxpayer who maintained a reserve for bad debts for such taxpayer's last taxable year beginning before 1-1-87, and who is required by the amendments made by this section to change its method of accounting for any taxable year—
   (A)   such change shall be treated as initiated by the taxpayer,
   (B)   such change shall be treated as made with the consent of the Secretary, and
   (C)   the net amount of adjustments required by section 481 of the '86 Code to be taken into account by the taxpayer shall—
   (i)   in the case of a taxpayer maintaining a reserve under section 166(f), be reduced by the balance in the suspense account under section 166(f)(4) of such Code as of the close of such last taxable year, and
   (ii)   be taken into account ratably in each of the first 4 taxable years beginning after 12-31-86.

   Sec. 108(g) in *italics* added by section 405(c), '86 TRA.
   Effective date   (Sec. 405(c), '86 TRA).—Applies to discharges of indebtedness occurring after 4-9-86, in taxable years ending after such date.
   【Footnote ¶2902】   Matter in *italics* in Sec. 111(a) and (c) added by section 1812(a)(1) and (2), '86 TRA, which

* * * * * * * * * * *

(c) **Treatment of Carryovers.**—For purposes of this section, an increase in a carryover which has not expired before the beginning of the taxable year in which the recovery or adjustment takes place shall be treated as reducing [2]tax imposed by this chapter.[3]

* * * * * * * * * * *

[For official explanation, see Committee Reports, ¶4146.]

〖¶2903〗 CODE SEC. 116. PARTIAL EXCLUSION OF DIVIDENDS RECEIVED BY INDIVIDUALS.

[Repealed by section 612(a), '86 TRA].[1]

[For official explanation, see Committee Reports, ¶3913.]

〖¶2904〗 CODE SEC. 117. [1]QUALIFIED SCHOLARSHIPS.

(a) *General Rule.*—*Gross income does not include any amount received as a qualified*

〖**Footnote ¶2902 continued**〗

struck out:

(1) "income subject to tax."

(2) "income subject to tax or reducing"

(3) ", as the case may be"

Effective date (Sec. 1881, '86 TRA and section 171(c), '84 TRA). —Applies to amounts recovered after 12-31-83, in taxable years ending after such date.

〖**Footnote ¶2903**〗 (1) **Effective date** (Sec. 612(c), '86 TRA).—Applies to taxable years beginning after 12-31-86.

〖**Footnote ¶2904**〗 Matter in *italics* in Sec. 117, other than the last sentence in (d)(3), and (d)(4), added by section 123(a), '86 TRA, which struck out:

(1) "SCHOLARSHIPS AND FELLOWSHIP GRANTS.

(a) **General Rule.**—In the case of an individual, gross income does not include—

(1) any amount received—

(A) as a scholarship at an educational organization described in section 170(b)(1)(A)(ii), or

(B) as a fellowship grant,

including the value of contributed services and accommodations; and

(2) any amount received to cover expenses for—

(A) travel,

(B) research,

(C) clerical help, or

(D) equipment,

which are incident to such a scholarship or to a fellowship grant, but only to the extent that the amount is so expended by the recipient.

(b) **Limitations.**—

(1) **Individuals who are candidates for degrees.**—In the case of an individual who is a candidate for a degree at an educational organization described in section 170(b)(1)(A)(ii), subsection (a) shall not apply to that portion of any amount received which represents payment for teaching, research, or other services in the nature of part-time employment required as a condition to receiving the scholarship or the fellowship grant. If teaching, research, or other services are required of all candidates (whether or not recipients of scholarships or fellowship grants) for a particular degree as a condition to receiving such degree, such teaching, research, or other services shall not be regarded as part-time employment within the meaning of this paragraph.

(2) **Individuals who are not candidates for degrees.**—In the case of an individual who is not a candidate for a degree at an educational organization described in section 170(b)(1)(A)(ii), subsection (a) shall apply only if the condition in subparagraph (A) is satisfied and then only within the limitations provided in subparagraph (B).

(A) Conditions for exclusion.—The grantor of the scholarship or fellowship grant is—

(i) an organization described in section 501(c)(3) which is exempt from tax under section 501(a),

(ii) a foreign government,

(iii) an international organization, or a binational or multinational educational and cultural foundation or commission created or continued pursuant to the Mutual Educational and Cultural Exchange Act of 1961, or

(iv) the United States, or any instrumentality or agency thereof, or a State, or a possession of the United States, or any political subdivision thereof, or the District of Columbia.

(B) Extent of exclusion.—The amount of the scholarship or fellowship grant excluded under subsection (a)(1) in any taxable year shall be limited to an amount equal to $300 times the number of months for which the recipient received amounts under the scholarship or fellowship grant during such taxable year, except that no exclusion shall be allowed under subsection (a) after the recipient has been entitled to exclude under this section for a period of 36 months (whether or not consecutive) amounts received as a scholarship or fellowship grant while not a candidate for a degree at an educational organization described in section 170(b)(1)(A)(ii).

(c) **Federal Grants for Tuition and Related Expenses not Includable Merely Because There is Requirement of Future Service as Federal Employee.**—

(1) In general.—If—

(A) an amount received by an individual under a Federal program would be excludable under subsections (a) and (b) as a scholarship or fellowship grant but for the fact that the individual is required to perform future service as a Federal employee, and

(B) the individual establishes that, in accordance with the terms of the grant, such amount was used for qualified tuition and related expenses,

scholarship by an individual who is a candidate for a degree at an educational organization described in section 170(b)(1)(A)(ii).

(b) *Qualified Scholarship.*—For purposes of this section—

(1) *In general.*—The term "qualified scholarship" means any amount received by an individual as a scholarship or fellowship grant to the extent the individual establishes that, in accordance with the conditions of the grant, such amount was used for qualified tuition and related expenses.

(2) *Qualified tuition and related expenses.*—For purposes of paragraph (1), the term "qualified tuition and related expenses" means—

(A) tuition and fees required for the enrollment or attendance of a student at an educational organization described in section 170(b)(1)(A)(ii), and

(B) fees, books, supplies, and equipment required for courses of instruction at such an educational organization.

(c) *Limitation.*—Subsections (a) and (d) shall not apply to that portion of any amount received which represents payment for teaching, research, or other services by the student required as a condition for receiving the qualified scholarship or qualified tuition reduction.

(d) *Qualified Tuition Reduction.*—

(1) *In general.*—Gross income shall not include any qualified tuition reduction.

(2) *Qualified tuition reduction.*—For purposes of this subsection, the term "qualified tuition reduction" means the amount of any reduction in tuition provided to an employee of an organization described in section 170(b)(1)(A)(ii) for the education (below the graduate level) at such organization (or another organization described in section 170(b)(1)(A)(ii)) of—

(A) such employee, or

(B) any person treated as an employee (or whose use is treated as an employee use) under the rules of section 132(f).

(3) *Reduction must not discriminate in favor of highly compensated, etc.*—Paragraph (1) shall apply with respect to any qualified tuition reduction provided with respect

---

[Footnote ¶2904 continued]

gross income shall not include such amount.

(2) **Qualified tuition and related expenses defined.**—For purposes of this subsection—

(A) In general.—The term 'qualified tuition and related expenses' means—

(i) tuition and fees required for the enrollment or attendance of a student at an institution of higher education, and

(ii) fees, books, supplies, and equipment required for courses of instruction at an institution of higher education.

(B) Institution of higher education.—The term 'institution of higher education' means an educational institution in any State which—

(i) admits as regular students only individuals having a certificate of graduation from a high school, or the recognized equivalent of such a certificate,

(ii) is legally authorized within such State to provide a program of education beyond high school,

(iii) provides an educational program for which it awards a bachelor's or higher degree, provides a program which is acceptable for full credit toward such a degree, or offers a program of training to prepare students for gainful employment in a recognized health profession, and

(iv) is a public or other nonprofit institution.

(3) **Service as Federal Employee.**—For purposes of this subsection, service in a health manpower shortage area shall be treated as service as a Federal employee.

(d) **Qualified Tuition Reduction.**—

(1) **In general.**—Gross income shall not include any qualified tuition reduction.

(2) **Qualified tuition reduction.**—For purposes of this subsection, the term 'qualified tuition reduction' means the amount of any reduction in tuition provided to an employee of an organization described in section 170(b)(1)(A)(ii) for the education (below the graduate level) at such organization (or another organization described in section 170(b)(1)(A)(ii)) of—

(A) such employee, or

(B) any person treated as an employee (or whose use is treated as an employee use) under the rules of section 132(f).

(3) **Reduction must discriminate in favor of highly compensated, etc.**—Paragraph (1) shall apply with respect to any qualified tuition reduction provided with respect to any officer, owner, or highly compensated employee only if such reduction is available on substantially the same terms to each member of a group of employees which is defined under a reasonable classification set up by the employer which does not discriminate in favor of officers, owners, or highly compensated employees."

Effective date (Sec. 151, '86 TRA).—Applies to taxable years beginning after 12-31-86.

to any[2] *highly compensated employee only if such reduction is available on substantially the same terms to each member of a group of employees which is defined under a reasonable classification set up by the employer which does not discriminate in favor of*[3] *highly compensated employees (within the meaning of section 414(q)). For purposes of this paragraph, the term "highly compensated employee" has the meaning given such term by section 414(q).*

(4) Exclusion of certain employees.—For purposes of this subsection, there may be excluded from consideration employees who may be excluded from consideration under section 89(h).

[*For official explanation, see Committee Reports, ¶3859; 3979; 4007.*]

[¶2905] CODE SEC. 118. CONTRIBUTIONS TO THE CAPITAL OF A CORPORATION.

(a) General Rule.—In the case of a corporation, gross income does not include any contribution to the capital of the taxpayer.

[1]*(b) Contributions in Aid of Construction, Etc.—For purposes of subsection (a), the term "contribution to the capital of the taxpayer" does not include any contribution in aid of construction or any other contribution as a customer or potential customer.*[2]

[Footnote ¶2904 continued]

The last sentence of Sec. 117(d)(3) in *italics* added by section 1114(b)(2)(A)—(C), '86 TRA, which struck out:
(2) "officer, owner, or"
(3) "officers, owners, or"
Effective date (Sec. 1114(c)(2), '86 TRA).—Applies to taxable years beginning after 12-31-87.

Sec. 117(d)(4) in *italics* added by section 1151(g)(2), '86 TRA.
Effective date (Sec. 1151(k), '86 TRA).—Generally applies to years beginning after the later of—
(A) 12-31-87, or
(B) the earlier of—
(i) the date which is 3 months after the date on which the Secretary of the Treasury or his delegate issues such regulations as are necessary to carry out the provisions of section 89 of the '86 Code (as added by this section), or
(ii) 12-31-88.
For special rules relating for collective bargaining plans, group-term insurance plans, church plans, and cafeteria plans, see footnote ¶2895.
[Footnote ¶2905] Matter in *italics* in Sec. 118(b)—(c) added by section 824(a), '86 TRA, which struck out:
(1) "**(b) Contributions in Aid of Construction.**—
(1) **General rule.**—For purposes of this section, the term 'contribution to the capital of the taxpayer' includes any amount of money or other property received from any person (whether or not a shareholder) by a regulated public utility which provides electric energy, gas (through a local distribution system or transportation by pipeline), water, or sewerage disposal services if—
(A) such amount is a contribution in aid of construction,
(B) where the contribution is in property which is other than electric energy, gas, steam, water, or sewerage disposal facilities, such amount meets the requirements of the expenditure rule of paragraph (2), and
(C) such amounts (or any property acquired or constructed with such amounts) are not included in the taxpayer's rate base for rate-making purposes.
(2) **Expenditure rule.**—An amount meets the requirements of this paragraph if—
(A) an amount equal to such amount is expended for the acquisition or construction of tangible property described in section 1231(b)—
(i) which was the purpose motivating the contribution, and
(ii) which is used predominantly in the trade or business of furnishing electric energy, gas, steam, water, or sewerage disposal services,
(B) the expenditure referred to in subparagraph (A) occurs before the end of the second taxable year after the year in which such amount was received, and
(C) accurate records are kept of the amount contributed and expenditures made on the basis of the project for which the contribution was made and on the basis of the year of contribution or expenditure.
(3) **Definitions.**—For purposes of this section—
(A) Contribution in aid of construction—The term 'contribution in aid of construction' shall be defined by regulations prescribed by the Secretary; except that such term shall not include amounts paid as customer connection fees (including amounts paid to connect the customer's line to an electric line, a gas main, a steam line, or a main water or sewer line and amounts paid as service charges for starting or stopping services.
(B) Predominately.—The term 'predominately' means 80 percent or more.
(C) Regulated public utility.—Ther term 'regulated public utility' has the meaning given such term by section 7701(a)(33); except that such term shall not include any such utility which is not required to provide electric energy, gas, water, or sewage disposal services to members of the general public (including in the case of a gas transmission utility, the provision of gas services by sale for resale to the general public) in its service area.
(4) **Disallowance of deductions and investment credit; adjusted basis.**—Notwithstanding any other provision of this subtitle, no deduction or credit shall be allowed for, or by reason of, the expenditure which constitutes a contribution in aid of construction to which this subsection applies. The adjusted basis of any property acquired with contributions in aid of construction to which this subsection applies shall be zero."
(2) "**(c) Statute of Limitations.**—If the taxpayer for any taxable year treats an amount as a contribution to the capital of the taxpayer described in subsection (b), then—
(1) the statutory period for the assessment of any deficiency attributable to any part of such amount shall not

³(c) Cross References.—

(1) For basis of property acquired by a corporation through a contribution to its capital, see section 362.

(2) For special rules in the case of contributions of indebtedness, see section 108(e)(6).

[For official explanation, see Committee Reports, ¶3946.]

[¶2906] CODE SEC. 119. MEALS OR LODGING FURNISHED FOR THE CONVENIENCE OF THE EMPLOYER.

* * * * * * * * * * * *

(d) *Lodging Furnished by Certain Educational Institutions to Employees.—*

(1) *In general.—In the case of an employee of an educational institution, gross income shall not include the value of qualified campus lodging furnished to such employee during the taxable year.*

(2) *Exception in cases of inadequate rent.—Paragraph (1) shall not apply to the extent of the excess of—*

(A) *the lesser of—*

(i) *5 percent of the appraised value (as of the close of the calendar year in which the taxable year begins) of the qualified campus lodging, or*

(ii) *the average of the rentals paid by individuals (other than employees or students of the educational institution) during such calendar year for lodging provided by the educational institution which is comparable to the qualified campus lodging provided to the employee, over*

(B) *the rent paid by the employee for the qualified campus lodging during such calendar year.*

(3) *Qualified campus lodging.—For purposes of this subsection, the term "qualified campus lodging" means lodging to which subsection (a) does not apply and which is—*

[Footnote ¶2905 continued]

expire before the expiration of 3 years from the date the Secretary is notified by the taxpayer (in such manner as the Secretary may prescribe) of—

(A) the amount of the expenditure referred to in subparagraph (A) of subsection (b)(2).

(B) the taxpayer's intention not to make the expenditures referred to in such subparagraph, or

(C) a failure to make such expenditure within the period described in subparagraph (B) of subsection (b)(2); and

(2) such deficiency may be assessed before the expiration of such 3-year period notwithstanding the provisions of any other law or rule of law which would otherwise prevent such assessment."

(3) "(d)"

Effective date (Sec. 824(c), '86 TRA).—(1) Generally applies to amounts received after 12-31-86, in taxable years ending after such date.

(2) Treatment of certain water supply projects.—The amendments made by this section shall not apply to amounts which are paid by the New Jersey Department of Environmental Protection for construction of alternative water supply projects in zones of drinking water contamination and which are designated by such department as being taken into account under this paragraph. Not more than $4,631,000 of such amounts may be designated under the preceding sentence.

(3) Treatment of certain contributions by transportation authority.—The amendments made by this section shall not apply to contributions in aid of construction by a qualified transportation authority which were clearly identified in master plan in existence on 9-13-84, and which are designated by such authority as being taken into account under this paragraph. Not more than $68,000,000 of such contributions may be designated under the preceding sentence. For purposes of this paragraph, a qualified transportation authority is an entity which was created on 2-20-67, and which was established by an interstate compact and consented to by Congress in Public Law 89-774, 80 Stat. 1324 (1966).

(4) Treatment of certain partnerships.—In the case of a partnership with a taxable year beginning 5-1-86, if such partnership realized net capital gain during the period beginning on the 1st day of such taxable year and ending on 5-29-86, pursuant to an indemnity agreement dated 5-6-86, then such partnership may elect to treat each asset to which such net capital gain relates as having been distributed to the partners of such partnership in proportion to their distributive share of the capital gain or loss realized by the partnership with respect to such asset and to treat each such asset as having been sold by each partner on the date of the sale of the asset by the partnership. If such an election is made, the consideration received by the partnership in connection with the sale of such assets shall be treated as having been received by the partners in connection with the deemed sale of such assets. In the case of a tiered partnership, for purposes of this paragraph each partnership shall be treated as having realized net capital gain equal to its proportionate share of the net capital gain of each partnership in which it is a partner, and the election provided by this paragraph shall apply to each tier.

[Footnote ¶2906] Sec. 119(d) in *italics* added by section 1164(a), '86 TRA.

Effective date (Sec. 1164(b), '86 TRA).—Applies to taxable years beginning after 12-31-85.

(A) located on, or in the proximity of, a campus of the educational institution, and

(B) furnished to the employee, his spouse, and any of his dependents by or on behalf of such institution for use as a residence.

(4) **Educational institution.**—For purposes of this paragraph, the term "educational institution" means an institution described in section 170(b)(1)(A)(ii).

[For official explanation, see Committee Reports, ¶4011.]

[¶2907] **CODE SEC. 120. AMOUNTS RECEIVED UNDER QUALIFIED GROUP LEGAL SERVICES PLANS.**

* * * * * * * * * * *

(b) **Qualified Group Legal Services Plan.**—For purposes of this section, a qualified group legal services plan is a separate [1]plan of an employer—

(1) under which the employer provides specified personal legal services to employees (or their spouses or dependents) through the prepayment of, or the provision in advance for, any portion of the legal fees for such services, and

(2) which meets the requirements of subsection (c) and section 89(k).

(c) **Requirements.**—

(1) **Discrimination.**—The contributions or benefits provided under the plan shall not discriminate in favor of employees who are [2]highly compensated employees (within the meaning of section 414(q)).

(2) **Eligibility.**—The plan shall benefit employees who qualify under a classification set up by the employer and found by the Secretary not to be discriminatory in favor of employees who are described in paragraph (1). [3]For purposes of this paragraph, there may be excluded from consideration employees who may be excluded from consideration under section 89(h)."

* * * * * * * * * * *

(d) **Other Definitions and Special Rules.**—For purposes of this section—

(1) [4]**Employee.**—The [5] term "employee" includes, for any year, an individual who is an employee within the meaning of section 401(c)(1) (relating to self-employed individuals).

* * * * * * * * * * *

[Footnote ¶2907] Matter in *italics* in Sec. 120(b) added by section 1151(c)(3), '86 TRA, which struck out:

(1) "written plan of an employer for the exclusive benefit of his employees or their spouses or dependents to provide such employees, spouses, or dependents with specified benefits consisting of personal legal services through prepayment of, or provision in advance for, legal fees in whole or in part by the employer, if the plan meets the requirements of subsection (c)."

Effective date (Sec. 1151(k)(1) '86 TRA).—Generally applies to years beginning after the later of—

(A) 12-31-87, or

(B) the earlier of—

(i) the date which is 3 months after the date on which the Secretary of the Treasury or his delegate issues such regulations as are necessary to carry out the provisions of section 89 of the '86 Code (as added by this section), or

(ii) 12-31-88.

For special rules for collective bargaining plans, group-term insurance plans, church plans and cafeteria plans, see footnote ¶2908.

Matter in *italics* in Sec. 120(c)(1) added by section 1114(b)(3)(A), '86 TRA, which struck out:

(2) "officers, shareholders, self-employed individuals, or highly compensated"

Effective date (Sec. 1114(c), '86 TRA).—(1) Generally applies to years beginning after 12-31-87. For transitional and special rules see footnote ¶3004.

Matter in *italics* in Sec. 120(c)(2) added by section 1151(g)(1), '86 TRA, which struck out:

(3) "For purposes of this paragraph, there shall be excluded from consideration employees not included in the plan who are included in a unit of employees covered by an agreement which the Secretary of Labor finds to be a collective bargaining agreement between employee representatives and one or more employers, if there is evidence that group legal services plan benefits were the subject of good faith bargaining between such employee representatives and such employer or employers."

Effective date (Sec. 1151(k)(1), '86 TRA).—See above.

Matter in *italics* in the heading of Sec. 120(d)(1) and (d)(1) added by section 1114(b)(3)(B)(i) and (ii), '86 TRA, which struck out:

(4) "Self-employed individual;"

(5) "term "self employed individual means, and the"

Effective date (Sec. 1114(c)(1) and (2), '86 TRA).—Generally applies to years beginning after 12-31-87. For transitional and special rules, see footnote ¶3004.

(e) **Termination.**—This section and section 501(c)(20) shall not apply to taxable years ending after [6]*December 31, 1987.*

(f) **Cross Reference.—**
For reporting and recordkeeping requirements, see section 6039D.

[For official explanation, see Committee Reports, ¶4007; ¶3979; ¶4009.]

≫**P-H CAUTION**→ There are two versions of Sec. 125. Sec. 125, generally effective after 12-31-87, follows. For Sec. 125, generally effective before 1-1-88, see ¶2908-A, below.

[¶2908] CODE SEC. 125. CAFETERIA PLANS. [1]

(a) *General Rule.*—*In the case of a cafeteria plan*—

(1) *amounts shall not be included in gross income of a participant in such plan solely because, under the plan, the participant may choose among the benefits of the plan, and*

[Footnote ¶2907 continued]

Matter in *italics* in Sec. 120(e) added by section 1162(b), '86 TRA, which struck out:
(6) "December 31, 1985"
Effective date (Sec. 1162(c)(2), '86 TRA).—Applies to taxable years beginning after 12-31-85.
[Footnote ¶2908] Matter in *italics* in Sec. 125 added by section 1151(d)(1), '86 TRA, which struck out:
(1) "**(a) In General.**—Except as provided in subsection (b), no amount shall be included in the gross income of a participant in a cafeteria plan solely because, under the plan, the participant may choose among the benefits of the plan.
(b) **Exception for Highly Compensated Participants and Key Employees.—**
(1) **Highly compensated Participants.**—In the case of a highly compensated participant, subsection (a) shall not apply to any benefit attributable to a plan year for which the plan discriminates in favor of—
(A) highly compensated individuals as to eligibility to participate, or
(B) highly compensated participants as to contributions and benefits.
(2) **Key employees.**—In the case of a key employee (within the meaning of section 416(i)(1)), subsection (a) shall not apply to any benefit attributable to a plan for which the statutory nontaxable benefits provided to key employees exceed 25 percent of the aggregate of such benefits provided for all employees under the plan. For purposes of the preceding sentence, statutory nontaxable benefits shall be determined without regard to the last sentence of subsection (f).
(3) **Year of inclusion.**—For purposes of determining the taxable year of inclusion, any benefit described in paragraph (1) or (2) shall be treated as received or accrued in the taxable year of the participant or key employee in which the plan year ends.
(c) **Discrimination as to Benefits or Contributions.**—For purposes of subparagraph (B) of subsection (b)(1), a cafeteria plan does not discriminate where qualified benefits and total benefits (or employer contributions allocable to qualified benefits and employer contributions for total benefits) do not discriminate in favor of highly compensated participants.
(d) **Cafeteria Plan Defined.**—For purposes of this section—
(1) **In general.**—The term 'cafeteria plan' means a written plan under which—
(A) All participants are employees, and
(B) the participants may choose among 2 or more benefits consisting of cash and qualified benefits.
(2) **Deferred compensation plans excluded.**—The term 'cafeteria plan' does not include any plan which provides for deferred compensation. The preceding sentence shall not apply in the case of a profit-sharing or stock bonus plan, which includes a qualified cash or deferred arrangement (as defined in section 401(k)(2)) to the extent of amounts which a covered employee may elect to have the employer pay as contributions to a trust under such plan on behalf of the employee.
(e) **Highly Compensated Participant and Individual Defined.**—For purposes of this section—
(1) **Highly compensated participant.**—The term 'highly compensated participant' means a participant who is—
(A) an officer,
(B) a shareholder owning more than 5 percent of the voting power or value of all classes of stock of the employer,
(C) highly compensated, or
(D) a spouse or dependent (within the meaning of section 152) of an individual described in subparagraph (A), (B), or (C).
(2) **Highly compensated individual.**—The term 'highly compensated individual' means an individual who is described in subparagraph (A), (B), (C), or (D) of paragraph (1).

   (2)   if the plan fails to meet the requirements of subsection (b) for any plan year—
      (A)   paragraph (1) shall not apply, and
      (B)   notwithstanding any other provision of part III of this subchapter, any qualified benefits received under such cafeteria plan by a highly compensated employee for such plan year shall be included in the gross income of such employee for the taxable year with or within which such plan year ends.

   (b)   Prohibition Against Discrimination as to Eligibility To Participate.—

⟦Footnote ¶2908 continued⟧

   (f)   **Qualified Benefits Defined.**—For purposes of this section, the term "qualified benefit" means any benefit which, with the application of subsection (a), is not includible in the gross income of the employee by reason of an express provision of this chapter (other than section 117, 124, 127, or 132). Such term includes any group term life insurance which is includible in gross income only because it exceeds the dollar limitation of section 79 and such term includes any benefit permitted under regulations.

   (g)   **Special Rules.—**

   (1)   **Collectively bargained plan not considered discriminatory.**—For purposes of this section, a plan shall not be treated as discriminatory if the plan is maintained under an agreement which the Secretary finds to be a collective bargaining agreement between employee representatives and one or more employers.

   (2)   **Health benefits.**—For purposes of subparagraph (B) of subsection (b)(1), a cafeteria plan which provides health benefits shall not be treated as discriminatory if—

      (A)   contributions under the plan on behalf of each participant include an amount which—

      (i)   equals 100 percent of the cost of the health benefit coverage under the plan of the majority of the highly compensated participants similarly situated, or

      (ii)   equals or exceeds 75 percent of the cost of the health benefit coverage of the participant (similarly situated) having the highest cost health benefit coverage under the plan, and

      (B)   contributions or benefits under the plan in excess of those described in subparagraph (A) bear a uniform relationship to compensation.

   (3)   **Certain participation eligibility rules not treated as discriminatory.**—For purposes of subparagraph (A) of subsection (b)(1), a classification shall not be treated as discriminatory if the plan—

      (A)   benefits a group of employees described in subparagraph (B) of section 410(b)(1), and

      (B)   meets the requirements of clauses (i) and (ii):

      (i)   No employee is required to complete more than 3 years of employment with the employer or employers maintaining the plan as a condition of participation in the plan, and the employment requirement for each employee is the same.

      (ii)   Any employee who has satisfied the employment requirement of clause (i) and who is otherwise entitled to participate in the plan commences participation no later than the first day of the first plan year beginning after the date the employment requirement was satisfied unless the employee was separated from service before the first day of that plan year.

   (4)   **Certain controlled groups, etc.**—All employees who are treated as employed by a single employer under subsection (b), (c), or (m) of section 414 shall be treated as employed by a single employer for purposes of this section.

   (h)   **Cross Reference.—**

   For reporting and recordkeeping requirements, see section 6039D.

   (i)   **Regulations.**—The Secretary shall prescribe such regulations as may be necessary to carry out the provisions of this section.

   Effective date (Sec. 1151(k), '86 TRA).—

   (1)   Generally applies to years beginning after the later of —

      (A)   12-31-87, or

      (B)   the earlier of—

      (i)   the date which is 3 months after the date on which the Secretary of the Treasury or his delegate issues such regulations as are necessary to carry out the provisions of Sec. 89 '86 Code (as added by this section), or

      (ii)   12-31-88.

   (2)   Special rule for collective bargaining plan.—In the case of a plan maintained pursuant to 1 or more collective bargaining agreements between employee representatives and 1 or more employers ratified before 3-1-86, the amendments made by this section shall not apply to employees covered by such an agreement in years beginning before the earlier of—

      (A)   the date on which the last of such collective bargaining agreements terminates (determined without regard to any extension thereof after 2-28-86, or

      (B)   1-1-91.

A plan shall not be required to take into account employees to which the preceding sentence applies for purposes of applying Sec. 89 '86 Code (as added by this section) to employees to which the preceding sentence does not apply for any year preceding the year described in the preceding sentence.

   (3)   Exception for certain group-term insurance plans.—In the case of a plan described in section 223(d)(2) '84 TRA, such plan shall be treated as meeting the requirements of Sec. 89 '86 Code (as added by this section) with respect to individuals described in section 223(d)(2) '84 TRA. An employer may elect to disregard such individuals in applying Sec. 89 '86 Code (as so added) to other employees of the employer.

   (4)   Special rule for church plans.—In the case of a church plan (within the meaning of section 414(e)(3) '86 Code maintaining an insured accident and health plan, the amendments made by this section shall apply to years beginning after 12-31-88.

(1) *Highly compensated employees.*—*A plan shall be treated as failing to meet the requirements of this subsection unless the plan is available to a group of employees as qualify under a classification set up by the employer and which the Secretary find not to be discriminatory in favor of highly compensated employees.*

(2) *Key employees.*—*In the case of a key employee (within the meaning of section 416(i)(1)), a plan shall be treated as failing to meet the requirements of this subsection if the qualified benefits provided to key employees under the plan exceed 25 percent of the aggregate of such benefits provided for all employees under the plan. For purposes of the preceding sentence, qualified benefits shall be determined without regard to the last sentence of subsection (e).*

(3) *Excludable employees.*—*For purposes of this subsection, there may be excluded from consideration employees who may be excluded from consideration under section 89(h).*

(c) *Cafeteria Plan Defined.*—*For purposes of this section—*

(1) *In general.*—*The term "cafeteria plan" means a plan which meets the requirements of section 89(k) and under which—*
   (A) *all participants are employees, and*
   (B) *the participants may choose—*
      (i) *among 2 or more benefits consisting of cash and qualified benefits, or*
      (ii) *among 2 or more qualified benefits.*

(2) *Deferred compensation plans excluded.*—
   (A) *In general.*—*The term "cafeteria plan" does not include any plan which provides for deferred compensation.*
   (B) *Exception for cash and deferred arrangements.*—*Subparagraph (A) shall not apply to a profit-sharing or stock bonus plan which includes a qualified cash or deferred arrangement (as defined in section 401(k)(2)) to the extent of amounts which a covered employee may elect to have the employer pay as contributions to a trust under such plan on behalf of the employee.*
   (C) *Exception for certain plans maintained by educational institutions.*—*Subparagraph (A) shall not apply to a plan maintained by an educational organization described in section 170(b)(1)(A))ii) to the extent of amounts which a covered employee may elect to have the employer pay as contributions for post-retirement group life insurance if—*
      (i) *all contributions for such insurance must be made before retirement, and*
      (ii) *such life insurance does not have a cash surrender value at any time.*

For purposes of section 79, any life insurance described in the preceding sentence shall be treated as group-term life insurance.

(d) *Highly Compensated Employee.*—*For purposes of this section, the term "highly compensated employee" has the meaning given such term by section 414(q).*

(e) *Qualified Benefits Defined.*—*For purposes of this section—*

(1) *In general.*—*The term "qualified benefit" means any benefit which, with the application of subsection (a), is not includible in the gross income of the employee by reason of an express provision of this chapter (other than section 117, 124, 127, or 132).*

(2) *Certain benefits included.*—*The term "qualified benefits" includes—*
   (A) *any group-term life insurance which is includible in gross income only because it exceeds the dollar limitation of section 79, and*
   (B) *any other benefit permitted under regulations.*

(f) *Collectively Bargained Plan Not Considered Discriminatory.*—*For purposes of this section, a plan shall not be treated as discriminatory if the plan is maintained under an agreement which the Secretary finds to be a collective bargaining agreement between employee representatives and one or more employers.*

(g) *Cross References.*—
For reporting and recordkeeping requirements, see section 6039D.

≫**P-H CAUTION→** There are two versions of Sec. 125. Sec. 125, generally effective before 1-1-88 follows. For Sec. 125, generally effective after 12-31-87 see ¶2908, above.

【¶2908-A】 **CODE SEC. 125. CAFETERIA PLANS.**

* * * * * * * * * * * * * *

(c) **Discrimination as to Benefits or Contributions.**—For purposes of subparagraph (B) of subsection (b)(1), a cafeteria plan does not discriminate where [1]*qualified* benefits and total benefits (or employer contributions allocable to [1]*qualified* benefits and employer contributions for total benefits) do not discriminate in favor of highly compensated participants.

(d) **Cafeteria Plan Defined.**—For purposes of this section—

(1) **In general.**—The term "cafeteria plan" means a written plan under which—

(A) All participants are employees, and

(B) the participants may choose among 2 or more benefits *consisting of cash and* [1]*qualified* benefits.

* * * * * * * * * * *

(f) [2]*Qualified Benefits Defined.—For purposes of this section, the term "qualified benefit" means any benefit which, with the application of subsection (a), is not includible in the gross income of the employee by reason of an express provision of this chapter (other than section 117, 124, 127, or 132). Such term includes any group term life insurance which is includible in gross income only because it exceeds the dollar limitation of section 79 and such term includes any other benefit permitted under regulations.*

[For official explanation, see Committee Reports, ¶3980; 4173.]

[¶2909] CODE SEC. 127. EDUCATIONAL ASSISTANCE PROGRAMS.

(a) **Exclusion From Gross Income.**—

* * * * * * * * * * *

(2) [1]*$5,250 maximum exclusion.*—If, but for this paragraph, this section would exclude from gross income more than [1]*$5,250* of educational assistance furnished to an individual during a calendar year, this section shall apply only to the first [1]*$5,250* of such assistance so furnished.

(b) **Educational Assistance Program.**—

(1) **In general.**—For purposes of this section, an educational assistance program is

---

[Footnote ¶2908-A] Matter in *italics* in Sec. 125(c), (d)(1)(B) and (f) added by section 1853(b)(1), '86 TRA, which struck out:

(1) "statutory nontaxable"

(2) "**Statutory Nontaxable Benefits Defined.**—For purposes of this section, the term 'nontaxable benefit' means any benefit which, with the application of subsection (a), is not includible in the gross income of the employee by reason of an express provision of this chapter (other than section 117, 124, 127, or 132). Such term includes any group term life insurance which is includible in gross income only because it exceeds the dollar limitation of section 79."

Effective date (Sec. 1881, '86 TRA, and section 531(h), '84 TRA).—Takes effect on 1-1-85.

[Footnote ¶2909] Matter in *italics* in Sec. 127(a)(2) added by section 1162(a)(2), '86 TRA, which struck out:

(1) "$5,000"

Effective date (Sec. 1162(c)(1), '86 TRA).—Applies to taxable years beginning after 12-31-85.

Matter in italics in Sec. 127(b)(1) added by section 1151(c)(4)(A), '86 TRA, which struck out:

(2) (1) "separate written plan of an employer for the exclusive benefit of his employees to provide such employees with educational assistance. The program must meet the requirements of paragraphs (2) through (6) of this subsection."

Effective date (Sec. 1151(k)(1)—(3), '86 TRA).—(1) Generally applies to years beginning after the later of—

(A) 12-31-87, or

(B) the earlier of —

(i) the date which is 3 months after the date on which the Secretary of the Treasury issues such regulations as are necessary to carry out the provisions of. Sec. 89 of the '86 Code (as added by this section), or

(ii) 12-31-88.

(2) Special rule for collective bargaining plan.—In the case of a plan maintained pursuant to 1 or more collective bargaining agreements between employee representatives and 1 or more employers ratified before 3-1-86, the amendments made by this section shall not apply to employees covered by such an agreement in years before the earlier of—

(A) the date on which the last of such collective bargaining agreements terminates (determined without regard to any extension thereof after 2-28-86), or

(B) 1-1-91.

A plan shall not be required to take into account employees to which the preceding sentence applies for purposes of applying section 89 of the '86 Code (as added by this section) to employees to which the preceding sentence does not apply for any year preceding the year described in the preceding sentence.

(3) Exception for certain group-term insurance plans.—In the case of a plan described in section 223(d)(2) of the '84 TRA, such plan shall be treated as meeting the requirements of section 89 of the '86 Code (as added by this section) with respect to individuals described in section 223(d)(2) of such Act. An employer may elect to disregard such individuals in applying section 89 of such Code (as so added) to other employees of the employer.

a [2]plan of an employer—
    (A) under which the employer provides employees with educational assistance, and
    (B) which meets the requirements of paragraphs (2) through (5) and section 89(k).

  (2) Eligibility.—The program shall benefit employees who qualify under a classification set up by the the employer and found by the Secretary not to be discriminatory in favor of employees who are[3] highly compensated employees (within the meaning of section 414(q), or their dependents. For purposes of this paragraph, there [4]may be excluded from consideration employees who may be excluded from consideration under section 89(h).

* * * * * * * * * * * *

  (6) [struck out][5]

* * * * * * * * * * * *

  (d) Termination.—This section shall not apply to taxable years beginning after [6]December 31, 1987.

[For official explanation, see Committee Reports, ¶4009, 4007, 3979.]

[¶2910] CODE SEC. 129. DEPENDENT CARE ASSISTANCE PROGRAMS.

  (a) *Exclusion.*—

    (1) In general.—Gross income of an employee does not include amounts paid or incurred by the employer for dependent care assistance provided to such employee if the assistance is furnished pursuant to a program which is described in subsection (d).

    (2) Limitation of exclusion.—The aggregate amount excluded from the gross income of the taxpayer under this section for any taxable year shall not exceed $5,000 ($2,500 in the case of a separate return by a married individual).
For purposes of the preceding sentence, marital status shall be determined under the rules of paragraphs (3) and (4) of section 21(e).

* * * * * * * * * * * *

  (c) Payments To Related Individuals.—No amount paid or incurred during the taxable year of an employee by an employer in providing dependent care assistance to such employee shall be excluded under subsection (a) if such amount was paid or incurred to an individual—
    (1) with respect to whom, for such taxble year, a deduction is allowable under [1] section 151(c) (relating to personal exemptions for dependents) to such employee or the spouse of such employee, or
    (2) who is a child of such employee (within the meaning of [2]section 151(c)(3)

[Footnote ¶2909 continued]

Matter in *italics* in the first sentence in Sec. 127(b)(2) added by section 1114(b)(4), '86 TRA, which struck out:
(3) "officers, owners, or highly compensated,"
Effective date (Sec. 1114(c)(2), '86 TRA).—Applies to years beginning after 12-31-87.

Matter in *italics* in the last sentence in Sec. 127(b)(2) added by section 1151(g)(3), '86 TRA, which struck out:
(4) "shall be excluded from consideration employees not included in the program who are included in a unit of employees covered by an agreement which the Secretary of Labor finds to be a collective bargaining agreement between employee representatives and one or more employers, if there is evidence that educational assistance benefits were the subject of good faith bargaining between such employee representatives and such employer."
Effective date (Sec. 1151(k)(1)—(3), '86 TRA).—See above.

Section 1151(c)(4)(B), '86 TRA, struck out Sec. 127(b)(6):
(5) **"Notification of employees.**—Reasonable notification of the availability and terms of the program must be provided to eligible employees"
Effective date (Sec. 1151(k)(1)—(3), '86 TRA).—See above.

Matter in *italics* in Sec. 127(d) added by section 1162(a)(1), '86 TRA, which struck out:
(6) "December 31, 1985"
Effective date (Sec. 1162(c)(1), '86 TRA).—See above.
[Footnote ¶2910] Matter in *italics* in Sec. 129(a), added by section 1163(a), '86 TRA.
Effective date (Sec. 1163(c), '86 TRA).—Applies to taxable years beginning after 12-31-86.

Matter in *italics* in Sec. 129(c)(1) and (2) added by section 104(b)(1), '86 TRA, which struck out:
(1) "section 151(e)"
(2) "section 151(e)(3)"
Effective date (Sec. 151(a), '86 TRA).—Applies to taxable years beginning after 12-31-86.

---

under the age of 19 at the close of such taxable year.

(d) Dependent Care Assistance Program.—

    (1) In general.—[3]*For purposes of this section, a dependent care assistance program is a plan of an employer—*

        (A) under which the employer provides employees with dependent care assistance, and

        (B) which meets the requirements of paragraphs (2) through (6) and section 89(k).

    (2) Discrimination.—The contributions or benefits provided under the plan shall not discriminate in favor of employees who are [4] *highly compensated employees (within the meaning of section 414(q)),* or their dependents.

    (3) Eligibility.—The program shall benefit employees who qualify under a classification set up by the employer and found by the Secretary not to be discriminatory in favor of employees described in paragraph (2), or their dependents.[5] *For purposes of this paragraph, there may be excluded from consideration employees who may be excluded from consideration under section 89(h).*

* * * * * * * * * * * *

    (5) No funding required.—A program referred to in the paragraph (1) is not required to be funded.[6]

    [7]**(6) Statement of expenses.—**The plan shall furnish to an employee, on or before January 31, a written statement showing the amounts paid or expenses incurred by the employer in providing dependent care assistance to such employee during the previous calendar year.

    (8) [should read (7)] Benefits.—

        (A) In general.—A plan meets the requirements of this paragraph if the average benefits provided to employees who are not highly compensated employees is at least 55 percent of the average benefits provided to highly compensated employees.

        (B) Salary reduction agreements.—For purposes of subparagraph (A), in the case of any benefits provided through a salary reduction agreement, there shall be disregarded any employees whose compensation (within the meaning of section 415(q)(7)) is less than $25,000.

(e) Definitions and Special Rules.—For purposes of this section—

* * * * * * * * * * * *

⟦Footnote ¶2910 continued⟧

Matter in *italics* in Sec. 129(d)(1) added by section 1151(c)(5)(A), '86 TRA, which struck out:

(3) "For purposes of this section a dependent care assistance program is a separate written plan of an employer for the exclusive benefit of his employees to provide such employees with dependent care assistance which meets the requirements of paragraphs (2) through (7) of this subsection."

Effective date (Sec. 1151(k)(1), '86 TRA).—

(1) Generally applies to years beginning after the later of—

(A) 12-31-87, or

(B) the earlier of—

(i) the date which is 3 months after the date on which the Secretary of the Treasury or his delegate issues such regulations as are necessary to carry out the provisions of Sec. 89 '86 Code (as added by this section), or

(ii) 12-31-88.

For Special Rules and Exceptions on collective bargaining plans, group term insurance plans, church plans and cafeteria plans, see ¶2908.

Matter in *italics* in Sec. 129(d)(2) added by section 1114(b)(4), '86 TRA, which struck out:

(4) "officers, owners, or highly compensated"

Effective date (Sec. 1114(c)(3), '86 TRA).—Applies to years beginning after 12-31-88.

Matter in *italics* in Sec. 129(d)(3) and (6)—(8) [should read (7)] added by section 1151(c)(5)(B), (f) and (g)(4), '86 TRA, which struck out:

(5) "For purposes of this paragraph, there shall be excluded from consideration employees not included in the program who are included in a unit of employees covered by an agreement which the Secretary of Labor finds to be a collective bargaining agreement between employee representatives and one or more employers, if there is evidence that dependent care benefits were the subject of good faith bargaining between such employee representatives and such employer or employers."

(6) "(6) **Notification of eligible employees.**—Reasonable notification of the availability and terms of the program shall be provided to eligible employees."

(7) "(7)"

Effective date (Sec. 1151(k)(1), '86 TRA). —See above.

Sec. 129(e)(8) in *italics* added by section 1163(b), '86 TRA.

Effective date (Sec. 1163(c), '86 TRA).—Applies to taxable years beginning after 12-31-86.

(8) *Treatment of onsite facilities.—In the case of an onsite facility, except to the extent provided in regulations, the amount excluded with respect to any dependent shall be based on—*
    (A) *utilization, and*
    (B) *the value of the services provided.*

[For official explanation, see Committee Reports, ¶4007; 4010.]

[¶2911]   CODE SEC. 130.   CERTAIN PERSONAL INJURY LIABILITY ASSIGNMENTS.

* * * * * * * * * * *

(c) **Qualified Assignment.**—For purposes of this section, the term "qualified assignment" means any assignment of a liability to make periodic payments as damages (whether by suit or agreement) on account of personal injury or sickness (*in a case involving physical injury or physical sickness*)—
    (1)   if the assignee assumes such liability from a person who is a party to the suit or agreement, and
    (2)   if—
        (A)   such periodic payments are fixed and determinable as to amount and time of payment,
        (B)   such periodic payments cannot be accelerated, deferred, increased, or decreased by the recipient of such payments,
        (C)   the assignee does not provide to the recipient of such payments rights against the assignee which are greater than those of a general creditor,
        (D)   the assignee's obligation on account of the personal injuries or sickness is not greater than the obligation of the person who assigned the liability, and
        (E)   such periodic payments are excludable from the gross income of the recipient under section 104(a)(2).

* * * * * * * * * * *

[For official explanation, see Committee Reports, ¶3955.]

[¶2912]   CODE SEC. 131.   CERTAIN FOSTER CARE PAYMENTS.

[1]*(a)   General Rule.—Gross income shall not include amounts received by a foster care provider during the taxable year as qualified foster care payments.*

[Footnote ¶2911]   Matter in *italics* in Sec. 130(c) added by section 1002(a), '86 TRA.
Effective date (Sec. 1002(b), '86 TRA).—Applies to assignments entered into after 12-31-86, in taxable years ending after such date.
[Footnote ¶2912]   Matter in *italics* in Sec. 131 added by section 1707(a), '86 TRA, which struck out:
(1)   "(a)   **General Rule.**—Gross income shall not include amounts received by a foster parent during the taxable year as qualified foster care payments.
(b)   **Qualified Foster Care Payment Defined.**—For purposes of this section—
(1)   **In general.**—The term "qualified foster care payment" means any amount—
(A)   which is paid by a State or political subdivision thereof or by a child-placing agency which is described in section 501(c)(3) and exempt from tax under section 501(a), and
(B)   which is—
(i)   paid to reimburse the foster parent for the expenses of caring for a qualified foster child in the foster parent's home, or
(ii)   a difficulty of care payment.
(2)   **Qualified foster child.**—The term "qualified foster child" means any individual who—
(A)   has not attained age 19, and
(B)   is living in a foster family in which such individual was placed by—
(i)   an agency of a State or political subdivision thereof, or
(ii)   an organization which is licensed by a State (or political subdivision thereof) as a child-placing agency and which is described in section 501(c)(3) and exempt from tax under section 501(a).
(c)   **Difficulty of Care Payments.**—For purposes of this section—
(1)   **Difficulty of care payments.**—The term "difficulty of care payments" means payments to individuals which are not described in subsection (b)(1)(B)(i), and which—
(A)   are compensation for providing the additional care of a qualified foster child which is—
(i) required by reason of a physical, mental, or emotional handicap of such child with respect to which the State has determined that there is a need for additional compensation, and
(ii)   provided in the home of the foster parent, and
(B)   are designated by the payor as compensation described in subparagraph (A).
(2)   **Limitation based on number of children.**—In the case of any foster home, difficulty of care payments for any period to which such payments relate shall not be excludable from gross income under subsection (a) to the extent such payments are made for more than 10 qualified foster children."
Effective date (Sec. 1707(b), '86 TRA).—Applies to taxable years beginning after 12-31-85.

(b) Qualified Foster Care Payment Defined.—For purposes of this section—

(1) In General.—The term "qualified foster care payment" means any amount—

(A) which is paid by a State or political subdivision thereof or by a placement agency which is described in section 501(c)(3) and exempt from tax under section 501(a), and

(B) which is—

(i) paid to the foster care provider for caring for a qualified foster individual in the foster care provider's home, or

(ii) a difficulty of care payment.

(2) Qualified foster individual.—The term "qualified foster individual" means any individual who is living in a foster family home in which such individual was placed by—

(A) an agency of a State or political subdivision thereof, or

(B) in the case of an individual who has not attained age 19, an organization which is licensed by a State (or political subdivision thereof) as a placement agency and which is described in section 501(c)(3) and exempt from tax under section 501(a).

(3) Limitation based on number of individuals over the age of 18.—In the case of any foster home in which there is a qualified foster care individual who has attained age 19, foster care payments (other than difficulty of care payments) for any period to which such payments relate shall not be excludable from gross income under subsection (a) to the extent such payments are made for more than 5 such qualified foster individuals.

(c) Difficulty of Care Payments.—For purposes of this section—

(1) Difficulty of care payments.—The term "difficulty of care payments" means payments to individuals which are not described in subsection (b)(1)(B)(i), and which—

(A) are compensation for providing the additional care of a qualified foster individual which is—

(i) required by reason of a physical, mental, or emotional handicap of such individual with respect to which the State has determined that there is a need for additional compensation, and

(ii) provided in the home of the foster care provider, and

(B) are designated by the payor as compensation described in subparagraph (A).

(2) Limitation based on number of individuals.—In the case of any foster home, difficulty of care payments for any period to which such payments relate shall not be excludable from gross income under subsection (a) to the extent such payments are made for more than—

(A) 10 qualified foster individuals who have not attained age 19, and

(B) 5 qualified foster individuals not described in subparagraph (A).

[For official explanation, see Committee Reports, ¶4129.]

【¶2913】   CODE SEC. 132.   CERTAIN FRINGE BENEFITS.

* * * * * * * * * * * *

(c) Qualified Employee Discount Defined.—For purposes of this section—

* * * * * * * * * * * *

(3) Employee discount defined.—The term "employee discount" means the amount by which—

(A) the price at which the property or services are provided [1]*by the employer to an employee for use by such employee,* is less than

* * * * * * * * * * * *

(e) De Minimis Fringe Defined.—For purposes of this section—

【Footnote ¶2913】   Matter in *italics* in Sec. 132(c)(3)(A) added by section 1853(a)(2), '86 TRA, which struck out:

(1) "to the employee by the employer"

Effective date (Sec. 1881, '86 TRA and section 531(h), '84 TRA).—Takes effect 1-1-85.

(2) **Treatment of certain eating facilities.**—The operation by an employer of any eating facility for employees shall be treated as a de minimis fringe if—

(A) such facility is located on or near the business premises of the employer, and

(B) revenue derived from such facility normally equals or exceeds the direct operating costs of such facility.

The preceding sentence shall apply with respect to any [2] highly compensated employee only if access to the facility is available on substantially the same terms to each member of a group of employees which is defined under a reasonable classification set up by the employer which does not discriminate in favor of [3] highly compensated employees.

(f) **Certain individuals Treated as Employees for Purposes of Subsection (a)(1) and (2).**—For purposes of paragraphs (1) and (2) of subsection (a)—

* * * * * * * * * * * *

(2) **Spouse and dependent children.**—

(A) **In General**—Any use by the spouse or a dependent child of the employee shall be treated as use by the employee.

(B) **Dependent Child.**—For purposes of subparagraph (A), the term "dependent child" means any child (as defined in section 151(e)(3)) of the employee—

(i) who is a dependent of the employee, or

(ii) both of whose parents are deceased *and who has not attained age 25*

For purposes of the preceding sentence, any child to whom section 152(e) applies shall be treated as the dependent of both parents.

* * * * * * * * * * * *

[4]*(g)* *Reciprocal Agreements.*—*For purposes of paragraph (1) of subsection (a), any service provided by an employer to an employee of another employer shall be treated as provided by the employer of such employee if—*

(1) such service is provided pursuant to a written agreement between such employers, and

(2) neither of such employers incurs any substantial additional costs (including foregone revenue) in providing such service or pursuant to such agreement.

(h) **Special rules**—

(1) **Exclusions under subsection (a)(1) and (2) apply to officers, etc., only if no discrimination.**—Paragraphs (1) and (2) of subsection (a) shall apply with respect to any fringe benefit described therein provided with respect to any [5] highly compensated employee only if such fringe benefit is available on substantially the same terms to

---

[Footnote ¶2913 continued]

Section 1114(b)(5)(A), '86 TRA struck out from Sec. 132(e)(2):

(2) "officer, owner, or"

(3) "officers, owners, or"

Effective date (Sec. 1114(c)(2), '86 TRA).—Applies to years beginning after 12-31-87.

Matter in *italics* is Sec. 132(f)(2)(B)(ii) added by section 1853(a)(1), '86 TRA.

Effective date (Sec. 1881, '86 TRA and section 531(h), '84 TRA).—Takes effect 1-1-85.

Matter in *italics* in Sec. 132(g) added by section 1151(e)(2), '86 TRA, which struck out:

(4) "(g) **Special Rules Relating to Employee.**—For purposes of this section—

(1) **Controlled Groups, etc.**—All employees treated as employed by a single employer under subsection (b), (c), or (m) of section 414 shall be treated as employed by a single employer for purposes of this section.

(2) **Reciprocal agreements.**—For purposes of paragraph (1) of subsection (a), any service provided by an employer to an employee of another employer shall be treated as provided by the employer of such employee if—

(A) such service is provided pursuant to a written agreement between such employers, and

(B) neither of such employers incurs any substantial additional cost (including forgone revenue) in providing such service or pursuant to such agreement."

Effective date (Sec. 1151(k)(1), '86 TRA).—(1) Generally applies to years beginning after the later of—

(A) 12-31-87, or

(B) the earlier of—

(i) the date which is 3 months after the date on which the Secretary of the Treasury or his delegate issues such regulations as are necessary to carry out the provisions of section 89 '86 Code (as added by this section), or

(ii) 12-31-88.

For special rules and exceptions, see footnote ¶2908.

Section 1114(b)(5)(A), '86 TRA, struck out from Sec. 132(h)(1):

(5) "officer, owner, or"

each member of a group of employees which is defined under a reasonable classification set up by the employer which does not discriminate in favor of [6] highly compensated employees. *For purposes of this paragraph and subsection (e), there may be excluded from consideration employees who may be excluded from consideration under section 89(h).*

*   *   *   *   *   *   *   *   *   *   *

(3) Auto salesmen.—

(A) In General.—For purposes of subsection (a)(3), qualified automobile demonstration use shall be treated as a working condition fringe.

(B) Qualified Automobile Demonstration Use.—For purposes of subparagraph (A), the term "qualified automobile demonstration use" means any use of an automobile by a full-time automobile salesman in the sales area is which the automobile dealer's sales office is located if—

    (i) such use [7]*is provided primarily to facilitate the salesman's performance of services for the employer, and*

    (ii) there are substantial restrictions on the personal use of such automobile by such salesman.

*   *   *   *   *   *   *   *   *   *   *

(7) Highly compensated employee.—For purposes of this section, the term "highly compensated employee" has the meaning given such term by section 414(q).

(i) Customers Not to Include Employees.—For purposes of this section (other than [8]*subsection (c)(2)*), the term "customers" shall only include customers who are not employees.

*   *   *   *   *   *   *   *   *   *   *

[For official explanation, see Committee Reports, ¶4173; 4007; 3979.]

[¶2914] CODE SEC. 133. INTEREST ON CERTAIN LOANS USED TO ACQUIRE EMPLOYER SECURITIES.

(a) In General.—Gross income does not include 50 percent of the interest received by—

    (1) a bank (within the meaning of section 581),

    (2) an insurance company to which subchapter L applies,[1]

    (3) a corporation actively engaged in the business of lending money, *or*

    (4) *a regulated investment company (as defined in section 851),* with respect to a securities acquisition loan.

(b) Securities Acquisition Loan.—

    [2]*(1) In general.—For purposes of this section, the term "securities acquisition loan"*

[Footnote ¶2913 continued]

(6) "officers, owners, or"
Effective date (Sec. 1114(c)(2), '86 TRA).—Applies to years beginning after 12-31-87.

Matter in *italics* in Sec. 132(h)(1) added by section 1151(g)(5), '86 TRA.
Effective date (Sec. 1151(k)(1), '86 TRA).—(1) Generally applies to years beginning after the later of—
(A) 12-31-87, or
(B) the earlier of—
(i) the date which is 3 months after the date on which the Secretary of the Treasury or his delegate issues such regulations as are necessary to carry out the provisions of section 89 '86 Code (as added by this section), or
(ii) 12-31-88.
For special rules and exceptions, see footnote ¶2908.

Matter in *italics* in Sec. 132(h)(3)(B)(i) added by section 1899A(5), '86 TRA, which struck out:
(7) "in"

Sec. 132(h)(7) added by section 1114(b)(5)(B), '86 TRA.
Effective date (Sec. 1114(c)(2), '86 TRA).—Applies to years beginning after 12-31-87.

Matter in *italics* in Sec. 132(i) added by section 1853(a)(3), '86 TRA, which struck out:
(8) "subsection (c)(2)(B)"
Effective date (Sec. 1881, '86 TRA and section 531(h), '84 TRA).—Takes effect 1-1-85.
[Footnote ¶2914] Matter in *italics* in Sec. 133(a) and (b)(1) added by section 1173(b)(1)(A) and (2), '86 TRA, which struck out:
(1) "or"
(2) "any loan to a corporation, or to an employee stock ownership plan, to the extent that the proceeds are used to acquire employer securities (within the meaning of section 409A(1)) for the plan."
Effective date (Sec. 1173(c)(2), '86 TRA).—(A) Applies to loans used to acquire employer securities after the date of the enactment of this Act, including loans used to refinance loans used to acquire employer securities be-

means—

(A) *any loan to a corporation or to an employee stock ownership plan to the extent that the proceeds are used to acquire employer securities for the plan, or are used to refinance such a loan, or*

(B) *any loan to a corporation to the extent that, within 30 days, employer securities are transferred to the plan in an amount equal to the proceeds of such loan and such securities are allocable to accounts of plan participants within 1 year of the date of such loan, except that this subparagraph shall not apply to any loan the commitment period of which exceeds 7 years.*

For purposes of this paragraph, the term "employer securities" has the meaning given such term by section 409(l).

(2) **Loans between related persons.**—The term "securities acquisition loan" shall not include—

(A) any loan made between corporations which are members of the same controlled group of corporations, or

(B) any loan made between an employee stock ownership plan and any person that is—

(i) the employer of any employees who are covered by the plan; or

(ii) a member of a controlled group of corporations which includes such employer.

For purposes of this paragraph, subparagraphs (A) and (B) shall not apply to any loan which, but for such subparagraphs, would be a securities acquisition loan if such loan was not originated by the employer of any employees who are covered by the plan or by any member of the controlled group of corporations which includes such employer, except that this section shall not apply to any interest received on such loan during such time as such loan is held by such employer (or any member of such controlled group)

(3) *Terms applicable to certain securities acquisition loans.—A loan to a corporation shall not fail to be treated as a securities acquisition loan merely because the proceeds of such loan are lent to an employee stock ownership plan sponsored by such corporation (or by any member of the controlled group of corporations which includes such corporation) if such loan includes—*

(A) *repayment terms which are substantially similar to the terms of the loan of such corporation from a lender described in subsection (a), or*

(B) *repayment terms providing for more rapid repayment of principal or interest on such loan but only if—*

(i) *allocations under the plan attributable to such repayment do not discriminate in favor of highly compensated employees (within the meaning of section 414(q)), and*

(ii) *the total commitment period of such loan to the corporation does not exceed 7 years*

[3](4) **Controlled group of corporations.**—For purposes of this paragraph, the term "controlled group of corporations" has the meaning given such term by section 409A(l)(4).

* * * * * * * * * * * *

(d) *Application With Section 483 and Original Issue Discount Rules.—In applying section 483 and subpart A of part V of subchapter P to any obligation to which this section applies, appropriate adjustments shall be made to the applicable Federal rate to take into account the exclusion under subsection (a).*

[For official explanation, see Committee Reports, ¶4018; 4174.]

【¶2915】 CODE SEC. 134. CERTAIN MILITARY BENEFITS.

(a) General Rule.—Gross income shall not include any qualified military benefit.

(b) Qualified Military Benefit.—For purposes of this section—

(1) In general.—The term "qualified military benefit" means any allowance or in-kind benefit which—

(A) is received by any member or former member of the uniformed services of the United States or any dependent of such member by reason of such member's status or service as a member of such uniformed services, and

(B) was excludable from gross income on September 9, 1986, under any provision of law or regulation thereunder which was in effect on such date (other than a provision of this title).

(2) No other benefit to be excludable except as provided by this title.—Notwithstandng any other provision of law, no benefit shall be treated as a qualified military benefit unless such benefit—

(A) is a benefit described in paragraph (1), or

(B) is excludable from gross income under this title without regard to any provision of law which is not contained in this title and which is not contained in a revenue Act.

(3) Limitations on modifications.—

(A) In general.—Except as provided in subparagraph (B), no modification or adjustment of any qualified military benefit after September 9, 1986, under any provision of law or regulation described in paragraph (1) shall be taken into account.

(B) Exception for certain adjustments to cash benefits.—Subparagraph (A) shall not apply to any adjustment to any qualified military benefit payable in cash which—

(i) is pursuant to a provision of law or regulation (as in effect on September 9, 1986), and

(ii) is determined by reference to any fluctuation in cost, price, currency, or other similar index.

[For official explanation, see Committee Reports, ¶4015.]

【¶2915-A】 CODE SEC. ¹135. CROSS REFERENCES TO OTHER ACTS.

* * * * * * * * * * *

[For official explanation, see Committee Reports, ¶4015.]

【¶2916】 CODE SEC. 141. PRIVATE ACTIVITY BOND; QUALIFIED BOND.

(a) Private Activity Bond.—For purposes of this title, the term "private activity bond" means any bond issued as part of an issue—

(1) which meets—

(A) the private business use test of paragraph (1) of subsection (b), and

(B) the private security or payment test of paragraph (2) of subsection (b), or

(2) which meets the private loan financing test of subsection (c).

(b) Private Business Tests.—

(1) Private business use test.—Except as otherwise provided in this subsection, an issue meets the test of this paragraph if more than 10 percent of the proceeds of the issue are to be used for any private business use.

(2) Private security or payment test.—Except as otherwise provided in this subsection, an issue meets the test of this paragraph if the payment of the principal of, or the interest on, more than 10 percent of the proceeds of such issue is (under the terms of such issue or any underlying arrangement) directly or indirectly—

【Footnote ¶2915】 Sec. 134 added by section 1168(a), '86 TRA.
Effective date (Sec. 1168(c), '86 TRA.)—Applies to taxable years beginning after 12-31-86.
【Footnote ¶2915-A】 Sec. 135 renumbered by section 1168(a), '86 TRA, which struck out:
(1) "134"
Effective date (Sec. 1168(c), '86 TRA).—Applies to taxable years beginning after 12-31-86.
【Footnote ¶2916】 Sec. 141 added by section 1301(b), '86 TRA.
Effective date (Sec. 1311(a), '86 TRA).—(a) Generally applies to bonds issued after 8-15-86. For special and transitional rules, see ¶2071—2077.

(A) secured by any interest in—
  (i) property used or to be used for a private business use, or
  (ii) payments in respect of such property, or
(B) to be derived from payments (whether or not to the issuer) in respect of property or borrowed money, used or to be used for a private business use.

(3) 5 percent test for private business use not related or disproportionate to government use financed by the issue.—
(A) In general.—An issue shall be treated as meeting the tests of paragraphs (1) and (2) if such tests would be met if such paragraphs were applied—
  (i) by substituting "5 percent" for "10 percent" each place it appears, and
  (ii) by taking into account only—
    (I) the proceeds of the issue which are to be used for any private business use which is not related to any government use of such proceeds,
    (II) the disproportionate related business use proceeds of the issue, and
    (III) payments, property, and borrowed money with respect to any use of proceeds described in subclause (I) or (II).
(B) Disproportionate related business use proceeds.—For purposes of subparagraph (A), the disproportionate related business use proceeds of an issue is an amount equal to the aggregate of the excesses (determined under the following sentence) for each private business use of the proceeds of an issue which is related to a government use of such proceeds. The excess determined under this sentence is the excess of—
  (i) the proceeds of the issue which are to be used for the private business use over
  (ii) the proceeds of the issue which are to be used for the government use to which such private business use relates.

(4) Lower limitation for certain output facilities.—An issue 5 percent or more of the proceeds of which are to be used with respect to any output facility (other than a facility for the furnishing of water) shall be treated as meeting the tests of paragraphs (1) and (2) if the nonqualified amount with respect to such issue exceeds the excess of—
(A) $15,000,000, over
(B) the aggregate nonqualified amounts with respect to all prior tax-exempt issues 5 percent or more of the proceeds of which are or will be used with respect to such facility (or any other facility which is part of the same project).
There shall not be taken into account under subparagraph (B) any bond which is not outstanding at the time of the later issue or which is to be redeemed (other than in an advance refunding) from the net proceeds of the later issue.

(5) Coordination with volume cap where nonqualified amount exceeds $15,000,000.—If the nonqualified amount with respect to an issue—
(A) exceeds $15,000,000, but
(B) does not exceed the amount which would cause a bond which is part of such issue to be treated as a private activity bond without regard to the paragraph,
such bond shall nonetheless be treated as a private activity bond unless the issuer allocates a portion of its volume cap under section 146 to such issue in an amount equal to the excess of such nonqualified amount over $15,000,000.

(6) Private business use defined.—
(A) In general.—For purposes of this subsection, the term "private business use" means use (directly or indirectly) in a trade or business carried on by any person other than a governmental unit. For purposes of the preceding sentence, use as a member of the general public shall not be taken into account.
(B) Clarification of trade or business.—For purposes of the 1st sentence of subparagraph (A), any activity carried on by a person other than a natural person shall be treated as a trade or business.

(7) Government use.—The term "government use" means any use other than a private business use.

(8) Nonqualified amount.—For purposes of this subsection, the term "nonqualified amount" means, with respect to an issue, the lesser of—
(A) the proceeds of such issue which are to be used for any private business use, or

(B) the proceeds of such issue with respect to which there are payments (or property or borrowed money) described in paragraph (2).

(9) **Exception for qualified 501(c)(3) bonds.**—There shall not be taken into account under this subsection or subsection (c) the portion of the proceeds of an issue which (if issued as a separate issue) would be treated as a qualified 501(c)(3) bond if the issuer elects to treat such portion as a qualified 501(c)(3) bond.

(c) **Private Loan Financing Test.—**

(1) **In general.**—An issue meets the test of this subsection if the amount of the proceeds of the issue which are to be used (directly or indirectly) to make or finance loans (other than loans described in paragraph (2)) to persons other than governmental units exceeds the lesser of—

    (A) 5 percent of such proceeds, or

    (B) $5,000,000.

(2) **Exception for tax assessment, etc., loans.**—For purposes of paragraph (1), a loan is described in this paragraph if such loan—

    (A) enables the borrower to finance any governmental tax or assessment of general application for a specific essential governmental function, or

    (B) is a nonpurpose investment (within the meaning of section 148(f)(6)(A)).

(d) **Qualified Bond.**—For purposes of this part, the term "qualified bond" means any private activity bond if—

(1) **In general.**—Such bond is—

    (A) an exempt facility bond,

    (B) a qualified mortgage bond,

    (C) a qualified veterans' mortgage bond,

    (D) a qualified small issue bond,

    (E) a qualified student loan bond,

    (F) a qualified redevelopment bond, or

    (G) a qualified 501(c)(3) bond.

(2) **Volume cap.**—Such bond is issued as part of an issue which meets the applicable requirements of section 146, and

(3) **Other requirements.**—Such bond meets the applicable requirements of each subsection of section 147.

[For official explanation, see Committee Reports, ¶4058.]

[¶2917] CODE SEC. 142. EXEMPT FACILITY BOND.

(a) **General Rule.**—For purposes of this part, the term "exempt facility bond" means any bond issued as part of an issue 95 percent or more of the net proceeds of which are to be used to provide—

    (1) airports,

    (2) docks and wharves,

    (3) mass commuting facilities,

    (4) facilities for the furnishing of water,

    (5) sewage facilities,

    (6) solid waste disposal facilities,

    (7) qualified residential rental projects,

    (8) facilities for the local furnishing of electric energy or gas,

    (9) local district heating or cooling facilities, or

    (10) qualified hazardous waste facilities.

(b) **Special Exempt Facility Bond Rules.**—For purposes of subsection (a)—

(1) **Certain facilities must be governmentally owned.—**

    (A) **In general.**—A facility shall be treated as described in paragraph (1), (2), or (3) of subsection (a) only if all of the property to be financed by the net proceeds of the issue is to be owned by a governmental unit.

    (B) **Safe harbor for leases and management contracts.**—For purposes of subparagraph (A), property leased by a governmental unit shall be treated as owned by such governmental unit if—

        (i) the lessee makes an irrevocable election (binding on the lessee and all successors in interest under the lease) not to claim depreciation or an investment credit with respect to such property,

---

[Footnote ¶2917] Sec. 142 added by section 1301(b), '86 TRA.
Effective date (Sec. 1311(a), '86 TRA).—Generally applies to bonds issued after 8-15-86. For transitional and special rules, see ¶2071—2077.

 (ii) the lease term (as defined in 168(i)(3)) is not more than 80 percent of the reasonably expected economic life of the property (as determined under section 147(b)), and

 (iii) the lessee has no option to purchase the property other than at fair market value (as of the time such option is exercised).

Rules similar to the rules of the preceding sentence shall apply to management contracts and similar types of operating agreements.

 (2) Limitation on office space.—An office shall not be treated as described in a paragraph of subsection (a) unless—

 (A) the office is located on the premises of a facility described in such a paragraph, and

 (B) not more than a de minimis amount of the functions to be performed at such office is not directly related to the day-to-day operations at such facility.

(c) Airports, Docks and Wharves, and Mass Commuting Facilities.—For purposes of subsection (a)—

 (1) Storage and training facilities.—Storage or training facilities directly related to a facility described in paragraph (1), (2), or (3) of subsection (a) shall be treated as described in the paragraph in which such facility is described.

 (2) Exception for certain private facilities.—Property shall not be treated as described in paragraph (1), (2), or (3) of subsection (a) if such property is described in any of the following subparagraphs and is to be used for any private business use (as defined in section 141(b)(6)).

 (A) Any lodging facility.

 (B) Any retail facility (including food and beverage facilities) in excess of a size necessary to serve passengers and employees at the exempt facility.

 (C) Any retail facility (other than parking) for passengers or the general public located outside the exempt facility terminal.

 (D) Any offfice building for individuals who are not employees of a governmental unit or of the operating authority for the exempt facility.

 (E) Any industrial park or manufacturing facility.

(d) Qualified Residential Rental Project.—For purposes of this section—

 (1) In general.—The term "qualified residential rental project" means any project for residential rental property if, at all times during the qualified project period, such project meets the requirements of subparagraph (A) or (B), whichever is elected by the issuer at the time of the issuance of the issue with respect to such project:

 (A) 20-50 test.—The project meets the requirements of this subparagraph if 20 percent or more of the residential units in such project are occupied by individuals whose income is 50 percent or less of area median gross income.

 (B) 40-60 test.—The project meets the requirements of this subparagraph if 40 percent or more of the residential units in such project are occupied by individuals whose income is 60 percent or less of area median gross income.

For purposes of this paragraph, any property shall not be treated as failing to be residential rental property merely because part of the building in which such property is located is used for purposes other than residential rental purposes.

 (2) Definitions and special rules.—For purposes of this subsection—

 (A) Qualified project period.—The term "qualified project period" means the period beginning on the 1st day on which 10 percent of the residential units in the project are occupied and ending on the latest of—

 (i) the date which is 15 years after the date on which 50 percent of the residential units in the project are occupied,

 (ii) the 1st day on which no tax-exempt private activity bond issued with respect to the project is outstanding, or

 (iii) the date on which any assistance provided with respect to the project under section 8 of the United States Housing Act of 1937 terminates.

 (B) Income of individuals; area median gross income.—The income of individuals and area median gross income shall be determined by the Secretary in a manner consistent with determinations of lower income families and area median gross income under section 8 of the United States Housing Act of 1937 (or, if such program is terminated, under such program as in effect immediately before such termination). Determinations under the preceding sentence shall include adjustments for family size.

(3) **Current income determinations.**—For purposes of this subsection—

(A) In general.—The determination of whether the income of a resident of a unit in a project exceeds the applicable income limit shall be made at least annually on the basis of the current income of the resident.

(B) Continuing resident's income may increase above the applicable limit.—If the income of a resident of a unit in a project did not exceed the applicable income limit upon commencement of such resident's occupancy of such unit (or as of any prior determination under subparagraph (A)), the income of such resident shall be treated as continuing to not exceed the applicable income limit. The preceding sentence shall cease to apply to any resident whose income as of the most recent determination under subparagraph (A) exceeds 140 percent of the applicable income limit if after such determination, but before the next determination, any residential unit of comparable or smaller size in the same project is occupied by a new resident whose income exceeds the applicable income limit.

(4) **Special rule in case of deep rent skewing.**—

(A) In general.—In the case of any project described in subparagraph (B), the 2d sentence of subparagraph (B) of paragraph (3) shall be applied by substituting—

(i) "170 percent" for "140 percent", and

(ii) "any low-income unit in the same project is occupied by a new resident whose income exceeds 40 percent of area median gross income" for "any residential unit of comparable or smaller size in the same project is occupied by a new resident whose income exceeds the applicable income limit".

(B) Deep rent skewed project.—A project is described in this subparagraph if the owner of the project elects to have this paragraph apply and, at all times during the qualified project period, such project meets the requirements of clauses (i), (ii), and (iii):

(i) The project meets the requirements of this clause if 15 percent or more of the low-income units in the project are occupied by individuals whose income is 40 percent or less of area median gross income.

(ii) The project meets the requirements of this clause if the gross rent with respect to each low-income unit in the project does not exceed 30 percent of the applicable income limit which applies to individuals occupying the unit.

(iii) The project meets the requirements of this clause if the gross rent with respect to each low-income unit in the project does not exceed 1/3 of the average rent with respect to units of comparable size which are not occupied by individuals who meet the applicable income limit.

(C) Definitions applicable to subparagraph (B).—For purposes of subparagraph (B)—

(i) Low-income unit.—The term "low-income unit" means any unit which is required to be occupied by individuals who meet the applicable income limit.

(ii) Gross rent.—The term "gross rent" includes—

(I) any payment under section 8 of the United States Housing Act of 1937, and

(II) any utility allowance determined by the Secretary after taking into account such determinations under such section 8.

(5) **Applicable income limit.**—For purposes of paragraphs (3) and (4), the term "applicable income limit" means—

(A) the limitation under subparagraph (A) or (B) of paragraph (1) which applies to the project, or

(B) in the case of a unit to which paragraph (4)(B)(i) applies, the limitation which applies to such unit.

(6) **Special rule for certain high cost housing area.**—In the case of a project located in a city having 5 boroughs and a population in excess of 5,000,000, subparagraph (B) of paragraph (1) shall be applied by substituting "25 percent" for "40 percent".

(7) **Certification to secretary.**—The operator of any project with respect to which an election was made under this subsection shall submit to the Secretary (at such time and in such manner as the Secretary shall prescribe) an annual certification as to whether such project continues to meet the requirements of this subsection. Any failure to comply with the provisions of the preceding sentence shall not affect the tax-

exempt status of any bond but shall subject the operator to penalty, as provided in section 6652(j).

(e) Facilities for the Furnishing of Water.—For purposes of subsection (a)(4), the term "facilities for the furnishing of water" means any facility for the furnishing of water if—

(1) the water is or will be made available to members of the general public (including electric utility, industrial, agricultural, or commercial users), and

(2) either the facility is operated by a governmental unit or the rates for the furnishing or sale of the water have been established or approved by a State or political subdivision thereof, by an agency or instrumentality of the United States, or by a public service or public utility commission or other similar body of any State or political subdivision thereof.

(f) Local Furnishing of Electric Energy or Gas.—For purposes of subsection (a)(8), the local furnishing of electric energy or gas from a facility shall only include furnishing solely within the area consisting of—

(1) a city and 1 contiguous county, or

(2) 2 contiguous counties.

(g) Local District Heating or Cooling Facility.—

(1) In general.—For purposes of subsection (a)(9), the term "local district heating or cooling facility" means property used as an integral part of a local district heating or cooling system.

(2) Local district heating or cooling system.—

(A) In general.—For purposes of paragraph (1), the term "local district heating or cooling system" means any local system consisting of a pipeline or network (which may be connected to a heating or cooling source) providing hot water, chilled water, or steam to 2 or more users for—

(i) residential, commercial, or industrial heating or cooling, or

(ii) process steam.

(B) Local system.—For purposes of this paragraph, a local system includes facilities furnishing heating and cooling to an area consisting of a city and 1 contiguous county.

(h) Qualified Hazardous Waste Facilities.—For purposes of subsection (a)(10), the term "qualified hazardous waste facility" means any facility for the disposal of hazardous waste by incineration or entombment but only if—

(1) the facility is subject to final permit requirements under subtitle C of title II of the Solid Waste Disposal Act (as in effect on the date of the enactment of the Tax Reform Act of 1986), and

(2) the portion of such facility which is to be provided by the issue does not exceed the portion of the facility which is to be used by persons other than—

(A) the owner or operator of such facility, and

(B) any related person (within the meaning of section 144(a)(3)) to such owner or operator.

[For official explanation, see Committee Reports, ¶4058.]

[¶2918] Reserved.

≫P-H CAUTION→ Sec. 143 added by '86 TRA, follows. For Sec. 143, redesignated as Sec. 7703, see ¶3430.

[¶2918-A] CODE SEC. 143. MORTGAGE REVENUE BONDS: QUALIFIED MORTGAGE BOND AND QUALIFIED VETERANS' MORTGAGE BOND.

(a) Qualified Mortgage Bond.—

(1) Qualified mortgage bond defined.—

(A) In general.—For purposes of this title, the term "qualified mortgage bond" means a bond which is issued as part of a qualified mortgage issue.

(B) Termination on December 31, 1988.—No bond issued after December 31, 1988, may be treated as a qualified mortgage bond.

(2) Qualified mortgage issue defined.—

[Footnote ¶2918-A] Sec. 143 added by section 1301(b), '86 TRA.
Effective date (Sec. 1311(a), '86 TRA).—Generally applies to bonds issued after 8-15-86. For transitional and special rules, see ¶2071—2077.

(A) Definition.—For purposes of this title, the term "qualified mortgage issue" means an issue by a State or political subdivision thereof of 1 or more bonds, but only if—

(i) all proceeds of such issue (exclusive of issuance costs and a reasonably required reserve) are to be used to finance owner-occupied residences,

(ii) such issue meets the requirements of subsections (c), (d), (e), (f), (g), (h), and (i), and

(iii) no bond which is part of such issue meets the private business tests of paragraphs (1) and (2) of section 141(b).

(B) Good faith effort to comply with mortgage eligibility requirements.—An issue which fails to meet 1 or more of the requirements of subsections (c), (d), (e), (f), and (i) shall be treated as meeting such requirements if—

(i) the issuer in good faith attempted to meet all such requirements before the mortgages were executed,

(ii) 95 percent or more of the proceeds devoted to owner-financing was devoted to residences with respect to which (at the time the mortgages were executed) all such requirements were met, and

(iii) any failure to meet the requirements of such subsections is corrected within a reasonable period after such failure is first discovered.

(C) Good faith effort to comply with other requirements.—An issue which fails to meet 1 or more of the requirements of subsections (g) and (h) shall be treated as meeting such requirements if—

(i) the issuer in good faith attempted to meet all such requirements, and

(ii) any failure to meet such requirements is due to inadvertent error after taking reasonable steps to comply with such requirements.

(b) Qualified Veterans' Mortgage Bond Defined.—For purposes of this part, the term "qualified veterans' mortgage bond" means any bond—

(1) which is issued as part of an issue 95 percent or more of the net proceeds of which are to be used to provide residences for veterans,

(2) the payment of the principal and interest on which is secured by the general obligation of a State,

(3) which is part of an issue which meets the requirements of subsections (c), (g), (i)(1), and (l), and

(4) which does not meet the private business tests of paragraphs (1) and (2) of section 141(b).

Rules similar to the rules of subparagraphs (B) and (C) of subsection (a)(2) shall apply to the requirements specified in paragraph (3) of this subsection.

(c) Residence Requirements.—

(1) **For a residence.**—A residence meets the requirements of this subsection only if—

(A) it is a single-family residence which can reasonably be expected to become the principal residence of the mortgagor within a reasonable time after the financing is provided, and

(B) it is located within the jurisdiction of the authority issuing the bond.

(2) **For an issue.**—An issue meets the requirements of this subsection only if all of the residences for which owner-financing is provided under the issue meet the requirements of paragraph (1).

(d) 3-Year Requirement.—

(1) **In general.**—An issue meets the requirements of this subsection only if 95 percent or more of the net proceeds of such issue are used to finance the residences of mortgagors who had no present ownership interest in their principal residences at any time during the 3-year period ending on the date their mortgage is executed.

(2) **Exceptions.**—For purposes of paragraph (1), the proceeds of an issue which are used to provide—

(A) financing with respect to targeted area residences, and

(B) qualified home improvement loans and qualified rehabilitation loans,

shall be treated as used as described in paragraph (1).

(3) **Mortgagor's interest in residence being financed.**—For purposes of paragraph (1), a mortgagor's interest in the residence with respect to which the financing is being provided shall not be taken into account.

(e) Purchase Price Requirement.—

(1) **In general.**—An issue meets the requirements of this subsection only if the acquisition cost of each residence the owner-financing of which is provided under the issue does not exceed 90 percent of the average area purchase price applicable to such residence.

(2) **Average area purchase price.**—For purposes of paragraph (1), the term "average area purchase price" means, with respect to any residence, the average purchase price of single family residences (in the statistical area in which the residence is located) which were purchased during the most recent 12-month period for which sufficient statistical information is available. The determination under the preceding sentence shall be made as of the date on which the commitment to provide the financing is made (or, if earlier, the date of the purchase of the residence).

(3) **Separate application to new residences and old residences.**—For purposes of this subsection, the determination of average area purchase price shall be made separately with respect to—

(A) residences which have not been previously occupied, and

(B) residences which have been previously occupied.

(4) **Special rule for 2 to 4 family residences.**—For purposes of this subsection, to the extent provided in regulations, the determination of average area purchase price shall be made separately with respect to 1 family, 2 family, 3 family, and 4 family residences.

(5) **Special rule for targeted area residences.**—In the case of a targeted area residence, paragraph (1) shall be applied by substituting "110 percent" for "90 percent."

(6) **Exception for qualified home improvement loans.**—Paragraph (1) shall not apply with respect to any qualified home improvement loan.

(f) **Income requirements.**—

(1) **In general.**—An issue meets the requirements of this subsection only if all owner-financing provided under the issue is provided for mortgagors whose family income is 115 percent or less of the applicable median family income.

(2) **Determination of family income.**—For purposes of this subsection, the family income of mortgagors, and area median gross income, shall be determined by the Secretary after taking into account the regulations prescribed under section 8 of the United States Housing Act of 1937 (or, if such program is terminated, under such program as in effect immediately before such termination).

(3) **Special rule for applying paragraph (1) in the case of targeted area residences.**—In the case of any financing provided under any issue for targeted area residences—

(A) ⅓ of the amount of such financing may be provided without regard to paragraph (1), and

(B) paragraph (1) shall be treated as satisfied with respect to the remainder of the owner financing if the family income of the mortgagor is 140 percent or less of the applicable median family income.

(4) **Applicable median family income.**—For purposes of this subsection, the term "applicable median family income" means, with respect to a residence, whichever of the following is the greater:

(A) the area median gross income for the area in which such residence is located, or

(B) the statewide median gross income for the State in which such residence is located.

(g) **Requirements Related to Arbitrage.**—

(1) **In general.**—An issue meets the requirements of this subsection only if such issue meets the requirements of paragraphs (2) and (3) of this subsection. Such requirements shall be in addition to the requirements of section 148 (other than subsection (f) thereof).

(2) **Effective rate of mortgage interest cannot exceed bond yield by more than 1,125 percentage points.**—

(A) In general.—An issue shall be treated as meeting the requirements of this paragraph only if the excess of—

(i) the effective rate of interest on the mortgages provided under the issue, over

(ii) the yield on the issue,

is not greater than 1,125 percentage points.

(B) Effective rate of mortgage interest.—

(i) In general.—In determining the effective rate of interest on any mortgage for purposes of this paragraph, there shall be taken into account all fees, charges and other amounts borne by the mortgagor which are attributable to the mortgage or to the bond issue.

(ii) Specification of some of the amounts to be treated as borne by the mortgagor.—For purposes of clause (i), the following items (among others) shall be treated as borne by the mortgagor:

(I) all points or similar charges paid by the seller of the property, and

(II) the excess of the amounts received from any person other than the mortgagor by any person in connection with the acquisition of the mortgagor's interest in the property over the usual and reasonable acquisition costs of a person acquiring like property where owner-financing is not provided through the use of qualified mortgage bonds or qualified veterans' mortgage bonds.

(iii) Specification of some of the amounts to be treated as not borne by the mortgagor.—For purposes of clause (i), the following items shall not be taken into account:

(I) any expected rebate of arbitrage profits, and

(II) any application fee, survey fee, credit report fee, insurance charge, or similar amount to the extent such amount does not exceed amounts charged in such area in cases where owner-financing is not provided through the use of qualified mortgage bonds or qualified veterans' mortgage bonds.

Subclause (II) shall not apply to origination fees, points, or similar amounts.

(iv) Prepayment assumptions.—In determining the effective rate of interest—

(I) it shall be assumed that the mortgage prepayment rate will be the rate set forth in the most recent applicable mortgage maturity experience table published by the Federal Housing Administration, and

(II) prepayments of principal shall be treated as received on the last day of the month in which the issuer reasonably expects to receive such prepayments.

(C) Yield on the issue.—For purposes of this subsection, the yield on an issue shall be determined on the basis of—

(i) the issue price (within the meaning of sections 1273 and 1274), and

(ii) an expected maturity for the bonds which is consistent with the assumptions required under subparagraph (B)(iv).

(3) Arbitrage and investment gains to be used to reduce costs of owner-financing.—

(A) In general.—An issue shall be treated as meeting the requirements of this paragraph only if an amount equal to the sum of—

(i) the excess of—

(I) the amount earned on all nonpurpose investments (other than investments attributable to an excess described in this clause), over

(II) the amount which would have been earned if such investments were invested at a rate equal to the yield on the issue, plus

(ii) any income attributable to the excess described in clause (i),

is paid or credited to the mortgagors as rapidly as may be practicable.

(B) Investment gains and losses.—For purposes of subparagraph (A), in determining the amount earned on all nonpurpose investments, any gain or loss on the disposition of such investments shall be taken into account.

(C) Reduction where issuer does not use full 1.125 percentage points under paragraph (2).—

(i) In general.—The amount required to be paid or credited to mortgagors under subparagraph (A) (determined under this paragraph without regard to this subparagraph) shall be reduced by the unused paragraph (2) amount.

(ii) Unused paragraph (2) amount.—For purposes of clause (i), the unused paragraph (2) amount is the amount which (if it were treated as an interest payment made by mortgagors) would result in the excess referred to in paragraph (2)(A) being equal to 1.125 percentage points. Such amount shall be fixed and determined as of the yield determination date.

(D) Election to pay United States.—Subparagraph (A) shall be satisfied with respect to any issue if the issuer elects before issuing the bonds to pay over to the United States—

(i) not less frequently than once each 5 years after the date of issue, an amount equal to 90 percent of the aggregate amount which would be required to be paid or credited to mortgagors under subparagraph (A) (and not theretofore paid to the United States), and

(ii) not later than 60 days after the redemption of the last bond, 100 percent of such aggregate amount not theretofore paid to the United States.

(E) Simplified accounting.—The Secretary shall permit any simplified system of accounting for purposes of this paragraph which the issuer establishes to the satisfaction of the Secretary will assure that the purposes of this paragraph are carried out.

(F) **Nonpurpose investment.**—For purposes of this paragraph, the term "nonpurpose investment" has the meaning given such term by section 148(f)(6)(A).

(h) **Portion of Loans Required To Be Placed in Targeted Areas.—**

(1) **In general.**—An issue meets the requirements of this subsection only if at least 20 percent of the proceeds of the issue which are devoted to providing owner-financing is made available (with reasonable diligence) for owner-financing of targeted area residences for at least 1 year after the date on which owner-financing is first made available with respect to targeted area residences.

(2) **Limitation.**—Nothing in paragraph (1) shall be treated as requiring the making available of an amount which exceeds 40 percent of the average annual aggregate principal amount of mortgages executed during the immediately preceding 3 calendar years for single-family, owner-occupied residences located in targeted areas within the jurisdiction of the issuing authority.

(i) **Other Requirements.—**

(1) **Mortgages must be new mortgages.—**

(A) In general.—An issue meets the requirements of this subsection only if no part of the proceeds of such issue is used to acquire or replace existing mortgages.

(B) Exceptions.—Under regulations prescribed by the Secretary, the replacement of—

(i) construction period loans,

(ii) bridge loans or similar temporary initial financing, and

(iii) in the case of a qualified rehabilitation, an existing mortgage,

shall not be treated as the acquisition or replacement of an existing mortgage for purposes of subparagraph (A).

(2) **Certain requirements must be met where mortgage is assumed.**—An issue meets the requirements of this subsection only if each mortgage with respect to which owner-financing has been provided under such issue may be assumed only if the requirements of subsections (c), (d), and (e), and the requirements of paragraph (1) or (3)(B) of subsection (f) (whichever applies), are met with respect to such assumption.

(j) **Targeted Area Residences.—**

(1) **In general.**—For purposes of this section, the term "targeted area residence" means a residence in an area which is either—

(A) a qualified census tract, or

(B) an area of chronic economic distress.

(2) **Qualified census tract.—**

(A) In general.—For purposes of paragraph (1), the term "qualified census tract" means a census tract in which 70 percent or more of the families have income which is 80 percent or less of the statewide median family income.

(B) Data used.—The determination under subparagraph (A) shall be made on the basis of the most recent decennial census for which data are available.

(3) **Area of chronic economic distress.—**

(A) In general.—For purposes of paragraph (1), the term "area of chronic economic distress" means an area of chronic economic distress—

(i) designated by the State as meeting the standards established by the State for purposes of this subsection, and

(ii) the designation of which has been approved by the Secretary and the Secretary of Housing and Urban Development.

(B) Criteria to be used in approving state designations.—The criteria used by the Secretary and the Secretary of Housing and Urban Development in evaluating any proposed designation of an area for purposes of this subsection shall be—

    (i) the condition of the housing stock, including the age of the housing and the number of abandoned and substandard residential units,

    (ii) the need of area residents for owner-financing under this section, as indicated by low per capita income, a high percentage of families in poverty, a high number of welfare recipients, and high unemployment rates,

    (iii) the potential for use of owner-financing under this section to improve housing conditions in the area, and

    (iv) the existence of a housing assistance plan which provides a displacement program and a public improvements and services program.

(k) **Other Definitions and Special Rules.—For purposes of this section—**

  (1) **Mortgage.—**The term "mortgage" means any owner-financing.

  (2) **Statistical area.—**

    (A) In general.—The term "statistical area" means—

      (i) a metropolitan statistical area, and

      (ii) any county (or the portion thereof) which is not within a metropolitan statistical area.

    (B) Metropolitan statistical area.—The term "metropolitan statistical area" includes the area defined as such by the Secretary of Commerce.

    (C) Designation where adequate statistical information not available.—For purposes of this paragraph, if there is insufficient recent statistical information with respect to a county (or portion thereof) described in subparagraph (A)(ii), the Secretary may substitute for such county (or portion thereof) another area for which there is sufficient recent statistical information.

    (D) Designation where no county.—In the case of any portion of a State which is not within a county, subparagraphs (A)(ii) and (C) shall be applied by substituting for "county" an area designated by the Secretary which is the equivalent of a county.

  (3) **Acquisition cost.—**

    (A) In general.—The term "acquisition cost" means the cost of acquiring the residence as a completed residential unit.

    (B) Exceptions.—The term "acquisition cost" does not include—

      (i) usual and reasonable settlement or financing costs,

      (ii) the value of services performed by the mortgagor or members of his family in completing the residence, and

      (iii) the cost of land which has been owned by the mortgagor for at least 2 years before the date on which construction of the residence begins.

    (C) Special rule for qualified rehabilitation loans.—In the case of a qualified rehabilitation loan, for purposes of subsection (e), the term "acquisition cost" includes the cost of the rehabilitation.

  (4) **Qualified home improvement loan.—**The term "qualified home improvement loan" means the financing (in an amount which does not exceed $15,000)—

    (A) of alterations, repairs, and improvements on or in connection with an existing residence by the owner thereof, but

    (B) only of such items as substantially protect or improve the basic livability or energy efficiency of the property.

  (5) **Qualified rehabilitation loan.—**

    (A) In general.—The term "qualified rehabilitation loan" means any owner-financing provided in connection with—

      (i) a qualified rehabilitation, or

      (ii) the acquisition of a residence with respect to which there has been a qualified rehabilitation,

but only if the mortgagor to whom such financing is provided is the first resident of the residence after the completion of the rehabilitation.

    (B) Qualified rehabilitation.—For purposes of subparagraph (A), the term "qualified rehabilitation" means any rehabilitation of a building if—

      (i) there is a period of at least 20 years between the date on which the building was first used and the date on which the physical work on such rehabilitation begins,

      (ii) in the rehabilitation process—

        (I) 50 percent or more of the existing external walls of such building are retained in place as external walls,

(II)   75 percent or more of the existing external walls of such building are retained in place as internal or external walls, and

(III)   75 percent or more of the existing internal structural framework of such a building is retained in place, and

(iii)   the expenditures for such rehabilitation are 25 percent or more of the mortgagor's adjusted basis in the residence.

For purposes of clause (iii), the mortgagor's adjusted basis shall be determined as of the completion of the rehabilitation or, if later, the date on which the mortgagor acquires the residence.

(6)   **Determinations on actuarial basis.**—All determinations of yield, effective interest rates, and amounts required to be paid or credited to mortgagors or paid to the United States under subsection (g) shall be made on an actuarial basis taking into account the present value of money.

(7)   **Single-family and owner-occupied residences include certain residences with 2 to 4 units.**—Except for purposes of subsection (h)(2), the terms "single-family" and "owner-occupied", when used with respect to residences, include 2, 3, or 4 family residences—

(A)   one unit of which is occupied by the owner of the units, and

(B)   which were first occupied at least 5 years before the mortgage is executed.

(8)   **Cooperative housing corporations.—**

(A)   In general.—In the case of any cooperative housing corporation—

(i)   each dwelling unit shall be treated as if it were actually owned by the person entitled to occupy such dwelling unit by reason of his ownership of stock in the corporation, and

(ii)   any indebtedness of the corporation allocable to the dwelling unit shall be treated as if it were indebtedness of the shareholder entitled to occupy the dwelling unit.

(B)   Adjustment to targeted area requirement.—In the case of any issue to provide financing to a cooperative housing corporation with respect to cooperative housing not located in a targeted area, to the extent provided in regulations, such issue may be combined with 1 or more other issues for purposes of determining whether the requirements of subsection (h) are met.

(C)   Cooperative housing corporation.—The term "cooperative housing corporatin" has the meaning given to such term by section 216(b)(1).

(9)   **Treatment of limited equity cooperative housing.—**

(A)   Treatment as residential rental property.—Except as provided in subparagraph (B), for purposes of this part—

(i)   any limited equity cooperative housing shall be treated as residential rental property and not as owner-occupied housing, and

(ii)   bonds issued to provide such housing shall be subject to the same requirements and limitations as bonds the proceeds of which are to be used to provide qualified residential rental projects (as defined in section 142(d)).

(B)   Bonds subject to qualified mortgage bond termination date.—Subparagraph (A) shall not apply to any bond ·issued after the date specified in subsection (a)(1)(B).

(C)   Limited equity cooperative housing.—For purposes of this paragraph, the term "limited equity cooperative housing" means any dwelling unit which a person is entitled to occupy by reason of his ownership of stock in a qualified cooperative housing corporation.

(D)   Qualified cooperative housing corporation.—For purposes of this paragraph, the term "qualified cooperative housing corporation" means any cooperative housing corporation (as defined in section 216(b)(1)) if—

(i)   the consideration paid for stock held by any stockholder entitled to occupy any house or apartment in a building owned or leased by the corporation may not exceed the sum of—

(I)   the consideration paid for such stock by the first such stockholder, as adjusted by a cost-of-living adjustment determined by the Secretary,

(II)   payments made by any stockholder for improvements to such house or apartment, and

(III)   payments (other than amounts taken into account under subclause (I) or (II) attributable to any stockholder to amortize the principal of the

Code §143(k)(9) ¶2918-A

corporation's indebtedness arising from the acquisition or development of real property, including improvements thereof,

(ii) the value of the corporation's assets (reduced by any corporate liabilities), to the extent such value exceeds the combined transfer values of the outstanding corporate stock, shall be used only for public benefit or charitable purposes, or directly to benefit the corporation itself, and shall not be used directly to benefit any stockholder, and

(iii) at the time of issuance of the issue, such corporation makes an election under this paragraph.

(E) Effect of election.—If a cooperative housing corporation makes an election under this paragraph, section 216 shall not apply with respect to such corporation (or any successor thereof) during the qualified project period (as defined in section 142(d)(2)).

(F) Corporation must continue to be qualified cooperative.—Subparagraph (A)(i) shall not apply to limited equity cooperative housing unless the cooperative housing corporation continues to be a qualified cooperative housing corporation at all times during the qualified project period (as defined in section 142(d)(2)).

(G) Election irrevocable.—Any election under this paragraph, once made, shall be irrevocable.

(l) Additional Requirements for Qualified Veterans' Mortgage Bonds.—An issue meets the requirements of this subsection only if it meets the requirements of paragraphs (1), (2), and (3).

(1) Veterans to whom financing may be provided.—An issue meets the requirements of this paragraph only if each mortgagor to whom financing is provided under the issue is a qualified veteran.

(2) Requirement that state program be in effect before June 22, 1984.—An issue meets the requirements of this paragraph only if it is a general obligation of a State which issued qualified veterans' mortgage bonds before June 22, 1984.

(3) Volume limitation.—

(A) In general.—An issue meets the requirements of this paragraph only if the aggregate amount of bonds issued pursuant thereto (when added to the aggregate amount of qualified veterans' mortgage bonds previously issued by the State during the calendar year) does not exceed the State veterans limit for such calendar year.

(B) State veterans limit.—A State veterans limit for any calendar year is the amount equal to—

(i) the aggregate amount of qualified veterans bonds issued by such State during the period beginning on January 1, 1979, and ending on June 22, 1984 (not including the amount of any qualified veterans bond issued by such State during the calendar year (or portion thereof) in such period for which the amount of such bonds so issued was the lowest), divided by

(ii) the number (not to exceed 5) of calendar years after 1979 and before 1985 during which the State issued qualified veterans bonds (determined by only taking into account bonds issued on or before June 22, 1984).

(C) Treatment of refunding issues.—

(i) In general.—For purposes of subparagraph (A), the term "qualified veterans' mortgage bond" shall not include any bond issued to refund another bond but only if the maturity date of the refunding bond is not later than the later of—

(I) the maturity date of the bond to be refunded, or

(II) the date 32 years after the date on which the refunded bond was issued (or in the case of a series of refundings, the date on which the original bond was issued).

The preceding sentence shall apply only to the extent that the amount of the refunding bond does not exceed the outstanding amount of the refunded bond.

(ii) Exception for advance refunding.—Clause (i) shall not apply to any bond issued to advance refund another bond.

(4) Qualified veteran.—For purposes of this subsection, the term "qualified veteran" means any veteran—

(A) who served on active duty at some time before January 1, 1977, and

(B) who applied for the financing before the later of—

(i) the date 30 years after the last date on which such veteran left active service, or

(ii) January 31, 1985.

(5) **Special rule for certain short-term bonds.**—In the case of any bond—

(A) which has a term of 1 year or less,

(B) which is authorized to be issued under O.R.S. 407.435 (as in effect on the date of the enactment of this subsection), to provide financing for property taxes, and

(C) which is redeemed at the end of such term, the amount taken into account under this subsection with respect to such bond shall be 1/15 of its principal amount.

[For official explanation, see Committee Reports, ¶4058.]

[¶2919] CODE SEC. 144. QUALIFIED SMALL ISSUE BOND; QUALIFIED STUDENT LOAN BONDS; QUALIFIED REDEVELOPMENT BOND.

(a) **Qualified Small Issue Bond.**—

(1) **In general.**—For purposes of this part, the term "qualified small issue bond" means any bond issued as part of an issue the aggregate authorized face amount of which is $1,000,000 or less and 95 percent or more of the net proceeds of which are to be used—

(A) for the acquisition, construction, reconstruction, or improvement of land or property of a character subject to the allowance for depreciation, or

(B) to redeem part or all of a prior issue which was issued for purposes described in subparagraph (A) or this subparagraph.

(2) **Certain prior issues taken into account.**—If—

(A) the proceeds of 2 or more issues of bonds (whether or not the issuer of each such issue is the same) are or will be used primarily with respect to facilities located in the same incorporated municipality or located in the same county (but not in any incorporated municipality),

(B) the principal user of such facilities is or will be the same person or 2 or more related persons, and

(C) but for this paragraph, paragraph (1) (or the corresponding provision of prior law) would apply to each such issue,

then, for purposes of paragraph (1), in determining the aggregate face amount of any later issue there shall be taken into account the aggregate face amount of tax-exempt bonds issued under all prior such issues and outstanding at the time of such later issue (not including as outstanding any bond which is to be redeemed (other than in an advance refunding) from the net proceeds of the later issue).

(3) **Related persons.**—For purposes of this subsection, a person is a related person to another person if—

(A) the relationship between such persons would result in a disallowance of losses under section 267 or 707(b), or

(B) such persons are members of the same controlled group of corporations (as defined in section 1563(a), except that "more than 50 percent" shall be substituted for "at least 80 percent" each place it appears therein).

(4) **$10,000,000 limit in certain cases—**

(A) **In general.**—At the election of the issuer with respect to any issue, this subsection shall be applied—

(i) by substituting "$10,000,000" for "$1,000,000" in paragraph (1), and

(ii) in determining the aggregate face amount of such issue, by taking into account not only the amount described in paragraph (2), but also the aggregate amount of capital expenditures with respect to facilities described in subparagraph (B) paid or incurred during the 6-year period beginning 3 years before the date of such issue and ending 3 years after such date (and financed otherwise than out of the proceeds of outstanding tax-exempt issues to which paragraph (1) (or the corresponding provision of prior law) applied), as if the aggregate amount of such capital expenditures constituted the face amount of a prior outstanding issue described in paragraph (2).

(B) **Facilities taken into account.**—For purposes of subparagraph (A)(ii), the facilities described in this subparagraph are facilities—

(i) located in the same incorporated municipality or located in the same county (but not in any incorporated municipality), and

[Footnote ¶2919] Sec. 144 added by section 1301(b), '86 TRA.
Effective date (Sec. 1311(a), '86 TRA).—Generally applies to bonds issued after 8-15-86. For transitional and special rules, see ¶2071—2077.

(ii) the principal user of which is or will be the same person or 2 or more related persons.

For purposes of clause (i), the determination of whether or not facilities are located in the same governmental unit shall be made as of the date of issue of the issue in question.

(C) Certain capital expenditures not taken into account.—For purposes of subparagraph (A)(ii), any capital expenditure—

(i) to replace property destroyed or damaged by fire, storm, or other casualty, to the extent of the fair market value of the property replaced,

(ii) required by a change made after the date of issue of the issue in question in a Federal or State law or local ordinance of general application or required by a change made after such date in rules and regulations of general application issued under such a law or ordinance,

(iii) required by circumstances which could not be reasonably foreseen on such date of issue or arising out of a mistake of law or fact (but the aggregate amount of expenditures not taken into account under this clause with respect to any issue shall not exceed $1,000,000), or

(iv) described in clause (i) or (ii) of section 41(b)(2)(A) for which a deduction was allowed under section 174(a),

shall not be taken into account.

(D) Limitation on loss of tax exemption.—In applying subparagraph (A)(ii) with respect to capital expenditures made after the date of any issue, no bond issued as a part of such issue shall cease to be treated as a qualified small issue bond by reason of any such expenditure for any period before the date on which such expenditure is paid or incurred.

(E) Certain refinancing issues.—In the case of any issue described in paragraph (1)(B), an election may be made under subparagraph (A) of this paragraph only if all of the prior issues being redeemed are issues to which paragraph (1) (or the corresponding provision of prior law) applied. In applying subparagraph (A)(ii) with respect to such a refinancing issue, capital expenditures shall be taken into account only for purposes of determining whether the prior issues being redeemed qualified (and would have continued to qualify) under paragrpah (1) (or the corresponding provision of prior law).

(F) Aggregate amount of capital expenditures where there is urban development action grant.—In the case of any issue 95 percent or more of the net proceeds of which are to be used to provide facilities with respect to which an urban development action grant has been made under section 119 of the Housing and Community Development Act of 1974, capital expenditures of not to exceed $10,000,000 shall not be taken into account for purposes of applying subparagraph (A)(ii).

(5) **Issues for residential purposes.**—This subsection shall not apply to any bond issued as part of an issue 5 percent or more of the net proceeds of which are to be used directly or indirectly to provide residential real property for family units.

(6) **Limitations on treatment of bonds as part of the same issue.**—

(A) In general.—For purposes of this subsection, separate lots of bonds which (but for this subparagraph) would be treated as part of the same issue shall be treated as separate issues unless the proceeds of such lots are to be used with respect to 2 or more facilities—

(i) which are located in more than 1 State, or

(ii) which have, or will have, as the same principal user the same person or related persons.

(B) Franchises.—For purposes of subparagraph (A), a person (other than a governmental unit) shall be considered a principal user of a facility if such person (or a group of related persons which includes such person)—

(i) guarantees, arranges, participates in, or assists with the issuance (or pays any portion of the cost of issuance) of any bond the proceeds of which are to be used to finance or refinance such facility, and

(ii) provides any property, or any franchise, trademark, or trade name (within the meaning of section 1253), which is to be used in connection with such facility.

(7) **Subsection not to apply if bonds issued with certain other tax-exempt bonds.**—
This subsection shall not apply to any bond issued as part of an issue (other than an

issue to which paragraph (4) applies) if the interest on any other bond which is part of such issue is excluded from gross income under any provision of law other than this subsection.

(8) Restrictions on financing certain facilities.—This subsection shall not apply to an issue if—

(A) more than 25 percent of the net proceeds of the issue are to be used to provide a facility the primary purpose of which is one of the following: retail food and beverage services, automobile sales or service, or the provision of recreation or entertainment; or

(B) any portion of the proceeds of the issue is to be used to provide the following: any private or commercial golf course, country club, massage parlor, tennis club, skating facility (including roller skating, skateboard, and ice skating), racquet sports facility (including any handball or racquetball court), hot tub facility, suntan facility, or racetrack.

(9) Aggregation of issues with respect to single project.—For purposes of this subsection, 2 or more issues part or all of the net proceeds of which are to be used with respect to a single building, an enclosed shopping mall, or a strip of offices, stores, or warehouses using substantial common facilities shall be treated as 1 issue (and any person who is a principal user with respect to any of such issues shall be treated as a principal user with respect to the aggregated issue).

(10) Aggregate limit per taxpayer.—

(A) **In general.**—This subsection shall not apply to any issue if the aggregate authorized face amount of such issue allocated to any test-period beneficiary (when increased by the outstanding tax-exempt facility-related bonds of such beneficiary) exceeds $40,000,000.

(B) **Outstanding tax-exempt facility-related bonds.**—

(i) **In general.**—For purposes of applying subparagraph (A) with respect to any issue, the outstanding tax-exempt facility-related bonds of any person who is a test-period beneficiary with respect to such issue is the aggregate amount of tax-exempt bonds referred to in clause (ii)—

(I) which are allocated to such beneficiary, and

(II) which are outstanding at the time of such later issue (not including as outstanding any bond which is to be redeemed (other than in an advance refunding) from the net proceeds of the later issue).

(ii) **Bonds taken into account.**—For purposes of clause (i), the bonds referred to in this clause are—

(I) exempt facility bonds, qualified small issue bonds, and qualified redevelopment bonds, and

(II) industrial development bonds (as defined in section 103(b)(2), as in effect on the day before the date of the enactment of the Tax Reform Act of 1986) to which section 141(a) does not apply.

(C) **Allocation of face amount of issue.**—

(i) **In general.**—Except as otherwise provided in regulations, the portion of the face amount of an issue allocated to any test-period beneficiary of a facility financed by the proceeds of such issue (other than an owner of such facility) is an amount which bears the same relationship to the entire face amount of such issue as the portion of such facility used by such beneficiary bears to the entire facility.

(ii) **Owners.**—Except as otherwise provided in regulations, the portion of the face amount of an issue allocated to any test-period beneficiary who is an owner of a facility financed by the proceeds of such issue is an amount which bears the same relationship to the entire face amount of such issue as the portion of such facility owned by such beneficiary bears to the entire facility.

(D) **Test-period beneficiary.**—For purposes of this paragraph, except as provided in regulations, the term "test-period beneficiary" means any person who is an owner or a principal user of facilities being financed by the issue at any time during the 3-year period beginning on the later of—

(i) the date such facilities were placed in service, or

(ii) the date of issue.

(E) Treatment of related persons.—For purposes of this paragraph, all persons who are related (within the meaning of paragraph (3)) to each other shall be treated as 1 person.

(11) Limitation on acquisition of depreciable farm property.—

(A) In general.—This subsection shall not apply to any issue if more than $250,000 of the net proceeds of such issue are to be used to provide depreciable farm property with respect to which the principal user is or will be the same person or 2 or more related persons.

(B) Depreciable farm property.—For purposes of this paragraph, the term "depreciable farm property" means property of a character subject to the allowance for depreciation which is to be used in a trade or business of farming.

(C) Prior issues taken into account.—In determining the amount of proceeds of an issue to be used as described in subparagraph (A), there shall be taken into account the aggregate amount of each prior issue to which paragraph (1) (or the corresponding provisions of prior law) applied which were or will be so used.

(12) Termination dates.—

(A) In general.—This subsection shall not apply to—

(i) any bond (other than a bond described in clause (ii)) issued after December 31, 1986, or

(ii) any bond issued to refund a bond issued on or before such date unless—

(I) the refunding bond has a maturity date not later than the maturity date of the refunded bond,

(II) the amount of the refunding bond does not exceed the outstanding amount of the refunded bond,

(III) the interest rate on the refunding bond is lower than the interest rate on the refunded bond, and

(IV) the net proceeds of the refunding bond are used to redeem the refunded bond not later than 90 days after the date of the issuance of the refunding bond.

(B) Bonds issued to finance manufacturing facilities and farm property.—In the case of any bond issued as part of an issue 95 percent or more of the net proceeds of which are to be used to provide—

(i) any manufacturing facility, or

(ii) any land or property in accordance with section 147(c)(2),

subparagraph (A) shall be applied by substituting "1989" for "1986".

(C) Manufacturing facility.—For purposes of this paragraph, the term "manufacturing facility "means any facility which is used in the manufacturing or production of tangible personal property (including the processing resulting in a change in the condition of such property). A rule similar to the rule of section 142(b)(2) shall apply for purposes of the preceding sentence.

(b) Qualified Student Loan Bond.—For purposes of this part—

(1) In general.—The term "qualified student loan bond" means any bond issued as part of an issue the applicable percentage or more of the net proceeds of which are to be used directly or indirectly to make or finance student loans under—

(A) a program of general application to which the Higher Education Act of 1965 applies if—

(i) limitations are imposed under the program on—

(I) the maximum amount of loans outstanding to any student, and

(II) the maximum rate of interest payable on any loan,

(ii) the loans are directly or indirectly guaranteed by the Federal Government,

(iii) the financing of loans under the program is not limited by Federal law to the proceeds of tax-exempt bonds, and

(iv) special allowance payments under section 438 of the Higher Education Act of 1965—

(I) are authorized to be paid with respect to loans made under the program, or

(II) would be authorized to be made with respect to loans under the program if such loans were not financed with the proceeds of tax-exempt bonds, or

(B) a program of general application approved by the State to which part B of title IV of the Higher Education Act of 1965 (relating to guaranteed student loans) does not apply if no loan under such program exceeds the difference between the **total cost** of attendance and other forms of student assistance (not including loans pursuant to section 428B(a)(1) of such Act (relating to parent loans) or subpart I of part C of title VII of the Public Health Service Act (relating to student assistance)) for which the student borrower may be eligible. A bond issued as part of an issue shall be treated as a qualified student loan bond only if no bond which is part of such issue meets the private business tests of paragraphs (1) and (2) of section 141(b).

(2) **Applicable percentage.**—For purposes of paragraph (1), the term "applicable percentage" means—

(A) 90 percent in the case of the program described in paragraph (1)(A), and

(B) 95 percent in the case of the program described in paragraph (1)(B).

(3) **Student borrowers must be residents of issuing states, etc.**—A student loan shall be treated as being made or financed under a program described in paragraph (1) with respect to an issue only if the student is—

(A) a resident of the State from which the volume cap under section 146 for such loan was derived, or

(B) enrolled at an educational institution located in such State.

(4) **Discrimination on basis of school location not permitted.**—A program shall not be treated as described in paragraph (1)(A) if such program discriminates on the basis of the location (in the United States) of the educational institution in which the student is enrolled.

(c) **Qualified Redevelopment Bond.**—For purposes of this part—

(1) **In general.**—The term "qualified redevelopment bond" means any bond issued as part of an issue 95 percent or more of the net proceeds of which are to be used for 1 or more redevelopment purposes in any designated blighted area.

(2) **Additional requirements.**—A bond shall not be treated as a qualified redevelopment bond unless—

(A) the issue described in paragraph (1) is issued pursuant to—

(i) a State law which authorizes the issuance of such bonds for redevelopment puposes in blighted areas, and

(ii) a redevelopment plan which is adopted before such issuance by the governing body described in paragraph (4)(A) with respect to the designated blighted area,

(B)(i) the payment of the principal and interest on such issue is primarily secured by taxes of general applicability imposed by a general purpose governmental unit, or

(ii) any increase in real property tax revenues (attributable to increases in assessed value) by reason of the carrying out of such purposes in such area is reserved exclusively for debt service on such issue (and similar issues) to the extent such increase does not exceed such a debt service,

(C) each interest in real property located in such area—

(i) which is acquired by a governmental unit with the proceeds of the issue, and

(ii) which is transferred to a person other than a governmental unit,

is transferred for fair market value,

(D) the financed area with respect to such issue meets the no additional charge requirements of paragraph (5), and

(E) the use of the proceeds of the issue meets the requirements of paragraph (1)—

(3) **Redevelopment purposes.**—For purposes of paragraph (1)—

(A) In general.—The term "redevelopment purposes" means, with respect to any designated blighted area—

(i) the acquisition (by a governmental unit having the power to exercise eminent domain) of real property located in such area,

(ii) the clearing and preparation for redevelopment of land in such area which was acquired by such governmental unit,

(iii) the rehabilitation of real property located in such area which was acquired by such governmental unit, and

(iv) the relocation of occupants of such real property.

Code §144(c)(3) ¶2919

(B) New construction not permitted.—The term "redevelopment purposes" does not include the construction (other than the rehabilitation) of any property or the enlargement of an existing building.

(4) **Designated blighted area.**—For purposes of this subsection—

(A) In general.—The term "designated blighted area" means any blighted area designated by the governing body of a local general purpose governmental unit in the jurisdiction of which such area is located.

(B) Blighted area.—The term "blighted area" means any area which the governing body described in subparagraph (A) determines to be a blighted area on the basis of the substantial presence of factors such as excessive vacant land on which structures were previously located, abandoned or vacant buildings, substandard structures, vacancies, and delinquencies in payment of real property taxes.

(C) Designated areas may not exceed 20 percent of total assessed value of real property in government's jurisdiction.—

(i) In general.—An area may be designated by a governmental unit as a blighted area only if the designation percentage with respect to such area, when added to the designation percentages of all other designated blighted areas within the jurisdiction of such governmental unit, does not exceed 20 percent.

(ii) Designation percentage.—For purposes of this subparagraph, the term "designation percentage" means, with respect to any area, the percentage (determined at the time such area is designated) which the assessed value of real property located in such area is of the total assessed value of all real property located within the jurisdiction of the governmental unit which designated such area.

(iii) Exception where bonds not outstanding.—The designation percentage of a previously designated blighted area shall not be taken into account under clause (i) if no qualified redevelopment bond (or similar bond) is or will be outstanding with respect to such area.

(D) Minimum designated area.—

(i) In general.—Except as provided in clause (ii), an area shall not be treated as a designated blighted area for purposes of this subsection unless such area is contiguous and compact and its area equals or exceeds 100 acres.

(ii) 10-acre minimum in certain cases.—Clause (i) shall be applied by substituting "10 acres" for "100 acres" if not more than 25 percent of the financed area is to be provided (pursuant to the issue and all other such issues) to 1 person. For purposes of the preceding sentence, all related persons (as defined in subsection (a)(3)) shall be treated as 1 person. For purposes of this clause, an area provided to a developer on a short-term interim basis shall not be treated as provided to such developer.

(5) **No additional charge requirements.**—The financed area with respect to any issue meets the requirements of this paragraph if, while any bond which is part of such issue is outstanding—

(A) no owner or user of property located in the financed area is subject to a charge or fee which similarly situated owners or users of comparable property located outside such area are not subject, and

(B) the assessment method or rate of real property taxes with respect to property located in the financed area does not differ from the assessment method or rate of real property taxes with respect to comparable property located outside such area.

For purposes of the preceding sentence, the term "comparable property" means property which is of the same type as the property to which it is being compared and which is located within the jurisdiction of the designating governmental unit.

(6) **Use of proceeds requirements.**—The use of the proceeds of an issue meets the requirements of this paragraph if—

(A) not more than 25 percent of the net proceeds of such issue are to be used to provide (including the provision of land for) facilities described in subsection (a)(8) or section 147(e), and

(B) no portion of the proceeds of such issue is to be used to provide (including the provision of land for) any private or commercial golf course, country club, massage parlor, hot tub facility, suntan facility, racetrack or other facility used for gambling, or any store the principal business of which is the sale of alcoholic beverages for consumption off premises.

(7) **Financed area.**—For purposes of this subsection, the term "financed area" means, with respect to any issue, the portion of the designated blighted area with respect to which the proceeds of such issue are to be used.

(8) **Restriction on acquisition of land not to apply.**—Section 147(c) (other than paragraphs (1)(B) and (2) thereof) shall not apply to any qualified redevelopment bond.

[For official explanation, see Committee Reports, ¶4058.]

〔¶2920〕 **CODE SEC. 145. QUALIFIED 501(c)(3) BOND.**

(a) **In General.**—For purposes of this part, except as otherwise provided in this section, the term "qualified 501(c)(3) bond" means any private activity bond issued as part of an issue if—

(1) all property which is to be provided by the net proceeds of the issue is to be owned by a 501(c)(3) organization or a governmental unit, and

(2) such bond would not be a private activity bond if—

(A) 501(c)(3) organizations were treated as governmental units with respect to their activities which do not constitute unrelated trades or businesses, determined by applying section 513(a), and

(B) paragraphs (1) and (2) of section 141(b) were applied by substituting "5 percent" for "10 percent" each place it appears and by substituting "net proceeds" for "proceeds" each place it appears.

(b) **$150,000,000 Limitation on Bonds Other Than Hospital Bonds.**—

(1) **In general.**—A bond (other than a qualified hospital bond) shall not be treated as a qualified 501(c)(3) bond if the aggregate authorized face amount of the issue (of which such bond is a part) allocated to any 501(c)(3) organization which is a test-period beneficiary (when increased by the outstanding tax-exempt nonhospital bonds of such organization) exceeds $150,000,000.

(2) **Outstanding tax-exempt nonhospital bonds.**—

(A) In general.—For purposes of applying paragraph (1) with respect to any issue, the outstanding tax-exempt nonhospital bonds of any organization which is a test-period beneficiary with respect to such issue is the aggregate amount of tax-exempt bonds referred to in subparagraph (B)—

(i) which are allocated to such organization, and

(ii) which are outstanding at the time of such later issue (not including as outstanding any bond which is to be redeemed (other than in an advance refunding) from the net proceeds of the later issue).

(B) Bonds taken into account.—For purposes of subparagraph (A), the bonds referred to in this subparagraph are—

(i) any qualified 501(c)(3) bond other than a qualified hospital bond, and

(ii) any bond to which section 141(a) does not apply if—

(I) such bond would have been an industrial development bond (as defined in section 103(b), as in effect on the day before the date of the enactment of the Tax Reform Act of 1986) if 501(c)(3) organizations were not exempt persons, and

(II) such bond was not described in paragraph (4), (5), or (6) of such section 103(b) (as in effect on the date such bond was issued).

(C) Only nonhospital portion of bonds taken into account.—

(i) In general.—A bond shall be taken into account under subparagraph (B)(ii) only to the extent that the proceeds of the issue of which such bond is a part are not used with respect to a hospital.

(ii) Special rule.—If 90 percent or more of the net proceeds of an issue are used with respect to a hospital, no bond which is part of such issue shall be taken into account under subparagraph (B)(ii).

(3) **Aggregation rule.**—For purposes of this subsection, 2 or more organizations under common management or control shall be treated as 1 organization.

(4) **Allocation of face amount of issue; test-period beneficiary.**—Rules similar to the rules of subparagraphs (C) and (D) of section 144(a)(10) shall apply for purposes of this subsection.

〔Footnote ¶2920〕 Sec. 145 added by section 1301(b), '86 TRA.

Effective date (Sec. 1311(a), '86 TRA).—Generally applies to bonds issued after 8-15-86. For transitional and special rules, see ¶2071—2077.

(c) **Qualified Hospital Bond.**—For purposes of this section, the term "qualified hospital bond" means any bond issued as part of an issue 95 percent or more of the net proceeds of which are to be used with respect to a hospital.

(d) **Election Out.**—This section shall not apply to an issue if—

(1) the issue elects not to have this section apply to such issue, and

(2) such issue is an issue of exempt facility bonds, or qualified redevelopment bonds, to which section 146 applies.

[For official explanation, see Committee Reports, ¶4058.]

[¶2921] CODE SEC. 146. VOLUME CAP.

(a) **General Rule.**—A private activity bond issued as part of an issue meets the requirements of this section if the aggregate face amount of the private activity bonds issued pursuant to such issue, when added to the aggregate face amount of tax-exempt private activity bonds previously issued by the issuing authority during the calendar year, does not exceed such authority's volume cap for such calendar year.

(b) **Volume Cap for State Agencies.**—For purposes of this section—

(1) **In general.**—The volume cap for any agency of the State authorized to issue tax-exempt private activity bonds for any calendar year shall be 50 percent of the State ceiling for such calendar year.

(2) **Special rule where state has more than 1 agency.**—If more than 1 agency of the State is authorized is issue tax-exempt private activity bonds, all such agencies shall be treated as a single agency.

(c) **Volume Cap for Other Issuers.**—For purposes of this section—

(1) **In general.**—The volume cap for any issuing authority (other than a State agency) for any calendar year shall be an amount which bears the same ratio to 50 percent of the State ceiling for such calendar year as—

(A) the population of the jurisdiction of such issuing authority, bears to

(B) the population of the entire State.

(2) **Overlapping jurisdictions.**—For purposes of paragraph (1)(A), if an area is within the jurisdiction of 2 or more governmental units, such area shall be treated as only within the jurisdiction of the unit having jurisdiction over the smallest geographical area unless such unit agrees to surrender all or part of such jurisdiction for such calendar year to the unit with overlapping jurisdiction which has the next smallest geographical area.

(d) **State Ceiling.**—For purposes of this section—

(1) **In general.**—The State ceiling applicable to any State for any calendar year shall be the greater of—

(A) an amount equal to $75 multiplied by the State population, or

(B) $250,000,000.

Subparagraph (B) shall not apply to any possession of the United States.

(2) **Adjustment after 1987.**—In the case of calendar years after 1987, paragraph (1) shall be applied by substituting—

(A) "$50" for "$75", and

(B) "$150,000,000" for "$250,000,000".

(3) **Special rule for states with constitutional home rules cities.**—For purposes of this section—

(A) **In general.**—The volume cap for any constitutional home rule city for any calendar year shall be determined under paragraph (1) of subsection (c) by substituting "100 percent" for "50 percent".

(B) **Coordination with other allocations.**—In the case of any State which contains 1 or more constitutional home rule cities, for purposes of applying subsections (b) and (c) with respect to issuing authorities in such State other than constitutional home rule cities, the State ceiling for any calendar year shall be reduced by the aggregate volume caps determined for such year for all constitutional home rule cities in such State.

(C) **Constitutional home rule city.**—For purposes of this section, the term "constitutional home rule city" means, with respect to any calendar year, any political subdivision of a State which, under a State constitution which was adopted in

---

[Footnote ¶2921] Sec. 146 added by section 1301(b), '86 TRA.
Effective date (Sec. 1311(a), '86 TRA).—Generally applies to bonds issued after 8-15-86. For transitional and special rules, see ¶2071—2077.

1970 and effective on July 1, 1971, had home rule powers on the 1st day of the calendar year.

(4) Special rule for possessions with populations of less than the population of the least populous state.—

(A) In general.—If the population of any possession of the United States for any calendar year is less than the population of the least populous State (other than a possession) for such calendar year, the limitation under paragraph (1)(A) shall not be less than the amount determined under subparagraph (B) for such calendar year.

(B) Limitation.—The limitation determined under this subparagraph, with respect a possession, for any calendar year is an amount equal to the product of—

(i) the fraction—

(I) the numerator of which is the amount applicable under paragraph (1)(B) for such calendar year, and

(II) the denominator of which is the State population of the least populous State (other than a possession) for such calendar year, and

(ii) the population of such possession for such calendar year,

(e) State May Provide for Different Allocation.—For purposes of this section—

(1) In general.—Except as provided in paragraph (3), a State may, by law provide a different formula for allocating the State ceiling among the governmental units (or other authorities) in such State having authority to issue tax-exempt private activity bonds.

(2) Interim authority for governor.—

(A) In general.—Except as otherwise provided in paragraph (3), the Governor of any State may proclaim a different formula for allocating the State ceiling amount the governmental units (or other authorities) in such State having authority to issue private activity bonds.

(B) Termination of authority.—The authority provided in subparagraph (A) shall not apply to bonds issued after the earlier of—

(i) the last day of the 1st calendar year after 1986 during which the legislature of the State met in regular session, or

(ii) the effective date of any State legislation with respect to the allocation of the State ceiling.

(3) State may not alter allocation to constitutional home rule cities.—Except as otherwise provided in a State constitutional amendment (or law changing the home rule provision adopted in the manner provided by the State constitution), the authority provided in this subsection shall not apply to that portion of the State ceiling which is allocated to any constitutional home rule city in the States unless such city agrees to such different allocation.

(f) Elective Carryforward of Unused Limitation for Specified Purpose.—

(1) In general.—If—

(A) an issuing authority's volume cap for any calendar year after 1985, exceeds

(B) the aggregate amount of tax-exempt private activity bonds issued during such calendar year by such authority, such authority may elect to treat all (or any portion) of such excess as a carryforward for 1 or more carryforward purposes.

(2) Election must identify purpose.—In any election under paragraph (1), the issuing authority shall—

(A) identify the purpose for which the carryforward is elected, and

(B) specify the portion of the excess described in paragraph (1) which is to be a carryforward for each such purpose.

(3) Use of carryforward.—

(A) In general.—If any issuing authority elects a carryforward under paragraph (1) with respect to any carryforward purpose, any private activity bonds issued by such authority with respect to such purpose during the 3 calendar years following the calendar year in which the carryforward arose shall not be taken into account under subsection (a) to the extent the amount of such bonds does not exceed the amount of the carryforward elected for such purpose.

(B) Order in which carryforward used.—Carryforwards elected with respect to any purpose shall be used in the order of the calendar years in which they arose.

(4) **Election.**—Any election under this paragraph (and any identification or specification contained therein), once made, shall be irrevocable.

(5) **Carryforward purpose.**—The term "carryforward purpose" means—

(A) the purpose of issuing bonds referred to in one of the clauses of section 141(d)(1)(A).

(B) the purpose of issuing qualified mortgage bonds or mortgage credit certificates,

(C) the purpose of issuing qualified student loan bonds, and

(D) the purpose of issuing qualified redevelopment bonds.

(g) **Exception for Certain Bonds.**—Only for purposes of this section, the term "private activity bond" shall not include—

(1) any qualified veterans' mortgage bond,

(2) any qualified 501(c)(3) bond, and

(3) any exempt facility bond issued as part of an issue described in paragraph (1) or (2) of section 142(a) (relating to airports and docks and wharves).

(h) **Exception for Government-Owned Solid Waste Disposal Facilities.**—

(1) **In general.**—Only for purposes of this section, the term "private activity bond" shall not include any exempt facility bond described in section 142(a)(6) which is issued as part of an issue if all of the property to be financed by the net proceeds of such issue is to be owned by a governmental unit.

(2) **Safe harbor for determination of government ownership.**—In determining ownership for purposes of paragraph (1), section 142(b)(1)(B) shall apply, except that a lease term shall be treated as satisfying clause (ii) thereof if it is not more than 20 years.

(i) **Treatment of Refunding Issues.**—For purposes of the volume cap imposed by this section—

(1) **In general.**—The term "private activity bond" shall not include any bond which is issued to refund another bond to the extent that the amount of such bond does not exceed the outstanding amount of the refunded bond.

(2) **Special rules for student loan bonds.**—In the case of any qualified student loan bond, paragraph (1) shall apply only if the maturity date of the refunding bond is not later than the later of—

(A) the maturity date of the bond to be refunded, or

(B) the date 17 years after the date on which the refunded bond was issued (or in the case of a series of refundings, the date on which the original bond was issued).

(3) **Special rules for qualified mortgage bonds.**—In the case of any qualified mortgage bond, paragraph (1) shall apply only if the maturity date of the refunding bond is not later than the later of—

(A) the maturity date of the bond to be refunded, or

(B) the date 32 years after the date on which the refunded bond was issued (or in the case of a series of refundings, the date on which the original bond was issued).

(4) **Exception for advance refunding.**—This subsection shall not apply to any bond issued to advance refund another bond.

(j) **Population.**—For purposes of this section, determinations of the population of any State (or issuing authority) shall be made with respect to any calendar year on the basis of the most recent census estimate of the resident population of such State (or issuing authority) released by the Bureau of Census before the beginning of such calendar year.

(k) **Facility Must Be Located Within State.**—

(1) **In General.**—Except as provided in paragraph (2), no portion of the State ceiling applicable to any State for any calendar year may be used with respect to financing for a facility located outside such State.

(2) **Exception for certain facilities where state will get proportionate share of benefits.**—Paragraph (1) shall not apply to any exempt facility bond described in paragraph (4), (5), (6), or (10) of section 142(a) if the issuer establishes that the State's share of the use of the facility (or its output) will equal or exceed the State's share of the private activity bonds issued to finance the facility.

(l) Issuer of Qualified Scholarship Funding Bonds.—In the case of a qualified scholarship funding bond, such bond shall be treated for purposes of this section as issued by a State or local issuing authority (whichever is appropriate).

(m) Treatment of Amounts Allocated to Private Activity Portion of Government Use Bonds.—

(1) In General.—The volume cap of an issuer shall be reduced by the amount allocated by the issuer to an issue under section 141(b)(5).

(2) Advance refundings.—Except as otherwise provided by the Secretary, any advance refunding of any part of an issue to which an amount was allocated under section 141(b)(5) (or would have been allocated if such section applied to such issue) shall be taken into account under this section to the extent of the amount of the volume cap which was (or would have been) so allocated.

(n) Reduction for Mortgage Credit Certificates, Etc.—The volume cap of any issuing authority for any calendar year shall be reduced by the sum of—

(1) the amount of qualified mortgage bonds which such authority elects not to issue under section 25(c)(2)(A)(ii) during such year, plus

(2) the amount of any reduction in such ceiling under section 25(f) applicable to such authority for such year.

[For official explanation, see Committee Reports, ¶4058.]

[¶2922] CODE SEC. 147. OTHER REQUIREMENTS APPLICABLE TO CERTAIN PRIVATE ACTIVITY BONDS.

(a) Substantial User Requirement.—

(1) In general.—Except as provided in subsection (h), a private activity bond shall not be a qualified bond for any period during which it is held by a person who is a substantial user of the facilities or by a related person of such a substantial user.

(2) Related person.—For purposes of paragraph (1), the following shall be treated as related persons—

(A) 2 or more persons if the relationship between such persons would result in a disallowance of losses under section 267 or 707(b),

(B) 2 or more persons which are members of the same controlled group of corporations (as defined in section 1563(a), except that "more than 50 percent" shall be substituted for "at least 80 percent" each place it appears therein),

(C) a partnership and each of its partners (and their spouses and minor children), and

(D) an S corporation and each of its shareholders (and their spouses and minor children).

(b) Maturity May Not Exceed 120 Percent of Economic Life.—

(1) General rule.—Except as provided in subsection (h), a private activity bond shall not be a qualified bond if it is issued as part of an issue and—

(A) the average maturity of the bonds issued as part of such issue, exceeds

(B) 120 percent of the average reasonably expected economic life of the facilities being financed with the net proceeds of such issue.

(2) Determination of averages.—For purposes of paragraph (1)—

(A) the average maturity of any issue shall be determined by taking into account the respective issue prices of the bonds issued as part of such issue, and

(B) the average reasonably expected economic life of the facilities being financed with any issue shall be determined by taking into account the respective cost of such facilities.

(3) Special rules.—

(A) Determination of economic life.—For purposes of this subsection, the reasonably expected economic life of any facility shall be determined as of the later of—

(i) the date on which the bonds are issued, or

(ii) the date on which the facility is placed in service (or expected to be placed in service).

(B) Treatment of land.—

[Footnote ¶2922] Sec. 147 added by section 1301(b), '86 TRA.
Effective date (Sec. 1311(a), '86 TRA).—Generally applies to bonds issued after 8-15-86. For transitional and special rules, see ¶2071—2077.

(i) Land not taken into account.—Except as provided in clause (ii), land shall not be taken into account under paragraph (1)(B).

(ii) Issues where 25 percent or more of proceeds used to finance land.—If 25 percent or more of the net proceeds of any issue is to be used to finance land, such land shall be taken into account under paragraph (1)(B) and shall be treated as having an economic life of 30 years.

(4) Special rule for pooled financing of 501(c)(3) organization.—

(A) In general.—At the election of the issuer, a qualified 501(c)(3) bond shall be treated as meeting the requirements of paragraph (1) if such bond meets the requirements of subparagraph (B).

(B) Requirements.—A qualified 501(c)(3) bond meets the requirements of this subparagraph if—

(i) 95 percent or more of the net proceeds of the issue of which such bond is a part are to be used to make or finance loans to 2 or more 501(c)(3) organizations or governmental units for acquisition of property to be used by such organizations,

(ii) each loan described in clause (i) satisfies the requirements of paragraph (1) (determined by treating each loan as a separate issue),

(iii) before such bond is issued, a demand survey was conducted which shows a demand for financing greater than an amount equal to 120 percent of the lendable proceeds of such issue, and

(iv) 95 percent or more of the net proceeds of such issue are to be loaned to 501(c)(3) organizations or governmental units within 1 year of issuance and, to the extent there are any unspent proceeds after such 1-year period, bonds issued as part of such issue are to be redeemed as soon as possible thereafter (and in no event later than 18 months after issuance).

A bond shall not meet the requirements of this subparagraph if the maturity date of any bond issued as part of such issue is more than 30 years after the date on which the bond was issued (or, in the case of a refunding or series of refundings, the date on which the original bond was issued).

(5) Special rule for certain FHA insured loans.—Paragraph (1) shall not apply to any bond issued as part of an issue 95 percent or more of the net proceeds of which are to be used to finance mortgage loans insured under FHA 242 or under a similar Federal Housing Administration program (as in effect on the date of the enactment of the Tax Reform Act of 1986) where the loan term approved by such Administration plus the maximum maturity of debentures which could be issued by such Administration in satisfaction of its obligations exceeds the term permitted under paragraph (1).

(c) Limitation on Use for Land Acquisition.—

(1) In general.—Except as provided in subsection (h), a private activity bond shall not be a qualified bond if—

(A) it is issued as part of an issue and 25 percent or more of the net proceeds of such issue are to be used (directly or indirectly) for the acquisition of land (or an interest therein), or

(B) any portion of the proceeds of such issue is to be used (directly or indirectly) for the acquisition of land (or an interest therein) to be used for farming purposes.

(2) Exception for first-time farmers.—

(A) In general.—If the requirements of subparagraph (B) are met with respect to any land, paragraph (1) shall not apply to such land, and subsection (d) shall not apply to property to be used thereon farming purposes, but only to the extent of expenditures (financed with the proceeds of the issue) not in excess of $250,000.

(B) Acquisition by first-time farmers.—The requirements of this subparagraph are met with respect to any land if—

(i) such land is to be used for farming purposes, and

(ii) such land is to be acquired by an individual who is a first-time farmer, who will be the principal user of such land, and who will materially and substantially participate on the farm of which such land is a part in the operation of such farm.

(C) First-time farmer.—For purposes of this paragraph—

(i) In general.—The term "first-time farmer" means any individual if such individual—

(I) has not at any time had any direct or indirect ownership interest in substantial farmland in the operation of which such individual materially participated, and

(II) has not received financing under this paragraph in an amount which, when added to the financing to be provided under this paragraph, exceeds $250,000.

(ii) Aggregation rules.—Any ownership or material participation, or financing received, by an individual's spouse or minor child shall be treated as ownership and material participation, or financing received, by the individual.

(iii) Insolvent farmer.—For purposes of clause (i), farmland which was previously owned by the individual and was disposed of while such individual was insolvent shall be disregarded if section 108 applied to indebtedness with respect to such farmland.

(D) Farm.—For purposes of this paragraph, the term "farm" has the meaning given such term by section 6420(c)(2).

(E) Substantial farmland.—For purposes of this paragraph, the term "substantial farmland" means any parcel of land unless—

(i) such parcel is smaller than 15 percent of the median size of a farm in the county in which such parcel is located, and

(ii) the fair market value of the land does not at any time while held by the individual exceed $125,000.

(F) Used equipment limitation.—For purposes of this paragraph, in no event may the amount of financing provided by reason of this paragraph to a first-time farmer for personal property—

(i) of a character subject to the allowance for depreciation,

(ii) the original use of which does not begin with such farmer, and

(iii) which is to be used for farming purposes,

exceed $62,500. A rule similar to the rule of subparagraph (C)(ii) shall apply for purposes of the preceding sentence.

(3) **Exception for certain land acquired for environmental purposes, etc.**—Any land acquired by a governmental unit (or issuing authority) in connection with an airport, mass commuting facility, dock or wharf shall not be taken into account under paragraph (1) if—

(A) such land is acquired for noise abatement or wetland preservation, or for future use as an airport, mass commuting facility, dock, or wharf, and

(B) there is no other significant use of such land.

(d) **Acquisition of Existing Property Not Permitted.—**

(1) **In general.**—Except as provided in subsection (h), a private activity bond shall not be a qualified bond if issued as part of an issue and any portion of the net proceeds of such issue is to be used for the acquisition of any property (or an interest therein) unless the 1st use of such property is pursuant to such acquisition.

(2) **Exception for certain rehabilitations.**—Paragraph (1) shall not apply with respect to any building (and the equipment therefor) if—

(A) the rehabilitation expenditures with respect to such building, equal or exceed

(B) 15 percent of the portion of the cost of acquiring such building (and equipment) financed with the net proceeds of the issue.

A rule similar to the rule of the preceding sentence shall apply in the case of structures other than a building except that subparagraph (B) shall be applied by substituting "100 percent" for "15 percent".

(3) **Rehabilitation expenditures.**—For purposes of this subsection—

(A) In general.—Except as provided in this paragraph, the term "rehabilitation expenditures" means any amount properly chargeable to capital account which is incurred by the person acquiring the building for property (or additions or improvements to property) in connection with the rehabilitation of a building. In the case of an integrated operation contained in a building before its acquisition, such term includes rehabilitating existing equipment in such bbuilding or replacing it with equipment having substantially the same function. For purposes of this subparagraph, any amount incurred by a successor to the person acquiring the build-

Code §147(d)(3) ¶2922

ing or by the seller under a sales contract with such person shall be treated as incurred by such person.

(B) Certain expenditures not included.—The term "rehabilitation expenditures" does not include any expenditure described in section 48(g)(2)(B).

(C) Period during which expenditures must be incurred.—The term "rehabilitation expenditures" shall not include any amount which is incurred after the date 2 years after the later of—

(i) the date on which the building was acquired, or

(ii) the date on which the bond was issued.

(4) Special rule for certain projects.—In the case of a project involving 2 or more buildings, this subsection shall be applied on a project basis.

(e) No Portion of Bonds May Be Issued for Skyboxes, Airplanes, Gambling Establishments, Etc.—A private activity bond shall not be treated as a qualified bond if issued as part of an issue and any portion of the proceeds of such issue is to be used to provide any airplane, skybox or other private luxury box, health club facility, facility primarily used for gambling, or store the principal business of which is the sale of alcoholic beverages for consumption off premises.

(f) Public Approval Required for Private Activity Bonds.—

(1) In general.—A private activity bond shall not be a qualified bond unless such bond satisfies the requirements of paragraph (2).

(2) Public approval requirement.—

(A) In general.—A bond shall satisfy the requirements of this paragraph if such bond is issued as a part of an issue which has been approved by—

(i) the governmental unit—

(I) which issued such bond, or

(II) on behalf of which such bond was issued, and

(ii) each governmental unit having jurisdiction over the area in which any facility, with respect to which financing is to be provided from the net proceeds of such issue, is located (except that if more than 1 governmental unit within a State has jurisdiction over the entire area within such State in which such facility is located, only 1 such unit need approve such issue).

(B) Approval by a governmental unit.—For purposes of subparagraph (A), an issue shall be treated as having been approved by any governmental unit if such issue is approved—

(i) by the applicable elected representative of such governmental unit after a public hearing following reasonable public notice, or

(ii) by voter referendum of such governmental unit.

(C) Special rules for approval of facility.—If there has been public approval under subparagraph (A) of the plan for financing a facility, such approval shall constitute approval under subparagraph (A) for any issue—

(i) which is issued pursuant to such plan within 3 years after the date of the 1st issue pursuant to the approval, and

(ii) all or substantially all of the proceeds of which are to be used to finance such facility or to refund previous financing under such plan.

(D) Refunding bonds.—No approval under subparagraph (A) shall be necessary with respect to any bond which is issued to refund (other than to advance refund) a bond approved under subparagraph (A) (or treated as approved under subparagraph (C)) unless the maturity date of such bond is later than the maturity date of the bond to be refunded.

(E) Applicable elected representative.—For purposes of this paragraph—

(i) In general.—The term "applicable elected representative" means with respect to any governmental unit—

(I) an elected legislative body of such unit, or

(II) the chief elected executive officer, the chief elected State legal officer of the executive branch, or any other elected official of such unit designated for purposes of this paragraph by such chief elected executive officer or by State law.

(ii) No applicable elected representative.—If (but for this clause) a governmental unit has no applicable elected representative, the applicable elected representative for purposes of clause (i) shall be the applicable elected representative of the governmental unit—

      (I) which is the next higher governmental unit with such a representative, and

      (II) from which the authority of the governmental unit with no such representative is derived.

  (3) Special rule for approval of airports.—If—

    (A) the proceeds of an issue are to be used to finance a facility or facilities located at an airport, and

    (B) the governmental unit issuing such bonds is the owner or operator of such airport,

such governmental unit shall be deemed to be the only governmental unit having jurisdiction over such airport for purposes of this subsection.

(g) Restriction on Issuance Costs Financed by Issue.—

  (1) In general.—A private activity bond shall not be a qualified bond if the issuance costs financed by the issue (of which such bond is a part) exceed 2 percent of the aggregate face amount of the issue.

  (2) Special rule for small mortgage revenue bond issues.—In the case of an issue of qualified mortgage bonds or qualified veterans' mortgage bonds, paragraph (1) shall be applied by substituting "3.5 percent" for "2 percent" if the aggregate authorized face amount of the issue does not exceed $20,000,000.

(h) Certain Rules Not To Apply to Mortgage Revenue Bonds, Qualified Student Loan Bonds, and Qualified 501(c)(3) Bonds.—

  (1) Mortgage revenue bonds and qualified student loan bonds.—Subsections (a), (b), (c), and (d) shall not apply to any qualified mortgage bond, qualified veterans' mortgage bond, or qualified student loan bond.

  (2) Qualified 501(c)(3) bonds.—Subsections (a), (c), and (d) shall not apply to any qualified 501(c)(3) bond and subsection (e) shall be applied as if it did not contain "health club facility" with respect to such a bond.

[For official explanation, see Committee Reports, ¶4058.]

【¶2923】 CODE SEC. 148. ARBITRAGE.

(a) Arbitrage Bond Defined.—For purposes of section 103, the term "arbitrage bond" means any bond issued as part of an issue any portion of the proceeds of which are reasonably expected (at the time of issuance of the bond) to be used directly or indirectly—

  (1) to acquire higher yielding investments, or

  (2) to replace funds which were used directly or indirectly to acquire higher yielding investments.

For purposes of this subsection, a bond shall be treated as an arbitrage bond if the issuer intentionally uses any portion of the proceeds of the issue of which such bond is a part in a manner described in paragraph (1) or (2).

(b) Higher Yielding Investments.—For purposes of this section—

  (1) In general.—The term "higher yielding investments" means any investment property which produces a yield over the term of the issue which is materially higher than the yield on the issue.

  (2) Investment property.—The term "investment property" means—

    (A) any security (within the meaning of section 165(g)(2)(A) or (B)),

    (B) any obligation,

    (C) any annuity contract, or

    (D) any investment-type property.

Such term shall not include any tax-exempt bond.

(c) Temporary Period Exception.—

  (1) In general.—For purposes of subsection (a), a bond shall not be treated as an arbitrage bond solely by reason of the fact that the proceeds of the issue of which such bond is a part may be invested in higher yielding investments for a reasonable temporary period until such proceeds are needed for the purpose for which such issue was issued.

  (2) Limitation on temporary period for pooled financings.—

【Footnote ¶2923】 Sec. 148 added by section 1301(b), '86 TRA.
Effective date (Sec. 1311(a), '86 TRA).—Generally applies to bonds issued after 8-15-86. For transitional and special rules, see ¶2071—2077.

(A) In general.—The temporary period referred to in paragraph (1) shall not exceed 6 months with respect to the proceeds of an issue which are to be used to make or finance loans (other than nonpurpose investments) to 2 or more persons.

(B) Special rule for certain student loan pools.—In the case of the proceeds of an issue to be used to make or finance loans under a program described in section 144(b)(1)(A), subparagraph (A) shall be applied by substituting "18 months" for "6 months". The preceding sentence shall not apply to any bond issued after December 31, 1988.

(C) Shorter temporary period for loan repayments, etc.—Subparagraph (A) shall be applied by substituting "3 months" for "6 months" with respect to the proceeds from the sale or repayment of any loan which are to be used to make or finance any loan. For puposes of the preceding sentence, a nonpurpose investment shall not be treated as a loan.

(D) Exception for mortgage revenue bonds.—This paragraph shall not apply to any qualified mortgage bond or qualified veterans' mortgage bond.

(d) **Special Rules for Reasonably Required Reserve or Replacement Fund.—**

(1) **In general.**—For purposes of subsection (a), a bond shall not be treated as an arbitrage bond solely by reason of the fact that an amount of the proceeds of the issue of which such bond is a part may be invested in higher yielding investments which are part of a reasonably required reserve or replacement fund. The amount referred to in the preceding sentence shall not exceed 10 percent of the proceeds of such issue unless the issuer establishes to the satisfaction of the Secretary that a higher amount is necessary.

(2) **Limitation on amount in reserve or replacement fund which may be financed by issue.**—A bond issued as part of an issue shall be treated as an arbitrage bond if the amount of the proceeds from the sale of such issue which is part of any fund described in paragraph (1) exceeds 10 percent of the proceeds of the issue (or such higher amount which the issuer establishes is necessary to the satisfaction of the Secretary).

(3) **Limitation on investment in nonpurpose investments.—**

(A) In general.—A bond which is part of an issue which does not meet the requirements of subparagraph (B) shall be treated as an arbitrage bond.

(B) Requirements.—An issue meets the requirements of this subparagraph only if—

(i) at no time during any bond year may the amount invested in nonpurpose investments with a yield materially higher than the yield on the issue exceed 150 percent of the debt service on the issue for the bond year, and

(ii) the aggregate amount invested as provided in clause (i) is promptly and appropriately reduced as the amount of outstanding bonds of the issue is reduced (or, in the case of a qualified mortgage bond or a qualified veterans' mortgage bond, as the mortgages are repaid).

(C) Exceptions for temporary period.—Subparagraph (B) shall not apply to—

(i) proceeds of the issue invested for an initial temporary period until such proceeds are needed for the governmental purpose of the issue, and

(ii) temporary investment periods related to debt service.

(D) Debt service defined.—For purposes of this paragraph, the debt service on the issue for any bond year is the scheduled amount of interest and amortization of principal payable for such year with respect to such issue. For purposes of the preceding sentence, there shall not be taken into account amounts scheduled with respect to any bond which has been redeemed before the beginning of the bond year.

(E) No disposition in case of loss.—This paragraph shall not require the sale or disposition of any investment if such sale or disposition would result in a loss which exceeds the amount which, but for such sale or disposition, would at the time of such sale or disposition—

(i) be paid to the United States, or,

(ii) in the case of a qualified mortgage bond or a qualified veterans' mortgage bond, be paid or credited mortgagors under section 143(g)(3)(A).

(F) Exception for governmental use bonds and qualified 501(c)(3) bonds.—This paragraph shall not apply to any bond which is not a private activity bond or which is a qualified 501(c)(3) bond.

(e) **Minor Portion May Be Invested in Higher Yielding Investments.**—Notwithstanding subsections (a), (c), and (d), a bond issued as part of an issue shall not be treated as an arbitrage bond solely by reason of the fact that an amount of the proceeds of such issue (in addition to the amounts under subsections (c) and (d)) is invested in higher yielding investments if such amount does not exceed the lesser of—

    (1) 5 percent of the proceeds of the issue, or

    (2) $100,000.

(f) Required Rebate to the United States.—

    (1) In general.—A bond which is part of an issue shall be treated as an arbitrage bond if the requirements of paragraphs (2) and (3) are not met with respect to such issue. The preceding sentence shall not apply to any qualified mortgage bond or qualified veterans' mortgage bond.

    (2) Rebate to United States.—An issue shall be treated as meeting the requirements of this paragraph only if an amount equal to the sum of—

        (A) the excess of—

            (i) the amount earned on all nonpurpose investments (other than investments attributable to an excess described in this subparagraph), over

            (ii) the amount which would have been earned if such nonpurpose investments were invested at a rate equal to the yield on the issue, plus

        (B) any income attributable to the excess described in subparagraph (A),

    is paid to the United States by the issuer in accordance with the requirements of paragraph (3).

    (3) Due date of payments under paragraph (2).—Except to the extent provided by the Secretary, the amount which is required to be paid to the United States by the issuer shall be paid in installments which are made at least once every 5 years. Each installment shall be in an amount which ensures that 90 percent of the amount described in paragraph (2) with respect to the issue at the time payment of such installment is required will have been paid to the United States. The last installment shall be made no later than 60 days after the day on which the last bond of the issue is redeemed and shall be in an amount sufficient to pay the remaining balance of the amount described in paragraph (2) with respect to such issue.

    (4) Special rules for applying paragraph (2).—

        (A) In general.—In determining the aggregate amount earned on nonpurpose investments for purposes of paragraph (2)—

            (i) any gain or loss on the disposition of a nonpurpose investment shall be taken into account, and

            (ii) unless the issuer otherwise elects, any amount earned on a bona fide debt service fund shall not be taken into account if the gross earnings on such fund for the bond year is less than $100,000.

        (B) Temporary investments.—Under regulations prescribed by the Secretary—

            (i) In general.—An issue shall, for the purpose of this subsection, be treated as meeting the requirements of paragraph (2) if the gross proceeds of such issue are expended for the governmental purpose for which the issue was issued by no later than the day which is 6 months after the date of issuance of such issue. Gross proceeds which are held in a bona fide debt service fund shall not be considered gross proceeds for purposes of this subparagraph only.

            (ii) Additional period for certain bonds.—

                (I) In general.—In the case of an issue described in subclause (II), clause (i) shall be applied by substituting "1 year" for "6 months" with respect to the portion of the proceeds of the issue which are not expended in accordance with clause (i) if such portion does not exceed the lesser of 5 percent of the proceeds of the issue or $100,000.

                (II) Issues to which subclause (I) applies.—An issue is described in this subclause if no bond which is part of such issue is a private activity bond (other than a qualified 501(c)(3) bond) or a tax or revenue anticipation bond.

            (iii) Safe harbor for determining when proceeds of tax and revenue anticipation bonds are expended.—

                (I) In general.—For purposes of clause (i), in the case of an issue of tax or revenue anticipation bonds, the net proceeds of such issue (including earnings thereon) shall be treated as expended for the governmental purpose of the issue on the 1st day after the date of issuance that the cumulative cash flow deficit to be financed by such issue exceeds 90 percent of the aggregate face amount of such issue.

(II) Cumulative cash flow deficit.—For purposes of subclause (I), the term "cumulative cash flow deficit" means, as of the date of computation, the excess of the expenses paid during the period described in subclause (III) which would ordinarily be paid out of or financed by anticipated tax or other revenues over the aggregate amount available (other than from the proceeds of the issue) during such period for the payment of such expenses.

(III) Period involved.—For purposes of subclause (II), the period described in this subclause is the period beginning on the date of issuance of the issue and ending on the earliest of the maturity date of the issue, the date 6 months after such date of issuance, or the date of the computation of cumulative cash flow deficit.

(C) Exception for small governmental units.—An issue shall, for purposes of this subsection, be treated as meeting the requirements of paragraphs (2) and (3) if—

(i) the issue is issued by governmental unit with general taxing powers,

(ii) no bond which is part of such issue is a private activity bond,

(iii) 95 percent or more of the net proceeds of such issue are to be used for local governmental activities of the issuer (or of a governmental unit the jurisdiction of which is entirely within the jurisdiction of the issuer), and

(iv) the aggregate face amount of all tax-exempt bonds (other than private activity bonds) issued by such unit (and all subordinate entities thereof) during the calendar year in which such issue is issued is not reasonably expected to exceed $5,000,000.

Clause (iv) shall not take into account any bond which is not outstanding at the time of a later issue or which is redeemed (other than in an advance refunding) from the net proceeds of the later issue.

(D) Exception for certain qualified student loan bonds.—

(i) In general.—In determining the aggregate amount earned on nonpurpose investments acquired with gross proceeds of an issue of bonds described in section 144(b)(1)(A), the amount earned from investment of net proceeds of such issue during the initial temporary period under subsection (c) shall not be taken into account to the extent that the amount so earned is used to pay the reasonable—

(I) administrative costs of such a program attributable to such issue and the costs of carrying such issue, and

(II) costs of issuing such issue,

but only to the extent such costs were financed with proceeds of such issue and for which the issuer was not reimbursed.

(ii) Only arbitrage on amounts loaned during temporary period taken into account for administrative costs, etc.—The amount earned from investment of net proceeds of an issue during the initial temporary period under subsection (c) shall be taken into account under clause (i)(I) only to the extent attributable to proceeds which were used to make or finance (not later than the close of such period) student loans under a program described in section 144(b)(1)(A).

(iii) Election.—This subparagraph shall not apply to any issue if the issuer elects not to have this subparagraph apply to such issue.

(iv) Termination.—This subparagraph shall not apply to any bond issued after December 31, 1988.

(5) Exemption from gross income of sum rebated.—Gross income shall not include the sum described in paragraph (2). Notwithstanding any other provision of this title, no deduction shall be allowed for any amount paid to the United States under paragraph (2).

(6) Definitions.—For purposes of this subsection and subsections (c) and (d)—

(A) Nonpurpose investment.—The term "nonpurpose investment" means any investment property which—

(i) is acquired with the gross proceeds of an issue, and

(ii) is not acquired in order to carry out the governmental purpose of the issue.

(B) Gross proceeds.—Except as otherwise provided by the Secretary, the gross proceeds of an issue include—

(i) amounts received (including repayments of principal) as a result of investing the original proceeds of the issue, and

(ii) amounts to be used to pay debt service on the issue.

(7) **Penalty in lieu of loss of tax exemption.**—In the case of an issue which would (but for this paragraph) fail to meet the requirements of paragraph (2) or (3), the Secretary may treat such issue as not failing to meet such requirements if—

(A) no bond which is part of such issue is a private activity bond (other than a qualified 501(c)(3) bond),

(B) the failure to meet such requirements is due to reasonable cause and not to willful neglect, and

(C) the issuer pays to the United States a penalty in an amount equal to the sum of—

(i) 50 percent of the amount which was not paid in accordance with paragraphs (2) and (3), plus

(ii) interest (at the underpayment rate established under section 6621) on the portion of the amount which was not paid on the date required under paragraph (3) for the period beginning on such date.

The Secretary may waive all or any portion of the penalty under this paragraph.

(g) **Student Loan Incentive Payments.**—Except to the extent otherwise provided in regulations, payments made by the Secretary of Education pursuant to section 438 of the Higher Education Act of 1965 are not to be taken into account, for purposes of subsection (a)(1), in determining yields on student loan notes.

(h) **Determinations of Yield.**—For purposes of this section, the yield on an issue shall be determined on the basis of the issue price (within the meaning of sections 1273 and 1274).

(i) Regulations.—The Secretary shall prescribe such regulations as may be necessary or appropriate to carry out the purposes of this section.

[For official explanation, see Committee Reports, ¶4058.]

【¶2924】 **CODE SEC. 149. BONDS MUST BE REGISTERED TO BE TAX EXEMPT; OTHER REQUIREMENTS.**

(a) **Bonds Must Be Registered To Be Tax Exempt.**—

(1) **General rule.**—Nothing in section 103(a) or in any other provision of law shall be construed to provide an exemption from Federal income tax for interest on any registration-required bond unless such bond is in registered form.

(2) **Registration-required bond.**—For purposes of paragraph (1), the term "registration-required bond" means any bond other than a bond which—

(A) is not of a type offered to the public,

(B) has a maturity (at issue) of not more than 1 year, or

(C) is described in section 163(f)(2)(B).

(3) **Special rules.**—

(A) Book entries permitted.—For purposes of paragraph (1), a book entry bond shall be treated as in registered form if the right to the principal of, and stated interest on, such bond may be transferred only through a book entry consistent with regulations prescribed by the Secretary.

(B) Nominees.—The Secretary shall prescribe such regulations as may be necessary to carry out the purpose of paragraph (1) where there is a nominee or chain of nominees.

(b) **Federally Guaranteed Bond Is Not Tax Exempt.**—

(1) **In general.**—Section 103(a) shall not apply to any State or local bond if such bond is federally guaranteed.

(2) **Federally guaranteed defined.**—For purposes of paragraph (1), a bond is federally guaranteed if—

(A) the payment of principal or interest with respect to such bond is guaranteed (in whole or in part) by the United States (or any agency or instrumentality thereof),

(B) such bond is issued as part of an issue and 5 percent or more of the proceeds of such issue is to be—

(i) used in making loans the payment of principal or interest with respect to which are to be guaranteed (in whole or in part) by the United States (or any agency or instrumentality thereof), or

【Footnote ¶2924】 Sec. 149 added by section 1301(b), '86 TRA.
Effective date (Sec. 1311(a), '86 TRA).—Generally applies to bonds issued after 8-15-86. For transitional and special rules, see ¶2071—2077.

    (ii)   invested (directly or indirectly) in federally insured deposits or accounts, or

    (C)   the payment of principal or interest on such bond is otherwise indirectly guaranteed (in whole or in part) by the United States (or an agency or instrumentality thereof).

(3)   Exceptions.—

    (A)   Certain insurance programs.—A bond shall not be treated as federally guaranteed by reason of—

        (i)   any guarantee by the Federal Housing Administration, the Veterans' Administration, the Federal National Mortgage Association, the Federal Home Loan Mortgage Corporation, or the Government National Mortgage Association,

        (ii)   any guarantee of student loans and any guarantee by the Student Loan Marketing Association to finance student loans, or

        (iii)   any guarantee by the Bonneville Power Authority pursuant to the Northwest Power Act (16 U.S.C. 839d) as in effect on the date of the enactment of the Tax Reform Act of 1984 with respect to any bond issued before July 1, 1989.

    (B)   Debt service, etc.—Paragraph (1) shall not apply to—

        (i)   proceeds of the issue invested for an initial temporary period until such proceeds are needed for the purpose for which such issue was issued,

        (ii)   investments of a bona fide debt service fund,

        (iii)   investments of a reserve which meet the requirements of section 148(d),

        (iv)   investments in bonds issued by the United States Treasury, or

        (v)   other investments permitted under regulations.

    (C)   Exception for housing programs.—

        (i)   In general.—Except as provided in clause (ii), paragraph (1) shall not apply to—

            (I)   a private activity bond for a qualified residential rental project or a housing program obligation under section 11(b) of the United States Housing Act of 1937,

            (II)   a qualified mortgage bond, or

            (III)   a qualified veterans' mortgage bond.

        (ii)   Exception not to apply where bond invested in federally insured deposits or accounts.—Clause (i) shall not apply to any bond which is federally guaranteed within the meaning of paragraph (2)(B)(ii).

    (D)   Loans to, or guarantees by, financial institutions.—Except as provided in paragraph (2)(B)(ii), a bond which is issued as part of an issue shall not be treated as federally guaranteed merely by reason of the fact that the proceeds of such issue are used in making loans to a financial institution or there is a guarantee by a financial institution unless such guarantee constitutes a federally insured deposit or account.

(4)   Definitions.—For purposes of this subsection—

    (A)   Treatment of certain entities with authority to borrow from United States.—To the extent provided in regulations prescribed by the Secretary, any entity with statutory authority to borrow from the United States shall be treated as an instrumentality of the United States. Except in the case of an exempt facility bond, a qualified small issue bond, a qualified student loan bond, and a qualified redevelopment bond, nothing in the preceding sentence shall be construed as treating the District of Columbia or any possession of the United States as an instrumentality of the United States.

    (B)   Federally insured deposit or account.—The term "federally insured deposit or account" means any deposit or account in a financial institution to the extent such deposit or account is insured under Federal law by the Federal Deposit Insurance Corporation, the Federal Savings and Loan Insurance Corporation, the National Credit Union Administration, or any similar federally chartered corporation.

(c)   Tax Exemption Must Be Derived From This Title.—

    (1)   General Rule.—Except as provided in paragraph (2), no interest on any bond shall be exempt from taxation under this title unless such interest is exempt from tax under this title without regard to any provision of law which is not contained in this title and which is not contained in a revenue Act.

    (2)   Certain prior exemptions.—

(A) Prior exemptions continued.—For purposes of this title, notwithstanding any provision of this part, any bond the interest on which is exempt from taxation under this title by reason of any provision of law (other than a provision of this title) which is in effect on January 6, 1983, shall be treated as a bond described in section 103(a).

(B) Additional requirements for bonds issued after 1983.—Subparagraph (A) shall not apply to a bond (not described in subparagraph (C)) issued after 1983 if the appropriate requirements of this part (or the corresponding provisions of prior law) are not met with respect to such bond.

(C) Description of bond.—A bond is described in this subparagraph (and treated as described in subparagraph (A)) if—

(i) such bond is issued pursuant to the Northwest Power Act (16 U.S.C. 839d), as in effect on July 18, 1984;

(ii) such bond is issued pursuant to section 608(a)(6)(A) of Public Law 97-468, as in effect on the date of the enactment of the Tax Reform Act of 1986; or

(iii) such bond is issued before June 19, 1984 under section 11(b) of the United States Housing Act of 1937.

(d) Advance Refunding.—

(1) **In general.**—Nothing in section 103(a) or in any other provision of law shall be construed to provide an exemption from Federal income tax for interest on any bond issued as part of an issue described in paragraph (2), (3), or (4).

(2) **Certain private activity bonds.**—An issue is described in this paragraph if any bond (issued as part of such issue) is issued to advance refund a private activity bond (other than a qualified 501(c)(3) bond).

(3) **Other bonds.—**

(A) In general.—An issue is described in this paragraph if any bond (issued as part of such issue), hereinafter in this paragraph referred to as the "refunding bond", is issued to advance refund a bond unless—

(i) the refunding bond is only—

(I) the 1st advance refunding of the original bond if the original bond is issued after 1985, or

(II) the 1st or 2nd advance refunding of the original bond if the original bond was issued before 1986,

(ii) in the case of refunded bonds issued before 1986, the refunded bond is redeemed not later than the earliest date on which such bond may be redeemed at par or at a premium of 3 percent or less,

(iii) in the case of refunded bonds issued after 1985, the refunded bond is redeemed not later than the earliest date on which such bond may be redeemed,

(iv) the initial temporary period under section 148(c) ends—

(I) with respect to the proceeds of the refunding bond not later than 30 days after the date of issue of such bond, and

(II) with respect to the proceeds of the refunded bond on the date of issue of the refunding bond, and

(v) in the case of refunded bonds to which section 148(e) did not apply, on and after the date of issue of the refunding bond, the amount of proceeds of the refunded bond invested in higher yielding investments (as defined in section 148(b)) which are nonpurpose investments as defined in section 148(f)(6)(A) does not exceed—

(I) the amount so invested as part of a reasonably required reserve or replacement fund or during an allowable temporary period, and

(II) the amount which is equal to the lesser of 5 percent of the proceeds of the issue of which the refunded bond is a part or $100,000 (to the extent such amount is allocable to the refunded bond).

(B) Special rules for redemptions.—

(i) Issuer must redeem only if debt service savings.—Clause (ii) and (iii) of subparagraph (A) shall apply only if the issuer may realize present value debt service savings (determined without regard to administrative expenses) in connection with the issue of which the refunding bond is a part.

(ii) Redemptions not required before 90th day.—For purposes of clauses (ii) and (iii) of subparagraph (A), the earliest date referred to in such clauses shall not be earlier than the 90th day after the date of issuance of the refunding bond.

(4) Abusive transactions prohibited.—An issue is described in this paragraph if any bond (issued as part of such issue) is issued to advance refund another bond and a device is employed in connection with the issuance of such issue to obtain a material financial advantage (based on arbitrage) apart from savings attributable to lower interest rates.

(5) Advance refunding.—For purposes of this part, a bond shall be treated as issued to advance refund another bond if it is issued more than 90 days before the redemption of the refunded bond.

(6) Special rules for purposes of paragraph (3).—For purposes of paragraph (3), bonds issued before the date of the enactment of this subsection shall be taken into account under subparagraph (A)(i) thereof except—

    (A) a refunding which occurred before 1986 shall be treated as an advance refunding only if the refunding bond was issued more than 180 days before the redemption of the refunded bond, and

    (B) a bond issued before 1986, shall be treated as advance refunded no more than once before March 15, 1986.

(7) Regulations.—The Secretary shall prescribe such regulations as may be necessary or appropriate to carry out the purposes of this subsection.

(e) Information Reporting.—

(1) In general.—Nothing in section 103(a) or any other provision of law shall be construed to provide an exemption from Federal income tax for interest on any bond unless such bond satisfies the requirements of paragraph (2).

(2) Information reporting requirements.—A bond satisfies the requirements of this paragraph if the issuer submits to the Secretary not later than the 15th day of the 2d calendar month after the close of the calendar quarter in which the bond is issued (or such later time as the Secretary may prescribe with respect to any portion of the statement), a statement concerning the issue of which the bond is a part which contains—

    (A) the name and address of the issuer,

    (B) the date of issue, the amount of net proceeds of the issue, the stated interest rate, term, and face amount of each bond which is part of the issue, the amount of issuance costs of the issue, and the amount of reserves of the issue,

    (C) where required, the name of the applicable elected representative who approved the issue, or a description of the voter referendum by which the issue was approved,

    (D) the name, address, and employer identification number of—

        (i) each initial principal user of any facility provided with the proceeds of the issue,

        (ii) the common parent of any affiliated group of corporations (within the meaning of section 1504(a)) of which such initial principal user is a member, and

        (iii) if the issue is treated as a separate issue under section 144(a)(6)(A), any person treated as a principal user under section 144(a)(6)(B),

    (E) a description of any property to be financed from the proceeds of the issue.

    (F) a certification by a State official designated by State law (or, where there is no such official, the Governor) that the bond meets the requirements of section 146 (relating to cap on private activity bonds), if applicable, and

    (G) such other information as the Secretary may require. Subparagraphs (C) and (D) shall not apply to any bond which is not a private activity bond. The Secretary may provide that certain information specified in the 1st sentence need not be included in the statement with respect to an issue where the inclusion of such information is not necessary to carry out the purposes of this subsection.

(3) Extension of time.—The Secretary may grant an extension of time for the filing of any statement required under paragraph (2) if there is reasonable cause for the failure to file such statement in a timely fashion.

[For official explanation, see Committee Reports, ¶4058.]

[¶2925] CODE SEC. 150. DEFINITIONS AND SPECIAL RULES.

[Footnote ¶2925] Sec. 150 added by section 1301(b), '86 TRA.
Effective date (Sec. 1311(a) and (c), '86 TRA).—(a) Generally applies to bonds issued after 8-15-86.
  (c) Changes in use, etc., of facilities financed with private activity bonds.—Subsection (b) of section 150 of the '86 Code shall apply to changes in use (and ownership) after 8-15-86, but only with respect to financing (including

(a) **General Rule.**—For purposes of this part—

(1) **Bond.**—The term "bond" includes any obligation.

(2) **Governmental unit not to include federal government.**—The term "governmental unit" does not include the United States or any agency or instrumentality thereof.

(3) **Net proceeds.**—The term "net proceeds" means, with respect to any issue, the proceeds of such issue reduced by amounts in a reasonably required reserve or replacement fund.

(4) **501(c)(3) organization.**—The term "501(c)(3) organization" means any organization described in section 501(c)(3) and exempt from tax under section 501(a).

(5) **Ownership of property.**—Property shall be treated as owned by a governmental unit if it is owned on behalf of such unit.

(6) **Tax-exempt bond.**—The term "tax-exempt" means, with respect to any bond (or issue), that the interest on such bond (or on the bonds issued as part of such issue) is excluded from gross income.

(b) **Change in Use of Facilities Financed With Tax-Exempt Private Activity Bonds.**—

(1) **Mortgage revenue bonds.**—

(A) In general.—In the case of any residence with respect to which financing is provided from the proceeds of a qualified mortgage bond or qualified veterans' mortgage bond, if there is a continuous period of at least 1 year during which such residence is not the principal residence of at least 1 of the mortgagors who received such financing, then no deduction shall be allowed under this chapter for interest on such financing which accrues on or after the date such period began.

(B) Exception.—Subparagraph (A) shall not apply to the extent the Secretary determines that its application would result in undue hardship and that the failure to meet the requirements of subparagraph (A) resulted from circumstances beyond the mortgagor's control.

(2) **Qualified residential rental projects.**—In the case of any project for residential rental property—

(A) with respect to which financing is provided from the proceeds of any private activity bond which, when issued, purported to be a tax-exempt bond described paragraph (7) of section 142(a), and

(B) which does not meet the requirements of section 142(d),

no deduction shall be allowed under this chapter for interest on such financing which accrues during the period beginning on the 1st day of the taxable year in which such project fails to meet such requirements and ending on the date such project meets such requirements.

(3) **Qualified 501(c)(3) bonds.**—

(A) In general.—In the case of any facility with respect to which financing is provided from the proceeds of any private activity bond which, when issued, purported to be a tax-exempt qualified 501(c)(3) bond, if any portion of such facility—

(i) is used in a trade or business of any person other than a 501(c)(3) organization or a governmental unit, but

(ii) continues to be owned by a 501(c)(3) organization,

then the owner of such portion shall be treated for purposes of this title as engaged in an unrelated trade or business (as defined in section 513) with respect to such portion. The amount of gross income attributable to such portion for any period shall not be less than the fair rental value of such portion for such period.

(B) Denial of deduction for interest.—No deduction shall be allowed under this chapter for interest on financing described in subparagraph (A) which accrues during the period beginning on the date such facility is used as described in subparagraph (A)(i) and ending on the date such facility is not so used.

(4) **Certain exempt facility bonds.**—

(A) In general.—In the case of any facility with respect to which financing is provided from the proceeds of any private activity bond to which this paragraph applies, if such facility is not used for a purpose for which a tax-exempt bond

---

[Footnote ¶2929 continued]

refinancings) provided after such date.

For special and transitional rules see ¶2071—2077.

could be issued on the date of such issue, no deduction shall be allowed under this chapter for interest on such financing which accrues during the period beginning on the date such facility is not used and ending on the date such facility is so used.

(B) Bonds to which paragraph applies.—This paragraph applies to any private activity bond which, when issued, purported to be a tax-exempt exempt facility bond described in a paragraph (other than paragraph (7)) of section 142(a).

(5) **Facilities required to be owned by governmental units or 501(c)(3) organizations.**—If—

(A) financing is provided with respect to any facility from the proceeds of any private activity bond which, when issued, purported to be a tax-exempt bond,

(B) such facility is required to be owned by a governmental unit or a 501(c)(3) organization as a condition of such tax exemption, and

(C) such facility is not so owned,

then no deduction shall be allowed under this chapter for interest on such financing which accrues during the period beginning on the date such facility is not so owned and ending on the date such facility is so owned.

(c) **Exception and Special Rules for Purposes of Subsection (b).**—For purposes of subsection (b)—

(1) **Exception.**—Any use with respect to facilities financed with proceeds of an issue which are not required to be used for the exempt purpose of such issue shall not be taken into account.

(2) **Treatment of amounts other than interest.**—If the amounts payable for the use of a facility are not interest, subsection (b) shall apply to such amounts as if they were interest but only to the extent such amounts for any period do not exceed the amount of interest accrued on the bond financing for such period.

(3) **Use of portion of facility.**—In the case of any person which uses only a portion of the facility, only the interest accruing on the financing allocable to such portion shall be taken into account by such person.

(4) **Cessation with respect to portion of facility.**—In the case of any facility where part but not all of the facility is not used for an exempt purpose, only the interest accruing on the financing allocable to such part shall be taken into account.

(5) **Regulations.**—The Secretary shall prescribe such regulations as may be necessary or appropriate to carry out the purposes of this subsection and subsection (b).

(d) **Qualified Scholarship Funding Bond.**—For purposes of this part and section 103—

(1) **Treatment as state or local bond.**—A qualified scholarship funding bond shall be treated as a State or local bond.

(2) **Qualified scholarship funding bond defined.**—The term "qualified scholarship funding bond" means a bond issued by a corporation which—

(A) is a corporation not for profit established and operated exclusively for the purpose of acquiring student loan notes incurred under the Higher Education Act of 1965, and

(B) is organized at the request of the State or 1 or more political subdivisions thereof or is requested to exercise such power by 1 or more political subdivisions and required by its corporate charter and bylaws, or required by State law, to devote any income (after payment of expenses, debt service, and the creation of reserves for the same) to the purchase of additional student loan notes or to pay over any income to the United States.

(e) **Bonds of Certain Volunteer Fire Departments.**—For purposes of this part and section 103—

(1) **In general.**—A bond of a volunteer fire department shall be treated as a bond of a political subdivision of a State if—

(A) such department is a qualified volunteer fire department with respect to an area within the jurisdiction of such political subdivision, and

(B) such bond is issued as part of an issue 95 percent or more of the net proceeds of which are to be used for the acquisition, construction, reconstruction, or improvement of a firehouse or firetruck used or to be used by such department.

(2) **Qualified volunteer fire department.**—For purposes of this subsection, the term "qualified volunteer fire department" means, with respect to a political subdivision of a State, any organization—

(A) which is organized and operated to provide firefighting or emergency medical services for persons in an area (within the jurisdiction of such political subdivision) which is not provided with any other firefighting services, and

(B) which is required (by written agreement) by the political subdivision to furnish firefighting services in such area.

[For official explanation, see Committee Reports, ¶4058.]

[¶2926] CODE SEC. 151. ALLOWANCE OF DEDUCTIONS FOR PERSONAL EXEMPTIONS.

* * * * * * * * * * *

¹(c) ² **Additional Exemption for Dependents.—**

* * * * * * * * * * *

(5) **Certain income of handicapped dependents not taken into account.—**

* * * * * * * * * * *

(C) Permanent and total disability defined.—An individual shall be treated as permanently and totally disabled for purposes of this paragraph if such individual would be so treated under paragraph (3) of ³ *section 22(e).*

⁴ *(d)* **Exemption Amount.—**⁵ *For purposes of this section—*

(1) In general.—Except as provided in paragraph (2), the term "exemption amount" means—

(A) $1,900 for taxable years beginning during 1987,
(B) $1,950 for taxable years beginning during 1988, and
(C) $2,000 for taxable years beginning after December 31, 1988.

(2) Exemption amount disallowed in the case of certain dependents.—In the case of an individual with respect to whom a deduction under this section is allowable to another taxpayer for a taxable year beginning in the calendar year in which the individual's taxable year begins, the exemption amount applicable to such individual for such individual's taxable year shall be zero.

[Footnote ¶2926] Matter in *italics* in Sec. 151(c) added by section 103(b), '86 TRA, which struck out:
(1) **"(c) Additional Exemption for Taxpayer or Spouse Aged 65 or More.—**
(1) **For taxpayer.—**An additional exemption of the exemption amount for the taxpayer if he has attained the age of 65 before the close of his taxable year.
(2) **For spouse.—**An additional exemption of the exemption amount for the spouse of the taxpayer if a joint return is not made by the taxpayer and his spouse, and if the spouse has attained the age of 65 before the close of such taxable year, and, for the calendar year in which the taxable year of the taxpayer begins, has no gross income and is not the dependent of another taxpayer.
(d) **Additional Exemption for Blindness of Taxpayer or Spouse.—**
(1) **For taxpayer.—**An additional exemption of the exemption amount for the taxpayer if he is blind at the close of his taxable year.
(2) **For spouse.—**An additional exemption of the exemption amount for the spouse of the taxpayer if a separate return is made by the taxpayer, and if the spouse is blind and, for the calendar year in which the taxable year of the taxpayer begins, has no gross income and is not the dependent of another taxpayer. For purposes of this paragraph, the determination of whether the spouse is blind shall be made as of the close of the taxable year of the taxpayer; except that if the spouse dies during such taxable year such determination shall be made as of the time of such death.
(3) **Blindness defined.—**For purposes of this subsection, an individual is blind only if his central visual acuity does not exceed 20/200 in the better eye with correcting lenses, or if his visual acuity is greater than 20/200 but is accompanied by a limitation in the fields of vision such that the widest diameter of the visual field subtends an angle no greater than 20 degrees."
(2) **"(e)"**
Effective date (Sec. 151(a), '86 TRA).—Applies to taxable years beginning after 12-31-86.

Matter in *italics* in Sec. 151(c)(5)(C) (former (e)(5)(C)) added by section 1847(b)(3), '86 TRA, which struck out:
(3) "section 37(e)"
Effective date (Sec. 1881, '86 TRA and Sec. 475(a), '84 TRA).—Applies to taxable years beginning after 12-31-83, and to carrybacks from such years.

Matter in *italics* in Sec. 151(d) added by section 103(a) and (b), '86 TRA, which struck out:
(4) "(f)"
(5) "For purposes of this section, the term "exemption amount" means, with respect to any taxable year, $1,000 increased by an amount equal to $1,000 multiplied by the cost-of-living adjustment (as defined in section 1(f)(3)) for the calendar year in which the taxable year begins. If the amount determined under the preceding sentence is not a multiple of $10, such amount shall be rounded to the nearest multiple of $10 (or if such amount is a multiple of $5, such amount shall be increased to the next highest multiple of $10)."
Effective date (Sec. 151(a), '86 TRA).—Applies to taxable years beginning after 12-31-86.

(3) Inflation adjustment for years after 1989.—In the case of any taxable year beginning in a calendar year after 1989, the dollar amount contained in paragraph (1)(C) shall be increased by an amount equal to—

    (A) such dollar amount, multiplied by

    (B) the cost-of-living adjustment determined under section 1(f)(3), for the calendar year in which the taxable year begins, by substituting "calendar year 1988" for "calendar year 1987" in subparagraph (B) thereof.

[For official explanation, see Committee Reports, ¶3854; 4167.]

【¶2927】   **CODE SEC. 152. DEPENDENT DEFINED.**

(a) General Definition.—For purposes of this subtitle, the term "dependent" means any of the following individuals over half of whose support, for the calendar year in which the taxable year of the taxpayer begins, was received from the taxpayer (or is treated under subsection (c) or (e) as received from the taxpayer):

* * * * * * * * * * * *

(9) An individual (other than an individual who at any time during the taxable year was the spouse, determined without regard to *1section 7703*, of the taxpayer) who, for the taxable year of the taxpayer, has as his principal place of abode the home of the taxpayer and is a member of the taxpayer's household.

(d) Special Support Test in Case of Students.—For purposes of subsection (a), in the case of any individual who is—

    (1) a son, stepson, daughter, or stepdaughter of the taxpayer (within the meaning of this section), and

    (2) a student (within the meaning of section *2151(c)(4)*),

amounts received as scholarships for study at an educational organization described in section 170(b)(1)(A)(ii) shall not be taken into account in determining whether such individual received more than half of his support from the taxpayer.

(e) Support Test in Case of Child of Divorced Parents, etc.—

    (1) Custodial parent gets exemption.—Except as otherwise provided in this subsection, if—

        (A) a child (as defined in section *3151(c)(3)* receives over half of his support during the calendar year from his parents—

            (i) who are divorced or legally separated under a decree of divorce or separate maintenance,

            (ii) who are separated under a written separation agreement, or

            (iii) who live apart at all times during the last 6 months of the calendar year, and

        (B) such child is in the custody of one or both of his parents for more than one-half of the calendar year,

such child shall be treated, for purposes of subsection (a), as receiving over half of his support during the calendar year from the parent having custody for a greater portion of the calendar year (hereinafter in this subsection referred to as the "custodial parent").

* * * * * * * * * * * *

[For official explanation, see Committee Reports, ¶3854.]

【¶2928】   **SEC. 153. CROSS REFERENCES.**

* * * * * * * * * * * *

    (3) For exemptions of nonresident aliens, see section 873(b)(3).[1]

【Footnote ¶2927】 Matter in *italics* in Sec. 152(a)(9) added by section 1301(j)(8), '86 TRA, which struck out:
(1) "section 143"
Effective date (Sec. 1311(a), '86 TRA).—Applies to bonds issued after 8-15-86. For special and transitional rules, see ¶2071—2077.

Matter in *italics* in Sec. 152(d)(2) and (e)(1)(A) added by section 104(b)(1)(B) and (3), '86 TRA, which struck out:
(2) "151(e)(4)"
(3) "151(e)(3)"
Effective date (Sec. 151(a), '86 TRA).—Applies to taxable years beginning after 12-31-86.
【Footnote ¶2928】 Matter in *italics* in Sec. 153(4) (other than "section 7703") added by section 1272(d)(7), '86 TRA, which struck out:
(1) "(4) For exemptions of citizens deriving income mainly from sources within possessions of the United States, see section 931(e)."

²4 For determination of marital status, see ³*section 7703*.

[For official explanation, see Committee Reports, ¶3854.]

【¶2929】 CODE SEC. 162. TRADE OR BUSINESS EXPENSES.

* * * * * * * * * * * *

(k) Continuation coverage requirements of group health plans.—

(1) In general.—For purposes of subsection (i)(2) and section 106(b)(1), a group health plan meets the requirements of this subsection only if each qualified beneficiary who would lose coverage under the plan as a result of a qualifying event is entitled to elect, within the election period, continuation coverage under the plan.

(2) Continuation coverage.—For purposes of paragraph (1), the term 'continuation coverage' means coverage under the plan which meets the following requirements:

(A) Type of benefit coverage.—The coverage must consist of coverage which, as of the time the coverage is being provided, is identical to the coverage provided under the plan to similarly situated beneficiaries under the plan with respect to whom a qualifying event has not occurred. *If coverage under the plan is modified for any group of similarly situated beneficiaries, the coverage shall also be modified in the same manner for all individuals who are qualified beneficiaries under the plan pursuant to this subsection in connection with such group.*

(B) Period of coverage.—The coverage must extend for at least the period beginning on the date of the qualifying event and ending not earlier than the earliest of the following

¹*(i) Maximum required period—*

(I) General rule for terminations and reduced hours.—In the case of a qualifying event described in paragraph (3)(B), except as provided in subclause (II), the date which is 18 months after the date of the qualifying event.

(II) Special rule for multiple qualifying events.—If a qualifying event occurs during the 18 months after the date of a qualifying event described in paragraph (3)(B), the date which is 36 months after the date of the qualifying event described in paragraph (3)(B).

(III) General rule for other qualifying events.—In the case of a qualifying event not described in paragraph (3)(B), the date which is 36 months after the date of the qualifying event.

(ii) End of plan.—The date on which the employer ceases to provide any group health plan to any employee.

(iii) Failure to pay premium.—The date on which coverage ceases under the plan by reason of a failure to make timely payment of any premium required under the plan with respect to the qualified beneficiary. *The payment of any premium (other than any payment referred to in the last sentence of subparagraph (C)) shall be considered to be timely if made within 30 days after the date due or within such longer period as applies to or under the plan.*

(iv) ² *Group health plan coverage or medicare eligibility.—*The date on which the qualified beneficiary first becomes, after the date of the election—

³*(I) covered under any other group health plan (as an employee or otherwise), or*

(II) entitled to benefits under title XVIII of the Social Security Act.⁴

【Footnote ¶2928 continued】

(2) "(5)"

Effective date (Sec. 1277(a), '86 TRA).—Generally applies to taxable years beginning after 12-31-86. For special rules, see ¶2068.

"*section 7703*" in *italics* in Sec. 153(4) (former (5)) added by section 1301(j)(8), '86 TRA, which struck out:
(3) "section 143"
Effective date (Sec. 1311(a), '86 TRA).—Applies to bonds issued after 8-15-86. For special and transitional rules, see ¶2071—2077.

【Footnote ¶2929】 Matter in *italics* in Sec. 162(k)(2)(A), (2)(B)(i), (iii), (iv), (5)(B), and (7)(B)(iii) added by section 1895(d)(1)(A), (2)(A), (3)(A), (4)(A), (5)(A), and (d)(7), '86 TRA, which struck out:
(1) "(i) Maximum period.—In the case of—
(I) a qualifying event described in paragraph (3)(B) (relating to terminations and reduced hours), the date which is 18 months after the date of the qualifying event, and
(II) any qualifying event not described in subclause (I), the date which is 36 months after the date of the qualifying event."
(2) "Reemployment or medicare eligibility"
(3) "(I) a covered employee under any other group health plan, or"
(4) "(v) Remarriage of spouse.—In the case of an individual who is a qualified beneficiary by reason of being

Code §162(k)(2) ¶2929

(5) **Election.**—For purposes of this subsection.—

(A) Election period.—The term "election period" means the period which—

(i) begins not later than the date on which coverage terminates under the plan by reason of a qualifying event,

(ii) is of at least 60 days' duration, and

(iii) ends not earlier than 60 days after the later of—

(I) the date described in clause (i), or

(II) in the case of any qualified beneficiary who receives notice under paragraph (6)(D), the date of such notice.

(B) Effect of election on other beneficiaries.—Except as otherwise specified in an election, any election *of continuation coverage* by a qualified beneficiary described in clause (i)(I) or (ii) of paragraph (7)(B) shall be deemed to include an election of continuation coverage on behalf of any other qualified beneficiary who would lose coverage under the plan by reason of the qualifying event. *If there is a choice among types of coverage under the plan, each qualified beneficiary is entitled to make a separate selection among such types of coverage.*

(6) **Notice requirements.**—In accordance with regulations prescribed by the Secretary.—

(A) the group health plan shall provide, at the time of commencement of coverage under the plan, written notice to each covered employee and spouse of the employee (if any) of the rights provided under this subsection,

(B) the employer of an employee under a plan must notify the plan administrator of a qualifying event described in subparagraph (A), (B), or (D) of paragraph (3) with respect to such employee within 30 days of the date of the qualifying event,

(C) each covered employee or qualified beneficiary is responsible for notifying the plan administrator of the occurrence of any qualifying event described in subparagraph (C) or (E) of paragraph (3) *within 60 days after the date of the qualifying event,* and

(D) the plan administrator shall notify—

(i) in the case of a qualifying event described in subparagraph (A), (B), or (D) of paragraph (3), any qualified beneficiary with respect to such event, and

---

[Footnote ¶2929 continued]

the spouse of a covered employee, the date on which the beneficiary remarries and becomes covered under a group health plan."

Effective date (Sec. 1895(e), '86 TRA and section 10001, P.L. 99-272, COBRA).—(1) Generally applies to plan years beginning on or after 7-1-86.

(2) Special rule for collective bargaining agreements.—In the case of a group health plan maintained pursuant to one or more collective bargaining agreements between employee representatives and one or more employers ratified before the date of the enactment of this Act, the amendments made by this section shall not apply to plan years beginning before the later of—

(A) the date on which the last of the collective bargaining agreements relating to the plan terminates (determined without regard to any extension thereof agreed to after the date of the enactment of this Act), or

(B) January 1, 1987.

For purposes of subparagraph (A), any plan amendment made pursuant to a collective bargaining agreement relating to the plan which amends the plan solely to conform to any requirement added by this section shall not be treated as a termination of such collective bargaining agreement.

Matter in *italics* in Sec. 162(k)(6)(C) added by section 1895(d)(6)(A), '86 TRA.

Effective date (Sec. 1895(d)(6)(D), '86 TRA).—Applies only with respect to qualifying events occurring after the date of enactment of this Act.

Sec. 162(l) in *italics* added by section 613(a), '86 TRA, which also relettered former (l) as (m).

Effective date (Sec. 613(b), '86 TRA).—Applies to any amount paid or incurred after 2-28-86, in taxable years ending after such date.

Sec. 162(m) in *italics* added by section 1161(a), '86 TRA, which also relettered (n) as (m) [should read (m) relettered (n)].

Effective date (Sec. 1161(b), '86 TRA).—(1) Generally applies to taxable years beginning after 12-31-86.

(2) Transitional rule.—In the case of any year to which section 89 of '86 Code does not apply, section 162(m)(2)(B) of such Code shall be applied by substituting any nondiscrimination requirements otherwise applicable for the requirements of section 89 of such Code.

(3) Assistance.—The Secretary of the Treasury or his delegate shall provide guidance to self-employed individuals to assist them in meeting the requirements of section 89 of the '86 Code with respect to coverage required by the amendments made by this section.

(ii) in the case of a qualifying event described in subparagraph (C) or (E) of paragraph (3) where the covered employee notifies the plan administrator under subparagraph (C), any qualified beneficiary with respect to such event, of such beneficiary's rights under this subsection.

For purposes of subparagraph (D), any notification shall be made within 14 days of the date on which the plan administrator is notified under subparagraph (B) or (C), whichever is applicable, and any such notification to an individual who is a qualified beneficiary as the spouse of the covered employee shall be treated as notification to all other qualified beneficiaries residing with such spouse at the time such notification is made.

(7) **Definitions.**—For purposes of this subsection.—

(A) Covered employee.—The term "covered employee" means an individual who is (or was) provided coverage under a group health plan by virtue of the individual's employment or previous employment with an employer.

(B) Qualified beneficiary.—

(i) In general.—The term "qualified beneficiary" means, with respect to a covered employee under a group health plan, any other individual who, on the day before the qualifying event for that employee, is a beneficiary under the plan—

(I) as the spouse of the covered employee, or

(II) as the dependent child of the employee.

(ii) Special rule for terminations and reduced employment.—In the case of a qualifying event described in paragraph (3)(B), the term "qualified beneficiary" includes the covered employee.

(iii) Exception for nonresident aliens.—Notwithstanding clauses (i) and (ii), the term "qualified beneficiary" does not include an individual whose status as a covered employee is attributable to a period in which such individual was a nonresident alien who received no earned income (within the meaning of section 911(d)(2)) from the employer which constituted income from sources within the United States (within the meaning of section 861(a)(3)). If an individual is not a qualified beneficiary pursuant to the previous sentence, a spouse or dependent child of such individual shall not be considered a qualified beneficiary by virtue of the relationship to the individual.

(C) Plan administrator.—The term "plan administrator" has the meaning given the term "administrator" by section 3(16)(A) of the Employee Retirement Income Security Act of 1974.

(l) *Stock Redemption Expenses.*—

(1) *In General.*—Except as provided in paragraph (2), no deduction otherwise allowable shall be allowed under this chapter for any amount paid or incurred by a corporation in connection with the redemption of its stock.

(2) *Exceptions.*—Paragraph (1) shall not apply to—

(A) *Certain specific deductions.*—Any—

(i) deduction allowable under section 163 (relating to interest), or

(ii) deduction for dividends paid (within the meaning of section 561).

(B) *Stock of certain regulated investment companies.*—Any amount paid or incurred in connection with the redemption of any stock in a regulated investment company which issues only stock which is redeemable upon the demand of the shareholder.

(m) *Special Rules for Health Insurance Costs of Self-Employed Individuals.*—

(1) *In general.*—In the case of an individual who is an employee within the meaning of section 401(c)(1), there shall be allowed as a deduction under this section an amount equal to 25 percent of the amount paid during the taxable year for insurance which constitutes medical care for the taxpayer, his spouse, and dependents.

(2) *Limitations.*—

(A) *Dollar amount.*—No deduction shall be allowed under paragraph (1) to the extent that the amount of such deduction exceeds the taxpayer's earned income (within the meaning of section 401(c)).

(B) *Required coverage.*—Paragraph (1) shall not apply to any taxpayer for any taxable year unless coverage is provided under 1 or more plans meeting the requirements of section 89, treating such coverage as an employer-provided benefit.

Code §162(m)(2) ¶2929

(C) Other coverage.—Paragraph (1) shall not apply to any taxpayer who is eligible to participate in any subsidized health plan maintained by an employer of the taxpayer or of the spouse of the taxpayer.

(3) Coordination with medical deduction.—Any amount paid by a taxpayer for insurance to which paragraph (1) applies shall not be taken into account in computing the amount allowable to the taxpayer as a deduction under section 213(a).

(4) Termination.—This subsection shall not apply to any taxable year beginning after December 31, 1989.

(m) [should read (n)] *Cross References.—*

* * * * * * * * * * * *

[For official explanation, see Committee Reports, ¶3914; 4008; 4208.]

【¶2930】 **CODE SEC. 163. INTEREST.**

* * * * * * * * * * * *

[1]*(d) Limitation on Investment Interest.—*

【Footnote ¶2930】 Matter in *italics* in Sec. 163(d) added by section 511(a), '86 TRA, which struck out:

(1) **"(d) Limitation on Interest on Investment Indebtedness.—**

(1) **In general.**—In the case of a taxpayer other than a corporation, the amount of investment interest (as defined in paragraph (3)(D)) otherwise allowable as a deduction under this chapter shall be limited, in the following order, to—

(A) $10,000 ($5,000, in the case of a separate return by a married individual), plus

(B) the amount of the net investment income (as defined in paragraph (3)(A)), plus the amount (if any) by which the deductions allowable under this section (determined without regard to this subsection) and sections 162, 164(a)(1) or (2), or 212 attributable to property of the taxpayer subject to a net lease exceeds the rental income produced by such property for the taxable years.

In the case of a trust, the $10,000 amount specified in subparagraph (A) shall be zero.

(2) **Carryover of disallowed investment interest.**—The amount of disallowed investment interest for any taxable year shall be treated as investment interest paid or accrued in the succeeding taxable year.

(3) **Definitions.**—For purposes of this subsection—

(A) Net investment income.—The term "net investment income" means the excess of investment income over investment expenses. If the taxpayer has investment interest for the taxable year to which this subsection (as in effect before the Tax Reform Act of 1976) applies, the amount of the net investment income taken into account under this subsection shall be the amount of such income (determined without regard to this sentence) multiplied by a fraction the numerator of which is the excess of the investment interest for the taxable year over the investment interest to which such prior provision applies, and the denominator of which is the investment interest for the taxable year.

(B) Investment income.—The term "investment income" means—

(i) the gross income from interest, dividends, rents, and royalties,

(ii) the net short-term capital gain attributable to the disposition of property held for investment, and

(iii) any amount treated under section 1245, 1250, and 1254 as ordinary income,

but only to the extent such income, gain, and amounts are not derived from the conduct of a trade or business.

(C) Investment expenses.—The term "investment expenses" means the deductions allowable under sections 162, 164(a)(1) or (2), 166, 167, 171, 212, or 611 directly connected with the production of investment income. For purposes of this subparagraph, the deduction allowable under section 167 with respect to any property may be treated as the amount which would have been allowable had the taxpayer depreciated the property under the straight line method for each taxable year of its useful life for which the taxpayer has held the property, and the deduction allowable under section 611 with respect to any property may be treated as the amount which would have been allowable had the taxpayer determined the deduction under section 611 without regard to section 613 for each taxable year for which the taxpayer has held the property.

(D) Investment interest.—

(i) In general.—The term "investment interest" means interest paid or accrued on indebtedness incurred or continued to purchase or carry property held for investment.

(ii) Certain expenses incurred in connection with short sales.—For purposes of clause (i), the term "interest" includes any amount allowable as a deduction in connection with the personal property used in a short sale.

(E) Disallowed investment interest.—The term "disallowed investment interest" means with respect to any taxable year, the amount not allowable as a deduction solely by reason of the limitation in paragraph (1).

(4) **Special rules.**—

(A) Property subject to net lease.—For purposes of this subsection, property subject to a lease shall be treated as property held for investment, and not as property used in a trade or business, for a taxable year, if—

(i) for such taxable year the sum of the deductions of the lessor with respect to such property which are allowable solely by reason of section 162 (other than rents and reimbursed amounts with respect to such property) is less than 15 percent of the rental income produced by such property, or

(ii) the lessor is either guaranteed a specified return or is guaranteed in whole or in part against loss of income.

(B) Construction interest.—For purposes of this subsection, interest paid or accrued on indebtedness incurred or continued in the construction of property to be used in a trade or business shall not be treated as investment interest.

(5) **Exceptions.**—This subsection shall not apply with respect to investment interest, investment income, and investment expenses attributable to a specific item of property, if the indebtedness with respect to such property—

(A) is for a specified term, and

(B) was incurred before December 17, 1969, or is incurred after December 16, 1969, pursuant to a written

(1) In general.—In the case of a taxpayer other than a corporation, the amount allowed as a deduction under this chapter for investment interest for any taxable year shall not exceed the net investment income of the taxpayer for the taxable year.

(2) Carryforward of disallowed interest.—The amount not allowed as a deduction for any taxable year by reason of paragraph (1) shall be treated as investment interest paid or accrued by the taxpayer in the succeeding taxable year.

(3) Investment interest.—For purposes of this subsection—

(A) *In general.*—The term "investment interest" means any interest allowable as a deduction under this chapter (determined without regard to paragraph (1)) which is paid or accrued on indebtedness incurred or continued to purchase or carry property held for investment.

(B) *Exceptions.*—The term "investment interest" shall not include—

(i) any qualified residence interest (as defined in subsection (h)(3)), or

(ii) any interest which is taken into account under section 469 in computing income or loss from a passive activity of the taxpayer.

(C) *Personal property used in short sale.*—For purposes of this paragraph, the term "interest" includes any amount allowable as a deduction in connection with personal property used in a short sale.

(4) Net investment income.—For purposes of this subsection—

(A) *In general.*—The term "net investment income" means the excess of—

(i) investment income, over

(ii) investment expenses.

(B) *Investment income.*—The term "investment income" means the sum of—

(i) gross income (other than gain described in clause (ii)) from property held for investment, and

(ii) any net gain attributable to the disposition of property held for investment,

but only to the extent such amounts are not derived from the conduct of a trade or business.

(C) *Investment expenses.*—The term "investment expenses" means the deductions allowed under this chapter (other than for interest) which are directly connected with the production of investment income.

(D) *Income and expenses from passive activities.*—Investment income and investment expenses shall not include any income or expenses taken into account under section 469 in computing income or loss from a passive activity.

【Footnote ¶2930 continued】

contract or commitment which, on such date and at all times thereafter prior to the incurring of such indebtedness, is binding on the taxpayer.

For taxable years beginning after December 31, 1975, this paragraph shall be applied on an allocation basis rather than a specific item basis.

(6) **Real property leases.**—For purposes of paragraph (4)(A)—

(A) if a parcel of real property of the taxpayer is leased under two or more leases, paragraph (4)(A)(i) shall, at the election of the taxpayer, be applied by treating all leased portions of such property as subject to a single lease; and

(B) at the election of the taxpayer, paragraph (4)(A)(i) shall not apply with respect to real property of the taxpayer which has been in use for more than 5 years.

An election under subparagraph (A) or (B) shall be made at such time and in such manner as the Secretary prescribes by regulations.

(7) **Special rule where taxpayer owns 50 percent or more of enterprise.**—

(A) General rule.—In the case of any 50 percent owned corporation or partnership, the $10,000 figure specified in paragraph (1) shall be increased by the lesser of—

(i) $15,000 or

(ii) the interest paid or accrued during the taxable year on investment indebtedness incurred or continued in connection with the acquisition of the interest in such corporation or partnership.

In case of a separate return by a married individual, $7,500 shall be substituted for the $15,000 figure in clause (1).

(B) Ownership requirements.—This paragraph shall apply with respect to indebtedness only if the taxpayer, his spouse, and his children own 50 percent or more of the total value of all classes of stock of the corporation or 50 percent or more of all capital interests in the partnership, as the case may be.

Effective date (Sec. 511(e), '86 TRA).—Applies to taxable years beginning after 12-31-86.

Sec. 163(e)(2)(C) in *italics* added by section 1803(a)(4), '86 TRA.

Effective date (Sec. 1881, '86 TRA, and Sec. 44(a), '84 TRA amended by P.L. 98-612 and section 1803(b), '86 TRA).—(a) Generally applies to taxable years ending after 7-18-84. For amendments and special rules, see footnote ¶3030.

(E) Reduction in investment income during phase-in of passive loss rules.—Investment income of the taxpayer for any taxable year shall be reduced by the amount of the passive activity loss to which section 469(a) does not apply for such taxable year by reason of section 469(l). The preceding sentence shall not apply to any portion of such passive activity loss which is attributable to a rental real estate activity with respect to which the taxpayer actively participates (within the meaning of section 469(i)(6)) during such taxable year.

(5) *Property held for investment.—For purposes of this subsection—*
   (A) In general.—The term "property held for investment" shall include—
      (i) any property which produces income of a type described in section 469(e)(1), and
      (ii) any interest held by a taxpayer in an activity involving the conduct of a trade or business—
        (I) which is not a passive activity, and
        (II) with respect to which the taxpayer does not materially participate.
   (B) Investment expenses.—In the case of property described in subparagraph (A)(i), expenses shall be allocated to such property in the same manner as under section 469.
   (C) Terms.—For purposes of this paragraph, the terms "activity", "passive activity", and "materially participate" have the meanings given such terms by section 469.

(6) *Phase-in of disallowance.—In the case of any taxable year beginning in calendar years 1987 through 1990—*
   (A) In general.—The amount of interest disallowed under this subsection for any such taxable year shall be equal to the sum of—
      (i) the applicable percentage of the amount which (without regard to this paragraph) is not allowed as a deduction under this subsection for the taxable year to the extent such amount does not exceed the ceiling amount,
      (ii) the amount which (without regard to this paragraph) is not allowed as a deduction under this subsection in excess of the ceiling amount, plus
      (iii) the amount of any carryforward to such taxable year under paragraph (2) with respect to which a deduction was disallowed under this subsection for a preceding taxable year.

For purposes of this subparagraph, the amount under clause (i) or (ii) shall be computed without regard to the amount described in clause (iii).
   (B) Applicable percentage.—For purposes of this paragraph, the applicable percentage shall be determined in accordance with the following table:

In the case of taxable years beginning in:	The applicable percentage is:
1987	35
1988	60
1989	80
1990	90.

   (C) Ceiling amount.—For purposes of this paragraph, the term "ceiling amount" means—
      (i) $10,000 in the case of a taxpayer not described in clause (ii) or (iii),
      (ii) $5,000 in the case of a married individual filing a separate return, and
      (iii) zero in the case of a trust.

(e) **Original Issue Discount.—**

* * * * * * * * * * *

(2) **Definitions and special rules.—**For purposes of this subsection—

* * * * * * * * * * *

   (C) Short-term obligations.—In the case of an obligor of a short-term obligation (as defined in section 1283(a)(1)(A)) who uses the cash receipts and disbursements method of accounting, the original issue discount (and any other interest payable) on such obligation shall be deductible only when paid.

(3) **Special rule for original issue discount on obligation held by related foreign person.—**
   (A) In general.—If any debt instrument having original issue discount is held by a related foreign person, any portion of such original issue discount shall not be allowable as a deduction to the issuer until paid. *The preceding sentence shall not apply to the extent that the original issue discount is effectively connected with the*

conduct by such foreign related person of a trade or business within the United States unless such original issue discount is exempt from taxation (or is subject to a reduced rate of tax) pursuant to a treaty obligation of the United States.

(B) Related foreign person.—For purposes of subparagraph (A), the term "related foreign person" means any person—

(i) who is not a United States person, and

(ii) who is related (within the meaning of section 267(b)) to the issuer.

* * * * * * * * * * *

[2](5) **Cross References.**—* * *

(f) **Denial of Deduction for Interest on Certain Obligations Not in Registered Forml.**—

* * * * * * * * * * *

(3) **Book entries permitted, etc.**—For purposes of this subsection, rules similar to the rules of [3]section 149(a)(3) shall apply.

* * * * * * * * * * *

(h) *Disallowance of Deduction for Personal Interest.*—

(1) *In general.*—In the case of a taxpayer other than a corporation, no deduction shall be allowed under this chapter for personal interest paid or accrued during the taxable year.

(2) *Personal interest.*—For purposes of this subsection, the term "personal interest" means any interest allowable as a deduction under this chapter other than—

(A) interest paid or accrued on indebtedness incurred or continued in connection with the conduct of a trade or business (other than the trade or business of performing services as an employee),

(B) any investment interest (within the meaning of subsection (d)),

(C) any interest which is taken into account under section 469 in computing income or loss from a passive activity of the taxpayer,

(D) any qualified residence interest (within the meaning of paragraph (3)), and

(E) any interest payable under section 6601 on any unpaid portion of the tax imposed by section 2001 for the period during which an extension of time for payment of such tax is in effect under section 6163 or 6166.

(3) *Qualified residence interest.*—For purposes of this subsection—

(A) *In general.*—The term "qualified residence interest" means interest which is paid or accrued during the taxable year on indebtedness which is secured by any property which (at the time such interest is paid or accrued) is a qualified residence of the taxpayer.

(B) *Limitation on amount of interest.*—The term "qualified residence interest" shall not include any interest paid or accrued on indebtedness secured by any qualified residence which is allocable to that portion of the principal amount of such indebtedness which, when added to the outstanding aggregate principal amount of all other indebtedness previously incurred and secured by such qualified residence exceeds the lesser of—

(i) the fair market value of such qualified residence, or

(ii) the sum of—

(I) the taxpayer's basis in such qualified residence (adjusted only by the cost of any improvements to such residence), plus

(II) the aggregate amount of qualified indebtedness of the taxpayer with respect to such qualified residence.

(C) *Cost not less than balance of indebtedness incurred on or before August 16, 1986.*—The amount under subparagraph (B)(ii)(I) at any time after August 16, 1986, shall not be less than the outstanding aggregate principal amount (as of such time) of indebtedness which was incurred on or before August 16, 1986, and which was secured by the qualified residence on August 16, 1986.

(D) *Time for determination.*—Except as provided in regulations, any determination under subparagraph (B) shall be made as of the time the indebtedness is incurred.

(4) *Qualified indebtedness.*—For purposes of this subsection—

(A) *In general.*—The term "qualified indebtedness" means indebtedness secured by a qualified residence of the taxpayer which is incurred after August 16, 1986, to pay for—

(i) qualified medical expenses, or

(ii) qualified educational expenses,

which are paid or incurred within a reasonable period of time before or after such indebtedness is incurred.

(B) *Qualified medical expenses.*—For purposes of this paragraph, the term "qualified medical expenses" means amounts, not compensated for by insurance or otherwise, incurred for medical care (within the meaning of subparagraphs (A) and (B) of section 213(d)(1)) for the taxpayer, his spouse, or a dependent.

(C) *Qualified educational expenses.*—For purposes of this paragraph—

(i) *In general.*—The term "qualified educational expenses" means qualified tuition and related expenses of the taxpayer, his spouse, or a dependent for attendance at an educational institution described in section 170(b)(1)(A)(ii).

(ii) *Qualified tuition and related expenses.*—The term "qualified tuition and related expenses" has the meaning given such term by section 117(b), except that such term shall include any reasonable living expenses while away from home.

(D) *Dependent.*—For purposes of this paragraph, the term "dependent" has the meaning given such term by section 152.

(5) *Other definitions and special rules.*—

(A) *Qualified residence.*—For purposes of this subsection—

(i) *In general.*—The term "qualified residence" means—

(I) the principal residence (within the meaning of section 1034) of the taxpayer, and

(II) 1 other residence of the taxpayer which is selected by the taxpayer for purposes of this sebsection for the taxable year and which is used by the taxpayer as a residence (within the meaning of section 280A(d)(1)).

(ii) *Married individuals filing separate returns.*—If a married couple does not file a joint return for the taxable year—

(I) such couple shall be treated as 1 taxpayer for purposes of clause (i), and

(II) each individual shall be entitled to take into account 1 residence unless both individuals consent in writing to 1 individual taking into account the principal residence and 1 other residence.

(iii) *Residence not used or rented.*—For purposes of clause (i)(II), notwithstanding section 280A(d)(1), if the taxpayer does not rent or use a dwelling unit at any time during a taxable year, such unit may be treated as a residence for such taxable year.

(B) *Special rule for cooperative housing corporations.*—For purposes of this paragraph, any indebtedness secured by stock held by the taxpayer as a tenant-stockholder (as defined in section 216) in a cooperative housing corporation (as so defined) shall be treated as secured by the house or apartment which the taxpayer is entitled to occupy as such a tenant-stockholder. If stock described in the preceding sentence may not be used to secure indebtedness, indebtedness shall be treated as so secured if the taxpayer establishes to the satisfaction of the Secretary that such indebtedness was incurred to acquire such stock.

(6) *Phase-in of limitation.*—In the case of any taxable year beginning in calendar years 1987 through 1990, the amount of interest with respect to which a deduction is disallowed under this subsection shall be equal to the applicable percentage (within the meaning of subsection (d)(6)(B)) of the amount which (but for this subsection) would have been so disallowed.

[4](i)   **Cross references.**—

(1) For disallowance of certain amounts paid in connection with insurance, endownment or annuity contracts, see section 264.

(2) For disallowance of deduction for interest relating to tax-exempt income, see [5]*section 265(a)(2).*

* * * * * * * * * * * *

[For official explanation, see Committee Reports, ¶3905; ¶3949; ¶4058; ¶4137; ¶4149.]

【¶2931】 **CODE SEC. 164. TAXES.**

(a) **General Rule.**—Except as otherwise provided in this section, the following taxes shall be allowed as a deduction for the taxable year within which paid or accrued:

(1) State and local, and foreign, real property taxes.

(2) State and local personal property taxes.

(3) State and local, and foreign, income, war profits, and excess profits taxes.[1]

[2](4) The windfall profit tax imposed by section 4986.

(5) the GST tax imposed on income distributions.

In addition, there shall be allowed as a deduction State and local, and foreign, taxes not described in the preceding sentence which are paid or accrued within the taxable year in carrying on a trade or business or an activity described in section 212 (relating to expenses for production of income). *Notwithstanding the preceding sentence, any tax (not described in the first sentence of this subsection) which is paid or accrued by the taxpayer in connection with an acquisition or disposition of property shall be treated as part of the cost of the acquired property or, in the case of a disposition, as a reduction in the amount realized on the disposition.*

(b) **Definitions and Special Rules.**—For purposes of this section—[3]

* * * * * * * * * * * *

[4]*(2)* **State or local taxes.**—

* * * * * * * * * * * *

【Footnote ¶2930 continued】

Matter in *italics* in Sec. 163(i)(2) [former Sec. 163(h)(2) (reads (h)(12) in '86 TRA)] amended by Sec. 902(e)(1), '86 TRA, which struck out:

(5) "section 265(2)"

Effective date (Sec. 902(f)(1), '86 TRA).—Generally applies to taxable years ending after 12-31-86.

For transitional rules see footnote ¶2963

【Footnote ¶2931】 Matter in *italics* in Sec. 164(a), except (5), added by section 134(a) '86 TRA, which struck out:

(1) "(4) State and local general sales taxes."

(2) "(5)"

Effective date (Sec. 151(a), '86 TRA).—Applies to taxable years beginning after 12-31-86.

Sec. 164(a)(5) in *italics* added by section 1432(a)(1), '86 TRA.

Effective date (Sec. 1433(a), '86 TRA).—Generally applies to any generation-skipping transfer (within the meaning of section 2611 of the '86 Code) made after the date of the enactment of this Act. For special rules, see footnote ¶3252.

Matter in *italics* in Sec. 164(b)(2) and (3) added by section 134(b), '86 TRA, which struck out:

(3) "(2) **General sales taxes.**—

(A) In General.—The term 'general sales tax' means a tax imposed at one rate in respect to the sale at retail of a broad range of classes of items.

(B) Special rules for food, etc.—In the case of items of food, clothing, medical supplies, and motor vehicles—

(i) the fact that the tax does not apply in respect of some or all of such items shall not be taken into account in determining whether the tax applies in respect of a broad range of classes of items, and

(ii) the fact that the rate of tax applicable in respect of some or all of such items is lower than the general rate of tax shall not be taken into account in determining whether the tax is imposed at one rate.

(C) Items taxed at different rates.—Except in the case of a lower rate of tax applicable in respect of an item described in subparagraph (B), no deduction shall be allowed under this section for any general sales tax imposed in respect of an item at a rate other than the general rate of tax.

(D) Compensating use taxes.—A compensating use tax in respect of an item shall be treated as a general sales tax. For purposes of the preceding sentence, the term 'compensating use tax' means, in respect of any item, a tax which—

(i) is imposed on the use, storage, or consumption of such item, and

(ii) is complementary to a general sales tax, but only if a deduction is allowable under subsection (a)(4), in respect of items sold at retail in the taxing jurisdiction which are similar to such item.

(E) Special rule for motor vehicles.—In the case of motor vehicles, if the rate of tax exceeds the general rate, such excess shall be disregarded and the general rule shall be treated as the rate of tax."

(4) "(3)"

[5](3)   **Foreign taxes.—**

* * * * * * * * * * * *

(4)   *Special rules for GST tax.—*

(A)   *In general.—The GST tax imposed on income distributions is—*
(i)   *the tax imposed by section 2601, and*
(ii)   *any State tax described in section 2604,*

but only to the extent such tax is imposed on a transfer which is included in the gross income of the distributee and to which section 666 does not apply.

(B)   *Special rule for tax paid before due date.—Any tax referred to in subparagraph (A) imposed with respect to a transfer occurring during the taxable year of the distributee (or, in the case of a taxable termination, the trust) which is paid not later than the time prescribed by law (including extensions) for filing the return with respect to such transfer shall be treated as having been paid on the last day of the taxable year in which the transfer was made.[6]*

* * * * * * * * * * * *

〔¶2932〕   CODE SEC. 165.   LOSSES.

(a)   **General Rule.—**There shall be allowed as a deduction any loss sustained during the taxable year and not compensated for by insurance or otherwise.

* * * * * * * * * * * *

(c)   **Limitation on Losses of Individuals.—**In the case of an individual, the deduction under subsection (a) shall be limited to—
(1)   losses incurred in a trade or business;
(2)   losses incurred in any transaction entered into for profit, though not connected with a trade or business; and
(3)   except as provided in subsection (h), losses of property not connected with a trade or business or a transaction entered into for profit, if such losses arise from fire, storm, shipwreck, or other casualty, or from theft.

* * * * * * * * * * * *

(h)   **Treatment of Casualty Gains and Losses.—**

* * * * * * * * * * * *

(4)   **Special Rules.—**

* * * * * * * * * * * *

(E)   *Claim required to be filed in certain cases.—Any loss of an individual described in subsection (c)(3) to the extent covered by insurance shall be taken into account under this section only if the individual files a timely insurance claim with respect to such loss.*

* * * * * * * * * * * *

(l)   *Treatment of Certain Losses in Insolvent Financial Institutions.—*

(1)   *In general.—If—*
(A)   *as of the close of the taxable year, it can reasonably be estimated that there is a loss on a qualified individual's deposit in a qualified financial institution, and*
(B)   *such loss is on account of the bankruptcy or insolvency of such institution,*

then the taxpayer may elect to treat the amount so estimated as a loss described in subsection (c)(3) incurred during the taxable year.

〔Footnote ¶2931 continued〕

(5)   "(4)"
Effective date   (Sec. 151(a), '86 TRA).—Applies to taxable years beginning after 12-31-86.

Matter in *italics* in Sec. 164(b)(4) added by section 1432(a)(2), '86 TRA.
Effective date   (Sec. 1433(a), '86 TRA).—Generally applies to any generation-skipping transfer (within the meaning of section 2611 of the '86 Code) made after the date of the enactment of this Act. For special rules, see footnote ¶3252.

Sec. 164(b)(5) struck out by section 134(b)(1), '86 TRA:
(6)   "(5)   **Separately stated general sales taxes.—**If the amount of any general sales tax is separately stated, then, to the extent that the amount so stated is paid by the consumer (otherwise than in connection with the consumer's trade or business) to his seller, such amount shall be treated as a tax imposed on, and paid by, such consumer."
Effective date   (Sec. 151(a), '86 TRA).—Applies to taxable years beginning after 12-31-86.
〔Footnote ¶2932〕   Sec. 165(h)(4)(E) in *italics* added by section 1004(a), '86 TRA.
Effective date (Sec.1004(b), '86 TRA).—Applies to losses sustained in taxable years beginning after 12-31-86.

(2) *Qualified individual defined.*—For purposes of this subsection, the term "qualified individual" means any individual, except an individual—

(A) who owns at least 1 percent in value of the outstanding stock of the qualified financial institution,

(B) who is an officer of the qualified financial institution,

(C) who is a sibling (whether by the whole or half blood), spouse, aunt, uncle, nephew, niece, ancestor, or lineal descendant of an individual described in subparagraph (A) or (B), or

(D) who otherwise is a related person (as defined in section 267(b)) with respect to an individual described in subparagraph (A) or (B).

(3) *Qualified financial institution.*—For purposes of this subsection, the term "qualified financial institution" means—

(A) any bank (as defined in section 581),

(B) any institution described in section 591,

(C) any credit union the deposits or accounts in which are insured under Federal or State law or are protected or guaranteed under State law, or

(D) any similar institution chartered and supervised under Federal or State law.

(4) *Deposit.*—For purposes of this subsection, the term "deposit" means any deposit, withdrawable account, or withdrawable or repurchasable share.

(5) *Election.*—Any election by the taxpayer under this subsection may be revoked only with the consent of the Secretary and shall apply to all losses of the taxpayer on deposits in the institution with respect to which such election was made.

(6) *Coordination with section 166.*—Section 166 shall not apply to any loss to which an election under this subsection applies.

[1](m)   **Cross References.**—

* * * * * * * * * * * *

[¶2933]   CODE SEC. 166.   BAD DEBTS.

* * * * * * * * * * * *

(c)   **[Repealed]**[1]

* * * * * * * * * * * *

[2](f)   [3]**Cross Reference.**—

[Footnote ¶2932 continued]

Matter in *italics* in Sec. 165(*l*) and (m) added by section 905(a), '86 TRA, which struck out:

(1)   "(*l*)"

Effective date (Sec. 905(c)(1), '86 TRA).—Applies to taxable years beginning after 12-31-82.

[Footnote ¶2933]   Section 805(a), '86 TRA, repealed Sec. 166(c):

(1)   "(c)   **Reserve for Bad Debts.**—In lieu of any deduction under subsection (a), there shall be allowed (in the discretion of the Secretary) a deduction for a reasonable addition to a reserve for bad debts."

Effective date (Sec. 805(d), '86 TRA).—(1) Generally applies to taxable years beginning after 12-31-86.

(2)   Change in method of accounting.—In the case of any taxpayer who maintained a reserve for bad debts for such taxpayer's last taxable year beginning before 1-1-87, and who is required by the amendments made by this section to change its method of accounting for any taxable year—

(A)   such change shall be treated as initiated by the taxpayer,

(B)   such change shall be treated as made with the consent of the Secretary, and

(C)   the net amount of adjustments required by section 481 of the '86 Code to be taken into account by the taxpayer shall—

(i)   in the case of a taxpayer maintaining a reserve under section 166(f), be reduced by the balance in the suspense account under section 166(f)(4) of such Code as of the close of such last taxable year, and

(ii)   be taken into account ratably in each of the first 4 taxable years beginning after 12-31-86.

Matter in *italics* in Sec. 166(f) added by section 805(b), '86 TRA, which struck out:

(2)   "(f)   **Reserve for Certain Guaranteed Debt Obligations.**—

(1)   **Allowance of deduction.**—In the case of a taxpayer who is a dealer in property in lieu of any deduction under subsection (a), there shall be allowed (in the discretion of the Secretary) for any taxable year ending after October 21, 1965, a deduction—

(A)   for a reasonable addition to a reserve for bad debts which may arise out of his liability as a guarantor, endorser, or indemnitor of debt obligations arising out of the sale by him of real property or tangible personal property (including related services) in the ordinary course of his trade or business; and

(B)   for the amount of any reduction in the suspense account required by paragraph (4)(B)(i).

(2)   **Deduction disallowed in other cases.**—Except as provided in paragraph (1), no deduction shall be allowed to a taxpayer for any addition to a reserve for bad debts which may arise out of his liability as guarantor, endorser, or indemnitor of debt obligations.

(1) For disallowance of deduction for worthlessness of debts owed by political parties and similar organizations, see section 271.

(2) For special rule for banks with respect to worthless securities, see section 582.[4]

* * * * * * * * * * * *

[¶2934] CODE SEC. 167. DEPRECIATION.

* * * * * * * * * * * *

(c) **Limitations on Use of Certain Methods and Rates.**—Paragraphs (2), (3), and (4) of subsection (b) shall apply only in the case of property (other than intangible property) described in subsection (a) with a useful life of 3 years or more—

(1) the construction, reconstruction, or erection of which is completed after December 31, 1953, and then only to that portion of the basis which is properly attributable to such construction, reconstruction, or erection after December 31, 1953, or

(2) acquired after December 31, 1953, if the original use of such property commences with the taxpayer and commences after such date.

Paragraphs (2), (3), and (4) of subsection (b) shall not apply to any motion picture film, video tape, or sound recording.

* * * * * * * * * * * *

(m) **Class Lives.**—

* * * * * * * * * * * *

(4) **Termination.**—This subsection shall not apply with respect to [1]*any property to which section 168 applies.*

* * * * * * * * * * * *

(q) **Retirement or Replacement of Certain Boilers, Etc., Fueled by Oil or Gas.**—

* * * * * * * * * * * *

[Footnote ¶2933 continued]

(3) **Opening balance.**—The opening balance of a reserve described in paragraph (1)(A) for the first taxable year ending after October 21, 1965, for which a taxpayer maintains such reserve shall, under regulations prescribed by the Secretary, be determined as if the taxpayer had maintained such reserve for the preceding taxable years.

(4) **Suspense account.**—(A) Requirement.—Except as provided by subparagraph (C), each taxpayer who maintains a reserve described in paragraph (1)(A) shall, for purposes of this subsection and section 81, establish and maintain a suspense account. The initial balance of such account shall be equal to the opening balance described in paragraph (3).

(B) Adjustments.—At the close of each taxable year the suspense account shall be—

(i) reduced by the excess of the suspense account at the beginning of the year over the reserve described in paragraph (1)(A) (after making the addition for such year provided in such paragraph), or

(ii) increased (but not to an amount greater than the initial balance of the suspense account) by the excess of the reserve described in paragraph (1)(A) (after making the addition for such year provided in such paragraph) over the suspense account at the beginning of such year.

(C) Limitations.—Subparagraphs (A) and (B) shall not apply in the case of the taxpayer who maintained for his last taxable year ending before October 22, 1965, a reserve for bad debts under subsection (c) which included debt obligations described in paragraph (1)(A).

(D) Section 381 acquisitions.—The application of this paragraph in any acquisition to which section 381(a) applies shall be determined under regulations prescribed by the Secretary."

(3) "(g)"

Effective date (Sec. 805(d), '86 TRA).—(1) Generally applies to taxable years beginning after 12-31-86. For transitional and special rules, see above.

Section 901(d)(4)(A), '86 TRA, struck out Sec. 166(f)(3) and (4) (former (g)(3) and (4)):

(4) "(3) For special rule for bad debt reserves of certain mutual savings banks, domestic building and loan associations, and cooperative banks, see section 593.

(4) For special rule for bad debt reserves of banks, small business investment companies, etc., see sections 585 and 586."

Effective date (Sec. 901(e), '86 TRA).—Applies to taxable years beginning after 12-31-86.

[Footnote ¶2934] Matter in *italics* in Sec. 167(c) added by section 1809(d)(1), '86 TRA.

Effective date (Sec. 1809(d)(1), '86 TRA).—Applies to property placed in service by taxpayer after 3-28-85.

Matter in *italics* in Sec. 167(m)(4) added by section 201(d)(1), '86 TRA, which struck out:

(1) "recovery property (within the meaning of section 168) placed in service after December 31, 1980."

Effective date (Sec. 203(a)(1), '86 TRA).—(A) Generally applies to property placed in service after 12-31-86, in taxable years ending after such date.

(B) Election to have amendments made by section 201 apply.—A taxpayer may elect (at such time and in such manner as the Secretary of the Treasury or his delegate may prescribe) to have the amendments made by section 201 apply to any property placed in service after 7-31-86 and before 1-1-87.

For transitional and special rules, see ¶2007—2008.

---

(2) Interest.—If the retirement or replacement of any combustor does not occur on or before the date referred to in paragraph (1)(B)—

(A) this subsection shall cease to apply with respect to such combustor as of such date, and

(B) interest at the [2]*underpayment rate established* under section 6621 on the amount of the tax benefit arising from the application of this subsection with respect to such combustor shall be due and payable for the period during which such tax benefit was available to the taxpayer and ending on the date referred to in paragraph(1)(B).

* * * * * * * * * * *

[For official explanation, see Committee Reports, ¶3870; 4075; 4143.]

≫**P-H CAUTION→** There are two versions of Sec. 168. Sec. 168, generally effective after 12-31-86, follows. For Sec. 168, generally effective before 1-1-87, see ¶2935-A, below.

【¶2935】 CODE SEC. 168. ACCELERATED COST RECOVERY SYSTEM.

(a) General Rule.—Except as otherwise provided in this section, the depreciation deduction provided by section 167(a) for any tangible property shall be determined by using—

(1) the applicable depreciation method,
(2) the applicable recovery period, and
(3) the applicable convention.

(b) Applicable Depreciation Method.—For purposes of this section—

(1) In general.—Except as provided in paragraphs (2) and (3), the applicable depreciation method is—

(A) the 200 percent declining balance method,

(B) switching to the straight line method for the 1st taxable year for which using the straight line method with respect to the adjusted basis as of the beginning of such year will yield a larger allowance.

(2) 15-year and 20-year property.—In the case of 15-year and 20-year property, paragraph (1) shall be applied by substituting "150 percent" for "200 percent."

(3) Property to which straight line method applies.—The applicable depreciation method shall be the straight line method in the case of the following property:

(A) Nonresidential real property.
(B) Residential rental property.
(C) Property with respect to which the taxpayer elects under paragraph (5) to have the provisions of this paragraph apply.

(4) Salvage value treated as zero.—Salvage value shall be treated as zero.

(5) Election.—An election under paragraph (3)(C) may be made with respect to 1 or more classes of property for any taxable year and once made with respect to any class shall apply to all property in such class placed in service during such taxable year. Such an election, once made, shall be irrevocable.

(c) Applicable Recovery Period.—For purposes of this section, the applicable recovery period shall be determined in accordance with the following table:

In the case of:	The applicable recovery period is:
3-year property	3 years
5-year property	5 years
7-year property	7 years
10-year property	10 years
15-year property	15 years
20-year property	20 years
Residential rental property	27.5 years
Nonresidential real property	31.5 years

(d)   Applicable Convention.—For purposes of this section—

(1)   **In general.**—Except as otherwise provided in this subsection, the applicable convention is the half-year convention.

(2)   **Real property.**—In the case of—

(A)   nonresidential real property, and

(B)   residential rental property,

the applicable convention is the mid-month convention.

(3)   **Special rule where substantial property placed in service during last 3 months of taxable year.**—

(A)   In general.—Except as provided in regulations, if during any taxable year—

(i)   the aggregate bases of property to which this section applies and which are placed in service during the last 3 months of the taxable year, exceed

(ii)   **40** percent of the aggregate bases of property to which this section applies placed in service during such taxable year,

the applicable convention for all property to which this section applies placed in service during such taxable year shall be the mid-quarter convention.

(B)   Certain real property not taken into account.—For purposes of subparagraph (A), nonresidential real property and residential rental property shall not be taken into account.

(4)   **Definitions.**—

(A)   Half-year convention.—The half-year convention is a convention which treats all property placed in service during any taxable year (or disposed of during any taxable year) as placed in service (or disposed of) on the mid-point of such taxable year.

(B)   Mid-month convention.—The mid-month convention is a convention which treats all property placed in service during any month (or disposed of during any month) as placed in service (or disposed of) on the midpoint of such month.

(C)   Mid-quarter convention.—The mid-quarter convention is a convention which treats all property placed in service during any quarter of a taxable year (or disposed of during any quarter of a taxable year) as placed in service (or disposed of) on the mid-point of such quarter.

(e)   Classification of Property.—For purposes of this section—

(1)   **In general.**—Except as otherwise provided in this subsection, property shall be classified under the following table:

Property shall be treated as:	If such property has a class life (in years) of:
3-year property	4 or less
5-year property	More than 4 but less than 10
7-year property	10 or more but less than 16
10-year property	16 or more but less than 20
15-year property	20 or more but less than 25
20-year property	25 or more.

(2)   **Residential rental or nonresidential real property.**—

(A)   Residential rental property.—The term "residential rental property" has the meaning given such term by section 167(j)(2)(B).

(B)   Nonresidential real property.—The term "nonresidential real property" means section 1250 property which is not—

(i)   residential rental property, or

(ii)   property with a class life of less than 27.5 years.

(3)   **Classification of certain property.**—

(A)   3-year property.—The term "3-year property" includes—

(i) any race horse which is more than 2 years old at the time it is placed in service, and

(ii) any horse other than a race horse which is more than 12 years old at the time it is placed in service.

(B) 5-year property.—The term "5-year property" includes—
(i) any automobile or light general purpose truck,
(ii) any semi-conductor manufacturing equipment,
(iii) any computer-based telephone central office switching equipment,
(iv) any qualified technological equipment,
(v) any property used in connection with research and experimentation, and
(vi) any property which—
(I) is described in paragraph (3)(A)(viii), (3)(A)(ix), or (4) of section 48(l), or
(II) is described in paragraph (15) of section 48(l) and is a qualifying small power production facility within the meaning of section 3(17)(C) of the Federal Power Act (16 U.S.C. 796(17)(C)), as in effect on September 1, 1986.

(C) 7-year property.—The term "7-year property" includes—
(i) any railroad track,
(ii) any single-purpose agricultural or horticultural structure (within the meaning of section 48(p)), and
(iii) any property which—
(I) does not have a class life, and
(II) is not otherwise classified under paragraph (2) or this paragraph.

(D) 15-year property.—The term "15-year property" includes—
(i) any municipal wastewater treatment plant, and
(ii) any telephone distribution plant and comparable equipment used for 2-way exchange of voice and data communications.

(E) 20-year property.—The term "20-year property" includes any municipal sewers.

(f) **Property To Which Section Does Not Apply.**—This section shall not apply to —

(1) **Certain methods of depreciation.**—Any property if—
(A) the taxpayer elects to exclude such property from the application of this section, and
(B) for the 1st taxable year for which a depreciation deduction would be allowable with respect to such property in the hands of the taxpayer, the property is properly depreciated under the unit-of-production method or any method of depreciation not expressed in a term of years (other than the retirement-replacement-betterment method or similar method).

(2) **Certain public utility property.**—Any public utility property (within the meaning of section 167(l)(3)(A)) if the taxpayer does not use a normalization method of accounting.

(3) **Films and video tape.**—Any motion picture film or video tape.

(4) **Sound recordings.**—Any sound recording described in section 48(r)(5).

(5) **Certain property placed in service in churning transactions.—**
(A) In general.—Property—
(i) described in paragraph (4) of section 168(e) (as in effect before the amendments made by the Tax Reform Act of 1986), or
(ii) which would be described in such paragraph if such paragraph were applied by substituting "1987" for "1981" and "1986" for "1980" each place such terms appear.
(B) Subparagraph (A)(II) not to apply.—Clause (ii) of subparagraph (A) shall not apply to—
(i) any residential rental property or nonresidential real property, or
(ii) any property if, for the 1st full taxable year in which such property is placed in service—
(I) the amount allowable as a deduction under this section (as in effect before the date of the enactment of this paragraph) with respect to such property is greater than

(II)   the amount allowable as a deduction under this section (as in effect on or after such date and using the half-year convention) for such taxable year.

(g)   **Alternative Depreciation System for Certain Property.—**

(1)   **In general.—**In the case of —

(A)   any tangible property which during the taxable year is used predominantly outside the United States,

(B)   any tax-exempt use property,

(C)   any tax-exempt bond financed property,

(D)   any imported property covered by an Executive order under paragraph (6), and

(E)   any property to which an election under paragraph (7) applies,

the depreciation deduction provided by section 167(a) shall be determined under the alternative depreciation system.

(2)   **Alternative depreciation system.—**For purposes of paragraph (1), the alternative depreciationn system is depreciation determined by using—

(A)   the straight line method (without regard to salvage value),

(B)   the applicable convention determined under subsection (d), and

(C)   a recovery period determined under the following table:

In the case of:	The recovery period shall be:
(i) Property not described in clause (ii) or (iii)	The class life.
(ii) Personal property with no class life	12 years.
(iii) Nonresidential real and residential rental property	40 years.

(3)   **Special rules for determining class life.—**

(A)   Tax-exempt use property subject to lease.—In the case of any tax-exempt use property subject to a lease, the recovery period used for purposes of paragraph (2) shall in no event be less than 125 percent of the lease term.

(B)   Special rule for certain property assigned to classes.—For purposes of paragraph (2), in the case of property described in any of the following subparagraphs of subsection (e)(3), the class life shall be determined as follows:

If property is described in subparagraph:	The class life is:
(B)(ii)	5
(B)(iii)	9.5
(C)(i)	10
(C)(ii)	15
(D)(i)	24
(D)(ii)	24
(E)	50.

(C)   Qualified technological equipment.—In the case of any qualified technological equipment, the recovery period used for purposes of paragraph (2) shall be 5 years.

(D)   Automobiles, etc.—In the case of any automobile or light general purpose truck, the recovery period used for purposes of paragraph (2) shall be 5 years.

(E)   Certain real property.—In the case of any section 1245 property which is real property with no class life, the recovery period used for purposes of paragraph (2) shall be 40 years.

(4)   **Property used predominantly outside the United States.—**For purposes of this subsection, rules similar to the rules under section 48 (a)(2) (including the exceptions contained in subparagraph (B) thereof) shall apply in determining whether property is used predominantly outside the United States. In addition to the exceptions contained in such subparagraph (B), there shall be excepted any satellite or other spacecraft (or any interest therein) held by a United States person if such satellite or spacecraft was launched from within the United States.

(5)   **Tax-exempt bond financed property.—**For purposes of this subsection—

(A)   In general.—Except as otherwise provided in this paragraph, the term "tax-exempt bond financed property" means any property to the extent such property is financed (directly or indirectly) by an obligation the interest on which is exempt from tax under section 103(a).

(B)   Allocation of bond proceeds.—For purposes of subparagraph (A), the proceeds of any obligation shall be treated as used to finance property acquired in connection with the issuance of such obligation in the order in which such property is placed in service.

(C) Qualified residential rental projects.—The term "tax-exempt bond financed property" shall not include any qualified residential rental project (within the meaning of section 142(a)(7)).

(6) Imported property.—

(A) Countries maintaining trade restrictions or engaging in discriminatory acts.—If the President determines that a foreign country—

(i) maintains nontariff trade restrictions, including variable import fees, which substantially burden United States commerce in a manner inconsistent with provisions of trade agreements, or

(ii) engages in discriminatory or other acts (including tolerance of international cartels) or policies unjustifiably restricting United States commerce,

the President may by Executive order provide for the application of paragraph (1)(D) to any article or class of articles manufactured or produced in such foreign country for such period as may be provided by such Executive order. Any period specified in the preceding sentence shall not apply to any property ordered before (or the construction, reconstruction, or erection of which began before) the date of the Executive order unless the President determines an earlier date to be in the public interest and specifies such date in the Executive order.

(B) Imported property.—For purposes of this subsection, the term "imported property" means any property if—

(i) such property was completed outside the United States, or

(ii) less than 50 percent of the basis of such property is attributable to value added within the United States.

For purposes of this subparagraph, the term "United States" includes the Commonwealth of Puerto Rico and the possessions of the United States.

(7) Election to use alternative depreciation system.—

(A) In general.—If the taxpayer makes an election under this paragraph with respect to any class of property for any taxable year, the alternative depreciation system under this subsection shall apply to all property in such class placed in service during such taxable year. Notwithstanding the preceding sentence, in the case of nonresidential real property or residential rental property, such election may be made separately with respect to each property.

(B) Election irrevocable.—An election under subparagraph (A), once made, shall be irrevocable.

(h) Tax-Exempt Use Property.—

(1) In general.—For purposes of this section—

(A) Property other than nonresidential real property.—Except as otherwise provided in this subsection, the term "tax-exempt use property" means that portion of any tangible property (other than nonresidential real property) leased to a tax-exempt entity.

(B) Nonresidential real property.—

(i) In general.—In the case of nonresidential real property, the term "tax-exempt use property" means that portion of the property leased to a tax-exempt entity in a disqualified lease.

(ii) Disqualified lease.—For purposes of this subparagraph, the term "disqualified lease" means any lease of the property to a tax-exempt entity, but only if—

(I) part or all of the property was financed (directly or indirectly) by an obligation the interest on which is exempt from tax under section 103(a) and such entity (or a related entity) participated in such financing.

(II) under such lease there is a fixed or determinable price purchase or sale option which involves such entity (or a related entity) or there is the equivalent of such an option.

(III) such lease has a lease term in excess of 20 years, or

(IV) such lease occurs after a sale (or other transfer) of the property by, or lease of the property from, such entity (or a related entity) and such property has been used by such entity (or a related entity) before such sale (or other transfer) or lease.

Code §168(h)(1) ¶2935

(iii) 35-percent threshold test.—Clause (i) shall apply to any property only if the portion of such property leased to tax-exempt entities in disqualified leases is more than 35 percent of the property.

(iv) Treatment of improvements.—For purposes of this subparagraph, improvements to a property (other than land) shall not be treated as a separate property.

(v) Leasebacks during 1st 3 months of use not taken into account.—Subclause (IV) of clause (ii) shall not apply to any property which is leased within 3 months after the date such property is first used by the tax-exempt entity (or a related entity).

(C) Exception for short-term leases.—

(i) In general.—Property shall not be treated as tax-exempt use property merely by reason of a short-term lease.

(ii) Short-term lease.—For purposes of clause (i), the term "short-term lease" means any lease the term of which is—

(I) less than 3 years, and

(II) less than the greater of 1 year or 30 percent of the property's present class life.

In the case of nonresidential real property and property with no present class life, subclause (II) shall not apply.

(D) Exception where property used in unrelated trade or business.—The term "tax-exempt use property" shall not include any portion of a property if such portion is predominantly used by the tax-exempt entity (directly or through a partnership of which such entity is a partner) in an unrelated trade or business the income of which is subject to tax under section 511. For purposes of subparagraph (B)(iii), any portion of a property so used shall not be treated as leased to a tax-exempt entity in a disqualified lease.

(E) Nonresidential real property defined.—For purposes of this paragraph, the term "nonresidential real property" includes residential rental property.

(2) **Tax-exempt entity.**—

(A) In general.—For purposes of this subsection, the term "tax-exempt entity" means—

(i) the United States, any State or political subdivision thereof, any possession of the United States, or any agency or instrumentality of any of the foregoing,

(ii) an organization (other than a cooperative described in section 521) which is exempt from tax imposed by this chapter, and

(iii) any foreign person or entity.

(B) Exceptions for certain property subject to United States tax and used by foreign person or entity.—

(i) Income from property subject to United States tax.—Clause (iii) of subparagraph (A) shall not apply with respect to any property if more than 50 percent of the gross income for the taxable year derived by the foreign person or entity from the use of such property is—

(I) subject to tax under this chapter, or

(II) included under section 951 in the gross income of a United States shareholder for the taxable year with or within which ends the taxable year of the controlled foreign corporation in which such income was derived.

For purposes of the preceding sentence, any exclusion or exemption shall not apply for purposes of determining the amount of the gross income so derived, but shall apply for purposes of determining the portion of such gross income subject to tax under this chapter.

(ii) Movies and sound recordings.—Clause (iii) of subparagraph (A) shall not apply with respect to any qualified film (as defined in section 48(k)(1)(B)) or any sound recording (as defined in section 48(r)(5)).

(C) Foreign person or entity.—For purposes of this paragraph, the term "foreign person or entity" means—

(i) any foreign government, any international organization, or any agency or instrumentality of any of the foregoing, and

(ii) any person who is not a United States person.

Such term does not include any foreign partnership or other foreign pass-thru entity.

(D) Treatment of certain taxable instrumentalities.—For purposes of this subsection, a corporation shall not be treated as an instrumentality of the United States or of any State or political subdivision thereof if—

(i) all of the activities of such corporation are subject to tax under this chapter, and

(ii) a majority of the board of directors of such corporation is not selected by the United States or any State or political subdivision thereof.

(E) Certain previously tax-exempt organizations.—

(i) In general.—For purposes of this subsection, an organization shall be treated as an organization described in subparagraph (A)(ii) with respect to any property (other than property held by such organization) if such organization was an organization (other than a cooperative described in section 521) exempt from tax imposed by this chapter at any time during the 5-year period ending on the date such property was first used by such organization. The preceding sentence and subparagraph (D)(ii) shall not apply to the Federal Home Loan Mortgage Corporation.

(ii) Election not to have clause (I) apply.—

(I) In general.—In the case of an organization formerly exempt from tax under section 501(a) as an organization described in section 501(c)(12), clause (i) shall not apply to such organization with respect to any property if such organization elects not to be exempt from tax under section 501(a) during the tax-exempt use period with respect to such property.

(II) Tax-exempt use period.—For purposes of subclause (I), the term "tax-exempt use period" means the period beginning with the taxable year in which the property described in subclause (I) is first used by the organization and ending with the close of the 15th taxable year following the last taxable year of the applicable recovery period of such property.

(III) Election.—Any election under subclause (I), once made, shall be irrevocable.

(iii) Treatment of successor organizations.—Any organization which is engaged in activities substantially similar to those engaged in by a predecessor organization shall succeed to the treatment under this subparagraph of such predecessor organization.

(iv) First used.—For purposes of this subparagraph, property shall be treated as first used by the organization—

(I) when the property is first placed in service under a lease to such organization, or

(II) in the case of property leased to (or held by) a partnership (or other pass-thru entity) in which the organization is a member, the later of when such property is first used by such partnership or pass-thru entity or when such organization is first a member of such partnership or pass-thru entity.

(3) Special rules for certain high technology equipment.—

(A) Exemption where lease term is 5 years or less.—For purposes of this section, the term "tax-exempt use property" shall not include any qualified technological equipment if the lease to the tax-exempt entity has a lease term of 5 years or less.

(B) Exception for certain property.—

(i) In general.—For purposes of subparagraph (A), the term "qualified technological equipment" shall not include any property leased to a tax-exempt entity if—

(I) part or all of the property was financed (directly or indirectly) by an obligation the interest on which is exempt from tax under section 103(a),

(II) such lease occurs after a sale (or other transfer) of the property by, or lease of such property from, such entity (or related entity) and such property has been used by such entity (or a related entity) before such sale (or other transfer) or lease, or

(III) such tax-exempt entity is the United States or any agency or instrumentality of the United States.

(ii) Leasebacks during 1st 3 months of use not taken into account.—Subclause (II) of clause (i) shall not apply to any property which is leased within 3 months after the date such property is first used by the tax-exempt entity (or a related entity).

(4) **Related entities.**—For purposes of this subsection—

(A)(i) Each governmental unit and each agency or instrumentality of a governmental unit is related to each other such unit, agency, or instrumentality which directly or indirectly derives its powers, rights, and duties in whole or in part from the same sovereign authority.

(ii) For purposes of clause (i), the United States, each State, and each possession of the United States shall be treated as a separate sovereign authority.

(B) Any entity not described in subparagraph (A)(i) is related to any other entity if the 2 entities have—

(i) significant common purposes and substantial common membership, or

(ii) directly or indirectly substantial common direction or control.

(C)(i) An entity is related to another entity if either entity owns (directly or through 1 or more entities) a 50 percent or greater interest in the capital or profits of the other entity.

(ii) For purposes of clause (i), entities treated as related under subparagraph (A) or (B) shall be treated as 1 entity.

(D) An entity is related to another entity with respect to a transaction if such transaction is part of an attempt by such entities to avoid the application of this subsection.

(5) **Tax-exempt use of property leased to partnerships, etc., determined at partner level.**—For purposes of this subsection—

(A) **In general.**—In the case of any property which is leased to a partnership, the determination of whether any portion of such property is tax-exempt use property shall be made by treating each tax-exempt entity partner's proportionate share (determined under paragraph (6)(C)) of such property as being leased to such partner.

(B) **Other pass-thru entities; tiered entities.**—Rules similar to the rules of subparagraph (A) shall also apply in the case of any pass-thru entity other than a partnership and in the case of tiered partnerships and other entities.

(C) **Presumption with respect to foreign entities.**—Unless it is otherwise established to the satisfaction of the Secretary, it shall be presumed that the partners of a foreign partnership (and the beneficiaries of any other foreign pass-thru entity) are persons who are not United States persons.

(6) **Treatment of property owned by partnerships, etc.—**

(A) **In general.**—For purposes of this subsection, if—

(i) any property which (but for this subparagraph) is not tax-exempt use property is owned by a partnership which has both a tax-exempt entity and a person who is not a tax-exempt entity as partners, and

(ii) any allocation to the tax-exempt entity of partnership items is not a qualified allocation,

an amount equal to such tax-exempt entity's proportionate share of such property shall (except as provided in paragraph (1)(D)) be treated as tax-exempt use property.

(B) **Qualified allocation.**—For purposes of subparagraph (A), the term "qualified allocation" means any allocation to a tax-exempt entity which—

(i) is consistent with such entity's being allocated the same distributive share of each item of income, gain, loss, deduction, credit, and basis and such share remains the same during the entire period the entity is a partner in the partnership, and

(ii) has substantial economic effect within the meaning of section 704(b)(2).

For purposes of this subparagraph, items allocated under section 704(c) shall not be taken into account.

(C) **Determination of proportionate share.—**

(i) **In general.**—For purposes of subparagraph (A), a tax-exempt entity's proportionate share of any property owned by a partnership shall be determined on the basis of such entity's share of partnership items of income or gain (excluding gain allocated under section 704(c)), whichever results in the largest proportionate share.

(ii) **Determination where allocations vary.**—For purposes of clause (i), if a tax-exempt entity's share of partnership items of income or gain (excluding gain allocated under section 704(c)) may vary during the period such entity is a partner in the partnership, such share shall be the highest share such entity may receive.

(D) Determination of whether property used in unrelated trade or business.—For purposes of this subsection, in the case of any property which is owned by a partnership which has both a tax-exempt entity and a person who is not a tax-exempt entity as partners, the determination of whether such property is used in an unrelated trade or business of such an entity shall be made without regard to section 514.

(E) Other pass-thru entities; tiered entities.—Rules similar to the rules of subparagraphs (A), (B), (C), and (D) shall also apply in the case of any pass-thru entity other than a partnership and in the case of tiered partnerships and other entities.

(F) Treatment of certain taxable entities.—

(i) In general.—For purposes of this paragraph and paragraph (5), except as otherwise provided in this subparagraph, any tax-exempt controlled entity shall be treated as a tax-exempt entity.

(ii) Election.—If a tax-exempt controlled entity makes an election under this clause—

(I) such entity shall not be treated as a tax-exempt entity for purposes of this paragraph and paragraph (5), and

(II) any gain recognized by a tax-exempt entity on any disposition of an interest in such entity (and any dividend or interest received or accrued by a tax-exempt entity from such tax-exempt controlled entity) shall be treated as unrelated business taxable income for purposes of section 511.

Any such election shall be irrevocable and shall bind all tax-exempt entities holding interests in such tax-exempt controlled entity. For purposes of subclause (II), there shall only be taken into account dividends which are properly allocable to income of the tax-exempt controlled entity which was not subject to tax under this chapter.

(iii) Tax-exempt controlled entity.—

(I) General.—The term "tax-exempt controlled entity" means any corporation (which is not a tax-exempt entity determined without regard to this subparagraph and paragraph (2)(E)) if 50 percent or more (in value) of the stock in such corporation is held by 1 or more tax-exempt entities (other than a foreign person or entity).

(II) Only 5-percent shareholders taken into account in case of publicly traded stock.—For purposes of subclause (I), in the case of a corporation the stock of which is publicly traded on an established securities market, stock held by a tax-exempt entity shall not be taken into account unless such entity holds at least 5 percent (in value) of the stock in such corporation. For purposes of this subclause, related entities (within the meaning of paragraph (4)) shall be treated as 1 entity.

(III) Section 318 to apply.—For purposes of this clause, a tax-exempt entity shall be treated as holding stock which it holds through application of section 318 (determined without regard to the 50-percent limitation contained in subsection (a)(2)(C) thereof).

(G) Regulations—For purposes of determining whether there is a qualified allocation under subparagraph (B), the regulations prescribed under paragraph (8) for purposes of this paragraph—

(i) shall set forth the proper treatment for partnership guaranteed payments, and

(ii) may provide for the exclusion or segregation of items.

(7) **Lease**—For purposes of this subsection, the term "lease" includes any grant of a right to use property.

(8) **Regulations.**—The Secretary shall prescribe such regulations as may be necessary or appropriate to carry out the purposes of this subsection.

(i) **Definitions and Special Rules.**—For purposes of this section—

(1) **Class life.**—

(A) In general.—Except as provided in this section, the term "class life" means the class life (if any) which would be applicable with respect to any property as of January 1, 1986, under subsection (m) of section 167 (determined without regard to paragraph (4) thereof and as if the taxpayer had made an election under such subsection).

(B) Secretarial Authority.—The Secretary, through an office established in the Treasury—

(i) shall monitor and analyze actual experience with respect to all depreciable assets, and

(ii) except in the case of residential rental property or nonresidential real property—

(I) may prescribe a new class life for any property,

(II) in the case of assigned property, may modify any assigned item, or

(III) may prescribe a class life for any property which does not have a class life within the meaning of subparagraph (A).

Any class life or assigned item prescribed or modified under the preceding sentence shall reasonably reflect the anticipated useful life, and the anticipated decline in value over time, of the property to the industry or other group.

(C) Effect of modification.—Any class life or assigned item with respect to any property prescribed or modified under subparagraph (B) shall be used in classifying such property under subsection (e) and in applying subsection (g).

(D) No modification of assigned property before January 1, 1992.—

(i) In general.—Except as otherwise provided in this subparagraph, the Secretary may not modify an assigned item under subparagraph (B)(ii)(II) for any assigned property which is placed in service before January 1, 1992.

(ii) Exception for shorter class life.—In the case of assigned property which is placed in service before January 1, 1992, and for which the assigned item reflects a class life which is shorter than the class life under subparagraph (A), the Secretary may modify such assigned item under subparagraph (B)(ii)(II) if such modification results in an item which reflects a shorter class life than such assigned item.

(E) Assigned property and item.—For purposes of this paragraph—

(i) Assigned property.—The term "assigned property" means property for which a class life, classification, or recovery period is assigned under subsection (e)(3) or subparagraph (B), (C), or (D) of subsection (g)(3).

(ii) Assigned item.—The term "assigned item" means the class life, classification, or recovery period assigned under subsection (e)(3) or subparagraph (B), (C), or (D) of subsection (g)(3).

(2) **Qualified technological equipment.—**

(A) In general.—The term "qualified technological equipment" means—

(i) any computer or peripheral equipment,

(ii) any high technology telephone station equipment installed on the customer's premises, and

(iii) any high technology medical equipment.

(B) Computer or peripheral equipment defined.—For purposes of this paragraph—

(i) In general.—The term "computer or peripheral equipment" means—

(I) any computer, and

(II) any related peripheral equipment.

(ii) Computer.—The term "computer" means a programmable electronically activated device which—

(I) is capable of accepting information, applying prescribed processes to the information, and supplying the results of these processes with or without human intervention, and

(II) consists of a central processing unit containing extensive storage, logic, arithmetic, and control capabilities.

(iii) Related peripheral equipment.—The term "related peripheral equipment" means any auxiliary machine (whether on-line or off-line) which is designed to be placed under the control of the central processing unit of a computer.

(iv) Exceptions.—The term "computer or peripheral equipment" shall not include—

(I) any equipment which is an integral part of other property which is not a computer,

(II) typewriters, calculators, adding and accounting machines, copiers, duplicating equipment, and similar equipment, and

(III) equipment of a kind used primarily for amusement or entertainment of the user.

(C) High technology medical equipment.—For purposes of this paragraph, the term "high technology medical equipment" means any electronic, electromechanical, or computer-based high technology equipment used in the screening, monitoring, observation, diagnosis, or treatment of patients in a laboratory, medical, or hospital environment.

(3) Lease term.—

(A) In general.—In determining a lease term—

(i) there shall be taken into account options to renew, and

(ii) 2 or more successive leases which are part of the same transaction (or a series of related transactions) with respect to the same or substantially similar property shall be treated as 1 lease.

(B) Special rule for fair rental options on nonresidential real property or residential rental property.—For purposes of clause (i) of subparagraph (A), in the case of nonresidential real property or residential rental property, there shall not be taken into account any option to renew at fair market value, determined at the time of renewal.

(4) General asset accounts.—Under regulations, a taxpayer may maintain 1 or more general asset accounts for any property to which this section applies. Except as provided in regulations, all proceeds realized on any disposition of property in a general asset account shall be included in income as ordinary income.

(5) Changes in use.—The Secretary shall, by regulations, provide for the method of determining the deduction allowable under section 167(a) with respect to any tangible property for any taxable year (and the succeeding taxable years) during which such property changes status under this section but continues to be held by the same person.

(6) Treatments of additions or improvements to property.—In the case of any addition to (or improvement of) any property—

(A) any deduction under subsection (a) for such addition or improvement shall be computed in the same manner as the deduction for such property would be computed if such property had been placed in service at the same time as such addition or improvement, and

(B) the applicable recovery period for such addition or improvement shall begin on the later of—

(i) the date on which such addition (or improvement) is placed in service, or

(ii) the date on which the property with respect to which such addition (or improvement) was made is placed in service.

(7) Treatment of certain transferees.—

(A) In general.—In the case of any property transferred in a transaction described in subparagraph (B), the transferee shall be treated as the transferor for purposes of computing the depreciation deduction determined under this section with respect to so much of the basis in the hands of the transferee as does not exceed the adjusted basis in the hands of the transferor.

(B) Transactions covered.—The transactions described in this subparagraph are any transaction described in section 332, 351, 361, 371(a), 374(a), 721, or 731. Subparagraph (A) shall not apply in the case of a termination of a partnership under section 708(b)(1)(B).

(C) Property reacquired by the taxpayer.—Under regulations, property which is disposed of and then reacquired by the taxpayer shall be treated for purposes of computing the deduction allowable under subsection (a) as if such property had not been disposed of.

(D) Exception.—This paragraph shall not apply to any transaction to which subsection (f)(5) applies (relating to churning transactions).

(8) Treatment of leasehold improvements.—In the case of any building erected (or improvements made) on leased property, if such building or improvement is property to which this section applies, the depreciation deduction shall be determined under the provisions of this section.

(9) Normalization rules.—

(A) In general.—In order to use a normalization method of accounting with respect to any public utility property for purposes of subsection (f)(2)—

(i) the taxpayer must, in computing its tax expense for purposes of establishing its cost of service for rate-making purposes and reflecting operating results in its regulated books of account, use a method of depreciation with respect to such property that is the same as, and a depreciation period for such property that is no shorter than, the method and period used to compute its depreciation expense for such purposes; and

(ii) if the amount allowable as a deduction under this section with respect to such property differs from the amount that would be allowable as a deduction under section 167 (determined without regard to section 167(l)) using the method (including the period, first and last year convention, and salvage value) used to compute regulated tax expense under clause (i), the taxpayer must make adjustments to a reserve to reflect the deferral of taxes resulting from such difference.

(B) Use of inconsistent estimates and projections, etc.—

(i) In general.—One way in which the requirements of subparagraph (A) are not met is if the taxpayer, for ratemaking purposes, uses a procedure or adjustment which is inconsistent with the requirements of subparagraph (A).

(ii) Use of inconsistent estimates and projections.—The procedures and adjustments which are to be treated as inconsistent for purposes of clause (i) shall include any procedure or adjustment for ratemaking purposes which uses an estimate or projection of the taxpayer's tax expense, depreciation expense, or reserve for deferred taxes under subparagraph (A)(ii) unless such estimate or projection is also used, for ratemaking purposes, with respect to the other 2 such items and with respect to the rate base.

(iii) Regulatory authority.—The Secretary may by regulations prescribe procedures and adjustments (in addition to those specified in clause (ii)) which are to be treated as inconsistent for purposes of clause (i).

(C) Public utility property which does not meet normalization rules.—In the case of any public utility property to which this section does not apply by reason of subsection (f)(2), the allowance for depreciation under section 167(a) shall be an amount computed using the method and period referred to in subparagraph (A)(i).

(10) Public utility property.—The term "public utility property" has the meaning given such term by section 167(l)(3)(A).

(11) Research and experimentation.—The term "research and experimentation" has the same meaning as the term research and experimental has under section 174.

(12) Section 1245 and 1250 property.—The terms "section 1245 property" and "section 1250 property" have the meanings given such terms by sections 1245(a)(3) and 1250(c), respectively.

[For official explanation, see Committee Reports, ¶3870.]

≫**P-H CAUTION→** There are two versions of Sec. 168. Sec. 168, generally effective before 1-1-87, follows. For Sec. 168, generally effective after 12-31-86, see ¶2935, above.

[¶2935-A] CODE SEC. 168. ACCELERATED COST RECOVERY SYSTEM.

(a) Allowance of Deduction.—There shall be allowed as a deduction for any taxable year the amount determined under this section with respect to recovery property.

(b) Amount of Deduction.—

*   *   *   *   *   *   *   *   *   *   *

(2) 19-year real property.—

(A) In general.—In the case of 19-year real property, the applicable percentage shall be determined in accordance with a table prescribed by the Secretary. In prescribing such table, the Secretary shall—

(i) assign to the property a 19-year recovery period, and

(ii) assign percentages generally determined in accordance with use of the 175 percent declining balance method, switching to the method described in section 167(b)(1) at a time to maximize the deduction allowable under subsection (a).[1]

[2](B) *Mid-month convention for 19-year real property.—In the case of 19-year real*

---

property, the amount of the deduction determined under any provision of this section (or for purposes of section 57(a)(12)(B) or 312(k)) for any taxable year shall be determined on the basis of the number of months (using a mid-month convention) in which the property is in service.

(3) Election of different recovery percentage.—

(A) In general.—Except as provided in subsection (f)(2), in lieu of any applicable percentage under paragraph (1), (2), or (4), the taxpayer may elect, with respect to one or more classes of recovery property placed in service during the taxable year, the applicable percentage determined by use of the straight line method over the recovery period elected by the taxpayer in accordance with the following table:

In the case of:	The taxpayer may elect a recovery period of:
3-year property	3, 5, or 12 years.
5-year property	5, 12, or 25 years.
10-year property	10, 25, or 35 years.
19-year real property [3]	19, 35, or 45 years.
15-year public utility property	15, 35, or 45 years.
Low-income housing	*15, 35, or 45 years.*

* * * * * * * * * * * *

(4) Low-income housing.—

(A) In general.—In the case of low-income housing, the applicable percentage shall be determined in accordance with the table prescribed in paragraph (2) (without regard to the mid-month convention), except that in prescribing such table, the Secretary shall—

    (i) assign to the property a 15-year recovery period, and

    (ii) assign percentages generally determined in accordance with use of the 200 percent declining balance method, switching to the method described in section 167(b)(1) at a time to maximize the deduction allowable under subsection (a).

[4]*(B) Monthly convention.—In the case of low-income housing, the amount of the deduction determined under any provision of this section (or for purposes of section 57(a)(12)(B) or 312(k)) for any taxable year shall be determined on the basis of the number of months (treating all property placed in service or disposed of during any month as placed in service or disposed of on the first day of such month) in which the property is in service.*

* * * * * * * * * * * *

(f) Special Rules for Application of This Section.—For purposes of this section—

* * * * * * * * * * * *

(2) Recovery property used predominantly outside the United States.—

(A) In general.—Except as provided in subparagraphs (B) and (C), in the case of recovery property which, during the taxable year, is used predominantly outside the United States, the recovery deduction for the taxable year shall be, in lieu of the amount determined under subsection (b), the amount determined by applying to the unadjusted basis of such property the applicable percentage determined under tables prescribed by the Secretary. For purposes of the preceding sentence, in prescribing such tables, the Secretary shall—

    (i) assign the property described in this subparagraph to classes in accordance with the present class life (or 12 year in the case of personal property with no present class life) of such property; and

    (ii) assign percentages (taking into account the half-year convention) determined in accordance with use of the method of depreciation described in section

---

[Footnote ¶2935-A continued]

tion allowable under subsection (a) for the taxable year in which the disposition occurs shall reflect only the months (using a mid-month convention) during such year the property was in service."

(3) "and low income housing"

(4) "(B) Special rule for year of disposition.—In the case of a disposition of low-income housing, the deduction allowable under subsection (a) for the taxable year in which the disposition occurs shall reflect only the months during such year the property was placed in service."

167(b)(2), switching to the method described in section 167(b)(1) at a time to maximize the deduction allowable under subsection (a).

[5]*(B) Real property.—Except as provided in subparagraph (C), in the case of 19-year real property or low-income housing which, during the taxable year, is predominantly used outside the United States, the recovery deduction for the taxable year shall be, in lieu of the amount determined under subsection (b), the amount determined by applying to the unadjusted basis of such property the applicable percentage determined under tables prescribed by the Secretary. For purposes of the preceding sentence, in prescribing such tables, the Secretary shall—*

(i) assign to the property described in this subparagraph a 35-year recovery period, and

(ii) assign percentages determined in accordance with the use of the method of depreciation described in section 167(j)(1)(B), switching to the method described in section 167(b)(1) at a time to maximize the deduction allowable under subsection (a).

* * * * * * * * * * *

(10) Transferee bound by transferor's period and method in certain cases.—

(A) In general.—In the case of recovery property transferred in a transaction described in subparagraph (B), [6] for purposes of computing the deduction allowable under subsection (a) with respect to so much of the basis in the hands of the transferee as does not exceed the adjusted basis in the hands of the transferor—

(i) if the transaction is described in subparagraph (B)(i), the transferee shall be treated in the same manner as the transferor, or

---

[**Footnote ¶2935-A continued**]

(5) "(B) Real property.—

(i) In general.—Except as provided in subparagraph (C), in the case of 19-year real property or low-income housing which, during the taxable year, is predominantly used outside the United States, the recovery deduction for the taxable year shall be, in lieu of the amount determined under subsection (b), the amount determined by applying to the unadjusted basis of such property the applicable percentage determined under tables prescribed by the Secretary. For purposes of the preceding sentence in prescribing such tables, the Secretary shall—

(I) assign to the property described in this subparagraph a 35-year recovery period; and

(II) assign percentages (taking into account the next to the last sentence of subsection (b)(2)(A)) determined in accordance with use of the method of depreciation described in section 167(j)(1)(B), switching to the method described in section 167(b)(1) at a time to maximize the deduction allowable under subsection (a).

(ii) Special rule for disposition.—In the case of a disposition of 19-year real property or low-income housing described in clause (i), subsection (b)(2)(B) shall apply."

Effective date (Sec. 1881, '86 TRA and 111(g), '84 TRA).—(1) Generally applies with respect to property placed in service by the taxpayer after 3-15-84.

(2) Exception.—The amendments shall not apply to property placed in service by the taxpayer before 1-1-87, if—

(A) the taxpayer or a qualified person entered into a binding contract to purchase or construct such property before 3-16-84, or

(B) construction of such property was commenced by or for the taxpayer or a qualified person before 3-16-84. For purposes of this paragraph the term "qualified person" means any person who transfers his rights in such a contract or such property to the taxpayer, but only if the property is not placed in service by such person before such rights are transferred to the taxpayer.

(3) Special rules for application of paragraph (2).—

(A) Certain inventory.—In the case of any property which—

(i) is held by a person as property described in section 1221(1), and

(ii) is disposed of by such person before 1-1-85,

such person shall not, for purposes of paragraph (2), be treated as having placed such property in service before such property is disposed of merely because such person rented such property or held such property for rental. No deduction for depreciation or amortization shall be allowed to such person with respect to such property.

(B) Certain property financed by bonds.—In the case of any property with respect to which—

(i) bonds were issued to finance such property before 1984, and

(ii) An architectural contract was entered into before 3-16-84,

paragraph (2) shall be applied by substituting "May 2" for "March 16".

(4) Special rule for components.—For purposes of applying section 168(f)(1)(B) of the '54 Code (as amended by this section) to components placed in service after 12-31-86, property to which paragraph (2) applies shall be treated as placed in service by the taxpayer before 3-16-84.

(5) Special rule for mid-month convention.—In the case of the amendment made by subsection (d)—

(A) paragraph (1) shall be applied by substituting "June 22, 1984" for "March 15, 1984", and

(B) paragraph (2) shall be applied by substituting "June 23, 1984" for "March 16, 1984" each place it appears.

Matter in *italics* in Sec. 168(f)(10) added by section 1809(b)(1) and (2), '86 TRA, which struck out:

(6) "the transferee shall be treated as the transferor"

Effective date (Sec. 1809(b)(3), '86 TRA).—Applies to property placed in service by the transferee after 12-31-85, in taxable years ending after such date.

(ii) if the transaction is described in clause (ii) or (iii) of subparagraph (B) and the transferor made an election with respect to such property under subsection (b)(3) or (f)(2)(C), the transferee shall be treated as having made the same election (or its equivalent).

(B) Transfers covered.—The transactions described in this subparagraph are—

(i) a transaction described in section 332, 351, 361, 371(a), 374(a), 721, or 731;

(ii) an acquisition (other than described in clause (i)) from a related person (as defined in subparagraph (D) of subsection (e)(4)); and

(iii) an acquisition followed by a leaseback to the person from whom the property is acquired.

Clause (i) shall not apply in the case of the termination of a partnership under section 708(b)(1)(B).

* * * * * * * * * * *

(12) **Limitations on property financed with tax-exempt bonds.—**

(A) In general.—Notwithstanding any other provision of this section, to the extent that any property is financed by the proceeds of an industrial development bond (within the meaning of section 103(b)(2)) the interest of which is exempt from taxation under 103(a), the deduction allowed under subsection (a) (and any deduction allowable in lieu of the deduction allowable under subsection (a)) for any taxable year with respect to such property shall be determined under subparagraph (B).

(B) Recovery method.—

(i) In general.—Except as provided in clause (ii), the amount of the deduction allowed with respect to property described in subparagraph (A) shall be determined by using the straight-line method (with a half-year convention and without regard to salvage value) and a recovery period determined in accordance with the following table:

In the case of:	The recovery period is:
3-year property	3 years.
5-year property	5 years.
10-year property	10 years.
15-year public utility property	15 years.

(ii) 19-year real property.—In the case of 19-year real property, the amount of the deduction allowed shall be determined by using the straight-line method [7] (without regard to salvage value) and a recovery period of 19 years.

[8]*(C) Exception for low- and moderate-income housing.—Subparagraph (A) shall not apply to—*

(i) any low-income housing, and

(ii) any other recovery property which is placed in service in connection with projects for residential rental property financed by the proceeds of obligations described in section 103(b)(4)(A).

* * * * * * * * * * *

[9]*(14) **Motor vehicle operating leases.—***

* * * * * * * * * * *

[10]*(15) **Special rules for sound recordings.—***

[Footnote ¶2935-A continued]

Matter in *italics* in Sec. 168(f)(12)(B)(ii) and (C) added by section 1809(a)(4), '86 TRA, which struck out:

(7) "determined on the basis of the number of months in the year in which such property was in service and"

(8) "(C) Exception for projects for residential rental property.—Subparagraph (A) shall not apply to any recovery property which is placed in service in connection with projects for residential rental property financed by the proceeds of obligations described in section 103(b)(4)(A)."

Effective date (Sec. 1881, '86 TRA and Sec. 111(g)(1)—(5), '84 TRA).—Generally applies with respect to property placed in service by taxpayer after 3-15-84. For the exception and special rules, see above.

Matter in *italics* in Sec. 168(f)(14) and (15) added by section 1802(b)(1), which struck out:

(9) "(13)"

(10) "(14)"

Effective date (Sec. 1881, '86 TRA and section 32(c), '84 TRA, amended by section 1802(b)(2), '86 TRA).—Applies to agreements described in Sec. 168(f)(14) of the '54 Code (as added by subsection (a)) entered into more than 90 days after 7-18-84.

---

* * * * * * * * * * *

(j) Property Leased to Governments and Other Tax-Exempt Entities.—

* * * * * * * * * * * *

(2) Operating rules.—

(A) Recovery period must at least equal 125 percent of lease term.—In the case of any tax-exempt use property, the recovery period used for purposes of paragraph (1) shall not be less than 125 percent of the lease term.

(B) Conventions.—

(i) Property other than 19-year real property.—In the case of property other than 19-year real property, the half-year convention shall apply for purposes of paragraph (1).

(ii) [11]*Cross reference.—*

For other applicable conventions, see paragraphs (2)(B) and (4)(B) of subsection (b).

* * * * * * * * * * *

(3) Tax-exempt use property.—For purposes of this subsection—

* * * * * * * * * * * *

(D) Exception where property used in unrelated trade or business.—The term "tax-exempt use property" shall not include any portion of a property if such portion is predominantly used by the tax-exempt entity (directly or through a partnership of which such entity is a partner) in an unrelated trade or business the income of which is subject to tax under section 511. *For purposes of subparagraph (B)(iii), any portion of a property so used shall not be treated as leased to a tax-exempt entity in a disqualified lease.*

(4) Tax-exempt entity.—

* * * * * * * * * * *

(E) Certain previously tax-exempt organizations.—

(i) In general.—For purposes of this subsection and paragraph (4) of section 48(a), an organization shall be treated as an organization described in subparagraph (A)(ii) with respect to [12]*any property (other than property held by such organization)* if such organization was an organization (other than a cooperative described in section 521) exempt from tax imposed by this chapter at any time during the 5-year period ending on the date such property was [13]*first used by* such organization. The preceding sentence *and subparagraph (D)(ii)* shall not apply to the Federal Home Loan Mortgage Corporation.

(ii) Election not to have clause (i) apply.—

(I) In general.—In the case of an organization formerly exempt from tax under section 501(a) as an organization described in section 501(c)(12), clause (i) shall not apply to such organization with respect to any property [14] if such organization elects not to be exempt from tax under section 501(a) during the tax-exempt use period with respect to such property.

(II) Tax-exempt use period.—For purposes of subclause (I), the term "tax-exempt use period" means the period beginning with the taxable year in which the property described in subclause (I) is [15]*first used by the organiza-*

⌈**Footnote ¶2935-A continued**⌉

Matter in *italics* in 168(j)(2)(B)(ii) added by section 1809(a)(2)(C)(i), '86 TRA, which struck out:

(11) "19-year real property.—In the case of 19-year real property, the amount determined under paragraph (1) shall be determined on the basis of the number of months (using a mid-month convention) in the year in which the property is in service."

Effective date (Sec. 1809(a)(2)(C)(i), '86 TRA).—(i) Effective on and after the date of the enactment of this Act.

Matter in *italics* in Sec. 168(j)(3)(D), (4)(E)(i), (ii)(I), (II) and (iv) added by section 1802(a)(1), (2)(a)—(D) and (G), '86 TRA, which struck out:

(12) "any property of which such organization is the lessee"

(13) "first leased to"

(14) "of which such organization is the lessee"

(15) "placed in service under the lease"

Effective date (Sec. 1881, '86 TRA and Sec. 31(g), '84 TRA, as amended by Sec. 1802(a)(2)(F) and (10), '86 TRA).—

(1) In general.—Except as otherwise provided in this subsection, the amendments made by this section shall apply—

(A) to property placed in service by the taxpayer after 5-23-83, in taxable years ending after such date, and

(B) to property placed in service by the taxpayer on or before 5-23-83, if the lease to the tax-exempt entity is

[Footnote ¶2935-A continued]

entered into after 5-23-83.

(2) Leases entered into on or before May 23, 1983.—The amendments made by this section shall not apply with respect to any property leased to a tax-exempt entity if the property is leased pursuant to—

(A) to lease entered into on or before 5-23-83 (or a sublease under such a lease), or

(B) any renewal or extension of a lease entered into on or before 5-23-83, if such renewal or extension is pursuant to an option exercisable by the tax-exempt entity which was held by the tax-exempt entity on 5-23-83.

(3) Binding contracts, etc.—

(A) The amendments made by this section shall not apply with respect to any property leased to a tax-exempt entity if such lease is pursuant to 1 or more written binding contracts which, on 5-23-83, and all times thereafter, required—

(i) the taxpayer (or his predecessor in interest under the contract) to acquire, construct, reconstruct, or rehabilitate such property, and

(ii) the tax-exempt entity (or a tax-exempt predecessor thereof) to be the lessee of such property.

(B) Paragraph (9) of section 168(j) of the '54 Code (as added by this section) shall not apply with respect to any property owned by a partnership if—

(i) such property was acquired by such partnership on or before 10-21-83, or

(ii) such partnership entered into a written binding contract which, on 10-21-83, and at all times thereafter, required the partnership to acquire or construct such property.

(C) The amendments made by this section shall not apply with respect to any property leased to a tax-exempt entity (other than any foreign person or entity)—

(i) if—

(I) on or before 5-23-83, the taxpayer (or his predecessor in interest under the contract) or the tax-exempt entity entered into a written, binding contract to acquire, construct, reconstruct, or rehabilitate such property and such property had not previously been used by the tax-exempt entity, or

(II) the taxpayer or the tax-exempt entity acquired the property after 6-30-82, and on or before 5-23-83, or completed the construction, reconstruction, or rehabilitation of the property after 12-31-82, and on or before 5-23-83, and

(ii) if such lease is pursuant to a written binding contract entered into before 1-1-85, which requires the tax-exempt entity to be the lessee of such property.

(4) Official governmental action on or before November 1, 1983.—

(A) In general.—The amendments made by this section shall not apply with respect to any property leased to a tax-exempt entity (other than the United States, any agency or instrumentality thereof, or any foreign person or entity) if—

(i) on or before 11-1-83, there was significant official governmental action with respect to the project or its design, and

(ii) the lease to the tax-exempt entity is pursuant to a written binding contract entered into before 1-1-85, which requires the tax-exempt entity to be the lessee of the property.

(B) Significant official governmental action.—For purposes of subparagraph (A), the term "significant official governmental action" does not include granting of permits, zoning changes, environmental impact statements, or similar governmental actions.

(C) Special rules for credit unions.—In the case of any property leased to a credit union pursuant to a written binding contract with an expiration date of 12-31-84, which was entered into by such organization on 8-23-84—

(i) such credit union shall not be treated as an agency or instrumentality of the United States; and

(ii) clause (ii) of subparagraph (A) shall be applied by substituting "January 1, 1987" for "January 1, 1985".

(D) Special rule for Greenville Auditorium Board.—For purposes of this paragraph, significant official governmental action taken by the Greenville County Auditorium Board of Greenville, South Carolina, before 5-23-83, shall be treated as significant official governmental action with respect to the coliseum facility subject to a binding contract to lease which was in effect on 1-1-85.

(E) Treatment of certain historic structures.—If—

(i) On 6-16-82, the legislative body of the local governmental unit adopted a bond ordinance to provide funds to renovate elevators in a deteriorating building owned by the local governmental unit and listed in the National Register, and

(ii) the chief executive officer of the local governmental unit, in connection with the renovation of such building, made an application on 6-1-83, to a State agency for a Federal historic preservation grant and made an application on 6-17-83, to the Economic Development Administration of the United States Department of Commerce for a grant,

the requirements of clause (i) and (ii) of subparagraph (A) shall be treated as met.

(5) Mass commuting vehicles.—The amendments made by this section shall not apply to any qualified mass commuting vehicle (as defined in section 103(b)(9) of the '54 Code which is financed in whole or in part by obligations the interest on which is excludable from gross income under section 103(a) of such Code if—

(A) such vehicle is placed in service before 1-1-88, or

(B) such vehicle is placed in service on or after such date—

(i) pursuant to a binding contract or commitment entered into before 4-1-83, and

(ii) solely because of conditions which, as determined by the Secretary of the Treasury or his delegate, are not within the control of the lessor or lessee.

(6) Certain Turbines and Boilers.—The amendments made by this section shall not apply to any property described in section 208(d)(3)(E) of the '82 TEFRA.

(7) Certain facilities for which ruling requests filed on or before May 23, 1983.—The amendments made by this section shall not apply with respect to any facilities described in clause (ii) of section 168(f)(12)(C) of the '54 Code

[Footnote ¶2935-A continued]

(relating to certain sewage or solid waste disposal facilities), as in effect on the day before 7-18-84 if a ruling request with respect to the lease of such facility to the tax-exempt entity filed with the Internal Revenue Service on or before 5-23-83.

(8) Recovery period for certain qualified sewage facilities.—

(A) In general.—In the case of any property (other than 15-year real property) which is a part of a qualified sewage facility, the recovery period used for purposes of paragraph (1) of section 168(j) of the '54 Code (as added by this section) shall be 12 years. For purposes of the preceding sentence, the term "15-year real property" includes 18-year real property.

(B) Qualified sewage facility.—For purposes of subparagraph (A), the term "qualified sewage facility" means any facility which is part of the sewer system of a city, if—

(i) on 6-15-83, the City Council approved a resolution under which the city authorized the procurement of equity investments for such facility, and

(ii) on 7-12-83, the Industrial Development Board of the city approved a resolution to issue a $100,000,000 industrial development bond issue to provide funds to purchase such facility.

(9) Property used by the postal service.—In the case of property used by the United States Postal Service, paragraphs (1) and (2) shall be applied by substituting "October 31" for "May 23".

(10) Existing appropriations.—The amendments made by this section shall not apply to personal property leased to or used by the United States if—

(A) an express appropriation has been made for rentals under such lease for the fiscal year 1983 before 5-23-83, and

(B) the United States or an agency or instrumentality thereof has not provided an indemnification against the loss of all or a portion of the tax benefits claimed under the lease or service contract.

(11) Special rule for certain partnerships.—

(A) Partnerships for which qualifying action existed before 10-21-83.—Paragraph (9) of section 168(j) of the '54 Code (as added by this section) shall not apply to any property acquired, directly or indirectly, before 1-1-85, by any partnership described in subparagraph (B).

(B) Application filed before 10-21-83.—A partnership is described in this subparagraph if—

(i) before 10-21-83, the partnership was organized, a request for exemption with respect to such partnership was filed with the Department of Labor, and a private placement memorandum stating the maximum number of units in the partnership that would be offered had been circulated,

(ii) the interest in the property to be acquired, directly or indirectly (including through acquiring an interest in another partnership) by such partnership was described in such private placement memorandum, and

(iii) the marketing of partnership units in such partnership is completed not later than two years after the later of 7-18-84 or the date of publication in the Federal Register of such exemption by the Department of Labor and the aggregate number of units in such partnership sold does not exceed the amount described in clause (i).

(C) Partnerships for which qualifying action existed before 3-6-84.—Paragraph (9) of section 168(j) of the '54 Code (as added by this section) shall not apply to any property acquired directly or indirectly, before 1-1-86, by any partnership described in subparagraph (D). For purposes of this subparagraph, property shall be deemed to have been acquired prior to 1-1-86, if the partnership had entered into a written binding contract to acquire such property prior to 1-1-86 and the closing of such contract takes place within 6 months of the date of such contract (24 months in the case of new construction.)

(D) Partnership organized before 3-6-84.—A partnership is described in this subparagraph if—

(i) before 3-6-84, the partnership was organized and publicly announced the maximum amount (as shown in the registration statement, prospectus or partnership agreement, whichever is greater) of interests which would be sold in the partnership, and

(ii) the marketing or partnership interests in such partnership was completed not later than the 90th day after 7-18-84 and the aggregate amount of interest in such partnership sold does not exceed the maximum amount described in clause (i).

(12) Special rule for amendment made by subsection (c)(2).—The amendment made by subsection (c)(2) to the extent it relates to subsection (f)(12) of section 168 of the '54 Code shall take effect as if it had been included in the amendments made by section 216(a) of '82 TEFRA.

(13) Special rule for service contracts not involving tax-exempt entities.—In the case of a service contract or other arrangement described in section 7701(e) of the '54 Code (as added by this section) with respect to which no party is a tax-exempt entity, such section 7701(e) shall not apply to—

(A) such contract or other arrangement if such contract or other arrangement was entered into before 11-5-83, or

(B) any renewal or other extension of such contract or other arrangement pursuant to an option contained in such contract or other arrangement on 11-5-83.

(14) Property leased to section 593 organizations.—For purposes of the amendment made by subsection (f), paragraphs (1), (2), and (4) shall be applied by substituting—

(A) "11-5-83" for "5-23-83" and "11-1-83", as the case may be, and

(B) "organization described in section 593 of the '54 Code" for "tax-exempt entity".

(15) Special rules relating to foreign persons or entities—

(A) In general.—In the case of tax-exempt use property which is used by a foreign person or entity, the amendments made by this section shall not apply to any property which—

(i) is placed in service by the taxpayer before 1-1-84, and

(ii) is used by such foreign person or entity pursuant to a lease entered into before 1-1-84.

(B) Special rule for subleases.—If tax-exempt use property is being used by a foreign person or entity pursuant to a sublease under a lease described in subparagraph (A)(ii), subparagraph (A) shall apply to such property only if such property was used before 1-1-84, by any foreign person or entity pursuant to such lease.

(C) Binding contracts, etc.—The amendments made by this section shall not apply with respect to any prop-

【Footnote ¶2935-A continued】

erty (other than aircraft described in subparagraph (D)) leased to a foreign person or entity—

(i) if—

(I) on or before 5-23-83, the taxpayer (or a predecessor in interest under the contract) or the foreign person or entity entered into a written binding contract to acquire, construct, or rehabilitate such property and such property had not previously been used by the foreign person or entity, or

(II) the taxpayer or the foreign person or entity acquired the property or completed the construction, reconstruction, or rehabilitation of the property after 12-31-82 and on or before 5-23-83, and

(ii) if such lease is pursuant to a written binding contract entered into before 1-1-84, which requires the foreign person or entity to be the lessee of such property.

(D) Certain aircraft.—The amendments made by this section shall not apply with respect to any wide-body, four-engine, commerical aircraft used by a foreign person or entity if—

(i) on or before 11-1-83, the foreign person or entity entered into a written binding contract to acquire such aircraft, and

(ii) such aircraft is originally placed in service by such foreign person or entity (or its successor in interest under the contract) after 5-23-83, and before 1-1-86.

(E) Use after 1983.—Qualified container equipment placed in service before 1-1-84, which is used before such date by a foreign person shall not, for purposes of section 47 of the '54 Code, be treated as ceasing to be section 38 property by reason of the use of such equipment before 1-1-85, by a foreign person or entity. For purposes of this subparagraph the term "qualified container equipment" means any container, container chassis, or container trailer of a United States person with a present class life of not more than 6 years.

(16) Organizations electing exemption from rules relating to previously tax-exempt organizations must elect taxation of exempt arbitrage profits.—

(A) In general.—An organization may make the election under section 168(j)(4)(E)(ii) of the '54 Code (relating to election not to have rules relating to previously tax-exempt organizations apply) only if such organization elects the tax treatment of exempt arbitrage profits described in subparagraph (B).

(B) Taxation of exempt arbitrage profits.—

(i) In general.—In the case of an organization which elects the application of this subparagraph, there is hereby imposed a tax on the exempt arbitrage profits of such organization.

(ii) Rate of tax, etc.—The tax imposed by clause (i)—

(I) shall be the amount of tax which would be imposed by section 11 of such Code if the exempt arbitrage profits were taxable income (and there were no other taxable income), and

(II) shall be imposed for the first taxable year of the tax-exempt use period (as defined in section 168(j)(4)(E)-(ii) of such Code).

(C) Exempt arbitrage profits.—

(i) In general.—For purposes of this paragraph, the term exempt arbitrage profits means the aggregate amount described in clauses (i) and (ii) of subparagraph (D) of section 103(c)(6) of such Code for all taxable years for which the organization was exempt from tax under section 501(a) of such Code with respect to obligations—

(I) associated with property described in section 168(j)(4)(E)(i), and

(II) issued before 1-1-85.

(ii) Application of section 103(b)(6).—For purposes of this paragraph, section 103(b)(6) of such Code shall apply to obligations issued before 1-1-85, but the amount described in clauses (i) and (ii) of subparagraph (D) thereof shall be determined without regard to clauses (i)(II) and (ii) of subparagraph (F) thereof.

(D) Other laws applicable.—

(i) In general.—Except as provided in clause (ii), all provisions of law, including penalties, applicable with respect to the tax imposed by section 11 of such Code shall apply with respect to the tax imposed by this paragraph.

(ii) No credits against tax, etc.—The tax imposed by this paragraph shall not be treated as imposed by section 11 of such Code for purposes of—

(I) part VI of subchapter A of chapter 1 of such Code (relating to minimum tax preferences), and

(II) determining the amount of any credit allowable under subpart A of part IV of such subchapter.

(E) Election.—Any election under subparagraph (A)—

(i) shall be made at such time and in such manner as the Secretary may prescribe,

(ii) shall apply to any successor organization which is engaged in substantially similar activities, and

(iii) once made, shall be irrevocable.

(17) Certain transitional leased property.—The amendments made by this section shall not apply to property described in section 168(c)(2)(D) of the '54 Code, as in effect on the day before 7-18-84, and which is described in any of the following subparagraphs:

(A) Property is described in this subparagraph if such property is leased to a university, and—

(i) on 6-16-83, the Board of Administrators of the university adopted a resolution approving the rehabilitation of the property in connection with an overall campus development program; and

(ii) the property houses a basketball arena and university offices.

(B) Property is described in this subparagraph if such property is leased to a charitable organization, and—

(i) on 8-21-81, the charitable organization acquired the property, with a view towards rehabilitating the property; and

(ii) on 6-12-82, an arson fire caused substantial damage to the property, delaying the planned rehabilitation.

(C) Property is described in this subparagraph if such property is leased to a corporation that is described in section 501(c)(3) of the '54 Code (relating to organizations exempt from tax) pursuant to a contract—

(i) which was entered into on 8-3-83; and

(ii) under which the corporation first occupied the property on 12-22-83.

(D) Property is described in this subparagraph if such property is leased to an educational institution for use as

[Footnote ¶2935-A continued]

an Arts and Humanities Center and with respect to which—

(i) in November 1982, an architect was engaged to design a planned renovation;

(ii) in January 1983, the architectural plans were completed;

(iii) in December 1983, a demolition contract was entered into; and

(iv) in March 1984, a renovation contract was entered into.

(E) Property is described in this subparagraph if such property is used by a college as a dormitory, and—

(i) in October 1981, the college purchased the property with a view towards renovating the property;

(ii) renovation plans were delayed because of a zoning dispute; and

(iii) in May 1983, the court of highest jurisdiction in the State in which the college is located resolved the zoning dispute in favor of the college.

(F) Property is described in this subparagraph if such property is a fraternity house related to a university with respect to which—

(i) in August 1982, the university retained attorneys to advise the university regarding the rehabilitation of the property;

(ii) on 1-1-83, the governing body of the university established a committee to develop rehabilitation plans;

(iii) on 1-10-84, the governor of the state in which the university is located approved historic district designation for an area that includes the property; and

(iv) on 2-2-84, historic preservation certification applications for the property were filed with a historic landmarks commission.

(G) Property is described in this subparagraph if such property is leased to a retirement community with respect to which—

(i) on 1-5-77, a certificate of incorporation was filed with the appropriate authority of the state in which the retirement community is located; and

(ii) on 11-22-83, the Board of Trustees adopted a resolution evidencing the intention to begin immediate construction of the property.

(H) Property is described in this subparagraph if such property is used by a university, and—

(i) in July 1982, the Board of Trustees of the university adopted a master plan for the financing of the property; and

(ii) as of 8-1-83, at least $60,000 in private expenditures had been expended in connection with the property. In the case of Clemson University, the preceding sentence applies only to the Continuing Education Center and the component housing project.

(I) Property is described in this subparagraph if such property is used by a university as a fine arts center and the Board of Trustees of such university authorized the sale-leaseback agreement with respect to such property on 3-7-84.

(J) Property is described in this subparagraph if such property is used by a tax-exempt entity as an international trade center, and

(i) prior to 1982, an environmental impact study for such property was completed;

(ii) on 6-24-81, a developer made a written commitment to provide one-third of the financing for the development of such property; and

(iii) on 10-20-83, such developer was approved by the Board of Directors of the tax-exempt entity.

(K) Property is described in this subparagraph if such property is used by university of osteopathic medicine and health sciences, and on or before 12-31-83, the Board of Trustees of such university approved the construction of such property.

(L) Property is described in this subparagraph if such property is used by a tax-exempt entity, and—

(i) such use is pursuant to a lease with a taxpayer which placed substantial improvements in service;

(ii) on 5-23-83, there existed architectural plans and specifications (within the meaning of sec. 48(g)(1)(C)(ii) of the '54 Code); and

(iii) prior to 5-23-83, at least 10 percent of the total cost of such improvements was actually paid or incurred. Property is described in this subparagraph if such property was leased to a tax-exempt entity pursuant to a lease recorded in the Registry of Deeds of Essex County, New Jersey, on 5-7-84, and a deed of such property was recorded in the Registry of Deeds of Essex County, New Jersey, on 5-7-85.

(M) Property is described in this subparagraph if such property is used as a convention center, on 6-2-83, the City Council of the city in which the center is located provided for over $6 million for the project.

(18) Special rule for amendment made by subsection (c)(1).—

(A) In general.—The amendment made by subsection (c)(1) shall not apply to property—

(i) leased by the taxpayer on or before 11-1-83, or

(ii) leased by the taxpayer after 11-1-83, if on or before such date the taxpayer entered into a written binding contract requiring the taxpayer to lease such property.

(B) Limitation.—Subparagraph (A) shall apply to the amendment made by subsection (c)(1) only to the extent such amendment relates to property described in subclause (II), (III), or (IV) of section 168(j)(3)(B)(ii) of the '54 Code (as added by this section).

(19) Special rule for certain energy management contracts.—

(A) In general.—The amendments made by subsection (c) shall not apply to property used pursuant to an energy management contract that was entered into prior to 5-1-84.

(B) Definition of energy management contract.—For purposes of subparagraph (A), the term "energy management contract" means a contract for the providing of energy conservation or energy management services.

(20) Definitions.—For purposes of this subsection—

(A) Tax-exempt entity.—The term "tax-exempt entity" has the same meaning as when used in section 168(j) of '54 Code (as added by this section), except that such term shall include any related entity (within the meaning of such section).

(R) Treatment of improvements.—

tion and ending with the close of the 15th taxable year following the last taxable year of the recovery period of such property.

(III) Election.—Any election under subclause (I), once made, shall be irrevocable.

(iii) Treatment of successor organizations.—Any organization which is engaged in activities substantially similar to those engaged in by a predecessor organization shall succeed to the treatment under this subparagraph of such predecessor organization.

(iv) *First used.—For purposes of this subparagraph, property shall be treated as first used by the organization—*

(I) *when the property is first placed in service under a lease to such organization, or*

(II) *in the case of property leased to (or held by) a partnership (or other pass-thru entity) in which the organization is a member, the later of when such property is first used by such partnerhip or pass-thru entity or when such organization is first a member of such partnership or pass-thru entity.*

(5) Special rules for certain high technology equipment.—

* * * * * * * * * * * *

(C) Qualified technological equipment.—For purposes of this paragraph—

* * * * * * * * * * * *

(iv) [Repealed][16]

* * * * * * * * * * * *

(8) Tax-exempt use of property leased to partnerships, etc., determined at partner level.—For purposes of this subsection[17]—

(9) Treatment of property owned by partnerships, etc.—
(A) In general.—For purposes of this subsection[17], if—
(i) any property which (but for this subparagraph) is not tax-exempt use property is owned by a partnership which has both a tax-exempt entity and a person who is not a tax-exempt entity as partners, and

---

⌈Footnote ¶2935-A continued⌋

(i) In general.—For purposes of this subsection, an improvement to property shall not be treated as a separate property unless such improvement is a substantial improvement with respect to such property.

** (ii) Substantial improvement.—For purposes of clause (i), the term "substantial improvement" has the meaning given such term by section 168(f)(1)(C) of such Code determined—

(I) by substituting "property" for "building" each place it appears therein,

(II) by substituting "20 percent" for "25 percent" in clause (ii) thereof, and

(III) without regard to clause (iii) thereof.

(C) Foreign person or entity.—The term "foreign person or entity" has the meaning given to such term by subparagraph (C) of section 168(j)(4) of such Code (as added by this section). For purposes of this subparagraph and subparagraph (A), such subparagraph (C) shall be applied without regard to the last sentence thereof.

(D) Leases and subleases.—The determination of whether there is a lease or sublease to a tax-exempt entity shall take into account sections 168(j)(6)(A), 168(j)(8)(A), and 7701(e) of the '54 Code (as added by this section).

** (ii) The amendment made by clause (i) of Sec. 1802(10)(D), '86 TRA, to Sec. 31(g)(20)(B) of '84 TRA, shall not apply to any property if—

(I) on or before 3-28-85, the taxpayer (or a predecessor in interest under the contract) or the tax-exempt entity entered into a written binding contract to acquire, construct, or rehabilitate the property, or

(II) the taxpayer or the tax-exempt entity began the construction, reconstruction, or rehabilitation of the property on or before 3-28-85.

Section 1802(a)(3), 'TRA, repealed Sec. 168(j)(5)(C)(iv):

(16) "(iv) Property not subject to rapid obsolescence may be excluded.—The term "qualified technological equipment" shall not include any equipment described in subclause (II) or (III) of clause (i)—

(I) which the Secretary determines by regulations is not subject to rapid obsolescence, and

(II) which is placed in service after the date on which final regulations implementing such determination are published in the Federal Register."

Effective date (Sec. 1881, '86 TRA and Sec. 31(g), '84 TRA, as amended by Sec. 1802(a)(2)(F) and (10), '86 TRA).—See above.

Matter in *italics* in Sec. 168(j)(8), (9)(A), (B)(i) and (D), (E), relettering of (F) and (G) added by section 1802(a)(2)(E)(i), (4)(A), (B) and (7), '86 TRA, which struck out:

(17) "and paragraphs (4) and (5) of section 48(a)"

(ii) any allocation to the tax-exempt entity of partnership items is not a qualified allocation,

an amount equal to such tax-exempt entity's proportionate share of such property shall (except as provided in paragraph (3)(D)) be treated as tax-exempt use property.

(B) Qualified allocation.—For purposes of subparagraph (A), the term "qualified allocation" means any allocation to a tax-exempt entity which—

(i) is consistent with such entity's being allocated the same distributive share of each item of income, gain, [18]*loss deduction*, credit, and basis and such share remains the same during the entire period the entity is a partner in the partnership, and

(ii) has substantial economic effect within the meaning of section 704(b)(2).

* * * * * * * * * * * *

(D) Determination of whether property used in unrelated trade or business.—For purposes of this subsection, in the case of any property which is owned by a partnership which has both a tax-exempt entity and a person who is not a tax-exempt entity as partners, the determination of whether such property is used in an unrelated trade or business of such an entity shall be made without regard to section 514.

[19]**(E)* Other pass-thru entities; tiered entities.—Rules similar to the rules of subparagraphs (A), (B), [20]*(C)*, and (D) shall also apply in the case of any pass-thru entity other than a partnership and in the case of tiered partnerships and other entities.

[21]**(F) Treatment of certain taxable entities.—*

(i) In general.—For purposes of this paragraph, except as otherwise provided in this subparagrraph, any tax-exempt controlled entity shall be treated as a tax-exempt entity.

(ii) Election.—If a tax-exempt controlled entity makes an election under this clause—

(I) such entity shall not be treated as a tax-exempt entity for purposes of this paragraph, and

(II) any gain recognized by a tax-exempt entity on any disposition of an interest in such entity (and any dividend or interest received or accrued by a tax-exempt entity from such tax-exempt controlled entity) shall be treated as unrelated business taxable income for purposes of section 511.

Any such election shall be irrevocable and shall bind all tax-exempt entities holding interests in such tax-exempt controlled entity. For purposes of subclause (II), there shall only be taken into account dividends which are properly allocable to income of the tax-exempt controlled entity which was not subject to tax under this chapter.

(iii) Tax-exempt controlled entity.—The term "tax-exempt controlled entity" means any corporation (which is not a tax-exempt entity determined without regard to this subparagraph and pargraph (4)(E)) if 50 percent or more (by value) of the stock in such corporation is held (directly or through the application of section 318 determined without regard to the 50-percent limitation contained in subsection (a)(2)(C) thereof) by 1 or more tax-exempt entities.

[21]*(G)* Regulations.—

* * * * * * * * * * * *

[For official explanation, see Committee Reports, ¶4136; 4143.]

〔Footnote ¶2935-A continued〕

(18) "loss deduction"
(19) "(D)"
(20) "and (C)"
(21) "(E)"
Effective date (Sec. 1881, '86 TRA, and Sec. 31(g), '84 TRA, as amended by Sec. 1802(a)(2)(F) and (10), '86 TRA).—See above.

---

* Sec. 168(j)(9)(F), added by section 1802(a)(2)(E)(i), '86 TRA.
Effective date (Sec. 1802(a)(2)(E)(ii), '86 TRA).—

(I) Except as otherwise provided in this clause, the amendment made by clause (i) shall apply to property placed in service after 9-27-85; except that such amendment shall not apply to any property acquired pursuant to a binding written contract in effect on such date (and at all times thereafter).

(II) If an election under this subclause is made with respect to any property, the amendment made by clause (i) shall apply to such property whether or not placed in service on or before 9-27-85.

[¶2936] CODE SEC. 170. CHARITABLE, ETC., CONTRIBUTIONS AND GIFTS.

* * * * * * * * * * * * *

(b) Percentage Limitations.—

(1) **Individuals.**—In the case of an individual, the deduction provided in subsection (a) shall be limited as provided in the succeeding subparagraphs.

(C) Special limitation with respect to contributions described in subparagraph (A) of certain capital gain property.—

* * * * * * * * * * * *

(iv) For purposes of this ¹*paragraph,* the term "capital gain property" means, with respect to any contribution, any capital asset the sale of which at its fair market value at the time of the contribution would have resulted in gain which would have been long-term capital gain. For purposes of the preceding sentence, any property which is property used in the trade or business (as defined in section 1231(b)) shall be treated as a capital asset.

* * * * * * * * * *

(e) Certain Contributions of Ordinary Income and Capital Gain Property.—

(1) **General rule.**—The amount of any charitable contribution of property otherwise taken into account under this section shall be reduced by the sum of—

(A) the amount of gain which would not have been long-term capital gain if the property contributed had been sold by the taxpayer at its fair market value (determined at the time of such contribution), and

(B) in the case of a charitable contribution—

(i) of tangible personal property, if the use by the donees is unrelated to the purpose or function constituting the basis for its exemption under section 501 (or, in the case of a governmental unit, to any purpose or function described in subsection (c)), or

(ii) to or for the use of a private foundation (as defined in section 509(a)), other than a private foundation described in subsection (b)(1)(E), ² the amount of gain which would have been long-term capital gain if the property contributed had been sold by the taxpayer at its fair market value (determined at the time of such contribution).

For purpose of applying this paragraph (other than in the case of gain to which section 617(d)(1), 1245(a), 1250(a), 1252(a) or 1254(a) applies), property which is property used in the trade or business (as defined in section 1231(b)) shall be treated as a capital asset.

* * * * * * * * * * * *

(4) **Special rate for contributions of scientific property used for research.**—

(A) Limit on reduction.—In the case of a qualified research contribution, the reduction under paragraph (1)(A) shall be no greater than the amount determined under paragraph (3)(B).

(B) Qualified research contributions.—For purposes of this paragraph, the term "qualified research contribution" means a charitable contribution by a corporation of tangible personal property described in paragraph (1) of section 1221, but only if—

(i) ³*the contribution is to an organization described in subparagraph (A) or subparagraph (B) of section 41(e)(6),*

(ii) the property is constructed by the taxpayer,

(iii) the contribution is made not later than 2 years after the date the construction of the property is substantially completed,

---

[Footnote ¶2936] Matter in *italics* in Sec. 170(b)(1)(C)(iv) added by section 1831, '86 TRA, which struck out:
(1) "subparagraph"
Effective date (Sec. 1881, '86 TRA, and section 301(d)(1), '84 TRA).—Applies to contributions made in taxable years ending after 7-18-84.

Section 301(b)(2), '86 TRA, struck out from Sec. 170(e)(1):
(2) "40 percent (28/46, in the case of a corporation) of"
Effective date (Sec. 301(c), '86 TRA).—Applies to taxable years beginning after 12-31-86.

Matter in *italics* in Sec. 170(e)(4)(B)(i) added by section 231(f), '86 TRA, which struck out:
(3) "the contribution is to an educational organization which is described in subsection (b)(1)(A)(ii) of this section and which is an institution of higher education (as defined in section 3304(f)),"
Effective date (Sec. 231(g)(1), '86 TRA).—Applies to taxable years beginning after 12-31-86.

    (iv)   the original use of the property is by the donee,

    (v)   the property is scientific equipment or apparatus substantially all of the use of which by the donee is for research or experimentation (within the meaning of section 174), or for research training, in the United States in physical or biological sciences,

    (vi)   the property is not transferred by the donee in exchange for money, other property, or services, and

    (vii)   The taxpayer receives from the donee a written statement representing that its use and disposition of the property will be in accordance with the provisions of clauses (v) and (vi).

*   *   *   *   *   *   *   *   *   *   *

    (k)   *Denial of Deduction for Certain Travel Expenses.—No deduction shall be allowed under this section for traveling expenses (including amounts expended for meals and lodging) while away from home, whether paid directly or by reimbursement, unless there is no significant element of personal pleasure, recreation, or vacation in such travel.*

[4]*(l)*   **Disallowance of Deductions in Certain Cases.—** *   *   *

[5]*(m)*   **Other Cross References.—**

*   *   *   *   *   *   *   *   *   *   *

[For official explanation, see Committee Reports, ¶3866; 3872; 3885.]

[¶2937]   CODE SEC. 171.   AMORTIZABLE BOND PREMIUM.

    (a)   General Rule.—In the case of any bond, as defined in subsection (d), the following rules shall apply to the amortizable bond premium (determined under subsection (b)) on the bond:

    (1)   Taxable bonds.—In the case of a bond (other than a bond the interest on which is excludable from gross income), the amount of the amortizable bond premium for the taxable year shall be allowed as a deduction.

    (2)   Tax-exempt bonds.—In the case of any bond the interest on which is excludable from gross income, no deduction shall be allowed for the amortizable bond premium for the taxable year.

    (3)   Cross reference.—

    For adjustment to basis on account of amortizable bond premium, see section 1016(a)(5).

    (b)   Amortizable Bond Premium.—

    (1)   Amount of bond premium.—For purposes of paragraph (2), the amount of bond premium, in the case of the holder of any bond, shall be determined—

    (A)   with reference to the amount of the basis (for determining loss on sale or exchange) of such bond,

    (B)   (i)   with reference to the amount payable on maturity or on earlier call date, in the case of any bond other than a bond to which clause (ii) applies, or

    (ii)   with reference to the amount payable on maturity (or if it results in a smaller amortizable bond premium attributable to the period to earlier call date, with reference to the amount payable on earlier call date), in the case of any bond described in subsection (a)(1) which is acquired after December 31, 1957, and

    (C)   with adjustments proper to reflect unamortized bond premiums, with respect to the bond, for the period before the date as of which subsection (a) becomes applicable with respect to the taxpayer with respect to such bond.

In no case shall the amount of bond premium on a convertible bond include any amount attributable to the conversion features of the bond.

    (2)   Amount amortizable.—The amortizable bond premium of the taxable year shall be the amount of the bond premium attributable to such year. In the case of a bond to which paragraph (1)(B)(ii) applies and which has a call date, the amount of bond premium attributable to the taxable year in which the bond is called shall include an amount equal to the excess of the amount of the adjusted basis (for determining loss

[Footnote ¶2936 continued]

Matter in *italics* in Sec. 170(k)—(m) added by section 142(d), '86 TRA, which struck out:

(4)   "(k)"

(5)   "(l)"

Effective date (Sec. 151(a), '86 TRA).—Applies to taxable years beginning after 12-31-86.

on sale or exchange) of such bond as of the beginning of the taxable year over the amount received on redemption of the bond or (if greater) the amount payable on maturity.

[1](3) *Method of determination.—*

(A) In general.—Except as provided in regulations prescribed by the Secretary the determinations required under paragraphs (1) and (2) shall be made on the basis of the taxpayer's yield maturity determined by—

(i) using the taxpayer's basis (for purposes of determining loss on sale or exchange) of the obligation, and

(ii) compounding at the close of each accrual period (as defined in section 1272(a)(5)).

(B) Special rule where earlier call date is used.—For purposes of subparagraph (A), if the amount payable on an earlier call date is used under paragraph (1)(B)(ii) in determining the amortizable bond premium attributable to the period before the earlier call date, such bond shall be treated as maturing on such date for the amount so payable and then reissued on such date for the amount so payable.

(4) Treatment of certain bonds acquired in exchange for other property.—

(A) In general.—If—

(i) a bond is acquired by any person in exchange for other property, and

(ii) the basis of such bond is determined (in whole or in part) by reference to the basis of such other property,

for purposes of applying this subsection to such bond while held by such person, the basis of such bond shall not exceed its fair market value immediately after the exchange. A similar rule shall apply in the case of such bond while held by any other person whose basis is determined (in whole or in part) by reference to the basis in the hands of the person referred to in clause (i).

(B) Special rule where bond exchanged in reorganization.—Subparagraph (A) shall not apply to an exchange by the taxpayer of a bond for another bond if such exchange is a part of a reorganization (as defined in section 368). If any portion of the basis of the taxpayer in a bond transferred in such an exchange is not taken into account in determining bond premium by reason of this paragraph, such portion shall not be taken into account in determining the amount of bond premium on any bond received in the exchange.

* * * * * * * * * * *

(d) Bond Defined.—For purposes of this section, the term "bond" means any bond, debenture, note, or certificate or other evidence of indebtedness,[2] but does not include any such obligation which constitutes stock in trade of the taxpayer or any such obligation of a kind which would properly be included in the inventory of the taxpayer if on hand at the close of the taxable year, or any such obligation held by the taxpayer primarily for sale to customers in the ordinary course of his trade or business.

⟦**Footnote ¶2937**⟧ Matter in *italics* in Sec. 171(b)(3) added by section 1803(a)(11)(A), '86 TRA, which struck out:

(1) "**(3) Method of determination.—**The determinations required under paragraphs (1) and (2) shall be made—

(A) in accordance with the method of amortizing bond premium regularly employed by the holder of the bond, if such method is reasonable;

(B) in all other cases, in accordance with regulations prescribing reasonable methods of amortizing bond premium prescribed by the Secretary."

Effective date (Sec. 1803(a)(11)(C), '86 TRA).—(i) Applies to obligations issued after 9-27-85.

(ii) In the case of a taxpayer with respect to whom an election is in effect on the date of the enactment of this Act under section 171(c) of the '54 Code such election shall apply to obligations issued after 9-27-85, only if the taxpayer chooses (at such time and in such manner as may be prescribed by the Secretary of the Treasury or his delegate) to have such election apply with respect to such obligations.

Sec. 171(b)(4) added by section 1803(a)(12)(A), '86 TRA.
Effective date (Sec. 1803(a)(12)(B), '86 TRA).—Applies to exchanges after 5-6-86.

Section 1803(a)(11)(B), '86 TRA, struck out from Sec. 171(d):
(2) "issued by any corporation and bearing interest (including any like obligation issued by a government or political subdivision thereof),"
Effective date (Sec. 1803(a)(11)(C), '86 TRA).—Applies to obligations issued after 9-27-85. For special rule, see above.

(e) Treatment as interest.—*Except as provided in regulations the amount of any amortizable bond premium with respect to which a deduction is allowed under subsection (a)(1) for any taxable year shall be treated as interest for purposes of this title.*

[3]*(f)* **Dealers in Tax-Exempt Securities.**—

For special rules applicable in the case of dealers in securities, with respect to premium attributable to certain wholly tax-exempt securities, see section 75.

[For official explanation, see Committee Reports, ¶3923; 4137.]

〖¶2938〗 CODE SEC. 172. NET OPERATING LOSS DEDUCTION.

* * * * * * * * * * *

(b) Net Operating Loss Carrybacks and Carryovers.—

   (1) Years to which loss may be carried.—

     (A) Except as provided in subparagraphs (D) (E), (F), (G), (H), (I), (J), [1] *(K), (L), and (M)*, a net operating loss for any taxable year shall be a net operating loss carryback to each of the 3 taxable years preceding the taxable year of such loss.

     (B) Except as provided in subparagraphs (C), (D), and (E) a net operating loss for any taxable year ending after December 31, 1955, shall be a net operating loss carryover to each of the 5 taxable years following the taxable year of such loss. Except as provided in subparagraphs (C), (D), (E), (F), (G), (H), [1] (J), *(L), and (M)*, a net operating loss for any taxable year ending after December 31, 1975, shall be a net operating loss carryover to each of the 15 years following the taxable year of such loss.

     (C) In the case of a taxpayer which is a regulated transportation corporation (as defined in subsection (g)(1), a net operating loss for any taxable year ending after December 31, 1955, and before January 1, 1976, shall (except as provided in subsection (g)) be a net operating loss carryover to each of the 7 taxable years following the taxable year of such loss.

     (D) In the case of a taxpayer which has a foreign expropriation loss (as defined in subsection (h)) for any taxable year ending after December 31, 1958, the portion of the net operating loss for such year attributable to such foreign expropriation loss shall not be a net operating loss carryback to any taxable year preceding the taxable year of such loss and shall be a net operating loss carryover to each of the 10 taxable years following the taxable year of such loss (or, with respect to that portion of the net operating loss for such year attributable to a Cuban expropriation loss, to each of the 20 taxable years following the taxable year of such loss).

     (E)(i) A net operating loss for a REIT year—

       (I) shall not be a net operating loss carryback to any taxable year preceding the taxable year of such loss, and

       (II) shall be a net operating loss carryover to each of the 15 taxable years following the taxable year of the loss.

      (ii) In the case of any net operating loss for a taxable year which is not a REIT year, such losses shall not be carried back to any taxable year which is a REIT year.

      (iii) For purposes of this subparagraph, the term "REIT year" means any taxable year for which the provisions of part II of subchapter M (relating to real estate investment trusts) apply to the taxpayer.

     (F) In the case of a financial institution [2]*referred to in section 582(c)(5)*, a net

---

〖Footnote ¶2937 continued〗

Matter in *italics* in Sec. 171(e) and (f) added by section 643(a), '86 TRA, which struck out:

(3) "(e)"

Effective date (Sec. 643(b), '86 TRA).—(1) Generally applies to obligations acquired after the date of enactment, in taxable years ending after such date.

(2) Revocation of election.—In the case of a taxpayer with respect to whom an election is in effect on the date of enactment of this Act under section 171(c) of the '86 Code, such election shall apply to obligations issued after the date of the enactment of this Act only if the taxpayer chooses (at such time and in such manner as may be prescribed by the Secretary of the Treasury or his delegate) to have such election apply with respect to such obligations.

   〖Footnote ¶2938〗 Matter in *italics* in Sec. 172(b)(1)(A) and (B) added by section 903(b)(2)(A) and (B), '86 TRA, which struck out:

(1) "and"

Effective date (Sec. 903(c)(1), '86 TRA).—Applies to losses incurred in taxable years beginning after 12-31-86.

"*referred to in section 582(c)(5)*" in *italics* in Sec. 172(b)(1)(F) added by section 901(d)(4)(B), '86 TRA, which struck out:

(2) "to which section 585, 586, or 593 applies"

Effective date (Sec. 901(e), '86 TRA).—Applies to taxable years beginning after 12-31-86.

operating loss for any taxable year beginning after December 31, 1975, *and before January 1, 1987,* shall be a net operating loss carryback to each of the 10 taxable years preceding the taxable year of such loss and shall be a net operating loss carryover to each of the 5 taxable years following the taxable year of such loss.

(G) In the case of a Bank for Cooperatives (organized and chartered pursuant to section 2 of the Farm Credit Act of 1933 (12 U.S.C. 1134)), a net operating loss for any taxable year beginning after December 31, 1969, *and before January 1, 1987,* shall be a net operating loss carryback to each of the 10 taxable years preceding the taxable year of such loss and shall be a net operating loss carryover to each of the 5 taxable years following the taxable year of such loss.

(H) In the case of a net operating loss of the Federal National Mortgage Association for any taxable year beginning after December 31, 1981, *and before January 1, 1987,* or a net operating loss of the Federal Home Loan Mortgage Corporation for any taxable year beginning after December 31, 1984 *and before January 1, 1987—*

(i) such loss, to the extent it exceeds the mortgage disposition loss (within the meaning of subsection (i)), shall be—

(I) a net operating loss carryback to each of the 10 taxable years preceding the taxable year of the loss, and

(II) a net operating loss carryover to each of the 5 taxable years following the taxable year of the loss, and

(ii) the mortgage disposition loss shall be—

(I) a net operating loss carryback to each of the 3 taxable years preceding the taxable year of the loss, and

(II) a net operating loss carryover to each of the 15 taxable years following the taxable year of the loss.

(I) Product liability losses.—In the case of a taxpayer which has a product liability loss (as defined in subsection (j) for a taxable year beginning after September 30, 1979 (referred to in this subparagraph as the "loss year"), the product liability loss shall be a net operating loss carryback to each of the 10 taxable years preceding the loss year. [3]

[4] *(J)* Special rule for deferred statutory or tort liability losses.—In the case of a taxpayer which has a deferred statutory or tort liability loss (as defined in subsection (k)) for any taxable year beginning after December 31, 1983, the deferred statutory or tort liability loss shall be a net operating loss carryback to each of the 10 taxable years preceding the taxable year of such loss.

(L) [should read (K)] Bad debt losses of commercial banks.—In the case of any bank (as defined in section 585(a)(2)), the portion of the net operating loss for any taxable year beginning after December 31, 1986, and before January 1, 1994, which is attributable to the deduction allowed under section 166(a) shall be a net operating loss carryback to each of the 10 taxable years preceding the taxable year of the loss and a net operating loss carryover to each of the 5 taxable years following the taxable year of such loss.

(M) [Should read (L)] Losses of thrift institutions.—In the case of an organization to which section 593 applies, in lieu of applying subparagraph (F), a net operat-

ing loss for any taxable year beginning after December 31, 1981, and before January 1, 1986, shall be a net operating loss carryback to each of the 10 taxable years preceding the taxable year of such loss and shall be a net operating loss carryover to each of the 8 taxable years following the taxable year of such loss.

(d) **Modifications.**—The modifications referred to in this section are as follows:

* * * * * * * * * *

(2) **Capital gains and losses of taxpayers other than corporations.**—[5] *In the case of a taxpayer other than a corporation, the amount deductible on account of losses from sales or exchanges of capital assets shall not exceed the amount includible on account of gains from sales or exchanges of capital assets.*

* * * * * * * * * *

(6) *Modifications related to real estate investment trusts.*—In the case of any taxable year for which part II of subchapter M (relating to real estate investment trusts) applies to the taxpayer—
    (A) the net operating loss for such taxable year shall be computed by taking into account the adjustment described in section 857(b)(2) (other than the deduction for dividends paid described in section 857(b)(2)(B)); and
    (B) where such taxable year is a "prior taxable year" referred to in paragraph (2) of subsection (b), the term "taxable income" in such paragraph shall mean "real estate investment trust taxable income" (as defined in section 857(b)(2)).[6]

(e) **Law Applicable to Computations.**—In determining the amount of any net operating loss carryback or carryover to any taxable year, the necessary computations involving any other taxable year shall be made under the law applicable to such other taxable year.

* * * * * * * * * *

(k) **Definitions and Special Rules Relating to Deferred Statutory or Tort Liability Losses.**—For purposes of this section—

* * * * * * * * * *

(2) **Special rule for nuclear powerplants.**—Except as provided in regulations prescribed by the Secretary, that portion of a deferred statutory or tort liability loss which is attributable to amounts incurred in the decommissioning of a nuclear powerplant (or any unit thereof) may, for purposes of [7]*subsection (b)(1)(J)* be carried back to each of the taxable years during the period—
    (A) beginning with the taxable year in which such plant (or unit thereof) was placed in service, and
    (B) ending with the taxable year preceding the loss year.

* * * * * * * * * *

(4) **No carryback to taxable years beginning before January 1, 1984.**—No deferred statutory or tort liability loss may be carried back to a taxable year beginning before January 1, 1984, unless such loss may be carried back to such year without regard to [7]*subsection (b)(1)(J).*

(l) *Rules Relating to Bad Debt Losses of Commerical Banks.*—For purposes of this section—

[Footnote ¶2938 continued]

Section 301(b)(3), '86 TRA, struck out from Sec. 172(d)(2):
(5) "In the case of a taxpayer other than a corporation—
(A) the amount deductible on account of losses from sales or exchanges of capital assets shall not exceed the amount includible on account of gains from sales or exchanges of capital assets; and
(B) the deduction for long-term capital gains provided by section 1202 shall not be allowed."
Effective date (Sec. 301(c), '86 TRA).—Applies to taxable years beginning after 12-31-86.

Matter in *italics* in Sec. 172(d)(6) added by section 1899A(6), '86 TRA.

Section 104(b)(4), '86 TRA, struck out from Sec. 172(d)(7):
(6) "(7) **Zero bracket amount.**—In the case of a taxpayer other than a corporation, the zero bracket amount shall be treated as a deduction allowed by this chapter. For purposes of subsection (c)—
(A) the deduction provided by the preceding sentence shall be in lieu of any itemized deductions of the taxpayer, and
(B) such sentence shall not apply to an individual who elects to itemize deductions."
Effective date (Sec. 151(a), '86 TRA).—Applies to taxable years beginning after 12-31-86.

Matter in *italics* in Sec. 172(k)(2) and (4) added by section 1303(b)(2), '86 TRA, which struck out:
(7) "subsection (b)(1)(K)"
Effective date (Sec. 1311(d), '86 TRA).—Takes effect on the date of enactment of this Act.

---

(1) *Portion attributable to deduction for bad debts.—The portion of the net operating loss for any taxable year which is attributable to the deduction allowed under section 166(a) shall be the excess of—*

    (i) *the net operating loss for such taxable year, over*

    (ii) *the net operating loss for such taxable year determined without regard to the amount allowed as a deduction under section 166(a) for such taxable year.*

(2) *Coordination with subsection (b)(2).—In applying paragraph (2) of subsection (b), the portion of the net operating loss for any taxable year which is attributable to the deduction allowed under section 166(a) shall be treated in a manner similar to the manner in which a foreign expropriation loss is treated.*

[8]*(m)* **Cross References.—** * * *

[For official explanation, see Committee Reports, ¶3950; 3948; 4059; 3885.]

【2939】 **CODE SEC. 173. CIRCULATION EXPENDITURES.**

     * * * * * * * * * * * *

(b) **Cross Reference.—For election of amortization of expenditures allowable as a deduction under subsection (a), see**[1]*section 59(d).*

[For official explanation, see Committee Reports, ¶3932.]

【¶2940】 **CODE SEC. 174. RESEARCH AND EXPERIMENTAL EXPENDITURES.**

     * * * * * * * * * * * *

(e) **Cross References.—**

    (1) **For adjustments to basis of property for amounts allowed as deductions as deferred expenses under subsection (b), see section 1016(a)(14).**

    (2) **For election of 10-year amortization of expenditures allowable as a deduction under subsection (a), see** [1]*section 59(d).*

【¶2941】 **CODE SEC. 175. SOIL AND WATER CONSERVATION EXPENDITURES.**

(a) **In General.—**A taxpayer engaged in the business of farming may treat expenditures which are paid or incurred by him during the taxable year for the purpose of soil or water conservation in respect of land used in farming, or for the prevention of erosion of land used in farming, as expenses which are not chargeable to capital account. The expenditures so treated shall be allowed as a deduction.

     * * * * * * * * * * * *

(c) **Definitions.—**For purposes of subsection (a)—

     * * * * * * * * * * * *

    (3) *Additional limitations.—*

        (A) *Expenditures must be consistent with soil conservation plan.—Notwithstanding any other provision of this section, subsection (a) shall not apply to any expenditures unless such expenditures are consistent with—*

        (i) *the plan (if any) approved by the Soil Conservation Service of the Department of Agriculture for the area in which the land is located, or*

        (ii) *if there is no plan described in clause (i), any soil conservation plan of a comparable State agency.*

【Footnote ¶2938 continued】

Matter in *italics* in Sec. 172(l) and (m) added by section 903(b)(2)(C), '86 TRA, which struck out:

(8) "(l)"

Effective date (Sec. 903(c)(1), '86 TRA).—Applies to losses incurred in taxable years beginning after 12-31-86.

【Footnote ¶2939】 Matter in *italics* in Sec. 173(b) by section 701(e)(4)(D), '86 TRA, which struck out:

(1) "section 58(i)"

Effective date (Sec. 701(f)(1), '86 TRA).—Generally applies to taxable years beginning after 12-31-86.

For special rules, see footnote ¶2879.

【Footnote ¶2940】 Matter in *italics* in Sec. 174(e)(2) added by section 701(e)(4)(D), '86 TRA, which struck out:

(1) "section 58(i)"

Effective date (Sec. 701(f)(1), '86 TRA).—Generally applies to taxable years beginning after 12-31-86. For special rules, see footnote ¶2879.

【Footnote ¶2941】 Sec. 175(c)(3) in *italics* added by section 401(a), '86 TRA.

Effective date (Sec. 401(b), '86 TRA).—

Applies to amounts paid or incurred after 12-31-86, in taxable years ending after such date.

(B)   *Certain wetland, etc., activities not qualified.—Subsection (a) shall not apply to any expenditures in connection with the draining or filling of wetlands or land preparation for center pivot irrigation systems.*

* * * * * * * * * * *

[For official explanation, see Committee Reports, ¶3890.]

[¶2942]   CODE SEC. 177. TRADEMARK AND TRADE NAME EXPENDI-TURES.

[Repealed by section 241(a), '86 TRA].[1]

[For official explanation, see Committee Reports, ¶3874.]

≫**P-H CAUTION→**   There are two versions of Sec. 178. Sec. 178, generally effective after 12-31-86, follows. For Sec. 178, generally effec-tive before 1-1-87, see ¶2943-A below.

[¶2943]   CODE SEC. 178.   *AMORTIZATION OF COST OF ACQUIRING A LEASE.*

(a)   *General Rule.—In determining the amount of the deduction allowable to a lessee of a lease for any taxable year for amortization under section 167, 169, 179, 185, 190, 193, or 194 in respect of any cost of acquiring the lease, the term of the lease shall be treated as including all renewal options (and any other period for which the parties reasonably expect the lease to be renewed) if less than 75 percent of such cost is attributable to the period of the term of the lease remaining on the date of its acquisition.*

(b)   *Certain Periods Excluded.—For purposes of subsection (a), in determining the per-iod of the term of the lease remaining on the date of acquisition, there shall not be taken into account any period for which the lease may subsequently be renewed, extended, or con-tinued pursuant to an option exercisable by the lessee.*

[For official explanation, see Committee Reports, ¶3870.]

[Footnote ¶2942]   (1)   Effective date   (Sec. 241(c), '86 TRA).—(1)   Generally applies to expenditures paid or incurred after 12-31-86.

(2)   Transitional rule.—The amendments made by this section shall not apply to any expenditure incurred—

(A)   pursuant to a binding contract entered into before 3-2-86.

(B)   with respect to the development, protection, expansion, registration, or defense of a trademark or trade name commenced before 3-2-86, but only if not less than the lesser of $1,000,000 or 5 percent of the aggregate cost of such development, protection, expansion, registration, or defense has been incurred or committed before such date.

The preceding sentence shall not apply to any expenditure with respect to a trademark or trade name placed in service after 12-31-87.

[Footnote ¶2943]   Matter in *italics* in Sec. 178 added by section 201(d)(2)(A), '86 TRA, which struck out:

(1)   "**DEPRECIATION OR AMORTIZATION OF IMPROVEMENTS MADE BY LESSEE ON LES-SOR'S PROPERTY.**

(a)   **General Rule.**—Except as provided in subsection (b), in determining the amount allowable to a lessee as a deduction for any taxable year for exhaustion, wear and tear, obsolescence, or amortization—

(1)   in respect of any building erected (or other improvement made) on the leased property, if the portion of the term of the lease (excluding any period for which the lease may subsequently be renewed, extended, or continued pursuant to an option exercisable by the lessee) remaining upon the completion of such building or other improve-ment is less than 60 percent of the useful life of such building or other improvement, or

(2)   in respect of any cost of acquiring the lease, if less than 75 percent of such cost is attributable to the por-tion of the term of the lease (excluding any period for which the lease may subsequently be renewed, extended, or continued pursuant to an option exercisable by the lessee) remaining on the date of its acquisition,

the term of the lease shall be treated as including any period for which the lease may be renewed, extended, or continued pursuant to an option exercisable by the lessee, unless the lessee establishes that (as of the close of the taxable year) it is more probable that the lease will not be renewed, extended, or continued for such period than that the lease will be so renewed, extended, or continued.

(b)   **Related Lessee and Lessor.—**

(1)   **General rule.**—If a lessee and lessor are related persons (as determined under paragraph (2)) at any time during the taxable year then, in determining the amount allowable to the lessee as a deduction for such taxable year for exhaustion, wear and tear, obsolescence, or amortization in respect of any building erected (or other im-provement made) on the leased property, the lease shall be treated as including a period of not less duration than the remaining useful life of such improvement.

(2)   **Related persons defined.**—For purposes of paragraph (1), a lessor and lessee shall be considered to be re-lated persons if—

(A)   the lessor and the lessee are members of an affiliated group (as defined in section 1504), or

(B)   the relationship between the lessor and lessee is one described in subsection (b) of section 267, except that, for purposes of this subparagraph, the phrase "80 percent or more" shall be substituted for the phrase "more than 50 percent" each place it appears in such subsection and subsection (f)(1)(A) of such section shall not apply.

For purposes of determining the ownership of stock in applying subparagraph (B), the rules of subsection (c) of section 267 shall apply, except that the family of an individual shall include only his spouse, ancestors, and lineal descendants.

(c)   **Reasonable Certainty Test.**—In any case in which neither subsection (a) nor subsection (b) applies, the determination as to the amount allowable to a lessee as a deduction for any taxable year for exhaustion, wear and

➤➤**P-H CAUTION**➤ There are two versions of Sec. 178. Sec. 178, generally effective before 1-1-87, follows. For Sec. 178, generally effective after 12-31-86, See ¶2943 above.

〔¶2943-A〕 CODE SEC. 178. DEPRECIATION OR AMORTIZATION OF IMPROVEMENTS MADE BY LESSEE ON LESSOR'S PROPERTY.

* * * * * * * * * * *

(b) Related Lessee and Lessor.—

* * * * * * * * * * * *

(2) **Related persons defined.**—For purposes of paragraph (1), a lessor and lessee shall be considered to be related persons if—

(A) the lessor and the lessee are members of an affiliated group (as defined in section 1504), or

(B) the relationship between the lessor and lessee is one described in subsection (b) of section 267, except that, for purposes of this subparagraph, the phrase "80 percent or more" shall be substituted for the phrase "more than 50 percent" each place it appears in such subsection *and subsection (f)(1)(A) of such section shall not apply.*

For purposes of determining the ownership of stock in applying subparagraph (B), the rules of subsection (c) of section 267 shall apply, except that the family of an individual shall include only his spouse, ancestors, and lineal descendants.

[For official explanation, see Committee Reports, ¶4146.]

〔¶2944〕 CODE SEC. 179. ELECTION TO EXPENSE CERTAIN DEPRECIABLE BUSINESS ASSETS.

(a) **Treatment as Expenses.**—A taxpayer may elect to treat the cost of any section 179 property as an expense which is not chargeable to capital account. Any cost so treated shall be allowed as a deduction for the taxable year in which the section 179 property is placed in service.

[1]*(b) Limitations.—*

〔Footnote ¶2943 continued〕

tear, obsolescence, or amortization—

(1) in respect of any building erected (or other improvement made) on the leased property, or

(2) in respect of any cost of acquiring the lease,

shall be made with reference to the term of the lease (excluding any period for which the lease may subsequently be renewed, extended, or continued pursuant to an option exercisable by the lessee), unless the lease has been renewed, extended, or continued or the facts show with reasonable certainty that the lease will be renewed, extended, or continued."

Effective date (Sec. 203(a)(1), '86 TRA).—

(A) In general.—Except as provided in this section, section 204, and section 251(d), the amendments made by section 201 shall apply to property placed in service after 12-31-86, in taxable years ending after such date.

(B) Election to have amendments made by section 201 apply.—A taxpayer may elect (at such time and in such manner as the Secretary of the Treasury or his delegate may prescribe) to have the amendments made by section 201 apply to any property placed in service after 7-31-86, and before 1-1-87.

For special and transitional rules, see ¶2007—2008.

〔Footnote ¶2943-A〕 Matter in *italics* in Sec. 178(b)(2)(B) added by section 1812(c)(4)(B), '86 TRA.

Effective date (Sec. 1881, '86 TRA and Sec. 174(c)(2)(A), '84 TRA).—Applies to transactions after 12-31-83, in taxable years ending after such date.

〔Footnote ¶2944〕 Matter in *italics* in Sec. 179(b) and (d)(1) added by section 202(a) and (b), '86 TRA, which struck out:

(1) "(b) Dollar Limitation.—

(1) In general.—The aggregate cost which may be taken into account under subsection (a) for any taxable year shall not exceed the following applicable amount:

If the taxable year begins in:	The applicable amount is:
1983, 1984, 1985, 1986, or 1987	$5,000
1988 or 1989	7,500
1990 or thereafter	10,000.

(2) **Married individuals filing separately.**—In the case of a husband and wife filing separate returns for a taxable year, the applicable amount under paragraph (1) shall be equal to 50 percent of the amount otherwise determined under paragraph (1)."

Effective date (Sec. 203(a)(2) and (b), '86 TRA).—(a)(2) Generally applies to property placed in service after 12-31-86, in taxable years ending after such date. For transitional rules and special rules, see footnote ¶2007—2008.

(1) Dollar limitation.—*The aggregate cost which may be taken into account under subsection (a) for any taxable year shall not exceed $10,000.*

(2) Reduction in limitation.—*The limitation under paragraph (1) for any taxable year shall be reduced (but not below zero) by the amount by which the cost of section 179 property placed in service during such taxable year exceeds $200,000.*

(3) Limitation based on income from trade or business.—

(A) In general.—*The aggregate cost of section 179 property taken into account under subsection (a) for any taxable year shall not exceed the aggregate amount of taxable income of the taxpayer for such taxable year which is derived from the active conduct by the taxpayer of any trade or business during such taxable year.*

(B) Carryover of unused cost.—*The amount of any cost which (but for subparagraph (A)) would have been allowed as a deduction under subsection (a) for any taxable year shall be carried to the succeeding taxable year and added to the amount allowable as a deduction under subsection (a) for such succeeding taxable year.*

(C) Computation of taxable income.—*For purposes of this paragraph, taxable income derived from the conduct of a trade or business shall be computed without regard to the cost of any section 179 property.*

(4) Married individuals filing separately.—*In the case of a husband and wife filing separate returns for the taxable year—*

(A) such individuals shall be treated as 1 taxpayer for purposes of paragraphs (1) and (2), and

(B) unless such individuals elect otherwise, 50 percent of the cost of which may be taken into account under subsection (a) for such taxable year (before application of paragraph (3)) shall be allocated to each such individual.

* * * * * * * * * * *

(d) Definitions and Special Rules.—

(1) Section 179 property.—For purposes of this section, the term "section 179 property" means any recovery property which is section 38 property and which is acquired by purchase for use *in the active conduct of* in ["in" should have been deleted] a trade or business.

* * * * * * * * * *

[2]*(8) Treatment of partnerships and s corporations.*—*In the case of a partnership, the limitations of subsection (b) shall apply with respect to the partnership and with respect to each partner. A similar rule shall apply in the case of an S corporation and its shareholders.*

(10) Recapture in certain cases.—The Secretary shall, by regulations provide for recapturing the benefit under any deduction allowable under subsection (a) with respect to any property which is not used predominantly in a trade or business at any time[3].

[For official explanation, see Committee Reports, ¶3870.]

[¶2945] **CODE SEC. 182. EXPENDITURES BY FARMERS FOR CLEARING LAND.**

[Repealed by section 402(a), '86 TRA].[1]

[Footnote ¶2944 continued]

Matter in *italics* in Sec. 179(d)(8) added by section 201(d)(3), '86 TRA, which struck out:

(2) "(8) **Dollar limitation in case of partnerships and S corporations.**—In the case of a partnership, the dollar limitation contained in subsection (b)(1) shall apply with respect to the partnership and with respect to each partner. A similar rule shall apply in the case of an S corporation and its shareholders."

Effective date (Sec. 203(a)(1) and (b), '86 TRA).—(a)(1)(A) Generally applies to property placed in service after 12-31-86, in taxable years ending after such date.

(B) Election to have amendments made by section 201 apply.—A taxpayer may elect (at such time and in such manner as the Secretary of the Treasury or his delegate may prescribe) to have the amendments made by section 201 apply to any property placed in service after July 31, 1986, and before 1-1-87. For transitional rules and special rules, see footnote ¶2007—2008.

Matter in *italics* in Sec. 179(d)(10) added by section 202(c), '86 TRA, which struck out:

(3) "before the close of the second taxable year following the taxable year in which it is placed in service by the taxpayer."

Effective date (Sec. 203(a)(2) and (b) '86 TRA).—See above.

[Footnote ¶2945] (1) **Effective date** (Sec. 402(c), '86 TRA).—Applies to amounts paid or incurred after 12-31-85, in taxable years ending after such date.

[For official explanation, see Committee Reports, ¶3891.]

〖¶2946〗 CODE SEC. 183. ACTIVITIES NOT ENGAGED IN FOR PROFIT.

* * * * * * * * * * * *

(d) Presumption.—If the gross income derived from an activity for [1]*3 or more* of the taxable years in the period of 5 consecutive taxable years which ends with the taxable year exceeds the deductions attributable to such activity (determined without regard to whether or not such activity is engaged in for profit), then, unless the Secretary establishes to the contrary, such activity shall be presumed for purposes of this chapter for such taxable year to be an activity engaged in for profit. In the case of an activity which consists in major part of the breeding, training, showing, or racing of horses, the preceding sentence shall be applied by substituting [2]*"2" for "3" and "7" for "5".*

* * * * * * * * * * * *

[For official explanation, see Committee Reports, ¶3867.]

〖¶2947〗 CODE SEC. 185. AMORTIZATION OF RAILROAD GRADING AND TUNNEL BORES. [Repealed by section 242(a), '86 TRA].[1]

[For official explanation, see Committee Reports, ¶3875.]

〖¶2948〗 CODE SEC. 189. AMORTIZATION OF REAL PROPERTY CONSTRUCTION PERIOD INTEREST AND TAXES.

[Repealed by section 803(b)(1), '86 TRA].[1]

[For official explanation, see Committee Reports, ¶3937.]

〖¶2949〗 CODE SEC. 190. EXPENDITURES TO REMOVE ARCHITECTURAL AND TRANSPORTATION BARRIERS TO THE HANDICAPPED AND ELDERLY.

* * * * * * * * * * *

(d) Application of Section.—This section shall apply to—
　(1)　taxable years beginning after December 31, 1976, and before January 2, 1983, and
　(2)　taxable years beginning after December 31, 1983.[1]

[For official explanation, see Committee Reports, ¶3877.]

〖¶2950〗 CODE SEC. 194. AMORTIZATION OF REFORESTATION EXPENDITURES.

* * * * * * * * * * *

(b) Limitations.—

　(1) Maximum dollar amount.—The aggregate amount of amortizable basis acquired during the taxable year which may be taken into account under subsection (a) for such taxable year shall not exceed $10,000 ($5,000 in the case of a separate return by a married individual (as defined in section [1]*7703*)).

* * * * * * * * * * *

〖Footnote ¶2946〗 Matter in *italics* in Sec. 183(d) added by section 143(a), '86 TRA, which struck out:
(1) "2 or more"
(2) "the period of 7 consecutive taxable years for the period of 5 consecutive taxable years."
Effective date (Sec. 151(a), '86 TRA).—Applies to taxable years beginning after 12-31-85.
〖Footnote ¶2947〗 **(1) Effective date** (Sec. 242(c), '86 TRA).—(1) Generally applies to that portion of the basis of any property which is attributable to expenditures paid or incurred after 12-31-86.
(2) Transitional rule.—The amendments made by this section shall not apply to any expenditure incurred—
(A) pursuant to a binding contract entered into before 3-2-86, or
(B) with respect to any improvement commenced before 3-2-86, but only if not less than the lesser of $1,000,000 or 5 percent of the aggregate cost of such improvement has been incurred or committed before such date.
The preceding sentence shall not apply to any expenditure with respect to an improvement placed in service after 12-31-87.
〖Footnote ¶2948〗 **(1) Effective date** (Sec. 803(d), '86 TRA).—(1) Generally applies to costs incurred after 12-31-86, in taxable years ending after such date. For special and transitional rules, see footnote ¶2961-A.
〖Footnote ¶2949〗 Section 244, '86 TRA, struck out from Sec. 190(d)(2):
(1) ", and before January 1, 1986"
〖Footnote ¶2950〗 Matter in *italics* in Sec. 194(b)(1) added by section 1301(j)(8), '86 TRA, which struck out:
(1) "143"
Effective date (Sec. 1311(a), '86 TRA).—Generally applies to bonds issued after 8-15-86. For transitional and special rules, see ¶2071—2077.

[For official explanation, see Committee Reports, ¶4058.]

[¶2951] CODE SEC. 213. MEDICAL, DENTAL, ETC., EXPENSES.

(a) Allowance of Deduction.—There shall be allowed as a deduction the expenses paid during the taxable year, not compensated for by insurance or otherwise, for medical care of the taxpayer, his spouse, or dependent (as defined in section 152), to the extent that such expenses exceed [1]*7.5 percent of adjusted gross income."*

* * * * * * * * * * * *

[For official explanation, see Committee Reports, ¶3862.]

[¶2952] CODE SEC. 216. DEDUCTION OF TAXES, INTEREST, AND BUSINESS DEPRECIATION BY COOPERATIVE HOUSING, CORPORATION TENANT-STOCKHOLDER.

(a) Allowance of Deduction.—In the case of a tenant-stockholder (as defined in subsection (b)(2), there shall be allowed as a deduction amounts (not otherwise deductible) paid or accrued to a cooperative housing corporation within the taxable year, but only to the extent that such amounts represent the tenant-stockholder's proportionate share of—

(1) the real estate taxes allowable as a deduction to the corporation under section 164 which are paid or incurred by the corporation on the houses or apartment building and on the land on which such houses (or building) are situated, or

(2) the interest allowable as a deduction to the corporate under section 163 which is paid or incurred by the corporation on its indebtedness contracted—

(A) in the acquisition, construction, alteration, rehabilitation, or maintenance of the houses or apartment building, or

(B) in the acquisition of the land on which the houses (or apartment building) are situated.

(b) Definitions.—For purposes of this section—

* * * * * * * * * * * *

(2) **Tenant-stockholder.**—The term "tenant-stockholder" means [1]*a person who is a* stockholder in a cooperative housing corporation, and whose stock is fully paid-up in an amount not less than an amount shown to the satisfaction of the Secretary as bearing a reasonable relationship to the portion of the value of the corporation's equity in the houses or apartment building and the land on which situated which is attributable to the house or apartment which such [2]*person is entitled to occupy.*

(3) [3]Tenant-stockholder's proportionate share.—

(A) In general.—Except as provided in subparagraph (B), the term "tenant-stockholder's proportionate share" means that proportion which the stock of the cooperative housing corporation owned by the tenant-stockholder is of the total outstanding stock of the corporation (including any stock held by the corporation).

(B) Special rule where allocation of taxes or interest reflect cost to corporation of stockholder's unit.—

(i) In general.—If, for any taxable year—

(I) each dwelling unit owned or leased by a cooperative housing corporation is separately allocated a share of such corporation's real estate taxes described in subsection (a)(1) or a share of such corporation's interest described in subsection (a)(2), and

(II) such allocations reasonably reflect the cost to such corporation of such taxes, or of such interest, attributable to the tenant-stockholder's dwelling unit (and such unit's share of the common areas).

then the term "tenant-stockholder's proportionate share" means the shares determined in accordance with the allocations described in subclause (II).

(ii) Election by corporation required.—Clause (i) shall apply with respect to any cooperative housing corporation only if such corporation elects its application.

[Footnote ¶2951] Matter in *italics* in Sec. 213(a) added by section 133, '86 TRA, which struck out:
(1) "5"
Effective date (Sec. 151(a), '86 TRA).—Applies to taxable years beginning after 12-31-86.
[Footnote ¶2952] Matter in *italics* in Sec. 216(b)(2)—(6), (c) and (d) added by section 644(a)—(d), '86 TRA, which struck out:
(1) "an individual"
(2) "individual"
(3) "The term "tenant-stockholder's proportionate share" means that proportion which the stock of the cooperative housing corporation owned by the tenant-stockholder is of the total outstanding stock of the corporation (including any stock held by the corporation)."

Such an election, once made, may be revoked only with the consent of the Secretary.

* * * * * * * * * * * *

[4](5) *Prior approval of occupancy.*—*For purposes of this section, in the following cases there shall not be taken into account the fact that (by agreement with the cooperative housing corporation) the person or his nominee may not occupy the house or apartment without the prior approval of such corporation:*

 (A) In any case where a person acquires stock of a cooperative housing corporation by operation of law.

 (B) In any case where a person other than an individual acquires stock of a cooperative housing corporation.

 (C) In any case where the original seller acquires any stock of the cooperative housing corporation from the corporation not later than 1 year after the date on which the apartments or houses (or leaseholds therein) are transferred by the original seller to the corporation.

[5](6) *Original seller defined.*—*For purposes of paragraph (5), the term "original seller" means the person from whom the corporation has acquired the apartments or houses (or leaseholds therein).*

(c)   Treatment as Property Subject to Depreciation.—

 (1)   In general.—So much of the stock of a tenant-stockholder in a cooperative housing corporation as is allocable, under regulations prescribed by the Secretary, to a proprietary lease or right of tenancy in property subject to the allowance for depreciation under section 167(a) shall, to the extent such proprietary lease or right of tenancy is used by such tenant-stockholder in a trade or business or for the production of income, be treated as property subject to the allowance for depreciation *under section 167(a).* The preceding sentence shall not be construed to limit or deny a deduction for depreciation under *section 167(a)* by a cooperative housing corporation with respect to property owned by such a corporation and leased to tenant stockholders.

 (2)   *Deduction limited to adjusted basis in stock.*—

  (A) In general.—*The amount of any deduction for depreciation allowable under section 167(a) to a tenant-stockholder with respect to any stock for any taxable year by reason of paragraph (1) shall not exceed the adjusted basis of such stock as of the close of the taxable year of the tenant-stockholder in which such deduction was incurred.*

  (B) Carryforward of disallowed amount.—*The amount of any deduction which is not allowed by reason of subparagraph (A) shall, subject to the provisions of subparagraph (A), be treated as a deduction allowable under section 167(a) in the succeeding taxable year.*

⸢Footnote ¶2952 continued⸥

(4)   "**(5)   Stock acquired through foreclosure by lending institution.**—If a bank or other lending institution acquires by foreclosure (or by instrument in lieu of foreclosure) the stock of a tenant stockholder, and a lease or the right to occupy an apartment or house to which such stock is appurtenant, such bank or other lending institution shall be treated as a tenant-stockholder for a period not to exceed three years from the date of acquisition. The preceding sentence shall apply even though, by agreement with the cooperative housing corporation, the bank (or other lending institution) or its nominee may not occupy the house or apartment without the prior approval of such corporation."

(5)   "**(6)   Stock owned by person from whom the corporation acquired its property.**—

(A)   In general.—If the original seller acquires any stock of the corporation from the corporation or by foreclosure, the original seller shall be treated as a tenant-stockholder for a period not to exceed 3 years from the date of acquisition of such stock.

(B)   Stock acquisition must take place not later than 1 year after transfer of dwelling units.—Except in the case of an acquisition of stock of a corporation by foreclosure, subparagraph (A) shall apply only if the acquisition of stock occurs not later than 1 year after the date on which the apartments or houses (or leaseholds therein) are transferred by the original seller to the corporation. For purposes of this subparagraph and subparagraph (A), the term "by foreclosure" means by foreclosure (or by instrument in lieu of foreclosure) of any purchase-money security interest in the stock held by the original seller.

(C)   Original seller must have right to occupy apartment or house.—Subparagraph (A) shall apply with respect to any acquisition of stock only if, together with such acquisition, the original seller acquires the right to occupy an apartment or house to which such stock is appurtenant. For purposes of the preceding sentence, there shall not be taken into account the fact that, by agreement with the corporation, the original seller or its nominee may not occupy the house or apartment without the prior approval of the corporation.

(D)   Original seller defined.—For purposes of this paragraph, the term "original seller" means the person from whom the corporation has acquired the apartments or houses (or leaseholds therein). The estate of an original seller shall succeed to, and take into account, the tax treatment of the original seller under this paragraph."

Effective date   (Sec. 644(f)(1), '86 TRA).—Applies to taxable years beginning after 12-31-86.

(d)   *Disallowance of Deduction for Certain Payments to the Corporation.—No deduction shall be allowed to a stockholder in a cooperative housing corporation for any amount paid or accrued to such corporation during any taxable year (in excess of the stockholder's proportionate share of the items described in subsections (a)(1) and (a)(2)) to the extent that, under regulations prescribed by the Secretary, such amount is properly allocable to amounts paid or incurred at any time by the corporation which are chargeable to the corporation's capital account. The stockholder's adjusted basis in the stock in the corporation shall be increased by the amount of such disallowance.*

[For official explanation, see Committee Reports, ¶3924.]

[¶2953]   **CODE SEC. 219.   RETIREMENT SAVINGS.**

(a)   **Allowance of Deduction.**—In the case of an individual, there shall be allowed as a deduction an amount equal to the qualified retirement contributions of the individual for the taxable year.

(b)   **Maximum Amount of Deduction.—**

*   *   *   *   *   *   *   *   *   *   *

⟫P-H CAUTION→   There are two versions of Sec. 219(b)(2). Sec. 219(b)(2), generally effective after 12-31-86, follows. For Sec. 219(b)(2), generally effective before 1-1-87, see below.

▲ **(2)**   **Special** [1]*rule* **for employer contributions under simplified employee pensions.—**[2]*This section shall not apply with respect to an employer contribution to a simplified employee pension.*

⟫P-H CAUTION→   There are two versions of Sec. 219(b)(2). Sec. 219(b)(2)(C), generally effective before 1-1-87, follows. Sec. 219(b)(2), generally effective after 12-31-86, see above.

▲▲ **(2)**   **Special rules for employer contributions under simplified employee pensions.—**

*   *   *   *   *   *   *   *   *   *   *

(C)   Special rule for applying subparagraph (A)(ii).—In the case of an employee who is an officer, shareholder, or owner-employee described in section 408(k)(3), the [3]*dollar limitation in effect under section 415(c)(1)(A)* shall be reduced by the amount of tax taken into account with respect to such individual under subparagraph (D) of section 408(k)(3).

[4]*(3)*   *Plans under section 501(c)(18).—Notwithstanding paragraph (1), the amount*

[Footnote ¶2953]   ▲ Matter in *italics* in Sec. 219(b)(2), preceded by a triangle, added by section 1108(g)(2), '86 TRA, which struck out:

(1)   "rules"

(2)   "(A)   Limitation.—If there is an employer contribution on behalf of the employee to a simplified employee pension, an employee shall be allowed as a deduction under subsection (a) (in addition to the amount allowable under paragraph (1)) an amount equal to the lesser of—

(i)   15 percent of the compensation from such employer includible in the employee's gross income for the taxable year (determined without regard to the employer contribution to the simplified employee pension), or

(ii)   the amount contributed by such employer to the simplified employee pension and included in gross income (but not in excess of the limitation in effect under section 415(c)(1)(A)).

(B)   Certain limitations do not apply to employer contribution.—Paragraph (1) of this subsection and paragraph (1) of subsection (d) shall not apply with respect to the employer contribution to a simplified employee pension.

(C)   Special rule for applying subparagraph (A)(ii).—In the case of an employee who is an officer, shareholder, or owner-employee described in section 408(k)(3), the dollar limitation in effect under Section 415(c)(1)(A) shall be reduced by the amount of tax taken into account with respect to such individual under subparagraph (D) of section 408(k)(3)."

Effective date (Sec. 1108(h), '86 TRA).—Applies to years beginning after 12-31-86.

▲▲ Matter in *italics* in Sec. 219(b)(2)(C), preceded by two triangles, added by section 1875(c)(6)(B), '86 TRA, which struck out:

(3)   "$15,000 amount specified in subparagraph (A)(ii)"

Effective date (Sec. 1881, '86 TRA, Sec. 715, '84 TRA and section 241(a), '82 TEFRA).—Applies to years beginning after 12-31-83.

Section 1101(b)(2)(A), '86 TRA, struck out from Sec. 219(b)(3):

(4)   "(3)   **Special rule for individual retirement plans.**—If the individual has paid any qualified voluntary employee contributions for the taxable year, the amount of the qualified retirement contributions (other than employer contributions to a simplified employee pension) which are paid for the taxable year to an individual retirement plan and which are allowable as a deduction under subsection (a) for such taxable year shall not exceed—

(A)   the amount determined under paragraph (1) for such taxable year, reduced by

(B)   the amount of the qualified voluntary employee contributions for the taxable year."

allowable as a deduction under subsection (a) with respect to any contributions on behalf of an employee to a plan described in section 501(c)(18) shall not exceed the lessor of—

    (A) $7,000, or

    (B) an amount equal to 25 percent of the compensation (as defined in section 415(c)(3)) includible in the individual's gross income for such taxable year.

(c) Special Rules for Certain Married Individuals.—

    (1) In general.—In the case of any individual with respect to whom a deduction is otherwise allowable under subsection (a)—

    (A) who files a joint return under section 6013 for a taxable year, and

    (B) whose spouse—

        (i) has no compensation (determined without regard to section 911) for [5]the taxable year, or

        (ii) elects to be treated for purposes of subsection (b)(1)(B) as having no compensation for the taxable year,

there shall be allowed as a deduction any amount paid in cash for the taxable year by or on behalf of the individual to an individual retirement plan established for the benefit of his spouse.

    (2) Limitation.—The amount allowable as a deduction under paragraph (1) shall not exceed the excess of—

    (A) the lesser of—

        (i) $2,250, or

        (ii) any amount equal to the compensation includible in the individual's gross income for the taxable year, over

    (B) the amount as a deduction under subsection (a) for the taxable year.[6]

In no event shall the amount allowable as a deduction under paragraph (1) exceed $2,000.

* * * * * * * * * * * * *

[7]*(e) Qualified Retirement Contribution.—For purposes of this section, the term "quali-*

⸢Footnote ¶2953 continued⸥

Effective date (Sec. 1101(c), '86 TRA).—Applies to contributions for taxable years beginning after 12-31-86.

Sec. 219(b)(3) in *italics* added by section 1109(b), '86 TRA.
Effective date (Sec. 1109(c), '86 TRA).—Applies to taxable years beginning after 12-31-86.

Matter in *italics* in Sec. 219(c)(1)(B) added by section 1103(a), '86 TRA, which struck out:
(5) "such"
Effective date (Sec. 1103(b), '86 TRA).—Applies to taxable years beginning before, on, or after 12-31-85.

Section 1108(g)(3), '86 TRA, struck out from Sec. 219(c)(2)(B):
(6) "(determined without regard to so much of the employer contributions to a simplified employee pension as is allowable by reason of paragraph (2) of subsection (b))"
Effective date (Sec. 1108(h), '86 TRA).—Applies to years beginning after 12-31-86.

Matter in *italics* in Sec. 219(e) added by section 1101(b)(1), '86 TRA, which struck out:
(7) **"(e)** **Definition of Retirement Savings Contributions, Etc.**—For purposes of this section—
(1) **Qualified retirement contribution.**—The term "qualified retirement contribution" means—
(A) any qualified voluntary employee contribution paid in cash by the individual for the taxable year, and
(B) any amount paid in cash for the taxable year by or on behalf of such individual for his benefit to an individual retirement plan.
(2) **Qualified voluntary employee contribution.—**
(A) In general.—The term "qualified voluntary employee contribution" means any voluntary contribution.—
(i) which is made by an individual as an employee under a qualified employer plan or government plan, which plan allows an employee to make contributions which may be treated as qualified voluntary employee contributions under this section, and
(ii) with respect to which the individual has not designated such contribution as a contribution which should not be taken into account under this section.
(B) Voluntary contribution.—For purposes of subparagraph (A), the term "voluntary contribution" means any contribution which is not a mandatory contribution (within the meaning of section 411(c)(2)(C).
(C) Designation.—For purposes of determining whether or not an individual has made a designation described in subparagraph (A)(ii) with respect to any contribution during any calendar year under a qualified employer plan or government plan, such individual shall be treated as having made such designation if he notifies the plan administrator of such plan, not later than the earlier of—
(i) April 15 of the succeeding calendar year, or
(ii) the time prescribed by the plan administrator, that the individual does not want such contribution taken

fied retirement contribution" means—

(1) any amount paid in cash for the taxable year by or on behalf of an individual to an individual retirement plan for such individual's benefit, and

(2) any amount contributed on behalf of any individual to a plan described in section 501(c)(18).

≫P-H CAUTION→ There are two versions of Sec. 219(f)(1). Sec. 219(f)(1), generally effective after 12-31-86, follows. For Sec. 219(f)(1), effective before 1-1-87, see below.

▲**(f)**   **Other Definitions and Special Rules.—**

(1) Compensation.—For purposes of this section, the term "compensation" includes earned income as defined in section 401(c)(2) reduced by any amount allowable as a deduction to the individual in computing adjusted gross income under [8] *paragraph (6)* of section 62. The term "compensation" does not include any amount received as a pension or annuity and does not include any amount received as deferred compensation. The term "compensation" shall include any amount includible in the individual's gross income under section 71 with respect to a divorce or separation instrument described in subparagraph (A) of section 71(b)(2).

≫P-H CAUTION→ There are two versions of Sec. 219(f)(1). Sec. (f)(1), generally effective before 1-1-87, follows. For Sec. 219(f)(1), generally effective after 12-31-86, see above.

▲▲**(f)**   **Other Definitions and Special Rules.—**

(1) Compensation.—For purposes of this section, the term "compensation" includes earned income as defined in section 401(c)(2). [9] The term "compensation" does not include any amount received as a pension or annuity and does not include any amount received as deferred compensation. The term "compensation" shall include any amount includible in the individual's gross income under section 71 with respect to a divorce or separation instrument described in subparagraph (A) of section 71(b)(2).

* * * * * * * * * * * *

[10] **(3)** *Time when contributions deemed made.*—For purposes of this section, a

---

⟦Footnote ¶2953 continued⟧

into account under this section. Any designation or notification referred to in the preceding sentence shall be made in such manner as the Secretary shall by regulations prescribe and, after the last date on which such designation or notification may be made, shall be irrevocable for such taxable year.

(3) **Qualified employer plan.—**The term "qualified employer plan" means—

(A) a plan described in section 401(a) which includes a trust exempt from tax under section 501(a),

(B) an annuity plan described in section 403(a), and

(C) a plan under, which amounts are contributed by an individual's employer for an annuity contract described in section 403(b).

(4) **Government plan.—**The term "government plan" means any plan, whether or not qualified, established and maintained for its employees by the United States, by a State or political subdivision thereof, or by an agency or instrumentality of any of the foregoing.

(5) **Payment for certain plans.—**The term "amounts paid to an individual retirement plan" includes amounts paid for an individual retirement annuity or a retirement bond."

Effective date (Sec. 1101(c), '86 TRA).—Applies to contributions for taxable years beginning after 12-31-86.

▲ Matter in *italics* in Sec. 219(f)(1), preceded by a single triangle added by section 301(b)(4), '86 TRA, which struck out:

(8) "paragraph (7)"

Effective date (Sec. 301(c), '86 TRA).—Applies to taxable years beginning after 12-31-86.

▲▲ Section 1875(c)(4), '86 TRA, struck out from Sec. 219(f)(1), preceded by two triangles:

(9) "reduced by any amount allowable as a deduction to the individual in computing adjusted gross income under paragraph (7) of section 62"

Effective date (Sec. 1881, '86 TRA, Sec. 715, '86 TRA and section 241(a), '82 TEFRA).—Applies to years beginning after 12-31-83.

Matter in *italics* in Sec. 219(f)(3) added by section 1101(a)(2), '86 TRA, which struck out:

(10) "(3) **Time when contributions deemed made.—**

(A) Individual retirement plans.—For purposes of this section, a taxpayer shall be deemed to have made a contribution to an individual retirement plan on the last day of the preceding taxable year if the contribution is made on account of such taxable year and is made not later than the time prescribed by law for filing the return for such taxable year (not including extensions thereof).

(B) Qualified employer or governmental plans.—For purposes of this section if a qualified employer or govern-

taxpayer shall be deemed to have made a contribution to an individual retirement plan on the last day of the preceding taxable year if the contribution is made on account of such taxable year and is made not later than the time prescribed by law for filing the return for such taxable year (not including extensions thereof).

* * * * * * * * * * * *

(7)   Election not to deduct contributions.—
For election not to deduct contributions to individual retirement plans, see section 408(o)(2)(B)(ii).

(g)   Limitation on Deduction for Active Participants in Certain Pension Plans.—

(1)   In general.—If (for any part of any plan year ending with or within a taxable year) an individual or the individual's spouse is an active participant, each of the dollar limitations contained in subsections (b)(1)(A) and (c)(2) for such taxable year shall be reduced (but not below zero) by the amount determined under paragraph (2).

(2)   Amount of reduction.—
(A)   In general.—The amount determined under this paragraph with respect to any dollar limitation shall be the amount which bears the same ratio to such limitation as—
(i)   the excess of—
(I)   the taxpayer's adjusted gross income for such taxable year, over
(II)   the applicable dollar amount, bears to
(ii) $10,000.
(B)   No reduction below $200 until complete phase-out.—No dollar limitation shall be reduced below $200 under paragraph (1) unless (without regard to this subparagraph) such limitation is reduced to zero.
(C)   Rounding.—Any amount determined under this paragraph which is not a multiple of $10 shall be rounded to the next lowest $10.

(3)   Adjusted gross income; applicable dollar amount.—For purposes of this subsection—
(A)   Adjusted gross income.—Adjusted gross income of any taxpayer shall be determined—
(i)   after application of sections 86 and 469, and
(ii)   without regard to section 911 or the deduction allowable under this section.
(B)   Applicable dollar amount.—The term "applicable dollar amount" means—
(i)   in the case of a taxpayer filing a joint return, $40,000,
(ii)   in the case of any other taxpayer (other than a married individual filing a separate return, $25,000, and
(iii)   in the case of a married individual filing a separate return, zero.

(4)   Special rule for married individuals filing separately.—In the case of a married individual filing a separate return for any taxable year, paragrapyh (1) shall be applied without regard to whether such individual's spouse is an active participant for any plan year ending with or within such taxable year.

(5)   Active participant.—For purposes of this subsection, the term "active participant" means, with respect to any plan year, an individual—
(A)   who is an active participant in—
(i)   a plan described in section 401(a) which includes a trust exempt from tax under section 501(a),
(ii)   an annuity plan described in section 403(a),

⟦Footnote ¶2953 continued⟧

ment plan elects to have the provisions of this subparagraph apply, a taxpayer shall be deemed to have made a voluntary contribution to such plan on the last day of the preceding calendar year (if, without regard to this paragraph, such contribution may be made on such date) if the contribution is made on account of the taxable year which includes such last day and by April 15 of the calendar year or such earlier time as is provided by the plan administrator."

Effective date (Sec. 1101(c), '86 TRA).—Applies to contributions for taxable years beginning after 12-31-86.

Sec. 219(f)(7) in *italics* added by section 1102(f), '86 TRA.
Effective date (Sec. 1102(g), '86 TRA).—Applies to contributions and distributions for taxable years beginning after 12-31-86.

Code §219(g)(5) ¶2953

     (iii)   a plan established for its employees by the United States, by a State or political subdivision thereof, or by an agency or instrumentality of any of the foregoing,

     (iv)   an annuity contract described in section 403(b), or

     (v)   a simplified employee pension (within the meaning of section 408(k)), or

  (B)   who makes deductible contributions to a trust described in section 501(c)(18).

The determination of whether an individual is an active participant shall be made without regard to whether or not such individual's rights under a plan, trust, or contract are nonforfeitable. An eligible deferred compensation plan (within the meaning of section 457(b)) shall not be treated as a plan described in subparagraph (A)(iii).

  (6)   Certain individuals not treated as active participants.—For purposes of this subsection, any individual described in any of the following subparagraphs shall not be treated as an active participant for any taxable year solely because of any participation so described:

    (A)   Members of reserve components.—Participation in a plan described in subparagraph (A)(iii) of paragraph (5) by reason of service as a member of a reserve component of the Armed Forces (as defined in section 261(a) of title 10), unless such individual has served in excess of 90 days on active duty (other than active duty for training) during the year.

    (B)   Volunteer firefighters.—A volunteer firefighter—

     (i)   who is a participant in a plan described in subparagraph (A)(iii) of paragraph (5) based on his activity as a volunteer firefighter, and

     (ii)   whose accrued benefit as of the beginning of the taxable year is not more than an annual benefit of $1,800 (when expressed as a single life annuity commencing at age 65).

[11]*(h)*   **Cross Reference.—For failure to provide required reports, see section** [12]**6652(g).**

[For official explanation, see Committee Reports, ¶3885; 3968; 3969; 3970; 3974; 3975; 4071; 4189.]

[¶2954]   CODE SEC. [1]**220.   CROSS** [2] [3]*REFERENCE.*
  For deductions in respect of a decedent, see section 691.

[For official explanation, see Committee Reports, ¶3864; 3885.]

[¶2955]   CODE SEC. 221.   DEDUCTION FOR TWO-EARNER MARRIED COUPLES.
[Repealed by section 131(a), '86 TRA].[1]

[For official explanation, see Committee Reports, ¶3860.]

[¶2956]   CODE SEC. 222.   ADOPTION EXPENSES.   [Repealed by section 135(a), '86 TRA].[1]

[For official explanation, see Committee Reports, ¶3864.]

[Footnote ¶2953 continued]

Matter in *italics* in Sec. 219(g) and (h) (except for the phrase "section 6652(g)") added by section 1101(a)(1), '86 TRA, which struck out:

(11) "g"
Effective date (Sec. 1101(c), '86 TRA).—Applies to contributions for taxable years beginning after 12-31-86.

The phrase *"section 6652(g)"* in *italics* in Sec. 219(h) formerly (g)) added by section 1501(d)(1)(B), '86 TRA, which struck out:

(12) "6652(h)"
Effective date (Sec. 1501(e), '86 TRA).—Applies to returns, the due date for which (determined without regard to extensions) is after 12-31-86.

[Footnote ¶2954]   Matter in *italics* in the title of Sec. 220 (former 223) added by section 135(b)(1), '86 TRA, which struck out:

(1) "223"
Effective date (Sec. 151(a), '86 TRA).—Applies to taxable years beginning after 12-31-86.

Matter in *italics* in Sec. 220 (former 223) added by section 301(b)(5)(A), '86 TRA, which struck out:

(2) "REFERENCES.
(1) For deduction for long-term capital gains in the case of a taxpayer other than a corporation, see section 1202."
(3) "(2)"
Effective date (Sec. 301(c), '86 TRA).—Applies to taxable years beginning after 12-31-86.

[Footnote ¶2955]   (1)   **Effective date** (Sec. 151(a), '86 TRA).—Applies to taxable years beginning after 12-31-86.

[Footnote ¶2956]   (1)   **Effective date** (Sec. 151(a), '86 TRA).—Applies to taxable years beginning after 12-31-86.

[¶2957] CODE SEC. 243. DIVIDENDS RECEIVED BY CORPORATIONS.

(a) General Rule.—In the case of a corporation, there shall be allowed as a deduction an amount equal to the following percentages of the amount received as dividends from a domestic corporation which is subject to taxation under this chapter:

(1) *80 percent* in the case of dividends other than dividends described in paragraph (2) or (3);

(2) 100 percent, in the case of dividends received by a small business investment company operating under the Small Business Investment Act of 1958 (15 U.S.C. 661 and following); and

(3) 100 percent, in the case of qualifying dividends (as defined in subsection (b)(1)).

(b) Qualifying Dividends.—

* * * * * * * * * * * * *

(3) **Effect of Election.**—If an election by an affiliated group is effective with respect to a taxable year of the common parent corporation, then under regulations prescribed by the Secretary—

(A) no member of such affiliated group may consent to an election under section 1562 for such taxable year,

(B) the members of such affiliated group shall be treated as one taxpayer for purposes of making the credit) and election under section 901(a) (relating to allowance of foreign tax credit), and

(C) the members of such affiliated group shall be limited to one—

(i) minimum accumulated earnings credit under section 535(c)(2) or (3), *and*[2]

[3](ii) surtax exemption, and one amount under sections 6154(c)(2) and sections 6655(e)(2), for purposes of estimated tax payment requirements under section 6154 and the addition to the tax under section 6655 for failure to pay estimated tax.

* * * * * * * * * * * * *

[For official explanation, see Committee Reports, ¶3896; 3912]

[¶2958] CODE SEC. 244. DIVIDENDS RECEIVED ON CERTAIN PREFERRED STOCK.

(a) General Rule.—In the case of a corporation, there shall be allowed as a deduction an amount computed as follows:

(1) First determine the amount received as dividends on the preferred stock of a public utility which is subject to taxation under this chapter and with respect to which the deduction provided in section 247 for dividends paid is allowable.

(2) Then multiply the amount determined under paragraph (1) by the fraction—

(A) the numerator of which is 14 percent, and

(B) the denominator of which is that percentage which equals the highest rate of tax specified in section 11(b).

(3) Finally ascertain the amount which is *80 percent* of the excess of—

(A) the amount determined under paragraph (1), over

[Footnote ¶2957] Matter in *italics* in Sec. 243(a)(1) added by section 611(a)(1), '86 TRA, which struck out:
(1) "85 percent"
Effective date (Sec. 611(b)(1), '86 TRA).—Applies to dividends received or accrued after 12-31-86, in taxable years ending after such date.

Matter in *italics* in Sec. 243(b)(3)(C) added by section 411(b)(2)(C)(iv), '86 TRA, which struck out:
(2) "(ii) $400,000 limitation for certain expenditures under section 617(h)(1), and"
(3) "(iii)"
Effective date (Sec. 411(c), '86 TRA).—(1) Generally applies to costs paid or incurred after 12-31-86, in taxable years ending after such date.
(2) Transition rule.—Does not apply with respect to intangible drilling and development costs incurred by United States companies pursuant to a minority interest in a license for Netherlands or United Kingdom North Sea development if such interest was acquired on or before 12-31-85.
[Footnote ¶2958] Matter in *italics* in Sec. 244(a)(3) and (b)(2) added by section 611(a)(2), '86 TRA, which struck out:
(1) "85 percent"
Effective date (Sec. 611(b)(1), '86 TRA).—Applies to dividends received or accrued after 12-31-86, in taxable years ending after such date.

(B) the amount determined under paragraph (2).

(b) Exception.—If the dividends described in subsection (a)(1) are qualifying dividends (a) defined in section 243(b)(1), but determined without regard to section 243(c)(4))—

(1) subsection (a) shall be applied separately to such qualifying dividends, and

(2) for purposes of subsection (a)(3), the percentage applicable to such qualifying dividends shall be 100 percent in lieu of [1]80 percent.

[For official explanation, see Committee Reports, ¶3912.]

[¶2959] CODE SEC. 245. DIVIDENDS RECEIVED FROM CERTAIN FOREIGN CORPORATIONS.

[1]*(a)   Dividends from 10-Percent Owned Foreign Corporations.—*

(1)   In General.—In the case of dividends received by a corporation from a qualified 10-percent owned foreign corporation, there shall be allowed as a deduction an amount equal to the percent (specified in section 243 for the taxable year) of the U.S. source portion of such dividends.

(2)   Qualified 10-Percent owned foreign corporation.—For purposes of this subsection, the term "qualified 10-percent owned foreign corporation" means any foreign corporation (other than a foreign personal holding company passive foreign investment company) if at least 10 percent of the stock of such corporation (by vote and value) is owned by the taxpayer.

(3)   U.S.-source portion.—For purposes of this subsection, the U.S.-source portion of any dividend is an amount which bears the same ratio to such dividend as—

(A)   the post-1986 undistributed U.S. earnings, bears to

(B)   the total post-1986 undistributed earnings.

(4)   Post-1986 undistributed earnings.—For purposes of this subsection, the term "post-1986 undistributed earnings" has the meaning given to such term by section 902(c)(1).

(5)   Post-1986 undistributed U.S. earnings.—For purposes of this subsection, the term "post-1986 undistributed U.S. earnings" means the portion of the post-1986 undistributed earnings which is attributable to—

(A)   income of the qualified 10-percent owned foreign corporation which is effectively connected with the conduct of a trade or business within the United States and subject to tax under this chapter, or

---

[Footnote ¶2959]   Matter in *italics* in Sec. 245(a) added by section 1226(a), '86 TRA, which struck out:

(1)   "General Rules.—In the case of dividends received from a foreign corporation (other than a foreign personal holding company) which is subject to taxation under this chapter, if, for an uninterrupted period of not less than 36 months ending with the close of such foreign corporation's taxable year in which such dividends are paid (or, if the corporation has not been in existence for 36 months at the close of such taxable year, for the period the foreign corporation has been in existence as of the close of such taxable year) such foreign corporation has been engaged in trade or business within the United States and if 50 percent or more of the gross income of such corporation from all sources for such period is effectively connected with the conduct of a trade or business within the United States, there shall be allowed as a deduction in the case of a corporation—

(1)   An amount equal to the percent (specified in section 243 for the taxable year) of the dividends received out of its earnings and profits specified in paragraph (2) of the first sentence of section 316(a), but such amount shall not exceed an amount which bears the same ratio to such percent of such dividends received out of such earnings and profits as the gross income of such foreign corporation for the taxable year which is effectively connected with the conduct of a trade or business within the United States bears to its gross income from all sources for such taxable year, and

(2)   An amount equal to the percent (specified in section 243 for the taxable year) of the dividends received out of that part of its earnings and profits specified in paragraph (1) of the first sentence of section 316(a) accumulated after the beginning of such uninterrupted period, but such amount shall not exceed an amount which bears the same ratio to such percent of such dividends received out of such accumulated earnings and profits as the gross income of such foreign corporation, which is effectively connected with the conduct of a trade or business within the United States, for the portion of such uninterrupted period ending at the beginning of such taxable year bears to its gross income from all sources for such portion of such uninterrupted period.

For purposes of this subsection, the gross income of the foreign corporation for any period before the first taxable year beginning after December 31, 1966, which is effectively connected with the conduct of a trade or business within the United States is an amount equal to the gross income for such period from sources within the United States. For purposes of paragraph (2), there shall not be taken into account any taxable year within such uninterrupted period if, with respect to dividends paid out of the earnings and profits of such year, the deduction provided by subsection (b) would be allowable."

Effective date (Sec. 1226(c)(1), '86 TRA).—(1)   Applies to distributions out of earnings and profits for taxable years beginning after 12-31-86.

(B) any dividend received (directly or through a wholly owned foreign corporation) from a domestic corporation at least 80 percent of the stock of which (by vote and value) is owned (directly or through such wholly owned foreign corporation) by the qualified 10-percent owned foreign corporation.

(6) Special rule.—If the 1st day on which the requirements of paragraph (2) are met with respect to any foreign corporation is in a taxable year of such corporation beginning after December 31, 1986, the post-1986 undistributed earnings and the post-1986 undistributed U.S. earnings of such corporation shall be determined by only taking into account periods beginning on and after the 1st day of the 1st taxable year in which such requirements are met.

*(7) **Coordination with subsection (b).**—Earnings and profits of any qualified 10-percent owned foreign corporation for any taxable year shall not be taken into account under this subsection if the deduction provided by subsection (b) would be allowable with respect to dividends paid out of such earnings and profits.*

*(8) **Coordination with section 902.**—In the case of a dividend received by a corporation from a qualified 10-percent owned foreign corporation, no credit shall be allowed under section 901 for any taxes treated as paid under section 902 with respect to the U.S.-source portion of such dividend.*

*(9) **Coordination with section 904.**—For purposes of section 904, the U.S.-source portion of any dividend received by a corporation from a qualified 10-percent owned foreign corporation shall be treated as from sources in the United States.*

* * * * * * * * * * * *

(c) Certain Dividends Received From FSC.—

(1) In General.—In the case of a domestic corporation, there shall be allowed as a deduction an amount equal to[2]—

(A) 100 percent of any dividend received by such corporation from another corporation which is distributed out of earnings and profits attributable to foreign trade income for a period during which such other corporation was a FSC, and

(B) 85 percent of any dividend received by such corporation from another corporation which is distributed out of earnings and profits attributable to qualified interest and carrying charges received or accrued by such other corporation while such other corporation was a FSC.

The deduction allowable under the preceding sentence with respect to any dividend shall be in lieu of any deduction allowable under subsection (a) or (b) with respect to such dividend.

(2) Exception for certain dividends.—Paragraph (1) shall not apply to any dividend which is distributed out of earnings and profits attributable to foreign trade income which—

(A) is section 923(a)(2) non-exempt income (within the meaning of section 927(d)(6)), or

(B) would not, but for section 923(a)(4), be treated as exempt foreign trade income.

(3) Coordination with subsections (a) and (b).—*The gross income giving rise to the earnings and profits described in subparagraph (A) or (B) of paragraph (1) (and not described in paragraph (2)) shall not be taken into account under subsections (a) and (b).*

[3]*(4) **Definitions.**—For purposes of this subsection, the terms "foreign trade income"*

⟦Footnote ¶2959 continued⟧
accounting which was entered into before 1-1-85, or

(C)   in the case of any contract other than a lease or contract described in subparagraph (A) or (B), any contract which was entered into before 1-1-85; except that this subparagraph shall only apply to the first 3 taxable years of the FSC ending after 1-1-85, or such later taxable years as the Secretary of the Treasury or his delegate may prescribe.

(3)   Section 801(d)(10).—The amendment made by section 801(d)(10) shall apply to distributions on or after 6-22-84.

(4)   Section 803.—The amendments made by section 803 shall apply to taxable years beginning after 12-31-84.

(b)   Transition Rules for DISC's.—

(1)   Close of 1984 taxable years of DISC's.—

(A)   In General.—For purposes of applying the '54 Code, the taxable year of each DISC which begins before 1-1-85, and which (but for this paragraph) would include 1-1-85, shall close on 12-31-84. For purposes of such Code, the requirements of section 992(a)(i)(B) of such Code (relating to percentage of qualified export assets on last day of the taxable year) shall not apply to any taxable year ending on 12-31-84.

(B)   Underpayments of estimated tax.—To the extent provided in regulations prescribed by the Secretary of the Treasury or his delegate, no addition to tax shall be made under section 6654 or 6655 of such Code with respect to any underpayment of any installment required to be paid before 4-13-85, to the extent the underpayment was created or increased by reason of subparagraph (A).

(2)   Exemption of accumulated a DISC income from tax.—

(A)   In general.—For purposes of applying the '54 Code with respect to actual distributions made after 12-31-84, by a DISC or former DISC which was a DISC on 12-31-84, any accumulated DISC income of a DISC or former DISC (within the meaning of section 996(f)(1) of such Code) which is derived before 1-1-85, shall be treated as previously taxed income (within the meaning of section 996(f)(2) of such Code) with respect to which there had previously been a deemed distribution to which section 996(e)(1) of such Code applied.

For purposes of the preceding sentence, the term 'actual distribution' includes a distribution in liquidation, and the earnings and profits of any corporation receiving a distribution not included in gross income by reason of the preceding sentence shall be increased by the amount of such distribution.

(B)   Exception for distribution of amounts previously disqualified.—Subparagraph (A) shall not apply to the distribution of any accumulated DISC income of a DISC or former DISC to which section 995(b)(2) of such Code applied by reason of any revocation or disqualification (other than a revocation which under regulations prescribed by the Secretary results solely from the provisions of this title.

(C)   Treatment of distribution of accumulated DISC income received by cooperatives.—In the case of any actual distribution received by an organization described in section 1381 of such Code and excluded from the gross income of such corporation by reason of subparagraph (A)—

(i)   such amount shall not be included in the gross income of any member of such organization when distributed in the form of a patronage dividend or otherwise, and

(ii)   no deduction shall be allowed to such organization by reason of any such distribution.

(3)   Installment treatment of certain deemed distributions of shareholders.—

(A)   In general.—Notwithstanding section 995(b) of such Code, if a shareholder of a DISC elects the application of this paragraph, any qualified distribution shall be treated, for purposes of such Code, as received by such shareholder in 10 equal installments on the last day of each of the 10 taxable years of such shareholder which begins after the first taxable year of such shareholder beginning in 1984. The preceding sentence shall apply without regard to whether the DISC exists after 12-31-84.

(B)   Qualified distribution.—The term "qualified distribution" means any distribution which a shareholder is deemed to have received by reason of section 995(b) of such Code with respect to income derived by the DISC in the first taxable year of the DISC beginning—

(i)   in 1984, and

(ii)   after the date in 1984 on which the taxable year of such shareholder begins.

(C)   Shorter period for installments.—The Secretary of the Treasury or his delegate may by regulations provide for the election by any shareholder to be treated as receiving a qualified distribution over such shorter period as the taxpayer may elect.

(D)   Elections.—Any election under this paragraph shall be made at such time and in such manner as the Secretary of the Treasury or his delegate may prescribe.

(4)   Treatment of transfers from DISC to FSC.—Except to the extent provided in regulations, section 367 of such Code shall not apply to transfers made before 1-1-86 (or, if later, the date 1 year after the date on which the corporation ceases to be a DISC), to a FSC of qualified export assets (as defined in section 993(b) of such Code) held on 8-4-83, by a DISC in a transaction described in section 351 or 368(a)(1) of such Code.

(5)   Deemed termination of a disc.—Under regulations prescribed by the Secretary, if any controlled group of corporations of which a DISC is a member establishes a FSC, then any DISC which is a member of such group shall be treated as having terminated its DISC status.

(6)   Definitions.—For purposes of this subsection, the terms "DISC" and "former DISC" have the respective meanings given to such terms by section 992 of such Code.

(c)   Special Rule for Export Trade Corporations.—

(1)   In general.—If, before 1-1-85, any export trade corporation—

(A)   makes an election under section 927(f)(1) of the '54 Code to be treated as a FSC, or

(B)   elects not to be treated as an export trade corporation with respect to taxable years beginning after 12-31-84,

rules similar to the rules of paragraphs (2) and (4) of subsection (b) shall apply to such export trade corporation.

(2)   Treatment of transfers to FSC.—In the case of any export trade corporation which—

(A)   makes an election described in paragraph (1), and

(B)   transfers before 1-1-86, any portion of its property to a FSC in a transaction described in section 351 or

and "exempt foreign trade income" have the meaning given such terms by section 923. For purposes of this subsection, the term "qualified interest and carrying charges" means any interest or carrying charges (as defined in section 927(d)(1)) derived from a transaction which results in foreign trade income.

* * * * * * * * * * *

[For official explanation, see Committee Reports, ¶4039; 4190.]

〖¶2960〗 CODE SEC. 246. RULES APPLYING TO DEDUCTIONS FOR DIVIDENDS RECEIVED.

(a) Deduction Not Allowed for Dividends From Certain Corporations.—

* * * * * * * * * * *

(2) Subsection not to apply to certain dividends of federal home loan banks.—

(A) Dividends out of current earnings and profits.—In the case of any dividend paid by any FHLB out of earnings and profits of the FHLB for the taxable year in which such dividend was paid, paragraph (1) shall not apply to that portion of such dividend which bears the same ratio to the total dividend as—

(i) the dividends received by the FHLB from the FHLMC during such taxable year, bears to

(ii) the total earnings and profits of the FHLB for such taxable year.

(B) Dividends out of accumulated earnings and profits.—[1]*In the case of any dividend which is paid out of any accumulated earnings and profits of any FHLB, paragraph (1) shall not apply to that portion of the dividend which bears the same ratio to the total dividend as—*

(i) the amount of dividends received by such FHLB from the FHLMC which are out of earnings and profits of the FHLMC—

(I) for taxable years ending after December 31, 1984, and

[2]*(II) which were not previously treated as distributed under subparagraph (A) or this subparagraph, bears to*

(ii) the total accumulated earnings and profits of the FHLB as of the time such dividend is paid.

For purposes of clause (ii), the accumulated earnings and profits of the FHLB as of January 1, 1985, shall be treated as equal to its retained earnings as of such date.

(C) Coordination with section 243.—To the extent that paragraph (1) does not apply to any dividend by reason of subparagraph (A) or (B) of this paragraph, the requirement contained in section 243(a) that the corporation paying the dividend be subject to taxation under this chapter shall not apply.

[3]*(D)* Definitions.—For purposes of this paragraph—

(i) FHLB.—The term "FHLB" means any Federal Home Loan Bank.

(ii) FHLMC.—The term "FHLMC" means the Federal Home Loan Mortgage Corporation.

(iii) Taxable year of FHLB.—The taxable year of an FHLB shall, except as provided in regulations prescribed by the Secretary, be treated as the calendar year.

(iv) Earnings and profits.—The earnings and profits of any FHLB for any taxable year shall be treated as equal to the sum of—

(I) any dividends received by the FHLB from the FHLMC during such taxable year, and

(II) the total earnings and profits (determined without regard to dividends described in subclause (I)) of the FHLB as reported in its annual financial statement prepared in accordance with section 20 of the Federal Home Loan Bank Act (12 U.S.C. 1440).

(b) Limitation on Aggregate Amount of Deductions.—

(1) General rule.—Except as provided in paragraph (2), the aggregate amount of the deductions allowed by sections 243(a)(1), 244(a), and subsection (a) or (b) of section 245 shall not exceed [4]*80 percent* of the taxable income computed without regard to the deductions allowed by sections 172, 243(a)(1), 244(a), subsection (a) or (b) of section 245 and 247, without regard to any adjustment under section 1059, and without regard to any capital loss carryback to the taxable year under section 1212(a)(1).

(c) Exclusion of Certain Dividends.—

(1) In general.—No deduction shall be allowed under section 243, 244, or 245, in respect of any dividend on any share of stock—

(A) which is [5]*held by the taxpayer for 45 days or less, or*

【Footnote ¶2960 continued】

(A) In general.—Paragraph (2) shall not apply to any right to receive income with respect to any mortgage pool participation certificate or other similar interest in any mortgage (not including any mortgage).

(B) Treatment of certain sales after March 15, 1984, and before January 1, 1985.—If any gain is realized on the sale or exchange of any right described in subparagraph (A) after 3-15-84, and before 1-1-85, the gain shall not be recognized when realized but shall be recognized 1-1-85.

(4) Clarification of earnings and profits of federal home loan mortgage corporation.—

(A) Treatment of distribution of preferred stock, etc.—For purposes of the '54 Code, the distribution of preferred stock by the Federal Home Loan Mortgage Corporation during December of 1984, and the other distributions of such stock by Federal Home Loan Banks during January of 1985, shall be treated as if they were distributions of money equal to the fair market value of the stock on the date of the distribution by the Federal Home Loan Banks (and such stock shall be treated as if it were purchased with the money treated as so distributed). No deduction shall be allowed under section 243 of the '54 Code with respect to any dividend paid by the Federal Home Loan Mortgage Corporation out of earnings and profits accumulated before 1-1-85.

(B) Section 246(a) not to apply to distributions out of earnings and profits accumulated during 1985.—Subsection (a) of section 246 of the '54 Code shall not apply to any dividend paid by the Federal Home Loan Mortgage Corporation during 1985 out of earnings and profits accumulated after 12-31-84.

(5) Adjusted basis.—For purposes of this subsection, the adjusted basis of any asset shall be determined under part II of subchapter O of the '54 Code.

(6) No carrybacks for years before 1985.—No net operating loss, capital loss, or excess credit of the Federal Home Loan Mortgage Corporation for any taxable year beginning after 12-31-84, shall be allowed as a carryback to any taxable year beginning before 1-1-85.

(7) No deduction allowed for interest on replacement obligations.—

(A) In general.—The Federal Home Loan Mortgage Corporation shall not be allowed any deduction for interest accruing after 12-31-84, on any replacement obligation.

(B) Replacement obligation defined.—For purposes of subparagraph (A), the term "replacement obligation" means any obligation to any person created after 3-15-84, which the Secretary of the Treasury or his delegate determines replaces any equity or debt interest of a Federal Home Loan Bank or any other person in the Federal Home Loan Mortgage Corporation existing on such date. The preceding sentence shall not apply to any obligation with respect to which the Federal Home Loan Mortgage Corporation establishes that there is no tax avoidance effect.

Matter in *italics* in Sec. 246(b)(1) added by section 611(a)(3), '86 TRA, which struck out:

(4) "85 percent"

Effective date (Sec. 611(b)(2), '86 TRA).—Applies to taxable years beginning after 12-31-86.

Matter in *italics* in Sec. 246(c)(1)(A) and (4) added by section 1804(b)(1)(A) and (B), '86 TRA, which struck out:

(5) "sold or otherwise disposed of in any case in which the taxpayer has held such share for 45 days or less, or"

(B) to the extent that the taxpayer is under an obligation (whether pursuant to a short sale or otherwise) to make related payments with respect to positions in substantially similar or related property.

* * * * * * * * * * * *

(4) Holding period reduced for periods where risk of loss diminished.—The holding periods determined [6]*for purposes of this subsection* shall be appropriately reduced (in the manner provided in regulations prescribed by the Secretary) for any period (during such periods) in which—

(A) the taxpayer has an option to sell, is under a contractual obligation to sell, or has made (and not closed) a short sale of, substantially identical stock or securities,

(B) the taxpayer is the grantor of an option to buy substantially identical stock or securities, or

(C) under regulations prescribed by the Secretary, a taxpayer has diminished his risk of loss by holding 1 or more other positions with respect to substantially similar or related property.

The preceding sentence shall not apply in the case of any qualified covered call (as defined in section 1092(c)(4) but without regard to the requirement that gain or loss with respect to the option not be ordinary income or loss).

* * * * * * * * * * * *

(e) Certain Distributions to Satisfy Requirements.—No deduction shall be allowed under section 243(a) with respect to a dividend received pursuant to a distribution described in section 936(h)(4)[7].

* * * * * * * * * * * *

[For official explanation, see Committee Reports, ¶3912; 4057; 4138; 4146.]

[¶2960-A] CODE SEC. 246A. DIVIDENDS RECEIVED DEDUCTION REDUCED WHERE PORTFOLIO STOCK IS DEBT FINANCED.

(a) General Rule.—In the case of any dividend on debt-financed portfolio stock, there shall be substituted for the percentage which (but for this subsection) would be used in determining the amount of the deduction allowable under section 243, 244, [1]*or 245(a)* a percentage equal to the product of—

(1) [2]*80 percent* and

[Footnote ¶2960 continued]

(6) "under paragraph (3)"
Effective date (Sec. 1804(b)(1)(C), '86 TRA).—Applies to stock acquired after 3-1-86.

Section 1275(a)(2)(B), '86 TRA, struck out from Sec. 246(e):
(7) "or 934(e)(3)"
Effective date (Sec. 1277(a), (b), (c)(1) and (d), '86 TRA).—(a) Generally applies to taxable years beginning after 12-31-86.

(b) Special Rule for Guam, American Samoa, and the Northern Mariana Islands.—The amendments made by this subtitle shall apply with respect to Guam, American Samoa, or the Northern Mariana Islands (and to residents thereof and corporations created or organized therein) only if (and so long as) an implementing agreement under section 1271 is in effect between the United States and such possession.

(c) Special Rules for the Virgin Islands.—

(1) In general.—The amendments made by section 1275(c) shall apply with respect to the Virgin Islands (and residents thereof and corporations created or organized therein) only if (and so long as) an implementing agreement is in effect between the United States and the Virgin Islands with respect to the establishment of rules under which the evasion or avoidance of United States income tax shall not be permitted or facilitated by such possession. Any such implementing agreement shall be executed on behalf of the United States by the Secretary of the Treasury, after consultation with the Secretary of the Interior.

* * * * * * * * * * * *

(d) Report on Implementing Agreements.—If, during the 1 year period beginning on the date of the enactment of this Act, any implementing agreement described in subsection (b) or (c) is not executed, the Secretary of the Treasury or his delegate shall report to the Committee on Finance of the United States Senate, the Committee on Ways and Means, and the Committee on Interior and Insular Affairs of the House of Representatives with respect to—

[Footnote ¶2960-A] Matter in *italics* in Sec. 246A(a) (except *"80 percent"* in (a)(1)) added by section 1804(a), '86 TRA, which struck out:
(1) "or 245"
Effective date (Sec. 1881, '86 TRA and Sec. 51(c), '84 TRA).—Applies with respect to stock the holding period for which begins after 7-18-84, in taxable years ending after such date.

---

(2) 100 percent minus the average indebtedness percentage.

The preceding sentence shall be applied before any determination of a ratio under paragraph (1) or (2) of section 245(a).

* * * * * * * * * * * *

[For official explanation, see Committee Reports, ¶3912; 4138.]

〚¶2961〛 CODE SEC. 263. CAPITAL EXPENDITURES.

(a) **General Rule.**—No deduction shall be allowed for—

(1) Any amount paid out for new buildings or for permanent improvements or betterments made to increase the value of any property or estate. This paragraph shall not apply to—

(A) expenditures for the development of mines or deposits deductible under section 616,

(B) research and experimental expenditures deductible under section 174,

(C) soil and water conservation expenditures deductible under section 175, or

(D) expenditures by farmers for fertilizers, etc., deductible under section 180[1]

[2]*(E)* expenditures for removal of architectural and transportational barriers to the handicapped and elderly which the taxpayer elects to deduct under section 190.

[3]*(F)* expenditures for tertiary injectants with respect to which a deduction is allowed under section 193 or

[4]*(G)* expenditures for which a deduction is allowed under section 179.

(2) Any amount expended in restoring property or in making good the exhaustion thereof for which an allowance is or has been made.

* * * * * * * * * * * *

(c) **Intangible Drilling and Development Costs in the Case of Oil and Gas Wells and Geothermal Wells.**—Notwithstanding subsection (a), *and except as provided in subsection (i),* regulations shall be prescribed by the Secretary under this subtitle corresponding to the regulations which granted the option to deduct as expenses intangible drilling and development costs in the case of oil and gas wells and which were recognized and approved by the Congress in House Concurrent Resolution 50, Seventy-ninth Congress. Such regulations shall also grant the option to deduct as expenses intangible drilling and development costs in the case of wells drilled for any geothermal deposit (as defined in section 613(e)(3)) to the same extent and in the same manner as such expenses are deductible in the case of oil and gas wells. This subsection shall not apply with respect to any costs to which any deduction is allowed under [5]*section 59(d).*

* * * * * * * * * * * *

(g) **Certain Interest and Carrying Costs in the Case of Straddles.—**

〚**Footnote ¶2960-A continued**〛

"*80 percent*" in *italics* in Sec. 246A(a)(1) added by section 611(a)(4), '86 TRA, which struck out:

(2) "85 percent"

Effective date Sec. 611(b)(1), '86 TRA.—Applies to dividends received or accrued after 12-31-86, in taxable years ending after such date.

〚**Footnote ¶2961**〛 Matter in *italics* in Sec. 263(a)(1)(E)—(G) added by section 402(b)(1), '86 TRA, which struck out:

(1) "(E) expenditures by farmers for clearing land deductible under section 182,"

(2) "(F)"

(3) "(G)"

(4) "(H)"

Effective date (Sec. 402(c), '86 TRA).—Applies to amounts paid or incurred after 12-31-85, in taxable years ending after such date.

Matter in *italics* in Sec. 263(c) [except "section 59(d)"] and (i) added by section 411(b)(1)(A) and (B), '86 TRA.

Effective date (Sec. 411(c), '86 TRA).—(1) Generally applies to costs paid or incurred after 12-31-86, in taxable years ending after such date.

(2) **Transition rule.**—The amendments made by this section shall not apply with respect to intangible drilling and development costs incurred by United States companies pursuant to a minority interest in a license for Netherlands or United Kingdom North Sea development if such interest was acquired on or before 12-31-85.

"section 59(d)" in *italics* in Sec. 263(c) added by section 701(e)(4)(D), '86 TRA, which struck out:

(5) "section 58(i)"

Effective date (sec. 701(f)(1), '86 TRA).—Applies to taxable years beginning after 12-31-86. For special rules, etc., see footnote ¶2879.

(1) General rule.—No deduction shall be allowed for interest and carrying charges properly allocable to personal property which is part of a straddle (as defined in section 1092(c)). Any amount not allowable as a deduction by reason of the preceding sentence shall be chargeable to the capital account with respect to the personal property to which such amount relates.

(2) Interest and carrying charges defined.—For purposes of paragraph (1), the term "interest and carrying charges" means the excess of—

(A) the sum of—

(i) interest on indebtedness incurred or continued to purchase or carry the personal property, and

(ii) all other amounts (including charges to insure, store, or transport the personal property) paid or incurred to carry the personal property, over

(B) the sum of—

(i) the amount of interest (including original issue discount) includible in gross income for the taxable year with respect to the property described in subparagraph (A),

(ii) any amount treated as ordinary income under section 1271(a)(3)(A), 1278, or 1281(a) with respect to such property for the taxable year,[6]

(iii) the excess of any dividends includible in gross income with respect to such property for the taxable year over the amount of any deduction allowable with respect to such individuals under section 243, 244, or 245[7] and,

---

【Footnote ¶2961 continued】

Matter in *italics* in Sec. 263(g)(2)(B)(ii)—(iv) added by section 1808(b), '86 TRA, which struck out:

(6) "and"

(7) "."

Effective date (Sec. 1881, '86 TRA and Sec. 102(f)—(i), '84 TRA).—(1) Generally applies to positions established after 7-18-84, in taxable years ending after such date.

(2) Special rule for options on regulated futures contracts.—In the case of any option with respect to a regulated futures contract (within the meaning of section 1256 of the '54 Code, the amendments made by this section shall apply to positions established after 10-31-83, in taxable years ending after such date.

(3) Special rule for self-employment tax.—Except as provided in section (g)(2), the amendments made by subsection (c) shall apply to taxable years beginning after the date of the enactment of this Act.

(4) Gains or losses from certain terminations.—The amendment made by subsection (d)(9) shall apply as if included in the amendment made by section 505(a) of the '81 ERTA, as amended by section 105(e) of the Technical Corrections Act of 1982.

(g) Elections With Respect to Property Held on or Before the Date of the Enactment of This Act.—At the election of the taxpayer—

(1) the amendments made by this section shall apply to all section 1256 contracts held by the taxpayer on 7-18-84, effective for periods after such date in taxable years ending after such date, or

(2) in lieu of an election under paragraph (1), the amendments made by this section shall apply to all section 1256 contracts held by the taxpayer at any time during the taxable year of the taxpayer which includes the date of the enactment of this Act.

(h) Elections for Installment Payment of Tax Attributable to Stock Options.—

(1) In general.—If the taxpayer makes an election under subsection (g)(2) and under this subsection—

(A) the taxpayer may pay part or all the tax for the taxable year referred to in subsection (g)(2) in 2 or more (but not exceeding 5) equal installments, and

(B) the maximum amount of tax which may be paid in installments under this subsection shall be the excess of—

(i) the tax for such taxable year determined by taking into account subsection (g)(2), over

(ii) the tax for such taxable year determined by taking into account subsection (g)(2) and by treating—

(I) all section 1256 contracts which are stock options, and

(II) any stock which was a part of a straddle including any such stock options,

as having been acquired for a purchase price equal to their fair market value on the last business day of the preceding taxable year. Stock options and stock shall be taken into account under subparagraph (B)(ii) only if such options or stock were held on the last day of the preceding taxable year and only if income on such options or stock would have been ordinary income if such options or stock were sold at a gain on such last day.

(2) Date for payment of installment.—

(A) If an election is made under this subsection, the first installment under paragraph (1) shall be paid on or before the due date for filing the return for the taxable year described in paragraph (1), and each succeeding installment shall be paid on or before the date which is 1 year after the date prescribed for payment of the preceding installment.

(B) If a bankruptcy case or insolvency proceeding involving the taxpayer is commenced before the final installment is paid, the total amount of any unpaid installments shall be treated as due and payable on the day preceding the day on which such case or proceeding is commenced.

(3) Interest imposed.—For purposes of section 6601 of the '54 Code, the time for payment of any tax with respect to which an election is made under this subsection shall be determined without regard to this subsection.

(4) Form of election.—An election under this subsection shall be made not later than the time for filing the

(iv) any amount which is a payment with respect to a security loan (within the meaning of section 512(a)(5)) includible in gross income with respect to such property for the taxable year.

For purposes of subparagraph (A), the term "interest" includes any amount paid or incurred in connection with personal proprty used in a short sale.

(3) Exception for hedging transactions.—This subsecton shall not apply in the case of a hedging transaction (as defined in secton 1256(e)).

(4) Application with other provisions.—
  (A) Subsection (c).—In the case of any short sale, this subsection shall be applied after subsection (h).

(i) Special Rules for Intangible Drilling and Development Costs Incurred Outside the United States.—In the case of intangible drilling and development costs paid or incurred with respect to an oil, gas, or geothermal well located outside the United States—
  (1) subsection (c) shall not apply, and
  (2) such costs shall—
    (A) at the election of the taxpayer, be included in adjusted basis for purposes of computing the amount of any deduction allowable under section 611 (determined without regard to section 613), or
    (B) if subparagraph (A) does not apply, be allowed as a deduction ratably over the 10-taxable year period beginning with the taxable year in which such costs were paid or incurred.

This subsection shall not apply to costs paid or incurred with respect to a nonproductive well.

[For official explanation, see Committee Reports, ¶3891; 3896; 3931; 4142.]

〖¶2961-A〗 CODE SEC. 263A. CAPITALIZATION AND INCLUSION IN INVENTORY COSTS OF CERTAIN EXPENSES.

(a) Nondeductibility of Certain Direct and Indirect Costs.—

(1) In general.—In the case of any property to which this section applies, any costs described in paragraph (2)—
  (A) in the case of property which is inventory in the hands of the taxpayer, shall be included in inventory costs, and
  (B) in the case of any other property, shall be capitalized.

〖Footnote ¶2961 continued〗
return for the taxable year described in paragraph (1) and shall be made in the manner and form required by regulations prescribed by Secretary of the Treasury or his delegate. The election shall set forth—
  (A) the amount determined under paragraph (1)(B) and the number of installments elected by the taxpayer,
  (B) the property described in paragraph (1)(B)(ii), and the date on which such property was acquired,
  (C) the fair market value of the property described in paragraph (1)(B)(ii) on the last business day of the taxable year preceding the taxable year described in paragraph (1), and
  (D) such other information for purposes of carrying out the provisions of this subsection as may be required by such regulations.
  (5) Delay of identification requirement.—Section 1256(e)(2)(C) of the '54 Code shall not apply to any stock option or stock acquired on or before the 60th day after 7-18-84.
  (i) Definitions.—For purposes of subsections (g) and (h)—
  (1) Section 1256 contract.—The term "section 1256 contract" has the meaning given to such term by section 1256(b) of the '54 Code (as amended by this section).
  (2) Stock option.—The term "stock option" means any option to buy or sell stock.
  〖Footnote ¶2961-A〗 Sec. 263A added by section 803(a), '86 TRA.
  Effective date (Sec. 803(d), '86 TRA).—(1) Generally applies to costs incurred after 12-31-86, in taxable years ending after such date.
  (2) Special rule for inventory property.—In the case of any property which is inventory in the hands of the taxpayer—
  (A) In general.—The amendments made by this section shall apply to taxable years beginning after 12-31-86.
  (B) Change in method of accounting.—If the taxpayer is required by the amendments made by this section to change its method of accounting with respect to such property for any taxable year—
  (i) such change shall be treated as initiated by the taxpayer,
  (ii) such change shall be treated as made with the consent of the Secretary, and
  (iii) the period for taking into account the adjustments under section 481 by reason of such change shall not exceed 4 years.
  (3) Special rule for self-constructed property.—The amendments made by this section shall not apply to any property which is produced by the taxpayer for use by the taxpayer if substantial construction had occurred before 3-1-86.
  (4) Transitional rule for capitalization of interest and taxes.—
  (A) Transition property exempted from interest capitalization.—Section 263A(f) of the '86 Code (as added by

(2) Allocable costs.—The costs described in this paragraph with respect to any property are—

   (A) the direct costs of such property, and

   (B) such property's proper share of those indirect costs (including taxes) part or all of which are allocable to such property.

(b) Property to Which Section Applies.—Except as otherwise provided in this section, this section shall apply to—

   (1) Property produced by taxpayer.—Real or tangible personal property produced by the taxpayer.

   (2) Property acquired for resale.—

     (A) In general.—Real or personal property described in section 1221(1) which is acquired by the taxpayer for resale.

     (B) Exception for taxpayer with gross receipts of $10,000,000 or less.—Subparagraph (A) shall not apply to any personal property acquired during any taxable year by the taxpayer for resale if the average annual gross receipts of the taxpayer (or any predecessor) for the 3-taxable year period ending with the taxable year preceding such taxable year do not exceed $10,000,000.

     (C) Aggregation rules, etc.—For purposes of subparagraph (B), rules similar to the rules of paragraphs (2) and (3) of section 448(c) shall apply.

For purposes of paragraph (1), the term "tangible personal property" shall include a film, sound recording, video tape, book, or similar property.

(c) General Exceptions.—

   (1) Personal use property.—This section shall not apply to any property produced by the taxpayer for use by the taxpayer other than in a trade or business or an activity conducted for profit.

   (2) Research and experimental expenditures.—This section shall not apply to any amount allowable as a deduction under section 174.

   (3) Certain development and other costs of oil and gas wells or other mineral property.—This section shall not apply to any cost allowable as a deduction under section 263(c), 616(a), or 617(a).

   (4) Coordination with long-term contract rules.—This section shall not apply to any property produced by the taxpayer pursuant to a long-term contract.

   (5) Timber and certain ornamental trees.—This section shall not apply to—

     (A) trees raised, harvested, or grown by the taxpayer other than trees described in clause (ii) of subsection (e)(4)(B) (after application of the last sentence thereof), and

     (B) any real property underlying such trees.

⟦Footnote ¶2961-A continued⟧

this section) and the amendment made by subsection (b)(1) shall not apply to any property—

   (i) to which the amendments made by section 201 do not apply by reason of sections 203(a)(1)(D) and (E) and 203(a)(5)(A), and

   (ii) to which the amendments made by section 251 do not apply by reason of section 251(d)(3)(M).

   (B) Interest and taxes.—Section 263A of such Code shall not apply to property described in the matter following subparagraph (B) of section 207(e)(2) of the '82 TEFRA to the extent it would require the capitalization of interest and taxes paid or incurred in connection with such property which are not required to be capitalized under section 189 of such Code (as in effect before the amendment made by subsection (b)(1)).

   (5) Transition rule concerning capitalization of inventory rules.—In the case of a corporation which on the date of the enactment of this Act was a member of an affiliated group of corporations (within the meaning of section 1504(a) of the '86 Code), the parent of which—

   (A) was incorporated in California on 4-15-25,

   (B) adopted LIFO accounting as of the close of the taxable year ended 12-31-50, and

   (C) was, on 5-22-86, merged into a Delaware corporation incorporated on 3-12-86,

the amendments made by this section shall apply under a cut-off method whereby the uniform capitalization rules are applied only in costing layers of inventory acquired during taxable years beginning on or after 1-1-87.

   (6) Treatment of certain rehabilitation project.—The amendments made by this section shall not apply to interest and taxes paid or incurred with respect to the rehabilitation and conversion of a certified historic building which was formerly a factory into an apartment project with 155 units, 39 units of which are for low-income families, if the project was approved for annual interest assistance on 6-10-86, by the housing authority of the State in which the project is located.

   (7) Special rule for casualty losses.—Section 263A(d)(2) of the '86 Code (as added by this section) shall apply to expenses incurred on or after the date of the enactment of this Act.

(d) **Exception for Farming Businesses.—**

(1) **Section to apply only if preproductive period is more than 2 years.—**

(A) In general.—This section shall not apply to any plant or animal which is produced by the taxpayer in a farming business and which has a preproductive period of 2 years or less.

(B) Exception for taxpayers required to use accrual method.—Subparagraph (A) shall not apply to any corporation, partnership, or tax shelter required to use an accrual method of accounting under section 447 or 448(a)(3).

(2) **Treatment of certain plants lost by reason of casualty.—**

(A) In general.—If plants bearing an edible crop for human consumption were lost or damaged (while in the hands of the taxpayer) by reason of freezing temperatures, disease, drought, pests, or casualty, this section shall not apply to any costs of the taxpayer of replanting plants bearing the same type of crop (whether on the same parcel of land on which such lost or damaged plants were located or any other parcel of land of the same acreage in the United States).

(B) Special rule for person with minority interest who materially participates.— Subparagraph (A) shall apply to amounts paid or incurred by a person (other than the taxpayer described in subparagraph (A)) if—

(i) the taxpayer described in subparagraph (A) has an equity interest of more than 50 percent in such grove, orchard, or vineyard, and

(ii) such other person holds any art of the remaining equity interest and materially participates in the planting, maintenance, cultivation, or development of such grove, orchard, or vineyard during the 4-taxable year period beginning with the taxable year in which the grove, orchard or vineyard was lost or damaged.

The determination of whether an individual materially participates in any activity shall be made in a manner similar to the manner in which such determination is made under section 2032A(e)(6).

(3) **Election to have this section not apply.—**

(A) In general.—If a taxpayer makes an election under this paragraph, this section shall not apply to any plant or animal produced in any farming business carried on by such taxpayer.

(B) Certain persons not eligible.—No election may be made under this paragraph—

(i) by a corporation, partnership, or tax shelter, if such corporation, partnership, or tax shelter is required to use an accrual method of accounting under section 447 or 448(a)(3), or

(ii) with respect to the planting, cultivation, maintenance, or development of pistachio trees.

(C) Special rules for citrus and almond growers.—An election under this paragraph shall not apply with respect to any item which is attributable to the planting, cultivation, maintenance, or development of any citrus or almond grove (or part thereof) and which is incurred before the close of the 4th taxable year beginning with the taxable year in which the trees were planted. For purposes of the preceding sentence, the portion of a citrus or almond grove planted in 1 taxable year shall be treated separately from the portion of such grove planted in another taxable year.

(D) Election.—Unless the Secretary otherwise consents, an election under this paragraph may be made only for the taxpayer's 1st taxable year which begins after December 31, 1986, and during which the taxpayer engages in a farming business. Any such election, once made, may be revoked only with the consent of the Secretary.

(e) **Definitions and Special Rules for Purposes of Subsection (d).—**

(1) **Recapture of expensed amounts on disposition.—**

(A) In general.—In the case of any plant or animal with respect to which amounts would have been capitalized under subsection (a) but for an election under subsection (d)(3)—

(i) such plant or animal (if not otherwise section 1245 property) shall be treated as section 1245 property, and

(ii) for purposes of section 1245, the recapture amount shall be treated as a deduction allowed for depreciation with respect to such property.

(B) Recapture amount.—For purposes of subparagraph (A), the term "recapture amount" means any amount allowable as a deduction to the taxpayer which, but for an election under subsection (d)(3), would have been capitalized with respect to the plant or animal.

(2) Effects of election on depreciation.—

(A) In general.—If the taxpayer (or any related person) makes an election under subsection (d)(3), the provisions of section 168(g)(2) (relating to alternative depreciation) shall apply to all property of the taxpayer used predominantly in the farming business and placed in service in any taxable year during which any such election is in effect.

(B) Related person.—For purposes of subparagraph (A), the term "related person" means—

(i) the taxpayer and members of the taxpayer's family,

(ii) any corporation (including an S corporation) if 50 percent or more (in value) of the stock of such corporation is owned (directly or through the application of section 318) by the taxpayer or members of the taxpayer's family,

(iii) a corporation and any other corporation which is a member of the same controlled group described in section 1563(a)(1), and

(iv) any partnership if 50 percent or more (in value) of the interests in such partnership is owned directly or indirectly by the taxpayer or members of the taxpayer's family.

(C) Members of family.—For purposes of this paragraph, the term "family" means the taxpayer, the spouse of the taxpayer, and any of their children who have not attained age 18 before the close of the taxable year.

(3) Preproductive period.—

(A) In general.—For purposes of this section, the term "preproductive period" means—

(i) in the case of a plant or animal which will have more than 1 crop or yield, the period before the 1st marketable crop or yield from such plant or animal, or

(ii) in the case of any other plant or animal, the period before such plant or animal is reasonably expected to be disposed of.

For purposes of this subparagraph, use by the taxpayer in a farming business of any supply produced in such business shall be treated as a disposition.

(B) Rule for determining period.—In the case of a plant grown in commercial quantities in the United States, the preproductive period for such plant if grown in the United States shall be based on the nationwide weighted average preproductive period for such plant.

(4) Farming business.—For purposes of this section—

(A) In general.—The term "farming business" means the trade or business of farming.

(B) Certain trades and businesses included.—The term "farming business" shall include the trade or business of—

(i) operating a nursery or sod farm, or

(ii) the raising or harvesting of trees bearing fruit, nuts, or other crops, or ornamental trees.

For purposes of clause (ii), an evergreen tree which is more than 6 years old at the time severed from the roots shall not be treated as an ornamental tree.

(5) Certain inventory valuation methods permitted.—The Secretary shall by regulations permit the taxpayer to use reasonable inventory valuation methods to compute the amount required to be capitalized under subsection (a) in the case of any plant or animal.

(f) Special Rules for Allocation of Interest to Property Produced by the Taxpayer.—

(1) Interest capitalized only in certain cases.—Subsection (a) shall only apply to interest costs which are—

(A) paid or incurred during the production period, and

(B) allocable to property which is described in subsection (b)(1) and which has—

(i) a long useful life,

(ii) an estimated production period exceeding 2 years, or

(iii) an estimated production period exceeding 1 year and a cost exceeding $1,000,000.

Code §263A(f)(1) ¶2961-A

(2) **Allocation rules.—**

(A) In general.—In. determining the amount of interest required to be capitalized under subsection (a) with respect to any property—

(i) interest on any indebtedness directly attributable to production expenditures with respect to such property shall be assigned to such property, and

(ii) interest on any other indebtedness shall be assigned to such property to the extent that the taxpayer's interest costs could have been reduced if production expenditures (not attributable to indebtedness described in clause (i)) had not been incurred.

(B) Exception for qualified residence interest.—Subparagraph (A) shall not apply to any qualified residence interest (within the meaning of section 163(h)).

(C) Special rule for flow-through entities.—Except as provided in regulations, in the case of any flow-through entity, this paragraph shall be applied first at the entity level and then at the beneficiary level.

(3) **Interest relating to property used to produce property.—**This subsection shall apply to any interest on indebtedness incurred or continued in connection with property used to produce property to which this subsection applies to the extent such interest is allocable to the produced property.

(4) **Definitions.—**For purposes of this subsection—

(A) Long useful life.—Property has a long useful life if such property is—

(i) real property, or

(ii) property with a class life of 20 years or more (as determined under section 168).

(B) Production period.—The term "production period" means, when used with respect to any property, the period—

(i) beginning on the date on which production of the property begins, and

(ii) ending on the date on which the property is ready to be placed in service or is ready to be held for sale.

(C) Production expenditures.—The term "production expenditures" means the costs (whether or not incurred during the production period) required to be capitalized under subsection (a) with respect to the property.

(g) **Production.—**For purposes of this section—

(1) **In general.—**The term "produce" includes construct, build, install, manufacture, develop, or improve.

(2) **Treatment of property produced under contract for the taxpayer.—**The taxpayer shall be treated as producing any property produced for the taxpayer under a contract with the taxpayer; except that only costs paid or incurred by the taxpayer (whether under such contract or otherwise) shall be taken into account in applying subsection (a) to the taxpayer.

(h) **Regulations.—**The Secretary shall prescribe such regulations as may be necessary or appropriate to carry out the purposes of this section, including—

(1) regulations to prevent the use of related parties, pass-thru entities, or intermediaries to avoid the application of this section, and

(2) regulations providing for simplified procedures for the application of this section in the case of property described in subsecton (b)(2).

[For official explanation, see Committee Reports, ¶3937.]

⟦¶2962⟧ CODE SEC. 264. CERTAIN AMOUNTS PAID IN CONNECTION WITH INSURANCE CONTRACTS.

(a) **General Rule.—**No deduction shall be allowed for—

* * * * * * * * * * * *

(4) Any interest paid or accrued on any indebtedness with respect to 1 or more life insurance policies owned by the taxpayer covering the life of any individual who—

(A) is an officer or employee of, or

(B) is financially interest in,

any trade or business carried on by the taxpayer to the extent that the aggregate amount of such indebtedness with respect to policies covering such individual exceeds $50,000.

Paragraph (2) shall apply in respect of annuity contracts only as to contracts purchased after March 1, 1954. Paragraph (3) shall apply only in respect of contracts

⟦Footnote ¶2962⟧   Matter in *italics* in Sec. 264(a) and (4) added by section 1003(a) and (b), '86 TRA.
Effective date (Sec. 1003(c), '86 TRA).—Applies to contracts purchased after 6-20-86, in taxable years ending after such date.

purchased after August 6, 1963. *Paragraph (4) shall apply with respect to contracts purchased afer June 20, 1986.*

* * * * * * * * * * *

[For official explanation, see Committee Reports, ¶3956.]

〖¶2963〗 CODE SEC. 265. EXPENSES AND INTEREST RELATING TO TAX-EXEMPT INCOME.

(a)   *General Rule.*—No deduction shall be allowed for—

* * * * * * * * * * *

(2)   Interest.—Interest on indebtedness incurred or continued to purchase or carry obligations the interest on which is wholly exempt from the taxes imposed by this subtitle, or to purchase or carry any certificate to the extent the interest on such certificate is excludable under section 128.[1]

* * * * * * * * * * *

(6)   Section not to apply with respect to parsonage and military housing allowances.—No deduction shall be denied under this section for interest on a mortgage on, or real property taxes on, the home of the taxpayer by reason of the receipt of an amount as—

(A) a military housing allowance, or

(B) a parsonage allowance excludable from gross income under section 107.

〖Footnote ¶2963〗   Matter in *italics* in this Sec. 265(a) and (b) added by section 902(a), (b) and (d), '86 TRA, which struck out:

(1) "In applying the preceding sentence to a financial institution (other than a bank) which is a face-amount certificate company registered under the Investment Company Act of 1940 (15 U.S.C. 80a-1 and following) and which is subject to the banking laws of the State in which such institution is incorporated, interest on face-amount certificates (as defined in section 2(a)(15) of such Act), issued by such institution, and interest on amounts received for the purchase of such certificates to be issued by such institution, shall not be considered as interest on indebtedness incurred or continued to purchase or carry obligations the interest on which is wholly exempt from the taxes imposed by this subtitle, to the extent that the average amount of such obligations held by such institution during the taxable year (as determined under regulations prescribed by the Secretary) does not exceed 15 percent of the average of the total assets held by such institution during the taxable year (as so determined)."

Effective date (Sec. 902(f) '86 TRA).—(1) Generally applies to taxable years ending afer 12-31-86.

(2) Obligations acquired pursuant to certain commitments.—For purposes of sections 265(b) and 291(e)(1)(B) of the '86 Code, any tax-exempt obligation which is acquired after 8-7-86, pursuant to a direct or indirect written commitment—

(A) to purchase or repurchase such obligation, and

(B) entered into on or before 9-25-85, shall be treated as an obligation acquired before 8-8-86.

(3) Transitional rules.—For purposes of sections 265(b) and 291(e)(1)(B) of the '86 Code, obligations with respect to any of the following projects shall be treated as obligations acquired before 8-8-86, in the hands of the first and any subsequent financial institution acquiring such obligations:

(A) Park Forest, Illinois, redevelopment project.

(B) Clinton, Tennessee, Carriage Trace project.

(C) Savannah, Geogia, Mall Terrace Warehouse project.

(D) Chattanooga, Tennessee, Warehouse Row project.

(E) Dalton, Georgia, Towne Square project.

(F) Milwaukee, Wisconsin, Standard Electric Supply Company—distribution company.

(G) Wausau, Wisconsin, urban renewal project.

(H) Cassville, Missouri, UDAG project.

(I) Outlook Envelope Company—plant expansion.

(J) Woodstock, Connecticut, Crabtree Warehouse partnership.

(K) Louisville, Kentucky, Speed Mansion renovation project.

(L) Charleston, South Carolina, waterfront project.

(M) New Orleans, Louisiana, Upper Pontabla Building renovation.

(N) Woodward Wight Building.

(O) Minneapolis, Minnesota, Miller Milling Company—flour mill project.

(P) Birmingham, Alabama, Club Apartments.

(Q) Charlotte, North Carolina—qualified mortgage bonds acquired by NCNB bank ($5,250,000).

(R) Grand Rapids, Michigan, Central Bank project.

(S) Ruppman Marketing Services, Inc.—building project.

(4) Additional transitional rule.—Obligations issued pursuant to an allocation of a State's volume limitation for private activity bonds, which allocation was made by Executive Order 25 signed by the Governor of the State on 5-22-86 (as such order may be amended before 1-1-87), shall be treated as acquired on or before 8-7-86, in the hands of the first and any subsequent financial institution acquiring such obligation. The aggregate face amount of obligations to which this subparagraph applies shall not exceed $200,000,000.

Sec. 265(a)(6) in *italics* added by section 144, '86 TRA.

Effective date (Sec. 155(e), '86 TRA).—Applies to taxable years beginning before, on, or after, 12-31-86.

Code §265(a)(6) ¶2963

(b) Pro Rata Allocation of Interest Expense of Financial Institutions to Tax-Exempt Interest—

(1) In general.—In the case of a financial institution, no deduction shall be allowed for that portion of the taxpayer's interest expense which is allocable to tax-exempt interest.

(2) Allocation.—For purposes of paragraph (1), the portion of the taxpayer's interest expense which is allocable to tax-exempt interest is an amount which bears the same ratio to such interest expense as—

  (A) the taxpayer's average adjusted bases (within the meaning of section 1016) of tax-exempt obligations acquired after August 7, 1986, bears to

  (B) such average adjusted bases for all assets of the taxpayer.

(3) Exception for certain tax-exempt obligations.—

  (A) In general.—Any qualified tax-exempt obligation acquired after August 7, 1986, shall be treated for purposes of paragraph (2) and section 291(e)(1)(B) as if it were acquired on August 7, 1986.

  (B) Qualified tax-exempt obligation.—For purposes of subparagraph (A), the term "qualified tax-exempt obligation" means a tax-exempt obligation which—

  (i) is not a private activity bond (as defined in section 141), and

  (ii) is designated by the issuer for purposes of this paragraph.

For purposes of the preceding sentence and subparagraph (C), a qualified 501(c)(3) bond (as defined in section 145) shall not be treated as a private activity bond.

  (C) Limitation on issuer.—An obligation issued by an issuer during any calendar year shall not be treated as a qualified tax-exempt obligation unless the reasonably anticipated amount of qualified tax-exempt obligations (other than private activity bonds) which will be issued by such issuer during such calendar year does not exceed $10,000,000.

  (D) Overall $10,000,000 Limitation.—Not more than $10,000,000 of obligations issued by an issuer during any calendar year may be designated by such issuer for purposes of this paragraph.

  (E) Aggregation of issuers.—For purposes of subparagraphs (C) and (D), an issuer and all subordinate entities thereof shall be treated as 1 issuer.

(4) Definitions.—For purposes of this subsection—

  (A) Interest expense.—The term "interest expense" means the aggregate amount allowable to the taxpayer as a deduction for interest for the taxable year (determined without regard to this subsection and section 291). For purposes of the preceding sentence, the term "interest" includes amounts (whether or not designated as interest) paid in respect of deposits, investment certificates, or withdrawable or repurchasable shares.

  (B) Tax-exempt obligation.—The term "tax-exempt obligation" means any obligation the interest on which is wholly exempt from taxes imposed by this subtitle. Such term includes shares of stock of a regulated investment company which during the taxable year of the holder thereof distributes exempt-interest dividends.

(5) Financial institution.—For purposes of this subsection, the term "financial institution" means any person who—

  (A) accepts deposits from the public in the ordinary course of such person's trade or business, and is subject to Federal or State supervision as a financial institution, or

  (B) is a corporation described in section 585(a)(2).

(6) Special rules.—

  (A) Coordination with subsection (a).—If interest on any indebtedness is disallowed under subsection (a) with respect to any tax-exempt obligation—

  (i) such disallowed interest shall not be taken into account for purposes of applying this subsection, and

  (ii) for purposes of applying paragraph (2), the adjusted basis of such tax-exempt obligation shall be reduced (but not below zero) by the amount of such indebtedness.

  (B) Coordination with section 263A.—This section shall be applied before the application of section 263A (relating to capitalization of certain expenses where taxpayer produces property).

[For official explanation, see Committee Reports, ¶3868; 3949.]

【¶2964】 CODE SEC. 267. LOSSES, EXPENSES, AND INTEREST WITH A RESPECT TO TRANSACTIONS BETWEEN RELATED TAXPAYERS.

(a) In general.—

(1) Deduction for losses disallowed.—No deduction shall be allowed in respect to any loss from the sale or exchange of property (other than a loss in case of a distribution in corporate liquidation), directly or indirectly, between persons specified in any of the paragraphs of subsection (b).

(2) Matching of deduction any payee income item in the case of expenses and interest.—If

(A) by reason of the method of accounting of the person to whom the payment is to be made, the amount thereof is not (unless paid) includible in the gross income of such person, and

(B) at the close of the taxable year of the taxpayer for which (but for this paragraph) the amount would be deductible under this chapter, both the taxpayer and the person to whom the payment is to be made are persons specified in any of the paragraphs of subsection (b), then any deduction allowable under this chapter in respect of such amount shall be allowable as of the day as of which such amount is includible in the gross income of the person to whom the payment is made (or, if later, as of the day on which it would be so allowable but for this paragraph). *For purposes of this paragraph, in the case of a personal service corporation (within the meaning of section 441(i)(2)), such corporation and any employee-owner (within the meaning of section 269A(b)(2), as modified by section 441(i)(2)) shall be treated as persons specified in subsection (b).*

(3) Payments to foreign persons.—*The Secretary shall by regulations apply the matching principle of paragraph (2) in cases in which the person to whom the payment is to be made is not a United States person.*

(b) Relationships.—The persons referred to in subsection (a) are:

(1) Members of a family, as defined in subsection (c)(4);

(2) An individual and a corporation more than 50 percent in value of the outstanding stock of which is owned, directly or indirectly, by or for such individual;

(3) Two corporations which are members of the same controlled group (as defined in subsection (f));

(4) A grantor and a fiduciary of any trust;

(5) A fiduciary of a trust and a fiduciary of another trust, if the same person is a grantor of both trusts;

(6) A fiduciary of a trust and a beneficiary of such trust;

(7) A fiduciary of a trust and a beneficiary of another trust, if the same person is a grantor of both trusts;

(8) A fiduciary of a trust and a corporation more than 50 percent in value of the outstanding stock of which is owned, directly or indirectly, by or for the trust or by or for a person who is a grantor of the trust;

(9) A person and an organization to which section 501 (relating to certain educational and charitable organizations which are exempt from tax) applies and which is controlled directly or indirectly by such person or (if such person is an individual) by members of the family of such individual;

(10) A corporation and a partnership if the same persons own—

(A) more than 50 percent in value of the outstanding stock of the corporation, and

(B) more than 50 percent of the capital interest, or the profits interest, in the partnership;

【Footnote ¶2964】 Matter in *italics* in Sec. 267(a)(2) added by section 806(c)(2), '86 TRA.

Effective date (Sec. 806(e), '86 TRA).—(1) Generally applies to taxable years beginning after 12-31-86.

(2) Change in accounting period.—In the case of any taxpayer required by the amendments made by this section to change its accounting period for any taxable year—

(A) such change shall be treated as initiated by the taxpayer,

(B) such change shall be treated as having been made with the consent of the Secretary, and

(C) with respect to any partner or shareholder of an S corporation which is required to include the items from more than 1 taxable year of the partnership or S corporation in any 1 taxable year, income in excess of expenses of such partnership or corporation for the short taxable year required by such amendments shall be taken into account ratably in each of the first 4 taxable years (including such short taxable year) beginning after 12-31-86, unless such partner or shareholder elects to include all such income in the short taxable year.

Shareholder (C) shall apply to a shareholder of an S corporation only if such corporation was an S corporation for a taxable year beginning in 1986.

(11) An S corporation and another S corporation if the same persons own more than 50 percent in value of the outstanding stock of each corporation; or

(12) An S corporation and a C corporation, if the same persons [1]*own* more than 50 percent in value of the outstanding stock of each corporation.

* * * * * * * * * * * * *

(e) **Special rules for pass-thru entities.—**

* * * * * * * * * * * *

(5) **Exception for certain expenses and interest of partnerships owning low-income housing.—**

* * * * * * * * * * * *

(D) Low-income housing.—For purposes of this paragraph, the term "low-income housing" means—

(i) any interest in [2]*property described in clause (i), (ii), (iii), or (iv) of section 1250(a)(1)(B),* and

(ii) any interest in a partnership owning [3]*such property.*

(6) *Cross reference.—*
For additional rules relating to partnerships, see section 707(b).

* * * * * * * * * * * *

(f) **Controlled group defined; special rules applicable to controlled groups.—**

* * * * * * * * * * * *

(3) **Loss deferral rules not to apply in certain cases.—**
(A) Transfer to DISC.—For purposes of applying subsection (a)(1), the term "controlled group" shall not include a DISC.

【Footnote ¶2964 continued】

Matter in *italics* in Sec. 267(a)(3) and (b)(12) added by section 1812(c)(1) and (4)(A), '86 TRA, which struck out:
(1) "owns"
Effective date (Sec. 1881, '86 TRA and section 174(c)(1) and (3), '84 TRA).—(1) Generally applies to amounts allowable as deductions under chapter 1 of the '54 Code for taxable years beginning after 12-31-83. For purposes of the preceding sentence, the allowability of a deduction shall be determined without regard to any disallowance or postponement of deductions under section 267 of such Code.
(3) Exception for existing indebtedness, etc.—
(A) In general.—The amendments shall not apply to any amount paid or incurred—
(i) on indebtedness incurred on or before 9-29-83, or
(ii) pursuant to a contract which was binding on 9-29-83, and at all times thereafter before the amount is paid or incurred.
(B) Treatment of renegotiations, extensions, etc.—If any indebtedness (or contract described in subparagraph (A)) is renegotiated, extended, renewed, or revised after 9-29-83, subparagraph (A) shall not apply to any amount paid or incurred on such indebtedness (or pursuant to such contract) after the date of such renegotiation, extension, renewal, or revision.

Matter in *italics* in Sec. 267(e)(5)(D) added by section 803(b)(5), '86 TRA, which struck out:
(2) "low-income housing (as defined in paragraph (5) of section 189(e))
(3) low-income housing (as so defined)"
Effective date (Sec. 803(d), '86 TRA).—(1) Generally applies to taxable years beginning after 12-31-86. For special and transitional rules, see footnote ¶2961-A.

Matter in *italics* in Sec. 267(e)(6) and (f)(3)(B) added by section 1812, '86 TRA.
Effective date (Sec. 1881, '86 TRA and section 174(c)(1) and (3), '84 TRA).—(1) Generally applies to amounts allowable as deductions under chapter 1 of the '54 Code for taxable years beginning after 12-31-83. For purposes of the preceding sentence, the allowability of a deduction shall be determined without regard to any disallowance or postponement of deductions under section 267 of such Code.
For special rules, see above.

Sec. 267(g) in italics added by section 1842(a), '86 TRA.
Effective date (Sec. 1881, '86 TRA and section 421(d), '84 TRA).—(1) Generally applies to transfers after 7-18-84 in taxable years ending after such date.
(2) Election to have amendments apply to transfers after 1983.—If both spouses or former spouses make an election under this paragraph, the amendments made by this section shall apply to all transfers made by such spouses (or former spouses) after 12-31-83.
(3) Exception for transfers purusant to existing degrees.—Except in the case of an election under paragraph (2), the amendments made by this section shall not apply to transfers under any instrument in effect on or before 7-18-84 unless both spouses (or former spouses) elect to have such amendments apply to tranfers under such instrument.
(4) Election.—Any election under paragraph (2) or (3) shall be made in such manner, as such time, and subject to such conditions, as the Secretary of the Treasury or his delegate may by regulations prescribe.

(B) Certain sales of inventory.—Except to the extent provided in regulations prescribed by the Secretary, subsection (a)(1) shall not apply to the sale or exchange of property between members of the same controlled group *(or persons described in subsection (b)(10))* if—

(i) such property in the hands of the tranferor is property described in section 1221(1), and

(ii) such sale or exchange is in the ordinary course of the transferor's trade or business,

(iii) such property in the hands of the transferee is property described in section 1221(1), and

(iv) the tranferee or the transferor is a foreign corporation.

* * * * * * * * * * * * *

(g) *Coordination With Section 1041.—Subsection (a)(1) shall not apply to any transfer described in section 1041(a) (relating to transfers of property between spouses or incident to divorce).*

[For official explanation, see Committee Reports, ¶3935; 3940; 4146; 4161.]

[¶2965] CODE SEC. 269A. PERSONAL SERVICE CORPORATIONS FORMED OR AVAILED OF TO AVOID OR EVADE INCOME TAX.

* * * * * * * * * * * * *

(b) **Definitions.**—For purposes of this section—

* * * * * * * * * * * * *

(3) **Related persons.**—All related persons (within the meaning of [1]*section 144(a)(3)*) shall be treated as 1 entity.

[For official explanation, see Committee Reports, ¶4058.]

[¶2965-A] CODE SEC. 269B STAPLED ENTITIES.

* * * * * * * * * * * * *

(b) **Secretary to Prescribe Regulations.**—The Secretary will prescribe such regulations as may be necessary to prevent avoidance or evasion of Federal income tax through the use of stapled entities. Such regulations may include (but shall not be limited to) regulations providing the extent to which 1 of such entities shall be treated as owning the other entity (to the extent of the stapled interest) *and regulations providing that any tax imposed*

[Footnote ¶2965] Matter in *italics* in Sec. 269A(b)(3) added by section 1301(j)(4), '86 TRA, which struck out:
(1) "section 103(b)(6)(C)"
Effective date (Sec. 1311(a), '86 TRA).—Generally applies to bonds issued after 8-15-86.
For special and transitional rules, see ¶2071-2077.
[Footnote ¶2965-A] Matter in *italics* in Sec. 269B(b) and (e) added by section 1810(j), '86 TRA.
Effective date (Sec. 1881, '86 TRA and Section 136(c), '84 TRA).—(1) Generally takes effect on 7-18-84.
(2) Interests stapled as of June 30, 1983.—Except as otherwise provided in this subsection, in the case of any interests which on 6-30-83, were stapled interests (as defined in section 269B(c)(3) of the '54 Code (as added by this section)), the amendments made by this section shall take effect on 1-1-85 (1-1-87, in the case of stapled interests in a foreign corporation).
(3) Certain stapled entities which include real estate investment trust.—Paragraph (3) of section 269B(a) of such Code shall not apply in determining the application of the provisions of part II of subchapter M of chapter 1 of such Code to any real estate investment trust which is part of a group of stapled entities if—
(A) all members of such group were stapled entities as of 6-30-83, and
(B) as of 6-30-83, such group included one or more real estate investment trusts.
(4) Certain stapled entities which include Puerto Rican corporations.—
(A) Paragraph (1) of section 269B(a) of such Code shall not apply to a domestic corporation and a qualified Puerto Rican corporation which, on 6-30-83, were stapled entities.
(B) For purposes of subparagraph (A), the term "qualified Puerto Rican corporation" means any corporation organized in Puerto Rico—
(i) which is described in section 957(c) of such Code or would be so described if any dividends it received from any other corporation described in such section 957(c) were treated as gross income of the type described in such section 957(c), and
(ii) does not, at any time during the taxable year, own (within the meaning of section 958 of such Code but before applying paragraph (2) of section 269B(a) of such Code) any stock of any corporation which is not described in such section 957(c).
(5) Treaty rule not to apply to stapled entities entitled to treaty benefits as of June 30, 1983.—In the case of any entity which was a stapled entity as of 6-30-83, subsection (d) of section 269B of such Code shall not apply to any treaty benefit to which such entity was entitled as of 6-30-83.
(6) Elections to treat stapled foreign entities as subsidiaries.—
(A) In general.—In the case of any foreign corporation and domestic corporation which as of 6-30-83, were stapled entities, such domestic corporation may elect (in lieu of applying paragraph (1) of section 269B(a) of such

on the foreign corporation referred to in subsection (a)(1) may, if not paid by such corporation, be collected from the domestic corporation referred to in such subsection or the shareholders of such foreign corporation.

* * * * * * * * * * * * *

(e) Subsection (a)(1) Not to Apply in Certain Cases.—

(1) In general.—Subsection (a)(1) shall not apply if it is established to the satisfaction of the Secretary that the domestic corporation and the foreign corporation referred to in such subsection are foreign owned.

(2) Foreign owned.—For purposes of paragraph (1), a corporation is foreign owned if less than 50 percent of—

(A) the total combined voting power of all classes of stock of such corporation entitled to vote, and

(B) the total value of the stock of the corporation,

is held directly (or indirectly through applying paragraphs (2) and (3) of section 958(a) and paragraph (4) of section 318(a)) by United States persons (as defined in section 7701(a)(30)).

[For official explanation, see Committee Reports, ¶4144.]

【¶2966】 CODE SEC. 274. DISALLOWANCE OF CERTAIN ENTERTAINMENT, ETC., EXPENSES.

* * * * * * * * * * * * *

(b) Gifts.—

(1) Limitation.—No deduction shall be allowed under section 162 or section 212 for any expense for gifts made directly or indirectly to any individual to the extent that such expense, when added to prior expenses of the taxpayer for gifts made to such individual during the same taxable year, exceeds $25. For purposes of this section, the term "gift" means any item excludable from gross income of the recipient under section 102 which is not excludable from his gross income under any other provision of this chapter, but such term does not include—

(A) an item having a cost to the taxpayer not in excess of $4.00 on which the name of the taxpayer is clearly and permanently imprinted and which is one of a number of identical items distributed generally by the taxpayer, *or*

(B) a sign, display rack, or other promotional material to be used on the business premises of the recipient.[1]

(2) Special rules.—

【Footnote ¶2965-A continued】

Code) to be treated as owning all interests in the foreign corporation which constitute stapled interests with respect to stock of the domestic corporation.

(B) Election.—Any election under subparagraph (A) shall be made not later than 180 days after the date of the enactment of this Act and shall be made in such manner as the Secretary of the Treasury or his delegate shall prescribe.

(C) Election irrevocable.—Any election under subparagraph (A), once made, may be revoked only with the consent of the Secretary of the Treasury or his delegate.

(7) Other stapled entities which include real estate investment trust.—

(A) In general.—Paragraph (3) of section 269B(a) of such Code shall not apply in determining the application of the provisions of part II of subchapter M of chapter 1 of such Code to any qualified real estate investment trust which is a part of a group of stapled entities—

(i) which was created pursuant to a written board of directors resolution adopted on 4-5-84, and

(ii) all members of such group were stapled entities as of 6-16-85.

(B) Qualified real estate investment trust.—The term "qualified real estate investment trust" means any real estate trust—

(i) at least 75 percent of the gross income of which is derived from interest on obligations secured by mortgages on real property (as defined in section 856 of such Code),

(ii) with respect to which the interest on the obligations described in clause (i) made or acquired by such trust (other than to persons who are independent contractors, as defined in section 856(d)(3) of such Code) is at an arm's length rate or a rate not more than 1 percentage point greater than the associated borrowing cost of the trust, and

(iii) with respect to which any real property held by the trust is not used in the trade or business of any other member of the group of stapled entities.

【Footnote ¶2966】 Matter in *italics* in Sec. 274(b) added by section 122(c) '86 TRA, which struck out:

(1) "or

(C) an item of tangible personal property which is awarded to an employee by reason of length of service, productivity, or safety achievement, but only to the extent that—

(i) the cost of such item to the taxpayer does not exceed $400, or

(ii) such item is a qualified plan award"

(A) In the case of a gift by a partnership, the limitation contained in paragraph (1) shall apply to the partnership as well as to each member thereof.

(B) For purposes of paragraph (1), a husband and wife shall be treated as one taxpayer.[2]

* * * * * * * * * * * *

(e) **Specific Exceptions to Application of Subsection (a).**—Subsection (a) shall not apply to—[3]

[4]*(1)* **Food and beverages for employees.**—Expenses for food and beverages (and facilities used in connection therewith) furnished on the business premises of the taxpayer primarily for his employees.

[5]*(2)* **Expenses treated as compensation.**—Expenses for goods, services and facilities, to the extent that the expenses are treated by the taxpayer, with respect to the recipient of the entertainment, amusement, or recreation, as compensation to an employee on the taxpayer's return of tax under this chapter and as wages to such employee for purposes of chapter 24 (relating to withholding of income tax at source on wages).

[6]*(3)* **Reimbursed expenses.**—Expenses paid or incurred by the taxpayer, in connection with the performance by him of services for another person (whether or not such other person is his employer), under a reimbursement or other expense allowance arrangement with such other person, but this paragraph shall apply—

(A) where the services are performed for an employer, only if the employer has treated such expenses in the manner provided in [7]*paragraph (2)*, or

(B) where the services are performed for a person other than an employer, only if the taxpayer accounts (to the extent provided by subsection (d)) to such person.

[8]*(4)* **Recreational, etc., expenses for employees.**—Expenses for recreational, social, or similar activities (including facilities therefor) primarily for the benefit of employees (other than employees who are [9] highly compensated employees). For purposes of this paragraph, an individual owning less than a 10-percent interest in the taxpayer's trade or business shall not be considered a shareholder or other owner, and for such purposes an individual shall be treated as owning any interest owned by a member of his family (within the meaning of section 267(c)(4)).

[10]*(5)* **Employee, stockholder, etc., business meetings.**—Expenses incurred by a tax-

---

⟦Footnote ¶2966 continued⟧

(2) "**(3) Qualified plan award.**—For purposes of this subsection—

(A) In general.—The term "qualified plan award" means an item which is awarded as part of a permanent, written plan or program of the taxpayer which does not discriminate in favor of officers, shareholders, or highly compensated employees as to eligibility or benefits.

(B) Average amount of awards.—An item shall not be treated as a qualified plan award for any taxable year if the average cost of all items awarded under all plans described in subparagraph (A) of the taxpayer during the taxable year exceeds $400.

(C) Maximum amount per item.—An item shall not be treated as a qualified plan award under this paragraph to the extent that the cost of such item exceeds $1,600."

Effective date (Sec. 151(c), '86 TRA).—Applies to prizes and awards granted after 12-31-86.

Matter in *italics* in Sec. 274(e)(1)—(5) added by section 142(a)(2), '86 TRA, which struck out:

(3) "**(1) Business meals.**—Expenses for food and beverages furnished to any individual under circumstances which (taking into account the surroundings in which furnished, the taxpayer's trade, business or income-producing activity and the relationship to such trade, business, or activity of the persons to whom the food and beverages are furnished) are of a type generally considered to be conducive to a business discussion."

(4) "**(2)**"

(5) "**(3)**"

(6) "**(4)**"

(7) "paragraph 3"

(8) "**(5)**"

Effective date (Sec. 151(a), '86 TRA).—Applies to taxable years beginning after 12-31-86.

Section 1114(b)(6), '86 TRA, struck out from Sec. 274(e)(5):

(9) "officers, shareholders or other owners, or"

Effective date (Sec. 1114(c)(1), '86 TRA).—Applies to years beginning after 12-31-86.

Matter in *italics* in Sec. 274(e)(6)—(10) and (h)(1)—(5) and (7) added by section 142(a)(1) and (c), '86 TRA, which struck out:

(10) "**(6)**"

payer which are directly related to business meetings of his employees, stockholders, agents, or directors.

[11](6) **Meetings of business leagues, etc.**—Expenses directly related and necessary to attendance at a business meeting or convention of any organization described in section 501(c)(6) (relating to business leagues, chambers of commerce, real estate boards, and boards of trade) and exempt from taxation under section 501(a).

[12](7) **Items available to public.**—Expenses for goods, services, and facilities made available by the taxpayer to the general public.

[13](8) **Entertainment sold to customers.**—Expenses for goods or services (including the use of facilities) which are sold by the taxpayer in a bona fide transaction for an adequate and full consideration in money or money's worth.

[14](9) **Expenses includible in income of persons who are not employees.**—Expenses paid or incurred by the taxpayer for goods, services, and facilities to the extent that the expenses are includible in the gross income of a recipient of the entertainment, amusement, or recreation who is not an employee of the taxpayer as compensation for services rendered or as a prize or award under section 74. The preceding sentence shall not apply to any amount paid or incurred by the taxpayer if such amount is required to be included (or would be so required except that the amount is less than $600) in any information return filed by such taxpayer under part III of subchapter A of chapter 61 and is not so included.

For purposes of this subsection, any item referred to in subsection (a) shall be treated as an expense.

* * * * * * * * * * * * *

(h) Attendance at Conventions, Etc.—

(1) **In general.**—In the case of any individual who attends a convention, seminar, or similar meeting which is held outside the North American area, no deduction shall be allowed under section 162[15] for expenses allocable to such meeting unless the taxpayer establishes that the meeting is directly related to the active conduct of his trade or business[16] that, after taking into account in the manner provided by regulations prescribed by the Secretary—

    (A) the purpose of such meeting and the activities taking place at such meeting,

    (B) the purposes and activities of the sponsoring organizations or groups,

    (C) the residences of the active members of the sponsoring organization and the places at which other meetings of the sponsoring organization or groups have been held or will be held, and

    (D) such other relevant factors as the taxpayer may present,

it is as reasonable for the meeting to be held outside the North American area as within the North American area.

(2) **Conventions on cruise ships.**—In the case of any individual who attends a convention, seminar, or other meeting which is held on any cruise ship, no deduction shall be allowed under section 162[15] for expenses allocable to such meeting, unless the taxpayer meets the requirements of paragraph (5) and establishes that the meeting is directly related to the active conduct of his trade or business that —

    (A) the cruise ship is a vessel registered in the United States; and

    (B) all ports of call of such cruise ship are located in the United States or in possessions of the United States.

With respect to cruises beginning in any calendar year, not more than $2,000 of the expenses attributable to an individual attending one or more meetings may be taken into account under section 162[15] by reason of the preceding sentence.

* * * * * * * * * * * * *

(4) **Subsection to apply to employer as well as to traveler.—**

    (A) Except as provided in subparagraph (B), this subsection shall apply to deductions otherwise allowable under section 162[15] to any person, whether or not such person is the individual attending the convention, seminar, or similar meeting.

[Footnote ¶2966 continued]

(11) "(7)"
(12) "(8)"
(13) "(9)"
(14) "(10)"
(15) "or 212"
(16) "or to an activity described in section 212 and"
Effective date (Sec. 151(a), '86 TRA).—Applies to taxable years beginning after 12-31-86.

(B) This subsection shall not deny a deduction to any person other than the individual attending the convention, seminar, or similar meeting with respect to any amount paid by such person to or on behalf of such individual if includible in the gross income of such individual. The preceding sentence shall not apply if the amount is required to be included in any information return filed by such person under part III of subchapter A of chapter 61 and is not so included.

(5) Reporting requirements.—No deduction shall be allowed under section 162[15] for expenses allocable to attendance at a convention, seminar, or similar meeting on any cruise ship unless the taxpayer claiming the deduction attaches to the return of tax on which the deduction is claimed—

(A) a written statement signed by the individual attending the meeting which includes—

(i) information with respect to the total days of the trip, excluding the days of transportation to and from the cruise ship port, and the number of hours of each day of the trip which such individual devoted to scheduled business activities.

(ii) a program of the scheduled business activities of the meeting, and

(iii) such other information as may be required in regulations prescribed by the Secretary; and

(B) a written statement signed by an officer of the organization or group sponsoring the meeting which includes—

(i) a schedule of the business activities of each day of the meeting,

(ii) the number of hours which the individual attending the meeting attended such scheduled business activities, and

(iii) such other information as may be required in regulations prescribed by the Secretary.

* * * * * * * * * * * *

(7) Seminars, etc. for section 212 purposes.—No deduction shall be allowed under section 212 for expenses allocable to a convention, seminar, or similar meeting.

* * * * * * * * * * * *

(j) Employee Achievement Awards.—

(1) General Rule—No deduction shall be allowed under section 162 or section 212 for the cost of an employee achievement award except to the extent that such cost does not exceed the deduction limitations of paragraph (2).

(2) Deduction limitations.—The deduction for the cost of an employee achievement award made by an employer to an employee.—

(A) which is not a qualified plan award, when added to the cost to the employer for all other employee achievement awards made to such employee during the taxable year which are not qualified plan awards, shall not exceed $400, and

(B) which is a qualified plan award, when added to the cost to the employer for all other employee achievement awards made to such employee during the taxable year (including employee achievement awards which are not qualified plan awards), shall not exceed $1,600.

(3) Definitions.—For purposes of this subsection—

(A) Employee achievement award.—The term "employee achievement award" means an item of tangible personal property which is—

(i) transferred by an employer to an employee for length of service achievement or safety achievement,

(ii) awarded as part of a meaningful presentation, and

(iii) awarded under conditions and circumstances that do not create a significant likelihood of the payment of disguised compensation.

(B) Qualified plan award.—

(i) In general.—The term "qualified plan award" means an employee achievement award awarded as part of an established written plan or program of the taxpayer which does not discriminate in favor of highly compensated employees (within the meaning of section 414(q)) as to eligibility or benefits.

(ii) Limitation.—An employee achievement award shall not be treated as a qualified plan award for any taxable year if the average cost of all employee achievement awards which are provided by the employer during the year, and which would be qualified plan awards but for this subparagraph, exceeds $400.

Code §274(j)(3) ¶2966

For purposes of the preceding sentence, average cost shall be determined by includ-ing the entire cost of qualified plan awards, without taking into account employee achievement awards of nominal value.

(4) *Special rules.*—*For purposes of this subsection*—

(A) *Partnerships.*—*In the case of an employee achievement award made by a partnership, the deduction limitations contained in paragraph (2) shall apply to the partnership as well as to each member thereof.*

(B) *Length of service awards.*—*An item shall not be treated as having been pro-vided for length of service achievement if the item is received during the recipient's 1st 5 years of employment or if the recipient received a length of service achievement award (other than an award excludable under section 132(e)(1)) during that year or any of the prior 4 years.*

(C) *Safety achievement awards.*—*An item provided by an employer to an em-ployee shall not be treated as having been provided for safety achievement if*—

(i) *during the taxable year, employee achievement awards (other than awards excludable under section 132(e)(1)) for safety achievement have previously been awarded by the employer to more than 10 percent of the employees of the em-ployer (excluding employees described in clause (ii)), or*

(ii) *such item is awarded to a manager, administrator, clerical employee, or other professional employee.*

(k) *Business meals.*—

(1) *In general.*—*No deduction shall be allowed under this chapter for the expense of any food or beverages unless*—

(A) *such expense is not lavish or extravagant under the circumstances, and*

(B) *the taxpayer (or an employee of the taxpayer) is present at the furnishing of such food or beverages.*

(2) *Exceptions.*—*Paragraph (1) shall not apply to any expense if subsection (a) does not apply to such expense by reason of paragraph (2), (3), (4), (7), (8), or (9) of subsec-tion (e).*

(l) *Additional Limitations on Entertainment Tickets.*—

(1) *Entertainment tickets.*—

(A) *In general.*—*In determining the amount allowable as a deduction under this chapter for any ticket for any activity or facility described in subsection (d)(2), the amount taken into account shall not exceed the face value of such ticket.*

(B) *Exception for certain charitable sports events.*—*Subparagraph (A) shall not apply to any ticket for any sports event*—

(i) *which is organized for the primary purpose of benefiting an organization which is described in section 501(c)(3) and exempt from tax under section 501(a),*

(ii) *all of the net proceeds of which are contributed to such organization, and*

(iii) *which utilizes volunteers for substantially all of the work performed in carrying out such event.*

(2) *Skyboxes, etc.*—

(A) *In general.*—*In the case of a skybox or other private luxury box leased for more than 1 event, the amount allowable as a deduction under this chapter with re-spect to such events shall not exceed the sum of the face value of non-luxury box seat tickets for the seats in such box covered by the lease. For purposes of the preceding sentence, 2 or more related leases shall be treated as 1 lease.*

(B) *Phasein.*—*In the case of*—

(i) *a taxable year beginning in 1987, the amount disallowed under subpara-graph (A) shall be 1/3 of the amount which would be disallowed without regard to this subparagraph, and*

(ii) *in the case of a taxable year beginning in 1988, the amount disallowed under subparagraph (A) shall be 2/3 of the amount which would have been disal-lowed without regard to this subparagraph.*

(m) *Additional Limitations on Travel Expenses.*—

(1) *Luxury water transportation.*—

(A) *In general.*—*No deduction shall be allowed under this chapter for expenses incurred for transportation by water to the extent such expenses exceed twice the ag-gregate per diem amounts for days of such transportation. For purposes of the preced-ing sentence, the term "per diem amounts" means the highest amount generally al-lowable with respect to a day to employees of the executive branch of the Federal Government for per diem while away from home but serving in the United States.*

  (B) *Exceptions.—Subparagraph (A) shall not apply to—*
   (i) *any expense allocable to a convention, seminar, or other meeting which is held on any cruise ship, and*
   (ii) *any expense to which subsection (a) does not apply by reason of paragraph (2), (3), (4), (7), (8), or (9) of subsection (e).*

  (2) *Travel as form of education.—No deduction shall be allowed under this chapter for expenses for travel as a form of education.*

 (n) *Only 80 Percent of Meal and Entertainment Expenses Allowed as Deduction.—*
  (1) *In general—The amount allowable as a deduction under this chapter for—*
   (A) *any expense for food or beverages, and*
   (B) *any item with respect to an activity which is of a type generally considered to constitute entertainment, amusement, or recreation, or with respect to a facility used in connection with such activity,*

shall not exceed 80 percent of the amount of such expense or item which would (but for this paragraph) be allowable as a deduction under this chapter.

  (2) *Exceptions.—Paragraph (1) shall not apply to any expense if—*
   (A) *subsection (a) does not apply to such expense by reason of paragraph (2), (3), (4), (7), (8), or (9) of subsection (e),*
   (B) *in the case of an expense for food or beverages, such expense is excludable from the gross income of the recipient under section 132 by reason of subsection (e) thereof (relating to de minimis fringes),*
   (C) *such expense is covered by a package involving a ticket described in subsection (l)(1)(B), or*
   (D) *in the case of an expense for food or beverages before January 1, 1989, such expense is an integral part of a qualified meeting.*

  (3) *Qualified meeting.—For purposes of paragraph (2)(D), the term "qualified meeting" means any convention, seminar, annual meeting, or similar business program with respect to which—*
   (A) *an expense for food or beverages is not separately stated,*
   (B) *more than 50 percent of the participants are away from home,*
   (C) *at least 40 individuals attend, and*
   (D) *such food and beverages are part of a program which includes a speaker.*

 *(o) **Regulatory Authority.**—The secretary shall prescribe such regulations as he may deem necessary to carry out the purposes of this section, including regulations prescribing whether subsection (a) or subsection (b) applies in cases where both such subsections would otherwise apply.

[For official explanation, see Committee Reports, ¶3858; 3866; 3979.]

[¶2967] CODE SEC. 277. DEDUCTIONS INCURRED BY CERTAIN MEMBERSHIP ORGANIZATIONS IN TRANSACTIONS WITH MEMBERS.

 (a) **General Rule.**—In the case of a social club or membership organization which is operated primarily to furnish services or goods to members and which is not exempt from taxation, deductions for the taxable year attributable to furnishing services, insurances, goods, or other items of value to members shall be allowed only to the extent of income derived during such year from members or transactions with members (including income derived during such year from institutes and trade shows which are primarily for the education of members). If for any taxable year such deductions exceed such income, the excess shall be treated as a deduction attributable to furnishing services, insurance goods, or other items of value to members paid or incurred in the succeeding taxable year. The deductions provided by sections 243, 244, and 245 (relating to dividends received by corporations) shall not be allowed to any organization to which this section applies for the taxable year.

 (b) **Exceptions.**—Subsection (a) shall not apply to any organization—
  (1) which for the taxable year is subject to taxation under subchapter H or L,

---

[Footnote ¶2966 continued]

 * Former Sec. 274(j) was relettered (k), by section 122(d), '86 TRA, and was further relettered (o) by section 142(a)(1), '86 TRA.

Effective date (Sec. 151(a), '86 TRA).—Applies to taxable years beginning after 12-31-86.
Matter in *italics* in Sec. 274(j)—(n) added by section 142 (a)(1) and (b), '86 TRA.
Effective date (Sec. 151(a), '86 TRA).—Applies to taxable years beginning after 12-31-86.

(2) which has made an election before October 9, 1969, under section 456(c) or which is affiliated with such an organization,[1]

(3) which for each day of any taxable year is a national securities exchange subject to regulation under the Securities Exchange Act of 1934 or a contract market subject to regulation under the Commodity Exchange Act[2], *or*

(4) *which is engaged primarily in the gathering and distribution of news to its members for publication.*

[For official explanation, see Committee Reports, ¶4117.]

[¶2968] CODE SEC. 278. CAPITAL EXPENDITURES INCURRED IN PLANTING AND DEVELOPING CITRUS AND ALMOND GROVES; *CERTAIN CAPITAL EXPENDITURES OF FARMING SYNDICATES.*

[Repealed by section 803(b)(6), '86 TRA].[1]

[For official explanation, see Committee Reports, ¶3937.]

[¶2969] CODE SEC. 280. CERTAIN EXPENDITURES INCURRED IN PRODUCTION OF FILMS, BOOKS, RECORDS, OR SIMILAR PROPERTY.

[Repealed by section 803(b)(2)(A), '86 TRA].[1]

[For official explanation, see Committee Reports, ¶3937.]

[¶2969-A] CODE SEC. 280A. DISALLOWANCE OF CERTAIN EXPENSES IN CONNECTION WITH BUSINESS USE OF HOME, RENTAL OF VACATION HOMES, ETC.

* * * * * * * * * * * * *

(c) Exceptions for Certain Business or Rental Use; Limitation on Deductions for Such Use.—

* * * * * * * * * * * * *

(5) Limitation on deductions.—In the case of a use described in paragraph (1), (2), or (4) and in the case of a use described in paragraph (3) where the dwelling unit is used by the taxpayer during the taxable year as a residence, the deductions allowed under this chapter for the taxable year by reason of being attributed to such use shall not exceed the excess of—

(A) the gross income derived from such use for the taxable year, over[1]

(B) *the sum of—*

(i) *the deductions allocable to such use which are allowable under this chapter for the taxable year whether or not such unit (or portion thereof) was so used, and*

(ii) *the deductions allocable to the trade or business in which such use occurs (but which are not allocable to such use) for such taxable year.*

Any amount not allowable as a deduction under this chapter by reason of the preceding sentence shall be taken into account as a deduction (allocable to such use) under this chapter for the succeeding taxable year.

(6) *Treatment of rental to employer.—Paragraphs (1) and (3) shall not apply to any item which is attributable to the rental of the dwelling unit (or any portion thereof) by the taxpayer to his employer during any period in which the taxpayer uses the dwelling unit (or portion) in performing services as an employee of the employer.*

* * * * * * * * * * * * *

[For official explanation, see Committee Reports, ¶3867.]

[¶2969-B] CODE SEC. 280C. CERTAIN EXPENSES FOR WHICH CREDITS ARE ALLOWABLE.

* * * * * * * * * * * * *

[Footnote ¶2967] Matter in *italics* in Sec. 277(b) added by section 1604(a), '86 TRA, which struck out:

(1) "or"

(2) "."

Effective date (Sec. 1604(b), '86 TRA). —Applies to taxable years beginning after the date of the enactment of this Act.

[Footnote ¶2968] (1) **Effective date** (Sec. 803(d), '86 TRA).—(1) Generally applies to costs incurred after 12-31-86, in taxable years ending after such date. For special and transitional rules, see footnote ¶2961-A.

[Footnote ¶2969] (1) **Effective date** (Sec. 803(d), '86 TRA).—(1) Generally applies to costs incurred after 12-31-86, in taxable years ending after such date. For special and transitional rules, see footnote ¶2961-A.

[Footnote ¶2969-A] Matter in *italics* in Sec. 280(c)(5)(B) and (6) added by section 143(b) and (c), '86 TRA, which struck out:

(1) "(B) the deductions allocable to such use which are allowable under this chapter for the taxable year whether or not such unit (or portion thereof) was so used"

Effective date (Sec. 151(a), '86 TRA).—Applies to taxable years beginning after 12-31-86.

(b) Credit for Qualified Clinical Testing Expenses for Certain Drugs.—

(1) In general.—No deduction shall be allowed for that portion of the qualified clinical testing expenses (as defined in [1]*section 28(b)*) otherwise allowable as a deduction for the taxable year which is equal to the amount of the credit allowable for the taxable year under [2]*section 28* (determined without regard to subsection (d)(2) thereof).

(2) Similar rule where taxpayer capitalizes rather than deducts expenses. If—

(A) the amount of the credit allowable for the taxable year under [2]*section 28* (determined without regard to subsection (d)(2) thereof), exceeds

(B) the amount allowable as a deduction for the taxable year for qualified clinical testing expenses (determined without regard to paragraph (1)),

the amount chargeable to capital account for the taxable year for such expenses shall be reduced by the amount of such excess.

(3) Controlled groups.—In the case of a corporation which is a member of a controlled group of corporations (within the meaning of [3]*section 41(f)(5)*) or a trade or business which is treated as being under common control with other trades or business (within the meaning of [4]*section 41(f)(1)(B)*, this subsection shall be applied under rules prescribed by the Secretary similar to the rules applicable under subparagraphs (A) and (B) of [5]*section 41(f)(1)*.

[For official explanation, see Committee Reports, ¶4161; 3872.]

[¶2969-C] CODE SEC. 280F. LIMITATION ON INVESTMENT TAX CREDIT AND DEPECIATION FOR LUXURY AUTOMOBILES; LIMITATION WHERE CERTAIN PROPERTY USED FOR PERSONAL PURPOSES.

(a) Limitation on Amount of Investment Tax Credit and Depreciation for Luxury Automobiles.—

(1) Investment tax credit.—The amount of the credit determined under section 46(a) for any passenger automobile shall not exceed $675.

(2) Depreciation.—

(A) Limitation.—The amount of the [1]*depreciation* deduction for any taxable year for any passenger automobile shall not exceed—

[2]*(i) $2,560 for the 1st taxable year in the recovery period,*
(ii) $4,100 for the 2nd taxable year in the recovery period,
(iii) $2,450 for the 3rd taxable year in the recovery period, and
(iv) $1,475 for each succeeding taxable year in the recovery period.

(B) Disallowed deductions allowed for years after recovery period.—

(i) In general.—Except as provided in clause (ii), the unrecovered basis of any passenger automobile shall be treated as an expense for the 1st taxable year after the recovery period. Any excess of the unrecovered basis over the limitation of clause (ii) shall be treated as an expense in the succeeding taxable year.

(ii) [3]*$1,475* limitation.—The amount treated as an expense under clause (i) for any taxable year shall not exceed [3]*$1,475*.

(iii) Property must be depreciable.—No amount shall be allowable as a deduction by reason of this subparagraph with respect to any property for any

---

[Footnote ¶2969-B] Matter in *italics* in Sec. 280C(b)(1) and (2) added by section 1847(b)(8), '86 TRA, which struck out:

(1) "section 29(b)"
(2) "section 29"

Effective date (Sec. 1881, '86 TRA and Sec. 475(a), '84 TRA).—Applies to taxable years beginning after 12-31-83, and to carrybacks from such years.

Matter in *italics* in Sec. 280C(b)(3) added by section 231(d)(3)(E), '86 TRA, which struck out:

(3) "section 30(f)(5)"
(4) "section 30(f)(1)(B)"
(5) "section 30(f)(1)"

Effective date (Sec. 231(g)(1), '86 TRA).—Applies to taxable years beginning after 12-31-85.

[Footnote ¶2969-C] Matter in *italics* in Sec. 280F(a)(2), (3), (b)(2), (3)(A), (4), (c)(4), (d)(1) and (2) added by section 201(d)(4)(A)—(F), (J) and (K), '86 TRA, which struck out:

(1) "recovery"
(2) "(i) $3,200 for the first taxable year in the recovery period, and
(ii) $4,800 for each succeeding taxable year in the recovery period."
(3) "$4,800"

taxable year unless a depreciation deduction would be allowable with respect to such property for such taxable year.

(iv) Amount treated as [1]*depreciation* deduction.—For purposes of this subtitle, any amount allowable as a deduction by reason of this subparagraph shall be treated as a [1]*depreciation* deduction allowable under section 168.

(3) Coordination with reductions in amount allowable by reason of personal use, etc.—This subsection shall be applied before—

(A) the application of subsection (b), and

(B) the application of any other reduction in the amount of the credit determined under section 46(a) or any [1]*depreciation* deduction allowable under section 168 by reason of any use not qualifying the property for such credit or recovery deduction.

* * * * * * * * * * * *

(b) Limitation Where Business Use of Listed Property Not Greater Than 50 Percent.—

* * * * * * * * * * * *

(2) Depreciation.—If any listed property is not predominantly used in a qualified business use for any taxable year, the deduction allowed under section 168 with respect to such property for such taxable year and any subsequent taxable year shall be determined under the [4]*section 168(g) (relating to alternative depreciation system)*.

(3) Recapture.—

(A) Where business use percentage does not exceed 50 percent.—If—

(i) property is predominantly used in a qualified business use in a taxable year in which it is placed in service, and

(ii) such property is not predominantly used in a qualified business use for any subsequent taxable year,

then any excess depreciation shall be included in gross income for the taxable year referred to in clause (ii), and the [1]*depreciation* deduction for the taxable year referred to in clause (ii) and any subsequent taxable years shall be determined under [5]*section 168(g) (relating to alternative depreciation system)*.

(B) Excess depreciation.—For purposes of subparagraph (A), the term "excess depreciation" means the excess (if any) of—

(i) the amount of the [1]*depreciation* deductions allowable with respect to the property for taxable years before the 1st taxable year in which the property was not predominantly used in a qualified business use, over

(ii) the amount which would have been so allowable if the property had not been predominantly used in a qualified ~usiness use for the taxable year in which it was placed in service.

[6]**(4) Property predominantly used in qualified business use.**—*For purposes of this subsection, property shall be treated as predominantly used in a qualified business use for any taxable year if the business use percentage for such taxable year exceeds 50 percent.*

(c) Treatment of Leases.—

* * * * * * * * * * * *

(4) Lease term.—In determining the term of any lease for purposes of paragraph (2), the rules of [7]*section 168(i)(3)(A)* shall apply.

* * * * * * * * * * * *

⟦Footnote ¶2969-C continued⟧

(4) "straight line method over the earnings and profits life for such property"

(5) "the straight line method over the earnings and profits life"

(6) "**(4) Definitions.**—For purposes of this subsection—

(A) Property predominantly used in qualified business use.—Property shall be treated as predominantly used in a qualified business use for any taxable year if the business use percentage for such taxable year exceeds 50 percent.

(B) Straight line method over earnings and profits life.—The amount determined under the straight line method over the earnings and profits life with respect to any property shall be the amount which would be determined with respect to such property under the principles of section 312(k)(3). If the recovery period applicable to any property under section 168 is longer than the recovery period applicable to such property under section 312(k)(3), such longer recovery period shall be used for purposes of the preceding sentence."

(7) "section 168(j)(6)(B)"

Effective date (Sec. 203(a)(1)(A), '86 TRA).—Generally applies to property placed in service after 12-31-86, in taxable years ending after such date. For transitional and special rules, see ¶2007—2008.

Section 1812(e)(5), '86 TRA, struck out from Sec. 280F(d)(2):

(d) Definitions and Special Rules.—For purposes of this section—

(1) Coordination with section 179.—Any deduction allowable under section 179 with respect to any listed property shall be subject to the limitations of subsections (a) and (b) in the same manner as if it were a [1]*depreciation* deduction allowable under section 168.

(2) Subsequent depreciation deductions reduced for deductions allocable to personal use.—Solely for purposes of determining the amount of the [1]*depreciation* deduction for subsequent taxable years, if less than 100 percent of the use of any listed property during any taxable year is [8] use [9]*in a trade or business (including the holding for the production of income)*, all of the use of such property during such taxable year shall be treated as use so described.

(3) Deductions of employee.—

(A) In general.—Any employee use of listed property shall not be treated as use in a trade or business for purposes of determining the amount of any credit allowable under section 38 to the employee or the amount of any recovery deduction allowable to the employee *(or the amount of any deduction allowable to the employee for rentals or other payments under a lease of listed property)* unless such use is for the convenience of the employer and required as a condition of employment.

(B) · Employee use.—For purposes of subparagraph (A), the term "employee use" means any use in connection with the performance of services as an employee.

(4) Listed property.—

(A) In general.—Except as provided in subparagraph (B), the term "listed property" means—

(i) any passenger automobile,

(ii) any other property used as a means of transportation,

(iii) any property of a type generally used for purposes of entertainment, recreation, or amusement,

(iv) any computer or peripheral equipment (as defined in [10]*section 168(i)(2)(B)*, and

(v) any other property of a type specified by the Secretary by regulations.

(B) Exception for certain computers.—The term "listed property" shall not include any computer or peripheral equipment (as so defined) used exclusively at a regular business establishment *and owned or leased by the person operating such establishment.* For purposes of the preceding sentence, any portion of a dwelling

---

⟦Footnote ¶2969-C continued⟧

(8) "not"
Effective date (Sec. 1881, '86 TRA and section 179(d)(1), '84 TRA).—
(1)(A) Generally applies to—,
(i) property placed in service after 6-18-84, in taxable years ending after such date, and
(ii) property leased after 6-18-84, in taxable years ending after such date.
(B) shall not apply to any property—
(i) acquired by the taxpayer pursuant to a binding contract in effect on 6-18-84, and at all times thereafter (or under construction on such date) but only if the property is placed in service before 1-1-85 (1-1-87, in the case of 15-year real property), or
(ii) of which the taxpayer is the lessee but only if the lease is pursuant to a binding contract in effect on 6-18-84, and at all times thereafter and only if the taxpayer first uses such property under the lease before 1-1-85 (1-1-87, in the case of 15-year real property).
For purposes of the preceding sentence, the term "15-year real property" includes 18-year real property.

Matter in *italics* in Sec. 280F(d)(2) added by section 201(d)(4)(F)(ii), '86 TRA, which struck out:
(9) "described in section 168(c)(1) (defining recovery property)"
Effective date (Sec. 203(a)(1)(A), '86 TRA).—Generally applies to property placed in service after 12-31-86, in taxable years ending after such date. For transitional and special rules, see ¶2007—2008.

Matter in *italics* in Sec. 280F(d)(3)(A) added by section 1812(e)(2), '86 TRA.
Effective date (Sec. 1881, '86 TRA and section 179(d)(1), '84 TRA).—See above.

Matter in *italics* in Sec. 280F(d)(4)(A)(iv) added by section 201(d)(4)(G), '86 TRA, which struck out:
(10) "section 168(j)(5)(D)"
Effective date (Sec. 203(a)(1)(A), '86 TRA).—Generally applies to property placed in service after 12-31-86, in taxable years ending after such date. For transitional and special rules, see ¶2007—2008.

Matter in *italics* in Sec. 280F(d)(4)(B), (C) and (5)(A) added by section 1812(e)(1), (3) and (4), '86 TRA.
Effective date (Sec. 1881, '86 TRA and section 179(d)(1), '84 TRA).—See above.

unit shall be treated as a regular business establishment if (and only if) the requirements of section 280A(c)(1) are met with respect to such portion.

(C) Exception for property used in business of transporting persons or property.— Except to the extent provided in regulations, clause (ii) of subparagraph (A) shall not apply to any property substantially all of the use of which is in a trade or business of providing to unrelated persons services consisting of the transportation of persons or property for compensation or hire.

(5) Passenger automobile.—

(A) In general.—Except as provided in subparagraph (B), the term "passenger automobile" means any 4-wheeled vehicle

(i) which is manufactured primarily for use on public streets, roads, and highways, and

(ii) which is rated at 6,000 pounds *unloaded* gross vehicle weight or less.

In the case of a truck or van, clause (ii) shall be applied by substituting "gross vehicle weight" for "unloaded gross vehicle weight".

* * * * * * * * * * * *

(8) Unrecovered basis.—[11]*For purposes of subsection (a)(2), the term "unrecovered basis" means the adjusted basis of the passenger automobile determined after the application of subsection (a) and as if all use during the recovery period were use in a trade or business (including the holding of property for the production of income).*

* * * * * * * * * * * *

(10) Special rule for property acquired in nonrecognition transactions.—For purposes of subsection (a)(2) [12]any property acquired in a nonrecognition transaction shall be treated as a single property originally placed in service in the taxable year in which it was placed in service after being so acquired.

* * * * * * * * * * * *

[For official explanation, see Committee Reports, ¶3870; 4146.]

[¶2969-D] CODE SEC. 280G. GOLDEN PARACHUTE PAYMENTS.—

(a) General Rule.—No deduction shall be allowed under this chapter for any excess parachute payment.

(b) Excess Parachute Payment.—For purposes of this section—

(1) In general.—The term "excess parachute payment" means an amount equal to the excess of any parachute payment over the portion of the base amount allocated to such payment.

(2) Parachute payment defined.—

(A) In general.—The term "parachute payment" means any payment in the nature of compensation to (or for the benefit of) a disqualified individual if—

(i) such payment is contingent on a change—

(I) in the ownership or effective control of the corporation, or

(II) in the ownership of a substantial portion of the assets of the corporation, and

(ii) the aggregate present value of the payments in the nature of compensation to (or for the benefit of) such individual which are contingent on such change equals or exceeds an amount equal to 3 times the base amount.

For purposes of clause (ii), payments not treated as parachute payments under paragraph (4)(A), (5), or (6) shall not be taken into account.

(B) Agreements.—The term "parachute payment" shall also include any payment in the nature of compensation to (or for the benefit of) a disqualified individual if such payment is *made pursuant to an agreement which violates any generally enforced securities laws or regulations. In any proceeding involving the issue of whether any payment made to a disqualified individual is a parachute payment on account of a violation of any generally enforced securities laws or regulations, the*

[Footnote ¶2969-C continued]

Matter in *italics* in Sec. 280F(d)(8) and (10) added by section 201(d)(4)(H) and (I), '86 TRA, which struck out:

(11) "For purposes of subsection (a)(2), the term "unrecovered basis" means the excess (if any) of—

(A) the unadjusted basis (as defined in section 168(d)(1)(A)) of the passenger automobile, over

(B) the amount of the recovery deductions which would have been allowable for taxable years in the recovery period determined after the application of subsection (a) and as if all use during the recovery period were use described in section 168(c)(1)."

(12) ", not withstanding any regulations prescribed under section 168(f)(7),"

Effective date (Sec. 203(a)(1)(A), '86 TRA).—Generally applies to property placed in service after 12-31-86, in taxable years ending after such date. For transitional and special rules, see ¶2007—2008.

burden of proof with respect to establishing the occurrence of a violation of such a law or regulation shall be upon the Secretary.

* * * * * * * * * * * *

[1]*(4) Treatment of amounts which taxpayer establishes as reasonable compensation.—In the case of any payment described in paragraph (2)(A)—*

    (A) the amount treated as a parachute payment shall not include the portion of such payment which the taxpayer establishes by clear and convincing evidence is reasonable compensation for personal services to be rendered on or after the date of the change described in paragraph (2)(A)(i), and

    (B) the amount treated as an excess parachute payment shall be reduced by the portion of such payment which the taxpayer establishes by clear and convincing evidence is reasonable compensation for personal services actually rendered before the date of the change described in paragraph (2)(A)(i).

For purposes of subparagraph (B), reasonable compensation for services actually rendered before the date of the change described in paragraph (2)(A)(i) shall be first offset against the base amount.

    (5) **Exemption for small business corporations, etc.—**

      (A) **In general.—**Notwithstanding paragraph (2), the term "parachute payment" does not include—

        (i) any payment to a disqualified individual with respect to a corporation which (immediately before the change described in paragraph (2)(A)(i)) was a small business corporation (as defined in section 1361(b)), and

        (ii) any payment to a disqualified individual with respect to a corporation (other than a corporation described in clause (i)) if—

          (I) immediately before the change described in paragraph (2)(A)(i), no stock in such corporation was readily tradeable on an established securities market or otherwise, and

          (II) the shareholder approval requirements of subparagraph (B) are met with respect to such payment.

The Secretary may, by regulations, prescribe that the requirements of subclause (I) of clause (ii) are not met where a substantial portion of the assets of any entity consists (directly or indirectly) of stock in such corporation and interests in such other entity are readily tradeable on an established securities market, or otherwise.

      (B) **Shareholder approval requirements.—**The shareholder approval requirements of this subparagraph are met with respect to any payment if—

        (i) such payment was approved by a vote of the persons who owned, immediately before the change described in paragraph (2)(A)(i), more than 75 percent of the voting power of all outstanding stock of the corporation, and

        (ii) there was adequate disclosure to shareholders of all material facts concerning all payments which (but for this paragraph) would be parachute payments with respect to a disqualified individual.

    (6) **Exemption for payments under qualified plans.—**Notwithstanding paragraph (2), the term "parachute payment" shall not include any payment to or from—

      (A) a plan described in section 401(a) which includes a trust exempt from tax under section 501(a),

      (B) an annuity plan described in section 403(a), or

      (C) a simplified employee pension (as defined in section 408(k)).

(c) **Disqualified Individuals.—**For purposes of this section, the term "disqualified individual" means any individual who is—

    (1) an employee, independent contractor, or other person specified in regulations by the Secretary who performs personal services for any corporation, and

    (2) is an officer, shareholder, or highly-compensated individual.

For purposes of this section, a personal service corporation (or similar entity) shall be treated as an individual. *For purposes of paragraph (2), the term "highly-compensated individual" only includes an individual who is (or would be if the individual were an employee)*

[Footnote ¶2969-D] Matter in *italics* in Sec. 280G(b)(2)(A), (B), (b)(4)—(6), (c), (d)(2) and (5) added by section 1804(j), '86 TRA which struck out:

  (1) **"(4) Excess parachute payments reduced to extent taxpayer establishes reasonable compensation.—**In the case of any parachute payment described in paragraph (2)(A), the amount of any excess parachute payment shall be reduced by the portion of such payment which the taxpayer establishes by clear and convincing evidence is reasonable compensation for personal services actually rendered. For purposes of the preceding sentence, reasonable compensation shall be first offset against the base amount."

a member of the group consisting of the highest paid 1 percent of the employees of the corporation or, if less, the highest paid 250 employees of the corporation.

(d) **Other Definitions and Special Rules.**—For purposes of this section—

* * * * * * * * * * * *

(2) **Base period.**—The term "base period" means the period consisting of the most recent 5 taxable years ending before the date on which the change in ownership or control described in paragraph (2)(A) of subsection (b) occurs (or such portion of such period during which the disqualified individual [2]*performed personal services for the corporation*).

* * * * * * * * * * * *

(5) *Treatment of affiliated groups.—Except as otherwise provided in regulations, all members of the same affiliated group (as defined in section 1504, determined without regard to section 1504(b)) shall be treated as 1 corporation for purposes of this section. Any person who is an officer or any member of such group shall be treated as an officer of such 1 corporation.*

* * * * * * * * * * * *

[For official explanation, see Committee Reports, ¶4138.]

[¶2970] CODE SEC. 291. SPECIAL RULES RELATING TO CORPORATE PREFERENCE ITEMS.

(a) [1]**Reduction in Certain Preference Items, etc.**—For purposes of this subtitle, in the case of a corporation—

(1) **Section 1250 capital gain treatment.**—In the case of section 1250 property which is disposed of during the taxable year, 20 percent of the excess (if any) of—

(A) the amount which would be treated as ordinary income if such property was section 1245 property [2]*over*

(B) the amount treated as ordinary income under section 1250 (determined without regard to this paragraph),

shall be treated as gain which is ordinary income under section 1250 and shall be recognized notwithstanding any other provision of this title. Under regulations prescribed by the Secretary, the provisions of this paragraph shall not apply to the disposition of any property to the extent section 1250(a) does not apply to such disposition by reason of section 1250(d).

(2) **Reduction in percentage depletion.**—In the case of iron ore and coal (including lignite), the amount allowable as a deduction under section 613 with respect to any property (as defined in section 614) shall be reduced by [3]*20 percent of the amount of the excess (if any) of—*

(A) the amount of the deduction allowable under section 613 for the taxable year (determined without regard to this paragraph), over

---

[Footnote ¶2969-D continued]

(2) "was an employee of"

Effective date (Sec. 1881, '86 TRA and Sec. 67(e), '84 TRA).—(1) Generally applies to payments under agreements entered into or renewed after 6-14-84, in taxable years ending after such date.

(2) Special rule for contract amendments.—In the case of any contract entered into before 6-15-84, any amendment to such contract after 6-14-84, which amends such contract in any significant relevant aspect shall be treated as a new contract.

[Footnote ¶2970] Section 1804(k)(3)(A), '86 TRA, struck out from heading of Sec. 291(a):

(1) "20 Percent"

Effective date (Sec. 1881, '86 TRA and section 68(e)(1), '84 TRA).—Applies to taxable years beginning after 12-31-84.

Section 201(d)(5)(A), '86 TRA, struck out from Sec. 291(a)(1)(A):

(2) "or section 1245 recovery property"

Effective date (Sec. 203(a)(1), '86 TRA).—(1) Generally applies to property placed in service after 12-31-86, in taxable years ending after such date.

(B) Election to have amendments made by section 201 apply.—A taxpayer may elect (at such time and in such manner as the Secretary of the Treasury or his delegate may prescribe) to have the amendments made by section 201 apply to any property placed in service after 7-31-86, and before 1-1-87.

For transitional rules and special rules, see ¶2007—2008.

Matter in *italics* in Sec. 291(a)(2) added by section 412(b)(1), '86 TRA, which struck out:

(3) "15 percent"

Effective date (Sec. 412(b)(2), '86 TRA).—Applies to taxable years beginning after 12-31-86.

(B) the adjusted basis of the property at the close of the taxable year (determined without regard to the depletion deduction for the taxable year).

* * * * * * * * * * * *

≫P-H CAUTION→ There are two versions of Sec. 291(a)(4). Sec. 291(a)(4), generally effective after 12-31-84, follows. For Sec. 291(a)(4), generally effective before 1-1-85, see below.

▲ [4](4) *Certain FSC income.—In the case of taxable years beginning after December 31, 1984, section 923(a) shall be applied with respect to any FSC by substituting—*
(A) *"30 percent" for "32 percent" in paragraph (2), and*
(B) *"15/23" for "16/23" in paragraph (3).*
If all of the stock in the FSC is not held by 1 or more C corporations throughout the taxable year, under regulations, proper adjustments shall be made in the application of the preceding sentence to take into account stock held by persons other than C corporations.

≫P-H CAUTION→ There are two versions of Sec. 291(a)(4). Sec. 291(a)(4), generally effective before 1-1-85, follows. For Sec. 291(a)(4), generally effective after 12-31-84, see above.

▲ ▲ **(4) Certain deferred disc income.—**If [5]a *C Corporation* is a shareholder of a DISC, in the case of taxable years beginning after December 31, 1982, section 995(b)(1)(F)(i) shall be applied with respect to such corporation by substituting "57.5 percent" for "one-half."

* * * * * * * * * * * *

(b) **Special Rules for Treatment of Intangible Drilling Costs and Mineral Exploration and Development Costs.—**For purposes of this subtitle, in the case of a corporation—

(1) **In general.—**The amount allowable as a deduction for any taxable year (determined without regard to this section)—
(A) under section 263(c) in the case of an integrated oil company, or
(B) under section 616(a) or [6]*617(a),* shall be reduced by [7]*30 percent.*

[8](2) *Amortization of amounts not allowable as deductions under paragraph (1).—*

⟦Footnote ¶2970 continued⟧

▲ Matter in *italics* in Sec. 291(a)(4), preceded by a triangle, added by section 1876(b)(1), '86 TRA, which struck out:
(4) **"(4) Certain deferred FSC income.—**If a C corporation is a shareholder of the FSC, in the case of taxable years beginning after December 31, 1984, section 923(a) shall be applied with respect to such corporation by substituting—
(A) "30 percent" for "32 percent" in paragraph (2), and
(B) "15/23" for "16/23" in paragraph (3).
Effective date (Sec. 1881, '86 TRA and section 805(a), '84 TRA).—(a) Generally applies to transaction after 12-31-84, in taxable years ending after such date. For special rules, see footnote ¶2959.

▲ ▲ Matter in *italics* in Sec. 291(a)(4), [as in effect before '84 TRA] preceded by two triangles added by section 1804(k)(1), '86 TRA, which struck out:
(5) "a corporation"
Effective date (Sec. 1804(k)(1), '86 TRA).—Takes effect with respect to taxable years beginning after 12-31-82.

Matter in *italics* in Sec. 291(b), added by section 411(a) and (b)(2)(C)(ii), '86 TRA, which struck out:
(6) "617"
(7) "20 percent"
(8) **"(2) Special rule for amounts not allowable as deductions under paragraph (1).—**
(A) Intangible drilling costs.—The amount not allowable as a deduction under section 263(c) for any taxable year by reason of paragraph (1) shall be allowable as a deduction ratably over the 36-month period beginning with the month in which the costs are paid or incurred.
(B) Mineral exploration and development costs.—In the case of any amount not allowable as a deduction under section 616(a) or 617 for any taxable year by reason of paragraph (1)—
(i) the applicable percentage of the amount not so allowable as a deduction shall be allowable as a deduction for the taxable year in which the costs are paid or incurred and in each of the 4 succeeding taxable years, and
(ii) in the case of a deposit located in the United States, such costs shall be treated, for purposes of determining the amount of the credit allowable under section 38 for the taxable year in which paid or incurred, as qualified investment (within the meaning of subsections (c) and (d) of section 46) with respect to property placed in service during such year.
(3) Applicable percentage.—For purposes of paragraph (2)(B), the term "applicable percentage" means the percentage determined in accordance with the following table:

The amount not allowable as a deduction under section 263(c), 616(a), or 617(a) (as the case may be) for any taxable year by reason of paragraph (1) shall be allowable as a deduction ratably over the 60-month period beginning with the month in which the costs are paid or incurred.

(3) Dispositions.—For purposes of section 1254, any deduction under paragraph (2) shall be treated as a deduction allowable under section 263(c), 616(a), or 617(a) (whichever is appropriate).

(4) Integrated oil company defined.—For purposes of this subsection, the term "integrated oil company" means, with respect to any taxable year, any producer (within the meaning of section 4996(a)(1)) of crude oil other than an independent producer (within the meaning of section 4992(b)).

(5) Coordination with cost depletion.—The portion of the adjusted basis of any property which is attributable to amounts to which paragraph (1) applied shall not be taken into account for purposes of determining depletion under section 611.

(c) Special Rules Relating to Pollution Control Facilities.—For purposes of subtitle—
[9]*(1) Accelerated cost recovery deduction.—Section 168 shall apply with respect to that portion of the basis of any property not taken into account under section 169 by reason of subsection (a)(5).*

* * * * * * * * * * * * *

(e) Definitions.—For purposes of this section—

(1) Financial institution preference item.—The term "financial institution preference item" includes the following:

(A) Excess reserves for losses on bad debts of financial institutions.—In the case of a financial institution to which section 585 [10] applies, the excess of—

⟦Footnote ¶2970 continued⟧

Taxable Year:	Applicable Percentage:
1	15
2	22
3	21
4	21
5	21

(4) Dispositions.—

(A) Oil, gas, and geothermal property.—In the case of any disposition of any oil, gas, or geothermal property to which section 1254 applies (determined without regard to this section) any deduction under paragraph (2)(A) with respect to intangible drilling and development costs under section 263(c) which are allocable to such property shall, for purposes of section 1254, be treated as a deduction allowable under section 263(c).

(B) Application of section 617(d).—In the case of any disposition of mining property to which section 617(d) applies (determined without regard to this section), any amount allowable as a deduction under paragraph (2)(B) which is allocable to such property shall, for purposes of section 617(d), be treated as a deduction allowable under section 617(a).

(C) Recapture of investment credit.—In the case of any disposition of any property to which the credit allowable under section 38 by reason of paragraph (2)(B) is allocable, such disposition shall, for purposes of section 47, be treated as a disposition of section 38 recovery property which is not 3-year property.

(5) Integrated oil company defined.—For purposes of this subsection, the term "integrated oil company" means, with respect to any taxable year, any producer (within the meaning of section 4992(b)).

(6) Coordination with cost depletion.—The portion of the adjusted basis of any property which is attributable to amounts to which paragraph (1) applied shall not be taken into account for purposes of determining under section 611."

Effective date (Sec. 411(c), '86 TRA).—(1) Generally applies to costs paid or incurred after 12-31-86, in taxable years ending after such date.

(2) Transitional rule.—The amendments made by this section shall not apply with respect to intangible drilling and development costs incurred by United States companies pursuant to a minority interest in a license for Netherlands or United Kingdom North Sea development if such interest was acquired on or before 12-31-85.

Matter in *italics* in Sec. 291(c)(1) added by section 201(d)(5)(B), '86 TRA, which struck out:

(9) **"(1) Accelerated cost recovery reduction.**—For purposes of subclause (I) of section 168(d)(1)(A)(ii), a taxpayer shall not be treated as electing the amortization deduction under section 169 with respect to that portion of the basis not taken into account under section 169 by reason of subsection (a)(5)."

Effective date (Sec. 203(a)(1) and (b)—(e), 86 TRA).—Generally applies to property placed in service after 12-31-86, in taxable years ending after such date. For Elections, see above. For transitional rules and special rules, see ¶2007—2008.

Section 901(b)(4), '86 TRA, struck out from 291(e)(1)(A):
(10) "or 593"

(i)   the amount which would, but for this section, be allowable as a deduction for the taxable year for a reasonable addition to a reserve for bad debts, over

(ii)   the amount which would have been allowable had such institution maintained its bad debt reserve for all taxable years on the basis of actual experience.

(B)   Interest on debt to carry tax-exempt obligations acquired after December 31, 1982, *and before August 8, 1986.*—

(i)   In general.—In the case of a financial institution [11]*which is a bank (as defined in section 585(a)(2) or to which 593 applies,* the amount of interest on indebtedness incurred or continued to purchase or carry obligations acquired after December 31, 1982, *and before August 8, 1986,* the interest on which is exempt from taxes for the taxable year, to the extent that a deduction would [12] *(but for this paragraph or section 265(b))* be allowable with respect to such interest for such taxable year.

(ii)   Determination of interest allocable to indebtedness on tax-exempt obligations.—Unless the taxpayer (under regulations prescribed by the Secretary) establishes otherwise, the amount determined under clause (i) shall be an amount which bears the same ratio to the aggregate amount allowable (determined without regard to this section *and section 265(b))* to the taxpayer as a deduction for interest for the taxable year as—

(I)   the taxpayer's average adjusted basis (within the meaning of section 1016) of obligations described in clause (i), bears to

(II)   such average adjusted basis for all assets of the taxpayer.

(iii)   Interest.—For purposes of this subparagraph, the term "interest" includes amounts (whether or not designated as interest) paid in respect of deposits, investment certificates, or withdrawable or repurchasable shares.

(iv)   Special rules for obligations to which section 133 applies.—In the case of an obligation to which section 133 applies, interest on such obligation shall not be treated as exempt from taxes for purposes of this subparagraph.

(iv)   [should read (v)]   Application of subparagraph to certain obligations issued after August 7, 1986.—

For application of this subparagraph to certain obligations issued after August 7, 1986, see section 265(b)(3).

(2)   **Section 1245 and 1250 property.**—The terms "section 1245 property", [13]and

---

⟦Footnote ¶2970 continued⟧

Effective date (Sec. 901(e), '86 TRA).—Applies to taxable years beginning after 12-31-86.

Matter in *italics* in the heading of Sec. 291(e)(1)(B) added by section 902(c)(2)(C), '86 TRA.
Effective date (Sec. 902(f), '86 TRA).—Generally applies to taxable years ending after 12-31-86. For exceptions and transitional rules, see footnote ¶2963.

The phrase "*which is a bank (as defined in section 585(a)(2) or to which 593 applies*" in *italics* in Sec. 291(e)(1)(B)(i) added by section 901(d)(4)(C), '86 TRA, which struck out:
(11)   "to which section 585 or 593 applies"
Effective date (Sec. 901(e), '86 TRA).—Applies to taxable years beginning after 12-31-86.

Matter in *italics* in Sec. 291(e)(1)(B)(i) and (ii) (except for the phrase "*which is a bank (as defined in section 585(a)(2) or to which 593 applies*") added by section 902(c)(1), (2)(A) and (B), '86 TRA, which struck out:
(12)   "(but for this paragraph)"
Effective date   (Sec. 902(f), '86 TRA).—Generally applies to taxable years ending after 12-31-86. For exceptions and transitional rules, see footnote ¶2963.

Sec. 291(e)(1)(B)(iv) in *italics,* added by section 1854(c)(1), '86 TRA.
Effective date (Sec. 1881, '86 TRA and section 543(c), '84 TRA).—Applies to loans used to acquire employer securities after 7-18-84.

Sec. 291(e)(1)(B)(iv) [should read (v)] in *italics,* preceded by single triangle, added by section 902(c)(2)(D), '86 TRA.
Effective date   (Sec. 902(f), '86 TRA).—(1)   Generally applies to taxable years ending after 12-31-86. For exceptions and transitional rules, see footnote ¶2963.

Section 201(d)(5)(C) struck out from Sec. 291(e)(2):
(13)   ", 'section 1245 recovery property',"

"section 1250 property" have the meanings given such terms by section 1245(a)(3) [14] and 1250(c), respectively.

[For official explanation, see Committee Reports, ¶3870; 3896; 3897; 3948; 3949; 4138; 4174; 4190.]

[¶2971]   CODE SEC. 301.   DISTRIBUTIONS OF PROPERTY.

* * * * * * * * * * * *

(f) Special Rule for Certain Distributions Received by 20 Percent Corporate Shareholder.—

* * * * * * * * * * * *

(3) Regulations.—The Secretary shall prescribe such regulations as may be necessary or appropriate to carry out the purposes of this [1]*subsection.*

(g) Special Rules.—

* * * * * * * * * * * *

(4) [struck out][2]

[For official explanation, see Committee Reports, ¶3913; 4138.]

[¶2972]   CODE SEC. 303.   DISTRIBUTIONS IN REDEMPTION OF STOCK TO PAY DEATH TAXES.

* * * * * * * * * * * *

(d) Special Rules for Generation-Skipping Transfers.—

[1]*Where stock in a corporation is the subject of a generation-skipping transfer (within the*

【Footnote ¶2970 continued】

(14) ", 1245(a)(5),"
Effective date (Sec. 203(a)(1), '86 TRA).—(1) Generally applies to property placed in service after 12-31-86, in taxable years ending after such date. For special election, see above. For transitional rules and special rules, see ¶2007—2008.
【Footnote ¶2971】 Matter in *italics* in Sec. 301(f)(3) added by section 1804(f)(2)(B), '86 TRA, which struck out:
(1) "section"
Effective date (Sec. 1881, '86 TRA and Sec. 61(e)(4), '84 TRA).—Applies to distributions after 7-18-84, in taxable years ending after such date.

Sec. 301(g)(4) struck out by section 612(b)(1), '86 TRA:
(2) **"For partial exclusion from gross income of dividends received by individuals, see section 116."**
Effective date (Sec. 612(c), '86 TRA).—Applies to taxable years beginning after 12-31-86.
【Footnote ¶2972】 Matter in *italics* in Sec. 303(d) added by section 1432(b), '86 TRA, which struck out:
(1) "Under regulations prescribed by the Secretary, where stock in a corporation is subject to tax under section 2601 as a result of a generation-skipping transfer (within the meaning of section 2611(a)), which occurs at or after the death of the deemed transferor (within the meaning of section 2612)—
(1) the stock shall be deemed to be included in the gross estate of the deemed transferor;
(2) Taxes of the kind referred to in subsection (a)(1) which are imposed because of the generation-skipping transfer shall be treated as imposed because of the deemed transferor's death (and for this purpose the tax imposed by section 2601 shall be treated as an estate tax);"
Effective date (Sec. 1433(a), (b), (c) and (d), '86 TRA).—(a) General Rule.—Except as provided in subsection (b), the amendments made by this part shall apply to any generation-skipping transfer (within the meaning of section 2611 of the '86 Code) made after the date of the enactment of this Act.
(b) Special Rules.—
(1) Treatment of certain inter vivos transfers made after September 25, 1985.—For purposes of subsection (a) (and chapter 13 of the '86 Code as amended by this part), any inter vivos transfer after 9-25-85, and on or before the date of the enactment of this Act shall be treated as if it were made on the 1st day after the date of enactment of this Act.
(2) Exceptions.—The amendments made by this part shall not apply to—
(A) Any generation-skipping transfer under a trust which was irrevocable on 9-25-85, but only to the extent that such transfer is not made out of corpus added to the trust after 9-25-85,
(B) any generation-skipping transfer under a will executed before the date of the enactment of this Act if the decedent dies before 1-1-87, and
(C) any generation-skipping transfer—
(i) under a trust to the extent such trust consists of property included in the gross estate of a decedent (other than property transferred by the decedent during his life after the date of the enactment of this Act), or reinvestments thereof, or
(ii) which is a direct skip which occurs by reason of the death of any decedent;
but only if such decedent was, on the date of the enactment of this Act, under a mental disability to change the disposition of his property and did not regain his competence to dispose of such property before the date of his death.
(3) Treatment of certain transfers to grandchildren.—For purposes of chapter 13 of the '86 Code, the term "direct skip" shall not include any transfer before 1-1-90, from a transferor to a grandchild of the transferor to the extent that the aggregate transfers from such transferor to such grandchild do not exed $2,000,000.

meaning of section 2611(a)) occurring at the same time as and as a result of the death of an individual—

    (1) the stock shall be deemed to be included in the gross estate of such individual;

    (2) taxes of the kind referred to in subsection (a)(1) which are imposed because of the generation-skipping transfer shall be treated as imposed because of such individual's death (and for this purpose the tax imposed by section 2601 shall be treated as an estate tax);

    (3) the period of distribution shall be measured from the date of the generation-skipping transfer; and

    (4) the relationship of stock to the decedent's estate shall be measured with reference solely to the amount of the generation-skipping transfer.

[For official explanation, see Committee Reports, ¶4068.]

〔¶2973〕 CODE SEC. 304. REDEMPTION THROUGH USE OF RELATED CORPORATIONS.

  (a) Treatment of Certain Stock Purchases.—

    (1) Acquisition by related corporation (other than subsidiary).—For purposes of sections 302 and 303, if—

    (A) one or more persons are in control of each of two corporations, and

    (B) in return for property, one of the corporations acquires stock in the other corporation from the person (or persons) so in control,

then (unless paragraph (2) applies) such property shall be treated as a distribution in redemption of the stock of the corporation acquiring such stock. [1]*To the extent that such distribution is treated as a distribution to which section 301 applies* stock so acquired shall be treated as having been transferred by the person from whom acquired and as having been received by the corporation acquiring it, as a contribution to the capital of such corporation.

〔Footnote ¶2972 continued〕

  (c) Repeal of Existing Tax on Generation-Skipping Transfers.—

  (1) In general.—In the case of any tax imposed by chapter 13 of the '54 Code (as in effect on the day before the date of the enactment of this Act), such tax (including interest, additions to tax, and additional amounts) shall not be assessed and if assessed, the assessment shall be abated, and if collected, shall be credited or refunded (with interest) as an overpayment.

  (2) Waiver of statute of limitations.—If on the date of the enactment of this Act (or at any time within 1 year after such date of enactment) refund or credit of any overpayment of tax resulting from the application of paragraph (1) is barred by any law or rule of law, refund or credit of such overpayment shall, nevertheless, be made or allowed if claim therefore is filed before the date 1 year after the date of the enactment of this Act.

  (d) Election for Certain Transfers Benefiting Grandchild.—

  (1) In general.—For purposes of chapter 13 of the '86 Code (as amended by this Act) and subsection (b) of this section, any transfer in trust for the benefit of a grandchild of a transferor shall be treated as a direct skip if—

  (A) the transfer occurs before the date of enactment of this Act,

  (B) the transfer would be a direct skip except for the fact that the trust instrument provides that, if the grandchild dies before vesting of the interest transferred, the interest is transferred to the grandchild's heir (rather than the grandchild's estate), and

  (C) an election under this subsection applies to such transfer.

Any transfer treated as a direct skip by reason of the preceding sentence shall be subject to Federal estate tax on the grandchild's death in the same manner as if the contingent gift over had been to the grandchild's estate.

  (2) Election.—An election under paragraph (1) shall be made at such time and in such manner as the Secretary of the Treasury or his delegate may prescribe.

  〔Footnote ¶2973〕 Matter in *italics* in Sec. 304(a)(1) added by section 1875(b), '86 TRA, which struck out:

  (1) "In any such case"

  Effective date (Sec. 1881, '86 TRA and Sec. 712(*l*)(7), '84 TRA).—(A) Generally applies to stock acquired after 6-18-84, in taxable years ending after such date.

  (B) Election by taxpayer to have amendments apply earlier.—Any taxpayer may elect, at such time and in such manner as the Secretary of the Treasury or his delegate may prescribe, to have the amendments apply as if included in section 226 of '82 TEFRA.

  (C) Special rule for certain transfers to form bank holding company.—Except as provided in subparagraph (D), the amendments shall not apply to transfers pursuant to an application to form a BHC (as defined in section 304(b)(3)(D)(ii) '54 Code) filed with the Federal Reserve Board before 6-18-84, if—

  (i) such BHC was formed not later then the 90th day after the date of the last required approval of any regulatory authority to form such BHC, and

  (ii) such BHC did not elect (at such time and in such manner as the Secretary of the Treasury or his delegate shall prescribe) not to have the provisions of this subparagraph apply.

  (D) Amendments to apply to certain liabilities incurred before 10-20-83.—The amendment made by paragraph (3)(A) of 712(*l*)(3) of '84 TRA, shall apply to the acquisition of any stock to the extent the liability assumed, or to which such stock is subject, was incurred by the transferor after 10-20-83.

* * * * * * * * * * * *

[For official explanation, see Committee Reports, ¶4189.]

〔¶2974〕 CODE SEC. 311. TAXABILITY OF CORPORATION ON DISTRIBU-TION.

¹(a)   General Rule.—Except as provided in subsection (b), no gain or loss shall be recog-

〔Footnote ¶2974〕 Matter in *italics* in Sec. 311 added by section 631(c), '86 TRA, which struck out:

(1) **"(a) General Rule.**—Except as provided in subsections (b), (c), and (d) of this section and section 453B, no gain or loss shall be recognized to a corporation on the distribution, with respect to its stock, of—

(1) its stock (or rights to acquire its stock), or

(2) property.

(b) LIFO Inventory.—

(1) **Recognition of gain.**—If a corporation inventorying goods under the method provided in section 472 (relating to last-in, first-out inventories) distributes inventory assets (as defined in paragraph (2(A)), then the amount (if any) by which—

(A) the inventory amount (as defined in paragraph (2)(B)) of such assets under a method authorized by section 471 (relating to general rule for inventories), exceeds

(B) the inventory amount of such assets under the method provided in section 472,

shall be treated as gain to the corporation recognized from the sale of such inventory assets.

(2) **Definitions.**—For purposes of paragraph (1)—

(A) Inventory assets.—The term 'inventory assets' means stock in trade of the corporation, or other property of a kind which would properly be included in the inventory of the corporation if on hand at the close of the taxable year.

(B) Inventory amount.—The term 'inventory amount' means, in the case of inventory assets distributed during a taxable year, the amount of such inventory assets determined as if the taxable year closed at the time of such distribution.

(3) **Method of determining inventory amount.**—For purposes of this subsection, the inventory amount of assets under a method authorized by section 471 shall be determined—

(A) if the corporation uses the retail method of valuing inventories under section 472, by using such method, or

(B) if subparagraph (A) does not apply, by using cost or market, whichever is lower.

(c) Liability in Excess of Basis.—If—

(1) a corporation distributes property to a shareholder with respect to its stock,

(2) such property is subject to a liability, or the shareholder assumes a liability of the corporation in connection with the distribution, and

(3) the amount of such liability exceeds the adjusted basis (in the hands of the distributing corporation) and such property,

then gain shall be recognized to the distributing corporation in an amount equal to such excess as if the property distributed had been sold at the time of the distribution. In the case of a distribution of property subject to a liability which is not assumed by the shareholder, the amount of gain to be recognized under the preceding sentence shall not exceed the excess, if any, of the fair market value of such property over its adjusted basis.

(d) Distributions of Appreciated Property.—

(1) **In general.**—If—

(A) a corporation distributes property (other than an obligation of such corporation) to a shareholder in a distribution to which subpart A applies, and

(B) the fair market value of such property exceeds its adjusted basis (in the hands of the distributing corporation),

then gain shall be recognized to the distributing corporation in an amount equal to such excess as if the property distributed had been sold at the time of the distribution. This subsection shall be applied after the application of subsections (b) and (c).

(2) **Exceptions and limitations.**—Paragraph (1) shall not apply to—

(A) a distribution which is made with respect to qualified stock if—

(i) section 302(b)(4) applies to such distribution, or

(ii) such distribution is a qualified dividend;

(B) a distribution of stock or an obligation of a corporation if the requirements of paragraph (2) of subsection (e) are met with respect to the distribution;

(C) a distribution to the extent that section 303(a) (relating to distributions in redemption of stock to pay death taxes) applies to such distribution;

(D) a distribution to a private foundation in redemption of stock which is described in section 537(b)(2)(A) and (B); and

(E) a distribution by a corporation to which part I of subchapter M (relating to regulated investment companies) applies, if such distribution is in redemption of its stock upon the demand of the shareholder.

(e) Definitions and Special Rules for Subsection (d)(2).—For purposes of subsection (d)(2) and this subsection—

(1) **Qualified stock.—**

(A) In general.—The term 'qualified stock' means stock held by a person (other than a corporation) who at all times during the lesser of—

(i) the 5-year period ending on the date of distribution, or

(ii) the period during which the distributing corporation (or a predecessor corporation) was in existence,

Held at least 10 percent in value of the outstanding stock of the distributing corporation (or predecessor corporation).

(B) Determination of stock held.—Section 318 shall apply in determining ownership of stock under subpara-

nized to a corporation on the distribution, with respect to its stock, of—

(1) its stock (or rights to acquire its stock), or

(2) property.

(b) **Distributions of Appreciated Property.**—

(1) *In general.*—If—

(A) a corporation distributes property (other than an obligation of such corporation) to a shareholder in a distribution to which subpart A applies, and

(B) the fair market value of such property exceeds its adjusted basis (in the hands of the distributing corporation),

then gain shall be recognized to the distributing corporation as if such property were sold to the distributee at its fair market value.

(2) *Treatment of liabilities in excess of basis.*—Rules similar to the rules of section 336(b) shall apply for purposes of this subsection.

[For official explanation, see Committee Reports, ¶3917.]

[¶2975] CODE SEC. 312. EFFECT ON EARNINGS AND PROFITS.

[1]*(b) Distributions of Appreciated Property.*—On the distribution by a corporation, with

---

[Footnote ¶2974 continued]

graph (A); except that in applying sections 318(a)(1), the term 'family' includes any individual described in section 267(c)(4) and any spouse of any such individual.

(C) Rules for passthru entities.—In the case of an S corporation, partnership, trust, or estate—

(i) the determination of whether subparagraph (A) is satisfied shall be made at the shareholder, partner, or beneficiary level (rather than at the entity level), and

(ii) the distribution shall be treated as made directly to the shareholders, partners, or beneficiaries in proportion to their respective interests in the entity.

(2) **Distributions of stock or obligations of controlled corporations.**—

(A) Requirements.—A distribution of stock or an obligation of a corporation (hereinafter in this paragraph referred to as the 'controlled corporation' meets the requirements of this paragraph if—

(i) such distribution is made with respect to qualified stock,

(ii) substantially all of the assets of the controlled corporation consists of the assets of 1 or more qualified businesses,

(iii) no substantial part of the controlled corporation's nonbusiness assets were acquired from the distributing corporation, in a transaction to which section 351 applied or as a contribution to capital, within the 5-year period ending on the date of the distribution, and

(iv) more than 50 percent in value of the outstanding stock of the controlled corporation is distributed by the distributing corporation with respect to qualified stock.

(B) Definitions.—For purposes of subparagraph (A)—

(i) Qualified business.—The term 'qualified business' means any trade or business which—

(I) was actively conducted throughout the 5-year period ending on the date of the distribution, and

(II) was not acquired by any person within such period in a transaction in which gain or loss was recognized in whole or in part.

(ii) Nonbusiness asset.—The term "nonbusiness asset" means any asset not used in the active conduct of a trade or business.

(3) **Qualified dividend.**—the term 'qualified dividend' means any distribution of property to a shareholder other than a corporation if—

(A) such distribution is a dividend,

(B) such property was used by the distributing corporation in the active conduct of a qualified business (as defined in paragraph (2)), and

(C) such property is not property described in paragraph (1) or (4) of section 1221."

Effective date (Sec. 633(a), '86 TRA).—Generally applies to—

(1) any distribution in complete liquidation, and any sale or exchange, made by a corporation after 7-31-86, unless such corporation is completely liquidated before 1-1-87,

(2) any transaction described in section 338 of the '86 Code for which the acquisition date occurs after 12-31-86, and

(3) any distribution (not in complete liquidation) made after 12-31-86.

For transitional and special rules, see ¶2023.

[Footnote ¶2975] Matter in *italics* in Sec. 312(b) and (c) added by section 1804(f)(1)(A)—(C), '86 TRA, which struck out:

(1) "Certain Inventory Assets."

(1) **In General.**—On the distribution by a corporation, with respect to its stock, of inventory assets (as defined in paragraph (2)(A)) the fair market value of which exceeds the adjusted basis thereof, the earnings and profits of the corporation—

(A) shall be increased by the amount of such excess; and

(B) shall be decreased by whichever of the following is the lesser:

(i) the fair market value of the inventory assets distributed, or

(ii) the earnings and profits (as increased under subparagraph (A)).

(2) **Definitions.**—

(A) Inventory assets.—For purposes of paragraph (1), the term 'inventory assets' means—

respect to its stock, of any property the fair market value of which exceeds the adjusted basis thereof—

(1) the earnings and profits of the corporation shall be increased by the amount of such excess, and

(2) subsection (a)(3) shall be applied by substituting "fair market value" for "adjusted basis".

For purposes of this subsection and subsection (a), the adjusted basis of any property is its adjusted basis as determined for purposes of computing earnings and profits.

(c) **Adjustments for Liabilities**[2].—In making the adjustments to the earnings and profits of a corporation under subsection (a) or (b) proper adjustment shall be made for—

(1) the amount of any liability to which the property distributed is subject, *and*

(2) the amount of any liability of the corporation assumed by a shareholder in connection with the distribution[3].[4]

* * * * * * * * * * * *

(k) **Effect of Depreciation on Earnings and Profits.—**

* * * * * * * * * * * *

≫P-H CAUTION→ There are two versions of Sec. 312(k)(3). Sec. 312(k)(3), generally effective for property placed in service after 12-31-86, follows. For Sec. 312(k)(3), generally effective for property placed in service before 1-1-87, see below.

▲ [5]*(3) Exception for tangible property.—*

[Footnote ¶2975 continued]

(i) stock in trade of the corporation, or other property of a kind which would properly be included in the inventory of the corporation if on hand at the close of the taxable year;

(ii) property held by the corporation primarily for sale to customers in the ordinary course of its trade or business; and

(iii) unrealized receivable or fees, except receivable from sales or exchanges of assets other than assets described in this subparagraph.

(B) Unrealized receivable or fees.—For purposes of subparagraph (A)(iii), the term 'unrealized receivable or fees' means, to the extent not previously includible in income under the method of accounting used by the corporation, any rights (contractual or otherwise) to payment for—

(i) goods delivered, or to be delivered, to the extent that the proceeds therefrom would be treated as amounts received from the sale or exchange of property other than a capital asset, or

(ii) services rendered or to be rendered."

(2) ", etc"

(3) ", and"

(4) "(3) any gain recognized to the corporation on the distribution"

Effective date (Sec. 1881, '86 TRA, and section 61(e)(1)(B), '84 TRA).—Applies to distributions after 9-30-84; except that such provisions shall not apply to any distribution to which the amendments made by section 54(a), '84 TRA, do not apply.

▲ Matter in *italics* in Sec. 312(k)(3) preceeded by a triangle, added by section 201(b), '86 TRA, which struck out:

(5) "(3) Exception for recovery and section 179 property.—

(A) Recovery Property.—Except as provided in subparagraphs (B) and (C), in the case of recovery property (within the meaning of section 168), the adjustment to earnings and profits for depreciation for any taxable year shall be the amount determined under the straight-line method (using a half year convention in the case of property other than the 19-year real property and low-income housing without regard to salvage value) and using a recovery period determined in accordance with the following table:

In the case of:	The applicable recovery period is:
3-year property	5 years.
5-year property	12 years.
10-year property	25 years.
19-year real property and low-income housing	40 years.
15-year public utility property	35 years.

For purposes of this subparagraph, no adjustment shall be allowed in the year of disposition (except with respect to 19-year real property and low-income housing).

(B) Treatment of amounts deductible under section 179.—For purposes of computing the earnings and profits of a corporation, any amount deductible under section 179 shall be allowed as a deduction ratably over the period

(A) In general.—Except as provided in subparagraph (B), in the case of tangible property to which section 168 applies, the adjustment to earnings and profits for depreciation for any taxable year shall be determined under the alternative depreciation system (within the meaning of section 168(g)(2)).

(B) Treatment of amounts deductible under section 179.—For purposes of computing the earnings and profits of a corporation, any amount deductible under section 179 shall be allowed as a deduction ratably over the period of 5 taxable years (beginning with the taxable year for which such amount is deductible under section 179).

≫P-H CAUTION→ There are two versions of Sec. 312(k)(3). Sec. 312(k)(3), generally effective for property placed in service before 1-1-87, follows. For Sec. 312(k)(3), generally effective for property placed in service after 12-31-86, see above.

▲ ▲ **(3) Exception for recovery and section 179 property.—**
(A) Recovery Property.—Except as provided in subparagraphs (B) and (C), in the case of recovery property (within the meaning of section 168), the adjustment to earnings and profits for depreciation for any taxable year shall be the amount determined under the straight-line method (using a half year convention in the case of property other than the 19-year real property and low-income housing without regard to salvage value) and using a recovery period determined in accordance with the following table:

In the case of:	The applicable recovery period is:
3-year property	5 years.
5-year property	12 years.
10-year property	25 years.
19-year real property and low income housing	40 years.
15-year public utility property	35 years.

For purposes of this subparagrah, no adjustment shall be allowed in the year of disposition (except with respect to 19-year real property and low-income housing)[6].

(B) Treatment of amounts deductible under section 179.—For purposes of computing the earnings and profits of a corporation, any amount deductible under section 179 shall be allowed as a deduction ratably over the period of 5 years (beginning with the year for which such amount is deductible under section 179).

(C) Flexibility.—In any case where a different recovery percentage is elected under section 168(b)(3) or (f)(2)(C) based on a recovery period longer than the recovery period provided in subparagraph (A), the adjustment to earnings and profits shall be based on such longer period under rules similar to those provided in subparagraph (A).

(4) Certain foreign corporations.—The provisions of paragraphs (1) and (3) shall not apply in computing the earnings and profits of a foreign corporation for any taxable year for which less than 20 percent of the gross income from all souces of such corporation is derived from sources within the United States.[7]

[Footnote ¶2975 continued]

of 5 years (beginning with the year for which such amount is deductible under section 179).

(C) Flexibility.—In any case where a different recovery percentage is elected under section 168(b)(3) or (f)(2)(C) based on a recovery period longer than the recovery period provided in subparagraph (A), the adjustment to earnings and profits shall be based on such longer period under rules similar to those provided in subparagraph (A)."

Effective date (Sec. 203 '86 TRA).—Generally applies to property placed in service after 12-31-86, in taxable years ending after such date. For transitional rules and special rules see ¶2007—2008.

▲ ▲ Section 1809(a)(2)(C)(ii), '86 TRA, struck out from Sec. 312(k)(3)(A), preceded by two triangles,:

(6) ", and rules similiar to the rules under the next to the last sentence of section 168(b)(2)(A) and section 168(b)(2)(B) shall apply"

Effective date (Sec. 1881, '86 TRA, and section 111(g)(1)—(3), '84 TRA).—(1) Applies to property placed in service by the taxpayer after 3-15-84. For special and transitional rules see footnote ¶2935-A.

Section 201(d)(b), '86 TRA, struck out from Sec. 312(k)(4):

(7) "In determining the earnings and profits of such corporation in the case of recovery property (within the meaning of section 168), the rules of section 168(f)(2) shall apply."

Effective date (Sec. 203, 86 TRA).—Generally applies to property placed in service after 12-31-86, in taxable years ending after such date. For transitional and special rules, see ¶2007—2008.

(5) **Basis adjustment not taken into account.**—In computing the earnings and profits of a corporation for any taxable year, the allowance for depreciation (and amortization, if any) shall be computed without regard to any basis adjustment under section 48(q).

* * * * * * * * * * * *

(n) **Adjustments to Earnings and Profits to more accurately reflect Economic Gain and Loss.**—For purposes of computing the earnings and profits of a corporation, the following adjustments shall be made:

(1) **Construction period carrying charges.**—

* * * * * * * * * * * *

(B) Construction period carrying charges defined.—For purpoes of this paragraph, the term "construction period carrying charges" means all—

    (i)   interest paid or accrued on indebtedness incurred or continued to acquire, construct, or carry property,

    (ii)   property taxes, and

    (iii)   similar carrying charges,

to the extent such interest, taxes, or charges are attributable to the construction period for such property and would be allowable as a deduction in determining taxable income under this chapter for the taxable year in which paid or incurred[8].

    [9]*(C)*   *Construction period.—The term "construction period" has the meaning given the term production period under section 236A(f)(4)(B).*

* * * * * * * * * * * *

(3) **Certain amortization provisions not to apply.**—Section 173, [10] and 248 shall not apply.[11]

* * * * * * * * * * * *

    [12]*(4)*   *LIFO inventory adjustments.—*

[Footnote ¶2975 continued]

Matter in *italics* in Sec. 312(n)(1)(B) and (C) added by section 803(b)(3), '86 TRA, which struck out:

(8)   "(determined without regard to section 189)"

(9)   "(C) Construction period.—The term 'construction period' has the meaning given such term by section 189(e)(2) (determined without regard to any real property limitation)."

Effective date (Sec. 803(d)(1), '86 TRA).—(1) Generally applies to costs incurred after 12-31-86, in taxable years ending after such date. For special and transitional rules, see footnote ¶2961-A.

Section 241(b)(1), '86 TRA, struck out from Sec. 312(n)(3):

(10)   ",177,"

Effective date (Sec. 241(c), '86 TRA).—(1) Generally applies to expenditures paid or incurred after 12-31-86.

(2) Transitional rule.—The amendments made by this section shall not apply to any expenditure incurred—

(A)   pursuant to a binding contract entered into before 3-2-86 or

(B)   with respect to the development, protection, expansion, registration, or defense of a trademark or trade name commenced before 3-2-86, but only if not less than the lesser of $1,000,000 or 5 percent of the aggregate cost of such development, protection, expansion, registration, or defense has been incurred or committed before such date.

The preceding sentence shall not apply to any expenditure with respect to a trademark or trade name placed in service after 12-31-87.

Section 1804(f)(1)(D) '86 TRA, struck out Sec. 312(n)(4):

(11)   "**(4)**   **Certain untaxed appreciation of distributed property.**—In the case of any distribution of property by a corporation described in section 311(d), earnings and profits shall be increased by the amount of any gain which would be includible in gross income for any taxable year if section 311(d)(2) did not apply."

Effective date (Sec. 1881, '86 TRA, and section 61(e)(1), '84 TRA).—Applies to distributions after 9-30-84; except that such provisions shall not apply to any distribution to which the amendments made by section 54(a), '84 TRA do not apply.

Matter in *italics* in Sec. 312(n)(4) added by section 631(e)(1), '86 TRA, which struck out:

(12)   "LIFO inventory adjustments.—Earnings and profits shall be increased or decreased by the amount of any increase or decrease in the LIFO recapture amount (determined under section 336(b)(3)) as of the close of each taxable year; except that any decrease below the LIFO recapture amount as of the close of the taxable year preceding the first taxable year to which this paragraph applies to the taxpayer shall be taken into account only to the extent provided in regulations prescribed by the Secretary."

Effective date (Sec. 633(a), '86 TRA).—(1) Generally applies to any distribution in complete liquidation, and any sale or exchange, made by a corporation after 7-31-86, unless such corporation is completely liquidated before 1-1-87.

(A) *In general.—Earnings and profits shall be increased or decreased by the amount of any increase or decrease in the LIFO recapture amount as of the close of each taxable year; except that any decrease below the LIFO recapture amount as of the close of the taxable year preceding the 1st taxable year to which this paragraph applies to the taxpayer shall be taken into account only to the extent provided in regulations prescribed by the Secretary.*

(B) *LIFO recapture amount.—For purposes of this paragraph, the term "LIFO recapture amount" means the amount (if any) by which—*

(i) *the inventory amount of the inventory assets under the first-in, first-out method authorized by section 471, exceeds*

(ii) *the inventory amount of such assets under the LIFO method.*

(C) *Definitions.—For purposes of this paragraph—*

(i) *LIFO method.—The term "LIFO method" means the method authorized by section 472 (relating to last-in, first-out inventories).*

(ii) *Inventory assets.—The term "inventory assets" means stock in trade of the corporation, or other property of a kind which would properly be included in the inventory of the corporation if on hand at the close of the taxable year.*

(iii) *Inventory amount.—The inventory amount of assets under the first-in, first-out method authorized by section 471 shall be determined—*

(I) *if the corporation uses the retail method of valuing inventories under section 472, by using such method, or*

(II) *if subclause (I) does not apply, by using cost or market, whichever is lower.*

[13](5) **Installment sales.—**

*   *   *   *   *   *   *   *   *   *   *

[14](6) **Completed contract method of accounting.—**

*   *   *   *   *   *   *   *   *   *   *

[15](7) **Redemptions.—**

*   *   *   *   *   *   *   *   *   *   *

[16](8) **Special rule for certain foreign corporations.—**In the case of a foreign corporation described in [17]*subsection (k)(4)—*

(A) *paragraphs (4) and (6) shall apply only in the case of taxable years beginning after December 31, 1985, and*

(B) *Paragraph (5) shall apply only in the case of taxable years beginning after December 31, 1987.*

*   *   *   *   *   *   *   *   *   *   *

[For official explanation, see Committee Reports, ¶4138.]

〔¶2976〕   CODE SEC. 318.   CONSTRUCTIVE OWNERSHIP OF STOCK.

*   *   *   *   *   *   *   *   *   *   *

〔Footnote ¶2975 continued〕

(2) Any transaction described in section 338 of the '86 Code for which the acquisition date occurs after 12-31-86 and

(3) any distribution (not in complete liquidation) made after 12-31-86.

For special and transitional rules, see ¶2023.

Matter in *italics* in Sec. 312(n)(5) and (6) added by section 1804(f)(1)(D), which struck out:

(13) "(6)"

(14) "(7)"

Effective date (Sec. 1881, '86 TRA and section 61(e)(1)(D)—(E), '84 TRA).—Shall apply to sales and contracts after 9-30-84, in taxable years ending after such date.

Matter in *italics* in Sec. 312(n)(7) added by section 1804(f)(1)(D), '86 TRA, which struck out:

(15) "(8)"

Effective date (Sec. 1804(f)(3), '86 TRA).—Applies to distributions in taxable years beginning after 9-30-84.

Matter in *italics* in Sec. 312(n)(8) added by section 1804(f)(1)(D) and (E), which struck out:

(16) "(9)"

(17) "subsection (k)(4), paragraphs (5), (6), and (7) shall apply only in the case of taxable years beginning after December 31, 1985."

Effective date (Sec, 1881, '86 TRA and section 61(e)(1)(B)—(E), '84 TRA).—See above.

(b) Cross References.—

For provisions to which the rules contained in subsection (a) apply, see—

* * * * * * * * * * * *

(5) [1]*section 382(l)(3) (relating to special limitations on net operating loss carryovers);*

* * * * * * * * * * * *

[For official explanation, see Committee Reports, ¶3916.]

〖¶2977〗 CODE SEC. 332. COMPLETE LIQUIDATIONS OF SUBSIDIARIES.

(a) **General Rule.**—No gain or loss shall be recognized on the receipt by a corporation of property distributed in complete liquidation of another corporation.

(b) **Liquidations to Which Section Applies.**—For purposes of subsection (a), a distribution shall be considered to be in complete liquidation only if—

(1) *the corporation receiving such property was, on the date of the adoption of the plan of liquidation, and has continued to be at all times until the receipt of the property, the owner of stock (in such other corporation) meeting the requirements of section 1504(a)(2); and either*

(2) the distribution is by such other corporation in complete cancellation or redemption of all its stock, and the transfer of all the property occurs within the taxable year; in such case the adoption by the shareholders of the resolution under which is authorized the distribution of all the assets of such corporation in complete cancellation or redemption of all its stock shall be considered an adoption of a plan of liquidation, even though no time for the completion of the transfer of the property is specified in such resolution; or

(3) such distribution is one of a series of distributions by such other corporation in complete cancellation or redemption of all its stock in accordance with a plan of liquidation under which the transfer of all the property under the liquidation is to be completed within 3 years from the close of the taxable year during which is made the first of the series of distributions under the plan, except that if such transfer is not completed within such period, or if the taxpayer does not continue qualified under paragraph (1) until the completion of such transfer, no distribution under the plan shall be considered a distribution in complete liquidation.

If such transfer of all the property does not occur within the taxable year, the Secretary may require of the taxpayer such bond, or waiver of the statute of limitations on assessment and collection, or both, as he may deem necessary to insure, if the transfer of the property is not completed within such 3-year period, or if the taxpayer does not continue qualified under paragraph (1) until the completion of such transfer, the assessment and collection of all income taxes then imposed by law for such taxable year or subsequent

---

〖Footnote ¶2976〗 Matter in *italics* in Sec. 318(b)(5) added by section 621(c)(1), '86 TRA, which struck out:

(1) "section 382(a)(3)"

Effective date (Sec. 621(f)(1) and (3)—(5), '86 TRA).—(1) Generally applies to any ownership change following—

(A) an owner shift involving a 5-percent shareholder occurring after 12-31-86, or

(B) an equity structure shift occurring pursuant to a plan of reorganization adopted after 12-31-86.

For transitional and special rules, see ¶2022.

〖Footnote ¶2977〗 Matter in *italics* in Sec. 332(b)(1) added by section 1804(e)(6)(A), '86 TRA, which struck out:

(1) "(1) the corporation receiving such property was, on the date of the adoption of the plan of liquidation, and has continued to be at all times until the receipt of the property, the owner of stock (in such other corporation) possessing at least 80 percent of the total combined voting power of all classes of stock entitled to vote and the owner of at least 80 percent of the total number of shares of all other classes of stock (except nonvoting stock which is limited and preferred as to dividends); and either"

Effective date (Sec. 1804(e)(6)(B), '86 TRA).—(i) Generally applies with respect to plans of complete liquidation adopted after 3-28-85.

(ii) Certain distributions made after December 31, 1984.—Except as provided in clause (iii), the amendment made by subparagraph (A) shall also apply with respect to plans of complete liquidations adopted on or before 3-28-85, pursuant to which any distribution is made in a taxable year beginning after 12-31-84 (12-31-83, in the case of an affiliated group to which an election under section 60(b)(7) of '84 TRA applies), but only if the liquidating corporation and any corporation which receives a distribution in complete liquidation of such corporation are members of an affiliated group of corporations filing a consolidated return for the taxable year which includes the date of the distribution.

(iii) Transitional rule for affiliated groups.—The amendment made by subparagraph (A) shall not apply with respect to plans of complete liquidation if the liquidating corporation is a member of an affiliated group of corporations under section 60(b)(2), (5), (6), or (8) of '84 TRA, for all taxable years which include the date of any distribution pursuant to such plan.

taxable years, to the extent attributable to property so received. A distribution otherwise constituting a distribution in complete liquidation within the meaning of this subsection shall not be considered as not constituting such a distribution merely because it does not constitute a distribution or liquidation within the meaning of the corporate law under which the distribution is made; and for purposes of this subsection a transfer of property of such other corporation to the taxpayer shall not be considered as not constituting a distribution (or one of a series of distributions) in complete cancellation or redemption of all the stock of such other corporation, merely because the carrying out of the plan involves (A) the transfer under the plan to the taxpayer by such other corporation of property, not attributable to shares owned by the taxpayer, on an exchange described in section 361, and (B) the complete cancellation or redemption under the plan, as a result of exchanges described in section 354, of the shares not owned by the taxpayer.

(c)   [Repealed][2]

[For official explanation, see Committee Reports, ¶3917; 4138.]

[¶2978]   CODE SEC. 333.   ELECTION AS TO RECOGNITION OF GAIN IN CERTAIN LIQUIDATIONS.   [Repealed by section 631(e)(3), '86 TRA].

[For official explanation, see Committee Reports, ¶3916.]

[¶2979]   CODE SEC. 334.   BASIS OF PROPERTY RECEIVED IN LIQUIDATIONS.

(a)   General Rule.—If property is received in a distribution in complete liquidation[1], and if gain or loss is recognized on receipt of such property, then the basis of the property in the hands of the distributee shall be the fair market value property at the time of the distribution.

$$* * * * * * * * * * * *$$

(c)   [struck out][2]

[For official explanation, see Committee Reports, ¶3916.]

[Footnote ¶2977 continued]

Section 631(e)(2), '86 TRA, struck out Sec. 332(c).

(2)   "Special Rule for Indebtedness of Subsidiary to Parent.—If—

(1)   a corporation is liquidated and subsection (a) applies to such liquidation, and

(2)   on the date of the adoption of the plan of liquidation, such corporation was indebted to the corporation which meets the 80 percent stock ownership requirements specified in subsection (b),

then no gain or loss shall be recognized to the corporation so indebted because of the transfer of property in satisfaction of such indebtedness."

Effective date (Sec. 633(a), '86 TRA).—(a)   Generally applies to—

(1)   any distribution in complete liquidation, and any sale or exchange, made by a corporation after 7-31-86, unless such corporation is completely liquidated before 1-1-87,

(2)   any transaction described in section 338 of the '86 Code for which the acquisition date occurs after 12-31-86, and

(3)   any distribution (not in complete liquidation) made after 12-31-86.

For transitional and special rules, see ¶2023.

[Footnote ¶2978]   Effective date (Sec. 633(a), '86 TRA).—(1)   Generally applies to any distribution in complete liquidation, and any sale or exchange, made by a corporation after 7-31-86, unless such corporation is completely liquidated before 1-1-87,

(2)   any transaction described in section 338 of the '86 Code for which the acquisition date occurs after 12-31-86, and

(3)   any distribution (not in complete liquidation) made after 12-31-86.

For special and transition rules, see ¶2023.

[Footnote ¶2979]   Section 631(e)(4), '86 TRA, struck out from Sec. 334(a) and (c):

(1)   "(other than a distribution to which section 333 applies)"

(2)   "(c)   Property Received in Liquidation Under Section 333.—**If—

(1)   property was acquired by a shareholder in the liquidation of a corporation in cancellation or redemption of stock, and

(2)   with respect to such acquisition—

(A)   gain was realized, but

(B)   as a result of an election made by the shareholder under section 333, the extent to which gain was recognized was determined under section 333,

then the basis shall be the same as the basis of such stock cancelled or redeemed in the liquidation, decreased in the amount of any money received by the shareholder, and increased in the amount of gain recognized to him."

Effective date (Sec. 633, '86 TRA).—Generally applies to—

(1)   any distribution in complete liquidation, and any sale or exchange, made by a corporation after 7-31-86, unless such corporation is completely liquidated before 1-1-87,

(2)   any transaction described in section 338 of the '86 Code for which the acquisition date occurs after 12-31-86, and

(3)   any distribution (not in complete liquidation) made after 12-31-86.

For special and transitional rules, see ¶2023.

⟦¶2980⟧ CODE SEC. 336. [1]*GAIN OR LOSS RECOGNIZED ON PROPERTY DISTRIBUTED IN COMPLETE LIQUIDATION.*

(a)   General Rule.—Except as otherwise provided in this section or section 337, gain or loss shall be recognized to a liquidating corporation on the distribution of property in complete liquidation as if such property were sold to the distributee at its fair market value.

(b)   Treatment of Liabilities in Excess of Basis.—If any property distributed in the liquidation is subject to a liability or the shareholder assumes a liability of the liquidating corporation in connection with the distribution, for purposes of subsection (a) and section 337, the fair market value of such property shall be treated as not less than the amount of such liability.

(c)   Exception for Certain Liquidations to Which Part III Applies.—This section shall not apply with respect to any distribution of property to the extent there is nonrecognition of gain or loss with respect to such property to the recipient under part III.

(d)   Limitations on Recognition of Loss.—

(1)   No loss recognized in certain distributions to related persons.—

(A)   In general.—No loss shall be recognized to a liquidating corporation on the distribution of any property to a related person (within the meaning of section 267) if—

(i)   such distribution is not pro rata, or

(ii)   such property is disqualified property.

(B)   Disqualified property.—For purposes of subparagraph (A), the term "disqualified property" means any property which is acquired by the liquidating corporation in a transaction to which section 351 applied, or as a contribution to capital, during the 5-year period ending on the date of the distribution. Such term includes any property if the adjusted basis of such property is determined (in whole or in part) by reference to the adjusted basis of property described in the preceding sentence.

(2)   Special rule for certain property acquired in certain carryover basis transactions.—

(A)   In general.—For purposes of determining the amount of loss recognized by any liquidating corporation on any sale, exchange, or distribution of property described in subparagraph (B), the adjusted basis of such property shall be reduced (but not below zero) by the excess (if any) of—

(i)   the adjusted basis of such property immediately after its acquisition by such corporation, over

(ii)   the fair market value of such property as of such time.

(B)   Description of Property.—

⟦Footnote ¶2980⟧   Section 631(a), '86 TRA, struck out from Sec. 336:

(1)   "DISTRIBUTIONS OF PROPERTY IN LIQUIDATION.

(a)   General Rule.—Except as provided in subsection (b) of this section and in section 453B (relating to disposition of installment obligations), no gain or loss shall be recognized to a corporation on the distribution of property in complete liquidation.

(b)   LIFO Inventory.—

(1)   In general.—If a corporation inventorying goods under the LIFO method distributes inventory assets in complete liquidation, then the LIFO recapture amount with respect to such assets shall be treated as gain to the corporation recognized from the sale of such inventory assets.

(2)   Exception where basis determined under section 334(b).—Paragraph (1) shall not apply to any liquidation under section 332 for which the basis of property received is determined under section 334(b).

(3)   LIFO recapture amount.—For purposes of this subsection the term 'LIFO recapture amount' means the amount (if any) by which—

(A)   the inventory amount of the inventory assets under the first-in, first-out method authorized by section 471, exceeds

(B)   the inventory amount of such assets under the LIFO method.

(4)   Definitions.—For purposes of this subsection—

(A)   LIFO method.—The term 'LIFO method' means the method authorized by section 472 (relating to last-in, first-out inventories).

(B)   Other definitions.—The term 'inventory assets' has the meaning given to such term by subparagraph (A) of section 311(b)(2), and the term 'inventory amount' has the meaning given to such term by subparagraph B of section 311(b)(2) (as modified by paragraph (3) of section 311(b))."

Effective date (Sec. 633, '86 TRA).—(1)   Generally applies to—

(1)   any distribution in complete liquidation, and any sale or exchange, made by a corporation after 7-31-86, unless such corporation is completely liquidated before 1-1-87,

(2)   any transaction described in section 338 of the '86 Code for which the acquisition date occurs after 12-31-86, and

(3)   any distribution (not in complete liquidation) made after 12-31-86.

For special and transitional rules, see ¶2023.

(i) In general.—For purposes of subparagraph (A), property is described in this subparagraph if—

(I) such property is acquired by the liquidating corporation in a transaction to which section 351 applied or as a contribution to capital, and

(II) the acquisition of such property by the liquidating corporation was part of a plan a principal purpose of which was to recognize loss by the liquidating corporation with respect to such property in connection with the liquidation.

Other property shall be treated as so described if the adjusted basis of such other property is determined (in whole or in part) by reference to the adjusted basis of property described in the preceding sentence.

(ii) Certain acquisitions treated as part of plan.—For purposes of clause (i), any property described in clause (i)(I) acquired by the liquidating corporation during the 2-year period ending on the date of the adoption of the plan of complete liquidation shall, except as provided in regulations, be treated as part of a plan described in clause (i)(II).

(C) Recapture in lieu of disallowance.—The Secretary may prescribe regulations under which, in lieu of disallowing a loss under subparagraph (A) for a prior taxable year, the gross income of the liquidating corporation for the taxable year in which the plan of complete liquidation is adopted shall be increased by the amount of the disallowed loss.

(3) Special rule in case of liquidation to which section 332 applies.—In the case of any liquidation to which section 332 applies, no loss shall be recognized to the liquidating corporation on any distribution in such liquidation.

(e) Certain Stock Sales and Distributions May Be Treated As Asset Transfers.—Under regulations prescribed by the Secretary, if—

(1) a corporation owns stock in another corporation meeting the requirements of section 1504(a)(2), and

(2) such corporation sells, exchanges, or distributes all of such stock,

such corporation may elect to treat such sale, exchange, or distribution as a disposition of all of the assets of such other corporation, and no gain or loss shall be recognized on the sale, exchange, or distribution of such stock.

[For official explanation, see Committee Reports, ¶3916.]

≫**P-H CAUTION→** There are two versions of Sec. 337. Sec. 337 generally effective for any sale or exchange after 7-31-86, follows. For Sec. 337, generally effective for any sale or exchange before 8-1-86, see ¶2981-A, below.

[¶2981] CODE SEC. 337. [1]*NONRECOGNITION FOR PROPERTY DISTRIBUTED TO PARENT IN COMPLETE LIQUIDATION OF SUBSIDIARY.*

(a) In General.—No gain or loss shall be recognized to the liquidating corporation on the distribution to the 80-percent distributee of any property in a complete liquidation to which section 332 applies.

(b) Treatment of Indebtedness of Subsidiary, Etc.—

(1) Indebtedness of subsidiary to parent.—If—

(A) a corporation is liquidated in a liquidation to which section 332 applies, and

---

[Footnote ¶2981] Matter in *italics* in Sec. 337 added by section 631(a), '86 TRA, which struck out:

(1) "GAIN OR LOSS ON SALES OR EXCHANGES IN CONNECTION WITH CERTAIN LIQUIDATIONS.

(a) **General Rule.**—If, within the 12-month period beginning on the date on which a corporation adopts a plan of complete liquidation, all of the assets of the corporation are distributed in complete liquidation, less assets retained to meet claims, then no gain or loss shall be recognized to such corporation from the sale or exchange by it of property within such 12-month period.

(b) **Property Defined.—**

(1) **In general.**—For purposes of subsection (a), the term "property" does not include—

(A) stock in trade of the corporation, or other property of a kind which would properly be included in the inventory of the corporation if on hand at the close of the taxable year, and property held by the corporation primarily for sales to customers in the ordinary course of its trade or business.

(B) installment obligations acquired in respect of the sale or exchange (without regard to whether such sale or exchange occurred before, on, or after the date of the adoption of the plan referred to in subsection (a)) of stock in trade or other property described in subparagraph (A) of this paragraph, and

(C) installment obligations acquired in respect of property (other than property described in subparagraph (A)) sold or exchanged before the date of the adoption of such plan of liquidation.

      (B) *on the date of the adoption of the plan of liquidation, such corporation was indebted to the 80-percent distributee,*

for purposes of this section and section 336, any transfer of property to the 80-percent distributee in satisfaction of such indebtedness shall be treated as a distribution to such distributee in such liquidation.

      (2) *Treatment of tax exempt distributee.—*

[**Footnote ¶2981 continued**]

    (2) **Nonrecognition with respect to inventory in certain cases.**—Notwithstanding paragraph (1) of this subsection, if substantially all of the property described in subparagraph (A) of such paragraph (1) which is attributable to a trade or business of the corporation is, in accordance with this section, sold or exchanged to one person in one transaction, then for purposes of subsection (a) the term "property" includes—

    (A) such property so sold or exchanged, and

    (B) installment obligations acquired in respect of such sale or exchange.

    (c) **Limitations.—**

    (1) **Collapsible corporations and liquidations to which section 333 applies.**—This section shall not apply to any sale or exchange—

    (A) made by a collapsible corporation (as defined in section 341(b)), or

    (B) following the adoption of a plan of complete liquidation, if section 333 applies with respect to such liquidation.

    (2) **Liquidations to which section 332 applies.**—In the case of any sale or exchange following the adoption of a plan of complete liquidation, if section 332 applies with respect to such liquidation, this section shall not apply.

    (3) **Special rule for affiliated group.—**

    (A) In general.—Paragraph (2) shall not apply to a sale or exchange by a corporation (hereinafter in this paragraph referred to as the "selling corporation") if—

    (i) within the 12-month period beginning on the date of the adoption of a plan of complete liquidation by the selling corporation, the selling corporation and each distributee corporation is completely liquidated, and

    (ii) none of the complete liquidations referred to in clause (i) is a liquidation with respect to which section 333 applies.

    (B) Distributee corporation.—For purposes of subparagraph (A), the term "distributee corporation" means any corporation which receives a distribution to which section 332 applies in a complete liquidation of the selling corporation. Such term also includes any other corporation which receives a distribution to which section 332 applies in a complete liquidation of a corporation which is a distributee corporation under the preceding sentence or prior application of this sentence

    (d) **Special rule for certain minority shareholders.**—If a corporation adopts a plan of complete liquidation, and if subsection (a) does not apply to sales or exchanges of property by such corporation, solely by reason of the application of subsection (c)(2), then for the first taxable year of any shareholder (other than a corporation which meets the 80-percent stock ownership requirement specified in section 332(b)(1) in which he receives a distribution in complete liquidation—

    (1) the amount realized by such shareholder on the distribution shall be increased by his proportionate share of the amount by which the tax imposed by this subtitle on such corporation would have been reduced if subsection (c)(2) had not been applicable, and

    (2) for purposes of this title, such shareholder shall be deemed to have paid, on the last day prescribed by law for the payment of the tax imposed by this subtitle on such shareholder for such taxable year, an amount of tax equal to the amount of the increase described in paragraph (1).

    (e) **Special Rule for Involuntary Conversions.**—If—

    (1) there is an involuntary conversion (within the meaning of section 1033) of property of a distributing corporation and there is a complete liquidation of such corporation which qualifies under subsection (a),

    (2) the disposition of the converted property (within the meaning of clause (ii) of section 1033(a)(2)(E)) occurs during the 60-day period which ends on the day before the first day of the 12-month period, and

    (3) such corporation elects the application of this subsection at such time and in such manner as the Secretary may by regulations prescribe,

then for purposes of this section such disposition shall be treated as a sale or exchange occurring within the 12-month period.

    (f) **Special Rule for LIFO Inventories.—**

    (1) **In General.**—In the case of a corporation inventorying goods under the LIFO method, this section shall apply to gain from the sale or exchange of inventory assets (which under subsection (b)(2) constitutes property) only to the extent that such gain exceeds the LIFO recapture amount with respect to such assets.

    (2) **Definitions.**—The terms used in this subsection shall have the same meaning as when used in section 336(b).

    (3) **Cross reference.—**

For treatment of gain from the sale or exchange of an installment obligation as gain resulting from the sale or exchange of the property in respect of which the obligation was received, see the last sentence of section 453(d)(1).

    (g) **Title 11 or Similar Cases.**—If a corporation completely liquidates pursuant to a plan of complete liquidation adopted in a title 11 or similar case (within the meaning of section 368(a)(3)(A))—

    (1) for purposes of subsection (a), the term "property" shall not include any item acquired on or after the date of the adoption of the plan of liquidation if such item is not property within the meaning of subsection (b)(2), and

    (2) subsection (a) shall apply to sales and exchanges by the corporation of property within the period beginning on the date of the adoption of the plan and ending on the date of the termination of the case.

    Effective date (Sec. 633, '86 TRA).—Generally applies to any distribution in complete liquidation, and any sale or exchange made by a corporation after 7-31-86. For special and transitional rules, see ¶2023.

(A) In general.—Except as provided in subparagraph (B), paragraph (1) and subsection (a) shall not apply where the 80-percent distributee is an organization (other than a cooperative described in section 521) which is exempt from the tax imposed by this chapter.

(B) Exception where property will be used in unrelated business.—

(i) In general.—Subparagraph (A) shall not apply to any distribution of property to an organization described in section 511(a)(2) or 511(b)(2) if, immediately after such distribution, such organization uses such property in an unrelated trade or business (as defined in section 513).

(ii) Later disposition or change in use.—If any property to which clause (i) applied is disposed of by the organization acquiring such property, notwithstanding any other provision of law, any gain (not in excess of the amount not recognized by reason of clause (i) shall be included in such organization's unrelated business taxable income. For purposes of the preceding sentence, if such property ceases to be used in an unrelated trade or business of such organization, such organization shall be treated as having disposed of such property on the date of such cessation.

(c) 80-Percent Distributee.—For purposes of this section, the term "80-percent distributee" means only the corporation which meets the 80-percent stock ownership requirements specified in section 332(b).

(d) Regulations.—The Secretary shall prescribe such regulations as may be necessary or appropriate to carry out the purposes of the amendments made to this subpart by the Tax Reform Act of 1986, including—

(1) regulations to ensure that such purposes may not be circumvented through the use of any provision of law or regulations (including the consolidated return regulations and part III of this subchapter), and

(2) regulations providing for appropriate coordination of the provisions of this section with the provisions of this title relating to taxation of foreign corporations and their shareholders.

[For official explanation, see Committee Reports, ¶3917.]

»**P-H CAUTION**→ There are two versions of Sec. 337. Sec. 337 generally effective for any sale or exchange before 8-1-86, follows. For Sec. 337, generally effective for any sale or exchange after 7-31-86, see ¶2981, above.

[¶2981-A] CODE SEC. 337. GAIN OR LOSS ON SALES OR EXCHANGES IN CONNECTION WITH CERTAIN LIQUIDATIONS.

* * * * * * * * * * * *

(c) Limitations.—

* * * * * * * * * * * *

(3) Special rule for affiliated group.—

(A) In general.—Paragraph (2) shall not apply to a sale or exchange by a corporation (hereinafter in this paragraph referred to as the "selling corporation"(if—

(i) within the 12-month period beginning on the date of the adoption of a plan of complete liquidation by the selling corporation, the selling corporation and each distributee corporation is completely liquidated, and

(ii) none of the complete liquidations referred to in clause (i) is a liquidation with respect to which section 333 applies.

[1]*(B) Distributee corporation.—For purposes of subparagraph (A), the term "distributee corporation" means any corporation which receives a distribution to which*

[Footnote ¶2981-A] Matter in *italics* in Sec. 337(c)(3)(B) added by section 1804(e)(7)(A), '86 TRA, which struck out:

(1) "(B) Definitions.—For purposes of subparagraph (A)—

(i) The term "distributee corporation" means a corporation in the chain of includible corporations to which the selling corporation or a corporation above the selling corporation in such chain makes a distribution in complete liquidation within the 12-month period referred to in subparagraph (A)(i).

(ii) The term "chain of includible corporation" includes, in the case of any distribution, any corporation which (at the time of such distribution) is in a chain of includible corporations for purposes of section 1504(a) (determined without regard to the exceptions contained in section 1504(b)). Such term includes, where appropriate, the common parent corporation."

Effective date (Sec. 1804(e)(7)(B), '86 TRA).—Applies in the case of plans of complete liquidation pursuant to which any distribution is made in a taxable year beginning after 12-31-84 (12-31-83, in the case of an affiliated group to which an election under section 60(b)(7) of '84 TRA applies).

section 332 applies in a complete liquidation of the selling corporation. Such term also includes any other corporation which receives a distribution to which section 332 applies in a complete liquidation of a corporation which is a distributee corporation under the preceding sentence or prior application of this sentence.

[For official explanation, see Committee Reports, ¶4138.]

【¶2982】 CODE SEC. 338. CERTAIN STOCK PURCHASES TREATED AS ASSET ACQUISITIONS.

(a)   General Rule.—For purposes of this subtitle, if a purchasing corporation makes an election under this section (or is treated under subsection (e) as having made such an election), then, in the case of any qualified stock purchase, the target corporation—

(1)   shall be treated as having sold all of its assets at the close of the acquisition date at fair market value in a single transaction [1] and

(2)   shall be treated as a new corporation which purchased all of the assets referred to in paragraph (1) as of the beginning of the day after the acquisition date.

* * * * * * * * * * * *

(c)   [Repealed][2]

(d)   Purchasing Corporation: Target Corporation; Qualified Stock Purchase.—For purposes of this section—

* * * * * * * * * * * *

[3]*(3)   Qualified stock purchase.—The term "qualified stock purchase" means any transaction or series of transactions in which stock (meeting the requirements of section 1504(a)(2)) of 1 corporation is acquired by another corporation by purchase during the 12-month acquisition period.*

* * * * * * * * * * * *

(h)   Definitions and Special Rules.—For purposes of this section—

* * * * * * * * * * * *

(3)   Purchase.—

* * * * * * * * * * * *

(C)   Certain stock acquisitions from related corporations.—

【Footnote ¶2982】   Matter in *italics* in Sec. 338(a), added by section 631(b)(1), '86 TRA, which struck out:
(1)   "to which section 337 applies"
Effective date (Sec. 633, '86 TRA).—Generally applies to:
(1)   any distribution in complete liquidation, and any sale or exchange, made by a corporation after 7-31-86, unless such corporation is completely liquidated before 1-1-87,
(2)   any transaction described in section 338 of the '86 Code for which the acquisition date occurs after 12-31-86, and
(3)   any distribution (not in complete liquidation) made after 12-31-86.
For special and transitional rules, see ¶2023.

Sec. 338(c) repealed by section 631(b)(2), '86 TRA:
(2)   "(c)   Special Rules.—
(1)   Coordination with section 337 where purchasing corporation holds less than 100 percent of stock.—If during the 1-year period beginning on the acquisition date the maximum percentage (by value) of stock in the target corporation held by the purchasing corporation is less than 100 percent then in applying section 337 for purposes of subsection (a)(1), the nonrecognition of gain or loss shall be limited to an amount determined by applying such maximum percentage to such gain or loss. The preceding sentence shall not apply if the target corporation is liquidated during such 1-year period and section does not apply to each liquidation.
(2)   Certain redemptions where election made.—If, in connection with a qualified stock purchase with respect to which an election is made under this section, the target corportion makes a distribution in complete redemption of all of the stock of a shareholder which qualifies under section 302(b)(3) (determined without regard to the application of section 302(c)(2)(A)(ii)), section 336 shall apply to such distribution as if it were a distribution in complete liquidation."
Effective date (Sec. 633, '86 TRA).—See above.

Matter in *italics* in Sec. 338(d)(3) added by section 1804(e)(8)(A), '86 TRA, which struck out:
(3)   "Qualified stock purchase.—The term 'qualified stock purchase' means any transaction or series of transactions in which stock of 1 corporation possessing—
(A)   at least 80 percent of total combined voting power of all classes of stock entitled to vote, and
(B)   at least 80 percent of the total number of shares of all other classes of stock (except nonvoting stock which is limited and preferred as to dividends),
is acquired by another corporation by purchase during the 12-month acquisition period."
Effective date (Sec. 1804(e)(8)(B), '86 TRA).—Applies in cases where the 12-month acquisition period (as defined in section 338(h)(1) of the '54 Code) begins after 12-31-85.

(i) In general.—Clause (iii) of subparagraph (A) shall not apply to an acquisition of stock from a related corporation if at least 50 percent in value of the stock of such related corporation was acquired by purchase (within the meaning of [4]*subparagraphs* (A) and (B)).

* * * * * * * * * * * *

(6) Target affiliate.—

* * * * * * * * * * * *

(B) Certain foreign corporations, etc.—Except as otherwise provided in regulations (and subject to such conditions as may be provided in regulations)—
(i) the term "target affiliate" does not include a foreign corporation, a DISC,[5] or a corporation to which an election under section 936 applies, and

* * * * * * * * * * * *

(10) Elective recognition of gain or loss by target corporation, together with non-recognition of gain or loss on stock sold by selling consolidated group.—

* * * * * * * * * * * *

(B) Selling consolidated group.—For purposes of subparagraph (A), the term "selling consolidated group" means any group of corporations which (for the taxable period which includes the transaction)—
(i) includes the target corporation, and
(ii) files a consolidated return.

To the extent provided in regulations, such term also includes any affiliated group of corporations which includes the target corporation (whether or not such group files a consolidated return).

* * * * * * * * * * * *

(12) [Repealed][6]

* * * * * * * * * * * *

[For official explanation, see Committee Reports, ¶3917; 4057; 4138.]

〖¶2983〗 CODE SEC. 341. COLLAPSIBLE CORPORATIONS.

(a) Treatment of Gain to Shareholders.—Gain from—
(1) the sale or exchange of stock of a collapsible corporation,
(2) a distribution—
(A) in complete liquidation of a collapsible corporation if such distribution is treated under this part as in part or full payment in exchange for stock, or
(B) in partial liquidation (within the meaning of section 302(e)) of a collapsible corporation if such distribution is treated under section 302(b)(4) as in part or full payment in exchange for the stock, and
(3) a distribution made by a collapsible corporation which, under section 301(c)(3)(A), is treated, to the extent it exceeds the basis of the stock, in the same manner as a gain from the sale or exchange of property,

---

〖Footnote ¶2982 continued〗

Matter in *italics* in Sec. 338(h)(3)(C)(i) added by section 1899A(7), '86 TRA, which struck out:
(4) "subparagraph"

Matter in *italics* in Sec. 338(h)(6)(B)(i) added by section 1275(c)(6), '86 TRA, which struck out:
(5) "a corporation described in section 934(b),"
Effective date (Sec. 1277, '86 TRA).—Generally applies to taxable years beginning after 12-31-86. For special rules and exceptions, see ¶2068.

Matter in italics in Sec. 338(h)(10)(B), added by section 631(b)(3), 186 TRA.
Effective date (Sec. 633, '86 TRA).—See above.

Sec. 338(h)(12) repealed by section 631(e)(5)), '86 TRA:
(6) (12) Section 337 to apply where target had adopted plan for complete liquidation.—If—
(A) during the 12-month period ending on the acquisition date the target corporation adopted a plan of complete liquidation.
(B) such plan was not rescinded before the close of the acquisition date, and
(C) the purchasing corporation makes an election under this section (or is treated under subsection (c) as having made such an election) with respect to the target corporation,
then, subject to rules similar to the rules of subsection (c)(1), for purposes of section 337 (and other provisions which relate to section 337), the target corporation shall be treated as having distributed all of its assets as of the close of the acquisition date.
Effective date (Sec. 633, '86 TRA).—See above.

to the extent that it would be considered (but for the provisions of this section) as gain from the sale or exchange of a capital asset [1] shall, except as otherwise provided in this section, be considered as ordinary income.

* * * * * * * * * * * *

(e) **Exceptions to Application of Section.—**

* * * * * * * * * * * *

(2) [struck out][2]

(3) [struck out][3]

(4) [struck out][4]

(5) **Subsection (e) asset defined.—**

(A) For purposes of [5] *paragraph (1)*, the term "subsection (e) asset" means, with respect to property held by any corporation—

(i) property (except property used in the trade or business, as defined in paragraph (9)) which in the hands of the corporation is, or, in the hands of a shareholder who owns more than 20 percent in value of the outstanding stock of the corporation, would be, property gain from the sale or exchange of which would under any provision of this chapter be considered in whole or in part as ordinary income;

(ii) property used in the trade or business (as defined in paragraph (9)), but only if the unrealized depreciation on all such property on which there is unreal-

---

⟦Footnote ¶2983⟧ Section 1084(i)(1), '86 TRA, struck out from Sec. 341(a)

(1) "held for more than 6 months"

Effective date (Sec. 1804(i)(2), '86 TRA).—Applies with respect to sales, exchanges, and distributions after 9-27-85.

Matter in *italics* in Sec. 341(e)(5) added by section 631(e)(6), '86 TRA, which struck out:

(2) **"(2) Distributions in liquidation.**—For purposes of subsection (a)(2), a corporation shall not be considered to be a collapsible corporation with respect to any distribution to a shareholder pursuant to a plan of complete liquidation if, by reason of the application of paragraph (4) of this subsection, 337(a) applies to sales or exchanges of property by the corporation within the 12-month period beginning on the date of the adoption of such plan, and if, at all times after the adoption of the plan of liquidation, the sum of—

(A) the net unrealized appreciation in subsection (e) assets of the corporation (as defined in paragraph (5)(A)), plus

(B) if the shareholder owns more than 5 percent in value of the outstanding stock of the corporation, the net unrealized appreciation in assets of the corporation described in paragraph (1)(B) (other than assets described in subparagraph (A) of this paragraph), plus

(C) if the shareholder owns more than 20 percent in value of the outstanding stock of the corporation and owns, or at any time during the preceding 3-year period owned, more than 20 percent in value of the outstanding stock of any other corporation more than 70 percent in value of the assets of which are, or were at any time during which such shareholder owned during such 3-year period more than 20 percent in value of the outstanding stock, assets similar or related in service or use to assets comprising more than 70 percent in value of the assets of the corporation, the net unrealized appreciation in assets of the corporation described in paragraph (1)(C) (other than assets described in subparagraph (A) of this paragraph),

does not exceed an amount equal to 15 percent of the net worth of the corporation."

(3) **"(3) Recognition of gain in certain liquidations.**—For purposes of section 333, a corporation shall not be considered to be a collapsible corporation if at all times after the adoption of the plan of liquidation, the net unrealized appreciation in subsection (e) assets of the corporation (as defined in paragraph (5)(B)) does not exceed an amount equal to 15 percent of the net worth of the corporation."

(4) **"(4) Gain or loss on sales or exchanges in connection with certain liquidations.**—For purposes of section 337, a corporation shall not be considered to be a collapsible corporation with respect to any sale or exchange by it of property within the 12-month period beginning on the date of the adoption of a plan of complete liquidation, if—

(A) at all times after the adoption of such plan, the net unrealized appreciation in subsection (e) assets of the corporation (as defined in paragraph (5)(A)) does not exceed an amount equal to 15 percent of the net worth of the corporation,

(B) within the 12-month period beginning on the date of the adoption of such plan, the corporation sells substantially all of the properties held by it on such date, and

(C) following the adoption of such plan, no distribution is made of any property which in the hands of the corporation or in the hands of the distributee is property in respect of which a deduction for exhaustion, wear and tear, obsolescence, amortization, or depletion is allowable.

This paragraph shall not apply with respect to any sale or exchange of property by the corporation to any shareholder who owns more than 20 percent in value of the outstanding stock of the corporation or to any person related to such shareholder (within the meaning of paragraph (8)), if such property in the hands of the corporation or in the hands of such shareholder or related person is property in respect of which a deduction for exhaustion, wear and tear, obsolescence, amortization, or depletion is allowable."

(5) "paragraphs (1), (2), and (4)"

ized depreciation exceeds the unrealized appreciation on all such property on which there is unrealized appreciation;

(iii) if there is net unrealized appreciation on all property used in the trade or business (as defined in paragraph (9)), which, in the hands of a shareholder who owns more than 20 percent in value of the outstanding stock of the corporation, would be property gain from the sale or exchange of which would under any provision of this chapter be considered in whole or in part as ordinary income; and

(iv) property (unless included under clause (i), (ii), or (iii) which consists of a copyright, a literary, musical, or artistic composition, a letter or memorandum, or similar property, or any interest in any such property, if the property was created in whole or in part by the personal efforts of, or (in the case of a letter, memorandum, or similar property) was prepared, or produced in whole or in part for, any individual who owns more than 5 percent in value of the stock of the corporation.

The determination as to whether property of the corporation in the hands of the corporation, is, or in the hands of a shareholder would be, property gain from the sale or exchange of which would under any provision of this chapter be considered in whole or in part as ordinary income shall be made as if all property of the corporation had been sold or exchanged to one person in one transaction.[6]

* * * * * * * * * * *

(12) **Nonapplication of Section 1245(a)** *etc.*—For purposes of this subsection, the determination of whether gain from the sale or exchange of property would under any provision of this chapter be considered as ordinary income shall be made without regard to the application of sections 617(d)(1), 1245(a), 1250(a), 1252(a), 1254(a), and 1276(a).

* * * * * * * * * * *

[For official explanation, see Committee Reports, ¶3917; 4138.]

【¶2984】 **CODE SEC. 346. DEFINITION AND SPECIAL RULE.**

(a) **Complete Liquidation.**—For purposes of this subchapter, a distribution shall be treated as in complete liquidation of a corporation if the distribution is one of a series of distributions in redemption of all of the stock of the corporation pursuant to a plan.

(b) **Transactions Which Might Reach Same Result as Partial Liquidations.**—The Secretary shall prescribe such regulations as may be necessary to ensure that the purposes of subsections (a) and (b) of section 226 of the Tax Equity and Fiscal Responsibility Act of 1982 (which repeal the special tax treatment for partial liquidations) may not be circumvented through the use of section 335, 351, [1] or any other provision of law or regulations (including the consolidated return regulations).

【¶2985】 **CODE SEC. 361. NONRECOGNITION OF GAIN OR LOSS TO** [1]

【Footnote ¶2983 continued】

(6) "(B) For purposes of paragraph (3), the term 'subsection (e) asset' means, with respect to property held by any corporation, property described in clauses (i), (ii), (iii), and (iv) of subparagraph (A), except that clauses (i) and (iii) shall apply in respect of any shareholder who owns more than 5 percent in value of the outstanding stock of the corporation (in lieu of any shareholder who owns more than 20 percent in value of such stock)."

Effective date (Sec. 633, '86 TRA).—(a) Generally applies to—

(1) any distribution in complete liquidation, and any sale or exchange, made by a corporation after 7-31-86, unless such corporation is completely liquidated before 1-1-87,

(2) any transaction described in section 338 '86 Code for which the acquisition date occurs after 12-31-86, and

(3) any distribution (not in complete liquidation) made after 12-31-86.

For Special and transitional rules, see footnote ¶2023.

Matter in *italics* in Sec. 341(e)(12) added by section 1899A(8), '86 TRA.

【Footnote ¶2984】 Section 631(e)(7), '86 TRA, struck out from Sec. 346(b):

(1) "337,"

Effective date (Sec. 633(a), '86 TRA).—Generally applies to—

(1) any distribution in complete liquidation, and any sale or exchange, made by a corporation after 7-31-86, unless such corporation is completely liquidated before 1-1-87,

(2) an transaction described in Sec. 338 of the '86 Code for which the acquisition date occurs after 12-31-86, and

(3) any distribution (not in complete liquidation) made after 12-31-86.

For special rules, see ¶2023.

【Footnote ¶2985】 Matter in *italics* in Sec. 361 added by section 1804(g)(1), '86 TRA, which struck out:

(1) "CORPORATIONS.

(a) **General Rule.**—No gain or loss shall be recognized if a corporation a party to a reorganization exchanges

TRANSFEROR CORPORATION; OTHER TREATMENT OF TRANSFEROR CORPORATION; ETC.

    (a)   General Rule.—No gain or loss shall be recognized to a transferor corporation which is a party to a reorganization on any exchange of property pursuant to the plan of reorganization.

    (b)   Other Treatment of Transferor Corporation.—In the case of a transferor corporation which is a party to a reorganization—

        (1)   sections 336 and 337 shall not apply with respect to any liquidation of such corporation pursuant to the plan of reorganization,

        (2)   the basis of the property (other than stock and securities described in paragraph (3)) received by the corporation pursuant to such plan of reorganization shall be the same as it would be in the hands of the transferor of such property, adjusted by the amount of gain or loss recognized to such transferor on such transfer, and

        (3)   no gain or loss shall be recognized by such corporation on any disposition (pursuant to the plan of reorganization) of stock or securities which were received pursuant to such plan and which are in another corporation which is a party to such reorganization.

For purposes of paragraph (3), if the transferor corporation is merged, consolidated, or liquidated pursuant to the plan of reorganization, or if a transaction meets the requirements of section 368(a)(1)(C) pursuant to a waiver granted by the Secretary under section 368(a)(2)(G)(ii), any distribution of such stock or securities by the transferor corporation to its creditors in connection with such transaction shall be treated as pursuant to such plan of reorganization.

    (c)   Treatment of Distributions of Appreciated Property.—Notwithstanding any other provisions of this subtitle, gain shall be recognized on the distribution of property (other than property permitted by section 354, 355, or 356 to be received without the recognition of gain) pursuant to a plan of reorganization in the same manner as if such property had been sold to the distributee at its fair market value.

[For official explanation, see Committee Reports, ¶4138.]

[¶2986]   **CODE SEC. 362. BASIS TO CORPORATIONS.**

       *   *   *   *   *   *   *   *   *   *   *   *

    (c)   Special Rule for Certain Contributions to Capital.—

       *   *   *   *   *   *   *   *   *   *   *   *

        (3)   [struck out][1]

[For official explanation, see Committee Reports, ¶3946.]

[¶2987]   **CODE SEC. 367. FOREIGN CORPORATIONS.**

    (a)   Transfers of Property From the United States.—

        (1)   General rule.—If, in connection with any exchange described in section 332, 351, 354, [1] *356,* or 361, a United States person transfers property to a foreign corpo-

---

[Footnote ¶2985 continued]

property, in pursuance of the plan of reorganization, solely for stock or securities in another corporation a party to the reorganization.

  (b)   Exchanges Not Solely in Kind.—

  (1)   Gain.—If subsection (a) would apply to an exchange but for the fact that the property received in exchange consists not only of stock or securities permitted by subsection (a) to be received without the recognition of gain, but also of other property or money, then—

  (A)   If the corporation receiving such other property or money distributes it in pursuance of the plan of reorganization, no gain to the corporation shall be recognized from the exchange, but

  (B)   If the corporation receiving such other property or money does not distribute it in pursuance of the plan of reorganization, the gain, if any, to the corporation shall be recognized, but in an amount not in excess of the sum of such money and the fair market value of such property so received, which is not so distributed.

  (2)   Loss.—If subsection (a) would apply to an exchange but for the fact that the property received in exchange consists not only of property permitted by subsection (a) to be received without the recognition of gain or loss, but also of other property or money, then no loss from the exchange shall be recognized."

Effective date (Sec. 1804(g)(4), '86 TRA).—Applies to plans of reorganizations adopted after the date of enactment.

  [Footnote ¶2986]   Section 824(b), '86 TRA, struck out from Sec. 362(c)(3):

  (1)   "(3)   Exception for contributions in aid of construction .—The provisions of this subsection shall not apply to contributions in aid of construction to which section 118(b) applies"

Effective date (Sec. 824(c), '86 TRA).—Generally applies to amounts received after 12-31-86, in taxable years ending after such date. For special rules, see footnote ¶2905.

  [Footnote ¶2987]   Matter in *italics* in Sec. 367(a)(1) added by section 1810(g)(4)(A), '86 TRA, which struck out:

  (1)   "355,"

ration, such foreign corporation shall not, for purposes of determining the extent to which gain shall be recognized on such transfer, be considered to be a corporation.

* * * * * * * * * * * *

(d)   Special Rules Relating to Transfers of Intangibles.—

* * * * * * * * * * * *

(2)   Transfer of intangibles as transfer pursuant to sale of contingent payments.—
(A)   In general.—If paragraph (1) applies to any transfer, the United States person transferring such property shall be treated as—
(i)   having sold such property in exchange for payments which are contingent upon the productivity, use, or disposition of such property, and
(ii)   receiving amounts which reasonably reflect the amounts which would have been received—
(I)   annually in the form of such payments over the useful life of such property, or
(II)   in the case of a disposition following such transfer (whether direct or indirect), at the time of the disposition.

The amounts taken into account under clause (ii) shall be commensurate with the income attributable to the intangible.

* * * * * * * * * * * *

≫**P-H CAUTION**→ There are two versions of Sec. 367(e). Sec. 367(e), generally effective for any sale or exchange after 7-31-86, follows. For Sec. 367(e), generally effective for any sale or exchange before 8-1-86, see below.

▲ **(e)   Treatment of** [2]*Distributions Described in Section 355 or Liquidations Under Section 332.—*

(1)   Distributions described in section 355.—In the case of any distribution described in section 355 (or so much of section 356 as relates to section 355) by a domestic corpo-

---

⟦Footnote ¶2987 continued⟧

Effective date (Sec. 1881, '86 TRA and Sec. 131(g), '84 TRA).—(1) Generally applies to transfers or exchanges after 12-31-84, in taxable years ending after such date.
(2) Special rule for certain transfers of intangibles.—
(A) In general.—If, after 6-6-84, and before 1-1-85, a United States person transfers any intangible property (within the meaning of section 936(h)(3)(B) of the '54 Code) to a foreign corporation or in a transfer described in section 1491, such transfer shall be treated for purposes of sections 367(a), 1492(2), and 1494(b) of such Code as pursuant to a plan having as 1 of its principal purposes the avoidance of Federal income tax.
(B) Waiver.—Subject to such terms and conditions as the Secretary of the Treasury or his delegate may prescribe, the Secretary may waive the application of subparagraph (A) with respect to any transfer.
(3) Ruling request before 3-1-84.—The amendments made by this section (and the provisions of paragraph (2) of this subsection) shall not apply to any transfer or exchange of property described in a request filed before 3-1-84, under section 367(a), 1492(2), or 1494(b) of the '54 Code (as in effect before such amendments).

Matter in *italics* in Sec. 367(d)(2)(A) added by section 1231(e)(2), '86 TRA.
Effective date (Sec. 1231(g)(2), '86 TRA).—(A) Generally applies to taxable years beginning after 12-31-86, but only with respect to transfers after 11-16-85, or licenses granted after such date (or before such date with respect to property not in existence or owned by the taxpayer on such date).
(B) Special rule for section 936.—For purposes of section 936(h)(5)(C) of the '86 Code the amendments made by subsection (e) shall apply to taxable years beginning after 12-31-86, without regard to when the transfer (or license) was made.

▲ Matter in *italics* in Sec. 367(e), preceded by a triangle, added by section 631(d)(1), '86 TRA, which struck out:
(2)   "Distributions Described in section 336 or 355—In the case of any distribution described in section 336 or 355 (or so much of section 356 as relates to section 355) by a domestic corporation which is made to a person who is not a United States person, to the extent provided in regulations, gain shall be recognized under principles similar to the principles of this section."
Effective date (Sec. 633, '86 TRA).—Generally applies to—
(1) any distribution in complete liquidation, and any sale or exchange, made by a corporation after 7-31-86, unless such corporation is completely liquidated before 1-1-87,
(2) any transaction described in section 338 of the '86 Code for which the acquisition date occurs after 12-31-86, and
(3) any distribution (not in complete liquidation) made after 12-31-86.
For special and transitional rules, see ¶2023.

Code §367(e) (1) ¶2987

ration to a person who is not a United States person, to the extent provided in regulations, gain shall be recognized under principles similar to the principles of this section.

(2) Liquidations under section 332.—In the case of any liquidation to which section 332 applies, except as provided in regulations, subsections (a) and (b)(1) of section 337 shall not apply where the 80-percent distributee (as defined in section 337(c)) is a foreign corporation.

≫**P-H CAUTION**→ There are two versions of Sec. 367(e). Sec. 367(e), generally before 8-1-86, follows. For Sec. 367(e), generally effective for any sale or exchange after 7-31-86, see above.

▲ ▲ **(e) Treatment of** [3]*Distributions Described in Section 336 or 355.—In the case of any distribution described in section 336 or 355 (or so much of section 356 as relates to section 355) by a domestic corporation which is made to a person who is not a United States person, to the extent provided in regulations, gain shall be recognized under principles similar to the principles of this section.*[4]

[For official explanation, see Committee Reports, ¶3917; 4041; 4144.]

【¶2988】 CODE SEC. 368. DEFINITIONS RELATING TO CORPORATE REORGANIZATIONS.

(a) Reorganization.—

(1) In general.—For purposes of parts I and II of this part, the term "reorganization" means—

(A) a statutory merger or consolidation;

(B) the acquisition by one corporation, in exchange solely for all or a part of its voting stock (or in exchange solely for all or part of the voting stock of a corporation which is in control of the acquiring corporation), of stock of another corporation if, immediately after the acquisition, the acquiring corporation has control of such other corporation (whether or not such acquiring corporation had control immediately before the acquisition);

(C) the acquisition by one corporation, in exchange solely for all or a part of its voting stock (in exchange for all or a part of the voting stock of a corporation which is in control of the acquiring corporation), of substantially all of the properties of another corporation, but in determining whether the exchange is solely for stock the assumption by the acquiring corporation of a liability of the other, or the fact that property acquired is subject to a liability, shall be disregarded;

【Footnote ¶2987 continued】

▲ ▲ Matter in *italics* in Sec. 367(e), preceded by two triangles, added by section 1810(g)(4)(B), '86 TRA, which struck out:

(3) "Liquidations Under Section 336"
Effective date (Sec. 1881, '86 TRA and Sec. 131(g), '84 TRA).—Generally applies to transfers or exchanges after 12-31-84, in taxable years ending after such date. For special rules, see above.

Section 1810(g)(1), '86 TRA, repealed Sec. 367(f):
(4) "(f) Transitional Rule.—In the case of any exchange beginning before January 1, 1978—
(1) subsection (a) shall be applied without regard to whether or not there is a transfer of property described in subsection (a)(1), and
(2) subsection (b) shall not apply."
Effective date (Sec. 1881, '86 TRA and Sec. 131(g), '86 TRA).—See above.
【Footnote ¶2988】 Matter in *italics* is Sec. 368(a)(2)(A) added by section 1804(h)(3), '86 TRA.
Effective date (Sec. 1881, '86 TRA and section 64(b), '84 TRA).—Applies to transactions pursuant to plans adopted after 7-18-84.

Matter in *italics* in Sec. 368(a)(2)(F)(ii) added by section 1879(l)(1). '86 TRA, which struck out:
(1) "(ii) A corporation meets the requirement of this clause if not more than 25 percent of the value of its total assets is invested in the stock and securities of any one issuer, and not more than 50 percent of the value of its total assets is invested in the stock and securities of 5 or fewer issuers. For purposes of this clause, all members of a controlled group of corporations (within the meaning of section 1563(a)) shall be treated as one issuer."
Effective date (Sec. 1879(l)(2), '86 TRA and section 2131(f)(1), '76 TRA).—Generally applies for transfers made after 2-17-76, in taxable years ending after such date.

Matter in *italics* in Sec. 368(a)(2)(G)(i) added by section 1804(g)(2), '86 TRA.
Effective date (Sec. 1804(g)(4), '86 TRA).—Applies to plans of reorganizations adopted after date of enactment of this Act.

Sec. 368(a)(2)(H) in *italics* added by section 1804(h)(2), '86 TRA.
Effective date (Sec. 1881, '86 TRA and section 64(b), '84 TRA).—Applies to transactions pursuant to plans adopted after 7-18-84.

(D) a transfer by a corporation of all or part of its assets to another corporation if immediately after the transfer the transferor, or one or more of its shareholders (including persons who were shareholders immediately before the transfer), or any combination thereof, is in control of the corporation to which the assets are transferred; but only if, in pursuance of the plan, stock or securities of the corporation to which the assets are transferred are distributed in a transaction which qualifies under section 354, 355, or 356;

(E) a recapitalization;

(F) a mere change in identity, form, or place of organization of one corporation, however effected; or

(G) a transfer by a corporation of all or part of its assets to another corporation in a title 11 or similar case; but only if, in pursuance of the plan, stock or securities of the corporation to which the assets are transferred are distributed in a transaction which qualifies under section 354, 355, or 356.

(2) **Special rules relating to paragraph (1).—**

(A) Reorganizations described in both paragraph (1)(C) and paragraph(1)(D).—If a transaction is described in both paragraph (1)(C) and paragraph (1)(D), then, for purposes of this subchapter *(other than for purposes of subparagraph (C))*, such transaction shall be be treated as described only in paragraph (1)(D).

* * * * * * * * * * * *

(F) Certain transactions involving 2 or more investment companies.—

* * * * * * * * * * * *

(ii) A corporation meets the requirements of this clause if not more than 25 percent of the value of its total assets is invested in the stock and securities of any one issuer (other than stock in a regulated investment company, a real estate investment trust, or an investment company which meets the requirements of this clause (ii)), and not more than 50 percent of the value of its total assets is invested in the stock and securities of 5 or fewer issuers (other than stock in a regulated investment company, a real estate investment trust, or an investment company which meets the requirements of this clause (ii)). For purposes of this clause, all members of a controlled group of corporations (within the meaning of section 1563(a)) shall be treated as one issuer.

* * * * * * * * * * * *

(G) Distribution requirement for paragraph (1)(C).—

(i) In general.—A transaction shall fail to meet the requirements of paragraph (1)(C) unless the acquired corporation distributes the stock, securities, and other properties it receives, as well as its other properties, in pursuance of the plan of reorganization. For purposes of the preceding sentence, if the acquired corporation is liquidated pursuant to the plan of reorganization, any distribution to its creditors in connection with such liquidation shall be treated as pursuant to the plan of reorganization.

* * * * * * * * * * * *

(H) Special rule for determining whether certain transactions are qualified under paragraph (1)(d).—In the case of any transaction with respect to which the requirements of subparagraphs (A) and (B) of section 354(b)(1) are met, for purposes of determining whether such transaction qualifies under subparagraph (D) of paragraph (1), the term "control" has the meaning given to such term by section 304(c).

(3) *Additional rules relating to title 11 and similar cases.—*

* * * * * * * * * * * *

[2](D) *Agency receivership proceedings which involve financial institutions.—For*

[**Footnote ¶2988 continued**]

Matter in *italics* in Sec. 368(a)(3)(D) added by section 904(a), '86 TRA, which struck out:

(2) "(D) Agency proceedings which involve financial institutions.—

(i) For purpose of subparagraphs (A) and (B)—

(I) In the case of a receivership, foreclosure, or similar proceeding before a Federal or State agency involving a financial institution to which section 585 applies, the agency shall be treated as a court, and

(II) In the case of a financial institution to which section 593 applies, the term "title 11 or similar case" means only a case in which the Board (which will be treated as the court in such case) makes the certification described in clause (ii).

(ii) A transaction otherwise meeting the requirements of subparagraph (G) to paragraph (1), in which the

purposes of subparagraphs (A) and (B), in the case of a receivership, foreclosure, or similar proceeding before a Federal or State agency involving a financial institution referred to in section 581 or 591, the agency shall be treated as a court.

* * * * * * * * * * * *

[3](c) *Control Defined.—For purposes of part I (other than section 304), part II, this part, and part V, the term "control" means the ownership of stock possessing at least 80 percent of the total combined voting power of all classes of stock entitled to vote and at least 80 percent of the total number of shares of all other classes of stock of the corporation.*

[For official explanation, see Committee Reports, ¶3951; 4138; 4193.]

[¶2989] CODE SEC. 374. GAIN OR LOSS NOT RECOGNIZED IN CERTAIN RAILROAD REORGANIZATIONS.

* * * * * * * * * * * *

(e) Use of Expired Net Operating Loss Carryovers to Offset Income Arising From Certain Railroad Reorganization Proceedings.—

   (1) In general.—If—

     (A) any corporation receives or accrues any amount pursuant to—

       (i) an award in (or settlement of) a proceeding under section 77 of the Bankruptcy Act,

       (ii) an award in (or settlement of) a proceeding before the special court to carry out section 303(c), 305, or 306 of the Regional Rail Reorganization Act of 1973.

       (iii) an award in (or settlement of) a proceeding in the [1]*United States Claims Court* under section 1491 of title 28 of the United States Code, to the extent such proceeding involves a claim arising under the Regional Rail Reorganization Act of 1973, or

       (iv) a redemption of a certificate of value of the United States Railway Association issued under section 306 of such Act to such corporation (or issued to another member of the same affiliated group (within the meaning of section 1504) as such corporation for their taxable years which included March 31, 1976),

     (B) any portion of such amount is includible in the gross income of such corporation for the taxable year in which such portion is received or accrued, and such taxable year begins not more than 5 years after the date of such award, settlement, or redemption, and

     (C) the net operating loss of such corporation for any taxable year—

[Footnote ¶2988 continued]

transferor corporation is a financial institution to which section 593 applies, will not be disqualified as a reorganization if no stock or securities of the corporation to which the assets are transferred (transferee) are received or distributed, but only if all of the following conditions are met:

   (I) substantially all of the liabilities of the transferor immediately before the transfer become, as a result of the transfer, liabilities of the transferee, and

   (III) the Board certifies that the grounds set forth in section 1464(d)(6)(A)(i), (ii), or (iii) of title 12, United States Code, exist with respect to the transferor or will exist in the near future in the absence of action by the Board.

   (iii) For purposes of this subparagraph, the "Board" means the Federal Home Loan Bank Board or the Federal Savings and Loan Insurance Corporation or, if neither has supervisory authority with respect to the transferor, the equivalent state authority."

Effective date (Sec. 904(c)(1), '86 TRA).—Applies to acquisitions after 12-31-88, in taxable years ending after such date.

Matter in italics in Sec. 368(c) added by section 1804(h)(1), '86 TRA, which struck out:

   (3) "(c) Control Defined.—

   (1) In general.—For purposes of part I (other than section 304), part II, this part, and part V, the term "control" means the ownership of stock possessing at least 80 percent of the total combined voting power of all classes of stock entitled to vote ʍnd at least 80 percent of the total number of shares of all other classes of stock of the corporation.

   (2) Special rule for determining whether certain transactions are described in subsection (a)(1)(D).—In the case of any transactions with respect to which the requirements of subparagraphs (A) and (B) of section 354(b)(1) are met, for purposes of determining whether such transaction is described in subparagraph (D) of subsection (a)(1), the term "control" has the meaning given to such term by section 304(c)."

Effective date (Sec. 1881, '86 TRA and section 64(b), '84 TRA).—Applies to transactions pursuant to plans adopted after 7-18-84.

   [Footnote ¶2989] Matter in *italics* in Sec. 374(e)(1)(A)(iii) added by section 1899A(9), '86 TRA, which struck out:

   (1) "Court of Claims".

(i) was a net operating loss carryover to, or arose in, the first taxable year of such corporation ending after March 31, 1976 (or, in the case of a proceeding referred to in subparagraph (A)(i) which began after March 31, 1976, ending after the beginning of such proceeding), but

(ii) solely by reason of the lapse of time, is not a net operating loss carryover to the taxable year referred to in subparagraph (B),

then such net operating loss shall be a net operating loss carryover to the taxable year described in subparagraph (B) but only for use (to the extent not theretofore used under this subsection to offset other amounts) to offset the portion referred to in subparagraph (B).

* * * * * * * * * * * * *

[¶2990]   CODE SEC. 381.   CARRYOVERS IN CERTAIN CORPORATE ACQUISITIONS.

(a) **General Rule.**—In the case of the acquisition of assets of a corporation by another corporation—

(1) in a distribution to such other corporation to which section 332 relating to liquidations of subsidiaries applies, or

(2) in a transfer to which section 361 (relating to nonrecognition of gain or loss to corporation) applies, but only if the transfer is in connection with a reorganization described in subparagraph (A), (C), (D) (F), or (G) of section 368(a)(1), the acquiring corporation shall succeed to and take into account, as of the close of the day of distribution or transfer, the items described in subsection (c) of the distributor or transferor corporation, subject to the conditions and limitations specified in subsections (b) and (c). For purposes of the preceding sentence, a reorganization shall be treated as meeting the requirements of subparagraph (D) or (G) of section 368(a)(1) only if the requirements or subparagraph (A) and (B) of section 354(b)(1) are met.

* * * * * * * * * * * *

(c) **Items of the Distributor or Transferor Corporation.**—The items referred to in subsection (a) are:

* * * * * * * * * * * *

(10) **Treatment of certain mining development and exploration expenses of distributor or transferor corporation.**—The acquiring corporation shall be entitled to deduct, as if it were the distributor or transferor corporation, expenses, deferred under section 616 (relating to certain development expenditures) if the distributor or transferor corporation has so elected.[1]

* * * * * * * * * * * *

(12) [2]*Recovery of tax benefit items.—If the acquiring corporation is entitled to the recovery of any amounts previously deducted by (or allowable as credits to) the distributor or transferor corporation, the acquiring corporation shall succeed to the treatment*

[Footnote ¶2990]   Section 411(b)(2)(C)(iii), '86 TRA, struck out from Sec. 381(c)(10):

(1) "For the purpose of applying the limitation provided in section 617(h), if, for any taxable year, the distributor or transferor corporation was allowed a deduction under section 617(a), the acquiring corporation shall be deemed to have been allowed such deduction."

Effective date (Sec. 411(c), '86 TRA).—(1) Generally applies to costs paid or incurred after 12-31-86 in taxable years ending after such date.

(2) Transition rule.—The amendments made by this section shall not apply with respect to intangible drilling and development costs incurred by United States companies pursuant to a minority interest in a license for Netherlands or United Kingdom North Sea development if such interest was acquired on or before 12-31-85.

Matter in *italics* in Sec. 381(c)(12) added by section 1812(a)(3), '86 TRA, which struck out:

(2) **"Recovery of bad debts, prior taxes, or delinquency amounts.**—If the acquiring corporation is entitled to the recovery of bad debts, prior taxes, or delinquency amounts previously deducted or credited by the distributor or transferor corporation, the acquiring corporation shall include in its income such amounts as would have been includible by the distributor or transferor corporation in accordance with section 111 (relating to the recovery of bad debts, prior taxes, and delinquency amounts)."

Effective date (Sec. 1881, '86 TRA and section 171(c), '84 TRA).—Applies to amounts recovered after 12-31-83, in taxable years ending after such date.

Matter in *italics* 381(c)(25) added by section 231(d)(3)(F), '86 TRA, which struck out:

(3) "(25) **Credit under section 30.**—The acquiring corporation shall take into account (to the extent proper to carry out the purposes of this section and section 30, and under such regulations as may be prescribed by the Secretary) the items required to be taken into account for purposes of section 30 in respect of the distributor or transferor corporation."

under section 111 which would apply to such amounts in the hands of the distributor or transferor corporation.

* * * * * * * * * * *

[3] *(25)* [4]**Credit under section 38.**—The acquiring corporation shall take into account (to the extent proper to carry out the purposes of this section and section 38, and under such regulations as may be prescribed by the Secretary) the items required to be taken into account for purposes of section 38 in respect of the distributor or transferor corporation.

(27) *[should read (26)]* *Credit under section 53.—The acquiring corporation shall take into account (to the extent proper to carry out the purposes of this section and section 53, and under such regulations as may be prescribed by the Secretary) the items required to be taken into account for purposes of section 53 in respect of the distributor or transferor corporation.*

* * * * * * * * * * *

[¶2991] **CODE SEC. 382.** [1]*LIMITATION ON NET OPERATING LOSS CARRYFORWARDS AND CERTAIN BUILT-IN LOSSES FOLLOWING OWNERSHIP CHANGE.*

(a) *General Rule.—The amount of the taxable income of any new loss corporation for any post-change year which may be offset by pre-change losses shall not exceed the section 382 limitation for such year.*

(b) *Section 382 Limitation.—For purposes of this section—*

(1) *In general.—Except as otherwise provided in this section, the section 382 limitation for any post-change year is an amount equal to—*

(A) *the value of the old loss corporation, multiplied by*

(B) *the long-term tax-exempt rate.*

[Footnote ¶2990 continued]
(4) "(26)"
Effective date (Sec. 231(g)(1), '86 TRA).—(1) Applies to taxable years beginning after 12-31-85.

Matter in *italics* in section 381(c)(27) [should read (26)] added by section 701(e)(1), '86 TRA.
Effective date (Sec. 701(f), '86 TRA).—(1) Applies to taxable years beginning after 12-31-86. For special transitional rules, see footnote ¶2879.
[Footnote ¶2991] Matter in *italics* in Sec. 382 added by section 621(a), '86 TRA, which struck out:
(1) "**SPECIAL LIMITATIONS ON NET OPERATING LOSS CARRYOVER.**
(a) **Certain Acquisitions of Stock of a Corporation.—**
(1) **In General.—**If—
(A) on the last day of a taxable year of a corporation,
(B) any one or more of the persons described in paragraph (4)(B) own, directly or indirectly, a percentage of the total fair market value of the participating stock or of all the stock of the corporation which exceeds by more than 60 percentage points the percentage of such stock owned by such person or persons at—
(i) the beginning of such taxable year, or
(ii) the beginning of the first or second preceding taxable year, and
(C) such increase in percentage points is attributable to—
(i) a purchase by such person or persons of such stock, or of the stock of another corporation owning stock in such corporation, or of an interest in a partnership or trust owning stock in such corporation,
(ii) an acquisition (by contribution, merger, or consolidation) of an interest in a partnership owning stock in such corporation, or an acquisition (by contribution, merger, or consolidation) by a partnership of such stock,
(iii) an exchange to which section 351 (relating to transfer to corporation controlled by transferor) applies, or an acquisition by a corporation of such stock in an exchange in which section 351 applies to the transferor,
(iv) a contribution to the capital of such corporation,
(v) a decrease in the amount of such stock outstanding or in the amount of stock outstanding of another corporation owning stock in such corporation (except a decrease resulting from a redemption to pay death taxes to which section 303 applies),
(vi) a liquidation of the interest of a partner in a partnership owning stock in such corporation, or
(vii) any combination of the transactions described in clauses (i) through (vi),
then the net operating loss carryover, if any, from such taxable year and the net operating loss carryovers, if any, from prior taxable years to such taxable year and subsequent taxable years of such corporation shall be reduced by the percentage determined under paragraph (2).
(2) **Reduction of net operating loss carryover.—**The reduction applicable under paragraph (1) shall be the sum of the percentages determined by multiplying—
(A) by three and one-half the increase in percentage points (including fractions thereof) in excess of 60 and up to and including 80, and
(B) by one and one-half the increase in percentage points (including fractions thereof) in excess of 80.
The reduction under this paragraph shall be determined by reference to the increase in percentage points of the total fair market value of the participating stock or of all the stock, whichever increase is greater.
(3) **Minimum ownership rule.—**Notwithstanding the provisions of paragraph (1), a net operating loss carryover from a taxable year shall not be reduced under this subsection if, at all times during the last half of such taxable year, any of the persons described in paragraph (4)(B) (determined on the last day of the taxable year referred to in paragraph (1)(A)) owned at least 40 percent of the total fair market value of the participating stock and of all the stock of the corporation. For purposes of the preceding sentence, persons owning stock of a corporation on the last day of its first taxable year shall be considered to have owned such stock at all times during the last half of

(2) *Carryforward of unused limitation.—If the section 382 limitation for any post-change year exceeds the taxble income of the new loss corporation for such year which was offset by pre-change losses, the section 382 limitation for the next post-change year shall be increased by the amount of such excess.*

(3) *Special rule for post-change year which includes change date.—In the case of any post-change year which includes the change date—*

(A) *Limitation does not apply to taxable income before change.—Subsection (a) shall not apply to the portion of the taxable income for such year which is allocable to the period in such year on or before the change date. Except as provided in subsection (h)(5) and in regulations, taxable income shall be allocated ratably to each day in the year.*

(B) *Limitation for period after change.—For purposes of applying the limitation of subsection (a) to the remainder of the taxable income for such year, the section 382 limitation shall be an amount which bears the same ratio to such limitation (determined without regard to this paragraph) as—*

(i) *the number of days in such year after the change date, bears to*

(ii) *the total number of days in such year.*

(c) *Carryforwards Disallowed if Continuity of Business Requirements Not Met.—*

(1) *In general.—Except as provided in paragraph (2), if the new loss corporation does not continue the business enterprise of the old loss corporation at all times during the 2-year period beginning on the change date, the section 382 limitation for any post-change year shall be zero.*

(2) *Exception for certain gains.—The section 382 limitation for any post-change year shall not be less than the sum of—*

⟦Footnote ¶2991 continued⟧

such first taxable year.

(4) Operating rules.—For purposes of this subsection—

(A) Definition of purchase.—The term "purchase" means an acquisition of stock the basis of which is determined by reference to its cost to the holder thereof.

(B) Description of person or persons.—The person or persons referred to in paragraph (1)(B) shall be the 15 persons (or such lesser number as there are persons owning the stock on the last day of the taxable year) who own the greatest percentage of the total fair market value of all the stock on the last day of that year, except that if any other person owns the same percentage of such stock at such time as is owned by one of the 15 persons, that other person shall also be included. If any of the persons are so related that the stock owned by one is attributed to the other under the rules specified in subparagraph (C), such persons shall be considered as only one person solely for the purpose of selecting the 15 persons (more or less) who own the greatest percentage of the total fair market value of all the stock.

(C) Constructive ownership.—Section 318 (relating to constructive ownership of stock) shall apply in determining the ownership of stock, except that section 318(a)(2)(C) and 318(a)(3)(C) shall be applied without regard to the 50 percent limitation contained therein.

(D) Short taxable years.—If one of the taxable years of the corporation referred to in paragraph (1)(B) is a short taxable year, then such paragraph and paragraph (6) shall be applied by substituting "first, second, or third" for "first or second" each time such phrase occurs.

(5) Exceptions.—This subsection shall not apply to a purchase or other acquisition of stock (or of an interest in a partnership or trust owning stock in the corporation)—

(A) from a person whose ownership of stock would be attributed to the holder by application of paragraph (4)(C) to the extent that such stock would be so attributed;

(B) if (and to the extent) the basis thereof is determined under section 1014 or 1023 (relating to property acquired from a decedent), or section 1015(a) or (b) (relating to property acquired by gift or transfers in trust);

(C) by a security holder or creditor in exchange for the relinquishment or extinguishment in whole or part of a claim against the corporation, unless the claim was acquired for the purpose of acquiring such stock;

(D) by one or more persons who were full-time employees of the corporation at all times during the period of 36 months ending on the last day of the taxable year of the corporation (or at all times during the period of the corporation's existence, if shorter);

(E) by a trust described in section 401(a) which is exempt from tax under section 501(a) and which benefits exclusively the employees (or their beneficiaries) of the corporation, including a member of a controlled group of corporations (within the meaning of section 1563(a) determined without regard to section 1563(a)(4) and (e)(3)(C)) which includes such corporation;

(F) by an employee stock ownership plan meeting the requirements of section 301(d) of the Tax Reduction Act of 1975; or

(G) in a recapitalization described in section 368(a)(1)(E).

(6) Successive applications of subsection.—If—

(A) a net operating loss carryover is reduced under this subsection at the end of a taxable year of a corporation, and

(B) any person described in paragraph (4)(B) who owns stock of the corporation on the last day of such taxable year does not own, on the last day of the first or second succeeding taxable year of the corporation, a greater percentage of the total fair market value of the participating stock or of all the stock of the corporation than such person owned on the last day of such taxable year,

then, for purposes of applying this subsection as of the end of the first or second succeeding taxable year (as the case may be), stock owned by such person at the end of such succeeding taxable year shall be considered owned

Code §382(c)(2) ¶2991

(A)   any increase in such limitation under—
    (i)   subsection (h)(1)(A) for recognized built-in gains for such year, and
    (ii)   subsection (h)(1)(C) for gain recognized by reason of an election under section 338, plus

(B)   any increase in such limitation under subsection (b)(2) for amounts described in subparagraph (A) which are carried forward to such year.

(d)   *Pre-Change Loss and Post-Change Year.*—For purposes of this section—

(1)   *Pre-change loss.*—The term "pre-change loss" means—
    (A)   any net operating loss carryforward of the old loss corporation to the taxable year ending with the ownership change or in which the change date occurs, and
    (B)   the net operating loss of the old loss corporation for the taxable year in which the ownership change occurs to the extent such loss is allocable to the period in such year on or before the change date.
Except as provided in subsection (h)(5) and in regulations, the net operating loss shall, for purposes of subparagraph (B), be allocated ratably to each day in the year.

(2)   *Post-change year.*—The term "post-change" means any taxable year ending after the change date.

(e)   *Value of Old Loss Corporation.*—For purposes of this section—

(1)   *In general.*—Except as otherwise provided in this subsection, the value of the old loss corporation is the value of the stock of such corporation (including any stock described in section 1504(a)(4)) immediately before the ownership change.

(2)   *Special rule in the case of redemption.*—If a redemption occurs in connection with an ownership change, the value under paragraph (1) shall be determined after taking such redemption into account.

(f)   *Long-Term Tax-Exempt Rate.*—For purposes of this section—

(1)   *In general.*—The long-term tax-exempt rate shall be the highest of the adjusted Federal long-term rates in effect for any month in the 3-calendar-month period ending with the calendar month in which the change date occurs.

(2)   *Adjusted federal long-term rate.*—For purposes of paragraph (1), the term "adjusted Federal long-term rate" means the Federal long-term rate determined under section 1274(d), except that—
    (A)   paragraphs (2) and (3) thereof shall not apply, and
    (B)   such rate shall be properly adjusted for differences between rates on long-term taxable and tax-exempt obligations.

(g)   **Ownership Change.**—For purposes of this section—

(1)   *In general.*—There is an ownership change if, immediately after any owner shift involving a 5-percent shareholder or any equity structure shift—

[Footnote ¶2991 continued]

by such person at the beginning of the first or second preceding taxable year. Other rules relating to the manner and extent of successive applications of this section in the case of increases in ownership and transfers of stock by the persons described in paragraph (4)(B) shall be prescribed by regulations issued by the Secretary.

(b)   **Reorganizations.—**

(1)   **In general.—**If one corporation acquires the stock or assets of another corporation in a reorganization described in subparagraph (A), (B), (C), or (F) of section 368(a)(1) or subparagraph (D) or (G) of section 368(a)(1) (but only if the requirements of section 354(b)(1) are met), and if—

(A)   the acquiring or acquired corporation has a net operating loss for the taxable year which includes the date of the acquisition, or a net operating loss carryover from a prior taxable year to such taxable year, and

(B)   the shareholders (immediately before the reorganization) of such corporation (the "loss corporation"), as the result of owning stock of the loss corporation, own (immediately after the reorganization) less than 40 percent of the total fair market value of the participating stock or of all the stock of the acquiring corporation,

then the net operating loss carryover (if any) of the loss corporation from the taxable year which includes the date of the acquisition, and the net operating loss carryovers (if any) of the loss corporation from prior taxable years to such taxable year and subsequent taxable years, shall be reduced by the percentage determined under paragraph (2).

(2)   **Reduction of net operating loss carryover.—**

(A)   Ownership of 20 percent or more.—If such shareholders own less than 40 percent, but not less than 20 percent, of the total fair market value of the participating stock or of all the stock of the acquiring corporation, the reduction applicable under paragraph (1) shall be the percentage equal to the number of percentage points (including fractions thereof) less than 40 percent, multiplied by three and one-half.

(B)   Ownership of less than 20 percent.—If such shareholders own less than 20 percent of the total fair market value of the participating stock or of all the stock of the acquiring corporation, the reduction applicable under paragraph (1) shall be the sum of—

(i)   the percentage that would be determined under subparagraph (A) of the shareholders owned 20 percent of such stock, plus

(ii)   the percentage equal to the number of percentage points (including fractions thereof) of such stock less than

    (A) the percentage of the stock of the new loss corporation owned by 1 or more 5-percent shareholders has increased by more than 50 percentage points, over

    (B) the lowest percentage of stock of the old loss corporation (or any predecessor corporation) owned by such shareholders at any time during the testing period.

    (2) *Owner shift involving 5-percent shareholder.*—There is an owner shift involving a 5-percent shareholder if—

    (A) there is any change in the respective ownership of stock of a corporation, and

    (B) such change affects the percentage of stock of such corporation owned by any person who is a 5-percent shareholder before or after such change.

    (3) *Equity structure shift defined.*—

    (A) *In general.*—The term "equity structure shift" means any reorganization (within the meaning of section 368). Such term shall not include—

        (i) any reorganization described in subparagraph (D) or (G) of section 368(a)(1) unless the requirements of section 354(b)(1) are met, and

        (ii) any reorganization described in subparagraph (F) of section 368(a)(1)

    (B) *Taxable reorganization-type transactions, etc.*—To the extent provided in regulations, the term "equity structure shift" includes taxable reorganization-type transactions, public offerings, and similar transactions.

    (4) *Special rules for application of subsection.*—

    (A) *Treatment of less than 5-percent shareholders.*—Except as provided in subparagraphs (B)(i) and (C), in determining whether an ownership change has occurred, all stock owned by shareholders of a corporation who are not 5-percent shareholders of such corporation shall be treated as stock owned by 1 5-percent shareholder of such corporation.

    (B) *Coordination with equity structure shifts.*—For purposes of determining whether an equity structure shift (or subsequent transaction) is an ownership change—

        (i) *Less than 5-percent shareholders.*—Subparagraph (A) shall be applied separately with respect to each group of shareholders (immediately before such equity structure shift) of each corporation which was a party to the reorganization involved in such equity structure shift.

        (ii) *Acquisitions of stock.*—Unless a different proportion is established, acquisitions of stock after such equity structure shift shall be treated as being made proportionately from all shareholders immediately before such acquisition.

    (C) *Coordination with other owner shifts.*—Except as provided in regulations, the rules of subparagraph (B) shall apply in determining whether there has been an owner shift involving a 5-percent shareholder and whether such shift (or subsequent transaction) results in an ownership change.

〔Footnote ¶2991 continued〕

20 percent, multiplied by one and one-half.

The reduction under this paragraph shall be determined by reference to the lesser of the percentage of the total fair market value of the participating stock or of all the stock of the acquiring corporation owned by such shareholders.

  (3) **Losses of controlled corporations.**—For purposes of this subsection—

  (A) Holding companies.—If, immediately before the reorganization, the acquiring or acquired corporation controls a corporation which has a net operating loss for the taxable year which includes the date of the acquisition, or a net operating loss carryover from a prior taxable year to such taxable year, the acquiring or acquired corporation, as the case may be, shall be treated as the loss corporation (whether or not such corporation is a loss corporation). The reduction, if any, so determined under paragraph (2) shall be applied to the losses of such controlled corporation.

  (B) Triangular reorganizations.—Except as otherwise provided in paragraph (5), if the shareholders of the loss corporation (immediately before the reorganization) own, as a result of the reorganization, stock in a corporation controlling the acquiring corporation, such shareholders shall be treated as owning (immediately after the reorganization) a percentage of the total fair market value of the participating stock and of all the stock of the acquiring corporation owned by the controlling corporation equal to the percentage of the total fair market value of the participating stock and of all the stock, respectively, of the controlling corporation owned by such shareholders.

  (4) **Special rules.**—For purposes of applying paragraph (1)(B)—

  (A) Certain related transactions.—If, immediately before the reorganization—

  (i) one or more shareholders of the loss corporation own stock of such corporation which such shareholder acquired during the 36-month period ending on the date of the acquisition in a transaction described in paragraph (1) or in subsection (a)(1)(C) (unless excepted by subsection (a)(5)), and

  (ii) such shareholders own more than 50 percent of the total fair market value of the stock of another corporation a party to the reorganization, or any such shareholder is a corporation controlled by another corporation a party to the reorganization,

then such shareholders shall not be treated as shareholders of the loss corporation with respect to such stock.

Code §382(g)(4) ¶2991

(h) Special Rules for Built-In Gains and Losses and Section 338 Gains.—For purposes of this section—

    (1) In general.—

        (A) Net unrealized built-in gain.—

            (i) In general.—If the old loss corporation has a net unrealized built-in gain, the section 382 limitation for any recognition period taxable year shall be increased by the recognized built-in gains for such taxable year.

            (ii) Limitation.—The increase under clause (i) for any recognition period taxable year shall not exceed—

                (I) the net unrealized built-in gain, reduced by

                (II) recognized built-in gains for prior years ending in the recognition period.

        (B) Net unrealized built-in loss.—

            (i) In general.—If the old loss corporation has a net unrealized built-in loss, the recognized built-in loss for any recognition period taxable year shall be subject to limitation under this section in the same manner as if such loss were a pre-change loss.

            (ii) Limitation.—Clause (i) shall apply to recognized built-in losses for any recognition period taxable year only to the extent such losses do not exceed—

                (I) the net unrealized built-in loss, reduced by

                (II) recognized built-in losses for prior taxable years ending in the recognition period.

        (C) Section 338 gain.—The section 382 limitation for any taxable year in which gain is recognized by reason of an election under section 338 shall be increased by the excess of—

            (i) the amount of such gain, over

            (ii) the portion of such gain taken into account in computing recognized built-in gains for such taxable year.

    (2) Recognized built-in gain and loss.—

        (A) Recognized built-in gain.—The term "recognized built-in gain" means any gain recognized during the recognition period on the disposition of any asset to the extent the new loss corporation establishes that—

            (i) such asset was held by the old loss corporation immediately before the change date, and

            (ii) such gain does not exceed the excess of—

                (I) the fair market value of such asset on the change date over

                (II) the adjusted basis of such asset on such date.

        (B) Recognized built-in loss.—The term "recognized built-in loss" means any loss recognized during the recognition period on the disposition of any asset except to the extent the new loss corporation establishes that—

〖Footnote ¶2991 continued〗

(B)   Certain prior ownership of loss corporation.—If, immediately before the reorganization, the acquiring or acquired corporation owns stock of the loss corporation, then paragraph (1)(B) shall be applied by treating the shareholders of the loss corporation as owning an additional amount of the total fair market value of the participating stock and of all the stock of the acquiring corporation, as a result of owning stock in the loss corporation, equal to the total fair market value of the participating stock and of all the stock of the loss corporation, respectively, owned (immediately before the reorganization) by the acquiring or acquired corporation. This subparagraph shall not apply to stock of the loss corporation owned by the acquiring or acquired corporation if such stock was acquired by such corporation within the 36-month period ending on the date of the reorganization in a transaction described in subsection (a)(1)(C) (unless excepted by subsection (a)(5)); or to a reorganization described in section 368(a)(1)(B) or (C) to the extent the acquired corporation does not distribute the stock received by it to its own shareholders.

(C)   Certain asset acquisitions.—If a loss corporation receives stock of the acquiring corporation in a reorganization described in section 368(a)(1)(C) and does not distribute such stock to its shareholders, paragraph (1)(B) shall be applied by treating the shareholders of the loss corporation as owning (immediately after the reorganization) such undistributed stock in proportion to the fair market value of the stock which such shareholders own in the loss corporation.

(5)   Certain stock-for-stock reorganizations.—In the case of a reorganization described in section 368(a)(1)(B) in which the acquired corporation is a loss corporation—

(A)   Stock which is exchanged.—Paragraphs (1)(B) and (2) shall be applied by reference to the ownership of stock of the loss corporation (rather than the acquiring corporation) immediately after the reorganization. Shareholders of the loss corporation who exchange stock of the loss corporation shall be treated as owning (immediately after the reorganization) a percentage of the total fair market value of the participating stock and of all the stock of the loss corporation acquired in the exchange by the acquiring corporation which is equal to the percentage of the total fair market value of the participating stock and of all the stock, respectively, of the acquiring corporation owned (immediately after the reorganization) by such shareholders.

(B)   Stock which is not exchanged.—Stock of the loss corporation owned by shareholders immediately before

(i)   such asset was not held by the old loss corporation immediately before the change date, or

(ii)   such loss exceeds the excess of—

(I)   the adjusted basis of such asset on the change date, over

(II)   the fair market value of such asset on such date.

(3)   *Net unrealized built-in gain and loss defined.*—

(A)   *Net unrealized built-in gain and loss.*—

(i)   *In general.*—The terms "net unrealized built-in gain" and "net unrealized built-in loss" mean, with respect to any old loss corporation, the amount by which—

(I)   the fair market value of the assets of such corporation immediately before an ownership change is more or less, respectively, than

(II)   the aggregate adjusted basis of such assets at such time.

(ii)   *Special rule for redemptions.*—If a redemption occurs in connection with an ownership change, determinations under clause (i) shall be made after taking such redemption into account.

(B)   *Threshold requirement.*—

(i)   If the amount of the net unrealized built-in gain or net unrealized built-in loss (determined without regard to this subparagraph) of any old loss corporation is not greater than 25 percent of the amount determined for purposes of subparagraph (A)(i)(I), the net unrealized built-in gain or net unrealized built-in loss shall be zero.

(ii)   *Cash and cash items not taken into account.*—In computing any net unrealized built-in gain or net unrealized built-in loss under clause (i), there shall not be taken into account—

(I)   any cash or cash item, or

(II)   any marketable security which has a value which does not substantially differ from adjusted basis.

(4)   *Disallowed loss treated as a net operating loss.*—If a deduction for any portion of a recognized built-in loss is disallowed for any post-change year, such portion—

(A)   shall be carried forward to subsequent taxable years under rules similar to the rules for the carrying forward of net operating losses, but

(B)   shall be subject to limitation under this section in the same manner as a pre-change loss.

(5)   *Special rules for post-change year which includes change date.*—For purposes of subsection (b)(3)—

(A)   in applying subparagraph (A) thereof, taxable income shall be computed without regard to recognized built-in gains and losses, and gain described in paragraph

---

⟦Footnote ¶2991 continued⟧

the reorganization which was not exchanged in the reorganization shall be taken into account in applying paragraph (1)(B). For purposes of the preceding sentence, the acquiring corporation (or a corporation controlled by the acquiring corporation) shall not be treated as a shareholder of the loss corporation with respect to stock of the loss corporation acquired in a transaction described in paragraph (1), or in subsection (a)(1)(C) (unless excepted by subsection (a)(5)), during the 36-month period ending on the date of the exchange.

(C)   Triangular exchanges.—For purposes of applying the rules in this paragraph, if the shareholders of the loss corporation receive stock of a corporation controlling the acquiring corporation, such shareholders shall be treated as owning a percentage of the participating stock and of all the stock of the acquiring corporation owned by the controlling corporation equal to the percentage of the total fair market value of the participating stock and of all the stock, respectively, which such shareholders own of the controlling corporation immediately after the reorganization.

(6)   Exceptions.—The limitations in this subsection shall not apply—

(A)   if the same persons own substantially all the stock of the acquiring corporation and of the other corporation in substantially the same proportions; or

(B)   to a net operating loss carryover from a taxable year if the acquiring or acquired corporation owned at least 40 percent of the total fair market value of the participating stock and of all the stock of the loss corporation at all times during the last half of such taxable year.

for purposes of subparagraph (A), if the acquiring or acquired corporation is controlled by another corporation, the shareholders of the controlling corporation shall be considered as also owning the stock owned by the controlling corporation in that proportion which the total fair market value of the stock which each shareholder owns in the controlling corporation bears to the total fair market value of all the stock in the controlling corporation.

(c)   Rules Relating to Stock.—For purposes of this section—

(1)(C), for the year, and

(B)   in applying subparagraph (B) thereof, the section 382 limitation shall be computed without regard to recognized built-in gains, and gain described in paragraph (1)(C), for the year.

(6)   Secretary may treat certain deductions as built-in losses.—The Secretary may by regulation treat amounts which accrue on or before the change date but which are allowable as a deduction after such date as recognized built-in losses.

(7)   Recognition period, etc.—

(A)   Recognition period.—The term "recognition period" means, with respect to any ownership change, the 5-year period beginning on the change date.

(B)   Recognition period taxable year.—The term "recognition period taxable year" means any taxable year any portion of which is in the recognition period.

(8)   Determination of fair market value in certain cases.—If 80 percent or more in value of the stock of a corporation is acquired in 1 transaction (or in a series of related transactions during any 12-month period), for purposes of determining the net unrealized built-in-loss, the fair market value of the assets of such corporation shall not exceed the grossed up amount paid for such stock properly adjusted for indebtedness of the corporation and other relevant items.

(9)   Tax-free exchanges or transfers.—The Secretary shall prescribe such regulations as may be necessary to carry out the purposes of this subsection where property held on the change date is transferred in a transaction where gain or loss is not recognized (in whole or in part).

(i)   Testing Period.—For purposes of this section—

(1)   3-year period.—Except as otherwise provided in this section, the testing period is the 3-year period ending on the day of any owner shift involving a 5-percent shareholder or equity structure shift.

(2)   Shorter period where there has been recent ownership change.—If there has been an ownership change under this section, the testing period for determining whether a 2nd ownership change has occurred shall not begin before the 1st day following the change date for such earlier ownership change.

(3)   Shorter period where all losses arise after 3-year period begins.—The testing period shall not begin before the 1st day of the 1st taxable year from which there is a carryforward of a loss or of an excess credit to the 1st post-change year. Except as provided in regulations, this paragraph shall not apply to any loss corporation which has a net unrealized built-in loss (determined after application of subsection (h)(3)(B)).

(j)   Change Date.—For purposes of this section, the change date is—

(1)   in the case where the last component of an ownership change is an owner shift involving a 5-percent shareholder, the date on which such shift occurs, and

(2)   in the case where the last component of an ownership change is an equity structure shift, the date of the reorganization.

(k)   Definitions and Special Rules.—For purposes of this section—

⌊Footnote ¶2991 continued⌋

(1)   The term "stock" means all shares of stock, except stock which—

(A)   is not entitled to vote,

(B)   is fixed and preferred as to dividends and does not participate in corporate growth to any significant extent,

(C)   has redemption and liquidation rights which do not exceed the paid-in capital or par value represented by such stock (except for a reasonable redemption premium in excess of such paid-in capital or par value), and

(D)   is not convertible into another class of stock.

(2)   The term "participating stock" means stock (including common stock) which represents an interest in the earnings and assets of the issuing corporation which is not limited to a stated amount of money or property or percentage of paid-in capital or par value, or by any similar formula.

(3)   The Secretary shall prescribe regulations under which—

(A)   stock or convertible securities shall be treated as stock or participating stock, or

(B)   stock (however denoted) shall not be treated as stock or participating stock,

by reason of conversion and call rights, rights in earnings and assets, priorities and preferences as to distributions of earnings or assets, and similar factors."

Effective date (Sec. 621(f), '86 TRA).—Generally applies to any ownership change following—

(A)   an owner shift involving a 5-percent shareholder occurring after 12-31-86, or

(B)   an equity structure shift occurring pursuant to a plan of reorganization adopted after December 31, 1986.

For transitional and special rules, see ¶2022.

(1) *Loss corporation.*—The term "loss corporation" means a corporation entitled to use a net operating loss carryover. Except to the extent provided in regulations, such term includes any corporation with a net unrealized built-in loss.

(2) *Old loss corporation.*—The term "old loss corporation" means any corporation with respect to which there is an ownership change—
  (A) which (before the ownership change) was a loss corporation, or
  (B) with respect to which there is a pre-change loss described in subsection (d)(1)(B).

(3) *New loss corporation.*—The term "new loss corporation" means a corporation which (after an ownership change) is a loss corporation. Nothing in this section shall be treated as implying that the same corporation may not be both the old loss corporation and the new loss corporation.

(4) *Taxable income.*—Taxable income shall be computed with the modifications set forth in section 172(d).

(5) *Value.*—The term "value" means fair market value.

(6) *Rules relating to stock.*—
  (A) *Preferred stock.*—Except as provided in regulations and subsection (e), the term "stock" means stock other than stock described in section 1504(a)(4).
  (B) *Treatment of certain rights, etc.*—The Secretary shall prescribe such regulations as may be necessary—
    (i) to treat warrants, options, contracts to acquire stock, convertible debt interests, and other similar interests as stock, and
    (ii) to treat stock as not stock.
  (C) *Determinations on basis of value.*—Determinations of the percentage of stock of any corporation held by any person shall be made on the basis of value.

(7) *5-percent shareholder.*—The term "5-percent shareholder" means any person holding 5 percent or more of the stock of the corporation at any time during the testing period.

(l) *Certain Additional Operating Rules.*—For purposes of this section—

  (1) *Certain capital contributions not taken into account.*—
    (A) *In general.*—Any capital contribution received by an old loss corporation as part of a plan a principal purpose of which is to avoid or increase any limitation under this section shall not be taken into account for purposes of this section.
    (B) *Certain contributions treated as part of plan.*—For purposes of subparagraph (A), any capital contribution made during the 2-year period ending on the change date shall, except as provided in regulations, be treated as part of a plan described in subparagraph (A).

  (2) *Ordering rules for application of section.*—
    (A) *Coordination with section 172(b) carryover rules.*—In the case of any pre-change loss for any taxable year (hereinafter in this subparagraph referred to as the "loss year") subject to limitation under this section, for purposes of determining under the 2nd sentence of section 172(b)(2) the amount of such loss which may be carried to any taxable year, taxable income for any taxable year shall be treated as not greater than—
      (i) the section 382 limitation for such taxable year, reduced by
      (ii) the unused pre-change losses for taxable years preceding the loss year.
  Similar rules shall apply in the case of any credit or loss subject to limitation under section 383.
    (B) *Ordering rule for losses carried from same taxable year.*—In any case in which—
      (i) a pre-change loss of a loss corporation for any taxable year is subject to a section 382 limitation, and
      (ii) a net operating loss of such corporation from such taxable year is not subject to such limitation,
  taxable income shall be treated as having been offset first by the loss subject to such limitation.

  (3) *Operating rules relating to ownership of stock.*—
    (A) *Constructive ownership.*—Section 318 (relating to constructive ownership of stock) shall apply in determining ownership of stock, except that—

(i) paragraphs (1) and (5)(B) of section 318(a) shall not apply and an individual and all members of his family described in paragraph (1) of section 318(a) shall be treated as 1 individual for purposes of applying this section,

(ii) paragraph (2) of section 318(a) shall be applied—

(I) without regard to the 50-percent limitation contained in subparagraph (C) thereof, and

(II) except as provided in regulations, by treating stock attributed thereunder as no longer being held by the entity from which attributed,

(iii) paragraph (3) of section 318(a) shall be applied only to the extent provided in regulations, and

(iv) except to the extent provided in regulations, paragraph (4) of section 318(a) shall apply to an option if such application results in an ownership change.

A rule similar to the rule of clause (iv) shall apply in the case of any contingent purchase, warrant, convertible debt, put, stock subject to a risk of forfeiture, contract to acquire stock, or similar interests.

(B) *Stock acquired by reason of death, gift, divorce, separation, etc.*—If—

(i) the basis of any stock in the hands of any person is determined—

(I) under section 1014 (relating to property acquired from a decedent),

(II) section 1015 (relating to property acquired by a gift or transfer in trust), or

(III) section 1041(b)(2) (relating to transfers of property between spouses or incident to divorce,

(ii) stock is received by any person in satisfaction of a right to receive a pecuniary bequest, or

(iii) stock is acquired by a person pursuant to any divorce or separation instrument (within the meaning of section 71(b)(2)),

such person shall be treated as owning such stock during the period such stock was owned by the person from whom it was acquired.

(C) *Special rule for employee stock ownership plans.*—

(i) *In general.*—Except as provided in clause (ii), the acquisition of employer securities (within the meaning of section 409(l)) by—

(I) a tax credit employee stock ownership plan or an employee stock ownership plan (within the meaning of section 4975(e)(7)), or

(II) a participant of any such plan pursuant to the requirements of section 409(h),

shall not be taken into account in determining whether an ownership change has occurred.

(ii) *Ownership and allocation requirements.*—Subclause (I) of clause (i) shall not apply to any acquisition unless—

(I) immediately after such acquisition the plan holds stock meeting the requirements of section 1042(b)(2), except that such section shall be applied by substituting "50 percent" for "30 percent", and

(II) the plan meets requirements similar to the requirements of section 409(n).

(D) *Certain changes in percentage ownership which are attributable to fluctuations in value not taken into account.*—Except as provided in regulations, any change in proportionate ownership which is attributable solely to fluctuations in the relative fair market values of different classes of stock shall not be taken into account.

(4) *Reduction in value where substantial nonbusiness assets.*—

(A) *In general.*—If, immediately after an ownership change, the new loss corporation has substantial nonbusiness assets, the value of the old loss corporation shall be reduced by the excess (if any) of—

(i) the fair market value of the nonbusiness assets of the old loss corporation, over

(ii) the nonbusiness asset share of indebtedness for which such corporation is liable.

(B) *Corporation having substantial nonbusiness assets.*—For purposes of subparagraph (A)—

(i) *In general.*—The old loss corporation shall be treated as having substantial nonbusiness assets if at least $\frac{1}{3}$ of the value of the total assets of such corporation consists of nonbusiness assets.

(ii) *Exception for certain investment entities.*—A regulated investment company to which part I of subchapter M applies, a real estate investment trust to which part II of subchapter M applies, or a real estate mortgage pool to which part IV of subchapter M applies, shall not be treated as a new loss corporation having substantial nonbusiness assets.

(C) *Nonbusiness assets.*—For purposes of this paragraph, the term "nonbusiness assets" means assets held for investment.

(D) *Nonbusiness asset share.*—For purposes of this paragraph, the nonbusiness asset share of the indebtedness of the corporation is an amount which bears the same ratio to such indebtedness as—

   (i)   the fair market value of the nonbusiness assets of the corporation, bears to

   (ii)   the fair market value of all assets of such corporation.

(E) *Treatment of subsidiaries.*—For purposes of this paragraph, stock and securities in any subsidiary corporation shall be disregarded and the parent corporation shall be deemed to own its ratable share of the subsidiary's assets. For purposes of the preceding sentence, a corporation shall be treated as a subsidiary if the parent owns 50 percent or more of the combined voting power of all classes of stock entitled to vote, and 50 percent or more of the total value of shares of all classes of stock.

(5)   *Title 11 or similar case.*—

   (A)   *In general.*—Subsection (a) shall not apply to any ownership change if—

      (i)   the old loss corporation is (immediately before such ownership change) under the jurisdiction of the court in a title 11 or similar case, and

      (ii)   the shareholders and creditors of the old loss corporation (determined immediately before such ownership change) own (immediately after such ownership change) stock of the new loss corporation (or stock of controlling corporation if also in bankruptcy) which meets the requirements of section 1504(a)(2) (determined by substituting "50 percent" for "80 percent" each place it appears).

   (B)   *Reduction for interest payments to creditors becoming shareholders.*—In any case to which subparagraph (A) applies, the net operating loss deduction under section 172(a) for any post-change year shall be determined as if no deduction was allowable under this chapter for the interest paid or accrued by the old loss corporation on indebtedness which was converted into stock pursuant to title 11 or similar case during—

      (i)   any taxable year ending during the 3-year period preceding the taxable year in which the ownership change occurs, and

      (ii)   the period of the taxable year in which the ownership change occurs on or before the change date.

   (C)   *Reduction of carryforwards where discharge of indebtedness.*—In any case to which subparagraph (A) applies, the pre-change losses and excess credits (within the meaning of section 383(a)(2)) which may be carried to a post-change year shall be computed as if 50 percent of the amount which, but for the application of section 108(e)(10)(B), would have been includible in gross income for any taxable year had been so included.

   (D)   *Section 382 limitation zero if another change within 2 years.*—If, during the 2-year period immediately following an ownership change to which this paragraph applies, an ownership change of the new loss corporation occurs, this paragraph shall not apply and the section 382 limitation with respect to the 2nd ownership change for any post-change year ending after the change date of the 2nd ownership change shall be zero.

   (E)   *Only certain stock of creditors taken into account.*—For purposes of subparagraph (A)(ii), stock transferred to a creditor in satisfaction of indebtedness shall be taken into account only if such indebtedness—

      (i)   was held by the creditor at least 18 months before the date of the filing of the title 11 or similar case, or

      (ii)   arose in the ordinary course of the trade or business of the old loss corporation and is held by the person who at all times held the beneficial interest in such indebtedness.

   (F)   *Special rule for certain financial institutions.*—

      (i)   *In general.*—In the case of any ownership change to which this subparagraph applies, this paragraph shall be applied—

         (I)   by substituting "20 percent" for "50 percent" in subparagraph (A)(ii), and

         (II)   without regard to subparagraphs (B) and (C).

    (ii) Special rule for depositors.—For purposes of applying this paragraph to an ownership change to which this subparagraph applies—

       (I) a depositor in the old loss corporation shall be treated as a stockholder in such loss corporation immediately before the change,

       (II) deposits which, after the change, become deposits of the new loss corporaton shall be treated as stock of the new loss corporation, and

       (III) the fair market value of the outstanding stock of the new loss corporation shall include deposits described in subclause (II).

    (iii) Changes to whch subparagraph applies.—

   This subparagraph shall apply to—

       (I) an equity structure shift which is a reorganization described in section 368(a)(3)(D)(ii), or

       (II) any other equity structure shift (or transaction to which section 351 applies) which occurs as an integral part of a transaction involving a change to which subclause (I) applies.

   This subparagraph shall not apply to any equity structure shift or transaction occurring after December 31, 1988.

    (G) Title 11 or similar case.—For purposes of this paragraph, the term "title 11 or similar case" has the meaning given such term by section 368(a)(3)(A).

    (H) Election not to have paragraph apply.—A new loss corporation may elect, subject to such terms and conditions as the Secretary may prescribe, not to have the provisions of this paragraph apply.

   (6) Special rule for insolvency transactions.—*If paragraph (5) does not apply to any reorganization described in subparagraph (G) of section 368(a)(1) or any exchange of debt for stock in a title 11 or similar case (as defined in section 368(a)(3)(A)), the value under subsection (e) shall be the value of the new loss corporation immediately after the ownership change.*

   (7) Coordination with alternative minimum tax.—*The Secretary shall be regulation provide for the application of this section to the alternative tax net operating loss deduction under section 56(d).*

   (m) Regulations.—*The Secretary shall prescribe such regulations as may be necessary or appropriate to carry out the purposes of this section and section 383, including (but not limited to) regulations—*

    (1) providing for the application of this section and section 383 where an ownership change with respect to the old loss corporation is followed by an ownership change with respect to the new loss corporation, and

    (2) providing for the application of this section and section 383 in the case of a short taxable year,

    (3) providing for such adjustments to the application of this section and section 383 as is necessary to prevent the avoidance of the purposes of this section and section 383, including the avoidance of such purposes through the use of related persons, pass-thru entities, or other intermediaries.

    (4) providing for the treatment of corporate contractions as redemptions for purposes of subsections (e)(2) and (h)(3)(A), and

    (5) providing for the application of subsection (g)(4) where there is only 1 corporation involved.

[For official explanation, see Committee Reports, ¶3916.]

〔¶2992〕 CODE SEC. 383. SPECIAL LIMITATIONS ON [1]CERTAIN EXCESS CREDITS, ETC.

   (a) Excess Credits.—

〔Footnote ¶2992〕   Matter in *italics* in Sec. 383 added by section 621(b), '86 TRA, which struck out:

(1) "SPECIAL LIMITATIONS ON UNUSED BUSINESS CREDITS, RESEARCH CREDITS, FOREIGN TAXES AND CAPITAL LOSSES.

   In the case of a change of ownership of a corporation in the manner described in section 382(a) or (b), the limitations provided in section 382 in such cases with respect to net operating losses shall apply in the same manner, as provided under regulations prescribed by the Secretary, with respect to any unused, business credit of the corporation under section 39, to any unused credit of the corporation under section 30(g)(2), to any excess foreign taxes of the corporation under section 904(c), and to any net capital loss of the corporation under section 1212."

Effective date (Sec. 621(f), '86 TRA).—(1) Generally applies to any ownership change following—

(A)   an owner shift involving a 5-percent shareholder occurring after 12-31-86, or

(B)   an equity structure shift occuring pursuant to a plan of reorganization adopted after 12-31-86.

For special rules, see ¶2022.

(1) *In General.—Under regulations, if an ownership change occurs with respect to a corporation, the amount of any excess credit for any taxable year which may be used in any post-change year shall be limited to an amount determined on the basis of the tax liability which is attributable to so much of the taxable income as does not exceed the section 382 limitation for such post-change year to the extent available after the application of section 382 and subsections (b) and (c) of this section.*

(2) *Excess Credit.—For purposes of paragraph (1), the term "excess credit" means—*
 (A) *any unused general business credit of the corporation under section 39, and*
 (B) *any unused minimum tax credit of the corporation under section 53.*

(b) *Limitation on Net Capital Loss.—If an ownership change occurs with respect to a corporation, the amount of any net capital loss under section 1212 for any taxable year before the 1st post-change year shall be limited under regulations which shall be based on the principles applicable under section 382. Such regulations shall provide that any such net capital loss used in a post-change year shall reduce the section 382 limitation which is applied to pre-change losses under section 382 for such year.*

(c) *Foreign Tax Credits.—If an ownership change occurs with respect to a corporation, the amount of any excess foreign taxes under section 904(c) for any taxable year before the 1st post-change taxable year shall be limited under regulations which shall be consistent with purposes of this section and section 382.*

(d) *Pro Ration Rules for Year Which Includes Change.—For purposes of this section, rules similar to the rules of subsections (b)(3) and (d)(1)(B) of section 382 shall apply.*

(e) *Definitions.—Terms used in this section shall have the same respective meanings as when used in section 382, except that appropriate adjustments shall be made to take into account that the limitations of this section apply to credits and net capital losses.*

[For official explanation, see Committee Reports, ¶3916.]

[¶2993] CODE SEC. 386. TRANSFERS OF PARTNERSHIPS AND TRUST INTERESTS BY CORPORATIONS.

* * * * * * * * * * * *

(d) *Limitation on Amount of Gain Recognized in Case of Non-Liquidating Distributions.—In the case of any distribution by a corporation to which section 311 applies, the amount of any gain recognized by reason of subsection (a) shall not exceed the amount of the gain which would have been recognized if the partnership interest had been sold. The Secretary may by regulations provide that the amount of such gain shall be computed without regard to any loss attributable to property contributed to the partnership for the principal purpose of recognizing such loss on the distribution.*

[1](e) **Extension To Trust.**—Under regulations, rules similar to the rules of this section shall also apply in the case of the distribution or sale or exchange by a corporation of an interest in a trust.

[For official explanation, see Committee Reports, ¶4139.]

[¶2994] CODE SEC. 401. QUALIFIED PENSION, PROFIT-SHARING, AND STOCK BONUS PLANS.

(a) **Requirements for Qualification.**—A trust created or organized in the United States and forming part of a stock bonus, pension, or profit-sharing plan of an employer for the exclusive benefit of his employees or their beneficiaries shall constitute a qualified trust under this section—

(1) if contributions are made to the trust by such employer, or employees, or both, or by another employer who is entitled to deduct his contributions, under section 404(a)(3)(B) (relating to deduction for contributions to profit-sharing and stock bonus plans), for the purpose of distributing to such employees or their beneficiaries the corpus and income of the fund accumulated by the trust in accordance with such plan;

(2) if under the trust instrument it is impossible, at any time prior to the satisfaction of all liabilities with respect to employees and their beneficiaries under the trust, for any part of the corpus or income to be (within the taxable year or thereafter) used for, or diverted to, purposes other than for the exclusive benefit of his employees or

---

[Footnote ¶2993] Matter in *italics* in Sec. 386(d) and (e) added by section 1805(c)(1), '86 TRA, which struck out:

(1) "(d)"

Effective date (Sec. 1581, '86 TRA and section 75(e), '84 TRA).—Applies to distributions, sales, and exchanges made after 3-31-84, in taxable years ending after such date.

their beneficiaries; (but this paragraph shall not be construed, in the case of a multiemployer plan, to prohibit the return of a contribution within 6 months after the plan administrator determines that the contribution was made by a mistake of fact of law (other than a mistake relating to whether the plan is described in section 401(a) or the trust which is part of such plan is exempt from taxation under section 501(a), or the return of any withdrawal liability payment determined to be an overpayment within 6 months of such determination);

(3) if the plan of which such trust is a part satisfies the requirements of section 410 (relating to minimum participation standards); and

[1](4) *if the contributions or benefits provided under the plan do not discriminate in favor of highly compensated employees (within the meaning of section 414(q)). For purposes of this paragraph, there shall be excluded from consideration employees described in section 410(b)(3)(A) and (C).*

[2](5) *Special rules relating to nondiscrimination requirements.—*

    (A) Salaried or clerical employees.—A classification shall not be considered discriminatory within the meaning of paragraph (4) or section 410(b)(2)(A)(i) merely because it is limited to salaried or clerical employees.

    (B) Contributions and benefits may bear uniform relationship to compensation.— A plan shall not be considered discriminatory within the meaning of paragraph (4) merely because the contributions or benefits of, or on behalf of, the employees under

---

⟦**Footnote ¶2994**⟧   Matter in *italics* in Sec. 401(a)(4) added by section 1114(b)(7), '86 TRA, which struck out:

(1)   "(4) if the contributions or the benefits provided under the plan do not discriminate in favor of employees who are—

(A)   officers,

(B)   shareholders, or

(C)   highly compensated.

For purposes of this paragraph, there shall be excluded from consideration employees described in section 410(b)(3)(A) and (C)."

Effective date (Sec. 1114(c)(3), '86 TRA).—Applies to years beginning after 12-31-88.

Matter in *italics* in Sec. 401(a)(5) added by section 1111(b), '86 TRA, which struck out:

(2)   "(5) A classification shall not be considered discriminatory within the meaning of paragraph (4) or section 510(b) (without regard to paragraph (1)(A) thereof) merely because it excludes employees the whole of whose remuneration constitutes "wages" under section 3121(a)(1) (relating to the Federal Insurance Contributions Act) or merely because it is limited to salaried or clerical employees. Neither shall a plan be considered discriminatory within the meaning of such provisions merely because the contributions or benefits of or on behalf of the employees under the plan bear a uniform relationship to the total compensation, or the basic or regular rate of compensation, of such employees, or merely because the contributions or benefits based on that part of an employee's remuneration which is excluded from 'wages' by section 3121(a)(1) differ from the contributions of benefits based on employee's remuneration not so excluded, or differ because of any retirement benefits created under State or Federal law. For purposes of this paragraph and paragraph (10), the total compensation of an individual who is an employee within the meaning of subsection (c)(1) means such individual's earned income (as defined in subsection (c)(2)), and the basic or regular rate of compensation of such an individual shall be determined, under regulations prescribed by the Secretary, with respect to that portion of his earned income which bears the same ratio to his earned income as the basic or regular compensation of the employees under the plan bears to the total compensation of such employees. For purposes of determining whether two or more plans of an employer satisfy the requirements of paragraph (4) when considered as a single plan, if the amount of contributions on behalf of the employees allowed as a deduction under section 404 for the taxable year with respect to such plan, taken together, bears a uniform relationship to the total compensation, or the basic or regular rate of compensation, of such employees, the plans shall not be considered discriminatory merely because the rights of employees to, or derived from, the employer contributions under the separate plans do not become nonforfeitable at the same rate. For the purposes of determining whether two or more plans of an employer satisfy the requirements of paragraph (4) when considered as a single plan, if the employees' rights to benefits under the separate plans do not become nonforfeitable at the same rate, but the levels of benefits provided by the separate plans satisfy the requirements of regulations prescribed by the Secretary to take account of the differences in such rates, the plans shall not be considered discriminatory merely because of the difference in such rates. For purposes of determining whether one or more plans of an employer satisfy the requirements of paragraph (4) and of section 410(b), an employer may take into account all simplified employee pensions to which only the employer contributes."

Effective date (Sec. 1111(c)(2) and (3), '86 TRA).—(2) Applies to years beginning after 12-31-88.

(3) Special rule for collective bargaining agreements.—In the case of a plan maintained pursuant to 1 or more collective bargaining agreements between employee representatives and 1 or more employers ratified before 3-1-86, the amendments made by this section shall not apply to benefits pursuant to, and individuals covered by, any such agreement in plan years beginning before the earlier of—

(A)   the later of—

(i)   1-1-89, or

(ii)   the date on which the last of such collective bargaining agreements terminates (determined without regard to any extension thereof after 2-28-86, or

(B)   1-1-91.

the plan bear a uniform relationship to the compensation (within the meaning of section 414(s)) of such employees.

(C) Certain disparity permitted.—A plan shall not be considered discriminatory within the meaning of paragraph (4) merely because the contributions or benefits of, or on behalf of, the employees under the plan favor highly compensated employees (as defined in section 414(q)) in the manner permitted under subsection (l).

(D) Integrated defined benefit plan.—

(i) In general.—A defined benefit plan shall not be considered discriminatory within the meaning of paragraph (4) merely because the plan provides that the employer-derived accrued retirement benefit for any participant under the plan may not exceed the excess (if any) of—

(I) the participant's final pay with the employer, over

(II) the employer-derived retirement benefit created under Federal law attributable to service by the participant with the employer.

For purposes of this clause, the employer-derived retirement benefit created under Federal law shall be treated as accruing ratably over 35 years.

(ii) Final pay.—For purposes of this subparagraph, the participant's final pay is the compensation (as defined in section 414(q)(7)) paid to the participant by the employer for any year—

(I) which ends during the 5-year period ending with the year in which the participant separated from service for the employer, and

(II) for which the participant's total compensation from the employer was highest.

(E) 2 or more plans treated as single plan.—For purposes of determining whether 2 or more plans of an employer satisfy the requirements of paragraph (4) when considered as a single plan—

(i) Contributions.—If the amount of contributions on behalf of the employees allowed as a deduction under section 404 for the taxable year with respect to such plans, taken together, bears a uniform relationship to the compensation (within the meaning of section 414(s)) of such employees, the plans shall not be considered discriminatory merely because the rights of employees to, or derived from, the employer contributions under the separate plans do not become nonforfeitable at the same rate.

(ii) Benefits.—If the employees' rights to benefits under the separate plans do not become nonforfeitable at the same rate, but the levels of benefits provided by the separate plans satisfy the requirements of regulations prescribed by the Secretary to take account of the differences in such rates, the plans shall not be considered discriminatory merely because of the difference in such rates.

(6) A plan shall be considered as meeting the requirements of paragraph (3) during the whole of any taxable year of the plan if on one day in each quarter it satisfied such requirements.

(7) A trust shall not constitute a qualified trust under this section unless the plan of which such trust is a part satisfies the requirements of section 411 (relating to minimum vesting standards).

(8) A trust forming part of a [3]*defined benefit plan* shall not constitute a qualified trust under this section unless the plan provides that forfeitures must not be applied to increase the benefits any employee would otherwise receive under the plan.

(9) Required distributions.—

* * * * * * * * * * * * *

≫**P-H CAUTION**→ There are two versions of Sec. 401(a)(9)(C). Sec. 401(a)(9)(C), generally effective after 12-31-88, follows. For Sec. 401(a)(9)(C), generally effective before 1-1-89, see below.

[4]▲ *(C) Required beginning date.—For purposes of this paragraph, the term*

⟦Footnote ¶2994 continued⟧

Matter in *italics* in Sec. 401(a)(8) added by section 1119(a), '86 TRA, which struck out:

(3) "pension plan"

Effective date (Sec. 1119(b), '86 TRA).—Applies to plan years beginning after 12-31-85.

▲ Matter in *italics* in Sec. 401(a)(9)(C), preceded by a triangle, added by section 1121(b), '86 TRA, which struck out:

(4) "(C) Required beginning date.—For purposes of this paragraph, the term "required beginning date" means April 1 of the calendar year following the later of—

(i) the calendar year in which the employee attains age 70½ or

"required beginning date" means April 1 of the calendar year following the calendar year in which the employee attains age 70½.

≫**P-H CAUTION→** There are two versions of Sec. 401(a)(9)(C). For Sec. 401(a)(9)(C), generally effective before 1-1-89, follows. For Sec. 401(a)(9)(C), generally effective after 12-31-88, see above.

▲▲ (C) Required beginning date.—For purposes of this paragraph, the term "required beginning date" means April 1 of the calendar year following the later of—

(i) the calendar year in which the employee attains age 70½ or

(ii) the calendar year in which the employee retires.

⁵Clause (ii) shall not apply in the case of an employee who is a 5-percent owner (as defined in section 416(i)(1)(B)) at any time during the 5-plan-year period ending in the

---

⟦Footnote ¶2994 continued⟧

▲ Matter in *italics* in Sec. 401(a)(9)(C), preceded by a triangle, added by section 1121(b), '86 TRA, which struck out:

(4) "(C) Required beginning date.—For purposes of this paragraph, the term "required beginning date" means April 1 of the calendar year following the later of—

(i) the calendar year in which the employee attains age 70½ or

(ii) the calendar year in which the employee retires.

Clause (ii) shall not apply in the case of an employee who is a 5-percent owner (as defined in section 416(i)(1)(B)) at any time during the 5-plan-year period ending in the calendar year in which the employee attains age 70½. If the employee becomes a 5-percent owner during any subsequent plan year, the required beginning date shall be April 1 of the calendar year following the calendar year in which such subsequent plan year ends.

Effective date (Sec. 1121(d)(1), (3) and (4), '86 TRA).—(1) Generally applies to years beginning after 12-31-88.

* * * * * * * * * *

(3) Collective bargaining agreements.—In the case of a plan maintained pursuant to 1 or more collective bargaining agreements between employee representatives and 1 or more employers ratified before 3-1-86, the amendments made by this section shall not apply to distributions to individuals covered by such agreements in plan years beginning before the earlier of—

(A) the later of—

(i) the date on which the last of such collective bargaining agreements terminates (determined without regard to any extension thereof after 2-28-86), or

(ii) 1-1-89, or

(B) 1-1-91.

(4) Transition rules.—

(A) The amendments made by subsections (a) and (b) shall not apply with respect to any benefits with respect to which a designation is in effect under section 242(b)(2) '82 TEFRA.

(B)(i) Except as provided in clause (ii), the amendment made by subsection (b) shall not apply in the case of any individual who has attained age 70½ before 1-1-88.

(ii) Clause (i) shall not apply to any individual who is a 5-percent owner (as defined in section 416(i) '86 Code), at any time during—

(I) the plan year ending with or within the calendar year in which such owner attains age 66½, and

(II) any subsequent plan year.

▲▲ Matter in *italics* in Sec. 401(a)(9)(C), preceded by two triangles, added by section 1852(a)(4)(A), '86 TRA, which struck out:

(5) "Except as provided in section 409A(d), clause (ii) shall not apply in the case of an employee who is a 5-percent owner (as defined in section 416) with respect to the plan year ending in the calendar year in which the employee attains 70½."

Effective date (Sec. 1881, '86 TRA and section 521(e)(1), (3) and (5), '84 TRA).—(1) Generally applies to years beginning after 12-31-84.

* * * * * * * * * * * *

(3) Transition rules.—A trust forming part of a plan shall not be disqualified under paragraph (9) of section 401(a) '54 Code, as amended by subsection (a)(1), by reason of distributions under a designation (before 1-1-84) by any employee in accordance with a designation described in section 242(b)(2) '82 TEFRA (as in effect before the amendments made by this Act).

(5) Special rule for collective bargaining agreements.—In the case of a plan maintained pursuant to one or more collective bargaining agreements ratified on or before the date of the enactment of this Act between employee representatives and one or more employers, the amendments made by this section shall not apply to years beginning before the earlier of—

(A) the date on which the last of the collective bargaining agreements relating to the plan terminates (determined without regard to any extension thereof agreed to after the date of the enactment of this Act), or

(B) 1-1-88

For purposes of subparagraph (A), any plan amendment made pursuant to a collective bargaining agreement relating to the plan which amends the plan solely to conform to any requirement added by this section shall not be treated as a termination of such collective bargaining agreement.

Sec. 401(a)(9)(G) in *italics* added by section 1852(a)(6), '86 TRA.

Effective date (Sec. 1881, '86 TRA and section 521(e)(1), (3) and (5), '84 TRA).—Generally applies to years beginning after 12-31-84. For special rules, see above.

---

*calendar year in which the employee attains age 70½. If the employee becomes a
5-percent owner during any subsequent plan year, the required beginning date shall be
April 1 of the calendar year following the calendar year in which such subsequent plan
year ends.*

* * * * * * * * * * *

*(G) Treatment of incidental death benefit distributions.—For purposes of this ti-
tle, any distribution required under the incidental death benefit requirements of this
subsection shall be treated as a distribution required under this paragraph.*

* * * * * * * * * * *

(11) Requirement of joint and survivor annuity and preretirement survivior annuity.—
    (A) In general.—In the case of any plan to which this paragraph applies, ex-
cept as provided in section 417, a trust forming part of such plan shall not constitute a qualified trust under this section unless—
        (i) in the case of a vested participant [6]*who does not die before the annuity
starting date*, the accrued benefit payable to such participant is provided in the
form of a qualified joint and survivor annuity, and
        (ii) in the case of a vested participant who dies before the annuity starting
date and who has a surviving spouse, a qualified preretirement survivor annuity
is provided to the surviving spouse of such participant.
    (B) Plans to which paragraph applies.—This paragraph shall apply to—
        (i) any defined benefit plan.
        (ii) any defined contribution plan which is subject to the funding standards of
section 412, and
        (iii) any participant under any other defined contribution plan unless—
            (I) such plan provides that [7]*the participant's nonforfeitable accrued benefit
(reduced by any security interest held by the plan by reason of a loan outstanding to such participant) is payable in full*, on the death of the participant, to the participant's surviving spouse (or, if there is no surviving spouse
or the surviving spouse consents in the manner required under [8]*section
417(a)(2)*, to a designated beneficiary),
            (II) such participant does not elect a payment of benefits in the form of a
life annuity, and
           (III) with respect to such participant, such plan is not a direct or [9]*indirect*

[Footnote ¶2994 continued]

Matter in *italics* in Sec. 401(a)(11)(A)(i), (B), (iii)(I), and (III) added by section 1898(b)(2), (3)(A), (7)(A) and
(13)(A), '86 TRA, which struck out:
  (6) "who retires under the plan"
  (7) "the participant's nonforfeitable accrued benefit."
  (8) "section 417(a)(2)(A)"
  (9) "indirect transferee"
Effective date (Sec. 1898(j), '86 TRA, and sections 302 and 303, Retirement Equity Act of 1984, P.L. 98-397,
8-23-84, as amended by sections 1145(c), and 1898(g) and (h), '86 TRA).—
SEC. 302. GENERAL EFFECTIVE DATES.
  (a) In General.—Except as otherwise provided in this section or section 303, the amendments shall apply to
plan year beginning after 12-31-84.
  (b) Special Rules for Collective Bargaining Agreements.—In the case of a plan maintained pursuant to 1 or
more collective bargaining agreements between employee representatives and 1 or more employers ratified before
8-23-84 except as provided in subsection (d) or section 303, the amendments shall not apply to plan years beginning before the earlier of—
  (1) the date on which the last of the collective bargaining agreements relating to the plan terminates (determined without regard to any extension thereof agreed to after 8-23-84), or
  (2) 7-1-88.
For purposes of paragraph (1), any plan amendment made pursuant to a collective bargaining agreement relating
to the plan which amends the plan solely to conform to any requirement added by title I or II shall not be treated
as a termination of such collective bargaining agreement.
  (c) Notice requirement.—The amendments made by section 207 of P.L. 98-397, shall apply to distributions
after 12-31-84.
  (d) Special Rules for Treatment of Plan Amendments.—
  (1) In general.—Except as provided in paragraph (2), the amendments made by section 301 of P.L. 98-397,
shall apply to plan amendments made after 7-30-84.
  (2) Special rule for collective bargaining agreements.—In the case of a plan maintained pursuant to 1 or more
collective bargaining agreements entered into before 1-1-85, which are—
  (A) between employee representatives and 1 or more employers, and
  (B) successor agreements to 1 or more collective bargaining agreements which terminate after 7-30-84, and
before 1-1-85,

⸢Footnote ¶2994 continued⸣

the amendments made by section 301 of P.L. 98-397, shall not apply to plan amendments adopted before 4-1-85, pursuant to such successor agreements (without regard to any modification or reopening after 12-31-84).

SEC. 303. TRANSITIONAL RULES.

(a) Amendments Relating to Vesting Rules; Breaks in Service; Maternity or Paternity Leave.—

(1) Minimum age for vesting.—The amendments made by sections 102(b) and 202(b) of P.L. 98-397, shall apply in the case of participants who have at least 1 hour of service under the plan on or after the first day of the first plan year to which the amendments made by this Act apply.

(2) Break in the service rules.—If, as of the day before the first day of the first plan year to which the amendments apply, section 202(a) or (b) or 203(b) of the Employee Retirement Income Security Act of 1974 or section 410(a) or 411(a) of the '54 Code (as in effect on the day before 8-23-84 would not require any service to be taken into account, nothing in the amendments made by subsections (c) and (d) of section 102 of P.L. 98-397, and subsections (c) and (d) of section 202 of P.L. 98-397, shall be construed as requiring such service to be taken into account under such section 202(a) or (b), 203(b), 410(a), or 411(a); as the case may be.

(3) Maternity or paternity leave.—The amendments made by section 102(e) and 202(e) P.L. 98-397, shall apply in the case of absences from work which begin on or after the first day of the first plan year to which the amendments apply.

(b) Special Rule for Amendments Relating to Maternity or Paternity Absences.—If a plan is administered in a manner which would meet the amendments made by section 102(e) and 202(e) P.L. 98-397, (relating to certain maternity or paternity absences not treated as breaks in service), such plan need not be amended to meet such requirements until the earlier of—

(1) the date on which such plan is first otherwise amended after 8-23-84, or

(2) the beginning of the first plan year beginning after 12-31-86.

(c) Requirement of Joint and Survivor Annuity and Preretirement Survivor Annuity.—

(1) Requirement that participant have at least 1 hour of service or paid leave on or after 8-23-84.—The amendments made by sections 103 and 203 of P.L. 98-397 shall apply only in the case of participants who have at least 1 hour of service under the plan on or after 8-23-84 or have at least 1 hour of paid leave on or after 8-23-84.

(2) Requirement that preretirement survivor annuity be provided in case of certain participants dying on or after 8-23-84.—In the case of any participant—

(A) who has at least 1 hour of service under the plan on or after 8-23-84 or has at least 1 hour of paid leave on or after such 8-23-84,

(B) who dies before the annuity starting date, and

(C) who dies on or after the date of 8-23-84 and before the first day of the first plan year to which the amendments apply,

the amendments made by sections 103 and 203 of P.L. 98-397 shall be treated as in effect as of the time of such participant's death. In the case of a profit-sharing or stock bonus plan to which this paragraph applies, the plan shall be treated as meeting the requirements of the amendments made by section 103 and 203, P.L. 98-397 with respect to any participant if the plan made a distribution in a form other than a life annuity to the surviving spouse of the participant of such participant's nonforfeitable benefit."

(3) Spousal consent required for certain elections after December 31, 1984.—Any election after 12-31-84, and before the first day of the first plan year to which the amendments apply not to take a joint and survivor annuity shall not be effective unless the requirements of section 205(c)(2) of the Employee Retirement Income Security Act of 1974 (as amended by section 103 of P.L. 98-397) and section 417(a)(2) of the Internal Revenue Code of 1954 (as added by section 203) are met with respect to such election.

(4) Elimination of double death benefits.—

"(A) In general.—In the case of a participant described in paragraph (2), death benefits (other than a qualified joint and survivor annuity or a qualified preretirement survivor annuity) payable to any beneficiary shall be reduced by the amount payable to the surviving spouse of such participant by reason of paragraph (2). The reduction under the preceding sentence shall be made on the basis of the respective present values (as of the date of the participant's death) of such death benefits and the amount so payable to the surviving spouse.

(B) Spouse may waive provisions of paragraph (2).—In the case of any participant described in paragraph (2), the surviving spouse of such participant may waive the provisions of paragraph (2). Such waiver shall be made on or before the close of the second plan year to which the amendments made by section 103 of this Act apply. Such a waiver shall not be treated as a transfer of property for purposes of chapter 12 of the Internal Revenue Code of 1954 and shall not be treated as an assignment or alienation for purposes of section 401(a)(13) of the Internal Revenue Code of 1954 or section 206(d) of the Employee Retirement Income Security Act of 1974."

(d) Amendments Relating to Assignments in Divorce, Etc., Proceedings.—The amendments made by sections 104 and 204 of P.L. 98-397 shall take effect on 1-1-85 except that in the case of a domestic relations orders entered before such date, the plan administrator—

(1) shall treat such order as a qualified domestic relations order if such administrator is paying benefits pursuant to such order on such date, and

(2) may treat any other such order entered before such date as a qualified domestic relations order even if such order does not meet the requirements of such amendments.

(e) Treatment of Certain Participants Who Separate From Service Before Date of Enactment.—

(1) Joint and survivor annuity provisions of employee retirement income security act of 1974 apply to certain participants.—If—

(A) a participant had at least 1 hour of service under the plan on or after 9-2-74

(B) section 205 of the Employee Retirement Income Security Act of 1974 and section 401(a)(11) of the Internal Revenue Code of 1954 (as in effect on the day before 8-23-84 would not (but for this paragraph) apply to such participant,

(C) the amendments made by section 103 and 203 of P.L 98-397 do not apply to such participant, and

(D) as of 8-23-84, the participant's annuity starting date has not occurred and the participant is alive,

transferee (in a transfer after December 31, 1984) of a plan which is described in clause (i) or (ii) or to which this clause applied with respect to the participant.

Clause (iii)(III) shall apply only with respect to the transferred assets (and income therefrom) if the plan separately accounts for such assets and any income therefrom.

 (C) Exception for certain ESOP benefits—

  (i) In general.—In the case of—

   (I) a tax credit employee stock ownership plan (as defined in section 409(a)), or

   (II) an employee stock ownership plan (as defined in section 4975(e)(7)),

subparagraph (A) shall not apply to that portion of the employee's accrued benefit to which the requirements of section 409(h) apply.

  (ii) Nonforfeitable benefit must be paid in full, etc.—In the case of any participant, clause (i) shall apply only if the requirements of subclauses (I), (II), and (III) of subparagraph (B)(iii) are met with respect to such participant.

 (D) Special rule where participant and spouse married less than 1 year.—A plan shall not be treated as failing to meet the requirements of subparagraphs (B)(iii) or (C) merely because the plan provides that benefits will not be payable to the surviving spouse of the participant unless the participant and such spouse had been married throughout the 1-year period ending on the earlier of the participant's annuity starting date or the date of the participant's death.

 (E) Exception for plans described in section 404(C).—This paragraph shall not apply to a plan which the Secretary has determined is a plan described in section 404(c) (or a continuation thereof) in which participation is substantially limited to individuals who, before January 1, 1976, ceased employment covered by the plan.

 [10]*(E)* [should read (F)] Cross reference.—For—

⟦Footnote ¶2994 continued⟧

then such participant may elect to have section 205 of the Employee Retirement Income Security Act of 1974 and section 401(a)(11) of the '54 Code (as in effect on the day before 8-23-84) apply.

(2) Treatment of certain participants who perform service on or after January 1, 1976.—If—

(A) a participant had a least 1 hour of service in any plan year beginning on or after January 1, 1976,

(B) the amendments made by section 103 and 203, P.L. 98-397 would not (but for this paragraph) apply to such participant,

(C) when such participant separated from service, such participant had a least 10 years of service under the plan and had a nonforfeitable right to all (or any portion) of such participant's accrued benefit derived from employer contributions, and

(D) as of the 8-23-84 such participant's annuity starting date has not occurred and such participant is alive,

then such participant may elect to have the qualified preretirement survivor annuity requirements of the amendments made by sections 103 and 203 of P.L. 98-397 apply.

(3) Period during which election may be made.—An election under paragraph (1) or (2) may be made by any participant during the period—

(A) beginning on 8-23-84, and

(B) ending on the earlier of the participant's annuity starting date or the date of the participant's death.

(4) Requirement of notice.—

(A) In general.—

(i) Time and manner.—Every plan shall give notice of the provisions of this subsection at such time or times and in such manner or manners as the Secretary of the Treasury may prescribe.

(ii) Penalty.—If any plan fails to meet the requirements of clause (i), such plan shall pay a civil penalty to the Secretary of the Treasury equal to $1 per participant for each day during the period beginning with the first day on which such failure occurs and ending on the day before notice is given by the plan; except that the amount of such penalty imposed on any plan shall not exceed $2,500.

(B) Responsibilities of secretary of labor.—The Secretary of Labor shall take such steps (by public announcements and otherwise) as may be necessary or appropriate to bring to public attention the provisions of this subsection.

(f) The amendments made by section 301 of P.L. 98-397 shall not apply to the termination of a defined benefit plan if such termination—

(1) is pursuant to a resolution directing the termination of such plan which was adopted by the Board of Directors of a corporation on 7-24-84, and

(2) occurred on 11-30-84."

Matter in *italics* in Sec. 401(a)(11)(D) added by section 1898(b)(14)(A), '86 TRA, which struck out:

(10) "(D)"

Effective date (Sec. 1898(j), '86 TRA and sections 302 and 303, Retirement Equity Act of 1984, P.L. 98-397, 8-23-84, amended by sections 1145(c), 1898(g) and (h)).—(a) Generally applies to plan years beginning after 12-31-84. For transitional rules, see above.

Matter in *italics* in Sec. 401(a)(11)(E), added by section 1145(a), '86 TRA.

Effective date (Sec. 1145(d), '86 TRA and sections 302 and 303, Retirement Equity Act of 1984, P.L. 98-397,

(i) provisions under which participants may elect to waive the requirements of this paragraph, and

(ii) other definitions and special rules for purposes of this paragraph see section 417.[1]

* * * * * * * * * * *

(17) A trust shall not constitute a qualified trust under this section unless, under the plan of which such trust is a part, the annual compensation of each employee taken into account under the plan for any year does not exceed $200,000. The Secretary shall adjust the $200,000 amount at the same time and in the same manner as under section 415(d).

* * * * * * * * * * *

(20) A trust forming part of a pension plan shall not be treated as failing to constitute a qualified trust under this section merely because the pension plan of which such trust is a part makes a [11]*qualified total distribution described in section 402(a)(5)(E)(i)(I).* This paragraph shall not apply to a defined benefit plan unless the employer maintaining such plan files a notice with the Pension Benefit Guaranty Corporation (at the time and in the manner prescribed by the Pension Benefit Guaranty Corporation) notifying the Corporation of such payment or distribution and the Corporation has approved such payment or distribution or, within 90 days after the date on which such notice was filed, has failed to disapprove such payment or distribution.

(21) [Repealed][12]

(22) *If* [13]a defined contributions plan (other than a profit-sharing plan)—

(A) is established by an employer whose stock is not publicly traded, and

(B) after acquiring securities of the employer, more than 10 percent of the total assets of the plan are securities of the employer,

any trust forming part of such plan shall not constitute a qualified trust under this section unless the plan meets the requirements of subsection (e) of section 409. *The requirements of subsection (e) of section 409 shall not apply to any employees of an employer who are participants in any defined contribution plan established and maintained by such employer if the stock of such employer is not publicly traded and the*

⟦Footnote ¶2994 continued⟧

8-23-84, amended by sections 1145(c), 1898(g) and (h), '86 TRA.—(a) Generally applies to plan years beginning after 12-31-84. For transitional rules, see above.

Sec. 401(a)(17) in *italics* added by section 1106(d)(1), '86 TRA.
Effective date (Sec. 1106(i)(5), '86 TRA).—(A) Generally applies to benefits accruing in years beginning after 12-31-88.
(B) Collective bargaining agreements.—In the case of a plan described in paragraph (2), the amendments made by subsection (d) shall apply to benefits accruing in years beginning on or after the earlier of—
(i) the later of—
(I) the date determined under paragraph (2)(A), or
(II) 1-1-89, or
(ii) 1-1-91.

Matter in *italics* in Sec. 401(a)(20) added by section 1852(b)(8), '86 TRA, which struck out:
(11) "qualifying rollover distribution (determined as if section 402(a)(5)(D)(i) did not contain subclause (II) thereof) described in section 402(a)(5)(A)(i) or 403(a)(4)(A)(i)"
Effective date (Sec. 1881, '86 TRA and 522(e), '84 TRA).—Applies to distributions made after 7-18-84, in taxable years ending after such date.

Sec. 401(a)(21) repealed by section 1171(b)(5), '86 TRA:
(12) "(21) A trust forming part of a tax credit employee stock ownership plan shall not fail to be considered a permanent program merely because employer contributions under the plan are determined solely by reference to the amount of credit which would be allowable under section 41 if the employer made the transfer described in section 41(c)(1)(B).
Effective date (Sec. 1171(c)(1), '86 TRA).—Applies to compensation paid or accrued after 12-31-86, in taxable years ending after such date.

Matter in *italics* in Sec. 401(a)(22) (except for the last sentence in *italics*) added by section 1899A(10), '86 TRA, which struck out:
(13) "if"

The last sentence in *italics* in Sec. 401(a)(22) added by 1176(a), '86 TRA.
Effective date (sec. 1176(c), '86 TRA.—Takes effect 12-31-86.

trade or business of such employer consists of publishing on a regular basis a newspaper for general circulation.

[14]*(23)   A stock bonus plan shall not be treated as meeting the requirements of this section unless such plan meets the requirements of subsections (h) and (o) of section 409, except that in applying section 409(h) for purposes of this paragraph, the term "employer securities" shall include any securities of the employer held by the plan.*

* * * * * * * * * * * *

(26)   Additional participation requirements.—

(A)   In general.—A trust shall not constitute a qualified trust under this subsection unless such trust is part of a plan which on each day of the plan year benefits the lesser of—

(i)   50 employees of the employer, or

(ii)   40 percent or more of all employees of the employer.

(B)   Treatment of excludable employees.—

(i)   In general.—A plan may exclude from consideration under this paragraph employees described in paragraphs (3) and (4)(A) of section 410(b).

(ii)   Separate application for certain excludable employees.—If employees described in section 410(b)(4)(B) are covered under a plan which meets the requirements of subparagraph (A) separately with respect to such employees, such employees may be excluded from consideration in determining whether any plan of the employer meets such requirements if—

(I)   the benefits for such employees are provided under the same plan as benefits for other employees,

---

⌈**Footnote ¶2994 continued**⌉

Matter in *italics* in Sec. 401(a)(23) added by section 1174(c)(2)(A), '86 TRA, which struck out:

(14)   "(23)   A stock bonus plan which otherwise meets the requirements of this section shall not be considered to fail to meet the requirements of this section because it provides a cash distribution option to participants if that option meets the requirements of section 409(h), except that in applying section 409(h) for purposes of this paragraph, the term "employer securities" shall include any securities of the employer held by the plan.

Effective date (Sec. 1174(c)(2)(B), '86 TRA).—Applies to distributions attributable to stock acquired after 12-31-86.

Sec. 401(a)(26) in *italics* added by section 1112(b), '86 TRA.

Effective date (Sec. 1112(e), '86 TRA).—(1) Generally applies to plan years beginning after 12-31-88.

(2)   Special rule for collective bargaining agreements.—In the case of a plan maintained pursuant to 1 or more collective bargaining agreements between employee representatives and 1 or more employers ratified before 3-1-86, the amendments made by this section shall not apply to employees covered by any such agreement in plan years beginning before the earlier of—

(A)   the later of—

(i)   1-1-89, or

(ii)   the date on which the last of such collective bargaining agreement terminates (determined without regard to any extension thereof after 2-28-86), or

(B)   1-1-91.

(3)   Waiver of excise tax on reversions.—

(A)   In general.—If—

(i)   a plan is in existence on 8-16-86,

(ii)   such plan would fail to meet the requirements of section 401(a)(26) '86 Code (as added by subsection (b)) if such section were in effect for the plan year including 8-16-86, and

(iii)   there is no transfer of assets to or liabilities from a plan or merger or spinoff or merger involving such plan after 8-16-86,

then no tax shall be imposed under sec. 4980 of such Code on any employer reversion by reason of the termination or merger of such plan before the 1st year to which the amendment made by subsection (b) applies.

(B)   Determination of amount of reversion.—For purposes of the '86 Code, in determining the present value of the accrued benefit of any highly compensated employee (within the meaning of section 414(q) of such Code) on the termination or merger of any plan to which subparagraph (A) applies, the plan shall use the highest interest rate which may be used for calculating present value under section 411(a)(11)(B) of such Code.

(C)   Special rule for plans which may not terminate.—To the extent provided in regulations prescribed by the Secretary of the Treasury or his delegate, if a plan is prohibited from terminating under title IV of the Employee Retirement Income Security Act of 1974 before the 1st year to which the amendment made by subsection (b) applies, subparagraph (A) shall be applied by substituting "the 1st year in which the plan is able to terminate" for "the 1st year to which the amendment made by subsection (b) applies".

Sec. 401(a)(27) in *italics* added by section 1136(a), '86 TRA.

Effective date (Sec. 1136(c), '86 TRA).—Applies to years beginning after 12-31-85.

Sec. 401(a)(28) in *italics* added by section 1175(a)(1), '86 TRA.

Effective date (Sec. 1175(a)(2), '86 TRA).—Applies to stock acquired after 12-31-86.

    *(II) the benefits provided to such employees are not greater than compara-
ble benefits provided to other employees under the plan, and*

    *(III) no highly compensated employee (within the meaning of section
414(q)) is included in the group of such employees for more than 1 year.*

    *(C) Eligibility to participate.—In the case of contributions under section 401(k) or
401(m), employees who are eligible to contribute (or may elect to have contributions
made on their behalf) shall be treated as benefiting under the plan.*

    *(D) Special rule for collective bargaining units.—Except to the extent provided in
regulations, a plan covering only employees described in section 410(b)(3)(A) may
exclude from consideration any employees who are not included in the unit or units
in which the covered employees are included.*

    *(E) Paragraph not to apply to multiemployer plans.—Except to the extent pro-
vided in regulations, this paragraph shall not apply to employees in a multiemployer
plan (within the meaning of section 414(f)) who are covered by collective bargaining
agreements.*

    *(F) Regulations.—The Secretary may by regulation provide that any separate ben-
efit structure, any separate trust, or any other separate arrangement is to be treated
as a separate plan for purposes of applying this paragraph.*

  *(27) The determination of whether the plan under which any contributions are made
is a profit-sharing plan shall be made without regard to current or accumulated profits
of the employer and without regard to whether the employer is a tax-exempt organization.*

  (28) Additional requirements relating to employee stock ownership plans.—

    *(A) In general.—In the case of a trust which is part of an employee stock owner-
ship plan (within the meaning of section 4975(e)(7)) or a plan which meets the requirements of section 409(a), such trust shall not constitute a qualified trust under
this section unless such plan meets the requirements of subparagraphs (B) and (C).*

    (B) Diversification of investments.—

      *(i) In general.—A plan meets the requirements of this subparagraph if each
qualified participant in the plan may elect within 90 days after the close of each
plan year in the qualified election period to direct the plan as to the investment of
at least 25 percent of the participant's account in the plan (to the extent such portion exceeds the amount to which a prior election under this subparagraph applies). In the case of the election year in which the participant can make his last
election, the preceding sentence shall be applied by substituting "50 percent" for
"25 percent".*

      *(ii) Method of meeting requirements.—A plan shall be treated as meeting the
requirements of clause (i) if—*

        *(I) the portion of the participant's account covered by the election under
clause (i) is distributed within 90 days after the period during which the election may be made, or*

        *(II) the plan offers at least 3 investment options (not inconsistent with regu-
lations prescribed by the Secretary) to each participant making an election under clause (i).*

      *(iii) Qualified participant.—For purposes of this subparagraph, the term "qual-
ified participant" means any employee who has completed at least 10 years of participation under the plan and has attained age 55.*

      *(iv) Qualified election period.—For purposes of this subparagraph, the term
"qualified election period" means the 5-plan-year period beginning with the plan
year after the plan year in which the participant attains age 55 (or, if later, beginning with the plan year after the 1st plan year in which the individual 1st became
a qualified participant).*

    *(C) Use of independent appraiser.—A plan meets the requirements of the sub-
paragraph if all valuations of employer securities which are not readily tradable on
an established securities market with respect to activities carried on by the plan are by
an independent appraiser. For purposes of the preceding sentence, the term 'independent appraiser' means any appraiser meeting requirements similar to the requirements
of the regulations prescribed under section 170(a)(1).*

* * * * * * * * * * * *

  *(c) Definitions and Rules Relating to Self-Employed Individuals and Owner-
Employees.—For purposes of this section—*

* * * * * * * * * * * *

(2) *Earned income.—*

(A) *In general.—The term "earned income" means the net earnings from self-employment (as defined in section 1402(a)), but such net earnings shall be determined—*

(i) *only with respect to a trade or business in which personal services of the taxpayer are a material income-producing factor,*

(ii) *without regard to paragraphs (4) and (5) of section 1402(c),*

(iii) *in the case of any individual who is treated as an employee under section 3121(d)(3)(A), (C), or (D), without regard to paragraph (2) of section 1402(c),*

(iv) *without regard to items which are not included in gross income for purposes of this chapter, and the deductions properly allocable to or chargeable against such items, and*

(v) *with regard to the deductions allowed by* [15]*section 404 to the taxpayer."*

For purposes of this subparagraph, section 1402, as in effect for a taxable year ending on December 31, 1962, shall be treated as having been in effect for all taxable years ending before such date.

(B) [Struck out by section 204(c), P.L. 89-809, 11-13-66]

(C) Income from disposition of certain property.—For purposes of this section, the term "earned income" includes gains (other than any gain which is treated under any provision of this chapter as gain from the sale or exchange of a capital asset) and net earnings derived from the sale or other disposition of, the transfer of any interest in, or the licensing of the use of property (other than good will) by an individual whose personal efforts created such property.

* * * * * * * * * * *

(6) *Special rule for certain fishermen.—For purposes of this subsection, the term "self-employed individual" includes an individual described in section 3121(b)(20) (relating to certain fishermen).*

* * * * * * * * * * *

(h) **Medical, etc., Benefits for Retired Employees and Their Spouses and Dependents.—**Under regulations prescribed by the Secretary, a pension or annuity plan may provide for the payment of benefits for sickness, accident, hospitalization, and medical expenses of retired employees, their spouses and their dependents, but only if—

(1) such benefits are subordinate to the retirement benefits provided by the plan,

(2) a separate account is established and maintained for such benefit,

(3) the employer's contributions to such separate account are reasonable and ascertainable,

(4) it is impossible, at any time prior to the satisfaction of all liabilities under the plan to provide such benefits, for any part of the corpus or income of such separate account to be (within the taxable year or thereafter) used for, or diverted to, any purposes other than the providing of such benefits,

(5) notwithstanding the provisions of subsection (a)(2), upon the satisfaction of all liabilities under the plan to provide such benefits, any amount remaining in such separate account must, under the terms of the plan, be returned to the employer, and

(6) in the case of an employee who is a [16]*key employee,* a separate account is established and maintained for such benefits payable to such employee (and his spouse and dependents) and such benefits (to the extent attributable to plan years beginning after March 31, 1984, for which the employee is a [16]*key employee)* are only payable to such employee (and his spouse and dependents) from such separate account.

[17]*For purposes of paragraph (6), the term 'key employee' means any employee, who at*

---

any time during the plan year or any preceding plan year during which contributions were made on behalf of such employee, is or was a key employee as defined in section 416(i).

* * * * * * * * * * * *

(k) Cash or Deferred Arrangements.—

(1) **General Rule.**—A profit-sharing or stock bonus plan [18], *a pre-ERISA money purchase plan, or a rural electric cooperative plan* shall not be considered as not satisfying the requirements of subsection (a) merely because the plan includes a qualified cash or deferred arrangement.

(2) **Qualified cash or deferred arrangement.**—A qualified cash or deferred arrangement is any arrangement which is part of a profit-sharing or stock bonus plan [18], *a pre-ERISA money purchase plan, or a rural electric cooperative plan* which meets the requirements of subsection (a)—

(A) under which a covered employee may elect to have the employer make payments as contributions to a trust under the plan on behalf of the employee, or to the employee directly in cash;

[19]*(B) under which—*

(i) amounts held by the trust which are attributable to employer contributions made pursuant to the employee's election may not be distributable to participants or other beneficiaries earlier than—

(I) separation from service, death, or disability,

(II) termination of the plan without establishment of a successor plan,

(III) the date of the sale by a corporation of substantially all of the assets (within the meaning of section 409(d)(2)) used by such corporation in a trade or business of such corporation with respect to an employee who continues employment with the corporation acquiring such assets,

(IV) the date of the sale by a corporation of such corporation's interest in a subsidiary (within the meaning of section 409(d)(3)) with respect to an employee who continues employment with such subsidiary,

(V) in the case of a profit-sharing or stock bonus plan, the attainment of age 59½, or

(VI) in the case of contributions to a profit-sharing or stock bonus plan to which section 402(a)(8) applies, upon hardship of the employee, and

(ii) amounts will not be distributable merely by reason of the completion of a stated period of participation or the lapse of a fixed number of years;[20]

⟦Footnote ¶2994 continued⟧

was a 5-percent owner (as defined in section 416(i)(1)(B)).

Effective date (Sec. 1881, '86 TRA and section 528(c), '84 TRA).—Applies to years beginning after 3-31-84.

Matter in *italics* in Section 401(k)(1) and (2) added by section 1879(g)(1), '86 TRA, which struck out:

(18) "(or a pre-ERISA money purchase plan)"

Effective date (Sec. 1879(g)(3), '86 TRA).—Applies to plan years beginning after 12-31-84.

Matter in *italics* in 401(k)(2)(B) added by section 1116(b)(1) and (2), '86 TRA, which struck out:

(19) "(B) under which amounts held by the trust which are attributable to employer contributions made pursuant to the employee's election may not be distributable to participants or other beneficiaries earlier than upon retirement, death, disability, or separation from service (or in the case of a profit-sharing or stock bonus plan, hardship or the attainment of age 59½), and will not be distributable merely by reason of the completion of a stated period of participation or the lapse of a fixed number of years; and

(20) "and"

Effective date (Sec. 1116(f), '86 TRA).—(1) Generally applies to years beginning after 12-31-88.

(2) Nondiscrimination rules.—

(A) In general.—Except as provided in subparagraph (B), the amendments made by subsections (a), (b)(4), and (d), and the provisions of section 401(k)(4)(B) '86 Code (as added by this section), shall apply to years beginning after 12-31-86.

(B) Transition rules for certain governmental and tax-exempt plans.—Subparagraph (B) of section 401(k)(4) of the '86 Code (relating to governments and tax-exempt organizations not eligible for cash or deferred arrangements), as added by this section, shall not apply to any cash or deferred arrangement adopted by—

(i) a State or local government (or political subdivision thereof) before 5-6-86, or

(ii) a tax-exempt organization before 7-2-86.

In the case of an arrangement described in clause (i), the amendments made by subsections (a), (b)(4), and (d) shall apply to years beginning after 12-31-88.

(3) Aggregation and excess contributions.—The amendments made by subsections (c) and (e) shall apply to years beginning after 12-31-86,

(4) Collective bargaining agreements.—

(A) In general.—In the case of a plan maintained pursuant to 1 or more collective bargaining agreements be-

(C) which provides that an employee's right to his accrued benefit derived from employer contributions made to the trust pursuant to his election [21]*is* nonforfeitable[22], *and*

[Footnote ¶2994 continued]

tween employee representatives and 1 or more employers ratified before 3-1-86, the amendments made by this section shall not apply to years beginning before the earlier of—

(i) the later of—

(I) 1-1-89, or

(II) the date on which the last of such collective bargaining agreements terminates (determined without regard to any extension thereof after 2-28-86), or

(ii) 1-1-91.

(B) Special rule for nondiscrimination rules.—In the case of a plan described in subparagraph (A), the amendments and provisions described in paragraph (2) shall not apply to years beginning before the earlier of—

(i) the date determined under subparagraph (A)(i)(II), or

(ii) 1-1-89.

(5) Special rule for qualified offset arrangements.—

(A) In general.—A cash or deferred arrangement shall not be treated as failing to meet the requirements of section 401(k)(4) '86 Coe (as added by this section) to the extent such arrangement is part of a qualified offset arrangement consisting of such cash of deferred arrangement and a defined benefit plan.

(B) Qualified offset arrangement.—For purposes of subparagraph (A), a cash or deferred arrangement is part of a qualified offset arrangement with a defined benefit plan to the extent such offset arrangement satisfies each of the following conditions with respect to the employer maintaining the arrangement on 4-16-86, and at all times thereafter:

(i) The benefit under the defined benefit plan is directly and uniformly conditioned on the initial elective deferrals (up to 4 percent of compensation).

(ii) The benefit provided under the defined benefit plan (before the offset) is at least 60 percent of an employee's cumulative elective deferrals (up to 4 percent of compensation).

(iii) The benefit under the defined benefit plan is reduced by the benefit attributable to the employee's elective deferrals under the plan (up to 4 percent of compensation) and the income allocable thereto. The interest rate used to calculate the reduction shall not exceed the greater of the rate under section 411(a)(11)(B)(ii) of such Code or the interest rate applicable under section 411(c)(2)(C)(iii) of such Code, taking into account section 411(c)(2)(D) of such Code.

For purposes of applying section 401(k)(3) of such Code to the cash or deferred arrangement, the benefits under the defined benefit plan conditioned on initial elective deferrals may be treated as matching contributions under such rules as the Secretary of the Treeasury or his delegate may prescribe. The Secretary shall provide rules for the application of this paragraph in the case of successor plans.

(C) Definition of employer.—For purposes of this paragraph, the term "employer" includes any research and development center which is federally funded and engaged in cancer research, but only with respect to employees of contractor-operators whose salaries are reimbursed as direct costs against the operator's contract to perform work at such center.

(6) Withdrawals on sale of assets.—Subclauses (II), (III), and (IV) of section 401(k)(2)(B)(i) '86 Code (as added by subsection (b)(1)) shall apply to distributions after 12-31-84.

(7) Distributions before plan amendment.—

(A) In general.—If a plan amendment is required to allow a plan to make any distribution described in section 401(k)(8) '86 Code, any such distribution which is made before the close of the 1st plan year for which such amendment is required to be in effect under section 1140, shall be treated as made in accordance with the provisions of such plan.

(B) Distributions pursuant to model amendment.—

(i) Secretary to prescribe amendment.—The Secretary of the Treasury or his delegate shall prescribe an amendment which allows a plan to make any distribution described in section 401(k)(8) of such Code.

(ii) Adoption by plan.—If a plan adopts the amendment prescribed under clause (i) and makes a distribution in accordance with such amendment, such distribution shall be treated as made in accordance with the provisions of the plan.

The phrase "*is*" in italics in Sec. 401(k)(2)(C) added by section 1852(g)(3), '86 TRA, which struck out:

(21) "are"

Effective date (Sec. 1881, '86 TRA and section 527(c)(2), '84 TRA).—(A) Generally applies with respect to plan years beginning after 7-18-84.

(B) Transitional rule.—Rules similar to the rules under section 135(c)(2) of the Revenue Act of 1978 shall apply with respect to any pre-ERISA money purchase plan (as defined in section 401(k)(5) of the '54 Code for plan years beginning after 12-31-79 and on or before the date of the enactment of this Act.

The phrase "*and*" in italics in Sec. 401(k)(2)(C) and Sec. 401(k)(2)(D) in *italics* added by section 1116(b)(2), '86 TRA, which struck out:

(22) "."

Effective date (Sec. 1116(f), '86 TRA).—Generally applies to years beginning after 12-31-88. For special and transitional rules, see above.

(D)   which does not require, as a condition of participation in the arrangement, that an employee complete a period of service with the employer (or employers) maintaining the plan extending beyond the period permitted under section 410(a)(1) (determined without regard to subparagraph (B)(i) thereof).

(3)   Application of participation and discrimination standards.—

(A)   A cash or deferred arrangement shall not be treated as a qualified cash or deferred arrangement unless—

(i)   those employees eligible to benefit under the arrangement satisfy the provisions of [23] section 410(b)(1), and

(ii)   the actual deferral percentage for highly compensated employees (as defined in [24]*paragraph (5))* for such year bears a relationship to the actual deferral percentage for all other eligible employees for such plan year which meets either of the following tests:

(I)   The actual deferral percentage for the group of highly compensated employees is not more than the actual deferral percentage of all other eligible employees multipled by [25]*1.25.*

(II)   The excess of the actual deferral percentage for the group of highly compensated employees over that of all other eligible employees is not more than [26]*2 percentage points,* and the actual deferral percentage for the group of highly compensated employees is not more than the actual deferral percentage of all other eligible employees multiplied by [27]*2.*

If 2 or more plans which include cash or deferred arrangements are considered as 1 plan for purposes of section 401(a)(4) or 410(b), the cash or deferred arrangements included in such plans shall be treated as 1 arrangement for purposes of this subparagraph.

[28]*If* [29]*any highly compensated employee is a participant under 2 or more cash or deferred arrangements of the employer, for purposes of determining the deferral percentage with respect to such employee, all such cash or deferred arrangements shall be treated as 1 cash or deferred arrangement.*

(B)   For purposes of subparagraph (A), the actual deferral percentage for a specified group of employees for a plan year shall be the average of the ratios (calculated separately for each employee in such group) of—

(i)   the amount of employer contributions actually paid over to the trust on behalf of each such employee for such plan year, to

(ii)   the employee's compensation for such plan year.[30]

»P-H CAUTION→   There are two versions of Sec. 401(k)(3)(C). Sec. 401(k)(3)(C), generally effective after 12-31-88, follows. For Sec. 401(k)(3)(C), generally effective before 1-1-89, see below.

【Footnote ¶2994 continued】

Section 1112(d), '86 TRA, struck out from Sec. 401(k)(3)(A):
(23)   "subparagraph (A) or (B) of"
Effective date (Sec. 1112(e), '86 TRA).—(1) Generally applies to plan years beginning after 12-31-88. For special rules, see above.

Matter in *italics* in Sec. 401(k)(3)(A)(ii) added by section 1116(a) and (c)(2), '86 TRA, which struck out:
(24)   "paragraph (4)"
(25)   "1.5"
(26)   "3 percentage points"
(27)   "2.5"
Effective date (Sec. 1116(f), '86 TRA).—Generally applies to years beginning after 12-31-88. For special and transitional rules, see above.

The last sentence in *italics* in Sec. 401(k)(3)(A) (except the phrase *"any highly compensated employee"*) added by section 1852(g)(2), '86 TRA, which struck out:
(28)   "The deferral percentage taken into account under this subparagraph for any employee who is a participant under 2 or more cash or deferred arrangements of the employer shall be the sum of the deferral percentages for such employee under each of such arrangements.
Effective date (Sec. 1881, '86 TRA and section 527(c)(2), '84 TRA).—Generally applies with respect to plan years beginning after 7-18-84. For transitional rules, see above.

The phrase *"any highly compensated employee"* in *italics* in the last sentence of Sec. 401(k)(3)(A) added by section 1116(b)(4) and (d)(3), '86 TRA, which struck out:
(29)   "an [should read any] employee"
(30)   "For purposes of the preceding sentence, the compensation of any employee for a plan year shall be the amount of his compensation which is taken into account under the plan in calculating the contribution which may be made on his behalf for such plan year.
Effective date (Sec. 1116(f), '86 TRA).—Generally applies to years beginning after 12-31-88. For special and transitional rules, see above.

▲ [30a]*(C)   For purposes of subparagraph (B), the employer contributions on behalf of any employee—*

(i)   shall include any employer contributions made pursuant to the employee's election under paragraph (2), and

(ii)   under such rules as the Secretary may prescribe, may, at the election of the employer, include—

(I)   matching contributions (as defined in 401(m)(4)(A) which meets the requirements of paragraph (2) (B and (C)), and

(II)   qualified nonelective contributions (within the meaning of section 401(m)(4)(C)).

⇒**P-H CAUTION→** There are two versions of Sec. 401(k)(3)(C). Sec. 401(k)(3)(C), generally effective before 1-1-89, follows. For Sec. 401(k)(3)(C), generally effective after 12-31-88, see above.

▲▲*(C)   A cash or deferred arrangement shall be treated as meeting the requirements of subsection (a)(4) with respect to contributions if the requirements of subparagraph (A)(ii) are met.*

(4)   Other requirements.—

(A)   Benefits (other than matching contributions) must not be contingent on election to defer.—A cash or deferred arrangement of any employer shall not be treated as a qualified cash or deferred arrangement if any other benefit provided by such employer is conditioned (directly or indirectly) on the employee electing to have the employer make or not make contributions under the arrangement in lieu of receiving cash. The preceding sentence shall not apply to any matching contribution (as defined in section 401(m) made by reason of such an election.

(B)   State and local governments and tax-exempt organizations not eligible.—A cash or deferred arrangement shall not be treated as a qualified cash or deferred arrangement if it is part of a plan maintained by—

(i)   a State or local government or political subdivision thereof, or any agency or instrumentality thereof, or

(ii)   any organization exempt from tax under this subtitle.

(C)   Coordination with other plans.—Except as provided in section 401(m), any employer contribution made pursuant to an employee's election under a qualified cash or deferred arrangement shall not be taken into account for purposes of determining whether any other plan meets the requirements of section 401(a) or 410(b). This subparagraph shall not apply for purposes of determining whether a plan meets the average benefit requirement of section 410(b)(2)(A)(ii).

[31]*(5)   Highly compensated employee.—For purposes of this subsection, the term "highly compensated employee" has the meaning given such term by section 414(q).*

[32]*(6)   **Pre-ERISA money purchase plan.**—For purposes of this subsection, the term*

⟦Footnote ¶2994 continued⟧

▲ Sec. 401(k)(3)(C), in *italics*, preceded by a triangle, added by section 1116(e), '86 TRA, which struck out:

(30a) "(C) A cash or deferred arrangement shall be treated as meeting the requirements of subsection (a)(4) with respect to contributions if the requirements of subparagraph (A)(ii) are met."

Effective date (Sec. 1116(f), '86 TRA).—Generally applies to years beginning after 12-31-88. For special and transitional rules, see above.

▲▲ Sec. 401(k)(3)(C) in *italics* preceded by two triangles, added by section 1852(g)(1), '86 TRA.

Effective date (Sec. 1181, '86 TRA and section 527(c)(1), '84 TRA).—(A) Generally applies to plan years beginning after 12-31-84.

(B) Exception for certain existing plans.—The amendment made by subsection (a) shall not apply to any plan—

(i)   which was maintaind by a State on 6-8-84, and

(ii) with respect to which a determination letter had been issued by the Secretary on 12-6-82.

Matter in *italics* in Sec. 401(k)(4)—(6) added by section 1116(b)(3) and (d)(1), '86 TRA, which struck out:

(31) "(4) **Highly compensated employee.**—for purposes of this subsection, the term "highly compensated employee" means any employee who is more highly compensated than two-thirds of all eligible employees, taking into account only compensation which is considered in applying paragraph (3).

(32) "(5)"

Effective date (Sec. 1116(f)(1), '86 TRA).—Generally applies to years beginning after 12-31-88. For special and transitional rules, see above.

Sec. 401(k)(7) [formerly redesignated as (6) by section 1116(b)(3), '86 TRA], in *italics* added by section 1879(g)(2), '86 TRA.

"pre-ERISA money purchase plan" means a pension plan—

(A) which is a defined contribution plan (as defined in section 414(i)),

(B) which was in existence on June 27, 1974, and which, on such date, included a salary reduction arrangement, and

(C) under which neither the employee contributions nor the employer contributions may exceed the levels provided for by the contribution formula in effect under the plan on such date.

(7) *Rural electric cooperative plan.—For purposes of this subsection, the term "rural electric cooperative plan" means any pension plan—*

(A) *which is a defined contribution plan (as defined in section 414(i)), and*

(B) *which is established and maintained by a rural electric cooperative (as defined in section 457(d)(9)(B)) or a national association of such rural electric cooperatives.*

(8) *Arrangement not disqualified if excess contributions distributed.—*

(A) *In general.—A cash or deferred arrangement shall not be treated as failing to meet the requirements of clause (ii) of paragraph (3)(A) for any plan year if, before the close of the following plan year—*

(i) *the amount of the excess contributions for such plan year (and any income allocable to such contributions) is distributed, or*

(ii) *to the extent provided in regulations, the employee elects to treat the amount of the excess contributions as an amount distributed to the employee and then contributed by the employee to the plan.*

Any distribution of excess contributions (and income) may be made without regard to any other provision of law.

(B) *Excess contributions.—For purposes of subparagraph (A), the term "excess contributions" means, with respect to any plan year, the excess of—*

(i) *the aggregate amount of employer contributions actually paid over to the trust on behalf of highly compensated employees for such plan year, over*

(ii) *the maximum amount of such contributions permitted under the limitations of clause (ii) of paragraph (3)(A) (determined by reducing contributions made on behalf of highly compensated employees in order of the actual deferral percentages beginning with the highest of such percentages).*

(C) *Method of distributing excess contributions.—Any distribution of the excess contributions for any plan year shall be made to highly compensated employees on the basis of the respective portions of the excess contributions attributable to each of such employees.*

(D) *Additional tax under section 72(t) not to apply.—No tax shall be imposed under section 72(t) on any amount required to be distributed under this paragraph.*

(E) *Cross reference.—*

For excise tax on certain excess contributions, see section 4979.

(9) *Compensation.—For purposes of this subsection, the term "compensation" has the meaning given such term by section 414(s).*

[33](l) *Permitted Disparity in Plan Contributions or Benefits.—*

⟦Footnote ¶2994 continued⟧

Effective date (Sec. 1879(g)(3), '86 TRA).—Applies to plan years beginning after 12-31-84.

Sec. 401(k)(8) and (9) added by section 1116(c)(1) and (d)(2), '86 TRA.
Effective date (Sec. 1116(f)(1), '86 TRA).—Generally applies to years beginning after 12-31-88. For special and transitional rules, see above.

Matter in *italics* in Sec. 401(l) added by section 1111(a), '86 TRA, which struck out:

(33) "(l) **Nondiscriminatory Coordination of Defined Contribution Plans With OASDI.—**

(1) **In general.—**Notwithstanding subsection (a)(5), the coordination of a defined contribution plan with OASDI meets the requirements of subsection (a)(4) only if the total contributions with respect to each participant, when increased by the OASDI contributions, bear a uniform relationship—

(A) to the total compensation of such employee, or

(B) to the basic or regular rate of compensation of such employee.

(2) **Definitions.—**For purposes of paragraph (1)—

(A) OASDI contributions.—The term "OASDI contributions" means the product of—

(i) so much of the remuneration paid by the employer to the employee during the plan year as—

(I) constitutes wages (within the meaning of section 3121(a) without regard to paragraph (1) thereof), and

(II) does not exceed the contribution and benefit base applicable under OASDI at the beginning of the plan year, multiplied by

(ii) the rate of tax applicable under section 3111(a) (relating to employer's OASDI tax) at the beginning of the plan year.

(1) In general.—The requirements of this subsection are met with respect to a plan if—

(A) in the case of a defined contribution plan, the requirements of paragraph (2) are met, and

(B) in the case of a defined benefit plan, the requirements of paragraph (3) are met.

(2) Defined contribution plan.—

(A) In general.—A defined contribution plan meets the requirements of this paragraph if the excess contribution percentage does not exceed the base contribution percentage by more than the lesser of—

(i) the base contribution percentage, or

(ii) the greater of—

(I) 5.7 percentage points, or

(II) the percentage equal to the portion of the rate of tax under section 3111(a) (in effect as of the beginning of the year) which is attributable to old-age insurance.

(B) Contribution percentages.—For purposes of this paragraph—

(i) Excess contribution percentage.—The term "excess contribution percentage" means the percentage of compensation which is contributed under the plan with respect to that portion of each participant's compensation in excess of the integration level.

(ii) Base contribution percentage.—The term "base contribution percentage" means the percentage of compensation contributed under the plan with respect to that portion of each participant's compensation not in excess of the integration level.

(3) Defined benefit plan.—A defined benefit plan meets the requirements of this paragraph if—

(A) Excess plans.—

(i) In general.—In the case of a plan other than an offset plan—

(I) the excess benefit percentage does not exceed the base benefit percentage by more than the maximum excess allowance,

(II) any optional form of benefit, preretirement benefit, actuarial factor, or other benefit or feature provided with respect to compensation in excess of the integration level is provided with respect to compensation not in excess of such level, and

(III) benefits are based on average annual compensation.

(ii) Benefit percentages.—For purposes of this subparagraph, the excess and base benefit percentages shall be computed in the same manner as the excess and base contribution percentages under paragraph (2)(B), except that such determination shall be made on the basis of benefits rather than contributions.

(B) Offset plans.—In the case of an offset plan, the plan provides that—

(i) a participant's accrued benefit attributable to employer contributions (within the meaning of section 411(c)(1)) may not be reduced (by reason of the offset) by more than the maximum offset allowance, and

(ii) benefits are based on average annual compensation.

[Footnote ¶2994 continued]

In the case of an individual who is an employee within the meaning of subsection (c)(1), the preceding sentence shall be applied by taking into account his earned income (as defined in subsection (c)(2)).

(B) OASDI.—The term "OASDI" means the system of old-age, survivors, and disability insurance established under Title II of the Social Security Act and the Federal Insurance Contributions Act.

(C) Remuneration.—The term "remuneration" means—

(i) total compensation, or

(ii) basic or regular rate of compensation,

whichever is used in determining contributions or benefits under the plan.

(3) Determination of compensation, etc., of self-employed individuals.—For purposes of this subsection, in the case of an individual who is an employee within the meaning of subsection (c)(1)—

(A) his total compensation shall include his earned income (as defined in subsection (c)(2)), and

(B) his basic or regular rate of compensation shall be determined (under regulations prescribed by the Secretary) with respect to that portion of his earned income which bears the same ratio to his earned income as the basic or regular compensation of the employees under the plan (other than employees within the meaning of subsection (c)(1)) bears to the total compensation of such employees.

Effective date (Sec. 1111(c)(1), '86 TRA).—Generally applies to benefits attributable to plan years beginning after 12-31-88. For special rule for collective bargaining agreements, see above.

(4) *Definitions relating to paragraph (3).—For purposes of paragraph (3)—*

(A) *Maximum excess allowance.—The maximum excess allowance is equal to—*

(i) in the case of benefits attributable to any year of service with the employer taken into account under the plan, 3/4 of a percentage point, and

(ii) in the case of total benefits, 3/4 of a percentage point, multiplied by the participant's years of service (not in excess of 35) with the employer taken into account under the plan.

In no event shall the maximum excess allowance exceed the base benefit percentage.

(B) *Maximum offset allowance.—The maximum offset allowance is equal to—*

(i) in the case of benefits attributable to any year of service with the employer taken into account under the plan, 3/4 percent of the participant's final average compensation, and

(ii) in the case of total benefits, 3/4 percent of the participant's final average compensation, multiplied by the participant's years of service (not in excess of 35) with the employer taken into account under the plan.

In no event shall the maximum offset allowance exceed 50 percent of the benefit which would have accrued without regard to the offset reduction.

(C) *Reductions.—*

(i) *In general.—The Secretary shall prescribe regulations requiring the reduction of the 3/4 percentage factor under subparagraph (A) or (B)—*

(I) in the case of a plan other than an offset plan which has an integration level in excess of covered compensation, or

(II) with respect to any participant in an offset plan who has final average compensation in excess of covered compensation.

(ii) *Basis of reductions.—Any reductions under clause (i) shall be based on the percentages of compensation replaced by the employer-derived portions of primary insurance amounts under the Social Security Act for participants with compensation in excess of covered compensation.*

(D) *Offset plan.—The term "offset plan" means any plan with respect to which the benefit attributable to employer contributions for each participant is reduced by an amount specified in the plan.*

(5) *Other definitions and special rules.—For purposes of this subsection—*

(A) *Integration level.—*

(i) *In general.—The term "integration level" means the amount of compensation specified under the plan (by dollar amount or formula) at or below which the rate at which contributions or benefits are provided (expressed as a percentage) is less than such rate above such amount.*

(ii) *Limitation.—The integration level for any year may not exceed the contribution and benefit base in effect under section 230 of the Social Security Act for such year.*

(iii) *Level to apply to all participants.—A plan's integration level shall apply with respect to all participants in the plan.*

(iv) *Multiple integration levels.—Under rules prescribed by the Secretary, a defined benefit plan may specify multiple integration levels.*

(B) *Compensation.—The term "compensation" has the meaning given such term by section 414(s).*

(C) *Average annual compensation.—The term "average annual compensation" means the greater of—*

(i) the participant's final average compensation (determined without regard to subparagraph (D)(ii)), or

(ii) the participant's highest average annual compensation for any other period of at least 3 consecutive years.

(D) *Final average compensation.—*

(i) *In general.—The term "final average compensation" means the participant's average annual compensation for—*

(I) the 3-consecutive year period ending with the current year, or

(II) if shorter, the participant's full period of service.

(ii) Limitation.—A participant's final average compensation shall be determined by not taking into account in any year compensation in excess of the contribution and benefit base in effect under section 230 of the Social Security Act for such year.

(E) Covered compensation.—

(i) In general.—The term "covered compensation" means, with respect to an employee, the average of the contribution and benefit bases in effect under section 230 of the Social Security Act for each year in the 35-year period ending with the year in which the employee attains age 65.

(ii) Computation for any year.—For purposes of clause (i), the determination for any year preceding the year in which the employee attains age 65 shall be made by assuming that there is no increase in the bases described in clause (i) after the determination year and before the employee attains age 65.

(F) Regulations.—The Secretary shall prescribe such regulations as are necessary or appropriate to carry out the purposes of this subsection, including—

(i) in the case of a defined benefit plan which provides for unreduced benefits commencing before the social security retirement age (as defined in section 415(b)(8)), rules providing for the reduction of the maximum excess allowance and the maximum offset allowance, and

(ii) in the case of an employee covered by 2 or more plans of the employer which fail to meet the requirements of subsection (a)(4) (without regard to this subsection), rules preventing the multiple use of the disparity permitted under this subsection with respect to any employee.

For purposes of clause (i), unreduced benefits shall not include benefits for disability (within the meaning of section 223(d) of the Social Security Act).

(6) Special rule for plan maintained by railroads.—In determining whether a plan which includes employees of a railroad employer who are entitled to benefits under the Railroad Retirement Act of 1974 meets the requirements of this subsection, rules similar to the rules set forth in this subsection shall apply. Such rules shall take into account the employer-derived portion of the employees' tier 2 railroad retirement benefits and any supplemental annuity under the Railroad Retirement Act of 1974.

(m) Nondiscrimination Test for Matching Contributions and Employee Contributions.—

(1) In general.—A plan shall be treated as meeting the requirements of subsection (a)(4) with respect to the amount of any matching contribution or employee contribution for any plan year only if the contribution percentage requirement of paragraph (2) of this subsection is met for such plan year.

(2) Requirements.—

【Footnote ¶2994 continued】

Sec. 401(m) in *italics* added by section 1117(a), '86 TRA.

Effective date (Sec. 1117(d), '86 TRA.—(1) Generally applies to plan years beginning after 12-31-86.

(2) Collective bargaining agreements.—In the case of a plan maintained pursuant to 1 or more collective bargaining agreements between employee representatives and 1 or more employers ratified before 3-1-86, the amendments made by this section shall not apply to plan years beginning before the earlier of—

(a) 1-1-89,

(B) the date on which the last of such collective bargaining agreements terminates (determined without regard to any extension thereof after 2-28-86).

(3) Annuity contracts.—In the case of an annuity contract under section 403(b) '86 Code—

(A) the amendments made by this section shall apply to plan years beginning after 12-31-88, and

(B) in the case of a collective bargaining agreement described in paragraph (2), the amendments made by this section shall not apply to years beginning before the earlier of—

(i) the later of—

(I) 1-1-89, or

(II) the date determined under paragraph (2)(B), or

(ii) 1-1-91.

Sec. 401(n) [formerly redesignated as (m) by section 1117(a), '86 TRA], added by section 1898(c)(3), '86 TRA.

Effective date (Sec. 1898(j), '86 TRA and Sec. 302 and 303, Retirement Equity Act of 1984, P.L. 98-397, 8-23-84, as amended by sections 1145(c), 1898(g), and (h), of '86 TRA.—Applies to plan years beginning after 12-31-84. For special and transitional rules, see above.

(A) *Contribution percentage requirement.—A plan meets the contribution percentage requirement of this paragraph for any plan year only if the contribution percentage for eligible highly compensated employees does not exceed the greater of—*
    (i) *125 percent of such percentage for all other eligible employees, or*
    (ii) *the lesser of 200 percent of such percentage for all other eligible employees, or such percentage for all other eligible employees plus 2 percentage points.*

(B) *Multiple plans treated as a single plan.—If two or more plans of an employer to which matching contributions, employee contributions, or elective deferrals are made are treated as one plan for purposes of section 410(b), such plans shall be treated as one plan for purposes of this subsection. If a highly compensated employee participates in two or more plans of an employer to which such contributions are made, all such contributions shall be aggregated for purposes of this subsection.*

(3) *Contribution percentage.—For purposes of this paragraph (2), the contribution percentage for a specified group of employees for a plan year shall be the average of the ratios (calculated separately for each employee in such group) of—*
    (A) *the sum of the matching contributions and employee contributions paid under the plan on behalf of each such employee for such plan year, to*
    (B) *the employee's compensation (within the meaning of section 414(s)) for such plan year.*

Under regulations, an employer may elect to take into account (in computing the contribution percentage) elective deferrals and qualified nonelective contributions under the plan or any other plan of the employer.

(4) *Definitions.—For purposes of this subsection—*
    (A) *Matching contribution.—The term "matching contribution" means—*
        (i) *any employer contribution made to the plan on behalf of an employee on account of an employee contribution made by such employee, and*
        (ii) *any employer contribution made to the plan on behalf of an employee on account of an employee's elective deferral.*
    (B) *Elective deferral.—The term "elective deferral" means any employer contribution described in section 402(g)(3)(A).*
    (C) *Qualified nonelective contributions.—The term "qualified nonelective contribution" means any employer contribution (other than a matching contribution) with respect to which—*
        (i) *the employee may not elect to have the contribution paid to the employee in cash instead of being contributed to the plan, and*
        (ii) *the requirements of subparagraphs (B) and (C) of subsection (k)(2) are met.*

(5) *Employees taken into consideration.—*
    (A) *In general.—Any employee who is eligible to make an employee contribution (or, if the employer takes elective contributions into account, elective contributions) or to receive a matching contribution under the plan being tested under paragraph (1) shall be considered an eligible employee for purposes of this subsection.*
    (B) *Certain nonparticipants.—If an employee contribution is required as a condition of participation in the plan, any employee who would be a participant in the plan if such employee made such a contribution shall be treated as an eligible employee on behalf of whom no employer contributions are made.*

(6) *Plan not disqualified if excess aggregate contributions distributed before end of following plan year.—*
    (A) *In general.—A plan shall not be treated as failing to meet the requirements of paragraph (1) for any plan year if, before the close of the following plan year, the amount of the excess aggregate contributions for such plan year (and any income allocable to such contributions) is distributed (or, if forfeitable, is forfeited). Such contributions (and such income) may be distributed without regard to any other provision of law.*
    (B) *Excess aggregate contributions.—For purposes of subparagraph (A), the term "excess aggregate contributions" means, with respect to any plan year, the excess of—*
        (i) *the aggregate amount of the matching contributions and employee contributions (and any qualified nonelective contribution or elective contribution taken into account in computing the contribution percentage) actually made on behalf of highly compensated employees for such plan year, over*
        (ii) *the maximum amount of such contributions permitted under the limitations of paragraph (2)(A) (determined by reducing contributions made on behalf*

of highly compensated employees in order of their contribution percentages beginning with the highest of such percentages).

(C)   *Method of distributing excess contributions.*—Any distribution of the excess aggregate contributions for any plan year shall be made to highly compensated employees on the basis of the respective portions of such amounts attributable to each of such employees. Forfeitures of excess aggregate contributions may not be allocated to participants whose contributions are reduced under this paragraph.

(D)   *Coordination with subsection (k) and 402(g).*—The determination of the amount of excess aggregate contributions with respect to a plan shall be made after—

(i)   first determining the excess deferrals (within the meaning of section 402(g)), and

(ii)   then determining the excess contributions under subsection (k).

(7)   *Treatment of distributions.*—

(A)   *Additional tax of section 72(t) not applicable.*—No tax shall be imposed under section 72(t) on any amount required to be distributed under paragraph (8).

(B)   *Exclusion of employee contributions.*—Any distribution attributable to employee contributions shall not be included in gross income except to the extent attributable to income on such contributions.

(8)   *Highly compensated employee.*—For purposes of this subsection, the term "highly compensated employee" has the meaning given to such term by section 414(q).

(9)   *Regulations.*—The Secretary shall prescribe such regulations as may be necessary to carry out the purposes of this subsection and subsection (k) including—

(A)   such regulations as may be necessary to prevent the multiple use of the alternative limitation with respect to any highly compensated employee, and

(B)   regulations permitting appropriate aggregation of plans and contributions.

For purposes of the preceding sentence, the term "alternative limitation" means the limitation of section 401(k)(3)(A)(ii)(II) and the limitation of paragraph (2)(A)(ii) of this subsection."

(10)   *Cross reference.*—

For excise tax on certain excess contributions, see section 4979.

(n)   **Coordination With Qualified Domestic Relations Orders.**—The Secretary shall prescribe such rules or regulations as may be necessary to coordinate the requirements of subsection (a)(13)(B) and section 414(p) (and the regulations issued by the Secretary of Labor thereunder) with the other provisions of this chapter.

[34](o)   **Cross Reference.**—

For exemption from tax of a trust qualified under this section, see section 501(a).

[For official explanation, see Committee Reports, ¶3979; 3976; 3984; 3986; 4172; 4211; 4005; 3972; 4016; 4021;   4019; 3977; 3995; 4020; 4161; 4002; 4193; 3981; 3977; 3982.]

[¶2995]   CODE SEC. 402.   TAXABILITY OF BENEFICIARY OF EMPLOYEES' TRUST.

(a)   **Taxability of Beneficiary of Exempt Trust.**—

(1)   **General rule.**—Except as provided in paragraphs (2) and (4), the amount actually distributed to any distributee by any employees' trust described in section 401(a) which is exempt from tax under section 501(a) shall be taxable to him, in the year in which so distributed under section 72 (relating to annuities). The amount actually distributed to any distributee shall not include net unrealized appreciation in securities of the employer corporation attributable to the amount contributed by the employee (other than deductible employee contributions within the meaning of section 72(o)(5)). Such net unrealized appreciation and the resulting adjustments to basis of such securities shall be determined in accordance with regulations prescribed by the Secretary.

(2)   **[Repealed]**[1]

---

(5)   Rollover amounts.—

* * * * * * * * * * * * *

(D)   Special rules for partial distributions

≫P-H CAUTION→   There are two versions of Sec. 402(a)(5)(D)(i). Sec. 402(a)(5)(D)(i), generally effective for amounts distributed after 12-31-86, follows. For Sec. 402(a)(5)(D)(i), generally effective for distributions made before 1-1-87, see below.

▲(i)   Requirements.—Subparagraph (A) shall apply to a partial distribution only if [2] *the employee elects to have subparagraph (A) apply to such distribution and such distribution would be a lump sum distribution if subsection (e)(4)(A) were applied—*

(I)   by substituting "50 percent of the balance to the credit of an employee" for "the balance to the credit of an employee",

(II)   without regard to clause (ii) thereof, the second sentence thereof, and subparagraph (B) of subsection (e)(4).

Any distribution described in section 401(a)(28)(B)(ii) shall be treated as meeting the requirements of this clause.

≫P-H CAUTION→   There are two versions of Sec. 402(a)(5)(D)(i). Sec. 402(a)(5)(D)(i), generally effective for distributions made before 1-1-87, in taxable years ending after such date, follows. For Sec. 402(a)(5)(D)(i), generally effective for amounts distributed after 12-31-86, in taxable years ending after such date, see above.

▲ ▲(i)   Requirements.—Subparagraph (A) shall apply to a partial distribution only if—

(I)   such distribution is of an amount equal to at least 50 percent of the balance to the credit of the employee in a qualified trust (determined immediately before such distribution and without regard to subsection (e)(4)(C)),

(II)   such distribution is not one of a series of periodic payments, and

(III)   the employee elects (at such time and in such manner as the Secretary shall by regulations prescribe) to have subparagraph (A) apply to such partial distribution.

⟦Footnote ¶2995 continued⟧

able amount multiplied by a fraction—

(A)   the numerator of which is the number of calendar years of active participation by the employee in such plan before January 1, 1974, and

(B)   the denominator of which is the number of calendar years of active participation by the employee in such plan,

shall be treated as a gain from the sale or exchange of a capital asset held for more than 6 months. For purposes of computing the fraction described in this paragraph and the fraction under subsection (e)(4)(E), the Secretary may prescribe regulations under which plan years may be used in lieu of calendar years. For purposes of this paragraph, in the case of an individual who is an employee without regard to section 401(c)(1), determination of whether or not any distribution is a lump sum distribution shall be made without regard to the requirement that an election be made under subsection (e)(4)(B), but no distribution to any taxpayer other than an individual, estate, or trust may be treated as a lump sum distribution under this paragraph."

Effective date (Sec. 1122(h), '86 TRA).—Generally applies to amounts distributed after 12-31-86, in taxable years ending after such date. For special rules, see ¶2043.

▲Matter in *italics* in Sec. 402(a)(5)(D)(i), preceded by a triangle, added by section 1122(e)(1), '86 TRA, which struck out:

(2)   "(I)   such distribution is of an amount equal to at least 50 percent of the balance to the credit of the employee in a qualified trust (determined immediately before such distribution and without regard to Subsection (e)(4)(C)),

(II)   such distribution is not one of a series of periodic payments, and

(III)   the employee elects (at such time and in such manner as the Secretary shall by regulations prescribe) to have subparagraph (A) apply to such partial distribution.

For purposes of subclause (I), the balance to the credit of the employee shall not include any accumulated deductible employee contributions (within the meaning of section 72(o)(5))."

Effective date (Sec. 1122(h), '86 TRA).—Generally applies to amounts distributed after 12-31-86, in taxable years ending after such date. For special rules, see ¶2043.

▲ ▲Matter in *italics* in Sec. 402(a)(5)(D)(i), preceded by two triangles, added by section 1852(b)(2), '86 TRA.

Effective date (Sec. 1881, '86 TRA and section 522(e), '84 TRA).—Applies to distributions made after 7-18-84, in taxable years ending after such date.

For purposes of subclause (I), the balance to the credit of the employee shall not include any accumulated deductible employee contributions (within the meaning of section 71(o)(5)).

(ii) Partial distributions may be transferred only to individual retirement plans.—In the case of a partial distribution, a *trust or* plan described in subclause *(III) or* (IV) [3] of subparagraph (E)(iv) shall not be treated as an eligible retirement plan.

(iii) Denial of 10-year averaging [4]*for subsequent distributions.—If an election under clause (i) is made with respect to any partial distribution paid to any employee, paragraphs (1) and (3) of subsection (e) shall not apply to any distribution (paid after such partial distribution) of the balance to the credit of such employee under the plan under which such partial distribution was made (or under any other plan which, under subsection (e)(4)(C), would be aggregated with such plan).*

(iv) Special rule for unrelated appreciation.—If an election under clause (i) is made with respect to any partial distribution, the second and third sentences of paragraph (1) shall not apply to such distribution.

(E) Definitions. For purposes of this paragraph—

(i) Qualifying total rollover distribution.—The term "qualified total distribution" means 1 or more distributions—

(I) within 1 taxable year of the employee on account of a termination of the plan of which the trust is a part or, in the case of a profit-sharing or stock bonus plan, a complete discontinuance of contributions under such plan,

(II) which constitute a lump sum distribution within the meaning of subsection (e)(4)(A) (determined without reference to, subparagraphs (B) and (H) of subsection (e)(4)), or

(III) which constitute a distribution of accumulated deductible employee contributions (within the meaning of section 72(o)(5)).

(ii) Employee contributions.—The term "employee contributions" means—

(I) the excess of the amounts considered contributed by the employee (determined by applying section 72(f)), over

(II) any amounts theretofore distributed to the employee which were not includible in gross income (determined without regard to this paragraph).

(iii) Qualified trust.—The term "qualifed trust" means an employees' trust described in section 401(a) which is exempt from tax under section 501(a).

(iv) Eligible retirement plan.—The term "eligible retirement plan" means—

(I) an individual retirement account described in section 408(a),

(II) an individual retirement annuity described in section 408(b) (other than an endowment contract),

(III) a qualified trust, and

(IV) an annuity plan described in section 403(a),

(v) Partial distribution.—The term "partial distribution" means any distribution to an employee of *all or* any portion of the balance to the credit of such

---

⟦Footnote ¶2995 continued⟧

Matter in *italics* in Sec. 402(a)(5)(D)(ii), added by section 1852(b)(5), '86 TRA, which struck out:
(3) "or (V)"
Effective date (Sec. 1881, '86 TRA and section 522(e), '84 TRA.—Applies to distributions made after 7-18-84, in taxable years ending after such date.

Matter in *italics* in Sec. 402(a)(5)(D)(iii) added by section 1122(b)(2)(A), '86 TRA, which struck out:
(4) "and capital gains treatment for subsequent distributions.—If an election under clause (i) is made with respect to any partial distribution paid to any employee—
(I) paragraph (2) of this subsection,
(II) paragraphs (1) and (3) of subsection (e), and
(III) paragraph (2) of section 403(a),
shall not apply to any distribution (paid after such partial distribution) of the balance to the credit of such employee under the plan under which such partial distribution was made (or under any other plan which, under subsection (e)(4)(C), would be aggregated with such plan)."
Effective date (Sec. 1122(h), '86 TRA).—Generally applies to amounts distributed ater 12-31-86, in taxable years ending after such date. For special rules, see ¶2043.

Matter in *italics* in Sec. 402(a)(5)(E)(v) added by section 1852(b)(1).
Effective date (Sec. 1881, '86 TRA and section 522(e), '84 TRA).—Applies to distributions made after 7-18-84, in taxable years ending after such date.

---

employee in a qualified trust; except that such term shall not include any distribution which is a qualified total distribution.

➤➤P-H CAUTION→ **There are two versions of Sec. 402(a)(5)(F). Section 402(5)(F), generally effective after 12-31-88, follows. For Sec. 402(a)(5)(F), generally effective before 1-1-89, see below.**

▲(F) [5]*Transfer treated as rollover contribution under section 408.—For purposes of this title, a transfer described in subparagraph (A) to an eligible retirement plan described in subclause (I) or (II) of subparagraph (E)(iv) shall be treated as a rollover contribution described in section 408(d)(3).*

➤➤P-H CAUTION→ **There are two versions of Sec. 402(a)(5)(F). Sec. 402(a)(5)(F), generally effective for years beginning before 1-1-89, follows. For Sec. 402(a)(5)(F), generally effective for years beginning after 12-31-88, see below.**

▲▲(F) Special rules.—
(i) Transfer treated as rollover contribution under section 408.—For purposes of this title a transfer [6]*resulting in any portion of a distribution being excluded from gross income under* subparagraph (A) to an eligible retirement plan described in subclause (I) or (II) of subparagraph (E)(iv) shall be treated as a rollover contribution described in section 408(d)(3).
(ii) [7]*5-percent owners.—An eligible retirement plan described in subclause (III)*

[Footnote ¶2995 continued]

▲Matter in *italics* in Sec. 402(a)(5)(F), preceded by a triangle, added by section 1121(c)(1), '86 TRA, which struck out:
(5) "Special rules.—
(i) Transfer treated as rollover contribution under section 408.—For purposes of this title a transfer resulting in any portion of a distribution being excluded from gross income under subparagraph (A) to an eligible retirement plan described in subclause (I) or (II) of subparagraph (E)(iv) shall be treated as a rollover contribution described in section 408(d)(3).
(ii) 5-percent owners.—An eligible retirement plan described in subclause (III) or (IV) of subparagraph (E)(iv) shall not be treated as an eligible retirement plan for the transfer of a distribution if the employee is a 5-percent owner at the time such distribution is made. For purposes of the preceding sentence, the term "5-percent owner" means any individual who is a 5-percent owner (as defined in section 416(i)(1)(B)) at any time during the 5 plan years preceding the plan year in which the distribution is made.
Effective date (Sec. 1121(d)(2), (3), '86 TRA). (2) Applies to years beginning after 12-31-88.
(3) Collective bargaining agreements.—In the case of a plan maintained pursuant to 1 or more collective bargaining agreements between employee representatives and 1 or more employers ratified before 3-1-86, the amendments made by this section shall not apply to distributions to individuals covered by such agreements in plan years beginning before the earlier of—
(A) the later of—
(i) the date on which the last of such collective bargaining agreements terminates (determined without regard to any extension thereof after 2-28-86, or
(ii) 1-1-89, or
(B) January 1, 1991.
(4) Transition rules.—
(A) The amendments made by subsections (a) and (b) shall not apply with respect to any benefits with respect to which a designation is in effect under section 242(b)(2) of '82 TEFRA.
(B)(i) Except as provided in clause (ii), the amendment made by subsection (b) shall not apply in the case of any individual who has attained age 70½ before 1-1-88.
(ii) Clause (i) shall not apply to any individual who is a 5-percent owner (as defined in section 416(i) of the '86 Code), at any time during—
(I) the plan year ending with or within the calendar year in which such owner attains age 66½, and
(II) any subsequent plan year.

▲▲Matter in *italics* in Sec. 402(a)(5)(F)(i), preceded by two triangles, added by section 1852(b)(6), '86 TRA, which struck out"
(6) "described"
Effective date (Sec. 1881, '86 TRA and section 522(e), '84 TRA).—Applies to distributions made after 7-18-84, in taxable years ending after such date.

▲▲Matter in *italics* in Sec. 402(a)(5)(F)(ii), preceded by two triangles, added by section 1875(c)(1)(A), '86 TRA), which struck out:
(7) "Key employees.—An eligible retirement plan described in subclause (III) or (IV) of subparagraph (E)(iv) shall not be treated as an eligible retirement plan for the transfer of a distribution if any part of the distribution is attributable to contributions made on behalf of the employee while he was a key employee in a top-heavy plan. For purposes of the preceding sentence, the terms "key employee" and "top-heavy plan" have the same respective meanings as when used in section 416."
Effective date (Sec. 1875(c)(1)(B), '86 TRA).—Applies to distributions after the enactment date. Applies also to

or (IV) of subparagraph (E)(iv) shall not be treated as an eligible retirement plan for the transfer of a distribution if the employee is a 5-percent owner at the time such distribution is made. For purposes of the preceding sentence, the term "5-percent owner" means any individual who is a 5-percent owner (as defined in section 416(i)(1)(B)) at any time during the 5 plan years preceding the plan year in which the distribution is made.

(G) Required distributions not eligible for rollover treatment.—Subparagraph (A) shall not apply to any distribution to the extent such distribution is required under section 401(a)(9).

(6) Special rollover rules.—

* * * * * * * * * * * *

(D) Sales of distributed property.—For purposes of subparagraphs (5) and (7)—

* * * * * * * * * * * *

(v) Nonrecognition of gain or loss.—In the case of any sale described in clause (i), to the extent that an amount equal to the proceeds is transferred pursuant to paragraph (5)(B) or (7)[8] (as the case may be), neither gain nor loss on such sale shall be recognized.

* * * * * * * * * * * *

(F) Qualified domestic relations order.—If—
(i) within 1 taxable year of the recipient, the balance to the credit of the recipient by reason of any qualified domestic relations order (within the meaning of section 414(p)) is distributed or paid to the recipient,
(ii) the recipient transfers any portion of the property the recipient receives in such distributions to an eligible retirement plan described in subclause (I) or (II) of paragraph (5)(E)(iv), and
(iii) in the case of a distribution of property other than money, the amount so transferred consists of the property distributed,
then the portion of the distribution so transferred shall be treated as a distribution described in paragraph (5)[9].
(G) Payments from certain pension plan termination trusts.—If—
(i) any amount is paid or distributed to a recipient from a trust described in section 501(c)(24),

---

【Footnote ¶2995 continued】
distributions after 1983 and on or before the enactment date to individuals who are not 5-percent owners (as defined in section 402(a)(5)(F)(ii) of the '54 Code (as amended by section 1875(c)(1)(A), '86 TRA.

Sec. 402(a)(5)(G) in *italics* added by section 1852(a)(5)(A), '86 TRA.
Effective date (Sec. 1881, '86 TRA and section 521(e), '84 TRA).—Generally applies to years beginning after 12-31-84. For special rules, see footnote ¶2994.

Matter in *italics* in Sec. 402(a)(6)(D)(v) added by section 1852(b)(7), '86 TRA, which struck out:
(8) "(B)"
Effective date (Sec. 1881, '86 TRA and section 522(e), '84 TRA).—Applies to distributions made after 7-18-84 in taxable years ending after such date.

Matter in *italics* in Sec. 402(a)(6)(G) [should read (H)] added by section 1898(a)(3) and (c)(7)(A)(i), '86 TRA, which struck out:
(9) "(A)"
Effective date (Sec. 1898(j), '86 TRA and section 302 and 303, '84 Retirement Equity Act, as amended by '86 TRA).—(a) Generally applies to plan years beginning after 12-31-84. For '86 TRA amendments, and special and transitional rules, see footnote ¶2994.

Section 402(a)(6)(H) [(should read (I)] in *italics* added by section 1122(e)(2)(A), '86 TRA.
Effective date (Sec. 1122(h), '86 TRA).—Generally applies to amounts distributed after 12-31-86, in taxable years ending after such date. For special rules, see ¶2043.

Matter in *italics* in Sec. 402(a)(7) added by section 1852(b)(4), '86 TRA.
Effective date (Sec. 1881, '86 TRA and section 522(a), '84 TRA).—Applies to distributions made after 7-18-84, in taxable years ending after such date.

Matter in *italics* in Sec. 402(a)(9) added by section 1898(c)(1)(A), '86 TRA, which struck out:

(ii)   the recipient transfers any portion of the property received in such distribution to an eligible retirement plan described in subclause (I) or (II) of paragraph (5)(E)(iv), and

(iii)   in the case of a distribution of property other than money, the amount so transferred consists of the property distributed,

then the portion of the distribution so transferred shall be treated as a distribution described in paragraph (5)(A).

(G)   [should read (H)] Treatment of potential future vesting.—

(i)   In general.—For purposes of paragraph (5), in determining whether any portion of a distribution on account of the employee's separation from service may be transferred in a transfer to which paragraph (5)(A) applies, the balance to the credit of the employee shall be determined without regard to any increase in vesting which may occur if the employee is re-employed by the employer.

(ii)   Treatment of subsequent distributions.—If—

(I)   any portion of a distribution is transferred in a transfer to which paragraph (5)(A) applies by reason of clause (i),

(II)   the employee is subsequently re-employed by the employer, and

(III)   as a result of service performed after being so re-employed, there is an increase in the employee's vesting for benefits accrued before the separation referred to in clause (i),

then the provisions of paragraph (5)(D)(iii) shall apply to any distribution from the plan after the distribution referred to in clause (i). The preceding sentence shall not apply if the distribution referred to in subclause (I) is made without the consent of the participant.

(H)   [should read (I)] Special rule for frozen deposits.—

(i)   In general.—The 60-day period described in paragraph (5)(C) shall not—

(I)   include any period during which the amount transferred to the employee is a frozen deposit, or

(II)   end earlier than 10 days after such amount ceases to be a frozen deposit.

(ii)   Frozen deposit.—For purposes of this subparagraph, the term "frozen deposit" means any deposit which may not be withdrawn because of—

(I)   the bankruptcy or insolvency of any financial institution, or

(II)   any requirement imposed by the State in which such institution is located by reason of the bankruptcy or insolvency (or threat thereof) of 1 or more financial institutions in such State.

(7)   Rollover where spouse receives distributions after death of employee.—If any distribution attributable to an employee is paid to the spouse of the employee after the employee's death, paragraph (5) shall apply to such distribution in the same manner as if the spouse were the employee; *except that a trust or plan described in subclause (III) or (IV) of paragraph (5)(E)(iv) shall not be treated as an eligible retirement plan with respect to such distribution.*

* * * * * * * * * * *

(9)   Alternate payee under qualified domestic relations order treated as distributee.—For purposes of subsection (a)(1) and section 72, [10] *any* alternate payee *who is the spouse or former spouse of the participant* shall be treated as the distributee of any distribution or payment made to the alternate payee under a qualified domestic relations order (as defined in section 414(p)).

(b)   Taxability of Beneficiary of Nonexempt Trust.

*(1)   In general—*Contributions to an employees' trust made by an employer during a taxable year of the employer which ends within or with a taxable year of the trust for which the trust is not exempt from tax under section 501(a) shall be included in the gross income of the employee in accordance with section 83 (relating to property transferred in connection with performance of services), except that the value of the employee's interest in the trust shall be substituted for the fair market value of the property for purposes of applying such section. The amount actually distributed or made available to any distributee by any such trust shall be taxable to him in the year

【Footnote ¶2995 continued】

(10)   "the"
Effective date (Sec. 1898(c)(1)(C), '86 TRA).—Applies to payments made after the enactment date.

———

Matter in *italics* in the heading of Sec. 402(b)(1) added by section 1112(c)(2), '86 TRA.
Effective date (Sec. 1112(e), '86 TRA).—Generally applies to plan years beginning after 12-31-88. For special rules, see footnote ¶2994.

———

Matter in *italics* in Sec. 402(b)(1), except the heading, added by section 1852(c)(5), '86 TRA, which struck out:

in which so distributed or made available, under section 72 (relating to annuities), except that distributions of income of such trust before the annuity starting date (as defined in section 72(c)(4)) shall be included in the gross income of the employee without regard to [11] *section 72(e)(5)* (relating to amount not received as annuities). A beneficiary of any such trust shall not be considered the owner of any portion of such trust under subpart E of part I of subchapter J (relating to grantors and others treated as substantial owners).

(2) *Failure to meet requirements of section 410(b).—*

(A) *In general.—In the case of a trust which is not exempt from tax under section 501(a) solely because such trust is part of a plan which fails to meet the requirements of section 410(b)—*

(i) *such trust shall be treated as exempt from tax under section 501(a) for purposes of applying paragraph (1) to employees who are not highly compensated employees, and*

(ii) *paragraph (1) shall be applied to the vested accrued benefit (other than employee contributions) of any highly compensated employee as of the close of the employer's taxable year described in paragraph (1) (rather than contributions made during such year).*

(B) *Failure in more than 1 year.—If a plan fails to meet the requirements of section 410(b) for more than 1 taxable year, any portion of the vested accrued benefit to which subparagraph (A) applies shall be included in gross income only once.*

(C) *Highly compensated employee.—For purposes of this paragraph, the term "highly compensated employee" has the meaning given such term by section 414(q).*

* * * * * * * * * * * *

(e) **Tax on Lump Sum Distributions.—**

(1) **Imposition of separate tax on lump sum distributions.—**

(A) Separate tax.—There is hereby imposed a tax (in the amount determined under subparagraph (B)) on the ordinary income portion of a lump sum distribution.[12]

[13]*(B)* [14]*Amount of* tax.—The [14]*amount of* tax *imposed by subparagraph (A)* for any taxable year is an amount equal to [15]5 *times* the tax which would be imposed by subsection (c) of section 1 if the recipient were an individual referred to in such subsection and the taxable income were an amount equal to [16] [17]1/5 of the excess of—

(i) the total taxable amount of the lump sum distribution for the taxable year, over

(ii) the minimum distribution allowance.

[18]*(C)* Minimum distribution allowance.—For purposes of this paragraph, the minimum distribution allowance for the taxable year is an amount equal to—

(i) the lesser of $10,000 or one-half of the total taxable amount of the lump sum distribution for the taxable year, reduced (but not below zero) by

---

〔Footnote ¶2995 continued〕

(11) "section (72)(e)(1)"

Effective date (Sec. 1881, '86 TRA and section 523(c), '84 TRA).—Applies to any amount received or loan made after 10-16-84.

Sec. 402(b)(2) added by section 1112(c)(1), '86 TRA.

Effective date (Sec. 1112(e), '86 TRA).—Generally applies to plan years beginning after 12-31-88. For special rules, see footnote ¶2994.

Matter in *italics* in Sec. 402(e)(1)(B)—(D) added by section 1122(b)(2)(B), '86 TRA, which struck out:

(12) "(B) Amount of tax.—The amount of tax imposed by subparagraph (A) for any taxable year shall be an amount equal to the amount of the initial separate tax for such taxable year multiplied by a fraction, the numerator of which is the ordinary income portion of the lump sum distribution for the taxable year and the denominator of which is the total taxable amount of such distribution for such year.

(13) "(C)"

(14) "amount of"

(15) "10 times"

Effective date (Sec. 1122(h), '86 TRA).—Generally applies to amounts distributed after 12-31-86, in taxable years ending after such date. For special rules, see ¶2043.

Section 104(b), '86 TRA, struck out from Sec. 402(e)(1)(B):

(16) "the zero bracket amount applicable to such an individual for the taxable year plus"

Effective date (Sec. 151(a), '86 TRA).—Applies to taxable years beginning after 12-31-86.

Matter in *italics* in Sec. 402(e)(1)(B)—(D); (e)(3), (4)(B), and (E) added by section 1122(a)(1), (b)(2)(C), and (D), '86 TRA, which struck out:

(17) one-tenth

(18) "(D)"

(ii)   20 percent of the amount (if any) by which such total taxable amount exceeds $20,000.

[19]*(D)   Liability for tax.*—The recipient shall be liable for the tax imposed by this paragraph.

(2)   Multiple distributions and distributions of annuity contracts.—In the case of any recipient of a lump sum distribution for the taxable year with respect to whom during the 6-taxable-year period ending on the last day of the taxable year there has been one or more other lump sum distributions after December 31, 1973, or if the distribution (or any part thereof) is an annuity contract, in computing the tax imposed by paragraph (1)(A), the total taxable amounts of all such distributions during such 6-taxable-year period shall be aggregated, but the amount of tax so computed shall be reduced (but not below zero) by the sum of—

(A)   the amount of the tax imposed by paragraph (1)(A) paid with respect to such other distributions, plus

(B)   that portion of the tax on the aggregated total taxable amounts which is attributable to annuity contracts.

For purposes of this paragraph, a beneficiary of a trust to which a lump sum distribution is made shall be treated as the recipient of such distribution if the beneficiary is an employee (including an employee within the meaning of section 401(c)(1)) with respect to the plan under which the distribution is made or if the beneficiary is treated as the owner of such trust for purposes of subpart E of part I of subchapter J. In the case of the distribution of an annuity contract, the taxable amount of such distribution shall be deemed to be the current actuarial value of the contract, determined on the date of such distribution. In the case of a lump sum distribution with respect to any individual which is made only to two or more trusts, the tax imposed by paragraph (1)(A) shall be computed as if such distribution was made to a single trust, but the liability for such tax shall be apportioned among such trusts according to the relative amounts received by each. The Secretary shall prescribe such regulations as may be necessary to carry out the purpose of this paragraph.

(3)   Allowance of deduction.—The [20]*total taxable amount* of a lump sum distribution for the taxable year shall be allowed as a deduction from gross income for such taxable year, but only to the extent included in the taxpayer's gross income for such taxable year.

(4)   Definitions and special rules.—

(A)   Lump sum distribution.—For purposes of this section and section 403, the term "lump sum distribution" means the distribution or payment within one taxable year of the recipient of the balance to the credit of an employee which becomes payable to the recipient—

(i)   on account of the employee's death,

(ii)   after the employee attains age 59 1/2,

(iii)   on account of the employee's separation from the service, or

(iv)   after the employee has become disabled (within the meaning of section 72(m)(7))

from a trust which forms a part of a plan described in section 401(a) and which is exempt from tax under section 501 or from a plan described in section 403(a). Clause (iii) of this subparagraph shall be applied only with respect to an individual who is an employee without regard to section 401(c)(1), and clause (iv) shall be applied only with respect to an employee within the meaning of section 401(c)(1). Except for purposes of subsection (a)(2) and section 403(a)(2), a distribution of an annuity contract from a trust or annuity plan referred to in the first sentence of this subparagraph shall be treated as a lump sum distribution. For purposes of this subparagraph, a distribution to two or more trusts shall be treated as a distribution to one recipient. For purposes of this subsection, subsection (a)(2) of this section and subsection (a)(2) of section 403, the balance to the credit of the employee does not include the accumulated deductible employee contributions under the plan (within the meaning of section 72(o)(5)).

(B)   [21]*Averaging to apply to 1 lump sum distribution after age 59 1/2—Paragraph*

[Footnote ¶2995 continued]

(19)   "(E)"

(20)   "ordinary income portion"

(21)   "Election of lump sum treatment.—For purposes of this section and section 403, no amount which is not an annuity contract may be treated as a lump sum distribution under subparagraph (A) unless the taxpayer elects for the taxable year to have all such amounts received during such year so treated at the time and in the manner provided under regulations prescribed by the Secretary. Not more than one election may be made under this subparagraph with respect to any individual after such individual has attained age 59 1/2. No election may be made

(1) shall apply to a lump sum distribution with respect to an employee under subparagraph (A) only if—

    (i) such amount is received on or after the taxpayer has attained age 59½, and

    (ii) The taxpayer elects for the taxable year to have all such amounts received during such taxable year so treated.

Not more than 1 election may be made under this subparagraph by any taxpayer with respect to any employee. No election may be made under this subparagraph by any taxpayer other than an individual, an estate, or a trust. In the case of a lump sum distribution made with respect to an employee to 2 or more trusts, the election under this subparagraph shall be made by the personal representative of the taxpayer.

    *   *   *   *   *   *   *   *   *   *   *

    (E) [Struck out][22]

    (F) [Struck out][23]

    (G) Community property law.—The provisions of this subsection, other than paragraph (3), shall be applied without regard to community property laws.

    (H) Minimum period of service.—For purposes of this subsection [24] no amount

---

[Footnote ¶2995 continued]

under this subparagraph by any taxpayer other than an individual, an estate, or a trust. In the case of a lump sum distribution made with respect to an employee to two or more trusts, the election under this subparagraph shall be made by the personal representative of the employee."

(22) "Ordinary income portion.—For purposes of this section, the term "ordinary income portion" means, with respect to a lump sum distribution, so much of the total taxable amount of such distribution as is equal to the product of such total taxable amount multiplied by a fraction—

(i) the numerator of which is the number of calendar years of active participation by the employee in such plan after December 31, 1973, and

(ii) the denominator of which is the number of calendar years of active participation by the employee in such plan."

Effective date (Sec. 1122(h), '86 TRA).—Generally applies to amounts distributed after 12-31-86, in taxable years ending after such date. For special rules, see ¶2043.

Sec. 402(e)(4)(F) struck out by section 1852(b)(3)(B), '86 TRA.

(23) "Employee.—For purposes of this subsection and subsection (a)(2), except as otherwise provided in subparagraph (A), the term "employee" includes an individual who is an employee within the meaning of section 401(c)(1) and the employer of such individual is the person treated as his employee under section 401(c)(4)."

Effective date (Sec. 1881, '86 TRA and section 523(c), '84 TRA).—Applies to any amount received or loan made after 10-16-84.

Matter in *italics* in Sec. 402(e)(4)(H) and (J) added by section 1122(b)(2)(E) and (g), '86 TRA, which struck out:

(24) "(but not for purposes of subsection (a)(2) or section 403(a)(2)(A))"

Effective date (Sec. 1122(h), '86 TRA).—Generally applies to amounts distributed after 12-31-86, in taxable years ending after such date. For special rules, see ¶2403.

Sec. 402(e)(4)(N) in *italics* added by section 1106(c)(2), '86 TRA.

Effective date (Sec. 1106(i), '86 TRA).—(1) Generally applies to years beginning after 12-31-86.

(2) Collective bargaining agreements.—In the case of a plan maintained pursuant to 1 or more collective bargaining agreements between employee representatives and 1 or more employers ratified before 3-1-86, the amendments made by this section (other than subsection (d)) shall not apply to contributions or benefits pursuant to such agreement in years beginning before the earlier of—

(A) the date on which the last of such collective bargaining agreements terminates (determined without regard to any extension thereof after 2-28-86), or

(B) January 1, 1989.

(3) Right to higher accrued defined benefit preserved.—

(A) In general.—In the case of an individual who is a participant (as of the 1st day of the 1st year to which the amendments made by this section apply) in a defined benefit plan which is in existence on 5-6-86, and with respect to which the requirements of section 415 of the '86 Code have been met for all plan years, if such individual's current accrued benefit under the plan exceeds the limitation of subsection (b) of section 415 of such Code (as amended by this section), then (in the case of such plan), for purposes of subsections (b) and (e) of such section, the limitation of such subsection (b)(1)(A) with respect to such individual shall be equal to such current accrued benefit.

(B) Current accrued benefit defined.—

(i) In general.—For purposes of this paragraph, the term "current accrued benefit" means the individual's accrued benefit (at the close of the last year to which the amendments made by this section do not apply) when expressed as an annual benefit (within the meaning of section 415(b)(2) of such Code).

(ii) Special rule.—For purposes of determining the amount of any individual's current accrued benefit—

(I) no change in the terms and conditions of the plan after 5-6-86, and

(II) no cost-of-living adjustment occurring after 5-6-86,

shall be taken into account. For purposes of subclause (I), any change in the terms and conditions of the plan

distributed to an employee from or under a plan may be treated as a lump sum distributed under subparagraph (A) unless he has been a participant in the plan for 5 or more taxable years before the taxable year in which such amounts are distributed.

(I)   Amounts subject to penalty.—This subsection shall not apply to amounts described in clause (ii) of subparagraph (A) of section 72(m)(5) to the extent that section 72(m)(5) applies to such amounts.

(J)   Unrealized appreciation of employer securities.—In the case of any distribution including securities of the employer corporation which, without regard to the requirement of subparagraph (H), would be treated as a lump sum distribution under subparagraph (A), there shall be excluded from gross income the net unrealized appreciation attributable to that part of the distribution which consists of securities of the employer corporation so distributed. In the case of any such distribution or any lump sum distribution including securities of the employer corporation, the amount of net unrealized appreciation of such securities and the resulting adjustments to the basis of such securities shall be determined under regulations prescribed by the Secretary. This subparagraph shall not apply to distributions of accumulated deductible employee contributions (within the meaning of section 77(o)(5)). *To the extent provided by the Secretary, a taxpayer may elect before any distribution not to have this paragraph apply with respect to such distribution.*

(K)   Securities.—For purposes of this subsection, the terms "securities" and "securities of the employer corporation" have the respective meanings provided by subsection (a)(3).

(L)   Election to treat pre-1974 participation as post-1973 participation.—For purposes of subparagraph (E) subsection (a)(2), and section 403(a)(2), if a taxpayer elects (at the time and in the manner provided under regulations prescribed by the Secretary), all calendar years of an employee's active participation in all plans in which the employee has been an active participant shall be considered years of active participation by such employee after December 31, 1973. An election made under this subparagraph, once made, shall be irrevocable and shall apply to all lump-sum distributions received by the taxpayer with respect to the employee. This subparagraph shall not apply if the taxpayer received a lump-sum distribution in a previous taxable year of the employee beginning after December 31, 1975, unless no portion of such lump-sum distribution was treated under subsection (a)(2) or section 403(a)(2) as gain from the sale or exchange of a capital asset held for more than 6 *months.*

(M)   Balance to credit of employee not to include amounts payable under qualified domestic relations order.—For purposes of this subsection, subsection (a)(2) of this section, and section 403(a)(2), the balance to the credit of an employee shall not include any amount payable to an alternate payee under a qualified domestic relations order (within the meaning of section 414(p)).

(N)   Transfers to cost-of-living arrangement not treated as distribution.—For purposes of this subsection, the balance to the credit of an employee under a defined contribution plan shall not include any amount transferred from such defined contribution plan to a qualified cost-of-living arrangement (within the meaning of section 415(k)(2)) under a defined benefit plan.

(5)   Special rule where portion of lump-sum distribution attributable to rollover of bond purchased under qualified bond purchase plan.—If any portion of a lump-sum distribution is attributable to a transfer described in section 405(d)(3)(A)(ii) (as in effect before its repeal by the Tax Reform Act of 1984), paragraphs (1) and (3) of this subsection and paragraph (2) of subsection (a) shall not apply to such portion.

(6)   Treatment of potential future vesting.—

(A)   In general.—For purposes of determining whether any distribution which becomes payable to the recipient on account of the employee's separation from service is a lump sum distribution, the balance to the credit of the employee shall be deter-

mined *without regard to any increase in vesting which may occur if the employee is re-employed by the employer.*

(B) Recapture in certain cases.—If—

(i) an amount is treated as a lump sum distribution by reason of subparagraph (A),

(ii) special lump sum treatment applies to such distribution,

(iii) the employee is subsequently re-employed by the employer; and

(iv) as a result of services performed after being so re-employed, there is an increase in the employee's vesting for benefits accrued before the separation referred to in subparagraph (A),

under regulations prescribed by the Secretary, the tax imposed by this chapter for the taxable year (in which the increase in vesting first occurs) shall be increased by the reduction in tax which resulted from the special lump sum treatment (and any election under paragraph (4)(B) shall not be taken into account for purposes of determining whether the employee may make another election under paragraph (4)(B)).

(C) Special lump sum treatment.—For purposes of this paragraph, special lump sum treatment applies to any distribution if any portion of such distribution—

(i) is taxed under this subsection by reason of an election under paragraph (4)(B), or

(ii) is treated as long-term capital gain under subsection (a)(2) of this section or section 403(a)(2).

(D) Vesting.—For purposes of this paragraph the term "vesting" means the portion of the accrued benefits derived from employer contributions to which the participant has a nonforfeitable right.

(f) **Written Explanation to Recipients of Distributions Eligible for Rollover Treatment.—**

(1) **In general.**—The plan administrator of any plan shall, when making a [25]*eligible* rollover distribution, provide a written explanation to the recipient—

(A) of the provisions under which such distributions will be subject to tax if transferred to an eligible retirement plan within 60 days after the date on which the recipient received the distribution, and,

(B) if applicable, the provisions of subsection (a)(2) and (e) of this section.

(2) **Definitions.**—[26]*For purposes of this subsection—*

【Footnote ¶2995 continued】

Matter in *italics* in Sec. 402(e)(6), (f)(1) and (2) added by section 1898(a)(2) and (e), '86 TRA, which struck out:

(25) "qualifying"

(26) "For purposes of this subsection, the terms "qualifying rollover distribution" and "eligible retirement plan" have the respective meanings given such terms by subsection (a)(5)(E)."

Effective date (Sec. 1898(j), '86 TRA and section 302 and 303, '84 Retirement Equity Act as amended by '86 TRA).— Generally applies to plan years beginning after 12-31-84. For '86 TRA amendments and special transitional rules, see footnote ¶2994.

Sec. 402(g) in *italics* added by section 1852(b)(3)(A), '86 TRA.

Effective date (Sec. 1881, '86 TRA and section 522(e), '84 TRA).—Applies to distributions made after 7-18-84, in taxable years ending after such date.

Sec. 402(g) [should read (h)] in *italics* added by section 1854(f)(2), '86 TRA.

Effective date (Sec. 1854(f)(4)(C), '86 TRA.—Applies to any transaction occurring after 12-31-84, except that in the case of any transaction occurring before Enactment date, the period under which proceeds are required to be invested under section 402(g) [should read (i)] of the '54 Code shall not end before the earlier of 1 year after the date of such transaction or 180 days after Enactment date.

Sec. 402(g) [should read (i)] in *italics* added by section 1105(a), '86 TRA.

Effective date (Sec. 1105(c)(1)—(3), '86 TRA).—(1) Generally applies to taxable years beginning after 12-31-86.

(2) Deferrals under collective bargaining agreements.—In the case of a plan maintained pursuant to 1 or more collective bargaining agreements between employee representatives and 1 or more employers ratified before 3-1-86, the amendment made by subsection (a) shall not apply to contributions made pursuant to such an agreement for taxable years beginning before the earlier of—

(A) the date on which the last of such collective bargaining agreements terminates (determined without regard to any extension thereof after 2-28-86), or

(B) January 1, 1989.

Such contributions shall be taken into account for purposes of applying the amendment made by this section to other plans.

(3) Distributions made before plan amendment.—

(A) In general.—If a plan amendment is required to allow the plan to make any distribution described in sec-

(A) *Eligible rollover distribution.—The term "eligible rollover distribution" means any distribution any portion of which may be excluded from gross income under subsection (a)(5) of this section or subsection (a)(4) of section 403 if transferred to an eligible retirement plan in accordance with the requirements of such subsection.*

(B) *Eligible retirement plan.—The term "eligible retirement plan" has the meaning given such term by subsection (a)(5)(E)(iv).*

(g) *Treatment of Self-employed Individuals.—For purposes of this section, except as otherwise provided in subparagraph (A) of subsection (e)(4), the term "employee" includes a self-employed individual (as defined in section 401(c)(1)(B)) and the employer of such individual shall be the person treated as his employer under section 401(c)(4).*

(g) *[should read (h)] Effect of Disposition of Stock by Plan on Net Unrealized Appreciation.—*

(1) *In general.—For purposes of subsection (a)(1) or (e)(4)(J), in the case of any transaction to which this subsection applies, the determination of net unrealized appreciation shall be made without regard to such transaction.*

(2) *Transaction to which subsection applies.—This subsection shall apply to any transaction in which—*

(A) *the plan trustee exchanges the plan's securities of the employer corporation for other such securities, or*

(B) *the plan trustee disposes of securities of the employer corporation and uses the proceeds of such disposition to acquire securities of the employer corporation within 90 days (or such longer period as the Secretary may prescribe), except that this subparagraph shall not apply to any employee with respect to whom a distribution of money was made during the period after such disposition and before such acquisition.*

(g) *[should read (i)] Limitation on Exclusion for Elective Deferrals.—*

(1) *In general.—Notwithstanding subsections (a)(8) and (h)(1)(B), the elective deferrals of any individual for any taxable year shall be included in such individual's gross income to the extent the amount of such deferrals for the taxable year exceeds $7,000.*

(2) *Required distribution of excess deferrals.—*

(A) *In general.—If any amount (hereinafter in this paragraph referred to as "excess deferrals") is included in the gross income of an individual under paragraph (1) for any taxable year—*

(i) *not later than the 1st March 1 following the close of the taxable year, the individual may allocate the amount of such excess deferrals among the plans under which the deferrals were made and may notify each such plan of the portion allocated to it, and*

(ii) *not later than the 1st April 15 following the close of the taxable year, each such plan may distribute to the individual the amount allocated to it under clause (i) (and any income allocable to such amount).*

The distribution described in clause (ii) may be made notwithstanding any other provision of law.

(B) *Treatment of distribution under section 401(k).—Except to the extent provided under rules prescribed by the Secretary, notwithstanding the distribution of any portion of an excess deferral from a plan under subparagraph (A)(ii), such portion shall, for purposes of applying section 401(k)(3)(A)(ii), be treated as an employer contribution.*

(C) *Taxation of distribution.—In the case of a distribution to which subparagraph (A) applies—*

(i) *except as provided in clause (ii), such distribution shall not be included in gross income (and no tax shall be imposed under section 72(t)), and*

【Footnote ¶2995 continued】

tion 402(g)(2)(A)(ii) of the '86 Code, any such distribution which is made before the close of the 1st plan year for which such amendment is required to be in effect under section 1140 shall be treated as made in accordance with the provisions of such plan.

(B) Distributions pursuant to model amendment.—

(i) Secretary to prescribe amendment.—The Secretary of the Treasury or his delegate shall prescribe an amendment which allows a plan to make any distribution described in section 402(g)(2)(A)(ii) of such Code.

(ii) Adoption by plan.—If a plan adopts the amendment prescribed under clause (i) and makes a distribution in accordance with such amendment, such distribution shall be treated as made in accordance with the provisions of the plan.

(ii) any income on the excess deferral shall, for purposes of this chapter, be treated as earned and received in the taxable year in which such excess deferral is made.

(3) Elective deferrals.—For purposes of this paragraph, the term "elective deferrals" means, with respect to any taxable year, the sum of—

(A) any employer contribution under a qualified cash or deferred arrangement (as defined in section 401(k)) to the extent not includible in gross income for the taxable year under subsection (a)(8) (determined without regard to this subsection),

(B) any employer contribution to the extent not includible in gross income for the taxable year under subsection (h)(1)(B) (determined without regard to this subsection), and

(C) any employer contribution to purchase an annuity contract under section 403(b) under a salary reduction agreement (within the meaning of section 3121(a)(5)(D)).

(4) Increase in limit for amounts contributed under section 403(b) contracts.—The limitation under paragraph (1) shall be increased (but not to an amount in excess of $9,500) by the amount of any employer contributions for the taxable year described in paragraph (3)(C).

(5) Cost-of-living adjustment.—The secretary shall adjust the $7,000 amount under paragraph (1) at the same time and in the same manner as under section 415(d).

(6) Disregard of community property laws.—This subsection shall be applied without regard to community property laws.

(7) Coordination with section 72.—For purposes of applying section 72, any amount includible in gross income for any taxable year under this subsection but which is not distributed from the plan during such taxable year shall not be treated as investment in the contract.

(8) Special rule for certain organizations.—

(A) In general.—In the case of a qualified employee of a qualified organization, with respect to employer contributions described in paragraph (3)(C) made by such organization, the limitation of paragraph (1) for any taxable year shall be increased by whichever of the following is the least:

(i) $3,000,

(ii) $15,000 reduced by amounts not included in gross income for prior taxable years by reason of this paragraph, or

(iii) the excess of $5,000 multiplied by the number of years of service of the employee with the qualified organization over the employer contributions described in paragraph (3) made by the organization on behalf of such employee for prior taxable years.

(B) Qualified organization.—For purposes of this paragraph, the term "qualified organization" means any educational organization, hospital, home health service agency, health and welfare service agency, church, or convention or association of churches. Such term includes any organization described in section 414(e)(3)(B)(ii). Terms used in this subparagraph shall have the same meaning as when used in section 415(c)(4).

(C) Qualified employee.—For purposes of this paragraph, the term "qualified employee" means any employee who has completed 15 years of service with the qualified organization.

(h) [should read (j)] Special Rules for Simplified Employee Pensions.—For purposes of this chapter—

(1) In general.—Except as provided in paragraph (2), contributions made by an employer on behalf of an employee to an individual retirement plan pursuant to a simplified employee pension (as defined in section 408(k))—

(A) shall not be treated as distributed or made available to the employee or as contributions made by the employee, and

(B) if such contributions are made pursuant to an arrangement under section 408(k)(6) under which an employee may elect to have the employer make contributions to the simplified employee pension on behalf of the employee, shall not be treated as distributed or made available or as contributions made by the employee merely because the simplified employee pension includes provisions for such election.

⌈Footnote ¶2995 continued⌉

Sec. 402(h) [should read (j)] in *italics*, added by section 1108(b), '86 TRA.

Effective date (Sec. 1108(h), '86 TRA).—Applies to taxable years beginning after 12-31-86.

(2) *Limitations on employer contributions.*—*Contributions made by an employer to a simplified employee pension with respect to an employee for any year shall be treated as distributed or made available to such employee and as contributions made by the employee to the extent such contributions exceed the lesser of—*

(A) 15 percent of the compensation (within the meaning of section 414(s)) from such employer includible in the employee's gross income for the year (determined without regard to the employer contributions to the simplified employee pension), or

(B) the limitation in effect under 415(c)(1)(A), reduced in the case of any highly compensated employee (within the meaning of section 414(q)) by the amount taken into account with respect to such employee under section 408(k)(3)(D).

(3) *Distributions.*—*Any amount paid or distributed out of an individual retirement plan pursuant to a simplified employee pension shall be included in gross income by the payee or distributee, as the case may be, in accordance with the provisions of section 408(d).*

[For official explanation, see Committee Reports, ¶3971; 3972; 3977; 3986; 3987; 4172; 4174; 4189; 4211.]

[¶2996] CODE SEC. 403. TAXATION OF EMPLOYEE ANNUITIES.

(a) Taxability of Beneficiary Under a Qualified Annuity Plan.—

[1](1) *Distributee taxable under section 72.*—*If an annuity contract is purchased by an employer for an employee under a plan which meets the requirements of section 404(a)(2) (whether or not the employer deducts the amounts paid for the contract under such section), the amount actually distributed to any distributee under the contract shall be taxable to the distributee (in the year in which so distributed) under section 72 (relating to annuities).*

(2) **[Repealed]**[2]

* * * * * * * * * * * *

(4) **Rollover amounts.—**
   (A) General rule.—If—
      (i) any portion of the balance to the credit of an employee in an employee annuity described in paragraph (1) is paid to him,
      (ii) the employee transfers any portion of the property he receives in such distribution to an eligible retirement plan, and
      (iii) in the case of a distribution of property other than money, the amount so transferred consists of the property (other than money) distributed,

then such distribution (to the extent so transferred) shall not be includible in gross income for the taxable year in which paid.

[Footnote ¶2996] Matter in *italics* in Sec. 403(a)(1) added by section 1122(d)(1), '86 TRA, which struck out.

(1) "(1) **General rule.**—Except as provided in paragraph (2), if an annuity contract is purchased by an employer for an employee under a plan which meets the requirements of section 404(a)(2) (whether or not the employer deducts the amounts paid for the contract under such section), the employee shall include in his gross income the amounts received under such contract for the year received as provided in section 72 (relating to annuities)."

Effective date (Sec. 1122(h)(7), '86 TRA).—Applies to taxable years beginning after 12-31-85.

Section 1122(b)(1)(B), '86 TRA, repealed Sec. 403(a)(2):

(2) "(2) **Capital gains treatment for certain distributions.**—

(A) General rule.—If—

(i) an annuity contract is purchased by an employer for an employee under a plan described in paragraph (1);

(ii) such plan requires that refunds of contributions with respect to annuity contracts purchased under such plan be used to reduce subsequent premiums on the contracts under the plan; and

(iii) a lump sum distribution (as defined in section 402(e)(4)(A)) is paid to the recipient,

so much of the total taxable amount (as defined in section 402(e)(4)(D)) of such distribution as is equal to the product of such total taxable amount multiplied by the fraction described in section 402(a)(2) shall be treated as a gain from the sale or exchange of a capital asset held for more than 6 months. For purposes of this paragraph, in the case of an individual who is an employee without regard to section 401(c)(1), determination of whether or not any distribution is a lump sum distribution shall be made without regard to the requirement that an election be made under subsection (e)(4)(B) of section 402, but no distribution to any taxpayer other than an individual, estate, or trust may be treated as a lump sum distribution under this paragraph.

(B) Cross reference.—

For imposition of separate tax on ordinary income portion of lump sum distribution, see section 402(e)."

Effective date (Sec. 1122(h)(1), '86 TRA).—Generally applies to amounts distributed after 12-31-86, in taxable years ending after such date. For special and transitional rules, see ¶2043.

(B)   Certain rules made applicable.—Rules similar to the rules of subparagraphs (B) *³through (G)* of section 402(a)(5) and of paragraphs (6) and (7) of section 402(a) shall apply for purposes of subparagraph (A).

(b) Taxability of Beneficiary Under Annuity Purchased by Section 501(c)(3) Organization or Public School.—

    (1)   General rule.—If—

      (A)   an annuity contract is purchased—

        (i)   for an employee by an employer described in section 501(c)(3) which is exempt from tax under section 501(a), or

        (ii)   for an employee (other than an employee described in clause (i)), who performs services for an educational organization described in section 170(b)(1)(A)(ii) by an employer which is a State, a political subdivision of a State, or an agency or instrumentality of any one or more of the foregoing,

      (B)   such annuity contract is not subject to subsection (a), ⁴

      (C)   the employee's rights under the contract are nonforfeitable, except for failure to pay future premiums, and

      (D)   except in the case of a contract purchased by a church, such contract is purchased under a plan which meets the nondiscrimination requirements of paragraph (10),

then amounts contributed by such employer for such annuity contract on or after such rights become nonforfeitable shall be excluded from the gross income of the employee for the taxable year to the extent that the aggregate of such amounts does not exceed the exclusion allowance for such taxable year. *⁵The amount actually distributed to any distributee under such contract shall be taxable to the distributee (in the year in which so distributed) under section 72 (relating to annuities).* For purposes of applying the rules of this subsection to amounts contributed by an employer for a taxable year, amounts transferred to a contract described in this paragraph by reason of a rollover contribution described in paragraph (8) of this subsection or section 408(d)(3)(A)(iii) shall not be considered contributed by such employer.

     *   *   *   *   *   *   *   *   *   *   *

    (7)   Custodial accounts for regulated investment company stock.—

      (A)   Amounts paid treated as contributions.—For purposes of this title, amounts paid by an employer described in paragraph (1)(A) to a custodial account which satisfies the requirements of section 401(f)(2) shall be treated as amounts contributed by him for an annuity contract for his employee if—

        (i)   the amounts are to be invested in regulated investment company stock to be held in that custodial account, and

        (ii)   under the custodial account no such amounts may be paid or made available to any distributee before the employee dies, attains age 59½, separates

---

[**Footnote ¶2996 continued**]

Matter in *italics* in Sec. 403(a)(4)(B), (b)(8)(C) and (D) added by section 1852(a)(5)(B)(i)(5)(B)(ii) and (b)(10), '86 TRA, which struck out:
(3)   "through (F)"
Effective date (Sec. 1881, '86 TRA and section 521(e), '84 TRA).— Generally applies to years beginning after 12-31-84. For special and transitional rules, see footnote ¶2994.

Matter in *italics* in Sec. 403(b)(1)(B)—(D) added by section 1120(a), '86 TRA, which struck out;
(4)   "and"
Effective date (Sec. 1120(c), '86 TRA).—Applies to years beginning after 12-31-88.

Matter in *italics* in Sec. 403(b)(1) added by section 1122(d)(2), '86 TRA, which struck out:
(5)   "The employee shall include in his gross income the amounts received under such contract for the year received as provided in section 72 (relating to annuities)"
Effective date (Sec. 1122(h)(7), '86 TRA).—Applies to taxable years beginning after 12-31-85.

Matter in *italics* in Sec. 403(b)(7)(ii) [should read 403(b)(7)(A)(ii)] added by section 1123(c)(2), '86 TRA.
Effective date (Sec. 1123(e)(2)—(4), '86 TRA).—(2)   Generally applies to taxable years beginning after 12-31-88.
(3)   Exception where distribution commences.—The amendments made by this section shall not apply to distributions to any employee from a plan maintained by any employer if—
(A)   as of 3-1-86, the employee separated from service with the employer,
(B)   as of 3-1-86, the accrued benefit of the employee was in pay status pursuant to a written election providing a specific schedule for the distribution of the entire accrued benefit of the employee, and
(C)   such distribution is made pursuant to such written election.
(4)   Transition rule.—The amendments made by this section shall not apply with respect to any benefits with respect to which a designation is an effect under section 242(b)(2) of the '82 TEFRA.

---

from service, becomes disabled (within the meaning of section 72(m)(7)), or *in the case of contributions made pursuant to a salary reduction agreement (within the meaning of section 3121(a)(1)(D))* encounters financial hardship.

(B) Account treated as plan.—For purposes of this title, a custodial account which satisfies the requirements of section 401(f)(2) shall be treated as an organization described in section 401(a) solely for purposes of subchapter F and subtitle F with respect to amounts received by it (and income from investment thereof).

(C) Regulated investment company.—For purposes of this paragraph, the term "regulated investment company" means a domestic corporation which is a regulated investment company within the meaning of section 851(a).[6]

(8) Rollover amounts.—
   (A) General rule.—If—
      (i) any portion of the balance to the credit of an employee in an annuity contract described in paragraph (1) is paid to him.
      (ii) the employee transfers any portion of the property he receives in such distribution to an individual retirement plan or to an annuity contract described in paragraph (1), and
      (iii) in the case of a distribution of property other than money, the property so transferred consists of the property distributed,
   then such distribution (to the extent so transferred) shall not be includible in gross income for the taxable year in which paid.

* * * * * * * * * * *

   (C) Certain rules made applicable.—Rules similar to the rules of subparagraphs (B), (C), *and (F)(i)* of section 402(a)(5) and of paragraphs (6) and (7) of section 402(a) shall apply for purposes of subparagraph (A).
   (D) Required distributions not eligible for rollover treatment.—Subparagraph (A) shall not apply to any distribution to the extent such distribution is required under paragraph (10).

* * * * * * * * * * *

   (10) Distribution requirements.—Under regulations prescribed by the Secretary, this subsection shall not apply to any annuity contract (or to any custodial account described in paragraph (7) or retirement income account described in paragraph (9)) unless requirements similar to the requirements of section 401(a)(9) are met (and requirements similar to the incidental death benefit requirements of section 401(a) are met) with respect to such annuity contract (or custodial account or retirement income account).

   (10) [should read (11)] Nondiscrimination requirements.—
      (A) In general.—For purposes of paragraph (1)(D), a plan meets the nondiscrimination requirements of this paragraph if—
         (i) with respect to contributions not made pursuant to a salary reduction agreement, such plan meets the requirements of paragraphs (4), (5), and (26) of section 401(a) and section 410(b) in the same manner as if such plan were described in section 401(a), and
         (ii) all employees of the organization may elect to have the employer make contributions of more than $200 pursuant to a salary reduction agreement if any employee of the organization may elect to have the organization make contributions for such contracts pursuant to such agreement.

⟦Footnote ¶2996 continued⟧

Section 1852(a)(3)(B), '86 TRA, struck out 403(b)(7)(D):
(6) "(D) Distribution requirements.—For purposes of determining when the interest of an employee in a custodial account must be distributed, such account shall be treated in the same manner as an annuity contract."
Effective date (Sec. 1881, '86 TRA and 521(e), '84 TRA).—Generally applies to years beginning after 12-31-84. For special and transitional rules, see footnote ¶2994.

Sec. 403(b)(10) in *italics* added by section 1852(a)(3)(A), '86 TRA.
Effective date (Sec. 1881, '86 TRA and section 521(e), '84 TRA).—Generally applies to years beginning after 12-31-84. For special rules and transitional rules, see footnote ¶2994.

Sec. 403(b)(10) [should read (11)] italics added by section 1120(b), '86 TRA.
Effective date (Sec. 1120(c), '86 TRA).—Applies to years beginning after 12-31-88.

Sec. 403(b)(11) [should read (12)] in *italics* added by section 1123(c)(1), '86 TRA.
Effective date (Sec. 1123(e)(2)—(4), '86 TRA).—Generally applies to taxable years beginning after 12-31-88. For exception and transitional rule, see above.

For purposes of clause (ii), there may be excluded any employee who is a participant in an eligible deferred compensation plan (within the meaning of section 457) or a qualified cash or deferred arrangement of the organization or another annuity contract described in this subsection. Any nonresident alien described in section 410(b)(3)(C) may also be excluded. For purposes of this subparagraph, students who normally work less than 20 hours per week may (subject to the conditions applicable under section 410(b)(4)) be excluded.

    (B) Church.—For purposes of paragraph (1)(D), the term "church" has the meaning given to such term by section 3121(w)(3)(A). Such term shall include any qualified church-controlled organization (as defined in section 3121(w)(3)(B)).

    (11) [should read (12)] Requirement that distributions not begin before age 59½, separation from service, death, or disability.—This subsection shall not apply to any annuity contract unless under such contract distributions attributable to contributions made pursuant to a salary reduction agreement (within the meaning of section 402(g)(3)(C)) may be paid only—

        (A) when the employee attains age 59½, separates from service, dies, or becomes disabled (within the meaning of section 72(m)(7)), or

        (B) in the case of hardship.

Such contract may not provide for the distribution of any income attributable to such contributions in the case of hardship.

  (c) Taxability of Beneficiary Under Nonqualified Annuities or Under Annuities Purchased by Exempt Organizations.—Premiums paid by an employer for an annuity contract which is not subject to subsection (a) shall be included in the gross income of the employee in accordance with section 83 (relating to property transferred in connection with performance of services), except that the value of such contract shall be substituted for the fair market value of the property for purposes of applying such section. [7]*In the case of any portion of any contract which is attributable to premiums to which this subsection applies, the amount actually paid or made available under such contract to any beneficiary which is attributable to such premiums shall be taxable to the beneficiary (in the year in which so paid or made available) under section 72 (relating to annuities).*

[For official explanation, see Committee Reports, ¶3985; 3987; 3988; 4172.]

[¶2997] CODE SEC. 404. DEDUCTION FOR CONTRIBUTIONS OF AN EMPLOYER TO AN EMPLOYEES' TRUST OR ANNUITY PLAN AND COMPENSATION UNDER A DEFERRED-PAYMENT PLAN.

  (a) General Rule.—If contributions are paid by an employer to or under a stock bonus, pension, profit-sharing or annuity plan, or if compensation is paid or accrued on account of any employee under a plan deferring the receipt of such compensation, such contributions or compensation shall not be deductible under [1]*this chapter; but, if they*

[Footnote ¶2996 continued]

  Matter in *italics* in Sec. 403(c) added by section 1122(d)(3), '86 TRA, which struck out:

  (7) "The preceding sentence shall not apply to that portion of the premiums paid which is excluded from gross income under subsection (b). The amount actually paid or made available to any beneficiary under such contract shall be taxable to him in the year in which so paid or made available to him under section 72 (relating to annuities)."

  Effective date (Sec. 1122(h)(7), '86 TRA)—Applies to taxable years beginning after 12-31-85.

  [Footnote ¶2997] Matter in *italics* in Sec. 404(a) added by section 1851(b)(2)(C), '86 TRA, which struck out:

  (1) "section 162 (relating to trade or business expenses) or section 212 (relating to expenses for the production of income); but if they satisfy the conditions of either of such sections"

  Effective date (Sec. 1881, '86 TRA and section 512(c), '84 TRA).—(1) Generally applies to amounts paid or incurred after 7-18-84 in taxable years ending after such date.

  (2) Exception for certain extended vacation pay plans.—In the case of any extended vacation pay plan maintained pursuant to a collective bargaining agreement—

  (A) between employee representatives and 1 or more employers, and

  (B) in effect on 6-22-84,

the amendments made by this section shall not apply before the date on which such collective bargaining agreement terminates (determined without regard to any extension thereof agreed to after 6-22-84). For purposes of the preceding sentence, any plan amendment made pursuant to a collective bargaining agreement relating to the plan which amends the plan solely to conform to any requirement added by this section shall not be treated as a termination of such collective bargaining agreement.

  Section 1112(d)(2), '86 TRA, amended Sec. 404(a)(2) by striking out "and (22)" and inserting in lieu thereof "(22), and (26)".

  Effective date (Sec. 1112(e), '86 TRA).—Generally applies to plan years beginning after 12-31-88. For special rules, etc. see ¶2994.

  Section 1136(b), '86 TRA, amended Sec. 404(a)(2) by striking out "and (26)" and inserting in lieu thereof "(26), and (27)".

would otherwise be deductible, they shall be deductible under this section, subject, however, to the following limitations as to amounts deductible in any years:

* * * * * * * * * * *

(2) **Employees' annuities.**—In the taxable year when paid, in an amount determined in accordance with paragraph (1), if the contributions are paid toward the purchase of retirement annuities, or retirement annuities and medical benefits as described in Sec. 401(h), and such purchase is a part of a plan which meets the requirements of section 401(a)(3), (4), (5), (6), (7), (8), (9), (11), (12), (13), (14), (15), (16), (19), (20), (22), *(26) and (27)* and, if applicable the requirements of section 401(a)(10) and of section 401(d), and if refunds of premiums, if any, are applied within the current taxable or next succeeding taxable year towards the purchase of such retirement annuities, or such retirement annuities and medical benefits.

(3) **Stock bonus and profit-sharing trusts.—**
    (A) Limits on deductible contributions.—
        [2]*(i) In general.—In the taxable year when paid, if the contributions are paid into a stock bonus or profit-sharing trust, and if such taxable year ends within or with a taxable year of the trust with respect to which the trust is exempt under section 501(a), in an amount not in excess of 15 percent of the compensation otherwise paid or accrued during the taxable year to the beneficiaries under the stock bonus or profit-sharing plan.*

        (ii) Carryover of excess contributions.—Any amount paid into the trust in any taxable year in excess of the limitation of clause (i) (or the corresponding provision of prior law) shall be deductible in the succeeding taxable years in order of time, but the amount so deductible under this clause in any 1 such succeeding taxable year together with the amount allowable under clause (i) shall not exceed 15 percent of the compensation otherwise paid or accrued during such taxable year to the beneficiaries under the plan.

        (iii) Certain retirement plans excluded.—For purposes of this subparagraph, the term "stock bonus or profit-sharing trust" shall not include any trust designed to provide benefits upon retirement and covering a period of years, if under the plan the amounts to be contributed by the employer can be determined actuarially as provided in paragraph (1).

        (iv) 2 or more trusts treated as 1 trust.—If the contributions are made to 2 or more stock bonus or profit-sharing trusts, such trusts shall be considered a single trust for purposes of applying the limitations in this subparagraph.

        (v) Pre-87 limitation carryforwards.—
            (I) In general.—The limitation of clause (i) for any taxable year shall be increased by the unused pre-87 limitation carryforward (but not to an amount in excess of 25 percent of the compensation described in clause (i)).

            (II) Unused pre-87 limitation carryforwards.—For purposes of subclause (I), the term "unused pre-87 limitation carryforwards" means the amount by

---

Matter in *italics* in Sec. 404(a)(3)(A) and (7) added by section 1131(a) and (b), '86 TRA, which struck out:

(2) "In the taxable year when paid, if the contributions are paid into a stock bonus or profit-sharing trust, and if such taxable year ends within or with a taxable year of the trust with respect to which the trust is exempt under section 501(a), in an amount not in excess of 15 percent of the compensation otherwise paid or accrued during the taxable year to all employees under the stock bonus or profit-sharing plan. If in any taxable year there is paid into the trust, or a similar trust then in effect, amounts less than the amounts deductible under the preceding sentence, the excess, or if no amount is paid, the amounts deductible, shall be carried forward and be deductible when paid in the succeeding taxable years in order of time, but the amount so deductible under this sentence in any such succeeding taxable year shall not exceed 15 percent of the compensation otherwise paid or accrued during such succeeding taxable year to the beneficiaries under the plan, but the amount so deductible under this sentence in any one succeeding taxable year together with the amount so deductible under the first sentence of this subparagraph shall not exceed 25 percent of the compensation otherwise paid or accrued during such taxable year to the beneficiaries under the plan. In addition, any amount paid into the trust in any taxable year in excess of the amount allowable with respect to such year under the preceding provisions of this subparagraph shall be deductible in the suceeding taxable years in order of time, but the amount so deductible under this sentence in any one such succeeding taxable year together with the amount allowable under the first sentence of this subparagraph shall not exceed 15 percent of the compensation otherwise paid or accrued during such taxable year to the beneficiaries under the plan. The term "stock bonus or profit-sharing trust," as used in this subparagraph, shall not include any trust designed to provide benefits upon retirement and covering a period of years, if under the plan the amounts to be contributed by the employer can be determined actuarially as provided in paragraph (1). If the contributions are made to 2 or more stock bonus or profit-sharing trusts, such trusts shall be considered a single trust for purposes of applying the limitations in this subparagraph."

which the limitation of the first sentence of this subparagraph (as in effect on the day before the date of the enactment of the Tax Reform Act of 1986) for any taxable year beginning before January 1, 1987, exceeded the amount paid to the trust for such taxable year (to the extent such excess was not taken into account in prior taxable years).

* * * * * * * * * * * *

[3](7) *Limitation of deductions where combination of defined contribution plan and defined benefit plan.*—

(A) In general.—*If amounts are deductible under the foregoing provisions of this subsection (other than paragraph (5)) in connection with 1 or more defined contribution plans and 1 or more defined benefit plans, the total amount deductible in a taxable year under such plans shall not exceed the greater of*—

(i) 25 percent of the compensation otherwise paid or accrued during the taxable year to the beneficiaries under such plans, or

(ii) the amount of contributions made to or under the defined benefit plans to the extent such contributions do not exceed the amount of employer contributions necessary to satisfy the minimum funding standard provided by section 412 with respect to any such defined benefit plans for the plan year which ends with or within such taxable year (or for any prior plan year).

A defined contribution plan which is a pension plan shall not be treated as failing to provide definitely determinable benefits merely by limiting employer contributions to amounts deductible under this section.

(B) Carryover of contributions in excess of the deductible limit.—*Any amount paid under the plans in any taxable year in excess of the limitation of subparagraph (A) shall be deductible in the succeeding taxable years in order of time, but the amount so deductible under this subparagraph in any 1 such succeeding taxable year together with the amount allowable under subparagraph (A) shall not exceed 25 percent of the compensation otherwise paid or accrued during such taxable year to the beneficiaries under the plans.*

(C) Paragraph not to apply in certain cases.—*This paragraph shall not have the effect of reducing the amount otherwise deductible under paragraphs (1), (2), and (3), if no employee is a beneficiary under more than 1 trust or under a trust and an annuity plan.*

(D) Section 412(i) plans.—*For purposes of this paragraph, any plan described in section 412(i) shall be treated as a defined benefit plan.*

(8) Self-employed individuals.—In the case of a plan included in paragraph (1), (2), or (3) which provides contributions or benefits for employees some or all of whom are employees within the meaning of section 401(c)(1), for purposes of this section—

(A) the term "employee" includes an individual who is an employee within the meaning of section 401(c)(1), and the employer of such individual is the person treated as his employer under section 401(c)(4);

(B) the term "earned income" has the meaning assigned to it by section 401(c)(2);

[Footnote ¶2997 continued]

(3) "(7) **Limit on deductions.**—If amounts are deductible under paragraphs (1) and (3), or (2) and (3), or (1), (2), and (3), in connection with 2 or more trusts, or one or more trusts and an annuity plan, the total amount deductible in a taxable year under such trusts and plans shall not exceed the greater of 25 percent of the compensation otherwise paid or accrued during the taxable year to the beneficiaries of the trusts or plans, or the amount of contributions made to or under the trusts or plans to the extent such contributions do not exceed the amount of employer contributions necessary to satisfy the minimum funding standard provided by section 412 for the plan year which ends with or within such taxable year (or for any prior plan year). In addition, any amount paid into such trust or under such annuity plans in any taxable year in excess of the amount allowable with respect to such year under the preceding provisions of this paragraph shall be deductible in the succeeding taxable years in order of time, but the amount so deductible under this sentence in any one such succeeding taxable year together with the amount allowable under the first sentence of this paragraph shall not exceed 25 percent of the compensation otherwise paid or accrued during such taxable years to the beneficiaries under the trusts or plans. This paragraph shall not have the effect of reducing the amount otherwise deductible under paragraphs (1), (2), and (3), if no employee is a beneficiary under more than one trust, or a trust and an annuity plan."

Effective date. (Sec. 1131(d), 'TRA).—Applies to taxable years beginning after 12-31-86.

Matter in *italics* in Sec. 404(a)(8)(C) added by section 1875(c)(7)(A), '86 TRA.

Effective date (Sec. 1881, '86 TRA and section 715, '84 TRA, and section 241(a), '82 TEFRA.—Applies to years beginning after 12-31-83.

(C) the contributions to such plan on behalf of an individual who is an employee within the meaning of section 401(c)(1) shall be considered to satisfy the conditions of section 162 or 212 to the extent that such contributions do not exceed the earned income of such individual *(determined without regard to the deductions allowed by this section)* derived from the trade or business with respect to which such plan is established, and to the extent that such contributions are not allocable (determined in accordance with regulations prescribed by the Secretary) to the purchase of life, accident, health, or other insurance: and

≫**P-H CAUTION**→ There are two versions of Sec. 404(a)(8)(D). Sec. 404(a)(8)(D), as amended by Sec. 1848(c) '86 TRA, follows. For Sec. 404(a)(8)(D), as amended by Sec. 1875(c)(7)(B), '86 TRA, see below.

▲ (D) any reference to compensation shall, in the case of an individual who is an employee within the meaning of section 401(c)(1), be considered to be a reference to the earned income of such individual (determined without regard to the [4]*deduction* allowed by this section[5]) derived from the trade or business with respect to which the plan is established.

≫**P-H CAUTION**→ There are two versions of Sec. 404(a)(8)(D). Sec. 404(a)(8)(D), as amended by Sec. 1875(c)(7)(B), follows. For Sec. 404(a)(8)(D), as amended by Sec. 1848(c), see above.

▲ ▲ (D) any reference to compensation shall, in the case of an individual who is an employee within the meaning of section 401(c)(1), be considered to be a reference to the earned income of such individual[6] derived from the trade or business with respect to which the plan is established.

* * * * * * * * * * *

(b) Method of Contributions, Etc., Having the Effect of a Plan; [7]*Certain* Deferred Benefits.—
(1) Method of contributions, etc., having the effect of a plan.—If—
(A) there is no plan, but
(B) there is a method or arrangement of employer contributions or compensation which has the effect of a stock bonus, pension, profit-sharing, or annuity plan, or other plan deferring the receipt of compensation (including a plan described in paragraph (2)),
subsection (a) shall apply if there were such a plan.
(2) Plans providing [7]*certain* **deferred benefits.—**
(A) In general.—For purposes of this section, any plan providing for deferred benefits (other than compensation) for employees, their spouses, or their dependents shall be treated as a plan deferring the receipt of compensation. In the case of such a plan, for purposes of this section, the determination of when an amount is includible in gross income shall be made without regard to any provisions of this chapter excluding such benefits from gross income.
(B) Exception for certain benefits.—Subparagraph (A) shall not apply to—
(i) any benefit provided through a welfare benefit fund (as defined in section 419(e)), or
(ii)[8] any benefit with respect to which an election under section 463 applies.

* * * * * * * * * * *

(d) Deductibility of Payments of Deferred Compensation, Etc., to Independent Contractors.—If a plan would be described in so much of subsection (a) as precedes paragraph (1) thereof (as modified by subsection (b)) but for the fact that there is no employer-employee relationship, the contributions or compensation—

─────────────────────────

【Footnote ¶2997 continued】

▲ Section 1848(c), '86 TRA, struck out from Sec. 404(a)(8)(D), preceded by a single triangle:
(4) "deductions"
(5) "and section 405(c)"
Effective date (Sec. 1881, '86 TRA and section 491(f)(1), '84 TRA).—Applies to obligations issued after 12-31-83.

─────────

▲ ▲ Section 1875(c)(7)(B), '86 TRA, struck out from Sec. 404(a)(8)(D), preceded by two triangles:
(6) "(determined without regard to the deductions allowed by this section and section 405(c))"
Effective date (Sec. 1875(c)(7)(B), '86 TRA).—Applies to taxable years beginning after 12-31-84.

─────────

Matter in *italics* in the headings of Sec. 404(b), (2)(B)(ii) and (d) added by section 1851(b)(2)(A)—(C), '86 TRA, which struck out:
(7) "**Unfunded**"
(8) "to"

(1)   shall not be deductible by the payor thereof [9]*under this chapter,* but

(2)   shall (if they would be deductible [9]*under this chapter* but for paragraph (1)) be deductible under this subsection for the taxable year in which an amount attributable to the contribution or compensation is includible in the gross income of the persons participating in the plan.

* * * * * * * * * * * *

(h) Special Rules for Simplified Employee Pensions.—

(1) In general.—Employer contributions to a simplified employee pension shall be treated as if they are made to a plan subject to the requirements of this section. Employer contributions to a simplified employee pension are subject to the following limitations:

[10]*(A)   Contributions made for a year are deductible—*

    (i)   in the case of a simplified employee pension maintained on a calendar year basis, for the taxable year with or within which the calendar year ends, or

    (ii)   in the case of a simplified employee pension which is maintained on the basis of the taxable year of the employer, for such taxable year.

(B)   Contributions shall be treated for purposes of this subsection as if they were made for a taxable year if such contributions are made on account of such taxable year and are made not later than the time prescribed by law for filing the return for such taxable year (including extensions thereof).

* * * * * * * * * * * *

(i)   [Repealed][11]

* * * * * * * * * * * *

(k) Dividends Paid Deductions.—In addition to the deductions provided under subsection (a), there shall be allowed as a deduction to a corporation the amount of any dividend paid in cash by such corporation [12]*with respect to the stock of such corporation* if—

(1)   such stock is held on the record date for the dividend by a tax credit employee stock ownership plan (as defined in section 409) or an employee stock ownership plan (as defined in section 4975(e)(7)) which is maintained by such corporation or by any

---

[Footnote ¶2997 continued]

(9)   "under section 162 or 212"

Effective date (Sec. 1881, '86 TRA and section 512(c), '84 TRA).—Generally applies to amounts paid or incurred after 7-18-84 in taxable years ending after such date. For exception, see above.

Matter in *italics* in Sec. 404(h)(1)(A) and (B) added by section 1108(c), '86 TRA, which struck out:

(10)   "(A)   Contributions made for a calendar year are deductible for the taxable year with which or within which the calendar year ends.

(B)   Contributions made within 3½ months after the close of a calendar year are treated as if they were made on the last day of such calendar year if they are made on account of such calendar year."

Effective date (Sec. 1108(h), '86 TRA).—Applies for taxable years beginning after 12-31-86.

Sec. 404(i) repealed by: section 1171(b)(6), '86 TRA

(11)   "(i)   **Deductibility of Unused Portion of Employee Stock Ownership Credit.—**

(1)   **Unused credit carryovers.—**If any portion of the employee stock ownership credit determined under section 41 for any taxable year has not, after the application of section 38(c), been allowed under section 38 for any taxable year, such portion shall be allowed as a deduction (without regard to any limitations provided under this section) for the last taxable year to which such portion could have been allowed as a credit under section 39.

(2)   **Reductions in credit.—**There shall be allowed as a deduction (subject to the limitations provided under this section) an amount equal to any reduction of the credit allowed under section 41 resulting from a final determination of such credit to the extent such reduction is not taken into account under section 41(c)(3)."

Effective date (Sec. 1171(c), '86 TRA).—(1) Generally applies to compensation paid or accrued after 12-31-86, in taxable years ending after such date.

(2)   **Sections 404(i) and 6699 to continue to apply to pre-1987 credits.—**The provisions of sections 404(i) and 6699 of the '86 Code shall continue to apply with respect to credits under section 41 of such Code attributable to compensation paid or accrued before 1-1-87 (or under section 38 of such Code with respect to qualified investment before 1-1-83).

Matter in *italics* in Sec. 404(k), [except the last sentence, and (2)(C)] added by section 1854(b)(2)—(5), '86 TRA, which struck out:

(12)   "during the taxable year"

Effective date (Sec. 1881, '86 TRA and section 542(d), '84 TRA and section 1854(b)(6), '86 TRA).—Generally applies to taxable years beginning after 7-18-84. For exception, see footnote ¶2887.

---

other corporation that is a member of a controlled group of corporations (within the meaning of section 409(1)(4)) that includes such corporation, and

(2) in accordance with the plan provisions—

(A) the dividend is paid in cash to the participants in the plan *or their beneficiaries,* [13]

(B) the dividend is paid to the plan and is distributed in cash to participants in the plan *or their beneficiaries* not later than 90 days after the close of the plan year in which paid [14], *or*

(C) *the dividend with respect to employer securities is used to make payments on a loan described in section 404(a)(9).*

Any deduction under subparagraph (A) or (B) of paragraph (2) shall be allowed in the taxable year of the corporation in which the dividend is paid or distributed to the participant under paragraph (2). A plan to which this subsection applies shall not be treated as violating the requirements of section 401, 409, or 4975(e)(7) merely by reason of any distribution described in paragraph (2). The Secretary may disallow the deduction under this subsection for any dividend if the Secretary determines that such dividend constitutes, in substance, an avoidance of taxation. Any deduction under paragraph (2)(C) shall be allowable in the taxable year of the corporation in which the dividend is used to repay the loan described in such paragraph.

(l) **Limitation on Amount of Annual Compensation Taken Into Account.**—*For purposes of applying the limitations of this section, the amount of annual compensation of each employee taken into account under the plan for any year shall not exceed $200,000. The Secretary shall adjust the $200,000 amount at the same time and in the same manner as under section 415(d).*

[For official explanation, see Committee Reports, ¶3972; 3974; 3977; 3990; 3995; 4016; 4018; 4161; 4171; 4174; 4189.]

[¶2997-A] CODE SEC. 404A. DEDUCTION FOR CERTAIN FOREIGN DEFERRED COMPENSATION PLANS.

(a) **General Rule.**—Amounts paid or accrued by an employer under a qualified foreign plan—

(1) shall not be allowable as a deduction under [1]*this chapter,* but

(2) if they [2]*would otherwise be deductible,* shall be allowed as a deduction under

---

this section for the taxable year for which such amounts are properly taken into account under this section.

* * * * * * * * * * * *

(g) Other Special Rules.—

　(1) No deduction for certain amounts.—Except as provided in section 404(a)(5), no deduction shall be allowed under this section for any item to the extent such item is attributable to services—

　　(A) performed by a citizen or resident of the United States who is [3]*a highly compensated employee (within the meaning of section 414(q)),* or

　　(B) performed in the United States the compensation for which is subject to tax under this chapter.

* * * * * * * * * * *

[For official explanation, see Committee Reports, ¶3979; 4171.]

[¶2998] CODE SEC. 406. EMPLOYEES OF FOREIGN AFFILIATES COVERED BY SECTION 3121(1) AGREEMENTS

* * * * * * * * * *

(b) Special Rules for Application of Section 401(a).—

　(1) Nondiscrimination requirements.—For purposes of applying section 401(a)(4) and section 410(b) [1] with respect to an individual who is treated as an employee of an American employer under subsection (a)—

　　(A) if such individual is [2]*a highly compensated employee (within the meaning of secton 414(q)),* he shall be treated as having such capacity with respect to such American employer; and

　　(B) the determination of whether such individual is a highly compensated employee *(as so defined)* shall be made by treating such individual's total compensation (determined with the application of paragraph (2) of this subsection) as compensation paid by such American employer and by determining such individual's status with regard to such American employer.

* * * * * * * * * * *

(e) Treatment as Employee Under Related Provisions.—An individual who is treated as an employee of an American employer under subsection (a) shall also be treated as an employee of such American employer, with respect to the plan described in subsection (a)(2), for purposes of applying the following provisions of this title:

　(1) Section 72(d) (relating to employees' annuities).

　(2) Section 72(f) (relating to special rules for computing employees' contributions).

　(3) Section 101(b) (relating to employees' death benefits).

　(4) Section 2039 (relating to annuities).[3]

[Footnote ¶2997-A continued]

preceding sentence, any plan amendment made pursuant to a collective bargaining agreement relating to the plan which amends the plan solely to conform to any requirement added by this section shall not be treated as a termination of such collective bargaining agreement.

Matter in *italics* in Sec. 404A(g)(1)(A) added by section 1114(b)(8), '86 TRA, which struck out:

(3) "an officer, shareholder, or"

Effective date (Sec. 1114(c), '86 TRA).—Generally to years beginning after 12-31-88. For special rules, see footnote ¶3004.

[Footnote ¶2998] Section 1112(d)(3), '86 TRA, struck out from Sec. 406(b)(1):

(1) "(without regard to paragraph (1)(A) thereof)"

Effective date (Sec. 1112(e), '86 TRA).—Generally applies to plan years beginning after 12-31-88. For special rules, see footnote ¶2994.

Matter in *italics* in Sec. 406(b)(1)(A) and (B) added by section 1114(b)(9)(A) and (C). '86 TRA, which struck out:

(2) "an officer, shareholder, or person whose principal duties consist in supervising the work of other employees of a foreign affiliate of such American employer"

Effective date (Sec. 1114(c)(3), '86 TRA).—Applies to years beginning after 12-31-88. For special rule for determining highly compensated employees, see footnote ¶3004.

Section 1852(e)(2), '86 TRA, struck out from Sec. 406(e):

(3) "(5) Section 2517 (relating to certain annuities under qualified plans)."

Effective date (Sec. 1852(e)(2)(E), '86 TRA).—Applies to transfers after the date of the enactment of this Act.

[For official explanation, see Committee Reports, ¶3977; 3979.]

〔¶2999〕 CODE SEC. 407. CERTAIN EMPLOYEES OF DOMESTIC SUBSIDIARIES ENGAGED IN BUSINESS OUTSIDE THE UNITED STATES.

* * * * * * * * * *

(b) Special Rules for Application of Section 401.—

    (1) Nondiscrimination requirements.—For purposes of applying section 401(a)(4) and section 410(b) [1] with respect to an individual who is treated as an employee of domestic parent corporation under subsection (a)—

        (A) if such individual is [2]*a highly compensated employee (within the meaning of section 414(q))* he shall be treated as having such capacity with respect to such domestic parent corporation; and

        (B) the determination of whether such individual is a highly compensated employee *(as so defined)* shall be made by treating such individual's total compensation (determined with the application of paragraph (2) of this subsection) as compensation paid by such domestic parent corporation and by determining such individual's status with regard to such domestic parent corporation.

* * * * * * * * * *

(e) Treatment as Employee Under Related Provisions.—An individual who is treated as an employee of a domestic parent corporation under subsection (a) shall also be treated as an employee of such domestic parent corporation, with respect to the plan described in subsection (a)(1)(A), for purposes of applying the following provisions of this title:

    (1) Section 72(d) (relating to employees' annuities).

    (2) Section 72(f) (relating to special rules for computing employees' contributions).

    (3) Section 101(b) (relating to employees' death benefits).

    (4) Section 2039 (relating to annuities).[3]

[For official explanation, see Committee Reports, ¶3977; 3979; 4172.]

〔¶3000〕 CODE SEC. 408. INDIVIDUAL RETIREMENT ACCOUNTS.

    (a) Individual Retirement Account.—For purposes of this section, the term "individual retirement account" means a trust created or organized in the United States for the exclusive benefit of an individual or his beneficiaries, but only if the written governing instrument creating the trust meets the following requirements:

    (1) Except in the case of a rollover contribution described in subsection (d)(3), in section 402(a)(5), 402(a)(7), 403(a)(4), or 403(b)(8), no contribution will be accepted unless it is in cash, and contributions will not be accepted for the taxable year in excess of $2,000 on behalf of any individual

    (2) The trustee is a bank (as defined in subsection (n)) or such other person who demonstrates to the satisfaction of the Secretary that the manner in which such other person will administer the trust will be consistent with the requirements of this section.

    (3) No part of the trust funds will be invested in life insurance contracts.

    (4) The interest of an individual in the balance in his account is nonforfeitable.

    (5) The assets of the trust will not be commingled with other property except in a common trust fund or common investment fund.

    (6) Under regulations prescribed by the Secretary, rules similar to the rules of section 401(a)(9) [1]*(without regard to subparagraph (C)(ii) thereof) and the incidental death*

〔Footnote ¶2999〕 Section 1112(d)(3), '86 TRA, struck out from Sec. 407(b)(1):

(1) "(without regard to paragraph (1)(A) thereof"

Effective date (Sec. 1112(e), '86 TRA).—Generally applies to plan years beginning after 12-31-88. For special rules, see footnote ¶2994.

Matter in *italics* in Sec. 407(b)(1)(A) and (B) added by section 1114(b)(9)(B) and (C), '86 TRA, which struck out:

(2) "an officer, shareholder, or person whose principal duties consist of supervising the work of other employees of a domestic subsidiary"

Effective date (Sec. 1114(c)(3), '86 TRA).—Applies to years beginning after 12-31-88.

Section 1852(e)(2)(D), '86 TRA, struck out from Sec. 407(e):

(3) "(5) section 2517 (relating to certain annuities under qualified plans)."

Effective date (Sec. 1852(e)(2)(E), '86 TRA).—Applies to transfers after the date of the enactment of this Act.

    〔Footnote ¶3000〕 Matter in *italics* in Sec. 408(a)(6), (b)(3) and (c)(1), added by section 1852(a)(1), and (7)(A). '86 TRA, which struck out:

(1) "(relating to required distributions)"

benefit requirements of section 401(a) shall apply to the distribution of the entire interest of an individual for whose benefit the trust maintained.

(b) Individual Retirement Annuity.—For purposes of this section, the term "individual retirement annuity" means an annuity contract, or an endowment contract (as determined under regulations prescribed by the Secretary), issued by an insurance company which meets the following requirements:

* * * * * * * * * * *

(3) Under regulations prescribed by the Secretary, rules similar to the rules of section 401(a)(9) [1]*(without regard to subparagraph (C)(ii) thereof) and the incidental death benefit requirements of section 401(a),* shall apply to the distribution of the entire interest of the owner.

* * * * * * * * * * *

(c) Accounts Established by Employers and Certain Associations of Employees.—A trust created or organized in the United States by an employer for the exclusive benefit of his employees or their beneficiaries, or by an association of employees (which may include employees within the meaning of section 401(c)(1)) for the exclusive benefit of its members or their beneficiaries, shall be treated as an individual retirement account (described in subsection (a)), but only if the written governing instrument creating the trust meets the following requirements:

(1) The trust satisfies the requirements of paragraphs (1) [2]*through (6)* of subsection (a).

(2) There is a separate accounting for the interest of each employee or member (or spouse of an employee or member).

The assets of the trust may be held in a common fund for the account of all individuals who have an interest in the trust.

(d) Tax Treatment of Distributions.—

[3]*(1) In general.*—*Except as otherwise provided in this subsection, any amount paid or distributed out of an individual retirement plan shall be included in gross income by the payee or distributee, as the case may be, in the manner provided under section 72.*

(2) Special rules for applying section 72.—*For purpose of applying section 72 to any amount described in paragraph (1)*—

(A) all individual retirement plans shall be treated as 1 contract,

(B) all distributions during any taxable year shall be treated as 1 distribution, and

(C) the value of the contract, income on the contract, and investment in the contract shall be computed as of the close of the calendar year with or within which the taxable year ends.

For purposes of subparagraph (C), the value of the contract shall be increased by the amount of any distributions during the calendar year.

(3) Rollover contribution.—An amount is described in this paragraph as a rollover contribution if it meets the requirements of subparagraphs (A) and (B).

[Footnote ¶3000 continued]

(2) "through (7)"

Effective date (Sec. 1881, '86 TRA and 521(e)(1), (5), '84 TRA).—Generally applies to years beginning after 12-31-84. For special rule for collective bargaining agreements see footnote ¶2994.

Matter in *italics* in Sec. 408(d)(1) and (2) added by section 1102(c), '86 TRA, which struck out:

(3) "**(1) In general.**—Except as otherwise provided in this subsection, any amount paid or distributed out of an individual retirement account or under an individual retirement annuity shall be included in gross income by the payee or distributee, as the case may be, for the taxable year in which the payment or distribution is received. Notwithstanding any other provision of this title (including chapters 11 and 12), the basis of any person in such an account or annuity is zero.

(2) **Distributions of annuity contracts.**—Paragraph (1) does not apply to any annuity contract which meets the requirements of paragraphs (1), (3), (4), and (5) of subsection (b) and which is distributed from an individual retirement account. Section 72 applies to any such annuity contract, and for purposes of section 72 the investment in such contract in zero."

Effective date (Sec. 1102(g), '86 TRA).—Applies to contributions and distributions for taxable years beginning after 12-31-86.

Sec. 408(d)(3)(E) in *italics* added by section 1852(a)(5)(C), '86 TRA.

Effective date (Sec. 1881, '86 TRA, and Sec. 521(e)(1), '84 TRA).—Applies to years beginning after 12-31-84.

Code §408(d)(3) ¶3000

(A) In general.—Paragraph (1) does not apply to any amount paid or distributed out of an individual retirement account or individual retirement annuity to the individual for whose benefit the account or annuity is maintained if—

(i) The entire amount received (including money and any other property) is paid into an individual retirement account or individual retirement annuity (other than an endowment contract) for the benefit of such individual not later than the 60th day after the day on which he receives the payment or distribution;

*(ii) the entire amount received (including money and any other property) represents the entire amount in the account or the entire value of the annuity and no amount in the account and no part of the value of the annuity is attributable to any source other than a rollover contribution of a qualified total distribution (as defined in section 402(a)(5)(E)(i)) from an employee's trust described in section 401(a) which is exempt from tax under section 501(a)[4], or an annuity plan described in section 403(a),[5] and any earnings on such sums and the entire amount thereof is paid into another such trust (for the benefit of such individual) or annuity plan not later than the 60th day on which he receives the payment or distribution; or

(iii) (I) the entire amount received (including money and other property) represents the entire interest in the account or the entire value of the annuity.

(II) no amount in the account and no part of the value of the annuity is attributable to any source other than a rollover contribution from an annuity contract described in section 403(b) and any earnings on such rollover, and

(III) the entire amount thereof is paid into another annuity contract described in section 403(b) (for the benefit of such individual) not later than the 60th day after her receives the payment or distribution.

Clause (ii) shall not apply during the 5-year period beginning on the date of the qualified total distribution referred to in such clause if the individual was treated as a 5-percent owner with respect to such distribution under section 402(a)(5)(F)(ii).

* * * * * * * * * * *

(E) Denial of rollover treatment for required distributions.—This subparagraph shall not apply to any amount to the extent such amount is required to be distributed under subsection (a)(6) or (b)(3).

(F) Frozen deposits.—For purposes of this paragraph, rules similar to the rules of section 402(a)(6)(H) (relating to frozen deposits) shall apply.

* * * * * * * * * * *

(5) **Certain distributions to excess contributions after due date for taxable year.—**

(A) In general.—In the case of any individual, if the aggregate contributions (other than rollover contributions) paid for any taxable year to an individual retirement account or for an individual retirement annuity do not exceed $2,250 paragraph (1) shall not apply to the distribution of any such contribution to the extent that such contribution exceeds the amount allowable as a deduction under section 219 for the taxable year for which the contribution was paid—

(i) if such distribution is received after the date described in paragraph (4),

(ii) but only to the extent that no deduction has been allowed under section 219 with respect to such excess contribution. If employer contributions on behalf of the individual are paid for the taxable year to a simplified employee pension, the dollar limitation of the preceding sentence shall be increased by the lesser of the amount of such contributions or [8]*the dollar limitation in effect*

Matter in *italics* in Sec. 408(d)(3)(A), added by section 1875(c)(8), '86 TRA which stuck out:

(4) "(other than a trust forming part of a plan under which the individual was an employee within the meaning of section 401(c)(1) at the time contributions were made on his behalf under the plan)."

(5) "(other than a plan under which the individual was an employee within the meaning of section 401(c)(1) at the time contributions were made on his behalf under the plan)"

Effective date (Sec. 1881, '86 TRA, section 715, '84 TRA and section 243(c). '82 TEFRA, as amended by section 713(g)(1), '84 TRA).—Applies with respect to individuals dying after 12-31-83.

---

*Section 408(d)(3)(A)(ii) is also amended by Section 1121(c)(2), '86 TRA, by striking out the third and fourth parenthetical phrases, effective under section 1121(d)(2), '86 TRA, for years beginning after 12-31-86.

Sec. 408(d)(3)(F) in *italics* added by section 1122(e)(2)(B), '86 TRA

Effective date (Sec. 1122(h)(8), '86 TRA).—Applies to amounts transferred to an employee before, on, or after

under section 415(c)(1)(A) for such taxable year.

(B)   Excess rollover contributions attributable to erroneous information.—If—
   (i)   the taxpayer reasonably relies on information supplied pursuant to subtitle F for determining the amount of a rollover contribution, but
   (ii)   the information was erroneous, subparagraph (A) shall be applied by increasing the dollar limit set forth therein by the portion of the excess contribution which was attributable to such information.

For purposes of this paragraph, the amount allowable as a deduction under section 219 (after application of section 408(o)(2)(B)(ii)) shall be increased by the nondeductible limit under section 408(o)(2)(B).

* * * * * * * * * * * *

(f)   **[Repealed]**[9]

* * * * * * * * * * * *

(i)   **Reports.**—The trustee of an individual retirement account and the issuer of an endowment contract described in subsection (b) or an individual retirement annuity shall make such reports regarding such account, contract, or annuity to the Secretary, and to the individuals for whom the account, contract, or annuity is, or is to be, maintained with respect to the contributions (and the years in which they relate), distributions and such other matters as the Secretary may require under regulations. [10]*The reports required by this subsection—*

⟦Footnote ¶3000 continued⟧

the date of the enactment of this Act, except that in the case of an amount transferred on or before such date, the 60-day period referred to in section 402(a)(5)(C) of the '86 Code shall not expire before the 60th day after the date of the enactment of this Act:

Matter in *italics* in Sec. 408(d)(5)(A)(ii) added by section 1875(c)(6)(A), '86 TRA, which struck out:
(8)   "$15,000"
Effective date (Sec. 1881, '86 TRA, section 715, '84 TRA, and section 243(c), '82 TEFRA, as amended by Sec. 713(g)(1), '84 TRA).—Applies with respect to individuals dying after 12-31-83.

The last sentence in *italics* in Sec. 408(d)(5) added by Sec. 1102(b)(2), '86 TRA.
Effective date (Sec. 1102(g), '86 TRA).—Applies to contributions and distributions for taxable years beginning after 12-31-86.

Sec. 408(f) repealed by section 1123(d)(2), '86 TRA.
(9)   "**(f)   Additional Tax on Certain Amounts Included in Gross Income Before Age 59½.**—
(1)   **Early distribution from an individual retirement account, etc.**—If a distribution from an individual retirement account or under an individual retirement annuity to the individual for whose benefit such account or annuity was established is made before such individual attains age 59½, his tax under this chapter for the taxable year in which such distribution is received shall be increased by an amount equal to 10 percent of the amount of the distribution which is includible in his gross income for such taxable year.
(2)   **Disqualification cases.**—If an amount is includible in gross income for a taxable year under subsection (e) and the taxpayer has not attained age 59½ before the beginning of such taxable year, his tax under this chapter for such taxable year shall be increased by an amount equal to 10 percent of such amount so required to be included in his gross income.
(3)   **Disability cases.**—Paragraphs (1) and (2) do not apply if the amount paid or distributed, or the disqualification of the account or annuity under subsection (e), is attributable to the taxpayer becoming disabled within the meaning of section 72(m)(7)."
Effective date (Sec. 1123(e)(1), (3) and (4) '86 TRA).—(1) Generally applies to taxable years beginning after 12-31-86.

* * * * * * * * * * * *

(3)   Exception where distribution commences.—The amendments shall not apply to distributions to any employee from a plan maintained by any employer if—
(A)   as of 3-1-86, the employee separated from service with the employer,
(B)   as of 3-1-86, the accrued benefit of the employee was in pay status pursuant to a written election providing a specific schedule for the distribution of the entire accrued benefit of the employee, and
(C)   such distribution is made pursuant to such written election.
(4)   Transition rule.—The amendments shall not apply with respect to any benefits with respect to which a designation is in effect under section 242(b)(2) of '82 TEFRA.

Matter in *italics* in Sec. 408(i) added by section 1102(e)(2), '86 TRA, which struck out:
(10)   "The reports required by this subsection shall be filed at such time and in such manner and furnished to such individuals at such time and in such manner as may be required by those regulations."
Effective date (Sec. 1102(g), '86 TRA).—Applies to contributions and distributions for taxable years beginning after 12-31-86.

---

(1) shall be filed at such time and in such manner as the Secretary prescribes in such regulations, and

    (2) shall be furnished to individuals—

       (A) not later than January 31 of the calendar year following the calendar year to which such reports relate, and

       (B) in such manner as the Secretary prescribes in such regulations.

*   *   *   *   *   *   *   *   *   *   *   *

(k) Simplified Employee Pension Defined.—

*   *   *   *   *   *   *   *   *   *   *   *

≫**P-H CAUTION**→ There are two versions of Sec. 408(k)(2). Sec. 408(k)(2), generally effective after 12-31-86, follows. For Sec. 408(k)(2), generally effective after enactment date, see below.

[11]▲ *(2) Participation requirements.—This paragraph is satisfied with respect to a simplified employee pension for a year only if for such year the employer contributes to the simplified employee pension of each employee who—*

    (A) has attained age 21,

    (B) has perfomed service for the employer during at least 3 of the immediately preceding 5 years, and

    (C) received at least $300 in compensation (within the meaning of section 414(q)(7)) from the employer for the year.

For purposes of this paragraph, there shall be excluded from consideration employees described in subparagraph (A) or (C) of section 410(b)(3). For purposes of any arrangement described in subsection (k)(6), any employee who is eligible to have employer contributions made on the employee's behalf under such arrangement shall be treated as if such a contribution was made.

≫**P-H CAUTION**→ There are two versions of Sec. 408(k)(2). Sec. 408(k)(2), effective after the date of the enactment of this Act, follows. For Sec. 408(k)(2)(A), effective after 12-31-86, see above.

▲ ▲ **(2) Participation requirements.**—This paragraph is satisfied with respect to a simplified employee pension for a calendar year only if for such year the employer contributes to the simplified employee pension of each employee who—

    (A) has attained [12]*age 21* , and

    (B) has performed service for the employer during at least 3 of the immediately preceding 5 calendar years.

For purposes of this paragraph, there shall be excluded from consideration employees described in subparagraph (A) or (C) of section 410(b)(3).

    (3) Contributions may not discriminate in favor of the highly compensated, etc.—

       (A) In general.—The requirements of this paragraph are met with respect to a simplified pension for a [13] year if for such year the contributions made by the employer to simplified employee pensions for his employees do not discriminate in favor of [14]*any highly compensated employee (within the meaning of section 414(q))*

⟦Footnote ¶3000 continued⟧

  ▲ Matter in *italics* in Sec. 408(k)(2), preceded by a triangle, added by section 1108(d), '86 TRA, which struck out:

  (11) "**(2) Participation requirements.**—This paragraph is satisfied with respect to a simplified employee pension for a calendar year only if for such year the employer contributes to the simplified employee pension of each employee who—

(A) has attained age 21, and

(B) has performed service for the employee during at least 3 of the immediately preceding 5 calendar years.

For purposes of this paragraph, there shall be excluded from consideration employees, described in subparagraph (A) or (C) of section 410(b)(3)."

Effective date (Sec. 1108(h), '86 TRA).—Applies to years beginning after 12-31-86.

  ▲ ▲ Matter in *italics* in Sec. 408(k)(2), preceded by two triangles, added by section 1898(a)(5), '86 TRA, which struck out:

(12) "age 25"

Effective date (Sec. 1898(a)(5), '86 TRA).—Applies to plan years beginning after the date of enactment of this Act.

Matter in *italics* in Sec. 408(k)(3)(A), (C), (D), and (k)(6)—(9) added by section 1108(a), (e), (f), (g)(1), (4), and (6), '86 TRA, which struck out:

(13) "calendar"

(14) "any employee who is—

(i) an officer,

(B) Special Rules.—For purposes of subparagraph (A)—

(i) there shall be excluded from consideration employees described in subparagraph (A) or (C) of section 410(b)(3), and

(ii) an individual shall be considered a shareholder if he owns (with the application of section 318) more than 10 percent of the value of the stock of the employer.

(C) Contributions must bear a uniform relationship to total compensation.— For purposes of subparagraph (A), *and except as provided in subparagraph (D),* employer contributions to simplified employee pensions *(other than contributions under an arrangement described in paragraph (6))* shall be considered discriminatory unless contributions thereto bear a uniform relationship to the total compensation (not in excess of the first $200,000) of each employee maintaining a simplified employee pension.[15]

[16](D) *Permitted disparity.—For purposes of subparagraph (C), the rules of section 401(1)(2) shall apply to contributions to simplified employee pensions (other than contributions under an arrangement described in paragraph (6)).*

* * * * * * * * * * *

(6) *Employee may elect salary reduction arrangement.—*

(A) *In general.—A simplified employee pension shall not fail to meet the requirements of this subsection for a year merely because, under the terms of the pension—*

(i) *an employee may elect to have the employer make payments—*

(I) *as elective employer contributions to the simplified employee pension on behalf of the employee, or*

(II) *to the employee directly in cash,*

(ii) *an election described in clause (i)(I) is made or is in effect with respect to not less than 50 percent of the employees of the employer, and*

(iii) *the deferral percentage for such year of each highly compensated employee eligible to participate is not more than the product derived by multiplying the average of the deferral percentages for such year of all employees (other than highly compensated employees) eligible to participate by 1.25.*

(B) *Exception where more than 25 employees.—This paragraph shall not apply with respect to any year in the case of a simplified employee pension maintained by an employer with more than 25 employees at any time during the preceding year.*

(C) *Distributions of excess contributions.—*

(i) *In general.—Rules similar to the rules of section 401(k)(8) shall apply to any excess contribution under this paragraph. Any excess contribution under a simplified employee pension shall be treated as an excess contribution for purposes of section 4979.*

(ii) a shareholder,

(iii) a self-employed individual, or

(iv) highly compensated."

(15) "The Secretary shall annually adjust the $200,000 amount contained in the preceding sentence at the same time and in the same manner as he adjusts the dollar amount contained in section 415(c)(1)(A)."

(16) "(D) Treatment of certain contributions and taxes.—Except as provided in this subparagraph, employer contributions do not meet the requirements of this paragraph unless such contributions meet the requirements of this paragraph without taking into account contributions or benefits under chapter 2 (relating to tax on self-employment income), chapter 21 (relating to Federal Insurance Contribution Act), title II of the Social Security Act, or any other Federal or State law. If the employer does not maintain an integrated plan at any time during the taxable year, OASDI contributions (as defined in section 401(l)(2)) may, for purposes of this paragraph, be taken into account as contributions by the employer to the employee's simplified employee pension, but only if such contributions are so taken into account with respect to each employee maintaining a simplified employee pension.

(E) Integrated plan defined.—For purposes of subparagraph (D), the term "integrated plan" means a plan which meets the requirements of section 401(a) or 403(a) but would not meet such requirements if contributions or benefits under chapter 2 (relating to tax on self-employment income), chapter 21 (relating to Federal Insurance Contributions Act), title II of the Social Security Act, or any other Federal or State law were not taken into account."

Effective date (Sec. 1108(h), '86 TRA).—Applies to taxable years beginning after 12-31-86.

(ii) *Excess contribution.—For purposes of clause (i), the term "excess contribution" means, with respect to a highly compensated employee, the excess of elective employer contributions under this paragraph over the maximum amount of such contributions allowable under subparagraph (A)(iii).*

(D) *Deferral percentage.—for purposes of this paragraph, the deferral percentage for an employee for a year shall be the ratio of—*

(i) *the amount of elective employer contributions actually paid over to the simplified employee pension on behalf of the employee for the year, to*

(ii) *the employee's compensation (within the meaning of section 414(s)) for the year.*

(E) *Exception for state and local and tax-exempt pensions.—This paragraph shall not apply to a simplified employee pension maintained by—*

(i) *a State or local government or political subdivision thereof, or any agency or instrumentality thereof, or*

(ii) *an organization exempt from tax under this title.*

(F) *Highly compensated employee.—For purposes of this paragraph, the term "highly compensated employee" has the meaning given such term by section 414(q).*

(7) **Definitions.**—For purposes of this subsection and subsection (1)—

(A) Employee, employer, or owner-employee.—The terms "employee", "employer", and "owner-employee" shall have the respective meanings given such terms by section 401(c).

(B) Compensation.—The term "compensation" means, in the case of an employee within the meaning of section 401(c)(1), earned income within the meaning of section 401(c)(2).

(C) Year.—The term "year" means—

(i) the calendar year, or

(ii) if the employer elects, subject to such terms and conditions as the Secretary may prescribe, to maintain the simplified employee pension on the basis of the employer's taxable year, the employer's taxable year.

(8) *Cost-of-living adjustment.—The Secretary shall adjust the $300 amount in paragraph (2)(C) and the $200,000 amount in paragraph (3)(C) at the same time and in the same manner as under section 415(d).*

(9) *Cross Reference.—*
For excise tax on certain excess contributions, see section 4979.

* * * * * * * * * * *

(m) **Investment in Collectibles Treated as Distributions.—**

(1) **In general.**—The acquisition by an individual retirement account or by an individually-directed account under a plan described in section 401(a) of any collectible shall be treated (for purposes of this section and section 402) as a distribution from such account in an amount equal to the cost to such account of such collectible.

(2) **Collectible defined.**—For purposes of this subsection, the term "collectible" means—

(A) any work of art,

(B) any rug or antique,

(C) any metal or gem,

(D) any stamp or coin,

(E) any alcoholic beverage, or

(F) any other tangible personal property specified by the Secretary for purposes of this subsection.

(3) *Exception for certain coins.—In the case of an individual retirement account, paragraph (2) shall not apply to any gold coin described in paragraph (7), (8), (9), or (10) of section 5112(a) of title 31 or any silver coin described in section 5112(e) of title 31.*

* * * * * * * * * * *

[Footnote ¶3000 continued]

Sec. 408(m)(3) in *italics* added by section 1144(a), '86 TRA.
Effective date (Sec. 1144(b), '86 TRA).—Applies to acquisitions after 12-31-85.

(o) Definitions and Rules Relating to Nondeductible Contributions to Individual Retirement Plans.—

(1) In general.—Subject to the provisions of this subsection, designated nondeductible contributions may be made on behalf of an individual to an individual retirement plan.

(2) Limits on amounts which may be contributed.—

(A) In general.—The amount of the designated nondeductible contributions made on behalf of any individual for any taxable year shall not exceed the nondeductible limit for such taxable year.

(B) Nondeductible limit.—For purposes of this paragraph—

(i) In general.—The term "nondeductible limit" means the excess of—

(I) the amount allowable as a deduction under section 219 (determined without regard to section 219(g)), over

(II) the amount allowable as a deduction under section 219 (determined with regard to section 219(g)).

(ii) Taxpayer may elect to treat deductible contributions as nondeductible.—If a taxpayer elects not to deduct an amount which (without regard to this clause) is allowable as a deduction under section 219 for any taxable year, the nondeductible limit for such taxable year shall be increased by such amount.

(C) Designated nondeductible contributions.—

(i) In general.—For purposes of this paragraph, the term "designated nondeductible contribution" means any contribution to an individual retirement plan for the taxable year which is designated (in such manner as the Secretary may prescribe) as a contribution for which a deduction is not allowable under section 219.

(ii) Designation.—Any designation under clause (i) shall be made on the return of tax imposed by chapter 1 for the taxable year.

(3) Time when contributions made.—In determining for which taxable year a designated nondeductible contribution is made, the rule of section 219(f)(3) shall apply.

(4) Individual required to report amount of designated nondeductible contributions.—

(A) In general.—Any individual who—

(i) makes a designated nondeductible contribution to any individual retirement plan for any taxable year, or

(ii) receives any amount from any individual retirement plan for any taxable year,

shall include on his return of the tax imposed by chapter 1 for such taxable year and any succeeding taxable year (or on such other form as the Secretary may prescribe for any such taxable year) information described in subparagraph (B).

(B) Information required to be supplied.—The following information is described in this subparagraph:

(i) The amount of designated nondeductible contributions for the taxable year,

(ii) The amount of distributions from individual retirement plans for the taxable year,

(iii) The excess (if any) of—

(I) the aggregate amount of designated nondeductible contributions for all preceding taxable years, over

(II) the aggregate amount of distributions from individual retirement plans which was excludable from gross income for such taxable years.

(iv) The aggregate balance of all individual retirement plans of the individual as of the close of the calendar year with or within which the taxable year ends.

(v) Such other information as the Secretary may prescribe.

(C) Penalty for reporting contributions not made.—

For penalty where individual reports designated nondeductible contributions not made, see section 6693(b).

[17](p) **Cross References.—**

* * * * * * * * * * * * *

[For official explanation, see Committee Reports, ¶3969; 3974; 3986; 3988; 4172; 4189.]

⟦Footnote ¶3000 continued⟧

Matter in *italics* in Sec. 408(o), and (p) added by section 1102(a), '86 TRA, which struck out:
(17) "(o)"

Effective date (Sec. 1102(g), '86 TRA).—Applies to contributions and distributions for taxable years beginning after 12-31-86.

[¶3001] CODE SEC. 409. QUALIFICATIONS FOR TAX CREDIT EMPLOYEE STOCK OWNERSHIP PLANS.

(a) **Tax Credit Employee Stock Ownership Plans Defined.**—Except as otherwise provided in this title, for purposes of this title, the term tax credit employee stock ownership plan means a defined contribution plan which—

(1) meets the requirements of section 401(a),

(2) is designed to invest primarily in employer securities, and

(3) meets the requirements of subsections (b), (c), (d), (e), (f), (g), [1]*(h), and (o)* of this section.

* * * * * * * * * * * *

(d) **Employer Securities Must Stay in the Plan.**—A plan meets the requirements of this subsection only if it provides that no employer security allocated to a [2]*participant's* account under subsection (b) (or allocated to a [2]*participant's* account in connection with matched employer and employee contributions) may be distributed from that account before the end of the 84th month beginning after the month in which the security is allocated to the account. To the extent provided in the plan, the preceding sentence shall not apply in the case of—

(1) death, disability, [3]*separation from service, or termination of the plan;*

(2) a transfer of a participant to the employment of an acquiring employer from the employment of the selling corporation in the case of a sale to the acquiring corporation of substantially all of the assets used by the selling corporation in a trade or business conducted by the selling corporation, or

(3) with respect to the stock of a selling corporation, a disposition of such selling corporation's interest in a subsidiary when the participant continues employment with such subsidiary.

This subsection shall not apply to any distribution required under section 401(a)(9).

(e) **Voting Rights.**—

* * * * * * * * * * * *

(2) **Requirements where employer has a registration-type class of securities.**—If the employer has a registration-type class of securities, the plan meets the requirements of this paragraph only if each participant *or beneficiary* in the plan is entitled to direct the plan as to the manner in which [4]*securities of the employer* which are entitled to vote and are allocated to the account of such participant *or beneficiary* are to be voted.

(3) **Requirement for other employers.**—If the employer does not have a registration-type class of securities, the plan meets the requirements of this paragraph only if each participant *or beneficiary* in the plan is entitled to direct the plan as to the manner in which voting rights under [4]*securities of the employer* which are allocated to the account of such participant *or beneficiary* are to be exercised with respect to [5]*any corporate matter which involves the voting of such shares with respect to the approval or disapproval of any corporate merger or consolidation, recapitalization, reclassification, liquidation, dissolution, sale of substantially all assets of a trade or business, or such similar transaction as the Secretary may prescribe in regulations.*

[Footnote ¶3001] Matter in *italics* in Sec. 409(a)(3) added by section 1174(b)(2), '86 TRA, which struck out:
(1) "and (h)"
Effective date (Sec. 1174(b)(3), '86 TRA).—Applies to distributions attributable to stock acquired after 12-31-86.

Matter in *italics* in the first sentence of Sec. 409(d) added by section 1899A(11), '86 TRA, which struck out:
(2) "participants's"

Matter in *italics* in Sec. 409(d)(1) added by section 1174(a)(1), '86 TRA, which struck out:
(3) "or separation from service"
Effective date (Sec. 1174(a)(2), '86 TRA).—Applies to plan terminations after 12-31-84.

Matter in *italics* in the last sentence of Sec. 409(d) added by section 1852(a)(4)(B), '86 TRA.
Effective date (Sec. 1881, '86 TRA and section 521(e), '84 TRA).— Generally applies to years beginning after 12-31-84. For special and transitional rules see footnote ¶2994.

Matter in *italics* in Sec. 409(e)(2), (3) added by section 1854(f)(1)(B)—(D), '86 TRA, which struck out:
(4) "employer securities"
(5) "a corporate matter which (by law or charter) must be decided by more than a majority vote of outstanding common shares voted."
Effective date (Sec. 1854(f)(4)(B), '86 TRA).—Applies after 12-31-86 to stock acquired after 12-31-79.

* * * * * * * * * * * *

(5) *1 vote per participant.*—*A plan meets the requirements of paragraph (2) or (3) with respect to an issue if—*

(A) *the plan permits each participant 1 vote with respect to such issue, and*

(B) *the trustee votes the shares held by the plan in the proportion determined after application of subparagraph (A).*

* * * * * * * * * * * *

(h) Right to Demand Employer Securities; Put Option.—

* * * * * * * * * * * *

(2) **Plan may distribute cash in certain cases.**—A plan which otherwise meets the requirements of this subsection or of section 4975(e)(7) shall not be considered to have failed to meet the requirements of section 401(a) merely because under the plan the benefits may be distributed in cash, *except that such plan may distribute employer securities subject to a requirement that such securities may be resold to the employer under terms which meet the requirements of section 409(o)* or in the form of employer securities. In the case of an employer whose charter or bylaws restrict the ownership of substantially all outstanding employer securities to employees or to a trust described in section 401(a), a plan which otherwise meets the requirements of this subsection or section 4975(e)(7) shall not be considered to have failed to meet the requirements of this subsection or of section 401(a) merely because it does not permit a participant to exercise the right described in paragraph (1)(A) if such plan provides that participants entitled to a distribution from the plans shall have a right to receive such distribution in cash.

* * * * * * * * * * * *

(5) *Payment requirement for total distribution.*—*If an employer is required to repurchase employer securities which are distributed to the employee as part of a total distribution, the requirements of paragraph (1)(B) shall be treated as met if—*

(A) *the amount to be paid for the employer securities is paid in substantially equal periodic payments (not less frequently than annually) over a period beginning not later than 30 days after the exercise of the put option described in paragraph (4) and not exceeding 5 years, and*

(B) *there is adequate security provided and reasonable interest paid on the unpaid amounts referred to in subparagraph (A),*

For purposes of this paragraph, the term "total distribution" means the distribution, within 1 taxable year to the recipient of the balance to the credit of the recipient's account.

(6) *Payment requirement for installment distributions.*—*If an employer is required to repurchase employer securities as part of an installment distribution, the requirements of paragraph (1)(B) shall be treated as met if the amount to be paid for the employer securities is paid not later than 30 days after the exercise of the put option described in paragraph (4).*

* * * * * * * * * * * *

[Footnote ¶3001 continued]

Matter in *italics* in Sec. 409(e)(5) and (h)(2) added by section 1854(f)(1)(A) and (3)(C), '86 TRA.
Effective date (Sec. 1854(f)(4)(A) '86 TRA).—Takes effect on date of enactment of this Act.

Matter in *italics* in Sec. 409(h)(5) and (6) added by section 1174(c)(1)(A), '86 TRA.
Effective date (Sec. 1174(c)(1)(B) '86 TRA).—Applies to distributions attributable to stock acquired after 12-31-86, except that a plan may elect to have such amendment apply to all distributions after the date of enactment of this Act.

(l) **Employer Securities Defined.**—For purposes of this section—

* * * * * * * * * *

(4) [should read (5)] Nonvoting common stock may be acquired in certain cases.— Nonvoting common stock of an employer described in the last sentence of section 401(a)(22) shall be treated as employer securities if an employer has a class of nonvoting common stock outstanding and the specific shares that the plan acquires have been issued and outstanding for at least 24 months.

* * * * * * * * * *

(n) Securities Received in Certain Transactions.—

(1) In general.—A plan to which section 1042 applies and an eligible worker-owned cooperative (within the meaning of section 1042(c)) shall provide that no portion of the assets of the plan or cooperative attributable to (or allocable in lieu of) employer securities acquired by the plan or cooperative in a sale to which section 1042 or section 2057 applies may accrue (or be allocated directly or indirectly under any plan of the employer meeting the requirements of section 401(a))—

(A) during the nonallocation period, for the benefit of—

(i) any taxpayer who makes an election under section 1042(a) with respect to employer securities or any decedent if the executor of the estate of such decedent makes a qualified sale to which section 2057 applies,

(ii) any individual who is related to the taxpayer or the decedent (within the meaning of section 267(b)), or

(B) for the benefit of any other person who owns (after application of section 318(a)) more than 25 percent of—

(i) any class of outstanding stock of the corporation which issued such employer securities or of any corporation which is a member of the same controlled group of corporations (within the meaning of subsection (l)(4)) as such corporation, or

(ii) the total value of any class of outstanding stock of any such corporation.

For purposes of subparagraph (B), section 318(a) shall be applied without regard to the employee trust exception in paragraph (2)(B)(i).

(2) Failure to meet requirements.—If a plan fails to meet the requirements of paragraph (1)—

(A) the plan shall be treated as having distributed to the person described in paragraph (1) the amount allocated to the account of such person in violation of paragraph (1) at the time of such allocation,

(B) the provisions of section 4979A shall apply, and

(C) the statutory period for the assessment of any tax imposed by section 4979A shall not expire before the date which is 3 years from the later of—

(i) the 1st allocation of employer securities in connection with a sale to the plan to which section 1042 applies, or

(ii) the date on which the Secretary is notified of such failure.

(3) Definitions and special rules.—For purposes of this subsection—

(A) Lineal descendants.—Paragraph (1)(A)(ii) shall not apply to any individual if—

(i) such individual is a lineal descendant of the taxpayer, and

(ii) the aggregate amount allocated to the benefit of all such lineal descendants during the nonallocation period does not exceed more than 5 percent of the employer securities (or amounts allocated in lieu thereof) held by the plan which are attributable to a sale to the plan by any person related to such descendants (within the meaning of section 267(c)(4)) in a transaction to which section 1042 applied.

⟦Footnote ¶3001 continued⟧

Matter in *italics* in Sec. 409(l)(4) [should read (5)] added by section 1176(b), '86 TRA.
Effective date (Sec. 1176(a), '86 TRA).—Applies to acquisitions of securities after 12-31-86.

Matter in *italics* in Sec. 409(n), except the phrases: *"or section 2057"*, *"or the decedent"*, and *"or any decedent if the executor of the estate of such decedent makes a qualified sale to which section 2057 applies,"* added by section 1854(a)(3)(A), '86 TRA.
Effective date (Sec. 1854(a)(3)(C), '86 TRA).—Applies to sales of securities after date of enactment of this Act.

The phrases *"or section 2057"*, *"or the decedent"*, and *"or any decedent if the executor of the estate of such decedent makes a qualified sale to which section 2057 applies,"* in Sec. 409(n) added by section 1172(b)(1), '86 TRA.
Effective date (Sec. 1172(c), '86 TRA).—Applies to sales after the date of the enactment of this Act with respect to which an election is made by the executor of an estate who is required to file the return of the tax imposed by the '86 Code on a date (including extensions) after the date of the enactment of this Act.

(B) *25-percent shareholders.—A person shall be treated as failing to meet the stock ownership limitation under paragraph (1)(B) if such person fails such limitation—*

(i) *at any time during the 1-year period ending on the date of sale of qualified securities to the plan or cooperative, or*

(ii) *on the date as of which qualified securities are allocated to participants in the plan or cooperative.*

(C) *Nonallocation period.—The term "nonallocation period" means the 10-year period beginning on the later of—*

(i) *the date of the sale of the qualified securities, or*

(ii) *the date of the plan allocation attributable to the final payment of acquisition indebtedness incurred in connection with such sale.*

(o) **Distribution and Payment Requirements.**—*A plan meets the requirements of this subsection if—*

(1) **Distribution requirement.**—

(A) *In general.—The plan provides that, unless the participant otherwise elects, the distribution of the participant's account balance in the plan will commence not later than 1 year after the close of the plan year—*

(i) *in which the participant separates from service by reason of the attainment of normal retirement age under the plan, disability, or death, or*

(ii) *which is the 5th plan year following the plan year in which the participant otherwise separates from services, except that this clause shall not apply if the participant is reemployed by the employer before such year.*

(B) *Exception for certain financed securities.—For purposes of this subsection, the account balance of a participant shall not include any employer securities acquired with the proceeds of the loan described in section 404(a)(9) until the close of the plan year in which such loan is repaid in full.*

(C) *Limited distribution period.—The plan provides that, unless the participant elects otherwise, the distribution of the participant's account balance will be in substantially equal periodic payments (not less frequently than annually) over a period not longer than the greater of—*

(i) *5 years, or*

(ii) *in the case of a participant with an account balance in excess of $500,000 5 years plus 1 additional year (but not more than 5 additional years) for each $100,000 or fraction thereof by which such balance exceeds $500,000.*

(2) **Cost-of-living adjustment.**—*The Secretary shall adjust the dollar amounts under paragraph (1)(C) at the same time and in the same manner as under section 415(d).*

*(p) Cross References.—

[For official explanation, see Committee Reports, ¶4019; 4021; 4172; 4174.]

〖¶3002〗 CODE SEC. 410. MINIMUM PARTICIPATION STANDARDS

(a) **Participation.—**

(1) **Minimum age and service conditions.—**

(A) General Rule.—A trust shall not constitute a qualified trust under section 401(a) if the plan of which it is a part requires, as a condition of participation in the plan, that an employee complete a period of service with the employer or employers maintaining the plan extending beyond the later of the following dates—

(i) the date on which the employee attains the age of 21; or

(ii) the date on which he completes 1 year of service.

(B) Special rules for certain plans.—

(i) In the case of any plan which provides that after not more than [1]2 *years of service* each participant has a right to 100 percent of his accrued benefit under the plan which is nonforfeitable (within the meaning of section 411) at the

---

〖Footnote ¶3001 continued〗

Matter in *italics* in Sec. 409(o) added by section 1174(b)(1), '86 TRA.

Effective date (Sec. 1174(b)(3), '86 TRA).—Applies to distributions attributable to stock acquired after 12-31-86.

---

* Former Sec. 409(n) was relettered (o), by section 1854(a)(3)(A), '86 TRA, and was further relettered as (p) by section 1174(b)(1), '86 TRA.

Effective date (Sec. 1174(b)(3), '86 TRA).—Applies to distributions attributable to stock acquired after 12-31-86.

〖Footnote ¶3002〗 Matter in *italics* in Sec. 410(a)(1)(B) and (5)(B) added by section 1113(c) and (d)(A), '86 TRA, which struck out:

(1) "3 years"

time such benefit accrues, clause (ii) of subparagraph (A) shall be applied by substituting [1] "*2 years* of service" for "1 year of service."

*   *   *   *   *   *   *   *   *   *   *   *

(5) Breaks in service.—

*   *   *   *   *   *   *   *   *   *   *   *

(B) Employees under [2]*2-year* 100 percent vesting.—In the case of any employee who has any 1-year break in service (as defined in section 411(a)(6)(A)) under a plan to which the service requirements of clause (i) of paragraph (1)(B) apply, if such employee has not satisfied such requirements, service before such break shall not be required to be taken into account.

*   *   *   *   *   *   *   *   *   *   *   *

[3]*(b) Minimum Coverage Requirements.—*

⟦Footnote ¶3002 continued⟧

(2) "3-year"
Effective date (Sec. 1113(e), '86 TRA).—(1) Applies to plan years beginning after 12-31-88.
(2) Special rule for collective bargaining agreements.—In the case of a plan maintained pursuant to 1 or more collective bargaining agreements between employee representatives and 1 or more employers ratified before 4-1-86, the amendments made by this section shall not apply to employees covered by any such agreement in plan years beginning before the earlier of—
(A) the later of—
(i) 1-1-89, or
(ii) the date on which the last of such collective bargaining agreements terminates (determined without regard to any extension thereof after 2-28-86, or
(B) 1-1-89.
(3) Participation required.—The amendments made by this section shall not apply to any employee who does not have 1 hour of service in any plan year to which the amendments made by this section apply.

Matter in *italics* in Sec. 410(b) added by section 1112(a) '86 TRA, which struck out:
(3) "(b) Eligibility.—
(1) **In general.**—A trust shall not constitute a qualified trust under section 401(a) unless the trust, or two or more trusts, or the trust or trusts and annuity plan or plans are designated by the employer as constituting parts of a plan intended to qualify under section 401(a) which benefits either—
(A) 70 percent or more of all employees, or 80 percent or more of all the employees who are eligible to benefit under the plan if 70 percent or more of all the employees are eligible to benefit under the plan, excluding in each case employees who have not satisfied the minimum age and service requirements, if any, prescribed by the plan as a condition of participation, or
(B) such employees as qualify under a classification set up by the employer and found by the Secretary not to be discriminatory in favor of employees who are officers, shareholders, or highly compensated.
(2) **Special rule for certain plans.**—A trust which is part of a tax credit employees stock ownership plan which is the only plan of an employer intended to qualify under section 401(a) shall not be treated as not a qualified trust under section 401(a) solely because it fails to meet the requirements of paragraph (1) if—
(A) it benefits 50 percent or more of all the employees who are eligible under the plan (excluding employees who have not satisfied the minimum age and service requirements; if any, prescribed by the plan as a condition of participation), and
(B) the sum of the amounts allocated to each participant's account for the year does not exceed 2 percent of the compensation of that participant for the year.
(3) **Exclusion of certain employees.**—For purposes of paragraphs (1) and (2), there shall be excluded from consideration—
(A) employees not included in the plan who are included in a unit of employees covered by an agreement which the Secretary of Labor finds to be a collective bargaining agreement between employee representatives and one or more employers, if there is evidence that retirement benefits were the subject of good faith bargaining between such employee representatives and such employer or employers,
(B) in the case of a trust established or maintained pursuant to an agreement which the Secretary of Labor finds to be a collective bargaining agreement between air pilots represented in accordance with title II of the Railway Labor Act and one or more employers, all employees not covered by such agreement, and
(C) employees who are nonresident aliens and who receive no earned income (within the meaning of section 911(d)(2)) from the employer which constitutes income from sources within the United States (within the meaning of section 861(a)(3)).
Subparagraph (B) shall not apply in the case of plan which provides contributions or benefits for employees whose principal duties are not customarily performed aboard aircraft in flight.))"
Effective date (Sec. 1112(e), '86 TRA).—(1) Applies to plan years beginning after 12-31-88.
(2) Special rule for collective bargaining agreements.—In the case of a plan maintained pursuant to 1 or more collective bargaining agreements between employee representatives and 1 or more employers ratified before 4-1-86, the amendments made by this section shall not apply to employees covered by any such agreement in plan years beginning before the earlier of—
(A) the later of—
(i) 1-1-89, or
(ii) the date on which the last of such collective bargaining agreement terminates (determined without regard to

(1) In general.—A trust shall not constitute a qualified trust under section 401(a) unless such trust is designated by the employer as part of a plan which meets 1 of the following requirements:

(A) The plan benefits at least 70 percent of employees who are not highly compensated employees.

(B) The plan benefits—

(i) a percentage of employees who are not highly compensated employees which is at least 70 percent of

(ii) the percentage of highly compensated employees benefitting under the plan.

(C) The plan meets the requirements of paragraph (2).

(2) Average benefit percentage test.—

(A) In general.—A plan shall be treated as meeting the requirements of this paragraph if—

(i) the plan benefits such employees as qualify under a classification set up by the employer and found by the Secretary not to be discriminatory in favor of highly compensated employees, and

(ii) the average benefit percentage for employees who are not highly compensated employees is at least 70 percent of the average benefit percentage for highly compensated employees.

(B) Average benefit percentage.—For purposes of this paragraph, the term "average benefit percentage" means, with respect to any group, the average of the benefit percentages calculated separately with respect to each employee in such group (whether or not a participant in any plan).

(C) Benefit percentage.—For purposes of this paragraph—

(i) In general.—The term "benefit percentage" means the employer-provided contribution or benefit of an employee under all qualified plans maintained by the employer, expressed as a percentage of such employee's compensation (within the meaning of section 414(s)).

(ii) Period for computing percentage.—At the election of an employer, the benefit percentage for any plan year shall be computed on the basis of contributions or benefits for—

(I) such plan year, or

(II) any consecutive plan year period (not greater than 3 years) which ends with such plan year and which is specified in such election.

An election under this clause, once made, may be revoked or modified only with the consent of the Secretary.

(D) Employees taken into account.—For purposes of determining who is an employee for purposes of determining the average benefit percentage under subparagraph (B)—

(i) except as provided in clause (ii), paragraph (4)(A) shall not apply, or

---

[Footnote ¶3002 continued]

any extension thereof after 2-28-86, or

(B) 1-1-89.

(3) Waiver of excise tax on reversions.—

(A) If general.—If—

(i) a plan is in existence on 8-16-86,

(ii) such plan would fail to meet the requirements of section 401(a)(26) of the '86 Code (as added by subsection (b)) if such section were in effect for the plan year including 8-16-86, and

(iii) there is no transfer of assets to or liabilities from a plan or merger or spinoff or merger involving such plan after 8-16-86,

then no tax shall be imposed under section 4980 of such Code on any employer reversion by reason of the termination or merger of such plan before the 1st year to which the amendment made by subsection (b) applies.

(B) Determination of amount of reversion.—For purposes of the '86 Code, in determining the present value of the accrued benefit of any highly compensated employee (within the meaning of section 414(q) of such Code) on the termination or merger of any plan to which subparagraph (A) applies, the plan shall use the highest interest rate which may be used for calculating present value under section 411(a)(11)(B) of such Code.

(C) Special rule for plans which may not terminate.—To the extent provided in regulations prescribed by the Secretary of the Treasury or his delegate, if a plan is prohibited from terminating under title IV of the Employee Retirement Income Security Act of 1974 before the 1st year to which the amendment made by subsection (b) applies, subparagraph (A) shall be applied by substituting "the 1st year in which the plan is able to terminate" for "the 1st year to which the amendment made by subsection (b) applies. "

Code §410(b)(2) ¶3002

(ii) if the employer elects, paragraph (4)(A) shall be applied by using the lowest age and service requirements of all qualified plans maintained by the employer.

(E) Qualified plan.—For purposes of this paragraph, the term "qualified plan" means any plan which (without regard to this subsection) meets the requirements of section 401(a).

(3) *Exclusion of certain employees.—For purposes of this subsection, there shall be excluded from consideration—*

(A) employees who are included in a unit of employees covered by an agreement which the Secretary of Labor finds to be a collective bargaining agreement between employee representatives and one or more employers, if there is evidence that retirement benefits were the subject of good faith bargaining between such employee representatives and such employer or employers,

(B) in the case of a trust established or maintained pursuant to an agreement which the Secretary of Labor finds to be a collective bargaining agreement between air pilots represented in accordance with title II of the Railway Labor Act and one or more employers, all employees not covered by such agreement, and

(C) employees who are nonresident aliens and who receive no earned income (within the meaning of section 911(d)(2)) from the employer which constitutes income from sources within the United States (within the meaning of section 861(a)(3)).

Subparagraph (A) shall not apply with respect to coverage of employees under a plan pursuant to an agreement under such subparagraph. Subparagraph (B) shall not apply in the case of a plan which provides contributions or benefits for employees whose principal duties are not customarily performed aboard aircraft in flight.

(4) *Exclusion of employees not meeting age and service requirements.—*

(A) In general.—If a plan—

(i) prescribes minimum age and service requirements as a condition of participation, and

(ii) excludes all employees not meeting such requirements from participation,

then such employees shall be excluded from consideration for purposes of this subsection.

(B) Requirements may be met separately with respect to excluded group.—If employees do not meet the minimum age or service requirements of subsection (a)(1) (without regard to subparagraph (B) thereof) and are covered under a plan of the employer which meets the requirements of paragraph (1) separately with respect to such employees, such employees may be excluded from consideration in determining whether any plan of the employer meets the requirements of paragraph (1).

(5) *Line of business exception.—*

(A) In general.—If, under section 414(r), an employer is treated as operating separate lines of business for a year, the employer may apply the requirements of this subsection for such year separately with respect to employees in each separate line of business.

(B) Plan must be nondiscriminatory.—Subparagraph (A) shall not apply with respect to any plan maintained by an employer unless such plan benefits such employees as qualify under a classification set up by the employer and found by the Secretary not to be discriminatory in favor of highly compensated employees.

(6) *Definitions and special rules.—For purposes of this subsection—*

(A) Highly compensated employee.—The term "highly compensated employee" has the meaning given such term by section 414(q).

(B) Aggregation rules.—An employer may elect to designate—

(i) 2 or more trusts,

(ii) 1 or more trusts and 1 or more annuity plans, or

(iii) 2 or more annuity plans,

as part of 1 plan intended to qualify under section 401(a) to determine whether the requirements of this subsection are met with respect to such trusts or annuity plans. If an employer elects to treat any trusts or annuity plans as 1 plan under this subparagraph, such trusts or annuity plans shall be treated as 1 plan for purposes of section 401(a)(4).

(C) Special rules for certain dispositions or acquisitions.—

(i) In general.—If a person becomes, or ceases to be, a member of a group described in subsection (b), (c), (m), or (o) of section 414, then the requirements of this subsection shall be treated as having been met during the transition period

with respect to any plan covering employees of such person or any other member of such group if—

    (I) *such requirements were met immediately before each such change, and*

    (II) *the coverage under such plan is not significantly changed during the transition period (other than by reason of the change in members of a group).*

  (ii) *Transition period.—For purposes of clause (i), the term "transition period" means the period—*

    (I) *beginning on the date of the change in members of a group, and*

    (II) *ending on the last day of the 1st plan year beginning after the date of such change.*

  (D) *Special rule for certain employee stock ownership plans.—A trust which is part of a tax credit employee stock ownership plan which is the only plan of an employer intended to qualify under section 401(a) shall not be treated as not a qualified trust under section 401(a) solely because it fails to meet the requirements of this subsection if—*

    (i) *such plan benefits 50 percent or more of all the employees who are eligible under a nondiscriminatory classification under the plan, and*

    (ii) *the sum of the amounts allocated to each participant's account for the year does not exceed 2 percent of the compensation of that participant for the year.*

  (E) *Eligibility to contribute.—In the case of contributions which are subject to section 401(k) or 401(m), employees who are eligible to contribute (or elect to have contributions made on their behalf) shall be treated as benefiting under the plan (other than for purposes of paragraph (2)(A)(ii)).*

  (F) *Regulations.—The Secretary shall prescribe such regulations as may be necessary or appropriate to carry out the purposes of this subsection.*

*   *   *   *   *   *   *   *   *   *   *   *

[For official explanation, see Committee Reports, ¶3977; 3978.]

[¶3003] CODE SEC. 411. MINIMUM VESTING STANDARDS.

  (a) **General Rule.**—A trust shall not constitute a qualified trust under section 401(a) unless the plan of which such trust is a part provides that an employee's right to his normal retirement benefit is nonforfeitable upon the attainment of normal retirement age (as defined in paragraph (8)) and in addition satisfies the requirements of paragarphs (1)[1], (2), *and (11)* of this subsection and the requirements of paragraph (2) of subsection (b), and in the case of a defined benefit plan, also satisfies the requirements of paragraph (1) of subsection (b).

*   *   *   *   *   *   *   *   *   *   *   *

  (2) **Employer contributions.**—A plan satisfies the requirements of this paragraph if it satisfies the requirements of subparagraph (A), (B), or (C).

  (A) [2]*5-year vesting.—A plan satisfies the requirements of this subparagraph if an*

Years of service:		Nonforfeitable percentage
5	....	25
6	....	30
7	....	35
8	....	40
9	....	45
10	....	50
11	....	60
12	....	70

employee who has completed at least 5 years of service has a nonforfeitable right to 100 percent of the employee's accrued benefit derived from employer contributions.

(B) 3 to 7 year vesting.—A plan satisfies the requirements of this subparagraph if an employee has a nonforfeitable right to a percentage of the employee's accrued benefit derived from employer contributions determined under the following table:

Years of service:		The nonforfeitable percentage is:
3	. . . .	20
4	. . . .	40
5	. . . .	60
6	. . . .	80
7 or more	. . . .	100.

(C) Multiemployer plans.—A plan satisfies the requirements of this subparagraph if—

(i) the plan is a multiemployer plan (within the meaning of section 414(f)), and

(ii) under the plan—

(I) an employee who is covered pursuant to a collective bargaining agreement described in section 414(f)(1)(B) and who has completed at least 10 years of service has a nonforfeitable right to 100 percent of the employee's accrued benefit derived from employer contributions, and

(II) the requirements of subparagraph (A) or (B) are met with respect to employees not described in subclause (I).

(3) **Certain permitted forfeitures, suspensions, etc.**—For purposes of this subsection—

* * * * * * * * * * * *

(D) Withdrawal of mandatory contribution.—

〔Footnote ¶3003 continued〕

13	. . . .	80
14	. . . .	90
15 or more	. . . .	100.

(C) Rule of 45.—

(i) A plan satisfies the requirements of this subparagraph if an employee who is not separated from the service, who has completed at least 5 years of service, and with respect to whom the sum of his age and years of service equals or exceeds 45, has a nonforfeitable right to a percentage of his accrued benefit derived from employer contributions determined under the following table:

If years of service equal or exceed—	and sum of age and service equals or exceeds—	then the nonforfeitable percentage is—
5	45	50
6	47	60
7	49	70
8	51	80
9	53	90
10	55	100.

(ii) Notwithstanding clause (i), a plan shall not be treated as satisfying the requirements of this subparagraph unless any employee who has completed at least 10 years of service has a nonforfeitable right to not less than 50 percent of his accrued benefit derived from employer contributions and to not less than an additional 10 percent for each additional year of service thereafter."

Effective date (Sec. 1113(e), '86 TRA).—(1) Generally applies to plan years beginning after 12-31-88.

(2) Special rule for collective bargaining agreements.—In the case of a plan maintained pursuant to 1 or more collective bargaining agreements between employee representatives and 1 or more employers ratified before 3-1-86, the amendments made by this section shall not apply to employees covered by any such agreement in plan years beginning before the earlier of—

(A) the later of—

(i) 1-1-89, or

(ii) the date on which the last of such collective bargaining agreements terminates (determined without regard to any extension thereof after 2-28-86), or

(B) 1-1-91.

(3) Participation required.—The amendments made by this section shall not apply to any employee who does not have 1 hour of service in any plan year to which the amendments made by this section apply.

(i) A right to an accrued benefit derived from employer contributions shall not be treated as forfeitable solely because the plan provides that, in the case of a participant who does not have a nonforfeitable right to at least 50 percent of his accrued benefit derived from employer contributions, such accrued benefit may be forfeited on account of the withdrawal by the participant of any amount attributable to the benefit derived from mandatory contributions (as defined in subsection (c)(2)(C)) made by such participant).

(ii) Clause (i) shall not apply to a plan unless the plan provides that any accrued benefit forfeited under a plan provision described in such clause shall be restored upon repayment by the participant of the full amount of the withdrawal described in such clause plus, in the case of a defined benefit plan, interest. Such interest shall be computed on such amount at the rate determined for purposes of subsection (c)(2)(C) on the date of such repayment (computed annually from the date of such withdrawal). [3]*The plan provision required under this clause may provide that such repayment must be made (I) in the case of a withdrawal on account of separation from service, before the earlier of 5 years after the first date on which the participant is subsequently re-employed by the employer, or the close of the first period of 5 consecutive 1-year breaks in service commencing after the withdrawal; or (II) in the case of any other withdrawal, 5 years after the date of the withdrawal.*

* * * * * * * * * * * *

(7) **Accrued benefit.—**

(A) In general.—For purposes of this section, the term "accrued benefit" means—

(i) in the case of a defined benefit plan, the employee's accrued benefit determined under the plan and, except as provided in subsection (c)(3), expressed in the form of an annual benefit commencing at normal retirement age, or

(ii) in the case of a plan which is not a defined benefit plan, the balance of the employee's account.

(B) Effect of certain distributions.—Notwithstanding paragraph (4), for purposes of determining the employee's accrued benefit under the plan, the plan may disregard service performed by the employee with respect to which he has received—

(i) a distribution of the present value of his entire nonforfeitable benefit if such distribution was in an amount (not more than $3,500) permitted under regulations prescribed by the Secretary, or

(ii) a distribution of the present value of his nonforfeitable benefit attributable to such service which he elected to receive.

Clause (i) of this subparagraph shall apply only if such distribution was made on termination of the employee's participation in the plan. Clause (ii) of this subparagraph shall apply only if such distribution was made on termination of the employee's participation in the plan or under such other circumstances as may be provided under regulations prescribed by the Secretary.

(C) Repayment of subparagraph (B) distributions.—For purposes of determining the employee's accrued benefit under a plan, the plan may not disregard service as provided in subparagraph (B) unless the plan provides an opportunity for the participant to repay the full amount of the distribution described in such subparagraph (B) with, in the case of a defined benefit plan, interest at the rate determined for purposes of subsection (c)(2)(C) and provides that upon such repayment the employee's accrued benefit shall be recomputed by taking into account service so disregarded. This subparagraph shall apply only in the case of a participant who—

(i) received such a distribution in any plan year to which this section applies, which distribution was less than the present value of his accrued benefit,

(ii) resumes employment covered under the plan, and

(iii) repays the full amount of such distribution with, in the case of a defined benefit plan, interest at the rate determined for purposes of subsection (c)(2)(C).

[4]*The plan provision required under this subparagraph may provide that such repayment*

---

must be made (I) in the case of a withdrawal on account of separation from service, before the earlier of 5 years after the first date on which the participant is subsequently re-employed by the employer, or the close of the first period of 5 consecutive 1-year breaks in service commencing after the withdrawal; or (II) in the case of any other withdrawal, 5 years after the date of the withdrawal.

* * * * * * * * * * * *

(10) Changes in vesting schedule.—

(A) General rule.—A plan amendment changing any vesting schedule under the plan shall be treated as not satisfying the requirements of paragraph (2) if the non-forfeitable percentage of the accrued benefit derived from employer contributions (determined as of the later of the date such amendment is adopted, or the date such amendment becomes effective) of any employee who is a participant in the plan is less than such nonforfeitable percentage computed under the plan without regard to such amendment.

(B) Election of former schedule.—A plan amendment changing any vesting schedule under the plan shall be treated as not satisfying the requirements of paragraph (2) unless each participant having not less than [5]*3 years* of service is permitted to elect, within a reasonable period after the adoption of such amendment, to have his nonforfeitable percentage computed under the plan without regard to such amendment.

(11) Restrictions on certain mandatory distributions.—

(A) In general.—If the present value of any *vested* accrued benefit exceeds $3,500 [6]*a plan meets the requirements of this paragraph only if such plan provides that such benefit may not* be immediately distributed without consent of the participant.

(B) Determination of present value.—[7]*(i) In general.—For purposes of*

[**Footnote ¶3003 continued**]

ing after such withdrawal."
Effective date (Sec. 1898(j), '86 TRA and section 302, '84 Retirement Equity Act, amended by '86 TRA).—See above.

Matter in *italics* in Sec. 411(a)(10)(B) added by section 1113(d)(B), '86 TRA, which struck out:
(5) "5 years"
Effective date (Sec. 1113(e), '86 TRA).—See above.

Matter in *italics* in Sec. 411(a)(11)(A) added by section 1898(d)(1)(A)(i), '86 TRA, which struck out:
(6) "such benefit shall not be treated as nonforfeitable if the plan provides that the present value of such benefit could"
Effective date (Sec. 1898(j), '86 TRA and section 302, '84 Retirement Equity Act, amended by '86 TRA).—See above.

Matter in *italics* in Sec. 411(a)(11)(B) added by Sec. 1139(a), '86 TRA, which struck out:
(7) "For purposes of subparagraph (A), the present value shall be calculated by using an interest rate not greater than the interest rate which would be used (as of the date of the distribution) by the Pension Benefit Guaranty Corporation for purposes of determining the present value of a lump sum distribution on plan termination."
Effective date (Sec. 1139(d), '86 TRA).—(1) Generally applies to distributions in plan years beginning after 12-31-84, except that such amendments shall not apply to any distributions in plan years beginning after 12-31-84, and before before 1-1-87, if such distributions were made in accordance with the requirements of the regulations issued under the Retirement Equity Act of 1984.
(2) Reduction in accrued benefits.—
(A) In general.—If a plan—
(i) adopts a plan amendment before the close of the first plan year beginning on or before 1-1-89, which provides for the calculation of the present value of the accrued benefits in the manner provided by the amendments made by this section, and
(ii) the plan reduces the accrued benefits for any plan year to which such plan amendment applies in accordance with such plan amendment,
such reduction shall not be treated as a violation of section 411(d)(6) of the '86 Code or section 204(g) of the '74 ERISA (29 U.S.C. 1054(g)).
(B) Special rule.—In the case of a plan maintained by a corporation incorporated on 4-11-34, which is head-quartered in Tarrant County, Texas—
(i) such plan may be amended to remove the option of an employee to receive a lump sum distribution (within the meaning of section 402(e)(5) of such Code) if such amendment—
(I) is adopted within 1 year of the date of the enactment of this Act, and
(II) is not effective until 2 years after the employees are notified of such amendment, and
(ii) the present value of any vested accrued benefit of such plan determined during the 3-year period beginning on the date of the enactment of this Act shall be determined under the applicable interest rate (within the meaning of section 411(a)(11)(B)(ii) of such Code, except that if such value (as so determined) exceeds $50,000, then the value of any excess over $50,000 shall be determined by using the interest rate specified in the plan as of 8-16-86.

subparagraph (A), the present value shall be calculated—

    (I)   by using an interest rate no greater than the applicable interest rate if the vested accrued benefit (using such rate) is not in excess of $25,000, and

    (II)   by using an interest rate no greater than 120 percent of the applicable interest rate if the vested accrued benefit exceeds $25,000 (as determined under subclause (I)).

In no event shall the present value determined under subclause (II) be less than $25,000.

    (ii)   Applicable interest rate.—For purposes of clause (i), the term "applicable interest rate" means the interest rate which would be used (as of the date of the distribution) by the Pension Benefit Guaranty Corporation for purposes of determining the present value of a lump sum distribution on plan termination.

    (C)   Dividend distributions of ESOPs arrangement.—This paragraph shall not apply to any distribution of dividends to which section 404(k) applies.

*   *   *   *   *   *   *   *   *   *   *

(d) Special Rules.—

    (1) Coordination with section 401(a)(4).—A plan which satisfies the requirements of this section shall be treated as satisfying any vesting requirements resulting from the application of section 401(a)(4) unless—

    (A)   there has been a pattern of abuse under the plan (such as dismissal of employees before their accrued benefits become nonforfeitable) tending to discriminate in favor of employees who are [8]highly compensated *employees (within the meaning of section 414(q)*, or

    (B)   there have been, or there is reason to believe there will be, an accrual of benefits or forfeitures tending to discriminate in favor of employees who are [8]highly compensated *employees (within the meaning of 414(q))*.

*   *   *   *   *   *   *   *   *   *   *

≫P-H CAUTION→ There are two versions of Sec. 411(d)(4). Sec 411(d)(4), repealed generally effective for plan years after 12-31-88, follows. For Sec. 411(d)(4), generally effective for plan years before 1-1-89, see below.

▲ (4) [Repealed][9]

Sec. 411(a)(11)(C) in *italics* added by section 1898(d)(2)(A), '86 TRA.
Effective date (Sec. 1898(j), '86 TRA and section 302, '84 Retirement Equity Act, amended by '86 TRA).—See above.

Matter in *italics* in Sec. 411(d)(1)(A) and (B) added by section 1114(b)(10), '86 TRA, which struck out:
(8) "officers, shareholders, or"
Effective date (Sec. 1114(c)(3), '86 TRA).—Generally applies to years beginning after 12-31-88. For special rule determining highly compensated employees, see footnote ¶3004.

▲ Sec. 1113(b), '86 TRA, repealed section 411(d)(4), preceded by a triangle:
(9) **"(4) Class year plans.**—
(A)   In general.—The requirements of subsection (a)(2) shall be treated as satisfied in the case of a class-year plan if such plan provides that 100 percent of each employee's right to or derived from the contributions of the employer on the employee's behalf with respect to any plan year is nonforfeitable not later than when such participant was performing services for the employer as of the close of each of 5 plan years (whether or not consecutive) after the plan year for which the contributions were made.
(B)   5-year break in service.—For purposes of subparagraph (A) if—
(i)   any contributions are made on behalf of a participant with respect to any plan year, and
(ii)   before such participant meets the requirements of subparagraph (A), such participant was not performing services for the employer as of the close of each of any 5 consecutive plan years after such plan year.
then the plan may provide that the participant forfeits any right to or derived from the contributions made with respect to such plan year,
(C)   Class-year plan.—For purposes of this section, the term 'class-year plan' means a profit-sharing, stock bonus, or money purchase plan which provides for the separate nonforfeitability of employees' rights to or derived from the contributions for each plan year."
Effective date (Sec. 1113(e), '86 TRA).—Generally applies to plan years beginning after 12-31-88. For special rules, see above.

≫**P-H CAUTION**→ There are two versions of Sec. 411(d)(4). Sec. 411(d)-(4), generally effective for plan years before 1-1-89, follows. For Sec. 411(d)(4), repealed generally effective for plan years after 12-31-88, see above.

▲ ▲ **(4)** [10]*Class-year plans.—*

(A) *In general.—The requirements of subsection (a)(2) shall be treated as satisfied in the case of a class-year plan if such plan provides that 100 percent of each employee's right to or derived from the contributions of the employer on the employee's behalf with respect to any plan year is nonforfeitable not later than when such participant was performing services for the employer as of the close of each of 5 plan years (whether or not consecutive) after the plan year for which the contributions were made.*

(B) *5-year break in service.—For purposes of subparagraph (A) if—*

(i) *any contributions are made on behalf of a participant with respect to any plan year, and*

(ii) *before such participant meets the requirements of subparagraph (A), such participant was not performing services for the employer as of the close of each of any 5 consecutive plan years after such plan year,*

then the plan may provide that the participant forfeits any right to or derived from the contributions made with respect to such plan year.

(C) *Class-year plan.—For purposes of this section, the term "class-year plan" means a profit-sharing, stock bonus, or money purchase plan which provides for the separate nonforfeitability of employees' rights to or derived from the contributions for each plan year.*

* * * * * * * * * * * *

(6) Accrued benefit not to be decreased by amendment.—

* * * * * * * * * * * *

(C) *Special rule for ESOPs.—For purposes of this paragraph, any—*

(i) *tax credit employee stock ownership plan (as defined in section 409(a)), or*

(ii) *employee stock ownership plan (as defined in section 4975(e)(7)),*

shall not be treated as failing to meet the requirements of this paragraph merely because it modifies distribution options in a nondiscriminatory manner.

* * * * * * * * * * * *

[For official explanation, see Committee Reports, ¶4211; 3978; 3998; 3979.]

[¶3004] CODE SEC. 414. DEFINITIONS AND SPECIAL RULES.

* * * * * * * * * * * *

(k) Certain Plans.—A defined benefit plan which provides a benefit derived from employer contributions which is based partly on the balance of the separate account of a participant shall—

(1) for purposes of section 410 (relating to minimum participation standards), be treated as a defined contribution plan.

(2) for purposes of sections 411(a)(7)(A)(relating to minimum vesting standards) [1],

---

415 (relating to limitations on benefits and contributions under qualified plans), *and 401(m) (relating to nondiscrimination tests for matching requirements and employee contributions)* be treated as consisting of a defined contribution plan to the extent benefits are based on the separate account of a participant and as a defined benefit plan with respect to the remaining portion of benefits under the plan, and

(3) for purposes of section 4975 (relating to tax on prohibited transactions), be treated as a defined benefit plan.

(m) Employees of an Affiliated Service Group.—

(1) **In general.**—For purposes of the employee benefit requirements listed in paragraph (4), except to the extent otherwise provided in regulations, all employees of the members of an affiliated service group shall be treated as employed by a single employer.

(2) **Affiliated service group.**—For purposes of this subsection, the term "affiliated service group" means a group consisting of a service organization (hereinafter in this paragraph referred to as the "first organization") and one or more of the following:

(A) any service organization which—

(i) is a shareholder or partner in the first organization, and

(ii) regularly performs services for the first organization or is regularly associated with the first organization in performing services for third persons, and

(B) any other organization if—

(i) a significant portion of the business of such organization is the performance of services (for the first organization, for organizations described in subparagraph (A), or for both) of a type historically performed in such service field by employees, and

(ii) 10 percent or more of the interests in such organization is held by persons who are [2]*highly compensated employees (within the meaning of section 414(q))* of the first organization or an organization described in subparagraph (A).

* * * * * * * * * * *

(5) **Certain organizations performing management functions.**—For purposes of this subsection, the term "affiliated service group" also includes a group consisting of— -

(A) an organization the principal business of which is performing, on a regular and continuing basis, management functions for 1 organization (or for 1 organization and other organizations related to such 1 organization), and

(B) the organization (and related organizations) for which such functions are so performed by the organization described in subparagraph (A).

For purposes of this paragraph, the term "related organizations" has the same meaning as the term "related persons" when used in [3]*section 144(a)(3).*

【Footnote ¶3004 continued】

(3) Annuity contracts.—In the case of an annuity contract under section 403(b) of the '86 Code—

(A) the amendments made by this section shall apply to plan years beginning after 12-31-88, and

(B) in the case of a collective bargaining agreement described in paragraph (2), the amendments made by this section shall not apply to years beginning before the earlier of—

(i) the later of—

(I) 1-1-89, or

(II) the date determined under paragraph (2)(B), or

(ii) 1-1-91.

Matter in *italics* in Sec. 414(m)(2)(B)(ii) added by section 1114(b)(11), '86 TRA, which struck out:

(2) "officers, highly compensated employees, or owners"

Effective date (Sec. 1114(c)(3) and (4), '86 TRA).—(3) Applies to years beginning after 12-31-88.

(4) Special rule for determining highly compensated employees.—For purposes of sections 401(k) and 401(m) of the '86 Code, in the case of an employer incorporated on 12-15-24, if more than 50 percent of its employees in the top-paid group (within the meaning of section 414(q)(4) of such Code) earn less than $25,000 (indexed at the same time and in the same manner as under section 415(d) of such Code), then the highly compensated employees shall include employees described in section 414(q)(1)(C) of such Code determined without regard to the level of compensation of such employees.

Matter in *italics* in Sec. 414(m)(5) added by section 1301(j)(4), '86 TRA, which struck out:

(3) "section 103(b)(6)(C)"

Effective date (Sec. 1311(a), '86 TRA).—Generally applies to bonds issued after 8-15-86. For special and transitional rules, see ¶2071—2077.

---

* * * * * * * * * * * *

(n) Employee Leasing.—

(1) In general.—For purposes of the [4]*requirements* listed in paragraph (3), [5] with respect to any person (hereinafter in this subsection referred to as the "recipient") for whom a leased employee performs services—

    (A) the leased employee shall be treated as an employee of the recipient, but

    (B) contributions or benefits provided by the leasing organization which are attributable to services performed for the recipient shall be treated as provided by the recipient.

(2) Leased employee.—For purposes of paragraph (1), the term "leased employee" means any person who is not an employee of the recipient and who provides services to the recipient if—

    (A) such services are provided pursuant to an agreement between the recipient and any other person (in this subsection referred to as the "leasing organization").

    (B) such person has performed such services for the recipient (or for the recipient and related persons) on a substantially full-time basis for a period of at least 1 year *(6 months in the case of core health benefits)*, and

    (C) such services are of a type historically performed, in the business field of the recipient, by employees.

(3) [6]*Requirements*.—For purposes of this subsection, the [4]*requirements* listed in this paragraph are—

    (A) paragraphs (3), (4), (7), and (16) of section 401(a), [7]

    (B) sections 408(k), 410, 411, 415, and 416[8] *and,*

    (C) *sections 79, 89, 106, 117(d), 120, 125, 127, 129, 132, 274(j), and 505.*

[9]*(4) Time when first considered as employee.—*

    (A) In general.—In the case of any leased employee, paragraph (1) shall apply only for purposes of determining whether the requirements listed in paragraph (3) are met for periods after the close of the period referred to in paragraph (2)(B).

    (B) Years of service.—In the case of a person who is an employee of the recipient (whether by reason of this subsection or otherwise), for purposes of the requirements listed in paragraph (3), years of service for the recipient shall be determined by taking into account any period for which such employee would have been a leased employee but for the requirements of paragraph (2)(B).

[10]*(5) Safe harbor.—*

⟦Footnote ¶3004 continued⟧

Matter in *italics* in Sec. 414(n)(1) and (n)(3) added by section 1151(i)(1) and (3)(B), '86 TRA, which struck out:
(4) "pension requirements"
Effective date (Sec. 1151(k)(1), '86 TRA).—Generally applies to years beginning after the later of—
(A) 12-31-87, or
(B) the earlier of—
(i) the date which is 3 months after the date on which the Secretary of the Treasury or his delegate issues such regulations as are necessary to carry out the provisions of Sec. 89 of the '86 Code (as added by this section), or
(ii) 12-31-88.
For special and transitional rules, see footnote ¶2895.

Section 1146(b)(2), '86 TRA, struck out from Sec. 414(n)(1):
(5) "except to the extent otherwise provided in regulations"
Effective date (Sec. 1146(c)(1), '86 TRA).—Applies to taxable years beginning after 12-31-83.

Matter in italics in Sec. 414(n)(2)(B) and (3) added by section 1151(i)(2) and (3)(A) and (C), '86 TRA, which struck out:
(6) "Pension requirements"
(7) "and"
(8) "."
Effective date (Sec. 1151(k)(1), '86 TRA).—See above.

Matter in *italics* in Sec. 414(n)(4) added by section 1146(a)(2), '86 TRA, which struck out:
(9) "(4) Time when leased employee is first considered employee.—In the case of any leased employee, paragraph (1) shall apply only for purposes of determining whether the pension requirements listed in paragraph (3) are met for periods after the close of the 1-year period referred to in paragraph (2), except that years of service for the recipient shall be determined by taking into account the entire period for which the leased employee performed services for the recipient (or related persons)."
Effective date (Sec. 1146(c)(1), '86 TRA).—Applies to taxable years beginning after 12-31-83.

Matter in *italics* in Sec. 414(n)(5) added by section 1146(a)(1), '86 TRA, which struck out:
(10) "(5) Safe harbor.—This subsection shall not apply to any leased employee if such employee is covered by

(A) *In general.—In the case of requirements described in subparagraphs (A) and (B) of paragraph (3), this subsection shall not apply to any leased employee with respect to services performed for a recipient if—*

    (i) such employee is covered by a plan which is maintained by the leasing organization and meets the requirements of subparagraph (B), and

    (ii) leased employees (determined without regard to this paragraph) do not constitute more than 20 percent of the recipient's nonhighly compensated work force.

(B) *Plan requirements.—A plan meets the requirements of this subparagraph if—*

    (i) such plan is a money purchase pension plan with a nonintegrated employer contribution rate for each participant of at least 10 percent of compensation,

    (ii) such plan provides for full and immediate vesting, and

    (iii) each employee of the leasing organization (other than employees who perform substantially all of their services for the leasing organization) immediately participates in such plan.

Clause (iii) shall not apply to any individual whose compensation from the leasing organization in each plan year during the 4-year period ending with the plan year is less than $1,000.

(C) *Definitions.—For purposes of this paragraph—*

    (i) Highly compensated employee.—The term "highly compensated employee" has the meaning given such term by section 414(q).

    (ii) Nonhighly compensated work force.—The term "nonhighly compensated work force" means the aggregate number of individuals (other than highly compensated employees)—

        (I) who are employees of the recipient (without regard to this subsection) and have performed services for the recipient (or for the recipient and related persons) on a substantially full-time basis for a period of at least 1 year, or

        (II) who are leased employees with respect to the recipient (determined without regard to this paragraph).

    (iii) Compensation.—The term "compensation" has the same meaning as when used in section 415; except that such term shall include—

        (I) any employer contribution under a qualified cash or deferred arrangement to the extent not included in gross income under section 402(a)(8) or 402(h)(1)(B),

        (II) any amount which the employee would have received in cash but for an election under a cafeteria plan (within the meaning of section 125), and

        (III) any amount contributed to an annuity contract described in section 403(b) pursuant to a salary reduction agreement (within the meaning of section 3121(a)(5)(D)).

[11]*(6) Other rules.—For purposes of this subsection—*

    (A) *Related persons.—The term "related persons" has the same meaning as when used in* [12] *section 144(a)(3).*

⟦Footnote ¶3004 continued⟧

a plan which is maintained by the leasing organization if, with respect to such employee, such plan—

(A) is a money purchase pension plan with a nonintegrated employer contribution rate of at least 7½ percent, and

(B) provides for immediate participation and for full and immediate vesting."

Effective date (Sec. 1146(c)(2), '86 TRA)—Applies to services performed after 12-31-86.

Matter in *italics* in Sec. 414(n)(6) except for the phrase *"section 144(a)(3)"* added by section 1146(a)(3), '86 TRA, which struck out:

(11) **"(6) Related persons.**—For purposes of this subsection, the term "related persons" has the same meaning as when used in section 103(b)(6)(C)."

Effective date (Sec. 1146(c)(1), '86 TRA).—Applies to taxable years beginning after 12-31-83.

The phrase *"section 144(a)(3)"* in italics in Sec. 414(n)(6) added by section 1301(j)(4), '86 TRA, which struck out:

(12) "section 103(b)(6)(C)"

Effective date (Sec. 1311(a), '86 TRA).—Generally applies to bonds issued after 8-15-86. For special and transitional rules see ¶2071—2077.

Matter in italics in 414(o) added by section 1146(b)(1), '86 TRA.

Effective date (Sec. 1146(c)(1) and (3), '86 TRA).—Generally applies to taxable years beginning after 12-31-83.

(B) Employees of entities under common control.—The rules of subsection (b), (c), (m), and (o) shall apply.

(o) Regulations.—The Secretary shall prescribe such regulations (which may provide rules in addition to the rules contained in subsections (m) and (n)) as may be necessary to prevent the avoidance of any employee benefit requirement listed in subsection (m)(4) or (n)(3) through the use of—

    (1) separate organizations,

    (2) employee leasing, or

    (3) other arrangements.

The regulations prescribed under subsection (n) shall include provisions to minimize the recordkeeping requirements of subsection (n) in the case of an employer which has no top-heavy plans (within the meaning of section 416(g)) and which uses the services of persons (other than employees) for an insignificant percentage of the employer's total workload.

(p) Qualified Domestic Relations Order Defined.—For purposes of this subsection and section 401(a)(13)—

    (1) In general.—

        (A) Qualified domestic relations order.—The term "qualified domestic relations order" means a domestic relations order—

            (i) which creates or recognizes the existence of an alternate payee's right to, or assigns to an alternate payee the right to, receive all or a portion of the benefits payable with respect to a participant under a plan, and

            (ii) with respect to which the requirements of paragraphs (2) and (3) are met.

        (B) Domestic relations order.—The term "domestic relations order" means any judgment, decree, or order (including approval of a property settlement agreement) which—

            (i) relates to the provision of child support, alimony payments, or marital property rights to a spouse, *former spouse,* child, or other dependent of a participant, and

            (ii) is made pursuant to a State domestic relations law (including a community property law).

    (2) Order must clearly specify certain facts.—A domestic relations order meets the requirements of this paragraph only if such clearly specifies—

        (A) the name and the last known mailing address (if any) of the participant and the name and mailing address of each alternate payee covered by the order,

        (B) the amount or percentage of the participant's benefits to be paid by the plan to each such alternate payee, or the manner in which such amount or percentage is to be determined,

        (C) the number of payments or period to which such order applies, and

        (D) each plan to which such order applies.

    (3) Order may not alter amount, form, etc., of benefits.—A domestic relations order meets the requirements of this paragraph only if such order—

        (A) does not require a plan to provide any type or form of benefit, or any option, not otherwise provided under the plan,

        (B) does not require the plan to provide increased benefit [13](determined on the

---

〖Footnote ¶3004 continued〗

    * * * * * * * * * * * *

(3) Recordkeeping requirements.—In the case of years beginning before the date of the enactment of this Act, the last sentence of section 414(o) shall be applied without regard to the requirement that an insignificant percentage of the workload be performed by persons other than employees.

Matter in *italics* **in Sec. 414(p)(1)(B)(i) added by section 1898(c)(7)(A)(ii), '86 TRA.**

Effective date (Sec. 1898(j), '86 TRA, and Sec. 303(d), Retirement Equity Act of 1984, P.L. 98-397, 8-23-84).— Generally takes effect on 1-1-85, except that in the case of a domestic relations order entered before such date, the plan administrator—

(1) shall treat such order as a qualified domestic relations order if such administrator is paying benefits pursuant to such order on such date, and

(2) may treat any other such order entered before such date as a qualified domestic relations order even if such order does not meet the requirements of such amendments.

For special and transitional rules see footnote ¶2994.

Section 1899A(12), '86 TRA struck out from Sec. 414(p)(3)(B):

(13) ","

basis of actuarial value), and

(C)　does not require the payment of benefits to an alternate payee which are required to be paid to another alternate payee under another order previously determined to be a qualified domestic relations order.

(4)　Exception for certain payments made after earliest retirement age.—

(A)　In general.—[14]*A* domestic relations order shall not be treated as failing to meet the requirements of subparagraph (A) of paragraph (3) solely because such order requires that payment of benefits be made to an alternate payee—

(i)　*in the case of any payment before a participant has separated from service* on or after the date on which the participant attains (or would have attained) the earliest retirement age,

(ii)　as if the participant had retired on the date on which such payment is to begin under such order (but taking into account only the present value of the benefits actually accrued and not taking into account the present value of any employer subsidy for early retirement), and

(iii)　in any form in which such benefits may be paid under the plan to the participant (other than in the form of a joint and survivor annuity with respect to the alternate payee and his or her subsequent spouse).

For purposes of clause (ii), the interest rate assumption used in determining the present value shall be the interest rate specified in the plan or, if no rate is specified, 5 percent.

[15]*(B)　Earliest retirement age.—For purposes of this paragraph, the term "earliest retirement age" means earlier of—*

(i)　in the date on which the participant is entitled to a distribution under the plan, or

(ii)　in the later of—

(I)　the date the participant attains age 50, or

(II)　the earliest date on which the participant could begin receiving benefits under the plan if the participant separated from service.

(5)　Treatment of former spouse as surviving spouse for purposes of determining survivor benefits.—To the extent provided in qualified domestic relations order—

(A)　the former spouse of a participant shall be treated as a surviving spouse of such participant for purposes of sections 401(a)(11) and 417 *(and any spouse of the participant shall not be treated as a spouse of the participant for such purposes)*, and

(B)　if married for at least 1 year, the surviving *former* spouse shall be treated as meeting the requirements of section 417(d).[16]

(6)　Plan procedures with respect to orders.—

(A)　Notice and determination by administrator.—In the case of any domestic relations order received by a plan—

(i)　the plan administrator shall promptly notify the participant and [17]*each alternate payee* of the receipt of such order and the plan's procedures for determining the qualified status of domestic relations orders, and

(ii)　within a reasonable period after receipt of such order, the plan administrator shall determine whether such order is a qualified domestic relations order and notify the participant and each alternate payee of such determination.

(B)　Plan to establish reasonable procedures.—Each plan shall establish reasonable procedures to determine the qualified status of domestic relations orders and to administer distributions under such qualified orders.

(7)　Procedures for period during which determination is being made.—

【Footnote ¶3004 continued】

Matter in *italics* in Sec. 414(p)(4)—(7), (9) and (10) added by section 1898(c)(2)(A), (4)(A), (6)(A) and (7)(A)-(ii)—(vii), '86 TRA, which struck out from:

(14)　"In the case of any payment before a participant has separated from service, a"

(15)　"(B)　Earliest retirement age.—For purposes of this paragraph, the term "earliest retirement age" has the meaning given such term by section 417(f)(3), except that in the case of any defined contribution plan, the earliest retirement age shall be the date which is 10 years before the normal retirement age (within the meaning of section 411(a)(8))."

(16)　"A plan shall not be treated as failing to meet the requirements of subsection (a) or (k) of section 401 which prohibit payment of benefits before termination of employment solely by reason of payments to an alternate payee pursuant to a qualified domestic relations order."

(17)　"any other alternate payee"

(A) In general.—During any period in which the issue of whether a domestic relations order is a qualifed domestic relations order is being determined (by the plan administrator, by a court of competent jurisdiction, or otherwise), the plan administrator [18]*shall separately account for the amounts (hereinafter in this paragraph referred to as the "segregated amounts")*, which would have been payable to the alternate payee during such period if the order had been determined to be a qualified domestic relations order.

(B) Payment to alternate payee if order determined to be qualified domestic relations order.—If within [19]*the 18 month period described in subparagraph (E)* the order (or modification thereof) is determined to be a qualified domestic relations order, the plan administrator shall pay the segregated amounts ([20]*including any interest* thereon) to the person or persons entitled thereto.

(C) Payment to plan participant in certain cases.—if within [19]*the 18 month period described in subparagraph (E)*—

    (i) it is determined that the order is not a qualified domestic relations order, or

    (ii) the issue as to whether such order is a qualifed domestic relations order is not resolved,

then the plan administrator shall pay the segregated amounts ([20]*including any interest* thereon) to the person or persons who would have been entitled to such amounts if there had been no order.

(D) Subsequent determination or order to be applied prospectively only.—Any determination that an order is a qualified domestic relations order which is made after the close of the 18-month period *described in subparagraph (E)* shall be applied prospectively only.

(E) Determination of 18-month period.—For purposes of this paragraph, the 18-month period described in this subparagraph is the 18-month period beginning with the date on which the first payment would be required to be made under the domestic relations order.

(8) **Alternate payee defined.**—The term "alternate payee" means any spouse, former spouse, child or other dependent of a participant who is recognized by a domestic relations order as having a right to receive all, or a portion of, the benefits payable under a plan with respect to such participant.

(9) **Subsection not to apply to plans to which section 401(a)(13) does not apply.**—This subsection shall not apply to any plan to which section 401(a)(13) does not apply.

(10) **Waiver of certain distribution requirements.**—With respect to the requirements of subsections (a) and (k) of section 401 and section 409(d), a plan shall not be treated as failing to meet such requirements solely by reason of payments to an alternative payee pursuant to a qualified domestic relations order.

[21]*(11)* **Consultation with the secretary.**—in prescribing regulations under this sub-

---

⟦Footnote ¶3004 continued⟧

(18) "shall segregate in a separate account in the plan or in an escrow account the amounts"
(19) "18 months"
(20) "plus any interest"
(21) "(9)"
Effective date (Sec. 1898(j), '86 TRA and Sec. 303(d), P.L. 98-397, 8-23-84).—See above.

Sec. 414(q) in *italics* added by section 1114(a), '86 TRA.
Effective date (Sec. 1114(c)(1) and (4), '86 TRA).—(1) Generally applies to years beginning after 12-31-86.
(4) Special rule for determining highly compensated employees.—For purposes of sections 401(k) and 401(m) of the '86 Code, in the case of an employer incorporated on 12-15-24, if more than 50 percent of its employees in the top-paid group (within the meaning of section 414(q)(4) of such Code) earn less than $25,000 (indexed at the same time and in the same manner as under section 415(d) of such Code), then the highly compensated employees shall include employees described in section 414(q)(1)(C) of such Code determined without regard to the level of compensation of such employees.

Sec. 414(r) and (s) in *italics* added by section 1115(a), '86 TRA.
Effective date (Sec. 1115(b), '86 TRA).—Applies to years beginning after 12-31-86.

Sec. 414(t) in *italics* added by section 1151(e)(1), '86 TRA.
Effective date (Sec. 1151(k)(1), '86 TRA).—Generally applies to years beginning after the later of—
(A) 12-31-87, or
(B) the earlier of—
(i) the date which is 3 months after the date on which the Secretary of the Treasury or his delegate issues such regulations as are necessary to carry out the provisions of section 89 of the '86 Code (as added by this section), or
(ii) 12-31-88.

section and section 401(a)(13), the Secretary of Labor shall consult with the Secretary.

(q)   Highly Compensated Employee.—

(1)   In general.—The term "highly compensated employee" means any employee who, during the year or the preceding year—

(A)   was at any time a 5-percent owner,

(B)   received compensation from the employer in excess of $75,000,

(C)   received compensation from the employer in excess of $50,000 and was in the top-paid group of employees for such year, or

(D)   was at any time an officer and received compensation greater than 150 percent of the amount in effect under section 415(c)(1)(A) for such year.

(2)   Special rule for current year.—In the case of the year for which the relevant determination is being made, an employee not described in subparagraph (B), (C), or (D) of paragraph (1) for the preceding year (without regard to this paragraph) shall not be treated as described in subparagraph (B), (C), or (D) of paragraph (1) unless such employee is a member of the group consisting of the 100 employees paid the greatest compensation during the year for which such determination is being made.

(3)   5-percent owner.—An employee shall be treated as a 5-percent owner for any year if at any time during such year such employee was a 5-percent owner (as defined in section 416(i)(1)) of the employer.

(4)   Top-paid group.—An employee is in the top-paid group of employees for any year if such employee is in the group consisting of the top 20 percent of the employees when ranked on the basis of compensation paid during such year.

(5)   Special rules for treatment of officers.—

(A)   Not more than 50 officers taken into account.—For purposes of paragraph (1)(D), no more than 50 employees (or, if lesser, the greater of 3 employees or 10 percent of the employees) shall be treated as officers.

(B)   At least 1 officer taken into account.—If for any year no officer of the employer is described in paragraph (1)(D), the highest paid officer of the employer for such year shall be treated as described in such paragraph.

(6)   Treatment of certain family members.—

(A)   In general.—If any individual is a member of the family of a 5-percent owner or of a highly compensated employee in the group consisting of the 10 highly compensated employees paid the greatest compensation during the year, then—

(i)   such individual shall not be considered a separate employee, and

(ii)   any compensation paid to such individual (and any applicable contribution or benefit on behalf of such individual) shall be treated as if it were paid to (or on behalf of) the 5-percent owner or highly compensated employee.

(B)   Family.—For purposes of subparagraph (A), the term "family" means, with respect to any employee, such employee's spouse and lineal ascendants or descendants and the spouses of lineal ascendants or descendants.

(7)   Compensation.—For purposes of this subsection—

(A)   In general.—The term "compensation" means compensation within the meaning of section 415(c)(3).

(B)   Certain provisions not taken into account.—The determination under subparagraph (A) shall be made—

(i)   without regard to sections 125, 402(a)(8), and 402(h)(1)(B), and

(ii)   in the case of employer contributions made pursuant to a salary reduction agreement, without regard to section 403(b).

(8)   Excluded employees.—For purposes of subsection (r) and for purposes of determining the number of employees in the top-paid group under paragraph (4), the following employees shall be excluded—

(A)   employees who have not completed 6 months of service,

(B)   employees who normally work less than $17\frac{1}{2}$ hours per week,

(C)   employees who normally work during not more than 6 months during any year,

(D)   employees who have not attained age 21,

(E) except to the extent provided in regulations, employees who are included in a unit of employees covered by an agreement which the Secretary of Labor finds to be a collective bargaining agreement between employee representatives and the employer, and

(F) employees who are nonresident aliens and who receive no earned income (within the meaning of section 911(d)(2)) from the employer which constitutes income from sources within the United States (within the meaning of section 861(a)(3)).

The employer may elect to apply subparagraph (A), (B), (C), or (D) by substituting a shorter period of service, smaller number of hours or months, or lower age for the period of service, number of hours or months, or age (as the case may be) than that specified in such subparagraph.

(9) *Former employees.*—A former employee shall be treated as a highly compensated employee if—

(A) such employee was a highly compensated employee when such employee separated from service, or

(B) such employee was a highly compensated employee at any time after attaining age 55.

(10) *Coordination with other provisions.*—Subsections (b), (c), (m), (n), and (o) shall be applied before the application of this section.

(r) *Special Rules for Separate Line of Business.*—

(1) *In general.*—For purposes of sections 89 and 410(b), an employer shall be treated as operating separate lines of business during any year if the employer for bona fide business reasons operates separate lines of business.

(2) *Line of business must have 50 employees, etc.*—A line of business shall not be treated as separate under paragraph (1) unless—

(A) such line of business has at least 50 employees who are not excluded under subsection (q)(8),

(B) the employer notifies the Secretary that such line of business is being treated as separate for purposes of paragraph (1), and

(C) such line of business meets guidelines prescribed by the Secretary or the employer receives a determination from the Secretary that such line of business may be treated as separate for purposes of paragraph (1).

(3) *Safe harbor rule.*—The requirements of subparagraph (C) of paragraph (2) shall not apply to any line of business if the highly compensated employee percentage with respect to such line of business is—

(A) not less than one-half, and

(B) not more than twice,

the percentage which highly compensated employees are of all employees of the employer. An employer shall be treated as meeting the requirements of subparagraph (A) if at least 10 percent of all highly compensated employees of the employer perform services solely for such line of business.

(4) *Highly compensated employee percentage defined.*—For purposes of this subsection, the term "highly compensated employee percentage" means the percentage which highly compensated employees performing services for the line of business are of all employees performing services for the line of business.

(5) *Allocation of benefits to line of business.*—For purposes of this subsection, benefits which are attributable to services provided to a line of business shall be treated as provided by such line of business.

(6) *Headquarters personnel, etc.*—The Secretary shall prescribe rules providing for—

(A) the allocation of headquarters personnel among the lines of business of the employer, and

(B) the treatment of other employees providing services for more than 1 line of business of the employer or not in lines of business meeting the requirements of paragraph (2).

(7) *Separate operating units.*—for purposes of this subsection, the term "separate line of business" includes an operating unit in a separate geographic area separately operated for a bona fide business reason.

(8) *Affiliated service group.*—This subsection shall not apply in the case of any affiliated service group (within the meaning of section 414(m)).

(s) *Compensation.*—For purposes of this part—

(1) *In general.—The* term *"compensation" means compensation for service performed for an employer which (taking into account the provisions of this chapter) is currently includible in gross income.*

(2) *Self-employed individuals.—The Secretary shall prescribe regulations for the determination of the compensation of an employee who is a self-employed individual (within the meaning of section 401(c)(1)) which are based on the principles of paragraph (1).*

(3) *Employer may elect to treat certain deferrals as compensation.—An employer may elect to include as compensation any amount which is contributed by the employer pursuant to a salary reduction agreement and which is not includible in the gross income of an employee under section 125, 402(a)(8), 402(h), or 403(b).*

(4) *Alternative determination of compensation.—The Secretary shall by regulation provide for alternative methods of determining compensation which may be used by an employer, except that such regulations shall provide that an employer may not use an alternative method if the use of such method discriminates in favor of highly compensated employees (within the meaning of subsection (q)).*

(t) *Application of Controlled Group Rules to Certain Employee Benefits.—*

(1) *In general.—All employees who are treated as employed by a single employer under subsection (b), (c), or (m) of section 414 shall be treated as employed by a single employer for purposes of an applicable section. The provisions of subsection (o) of section 414 shall apply with respect to the requirements of an applicable section.*

(2) *Applicable section.—For purposes of this subsection, the term "applicable section" means section 79, 89, 106, 117(d), 120, 125, 127, 129, 132, 274(j), or 505.*

[For official explanation, see Committee Reports, ¶3979; 3980; 3982; 4005; 4007; 4058; 4211.]

【¶3005】 CODE SEC. 415. LIMITATIONS ON BENEFITS AND CONTRIBUTION UNDER QUALIFIED PLANS.

* * * * * * * * * * *

(b) **Limitation for Defined Benefit Plans.—**

* * * * * * * * * * *

(2) **Annual benefit.—**

* * * * * * * * * * *

(B) Adjustment for certain other forms of benefit.—If the benefit under the plan is payable in any form other than the form described in subparagraph (A), or if the employees contribute to the plan or make rollover contributions (as defined in sections 402(a)(5), 403(a)(4) and 408(d)(3), the determinations as to whether the limitation described in paragraph (1) has been satisfied shall be made, in accordance with regulations prescribed by the Secretary, by adjusting such benefit so that it is equivalent to the benefit described in subparagraph (A). For purposes of this subparagraph any ancillary benefit which is not directly related to retirement income benefits shall not be taken into account; and that portion of any joint and survivor annuity which constitutes a qualified joint and survivor annuity (as defined in [1]*section 417* shall not be taken into account.

(C) Adjustment to $90,000 limit where benefit begins before [2]*the social security retirement age.*—If the retirement income benefit under the plan begins before [2]*the social security retirement age,* the determination as to whether the $90,000 limitation set forth in paragraph (1)(A) has been satisfied shall be made, in accordance with regulations prescribed by the Secretary, by reducing the limitation of paragraph (1)(A) so that such limitation (as so reduced) equals an annual benefit (beginning when such retirement income benefit begins) which is equivalent to a $90,000 annual benefit beginning at [2]*the social security retirement age.* [3]*The reduc-*

【Footnote ¶3005】 Matter in *italics* in Sec. 415(b)(2)(B) added by section 1898(b)(15)(C), '86 TRA, which struck out:

(1) "section 401(a)(11)(G)(iii)"

Effective date (Sec. 1898(j), '86 TRA, and section 303(c) and (e), P.L. 98-397, 8-23-84, as amended by sections 1145(c), and 1898(g) and (h), '86 TRA).—See footnote ¶2994.

Matter in *italics* Sec. 415(b)(2)(C) and (D) added by section 1106(b)(1)(A), which struck out:

(2) "age 62"

(3) "The reduction under this subparagraph shall not reduce the limitation of paragraph (1)(A) below—

tion under this subparagraph shall be made in such manner as the Secretary may prescribe which is consistent with the reduction for old-age insurance benefits commencing before the social security retirement age under the Social Security Act.

(D)   Adjustment to $90,000 limitation where benefit after [4]*the social security retirement age.*—If the retirement income benefit under the plan begins after [4]*the social security retirement age,* the determination as to whether the $90,000 limitation set forth in paragraph (1)(A) has been satisfied shall be made, in accordance with regulations prescribed by the Secretary, by increasing the limitation of paragraph (I)(A) so that such limitation (as so increased) equals an annual benefit (beginning when such retirement income benefit begins) which is equivalent to a $90,000 annual benefit beginning at [4]*the social security retirement age.*

(E)   Limitation on certain assumptions.—

(i)   For purposes of adjusting any benefit or limitation under subparagraph (B) or (C), the interest rate assumption shall not be less than the greater of 5 percent or the rate specified in the plan.

(ii)   For purposes of adjusting any limitation under subparagraph (D), the interest rate assumption shall not be greater than the lesser of 5 percent or the rate specified in the plan.

(iii)   For purposes of [5]*this subsection,* no adjustments under subsection (d)(1)

【Footnote ¶3005 continued】

(i)   if the benefit begins at or after age 55, $75,000, or

(ii)   if the benefit begins before age 55, the amount which is equivalent of the $75,000 limitation for age 55."

(4)   "age 65"

Effective date (Sec. 1106(i)(1)—(4), '86 TRA).—(1) Generally applies to years beginning after 12-31-86.

(2)   Collective bargaining agreements.—In the case of a plan maintained pursuant to 1 or more collective bargaining agreements between employee representatives and 1 or more employers ratified before 3-1-86, the amendments made by this section (other than subsection (d)) shall not apply to contributions or benefits pursuant to such agreement in years beginning before the earlier of—

(A)   the date on which the last of such collective bargaining agreements terminates (determined without regard to any extension thereof after 2-28-86, or

(B)   1-1-89.

(3)   Right to higher accrued defined benefit preserved.—

(A)   In general.—In the case of an individual who is a participant (as of the 1st day of the 1st year to which the amendments made by this section apply) in a defined benefit plan which is in existence on 5-6-86, and with respect to which the requirements of section 415 of the '86 Code have been met for all plan years, if such individual's current accrued benefit under the plan exceeds the limitation of subsection (b) of section 415 of such Code (as amended by this section), then (in the case of such plan), for purposes of subsections (b) and (e) of such section, the limitation of such subsection (b)(1)(A) with respect to such individual shall be equal to such current accrued benefit.

(B)   Current accrued benefit defined.—

(i)   In general.—For purposes of this paragraph, the term "current accrued benefit" means the individual's accrued benefit (at the close of the last year to which the amendments made by this section do not apply) when expressed as an annual benefit (within the meaning of section 415(b)(2) of such Code).

(ii)   Special rule.—For purposes of determining the amount of any individual's current accrued benefit—

(I)   no change in the terms and conditions of the plan after 5-5-86, and

(II)   no cost-of-living adjustment occurring after 5-5-86, shall be taken into account. For purposes of subclause (I), and change in the terms and conditions of the plan pursuant to a collective bargaining agreement ratified before 5-6-86, shall be treated as a change made before 5-6-86.

(4)   Transition rule where the sum of defined contribution and defined benefit plan fractions exceeds 1.0.—In the case of a plan which satisfied the requirements of section 415 of the '86 Code for its last year beginning before 1-1-87, the Secretary of the Treasury or his delegate shall prescribe regulations under which an amount is subtracted from the numerator of the defined contribution plan fraction (not exceeding such numerator) so that the sum of the defined benefit plan fraction and the defined contribution plan fraction computed under section 415(e)(1) of such Code does not exceed 1.0 for such year.

* * * * * * * * * * * *

Special rule (Sec. 1106(h), '86 TRA).—(h) Plans May Incorporate Section 415 Limitations by Reference.—Notwithstanding any other provision of law, except as provided in regulations prescribed by the Secretary of the Treasury or his delegate, a plan may incorporate by reference the limitations under section 415 of the '86 Code.

Matter in *italics* in Sec. 415(b)(2)(E)(iii) added by section 1875(c)(9), '86 TRA, which struck out:

(5)   "adjusting any benefit or limitation under subparagraph (B), (C), or (D)"

Effective date (Sec. 1881, '86 TRA, section 715, '84 TRA and section 235(g), '82 TEFRA, as amended by section 306(a)(10), '82 TCA and section 713(a)(2), (4), and (f)(3), '84 TRA).—

(1)   In general—

(A)   New plans.—In the case of any plan which is not in existence on 7-1-82, the amendments made by this section shall apply to years ending after 7-1-82.

(B)   Existing plans.—

(i)   In the case of any plan which is in existence on 7-1-82, the amendments made by the section shall apply to

shall be taken into account before the year for which such adjustment first takes effect.

(F) Plans maintained by governments and tax-exempt organizations.—In the case of a governmental plan (within the meaning of section 414(d)), a plan maintained by an organization (other than a governmental unit) exempt from tax under this subtitle, or a qualified merchant marine plan—

(i) subparagraph (C) shall be applied—

(I) by substituting "age 62" for "social security retirement age" each place it appears, and

(II) as if the last sentence thereof read as follows: "The reduction under this subparagraph shall not reduce the limitation of paragraph (1)(A) below (i) $75,000 if the benefit begins at or after age 55, or (ii) if the benefit begins before age 55, the equivalent of the $75,000 limitation for age 55.", and

(ii) subparagraph (D) shall be applied by substituting "age 65" for "social security retirement age" each place it appears.

⟦Footnote ¶3005 continued⟧

years beginning after 12-31-82.

(ii) Plan requirements.—A plan shall not be treated as failing to meet the requirements of section 401(a)(16) of the '54 Code for any year beginning before 1-1-84, merely because such plan provides for benefit or contribution limits which are in excess of the limitations under Section 415 of such Code, as amended by the section. The preceding sentence shall not apply to any plan which provides such limits in excess of the limitation under section 415 of such Code before such amendments.

(2) Amendments related to cost-of-living adjustments.—

(A) In general.—Except as provided in subparagraph (B), the amendments made by subsection (b), '82 TEFRA, shall apply to adjustments for years beginning after 12-31-82.

(B) Adjustment procedures.—The amendment made by subsection (b)(1) and (b)(2)(B), '82 TEFRA, shall apply in adjustments for years beginning after 12-31-85.

(3) Transition rule where the sum of defined contribution and defined benefit plan fractions exceeds 1.0—in the case of a plan which satisfied the requirements of section 415 of the '54 Code for the last year beginning before 1-1-83, the Secretary of the Treasury or his delegate shall prescribe regulations under which an amount is subtracted from the numerator of the defined contribution plan fraction (not exceeding such numerator) so that the sum of the defined benefit plan fraction and the defined contribution plan fraction computed under section 415(c)(1) of the '54 Code (as amended by '82 TEFRA) does not exceed 1.0 for such year.

A similar rule shall apply with respect to the last plan year beginning before 1-1-84, for purposes of applying section 416(h) '54 Code.

(4) Right to higher accrued defined benefit preserved.—

(A) In general.—In the case of an individual who is a participant before 1-1-83, in a defined benefit plan which is in existence on 7-1-82, and with respect to which the requirements of section 415 of such Code have been met for all years, if such individuals's current accrued benefit under such plan exceeds the limitation of subsection (b) of section 415 of the '54 Code (as amended by this section), then (in the case of such plan) for purposes of subsections (b) and (c) of such section, the limitation of such subsection (b) with respect to such individual shall be equal to such current accrued benefit.

(B) Current accrued benefit defined.—

(i) In general.—For purposes of this paragraph, the term "current accrued benefit" means the individual's accrued benefit (at the close of the last year beginning before 1-1-83) when expressed as an annual benefit (within the meaning of section 415(b)(2) of such Code as in effect before the amendments made by '82 TEFRA).

In the case of any plan described in the first sentence of paragraph (5), the preceding sentence shall be applied by substituting for "January 1, 1983" the applicable date determined under paragraph (5).

(ii) Special rule.—For purposes of determining the amount of any individual's current accrued benefit—

(I) no change in the terms and conditions of the plan after 7-1-82, and

(II) no cost-of-living adjustment occuring after 7-1-82,

shall be taken into account.

For purposes of subclause (I), any change in the terms and conditions of the plan pursuant to a collective bargaining agreement entered into before 7-1-82, and ratified before 9-3-82, shall be treated as a change made before 7-1-82.

(5) Special rule for collective bargaining agreements.—In the case of a plan maintained on 9-3-82 pursuant to 1 or more collective bargaining agreements between employee representatives and 1 or more employers, the amendments made by this section and section 242 (relating to age 70½) shall not apply to years beginning before the earlier of—

(A) the date on which the last of the collective bargaining agreements relating to the plan terminates (determined without regard to any extension thereof agreed to after 9-3-82), or

(B) 1-1-86.

For purposes of subparagraph (A), any plan amendment made pursuant to a collective bargaining agreement relating to the plan which amends the plan solely to conform to any requirement added by this section and section 242 shall not be treated as a termination of such collective bargaining agreement.

In the case of any plan described in the first sentence of this paragraph, paragraphs (2) and (3) of section 242(b) shall be applied by substituting for "January 1, 1984" the applicable date under this paragraph.

For purposes of this subparagraph, the term "qualified merchant marine plan" means a plan in existence on January 1, 1986, the participants in which are merchant marine officers holding licenses issued by the Secretary of Transportation under title 46, United States Code.

(G) Special limitation for qualified police or firefighters.—In the case of a qualified participant—

    (i) subparagraph (C) shall not reduce the limitation of paragraph (1)(A) to an amount less than $50,000, and

    (ii) the rules of subparagraph (F) shall apply.

The Secretary shall adjust the $50,000 amount in clause (i) at the same time and in the same manner as under section 415(d).

(H) Qualified participant defined.—For purposes of subparagraph (G), the term "qualified participant" means a participant—

    (i) in a defined benefit plan which is maintained by a State or political subdivision thereof,

    (ii) with respect to whom the period of service taken into account in determining the amount of the benefit under such defined benefit plan includes at least 20 years of service of the participant—

        (I) as a full-time employee of any police department or fire department which is organized and operated by the State or political subdivision maintaining such defined benefit plan to provide police protection, firefighting services, or emergency medical services for any area within the jurisdiction of such State or political subdivision, or

        (II) as a member of the Armed Forces of the United States.

(3) Average compensation for high 3 years.—For purposes of paragraph (1), a participant's high 3 years shall be the period of consecutive calendar years (not more than 3) during which the participant both was an active participant in the plan and had the greatest aggregate compensation from the employer. In the case of an employee within the meaning of section 401(c)(1), the preceding sentence shall be applied by substituting for "compensation from the employer" the following: "the participant's earned income (within the meaning of section 401(c)(2) but determined without regard to any exclusion under section 911)".

(4) Total annual benefits not in excess of $10,000.—Notwithstanding the preceding provisions of this subsection, the benefits payable with respect to a participant under any defined benefit plan shall be deemed not to exceed the limitation of this subsection if—

    (A) the retirement benefits payable with respect to such participant under such plan and under all other defined benefit plans of the employer do not exceed $10,000 for the plan year, or for any prior plan year, and

    (B) the employer has not at any time maintained a defined contribution plan in which the participant participated.

[6](5) *Reduction for participation or service of less than 10 years.—*

    (A) Dollar limitation.—In the case of an employee who has less than 10 years of participation in a defined benefit plan, the limitation referred to in paragraph (1)(A) shall be the limitation determined under such paragraph (without regard to this paragraph) multiplied by a fraction—

        (i) the numerator of which is the number of years (or part thereof) of participation in the defined benefit plan of the employer, and

        (ii) the denominator of which is 10.

    (B) Compensation and benefits limitations.—The provisions of subparagraph (A) shall apply to the limitations under paragraphs (1)(B) and (4), except that such subparagraph shall be applied with respect to years of service with an employer rather than years of participation in a plan.

    (C) Limitation on reduction.—In no event shall subparagraph (A) or (B) reduce the limitations referred to in paragraphs (1) and (4) to an amount less that 1/10 of such limitation (determined without regard to this paragraph).

⟦Footnote ¶3005 continued⟧

Matter in *italics* in Sec. 415(b)(2)(F)—(H), (5), (8), (9), (c)(1)(A), and (2)(B) added by section 1106(a), (b)(1)(B), (2), (3), (e)(1) and (f), '86 TRA which struck out:

(6) "**(5) Reduction for service less than 10 years.**—In the case of an employee who has less than 10 years of service with the employer, the limitation referred to in paragraph (1), and the limitation referred to in paragraph (4), shall be the limitation determined under such paragraph (without regard to this paragraph), multiplied by a fraction, the numerator of which is the number of years (or part thereof) of service with the employer and the denominator of which is 10."

(D) Application to changes in benefit structure.—To the extent provided in regulations, this paragraph shall be applied separately with respect to each change in the benefit structure of a plan.

* * * * * * * * * * * *

(8) Social security retirement age defined.—For purposes of this subsection, the term "social security retirement age" means the age used as the retirement age under section 216(l) of the Social Security Act, except that such section shall be applied—
(A) without regard to the age increase factor, and
(B) as if the early retirement age under section 216(l)(2) of such Act were 62.

(9) Special rule for commercial airline pilots.—
(A) In general.—Except as provided in subparagraph (B), in the case of any participant who is a commercial airline pilot—
(i) the rule of paragraph (2)(F)(i)(II) shall apply, and
(ii) if, as of the time of the participant's retirement, regulations prescribed by the Federal Aviation Administration require an individual to separate from service as a commercial airline pilot after attaining any age occurring on or after age 60 and before the social security retirement age, paragraph (2)(C) (after application of clause (i)) shall be applied by substituting such age for the social security retirement age.
(B) Individuals who separate from service before age 60.—If a participant described in subparagraph (A) separates from service before age 60, the rules of paragraph (2)(F) shall apply.

(c) Limitation for Defined Contribution Plans.—

(1) In general.—Contributions and other additions with respect to a participant exceed the limitation of this subsection if, when expressed as an annual addition (within the meaning of paragraph (2)) to the participant's account, such annual addition is greater than the lesser of—
(A) $30,000 *(or, if greater, ¼ of the dollar limitation in effect under subsection (b)(1)(A))*, or
(B) 25 percent of the participant's compensation.

(2) Annual addition.—For purposes of paragraph (1), the term "annual addition" means the sum of any year of—
(A) employer contributions,
[7]*(B) the employee contributions, and*
(C) forfeitures.

For the purposes of this paragraph, employee contributions under subparagraph (B) are determined without regard to any rollover contributions (as defined in sections 402(a)(5), 403(a)(4), 403(b)(8), and 408(d)(3)) without regard to employee contributions to a simplified employee pension [8]*which are excludable from gross income under section 408(k)(6). Subparagraph (B) of paragraph (1) shall not apply to any contribution for medical benefits (within the meaning of section 419A(f)(2)) after separation from service which is treated as an annual addition.*

(3) Participant's compensation.—For purposes of paragraph (1)—

(A) **In general.**—The term "participant's compensation" means the compensation of the participant from the employer for the year.

[Footnote ¶3005 continued]

(7) "(B) the lesser of—
(i) the amount of the employee contributions in excess of 6 percent of his compensation, or
(ii) one-half of the employee contributions, and"
Effective date (Sec. 1106(i)(1)—(4) and (6), '86 TRA).—For (i)(1)—(4), see above.
* * * * * * * * * * * *

(6) Special rule for amendment made of subsection (e).—The amendment made by subsection (e) shall not require the recomputation, for purposes of secton 415(c) of the'86 Code, of the annual addition for any year beginning before 1987.

Matter in *italics* in Sec. 415(c)(2) (except for the last sentence) added by section 1108(g)(5), '86 TRA, which struck out:
(8) "allowable as a deduction under section 219(a), and without regard to deductible employee contributions within the meaning of section 72(o)(5)."
Effective date (Sec. 1108, '86 TRA).—Applies to years beginning after 12-31-86.

Matter in *italics* in the last sentence of Sec. 415(c)(2) added by section 1106(e)(2), '86 TRA.
Effective date (Sec. 1106(i)(1)—(4) and (6), '86 TRA).—See above.

(B) Special rule for self-employed individuals.—In the case of an employee within the meaning of section 401(c)(1), subparagraph (A) shall be applied by substituting "the participant's earned income (within the meaning of section 401(c)(2) but determined without regard to any exclusion under section 911) for "compensation of the participant from the employer.

(C) Special rules for permanent and total disability.—In the case of a participant [9]*any defined contribution plan*—

(i) who is permanently and totally disabled (as defined in [10]*section 22(e)(3)),*

(ii) who is not [10a]*a highly compensated employee (within the meaning of section 414(q)),* and

(iii) with respect to whom the employer elects, at such time and in such manner as the Secretary may prescribe, to have this subparagraph apply,

the term "participant's compensation" means the compensation the participant would have received for the year if the participant was paid at the rate of compensation paid immediately before becoming permanently and totally disabled. This subparagraph shall apply only if contributions made with respect to amounts treated as compensation under this subparagraph are nonforfeitable when made.

(4) Special election for section 403(b) contracts purchased by educational organizations, hospitals, home health service agencies, and certain churches, etc.—

(A) In the case of amounts contributed for an annuity contract described in section 403(b) for the year in which occurs a participant's separation from the service with an educational organization, a hospital, a home health service agency, *a health and welfare service agency* or a church, convention or association of churches, or an organization described in section 414(e)(3)(B) (ii), at the election of the participant there is substituted for the amount specified in paragraph (1)(B) the amount of the exclusion allowance which would be determined under section 403(b)(2) (without regard to this section) for the participant's taxable year in which such separation occurs if the participant's years of service were computed only by taking into account his service for the employer (as determined for purposes of section 403(b)(2)) during the period of years (not exceeding ten) ending on the date of such separation.

(B) In the case of amounts contributed for an annuity contract described in section 403(b) for any year in the case of a participant who is an employee of an educational organization, a hospital, a home health service agency, *a health and welfare service agency* or a church, convention or association of churches, or an organization described in section 414(e)(3)(B)(ii), at the election of the participant there is substituted for the amount specified in paragraph (1)(B) the least of—

(i) 25 percent of the participant's includible compensation (as defined in section 403(b)(3)) plus $4,000,

(ii) the amount of the exclusion allowance determined for the year under section 403(b)(2), or

(iii) $15,000.

(C) In the case of amounts contributed for an annuity contract described in section 403(b) for any year for a participant who is an employee of an educational organization, a hospital, a home health service agency, *a health and welfare service agency* or a church, convention or association of churches, or an organization described in section 414(e)(3)(B)(ii), at the election of the participant the provisions of section 403(b)(2)(A) shall not apply.

(D) (i) The provisions of this paragraph apply only if the participant elects its application at the time and in the manner provided under regulations prescribed by the Secretary. Not more than one election may be made under subparagraph (A) by any participant. A participant who elects to have the provisions of subparagraph (A), (B), or (C) of this paragraph apply to him may not elect to have any

〔Footnote ¶3005 continued〕

Matter in *italics* in Sec. 415(c)(3)(C) added by section 1875(c)(11), '86 TRA, which struck out:
(9) "a profit sharing or stock bonus plan"
Effective date (Sec. 1881, '86 TRA and Sec. 715, '84 TRA and section 253(c), '82 TEFRA).—Applies to taxable years beginning after 12-31-81.

Matter in *italics* in Sec. 415(c)(3)(C)(i) added by section 1847(b)(4), '86 TRA, which struck out:
(10) "section 37(e)(3)"
Effective date (Sec. 1881, '86 TRA and 475(a), '84 TRA).—Applies to taxable years beginning after 12-31-83, and to carrybacks from such years.

Matter in *italics* in Sec. 415(c)(3)(C)(ii) added by section 1114(b)(12), '86 TRA, which struck out:
(10a) "an officer, owner, or highly compensated"
Effective date (Sec. 1114(c)(3), '86 TRA).—Applies to years beginning after 12-31-88.

other subparagraph of this paragraph apply to him. Any election made under this paragraph is irrevocable.

(ii) For purposes of this paragraph the term "educational oganization" means an educational organization described in section 170(b)(1)(A)(ii).

(iii) For purposes of this paragraph the term "home health service agency" means an organization described in subsection 501(c)(3) which is exempt from tax under section 501(a) and which has been determined by the Secretary of Health, Education, and Welfare to be a home health agency (as defined in section 1861(o) of the Social Security Act).

(6) Special limitation for employee stock ownership plan.—

(A) In the case of an employee stock ownership plan (as defined in subparagraph (B)), under which no more than one-third of the employer contributions for a year are allocated to [11]*highly compensated employees (within the meaning of section 414(q)),* the amount described in subsection (c)(1)(A) (as adjusted for such year pursuant to subsection (d)(1)) for a year with respect to any participant shall be equal to the sum of (i) the amount described in subsection (c)(1)(A) (as so adjusted) determined without regard to this paragraph and (ii) the lesser of the amount determined under clause (i) or the amount of employer securities contributed, or purchased with cash contributed, to the employee stock ownership plan.

(B) For purposes of this paragraph—

(i) the term "employee stock ownership plan" means an employee stock ownership plan (within the meaning of section 4975(e)(7) or a tax credit employee stock ownership plan.

(ii) the term "employer securities" has the meaning given to such term by section 409.[12]

(C) In the case of an employee stock ownership plan (as described in section, 4975(e)(7)), under which no more than one-third of the employer contributions for a year which are deductible under paragraph (9) of section 404(a) are allocated to [11]*highly compensated employees (within the meaning of section 414(q)),* the limitations imposed by this section shall not apply to—

(i) forfeitures of employer securities under an employee stock ownership plan (as described in section 4975(e)(7)) if such securities were acquired with the proceeds of a loan (as described in section 404(a)(9)(A)), or

(ii) employer contributions to such an employee stock ownership plan which are deductible under section 404(a)(9)(B) and charged against the participant's account.

* * * * * * * * * * * *

(d) Cost-of-Living Adjustments.—

(1) **In general.**—The Secretary shall adjust annually—

(A) the $90,000 amount in subsection (b)(1)(A), *and* [13]

[14]*(B)* in the case of a participant who is separated from service, the amount taken into account under subsection (b)(1)(B),

for increases in the cost of living in accordance with regulations prescribed by the Secretary. Such regulations shall provide for adjustment procedures which are similar to the

---

procedures used to adjust benefit amounts under section 215(i)(2)(A) of the Social Security Act.

(2) **Base periods.**—The base period taken into account—

(A) for purposes of [15]*subparagraph (A)* of paragraph (1) is the calendar quarter beginning October 1, 1986, and

(B) for purposes of [16]*subparagraph (B)* of paragraph (1) is the last calendar quarter of the calendar year before the calendar year in which the participant is separated from service.

(3) **Freeze on adjustment to defined contribution and benefit limits.**—The Secretary shall not make any adjustment under subparagraph (A) [17] of paragraph (1) with respect to any year beginning after December 31, 1982, and before January 1, 1988.

* * * * * * * * * * * *

(j) **Regulations; Definition of Year.**—The Secretary shall prescribe such regulations as may be necessary to carry out the purposes of this section, including, but not limited to, regulations defining the term "year" for purposes of any provision of this section.

(k) [18]*Definitions of Defined Contribution Plan and Defined Benefit Plan.*—For purposes of this title, the term "defined contribution plan" or "defined benefit plan" means a defined contribution plan (within the meaning of section 414(i)) or a defined benefit plan (within the meaning of section 414(j)), whichever applies, which is—

[19]*(1)* a plan described in section 401(a) which include a trust which is exempt from tax under section 501(a),

[20]*(2)* an annuity plan described in section 403(a),

[21]*(3)* an annuity contract described in section 403(b).

[22]*(4)* an individual retirement account described in section 408(a),

[23]*(5)* an individual retirement annuity described in section 408(b); or

[24]*(6)* a simplified employee pension.

(2) Contributions to provide cost-of-living protection under deferred benefit plans.—

(A) In general.—In the case of a defined benefit plan which maintains a qualified cost-of-living arrangement—

(i) any contribution made directly by an employee under such arrangement—

(I) shall not be treated as an annual addition for purposes of subsection (c), but

(II) shall be so treated for purposes of subsection (e), and

(ii) any benefit under such arrangement which is allocable to an employer contribution which was transferred from a defined contribution plan and to which the requirements of subsection (c) were applied shall, for purposes of subsection (b), be treated as a benefit derived from an employee contribution (and subsections (c) and (e) shall not again apply to such contribution by reason of such transfer),

(B) Qualified cost-of-living arrangement defined.—For purposes of this paragraph, the term "qualified cost-of-living arrangement" means an arrangement under a defined benefit plan which—

(i) provides a cost-of-living adjustment to a benefit provided under such plan or a separate plan subject to the requirements of section 412, and

(ii) meets the requirements of subparagraphs (C), (D), (E), and (F) and such other requirements as the Secretary may prescribe.

[**Footnote ¶3005 continued**]

(15) "subparagraphs (A) and (B)".
(16) "subparagraph (C)".
(17) "or (B)".
Effective date (Sec. 1106(i)(1)—(4), '86 TRA).—See above.

Matter in *italics* in Sec. 415(k)(1)—(6) added by section 1899A(13), '86 TRA, which struck out:
(18) **"(k) Special Rules.—**
(1) Defined benefit plan and defined contribution plan."
(19) "(A)".
(20) "(B)".
(21) "(C)".
(22) "(D)".
(23) "(E)".
(24) "(F)"

Sec. 415(k)(2) [starting with **"Contributions to provide . . ."**] in *italics* added by section 1106(c)(1), '86 TRA.
Effective date (Sec. 1106(i)(1)—(4), '86 TRA).—See above.

    (ii) meets the requirements of subparagraphs (C), (D), (E), and (F) and such other requirements as the Secretary may prescribe.

   (C) Determination of amount of benefit.—An arrangement meets the requirement of this subparagraph only if the cost-of-living adjustment of participants is based—

    (i) on increases in the cost-of-living after the annuity starting date, and

    (ii) on average cost-of-living increases determined by reference to 1 or more indexes prescribed by the Secretary, except that the arrangement may provide that the increase for any year will not be less than 3 percent of the retirement benefit (determined without regard to the arrangement).

   (D) Arrangement elective; time for election.—An arrangement meets the requirements of this subparagraph only if it is elective, it is available under the same terms to all participants, and it provides that such election may be made in—

    (i) the year in which the participant—

     (I) attains the earliest retirement age under the defined benefit plan (determined without regard to any requirement of separation from service), or

     (II) separates from service, or

    (ii) both such years,

   (E) Nondiscrimination requirements.—An arrangement shall not meet the requirements of this subparagraph if the Secretary finds that a pattern of discrimination exists with respect to participation.

   (F) Special rules for key employees.—

    (i) In general.—An arrangement shall not meet the requirements of this paragraph if any key employee is eligible to participate.

    (ii) Key employee.—For purposes of this subparagraph, the term "key employee" has the meaning given such term by section 416(i)(1), except that in the case of a plan other than a top-heavy plan (within the meaning of section 416(g)), such term shall not include an individual who is a key employee solely by reason of section 416(i0(1)(A)(i).

(l) Treatment of Certain Medical Benefits.—

   (1) In general.—For purposes of this section, contributions allocated to any individual medical account which is part of a [25]*pension or annuity* plan shall be treated as an annual addition to a defined contribution plan for purposes of subsection (c). *Subparagraph (B) of subsection (c)(1) shall not apply to any amount treated as an annual addition under the preceding sentence.*

   (2) Individual medical benefit account.—For purposes of paragraph (1), the term "individual medical benefit account" means any separate account—

    (A) which is established for a participant under a [25]*pension or annuity* plan, and

    (B) from which benefits described in section 401(h) are payable solely to such participant, his spouse, or his dependents.

[For official explanation, see Committee Reports, ¶3972; 3974; 3979; 4019; 4161; 4172; 4189; 4211.]

【¶3006】 CODE SEC. 416. SPECIAL RULES FOR TOP-HEAVY PLANS.

   (a) General Rule.—A trust shall not constitute a qualified trust under section 401(a) for any plan year if the plan of which it is a part is a top-heavy plan for such plan year unless such plan meets—

   (1) the vesting requirements of subsection (b), *and*

   (2) the minimum benefit requirements of subsection (c)[1] .[2]

   *   *   *   *   *   *   *   *   *   *   *   *

   (c) Plan must Provide Minimum Benefits.—

【Footnote ¶3005 continued】

Matter in *italics* in Sec. 415(l) added by section 1852(h)(2) and (3), '86 TRA, which struck out:

(25) "defined benefit"

Effective date (Sec. 1881, '86 TRA and 528(c), '84 TRA).—Applies to years beginning after 3-31-84.

【Footnote ¶3006】 Matter in *italics* in Sec. 416(a)(1), (2), (c)(2) and (d) by section 1106(d)(3)(A) and, (B) '86 TRA, which struck out:

(1) ", and"

(2) "(3) the limitation on compensation requirement of subsection (d)."

(3) "(ii) Determination of percentage.—The determination referred to in clause (i) shall be determined for each key employee by dividing the contributions for such employee by so much of his total compensation for the year as does not exceed $200,000."

Code §416(c) ¶3006

* * * * * * * * * * * * *

   (2) **Defined contribution plans.—**

* * * * * * * * * * * *

    (B) Special rule where maximum contribution less than 3 percent.—

      (i) In general.—The percentage referred to in subparagraph (A) for any year shall not exceed the percentage at which contributions are made (or required to be made) under the plan for the year for the key employee for whom such percentage is the highest for the year.[3]

      [4]*(ii)* *Treatment of aggregation groups.—*

        (I) *For purposes of this subparagraph, all defined contribution plans required to be included in an aggregation group under subsection (g)(2)(A)(i) shall be treated as one plan.*

        (II) *This subparagraph shall not apply to any plan required to be included in an aggregation group if such plan enables a defined benefit plan required to be included in such group to meet the requirements of section 401(a)(4) or 410.*

  (d) **[Repealed]**[5]

* * * * * * * * * * * *

  (g) **Top-Heavy Plan Defined.**—For purposes of this section—

* * * * * * * * * * * *

    (4) **Other special rules.**—For purposes of this subsection—

* * * * * * * * * * * *

    (E) Benefits not taken into account if employee not employed for last 5 years.—[6]*If any individual has not performed services for the employer maintaining the plan at any time during the 5-year period ending on the determination date, any accrued benefit for such individual (and the account of such individual) shall not be taken into account.*

    (F) *Accrued benefits treated as accruing ratably.—The accrued benefit of any employee (other than a key employee) shall be determined—*

      (i) under the method which is used for accrual purposes for all plans of the employer, or

      (ii) if there is no method described in clause (i), as if such benefit accrued not more rapidly than the slowest accrual rate permitted under section 411(b)(1)(C).

* * * * * * * * * * * *

  (i) **Definitions.**—For purposes of this section—

⟦Footnote ¶3006 continued⟧

  (4) "(iii)"

  (5) **"(d) Not More Than $200,000 in Annual Compensation Taken Into Account.—**

  (1) **In general.**—A plan meets the requirements of this subsection if the annual compensation of each employee taken into account under the plan does not exceed the first $200,000.

  (2) **Cost-of-living adjustments.**—The Secretary shall annually adjust the $200,000 amount contained in paragraph (1) of this subsection and in clause (ii) of subsection (c)(2)(B) at the same time and in the same manner as he adjusts the dollar amount contained in section 415(c)(1)(A)."

Effective date (Sec. 1106(i)(5), '86 TRA).—Generally applies to benefits accruing in years beginning after 12-31-88.

For special rules on collective bargaining agreements, see footnote ¶3005.

Matter in *italics* in Sec. 416(g)(4)(E) added by section 1852(d)(2), '86 TRA, which struck out:

  (6) "If any individual has not received any compensation from any employer maintaining the plan (other than benefits under the plan) at any time during the 5-year period ending on the determination date, any accrued benefit for such individual (and the account of such individual shall not be taken into account."

Effective date (Sec. 1881, '86 TRA and 524(b)(2), '84 TRA).—Applies to plan years beginning after 12-31-84.

Sec. 416(g)(4)(F) in *italics* added by section 1118(a), '86 TRA.

Effective date (Sec. 1118(b), '86 TRA).—Applies to plan years beginning after 12-31-86.

Matter in *italics* in Sec. 416(i)(1)(A) added by section 1852(d)(1), '86 TRA.

Effective date (Sec. 1881, '86 TRA and Sec. 524(a)(2), '84 TRA). Applies to plan years beginning after 12-31-83.

(1) **Key employee.—**

(A) In general.—The term "key employee" means an employee who, at any time during the plan year or any of the 4 preceding plan years, is—

(i) an officer of the employer having an annual compensation greater than 150 percent of the amount in effect under section 415(c)(1)(A) for any such plan year.

(ii) 1 of the 10 employees having annual compensation from the employer of more than the limitation in effect under section 415(c)(1)(A) and owning (or considered as owning within the meaning of section 318) the largest interest in the employer.

(iii) a 5-percent owner of the employer, or

(iv) a 1-percent owner of the employer having an annual compensation from the employer of more than $150,000.

For purposes of clause (i), no more than 50 employees (or, if lesser, the greater of 3 or 10 percent of the employees) shall be treated as officers. For purposes of clause (ii), if 2 employees have the same interest in the employer, the employee having greater annual compensation from the employer shall be treated as having a larger interest. *Such term shall not include any officer or employee of an entity referred to in section 414(d) (relating to governmental plans).*

* * * * * * * * * * *

[For official explanation, see Committee Reports, ¶3972; 3983; 4172.]

⟦¶3007⟧ CODE SEC. 417. DEFINITIONS AND SPECIAL RULES FOR PURPOSES OF MINIMUM SURVIVOR ANNUITY REQUIREMENTS.

(a) **Election To Waive Qualified Joint and Survivor Annuity or Qualified Preretirement Survivor Annuity.—**

(1) **In general.—**A plan meets the requirements of [1]*section 401(a)(11)* only if—

(A) under the plan, each participant—

(i) may elect at any time during the applicable election period to waive the qualified joint and survivor annuity form of benefit or the qualified preretirement survivor annuity form of benefit (or both), and

(ii) may revoke any such election at any time during the applicable election period, and

(B) the plan meets the requirements of [2]*paragraphs (2), (3), and (4) of this* subsection.

(2) **Spouse must consent to election.—**Each plan shall provide that an election under paragraph (1)(A)(i) shall not take effect unless—

(A)*(i)* the spouse of the participant consents in writing to such election.

(ii) such election designates a beneficiary (or a form of benefits) which may not be changed without spousal consent (or the consent of the spouse expressly permits designations by the participant without any requirement of further consent by the spouse), and

(iii) [3] the spouse's consent acknowledges the effect of such election and is witnessed by a plan representative or a notary public, or

(B) it is established to the satisfaction of a plan representative that the consent required under subparagraph (A) may not be obtained because there is no spouse,

---

⟦**Footnote ¶3007**⟧ *"section 401(a)(11)"* in *italics* in Sec. 417(a)(1) added by section 1898(b)(15)(A), '86 TRA, which struck out:

(1) "section 401(a)(ii)"

Effective date (Sec. 1898(j), '86 TRA, and section 302(a) and (b) and 303(c) and (e), P.L. 98-397, 8-23-84, as amended by section 1145(c) and 1898(g) and (h), '86 TRA).—Generally applies to plan years beginning after 12-31-84. For transitional and special rules, see footnote ¶2994.

Matter in *italics* in Sec. 417(a)(1)(B) added by section 1898(b)(4)(A)(i), '86 TRA, which struck out:

(2) "paragraphs (2) and (3)"

Effective date (Sec. 1898(b)(4)(C), '86 TRA).—(i) Applies with respect to loans made after 8-18-85.

(ii) In the case of any loan which was made on or before 8-18-85, and which is secured by a portion of the participant's accrued benefit, nothing in the amendments made by sections 103 and 203 of the Retirement Equity Act of 1984 shall prevent any distribution required by reason of a failure to comply with the terms of such loan.

(iii) For purposes of this subparagraph, any loan which is revised, extended, renewed, or renegotiated after 8-18-85, shall be treated as made after 8-18-85.

Matter in *italics* in Sec. 417(a)(2)(A) and (3)(B) added by section 1898(b)(5)(A) and (6)(A), '86 TRA, which struck out:

(3) "and "

because the spouse cannot be located, or because of such other circumstances as the Secretary may by regulations prescribe.

Any consent by a spouse (or establishment that the consent of a spouse may not be obtained) under the preceding sentence shall be effective only with respect to such spouse.

(3) **Plan to provide written explanations.—**

* * * * * * * * * * * *

(B) Explanation of qualified preretirement survivor annuity.—

[4]*(i) In general. Each plan shall provide to each participant, within the applicable period with respect to such participant (and consistent with such regulations as the Secretary may prescribe), a written explanation with respect to the qualified preretirement survivor annuity comparable to that required under subparagraph (A).*

(ii) Applicable period.—For purposes of clause (i), the term "applicable period" means, with respect to a participant, whichever of the following periods ends last:

(I) The period beginning with the first day of the plan year in which the participant attains age 32 and ending with the close of the plan year preceding the plan year in which the participant attains age 35.

(II) A reasonable period after the individual becomes a participant.

(III) A reasonable period ending after paragraph (5) ceases to apply to the participant.

(IV) A reasonable period ending after section 401(a)(11) applies to the participant.

(V) A reasonable period after separation from service in case of a participant who separates before attaining age 35.

(4) *Requirement of special consent for using plan assets as security for loans.—*
Each plan shall provide that, if section 401(a)(11) applies to a participant when part or all of the participant's accrued benefit is to be used as security for a loan, no portion of the participant's accrued benefit may be used as security for such loan unless—

(A) the spouse of the participant (if any) consents in writing to such use during the 90-day period ending on the date on which the loan is to be so secured, and

(B) requirements comparable to the requirements of paragraph (2) are met with respect to such consent.

[5]*(5)* **Special rules where plan fully subsidizes costs.—**

(A) In general.—The requirements of this subsection shall not apply with respect to the qualified joint and survivor annuity form of benefit or the qualified preretirement survivor annuity form of benefit, as the case may be, *if such benefit may not be waived (or another beneficiary selected) and* if the plan fully subsidizes the costs of such benefit.

* * * * * * * * * * * *

[6]*(6)* **Applicable election period defined.**

* * * * * * * * * * * *

(c) **Definition of Qualified Preretirement Survivor Annuity.—**For purposes of this section and section 401(a)(11)—

⟦Footnote ¶3007 continued⟧

(4) "Each plan shall provide to each participant, within the period beginning with the first day of the plan year in which the participant attains age 32 and ending with the close of the plan year preceding the plan year in which such participant attains age 35 (and consistent with such regulations as the Secretary may prescribe), a written explanation with respect to the qualified preretirement survivor annuity comparable to that required under subparagraph (A)."

Effective date (Sec. 1898(j), '86 TRA, and section 302(a) and (b) and 303(c) and (e), P.L. 98-397, 8-23-84, as amended by section 1145(c) and 1898(g) and (h), '86 TRA).—See above.

Matter in *italics* in Sec. 417(a)(4) and "(5)" in *italics* in (a)(5) added by section 1898(b)(4)(A)(ii) '86 TRA, which struck out:
(5) "(4)"
Effective date (Sec. 1898(b)(4)(C), '86 TRA).—See above.

Matter in *italics* in Sec. 417(a)(5)(A), added by section 1898(b)(11)(A), '86 TRA.
Effective date (Sec. 1898(j), '86 TRA and section 302(a) and (b) and 303(c) and (e), P.L. 98-397, 8-23-84, as amended by section 1145(c) and 1898(g) and (h), '86 TRA).—See above.

Matter in *italics* in Sec. 417(a)(6) added by section 1898(b)(4)(A)(ii), '86 TRA, which struck out:
(6) "(5)"
Effective date (Sec. 1898(b)(4)(C), '86 TRA).—See above.

(1) **In general.**—Except as provided in paragraph (2), the term "qualified preretirement survivor annuity" means a survivor annuity [7]*for* the life of the surviving spouse of the participant if—

(A) the payments to the surviving spouse under such annuity are not less than the amounts which would be payable as a survivor annuity under the qualified joint and survivor annuity under the plan (or the actuarial equivalent thereof) if—

(i) in the case of a participant who dies after the date on which the participant attained the earliest retirement age, such participant had retired with an immediate qualified joint and survivor annuity on the day before the participant's death, or

(ii) in the case of a participant who dies on or before the date on which the participant would have attained the earliest retirement age, such participant had—

(I) separated from service on the date of death,

(II) survived to the earliest retirement age,

(III) retired with an immediate qualified joint and survivor annuity at the earliest retirement age, and

(IV) died on the day after the day on which such participant would have attained the earliest retirement age, and

(B) under the plan, the earliest period for which the surviving spouse may receive a payment under such annuity is not later than the month in which the participant would have attained the earliest retirement age under the plan.

In the case of an individual who separated from service before the date of such individual's death, subparagraph (A)(ii)(I) shall not apply.

(2) **Special rule for defined contribution plans.**—In the case of any defined contribution plan or participant described in clause (ii) or (iii) of section 401(a)(11)(B), the term "qualified preretirement survivor annuity" means an annuity for the life of the surviving spouse the actuarial equivalent of which is not less than 50 percent of *the portion of* the account of the participant [8]*(as of the date of death) to which the participant had a nonforfeitable right (within the meaning of section 411(a)).*

(3) *Security interests taken into account.—For purposes of paragraphs (1) and (2), any security interest held by the plan by reason of a loan outstanding to the participant shall be taken into account in determining the amount of the qualified preretirement survivor annuity.*

* * * * * * * * * * * *

(e) **Restrictions on Cash-Outs.—**

* * * * * * * * * * * *

(3) **Determination of present value.—**

[9]*(A) In general.—For purposes of paragraphs (1) and (2), the present value shall be calculated—*

(i) by using an interest rate no greater than the applicable interest rate if the vested accrued benefit (using such rate) is not in excess of $25,000, and

(ii) by using an interest rate no greater than 120 percent of the applicable interest rate if the vested accrued benefit exceeds $25,000 (as determined under clause (i)).

[Footnote ¶3007 continued]

Matter in *italics* in Sec. 417(c) added by section 1898(b)(1)(A), (9)(A), and (15)(B), '86 TRA, which struck out:

(7) "or"

(8) "as of the date of death"

Effective date (Sec. 1898(j), '86 TRA and section 302(a) and (b) and 303(c) and (e), P.L. 98-397, 8-23-84, as amended by section 1145(c) and 1898(g) and (h), '86 TRA.—See above.

Matter in *italics* in Sec. 417(e)(3) added by section 1139(b), '86 TRA, which struck out:

(9) "For purposes of paragraphs (1) and (2), the present value of a qualified joint and survivor annuity or a qualified preretirement survivor annuity shall be determined as of the date of the distribution and by using an interest rate not greater than the interest rate which would be used (as of the date of the distribution) by the Pension Benefit Guaranty Corporation for purposes of determining the present value of a lump sum distribution on plan termination."

Effective date (Sec. 1139(d)(1), '86 TRA).—Generally applies to distributions in plan years beginning after 12-31-84, except that such amendments shall not apply to any distributions in plan years beginning after 12-31-84, and before 1-1-87, if such distributions were made in accordance with the requirements of the regulations issued under the Retirement Equity Act of 1984. For transitional and special rules, see footnote ¶3003.

Code §417(e)(3) ¶3007

In no event shall the present value determined under subclause (II) be less than $25,000.

(B) *Applicable interest rate.—For purposes of subparagraph (A), the term "applicable interest rate" means the interest rate which would be used (as of the date of the distribution) by the Pension Benefit Guaranty Corporation for purposes of determining the present value of a lump sum distribution on plan termination.*

(f) **Other Definitions and Special Rules.**—For purposes of this section and section 401(a)(11)—

(1) **Vested participant.**—The term "vested participant" means any participant who has a nonforfeitable right (within the meaning of section 411(a)) to any portion of [10] *such participant's accrued benefit.*

(2) **Annuity starting date.**—

[11]*(A) In general.—The term "annuity starting date" means—*

(i) the first day of the first period for which an amount is payable as an annuity, or

(ii) in the case of a benefit not payable in the form of an annuity, the first day on which all events have occurred which entitle the participant to such benefit.

(B) Special rule for disability benefits.—For purposes of subparagraph (A), the first day of the first period for which a benefit is to be received by reason of disability shall be treated as the annuity starting date only if such benefit is not an auxiliary benefit.

* * * * * * * * * * * *

(5) Distributions by reason of security interests.—If the use of any participant's accrued benefit (or any portion thereof) as security for a loan meets the requirements of subsection (a)(4), nothing in this section or section 411(a)(11) shall prevent any distribution required by reason of a failure to comply with the terms of such loan.

(6) Requirements for certain spousal consents.—No consent of a spouse shall be effective for purposes of subsection (e)(1) or (e)(2) (as the case may be) unless requirements comparable to the requirements for spousal consent to an election under subsection (a)(1)(A) are met.

[12]*(7)* **Consultation with the secretary of labor.**—In prescribing regulations under this section and section 401(a)(11), the Secretary shall consult with the Secretary of Labor.

[For official explanation, see Committee Reports, ¶3998; 4211.]

[¶3008] **CODE SEC. 419. TREATMENT OF FUNDED WELFARE BENEFIT PLANS.**

(a) **General rule.**—Contributions paid or accrued by an employer to a welfare benefit fund—

(1) shall not be deductible under [1]*this subchapter,* but

(2) if they [2]*would otherwise be deductible,* shall (subject to the limitation of subsection (b)) be deductible under this section for the taxable year in which paid.

* * * * * * * * * * * *

(e) **Welfare benefit fund.**—For purposes of this section—

* * * * * * * * * * * *

[Footnote ¶3007 continued]

Matter in *italics* in Sec. 417(f)(1) and (2) added by section 1898(b)(8)(A) and (12)(A), '86 TRA, which struck out:

(10) "the accrued benefit derived from employer contributions"

(11) "The term "annuity starting date" means the first day of the first period for which an amount is received as an annuity (whether by reason of retirement or disability)."

Effective date (Sec. 1898(j), '86 TRA, and section 302(a) and (b) and 303(c) and (e), P.L. 98-397, 8-23-84, as amended by section 1145(c) and 1898(g) and (h), '84 TRA).—See above.

Sec. 417(f)(5) in *italics* added by section 1898(b)(4)(A)(iii), '86 TRA. [Section 1898(b)(4)(A)(iii), '86 TRA, also renumbered former Sec. 417(f)(5) as (6)]

Effective date (Sec. 1898(b)(4)(C), '86 TRA).—See above.

Matter in *italics* in Sec. 417(f)(6) and (7) added by section 1898(b)(10)(A), '86 TRA, which struck out:

(12) "(6)"

Effective date (Sec. 1898(j), '86 TRA and section 302(a) and (b) and 303(c) and (e), P.L. 98-397, 8-23-84, as amended by section 1145(c) and 1898(g) and (h), '86 TRA).—See above.

[Footnote ¶3008] Matter in *italics* in Sec. 419(a), (e)(4) and (g)(1) added by section 1851(a)(1), (8)(A) and (b)(2)(C), '86 TRA, which struck out:

(1) "section 162 or 212"

(2) "satisfy the requirements of such sections"

(4) Treatment of amounts held pursuant to certain insurance contracts.—

(A) In general.—Notwithstanding paragraph (3)(C), the term "fund" shall not include amounts held by an insurance company pursuant to an insurance contract if—

(i)   such contract is a life insurance contract described in section 264(a)(1), or

(ii) such contract is a qualified nonguaranteed contract.

(B) Qualified nonguaranteed contract.—

(i) In general.—For purposes of this paragraph, the term "qualified non-guaranteed contract" means any insurance contract (including a reasonable premium stabilization reserve held thereunder) if—

(I)   there is no guarantee of a renewal of such contract, and

(II) other than insurance protection, the only payments to which the employer or employees are entitled are experience rated refunds or policy dividends which are not guaranteed and which are determined by factors other than the amount of welfare benefits paid to (or on behalf of) the employees of the employer or their beneficiaries.

(ii) Limitation.—In the case of any qualified nonguaranteed contract, subparagraph (A) shall not apply unless the amount of any experience rated refund or policy dividend payable to an employer with respect to a policy year is treated by the employer as received or accrued in the taxable year in which the policy year ends.

* * * * * * * * * * * *

(g) **Extension to plans for independent contractors.**—If any fund would be a welfare benefit fund (as modified by subsection (f)) but for the fact that there is no employee-employer relationship—

(1)   this section shall apply as if there were such a [3]*relationship* and

(2)   any reference in this section to the employer shall be treated as a reference to the person for whom services are provided, and any reference in this section to an employee shall be treated as a reference to the person providing the services.

[For official explanation, see Committee Reports, ¶4171.]

[¶3008-A] CODE SEC. 419A. QUALIFIED ASSET ACCOUNT; LIMITATION OF ADDITIONS TO ACCOUNT.

(a) **General Rule.**—For purposes of this subpart *and section 512,* the term "qualified asset account" means any account consisting of assets set aside to provide for the payment of—

(1)   disability benefits,

(2)   medical benefits,

(3)   SUB or severance pay benefits, or

(4)   life insurance benefits.

[Footnote ¶3008 continued]

(3) "plan"

Effective date (Sec. 1881, '86 TRA and Sec. 511(e), '84 TRA, as amended by section 1851(a)(14), '86 TRA).—

(1) Generally applies to contributions paid or accrued after 12-31-85, in taxable years ending after such date.

(2) Special rule for collective bargaining agreements.—In the case of plan maintained pursuant to 1 or more collective bargaining agreements—

(A) between employee representatives and 1 or more employers, and

(B) in effect on 7-1-85 (or ratified on or before such date),

the amendments made by this section shall not apply to years beginning before the date on which the last of the collective bargaining agreements relating to the plan terminates (determined without regard to any extension thereof agreed to after 7-1-85).

(3) Special rule for paragraph (2).—For purposes of paragraph (2), any plan amendment made pursuant to a collective bargaining agreement relating to the plan which amends the plan solely to conform to any requirement added by this section shall not be treated as a termination of such collective bargaining agreement.

(4) Special effective date for contributions of facilities.—Notwithstanding paragraphs (1) and (2), the amendments made by this section shall apply in the case of—

(A) any contribution after 6-22-84, of a facility to a welfare benefit fund, and

(B) any other contribution after 6-22-84, to a welfare benefit fund to be used to acquire or improve a facility.

(5) Binding contract exceptions to paragraph (4).—Paragraph (4) shall not apply to any facility placed in service before 1-1-87—

(A) which is acquired or improved by the fund (or contributed to the fund) pursuant to a binding contract in effect on 6-22-84, and at all times thereafter, or

(B) the construction of which by or for the fund began before 6-22-84.

Code §419A(a) ¶3008-A

(b) **Limitation on Additions to Account.**—No addition to any qualified asset account may be taken into account under section 419(c)(1)(B) to the extent such addition results in the amount in such account exceeding the account limit.

(c) **Account Limit.**—For purposes of this section—

* * * * * * * * * * *

(5) **Special limitation where no actuarial certification.**—

(A) In general.—Unless there is an actuarial certification of the account limit determined under [1] *this subsection* for any taxable year, the account limit for such taxable year shall not exceed the sum of the safe harbor limits for such taxable year.

* * * * * * * * * * *

(d) **Requirement of Separate Accounts for Post-Retirement Medical or Life Insurance Benefits Provided to Key Employees.**—

(1) **In general.**—In the case of any employee who is a key employee—

(A) a separate account shall be established for any medical benefits or life insurance benefits provided with respect to such employee after retirement, and

(B) medical benefits and life insurance benefits provided with respect to such employee after retirement may only be paid from such separate account.

The requirements of this paragraph shall apply to the first taxable year for which a reserve is taken into account under subsection (c)(2) and to all subsequent taxable years.

(2) **Coordination with section 415.**—For purposes of section 415, any amount attributable to medical benefits allocated to an account established under paragraph (1) shall be treated as an annual addition to a defined contribution plan for purposes of section 415(c).

Subparagraph (B) of section 415(c)(1) shall not apply to any amount treated as an annual addition under the preceding sentence.

(3) **Key employee.**—For purposes of this section, the term "key employee" means any employee who, at any time during the plan year or any preceding plan year, is or was a key employee as defined in section 416(i).

(e) **Special Limitations on Reserves for Medical Benefits or Life Insurance Benefits Provided to Retired Employees.**—

[2]*(1) Reserve must be nondiscriminatory.—No reserve may be taken into account under subsection (c)(2) for post-retirement medical benefits or life insurance benefits to be provided to covered employees unless the plan meets the requirements of section 505(b) with respect to such benefits (whether or not such requirements apply to such plan). The preceding sentence shall not apply to any plan maintained pursuant to an agreement between employee representatives and 1 or more employers if the Secretary finds that such agreement is a collective bargaining agreement and that post-retirement medical benefits or life insurance benefits were the subject of good faith bargaining between such employee representatives and such employer or employers.*

(2) Limitation on amount of life insurance benefits.—Life insurance benefits shall not be taken into account under subsection (c)(2) to the extent the aggregate amount of such benefits to be provided with respect to the employee exceeds $50,000.

≫**P-H CAUTION**→ There are two versions of Sec 419A(f)(5). Sec. 419A(f)(5), as amended by section 1851(a)(13) '86 TRA, follows. For Sec. 419A(f)(5), as amended by section 1851(a)(4) '86 TRA, see below.

(f) **Definitions and Other Special Rules.**—For purposes of this section—

* * * * * * * * * * *

【**Footnote ¶3008-A】** Matter in *italics* in Sec. 419A(a) [law reads (b)], (c)(5)(A), (d)(1), (2), and (e) added by section 1851(a)(2), (3)(A), (5), and (6)(B), '86 TRA, which struck out:

(1) "paragraph (1)"

(2) "**(1) Benefits must be nondiscriminatory.**—No reserve may be taken into account under subsection (c)(2) for post-retirement medical benefits or life insurance benefits to be provided to covered employees unless the plan meets the requirements of section 505(b)(1) with respect to such benefits.

(2) **Taxable life insurance benefits not taken into account.**—No life insurance benefit may be taken into account under subsection (c)(2) to the extent—

(A) such benefit is includible in gross income under section 79, or

(B) such benefit would be includible in gross income under section 101(b) (determined by substituting "$50,000" for "$5,000")."

Effective date (Sec. 1881, '86 TRA and section 511(e), '84 TRA as amended by section 1851(a)(14), '86 TRA)—(1) Generally applies to contributions paid or accrued after 12-31-85, in taxable years ending after such date. For special rules, see footnote ¶3008.

▲ **(5)** [3]*Special rule for collective bargained and employee pay-all plans.—No accounts limits shall apply in the case of any qualified asset account under a separate welfare benefit fund—*

(A) under a collective bargaining agreement, or

(B) an employee pay-all plan under section 501(c)(9) if—

(i) such plan has at least 50 employees (determined without regard to subsection (h)(1)), and

(ii) no employee is entitled to a refund with respect to amounts in the fund, other than a refund based on the experience of the entire fund.

≫**P-H CAUTION→** There are two versions of Sec. 419A(f)(5). Sec. 419A(f)(5), as amended by section 1851(a)(4), follows. For Sec. 419A(f)(5), as amended by section 1851(a)(13), see above.

(f) Definitions and Other Special Rules.—For purposes of this section—

▲▲ **(5) Higher limit in case of collectively bargained plans.**—Not later than July 1, 1985, the Secretary shall by regulations provide for special account limits in the case of any qualified asset account under a welfare benefit fund [4]*maintained pursuant to* a collective bargaining agreement.

* * * * * * * * * * *

(7) Adjustments for existing excess reserves.—

(A) Increase in account limit.—The account limit for any of the first 4 taxable years to which this section applies shall be increased by the applicable percentage of any existing excess reserves.

(B) Applicable percentage.—For purposes of subparagraph (A)—

In the case of:	The applicable percentage is:
The first taxable year to which this section applies	80
The second taxable year to which this section applies	60
The third taxable year to which this section applies	40
The fourth taxable year to which this section applies	20

(C) Existing excess reserve.—For purposes of [5]*computing the increase under subparagraph (A) for any taxable year, the term "existing excess reserve" means the excess (if any) of—*

(i) the amount of assets set aside at the close of the first taxable year ending after July 18, 1984, for purposes described in subsection (a), over

(ii) the account limit determined under this section (without regard to this paragraph) for the taxable year for which such increase is being computed.

(D) Funds to which paragraph applies.—This paragraph shall apply only to a welfare benefit fund which, as of July 18, 1984, had assets set aside for purposes described in subsection (a).

⟦Footnote ¶3008-A continued⟧

▲ Matter in *italics* in Sec. 419A(f)(5), preceded by a triangle, added by section 1851(a)(13), '86 TRA, which struck out:

(3) "Higher limit in case of collectively bargained plans.—Not later than July 1, 1985, the Secretary shall by regulations provide for special account limits in the case of any qualified asset account under a welfare benefit fund established under a collective bargaining agreement."

Effective date (Sec. 1881, '86 TRA and Sec. 511(e), '84 TRA, as amended by Sec. 1851(a)(14), '86 TRA).—See above.

▲▲ Matter in *italics* in 419A(f)(5), preceded by two triangles, added by section 1851(a)(4), '86 TRA, which struck out:

(4) "established under"

Effective date (Sec. 1881, '86 TRA and Sec. 511(e), '84 TRA, as amended by Sec. 1851(a)(14), '86 TRA). See above.

Matter in *italics* in Sec. 419A(f)(7)(C), (D), (g)(3) and (h)(1) added by section 1851(a)(6)(A), (7), and (9), which struck out:

(5) "this paragraph, the term "existing excess reserve" means the excess (if any) of—

(i) the amount of assets set aside for purposes described in subsection (a) as of the close of the first taxable year ending after the date of the enactment of the Tax Reform Act of 1984, over

(ii) the account limit which would have applied under this section to such taxable year if this section had applied to such taxable year."

(g) Employer Taxed on Income of Welfare Benefit Fund in Certain Cases.—

(1) In general.—In the case of any welfare benefit fund which is not an organization described in paragraph (7), (9), (17), or (20) of section 501(c), the employer shall include in gross income for any taxable year an amount equal to such fund's deemed unrelated income for the fund's taxable year ending within the employer's taxable year.

* * * * * * * * * * *

(3) Coordination with section 419.—If any amount is included in the gross income of an employer for any taxable year under paragraph (1) with respect to any welfare benefit fund—

(A) the amount of the tax imposed by this chapter which is attributable to the amount so included shall be treated as a contribution paid to such welfare benefit fund on the last day of such taxable year, and

(B) the tax so attributable shall be treated as imposed on the fund for purposes of section 419(c)(4)(A).

(h) Aggregation Rules.—For purposes of this subpart—

(1) Aggregation of funds.—
⁶ *Mandated aggregation.—For purposes of subsections (c)(4), (d)(2), and (e)(2), all welfare benefit funds of an employer shall be treated as 1 fund.*

(B) Permissive aggregation for purposes not specified in subparagraph (A).—For purposes of this section (other than the provisions specified in subparagraph (A)), at the election of the employer, 2 or more welfare benefit funds of such employer may (to the extent not inconsistent with the purposes of this subpart and section 512) be treated as 1 fund.

* * * * * * * * * * *

[For official explanation, see Committee Reports, ¶4171.]

[¶3009]   CODE SEC. 422A.   INCENTIVE STOCK OPTIONS.

* * * * * * * * * * *

(b) Incentive Stock Option.—For purposes of this part, the term "incentive stock option" means an option granted to an individual for any reason connected with his employment by a corporation, if granted by the employer corporation or its parent subsidiary corporation, to purchase stock of any of such corporations, but only if—

(1) the option is granted pursuant to a plan which includes the aggregate number of shares which may be issued under options and the employees (or class of employees) eligible to receive options, and which is approved by the stockholders of the granting corporation within 12 months before or after the date such plan is adopted;

(2) such option is granted within 10 years from the date such plan is adopted, or the date such plan is approved by the stockholders, whichever is earlier;

(3) such option by its terms is not exercisable after the expiration of ten years from the date such option is granted;

(4) the option price is not less than the fair market value of the stock at the time such option is granted;

(5) such option by its terms is not transferable by such individual otherwise than by will or the laws of descent and distribution, and is exercisable, during his lifetime, only by him;

(6) *such individual, at the time the option is granted, does not own stock possessing more than 10 percent of the total combined voting power of all classes of stock of the employer corporation or of its parent or subsidiary corporation; and*

¹*(7) under the terms of the plan the aggregate fair market value (determined at the*

[Footnote ¶3008-A continued]

(6) "At the election of the employer, 2 or more welfare benefit funds of such employer may be treated as 1 fund."

Effective date (Sec. 1881, '86 TRA and Sec. 511(e), '84 TRA, as amended by Sec. 1851(a)(14), '86 TRA).—See above.

[Footnote ¶3009]   Matter in *italics* in Sec. 422A(b)(6), (7), (c)(1), and (4)—(7) added by section 321(a) and (b), '86 TRA, which struck out:

(1) "(7) such option by its terms is not exercisable while there is outstanding (within the meaning of subsection (c)(7)) any incentive stock option which was granted, before the granting of such option, to such individual to purchase stock in his employer corporation or in a corporation which (at the time of the granting of such option) is a parent or subsidiary corporation of the employer corporation, or in a predecessor corporation of any of such corporations; and

(8) in the case of an option granted after December 31, 1980, under the terms of the plan the aggregate fair market value (determined as of the time the option is granted) of the stock for which any employee may be granted incentive stock options in any calendar year (under all such plans of his employer corporation and its parent and subsidiary corporation) shall not exceed $100,000 plus any unused limit carryover to such year."

time the option is granted) of the stock with respect to which incentive stock options are exercisable for the 1st time by such individual during any calendar year (under all such plans of the individual's employer corporation and its parent and subsidiary corporations) shall not exceed $100,000.

(c) **Special rules.—**

(1) **Good faith efforts to value stock.—**If a share of stock is transferred pursuant to the exercise by an individual of an option which would fail to qualify as an incentive stock option under subsection (b) because there was a failure in an attempt, made in good faith, to meet the requirement of subsection (b)(4), the requirement of subsection (b)(4) shall be considered to have been met. To the extent provided in regulations by the Secretary, a similar rule shall apply for purposes of [2]*paragraph (7) of subsection (b).*

* * * * * * * * * * * *

(3) **Certain transfers by insolvent individuals.—**If an insolvent individual holds a share of stock acquired pursuant to his exercise of an incentvie stock option, and if such share is transferred to a trustee, receiver, or other similar fiduciary in any proceeding under title II or any other similar insolvency proceeding, neither such transfer, nor any other transfer of such share for the benefit of his creditors in such proceeding, shall constitute a disposition of such share for purposes of subsection (a)(1).[3]

[4]*(4)* **Permissible provisions.—**An option which meets the requirements of subsection (b) shall be treated as an incentive stock option even if—

(A) the employee may pay for the stock with stock of the corporation granting the option,

(B) the employee has a right to receive property at the time of exercise of the option, or

(C) the option is subject to any condition not inconsistent with the provisions of subsection (b).

Subparagraph (B) shall apply to a transfer of property (other than cash) only if section 83 applies to the property so transferred.

[5]*(5)* **Coordination with section 422 and 424.—**Sections 422 and 424 shall not apply to an incentive stock option.[6]

[7]*(6)* **10-percent shareholder rule.—**Subsection (b)(6) shall not apply if at the time such option is granted the option price is at least 110 percent of the fair market value of the stock subject to the option and such option by its terms is not exercisable after the expiration of 5 years from the date such option is granted.

[8]*(7)* **Special rule when disabled.—**For purposes of subsection (a)(2), in the case of an employee who is disabled (within the meaning of [9]*section 22(e)(3)*, the 3-month

---

[Footnote ¶3009 continued]

(2) "paragraph (8) of subsection (b) and paragraph (4) of this subsection"

(3) "(4) **Carryover of unused limit.—**

(A) In general.—If—

(i) $100,000 exceeds,

(ii) the aggregate fair market value (determined as of the time the option is granted) of the stock for which an employee was granted incentive stock options in any calendar year after 1980 (under all plans described in subsection (b) of his employer corporation and its parent and subsidiary corporations),

one-half of such excess shall be unused limit carryover to each of the 3 succeeding calendar years.

(B) Amount carried to each year.—The amount of the unused limit carryover from any calendar year which may be taken into account in any succeeding calendar year shall be the amount of such carryover reduced by the amount of such carryover which was used in prior calendar years.

(C) Special rules.—For purposes of subparagraph (B)—

(i) the amount of options granted during any calendar year shall be treated as first using up the $100,000 limitation of subsection (b)(8), and

(ii) then shall be treated as using up unused limit carryovers to such year in the order of the calendar years in which the carryovers arose."

(4) "(5)"

(5) "(6)"

(6) "(7) **Options outstanding.—**For purposes of subsection (b)(7), any incentive stock option shall be treated as outstanding until such option is exercised in full or expires by reason of lapse of time."

(7) "(8)"

(8) "(9)"

Effective date (Sec. 321(c), '86 TRA).—Applies to options granted after 12-31-86.

"section 22(e)(3)" in *italics* in Sec. 422A(c)(7) [former (9)] added by section 1847(b)(5), '86 TRA, which struck out:

period of subsection (a)(2) shall be 1 year.

[10] **(8)** **Fair market value.**—For purposes of this section, the fair market value of stock shall be determined without regard to any restriction other than a restriction which, by its terms, will never lapse.

[For official explanation, see Committee Reports, ¶3888; 4161.]

[¶3010] **CODE SEC. 423.** **EMPLOYEE STOCK PURCHASE PLANS.**

*   *   *   *   *   *   *   *   *   *   *   *

(b) **Employee Stock Purchase Plan.**—For purposes of this part, the term "employee stock purchase plan" means a plan which meets the following requirements:

*   *   *   *   *   *   *   *   *   *   *   *

(4) Under the terms of the plan, options are to be granted to all employees of any corporation whose employees are granted any of such options by reason of their employment by such corporation, except that there may be excluded—

    (A) employees who have been employed less than 2 years,

    (B) employees whose customary employment is 20 hours or less per week,

    (C) employees whose customary employment is for not more than 5 months in any calendar year, and

    (D) [1] *highly compensated employees (within the meaning of Sec. 414(q));*

*   *   *   *   *   *   *   *   *   *   *   *

[For official explanation, see Committee Reports, ¶3979.]

[¶3011] **CODE SEC. 441.** **PERIOD FOR COMPUTATION OF TAXABLE INCOME.**

*   *   *   *   *   *   *   *   *   *   *   *

(f) **Election of Year Consisting of 52-53 Weeks.**—

*   *   *   *   *   *   *   *   *   *   *   *

(2) **Special rules for 52-53 week year.**—

*   *   *   *   *   *   *   *   *   *   *   *

(B) Change in accounting period. In the case of a change from or to a taxable year described in paragraph (1)—

    (i) if such change results in a short period (within the meaning of section 443) of 359 days or more, or of less than 7 days, section 443(b) (relating to alternative tax computation shall not apply.

    (ii) if such change results in a short period of less than 7 days, such short period shall, for purposes of this subtitle, be added to and deemed a part of the following taxable year; and

    (iii) if such change results in a short period to which subsection (b) of section 443 applies, the taxable income for such short period shall be placed on an annual basis for purposes of such subsection by multiplying the gross income for such short period (minus the deductions allowed by this chapter for the short period, but only the adjusted amount of the deductions for personal exemptions as described in section 443(c)) by 365, by dividing the result by the number of days in the short period, [1]and the tax shall be the same part of the tax computed on the annual basis as the number of days in the short period is of 365 days.

[Footnote ¶3009 continued]

(9) "section 37(e)(3)"

Effective date (Sec. 1881, '86 TRA and Sec. 475(a), '84 TRA).—Applies to taxable years beginning after 12-31-83, and to carrybacks from such years.

Matter in *italics* in Sec. 422A(c)(8), added by section 321(b)(1)(B), '86 TRA, which struck out:

(10) "(10)"

Effective date (Sec. 321(c), '86 TRA).—Applies to options granted after 12-31-86.

[Footnote ¶3010] Matter in *italics* in Sec. 423(b)(4)(D) added by section 1114(b)(13), '86 TRA, which struck out:

(1) "officers, persons whose principal duties consist of supervising the work of other employees, or highly compensated employees;"

Effective date (Sec. 1114(c)(1), (4), '86 TRA).—Applies to years beginning after 12-31-86.

[Footnote ¶3011] Section 104(b)(6), '86 TRA, struck out from Sec. 441(f)(2)(B)(iii):

(1) "and by adding the zero bracket amount,"

Effective date (Sec. 151(a), '86 TRA).—Applies to taxable years beginning after 12-31-86.

(3) Special rule for partnerships, S corporations, and personal service corporations.—*The Secretary may by regulation provide terms and conditions for the application of this subsection to a partnership, S corporation, or personal service corporation (within the meaning of section 441(i)(2)).*

[2](4) **Regulations.**—The Secretary shall prescribe such regulations as he deems necessary for the application of this subsection.

* * * * * * * * * * *

(i) Taxable year of Personal Service Corporations.—

(1) In general.—*For purposes of this subtitle, the taxable year of any personal service corporation shall be the calendar year unless the corporation establishes, to the satisfaction of the Secretary, a business purpose for having a different period for its taxable year. For purposes of this paragraph, any deferral of income to shareholders shall not be treated as a business purpose.*

(2) Personal service corporation.—*For purposes of this subsection, the term "personal service corporation" has the meaning given such term by section 269A(b)(1), except that section 269A(b)(2) shall be applied*—
    (A) by substituting "any" for "more than 10 percent," and
    (B) by substituting "any" for "50 percent or more in value" in section 318(a)(2)(C).

[For official explanation, see Committee Reports, ¶3940.]

⟦¶3012⟧ CODE SEC. 443. RETURNS FOR A PERIOD OF LESS THAN 12 MONTHS.

* * * * * * * * * * *

(b) Computation of Tax on Change of Annual Accounting period.—

(1) General rule.—If a return is made under paragraph (1) of subsection (a), the taxable income for the short period shall be placed on an annual basis by multiplying the modified taxable income for such short period by 12, dividing the result by the number of months in the short period.[1] The tax shall be the same part of the tax computed on the annual basis as the number of months in the short period is of 12 months.

(2) Exception.—
    (A) Computation based on 12-month period.—If the taxpayer applies for the benefits of this paragraph and establishes the amount of his taxable income for the 12-month period described in subparagraph (B), computed as if that period were a taxable year and under the law applicable to that year, then the tax for the short period, computed under paragraph (1), shall be reduced to the greater of the following:
        (i) an amount which bears the same ratio to the tax computed on the taxable income for the 12-month period as the modified taxable income computed on the basis of the short period bears to the modified taxable income for the 12-month period; or
        (ii) the tax computed on the [2] modified taxable income for the short period[3].

⟦Footnote ¶3011 continued⟧

Matter in *italics* in Sec. 441(f)(3), (4), and (i) added by section 806(c)(1) and (d), '86 TRA, which struck out:
(2) "(3)"
Effective date (Sec. 806(e), '86 TRA).—
(1) Generally applies to taxable years beginning after 12-31-86.
(2) Change in accounting period.—In the case of any taxpayer required by the amendments made by this section to change its accounting period for any taxable year—
(A) such change shall be treated as initiated by the taxpayer,
(B) such change shall be treated as having been made with the consent of the Secretary, and
(C) with respect to any partner or shareholder of an S corporation which is required to include the items from more than 1 taxable year of the partnership or S corporation in any 1 taxable year, income in excess of expenses of such partnership or corporation for the short taxable year required by such amendments shall be taken into account ratably in each of the first 4 taxable years (including such short taxable year) beginning after 12-31-86, unless such partner or shareholder elects to include all such income in the short taxable year.
Subparagraph (C) shall apply to a shareholder of an S corporation only if such corporation was an S corporation for a taxable year beginning in 1986.
⟦Footnote ¶3012⟧ Section 104(b)(7), '86 TRA, struck out from Sec. 443(b)(1) and (2)(A)(ii):
(1) ", and adding the zero bracket amount"
(2) "sum of the"
(3) "plus the zero bracket amount"

* * * * * * * * * * * *

(d)   **Adjustment in Computing Minimum Tax** [4]*and* **Tax Preferences.**—[5]*If a return is made for a short period by reason of subsection (a)—*

(1)   the alternative minimum taxable income for the short period shall be placed on an annual basis by multiplying such amount by 12 and dividing the result by the number of months in the short period, and

(2)   the amount computed under paragraph (1) of section 55(a) shall bear the same relation to the tax computed on the annual basis as the number of months in the short period bears to 12.

* * * * * * * * * * * *

[For official explanation, see Committee Reports, ¶3931.]

〖¶3013〗   CODE SEC. 447.   METHOD OF ACCOUNTING FOR CORPORATIONS ENGAGED IN FARMING.

(a)   **General Rule.**—Except as otherwise provided by law, the taxable income from farming of—

(1)   a corporation engaged in the trade or business of farming, or

(2)   a partnership engaged in the trade or business of farming, if a corporation is a partner in such partnership,

shall be computed on an accrual method of accounting [1]. This section shall not apply to the trade or business of operating a nursery or sod farm or to the raising or harvesting of trees (other than fruit and nut trees).

(b)   [2]*Preproduction Period of Expenses.*—

For rules requiring capitalization of certain preproductive period of expenses, see section 263A.

* * * * * * * * * * * *

(g)   **Certain Annual Accrual Accounting Methods.**—

(1)   **In general.**—[3]*Notwithstanding subsection (a) or section 263(A), if—*

〖Footnote ¶3012 continued〗

Effective date (Sec. 151(a), '86 TRA).—Applies to taxable years beginning after 12-31-86.

Matter in *italics* in Sec. 443(d) added by section 701(e)(3), '86 TRA, which struck out:

(4)   "for"

(5)   "If a return is made for a short period by reason of subsection (a), then—

(1)   in the case of a taxpayer other than a corporation, the alternative minimum taxable income for the short period shall be placed on an annual basis by multiplying that amount by 12 and dividing the result by the number of months in the short period, and the amount computed under paragraph (1) of section 55(a) shall be the same part of the tax computed on the annual basis as the number of months in the short period is of 12 months; and

(2)   the $10,000 amount specified in section 56 (relating to minimum tax for tax preferences), modified as provided by section 58, shall be reduced to the amount which bears the same ratio to such specified amount as the number of days in the short period bears to 365."

Effective date (Sec. 701(f)(1), '86 TRA).—Generally applies to taxable years beginning after 12-31-86. For special rules, see footnote ¶2879.

〖Footnote ¶3013〗   Matter in *italics* in Sec. 447(a), (b), and (g)(1) added by section 803(b)(7), '86 TRA, which struck out:

(1)   "and with capitalization of preproductive period expenses described in subsection (b)"

(2)   "**Preproductive Period Expenses.**—

(1)   **In general.**—For purposes of this section, the term 'preproductive period expenses' means any amount which is attributable to crops, animals, or any other property having a crop or yield during the preproductive period of such property.

(2)   **Exceptions.**—Paragraph (1) shall not apply—

(A)   to taxes and interest, and

(B)   to any amount incurred on account of fire, storm, flood, or other casualty or on account of disease or drought.

(3)   **Preproductive period defined.**—For purposes of this subsection, the term "preproductive period" means—

(A)   in the case of property having a useful life of more than 1 year which will have more than 1 crop or yield, the period before the disposition of the first such marketable crop or yield, or

(B)   in the case of any other property, the period before such property is disposed of.

For purposes of this section, the use by the taxpayer in the trade or business of farming of any supply produced in such trade or business shall be treated as a disposition."

(3)   "If—"

Effective date (Sec. 803(d), '86 TRA).—Generally applies to costs incurred after 12-31-86, in taxable years ending after such date. For special rules, see footnote ¶2961-A.

(A)   for its 10 taxable years ending with its first taxable year beginning after December 31, 1975, a corporation or qualified partnership used an annual accrual method of accounting with respect to its trade or business of farming,

(B)   such corporation raises crops which are harvested not less than 12 months after planting, and

(C)   such corporation has used such method of accounting for all taxable years intervening between its first taxable year beginning after December 31, 1975, and the taxable year,

such corporation may continue to employ such method of accounting for the taxable year with respect to its trade or business of farming.

* * * * * * * * * * * *

[For official explanation, see Committee Reports, ¶3937.]

〔¶3014〕   CODE SEC. 448.   LIMITATION ON USE OF CASH METHOD OF AC-COUNTING.

(a)   **General Rule.**—Except as otherwise provided in this section, in the case of a—

(1)   C corporation,

(2)   partnership which has a C corporation as a partner, or

(3)   tax shelter,

taxable income shall not be computed under the cash receipts and disbursements method of accounting.

(b)   **Exceptions.**—

(1)   **Farming business.**—Paragraphs (1) and (2) of subsection (a) shall not apply to any farming business.

(2)   **Qualified personal service corporations.**—Paragraphs (1) and (2) of subsection (a) shall not apply to a qualified personal service corporation, and such a corporation shall be treated as an individual for purposes of determining whether paragraph (2) of subsection (a) applies to any partnership.

(3)   **Entities with gross receipts of not more than $5,000,000.**—Paragraphs (1) and (2) of subsection (a) shall not apply to any corporation or partnership for any taxable year if, for all prior taxable years beginning after December 31, 1985, such entity (or any predecessor) met the $5,000,000 gross receipts test of subsection (c).

(c)   **$5,000,000 Gross Receipts Test.**—For purposes of this section—

(1)   **In general.**—A corporation or partnership meets the $5,000,000 gross receipts test of this subsection for any prior taxable year if the average annual gross receipts of such entity for the 3-taxable-year period ending with such prior taxable year does not exceed $5,000,000.

(2)   **Aggregation rules.**—All persons treated as a single employer under subsection (a) or (b) of section 52 or subsection (m) or (o) of section 414 shall be treated as one person for purposes of paragraph (1).

(3)   **Special rules.**—For purposes of this subsection—

(A)   Not in existence for entire 3-year period.—If the entity was not in existence for the entire 3-year period referred to in paragraph (1), such paragraph shall be

〔Footnote ¶3014〕 Sec. 448 added by section 801(a), '86 TRA.

Effective date (Sec. 801(d), '86 TRA).—(1) Generally applies to taxable years beginning after 12-31-86.

(2)   Election to retain cash method for certain transactions.—A taxpayer may elect not to have the amendments made by this section apply to any loan or lease, or any transaction with a related party (within the meaning of section 267(b) of the '54 code, as in effect before the enactment of this Act), entered into on or before 9-25-85. Any election under the preceding sentence may be made separately with respect to each transaction.

(3)   Certain contracts.—The Amendments made by this section shall not apply to—

(A)   contracts for the acquisition or transfer of real property, and

(B)   contracts for services related to the acquisition or development of real property,

but only if such contracts were entered into before 9-25-85, and the sole element of the contract which has not been performed as of 9-25-85, is payment for such property or services.

(4)   Treatment of affiliated group providing engineering services.—Each member of an affiliated group of corporations (within the meaning of Sec. 1504(a) of the '86 code shall be allowed to use the cash receipts and disbursements method of accounting for any trade or business of providing engineering services with respect to taxable years ending after 12-31-86, if the common parent of such group—

(A)   was incorporated in the State of Delaware in 1970,

(B)   was the successor to a corporation that was incorporated in the State of Illinois in 1949, and

(C)   used the completed contract method of accounting for a substantial part of its income from the performance of engineering services.

applied on the basis of the period during which such entity (or trade or business) was in existence.

(B) Short taxable years.—Gross receipts for any taxable year of less than 12 months shall be annualized by multiplying the gross receipts for the short period by 12 and dividing the result by the number of months in the short period.

(C) Gross receipts.—Gross receipts for any taxable year shall be reduced by returns and allowances made during such year.

(d) **Definitions and Special Rules.**—For purposes of this section—

(1) **Farming business.—**

(A) In general.—The term "farming business" means the trade or business of farming (within the meaning of section 263A(e)(4)).

(B) Timber and ornamental trees.—The term "farming business" includes the raising, harvesting, or growing of trees to which section 263A(c)(5) applies.

(2) **Qualified personal service corporation.**—The term "qualified personal service corporation" means any corporation—

(A) substantially all of the activities of which involve the performance of services in the fields of health, law, engineering, architecture, accounting, actuarial science, performing arts, or consulting, and

(B) substantially all of the stock of which (by value) is held directly or indirectly by—

(i) employees performing services for such corporation in connection with the activities involving a field referred to in subparagraph (A),

(ii) retired employees who had performed such services for such corporation,

(iii) the estate of any individual described in clause (i) or (ii), or

(iv) any other person who acquired such stock by reason of the death of an individual described in clause (i) or (ii) (but only for the 2-year period beginning on the date of the death of such individual).

(3) **Tax shelter defined.**—The term "tax shelter" has the meaning given such term by section 461(i)(3) (determined after application of paragraph (4) thereof).

(4) **Special rules for application of paragraph (2).**—For purposes of paragraph (2)—

(A) community property laws shall be disregarded,

(B) stock held by a plan described in section 401(a) which is exempt from tax under section 501(a) shall be treated as held by an employee described in paragraph (2)(B)(i), and

(C) at the election of the common parent of an affiliated group (within the meaning of section 1504(a)), all members of such group may be treated as 1 taxpayer for purposes of paragraph (2)(B) if substantially all of the activities of all such members involve the performance of services in the same field described in paragraph (2)(A).

(5) **Special rule for services.**—In the case of any person using an accrual method of accounting with respect to amounts to be received for the performance of services by such person, such person shall not be required to accrue any portion of such amounts which (on the basis of experience) will not be collected. This paragraph shall not apply to any amount if interest is required to be paid on such amount or there is any penalty for failure to timely pay such amount.

(6) **Treatment of certain trusts subject to tax on unrelated business income.**—For purposes of this section, a trust subject to tax under section 511(b) shall be treated as a C corporation with respect to its activities constituting an unrelated trade or business.

(7) **Coordination with section 481.**—In the case of any taxpayer required by this section to change its method of accounting for any taxable year—

(A) such change shall be treated as initiated by the taxpayer,

(B) such change shall be treated as made with the consent of the Secretary, and

(C) the period for taking into account the adjustments under section 481 by reason of such change—

(i) except as provided in clause (ii), shall not exceed 4 years, and

(ii) in the case of a hospital, shall be 10 years.

[For official explanation, see Committee Reports, ¶3935.]

〔¶3015〕 CODE SEC 451. GENERAL RULE FOR TAXABLE YEAR OF INCLU-SION.

* * * * * * * * * * * *

(f) Special Rule for Utility Services.—

(1) *In general.*—*In the case of a taxpayer the taxable income of which is computed under an accrual method of accounting, any income attributable to the sale or furnishing of utility services to customers shall be included in gross income not later than the taxable year in which such services are provided to such customers.*

(2) *Definition and special rule.*—*For purposes of this subsection—*

(A) *Utility services.*—*The term "utility services" includes—*

(i) *the providing of electrical energy, water, or sewage disposal,*

(ii) *the furnishing of gas or steam through a local distribution system,*

(iii) *telephone or other communication services, and*

(iv) *the transporting of gas or steam by pipeline,*

(B) *Year in which services provided.*—*The taxable year in which services are treated as provided to customers shall not, in any manner, be determined by reference to—*

(i) *the period in which the customers meters are read, or*

(ii) *the period in which the taxpayer bills (or may bill) the customers for such service.*

(f) [should read (g)] Treatment of Interest on Frozen Deposits in Certain Financial Institutions.—

(1) *In general.*—*In the case of interest credited during any calendar year on a frozen deposit in a qualified financial institution, the amount of such interest includible in the gross income of a qualified individual shall not exceed the sum of—*

(A) *the net amount withdrawn by such individual from such deposit during such calendar year, and*

(B) *the amount of such deposit which is withdrawable as of the close of the taxable year (determined without regard to any penalty for premature withdrawals of a time deposit).*

(2) *Interest tested each year.*—*Any interest not included in gross income by reason of paragraph (1) shall be treated as credited in the next calendar year.*

(3) *Deferral of interest deduction.*—*No deduction shall be allowed to any qualified financial institution for interest not includible in gross income under paragraph (1) until such interest is includible in gross income.*

(4) *Frozen deposit.*—*For purposes of this subsection, the term "frozen deposit" means any deposit if, as of the close of the calendar year, any portion of such deposit may not be withdrawn because of—*

(A) *the bankruptcy or insolvency of the qualified financial institution (or threat thereof), or*

(B) *any requirement imposed by the State in which such institution is located by reason of the bankruptcy or insolvency (or threat thereof) of 1 or more financial institutions in the State.*

〔**Footnote ¶3015**〕 Matter in *italics* in Sec. 451(f) added by section 821(a), '86 TRA.

Effective date (Sec. 821(b), '86 TRA.—(1) Generally applies to taxable years beginning after 12-31-86.

(2) Change in method of accounting.—If a taxpayer is required by the amendments made by this section to change its method of accounting for any taxable year—

(A) such change shall be treated as initiated by the taxpayer,

(B) such change shall be treated as having been made with consent of the Secretary, and

(C) the adjustments under section 481 of the '54 Code by reason of such change shall be taken into account ratably over a period no longer than the first 4 taxable years beginning after 12-31-86,

(3) Special rule for certain cycle billing.—If a taxpayer for any taxable year beginning before 8-16-86, for purposes of chapter 1 of the '86 Code took into account income from services described in section 451(f) of such Code (as added by subsection (a)) on the basis of the period in which the customers' meters were read, then such treatment for such year shall be deemed to be proper.

Matter in *italics* in Sec. 415(f) [should read (g)] added by section 905(b), '86 TRA.

Effective date (Sec. 905(c), '86 TRA.—(1) Generally applies to taxable years beginning after 12-31-82.

(2) Special rules for subsection (b).—

(A) The amendment made by subsection (b) shall apply to taxable years beginning after 12-31-82, and before 1-1-87, only if the qualified individual elects to have such amendment apply for all such taxable years.

(B) In the case of interest attributable to the period beginning 1-1-83, and ending 12-31-87, the interest deduction of financial institutions shall be determined without regard to paragraph (3) of section 451(f) [should read (g)] of the '86 Code (as added by subsection (b)).

(5) *Other definitions.—For purposes of this subsection, the terms "qualified individual", "qualified financial institution", and "deposit" have the same respective meanings as when used in section 165(1).*

[For official explanation, see Committee Reports, ¶3941.]

[¶3016]   CODE SEC. 453.   INSTALLMENT METHOD.

* * * * * * * * * * * * *

(f) **Definitions and Special Rules.**—For purposes of this section—

¹(1)   *Related person.*—*Except for purposes of subsection (g) and (h), the term "related person" means—*

(A)   *a person whose stock would be attributed under section 318(a) (other than paragraph (4) thereof) to the person first disposing of the property, or*

(B)   *a person who bears a relationship described in section 267(b) to the person first disposing of the property.*

* * * * * * * * * * * *

(8)   *Payments to be received defined.—The term "payment to be received" includes—*

(A)   the aggregate amount of all payments which are not contingent as to amount, and

(B)   the fair market value of all payments which are contingent as to amount.

(g)   **Sale of Depreciable Property to** ²*Controlled* **Entity.—**

³(1)   *In general.—In the case of an installment sale of depreciable property between related persons (within the meaning of section 1239(b))—*

(A)   *subsection (a) shall not apply, and*

(B)   *for purposes of this title—*

(i)   *except as provided in clause (ii), all payments to be received shall be treated as received in the year of the disposition, and*

(ii)   *in the case of any payments which are contingent as to amount but with respect to which the fair market value may not be reasonably ascertained—*

(I)   *the basis shall be recovered ratably, and*

(II)   *the purchaser may not increase the basis of any property acquired in such sale by any amount before such time as the seller includes such amount in income.*

* * * * * * * * * * * *

(h)   **Use of Installment Method by Shareholders in** ⁴*Certain* **Liquidations.—**

(1)   **Receipt of obligations not treated as receipt of payment.—**

⁵(A)   *In general.—If, in a liquidation to which section 331 applies, the shareholder receives (in exchange for the shareholder's stock) an installment obligation acquired in respect of a sale or exchange by the corporation during the 12-month period beginning on the date a plan of complete liquidation is adopted and the liquidation is completed during such 12-month period, then, for purposes of this section, the receipt of*

[**Footnote ¶3016**]   Matter in *italics* in Sec. 453(f)(1), (8), and (g) added by section 642(a)(1)(D), (3), (b)(1) and (2), '86 TRA, which struck out:

(1)   **"(1)   Related person.**—Except for purposes of subsections (g) and (h), the term 'related person' means a person whose stock would be attributed under section 318(a) (other than paragraph (4) thereof) to the person first disposing of the property."

(2)   **"80-Percent Owner"**

(3)   **"(1)   In general.**—In the case of an installment sale of depreciable property between related persons within the meaning of section 1239(b), subsection (a) shall not apply, and, for purposes of this title, all payments to be received shall be deemed received in the year of the disposition."

Effective date (Sec. 642(c), '86 TRA).—(1) Generally applies to sales after the date of enactment of this Act, in taxable years ending after such date.

(2)   Traditional rule for binding contracts.—The amendments made by this section shall not apply to sales made after 8-14-86, which are made pursuant to a binding contract in effect on 8-14-86, and at all times thereafter.

Matter in *italics* in Sec. 453(h) and (1)(A), (B) and (E) added by section 631(e)(8), '86 TRA, which struck out:

(4)   **"Section 337"**

(5)   "(A)   In general.—If, in connection with a liquidation to which section 337 applies, in a transaction to which section 331 applies the shareholder receives (in exchange for the shareholder's stock) an installment obligation acquired in respect of a sale or exchange by the corporation during the 12-month period set forth in section 337(a), then, for purposes of this section, the receipt of payments under such obligation (but not the receipt of such obligation) by the shareholder shall be treated as the receipt of payment for the stock.

(B)   Obligations attributable to sale of inventory must result from bulk sale.—Subparagraph (A) shall not apply to an installment obligation described in section 337(b)(1)(D) unless such obligation is also described in section 337(b)(2)(B)."

payments under such obligation (but not the receipt of such obligation) by the share-holder shall be treated as the receipt of payment for the stock.

(B) Obligations attributable to sale of inventory must result from bulk sale.—Subparagraph (A) shall not apply to an installment obligation acquired in respect of a sale or exchange of—

(i) stock in trade of the corporation,

(ii) other property of a kind which would properly be included in the inventory of the corporation if on hand at the close of the taxable year, and

(iii) property held by the corporation primarily for sale to customers in the ordinary course of its trade or business,

unless such sale or exchange is to one person and involves substantially all of such property attributable to a trade or business of the corporation.

* * * * * * * * * * *

(D) Coordination with subsection (e)(1)(A).—For purposes of subsection (e)(1) (A), disposition of property by the corporation shall be treated also as disposition of such property by the shareholder.

[6](E) *Sales by liquidating subsidiaries.—For purposes of subparagraph (A), in the case of a controlling corporate shareholder (within the meaning of section 368(c)(1)) of a selling corporation, an obligation acquired in respect of a sale or exchange by the selling corporation shall be treated as so acquired by such controlling corporate share-holder. The preceding sentence shall be applied successively to each controlling corporate shareholder above such controlling corporate shareholder.*

* * * * * * * * * * *

(i) **Recognition of Recapture Income in Year of Disposition.—**

(1) **In general.—**In the case of any installment sale of property to which subsection (a) applies—

(A) nonwithstanding subsection (a), any recapture income shall be recognized in the year of the disposition and

(B) any gain in excess of the recapture income shall be taken into account under the installment method.

(2) **Recapture income.—**For purposes of paragraph 1, the term "recapture income" means, with respect to any installment sale, the aggregate amount which would be treated as ordinary income under section 1245 or 1250 *(or so much of section 751 as*

[Footnote ¶3016 continued]

(6) "(E) Sales by liquidating subsidiary.—For purposes of subparagraph (A), in any case to which section 337(c)(3) applies, an obligation acquired in respect of a sale or exchange by the selling corporation shall be treated as so acquired by the corporation distributing the obligation to the shareholder."

Effective date (Sec. 633(a) '86 TRA).—(a) Generally applies to—

(1) any distribution in complete liquidation, and any sale or exchange, made by a corporation after 7-31-86, unless such corporation is completely liquidated before 1-1-87,

(2) any transaction described in section 338 '86 Code for which the acquisition date occurs after 12-31-86, and

(3) any distribution (not in complete liquidation) made after 12-31-86.

For special and transitional rules, see ¶2023.

Matter in *italics* in Sec. 453(i)(2) added by 1809(c), 86 TRA.

Effective date (Sec. 1881, '86 TRA and section 112(b), 'TRA).—(1) Generally applies with respect to dispositions made after 6-6-84.

(2) Exception.—The amendments made by this section shall not apply with respect to any disposition conducted pursuant to a contract which was binding on 3-22-84, and at all times thereafter.

(3) Special rule for certain disposition before October 1, 1984.—The amendments made by this section shall not apply to any disposition before 10-1-84, of all or substantially all of the personal property of a cable television business pursuant to a written offer delivered by the seller on 6-30-84, but only if the last payment under the installment contract is due no later than 10-1-89.

Sec. 453(j) [should read (k)] added by section 812(a), '86 TRA.

Effective date (Sec. 812(c), '86 TRA).—(1) Generally applies to taxable years beginning after 12-31-86.

(2) Change in method of accounting.—In the case of any taxpayer who made sales under a revolving credit plan and was on the installment method under section 453 or 453A '86 Code for such taxpayer's last taxable year beginning before 1-1-87, the amendments made by this section shall be treated as a change in method of accounting for its 1st taxable year beginning after 12-31-86, and—

(A) such change shall be treated as initiated by the taxpayer,

(B) such change shall be treated as having been made with the consent of the Secretary and

(C) the period for taking into account adjustments under section 481 of such Code by reason of such change shall not exceed 4 years.

Code §453(i)(2) ¶3016

relates to section 1245 or 1250) for the taxable year of the disposition if all payments to be received were received in the taxable year of disposition.

* * * * * * * * * * * *

(j)   [should read (k)] Current Inclusion in Case of Revolving Credit Plans, Etc.—In the case of—

(1)   any disposition of personal property under a revolving credit plan, or

(2)   any installment obligation arising out of a sale of—

(A)   stock or securities which are traded on an established securities market, or

(B)   to the extent provided in regulations, property (other than stock or securities) of a kind regularly traded on an established market,

subsection (a) and section 453A shall not apply, and, for purposes of this title, all payments to be received shall be treated as received in the year of disposition. The Secretary may provide for the application of this subsection in whole or in part for transactions in which the rules of this subsection otherwise would be avoided through the use of related parties, pass-thru entities, or intermediaries.

[For official explanation, see Committee Reports, ¶3917; ¶3922; ¶3941; ¶4143.]

〔¶3016-A〕 CODE SEC. 453A. INSTALLMENT METHOD FOR DEALERS IN PERSONAL PROPERTY.

(a)   General Rule.—

* * * * * * * * * * * *

(2)   Total contract price.—For purposes of paragraph (1), the total contract price of all sales of personal property on the installment plan includes the amount of carrying charges or interest which is determined with respect to such sales and is added on the books of account of the seller to the established cash selling price of such property.[1]

* * * * * * * * * * * *

(c)   Cross Reference.—

For disallowance of use of installment method for certain obligations, see section 453(j).

[For official explanation, see Committee Reports, ¶3941.]

〔¶3016-B〕 CODE SEC. 453B. GAIN OR LOSS ON DISPOSITION OF INSTALLMENT OBLIGATIONS.

* * * * * * * * * * * *

[1]*(d)   Effect of Distribution in Liquidations to Which Section 322 Applies.—If—*

〔Footnote ¶3016-A〕   Matter in *italics* in Sec. 453(a)(2) and (c) added by section 812(b), '86 TRA, which struck out:

"(1)   "This paragraph shall not apply with respect to sales of personal property under a revolving credit type plan."

Effective date (Sec. 812(c), '86 TRA).—Generally applies to taxable years beginning after 12-31-86. For change in method of accounting, see footnote ¶3016.

〔Footnote ¶3016-B〕   Matter in *italics* in Sec. 435B(d) added by section 631(e)(9), '86 TRA, which struck out:

(1)   "**(d)   Effect of Distribution in Certain Liquidations.—**

(1)   Liquidations to which section 322 applies,—If—

(A)   an installment obligation is distributed in a liquidation to which section 332 (relating to complete liquidations of subsidiaries) applies, and

(B)   the basis of such obligation in the hands of the distributee is determined under section 334(b)(1),

then no gain or loss with respect to the distribution of such obligation shall be recognized by the distributing corporation.

(2)   Liquidations to which section 337 applies.—If—

(A)   an installment obligation is distributed by a corporation in the course of a liquidation, and

(B)   under section 337 (relating to gain or loss on sales or exchanges in connection with certain liquidations) no gain or loss would have been recognized to the corporation if the corporation had sold or exchanged such installment obligation on the day of such distribution,

then no gain or loss shall be recognized to such corporation by reason of such distribution. The preceding sentence shall not apply to the extent that under subsection (a) gain to the distributing corporation would be considered as gain to which section 341(f), 617(d)(1), 1245(a), 1250(a), 1252(a), 1254(a) or 1276(a) applies. In the case of any installment obligation which would have met the requirements of subparagraphs (A) and (B) of the first sentence of this paragraph but for section 337(f), gain shall be recognized to such corporation by reason of such distribution only to the extent gain would have been recognized under section 337(f) if such corporation had sold or exchanged such installment obligation on the date of such distribution"

Effective date (Sec. 633(a), '86 TRA).—(a) Generally applies to—

(1)   any distribution in complete liquidation, and any sale or exchange, made by a corporation after 7-31-86, such corporation is completely liquidated before 1-1-87,

(2)   any transaction described in section 338 '86 Code for which the acquisition date occurs after 12-31-86,

(3)   any distribution (not in complete liquidation) made after 12-31-86.

For special rules and transitional rules see ¶2023.

(1) an installment obligation is distributed in a liquidation to which section 332 (relating to complete liquidations of subsidiaries) applies, and

(2) the basis of such obligation in the hands of the distributee is determined under section 334(b)(1),

then no gain or loss with respect to the distribution of such obligation shall be recognized by the distributing corporation.

(e)   Life Insurance Companies.—

* * * * * * * * * * *

(2)   Special rule where life insurance company elects to treat income as not related to insurance business.—Paragraph (1) shall not apply to any transfer or deemed transfer of an installment obligation if the life insurance company elects (at such time and in such manner as the Secretary may by regulations prescribe) to determine its life insurance company taxable income—

(A) by returning the income on such installment obligation under the installment method prescribed in section 453, and

(B) as if such income were an item attributable to a noninsurance business (as defined in ²*section 806(b)(3)*).

* * * * * * * * * * *

(g)   Transfers Between Spouses or Incident to Divorce.—In the case of any transfer described in subsection (a) of section 1041 *(other than a transfer in trust)*—

(1) subsection (a) of this section shall not apply; and

(2) the same tax treatment with respect to the transferred installment obligation shall apply to the transferee as would have applied to the transferor.

[For official explanation, see Committee Reports, ¶3917; 3958; 4161.]

〖¶3016-C〗 CODE SEC. 453C.   CERTAIN INDEBTEDNESS TREATED AS PAYMENT ON INSTALLMENT OBLIGATIONS.

(a)   General Rule.—For purposes of sections 453 and 453A, if a taxpayer has allocable installment indebtedness for any taxable year, such indebtedness—

(1) shall be allocated on a pro rate basis to any applicable installment obligation of the taxpayer which—

(A) arises in such taxable year, and

(B) is outstanding as of the close of such taxable year, and

〖Footnote ¶3016-B continued〗

Matter in *italics* in Sec. 453B(e)(2)(B) added by section 1011(b)(1), '86 TRA, which struck out:

(2) "section 806(c)(3)"

Effective date (Sec. 1011(c), '86 TRA.—Applies to taxable years beginning after 12-31-86.

Matter in *italics* in Sec. 453B(g) added by section 1842(c), '86 TRA.

Effective date (Sec. 1881, '86 TRA and Sec. 421(d), '84 TRA).—(1) Generally applies to transfers after 7-18-84 in taxable years ending after such date.

(2)   Election to have amendments apply to transfers after 1983.—If both spouses or former spouses make an election under this paragraph, the amendments made by this section shall apply to all transfers made by such spouses (or former spouses) after 12-31-83.

(3)   Exception for transfers pursuant to existing decrees.—Except in the case of an election under paragraph (2), the amendments made by this section shall not apply to transfers under any instrument in effect on or before 7-18-84 unless both spouses (or former spouses) elect to have such amendments apply to transfers under such instrument.

(4)   Election.—Any election under paragraph (2) or (3) shall be made in such manner, at such time, and subject to such conditions, as the Secretary of the Treasury or his delegate may by regulations prescribe.

〖Footnote ¶3016-C〗 Sec. 453C added by section 811(a), '86 TRA.

Effective date (Sec. 811(c), '86 TRA).—(1) Generally applies to taxable years ending after 12-31-86, with respect to dispositions after 2-28-86.

(2)   Exception for certain sales of property by a manufacturer to a dealer.—

(A)   In general.—The amendments made by this section shall not apply to any installment obligation arising from the disposition of tangible personal property by a manufacturer (or any affiliate) to a dealer if—

(i)   the dealer is obligated to pay on such obligation only when the dealer resells (or rents) the property,

(ii)   the manufacturer has the right to repurchase the property at a fixed (or ascertainable) price after no later than the 9-month period beginning with the date of the sale, and

(iii)   such disposition is in a taxable year with respect to which the requirements of subparagraph (B) are met.

(B)   Receivables must be at least 50 percent of total sales.—

(i)   In general.—The requirements of this subparagraph are met with respect to any taxable year if for such taxable year and the preceding taxable year the aggregate face amount of installment obligations described in subparagraph (A) is at least 50 percent of the total sales to dealers giving rise to such obligations.

(2) shall be treated as a payment received on such obligation as of the close of such taxable year.

(b) Allocable Installment Indebtedness.—For purposes of this section—

    (1) In general.—The term "allocable installment indebtedness" means, with respect to any taxable year, the excess (if any) of—

        (A) the installment percentage of the taxpayer's average quarterly indebtedness for such taxable year, over

        (B) the aggregate amount treated as allocable installment indebtedness with respect to applicable installment obligations which—

            (i) are outstanding as of the close of such taxable year, but

            (ii) did not arise during such taxable year.

⟦Footnote ¶3016-C continued⟧

(ii) Taxpayer must fail for 2 consecutive years.—A taxpayer shall be treated as failing to meet the requirements of clause (i) only if the taxpayer fails to meet the 50-percent test for both the taxable year and the preceding taxable year.

(C) Transition rule.—An obligation issued before the date of the enactment of this Act shall be treated as described in subparagraph (A) if, within 60 days after such date, the taxpayer modifies the terms of such obligation to conform to the requirements of subparagraph (A).

(D) Application with other obligations.—In applying section 453C of the '86 Code to any installment obligations to which the amendments made by this section apply, obligations described in subparagraph (A) shall not be treated as applicable installment obligations (within the meaning of section 453C(e)(1) of such Code).

(E) Other requirements.—This paragraph shall apply only if the taxpayer meets the requirements of subparagraphs (A) and (B) for its first taxable year beginning after the date of the enactment of this Act.

(3) Exception for certain obligations.—In applying the amendments made by this section to any installment obligation of a corporation incorporated on 1-13-28, the following indebtedness shall not be taken into account in determining the allocable installment indebtedness of such corporation under section 453C of the '86 Code (as added by this section):

(A) 12⅝ percent subordinated debentures with a total face amount of $175,000,000 issued pursuant to a trust indenture dated as of 9-1-85.

(B) A revolving credit term loan in the maximum amount of $130,000,000 made pursuant to a revolving credit and security agreement dated as of 9-6-85, payable in various stages with final payment due on 8-31-92.

This paragraph shall also apply to indebtedness which replaces indebtedness described in this paragraph if su8ch indebtedness does not exceed the amount and maturity of the indebtedness it replaces.

(4) Special rule for residential condominium project.—For purposes of applying the amendments made by this section, the term applicable installment obligation (within the meaning of section 453(C)(e)(1) of the '86 Code shall not include any obligation arising in connection with sales from a residential condominium project—

(A) for which a contract to purchase land for the project was entered into at least 5 years before the date of the enactment of this Act,

(B) with respect to which land for the project was purchased before 9-26-85,

(C) with respect to which building permits for the project were obtained, and construction commenced, before 9-26-85,

(D) in conjunction with which not less than 80 units of low-income housing are deeded to a tax-exempt organization designated by a local government, and

(E) with respect to which at least $1,000,000 of expenses were incurred before 9-26-85.

(D) the portion of the net adjustment taken into account in the 1st taxable year of the taxpayer ending after 12-31-86, shall not exceed 15 percent of such adjustment, and

(E) the remaining portion of such adjustment shall be taken into account ratably in the 2nd, 3rd, and 4th years ending after 12-31-86.

(5) Special rule for qualified buyout.—The amendments made by this section shall apply for taxable years ending after 12-31-91, to a corporation if—

(A) such corporation was incorporated on 5-25-84, for the purpose of acquiring all of the stock of another corporation,

(B) such acquisition took place on 10-23-85,

(C) in connection with such acquisition the corporation incurred indebtedness of approximately $151,000,000, and

(D) substantially all of the stock of the corporation is owned directly on indirectly by employees of the corporation the stock of which was acquired on 10-23-85.

(6) Special rule for sales of real property by dealers.—In the case of installment obligations arising from the sale of real property in the ordinary course of the trade or business of the taxpayer, any gain attributable to allocable installment indebtedness allocated to any such installment obligations which arise (or are deemed to arise)—

(A) in the 1st taxable year of the taxpayer ending after 12-31-86, shall be taken into account ratably over the 3 taxable years beginning with such 1st taxable year, and

(B) in the 2nd taxable year of the taxpayer ending after 12-31-86, shall be taken into account ratably over the 2 taxable years beginning with such 2nd taxable year.

(7) Special rule for sales of personal property by dealers.—In the case of installment obligations arising from the sale of personal property in the ordinary course of the trade or business of the taxpayer, solely for purposes of determining the time for payment of tax and interest payable with respect to such tax—

(A) any increase in tax imposed by chapter 1 of the '86 Code for the 1st taxable year of the taxpayer ending after 12-31-86, by reason of the amendments made by this section shall be treated as imposed ratably over the 3 taxable years beginning with such 1st taxable year, and

(B) any increase in tax imposed by such chapter 1 for the 2nd taxable year of the taxpayer ending after 12-31-86, (determined without regard to subparagraph (A)) by reason of the amendments made by this section shall be treated as imposed ratably over the 2 taxable years beginning with such 2nd taxable year.

(2) **Installment percentage.**—The term "installment percentage" means the percentage (not in excess of 100 percent) determined by dividing—

(A) the face amount of all applicable installment obligations of the taxpayer outstanding as of the close of the taxable year, by

(B) the sum of—

(i) the aggregate adjusted bases of all assets not described in clause (ii) held as of the close of the taxable year, and

(ii) the face amount of all installment obligations outstanding as of such time.

For purposes of subparagraph (B)(i), a taxpayer may elect to compute the aggregate adjusted bases of all assets using the deduction for depreciation which is used in computing earnings and profits under section 312(k).

(3) **Special rules for personal use property.**—For purposes of this subsection—

(A) for purposes of paragraph (2)(B), there shall not be taken into account any personal use property (within the meaning of section 1275(b)(3)) held by an individual or any installment obligation arising from the sale of such property, and

(B) for purposes of computing the taxpayer's average quarterly indebtedness under paragraph (1)(A), thee shall not be taken into account any indebtedness with respect to which substantially all of the property securing such indebtedness is property described in subparagraph (A).

(4) **Special rule for casual sales.**—If the taxpayer has no applicable installment obligations described in subclause (I) or (II) of subsection (e)(1)(A)(i) outstanding at any time during the taxable year, then the taxpayer's allocable installment indebtedness for such taxable yer shall be computed by using the taxpayer's indebtedness as of the close of such taxable year in lieu of the taxpayer's average quarterly indebtedness.

(c) **Treatment of Subsequent Payments.**—

(1) **Payments treated as receipt of tax paid amounts.**—If any amount is treated as received under subsection (a) (after application of subsection (d)(2)) with respect to any applicable installment obligation, subsequent payments received on such obligation shall not be taken into account for purposes of sections 453 and 453A to the extent that the aggregate amount of such subsequent payments does not exceed the aggregate amount treated as received on such obligation under subsection (a).

(2) **Reduction of allocable installment indebtedness.**—For purposes of applying subsection (b)(1)(B) for the taxable year in which any payment to which paragraph (1) of this subsection applies was received (and for any subsequent taxable year), the allocable installment indebtedness with respect to the applicable installment obligation shall be reduced (but not below zero) by the amount of such payment not taken into account by reason of paragraph (1).

(d) **Limitation Based on Total Contract Price.**—

(1) **In general.**—The amount treated as received under subsection (a) (after application of paragraph (2)) with respect to any applicable installment obligation for any taxable year shall not exceed the excess (if any) of—

(A) the total contract price, over

(B) any portion of the total contract price received under the contract before the close of such taxable year—

(i) including amounts so treated under subsection (a) for all preceding taxable years (after application of paragraph (2)), but

(ii) not including amounts not taken into account by reason of subsection (c).

[Footnote ¶3016-C continued]

(8) Treatment of certain installment obligations.—Notwithstanding the amendments made by subtitle B of title III, gain with respect to installment payments received pursuant to notes issued in accordance with a note agreement dated as of 8-29-80,

(A) such note agreement was executed pursuant to an agreement of purchase and sale dated 4-25-80,

(B) more than $\frac{1}{2}$ of the installment payments of the aggregate principal of such notes have been received by 8-29-86, and

(C) the last installment payment of the principal of such notes is due 8-29-89,

shall be taxed at a rate of 28 percent.

Code §453C(d)(1) ¶3016-C

(2) **Excess allocable installment indebtedness.**—If, after application of paragraph (1), the allocable installment indebtedness for any taxable year exceeds the amount which may be allocated to applicable installment obligations arising in (and outstanding as of the close of) such taxable year, such excess shall—

(A) subject to the limitations of paragraph (1), be allocated to applicable installment obligations outstanding as of the close of such taxable year which arose in preceding taxable years, beginning with applicable installment obligations arising in the earliest preceding taxable year, and

(B) be treated as a payment under subsection (a)(2).

(e) **Definitions and Special Rules.**—For purposes of this section—

(1) **Applicable installment obligation.**—

(A) **In general.**—The term "applicable installment obligation" means any obligation—

(i) which arises from the disposition—

(I) after February 28, 1986, of personal property under the installment method by a person who regularly sells or otherwise disposes of personal property of the same type on the installment plan,

(II) after February 28, 1986, of real property under the installment method which is held by the taxpayer for sale to customers in the ordinary course of the taxpayer's trade or business, or

(III) after August 16, 1986, of real property under the installment method which is property used in the taxpayer's trade or business or property held for the production of rental income, but only if the sales price of such property exceeds $150,000 (determined after application of the rule under the last sentence of section 1274(c)(3)(A)(ii)), and

(ii) which is held by the seller or a member of the same affiliated group (within the meaning of section 1504(a), but without regard to section 1504(b)) as the seller.

(B) **Exception for personal use and farm property.**—The term "applicable installment obligation" shall not include any obligation which arises from the disposition—

(i) by an individual of personal use property (within the meaning of section 1275(b)(3)), or

(ii) of any property used or produced in the trade or business of farming (within the meaning of section 2032A(e)(4)or (5)).

(2) **Aggregation rules.**—For purposes of this section, all persons treated as a single employer under section 52 shall be treated as 1 taxpayer. The Secretary shall prescribe regulations for the treatment under this section of transactions between such persons.

(3) **Aggregation of obligations.**—The Secretary may by regulations provide that all (or any portion of) applicable installment obligations of a taxpayer may be treated as 1 obligation.

(4) **Exception for sales of timeshares and residential lots.**—

(A) **In general.**—If a taxpayer elects the application of this paragraph, this section shall not apply to any installment obligation which—

(i) arises from a sale in the ordinary course of the taxpayer's trade or business to an individual of—

(I) a timeshare right to use or a timeshare ownership interest in residential real property for not more than 6 weeks, or a right to use specified campgrounds for recreational purposes, or

(II) any residential lot but only if the taxpayer (or any related person) is not to make any improvements with respect to such lot, and

(ii) which is not guaranteed by any person other than an individual.

For purposes of clause (i)(I), a timeshare right to use (or timeshare ownership interest in) property held by the spouse, children, grandchildren, or parents of an individual shall be treated as held by such individual.

(B) **Interest on deferred tax.**—If subparagraph (A) applies to any installment obligation, interest shall be paid on the portion of any tax for any taxable year (determined without regard to any deduction allowable for such interest) which is attributable to the receipt of payments on such obligation in such year (other than payments received in the taxable year of the sale). Such interest shall be computed for the period from the date of the sale to the date on which the payment is received using the applicable Federal rate under section 1274 (without regard to subsection (d)(2) or (3) thereof) in effect at the time of the sale, compounded semiannually.

(C) Time for payment.—Any interest payable under this paragraph with respect to a payment shall be treated as an addition to tax for the taxable year in which the payment is received, except that the amount of such interest shall be taken into account in computing the amount of any deduction allowable to the taxpayer for interest paid or accrued during such taxable year.

(5) **Regulations.**—The Secretary shall prescribe regulations as may be necessary to carry out the purposes of this section, including regulations—

(A) disallowing the use of the installment method in whole or in part for transactions in which the rules of this section otherwise would be avoided through the use of related parties, pass-through entities, or intermediaries,

(B) providing for the proper treatment of reserves (including consistent treatment with assets held in the reserves), and

(C) providing that subsection (b)(4) shall not apply where necessary to prevent the avoidance of the application of this section.

[For official explanation, see Committee Reports, ¶3941.]

[¶3017] CODE SEC. 457. DEFERRED COMPENSATION PLANS [1]*OF STATE AND LOCAL GOVERNMENTS AND TAX-EXEMPT ORGANIZATIONS.*

(a) *Year of Inclusion in Gross Income.—In the case of a participant in an eligible deferred compensation plan, any amount of compensation deferred under the plan, and any income attributable to the amounts so deferred, shall be includible in gross income only for the taxable year in which such compensation or other income is paid or otherwise made available to the participant or other beneficiary.*

(b) *Eligible Deferred Compensation Plan Defined.—For purposes of this section, the term "eligible deferred compensation plan" means a plan established and maintained by an eligible employer—*

(1) *in which only individuals who perform service for the employer may be participants,*

(2) *which provides that (except as provided in paragraph (3)) the maximum amount*

[Footnote ¶3017] Matter in *italics* in Sec. 457 added by section 1107(a), '86 TRA, which struck out:

(1) **"WITH RESPECT TO SERVICE FOR STATE AND LOCAL GOVERNMENTS.**

(a) **Year of Inclusion in Gross Income.**—In the case of a participant in an eligible State deferred compensation plan, any amount of compensation deferred under the plan, and any income attributable to the amounts so deferred, shall be includible in gross income only for the taxable year in which such compensation or other income is paid or otherwise made available to the participant or other beneficiary.

(b) **Eligible State Deferred Compensation Plan Defined.**—For purposes of this section, the term "eligible State deferred compensation plan" means a plan established and maintained by a State—

(1) in which only individuals who perform service for the State may be participants,

(2) which provides that (except as provided in paragraph (3)) the maximum that may be deferred under the plan for the taxable year shall not exceed the lesser of—

(A) $7,500, or

(B) 33⅓ percent of the participant's includible compensation,

(3) which may provide that, for 1 or more of the participant's last 3 taxable years ending before he attains normal retirement age under the plan, the ceiling set forth in paragraph (2) shall be the lesser of—

(A) $15,000, or

(B) the sum of—

(i) the plan ceiling established for purposes of paragraph (2) for the taxable year (determined without regard to this paragraph), plus

(ii) so much of the plan ceiling established for purposes of paragraph (2) for taxable years before the taxable year as has not theretofore been used under paragraph (2) or this paragraph,

(4) which provides that compensation will be deferred for any calendar month only if an agreement providing for such deferral has been entered into before the beginning of such month,

(5) which does not provide that amounts payable under the plan will be made available to participants or other beneficiaries earlier than when the participant is separated from service with the State or is faced with an unforeseeable emergency (determined in the manner prescribed by the Secretary by regulation), and

(6) which provides that—

(A) all amounts of compensation deferred under the plan,

(B) all property and rights purchased with such amounts, and

(C) all income attributable to such amounts, property, or rights, shall remain (until made available to the participant or other beneficiary) solely the property and rights of the State (without being restricted to the provision of benefits under the plan) subject only to the claims of the State's general creditors.

A plan which is administered in a manner which is inconsistent with the requirements of any of the preceding paragraphs shall be treated as not meeting the requirements of such paragraph as of the first plan year beginning more than 180 days after the date of notification by the Secretary of the inconsistency unless the State corrects the inconsistency before the first day of such plan year.

which may be deferred under the plan for the taxable year shall not exceed the lesser of—

 (A) $7,500, or

 (B) 33⅓ percent of the participant's includible compensation,

 (3) which may provide that, for 1 or more of the participant's last 3 taxable years ending before he attains normal retirement age under the plan, the ceiling set forth in paragraph (2) shall be the lesser of—

 (A) $15,000, or

 (B) the sum of—

  (i) the plan ceiling established for purposes of paragraph (2) for the taxable year (determined without regard to this paragraph), plus

  (ii) so much of the plan ceiling established for purposes of paragraph (2) for the taxable years before the taxable year as has not previously been used under paragraph (2) or this paragraph,

 (4) which provides that compensation will be deferred for any calendar month only if an agreement providing for such deferral has been entered into before the beginning of such month,

 (5) which meets the distribution requirements of subsection (d), and

 (6) which provides that—

 (A) all amounts of compensation deferred under the plan,

 (B) all property and rights purchased with such amounts, and

 (C) all income attributable to such amounts, property, or rights,

shall remain (until made available to the participant or other beneficiary) solely the property and rights of the employer (without being restricted to the provision of benefits under the plan), subject only to the claims of the employer's general creditors.

〔Footnote ¶3017 continued〕

 (c) **Individuals who Are Participants in More Than One Plan.—**

 (1) **In general.—**The maximum amount of the compensation of any one individual which may be deferred under subsection (a) during any taxable year shall not exceed $7,500 (as modified by any adjustment provided under subsection (b)(3)).

 (2) **Coordination with section 403(b).—**In applying paragraph (1) of this subsection and paragraphs (2) and (3) of subsection (b), an amount excluded during a taxable year under section 403(b) shall be treated as an amount deferred under subsection (a). In applying clause (ii) of section 403(b)(2)(A), an amount deferred under subsection (a) for any year of service shall be taken into account as if described in such clause.

 (d) **Other Definitions and Special Rules.—**For purposes of this section—

 (1) **State.—**The term 'State' means a State, a political subdivision of a State, and an agency or instrumentality of a State or political subdivision of a State.

 (2) **Performance of service.—**The performance of service includes performance of service as an independent contractor.

 (3) **Participant.—**The term 'participant' means an individual who is eligible to defer compensation under the plan.

 (4) **Beneficiary.—**The term 'beneficiary' means a beneficiary of the participant, his estate, or any other person whose interest in the plan is derived from the participant.

 (5) **Includible compensation.—**The term 'includible compensation' means compensation for service performed for the State which (taking into account the provisions of this section and section 403(b)) is currently includible in gross income.

 (6) **Compensation taken into account at present value.—**Compensation shall be taken into account at its present value.

 (7) **Community property laws.—**The amount of includible compensation shall be determined without regard to any community property laws.

 (8) **Income attributable.—**Gains from the disposition of property shall be treated as income attributable to such property.

 (9) **Section to apply to rural electric cooperatives.—**

 (A) **In general.—**This section shall apply with respect to any participant in a plan of a rural electric cooperative in the same manner and to the same extent as if such plan were a plan of a State.

 (B) **Rural electric cooperative defined.—**For purposes of subparagraph (A), the term 'rural electric cooperative' means—

 (i) any organization which is exempt from tax under section 501(a) and which is engaged primarily in providing electric service on a mutual or cooperative basis, and

 (ii) any organization described in paragraph (4) or (6) of section 501(c) which is exempt from tax under section 501(a) and at least 80 percent of the members of which are organizations described in clause (i).

 (e) **Tax Treatment of Participants Where Plan or Arrangement of State is not Eligible.—**

 (1) **In general.—**In the case of a plan of a State providing for a deferral of compensation, if such plan is not an eligible State deferred compensation plan, then—

 (A) the compensation shall be included in the gross income of the participant or beneficiary for the first taxable year in which there is no substantial risk of forfeiture of the rights to such compensation, and

 (B) the tax treatment of any amount made available under the plan to a participant or beneficiary shall be determined under section 72 (relating to annuities, etc.).

A plan which is established and maintained by an employer which is described in subsection (e)(1)(A) and which is administered in a manner which is inconsistent with the requirements of any of the preceding paragraphs shall be treated as not meeting the requirements of such paragraph as of the 1st plan year beginning more than 180 days after the date of notification by the Secretary of the inconsistency unless the employer corrects the inconsistency before the 1st day of such plan year.

(c) Individuals Who Are Participants in More Than 1 Plan.—

(1) In general.—The maximum amount of the compensation of any one individual which may be deferred under subsection (a) during any taxable year shall not exceed $7,500 (as modified by any adjustment provided under subsection (b)(3)).

(2) Coordination with certain other deferrals.—In applying paragraph (1) of this subsection and paragraphs (2) and (3) of subsection (b)—

(A) any amount excluded from gross income under section 403(b) for the taxable year, and

(B) any amount—

(i) excluded from gross income under section 402(a)(8) or section 402(h)(1)(B) for the taxable year, or

(ii) with respect to which a deduction is allowable by reason of a contribution to an organization described in section 501(c)(18) for the taxable year,

shall be treated as an amount deferred under subsection (a). In applying section 402(g)(8)(A)(iii) or 403(b)(2)(A)(ii), an amount deferred under subsection (a) for any year of service shall be taken into account as if described in section 402(g)(3)(C) or 403(b)(2)(A)-(ii), respectively. Subparagraph (B) shall not apply in the case of a participant in a rural electric cooperative plan (as defined in section 401(k)(7)).

(d) Distribution Requirements.—

(1) In general.—For purposes of subsection (b)(5), a plan meets the distribution requirements of this subsection if—

⟦Footnote ¶3017 continued⟧

(2) Exceptions.—Paragraph (1) shall not apply to—

(A) a plan described in section 401(a) which includes a trust exempt from tax under section 501(a),

(B) an annuity plan or contract described in section 403,

(C) that portion of any plan which consists of a transfer of property described in section 83, and

(D) that portion of any plan which consists of a trust to which section 402(b) applies.

(3) Definitions.—For purposes of this subsection—

(A) Plan includes arrangements, etc.—The term 'plan' includes any agreement or arrangement.

(B) Substantial risk of forfeiture.—The rights of a person to compensation are subject to a substantial risk of forfeiture if such person's rights to such compensation are conditioned upon the future performance of substantial services by any individual."

Effective date (Sec. 1107(c), '86 TRA).—(1) Generally applies to taxable years beginning after 12-31-88.

(2) Transfers and cash-outs.—Paragraphs (9) and (10) of section 457(e) of the '86 Code (as amended by this section) shall apply to taxable years beginning after 12-31-86.

(3) Application to tax-exempt organizations.—

(A) In general.—Except as provided in subparagraph (B), the application of section 457 of the '86 Code by reason of the amendments made by this section to eligible deferred compensaton plans established and maintained by organizations exempt from tax shall apply to taxable years beginning after 12-31-86.

(B) Existing deferrals and arrangements.—Section 457 of such Code shall not apply to amounts deferred under a plan described in subparagraph (A) which—

(i) were deferred from taxable years beginning before 1-1-87, or

(ii) are deferred from taxable years beginning after 12-31-86, pursuant to an agreement which —

(I) was in writing on 8-16-86,

(II) on such date provides for a deferral for each taxable year covered by the agreement of a fixed amount or of an amount determined pursuant to a fixed formula.

Clause (ii) shall not apply to any taxable year ending after the date on which any modification to the amount or formula described in subclause (II) is effective. Amounts described in the first sentence shall be taken into account for applying section 457 to other amounts deferred under any eligible deferred compensation plan.

(4) Deferred compensation plans for state judges.—The amendments made by this section shall not apply to any qualified State judicial plan (as defined in section 131(c)(3)(B) of the Revenue Act of 1978 as amended by section 252 of '82 TEFRA).

(5) Special rule for certain deferred compensation plans.—The amendments made by this section shall not apply to employees on 8-16-86, of—

(A) a deferred compensation plan of a nonprofit corporation organized under the laws of the State of Alabama with respect to which the IRS issued a ruling dated 3-17-76, that the plan would not affect the tax-exempt status of the corporation, or

(B) a deferred compensation plan with respect to which a letter dated 11-6-75, submitted the original plan to the IRS, an amendment was submitted on 11-19-75, and the IRS responded with a letter dated 12-24-75, but only with respect to deferrals under such plan.

(A) the plan provides that amounts payable under the plan will be made available to participants or other beneficiaries not earlier than when the participant is separated from service with the employer or is faced with an unforeseeable emergency (determined in the manner prescribed by the Secretary by regulation), and

(B) the plan meets the minimum distribution requirements of paragraph (2).

(2) **Minimum distribution requirements.**—A plan meets the minimum distribution requirements of this paragraph if such plan meets the requirements of subparagraph (A), (B), and (C):

(A) Application of section 401(a)(9).—A plan meets the requirements of this subparagraph if the plan meets the requirements of section 401(a)(9).

(B) **Additional distribution requirements.**—A plan meets the requirements of this subparagraph if—

(i) in the case of a distribution beginning before the death of the participant such distribution will be made in a form under which—

(I) at least ⅔ of the total amount payable with respect to the participant will be paid during the life expectancy of such participant (determined as of the commencement of the distribution), and

(II) any amount not distributed to the participant during his life will be distributed after the death of the participant at least as rapidly as under the method of distribution being used under subclause (I) as of the date of his death, or

(ii) in the case of a distribution which does not begin before the death of the participant, the entire amount payable with respect to the participant will be paid during a period not to exceed 15 years (or the life expectancy of the surviving spouse if such spouse is the beneficiary).

(C) Nonincreasing benefits.—A plan meets the requirements of this subparagraph if any distribution payable over a period of more than 1 year can only be made in substantially nonincreasing amounts (paid not less frequently than annually).

(e) **Other Definitions and Special Rules.**—For purposes of this section—

(1) **Eligible employer.**—The term "eligible employer" means—

(A) a State, political subdivision of a State, and any agency or instrumentality of a State or political subdivision of a State, and

(B) any other organization (other than a governmental unit) exempt from tax under this subtitle.

(2) **Performance of service.**—The performance of service includes performance of service as an independent contractor and the person (or governmental unit) for whom such services are performed shall be treated as the employer.

(3) **Participant.**—The term "participant" means an individual who is eligible to defer compensation under the plan.

(4) **Beneficiary.**—The term "beneficiary" means a beneficiary of the participant, his estate, or any other person whose interest in the plan is derived from the participant.

(5) **Includible compensation.**—The term "includible compensation" means compensation for service performed for the employer which (taking into account the provisions of this section and other provisions of this chapter) is currently includible in gross income.

(6) **Compensation taken into account at present value.**—Compensation shall be taken into account at its present value.

(7) **Community property laws.**—The amount of includible compensation shall be determined without regard to any community property laws.

(8) **Income attributable.**—Gains from the disposition of property shall be treated as income attributable to such property.

(9) **Benefits not treated as made available by reason of certain elections.**—If—

(A) the total amount payable to a participant under the plan does not exceed $3,500; and

(B) no additional amounts may be deferred under the plan with respect to the participant,

the amount payable to the participant under the plan shall not be treated as made available merely because such participant may elect to receive a lump sum payable within 60 days of the election.

(10) **Transfer between plans.**—A participant shall not be required to include in gross income any portion of the entire amount payable to such participant solely by reason of

the transfer of such portion from 1 eligible deferred compensation plan to another eligible deferred compensation plan.

(f) Tax Treatment of Participants Where Plan or Arrangement of Employer Is Not Eligible.—

(1) *In general.*—In the case of a plan of eligible employer providing for a deferral of compensation, if such plan is not an eligible deferred compensation plan, then—

(A) the compensation shall be included in the gross income of the participant or beneficiary for the 1st taxable year in which there is no substantial risk of forfeiture of the rights to such compensation, and

(B) the tax treatment of any amount made available under the plan to a participant or beneficiary shall be determined under section 72 (relating to annuities, etc.).

(2) *Exceptions.*—Paragraph (1) shall not apply to—

(A) a plan described in section 401(a) which includes a trust exempt from tax under section 501(a),

(B) an annuity plan or contract described in section 403,

(C) that portion of any plan which consists of a transfer of property described in section 83, and

(D) that portion of any plan which consists of a trust to which section 402(b) applies.

(3) *Definitions.*—For purposes of this subsection—

(A) *Plan includes arrangements, etc.*—The term "plan" includes any agreement or arrangement.

(B) *Substantial risk of forfeiture.*—The rights of a person to compensation are subject to a substantial risk of forfeiture if such person's rights to such compensation are conditioned upon the future performance of substantial services by any individual.

[For official explanation, see Committee Reports, ¶3973.]

〔¶3018〕 CODE SEC. 460. SPECIAL RULES FOR LONG-TERM CONTRACTS.

(a) Percentage of Completion-Capitalized Cost Method.—

(1) In general.—In the case of any long-term contract—

(A) 40 percent of the items with respect to such contract shall be taken into account under the percentage of completion method (as modified by subsection (b)), and

(B) 60 percent of the items with respect to such contract shall be taken into account under the taxpayer's normal method of accounting.

(2) 40 percent look-back method to apply.—Upon completion of any long-term contract, the taxpayer shall pay (or shall be entitled to receive) interest determined by applying the look-back method of subsection (b)(3) to 40 percent of the items with respect to the contract.

(b) Percentage of Completion Method.—

(1) Subsection (a) not to apply where percentage of completion method used.—Subsection (a) shall not apply to any long-term contract with respect to which amounts includible in gross income are determined under the percentage of completion method.

(2) Requirements of percentage of completion method.—In the case of any long-term contract with respect to which the percentage of completion method is used—

(A) the percentage of completion shall be determined by comparing costs allocated to the contract under subsection (c) and incurred before the close of the taxable year with the estimated total contract costs, and

---

〔Footnote ¶3018〕 Sec. 460 added by section 804(a), '86 TRA.

Effective date (Sec. 804(d), '86 TRA).—(1) Generally applies to any contract entered into after 2-28-86.

(2) Clarification of treatment of independent research and development expenses.—

(A) In general.—For periods before, on, or after the date of enactment of this Act—

(i) any independent research and development expenses taken into account in determining the total contract price shall not be severable from the contract, and

(ii) any independent research and development expenses shall not be treated as amounts chargeable to capital account.

(B) Independent research and development expenses.—For purposes of subparagraph (A), the term "independent research and development expenses" has the meaning given to such term by section 263A(c)(5) of the '86 Code, as added by this section.

(B) upon completion of the contract, the taxpayer shall pay (or shall be entitled to receive) interest computed under the look-back method of paragraph (3).

(3) Look-back method.—The interest computed under the look-back method of this subparagraph shall be determined by—

(A) first allocating income under the contract among taxable years before the year in which the contract is completed on the basis of the actual contract price and costs instead of the estimated contract price and costs,

(B) second, determining (solely for purposes of computing such interest) the overpayment or underpayment of tax for each taxable year referred to in paragraph (1) which would result solely from the application of paragraph (1), and

(C) then using the overpayment rate established by section 6621, compounded daily, on the overpayment or underpayment determined under paragraph (1).

(c) Allocation of Costs to Contract.—

(1) Direct and certain indirect costs.—In the case of a long-term contract, all costs (including research and experimental costs) which directly benefit, or are incurred by reason of, the long-term contract activities of the taxpayer shall be allocated to such contract in the same manner as costs are allocated to extended period long-term contracts under section 451 and the regulations thereunder.

(2) Costs indentified under cost-plus and certain federal contracts.—In the case of a cost-plus long-term contract or a Federal long-term contract, any cost not allocated to such contract under paragraph (1) shall be allocated to such contract if such cost is identified by the taxpayer (or a related person), pursuant to the contract or Federal, State, or local law or regulation, as being attributable to such contract.

(3) Allocation of production period interest to contract.—

(A) In general.—Except as provided in subparagraphs (B) and (C), in the case of a long-term contract, interest costs shall be allocated to the contract in the same manner as interest costs are allocated to property produced by the taxpayer under section 263A(f).

(B) Production period.—In applying section 263A(f) for purposes of subparagraph (A), the production period shall be the period—

(i) beginning on the later of—

(I) the contract commencement date, or

(II) in the case of a taxpayer who uses an accrual method with respect to long-term contracts, the date by which at least 5 percent of the total estimated costs (including design and planning costs) under the contract have been incurred, and

(ii) ending on the contract completion date.

(C) Application of de minimis rule.—In applying section 263A(f) for purposes of subparagraph (A), paragraph (1)(B)(iii) of such section shall be applied on a contract-by-contract basis; except that, in the case of a taxpayer described in subparagraph (B)(i)(II) of this paragraph, paragraph (1)(B)(iii) of section 263A(f) shall be applied on a property-by-property basis.

(4) Certain costs not included.—This subsection shall not apply to any—

(A) independent research and development expenses,

(B) expenses for unsuccessful bids and proposals, and

(C) marketing, selling, and advertising expenses.

(5) Independent research and development expenses.—For purposes of paragraph (4), the term "independent research and development expenses" means any expenses incurred in the performance of research or development, except that such term shall not include—

(A) any expenses which are directly attributable to a long-term contract in existence when such expenses are incurred, or

(B) any expenses under an agreement to perform research or development.

(d) Federal Long-Term Contract.—For purposes of this section—

(1) In general.—The term "Federal long-term contract" means any long-term contract—

(A) to which the United States (or any agency or instrumentality thereof) is a party, or

(B) which is a subcontract under a contract described in subparagraph (A).

(2) **Special rules for certain taxable entities.**—For purposes of paragraph (1), the rules of section 168(h)(2)(D) (relating to certain taxable entities not treated as instrumentalities) shall apply.

(e) **Exception for Certain Construction Contracts.—**

(1) **In general.**—Subsections (a), (b), and (c)(1) and (2) shall not apply to any construction contract entered into by a taxpayer—

(A) who estimates (at the time such contract is entered into) that such contract will be completed within the 2-year period beginning on the contract commencement date of such contract, and

(B) whose average annual gross receipts for the 3 taxable years preceding the taxable year in which such contract is entered into do not exceed $10,000,000.

(2) **Determination of taxpayer's gross receipts.**—For purposes of paragraph (1), the gross receipts of—

(A) all trades or businesses (whether or not incorporated) which are under common control with the taxpayer (within the meaning of section 52(b)), and

(B) all members of any controlled group of corporations of which the taxpayer is a member,

for the 3 taxable years of such persons preceding the taxable year in which the contract described in paragraph (1) is entered into shall be included in the gross receipts of the taxpayer for the period described in paragraph (1)(B). The Secretary shall prescribe regulations which provide attribution rules that take into account, in addition to the persons and entities described in the preceding sentence, taxpayers who engage in construction contracts through partnerships, joint ventures, and corporations.

(3) **Controlled group of corporations.**—For purposes of this subsection, the term "controlled group of corporations" has the meaning given to such term by section 1563(a), except that—

(A) "more than 50 percent" shall be substituted for "at least 80 percent" each place it appears in section 1563(a)(1), and

(B) The determination shall be made without regard to subsections (a)(4) and (e)(3)(C) of section 1563.

(4) **Construction contract.**—For purposes of this subsection, the term "construction contract" means any contract for the building, construction, reconstruction, or rehabilitation of, or the installation of any integral component to, or improvements of, real property.

(f) **Long-Term Contract.**—For purposes of this section—

(1) **In general.**—The term "long-term contract" means any contract for the manufacture, building, installation, or construction of property if such contract is not completed within the taxable year in which such contract is entered into.

(2) **Special rule for manufacturing contracts.**—A contract for the manufacture of property shall not be treated as a long-term contract unless such contract involves the manufacture of—

(A) any unique item of a type which is not normally included in the finished goods inventory of the taxpayer, or

(B) any item which normally requires more than 12 calendar months to complete (without regard to the period of the contract).

(3) **Aggregation, etc.**—For purposes of this subsection, under regulations prescribed by the Secretary—

(A) 2 or more contracts which are interdependent (by reason of pricing or otherwise) may be treated as 1 contract, and

(B) a contract which is properly treated as an aggregation of separate contracts may be so treated.

(g) **Contract Commencement Date.**—For purposes of this section, the term "contract commencement date" means, with respect to any contract, the first date on which any costs (other than bidding expenses or expenses incurred in connection with negotiating the contract) allocable to such contract are incurred.

[For official explanation, see Committee Reports, ¶3937.]

[¶3019] **CODE SEC. 461. GENERAL RULE FOR TAXABLE YEAR OF DEDUCTION.**

* * * * * * * * * * * *

(h) **Certain Liabilities Not Incurred Before Economic Performance.—**

* * * * * * * * * * *

(5) **Subsection not to apply to certain cases to which other provisions of this title specifically apply.**—This subsection shall not apply to any item to which any of the following provisions apply:[1]

[2](A) Section 463 (relating to vacation pay).

[3]*(B)* [former (C) struck out][4]

[5]**(C)* any other provisions of this title which specifically provides for a deduction for a reserve for estimated expenses.

≫**P-H CAUTION→** There are two versions of Sec. 461(i). Sec. 461(i), generally effective after 12-31-86, follows. For Sec. 461(i), generally effective before 1-1-87, see below.

▲ [6]*"(i) Special Rules for Tax Shelters.—*

⟦Footnote ¶3019⟧ Matter in *italics* in Sec. 461(h)(5)(A) and (B) added by section 805(c)(5), '86 TRA, which struck out:

(1) "(A) Subsection (c) or (f) of section 166 (relating to reserves for bad debts)."

(2) "(B)"

(3) "(C)"

Effective date (Sec. 805(d), '86 TRA)—(1) Generally applies to taxable years beginning after 12-31-86.

(2) Change in method of accounting.—In the case of any taxpayer who maintained a reserve for bad debts for such taxpayer's last taxable year beginning before 1-1-87, and who is required by the amendments made by this section to change its method of accounting for any taxable year—

(A) such change shall be treated as initiated by the taxpayer,

(B) such change shall be treated as made with the consent of the Secretary, and

(C) the net amount of adjustments required by section 481 of the '86 Code to be taken into account by the taxpayer shall—

(i) in the case of a taxpayer maintaining a reserve under section 166(f), be reduced by the balance in the suspense account under section 166(f)(4) of such Code as of the close of such last taxable year, and

(ii) be taken into account ratably in each of the first 4 taxable years beginning after 12-31-86.

Section 823(b)(1), '86 TRA, struck out Sec. 461(h)(5)(B) [former (C)]:

(4) "Section 466 (relating to discount coupons)."

Effective date (Sec. 823(c), '86 TRA).—(1) Generally applies to taxable years beginning after 12-31-86.

(2) Change in method of accounting.—In the case of any taxpayer who elected to have section 466 of the '54 Code apply for such taxpayer's last taxable year beginning before 1-1-87, and is required to change its method of accounting by reason of the amendments made by this section for any taxable year—

(A) such change shall be treated as initiated by the taxpayer,

(B) such change shall be treated as having been made with the consent of the Secretary, and

(C) the net amount of adjustments required by section 481 of the '86 Code to be taken into account by the taxpayer shall—

(i) be reduced by the balance in the suspense account under section 466(e) of such Code as of the close of such last taxable year, and

(ii) be taken into account over a period not longer than 4 years.

Matter in *italics* in Sec. 461(h)(5)(C) added by section 805(c)(5), '86 TRA, which struck out:

(5) "(D)"

Effective date (Sec. 805(d), '86 TRA).—(1) Generally applies to taxable years beginning after 12-31-86. For special rule, see above.

*Sec. 461(h)(5)(D) was also relettered (C) by section 823(b)(1), '86 TRA.

Effective date (Sec. 823(c), '86 TRA).—(1) Generally applies to taxable years beginning after 12-31-86. For special rule, see above.

▲ Matter in *italics* in Sec. 461(i), preceded by a triangle, added by section 801(b), '86 TRA, which struck out:

(6) "(i) **Tax Shelters May Not Deduct Items Earlier Than When Economic Performance Occurs.—**

(1) **In general.**—In the case of a tax shelter computing taxable income under the cash receipts and disbursements method of accounting, such tax shelter shall not be allowed a deduction under this chapter with respect to any item any earlier than the time when such item would be treated as incurred under subsection (h) (determined without regard to paragraph (3) thereof).

(2) **Exception (to extent of cash basis) when economic performance occurs on or before the 90th day after the close of the taxable year.**

(A) In general. Paragraph (1) shall not apply to any item if economic performance with respect to such item occurs before the close of the 90th day after the close of the taxable year.

(B) Deduction limited to cash basis.—

(i) Tax shelter partnerships.—In the case of a tax shelter which is a partnership, in applying section 704(d) to a deduction or loss for any taxable year attributable to an item, which is deductible by reason of subparagraph (A), the term 'cash basis' shall be substituted for the term 'adjusted basis'.

(ii) Other tax shelters.—Under regulations prescribed by the Secretary, in the case of a tax shelter other than a partnership, the aggregate amount of the deductions allowable by reason of subparagraph (A) for any taxable year

(1) Recurring Item Exception not to apply.—In the case of a tax shelter, economic performance shall be determined without regard to paragraph (3) of subsection (h).

(2) Special rule for spudding of oil or gas wells.—In the case of a tax shelter, economic performance with respect to the act of drilling an oil or gas well shall be treated as having occurred within a taxable year if drilling of the well commences before the close of the 90th day after the close of the taxable year.

* * * * * * * * * * * *

[7]*(4) Special rules for farming.*—In the case of the trade or business of farming (as defined in section 464(e)), in determining whether an entity is a tax shelter, the definition of farming syndicate in section 464(c) shall be substituted for subparagraphs (A) and (B) of paragraph (3).

* * * * * * * * * * * *

≫**P-H CAUTION**→ There are two versions of Sec. 461(i). Sec. 461(i), generally effective before 1-1-87, follows. For Sec. 461(i), generally effective after 12-31-86, see above.

▲ ▲ **(i) Tax Shelters May Not Deduct Items Earlier Than When Economic Performance Occurs.**—

(1) In general.—In the case of a tax shelter computing taxable income under the cash receipts and disbursements method of accounting, such tax shelter shall not be allowed a deduction under this chapter with respect to any item any earlier than the time when such item would be treated as incurred under subsection (h) (determined without regard to paragraph (3) thereof).

(2) Exception (to extent of cash basis) when economic performance occurs [8]*on or*

【Footnote ¶3019 continued】

shall be limited in a manner similar to the limitation under clause (i).

(C) Cash basis defined.—For purposes of subparagraph (B), a partner's cash basis in a partnership shall be equal to the adjusted basis of such partner's interest in the partnership, determined without regard to—

(i) any liability of the partnership, and

(ii) any amount borrowed by the partner with respect to such partnership which—

(1) was arranged by the partnership or by any person who participated in the organization, sale, or management of the partnership (or any person related to such person within the meaning of section 168(e)(4)), or

(II) was secured by any assets of the partnership.

(D) Special cash basis rule for spudding of oil or gas wells.—Solely for purposes of applying subparagraph (A), economic performance with respect to the act of drilling of an oil or gas well shall be treated as occurring when the drilling of the well is commenced.

(7) "**(4) Special rules for farming.**—In the case of a trade or business of farming (as defined in section 464(e))—

(A) any tax shelter described in paragraph (3)(C) shall be treated as a farming syndicate for purposes of section 464; except that this subparagraph shall not apply for purposes of determining the income of an individual meeting the requirements of section 464(e)(2).

(B) section 464 shall be applied before this subsection, and

(C) in determining whether an entity is a tax shelter, the definition of farming syndicate in section 464(c) shall be substituted for paragraphs (A) and (B) of paragraph (3)."

Effective date (Sec. 801(d), '86 TRA).—(1) Generally applies to taxable years beginning after 12-31-86.

(2) Election to retain cash method for certain transactions.—A taxpayer may elect not to have the amendments made by this section apply to any loan or lease, or any transaction with a related party (within the meaning of section 267(b) of the '54 Code, as in effect before the enactment of this Act), entered into on or before 9-25-85. Any election under the preceding sentence may be made separately with respect to each transaction.

(3) Certain contracts.—The Amendments made by this section shall not apply to—

(A) contracts for the acquisition or transfer of real property, and

(B) contracts for services related to the acquisition or development of real property,

but only if such contracts were entered into before 9-25-85, and the sole element of the contract which has not been performed as of 9-25-85, is payment for such property or services.

(4) Treatment of affiliated group providing engineering services.—Each member of an affiliated group of corporations (within the meaning of section 1504(a) of the '86 Code) shall be allowed to use the cash receipts and disbursements method of accounting for any trade or business of providing engineering services with respect to taxable years ending after 12-31-86, if the common parent of such group—

(A) was incorporated in the State of Delaware in 1970,

(B) was the successor to a corporation that was incorporated in the State of Illinois in 1949, and

(C) used the completed contract method of accounting for a substantial part of its income from the performance of engineering services.

▲ ▲ Matter in *italics* in Sec. 461(i), preceded by two triangles, added by section 1807(a)(1) and (2), '86 TRA,

before the 90th day **after the close of the taxable year.**

(A) In general.—Paragraph (1) shall not apply to any item if economic performance with respect to such item occurs [9]*before the close of the 90th day* of the taxable year.

(B) Deduction limited to cash basis.—

(i) Tax shelter partnerships.—In the case of a tax shelter which is a partnership, in applying section 704(d) to a deduction or loss for any taxable year attributable to an item, which is deductible by reason of subparagraph (A), the term "cash basis" shall be substituted for the term "adjusted basis".

(ii) Other tax shelters.—Under regulations prescribed by the Secretary, in the case of a tax shelter other than a partnership, the aggregate amount of the deductions allowable by reason of subparagraph (A) for any taxable year shall be limited in a manner similar to the limitation under clause (i).

* * * * * * * * * * *

(4) **Special rules for farming.**—In the case of a trade or business of farming (as defined in section 464(e))—

[10]*(A) any tax shelter described in paragraph (3)(C) shall be treated as a farming*

[**Footnote ¶3019 continued**]

which struck out:

(8) "within 90 days"

(9) "within 90 days"

(10) "(A) section 464 shall be applied to any tax shelter described in paragraph (3)(C)."

Effective date (Sec. 1881, '86 TRA and Sec. 91(g)(1)—(3), (h) and (i), '84 TRA, as amended by 1807(a)(6), '86 TRA).—

(g)(1) **In general.**—Except as provided in this subsection and subsections (h) and (i), the amendments made by this section shall apply to amounts with respect to which a deduction would be allowable under chapter 1 of the '54 Code (determined without regard to such amendments) after—

(A) in the case of amounts to which section 461(h) of such Code (as added by such amendments) applies, 7-18-84, and

(B) in the case of amounts to which section 461(i) of such Code (as so added) applies after 3-31-84.

(2) Taxpayer may elect earlier applications.—"

(A) In general.—In the case of amounts described in paragraph (1)(A), a taxpayer may elect to have the amendments made by this section apply to amounts which—

(i) are incurred on or before 7-18-84 (determined without regard to such amendments), and

(ii) are incurred after 7-18-84 (determined with regard to such amendments).

The Secretary of the Treasury or his delegate may by regulations provide that (in lieu of an election under the preceding sentence) a taxpayer may (subject to such conditions as such regulations may provide) elect to have subsection (h) of section 461 of such Code apply to the taxpayer's entire taxable year in which occurs 7-19-84.

(B) Election treated as change in the method of accounting.—For purposes of section 481 of the '54 Code, if an election is made under subparagraph (A) with respect to any amount, the application of the amendments made by this section shall be treated as a change in method of accounting—

(i) initiated by the taxpayer.

(ii) made with the consent of the Secretary of the Treasury, and

(iii) with respect to which section 481 of such Code shall be applied by substituting a 3-year adjustment period for a 10-year adjustment period.

(3) Section 461(h) to Apply in Certain Cases.—Notwithstanding paragraph (1) Sec. 461(h) of the '54 Code (as added by this section) shall be treated as being in effect to the extent necessary to carry out any amendments made by this section which take effect before Sec. 461(h).

* * * * * * * * * * *

(h) Exception for Certain Existing Activities and Contracts.—If—

(1) Existing Accounting Practices.—If, on 3-1-84, any taxpayer was regularly computing his deduction for mining reclamation activities under a current cost method of accounting (as determined by the Secretary of the Treasury of his delegate), the liability for reclamation activities—

(A) for land disturbed before 7-18-84, or

(B) to which paragraph (2) applies,

shall be treated as having been incurred when the land was disturbed.

(2) Fixed Price Supply Contract.—

(A) In General.—In the case of any fixed price supply contract entered into before 3-1-84, the amendments made by section 91(b), '84 TRA, which added new Code Sec. 468, shall not apply to any minerals extracted from such property which are sold pursuant to such contract.

(B) No Extension or Renegotiation.—Subparagraph (A) shall not apply—

(i) to any extension of any contract beyond the period such contract was in effect on 3-1-84, or

(ii) to any renegotiation of, or other change in, the terms and conditions of such contract in effect on 3-1-84.

(i) Transitional Rule for Accrued Vacation Pay.—

(1) In General.—In the case of any taxpayer—

(A) with respect to whom a deduction was allowable (other than under Sec. 463 of the '54 Code) for vested accrued vacation pay for the last taxable year ending before 7-18-84, and

(B) who elects the application of Sec. 463 of such Code for the first taxable year ending after 7-18-84, *syndicate for purposes of section 464; except that this subparagraph shall not apply for purposes of determining the income of an individual meeting the requirements of section 464(c)(2).*

   (B)   section 464 shall be applied before this subsection, and

   (C)   in determining whether an entity is a tax shelter, the definition of farming syndicate in section 464(c) shall be substituted for paragraphs (A) and (B) for paragraph (3).

* * * * * * * * * * *

[For official explanation, see Committee Reports, ¶3935; 3939; 3945; 4141.]

[¶3020]   CODE SEC. 463.   ACCRUAL OF VACATION PAY.

   (a) **Allowance of Deduction.**—At the election of a taxpayer whose taxable income is computed under an accrual method of accounting, if the conditions of section 162(a) are otherwise satisfied, the deduction allowable under section 162(a) with respect to vacation pay shall be an amount equal to the sum of—

   (1) a reasonable addition to an account representing the taxpayer's liability for vacation pay earned by employees before the close of the taxable year and [1]*paid during the taxable year or within 8½ months* following the close of the taxable year; plus

   (2) the amount (if any) of the reduction at the close of the taxable year in the suspense account provided in subsection (c)(2).

Such liability for vacation pay earned before the close of the taxable year shall include amounts which, because of contingencies, would not (but for this section) be deductible under section 162(a) as an accrued expense. All payments with respect to vacation pay shall be charged to such account.

* * * * * * * * * * *

[For official explanation, see Committee Reports, ¶4021.]

[¶3021]   CODE SEC. 464.   LIMITATIONS ON DEDUCTIONS [1]*FOR CERTAIN FARMING.*

   (a) **General Rule.**—In the case of any farming syndicate (as defined in subsection (c)), a deduction (otherwise allowable under this chapter) for amounts paid for feed, seed, fertilizer, or other similar farm supplies shall only be allowed in the taxable year in which such feed, seed, fertilizer, or other supplies are actually used or consumed, or, if later, in the taxable year for which allowable as a deduction (determined without regard to this section).

* * * * * * * * * * *

   (d)[2] *Exception.*—*Subsection (a) shall not apply to any amount paid for supplies which*

[Footnote ¶3019 continued]

then, for purposes of Sec. 463(b) of such Code, the opening balance of the taxpayer with respect to any vested accrued vacation pay shall be determined under Sec. 463(b)(1) of such Code.

   (2) **Vested Accrued Vacation Pay.**—For purposes of this subsection, the term "vested accrued vacation pay" means any amount allowable under Sec. 162(a) of such Code with respect to vacation pay of employees of the taxpayer (determined without regard to Sec. 463 of such Code).

See Sec. 1807(a)(8), '86 TRA, ¶2106 for transitional rule for certain amounts.

   [Footnote ¶3020] Matter in *italics* in Sec. 463(a)(1) added by section 1165(a), '86 TRA, which struck out:

   (1) "expected to be paid during the taxable years or within 12 months"

Effective date (Sec. 1165(b), '86 TRA).—Applies to taxable years beginning after 12-31-86.

   [Footnote ¶3021] Matter in *italics* in the heading of Sec. 464 added by section 404(b)(1), '86 TRA, which struck out:

   (1) "IN CASE OF FARMING SYNDICATES"

Effective date (Sec. 404(c), '86 TRA).—Applies to amounts paid or incurred after 3-1-86, in taxable years beginning after such date.

Matter in *italics* in Sec. 464(d), added by section 803(b)(8), '86 TRA, which struck out:

   (2) "**Exceptions.**—Subsection (a) shall not apply to—

   (1) any amount paid for supplies which are on hand at the close of the taxable year on account of fire, storm, flood, or other casualty or an account of disease or drought; and

   (2) any amount required to be charged to capital account under section 278."

Effective date (Sec. 803(d)(1), '86 TRA).—Generally applies to costs incurred after 12-31-86, in taxable years ending after such date. For special and transitional rules, see footnote ¶2961-A.

Sec. 464(f) in *italics* added by section 404(a), '86 TRA.

Effective date (Sec. 404(c), '86 TRA).—Applies to amounts paid or incurred after 3-1-86, in taxable years begin-

are on hand at the close of the taxable year on account of fire, storm, or other casualty, or on account of disease or drought.

* * * * * * * * * * * *

(f) Subsections (a) and (b) To Apply to Certain Persons Prepaying 50 Percent or More of Certain Farming Expenses.—

(1) In general.—In the case of a taxpayer to whom this subsection applies, subsections (a) and (b) shall apply to the excess prepaid farm supplies of such taxpayer in the same manner as if such taxpayer were a farming syndicate.

(2) Taxpayer to whom subsection applies.—This subsection applies to any taxpayer for any taxable year if such taxpayer—

(A) does not use an accrual method of accounting,

(B) has excess prepaid farm supplies for the taxable year, and

(C) is not a qualified farm-related taxpayer.

(3) Qualified farm-related taxpayer.—

(A) In general.—For purposes of this subsection, the term "qualified farm-related taxpayer" means any farm-related taxpayer if—

(i)(I) the aggregate prepaid farm supplies for the 3 taxable years preceding the taxable year are less than 50 percent of,

(II) the aggregate deductible farming expenses (other than prepaid farm supplies) for such 3 taxable years, or

(ii) the taxpayer has excess prepaid farm supplies for the taxable year by reason of any change in business operation directly attributable to extraordinary circumstances.

(B) Farm-related taxpayer.—For purposes of this paragraph, the term "farm-related taxpayer" means any taxpayer—

(i) whose principal residence (within the meaning of section 1034) is on a farm,

(ii) who has a principal occupation of farming, or

(iii) who is a member of the family (within the meaning of subsection (c)(2)(E)) of a taxpayer described in clause (i) or (ii).

(4) Definitions.—For purposes of this subsection—

(A) Excess prepaid farm supplies.—The term "excess prepaid farm supplies" means the prepaid farm supplies for the taxable year to the extent the amount of such supplies exceeds 50 percent of the deductible farming expenses for the taxable year (other than prepaid farm supplies).

(B) Prepaid farm supplies.—The term "prepaid farm supplies" means any amounts which are described in subsection (a) or (b) and would be allowable for a subsequent taxable year under the rules of subsections (a) and (b).

(C) Deductible farming expenses.—The term "deductible farming expenses" means any amount allowable as a deduction under this chapter (including any amount allowable as a deduction for depreciation or amortization) which is properly allocable to the trade or business of farming.

[For official explanation, see Committee Reports, ¶3893; 3937.]

〔¶3022〕 CODE SEC. 465. DEDUCTIONS LIMITED TO AMOUNT AT RISK.

* * * * * * * * * * * *

(b) Amounts Considered at Risk.—

* * * * * * * * * * * *

(3) Certain borrowed amounts excluded.—

(A) In general.—Except to the extent provided in regulations, for purposes of paragraph (1)(B), amounts borrowed shall not be considered to be at risk with respect to an activity if such amounts are borrowed from any person who has an interest in such activity or from a related person to a person (other than the taxpayer) having such an interest.

(B) Exceptions.—

(i) Interest as creditor.—Subparagraph (A) shall not apply to an interest as a creditor in the activity.

(ii) Interest as shareholder with respect to amounts borrowed by corporation.—In the case of amounts borrowed by a corporation from a shareholder, subparagraph (A) shall not apply to an interest as a shareholder.

[1]*(C) Related person.—For purposes of this subsection, a person (hereinafter in this paragraph referred to as the "related person" is related to any person if—*

(i) the related person bears a relationship to such person specified in section 267(b) or section 707(b)(1), or

(ii) the related person and such person are engaged in trades or business under common control (with the meaning of subsections (a) and (b) of section 52).

For purposes of clause (i), in applying section 267(b) or 707(b)(1), "10 percent" shall be substituted for "50 percent."

* * * * * * * * * * * *

(6) Qualifed nonrecourse financing treated as amount at risk.—For purposes of this section—

(A) In general.—Notwithstanding any other provision of this subsection, in the case of an activity of holding real property, a taxpayer shall be considered at risk with respect to the taxpayer's share of any qualified nonrecourse financing which is secured by real property used in such activity.

(B) Qualified nonrecourse financing.—For purposes of this paragraph, the term "qualified nonrecourse financing" means any financing—

(i) which is borrowed by the taxpayer with respect to the activity of holding real property,

(ii) which is borrowed by the taxpayer from a qualified person or represents a loan from any Federal, State or local government or instrumentality thereof, or is guaranteed by any Federal, State, or local government.

(iii) except to the extent provided in regulations, with respect to which no person is personally liable for repayment, and

(iv) which is not convertible debt.

(C) Special rule for partnerships.—In the case of a partnership, a partner's share of any qualifed nonrecourse financing of such partnership shall be determined on the basis of the partner's share of liabilities of such partnership incurred in connection with such financing (within the meaning of section 752).

(D) Qualified person defined.—For purposes of this paragraph—

(i) In general.—The term "qualified person" has the meaning given such term by section 46(c)(8)(D)(iv).

(ii) Certain commercially reasonable financing from related persons.—For purposes of clause (i) section 46(c)(8)(D)(iv) shall be applied without regard to subclause (I) thereof (relating to financing from related persons) if the financing from the related person is commercially reasonable and on substantially the same terms as loans involving unrelated persons.

(E) Activity of holding real property.—For purposes of this paragraph—

(i) Incidental personal property and services.—The activity of holding real property includes the holding of personal property and the providing of services which are incidental to making real property available as living accommodations.

(ii) Mineral property.—The activity of holding real property shall not include the holding of mineral property.

(c) **Activities to Which Section Applies.—**

* * * * * * * * * * * *

(3) **Extension to other activities.—**
(A) In general.—In the case of taxable years beginning after December 31, 1978, this section also applies to each activity—

[Footnote ¶3022] Matter in *italics* in Sec. 465(b)(3)(C) added by section 201(d)(7)(A), '86 TRA, which struck out:

(1) (C) Related person defined.—For purposes of subparagraph (A), the term (related person) has the meaning given such term by section 168(e)(4).

Effective date (Sec. 203, '86 TRA).—(A) Generally applies to property placed in service after 12-31-86, in taxable years ending after such date.

(B) Election to have amendments made by section 201 apply.—A taxpayer may elect (at such time and in such manner as the Secretary of the Treasury or his delegate may prescribe) to have the amendments made by section 201 apply to any property placed in service after 7-31-86, and before 1-1-87.

For special and transitional rules, see ¶2007—2008.

(i) engaged in by the taxpayer in carrying on a trade or business or for the production of income, and

(ii) which is not described in paragraph (1).

* * * * * * * * * * * *

(C) Aggregation or separation of activities under regulations.—The Secretary shall prescribe regulations under which activities described in subparagraph (A) shall be aggregated or treated as separate activities.[2]

[3](D) Application of subsection (b)(3).—In the case of an activity described in subparagraph (A), subsection (b)(3) shall apply only to the extent provided in regulations prescribed by the Secretary.

* * * * * * * * * * * *

(7) **Exclusion of active businesses of qualified C corporations.—**

* * * * * * * * * * * *

(D) Special rules for application of subparagraph (C).—

* * * * * * * * * * * *

(v) Special rule for life insurance companies.—

(I) In general.—Clause (iii) of subparagraph (C) shall not apply to any insurance business of a qualified life insurance company.

(II) Insurance business.—For purposes of subclause (I), the term "insurance business" means any business which is not a noninsurance business (within the meaning of [4]*section 806(b)(3)).*

(III) Qualified life insurance company.—For purposes of subclause (I), the term "qualified life insurance company" means any company which would be a life insurance company as defined in section 816 if unearned premiums were not taken into account under subsections (a)(2) and (c)(2) of section 816.

* * * * * * * * * * * *

[For official explanation, see Committee Reports, ¶3870; 3904; 3958.]

[¶3023] CODE SEC. 466. QUALIFIED DISCOUNT COUPONS REDEEMED AFTER CLOSE OF TAXABLE YEAR. [Repealed by section 823(a), '86 TRA]. [1]

[For official explanation, see Committee Reports, ¶3945.]

[Footnote ¶3022 continued]

Matter in *italics* in Sec. 465(b)(6) and (c)(3)(D) added by section 503(a) and (b), '86 TRA which struck out:

(2) "(D) Exclusion for real property.—In the case of activities described in subparagraph (A), the holding of real property (other than mineral property) shall be treated as a separate activity, and subsection (a) shall not apply to losses from such activity. For purposes of the preceding sentence, personal property and services which are incidental to making real property available as living accommodations shall be treated as part of the activity of holding such real property."

(3) "E"

Effective date (Sec. 503(c), '86 TRA).—(1) Generally applies to losses incurred after 12-31-86, with respect to property placed in service by the taxpayer after 12-31-86.

(2) Special rule for losses of S corporation, partnership, or pass-thru entity.—In the case of an interest in an S corporation, a partnership, or other pass-thru entity acquired after 12-31-86, the amendments made by this section shall apply to losses after 12-31-86, which are attributable to property placed in service by the S corporation, partnership, or pass-thru entity on, before, or after 1-1-86.

(3) Special rule for Athletic stadium.—The amendments made by this section shall not apply to any losses incurred by a taxpayer with respect to the holding of a multi-use athletic stadium in Pittsburgh, Pennsylvania, which the taxpayer acquired in a sale for which a letter of understanding was entered into before 4-16-86.

Matter in *italics* in Sec. 465(c)(7)(v) added by section 1011(b)(1), '86 TRA which struck out:

(4) "section 806(c)(3)"

Effective date (Sec. 1011(c)(1), '86 TRA).—Applies to taxable years beginning after 12-31-86.

[Footnote ¶3023] (1) **Effective date** (Sec. 823(c), '86 TRA).—(1) Generally applies to taxable years beginning after 12-31-86.

(2) Change in method of accounting.—In the case of any taxpayer who elected to have section 466 of the '54 Code apply for such taxpayer's last taxable year beginning before 1-1-87, and is required to change its method of accounting by reason of the amendments made by this section for any taxable year—

(A) such change shall be treated as initiated by the taxpayer,

(B) such change shall be treated as having been made with the consent of the Secretary, and

(C) the net amount of adjustments required by section 481 of the '86 code to be taken into account by the taxpayer shall—

(i) be reduced by the balance in the suspense account under section 466(e) of such Code as of the close of such last taxable year, and

(ii) be taken into account over a period not longer than 4 years.

〔¶3024〕 CODE SEC. 467. CERTAIN PAYMENTS FOR THE USE OF PROPERTY OR SERVICES.

* * * * * * * * * * * *

(b) Accrual Of Rental Payments.—

* * * * * * * * * * * *

    (2) Constant rental accrual in case of certain tax avoidance transactions, etc.—In the case of any section 467 rental agreement to which this paragraph applies, the portion of the rent which accrues during any taxable year shall be that portion of the constant rental amount with respect to such agreement which is allocable to such taxable year.

* * * * * * * * * * * *

    (4) Disqualified leaseback or long-term agreement.—For purposes of this subsection, the term "disqualified leaseback or long-term agreement" means any section 467 rental agreement if—

      (A) such agreement is part of a leaseback transaction or such agreement is for a term in excess of 75 percent of the statutory ¹*recovery* period for the property, and

      (B) a principal purpose for providing increasing rents under the agreement is the avoidance of tax imposed by this subtitle.

* * * * * * * * * * * *

(c) Recapture of Prior Understated Inclusions Under Leaseback or Long-Term Agreements.—

* * * * * * * * * * * *

    (4) Leaseback or long-term agreement.—For purposes of this subsection, the term "leaseback or long-term agreement" means any agreement described in ²*subsection (b)(4)(A)*.

    (5) Special rules.—Under regulations prescribed by the Secretary—

      (A) exceptions similar to the exceptions applicable under section 1245 or 1250

〔Footnote ¶3024〕   Matter in *italics* in Sec. 467(b)(4)(A) and (c)(4) added by section 1807(b)(1)(A) and (B), '86 TRA, which struck out:

    (1)   "recover"

    (2)   "subsection (b)(3)(A)"

Effective date (Sec. 1881, '86 TRA and Sec. 92(c), '84 TRA).—

    (1)   In general.—Except as otherwise provided in this subsection, the amendments made by this section shall apply with respect to agreements entered into after 6-8-84.

    (2)   Exceptions.—The amendments made by this section shall not apply—

    (A)   to any agreement entered into pursuant to a written agreement which was binding on 6-8-84, and at all times thereafter,

    (B)   subject to the provisions of paragraph (3), to any agreement to lease property if—

    (i)   there was in effect a firm plan, evidenced by a board of directors' resolution, memorandum of agreement, or letter of intent on 3-15-84, to enter into such an agreement, and

    (ii)   construction of the property was commenced (but such property was not placed in service) on or before 3-15-84,

    (C)   to any agreement to lease property if—

    (i)   the lessee of such property adopted a firm plan to lease the property, evidenced by a resolution of the Finance Committee of the Board of Directors of such lessee, on 2-10-84,

    (ii)   the sum of the present values of the rents payable by the lessee under the lease at the inception thereof equals at least $91,223,034, assuming (for purposes of this clause)—

    (I)   the annual discount rate is 12.6 percent,

    (II)   the initial payment of rent occurs 12 months after the commencement of the lease, and

    (III)   subsequent payments of rents occur on the anniversary date of the initial payment, and

    (iii)   during—

    (I)   the first 5 years of the lease, at least 9 percent of the rents payable by the lessee under the agreement are paid, and

    (II)   the second 5 years of the lease, at least 16.25 percent of the rents payable by the lessee under the agreement are paid.

Paragraph (3)(B)(ii)(II) shall apply for purposes of clauses (ii) and (iii) of subparagraph (C), as if, as of the beginning of the last stage, the separate agreements were treated at 1 single agreement, relating to all property covered by the agreements, including any property placed in service before the property to which the agreement for the last stage relates. If the lessor under the agreement described in subparagraph (C) lease the property from another person, this exception shall also apply to any agreement between the lessor and such person which is integrally related to, and entered into at the same time as, such agreement, and which calls for comparable payments of rent over the primary term of the agreement.

    (3)   Schedule Of Deemed Rental Payments.—

    (A)   In General.—In any case to which paragraph (2)(B) applies, for purposes of the '54 Code, the lessor shall be treated as having received or accrued (and the lessee shall be treated as having paid or incurred) rents equal to the greater of—

(whichever is appropriate) shall apply for purposes of this subsection.

(B)   any transferee in a disposition excepted by reason of subparagraph (A) who has a transferred basis in the property shall be treated in the same manner as the transferor, and

(C)   for purposes of Sections [3]170(e), 341(e)(12), [4]and 751(c), amounts treated as ordinary income under this section shall be treated in the same manner as a amounts treated as ordinary income under section 1245 or 1250.

(d)   Section 467 Rental Agreements.—

* * * * * * * * * * * *

(2)   Section not to apply to agreements involving payments of $250,000 or less.— This section shall not apply to any amount to be paid for the use of property if the sum of the following amounts does not exceed $250,000—

(A)   the aggregate amount of payments received as consideration for such use of property, and

(B)   the aggregate value of any other consideration to be received for such use of property.

For purposes of the preceding sentence, rules similar to the rules of clauses (ii) and (iii) of [5]*section 1274(c)(4)(C)* shall apply.

(e)   Definitions.—For purposes of this section—

⟫**P-H CAUTION→**   There are two versions of Sec. 467(e)(3). Sec. 467(e)(3), generally effective after 12-31-86, follows. For Sec. 467(e)(3), generally effective before 1-1-87, see below.

▲**(3)   Statutory recovery period.—**

[**Footnote ¶3024 continued**]

(i)   the amount of rents actually paid under the agreement during the taxable year, of

(ii)   the amount of rents determined in accordance with the schedule under subparagraph (B) for such taxable year.

(B)   Schedule.—

(i)   In General.—The schedule under this subparagraph is as follows:

Portion of lease term:	Cumulative percentage of total rent deemed paid:
1st ⅕	10
2nd ⅕	25
3rd ⅕	45
4th ⅕	70
Last ⅕	100

(ii)   Operating rules.—For purposes of this schedule—

(I)   the rent allocable to each taxable year within any portion of a lease term described in such schedule shall be a level pro rata amount properly allocable to such taxable year, and

(II)   any agreement relating to property which is to be placed in service in 2 or more stages shall be treated as 2 or more separate agreements.

(C)   Paragraph not to apply.—This paragraph shall not apply to any agreement if the sum of the present values of all payments under the agreement is greater than the sum of the present value of all the payments deemed to be paid or received under the schedule under subparagraph (B). For purposes of computing any present value under this subparagraph, the annual discount rate shall be equal to 12 percent, compounded semiannually.

Sec. 511(d)(2)(A), '86 TRA, struck out from Sec. 467(c)(5):
(3)   "163(d)"
Effective date (Sec. 511(e), '86 TRA).—Applies to taxable years beginning after 12-31-86.

Sec. 631(e)(10), '86 TRA, struck out from Sec. 467(c)(5):
(4)   "453B(d)(2)"
Effective date (Sec. 633, '86 TRA).—(a)   Generally applies to—
(1)   any distribution in complete liquidation, and any sale or exchange, made by a corporation after 7-31-86, unless such corporation is completely liquidated before 1-1-87,
(2)   any transaction described in section 338, '86 Code, for which the acquisition date occurs after 12-31-86, and
(3)   any distribution (not in complete liquidation) made after 12-31-86.
For special and transitional rules, see ¶2023.

Matter in *italics* in Sec. 467(d)(2) added by section 1807(b)(2)(C), '86 TRA, which struck out:
(5)   "section 1274(c)(2)(C)"
Effective date (Sec. 1881, '86 TRA, and Sec. 92(c), '84 TRA).—Generally applies with respect to agreements entered into after 6-8-84. For exceptions and special rules, see above.

(A) In general.—

⁶*In the case of:*	*The statutory recovery period is:*
3-year property	*3 years*
5-year property	*5 years*
7-year property	*7 years*
10-year property	*10 years*
15-year and 20-year property	*15 years*
Residential rental property and nonresidential real property	*19 years.*

(B) *Special rule for property not depreciable under section 168.—In the case of property to which section 168 does not apply, subparagraph (A) shall be applied as if section 168 applies to such property.*

≫**P-H CAUTION→** There are two versions of Sec. 467(e)(3). Sec. 467(e)(3), generally effective before 1-1-87, follows. For Sec. 467(e)(3), generally effective after 12-31-86, see above.

▲▲(3) **Statutory recovery period.—**
(A) In general.—

In the case of property which is:	The statutory recovery period is:
3-year property	3 years
5-year property	5 years
10-year property	10 years
Low-income housing	15 years
15-year public utility property	15 years
⁷19-year real property	⁸19 years

* * * * * * * * * * * *

≫**P-H CAUTION→** There are two versions of Sec. 467(e)(5), generally effective after 12-31-86, follows. For Sec. 467(e)(5), generally effective before 1-1-87, see below.

【Footnote ¶3024 continued】

▲ Matter in *italics* in Sec. 467(e)(3) preceded by a triangle added by section 201(d)(8)(A), '86 TRA, which struck out:

(6)

"In the case of property which is:	The statutory recovery period is:
3-year property	3 years
5-year property	5 years
10-year property	10 years
Low-income housing	15 years
15-year public utility property	15 years
19-year real property	19 years

(B) Special rule for property which is not recovery property.—In the case of any property which is not recovery property, subparagraph (A) shall be applied as if such property were recovery property."

Effective date (Sec. 203(a), '86 TRA).—Generally applies to property placed in service after 12-31-86, in taxable years ending after such date.

For transitional and special rules, see ¶2007—2008.

▲▲Matter in *italics* in Sec. 467(e)(3), preceded by two triangles added by section 1879(f)(1)(A) and (B), '86 TRA, which struck out:

(7) "18-year real property"

(8) "18 years"

Effective date (Sec. 1881, '86 TRA and section 105(b)(1) and (2), P.L. 99-121).—(1) Generally applies with respect to property placed in service by the taxpayer after 5-8-85.

(2) Exception.—The amendments made by section 103 shall not apply to property placed in service by the taxpayer before 1-1-87, if—

(A) the taxpayer or a qualified person entered into a binding contract to purchase or construct such property before 5-9-85, or

(B) construction of such property was commenced by or for the taxpayer or qualified person before 5-9-85.

For purposes of this paragraph, the term "qualified person" means any person whose rights in such a contract or such property are transferred to the taxpayer, but only if such property is not placed in service before such rights are transferred to the taxpayer.

▲ **(5) Related person.**—The term "related person" has the meaning given to such term by [9]*section 465(b)(3)(C).*

➤➤**P-H CAUTION**➤ There are two versions of Sec. 467(e)(5). Sec. 467(e)(5), generally effective before 1-1-87, follows. For Sec. 467(e)(5), generally effective after 12-31-86, see above.

▲ ▲ **(5) Related person.**—The term "related person" has the meaning given to such term by [10]*section 168(e)(4)(D).*

* * * * * * * * * * * *

(g) Comparable Rules for Services.—Under regulations prescribed by the Secretary, rules comparable to the rules of subsection (a)(2) shall also apply in the case of payments for services which meet requirements comparable to the requirements of subsection (d). *The preceding sentence shall not apply to any amount to which section 404 or 404A (or any other provision specified in regulations) applies.*

* * * * * * * * * * * *

[For official explanation, see Committee Reports, ¶3870; 3905; 3917; 4141; 4193.]

[¶3025] CODE SEC. 468. SPECIAL RULES FOR MINING AND SOLID WASTE RECLAMATION AND CLOSING COSTS.

(a) Establishment of Reserves for Reclamation and Closing Costs.—

(1) Allowance of deduction.—If a taxpayer elects the application of this [1]*section* with respect to any mining or solid waste disposal property, the amount of any deduction for qualified reclamation or closing costs for any taxable year to which such election applies shall be equal to the current reclamation or closing costs allocable to—

(A) in the case of qualified reclamation costs, the portion of the reserve property which was disturbed during such taxable year, and

(B) in the case of qualified closing costs, the production from the reserve property during such taxable year.

(2) Opening balance and adjustments to reserve.—

* * * * * * * * * * * *

(D) Reserve increased by amount deducted.—A reserve shall be increased each taxable year by the amount allowable as a deduction under paragraph (1) for such taxable year which is allocable to such reserve.

* * * * * * * * * * * *

(d) Definitions and Special Rules Relating to Reclamation and Closing Costs.—For purposes of this section—

* * * * * * * * * * * *

(2) Qualified reclamation or closing costs.—The term "qualified reclamation or closing costs" means any of the following expenses:

* * * * * * * * * * * *

(B) Solid waste disposal and closing costs.—

[Footnote ¶3024 continued]

▲ Matter in *italics* in Sec. 467(e)(5), preceded by a triangle, added by section 201(d)(8)(B), '86 TRA, which struck out:

(9) "section 168(e)(4)(D)"

Effective date (Sec. 203(a), '86 TRA).—Generally applies to property placed in service after 12-31-86, in taxable years ending after such date. For transitional and special rules, see ¶2007—2008.

▲ ▲ Matter in *italics* in Sec. 467(e)(5), preceded by two triangles, added by section 1807(b)(2)(D), '86 TRA, which struck out:

(10) "168(d)(4)(D)"

Effective date (Sec. 1881, '86 TRA, and Sec. 92(c), '84 TRA).—Generally applies with respect to agreements entered into after 6-8-84. For exceptions and special rules, see above.

Matter in *italics* in Sec. 467(g) added by section 1807(b)(1), '86 TRA.

Effective date (Sec. 1881, '86 TRA, and Sec. 92(c), '84 TRA).—Generally applies with respect to agreements entered into after 6-8-84. For exceptions and special rules, see above.

[Footnote ¶3025] Matter in *italics* in Sec. 468(a)(1) and (2)(D) added by section 1807(a)(3)(A) and (C), '86 TRA, which struck out:

(1) "subsection"

Effective date (Sec. 1881, '86 TRA and Sec. 91(g)(4), '84 TRA, as added by 1807(a)(3)(B), '86 TRA).—Generally takes effect on 7-18-84. For exceptions and special rules, see footnote ¶3019.

Matter in *italics* in Sec. 468(d)(2)(B)(ii) added by section 1899A(14).

    (i)   In general.—Any expenses incurred for any land reclamation or closing activity in connection with any solid waste disposal site which is conducted in accordance with any permit issued pursuant to—

        (I)   any provision of the Solid Waste Disposal Act (as in effect on January 1, 1984) requiring such activity, or

        (II)   any other Federal, State, or local law which imposes requirements substantially similar to the requirements imposed by the Solid Waste Disposal Act (as so in effect).

    (ii)   Exception for certain hazardous waste sites.—Clause (i) shall not apply to that portion of any property which is disturbed after the property is listed in the national contingency plan established under section 105 of the Comprehensive Environmental *Response* Compensation, and Liability Act of 1980.

* * * * * * * * * * *

[For official explanation, see Committee Reports, ¶4141.]

【¶3025-A】 CODE SEC. 468A. SPECIAL RULES FOR NUCLEAR DECOMMISSIONING COSTS.

(a)   In General.—If the taxpayer elects the application of this [1]*section,* there shall be allowed as a deduction for any taxable year the amount of payments made by the taxpayer to a Nuclear Decommissioning Reserve Fund (hereinafter referred to as the "Fund") during such taxable year.

* * * * * * * * * * *

(c)   Income and Deductions of the Taxpayer.—

    (1)   Inclusion of amounts distributed.—There shall be includible in the gross income of the taxpayer for any taxable year—

        (A)   any amount distributed from the Fund during such taxable year, other than any amount distributed to pay costs described in [2]*subsection (e)(4)(B),* and

        (B)   except to the extent provided in regulations, amounts properly includible in gross income in the case of any deemed distribution under subsection (e)(6), any termination under subsection (e)(7), or the disposition of any interest in the nuclear powerplant.

* * * * * * * * * * *

(d)   Ruling Amount.—For purposes of this [1]*section*—

* * * * * * * * * * *

(e)   Nuclear Decommissioning [3]*Reserve* Fund.—

    (1)   In general.—Each taxpayer who elects the application of this [1]*section* shall establish a Nuclear Decommissioning [4]*Reserve* Fund with respect to each nuclear powerplant to which such election applies.

    (2)   Taxation of fund.—

        [5]*(A)   In general.—There is hereby imposed on the gross income of the Fund for any taxable year a tax at a rate equal to the highest rate of tax specified in section 11(b), except that—*

            (i)   there shall not be included in the gross income of the Fund any payment to the Fund with respect to which a deduction is allowable under subsection (a), and

            (ii)   there shall be allowed as a deduction to the Fund any amount paid by the Fund which is described in paragraph (4)(B) (other than an amount paid to the taxpayer) and which would be deductible under this chapter for purposes of determining the taxable income of a corporation.

【Footnote ¶3025-A】   Matter in *italics* in Sec. 468A added by section 1807(a)(4)(A)(i), (B)—(E)(i)—(vi), '86 TRA, which struck out:

(1)   "subsection"

(2)   "subsection (e)(2)(B)"

(3)   **"Trust"**

(4)   **"Trust"**

(5)   "There is imposed on the gross income of the Fund for any taxable year a tax at a rate equal to the maximum rate in effect under section 11(b), except that.—

(A)   there shall not be included in the gross income of the Fund any payment to the Fund with respect to which a deduction is allowable under subsection (a), and

(B)   there shall be allowed as a deduction any amount paid by the Fund described in paragraph (4)(B) (other than to the taxpayer)."

Code §468A(e)(2) ¶3025-A

    (B)   Tax in lieu of other taxation.—The tax imposed by subparagraph (A) shall be in lieu of any other taxation under this subtitle of the income from assets in the Fund.

    (C)   Fund treated as corporation.—For purposes of subtitle F—

        (i)   the Fund shall be treated as if it were a corporation, and

        (ii)   any tax imposed by this paragraph shall be treated as a tax imposed by section 11.

*   *   *   *   *   *   *   *   *   *   *   *

    (4)   Use of fund.—The Fund shall be used exclusively for—

    (A)   satisfying, in whole or in part, any liability of any person contributing to the Fund for the decommissioning of a nuclear powerplant (or unit thereof), [6]

    (B)   to pay administrative costs (including taxes) and other incidental expenses of the Fund (including legal, accounting, actuarial, and trustee expenses) in connection with the operation of the Fund [7], *and*

    (C)   to the extent that a portion of the Fund is not currently needed for purposes described in subparagraph (A) or (B), making investments described in section 501(c)(21)(B)(ii).

*   *   *   *   *   *   *   *   *   *   *   *

    (6)   Disqualification of fund.—In any case in which the Fund violates any provision of this [1]*section* or section 4951, the Secretary may disqualify such Fund from the application of this [1]*section*. In any case to which this [8]*paragraph* applies, the Fund shall be treated as having distributed all of its funds on the date such determination takes effect.

    (7)   Termination upon completion.—Upon substantial completion of the nuclear decommissioning of the nuclear powerplant with respect to which a Fund relates, the taxpayer shall terminate such Fund.

    (f)   Nuclear Powerplant.—[9]*For purposes of this section, the* term "nuclear powerplant" includes any unit thereof.

    (g)   Time When Payments Deemed Made.—For purposes of this section, a taxpayer shall be deemed to have made a payment to the Fund on the last day of a taxable year if such payment is made on account of such taxable year and is made within $2\frac{1}{2}$ months after the close of such taxable year.

    [For official explanation, see Committee Reports, ¶4141.]

〔¶3025-B〕   CODE SEC. 468B.   SPECIAL RULES FOR DESIGNATED SETTLEMENT FUNDS.

    (a)   In General—For purposes of section 461(h), economic performance shall be deemed to occur as qualified payments are made by the taxpayer to a designated settlement fund.

〔Footnote ¶3025-A continued〕

  (6)   "and"

  (7)   "."

  (8)   "subparagraph"

  (9)   "The"

  Effective date (Sec. 1881, '86 TRA and Sec. 91(g)(5), '84 TRA, as added by section 1807(a)(4)(F), '86 TRA, and section 1807(a)(4)(A)(ii), '86 TRA).—Takes effect on 7-18-84, with respect to taxable years ending after such date.

  (ii)   Transitional rule.—To the extent provided in regulations prescribed by the Secretary of the Treasury or his delegate, subsection (g) of section 468A '54 Code (as added by clause (i)) shall be applied with respect to any payment on account of a taxable year beginning before 1-1-87, as if it did not contain the requirement that the payment be made within $2\frac{1}{2}$ months after the close of the taxable year. Such regulations may provide that, to the extent such payment to the Fund is made more than $2\frac{1}{2}$ months after the close of the taxable year, any adjustment to the tax attributable to such payment shall not affect the amount of interest payable with respect to periods before the payment is made. Such regulations may provide appropriate adjustments to the deduction allowed under such section 468A for any such taxable year to take into account the fact that the payment to the Fund is made more than $2\frac{1}{2}$ months after the close of the taxable year.

  〔Footnote ¶3025-B〕   Sec. 468B added by section 1807(a)(7)(A), '86 TRA.

  Effective date (Sec. 1881, '86 TRA and section 91(g)(1), '84 TRA, as amended by 1807(a)(3)(B), (4)(F), (5) and (6), '86 TRA).—(g)(1)

  (g)(1)   In general.—Except as provided in this subsection and subsections (h) and (i), the amendments made by this section shall apply to amounts with respect to which a deduction would be allowable under chapter 1 of the '54 Code (determined without regard to such amendments) after—

  (A)   in the case of amounts to which section 461(h) of such Code (as added by such amendments) applies, 7-18-84, and

(b) Taxation of Designated Settlement Fund.—

(1) **In general.**—There is imposed on the gross income of any designated settlement fund for any taxable year a tax at a rate equal to the maximum rate in effect for such taxable year under section 1(e).

(2) **Certain expenses allowed.**—For purposes of paragraph (1), gross income for any taxable year shall be reduced by the amount of any administrative costs (including State and local taxes) and other incidental expenses of the designated settlement fund (including legal, accounting, and actuarial expenses)—

(A) which are incurred in connection with the operation of the fund, and

(B) which would be deductible under this chapter for purposes of determining the taxable income of the corporation,

no other deduction shall be allowed to the fund.

(3) **Transfers to the fund.**—In the case of any qualified payment made to the fund—

(A) the amount of such payment shall not be treated as income of the designated settlement fund,

(B) the basis of the fund in any property which constitutes a qualified payment shall be equal to the fair market value of such property at the time of payment, and

(C) the fund shall be treated as the owner of the property in the fund (and any earnings thereon).

(4) **Tax in lieu of other taxation.**—The tax imposed by paragraph (1) shall be in lieu of any other taxation under this subtitle of income from assets in the designated settlement fund.

(5) **Coordination with subtitle F.**—For purposes of subtitle F—

(A) a designated settlement fund shall be treated as a corporation, and

(B) any tax imposed by this subsection shall be treated as a tax imposed by section 11.

(c) Deductions not Allowed for Transfer of Insurance Amounts.—No deduction shall be allowable for any qualified payment by the taxpayer of any amounts received from the settlement of any insurance claim to the extent such amounts are excluded from the gross income of the taxpayer.

(d) Definitions.—For purposes of this section—

(1) **Qualified payment.**—The term "qualified payment" means any money or property which is transferred to any designated settlement fund pursuant to a court order, other than—

(A) any amount which may be transferred from the fund to the taxpayer, or

(B) the transfer of any stock or indebtedness of the taxpayer (or any related person).

(2) **Designated settlement fund.**—The term "designated settlement fund" means any fund—

(A) which is established pursuant to a court order,

(B) with respect to which no amounts may be transferred other than in the form of qualified payments,

(C) which is administered by persons a majority of whom are independent of the taxpayer,

(D) which is established for the principal purpose of resolving and satisfying present and future claims against the taxpayer (or any related person or formerly related person) arising out of personal injury, death, or property damage,

(E) under the terms of which the taxpayer may not hold any beneficial interest in the income or corpus of the fund, and

(F) with respect to which an election is made under this section by the taxpayer.

An election under this section shall be made at such time and in such manner as the Secretary shall by regulation prescribe. Such an election, once made, may be revoked only with the consent of the Secretary.

[Footnote ¶3025-B continued]

(B) in the case of amounts to which section 461(i) of such Code (as so added) applies after 3-31-84.

For special and transitional rules see footnote ¶3019.

See Sec. 1807(a)(7)(C) and (D), '86 TRA, 2106 for special rule for taxpayer in bankruptcy reorganization and clarification of law with repsect to certain funds.

Code §468B(d)(2) ¶3025-B

(3) **Related person.**—The term "related person" means a person related to the taxpayer within the meaning of section 267(b).

(e) **Nonapplicability of section.**—This section shall not apply with respect to any liability of the taxpayer arising under any workers' compensation Act or any contested liability of the taxpayer within the meaning of section 461(f).

(f) **Other funds.**—Except as provided in regulations, any payment in respect of a liability described in subsection (d)(2)(D) (and not described in subsection (e)) to a trust fund or escrow fund which is not a designated settlement fund shall not be treated as constituting economic performance.

[For official explanation, see Committee Reports, ¶4141.]

[¶3026] CODE SEC. 469. PASSIVE ACTIVITY LOSSES AND CREDITS LIMITED.

(a) **Disallowance.**—

(1) **In general.**—If for any taxable year the taxpayer is described in paragraph (2), neither—
    (A)   the passive activity loss, nor
    (B)   the passive activity credit,
for the taxable year shall be allowed.

(2) **Persons described.**—The following are described in this paragraph:
    (A)   any individual, estate, or trust,
    (B)   any closely held C corporation, and
    (C)   any personal service corporation.

(b) **Disallowed Loss Or Credit Carried To Next Year.**—Except as otherwise provided in this section, any loss or credit from an activity which is disallowed under subsection (a) shall be treated as a deduction or credit allocable to such activity in the next taxable year.

(c) **Passive Activity Defined.**—For purposes of this section—

(1) **In general.**—The term "passive activity" means any activity—
    (A)   which involves the conduct of any trade or business, and
    (B)   in which the taxpayer does not materially participate.

(2) **Passive activity includes any rental activity.**—The term "passive activity" includes any rental activity.

(3) **Working interests in oil and gas property.**—
    (A)   **In general.**—The term "passive activity" shall not include any working interest in any oil or gas property which the taxpayer holds directly or through an entity which does not limit the liability of the taxpayer with respect to such interest.
    (B)   **Income in subsequent years.**—If any taxpayer has any loss for any taxable year from a working interest in any oil or gas property which is treated as a loss which is not from a passive activity, then any net income from such property (or any property the basis of which is determined in whole or in part by reference to the basis of such property) for any succeeding taxable year shall be treated as income of the taxpayer which is not from a passive activity.

(4) **Material participation not required for paragraphs (2) and (3).**—Paragraphs (2) and (3) shall be applied without regard to whether or not the taxpayer materially participates in the activity.

(5) **Trade or business includes research and experimentation activity.**—For purposes of paragraph (1)(A), the term "trade or business" includes any activity involving research or experimentation (within the meaning of section 174).

[Footnote ¶3026] Sec. 469 added by section 501(a), '86 TRA.

Effective date (Sec. 501(c), '86 TRA.—(1) Generally applies to taxable years beginning after 12-31-86.

(2) Special rule for carryovers.—The amendments made by this section shall not apply to any loss, deduction, or credit carried to a taxable year beginning after 12-31-86, from a taxable year beginning before 1-1-87.

(3) Special rule for low-income housing.—

(A) In general.—Except as provided in subparagraph (B), section 469(i)(6)(B)(i) of the '86 Code (as added by this section) shall not apply to any property placed in service after 12-31-89.

(B) Exception where at least 10 percent of costs incurred.—In the case of property placed in service after 12-31-89, and before 1-1-91, section 469(i)(6)(B)(i) of such Code shall apply to such property if at least 10 percent of the costs of such property were incurred before 1-1-89.

For transitional rule, see ¶2020.

(6)   Activity in connection with trade or business or production of income.—To the extent provided in regulations, for purposes of paragraph (1)(A), the term "trade or business" includes—

   (A)   any activity in connection with a trade or business, or

   (B)   any activity with respect to which expenses are allowable as a deduction under section 212.

(d)   Passive Activity Loss and Credit Defined.—For purposes of this section—

   (1)   Passive activity loss.—The term "passive activity loss" means the amount (if any) by which—

   (A)   the aggregate losses from all passive activities for the taxable year, exceed

   (B)   the aggregate income from all passive activities for such year.

   (2)   Passive activity credit.—The term "passive activity credit" means the amount (if any) by which—

   (A)   the sum of the credits from all passive activities allowable for the taxable year under—

   (i)   subpart D of part IV of subchapter A, or

   (ii)   subpart B (other than section 27(a)) of such part IV, exceeds

   (B)   the regular tax liability of the taxpayer for the taxable year allocable to all passive activities.

(e)   Special Rules for Determining Income or Loss From a Passive Activity.—For purposes of this section—

   (1)   Certain income not treated as income from passive activity.—In determining the income or loss from any activity—

   (A)   In general.—There shall not be taken into account—

   (i)   any—

   (I)   gross income from interest, dividends, annuities, or royalties not derived in the ordinary course of a trade or business,

   (II)   expenses (other than interest) which are clearly and directly allocable to such gross income, and

   (III)   interest expense properly allocable to such gross income, and

   (ii)   gain or loss attributable to the disposition of property—

   (I)   producing income of a type described in clause (i), or

   (II)   held for investment.

For purposes of clause (ii), any interest in a passive activity shall not be treated as property held for investment.

   (B)   Return on working capital.—For purposes of subparagraph (A), any income, gain, or loss which is attributable to an investment of working capital shall be treated as not derived in the ordinary course of a trade or business.

   (2)   Passive losses of certain closely held corporations may offset active income.—

   (A)   In general.—If a closely held C corporation (other than a personal service corporation) has net active income for any taxable year, the passive activity loss of such taxpayer for such taxable year (determined without regard to this paragraph)—

   (i)   shall be allowable as a deduction against net active income, and

   (ii)   shall not be taken into account under subsection (a) to the extent so allowable as a deduction.

A similar rule shall apply in the case of any passive activity credit of the taxpayer.

   (B)   Net active income.—For purposes of this paragraph, the term "net active income" means the taxable income of the taxpayer for the taxable year determined without regard to—

   (i)   any income or loss from a passive activity, and

   (ii)   any item of gross income, expense, gain, or loss described in paragraph (1)(A).

   (3)   Compensation for personal services.—Earned income (within the meaning of section 911(d)(2)(A)) shall not be taken into account in computing the income or loss from a passive activity for any taxable year.

   (4)   Dividends reduced by dividends received deduction.—For purposes of paragraphs (1) and (2), income from dividends shall be reduced by the amount of any dividends received deduction under section 243, 244, or 245.

Code §469(e)(4)   ¶3026

(f)   **Treatment of Former Passive Activities.**—For purposes of this section—

(1)   **In general.**—If an activity is a former passive activity for any taxable year—

(A)   any unused deduction allocable to such activity under subsection (b) shall be offset against the income from such activity for the taxable year,

(B)   any unused credit allocable to such activity under subsection (b) shall be offset against the regular tax liability (computed after the application of paragraph (1)) allocable to such activity for the taxable year, and

(C)   any such deduction or credit remaining after the application of subparagraphs (A) and (B) shall continue to be treated as arising from a passive activity.

(2)   **Change in status of closely held C corporation or personal service corporation.**—If a taxpayer ceases for any taxable year to be a closely held C corporation or personal service corporation, this section shall continue to apply to losses and credits to which this section applied for any preceding taxable year in the same manner as if such taxpayer continued to be a closely held C corporation or personal service corporation, whichever is applicable.

(3)   **Former passive activity.**—The term "former passive activity" means any activity which, with respect to the taxpayer—

(A)   is not a passive activity for the taxable year, but

(B)   was a passive activity for any prior taxable year.

(g)   **Dispositions of Entire Interest in Passive Activity.**—If during the taxable year a taxpayer disposes of his entire interest in any passive activity (or former passive activity), the following rules shall apply:

(1)   **Fully taxable transaction.**—

(A)   In general.—If all gain or loss realized on such disposition is recognized, any loss from such activity which has not previously been allowed as a deduction (and in the case of a passive activity for the taxable year, any loss realized on such disposition) shall not be treated as a passive activity loss and shall be allowable as a deduction against income in the following order:

(i)   Income or gain from the passive activity for the taxable year (including any gain recognized on the disposition).

(ii)   Net income or gain for the taxable year from all passive activities.

(iii)   Any other income or gain.

(B)   Subparagraph (a) not to apply to disposition involving related party.—If the taxpayer and the person acquiring the interest bear a relationship to each other described in section 267(b) or section 707(b)(1), then subparagraph (A) shall not apply to any loss of the taxpayer until the taxable year in which such interest is acquired (in a transaction described in subparagraph (A)) by another person who does not bear such a relationship to the taxpayer.

(C)   Coordination with section 1211.—In the case of any loss realized on the disposition of an interest in a passive activity, section 1211 shall be applied before subparagraph (A) is applied.

(2)   **Disposition by death.**—If an interest in the activity is transferred by reason of the death of the taxpayer—

(A)   paragraph (1) shall apply to such losses to the extent such losses are greater than the excess (if any) of—

(i)   the basis of such property in the hands of the transferee, over

(ii)   the adjusted basis of such property immediately before the death of the taxpayer, and

(B)   any losses to the extent of the excess described in subparagraph (A) shall not be allowed as a deduction for any taxable year.

(3)   **Installment sale of entire interest.**—In the case of an installment sale of an entire interest in an activity to which section 453 applies, paragraph (1) shall apply to the portion of such losses for each taxable year which bears the same ratio to all such losses as the gain recognized on such sale during such taxable year bears to the gross profit from such sale realized (or to be realized) when payment is completed.

(h)   **Material Participation Defined.**—For purposes of this section—

(1)   **In general.**—A taxpayer shall be treated as materially participating in an activity only if the taxpayer is involved in the operations of the activity on a basis which is—

(A)   regular,

(B)   continuous, and

(C) substantial.

(2) **Interests in limited partnerships.**—Except as provided in regulations, no interest in a limited partnership as a limited partner shall be treated as an interest with respect to which a taxpayer materially participates.

(3) **Treatment of certain retired individuals and surviving spouses.**—A taxpayer shall be treated as materially participating in any farming activity for a taxable year if paragraph (4) or (5) of section 2032A(b) would cause the requirements of section 2032A(b)(1)(C)(ii) to be met with respect to real property used in such activity if such taxpayer had died during the taxable year.

(4) **Certain closely held C corporations and personal service corporations.**—A closely held C corporation or personal service corporation shall be treated as materially participating in an activity if—

   (A) 1 or more shareholders holding stock representing more than 50 percent (by value) of the outstanding stock of such corporation materially participate in such activity, or

   (B) in the case of a closely held C corporation (other than a personal service corporation), the requirements of section 465(c)(7)(C) (without regard to clause (iv)) are met with respect to such activity.

(5) **Participation by spouse.**—In determining whether a taxpayer materially participates, the participation of the spouse of the taxpayer shall be taken into account.

(i) $25,000 Offset for Rental Real Estate Activities.—

(1) **In general.**—In the case of any natural person, subsection (a) shall not apply to that portion of the passive activity loss or the deduction equivalent (within the meaning of subsection (j)(5)) of the passive activity credit for any taxable year which is attributable to all rental real estate activities with respect to which such individual actively participated in the taxable year in which such portion of such loss or credit arose.

(2) **Dollar limitation.**—The aggregate amount to which paragraph (1) applies for any taxable year shall not exceed $25,000.

(3) **Phase-out of exemption.**—

   (A) **In general.**—In the case of any taxpayer, the $25,000 amount under paragraph (2) shall be reduced (but not below zero) by 50 percent of the amount by which the adjusted gross income of the taxpayer for the taxable year exceeds $100,000.

   (B) **Special phase-out of low-income housing and rehabilitation credits.**—In the case of any portion of the passive activity credit for any taxable year which is attributable to any credit to which paragraph (6)(B) applies, subparagraph (A) shall be applied by substituting "$200,000" for "$100,000".

   (C) **Ordering rule to reflect separate phase-outs.**—If subparagraph (B) applies for any taxable year, paragraph (1) shall be applied—

      (i) first to the passive activity loss,

      (ii) second to the portion of the passive activity credit to which subparagraph (B) does not apply, and

      (iii) then to the portion of such credit to which subparagraph (B) applies.

   (D) **Adjusted gross income.**—For purposes of this paragraph, adjusted gross income shall be determined without regard to—

      (i) any amount includible in gross income under section 86,

      (ii) any amount allowable as a deduction under section 219, and

      (iii) any passive activity loss.

(4) **Special rule for estates.**—

   (A) **In general.**—In the case of taxable years of an estate ending less than 2 years after the date of the death of the decedent, this subsection shall apply to all rental real estate activities with respect to which such decedent actively participated before his death.

   (B) **Reduction for surviving spouse's exemption.**—For purposes of subparagraph (A), the $25,000 amount under paragraph (2) shall be reduced by the amount of the exemption under paragraph (1) (without regard to paragraph (3)) allowable to the surviving spouse of the decedent for the taxable year ending with or within the taxable year of the estate.

(5) **Married individuals filing separately.**—

(A) In general.—Except as provided in subparagraph (B), in the case of any married individual filing a separate return, this subsection shall be applied by substituting—

    (i) "$12,500" for "$25,000" each place it appears,

    (ii) "$50,000" for "$100,000" in paragraph (3)(A), and

    (iii) "$100,000" for "$200,000" in paragraph (3)(B).

(B) Taxpayers not living apart.—This subsection shall not apply to a taxpayer who—

    (i) is a married individual filing a separate return for any taxable year, and

    (ii) does not live apart from his spouse at all times during such taxable year.

(6) Active participation.—

(A) In general.—An individual shall not be treated as actively participating with respect to any interest in any rental real estate activity for any period if, at any time during such period, such interest (including any interest of the spouse of the individual) is less than 10 percent (by value) of all interests in such activity.

(B) No participation requirement for low-income housing or rehabilitation credit.—Paragraphs (1) and (4)(A) shall be applied without regard to the active participation requirement in the case of—

    (i) any credit determined under section 42 for any taxable year, or

    (ii) any rehabilitation investment credit (within the meaning of section 48(o)).

(C) Interest as a limited partner.—No interest as a limited partner in a limited partnership shall be treated as an interest with respect to which the taxpayer actively participates.

(D) Participation by spouse.—In determining whether a taxpayer actively participates, the participation of the spouse of the taxpayer shall be taken into account.

(j) **Other Definitions and Special Rules.**—For purposes of this section—

(1) Closely held C corporation.—The term "closely held C Corporation" means any C corporation described in section 465(a)(1)(B).

(2) Personal Service Corporation.—The term "personal service corporation" has the meaning given such term by section 269A(b)(1), except that section 269A(b)(2) shall be applied—

(A) by substituting "any" for "more than 10 percent", and

(B) by substituting "any" for "50 percent or more in value" in section 318(a)(2)(C).

A corporation shall not be treated as a personal service corporation unless more than 10 percent of the stock (by value) in such corporation is held by employee-owners (within the meaning of section 269A(b)(2), as modified by the preceding sentence).

(3) Regular tax liability.—The term "regular tax liability" has the meaning given such term by section 26(b).

(4) Allocation of passive activity loss and credit.—The passive activity loss and the passive activity credit (and the $25,000 amount under subsection (i)) shall be allocated to activities, and within activities, on a pro rata basis in such manner as the Secretary may prescribe.

(5) Deduction equivalent.—The deduction equivalent of credits from a passive activity for any taxable year is the amount which (if allowed as a deduction) would reduce the regular tax liability for such taxable year by an amount equal to such credits.

(6) Special rule for gifts.—In the case of a disposition of any interest in a passive activity by gift—

(A) the basis of such interest immediately before the transfer shall be increased by the amount of any passive activity losses allocable to such interest, and

(B) such losses shall not be allowable as a deduction for any taxable year.

(7) Qualified residence interest.—The passive activity loss of a taxpayer shall be computed without regard to qualified residence interest (within the meaning of section 163(h)(3)).

(8) Rental activity.—The term "rental activity" means any activity where payments are principally for the use of tangible property.

(9) Election to increase basis of property by amount of disallowed credit.—For purposes of determining gain or loss from a disposition of any property to which subsection (g)(1) applies, the transferor may elect to increase the basis of such property immediately before the transfer by an amount equal to the portion of any unused credit allowable under this chapter which reduced the basis of such property for the taxable year in which such credit arose. If the taxpayer elects the application of this paragraph, such portion of the passive activity credit of such taxpayer shall not be allowed for any taxable year.

(k) Regulations.—The Secretary shall prescribe such regulations as may be necessary or appropriate to carry out provisions of this section, including regulations—

(1)   which specify what constitutes an activity, material participation, or active participation for purposes of this section,

(2)   which provide that certain items of gross income will not be taken into account in determining income or loss from any activity (and the treatment of expenses allocable to such income),

(3)   requiring net income or gain from a limited partnership or other passive activity to be treated as not from a passive activity,

(4)   which provide for the determination of the allocation of interest expense for purposes of this section, and

(5)   which deal with changes in marital status and changes between joint returns and separate returns.

(l) Phase-In of Disallowance of Losses and Credits for Interests Held Before Date of Enactment.—

(1) **In general.**—In the case of any passive activity loss or credit for any taxable year beginning in calendar years 1987 through 1990 which—

(A)   is attributable to a pre-enactment interest, but

(B)   is not attributable to a carryforward to such taxable year of any loss or credit which was disallowed under this section for a preceding taxable year,

there shall be disallowed under subsection (a) only the applicable percentage of the amount which (but for this subsection) would have been disallowed under subsection (a) for such taxable year.

(2) **Applicable percentage.**—For purposes of this subsection, the applicable percentage shall be determined in accordance with the following table:

In the case of taxable years beginning in:	The applicable percentage is:
1987	35
1988	60
1989	80
1990	90.

(3) **Portion of loss or credit attributable to pre-enactment interests.**—For purposes of this subsection—

(A) **In general.**—The portion of the passive activity loss for any taxable year which is attributable to pre-enactment interests shall be equal to the lesser of—

(i)   the passive activity loss for such taxable year, or

(ii)   the passive activity loss for such taxable year determined by taking into account only pre-enactment interests.

For purposes of this subparagraph, the deduction equivalent (within the meaning of subsection (j)(5)) of a passive activity credit shall be taken into account.

(B) **Pre-enactment interest.—**

(i) **In general.**—The term "pre-enactment interest" means any interest in a passive activity held by a taxpayer on the date of the enactment of the Tax Reform Act of 1986, and at all times thereafter.

(ii) **Binding contract exception.**—For purposes of clause (i), any interest acquired after such date of enactment pursuant to a written binding contract in effect on such date, and at all times thereafter, shall be treated as held on such date.

(iii) **Interest in activities.**—The term "pre-enactment interest" shall not include an interest in a passive activity unless such activity was being conducted on such date of enactment. The preceding sentence shall not apply to an activity commencing after such date if—

(I)   the property used in such activity is acquired pursuant to a written binding contract in effect on August 16, 1986, and at all times thereafter, or

(II)   construction of property used in such activity began on or before August 16, 1986.

Code §469(l)(3) ¶3026

[For official explanation, see Committee Reports, ¶3902.]

⟦¶3027⟧ CODE SEC. 471. GENERAL RULE FOR INVENTORIES.

(a) *General Rule.*—Whenever in the opinion of the Secretary the use of inventories is necessary in order clearly to determine the income of any taxpayer, inventories shall be taken by such taxpayer on such basis as the Secretary may prescribe as conforming as nearly as may be to the best accounting practice in the trade or business and as most clearly reflecting the income.

(b) *Cross Reference.—*

For rules relating to capitalization of direct and indirect costs of property, see section 263A.

[For official explanation, see Committee Reports, ¶3937.]

⟦¶3028⟧ CODE SEC. 474.[1] *SIMPLIFIED DOLLAR-VALUE LIFO METHOD FOR CERTAIN SMALL BUSINESSES.*

(a) *General Rule.*—*An eligible small business may elect to use the simplified dollar-value method of pricing inventories for purposes of the LIFO method.*

(b) *Simplified Dollar-Value Method of Pricing Inventories.—For purposes of this section—*

    (1) In general.—The simplified dollar-value method of pricing inventories is a dollar-value method of pricing inventories under which—
        (A) the taxpayer maintains a separate inventory pool for items in each major category in the applicable Government price index, and
        (B) the adjustment for each such separate pool is based on the change from the preceding taxable year in the component of such index for the major category.

⟦**Footnote ¶3027**⟧   Matter in *italics* in Sec. 471 added by section 803(b)(4), '86 TRA.

Effective date (Sec. 803(d), '86 TRA).—Generally applies to costs incurred after 12-31-86, in taxable years ending after such date. For transitional and special rules, see footnote ¶2961-A.

⟦**Footnote ¶3028**⟧   Matter in *italics* in Sec. 474 added by section 802(a), '86 TRA, which struck out:

(1) "ELECTION BY CERTAIN SMALL BUSINESSES TO USE ONE INVENTORY POOL.

(a) **In General.**—A taxpayer which is an eligible small business and which uses the dollar-value method of pricing inventories under the method provided by section 472(b) may elect to use one inventory pool for any trade or business of such taxpayer.

(b) **Eligible Small Business Defined.**—For purposes of this section, a taxpayer is an eligible small business for any taxable year if the average annual gross receipts of the taxpayer do not exceed $2,000,000 for the 3-taxable year period ending with the taxable year.

(c) **Special Rules.**—For purposes of this section—

(1) **Controlled Groups.**

(A) **In general.**—In the case of a taxpayer which is a member of a controlled group, all persons which are component members of such group at any time during the calendar year shall be treated as one taxpayer for such year for purposes of determining the gross receipts of the taxpayer.

(B) **Controlled group defined.**—For purposes of subparagraph (A), persons shall be treated as being members of a controlled group if such persons would be treated as a single employer under the regulations prescribed under section 52(b).

(2) **Election.—**

(A) **In general.**—The election under this section may be made without the consent of the Secretary and shall be made at such time and in such manner as the Secretary may by regulations prescribe.

(B) **Period to which election applies.**—The election under this section shall apply—

(i) to the taxable year for which it is made, and

(ii) to all subsequent taxable years for which the taxpayer is an eligible small business,

unless the taxpayer secures the consent of the Secretary to the revocation of such election.

(3) **Transitional Rules.**—In the case of a taxpayer who changes the number of inventory pools maintained by him in a taxable year by reason of an election (or cessation thereof) under this section—

(A) the inventory pools combined or separated shall be combined or separated in the manner provided by regulations under section 472;

(B) the aggregate dollar value of the taxpayer's inventory as of the beginning of the first taxable year—

(i) for which an election under this section is in effect, or

(ii) after such election ceases to apply,

shall be the same as the aggregate dollar value as of the close of the taxable year preceding the taxable year described in clause (i) or (ii) (as the case may be), and

(C) the first taxable year for which an election under this section is in effect or after such election ceases to apply (as the case may be) shall be treated as a new base year in accordance with procedures provided by regulations under section 472."

Effective date (Sec. 802(c), '86 TRA).—(1) Generally applies to taxable years beginning after 12-31-86.

(2) Treatment of taxpayers who made elections under existing section 474.—The amendments made by this section shall not apply to any taxpayer who made an election under section 474 of the '54 Code (as in effect on the day before the date of the enactment of this Act) for any period during which such election is in effect. Notwithstanding any provision of such section 474 (as so in effect), an election under such section may be revoked without the consent of the Secretary.

(2) *Applicable government price index.*—The term "applicable Government price index" means—

(A) except as provided in subparagraph (B), the Producer Price Index published by the Bureau of Labor Statistics, or

(B) in the case of a retailer using the retail method, the Consumer Price Index published by the Bureau of Labor Statistics.

(3) *Major category.*—The term "major category" means—

(A) in the case of the Producer Price Index, any of the 2-digit standard industrial classifications in the Producer Prices Data Report, or

(B) in the case of the Consumer Price Index, any of the general expenditure categories in the Consumer Price Index Detailed Report.

(c) *Eligible Small Business.*—For purposes of this section, a taxpayer is an eligible small business for any taxable year if the average annual gross receipts of the taxpayer for the 3 preceding taxable years do not exceed $5,000,000. For purposes of the preceding sentence, rules similar to the rules of section 448(c)(3) shall apply.

(d) *Special Rules.*—For purposes of this section—

(1) *Controlled groups.*—

(A) *In general.*—In the case of a taxpayer which is a member of a controlled group, all persons which are component members of such group shall be treated as 1 taxpayer for purposes of determining the gross receipts of the taxpayer.

(B) *Controlled group defined.*—For purposes of subparagraph (A), persons shall be treated as being component members of a controlled group if such persons would be treated as a single employer under section 52.

(2) *Election.*—

(A) *In general.*—The election under this section may be made without the consent of the Secretary.

(B) *Period to which election applies.*—The election under this section shall apply—

(i) to the taxable year for which it is made, and

(ii) to all subsequent taxable years for which the taxpayer is an eligible small business,

unless the taxpayer secures the consent of the Secretary to the revocation of such election.

(3) *LIFO method.*—The term "LIFO method" means the method provided by section 472(b).

(4) *Transitional rules.*—

(A) *In general.*—In the case of a year of change under this section—

(i) the inventory pools shall—

(I) in the case of the 1st taxable year to which such an election applies, be established in accordance with the major categories in the applicable Government price index, or

(II) in the case of the 1st taxable year after such election ceases to apply, be established in the manner provided by regulations under section 472;

(ii) the aggregate dollar amount of the taxpayer's inventory as of the beginning of the year of change shall be the same as the aggregate dollar value as of the close of the taxable year preceding the year of change, and

(iii) The year of change shall be treated as a new base year in accordance with procedures provided by regulations under section 472.

(B) *Year of change.*—For purposes of this paragraph, the year of change under this section is—

(i) the 1st taxable year to which an election under this section applies, or

(ii) in the case of a cessation of such an election, the 1st taxable year after such election ceases to apply.

[For official explanation, see Committee Reports, ¶3936.]

〔¶3029〕 CODE SEC. 482. ALLOCATION OF INCOME AND DEDUCTIONS AMONG TAXPAYERS.

〔**Footnote ¶3029**〕 Matter in *italics* in Sec. 482 added by section 1231(e)(1), '86 TRA.

Effective date Sec. 1231(g)(2), '86 TRA).—(A) Generally applies to taxable years beginning after 12-31-86, but only with respect to transfers after 11-16-85, or licenses granted after such date (or before such date with respect to property not in existence or owned by the taxpayer on such date).

In any case of two or more organizations, trades, or businesses (whether or not incorporated, whether or not organized in the United States, and whether or not affiliated) owned or controlled directly or indirectly by the same interests, the Secretary may distribute, apportion, or allocate gross income, deductions, credits, or allowances between or among such organizations, trades, or businesses, if he determines that such distribution, apportionment, or allocation is necessary in order to prevent evasion of taxes or clearly to reflect the income of any of such organizations, trades, or businesses. *In the case of any transfer (or license) of intangible property (within the meaning of section 936(h)(3)(B)), the income with respect to such transfer or license shall be commensurate with the income attributable to the intangible.*

[For official explanation, see Committee Reports, ¶4041.]

〔¶3030〕 CODE SEC. 483. INTEREST ON CERTAIN DEFFERED PAYMENTS.

* * * * * * * * * * * *

(d) Exceptions and Limitations.—

(1) **Coordination with original issue discount rules.—**This section shall not apply to any debt instrument ¹*for which an issue price is determined under section 1273(b)*

〔Footnote ¶3029 continued〕

(B) Special rule for section 936.—For purposes of section 936(h)(5)(C) of the '86 Code the amendments made by subsection (e) shall apply to taxable years beginning after 12-31-86, without regard to when the transfer (or license) was made.

〔Footnote ¶3030〕 Matter in *italics* in Sec. 483(d)(1) added by section 1803(a)(14)(B), '86 TRA, which struck out:

(1) "to which section 1272 applies"

Effective date (Sec. 1881, '86 TRA and Sec. 44, '84 TRA as amended by section 2 of Public Law 98-612 and as amended by Sec. 1803(b), '86 TRA).—(a) Generally applies to taxable years ending after 7-18-84.

(b) Treatment of Debt Instruments Received in Exchange for Property.—

(1) In general.—

(A) Except as otherwise provided in this subsection, section 1274 of the '54 Code (as added by section 41) and the amendment made by section 41(b) (relating to amendment of section 483) shall apply to sales or exchanges after 12-31-84.

(B) Section 1274 of such Code and the amendment made by section 41(b) shall not apply to any sale or exchange pursuant to a written contract which was binding on 4-1-84, and at all times thereafter before the sale or exchange.

(2) Revision of section 482 regulations.—Not later than 180 days after the date of the enactment of this Act, the Secretary of the Treasury or his delegate shall modify the safe harbor interest rates applicable under the regulations prescribed under section 482 of the '54 Code so that such rates are consistent with the rates applicable under section 483 of such Code by reason of the amendments made by section 41.

(3) Clarification of interest accrual; fair market value rule in case of potentially abusive situations.—

(A) In general.—

(i) Clarification of interest accrual.—In the case of any sale or exchange—

(I) after 4-1-84, nothing in section 483 of the '54 Code shall permit any interest to be deductible before the period to which such interest is properly allocable, or

(II) after 6-8-84, notwithstanding section 483 of the '54 Code or any other provision of law, no interest shall be deductible before the period to which such interest is properly allocable.

(ii) Fair market rule.—In the case of any sale or exchange after 3-1-84, and such section 483 shall be treated as including provisions similar to the provisions of section 1274(b)(3) of such Code (as added by section 41).

(B) Exception for binding contracts.—

(i) Subparagraph (A)(i)(I) shall not apply to any sale or exchange pursuant to a written contract which was binding on 3-1-84, and at all times thereafter before the sale or exchange.

(ii) Subparagraph (A)(i)(II) shall not apply to any sale or exchange pursuant to a written contract which was binding on 6-8-84, and at all times thereafter before the sale or exchange.

(C) Interest accrual rule not to apply where substantially equal annual payments.—Clause (i) of subparagraph (A) shall not apply to any debt instrument with substantially equal annual payments.

(4) Special rules for sales after December 31, 1984, and before July 1, 1985.—

(A) In general.—In the case of any sale or exchange after 12-31-84, and before 7-1-85, of property other than new section 38 property—

(i) sections 483(c)(1)(B) and 1274(c)(3) of the '54 Code shall be applied by substituting the testing rate determined under subparagraph (B) for 110 percent of the applicable Federal rate determined under section 1274(d) of such Code, and

(ii) sections 483(b) and 1274(b) of such Code shall be applied by substituting the imputation rate determined under subparagraph (C) for 120 percent of the applicable Federal rate determined under section 1274(d) of such Code.

(B) Testing rate.—For purposes of this paragraph—

(i) In general.—The testing rate determined under this subparagraph is the sum of—

(I) 9 percent, plus

(II) if the borrowed amount exceeds $2,000,000, the excess determined under clause (ii) multiplied by a fraction the numerator of which is the borrowed amount to the extent it exceeds $2,000,000, and the denominator of which is the borrowed amount.

[Footnote ¶3030 continued]

(ii) Excess.—For purposes of clause (i), the excess determined under this clause is the excess of 110 percent of the applicable Federal rate determined under section 1274(d) of such Code over 9 percent.

(C) Imputation rate.—For purposes of this paragraph—

(i) In general.—The imputation rate determined under this subparagraph is the sum of—

(I) 10 percent, plus

(II) if the borrowed amount exceeds $2,000,000, the excess determined under clause (ii) multiplied by a fraction the numerator of which is the borrowed amount to the extent it exceeds $2,000,000, and the denominator of which is the borrowed amount.

(ii) Excess.—For purposes of clause (i), the excess determined under this clause is the excess of 120 percent of the applicable Federal rate determined under section 1274(d) of such Code over 10 percent.

(D) Borrowed amount.—For purposes of this paragraph, the term "borrowed amount" means the stated principal amount.

(E) Aggregation rules.—For purposes of this paragraph—

(i) all sales or exchanges which are part of the same transaction (or a series of related transactions) shall be treated as one sale or exchange, and

(ii) all debt instruments arising from the same transaction (or a series of related transactions) shall be treated as one debt instrument.

(F) Cash method of accounting.—In the case of any sale or exchange before 7-1-85, of property (other than new section 38 property) used in the active business of farming and in which the borrowed amount does not exceed $2,000,000—

(i) section 1274 of the '54 Code shall not apply, and

(ii) interest on the obligation issued in connection with such sale or exchange shall be taken into account by both buyer and seller on the cash receipts and disbursements method of accounting.

(G) Clarification of application of this paragraph, etc.—This paragraph and paragraphs (5), (6), and (7) shall apply only in the case of sales or exchanges to which section 1274 or 483 of the '54 Code (as amended by section 41) applies.

The Secretary of the Treasury or his delegate may by regulation prescribe rules to prevent the mismatching of interest income and interest deductions in connection with obligations on which interest is computed on the cash receipts and disbursements method of accounting. [Added by Sec. 2 of P.L. 98-612, 10-31-84.]

(5) General rule for assumptions of loans.—Except as provided in paragraphs (6) and (7), if any person—

(A) assumes, in connection with the sale or exchange of property, any debt obligation, or

(B) acquires any property subject to any debt obligation, sections 1274 and 483 of the '54 Code shall apply to such debt obligation by reason of such assumption (or such acquisition). [Added by Sec. 2 of P.L. 98-612, 10-31-84.]

(6) Exception for assumptions of loans made on or before October 15, 1984.—

(A) In general.—If any person—

(i) assumes, in connection with the sale or exchange of property, any debt obligation described in subparagraph (B) and issued on or before 10-15-84, or

(ii) acquires any property subject to any such debt obligation issued on or before 10-15-84,

sections 1274 and 483 of '54 Code shall not be applied to such debt obligation by reason of such assumption (or such acquisition) unless the terms and conditions of such debt obligation are modified in connection with the assumption (or acquisition),

(B) Obligations described in this subparagraph.—A debt obligation is described in this subparagraph if such obligation—

(i) was issued on or before 10-15-84, and

(ii) was assumed (or property was taken subject to such obligation) in connection with the sale or exchange of property (including a deemed sale under section 338(a)) the sales price of which is not greater than $100,000,000.

(C) Regulations.—The Secretary shall prescribe such regulations as may be appropriate to effect the purpose of this paragraph and paragraph (5), including regulations relating to tax-exempt obligations, government subsidized loans, or other instruments.

(D) Certain exempt transactions.—The Secretary shall prescribe regulations under which any transaction shall be exempt from the application of this paragraph if such exemption is not likely to significantly reduce the tax liability of the purchaser by reason of the overstatement of the adjusted basis of the acquired asset. [Added by Sec. 2 of PL 98-612, 10-31-84.]

(7) Exception for assumptions of loans with respect to certain property.—

(A) In general.—If any person—

(i) assumes, in connection with the sale or exchange of property described in subparagraph (B), any debt obligation, or

(ii) acquires any such property subject to any such debt obligation,

sections 1274 and 483 of the '54 Code shall not be applied to such debt obligation by reason of such assumption (or such acquisition) unless the terms and conditions of such debt obligation are modified in connection with the assumption (or acquisition).

(B) Sales or exchanges to which this paragraph applies.—This paragraph shall apply to any of the following sales or exchanges:

(i) Residences.—Any sale or exchange of a residence by an individual, an estate, or a testamentary trust, but only if—

(I) either—

(aa) such residence on the date of such sale or exchange (or in the case of an estate or testamentary trust, on the date of death of the decedent) was the principal residence (within the meaning of section 1034) of the individ-

Code §483(d)(1) ¶3030

[Footnote ¶3030 continued]

ual or decedent, or

(bb)   during the 2-year period ending on such date, no substantial portion of such residence was of a character subject to an allowance under this title for depreciation (or amortization in lieu thereof) in the hands of such individual or decedent, and

(II)   such residence was not at any time, in the hands of such individual, estate, testamentary trust, or decedent, described in section 1221(1) (relating to inventory, etc.).

(ii)   Farms.—Any sale or exchange by a qualified person of—

(I)   real property which was used as a farm (within the meaning of section 6420(c)(2)) at all times during the 3-year period ending on the date of such sale or exchange, or

(II)   tangible personal property which was used in the active conduct of the trade or business of farming on such farm and is sold in connection with the sale of such farm, but only if such property is sold or exchanged for use in the active conduct of the trade or business of farming by the transferee of such property.

(iii)   Trades or businesses.—

(I)   In general.—Any sale or exchange by a qualified person of any trade or business.

(II)   Application with subparagraph (b).—This subparagraph shall not apply to any sale or exchange of any property described in subparagraph (B).

(III)   New section 38 property.—This subparagraph shall not apply to the sale or exchange of any property which, in the hands of the transferee, is new section 38 property.

(iv)   Sale of business real estate.—Any sale or exchange of any real property used in an active trade or business by a person who would be a qualified person if he disposed of his entire interest.

This subparagraph shall not apply to any transaction described in the last sentence of paragraph (6)(B) (relating to transaction in excess of $100,000,000).

(C)   Definitions.—For purposes of this paragraph—

(i)   Qualified person defined.—The term "qualified person" means—

(I)   a person who—

(aa)   is an individual estate, or testamentary trust,

(bb)   is a corporation which immediately prior to the date of the sale or exchange has 35 or fewer shareholders, or

(cc)   is a partnership which immediately prior to the date of the sale or exchange has 35 or fewer partners,

(II)   is a 10-percent owner of a farm or a trade or business,

(III)   pursuant to a plan disposes of—

(aa)   an interest in a farm or farm property, or

(bb)   his entire interest in a trade or business and all substantially similar trades or businesses, and

(IV)   the ownership interest of whom may be readily established by reason of qualified allocations (of the type described in section 168(j)(9)(B), one class of stock, or the like).

(ii)   10-percent owner defined.—The term "10-percent owner" means a person having at least a 10-percent ownership interest, applying the attribution rules of section 318 (other than subsection (a)(4)).

(iii)   Trade or business defined.—

(I)   In general.—The term "trade or business" means any trade or business, including any line of business, qualifying as an active trade or business within the meaning of section 355.

(II)   Rental of real property.—For purpose of this clause, the holding of real property for rental shall not be treated as an active trade or business. [Added by Sec. 2 of PL 98-612, 10-31-84.]

(c)   Market Discount Rules.—

(1)   Ordinary income treatment.—Section 1276 of the '54 Code (as added by section 41) shall apply to obligations issued after 7-18-84 in taxable years ending after such date.

* * * * * * * * * * * *

(d)   Rules Relating to Discount on Short-Term Obligations.—Subpart C of part V of subchapter P of chapter 1 of such Code (as added by section 41) shall apply to obligations acquired after 7-18-84.

(e)   5-Year Spread of Adjustments Required by Reason of Accrual of Discount on Certain Short-Term Obligations.—

(1)   Election to have section 1281 apply to all obligations held during taxable year.—A taxpayer may elect for his first taxable year ending after the date of the enactment of this Act to have section 1281 of the '54 Code apply to all short-term obligations described in subsection (b) of such section which were held by the taxpayer at any time during such first taxable year.

(2)   5-year spread.—

(A)   In general.—In the case of any taxpayer who makes an election under paragraph (1)—

(i)   the provisions of section 1281 of the '54 Code (as added by section 41) shall be treated as a change in the method of accounting of the taxpayer,

(ii)   such change shall be treated as having been made with the consent of the Secretary, and

(iii)   the net amount of the adjustments required by section 481(a) of such Code to be taken into account by the taxpayer in computing taxable income (hereinafter in this paragraph referred to as the "net adjustments") shall be taken into account during the spread period with the amount taken into account in each taxable year in such period determined under subparagraph (B).

(B)   Amount taken into account during each year of spread period.—

(i)   First year.—The amount taken into account for the first taxable year in the spread period shall be the sum of—

(I)   one-fifth of the net adjustments, and

(II)   the excess (if any) of—

(a)   the cash basis income over the accrual basis income, over

(b)   one-fifth of the net adjustments.

(other than paragraph (4) thereof) or section 1274.

* * * * * * * * * * *

[For official explanation, see Committee Reports, ¶4137.]

[¶3031] CODE SEC. 501. EXEMPTION FROM TAX ON CORPORATIONS, CERTAIN TRUSTS, ETC.

(a) Exemption From Taxation.—An organization described in subsection (c) or (d) or section 401(a) shall be exempt from taxation under this subtitle unless such exemption is denied under section 502 or 503.

* * * * * * * * * * *

(c) List of Exempt Organizations.—The following organizations are referred to in subsection (a):

(1) any corporation organized under Act of Congress which is an instrumentality of the United States but only if such corporation—

(A) is exempt from Federal income taxes—

(i) under such Act as amended and supplemented before [1]*July 18, 1984,* or

(ii) under this title without regard to any provision of law which is not contained in this title and which is not contained in a revenue Act, or

(B) is described in subsection (1).

* * * * * * * * * * *

(14) (A) Credit unions without capital stock organized and operated for mutual purposes and without profit.

(B) Corporations or associations without capital stock organized before September 1, 1957, and operated for mutual purposes and without profit for the purpose of providing reserve funds for, and insurance of shares or deposits in—

(i) domestic building and loan associations,

(ii) cooperative banks without capital stock organized and operated for mutual purposes and without profit, [2]

(iii) mutual savings banks not having capital stock represented by shares [3]

[Footnote ¶3030 continued]

(ii) For subsequent years in spread period.—The amount taken into account in the second or any succeeding taxable year in the spread period shall be the sum of—

(I) the portion of the net adjustments not taken into account in the preceding taxable year of the spread period divided by the number of remaining taxable years in the spread period (including the year for which the determination is being made), and

(II) the excess (if any) of—

(a) the excess of the cash basis income over the accrual basis income, over

(b) one-fifth of the net adjustments, multiplied by 5 minus the number of years remaining in the spread period (not including the current year).

The excess described in subparagraph (B)(ii)(II)(a) shall be reduced by any amount taken into account under this subclause or clause (i)(II) in any prior year.

(C) Spread period.—For purposes of this paragraph, the term "spread period" means the period consisting of the 5 taxable years beginning with the year for which the election is made under paragraph (1).

(D) Cash basis income.—For purposes of this paragraph, the term "cash basis income" means for any taxable year the aggregate amount which would be includible in the gross income of the taxpayer with respect to short-term obligations described in subsection (b) of section 1281 of such Code if the provisions of section 1281 of such Code did not apply to such taxable year and all prior taxable years within the spread period.

(E) Accrual basis income.—For purposes of this paragraph, the term "accrual basis income" means for any taxable year the aggregate amount includible in gross income under section 1281(a) of such Code for such a taxable year and all prior taxable years within the spread period.

* * * * * * * * * * *

(j) Clarification That Prior Effective Date Rules Not Affected.—Nothing in the amendment made by section 41(a) shall affect the application of any effective date provision (including any transititonal rule) for any provision which was a predecessor to any provision contained in part V of subchapter P of chapter 1 of the '54 Code (as added by section 41).

[Footnote ¶3031] Matter in *italics* in Sec. 501(c)(1)(A)(i) added by 1899A(15), '86 TRA, which struck out:

(1) "the date of the enactment of the Tax Reform Act of 1984"

Matter in *italics* in Sec. 501(c)(14)(B)(ii)—(iv) added by section 1879(k)(1), '86 TRA, which struck out:

(2) "or"

(3) "."

Effective date (Sec. 1879(k)(2), '86 TRA).—Applies to taxable years ending after 8-13-81.

---

and

    (iv)   mutual savings banks described in section 591(b)

    (C)   Corporations or associations organized before September 1, 1957, and operated for mutual purposes and without profit for the purpose of providing reserve funds for associations or banks described in clause (i), (ii), or (iii) of subparagraph (B); but only if 85 percent or more of the income is attributable to providing such reserve funds and to investments. This subparagraph shall not apply to any corporation or association entitled to exemption under subparagraph (B).

    (15) *[4](A) Insurance companies or associations other than life (including interinsurers and reciprocal underwriters) if the net written premiums (or, if greater, direct written premiums) for the taxable year do not exceed $350,000.*

    (B) For purposes of subparagraph (A), in determining whether any company or association is described in subparagraph (A), such company or association shall be treated as receiving during the taxable year amounts described in subparagraph (A) which are received during such year by all other companies or associations which are members of the same controlled group as the insurance company or association for which the determination is being made.

    (C) For purposes of subparagraph (B), the term "controlled group" has the meaning given such term by section 831(b)(2)(B)(ii).

*   *   *   *   *   *   *   *   *   *   *

    (17) (A) A trust or trusts forming part of a plan providing for the payment of supplemental unemployment compensation benefits, if—

    (i) under the plan, it is impossible, at any time prior to the satisfaction of all liabilities with respect to employees under the plan, for any part of the corpus or income to be (within the taxable year or thereafter) used for, or diverted to, any purpose other than the providing of supplemental unemployment compensation benefits,

    (ii) such benefits are payable to employees under a classification which is set forth in the plan and which is found by the Secretary not to be discriminatory in favor of employees who are [5]*highly compensated employees within the meaning of section 414(q)),* and

    (iii) such benefits do not discriminate in favor of employees who are [5]*highly compensated employees within the meaning of section 414(q)).* A plan shall not be considered discriminatory within the meaning of this clause merely because the benefits received under the plan bear a uniform relationship to the total compensation, or the basic or regular rate of compensation, of the employees covered by the plan.

    (B) In determining whether a plan meets the requirements of subparagraph (A), any benefits provided under any other plan shall not be taken into consideration, except that a plan shall not be considered discriminatory—

    (i) merely because the benefits under the plan which are first determined in a nondiscriminatory manner within the meaning of subparagraph (A) are then reduced by any sick, accident, or unemployment compensation benefits received under State or Federal law (or reduced by a portion of such benefits if determined in a nondiscriminatory manner), or

    (ii) merely because the plan provides only for employees who are not eligible to receive sick, accident, or unemployment compensation benefits under State or Federal law the same benefits (or a portion of such benefits if determined in a

---

⟦Footnote ¶3031 continued⟧

Matter in *italics* in Sec. 501(c)(15) added by section 1024(b), '86 TRA, which struck out:

(4) "Mutual insurance companies or associations other than life or marine (including interinsurers and reciprocal underwriters) if the gross amount received during the taxable year from the items described in section 822(b) (other than paragraph (1)(D) thereof) and premiums (including deposits and assessments) does not exceed $150,000."

Effective date (Sec. 1024(e), '86 TRA).—Applies to taxable years beginning after 12-31-86.

Matter in *italics* in Sec. 501(c)(17)(A), (18)(B) and (C) added by 1114(b)(14), '86 TRA, which struck out:

(5) "officers, shareholders, persons whose principal duties consist of supervising the work of other employees, or highly compensated employees"

Effective date (Sec. 1114(c)(1) and (4), '86 TRA).—(1) Applies to years beginning after 12-31-86.

(4) Special rule for determining highly compensated employees.—For purposes of section 401(k) and 401(m) of the Code '86, in the case of an employer incorporated on 12-15-24, if more than 50 percent of its employees in the top-paid group (within the meaning of section 414(q)(4) of such Code) earn less than $25,000 (indexed at the same time and in the same manner as under section 415(d) of such Code), then the highly compensated employees shall include employees described in section 414(q)(1)(C) of such Code determined without regard to the level of compensation of such employees.

nondiscriminatory manner) which such employees would receive under such laws if such employees were eligible for such benefits, or

(iii)   merely because the plan provides only for employees who are not eligible under another plan (which meets the requirements of subparagraph (A)) of supplemental unemployment compensation benefits provided wholly by the employer the same benefits (or a portion of such benefits if determined in a nondiscriminatory manner) which such employees would receive under such other plan if such employees were eligible under such other plan, but only if the employees eligible under both plans would make a classification which would be nondiscriminatory within the meaning of subparagraph (A).

(C)   A plan shall be considered to meet the requirements of subparagraph (A) during the whole of any year of the plan if on one day in each quarter it satisfies such requirements.

(D)   The term "supplemental unemployment compensation benefits" means only—

(i)   benefits which are paid to an employee because of his involuntary separation from the employment of the employer (whether or not such separation is temporary) resulting directly from a reduction in force, the discontinuance of a plan or operation, or other similar conditions, and

(ii)   sick and accident benefits subordinate to the benefits described in clause (i).

(E)   Exemption shall not be denied under subsection (a) to any organization entitled to such exemption as an association described in paragraph (9) of this subsection merely because such organization provides for the payment of supplemental unemployment benefits (as defined in subparagraph (D)(i)).

(18)   A trust or trusts created before June 25, 1959, forming part of a plan providing for the payment of benefits under a pension plan funded only by contributions of employees, if—

(A)   under the plan, it is impossible, at any time prior to the satisfaction of all liabilities with respect to employees under the plan, for any part of the corpus or income to be (within the taxable year or thereafter) used for, or diverted to, any purpose other than the providing of benefits under the plan,

(B)   such benefits are payable to employees under a classification which is set forth in the plan and which is found by the Secretary not to be discriminatory in favor of employees who are [5]*highly compensated employees within the meaning of section 414(q),* [6]

(C)   such benefits do not discriminate in favor of employees who are [5]*highly compensated employees within the meaning of section 414(q).* A plan shall not be considered discriminatory within the meaning of this subparagraph merely because the benefits received under the plan bear a uniform relationship to the total compensation, or the basic or regular rate of compensation, of the employees covered by the plan[7], *and*

(D)   in the case of a plan under which an employee may designate certain contributions as deductible—

(i)   such contributions do not exceed the amount with respect to which a deduction is allowable under section 219(b)(3),

(ii)   requirements similar to the requirements of section 401(k)(3)(A)(ii) are met with respect to such elective contributions, and

(iii)   such contributions are treated as elective deferrals for purposes of secton 402(g) (other than paragraph (4) thereof).

⟦Footnote ¶3031 continued⟧

Section 1109(a), '86 TRA, struck out from Sec. 501(c)(18)(B):
(6) "and"
Effective date (Sec. 1109(c), '86 TRA).—Applies to taxable years beginning after 12-31-86.

Sec. 501(c)(18)(D), in *italics* added by section 1109(a), '86 TRA which struck out:
(7) "."
Effective date (Sec. 1109(c), '86 TRA).—Applies to taxable years beginning after 12-31-86.

Sec. 501(c)(25) in *italics* added by section 1603(a), '86 TRA.
Effective date (Sec. 1603(c), '86 TRA).—Applies to taxable years beginning after 12-31-86.

For purposes of subparagraph (D)(ii), rules similar to the rules of section 401(k)(8) shall apply. For purposes of section 4979, any excess contribution under clause (ii) shall be treated as an excess contribution under a cash or deferred arrangement.

* * * * * * * * * * *

(25)(A) Any corporation or trust which—

 (i) has no more than 35 shareholders or beneficiaries,

 (ii) has only 1 class of stock or beneficial interest, and

 (iii) is organized for the exclusive purposes of—

  (I) acquiring real property and holding title to, and collecting income from, such property, and

  (II) remitting the entire amount of income from such property (less expenses) to 1 or more organizations described in subparagraph (C) which are shareholders of such corporation or beneficiaries of such trust.

(B) A corporation or trust shall be described in subparagraph (A) without regard to whether the corporation or trust is organized by 1 or more organizations described in subparagraph (C).

(C) An organization is described in this subparagraph if such organization is—

 (i) a qualified pension, profit sharing or stock bonus plan that meets the requirements of section 401(a).

 (ii) a governmental plan (within the meaning of section 414(d)).

 (iii) the United States, any State or political subdivision thereof, or any agency or instrumentality of any of the foregoing.

 (iv) any organization described in paragraph (3), or

 (v) any organization described in this paragraph.

(D) A corporation or trust described in this paragraph must permit its shareholders or beneficiaries—

 (i) to dismiss the corporation's or trust's investment adviser, following reasonable notice, upon a vote of the shareholders or beneficiaries holding a majority of interest in the corporation or trust, and

 (ii) to terminate their interest in the corporation or trust by either, or both, of the following alternatives, as determined by the corporation or trust:

  (I) by selling or exchanging their stock in the corporation or interest in the trust (subject to any Federal or State securities law) to any organization described in subparagraph (C) so long as the sale or exchange does not increase the number of shareholders or beneficiaries in such corporation or trust above 35, or

  (II) by having their stock or interest redeemed by the corporation or trust after the shareholder or beneficiary has provided 90 days notice to such corporation or trust.

* * * * * * * * * * *

(m) *Certain Organizations Providing Commercial-Type Insurance Not Exempt From Tax.—*

(1) *Denial of tax exemption where providing commercial-type insurance is substantial part of activities.—An* organization described in paragraph (3) or (4) of subsection (c) shall be exempt from tax under subsection (a) only if no substantial part of its activities consists of providing commercial-type insurance.

(2) *Other organizations taxed as insurance companies on insurance business.—In* the case of an organization described in paragraph (3) or (4) of subsection (c) which is exempt from tax under section (a) after application of paragraph (1) of this subsection—

 (A) the activity of providing commercial-type insurance shall be treated as an unrelated trade or business (as defined in section 513), and

 (B) in lieu of the tax imposed by section 511 with respect to such activity, such organization shall be treated as an insurance company for purposes of applying subchapter L with respect to such activity.

(3) *Commercial-type insurance.—For* purposes of this subsection, the term "commercial-type insurance" shall not include—

 (A) insurance provided at substantially below cost to a class of charitable recipients,

 (B) incidental health insurance provided by a health maintenance organization of a kind customarily provided by such organizations, and

 (C) property or casualty insurance provided (directly or through an organization described in section 414(e)(3)(B)(ii)) by a church or convention or association of churches for such church or convention or association of churches, and

    (D) providing retirement or welfare benefits (or both) by a church or a convention or association of churches (directly or through an organization described in section 414(e)(3)(A) or 414(e)(3)(B)(ii)) for the employees (including employees described in section 414(e)(3)(B)) of such church or convention or association of churches or the beneficiaries of such employees.

    (4) Insurance includes annuities.—*For purposes of this subsection, the issuance of annuity contracts shall be treated as providing insurance.*

[8]*(n)* **Cross Reference.—**
For nonexemption of Communist-controlled organizations, see section 11(b) of the Internal Security Act of 1950 (64 Stat. 997; 50 U.S.C. 790(b)).

[For official explanation, see Committee Reports, ¶3959; 3964; 3979; 4116; 4193.]

[¶3032] CODE SEC. 505. ADDITIONAL REQUIREMENTS FOR ORGANIZATIONS DESCRIBED IN PARAGRAPH (9), (17), OR (20) OF SECTION 501(c).

    (a) Certain Requirements Must Be Met in the Case of Organizations Described in Paragraph (9) or (20) of Section 501(c).—

       (1) Voluntary employees' beneficiary associations, etc.—An organization described in paragraph (9) or (20) of subsection (c) of section 501 which is part of a plan [1] shall not be exempt from tax under section 501(a) unless such plan meets the requirements of subsection (b) of this section.

       (2) Exception for collective bargaining agreements.—Paragraph (1) shall not apply to any organization which is part of a plan maintained pursuant to [2]*an agreement between employee representatives and 1 or more employers if the Secretary finds that such agreement is a collective bargaining agreement and that such plan was the subject of good faith bargaining between such employee representatives and such employer or employers.*

    (b) Nondiscrimination Requirements.—

       (1) In general.—Except as [3]*otherwise provided in this subsection,* a plan meets the requirements of this subsection only if—

[Footnote ¶3031 continued]

  Matter in *italics* in Sec. 501(m) and (n) added by section 1012(a), '86 TRA, which struck out:
(8) "(m)"
Effective date (Sec. 1012(c)(1), (2), and (4), '86 TRA)—(1) Generally applies to taxable years after 12-31-86.

  (2) Study of fraternal beneficiary associations.—The Secretary of the Treasury or his delegate shall conduct a study of organizations described in section 501(c)(8) of the '86 Code and which received gross annual insurance premiums in excess of $25,000,000 for the taxable years of such organizations which ended during 1984. Not later than 1-1-88, the Secretary of the Treasury shall submit to the Committee on Ways and Means of the House of Representatives, the Committee on Finance of the Senate, and the Joint Committee on Taxation the results of such study, together with such recommendations as he determines to be appropriate. The Secretary of the Treasury shall have authority to require the furnishing of such information as may be necessary to carry out the purposes of this paragraph.

          *   *   *   *   *   *   *   *   *   *   *   *

  (4) Other special rules.—
  (A) The amendments made by this section shall not apply with respect to that portion of the business of Mutual of America which is attributable to pension business.
  (B) The amendments made by this section shall not apply to that portion of the business of the Teachers Insurance Annuity Association-College Retirement Equities Fund which is attributable to pension business.
  (C) The amendments made by this section shall not apply to—
  (i) the retirement fund of the YMCA,
  (ii) the Missouri Hospital Association,
  (iii) administrative services performed by municipal leagues, and
  (iv) dental benefit coverage provided by Delta Dental Plans Association through contracts with independent professional service providers so long as the provision of such coverage is the principal activity of such Association.
  (D) For purposes of this paragraph, the term "pension business" means the administration of any plan described in section 401(a) of the Internal Revenue Code of 1954 which includes a trust exempt from tax under section 501(a), any plan under which amounts are contributed by an individual's employer for an annuity contract described in section 403(b) of such Code, any individual retirement plan described in section 408 of such Code, and any eligible deferred compensation plan to which section 457(a) of such Code applies.
  [Footnote ¶3032] Matter in *italics* in Sec. 505(a) and (b)(1) added by section 1851(c), '86 TRA, which struck out:
  (1) "of an employer"
  (2) "1 or more collective bargaining agreements between 1 or more employee organizations and 1 or more employers."
  (3) "provided in paragraph (2)"

(A) each class of benefits under the plan is provided under a classification of employees which is set forth in the plan and which is found by the Secretary not to be discriminatory in favor of employees who are highly compensated individuals, and

(B) in the case of each class of benefits, such benefits do not discriminate in favor of employees who are highly compensated *4individuals.*

A life insurance, disability, severance pay, or supplemental unemployment compensation benefit shall not be considered to fail to meet the requirements of subparagraph (B) merely because the benefits available bear a uniform relationship to the total compensation, or the basic or regular rate of compensation, of employees covered by the plan.

(2) **Exclusion of certain employees.**—For purposes of paragraph (1), there may be excluded from consideration *5employees who may be excluded from consideration under section 89(h).*

* * * * * * * * * * *

6(5) Highly compensated individual.—For purposes of this subsection, the determination as to whether an individual is a highly compensated individual shall be made under rules similar to the rules for determining whether an individual is a highly compensated emloyee (within the meaning of section 414(q)).

(6) Compensation.—For purposes of this subsection, the term "compensation" has the meaning given such term by section 414(s).

(c) **Requirement That Organization Notify Secretary That It Is Applying for Tax-Exempt Status.—**

* * * * * * * * * * *

(2) **Special rule for existing organizations.**—In the case of any organization in existence on the *7July 18, 1984,* the time for giving notice under paragraph (1) shall not expire before the date 1 year after such date of the enactment.

[For official explanation, see Committee Reports, ¶3979; 4007; 4171.]

〖Footnote ¶3032 continued〗

(4) "employees"
Effective date (Sec. 1881, '86 TRA and section 513(c), '84 TRA).—(1) Generally applies to years beginning after 12-31-84.

(2) Treatment of certain benefits in pay status as of January 1, 1985.—For purposes of determining whether a plan meets the requirements of section 505(b) '54 Code (as added by subsection (a)), there may (at the election of the employer) be excluded from consideration all disability or severance payments payable to individuals who are in pay status as of 1-1-85. The preceding sentence shall not apply to any payment to the extent such payment is increased by any plan amendment adopted after 6-22-84.

Matter in *italics* in Sec. 505(b)(2) added by section 1151(g)(6), '86 TRA, which struck out:
(5) "(A) employees who have not completed 3 years of service,
(B) employees who have not attained age 21,
(C) seasonal employees or less than half-time employees,
(D) employees not included in the plan who are included in a unit of employees covered by an agreement between employee representatives and 1 or more employers which the Secretary finds to be a collective bargaining agreement if the class of benefits involved was the subject of good faith bargaining between such employee representatives and such employer or employers, and
(E) employees who are nonresident aliens and who receive no earned income (within the meaning of section 911(d)(2)) from the employer which constitutes income from sources within the United States (within the meaning of section 861(a)(3))."
Effective date (Sec. 1151(k), '86 TRA).—(1) Generally applies to years beginning the later of—
(A) 12-31-87,
(B) the earlier of—
(i) the date which is 3 months after the date on which the Secretary of the Treasury or his delegate issues such regulations as are necessary to carry out the provisions of section 89 of the '86 Code (as added by this section), or
(ii) 12-31-88.
For special rules and transitional rules see footnote ¶2895.

Matter in *italics* in Sec. 505(b)(5) added by section 1114(b)(16), '86 TRA, which struck out:
(6) "(5) **Highly compensated individual.**—For purposes of this subsection, the term 'highly compensated individual' has the meaning given such term by section 105(h)(5). For purposes of the preceding sentence, section 105(h)(5) shall be applied by substituting '10 percent' for '25 percent'."
Effective date (Sec. 1114(c)(2), '86 TRA).—Applies to years beginning after 12-31-87.

Sec. 505(b)(6) in *italics* added by section 1151(j)(3), '86 TRA.
Effective date (Sec. 1151(k)(1), '86 TRA).—See above.

Matter in *italics* in Sec. 505(c)(2) added by section 1899A(16), '86 TRA, which struck out:
(7) "the date of the enactment of the Tax Reform Act of 1984."

[¶3033] CODE SEC. 512. UNRELATED BUSINESS TAXABLE INCOME.

(a) **Definition.**—For purposes of this title.

* * * * * * * * * * * *

(3) **Special rules applicable to organizations described in paragraph (7), (9), (17), or (20) of section 501(c).**—

* * * * * * * * * * * *

(E) Limitation on amount of setaside in the case of organizations described in paragraph (9), (17), or (20) of section 501(c).—

(i) In general.—In the case of any organization described in paragraph (9), (17), or (20) of section 501(c), a set-aside for any purpose specified in clause (ii) of subparagraph (B) may be taken into account under subparagraph (B) only to the extent that such set-aside does not result in an amount of assets set aside for such purpose in excess of the account limit [1]*determined under section 419A (without regard to subsection (f)(6) thereof)* for the taxable year (not taking into account any reserve described in section 419A(c)(2)(A) for post-retirement medical benefits).[2]

[3]*(ii)* Treatment of existing reserves for post-retirement medical or life insurance benefits.—

(I) Clause (i) shall not apply to any income attributable to [4]*an* existing reserve for post-retirement medical or life insurance benefits.

[5]*(II) For purposes of subclause (II), the term "reserve for post-retirement medical or life insurance benefits" means the greater of the amount of assets set aside for purposes of post-retirement medical or life insurance benefits to be provided to covered employees as of the close of the last plan year ending before the date of the enactment of the Tax Reform Act of 1984 or on July 18, 1984,*

(III) All payments during plan years ending on or after the date of the enactment of the Tax Reform Act of 1984 of post-retirement medical benefits or life insurance benefits shall be charged against the reserve referred to in subclause (II). Except to the extent provided in regulations prescribed by the Secretary, all plans of an employer shall be treated as 1 plan for purposes of the preceding sentence.

[6]*(iii)* Treatment of tax exempt organizations.—This [7]*subparagraph* shall not apply to any organization if substantially all of the contributions to such organization are made by employers who were exempt from tax under this chapter throughout the 5-taxable year period ending with the taxable year in which the contributions are made.

* * * * * * * * * * * *

[For official explanation, see Committee Reports, ¶4147.]

[¶3034] CODE SEC. 513. UNRELATED TRADE OR BUSINESS.

* * * * * * * * * * * *

(d) **Certain Activities of Trade Shows, State Fairs, Etc.—**

* * * * * * * * * * * *

(3) **Qualified convention and trade show activities.—**

[Footnote ¶3033] Matter in *italics* in Sec. 512(a)(3)(E) added by section 1851(a)(10), '86 TRA, which struck out:

(1) "determined under section 419(A)(c)"

(2) "(ii) No set aside for facilities.—No set aside for assets used in the provision of benefits described in clause (ii) of subparagraph (B) shall be taken into account."

(3) "(iii)"

(4) "a"

(5) "(II) For purposes of subclause (I), the term 'existing reserve or post-retirement medical or life insurance benefit' means the amount of assets set aside as of the close of the last plan year ending before the date of the enactment of the post-retirement medical benefits or life insurance benefits to be provided to covered employees."

(6) "(iv)"

(7) "paragraph"

Effective date (Sec. 1881, '86 TRA and section 511(e)(6), '84 TRA, as added by section 1851(a)(12), '86 TRA).—Shall apply with respect to taxable years ending after 12-31-85. For purposes of Sec. 15 of '54 code, such amendments shall be treated as a change in the rate of a tax imposed by chapter 1 of such code.

* * * * * * * * * * *

(B) Qualified convention and trade show activity.—The term "qualified convention and trade show activity" means a convention and trade show activity carried out by a qualifying organization described in subparagraph (C) in conjunction with an international, national, State, regional, or local convention, annual meeting, or show conducted by an organization described in subparagraph (C) if one of the purposes of such organization in sponsoring the activity is the promotion and stimulation of interest in, and demand for, the products and services of that industry in general *or to educate persons in attendance regarding new developments or products and services related to the exempt activities of the organization* and the show is designed to achieve such purpose through the character of the exhibits and the extent of the industry products displayed.

(C) Qualifying organizations.—For purposes of this paragraph, the term "qualifying organization" means an organization described in section [1]*501(c)(3), (4), (5), or (6)* which regularly conducts as one of its substantial exempt purposes a show which stimulates interest in, and demand for, the products of a particular industry or segment of such industry *or which educates persons in attendance regarding new developments or products and services related to the exempt activities of the organization.*

* * * * *. * * * * * *

(h) *Certain Distributions of Low Cost Articles Without Obligation To Purchase and Exchanges and Rentals of Member Lists.—*

(1) *In general.—In the case of an organization which is described in section 501 and contributions to which are deductible under paragraph (2) or (3) of section 170(c), the term "unrelated trade or business" does not include—*

(A) *activities relating to the distribution of low cost articles if the distribution of such articles is incidental to the solicitation of charitable contributions, or*

(B) *any trade or business which consists of—*

(i) *exchanging with another such organization names and addresses of donors to (or members of) such organization, or*

(ii) *renting such names and addresses to another such organization.*

(2) *Low cost article defined.—For purposes of this subsection—*

(A) *In general.—The term "low cost article" means any article which has a cost not in excess of $5 to the organization which distributes such item (or on whose behalf such item is distributed).*

(B) *Aggregation rule.—If more than 1 item is distributed by or on behalf of an organization to a single distributee in any calendar year, the aggregate of the items so distributed in such calendar year to such distributee shall be treated as 1 article for purposes of subparagraph (A).*

(C) *Indexation of $5 amount.—In the case of any taxable year beginning in a calendar year after 1987, the $5 amount in subparagraph (A) shall be increased by an amount equal to—*

(i) *$5, multiplied by*

(ii) *the cost-of-living adjustment determined under section 1(f)(3) for the calendar year in which the taxable year begins.*

(3) *Distribution which is incidental to the solicitation of charitable contributions described.—For purposes of this subsection, any distribution of low cost articles by an organization shall be treated as a distribution incidental to the solicitation of charitable contributions only if—*

(A) *such distribution is not made at the request of the distributee,*

(B) *such distribution is made without the express consent of the distributee, and*

(C) *the articles so distributed are accompanied by—*

(i) *a request for a charitable contribution (as defined in section 170(c)) by the distributee to such organization, and*

  (ii) *a statement that the distributee may retain the low cost article regardless of whether such distributee makes a charitable contribution to such organization.*

[For official explanation, see Committee Reports, ¶4115.]

【¶3035】 **CODE SEC. 514. UNRELATED DEBT-FINANCED INCOME.**

＊ ＊ ＊ ＊ ＊ ＊ ＊ ＊ ＊ ＊

(c) Acquisition Indebtedness.—

＊ ＊ ＊ ＊ ＊ ＊ ＊ ＊ ＊ ＊

  (9) Real property acquired by a qualified organization—
   (A) In general.—Except as provided in subparagraph (B), the term "acquisition indebtedness" does not for purposes of this section, include indebtedness incurred by a qualified organization in acquiring or improving any real property.
   (B) Exceptions.—The provisions of subparagraph (A) shall not apply in any case in which—
    (i) the price for the acquisition or improvement is not a fixed amount determined as of the date of the acquisition or the completion of the improvement;
    (ii) the amount of any indebtedness or any other amount payable with respect to such indebtedness, or the time for making any payment of any such amount, is dependent, in whole or in part, upon any revenue, income, or profits derived from such real property;
    (iii) the real property is at any time after the acquisition leased by the qualified organization to the person selling such property to such organization or to any person who bears a relationship described in section 267(b) or 707(b) to such person;
    (iv) the real property is acquired by a qualified trust from, or is at any time after the acquisition leased by such trust to, any person who—
     (I) bears a relationship which is described in subparagraph (C), (E), or (G) of section 4975(e)(2) to any plan with respect to which such trust was formed, or
     (II) bears a relationship which is described in subparagraph (F) or (H) of section 4975(e)(2) to any person described in subclause (I);
    (v) any person described in clause (iii) or (iv) provides the qualified organization with financing in connection with the acquisition or improvement; or
    ¹(vi) *the real property is held by a partnership (which does not fail to meet the*

【Footnote ¶3035】 Matter in *italics* in Sec. 514(c)(9)(B)(vi) except "section 168(h)(6)" added by section 1878(e)(1) and (3), '86 TRA, which struck out:
 (1) "(vi) the real property is held by a partnership unless the partnership meets the requirements of clauses (i) through (v) and unless—
 (I) all of the partners of the partnership are qualified organizations, or
 (II) each allocation to a partner of the partnership which is a qualified organization is a qualified allocation (within the meaning of section 168(j)(9)).
For purposes of clause (vi)(I), an organization shall not be treated as a qualified organization if any income of such organization would be unrelated business taxable income (determined without regard to this paragraph)."
 Effective date (Sec. 1881, '86 TRA and Sec. 1034(c)(1)—(3), '84 TRA).—(1) Generally applies to indebtedness incurred after 7-18-84.
 (2) Exception for indebtedness on certain property acquired before January 1, 1985.—
 (A) The amendment made by subsection (a) shall not apply to any indebtedness incurred before 1-1-85, by a partnership described in subparagraph (B) if such indebtedness is incurred with respect to property acquired (directly or indirectly) by such partnership before such date.
 (B) A partnership is described in this subparagraph if—
 (i) before 10-21-83, the partnership was organized, a request for exemption with respect to such partnership was filed with the Department of Labor, and a private placement memorandum stating the maximum number of units in the partnership that would be offered had been circulated.
 (ii) the interest in the property to be acquired, directly or indirectly (including through acquiring an interest in another partnership) by such partnership was described in such private placement memorandum, and
 (iii) the marketing of partnership interests in such partnership is completed not later than 2 years after the later of 7-18-84 or the date of publication in the Federal Register of such exemption by the Department of Labor and the aggregate number of units in such partnership sold does not exceed the amount described in clause (i).
 (3) Exception for indebtedness on certain property acquired before January 1, 1986.—
 (A) The amendment made by subsection (a) shall not apply to any indebtedness incurred before 1-1-86, by a partnership described in subparagraph (B) if such indebtedness is incurred with respect to property acquired (directly or indirectly) by such partnership before such date.
 (B) a partnership is described in this paragraph if—
 (i) before 3-6-84, the partnership was organized and publicly announced, the maximum amount of interests which would be sold in such partnership, and
 (ii) the marketing of partnership interests in such partnership is completed not later than the 90th day after

requirements of clauses (i) through (v)), and—

(I) any partner of the partnership is not a qualified organization, and

(II) the principal purpose of any allocation to any partner of the partnership which is a qualified organization which is not a qualified allocation (within the meaning of ²section 168(h)(6)) is the avoidance of income tax.

For purposes of subclause (I) of clause (vi), an organization shall not be treated as a qualified organization if any income of such organization would be unrelated business taxable income (determined without regard to this paragraph). For purposes of clause (vi), an interest in a mortgage shall in no event be treated as real property.

(C) Qualified organization.—For purposes of this paragraph, the term "qualified organization" means—

(i) an organization described in section 170(b)(1)(A)(ii) and its affiliated support organizations described in ³*section 509(a)(3);* ⁴

(ii) any trust which constitutes a qualified trust under section 401⁵; *or*

(iii) an organization described in section 501(c)(25).

* * * * * * * * * * * *

[For official explanation, see Committee Reports, ¶3870; 4116; 4192.]

⟦¶3036⟧ CODE SEC. 527. POLITICAL ORGANIZATIONS.

* * * * * * * * * * * *

(g) Treatment of Newsletter Funds.—

(1) In general.—For purposes of this section, a fund established and maintained by an individual who holds, has been elected to, or is a candidate (within the meaning of ¹*paragraph (3)* for nomination or election to, any Federal, State, or local elective public office for use by such individual exclusively for the preparation and circulation of such individual's newsletter shall, except as provided in paragraph (2), be treated as if such fund constituted a political organization.

* * * * * * * * * * * *

(3) Candidate.—For purposes of paragraph (1), the term "candidate" means, with respect to any Federal, State, or local elective public office, an individual who—

⟦Footnote ¶3035 continued⟧

7-18-84 and the aggregate amount of interests in such partnership sold does not exceed the maximum amount described in clause (i).

For purposes of clause (i), the maximum amount taken into account shall be the greatest of the amounts shown in the registration statement, prospectus, or partnership agreement.

(C) Binding contracts.—For purposes of this paragraph, property shall be deemed to have been acquired before 1-1-86, if such property is acquired pursuant to a written contract which, on 1-1-86, and at all times thereafter, required the acquisition of such property and such property is placed in service not later than 6 months after the date such contract was entered into.

"section 168(h)(6)" in *italics* in Sec. 514(c)(9)(B)(vi)(II) added by section 201(d)(9), '86 TRA, which struck out:
(2) "section 168(j)(9)"
Effective date (Sec. 203(a), '86 TRA).—(1) Generally applies to property placed in service after 12-31-86, in taxable years ending after such date.

(B) Election to have amendments made by section 201 apply.—A taxpayer may elect (at such time and in such manner as the Secretary of the Treasury or his delegate may prescribe) to have the amendments made by section 201 apply to any property placed in service after 7-31-86, and before 1-1-87.

For special and transitional rules see ¶2007 and 2008.

Matter in *italics* in Sec. 514(c)(9)(C)(i) added by section 1878(e)(2), '86 TRA, which struck out:
(3) "section 509(a)"
Effective date (Sec. 1881, '86 TRA and section 1034(c)(1)—(3), '84 TRA).—See above.

Section 1603(b)(1), '86 TRA, struck out from Sec. 514(c)(9)(C)(i):
(4) "or"
Effective date (Sec. 1603(c), '86 TRA).—Applies to taxable years beginning after 12-31-86.

Matter in *italics* in Sec. 514(c)(9)(C)(ii) and (iii) added by section 1603(b)(2) and (3), '86 TRA, which struck out:
(5) "."
Effective date (Sec. 1603(c), '86 TRA).—Applies to taxable years beginning after 12-31-86.

⟦Footnote ¶3036⟧ Matter in *italics* in Sec. 527(g)(1) and 3 added by section 112(b)(1), '86 TRA, which struck out:
(1) "section 24(c)(2)"
Effective date (Sec. 151(a), '86 TRA).—Applies to taxable years beginning after 12-31-86.

    (A) publicly announces that he is a candidate for nomination or election to such office, and

    (B) meets the qualifications prescribed by law to hold such office.

*   *   *   *   *   *   *   *   *   *   *

[For official explanation, see Committee Reports, ¶3856.]

【¶3037】 CODE SEC. 532. CORPORATIONS SUBJECT TO ACCUMULATED EARNINGS TAX.

  (a) General Rule.—The accumulated earnings tax imposed by section 531 shall apply to every corporation (other than those described in subsection (b)) formed or availed of for the purpose of avoiding the income tax with respect to its shareholders or the shareholders of any other corporation, by permitting earnings and profits to accumulate instead of being divided or distributed.

  (b) Exceptions.—The accumulated earnings tax imposed by section 531 shall not apply to—

    (1) a personal holding company (as defined in section 542),

    (2) a foreign personal holding company (as defined in section 552),·[1]

    (3) a corporation exempt from tax under subchapter F (section 501 and following)[2], *or*

    (4) a passive foreign investment company (as defined in section 1296).

*   *   *   *   *   *   *   *   *   *   *

[For official explanation, see Committee Reports, ¶4045.]

【¶3038】 CODE SEC. 535. ACCUMULATED TAXABLE INCOME.

  (a) Definition.—For purposes of this subtitle, the term "accumulated taxable income" means the taxable income, adjusted in the manner provided in subsection (b), minus the sum of the dividends paid deduction (as defined in section 561) and the accumulated earnings credit (as defined in subsection (c)).

  (b) Adjustments to Taxable Income.—For purposes of subsection (a), taxable income shall be adjusted as follows:

*   *   *   *   *   *   *   *   *   *   *

  (5) Capital losses.—

*   *   *   *   *   *   *   *   *   *   *

    (C) Nonrecaptured capital gains deductions.—For purposes of subparagraph (B), the term "nonrecaptured capital gains deductions" means the excess of—

      (i) the aggregate amount allowable as a deduction under paragraph (6) for preceding taxable years beginning after[1]*July 18, 1984,* over

      (ii) the aggregate of the reductions under subparagraph (B) for preceding taxable years.

*   *   *   *   *   *   *   *   *   *   *

  (8) Special rules for mere holding or investment companies.—In the case of a mere holding or investment company—

*   *   *   *   *   *   *   *   *   *   *

    (C) Earnings and profits.—For purposes of subchapter C, the accumulated earnings and profits at any time shall not be less than they would be if this subsection had applied to the computation of earnings and profits for all taxable years beginning after[1]*July 18, 1984.*

【Footnote ¶3037】 Matter in *italics* in Sec. 532(b)(3) and (4) added by section 1235(f)(1), '86 TRA, which struck out:

  (1) "or"

  (2) "."

Effective date (Sec. 1235(h), '86 TRA).—Applies to taxable years of foreign corporations beginning after 12-31-86.

  【Footnote ¶3038】 Matter in *italics* in Sec. 535(b)(5)(C)(i) and (8)(C) added by section 1899A(17), '86 TRA, which struck out:

  (1) "the date of the enactment of the Tax Reform Act of 1984"

Sec. 535(b)(9) in *italics* added by section 1225(a), '86 TRA.

Effective date (Sec. 1225(c), '86 TRA).—Applies to gains and losses realized on or after 3-1-86.

(9) *Special rule for capital gains and losses of foreign corporations.—In the case of a foreign corporation, paragraph (6) shall be applied by taking into account only gains and losses which are effectively connected with the conduct of a trade or business within the United States and are not exempt from tax under treaty.*

* * * * * * * * * * * *

[For official explanation, see Committee Reports, ¶4038.]

【¶3039】 CODE SEC. 541. IMPOSITION OF PERSONAL HOLDING COMPANY TAX.

In addition to other taxes imposed by this chapter, there is hereby imposed for each taxable year on the undistributed personal holding company income (as defined in section 545) of every personal holding company (as defined in section 542) a personal holding company tax equal to [1]*28 percent (38.5 percent in the case of taxable years beginning in 1987)* of the undistributed personal holding company income.

【¶3040】 CODE SEC. 542. DEFINITION OF PERSONAL HOLDING COMPANY.

* * * * * * * * * * * *

(c) **Exceptions.**—The term "personal holding company" as defined in subsection (a) does not include—

* * * * * * * * * * * *

(8) a small business investment company which is licensed by the Small Business Administration and operating under the Small Business Investment Act of 1958 (15 U.S.C. 661 and following) and which is actively engaged in the business of providing funds to small business concerns under that Act. This paragraph shall not apply if any shareholder of the small business investment company owns at any time during the taxable year directly or indirectly (including, in the case of an individual, ownership by the members of his family as defined in section 544(a)(2)) a 5 percentum or more proprietary interest in a small business concern to which funds are provided by the investment company or 5 percentum or more in value of the outstanding stock of such concern; [1]

(9) a corporation which is subject to the jurisdiction of the court in a title 11 or similar case (within the meaning of section 368(a)(3)(A)) unless a major purpose of instituting or continuing such case is the avoidance of the tax imposed by section 541 [2]*; and*

(10) *a passive foreign investment company (as defined in section 1296).*

* * * * * * * * * * * *

[For official explanation, see Committee Reports, ¶4045.]

【¶3041】 CODE SEC. 543. PERSONAL HOLDING COMPANY INCOME.

(a) **General Rule.**—For purposes of this subtitle, the term "personal holding company income" means the portion of the adjusted ordinary gross income which consists of:

(1) **Dividends, etc.**—Dividends, interest, royalties (other than mineral, oil, or gas royalties or copyright royalties), and annuities. This paragraph shall not apply to—

(A) interest constituting rent (as defined in subsection (b)(3)), [1]

(B) interest on amounts set aside in a reserve fund under section 511 or 607 of the Merchant Marine Act, 1936, [2]*(46 U.S.C. App.* 1161 or 1177) [3]*, and*

【Footnote ¶3039】 Matter in *italics* in Sec. 541 added by section 104(b)(8), '86 TRA, which struck out:
(1) "50 percent"
Effective date (Sec. 151(a), '86 TRA).—Applies to taxable years beginning after 12-31-86.
【Footnote ¶3040】 Matter in *italics* in Sec. 542(c)(9) and (10) added by section 1235(f)(2), '86 TRA, which struck out:
(1) "and"
(2) "."
Effective date (Sec. 1235(h), '86 TRA).—Applies to taxable years of foreign corporations beginning after 12-31-86.
【Footnote ¶3041】 Section 645(a)(1)(A), '86 TRA, struck out from Sec. 543(a)(1)(A):
(1) "and"
Effective date (Sec. 645(e), '86 TRA).—Applies to royalities received before, on, and after 12-31-86.

Matter in *italics* in Sec. 543(a)(1)(B) (except "*, and*") added by section 1899A(18), '86 TRA, which struck out:
(2) "46 U.S.C."

Matter in *italics* in Sec. 543(a)(1)(B) (except "*46 U.S.C. App.*"), (C), (4), (b)(3), and (d) added by section 645(a)(1)(B)—(C), (2), (4), '86 TRA, which struck out:
(3) "."

(C) active business computer software royalties (within the meaning of subsection *(d))*.

* * * * * * * * * * * * *

(4) Copyright royalties—Copyright royalties; except that copyright royalties shall not be included If—

(A) such royalties (exclusive of royalties received for the use of, or right to use, copyrights or interests in copyrights on works created in whole, or in part, by any shareholder) constitute 50 percent or more of the ordinary gross income,

(B) the personal holding company income for the taxable year computed—

(i) without regard to copyright royalties, other than royalties received for the use of, or right to use, copyrights or interests in copyrights in works created in whole, or in part, by any shareholder owning more than 10 percent of the total outstanding capital stock of the corporation.

(ii) without regard to dividends from any corporation in which the taxpayer owns at least 50 percent of all classes of stock entitled to vote and at least 50 percent of the total value of all classes of stock and which corporation meets the requirements of this subparagraph and subparagraphs (A) and (C), and

(iii) by including as personal holding company income the adjusted income from rents and the adjusted income from mineral oil, and gas royalties.

is not more than 10 percent of the ordinary gross income, and

(C) the sum of the deductions which are properly allocable to such royalties and which are allowable under section 162, other than—

(i) deductions for compensation for personal service rendered by the shareholders,

(ii) deductions for royalties, paid or accrued, and

(iii) deductions which are specifically allowable under sections other than section 162,

equals or exceeds 25 percent of the amount by which the ordinary gross income exceeds the sum of the royalties paid or accrued and the amounts allowable as deductions under section 167 (relating to depreciation) with respect to copyright royalties.

For purposes of this subsection, the term "copyright royalties" means compensation, however designated, for the use of, or the right to use, copyrights in works protected by copyright issued under title 17 of the United States Code out from Sec. 543(a)(4): and to which copyright protection is also extended by the laws of any country other than the United States of America by virtue of any international treaty, convention, or agreement, or interests in any such copyrighted works, and includes payments from any person for performing rights in any such copyrighted work and payments (other than produced film rents as defined in paragraph (5)(B)) received for the use of, or right to use, films. For purposes of this paragraph, the term "shareholder" shall include any person who owns stock within the meaning of section 544. *This paragraph shall not apply to active business computer software royalties.*

* * * * * * * * * * * *

(b) Definitions.—For purposes of this part—

* * * * * * * * * * * *

(3) Adjusted income from rents.—The term "adjusted income from rents" means the gross income from rents, reduced by the amount subtracted under paragraph (2)(A) of this subsection. For purposes of the preceding sentence, the term "rents" means compensation, however designated, for the use of, or right to use, property, and the interest on debts owed to the corporation, to the extent such debts represent the price for which real property held primarily for sale to customers in the ordinary course of its trade or business was sold or exchanged by the corporation; but such term does not include—

(A) amounts constituting personal holding company income under subsection (a)(6),

(B) copyright royalties (as defined in subsection (a)(4)),

(C) produced film rents (as defined in subsection (a)(5)(B)), [4]

[Footnote ¶3041 continued]

(4) "or"

Effective date (Sec. 645(e), '86 TRA).—Applied to royalties received before, on, and after 12-31-86.

(D)   compensation, however designated, for the use of, or the right to use, any tangible personal property manufactured or produced by the taxpayer, if during the taxable year the taxpayer is engaged in substantial manufacturing or production of tangible personal property of the same type[3], *or*

(E)   active business computer software royalties (as defined in subsection (d)).

* * * * * * * * * * * *

(c)   **Gross Income of Insurance Companies Other Than Life or Mutual.**—In the case of an insurance company other than life or mutual, the term "gross income" as used in this part means the gross income, as defined in section 832(b)(1), increased by the amount of losses incurred as defined in section 832(b)(5), and the amount of expenses incurred, as defined in section 832(b)(6), and decreased by the amount deductible under section 832(c)(7) relating to tax-free interest).

(d)   Active Business Computer Software Royalties.—

(1)   In general.—For purposes of this section, the term "active business computer software royalties" means any royalties—
(A)   received by any corporation during the taxable year in connection with the licensing of computer software, and
(B)   with respect to which the requirements of paragraphs (2), (3), (4), and (5) are met.

(2)   Royalties must be received by corporation actively engaged in computer software business.—The requirements of this paragraph are met if the royalties described in paragraph (1)—
(A)   are received by a corporation engaged in the active conduct of the trade or business of developing, manufacturing, or producing computer software, and
(B)   are attributable to computer software which—
(i)   is developed, manufactured, or produced by such corporation (or its predecessor) in connection with the trade or business described in subparagraph (A), or
(ii)   is directly related to such trade or business.

(3)   Royalties must constitute at least 50 percent of income.—The requirements of this paragraph are met if the royalties described in paragraph (1) constitute at least 50 percent of the ordinary gross income of the corporation for the taxable year.

(4)   Deductions under sections 162 and 174 relating to royalties must equal or exceed 25 percent of ordinary gross income.—
(A)   In general.—The requirements of this paragraph are met if—
(i)   the sum of the deductions allowable to the corporation under sections 162, 174, and 195 for the taxable year which are properly allocable to the trade or business described in paragraph (2) equals or exceeds 25 percent of the ordinary gross income of such corporation for such taxable year, or
(ii)   the average of such deductions for the 5-taxable year period ending with such taxable year equals or exceeds 25 percent of the average ordinary gross income of such corporation for such period.

If a corporation has not been in existence during the 5-taxable year period described in clause (ii), then the period of existence of such corporation shall be substituted for such 5-taxable year period.

(B)   Deductions allowable under section 162.—For purposes of subparagraph (A), a deduction shall not be treated as allowable under section 162 if it is specifically allowable under another section.
(C)   Limitation on allowable deductions.—For purposes of subparagraph (A), no deduction shall be taken into account with respect to compensation for personal services rendered by the 5 individual shareholders holding the largest percentage (by value) of the outstanding stock of the corporation. For purposes of the preceding sentence—
(i)   individuals holding less than 5 percent (by value) of the stock of such corporation shall not be taken into account, and
(ii)   stock deemed to be owned by a shareholder solely by attribution from a partner under section 544(a)(2) shall be disregarded.

(5)   Dividends must equal or exceed excess of personal holding company income over 10 percent of ordinary gross income.—
(A)   In general.—The requirements of this paragraph are met if the sum of—
(i)   the dividends paid during the taxable year (determined under section 562),

    (ii) *the dividends considered as paid on the last day of the taxable year under section 563(c) (as limited by the second sentence of section 563(b)), and*

    (iii) *the consent dividends for the taxable year (determined under section 565),*

equals or exceeds the amount, if any, by which the personal holding company income for the taxable year exceeds 10 percent of the ordinary gross income of such corporation for such taxable year.

    (B) Computation of personal holding company income.—*For purposes of this paragraph, personal holding company income shall be computed*—

    (i) *without regard to amounts described in subsection (a)(1)(C),*

    (ii) *without regard to interest income during any taxable year*—

    (I) *which is in the 5-taxable year period beginning with the later of the 1st taxable year of the corporation or the 1st taxable year in which the corporation conducted the trade or business described in paragraph (2)(A), and*

    (II) *during which the corporation meets the requirements of paragraphs (2), (3), and (4), and*

    (iii) *by including adjusted income from rents and adjusted income from mineral, oil, and gas royalties (within the meaning of paragraphs (2) and (3) of subsection (a)).*

  (6) Special rules for affiliated group members.—

    (A) In general.—*In any case in which*—

    (i) *the taxpayer receives royalties in connection with the licensing of computer software, and*

    (ii) *another corporation which is a member of the same affiliated group as the taxpayer meets the requirements of paragraphs (2), (3), (4), and (5) with respect to such computer software,*

the taxpayer shall be treated as having met such requirements.

    (B) Affiliated group.—*For purposes of this paragraph, the term "affiliated group" has the meaning given such term by section 1504(a).*

[For official explanation, see Committee Reports, ¶3925.]

[¶3042] CODE SEC. 545. UNDISTRIBUTED PERSONAL HOLDING COMPANY INCOME.

  (a) Definition.—For purposes of this part, the term "undistributed personal holding company income" means the taxable income of a personal holding company adjusted in the manner provided in subsections (b), (c), and (d), minus the dividends paid deduction as defined in section 561. In the case of a personal holding company which is a foreign corporation, not more than 10 percent in value of the outstanding stock of which is owned (within the meaning of section 958(a)) during the last half of the taxable year by United States persons, the term "undistributed personal holding company income" means the amount determined by multiplying the undistributed personal holding company income (determined without regard to this sentence) by the percentage in value of its outstanding stock which is the greatest percentage in value of its outstanding stock so owned by United States persons on any one day during such period.

  (b) Adjustments to Taxable Income.—For the purposes of subsection (a), the taxable income shall be adjusted as followed:

* * * * * * * * * * *

  (7) Special rule for capital gains and losses of foreign corporations.—*In the case of a foreign corporation, paragraph (5) shall be applied by taking into account only gains and losses which are effectively connected with the conduct of a trade or business within the United States and are not exempt from tax under treaty.*

* * * * * * * * * * *

[For official explanation, see Committee Reports, ¶4038.]

[¶3043] CODE SEC. 551. FOREIGN PERSONAL HOLDING COMPANY INCOME TAXED TO UNITED STATES SHAREHOLDERS.

* * * * * * * * * * *

[Footnote ¶3042] Sec. 545(b)(7) in *italics* added by section 1225(b), '86 TRA.
Effective date (Sec. 1225(c), '86 TRA).—Applies to gains and losses realized on or after 3-1-86.

(f) **Stock held through foreign entity.**—For purposes of this section, stock of a foreign personal holding company owned (directly or through the application of this subsection) by—

    (1)   a partnership, estate, or trust which is not a United States shareholder *or an estate or trust which is a foreign estate or trust,* or

    (2)   a foreign corporation which is not a foreign personal holding company,

shall be considered as being owned proportionately by its partners, beneficiaries, or shareholders. In any case to which the preceding sentence applies, the Secretary may by regulations provide for such adjustments in the application of this part as may be necessary to carry out the purposes of the preceding sentence.

(g)   *Coordination With Passive Foreign Investment Company Provisions.*—*If, but for this subsection, an amount would be included in the gross income of any person under subsection (a) and under section 1293 (relating to current taxation of income from certain passive foreign investment companies), such amount shall be included in the gross income of such person only under subsection (a).*

¹*(h)*   **Cross References.**—

    (1)   **For basis of stock or securities in a foreign personal holding company acquired from a decedent, see section 1014(b)(5).**

    (2)   **For period of limitation on assessment and collection without assessment, in case of failure to include in gross income the amount properly includible therein under subsection (b), see section 6501.**

[For official explanation, see Committee Reports, ¶4045; 4144.]

〖¶3044〗   **CODE SEC. 552. DEFINITION OF FOREIGN PERSONAL HOLDING COMPANY.**

(a)   **General Rule.**—For purposes of this subtitle, the term "foreign personal holding company" means any foreign corporation if—

    (1)   **Gross income requirement.**—At least 60 percent of its gross income (as defined in section 555(a) for the taxable year is foreign personal holding company income as defined in section 553; but if the corporation is a foreign personal holding company with respect to any taxable year ending after August 26, 1937, then, for each subsequent taxable year, the minimum percentage shall be 50 percent in lieu of 60 percent, until a taxable year during the whole of which the stock ownership required by paragraph (2) does not exist, or until the expiration of three consecutive taxable years in each of which less than 50 percent of the gross income is foreign personal holding company income. For purposes of this paragraph, there shall be included in the gross income the amount includible therein as a dividend by reason of the application of section 555(c)(2); and

    (2)   **Stock ownership requirement.**—¹*At any time during the taxable year more than*

〖Footnote ¶3043〗   Matter in *italics* in Sec. 551(f)(1) added by section 1810(h)(2), '86 TRA.

Effective date (Sec. 1881, '86 TRA and Sec. 132(d)(1), '84 TRA).—(A)   Generally applies to taxable years of foreign corporations beginning after 12-31-83.

(B)   1-year extension for certain trusts created before 6-30-53.—

(i)   In general.—The amendment made by subsection (b) shall apply to taxable years of a foreign corporation beginning after 12-31-84, with respect to stock of such corporation which is held (directly or indirectly, within the meaning of section 554 of the '54 Code) by a trust created before 6-30-53, if—

(I) none of the beneficiaries of such trust was a citizen or resident of the United States at the time of its creation or within 5 years thereafter, and

(II) such trust does not, after 7-1-83, acquire (directly or indirectly) stock of any foreign personal holding company other than a company described in clause (ii).

(ii)   Description of company.—A company is described in this clause if—

(I)   substantially all of the assets of such company are stock or assets previously held by such trust, or

(II)   such company ceases to be a foreign personal holding company before 1-1-85.

Sec. 551(g) and (h) in *italics* added by section 1235(e), '86 TRA, which struck out:

(1)   "(g)"

Effective date (Sec. 1235(h), '86 TRA).—Applies to taxable years of foreign corporations beginning after 12-31-86.

〖Footnote ¶3044〗   Matter in *italics* in Sec. 552(a)(2) added by section 1222(b), '86 TRA, which struck out:

(1)   "At any time during the taxable year more than 50 percent in value of its outstanding stock is owned, directly or indirectly, by or for not more than five individuals who are citizens or residents of the United States, hereinafter called 'United States group'."

Effective date (Sec. 1222(c), '86 TRA).—Applies to taxable years of foreign corporations beginning after 12-31-86; except that for purposes of applying sections 951(a)(1)(B) and 956 of the '86 Code, such amendments shall take effect on 8-16-86.

(2)   Transitional rule.—In the case of any corporation treated as a controlled foreign corporation by reason of

50 percent of—

    (A) the total combined voting power of all classes of stock of such corporation entitled to vote, or

    (B) the total value of the stock of such corporation,

is owned (directly or indirectly) by or for not more than 5 individuals who are citizens or residents of the United States (hereinafter in this part referred to as the "United States group").

*   *   *   *   *   *   *   *   *   *   *

(c) Certain Dividends and Interest Not Taken Into Account.—For purposes of subsection (a)(1) and section 553(a)(1), gross income and foreign personal holding company income shall not include any dividends and interest which—

    (1) are described in subparagraph (A) of section 954(c)(4), and

    (2) are received from a related person which is not a foreign personal holding company (determined without regard to this subsection).

For purposes of the preceding sentence, the term "related person" has the meaning given such term by section 954(d)(3) (determined by substituting "foreign personal holding company" for "controlled foreign corporation" each place it appears).

[For official explanation, see Committee Reports, ¶4035; 4144.]

[¶3045] CODE SEC. 553. FOREIGN PERSONAL HOLDING COMPANY INCOME.

(a) Foreign Personal Holding Company Income.—For purposes of this subtitle, the term "foreign personal holding company income" means that portion of the gross income, determined for purposes of section 552, which consists of:

    (1) Dividends, etc.—Dividends, interest, royalties, and annuities. *This paragraph shall not apply to active business computer software royalties (as defined in section 543(d)).*

*   *   *   *   *   *   *   *   *   *   *

[For official explanation, see Committee Reports, ¶3925.]

[¶3046] CODE SEC. 562. RULES APPLICABLE IN DETERMINING DIVIDENDS ELIGIBLE FOR DIVIDENDS PAID DEDUCTION.

*   *   *   *   *   *   *   *   *   *   *

(b) Distributions in Liquidation.—

    (1) Except in the case of a personal holding company described in section 542 or a foreign personal holding company described in section 552—

    (A) in the case of amounts distributed in liquidation, the part of such distribution which is properly chargeable to earnings and profits accumulated after February 28, 1913, shall be treated as a dividend for purposes of computing the dividends paid deduction,

    (B) in the case of a complete liquidation occurring within 24 months after the adoption of a plan of liquidation, any distribution within such period pursuant to such plan shall, to the extent of the earnings and profits (computed without regard to capital losses) of the corporation for the taxable year in which such distribution is made, be treated as a dividend for purposes of computing the dividends paid deduction.

[Footnote ¶3044 continued]

the amendments made by this section, property acquired before 8-16-86, shall not be taken into account under section 956(b) '86 Code.

    (3) Special rule for beneficiary of trust.—In the case of an individual—

    (A) who is a beneficiary of a trust which was established on 12-7-79, under the laws of a foreign jurisdiction, and

    (B) who was not a citizen or resident of the United States on the date the trust was established,

amounts which are included in the gross income of such beneficiary under section 951(a) '86 Code with respect to stock held by the trust (and treated as distributed to the trust) shall be treated as the first amounts which are distributed by the trust to such beneficiary and as amounts to which section 959(a) of such Code applies.

Matter in *italics* in Sec. 552(c) added by section 1810(h)(1), '86 TRA.

Effective date (Sec. 1881, '86 TRA and section 132(d)(2)(B), '84 TRA).—Applies to taxable years of foreign corporations beginning after 3-15-84.

[Footnote ¶3045] Matter in *italics* in Sec. 553(a)(1) added by section 645(a)(3), '86 TRA.

Effective date (Sec. 645(e), '86 TRA).—Applies to royalties received before, on, and after 12-31-86.

For purposes of subparagraph (A), a liquidation includes a redemption of stock to which section 302 applies. *Except to the extent provided in regulations, the preceding sentence shall not apply in the case of any mere holding or investment company which is not a regulated investment company.*

* * * * * * * * * * *

(c) **Preferential Dividends.**—The amount of any distribution shall not be considered as a dividend for purposes of computing the dividends paid deduction, unless such distribution is pro rata, with no preference to any share of stock as compared with other shares of the same class, and with no preference to one class of stock as compared with another class except to the extent that the former is entitled (without reference to waivers of their rights by shareholders) to such preference. *In the case of a distribution by a regulated investment company to a shareholder who made an initial investment of at least $10,000,000 in such company, such distribution shall not be treated as not being pro rata or as being preferential solely by reason of an increase in the distribution by reason of reductions in administrative expenses of the company.*

* * * * * * * * * * *

[For official explanation, see Committee Reports, ¶3928; 4138.]

〖¶3047〗 CODE SEC. 582. BAD DEBTS, LOSSES, AND GAINS WITH RESPECT TO SECURITIES HELD BY FINANCIAL INSTITUTIONS.

* * * * * * * * * * *

(c) **Bond, etc., Losses and Gains of Financial Institutions.**—

(1) **General rule.**—For purposes of this subtitle, in the case of [1] *a financial institution referred to in paragraph (5)*, the sale or exchange of a bond, debenture, note, or certificate or other evidence of indebtedness shall not be considered a sale or exchange of a capital asset. *For purposes of the preceding sentence, any regular or residual interest in a REMIC shall be treated as evidence of indebtedness.*

* * * * * * * * * * *

(5) Financial institutions to which paragraph (1) applies.—

(A) In general.—For purposes of paragraph (1), the financial institutions referred to in this paragraph are—
  (i) any bank (and any corporation which would be a bank except for the fact it is a foreign corporation),
  (ii) any financial institution referred to in section 591,
  (iii) any small business investment company operating under the Small Business Investment Act of 1958, and
  (iv) any business development corporation.

(B) Business development corporation.—For purposes of subparagraph (A), the term "business development corporation" means a corporation which was created by or pursuant to an act of a State legislature for purposes of promoting, maintaining, and assisting the economy and industry within such State on a regional or statewide basis by making loans to be used in trades and businesses which would generally not be made by banks within such region or State in the ordinary course of their business (except on the basis of a partial participation), and which is operated primarily for such purposes.

(C) Limitations on foreign banks.—In the case of a foreign corporation referred to in subparagraph (A)(i), paragraph (1) shall only apply to gains and losses which are effectively connected with the conduct of a banking business in the United States.

[For official explanation, see Committee Reports, ¶3930; 3948.]

〖Footnote ¶3046〗   Matter in *italics* in Sec. 562(b)(1) added by section 1804(d)(1), '86 TRA.
Effective date (Sec. 1804(d)(2), '86 TRA).—Applies to distributions after 9-27-85.

Matter in *italics* in Sec. 562(c) added by section 657(a), '86 TRA.
Effective date (Sec. 657(b), '86 TRA).—Applies to distributions after the date of the enactment of this Act.
〖Footnote ¶3047〗   Matter in *italics* in Sec. 582(c)(1) and (5) added by section 901(d)(3), '86 TRA, which struck out:
(1)   "a financial institution to which section 585, 586, or 593 applies,"
Effective date (Sec. 901(e), '86 TRA).—Applies to taxable years beginning after 12-31-86.

The last sentence in *italics* in Sec. 582(c)(1) added by section 671(b)(4), '86 TRA.
Effective date (Sec. 675, '86 TRA).—Applies to taxable years beginning after 12-31-86.

〖¶3048〗 CODE SEC. 584. COMMON TRUST FUNDS.

* * * * * * * * * * *

(c) Income of Participants in Fund.—[1]*Each participant in the common trust fund in computing its taxable income shall include, whether or not distributed and whether or not distributable—*

(1) as part of its gains and losses from sales or exchanges of capital assets held for not more than 6 months, its proportionate share of the gains and losses of the common trust fund from sales or exchanges of capital assets held for not more than 6 months,

(2) as part of its gains and losses from sales or exchanges of capital assets held for more than 6 months, its proportionate share of the gains and losses of the common trust fund from sales or exchanges of capital assets held for more than 6 months, and

(3) its proportionate share of the ordinary taxable income or the ordinary net loss of the common trust fund, computed as provided in subsection (d).

* * * * * * * * * * *

[For official explanation, see Committee Reports, ¶3913.]

〖¶3049〗 CODE SEC. 585. RESERVES FOR LOSSES ON LOANS OF BANKS.

[1]*(a) Reserve for bad debts.*—

(1) In General.—*Except as provided in subsection (c), a bank shall be allowed a deduction for a reasonable addition to a reserve for bad debts. Such deduction shall be in lieu of any deduction under section 166(a).*

(2) Bank.—*For purposes of this section—*

(A) In general.—*The term "bank" means any bank (as defined in section 581) other than an organization to which section 593 applies.*

(B) Banking business of United States branch of foreign corporation.—*The term "bank" also includes any corporation to which subparagraph (A) would apply except for the fact that it is a foreign corporation. In the case of any such foreign corporation, this section shall apply only with respect to loans outstanding the interest on which is effectively connected with the conduct of a banking business within the United States.*

(b) Addition to Reserve for Bad Debts.—

(1) General rule.—For purposes of [2]*subsection(a)*, the reasonable addition to the reserve for bad debts of any financial institution to which this section applies shall be an amount determined by the taxpayer which shall not exceed the greater of—

〖Footnote ¶3048〗 Matter in *italics* in Sec. 584(c) added by section 612(b)(2)(A), '86 TRA, which struck out:

(1) "(1) **Inclusions in taxable income.**—Each participant in the common trust fund in computing its taxable income shall include, whether or not distributed and whether or not distributable—

(A) as part of its gains and losses from sales or exchanges of capital assets held for not more than 6 months its proportionate share of the gains and losses of the common trust fund from sales or exchanges of capital assets held for not more than 6 months,

(B) as part of its gains and losses from sales or exchanges of capital assets held for more than 6 months its proportionate share of the gains and losses of the common trust fund from sales or exchanges of capital assets held for more than 6 months;

(C) its proportionate share of the ordinary taxable income or the ordinary net loss of the common trust fund, computed as provided in subsection (d).

(2) **Dividends or interest received.**—The proportionate share of each participant in the amount of dividends or interest received by the common trust fund and to which section 116 or 128 applies shall be considered for purposes of such section as having been received by such participant."

Effective date (Sec. 612(c), '86 TRA).—Applies to taxable years beginning after 12-31-86.

***Special rule**—(Section 612(b)(2)(B), '86 TRA).—(B) If the amendments made by section 1001 of the '84 TRA cease to apply, effective with respect to property to which such amendments do not apply, subsection (c) of section 584 is amended by striking out "6 months" each place it appears and inserting in lieu thereof "1 year".

〖Footnote ¶3049〗 Matter in *italics* in Sec. 585(a), (b)(1), and (c) added by section 901(a) and (d)(1), '86 TRA, which struck out:

(1) "(a) **Institutions to Which Section Applies.**—This section shall apply to the following financial institutions:

(1) any bank (as defined in section 581) other than an organization to which section 593 applies, and

(2) any corporation to which paragraph (1) would apply except for the fact that it is a foreign corporation, and in the case of any such foreign corporation this section shall apply only with respect to loans outstanding the interest on which is effectively connected with the conduct of a banking business within the United States."

(2) "section 166(c)"

Effective date (Sec. 901(e), '86 TRA).—Applies to taxable years beginning after 12-31-86.

(A) for taxable years beginning before 1988 the addition to the reserve for losses on loans determined under the percentage method as provided in paragraph (2), or

(B) the addition to the reserve for losses on loans determined under the experience method as provided in paragraph (3).

* * * * * * * * * * *

(c) Section not to apply to large banks.—

(1) In general.—In the case of a large bank, this section shall not apply (and no deduction shall be allowed under any other provision of this subtitle for any addition to a reserve for bad debts).

(2) Large banks.—For purposes of this subsection, a bank is a large bank if, for the taxable year (or for any preceding taxable year beginning after December 31, 1986)—

(A) the average adjusted bases of all assets of such bank exceeded $500,000,000, or

(B) such bank was a member of a parent-subsidiary controlled group and the average adjusted bases of all assets of such group exceeded $500,000,000.

(3) 4-year spread of adjustments.—

(A) In general.—Except as provided in paragraph (4), in the case of any bank which for its last taxable year before the disqualification year maintained a reserve for bad debts—

(i) the provisions of this subsection shall be treated as a change in the method of accounting of such bank for the disqualification year,

(ii) such change shall be treated as having been made with the consent of the Secretary, and

(iii) the net amount of adjustments required by section 481(a) to be taken into account by the taxpayer shall be taken into account in each of the 4 taxable years beginning with the disqualification year with—

(I) the amount taken into account for the 1st or such taxable years being the greater of 10 percent of such net amount or such greater amount as the taxpayer may designate, and

(II) the amount taken into account in each of the 3 succeeding taxable years being equal to the applicable fraction (determined in accordance with the following table for the taxable year involved) of the portion of such net amount not taken into account under subclause (I).

If the case of the—	The applicable fraction is —
1st succeeding year	2/9
2nd succeeding year.	1/3
3rd succeeding year.	4/9

(B) Suspension of recapture for taxable year for which bank is financially troubled.—

(i) In general.—In the case of a bank which is a financially troubled bank for any taxable year—

(I) no adjustment shall be taken into account under subparagraph (A) for such taxable year, and

(II) such taxable year shall be disregarded in determining whether any other taxable year is a taxable year for which an adjustment is required to be taken into account under subparagraph (A) or the amount of such adjustment.

(ii) Exception for elective recapture for 1st year.—Clause (i) shall not apply to the 1st taxable year referred to in subparagraph (A)(iii)(I) if the taxpayer designates an amount in accordance with such subparagraph.

(iii) Financially troubled bank.—For purposes of clause (i), the term "financially troubled bank" means any bank if, for the taxable year, the nonperforming loan percentage of such bank exceeds 75 percent.

(iv) Nonperforming loan percentage.—For purposes of clause (iii), the term "nonperforming loan percentage" means the percentage determined by dividing—

(I) the sum of the outstanding balances of nonperforming loans of the bank as of the close of each quarter of the taxable year, by

(II) the sum of the amounts of equity of the bank as of the close of each such quarter.

In the case of a bank which is a member of a parent-subsidiary controlled group for the taxable year, the preceding sentence shall be applied with respect to such group.

(v) Other definitions.—For purposes of this subparagraph—

(I) Nonperforming loans.—The term "nonperforming loan" means any loan which is considered to be nonperforming by the primary Federal regulatory agency with respect to the bank.

(II) Equity.—The term "equity" means the equity of the bank as determined for Federal regulatory purposes.

(C) Coordination with estimated tax payments.—For purposes of applying section 6655(d)(3) with respect to any installment, the determination under subparagraph (B) of whether an adjustment is required to be taken into account under subparagraph (A) shall be made as of the last day prescribed for payment of such installment.

(4) Elective cut-off method.—If a bank makes an election under this paragraph for the disqualification year—

(A) the provisions of this subsection shall not be treated as a change in the method of accounting of the taxpayer for purposes of section 481,

(B) the taxpayer shall continue to maintain its reserve for loans held by the bank as of the 1st day of the disqualification year and charge against such reserve any losses resulting from loans held by the bank as of such 1st day, and

(C) no deduction shall be allowed under this section (or any other provision of this subtitle) for any addition to such reserve for the disqualification year or any subsequent taxable year.

(5) Definitions.—For purposes of this subsection—

(A) Parent-subsidiary controlled group.—The term "parent-subsidiary controlled group" means any controlled group of corporations described in section 1563(a)(1). In determining the average adjusted bases of assets held by such a group, interests held by one member of such group in another member of such group shall be disregarded.

(B) Disqualification year.—The term "disqualification year" means, with respect to any bank, the 1st taxable year beginning after December 31, 1986, for which such bank was a large bank if such bank maintained a reserve for bad debts for the preceding taxable year.

[For official explanation, see Committee Reports, ¶3948.]

[¶3050] CODE SEC. 586. RESERVES FOR LOSSES ON LOANS OF SMALL BUSINESS INVESTMENT COMPANIES, ETC. [Repealed by section 901(c), '86 TRA].[1]

[For official explanation, see Committee Reports, ¶3948.]

[¶3051] CODE SEC. 593. RESERVES FOR LOSSES ON LOANS.

[1](a) *Reserve for Bad Debts.—*

(1) In general.—Except as provided in paragraph (2), in the case of—

(A) any domestic building and loan association,

(B) any mutual savings bank, or

(C) any cooperative bank without capital stock organized and operated for mutual purposes and without profit,

there shall be allowed a deduction for a reasonable addition to a reserve for bad debts. Such deduction shall be in lieu of any deduction under section 166(a).

(2) Organization must meet 60-percent asset test of section 7701(a)(19).—This section shall apply to an association or bank referred to in paragraph (1) only if it meets the requirements of section 7701(a)(19)(C).

(b) Addition to Reserves for Bad Debts.—

(1) In general.—For purposes of [2]*subsection (a),* the reasonable addition for the taxable year to the reserve for bad debts of any taxpayer described in subsection (a) shall be an amount equal to the sum of—

(A) the amount determined to be a reasonable addition to the reserve for losses on nonqualifying loans, computed in the same manner as is provided with respect

---

[Footnote ¶3050] (1) **Effective date** (Sec. 901(e), '86 TRA).—Applies to taxable years beginning after 12-31-86.

[Footnote ¶3051] Matter in *italics* in Sec. 593(a), (b)(1) and (2) added by section 901(b)(1), (2), (d)(2)(A) and (B), '86 TRA, which struck out:

(1) **"(a) Organizations to which Section Applies.—**This section shall apply to any mutual savings bank, domestic building and loan association, or cooperative bank without capital stock organized and operated for mutual purposes and without profit."

(2) "section 166(c)"

to additions to the reserves for losses on loans of banks under section 585(b)(3), plus

(B)   the amount determined by the taxpayer to be a reasonable addition to the reserve for losses on qualifying real property loans, but such amount shall not exceed the amount determined under ³*paragraph (2) or (3), whichever is the larger,* but the amount determined under this subparagraph shall in no case be greater than the larger of—

(i)   the amount determined under ⁴*paragraph (3)*, or

(ii)   the amount which, when added to the amount determined under subparagraph (A), equals the amount by which 12 percent of the total deposits or withdrawable accounts of depositors of the taxpayer at the close of such year exceeds the sum of its surplus, undivided profits, and reserves at the beginning of such year (taking into account any portion thereof attributable to the period before the first taxable year beginning after December 31, 1951).

(2)   Percentage of taxable income method.—

⁵*"(A)   In general.—Subject to subparagraphs (B) and(C), the amount determined under this paragraph for the taxable year shall be an amount equal to 8 percent of the taxable income for such year.*

"(B)   Reduction for amounts referred to in paragraph (1)(A).—The amount determined under subparagraph (A) shall be reduced (but not below 0) by the amount determined under paragraph (1)(A).

⁶*(C)*   Overall limitation on paragraph.—The amount determined under this paragraph shall not exceed the amount necessary to increase the balance at the close of the taxable year of the reserve for losses on qualifying real property loans to 6 percent of such loans outstanding at such time.

⁷*(D)*   Computation of taxable income.—For purposes of this paragraph, taxable income shall be computed—

(i)   by excluding from gross income any amount included therein by reason of subsection (e),

(ii)   without regard to any deduction allowable for any addition to the reserve for bad debts,

(iii)   by excluding from gross income an amount equal to the net gain for the taxable year arising from the sale or exchange of stock of a corporation or of obligations the interest on which is excludable from gross income under section 103, *and* ⁸

〖Footnote ¶3051 continued〗

(3)   "paragraph (2), (3), or (4), whichever amount is the largest"

(4)   "paragraph (4)"

(5)   "(A)   In general.—Subject to subparagraphs (B), (C), and (D), the amount determined under this paragraph for the taxable year shall be an amount equal to the applicable percentage of the taxable income for such year (determined under the following table):

For a taxable year beginning in—	The applicable percentage under this paragraph shall be—
1976	43 percent.
1977	42 percent.
1978	41 percent.
1979 or thereafter	40 percent.

(B)   Reduction of applicable percentage in certain cases.—If, for the taxable year, the percentage of the assets of a taxpayer described in subsection (a), which are assets described in section 7701(a)(19)(C), is less than—

(i)   82 percent of the total assets in the case of a taxpayer other than a mutual savings bank which is not described in section 591(b), the applicable percentage for such year provided by subparagraph (A) shall be reduced by ¾ of 1 percentage point for each 1 percentage point of such difference, or

(ii)   72 percent of the total assets in the case of a mutual savings bank which is not described in section 591(b), the applicable percentage for such year provided by subparagraph (A) shall be reduced by 1½ percentage points for each 1 percentage point of such difference.

If, for the taxable year, the percentage of the assets of such taxpayer which are assets described in section 7701(a)(19)(C) is less than 60 percent (50 percent for a taxable year beginning before 1973 in the case of a mutual savings bank which is not described in section 591(b)), this paragraph shall not apply.

(C)   Reduction for amounts referred to in paragraph (1)(A).—The amount determined under subparagraph (A) shall be reduced by that portion of the amount referred to in paragraph (1)(A) for the taxable year (not in excess of 100 percent) which bears the same ratio to such amount as (i) 18 percent (28 percent in the case of mutual savings banks which are not described in section 591(b) bears to (ii) the percentage of the assets of the taxpayer for such year which are not assets described in section 7701(a)(19)(C)."

(6)   "(D)"

(7)   "(E)"

Effective date (Sec. 901(e), '86 TRA).—Applies to taxable years beginning after 12-31-86.

Matter in *italics* in Sec. 593(b)(2)(D)(iii) and (iv) [formerly (E)] added by section 311(b)(2), '86 TRA, which struck out:

(8)   "(iv)   by excluding from gross income an amount equal to the lesser of **18/46** of the net long-term capital

[9](iv) by excluding from gross income dividends with respect to which a deduction is allowable by part VIII of subchapter B, reduced by an amount equal to [10]8 *percent* of the dividends received deduction (determined without regard to section 596) for the taxable year. [11]

[12](3) **Experience method.**—The amount determined under this paragraph for the taxable year shall be computed in the same manner as is provided with respect to additions to the reserves for losses on loans of banks under section 585(b)(3).[13]

* * * * * * * * * * * *

(d) Loans Defined.—For purposes of this section—

* * * * * * * * * * * *

(4) Treatment of interests in REMIC's.—A regular or residual interest in a REMIC shall be treated as a qualifying real property loan; except that, if less than 95 percent of the assets of such REMIC are qualifying real property loans (determined as if the taxpayer held the assets of the REMIC), such interest shall be so treated only in the proportion which the assets of such REMIC consist of such loans.

(e) Distributions to Shareholders.—

(1) In General.—For purposes of this chapter, any distribution of property (as defined in section 317(a)) by a domestic building and loan association or an institution that is treated as a mutual savings bank under section 591(b) to a shareholder with respect to its stock, if such distribution is not allowable as a deduction under section 591, shall be treated as made—

【Footnote ¶3051 continued】

gain for the taxable year or [18]/₄₆ of the net long-term capital gain for the taxable year from the sale or exchange of property other than property described in clause (iii), and"

(9) "(v)"

Effective date (Sec. 311(c), (d), '86 TRA).—Applies to taxable years beginning after 12-31-86.

(d) Transitional Rules.—

(1) Taxable years which begin in 1986 and end in 1987.—In the case of any taxable year which begins before 1-1-87, and ends on or after such date, paragraph (2) of section 1201(a) of the '54 Code as in effect on the date before the date of enactment of this Act, shall be applied as if it read as follows:

(2) the sum of—

(A) 28 percent of the lesser of—

(i) the net capital gain determined by taking into account only gain or loss which is properly taken into account for the portion of the taxable year before 1-1-87, or

(ii) the net capital gain for the taxable year, and

(B) 34 percent of the excess (if any) of—

(i) the net capital gain for the taxable year, over

(ii) the amount of the net capital gain taken into account under subparagraph (A).

(2) Revocation of elections under section 631(a).—Any election under section 631(a) of the '54 Code made (whether by a corporation or a person other than a corporation) for a taxable year beginning before 1-1-87, may be revoked by the taxpayer for any taxable year ending after 12-31-86. For purposes of determining whether the taxpayer may make a further election under such section, such election (and any revocation under this paragraph) shall not be taken into account.

Matter in *italics* in Sec. 593(b)(2)(D)(vi) [formerly (E)(v)] added by section 901(b)(3) and (d)(2)(B) [should read (C)], '86 TRA, which struck out:

(10) "the applicable percentage (determined under subparagraphs (A) and (B))"

(11) "(3) **Percentage method.**—The amount determined under this paragraph to be a reasonable addition to the reserve for losses on qualifying real property loans shall be computed in the same manner as is provided with respect to additions to the reserves for losses on loans of banks under section 585(b)(2), reduced by the amount referred to in paragraph (1)(A) for the taxable year."

(12) "(4)"

(13) "(5) **Determination of reserve for percentage method.**—For purposes of paragraph (3), the amount deemed to be the balance of the reserve for losses on loans at the beginning of the taxable year shall be the total of the balances at such time of the reserve for losses on nonqualifying loans, the reserve for losses on qualifying real property loans, and the supplemental reserves for losses on loans."

Effective date (Sec. 901(e), '86 TRA).—Applies to taxable years beginning after 12-31-86.

Sec. 593(d)(4) in *italics* added by section 671(b)(2), '86 TRA.

Effective date (Sec. 675(a), '86 TRA).—Applies to taxable year beginning after 12-31-86.

(A) first out of its earnings and profits accumulated in taxable years beginning after December 31, 1951, to the extent thereof,

(B) then out of the reserve for losses on qualifying real property loans, to the extent additions to such reserve exceed the additions which would have been allowed under [14]*subsection (b)(3),*

(C) then out of the supplemental reserve for losses on loans, to the extent thereof,

(D) then out of such other accounts as may be proper.

This paragraph shall apply in the case of any distribution in redemption of stock or in partial or complete liquidation of the association or an institution that is treated as a mutual savings bank under section 591(b), except that any such distribution shall be treated as made first out of the amount referred to in subparagraph (B), second out of the amount referred to in subparagraph (C), third out of the amount referred to in subparagraph (A), and then out of such other accounts as may be proper. This paragraph shall not apply to any transaction to which section 381 (relating to carryovers in certain corporate acquisitions) applies, or to any distribution to the Federal Savings and Loan Insurance Corporation in redemption of an interest in an association or an institution that is treated as a mutual savings bank under section 591(b), if such interest was originally received by the Federal Savings and Loan Insurance Corporation in exchange for financial assistance pursuant to section 406(f) of the National Housing Act (12 U.S.C. sec. 1729(f)).

* * * * * * * * * * *

[For official explanation, see Committee Reports, ¶3948; 3887; 3930.]

〖¶3052〗 CODE SEC. 596. LIMITATION ON DIVIDENDS RECEIVED DEDUCTION.

In the case of an organization to which section 593 applies and which computes additions to the reserve for losses on loans for the taxable year under section 593(b)(2), the total amount allowed under sections 243, 244, and 245 (determined without regard to this section) for the taxable year as a deduction with respect to dividends received shall be reduced by [1]*an amount equal to 8 percent of such total amount.*

[For official explanation, see Committee Reports, ¶3948.]

〖¶3053〗 CODE SEC. 597. FSLIC FINANCIAL ASSISTANCE.

[Repealed by section 904(b)(1), '86 TRA].[1]

[For official explanation, see Committee Reports, ¶3951.]

〖¶3054〗 CODE SEC. 613. PERCENTAGE DEPLETION.

* * * * * * * * * * *

(e) **Percentage Depletion for Geothermal Deposits.—**

* * * * * * * * * * *

(4) *Percentage depletion not to include lease bonuses, etc.—In the case of any geothermal deposit, the term "gross income from the property" shall, for purposes of this section, not include any amount described in section 613A(d)(5).*

[For official explanation, see Committee Reports, ¶3897.]

〖Footnote ¶3051 continued〗

Matter in *italics* in Sec. 593(e)(1)(B) added by section 901(d)(2)(C) [should read (D)], '86 TRA, which struck out:

(14) "subsection (b)(4)"

Effective date (Sec. 901(e), '86 TRA).—Applies to taxble years beginning after 12-31-86.

〖Footnote ¶3052〗 Matter in *italics* in Sec. 596 added by section 901(d)(4)(D), '86 TRA, which struck out:

(1) "an amount equal to the applicable percentage for such year (determined under subparagraphs (A) and(B) of section 593(b)(2)) of such total amount."

Effective date (Sec. 901(e), '86 TRA).—Applies to taxable years beginning after 12-31-86.

〖Footnote ¶3053〗 Sec. 597 repealed by section 904(b)(1), '86 TRA.

Effective date (Sec. 904(c)(2), '86 TRA).—(A) Generally applies to transfers after 12-31-88, in taxable years ending after such date; except that such amendments shall not apply to transfers after such date pursuant to an acquisition to which the amendments made by subsection (a) do not apply.

(B) Clarification of treatment of amounts excluded under section 597.—Section 265(a)(1) of the '86 Code (as amended by this title) shall not deny any deduction by reason of such deduction being allocable to amounts excluded from gross income under section 597 of the '54 Code (as in effect on the day before the date of the enactment of this Act).

〖Footnote ¶3054〗 Sec. 613(e)(4) added by section 412(a)(2), '86 TRA.

Effective date (Sec. 412(a)(3), '86 TRA).—Applies to amounts received or accrued after 8-16-86, in taxable years ending after such date.

〖¶3054-A〗 CODE SEC. 613A. LIMITATIONS ON PERCENTAGE DEPLETION IN CASE OF OIL AND GAS WELLS.

* * * * * * * * * * * *

(d) Limitations on Application of Subsection (c).—

(1) **Limitation based on taxable income.**—The deduction for the taxable year attributable to the application of subsection (c) shall not exceed 65 percent of the taxpayer's taxable income [1] for the year computed without regard to—

   (A) any depletion on production from an oil or gas property which is subject to the provisions of subsection (c),

   (B) any net operating loss carryback to the taxable year under section 172,

   (C) any capital loss carryback to the taxable year under section 1212, and

   (D) in the case of a trust, any distributions to its beneficiary, except in the case of any trust where any beneficiary of such trust is a member of the family (as defined in section 267(c)(4)) of a settlor who created inter vivos and testamentary trust for members of the family and such settlor died within the last six days of the fifth month in 1970, and the law in the jurisdiction in which such trust was created requires all or a portion of the gross or net proceeds of any royalty or other interest in oil, gas, or other mineral representing any percentage depletion allowance to be allocated to the principal of the trust.

If an amount is disallowed as a deduction for the taxable year by reason of application of the preceding sentence, the disallowed amount shall be treated as an amount allowable as a deduction under subsection (c) for the following taxable year, subject to the application of the preceeding sentence to such taxable year. For purposes of basic adjustments and determining whether cost depletion exceeds percentage depletion with respect to the production from a property, any amount disallowed as a deduction on the application of this paragraph shall be allocated to the respective properties from which the oil or gas was produced in proportion to the percentage depletion otherwise allowable to such properties under subsection (c).

* * * * * * * * * * * *

(5) *Percentage depletion not allowed for lease bonuses, etc.—In the case of any oil or gas property to which subsection (c) applies, for purposes of section 613, the term "gross income from the property" shall not include any lease bonus, advance royalty, or other amount payable without regard to production from property.*

* * * * * * * * * * * *

[For official explanation, see Committee Reports, ¶3897.]

〖¶3055〗 CODE SEC 616. DEVELOPMENT EXPENDITURES.

(a) **In General.**—Except as provided in[1]*subsections (b) and (d)*, there shall be allowed as a deduction in computing taxable income all expenditures paid or incurred during the taxable year for the development of a mine or other natural deposit (other than an oil or gas well) if paid or incurred after the existence of ores or minerals in commercially marketable quantities has been disclosed. This section shall not apply to expenditures for the acquisition or improvement of property of a character which is subject to the allowance for depreciation provided in section 167, but allowances for depreciation shall be considered, for purposes of this section, as expenditures.

* * * * * * * * * * * *

〖Footnote ¶3054-A〗 Section 104(b)(9), '86 TRA, struck out from Sec. 613A(d)(1):
(1) "(reduced in the case of an individual by the zero bracket amount)"
Effective date (Sec. 151(a), '86 (TRA).—Applies to taxable years beginning after 12-31-86.
Sec. 613A(d)(5) added by section 412(a)(1), '86 TRA.

Effective date (Sec. 412(a)(3), '86 TRA).—Applies to amounts received or accrued after 8-16-86, in taxable years ending after such date.
〖Footnote ¶3055〗 Matter in *italics* in Sec. 616(a), (d) and (e) added by section 411(b)(2)(A) & (C)(i) '86 TRA, which struck out:
(1) "subsection (b)"
Effective date (Sec. 411(c) '86 TRA).—(1) Applies to costs paid or incurred after 12-31-86, in taxable years ending after such date.
(2) Transition rule.—The amendments made by this section shall not apply with respect to intangible drilling and development costs incurred by United States companies pursuant to a minority interest in a license for Netherlands or United Kingdom North Sea development if such interest was acquired on or before 12-31-85.

(d)   *Special Rules for Foreign Development.—In the case of any expenditures paid or incurred with respect to the development of a mine or other natural deposit (other than an oil, gas or geothermal well) located outside of the United States—*

     (1)   subsections (a) and (b) shall not apply, and

     (2)   such expenditures shall—

         (A)   at the election of the taxpayer, be included in adjusted basis for purposes of computing the amount of any deduction allowable under section 611 (without regard to section 613), or

         (B)   if subparagraph (A) does not apply, be allowed as a deduction ratably over the 10-taxable year period beginning with the taxable year in which such expenditures were paid or incurred.

²*(e)*   **Cross Reference.—**

For election of 10-year amortization of expenditures allowable as a deduction under subsection (a), see section 58(i).

[For official explanation, see Committee Reports, ¶3896.]

〔¶3056〕 CODE SEC. 617. DEDUCTION AND RECAPTURE OF CERTAIN MINING EXPLORATION EXPENDITURES.

*   *   *   *   *   *   *   *   *   *   *   *

(d)   Gain From Disposition of Certain Mining Property.—

*   *   *   *   *   *   *   *   *   *   *   *

     (5)   Coordination with section 1254.—This subsection shall not apply to any disposition to which section 1254 applies.

*   *   *   *   *   *   *   *   *   *   *   *

¹*(h)*   *Special Rules for Foreign Exploration.—In the case of any expenditures paid or incurred before the development stage for the purpose of ascertaining the existence, location, extent, or quality of any deposit of ore or other mineral (other than an oil, gas, or geothermal well) located outside the United States—*

     (1)   subsection (a) shall not apply, and

     (2)   such expenditures shall—

         (A)   at the election of the taxpayer, be included in adjusted basis for purposes of computing the amount of any deduction allowable under section 611 (without regard to section 613), or

         (B)   if subparagraph (A) does not apply, be allowed as a deduction ratably over the 10-taxable year period beginning with the taxable year in which such expenditures were paid or incurred.

〔Footnote ¶3056〕   Sec. 617(d)(5) added by section 413(b), '86 TRA.

Effective date (Sec. 413(c), '86 TRA),—(1)   Generally applies to any disposition of property which is placed in service by the taxpayer after 12-31-86.

(2)   Exception for binding contracts.—The amendments made by this section shall not apply to any disposition of property placed in service after 12-31-86, if such property was acquired pursuant to a written contract which was entered into before 9-26-85, and which was binding at all times thereafter.

Matter in *italics* in Sec. 617(h) added by section 411(b)(2)(B), '86 TRA, which struck out:

(1)   "(h)   Limitation.—

(1)   **In general.**—Subsection (a) shall apply to any amount paid or incurred after December 31, 1969, with respect to any deposit of ore or other mineral located outside the United States, only to the extent that such amount, when added to the amounts which are or have been deducted under subsection (a) and subsection (a) of section 615 (as in effect before the enactment of the Tax Reform Act of 1976), or the corresponding provisions of prior law, does not exceed $400,000.

(2)   **Amounts taken into account.**—For purposes of paragraph (1), there shall be taken into account amounts deducted and amounts treated as deferred expenses by—

(A)   the taxpayer, and

(B)   any individual or corporation who has transferred to the taxpayer any mineral property.

(3)   **Application of paragraph (2)(B).**—Paragraph (2)(B) shall apply with respect to all amounts deducted before the latest such transfer from the individual or corporation to the taxpayer.

Paragraph (2)(B) shall apply only if—

(A)   the taxpayer acquired any mineral property from the individual or corporation under circumstances which make paragraph (7), (8), (11), (15), (17), (20), of (22) of section 113(a) of the Internal Revenue Code of 1939 apply to such transfer; or

(B)   the taxpayer acquired any mineral property from the individual or corporation under circumstances which make section 334(b), 338, 362 (a) and (b), 372(a), 374(b)(1), 1051, or 1082 apply to such transfer."

Effective date (Sec. 411(c) '86 TRA).—Generally applies to costs paid or incurred after 12-31-86, in taxable years ending after such date.

For transitional rule, see footnote ¶3055.

* * * * * * * * * * * *

[For official explanation, see Committee Reports, ¶3896; 3898.]

【¶3057】 CODE SEC. 631. GAIN OR LOSS IN THE CASE OF TIMBER, COAL, OR DOMESTIC IRON ORE.

* * * * * * * * * * * *

(c) **Disposal of Coal or Domestic Iron Ore With a Retained Economic Interest.**—In the case of the disposal of coal (including lignite), or iron ore mined in the United States held for more than 6 months before such disposal, by the owner thereof under any form of contract by virtue of which such owner retains an economic interest in such coal or iron ore, the difference between the amount realized from the disposal of such coal or iron ore and the adjusted depletion basis thereof plus the deductions disallowed for the taxable year under section 272 shall be considered as though it were a gain or loss, as the case may be, on the sale of such coal or iron ore. [1]*If for the taxable year of such gain or loss the maximum rate of tax imposed by this chapter on any net capital gain is less than such maximum rate for ordinary income, such owner* shall not be entitled to the allowance for percentage depletion provided in section 613 with respect to such coal or iron ore. The subsection shall not apply to income realized by any owner as a co-adventurer, partner, or principal in the mining of such coal or iron ore, and the word "owner" means any person who owns an economic interest in coal or iron ore in place, including a sublessor. The date of disposal of such coal or iron ore shall be deemed to be the date such coal or iron ore is mined. In determining the gross income, the adjusted gross income, or the taxable income of the lessee the deductions allowable with respect to rents and royalties shall be determined without regard to the provisions of this subsection. This subsection shall have no application, for purposes of applying subchapter G, relating to corporations used to avoid income tax on shareholder (including the determinations of the amount of the deductions under section 535(b)(6) or section 545(b)(5). This subsection shall not apply to any disposal of iron ore or coal—

(1) to a person whose relationship to the person disposing of such iron ore or coal would result in the disallowance of losses under section 267 or 707(b), or

(2) to a person owned or controlled directly or indirectly by the same interests which own or control the person disposing of such iron ore or coal.

[For official explanation, see Committee Reports, ¶3887.]

【¶3058】 CODE SEC. 642. SPECIAL RULES FOR CREDITS AND DEDUCTIONS.[1]

(a) *Foreign Tax Credit Allowed.—An estate or trust shall be allowed the credit against tax for taxes imposed by foreign countries and possessions of the United States, to the extent allowed by section 901, only in respect of so much of the taxes described in such section as is not properly allocable under such section to the beneficiaries.*

* * * * * * * * * * * *

(c) **Deduction for Amounts Paid or Permanently Set Aside for a Charitable Purpose.—**

* * * * * * * * * * * *

(4) [2]*Coordination with section 681.*—[3]In the case of a trust, the deduction allowed

---

【Footnote ¶3057】 Matter in *italics* in Sec. 631(c) added by section 311(b)(3), '86 TRA, which struck out:

(1) "Such owner"

Effective date (Sec. 311(c), '86 TRA).—Applies to taxable years beginning after 12-31-86. For transitional rules, see ¶2017.

【Footnote ¶3058】 Matter in *italics* in Sec. 642(a) added by section 112(b)(2), '86 TRA, which struck out:

(1) "(a) **Credits Against Tax.—**

(1) **Foreign taxes.**—An estate or trust shall be allowed the credit against tax for taxes imposed by foreign countries and possessions of the United States, to the extent allowed by section 901, only in respect of so much of the taxes described in such section as is not properly allocable under such section to the beneficiaries.

(2) **Political contributions.**—An estate or trust shall not be allowed the credit against tax for political contributions provided by section 24."

Effective date (Sec. 151(a), '86 TRA).—Applies to taxable years beginning after 12-31-86.

Matter in *italics* in Sec. 642(c)(4) added by section 301(b)(6)(A) and (B), '86 TRA, which struck out:

(2) "**Adjustments**"

(3) "To the extent that the amount otherwise allowable as a deduction under this subsection consists of gain from the sale or exchange of capital assets held for more than 6 months, proper adjustment shall be made for any deduction allowable to the estate or trust under section 1202 (relating to deduction for excess of capital gains over

Code §642(c)(4) ¶3058

by this subsection shall be subject to section 681 (relating to unrelated business income).[4]

*   *   *   *   *   *   *   *   *   *   *

[For official explanation, see Committee Reports, ¶3856; 3885; 3913.]

[¶3059] CODE SEC. 643. DEFINITIONS APPLICABLE TO SUBPARTS A, B, C, AND D.

(a) Distributable Net Income.—For purposes of this part, the term "distributable net income" means, with respect to any taxable year, the taxable income of the estate or trust computed with the following modifications—

*   *   *   *   *   *   *   *   *   *   *

(3) **Capital gains and losses.**—Gains from the sale or exchange of capital assets shall be excluded to the extent that such gains are allocated to corpus and are not (A) paid, credited, or required to be distributed to any beneficiary during the taxable year, or (B) paid, permanently set aside, or to be used for the purposes specified in section 642(c). Losses from the sale or exchange of capital assets shall be excluded, except to the extent such losses are taken into account in determining the amount of gains from the sale or exchange of capital assets which are paid, credited, or required to be distributed to any beneficiary during the taxable year.[1]

*   *   *   *   *   *   *   *   *   *   *

(7) **[Repealed]**[2]

*   *   *   *   *   *   *   *   *   *   *

(d) Coordination With Back-up Withholding.—Except to the extent otherwise provided in regulations, this subchapter shall be applied with respect to payments subject to withholding under section 3406—

(1) by allocating between the estate or trust and its beneficiaries any credit allowable under section 31(c) (on the basis of their respective shares of any such payment taken into account under this subchapter),

(2) by treating each beneficiary to whom such credit is allocated as if an amount equal to such credit has been paid to him by the estate or trust, and

(3) by allowing the estate or trust a deduction in an amount equal to the credit so allocated to beneficiaries.

[3]*(e)* Treatment of Property Distributed in Kind.—

[Footnote ¶3058 continued]

capital losses)."

Effective date (Sec. 301(c), '86 TRA).—Applies to taxable years beginning after 12-31-86.

Section 612(b)(3), '86 TRA, struck out from Sec. 642(j):

(4) "(j) Cross Reference.—

For special rule for determining the time of receipt of dividends by a beneficiary under section 652 and 662, see section 116(c)(3)."

Effective date (Sec. 633(a), '86 TRA.—Generally applies to

(1) any distribution in complete liquidation, and any sale or exchange, made by a corporation after 7-31-86, unless such corporation is completely liquidated before 1-1-87,

(2) any transaction described in section 338 of the '86 Code for which the acquisition date occurs after 12-31-86, and

(3) any distribution (not in complete liquidation) made after 12-31-86. For special rules, see ¶2023.

[Footnote ¶3059] Section 301(b)(7), '86 TRA, struck out from Sec. 643(a)(3):

(1) "The deduction under section 1202 (relating to deduction for excess of capital gains over capital losses) shall not be taken into account."

Effective date (Sec. 301(c), '86 TRA).—Applies to taxable years beginning after 12-31-86.

Section 612(b)(4), '86 TRA, repealed Sec. 643(a)(7):

(2) "(7) Dividends or interest.—There shall be included the amount of any dividends or interest excluded from gross income pursuant to section 116 (relating to partial exclusion of dividends or section 128 (relating to certain interest).

If the estate or trust is allowed a deduction under section 642(c), the amount of the modifications specified in paragraphs (5) and (6) shall be reduced to the extent that the amount of income which is paid, permanently set aside, or to be used for the purposes specified in section 642(c) is deemed to consist of items specified in those paragraphs. For this purpose, such amount shall (in the absence of specific provisions in the governing instrument) be deemed to consist of the same proportion of each class of items of income of the estate or trust as the total of each class bears to the total of all classes."

Effective date (Sec. 612(c), '86 TRA).—Applies to taxable years beginning after 12-31-86.

Matter in *italics* in Sec. 643(e) added by section 1806(a) and (c)(1), '86 TRA, which struck out:

(3) "(d)"

* * * * * * * * * * * *

(3) Election to recognize gain.—

   (A) In general.—In the case of any distribution of property (other than cash) to which an election under this paragraph applies—

     (i) paragraph (2) shall not apply.

     (ii) gain or loss shall be recognized by the estate or trust in the same manner as if such property had been sold to the distributee at its fair market value, and

     (iii) the amount taken into account under sections 661(a)(2) and 662(a)(2) shall be the fair market value of such property.

   (B) Election.—Any election under this paragraph shall [4]*apply to all distributions made by the estate or trust during a taxable year and shall be made on the return of such estate or trust for such taxable year.*

Any such election, once made, may be revoked only with the consent of the Secretary.

* * * * * * * * * * * *

[5]*(f)* **Treatment of Multiple Trusts.—**For purposes of this subchapter, under regulations prescribed by the Secretary, 2 or more trusts shall be treated as 1 trust if—

   (1) such trusts have substantially the same grantor or grantors and substantially the same primary beneficiary or beneficiaries, and

   (2) a principal purpose of such trusts is the avoidance of the tax imposed by this chapter.

For purposes of the preceding sentence, a husband and wife shall be treated as 1 person.

(g) *Certain Payments of Estimated Tax Treated as Paid by Beneficiary.—*

   (1) In general.—In the case of a trust—

     (A) the trustee may elect to treat any portion of a payment of estimated tax made by such trust for any taxable year of the trust as a payment made by a beneficiary of such trust,

     (B) any amount so treated shall be treated as paid or credited to the beneficiary on the last day of such taxable year, and

     (C) for purposes of subtitle F, the amount so treated—

       (i) shall not be treated as a payment of estimated tax made by the trust, but

       (ii) shall be treated as a payment of estimated tax made by such beneficiary on January 15 following the taxable year.

The preceding sentence shall apply only to the extent the payments of estimated tax made by the trust for the taxable year exceed the tax imposed by this chapter shown on its return for the taxable year.

   (2) Time for making election.—An election under paragraph (1) may be made—

     (A) only on the trust's return of the tax imposed by this chapter for the taxable year, and

     (B) only if such return is filed on or before the 65th day after the close of the taxable year.

[For official explanation, see Committee Reports, ¶3885; ¶3913; ¶4063; ¶4140.]

⟦Footnote ¶3059 continued⟧

   (4) "be made by the estate or trust on its return for the taxable year for which the distribution was made."

Effective date (Sec. 1881, '86 TRA, and section 81(b), '84 TRA).—(1) Generally applies to distributions after 6-1-84, in taxable years ending after such date.

   (2) Time for making election.—In the case of any distribution before 7-18-84—

   (A) the time for making an election under section 643(d)(3) of the '54 Code (as added by this section) shall not expire before 1-1-85, and

   (B) the requirement that such election be made on the return of the estate or trust shall not apply.

   Matter in *italics* in Sec. 643(f) added by section 1806(c)(2), '86 TRA, which struck out:

   (5) "(e)"

Effective date (Sec. 1881, '86 TRA, and section 82(b), '84 TRA).—Applies to taxable years beginning after 3-1-84.

   Sec. 643(g) in *italics* added by section 1404(b), '86 TRA.

Effective date (Sec. 1404(d), '86 TRA).—Applies to taxable years beginning after 12-31-86.

〔¶3060〕 CODE SEC. 644. SPECIAL RULE FOR GAIN ON PROPERTY TRANSFERRED TO TRUST AT LESS THAN FAIR MARKET VALUE.

(a) **Imposition of Tax.—**

* * * * * * * * * * * *

(2) **Amount of tax.—**The amount of the tax imposed by paragraph (1) on any includible gain recognized on the sale or exchange of any property shall be equal to the sum of—

(A) the excess of—

(i) the tax which would have been imposed under this chapter for the taxable year of the transferor in which the sale or exchange of such property occurs had the amount of the includible gain realized on such sale or exchange, reduced by any deductions properly allocable to such gain, been included in the gross income of the transferor for such taxable year, over

(ii) the tax actually imposed under this chapter for such taxable year on the transferor, plus

(B) if such sale or exchange occurs in a taxable year of the transferor which begins after the beginning of the taxable year of the trust in which such sale or exchange occurs, an amount equal to the amount determined under subparagraph (A) multiplied by [1]*The underpayment rate* established under section 6621. The determination of tax under clause (i) of subparagraph (A) shall be made by not taking into account any carryback, and by not taking into account any loss or deduction to the extent that such loss or deduction may be carried by the transferor to any other taxable year.

* * * * * * * * * * *

[For official explanation, see Committee Reports, ¶4075.]

〔¶3061〕 SEC. 645. TAXABLE YEAR OF TRUSTS.

(a) **In General.—**For purposes of this subtitle, the taxable year of any trust shall be the calendar year.

(b) **Exception for Trusts Exempt From Tax and Charitable Trusts.—**Subsection (a) shall not apply to a trust exempt from taxation under section 501(a) or to a trust described in section 4947(a)(1).

[For official explanation, see Committee Reports, ¶4062.]

〔¶3062〕 CODE SEC. 665. DEFINITIONS APPLICABLE TO SUBPART D.

* * * * * * * * * * * *

(d) **Taxes Imposed on the Trust.—**For purposes of this subpart—

(1) **In general.—**The term "taxes imposed on the trust" means the amount of the taxes which are imposed for any taxable year of the trust under this chapter (without regard to this subpart or [1] part IV of subchapter A) and which, under regulations prescribed by the Secretary, are properly allocable to the undistributed portions of distributable net income and gains in excess of losses from sales or exchanges of capital assets. The amount determined in the preceding sentence shall be reduced by any amount of such taxes deemed distributed under section 666(b) and (c) or 669(d) and (e) to any beneficiary.

〔Footnote ¶3060〕 Matter in *italics* in Sec. 644(a)(2)(B) added by section 1511(c)(5), '86 TRA, which struck out:

(1) "the annual rate"

Effective date (Sec. 1511(d), '86 TRA).—Applies for purposes of determining interest for periods after 12-31-86.

〔Footnote ¶3061〕 Sec. 645 added by section 1403(a), '86 TRA.

Effective date (Sec. 1403(c), '86 TRA).—(1) Generally applies to taxable years beginning after 12-31-86.

(2) Transition rule.—With respect to any trust beneficiary who is required to include in gross income amounts under sections 652(a) or 662(a) of the '86 Code in the 1st taxable year of the beneficiary beginning after 12-31-86, by reason of any short taxable year of the trust required by the amendments made by this section, such income shall be ratably included in the income of the trust beneficiary over the 4-taxable year period beginning with such taxable year.

〔Footnote ¶3062〕 Matter in *italics* in Sec. 665(d)(1) added by section 1847(b)(16), '86 TRA, which struck out:

(1) "subpart A of"

Effective date (Sec. 1881, '86 TRA and Sec. 475, '84 TRA).—(a) Generally applies to taxable years beginning after 12-31-83, and to carrybacks from such years.

(b) Tax-Free Covenant Bonds.—The amendments made by subsections (j) and (r)(29) of section 474 shall not apply with respect to obligations issued before 1-1-84.

(c) Clarification of Effect of Amendments of Investment Tax Credit.—Nothing in the amendments made by section 474(o) shall be construed as reducing the amount of any credit allowable for qualified investment in taxable years beginning before 1-1-84.

[For official explanation, see Committee Reports, ¶4161.]

⟦¶3063⟧　CODE SEC. 667.　TREATMENT OF AMOUNTS DEEMED DISTRIBUTED BY TRUST IN PRECEDING YEARS.

* * * * * * * * * * * * *

(b)　Tax on Distribution.—

(1)　In general.—The partial tax imposed by subsection (a)(2) shall be determined—

(A)　by determining the number of preceding taxable years of the trust on the last day of which an amount is deemed under section 666(a) to have been distributed,

(B)　by taking from the 5 taxable years immediately preceding the year of the accumulation distribution the 1 taxable year for which the beneficiary's taxable income was the highest and the 1 taxable year for which his taxable income was the lowest,

(C)　by adding to the beneficiary's taxable income for each of the 3 taxable years remaining after the application of subparagraph (B) an amount determined by dividing the amount deemed distributed under section 666 and required to be included in income under subsection (a) by the number of preceding taxable years determined under subparagraph (A), and

(D)　by determining the average increase in tax for the 3 taxable years referred to in subparagraph (C) resulting from the application of such subparagraph.

The partial tax imposed by subsection (a)(2) shall be the excess (if any) of the average increase in tax determined under subparagraph (D), multiplied by the number of preceding taxable years determined under subparagraph (A), over the amount of taxes (other than the amount of taxes described in section 665(d)(2) deemed distributed to the beneficiary under sections 666(b) and (c).

(2)　Treatment of loss years.—[1]*For purposes of paragraph (1), the taxable income of the beneficiary for any taxable year shall be deemed to be not less than zero.*

* * * * * * * * * * * * *

⟦¶3064⟧　CODE SEC. 672.　DEFINITIONS AND RULES.

* * * * * * * * * * * * *

(e)　Grantor Treated as Holding Any Power or Interest of Grantor's Spouse.—For purposes of this subpart, if a grantor's spouse is living with the grantor at the time of the creation of any power or interest held by such spouse, the grantor shall be treated as holding such power or interest.

[For official explanation, see Committee Reports, ¶3930.]

⟦¶3065⟧　CODE SEC. 673.　REVERSIONARY INTERESTS.

[1]*(a)　General Rule.—The grantor shall be treated as the owner of any portion of a trust*

⟦**Footnote ¶3063**⟧　Matter in *italics* in Sec. 667(b)(2) added by section 104(b)(10), '86 TRA, which struck out:

(1)　"For purposes of paragraph (1), the taxable income of the beneficiary for any taxable year shall be deemed to be not less than—

(A)　in the case of a beneficiary who is an individual, the zero bracke amount for such year, or

(B)　in the case of a beneficiary who is a corporation, zero."

Effective date (Sec. 151(a), '86 TRA).—Applies to taxable years beginning after 12-31-86.

⟦**Footnote ¶3064**⟧　Sec. 672(e) in *italics* added by section 1401(a), '86 TRA.

Effective date (Sec. 1401(b), '86 TRA).—Applies with respect to transfers in trust made after 3-1-86.

⟦**Footnote ¶3065**⟧　Matter in *italics* in Sec. 673 added by section 1402(a), '86 TRA, which struck out:

(1)　"(a)　General Rule.—The grantor shall be treated as the owner of any portion of a trust in which he has a revisionary interest in either the corpus or the income therefrom if, as of the inception of that portion of the trust, the interest will or may reasonably be expected to take effect in possession or enjoyment within 10 years commencing with the date of the transfer of that portion of the trust.

(b)　[Repealed]

(c)　**Reversionary Interest Taking Effect at Death of Income Beneficiary.**—The grantor shall not be treated under subsection (a) as the owner of any portion of a trust where his reversionary interest in such portion is not to take effect in possession or enjoyment until the death of the person or persons to whom the income therefrom is payable.

(d)　**Postponement of Date Specified for Reacquisition.**—Any postponement of the date specified for the reacquisition of possession or enjoyment of the reversionary interest shall be treated as a new transfer in trust commencing with the date on which the postponement is effected and terminating with the date prescribed by the post-

in which he has a reversionary interest in either the corpus or the income therefrom, if, as of the inception of that portion of the trust, the value of such interest exceeds 5 percent of the value of such portion.

(b) Reversionary Interest Taking Effect at Death of Minor Lineal Descendant Beneficiary.—In the case of any beneficiary who—

     (1) is a lineal descendant of the grantor, and

     (2) holds all of the present interests in any portion of a trust, the grantor shall not be treated under subsection (a) as the owner of such portion solely by reason of a reversionary interest in such portion which takes effect upon the death of such beneficiary before such beneficiary attains age 21.

[For official explanation, see Committee Reports, ¶4061.]

[¶3066]   **CODE SEC. 674. POWER TO CONTROL BENEFICIAL ENJOYMENT.**

*   *   *   *   *   *   *   *   *   *   *   *

    (b) Exceptions for Certain Powers.—Subsection (a) shall not apply to the following powers regardless of by whom held.

*   *   *   *   *   *   *   *   *   *   *   *

    (2) Power affecting beneficial enjoyment only after [1]*occurrence of event.*—A power, the exercise of which can only affect the beneficial enjoyment of the income for a period commencing after the [2]*occurrence of an event* such that a grantor would not be treated as the owner under section 673 if the power were a reversionary interest; but the grantor may be treated as the owner after the [3]*occurrence of the event* unless the power is relinquished.

*   *   *   *   *   *   *   *   *   *   *   *

[For official explanation, see Committee Reports, ¶4061.]

[¶3067]   **CODE SEC. 676. POWER TO REVOKE.**

*   *   *   *   *   *   *   *   *   *   *   *

    (b) Power Affecting Beneficial Enjoyment Only After [1]*Occurrence of Event.* —Subsection (a) shall not apply to a power the exercise of which can only affect the beneficial enjoyment of the income for a period commencing after the [2]*occurrence of an event* such that a grantor would not be treated as the owner under section 673 if the power were a reversionary interest. But the grantor may be treated as the owner after the [3]*occurrence of*

[Footnote ¶3065 continued]

ponement. However, income for any period shall not be included in the income of the grantor by reason of the preceding sentence if such income would not be so includible in the absence of such postponement."

    Effective date (Sec. 1402(c), '86 TRA).—(1) Generally applies with respect to transfers in trust made after 3-1-86.

    (2) Transfers pursuant to property settlement agreement.—The amendments made by this section shall not apply to any transfer in trust made after 3-1-86, pursuant to a binding property settlement agreement entered into on or before 3-1-86, which required the taxpayer to establish a grantor trust and for the transfer of a specified sum of money or property to the trust by the taxpayer. This paragraph shall apply only to the extent of the amount required to be transferred under the agreement described in the preceding sentence.

    [Footnote ¶3066]   Matter in *italics* in Sec. 674(b)(2) added by section 1402(b)(1), '86 TRA, which struck out:

    (1) "expiration of 10-year period"

    (2) "expiration of a period"

    (3) "expiration of the period"

    Effective date (Sec. 1402(c), '86 TRA).—(1) Generally applies with respect to transfers in trust made after 3-1-86.

    (2) Transfers pursuant to property settlement agreement.—The amendments made by this section shall not apply to any transfer in trust made after 3-1-86, pursuant to a binding property settlement agreement entered into on or before 3-1-86, which required the taxpayer to establish a grantor trust and for the transfer of a specified sum of money or property to the trust by the taxpayer. This paragraph shall apply only to the extent of the amount required to be transferred under the agreement described in the preceding sentence.

    [Footnote ¶3067]   Matter in *italics* in Sec. 676(b) added by section 1402(b)(2), '86 TRA, which struck out:

    (1) "Expiration of 10-Year Period"

    (2) "expiration of a period"

    (3) "expiration of such period"

    Effective date (Sec. 1402(c), '86 TRA).—(1) Generally applies with respect to transfers in trust made after 3-1-86.

    (2) Transfers pursuant to property settlement agreement.—The amendments made by this section shall not apply to any transfer in trust made after 3-1-86, pursuant to a binding property settlement agreement entered into on or before 3-1-86, which required the taxpayer to establish a grantor trust and for the transfer of a specified sum of money or property to the trust by the taxpayer. This paragraph shall apply only to the extent of the amount required to be transferred under the agreement described in the preceding sentence.

such event unless the power is relinquished.

[For official explanation, see Committee Reports, ¶4061.]

〔¶3068〕 CODE SEC. 677. INCOME FOR BENEFIT OF GRANTOR.

(a) General Rule.—The grantor shall be treated as the owner of any portion of a trust, whether or not he is treated as such owner under section 674, whose income without the approval or consent of any adverse party is, or, in the discretion of the grantor or a nonadverse party, or both, may be—

(1) distributed to the grantor or the grantor's spouse;

(2) held or accumulated for future distribution to the grantor or the grantor's spouse; or

(3) applied to the payment of premiums on policies of insurance on the life of the grantor or the grantor's spouse (except policies of insurance irrevocably payable for a purpose specified in section 170(c) (relating to definition of charitable contributions)).

This subsection shall not apply to a power the exercise of which can only affect the beneficial enjoyment of the income for a period commencing after the [1]*occurrence of an event* such that the grantor would not be treated as the owner under section 673 if the power were a reversionary interest; but the grantor may be treated as the owner after the [2]*occurrence of the event* unless the power is relinquished.

* * * * * * * * * * * *

[For official explanation, see Committee Reports, ¶4061.]

〔¶3069〕 CODE SEC. 691. RECIPIENTS OF INCOME IN RESPECT OF DECENDENTS.

* * * * * * * * * * * *

(c) Deduction for Estate Tax.—

[1]*(3) Special rule for generation-skipping transfers.—In the case of any tax imposed by chapter 13 on a taxable termination or a direct skip occurring as a result of the death of the transferor, there shall be allowed a deduction (under principles similar to the principles of this subsection) for the portion of such tax attributable to items of gross income of the trust which were not properly includible in the gross income of the trust for periods before the date of such termination.*

(4) Coordination with capital gain [2]*provisions.*—For purposes of sections [3]*1(j), 1201,* and 1211, the amount of any gain taken into account with respect to any item described

---

〔Footnote ¶3068〕 Matter in *italics* in Sec. 677(a) added by section 1402(b)(3), '86 TRA, which struck out:
(1) "expiration of a period"
(2) "expiration of the period"
Effective date (Sec. 1402(c), '86 TRA).—(1) Generally applies with respect to transfers in trust made after 3-1-86.
(2) Transfers pursuant to property settlement agreement.—The amendments made by this section shall not apply to any transfer in trust made after 3-1-86, pursuant to a binding property settlement agreement entered into on or before 3-1-86, which required the taxpayer to establish a grantor trust and for the transfer of a specified sum of money or property to the trust by the taxpayer. This paragraph shall apply only to the extent of the amount required to be transferred under the agreement described in the preceding sentence.
〔Footnote ¶3069〕 Matter in *italics* in Sec. 691(c)(3) added by section 1432(a)(3), '86 TRA, which struck out:
(1) "**(3) Special rule for generation-skipping transfers.**—For purposes of this section—
(A) the tax imposed by section 2601 or any State inheritance tax described in section 2602(c)(5)(B) on any generation-skipping transfer shall be treated as a tax imposed by section 2001 on the estate of the deemed transferor (as defined in section 2612(a));
(B) any property transferred in such a transfer shall be treated as if it were included in the gross estate of the deemed transferor at the value of such property taken into account for purposes of tax imposed by section 2601; and
(C) under regulations prescribed by the Secretary, any item of gross income subject to the tax imposed under section 2601 shall be treated as income described in subsection (a) if such item is not properly includible in the gross income of the trust on or before the date of the generation-skipping transfer (within the meaning of section 2611(a)) and if such transfer occurs at or after the death of the deemed transferor (as so defined)."
Effective date (Sec. 1433(a), '86 TRA).—Generally applies to any generation-skipping transfer (within the meaning of section 2611 of the '86 Code) made after the date of the enactment of this Act. For transitional and special rules, see ¶2081.

Matter in *italics* in Sec. 691(c)(4) added by section 301(b)(8), '86 TRA, which struck out:
(2) "**deduction, etc.**"
(3) "1201, 1202, and 1211, and for purposes of 57(a)(9)"
Effective date (Sec. 301(c), '86 TRA).—Applies to taxable years beginning after 12-31-86.

in subsection (a)(1) shall be reduced (but not below zero) by the amount of the deduction allowable under paragraph (1) of this subsection with respect to such item.

* * * * * * * * * * * *

[For official explanation, see Committee Reports, ¶3885; ¶4068.]

⟦¶3070⟧ CODE SEC. 692. INCOME TAXES OF MEMBERS OF ARMED FORCES ON DEATH.

(a) General Rule.—In the case of any individual who dies while in active service as a member of the Armed Forces of the United States, if such death occurred while serving in a combat zone (as determined under section 112) or as a result of wounds, disease, or injury incurred while so serving—

(1) any tax imposed by this subtitle shall not apply with respect to the taxable year in which falls the date of his death, or with respect to any prior taxable year ending on or after the first day he so served in a combat zone after June 24, 1950; and

(2) any tax under this subtitle and under the corresponding provisions of prior revenue laws for taxable years preceding those specified in paragraph (1) which is unpaid at the date of his death (including interest, additions to the tax, and additional amounts) shall not be assessed, and if assessed the assessment shall be abated, and if collected shall be credited or refunded as an overpayment.

(b) Individuals in Missing Status.—For purposes of this section, in the case of an individual who was in a missing status within the meaning of section 6013(f)(3)(A), the date of his death shall be treated as being not earlier than the date on which a determination of his death is made under section 556 of title 37 of the United States Code. [1]*Except in the case of the combat zone designated for purposes of the Vietnam conflict, the preceding sentence shall not cause subsection (a)(1) to apply for any taxable year beginning more than 2 years after the date designated under section 112 as the date of termination of combatant activities in a combat zone.*

* * * * * * * * * * * *

[For official explanation, see Committee Reports, ¶4130.]

⟦¶3071⟧ CODE SEC. 702. INCOME AND CREDITS OF PARTNER.

(a) General Rule.—In determining his income tax, each partner shall take into account separately his distributive share of the partnership's—

(1) gains and losses from sales or exchanges of capital assets held for not more than 6 months,

(2) gains and losses from sales or exchanges of capital assets held for more than 6 months,

(3) gains and losses from sales or exchanges of property described in section 1231 (relating to certain property used in a trade or business and involuntary conversions),

(4) charitable contributions (as defined in section 170(c)),

[1]*(5) dividends with respect to which there is a deduction under part VIII of subchapter B,*

(6) taxes, described in section 901, paid or accrued to foreign countries and to possessions of the United States,

(7) other items of income, gain, loss, deduction, or credit, to the extent provided by regulations prescribed by the Secretary, and

(8) taxable income or loss, exclusive of items requiring separate computation under other paragraphs of this subsection.

* * * * * * * * * * * *

[For official explanation, see Committee Reports, ¶3913.]

⟦¶3072⟧ CODE SEC. 703. PARTNERSHIP COMPUTATIONS.

⟦Footnote ¶3070⟧ Matter in *italics* in Sec. 692(b) by section 1708(a)(2), '86 TRA, which struck out:

(1) "The preceding sentence shall not cause subsection (a)(1) to apply for any taxable year beginning—

(1) December 31, 1982, in the case of service in the combat zone designated for purposes of the Vietnam conflict, or

(2) more than 2 years after the date designated under section 112 as the date of termination of combatant activities in that zone, in the case of any combat zone other than that referred to in paragraph (1)."

Effective date (Sec. 1708(b), '86 TRA).—Applies to taxable years beginning after 12-31-82.

⟦Footnote ¶3071⟧ Matter in *italics* in Sec. 702(a)(5) added by section 612(b)(5), '86 TRA, which struck out:

(1) "(5) dividends or interest with respect to which there is an exclusion under section 116 or 128 or a deduction under part VIII of subchapter B,"

Effective date (Sec. 612(c), '86 TRA).—Applies to taxable years beginning after 12-31-86.

* * * * * * * * * * *

(b)   Elections of the partnership.—Any election affecting the computation of taxable income derived from a partnership shall be made by the partnership, except that any election under—[1]

[2]*(1)   subsection (b)(5) or (d)(4) of section 108 (relating to income from discharge of indebtedness),*[3]

[4]*(2)   section 617 (relating to deduction and recapture of certain mining exploration expenditures, or*

[5]*(3)   section 901 (relating to taxes of foreign countries and possessions of the United States),*

shall be made by each partner separately.

[For official explanation, see Committee Reports, ¶3931; 3905.]

〔¶3073〕   CODE SEC. 706.   TAXABLE YEARS OF PARTNER AND PARTNER-SHIP.

* * * * * * * * * * *

(b)   **[1]Taxable Year.—**

[2]*(1)   Partnership's taxable year.—*

(A)   Partnership treated as taxpayer.—The taxable year of a partnership shall be determined as though the partnership were a taxpayer.

(B)   Taxable year determined by reference to partners.—Except as provided in subparagraph (C), a partnership shall not have a taxable year other than—

(i)   the taxable year of 1 or more of its partners who have an aggregate interest in partnership profits and capital of greater than 50 percent,

(ii)   if there is no taxable year described in clause (i), the taxable year of all the principal partners of the partnership, or

(iii)   if there is no taxable year described in clause (i) or (ii), the calendar year of such other period as the Secretary may prescribe in regulations.

(C)   Business purpose.—A partnership may have a taxable year not described in subparagraph (B) if it establishes, to the satisfaction of the Secretary, a business purpose therefor. For purposes of this subparagraph, any deferral of income to partners shall not be treated as a business purpose.

〔Footnote ¶3072〕   Matter in *italics* in Sec. 703(b)(1) added by section 701(e)(4)(E), '86 TRA, which struck out:

(1)   "(1) section 57(c) (defining net lease),"

(2)   "(2)"

Effective date (Sec. 701(f)(1), '86 TRA).—Generally applies to taxable years beginning after 12-31-86. For transitional and special rules, see footnote ¶2879.

Section 511(d)(2)(B), '86 TRA, struck out Sec. 703(b)(3):

(3)   "(3) section 163(d) (relating to limitation of interest on investment indebtedness),"

Effective date (Sec. 511(e), '86 TRA).—Applies to taxable years beginning after 12-31-86.

Matter in *italics* in Sec. 703(b)(2) (former (3)) and (3) (former (4)) (as amended by Sec. 511(d)(2)(B), '86 TRA), added by section 701(e)(4)(E), '86 TRA, which struck out:

(4)   "(4)"

(5)   "(5)"

Effective date (Sec. 701(f)(1), '86 TRA).—See above.

〔Footnote ¶3073〕   Matter in *italics* in Sec. 706(b)(1), (4) added by section 806(a), '86 TRA, which struck out:

(1)   "Adoption of"

(2)   "(1) Partnership's taxable year.—The taxable year of a partnership shall be determined as though the partnership were a taxpayer. A partnership may not change to, or adopt, a taxable year other than that of all its principal partners unless it establishes, to the satisfaction of the Secretary, a business purpose therefor."

Effective date (Sec. 806(e), '86 TRA).—(1) Generally applies to taxable years beginning after 12-31-86.

(2) Change in accounting period.—In the case of any taxpayer required by the amendments made by this section to change its accounting period for any taxable year—

(A)   such change shall be treated as initiated by the taxpayer,

(B)   such change shall be treated as having been made with the consent of the Secretary, and

(C)   with respect to any partner or shareholder of an S corporation which is required to include the items from more than 1 taxable year of the partnership or S corporation in any 1 taxable year, income in excess of expenses of such partnership or corporation for the short taxable year required by such amendments shall be taken into account ratably in each of the first 4 taxable years (including such short taxable year) beginning after 12-31-86, unless such partner or shareholder elects to include all such income in the short taxable year.

Subparagraph (C) shall apply to a shareholder of an S corporation only if such corporation was an S corporation for a taxable year beginning in 1986.

---

* * * * * * * * * * *

(4) Application of majority interest rule.—Clause (i) of paragraph (1)(B) shall not apply to any taxable year of a partnership unless the period which constitutes the taxable year of 1 or more of its partners who have an aggregate interest in partnership profits and capital of greater than 50 percent has been the same for—

    (A) the 3-taxable year period of such partner or partners ending on or before the beginning of such taxable year of the partnership, or

    (B) if the partnership has not been in existence during all of such 3-taxable year period, the taxable years of such partner or partners ending with or within the period of existence.

This paragraph shall apply without regard to whether the same partners or interests are taken into account in determining the 50 percent interest during any period.

* * * * * * * * * * *

(d) Determination of Distributive Share When Partner's Interest Changes.—

* * * * * * * * * * *

(2) Certain cash basis items prorated over period to which attributable.—

    (A) In general.—If during any taxable year of the partnership there is a change in any partner's interest in the partnership, then (except to the extent provided in regulations) each partner's distributive share of any allocable cash basis item shall be determined—

        (i) by assigning the appropriate portion of [3]such item to each day in the period to which it is attributable, and

        (ii) by allocating the portion assigned to any such day among the partners in proportion to their interests in the partnership at the close of such day.

    (B) Allocable cash basis item.—For purposes of this paragraph, the term "allocable cash basis item" means any of the following items [4]with respect to which the partnership uses the cash receipts and disbursements method of accounting:

        (i) Interest.

        (ii) Taxes.

        (iii) Payments for services or for the use of property.

        (iv) Any other item of a kind specified in regulations prescribed by the Secretary as being an item with respect to which the application of this paragraph is appropriate to avoid significant misstatements of the income of the partners.

    (C) Items attributable to periods not within taxable year.—If any portion of any allocable cash basis item is attributable to—

        (i) any period before the beginning of the taxable year, such portion shall be assigned under subparagraph (A)(i) to the first day of [5]the taxable year, or

        (ii) any period after the close of the taxable year, such portion shall be assigned under subparagraph (A)(i) to the last day of the taxable year.

* * * * * * * * * * *

[For official explanation, see Committee Reports, ¶3940; 4139.]

[¶3074]   CODE SEC. 707.   TRANSACTIONS BETWEEN PARTNER AND PARTNERSHIP.

(a) Partner Not Acting in Capacity as Partner.—

* * * * * * * * * * *

(2) Treatment of payments to partners for property or services.—Under regulations prescribed by the Secretary—

* * * * * * * * * * *

    (B) Treatment of certain property transfers.—If—

        (i) there is a direct or indirect transfer of money or other property by a partner to a partnership,

        (ii) there is a related direct or indirect transfer of money or other property by the partnership to such partner (or another partner), and

---

[Footnote ¶3073 continued]

Matter in *italics* in Sec. 706(d)(2)(A)(i), (B) and (C)(1) added by section 1805(a), '86 TRA, which struck out:

(3)   "each"

(4)   "which are described in paragraph (1) and"

(5)   "such"

Effective date   (Sec. 1881, '86 TRA and Sec. 72(c)(1), '84 TRA).—Applies to amounts attributable to periods after 3-31-84.

(iii) the transfer described in clauses (i) and (ii), when viewed together, are properly characterized as a ¹*sale or exchange of property,*

such transfers shall be treated either as a transaction described in paragraph (1) or as a transaction between 2 or more partners acting other than in their capacity as members of the partnership.

(b) Certain Sales or Exchanges of Property With Respect to Controlled Partnerships.—

(1) Losses disallowed.—No deduction shall be allowed in respect of losses from sales or exchanges of property (other than an interest in the partnership), directly or indirectly, between—

(A) a partnership and ²*a person* owning, directly or indirectly, more than 50 percent of the capital interest, or the profits interest, in such partnership, or

(B) two partnerships in which the same persons own, directly or indirectly, more than 50 percent of the capital interests or profits interests.

In the case of a subsequent sale or exchange by a transferee described in this paragraph, section 267(d) shall be applicable as if the loss were disallowed under section 267(a)(1). *For purposes of section 267(a)(2), partnerships described in subparagraph (B) of this paragraph shall be treated as persons specified in section 267(b).*

(2) Gains treated as ordinary income.—In the case of a sale or exchange, directly or indirectly, of property, which in the hands of the transferee, is property other than a capital asset as defined in section 1221—

(A) between a partnership and ²*a person* owning, directly or indirectly, more than ³*50 percent* of the capital interest, or profits interest, in such partnership, or

(B) between two partnerships in which the same persons own, directly or indirectly, more than ³*50 percent* of the capital interests or profits interests,

any gain recognized shall be considered as ordinary income.

* * * * * * * * * * * *

[For official explanation, see Committee Reports, ¶3922; 4139; 4146.]

〔¶3075〕 CODE SEC. 751. UNREALIZED RECEIVABLES AND INVENTORY ITEMS.

* * * * * * * * * * * *

(c) Unrealized Receivables.—For purposes of this subchapter, the term "unrealized receivables" includes, to the extent not previously includible in income under the method

---

〔Footnote ¶3074〕 Matter in *italics* in Sec. 707(a)(2)(B)(iii) added by section 1805(b), '86 TRA, which struck out:

(1) "sale of property"

Effective date (Sec. 1881, '86 TRA and Sec. 73(b), '84 TRA).—(1) Generally applies

(A) in the case of arrangements described in section 707(a)(2)(A) of the '54 Code (as amended by section 73(a), '84 TRA to Sec. 707(a)), to services performed or property transferred after 2-29-84, and

(B) in the case of transfers described in section 707(a)(2)(B) of such Code (as so amended), to property transferred after 3-31-84.

(2) Binding contract exception.—The amendment made by section 73(a), '84 TRA to Sec. 707(a) shall not apply to a transfer of property described in section 707(a)(2)(B)(i) if such transfer is pursuant to a binding contract in effect on 3-31-84, and at all times thereafter before the transfer.

(3) Exception for certain transfers.—The amendment made by section 73(a), '84 TRA to Sec. 707(a) shall not apply to a transfer of property described in section 707(a)(2)(B)(i) that is made before 12-31-84, if—

(A) such transfer was proposed in a written private offering memorandum circulated before 2-28-84;

(B) the out-of-pocket costs incurred with respect to such offering exceeded $250,000 as of 2-28-84;

(C) the encumbrances placed on such property in anticipation of such transfer all constitute obligations for which neither the partnership nor any partner is liable, and

(D) the transferor of such property is the sole general partner of the partnership.

Matter in *italics* in Sec. 707(b)(1)(A) and (2)(A) added by section 1812(c)(3)(A) and (B), '86 TRA, which struck out:

(2) "a partner"

Effective date (Sec. 1812(c)(3)(A), '86 TRA).—Effective with respect to sales or exchanges after 9-27-85.

Matter in *italics* in Sec. 707(b)(2) added by section 642(a)(2), '86 TRA, which struck out:

(3) "80 percent"

Effective date (Sec. 642(c), '86 TRA).—(1) Generally applies to sales after the date of the enactment of this Act, in taxable years ending after such date.

(2) Traditional rule for binding contracts.—The amendments made by this section shall not apply to sales made after 8-14-86, which are made pursuant to a binding contract in effect on 8-14-86, and at all time thereafter.

of accounting used by the partnership, any rights (contractual or otherwise) to payment for—

    (1)   goods delivered, or to be delivered, to the extent the proceeds therefrom would be treated as amounts received from the sale or exchange of property other than a capital asset, or

    (2)   services rendered, or to be rendered.

For purposes of this section and sections 731, 736 and 741, such term also includes mining property (as defined in [1]*section 617(f)(2)) stock* in a DISC (as described in section 992(a)), section 1245 property (as defined in section 1245(a)(3)),[2] stock in certain foreign corporations (as described in section 1248), section 1250 property (as defined in section 1250(c)), farmland (as defined in section 1252(a)), franchises, trademarks, or trade names (referred to in section 1253(a)), and an oil, gas, or geothermal property (described in section 1254) but only to the extent of the amount which would be treated as gain to which section 617(d)(1), 995(c), 1245(a), 1248(a), 1250(a), 1252(a), 1253(a) or 1254(a) would apply if (at the time of the transaction described in this section or section 731, 736, or 741, as the case may be) such property had been sold by the partnership at its fair market value. For purposes of this section and sections 731, 736, and 741, such term also includes any market discount bond (as defined in section 1278 and any short-term obligation (as defined in section 1283) but only to the extent of the amount which would be treated as ordinary income if (at the time of the transaction described in this section or section 731, 736, or 741, as the case may be) such property had been sold by the partnership.

*   *   *   *   *   *   *   *   *   *   *

[For official explanation, see Committee Reports, ¶3870.]

[¶3076]   CODE SEC. 761. TERMS DEFINED.

*   *   *   *   *   *   *   *   *   *   *

    (e)   **Distributions** *of Partnership Interests* **treated as exchanges.**—[1]*Except as otherwise provided in regulations for purposes of—*

    (1)   section 708 (relating to continuation of partnership),

    (2)   section 743 (relating to optional adjustment to basis of partnership property), and

    (3)   any other provisions of this subchapter specified in regulations prescribed by the Secretary,

any distributiion *of an interest in a partnership* (not otherwise treated as an exchange) shall be treated as an exchange.

*   *   *   *   *   *   *   *   *   *   *

[For official explanation, see Committee Reports, ¶4139.]

[¶3077]   CODE SEC. 801.   TAX IMPOSED.—

    (a)   **Tax Imposed.—**

*   *   *   *   *   *   *   *   *   *   *

    (2)   **Alternative tax in case of capital gains.—**

*   *   *   *   *   *   *   *   *   *   *

    (C)   Net capital gain not taken into account in determining [1] small life insurance company deduction.—For purposes of subparagraph (B)(i), the [2]*amount allowable as a deduction under paragraph (2)* of section 804 shall be determined by re-

---

[Footnote ¶3075]   Matter in *italics* in Sec. 751(c) added by section 1899(A)(19), '86 TRA, which struck out:

(1)   "section 617(f)(2), stock"

Section 201(d)(10), '86 TRA, struck out from Sec. 751(c):

(2)   "section 1245 recovery property (as defined in section 1245(a)(5)),"

Effective date (Sec. 203, '86 TRA).— Generally applies to property placed in service after 12-31-86, in taxable years ending after such date.

For transitional and special rules see footnote ¶2007—2008.

[Footnote ¶3076]   Matter in *italics* in Sec. 761(e) added by section 1805(c)(2), '86 TRA, which struck out:

(1)   "For purposes of"

Effective date (Sec. 1881, '86 TRA and section 75(e), '84 TRA).—Applies to distributions, sales, and exchanges made after 3-31-84, in taxable years ending after such date.

[Footnote ¶3077]   Matter in *italics* in Sec. 801(a)(2)(C) added by section 1011(b)(3),'86 TRA, which struck out:

(1)   "special life insurance company deduction and"

(2)   "amounts allowable as deductions under paragraphs (2) and (3)"

Effective date (Sec. 1011(c)(1), '86 TRA).—Applies to taxable years beginning after 12-31-86.

ducing the tentative LICTI by the amount of the net capital gain (determined without regard to items attributable to noninsurance businesses).

* * * * * * * * * * * *

[For official explanation, see Committee Reports, ¶3958.]

〔¶3078〕 CODE SEC. 804. LIFE INSURANCE DEDUCTIONS.

For purposes of this part, the term "life insurance deductions" means—
(1) the general deductions provided in section 805, *and*

[1]*(2) the small life insurance company deduction (if any) determined under section 806(a).*

[For official explanation, see Committee Reports, ¶3958.]

〔¶3079〕 CODE SEC. 805. GENERAL DEDUCTIONS.

(a) **General Rule.**—For purposes of this part, there shall be allowed the following deductions:

* * * * * * * * * * * *

(4) **Dividends received by company.**—
(A) In general.—The deductions provided by sections 243, 244, and 245 (as modified by subparagraph (B))—
(i) for 100 percent dividends received, and
(ii) for the life insurance company's share of the dividends (other than 100 percent dividends) received.
(B) Application of section 246(b).—In applying section 246(b) (relating to limitation on aggregate amount of deductions for dividends received) for purposes of subparagraph (A), the limit on the aggregate amount of the deductions allowed by sections 243(a)(1), 244(a), and 245 shall be [1]*80 percent* of the life insurance company taxable income, computed without regard to—
(i) [2] the small life insurance company deduction,
(ii) the operations loss deduction provided by section 810,
(iii) the deductions allowed by sections 243(a)(1), 244(a), and 245, and
(iv) any capital loss carryback to the taxable year under section 1212(a)(1),

but such limit shall not apply for any taxable year for which there is a loss from operations.
[3]*(C) 100 percent dividend.—For purposes of subparagraph (A)—*
(i) In general.—Except as provided in clause (ii), the term "100 percent dividend" means any dividend if the percentage used for purposes of determining the deduction allowable under section 243, 244, or 245(b) is 100 percent.
(ii) Treatment of dividends from noninsurance companies.—The term "100 percent dividend" does not include any distribution by a corporation which is not an insurance company to the extent such distribution is out of tax-exempt interest or out of dividends which are not 100 percent dividends (determined with the application of this clause as if it applies to distributions by all corporations including insurance companies).
(D) Special rules for certain dividends from insurance companies.—

(i)   *In general.—In the case of any 100 percent dividend paid to any life insurance company out of the earnings and profits for any taxable year beginning after December 31, 1983, of another life insurance company if—*

(I)   *the paying company's share determined under section 812 for such taxable year, exceeds*

(II)   *the receiving company's share determined under section 812 for its taxable year in which the dividend is received or accrued,*

the deduction allowed under section 243, 244, or 245(b) (as the case may be) shall be reduced as provided in clause (ii).

(ii)   *Amount of reduction.—The reduction under this clause for a dividend is an amount equal to—*

(I)   *the portion of such dividend attributable to prorated amounts, multiplied by*

(II)   *the percentage obtained by subtracting the share described in subclause (II) of clause (i) from the share described in subclause (I) of such clause.*

(iii)   *Prorated amounts.—For purposes of this subparagraph, the term "prorated amounts" means tax-exempt interest and dividends other than 100 percent dividends.*

(iv)   *Portion of dividend attributable to prorated amounts.—For purposes of this subparagraph, in determining the portion of any dividend attributable to prorated amounts—*

(I)   *any dividend by the paying corporation shall be treated as paid first out of earnings and profits for taxable years beginning after December 31, 1983, attributable to prorated amounts (to the extent thereof), and*

(II)   *by determining the portion of earnings and profits so attributable without any reduction for the tax imposed by this chapter.*

(v)   *Subparagraph to apply to dividends from other insurance companies.—Rules similar to the rules of this subsection shall apply in the case of 100 percent dividends paid by an insurance company which is not a life insurance company.*

[4](E)   Certain dividends received by foreign corporations.—Subparagraph (A)(i) (and not subparagraph (A)(ii)) shall apply to any dividend received by a foreign corporation from a domestic corporation which would be a 100 percent dividend if section 1504(b)(3) did not apply for purposes of applying section 243(b)(5).

* * * * * * * * * * * *

(b)   Modifications.—The modifications referred to in subsection (a)(8) are as follows:

(1)   Interest.—In applying section 163 (relating to deduction for interest), no deduction shall be allowed for interest in respect of items described in section 807(c).[5]

[6](2)   **Charitable, etc., contributions and gifts.**—In applying section 170—

(A)   the limit on the total deductions under such section provided by section 170(b)(2) shall be 10 percent of the life insurance company taxable income computed without regard to—

(i)   the deduction provided by section 170,

(ii)   the deductions provided by paragraphs (3) and (4) of subsection (a),

(iii)   [2]the small life insurance company deduction,

(iv)   any operations loss carryback to the taxable year under section 810, and

(v)   any capital loss carryback to the taxable year under section 1212(a)(1), and

(B)   under regulations prescribed by the Secretary, a rule similar to the rule contained in section 170(d)(2)(B) (relating to special rule for net operating loss carryovers) shall be applied.

[7](3)   **Amortizable bond premium.—**

(A)   In general.—Section 17 shall not apply.

(B)   Cross reference.—

For rules relating to amortizable bond premium, see section 811(b).

【Footnote ¶3079 continued】

(4)   "(D)"

Effective date (Sec. 1881, '86 TRA and Sec. 215, '84 TRA).—Applies to taxable years beginning after 12-31-83. For special and transitional rules, see footnote ¶3081.

Matter in *italics* in Sec. 805(b)(2)—(5) added by section 805(c)(6), '86 TRA, which struck out:

(5)   "(2) **Bad debts.**—Section 166(c) (relating to reserve for bad debts) shall not apply."

(6)   "(3)"

(7)   "(4)"

[8](4) **Net operating loss deduction.**—Except as provided by section 844, the deduction for net operating losses provided in section 172 shall not be allowed.

[9](5) **Dividends received deduction.**—Except as provided in subsection (a)(4), the deductions for dividends received provided by sections 243, 244, and 245 shall not be allowed.

[For official explanation, see Committee Reports, ¶3912; 3939; 3958; 4147.]

【¶3080】 CODE SEC. 806. [1]*SMALL LIFE INSURANCE COMPANY DEDUCTION.*[2]

[3]*(a)* **Small Life Insurance Company Deduction.**

*   *   *   *   *   *   *   *   *   *   *

[4]*(b)* **Tentative LICTI.**—For purposes of this part—

(1) **In general.**—The term "tentative LICTI" means life insurance company taxable income determined [5]*without regard to the small life insurance company deduction.*

*   *   *   *   *   *   *   *   *   *   *   *

[6]*(c)* **Special Rule for Controlled Groups.**—

(1) [7]*Small* **life insurance company deduction determined on controlled group basis.**—For purposes of [8]*subsection (a)*—
    (A) all life insurance companies which are members of the same controlled group shall be treated as 1 life insurance company, and
    (B) [9]any small life insurance company deduction determined with respect to such group shall be allocated among the life insurance companies which are members of such group in proportion to their respective tenative LICTI's.

(2) **Nonlife insurance members included for asset test.**—For purposes of [10]*subsection (a)(3),* all members of the same controlled group (whether or not life insurance companies) shall be treated as 1 company.

(3) **Controlled group.**—For purposes of this subsection, the term "controlled group" means any controlled group of corporations (as defined in section 1563(a)); except that subsections (a)(4) and (b)(2)(D) of section 1563 shall not apply.[11]

【Footnote ¶3079 continued】

(8) "(5)"
(9) "(6)"
Effective date (Sec. 805(d), '86 TRA).—Applies to taxable years beginning after 12-31-86. For special rules, see footnote ¶2959.
【Footnote ¶3080】 Matter in *italics* in the heading of Sec. 806, and (a)—(c) added by section 1011(a), (b)(5)—(8) and (11)(A), '86 TRA, which struck out:
(1) "SPECIAL DEDUCTIONS"
(2) "(a) **Special Life Insurance Company Deduction.**—For purposes of section 804, the special life insurance company deduction for any taxable year is 20 percent of the excess of the tentative LICTI for such taxable year over the small life insurance company deduction (if any)."
(3) "(b)"
(4) "(c)"
(5) "without regard to—
(A) the special life insurance company deduction, and
(B) the small life insurance company deduction."
(6) "(d)"
(7) "Special life insurance company deduction and small"
(8) "subsections (a) and (b)"
(9) "any special life insurance company deduction and"
(10) "subsection (b)(3)"
(11) "(4) **Election with respect to loss from operations of member of group.**—
(A) In general.—Any life insurance company which is a member of a controlled group may elect to have its loss from operations for any taxable year not taken into account for purposes of determining the amount of the special life insurance company deduction for the life insurance companies which are members of such group and which do not file a consolidated return with such life insurance company for the taxable year.
(B) Limitation on amount of loss which may offset nonlife income.—In the case of that portion of any loss from operations for any taxable year of a life insurance company which (but for subparagraph (A)), would have reduced tentative LICTI of other life insurance companies for such year—
(i) only 80 percent of such portion may be used to offset nonlife income, and
(ii) to the extent such portion is used to offset nonlife income, the loss shall be treated as used at a rate of $1 for each 80 cents of income so offset.
For purposes of the preceding sentence, any such portion shall be used before the remaining portion of the loss from the same year and shall be treated as first being offset against income which is not nonlife income.
(C) Nonlife income.—
(i) In general.—The term "nonlife income" means the portion of the life insurance company's taxable income for which the special life insurance company deduction was not allowable and any income of a corporation not

[12]*(4)* **Adjustments to prevent excess detriment or benefit.**—Under regulations prescribed by the Secretary, proper adjustments shall be made in the application of this subsection to prevent any excess detriment or benefit (whether from year-to-year or otherwise) arising from the application of this subsection.

[For official explanation, see Committee Reports, ¶3958.]

【¶3081】 **CODE SEC. 807.   RULES FOR CERTAIN RESERVES.**

* * * * * * * * * * * *

【Footnote ¶3080 continued】

subject to tax under this part.

(ii) Special rule for taxable years beginning before January 1, 1984.—In the case of a taxable year beginning before January 1, 1984, all life insurance company taxable income shall be treated as nonlife income."

(12) "(5)"

Effective date (Sec. 1011(c)(1), '86 TRA).—Applies to taxable years beginning after 12-31-86.

【Footnote ¶3081】 The second to the last sentence in *italics* in Sec. 807(c) added by section 1821(a), '86 TRA.

Effective date (Sec. 1881, '86 TRA and Sec. 215—219, '84 TRA, amended by section 1011(c)(2), '86 TRA).— Applies to taxable years beginning after 12-31-83.

Transitional Rules.

SEC. 216. '84 TRA. RESERVES COMPUTED ON NEW BASIS; FRESH START.

(a) Recomputation of Reserves.—

(1) General.—As of the beginning of the first taxable year beginning after 12-31-83, for purposes of subchapter L of the '54 Code (other than section 816 thereof), the reserve for any contract shall be recomputed as if the amendments made by this subtitle had applied to such contract when it was issued.

(2) Premiums earned.—For the first taxable year beginning after 12-31-83, in determining "premiums earned on insurance contracts during the taxable year" as provided in section 832(b)(4) of the '54 Code, life insurance reserves which are included in unearned premiums on outstanding business at the end of the preceding taxable year shall be determined as provided in section 807 of the '54 Code, as amended by this subtitle, as though section 807 was applicable to such reserves in such preceding taxable year.

(3) Issuance date for group contracts.—For purposes of this subsection, the issuance date of any group contract shall be determined under section 807(e)(2) of the '54 Code (as added by this subtitle), except that if such issuance date cannot be determined, the issuance date shall be determined on the basis prescribed by the Secretary of the Treasury or his delegate for purposes of this subsection.

(b) Fresh Start.—

(1) In general.—Except as provided in paragraph (2), in the case of any insurance company, any change in the method of accounting (and any change in the method of computing reserves) between such company's first taxable year beginning after 12-31-83, and the preceding taxable year which is required solely by the amendments made by this subtitle shall be treated as not being a change in the method of accounting (or change in the method of computing reserves) for purposes of the '54 Code.

(2) Treatment of adjustments from years before 1984.—

(A) Adjustments attributable to decreases in reserves.—No adjustment under section 810(d) of the '54 Code (as in effect on the day before 7-18-84) attributable to any decrease in reserves as a result of a change in a taxable year beginning before 1984 shall be taken into account in any taxable year beginning after 1983.

(B) Adjustments attributable to increases in reserves.—

(i) In general.—Any adjustment under section 810(d) of the '54 Code (as so in effect) attributable to an increase in reserves as a result of a change in a taxable year beginning before 1984 shall be taken into account in taxable years beginning after 1983 to the extent that—

(I) the amount of the adjustments which would be taken into account under such section in taxable years beginning after 1983 without regard to this subparagraph, exceeds

(II) the amount of any fresh start adjustment attributable to contracts for which there was such an increase in reserves as a result of such change.

(ii) Fresh start adjustment.—For purposes of clause (i), the fresh start adjustment with respect to any contract is the excess (if any) of—

(I) the reserve attributable to such contract as of the close of the taxpayer's last taxable year beginning before 1-1-84; over

(II) the reserve for such contract as of the beginning of the taxpayer's first taxable year beginning after 1983 as recomputed under subsection (a) of this section.

(C) Related income inclusions not taken into account to the extent deduction disallowed under subparagraph (b)—No premium shall be included in income to the extent such premium is directly related to an increase in a reserve for which a deduction is disallowed by subparagraph (B).

(3) Reinsurance transactions, and reserve strengthening, after September 27, 1983.—

(A) In general.—Paragraph (1) shall not apply (and section 807(f) of the '54 Code as amended by this subtitle shall apply)—

(i) to any reserve transferred pursuant to—

(I) a reinsurance agreement entered into after 9-27-83, and before 1-1-84, or

(II) a modification of a reinsurance agreement made after 9-27-83, and before 1-1-84, and

(ii) to any reserve strengthening reported for Federal income tax purposes after 9-27-83, for a taxable year ending before 1-1-84.

Clause (ii) shall not apply to the computation of reserves on any contract issued if such computation employs the reserve practice used for purposes of the most recent annual statement filed before 9-27-83, for the type of contract with respect to which such reserves are set up.

[Footnote ¶3081 continued]

(B) Treatment of reserve attributable to section 818(c) election.—In the case of any reserve described in sub-paragraph (A), for purposes of section 807(f) of the '54 Code, any change in the treatment of any contract to which an election under section 818(c) of such Code (as in effect on the day before 7-18-84) applied shall be treated as a change in the basis for determining the amount of any reserve.

(C) 10-year spread inapplicable where no 10-year spread under prior law.—In the case of any item to which section 807(f) of such Code applies by reason of subparagraph (A) or (B), such item shall be taken into account for the first taxable year beginning after 12-31-83 (in lieu of over the 10-year period otherwise provided in such section) unless the item was required to have been taken into account over a period of 10 taxable years under section 810(d) of such Code (as in effect on the day before 7-18-84).

(D) Disallowance of special life insurance company deduction and small life insurance company deduction.—Any amount included in income under section 807(f) of such Code by reason of subparagraph (A) or (B) (and any income attributable to expenses transferred in connection with the transfer of reserves described in subparagraph (A)) shall not be taken into account for purposes of determining the amount of special life insurance company deduction and the small life insurance company deduction.

(E) Disallowance of deductions under section 809(d).—No deduction shall be allowed under paragraph (5) or (6) of section 809(d) of such Code (as in effect before the amendments made by this subtitle) with respect to any amount described in either such paragraph which is transferred in connection with the transfer of reserves described in subparagraph (A).

(4) Elections under section 818(c) after September 27, 1983, not to take effect.—

(A) In general.—Except as provided in subparagraph (B), any election after 9-27-83, under section 818(c) of the '54 Code (as in effect on the day before 7-18-84) shall not take effect.

(B) Exception for certain contracts issued under plan of insurance first filed after 3-1-82, and before 9-28-83.—Subparagraph (A) shall not apply to any election under such section 818(c) if more than 95 percent of the reserves computed in accordance with such election are attributable to risks under life insurance contracts issued by the taxpayer under a plan of insurance first filed after 3-1-82, and before 9-28-83.

(5) Recapture of reinsurance after December 31, 1983.—If (A) insurance or annuity contracts in force on 12-31-83, are subject to a conventional coinsurance agreement entered into after 12-31-81, and before 1-1-84, and (B) such contracts are recaptured by the reinsured in any taxable year beginning after 12-31-83, then—

(i) if the amount of the reserves with respect to the recaptured contracts, computed at the date of recapture, that the reinsurer would have taken into account under section 810(c) of the '54 Code (as in effect on the day before 7-18-84) exceeds the amount of the reserves with respect to the recaptured contracts, computed at the date of recapture, taken into account by the reinsurer under section 807(c) of the '54 Code (as amended by this subtitle), such excess (but not greater than the amount of such excess if computed on 1-1-84) shall be taken into account by the reinsurer under the method described in section 807(f)(1)(B)(ii) of the '54 Code (as amended by this subtitle) commencing with the taxable year of recapture, and

(ii) the amount, if any, taken into account by the reinsurer under clause (i) for purposes of part I of subchapter L of chapter 1 of the '54 Code shall be taken into account by the reinsured under the method described in section 807(f)(1)(B)(ii) of the '54 Code (as amended by this subtitle) commencing with the taxable year of recapture.

The excess described in clause (i) shall be reduced by any portion of such excess to which section 807(f) of the '54 Code applies by reason of paragraph (3) of this subsection. For purposes of this paragraph, the term "reinsurer" refers to the taxpayer that held reserves with respect to the recaptured contracts as of the end of the taxable year preceding the first taxable year beginning after 12-31-83, and the term "reinsured" refers to the taxpayer to which such reserves are ultimately transferred upon termination.

(c) Election Not To Have Reserves Recomputed.—

(1) In general.—If a qualified life insurance company makes an election under this paragraph—

(A) subsection (a) shall not apply to such company, and

(B) as of the beginning of the first taxable year beginning after 12-31-83, and thereafter, the reserve for any contract issued before the first day of such taxable year by such company shall be the statutory reserve for such contract (within the meaning of section 809(b)(4)(B)(i) of the '54 Code).

(2) Election with respect to contracts issued after 1983 and before 1989.—

(A) In general.—If—

(i) a qualified life insurance company makes an election under paragraph (1), and

(ii) the tentative LICTI (within the meaning of section 806(c) of such Code) of such company for its first taxable year beginning after 12-31-83, does not exceed $3,000,000,

such company may elect under this paragraph to have the reserve for any contract issued on or after the first day of such first taxable year and before 1-1-89, be equal to the statutory reserve for such contract, adjusted as provided in subparagraph (B).

(B) Adjustment to reserves.—If this paragraph applies to any contract, the statutory reserves for such contract shall be adjusted as provided under section 805(c)(1) of such Code (as in effect for taxable years beginning in 1982 and 1983), except that section 805(c)(1)(B)(ii) of such Code (as so in effect) shall be applied by substituting—

(i) the prevailing State assumed interest rate (within the meaning of section 807(c)(4) of such Code), for

(ii) the adjusted reserves rate.

(3) Qualified life insurance company.—For purposes of this subsection, the term "qualified life insurance company" means any life insurance company which, as of 12-31-83, had assets of less than $100,000,000 (determined in the same manner as under section 806(b)(3) of such Code).

(4) Special rules for controlled groups.—For purposes of applying the dollar limitations of paragraph (2) and (3), rules similar to the rules of section 806(d) of such Code shall apply.

(5) Elections.—Any election under paragraph (1) or (2)—

(A) shall be made at such time and in such manner as the Secretary of the Treasury may prescribe, and

⟦Footnote ¶3081 continued⟧

(B)   once made, shall be irrevocable.

SEC. 217. '84 TRA, OTHER SPECIAL RULES.

(a)   New Section 814 Treated as Continuation of Section 819A.—For purposes of section 814 of the '54 Code (relating to contiguous country branches of domestic life insurance companies)—

(1)   any election under section 819A of such Code (as in effect on the day before 7-18-84) shall be treated as an election under such section 814, and

(2)   any reference to a provision of such section 814 shall be treated as including a reference to the corresponding provision of such section 819A.

(b)   Treatment of Election Under Section 453B(e)(2).—If an election is made under section 453B(e)(2) before 1-1-84, with respect to any installment obligation, any income from such obligation shall be treated as attributable to a noninsurance business (as defined in section 806(c)(3) of the '54 Code).

(c)   Determination of Tentative LICTI Where Corporation Made Certain Acquisitions in 1980, 1981, 1982, and 1983.—If—

(1)   a corporation domiciled or having its principal place of business in Alabama, Arkansas, Oklahoma, or Texas acquired the assets of 1 or more insurance companies after 1979 and before 4-1-83, and

(2)   the basis of such assets in the hands of the corporation were determined under section 334(b)(2) of the '54 Code or such corporation made an election under section 338 of such Code with respect to such assets,

then the tentative LICTI of the corporation holding such assets for taxable years beginning after 12-31-83, shall, for purposes of determining the amount of the special deductions under section 806 of such Code, be increased by the deduction allowable under chapter 1 of such Code for the amortization of the cost of insurance contracts acquired in such asset acquisition (and any portion of any operations loss deduction attributable to such amortization).

(d)   Effective Date for New Section 845.—

(1)   Subsection (a) of section 845 of the '54 Code (as added by this title) shall apply with respect to any risk reinsured on or after 9-27-83.

(2)   Subsection (b) of such Code (as so added) shall apply with respect to risks reinsured afteer 12-31-83.

(e)   Treatment of Certain Companies Operating Both as Stock and Mutual Company.—If, during the 10-year period ending on 12-31-83, a company has, as authorized by the law of the State in which the company is domiciled, been operating as a mutual life insurance company with shareholders, such company shall be treated as a stock life insurance company.

(f)   Treatment of Certain Assessment Life Insurance Companies.—

(1)   Mortality and morbidity tables.—In the case of a contract issued by an assessment life insurance company, the mortality and morbidity tables used in computing statutory reserves for such contract shall be used for purposes of paragraph (2)(C) of section 807(d) of the '54 Code (as amended by this subtitle) if such tables were—

(A)   in use since 1965, and

(B)   developed on the basis of the experience of assessment life insurance companies in the State in which such assessment life insurance company is domiciled.

(2)   Treatment of certain mutual assessment life insurance companies.—In the case of any contract issued by a mutual assessment life insurance company which—

(A)   has been in existence since 1965, and

(B)   operates under chapter 13 or 14 of the Texas Insurance Code,

for purposes of part I of subchapter L of chapter 1 of the '54 Code, the amount of the life insurance reserves for such contract shall be equal to the amount taken into account with respect to such contract in determining statutory reserves.

(3)   Statutory reserves.—For purposes of this subsection, the term "statutory reserves" has the meaning given to such term by section 809(b)(4)(B) of such Code.

(g)   Treatment of Reinsurance Agreements Required by NAIC.—Effective for taxable years beginning after 12-31-81, and before 1-1-84, subsections (c)(1)(F) and (d)(12) of section 809 of the '54 Code (as in effect on the day before 7-18-84) shall not apply to dividends to policyholders reimbursed to the taxpayer by a reinsurer in respect of accident and health policies reinsured under a reinsurance agreement entered into before 6-30-55, pursuant to the direction of the National Association of Insurance Commissioners and approved by the State insurance commissioner of the taxpayer's State of domicile. For purposes of subchapter L of chapter 1 of such Code (as in effect on the day before the date of the enactment of this Act) any such dividends shall be treated as dividends of the reinsurer and not the taxpayer.

(h)   Determination of Assets of Controlled Group for Purposes of Small Life Insurance Company Deduction for 1984.—

(1)   In general.—For purposes of applying paragraph (2) of section 806(d) of the '54 Code (relating to nonlife insurance members included for asset test) for the first taxable year beginning after 12-31-83, the members of the controlled group referred to in such paragraph shall be treated as including only those members of such group which are described in paragraph (2) of this subsection if—

(A)   an election under section 1504(c)(2) of such Code is not in effect for the controlled group for such taxable year,

(B)   during such taxable year, the controlled group does not include a member which is taxable under part I of subchapter L of chapter 1 of such Code and which became a member of such group after 9-27-83, and

(C)   the sum of the contributions to capital received by members of the controlled group which are taxable under such part I during such taxable year from the members of the controlled group which are not taxable under such part does not exceed the aggregate dividends paid during such taxable year by the members of such group which are taxable under such part I.

(2)   Members of group taken into account.—For purposes of paragraph (1), the members of the controlled group which are described in this paragraph are—

[Footnote ¶3081 continued]

(A) any financial institution to which section 585 or 593 of such Code applies,

(B) any lending or finance business (as defined by section 542(d)),

(C) any insurance company subject to tax imposed by subchapter L of chapter 1 of such Code, and

(D) any securities broker.

(i) Special Election To Treat Individual Noncancellable Accident and Health Contracts as Cancellable.—

(1) In general.—A mutual life insurance company may elect to treat all individual noncancellabel (or guaranteed renewable) accident and health insurance contracts as though they were cancellable for purposes of section 816 of subchapter L of chapter 1 of the '54 Code.

(2) Effect of election of subsidiaries of electing parent.—

(A) Treated as mutual life insurance company.—Any stock life insurance company whish is a member of an affiliated group which has a common parent which made an election under paragraph (1), for purposes of part I of subchapter L of the '54 Code, such stock life insurance company shall be treated as though it were a mutual life insurance company.

(B) Income of electing parent taken into account in determining small life insurance company deduction of any subsidiary.—For purposes of determining the amount of the small life insurance company deduction of any controlled group which includes a mutual company which made an election under paragraph (1), the taxable income of such electing company shall be taken into account under section 806(b)(2) of the '54 Code (relating to phase-out of small life insurance company deduction).

(3) Election.—An election under paragraph (1) shall apply to the company's first taxable year beginning after 12-31-83, and all taxable years thereafter.

(4) Time and manner.—An election under paragraph (1) shall be made—

(A) on the return of the taxpayer for its first taxable year beginning after 12-31-83, and

(B) in such manner as the Secretary of the Treasury or his delegate may prescribe.

(j) Reduction in Equity Base for Mutual Successor of Fraternal Benefit Society.—In the case of any mutual life insurance company which—

(1) is the successor to a fraternal benefit society, and

(2) which assumed the surplus of such fraternal benefit society in 1950 or in March of 1961,

for purposes of section 809 of the '54 Code (as amended by this subtitle), the equity base of such mutual life insurance company shall be reduced by the amount of the surplus so assumed plus earnings thereon, (i) for taxable years before 1984, at a 7 percent interest rate, and (ii) for taxable years 1984 and following, at the average mutual earnings rate for such year.

(k) Special Rule for Certain Debt-Financed Acquisition of Stock.—If—

(1) a life insurance company owns the stock of another corporation through a partnership of which it is a partner,

(2) the stock of the corporation was acquired on 1-14-81, and

(3) such stock acquired by debt financing,

then, for purposes of determining the small life insurance company deduction under section 806(a) of the '54 Code (as amended by this subtitle), the amount of tentative LICTI of such life insurance company shall be computed without taking into account any income, gain, loss, or deduction attributable to the ownership of such stock.

For purposes of determining taxable income, the amount of any income, gain, loss, or deduction attributable to the ownership of such stock shall be an amount equal to 46 times the amount of such income, gain, loss, or deduction, divided by 36.8.

(l) Treatment of Losses From Certain Guaranteed Interest Contracts.—

(1) In General.—For purposes of determining the amount of the special deductions under section 806 of the '54 Code (as amended by this subtitle), for any taxable year beginning before 1-1-88, the amount of tentative LICTI of any qualified life insurance company shall be computed without taking into account any income, gain, loss, or deduction attributable to a qualified GIC,

(2) Qualified life insurance company.—For purposes of this subsection, the term "qualified life insurance company" means any life insurance company if—

(A) the accrual of discount less amortization of premium for bonds and short-term investments (as shown in the first footnote to Exhibit 3 of its 1983 annual statement for life insurance companies approved by the National Association of Insurance Commissioners (but excluding separate accounts) filed in its state of domicile) exceeds $72,000,000 but does not exceed $73,000,000, and

(B) such life insurance company makes an election under this subsection on its return for its first taxable year beginning after 12-31-83.

(3) Qualified gic.—The term "qualified GIC" means any group contract—

(A) which is issued before 1-1-84,

(B) which specifies the contract maturity or renewal date,

(C) under which funds deposited by the contract holder plus interest guaranteed at the inception of the contract for the term of the contract and net of any specified expenses are paid as directed by the contract holder, and

(D) which is a pension plan contract (as defined in section 818(a) of the '54 Code).

(4) Scope of election.—An election under this subsection shall apply to all qualified GIC's of a qualified life insurance company. Any such election, once made, shall be irrevocable.

(5) Income on underlying assets taken into account.—In determining the amount of any income attributable to a qualified GIC, income on any asset attributable to such contract (as determined in the manner provided by the Secretary of the Treasury or his delegate) shall be taken into account.

(6) Limitation on tax benefit.—The amount of any reduction in tax for any taxable year by reason of this subsection for any qualified life insurance company (or controlled group within the meaning of section 806(d)(3) of the '54 Code) shall not exceed the applicable amount set forth in the following table:

* * * * * * * * * * * *

(c) **Items Taken Into Account.**—The items referred to in subsections (a) and (b) are as follows:

[Footnote ¶3081 continued]

In the case of taxable years beginning in:	The reduction may not exceed:
1984	$4,500,000
1985	$4,500,000
1986	$3,000,000
1987	$2,000,000

(m) Special Rule for Certain Interests in Oil and Gas Properties.—

(1) In General.—For purposes of section 806 of the '54 Code, the ownership by a qualified life insurance company of any undivided interest in operating mineral interests with respect to any oil or gas properties held on 12-31-83, shall be treated as an insurance business.

(2) Qualified life insurance company.—For purposes of paragraph (1), the term "qualified life insurance company" means a mutual life insurance company which—

(A) was originally incorporated in March of 1857, and

(B) has a cost to such company (as of 12-31-83) in the operating mineral interests decribed in paragraph (1) in excess of $250,000,000.

(n) Special Rule for Companies Using Net Level Reserve Method for Noncancellable Accident and Health Insurance Contracts.—A company shall be treated as meeting the requirement of section 807(d)(3)(A)(iii) of the '54 Code, as amended by this Act, with respect to any noncancellable accident and health insurance contract for any taxable year if such company—

(1) uses the net level reserve method to compute its tax reserves under section 807 of such Code on such contracts for such taxable year,

(2) was using the net level reserve method to compute its statutory reserves on such contracts as of 12-31-82, and

(3) has continuously used such method for computing such reserves on such contracts after 12-31-82, and through such taxable year.

SEC. 218. '84 TRA. UNDERPAYMENTS OF ESTIMATED TAX FOR 1984.

No addition to the tax shall be made under section 6655 of the '54 Code (relating to failure by corporation to pay estimated tax) with respect to any underpayment of an installment required to be paid before 7-18-84 to the extent—

(1) such underpayment was created or increased by any provision of this subtitle, and

(2) such underpayment is paid in full on or before the last date prescribed for payment of the first installment of estimated tax required to be paid after 7-18-84.

SEC. 219. '84 TRA. CLARIFICATION OF AUTHORITY TO REQUIRE CERTAIN INFORMATION.

Nothing in any provision of law shall be construed to prevent the Secretary of the Treasury or his delegate from requiring (from time to time) life insurance companies to provide such data with respect to taxable years beginning before 1-1-84, as may be necessary to carry out the provisions of section 809 of such Code (as added by this title).

The last sentence in italics in Sec. 807(c) added by section 1023(b), '86 TRA.

Effective date (Sec. 1023(e), '86 TRA).—(1) Applies to taxable years beginning after 12-31-86.

(2) Transitional rule.—For the first taxable year beginning after 12-31-86—

(A) the unpaid losses and the expenses unpaid (as defined in paragraphs (5)(B) and (6) of section 832(b) of the '86 Code) at the end of the preceding taxable year, and

(B) the unpaid losses as defined in sections 807(c)(2) and 805(a)(1) of such Code at the end of the preceding taxable year,

shall be determined as if the amendments made by this section had applied to such unpaid losses and expenses unpaid in the preceding taxable year and by using the interest rate and loss payment patterns applicable to accident years ending with calendar year 1987. For subsequent taxable years, such amendments shall be applied with respect to such unpaid losses and expenses unpaid by using the interest rate and loss payment patterns applicable to accident years ending with calendar year 1987.

(3) Fresh start.—

(A) In general.—Except as otherwise provided in this paragraph, any difference between—

(i) the amount determined to be the unpaid losses and expenses unpaid for the year preceding the 1st taxable year of an insurance company beginning after 12-31-86, determined without regard to paragraph (2), and

(ii) such amount determined with regard to paragraph (2),

shall not be taken into account for purposes of the '86 Code.

(B) Reserve strengthening in years after 1985.—Subparagraph (A) shall not apply to any reserve strengthening in a taxable year beginning in 1986, and such strengthening shall be treated as occurring in the taxpayer's 1st taxable year beginning after 12-31-86.

(C) Effect on earnings and profits.—The earnings and profits of any insurance company for its 1st taxable year beginning after 12-31-86, shall be increased by the amount of the difference determined under subparagraph (A) with respect to such company.

Matter in *italics* in Sec. 807(d)(5)(C) added by section 1821(s), '86 TRA.

Effective date (Sec. 1881, '86 TRA and Sec. 215, '84 TRA).—Applies to taxable years beginning after 12-31-83. For transitional rules, see above.

(1) The life insurance reserves (as defined in section 816(b)).

(2) The unearned premiums and unpaid losses included in total reserves under section 816(c)(2).

(3) The amounts (discounted at the appropriate rate of interest) necessary to satisfy the obligations under insurance and annuity contracts, but only if such obligations do not involve (at the time with respect to which the computation is made under this paragraph) life, accident, or health contingencies.

(4) Dividend accumulations, and other amounts, held at interest in connection with insurance and annuity contracts.

(5) Premiums received in advance, and liabilities for premium deposit funds.

(6) Reasonable special contingency reserves under contracts of group term life insurance or group accident and health insurance which are established and maintained for the provision of insurance on retired lives, for premium stabilization, or for a combination thereof.

For purposes of paragraph (3), the appropriate rate of interest for any obligation is the higher of the prevailing State assumed interest rate as of the time such obligation first did not involve life, accident, or health contingencies or the rate of interest assumed by the company (as of such time) in determining the guaranteed benefit. *In no case shall the amount determined under paragraph (3) for any contract be less than the net surrender value of such contract. For purposes of paragraph (2) and section 805(a)(1), the amount of the unpaid losses (other than losses on life insurance contracts) shall be the amount of the discounted unpaid losses as defined in section 846.*

(d) **Method of Computing Reserves for Purposes of Determining Income.—**

* * * * * * * * * * * *

(5) **Prevailing commissioners' standard tables.—**For purposes of this subsection—

* * * * * * * * * * * *

(C) Special rule for contracts for which there are no commissioners' standard tables.—If there are no commissioners' standard tables applicable to any contract when it is issued, the mortality and morbidity tables used for purposes of paragraph (2)(C) shall be determined under regulations prescribed by the Secretary. *When the Secretary by regulation changes the table applicable to a type of contract, the new table shall be treated (for purposes of subparagraph (B) and for purposes of determining the issue dates of contracts for which it shall be used) as if it were a new prevailing commissioners' standard table adopted by the twenty-sixth State as of a date (no earlier than the date the regulation is issued) specified by the Secretary.*

* * * * * * * * * * * *

[For official explanation, see Committee Reports, ¶3963; 4147.]

⟦¶3082⟧ CODE SEC. 808. POLICYHOLDER DIVIDENDS DEDUCTION.

* * * * * * * * * * * *

(d) **Definitions.—**For purposes of this section—

(1) **Excess interest.—**The term "excess interest" means any amount in the nature of interest—

(A) paid or credited to a policyholder in his capacity as such, and

[1]*(B) in excess of interest determined at the prevailing State assumed rate for such contract.*

* * * * * * * * * * * *

(f) *Coordination of 1984 Fresh-Start Adjustment With Acceleration of Policyholder Dividends Deduction Through Change in Business Practice.—*

(1) In general.—The amount determined under paragraph (1) of subsection (c) for the year of change shall (before any reduction under paragraph (2) of subsection (c)) be reduced by so much of the accelerated policyholder dividends deduction for such year as does not exceed the 1984 fresh-start adjustment for policyholder dividends (to the extent such adjustment was not previously taken into account under this subsection).

⟦**Footnote ¶3082**⟧ Matter in *italics* in Sec. 808(d)(1)(B) and (f) added by section 1821(b) and (c), '86 TRA, which struck out:

(1) "(B) determined at a rate in excess of the prevailing State assumed interest rate for such contract."

Effective date (Sec. 1881, '86 TRA and Sec. 215, '84 TRA).—Applies to taxable years beginning after 12-31-83. For transitional rules, see footnote ¶3081.

(2) *Year of change.*—*For purposes of this subsection, the term "year of change" means the taxable year in which the change in business practices which results in the accelerated policyholder dividends deduction takes effect.*

(3) *Accelerated policyholder dividends deduction defined.*—*For purposes of this subsection, the term "accelerated policyholder dividends deduction" means the amount which (but for this subsection) would be determined for the taxable year under paragraph (1) of subsection (c) but which would have been determined (under such paragraph) for a later taxable year under the business practices of the taxpayer as in effect at the close of the preceding taxable year.*

(4) *1984 Fresh Start adjustment for policyholder dividends.*—*For purposes of this subsection, the term "1984 fresh-start adjustment for policyholder dividends" means the amounts held as of December 31, 1983, by the taxpayer as reserves for dividends to policyholders under section 811(b) (as in effect on the day before the date of the enactment of the Tax Reform Act of 1984) other than for dividends which accrued before January 1, 1984. Such amounts shall be properly reduced to reflect the amount of previously nondeductible policyholder dividends (as determined under section 809(f) as in effect on the day before the date of the enactment of the Tax Reform Act of 1984).*

(5) *Separate application with respect to lines of business.*—*This subsection shall be applied separately with respect to each line of business of the taxpayer.*

(6) *Subsection not to apply to mere change in dividend amount.*—*This subsection shall not apply to a mere change in the amount of policyholder dividends.*

(7) *Subsection not to apply to policies issued after December 31, 1983.*—

(A) *In general.*—*This subsection shall not apply to any policyholder dividend paid or accrued with respect to a policy issued after December 31, 1983.*

(B) *Exchanges of substantially similar policies.*—*For purposes of subparagraph (A), any policy issued after December 31, 1983, in exchange for a substantially similar policy issued on or before such date shall be treated as issued before January 1, 1984. A similar rule shall apply in the case of a series of exchanges.*

(8) *Subsection to apply to policies provided under employee benefit plans.*—*This subsection shall not apply to any policyholder dividend paid or accrued with respect to a group policy issued in connection with a plan to provide welfare benefits to employes (within the meaning of section 419(e)(2)).*

[For official explanation, see Committee Reports, ¶4147.]

[¶3083] CODE SEC. 809. REDUCTION IN CERTAIN DEDUCTIONS OF MUTUAL LIFE INSURANCE COMPANIES.

* * * * * * * * * * * *

(b) **Average Equity Base.**—For purposes of this section—

* * * * * * * * * * * *

(2) **Equity base.**—The term "equity base" means an amount determined in the manner prescribed by regulations equal to—
(A) the surplus and capital,
(B) adjusted as provided in paragraphs (3), (4), (5), and (6) of this subsection.
No item shall be taken into account more than once in determining equity base.

* * * * * * * * * * * *

(c) **Differential Earnings Rate.**—

* * * * * * * * * * * *

(3) *Coordination with estimated tax payments.*—*For purposes of applying section 6655 with respect to any installment of estimated tax, the amount of tax shall be determined by using the lessor of*—
(A) *the differential earnings rate of the second tax year preceding the taxable year for which the installment is made, or*
(B) *the differential earnings rate for the taxable year for which the installment is made.*

(d) **Imputed Earnings Rate.**—

* * * * * * * * * * * *

(4) **Stock earnings rate.**—

* * * * * * * * * * * *

(C)   50 largest stock companies.—For purposes of this paragraph the term "50 largest stock companies" means a group (as determined by the Secretary) of stock life insurance companies which consists of the 50 largest *domestic* stock life insurance companies which are subject to tax under this part. [1]*the Secretary—*

(i)   shall, for purposes of determining the base period stock earnings rate, exclude from the group determined under the preceding sentence any company which had a negative equity base at any time during 1981, 1982, or 1983,

(ii)   shall exclude from such group for any calendar year any company which has a negative equity base, and

(iii)   may by regulations exclude any other company which otherwise would have been included in such group if the inclusion of the excluded company or companies would, by reason of the small equity base of such company, seriously distort the stock earnings rate.

The aggregate number of companies excluded by the Secretary under clause (iii) shall not exceed the excess of 2 over the number of companies excluded under clause (ii).

* * * * * * * * * * * *

(e)   Average Mutual Earnings Rate.—For purposes of this section, the average mutual earnings rate for any calendar year is the percentage (determined by the Secretary) which—

(1)   the aggregate statement gain or loss from operations for such year of *domestic* mutual life insurance companies, is of

(2)   their aggregate average equity bases for such year.

(f)   Recomputation in Subsequent Year.—

* * * * * * * * * * * *

(3)   Recomputed differential earnings amount.—For purposes of this subsection, the term "recomputed differential earnings amount" means, with respect to any taxable year, the amount which would be the differential earnings amount for such taxable year if the average mutual earnings rate taken into account under [2]*subsection (c)(1)(B)* were the average mutual earnings rate for the calendar year in which the taxable year begins.

* * * * * * * * * * * *

(5)   Subsection not to apply for purposes of estimated tax.—Section 6655 shall be applied to any taxable year without regard to any adjustments under this subsection for such year.

(g)   Definitions and Special Rules.—For purposes of this section—

[3]*(1)   Statement gain or loss from operations.—The term "statement gain or loss from operations" means the net gain or loss from operations required to be set forth in the annual statement, determined without regard to Federal income taxes, and—*

(A)   determined by substituting for the amount shown for policyholder dividends the amount of deduction for policyholder dividends determined under section 808 (without regard to section 808(c)(2)),

(B)   determined on the basis of the tax reserves rather than statutory reserves, and

(C)   properly adjusted for realized capital gains and losses and other relevant items.

* * * * * * * * * * * *

[For official explanation, see Committee Reports, ¶4147.]

⟦Footnote ¶3083⟧   Matter in *italics* in Sec. 809(b)(2), (c)(3), (d)(4)(C), (e)(1), (f)(3), (5), and (g)(1) added by section 1821(d)—(h) and (r), '86 TRA, which struck out:

(1)   "The Secretary may by regulations provide for exclusion from the group determined under the preceding sentence of any stock life insurance company if (i) the equity of such company is not great enough for such company to be 1 of the 50 largest stock life insurance companies if the determination were made on the basis of equity, and (ii) by reason of the small equity base of such company, it has an earnings rate which would seriously distort the stock earnings rate."

(2)   "subsection (c)(2)"

(3)   **"(1)   Statement gain or loss from operations.**—The term "statement gain or loss from operations" means the net gain or loss from operations required to be set forth in the annual statement—

(A)   determined with regard to policyholder dividends (as defined in section 808) but without regard to Federal income taxes,"

Effective date (Sec. 1881, '86 TRA and Sec. 215, '84 TRA).—Applies to taxable years beginning after 12-31-83. For transitional rules, see footnote ¶3081.

Code §809(g)(1)   ¶3083

[¶3084]　CODE SEC. 812.　DEFINITION OF COMPANY'S SHARE AND POLI-CYHOLDERS' SHARE.

(a)　General Rule.—

* * * * * * * * * * * *

(b)　Company's Share of Net Investment Income.—

* * * * * * * * * * * *

(2)　Policy interest.—For purposes of this subsection, the term "policy interest" means—

　(A)　required interest (at the prevailing State assumed rate *or, where such rate is not used, another appropriate rate*) on reserves under section 807(c) (other than paragraph (2) thereof).

　(B)　the deductible portion of excess interest,[1]

　(C)　the deductible portion of any amount (whether or not a policyholder dividend), and not taken into account under subparagraph (A) or (B), credited to—

　　(i)　a policyholder's fund under a pension plan contract for employees (other than retired employees), or

　　(ii)　a deferred annuity contract before the annuity starting date[2], *and*

　(D)　interest on amounts left on deposit with the company

(3)　Gross investment income's proportionate share of policyholder dividends.— For purposes of paragraph (1), the gross investment income's proportionate share of policyholder dividend is—

　(A)　the deduction for policyholders' dividends determined under sections 808 and 809 for the taxable year, but not including—

　　(i)　the deductible portion of excess interest,

　　(ii)　the deductible portion of policyholder dividends on contracts referred to in clauses (i) and (ii) of paragraph (2)(C), and

　　(iii)　the deductible portion of the premium and mortality charge adjustments with respect to contracts paying excess interest for such year,

　multiplied by

　(B)　the fraction—

　　(i)　the numerator of which is gross investment income for the taxable year (reduced by the policy interest for such year), and

　　(ii)　the denominator of which is life insurance gross income [3] reduced by the excess (if any) of the closing balance for the items described in section 807(c) over the opening balance for such items for the taxable year.

For purposes of subparagraph (B)(ii), life insurance gross income shall be determined by including tax-exempt interest and by applying section 807(a)(2)(B) as if it did not contain clause (i) thereof.

(c)　Net Investment Income.—[4]*For purposes of this section, the term "net investment income" means—*

　(1)　except as provided in paragraph (2), 90 percent of gross investment income; or

　(2)　in the case of gross investment income attributable to assets held in segregated asset accounts under variable contracts, 95 percent of gross investment income.

* * * * * * * * * * * *

(g)　*Treatment of Interest Partially Tax-Exempt under Section 133.—For purposes of this section and subsections (a) and (b) of section 807, the terms "gross investment income" and "tax-exempt interest" shall not include any interest received with respect to a securities acquisition loan (as defined in section 133(b)). Such interest shall not be included in life insurance gross income for purposes of subsection (b)(3).*

[For official explanation, see Committee Reports, ¶4147.]

[Footnote ¶3084]　Matter in *italics* in Sec. 812(b)(2), (3)(B), (c) and (g) added by section 1821(i), '86 TRA, which struck out:

(1)　"and"

(2)　"."

(3)　"(including tax-exempt interest)"

(4)　"For purposes of this section, the term "net investment income" means 90 percent of gross investment income."

Effective date (Sec. 1881, '86 TRA and Sec. 215, '84 TRA).—Applies to taxable years beginning after 12-31-83. For transitional rules, see footnote ¶3081.

〖¶3085〗 CODE SEC. 813. FOREIGN LIFE INSURANCE COMPANIES.

(a) Adjustment Where Surplus Held in the United States Is Less Than Specified Minimum.—

    (1) In general.—In the case of any foreign company taxable under this part, if—
        (A) the required surplus determined under paragraph (2), exceeds
        (B) the surplus held in the United States,

then its income effectively connected with the conduct of an insurance business within the United States shall be increased by an amount determined by multiplying such excess by such company's current investment yield.

The preceding sentence shall be applied before computing the amount of the special life insurance company deduction and the small life insurance company deduction, and any increase under the preceding sentence shall be treated as gross investment income.

* * * * * * * * * * * * *

    (4) Other definitions.—For purposes of this subsection—
        (A) Surplus held in the United States.—The surplus held in the United States is the excess of the assets (determined under [1]*section 806(a)(3)C*) held in the United States over the total insurance liabilities on United States business.

* * * * * * * * * * * * *

[For official explanation, see Committee Reports, ¶3958; 4147.]

〖¶3086〗 CODE SEC. 815. DISTRIBUTIONS TO SHAREHOLDERS FROM PRE-1984 POLICYHOLDERS SURPLUS ACCOUNT.

    (a) General Rule.—In the case of a stock life insurance company which has an existing policyholders surplus account, the tax imposed by section 801 for any taxable year shall be the amount which would be imposed by such section for such year on the sum of—
        (1) life insurance company taxable income for such year (but not less than zero), plus
        (2) the amount of direct and indirect distributions during such year to shareholders from such account.

For purposes of the preceding sentence, the term "indirect distribution" shall not include any bona fide loan with arms-length terms and conditions.

* * * * * * * * * * * * *

    (c) Shareholders Surplus Account.—

* * * * * * * * * * * *

    (2) Additions to account.—The amount added to the shareholders surplus account for any taxable year beginning after December 31, 1983, shall be the excess of—
        (A) the sum of—
            (i) the life insurance company's taxable income (but not below zero),
            (ii) the [1]*small life insurance company deduction* provided by section 806, and
            (iii) the deductions for dividends received provided by sections 243, 244, and 245 (as modified by section 805(a)(4)) and the amount of interest excluded from gross income under section 103, over
        (B) the taxes imposed for the taxable year by section 801 (determined without regard to this section).

* * * * * * * * * * * * *

〖Footnote ¶3085〗 Matter in *italics* in Sec. 813(a)(1) added by section 1821(j), '86 TRA.
Effective date (Sec. 1881, '86 TRA and Sec. 215, '84 TRA).—Applies to taxable years beginning after 12-31-83. For transitional rules, see footnote ¶3081.

Matter in *italics* in Sec. 813(a)(4)(A) added by section 1011(b)(9), '86 TRA, which struck out:
(1) "section 806(b)(3)(C)"
Effective date (Sec. 1011(c)(1), '86 TRA).—Applies to taxable years beginning after 12-31-86.
〖Footnote ¶3086〗 Matter in *italics* in Sec. 815(a) added by section 1821(k)(2), '86 TRA.
Effective date (Sec. 1881, '86 TRA and Sec. 215, '84 TRA).—Applies to taxable years beginning after 12-31-83. For special and transitional rules, see footnote ¶3081.

Matter in *italics* in Sec. 815(c)(2)(A)(ii) added by section 1011(b)(10), '86 TRA, which struck out:
(1) "special deductions"
Effective date (Sec. 1011(c)(1), '86 TRA).—Applies to taxable years beginning after 12-31-86.

(f) Other Rules Applicable to Policyholders Surplus Account Continued.—Except to the extent inconsistent with the provisions of this part, the provisions of subsections (d), (e), and (g) of section 815 (and of ²*sections 819(b), 6501(c)(6), 6501(k), 6511(d)(6),* 6601(d)(3), and 6611(f)(4) as in effect before the enactment of the Tax Reform Act of 1984 are hereby made applicable in respect of any policyholders surplus account for which there was a balance as of December 31, 1983.

[For official explanation, see Committee Reports, ¶3958; 4147.]

[¶3087] CODE SEC. 816.   LIFE INSURANCE COMPANY DEFINED.—

* * * * * * * * * * * *

(h) Treatment of Deficiency Reserves.—*For purposes of this section and section 813(a)(4)(B), the terms "life insurance reserves" and "total reserves" shall not include deficiency reserves.*

[For official explanation, see Committee Reports, ¶4147.]

[¶3088] CODE SEC. 817.   TREATMENT OF VARIABLE CONTRACTS.

* * * * * * * * * * * *

(d) Variable Contract Defined.—For purposes of this part, the term "variable contract" means a contract—

(1) which provides for the allocation of all or part of the amounts received under the contract to an account which, pursuant to State law or regulation, is segregated from the general asset accounts of the company,

(2) which—

(A) provides for the payment of annuities, or

(B) is a life insurance contract, and

(3) under which—

(A) in the case of an annuity contract, the amounts paid in, or the amount paid out, reflect the investment return and the market value of the segregated asset account, or

(B) in the case of a life insurance contract, the amount of the death benefit (or the period of coverage) is adjusted on the basis of the investment return and the market value of the segregated asset account.

If a contract ceases to reflect current investment return and current market value, such contract shall not be considered as meeting the requirements of paragraph (3) after such cessation. *Paragraph (3) shall be applied without regard to whether there is a guarantee, and obligations under such guarantee which exceed obligations under the contract without regard to such guarantee shall be accounted for as part of the company's general account.*

* * * * * * * * * * * *

(h) Treatment of Certain Nondiversified Contracts.—

(1) In general.—For purposes of subchapter L, section 72 (relating to annuities), and section 7702(a) (relating to definition of life insurance contract), a variable contract (other than a pension plan contract) which is otherwise described in this section and which is based on a segregated asset account shall not be treated as an annuity, endowment, or life insurance contract for any period (and any subsequent period) for which the investments made by such account are not, in accordance with regulations prescribed by the Secretary, adequately diversified.[1]

* * * * * * * * * * * *

[Footnote ¶3086 continued]

Matter in *italics* in Sec. 815(f) added by section 1821(k)(1), '86 TRA, which struck out:

(2) "sections 6501(c)(6)"

Effective date (Sec. 1881, '86 TRA and Sec. 215, '84 TRA).—Applies to taxable years beginning after 12-31-83. For special and transitional rules, at ¶3081.

[Footnote ¶3087] Sec. 816(h) in *italics* added by section 1821(l), '86 TRA.

Effective date (Sec. 1881, '86 TRA and Sec. 215, '84 TRA).—Applies to taxable years beginning after 12-31-83. For special and transitional rules, see footnote ¶3081.

[Footnote ¶3088] Matter in *italics* in Sec. 817(d) added by section 1821(t)(1), '86 TRA.

Effective date (Sec. 1821(t)(2), '86 TRA).—Applies—(A) to contracts issued after 12-31-86, and

(B) to contracts issued before 1-1-87, if such contract was treated as a variable contract on the taxpayer's return.

Matter in *italics* in Sec. 817(h) added by section 1821(m), '86 TRA, which struck out:

(1) "For purposes of this paragraph and paragraph (2), beneficial interests in a regulated investment company or in a trust shall not be treated as 1 investment if all of the beneficial interests in such compny or trust are held by 1 or more segregated asset accounts of 1 or more insurance companics."

²(3) *Special rule for investments in United States obligations.*—*To the extent that any segregated asset account with respect to a variable life insurance contract is invested in securities issued by the United States Treasury, the investments made by such account shall be treated as adequately diversified for purposes of paragraph (1).*

(4) *Look-through in certain cases.*—*For purposes of this subsection, if all of the beneficial interests in a regulated investment company or in a trust are held by 1 or more*—

(A) *insurance companies (or affiliated companies) in their general account or in segregated asset accounts, or*

(B) *fund managers (or affiliated companies) in connection with the creation or management of the regulated investment company or trust,*

the diversification requirements of paragraph (1) shall be applied by taking into account the assets held by such regulated investment company or trust.

(5) *Independent investment advisors permitted.*—*Nothing in this subsection shall be construed as prohibiting the use of independent investment advisors.*

[For official explanation, see Committee Reports, ¶4147.]

【¶3089】 CODE SEC. 818. OTHER DEFINITIONS AND SPECIAL RULES.

(a) **Pension Plan Contracts.**—For purposes of this part, the term "pension plan contract" means any contract—

(1) entered into with trusts which (as of the time the contracts were entered into) were deemed to be trusts described in section 401(a) and exempt from tax under section 501(a), (or trusts exempt from tax under section 165 of the Internal Revenue Code of 1939 or the corresponding provisions of prior revenue laws);

(2) entered into under plans which (as of the time the contracts were entered into) were deemed to be plans described in section 403(a), or plans meeting the requirements of paragraphs (3), (4), (5), and (6) of section 165(a) of the Internal Revenue Code of 1939;

(3) provided for employees of the life insurance company under a plan which, for the taxable year, meets the requirements of paragraphs (3), (4), (5), (6), (7), (8), (11), (12), (13), (14), (15), (16), *(17)*, (19), (20), (22), **(26)*, and (27) of section 401(a);

(4) purchased to provide retirement annuities for its employees by an organization which (as of the time the contracts were purchased) was an organization described in section 501(c)(3) which was exempt from tax under section 501(a) (or was an organization exempt from tax under section 101(6) of the Internal Revenue Code of 1939 or the corresponding provisions of prior revenue laws), or purchased to provide retirement annuities for employees described in section 403(b)(1)(A)(ii) by an employer which is a State, a political subdivision of a State, or an agency or instrumentality of any one or more of the foregoing;

(5) entered into with trusts which (at the time the contracts were entered into) were individual retirement accounts described in section 408(a) or under contracts entered into with individual retirement annuities described in section 408(b); or

(6) purchased by—

(A) a governmental plan (within the meaning of section 414(d)) *or an eligible State deferred compensation plan (within the meaning of section 457(b)),* or

---

【Footnote ¶3088 continued】

(2) "(3) **Special rule for variable life insurance contracts investing in United States obligations.**—In the case of a segregated asset account with respect to variable life insurance contracts, paragraph (1) shall not apply in the case of securities issued by the United States Treasury which are owned by a regulated investment company or by a trust all the beneficial interest in which are held by 1 or more segregated asset accounts of the company issuing the contract.

(4) **Independent investment advisors permitted.**—Nothing in this subsection shall be construed as prohibiting the use of independent investment advisors."

Effective date (Sec. 1881, '86 TRA and Sec. 215 '84 TRA).—Applies to taxable years beginning after 12-31-83. For special and transitional rules, see footnote ¶3081.

【Footnote ¶3089】 "*(17)*" in *italics* in Sec. 818(a)(3) added by section 1106(d)(3)(C), '86 TRA.

Effective date (Sec. 1106(i)(5)(A), '86 TRA).—Applies to benefits accruing in years beginning after 12-31-88.

---

* Sec. 1112(d)(4), '86 TRA, amended Sec. 818(a)(3) by striking out "and (22)" inserting in lieu thereof "(22), and (26)".

Effective date (Sec. 1112(e), '86 TRA).—(1) Generally applies to plan years beginning after 12-31-88. For special rules, see footnote ¶2994.

---

* Sec. 1136(b), '86 TRA, further amended Sec. 818(a)(3) by striking out "and (26)" and inserting in lieu thereof "(26), and (27)".

(B) the Government of the United States, the government of any State or political subdivision thereof, or by any agency or instrumentality of the foregoing, for use in satisfying an obligation of such government, political subdivision, or agency or instrumentality to provide a benefit under a plan described in subparagraph (A).

* * * * * * * * * * *

[1](e) *Special Rules for Consolidated Returns.*—

(1) *Items of companies other than life insurance companies.*—*If an election under section 1504(c)(2) is in effect with respect to an affiliated group for the taxable year, all items of the members of such group which are life insurance companies shall not be taken into account in determining the amount of the tentative LICTI of members of such group which are life insurance companies.*

(2) *Dividends within group.*—*In the case of a life insurance company filing or required to file a consolidated return under section 1501 with respect to any affiliated group for any taxable year, any determination under this part with respect to any dividend paid by one member of such group to another member of such group shall be made as if such group was not filing a consolidated return.*

* * * * * * * * * * *

[¶3090] CODE SEC. 821. TAX ON MUTUAL INSURANCE COMPANIES TO WHICH PART II APPLIES. [Repealed by section 1024(a)(1), '86 TRA].[1]

[For official explanation, see Committee Reports, ¶3964.]

[¶3091] CODE SEC. 823. DETERMINATION OF STATUTORY UNDERWRITING INCOME OR LOSS. [Repealed by section 1024(a)(1), '86 TRA].[1]

[For official explanation, see Committee Reports, ¶3964.]

[¶3092] CODE SEC. 824. ADJUSTMENTS TO PROVIDE PROTECTION AGAINST LOSSES. [Repealed by section 1024(a)(1), '86 TRA].[1]

[For official explanation, see Committee Reports, ¶3964.]

[¶3093] CODE SEC. 825. UNUSED LOSS DEDUCTION. [Repealed by section 1024(a)(1), '86 TRA].[1]

[For official explanation, see Committee Reports, ¶3964.]

[¶3095] CODE SEC. 831. TAX ON INSURANCE COMPANIES [1]*OTHER THAN LIFE INSURANCE COMPANIES.*

[Footnote ¶3089 continued]

Matter in *italics* in Sec. 818(a)(6)(A) and (e) added by section 1821(n) and (o), '86 TRA, which struck out:

(1) "**(e) Special Rule for Consolidated Returns.**—If an election under section 1504(c)(2) is in effect with respect to an affiliated group for the taxable year, all items of the members of such group which are not life insurance companies shall not be taken into account in determining the amount of the tentative LICTI of members of such group which are life insurance companies."

Effective date (Sec. 1881, '86 TRA and section 215, '84 TRA).—Generally applies to taxable years beginning after 12-31-83. For Transitional Rules, see footnote ¶3081.

[Footnote ¶3090] (1) **Effective date** (Sec. 1024(e), '86 TRA).—Generally applies to taxable years beginning after 12-31-86. For transitional rules, see footnote ¶3093.

[Footnote ¶3091] (1) **Effective date** (Sec. 1024(e), '86 TRA).—Generally applies to taxable years beginning after 12-31-86. For transitional rules, see footnote ¶3093.

[Footnote ¶3092] (1) **Effective date** (Sec. 1024(e) and (d)(1), '86 TRA).—(e) Generally applies to taxable years beginning after 12-31-86.

(d) Transitional Rules.—

(1) Treatment of amounts in protection against loss account.—In the case of any insurance company which had a protection against loss account for its last taxable year beginning before 1-1-87, there shall be included in the gross income of such company for any taxable year beginning after 12-31-86, the amount which would have been included in gross income for such taxable year under section 824 of the '54 Code (as in effect on the day before the date of the enactment of this Act). For purposes of the preceding sentence, no addition to such account shall be made for any taxable year beginning after 12-31-86.

[Footnote ¶3093] (1) **Effective date** (Sec. 1024(e) and (d)(2), '86 TRA).—(e) Generally applies to taxable years beginning after 12-31-86.

(d) Transitional Rules.—

* * * * * * * * * * * *

(2) Transitional rule for unused loss carryover under section 825.—Any unused loss carryover under section 825 of the '54 Code (as in effect on the day before the date of the enactment of this Act) which—

(A) is from a taxable year beginning before 1-1-87, and

(B) could have been carried under such section to a taxable year beginning after 12-31-86, but for the repeal made by subsection (a)(1),

shall be included in the net operating loss deduction under section 832(c)(10) of such Code without regard to the limitations of section 844(b) of such Code.

[Footnote ¶3095] Matter in *italics* in Sec. 831 added by section 1024(a)(4), '86 TRA, which struck out:

(1) "**(OTHER THAN LIFE OR MUTUAL), MUTUAL MARINE INSURANCE COMPANIES, AND CER-**

(a) **General Rule.**—*Taxes computed as provided in section 11 shall be imposed for each taxable year on the taxable income of every insurance company other than a life insurance company.*

(b) **Alternative Tax for Certain Small Companies.**—

(1) **In general.**—*In lieu of the tax otherwise applicable under subsection (a), there is hereby imposed for each taxable year on the income of every insurance company to which this subsection applies a tax computed by multiplying the taxable investment income of such company for such taxable year by the rates provided in section 11(b).*

(2) **Companies to which this subsection applies.**—

(A) **In general.**—*This subsection shall apply to every insurance company other than life (including interinsurers and reciprocal underwriters) if—*

(i) *the net written premiums (or, if greater, direct written premiums) for the taxable year exceed $350,000 but do not exceed $1,200,000, and*

(ii) *such company elects the application of this subsection for such taxable year.*

(B) **Controlled group rules.**—

(i) **In general.**—*For purposes of subparagraph (A), in determining whether any company is described in clause (i) of subparagraph (A), such company shall be treated as receiving during the taxable year amounts described in such clause (i) which are received during such year by all other companies which are members of the same controlled group as the insurance company for which the determination is being made.*

(ii) **Controlled group**—*For purposes of clause (i), the term "controlled group" means any controlled group of corporations (as defined in section 1563(a)); except that—*

(I) *"more than 50 percent" shall be substituted for "at least 80 percent" each place it appears in section 1563(a), and*

(II) *subsections (a)(4) and (b)(2)(D) of section 1563 shall not apply.*

(c) **Cross References.**—

(1) *For alternative tax in case of capital gains, see section 1201(a).*

(2) *For taxation of foreign corporations carrying on an insurance business within the United States, see section 842.*

(3) *For exemption from tax for certain insurance companies other than life, see section 501(c)(15).*

[For official explanation, see Committee Reports, ¶3964.]

⟦Footnote ¶3095 continued⟧

TAIN MUTUAL FIRE OR FLOOD INSURANCE COMPANIES.

(a) Imposition of Tax.—Taxes computed as provided in section 11 shall be imposed for each taxable year on the taxable income of—

(1) every insurance company (other than a life or mutual insurance company),

(2) every mutual marine insurance company, and

(3) every mutual fire or flood insurance company—

(A) exclusive issuing perpetual policies, or

(B) whose principal business is the issuance of policies for which the premium deposits are the same, regardless of the length of the term for which the policies are written, if the unabsorbed portion of such premium deposits not required for losses, expenses, or establishment of reserves is returned or credited to the policyholder on cancellation or expiration of the policy.

(b) Election for Multiple Line Company To Be Taxed on Total Income.—

(1) In general.—Any mutual insurance company engaged in writing marine, fire, and casualty insurance which for any 5-year period beginning after December 31, 1941, and ending before January 1, 1962, was subject to the tax imposed by section 831 (or the tax imposed by corresponding provisions of prior law) may elect, in such manner and at such time as the Secretary may by regulations prescribe, to be subject to the tax imposed by section 831, whether or not marine insurance is its predominant source of premium income.

(2) Effect of election.—If an election is made under paragraph (1), the electing company shall (in lieu of being subject to the tax imposed by section 821) be subject to the tax imposed by this section for taxable years beginning after December 31, 1961. Such election shall not be revoked except with the consent of the Secretary.

(c) Cross References

(1) For alternative tax in case of capital gains, see section 1201(a).

(2) For taxation of foreign corporations carrying on an insurance business within the United States, see section 842."

Effective date (Sec. 1024(e), '86 TRA).—Applies to taxable years beginning after 12-31-86.

〔¶3096〕 CODE SEC. 832.   INSURANCE COMPANY TAXABLE INCOME.

(a) **Definition of Taxable Income.**—In the case of an insurance company subject to the tax imposed by section 831, the term "taxable income" means the gross income as defined in subsection (b)(1) less the deductions allowed by subsection (c).

(b) **Definitions.**—In the case of an insurance company subject to the tax imposed by section 831—

(1) **Gross income.**—The term "gross income" means the sum of—

(A) the combined gross amount earned during the taxable year, from investment income and from underwriting income as provided in this subsection, computed on the basis of the underwriting and investment exhibit of the annual statement approved by the National Association of Insurance Commissioners.

(B) gain during the taxable year from the sale or other disposition of property,

(C) all other items constituting gross income under subchapter B, except that, in the case of a mutual fire insurance company [1]*exclusively issuing perpetual policies* the amount of single deposit premiums paid to such company shall not be included in gross income,

(D) in the case of a mutual fire or flood insurance company [2]*whose principal business is the issuance of policies—*

(i) *for which the premium deposits are the same (regardless of the length of the term for which the policies are written), and*

(ii) *under which the unabsorbed portion of such premium deposits not required for losses, expenses, or establishment of reserves is returned or credited to the policyholder on cancellation or expiration of the policy,*

an amount equal to 2 percent of the premiums earned on insurance contracts during the taxable year with respect to such policies after deduction of premium deposits returned or credited during the same taxable year, and

(E) in the case of a company which writes mortgage guaranty insurance, the amount required by subsection (e)(5) to be subtracted from the mortgage guaranty account.

* * * * * * * * * * * * *

(4) **Premiums earned.**—The term "premiums earned on insurance contracts during the taxable year" means an amount computed as follows:

(A) From the amount of gross premiums written on insurance contracts during the taxable year, deduct return premiums and premiums paid for reinsurance.

(B) [3]*To the result so obtained, add 80 percent of the unearned premiums on*

〔Footnote ¶3096〕 Matter in *italics* in Sec. 832(b)(1)(C) and (D) added by section 1024(c)(1) and (2), '86 TRA, which struck out:

(1) "described in section 831(a)(3)(A),"

(2) "described in section 831(a)(3)(B), an amount equal to 2 percent of the premiums earned on insurance contracts during the taxable year with respect to policies described in section 831(a)(3)(B) after deduction of premium deposits returned or credited during the same taxable year, and"

Effective date (Sec. 1024(e), (d), '86 TRA).—Generally applies to taxable years beginning after 12-31-86.

(d) Transitional Rules.—

(1) Treatment of amounts in protection against loss account.—In the case of any insurance company which had a protection against loss account for its last taxable year beginning before 1-1-87, there shall be included in the gross income of such company for any taxable year beginning after 12-31-86, the amount which would have been included in gross income for such taxable year under Sec. 824 of the '54 Code (as in effect on the day before the date of the enactment of this Act). For purposes of the preceding sentence, no addition to such account shall be made for any taxable year beginning after 12-31-86.

(2) Transitional rule for unused loss carryover under section 825.—Any unused loss carryover under Sec. 825 of the '54 Code (as in effect on the day before the date of the enactment of this Act) which—

(A) is from a taxable year beginning before 1-1-87, and

(B) could have been carried under such section to a taxable year beginning after 12-31-86 but for the repeal made by subsection (a)(1),

shall be included in the net operating loss deduction under Sec. 832(c)(10) of such Code without regard to the limitations of Sec. 844(b) of such Code.

Matter in *italics* in Sec. 832(b)(4)(B) and (C) added by section 1021(a), '86 TRA, which struck out:

(3) "To the result so obtained, add unearned premiums on outstanding business at the end of the preceding taxable year and deduct unearned premiums on outstanding business at the end of the taxable year."

Effective date (Sec. 1021(c), '86 TRA).—(1) **Generally** applies to taxable year beginning after 12-31-86.

(2) Special transitional rule for title insurance companies.—For the 1st taxable year beginning after 12-31-86, in the case of premiums attributable to title insurance—

(A) In general.—The unearned premiums at the end of the preceding taxable year as defined in paragraph (4) of section 832(b) shall be determined as if the amendments made by this section had applied to such unearned premiums in the preceding taxable year and by using the interest rate and premium recognition pattern applicable to years ending in calendar year 1987.

outstanding business at the end of the preceding taxable year and deduct 80 percent of the unearned premiums on outstanding business at the end of the taxable year.

(C) To the result so obtained, in the case of a taxable year beginning after December 31, 1986, and before January 1, 1993, add an amount equal to 3⅓ percent of unearned premiums on outstanding business at the end of the most recent taxable year beginning before January 1, 1987.

For purposes of this subsection, unearned premiums shall include life insurance reserves, as defined in section 816(b) but determined as provided in section 807, pertaining to the life, burial, or funeral insurance, or annuity business of an insurance company subject to the tax imposed by section 831 and not qualifying as a life insurance company under section 816. For purposes of this subsection, unearned premiums of mutual fire or flood insurance companies described in [4]*paragraph (1)(D)* means (with respect to the policies described in [4]*paragraph (1)(D)* the amount of unabsorbed premium deposits which the company would be obligated to return to its policyholders at the close of the taxable year if all of its policies were terminated at such time; and the determination of such amount shall be based on the schedule of unabsorbed premium deposit returns for each such company then in effect. [5]*Premiums paid by the subscriber of a mutual flood insurance company described in paragraph (1)(D) or issuing exclusively perpetual policies shall be treated, for purposes of computing the taxable income of such subscriber, in the same manner as premiums paid by a policyholder to a mutual fire insurance company described in subparagraph (C) or (D) of paragraph (1).*

(5) **Losses incurred.**—[6]

⟦Footnote ¶3096 continued⟧

(B) Fresh start.—Except as provided in subparagraph (C), any difference between—

(i) the amount determined to be unearned premiums for the year preceding the first taxable year of a title insurance company beginning after 12-31-86, determined without regard to subparagraph (A), and

(ii) such amount determined with regard to subparagraph (A),

shall not be taken into account for purposes of the '86 Code.

(C) Effect on earnings and profits.—The earnings and profits of any insurance company for its 1st taxable year beginning after 12-31-86, shall be increased by the amount of the difference determined under subparagraph (A) with respect to such company.

Matter in *italics* in Sec. 832(b)(4) [other than Sec. 832(b)(4)(B) and (C)] added by section 1024(c)(3)(A) and (B), '86 TRA, which struck out:

(4) "831(a)(3)(B)"

(5) "Premiums paid by the subscriber of a mutual flood insurance company referred to in paragraph (3) of section 831(a) shall be treated, for purposes of computing the taxable income of such subscriber, in the same manner as premiums paid by a policyholder to a mutual fire insurance company referred to in such paragraph (3)."

Effective date (Sec. 1024(e), (d) '86 TRA).—Generally applies to taxable years beginning after 12-31-86. For transitional rules, see above.

Sec. 832(b)(5) [other than Sec. 832(b)(5)(A)(ii)] added by section 1022(a), '86 TRA, which struck out:

(6) "The term 'losses incurred' means losses incurred during the taxable year on insurance contracts, computed as follows:

(A) To losses paid during the taxable year, add salvage and reinsurance recoverable outstanding at the end of the preceding taxable year and deduct salvage and reinsurance recoverable outstanding at the end of the taxable year.

(B) To the result so obtained, add all unpaid losses outstanding at the end of the taxable year and deduct unpaid losses outstanding at the end of the preceding taxable year."

Effective date (Sec. 1022(b), '86 TRA).—Applies to taxable years beginning after 12-31-86.

Sec. 832(b)(5)(A)(ii), added by section 1023(a)(1), '86 TRA.

Effective date (Sec. 1023(e), '86 TRA).—(1) Generally applies to taxable years beginning after 12-31-86.

(2) Transitional rule.—For the first taxable year beginning after 12-31-86—

(A)the unpaid losses and the expenses unpaid (as defined in paragraphs (5)(B) and (6) of Sec. 832(b) of the '86 Code at the end of the preceding taxable year, and

(B) the unpaid losses as defined in sections 807(c)(2) and 805(a)(1) of such Code at the end of the preceding taxable year,

shall be determined as if the amendments made by this section had applied to such unpaid losses and expenses unpaid in the preceding taxable year and by using the interest rate and loss payment patterns applicable to accident years ending with calendar year 1987. For subsequent taxable years, such amendments shall be applied with respect to such unpaid losses and expenses unpaid by using the interest rate and loss payment patterns applicable to accident years ending with calendar year 1987.

(3) Fresh start.—

(A) In general.—Except as otherwise provided in this paragraph, any difference between—

(i) the amount determined to be the unpaid losses and expenses unpaid for the year preceding the 1st taxable year of an insurance company beginning after 12-31-86, determined without regard to paragraph (2), and

(A) *In general.—The term "losses incurred" means losses incurred during the taxable year on insurance contracts, computed as follows:*

(i) *To losses paid during the taxable year, added salvage and reinsurance recoverable outstanding at the end of the preceding taxable year and deduct salvage and reinsurance recoverable outstanding at the end of the taxable year.*

"(ii) *To the result so obtained, add all unpaid losses on life insurance contracts plus all discounted unpaid losses (as defined in section 846) outstanding at the end of the taxable year and deduct unpaid losses on life insurance contracts plus all discounted unpaid losses outstanding at the end of the preceding taxable year."*

(B) *Reduction of deduction.—The amount which would (but for this subparagraph) be taken into account under subparagraph (A) shall be reduced by an amount equal to 15 percent of the sum of—*

(i) *tax-exempt interest received or accrued during such taxable year, and*

(ii) *the aggregate amount of deductions provided by sections 243, 244, and 245 for—*

(I) *dividends (other than 100 percent dividends) received during the taxable year, and*

(II) *100 percent dividends received during the taxable year to the extent attributable to prorated amounts.*

In the case of a 100 percent dividend paid by an insurance company, the portion attributable to prorated amounts shall be determined under subparagraph (E)(ii).

(C) *Exception for investments made before August 8, 1986.—*

(i) *In general.—Except as provided in clause (ii), subparagraph (B) shall not apply to any dividend or interest received or accrued on any stock or obligation acquired before August 8, 1986.*

(ii) *Special rule for 100 percent dividends.—For purposes of clause (i), the portion of any 100 percent dividend which is attributable to prorated amounts shall be treated as received with respect to stock acquired on the later of—*

(I) *the date the payor acquired the stock or obligation to which the prorated amounts are attributable, or*

(II) *the 1st day on which the payor and payee were members of the same affiliated group (as defined in section 243(b)(5)).*

(D) *Definitions.—For purposes of this paragraph—*

(i) *Prorated amounts.—The term "prorated amounts" means tax-exempt interest and dividends with respect to which a deduction is allowable under section 243, 244, or 245 (other than 100 percent dividends).*

(ii) *100 percent dividend.—*

(I) *In general.—The term "100 percent dividend" means any dividend if the percentage used for purposes of determining the deduction allowable under section 243, 244, or 245(b) is 100 percent.*

(II) *Certain dividends received by foreign corporations.—A dividend received by a foreign corporation from a domestic corporation which would be a 100 percent dividend if section 1504(b)(3) did not apply for purposes of applying section 243(b)(5) shall be treated as a 100 percent dividend.*

(E) *Special rules for dividends subject to proration at subsidiary level.—*

(i) *In general.—In the case of any 100 percent dividend paid to an insurance company to which this part applies by an insurance company, the amount of the decrease in the deductions of the payee company by reason of the portion of such dividend attributable to prorated amounts shall be reduced (but not below zero) by the amount of the decrease in the deductions (or increase in income) of the payor company attributable to the application of this section or section 805(a)(4)(A) to such amounts.*

【**Footnote ¶3096 continued**】

(ii) such amount determined with regard to paragraph (2),

shall not be taken into account for purposes of the '86 Code.

(B) Reserve strengthening in years after 1985.—Subparagraph (A) shall not apply to any reserve strengthening in a taxable year beginning in 1986, and such strengthening shall be treated as occurring in the taxpayer's 1st taxable year beginning after 12-31-86.

(C) Effect on earnings and profits.—The earnings and profits of any insurance company for its 1st taxable year beginning after 12-31-86, shall be increased by the amount of the difference determined under subparagraph (A) with respect to such company.

(ii) *Portion of dividend attributable to prorated amounts.—For purposes of this subparagraph, in determining the portion of any dividend attributable to prorated amounts—*

(I) *any dividend by the paying corporation shall be treated as paid first out of earnings and profits attributable to prorated amounts (to the extent thereof), and*

(II) *by determining the portion of earnings and profits so attributable without any reduction for the tax imposed by this chapter.*

(6) Expenses incurred.—The term "expenses incurred" means all expenses shown on the annual statement approved by the National Association of Insurance Commissioners, and shall be computed as follows: To all expenses paid during the taxable year, add expenses unpaid at the end of the taxable year and deduct expenses unpaid at the end of the preceding taxable year. *For purposes of this subchapter, the term "expenses unpaid" shall not include any unpaid loss adjustment expenses shown on the annual statement, but such unpaid loss adjustment expenses shall be included in unpaid losses.* For the purpose of computing the taxable income subject to the tax imposed by section 831, there shall be deducted from expenses incurred (as defined in this paragraph) all expenses incurred which are not allowed as deductions by subsection (c).

(7) *Special rules for applying paragraph (4).—*

(A) *Reduction not to apply to life insurance reserves.—Subparagraph (B) of paragraph (4) shall be applied with respect to amounts included in unearned premiums under the 2nd sentence of such paragraph by substituting "100 percent" for "80 percent" each place it appears in such subparagraph (B), and subparagraph (C) of paragraph (4) shall be applied by not taking such amounts into account.*

(B) *Special treatment of premiums attributable to insuring certain securities.—In the case of premiums attributable to insurance against default in the payment of principal or interest on securities described in section 165(g)(2)(C) with maturities of more than 5 years—*

(i) *subparagraph (B) of paragraph (4) shall be applied by substituting "90 percent" for "80 percent" each place it appears, and*

(ii) *subparagraph (C) of paragraph (4) shall be applied by substituting "1⅔ percent" for "3⅓ percent".*

(C) *Termination as nonlife insurance company.—Except as provided in section 381(c)(22) (relating to carryovers in certain corporate readjustments), if, for any taxable year beginning before January 1, 1993, the taxpayer ceases to be an insurance company taxable under this part, the aggregate adjustments which would be made under paragraph (4)(C) for such taxable year and subsequent taxable years but for such cessation shall be made for the taxable year preceding such cessation year.*

(8) *Special rules for applying paragraph (4) to title insurance premiums.—*

(A) *In general.—In the case of premiums attributable to title insurance—*

(i) *subparagraph (B) of paragraph (4) shall be applied by substituting "the discounted unearned premiums" for "80 percent of the unearned premiums" each place it appears, and*

(ii) *subparagraph (C) of paragraph (4) shall not apply.*

(B) *Method of discounting.—For purposes subparagraph (A), the amount of the discounted unearned premiums as of the end of any taxable year shall be the present value of such premiums (as of such time and separately with respect to premiums received in each calendar year) determined by using—*

(i) *the amount of the undiscounted unearned premiums at such time,*

(ii) *the applicable interest rate, and*

(iii) *the applicable statutory premium recognition pattern.*

(C) *Determination of applicable factors.—In determining the amount of the discounted unearned premiums as of the end of any taxable year—*

[Footnote ¶3096 continued]

Matter in *italics* in Sec. 832(b)(6) added by section 1023(a)(2), '86 TRA.
Effective date (Sec. 1023(e), '86 TRA.—Generally applies to taxable years beginning after 12-31-86. For transitional rules, see above.

Sec. 832(b)(7) and (8) in *italics* added by section 1021(b), '86 TRA.
Effective date (Sec. 1021(c), '86 TRA.—Generally applies to taxable years beginning after 12-31-86. For special transitional rule, see above.

    (i) Undiscounted unearned premiums.—The term "undiscounted unearned premiums" means the unearned premiums shown in the yearly statement filed by the taxpayer for the year ending with or within such taxable year.

    (ii) Applicable interest rate.—The term "applicable interest rate" means the annual rate determined under 846(c)(2) for the calendar year in which the premiums are received.

    (iii) Applicable statutory premium recognition pattern.—The term "applicable statutory premium recognition pattern" means the statutory premium recognition pattern—

        (I) which is in effect for the calendar year in which the premiums are received, and

        (II) which is based on the statutory premium recognition pattern which applies to premiums received by the taxpayer in such calendar year.

    For purposes of the preceding sentence, premiums received during any calendar year shall be treated as received in the middle of such year.

  (c) Deductions Allowed.—In computing the taxable income of an insurance company subject to the tax imposed by section 831, there shall be allowed as deductions:

    (1) all ordinary and necessary expenses incurred, as provided in section 162 (relating to trade or business expenses);

    (2) all interest, as provided in section 163;

    (3) taxes, as provided in section 164;

    (4) losses incurred, as defined in subsection (b)(5) of this section;

    (5) capital losses to the extent provided in subchapter P (sec. 1201 and following, relating to capital gains and losses) plus losses from capital assets sold or exchanged in order to obtain funds to meet abnormal insurance losses and to provide for the payment of dividends and similar distributions to policyholders. Capital assets shall be considered as sold or exchanged in order to obtain funds to meet abnormal insurance losses and to provide for the payment of dividends and similar distributions to policyholders to the extent that the gross receipts from their sale or exchange are not greater than the excess, if any, for the taxable year of the sum of dividends and similar distributions paid to policyholders in their capacity as such, losses paid, and expenses paid over the sum of the items described in Section [7]*834(b)* (other than paragraph (1)(D) thereof) and net premiums received. In the application of section 1212 for purposes of this section, the net capital loss for the taxable year shall be the amount by which losses for such year from sales or exchanges of capital assets exceeds the sum of the gains from such sales or exchanges and whichever of the following amounts is the lesser:

        (A) the taxable income (computed without regard to gains or losses from sales or exchanges of capital assets); or

        (B) losses from the sale or exchange of capital assets sold or exchanged to obtain funds to meet abnormal insurance losses and to provide for the payment of dividends and similar distributions to policyholders;

    (6) debts in the nature of agency balances and bills receivable which become worthless within the taxable year;

    (7) the amount of interest earned during the taxable year which under section 103 is excluded from gross income;

    (8) the depreciation deduction allowed by section 167 and the deduction allowed by section 611 (relating to depletion);

    (9) charitable, etc., contributions, as provided in section 170;

    (10) deductions (other than those specified in this subsection) as provided in part VI of subchapter B (sec. 161 and following, relating to itemized deductions for individuals and corporations and in part I of subchapter D sec. 401 and following, relating to pension, profit-sharing, stock bonus plans, etc.);

    (11) dividends and similar distributions paid or declared to policyholders in their capacity, as such, except in the case of a mutual fire insurance company described in [8] *subsection (b)(1)(C).* For purposes of the preceding sentence, the term "dividends and similar distributions" includes amounts returned or credited to policyholders on cancellation or expiration of policies described in [9]*subsection (b)(1)(D).*

[Footnote ¶3096 continued]

  Matter in *italics* in Sec. 832(c)(5), (11) and (f) added by section 1024(c)(4), (5)(A) and (B), and (6) '86 TRA, which struck out:

  (7) "822(b)"

  (8) "section 831(a)(3)(A)"

  (9) "section 831(a)(3)(B)"

  Effective date (Sec. 1024(e), (d) '86 TRA).—Applies to taxable years beginning after 12-31-86. For transitional rules, see above.

For purposes of this paragraph the term "paid or declared" shall be construed according to the method of accounting regularly employed in keeping the books of the insurance company;

(12) the special deductions allowed by part VIII of subchapter B (sec. 241 and following, relating to dividends received); and

(13) in the case of a company which writes mortgage guaranty insurance, the deduction allowed by subsection (e).

* * * * * * * * * * * *

(f) **Interinsurers.**—*In the case of a mutual insurance company which is an interinsurer or reciprocal underwriter*—

(1) there shall be allowed as a deduction the increase for the taxable year in savings credited to subscriber accounts, or

(2) there shall be included as an item of gross income the decrease for the taxable year in savings credited to subscriber accounts.

For purposes of the preceding sentence, the term "savings credited to subscriber accounts" means such portion of the surplus as is credited to the individual accounts of subscribers before the 16th day of the 3rd month following the close of the taxable year, but only if the company would be obligated to pay such amount promptly to such subscriber if he terminated his contract at the close of the company's taxable year. For purposes of determining his taxable income, the subscriber shall treat any such savings credited to his account as a dividend paid or declared.

[For official explanation, see Committee Reports, ¶3961; 3962; 3963; 3964.]

[¶3097] **CODE SEC. 833. TREATMENT OF BLUE CROSS AND BLUE SHIELD ORGANIZATIONS, ETC.**

(a) **General Rule.**—In the case of any organization to which this section applies—

(1) **Treated as stock company.**—Such organization shall be taxable under this part in the same manner as if it were a stock insurance company.

(2) **Special deduction allowed.**—The deduction determined under subsection (b) for any taxable year shall be allowed.

(3) **Reductions in unearned premium reserves not to apply.**—Subparagraph (B) of paragraph (4) of section 832(b) shall be applied by substituting "100 percent" for "80 percent", and subparagraph (C) of such paragraph (4) shall not apply.

(b) **Amount of Deduction.**—

(1) **In general.**—Except as provided in paragraph (2), the deduction determined under this subsection for any taxable year is the excess (if any) of—

(A) 25 percent of the sum of—

(i) the claims incurred during the taxable year, and

(ii) the expenses incurred during the taxable year in connection with the administration, adjustment, or settlement of claims, over

(B) the adjusted surplus as of the beginning of the taxable year.

(2) **Limitation.**—The deduction determined under paragraph (1) for any taxable year shall not exceed taxable income for such taxable year (determined without regard to such deduction).

(3) **Adjusted surplus.**—For purposes of this subsection—

(A) In general.—The adjusted surplus as of the beginning of any taxable year is an amount equal to the adjusted surplus as of the beginning of the preceding taxable year—

(i) increased by the amount of any adjusted taxable income for such preceding taxable year, or

---

[Footnote ¶3097]   Sec. 833 added by section 1012(b)(1), '86 TRA.

Effective date (Sec. 1012(c), '86 TRA).—(1) Generally applies to taxable years beginning after 12-31-86.

* * * * * * * * * * *

(3) Special rules for existing Blue Cross or Blue Shield Organizations.—

(A) In general.—In the case of any existing Blue Cross or Blue Shield organization (as defined in section 833(c)(2) of the '86 Code as added by this section)—

(i) no adjustment shall be made under section 481 (or any other provision) of such Code on account of a change in its method of accounting for its 1st taxable year beginning after 12-31-86, and

(ii) for purposes of determining gain or loss, the adjusted basis of any asset held on the 1st day of such taxable year shall be treated as equal to its fair market value as of such day. For other special rules, see footnote ¶3031.

* * * * * * * * * * *

(ii) decreased by the amount of any adjusted net operating loss for such preceding taxable year.

(B) Special rule.—The adjusted surplus as of the beginning of the organization's 1st taxable year beginning after December 31, 1986, shall be its surplus as of such time. For purposes of the preceding sentence and subsection (c)(3)(C), the term "surplus" means the excess of the total assets over total liabilities as shown on the annual statement

(C) Adjusted taxable income.—The term "adjusted taxable income" means taxable income determined—

(i) without regard to the deduction determined under this subsection,

(ii) without regard to any carryforward or carryback to such taxable year, and

(iii) by increasing gross income by an amount equal to the net exempt income for the taxable year.

(D) Adjusted net operating loss.—The term "adjusted net operating loss" means the net operating loss for any taxable year determined with the adjustments set forth in subparagraph (C).

(E) Net exempt income.—The term "net exempt income" means—

(i) any tax-exempt interest received or accrued during the taxable year, reduced by any amount (not otherwise deductible) which would have been allowable as a deduction for the taxable year if such interest were not tax-exempt, and

(ii) the aggregate amount allowed as a deduction for the taxable year under sections 243, 244, and 245.

The amount determined under clause (ii) shall be reduced by the amount of any decrease in deductions allowable for the taxable year by reason of section 832(b)(5)(B) to the extent such decrease is attributable to deductions under sections 243, 244, and 245.

(4) Only health-related items taken into account.—Any determination under this subsection shall be made by only taking into account items attributable to the health-related business of the taxpayer.

(c) Organizations To Which Section Applies.—

(1) In general.—This section shall apply to—

(A) any existing Blue Cross or Blue Shield organization, and

(B) any other organization meeting the requirements of paragraph (3).

(2) Existing Blue Cross or Blue Shield organization.—The term "existing Blue Cross or Blue Shield organization" means any Blue Cross or Blue Shield organization if—

(A) such organization was in existence on August 16, 1986,

(B) such organization is determined to be exempt from tax for its last taxable year beginning before January 1, 1987, and

(C) no material change has occurred in the operations of such organization or in its structure after August 16, 1986, and before the close of the taxable year.

To the extent permitted by the Secretary, any successor to an organization meeting the requirements of the preceding sentence, and any organization resulting from the merger or consolidation of organizations each of which met such requirements, shall be treated as an existing Blue Cross or Blue Shield organization.

(3) Other organizations.—

(A) In general.—An organization meets the requirements of this paragraph for any taxable year if—

(i) substantially all the activities of such organization involve the providing of health insurance,

(ii) at least 10 percent of the health insurance provided by such organization is provided to individuals and small groups (not taking into account any medicare supplemental coverage),

(iii) such organization provides continuous full-year open enrollment (including conversions) for individuals and small groups,

(iv) such organization's policies covering individuals provide full coverage of pre-existing conditions of high-risk individuals without a price differential (with a reasonable waiting period), and coverage is provided without regard to age, income, or employment status of individuals under age 65,

(v) at least 35 percent of its premiums are determined on a community rated basis, and

(vi) no part of its net earnings inures to the benefit of any private shareholder or individual.

(B) Small group defined.—For purposes of subparagraph (A), the term "small group" means the lesser of—

(i) 15 individuals, or

(ii) the number of individuals required for a small group under applicable State law.

(C) Special rule for determining adjusted surplus.—For purposes of subsection (b), the adjusted surplus of any organization meeting the requirements of this paragraph as of the beginning of the 1st taxable year for which it meets such requirements shall be its surplus as of such time.

[For official explanation, see Committee Reports, ¶3959.]

【¶3098】 CODE SEC. [1]*834.* DETERMINATION OF TAXABLE INVESTMENT INCOME.

(a) [2]*General Rule.—For purposes of section 831(b), the term "taxable investment income" means the gross investment income, minus the deductions provided in subsection (c).*

* * * * * * * * * * * *

(d) **Other Applicable Rules.—**

(1) **Rental value of real estate.**—The deduction under subsection (c)(3) or (4) on account of any real estate owned and occupied in whole or in part by a mutual insurance company subject to the tax imposed by section [3]*831* shall be limited to an amount which bears the same ratio to such deduction (computed without regard to this paragraph) as the rental value of the space not so occupied bears to the rental value of the entire property.

(2) **Amortization of premium and accrual of discount.**—The gross amount of income during the taxable year from interest and the deduction provided in subsection (c)(1) shall each be decreased to reflect the appropriate amortization of premium and increased to reflect the appropriate accrual of discount attributable to the taxable year on bonds, notes, debentures, or other evidences of indebtedness held by a mutual insurance company subject to the tax imposed by section [3]*831.* Such amortization and accrual shall be determined—

(A) in accordance with the method regularly employed by such company, if such method is reasonable, and

(B) in all other cases, in accordance with regulations prescribed by the Secretary.

No accrual of discount shall be required under this paragraph on any bond (as defined in section 171(d)), *except in the case of discount which is original issue discount (as defined in section 1273).*

(3) **Double deductions.**—*Nothing in this part shall permit the same item to be deducted more than once.*

* * * * * * * * * * * *

[For official explanation, see Committee Reports, ¶3964.]

【¶3099】 CODE SEC. [1]*835.* ELECTION BY RECIPROCAL.

【Footnote ¶3098】 Matter in *italics* in Sec. 834(a) and (d) added by section 1024(a)(3) and (c)(7) and (8), '86 TRA, which struck out:

(1) "822"

(2) "Definitions.—For purposes of this part—

(1) The term taxable investment income means the gross investment income, minus the deductions provided in subsection (c).

(2) The term "investment loss" means the amount by which the deductions provided in subsection (c) exceed the gross investment income."

(3) "821"

Effective date (Sec. 1024(e), '86 TRA).—Generally applies to taxable years beginning after 12-31-86. For transitional rules, see footnote ¶3102.

【Footnote ¶3099】 Matter in *italics* in title of Sec. 835 (former 826) added by section 1024(a)(3), 86 TRA, which struck out:

(1) "826"

Effective date (Sec. 1024(e), '86 TRA).—Generally applies to taxable years beginning after 12-31-86. For special rules, see footnote ¶3081.

* * * * * * * * * * * *

(c) **Exception.**—An election may not be made by a reciprocal under subsection (a) unless the attorney-in-fact of such reciprocal—

* * * * * * * * * * * *

(4) files its return on the calendar year basis.[2]

[3]*(d)* **Credit.**—Any reciprocal electing to be subject to the limitation provided in subsection (b) shall be credited with so much of the tax paid by the attorney-in-fact as is attributable, under regulations prescribed by the Secretary, to the income received by the attorney-in-fact from the reciprocal in such taxable year.

[4]*(e)* [5]*Benefits of Graduated Rates Denied.—Any increase in the taxable income of a reciprocal attributable to the limits provided in subsection (b) shall be taxed at the highest rate of tax specified in section 11(b).*

[6]*(f)* **Adjustment for Refund.**—If for any taxable year an attorney-in-fact is allowed a credit for refund for taxes paid with respect to which credit or refund to the reciprocal resulted under subsection (e), the taxes of such reciprocal for such taxable year shall be properly adjusted under regulations prescribed by the Secretary.

[7]*(g)* **Taxes of Attorney-in-Fact Unaffected.**—Nothing in this section shall increase or decrease the taxes imposed by this chapter on the income of the attorney-in-fact.

[For official explanation, see Committee Reports, ¶3964.]

[¶3100] CODE SEC. 841. CREDIT FOR FOREIGN TAXES.

The taxes imposed by foreign countries or possessions of the United States shall be allowed as a credit against the tax of a domestic insurance company subject to the tax imposed by section 801 [1] or 831, to the extent provided in the case of a domestic corporation in section 901 (relating to foreign tax credit). For purposes of the preceding sentence (and for purposes of applying section 906 with respect to a foreign corporation subject to tax under this subchapter), the term "taxable income" as used in section 904 means

(1) in the case of the tax imposed by section 801, the life insurance company taxable income (as defined in section 801(b)), and [2]

[3]*(2)* in the case of the tax imposed by section 831, the taxable income (as defined in section 832(a)).

[For official explanation, see Committee Reports, ¶3964.]

[¶3101] CODE SEC. 842. FOREIGN CORPORATIONS CARRYING ON INSURANCE BUSINESS.

If a foreign corporation carrying on an insurance business within the United States would qualify under part I [1]*or II* of this subchapter for the taxable year if (without regard to income not effectively connected with the conduct of any trade or business within

---

[Footnote ¶3099 continued]

Matter in *italics* in Sec. 835(d)—(g) (former 826) added by section 1024(c)(9), '86 TRA, which struck out:

(2) "**(d) Special Rule.**—In applying section 824(d)(1)(D), any amount which was added to the protection against loss account by reason of an election under this section shall be treated as having been added by reason of section 824(a)(1)(A)."

(3) "(e)"

(4) "(f)"

(5) "**Surtax Exemption Denied.**—Any increase in taxable income of a reciprocal attributable to the limitation provided in subsection (b) shall be taxed without regard to the surtax exemption provided in section 821(a)(2)."

(6) "(g)"

(7) "subsection (e)"

Effective date (Sec. 1024(e), '86 TRA).—Generally applies to taxable years beginning after 12-31-86. For transitional rules, see ¶3102.

[Footnote ¶3100] Matter in *italics* in Sec. 841 added by section 1024(c)(10), '86 TRA, which struck out:

(1) ", 821,"

(2) "(2) in the case of the tax imposed by section 821(a), the mutual insurance company taxable income (as defined in section 821(b)); and in the case of the tax imposed by section 821(c), the taxable investment income (as defined in section 822(a)), and"

(3) "(3)"

Effective date (Sec. 1024(e), '86 TRA).—Generally applies to taxable years beginning after 12-31-86. For transitional rules, see footnote ¶3102.

[Footnote ¶3101] Matter in *italics* in Sec. 842 added by section 1024(c)(11), '86 TRA, which struck out:

(1) ", II, or III"

Effective date (Sec. 1024(e), '86 TRA).—Generally applies to taxable years beginning after 12-31-86. For transitional rules, see footnote ¶3102.

the United States) it were a domestic corporation, such corporation shall be taxable under such part on its income effectively connected with its conduct of any trade or business within the United States. With respect to the remainder of its income, which is from sources within the United States, such a foreign corporation shall be taxable as provided in section 881.

[For official explanation, see Committee Reports, ¶3964.]

⊏¶3102⊐ CODE SEC. 844. SPECIAL LOSS CARRYOVER RULES.

(a) **General Rule.**—¹*If an insurance company—*

(1) is subject to the tax imposed by part I or II of this subchapter for the taxable year, and

(2) was subject to the tax imposed by a different part of this subchapter for the taxable year,

then any operations loss carryover under section 810 (or the corresponding provisions of prior law), *unused loss* or net operating loss carryover under section 172 (as the case may be) arising in such prior taxable year shall be included in its operations loss deduction under section 810(a) or net operating loss deduction under section 832(c)(10), as the case may be.

(b) **Limitation.**—*The amount included under section 810(a) or 832(c)(10) (as the case may be) by reason of the application of subsection (a) shall not exceed the amount that would have constituted the loss carryover under such section if for all relevant taxable years the company had been subject to the tax imposed by the part referred to in subsection (a)(1) rather than the part referred to in subsection (a)(2). For purposes of applying the preceding sentence, section 810(b)(1)(C) (relating to additional years to which losses may be carried by new life insurance companies) shall not apply.*

* * * * * * * * * * * * * *

[For official explanation, see Committee Reports, ¶3964.]

⊏¶3103⊐ CODE SEC. 846. DISCOUNTED UNPAID LOSSES DEFINED.

(a) **Discounted losses determined.—**

⊏Footnote ¶3102⊐ Matter in *italics* in Sec. 844(a) and (b) added by section 1024(c)(12), '86 TRA, which struck out:

(1) "If an insurance company—

(1) is subject to the tax imposed by part I, II, or III of this subchapter for the taxable year, and

(2) was subject to the tax imposed by a different part of this subchapter for a prior taxable year beginning after December 31, 1962,

then any operations loss carryover under section 810 (or the corresponding provisions of prior law), unused loss carryover under section 825, or net operating loss carryover under section 172, as the case may be, arising in such prior taxable year shall be included in its operations loss deduction under section 810(a), unused loss deduction under section 825(a), or net operating loss deduction under section 832(c)(10), as the case may be.

(b) **Limitation.**—The amount included under section 810(a), 825(a), or 832(c)(10), as the case may be, by reason of the application of subsection (a) shall not exceed the amount that would have constituted the loss carryover under such section if for all relevant taxable years such company had been subject to the tax imposed by the part referred to in subsection (a)(1) rather than the part referred to in subsection (a)(2). For purposes of applying the preceding sentence—

(1) in the case of a mutual insurance company which becomes a stock insurance company, an amount equal to 25 percent of the deduction under section 832(c)(11) (relating to dividends to policyholders) shall not be allowed, and

(2) section 810(b)(1)(C) (relating to additional years to which losses may be carried by new life insurance companies) shall not apply."

Effective date (Sec. 1024(e), (d) '86 TRA).—Applies to taxable years beginning after 12-31-86.

(d) Transitional Rules.—

(1) Treatment of amounts in protection against loss account.—In the case of any insurance company which had a protection against loss account for its last taxable year beginning before 1-1-87, there shall be included in the gross income of such company for any taxable year beginning after 12-31-86, the amount which would have been included in gross income for such taxable year under section 824 of the '54 Code (as in effect on the day before the date of the enactment of this Act). For purposes of the preceding sentence, no addition to such account shall be made for any taxable year beginning after 12-31-86.

(2) Transitional rule for unused loss carryover under section 825.—Any unused loss carryover under section 825 of the '54 Code (as in effect on the day before the date of the enactment of this Act) which—

(A) is from a taxable year beginning before 1-1-87, and

(B) could have been carried under such section to a taxable year beginning after 12-31-86, but for the repeal made by subsection (a)(1),

shall be included in the net operating loss deduction under section 832(c)(10) of such Code without regard to the limitations of section 844(b) of such Code.

The phrase, "unused loss" in *italics* in Sec. 844(a), was added by section 1899(a)(20), '86 TRA.

(1) **Separately computed for each accident year.**—The amount of the discounted unpaid losses as of the end of any taxable year shall be the sum of the discounted unpaid losses (as of such time) separately computed under this section with respect to unpaid losses in each line of business attributable to each accident year.

(2) **Method of discounting.**—The amount of the discounted unpaid losses as of the end of any taxable year attributable to any accident year shall be the present value of such losses (as of such time) determined by using—

(A) the amount of the undiscounted unpaid losses as of such time,

(B) the applicable interest rate, and

(C) the applicable loss payment pattern.

(3) **Limitation on amount of discounted losses.**—In no event shall the amount of the discounted unpaid losses with respect to any line of business attributable to any accident year exceed the aggregate amount of unpaid losses with respect to such line of business for such accident year included on the annual statement filed by the taxpayer for the year ending with or within the taxable year.

(4) **Determination of applicable factors.**—In determining the amount of the discounted unpaid losses attributable to any accident year—

(A) the applicable interest rate shall be the interest rate determined under subsection (c) for the calendar year with which such accident year ends, and

(B) the applicable loss payment pattern shall be the loss payment pattern determined under subsection (d) which is in effect for the calendar year with which such accident year ends.

(b) **Determination of undiscounted unpaid losses.**—For purposes of this section—

(1) **In general.**—Except as otherwise provided in this subsection, the term "undiscounted unpaid losses" means the unpaid losses shown in the annual statement filed by the taxpayer for the year ending with or within the taxable year of the taxpayer.

(2) **Adjustment if losses discounted on annual statement.**—If—

(A) the amount of unpaid losses shown in the annual statement is determined on a discounted basis, and

(B) the extent to which the losses were discounted can be determined on the basis of information disclosed on or with the annual statement,

the amount of the unpaid losses shall be determined without regard to any reduction attributable to such discounting.

(c) **Rate of interest.**—

(1) **In general.**—For purposes of this section, the rate of interest determined under this subsection shall be the annual rate determined by the Secretary under paragraph (2).

(2) **Determination of annual rate.**—

(A) **In general.**—The annual rate determined by the Secretary under this paragraph for any calendar year shall be a rate equal to the average of the applicable Federal mid-term rates (as defined in section 1274(d) but based on annual compounding) effective as of the beginning of each of the calendar months in the test period.

(B) **Test period.**—For purposes of subparagraph (A), the test period is the most recent 60-calendar-month period ending before the beginning of the calendar year for which the determination is made; except that there shall be excluded from the test period any month beginning before August 1, 1986.

(d) **Loss payment pattern.**—

(1) **In general.**—For each determination year, the Secretary shall determine a loss payment pattern for each line of business by reference to the historical loss payment pattern applicable to such line of business. Any loss payment pattern determined by the Secretary shall apply to the accident year ending with the determination year and to each of the 4 succeeding accident years.

(2) **Method of determination.**—Determinations under paragraph (1) for any determination year shall be made by the Secretary—

(A) by using the aggregate experience reported on the annual statements of insurance companies,

(B) on the basis of the most recent published aggregate data from such annual statements relating to loss payment patterns available on the 1st day of the determination year,

(C) as if all losses paid or treated as paid during any year are paid in the middle of such year, and

(D) in accordance with the computational rules prescribed in paragraph (3).

(3) Computational rules.—For purposes of this subsection—

(A) **In general.**—Except as otherwise provided in this paragraph, the loss payment pattern for any line of business shall be based on the assumption that all losses are paid—

(i) during the accident year and the 3 calendar years following the accident year, or

(ii) in the case of any line of business reported in the schedule or schedules of the annual statement relating to auto liability, other liability, medical malpractice, workers' compensation, and multiple peril lines, during the accident year and the 10 calendar years following the accident year.

(B) **Treatment of certain losses.**—Except as otherwise provided in this paragraph—

(i) in the case of any line of business not described in subparagraph (A)(ii), losses paid after the 1st year following the accident year shall be treated as paid equally in the 2nd and 3rd year following the accident year, and

(ii) in the case of a line of business described in subparagraph (A)(ii), losses paid after the close of the period applicable under subparagraph (A)(ii) shall be treated as paid in the last year of such period.

(C) **Special rule for certain long-tail lines.**—In the case of any long-tail line of business—

(i) the period taken into account under subparagraph (A)(ii) shall be extended (but not by more than 5 years) to the extent required under clause (ii), and

(ii) the amount of losses which would have been treated as paid in the 10th year after the accident year shall be treated as paid in such 10th year and each subsequent year in an amount equal to the amount of the losses treated as paid in the 9th year after the accident year (or, if lesser, the portion of the unpaid losses not theretofore taken into account).

Notwithstanding clause (ii), to the extent such unpaid losses have not been treated as paid before the last year of the extension, they shall be treated as paid in such last year.

(D) **Long-tail line of business.**—For purposes of subparagraph (C), the term "long-tail line of business" means any line of business described in subparagraph (A)(ii) if the amount of losses which (without regard to subparagraph (C)) would be treated as paid in the 10th year after the accident year exceeds the losses treated as paid in the 9th year after the accident year.

(E) **Special rule for international and reinsurance lines of business.**—Except as otherwise provided by regulations, any determination under subsection (a) with respect to unpaid losses relating to the international or reinsurance lines of business shall be made using, in lieu of the loss payment pattern applicable to the respective lines of business, a pattern determined by the Secretary under paragraphs (1) and (2) based on the combined losses for all lines of business described in subparagraph (A)(ii).

(F) **Adjustments if loss experience information available for longer periods.**—The Secretary shall make appropriate adjustments in the application of this paragraph if annual statement data with respect to payment of losses is available for longer periods after the accident year than the periods assumed under the rules of this paragraph.

(G) **Special rule for 9th year if negative or zero.**—If the amount of the losses treated as paid in the 9th year after the accident year is zero or a negative amount, subparagraphs (C)(ii) and (D) shall be applied by substituting the average of the losses treated as paid in the 7th, 8th, and 9th years after the accident year for the losses treated as paid in the 9th year after the accident year.

(4) Determination year.—For purposes of this section, the term "determination year" means calendar year 1987 and each 5th calendar year thereafter.

(e) Election to use company's historical payment pattern.—

(1) In general.—The taxpayer may elect to apply subsection (a)(2)(C) with respect to all lines of business by using a loss payment pattern determined by reference to the taxpayer's loss payment pattern for the most recent calendar year for which an annual statement was filed before the beginning of the accident year. Any such determination shall be made with the application of the rules of paragraphs (2)(C) and (3) of subsection (d).

(2) Election.—

(A) In general.—an election under paragraph (1) shall be made separately with respect to each determination year under subsection (d).

(B) Period for which election in effect.—Unless revoked with the consent of the Secretary, an election under paragraph (1) with respect to any determination year shall apply to accident years ending with the determination year and to each of the 4 succeeding accident years.

(C) Time for making election.—An election under paragraph (1) with respect to any determination year shall be made on the taxpayer's return for the taxable year in which (or with which) the determination year ends.

(3) No election for international or reinsurance business.—No election under this subsection shall apply to any international or reinsurance line of business.

(4) Regulations.—The Secretary shall prescribe such regulations as may be necessary or appropriate to carry out the purposes of this subsection including—

(A) regulations providing that a taxpayer may not make an election under this subsection if such taxpayer does not have sufficient historical experience for the line of business to determine a loss payment pattern, and

(B) regulations to prevent the avoidance (through the use of separate corporations or otherwise) of the requirement of this subsection that an election under this subsection applies to all lines of business of the taxpayer.

(f) Other definitions and special rules.—For purposes of this section—

(1) Accident year.—The term "accident year" means the calendar year in which the incident occurs which gives rise to the related unpaid loss.

(2) Unpaid loss adjustment expenses.—The term "unpaid losses" includes any unpaid loss adjustment expenses shown on the annual statement.

(3) Annual statement.—The term "annual statement" means the annual statement approved by the National Association of Insurance Commissioners which the taxpayer is required to file with insurance regulatory authorities of a State.

(4) Line of business.—The term "line of business" means a category for the reporting of loss payment patterns determined on the basis of the annual statement for fire and casualty insurance companies for the calendar year ending with or within the taxable year, except that the multiple peril lines shall be treated as a single line of business.

(5) Multiple peril lines.—The term "multiple peril lines" means the lines of business relating to farmowners multiple peril, homeowners multiple peril, commercial multiple peril, ocean marine, aircraft (all perils) and boiler and machinery.

【Footnote ¶3103】 Sec. 846 added by section 1023(c), '86 TRA;.

Effective date (Sec. 1023(e), '86 TRA).—(1) Generally applies to taxable years beginning after 12-31-86.

(2) Transitional rule.—For the first taxable year beginning after 12-31-86—

(A) the unpaid losses and the expenses unpaid (as defined in paragraphs (5)(B) and (6) of section 832(b) of the '86 Code) at the end of the preceding taxable year, and

(B) the unpaid losses as defined in sections 807(c)(2) and 805(a)(1) of such Code at the end of the preceding taxable year,

shall be determined as if the amendments made by this section had applied to such unpaid losses and expenses unpaid in the preceding taxable year and by using the interest rate and loss payment patterns applicable to accident years ending with calendar year 1987. For subsequent taxable years, such amendments shall be applied with respect to such unpaid losses and expenses unpaid by using the interest rate and loss payment patterns applicable to accident years ending with calendar year 1987.

(3) Fresh start.—

(A) In general.—Except as otherwise provided in this paragraph, any difference between—

(i) the amount determined to be the unpaid losses and expenses unpaid for the year preceding the 1st taxable year of an insurance company beginning after 12-31-86, determined without regard to paragraph (2), and

(ii) such amount determined with regard to paragraph (2),

shall not be taken into account for purposes of the '86 Code.

(B) Reserve strengthening in years after 1985.—Subparagraph (A) shall not apply to any reserve strengthening in a taxable year beginning in 1986, and such strengthening shall be treated as occurring in the taxpayer's 1st taxable year beginning after 12-31-86.

(C) Effect on earnings and profits.—The earnings and profits of any insurance company for its 1st taxable year beginning after 12-31-86, shall be increased by the amount of the difference determined under subparagraph (A) with respect to such company.

(6) **Special rule for certain accident and health insurance lines of business.**—Any determination under subsection (a) with respect to unpaid losses relating to accident and health insurance lines of businesses (other than credit disability insurance) shall be made—

    (A) in the case of unpaid losses relating to disability income, by using the general rules prescribed under section 807(d) applicable to noncancellable accident and health insurance contracts and using a mortality or morbidity table reflecting the taxpayer's experience; except that—

        (i) the prevailing State assumed interest rate shall be the rate in effect for the year in which the loss occurred rather than the year in which the contract was issued, and

        (ii) the limitation of subsection (a)(3) shall apply in lieu of the limitation of the last sentence of section 807(d)(1), and

    (B) in all other cases, by using an assumption (in lieu of a loss payment pattern) that unpaid losses are paid during the year following the accident year.

(g) **Regulations.**—The Secretary shall prescribe such regulations as may be necessary or appropriate to carry out the purposes of this section, including—

    (1) regulations providing proper treatment of allocated reinsurance, and

    (2) regulations providing proper treatment of salvage and reinsurance recoverable attributable to unpaid losses.

[For official explanation, see Committee Reports, ¶3963.]

[¶3104] CODE SEC. 851. DEFINITION OF REGULATED INVESTMENT COMPANY.

(a) **General Rule.**—For purposes of this subtitle, the term "regulated investment company" means any domestic corporation—

    (1) which, at all times during the taxable year, is registered under the Investment Company Act of 1940, as amended (15 U.S.C. 80 a-1 to 80 b-2), [1]*as a management company, business development company, or unit investment trust,* or

    (2) which is a common trust fund or similar fund excluded by section 3(c)(3) of such Act (15 U.S.C. 80 a-3(c)) from the definition of "investment company" and is not included in the definition of "common trust fund" by section 584(a).

(b) **Limitations.**—A corporation shall not be considered a regulated investment company for any taxable year unless—

    (1) it files with its return for the taxable year an election to be a regulated investment company or has made such election for a previous taxable year;

    (2) at least 90 percent of its gross income is derived from dividends, interest, payments with respect to securities loans (as defined in section 512(a)(5)), and gains from the sale or other disposition of stock or securities [2]*(as defined in section 2(a)(36) of the Investment Company Act of 1940, as amended) or foreign currencies, or other income (including but not limited to gains from options, futures, or forward contracts) derived with respect to its business of investing in such stock, securities, or currencies;.*

    (3) less than 30 percent of its gross income is derived from the sale or other disposition of stock or securities held for less than 3 months; and

    (4) at the close of each quarter of the taxable year—

        (A) at least 50 percent of the value of its total assets is represented by—

            (i) cash and cash items (including receivables), Government securities and securities of other regulated investment companies, and

            (ii) other securities for purposes of this calculation limited, except and to the extent provided in subsection (e), in respect of any one issuer to an amount not greater in value than 5 percent of the value of the total assets of the taxpayer and to not more than 10 percent of the outstanding voting securities of such issuer, and

---

[Footnote ¶3104] Matter in *italics* in Sec. 851(a)(1) added by section 652(a), '86 TRA, which struck out:
(1) "either as a management company or as a unit investment trust"
Effective date (Sec. 652(c), '86 TRA).—Applies to taxable years beginning after 12-31-86.

Matter in *italics* in Sec. 851(b) added by section 653(c), '86 TRA.
Effective date (Sec. 653(d), '86 TRA).—Applies to taxable years beginning after the date of the enactment of this Act.

Matter in *italics* in Sec. 851(b) added by section 1235(f)(3)(A) and (B), '86 TRA, which struck out:
(2) "section 951(a)(1)(A)(i)"

(B) not more than 25 percent of the value of its total assets is invested in the securities (other than Government securities or the securities of other regulated investment companies) of any one issuer, or of two or more issuers which the taxpayer controls and which are determined, under regulations prescribed by the Secretary, to be engaged in the same or similar trades or businesses or related trades or businesses.

For purposes of paragraph (2), there shall be treated as dividends amounts included in gross income under [3]*section 951(a)(1)(A)(i) or 1293(a)* for the taxable year to the extent that, under[4]*section 959(a)(1) or 1293(c) (as the case may be),* there is a distribution out of the earnings and profits of the taxable year which are attributable to the amounts so included. *For purposes of paragraph (2), the Secretary may by regulation exclude from qualifying income foreign currency gains which are not ancillary to the company's principal business of investing in stock or securities (or options and futures with respect to stock or securities).* For purposes of paragraphs (2) and (3), amounts excludable from gross income under section 103(a) shall be treated as included in gross income.

* * * * * * * * * * * *

(e) **Investment Companies Furnishing Capital to Development Corporations.—**

(1) **General Rule.—**If the Securities and Exchange Commission determines, in accordance with regulations issued by it, and certifies to the Secretary not earlier than 60 days prior to the close of the taxable year of a registered management company *or registered business development company,* that such investment company is principally engaged in the furnishing of capital to other corporations which are principally engaged in the development or exploitation of inventions, technological improvements, new processes, or products not previously generally available, such investment company may, in the computation of 50 percent of the value of its assets under subparagraph (A) of subsection (b)(4) for any quarter of such taxable year, include the value of any securities of an issuer, whether or not the investment company owns more than 10 percent of the outstanding voting securities of such issuer, the basis of which, when added to the basis of the investment company for securities of such issuer previously acquired, did not exceed 5 percent of the value of the total assets of the investment company at the time of the subsequent acquisition of securities. The preceding sentence shall not apply to the securities of an issuer if the investment company has continuously held any security of such issuer (or of any predecessor company of such issuer as determined under regulations prescribed by the Secretary) for 10 or more years preceding such quarter of such taxable year.

* * * * * * * * * * * *

(g) *Treatment of Certain Hedging Transactions.—*

(1) *In general.—In the case of any designated hedge, for purposes of subsection (b)(3), increases (and decreases) during the period of the hedge in the value of positions which are part of such hedge shall be netted.*

[Footnote ¶3104 continued]

(3) "section 959(a)(1)"
Effective date (Sec. 1235(h), '86 TRA).—Applies to taxable years of foreign corporations beginning after 12-31-86.

Matter in *italics* in Sec. 851(b)(2) and (g) added by section 653(a) and (b), '86 TRA, which struck out:
(4) ";"
Effective date (Sec. 653(d), '86 TRA).—Applies to taxable years beginning after—(the date of the enactment of this Act).

Matter in *italics* in Sec. 851(e)(1) added by section 652(b), '86 TRA.
Effective date (Sec. 652(c), '86 TRA).—Applies to taxable years beginning after 12-31-86.

Matter in *italics* in Sec. 851(q) added by section 654(a), '86 TRA.
Effective date (Sec. 654(b)(1), '86 TRA).—(1) Applies to taxable years beginning after—(the date of the enactment of this Act).

(2) Treatment of certain existing series funds.—In the case of a regulated investment company which has more than one fund on the date of the enactment of this act, and has before such date been treated for Federal income tax purposes as a single corporation—

(A) the amendment made by subsection (a), and the resulting treatment of each fund as a separate corporation, shall not give rise to the realization or recognition of income or loss by such regulated investment company, its funds, or its shareholders; and

(B) the tax attributes of such regulated investment company shall be appropriately allocated among its funds.

(2) *Designated hedge.—For purposes of this subsection there is a designated hedge where—*

(A) the taxpayer's risk of loss with respect to any position in property is reduced by reason of—

(i) the taxpayer having an option to sell, being under a contractual option to sell, or having made (and not closed) a short sale of substantially identical property,

(ii) the taxpayer being the grantor of an option to buy substantially identical property, or

(iii) under regulations prescribed by the Secretary, the taxpayer holding 1 or more other positions, and

(B) the positions which are part of the hedge are clearly identified by the taxpayer in the manner prescribed by regulations.

(q) *[should read (h)] Special rule for series funds.—*

(1) In general.—In the case of a regulated investment company (within the meaning of subsection (a)) having more than one fund, each fund of such regulated investment company shall be treated as a separate corporation for purposes of this title (except with respect to the definitional requirement of subsection (a)).

(2) Fund defined.—For purposes of paragraph (1) the term "fund" means a segregated portfolio of assets, the beneficial interests in which are owned by the holders of a class or series of stock of the regulated investment company that is preferred over all other classes or series in respect of such portfolio of assets.

[For official explanation, see Committee Reports, ¶3928; 4045.]

〔¶3105〕 CODE SEC. 852. TAXATION OF REGULATED INVESTMENT COMPANIES AND THEIR SHAREHOLDERS.

(a) **Requirements Applicable to Regulated Investment Companies.**—The provisions of this part shall not be applicable to a regulated investment company for a taxable year unless—

(1) the deduction for dividends paid during the taxable year (as defined in section 561, but without regard to capital gain dividends) equals or exceeds the sum of—

(A) *90 percent of its investment company taxable income for the taxable year determined without regard to subsection (b)(2)(D); and*

(B) *90 percent of the excess of (i) its interest income excludable from gross income under section 103(a) over (ii) its deductions disallowed under sections 265, 171(a)(2), and* [1]

[2](2) either—

(A) the provisions of this part applied to the investment company for all taxable years ending on or after November 8, 1983, or

(B) as of the close of the taxable year, the investment company has no earnings and profits accumulated in any taxable year to which the provisions of this part (or the corresponding provisions of prior law) did not apply to it.

(b) **Method of Taxation of Companies and Shareholders.—**

(1) **Imposition of tax on regulated investment companies.—**There is hereby imposed for each taxable year upon the investment company taxable income of every regulated investment company a tax computed as provided in section 11, as though the investment company taxable income were the taxable income referred to in section 11 [3]*or which fails to comply for the taxable year with regulations prescribed by the*

〔Footnote ¶3105〕 Matter in *italics* in Sec. 852(a) and (b)(1) added by section 1878(j), '86 TRA, which struck out:

(1) "(2) the investment company complies for such year with regulations prescribed by the Secretary for the purpose of ascertaining the actual ownership of its outstanding stock, and"

(2) "(3)"

(3) ", that tax shall be computed at the highest rate of tax specified in section 11(b)."

Effective date (Sec. 1881, '86 TRA and Sec. 1071(a)(5), '84 TRA).—

(A) Applies to taxable years beginning after 12-31-82.

(B) Investment companies which were regulated investment companies for years ending before 11-8-83.—In the case of any investment company to which the provisions of part I of subchapter M of chapter 1 of the '54 Code applied for any taxable year ending before 11-8-83, for purposes of section 852(a)(3)(B) of the '54 Code (as amended by this subsection), no earnings and profits accumulated in any taxable year ending before 1-1-84, shall be taken into account.

(C) Investment companies beginning business in 1983.—In the case of an investment company which began business in 1983 (and was not a successor corporation), earnings and profits accumulated during its first taxable

Secretary for the purpose of ascertaining the actual ownership of its stock, such tax shall be computed at the highest rate of tax specified in section 11(b).

* * * * * * * * * * * *

(3) **Capital gains.—**

(C) Definition of capital gain dividend.—For purposes of this part, a capital gain dividend is any dividend, or part thereof, which is designated by the company as a capital gain dividend in a written notice mailed to its shareholders not later than [4]60 *days* after the close of its taxable year. If the aggregate amount so designated with respect to a taxable year of the company (including capital gains dividends paid after the close of the taxable year described in section 885) is greater than the net capital gain of the taxable year, the portion of each distribution which shall be a capital gain dividend shall be only that proportion of the amount so designated; except that, if there is an increase in the excess described in subparagraph (A) of this paragraph for such year which results from a determination (as defined in section 860(e)), such designation may be made with respect to such increase at any time before the expiration of 120 days after the date of such determination. *For purposes of this subparagraph, the amount of the net capital gain for a taxable year (to which an election under section 4982(e)(4) does not apply) shall be determined without regard to any net capital loss attributable to transactions after October 31 of such year, and any such net capital loss shall be treated as arising on the 1st day of the next taxable year. To the extent provided in regulations, the preceding sentence shall apply also for purposes of computing regulated investment company taxable income.*

(D) Treatment by shareholders of undistributed capital gains.—

(i) Every shareholder of a regulated investment company at the close of the company's taxable year shall include, in computing his long-term capital gains on his return for his taxable year in which the last day of the company's taxable year falls, such amount as the company shall designate in respect of such shares in a written notice mailed to its shareholders at any time prior to the expiration of [4]60 *days* after close of its taxable year but the amount so includible by any shareholder shall not exceed that part of the amount subjected to tax in subparagraph (A) which he would have received if all of such amount had been distributed as capital gain dividends by the company to the holders of such shares at the close of its taxable year.

(ii) For purposes of this title, every such shareholder shall be deemed to have paid, for his taxable year under clause (i) the tax imposed by subparagraph (A) on the amounts required by this subparagraph to be included in respect of such shares in computing his long-term capital gains for that year and such shareholder shall be allowed credit or refund, as the case may be, for the tax so deemed to have been paid by him.

(iii) The adjusted basis of such shares in the hands of the shareholder shall be increased, with respect to the amounts required by this subparagraph to be included in computing his long-term capital gains, by [5]66 *percent* of so much of

---

[Footnote ¶3105 continued]

year shall not be taken into account for purposes of section 852(a)(3)(B) of such Code (as so amended).

(D) Investment companies registering before 11-8-83.—In the case of any investment company—

(i) which, during the period after 12-31-81, and before 11-8-83—

(I) was engaged in the active conduct of a trade or business,

(II) sold substantially all of its operating assets, and

(III) registered under the Investment Company Act of 1940 as either a management company or a unit investment trust, and

(ii) to which the provisions of part I of subchapter M of chapter 1 of the '54 Code applied for its first taxable year after 11-8-83,

for purposes of section 852(a)(3)(A) of such Code (as amended by paragraph (3)), the provisions of part I of subchapter M of chapter 1 of such Code shall be treated as applying to such investment company for its first taxable year ending after 11-8-83. For purposes of the preceding sentence, all members of an affiliated group (as defined in section 1504(a) of such Code) filing a consolidated return shall be treated as 1 taxpayer.

Matter in *italics* in Sec. 852(b)(3) and (5) added by section 655(a)(1), '86 TRA, which struck out:

(4) "45 days"

Effective date (Sec. 655(b), '86 TRA).—Applies to taxable years beginning after date of enactment of this Act.

Matter in *italics* in Sec. 852(b)(3)(D)(iii) added by section 311(h)(1), '86 TRA, which struck out:

(5) "72 percent"

such amounts as equals the amount subject to tax in accordance with section 1201(a).

(iv) In the event of such designation the tax imposed by subparagraph (A) shall be paid by the regulated investment company within 30 days after close of its taxable year.

(v) The earnings and profits of such regulated investment investment company, and the earnings and profits of any such shareholder which is a corporation, shall be appropriately adjusted in accordance with regulations prescribed by the Secretary.

(4) Loss on sale or exchange of stock held [6]*6 months or less.—*

(A) Loss attributable to capital gain dividend.—If—

(i) subparagaph (B) or (D) of paragraph (3) provides that any amount with respect to any share is to be treated as long-term capital gain, and

(ii) such share is held by the taxpayer for 6 months or less,

then any loss (to the extent not disallowed under subparagraph (B)) on the sale or exchange of such share shall, to the extent of the amount described in clause (i), be treated as a long-term capital loss.

(B) Loss attributable to exempt interest dividend.—If—

(i) a shareholder of a regulated investment company receives an exempt-interest dividend with respect to any share, and

(ii) such share is held by the taxpayer for [7]*6 months or less,*

then any loss on the sale or exchange of such share shall, to the extent of the amount of such exempt-interest dividend, be disallowed.

(C) Determinations of holding periods.—For purposes of this paragraph, the rules of paragraphs (3) and (4) of section 246(c) shall apply in determining the period for which the taxpayer [8]*has held any share of stock; except that "6 months" shall be substituted for each number of days specified in subparagraph (B) of section 246(c)(3).*

(D) Losses incurred under a periodic liquidation plan.—To the extent provided in regulations, [9]*subparagraphs (A) and (B)* shall not apply to losses incurred on the sale or exchange of shares of stock in a regulated investment company pursuant to a plan which provides for the periodic liquidation of such shares.

(E) Authority to shorten required holding period.—In the case of a regulated investment company which regularly distributes at least 90 percent of its net tax-exempt interest, the Secretary may by regulations prescribe that subparagraph (B) (and subparagraph (C) to the extent it relates to subparagraph (B)) shall be applied on the basis of a holding period requirement shorter than 6 months; except that such shorter holding period requirement shall not be shorter than the greater of 31 days of the period between regular distributions of exempt-interest dividends.

(5) Exempt-interest dividends.—If, at the close of each quarter of its taxable year, at least 50 percent of the value (as defined in section 851(c)(4)) of the total assets of the regulated investment company consists of obligations described in section 103(a), such a company shall be qualified to pay exempt-interest dividends, as defined herein, to its shareholders.

[Footnote ¶3105 continued]

Effective date (Sec. 311(c), '86 TRA).—Applies to taxable years beginning after 12-31-86.

Matter in *italics* in Sec. 852(b)(4) added by section 1804(c)(1)—(5), '86 TRA, which struck out:

(6) **"less than 31 days"**

(7) **"less than 31 days,"**

(8) "held any share of stock; except that for the number of days specified in subparagraph (b) of section 246(c)(3) there shall be substituted—

(i) '6 months' for purposes of subparagraph (A), and

(ii) '30 days' for purposes of subparagraph (B)."

(9) "subparagraph (A)"

Effective date (Sec. 1804(c)(6), '86 TRA).—Applies to stock with respect to which the taxpayer's holding period begins after 3-28-85.

Sec. 852(b)(5)(C) in *italics* added by section 1173(b)(1)(B), '86 TRA.

Effective date (Sec. 1173(c)(2)(A), '86 TRA).—Applies to loans used to acquire employer securities after the date of the enactment of this Act, including loans used to refinance loans used to acquire employer securities before such date of such loans were used to acquire employer securities after 5-23-84.

(A) Definition.—An exempt-interest dividend means any dividend or part thereof (other than a capital gain dividend) paid by a regulated investment company and designated by it as an exempt-interest dividend in a written notice mailed to its shareholders not later than [4]*60 days* after the close of its taxable year. If the aggregate amounts so designated with respect to a taxable year of the company (including exempt-interest dividends paid after the close of the taxable year as described in section 855) is greater than the excess of—

(i) the amount of interest excludable from gross income under section 103(a), over

(ii) the amounts disallowed as deductions under sections 265 and 171(a)(2),

the portion of such distribution which shall constitute an exempt-interest dividend shall be only that proportion of the amount so designated as the amount of such excess for such taxable year bears to the amount so designated.

* * * * * * * * * * * *

(C) Interest on certain loans used to acquire employer securities.—For purposes of this paragraph—

(i) 50 percent of the amount of any loan of the regulated investment company which qualifies as a securities acquisition loan (as defined in section 133) shall be treated as an obligation described in section 103(a), and

(ii) 50 percent of the interest received on such loan shall be treated as interest excludable from gross income under section 103.

(6) Section 311(b) not to apply to certain distributions.—Section 311(b) shall not apply to any distribution by a regulated investment company to which this part applies, if such distribution is in redemption of its stock upon the demand of the shareholder.

(6) [should read (7)] *Time certain dividends taken into account.*—For purposes of this title, any dividend declared by a regulated investment company in December of any calendar year and payable to shareholders of record on a specified date in such month shall be deemed—

(A) to have been received by each shareholder on such date, and

(B) to have been paid by such company on such date (or, if earlier, as provided in section 855).

The preceding sentence shall apply only if such dividend is actually paid by the company before February 1 of the following calendar year.

[10]**(c) Earnings and Profits.**—

(1) In general.—The earnings and profits of a regulated investment company for any taxable year (but not its accumulated earnings and profits) shall not be reduced by any amount which is not allowable as a deduction in computing its taxable income for such taxable year. For purposes of this subsection, the term "regulated investment company" includes a domestic corporation which is a regulated investment company determined without regard to the requirements of subsection (a).

(2) Coordination with tax on undistributed income.—A regulated investment company shall be treated as having sufficient earnings and profits to treat as a dividend any distribution (other than in a redemption to which section 302(a) applies) which is treated as a dividend by such company. The preceding sentence shall not apply to the extent that the amount distributed during any calendar year by the company exceeds the required distribution for such calendar year (as determined under section 4982).

* * * * * * * * * * * *

(e) Procedures Similar to Deficiency Dividend Procedures Made Applicable.—

---

* * * * * * * * * * * *

　　(3)　Interest charge.—

　　　　(A)　In general.—If paragarph (1) applies to any non-RIC year of an investment company, such investment company shall pay interest at the [11]*underpayment* rate established under section 6621—

　　　　　　(i)　on an amount equal to 50 percent of the amount referred to in paragraph (2)(A)(i),

　　　　　　(ii)　for the period—

　　　　　　　　(I)　which begins on the last day prescribed for payment of the tax imposed for the non-RIC year (determined without regard to extensions), and

　　　　　　　　(II)　which ends on the date the determination is made.

* * * * * * * * * * * *

[For official explanation, see Committee Reports, ¶3887; 3917; 3928; 4018; 4075; 4192; 4138.]

〔¶3106〕　CODE SEC. 853.　FOREIGN TAX CREDIT ALLOWED TO SHAREHOLDERS.

* * * * * * * * * * * *

　　(c)　Notice to Shareholders.—The amounts to be treated by the shareholder, for purposes of subsection (b)(2), as his proportionate share of—

　　　　(1)　taxes paid to any foreign country or possession of the United States, and

　　　　(2)　gross income derived from sources within any foreign country or possession of the United States, shall not exceed the amounts so designated by the company in a written notice mailed to its shareholders not later than [1]*60 days* after the close of its taxable year.

* * * * * * * * * * * *

[For official explanation, see Committee Reports, ¶3928.]

〔¶3107〕　CODE SEC. 854.　LIMITATIONS APPLICABLE TO DIVIDENDS RECEIVED FROM REGULATED INVESTMENT COMPANY.

　　(a)　Capital Gain Dividend.—For purposes of [1] section 243 (relating to deductions for dividends received by corporations), a capital gain dividend (as defined in section 852(b)(3)) received from a regulated investment company shall not be considered as a dividend.

　　(b)　Other Dividends.—

　　　　(1)　Amount treated as dividend.—

　　　　　　(A)　Deduction under section 243.—In any case in which—

　　　　　　　　(i)　a dividend is received from a regulated investment company (other than a dividend to which subsection (a) applies), and

　　　　　　　　(ii)　such investment company meets the requirements of section 852(a) for the taxable year during which it paid such dividend,

　　　　then, in computing any deduction under section 243, there shall be taken into account only that portion of such dividend designated under this subparagraph by the regulated investment company. [2]

　　　　　　[3]*(B)　Limitation.—*The aggregate amount which may be designated as dividends under subparagraph (A) [4] shall not exceed the aggregate dividends received by the

---

〔Footnote ¶3105 continued〕

Matter in *italics* in Sec. 852(e)(3)(A) added by section 1511(c)(6), '86 TRA, which struck out:

(11)　"annual"

Effective date (Sec. 1511(d), '86 TRA).—Applies for purposes of determining interest for periods after 12-31-86.

〔Footnote ¶3106〕　Matter in *italics* in Sec. 853(c) added by section 655(a)(3), '86 TRA, which struck out:

(1)　"45 days"

Effective date (Sec. 655(b) '86 TRA).—Applies to taxable years beginning after the date of the enactment of this Act.

〔Footnote ¶3107〕　Matter in *italics* in Sec. 854(a) and (b) added by section 612(b)(6), '86 TRA, which struck out:

(1)　"section 116 (relating to an exclusion for dividends received by individuals) and"

(2)　"(B) Exclusion under section 116.—If the aggregate dividends received by a regulated investment company during any taxable year are less than 95 percent of its gross income, then, in computing the exclusion under section 116, rules similar to the rules of subparagraph (A) shall apply."

(3)　"(C)"

(4)　"or (B)"

company for the taxable year.

(2) **Notice to shareholders.**—The amount of any distribution by a regulated invest-ment company which may be taken into account as a dividend for purposes of [5] the deduction under section 243 shall not exceed the amount so designated by the com-pany in a written notice to its shareholders mailed not later than [6]*60 days* after the close of its taxable year.

(3) **Definitions.**—For purposes of this subsection—

* * * * * * * * * * * * *

[7]*(B)(i)   The term "aggregate dividends received" includes only dividends received from domestic corporations.*

(ii)   For purposes of clause (i), the term "dividend" shall not include any dis-tribution from—

(I)   a corporation which, for the taxable year of the corporation in which the distribution is made, or for the next preceding taxable year of the corpora-tion, is a corporation exempt from tax under section 501 (relating to certain charitable, etc., organizations) or section 521 (relating to farmers' cooperative associations), or

(II)   a real estate investment trust which, for the taxable year of the trust in which the dividend is paid, qualifies under part II of subchapter M (section 856 and following).

(iii)   In determining the amount of any dividend for purposes of this subpara-graph, a dividend received from a regulated investment company shall be subject to the limitations prescribed in this section.

(4) **Special rule for computing deduction under section 243.**—For purposes of sub-paragraph (A) of paragraph (1), an amount shall be treated as a dividend for the pur-pose of paragraph (1) only if a deduction would have been allowable under section 243 to the regulated investment company determined—

(A)   as if section 243 applied to dividends received by a regulated investment company,

(B)   after the application of section 246 (but without regard to subsection (b) thereof), and

(C)   after the application of section 246A.

[For official explanation, see Committee Reports, ¶3913; 3928.]

[¶3108]   CODE SEC. 855.   DIVIDENDS PAID BY REGULATED INVESTMENT COMPANY AFTER CLOSE OF TAXABLE YEAR.

(a) **General Rule.**—For purposes of this chapter, if a regulated investment company—

(1)   declares a dividend prior to the time prescribed by law for the filing of its re-turn for a taxable year (including the period of any extension of time granted for filing such return), and

(2)   distributes the amount of such dividend to shareholders in the 12-month per-iod following the close of such taxable year and not later than the date of the first regular dividend payment made after such declaration

the amount so declared and distributed shall, to the extent the company elects in such return in accordance with regulations prescribed by the Secretary, be considered as hav-ing been paid during such taxable year, except as provided in subsections (b), (c), and (d).

(b) **Receipt by Shareholder.**—[1]*Except as provided in section 852(b)(6), amounts* to

【Footnote ¶3107 continued】

(5) "the exclusion under section 116 and"
Effective date (Sec. 612(c), '86 TRA).—Applies to taxable years beginning after 12-31-86.

Matter in *italics* in Sec. 854(b)(2) added by section 655(a)(4), '86 TRA, which struck out:
(6) "45 days"
Effective date (Sec. 655(b), '86 TRA).—Applies to taxable years beginning after the date of the enactment of this Act.

Matter in *italics* in Sec. 854(b)(3) added by section 612(b)(6), '86 TRA, which struck out:
(7) "(B)   The term 'aggregate dividends received' includes only dividends received from domestic corporations other than dividends described in section 116(b) (relating to dividends excluded from gross income). In determining the amount of any dividend for purposes of this subparagraph, the rules provided in section 116(c) (relating to certain distributions) shall apply."
Effective date (Sec. 612(c), '86 TRA).—Applies to taxable years beginning after 12-31-86.
【Footnote ¶3108】   Matter in *italics* in Sec. 855(b) added by section 651(h)(1)(B), '86 TRA, which struck out:
(1) "Amounts"

which subsection (a) is applicable shall be treated as received by the shareholder in the taxable year in which the distribution is made.

(c) **Notice to Shareholders.**—In the case of amounts to which subsection (a) is applicable, any notice to shareholders required under this part with respect to such amounts shall be made not later than [2]*60 days* after the close of the taxable year in which the distribution is made.

(d) **Foreign Tax Election.**—If an investment company to which section 853 is applicable for the taxable year makes a distribution as provided in subsection (a) of this section, the shareholders shall consider the amounts described in section 853(b)(2) allocable to such distribution as paid or received, as the case may be, in the taxable year in which the distribution is made.

[For official explanation, see Committee Reports, ¶3928.]

〔¶3109〕 CODE SEC. 856. DEFINTION OF REAL ESTATE INVESTMENT.

(a) **In General.**—For purposes of this title, the term "real estate investment trust" means a corporation, trust, or association—

(1)   which is managed by one or more trustees or directors;

(2)   the beneficial ownership of which is evidenced by transferable shares, or by transferable certificates of beneficial interest;

(3)   which (but for the provisions of this part) would be taxable as a domestic corporation;

(4)   which is neither (A) a financial institution [1]*referred to in section 582(c)(5)*, nor (B) an insurance company to which subchapter L applies;

(5)   the beneficial ownership of which is held by 100 or more persons;

(6)   [2]*which is not closely held (as determined under subsection (h)); and*

(7)   which meets the requirements of subsection (c).

* * * * * * * * * * * *

(c) **Limitations.**—A corporation, trust, or association shall not be considered a real estate investment trust for any taxable year unless—

* * * * * * * * * * * *

(3)   at least 75 percent of its gross income (excluding gross income from prohibited transactions) is derived from—

(A)   rents from real property;

(B)   interest on obligations secured by mortgages on real property or on interests in real property;

(C)   gain from the sale or other disposition of real property (including interest in real property and interest in mortgages on real property) which is not property described in section 1221(1);

(D)   dividends or other distributions on, and gain (other than gain from prohibited transactions) from the sale or other disposition of tranferable shares (or transferable certificates of beneficial interest) in other real estate investment trusts which meet the requirements of this part;

(E)   abatements and refunds of taxes on real property;

〔Footnote ¶3108 continued〕

Effective date (Sec. 651(d) '86 TRA).—Applies to calendar years beginning after 12-31-86.

Matter in *italics* in Sec. 855(c) added by section 655(a)(5), '86 TRA, which struck out:

(2) "45 days"

Effective date (Sec. 655(b) '86 TRA).—Applies to taxable years beginning after the date of the enactment of this Act.

〔Footnote ¶3109〕 Matter in *italics* in Sec. 856(a)(4) added by section 901(d)(4)(E), '86 TRA, which struck out:

(1) "to which section 585, 586, or 593 applies"

Effective date (Sec. 901(e), '86 TRA).—Applies to taxable years beginning after 12-31-86.

Matter in *italics* in Sec. 856(a)(6) added by section 661(a)(1), '86 TRA, which struck out:

(2) "which would not be a personal holding company (as defined in section 542) if all of its adjusted ordinary gross income (as defined in section 543(b)(2)) constituted personal holding company income (as defined in section 543); and"

Effective date (Sec. 669(a), '86 TRA).—Applies to taxable years beginning after 12-31-86.

(F)   income and gain derived from foreclosure property (as defined in subsection (e));

(G)   amounts (other than amounts the determination of which depends in whole or in part on the income or profits of any person) received or accrued as consideration for entering into agreements (i) to make loans secured by mortgages on real property or on interests in real property or (ii) to purchase or lease real property (including interests in real property and interests in mortgages on real property); [3]

(H)   gain from the sale or other disposition of a real estate asset which is not a prohibited transaction solely by reason of section 857(b)(6); *and*

(I)   *qualified temporary investment income;*

* * * * * * * * * * * * *

(6)   for purposes of this part—

* * * * * * * * * * * * *

(B)   The term "real estate assets" means real property (including interests in real property and interests in mortgages on real property) and shares (or transferable certificates of beneficial interest) in other real estate investment trusts which meet the requirements of this part. *Such term also includes any property (not otherwise a real estate asset) attributable to the temporary investment of new capital, but only if such property is stock or a debt instrument, and only for the 1-year period beginning on the date the real estate trust receives such capital.*

* * * * * * * * * * * *

A regular or residual interest in a REMIC shall be treated as an interest in real property, and any amount includible in gross income with respect to such an interest shall be treated as interest; except that, if less than 95 percent of the assets of such REMIC are interests in real property (determined as if the taxpayer held such assets), such interest shall be so treated only in the proportion which the assets of the REMIC consist of such interests.

[4]*(E)   Qualified temporary investment income.—*

(i)   In general.—The term "qualified temporary investment income" means any income which—

(I)   is attributable to stock or a debt instrument,

(II)   is attributable to the temporary investment of new capital, and

(III)   is received or accrued during the 1-year period beginning on the date on which the real estate investment trust receives such capital.

(ii)   New capital.—The term "new capital" means any amount received by the real estate investment trust—

(I)   in exchange for stock in such trust (other than amounts received pursuant to a dividend reinvestment plan), or

(II)   in a public offering of debt obligations of such trust which have maturities of at least 5 years.

[5]*(E)*   [should read F]   All other terms shall have the same meaning as when used in the Investment Company Act of 1940, as amended (15 U.S.C. 80a-1 and following).

* * * * * * * * * * * *

(d)   Rents From Real Property Defined.—

* * * * * * * * * * * *

(2)   [6]*Except as provided in section 857(b)(8), amounts* **excluded.**—For purposes of

---

⟦Footnote ¶3109 continued⟧

Matter in *italics* in Sec. 856(c)(3)(G), (H), and (I) added by section 662(b)(1) '86 TRA, which struck out:
(3)   "and"
Effective date (Sec. 669(a), '86 TRA).—Applies to taxable years beginning after 12-31-86.

Matter in *italics* in Sec. 856(c)(6)(B) added by section 662(b)(2), '86 TRA.
Effective date (Sec. 669(a), '86 TRA).—Applies to taxable years beginning after 12-31-86.

Matter in *italics* in Sec. 856(c)(6)(D) added by section 671(b)(1), '86 TRA, which struck out:
(4)   "(D)" (as added by Sec. 662(b)(3), '86 TRA)
Effective date (Sec. 675(a), '86 TRA).—Applies to taxable years beginning after 12-31-86.

Matter in *italics* in Sec. 856(E) added by section 662(b)(3), '86 TRA, which struck out:
(5)   "(D)" (should be (F))
Effective date (Sec. 669(a), '86 TRA).—Applies to taxable years beginning after 12-31-86.

paragraphs (2) and (3) of subsection (c), the term "rents from real property" does not include—

   (A) except as provided in[7]*paragraphs (4) and (6),* any amount received or accrued, directly or indirectly, with respect to any real or personal property, if the determination of such amount depends in whole or in part on the income or profits derived by any person from such property (except that any amount so received or accrued shall not be excluded from the term "rents from real property" solely by reason of being based on a fixed percentage or percentages of receipts or sales);

    * * * * * * * * * * * *

   (C) any amount received or accrued, directly or indirectly, with respect to any real or personal property if the real estate investment trust furnishes or renders services to the tenants of such property, or manages or operates such property, other than through an independent contractor from whom the trust itself does not derive or receive any income.

Subparagraph (C) shall not apply with respect to any amount if such amount would be excluded from unrelated business taxable income under section 512(b)(3) if received by an organization described in section 511(a)(2)

    * * * * * * * * * * * *

   (6) Special rule for certain property subleased by tenant of real estate investment trusts.—
     (A) In general.—If—
      (i) a real estate investment trust receives or accrues, with respect to real or personal property, amounts from a tenant which derives substantially all of its income with respect to such property from the subleasing of substantially all of such property, and
      (ii) such tenant receives or accrues, directly or indirectly, from subtenants only amounts which are qualified rents,
   then the amounts that the trust receives or accrues from the tenant shall not be excluded from the term "rents from real property" solely by reason of being based on the income or profits of such tenant.
     (B) Qualified rents.—For purposes of subparagraph (A), the term "qualified rents" means any amount which would be treated as rents from real property if received by the real estate investment trust.

    * * * * * * * * * * * *

  (f) Interest.—
   [8]*(1) In general.—For purposes of paragraphs (2)(B) and (3)(B) of subsection (c), the*

⟦Footnote ¶3109 continued⟧

Matter in *italics* in the heading of Sec. 856(d)(2) (erroneously designated as 856(b)) added by section 668(b)(1)(B), '86 TRA, which struck out:

(6) **"Amounts"**

Effective date (Sec. 669(b), '86 TRA).—Applies to calendar years beginning after 12-31-86.

Matter in *italics* in Sec. 856(d)(2)(A) and the last sentence of Sec. 856(d)(2) added by section 663(a) and (b)(3), '86 TRA which struck out:

(7) "paragraph 4"

Effective date (Sec. 669(a), '86 TRA).—Applies to taxable years beginning after 12-31-86.

Matter in *italics* in Sec. 856(d)(6) added by section 663(b)(1), '86 TRA.

Effective date (Sec. 669(a), '86 TRA).—Applies to taxable years beginning after 12-31-86.

Matter in *italics* in Sec. 856(f) added by section 663(b)(2), '86 TRA, which struck out:

(8) "For purposes of paragraphs (2)(B) and (3)(B) of subsection (c), the term 'interest' does not include any amount received or accrued, directly or indirectly, if the determination of such amount depends in whole or in part on the income or profits of any person except that:

(1) any amount so received or accrued shall not be excluded from the term 'interest' solely by reason of being based on a fixed percentage or percentages of receipts or sales, and

(2) where a real estate investment trust receives or accrues any amount which would be excluded from the term 'interest' solely because the debtor of the real estate investment trust receives or accrues any amount the determination of which depends in whole or in part on the income or profits of any person, only a proportionate part (determined pursuant to regulations prescribed by the Secretary) of the amount received or accrued by the real estate investment trust from such debtor will be excluded from the term 'interest.'

The provisions of this subsection shall apply only with respect to amounts received or accrued pursuant to loans

Code §856(f)(1) ¶3109

term "interest" does not include any amount received or accrued (directly or indirectly) if the determination of such amount depends (in whole or in part) on the income or profits of any person, except that—

    (A) any amount so received or accrued shall not be excluded from the term "interest" solely by reason of being based on a fixed percentage or percentages of receipts or sales, and

    (B) any amount so received or accrued with respect to an obligation secured by a mortgage on real property or an interest in real property shall not be excluded from the term "interest" solely by reason of being based on the income or profits of the debtor from such property, if—

        (i) the debtor derives substantially all of its gross income with respect to such property from the leasing of substantially all of its interests in such property to tenants, and

        (ii) the amounts received or accrued directly or indirectly by the debtor from such tenants are only qualified rents (as defined as subsection (d)(6)(B)).

    (2) *Special rule.*—Where a real estate investment trust receives or accrues any amount which would be excluded from the term "interest" solely because the debtor of the real estate investment trust receives or accrues any amount the determination of which depends (in whole or in part) on the income or profits of any person, only a proportionate part (determined under regulations prescribed by the Secretary) of the amount received or accrued by the real estate investment trust shall be excluded from the term "interest".

* * * * * * * * * * * *

(h) Closely Held Determinations.—

    (1) *Section 542(a)(2) applied.*

      (A) *In general.*—For purposes of subsection (a)(6), a corporation, trust, or association is closely held if the stock ownership requirement of section 542(a)(2) is met.

      (B) *Waiver of partnership attribution, etc.*—For purposes of subparagraph (A)—

        (i) paragraph (2) of section 544(a) shall be applied as if such paragraph did not contain the phrase "or by or for his partner", and

        (ii) sections 544(a)(4)(A) and 544(b)(1) shall be applied by substituting "the entity meet the stock ownership requirement of section 542(a)(2)" for "the corporation a personal holding company".

    (2) *Subsections (a)(5) and (6) not to apply to 1st year.*—Paragraphs (5) and (6) of subsection (a) shall not apply to the 1st taxable year for which an election is made under subsection (c)(1) by any corporation, trust, or association."

(i) Treatment of Certain Wholly Owned Subsidiaries.—

    (1) *In general.*—For purposes of this title—

      (A) a corporation which is a qualified REIT subsidiary shall not be treated as a separate corporation, and

      (B) all assets, liabilities, and items of income,, deduction, and credit of a qualified REIT subsidiary shall be treated as assets, liabilities, and such items (as the case may be) of the real estate investment trust.

    (2) *Qualified REIT subsidiary.*—For purposes of this subsection, the term "qualified REIT subsidiary" means any corporation if 100 percent of the stock of such corporation is held by the real estate investment trust at all times during the period such corporation was in existence.

    (3) *Treatment of termination of qualified subsidiary status.*—For purposes of this subtitle, if any corporation which was a qualified REIT subsidiary ceases to meet the requirements of paragraph (2), such corporation shall be treated as a new corporation

---

〔Footnote ¶3109 continued〕

made after May 27, 1976. For purposes of the preceding sentence, a loan is considered to be made before May 28, 1976, if such loan is made pursuant to a binding commitment entered into before May 28, 1976."

Effective date (Sec. 669(a) and (c), '86 TRA).—(a) Applies to taxable years beginning after 12-31-86.

* * * * * * * * * * * *

(c) Retention of Existing Transitional Rule.—The amendment made by section 663(b)(2) shall not apply with respect to amounts received or accrued pursuant to loans made before 5-28-76. For purposes of the preceding sentence, a loan is considered to be made before 5-28-76, if such loan is made pursuant to a binding commitment entered into before 5-28-76.

Matter in *italics* in Sec. 856(h), (i) and (j) added by sections 661(a)(2), 662(a) and (c), '86 TRA.
Effective date (Sec. 669(a), '86 TRA).—Applies to taxable years beginning after 12-31-86.

acquiring all of its assets (and assuming all of its liabilities) immediately before such cessation from the real estate investment trust in exchange for its stock.

(j) Treatment of Shared Appreciation Mortgages.—

(1) In general.—Solely for purposes of subsection (c) of this section and section 857(b)(6), any income derived from a shared appreciation provision shall be treated as gain recognized on the sale of the secured property.

(2) Treatment of income.—For purposes of applying subsection (c) of this section and section 857(b)(6) to any income described in paragraph (1)—

(A) the real estate investment trust shall be treated as holding the secured property for the period during which it held the shared appreciation provision (or, if shorter, for the period during which the secured property was held by the person holding such property), and

(B) the secured property shall be treated as property described in section 1221(1) if it is so described in the hands of the persons holding the secured property (or it would be so described if held by the real estate investment trust).

(3) Coordination with prohibited transactions safe harbor.—For purposes of section 857(b)(6)(C)—

(A) the real estate investment trust shall be treated as having sold the secured property when it recognizes any income described in paragraph (1), and

(B) any expenditures made by any holder of the secured property shall be treated as made by the real estate investment trust.

(4) Definitions.—For purposes of this subsection—

(A) Shared appreciation provision.—The term "shared appreciation provision" means any provision—

(i) which is in connection with an obligation which is held by the real estate investment trust and is secured by an interest in real property, and

(ii) which entitles the real estate investment trust to receive a specified portion of any gain realized on the sale or exchange of such real property (or of any gain which would be realized if the property were sold on a specified date).

(B) Secured property.—The term "secured property" means the real property referred to in subparagraph (A).

[For official explanation, see Committee Reports, ¶3948; 3929; 3930.]

【¶3110】 CODE SEC. 857. TAXATION OF REAL ESTATE INVESTMENT TRUSTS AND THEIR BENEFICIARIES.

(a) Requirements Applicable to Real Estate Investment Trusts.—The provisions of this part (other than subsection (d) of this section (and subsection (g) of section 856) shall not apply to a real estate investment trust for a taxable year unless—

(1) the deduction for dividends paid during the taxable year (as defined in section 561, but determined without regard to capital gains dividends) equals or exceeds—

(A) the sum of—

(i) 95 percent (90 percent for taxable years beginning before January 1, 1980) of the real estate investment trust taxable income for the taxable year (determined without regard to the deduction for dividends paid (as defined in section 561) and by excluding any net capital gain); and

(ii) 95 percent (90 percent for taxable years beginning before January 1, 1980) of the excess of the net income from foreclosure property over the tax imposed on such income by subsection (b)(4)(A); minus

(B) [1]*any excess noncash income (as determined under subsection (e));* [2]

(2) the real estate investment trust complies for such year with regulations prescribed by the Secretary for the purpose of ascertaining the actual ownership of the outstanding shares, or certificates of beneficial interest, of such trust [3], *and*

【Footnote ¶3110】 Matter in *italics* in Sec. 857(a)(1)(B) added by section 664(a), '86 TRA, which struck out:
(1) "the sum of—
(i) the amount of any penalty imposed on the real estate investment trust by section 6697 which is paid by such trust during the taxable year; and
(ii) the net loss derived from prohibited transactions; and"
Effective date (Sec. 669(a), '86 TRA).—Applies to taxable years beginning after 12-31-86.

Matter in *italics* in Sec. 857(a)(1)(B)(2) and (3) added by section 661(b), '86 TRA, which struck out:
(2) "and"
(3) "."

(3) either—

   (A) the provisions of this part apply to the real estate investment trust for all taxable years beginning after February 28, 1986, or

   (B) as of the close of the taxable year, the real estate investment trust has no earnings and profits accumulated in any non-REIT year.

For purposes of the preceding sentence, the term "non-REIT year" means any taxable year to which the provisions of this part did not apply with respect to the entity.

(b) Method of Taxation of Real Estate Investment Trusts and Holders of Shares or Certificates of Beneficial Interest.—

*   *   *   *   *   *   *   *   *   *   *   *   *

   (2) Real estate investment trust taxable income.—For purposes of this part, the term "real estate investment trust taxable income" means the taxable income of the real estate investment trust, adjusted as follows:

*   *   *   *   *   *   *   *   *   *   *   *   *

   (F) There shall be excluded an amount equal to any net income derived from prohibited transactions [4] .

   (3) Capital Gains.—

*   *   *   *   *   *   *   *   *   *   *   *   *

   (C) Definition of capital gain dividend.—For purposes of this part, a capital gain dividend is any dividend, or part thereof, which is designated by the real estate investment trust as a capital gain dividend in a written notice mailed to its shareholders or holders of beneficial interest at any time before the expiration of 30 days after [5]*the close of its taxable year (or mailed to its shareholders or holders of beneficial interests with its annual report for the taxable year)* except that, if there is an increase in the excess described in subparagraph (A)(ii) of this paragraph for such year which results from a determination (as defined in section 860(e)), such designation may be made with respect to such increase at any time before the expiration of 120 days after the date of such determination. If the aggregate amount so designated with respect to a taxable year of the trust (including capital gain dividends paid after the close of the taxable year described in section 858) is greater than the net capital gain of the taxable year, the portion of each distribution which shall be a capital gain dividend shall be only that proportion of the amount so designated which such net capital gain bears to the aggregate amount so designated [6] *For purposes of this subparagraph, the amount of the net capital gain for any taxable year which is not a calendar year shall be determined without regard to any net capital loss attributable to transactions after December 31 of such year, and any such net capital loss such be treated as arising on the 1st day of the next taxable year. To the extent provided in regulations, the preceding sentence shall apply also for purposes of computing real estate investment trust taxable income.*

   (D) Coordination with net operating loss provisions.—For purposes of section 172, if a real estate investment trust pays capital gain dividends during any taxable year,

---

the amount of the net capital gain for such taxable year (to the extent such gain does not exceed the amount of such capital gain dividends) shall be excluded in determining—

(i)   the net operating loss for the taxable year, and

(ii)   the amount of the net operating loss of any prior taxable year which may be carried through such taxable year under section 172(b)(2) to a succeeding taxable year.

* * * * * * * * * * * *

(6)   **Income from prohibited transactions.—**

(A)   Imposition of tax.—There is hereby imposed for each taxable year of every real estate investment trust a tax equal to 100 percent of the net income derived from prohibited transactions.

(B)   Definitions.—For purposes of this part—

(i)   the term "net income derived from prohibited transactions" means the excess of the gain from prohibited transactions over the deductions allowed by this chapter which are directly connected with prohibited transactions;

(ii)   [7]*in determining the amount of the net income derived from prohibited transactions, there shall not be taken into account any item attributable to any prohibited transaction for which there was a loss; and*

(iii)   the term "prohibited transaction" means a sale or other disposition of property described in section 1221(1) which is not foreclosure property.

(C)   Certain sales not to constitute prohibited transactions.—For purposes of this part, the term "prohibited transaction" does not include a sale of property which is a real estate asset as defined in section 856(c)(6)(B) if—

(i)   the trust has held the property for not less than 4 years;

(ii)   aggregate expenditures made by the trust, or any partner of the trust, during the 4-year period preceding the date of sale which are includible in the basis of the property do not exceed [8]*30 percent* of the net selling price of the property;

(iii)   [9]*(I)   during the taxable year the trust does not make more than 7 sales of property (other than foreclosure property), or (II) the aggregate adjusted bases (as determined for purposes of computing earnings and profits) of property (other than foreclosure property) sold during the taxable year does not exceed 10 percent of the aggregate bases (as so determined) of all of the assets of the trust as of the beginning of the taxable year;*[10]

(iv)   in the case of property, which consists of land or improvements, not acquired through foreclosure (or deed in lieu of foreclosure), or lease termination, the trust has held the property for not less than 4 years for production of rental income.[11]*; and*

(v)   *if the requirement of clause (iii)(I) is not satisfied, substantially all of the marketing and development expenditures with respect to the property were made through an independent contractor (as defined in section 856(d)(3)) from whom the trust itself does not derive or receive any income.*

* * * * * * * * * * * *

(8)   *Time certain dividends taken into account.—For purposes of this title, any dividend declared by a real estate investment trust in December of any calendar year and payable to shareholders of record on a specified date in such month shall be deemed—*

(A)   *to have been received by each shareholder on such date, and*

(B)   *to have been paid by such trust on such date (or, if earlier, as provided in section 858).*

[Footnote ¶3110 continued]

(7)   "the term 'net loss derived from prohibited transactions' means the excess of the deductions allowed by this chapter which are directly connected with prohibited transactions over the gain from prohibited transactions; and"

(8)   "20 percent"

(9)   "during the taxable year the trust does not make more than 5 sales of property (other than foreclosure property); and"

(10)   "and"

(11)   "."

Effective date (Sec. 669(a), '86 TRA)—Applies to taxable years beginning after 12-31-86.

Sec. 857(b)(8) in *italics* added by section 668(b)(1)(A), '86 TRA.

Effective date (Sec. 669(b), '86 TRA).—Applies to calendar years beginning after 12-31-86.

The preceding sentence shall apply only if such dividend is actually paid by the company before February 1 of the following calendar year.

(c) Restrictions Applicable to Dividends Received From Real Estate Investment Trusts.—For purposes of [12] section 243 (relating to deductions for dividends received by corporations), a dividend received from a real estate investment trust which meets the requirements of this part shall not be considered as a dividend.

(d) Earning and Profits.—

[13]*(1) In general.*—*The earnings and profits of a real estate investment trust for any taxable year (but not its accumulated earnings) shall not be reduced by any amount which is not allowable in computing its taxable income for such taxable year. For purposes of this subsection, the term "real estate investment trust" includes a domestic corporation, trust, or association which is a real estate investment trust determined without regard to the requirements of subsection (a).*

(2) Coordination with tax on undistributed income.—*A real estate investment trust shall be treated as having sufficient earnings and profits to treat as a dividend any distribution (other than in a redemption to which section 302(a) applies) which is treated as a dividend by such trust. The preceding sentence shall not apply to the extent that the amount distributed during any calendar year by the trust exceeds the required distribution for such calendar year (as determined under section 4981).*

(e) Excess Noncash Income.—

(1) In general.—*For purposes of subsection (a)(1)(B), the term "excess noncash income" means the excess (if any) of*—

    (A) the amount determined under paragraph (2) for the taxable year, over

    (B) 5 percent of the real estate investment trust taxable income for the taxable year determined without regard to the deduction for dividends paid (as defined in section 561) and by excluding any net capital gain.

(2) Determination of amount.—*The amount determined under this paragraph for the taxable year is the sum of*—

    (A) the amount (if any) by which—

        (i) the amounts includible in gross income under section 467 (relating to certain payments for the use of property or services), exceed

        (ii) the amounts which would have been includible in gross income without regard to such section,

    (B) in the case of a real estate investment trust using the cash receipts and disbursements method of accounting, the amount (if any) by which—

        (i) the amounts includible in gross income as original issue discount on instruments to which section 1274 (relating to certain debt instruments issued for property) applies, exceed

        (ii) the amount of money and the fair market value of other property received during the taxable year under such instruments; plus

    (C) any income on the disposition of a real estate asset if—

        (i) there is a determination (as defined in section 860(e)) that such income is not eligible for nonrecognition under section 1031, and

        (ii) failure to meet the requirements of section 1031 was due to reasonable cause and not to willful neglect.

[14]*(f) Cross Reference.*—

For provisions relating to excise tax based on certain real estate investment trust taxable income not distributed during the taxable year, see section 4981.

⟦Footnote ¶3110 continued⟧

Section 612(b)(7), '86 TRA, struck out from Sec. 857(c):

(12) "section 116 (relating to an exclusion for dividends received by individuals) and"

Effective date (Sec. 612(c), '86 TRA).—Applies to taxable years beginning after 12-31-86.

Matter in *italics* in Sec. 857(d) added by section 668(b)(2), '86 TRA which struck out:

(13) "The earnings and profits of a real estate investment trust for any taxable year (but not its accumulated earnings and profits) shall not be reduced by any amount which is not allowable as a deduction in computing its taxable income for such taxable year. For purposes of this subsection, the term 'real estate investment trust' includes a domestic corporation, trust, or association which is a real estate investment trust determined without regard to the requirements of subsection (a)."

Effective date (Sec. 669(b), '86 TRA).—Applies to calendar years beginning after 12-31-86.

Matter in *italics* in Sec. 857(e) and (f) added by section 664(b), '86 TRA, which struck out:

(14) "(e)"

Effective date (Sec. 669(a), '86 TRA).—Applies to taxable years beginning after 12-31-86.

[For official explanation, see Committee Reports, ¶3913; 3929.]

[¶3111] CODE SEC. 858. DIVIDENDS PAID BY REAL ESTATE INVESTMENT TRUST AFTER CLOSE OF TAXABLE YEAR.

* * * * * * * * * * * *

(c) **Notice to Shareholders.**—In the case of amounts to which subsection (a) applies, any notice to shareholders or holders of beneficial interests required under this part with respect to such amounts shall be made not later than 30 days after the close of the taxable year in which the distribution is made *(or mailed to its shareholders or holders of beneficial interests with its annual report for the taxable year).*

[For official explanation, see Committee Reports, ¶3929.]

[¶3112] CODE SEC. 859. ADOPTION OF ANNUAL ACCOUNTING PERIOD.

* * * * * * * * * * * *

(b) *Change of Accounting Period Without Approval.*—Notwithstanding section 442, an entity which has not engaged in any active trade or business may change its accounting period to a calendar year without the approval of the Secretary if such change is in connection with an election under section 856(c).

[For official explanation, see Committee Reports, ¶3929.]

[¶3113] CODE SEC. 860. DEDUCTION FOR DEFICIENCY DIVIDENDS.

* * * * * * * * * * * *

(j) **Penalty.—**

For assessable penalty with respect to liability for tax of a [1]*regulated investment company* which is allowed a deduction under section (a), see section 6697.

[For official explanation, see Committee Reports, ¶3929.]

[¶3113-A] CODE SEC. 860A. TAXATION OF REMICS.

(a) **General Rule.**—Except as otherwise provided in this part, a REMIC shall not be subject to taxation under this chapter (and shall not be treated as a corporation, partnership, or trust for purposes of this chapter).

(b) **Income Taxable to Holders.**—The income of any REMIC shall be taxable to the holders of interests in such REMIC as provided in this part.

[For official explanation, see Committee Reports, ¶3930.]

[¶3113-B] CODE SEC. 860B. TAXATION OF HOLDERS OF REGULAR INTERESTS.

(a) **General Rule.**—In determining the tax under this chapter of any holder of a regular interest in a REMIC, such interest (if not otherwise a debt instrument) shall be treated as a debt instrument.

(b) **Holders Must Use Accrual Method.**—The amounts includible in gross income with respect to any regular interest in a REMIC shall be determined under the accrual method of accounting.

(c) **Portion of Gain Treated as Ordinary Income.**—Gain on the disposition of a regular interest shall be treated as ordinary income to the extent such gain does not exceed the excess (if any) of—

(1) the amount which would have been includible in the gross income of the taxpayer with respect to such interest if the yield on such interest were 110 percent of the applicable Federal rate (as defined in section 1274(d) without regard to paragraph (2) thereof) as of the beginning of the taxpayer's holding period, over

---

[Footnote ¶3111] Matter in *italics* in Sec. 858(c) added by section 665(b)(2), '86 TRA.
Effective date (Sec. 669(a), '86 TRA).—Applies to taxable years beginning after 12-31-86.
[Footnote ¶3112] Matter in *italics* in Sec. 859 added by section 661(c)(1) and (2), '86 TRA.
Effective date (Sec. 669(a), '86 TRA).—Applies to taxable years beginning after 12-31-86.
[Footnote ¶3113] Matter in *italics* in Sec. 806(j) added by section 667(b)(1), '86 TRA, which struck out:
(1) "qualified investment entity"
Effective date (Sec. 669(a), '86 TRA).—Applies to taxable years beginning after 12-31-86.
[Footnote ¶3113-A] Sec. 860A added by section 671(a), '86 TRA.
Effective date (Sec. 675(a), '86 TRA).—Generally applies to taxable years beginning after 12-31-86.
[Footnote ¶3113-B] Sec. 860B added by section 671(a), '86 TRA.
Effective date (Sec. 675(a), '86 TRA).—Generally applies to taxable years beginning after 12-31-86.

(2) the amount actually includible in gross income with respect to such interest by the taxpayer.

(d) Cross Reference.—

For special rules in determining inclusion of original issue discount on regular interests, see section 1272(a)(6).

[For official explanation, see Committee Reports, ¶3930.]

[¶3113-C] CODE SEC. 860C. TAXATION OF RESIDUAL INTERESTS.

(a) Pass-Thru of Income or Loss.—

(1) In general.—In determining the tax under this chapter of any holder of a residual interest in a REMIC, such holder shall take into account his daily portion of the taxable income or net loss of such REMIC for each day during the taxable year on which such holder held such interest.

(2) Daily portion.—The daily portion referred to in paragraph (1) shall be determined—

(A) by allocating to each day in any calendar quarter its ratable portion of the taxable income (or net loss) for such quarter, and

(B) by allocating the amount so allocated to any day among the holders (on such day) of residual interest in proportion to their respective holdings on such day.

(b) Determination of Taxable Income or Net Loss.—For purposes of this section—

(1) Taxable income.—The taxable income of a REMIC shall be determined under an accrual method of accounting and in the same manner as in the case of an individual, except that—

(A) regular interests in such REMIC (if not otherwise debt instruments) shall be treated as indebtedness of such REMIC,

(B) market discount on any market discount bond shall be included in gross income for the taxable years to which it is attributable as determined under the rules of section 1276(b)(2) (and sections 1276(a) and 1277 shall not apply),

(C) there shall not be taken into account any item of income, gain, loss, or deduction allocable to a prohibited transaction, and

(D) the deductions referred to in section 703(a)(2) (other than any deduction under section 212) shall not be allowed.

(2) Net loss.—The net loss of any REMIC is the excess of—

(A) the deductions allowable in computing the taxable income of such REMIC, over

(B) its gross income.

Such amount shall be determined with the modifications set forth in paragraph (1).

(c) Distributions.—Any distribution by a REMIC—

(1) shall not be included in gross income to the extent it does not exceed the adjusted basis of the interest, and

(2) to the extent it exceeds the adjusted basis of the interest, shall be treated as gain from the sale or exchange of such interest.

(d) Basis Rules.—

(1) Increase in basis.—The basis of any person's residual interest in a REMIC shall be increased by the amount of the taxable income of such REMIC taken into account under subsection (a) by such person with respect to such interest.

(2) Decreases in basis.—The basis of any person's residual interest in a REMIC shall be decreased (but not below zero) by the sum of the following amounts:

(A) any distributions to such person with respect to such interest, and

(B) any net loss of such REMIC taken into account under subsection (a) by such person with respect to such interest.

(e) Special Rules.—

(1) Amounts treated as ordinary income.—Any amount included in the gross income of any holder of a residual interest in a REMIC by reason of subsection (a) shall be treated as ordinary income.

(2) Limitation on losses.—

(A) In general.—The amount of the net loss of any REMIC taken into account by a holder under subsection (a) with respect to any calendar quarter shall not ex-

[Footnote ¶3113-C] Sec. 860C added by section 671(a).
Effective date (Sec. 675(a), '86 TRA).—Generally applies to taxable years beginning after 12-31-86.

ceed the adjusted basis of such holder's residual interest in such REMIC as of the close of such calendar quarter (determined without regard to the adjustment under subsection (d)(2)(B) for such calendar quarter).

(B) Indefinite carryforward.—Any loss disallowed by reason of subparagraph (A) shall be treated as incurred by the REMIC in the succeeding calendar quarter with respect to such holder.

(3) Cross reference.—

For special treatment of income in excess of daily accruals, see section 860E.

[For official explanation, see Committee Reports, ¶3930.]

[¶3113-D] CODE SEC. 860D. REMIC DEFINED.

(a) General Rule.—For purposes of this title, the terms "real estate mortgage investment conduit" and "REMIC" mean any entity—

(1) to which an election to be treated as a REMIC applies for the taxable year and all prior taxable years,

(2) all of the interests in which are regular interests or residual interests,

(3) which has 1 (and only 1) class of residual interests (and all distributions, if any, with respect to such interests are pro rata),

(4) as of the close of the 4th month ending after the startup day and each quarter ending thereafter, substantially all of the assets of which consist of qualified mortgages and permitted investments, and

(5) which has a taxable year which is a calendar year.

(b) Election.—

(1) **In general.**—An entity (otherwise meeting the requirements of subsection (a)) may elect to be treated as a REMIC for its 1st taxable year. Such an election shall be made on its return for such 1st taxable year. Except as provided in paragraph (2), such an election shall apply to the taxable year for which made and all subsequent taxable years.

(2) **Termination.—**

(A) In general.—If any entity ceases to be a REMIC at any time during the taxable year, such entity shall not be treated as a REMIC for such taxable year or any succeeding taxable year.

(B) Inadvertent terminations.—If—

(i) an entity ceases to be a REMIC,

(ii) the Secretary determines that such cessation was inadvertent,

(iii) no later than a reasonable time after the discovery of the event resulting in such cessation, steps are taken so that such entity is once more a REMIC, and

(iv) such entity, and each person holding an interest in such entity at any time during the period specified pursuant to this subsection, agrees to make such adjustments (consistent with the treatment of such entity as a REMIC or a C corporation) as may be required by the Secretary with respect to such period,

then, notwithstanding such terminating event, such entity shall be treated as continuing to be a REMIC (or such cessation shall be disregarded for purposes of subparagraph (A)) whichever the Secretary determines to be appropriate.

[For official explanation, see Committee Reports, ¶3930.]

[¶3113-E] CODE SEC. 860E. TREATMENT OF INCOME IN EXCESS OF DAILY ACCRUALS ON RESIDUAL INTERESTS.

(a) Excess Inclusions May Not Be Offset by Net Operating Losses.—

(1) **In general.**—Except as provided in paragraph (2), the taxable income of any holder of a residual interest in a REMIC for any taxable year shall in no event be less than the excess inclusion for such taxable year.

(2) **Exception for certain financial institutions.**—Paragraph (1) shall not apply to any organization to which section 593 applies. The Secretary may by regulations provide that the preceding sentence shall not apply where necessary or appropriate to prevent avoidance of tax imposed by this chapter.

[Footnote ¶3113-D] Sec. 860D added by section 671(a), '86 TRA.
Effective date (Sec. 675(a), '86 TRA).—Generally applies to taxable years beginning after 12-31-86.
[Footnote ¶3113-E] Sec. 860E added by section 671(a), '86 TRA.
Effective date (Sec. 675(a), '86 TRA).—Generally applies to taxable years beginning after 12-31-86.

(b) Organizations Subject to Unrelated Business Tax.—If the holder of any residual interest in a REMIC is an organization subject to the tax imposed by section 511, the excess inclusion of such holder for any taxable year shall be treated as unrelated business taxable income of such holder for purposes of section 511.

(c) Excess Inclusion.—For purposes of this section—

(1) In general.—The term "excess inclusion" means with respect to any residual interest in a REMIC for any calendar quarter, the excess (if any) of—

(A) the amount taken into account with respect to such interest by the holder under section 860C(a), over

(B) the sum of the daily accruals with respect to such interest for days during such calendar quarter while held by such holder.

To the extent provided in regulations, if residual interests in a REMIC do not have significant value, the excess inclusions with respect to such interests shall be the amount determined under subparagraph (A) without regard to subparagraph (B).

(2) Determination of daily accruals.—

(A) **In general.**—For purposes of this subsection, the daily accrual with respect to any residual interest for any day in any calendar quarter shall be determined by allocating to each day in such quarter its ratable portion of the product of—

(i) the adjusted issue price of such interest at the beginning of such quarter, and

(ii) 120 percent of the long-term Federal rate (determined on the basis of compounding at the close of each calendar quarter and properly adjusted for the length of such quarter).

(B) **Adjusted issue price.**—For purposes of this paragraph, the adjusted issue price of any residual interest at the beginning of any calendar quarter is the issue price of residual interest—

(i) increased by the amount of daily accruals for prior quarters, and

(ii) decreased by any distribution made with respect to such interest before the beginning of such quarter.

(C) **Federal long-term rate.**—For purposes of this paragraph, the term "Federal long-term rate" means the Federal long-term rate which would have applied to the residual interest under section 1274(d) (determined without regard to paragraph (2) thereof) if it were a debt instrument.

(d) Treatment Of Residual Interests Held By Real Estate Investment Trusts.—If a residual interest in a REMIC is held by a real estate investment trust, under regulations prescribed by the Secretary—

(1) any excess of—

(A) the aggregate excess inclusions determined with respect to such interests, over

(B) the real estate investment trust taxable income (within the meaning of section 857(b)(2), excluding any net capital gain),

Shall be allocated among the shareholders of such trust in proportion to the dividends received by such shareholders received by such shareholders from trust, and

(2) any amount allocated to a shareholder under paragraph (1) shall be treated as an excess inclusion with respect to a residual interest held by such shareholder.

[For official explanation, see Committee Reports, ¶3930.]

[¶3113-F] CODE SEC. 860F. OTHER RULES.

(a) 100 Percent Tax on Prohibited Transactions.—

(1) Tax imposed.—There is hereby imposed for each taxable year of a REMIC a tax equal to 100 percent of the net income derived from prohibited transactions.

(2) Prohibited transaction.—For purposes of this part, the term "prohibited transaction" means—

(A) **Disposition of qualified mortgage.**—The disposition of any qualified mortgage transferred to the REMIC other than a disposition pursuant to—

(i) the substitution of a qualified replacement mortgage for a qualified mortgage,

(ii) a disposition incident to the foreclosure, default, or imminent default of the mortgage,

---

[**Footnote ¶3113-F**] Sec. 860F added by section 671(a), '86 TRA.
Effective date (Sec. 675(a), '86 TRA).—Applies to taxable years beginning after 12-31-86.

(iii) the bankruptcy or insolvency of the real estate mortgage pool, or

(iv) a qualified liquidation.

Notwithstanding the preceding sentence, the term "prohibited transaction" shall not include any disposition required to prevent default on a regular interest where the threatened default resulted from a default on 1 or more qualified mortgages.

(B) Income from nonpermitted assets.—The receipt of any income attributable to any asset which is neither a qualified mortgage nor a permitted investment.

(C) Compensation for services.—The receipt by the real estate mortgage pool of any amount representing a fee or other compensation for services.

(D) Gain from disposition of cash flow investments.—Gain from the disposition of any cash flow investment other than pursuant to any qualified liquidation described in subsection (b).

(3) **Determination of net income.**—For purposes of paragraph (1), the term "net income derived from prohibited transactions" means the excess of the gross income from prohibited transactions over the deductions allowed by this chapter which are directly connected with such transactions; except that there shall not be taken into account any item attributable to any prohibited transaction for which there was a loss.

(4) **Qualified liquidation.**—For purposes of this part—

(A) In general.—The term "qualified liquidation" means a transaction in which—

(i) the REMIC adopts a plan of complete liquidation,

(ii) such REMIC sells all its assets (other than cash) within the liquidation period, and

(iii) all proceeds of the liquidation (plus the cash), less assets retained to meet claims, are credited or distributed to holders of regular or residual interests on or before the last day of the liquidation period.

(B) Liquidation period.—The term "liquidation period" means the period—

(i) beginning on the date of the adoption of the plan of liquidation, and

(ii) ending at the close of the 90th day after such date.

(b) Treatment of Transfers to the REMIC.—

(1) **Treatment of transferor.—**

(A) Nonrecognition gain or loss.—No gain or loss shall be recognized to the transferor on the transfer of any property to a REMIC.

(B) Adjusted bases of interests.—The adjusted bases of the regular and residual interest received in a transfer described in subparagraph (A) shall be equal to the aggregate adjusted bases of the property transferred in such transfer. Such amount shall be allocated among such interests in proportion to their respective fair market values.

(C) Treatment of nonrecognized gain.—If the issue price of any regular or residual interest exceeds its adjusted basis as determined under subparagraph (B), for periods during which such interest is held by the transferor (or by any other person whose basis is determined in whole or in part by reference to the basis of such interest in the hand of the transferor)—

(i) in the case of a regular interest, such excess shall be included in gross income (as determined under rules similar to rules of section 1276(b)), and

(ii) in the case of a residual interest, such excess shall be included in gross income ratably over the anticipated period during which the real estate mortgage pool will be in existence.

(D) Treatment of nonrecognized loss.—If the adjusted basis of any regular or residual interest received in a transfer described in subparagraph (A) exceeds its issue price, for periods during which such interest is held by the transferor (or by any other person whose basis is determined in whole or in part by reference to the basis of such interest in the hand of the transferor)—

(i) in the case of a regular interest, such excess shall be allowable as a deduction under rules similar to the rules of section 171, and

(ii) in the case of a residual interest, such excess shall be allowable as a deduction ratably over the anticipated period during which the real estate mortgage pool will be in existence.

(2) **Basis to REMIC.**—The basis of any property received by a REMIC in a transfer described in paragraph (1)(A) shall be its fair market value immediately after such transfer.

Code §860F(b)(2) ¶3113-F

(c) Distributions of Property.—If a REMIC makes a distribution of property with respect to any regular or residual interest—

(1) notwithstanding any other provision of this subtitle, gain shall be recognized to such REMIC on the distribution in the same manner as if it had sold such property to the distributee at its fair market value, and

(2) the basis of the distributee in such property shall be its fair market value.

(d) Coordination With Wash Sale Rules.—For purposes of section 1091—

(1) any residual interest in a REMIC shall be treated as a security, and

(2) in applying such section to any loss claimed to have been sustained on the sale or other disposition of a residual interest in a REMIC—

(A) except as provided in regulations, any residual interest in any REMIC and any interest in a taxable mortgage pool (as defined in section 7701(i)) comparable to a residual interest in a REMIC shall be treated as substantially identical stock or securities, and

(B) subsections (a) and (e) of such section shall be applied by substituting "6 months" for "30 days" each place it appears.

(e) Treatment Under Subtitle F.—For purposes of subtitle F, a REMIC shall be treated as a partnership (and holders of residual interests in such REMIC shall be treated as partners). Any return required by reason of the preceding sentence shall include the amount of the daily accruals determined under section 860E(c).

[For official explanation, see Committee Reports, ¶3930.]

〔¶3113-G〕 CODE SEC. 860G. OTHER DEFINITIONS AND SPECIAL RULES.

(a) Definitions.—For purposes of this part—

(1) Regular Interest.—The term "regular interest" means an interest in a REMIC the terms of which are fixed on the startup day, and which—

(A) unconditionally entitles the holder to receive a specified principal amount (or other similar amount), and

(B) provides that interest payments (or other similar amounts), if any, at or before maturity are payable based on a fixed rate (or to the extent provided in regulations, at a variable rate).

An interest shall not fail to meet the requirements of subparagraph (A) merely because the timing (but not the amount) of the principal payments (or other similar amounts) may be contingent on the extent of prepayments on qualified mortgages and the amount of income from permitted investments.

(2) Residual Interest.—The term "residual interest" means an interest in a REMIC which is not a regular interest and is designated as a residual interest.

(3) Qualified Mortgage.—The term "qualified mortgage" means—

(A) any obligations (including any participation or certification of beneficial ownership therein) which is principally secured, directly or indirectly, by an interest in real property and which—

(i) is transferred to the REMIC on or before the startup day, or

(ii) is purchased by the REMIC within the 3-month period beginning on the startup day,

(B) any qualified replacement mortgage, and

(C) any regular interest in another REMIC transferred to the REMIC on or before the startup day.

(4) Qualified Replacement Mortgage.—The term "qualified replacement mortgage" means any obligation—

(A) which would be described in paragraph (3)(A) if it were transferred to the REMIC on or before the startup day, and

(B) which is received for—

(i) another obligation within the 3-month period beginning on the startup day, or

(ii) a defective obligation within the 2-year period beginning on the startup day.

(5) Permitted Investments.—The term "permitted investments" means any—

(A) cash flow investment,

(B) qualified reserve asset, or

(C) foreclosure property.

〔Footnote ¶3113-G〕 Sec. 860G added by section 671(a), '86 TRA.
Effective date (Sec. 675(a), '86 TRA).—Generally applies to taxable years beginning after 12-31-86.

(6) **Cash Flow Investment.**—The term "cash flow investment" means any investment of amounts received under qualified mortgages for a temporary period before distribution to holders of interests in the REMIC.

(7) **Qualified Reserve Asset.**—

(A) **In General.**—The term "qualified reserve asset" means any intangible property which is held for investment and as part of a qualified reserve fund.

(B) **Qualified Reserve Fund.**—For purposes of subparagraph (A), the term "qualified reserve fund" means any reasonably required reserve to provide for full payment of expenses of the REMIC or amounts due on regular interests in the event of defaults on qualified mortgages. The amount of any such reserve shall be promptly and appropriately reduced as payments of qualified mortgages are received.

(C) **Special Rule.**—A reserve shall not be treated as a qualified reserve for any taxable year (and all subsequent taxable years) if more than 30 percent of the gross income from the assets in such fund for the taxable year is derived from the sale or other disposition of property held for less than 3 months. For purposes of the preceding sentence, gain on the disposition of a qualified reserve asset shall not be taken into account if the disposition giving rise to such gain is required to prevent default on a regular interest where the threatened default resulted from a default on 1 or more qualified mortgages.

(8) **Foreclosure property.**—The term "foreclosure property" means property—

(A) which would be foreclosure property under section 856(e) if acquired by a real estate investment trust, and

(B) which is acquired in connection with the default or imminent default of a qualified mortgage held by the REMIC.

Property shall cease to be foreclosure property with respect to the REMIC on the date which is 1 year after the date such real estate mortgage pool acquired such property.

(9) **Startup Day.**—The term "startup day" means any day selected by a REMIC which is on or before the 1st day on which interests in such REMIC are issued.

(10) **Issue Price.**—The issue price of any regular or residual interest in a REMIC shall be determined under section 1273(b) in the same manner as if such interest were a debt instrument; except that if the interest is issued for property, paragraph (3) of section 1273(b) shall apply whether or not the requirements of such paragraph are met.

(b) **Treatment of Nonresident Aliens and Foreign Corporations.**—If the holder of a residual interest in a REMIC is a nonresident alien individual or a foreign corporation, for purposes of sections 871(a), 881, 1441, and 1442—

(1) amounts includible in the gross income of such holder under this part shall be taken into account when paid or distributed (or when the interest is disposed of), and

(2) no exemption from the taxes imposed by such sections (and no reduction in the rates of such taxes) shall apply to any excess inclusion.

The Secretary may by regulations provide that such amounts shall be taken into account earlier than as provided in paragraph (1) where necessary or appropriate to prevent the avoidance of tax imposed by this chapter.

(c) **Regulations.**—The Secretary shall prescribe such regulations as may be necessary or appropriate to carry out the purposes of this part, including regulations—

(1) to prevent unreasonable accumulations of assets in a REMIC,

(2) permitting determinations of the fair market value of property transferred to a REMIC and issue price of interests in a REMIC to be made earlier than otherwise provided, and

(3) requiring reporting to holders of residual interests of such information as frequently as is necessary or appropriate to permit such holders to compute their taxable income accurately.

[¶3114] CODE SEC. 861. INCOME FROM SOURCES WITHIN THE UNITED STATES.

(a) **Gross Income From Sources Within United States.**—The following items of gross income shall be treated as income from sources within the United States:

* (1) Interest.—Interest from the United States or the District of Columbia, and interest on bonds, notes, or other interest-bearing obligations of [1]*noncorporate residents or domestic corporations* not including—[2]

[3]*(A) interest from a resident alien individual or domestic corporation, if such individual or corporation meets the 80-percent foreign business requirements of subsection (c)(1),*[4]

[5,6]*(B) interest—*

⟦Footnote ¶3114⟧ Matter in *italics* in Sec. 861(a)(1) added by section 1241(b)(1)(A), '86 TRA, which struck out:

(1) "residents, corporate or otherwise,"

Effective date (Sec. 1241(e), '86 TRA).—Applies to taxable years beginning after 12-31-86.

---

* Sec. 861(a)(1), before its amendment by section 1241(b)(1)(B), was also amended by section 1214(c)(5)(A), '86 TRA which relettered subparagraphs (B), (C), (D), (F), (G), and (H) as subparagraphs (A), (B), (C), (D), (E), and (F).

Matter in *italics* in Sec. 861(a)(1)(A) added by section 1214(a)(1) and (c)(5)(A), '86 TRA, which struck out:

(2) "(A) interest on amounts described in subsection (c) received by a nonresident alien individual or a foreign corporation, if such interest is not effectively connected with the conduct of a trade or business within the United States."

(3) "(B) interest received from a resident alien individual or a domestic corporation, when it is shown to the satisfaction of the Secretary that less than 20 percent of the gross income from all sources of such individual or such corporation has been derived from sources within the United States, as determined under the provisions of this part, for the 3-year period ending with the close of the taxable year of such individual or such corporation preceding the payment of such interest, or for such part of such period as may be applicable,"

Effective date (Sec. 1214(d), '86 TRA).—(1) Generally applies to payments after 12-31-86.

(2) Treatment of certain interest.—

(A) In general.—The amendments made by this section shall not apply to any interest paid or accrued on any obligation outstanding on 12-31-85. The preceding sentence shall not apply to any interest paid pursuant to any extension or renewal of such an obligation agreed to after 12-31-85.

(B) Special rule for related payee.—If the payee of any interest to which subparagraph (A) applies is related (within the meaning of section 904(d)(2)(G) of the '86 Code) to the payor, such interest shall be treated for purposes of section 904 of such Code as if the payor were a controlled foreign corporation (within the meaning of section 957(a) of such Code).

(3) Transitional rule.—

(A) Years before 1988.—In applying the amendments made by this section to any payment made by a corporation in a taxable year of such corporation beginning before 1-1-88, the requirements of clause (ii) of section 861(c)(1)(B) of the '86 Code (relating to active business requirements), as amended by this section, shall not apply to gross income of such corporation for taxable years beginning before 1-1-87.

(B) Years after 1987.—In applying the amendments made by this section to any payment made by a corporation in a taxable year of such corporation beginning after 12-31-87, the testing period for purposes of section 861(c) of such Code (as so amended) shall not include any taxable year beginning before 1-1-87.

(4) Certain dividends.—

(A) In general.—The amendments made by this section shall not apply to any dividend paid before 1-1-91, by a qualified corporation with respect to stock which was outstanding on 5-31-85.

(B) Qualified corporation.—For purposes of subparagraph (A), the term "qualified corporation" means any business systems corporation which—

(i) was incorporated in Delaware in February, 1979,

(ii) is headquartered in Garden City, New York, and

(iii) the parent corporation of which is a resident of Sweden.

Sec. 861(a)(1)(B) and (C) [former (C) and (D)] struck out by section 1241(b)(1)(B), '86 TRA.

(4) "(B) interest received from a foreign corporation (other than interest paid or credited by a domestic branch of a foreign corporation, if such branch is engaged in the commercial banking business), when it is shown to the satisfaction of the Secretary that less than 50 percent of the gross income from all sources of such foreign corporation for the 3-year period ending with the close of its taxable year preceding the payment of such interest (or for such part of such period as the corporation has been in existence) was effectively connected with the conduct of a trade or business within the United States,

(C) in the case of interest received from a foreign corporation (other than interest paid or credited by a domestic branch of a foreign corporation, if such branch is engaged in the commercial banking business), 50 percent or more of the gross income of which from all sources for the 3-year period ending with the close of its taxable year preceding the payment of such interest (or for such part of such period as the corporation has been in existence) was effectively connected with the conduct of a trade or business within the United States, an amount of such interest which bears the same ratio to such interest as the gross income of such foreign corporation for such period which was not effectively connected with the conduct of a trade or business within the United States bears to its gross income from all sources,"

Effective date (Sec. 1241(e), '86 TRA).—Applies to taxable years beginning after 12-31-86.

Sec. 861(a)(1)(E) struck out by section 1214(c)(5)(A), '86 TRA.

(5) "(E) income derived by a foreign central bank of issue from bankers' acceptances,"

Effective date (Sec. 1214(d), '86 TRA).—Generally applies to payments after 12-31-86. For special and transitional rules, see above.

(i)   on deposits with a foreign branch of a domestic corporation or a domestic partnership, if such branch is engaged in the commercial banking business, and

(ii)   on amounts satisfying the requirements of [7]*subparagraph (B) of section 871(i)(3)* which are paid by a foreign branch of a domestic corporation or a domestic partnership,

[8]*(C)*   interest on a debt obligation which was part of an issue with respect to which an election has been made under subsection (c) of section 4912 (as in effect before July 1, 1974) and which, when issued (or treated as issued under subsection (c)(2) of such section), had a maturity not exceeding 15 years and, when issued, was purchased by one or more underwriters with a view to distribution through resale, but only with respect to interest attributable to periods after the date of such election, and

[9]*(D)*   interest on a debt obligation which was part of an issue which—

(i)   was part of an issue outstanding on April 1, 1971,

(ii)   was guaranteed by a United States person,

(iii)   was treated under chapter 41 as a debt obligation of a foreign obligor,

(iv)   as of June 30, 1974, had a maturity of not more than 15 years, and

(v)   when issued, was purchased by one or more underwriters for the purpose of distribution through resale.

(2)   **Dividends.**—The amount received as dividends.—

[10]*(A)   from a domestic corporation other than a corporation which has an election in effect under section 936, or*

(B)   from a foreign corporation unless less than [11]*25 percent* of the gross income from all sources of such foreign corporation for the 3-year period ending with the close of its taxable year preceding the declaration of such dividends (or for such part of such period as the corporation has been in existence) was effectively connected *(or treated as effectively connected other than under section 884(a)(2))* with the conduct of a trade or business within the United States; but only in an amount which bears the same ratio to such dividends as the gross income of the corporation for such period which was effectively connected *(or treated as effectively connected other than under section 884(a)(2))* with the conduct of a trade or business within the United States bears to its gross income from all sources; but dividends (other than dividends for which a deduction is allowable under section 245(b)) from a foreign corporation shall, for purposes of subpart A of part III

[Footnote ¶3114 continued]

Matter in *italics* in Sec. 861(a)(1)(B) [former (F)] added by section 1241(b)(1)(B), '86 TRA, which struck out:
(6)   "(D)"
Effective date (Sec. 1241(e), '86 TRA).—Applies to taxable years beginning after 12-31-86.

Matter in *italics* in Sec. 861(a)(1)(B)(ii) added by section 1214(c)(5)(B), '86 TRA, which struck out:
(7)   "paragraph (2) of subsection (c)"
Effective date (Sec. 1214(d), '86 TRA).—Generally applies to payments after 12-31-86. For special and transitional rules, see above.

Matter in *italics* in Sec. 861(a)(1)(C) and (D) [former (G) and (H)] added by section 1241(b)(1)(B), '86 TRA, which struck out:
(8)   "(E)"
(9)   "(F)"
Effective date (Sec. 1241(e), '86 TRA).—Applies to taxable years beginning after 12-31-86.

Matter in *italics* in Sec. 861(a)(2)(A) added by section 1214(b), '86 TRA, which struck out:
(10)   "(A)   from a domestic corporation other than a corporation which has an election in effect under section 936, and other than a corporation less than 20 percent of whose gross income is shown to the satisfaction of the Secretary to have been derived from sources within the United States, as determined under the provisions of this part, for the 3-year period ending with the close of the taxable year of such corporation preceding the declaration of such dividends (or for such part of such period as the corporation has been in existence), or"
Effective date (Sec. 1214(d), '86 TRA).—Generally applies to payments after 12-31-86. For special and transitional rules, see above.

Matter in *italics* in Sec. 861(a)(2)(B) added by section 1241(b)(2), '86 TRA, which struck out:
(11)   "50 percent"
Effective date (Sec. 1241(e), '86 TRA).—Applies to taxable years beginning after 12-31-86.

(relating to foreign tax credit), be treated as income from sources without the United States to the extent (and only to the extent) exceeding the amount which is 100/85th of the amount of the deduction allowable under section 245 in respect of such dividends, or

(C) from a foreign corporation to the extent that such amount is required by section 243(d) (relating to certain dividends from foreign corporations) to be treated as dividends from a domestic corporation which is subject to taxation under this chapter, and to such extent subparagraph (B) shall not apply to such amount, or

(D) from a DISC or former DISC (as defined in section 992(a)) except to the extent attributable (as determined under regulations prescribed by the Secretary) to qualified export receipts described in section 993(a)(1) (other than interest and gains described in section 995(b)(1)).

* * * * * * * * * * * *

(6) **Sale or Exchange of personal property.**—Gains, profits, and income derived from the purchase of [12]*inventory property (within the meaning of section 865(h)(1))* without the United States (other than within a possession of the United States) and its sale or exchange within the United States.

* * * * * * * * * * * *

(b) **Taxable Income From Sources Within United States.**—From the items of gross income specified in subsection (a) as being income from sources within the United States there shall be deducted the expenses, losses, and other deductions properly apportioned or allocated thereto and a ratable part of any expenses, losses or other deductions which cannot definitely be allocated to some item or class of gross income. The remainder, if any, shall be included in full as taxable income from sources within the United States. In the case of an individual who does not itemize deductions, an amount equal to the [13] *standard deduction* shall be considered a deduction which cannot definitely be allocated to some item or class of gross income.

[14]*(c)* *Foreign Business Requirements.*—

(1) *Foreign business requirements.*—

(A) *In general.*—*An individual or corporation meets the 80-percent foreign business requirements of this paragraph if it is shown to the satisfaction of the Secretary that at least 80 percent of the gross income from all sources of such individual or corporation for the testing period is active foreign business income.*

(B) *Active foreign business income.*—*For purposes of subparagraph (A), the term "active foreign business income" means gross income which*—

(i) *is derived from sources outside the United States (as determined under this subchapter), and*

(ii) *is attributable to the active conduct of a trade or business in a foreign country or possession of the United States by the individual or corporation (or by a subsidiary or chain of subsidiaries of such corporation).*

(C) *Testing period.*—*For purposes of this subsection, the term "testing period" means the 3-year period ending with the close of the taxable year of the individual or corporation preceding the payment (or such part of such period as may be applicable).*

⟦Footnote ¶3114 continued⟧

Matter in *italics* in Sec. 861(a)(6) added by section 1211(b)(1)(B), '86 TRA, which struck out:

(12) "personal property"

Effective date (Sec. 1211(c), '86 TRA).—(1) Generally applies to taxable years beginning after 12-31-86. (2) Special rule for foreign persons.—In the case of any foreign person other than any controlled foreign corporations (within the meaning of section 957(a) of the '54 Code), the amendments made by this section shall apply to transactions entered into after 3-18-86.

Matter in *italics* in Sec. 861(b) added by section 104(b)(11), '86 TRA, which struck out:

(13) "zero bracket amount"

Effective date (Sec. 151(a), '86 TRA).—Applies to taxable years beginning after 12-31-86.

Matter in *italics* in Sec. 861(c) and (d) added by section 1214(a)(2) and (c)(5)(C), '86 TRA, which struck out:

(14) **"(c) Interest on Deposits, Etc.**—For purposes of subsection (a)(1)(A), the amounts described in this subsection are—

(1) deposits with persons carrying on the banking business,

(2) deposits or withdrawable accounts with savings institutions chartered and supervised as savings and loan or similar associations under Federal or State law, but only to the extent that amounts paid or credited on such deposits or accounts are deductible under section 591 (determined without regard to section 265) in computing the taxable income of such institutions, and

(3) amounts held by an insurance company under an agreement to pay interest thereon."

If the individual or corporation has no gross income for such 3-year period (or part thereof), the testing period shall be the taxable year in which the payment is made.

   (2)   *Look-thru where related person receives interest.—*

      (A)   *In general.—In the case of interest received by a related person from a resident alien individual or domestic corporation meeting the 80-percent foreign business requirements of paragraph (1), subsection (a)(1)(A) shall apply only to a percentage of such interest equal to the percentage which—*

         (i)   *the gross income of such individual or corporation for the testing period from sources outside the United States (as determined under this subchapter), is of*

         (ii)   *the total gross income of such individual or corporation for the testing period.*

      (B)   *Related person.—For purposes of this paragraph, the term "related person" has the meaning given such term by section 954(d)(3), except that—*

         (i)   *such section shall be applied by substituting "the individual or corporation making the payment" for "controlled foreign corporation" each place it appears, and*

         (ii)   *such section shall be applied by substituting "10 percent" for "50 percent" each place it appears.*

[15]*(d)   Special Rule for Application of Subsection (a)(2)(B).—For purposes of subsection (a)(2)(B), if the foreign corporation has no gross income from any source for the 3-year period (or part thereof) specified, the requirements of such subsection shall be applied with respect to the taxable year of such corporation in which the payment of the dividend is made.*[16]

[17]*(e)*   **Income From Certain Railroad Rolling Stock Treated as Income From Sources**

⟦Footnote ¶3114 continued⟧

   (15)   **"(d)   Special Rules for Application of Paragraphs (1)(B), (1)(C), (1)(D), and (2)(B) of subsection (a).—**

   (1)   **New entities.—**For purposes of paragraphs (1)(B), (1)(C), (1)(D), and (2)(B) of subsection (a), if the resident alien individual, domestic corporation, or foreign corporation, as the case may be, has no gross income from any source for the 3-year period (or part thereof) specified, the 20 percent test or the 50 percent test, as the case may be, shall be applied with respect to the taxable year of the payor in which payment of the interest or dividends, as the case may be, is made.

   (2)   **Transition rule.—**For purposes of paragraphs (1)(C), (1)(D), and (2)(B) of subsection (a), the gross income of the foreign corporation for any period before the first taxable year beginning after December 31, 1966, which is effectively connected with the conduct of a trade or business within the United States is an amount equal to the gross income for such period from sources within the United States."

Effective date (Sec. 1214(d), '86 TRA).—Generally applies to payments after 12-31-86. For special and transitional rules, see above.

   Matter in *italics* in Sec. 861(e) added by section 1212(d), '86 TRA, which struck out:

   (16)   **"(e)   Income From Certain Leased Aircraft, Vessels, and Spacecraft Treated as Income From Sources Within the United States.—**

   (1)   **In General.—**For purposes of subsection (a) and section 862(a), if—

   (A)   a taxpayer owning a craft which is section 38 property (or would be section 38 property but for section 48(a)(5)) leases such craft to a United States person, other than a member of the same controlled group of corporations (as defined in section 1563) as the taxpayer, and

   (B)   such craft is manufactured or constructed in the United States,

then all amounts includible in gross income by the taxpayer with respect to such craft for any taxable year ending after the commencement of such lease (whether during or after the period of such lease), including gain from sale, exchange, or other disposition of such craft, shall be treated as income from sources within the United States.

   (2)   **Certain transfers involving carryover basis.—**If the taxpayer transfers or distributes a craft to which paragraph (1) applied and the basis of such craft in the hands of the transferee or distributee is determined by reference to its basis in the hands of the transferor or distributor, paragraph (1) shall continue to apply to such craft in the hands of the transferee or distributee.

   (3)   **Craft defined.—**For purposes of this subsection, the term 'craft' means a vessel, aircraft, or spacecraft."

   (17)   **"(f)"**

Effective date (Sec. 1212(f), '86 TRA).—(1) Generally applies to taxable years beginning after 12-31-86. (2) Special rule for certain leased property.—The amendments made by subsections (a) and (d) shall not apply to any income attributable to property held by the taxpayer on 1-1-86, if such property was first leased by the taxpayer before 1-1-86, in a lease to which section 863(c)(2)(B) or 861(e) of the '54 Code (as in effect on the day before the date of the enactment of this Act) applied.

   (3)   Special rule for certain ships leased by the United States Navy.—

   (A)   In general.—In the case of any property described in subparagraph (B), paragraph (2) shall be applied by substituting "1987" for "1986" each place it appears.

   (B)   Property to which paragraph applies.—Property described in this subparagraph consists of 4 ships which are to be leased by the United States Navy and which are the subject of IRS rulings issued on the following dates and which involved the following amount of financing, respectively:

Within the United States.

* * * * * * * * * * * *

[For official explanation, see Committee Reports, ¶4028; 4029; 4031; 4047.]

[¶3115] CODE SEC. 862. INCOME FROM SOURCES WITHOUT THE UNITED STATES.

(a) **Gross Income From Sources Without United States.**—The following items of gross income shall be treated as income from sources without the United States:

(1) interest other than that derived from sources within the United States as provided in section 861(a)(1);

(2) dividends other than those derived from sources within the United States as provided in section 861(a)(2);

(3) compensation for labor or personal services performed without the United States;

(4) rentals or royalties from property located without the United States or from any interest in such property, including rentals or royalties for the use of or for the privilege of using without the United States patents, copyrights, secret processes and formulas, good will, trade-marks, trade brands, franchises, and other like properties;

(5) gains, profits, and income from the sale or exchange of real property located without the United States;

(6) gains, profits, and income derived from the purchase of ¹*inventory property (within the meaning of section 865(h)(1))* within the United States and its sale or exchange without the United States;

(7) underwriting income other than that derived from sources within the United States as provided in section 861(a)(7); and

(8) gains, profits, and income from the disposition of a United States real property interest (as defined in section 897(c)) when the real property is located in the Virgin Islands.

(b) **Taxable Income From Sources Without United States.**—From the items of gross income specified in subsection (a) there shall be deducted the expenses, losses, and other deductions properly apportioned or allocated thereto, and a ratable part of any expenses, losses, or other deductions which cannot definitely be allocated to some item or class of gross income. The remainder, if any, shall be treated in full as taxable income from sources without the United States. In the case of an individual who does not itemize deductions, an amount equal to the ²*standard deduction* shall be considered a deduction which cannot definitely be allocated to some item or class of gross income.

* * * * * * * * * * * *

[For official explanation, see Committee Reports, ¶4028.]

[¶3116] CODE SEC. 863. ITEMS NOT SPECIFIED IN SECTION 861 OR 862.

* * * * * * * * * * * *

(b) **Income Partly From Within and Partly From Without the United States.**—In the case of gross income derived from sources partly within and partly without the United States, the taxable income may first be computed by deducting the expenses, losses, or other deductions apportioned or allocated thereto and a ratable part of any expenses, losses, or other deductions which cannot definitely be allocated to some item or class of gross income; and the portion of such taxable income attributable to sources within the

---

[Footnote ¶3114 continued]

February 5, 1986	$ 64,567,000
March 5, 1986	176,844,000
April 22, 1986	64,598,000
May 22, 1986	175,300,000.

[Footnote ¶3115] Matter in *italics* in Sec. 862(a)(6) added by section 1211(b)(1)(C), '86 TRA, which struck out:

(1) "personal property"

Effective date (Sec. 1211(c), '86 TRA).—(1) Generally applies to taxable years beginning after 12-31-86.

(2) Special rule for foreign persons.—In the case of any foreign person other than any controlled foreign corporations (within the meaning of section 957(a) of the '54 Code), the amendments made by this section shall apply to transactions entered into after 3-18-86.

Matter in *italics* in Sec. 862(b) added by section 104(b)(12), '86 TRA, which struck out:

(2) "zero bracket amount"

Effective date (Sec. 151(a), '86 TRA). —Applies to taxable years beginning after 12-31-86.

United States may be determined by processes or formulas of general apportionment prescribed by the Secretary. Gains, profits, and income—

(1) from [1] services rendered partly within and partly without the United States,

(2) from the sale or exchange of [2]*inventory property (within the meaning of section 865(h)(1))* produced (in whole or in part) by the taxpayer within and sold or exchanged without the United States, or produced (in whole or in part) by the taxpayer without and sold or exchanged within the United States, or

(3) derived from the purchase of [2]*inventory property (within the meaning of section 865(h)(1))* within a possession of the United States and its sale or exchange within the United States,

shall be treated as derived partly from sources within and partly from sources without the United States.

(c) Source Rule for Certain Transportation Income.—

* * * * * * * * * * * *

[3]*(2) Other transportation having United States connection.—*

(A) In general.—50 percent of all transportation income attributable to transportation which—

(i) is not described in paragraph (1), and

(ii) begins or ends in the United States,

shall be treated as from sources in the United States,

〔Footnote ¶3116〕 Section 1212(e), '86 TRA, struck out from Sec. 863(b)(1):

(1) "transportation or other"

Effective date (Sec. 1212(f)(1), '86 TRA).—Applies to taxable years beginning after 12-31-86.

Matter in *italics* in Sec. 863(b)(2) and (3) added by section 1211(b)(1)(A), '86 TRA, which struck out:

(2) "personal property"

Effective date (Sec. 1211(c), '86 TRA).—(1) Generally applies to taxable years beginning after 12-31-86.

(2) Special rule for foreign persons.—In the case of any foreign person other than any controlled foreign corporations (within the meaning of section 957(a) of the '54 Code), the amendments made by this section shall apply to transactions entered into after 3-18-86.

Matter in *italics* in Sec. 863(c)(2) added by section 1212(a), '86 TRA, which struck out:

(3) "(2) Transportation between United States and any possession.—

(A) In General.—50 percent of all transportation income attributable to transportation which—

(i) begins in the United States and ends in a possession of the United States, or

(ii) begins in a possession of the United States and ends in the United States, shall be treated as derived from sources within the United States.

(B) Special Rule For Certain Lessors of Aircraft.—If—

(i) the taxpayer owns an aircraft which is section 38 property and leases such aircraft to a United States person (other than a member of the same controlled group of corporations (as defined in section 1563) as the taxpayer), and

(ii) such United States person is a regularly scheduled air carrier,

subparagraph (A) shall be applied by substituting '100 percent' for '50 percent.' "

Effective date (Sec. 1212(f)(1), (2), and (3) '86 TRA).—(1) Generally applies to taxable years beginning after 12-31-86.

(2) Special rule for certain leased property.—The amendments made by subsections (a) and (d) shall not apply to any income attributable to property held by the taxpayer on 1-1-86, if such property was first leased by the taxpayer before 1-1-86, in a lease to which section 863(c)(2)(B) or 861(e) of the '54 Code (as in effect on—86) applied.

(3) Special rule for certain ships leased by the United States Navy.—

(A) In general.—In the case of any property described in subparagraph (B), paragraph (2) shall be applied by substituting "1987" for "1986" each place it appears.

(B) Property to which paragraph applies.—Property described in this subparagraph consists of 4 ships which are to be leased by the United States Navy and which are the subject of Internal Revenue Service rulings issued on the following dates and which involved the following amount of financing, respectively:

February 5, 1986	$ 64,567,000
March 5, 1986	176,844,000
April 22, 1986	64,598,000
May 22, 1986	175,300,000.

Sec. 863(d) and (e) in *italics* added by section 1213(a), '86 TRA.

Effective date (Sec. 1213(b), '86 TRA).—Applies to taxable years beginning after 12-31-86.

Code §863(c)(2) ¶3116

(B)　*Special rule for personal service income.—Subparagraph (A) shall not apply to any transportation income which is income derived from personal services performed by the taxpayer, unless such income is attributable to transportation which—*

(i)　*begins in the United States and ends in a possession of the United States, or*

(ii)　*begins in a possession of the United States and ends in the United States.*

* * * * * * * * * * *

(d)　*Source Rules for Space and Certain Ocean Activities.—*

(1)　*In general.—Except as provided in regulations, any income derived from a space or ocean activity—*

(A)　*if derived by a United States person, shall be sourced in the United States, and*

(B)　*if derived by a person other than a United States person, shall be sourced outside the United States.*

(2)　*Space or ocean activity.—For purposes of paragraph (1)—*

(A)　*In general.—The term "space or ocean activity" means—*

(i)　*any activity conducted in space, and*

(ii)　*any activity conducted on or under water not within the jurisdiction (as recognized by the United States) of a foreign country, possession of the United States, or the United States.*

Such term includes any activity conducted in Antarctica.

(B)　*Exception for certain activities.—The term "space or ocean activity" shall not include—*

(i)　*any activity giving rise to transportation income (as defined in section 863(c)),*

(ii)　*any activity giving rise to international communications income (as defined in subsection (e)(2)), and*

(iii)　*any activity with respect to mines, oil and gas wells, or other natural deposits to the extent within the United States or any foreign country or possession of the United States (as defined in section 638).*

For purposes of applying section 638, the jurisdiction of any foreign country shall not include any jurisdiction not recognized by the United States.

(e)　*International Communications Income.—*

(1)　*Source rules.—*

(A)　*United States persons.—In the case of any United States person, 50 percent of any international communications income shall be sourced in the United States and 50 percent of such income shall be sourced outside the United States.*

(B)　*Foreign persons.—*

(i)　*In general.—Except as provided in regulations or clause (ii), in the case of any person other than a United States person, any international communications income shall be sourced outside the United States.*

(ii)　*Special rule for income attributable to office or fixed place of business in the United States.—In the case of any person (other than a United States person) who maintains an office or other fixed place of business in the United States, any international communications income attributable to such office or other fixed place of business shall be sourced in the United States.*

(2)　*Definition.—For purposes of this section, the term "international communications income" includes all income derived from the transmission of communications or data from the United States to any foreign country or from any foreign country to the United States.*

[For official explanation, see Committee Reports, ¶4028; 4029; 4030.]

[¶3117]　CODE SEC. 864.　DEFINITIONS *AND SPECIAL RULES*.

* * * * * * * * * * *

(c)　**Effectively Connected Income, etc.—**

(1)　**General rule.**—For purposes of this title—

(A)　In the case of a nonresident alien individual or a foreign corporation engaged in trade or business within the United States during the taxable year, the

[Footnote ¶3117]　Matter in *italics* in the heading of Sec. 864 added by section 1215(b)(1), '86 TRA.
Effective date (Sec. 1215(c), '86 TRA).—(1)　Generally applies to taxable years beginning after 12-31-86. For special and transitional rules see ¶2058.

rules set forth in paragraphs (2), (3), [1]*(4), (6), and (7)* shall apply in determining the income, gain, or loss which shall be treated as effectively connected with the conduct of a trade or business within the United States.

(B) Except as provided in *paragraph (6) or (7) or in* section 871(d) or section 882(d) and (e), in the case of a nonresident alien individual or a foreign corporation not engaged in trade or business within the United States during the taxable year, no income, gain, or loss shall be treated as effectively connected with the conduct of a trade or business within the United States.

(2) Periodical, etc., income from sources within United States—factors.—In determining whether income from sources within the United States of the types described in section 871(a)(1) [2]*section 871(h), section 881(a),* or section 881(c), or whether gain or loss from sources within the United States from the sale or exchange of capital assets, is effectively connected with the conduct of a trade or business within the United States, the factors taken into account shall include whether—

(A) the income, gain or loss is derived from assets used in or held for use in the conduct of such trade or business, or

(B) the activities of such trade or business were a material factor in the realization of the income, gain, or loss.

In determining whether an asset is used or held for use in the conduct of such trade or business or whether the activities of such trade or business were a material factor in realizing an item of income, gain, or loss, due regard shall be given to whether or not such asset or income, gain, or loss was accounted for through such trade or business. In applying this paragraph and paragraph (4), interest referred to in section 861(a)(1)(A) shall be considered income from sources within the United States.

* * * * * * * * * * * *

(4) Income from sources without United States.—

* * * * * * * * * * * *

(B) Income, gain, or loss from sources without the United States shall be treated as effectively connected with the conduct of a trade or business within the United States by a nonresident alien individual or a foreign corporation if such person has an office or other fixed place of business within the United States to which such income, gain, or loss is attributable and such income, gain, or loss—

(i) Consists of rents or royalties for the use of or for the privilege of using intangible property described in section 862(a)(4) (including any gain or loss realized on the sale or exchange of such property) derived in the active conduct of such trade or business; *or*

(ii) consists of dividends or interest, or gain or loss from the sale or exchange of stock or notes, bonds, or other evidences of indebtedness, and either is derived in the active conduct of the banking, financing, or similar business within the United States or is received by a corporation the principal business of which is trading in stock or securities for its own account[3]. [4]

* * * * * * * * * * * *

⌈Footnote ¶3117 continued⌉

Matter in *italics* in Sec. 864(c)(1), (6) and (7) added by section 1242(a) and (b), '86 TRA, which struck out:
(1) "and (4)"
Effective date (Sec. 1242(c), '86 TRA).—Applies to taxable years beginning after 12-31-86.

Matter in *italics* in Sec. 864(c)(2) added by section 1899A(21), '86 TRA which struck out:
(2) "section 871(h) section 881(a)"

Matter in *italics* in Sec. 864(c)(4)(B) added by section 1211(b)(2), '86 TRA, which struck out:
(3) "; or"
(4) "(iii) is derived from the sale or exchange (without the United States) through such office or other fixed place of business of personal property described in section 1221(1), except that this clause shall not apply if the property is sold or exchanged for use, consumption, or disposition outside the United States and an office or other fixed place of business of the taxpayer outside the United States participated materially in such sale or exchange."
Effective date (Sec. 1211(c), '86 TRA.—(1) Generally applies to taxable years beginning after 12-31-86.
(2) Special rule for foreign persons.—In the case of any foreign person other than any controlled foreign corporations (within the meaning of section 957(a) of the '54 Code, the amendments made by this section shall apply to transactions entered into after 3-18-86.

---

(6) Treatment of Certain Deferred Payments, etc.—For purposes of this title, any income or gain of a nonresident alien individual or a foreign corporation for any taxable year which is attributable to a sale or exchange of property or the performance of services (or any other transaction) in any other taxable year shall be treated as effectively connected with the conduct of a trade or business within the United States if it would have been so treated if such income or gain were taken into account in such other taxable year.

(7) Treatment of certain property transactions.—For purposes of this title, if any property ceases to be used or held for use in connection with the conduct of a trade or business within the United States, the determination of whether any income or gain attributable to a sale or exchange of such property occurring within 10 years after such cessation is effectively connected with the conduct of a trade or business within the United States shall be made as if such sale or exchange occurred immediately before such cessation.

(d) Treatment of Related Person Factoring Income.—

*   *   *   *   *   *   *   *   *   *   *   *   *   *

≫P-H CAUTION→ There are two versions of Sec. 864(d)(5)(A)(i). Sec. 864(d)(5)(A)(i), generally effective after 12-31-86, follows. For Sec. 864(d)(5)(A)(i), generally effective before 1-1-87. See below.

▲ **(5) Certain provisions not to apply.—**

(A) Certain exceptions.—The following provisions shall not apply to any amont treated as interest under paragraph (1) or (6):

[5](i) Subparagraphs (A)(iii)(II), (B)(ii), and (C)(iii) of section 904(d)(2) (relating to exceptions for export financing interest).

≫P-H CAUTION→ There are two versions of Sec. 864(d)(5)(A)(i). Sec. 864(d)(5)(A)(i), generally effective before 1-1-87, follows. For Sec. 864(d)(5)(A)(i), generally effective after 12-31-86. See above.

▲▲**(5) Certain provisions not to apply.—**

(A) Certain exceptions.—The following provisions shall not apply to any amount treated as interest under paragraph (1) or (6):

(i) Subparagraphs (A), (B), (C), and (D) of section 904(d)(2) (relating to interest income to which separate limitation applies) *and subparagraph (j) of section 904(d)(3) (relating to interest from members of same affiliated group).*

(ii) Subparagraph (A) of section 954(b)(3) (relating to exception where foreign base company income is less than [6]*5 percent or 1,000,000).*

[7](iii) Subparagraph (B) of section 954(c)(2) (relating to certain export

---

【Footnote ¶3117 continued】

▲ Matter in italics in Sec. 864(d)(5)(A)(i), preceded by a triangle, added by section 1201(d)(4), '86 TRA, which struck out:

(5) "(i) Subparagraphs (A), (B), (C), and (D) of section 904(d)(2) (relating to interest income to which separate limitation applies) and subparagraph (J) of section 904(d)(3) (relating to interest from members of same affiliated group)."

Effective date (Sec. 1201(e), '86 TRA).—(1) Generally applies to taxable years beginning after 12-31-86. For special and transitional rules see ¶2055.

▲▲ Matter in *italics* in Sec. 864(d)(5)(A)(i) preceded by two triangles, added by section 1810(c)(3), '86 TRA.

Effective date (Sec. 1881, '86 TRA and 123(c), '84 TRA).—Applies to accounts receivable and evidences of indebtedness transferred after 3-1-84, in taxable years ending after such date.

(2) Transitional rule.—The amendments made by this section shall not apply to accounts receivable and evidences of indebtedness acquired after 3-1-84, and before 3-1-94, by a Belgian corporation in existence on 3-1-84, in any taxable year ending after such date, but only to the extent that the amount includible in gross income by reason of section 956 of the '54 Code with respect to such corporation for all such taxable years is not reduced by reason of this paragraph by more than the lesser of—

(A) $15,000,000 or

(B) the amount of the Belgian corporation's adjusted basis on 3-1-84 in stock of a foreign corporation formed to issue bonds outside the United States to the public.

Matter in *italics* in Sec. 864(d)(5)(A)(ii) added by section 1223(b)(1) which struck out:

(6) "10 percent"

Effective date (Sec. 1223(c), '86 TRA).—Applies to taxable years beginning after 12-31-86.

Matter in *italics* in Sec. 864(d)(5)(A)(iii) and (iv) added by section 1221(a)(2), '86 TRA, which struck out:

(7) "(iii) Subparagraph (B) of section 954(c)(3) (relating to certain income derived in active conduct of trade or business).

(iv) Subparagraphs (A) and (B) of section 954(c)(4) (relating to exception for certain income received from related persons)."

financing).

(iv) Clause (i) of section 954(c)(3)(A) (relating to certain income received from related persons).

(B) Special rules for possessions.—[8]*An amount treated as interest under paragraph (1) shall not be treated as income described in subparagraph (A) or (B) of section 936(a)(1) unless such amount is from sources within a possession of the United States (determined after the application of paragraph (1)).*

* * * * * * * * * * * *

(7) Exception for certain related persons doing business in same foreign country.— Paragraph (1) shall not apply to any trade or service receivable acquired by any person from a related person if—

(A) the person acquiring such receivable and such related person are created or organized under the laws of the same foreign country and such related person has a substantial part of its assets used in its trade or business located in such same foreign country, and

(B) such related person would not have derived any foreign base company income (as defined in section 954(a), determined without regard to section 954(b)(3)(A)), or any income effectively connected with the conduct of a trade or business within the United States, from such receivable if it had been collected by such related person.

[9]*(8)* **Regulations.**—The Secretary shall prescribe such regulations as may be necessary to prevent the avoidance of the provisions of this subsection or section 956(b)(3).

(e) Rules for Allocating Interest, Etc.—For purposes of this subchapter (except as provided in regulations)—

(1) Treatment of affiliated groups.—The taxable income of each member of an affiliated group from sources outside the United States shall be determined by allocating and apportioning interest expense of each member as if all members of such group were a single corporation.

(2) Gross income method may not be used for interest.—All allocations and apportionments of interest expense shall be made on the basis of assets rather than gross income.

(3) Tax-exempt assets not taken into account.—For purposes of allocating and apportioning any deductible expense, any tax-exempt asset (and any income from such an asset) shall not be taken into account. A similar rule shall apply in the case of any dividend (other than a qualifying dividend as defined in section 243(b)) for which a deduction is allowable under section 243 or 245(a) and any stock the dividends on which would be so deductible and would not be qualifying dividends (as so defined).

(4) Basis of stock in certain corporations adjusted for earnings and profits changes.—For purposes of allocating and apportioning expenses on the basis of assets, the adjusted basis of any asset which is stock in a corporation which is not included in the affiliated group and in which members of the affiliated group own 10 percent or more of

---

⟦Footnote ¶3117 continued⟧

Effective date (Sec. 1221(g), '86 TRA).—Generally applies to taxable years of foreign corporations beginning after 12-31-86. For special and transitional rules see ¶2060.

Matter in *italics* in Sec. 864(d)(5)(B) added by section 1275(c)(7), '86 TRA, which struck out:

(8) "(i) Puerto Rico and possessions tax credit.—Any amount treated as interest under paragraph (1) shall not be treated as income described in subparagraph (A) or (B) of section 936(a)(1) unless such amount is from sources within a possession of the United States (determined after the application of paragraph (1)).

(ii) Virgin Islands corporations.—Subsection (b) of section 934 shall not apply to any amount treated as interest under paragraph (1) unless such amount is from sources within the Virgin Islands (determined after the application of paragraph (1))."

Effective date (Sec. 1277, '86 TRA).—(a) Generally applies to taxable years beginning after 12-31-86. For special and transitional rules see ¶2068.

Matter in *italics* in Sec. 864(d)(7) and (8) added by section 1810(c)(2), '86 TRA, which struck out:

(9) "(7)"

Effective date (Sec. 1881, '86 TRA and Sec. 123(c), '84 TRA)—See above.

Sec. 864(e) in *italics* added by section 1215(a), '86 TRA.

Effective date (Sec. 1215(c), '86 TRA).—Applies to taxable years beginning after 12-31-86. For special and transitional rules see ¶2058.

the total combined voting power of all classes of stock entitled to vote in such corporation shall be—

    (A) increased by the amount of the earnings and profits of such corporation attributable to such stock and accumulated during the period the taxpayer held such stock, or

    (B) reduced (but not below zero) by any deficit in earnings and profits of such corporation attributable to such stock for such period.

    (5) *Affiliated group.*—For purposes of this subsection—

    (A) *In general.*—Except as provided in subparagraph (B), the term "affiliated group" has the meaning given such term by section 1504 (determined without regard to paragraph (4) of section 1504(b)).

    (B) *Treatment of certain financial institutions.*—For purposes of subparagraph (A), any corporation described in subparagraph (C) shall be treated as an includible corporation for purposes of section 1504 only for purposes of applying such section separately to corporations so described.

    (C) *Description.*—A corporation is described in this subparagraph if—

        (i) such corporation is a financial institution described in section 581 or 591,

        (ii) the business of such financial institution is predominantly with persons other than related persons (within the meaning of subsection (d)(4)) or their customers, and

        (iii) such financial institution is required by State or Federal law to be operated separately from any other entity which is not such an institution.

    (6) **Allocation and apportionment of other expenses.**—Expenses other than interest which are not directly allocable and apportioned to any specific income producing activity shall be allocated and apportioned as if all members of the affiliated group were a single corporation.

    (7) *Regulations.*—The Secretary shall prescribe such regulations as may be necessary or appropriate to carry out the purposes of this section, including regulations providing—

    (A) for the resourcing of income of any member of an affiliated group or modifications to the consolidated return regulations to the extent such resourcing or modification is necessary to carry out the purposes of this section,

    (B) for direct allocation of interest expense incurred to carry out an integrated financial transaction to any interest (or interest-type income) derived from such transaction, and

    (C) for the apportionment of expenses allocated to foreign source income among the members of the affiliated group and various categories of income described in section 904(d)(1).

[For official explanation, see Committee Reports, ¶4027; 4028; 4032; 4034; 4036; 4048; 4057; 4144.]

【¶3118】 CODE SEC. 865. SOURCE RULES FOR PERSONAL PROPERTY SALES.

    (a) General Rule.—Except as otherwise provided in this section, income from the sale of personal property—

    (1) by a United States resident shall be sourced in the United States, or

    (2) by a nonresident shall be sourced outside the United States.

    (b) Exception for Inventory Property.—In the case of income derived from the sale of inventory property—

    (1) this section shall not apply, and

    (2) such income shall be sourced under the rules of sections 861(a)(6), 862(a)(6), and 863(b).

    (c) Exception for Depreciable Personal Property.—

    (1) In general.—Gain (not in excess of the depreciation adjustments from the sale of depreciable personal property shall be allocated between sources in the United States and sources outside the United States—

    (A) by treating the same proportion of such gain as sourced in the United States as the United States depreciation adjustments with respect to such property bear to the total depreciation adjustments, and

---

【Footnote ¶3118】   Sec. 865 added by section 1211(a), '86 TRA.

Effective date (Sec. 1211(c), '86 TRA).—(1)   Generally applies to taxable years beginning after 12-31-86.

(2)   Special rule for foreign persons.—In the case of any foreign person other than any controlled foreign corporations (within the meaning of section 957(a) of the '54 Code), the amendments made by this section shall apply to transactions entered into after 3-18-86.

(B) by treating the remaining portion of such gain as sourced outside the United States.

(2) Gain in excess of depreciation.—Gain (in excess of the depreciation adjustments) from the sale of depreciable personal property shall be sourced as if such property were inventory property.

(3) United States depreciation adjustments.—For purposes of this subsection—

(A) In general.—The term "United States depreciation adjustments" means the portion of the depreciation adjustments to the adjusted basis of the property which are attributable to the depreciation deductions allowable in computing taxable income from sources in the United States.

(B) Special rule for certain property.—Except in the case of property of a kind described in section 48(a)(2)(B), if for any taxable year—

(i) such property is used predominantly in the United States, or

(ii) such property is used predominantly outside the United States,

all of the depreciation deductions allowable for such year shall be treated as having been allocated to income from sources in the United States (or, where clause (ii) applies, from sources outside the United States.)

(4) Other definitions.—For purposes of this subsection—

(A) Depreciable personal property.—The term "depreciable personal property" means any personal property if the adjusted basis of such property includes depreciation adjustments.

(B) Depreciable adjustments.—The term "depreciation adjustments" means adjustments reflected in the adjusted basis of any property on account of depreciation deductions (whether allowed with respect to such property or other property and whether allowed to the taxpayer or to any other person).

(C) Depreciation deductions.—The term "depreciation deductions" means any deductions for depreciation or amortization or any other deduction allowable under any provision of this chapter which treats an otherwise capital expenditure as a deductible expense.

(d) Exception for Intangibles.—

(1) In general.—In the case of any sale of an intangible—

(A) this section shall apply only to the extent the payments in consideration of such sale are not contingent on the productivity, use, or disposition of the intangible, and

(B) to the extent such payments are so contingent, the source of such payments shall be determined under this part in the same manner as if such payments were royalties.

(2) Intangible.—For purposes of paragraph (1), the term "intangible" means any patent, copyright, secret process or formula, goodwill, trademark, trade brand, or other like property.

(3) Special rule in the case of goodwill.—To the extent this section applies to the sale of goodwill, payments in consideration of such sale shall be treated as from sources in the country in which such goodwill was generated.

(e) Special Rules for Sales Through Offices or Fixed Places of Business.—

(1) Sales by residents.—

(A) In general.—In the case of income not sourced under subsection (b), (c), (d), or (f), if a United States resident maintains an office or other fixed place of business outside the United States, income from sales of personal property attributable to such office or other fixed place of business shall be sourced outside the United States.

(B) Tax must be imposed.—Subparagraph (A) shall not apply unless an income tax equal to at least 10 percent of the income from the sale is actually paid to a foreign country with respect to such income.

(2) Sales by nonresidents.—

(A) In general.—Notwithstanding any other provisions of this part, if a nonresident maintains an office or other fixed place of business in the United States, income from any sale of personal property (including inventory property) attributable to such office or other fixed place of business shall be sourced in the United States.

Code §865(e)(2) ¶3118

The preceding sentence shall not apply for purposes of section 971 (defining export trade corporation).

(B) Exception.—Subparagraph (A) shall not apply to—

(i) any sale of inventory property which is sold for use, disposition, or consumption outside the United States if an office or other fixed place of business of the taxpayer outside the United States Materially participated in the sale, or

(ii) any amount included in gross income under section 951(a)(1)(A).

(3) Sales attributable to an office or other fixed place of business.—The principles of section 864(c)(5) shall apply in determining whether a taxpayer has an office or other fixed place of business and whether a sale is attributable to such an office or other fixed place of business.

(f) Stock of Affiliates.—If—

(1) a United States resident sells stock in an affiliate which is a foreign corporation,

(2) such affiliate is engaged in the active conduct of a trade or business, and

(3) such sale occurs in the foreign country in which the affiliate derived more than 50 percent of its gross income for the 3-year period ending with the close of the affiliate's taxable year immediately preceding the year during which such sale occurred,

any gain from such sale shall be sourced outside the United States.

(g) United States Resident; Nonresident.—For purposes of this section—

(1) In general.—Except as otherwise provided in this subsection—

(A) United States resident.—The term "United States resident" means—

(i) any individual who has a tax home (as defined in section 911(d)(3)) in the United States, and

(ii) any corporation, partnership, trust, or estate which is a United States person (as defined in section 7701(a)(30)).

(B) Nonresident.—The term "nonresident" means any person other than a United States resident.

(2) Special rules for United States citizens and resident aliens.—For purposes of this section, a United States citizen or resident alien shall not be treated as a nonresident with respect to any sale of personal property unless an income tax equal to at least 10 percent of the gain derived from such sale is actually paid to a foreign country with respect to that gain.

(h) Other Definitions.—For purposes of this section—

(1) Inventory property.—The term "inventory property" means personal property described in paragraph (1) of section 1221.

(2) Sale includes exchange.—The term "sale" includes an exchange or any other disposition.

(3) Treatment of possessions.—Any possession of the United States shall be treated as a foreign country.

(4) Affiliate.—The term "affiliate" means a member of the same affiliated group (within the meaning of section 1504(a) without regard to section 1504(b)).

(i) Regulations.—The Secretary shall prescribe such regulations as may be necessary or appropriate to carry out the purpose of this section, including regulations—

(1) relating to the treatment of losses from sales of personal property, and

(2) applying the rules of this section to income derived from trading in futures contracts, forward contracts, options contracts, and other instruments.

(j) Cross References.—

(1) For provisions relating to the characterization as dividends for source purposes of gains from the sale of stock in certain foreign corporations, see section 1248.

(2) For sourcing of income from certain foreign currency transactions, see section 988.

[For official explanation, see Committee Reports, ¶4028.]

【¶3119】 CODE SEC. 871. TAX ON NONRESIDENT ALIEN INDIVIDUALS.

(a) Income Not Connected With United States Business—30 Percent Tax.—

(1) Income other than capital gains.—Except as provided in ¹*subsection (h)* there is

---

【Footnote ¶3119】 Matter in *italics* in Sec. 871(a)(1) added by section 1810(d)(3)(A), '86 TRA, which struck out:

(1) "subsection (i)"

hereby imposed for each taxable year a tax of 30 percent of the amount received from sources within the United States by a nonresident alien individual as—

(A)   interest (other than original issue discount as defined in section 1273), dividends, rents, salaries, wages, premiums, annuities, compensations, remunerations, emoluments, and other fixed or determinable annual or periodical gains, profits, and income,

(B)   gains described in section 402(a)(2), 403(a)(2), or 631(b) or (c), and gains on transfers described in section 1235 made on or before October 4, 1966,

(C)   in the case of [2]

(i)   a sale or exchange of an original issue discount obligation, the amount of the original issue discount accruing while such obligation was held by the nonresident alien individual (to the extent such discount was not theretofore taken into account under clause (ii)), and

(ii)   a payment on an original issue discount obligation, and amount equal to the original issue discount accruing while such obligation was held by the nonresident alien individual (except that such original issue discount shall be taken into account under this clause only to the extent such discount was not theretofore taken into account under this clause and only to the extent that the tax thereon does not exceed the payment less the tax imposed by subparagraph (A) thereon), and

(D)   gains from the sale or exchange after October 4, 1966, of patents, copyrights, secret processes and formulas, good will, trademarks, trade brands, franchises, and other like property, or of any interest in any such property, to the extent such gains are from payments which are contingent on the productivity, use, or disposition of the property or interest sold or exchanged, [3]

but only to the extent the amount so received is not effectively connected with the conduct of a trade or business within the United States.

(2)   **Capital gains of aliens present in the United States 183 days or more.**—In the case of a nonresident alien individual present in the United States for a period or periods aggregating 183 days or more during the taxable year, there is hereby imposed for such year a tax of 30 percent of the amount by which his gains, derived from sources within the United States, from the sale or exchange at any time during such year of capital assets exceed his losses, allocable to sources within the United States, from the sale or exchange at any time during such year of capital assets. For purposes of this paragraph, gains and losses shall be taken into account only if, and to the extent that, they would be recognized and taken into account if such gains and losses were effectively connected with the conduct of a trade or business within the United States, except that [4]such losses shall be determined without the benefits of the capital loss car-

---

⌈Footnote ¶3119 continued⌉

Effective date (Sec. 1881, '86 TRA and section 127(g)(1), '84 TRA).—Applies to interest received after 7-18-84, with respect to obligations issued after such date, in taxable years ending after such date.

Matter in *italics* in Sec. 871(a)(1)(C) added by section 1810(e)(2)(A), '86 TRA, which struck out:

(2)   "(i)   a sale or exchange of an original issue discount obligation, the amount of any gain not in excess of the original issue discount accruing while such obligation was held by the nonresident alien individual (to the extent such discount was not theretofore taken into account under clause (ii)), and

(ii)   the payment of interest on an original issue discount obligation, an amount equal to the original issue discount accrued on such obligation since the last payment of interest thereon (except that such original issue discount shall be taken into account under this clause only to the extent that the tax thereon does not exceed the interest payment less the tax imposed by subparagraph (A) thereon, and"

Effective date (Sec. 1881, '86 TRA and section 128(d)(1), '84 TRA).—Applies to payments made on or after 9-17-84, with respect to obligations issued after 3-31-72.

Section 1211(b)(4), '86 TRA struck out from Sec. 871(a)(1)(D):

(3)   "or from payments which are treated as being contingent under subsection (e),"

Effective date (Sec. 1211(c), '86 TRA).—(1) Generally applies to taxable years beginning after 12-31-86.

(2)   Special rule for foreign persons.—In the case of any foreign person other than any controlled foreign corporations (within the meaning of section 957(a) '54 Code the amendments made by this section shall apply to transactions entered into after 3-18-86.

Section 301(b)(9), '86 TRA, struck out from Sec. 871(a)(2):

(4)   "such gains and losses shall be determined without regard to section 1202 (relating to deduction for capital gains) and"

Effective date (Sec. 301(c), '86 TRA).—Applies to taxable years beginning after 12-31-86.

ryover provided in section 1212. Any gain or loss which is taken into account in determining the tax under papagraph (1) or subsection (b) shall not be taken into account in determining the tax under this paragraph. For purposes of the 183-day requirement of this paragraph, a nonresident alien individual not engaged in trade or business within the United States who has not established a taxable year for any prior period shall be treated as having a taxable year which is the calendar year.

(3) **Taxation of Social Security Benefits.**—For purposes of this section and section 1441—

(A) one-half of any social security benefit (as defined in section 86(d)) shall be included in gross income (notwithstanding section 207 of the Social Security Act), and

(B) section 86 shall not apply.

For treatment of certain citizens of possessions of the United States, see section 932(c).

* * * * * * * * * * * * *

(e) [Repealed] [5]

* * * * * * * * * * * * *

(h) **Repeal of Tax on Interest of Nonresident Alien Individuals Received From Certain Portfolio Debt Investments.**—

(2) **Portfolio interest.**—For purposes of this subsection, the term "portfolio interest" means any interest (including original issue discount) *which would be subject to tax under subsection (a) but for this subsection and* which is described in any of the following subparagraphs:

* * * * * * * * * * * * *

(B) Certain registered obligations.—Interest which is paid on an obligation—
(i) which is in registered form, and
(ii) with respect to which the United States person who would otherwise be required to deduct and withhold tax from such interest under section 1441(a) [6] *receives* a statement (which meets the requirements of paragraph (4)) that the beneficial owner of the obligation is not a United States person.

(3) **Portfolio interest not to include interest received by 10-percent shareholders.**— For purposes of this subsection—

* * * * * * * * * * * * *

(C) Attribution rules.—For purposes of determining ownership of stock under subparagraph (B)(i) the rules of section 318(a) shall apply, except that—
(i) Section 318(a)(2)(C) shall be applied without regard to the 50-percent limitation therein, [7]
(ii) *section 318(a)(3)(C) shall be applied—*
(I) without regard to the 50-percent limitation therein; and
(II) in any case where such section would not apply but for subclause (I), by considering a corporation as owning the stock (other than stock in such cor-

---

[Footnote ¶3119 continued]

Section 1211(b)(5), '86 TRA, repealed Sec. 871(e):

(5) "**Gains From Sale or Exchange of Certain Intangible Property.**—For purposes of subsection (a)(1)(D), and for purposes of sections 881(a)(4), 1441(b), and 1442(a)—

(1) **Payments treated as contingent on use, etc.**—If more than 50 percent of the gain for any taxable year from the sale or exchange of any patent, copyright, secret process or formula, good will, trademark, trade brand, franchise, or other like property, or of any interest in any such property, is from payments which are contingent on the productivity, use or disposition of such property or interest, all of the gain for the taxable year from the sale or exchange of such property or interest shall be treated as being from payments which are contingent on the productivity, use, or disposition of such property or interest.

(2) **Source rule.**—In determining whether gains described in subsection (a)(1)(D) and section 881(a)(4) are received from sources within the United States, such gains shall be treated as rentals or royalties for the use of, or privilege of using property or an interest in property."

Effective date (Sec. 1211(c), '86 TRA).—(1) Generally applies to taxable years beginning after 12-31-86. For special rule, see above.

Matter in *italics* in Sec. 871(h)(2), (B)(ii), and (3)(C) added by section 1810(d)(1)(A), (2), and (3)(B), '86 TRA, which struck out:

(6) "has received"

(7) "and"

poration) which is owned by or for any shareholder of such corporation in that proportion which the value of the stock which such shareholder owns in such corporation bears to the value of all stock in such corporation, and

[8]*(iii)* any stock which a person is treated as owning after application of section 318(a)(4) shall not, for purposes of applying paragraphs (2) and (3) of section 318(a), be treated as actually owned by such person.

Under regulations prescribed by the Secretary, rules similar to the rules of the preceding sentence shall be applied in determining the ownership of the capital or profits interest in a partnership for purposes of subparagraph (B)(ii).

* * * * * * * * * * * *

(i) Tax Not to Apply to Certain Interest and Dividends.—

(1) In general.—No tax shall be imposed under paragraph (1)(A) or (1)(C) of subsection (a) on any amount described in paragraph (2).

(2) Amounts to which paragraph (1) applies.—The amounts described in this paragraph are as follows:

(A) Interest on deposits, if such interest is not effectively connected with the conduct of a trade or business within the United States.

(B) A percentage of any dividend paid by a domestic corporation meeting the 80-percent foreign business requirements of section 861(c)(1) equal to the percentage determined for purposes of section 861(c)(2)(A).

(C) Income derived by a foreign central bank of issue from bankers' acceptances.

(3) Deposits.—For purposes of paragraph (2), the term "deposits" means amounts which are—

(A) deposits with persons carrying on the banking business,

(B) deposits or withdrawable accounts with savings institutions chartered and supervised as savings and loan or similar associations under Federal or State law, but only to the extent that amounts paid or credited on such deposits or accounts are deductible under section 591 (determined without regard to sections 265 and 291) in computing the taxable income of such institutions, and

(C) amounts held by an insurance company under an agreement to pay interest thereon.

[9]*(j)* **Cross References.—**

* * * * * * * * * * * *

[For official explanation, see Committee Reports, ¶¶3885; 4028; 4031; 4144.]

【¶3120】 **CODE SEC. 872. GROSS INCOME.**

* * * * * * * * * * * *

(b) Exclusions.—The following items shall not be included in gross income of a nonresident alien individual, and shall be exempt from taxation under this subtitle:

[1]*(1) Ships operated by certain nonresidents.—Gross income derived by an individual resident of a foreign country from the operation of a ship or ships if such foreign country grants an equivalent exemption to citizens of the United States and to corporations organized in the United States.*

【Footnote ¶3119 continued】

(8) "(ii)"
Effective date (Sec. 1881, '86 TRA and section 127(g)(1), '84 TRA).—Applies to interest received after 7-18-84, with respect to obligations issued after such date, in taxable years ending after such date.

Matter in *italics* in Sec. 871(i) and (j) added by section 1214(c)(1), '86 TRA, which struck out:
(9) "(i)"
Effective date (Sec. 1214(d), '86 TRA).—(1) Generally applies to payments after 12-31-86. For special and transitional rules, see footnote ¶3114.
【Footnote ¶3120】 Matter in *italics* in Sec. 872(b) added by section 1212(c)(1) and (2), '86 TRA, which struck out:
(1) "(1) Ships under foreign flag.—Earnings derived from the operation of a ship or ships documented under the laws of a foreign country which grants an equivalent exemption to citizens of the United States and to corporations organized in the United States.
(2) Aircraft of foreign registry.—Earnings derived from the operation of aircraft registered under the laws of a foreign country which grants an equivalent exemption to citizens of the United States and to corporations organized in the United States."
Effective date (Sec. 1212(f)(1), '86 TRA).—Generally applies to taxable years beginning after 12-31-86.

    (2) Aircraft operated by certain nonresidents.—Gross income derived by an individual resident of a foreign country from the operation of aircraft if such foreign country grants an equivalent exemption to citizens of the United States and to corporations organized in the United States.

* * * * * * * * * * *

    (5) Certain rental income.—Income to which paragraphs (1) and (2) apply shall include income which is derived from the rental on a full or bareboat basis of a ship or ships or aircraft, as the case may be.

    (6) Application to different types of transportation.—The Secretary may provide that this subsection be applied separately with respect to income from different types of transportation.

[For official explanation, see Committee Reports, ¶4029.]

⟦¶3121⟧ CODE SEC. 876. ALIEN RESIDENTS OF PUERTO RICO, [1]GUAM, AMERICAN SAMOA, OR THE NORTHERN MARIANA ISLANDS.

    (a) General Rules.—*This subpart shall not apply to any alien individual who is a bona fide resident of Puerto Rico, Guam, American Samoa, or the Northern Mariana Islands during the entire taxable year and such alien shall be subject to the tax imposed by section 1.*

    (b) Cross References.—
For exclusion from gross income of income derived from sources within—
    (1) Guam, American Samoa, and the Northern Mariana Islands, see section 931, and
    (2) Puerto Rico, see section 933.

[For official explanation, see Committee Reports, ¶4057.]

⟦¶3122⟧ CODE SEC. 877. EXPATRIATION TO AVOID TAX.

* * * * * * * * * * *

    (c) Special Rules of Source.—For purposes of subsection (b), the following items of gross income shall be treated as income from sources within the United States:

* * * * * * * * * * *

    (2) Stock or debt obligations.—Gains on the sale or exchange of stock issued by a domestic corporation or debt obligations of United States persons or of the United States, a State or political subdivision thereof, or the District of Columbia.

For purposes of this section, gain on the sale or exchange of property which has a basis determined in whole or in part by reference to property described in paragraph (1) or (2) shall be treated as gain described in paragraph (1) or (2).

* * * * * * * * * * *

[For official explanation, see Committee Reports, ¶4049.]

⟦¶3123⟧ CODE SEC. 879. TAX TREATMENT OF CERTAIN COMMUNITY INCOME IN THE CASE OF NONRESIDENT ALIEN INDIVIDUALS

* * * * * * * * * * *

    (c) Definitions and Special Rules.—For purposes of this section—

* * * * * * * * * * *

⟦**Footnote ¶3121**⟧ Matter in *italics* in Sec. 876 added by section 1272(b), '86 TRA, which struck out:

(1) "**(a) No application to Certain Alien Residents of Puerto Rico.**—This subpart shall not apply to an alien individual who is a bona fide resident of Puerto Rico during the entire taxable year, and such alien shall be subject to the tax imposed by section 1.

(b) Cross Reference.—
For exclusion from gross income of income derived from sources within Puerto Rico, see section 933."

Effective date (Sec. 1277(a) and (b), '86 TRA).—(a) Generally applies to taxable years beginning after 12-31-86.

(b) Special Rule for Guam, American Samoa, and the Northern Mariana Islands.—The amendments made by this subtitle shall apply with respect to Guam, American Samoa, or the Northern Mariana Islands (and to residents thereof and corporations created or organized therein) only if (and so long as) an implementing agreement under section 1271 is in effect between the United States and such possession.

For special rules see ¶2068.

⟦**Footnote ¶3122**⟧ Matter in *italics* in Sec. 877(c) added by section 1243(a), '86 TRA.

Effective date (Sec. 1243(b), '86 TRA).—Applies to sales or exchanges of property received in exchanges after 9-25-85.

(3) **Determination of marital status.**—The determination of marital status shall be made under [1]*section 7703(b).*

[For official explanation, see Committee Reports, ¶4058.]

【¶3124】 CODE SEC. 881. TAX ON INCOME OF FOREIGN CORPORATIONS NOT CONNECTED WITH UNITED STATES BUSINESS.

(a) **Imposition of Tax.**—Except as provided in subsection (c), there is hereby imposed for each taxable year a tax of 30 percent of the amount received from sources within the United States by a foreign corporation as—

(1) interest, (other than original issue discount as defined in section 1273, dividends, rents, salaries, wages, premiums, annuities, compensations, remuneration, emoluments, and other fixed or determinable annual or periodical gains, profits, and income,

(2) gains described in section 631(b) or (c),

(3) in the case of—

[1]*(A) a sale or exchange of an original issue discount obligation, the amount of the original issue discount accruing while such obligation was held by the foreign corporation (to the extent such discount was not theretofore taken into account under subparagraph (B)), and*

(B) a payment on an original issue discount obligation, an amount equal to the original issue discount accruing while such obligation was held by the foreign corporation (except that such original issue discount shall be taken into account under this subparagraph only to the extent such discount was not theretofore taken into account under this subparagraph and only to the extent that the tax thereon does not exceed the payment less the tax imposed by paragraph (1) thereon), and

(4) gains from the sale or exchange after October 4, 1966, of patents, copyrights, secret processes and formulas, good will, trademarks, trade brands, franchises, and other like property, or of any interest in any such property, to the extent such gains are from payments which are contingent on the productivity, use or disposition of the property or interest sold or exchanged,[2]

but only to the extent the amount so received is not effectively connected with the conduct of a trade or business within the United States.

(b) **Exception for certain Guam and Virgin Islands corporations.—**

[3]*(1) In general.—For purposes of this section and section 884, a corporation created*

【Footnote ¶3123】 Matter in *italics* in Sec. 879(c)(3) added by section 1301(j)(9), '86 TRA, which struck out:
(1) "section 143(a)"
Effective date (Sec. 1311(a), '86 TRA).—Applies to bonds issued after August 15, 1986.
For special and transitional rules, see footnote ¶2071-2077.

【Footnote ¶3124】 Matter in *italics* in Sec. 881(a)(3) added by section 1810(e)(2)(B), '86 TRA, which struck out:
(1) (A) a sale or exchange of an original issue discount obligation, the amount of any gain not in excess of the original issue discount accruing while such obligation was held by the foreign corporation (to the extent such discount was not therefore taken into account under subparagraph (B)), and
(B) the payment of interest on an original issue discount obligation, an amount equal to the original issue discount accrued on such obligation since the last payment of interest thereon (except that such original issue discount shall be taken into account under this subparagraph only to the extent that the tax thereon does not exceed the interest payment less the tax imposed by paragraph (1) thereon), and
Effective date (Sec. 1881, '86 TRA and section 128(d)(1), '84 TRA).—Applies to payments made on or after 9-16-84, the 60th day after 7-18-84, with respect to obligations issued after 3-31-72.

Section 1211(b)(6), '86 TRA, struck out from Sec. 881(a)(4):
(2) "or from payments which are treated as being so contingent under section 871(e),"
Effective date (Sec. 1211(c), '86 TRA).—(1) Generally applies to taxable years beginning after 12-31-86.
(2) Special rule for foreign persons.—In the case of any foreign person other than any controlled foreign corporations (within the meaning of section 957(a) '54 Code), the amendments made by this section shall apply to transactions entered into after 3-18-86.

Matter in *italics* in Sec. 881(b) added by section 1273(b)(1) and (2)(A), '86 TRA, which struck out:
(3) "(1) **In general.**—For purposes of this section, a corporation created or organized in Guam or the Virgin Islands or under the law of Guam or the Virgin Islands shall not be treated as a foreign corporation for any taxable year if—
(A) at all times during such taxable year less than 25 percent in value of the stock of such corporation is owned (directly or indirectly) by foreign persons, and
(B) at least 20 percent of the gross income of such corporation is shown to the satisfaction of the Secretary to have been derived from sources within Guam or the Virgin Islands (as the case may be) for the 3-year period ending with the close of the preceding taxable year of such corporation (or for such part of such period as the corporation has been in existence)."

or organized in Guam, American Samoa, the Northern Mariana Islands, or the Virgin Islands or under the law of any such possession shall not be treated as a foreign corporation for any taxable year if—

    (A) at all times during such taxable year less than 25 percent in value of the stock of such corporation is beneficially owned (directly or indirectly) by foreign persons,

    (B) at least 65 percent of the gross income of such corporation is shown to the satisfaction of the Secretary to be effectively connected with the conduct of a trade or business in such a possession or the United States for the 3-year period ending with the close of the taxable year of such corporation (or for such part of such period as the corporation or any predecessor has been in existence), and

    (C) no substantial part of the income of such corporation is used (directly or indirectly) to satisfy obligations to persons who are not bona fide residents of such a posession or the United States.[4]

[5]*(2)* **Definitions.—**

    (A) Foreign person.—For purposes of paragraph (1), the term "foreign person" means any person other than—

        (i) a United States person, or

        (ii) a person who would be a United States person if references to the United States in section 7701 included references to a possession of the United States.

    (B) Indirect ownership rules.—For purposes of paragraph (1), the rules of section 318(a)(2) shall apply except that "5 percent" shall be substituted for "50 percent" in subparagraph (C) thereof.[6]

(c) **Repeal of tax on interest of foreign corporations received from certain portfolio debt investments.—**

    (1) **In general.—**In the case of any portfolio interest received by a foreign corporation from sources within the United States, no tax shall be imposed under paragraph (1) or (3) of subsection (a).

    (2) **Portfolio interest.—**For purposes of this subsection, the term "portfolio interest" means any interest (including original issue discount) *which would be subject to tax under subsection (a) but for this subsection and* which is described in any of the following subparagraphs:

        (A) Certain obligations which are not registered.—Interest which is paid on any obligation which is described in section 871(h)(2)(A).

        (B) Certain registered obligations.—Interest which is paid on an obligation—

            (i) which is in registered form, and

            (ii) with respect to which the person who would otherwise be required to deduct and withhold tax from such interest under section 1442(a) [7]*receives a*

⌈Footnote ¶3124 continued⌋

(4) "(2) **Paragraph (1) not to apply to tax imposed in Guam.—**

For purposes of applying this subsection with respect to income tax liability incurred to Guam—

(A) paragraph (1) shall not apply, and

(B) for purposes of this section, the term 'foreign corporation' does not include a corporation created or organized in Guam under the law of Guam." [as amended by section 1899A(22), '86 TRA to correct spelling].

(5) "(3)"

(6) "(4) **Cross reference.—**

For tax imposed in the Virgin Islands, see sections 934 and 934A."

Effective date (Sec. 1277(a) and (b), '86 TRA).—(a) Generally applies to taxable years beginning after 12-31-86.

(b) Special Rule for Guam, American Samoa, and the Northern Mariana Islands.—The amendments made by this subtitle shall apply with respect to Guam, American Samoa, or the Northern Mariana Islands (and to residents thereof and corporations created or organized therein) only if (and so long as) an implementing agreement under section 1271 is in effect between the United States and such possession.

For other special and transitional rules, see ¶2068.

Matter in *italics* in Sec. 881(c)(2) and (b)(ii) added by section 1810(d)(1)(B) and (3)(C), '86 TRA, which struck out:

(7) "has received"

Effective date (Sec. 1881, '86 TRA and section 127(g)(1) and (3), '84 TRA).—(1) Generally applies to interest received after 7-18-84, with respect to obligations issued after such date in taxable years ending after such date.

      *   *   *   *   *   *   *   *

(3) Special rule for certain United States affiliate obligations.—

(A) In general.—For purposes of the '54 Code, payments of interest on a United States affiliate obligation to an applicable CFC in existence on or before 6-22-84, shall be treated as payments to a resident of the country in which the applicable CFC is incorporated.

(B) Exception.—Subparagraph (A) shall not apply to any applicable CFC which did not meet requirements which are based on the principles set forth in Revenue Rulings 69-501, 69-377, 70-645, and 73-110.

A COMPLETE GUIDE TO THE
TAX REFORM ACT OF 1986

Changes and Additions

p. 6—Change the third item from the bottom of the right-hand column to: "Extension of time for insolvent farmers to file for refunds . . . 1896"

p. 629—Change the sixth line down from the top to: "These can be only one class of residual interests. . . . "

p. 801—On the sixth line down from the top, change "Business" to "Businesses"

In the second paragraph, delete items (1) and (2) and the number "(3)". Sentence should read, "Starting in 1987, the new law allows nonaccrual of billings for services that, on the basis of experience, the taxpayer won't collect, unless interest or a late penalty is charged."

p. 1148—*Nondeductible interest.* Delete line six of paragraph and insert "will not be deductible even if it would be deductible under the general interest rules [¶510]. Moreover, these interest payments made after 12-31-86 will not increase the employee's basis in the plan."

Last paragraph of ¶1133—Change *Act Sec. 1133* to *Act Sec. 1134.*

p. 1893—Change heading to: [¶1896] "**Extension of Time for Insolvent Farmers to File for Refunds.**"

p. 1919—The effective date for Act Sec. 1004 should read "Losses sustained in TYBA 12-31-86"

p. 3226—In the ninth line down from the top, insert a comma between "*loss*" and "*deduction*".

p. 3230—In the 11th line down from the top, insert a comma between "(D)" and "(E)".

p. 3392—In the 6th, 18th, and 29th lines of Code Sec. 415(c)(4), insert a comma between "*agency*" and "or".

p. 3622—In the last line of text, the word "below" should read "above".

p. 3647—At [¶3212], "(b)" should read "(d)".

p. 3649—Delete the line of stars after the 1st line down from the top and add the following:

  (b) Computation of Corporation's Taxable Income.—The taxable income of an S corporation shall be computed in the same manner as in the case of an individual, except that—

    (1) the items described in section 1366(a)(1)(A) shall be separately stated,

p. 3655—In the 2nd line up from the bottom of the footnotes, insert a closing parenthesis after the word "States" and before the closing quotes.

p. 3658—In the seventh line of Code Sec. 1441(a), delete the superior figure [1].
In the 2nd line of Code Sec. 1441(b), delete the superior figure [2], and "*1273*" should read "*1273*".

p. 3695—In the last line of text, "*151(d)(2)(3)*" should read "*151(d)(2)* ".

p. 3730—In the 10th line up from the bottom of the footnotes, "1151(b)(3)" should read "1151(h)(3)" both times it appears.

p. 3751—In the third and fourth lines of Code Sec. 6401(b)(1), "*B, and D of such part IV*)," should read "B, and D of such part IV),".

p. 3754—^{7} *(1) "Gasoline used on farms.–"* should read ^{7} *(1)* **"Gasoline used on farms.–"**

p. 3757—In the 3rd line down from the top of the footnotes, insert "and (i)" after "Sec. 6427(h)".

In the last line of the footnotes, "12-31-86" should read "12-31-87".

p. 3903—In the first line of Code Sec. 7701(a)(17), "152(b)(4), 682 and ^{1} *2516,*" should read "152(b)(4) ^{1} , 682, *and 2516,*".

p. 3814—In the third line of Code Sec. 7703(b)(1), insert an opening parenthesis before the word "within".

Delete the last three lines of footnotes.

p. 4044—The 9th and 10th line in the first column should read "to [25], 13, and ten, respectively * * *."

p. 4470—At ⟦¶4125⟧, the first two lines of column one should read "(Sec. 4081– 4083, 6421, and 6427(h) of the Code)".

p. 4559—At ⟦¶4191⟧, the first line of column one should read "(Sec. 4051(d) and 6427(b) of the Code)".

statement which meets the requirements of section 871(h)(4) that the beneficial owner of the obligation is not a United States person.

(3) Portfolio interest shall not include interest received by certain persons.—For purposes of this subsection, the term "portfolio interest" shall not include any portfolio interest which—

(A) except in the case of interest paid on an obligation of the United States, is received by a bank on an extension of credit made pursuant to a loan agreement entered into in the ordinary course of its trade or business,

(B) is received by a 10-percent shareholder (within the meaning of section 871(h)(3)(B), or

(C) is received by a controlled foreign corporation from a related person (within the meaning of [8]*section 864(d)(4)*).

(4) Special rules for controlled foreign corporations.—

(A) In general.—In the case of any portfolio interest received by a controlled foreign corporation, the following provisions shall not apply:

(i) Subparagraph (A) of section 954(b)(3) (relating to exception where foreign base company income is [9]*less than 5 percent or $1,000,000*).

(ii) Paragraph (4) of section 954(b) (relating to corporations not formed or availed of to avoid tax).

(iii) Subparagraph (B) of section 954(c)(3) (relating to certain income derived in active conduct of trade or business).

(iv) Subparagraph (C) of section 954(c)(3) (relating to certain income derived by an insurance company).

(v) Subparagraphs (A) and (B) of section 954(c)(4) (relating to exception for certain income received from related persons).

(B) Controlled foreign corporation.—For purposes of this subsection, the term "controlled foreign corporation" has the meaning given to such term by section 957(a).

(5) Secretary may cease application of this subsection.—Under rules similar to the rules of section 871(h)(5), the Secretary may provide that this subsection shall not apply to payments of interest described in section 871(h)(5).

(6) Registered form.—For purposes of this subsection, the term "registered form" has the meaning given such term by section 163(f).

(d) Tax Not To Apply to Certain Interest and Dividends.—No tax shall be imposed under paragraph (1) or (3) of subsection (a) on any amount described in section 871(i)(2).

[10]*(e)* **Cross Reference.—**

For doubling of tax on corporations of certain foreign countries, see section 891.

For special rules for original issue discount, see section 871(g).

[For official explanation, see Committee Reports, ¶4028; 4031; 4036; 4057; 4144.]

[¶3125] CODE SEC. 882. TAX ON INCOME OF FOREIGN CORPORATIONS CONNECTED WITH UNITED STATES BUSINESS.

[Footnote ¶3124 continued]

(C) Definitions.—

(i) The term "applicable CFC" has the meaning given such term by section 121(b)(2)(D) of this Act, except that such section shall be applied by substituting "the date of interest payment" for "March 31, 1984," in clause (i) thereof.

(ii) The term "United States affiliate obligation" means an obligation described in section 121(b)(2)(F) of this Act which was issued before 6-22-84.

Matter in *italics* in Sec. 881(c)(3)(C) added by section 1899A(23), '86 TRA, which struck out:
(8) "section 864(d)(4)."

Matter in *italics* in Sec. 881(c)(4)(A) added by section 1223(b)(2), '86 TRA, which struck out:
(9) "less than 10 percent"
Effective date (Sec. 1223(c), '86 TRA).—(1) Applies to taxable years beginning after 12-31-86.

Matter in *italics* in Sec. 881(d) and (e) added by section 1214(c)(2), '86 TRA, which struck out:
(10) "(d)"
Effective date (Sec. 1214(d), '86 TRA).—(1) Generally applies to payments made after 12-31-86. For special and transitional rules, see footnote ¶3114.

(a)   Imposition of Tax.—

   (1)   In general.—A foreign corporation engaged in trade or business within the United States during the taxable year shall be taxable as provided in section 11, 55, or 1201(a) on its taxable income which is effectively connected with the conduct of a trade or business within the United States.

* * * * * * * * * * * *

(e)   Interest on United States Obligations Received by Banks Organized in Possessions.—In the case of a corporation created or organized in, or under the law of, a possession of the United States which is carrying on the banking business in a possession of the United States, interest on obligations of the United States shall—

   (1)   for purposes of this subpart, be treated as income which is effectively connected with the conduct of a trade or business within the United States, and

   (2)   shall be taxable as provided in subsection (a)(1) whether or not such corporation is engaged in trade or business within the United States during the taxable year.

The preceding sentence shall not apply to any Guam corporation which is treated as not being a foreign corporation by section 881(b)(1) for the taxable year.

* * * * * * * * * * * *

[*For official explanation, see Committee Reports,* ¶3931.]

〖¶3126〗   CODE SEC. 883.   EXCLUSIONS FROM GROSS INCOME.—

(a)   Income of Foreign Corporations from Ships and Aircraft.—The following items shall not be included in gross income of a foreign corporation, and shall be exempt from taxation under this subtitle:

   ¹*(1)   Ships operated by certain foreign corporations.—Gross income derived by a corporation organized in a foreign country from the operation of a ship or ships if such foreign country grants an equivalent exemption to citizens of the United States and to corporations organized in the United States.*

   ²*(2)   Aircraft operated by certain foreign corporations.—Gross income derived by a corporation organized in a foreign country from the operation of aircraft if such foreign country grants an equivalent exemption to citizens of the United States and to corporations organized in the United States.*

   (3)   Railroad rolling stock of foreign corporations.—Earnings derived from payments by a common carrier for the use on a temporary basis (not expected to exceed a total of 90 days in any taxable year) of railroad rolling stock owned by a corporation of a foreign country which grants an equivalent exemption to corporations organized in the United States.

   (4)   Special rules.—*The rules of paragraphs (5) and (6) of section 872(b) shall apply for purposes of this subsection.*

(b)   Earnings Derived from Communications Satellite System.—The earnings derived from the ownership or operation of a communications satellite system by a foreign entity designated by a foreign government to participate in such ownership or operation shall be exempt from taxation under this subtitle, if the United States, through its designated entity, participates in such system pursuant to the Communications Satellite Act of 1962 (47 U.S.C. 701 and following).

(c)   *Treatment of Certain Foreign Corporations.—*

【Footnote ¶3125】   Matter in *italics* in Sec. 882(a)(1) added by section 701(e)(4)(F), '86 TRA.

Effective date (Sec. 701(f)(1) and (2)(A), '86 TRA).—Generally applies to taxable years beginning after 12-31-86. For special rules, see footnote ¶2879.

Matter in *italics* in Sec. 882(e) added by section 1236(a), '86 TRA.

Effective date (Sec. 1236(b), '86 TRA).—Applies to taxable years beginning after 11-16-85.

【Footnote ¶3126】   Matter in *italics* in Sec. 883(a) and (c) added by section 1212(c)(3), (4), and (5), '86 TRA, which struck out:

   (1)   "**(1)   Ships under foreign flag.—**Earnings derived from the operation of a ship or ships documented under the laws of a foreign country which grants an equivalent exemption to citizens of the United States and to corporations organized in the United States."

   (2)   "**(2)   Aircraft of foreign registry.—**Earnings derived from the operation of aircraft registered under the laws of a foreign country which grants an equivalent exemption to citizens of the United States and to corporations organized in the United States."

Effective date (Sec. 1212(f)(1), '86 TRA).—(1) Applies to taxable years beginning after 12-31-86.

(1) *In general.—Paragraphs (1) and (2) of subsection (a) shall not apply to any foreign corporation if 50 percent or more of the value of the stock of such corporation is owned by individuals who are not residents of such foreign country or another foreign country meeting the requirements of such paragraphs (1) and (2).*

(2) **Treatment of controlled foreign corporations.—***Paragraph (1) shall not apply to any foreign corporation which is a controlled foreign corporation (as defined in section 957(a)).*

(3) **Exception for publicly traded corporations.—***Paragraph (1) shall not apply to any foreign corporation—*

(A) *the stock of which is primarily and regularly traded on an established securities market in the foreign country in which such corporation is organized, or*

(B) *which is wholly owned (either directly or indirectly) by another corporation meeting the requirements of subparagraph (A) and is organized in the same foreign country as such other corporation.*

(4) **Stock ownership through entities.—***For purposes of paragraph (1), stock owned (directly or indirectly) by or for a corporation, partnership, trust, or estate shall be treated as being owned proportionately by its shareholders, partners, or beneficiaries. Stock considered to be owned by a person by reason of the application of the preceding sentence shall, for purposes of applying such sentence, be treated as actually owned by such person.*

[For official explanation, see Committee Reports, ¶4029.]

〔¶3127〕 CODE SEC. 884. BRANCH PROFITS TAX.

(a) **Imposition of Tax.—**In addition to the tax imposed by section 882 for any taxable year, there is hereby imposed on any foreign corporation a tax equal to 30 percent of the dividend equivalent amount for the taxable year.

(b) **Dividend Equivalent Amount.—**For purposes of subsection (a), the term "dividend equivalent amount" means the foreign corporation's effectively connected earnings and profits for the taxable year adjusted as provided in this subsection:

(1) **Reduction for increase in U.S. net equity.—**If—

(A) the U.S. net equity of the foreign corporation as of the close of the taxable year, exceeds

(B) the U.S. net equity of the foreign corporation as of the close of the preceding taxable year,

the effectively connected earnings and profits for the taxable year shall be reduced (but not below zero) by the amount of such excess.

(2) **Increase for decrease in net equity.—**

(A) In general.—If—

(i) the U.S. net equity of the foreign corporation as of the close of the preceding taxable year, exceeds

(ii) the U.S. net equity of the foreign corporation as of the close of the taxable year,

the effectively connected earnings and profits for the taxable year shall be increased by the amount of such excess.

(B) Limitation.—The increase under subparagraph (A) for any taxable year shall not exceed the aggregate reductions under paragraph (1) for prior taxable years to the extent not previously taken into account under subparagraph (A).

(c) **U.S. Net Equity.—**For purposes of this section—

(1) **In general.—**The term "U.S. net equity" means—

(A) U.S. assets, reduced (including below zero) by

(B) U.S. liabilities.

(2) **U.S. assets and U.S. liabilities.—**For purposes of paragraph (1)—

(A) U.S. assets.—The term "U.S. assets" means the money and aggregate adjusted basis of property of the foreign corporation treated as connected with the conduct of a trade or business in the United States under regulations prescribed by the Secretary. For purposes of the preceding sentence, the adjusted basis of any property shall be its adjusted basis for purposes of computing earnings and profits.

〔Footnote ¶3127〕 Sec. 884 added by section 1241(a), '86 TRA.
Effective date (Sec. 1241(e), '86 TRA).—Applies to taxable years beginning after 12-31-86.

(B) U.S. liabilities.—The term "U.S. liabilities" means the liabilities of the foreign corporation treated as connected with the conduct of a trade or business in the United States under regulations prescribed by the Secretary.

(C) Regulations to be consistent with allocation of deductions.—The regulations prescribed under subparagraphs (A) and (B) shall be consistent with the allocation of deductions under section 882(c)(1).

(d) **Effectively Connected Earnings and Profits.**—For purposes of this section—

(1) **In general.**—The term "effectively connected earnings and profits" means earnings and profits (without diminution by reason of any distributions made during the taxable year) which are attributable to income which is effectively connected (or treated as effectively connected) with the conduct of a trade or business within the United States.

(2) **Exception for certain income.**—The term "effectively connected earnings and profits" shall not include any earnings and profits attributable to—

(A) income not includible in gross income under paragraph (1) or (2) of section 883(a),

(B) income treated as effectively connected with the conduct of a trade or business within the United States under section 921(d) or 926(b),

(C) gain on the disposition of a United States real property interest described in section 897(c)(1)(A)(ii), or

(D) income treated as effectively connected with the conduct of a trade or business within the United States under section 953(c)(3)(C).

Property and liabilities of the foreign corporation treated as connected with such income under regulations prescribed by the Secretary shall not be taken into account in determining the U.S. assets or U.S. liabilities of the foreign corporation.

(e) **Coordination With Income Tax Treaties; Etc.—**

(1) **Limitation on treaty exemption.**—No income tax treaty between the United States and a foreign country shall exempt any foreign corporation from the tax imposed by subsection (a) (or reduce the amount thereof) unless—

(A) such foreign corporation is a qualified resident of such foreign country, or

(B) such foreign corporation is not a qualified resident of such foreign country but such income tax treaty permits a withholding tax on dividends described in section 861(a)(2)(B) which are paid by such foreign corporation.

(2) **Treaty modifications.**—If a foreign corporation is a qualified resident of a foreign country with which the United States has an income tax treaty—

(A) the rate of tax under subsection (a) shall be the rate of tax specified in such treaty—

(i) on branch profits if so specified, or

(ii) if not so specified, on dividends paid by a domestic corporation to a corporation resident in such country which wholly owns such domestic corporation, and

(B) any other limitations under such treaty on the tax imposed by subsection (a) shall apply.

(3) **Coordination with 2nd tier withholding tax.—**

(A) **In general.**—If a foreign corporation is not exempt for any taxable year from the tax imposed by subsection (a) by reason of a treaty, no tax shall be imposed by section 871(a), 881(a), 1441, or 1442 on any dividends paid by such corporation during the taxable year.

(B) **Limitation on certain treaty benefits.**—No foreign corporation which is not a qualified resident of a foreign country shall be entitled to claim benefits under any income tax treaty between the United States and such foreign country with respect to dividends—

(i) which are paid by such foreign corporation and with respect to which such foreign corporation is otherwise required to deduct and withhold tax under section 1441 or 1442, or

(ii) which are received by such foreign corporation and are described in section 861(a)(2)(B).

(4) **Qualified resident.**—For purposes of this subsection—

(A) **In general.**—Except as otherwise provided in this paragraph, the term "qualified resident" means, with respect to any foreign country, any foreign corporation which is a resident of such foreign country unless—

(i) more than 50 percent (by value) of the stock of such foreign corporation is owned (within the meaning of section 883(c)(4)) by individuals who are not residents of such foreign country and who are not United States citizens or resident aliens, or

(ii) 50 percent or more of its income is used (directly or indirectly) to meet liabilities to persons who are not residents of such foreign country or the United States.

(B) Special rule for publicly traded corporations.—A foreign corporation which is a resident of a foreign country shall be treated as a qualified resident of such foreign country if—

(i) the stock of such corporation is primarily and regularly traded on an established securities market in such foreign country, or

(ii) such corporation is wholly owned (either directly or indirectly) by another foreign corporation which is organized in such foreign country and the stock of which is so traded.

(C) Secretary authority.—The Secretary may, in his sole discretion, treat a foreign corporation as being a qualified resident of a foreign country if such corporation establishes to the satisfaction of the Secretary that such corporation meets such requirements as the Secretary may establish to ensure that individuals who are not residents of such foreign country do not use the treaty between such foreign country and the United States in a manner inconsistent with the purposes of this subsection.

(f) Treatment of Interest Allocable to Effective Connected Income.—

(1) In general.—In the case of a foreign corporation engaged in a trade or business in the United States, for purposes of sections 871, 881, 1441, and 1442—

(A) any interest paid by such trade or business in the United States shall be treated as if it were paid by a domestic corporation, and

(B) to the extent the amount of interest allowable as a deduction under section 882 in computing the effectively connected taxable income of such foreign corporation exceeds the interest described in subparagraph (A), such foreign corporation shall be liable for tax under section 881(a) in the same manner as if such excess were interest paid to such foreign corporation by a wholly owned domestic corporation on the last day of such foreign corporation's taxable year.

Rules similar to the rules of subsection (e)(3)(B) shall apply to interest described in the preceding sentence.

(2) Effectively connected taxable income.—For purposes of this subsection, the term "effectively connected taxable income" means taxable income which is effectively connected (or treated as effectively connected) with the conduct of a trade or business within the United States.

(g) Regulations.—The Secretary shall prescribe such regulations as may be necessary or appropriate to carry out the purposes of this section, including regulations providing for appropriate adjustments in the determination of the dividend equivalent amount in connection with the distribution to shareholders or transfer to a controlled corporation of the taxpayer's U.S. assets and other adjustments in such determination as are necessary or appropriate to carry out the purposes of this section.

[For official explanation, see Committee Reports, ¶4047.]

〔¶3127-A〕 CODE SEC. ¹885. CROSS REFERENCES.

*   *   *   *   *   *   *   *   *   *   *   *

[For official explanation, see Committee Reports, ¶4047.]

〔¶3128〕 CODE SEC. 887. IMPOSITION OF TAX ON GROSS TRANSPORTATION INCOME OF NONRESIDENT ALIENS AND FOREIGN CORPORATIONS.

(a) Imposition of Tax.—In the case of any nonresident alien individual or foreign corporation, there is hereby imposed for each taxable year a tax equal to 4 percent of such individual's or corporation's United States source gross transportation income for such taxable year.

〔Footnote ¶3127-A〕 Matter in *italics* in Sec. 885 added by section 1241(a), '86 TRA, which struck out:
(1) "884"
Effective date (Sec. 1241(e), '86 TRA).—Applies to taxable years beginning after 12-31-86.
〔Footnote ¶3128〕 Sec. 887 added by section 1212(b)(1) '86 TRA.
Effective date (Sec. 1212(f)(1) '86 TRA).—Applies to taxable years beginning after 12-31-86.

(b) **United States Source Gross Transportation Income.—**

    (1) **In general.—**Except as provided in paragraph (2), the term "United States source gross transportation income" means any gross income which is transportation income (as defined in section 863(c)(3)) to the extent such income is treated as from sources in the United States under section 863(c).

    (2) **Exception for certain income effectively connected with business in the United States.—**The term "United States source gross transportation income" shall not include any income taxable under section 871(b) or 882.

    (3) **Determination of effectively connected income.—**For purposes of this chapter, transportation income of any taxpayer shall not be treated as effectively connected with the conduct of a trade or business in the United States unless—

        (A) the taxpayer has a fixed place of business in the United States involved in the earning of transportation income, and

        (B) substantially all of the United States source gross transportation income (determined without regard to pararagraph (2)) of the taxpayer is attributable to regularly scheduled transportation (or, in the case of income from the leasing of a vessel or aircraft, is attributable to a fixed place of business in the United States).

(c) **Coordination With Other Provisions.—**Any income taxable under this section shall not be taxable under section 871, 881, or 882.

[For official explanation, see Committee Reports, ¶4029.]

【¶3129】 **CODE SEC. 891. DOUBLING OF RATES OF TAX ON CITIZENS AND CORPORATIONS OF CERTAIN FOREIGN COUNTRIES.**

Whenever the President finds that, under the laws of any foreign country, citizens or corporations of the United States are being subjected to discriminatory or extraterritorial taxes, the President shall so proclaim and the rates of tax imposed by section 1, 3, 11, 801, [1]831, 852, 871, and 881 shall, for the taxable year during which such proclamation is made and for each taxable year thereafter, be doubled in the case of each citizen and corporation of such foreign country; but the tax at such doubled rate shall be considered as imposed by such sections as the case may be. In no case shall this section operate to increase the taxes imposed by such sections (computed without regard to this section) to an amount in excess of 80 percent of the taxable income of the taxpayer (computed without regard to the deductions allowable under section 151 and under part VIII of subchapter B). Whenever the President finds that the laws of any foreign country with respect to which the President has made a proclamation under the preceding provisions of this section have been modified so that discriminatory and extraterritorial taxes applicable to citizens and corporations of the United States have been removed, he shall so proclaim, and the provisions of this section providing for doubled rates of tax shall not apply to any citizen or corporation of such foreign country with respect to any taxable year beginning after such proclamation is made.

[For official explanation, see Committee Reports, ¶3964.]

【¶3130】 **CODE SEC. 892. INCOME OF FOREIGN GOVERNMENTS AND OF INTERNATIONAL ORGANIZATIONS.**

    [1]*(a)* *Foreign Governments.—*

        (1) *In general.—The income of foreign governments received from—*

            (A) *investments in the United States in—*

                (i) *stock, bonds, or other domestic securities owned by such foreign governments, or*

                (ii) *financial instruments held in the execution of governmental financial or monetary policy, or*

            (B) *interest on deposits in banks in the United States of moneys belonging to such foreign governments,*

【Footnote ¶3129】 Section 1024(c)(13), '86 TRA, struck out from Sec. 891:

(1) "821,"

Effective date (Sec. 1024(e), '86 TRA).—Applies to taxable years beginning after 12-31-86.

【Footnote ¶3130】 Matter in *italics* in Sec. 892 added by section 1247(a), '86 TRA, which struck out:

(1) "The income of foreign governments or international organizations received from investments in the United States in stocks, bonds, or other domestic securities, owned by such foreign governments or by international organizations, or from interest on deposits in banks in the United States of moneys belonging to such foreign governments or international organizations, or from any other source within the United States, shall not be included in gross income and shall be exempt from taxation under this subtitle."

Effective date (Sec. 1247(b), '86 TRA).—Applies to amounts received on or after 7-1-86, except that no amount shall be required to be deducted and withheld by reason of the amendment made by subsection (a) from any payment made before the date of the enactment of this Act.

(i) *Taxes Used to Provide Subsidies.*—Any income, war profits, or excess profits tax shall not be treated as a tax for purposes of this title to the extent—

(1) the amount of such tax is used (directly or indirectly) by the country imposing such tax to provide a subsidy by any means to the taxpayer, a related person (within the meaning of section 482), or any party to the transaction or to a related transaction, and

(2) such subsidy is determined (directly or indirectly) by reference to the amount of such tax, or the base used to compute the amount of such tax.

²*(j)* **Cross Reference.**—

    *   *   *   *   *   *   *   *   *   *   *   *   *   *

(3) **For right of estate or trust to the credit of taxes imposed by foreign countries and possessions of the United States under this section, see** ³*section 642(a).*

[For official explanation, see Committee Reports, ¶3856; 4027; 4190.]

【¶3133】 CODE SEC. 902. ¹*DEEMED PAID CREDIT WHERE DOMESTIC CORPORATION OWNS 10 PERCENT OR MORE OF VOTING STOCK OF FOREIGN CORPORATION.*

(a) *Taxes Paid by Foreign Corporation Treated as Paid by Domestic Corporation.*—For purposes of this subpart, a domestic corporation which owns 10 percent or more of the voting stock of a foreign corporation from which it receives dividends in any taxable year shall be deemed to have paid the same proportion of such foreign corporation's post-1986 foreign income taxes as—

(1) the amount of such dividends (determined without regard to section 78), bears to

(2) such foreign corporation's post-1986 undistributed earnings.

【Footnote ¶3132 continued】

Matter in *italics* in Sec. 901(i) and (j) added by section 1204(a), '86 TRA, which struck out:
(2) "(i)"
Effective date (Sec. 1204(b), '86 TRA).—Applies to foreign taxes paid or accrued in taxable years beginning after 12-31-86.

Matter in *italics* in Sec. 901(j)(3) (former (i)(3)) added by section 112(b)(3), '86 TRA, which struck out:
(3) "section 642(a)(1)"
Effective date (Sec. 151(a), '86 TRA).—Applies to taxable years beginning after 12-31-86.
【Footnote ¶3133】 Matter in *italics* in Sec. 902 added by section 1202(a), '86 TRA, which struck out:
(1) "CREDIT FOR CORPORATE STOCKHOLDER IN FOREIGN CORPORATION.
(a) **Treatment of Taxes Paid by Foreign Corporation.**—For purposes of this subpart, a domestic corporation which owns at least 10 percent of the voting stock of a foreign corporation from which it receives dividends in any taxable year shall be deemed to have paid the same proportion of any income, war profits, or excess profits taxes paid or deemed to be paid by such foreign corporation to any foreign country or to any possession of the United States, on or with respect to the accumulated profits of such foreign corporation from which such dividends were paid, which the amount of such dividends (determined without regard to section 78) bears to the amount of such accumulated profits in excess of such income, war profits, and excess profits taxes (other than those deemed paid).
(b) **Foreign Subsidiary of First and Second Foreign Corporation.**—
(1) **One tier.**—If the foreign corporation described in subsection (a) (hereinafter in this subsection referred to as the 'first foreign corporation') owns 10 percent or more of the voting stock of a second foreign corporation from which it receives dividends in any taxable year, it shall be deemed to have paid the same proportion of any income, war profits, or excess profits taxes paid or deemed to be paid by such second foreign corporation to any foreign country or to any possession of the United States on or with respect to the accumulated profits of such second foreign corporation from which such dividends were paid, which the amount of such dividends bears to the amount of such accumulated profits in excess of such income, war profits, and excess profits taxes (other than those deemed paid).
(2) **Two tiers.**—If such first foreign corporation owns 10 percent or more of the voting stock of a second foreign corporation which in turn, owns 10 percent or more of the voting stock of a third foreign corporation from which the second foreign corporation receives dividends in any taxable year, the second foreign corporation shall be deemed to have paid the same proportion of any income, war profits, or excess profits taxes paid by such third foreign corporation to any foreign country or to any possession of the United States, on or with respect to the accumulated profits of such third foreign corporation from which such dividends were paid, which the amount of such dividends bears to the amount of such accumulated profits in excess of such income, war profits, and excess profits taxes.
(3) **Voting stock requirement.**—For purposes of this subpart—
(A) Paragraph (1) shall not apply unless the percentage of voting stock owned by the domestic corporation in the first foreign corporation and the percentage of voting stock owned by the first foreign corporation in the second foreign corporation when multiplied together equal at least 5 percent, and
(B) Paragraph (2) shall not apply unless the percentage arrived at for purposes of applying paragraph (1) when multiplied by the percentage of voting stock owned by the second foreign corporation in the third foreign corporation is equal to at least 5 percent.
(c) **Applicable Rules.**—

(b) Deemed Taxes Increased in Case of Certain 2nd and 3rd Tier Foreign Corporations.—

    (1) 2nd tier.—If the foreign corporation described in subsection (a) (hereinafter in this section referred to as the "1st tier corporation") owns 10 percent or more of the voting stock of a 2nd foreign corporation from which it receives dividends in any taxable year, the 1st tier corporation shall be deemed to have paid the same proportion of such 2nd foreign corporation's post-1986 foreign income taxes as would be determined under subsection (a) if such 1st tier corporation were a domestic corporation.

    (2) 3rd tier.—If such 1st tier corporation owns 10 percent or more of the voting stock of a 2nd foreign corporation which, in turn, owns 10 percent or more of the voting stock of a 3rd foreign corporation from which the 2nd corporation receives dividends in any taxable year, such 2nd foreign corporation shall be deemed to have paid the same proportion of such 3rd foreign corporation's post-1986 foreign income taxes as would be determined under subsection (a) if such 2nd foreign corporation were a domestic corporation.

    (3) 5 percent stock requirement.—For purposes of this subpart—

        (A) For 2nd tier.—Paragraph (1) shall not apply unless the percentage of voting stock owned by the domestic corporation in the 1st tier corporation and the percentage of voting stock owned by the 1st tier corporation in the 2nd foreign corporation when multiplied together equal at least 5 percent.

        (B) For 3rd tier.—Paragraph (2) shall not apply unless the percentage arrived at for purposes of applying paragraph (1) when multiplied by the percentage of voting stock owned by the 2nd foreign corporation in the 3rd foreign corporation is equal to at least 5 percent.

(c) Definitions and Special Rules.—For purposes of this section—

    (1) Post-1986 undistributed earnings.—The term "post-1986 undistributed earnings" means the amount of the earnings and profits of the foreign corporation (computed in accordance with sections 964 and 986) accumulated in taxable years beginning after December 31, 1986,

        (A) as of the close of the taxable year of the foreign corporation in which the dividend is distributed, and

        (B) without diminution by reason of dividends distributed during such taxable year.

    (2) Post-1986 foreign income taxes.—The term "post-1986 foreign income taxes" means the sum of—

        (A) the foreign income taxes with respect to the taxable year of the foreign corporation in which the dividend is distributed, and

        (B) the foreign income taxes with respect to prior taxable years beginning after December 31, 1986, to the extent such foreign taxes were not deemed paid with respect to dividends distributed by the foreign corporation in prior taxable years.

    (3) Special rule where domestic corporation acquires 10 percent of foreign corporation after December 31, 1986.—

        (A) In general.—If the 1st day on which the ownership requirements of subparagraph (B) are met with respect to any foreign corporation is in a taxable year of such corporation beginning after December 31, 1986, the post-1986 undistributed earnings

---

⟦Footnote ¶3133 continued⟧

    (1) Accumulated profits defined.—For purposes of this section, the term 'accumulated profits' means, with respect to any foreign corporation, the amount of its gains, profits, or income computed without reduction by the amount of the income, war profits, and excess profits taxes imposed on or with respect to such profits or income by any foreign country or by any possession of the United States. The Secretary shall have full power to determine from the accumulated profits of what year or years such dividends were paid, treating dividends paid in the first 60 days of any year as having been paid from the accumulated profits of the preceding year or years (unless to his satisfaction shown otherwise), and in other respects treating dividends as having been paid from the most recently accumulated gains, profits, or earnings.

    (2) Accounting periods.—In the case of a foreign corporation the income, war profits, and excess profits taxes of which are determined on the basis of an accounting period of less than 1 year, the word "year" as used in this subsection, shall be construed to mean such accounting period.

    (d) Cross References.—

    (1) For inclusion in gross income of an amount equal to taxes deemed paid under subsection (a), see section 78.

    (2) For application of subsections (a) and (b) with respect to taxes deemed paid in a prior taxable year by a United States shareholder with respect to a controlled foreign corporation, see section 960.

    (3) For reduction of credit with respect to dividends paid out of accumulated profits for years for which certain information is not furnished, see section 6038."

    Effective date (Sec. 1202(e), '86 TRA).—Applies to distributions by foreign corporations out of, and to inclusions under section 951(a) of the '86 Code attributable to, earnings and profits for taxable years beginning after 12-31-86.

and the post-1986 foreign income taxes of such foreign corporation shall be determined by taking into account only periods beginning on and after the 1st day of the 1st taxable year in which such ownership requirements are met.

(B) Ownership requirements.—The ownership requirements of this subparagraph are met with respect to any foreign corporation if—

(i) 10 percent or more of the voting stock of such foreign corporation is owned by a domestic corporation,

(ii) the requirements of subsection (b)(3)(A) are met with respect to such foreign corporation and 10 percent or more of the voting stock of such foreign corporation is owned by another foreign corporation described in clause (i), or

(iii) the requirements of subsection (b)(3)(B) are met with respect to such foreign corporation and 10 percent or more of the voting stock of such foreign corporation is owned by another foreign corporation described in clause (ii).

(4) Foreign income taxes.—

(A) In general.—The term "foreign income taxes" means any income, war profits, or excess profits taxes paid by the foreign corporation to any foreign country or possession of the United States.

(B) Treatment of deemed taxes.—Except for purposes of determining the amount of the post-1986 foreign income taxes of a 3rd foreign corporation referred to in subsection (b)(2), the term "foreign income taxes" includes any such taxes deemed to be paid by the foreign corporation under this section.

(5) Accounting periods.—In the case of a foreign corporation the income, war profits, and excess profits taxes of which are determined on the basis of an accounting period of less than 1 year, the word "year" as used in this subsection shall be construed to mean such accounting period.

(6) Treatment of distributions from earnings before 1987.—

(A) In General.—In the case of any dividend paid by a foreign corporation out of accumulated profits (as defined in this section as in effect on the day before the date of the enactment of the Tax Reform Act of 1986) for taxable years beginning before the 1st taxable year taken into account in determining the post-1986 undistributed earnings of such corporation—

(i) this section (as amended by the Tax Reform Act of 1986) shall not apply, but

(ii) this section (as in effect on the day before the date of the enactment of such Act) shall apply.

(B) Dividends paid first out of post-1986 earnings.—Any dividend in a taxable year beginning after December 31, 1986, shall be treated as made out of post-1986 undistributed earnings to the extent thereof.

(7) Regulations.—The Secretary shall provide such regulations as may be necessary or appropriate to carry out the provisions of this section and section 960, including provisions which provide for the separate application of this section to reflect the separate application of section 904 to separate types of income and loss.

(d) Cross References.—

(1) For inclusion in gross income of an amount equal to taxes deemed paid under subsection (a), see section 78.

(2) For application of subsections (a) and (b) with respect to taxes deemed paid in a prior taxable year by a United States shareholder with respect to a controlled foreign corporation, see section 960.

(3) For reduction of credit with respect to dividends paid out of post-1986 undistributed earnings for years for which certain information is not furnished, see section 6038.

[For official explanation, see Committee Reports, ¶4027.]

【¶3134】 CODE SEC. 904. LIMITATION ON CREDIT.

(a) Limitation.—The total amount of the credit taken under section 901(a) shall not exceed the same proportion of the tax against which such credit is taken which the taxpayer's taxable income from sources without the United States (but not in excess of the taxpayer's entire taxable income) bears to his entire taxable income for the same taxable year.[1]

【Footnote ¶3134】 The last sentence in Sec. 904(a) struck out by section 104(b)(13), '86 TRA:

(1) "For purposes of the proceeding sentence, in the case of an individual the entire taxable income shall be reduced by an amount equal to the zero bracket amount."

(b)   **Taxable Income for Purpose of Computing Limitation.—**

*   *   *   *   *   *   *   *   *   *   *   *

(3)   **Definitions.—**For purposes of this subsection—

(A)   Foreign source capital gain net income.—The term "foreign source capital gain net income" means the lesser of—

(i)   capital gain net income from sources without the United States, or

(ii)   capital gain net income.

(B)   Foreign source net capital gain.—The term "foreign source net capital gain" means the lesser of—

(i)   net capital gain from sources without the United States, or

(ii)   net capital gain.[2]

[3]*(C)*   Section 1231 gains.—The term "gain from the sale or exchange of capital assets" includes any gain so treated under section 1231. [sic.]

[4]*(D)*   Rate differential portion.—The "rate differential portion" of foreign source net capital gain, net capital gain, or the excess of net capital gain from sources within the United States over net capital gain, as the case may be, is the same proportion of such amount as the excess of the highest rate of tax specified in section 11(b) over the alternative rate of tax under section 1201(a) bears to the highest rate of tax specified in section 11(b).

*   *   *   *   *   *   *   *   *   *   *   *

(d)   **Separate Application of Section With Respect to Certain** [5]*Categories of Income*

(1)   [6]*In general.*—The provisions of subsections (a), (b) and (c) *and sections 902, 907, and 960* shall be applied separately with respect to each of the following items of income:

[7]*(A)*   *passive income,*

⎡Footnote ¶3134 continued⎤

Effective date (Sec. 151(a), '86 TRA).—Applies to taxable years beginning after 12-31-86.

Matter in *italics* in Sec. 904(b)(3)(C) and (D) added by section 1211(b)(3), '86 TRA, which struck out:

(2)   "(C)   Exception for gain from the sale of certain personal property.—There shall be included as gain from sources within the United States any gain from sources without the United States from the sale or exchange of a capital asset which is personal property which—

(i)   in the case of an individual, is sold or exchanged outside of the country (or possession) of the individual's residence,

(ii)   in the case of a corporation, is stock in a second corporation sold or exchanged other than in a country (or possession) in which such second corporation derived more than 50 percent of its gross income for the 3-year period ending with the close of such second corporation's taxable year immediately preceding the year during which the sale or exchange occurred, or

(iii)   in the case of any taxpayer, is personal property (other than stock in a corporation) sold or exchanged other than in a country (or possession) in which such property is used in a trade or business of the taxpayer or in which such taxpayer derived more than 50 percent of its gross income for the 3-year period ending with the close of its taxable year immediately preceding the year during which the sale or exchange occurred,

unless such gain is subject to an income, war profits, or excess profits tax of a foreign country or possession of the United States, and the rate of tax applicable to such gain is 10 percent or more of the gain from the sale or exchange (computed under this chapter).

(D)   Gain from liquidation of certain foreign corporations.—Subparagraph (C) shall not apply with respect to a distribution in liquidation of a foreign corporation to which part II of subchapter C applies if such corporation derived less than 50 percent of its gross income from sources within the United States for the 3-year period ending with the close of such corporation's taxable year immediately preceding the year during which the distribution occurred."

(3)   "(E)"

(4)   "(F)"

Effective date (Sec. 1211(c), '86 TRA).—(1)   Generally applies to taxable years beginning after 12-31-86.

(2)   Special rule for foreign persons.—In the case of any foreign person other than any controlled foreign corporations (within the meaning of section 957(a) of the '54 Code), the amendments made by this section shall apply to transactions entered into after 3-18-86.

Matter in *italics* in Sec. 904(d) heading added by section 1201(d)(1), '86 TRA, which struck out:

(5)   **"Interest Income and Income From DISC, Former DISC, FSC, or Former FSC**

Effective date (Sec. 1201(e), '86 TRA).—Generally applies to taxable years beginning after 12-31-86. For special rules, see ¶2055.

Matter in *italics* in Sec. 904(d)(1) heading added by section 1899A(24), '86 TRA, which struck out:

(6)   **"In general.—"**

Matter in *italics* in Sec. 904(d)(1)(A)—(G), and subsection letter *"(H)"* added by section 1201(a) and (d)(3), '86 TRA, which struck out:

(7)   "(A)   the interest income described in paragraph (2),

(B) high withholding tax interest,

(C) financial services income,

(D) shipping income,

(E) dividends from each noncontrolled section 902 corporation,

[8]*(F)* dividends from a DISC or former DISC (as defined in section 992(a)) to the extent such dividends are treated as income from sources without the United States,

[9]*(G)* taxable income attributable to foreign trade income (within the meaning of section 923(b)),

[10]*(H)* distributions from a FSC (or former FSC) out of earnings and profits attributable to foreign trade income (within the meaning of section 923(b)) *or qualified interest and carrying charges as defined in section 245(c)),* and

[11]*(I)* income other than income described in [12]*any of the preceding paragraphs.*

≫P-H CAUTION→ There are two versions of Sec. 904(d)(2) and (3). Sec. 904(d)(2) and (3), generally effective after 12-31-86, follows. For Sec. 904(d)(2) and (3), generally effective before 1-1-87, see below.

▲[13]*(2)* *Definitions and special rules.—For purposes of this subsection—*

⟦Footnote ¶3134 continued⟧

TRA, which struck out:

(7) "(A) the interest income described in paragraph (2),

(8) "(B)"

(9) "(C)"

(10) "(D)"

Effective date (Sec. 1201(e), '86 TRA).—Generally applies to taxable years beginning after 12-31-86. For special rules, see ¶2055.

Matter in *italics* in Sec. 904(d)(1)(H) [former (D)], [except subsection letter "(H),"] added by section 1876(d)(2), '86 TRA.

Effective date (Sec. 1881, '86 TRA and section 805, '84 TRA, as amended by section 1876, '86 TRA).—Generally applies to transactions after 12-31-84, in taxable years ending after such date. For special and transitional rules, see footnote ¶2959.

Matter in *italics* in Sec. 904(d)(1)(I) [former (E)] added by section 1201(a) and (d)(2), '86 TRA, which struck out:

(11) "(E)"

(12) "subparagraph (A), (B), (C), or (D)."

Effective date (Sec. 1201(e), '86 TRA).—Generally applies to taxable years beginning after 12-31-86. For special rules, see ¶2055.

▲ Sec. 904(d)(2) and (3) in *italics*, preceded by a triangle, added by section 1201(b), '86 TRA, which struck out:

(13) "(2) **Interest income to which applicable.**—For purposes of this subsection, the interest income described in this paragraph is interest other than interest—

(A) derived from any transaction which is directly related to the active conduct by the taxpayer of a trade or business in a foreign country or a possession of the United States,

(B) derived in the conduct by the taxpayer of a banking, financing, or similar business,

(C) received from a corporation in which the taxpayer (or one or more includible corporations in an affiliated group, as defined in section 1504, of which the taxpayer is a member) owns, directly or indirectly, at least 10 percent of the voting stock, or

(D) received on obligations acquired as a result of the disposition of a trade or business actively conducted by the taxpayer in a foreign country or possession of the United States or as a result of the disposition of stock or obligations of a corporation in which the taxpayer owned at least 10 percent of the voting stock.

For purposes of subparagraph (C), stock owned, directly or indirectly, by or for a foreign corporation, shall be considered as being proportionately owned by its shareholders. For purposes of this subsection, interest (after the operation of section 904(d)(3)) received from a designated payor corporation described in section 904(d)(3)(E)(iii) by a taxpayer which owns directly or indirectly less than 10 percent of the voting stock of such designated payor corporation shall be treated as interest described in subparagraph (A) to the extent such interest would have been so treated had such taxpayer received it from other than a designated payor corporation.

(3) **Certain amounts attributable to United States-owned foreign corporation, etc., treated as interest.—**

(A) **In general.**—For purposes of this subsection, dividends and interest—

(i) paid or accrued by a designated payor corporation, and

(ii) attributable to any taxable year of such corporation,

shall be treated as interest income described in paragraph (2) to the extent that the aggregate amount of such dividends and interest does not exceed the separate limitation interest of the designated payor corporation for such taxable year.

(B) **Separate limitation interest.**—For purposes of this subsection, the term "separate limitation interest" means, with respect to any taxable year—

(A) passive income.—

   (i) In general.—Except as otherwise provided in this subparagraph, the term "passive income" means any income received or accrued by any person which is of a kind which would be foreign personal holding company income (as defined in section 954(c)).

   (ii) Certain amounts included.—The term "passive income" includes any amount includible in gross income under section 551 or section 1293 (relating to certain passive foreign investment companies).

   (iii) Exceptions.—The term "passive income" shall not include—

     (I) any income described in a subparagraph of paragraph (1) other than subparagraph (A),

     (II) any export financing interest,

     (III) any high-taxed income, and

     (IV) any foreign oil and gas extraction income (as defined in section 907(c)).

(B) High withholding tax interest.—

   (i) In general.—Except as otherwise provided in this subparagraph, the term "high withholding tax interest" means any interest if—

     (I) such interest is subject to a withholding tax of a foreign country or possession of the United States (or other tax determined on a gross basis), and

     (II) the rate of such tax applicable to such interest is at least 5 percent.

   (ii) Exception for export financing.—The term "high withholding tax interest" shall not include any export financing interest.

   (iii) Regulations.—The Secretary may be regulations provide that amounts (not otherwise high withholding tax interest) shall be treated as high withholding

---

⟦Footnote ¶3134 continued⟧

   (i) the aggregate amount of the interest income described in paragraph (2) (including amounts treated as so described by reason of this paragraph) which is received or accrued by the designated payor corporation during the taxable year, reduced by

   (ii) the deductions properly allocable (under regulations prescribed by the Secretary) to such income.

   (C) Exception where designated corporation has small amount of separate limitation interest.—Subparagraph (A) shall not apply to any amount attributable to the taxable year of a designated payor corporation, if—

   (i) such corporation has earnings and profits for such taxable year, and

   (ii) less than 10 percent of such earnings and profits is attributable to separate limitation interest.

The preceding sentence shall not apply to any amount includible in gross income under section 551 or 951.

   (D) Treatment of certain interest.—For purposes of this paragraph, the amount of the separate limitation interest and the earnings and profits of any designated payor corporation shall be determined without any reduction for interest paid or accrued to a United States shareholder (as defined in section 951(b)) or a related person (within the meaning of section 267(b)) to such a shareholder.

   (E) Designated payor corporation.—For purposes of this paragraph the term "designated payor corporation" means—

   (i) any United States-owned foreign corporation (within the meaning of subsection (g)(6)),

   (ii) any other foreign corporation in which a United States person is a United States shareholder (as defined in section 951(b)) at any time during the taxable year of such foreign corporation,

   (iii) any regulated investment company, and

   (iv) any other corporation formed or availed of for purposes of avoiding the provisions of this paragraph.

For purposes of this paragraph, the rules of paragraph (9) of subsection (g) shall apply.

   (F) Determination of year to which amount is attributable.—For purposes of determining whether an amount is attributable to a taxable year of a designated payor corporation—

   (i) any amount includible in gross income under section 551 or 951 in respect of such taxable year,

   (ii) any interest paid or accrued by such corporation during such taxable year, and

   (iii) any dividend paid out of the earnings and profits of such corporation for such taxable year,

shall be treated as attributable to such taxable year,

   (G) Ordering rules.—Subparagraph (A) shall be applied to amounts described therein in the order in which such amounts are described in subparagraph (F).

   (H) Dividend.—For purposes of this paragraph, the term "dividend" includes—

   (i) any amount includible in gross income under section 551 or 951, and

   (ii) any gain treated as ordinary income under section 1246 or as a dividend under section 1248.

   "(I) Interest and dividends from members of same affiliated group.—For purposes of this paragraph, dividends and interest received or accrued by the designated payor corporation from another member of the same affiliated group (determined under section 1504 without regard to subsection (b)(3) theeof) shall be treated as separate limitation interest if (and only if) such amounts are attributable (directly or indirectly) to separate limitation interest of any other member of such group."

   (J) Distributions through other entities.—The Secretary shall prescribe such regulations as may be necessary to carry out the purposes of this paragraph in the case of distributions or payments through 1 or more entities.

   Effective date (Sec. 1201(e), '86 TRA).—Generally applies to taxable years beginning after 12-31-86. For special rules, see ¶2055.

tax interest where necessary to prevent avoidance of the purposes of this subparagraph.

(C) Financial services income.—

(i) In general.—Except as otherwise provided in this subparagraph, the term "financial services income" means income received or accrued by any person which is not passive income (determined without regard to subparagraph (A)(iii)(I) and which—

(I) is derived in the active conduct of a banking, financing, or similar business, or derived from the investment by an insurance company of its unearned premiums or reserves ordinary and necessary for the proper conduct of its insurance business,

(II) is of a kind which would be insurance income as defined in section 953(a) determined without regard to those provisions of paragraph (1)(A) of such section which limit insurance income to income from countries other than the country in which the corporation was created or organized.

(ii) Special rule if entity predominantly engaged in banking, etc., business.—If, for any taxable year, an entity is predominantly engaged in the active conduct of a banking, insurance, financing, or similar business, the term "financial services income" includes any passive income (determined without regard to subparagraph (A)(iii)(I)) of such corporation for such taxable year. In the case of any entity described in the preceding sentence, the term "shipping income" shall not include any income treated as financial services income under the preceding sentence.

(iii) Exception for export financing.—The term "financial services income" does not include any export financing interest.

(iv) High withholding tax interest.—The term "financial services income" does not include any high withholding tax interest.

(D) Shipping income.—The term "shipping income" means any income received or accrued by any person which is of a kind which would be foreign base company shipping income (as defined in section 954(f)).

(E) Noncontrolled section 902 corporation.—

(i) In general.—The term "noncontrolled section 902 corporation" means any foreign corporation with respect to which the taxpayer meets the stock ownership requirements of section 902(a) (or, for purposes of applying paragraph (3), the requirements of section 902(b)). A controlled foreign corporation shall not be treated as a noncontrolled section 902 corporation with respect to any distribution out of its earnings and profits for periods during which it was a controlled foreign corporation.

(ii) Special rule for taxes on high-withholding tax interest.—If a foreign corporation is a noncontrolled section 902 corporation with respect to the taxpayer, taxes on high withholding tax interest (to the extent imposed at a rate in excess of 5 percent) shall not be treated as foreign taxes for purposes of determining the amount of foreign taxes deemed paid by the taxpayer under section 902.

(F) High-taxed income.—The term "high-taxed income" means any income which (but for this subparagraph) would be passive income if the sum of—

(i) the foreign income taxes paid or accrued by the taxpayer with respect to such income, and

(ii) the foreign income taxes deemed paid by the taxpayer with respect to such income under section 902 or 960,

exceeds the highest rate of tax specified in section 1 or 11 (whichever applies) multiplied by the amount of such income (determined with regard to section 78). For purposes of the preceding sentence, the term "foreign income taxes" means any income, war profits, or excess profits tax imposed by any foreign country or possession of the United States.

(G) Export financing interest.—For purposes of this paragraph, the term "export financing interest" means any interest derived from financing the sale (or other disposition) for use of consumption outside the United States of any property—

(i) which is manufactured, produced, grown, or extracted in the United States by the taxpayer or a related person, and

(ii) not more than 50 percent of the fair market value of which is attributable to products imported into the United States.

For purposes of clause (ii), the fair market value of any property imported into the United States shall be its appraised value, as determined by the Secretary under sec-

tion 402 of the Tariff Act of 1930 (19 U.S.C. 1401a) in connection with its importation.

(H) *Related person.*—For purposes of this paragraph, the term "related person" has the meaning given such term by section 954(d)(3), except that such section shall be applied by substituting 'the person with respect to whom the determination is being made' for 'controlled foreign corporation' each place it appears.

(I) *Transitional rule.*—For purposes of paragraph (1)—

(i) taxes paid or accrued in a taxable year beginning before January 1, 1987, with respect to income which was described in subparagraph (A) of paragraph (1) (as in effect on the day before the date of the enactment of the Tax Reform Act of 1986) shall be treated as taxes paid or accrued with respect to income described in subparagraph (A) of paragraph (1) (as in effect after such date),

(ii) taxes paid or accrued in a taxable year beginning before January 1, 1987, with respect to income which was described in subparagraph (E) of paragraph (1) (as in effect on the day before the date of the enactment of the Tax Reform Act of 1986) shall be treated as taxes paid or accrued with respect to income described in subparagraph (I) of paragraph(1) (as in effect after such date) except to the extent that—

(I) the taxpayer establishes to the satisfaction of the Secretary that such taxes were paid or accrued with respect to shipping income, or

(II) in the case of an entity meeting the requirements of subparagraph (C)(ii), the taxpayer establishes to the satisfaction of the Secretary that such taxes were paid or accrued with respect to financial services income, and

(iii) taxes paid or accrued in a taxable year beginning before January 1, 1987, with respect to income described in any other subparagraph of paragraph (1) (as so in effect before such date) shall be treated as taxes paid or accrued with respect to income described in the corresponding subparagraph of paragraph (1) (as so in effect after such date).

(3) *Look-thru in case of controlled foreign corporations.*—

(A) *In general.*—Except as otherwise provided in this paragraph, dividends, interest, rents, and royalties received or accrued by the taxpayer from a controlled foreign corporation in which the taxpayer is a United States shareholder shall not be treated as income in a separate category.

(B) *Subpart F inclusions.*—Any amount included in gross income under section 951(a)(1)(A) shall be treated as income in a separate category to the extent the amount so included is attributable to income in such category.

(C) *Interest, rents, and royalties.*—Any interest, rent, or royalty which is received or accrued from a controlled foreign corporation in which the taxpayer is a United States shareholder shall be treated as income in a separate category to the extent it is properly allocable (under regulations prescribed by the Secretary) to income of the controlled foreign corporation in such category.

(D) *Dividends.*—Any dividend paid out of the earnings and profits of any controlled foreign corporation in which the taxpayer is a United States shareholder shall be treated as income in a separate category in proportion to the ratio of—

(i) the portion of the earnings and profits attributable to income in such category, to

(ii) the total amount of earnings and profits.

(E) *Look-thru applies only where subpart F applies.*—If a controlled foreign corporation meets the requirements of section 954(b)(3)(A) (relating to de minimis rule) for any taxable year, for purposes of this paragraph, none of its income for such taxable year shall be treated as income in a separate category. Solely for purposes of applying subparagraph (D), income (other than high withholding tax interest and dividends from a noncontrolled section 902 corporation) of a controlled foreign corporation shall not be treated as income in a separate category if the requirements of section 954(b)(4) are met with respect to such income.

(F) *Separate category.*—For purposes of this paragraph, the term "separate category" means any category of income described in subparagraph (A), (B), (C), (D), or (E) of paragraph (1).

(G) *Dividend.*—For purposes of this paragraph, the term 'dividend' includes any amount included in gross income in section 951(a)(1)(B). Any amount included in gross income under section 78 to the extent attributable to amounts included in gross income in section 951(a)(1)(A) shall not be treated as a dividend but shall be treated as included in gross income under section 951(a)(1)(A).

≫P-H CAUTION→ There are two versions of Sec. 904(d)(2) and (3). Sec. 904(d)(2) and (3), generally effective before 1-1-87, follows. For Sec. 904(d)(2) and (3), generally effective after 12-31-86, see above.

▲ ▲ **(2) Interest income to which applicable.**—For purposes of this subsection, the interest income described in this paragraph is interest other than interest—

(A) derived from any transaction which is directly related to the active conduct by the taxpayer of a trade or business in a foreign country or a possession of the United States,

(B) derived in the conduct by the taxpayer of a banking, financing, or similar business,

(C) received from a corporation in which the taxpayer (or one or more includible corporations in an affiliated group, as defined in section 1504, of which the taxpayer is a member) owns, directly or indirectly, at least 10 percent of the voting stock, or

(D) received on obligations acquired as a result of the disposition of a trade or business actively conducted by the taxpayer in a foreign country or possession of the United States or as a result of the disposition of stock or obligations of a corporation in which the taxpayer owned at least 10 percent of the voting stock.

For purposes of subparagraph (C), stock owned, directly or indirectly, by or for a foreign corporation, shall be considered as being proportionately owned by its shareholders. *For purposes of this subsection, interest (after the operation of section 904(d)(3)) received from a designated payor corporation described in section 904(d)(3)(E)(iii) by a taxpayer which owns directly or indirectly less than 10 percent of the voting stock of such designated payor corporation shall be treated as interest described in subparagraph (A) to the extent such interest would have been so treated had such taxpayer received it from other than a designated payor corporation.*

(3) Certain amounts attributable to United States-owned foreign corporation, etc., treated as interest.—

* * * * * * * * * * * * *

(C) Exception where designated corporation has small amount of separate limitation interest.—Subparagraph (A) shall not apply to any amount attributable to the taxable year of a designated payor corporation, if—

(i) such corporation has earnings and profits for such taxable year, and

(ii) less than 10 percent of such earnings and profits is attributable to separate limitation interest.

The preceding sentence shall not apply to any amount includible in gross income under section 551 or 951.

* * * * * * * * * * * * *

(E) Designated payor corporation.—For purposes of this paragraph, the term "designated payor corporation" means—

(i) any United States-owned foreign corporation (within the meaning of subsection (g)(6)),

(ii) any other foreign corporation in which a United States person is a United States shareholder (as defined in section 951(b)) at any time during the taxable year of such foreign corporation, [14]

(iii) any regulated investment company [15]*and*

[Footnote ¶3134 continued]

▲ ▲ Matter in *italics* in Sec. 904(d)(2), (3)(C), (E)(ii), and (iii), preceded by two triangles, added by section 1810(b)(1), (3), and (4)(A), '86 TRA, which struck out:

(14) "and"

(15) "."

Effective date (Sec. 1881, '86 TRA and section 122(b), '84 TRA).—(1) Generally takes effect on 7-18-84.

(2) Special rules for interest income.—

(A) In general.—Interest income received or accrued by a designated payor corporation shall be taken into account for purposes of the amendment made by subsection (a) only in taxable years beginning after 7-18-84.

(B) Exception for investment after 6-22-84.—Notwithstanding subparagraph (A), the amendment made by subsection (a) shall apply to interest income received or accrued by a designated payor corporation after 7-18-84 if it is attributable to investment in the designated payor corporation after 6-22-84.

(3) Term obligations of designated payor corporation which is not applicable CFC.—In the case of any designated payor corporation which is not an applicable CFC (as defined in section 121(b)(2)(D)), any interest received or accrued by such corporation on a term obligation held by such corporation on 3-7-84, shall not be taken into account.

▲ ▲ Matter in italics in Sec. 904(d)(3)(E)(iv) and the last sentence in *italics* in Sec. 904(d)(3)(E), preceded by two triangles, added by section 1810(b)(4)(A), '86 TRA.

(iv) any other corporation formed or availed of for purposes of avoiding the provisions of this paragraph.

For purposes of this paragraph, the rules of paragraph (9) of subsection (g) shall apply.

* * * * * * * * * * *

[16]*(I) Interest and dividends from members of same affiliated group.—For purposes of this paragraph, dividends and interest received or accrued by the designated payor corporation from another member of the same affiliated group (determined under section 1504 without regard to subsection (b)(3) thereof) shall be treated as separate limitation interest if (and only if) such amounts are attributable (directly or indirectly) to separate limitation interest of any other member of such group.*

[17]*(J) Distributions through other entities.—The Secretary shall prescribe such regulations as may be necessary to carry out the purposes of this paragraph in the case of distributions or payments through 1 or more entities.*

(4) Controlled foreign corporation; United States shareholder.—For purposes of this subsection—

(A) Controlled foreign corporation.—The term "controlled foreign corporation" has the meaning given such term by section 957 (taking into account section 953(c)).

(B) United States shareholder.—The term "United States shareholder" has the meaning given such term by section 951(b) (taking into account section 953(c)).

(5) Regulations.—The Secretary shall prescribe such regulations as may be necessary or appropriate for the purposes of this subsection, including regulations—

(A) for the application of paragraph (3) and subsection (f)(5) in the case of income paid (or loans made) through 1 or more entities or between 2 or more chains of entities,

(B) preventing the manipulation of the character of income the effect of which is to avoid the purposes of this subsection, and

(C) providing that rules similar to the rules of paragraph (3)(C) shall apply to interest, rents, and royalties received or accrued from entities which would be controlled foreign corporations if they were foreign corporations.

* * * * * * * * * * *

(f) Recapture of Overall Foreign Loss.—

* * * * * * * * * * *

(5) Treatment of separate limitation losses.—

⟦Footnote ¶3134 continued⟧

Effective date (Sec. 1810(b)(4)(B), '86 TRA).—(i) The last sentence in Sec. 904(d)(3)(E) takes effect on 3-28-85. In the case of any taxable year ending after such date of any corporation treated as a designated payor corporation by reason of the amendment made by subparagraph (A)—

(I) only income received or accrued by such corporation after such date shall be taken into account under section 904(d)(3) of the '54 Code; except that

(II) subparagraph (C) of such section 904(d)(3) shall be applied by taking into account all income received or accrued by such corporation during such taxable year.

(ii) The amendment made by subparagraph (A) insofar as it adds clause (iv) to subparagraph (E) of section 904(d)(3) shall take effect on 12-31-85. For purposes of such amendment, the rule of the second sentence of clause (i) shall be applied by taking into account 12-31-85, in lieu of 3-28-85.

▲▲ Matter in *italics* in Sec. 904(d)(3)(I) and (J) [former (I)] preceded by two triangles added by section 1810(b)(2), '86 TRA, which struck out:

(16) "(J) Interest from members of same affiliated group.—For purposes of this paragraph, interest received or accrued by the designated payor corporation from another member of the same affiliated group (determined under section 1504 without regard to subsection (b)(3) thereof) shall not be treated as separate limitation interest, unless such interest is attributable directly or indirectly to separate limitation interest of such other member."

(17) "(I)"

Effective date (Sec. 1881, '86 TRA and section 122(b), '84 TRA).—(1) Generally takes effect on 7-18-84. For special rules, see above.

Sec 904(d)(4) and (5) in *italics* added by section 1201(b), '86 TRA.

Effective date (Sec. 1201(e), '86 TRA).—Generally applies to taxable years beginning after 12-31-86. For special rules, see ¶2055.

Sec. 904(f)(5) in *italics* added by section 1203(a), '86 TRA.

Effective date (Sec. 1203(b), '86 TRA).—Applies to losses incurred in taxable years beginning after 12-31-86.

(A) In general.—*The amount of the separate limitation losses for any taxable year shall reduce income from sources within the United States for such taxable year only to the extent the aggregate amount of such losses exceeds the aggregate amount of the separate limitation incomes for such taxable year.*

(B) Allocation of losses.—*The separate limitation losses for any taxable year (to the extent such losses do not exceed the separate limitation incomes for such year) shall be allocated among (and operate to reduce) such incomes on a proportionate basis.*

(C) Recharacterization of subsequent income.—If—

(i) a separate limitation loss from any income category (hereinafter in this subparagraph referred to as "the loss category") was allocated to income from any other category under subparagraph (B), and

(ii) the loss category has income for a subsequent taxable year,

such income (to the extent it does not exceed the aggregate separate limitation losses from the loss category not previously recharacterized under this subparagraph) shall be recharacterized as income from such other category in proportion to the prior reductions under subparagraph (B) in such other category not previously taken into account under this subparagraph. Nothing in the preceding sentence shall be construed as recharacterizing any tax.

(D) Special rules for losses from sources in the United States.—Any loss from sources in the United States for any taxable year (to the extent such loss does not exceed the separate limitation incomes from such year) shall be allocated among (and operate to reduce) such incomes on a proportionate basis. This subparagraph shall be applied after subparagraph (B).

(E) Definitions.—For purposes of this paragraph—

(i) Income category.—The term "income category" means each separate category of income described in subsection (d)(1).

(ii) Separate limitation income.—The term "separate limitation income" means, with respect to any income category, the taxable income from sources outside the United States, separately computed for such category.

(iii) Separate limitation loss.—The term "separate limitation loss" means, with respect to any income category, the loss from such category determined under the principles of section 907(c)(4)(B).

(g) Source rules in case of United States-Owned Foreign Corporations.—

(1) In general.—The following amounts which are derived from a United States owned foreign corporation and which would be treated as derived from sources outside the United States without regard to this subsection shall, for purposes of this section, be treated as derived from sources within the United States to the extent provided in this subsection:

(A) Any amount included in gross income under—

(i) section 951(a) (relating to amounts included in gross income of United States shareholders),[18]

(ii) section 551 (relating to foreign personal holding company income taxed to United States shareholders)[19], *or*

(iii) *section 1293 (relating to current taxation of income from qualified funds).*

(B) Interest.

(C) Dividends.

(2) Subpart F and foreign personal holding [20]*or passive foreign investment company.*—Any amount described in subparagraph (A) of paragraph (1) shall be treated as derived from sources within the United States to the extent such amount is attributable to income of the United States-owned foreign corporation from sources within the United States.

* * * * * * * * * * * * *

Matter in *italics* in Sec. 904(g)(1)(A)(i)—(iii) and (2) heading added by section 1235(f)(4), '86 TRA, which struck out:

(18) "or"

(19) "."

(20) "company inclusions"

Effective date (Sec. 1235(h), '86 TRA).—Applies to taxable years of foreign corporations beginning after 12-31-86.

---

    (9) Treatment of certain domestic corporations.—For purposes of this subsection—

        (A) in the case of interest treated as not from sources within the United States under section 861(a)(1)(B), the corporation paying such interest shall be treated as a United States-owned foreign corporation, and

        (B) in the case of any dividend treated as not from sources within the United States under section 861(a)(2)(A), the corporation paying such dividend shall be treated as a United States-owned foreign corporation.

    [21]*(10) Regulations.—*

    *   *   *   *   *   *   *   *   *   *   *   *

(i) Cross References.—

    *   *   *   *   *   *   *   *   *   *   *   *

    (2) For modification of limitation under subsection (a) for purposes of determining the amount of credit which can be taken [22]*against the alternative minimum tax, see section 59(a).*

[For official explanation, see Committee Reports, ¶3931; 4027; 4028; 4045; 4144; 4190.]

〖¶3135〗 CODE SEC. 906. NONRESIDENT ALIEN INDIVIDUALS AND FOR- EIGN CORPORATIONS.

    *   *   *   *   *   *   *   *   *   *   *   *

(b) Special Rules.—

    *   *   *   *   *   *   *   *   *   *   *   *

    (6) For purposes of section 902, any income, war profits, and excess profits taxes paid or accrued (or deemed paid or accrued) to any foreign country or possession of the United States with respect to income effectively connected with the conduct of a trade or business within the United States shall not be taken into account, and any accumulated profits attributable to such income shall not be taken into account.

    (6) [should read (7)] No credit shall be allowed under this section against the tax imposed by section 884.

[For official explanation, see Committee Reports, ¶4047; 4190.]

〖¶3136〗 CODE SEC. 911. CITIZENS OR RESIDENTS OF THE UNITED STATES LIVING ABROAD.

  (a) Exclusion From Gross Income.—At the election of a qualified individual (made separately with respect to paragraphs (1) and (2)), there shall be excluded from the gross income of such individual, and exempt from taxation under this subtitle, for any taxable year—

    (1) the foreign earned income of such individual, and

    (2) the housing cost amount of such individual.

  (b) Foreign Earned Income.—

    *   *   *   *   *   *   *   *   *   *   *   *

    (2) Limitation of foreign earned income.—

【Footnote ¶3134 continued】

Matter in *italics* in Sec. 904(g)(9) and (10) added by section 1810(a)(1)(A), '86 TRA, which struck out:
(21) "(9)"
Effective date (Sec. 1810(a)(1)(B), '86 TRA).—Takes effect on 3-28-85. In the case of any taxable year ending after such date of any corporation treated as a United States-owned foreign corporation by reason of the amend- ment made by subparagraph (A)—

(i) only income received or accrued by such corporation after such date shall be taken into account under sec- tion 904(g) of the '54 Code; except that

(ii) paragraph (5) of such section 904(g) shall be applied by taking into account all income received or accrued by such corporation during such taxable year.

Matter in *italics* in Sec. 904(i)(2) added by section 701(e)(4)(H), '86 TRA, which struck out:
(22) "by an individual against the alternative minimum tax, see section 55(c)"
Effective date (Sec. 701(f), '86 TRA).—Generally applies to taxable years beginning after 12-31-86. For special rules, see footnote ¶2879.
【Footnote ¶3135】 Sec. 906(b)(6) in *italics* added by section 1876(d)(3), '86 TRA.
Effective date (Sec. 1881, '86 TRA and Sec. 805, '84 TRA, as amended by section 1876, '86 TRA).—Generally applies to transactions after 12-31-84, in taxable years ending after such date. For special rule for certain contracts, see footnote ¶2959.

Sec. 906(b) (6) [should read (7)] in *italics* added by section 1241(c), '86 TRA.
Effective date (Sec. 1241(e), '86 TRA).—Applies to taxable years beginning after 12-31-86.

(A) In general.—The foreign earned income of an individual which may be excluded under subsection (a)(1) for any taxable year shall not exceed the amount of foreign earned income computed on a daily basis at [1]an annual rate *of $70,000.*

* * * * * * * * * * *

(d) **Definitions and Special Rules.**—For purposes of this section—

* * * * * * * * * * *

(8) *Limitation on income earned in restricted country.—*

(A) In general.—If travel (or any transaction in connection with such travel) with respect to any foreign country is subject to the regulations described in subparagraph (B) during any period—

(i) the term "foreign earned income" shall not include any income from sources within such country attributable to services performed during such period,

(ii) the term "housing expenses" shall not include any expenses allocable to such period for housing in such country or for housing of the spouse or dependents of the taxpayer in another country while the taxpayer is present in such country, and

(iii) an individual shall not be treated as a bona fide resident of, or as present in, a foreign country for any day during which such individual was present in such country during such period.

(B) Regulations.—For purposes of this paragraph, regulations are described in this subparagraph if such regulations—

(i) have been adopted pursuant to the Trading With the Enemy Act (50 U.S.C. App. 1 et seq.), or the International Emergency Economic Powers Act (50 U.S.C. 1701 et seq.), and

(ii) include provisions generally prohibiting citizens and residents of the United States from engaging in transactions related to travel to, from, or within a foreign country.

(C) Exception.—Subparagraph (A) shall not apply to any individual during any period in which such individual's activities are not in violation of the regulations described in subparagraph (B).

[2]**(9) Regulations.**—The secretary shall prescribe such regulations as may be necessary or appropriate to carry out the purposes of this section, including regulations providing rules—

(A) for cases where a husband and wife each have earned income from sources outside the United States, and

(B) for married individuals filing separate returns.

* * * * * * * * * * *

[For official explanation, see Committee Reports, ¶4043.]

〔¶3137〕 CODE SEC. 923. EXEMPT FOREIGN TRADE INCOME.

(a) **Exempt Foreign Trade Income.**—For purposes of this subpart—

* * * * * * * * * * *

〔Footnote ¶3136〕 Matter in *italics* in Sec. 911(b)(2)(A) added by section 1233(a), '86 TRA, which struck out:
(1) "the annual rate set forth in the following table for each day of the taxable year within the applicable period described in subparagraph (A) or (B) of subsection (d)(1):

In the case of taxable years beginning in:	The annual rate is:
1983, 1984, 1985, 1986, or 1987	$80,000
1988	85,000
1989	90,000
1990 and thereafter	95,000″

Effective date (Sec. 1233(c), '86 TRA).—Applies to taxable years beginning after 12-31-86.

Matter in *italics* in Sec. 911(d)(8) and (9) (former 8) added by section 1233(b), '86 TRA, which struck out:
(2) "(8)"
Effective date (Sec. 1233(c), '86 TRA).—Applies to taxable years beginning after 12-31-86.
〔Footnote ¶3137〕 Matter in *italics* in Sec. 923(a)(6) added by section 1876(b)(3), '86 TRA.
Effective date (Sec. 1881, '86 TRA and Sec. 805, '84 TRA, as amended by section 1876, '86 TRA).—Generally applies to transactions after 12-31-84, in taxable years ending after such date. For special rule for certain contracts, see footnote ¶2959.

(6) Cross reference.—

For reduction in amount of exempt foreign trade income, see section 291(a)(4).

* * * * * * * * * * * *

[For official explanation, see Committee Reports, ¶4190.]

【¶3138】 CODE SEC. 924. FOREIGN TRADING GROSS RECEIPTS.

* * * * * * * * * * * *

(c) Requirement That FSC Be Managed Outside the United States.—The management of a FSC meets the requirements of this subsection for the taxable year if—

    (1) all meetings of the board of directors of the corporation, and all meetings of the shareholders of the corporation, are outside the United States,

    [1]*(2) the principal bank account of the corporation is maintained in a foreign country which meets the requirements of section 927(e)(3) or in a possession of the United States at all times during the taxable year, and*

    (3) all dividends, legal and accounting fees, and salaries of officers and members of the board of directors of the corporation disbursed during the taxable year are disbursed out of bank accounts of the corporation maintained outside the United States.

* * * * * * * * * * * *

(f) Certain Receipts Not Included in Foreign Trading Gross Receipts.—

    (1) Certain receipts excluded on basis of use; subsidized receipts and receipts from related parties excluded.—The term "foreign trading gross receipts" shall not include receipts of a FSC from a transaction if—

        (A) the export property or services—

            (i) are for ultimate use in the United States, or

            (ii) are for use by the United States or any instrumentality thereof and such use of export property or services is required by law or regulation,

        (B) such transaction is accomplished by a subsidy granted by the United States or any instrumentality thereof, or

        (C) such receipts are from another FSC which is a member of the same controlled group of corporations of which such corporation is a member.

In the case of gross receipts of a FSC from a transaction involving any property, subparagraph (C) shall not apply if such FSC (and all other FSC's which are members of the same controlled group and which receive gross receipts from a transaction involving such property) do not use the pricing rules under paragraph (1) of section 925(a) (or the corresponding provisions of the regulations prescribed under section 925(b)) with respect to any transaction involving such property.

* * * * * * * * * * * *

[For official explanation, see Committee Reports, ¶4190.]

【¶3139】 CODE SEC. 927. OTHER DEFINITIONS AND SPECIAL RULES.

* * * * * * * * * * * *

(d) Other Definitions.—For purposes of this subpart—

* * * * * * * * * * * *

    (6) Section 923(a)(2) non-exempt income.—The term "section 923(a)(2) non-exempt income" means any foreign trade income from a transaction with respect to which paragraph (1) or (2) of section 925(a) does not apply and which is not exempt foreign trade income. *Such term shall not include any income which is effectively connected with the conduct of a trade or business within the United States (determined without regard to this subpart).*

(e) Special Rules.—

* * * * * * * * * * * *

【Footnote ¶3138】 Matter in *italics* in Sec. 924(c)(2) added by section 1876(e)(2), '86 TRA, which struck out: **(1)** "(2) the principal bank account of the corporation is maintained outside the United States at all times during the taxable year, and"
Effective date (Sec. 1876(e)(2), '86 TRA).—Effective for periods after 3-28-85.

Matter in *italics* in Sec. 924(f)(1) added by section 1876(l), '86 TRA.
Effective date (Sec. 1881, '86 TRA and Sec. 805, '84 TRA, as amended by section 1876, '86 TRA).—Generally applies to transactions after 12-31-84, in taxable years ending after such date. For special rule for certain contracts, see footnote ¶2959.

(2) Participation in international boycotts, etc.—Under regulations prescribed by the Secretary, the exempt foreign trade income of a FSC for any taxable year shall be limited under rules similar to the rules of [1]*clauses (ii) and (iii)* of section 995(b)(1)(F).

(3) Exchange of information requirements.—For purposes of this title, the term "FSC" shall not include any corporation which was created or organized under the laws of any foreign country [2]*unless there is* in effect between such country and the United States—

(A) a bilateral or multilateral agreement described in section 274(h)(6)(C) *(determined by treating any reference to a beneficiary country as being a reference to any foreign country and by applying such section without regard to clause (ii) thereof),*

(B) [3]*an income tax treaty which contains an exchange of information program—*

(i) which the Secretary certifies (and has not revoked such certification) is satisfactory in practice for purposes of this title, and

(ii) to which the FSC is subject.

* * * * * * * * * * * *

(5) [4]*Coordination with possessions taxation.—*

(A) Exemption.—No tax shall be imposed by any possession of the United States on any foreign trade income derived before 1-1-87. The preceding sentence shall not apply to any income attributable to the sale of property or the performance of services for ultimate use, consumption, or disposition within the possession.

(B) Clarification that possession may exempt certain income from tax.—Nothing in any provision of law shall be construed as prohibiting any possession of the United States from exempting from tax any foreign trade income of a FSC or any other income of a FSC described in paragraph (2) or (3) of section 921(d).

(C) No cover over of taxes imposed on FSC.—Nothing in any provision of law shall be construed as requiring any tax imposed by this title on a FSC to be covered over (or otherwise transferred) to any possession of the United States.

* * * * * * * * * * * *

[For official explanation, see Committee Reports, ¶4190.]

〖¶3140〗 CODE SEC. 931. INCOME FROM SOURCES WITHIN [1] *GUAM, AMERICAN SAMOA, OR THE NORTHERN MARIANA ISLANDS.*

(a) General Rule.—In the case of an individual who is a bona fide resident of a speci-

〖Footnote ¶3139〗 Matter in *italics* in Sec. 927(d)(6), (e)(2), (3) and (5) added by section 1876(a)(1), (e)(1), (f)(1), and (p)(5) '86 TRA, which struck out:

(1) "clauses (i) and (ii)"

(2) "unless, at the [same] time such corporation was created or organized, there was"

(3) "an income tax treaty with respect to which the Secretary certifies that the exchange of information program with such country under such treaty carries out the purposes of this paragraph."

(4) **Exemption from certain other taxes.**—No tax shall be imposed by any jurisdiction described in subsection (d)(5) on any foreign trade income derived before January 1, 1987."

Effective date (Sec. 1881, '86 TRA and Sec. 805, '84 TRA, as amended by section 1876, '86 TRA).—Applies to transactions after 12-31-84, in taxable years ending after such date. For special and transitional rules, see footnote ¶2959.

〖Footnote ¶3140〗 Matter in *italics* in Sec. 931 added by section 1272(a), '86 TRA, which struck out:

(1) "POSSESSIONS OF THE UNITED STATES.

(a) **General Rule.**—In the case of individual citizens of the United States gross income means only gross income from sources within the United States if the conditions of both paragraph (1) and paragraph (2) are satisfied:

(1) **Three-year period.**—If 80 percent or more of the gross income of such citizen (computed without the benefit of this section) for the 3-year period immediately preceding the close of the taxable year (or for such part of such period immediately preceding the close of such taxable year as may be applicable) was derived from sources within a possession of the United States; and

(2) **Trade or business.**—If 50 percent or more of his gross income (computed without the benefit of this section) for such period or such part thereof was derived from the active conduct of a trade or business within a possession of the United States either on his own account or as an employee or agent of another.

(b) **Amounts Received in United States.**—Notwithstanding subsection (a), there shall be included in gross income all amounts received by such citizens or corporations within the United States, whether derived from sources within or without the United States.

(c) **Definition.**—For purposes of this section, the term possession of the United States does not include the Commonwealth of Puerto Rico, the Virgin Islands of the United States, or Guam.

(d) **Deductions.—**

(1) **General rule.**—Except as otherwise provided in this subsection and subsection (e), in the case of a citizen of the United States entitled to the benefits of this section the deductions shall be allowed only if and to the extent that they are connected with income from sources within the United States; and the proper apportionment and

fied possession during the entire taxable year, gross income shall not include—

(1)   income derived from sources within any specified possession, and

(2)   income effectively connected with the conduct of a trade or business by such individual within any specified possession.

(b)   Deductions, Etc. Allocable to Excluded Amounts Not Allowable.—An individual shall not be allowed—

(1)   as a deduction from gross income any deductions (other than the deduction under section 151, relating to personal exemptions), or

(2)   any credit, properly allocable or chargeable against amounts excluded from gross income under this section.

(c)   Specified Possession.—For purposes of this section, the term "specified possession" means Guam, American Samoa, and the Northern Mariana Islands.

(d)   Special Rules.—For purposes of this section—

(1)   **Employees of the United States.**—Amounts paid for services performed as an employee of the United States (or any agency thereof) shall be treated as not described in paragraph (1) or (2) of subsection (a).

(2)   **Determination of source, etc.**—The determination as to whether income is described in paragraph (1) or (2) of subsection (a) shall be made under regulations prescribed by the Secretary.

(3)   **Determination of residency.**—For purposes of this section and section 876, the determination of whether an individual is a bona fide resident of Guam, American Samoa, or the Northern Mariana Islands shall be made under regulations prescribed by the Secretary.

⟦Footnote ¶3140 continued⟧

allocation of the deductions with respect to sources of income within and without the United States shall be determined as provided in part I, under regulations prescribed by the Secretary.

(2)   **Exceptions.**—The following deductions shall be allowed whether or not they are connected with income from sources within the United States:

(A)   The deductions, for loss not connected with the trade or business if incurred in transactions entered into for profit, allowed by section 165(c)(2), but only if the profit, if such transaction had resulted in a profit, would be taxable under this subtitle.

(B)   The deduction, for losses allowed by section 165(c)(3), but only if the loss is of property within the United States.

(C)   The deduction for charitable contributions and gifts allowed by section 170.

(e)   **Deduction for Personal Exemptions.**—A citizen of the United States entitled to the benefits of this section shall be allowed a deduction for only one exemption under section 151.

(f)   **Allowance of Deductions and Credits.**—A citizen of the United States entitled to the benefits of this section shall receive the benefit of the deductions and credits allowed to them in this subtitle only by filing or causing to be filed with the Secretary a true and accurate return of their total income received from all sources in the United States, in the manner prescribed in subtitle F, including therein all the information which the Secretary may deem necessary for the calculation of such deductions and credits.

(g)   **Foreign Tax Credit.**—A citizen of the United States entitled to the benefits of this section shall not be allowed the credits against the tax for taxes of foreign countries and possessions of the United States allowed by section 901.

(h)   **Employees of the United States.**—For purposes of this section, amounts paid for services performed by a citizen of the United States as an employee of the United States or any agency thereof shall be deemed to be derived from sources within the United States."

Effective date (Sec. 1277(a), (b), (d) and (e), '86 TRA).

(a)   Generally applies to taxable years beginning after 12-31-86.

(b)   Special Rule for Guam, American Samoa, and the Northern Mariana Islands.—The amendments made by this subtitle shall apply with respect to Guam, American Samoa, or the Northern Mariana Islands (and to residents thereof and corporations created or organized therein) only if (and so long as) an implementing agreement under section 1271 is in effect between the United States and such possession.

* * * * * * * * * * *

(d)   Report on Implementing Agreements.—If, during the 1-year period beginning on the date of the enactment of this Act, any implementing agreement described in subsection (b) or (c) is not executed, the Secretary of the Treasury or his delegate shall report to the Committee on Finance of the United States Senate, the Committee on Ways and Means, and the Committee on Interior and Insular Affairs of the House of Representatives with respect to—

(1)   the status of such negotiations, and

(2)   the reason why such agreement has not been executed.

(e)   Treatment of Certain United States Persons.—Except as otherwise provided in regulations prescribed by the Secretary of the Treasury or his delegate, if a United States person becomes a resident of Guam, American Samoa, or the Northern Mariana Islands, the rules of section 877(c) of the '54 Code shall apply to such person during the 10-year period beginning when such person became such a resident. The preceding sentence shall apply to dispositions after 12-31-85, in taxable years ending after such date.

[For official explanation, see Committee Reports, ¶4057.]

⟦¶3141⟧ CODE SEC. 932. CITIZENS OF POSSESSIONS OF THE UNITED STATES. [Repealed by section 1272(d)(1), '86 TRA, See New Sec. 932, below].[1]

[For official explanation, see Committee Reports, ¶4057.]

⟦¶3141-A⟧ CODE SEC. 932. COORDINATION OF UNITED STATES AND VIRGIN ISLANDS INCOME TAXES.

(a) Treatment of United States Residents.—

(1) Application of subsection.—This subsection shall apply to an individual for the taxable year if—

(A) such individual—

(i) is a citizen or resident of the United States (other than a bona fide resident of the Virgin Islands at the close of the taxable year), and

(ii) has income derived from sources within the Virgin Islands, or effectively connected with the conduct of a trade or business within such possession, for the taxable year, or

(B) such individual files a joint return for the taxable year with an individual described in subparagraph (A).

(2) Filing requirement.—Each individual to whom this subsection applies for the taxable year shall file his income tax return for the taxable year with both the United States and the Virgin Islands.

(3) Extent of income tax liability.—In the case of an individual to whom this subsection applies in a taxable year for purposes of so much of this title (other than this section and section 7654) as relates to the taxes imposed by this chapter, the United States shall be treated as including the Virgin Islands.

(b) Portion of United States Tax Liability Payable to the Virgin Islands.—

(1) In general.—Each individual to whom subsection (a) applies for the taxable year shall pay the applicable percentage of the taxes imposed by this chapter for such taxable year (determined without regard to paragraph (3)) to the Virgin Islands.

(2) Applicable percentage.—

(A) In general.—For purposes of paragraph (1), the term "applicable percentage" means the percentage which Virgin Islands adjusted gross income bears to adjusted gross income.

(B) Virgin Islands adjusted gross income.—For purposes of subparagraph (A), the term "Virgin Islands adjusted gross income" means adjusted gross income determined by taking into account only income derived from sources within the Virgin Islands and deductions properly apportioned or allocable thereto.

(3) Amounts paid allowed as credit.—There shall be allowed as a credit against the tax imposed by this chapter for the taxable year an amount equal to the taxes required to be paid to the Virgin Islands under paragraph (1) which are so paid.

(c) Treatment of Virgin Islands Residents.—

(1) Application of subsection.—This subsection shall apply to an individual for the taxable year if—

(A) such individual is a bona fide resident of the Virgin Islands at the close of the taxable year, or

(B) such individual files a joint return for the taxable year with an individual described in subparagraph (A).

(2) Filing requirement.—Each individual to whom this subsection applies for the taxable year shall file his income tax return for the taxable year with the Virgin Islands.

(3) Extent of income tax liability.—In the case of an individual to whom this subsection applies in a taxable year for purposes of so much of this title (other than this section and section 7654) as relates to the taxes imposed by this chapter, the Virgin Islands shall be treated as including the United States.

⟦Footnote ¶3141⟧ (1) **Effective date** (Sec. 1277, '86 TRA).—Generally applies to taxable years beginning after 12-31-86. For special rules and exceptions, see ¶2068.

⟦Footnote ¶3141-A⟧ New Sec. 932 added by section 1274(a), '86 TRA.

Effective date (Sec. 1277, '86 TRA).—Generally applies to taxable years beginning after 12-31-86. For special rules and exceptions, see ¶2068.

Code §932(c)(3) ¶3141-A

(4) Residents of the Virgin Islands.—In the case of an individual who is a bona fide resident of the Virgin Islands at the close of the taxable year and who, on his return of income tax to the Virgin Islands, reports income from all sources and identifies the source of each item shown on such return, for purposes of calculating income tax liability to the United States gross income tax shall not include any amount included in gross income on such return.

(d) Special Rule for Joint Returns.—In the case of a joint return, this section shall be applied on the basis of the residence of the spouse who has the greater adjusted gross income (determined without regard to community property laws) for the taxable year.

(e) Section Not to Apply to Tax Imposed in Virgin Islands.—This section shall not apply for purposes of determining income tax liability incurred to the Virgin Islands.

[For official explanation, see Committee Reports, ¶4057.]

〔¶3142〕 CODE SEC. 933. INCOME FROM SOURCES WITHIN PUERTO RICO.

The following items shall not be included in gross income and shall be exempt from taxation under this subtitle:

(1) Resident of Puerto Rico for entire taxable year.—In the case of an individual who is a bona fide resident of Puerto Rico during the entire taxable year, income derived from sources within Puerto Rico (except amounts received for services performed as an employee of the United States or any agency thereof); but such individual shall not be allowed as a deduction from his gross income any deductions (other than the deduction under section 151, relating to personal exemptions), *or any credit* properly allocable to or chargeable against amounts excluded from gross income under this paragraph.

(2) Taxable year of change of residence from Puerto Rico.—In the case of an individual citizen of the United States who has been a bona fide resident of Puerto Rico for a period of at least 2 years before the date on which he changes his residence from Puerto Rico, income derived from sources therein (except amounts received for services performed as an employee of the United States or any agency thereof) which is attributable to that part of such period of Puerto Rican residence before such date; but such individual shall not be allowed as a deduction from his gross income any deductions (other than the deduction for personal exemptions under section 151), *or any credit*, properly allocable to or chargeable against amounts excluded from gross income under this paragraph.

[For official explanation, see Committee Reports, ¶4057.]

〔¶3143〕 CODE SEC. 934. LIMITATION ON REDUCTION IN INCOME TAX LIABILITY INCURRED TO THE VIRGIN ISLANDS.

(a) General Rule.—Tax liability incurred to the Virgin Islands pursuant to this subtitle, as made applicable in the Virgin Islands by the Act entitled "An Act making appropriations for the naval service for the fiscal year ending June 30, 1922, and for other purposes", approved July 12, 1921 (48 U.S.C. 1397), or pursuant to section 28(a) of the Revised Organic Act of the Virgin Islands, approved July 22, 1954 (48 U.S.C. 1642), shall not be reduced or remitted in any way, directly or indirectly, whether by grant, subsidy, or other similar payment, by any law enacted in the Virgin Islands, except to the extent provided in subsection (b)[1].

[2]**(b)** *Reductions Permitted With Respect to Certain Income.*—

〔**Footnote ¶3142**〕 Matter in *italics* in Sec. 933(1) and (2) added by section 1272(d)(3), '86 TRA.

Effective date (Sec. 1277, '86 TRA)—(a) Generally applies to taxable years beginning after 12-31-86. For special rules, see ¶2068.

〔**Footnote ¶3143**〕 Matter in *italics* in Sec. 934(a) and (b) added by section 1275(a)(2)(A) and (c), '86 TRA, which struck out:

(1) "or in section 934A"

(2) "**(b) Exception for Certain Domestic and Virgin Islands Corporations.**—In the case of a domestic corporation or a Virgin Islands corporation, subsection (a) shall not apply (if the information required by subsection (d) is supplied) to the extent such corporation derived its income from sources without the United States if the conditions of both paragraph (1) and paragraph (2) are satisfied:

(1) **Three-year period.**—If 80 percent or more of the gross income of such corporation for the 3-year period immediately preceding the close of the taxable year (or for such part of such period immediately preceding the close of such taxable year as may be applicable) was derived from sources within the Virgin Islands; and

(2) **Trade or business.**—If 65 percent or more of the gross income of such corporation for such period or such part thereof was derived from the active conduct of a trade or business within the Virgin Islands.

For purposes of the preceding sentence, the gross income of a Virgin Islands corporation, and the sources from which the income of such corporation is derived, shall be determined as if such corporation were a domestic corporation.

⌈Footnote ¶3143 continued⌉

(c) **Exception for Certain Residents of the Virgin Islands.**—Subsection (a) shall not apply in the case of an individual citizen of the United States who is a bona fide resident of the Virgin Islands during the entire taxable year (if the information required by subsection (d) is supplied), to the extent his income is derived from sources within the Virgin Islands (except that subsection (a) shall apply in the case of amounts received for services performed as an employee of the United States or any agency thereof). For purposes of the preceding sentence, gain or loss from the sale or exchange of any security (as defined in section 165(g)(2) shall not be treated as derived from sources within the Virgin Islands.

(d) **Requirement to Supply Information.**—Subsections (b) and (c) shall apply only in the case of persons who supply (at such time and in such manner as the Secretary may by regulations prescribe) such information as the Secretary may by regulations prescribe for purposes of determining the applicability of such subsections.

(e) **Tax Treatment of Intangible Property Income of Certain Domestic Corporations.**—

(1) **In general.**—

(A) Income attributable to shareholder.—The intangible property income (within the meaning of section 936(h)(3)) for any taxable year of any domestic corporation which is described in subsection (b) and which is an inhabitant of the Virgin Islands (within the meaning of section 28(a) of the Revised Organic Act of the Virgin Islands (48 U.S.C. 1642)), shall be included on a pro rata basis in the gross income of all shareholders of such corporation at the close of the taxable year of such corporation as income from sources within the United States of the taxable year of such shareholder in which or with which the taxable year of such corporation ends.

(B) Exclusion from the income of the corporation.—Any intangible property income of a corporation described in subparagraph (A) which is included in the gross income of a shareholder of such corporation by reason of subparagraph (A) shall be excluded from the gross income of such corporation.

(2) **Foreign shareholders; shareholders not subject to tax; inhabitants of the Virgin Islands.**—

(A) In general.—Paragraph (1)(A) shall not apply with respect to any shareholder—

(i) who is not a United States person,

(ii) who is not subject to tax under this title on intangible property income which would be allocated to such shareholder (but for this subparagraph), or

(iii) who is an inhabitant of the Virgin Islands.

(B) Treatment of nonallocated intangible property income.—For purposes of this subtitle, intangible property income of a corporation described in paragraph (1)(A) which is not included in the gross income of a shareholder of such corporation by reason of subparagraph (A)—

(i) shall be treated as income from sources within the United States, and

(ii) shall not be taken into account for purposes of determining whether the conditions specified in paragraph (1) or (2) of subsection (b) are satisfied.

(3) **Distribution to meet qualification requirements.**—

(A) In general.—If the Secretary determines that a corporation does not satisfy a condition specified in paragraph (1) or (2) of subsection (b) for any taxable year by reason of the exclusion from gross income under paragraph (1)(B), such corporation shall nevertheless be treated as satisfying such condition for such year if it makes a pro rata distribution of property after the close of such taxable year to its shareholders (designated at the time of such distribution as a distribution to meet qualification requirements) with respect to their stock in an amount which is equal to—

(i) if the condition of subsection (b)(1) is not satisfied, that portion of the gross income for the period described in subsection (b)(1)—

(I) which was not derived from sources within the Virgin Islands, and

(II) which exceeds the amount of such income for such period which would enable such corporation to satisfy the condition of subsection (b)(1),

(ii) if the condition of subsection (b)(2) is not satisfied, that portion of the aggregate gross income for such period—

(I) which was not derived from the active conduct of a trade or business within the Virgin Islands, and

(II) which exceeds the amount of such income for such period which would enable such corporation to satisfy the conditions of subsection (b)(2), or

(iii) if neither of such conditions is satisfied, that portion of the gross income which exceeds the amount of gross income for such period which would enable such corporation to satisfy the conditions of paragraphs (1) and (2) of subsection (b).

(B) Effectively connected income.—In the case of a shareholder who is a nonresident alien individual, an inhabitant of the Virgin Islands, or a foreign corporation, trust, or estate, any distribution described in subparagraph (A) shall be treated as income which is effectively connected with the conduct of a trade or business conducted through a permanent establishment of such shareholder within the United States.

(C) Distribution denied in case of fraud or willful neglect.—Subparagraph (A) shall not apply to a corporation if the determination of the Secretary described in subparagraph (A) contains a finding that the failure of such corporation to satisfy the conditions in subsection (b) was due in whole or in part to fraud with intent to evade tax or willful neglect on the part of such corporation.

(4) **Certain provisions of section 936 to apply.**—

(A) In general.—The rules contained in paragraphs (5), (6), and (7) of section 936(h) shall apply to a domestic corporation described in paragraph (1)(A) of this subsection.

(B) Certain modifications.—For purposes of subparagraph (A), section 936(h) shall be applied by substituting wherever appropriate—

(i) "Virgin Islands" for "possession", and

(ii) qualification under paragraphs (1) and (2) of subsection (b) for qualification under section 936(a)(2).

(f) **Transitional Rule.**—In applying subsection (b)(2) with respect to taxable years beginning after December 31,

Code §934(b) ¶3143

(1) In general.—Except as provided in paragraph (2), subsection (a) shall not apply with respect to so much of the tax liability referred to in subsection (a) as is attributable to income derived from sources within the Virgin Islands or income effectively connected with the conduct of a trade or business within the Virgin Islands.

(2) Exception for liability paid by citizens or residents of the United States.—Paragraph (1) shall not apply to any liability payable to the Virgin Islands under section 932(b).

(3) Special rule for non-United States income of certain foreign corporations.—

(A) In general.—In the case of a qualified foreign corporation, subsection (a) shall not apply with respect to so much of the tax liability referred to in subsection (a) as is attributable to income which is derived from sources outside the United States and which is not effectively connected with the conduct of a trade or business within the United States.

(B) Qualified foreign corporation.—For purposes of subparagraph (A), the term "qualified foreign corporation" means any foreign corporation if less than 10 percent of—

(i) the total voting power of the stock of such corporation, and

(ii) the total value of the stock of such corporation, is owned or treated as owned (within the meaning of section 958) by 1 or more United States persons.

(4) Determination of income source, etc.—The determination as to whether income is derived from sources within the Virgin Islands or the United States or is effectively connected with the conduct of a trade or business within the Virgin Islands or the United States shall be made under regulations prescribed by the Secretary.[3]

[For official explanation, see Committee Reports, ¶4057; 4190.]

〔¶3144〕 CODE SEC. 934A. INCOME TAX RATE ON VIRGIN ISLANDS SOURCE INCOME.

[Repealed by section 1275(c)(3), '86 TRA.][1]

〔¶3145〕 CODE SEC. 935. COORDINATION OF UNITED STATES AND GUAM INDIVIDUAL INCOME TAXES.

[Repealed by section 1272(d)(2), '86 TRA].[1]

〔Footnote ¶3143 continued〕

1982, and before January 1, 1985, the following percentage shall be substituted for "65 percent":

For taxable years beginning in calendar year:	The percentage is:
1983	55
1984	60

Effective date (Sec. 1277(a), (c)(1) and (d), '86 TRA).—(a) Generally applies to taxable years beginning after 12-31-86.

* * * * * * * * * * * *

(c) Special Rules for the Virgin Islands.—

(1) In general.—The amendments made by section 1275(c) shall apply with respect to the Virgin Islands (and residents thereof and corporations created or organized therein) only if (and so long as) an implementing agreement is in effect between the United States and the Virgin Islands with respect to the establishment of rules under which the evasion or avoidance of United States income tax shall not be permitted or facilitated by such possession. Any such implementing agreement shall be executed on behalf of the United States by the Secretary of the Treasury, after consultation with the Secretary of the Interior.

(d) Report on Implementing Agreements.—If, during the 1-year period beginning on the date of the enactment of this Act, any implementing agreement described in subsection (b) or (c) is not executed, the Secretary of the Treasury or his delegate shall report to the Committee on Finance of the United States Senate, the Committee on Ways and Means, and the Committee on Interior and Insular Affairs of the House of Representatives with respect to—

(1) the status of such negotiations, and

(2) the reason why such agreement has not been executed.

Section 1876(f)(2), '86 TRA, struck out from Sec. 934(f):

(3) "(f) [should read (g)] FSC.—Section (a) shall not apply in the case of a Virgin Islands corporation which is a FSC.

Effective date (Sec. 1881, '86 TRA and section 805, '84 TRA, as amended by section 1876(h), (i), (n), (o) and (p)(4), '86 TRA).—(1) Generally applies to transactions after 12-31-84, in taxable years ending after such date. For special and transitional rules, see footnote ¶2959.

〔Footnote ¶3144〕 (1) **Effective date** (Sec. 1277(a), '86 TRA).—Generally applies to taxable years beginning after 12-31-86. For special rules, see ¶2068.

〔Footnote ¶3145〕 (1) **Effective date** (Sec. 1277(a), (b), (d) and (e), '86 TRA).—

(a) Generally applies to taxable years beginning after 12-31-86.

[For official explanation, see Committee Reports, ¶4057.]

[¶3146]   CODE SEC. 936.   PUERTO RICO AND POSSESSION TAX CREDIT.

(a) **Allowance of credit.—**

* * * * * * * * * * *

(2) **Conditions which must be satisfied.**—The conditions referred to in paragraph (1) are:

(A) 3-year period.—If 80 percent or more of the gross income of such domestic corporation for the 3-year period immediately preceding the close of the taxable year (or for such part of such period immediately preceding the close of such taxable year as may be applicable) was derived from sources within a possession of the United States (determined without regard to section 904(f); and

(B)   Trade or business.—If [1]75 *percent* or more of the gross income of such domestic corporation for such period or such part thereof was derived from the active conduct of a trade or business within a possession of the United States.[2]

(3) **Credit not allowed against certain taxes.**—The credit provided by paragraph (1) shall not be allowed against the tax imposed by—[3]

[4]*(A)*   section 531 (relating to the tax on accumulated earnings),

[5]*(B)*   section 541 (relating to personal holding company tax), or

[6]*(C)*   section 1351 (relating to recoveries of foreign expropriation losses).

(b) **Amounts Received in United States.**—In determining taxable income for purposes of subsection (a), there shall not be taken into account as income from sources without the United States any gross income which was received by such domestic corporation

---

⟦Footnote ¶3145 continued⟧

(b)   Special Rule for Guam, American Samoa, and the Northern Mariana Islands,—The amendments made by this subtitle shall apply with respect to Guam, American Samoa, or the Northern Mariana Islands (and to residents thereof and corporations created or organized therein) only if (and so long as) an implementing agreement under section 1271 is in effect between the United States and such possession.

* * * * * * * * * * *

(d)   Report on Implementing Agreements.—If, during the 1-year period beginning on the date of the enactment of this Act, any implementing agreement described in subsection (b) and (c) is not executed, the Secretary of the Treasury or his delegate shall report to the Committee on Finance of the United States Senate, the Committee on Ways and Means, and the Committee on Interior and Insular Affairs of the House of Representatives with respect to—

(1)   the status of such negotiations, and

(2)   the reason why such agreement has not been executed.

(e)   Treatment of Certain United States Persons.—Except as otherwise provided in regulations prescribed by the Secretary of the Treasury or his delegate, if a United States person becomes a resident of Guam, American Samoa, or the Northern Mariana Islands, the rules of section 877(c) of the '54 Code shall apply to such person during the 10-year period beginning when such person became such a resident. The preceding sentence shall apply to dispositions after 12-31-85, in taxable years ending after such date.

⟦Footnote ¶3146⟧   Matter in *italics* in Sec. 936(a)(2) added by section 1231(d), '86 TRA, which struck out:

(1)   "75 percent"

(2)   "(C)   Transitional rule.—In applying subparagraph (B) with respect to taxable years beginning after December 31, 1982, and before January 1, 1985, the following percentage shall be substituted for "65 percent":

For taxable years beginning in calendar year:	The percentage¹/ is:
1983	55
1984	60.

Effective date (Sec. 1231(g)(1), (4) '86 TRA).—Generally applies to taxable years beginning after 12-31-86. For special rules, see ¶2063.

Matter in *italics* in Sec. 936(a)(3) added by section 701(e)(4)(I), '86 TRA, which struck out:

(3)   "(A) section 56 (relating to corporate minimum tax),"

(4)   "(B)"

(5)   "(C)"

(6)   "(E)"

Effective date (Sec. 701(f), '86 TRA).—Generally applies to taxable years beginning after 12-31-86. For transitional and special rules, see footnote ¶2879.

---

within the United States, whether derived from sources within or without the United States. *This subsection shall not apply to any amount described in subsection (a)(1)(A)(i) received from a person who is not a related person (within the meaning of subsection (h)(3) but without regard to subparagraphs (D)(ii)(I) and (E)(i) thereof) with respect to the domestic corporation.*

* * * * * * * * * * * *

(d) **Definitions and special rules.**—For purposes of this section—

(1) **Possession.**—The term "possession of the United States" includes the Commonwealth of Puerto Rico [7]*and the Virgin Islands.*

(2) **Qualified possession source investment income.**—The term "qualified possession source investment income" means gross income which—

(A) is from sources within a possession of the United States in which a trade or business is actively conducted, and

(B) the taxpayer establishes to the satisfaction of the Secretary is attributable to the investment in such possession (for use therein) of funds derived from the active conduct of a trade or business in such possession, or from such investment,

less the deductions properly apportioned or allocated thereto.

* * * * * * * * * * * *

(4) Investment in qualified Caribbean Basin countries.—

(A) In general.—*For purposes of paragraph (2)(B), an investment in a financial institution shall, subject to such conditions as the Secretary may prescribe by regulations, be treated as for use in Puerto Rico to the extent used by such financial institution (or by the Government Development Bank for Puerto Rico or the Puerto Rico Economic Development Bank)—*

(i) for investment, consistent with the goals and purposes of the Caribbean Basin Economic Recovery Act, in—

(I) active business assets in a qualified Caribbean Basin country, or

(II) development projects in a qualified Caribbean Basin country, and

(ii) in accordance with a specific authorization granted by the Government Development Bank for Puerto Rico pursuant to regulations issued by the Secretary of the Treasury of Puerto Rico.

A similar rule shall apply in the case of a direct investment in the Government Development Bank for Puerto Rico or the Puerto Rico Economic Development Bank.

(B) Qualified Caribbean Basin country.—*For purposes of this subsection, the term "qualified Caribbean Basin country" means any beneficiary country (within the meaning of section 212(a)(1)(A) of the Caribbean Basin Economic Recovery Act) which meets the requirements of clauses (i) and (ii) of section 274(h)(6)(A).*

(C) Additional requirements.—*Subparagraph (A) shall not apply to any investment made by a financial institution (or by the Government Development Bank for Puerto Rico or the Puerto Rico Economic Development Bank) unless—*

(i) the person in whose trade or business such investment is made (or such other recipient of the investment) and the financial institution or such Bank certify to the Secretary and the Secretary of the Treasury of Puerto Rico that the proceeds of the loan will be promptly used to acquire active business assets or to make other authorized expenditures, and

(ii) the financial institution (or the Government Development Bank for Puerto Rico or the Puerto Rico Economic Development Bank) and the recipient of the investment funds agree to permit the Secretary and the Secretary of the Treasury of Puerto Rico to examine such of their books and records as may be necessary to ensure that the requirements of this paragraph are met.

* * * * * * * * * * * *

[Footnote ¶3146 continued]

Matter in *italics* in Sec. 936(b) added by section 1231(b), '86 TRA.
Effective date (Sec. 1231(g)(1), (4), '86 TRA).—Generally applies to taxable years beginning after 12-31-86. For transitional rules, see ¶2063.

Matter in *italics* in Sec. 936(d)(1) added by section 1275(a)(1), '86 TRA, which struck out:
(7) "but does not include the Virgin Islands of the United States"
Effective date (Sec. 1277, '86 TRA).—Generally applies to taxable years beginning after 12-31-86. For special rules, see ¶2068.

Sec. 936(d)(4) in *italics* added by section 1231(c), '86 TRA.
Effective date (Sec. 1231(g)(1), (4) '86 TRA.—Generally applies to taxable years beginning after 12-31-86. For transitional rules, see ¶2063.

(h) Tax Treatment of Intangible Property Income.—

* * * * * * * * * * *

(3) Intangible property income.—For purposes of this subsection—

* * * * * * * * * * *

(D) Related person.—

(i) In general.—A person (hereinafter referred to as the "related person") is related to any person if—

(I) the related person bears a relationship to such person specified in section 267(b) or section 707(b)(1), or

(II) the related person and such person are members of the same controlled group of corporations.

[1]*(ii) Special rule.—For purposes of clause (i), section 267(b) and section 707(b)(1) shall be applied by substituting "10 percent" for "50 percent".*

* * * * * * * * * * *

(5) Election out.—

* * * * * * * * * * *

(C) Methods of computation of taxable income.—If an election of one of the following methods is in effect pursuant to subparagraph (F) with respect to a product or type of service, an electing corporation shall compute its income derived from the active conduct of a trade or business in a possession with respect to such product or type of service in accordance with the method which is elected.

(i) Cost sharing.—

(I) Payment of cost sharing.—If an election of this method is in effect, the electing corporation must make a payment for its share of the cost (if any) of product area research which is paid or accrued by the affiliated group during that taxable year. Such share shall not be less than the same proportion *of 110 percent* of the cost of such product area research which the amount of "possession sales" bears to the amount of "total sales" of the affiliated group. The cost of product area research paid or accrued solely by the electing corporation in a taxable year (excluding amounts paid directly or indirectly to or on behalf of related persons and excluding amounts paid under any cost sharing agreements with related persons) will reduce (but not below zero) the amount of the electing corporation's cost sharing payment under this method for that year. *In the case of intangible property described in subsection (h)(3)(B)(i) which the electing corporation is treated as owning under subclause (II), in no event shall the payment required under this subclause be less than the inclusion or payment which would be required under section 367(d)(2)(A)(ii) or section 482 if the electing corporation were a foreign corporation.*

(a) Product area research.—For purposes of this section, the term "product area research" includes (notwithstanding any provision to the contrary) the research, development and experimental costs, losses, expenses and other related deductions—including amounts paid or accrued for the performance of research or similar activities by another person;

[Footnote ¶3146 continued]

Matter in *italics* in Sec. 936(h)(3)(D)(ii) added by section 1812(c)(4)(C), '86 TRA, which struck out:

(1) "(ii) Special rules.—For purposes of clause (i)—

(I) section 267(b) and section 707(b)(1) shall be applied by substituting "10 percent" for "50 percent", and

(II) section 267(b)(3) shall be applied without regard to whether a person was a personal holding company or a foreign personal holding company."

Effective date (Sec. 1881, '84 TRA and Sec. 174(c)(2), '84 TRA).—(A) Generally applies to transactions after 12-31-83, in taxable years ending after such date.

(B) Exception for transfers to foreign corporations on or before 3-1-84.—The amendments made by section 174(b)(2), '84 TRA shall not apply to property transferred to a foreign corporation on or before 3-1-84.

Matter in *italics* in Sec. 936(h)(5)(C)(i)(I) added by section 1231(a)(1), '86 TRA.

Effective date (Sec. 1231(g), '86 TRA).—Generally applies to taxable years beginning after 12-31-86.

Special rule for transfer of intangibles.—

* * * * * * * * * * *

(B) Special rule for section 936.—For purposes of section 936(h)(5)(C) of the '86 Code the amendments made by subsection (e) shall apply to taxable years beginning after 12-31-86, without regard to when the transfer (or license) was made.

For other special rules, see ¶2063.

qualified research expenses within the meaning of [8]*section 41(b);* amounts paid or accrued for the use of, or the right to use, research or any of the items specified in subsection (h)(3)(B)(i); and a proper allowance for amounts incurred for the acquisition of any of the items specified in subsection (h)(3)(B)(i)—which are properly apportioned or allocated to the same product area as that in which the electing corporation conducts its activities, and a ratable part of any such costs, losses, expenses and other deductions which cannot definitely be allocated to a particular product area.

* * * * * * * * * * * *

(ii) Profit split.—

* * * * * * * * * * * *

(II) Computation of combined taxable income.—Combined taxable income shall be computed separately for each product produced or type of service rendered, in whole or in part, by the electing corporation in a possession. Combined taxable income shall be computed (notwithstanding any provision to the contrary) for each such product or type of service rendered by deducting from the gross income of the affiliated group (other than foreign affiliates) derived from covered sales of such product or type of service all expenses, losses, and other deductions properly apportioned or allocated to gross income from such sales or services, and a ratable part of all expenses, losses, or other deductions which cannot definitely be allocated to some item or class of gross income, which are incurred by the affiliated group (other than foreign affiliates). Notwithstanding any other provision to the contrary, in computing the combined taxable income for each such product or type of service rendered, the research, development, and experimental costs, expenses and related deductions for the taxable year which would otherwise be apportioned or allocated to the gross income of the affiliated group (other than foreign affiliates) derived from covered sales of such product produced or type of service rendered, in whole or in part, by the electing corporation in a possession, shall not be less than the same proportion of the amount of the share of product area research determined under subparagraph (C)(i)(I) (without regard to [9]*the third and fourth sentences thereof, but substituting "120 percent" for "110 percent" in the second sentence thereof*) in the product area which includes such product or type of service, that such gross income from the product or type of service bears to such gross income from [10]*all products and types of services, within such product area, produced or rendered,* in whole or part, by the electing corporation in a possession.

* * * * * * * * * * * *

[For official explanation, see Committee Reports, ¶3872; 3931; 4041; 4057; 4146.]

⟦¶3147⟧ CODE SEC. 951. AMOUNTS INCLUDED IN GROSS INCOME OF UNITED STATES SHAREHOLDERS.

* * * * * * * * * * * *

(e) **Foreign Trade Income Not Taken Into Account.—**

⟦Footnote ¶3146 continued⟧

Matter in *italics* in Sec. 936(h)(5)(C)(i)(I)(a) added by section 231(d)(3)(G), '86 TRA, which struck out:
(8) "section 30(b)"
Effective date (Sec. 231(g), '86 TRA).—Applies to taxable years beginning after 12-31-85.

Matter in *italics* in Sec. 936(h)(5)(C)(ii)(II) added by section 1231(a)(2) and (f), '86 TRA, which struck out:
(9) "the third sentence thereof"
(10) "all products produced and types of service rendered"
Effective date (Sec. 1231(g), '86 TRA).—(1) Applies to taxable years beginning after 12-31-86.
(2) Special rule for transfer of intangibles.—

* * * * * * * * * * * *

(B) Special rule for section 936.—For purposes of section 936(h)(5)(C) of the '86 Code the amendments made by subsection (e) shall apply to taxable years beginning after 12-31-86 without regard to when the transfer (or license) was made.
For other special rules, see ¶2063.

* * * * * * * * * * * *

(1) In general.—The foreign trade income of a FSC and any deductions which are apportioned or allocated to such income shall not be taken into account under this subpart. [1]

* * * * * * * * * * * *

(f) Coordination With Passive Foreign Investment Company Provisions.—If, but for this subsection, an amount would be included in the gross income of a United States shareholder for any taxable year both under subsection (a)(1)(A)(i) and under section 1293 (relating to current taxation of income from certain passive foreign investment companies), such amount shall be included in the gross income of such shareholder only under subsection (a)(1)(A).

[For official explanation, see Committee Reports, ¶4045; 4190.]

〔¶3148〕 CODE SEC. 952. SUBPART F INCOME DEFINED.

(a) In General.—For purposes of this subpart, the term "subpart F income" means, in the case of any controlled foreign corporation, the sum of—

    (1) [1]*insurance income (as defined under section 953),*

    (2) the foreign base company income (as determined under section 954),

    (3) an amount equal to the product of—

        (A) the income of such corporation other than income which—

            (i) is attributable to earnings and profits of the foreign corporation included in the gross income of a United States person under section 951 (other than by reason of this paragraph), or

(b) Exclusion of United States Income.—In the case of a controlled foreign corporation, subpart F income does not include any item of income from sources within the United States which is effectively connected with the conduct by such corporation of a trade or business within the United States unless such item is exempt from taxation (or is subject to a reduced rate of tax) pursuant to a treaty obligation of the United States. *For purposes of the preceding sentence, income described in paragraph (2) or (3) of section 921(d) shall be treated as derived from sources within the United States.*

[2]*(c) Limitation.—*

〔Footnote ¶3147〕 Section 1876(c)(2), '86 TRA, struck out from Sec. 951(e)(1):

  (1) "For purposes of the preceding sentence, income described in paragraph (2) or (3) of section 921(d) shall be treated as derived from sources within the United States."

Effective date (Sec. 1881, '86 TRA and Sec. 805, '84 TRA, as amended by section 1876, '86 TRA).—Generally applies to transactions after 12-31-84, in taxable years ending after such date. For special rule for certain contracts, see footnote ¶2959.

Sec. 951(f) in *italics* added by section 1235(c), '86 TRA.

Effective date (Sec. 1235(h), '86 TRA).—Applies to taxable years of foreign corporations beginning after 12-31-86.

〔Footnote ¶3148〕 Matter in *italics* in Sec. 952(a)(1) added by section 1221(b)(3)(A), '86 TRA, which struck out:

  (1) "the income derived from the insurance of United States risks (as determined under section 953),"

Effective date (Sec. 1221(g), '86 TRA).—Generally applies to taxable years of foreign corporations beginning after 12-31-86. For exception and special rule, see ¶2060.

Matter in *italics* in Sec. 952(b) added by section 1876(c)(1), '86 TRA.

Effective date (Sec. 1881, '86 TRA and section 805, '84 TRA, as amended by section 1876(h), (i), (n), (o), and (p)(4), '86 TRA).—Generally applies to transactions after 12-31-84, in taxable years ending after such date. For special for certain contracts, see footnote ¶2959.

Matter in *italics* in Sec. 952(c) added by section 1221(f), '86 TRA, which struck out:

  (2) "**(c) Limitation.**—For purposes of subsection (a), the subpart F income of any controlled foreign corporation for any taxable year shall not exceed the earnings and profits of such corporation for such year reduced by the amount (if any) by which—

  (1) an amount equal to—

  (A) the sum of the deficits in earnings and profits for prior taxable years beginning after December 31, 1962, plus

  (B) the sum of the deficits in earnings and profits for taxable years beginning after December 31, 1959, and before January 1, 1963 (reduced by the sum of the earnings and profits for such taxable years); exceeds

  (2) an amount equal to the sum of the earnings and profits for prior taxable years beginning after December 31, 1962, allocated to other earnings and profits under section 959(c)(3).

For purposes of the preceding sentence, any deficit in earnings and profits for any prior taxable year shall be taken into account under paragraph (1) for any taxable year only to the extent it has not been taken into account under such paragraph for any preceding taxable year to reduce earnings and profits of such preceding year.

  (d) Special Rule in Case of Indirect Ownership.—For purposes of subsection (c), if—

(1)   In general.—

(A)   Subpart F income limited to current earnings and profits.—For purposes of subsection (a), the subpart F income of any controlled foreign corporation for any taxable year shall not exceed the earnings and profits of such corporation for such taxable year.

(B)   Certain prior year deficits may be taken into account.—

(i)   In general.—The amount included in the gross income of any United States shareholder under section 951(a)(1)(A)(i) for any taxable year and attributable to a qualified activity shall be reduced by the amount of such shareholder's pro rata share of any qualified deficit.

(ii)   Qualified deficit.—The term "qualified deficit" means any deficit in earnings and profits of the controlled foreign corporation for any prior taxable year which began after December 31, 1986, and for which the controlled foreign corporation was a controlled foreign corporation; but only to the extent such deficit—

(I)   is attributable to the same qualified activity as the activity giving rise to the income being offset, and

(II)   has not previously been taken into account under this subpararaph.

(iii)   Qualified activity.—For purposes of this paragraph, the term "qualified activity" means any activity giving rise to—

(I)   foreign base company shipping income,

(II)   foreign base company oil related income,

(III)   in the case of a qualified insurance company, insurance income or

(IV)   in the case of a qualified financial institution, foreign personal holding company income.

(iv)   Pro rata share.—For purposes of this paragraph, the shareholder's pro rata share of any deficit for any prior taxable year shall be determined under rules similar to rules under section 951(a)(2) for whichever of the following yields the smaller share:

(I)   the close of the taxable year, or

(II)   the close of the taxable year in which the deficit arose.

(v)   Qualified insurance company.—For purposes of this subparagraph, the term "qualified insurance company" means any controlled foreign corporation predominantly engaged in the active conduct of an insurance business in the taxable year and in the prior taxable years in which the deficit arose.

(vi)   Qualified financial institution.—For purposes of this paragraph, the term "qualified financial institution" means any controlled foreign corporation predominantly engaged in the active conduct of a banking, financing, or similar business in the taxable year and in the prior taxable year in which the deficit arose.

(2)   Recharacterization in subsequent taxable years.—If the subpart F income of any controlled foreign corporation for any taxable year was reduced by reason by paragraph (1)(A), any excess of the earnings and profits of such corporation for any subsequent taxable year over the subpart F income of such foreign corporation for such taxable year shall be recharacterized as subpart F income under rules similar to the rules applicable under section 904(f)(5).

[For official explanation, see Committee Reports, ¶4034; 4190.]

【¶3149】   CODE SEC. 953.   ¹INSURANCE INCOME.

(a)   **General Rule.—** ²*For purposes of section 952(a)(1), the term "insurance income"*

【Footnote ¶3148 continued】

(1)   a United States shareholder owns (within the meaning of section 958(a)) stock of a foreign corporation, and by reason of such ownership owns (within the meaning of such section) stock of any other foreign corporation, and

(2)   any of such foreign corporations has a deficit in earnings and profits for the taxable year,

then the earnings and profits for the taxable year of each such foreign corporation which is a controlled foreign corporation shall, with respect to such United States shareholder, be properly reduced to take into account any deficit described in paragraph (2) in such manner as the Secretary shall prescribe by regulations."

Effective date (Sec. 1221(g), '86 TRA).—Generally applies to taxable years of foreign corporations beginning after 12-31-86. For exception and special rule, see ¶2060.

【Footnote ¶3149】   Matter in *italics* in Sec. 953 added by section 1221(b)(1), (2), (3)(D), '86 TRA, which struck out:

(1)   "INCOME FROM INSURANCE OF UNITED STATES RISKS"

(2)   "For purposes of section 952(a)(1), the term "income derived from the insurance of United States risks" mean that income which—

(1)   is attributable to the reinsurance or the issuing of any insurance or annuity contract—

(A)   in connection with property in, or liability arising out of activity in, or in connection with the lives or

means any income which—

(1) is attributable to the issuing (or reinsuring) of any insurance or annuity contract—

(A) in connection with property in, liability arising out of activity in, or in connection with the lives or health of residents of, a country other than the country under the laws of which the controlled foreign corporation is created or organized, or

(B) in connection with risks not described in subparagraph (A) as the result of any arrangement whereby another corporation receives a substantially equal amount of premiums or other consideration in respect of issuing (or reinsuring) a contract described in subparagraph (A), and

(2) would (subject to the modifications provided by paragraphs (1) and (2) of subsection (b)) be taxed under subchapter L of this chapter if such income were the income of a domestic insurance company.

(b) Special Rules.—For purposes of subsection (a)—

(1) A corporation which would, if it were a domestic insurance corporation, be taxable under part II of subchapter L shall apply subsection (a) as if it were taxable under part III of subchapter L.

(2) The following provisions of subchapter L shall not apply:

(A) The special life insurance company deduction and the small life insurance company deduction.

(B) Section 805(a)(5) (relating to operations loss deduction).

(C) Section 832(c)(5) (relating to certain capital losses).

(3) The items referred to in—

(A) Section 803(a)(1) (relating to gross amount of premiums and other considerations).

(B) Section 803(a)(2) (relating to net decrease in reserves).

(C) Section 805(a)(2) (relating to net increase in reserves), and

(D) Section 832(b)(4) (relating to premiums earned on insurance contracts).

shall be taken into account only to the extent they are in respect of any reinsurance or the issuing of any insurance or annuity contract described in subsection (a)(1).

(4) All items of income, expenses, losses, and deductions (other than those taken into account under paragraph (3) shall be properly allocated or apportioned under regulations prescribed by the Secretary.

(c) Special Rule for Certain Captive Insurance Companies.—

(1) In general.—For purposes only of taking into account related person insurance income—

(A) the term "United States shareholder" means, with respect to any foreign corporation, a United States person (as defined in section 957(c)) who owns (within the meaning of section 958(a)) any stock of the foreign corporation, and

(B) the term "controlled foreign corporation" has the meaning given to such term by section 957(a) determined by substituting "25 percent or more" for "more than 50 percent".

(2) Related person insurance income.—For purposes of this subsection, the term "related person insurance income" means any insurance income attributable to a policy of insurance or reinsurance with respect to which the primary insured is a United States shareholder in the foreign corporation or a related person (within the meaning of section 954(d)(3)) to such a shareholder.

【Footnote ¶3149 continued】

health of residents of, the United States, or

(B) in connection with risks not included in subparagraph (A) as the result of any arrangement whereby another corporation receives a susbstantially equal amount of premiums or other consideration in respect to any reinsurance or the issuing of any insurance or annuity contract in connection with property in, or liability arising out of activity in, or in connection with the lives or health of residents of, the United States, and

(2) would (subject to the modifications provided by paragraphs (1) and (2) of subsection (b)) be taxed under subchapter L of this chapter if such income were the income of a domestic insurance corporation.

This section shall apply only in the case of a controlled foreign corporation which receives, during any taxable year, premiums or other consideration in respect of the reinsurance, and the issuing, of insurance and annuity contracts described in paragraph (1) in excess of 5 percent of the total of premiums and other consideration received during such taxable year in respect of all reinsurance and issuing of insurance and annuity contracts."

Effective date (Sec. 1221(g), '86 TRA).—Generally applies to taxable years of foreign corporations beginning after 12-31-86. For special rules, see ¶2060.

(3) *Exceptions.—*

(A) *Corporations not held by insureds.—Paragraph (1) shall not apply to any foreign corporation if at all times during the taxable year of such foreign corporation—*

    (i) *less than 20 percent of the total combined voting power of all classes of stock of such corporation entitled to vote, and*

    (ii) *less than 20 percent of the total value of such corporation,*

is owned (directly or indirectly under the principles of section 883(c)(4)) by persons who are the primary insured under any policy of insurance or reinsurance issued by such corporation or who are related persons (within the meaning of section 954(d)(3)) to any such primary insured.

(B) *De minimis exception.—Paragraph (1) shall not apply to any foreign corporation for a taxable year of such corporation if the related person insurance income of such corporation for such taxable year is less than 20 percent of its insurance income for such taxable year determined without regard to those provisions of subsection (a)(1) which limit insurance income to income from countries other than the country in which the corporation was created or organized.*

(C) *Election to treat income as effectively connected.—Paragraph (1) shall not apply to any foreign corporation for any taxable year if—*

    (i) *such corporation elects (at such time and in such manner as the Secretary may prescribe)—*

        (I) *to treat its related person insurance income for such taxable year as income effectively connected with the conduct of a trade or business in the United States, and*

        (II) *to waive all benefits with respect to related person insurance income under any income tax treaty between the United States and any foreign country, and*

    (ii) *such corporation meets such requirements as the Secretary shall prescribe to ensure that the tax imposed by this chapter on such income is paid.*

(D) *Special rules for subparagraph (c).—*

    (i) *Election irrevocable.—Any election under subparagraph (C) shall apply to the taxable year for which made and all subsequent taxable years unless revoked with the consent of the Secretary.*

    (ii) *Exemption from tax imposed by section 4371.—The tax imposed by section 4371 shall not apply with respect to any related person insurance income treated as effectively connected with the conduct of a trade or business within the United States under subparagraph (C).*

(4) *Treatment of mutual insurance companies.—In the case of a mutual insurance company—*

    (A) *this subsection shall apply,*

    (B) *policyholders of such company shall be treated as shareholders, and*

    (C) *appropriate adjustments in the application of this subpart shall be made under regulations prescribed by the Secretary.*

(5) *Regulations.—The Secretary shall prescribe such regulations as may be necessary to carry out the purposes of this subsection, including regulations preventing the avoidance of this subsection through cross insurance arrangements or otherwise.*

[For official explanation, see Committee Reports, ¶4034.]

【¶3150】 CODE SEC. 954. FOREIGN BASE COMPANY INCOME.

(a) **Foreign Base Company Income.**—For purposes of section 952(a)(2), the term "foreign base company income" means for any taxable year the sum of—

(1) the foreign personal holding company income for the taxable year (determined under subsection (c) and reduced as provided in subsection (b)(5)),

(2) the foreign base company sales income for the taxable year (determined under subsection (d) and reduced as provided in subsection (b)(5)),

(3) the foreign base company services income for the taxable year (determined under subsection (e) and reduced as provided in subsection (b)(5)),

(4) the foreign base company shipping income for the taxable year (determined under subsection (f) and reduced as provided in subsection (b)(5)), and

(5) *the foreign base company oil related income for the taxable year (determined* [1]

【Footnote ¶3150】 Matter in *italics* in Sec. 954 (a)(5) added by section 1221(c)(3)(A)(ii), '86 TRA, which struck out:

(1) "under subsection (h)"

under subsection (g) and reduced as provided in subsection (b)(5)).

(b)   Exclusions and Special Rules.—

* * * * * * * * * * * *

(2)   [Repealed][2]

[3]**(3)   De minimis, etc., rules.**—*For purposes of subsection (a) and section 953—*

(A)   De minimis rule.—If the sum of foreign base company income (determined without regard to paragraph (5)) and the gross insurance income for the taxable year is less than the lesser of—

(i)   5 percent of gross income, or

(ii) $1,000,000,

no part of the gross income for the taxable year shall be treated as foreign base company income or insurance income.

(B)   Foreign base company income and insurance income in excess of 70 percent of gross income.—If the sum of the foreign base company income (determined without regard to paragraph (5)) and the gross insurance income for the taxable year exceeds 70 percent of gross income, the entire gross income for the taxable year shall, subject to the provisions of paragraphs (4) and (5), be treated as foreign base company income or insurance income (whichever is appropriate).

(C)   Gross insurance income.—For purposes of subparagraphs (A) and (B), the term "gross insurance income" means any item of gross income taken into account in determining insurance income under section 953.

[4]**(4)   Exception for certain income subject to high foreign taxes.**—*For purposes of subsection (a) and section 953, foreign base company income and insurance income shall not include any item of income received by a controlled foreign corporation if the taxpayer establishes to the satisfaction of the Secretary that such income was subject to an effective rate of income tax imposed by a foreign country greater than 90 percent of the maximum rate of tax specified in section 11. The preceding sentence shall not apply to foreign base company oil-related income described in subsection (a)(5).*

(5)   Deductions to be taken into account.—For purposes of subsection (a), the foreign personal holding company income, the foreign base company sales income, the foreign base company services income, the foreign base company shipping income and

---

⟦Footnote ¶3150 continued⟧

Effective date (Sec. 1221(g)(1), '86 TRA).—Generally applies to taxable years of foreign corporations beginning after 12-31-86. For special and transitional rules, see ¶2060.

Sec. 954(b)(2) repealed by section 1221(c)(1), '86 TRA.

(2)   "**(2)   Exclusion for reinvested shipping income.**—For purposes of subsection (a), foreign base company income does not include foreign base company shipping income to the extent that the amount of such income does not exceed the increase for the taxable year in qualified investments in foreign base company shipping operations of the controlled foreign corporation (as determined under subsection (g))."

Effective date (Sec. 1221(g)(1), '86 TRA).—Generally applies to taxable years of foreign corporations beginning after 12-31-86. For special and transitional rules, see ¶2060.

Matter in *italics* in Sec. 954(b)(3) added by section 1223(a), '86 TRA, which struck out:

(3)   "**(3)   Special rule where foreign base company income is less than 10 percent or more than 70 percent of gross income.**—For purposes of subsection (a)—

(A)   If the foreign base company income (determined without regard to paragraphs (2) and (5)) is less than 10 percent of gross income, no part of the gross income of the taxable year shall be treated as foreign base company income.

(B)   If the foreign base company income (determined without regard to paragraphs (2) and (5)) exceeds 70 percent of gross income, the entire gross income of the taxable year shall, subject to the provisions of paragraphs (2), (4), and (5), be treated as foreign base company income."

Effective date (Sec. 1223(c), '86 TRA).—Applies to taxable year beginning after 12-31-86.

Matter in *italics* in Sec. 954(b)(4) added by section 1221(d), '86 TRA, which struck out:

(4)   "**(4)   Exception for foreign corporation not availed of to reduce taxes.**—For purposes of subsection (a), foreign base company income does not include any item of income received by a controlled foreign corporation if it is established to the satisfaction of the Secretary that neither—

(A)   the creation or organization of such controlled foreign corporation under the laws of the foreign country in which it is incorporated (or, in the case of a controlled foreign corporation which is an acquired corporation, the acquisition of such corporation created or organized under the laws of the foreign country in which it is incorporated), nor

(B)   the effecting of the transaction giving rise to such income through the controlled foreign corporation.

has as one of its significant purposes a substantial reduction of income, war profits, or excess profits or similar taxes. The preceding sentence shall not apply to foreign base company oil related income described in subsection (a)(5)."

Effective date (Sec. 1221(g), '86 TRA).—Generally applies to taxable years of foreign corporations beginning after 12-31-86. For special and transitional rules, see ¶2060.

---

the foreign base company oil related income shall be reduced, under regulations prescribed by the Secretary so as to take into account deductions (including taxes) properly allocable to such income. *Except to the extent provided in regulations prescribed by the Secretary, any interest which is paid or accrued by the controlled foreign corporation to any United States shareholder in such corporation (or any controlled foreign corporation related to such a shareholder) shall be allocated first to foreign personal holding company income which is passive income (within the meaning of section 904(d)(2)) of such corporation to the extent thereof. The Secretary may, by regulations, provide that the preceding sentence shall apply also to interest paid or accrued to other persons.*

* * * * * * * * * * *

(c) **Foreign Personal Holding Company Income.—**

[5]*(1) In general.—For purposes of subsection (a)(1), the term "foreign personal holding company income" means the portion of the gross income which consists of:*

    (A) Dividends, etc.—Dividends, interest, royalties, rents, and annuities.

    (B) Certain property transactions.—The excess of gains over losses from the sale or exchange of property—

        (i) which gives rise to income described in subparagraph (A) (after application of paragraph (2)(A)), or

        (ii) which does not give rise to any income.

This subparagraph shall not apply to gain from the sale or exchange of any property which, in the hands of the taxpayer, is property described in section 1221(1) or to gain from the sale or exchange of any property by a regular dealer in such property.

    (C) Commodities transactions.—The excess of gains over losses from transactions (including futures, forward and similar transactions) in any commodities. This subparagraph shall apply to gains or losses which—

        (i) arise out of bona fide hedging transactions reasonably necessary to the conduct of any business by a producer, processor, merchant, or handler of a commodity in the manner in which such business is customarily and usually conducted by others,

        (ii) are active business gains or losses from the sale of commodities, but only if substantially all of the controlled foreign corporation's business is as an active producer, processor, merchant, or handler of commodities, or

---

⟦Footnote ¶3150 continued⟧

Matter in *italics* in Sec. 954(b)(5) added by section 1201(c), '86 TRA.

Effective date (Sec. 1201(e), '86 TRA).—Generally applies to taxable years beginning after 12-31-86. For special and transitional rules, see ¶2055.

Matter in *italics* in Sec. 954(c) and (d) added by section 1221(a)(1) and (e), '86 TRA, which struck out:

(5) "(c) **Foreign Personal Holding Company Income.—**

(1) **In general.**—For purposes of subsection (a)(1), the term 'foreign personal holding company income' means the foreign personal holding company income (as defined in section 553), modified and adjusted as provided in paragraphs (2), (3), and (4).

(2) **Rents included without regard to 50 percent limitation.**—For purposes of paragraph (1), all rents shall be included in foreign personal holding company income without regard to whether or not such rents constitute 50 percent or more of gross income.

(3) **Certain income derived in active conduct of trade or business.**—For purposes of paragraph (1), foreign personal holding company income does not include—

(A) rents and royalties which are derived in the active conduct of a trade or business and which are received from a person other than a related person (within the meaning of subsection (d)(3)),

(B) dividends, interest, and gains from the sale or exchange of stock or securities derived in the conduct of a banking, financing, or similar business, or derived from the investments made by an insurance company of its unearned premiums or reserves ordinary and necessary for the proper conduct of its insurance business, and which are received from a person other than a related person (within the meaning of subsection (d)(3), or

(C) dividends, interest, and gains from the sale or exchange of stock or securities received from a person other than a related person (within the meaning of subsection (d)(3)) derived from investments made by an insurance company of an amount of its assets equal to one-third of its premiums earned on insurance contracts (other than life insurance and annuity contracts) during the taxable year (as defined in section 832(b)(4)) which are not directly or indirectly attributable to the insurance or reinsurance of risks of persons who are related persons (within the meaning of subsection (d)(3)).

(4) **Certain income received from related persons.**—For purposes of paragraph (1), foreign personal holding company income does not include—

(A) dividends and interest received from a related person which (i) is created or organized under the laws of the same foreign country under the laws of which the controlled foreign corporation is created or organized, and (ii) has a substantial part of its assets used in its trade or business located in such same foreign country.

(B) interest received in the conduct of a banking, financing, or similar business from a related person engaged in the conduct of a banking, financing, or similar business if the businesses of the recipient and the payor are predominantly with persons other than related persons; and

(C) rents, royalties, and similar amounts received from a related person for the use of, or the privilege of using, property within the country under the laws of which the controlled foreign corporation is created or organized.

(iii) *are foreign currency gains or losses (as defined in section 988(b)) attributable to any section 988 transactions.*

(D) *Foreign currency gains.—The excess of foreign currency gains over foreign currency losses (as defined in section 988(b)) attributable to any section 988 transactions. This subparagraph shall not apply in the case of any transaction directly related to the business needs of the controlled foreign corporation.*

(E) *Income equivalent to interest.—Any income equivalent to interest, including income from commitment fees (or similar amounts) for loans actually made.*

(2) *Exception for certain amounts.—*

(A) *Rents and royalties derived in active business.—Foreign personal holding company income shall not include rents and royalties which are derived in the active conduct of a trade or business and which are received from a person other than a related person (within the meaning of subsection (d)(3)).*

(B) *Certain export financing.—Foreign personal holding company income shall not include any interest which is derived in the conduct of a banking business and which is export financing interest (as defined in section 904(d)(2)(G)).*

(3) *Certain income received from related persons.—*

(A) *In general.—Except as provided in subparagraph (B), the term "foreign personal holding company income" does not include—*

(i) *dividends and interest received from a related person which (I) is created or organized under the laws of the same foreign country under the laws of which the controlled foreign corporation is created or organized, and (II) has a substantial part of its assets used in its trade or business located in such same foreign country, and*

(ii) *rents and royalties received from a related person for the use of, or the privilege of using, property within the country under the laws of which the controlled foreign corporation is created or organized.*

(B) *Exception not to apply to items which reduce subpart F income.—Subparagraph (A) shall not apply in the case of any interest, rent, or royalty to the extent such interest, rent, or royalty reduces the payor's subpart F income.*

(d) **Foreign Base Company Sales Income.—**

* * * * * * * * * * * * *

(3) **Related person defined.—**For purposes of this section, a person is a related person with respect to a controlled foreign corporation, if—

[6]*(A)* *such person is an individual, corporation, partnership, trust, or estate which controls, or is controlled by, the controlled foreign corporation, or*

(B) *such person is a corporation, partnership, trust, or estate which is controlled by the same person or persons which control the controlled foreign corporation. For purposes of the preceding sentence, control means, with respect to a corporation, the ownership, directly or indirectly, of stock possessing 50 percent or more of the total voting power of all classes of stock entitled to vote or of the total value of stock of such corporation. In the case of a partnership, trust, or estate, control means the ownership, directly or indirectly, of 50 percent or more (by value) of the beneficial interests in such partnership, trust, or estate. For purposes of this paragraph, rules similar to the rules of section 958 shall apply.*

≫**P-H CAUTION→** There are two versions of Sec. 954(e). Sec. 954(e), generally effective after 12-31-86, follows. For Sec. 954(e), generally effective before 1-1-87, see below.

▲**(e)** **Foreign Base Company Services Income.—**For purposes of subsection (a)(3), the term "foreign base company services income" means income (whether in the form of compensation, commissions, fees, or otherwise) derived in connection with the perfor-

---

【**Footnote ¶3150 continued**】

(6) "(A) such person is an individual, partnership, trust, or estate which controls the controlled foreign corporation;

(B) such person is a corporation which controls, or is controlled by, the controlled foreign corporation; or

(C) such person is a corporation which is controlled by the same person or persons which control the controlled foreign corporation."

For purposes of the preceding sentence, control means the ownership, directly or indirectly, of stock possessing more than 50 percent of the total combined voting power of all classes of stock entitled to vote. For purposes of this paragraph, the rules for determining ownership of stock prescribed by section 958 shall apply."

Effective date (Sec. 1221(g)(1), '86 TRA).—Generally applies to taxable years of foreign corporations beginning after 12-31-86. For special and transitional rules, see ¶2060.

Code §954(e) **¶3150**

mance of technical, managerial, engineering, architectural, scientific, skilled, industrial, commercial, or like services which—

(1) are performed for or on behalf of any related person (within the meaning of subsection (d)(3)), and

(2) are performed outside the country under the laws of which the controlled foreign corporation is created or organized.

The preceding sentence shall not apply to income derived in connection with the performance of services which are directly related to the sale or exchange by the controlled foreign corporation of property manufactured, produced, grown, or extracted by it and which are performed prior to the time of the sale or exchange, or of services directly related to an offer or effort to sell or exchange such property.[7]

≫**P-H CAUTION→** There are two versions of Sec. 954(e). Sec. 954(e), generally effective before 1-1-87, follows. For Sec. 954(e), generally effective after 12-31-86, see above.

▲▲ [8](e) *Foreign Base Company Services Income.—*

(1) In general.—For purposes of subsection (a)(3), the term "foreign base company services income" means income (whether in the form of compensation, commissions, fees, or otherwise) derived in connection with the performance of technical, managerial, engineering, architectural, scientific, skilled, industrial, commercial, or like services which—

(A) are performed for or on behalf of any related prson (within the meaning of subsection (d)(3)), and

(B) are performed outside the country under the laws of which the controlled foreign corporation is created or organized.

(2) Exception.—Paragraph (1) shall not apply to income derived in connection with the performance of services which are directly related to—

(A) the sale or exchange by the controlled foreign corporation of property manufactured, produced, grown, or extracted by it and which are performed before the time of the sale or exchange, or

(B) an offer or effort to sell or exchange such property.

(3) Treatment of certain insurance contracts.—For purposes of paragraph (1), in the case of any services performed with respect to any policy of insurance or reinsurance with respect to which the primary insured is a related person (within the meaning of section 864(d)(4))—

(A) such primary insured shall be treated as a related person for purposes of paragraph (1)(A) (whether or not the requirements of subsection (d)(3) are met),

(B) such services shall be treated as performed in the country within which the insured hazards, risks, losses, or liabilities occur, and

---

⟦Footnote ¶3150 continued⟧

▲ Section 1221(b)(3)(B), '86 TRA, struck out from Sec. 954(e), which is preceded by a single triangle:

(7) "For purposes of paragraph (2), any services performed with respect to any policy of insurance or reinsurance with respect to which the primary insured is a related person (within the meaning of section 864(d)(4) shall be treated as having been performed in the country within which the insured hazards, risks, losses, or liabilities occur, and except as provided in regulations prescribed by the Secretary, rules similar to the rules of section 953(b) shall be applied in determining the income from such services."

Effective date (Sec. 1221(g)(1), '86 TRA).—Generally applies to taxable years of foreign corporation beginning after 12-31-86. For special and transitional rules see ¶2060.

▲▲ Matter in *italics* in Sec. 954(e), preceded by two triangles added by section 1810(k), '86 TRA, which struck out:

(8) "(e) **Foreign Base Company Services Income.**—For purposes of subsection (a)(3), the term 'foreign base company services income' means income (whether in the form of compensation, commissions, fees, or otherwise) derived in connecton with the performance of technical, managerial, engineering, architectural, scientific, skilled, industrial, commercial, or like services which—

(1) are performed for or on behalf of any related person (within the meaning of subsection (d)(3)), and

(2) are performed outside the country under the laws of which the controlled foreign corporation is created or organized.

The preceding sentence shall not apply to income derived in connection with the performance of services which are directly related to the sale or exchange by the controlled foreign corporation of property manufactured, produced, grown, or extracted by it and which are performed prior to the time of the sale or exchange, or of services directly related to an offer or effort to sell or exchange such property. For purposes of paragraph (2), any services performed with respect to any policy of insurance or reinsurance with respect to which the primary insured is a related person (within the meaning of section 864(d)(4)) shall be treated as having been performed in the country within which the insured hazards, risks, losses, or liabilities occur, and except as provided in regulations prescribed by the Secretary, rules similar to the rules of section 953(b) shall be applied in determining the income from such services."

Effective date (Sec. 1881, '86 TRA and Sec. 137(b), '84 TRA).—Applies to taxable years of controlled foreign corporations beginning after 7-18-84.

(C)   except as otherwise provided in regulations by the Secretary, rules similar to the rules of section 953(b) shall be applied in determining the income from such services.

(f)   Foreign Base Company Shipping Income.—For purposes of subsection (a)(4), the term "foreign base company shipping income" means income derived from, or in connection with, the use (or hiring or leasing for use) of any aircraft or vessel in foreign commerce, or from, or in connection with, the performance of services directly related to the use of any such aircraft, or vessel or from the sale, exchange, or other disposition of any such aircraft or vessel. Such term includes, but is not limited to—

(1)   dividends and interest received from foreign corporation in respect of which taxes are deemed paid under section 902, and gain from the sale, exchange, or other disposition of stock or obligation of such a foreign corporation to the extent that such dividends, interest, and gains are attributable to foreign base company shipping income, and

(2)   that portion of the distributive share of the income of a partnership attributable to foreign base company shipping income. *Such term includes any income derived from a space or ocean activity (as defined in section 863(d)(2).[9]*

[10]**(g)   Foreign Base Company Oil Related Income.**—For purposes of this section—

(1)   In general.—Except as otherwise provided in this subsection, the term "foreign base company oil related income" means foreign oil related income (within the meaning of paragraphs (2) and (3) of section 907(c)) other than income derived from a source within a foreign country in connection with—

(A)   oil or gas which was extracted from an oil or gas well located in such foreign country, or

(B)   oil, gas or a primary product of oil and gas which is sold by the foreign corporation of a related person for use or consumption within such country or is loaded in such country on a vessel or aircraft as fuel for such vessel or aircraft.

* * * * * * * * * * * *

[For official explanation, see Committee Reports, ¶4027; 4034; 4036; 4144.]

[¶3151]   CODE SEC. 955.   WITHDRAWAL OF PREVIOUSLY EXCLUDED SUBPART F INCOME FROM QUALIFIED INVESTMENT.

(a)   General Rules.—

(1)   Amount withdrawn.—For purposes of this subpart, the amount of previously excluded subpart F income of any controlled foreign corporation withdrawn from investment in foreign base company shipping operations for any taxable year is an amount equal to the decrease in the amount of qualified investments in foreign base company shipping operations of the controlled foreign corporation for such year, but only to the extent that the amount of such decrease does not exceed an amount equal to—

(A)   the sum of the amounts excluded under section 954(b)(2) from the foreign base company income of such corporation for all prior taxable years *beginning before 1987,* reduced by

(B)   the sum of the amounts of previously excluded subpart F income withdrawn from investment in foreign base company shipping operations of such corporation determined under this subsection for all prior taxable years.

(2)   Decrease in qualified investments.—For purposes of paragraph (1), the amount of the decrease in qualified investments in foreign base company shipping operations of any controlled foreign corporations for any taxable year is the amount by which—

(A)   the amount of qualified investments in foreign base company shipping operations of the controlled foreign corporation[1]*as of the close of the last taxable year*

[Footnote ¶3150 continued]

Matter in *italics* in Sec. 954(f) and (g) added by section 1221(c)(2) and (c)(3)(A)(i), '86 TRA, which struck out:

(9)   "(g)   Increase in Qualified Investments in Foreign Base Company Shipping Operations.—For purposes of subsection (b)(2), the increase for any taxable year in qualified investments in foreign base company shipping operations of any controlled foreign corporation is the amount by which—

(1)   the qualified investments in foreign base company shipping operations (as defined in section 955(b)) of the controlled foreign corporation at the close of the taxable year, exceed

(2)   the qualified investments in foreign base company shipping operations (as so defined) of the controlled foreign corporation at the close of the preceding taxable year.

(10)   "(h)"

Effective date (Sec. 1221(g)(1), '86 TRA).—Generally applies to taxable years of foreign corporations beginning after 12-31-86. For special and transitional rules, see ¶2060.

[Footnote ¶3151]   Matter in *italics* in Sec. 955(a)(1), (2)(A) added by section 1221(c)(3)(B), (C), '86 TRA,

beginning before 1987, exceeds

(B)   the amount of qualified investments in foreign base company shipping operations of the controlled foreign corporation at the close of the taxable year,

to the extent that the amount of such decrease does not exceed the sum of the earnings and profits for the taxable year and the earnings and profits accumulated for prior taxable years beginning after December 31, 1975, and the amount of previously excluded subpart F income invested in less developed country corporations described in section 955(c)(2) (as in effect before the enactment of the Tax Reduction Act of 1975) to the extent attributable to earnings and profits accumulated for taxable years beginning after December 31, 1962. For purposes of this paragraph, if qualified investments in foreign base company shipping operations are disposed of by the controlled foreign corporation during the taxable year, the amount of the decrease in qualified investments in foreign base company shipping operations of such controlled foreign corporation for such year shall be reduced by an amount equal to the amount (if any) by which the losses on such dispositions during such year exceeds the gains on such dispositions during such year.

(3)   **Pro rata share of amount withdrawn.**—In the case of any United States shareholder, the pro rata share of the amount of previously excluded subpart F income of any controlled foreign corporation withdrawn from investment in foreign base company shipping operations for any taxable year is his pro rata share of the amount determined under paragraph (1).

* * * * * * * * * * * *

(4)   **Amount attributable to property.**—The amount taken into account under this subpart with respect to any property described in paragraph (1) shall be its adjusted basis, reduced by any liability to which such property is subject.

(5)   **Income excluded under prior law.**—Amounts invested in less developed country corporations described in section 955(c)(2) (as in effect before the enactment of the Tax Reduction Act of 1975) shall be treated as qualified investments in foreign base company shipping operations and shall not be treated as investments in less developed countries for purposes of section 951(a)(1)(A)(ii).

[For official explanation, see Committee Reports, ¶4034.]

【¶3152】   CODE SEC. 956.   INVESTMENT OF EARNINGS IN UNITED STATES PROPERTY.

(b)   **United States Property Defined.—**

* * * * * * * * * * * *

(3)   **Certain trade or service receivables acquired from related United States persons.—**

(A)   In general.—Notwithstanding paragraph (2) *(other than subparagraph (h) thereof),* the term "United States property" includes any trade or service receivable if—

(i)   such trade or service receivable is acquired (directly or indirectly) from a related person who is a United States person, and

(ii)   the obligor under such receivable is a United States person.

* * * * * * * * * * * *

[For official explanation, see Committee Reports, ¶4144.]

【Footnote ¶3151 continued】

which struck out:

(1)   "at the close of the preceding taxable year"

Effective date (Sec. 1221(g), '86 TRA). Generally applies to taxable years of foreign corporations beginning after 12-31-86. For special rules, see ¶2060.

【Footnote ¶3152】   Matter in *italics* in Sec. 956(b)(3)(A) added by section 1810(c)(1), '86 TRA.

Effective date (Sec. 1881, '86 TRA and Sec. 123(c), '84 TRA).—(1) Applies to accounts receivable and evidences of indebtedness transferred after 3-1-84, in taxable years ending after such date.

(2)   Transitional rule.—The amendments shall not apply to accounts receivable and evidences of indebtedness acquired after 3-1-84, and before 3-1-94, by a Belgian corporation in existence on 3-1-84, in any taxable year ending after such date, but only to the extent that the amount includible in gross income by reason of section 956 of the '54 Code with respect to such corporation for all such taxable years is not reduced by reason of this paragraph by more than the lesser of—

(A) $15,000,000 or

(B)   the amount of the Belgian corporation's adjusted basis on 3-1-84, in stock of a foreign corporation formed to issue bonds outside the United States to the public.

〔¶3153〕 CODE SEC. 957. CONTROLLED FOREIGN CORPORATIONS; UNITED STATES PERSONS.

(a) General Rule.—For purposes of this subpart, the term "controlled foreign corporation" means any foreign corporation [1]*if more than 50 percent of . . .*

(1) *the total combined voting power of all classes of stock of such corporation entitled to vote, or*

(2) *the total value of the stock of such corporation,*

is owned (within the meaning of section 958(a)), or is considered as owned by applying the rules of ownership of section 958(b), by United States shareholders on any day during the taxable year of such foreign corporation.

* * * * * * * * * * * *

(b) Special Rule for Insurance.—For purposes only of taking into account income described in section 953(a) (relating to [2]*insurance income*), the term "controlled foreign corporation" includes not only a foreign corporation as defined by subsection (a) but also one of which more than 25 percent of the total combined voting power of all classes of stock *(or more than 25 percent of the total value of stock)* is owned (within the meaning of section 958(a)), or is considered as owned by applying the rules of ownership of section 958(b), by United States shareholders on any day during the taxable year of such corporation, if the gross amount of premiums or other consideration in respect of the reinsurance or the issuing of insurance or annuity contracts described in section 953(a)(1) exceeds 75 percent of the gross amount of all premiums or other consideration in respect of all risks.[3]

〔Footnote ¶3153〕 Matter in *italics* in Sec. 957(a) added by section 1222(a)(1), '86 TRA, which struck out:

(1) "of which more than 50 percent of the total combined voting power of all classes of stock entitled to vote is owned (within the meaning of section 958(a)), or is considered as owned by applying the rules of ownership of section 958(b), by United State shareholders on any day during the taxable year of such foreign corporation."

Effective date (Sec. 1222(c), '86 TRA). (1) Generally applies to taxable years of foreign corporations beginning after 12-31-86; except that for purposes of applying sections 951(a)(1)(B) and 956 of the '86 Code, such amendments shall take effect on 8-16-86.

(2) Transitional rule.—In the case of any corporation treated as a controlled foreign corporation by reason of the amendments made by this section, property acquired before 8-16-86, shall not be taken into account under section 956(b) of the '86 Code.

(3) Special rule for beneficiary of trust.—In the case of an individual—

(A) who is a beneficiary of a trust which was established on 12-7-79, under the laws of a foreign jurisdiction, and

(B) who was not a citizen or resident of the United States on the date the trust was established,

amounts which are included in the gross income of such beneficiary under section 951(a) of the '86 Code with respect to stock held by the trust (and treated as distributed to the trust) shall be treated as the first amounts which are distributed by the trust to such beneficiary and as amounts to which section 959(a) of such Code applies.

"insurance income" in *italics* in Sec. 957(b) added by section 1221(b)(3)(C), '86 TRA, which struck out:

(2) "income derived from insurance of United States risks"

Effective date (Sec. 1221(g)(1), '86 TRA).—Applies to taxable years of foreign corporations beginning after 12-31-86. For transitional and special rules, see footnote ¶2060.

Matter in *italics* in Sec. 957(b) (except for *"insurance income"*) added by secton 1222(a)(2), '86 TRA.
Effective date (Sec. 1222(c), '86 TRA).—See above.

Matter in *italics* in Sec. 957(c) added by section 1224(a), '86 TRA, which struck out:

(3) **"(c) Corporations Organized in United States Possessions.**—For purposes of this subpart, the term 'controlled foreign corporation' does not include any corporation created or organized in the Commonwealth of Puerto Rico or a possession of the United States or under the laws of the Commonwealth of Puerto Rico or a possession of the United States if—

(1) 80 percent or more of the gross income of such corporation for the 3-year period immediately preceding the close of the taxable year (or for such part of such period immediately preceding the close of such taxable year as may be applicable) was derived from sources within the Commonwealth of Puerto Rico or a possession of the United States; and

(2) 50 percent or more of the gross income of such corporation for such period, or for such part thereof, was derived from the active conduct within the Commonwealth of Puerto Rico or a possession of the United States of any trades or businesses constituting the manufacture or processing of goods, wares, merchandise, or other tangible personal property; the processing of agricultural or horticultural products or commodities (including but not limited to livestock, poultry, or fur-bearing animals); the catching or taking of any kind of fish or the mining or extraction of natural resources, or any manufacturing or processing of any products or commodities obtained from such activities; or the ownership or operation of hotels.

For purposes of paragraphs (1) and (2), the determinations as to whether income was derived from sources within the Commonwealth of Puerto Rico or a possession of the United States and was derived from the active conduct of a described trade or business within the Commonwealth of Puerto Rico or a possession of the United States

[4](c) **United States Person.**—For purposes of this subpart, the term "United States person" has the meaning assigned to it by section 7701(a)(30) except that—

    (1) with respect to a corporation organized under the laws of the Commonwealth of Puerto Rico, such term does not include an individual who is a bona fide resident of Puerto Rico, if a dividend received by such individual during the taxable year from such corporation would, for purposes of section 933(1), be treated as income derived from sources within Puerto Rico, *and*

    [5]*(2) with respect to a corporation organized under the laws of Guam, American Samoa, or the Northern Mariana Islands—*

        (A) 80 percent or more of the gross income of which for the 3-year period ending at the close of the taxable year (or for such part of such period as such corporation or any predecessor has been in existence) was derived from sources within such a possession or was effectively connected with the conduct of a trade or business in such a possession, and

        (B) 50 percent or more of the gross income of which for such period (or part) was derived from the conduct of an active trade or business within such a possession,

    such term does not include an individual who is a bona fide resident of Guam, American Samoa, or the Northern Mariana Islands.

For purposes of subparagraphs (A) and (B) of paragraph (2), the determination as to whether income was derived from sources within a possession, was effectively connected with the conduct of a trade or business within a possession, or derived from the active conduct of a trade or business within a possession shall be made under regulations prescribed by the Secretary.

[For official explanation, see Committee Reports, ¶4034; 4035.]

〔¶3154〕 CODE SEC. 959. EXCLUSION FROM GROSS INCOME OF PREVIOUSLY TAXED EARNINGS AND PROFITS.

* * * * * * * * * * * *

    (d) **Distributions Excluded from Gross Income Not To Be Treated as Dividends.**— Except as provided in section 960(a)(3), any distribution excluded from gross income under subsection (a) shall be treated, for purposes of this chapter, as a distribution which is not a dividend; *except that such distributions shall immediately reduce earnings and profits.*

* * * * * * * * * * * *

[For official explanation, see Committee Reports, ¶4039.]

〔¶3155〕 CODE SEC. 960. SPECIAL RULES FOR FOREIGN TAX CREDIT.

    (a) **Taxes Paid by a Foreign Corporation.**—

    (1) **General rule.**—For purposes of subpart A of this part, if there is included, under section 951(a), in the gross income of a domestic corporation any amount attributable to earnings and profits—

〔Footnote ¶3153 continued〕
shall be made under regulations prescribed by the Secretary."

    (4) "(d)"

Effective date (Sec. 1224(b), '86 TRA). (1) Generally applies to taxable years of foreign corporations beginning after 12-31-86; except that for purposes of applying sections 951(a)(1)(B) and 956 of the '86 Code, such amendments shall take effect on 8-16-86,

    (2) Transitional rule.—In the case of any corporation treated as a controlled foreign corporation by reason of the amendment made by subsection (a), property acquired before 8-16-86, shall not be taken into account under section 956(b) of the '86 Code.

Matter in *italics* in Sec. 957(c) [former (d)] added by section 1273(a), '86 TRA, which struck out:

    (5) "(2) with respect to a corporation organized under the laws of the Virgin Islands, such term does not include an individual who is a bona fide resident of the Virgin Islands and whose income tax obligation under this subtitle for the taxable year is satisfied pursuant to section 28(a) of the Revised Organic Act of the Virgin Islands, approved July 22, 1954 (48 U.S.C. 1642), by paying tax on income derived from all sources both within and outside the Virgin Islands into the treasury of the Virgin Islands, and

    (3) with respect to a corporation organized under the laws of any other possession of the United States, such term does not include an individual who is a bona fide resident of any such other possession and whose income derived from sources within possessions of the United States is not, by reason of section 931(a), includible in gross income under this subtitle for the taxable year."

Effective date (Sec. 1277(a), '86 TRA).—Applies to taxable years beginning after 12-31-86. For transitional and special rules, see ¶2068.

  〔Footnote ¶3154〕 Matter in *italics* in Sec. 959(d) added by section 1226(b), '86 TRA.

Effective date (Sec. 1226(c)(2) '84 TRA). —Applies to distributions after the date of the enactment of this Act.

(A) of a foreign corporation (hereinafter in this subsection referred to as the "first foreign corporation") at least 10 percent of the voting stock of which is owned by such domestic corporation, or

(B) of a second foreign corporation (hereinafter in this subsection referred to as the "second foreign corporation") at least 10 percent of the voting stock of which is owned by the first foreign corporation, or

(C) of a third foreign corporation (hereinafter in this subsection referred to as the "third foreign corporation") at least 10 percent of the voting stock of which is owned by the second foreign corporation,

then, except to the extent provided in regulations, such domestic corporation shall be deemed to have paid a portion of such foreign corporation's post-1986 foreign income taxes determined under section 902 in the same manner as if the amount so included were a dividend paid by such foreign corporation (determined by applying section 902(c) in accordance with section 904(d)(3)(B)).

* * * * * * * * * * * *

[For official explanation, see Committee Reports, ¶4027.]

【¶3156】 CODE SEC. 985. FUNCTIONAL CURRENCY.

(a) In General.—Unless otherwise provided in regulations, all determinations under this subtitle shall be made in the taxpayer's functional currency.

(b) Functional Currency.—

(1) In General.—For purposes of this subtitle, the term "functional currency" means—

(A) except as provided in subparagraph (B), the dollar, or

(B) in the case of a qualified business unit, the currency of the economic environment in which a significant part of such unit's activities are conducted and which is used by such unit in keeping its books and records.

(2) Functional Currency Where Activities Primarily Conducted In Dollars.—The functional currency of any qualified business unit shall be the dollar if activities of such unit are primarily conducted in dollars.

(3) Election.—To the extent provided in regulations, the taxpayer may elect to use the dollar as the functional currency for any qualified business unit if—

(A) such unit keeps its books and records in dollars, or

(B) the taxpayer uses a method of accounting that approximates a separate transactions method.

Any such election shall apply to the taxable year for which made and all subsequent taxable years unless revoked with the consent of the Secretary.

(4) Change In Functional Currency Treated As A Change In Method Of Accounting.—Any change in the functional currency shall be treated as a change in the taxpayer's method of accounting for purposes of section 481 under procedures to be established by the Secretary.

[For official explanation, see Committee Reports, ¶4056.]

【¶3157】 CODE SEC. 986. DETERMINATION OF FOREIGN CORPORATION'S EARNINGS AND PROFITS AND FOREIGN TAXES.

【Footnote ¶3155】 Matter in *italics* in Sec. 960(a)(1) added by section 1202(b), '86 TRA, which struck out:

(1) "then under regulations prescribed by the Secretary, such domestic corporation shall be deemed to have paid the same proportion of the total income, war profits, and excess profits taxes paid (or deemed paid) by such foreign corporation to a foreign country or possession of the United States for the taxable year on or with respect to the earnings and profits of such foreign corporation which the amount of earnings and profits of such foreign corporation so included in gross income of the domestic corporation bears to the entire amount of the earnings and profits of such corporation for such taxable year. This paragraph shall not apply with respect to any amount included in the gross income of such domestic corporation attributable to earnings and profits of the second foreign corporation or of the third foreign corporation unless, in the case of the second foreign corporation, the percentage-of-voting-stock requirement of section 902(b)(3)(A) is satisfied, and in the case of the third foreign corporation, the percentage-of-voting-stock requirement of section 902(b)(3)(B) is satisfied."

Effective date (Sec. 1202(e), '86 TRA).—Applies to distributions by foreign corporations out of, and to inclusions under section 951(a) of the '86 Code attributable to, earnings and profits for taxable years beginning after 12-31-86.

【Footnote ¶3156】 Sec. 985 added by section 1261(a), '86 TRA.

Effective date (Sec. 1261(e)(1), '86 TRA).—Applies to taxable years beginning after 12-31-86.

【Footnote ¶3157】 Sec. 986 added by section 1261(a), '86 TRA.

Effective date (Sec. 1261(e), '86 TRA).—Applies to taxable years beginning after 12-31-86.

(a) **Earnings and Profits and Distributions.**—For purposes of determining the tax under this subtitle—

(1) of any shareholder of any foreign corporation, the earnings and profits of such corporation shall be determined in the corporation's functional currency, and

(2) in the case of any United States person, the earnings and profits determined under paragraph (1) (when distributed, deemed distributed, or otherwise taken into account under this subtitle) shall (if necessary) be translated into dollars using the appropriate exchange rate.

(b) **Foreign Taxes.**—

(1) **In general.**—In determining the amount of foreign taxes deemed paid under section 902 or 960—

(A) any foreign income taxes paid by a foreign corporation shall be translated into dollars using the exchange rates as of the time of payment, and

(B) any adjustment to the amount of foreign income taxes paid by a foreign corporation shall be translated into dollars using—

(i) except as provided in clause (ii), the appropriate exchange rate as of when such adjustment is made, and

(ii) in the case of any refund or credit of foreign taxes, using the exchange rate as of the time of original payment of such foreign income taxes.

(2) **Foreign income taxes.**—For purposes of paragraph (1), "foreign income taxes" means any income, war profits, or excess profits taxes paid to any foreign country or to any possession of the United States.

(c) **Previously Taxed Earnings and Profits.**—

(1) **In general.**—Foreign currency gain or loss with respect to distributions of previously taxed earnings and profits (as described in section 959 or 1293(c)) attributable to movements in exchange rates between the times of deemed and actual distribution shall be recognized and treated as ordinary income or loss from the same source as the associated income inclusion.

(2) **Distributions through tiers.**—The Secretary shall prescribe regulations with respect to the treatment of distributions of previously taxed earnings and profits through tiers of foreign corporations.

[For official explanation, see Committee Reports, ¶4056.]

【¶3158】 CODE SEC. 987. BRANCH TRANSACTIONS.

In the case of any taxpayer having 1 or more qualified business units with a functional currency other than the dollar, taxable income of such taxpayer shall be determined—

(1) by computing the taxable income or loss separately for each such unit in its functional currency,

(2) by translating the income or loss separately computed under paragraph (1) at the appropriate exchange rate,

(3) by making proper adjustments (as prescribed by the Secretary) for transfers of property between qualified business units of the taxpayer having different functional currencies, including—

(A) treating post-1986 remittances from each such unit as made on a pro rata basis out of post-1986 accumulated earnings, and

(B) treating gain or loss determined under this paragraph as ordinary income or loss, respectively, and sourcing such gain or loss by reference to the source of the income giving rise to post-1986 accumulated earnings, and

(4) by translating foreign income taxes paid by each qualified business unit of the taxpayer in the same manner as provided under section 986(b).

[For official explanation, see Committee Reports, ¶4056.]

【¶3159】 CODE SEC. 988. TREATMENT OF CERTAIN FOREIGN CURRENCY TRANSACTIONS.

(a) **General Rule.**—

(1) **Treatment as ordinary income or loss.**—

(A) **In general.**—Except as otherwise provided in this section, any foreign currency gain or loss attributable to a section 988 transaction shall be computed separately and treated as ordinary income or loss (as the case may be).

【Footnote ¶3158】 Sec. 987 added by section 1261(a), '86 TRA.
Effective date (Sec. 1261(e), '86 TRA).—Applies to taxable years beginning after 12-31-86.
【Footnote ¶3159】 Sec. 988 added by section 1261(a), '86 TRA.
Effective date (Sec. 1261(e), '86 TRA).—Applies to taxable years beginning after 12-31-86.

(B) Special rule for forward contracts, etc.—Except as provided in regulations, a taxpayer may elect to treat any foreign currency gain or loss attributable to a forward contract, a futures contract, or option described in subsection (c)(1)(B)(iii) which is a capital asset in the hands of the taxpayer and which is not a part of a straddle (within the meaning of section 1092(c), without regard to paragraph (4) thereof) as capital gain or loss (as the case may be) if the taxpayer makes such election and identifies such transaction before the close of the day on which such transaction is entered into (or such earlier time as the Secretary may prescribe).

(2) **Gain or loss treated as interest for certain purposes.**—To the extent provided in regulations, any amount treated as ordinary income or loss under paragraph (1) shall be treated as interest income or expense (as the case may be).

(3) **Source.**—
(A) In general.—Except as otherwise provided in regulations, in the case of any amount treated as ordinary income or loss under paragraph (1) (without regard to paragraph (1)(B)), the source of such amount shall be determined by reference to the residence of the taxpayer or the qualified business unit of the taxpayer on whose books the asset, liability, or item of income or expense is properly reflected.

(B) Residence.—For purposes of this subpart—
(i) In general.—The residence of any person shall be—
(I) in the case of an individual, the country in which such individual's tax home (as defined in section 911(d)(3)) is located,
(II) in the case of any corporation, partnership, trust, or estate which is a United States person (as defined in section 7701(a)(30)), the United States, and
(III) in the case of any corporation, partnership, trust, or estate which is not a United States person, a country other than the United States.

(ii) Exception.—In the case of a qualified business unit of any taxpayer (including an individual), the residence of such unit shall be the country in which the principal place of business of such qualified business unit is located.

(C) Special rule for certain related party loans.—Except to the extent provided in regulations, in the case of a loan by a United States person or a related person to a 10-percent owned foreign corporation which is denominated in a currency other than the dollar and bears interest at a rate at least 10 percentage points higher than the Federal mid-term rate (determined under section 1274(d)) at the time such loan is entered into, the following rules shall apply:
(i) For purposes of section 904 only, such loan shall be marked to market on an annual basis.
(ii) Any interest income earned with respect to such loan for the taxable year shall be treated as income from sources within the United States to the extent of any loss attributable to clause (i).

For purposes of this subparagraph, the term "related person" has the meaning given such term by section 954(d)(3), except that such section shall be applied by substituting "United States person" for "controlled foreign corporation" each place such term appears.

(D) 10-percent owned foreign corporation.—The term "10-percent owned foreign corporation" means any foreign corporation in which the United States person owns directly or indirectly at least 10 percent of the voting stock.

(b) **Foreign Currency Gain or Loss.**—For purposes of this section—
(1) Foreign currency gain.—The term "foreign currency gain" means any gain from a section 988 transaction to the extent such gain does not exceed gain realized by reason of changes in exchange rates on or after the booking date and before the payment date.

(2) Foreign currency loss.—The term "foreign currency loss" means any loss from a section 988 transaction to the extent such loss does not exceed the loss realized by reason of changes in exchange rates on or after the booking date and before the payment date.

(c) **Other Definitions.**—For purposes of this section—

(1) **Section 988 transaction.**—
(A) In general.—The term "section 988 transaction" means any transaction described in subparagraph (B) if the amount which the taxpayer is entitled to receive (or is required to pay) by reason of such transaction—

(i) is denominated in terms of a nonfunctional currency, or

(ii) is determined by reference to the value of 1 or more nonfunctional currencies.

(B) Description of transactions.—For purposes of subparagraph (A), the following transactions are described in this subparagraph:

(i) The acquisition of a debt instrument or becoming the obligor under a debt instrument.

(ii) Accruing (or otherwise taking into account) for purposes of this subtitle any item of expense or gross income or receipts which is to be paid or received after the date on which so accrued or taken into account.

(iii) Entering into or acquiring any forward contract, futures contract, option, or similar financial instrument if such instrument is not marked to market at the close of the taxable year under section 1256.

The Secretary may prescribe regulations excluding from the application of clause (ii) any class of items the taking into account of which is not necessary to carry out the purposes of this section by reason of the small amounts or short periods involved, or otherwise.

(C) Special rules for disposition of nonfunctional currency.—

(i) In general.—In the case of any disposition of any nonfunctional currency—

(I) such disposition shall be treated as a section 988 transaction, and

"(II) for purposes of determining the foreign currency gain or loss from such transaction, paragraphs (1) and (2) of subsection (b) shall be applied by substituting "acquisition date" for "booking date" and "disposition" for "payment date".

(ii) Nonfunctional currency.—For purposes of this section, the term "nonfunctional currency" includes coin or currency, and nonfunctional currency denominated demand or time deposits or similar instruments issued by a bank or other financial institution.—

(2) Booking date.—The term "booking date" means—

(A) in the case of a transaction described in paragraph (1)(B)(i), the date of acquisition or on which the taxpayer becomes the obligor,

(B) in the case of a transaction described in paragraph (1)(B)(ii), the date on which accrued or otherwise taken into account, or

(C) in the case of a transaction described in paragraph (1)(B)(iii), the date on which the position is entered into or acquired.

(3) Payment date.—The term "payment date" means—

(A) in the case of a transaction described in paragraph (1)(B)(i) or (ii), the date on which payment is made or received, or

(B) in the case of a transaction described in paragraph (1)(B)(iii), the date payment is made or received or the date the taxpayer's rights with respect to the position are terminated.

(4) Debt instrument.—The term "debt instrument" means a bond, debenture, note, or certificate or other evidence of indebtedness. To the extent provided in regulations, such term shall include preferred stock.

(d) Treatment of 988 Hedging Transactions.—

(1) In general.—To the extent provided in regulations, if any section 988 transaction is part of a 988 hedging transaction, all transactions which are part of such 988 hedging transaction shall be integrated and treated as a single transaction or otherwise treated consistently for purposes of this section. For purposes of the preceding sentence, the determination of whether any transaction is a section 988 transaction shall be determined without regard to whether such transaction would otherwise be marked-to-market under section 1256 and such term shall not include any transaction with respect to which an election is made under subsection (a)(1)(B). Sections 1092 and 1256 shall not apply to a transaction covered by this subsection.

(2) 988 hedging transaction.—For purposes of paragraph (1), the term "988 hedging transaction" means any transaction—

(A) entered into by the taxpayer primarily—

(i) to reduce risk of currency fluctuations with respect to property which is held or to be held by the taxpayer, or

(ii) to reduce risk of currency fluctuations with respect to borrowings made or to be made, or obligations incurred or to be incurred, by the taxpayer, and

   (B) identified by the Secretary or the taxpayer as being a 988 hedging transaction.

(e) **Application to Individuals.**—This section shall apply to section 988 transactions entered into by an individual only to the extent expenses properly allocable to such transactions meet the requirements of section 162 or 212 (other than that part of section 212 dealing with expenses incurred in connection with taxes).

[For official explanation, see Committee Reports, ¶4056.]

〖¶3160〗 **CODE SEC. 989. OTHER DEFINITIONS AND SPECIAL RULES.**

(a) **Qualified Business Unit.**—For purposes of this subpart, the term "qualified business unit" means any separate and clearly identified unit of a trade or business of a taxpayer which maintains separate books and records.

(b) **Appropriate Exchange Rate.**—Except as provided in regulations, for purposes of this subpart, the term "appropriate exchange rate" means—

   (1) in the case of an actual distribution of earnings and profits, the spot rate on the date such distribution is included in income,

   (2) in the case of an actual or deemed sale or exchange of stock in a foreign corporation treated as a dividend under section 1248, the spot rate on the date the deemed dividend is included in income,

   (3) in the case of any amounts included in income under section 951(a), 551(a), or 1293(a), the weighted average exchange rate for the taxable year of the foreign corporation, or

   (4) in the case of any other qualified business unit of a taxpayer, the weighted average exchange rate for the taxable year of such qualified business unit.

(c) **Regulations.**—The Secretary shall prescribe such regulations as may be necessary or appropriate to carry out the purposes of this subpart including regulations—

   (1) setting forth procedures to be followed by taxpayers with qualified business units using a net worth method of accounting before the enactment of this subpart,

   (2) limiting the recognition of foreign currency loss on certain remittances from qualified business units,

   (3) providing for the recharacterization of interest and principal payments with respect to obligations denominated in certain hyperinflationary currencies,

   (4) providing for alternative adjustments to the application of section 905(c), and

   (5) providing for the appropriate treatment of related party transactions (including transactions between qualified business units of the same taxpayer).

[For official explanation, see Committee Reports, ¶4056.]

〖¶3161〗 **CODE SEC. 995. TAXATION OF DISC INCOME TO SHAREHOLDERS.**

* * * * * * * * * * * *

(b) **Deemed Distributions.—**

   (1) **Distributions in qualified years.**—A shareholder of a DISC shall be treated as having received a distribution taxable as a dividend with respect to his stock in an amount which is equal to his pro rata share of the sum (or, if smaller, the earnings and profits for the taxable year) of—

     (A) the gross interest derived during the taxable year from producer's loans,

     (B) the gain recognized by the DISC during the taxable year on the sale or exchange of property, other than property which in the hands of the DISC is a qualified export asset, previously transferred to it in a transaction in which gain was not recognized in whole or in part, but only to the extent that the transferor's gain on the previous transfer was not recognized.

     (C) the gain (other than the gain described in subparagraph (B)) recognized by the DISC during the taxable year on the sale or exchange of property (other than property which in the hands of the DISC is stock in trade or other property described in section 1221(1)) previously transferred to it in a transaction in which gain was not recognized in whole or in part, but only to the extent that the transferor's gain on the previous transfer was not recognized and would have been treated as ordinary income if the property had been sold or exchanged rather than transferred to the DISC,

---

〖Footnote ¶3160〗 Sec. 989 added by section 1261(a), '86 TRA.
Effective date (Sec. 1261(e), '86 TRA).—Applies to taxable years beginning after 12-31-86.

(D) 50 percent of the taxable income of the DISC for the taxable year attributable to military property,

(E) the taxable income of the DISC attributable to qualified export receipts of the DISC for the taxable year which exceed $10,000,000,

(F) the sum of—

(i) *in the case of a shareholder which is a C corporation,* one-seventeenth of the excess of the taxable income of the DISC for the taxable year, before reduction for any distributions during the year, over the sum of the amounts deemed distributed for the taxable year under subparagraphs (A), (B), (C), (D), and (E),

(ii) an amount equal to $16/17$ *of the excess referred to in clause (i),* multiplied by the international boycott factor determined under section 999, and

(iii) any illegal bribe, kickback, or other payment (within the meaning of section 162(c)) paid by or on behalf of the DISC directly or indirectly to an official, employee, or agent in fact of a government, and

(G) the amount of foreign investment attributable to producer's loans (as defined in subsection (d)) of a DISC for the taxable year.

Distributions described in this paragraph shall be deemed to be received on the last day of the taxable year of the DISC in which the income was derived. In the case of a distribution described in subparagraph (G), earnings and profits for the taxable year shall include accumulated earnings and profits.

* * * * * * * * * * * *

(f) Interest on DISC-Related Deferred Tax Liability.—

* * * * * * * * * * * *

²*(4)* **Base period T-bill rate.—**For purposes of this subsection, the term "base period T-bill rate" means the annual rate of interest determined by the Secretary to be equivalent to the average investment yield of United States Treasury bills with maturities of 52 weeks which were auctioned during the 1-year period ending on September 30 of the calendar year ending with (or of the most recent calendar year ending before) the close of the taxable year of the shareholder.

³*(5)* **Short years.—**The Secretary shall prescribe such regulations as may be necessary for the application of this subsection to short years of the DISC, the shareholder, or both.

⁴*(6)* **Payment and assessment and collection of interest.—**The interest accrued during any taxable year which a shareholder is required to pay under paragraph (1) shall be treated, for purposes of this title, as interest payable under section 6601 and shall be paid by the shareholder at the time the tax imposed by this chapter for such taxable year is required to be paid.

(7) **DISC includes former DISC.—***For purposes of this subsection, the term "DISC" includes a former DISC.*

[For official explanation, see Committee Reports, ¶4190.]

【¶3162】 **CODE SEC. 996. RULES FOR ALLOCATION IN THE CASE IN DISTRIBUTIONS AND LOSSES.**

(a) Rules for Actual Distributions and Certain Deemed Distributions.—

* * * * * * * * * * * *

(2) Qualifying distributions.—Any actual distribution made pursuant to section 992(c) (relating to distributions to meet qualification requirements), and any deemed distribution pursuant to section 995(b)(1)(G) (relating to foreign investment attributable to producer's loans), shall be treated as made—

(A) first, out of accumulated DISC income, to the extent thereof,

(B) second, out of the earnings and profits described in paragraph (1)(C), to the extent thereof, and

(C) finally, out of previously taxed income.

【Footnote ¶3161】 Matter in *italics* in Sec. 995(b)(1)(F), (f)(4)—(7) added by section 1876(b)(2), (g), and (p)(1), '86 TRA, which struck out:

(1) "the amount determined under clause (i)"

(2) "(3)"

(3) "(4)"

(4) "(5)"

Effective date (Sec. 1881, '86 TRA and section 805(a), '84 TRA, as amended by section 1876, '86 TRA).—Generally applies to transactions after 12-31-84, in taxable years ending after such date. For special and transitional rules, see footnote ¶2959.

In the case of any amount of any actual distribution *to a C corporation* made pursuant to section 992(c) which is required to satisfy the condition of section 992(a)(1)(A), the preceding sentence shall apply to *¹16/17ths of such amount and paragraph (1) shall apply to the remaining 1/17th of such amount.*

* * * * * * * * * * * *

[For official explanation, see Committee Reports, ¶4190.]

【¶3163】 **CODE SEC. 1016. ADJUSTMENTS TO BASIS.**

(a) **General rule.**—Proper adjustment in respect of the property shall in all cases be made—

* * * * * * * * * * * *

¹(16)² in the case of any evidence of indebtedness referred to in section 811(b) (relating to amortization of premium and accrual of discount in the case of life insurance companies), to the extent of the adjustments required under section 811(b) (or the corresponding provisions of prior income tax laws) for the taxable year and all prior taxable years;

³(17) to the extent provided in section 1367 in the case of stock of, and indebtedness owed to, shareholders of an S corporation;

⁴(18) to the extent provided in section 961 in the case of stock in controlled foreign corporations (or foreign corporations which were controlled foreign corporations) and of property by reason of which a person is considered as owning such stock;

⁵(19) for amounts allowed as deductions for payments made on account of transfers of franchises, trademarks, or trade names under section 1253(d)(2);

⁶(20) to the extent provided in section 23(e), in the case of property with respect to which a credit has been allowed under *section 23;⁷*

⁸(22) [Repealed].

⁹(23) to the extent provided in section 48(q) in the case of expenditures with respect to which a credit has been allowed under section 38;

【Footnote ¶3162】 Matter in *italics* in Sec. 996(a)(2) added by section 1876(k), '86 TRA, which struck out:

(1) "one-half of such amount, and paragraph (1) shall apply to the remaining one-half of such amount"

Effective date (Sec. 1881, '86 TRA and Sec. 805, '84 TRA, as amended by section 1876, '86 TRA).—Generally applies to transactions after 12-31-84, in taxable years ending after such date. For special and transitional rules, see footnote ¶2959.

【Footnote ¶3163】 Matter in *italics* in Sec. 1016(a)(16)—(20) added by section 241(b)(2), '86 TRA, which struck out:

(1) "(16) for amounts allowed as deductions for expenditures treated as deferred expenses under Section 177 (relating to trade mark and trade name expenditures), and resulting in a reduction of the taxpayer's taxes under this subtitle, but not less than the amounts allowable under such section for the taxable year and prior years;"

(2) "(17)"

(3) "(18)"

(4) "(19)"

(5) "(20)"

(6) "(21)"

Effective date (Sec. 241(c), '86 TRA).—(1) Generally applies to expenditures paid or incurred after 12-31-86.

(2) Transitional rule.—The amendments made by this section shall not apply to any expenditure incurred—

(A) pursuant to a binding contract entered into before 3-2-86, or

(B) with respect to the development, protection, expansion, registration, or defense of a trademark or trade name commenced before 3-2-86, but only if less than the lesser of $1,000,000 or 5 percent of the aggregate cost of such development, protection, expansion, registration, or defense has been incurred or committed before such date. The preceding sentence shall not apply to any expenditure with respect to a trademark or trade name placed in service after 12-31-87.

Section 1303(b)(3), '86 TRA, struck out from Sec. 1016(a), paragraph (21) [formerly (22)] and redesignated paragraphs (23) through (27) as paragraphs (22) through (26) respectively. Paragraph (21) [formerly (22)] read as follows:

(7) "(22) to the extent provided in section 1395 in the case of stock of shareholders of a general stock ownership corporation (as defined in section 1391) which makes the election provided by section 1392;"

Effective date (Sec. 1311(d), '86 TRA).—Takes effect on the date of enactment.

[Ed. Sec. 241(b)(2), '86 TRA has already redesignated paragraphs (23) through (27) as paragraphs (22) through (26)—

Sec. 1899A(25), '86 TRA amended Sec. 1016(a)(23)—(25) [formerly (24)—(26)] by striking out the comma at the end thereof and inserting in lieu thereof a semicolon.

Matter in italics in Sec. 1016(a)(22)—(24) added by section 241(b)(2), '86 TRA, which struck out:

(8) "(23)"

(9) "(24)"

[10]*(24)* for amounts allowed as deductions under [11]*section 59(d)* (relating to optional 10-year writeoff of certain tax preferences);

[12]*(25)* to the extent provided in section 1059 (relating to reduction in basis for extraordinary dividends); and

[13]*(26)* in the case of qualified replacement property, the acquistion of which resulted under section 1042 in the nonrecognition of any part of the gain realized on the sale or exchange of any property, to the extent provided in section 1042(c).

* * * * * * * * * * * *

[For official explanation, see Committee Reports, ¶3874; 3931; 4059.]

〔¶3164〕   CODE SEC. 1017.   DISCHARGE OF INDEBTEDNESS.

(a)   General Rule.—If—

(1) an amount is excluded from gross income under subsection (a) of section 108 (relating to discharge of indebtedness), and

(2) under subsection (b)(2)(D) [1]*or (b)(5)* of section 108, any portion of such amount is to be applied to reduce basis,

then such portion shall be applied in reduction of the basis of any property held by the taxpayer at the beginning of the taxable year following the taxable year in which the discharge occurs.

(b)   Amount and Properties Determined Under Regulations.—

* * * * * * * * * * * *

(3)   Certain reductions may only be made on the basis of depreciable property.—

(A)   In general.—Any amount which under subsection (b)(5) [2] of section 108 is to be applied to reduce basis shall be applied only to reduce the basis of depreciable property held by the taxpayer.

* * * * * * * * * * *

(4)   Ordering rule in the case of qualified farm indebtedness.—Any amount which is excluded from gross income under section 108(a) by reason of the discharge of qualified farm indebtedness (within the meaning of section 108(g)(2)) and which under subsection (b) of section 108 is to be applied to reduce basis shall be applied—

(A)   first to reduce the tax attributes described in section 108(b)(2) (other than subparagraph (D) thereof),

(B)   then to reduce basis of property other than property described in subparagraph (C), and

(C)   then to reduce the basis of land used or held for use in the trade or business of farming.

* * * * * * * * * * * *

[For official explanation, see Committee Reports, ¶3894; 3944.]

〔Footnote ¶3163 continued〕

(10)   "(25)"

Effective date (Sec. 241(c), '86 TRA).—Generally applies to expenditures paid or incurred after 12-31-86. For transitional rules, see above.

"section 59(d)" in *italics* in Sec. 1016(a)(24) added by section 701(e)(4)(D), '86 TRA, which struck out:

(11)   "section 58(i)"

Effective date (Sec. 701(f), '86 TRA).—Generally applies to taxable years beginning after 12-31-86. For exceptions, see footnote ¶2879.

Matter in italics in Sec. 1016(a)(25) and (26), added by section 241(b)(2), '86 TRA, which struck out:

(12)   "(26)"

(13)   "(27)"

Effective date (Sec. 241(c), '86 TRA).—Generally applies to expenditures paid or incurred after 12-31-86. For transitional rules, see above.

〔Footnote ¶3164〕 Matter in *italics* in Sec. 1017(a)(2) and (b)(3)(A) added by section 822(b)(4) and (5), '86 TRA, which struck out:

(1)   ", (b)(5), or (c)(1)(A)"

(2)   "or (c)(1)(A)"

Effective date (Sec. 822(c), '86 TRA).—Applies to discharges after 12-31-86.

Matter in italics in Sec. 1017(b)(4) added by section 405(b), '86 TRA.

Effective date (Sec. 405(c), '86 TRA).—Applies to discharges of indebtedness occurring after 4-9-86, in taxable years ending after such date.

⟦¶3165⟧ CODE SEC. 1031. EXCHANGE OF PROPERTY HELD FOR PRODUCTIVE USE OR INVESTMENT.

(a) **Nonrecognition of Gain or Loss From Exchanges Solely in Kind.—**

* * * * * * * * * * * *

(3) **Requirement that property be identified and that exchange be completed not more than 180 days after transfer of exchanged property.**—For purposes of this subsection, any property received by the taxpayer shall be treated as property which is not like-kind property if—

(A)   such *prioperty is not identified as property to be received in the exchange on or* before the day which is 45 days after the date on which the taxpayer transfers the property relinquished in the exchange, or

(B)   such property is received after the earlier of—

(i)   the day which is 180 days after the date on which the taxpayer transfers the property relinquished in the exchange, or

(ii)   the due date (determined with regard to extension) for the transferor's return of the tax imposed by this chapter for the taxable year in which the transfer of the relinquished property occurs.

* * * * * * * * * * * *

[For official explanation, see Committee Reports, ¶4139.]

⟦¶3166⟧ CODE SEC. 1034. ROLLOVER OF GAIN ON SALE OF PRINCIPAL RESIDENCE.

* * * * * * * * * * * *

(h) **Members of Armed Forces.—**

* * * * * * * * * * * *

(2) **Members stationed outside the United States or required to reside in Government quarters.**—In the case of any taxpayer who, during any period of time the running of which is suspended by paragraph (1)—

(A)   is stationed outside of the United States, or

(B)   after returning from a tour of duty outside of the United States and pursuant to a determination by the Secretary of Defense that adequate off-base housing is not available at a remote base site, is required to reside in on-base Government quarters,

any such period of time as so suspended shall not expire before *the day which is 1 year after* the last day described in subparagraph (A) or (B), as the case may be, except that any such period of time as so suspended shall not extend beyond the date which is 8 years after the date of the sale of the old residence.

⟦Footnote ¶3165⟧   Matter in *italics* in Sec. 1031(a)(3)(A) added by section 1805(d), '86 TRA.
Effective date (Sec. 1881, '86 TRA and Sec. 77(b), '84 TRA).—
(1)   Generally applies to transfers made after 7-18-84 in taxable years ending after such date.
(2)   Binding contract exception for transfer of partnership interests.—Paragraph (2)(D) of section 1031(a) of the '54 Code (as amended by subsection (a)) shall not apply in the case of any exchange pursuant to a binding contract in effect on 3-1-84, and at all times thereafter before the exchange.
(3)   Requirement that property be identified within 45 days and that exchange be completed within 180 days.—Paragraph (3) of section 1031(a) of the '54 Code (as amended by subsection (a)) shall apply—
(A)   to transfers after 7-18-84, and
(B)   to transfers on or before 7-18-84 if the property to be received in the exchange is not received before 1-1-87.
In the case of any transfer on or before 7-18-84 which the taxpayer treated as part of a like-kind exchange, the period for assessing any deficiency of tax attributable to the amendment made by subsection (a) shall not expire before 1-1-88.
(4)   Special rule where property identified in binding contract.—If the property to be received in the exchange is identified in a binding contract in effect on 6-13-84, and at all times thereafter before the transfer, paragraph (3) shall be applied—
(A)   by substituting "January 1, 1989" for "January 1, 1987", and
(B)   by substituting "January 1, 1990" for "January 1, 1988".
(5)   Special rule for like kind exchange of partnership interests.—Paragraph (2)(D) of section 1031(a) of the '54 Code (as amended by subsection (a)) shall not apply to any exchange of an interest as general partner pursuant to a plan of reorganization of ownership interest under a contract which took effect on 3-29-84, and which was executed on or before 3-31-84, but only if all the exchanges contemplated by the reorganization plan are completed on or before 12-31-84.
⟦Footnote ¶3166⟧   Matter in *italics* in Sec. 1034(h)(2) added by section 1878(g), '86 TRA.
Effective date (Sec. 1881, '86 TRA and Sec. 1053(b), '84 TRA).—Applies to sales of old residences (within the meaning of section 1034 of the '54 Code) after 7-18-84.

* * * * * * * * * * * *

[For official explanation, see Committee Reports, ¶4192.]

[¶3167] **CODE SEC. 1035.** **CERTAIN EXCHANGES OF INSURANCE POLICIES.**

* * * * * * * * * * * *

(b) **Definitions.**—For the purposes of this section—

(1) **Endowment contract.**—A contract of endowment insurance is a contract with an insurance company [1] which depends in part on the life expectancy of the insured, but which may be payable in full in a single payment during his life.

[For official explanation, see Committee Reports, ¶4154.]

[¶3168] **CODE SEC. 1041.** **TRANSFERS OF PROPERTY BETWEEN SPOUSES OR INCIDENT TO DIVORCE.**

* * * * * * * * * * * *

(e)   Transfers in Trust Where Liability Exceeds Basis.—Subsection (a) shall not apply to the transfer of property in trust to the extent that—
(1)   the sum of the amount of the liabilities assumed, plus the amount of the liabilities to which the property is subject, exceeds
(2)   the total of the adjusted basis of the property transferred.
Proper adjustment shall be made under subsection (b) in the basis of the transferee in such property to take into account gain recognized by reason of the preceding sentence.

[For official explanation, see Committee Reports, ¶4161.]

[¶3169] **CODE SEC. 1042.** **SALES OF STOCK TO *EMPLOYEE* STOCK OWNERSHIP PLANS OR CERTAIN COOPERATIVES.**

(a) **Nonrecognition of Gain.**—If—
(1)   [1]*the taxpayer or executor elects in such form as the Secretary may prescribe,* the application of this section with respect to any sale of qualified securities,
(2)   the taxpayer purchases qualified replacement property within the replacement period, and
(3)   the requirements of subsection (b) are met with respect to such sale,
then the gain (if any) on such sale *which would be recognized as long term caital gain* shall be recognized only to the extent that the amount realized on such sale exceeds the cost to the taxpayer of such qualified replacement property.

(b) **Requirements to Qualify for Nonrecognition.**—A sale of qualified securities meets the requirements of this subsection if—

(1)   **Sale to employee organizations.**—The qualified securities are sold to—
(A)   an employee stock ownership plan (as defined in section 4975(e)(7)), or
(B)   an eligible worker-owned cooperative.

[Footnote ¶3167]   Section 1828, '86 TRA, struck out from Sec. 1035(b)(1):
(1) "subject to tax under subchapter L"
Effective date (Sec. 1881, '86 TRA and Sec. 224(b), '84 TRA).—Applies to all exchanges whether before, on, or after 7-18-84.
[Footnote ¶3168]   Sec. 1041(e) in *italics* added by section 1842(b), '86 TRA.
Effective date (Sec. 1881, '86 TRA and Sec. 421 (d), '84 TRA).—(1) Generally applies to transfers after 7-18-84 in taxable years ending after such date.
(2)   Election to have amendments apply to tranfers after 1983.—If both spouses or former spouses make an election under this paragraph, the amendments made by this section shall apply to all transfers made by such spouses (or former spouses) after 12-31-83.
(3)   Exception for transfers pursuant to existing decrees.—Except in the case of an election under paragraph (2), the amendments made by this section shall not apply to transfers under any instrument in effect on or before 7-18-84 unless both spouses (or former spouses) elect to have such amendments apply to transfers under such instrument.
(4)   Election.—Any election under paragraph (2) or (3) shall be made in such manner, at such time, and subject to such conditions, as the Secretary of the Treasury or his delegate may by regulations prescribe.
[Footnote ¶3169]   Matter in *italics* in the heading of Sec. 1042 added by section 1854(a)(11), '86 TRA.
Effective date (Sec. 1881, '86 TRA and section 541(c), '84 TRA).—Applies to sales of securities in taxable years beginning after 7-18-84.

Matter in *italics* in Sec. 1042(a)(1) added by section 1854(a)(1), '86 TRA, which struck out:
(1) "the taxpayer elects"
Effective date (Sec. 1881, '86 TRA and Section 541(c), '84 TRA).—Applies to sales of securities in taxable years beginning after 7-18-84.

   (2) [2]*Plan must hold 30 percent of stock after sale.—The plan or cooperative referred to in paragraph (1) owns (after application of section 318(a)(4)), immediately after the sale, at least 30 percent of—*
      (A) each class of outstanding stock of the corporation (other than stock described in section 1504(a)(4)) which issued the quailified securities, or
      (B) the total value of all outstanding stock of the corporation (other than stock described in section 1504(a)(4)).[3]

   [4]*(3)*   **Written statement required.—**
      (A)   In general.—The taxpayer files with the Secretary the written statement described in subparagraph (B).
      (B)   Statement.—A statement is described in this subparagraph if it is a verified written statement of—
         (i)   the employer whose employees are covered by the plan described in paragraph (1), or
         (ii)   any authorized officer of the cooperative described in paragraph (1).
   consenting to the application of * [5]*sections 4978 and 4979A* with respect to such employer or cooperative.

   (c)   **Definitions; Special Rules.—**For purposes of this [6]*section—*

   (1)   **Qualified securities.—**The term "qualified securities" means employer securities (as defined in section 409A(1)) which—
      (A)   are issued by a domestic corporation that has no [7]*stock outstanding that is* readily tradable on an established securities market, *and* [8]
   [9]*(B)*   were not received by the taxpayer in—
      (i)   a distribution from a plan described in section 401(a), or

---

〖Footnote ¶3169 continued〗

Matter in *italics* in Sec. 1042(b)(2) added by section 1854(a)(2)(A), '86 TRA, which struck out:
   "(2)   **Employees must own 30 percent of stock after sale.—**The plan or cooperative referred to in paragraph (1) owns, immediately after the sale, at least 30 percent of the total value of the employer securities (within the meaning of section 409(1) outstanding as of such time."
   Effective date (Sec. 1881, '86 TRA and section 541(c), '84 TRA).—Generally applies to sales of securities in taxable years beginning after 7-18-84. See special rule under section 1854(a)(2)(B) below:
   (B)(i)   The requirement that section 1042(b) of the '54 Code shall be applied with regard to section 318(a)(4) of such Code shall apply to sales after 5-6-86.
   (ii)   In the case of sales after 7-18-84, and before 7-18-84, paragraph (2) of section 1042(b) of such Code shall apply as if it read as follows:
   "(2)   Employees must own 30 percent of stock after sale.—The plan or cooperative referred to in paragraph (1) owns, immediately after the sale, at least 30 percent of the employer securities or 30 percent of the value of employer securities (within the meaning of section 409(1) outstanding at the time of sale."

Matter in *italics* in Sec. 1042(b)(3) added by section 1854(a)(3)(B), '86 TRA, which struck out:
   (3)   **"(3)**   **Plan maintained for benefit of employees.—**No portion of the assets of the plan or cooperative attributable to qualified securities acquired by the plan or cooperative described in paragraph (1) accrue under such plan, or are allocated by such cooperative, for the benefit of—
   (A)   the taxpayer,
   (B)   any person who is a member of the family of the taxpayer (within the meaning of section 267(c)(4)), or
   (C)   any other person who owns (after application of section 318(a)) more than 25 percent in value of any class of outstanding employer securities (within the meaning of section 409(1)."
   (4)   **"(4)"**
   Effective date (Sec. 1854(a)(3)(C), '86 TRA).—Applies to sales of securities after the date of enactment of this Act.

---

   * **(5)**   Sec. 1854(a)(9)(B), '86 TRA amended Sec. 1042(b)(3)(B) by striking out "section 4978(a)" and inserting in lieu thereof *"sections 4978 and 4979A"*.
   Effective date (Sec. 1854(a)(9)(D), '86 TRA).—Applies to sales of securities after the date of enactment of this Act.

---

   * **(5)**   Sec. 1854(f)(3)(B), '86 TRA amended Sec. 1042(b)(3)(B) by inserting *"and 4979A"* after "section 4978(a)"
   Effective date (Sec. 1854(f)(4)(A), '86 TRA).—Takes effect on the date of the enactment of this Act.

Matter in *italics* in Sec. 1042(c) added by section 1899A(26), '86 TRA, which stuck out:
   (6)   **"section.—"**

Matter in *italics* in Sec. 1042(c)(1)(A), (4) and (5) added by section 1854(a)(4), (5)(A) and (10), '86 TRA, which struck out:
   (7)   "securities outstanding that are"
   (8)   "(B)   at the time of the sale described in subsection (a)(1), have been held by the taxpayer for more than 1 year, and"
   (9)   "(C)"

(ii) a transfer pursuant to an option or other right to acquire stock to which section 83, 422, 422A, 423, or 424 applies.

* * * * * * * * * * *

(4) Qualified replacement property.—

[10]*(A) In general.—The term "qualified replacement property" means any security issued by a domestic operating corporation which—*

(i) did not, for the taxable year preceding the taxable year in which such security was purchased, have passive investment income (as defined in section 1362(d)(3)(D)) in excess of 25 percent of the gross receipts of such corporation for such preceding taxable year, and

(ii) is not the corporation which issued the qualified securities which such security is replacing or a member of the same controlled group of corporations (within the meaning of section 1563(a)(1)) as such corporation.

For purposes of clause (i), income which is described in section 954(c)(3) shall not be treated as passive investment income.

(B) Operating corporation.—For purposes of this paragraph—

(i) In general.—The term "operating corporation" means a corporation more than 50 percent of the assets of which were, at the time the security was purchased or before the close of the placement period, used in the active conduct of the trade or business.

(ii) Financial institutions and insurance companies.—The term "operating corporation" shall include—

(I) any financial institution described in section 581 or 593, and

(II) an insurance company subject to tax under subchapter L.

(C) Controlling and controlled corporations treated as 1 corporation.—

(i) In general.—For purposes of applying this paragraph, if—

(I) the corporation issuing the security owns stock representing control of 1 or more other corporations,

(II) 1 or more other corporations own stock representing control of the corporation issuing the security, or

(III) both,

then all such corporations shall be treated as 1 corporation.

(ii) Control.—For purposes of clause (i), the term "control" has the meaning given such term by section 304(c). In determining control, there shall be disregarded any qualified replacement property of the taxpayer with respect to the section 1042 sale being tested.

(D) Security defined.—For purposes of this paragraph, the term "security" has the meaning given such term by section 165(g)(2), except that such term shall not include any security issued by a government or political subdivision thereof.

(5) Securities [11]*sold* **by underwriter.—**No [12]*sale* of securities by an underwriter *to an employee stock ownership plan or eligible worker-owned cooperative* in the ordinary course of his trade or business as an underwriter, whether or not guaranteed, shall be treated as a sale for purposes of subsection (a).

* * * * * * * * * * *

【Footnote ¶3169 continued】

(10) The term qualified replacement property means any securities (as defined in section 165(g)(2)) issued by a domestic corporation which does not, for the taxable year in which such stock is issued, have passive investment income (as defined in section 1362(d)(3)(D)) that exceeds 25 percent of the gross receipts of such corporation for such taxable year.

(11) **"acquired"**

(12) **"acquisition"**

Effective date (Sec. 1881, '86 TRA and section 541(c), '84 TRA).—Applies to sales of securities in taxable years beginning after 7-18-84.

Matter in *italics* in Sec. 1042(c)(7) added by section 1854(a)(6)(A), '86 TRA.

Effective date (Sec. 1854(a)(6)(B) —(D), '86 TRA).—

(B) Generally applies to sales after 3-28-85, except that such amendment shall not apply to sales made before 7-1-85, if made pursuant to a binding contract in effect on 3-28-85, and at all times thereafter.

(C) Shall not apply to any sale occurring on 12-20-85, with respect to which—

(i) a commitment letter was issued by a bank on 10-31-84, and

(ii) a final purchase agreement was entered into on 11-5-85.

(D) In the case of a sale on 9-27-85, with respect to which a preliminary commitment letter was issued by a bank on 4-10-85, and with respect to which a commitment letter was issued by a bank on 6-28-85, the amendment shall apply but such sale shall be treated as having occurred on 9-27-86.

---

(7) *Section not to apply to gain of C corporation.*—Subsection (a) shall not apply to any gain on the sale of any qualified securities which is includible in the gross income of any C corporation.

(d) **Basis of Qualified Replacement Property.**—The basis of the taxpayer in qualified replacement property purchased by the taxpayer during the replacement period shall be reduced by the amount of gain not recognized by reason of such purchase and the application of subsection (a). If more than one item of qualified replacement property is purchased, the basis of each of such items shall be reduced by an amount determined by multiplying the total gain not recognized by reason of such purchase and the application of subsection (a) by a fraction—

(1) the numerator of which is the cost of such item of property, and

(2) the denominator of which is the total cost of all such items of property

Any reduction in basis under this subsection shall not be taken into account for purposes of section 1278(a)(2)(A)(ii) (relating to definition of market discount).

(e) *Recapture of Gain on Disposition of Qualified Replacement Property.*—

(1) *In general.*—If a taxpayer disposes of any qualified replacement property, then, notwithstanding any other provision of this title, gain (if any) shall be recognized to the extent of the gain which was not recognized under subsection (a) by reason of the acquisition by such taxpayer of such qualified replacement property.

(2) *Special rule for corporations controlled by the taxpayer.*—If—

(A) a corporation issuing qualified replacement property disposes of a substantial portion of its assets other than in the ordinary course of its trade or business, and

(B) any taxpayer owning stock representing control (within the meaning of section 304(c)) of such corporation at the time of such disposition holds any qualified replacement property of such corporation at such time,

then the taxpayer shall be treated as having disposed of such qualified replacement property at such time.

(3) *Recapture not to apply in certain cases.*—Paragraph (1) shall not apply to any transfer of qualified replacement property—

(A) in any reorganization (within the meaning of section 368) unless the person making the election under subsection (a)(1) owns stock representing control in the acquiring or acquired corporation and such property is substituted basis property in the hands of the transferee,

(B) by reason of the death of the person making such election,

(C) by gift, or

(D) in any transaction to which section 1042(a) applies.

[13](f) **Statute of Limitations.—**

* * * * * * * * * * * *

[For official explanation, see Committee Reports, ¶4174.]

[¶3170] CODE SEC. 1056. BASIS LIMITATION FOR PLAYER CONTRACTS TRANSFERRED IN CONNECTION WITH THE SALE OF A FRANCHISE.

(a) **General Rule.**—If a franchise to conduct any sports enterprise is sold or exchanged, and if, in connection with such sale or exchange, there is a transfer of a contract for the services of an athlete, the basis of such contract in the hands of the transferee shall not exceed the sum of—

(1) the adjusted basis of such contract in the hands of the transferor immediately before the transfer, plus

(2) the gain (if any) recognized by the transferor on the transfer of such contract.[1]

[Footnote ¶3169 continued]

Matter in *italics* in Sec. 1042(d) added by section 1854(a)(7), '86 TRA.

Effective date (Sec. 1881, '86 TRA and section 541(c), '84 TRA).—Applies to sales of securities in taxable years beginning after 7-18-84.

Matter in *italics* in Sec. 1042(e) and (f) added by section 1854(a)(8)(A), '86 TRA, which struck out:

(13) "(e)"

Effective date (Sec. 1854(a)(8)(B), '86 TRA).—Applies to dispositions after the date of the enactment of this Act, in taxable years ending after such date.

[Footnote ¶3170] Section 631(e)(13), '86 TRA, struck out from Sec. 1056(a):

(1) "For purposes of this section, gain realized by the transferor on the transfer of such contract, but not recognized by reason of section 337(a), shall be treated as recognized to the extent recognized by the transferor's shareholders."

Effective date (Sec. 633(a), '86 TRA).—(a) Generally applies to—

[For official explanation, see Committee Reports, ¶3917.]

⟦¶3171⟧ CODE SEC. 1059. CORPORATE SHAREHOLDERS BASIS IN STOCK REDUCED BY NONTAXED PORTION OF EXTRAORDINARY DIVIDENDS.

(a) General Rule.—[1]*If any corporation receives any extraordinary dividend with respect to any share of stock and such corporation has not held such stock for more than 2 years before the dividend announcement date—*

(1) Reduction in basis.—The basis of such corporation in such stock shall be reduced (but not below zero) by the nontaxed portion of such dividends.

(2) Recognition upon sale or disposition in certain cases.—In addition to any gain recognized under this chapter, there shall be treated as gain from the sale or exchange of any stock for the taxable year in which the sale or disposition of such stock occurs an amount equal to the aggregate nontaxed portions of any extraordinary dividends with respect to such stock which did not reduce the basis of such stock by reason of the limitation on reducing basis below zero.

(c) Extraordinary Dividend Defined.—For purposes of this section—

(1) In general.—The term "extraordinary dividend" means any dividend with respect to a share of stock if the amount of such dividend equals or exceeds the threshold percentage of the taxpayer's adjusted basis in such share of stock.[2]

* * * * * * * * * * * *

(4) Fair market value determination.—If the taxpayer establishes to the satisfaction of the Secretary the fair market value of any share of stock as of the day before the ex-dividend date, the taxpayer may elect to apply paragraphs (1) and (3) by substituting such value for the taxpayer's adjusted basis.

(d) Special Rules.—For purposes of this section—

[3]*(1) Time for reduction.—*

(A) In general.—Except as provided in subparagraph (B), any reduction in basis under subsection (a)(1) shall occur immediately before any sale or disposition of the stock.

(B) Special rule for computing extraordinary dividend.—In determining a taxpayer's adjusted basis for purposes of subsection (c)(1), any reduction in basis under subsection (a)(1) by reason of a prior distribution which was an extraordinary dividend shall be treated as occurring at the beginning of the ex-dividend date for such distribution.

* * * * * * * * * * *

(3) Determination of holding period.—For purposes of determining the holding period of stock under subsection (a)(2), rules similar to the rules of paragraphs (3) and (4) of section 246(c) shall apply; except that [4]"2 years" shall be substituted for the number of days specified in subparagraph (B) of section 246(c)(3).

* * * * * * * * * * *

(6) Dividend announcement date.—The term "dividend announcement date" means, with respect to any dividend, the date on which the corporation declares, announces, or agrees to, the payment of such dividend, whichever is the earliest.

⟦Footnote ¶3170 continued⟧

(1) any distribution in complete liquidation, and any sale or exchange, made by a corporation after 7-31-86, unless such corporation is completely liquidated before 1-1-87,

(2) any transaction described in sec. 338 of the '86 Code for which the acquisition date occurs after 12-31-86, and

(3) any distribution (not in complete liquidation) made after 12-31-86.

For special rules, see ¶2023.

⟦Footnote ¶3171⟧ Matter in *italics* in Sec. 1059(a), (c)(1), (4), (d)(1), (3), (6), (7), (e), and (f) added by section 614(a)—(e), '86 TRA, which struck out:

(1) "If any corporation—

(1) receives an extraordinary dividend with respect to any share of stock, and

(2) sells or otherwise disposes of such stock before such stock has been held for more than 1 year,

the basis of such corporation in such stock shall be reduced by the nontaxed portion of such dividend. If the nontaxed portion of such dividend exceeds such basis, such excess shall be treated as gain from the sale or exchange of such stock."

(2) "(determined without regard to this section)"

(3) "(1) **Time for reduction.—**Any reduction in basis under subsection (a) by reason of any distribution which is an extraordinary dividend shall occur at the beginning of the ex-dividend date for such distribution."

(4) "1 year"

   (7) *Exception where stock held during entire existence of corporation.*—*Subsection (a) shall not apply to any extraordinary dividend with respect to any share of stock of a corporation if—*

     (A) *such stock was held by the taxpayer during the entire period such corporation (and any predecessor corporation) was in existence,*

     (B) *except as provided in regulations, the only earnings and profits of such corporation were earnings and profits accumulated by such corporation (or any predecessor corporation) during such period, and*

     (C) *the application of this paragraph to such dividend is not inconsistent with the purposes of this section.*

  (e) *Special Rules for Certain Distributions.*—

   (1) *Treatment of partial liquidations and non-pro rata redemptions.*—*Except as otherwise provided in regulations, in the case of any redemption of stock which is—*

     (A) *part of a partial liquidation (within the meaning of section 302(e)) of the redeeming corporation, or*

     (B) *not pro rata as to all shareholders,*

any amount treated as a dividend under section 301 with respect to such redemption shall be treated as an extraordinary dividend for purposes of this section (without regard to the holding period of the stock).

   (2) *Qualifying dividends.*—*Except as provided in regulations, the term "extraordinary dividend" shall not include any qualifying dividend (within the meaning of section 243(b)(1)).*

   (3) *Qualified preferred dividends.*—

     (A) *In general.*—*A qualified preferred dividend shall be treated as an extraordinary dividend—*

       (i) *only if the actual rate of return of the taxpayer on the stock with respect to which such dividend was paid exceeds 15 percent, or*

       (ii) *if clause (i) does not apply, and the taxpayer disposes of such stock before the taxpayer has held such stock for more than 5 years, only to the extent the actual rate of return exceeds the stated rate of return.*

     (B) *Rate of return.*—*For purposes of subparagraph (A)—*

       (i) *Actual rate of return.*—*The actual rate of return shall be the rate of return for the period for which the taxpayer held the stock, determined—*

         (I) *by only taking into account dividends during such period, and*

         (II) *by using the lesser of the adjusted basis of the taxpayer in such stock or the liquidation preference of such stock.*

       (ii) *Stated rate of return.*—*The stated rate of return shall be the annual rate of the qualified preferred dividend payable with respect to any share of stock (expressed as a percentage of the amount described in subparagraph (B)(i)(II)).*

     (C) *Definitions and special rules.*—*For purposes of this paragraph—*

       (i) *Qualified preferred dividend.*—*The term "qualified preferred dividend" means any dividend payable with respect to any share of stock which—*

         (I) *provides for fixed preferred dividends payable not less frequently than annually, and*

         (II) *is not in arrears as to dividends at the time the taxpayer acquires the stock.*

       (ii) *Holding period.*—*In determining the holding period for purposes of subparagraph (A)(ii), subsection (d)(3) shall be applied by substituting "5 years" for "2 years".*

[5](f) **Regulations.**—The Secretary shall prescribe such regulations as may be appropriate to carry out the purposes of this section, including regulations providing for the application of this section in the case of stock dividends, stock splits, reorganizations, and other similar transactions.

[For official explanation, see Committee Reports, ¶3915.]

〖Footnote ¶3171 continued〗

  (5) "(e)"

  Effective date (Sec. 614(f), '86 TRA).—(1) Generally applies to dividends declared after 7-18-86, in taxable years ending after such date.

  (2) Aggregation.—For purposes of section 1059(c)(3) of the '86 Code, dividends declared after 7-18-86 shall not be aggregated with dividends declared on or before 7-18-86.

  (3) Redemptions.—Section 1059(e)(1) of the '86 Code (as added by subsection (e)) shall apply to dividends declared after the date of the enactment of this Act, in taxable years ending after such date.

【¶3171-A】 CODE SEC. 1059A. LIMITATION ON TAXPAYER'S BASIS OR IN-VENTORY COST IN PROPERTY IMPORTED FROM RELATED PERSONS.

(a) **In General.**—If any property is imported into the United States in a transaction (directly or indirectly) between related persons (within the meaning of section 482), the amount of any costs—

(1) which are taken into account in computing the basis or inventory cost of such property by the purchaser, and

(2) which are also taken into account in computing the customs value of such property,

shall not, for purposes of computing such basis or inventory cost for purposes of this chapter, be greater than the amount of such costs taken into account in computing such customs value.

(b) **Customs Value; Import.**—For purposes of this section—

(1) **Customs value.**—The term "custom value" means the value taken into account for purposes of determining the amount of any customs duties or any other duties which may be imposed on the importation of any property.

(2) **Import.**—Except as provided in regulations, the term "import" means the en-tering, or withdrawal from warehouse, for consumption.

[For official explanation, see Committee Reports, ¶4055.]

【¶3172】 CODE SEC. 1060. SPECIAL ALLOCATION RULES FOR CERTAIN ASSET ACQUISITIONS.

(a) **General Rule.**—In the case of any applicable asset acquisition, for purposes of determining both—

(1) the transferee's basis in such assets, and

(2) the gain or loss of the transferor with respect to such acquisition,

the consideration received for such assets shall be allocated among such assets acquired in such acquisition in the same manner as amounts are allocated to assets under section 338(b)(5).

(b) **Information Required To Be Furnished to Secretary.**—Under regulations, the transferor and transferee in an applicable asset acquisition shall, at such times and in such manner as may be provided in such regulations, furnish to the Secretary the follow-ing information:

(1) The amount of the consideration received for the assets which is allocated to goodwill or going concern value.

(2) Any modification of the amount described in paragraph (1).

(3) Any other information with respect to other assets transferred in such acquisi-tion as the Secretary may find necessary to carry out the provisions of this section.

(c) **Applicable Asset Acquisition.**—For purposes of this section, the term "applicable asset acquisition" means any transfer (whether directly or indirectly)—

(1) of assets which constitute a trade or business, and

(2) with respect to which the transferee's basis in such assets is determined wholly by reference to the consideration paid for such assets.

A transfer shall not be treated as failing to be an applicable asset acquisition merely be-cause section 1031 applies to a portion of the assets transferred.

[For official explanation, see Committee Reports, ¶3921.]

【¶3172-A】 CODE SEC. *1061.* CROSS REFERENCES.

(1) **For nonrecognition of gain in connection with the transfer of obsolete vessels to the Maritime Administration under section 510 of the Merchant Marine Act, 1936, see subsection (e) of that section, as amended August 4, 1939** [2]**(46 U.S.C. App. 1160).**

【Footnote ¶3171-A】 Sec. 1059A added by section 1248(a), '86 TRA.
Effective date (Sec. 1248(c), '86 TRA).—Applies to transactions entered into after 3-18-86.
【Footnote ¶3172】 Sec. 1060 added by section 641(a), '86 TRA.
Effective date (Sec. 641(c), '86 TRA).—Applies to any acquisition of assets after 5-6-86, unless such acquisition is pursuant to a binding contract which was in effect on 5-6-86, and at all times thereafter.
【Footnote ¶3172-A】 Matter in *italics* in Sec. 1061 (formerly Sec. 1060) added by section 641(a), '86 TRA, which struck out:
(1) "1060"
Effective date (Sec. 641(c), '86 TRA).—Applies to any acquisition of assets after 5-6-86, unless such acquisition is pursuant to a binding contract which was in effect on 5-6-86, and at all times thereafter.

Matter in *italics* in Sec. 1061(1) and (2) (formerly Sec. 1060) added by section 1899A(27), '86 TRA, which struck out:
(2) "(46 U.S.C."

(2) For recognition of gain or loss in connection with the construction of new vessels, see section 511 of such Act, as amended [2](46 U.S.C. App. 1161).

* * * * * * * * * * *

[For official explanation, see Committee Reports, ¶3921; 4213.]

【¶3173】 CODE SEC. 1082. BASIS FOR DETERMINING GAIN OR LOSS.

(a) **Exchanges Generally.—**

* * * * * * * * * * * *

(2) **Exchanges subject to the provisions of section 1081(b).—**The gain not recognized on a transfer by reason of section 1081(b) or the corresponding provisions of prior internal revenue laws shall be applied to reduce the basis for determining gain or loss on sale or exchange of the following categories of property in the hands of the transferor immediately after the transfer, and property acquired within 24 months after such transfer by an expenditure or investment to which section 1081(b) relates on account of the acquisition of which gain is not recognized under such subsection, in the following order:

(A) property of a character subject to the allowance for depreciation under section 167;

(B) property (not described in subparagraph (A)) with respect to deduction for amortization is allowable under section 169, 184,[1] or 188;

* * * * * * * * * * *

[For official explanation, see Committee Reports, ¶3875.]

【¶3174】 CODE SEC. 1092. STRADDLES

* * * * * * * * * * * *

(c) **Straddle Defined.—**For purposes of this section—

* * * * * * * * * * *

(4) **Exception for certain straddles consisting of qualified covered call options and the optioned stock.—**

(A) In general.—If—

(i) all the offsetting positions making up any straddle consist of 1 or more qualified covered call options and the stock to be purchased from the taxpayer under such options, and

(ii) such straddle is not part of a larger straddle, such straddle shall not be treated as a straddle for purposes of this section and section 263(g).

* * * * * * * * * * * *

(E) Special year end rule.—Subparagraph (A) shall not apply to any straddle for purposes of section 1092(a) if—

(i) the qualified covered call options referred to in such subparagraph are closed *or the stock is disposed of at a loss* during any taxable year.

(ii) gain on disposition of the stock to be purchased from the taxpayer under such options [1] *or gains on such options are* includible in gross income for a

---

【Footnote ¶3173】 Section 242(b)(1), '86 TRA, struck out from Sec. 1082(a)(2)(B):
(1) "185,"
Effective date (Sec. 242(c), '86 TRA).–Generally applies to that portion of the basis of any property which is attributable to expenditures paid or incurred after 12-31-86. For transitional rules, see footnote ¶2947.
【Footnote ¶3174】 Matter in *italics* in Sec. 1092(c)(4)(E) added by section 331(a), '86 TRA, which struck out:
(1) "is"
Effective date (Sec. 331(b), '86 TRA).—Applies to positions established on or after 1-1-87.

Matter in *italics* in Sec. 1092(d)(3)(A) added by section 1808(c), '86 TRA.
Effective date (Sec. 1881, '86 TRA and section 101(e)(1) and (2), '84 TRA).—(1) Generally applies to positions established after 12-31-83, in taxable years ending after such date.
(2) Special rule for offsetting position stock.—In the case of any stock of a corporation formed or availed of to take positions in personal property which offset positions taken by any shareholder, the amendments made by this section shall apply to positions established on or after 5-23-83, in taxable years ending on or after such date.

Sec. 1092(d)(7) in *italics* added by section 1261(b), '86 TRA.
Effective date (Sec. 1261(e), '86 TRA).—Applies to taxable years beginning after 12-31-86.

later taxable year, and

        (iii)   such stock *or option* was not held by the taxpayer for 30 days or more after the closing of such options *or the disposition of such stock.*

For purposes of the preceding sentence, the rules of paragraphs (3) (other than subparagraph (B) thereof) and (4) of section 246(c) shall apply in determining the period for which the taxpayer holds the stock.

* * * * * * * * * * *

(d)   Definitions and Special Rules.—For purposes of this section—

* * * * * * * * * * *

    (3)   Special rules for stock.—For purposes of paragraph (1)—

    (A)   In general.—Except as provided in subparagraph (B), the term "personal property" does not include stock. *The preceeding sentence shall not apply to any interest in stock.*

* * * * * * * * * * *

    (7)   Special rules for foreign currency.—

    (A)   Position to include interest in certain debt.—For purposes of paragraph (2), an obligor's interest in a nonfunctional currency denominated debt obligation is treated as a position in the nonfunctional currency.

    (B)   Actively traded requirement.—For purposes of paragraph (1), foreign currency for which there is an active interbank market is presumed to be actively traded.

* * * * * * * * * * *

[For official explanation, see Committee Reports, ¶3889; 4056; 4142.]

〖¶3175〗   CODE SEC. 1201.   ALTERNATIVE TAX FOR CORPORATIONS. [1]

  ≫P-H CAUTION→   There are two versions of Sec. 1201(a). Sec. 1201(a), as amended by section 311(a), '86 TRA follows. For Sec. 1201(a), as amended by 1024(c)(14), '86 TRA see below.

  ▲ [1](a)   *General rule.—If for any taxable year a corporation has a net capital gain and any rate of tax imposed by section 11, 511, or 831(a) (whichever is applicable) exceeds 34 percent (determined without regard to the last sentence of section 11(b)), then, in lieu of any such tax, there is hereby imposed a tax (if such tax is less than the tax imposed by such sections) which shall consist of the sum of—*

    (1)   a tax computed on the taxable income reduced by the amount of the net capital gain, at the rates and in the manner as if this subsection had not been enacted, plus

    (2)   a tax of 34 percent of the net capital gain.

  ≫P-H CAUTION→   There are two versions of Sec. 1201(a). Sec. 1201(a), as amended by section 1024(c)(14), '86 TRA, follows. For Sec. 1201(a), as amended by section 311(a), '86 TRA, see below.

〖Footnote ¶3175〗 ▲ Matter in *italics* in Sec. 1201(a), preceded by a triangle, as amended by section 1024(c)(14), '86 TRA, added by section 311(a), '86 TRA, struck out:

  (1) "(a)   Corporations.—If for any taxable year a corporation has a net gain, then, in lieu of the tax imposed by sections 11, 511, 831(a) or (b), there is hereby imposed a tax (if such tax is less than the tax imposed by such sections) which shall consist of the sum of—

  (1)   a tax computed on the taxable income reduced by the amount of the net capital gain, at the rates and in the manner as if this subsection had not been enacted, plus

  (2)   a tax of 28 percent of the net capital gain."

Effective date (Sec. 311(c) and (d), '86 TRA).—(c) Generally applies to taxable years beginning after 12-31-86.

  (d)   Transitional Rules.—

  (1)   Taxable years which begin in 1986 and end in 1987.—In the case of any taxable year which begins before 1-1-87, and ends on or after such date, paragraph (2) of section 1201(a) of the '54 Code, as in effect on the date before the date of enactment of this Act, shall be applied as if it read as follows:

  (2)   the sum of—

  (A)   28 percent of the lesser of—

  (i)   the net capital gain determined by taking into account only gain or loss which is properly taken into account for the portion of the taxable year before 1-1-87, or

  (ii)   the net capital gain for the taxable year, and

  (B)   34 percent of the excess (if any) of—

  (i)   the net capital gain for the taxable year, over

  (ii)   the amount of the net capital gain taken into account under subparagraph (A).

  (2)   Revocation of elections under section 631(a).—Any election under section 631(a) of the '54 Code made (whether by a corporation or a person other than a corporation) for a taxable year beginning before 1-1-87, may be revoked by the taxpayer for any taxable year ending after 12-31-86. For purposes of determining whether the taxpayer may make a further election under such section, such election (and any revocation under this paragraph) shall not be taken into account.

▲▲ **(a) Corporations.**—If for any taxable year a corporation has a net gain, then, in lieu of the tax imposed by sections 11, 511, [2]*831(a) or (b),* there is hereby imposed a tax (if such tax is less than the tax imposed by such sections) which shall consist of the sum of—

(1) a tax computed on the taxable income reduced by the amount of the net capital gain, at the rates and in the manner as if this subsection had not been enacted, plus

(2) a tax of 28 percent of the net capital gain.

[3]*(b) Cross References.*—

For computation of the alternative tax—

(1) *in the case of life insurance companies, see section 801(a)(2),*

(2) *in the case of regulated investment companies and their shareholders, see section 852(b)(3)(A) and (D), and*

(3) *in the case of real estate investment trusts, see section 857(b)(3)(A).*

[For official explanation, see Committee Reports, ¶3887; 3964.]

〖¶3176〗 CODE SEC. 1202. DEDUCTION FOR CAPITAL GAINS.

[Repealed by section 301(a), '86 TRA].[1]

[For official explanation, see Committee Reports, ¶3885.]

〖¶3177〗 CODE SEC. 1211. LIMITATION ON CAPITAL LOSSES.

* * * * * * * * * * * *

[1]*(b) Other Taxpayers.*—*In the case of a taxpayer other than a corporation, losses from sales or exchanges of capital assets shall be allowed only to the extent of the gains from such sales or exchanges, plus (if such losses exceed such gains) the lower of*—

(1) *$3,000 ($1,500 in the case of a married individual filing a separate return), or*

(2) *the excess of such losses over such gains.*

[For official explanation, see Committee Reports, ¶3885.]

〖¶3178〗 CODE SEC. 1212. CAPITAL LOSS CARRYBACKS AND CARRYOVERS.

〖**Footnote ¶3175 continued**〗

▲▲Matter in *italics* in Sec. 1201(a), preceded by two triangles, added by section 1024(c)(14), '86 TRA, which struck out:

(2) "821(a) or (c) and 831(a)"

Effective date (Sec. 1024(e), '86 TRA).—Applies to taxable years beginning after 12-31-86.

Matter in *italics* in Sec. 1201(b) added by section 311(a), '86 TRA, which struck out:

(3) "(c) [should read (b)] Transitional Rule.—If for any taxable year ending after December 31, 1978, and beginning before January 1, 1980, a corporation has a net capital gain, then subsection (a) shall be applied by substituting for the language of paragraph (2) the following:

(2) (A) a tax of 28 percent of the lesser of—

(i) the net capital gain for the taxable year, or

(ii) the net capital gain taking into account only gain or loss properly taken into account for the portion of the taxable year December 31, 1978, plus

(B) a tax of 30 percent of the excess of—

(i) the net capital gains for the taxable year, over

(ii) the amount of net capital gain taken into account under subparagraph (a).

(b) [should read (c)] Cross References.—

For computation of the alternative tax—

(1) in the case of life insurance companies, see section 801(a)(2).

(2) in the case of regulation investment companies and their shareholders, see section 852(b)(3)(A) and (D); and

(3) in the case of real estate investment trusts, see section 857(b)(3)(A)."

Effective date (Sec. 311(c) and (d), '86 TRA).—See above.

〖**Footnote ¶3176**〗 (1) **Effective date** (Sec. 301(c), '86 TRA).—Applies to taxable years beginning after 12-31-86.

〖**Footnote ¶3177**〗 Matter in *italics* in Sec. 1211(b) added by section 301(b)(10), '86 TRA, which struck out:

(1) "(1) **In general.**—In the case of a taxpayer other than a corporation, losses from sales or exchanges of capital assets shall be allowed only to the extent of the gains from such sales or exchanges, plus (if such losses exceed such gains) whichever of the following is smallest:

(A) the taxable income for the taxable year reduced (but not below zero) by the zero bracket amount,

(B) the applicable amount, or

(C) the sum of—

(i) the excess of the net short-term capital loss over the net long-term capital gain, and

(ii) one-half of the excess of the net long-term capital loss over the net short-term capital gain."

Effective date (Sec. 301(c), '86 TRA).—Applies to taxable years beginning after 12-31-86.

* * * * * * * * * * * * *

(b) Other Taxpayers.—

(1) In general.—If a taxpayer other than a corporation has a net capital loss for any taxable year—

    (A) the excess of the net short-term capital loss over the net long-term capital gain for such year shall be a short-term capital loss in the succeeding taxable year, and

    (B) the excess of the net long-term capital loss over the net short-term capital gain for such year shall be a long-term capital loss in the succeeding taxble year.

[1](2) *Special rule.—For purposes of determining the excess referred to in subparagraph (A) or (B) of paragraph (1), an amount equal to the amount allowed for the taxable year under paragraph (1) or (2) of section 1211(b) shall be treated as a short-term capital gain in such year.*

* * * * * * * * * * * * *

[For official explanation, see Committee Reports, ¶3885.]

【¶3179】 CODE SEC. 1239. GAIN FROM SALE OF DEPRECIABLE PROPERTY BETWEEN CERTAIN RELATED TAXPAYERS.

(a) Treatment of Gain as Ordinary Income.—In the case of a sale or exchange of property, directly or indirectly, between related persons, any gain recognized to the transferor shall be treated as ordinary income if such property is, in the hands of the transferee, of a character which is subject to the allowance for depreciation provided in section 167.

(b) Related Persons.—For purposes of subsection (a), the term "related person" means—

    (1) a person and all entities which are [1]*controlled* entities with respect to such person,

    (2) a taxpayer and any trust in which such taxpayer (or his spouse) is a beneficiary, unless such beneficiary's interest in the trust is a remote contingent interest (within the meaning of section 318(a)(3)(B)(i)).

(c) [2]*Controlled* Entity Defined.—

(1) General rule.—For purposes of this section, the term " [3]*controlled* entity" means, with respect to any person—

    (A) a corporation [4]*more than 50 percent of the* value of the outstanding stock of which is owned (directly or indirectly) by or for such person, [5]

    (B) a partnership [6]*more than 50 percent* of the capital interest or profits interest in which is owned (directly or indirectly) by or for such person, *and* [7]

    (C) any entity which is a related person to such person under paragraph (3), (10), (11), or (12) of section 267(b).

[8](2) *Constructive ownership.—For purposes of this section, ownership shall be deter-*

【Footnote ¶3178】 Matter in *italics* in Sec. 1212(b)(2) added by section 301(b)(11), '86 TRA, which struck out:

(1) "(2) Special rules.—

(A) For purposes of determining the excess referred to in paragraph (1)(A), an amount equal to the amount allowed for the taxable year under section 1211(b)(1)(A), (B), or (C) shall be treated as a short-term capital gain in such year.

(B) For purposes of determining the excess referred to in paragraph (1)(B), an amount equal to the sum of—

(i) the amount allowed for the taxable year under section 1211(b)(1)(A), (B), or (C), and

(ii) the excess of the amount described in clause (i) over the net short-term capital loss (determined without regard to this subsection) for such year, shall be treated as a short-term capital gain in such year."

Effective date (Sec. 301(c), '86 TRA).—Applies to taxable years beginning after 12-31-86.

【Footnote ¶3179】 Matter in *italics* in Sec. 1239(b) and (c) added by section 642(a)(1)(A)—(C), '86 TRA, which struck out:

(1) "80-percent owned"

(2) "80-Percent Owned"

(3) "80-percent owned"

(4) "80 percent or more in"

(5) "and"

(6) "80 percent or more"

(7) "."

(8) "(2) **Constructive ownership.**—For purposes of subparagraphs (A) and (B) of paragraph (1), the principles of section 318 shall apply, except that—

(A) the members of an individual's family shall consist only of such individual and such individual's spouse,

(B) paragraph (2)(C) of section 318(a) shall be applied without regard to the 50-percent limitation contained therein, and

(C) paragraph (3) of section 318(a) shall not apply."

mined in accordance with rules similar to the rules under section 267(c) (other than paragraph (3) thereof).

(d) Employer and Related Employee Association.—For purposes of subsection (a), the term "related person" also includes—

(1) an employer and any person related to the employer (within the meaning of subsection (b)), and

(2) a welfare benefit fund (within the meaning of section 419(e)) which is controlled directly or indirectly by persons referred to in paragraph (1).

(e) Patent Applications Treated as Depreciable Property.—For purposes of this section, a patent application shall be treated as property which, in the hands of the transferee, is of a character which is subject to the allowance for depreciation provided in section 167.

[For official explanation, see Committee Reports, ¶3922.]

【¶3180】 CODE SEC. 1245. GAIN FROM DISPOSITIONS OF CERTAIN DEPRECIABLE PROPERTY.

(a) General Rule.—

(1) Ordinary income.—Except as otherwise provided in this section, if section 1245 property is disposed of,[1] the amount by which the lower of—

(A) the recomputed basis of the property, or

(B) (i) in the case of a sale, exchange, or involuntary conversion, the amount realized, or

(ii) in the case of any other disposition, the fair market value of such property,

exceeds the adjusted basis of such property shall be treated as ordinary income. Such gain shall be recognized notwithstanding any other provision of this subtitle.

[2]*(2) Recomputed basis.—For purposes of this section—*

(A) In general.—The term "recomputed basis" means, with respect to any property, its adjusted basis recomputed by adding thereto all adjustments reflected in such adjusted basis on account of deductions (whether in respect of the same or other property) allowed or allowable to the taxpayer or to any other person for depreciation or amortization.

【Footnote ¶3179 continued】

Effective date (Sec. 642(c), '86 TRA).—(1) Generally applies to sales after the date of enactment of this Act, in taxable years ending after such date.

(2) **Transitional rule for binding contracts.**—The amendments made by this section shall not apply to sales made after 8-14-86, which are made pursuant to a binding contract in effect on 8-14-86, and at all times thereafter.

【Footnote ¶3180】 Matter in *italics* in Sec. 1245(a) added by section 201(d)(11), '86 TRA, which struck out:

(1) "during a taxable year beginning after December 31, 1962, or section 1245 recovery property is disposed of after December, 1980"

(2) "(2) **Recomputed basis.**—For purposes of this section, the term 'recomputed basis' means—

(A) with respect to any property referred to in paragraph (3)(A) or (B), its adjusted basis recomputed by adding thereto all adjustments, attributable to periods after December 31, 1961,

(B) with respect to any property referred to in paragraph (3)(C), its adjusted basis recomputed by adding thereto all adjustments, attributable to periods after June 30, 1963,

(C) with respect to livestock, its adjusted basis recomputed by adding thereto all adjustments attributble to periods after December 31, 1969,

(D) with respect to any property referred to in paragraph (3)(D), its adjusted basis recomputed by adding thereto all adjustments attributable to periods beginning with the first month for which a deduction for amortization is allowed under section 169, 185, 190, 193, or 194, or

(E) with respect to any section 1245 recovery property, the adjusted basis of such property recomputed by adding thereto all adjustments attributable to periods for which a deduction is allowed under section 168(a) (added by the Economic Recovery Tax Act of 1981) with respect to such property,

reflected in such adjustment basis on account of deductions (whether in respect of the same or other property) allowed or allowable to the taxpayer or to any other person for depreciation, or for amortization under section 168, (as in effect before its repeal by the Tax Reform Act of 1976), 169, 179, 184, 185, 188, 190, 193, 194,or (in the case of property described in paragraph (3)(C)) 191 (as in effect before its repeal by the Economic Recovery Tax Act of 1981). For purposes of the preceding sentence, if the taxpayer can establish by adequate records or other sufficient evidence that the amount allowed for depreciation, or for amortization under section 168 (as in effect before its repeal by the Tax Reform Act of 1976), 169, 179, 184, 185, 188, 190, 193, 194, or (in the case of property described in paragraph (3)(C)) 191 (as in effect before its repeal by the Economic Recovery Tax Act of 1981) for any period was less than the amount allowable, the amount added for such period shall be the amount allowed. For purposes of this section, any deduction allowable under section 179, 190, 194, shall be treated as if it were a deduction allowable for amortization."

(B) *Taxpayer may establish amount allowed.*—For purposes of subparagraph (A), if the taxpayer can establish by adequate records or other sufficient evidence that the amount allowed for depreciation or amortization for any period was less than the amount allowable, the amount added for such period shall be the amount allowed.

(C) *Certain deductions treated as amortization.*—Any deduction allowable under section 179, 190, or 193 shall be treated as if it were a deduction allowable for amortization.

(3) **Section 1245 property.**—For purposes of this section, the term "section 1245 property" means any property which is or has been property of a character subject to the allowance for depreciation provided in section 167 (or subject to the allowance of amortization provided in section 185) and is either—

(A) personal property,

(B) other property (not including a building or its structural components) but only if such other property is tangible and has an adjusted basis in which there are reflected adjustments described in paragraph (2) for a period in which such property (or other property)—

(i) was used as an integral part of manufacturing, production, or extraction or of furnishing transportation, communications, electrical energy, gas, water, or sewage disposal services.

(ii) constituted a research facility used in connection with any of the activities referred to in clause (i), or

(iii) constituted a facility used in connection with any of the activities referred to in clause (i) for the bulk storage of fungible commodities (including commodities in a liquid or gaseous state), [3]

[4](C) so much of any real property (other than any property described in subparagraph (B)) which has an adjusted basis in which there are reflected adjustments for amortization under section 169, 179, 188, 190, 193, or 194

[5](D) a single purpose agricultural or horticultural structure (as defined in section 48(p)), or

[6](E) a storage facility (not including a building or its structural components) used in connection with the distribution of petroleum or any primary product of petroleum.

(4) **Special rule for player contracts.—**

(A) *In general.*—For purposes of this section, if a franchise to conduct any sports enterprise is sold or exchanged, and if, in connection with such sale or exchange, there is a transfer of any player contracts, the recomputed basis of such player contracts in the hands of the transferor shall be the adjusted basis of such contracts increased by the greater of—

(i) the previously unrecaptured depreciation with respect to player contracts acquired by the transferor at the time of acquisition of such franchise, or

(ii) the previously unrecaptured depreciation with respect to the player contracts involved in such transfer.

(B) *Previously unrecaptured depreciation with respect to initial contracts.*—For purposes of subparagraph (A)(i), the term "previously unrecaptured depreciation" means the excess (if any) of—

(i) the sum of the deduction allowed or allowable to the taxpayer transferor for the depreciation attributable to periods after December 31, 1975, of any player contracts acquired by him at the time of acquisition of such franchise, plus the deduction allowed or allowable for losses incurred after December 31, 1975, with respect to such player contracts acquired at the time of such acquisition, over

(ii) the aggregate of the amounts described in clause (i) treated as ordinary income by reason of this section with respect to prior disposition of such player contracts acquired upon acquisition of the franchise.

(C) *Previously unrecaptured depreciation with respect to contracts transferred.*—For purposes of subparagraph (A)(ii), the term "previously unrecaptured depreciation" means the amount of any deduction allowed or allowable to the taxpayer transferor for the depreciation of any contracts involved in such transfer.

(D) *Player contract.*—For purposes of this paragraph, the term "player contract" means any contract for the services of an athlete which, in the hands of the

---

[**Footnote ¶3180 continued**]

(3) "(C) an elevator or an escalator,"
(4) "(D)"
(5) "(E)"
(6) "(F)"

taxpayer, is of a character subject to the allowance for depreciation provided in section 167. [7]

* * * * * * * * * * * *

[For official explanation, see Committee Reports, ¶3870.]

[¶3181] CODE SEC. 1246. GAIN ON FOREIGN INVESTMENT COMPANY STOCK

* * * * * * * * * * *

(f) Coordination With Section 1248.—This section shall not apply to any gain to the extent such gain is treated as ordinary income under section 1248 (determined without regard to section 1248(g)(3)).

[1]*(g)* **Information with Respect to Certain Foreign Investment Companies.—**

* * * * * * * * * * *

[For official explanation, see Committee Reports, ¶4045.]

[¶3182] CODE SEC. 1248. GAIN FROM CERTAIN SALES OR EXCHANGES OF STOCK IN CERTAIN FOREIGN CORPORATIONS.

* * * * * * * * * * *

(d) Exclusions From the and Profits.—For purposes of this section, the following amounts shall be excluded, with respect to any United States person, from the earnings and profits of a foreign corporation:

* * * * * * * * * * *

(6) Foreign trade income.—Earnings and profits of the foreign corporation attributable to foreign trade income [1]*of a FSC other than foreign trade income which—*

    (A) is section 923(a)(2) non-exempt income (within the meaning of section 927(d)(6)), or

    (B) would not (but for section 923(a)(4)) be treated as exempt foreign trade income.

[Footnote ¶3180 continued]

(7) "**(5) Section 1245 recovery property.**—For purposes of this section, the term section 1245 recovery property means recovery property (within the meaning of section 168) other than—

(A) 19-year real property and low-income housing which is residential rental property (as defined in section 167(j)(2)(B)),

(B) 19-year real property and low-income housing which is described in section 168(f)(2),

(C) 19-year real property and low-income housing with respect to which an election under subsection (b)(3) of section 168 to use a different recovery percentage is in effect, and

(D) low-income housing (within the meaning of section 168(c)(2)(F)).

If only a portion of a building (or other structure) is section 1245 recovery property, gain from any disposition of such building (or other structure) shall be allocated first to the portion of the building (or other structure) which is section 1245 recovery property (to the extent of the amount which may be treated as ordinary income under this section) and then to the portion of the building or other structure which is not section 1245 recovery property.

(6) **Special rule for qualified leased property.**—In any case in which—

(A) the lessor of qualified leased property (within the meaning of section 168(f)(8)(D)) is treated as the owner of such property for purposes of this subtitle under section 168(f)(8), and

(B) the lessee acquires such property.

the recomputed basis of the lessee under this subsection shall be determined by taking into account any adjustments which would be taken into account in determining the recomputed basis of the lessor."

Effective date (Sec. 203(a)(1), '86 TRA).—(A) Generally, except as provided in this section, section 204, and section 251(d), '86 TRA, the amendments made by section 201 shall apply to property placed in service after 12-31-86, in taxable years ending after such date.

(B) Election to have amendments made by section 201, '86 TRA apply.—A taxpayer may elect (at such time and in such manner as the Secretary of the Treasury or his delegate may prescribe) to have the amendments made by section 201 apply to any property placed in service after 7-31-86, and before 1-1-87.

For additional transitional and special rules, see ¶2007-2008.

[Footnote ¶3181] Matter in *italics* in Sec. 1246(f), and (g) added by section 1235(b), '86 TRA, which struck out:

(1) "(f)"

Effective date (Sec. 1235(h), '86 TRA).—Applies to taxable years of foreign corporations beginning after 12-31-86.

[Footnote ¶3182] Matter in *italics* in Sec. 1248(d)(6) added by section 1876(a)(2), '86 TRA, which struck out:

(1) "(within the meaning of section 923(b)) of a FSC."

Effective date (Sec. 1881, '86 TRA and section 805(a), '84 TRA, as amended by section 1876, '86 TRA).—Generally applies to transactions after 12-31-84, in taxable years ending after such date. For special and transitional rules, see footnote ¶2959.

For purposes of the preceding sentence, the terms "foreign trade income" and "exempt foreign trade income" have the respective meanings given such terms by section 923.

(e) **Sales or Exchanges of Stock in Certain Domestic Corporations.**—[2]*Except as provided in* regulations prescribed by the Secretary, if—

(1) a United States person sells or exchanges stock of a domestic corporation, or receives a distribution from a domestic corporation which, under section 302 or 331, is treated as an exchange of stock, and

(2) such domestic corporation was formed or availed of principally for the holding, directly or indirectly, of stock of one or more foreign corporations,

such sale or exchange shall, for purposes of this section, be treated as a sale or exchange of the stock of the foreign corporation or corporations held by the domestic corporation.

(f) **Certain Section 311, 336 or 337 Transactions.**—*Except as provided in regulations prescribed by the Secretary—*

(1) **In general.**—If—

(A) a domestic corporation satisfies the stock ownership requirements of subsection (a)(2) with respect to a foreign corporation, and

(B) such domestic corporation distributes, sells, or exchanges stock of such foreign corporation in a transaction to which section 311, 336, or 337 applies,

then, notwithstanding any other provision of this subtitle, an amount equal to the excess of the fair market value of such stock over its adjusted basis in the hands of the domestic corporation shall be included in the gross income of the domestic corporation as a dividend to the extent of the earnings and profits of the foreign corporation attributable (under regulations prescribed by the Secretary) to such stock which were accumulated in taxable years of such foreign corporation beginning after December 31, 1962, and during the period or periods the stock was held by such domestic corporation while such foreign corporation was a controlled foreign corporation. For purposes of subsections (c)(2), (d), and (h), a distribution, sale, or exchange of stock to which this subsection applies shall be treated as a sale of stock to which subsection (a) applies.

* * * * * * * * * * * *

(g) **Exceptions.**—This section shall not apply to—

(1) distributions to which section 303 (relating to distributions in redemption of stock to pay death taxes) applies; or[3]

[4](2) any amount to the extent that such amount is, under any other provision of this title, treated as—

(A) a dividend (other than an amount treated as a dividend under subsection (f)),

(B) ordinary income, or

(C) gain from the sale of an asset held for not more than 6 months.

* * * * * * * * * * * *

(i) **Treatment of Certain Indirect Transfers.**—

(1) **In general.**—If any shareholder of a 10-percent corporate shareholder of a foreign corporation exchanges stock of the 10-percent corporate shareholder for stock of

[Footnote ¶3182 continued]

Matter in *italics* in Sec. 1248(e) and (f) added by section 631(d)(2), '86 TRA, which struck out:

(2) "Under"

Effective date (Sec. 633(a), '86 TRA).—(a) Generally applies to—

(1) any distribution in complete liquidation, and any sale or exchange, made by a corporation after 7-31-86, unless such corporation is completely liquidated before 1-1-87,

(2) any transaction described in section 338 '86 Code for which the acquisition date occurs after 12-31-86 and

(3) any distribution (not in complete liquidation) made after 12-31-86.

For special and transitional rules see ¶2023.

Matter in *italics* in Sec. 1248(g)(1) and (2) added by section 1875(g)(1), '86 TRA, which struck out:

(3) "(2) gain realized on exchanges to which section 356 (relating to receipt of additional consideration in certain reorganizations) applies; or"

(4) "(3)"

Effective date (Sec. 1875(g)(2) and (3), '86 TRA).—(2) Applies to exchanges after 3-1-86.

(3) Transitional rule.—An exchange shall be treated as occurring on or before 3-1-86, if—

(A) on or before such date, the taxpayer adopts a plan of reorganization to which section 356 applies, and

(B) such plan or reorganization is implemented and distributions pursuant to such plan are completed on or before the date of enactment of this Act.

the foreign corporation, for purposes of this section, the stock of the foreign corporation received in such exchange shall be treated as if it had been—

    (A)   issued to the 10-percent corporate shareholder, and

    (B)   then distributed by the 10-percent corporate shareholder to such shareholder in redemption [5]*or liquidation (whichever is appropriate)*.

* * * * * * * * * * *

[For official explanation, see Committee Reports, ¶3917; 4189; 4190.]

[¶3183]   CODE SEC. 1250.   GAIN FROM DISPOSITIONS OF CERTAIN DEPRECIABLE REALTY.

* * * * * * * * * * *

  (b) **Additional Depreciation Defined.**—For purposes of this section—

* * * * * * * * * * *

    (3) **Depreciation adjustments.**—The term "depreciation adjustments" means, in respect to any property, all adjustments attributable to periods after December 31, 1963, reflected in the adjusted basis of such property on account of deductions (whether in respect of the same or other property) allowed or allowable to the taxpayer or to any other person for exhaustion, wear and tear, obsolescence, or amortization (other than amortization under section 168 (as in effect before its repeal by this Act), 169, 185 *(as in effect before its repeal by the Tax Reform Act of 1986)*, 188, 190, or 193). For purposes of the preceding sentence, if the taxpayer can establish by adequate records or other sufficient evidence that the amount allowed as a deduction for any period was less than the amount allowable, the amount taken into account for such period shall be the amount allowed.

* * * * * * * * * * *

[For official explanation, see Committee Reports, ¶3875.]

[¶3184]   CODE SEC. 1252.   GAIN FROM DISPOSITION OF FARM LAND.

  (a) **General Rule.**—

    (1) **Ordinary income.**—Except as otherwise provided in this section, if farm land which the taxpayer had held for less than 10 years is disposed of during a taxable year beginning after December 31, 1969, the lower of—

      (A)   the applicable percentage of the aggregate of the deductions allowed under sections 175 (relating to soil and water conservation expenditures) and 182 [1]*(as in*

[Footnote ¶3182 continued]

Matter in *italics* in Sec. 1248(i)(1)(B) added by section 1810(i)(l), '86 TRA, which struck out:

(5) "of his stock"

Effective date (Sec. 1881, '86 TRA and section 133(d), '84 TRA as amended by section 1810(i)(2), '86 TRA).—

(1) Subsection (a).—The amendment made by subsection (a) shall apply to exchanges after the date of the enactment of this Act in taxable years ending after such date.

(2) Subsections (b) and (c).—Except as provided in paragraph (3), the amendments made by subsections (b) and (c) shall apply with respect to transactions to which subsection (a) or (f) of section 1248 of the '54 Code applies occurring after the date of the enactment of this Act.

(3) Election of earlier date for certain transactions.—

(A) In general.—If the appropriate election is made under subparagraph (B), the amendments made by subsection (b) shall apply with respect to transactions to which subsection (a) or (f) of section 1248 of such Code applies occurring after 10-9-75.

(B) Election.—

(i) Subparagraph (A) shall apply with respect to transactions to which subsection (a) of section 1248 of such Code applies if the foreign corporation described in such subsection (or its successor in interest) so elects.

(ii) Subparagraph (A) shall apply with respect to transactions to which subsection (f) of section 1248 of such Code applies if the domestic corporation described in section 1248(f)(1) of such Code (or its successor) so elects.

(iii) Any election under clause (i) or (ii) shall be made not later than the date which is 1 year after 7-18-84. The date of enactment of the Tax Reform Act of 1985 [should read 1984] and shall be made in such manner as the Secretary of the Treasury or his delegate shall prescribe.

[Footnote ¶3183] Matter in *italics* in Sec. 1250(b)(3) added by section 242(b)(2), '86 TRA.

Effective date (Sec. 242(c), '86 TRA).—(1) Generally applies to that portion of the basis of any property which is attributable to expenditures paid or incurred after 12-31-86.

(2) Transitional rule.—The amendments made by this section shall not apply to any expenditure incurred—

(A) pursuant to a binding contract entered into before 3-2-86, or

(B) with respect to any improvement commenced before 3-2-86, but only if not less than the lesser of $1,000,000 or 5 percent of the aggregate cost of such improvement has been incurred or committed before such date.

The preceding sentence shall not apply to any expenditure with respect to an improvement placed in service after 12-31-87.

[Footnote ¶3184] Matter in *italics* in Sec. 1252(a)(1)(A) added by section 402(b)(2), '86 TRA, which struck *effect on the day before the date of the enactment of the Tax Reform Act of 1986)* for expenditures made by the taxpayer after December 31, 1969, with respect to the farm land or

    (B) the excess of—

        (i) the amount realized (in the case of a sale, exchange, or involuntary conversion), or the fair market value of the farm land (in the case of any other disposition), over

        (ii) the adjusted basis of such land,

shall be treated as ordinary inome. Such gain shall be recognized not withstanding any other provision of this subtitle.

* * * * * * * * * * *

[For official explanation, see Committee Reports, ¶3891.]

〔¶3185〕 CODE SEC. 1254. GAIN FROM DISPOSITION OF INTEREST IN OIL, GAS, OR GEOTHERMAL[1], *OR OTHER MINERAL PROPERTIES.*

  (a) *General Rule.—*

    (1) *Ordinary income.—If any section 1254 property is disposed of, the lesser of—*

      (A) The aggregate amount of—

        (i) expenditures which have been deducted by the taxpayer or any person under section 263, 616, or 617 with respect to such property and which, but for such deduction, would have been included in the adjusted basis of such property, and

        (ii) the deductions for depletion under section 611 which reduced the adjusted basis of such property, or

      (B) the excess of—

        (i) in the case of—

〔Footnote ¶3184 continued〕

out:

  (1) "(relating to expenditures by farmers for clearing land)"

  Effective date (Sec. 402(c), '86 TRA).—Applies to amounts paid or incurred after 12-31-85, in taxable years ending after such date.

  〔Footnote ¶3185〕   Matter in *italics* in Sec. 1254(a) added by section 413(a), '86 TRA, which struck out:

  (1) **"PROPERTY.**

  (a) **General Rule.—**

  (1) **Ordinary income.—**If oil, gas, or geothermal property is disposed of after December 31, 1975, the lower of—

  (A) the aggregate amount of expenditures after December 31, 1975, which are allocable to such property and which have been deducted as intangible drilling and development costs under section 263(c) by the taxpayer or any other person and which (but for being so deducted) would be reflected in the adjusted basis of such property, adjusted as provided in paragraph (4), or

  (B) the excess of—

  (i) the amount realized (in the case of a sale, exchange, or involuntary conversion), or the fair market value of the interest (in the case of any other disposition), over

  (ii) the adjusted basis of such interest,

shall be treated as gain which is ordinary income. Such gain shall be recognized notwithstanding any other provision of this subtitle.

  (2) **Disposition of portion of property.—**For purposes of paragraph (1)—

  (A) In the case of the disposition of a portion of an oil, gas, or geothermal property (other than an undivided interest), the entire amount of the aggregate expenditures described in paragraph (1)(A) with respect to such property shall be treated as allocable to such portion to the extent of the amount of the gain to which paragraph (1) applies.

  (B) In the case of the disposition of an undivided interest in an oil, gas, or geothermal property (or a portion thereof), a proportionate part of the expenditures described in paragraph (1)(A) with respect to such property shall be treated as allocable to such undivided interest to the extent of the amount of the gain to which paragraph (1) applies.

This paragraph shall not apply to any expenditures to the extent the taxpayer establishes to the satisfaction of the Secretary that such expenditures do not relate to the portion (or interest therein) disposed of.

  (3) **Oil, gas, or geothermal property.—**The term 'oil, gas, or geothermal property' means any property (within the meaning of section 614) with respect to which any expenditures described in paragraph (1)(A) are properly chargeable.

  (4) **Special rule for paragraph (1)(A).—**In applying paragraph (1)(A), the amount deducted for intangible drilling and development costs and allocable to the interest disposed of shall be reduced by the amount (if any) by which the deduction for depletion under section 611 with respect to such interest would have been increased if such costs incurred (after December 31, 1975) had been charged to capital account rather than deducted."

  Effective date (Sec. 413(c), '86 TRA).—(1) Generally applies to any disposition of property which is placed in service by the taxpayer after 12-31-86.

  (2) Exception for binding contracts.—The amendments made by this section shall not apply to any disposition of property placed in service after 12-31-86, if such property was acquired pursuant to a written contract which was entered into before 9-26-85, and which was binding at all times thereafter.

    (I) a sale, exchange, or involuntary conversion, the amount realized, or

    (II) in the case of any other disposition, the fair market value of such property, over

  (ii) the adjusted basis of such property,

shall be treated as gain which is ordinary income. Such gain shall be recognized notwithstanding any other provision of this subtitle.

  (2) *Disposition of portion of property.*—For purposes of paragraph (1)—

    (A) In the case of the disposition of a portion of section 1254 property (other than an undivided interest), the entire amount of the aggregate expenditures or deductions described in paragraph (1)(A) with respect to such property shall be treated as allocable to such portion to the extent of the amount of the gain to which paragraph (1) applies.

    (B) In the case of the disposition of an undivided interest in a section 1254 property (or a portion thereof), a proportionate part of the expenditures or deductions described in paragraph (1)(A) with respect to such property shall be treated as allocable to such undivided interest to the extent of the amount of the gain to which paragraph (1) applies.

This paragraph shall not apply to any expenditures to the extent the taxpayer establishes to the satisfaction of the Secretary that such expenditures do not relate to the portion (or interest therein) disposed of.

  (3) *Section 1254 property.*—The term "section 1254 property" means any property (within the meaning of section 614) if—

    (A) any expenditures described in paragraph (1)(A) are properly chargeable to such property, or

    (B) the adjusted basis of such property includes adjustments for deductions for depletion under section 611.

(b) Special Rules Under Regulations.—Under regulations prescribed by the Secretary—

  (1) rules similar to the rules of subsection (g) of section 617 and to the rules of subsections (b) and (c) of section 1245 shall be applied for purposes of this section; and

  (2) in the case of the sale or exchange of stock in an S corporation, rules similar to the rules of section 751 shall be applied to that portion of the excess of the amount realized over the adjusted basis of the stock which is attributable to expenditures referred to in subsection (a)(1)(A) of this section.

[For official explanation, see Committee Reports, ¶3898.]

[¶3186] CODE SEC. 1255. GAIN FROM DISPOSITION OF SECTION 126 PROPERTY.

* * * * * * * * * * * * *

(b) Special Rules.—Under regulations prescribed by the Secretary—

  (1) rules similar to the rules applicable under section 1245 shall be applied for purposes of this section, and

  (2) for purposes of [1]170(e), 341(e)(12), [2] and 751(c), amounts treated as ordinary income under this section shall be treated in the same manner as amounts treated as ordinary income under section 1245.

[For official explanation, see Committee Reports, ¶3905; 3917.]

[Footnote ¶3186] Section 511(d)(2)(A) [should read (c)(2)(A)], '86 TRA, struck out from Sec. 1255(b)(2):
(1) "section 163(d),"
Effective date (Sec. 511(e) [should read (d)], '86 TRA.—Applies to taxable years beginning after 12-31-86.

Section 631(e)(14), '86 TRA, struck out from Sec. 1255(b)(2):
(2) "453B(d)(2)"
Effective date (Sec. 633(a) and (c), '86 TRA.—Generally applies to—
  (1) any distribution in complete liquidation, and any sale or exchange made by a corporation after 7-31-86, unless such corporation is completely liquidated before 1-1-87,
  (2) any transaction described in section 338 of the '86 Code for which the acquisition date occurs after 12-31-86, and
  (3) any distribution (not in complete liquidation) made after 12-31-86.
For special and transitional rules see ¶2023.

【¶3187】   CODE SEC. 1256.   SECTION 1256 CONTRACTS MARKED TO MARKET.

*   *   *   *   *   *   *   *   *   *   *   *

(e)   **Mark to Market Not To Apply to Hedging Transactions.—**

*   *   *   *   *   *   *   *   *   *   *   *

(3)   **Special rule for syndicates.—**

*   *   *   *   *   *   *   *   *   *   *   *

(C)   Holding attributable to active management.—For purposes of subparagraph (B), an interest in an entity shall not be treated as held by a limited partner or a limited entrepreneur (within the meaning of section 464(e)(2))—

(i)   for any period if during such period such interest is held by an individual who actively participates at all times during such period in the management of such entity,

(ii)   for any period if during such period such interest is held by the spouse, children, grandchildren, and parents of an individual who actively participates at all times during such period in the management of such entity.

(iii)   if such interest is held by an individual who actively participated in the management of such entity for a period of not less than 5 years,

(iv)   if such interest is held by the estate of an individual who actively participated in the management of such entity or is held by the estate of an individual if with respect to such individual such interest was at any time described in clause (ii), or

(v)   if the Secretary determines (by regulations or otherwise) that such interest should be treated as held by an individual who actively participates in the management of such entity, and that such entity and such interest are not used (or to be used) for tax-avoidance purposes.

For purposes of this subparagraph, a legally adopted child of an individual shall be treated as a child of such individual by blood.[1]

[2]*(4)*   **Limitation on losses from hedging transactions.—**

(A)   In general.—

(i)   Limitation.—Any hedging loss for a taxable year which is allocable to any limited partner or limited entrepreneur (within the meaning of paragraph (3)) shall be allowed only to the extent of the taxable income of such limited partner or entrepreneur for such taxable year attributable to the trade or business in which the hedging transactions were entered into. For purposes of the preceding sentence, taxable income shall be determined by not taking into account items attributable to hedging transactions.

(ii)   Carryover of disallowed loss.—Any hedging loss disallowed under clause (i) shall be treated as a deduction attributable to a hedging transaction allowable in the first succeeding taxable year.

(B)   Exception where economic loss.—Subparagraph (A)(i) shall not apply to any hedging loss to the extent that such loss exceeds the aggregate unrecognized gains from hedging transactions as of the close of the taxable year attributable to the trade or business in which the hedging transactions were entered into.

(C)   Exception for certain hedging transactions.—In the case of any hedging transaction relating to property other than stock or securities, this paragraph shall apply only in the case of a taxpayer described in section 465(a)(1).

(D)   Hedging loss.—The term "hedging loss" means the excess of —

(i)   the deductions allowable under this chapter for the taxable year attributable to hedging transactions (determined without regard to subparagraph (A)(i), over

(ii)   income received or accrued by the taxpayer during such taxable year from such transactions.

(E)   Unrecognized gain.—The term "unrecognized gain" has the meaning given to such term by section 1092(a)(3).

*   *   *   *   *   *   *   *   *   *   *   *

[For official explanation, see Committee Reports, ¶4056.]

【Footnote ¶3187】   Matter in *italics* in Sec. 1256(e)(4) added by section 1261(c) '86 TRA, which struck out:

(1)   "(4)   **Special rule for banks.—**In the case of a bank (as defined in section 581), subparagraph (A) of paragraph (2) shall be applied without regard to clause (i) or (ii) thereof."

(2)   "(5)"

Effective date (Sec. 1261(e)(1), '86 TRA).—Applies to taxable years beginning after 12-31-86.

[¶3188] CODE SEC. 1257. DISPOSITION OF CONVERTED WETLANDS OR HIGHLY ERODIBLE CROPLANDS.

(a) **Gain Treated as Ordinary Income.**—Any gain on the disposition of converted wetland or highly erodible cropland shall be treated as ordinary income. Such gain shall be recognized notwithstanding any other provision of this subtitle, except that this section shall not apply to the extent such gain is recognized as ordinary income under any other provision of this part.

(b) **Loss Treated as Long-Term Capital Loss.**—Any loss recognized on the disposition of converted wetland or highly erodible cropland shall be treated as a long-term capital loss.

(c) **Definitions.**—For purposes of this section—

(1) **Converted wetland.**—The term "converted wetland" means any converted wetland (as defined in section 1201(4) of the Food Security Act of 1985 (16 U.S.C. 3801(4))) held—

(A) by the person whose activities resulted in such land being converted wetland, or

(B) by any other person who at any time used such land for farming purposes.

(2) **Highly erodible cropland.**—The term "highly erodible cropland" means any highly erodible cropland (as defined in section 1201(6) of the Food Security Act of 1985 (16 U.S.C. 3801(6))), if at any time the taxpayer used such land for farming purposes other than the grazing of animals).

(3) **Treatment of successors.**—If any land is converted wetland or highly erodible cropland in the hands of any person, such land shall be treated as converted wetland or highly erodible cropland in the hands of any other person whose adjusted basis in such land is determined (in whole or in part) by reference to the adjusted basis of such land in the hands of such person.

(d) **Special Rules.**—Under regulations prescribed by the Secretary, rules similar to the rules applicable under section 1245 shall apply for purposes of subsection (a). For purposes of sections 170(e), 341(e)(12), and 751(c), amounts treated as ordinary income under subsection (a) shall be treated in the same manner as amounts treated as ordinary income under section 1245.

[For official explanation, see Committee Reports, ¶3892.]

[¶3189] CODE SEC. 1271. TREATMENT OF AMOUNTS RECEIVED ON RETIREMENT OR SALE OR EXCHANGE OF DEBT INSTRUMENTS.

(a) **General Rule.**—For purposes of this title—

* * * * * * * * * * * *

(3) **Certain short-term government obligations.**—

(A) **In general.**—On the sale or exchange of any short-term Government obligation, any gain realized which does not exceed an amount equal to the ratable share of the acquisition discount shall be treated as ordinary income.

[1]*(B) Short-term government obligation.—For purposes of this paragraph, the term "short-term Government obligation" means any obligation of the United States or any of its possessions, or of a State or any political subdivision thereof, or of the District of Columbia, which has a fixed maturity date not more than 1 year from the date of issue. Such term does not include any tax-exempt obligation.*

* * * * * * * * * * * *

[Footnote ¶3188] Sec. 1257 added by section 403(a), '86 TRA.

Effective date (Sec. 403(c), '86 TRA). Applies to dispositions of converted wetland or highly erodible cropland (as defined in section 1257(c) of the '86 Code as added by this section) first used for farming after 3-1-86, in taxable years ending after that date.

[Footnote ¶3189] Matter in *italics* in Sec. 1271(a)(3)(B), (D), (E) and (4) added by section 1803(a)(1)(A), (2) and (3), '86 TRA, which struck out:

(1) "(B) Short-term government obligation.—For purposes of this paragraph, the (short-term Government obligation) means any obligation of the United States or any of its possessions, or of a State or any political subdivision thereof, or of the District of Columbia which is—

(i) issued on a discount basis, and

(ii) payable without interest at a fixed maturity date not more than 1 year from the date of issue.

Such term does not include any tax-exempt obligation."

Effective date (Sec. 1881, '86 TRA and Sec. 44(a), '84 TRA).—Applies to taxable years ending after 7-18-84. For transitional and special rules, see footnote ¶3030.

(D) *Ratable share.*—For purposes of this paragraph, *except as provided in subparagraph (E)*, the ratable share of the acquisition discount is an amount which bears the same ratio to such discount as—

(i) the number of days which the taxpayer held the obligation, bears to

(ii) the number of days after the date the taxpayer acquired the obligation and up to (and including) the date of its maturity.

(E) *Election of accrual on basis of constant interest rate.—At the election of the taxpayer with respect to any obligation, the ratable share of the acquisition discount is the portion of the acquisition discount accruing while the taxpayer held the obligation determined (under regulations prescribed by the Secretary) on the basis of—*

(i) the taxpayer's yield to maturity based on the taxpayer's cost of acquiring the obligation, and

(ii) compounding daily.

An election under this subparagraph, once made with respect to any obligation, shall be irrevocable.

(4) *Certain short-term nongovernment obligations.—*

(A) *In general.—On the sale or exchange of any short-term nongovernment obligation, any gain realized which does not exceed an amount equal to the ratable share of the original issue discount shall be treated as ordinary income.*

(B) *Short-term nongovernment obligation.—For purposes of this paragraph, the term "short-term nongovernment obligation" means any obligation which—*

(i) has a fixed maturity date not more than 1 year from the date of the issue, and

(ii) is not a short-term Government obligation (as defined in paragraph (3)(B) without regard to the last sentence thereof).

(C) *Ratable share.—For purposes of this paragraph, except as provided in subparagraph (D), the ratable share of the original issue discount is an amount which bears the same ratio to such discount as—*

(i) the number of days which the taxpayer held the obligation, bear to

(ii) the number of days after the date of original issue and up to (and including) the date of its maturity.

(D) *Election of accrual on basis of constant interest rate.—At the election of the taxpayer with respect to any obligation, the ratable share of the original issue discount is the portion of the original issue discount accruing while the taxpayer held the obligation determined (under regulations prescribed by the Secretary) on the basis of—*

(i) the yield to maturity based on the issue price of the obligation, and

(ii) compounding daily.

Any election under this subparagraph, once made with respect to any obligation, shall be irrevocable.

* * * * * * * * * * * *

[For official explanation, see Committee Reports, ¶4137.]

[¶3190] CODE SEC. 1272. CURRENT INCLUSION IN INCOME OF ORIGINAL ISSUE DISCOUNT.

* * * * * * * * * * * *

(6) *Determination of daily portions where principal subject to acceleration.—*

(A) *In general.—In the case of any debt instrument to which this paragraph applies, the daily portion of the original issue discount shall be determined by allocating to each day in any accrual period its ratable portion of the excess (if any) of—*

(i) the sum of (I) the present value determined under subparagraph (B) of all remaining payments under the debt instrument as of the close of such period, and (II) the payments during the accrual period of amounts included in the stated redemption price of the debt instrument, over

(ii) the adjusted issue price of such debt instrument at the beginning of such period.

(B) *Determination of present value.—For purposes of subparagraph (A), the present value shall be determined on the basis of—*

(i) the original yield to maturity (determined on the basis of compounding at the close of each accrual period and properly adjusted for the length of the accrual period),

(ii) events which have occurred before the close of the accrual period, and

(iii) a prepayment assumption determined in the manner prescribed by regulations.

    (C) Debt instruments to which paragraph applies.—This paragraph applies to—
        (i) any regular interest in a REMIC or qualified mortgage held by a REMIC, or
        (ii) any other debt instrument if payments under such debt instrument may be accelerated by reason of prepayments of other obligations securing such debt instrument (or, to the extent provided in regulations, by reason of other events).

[1]*(7) Reduction where subsequent holder pays acquisition premium.—*
    (A) Reduction.—For purposes of this subsection, in the case of any purchase after its original issue of a debt instrument to which this subsection applies, the daily portion for any day shall be reduced by an amount equal to the amount which would be the daily portion for such day (without regard to this paragraph) multiplied by the fraction determined under subparagraph (B).
    (B) Determination of fraction.—For purposes of subparagraph (A), the fraction determined under this subparagraph is a fraction—
        (i) the numerator of which is the excess (if any) of—
            (I) the cost of such debt instrument incurred by the purchaser, over
            (II) the issue price of such debt instrument, increased by the portion of original issue discount previously includible in the gross income of any holder (computed without regard to this paragraph), and
        (ii) the denominator of which is the sum of the daily portions for such debt instrument for all days after the date of such purchase and ending on the stated maturity date (computed without regard to this paragraph).

* * * * * * * * * * *

[For official explanation, see Committee Reports, ¶3930.]

[¶3191] CODE SEC. 1273. DETERMINATION OF AMOUNT OF ORIGINAL ISSUE DISCOUNT.

* * * * * * * * * * *

  (b) **Issue Price.**—For purposes of this subpart—

* * * * * * * * * * *

    (3) **Debt instruments issued for property where there is public trading.**—In the case of a debt instrument which is issued for property and which—
    (A) is part of an issue a portion of which is traded on an established securities market, or
    [1]*(B)(i) is issued for stock or securities which are traded on an established securities market, or*
        (ii) to the extent provided in regulations, is issued for property (other than stock or securities) of a kind regularly traded on an established market,
the issue price of such debt instrument shall be the fair market value of such property.

* * * * * * * * * * *

[For official explanation, see Committee Reports, ¶4137.]

[¶3192] CODE SEC. 1274. DETERMINATION OF ISSUE PRICE IN THE CASE OF CERTAIN DEBT INSTRUMENTS ISSUED FOR PROPERTY.

  (c) **Debt Instruments To Which Section Applies.**–

* * * * * * * * * * *

    (3) **Exceptions.**—This section shall not apply to—
    (A) Sales [1]*for $1,000,000 or less* of farms by individuals or small businesses.—

(i) In general.—Any debt instrument arising from the sale or exchange of a farm (within the meaning of section 6420(c)(2))—

(I) by an individual, estate, or testamentary trust,

(II) by a corporation which as of the date of the sale or exchange is a small business corporation (as defined in section 1244(c)(3)), or

(III) by a partnership which as of the date of the sale or exchange meets requirements similar to those of section 1244(c)(3).

* * * * * * * * * * *

[For official explanation, see Committee Reports, ¶4137.]

[¶3193] CODE SEC. 1275. OTHER DEFINITIONS AND SPECIAL RULES.

* * * * * * * * * * *

(a) **Definitions.**—For purposes of this subpart—

[1](5) **Treatment of obligations distributed** [2] *by corporations.*—Any debt obligation of a corporation distributed by such corporation with respect to its stock shall be treated as if it had been issued by such corporation for property.

* * * * * * * * * * *

[For official explanation, see Committee Reports, ¶4138.]

[¶3194] CODE SEC. 1276. DISPOSITION GAIN REPRESENTING ACCRUED MARKET DISCOUNT TREATED AS ORDINARY INCOME.

(a) **Ordinary Income.—**

* * * * * * * * * * *

(3) Treatment of partial principal payments.—

(A) In general.—Any partial principal payment on a market discount bond shall be included in gross income as ordinary income to the extent such payment does not exceed the accrued market discount on such bond.

(B) Adjustment.—If subparagraph (A) applies to any partial principal payment on any market discount bond, for purposes of applying this section to any disposition of (or subsequent partial principal payment on) such bond, the amount of accrued market discount shall be reduced by the amount of such partial principal payment included in gross income under subparagraph (A).

[1](4) **Gain treated as interest for certain purposes.**—Except for purposes of sections 871(a), 881, 1441, 1442, and 6049 (and such other provisions as may be specified in regulations), any amount treated as ordinary income under paragraph (1) shall be treated as interest for purposes of this title.

* * * * * * * * * * *

(c) **Treatment of Nonrecognition Transactions.**—Under regulations prescribed by the Secretary—

* * * * * * * * * * *

(3) **Paragraph (1) to apply to certain distributions by corporations or partnerships.**—For purposes of paragraph (1), if the basis of any market discount bond in the hands of a transferee is determined under section [2] 732(a), or 732(b), such property

---

[Footnote ¶3192 continued]

Effective date (Sec. 1881, '86 TRA and section 44(b)(1) '84 TRA, as amended by section 1803(b), '86 TRA).—Generally applies to sales or exchanges after 12-31-84. For special and transitional rules, see footnote ¶3030.

[Footnote ¶3193] Matter in *italics* in Sec. 1275(a)(5) added by section 1804(f)(2)(A), '86 TRA, which struck out:

(1) "(4)"

(2) "to"

Effective date (Sec. 1881, '86 TRA and Sec. 61(e)(3), '84 TRA.—Applies with respect to distributions declared after 3-15-84, in taxable years ending after such date.

[Footnote ¶3194] Matter in *italics* in Sec. 1276(a)(3) and (4) added by section 1803(a)(13)(A), '86 TRA, which struck out:

(1) "(3)"

Effective date (Sec. 1803(a)(13)(C), '86 TRA).—Applies to obligations acquired after 7-18-84.

Section 631(e)(15), '86 TRA, struck out from Sec. 1276(c)(3):

(2) "334(c),"

Effective date (Sec. 633(a), '86 TRA).—Applies to—(1) any distribution in complete liquidation, and any sale or exchange, made by a corporation after 7-31-86, unless such corporation is completely liquidated before 1-1-87,

(2) any transaction described in section 338 of the '86 Code for which the acquisition date occurs after

shall be treated as transferred basis property in the hands of such transferee.

(d) Special Rules.—Under regulations prescribed by the Secretary—

(1) rules similar to the rules of subsection (b) of section 1245 shall apply for purposes of this section; except that—

(A) paragraph (1) of such subsection shall not apply,[3]

(B) an exchange qualifying under section 354(a), 355(a), or 356(a) (determined without regard to subsection (a) of this section) shall be treated as an exchange described in paragraph (3) of such subsection, and

(C) *paragraph (3) of section 1245(b) shall be applied as if it did not contain a reference to section 351, and*

(2) appropriate adjustments shall be made to this basis of any property to reflect gain recognized under subsection (a).

(e) Section Not to Apply to Market Discount Bonds Issued on or Before Date of Enactment of Section.—This section shall not apply to any market discount bond issued on or before [4]*July 18, 1984.*

[For official explanation, see Committee Reports, ¶3917; 4137 .]

[¶3195] CODE SEC. 1277. DEFERRAL OF INTEREST DEDUCTION ALLOCABLE TO ACCRUED MARKET DISCOUNT.

* * * * * * * * * * * *

(b) Disallowed Deduction Allowed for Later Years.—

(1) Election to take into account in later year where net interest income from bond.—

* * * * * * * * * * * *

(B) Determination of disallowed interest expense.—For purposes of subparagraph (A), the amount of the disallowed interest expense—

(i) shall be determined as of the close of the preceding taxable year, and

(ii) shall not include any amount previously taken into account under subparagraph (A).

(C) Net interest income.—For purposes of [1]*this paragraph,* the term "net interest income" means the excess of the amount determined under paragraph (2) of subsection (c) over the amount determined under paragraph (1) of subsection (c).

(2) Remainder of disallowed interest expense allowed for year of disposition.—

* * * * * * * * * * * *

(C) Disallowed interest expense reduced for amounts previously taken into account under [2]*paragraph (1).*—For purposes of this paragraph, the amount of the disallowed interest expense shall not include any amount previously taken into account under paragraph (1).

* * * * * * * * * * * *

(c) Net Direct Interest Expense.—For purposes of this section, the term "net direct interest expense" means, with respect to any market discount bond, the excess (if any) of—

[Footnote ¶3194 continued]

12-31-86, and

(3) any distribution (not in complete liquidation) made after 12-31-86. For special and transitional rules, see ¶2023.

Matter in *italics* in Sec. 1276(d)(1)(A) and (C) added by section 1803(a)(5), '86 TRA, which struck out:

(3) "and"

Effective date (Sec. 1881, '86 TRA and Sec. 44(c)(1), '84 TRA, as amended by section 1803(b), '86 TRA).— Applies to obligations issued after 7-18-84 in taxable years ending after such date. For special and transitional rules, see footnote ¶3030.

Matter in *italics* in Sec. 1276(e) added by section 1899A(28), '86 TRA, which struck out:

(4) "the date of the enactment of this section"

[Footnote ¶3195] Matter in *italics* in Sec. 1277(b)(1) and (2) added by section 1899A(29) and (30), '86 TRA, which struck out:

(1) "this paragraph"

(2) "paragraph 1"

---

   (1) the amount of interest paid or accrued during the taxable year on indebtedness which is incurred or continued to purchase or carry such bond, over

   (2) the aggregate amount of interest (including original issue discount) includible in gross income for the taxable year with respect to such bond.

In the case of any financial institution [3]*which is a bank (as defined in section 585(a)(2)) or to which section 593 applies,* the determination of whether interest is described in paragraph (1) shall be made under principles similar to the principles of section 291(e)(1)(B)(ii). Under rules similar to the rules of [4]*section 265(a)(5),* short sale expenses shall be treated as interest for purposes of determining net direct interest expense.

  (d) Special Rule for Gain Recognized on Disposition of Market Discount Bonds Issued on or Before Date of Enactment of Section.—In the case of a market discount bond issued on or before [5]*July 18, 1984,* any gain recognized by the taxpayer on any disposition of such bond shall be treated as ordinary income to the extent the amount of such gain does not exceed the amount allowable with respect to such bond under subsection (b)(2) for the taxable year in which such bond is disposed of.

[For official explanation, see Committee Reports, ¶3948; 3949.]

【¶3196】 CODE SEC. 1278. DEFINITIONS AND SPECIAL RULES.

  (a) In General.—For purposes of this part—

* * * * * * * * * * * *

   (C) Treatment of bonds acquired at original issue.—

    (i) In general.—Except as otherwise provided in this subparagraph or in regulations, the term 'market discount bond' shall not include any bond acquired by the taxpayer at its original issue.

    (ii) Treatment of bonds acquired for less than issue price.—Clause (i) shall not apply to any bond if—

     (I) the basis of the taxpayer in such bond is determined under section 1012, and

     (II) such basis is less than the issue price of such bond determined under subpart A of this part.

    (iii) Bonds acquired in certain reorganizations.—Clause (i) shall not apply to any bond issued pursuant to a plan of reorganization (within the meaning of section 368(a)(1)) in exchange for another bond having market discount. Solely for purposes of section 1276, the preceding sentence shall not apply if such other bond was issued on or before July 18, 1984 (the date of the enactment of section 1276) and if the bond issued pursuant to such plan of reorganization has the same term and the same interest rate as such other bond had.

    (iv) Treatment of certain transferred basis property.—For purposes of clause (i), if the adjusted basis of any bond in the hands of the taxpayer is determined by reference to the adjusted basis of such bond in the hands of a person who acquired such bond at its original issue, such bond shall be treated as acquired by the taxpayer at its original issue.

  (4) Revised issue price.—The term "revised issue price" means [1] the sum of—
   (A) the issue price of the bond, and
   (B) the aggregate amount of the original issue discount includible in the gross income of all holders for periods before the acquisition of the bond by the taxpayer (determined without regard to section 1272(a)(6) or (b)(4)).

* * * * * * * * * * * *

【Footnote ¶3195 continued】

Matter in *italics* in Sec. 1277(c) added by section 901(d)(4)(F), '86 TRA, which struck out:
(3) "to which section 585 or"
Effective date (Sec. 901(e), '86 TRA).—Applies to taxable years beginning after 12-31-86.

Matter in *italics* in Sec. 1277(c) added by section 902(e)(2), '86 TRA, which struck out:
(4) "section 265(5)"
Effective date (Sec. 902(f), '86 TRA).—(1) Generally applies to taxable years ending after 12-31-86. For special and transitional rules, see footnote ¶2963.

Matter in *italics* in Sec. 1277(d) added by section 1899A(31), '86 TRA, which struck out:
(5) "the date of the enactment of this section"
【Footnote ¶3196】 Matter in *italics* in Sec. 1278(a)(1)(C) added by section 1803(a)(6), '86 TRA.
Effective date (Sec. 1881, '86 TRA and Sec. 44, '84 TRA, as amended by section 1803(b), '86 TRA).—Applies to taxable years ending 7-18-84. For special and transitional rules, see footnote ¶3030.

Matter in *italics* in Sec. 1278(a)(4) added by section 1899A(32), '86 TRA, which struck out:
(1) "of"

[For official explanation, see Committee Reports, ¶4137.]

[¶3197] **CODE SEC. 1281.   CURRENT INCLUSION IN INCOME OF DISCOUNT ON CERTAIN SHORT-TERM OBLIGATIONS.**

[1]*(a)   General Rule.—In the case of any short-term obligation to which this section applies, for purposes of this title—*

(1)   there shall be included in the gross income of the holder an amount equal to the sum of the daily portions of the acquisition discount for each day during the taxable year on which such holder held such obligation, and

(2)   any interest payable on the obligation (other than interest taken into account in determining the amount of the acquisition discount) shall be included in gross income as it accrues.

(b)   Short-Term Obligations to Which Section Applies.—

(1)   In general.—This section shall apply to any short-term obligation which—

(A)   is held by a taxpayer using an accrual method of accounting.

(B)   is held primarily for sale to customers in the ordinary course of the taxpayer's trade or business,

(C)   is held by a bank (as defined in section 581),

(D)   is held by a regulated investment company or a common trust fund, [2]

(E)   is identified by the taxpayer under section 1256(e)(2) as being part of a hedging transaction[3], *or*

(F)   is a stripped bond or stripped coupon held by the person who stripped the bond or coupon (or by any other person whose basis is determined by reference to the basis in the hands of such person).

* * * * * * * * * * *

[For official explanation, see Committee Reports, ¶4137.]

[¶3198] **CODE SEC. 1282.   DEFERRAL OF INTEREST DEDUCTION ALLOCABLE TO ACCRUED DISCOUNT.**

[1]*(a)   General Rule.—Except as otherwise provided in this section, the net direct interest expense with respect to any short-term obligation shall be allowed as a deduction for the taxable year only to the extent such expense exceeds the sum of—*

(1)   the daily portions of the acquisition discount for each day during the taxable year on which the taxpayer held such obligation, and

(2)   the amount of any interest payable on the obligation (other than interest taken into account in determining the amount of the acquisition discount) which accrues during the taxable year while the taxpayer held such obligation (and is not included in the gross income of the taxpayer for such taxable year by reason of the taxpayer's method of accounting).

* * * * * * * * * * *

[For official explanation, see Committee Reports, ¶4137.]

[Footnote ¶3197]   Matter in *italics* in Sec. 1281(a), added by section 1803(a)(8)(A), '86 TRA, which struck out:

(1)   "**In General.**—In the case of any short-term obligation to which this section applies, for purposes of this title, there shall be included in the gross income of the holder an amount equal to the sum of the daily portions of the acquisition discount for each day during the taxable year on which such holder held such obligation."

Effective date (Section 1803(a)(8)(A), '86 TRA).—Effective with respect to obligations acquired after 9-27-83.

Matter in *italics* in Sec. 1281(b)(1)(D)—(F), added by section 1803(a)(7), '86 TRA, which struck out:

(2)   "or"

(3)   "."

Effective date (Section 1881, '86 TRA, and section 44(a), (d) and (e), '84 TRA as amended by section 1803(b), '86 TRA).—Generally applies to taxable years ending after 7-18-84. For special and transitional rules, see footnote ¶3030.

[Footnote ¶3198]   Matter in *italics* in Sec. 1282(a) added by section 1803(a)(8)(B), '86 TRA, which struck out:

(1)   "(a)   General rule.—Except as otherwise provided in this section, the net direct interest expense with respect to any short-term obligation shall be allowed as a deduction for the taxable year only to the extent that such expense exceeds the sum of the daily portions of the acquisition discount for each day during the taxable year on which the taxpayer held such obligation."

Effective date (Sec. 1881, '86 TRA and Sec. 44(d), '84 TRA).—Applies to obligations acquired after 7-18-84. For exceptions and special rules, see footnote ¶3030.

〖¶3199〗 CODE SEC. 1283.   DEFINITIONS AND SPECIAL RULES.

* * * * * * * * * * * *

(d) Other Special Rules.—

* * * * * * * * * * *

(3) **Coordination with other provisions.**—Section 454(b) and [1]*paragraphs (3) and (4) of sectiion 1271(a)* shall not apply to any short-term obligation to which section 1281 applies.

[For official explanation, see Committee Reports, ¶4137.]

〖¶3200〗 CODE SEC. 1286.   TAX TREATMENT OF STRIPPED BONDS.

* * * * * * * * * * * *

(b) **Tax Treatment of Person Stripping Bond.**—For purposes of this subtitle, if any person strips 1 or more coupons from a bond and after July 1, 1982, disposes of the bond or such coupon—

(1) such person shall include in gross income an amount equal to the [1]*sum of—*

(A) the interest accrued on such bond while held by such person and before the time such coupon or bond was disposed of (to the extent such interest has not theretofore been included in such person's gross income), and

(B) the accrued market discount on such bond determined as of the time such coupon or bond was disposed of (to the extent such discount has not theretofore been included in such person's gross income),

(2) the basis of the bond and coupons shall be increased by [2]*the amount included in gross income under paragraph (1),*

(3) the basis of the bond and coupons immediately before the dispostion (as adjusted pursuant to paragraph (2)) shall be allocated among the items retained by such person and the items disposed of by such person on the basis of their respective fair market values, and

(4) for purposes of subsection (a), such person shall be treated as having purchased on the date of such disposition each such item which he retains for an amount equal to the basis allocated to such item under paragraph (3).

* * * * * * * * * * *

(d) **Special Rules for Tax-Exempt Obligations.**—In the case of any tax-exempt obligation (as defined in section 1275(a)(3)) [3]*from which 1 or more coupons have been stripped—*

(1) the amount of original issue discount determined under subsection (a) with respect to any stripped bond or stripped coupon from such obligation shall be the amount which produces a yield to maturity (as of the purchase date) equal to the lower of—

(A) the coupon rate of interest on such obligation before the separation of coupons, or

(B) the yield to maturity (on the basis of purchase price) of the stripped obligation or coupon,

(2) the amount of original issue discount determined under paragraph (1) shall be taken into account in determining the adjusted basis of the holder under section 1288,

(3) subsection (b)(1) shall not apply, and

〖Footnote ¶3199〗 Matter in *italics* in Sec. 1283(d)(3) added by section 1803(a)(1)(B), '86 TRA, which struck out:

(1) "section 1271(a)(3)"

Effective date (Sec. 1881, '86 TRA and Sec. 44(d), '84 TRA).—Applies to obligations acquired after 7-18-84. For exceptions and special rules, see footnote ¶3030.

〖Footnote ¶3200〗 Matter in *italics* in Sec. 1286(b)(1) and (2) added by section 1803(a)(13)(B), '86 TRA, which struck out:

(1) "interest accrued on such bond while held by such person and before the time that such coupon or bond was disposed of (to the extent such interest has not theretofore been included in such person's gross income),"

(2) "the amount of the accrued interest described in paragraph (1)"

Effective date (Sec. 1803(a)(13)(C), '86 TRA).—Applies to obligations acquired after the date of the enactment of this Act.

Matter in *italics* in Sec. 1286(d) added by section 1879(s)(1), '86 TRA, which struck out:

(3) "—

(1) subsections (a) and (b)(1) shall not apply.

(2) the rules of subsection (b)(4) shall apply for purposes of subsection (c), and

(3) subsection (c) shall be applied without regard to the requirement that the bond be purchased before July 2, 1982."

Effective date (Sec. 1879(s)(2), '86 TRA).—Applies to any purchase or sale of any stripped tax-exempt obligation or stripped coupon from such an obligation after the date of the enactment of this Act.

(4) subsection (b)(2) shall be applied by increasing the basis of the bond or coupon by the interest accrued but not paid before the time such bond or coupon was disposed of (and not previously reflected in basis).

* * * * * * * * * * * *

[For official explanation, see Committee Reports, ¶4137; 4193.]

【¶3201】 **CODE SEC. 1291. INTEREST ON TAX DEFERRAL.**

(a) Treatment of Distributions and Stock Dispositions.—

(1) Distributions.—If a United States person receives an excess distribution in respect of stock in a passive foreign investment company, then—

(A) the amount of the excess distribution shall be allocated ratably to each day in the taxpayer's holding period for the stock,

(B) with respect to such excess distribution, the taxpayer's gross income for the current year shall include (as ordinary income) only the amounts allocated under subparagraph (A) to—

(i) the current year, or

(ii) any period in the taxpayer's holding period before the 1st day of the 1st taxable year of the company for which it was a passive foreign investment company (or, if later, January 1, 1987), and

(C) the tax imposed by this chapter for the current year shall be increased by the deferred tax amount (determined under subsection (c)).

(2) Dispositions.—If the taxpayer disposes of stock in a passive foreign investment company, then the rules of paragraph (1) shall apply to any gain recognized on such disposition in the same manner as if such gain were an excess distribution.

(3) Definitions.—For purposes of this section—

(A) Holding period.—The taxpayer's holding period shall be determined under section 1223; except that, in the case of an excess distribution, such holding period shall be treated as ending on the date of such distribution.

(B) Current year.—The term "current year" means the taxable year in which the excess distribution or disposition occurs.

(4) Coordination with section 904.—Subparagraph (B) of paragraph (1) shall not apply for purposes of section 904.

(5) Section 902 not to apply.—Section 902 shall not apply to any dividend paid by a passive foreign investment company unless such company is a qualified electing fund.

(b) Excess Distribution.—

(1) In general.—For purposes of this section, the term "excess distribution" means any distribution in respect of stock received during any taxable year to the extent such distribution does not exceed its ratable portion of the total excess distribution (if any) for such taxable year.

(2) Total excess distribution.—For purposes of this subsection—

(A) In general.—The term "total excess distribution" means the excess (if any) of—

(i) the amount of the distributions in respect of the stock received by the taxpayer during the taxable year, over

(ii) 125 percent of the average amount received in respect of such stock by the taxpayer during the 3 preceding taxable years (or, if shorter, the portion of the taxpayer's holding period before the taxable year).

(B) No excess for 1st year.—The total excess distributions with respect to any stock shall be zero for the taxable year in which the taxpayer's holding period in such stock begins.

(3) Adjustments.—Under regulations prescribed by the Secretary—

(A) determinations under this subsection shall be made on a share-by-share basis, except that shares with the same holding period may be aggregated,

(B) proper adjustments shall be made for stock splits and stock dividends,

(C) if the taxpayer does not hold the stock during the entire taxable year, distributions received during such year shall be annualized,

---

【Footnote ¶3201】 Sec. 1291 added by section 1235(a), '86 TRA.

Effective date (Sec. 1235(h), '86 TRA).—Applies to taxable years of foreign corporations beginning after 12-31-86.

(D) if the taxpayer's holding period includes periods during which the stock was held by another person, distributions received by such other person shall be taken into account as if received by the taxpayer, and

(E) if the distributions are received in a foreign currency, determinations under this subsection shall be made in such currency and the amount of any excess distribution determined in such currency shall be translated into dollars.

(c) **Deferred Tax Amount.**—For purposes of this section—

(1) **In general.**—The term "deferred tax amount" means, with respect to any distribution or disposition to which subsection (a) applies, an amount equal to the sum of—

(A) the aggregate increases in taxes described in paragraph (2), plus

(B) the aggregate amount of interest (determined in the manner provided under paragraph (3)) on such increases in tax.

(2) **Aggregate increases in taxes.**—For purposes of paragraph (1)(A), the aggregate increases in taxes shall be determined by multiplying each amount allocated under subsection (a)(1)(A) to any taxable year (other than any taxable year referred to in subsection (a)(1)(B)) by the highest rate of tax in effect for such taxable year under section 1 or 11, whichever applies.

(3) **Computation of interest.**—

(A) In general.—The amount of interest referred to in paragraph (1)(B) on any increase determined under paragraph (2) for any taxable year shall be determined for the period—

(i) beginning on the due date for such taxable year, and

(ii) ending on the due date for the taxable year with or within which the distribution or disposition occurs,

by using the rates and method applicable under section 6621 for underpayments of tax for such period.

(B) Due date.—For purposes of this subsection, the term "due date" means the date prescribed by law (determined without regard to extensions) for filing the return of the tax imposed by this chapter for the taxable year.

(d) **Coordination With Subpart B.**—

(1) **In general.**—This section shall not apply with respect to—

(A) any distribution paid by a passive foreign investment company during a taxable year for which such company is a qualified electing fund, and

(B) any disposition of stock in a passive foreign investment company if such company is a qualified electing fund for each of its taxable years—

(i) which begins after December 31, 1986, and for which such company is a passive foreign investment company, and

(ii) which includes any portion of the taxpayer's holding period.

(2) **Election to recognize gain where company becomes qualified electing fund.**—

(A) In general.—If—

(i) a passive foreign investment company becomes a qualified electing fund for a taxable year which begins after December 31, 1986,

(ii) the taxpayer holds stock in such company on the first day of such taxable year, and

(iii) the taxpayer establishes to the satisfaction of the Secretary the fair market value of such stock on such first day,

the taxpayer may elect to recognize gain as if he sold such stock on such first day for such fair market value.

(B) Adjustments.—In the case of any stock to which subparagraph (A) applies—

(i) the adjusted basis of such stock shall be increased by the gain recognized under subparagraph (A), and

(ii) the taxpayer's holding period in such stock shall be treated as beginning on the first day referred to in subparagraph (A).

(e) **Certain Basis, Etc., Rules Made Applicable.**—Rules similar to the rules of subsections (c), (d), (e), and (f) of section 1246 shall apply for purposes of this section; except that—

(1) the reduction under subsection (e) of such section shall be the excess of the basis determined under section 1014 over the adjusted basis of the stock immediately before the decedent's death, and

(2) such a reduction shall not apply in the case of a decedent who was not a non-resident alien at all times during his holding period in the stock.

(f) Nonrecognition Provisions.—To the extent provided in regulations, gain shall be recognized on any disposition of stock in a passive foreign investment company.

[For official explanation, see Committee Reports, ¶4045.]

〔¶3202〕 CODE SEC. 1293. CURRENT TAXATION OF INCOME FROM QUALIFIED ELECTING FUNDS.

(a) Inclusion.—

(1) In general.—Every United States person who owns (or is treated under section 1297(a) as owning) stock of a qualified electing fund at any time during the taxable year of such fund shall include in gross income—

(A) as ordinary income, such shareholder's pro rata share of the ordinary earnings of such fund for such year, and

(B) as long-term capital gain, such shareholder's pro rata share of the net capital gain of such fund for such year.

(2) Year of inclusion.—The inclusion under paragraph (1) shall be for the taxable year of the shareholder in which or with which the taxable year of the fund ends.

(b) Pro Rata Share.—The pro rata share referred to in subsection (a) in the case of any shareholder is the amount which would have been distributed with respect to the shareholder's stock if, on each day during the taxable year of the fund, the fund had distributed to each shareholder a pro rata share of that day's ratable share of the fund's ordinary earnings and net capital gain for such year.

(c) Previously Taxed Amounts Distributed Tax Free.—If the taxpayer establishes to the satisfaction of the Secretary that any amount distributed by a passive foreign investment company is paid out of earnings and profits of the company which were included under subsection (a) in the income of any United States person, such amount shall be treated as a distribution which is not a dividend.

(d) Basis Adjustments.—The basis of the taxpayer's stock in a passive foreign investment company shall be—

(1) increased by any amount which is included in the income of the taxpayer under subsection (a) with respect to such stock, and

(2) decreased by any amount distributed with respect to such stock which is not includible in the income of the taxpayer by reason of subsection (c).

A similar rule shall apply also in the case of any property if by reason of holding such property the taxpayer is treated under section 1297(a) as owning stock in a qualified electing fund.

(e) Ordinary Earnings.—For purposes of this section—

(1) Ordinary earnings.—The term "ordinary earnings" means the excess of the earnings and profits of the qualified electing fund for the taxable year over its net capital gain for such taxable year.

(2) Limitation on net capital gain.—A qualified electing fund's net capital gain for any taxable year shall not exceed its earnings and profits for such taxable year.

(f) Foreign Tax Credit Allowed In the Case of 10-Percent Corporate Shareholder.— For purposes of section 960—

(1) any amount included in the gross income under subsection (a) shall be treated as if it were included under section 951(a), and

(2) any amount excluded from gross income under subsection (c) shall be treated in the same manner as amounts excluded from gross income under section 959.

[For official explanation, see Committee Reports, ¶4045.]

〔¶3203〕 CODE SEC. 1294. ELECTION TO EXTEND TIME FOR PAYMENT OF TAX ON UNDISTRIBUTED EARNINGS.

(a) Extension Allowed by Election.—

〔**Footnote ¶3202**〕 Sec. 1293 added by section 1235(a), '86 TRA.
Effective date (Sec. 1235(h), '86 TRA).—Applies to taxable years of foreign corporations beginning after 12-31-86.
〔**Footnote ¶3203**〕 Sec. 1294 added by section 1235(a), '86 TRA.
Effective date (Sec. 1235(h), '86 TRA).—Applies to taxable years of foreign corporations beginning after 12-31-86.

(1) **In general.**—At the election of the taxpayer, the time for payment of any undistributed PFIC earnings tax liability of the taxpayer for the taxable year shall be extended to the extent and subject to the limitations provided in this section.

(2) **Election not permitted where amounts otherwise includible under section 551 or 951.**—The taxpayer may not make an election under paragraph (1) with respect to the undistributed PFIC earnings tax liability attributable to a qualified electing fund for the taxable year if—

(A) any amount is includible in the gross income of the taxpayer under section 551 with respect to such fund for such taxable year, or

(B) any amount is includible in the gross income of the taxpayer under section 951 with respect to such fund for such taxable year.

(b) **Definitions.**—For purposes of this section—

(1) **Undistributed PFIC earnings tax liability.**—The term "undistributed PFIC earnings tax liability" means, in the case of any taxpayer, the excess of—

(A) the tax imposed by this chapter for the taxable year, over

(B) the tax which would be imposed by this chapter for such year without regard to the inclusion in gross income under section 1293 of the undistributed earnings of a qualified electing fund.

(2) **Undistributed earnings.**—The term "undistributed earnings" means, with respect to any qualified electing fund, the excess (if any) of—

(A) the amount includible in gross income by reason of section 1293(a) for the taxable year, over

(B) the amount not includible in gross income by reason of section 1293(c) for such taxable year.

(c) **Termination of Extension.**—

(1) **Distributions.**—

(A) **In general.**—If a distribution is not includible in gross income for the taxable year by reason of section 1293(c), then the extension under subsection (a) for payment of the undistributed PFIC earnings tax liability with respect to the earnings to which such distribution is attributable shall expire on the last date prescribed by law (determined without regard to extensions) for filing the return of tax for such taxable year.

(B) **Ordering rule.**—For purposes of subparagraph (A), a distribution shall be treated as made from the most recently accumulated earnings and profits.

(2) **Disposition, etc.**—If—

(A) stock in a passive foreign investment company is disposed of during the taxable year, or

(B) a passive foreign investment company ceases to be a qualified electing fund,

all extensions under subsection (a) for payment of undistributed PFIC earnings tax liability attributable to such stock (or, in the case of such a cessation, attributable to any stock in such company) which had not expired before the date of such disposition or cessation shall expire on the last date prescribed by law (determined without regard to extensions) for filing the return of tax for the taxable year in which such disposition or cessation occurs.

(3) **Jeopardy.**—If the Secretary believes that collection of an amount to which an extension under this section relates is in jeopardy, the Secretary shall immediately terminate such extension with respect to such amount, and notice and demand shall be made by him for payment of such amount.

(d) **Election.**—The election under subsection (a) shall be made not later than the time prescribed by law (including extensions) for filing the return of tax imposed by this chapter for the taxable year.

(e) **Authority to Require Bond.**—Section 6165 shall apply to any extension under this section as though the Secretary were extending the time for payment of the tax.

[For official explanation, see Committee Reports, ¶4045.]

〔¶3204〕 CODE SEC. 1295. QUALIFIED ELECTING FUND.

(a) **General Rule.**—For purposes of this part, the term "qualified electing fund" means any passive foreign investment company if—

〔**Footnote ¶3204**〕 Sec. 1295 added by section 1235(a), '86 TRA.

Effective date (Sec. 1235(h), '86 TRA).—Applies to taxable years of foreign corporations beginning after 12-31-86.

(1)   an election under subsection (b) applies to such company for the taxable year, and

(2)   such company complies for such taxable year with such requirements as the Secretary may prescribe for purposes of—

(A)   determining the ordinary earnings and net capital gain of such company for the taxable year,

(B)   ascertaining the ownership of its outstanding stock, and

(C)   otherwise carring out the purposes of this subpart.

(b)   Election.—

(1)   In general.—A passive foreign investment company may make an election under this subsection for any taxable year. Such an election, once made, shall apply to all subsequent taxable years of such company for which such company is a passive foreign investment company unless revoked with the consent of the Secretary.

(2)   When made.—An election under this subsection may be made for any taxable year at any time before the 15th day of the 3rd month of the following taxable year.

[For official explanation, see Committee Reports, ¶4045.]

〖¶3205〗   CODE SEC. 1296.   PASSIVE FOREIGN INVESTMENT COMPANY.

(a)   In General.—For purposes of this part, except as otherwise provided in this subpart from the term "passive foreign investment company" means any foreign corporation if—

(1)   75 percent or more of the gross income of such corporation for the taxable year is passive income, or

(2)   the average percentage of assets (by value) held by such corporation during the taxable year which produce passive income or which are held for the production of passive income is at least 50 percent.

(b)   Passive Income.—For purposes of this section—

(1)   In general.—Except as provided in paragraph (2), the term "passive income" has the meaning given such term by section 904(d)(2)(A) without regard to the exceptions contained in clause (iii) thereof.

(2)   Exception for certain banks and insurance companies.—Except as provided in regulations, the term "passive income" does not include any income—

(A)   derived in the active conduct of a banking business by an institution licensed to do business as a bank in the United States (or, to the extent provided in regulations, by any other corporation), or

(B)   derived in the active conduct of an insurance business by a corporation which would be subject to tax under subchapter L if it were a domestic corporation.

(c)   Look-Thru in the Case of 25-Percent Owned Corporations.—If a foreign corporation owns at least 25 percent (by value) of the stock of another corporation, for purposes of determining whether such foreign corporation is a passive foreign investment company, such foreign corporation shall be treated as if it—

(1)   held its proportionate share of the assets of such other corporation, and

(2)   received directly its proportionate share of the income of such other corporation.

(d)   Section 1247 Corporations.—For purposes of this part, the term "passive foreign investment company" does not include any foreign investment company to which section 1247 applies.

[For official explanation, see Committee Reports, ¶4045.]

〖¶3206〗   CODE SEC. 1297.   SPECIAL RULES.

(a)   Attribution of Ownership.—For purposes of this part—

(1)   Attribution to United States persons.—This subsection—

(A)   shall apply to the extent that the effect is to treat stock of a passive foreign investment company as owned by a United States person, and

---

〖Footnote ¶3205〗   Sec. 1296 added by section 1235(a), '86 TRA.
Effective date (Sec. 1235(h), '86 TRA).—Applies to taxable years of foreign corporations beginning after 12-31-86.
〖Footnote ¶3206〗   Sec. 1297 added by section 1235(a), '86 TRA.
Effective date (Sec. 1235(h), '86 TRA).—Applies to taxable years of foreign corporations beginning after 12-31-86.

(B)   except to the extent provided in regulations, shall not apply to treat stock owned (or treated as owned under this subsection) by a United States person as owned by any other person.

(2) Corporations.—

(A)   In general.—If 50 percent or more in value of the stock of a corporation is owned, directly or indirectly, by or for any person, such person shall be considered as owning the stock owned directly or indirectly by or for such corporation in that proportion which the value of the stock which such person so owns bears to the value of all stock in the corporation.

(B)   50-percent limitation not to apply to PFIC.—For purposes of determining whether a shareholder of a passive foreign investment company is treated as owning stock owned directly or indirectly by or for such company, subparagraph (A) shall be applied without regard to the 50-percent limitation contained therein.

(3) Partnerships, etc.—Stock owned, directly or indirectly, by or for a partnership, estate, or trust shall be considered as being owned proportionately by its partners or beneficiaries.

(4) Successive application.—Stock considered to be owned by a person by reason of the application of paragraph (2) or (3) shall, for purposes of applying such paragraphs, be considered as actually owned by such person.

(b) Other Special Rules.—For purposes of this part—

(1) Time for determination.—Stock held by a taxpayer shall be treated as stock in a passive foreign investment company if, at any time during the holding period of the taxpayer with respect to such stock, such corporation (or any predecessor) was a passive foreign investment corporation which was not a qualified electing fund. The preceding sentence shall not apply if the taxpayer elects to recognize gain (as of the last day of the last taxable year for which the company was a passive foreign investment company) under rules similar to the rules of section 1291(d)(2).

(2) Certain corporations not treated as PFIC's during start-up year.—A corporation shall not be treated as a passive foreign investment company for the first taxable year such corporation has gross income (hereinafter in this paragraph referred to as the "start-up year") if—

(A)   no predecessor of such corporation was a passive foreign investment company,

(B)   it is established to the satisfaction of the Secretary that such corporation will not be a passive foreign investment company for either of the 1st 2 taxable years following the start-up year, and

(C)   such corporation is not a passive foreign investment company for either of the 1st 2 taxable years following the start-up year.

(3) Certain corporations changing businesses.—A corporation shall not be treated as a passive foreign investment company for any taxable year if—

(A)   such corporation (and any predecessor) was not a passive foreign investment corporation for any prior taxable year,

(B)   it is established to the satisfaction of the Secretary that—

(i)   substantially all of the passive income of the corporation for the taxable year is attributable to proceeds from the disposition of 1 or more active trades or businesses, and

(ii)   such corporation will not be a passive foreign investment company for either of the 1st 2 taxable years following such taxable year, and

(C)   such corporation is not a passive foreign investment company for either of such 2 taxable years.

(4) Separate interests treated as separate corporations.—Under regulations prescribed by the Secretary, where necessary to carry out the purposes of this part, separate classes of stock (or other interests) in a corporation shall be treated as interests in separate corporations.

(5) Application of section where stock held by other entity.—Under regulations, in any case in which a United States person is treated as holding stock in a passive foreign investment company by reason of subsection (a), any disposition by the United States person or the person holding such stock which results in the United States person being treated as no longer holding such stock, shall be treated as a disposition by the United States person with respect to stock in the passive foreign investment company.

(6) Dispositions.—If a taxpayer uses any stock in a passive foreign investment company as security for a loan, the taxpayer shall be treated as having disposed of such stock.

(7) Coordination with section 1246.—Section 1246 shall not apply to earnings and profits of any company for any taxable year beginning after December 31, 1986, if such company is a passive foreign investment company for such taxable year.

(c) Regulations.—The Secretary shall prescribe such regulations as may be necessary or appropriate to carry out the purposes of this part.

[For official explanation, see Committee Reports, ¶4045.]

[¶3207] CODE SEC. 1301. LIMITATION ON TAX.
[Repealed by section 141(a), '86 TRA].[1]

[For official explanation, see Committee Reports, ¶3865.]

[¶3208] CODE SEC. 1302. DEFINITION OF AVERAGABLE INCOME; RELATED DEFINITIONS.
[Repealed by section 141(a), '86 TRA].[1]

[For official explanation, see Committee Reports, ¶3865.]

[¶3209] CODE SEC. 1303. ELIGIBLE INDIVIDUALS.
[Repealed by section 141(a), '86 TRA].[1]

[For official explanation, see Committee Reports, ¶3865.]

[¶3210] CODE SEC. 1304. SPECIAL RULES.
[Repealed by section 141(a), '84 TRA].[1]

[For official explanation, see Committee Reports, ¶3865.]

[¶3211] CODE SEC. 1305. REGULATIONS.
[Repealed by section 141(a), '86 TRA].[1]

[For official explanation, see Committee Reports, ¶3865.]

[¶3212] CODE SEC. 1351. TREATMENT OF RECOVERIES OF FOREIGN EXPROPRIATION LOSSES.

(a) Election.—

(1) In general.—This section shall apply only to recovery, by a domestic corporation subject to the tax imposed by section 11 or 801, of a foreign expropriation loss sustained by such corporation and only if such corporation was subject to the tax imposed by section 11 or 801, as the case may be, for the year of the loss and elects to have the provisions of this section apply with respect to such loss.

* * * * * * * * * * * *

(b) Adjustment for Prior Tax Benefits.—

(1) In general.—That part of the amount of a recovery of a foreign expropriation loss to which this section applies which, when added to the aggregate of the amounts of previous recoveries with respect to such loss, does not exceed the allowable deductions in prior taxable years on account of such loss shall be excluded from gross income for the taxable year of the recovery for purposes of computing the tax under this subtitle; but there shall be added to, and assessed and collected as a part of, the tax under this subtitle for all taxable years which would result by decreasing, in an amount equal to such part of the recovery so excluded, the deductions allowable in the prior taxable years on account of such loss. For purposes of this paragraph, if the loss to which the recovery relates was taken into account as a loss from the sale or exchange of a capital asset, the amount of the loss shall be treated as an allowable deduction even though there were no gains against which to allow such loss.

[Footnote ¶3207] (1) **Effective date** (Sec. 151(a), '86 TRA).—Applies to taxable years beginning after 12-31-86.

[Footnote ¶3208] (1) **Effective date** (Sec. 151(a), '86 TRA).—Applies to taxable years beginning after 12-31-86.

[Footnote ¶3209] (1) **Effective date** (Sec. 151(a), '86 TRA).—Applies to taxable years beginning after 12-31-86.

[Footnote ¶3210] (1) **Effective date** (Sec. 151(a), '86 TRA).—Applies to taxable years beginning after 12-31-86.

[Footnote ¶3211] (1) **Effective date** (Sec. 151(a), '86 TRA).—Applies to taxable years beginning after 12-31-86.

(2) **Computation.**—The increase in the tax for each taxable year referred to in paragraph (1) shall be computed in accordance with regulations prescribed by the Secretary. Such regulations shall give effect to previous recoveries of any kind (including recoveries described in section 111, relating to recovery of ¹*tax benefit items*) with respect to any prior taxable year, but shall otherwise treat the tax previously determined for any taxable year in accordance with the principles set forth in section 1314(a) (relating to correction of errors). Subject to the provisions of paragraph (3), all credits, allowable against the tax for any taxable year, and all carryovers and carrybacks affected by so decreasing the allowable deductions, shall be taken into account in computing increase in the tax.

* * * * * * * * * * * *

[For official explanation, see Committee Reports, ¶4146.]

〔¶3213〕 CODE SEC. 1361. S CORPORATION DEFINED.

* * * * * * * * * * * *

(b) **Small Business Corporation.**—

* * * * * * * * * * * *

(2) **Ineligible corporation defined.**—For purposes of paragraph (1), the term "ineligible corporation" means any corporation which is—
    (A) a member of an affiliated group (determined under section 1504 without regard to the exceptions contained in subsection (b) thereof),
    (B) a financial institution ¹*which is a bank (as defined in section 585(a)(2)) or to which section 593 applies,*
    (C) an insurance company subject to tax under subchapter L,
    (D) a corporation to which an election under section 936 applies, or
    (E) a DISC or former DISC.

* * * * * * * * * * * *

(d) **Special Rule for Qualified Subchapter S Trust.**—

* * * * * * * * * * * *

(3) **Qualified subchapter S trust.**—For purposes of this subsection, the term "qualified subchapter S trust" means a trust—
    (A) the terms of which require that—
       (i) during the life of the current income beneficiary, there shall be only 1 income beneficiary of the trust,
       (ii) any corpus distributed during the life of the current income beneficiary may be distributed only to such beneficiary,
       (iii) the income interest of the current income beneficiary in the trust shall terminate on the earlier of such beneficiary's death or the termination of the trust, and
       (iv) upon the termination of the trust during the life of the current income beneficiary, the trust shall distribute all of its assets to such beneficiary, and
    (B) all of the income (within the meaning of section 643(b)) of which is distributed (or required to be distributed) currently to 1 individual who is a citizen or resident of the United States. *A substantially separate and independent share of a trust treated as a separate trust under section 663(c) shall be treated as a separate trust for purposes of this subsection and subsection (c).*

* * * * * * * * * * * *

[For official explanation, see Committee Reports, ¶3948; 4193 .]

〔¶3214〕 CODE SEC. 1363. EFFECT OF ELECTION ON CORPORATION.

(a) **General Rule.**—Except as otherwise provided in this subchapter¹, an S

〔Footnote ¶3212〕 Matter in *italics* in Sec. 1351(d)(2) added by section 1812(a)(4), '86 TRA, which struck out:
(1) "bad debts, etc."
Effective date (Sec. 1881, '86 TRA and Sec. 171(c), '84 TRA).—Applies to amounts recovered after 12-31-83, in taxable years ending after such date.
〔Footnote ¶3213〕 Matter in *italics* in Sec. 1361(b)(2)(B) added by section 901(d)(4)(G), '86 TRA, which struck out:
(1) "to which section 585 or 593 applies"
Effective date (Sec. 901(e), '86 TRA).—Applies to taxable years beginning after 12-31-86.

Matter in *italics* in Sec. 1361(d)(3) added by section 1879(m)(1)(A), '86 TRA.
Effective date (Sec. 1879(m)(2), '86 TRA).—Applies to taxable years beginning after 12-31-82.
〔Footnote ¶3214〕 Section 701(e)(4)(J), '86 TRA, struck out from Sec. 1363(a):

corporation shall not be subject to the taxes imposed by this chapter.

* * * * * * * * * * * *

(2) the deductions referred to in section 703(a)(2) shall not be allowed to the corporation

(3) section 248 shall apply, and

(4) section 291 shall apply if the S corporation (or any predecessor) was a C corporation for any of the 3 immediately preceding taxable years.

(c) Elections of the S Corporation.—

(1) In general.—Except as provided in paragraph (2), any election affecting the computation of items derived from an S corporation shall be made by the corporation.

(2) Exceptions.—In the case of an S corporation, elections under the following provisions shall be made by each shareholder separately—[2]

[3]*(A)* section 617 (relating to deduction and recapture of certain mining exploration expenditures), and

[4]*(B)* section 901 (relating to taxes of foreign countries and possessions of the United States).

(d) Distribution of Appreciated Property.—Except as provided in subsection (e), if—

(1) an S corporation makes a distribution of property (other than an obligation of such corporation) with respect to its stock, and

(2) the fair market value of such property exceeds its adjusted basis in the hands of the S corporation,

then, notwithstanding any other provision of this subtitle, gain shall be recognized to the S corporation on the distribution in the same manner as if it had sold such property to the distributee at its fair market value.

[5]*(e) Subsection (d) Not to Apply to Reorganizations, Etc.*—*Subsection (d) shall not apply to any distribution to the extent it consists of property permitted by section 354, 355, or 356 to be received without the recognition of gain.*

[For official explanation, see Committee Reports, ¶3905; 3918; 3931.]

[¶3215] CODE SEC. 1366. PASS-THRU OF ITEMS TO SHAREHOLDERS.

* * * * * * * * * * * *

(f) Special Rules.—

* * * * * * * * * * * *

[1]*(2) Reduction in pass-thru for tax imposed on built-in gains.*—*If any tax is im-*

〖Footnote ¶3214 continued〗

(1) "and in section 58(d)"

Effective date (Sec. 701(f)(1), '86 TRA).—Applies to taxable years beginning after 12-31-86. For transitional and special rules, see ¶2879.

Matter in *italics* in Sec. 1363(c)(2) added by section 511(d) [should be (e)] (2)(C), '86 TRA, which struck out:

(2) "(A) section 163(d) (relating to limitation on interest on investment indebtedness)."

(3) "(B)"

(4) "(C)"

Effective date (Sec. 511(e) [should be (d)], '86 TRA).—Applies to taxable years beginning after 12-31-86.

Matter in *italics* in Sec. 3163(e) added by section 632(b), '86 TRA, which struck out:

(5) **"(e) Subsection (d) Not To Apply to Complete Liquidation and Reorganizations.**—Subsection (d) shall not apply to any distribution—

(1) of property in complete liquidation of the corporation, or

(2) to the extent it consists of property permitted by section 354, 355, or 356 to be received without the recognition of gain."

Effective date (Sec. 633(a), '86 TRA).—Applies to—

(1) any distribution in complete liquidation and any sale or exchange, made by a corporation after 7-31-86, unless such corporation is completely liquidated before 1-1-87,

(2) any transaction described in section 338 of the '86 Code for which the acquisition date occurs after 12-31-86, and

(3) any distribution (not in complete liquidation) made after 12-31-86.

For transitional and special rules, see ¶2023.

〖¶Footnote ¶3215〗 Matter in *italics* in Sec. 1366(f)(2) added by section 632(c)(2), '86 TRA, which struck out:

(1) (2) **Reduction in pass-thru for tax imposed on capital gain.**—If any tax is imposed under section 56 or 1374 for any taxable year on an S corporation, for purposes of subsection (a)—

posed under section 1374 for any taxable year on an S corporation, for purposes of sub-section (a), the amount of each recognized built-in gain (as defined in section 1374(d)(2)) for such taxable year shall be reduced by its proportionate share of such tax.

* * * * * * * * * * *

[For official explanation, see Committee Reports, ¶3918; 3931.]

[¶3216] CODE SEC. 1368. DISTRIBUTIONS.

* * * * * * * * * * *

(e) **Definitions and Special Rules.**—For purposes of this section—

    (1) **Accumulated adjustments account.—**

        (A) In general.—Except as provided in subparagraph (B), the term "accumu-lated adjustments account" means an account of the S corporation which is ad-justed for the S period in a manner similar to the adjustments under section 1367 (except that no adjustment shall be made for income (and related expenses) which is exempt from tax under this title and the phrase "(but not below zero)" shall be disregarded in section 1367(b)(2)(A)) [1]*and no adjustment shall be made for Federal taxes attributable to any taxable year in which the corporation was a C corporation.*

* * * * * * * * * * *

[For official explanation, see Committee Reports, ¶4193.]

[¶3217] CODE SEC. 1371. COORDINATION WITH SUBCHAPTER C.

* * * * * * * * * * *

(e) **Cash Distributions During Post-Termination Transition Period.—**

    (1) **In general.**—Any distribution of money by a corporation with respect to its stock during a post-termination transition period shall be applied against and reduce the adjusted basis of the stock, to the extent that the amount of the distribution does not exceed the accumulated adjustments account. *(within the meaning of section 1368(e)).*

    (2) **Election to distribute earnings first.**—An S corporation may elect to have par-agraph (1) not apply to all distributions made during a post-termination transition period described in section 1377(b)(1)(A). Such election shall not be effective unless all shareholders of the S corporation to whom distributions are made by the S corpora-tion during such post-termination transition period consent to such election[1].

[¶3218] CODE SEC. 1374. TAX IMPOSED ON CERTAIN [1]*BUILT-IN GAINS.*

[¶Footnote ¶3215 continued]

  (A) the amount of the corporation's long-term capital gains for the taxable year shall be reduced by the amount of such tax, and

  (B) if the amount of such tax exceeds the amount of such long-term capital gains, the corporation's gains from sales or exchanges of property described in section 1231 shall be reduced by the amount of such excess.

For purposes of the preceding sentence, the term "long-term capital gain" shall not include any gain from the sale or exchange of property described in section 1231.

  Effective date (Sec. 633(b), '86 TRA).—Applies to—taxable years beginning after 12-31-86, but only in cases where the 1st taxable year for which the corporation is an S corporation is pursuant to an election made after 12-31-86.

  Section 701(e)(4)(K), '86 TRA, also amended Sec. 1366(f)(2) by striking out "56 or".

  Effective date (Sec. 701(f), '86 TRA).—Generally applies to taxable years beginning after 12-31-86. For excep-tions and other special rules, see footnote ¶2879.

  [Footnote ¶3216] Matter in *italics* in Sec. 1368(e)(1)(A) added by section 1879(m)(1)(B), '86 TRA, which struck out:

  (1) "."

  Effective date (Sec. 1879(m)(2), '86 TRA).—Applies to taxable years beginning after 12-31-82.

  [Footnote ¶3217] Matter in *italics* in Sec. 1371(e)(1), (2) added by section 1899A(33), (34), '86 TRA, which struck out:

  (1) "(within the meaning of section 1368(e))"

  [Footnote ¶3218] Matter in *italics* in Sec. 1374 added by section 632(a), '86 TRA, which struck out:

  (1) "CAPITAL GAINS.

  (a) General Rule.—If for a taxable year of an S corporation—

  (1) the net capital gain of such corporation exceeds $25,000, and exceeds 50 percent of its taxable income for such year, and

  (2) the taxable income of such corporation for such year exceeds $25,000,

there is hereby imposed a tax (computed under subsection (b)) on the income of such corporation.

  (b) **Amount of Tax.**—The tax imposed by subsection (a) shall be the lower of—

  (1) an amount equal to the tax, determined as provided in section 1201(a), on the amount by which the net

---

⟦Footnote ¶3218 continued⟧

capital gain of the corporation for the taxable year exceeds $25,000, or

(2) an amount equal to the tax which would be imposed by section 11 on the taxable income of the corporation for the taxable year if the corporation were not an S corporation.

No credit shall be allowable under part IV of subchapter A of this chapter (other than under section 34) against the tax imposed by subsection (a).

(c) Exceptions.—

(1) **In general.—**Subsection (a) shall not apply to an S corporation for any taxable year if the election under section 1362(a) which is in effect with respect to such corporation for such taxable year has been in effect for the 3 immediately preceding taxable years.

(2) **New corporations.—**Subsection (a) shall not apply to an S corporation if—

(A) it has been in existence for less than 4 taxable years, and

(B) an election under section 1362(a) has been in effect with respect to such corporation for each of its taxable years.

To the extent provided in regulations, an S corporation and any predecesor corporation shall be treated as 1 corporation for purposes of this paragraph and paragraph (1).

(3) **Property with substituted basis.—**If—

(A) but for paragraph (1) or (2), subsection (a) would apply for the taxable year,

(B) any long-term capital gain is attributable to property acquired by the S corporation during the period beginning 3 years before the first day of the taxable year and ending on the last day of the taxable year, and

(C) the basis of such property is determined in whole or in part by reference to the basis of any property in the hands of another corporation which was not an S corporation throughout all of the period described in subparagraph (B) before the transfer by such other corporation and during which such other corporation was in existence, then subsection (a) shall apply for the taxable year, but the amount of the tax determined under subsection (b) shall not exceed a tax, determined as provided in section 1201(a), on the net capital gain attributable to property acquired as provided in subparagraph (B) and having a basis described in subparagraph (C).

(4) **Treatment of certain gains of options and commodities dealers.—**

(A) Exclusion of certain capital gains.—For purposes of this section, the net capital gain of any options dealer or commodities dealer shall be determined by not taking into account any gain or loss (in the normal course of the taxpayer's activity of dealing in or trading section 1256 contracts) from any section 1256 contract or property related to such a contract.

(B) Definitions.—For purposes of this paragraph—

(i) Options dealer.—The term 'options dealer' has the meaning given to such term by section 1256(g)(8).

(ii) Commodities dealer.—The term 'commodities dealer' means a person who is actively engaged in trading section 1256 contracts and is registered with a domestic board of trade which is designated as a contract market by the Commodities Futures Trading Commission.

(iii) Section 1256 contracts.—The term 'section 1256 contracts' has the meaning given to such term by section 1256(b).

(d) Determination of Taxable Income.—For purposes of this section, taxable income of the corporation shall be determined under section 63(a) without regard to—

(1) the deduction allowed by section 172 (relating to net operating loss deduction), and

(2) the deductions allowed by part VIII of subchapter B (other than the deduction allowed by section 248, relating to organization expenditures)."

Effective date (Sec. 633, '86 TRA).—Generally applies to—

(1) any distribution in complete liquidation, and any sale or exchange, made by a corporation after 7-31-86, unless such corporation is completely liquidated before 1-1-87,

(2) any transaction described in section 338 of the 86 Code for which the acquisition date occurs after 12-31-86, and

(a) General Rule.—*If for any taxable year beginning in the recognition period an S corporation has a recognized built-in gain, there is hereby imposed a tax (computed under subsection (b)) on the income of such corporation for such taxable year.*

(b) Amount of Tax.—

(1) In general.—*The tax imposed by subsection (a) shall be a tax computed by applying the highest rate of tax specified in section 11(b) to the lesser of*—

(A) the recognized built-in gains of the S corporation for the taxable year, or

(B) the amount which would be the taxable income of the corporation for such taxable year if such corporation were not an S corporation.

(2) Net operating loss carryforwards from C years allowed.—*Notwithstanding section 1371(b)(1), any net operating loss carryforward arising in a taxable year for which the corporation was a C corporation shall be allowed as a deduction against the lesser of the amounts referred to in subparagraph (A) or (B) of paragraph (1). For purposes of determining the amount of any such loss which may be carried to subsequent taxable years, the lesser of the amounts referred to in subparagraph (A) or (B) of paragraph (1) shall be treated as taxable income.*

(3) Credits.—

(A) In general.—*Except as provided in subparagraph (B), no credit shall be allowable under part IV of subchapter A of this chapter (other than under section 34) against the tax imposed by subsection (a).*

(B) Business credit carryforwards from C years allowed.—*Notwithstanding section 1371(b)(1), any business credit carryforward under section 39 arising in a taxable year for which the corporation was a C corporation shall be allowed as a credit against the tax imposed by subsection (a) in the same manner as if it were imposed by section 11.*

(4) Coordination with section 1201(a).—*For purposes of section 1201(a)*—

(A) the tax imposed by subsection (a) shall be treated as if it were imposed by section 11, and

(B) the lower of the amounts specified in subparagraphs (A) and (B) of paragraph (1) shall be treated as the taxable income.

(c) Limitations.—

(1) Corporations which were always S corporations.—*Subsection (a) shall not apply to any corporation if an election under section 1362(a) has been in effect with respect to such corporation for each of its taxable years. Except as provided in regulations, an S corporation and any predecessor corporation shall be treated as 1 corporation for purposes of the preceding sentence.*

(2) Limitation on amount of recognized built-in gains.—*The amount of the recognized built-in gains taken into account under this section for any taxable year shall not exceed the excess (if any) of*—

(A) the net unrealized built-in gain, over

(B) the recognized built-in gains for prior taxable years beginning in the recognition period.

(d) Definitions and Special Rules.—*For purposes of this section*—

(1) Net unrealized built-in gain.—*The term 'net unrealized built-in gain' means the amount (if any) by which*—

(A) the fair market value of the assets of the S corporation as of the beginning of its 1st taxable year for which an election under section 1362(a) is in effect, exceeds

(B) the aggregate adjusted bases of such assets at such time.

(2) Recognized built-in gain.—*The term 'recognized built-in gain' means any gain recognized during the recognition period on the disposition of any asset except to the extent that the S corporation establishes that*—

(A) such asset was not held by the S corporation as of the beginning of the 1st taxable year referred to in paragraph (1), or

(B) such gain exceeds the excess (if any) of—

【Footnote ¶3218 】

(3) any distribution (not in complete liquidation) made after 12-31-86.
For exceptions and special rules, see ¶2023.

(i) the fair market value of such asset as of the beginning of such 1st taxable year, over

(ii) the adjusted basis of the asset as of such time.

(3) **Recognition period.**—The term 'recognition period' means the 10-year period beginning with the 1st day of the 1st taxable year for which the corporation was an S corporation.

(4) **Taxable income.**—Taxable income of the corporation shall be determined under section 63(a)—

(A) without regard to the deductions allowed by part VIII of subchapter B (other than the deduction allowed by section 248, relating to organization expenditures), and

(B) without regard to the deduction under section 172.

[For official explanation, see Committee Reports, ¶3918.]

[¶3219] CODE SEC. 1375. TAX IMPOSED WHEN PASSIVE INVESTMENT INCOME OF CORPORATION HAVING SUBCHAPTER C EARNINGS AND PROFITS EXCEEDS 25 PERCENT OF GROSS RECEIPTS.

* * * * * * * * * * *

(b) **Definitions.**—For purposes of this section—

(1) **Excess net passive income.**—

(A) In general.—Except as provided in subparagraph (B), the term "excess net passive income" means an amount which bears the same ratio to the net passive income for the taxable year as—

(i) the amount by which the passive investment income for the taxable year exceeds 25 percent of the gross receipts for the taxable year, bears to

(ii) the passive investment income for the taxable year.

(B) Limitation.—The amount of the excess net passive income for any taxable year shall not exceed the corporation's taxable income for the taxable year (determined in accordance with section [1]*1374(d)(4))*.

(2) **Net passive income.**—The term "net passive income" means—

(A) passive investment income, reduced by

(B) the deductions allowable under this chapter which are directly connected with the production of such income (other than deductions allowable under section 172 and part VIII of subchapter B).

(3) **Passive investment income, etc.**—The terms "subchapter C earnings and profits", "passive investment income", and "gross receipts" shall have the same respective meanings as when used in paragraph (3) of section 1362(d).

(c) **Special Rules.**—

(1) **Disallowance of credit.**—No credit shall be allowed under part IV of subchapter A of this chapter (other than section 34) against the tax imposed by subsection (a).

* * * * * * * * * * *

[For official explanation, see Committee Reports, ¶3918.]

[¶3220] CODE SEC. 1378. TAXABLE YEAR OF S CORPORATION.

(a) **General Rule.**—[1]*For purposes of this subtitle, the taxable year of an S corporation shall be a permitted year.*

(b) **Permitted Year Defined.**—For purposes of this section, the term "permitted year" means a taxable year which—

(1) is a year ending December 31, or

(2) is any other accounting period for which the corporation establishes a business purpose to the satisfaction of the Secretary.

[Footnote ¶3219] Matter in *italics* in Sec. 1375(b)(1)(B) added by section 632(c)(3), '86 TRA, which struck out:

(1) "1374(d)"

Effective date (Sec. 633, '86 TRA).—Applies to—(1) any distribution in complete liquidation, and any sale or exchange, made by a corporation after 7-31-86, unless such corporation is completely liquidated before 1-1-87,

(2) any transaction described in section 338 of the '86 Code for which the acquisition date occurs after 12-31-86, and

(3) any distribution (not in complete liquidation) made after 12-31-86.

For transitional and special rules, see ¶2023.

[Footnote ¶3220] Matter in *italics* in Sec. 1378 added by section 806(b), '86 TRA, which struck out:

(1) "For purposes of this subtitle—

(1) an S corporation shall not change its taxable year to any accounting period other than a permitted year, and

(2) no corporation may make an election under section 1362(a) for any taxable year unless such taxable year is a permitted year."

For purposes of paragraph (2), any deferral of income to shareholders shall not be treated as a business purpose.[2]

[For official explanation, see Committee Reports, ¶3940.]

[¶3221] CODE SEC. 1391. DEFINITIONS.

[Repealed by section 1303(a), '86 TRA].[1]

[For official explanation, see Committee Reports, ¶4059.]

[¶3222] CODE SEC. 1392. ELECTION BY GSOC.

[Repealed by section 1303(a), '86 TRA].[1]

[For official explanation, see Committee Reports, ¶4059.]

[¶3223] CODE SEC. 1393. GSOC TAXABLE INCOME TAXED TO SHARE-HOLDERS.

[Repealed by section 1303(a), '86 TRA].[1]

[For official explanation, see Committee Reports, ¶4059.]

[¶3224] CODE SEC. 1394. RULES APPLICABLE TO DISTRIBUTIONS OF ELECTING GSOC.

[Repealed by section 1303(a), '86 TRA].[1]

[Footnote ¶3220 continued]

(2) **"(c) Existing S Corporations Required to Use Permitted Year After 50-Percent Shift in Ownership.—**

(1) **In general.**—A corporation which is an S corporation for a taxable year which includes December 31, 1982 (or which is an S corporation for a taxable year beginning during 1983 by reason of an election made on or before October 19, 1982), shall not be treated as an S corporation for any subsequent taxable year beginning after the first day on which more than 50 percent of the stock is newly owned stock unless such subsequent taxable year is a permitted year.

(2) **Newly owned stock.**—For purposes of paragraph (1), the stock held by any person on any day shall be treated as newly owned stock to the extent that—

(A) the percentage of the stock of such corporation owned by such person on such day, exceeds

(B) the percentage of the stock of such corporation owned by such person on December 31, 1982.

(3) **Stock acquired by reason of death, gift from family member, etc.—**

(A) In general.—For purposes of paragraph (2), if—

(i) a person acquired stock in the corporation after December 31, 1982, and

(ii) such stock was acquired by such person—

(I) by reason of the death of a qualified transferor,

(II) by reason of a gift from a qualified transferor who is a member of such person's family, or

(III) by reason of a qualified buy-sell agreement from a qualified transferor (or his estate) who was a member of such person's family,

then such stock shall be treated as held on December 31, 1982, by the person described in clause (i),

(B) Qualified transferor.—For purposes of subparagraph (A), the term 'qualified transferor' means a person—

(i) who (or whose estate) held the stock in the corporation (or predecessor stock) on December 31, 1982, or

(ii) who acquired the stock in an acquisition which meets the requirements of subparagraph (A).

(C) Family.—For purposes of subparagraph (A), the term 'family' has the meaning given such term by section 267(c)(4).

(D) Qualified buy-sell agreement.—For purposes of subparagraph (A), the term 'qualified buy-sell agreement' means any agreement which—

(i) has been continuously in existence since September 28, 1982, and

(ii) provides that on the death of any party to such agreement, the stock in the S corporation held by such party will be sold to surviving parties to such agreement who were parties to such agreement on September 28, 1982."

Effective date (Sec. 806(e), '86 TRA).—(1) Generally applies to taxable years beginning after 12-31-86. (2) Change in accounting period.—In the case of any taxpayer required by the amendments made by this section to change its accounting period for any taxable year—

(A) such change shall be treated as initiated by the taxpayer,

(B) such change shall be treated as having been made with the consent of the Secretary, and

(C) with respect to any partner or shareholder of an S corporation which is required to include the items from more than 1 taxable year of the partnership or S corporation in any 1 taxable year, income in excess of expenses of such partnership or corporation for the short taxable year required by such amendments shall be taken into account ratably in each of the first 4 taxable years (including such short taxable year) beginning after 12-31-86, unless such partner or shareholder elects to include all such income in the short taxable year.

Subparagraph (C) shall apply to a shareholder of an S corporation only if such corporation was an S corporation for a taxable year beginning in 1986.

[Footnote ¶3221] (1) **Effective date** (Sec. 1311(d), '86 TRA).—Shall take effect on the date of the enactment of this Act. For special and transitional rules, see 2071—2077.

[Footnote ¶3222] (1) **Effective date** (Sec. 1311(d), '86 TRA).—Shall take effect on the date of the enactment of this Act. For special and transitional rules, see ¶2071—2077.

[Footnote ¶3223] (1) **Effective date** (Sec. 1311(d), '86 TRA).—Takes effect on the date of the enactment of this Act. For special and transitional rules, see ¶2071—2077.

[Footnote ¶3224] (1) **Effective date** (Sec. 1311(d), '86 TRA).—Takes effect on the date of the enactment of

[For official explanation, see Committee Reports, ¶4059.]

【¶3225】 CODE SEC. 1395. ADJUSTMENT TO BASIS OF STOCK OF SHARE-HOLDERS.

[Repealed by section 1303(a), '86 TRA].[1]

[For official explanation, see Committee Reports, ¶4059.]

【¶3226】 CODE SEC. 1396. MINIMUM DISTRIBUTIONS.

[Repealed by section 1303(a), '86 TRA].[1]

[For official explanation, see Committee Reports, ¶4059.]

【¶3227】 CODE SEC. 1397. SPECIAL RULES APPLICABLE TO AN ELECTING GSOC.

[Repealed by section 1303(a), '86 TRA].[1]

【¶3228】 CODE SEC. 1398. RULES RELATING TO INDIVIDUALS' TITLE 11 CASES.

(c) **Computation and Payment of Tax;** [1]*Basic Standard Deduction.—*

* * * * * * * * * * *

[2]*(3) Basic standard deduction.—In the case of an estate which does not itemize deductions, the basic standard deduction for the estate for the taxable year shall be the same as for a married individual filing a separate return for such year.*

* * * * * * * * * * *

(d) **Taxable Year of Debtors.—**

(1) **General rule.—**Except as provided in paragraph (2), the taxable year of the debtor shall be determined without regard to the case under title 11 of the United States Code to which this section applies.

(2) **Election to terminate debtor's year when case commences.—**

(A) **In general.—**Notwithstanding section 442, the debtor may (without the approval of the Secretary) elect to treat the debtor's taxable year which includes the commencement date as 2 taxable years—

(i) the first of which ends on the day before the commencement date, and

(ii) the second of which begins on the commencement date.

(B) **Spouse may join in election.—**In the case of a married individual (within the meaning of [3]*section 7703,* the spouse may elect to have the debtor's election under subparagraph (A) also apply to the spouse, but only if the debtor and the spouse file a joint return for the taxable year referred to in subparagraph (A)(i).

(C) **No election where debtor has no assets.—**No election may be made under subparagraph (A) by a debtor who has no assets other than property which the debtor may treat as exempt property under section 522 of title 11 of the United States Code.

(D) **Time for making election.—**An election under subparagraph (A) or (B) may be made only on or before the due date for filing the return for the taxable year referred to in subparagraph (A)(i). Any such election, once made, shall be irrevocable.

(E) **Returns.—**A return shall be made for each of the taxable years specified in subparagraph (A).

【Footnote ¶3224 continued】
this Act. For special and transitional rules, see ¶2071—2077.
　【Footnote ¶3225】 **(1) Effective date** (Sec. 1311(d), '86 TRA).—Takes effect on the date of the enactment of this Act. For special and transitional rules, see ¶2071—2077.
　【Footnote ¶3226】 **(1) Effective date** (Sec. 1311(d), '86 TRA).—Takes effect on the date of the enactment of this Act. For special and transitional rules, see ¶2071—2077.
　【Footnote ¶3227】 **(1) Effective date** (Sec. 1311(d), '86 TRA).—Takes effect on the date of the enactment of this Act. For special and transitional rules, see ¶2071—2077.
　【Footnote ¶3228】 Matter in *italics* in Sec. 1398(c) added by section 104(b)(14), '86 TRA, which struck out:
(1) **"Zero Bracket Amount"**
(2) **"(3) Amount of zero bracket amount.—**The amount of the estate's zero bracket amount for the taxable year shall be the same as for a married individual filing a separate return for such year."
Effective date (Sec. 151(a), '86 TRA).—Applies to taxable years beginning after 12-31-86.

Matter in *italics* in Sec. 1398(d)(2)(B) added by section 1301(j)(8), '86 TRA, which struck out:
(3) "section 143"
Effective date (Sec. 1311(a), '86 TRA).—Applies to bonds issued after 8-15-86. For special and transitional rules, see ¶2071—2077.

(F) Annualization.—For purposes of subsections (b), (c), and (d) of section 443, a return filed for either of the taxable years referred to in subparagraph (A) shall be treated as a return made under paragraph (1) of subsection (a) of section 443.

(3) **Commencement date defined.**—For purposes of this subsection, the term "commencement date" means the day on which the case under title 11 of the United States Code to which this section applies commences.

(e) **Treatment of Income, Deductions, and Credits.**—

(1) **Estate's share of debtor's income.**—The gross income of the estate for each taxable year shall include the gross income of the debtor to which the estate is entitled under title 11 of the United States Code. The preceding sentence shall not apply to any amount received or accrued by the debtor before the commencement date (as defined in subsection (d)(3)).

(2) **Debtor's share of debtor's income.**—The gross income of the debtor for any taxable year shall not include any item to the extent that such item is included in the gross income of the estate by reason of paragraph (1).

(3) **Rule for making determinations with respect to deductions, credits, and employment taxes.**—Except as otherwise provided in this section, the determination of whether or not any amount paid or incurred by the estate—

(A) is allowable as a deduction or credit under this chapter, or

(B) is wages for purposes of subtitle C,

shall be made as if the amount were paid or incurred by the debtor and as if the debtor were still engaged in the trades and businesses, and in the activities, the debtor was engaged in before the commencement of the case.

* * * * * * * * * * * *

(g) **Estate Succeeds to Tax Attributes of Debtor.**—The estate shall succeed to and take into account the following items (determined as of the first day of the debtor's taxable year in which the case commences) of the debtor—

* * * * * * * * * * * *

[4]*(3) Recovery of tax benefit items.—Any amount to which section 111 (relating to recovery of tax benefit items) applies*

* * * * * * * * * * * *

[For official explanation, see Committee Reports, ¶4058, 4146.]

[¶3229] CODE SEC. 1402. DEFINITIONS.

(a) **Net Earnings From Self-Employment.**—The term "net earnings from self-employment" means the gross income derived by an individual from any trade or business carried on by such individual, less the deductions allowed by this subtitle which are attributable to such trade or business, plus his distributive share (whether or not distributed) of income or loss described in section 702(a)(8) from any trade or business carried on by a partnership of which he is a member; except that in computing such gross income and deductions and such distributive share of partnership ordinary income or loss—

* * * * * * * * * * * *

(8) an individual who is a duly ordained, commissioned, or licensed minister of a church or a member of a religious order shall compute his net earnings from self-employment derived from the performance of service described in subsection (c)(4) without regard to section 107 (relating to rental value of parsonages), section 119 (relating to meals and lodging furnished for the convenience of the employer), *and* section 911 (relating to citizens or residents of the United States living abroad);[1]

[2]*(9) the exclusion from gross income provided by section 931 shall not apply;*

---

* * * * * * * * * * *

[3](14)   in the case of church employee income, the special rules of subsection (j)(1) shall apply.

* * * * * * * * * * *

(b) Self-Employment Income.—The term "self-employment income" means the net earnings from self-employment derived by an individual (other than a nonresident alien individual, except as provided by an agreement under section 233 of the Social Security Act) during any taxable year; except that such term shall not include—

(1)   that part of the net earnings from self-employment which is in excess of (i) an amount equal to the contribution and benefit base (as determined under section 230 of the Social Security Act) which is effective for the calendar year in which such taxable year begins, minus (ii) the amount of the wages paid to such individual during such taxable years; or

(2)   the net earnings from self-employment, if such net earnings for the taxable year are less than $400.

For purposes of *[4]paragraph (1)*, the term "wages" (A) includes such remuneration paid to an employee for services included under an agreement entered into pursuant to the provisions of section 218 of the Social Security Act (relating to coverage of State employees), or under an agreement entered into pursuant to the provisions of section 3121(l) (relating to coverage of citizens of the United States who are employees of foreign affiliates of American employers), as would be wages under section 3121(a) if such services constituted employment under section 3121(b), (B) includes compensation which is subject to the tax imposed by section 3201 or 3211, and (c) includes, but only with respect to the tax imposed by section 1401(b), remuneration paid for medicare qualified government employment (as defined in section 3121(u)(3) which is subject to the taxes imposed by sections 3101(b) and 3111(b). An individual who is not a citizen of the United States but who is a resident of the Commonwealth of Puerto Rico, the Virgin Islands, Guam or American Samoa shall not, for purposes of this chapter be considered to be a nonresident alien individual. *In the case of church employee income, the special rules of subsection (j)(2) shall apply for purposes of paragraph (2).*

* * * * * * * * * * *

(e)   Ministers, Members of Religious Orders, and Christian Science Practitioners.—

(1)   **Exemption.**—*[5]Subject to paragraph (2), any* individual who is (A) a duly ordained, commissioned, or licensed minister of a church or a member of a religious order (other than a member of a religious order who has taken a vow of poverty as a member of such order) or (B) a Christian Science practitioner, upon filing an application (in such form and manner, and with such official, as may be prescribed by regulations made under this chapter) together with a statement that either he is conscientiously opposed to, or because of religious principles he is opposed to, the acceptance (with respect to services performed by him as such minister, member, or practitioner) of any public insurance which makes payments in the event of death, disability, old age, or retirement or makes payments toward the cost of, or provides services for, medical care (including the benefits of any insurance system established by the Social Security Act) *and, in the case of an individual described in subparagraph (A), that he*

<hr>

⟦Footnote ¶3229 continued⟧

within possessions of the United States) and 932 (relating to citizens of possessions of the United States) shall be deemed not to include the Virgin Islands, Guam, or American Samoa;"

Effective date (Sec. 1277, '86 TRA).—Generally applies to taxable years beginning after 12-31-86. For exceptions and special rules, see ¶2068.

<hr>

Matter in *italics* in Sec. 1402(a)(14) and (b) added by section 1882(b)(1)(B), '86 TRA, which struck out:

(3)   "(14)   with respect to remuneration for services which are treated as services in a trade or business under subsection (c)(2)(G)—

(A)   no deduction for trade or business expenses provided under this Code (other than the deduction under paragraph (12)) shall apply;

(B)   the provisions of subsection (b)(2) shall not apply; and

(C)   if the amount of such remuneration from an employer for the taxable year is less than $100, such remuneration from that employer shall not be included in self-employment income.

(4)   "clause (1)"

Effective date (Sec. 1882(b)(3), '86 TRA).—Applies to remuneration paid or derived in taxable years beginning after 12-31-85.

<hr>

Matter in *italics* in Sec. 1402(e)(1)—(4) added by section 1704(a)(1) and (2), '86 TRA, which struck out:

(5)   "Any"

has informed the ordaining, commissioning, or licensing body of the church or order that he is opposed to such insurance shall receive an exception from the tax imposed by this chapter with respect to services performed by him as such minister, member, or practitioner. Notwithstanding the preceding sentence, an exemption may not be granted to an individual under this subsection if he had filed an effective waiver certificate under this section as it was in effect before its amendment in 1967.

(2) Verification of application.—The Secretary may approve an application for an exemption filed pursuant to paragraph (1) only if the Secretary has verified that the individual applying for the exemption is aware of the grounds on which the individual may receive an exemption pursuant to this subsection and that the individual seeks exemption on such grounds. The Secretary (or the Secretary of Health and Human Services under an agreement with the Secretary) shall make such verification by such means as prescribed in regulations.

[6]*(3)* **Time for filing application.**—Any individual who desires to file an application pursuant to paragraph (1) must file such application on or before whichever of the following dates is later: (A) the due date of the return (including any extension thereof) for the second taxable year for which he has net earnings from self-employment (computed without regard to subsections (c)(4) and (c)(5) of $400 or more, any part of which was derived from the performance of service described in subsection (c)(4) or (c)(5); or (B) the due date of the return (including any extension thereof) for his second taxable year ending after 1967.

[7]*(4)* **Effective date of exemption.**—An exemption received by an individual pursuant to this subsection shall be effective for the first taxable year for which he has net earnings from self-employment (computed without regard to subsections (c)(4) and (c)(5) of $400 or more, any part of which was derived from the performance of service described in subsection (c)(4) or (c)(5), and for all succeeding taxable years. An exemption received pursuant to this subsection shall be irrevocable.

* * * * * * * * * * * *

(g) Members of Certain Religious Faiths.—

* * * * * * * * * * * *

(5) Subsection not to apply to certain church employees.—This subsection shall not apply with respect to services which are described in subparagraph (B) of section 3121(b)(8) (and are not described in subparagraph (A) of such section).

* * * * * * * * * * * *

(i) Special Rules for Options and Commodities Dealers.—

[8]*(1) In general.—Notwithstanding subsection (a)(3)(A), in determining the net earnings from self-employment of any options dealer or commodities dealer, there shall not be excluded any gain or loss (in the normal course of the taxpayer's activity of dealing in or trading section 1256 contracts) from section 1256 contracts or property related to such contracts.*

* * * * * * * * * * * *

⟦Footnote ¶3229 continued⟧

(6) "(2)"

(7) "(3)"

Effective date (Sec. 1704(a)(3), '86 TRA).—Applies to applications filed after 12-31-86.

Sec. 1402(g)(5) in *italics* added by section 1882(a), '86 TRA.
Effective date (Sec. 1882(a) and section 2603(e), '84 TRA).—Applies to services performed after 12-31-83.

Matter in *italics* in Sec. 1402(i)(1) added by section 301(b)(12), '86 TRA, which struck out:
(8) "(1) **In general.**—In determining the net earnings from self-employment of any options dealer or commodities dealer—
(A) notwithstanding subsection (a)(e)(A), there shall not be excluded any gain or loss (in the normal course of the taxpayer's activity of dealing in or trading section 1256 contracts) from section 1256 contracts or property related to such contacts, and
(B) the deduction provided by section 1202 shall not apply.
Effective date (Sec. 301(c), '86 TRA).—Applies to taxable years beginning after 12-31-86.

Sec. 1402(j) in *italics* added by section 1882(b)(1)(A), '86 TRA.
Effective date (Sec. 1882(b)(3), '86 TRA).—Applies to remuneration paid or derived in taxable years beginning after 12-31-85.

(j) Special Rules for Certain Church Employee Income.—

(1) Computation of net earnings.—In applying subsection (a)—

(A) church employee income shall not be reduced by any deduction;

(B) church employee income and deductions attributable to such income shall not be taken into account in determining the amount of other net earnings from self-employment.

(2) Computation of self-employment income.—

(A) Separate application of subsection (b)(2).—Paragraph (2) of subsection (b) shall be applied separately—

(i) to church employee income, and

(ii) to other net earnings from self-employment.

(B) $100 floor.—In applying paragraph (2) of subsection (b) to church employee income, "$100" shall be substituted for "$400".

(3) Coordination with subsection (a)(12).—Paragraph (1) shall not apply to any amount allowable as a deduction under subsection (a)(12), and paragraph (1) shall be applied before determining the amount so allowable.

(4) Church employee income defined.—For purposes of this section, the term "church employee income" means gross income for services which are described in section 3121(b)(8)(B) (and are not described in section 3121(b)(8)(A)).

[For official explanation, see Committee Reports, ¶3885; 4057; 4126; 4195; 4196.]

【¶3230】 CODE SEC. 1441. WITHHOLDING OF TAX ON NONRESIDENT ALIENS.

(a) General Rule.—Except as otherwise provided in subsection (c), all persons, in whatever capacity acting (including lessees or mortgagors of real or personal property, fiduciaries, employers, and all officers and employees of the United States) having the control, receipt, custody, disposal, or payment of any of the items of income specified in subsection (b) (to the extent that any of such items constitute gross income from sources within the United States), of any nonresident alien individual or of any foreign partnership shall ([1]except as otherwise provided in regulations prescribed by the Secretary under section 874) deduct and withhold from such items a tax equal to 30 percent thereof, except that in the case of any item of income specified in the second sentence of subsection (b), the tax shall be equal to 14 percent of such item.

(b) Income Items.—The items of income referred to in subsection (a) are interest (other than original issue discount as defined in section [2]1273), dividends, rent, salaries, wages, premiums, annuities compensations, remunerations, emoluments, or other fixed or determinable annual or periodical gains, profits, and income, gains described in section 402(a)(2), 403(a)(2), or 631(b) or (c), amounts subject to tax under section 871(a)(1)(C), gains subject to tax under section 871(a)(1)(D), and gains on transfers described in section 1235 made on or before October 4, 1966.[1] *The items of income referred to in subsection (a) from which tax shall be deducted and withheld at the rate of 14 percent are amounts which are received by a nonresident alien individual who is temporarily present in the United States as a nonimmigrant under subparagraph (F) or (J) of section 101(a)(15) of the Immigration and Nationality Act and which are incident to a qualified scholarship to which section 117(a) applies, but only to the extent such amounts are includible in gross income.*

In the case of a nonresident alien individual who is a member of a domestic partnership, the items of income referred to in subsection (a) shall be treated as referring to items specified in this subsection included in his distributive share of the income of such partnership.

(c) Exceptions.—

【Footnote ¶3230】 Matter in *italics* in Sec. 1441(b) added by section 123(b)(2), '86 TRA, which struck out:

(1) "The items of income referred to in subsection (a) from which tax shall be deducted and withheld at the rate of 14 percent are—

(1) that portion of any scholarship or fellowship grant which is received by a nonresident alien individual who is temporarily present in the United States as a nonimmigrant under subparagraph (F) or (J) of section 101(a)(15) of the Immigration and Nationality Act, as amended, and which is not excluded from gross income under section 177(a)(1) solely by reason of section 117(b)(2)(B); and

(2) amounts described in subparagraphs (A), (B), (C), and (D) of section 117(a)(2) which are received by any such nonresident alien individual and which are incident to a scholarship or fellowship grant to which section 177(a)(1) applies, but only to the extent such amounts are includible in gross income."

Effective date (Sec. 151(d), '86 TRA).—Applies to taxable years beginning after 12-31-86, but only in the case of scholarships and fellowships granted after 8-16-86.

* * * * * * * * * * * *

(9) Interest income from certain portfolio debt investments.—In the case of portfolio interest (within the meaning of [2]*section 871(h)*), no tax shall be required to be deducted and withheld from such interest unless the person required to deduct and withhold tax from such interest knows, or has reason to know, that such interest is not portfolio interest by reason of section 871(h)(3).

(10) Exception for certain interest and dividends.—No tax shall be required to be deducted and withheld under subsection (a) from any amount described in section 871(i)(2).

* * * * * * * * * * * *

[For official explanation, see Committee Reports, ¶3859; 4031; 4144.]

【¶3231】 CODE SEC. 1442. WITHHOLDING OF TAX ON FOREIGN CORPORATIONS.

(a) General Rule.—In the case of foreign corporations subject to taxation under this subtitle, there shall be deducted and withheld at the source in the same manner and on the same items of income as is provided in section 1441 a tax equal to 30 percent thereof. For purposes of the preceding sentence, the references in section 1441(b) to sections 871(a)(1)(C) and (D) shall be treated as referring to sections 881(a)(3) and (4), the reference in section 1441(c)(1) to section 871(b)(2) shall be treated as referring to section 842 or section 822(a)(2), as the case may be, the reference in section 1441(c)(5) to section 871(a)(1)(D) shall be treated as referring to section 881(a)(4), the reference in section 1441(c)(8) to section 871(a)(1)(C) shall be treated as referring to section 881(a)(3), and the references in section [1]*1441(c)(9)* to [2]*sections 871(h)* and 871(h)(3) shall be treated as referring to [3]*sections 881(c)* and 881(c)(3).

(b) Exemption.—Subject to such terms and conditions as may be provided by regulations prescribed by the Secretary, subsection (a) shall not apply in the case of a foreign corporation engaged in trade or business within the United States if the Secretary determines that the requirements of subsection (a) imposes an undue administrative burden and that the collection of the tax imposed by section 881 on such corporation will not be jeopardized by the exemption.

[4]*(c) Exception for Certain Possessions Corporations.—For purposes of this section, the term "foreign corporation" does not include a corporation created or organized in Guam, American Samoa, the Northern Mariana Islands, or the Virgin Islands or under the law of*

【Footnote ¶3230 continued】

Matter in *italics* in Sec. 1441(c)(9) added by section 1810(d)(3)(D), '86 TRA, which struck out:
(2) "871(h)(2)"
Effective date (Sec. 1881, '86 TRA and section 127(g)(1) and (3), '84 TRA).—(1) Generally applies to interest received after 7-18-84, with respect to obligations issued after such date, in taxable years ending after such date. For special rule for certain United States affiliate obligations, see footnote ¶3124.

Matter in *italics* in Sec. 1441(c)(10) added by section 1214(c)(3), '86 TRA.
Effective date (Sec. 1214(d), '86 TRA).—Generally applies to payments after 12-31-86. For special and transitional rules, see footnote ¶3114.
【Footnote ¶3231】 Matter in *italics* in Sec. 1442(a) added by section 1810(d)(3)(E), '86 TRA, which struck out:
(1) "section 1449(c)(9)"
(2) "sections 871(h)(2)"
(3) "sections 881(c)(2)"
Effective date (Sec. 1881, '86 TRA and section 127(g)(1) and (3), '84 TRA).—(1) Generally applies to interest received after 7-18-84, with respect to obligations issued after such date, in taxable years ending after such date. For special rule for certain U.S. affiliate obligations, see ¶3124.

Matter in *italics* in Sec. 1442(c) added by section 1273(b)(2)(B), '86 TRA, which struck out:
(4) "**(c) Exception for Certain Guam and Virgin Islands Corporations.**—
(1) In General.—For purposes of this section, the term "foreign corporation" does not include a corporation created or organized in Guam or the Virgin Islands or under the law of Guam or the Virgin Islands if the requirements of subparagraphs (A) and (B) of section 881(b)(1) are met with respect to such corporation.
(2) Paragraph (1) Not to Apply to Tax Imposed in Guam.—For purposes of applying this subsection with respect to income tax liability incurred in Guam—
(A) paragraph (1) shall not apply, and
(B) for purposes of this section, the term "foreign corporation" does not include a corporation created or organized in Guam or under the law of Guam.
(3) Cross Reference.—
For tax imposed in the Virgin Islands, see sections 934 and 934A.
Effective date (Sec. 1277(a) and (b), '86 TRA).—(a) Generally applies to taxable years beginning after 12-31-86. For special rules, see ¶2068.

any such possession if the requirements of subparagraphs (A), (B), and (C) of section 881(b)(1) are met with respect to such corporation.

[For official explanation, see Committee Reports, ¶4057; 4144.]

【¶3232】 CODE SEC. 1445. WITHHOLDING OF TAX ON DISPOSITIONS OF UNITED STATES REAL PROPERTY INTERESTS.

* * * * * * * * * * * *

(b) Exemptions.—

* * * * * * * * * * *

[1]*(3) Nonpublicly traded domestic corporation furnishes affidavit that interests in corporation not United States real property interests.—Except as provided in paragraph (7), this paragraph applies in the case of a disposition of any interest in any domestic corporation if the domestic corporation furnishes to the transferee an affidavit by the domestic corporation stating, under penalty of perjury, that—*
   (A)   the domestic corporation is not and has not been a United States real property holding corporation (as defined in section 897(c)(2)) during the applicable period specified in section 897(c)(1)(A)(ii), or
   (B)   as of the date of the disposition, interests in such corporation are not United States real property interests by reason of section 897(c)(1)(B).

* * * * * * * * * * * *

(d)   Liability of Transferor's Agents or Transferee's Agents—

   (1)   Notice of false affidavit; foreign corporations.—If—
   (A)   the transferor furnishes the transferee an affidavit described in [2]*paragraph (2)* of subsection (b) or a domestic corporation furnishes the transferee an affidavit described in paragraph (3) of subsection (b), and
   (B)   in the case of—
      [3]*(i)   any transferor's agent—*
         (I)   such agent has actual knowledge that such affidavit is false, or
         (II)   in the case of an affidavit described in subsection (b)(2) furnished by a corporation, such corporation is a foreign corporation, or
      (ii)   any transferee's agent, such agent has actual knowledge that such affidavit is false,

such agent shall so notify the transferee at such time and in such manner as the Secretary shall require by regulations.

* * * * * * * * * * * *

(e)   Special Rules Relating to Distributions, Etc., by Corporations, Partnerships, Trusts, or Estates.—

   (1)   Certain domestic partnerships, trusts, and estates.—[4]*In the case of any*

【Footnote ¶3232】   Matter in *italics* in Sec. 1445(b)(3), (d)(1) and (B)(i) added by section 1810(f)(2) and (3), '86 TRA, which struck out:

(1) "**(3)   Nonpublicly traded domestic corporation furnishes affidavit that it is not a United States real property holding corporation.**—Except as provided in paragraph (7), this paragraph applies in the case of a disposition of any interest in any domestic corporation, if the domestic corporation furnishes to the transferee an affidavit by the domestic corporation stating, under penalty or perjury, that the domestic corporation is not and has not been a United States real property holding corporation (as defined in section 897(c)(2)) during the applicable period specified in section 897(c)(1)(A)(ii)."

(2) "paragraph (2)(A)"

(3) "(i) any transferor's agent, the transferor is a foreign corporation or such agent has actual knowledge that such affidavit is false or"

Effective date (Sec. 1881, '86 TRA and 129(c)(1), '84 TRA).—Applies to any disposition on or after 1-1-85.

Matter in *italics* in Sec. 1445(e)(1) except "*34 percent*", added by Section 1810(f)(4)(A), '86 TRA, which struck out:

(4) "A domestic partnership, the trustee of a domestic trust, or the executor of a domestic estate shall be required to deduct and withhold under subsection(a) a tax equal to 10 percent of any amount of which such partnership, trustee, or executor has custody which is—

(A)   attributable to the disposition of a United States real property interest (as defined in section 897(c), other than a disposition described in paragraph (4) or (5)), and

(B)   either—

(i)   includible in the distributive share of a partner of the partnership who is a foreign person,

(ii)   includible in the income of a beneficiary of the trust or estate who is a foreign person, or

(iii)   includible in the income of a foreign person under the provisions of section 671."

Effective date (Sec. 1810(f)(4)(B), '86 TRA).—Applies to dispositions after the day 30 days after the date of the enactment of this Act.

disposition of a United States real property interest as defined in section 897(c) (other than a disposition described in paragraph (4) or (5)) by a domestic partnership, domestic trust, or domestic estate, such partnership, the trustee of such trust, or the executor of such estate (as the case may be) shall be required to deduct and withhold under subsection (a) a tax equal to [5]34 percent of the gain realized to the extent such gain—

    (A) is allocable to a foreign person who is a partner or beneficiary of such partnership, trust, or estate, or

    (B) is allocable to a portion of the trust treated as owned by a foreign person under subpart E of part I of subchapter J.

    (2) Certain distributions by foreign corporations.—In the case of any distribution by a foreign corporation on which gain is recognized under subsection (d) or (e) of section 897, the foreign corporation shall deduct and withhold under subsection (a) a tax equal to [5]34 *percent* of the amount of gain recognized on such distribution under such subsection.

    (3) Distributions by certain domestic corporations to foreign shareholders.—If a domestic corporation which is or has been a United States real property holding corporation (as defined in section 897(c)(2)) during the applicable period specified in section 897(c)(1)(A)(ii) distributes property to a foreign person in a transaction to which section 302 or part II of subchapter C applies, such corporation shall deduct and withhold under subsection (a) a tax equal to 10 percent of the amount realized by the foreign shareholder. *The preceding sentence shall not apply if, as of the date of the distribution, interests in such corporation are not United States real property interests by reason of section 897(c)(1)(B).*

    (4) Taxable distributions by domestic or foreign partnerships, trusts, or estates.— A domestic or foreign partnership, the trustee of a domestic or foreign trust, or the executor of a domestic or foreign estate shall be required to deduct and withhold under subsection (a) a tax equal to 10 percent of the fair market value (as of the time of the taxable distribution) of any United States real property interest distributed to a partner of the partnership or a beneficiary of the trust or estate, as the case may be, who is a foreign person in a transaction which would constitute a taxable distribution under the regulations promulgated by the Secretary pursuant to [6]*section 897.*

*   *   *   *   *   *   *   *   *   *   *

    (6) Regulations.—The Secretary shall prescribe such regulations as may be necessary to carry out the purposes of this subsection, including regulations providing for exceptions from provisions of this subsection *and regulations for the application of this subsection in the case of payments through 1 or more entities.*

*   *   *   *   *   *   *   *   *   *   *

[For official explanation, see Committee Reports, ¶3887; 4144.]

[¶3233] CODE SEC. 1446. WITHHOLDING TAX ON AMOUNTS PAID BY UNITED STATES PARTNERSHIPS TO FOREIGN PARTNERS.

    (a) General Rule.—Except as provided in this section, if a partnership has any income, gain, or loss which is effectively connected or treated as effectively connected with the conduct of a trade or business within the United States, any person described in section 1441(a) shall be required to deduct and withhold a tax equal to 20 percent of any amount distributed to a partner which is not a United States person.

⌈Footnote ¶3232 continued⌋

    "*34 percent*" in *italics* in Sec. 1445(e)(1) and (2) added by section 311(b)(4), '86 TRA, which struck out:
    (5) "*28 percent*"
    Effective date (Sec. 311(c) and (d), '86 TRA).—(c) Applies to taxable years beginning after 12-31-86. For transitional rules, see footnote ¶3175.

    Matter in *italics* in Sec. 1445(e)(3), (4) and (6) added by section 1810(f)(5), (6) and (8), '86 TRA, which struck out:
    (6) "section 897(g)"
    Effective date (Sec. 1881, '86 TRA and 129(c)(1), '84 TRA).—Applies to any disposition on or after 1-1-85.
    ⌈Footnote ¶3233⌋   Sec. 1446 added by section 1246(a), '86 TRA.
    Effective date (Sec. 1246(d), '86 TRA).—Applies to distributions after 12-31-87, (or, if earlier, the effective date (which shall not be earlier than 1-1-87) of the initial regulations issued under section 1446 of the '86 Code as added by this section).

(b) Limitation if Less than 80 Percent of Gross Income is Effectively Connected with United States Trade or Business.—

(1) In general.—If the effectively connected percentage is less than 80 percent, only the effectively connected percentage of any distribution shall be taken into account under subsection (a).

(2) Effectively connected percentage.—For purposes of paragraph (1) the term "effectively connected percentage" means the percentage of the gross income of the partnership for the 3 taxable years preceding the taxable year of the distribution which is effectively connected (or treated as effectively connected) with the conduct of a trade or business within the United States.

(c) Exceptions.—

(1) Amounts on which tax withheld.—Subsection (a) shall not apply to that portion of any distribution with respect to which a tax is required to be deducted and withheld under section 1441 or 1442 (or would be required to be deducted and withheld but for a treaty).

(2) Partnerships with certain allocations.—Except as provided in regulations, subsection (a) shall not apply to any partnership with respect to which substantially all income from sources within the United States and substantially all income which is effectively connected with the conduct of a trade or business within the United States is properly allocated to United States persons.

(3) Coordination with section 1445.—Under regulations proper adjustments shall be made in the amount required to be deducted and withheld under subsection (a) for amounts deducted and withheld under section 1445.

(d) Regulations.—The Secretary shall prescribe such regulations as may be necessary or appropriate to carry out the purposes of this section.

[For official explanation, see Committee Reports, ¶4052.]

[¶3234] CODE SEC. 1503. COMPUTATION AND PAYMENT OF TAX.

In any case in which a consolidated return is made or is required to be made, the tax shall be determined, computed, assessed, collected, and adjusted in accordance with the regulations under section 1502 prescribed before the last day prescribed by law for the filing of such return.

(c) [Should be Redesignated] Special Rule for Application of Certain Losses Against Income of Insurance Companies Taxed Under Section 801.—

(1) In general.—If an election under section 1504(c)(2) is in effect for the taxable year and the consolidated taxable income of the members of the group not taxed under section 801 results in a consolidated net operating loss for such taxable year, then under regulations prescribed by the Secretary, the amount of such loss which cannot be absorbed in the applicable carryback periods against the taxable income of such members not taxed under section 801 shall be taken into account in determining the consolidated taxable income of the affiliated group for such taxable years to the extent of 35 percent of such loss or 35 percent of the taxable income of the members taxed under section 801 whichever is less. The unused portions of such loss shall be available as a carryover, subject to the same limitations (applicable to the sum of the loss for the carryover year and the loss (or losses) carried over to such year), in applicable carryover years. For taxable years ending with or within calendar year 1981, "25 percent" shall be substituted for "35 percent" each place it appears in the first sentence of this subsection. For taxable years ending with or within calendar year 1982, "30 percent" shall be substituted for "35 percent" each place it appears in that sentence.

(2) Losses of recent nonlife affiliates.—Notwithstanding the provisions of paragraph (1), a net operating loss for a taxable year of a member of the group not taxed under section 801 shall not be taken into account in determining the taxable income of a member taxed under section 801 (either for the taxable year or as a carryover or carryback) if such taxable year precedes the sixth taxable year such members have been members of the same affiliated group (determined without regard to section 1504(b)(2)).

(d) Dual Consolidated Loss.—

[Footnote ¶3234] Sec. 1503(d) in *italics* added by section 1249(a), '86 TRA.

Effective date (Sec. 1249(b), '86 TRA).—Applies to net operating losses for taxable years beginning after 12-31-86.

(1) *In general.*—*The dual consolidated loss for any taxable year of any corporation shall not be allowed to reduce the taxable income of any other member of the affiliated group for the taxable year or any other taxable year.*

(2) *Dual consolidated loss.*—*For purposes of this section—*

(A) *In general.*—*Except as provided in subparagraph (B), the term "dual consolidated loss" means any net operating loss of a domestic corporation which is subject to an income tax of a foreign country, on its income without regard to whether such income is from sources in or outside of such foreign country, or is subject to such a tax on a residence basis.*

(B) *Special rule where loss not used under foreign law.*—*To the extent provided in regulations, the term "dual consolidated loss" shall not include any loss which, under the foreign income tax law, does not offset the income of any foreign corporation.*

[For official explanation, see Committee Reports, ¶4055.]

〔¶3235〕 CODE SEC. 1504. DEFINITIONS.

(a) **Affiliated group defined.**—For purposes of this subtitle—

* * * * * * * * * * * *

(4) **Stock not to include certain preferred stock.**—For purposes of this subsection, the term "stock" does not include any stock which—

(A) is not entitled to vote,

(B) is limited and preferred as to dividends and does not participate in corporate growth to any significant extent,

[1]*(C)* *has redemption and liquidation rights which do not exceed the issue price of*

〔Footnote ¶3235〕 Matter in *italics* in Sec. 1504(a)(4)(C) added by section 1804(e)(1), '86 TRA, which struck out:

(1) "(C) has redemption and liquidation rights which do not exceed the paid-in capital or par value represented by such stock (except for a reasonable redemption premium in excess of such paid-in capital or par value), and"

Effective date (Sec. 1881, '86 TRA and section 60(b), '84 TRA, as amended by section 1804(e)(2)—(5), '86 TRA).—(1) Generally applies to taxable years beginning after 12-31-84.

(2) Special rule for corporations affiliated on 6-22-84.—In the case of a corporation which on 6-22-84, is a member of an affiliated group which files a consolidated return for such corporation's taxable year which includes 6-22-84, for purposes of determining whether such corporation continues to be a member of such group for taxable years beginning before 1-1-88, the amendment made by subsection (a) shall not apply. The preceding sentence shall cease to apply as of the first day after 6-22-84, on which such corporation does not qualify as a member of such group under section 1504(a) '54 Code (as in effect on the day before the date of the enactment of this Act).

(3) Special rule not to apply to certain sell-downs after 6-22-84.—If—

(A) the requirements of paragraph (2) are satisfied with respect to a corporation,

(B) more than a de minimis amount of the stock of such corporation—

(i) is sold or exchanged (including in a redemption), or

(ii) is issued,

after 6-22-84 (other than in the ordinary course of business), and

(C) the requirements of the amendments made by subsection (a) are not satisfied after such sale, exchange, or issuance,

then the amendment made by subsection (a) shall apply for purposes of determining whether such corporation continues to be a member of the group. The preceding sentence shall not apply to any transaction if such transaction does not reduce the percentage of the fair market value of the stock of the corporation referred to in the preceding sentence held by members of the group determined without regard to this paragraph.

(4) Exception for certain sell-downs.—Subsection (b)(2) (and not subsection (b)(3)) will apply to a corporation if such corporation issues or sells stock after 6-22-84, pursuant to a registration statement filed with the Securities and Exchange Commission on or before 6-22-84, but only if the requirements of the amendment made by subsection (a) (substituting "more than 50 percent" for "at least 80 percent" in paragraph (2)(B) of section 1504(a) '54 Code) are satisfied immediately after such issuance or sale and at all times thereafter until the first day of the first taxable year beginning after 12-31-87. For purposes of the preceding sentence, if there is a letter of intent between a corporation and a securities underwriter entered into on or before 6-22-84, and the subsequent issuance or sale is effected pursuant to a registration statement filed with the Securities and Exchange Commission, such stock shall be treated as issued or sold pursuant to a registration statement filed with the Securities and Exchange Commission on or before 6-22-84.

(5) Native corporations.—

(A) In the case of a Native Corporation established under the Alaska Native Claims Settlement Act (43 U.S.C. 1601 et seq.), or a corporation all of whose stock is owned directly by such a corporation, during any taxable year (beginning after the effective date of these amendments and before 1992), or any part thereof, in which the Native Corporation is subject to the provisions of section 7(h)(1) of such Act (43 U.S.C. 1606(h)(1))—

(i) the amendment made by subsection (a) shall not apply, and

(ii) the requirements for affiliation under section 1504(a) '86 Code before the amendment made by subsection (a) shall be applied solely according to the provisions expressly contained therein, without regard to escrow arrangements, redemption rights, or similar provisions.

such stock (except for a reasonable redemption or liquidation premium), and

    (D)   is not convertible into another class of stock.

    (5) Regulations.—The Secretary shall prescribe such regulations as may be necessary or appropriate to carry out the purposes of this subsection, including (but not limited to) regulations—

    (A)   which treat warrants, obligations convertible into stock, and other similar interests as stock, and stock as not stock,

    (B)   which treat options to acquire or sell stock as having been exercised,

    (C)   which provide that the requirements of paragraph (2)(B) shall be treated as met if the affiliated group, in reliance on a good faith determination of value, treated such requirements as met,

    (D)   which disregard an inadvertent ceasing to meet the requirements of paragraph (2)(B) by reason of changes in relative values of different classes of stock,

    (E)   which provide that transfers of stock within the group shall not be taken into account in determining whether a corporation ceases to be a member of an affiliated group, and

    (F)   which disregard changes in voting power to the extent such changes are disproportionate to related changes in value.

    (b) Definition of "Includible Corporation".—As used in this chapter, the term "includible corporation" means any corporation except—

    (1)   Corporations exempt from taxation under section 501.

⸤**Footnote ¶3235 continued**⸥

    (B)   Except as provided in subparagraph (C), during the period described in subparagraph (A), no provision of the '86 Code (including sections 269 and 482) or principle of law shall apply to deny the benefit or use of losses incurred or credits earned by a corporation described in subparagraph (A) to the affiliated group of which the Native Corporation is the common parent.

    (C)   Losses incurred or credits earned by a corporation described in subparagraph (A) shall be subject to the general consolidated return regulations, including the provisions relating to separate return limitation years, and to sections 382 and 383 '86 Code.

    (D)   Losses incurred and credits earned by a corporation which is affiliated with a corporation described in subparagraph (A) shall be treated as having been incurred or earned in a separate return limitation year, unless the corporation incurring the losses or earning the credits satisfies the affiliation requirements of section 1504(a) without application of subparagraph (A).

    (6)   Treatment of certain corporations affiliated on 6-22-84.—In the case of an affiliated group which—

    (A)   has as its common parent a Minnesota corporation incorporated on 4-23-40, and

    (B)   has a member which is a New York corporation incorporated on 11-13-69,

for purposes of determining whether such New York corporation continues to be a member of such group, paragraph (2) shall be applied by substituting for 1-1-88 the earlier of 1-1-94, or the date on which the voting power of the preferred stock in such New York corporation terminates.

    (7)   Election to have amendments apply for years beginning after 1983.—If the common parent of any group makes an election under this paragraph, notwithstanding any other provision of this subsection, the amendments made by subsection (a) shall apply to such group for taxable years beginning after 12-31-83. Any such election, once made, shall be irrevocable.

    (8)   Treatment of certain affiliated groups.—If—

    (A)   a corporation (hereinafter in this paragraph referred to as the "parent") was incorporated in 1968 and filed consolidated returns as the parent of an affiliated group for each of its taxable years ending after 1969 and before 1985,

    (B)   another corporation (hereinafter in this paragraph referred to as the "subsidiary") became a member of the parent's affiliated group in 1978 by reason of a recapitalization pursuant to which the parent increased its voting interest in the subsidiary from not less than 56 percent to not less than 85 percent, and

    (C)   such subsidiary is engaged (or was on 9-27-85, engaged) in manufacturing and distributing a broad line of business systems and related supplies for binding, laminating, shredding, graphics, and providing secure identification,

then, for purposes of determining whether such subsidiary corporation is a member of the parent's affiliated group under section 1504(a) '54 Code (as amended by subsection (a)), paragraph (2)(B) of such section 1504(a) shall be applied by substituting "55 percent" for "80 percent".

    (9)   Treatment of certain corporations affiliated during 1971.—In the case of a group of corporations which filed a consolidated Federal income tax return for the taxable year beginning during 1971 and which—

    (A)   included as a common parent on 12-31-71, a Delaware corporation incorporated on 8-26-69, and

    (B)   included as a member thereof a Delaware corporation incorporated on 11-8-71,

for taxable years beginning after 12-31-70, and ending before 1-1-88, the requirements for affiliation for each member of such group under section 1504(a) '54 Code (before the amendment made by subsection (a)) shall be limited solely to the provisions expressly contained therein and by reference to stock issued under State law as common or preferred stock. During the period described in the preceding sentence, no provision of the '86 Code (including sections 269 and 482) or principle of law, except the general consolidated return regulations (including the provisions relating to separate return limitation years) and sections 382 and 383 of such Code, shall apply to deny the benefit or use of losses incurred or credits earned by members of such group.

---

(2) Insurance companies subject to taxation under section 801.[2]

(3) Foreign corporations.

(4) Corporations with respect to which an election under Section 936 (relating to possession tax credit) is in effect for the taxable year.

(5) [Struck out]

(6) Regulated investment companies and real estate investment trusts subject to tax under subchapter M of chapter 1.

[3]*(7) A DISC (as defined in section 992(a)(1)), or any other corporation which has accumulated DISC income which is derived after December 31, 1984.*

(c) Includible Insurance Companies.—Notwithstanding the provision of paragraph (2) of subsection (b)—

(1) Two or more domestic insurance companies each of which is subject to tax under section [2]801 shall be treated as includible corporations for purposes of applying subsection (a) to such insurance companies alone.

(2) (A) If an affiliated group (determined without regard to *subsection (b)(2))*[4] includes one or more domestic insurance companies taxed under subsection 801 [5] the common parent of such group may elect (pursuant to regulations prescribed by the Secretary) to treat all such companies as includible corporations for purposes of applying subsection (a) except that no such company shall be so treated until it has been a member of the affiliated group for the 5 taxable years immediately preceding the taxable year for which the consolidated return is filed.

(B) If an election under this paragraph is in effect for a taxable year—

(i) section 243(b)(6) and the exception provided under sectiion 243(b)(5) with respect to subsections (b)(2) and (c) of this section.

(ii) section 542(b)(5), and

(iii) subsection (a)(4) and (b)(2)(D) of section 1563, and the reference to section 1563(b)(2)(D) contained in section 1563(b)(3)(C), shall not be effective for such taxable year.

* * * * * * * * * * * *

[For official explanation, see Committee Reports, ¶3964; 4138.]

〔¶3236〕 CODE SEC. 1551. DISALLOWANCE OF THE BENEFITS OF THE GRADUATED CORPORATE RATES AND ACCUMULATED EARNINGS CREDIT.

* * * * * * * * * * * * *

(c) Authority of the Secretary Under This Section.—The provisions of [1]*section 269(c),* and the authority of the Secretary under such sections, shall, to the extent not inconsistent with the provisions of this section, be applicable to this section.

〔¶3237〕 CODE SEC. 1561. LIMITATIONS ON CERTAIN MULTIPLE TAX BENEFITS IN THE CASE OF CERTAIN CONTROLLED CORPORATIONS.

(a) General Rule.—The component members of a controlled group of corporations on a December 31, shall, for their taxable years which include such December 31, be limited for purposes of this subtitle to—

---

(1) amounts in each taxable income bracket in the tax table in section 11(b) which do not aggregate more than the maximum amount in such bracket to which a corporation is not a component member of a controlled group is entitled,[1]

(2) one $250,000 ($150,000 if any component member is a corporation described in section 535(c)(2)(B)) amount for purposes of computing the accumulated earnings credit under section 535(c)(2) and (3)[2], *and*

(3) one $40,000 exemption amount for purposes of computing the amount of the minimum tax.

The amounts specified in paragraph (1) *(and the amount specified in paragraph (3))* shall be divided equally among the component members of such group on such December 31 unless all of such component members consent (at such time and in such manner as the Secretary shall by regulations prescribe) to an apportionment plan providing for an unequal allocation of such amounts. The amounts specified in paragraph (2) shall be divided equally among the component members of such group on such December 31 unless the Secretary prescribes regulations permitting an unequal allocation of such amounts. Notwithstanding paragraph (1), in applying the last sentence of section 11(b) to such component members, the taxable income of all such component members shall be taken into account and any increase in tax under such last sentence shall be divided among such component members in the same manner as amounts under paragraph (1). *In applying section 55(d)(3), the alternative minimum taxable income of all component members shall be taken into account and any decrease in the exemption amount shall be allocated to the component members in the same manner as under paragraph (3).*

* * * * * * * * * * * *

[For official explanation, see Committee Reports, ¶3931.]

[¶3238] CODE SEC. 1563. DEFINITIONS AND SPECIAL RULES.

* * * * * * * * * * * *

(b) Component Member.—

* * * * * * * * * * * *

(2) **Excluded members.**—A corporation which is a member of a controlled group of corporations on December 31 of any taxable year shall be treated as an excluded member of such group for the taxable year including such December 31 if such corporation—

(A) is a member of such group for less than one-half the number of days in such taxable year which precede such December 31,

(B) is exempt from taxation under section 501(a) (except a corporation which is subject to tax on its unrelated business taxable income under section 511) for such taxable year,

(C) is a foreign corporation subject to tax under section 881 for such taxable year,

(D) is an insurance company subject to taxation under section 801 [1] (other than an insurance company which is a member of a controlled group described in subsection (a)(4)), or

(E) is a franchised corporation, as defined in subsection (f)(4).

* * * * * * * * * * * *

[¶3239] CODE SEC. 2013. CREDIT FOR TAX ON PRIOR TRANSFERS.

* * * * * * * * * * * *

(g) [Repealed][1]

[Footnote ¶3237] Matter in *italics* in Sec. 1561(a) added by section 701(e)(2), '86 TRA, which struck out:
(1) "and"
(2) "."
Effective date (Sec. 701(f)(1) and (2)(A), '86 TRA).—(1) Generally applies to taxable years beginning after 12-31-86. For special and transitional rules, see footnote ¶2879.

[Footnote ¶3238] Section 1024(c)(17), '86 TRA, struck out from Sec. 1563(b)(2)(D):
(1) "or section 821"
Effective date (Sec. 1024(e), '86 TRA).—Applies to taxable years beginning after 12-31-86.

[Footnote ¶3239] Section 1432(c)(2), '86 TRA, repealed Sec. 2013(g):
(1) "**(g) Treatment of Tax Imposed on Certain Generation-Skipping Transfers.**—If any property was transferred to the decedent in a transfer which is taxable under section 2601 (relating to tax imposed on generation-skipping transfers) and if the deemed transferor (as defined in section 2612) is not alive at the time of such transfer, for purposes of this section—
(1) such property shall be deemed to have passed to the decedent from the deemed transferor;
(2) the tax payable under section 2601 on such transfer shall be treated as a Federal estate tax payable with respect to the estate of the deemed transferor; and

[For official explanation, see Committee Reports, ¶4068.]

【¶3240】 CODE SEC. 2032. ALTERNATE VALUATION.

* * * * * * * * * * * *

(c) Election Must Decrease Gross Estate and Estate Tax.—No election may be made under this section with respect to an estate unless such election will decrease—

(1) the value of the gross estate, and

[1]*(2) the sum of the tax imposed by this chapter and the tax imposed by chapter 13 with respect to property includible in the decedent's gross estate (reduced by credits allowable against such taxes).*

* * * * * * * * * * * *

[For official explanation, see Committee Reports, ¶4068.]

【¶3241】 CODE SEC. 2032A. VALUATION OF CERTAIN FARM, ETC., REAL PROPERTY.

* * * * * * * * * * * *

(c) Tax Treatment of Dispositions and Failures To Use for Qualified Use.—

* * * * * * * * * * * *

(7) **Special rules.**—

* * * * * * * * * * * *

(D) Student.—For purposes of subparagraph (C), an individual shall be treated as a student with respect to periods during any calendar year if (and only if) such individual is a student (within the meaning of [1]*section 151(c)(4)*) for such calendar year.

* * * * * * * * * * * *

【¶3242】 CODE SEC. 2039. ANNUITIES.

(a) General.—The gross estate shall include the value of an annuity or other payment receivable by any beneficiary by reason of surviving the decedent under any form of contract or agreement entered into after March 3, 1931 (other than as insurance under policies on the life of the decedent), if, under such contract or agreement, an annuity or other payment was payable to the decedent, or the decedent possessed the right to receive such annuity or payment, either alone or in conjunction with another for his life or for any period not ascertainable without reference to his death or for any period which does not in fact end before his death.

* * * * * * * * * * * *

(c) [Repealed][1]

【Footnote ¶3239 continued】

(3) the amount of the taxable estate of the deemed transferor shall be increased by the value of such property as determined for purposes of the tax imposed by section 2601 on the transfer."

Effective date (Sec. 1433(a), '86 TRA).—Generally applies to any generation-skipping transfers made after the date of the enactment of this Act. For special rules and election for certain transfers benefitting grandchild, see footnote ¶3252.

【Footnote ¶3240】 Matter in *italics* in Sec. 2032(c)(2) added by section 1432(c)(1), '86 TRA, which struck out:

(1) "(2) the amount of the tax imposed by this chapter (reduced by credits allowable against such tax)."

Effective date (Sec. 1433(a), '86 TRA).—Generally applies to any generation-skipping transfers made after the date of the enactment of this Act. For special rules and transitional rules for transfers to grandchildren, see footnote ¶3252.

【Footnote ¶3241】 Matter in *italics* in Sec. 2032A(c)(7)(D) added by section 104(b)(3), '86 TRA, which struck out:

(1) "section 151(e)(4)"

Effective date (Sec. 151(a), '86 TRA).—Applies to taxable years beginning after 12-31-86.

【Footnote ¶3242】 Section 1852(e)(1)(A), '86 TRA, repealed Sec. 2039(c):

(1) "(c) **Exception of Certain Annuity Interests Created by Community Property Laws.**—

(1) **In general.**—In the case of an employee on whose behalf contributions or payments were made by his employer or former employer under a trust, plan, or contract to which this subsection applies, if the spouse of such employee predeceases such employee, then notwithstanding any provision of law, there shall be excluded from the gross estate of such spouse the value of any interest of such spouse in such trust, plan, or contract, to the extent such interest—

(A) is attributable to such contributions or payments, and

(B) arises solely by reason of such spouse's interest in community income under the community property laws of a State.

* * * * * * * * * * * *

(e) **Exclusion of Individual Retirement Accounts, Etc.**—Subject to the limitation of subsection (g), notwithstanding any other provison of this section or of any other provision of law, there shall be excluded from the value of the gross estate the value of an annuity receivable by any beneficiary (other than the executor) under—

(1) an individual retirement account described in section 408(a), or

(2) an individual retirement annuity described in section 408(b).

If any payment to an account described in paragraph (1) or for an annuity described in paragraph (2)[2] was not allowable as a deduction under section 219 and was not a rollover contribution described in section 402(a)(5), 403(a)(4), section 403(b)(8) (but only to the extent such contribution is attributable to a distribution from a contract described in subsection (c)(3)), or 408(d)(3), the preceding sentence shall not apply to that portion of the value of the amount receivable under such account or annuity (as the case may be) which bears the same ratio to the total value of the amount so receivable as the total amount which was paid to or for such account or annuity and which was not allowable as a deduction under section 219 and was not such a rollover contribution bears to the total amount paid to or for such account or annuity. For purposes of this subsection, the term "annuity" means an annuity contract or other arrangement providing for a series of substantially equal periodic contract or other arrangement providing for a series of substantially equal periodic payments to be made to a beneficiary (other than the executor) for his life or over a period extending for at least 36 months after the date of the decedent's death.

[For official explanation, see Committee Reports, ¶4161; 4172.]

[¶3243] CODE SEC. 2055. TRANSFERS FOR PUBLIC, CHARITABLE, AND RELIGIOUS USES.

* * * * * * * * * * * *

(f) *Special Rule for Irrevocable Transfers of Easements in Real Property.*—*A deduction shall be allowed under subsection (a) in respect of any transfer of a qualified real property interest (as defined in section 170(h)(2)(C)) which meets the requirements of section 170(h) (without regard to paragraph (4)(A) thereof).*

[1](g) **Cross References.**—

[Footnote ¶3242 continued]

(2) **Trusts, plans, and contracts to which subsection applies.**—This subsection shall apply to—

(A) any trust, plan, or contract which at the time of the decedent's separation from employment (by death or otherwise), or if earlier, at the time of termination of the plan—

(i) formed part of plan which met the requirements of section 401(a), or

(ii) was purchased pursuant to a plan described in section 403(a), or

(B) a retirement annuity contract purchased for an employee by an employer which is—

(i) an organization referred to in clause (ii) or (iv) of section 170(b)(1)(A), or

(ii) a religious organization (other than a trust) exempt from taxation under section 501(a).

(3) **Amount contributed by employee.**—For purposes of this subsection—

(A) contributions or payments made by the decedent's employer or former employer under a trust, plan, or contract described in paragraph (2)(A) shall not be considered to be contributed by the decedent, and

(B) contributions or payments made by the decedent's employer or former employer toward the purchase of an annuity contract described in paragraph (2)(B) shall not be considered to be contributed by the decedent to the extent excludable from gross income under section 403(b)."

Effective date (Sec. 1852(e)(1)(B), '86 TRA).—Applies to estates of decedents dying after the date of the enactment of this Act.

Section 1848(d), '86 TRA, struck out from Sec. 2039(e):

(2) "or a bond described in paragraph (3)"

Effective date (Sec. 1881, '86 TRA and section 491(f)(1), (4) and (5), '84 TRA).—(1) Generally applies to obligations issued after 12-31-83.

* * * * * * * * * * *

(4) Bonds under qualified bond purchase plans may be redeemed at any time.—Notwithstanding—

(A) subparagraph (D) of section 405(b)(1) of the '54 Code (as in effect before its repeal by this section), and

(B) the terms of any bond described in subsection (b) of such section 405,

such a bond may be redeemed at any time after the date of the enactment of this Act in the same manner as if the individual redeeming the bond had attained age 59½.

(5) Treatment of tax imposed under section 409(c).—For purposes of section 26(b) of the '54 Code (as amended by this Act), any tax imposed by section 409(c) of such Code (as in effect before its repeal by this section) shall be treated as a tax imposed by section 408(f) of such Code.

[Footnote ¶3243] Matter in *italics* in Sec. 2055(f) and (g) added by section 1422(a)(1) and (2), '86 TRA, which struck out:

(1) "(f)"

[For official explanation, see Committee Reports, ¶4066.]

**[¶3244] CODE SEC. 2057. SALES OF EMPLOYER SECURITIES TO EM-
PLOYEE STOCK OWNERSHIP PLANS OR WORKER-OWNED COOPERA-
TIVES.**

(a) **General Rule.**—For purposes of the tax imposed by section 2001, the value of the taxable estate shall be determined by deducting from the value of the gross estate an amount equal to 50 percent of the qualified proceeds of a qualified sale of employer securities.

(b) **Qualified Sale.**—For purposes of this section, the term "qualified sale" means any sale of employer securities by the executor of an estate to—

   (1) an employee stock ownership plan is described in section 4975(e)(7), or

   (2) an eligible worker-owned cooperative (within the meaning of section 1042(c)).

(c) **Qualified Proceeds.**—For purposes of this section—

   (1) **In general.**—The term "qualified proceeds" means the amount received by the estate from the sale of employer securities at any time before the date on which the return of the tax imposed by section 2001 is required to be filed (including any extensions).

   (2) **Proceeds from certain securities not qualified.**—The term "qualified proceeds" shall not include the proceeds from the sale of any employer securities if such securities were received by the decedent—

      (A) in a distribution from a plan exempt from tax under section 501(a) which meets the requirements of section 401(a), or

      (B) as a transfer pursuant to an option or other right to acquire stock to which section 83, 422, 422A, 423, or 424 applies.

(d) **Written Statement Required.**—

   (1) **In general.**—No deduction shall be allowed under subsection (a) unless the executor of the estate of the decedent files with the Secretary the statement described in paragraph (2).

   (2) **Statement.**—A statement is described in this paragraph if it is a verified written statement of—

      (A) the employer whose employees are covered by the plan described in subsection (b)(1), or

      (B) any authorized officer of the cooperative described in subsection (b)(2),

consenting to the application of section 4979A with respect to such employer or cooperative.

(e) **Employer Securities.**—For purposes of this section, the term "employer securities" has the meaning given such term by section 409(l).

(f) **Termination.**—This section shall not apply to any sale after December 31, 1991.

[For official explanation, see Committee Reports, ¶4017.]

[¶3245] CODE SEC. 2106. TAXABLE ESTATE.

(a) **Definition of Taxable Estate.**—For purposes of the tax imposed by section 2101, the value of the taxable estate of every decedent nonresident not a citizen of the United States shall be determined by deducting from the value of that part of his gross estate which at the time of his death is situated in the United States—

* * * * * * * * * * *

   (2) **Transfers for public, charitable, and religious uses.**—

* * * * * * * * * * *

      (F) Cross references.—

(i) For option as to time for valuation for purposes of deduction under this section, see section 2032.

(ii) For exemption of certain bequests for the benefit of the United States and for rules of construction for certain bequests, see [1] *section 2055(g).*

(iii) For treatment of gifts and bequests to or for the use of Indian tribal governments (or their subdivisions), see section 7871.

*   *   *   *   *   *   *   *   *   *   *

[For official explanation, see Committee Reports, ¶4066.]

[¶3246] CODE SEC. 2210. LIABILITY FOR PAYMENT IN CASE OF TRANS-FER OF EMPLOYER SECURITIES TO AN EMPLOYEE STOCK OWNERSHIP PLAN OR A WORKER-OWNED COOPERATIVE.

(a) **In General.**—If—

    (1) employer securities—

      (A) are acquired from the decedent by an employee stock ownership plan or by an eligible worker-owned cooperative from any decedent.

      (B) pass from the decedent to such a plan or cooperative, or

      (C) are transferred by the executor to such a plan or cooperative[1]

(2) the executor of the estate of the decedent may (without regard to this section) make an election under section 6166 with respect to that portion of the tax imposed by section 2001 which is attributable to employer securities, and

[2](3) the executor elects the application of this section and files the agreements described in subsection (e) before the due date (including extensions) for filing the return of tax imposed by section 2001,

then the executor is relieved of liability for payment of that portion of the tax imposed by section 2001 which such employee stock ownership plan or cooperative is required to pay under subsection (b).

*   *   *   *   *   *   *   *   *   *   *

(c) **Installment Payments.**—

    (1) **In general.**—If—

      (A) the executor of the estate of the decedent (without regard to this section) elects to have the provisions of section 6166 (relating to extensions of time for payment of estate tax where estate consists largely of interest in closely held business) apply to payment of that portion of the tax imposed by section 2001 with respect to such estate which is attributable to employer securities, and

      (B) the plan administrator or the cooperative provides to the executor of the agreement described in subsection (e)(1), then the plan administrator or *any authorized officer of* the cooperative may elect, before the due date (including extensions) for filing the return of such tax, to pay all or part of the tax described in subsection (b)(2) in installments under the provisions of section 6166.

*   *   *   *   *   *   *   *   *   *   *

(3) Special rules for application of section 6166(g).—In the case of any transfer of employer securities to an employee stock ownership plan or eligible worker-owned cooperative to which this section applies—

    (A) Transfer does not trigger acceleration.—Such transfer shall not be treated as a disposition or withdrawal to which section 6166(g) applies.

    (B) Separate application to estate and plan interests.—Section 6166(g) shall be applied separately to the interests held after such transfer by the estate and such plan or cooperative.

[Footnote ¶3245] Matter in *italics* in Sec. 2106(a)(2)(F)(ii) added by section 1422(c), '86 TRA, which struck out:

  (1) "section 2055(f)"

Effective date (Sec. 1422(e), '86 TRA).—Applies to transfers and contributions made after 12-31-86.

[Footnote ¶3246] Matter in *italics* in Sec. 2210(a)(1)—(3) added by section 1854(d)(1)(A), '86 TRA, which struck out:

  (1) "and"

  (2) "(2)"

Effective date (Sec. 1854(d)(1)(B), '86 TRA).—Applies to the estates of decedents dying after 9-27-85.

Matter in *italics* in Sec. 2210(c)(1), (3) and (d) added by section 1854(d)(2) and (4)—(5)(A), '86 TRA.

Effective date (Sec. 1881, '86 TRA and section 544(d), '84 TRA).—Applies to those estates of decedents which are required to file returns on a date (including any extensions) after 7-18-84.

(C)   Required distribution not taken into account.—In the case of any distribution of such securities by such plan which is described in section 4978(d)(1)—

(i)   such distribution shall not be treated as a disposition or withdrawal for purposes of section 6166(g), and

(ii)   such securities shall not be taken into account in applying section 6166(g) to any subsequent disposition or withdrawal.

(d)   Guarantee of Payments.—Any employer—

(1)   whose employees are covered by an employee stock ownership plan, and

(2)   who has entered into an agreement described in subsection (e)(2) which is in effect,

and any eligible worker-owned cooperative shall guarantee (in such manner as the Secretary [3]*may prescribe)* the payment of any amount [4]*such plan or cooperative, respectively,* is required to pay under subsection (b)[5].

* * * * * * * * * * * *

(g)   Definitions.—For purposes of this section—

* * * * * * * * * * * *

(3)   Eligible worker-owned cooperative.—The term "eligible worker-owned cooperative" has the meaning given to such term by [6] *section 1042(c)(2).*

* * * * * * * * * * * *

(5)   Tax imposed by section 2001.—The term *"tax imposed by section 2001"* includes *any interest, penalty, addition to tax, or additional amount relating to any tax imposed by section 2001.*

[For official explanation, see Committee Reports, ¶4174.]

〔¶3247〕   CODE SEC. 2503.   TAXABLE GIFTS.

* * * * * * * * * * * *

(f)   Waiver of Certain Pension Rights.—If any individual waives, before the death of a particpant, any survivor benefit, or right to such benefit, under section 401(a)(11) or 417, such waiver shall not be treated as a transfer of property by gift for purposes of this chapter.

[For official explanation, see Committee Reports, ¶4211.]

〔¶3248〕   CODE   SEC.   2515.   TREATMENT   OF   GENERATION-SKIPPING TRANSFER TAX.

In the case of any taxable gift which is a direct skip (within the meaning of chapter 13), the amount of such gift shall be increased by the amount of any tax imposed on the transferor under chapter 13 with respect to such gift.

[For official explanation, see Committee Reports, ¶4068.]

〔¶3249〕   CODE   SEC.   2517.   CERTAIN   ANNUITIES   UNDER   QUALIFIED PLANS.

[Repealed by section 1852(e)(2)(A), '86 TRA].[1]

[For official explanation, see Committee Reports, ¶4172.]

〔¶3250〕   CODE SEC. 2522.   CHARITABLE AND SIMILAR GIFTS.

〔Footnote ¶3246 continued〕

Matter in *italics* in Sec. 2210(d) added by section 1899A(37), '86 TRA, which struck out:
(3)   "may prescribe"

Matter in *italics* in Sec. 2210(d), (g)(3) and (5) added by section 1854(d)(3) and (5)(B)(C)—(6), '86 TRA, which struck out:
(4)   "such plan"
(5)   ", including any interest payable under section 6601 which is attributable to such amount"
(6)   "section 1041(b)(2)"
Effective date (Sec. 1881, '86 TRA and section 544(d), '84 TRA).—Applies to those estates of decedents which are required to file returns on a date (including any extensions) after 7-18-84.
〔Footnote ¶3247〕   Sec. 2503(f) in *italics* added by section 1898(h)(1)(B), '86 TRA.
Effective date (Sec. 1898(j), '86 TRA and sections 302 and 303, '84 Retirement Equity Act, P.L. 98-397, as amended by sections 1145(c), 1898(g), (h) of '86 TRA).—Generally applies to plan years beginning after 12-31-84.
For special and transitional rules see footnote ¶2994.
〔Footnote ¶3248〕   Sec. 2515 added by section 1432(d)(1), '86 TRA.
Effective date   (Sec. 1433(a), '86 TRA).—Applies to any generation-skipping transfers made after the date of the enactment of this Act. For special rules and election for certain transfers benefitting grandchild, see footnote ¶3252.
〔Footnote ¶3249〕 (1)   Effective date (Sec. 1852(e)(2)(E), '86 TRA).—Applies to transfers after the date of the enactment of this Act.

*   *   *   *   *   *   *   *   *   *   *

(d)   Special Rule for Irrevocable Transfers of Easements in Real Property.—A deduction shall be allowed under subsection (a) in respect of any transfer of a qualified real property interest (as defined in section 170(h)(2)(C)) which meets the requirements of section 170(h) (without regard to paragraph (4)(A) thereof).

[1](e)   **Cross Reference.—**

    (1)   **For treatment of certain organizations providing child care, see section 501(k).**

    (2)   **For exemption of certain gifts to or for the benefit of the United States and for rules of construction with respect to certain bequests see section 2055(f).**

    (3)   **For treatment of gifts to or for the use of Indian tribal governments (or their subdivisions), see section 7871.**

[For official explanation, see Committee Reports, ¶4066.]

⟦¶3251⟧   CODE SEC. 2523.   GIFT TO SPOUSE.

*   *   *   *   *   *   *   *   *   *   *

    (f)   Election With Respect to Life Estate for Donee Spouse.—

*   *   *   *   *   *   *   *   *   *   *

    (4)   Election.— [1]*(A).   Time and manner.—An election under this subsection with respect to any property shall be made on or before the date prescribed by section 6075(b) for filing a gift tax return with respect to the transfer (determined without regard to section 6019(2)) and shall be made in such manner as the Secretary shall by regulations prescribe.*

*   *   *   *   *   *   *   *   *   *   *

[For official explanation, see Committee Reports, ¶4193.]

⟦¶3252⟧   CODE SEC. 2601.   TAX IMPOSED.

⟦**Footnote ¶3250**⟧   Matter in *italics* in Sec. 2522(d) and (e) added by section 1422(b), '86 TRA, which struck out:

(1)   "(d)"

Effective date (Sec. 1422(e), '86 TRA).—Applies to transfers and contributions made after 12-31-86.

⟦**Footnote ¶3251**⟧   Matter in *italics* in Sec. 2523(f)(4)(A) added by section 1879(n)(1), '86 TRA, which struck out:

(1)   "(A)   Time and manner.—An election under this subsection with respect to any property shall be made on or before the first April 15th after the calendar year in which the interest was transferred and shall be made in such manner as the Secretary shall by regulations prescribe."

Effective date (Sec. 1879(n)(2), '86 TRA).—Applies to transfers made after 12-31-85.

⟦**Footnote ¶3252**⟧   Sec. 2601 added by section 1431(a), '86 TRA. Former Sec. 2601, as in effect before the amendment of Chapter 13 of Subtitle B of the Code by section 1431(a), '86 TRA, dealt with equivalent subject matter and read as follows:

FORMER CODE SEC. 2601.   TAX IMPOSED.

A tax is hereby imposed on every generation-skipping transfer in the amount determined under section 2602.

Effective date (Sec. 1433, '86 TRA).—(a) General rule.—Applies to any generation-skipping transfers made after the date of the enactment of this Act.

(b)   Special rules.—

(1)   Treatment of certain inter vivos transfers made after 9-25-85.—For purposes of subsection (a) (and chapter 13 of the '86 Code as amended by this part), any inter vivos transfer after 9-25-85, and on or before the date of the enactment of this Act shall be treated as if it were made on the 1st day after the date of enactment of this Act.

(2)   Exceptions.—The amendments made by this part shall not apply to—

(A)   any generation-skipping transfer under a trust which was irrevocable on 9-25-85, but only to the extent that such transfer is not made out of corpus added to the trust after 9-25-85,

(B)   any generation-skipping transfer under a will executed before the date of the enactment of this Act if the decedent dies before 1-1-87, and

(C)   any generation-skipping transfer—

(i)   under a trust to the extent such trust consists of property included in the gross estate of a decedent (other than property transferred by the decedent during his life after the date of the enactment of this Act), or reinvestments thereof, or

(ii)   which is a direct skip which occurs by reason of the death of any decedent;

but only if such decedent was, on the date of the enactment of this Act, under a mental disability to change the disposition of his property and did not regain his competence to dispose of such property before the date of his death.

(3)   Treatment of certain transfers to grandchildren.—For purposes of chapter 13 of the '86 Code, the term "direct skip" shall not include any transfer before 1-1-90, from a transferor to a grandchild of the transferor to the extent that the aggregate transfers from such transferor to such grandchild do not exceed $2,000,000.

(c)   Repeal of Existing Tax on Generation-Skipping Transfers.—

(1)   In general.—In the case of any tax imposed by chapter 13 of the '54 Code (as in effect on the day before the date of the enactment of this Act), such tax (including interest, additions to tax, and additional amounts) shall not be assessed and if assessed, the assessment shall be abated, and if collected, shall be credited or refunded (with interest) as an overpayment.

A tax is hereby imposed on every generation-skipping transfer (within the meaning of subchapter B).

[For official explanation, see Committee Reports, ¶4068.]

【¶3253】 CODE SEC. 2602. AMOUNT OF TAX.

【Footnote ¶3252 continued】

(2) Waiver of statute of limitations.—If on the date of the enactment of this Act (or at any time within 1 year after such date of enactment) refund or credit of any overpayment of tax resulting from the application of paragraph (1) is barred by any law or rule of law, refund or credit of such overpayment shall, nevertheless, be made or allowed if claim therefore is filed before the date 1 year after the date of the enactment of this Act.

(d) Election for Certain Transfers Benefitting Grandchild.—

(1) In general.—For purposes of chapter 13 of the '86 Code (as amended by this Act) and subsection (b) of this section, any transfer in trust for the benefit of a grandchild of a transferor shall be treated as a direct skip if—

(A) the transfer occurs before the date of enactment of this Act,

(B) the transfer would be a direct skip except for the fact that the trust instrument provides that, if the grandchild dies before vesting of the interest transferred, the interest is transferred to the grandchild's heir (rather than the grandchild's estate), and

(C) an election under this subsection applies to such transfer.

Any transfer treated as a direct skip by reason of the preceding sentence shall be subject to Federal estate tax on the grandchild's death in the same manner as if the contingent gift over had been to the grandchild's estate.

(2) Election.—An election under paragraph (1) shall be made at such time and in such manner as the Secretary of the Treasury or his delegate may prescribe.

【Footnote ¶3253】 Sec. 2602 added by section 1431(a), '86 TRA. Former Sec. 2602, as in effect before the amendment of Chapter 13 of Subtitle B of the Code by section 1431(a), '86 TRA, dealt with related subject matter and read as follows:

FORMER CODE SEC. 2602. AMOUNT OF TAX.

(a) **General Rule.**—The amount of the tax imposed by section 2601 with respect to any transfer shall be the excess of—

(1) a tentative tax computed in accordance with the rate schedule set forth in section 2001(c) (as in effect on the date of transfer) on the sum of—

(A) the fair market value of the property transferred determined as of the date of transfer (or in the case of an election under subsection (d), as of the applicable valuation date prescribed by section 2032),

(B) the aggregate fair market value (determined for purposes of this chapter) of all prior transfers of the deemed transferor to which this chapter applied,

(C) the amount of the adjusted taxable gifts (within the meaning of section 2001(b), as modified by section 2001(e)) made by the deemed transferor before this transfer, and

(D) if the deemed transferor has died at the same time as, or before, this transfer, the taxable estate of the deemed transferor, over

(2) a tentative tax (similarly computed) on the sum of the amounts determined under subparagraphs (B), (C), and (D) of paragraph (1).

(b) **Multiple Simultaneous Transfers.**—If two or more transfers which are taxable under section 2601 and which have the same deemed transferor occur by reason of the same event, the tax imposed by section 2601 on each such transfer shall be the amount which bears the same ratio to—

(1) the amount of the tax which would be imposed by section 2601 if the aggregate of such transfers were a single transfer, as

(2) the fair market value of the property transferred in such transfer bears to the aggregate fair market value of all property transferred in such transfers.

(c) **Deductions, Credits, Etc.—**

(1) **General rule.**—Except as otherwise provided in this subsection, no deduction, exclusion, exemption, or credit shall be allowed against the tax imposed by section 2601.

(2) **Charitable deductions allowed.**—The deduction under section 2055, 2106(a)(2), or 2522, whichever is appropriate, shall be allowed in determining the tax imposed by section 2601.

(3) **Unused portion of unified credit.**—If the generation-skipping transfer occurs at the same time as, or after, the death of the deemed transferor, then the portion of the credit under section 2010(a) (relating to unified credit) which exceeds the sum of—

(A) the tax imposed by section 2001, and

(B) the taxes theretofore imposed by section 2601 with respect to this deemed transferor,

shall be allowed as a credit against the tax imposed by section 2601. The amount of the credit allowed by the preceding sentence shall not exceed the amount of the tax imposed by section 2601.

(4) **Credit for prior transfers.**—The credit under section 2013 (relating to credit for tax on prior transfers) shall be allowed against the tax imposed by section 2601. For purposes of the preceding sentence, section 2013 shall be applied as if so much of the property subject to tax under section 2601 as is not taken into account for purposes of determining the credit allowable by section 2013 with respect to the estate of the deemed transferor passed from the transferor (as defined in section 2013) to the deemed transferor.

(5) **Coordination with estate tax.—**

(A) Certain expenses attributable to generation-skipping transfer.—If the generation-skipping transfer occurs at the same time as, or after, the death of the deemed transferor, for purposes of this section, the amount taken into account with respect to such transfer shall be reduced—

(i) in the case of a taxable termination, by any item referred to in section 2053 or 2054 to the extent that a deduction would have been allowable under such section for such item if the amount of the trust had been includ-

The amount of the tax imposed by section 2601 is—

(1) the taxable amount (determined under subchapter C), multiplied by

(2) the applicable rate (determined under subchapter E).

[For official explanation, see Committee Reports, ¶4068.]

[¶3254] CODE SEC. 2603. LIABILITY FOR TAX.

[Footnote ¶3253 continued]

ible in the deemed transferor's gross estate and if the deemed transferor had died immediately before such transfer; or

(ii) in the case of a taxable distribution, by any expense incurred in connection with the determination, collection, or refund of the tax imposed by section 2601 on such transfer.

(B) **Credit for state inheritance tax.**—If the generation-skipping transfer occurs at the same time as, or after, the death of the deemed transferor, there shall be allowed as a credit against the tax imposed by section 2601 an amount equal to that portion of the estate, inheritance, legacy, or succession tax actually paid to any State or the District of Columbia in respect of any property included in the generation-skipping transfer, but only to the extent of the lesser of—

(i) that portion of such taxes which is levied on such transfer, or

(ii) the excess of the limitation applicable under section 2011(b) if the adjusted taxable estate of the decedent had been increased by the amount of the transfer and all prior generation-skipping tranfers to which this subparagraph applied which had the same deemed transferor, over the sum of the amount allowable as a credit under section 2011 with respect to the estate of the decendent plus the aggregate amounts allowable under this subparagraph with respect to such prior generation-skipping transfers.

(d) **Alternate Valuation.**—

(1) **In general.**—In the case of—

(A) 1 or more generation-skipping transfers from the same trust which have the same deemed transferor and which are taxable terminations occurring at the same time as the death of such deemed transferor (or at the same time as the death of a beneficiary of the trust assigned to a higher generation than such deemed transferor); or

(B) 1 or more generation-skipping transfers from the same trust with different deemed transferors—

(i) which are taxable terminations occuring on the same day; and

(ii) which would, but for section 2613(b)(2), have occurred at the same time as the death of the individuals who are the deemed transferors with respect to the transfers;

the trustee may elect to value all of the property transferred in such transfers in accordance with section 2032.

(2) **Special rules.**—If the trustee makes an election under paragraph (1) with respect to any generation-skipping transfer, section 2032 shall be applied by taking into account (in lieu of the date of the decedent's death) the following date:

(A) in the case of any generation-skipping transfer described in paragraph (1)(A), the date of the death of the deemed transferor (or beneficiary) described in such paragraph, or

(B) in the case of any generation-skipping transfer described in paragraph (1)(B), the date on which such transfer occurred.

(e) **Transfers Within 3 Years of Death of Deemed Transferor.**—Under regulations prescribed by the Secretary, the principles of section 2035 shall apply with respect to transfers made during the 3-year period ending on the date of the deemed transferor's death. In the case of any transfer to which this subsection applies, the amount of the tax imposed by this chapter shall be determined as if the transfer occurred after the death of the deemed transferor and appropriate adjustments shall be made with respect to the amount of any prior transfer which is taken into account under subparagraph (B) or (C) of subsection (a)(1).

Effective date (Sec. 1433(a), '86 TRA).—Generally applies to any generation-skipping transfers made after the date of the enactment of this Act. For special rules and transitional rules for transfers to grandchildren, see footnote ¶3252.

[Footnote ¶3254] Sec. 2603 added by section 1431(a), '86 TRA. Former Sec. 2603, as in effect before the amendment of Chapter 13 of Subtitle B of the Code by section 1431(a), '86 TRA, dealt with related subject matter and read as follows:

FORMER CODE SEC. 2603. LIABILITY FOR TAX.

(a) **Personal Liability.**—

(1) **In general.**—If the tax imposed by section 2601 is not paid, when due then—

(A) except to the extent provided in paragraph (2), the trustee shall be personally liable for any portion of such tax which is attributable to a taxable termination, and

(B) the distributee of the property shall be personally liable for such tax to the extent provided in paragraph (3).

(2) **Limitation of personal liability of trustee who relies on certain information furnished by the Secretary.**—

(A) **Information with respect to rates.**—The trustee shall not be personally liable for any increase in the tax imposed by section 2601 which is attributable to the application to the transfer of rates of tax which exceed the rates of tax furnished by the Secretary to the trustee as being the rates at which the transfer may reasonably be expected to be taxed.

(B) **Amount of remaining exclusion.**—The trustee shall not be personally liable for any increase in the tax imposed by section 2601 which is attributable to the fact that—

(i) the amount furnished by the Secretary to the trustee as being the amount of the exclusion for a transfer to a grandchild of the grantor of the trust which may reasonably be expected to remain with respect to the deemed transferor, is less than

(ii) the amount of such exclusion remaining with respect to such deemed transferor.

(3) **Limitation on personal liability of distributee.**—The distributee of the property shall be personally liable for the tax imposed by section 2601 only to the extent of an amount equal to the fair market value (determined as of

(a) Personal Liability.—

(1) Taxable distributions.—In the case of a taxable distribution, the tax imposed by section 2601 shall be paid by the transferee.

(2) Taxable termination.—In the case of a taxable termination or a direct skip from a trust, the tax shall be paid by the trustee.

(3) Direct skip.—In the case of a direct skip (other than a direct skip from a trust), the tax shall be paid by the transferor.

(b) Source of Tax.—Unless otherwise directed pursuant to the governing instrument by specific reference to the tax imposed by this chapter, the tax imposed by this chapter on a generation-skipping transfer shall be charged to the property constituting such transfer.

(c) Cross Reference.—

For provisions making estate and gift tax provisions with respect to transferee liability, liens, and related matters applicable to the tax imposed by section 2601, see section 2661.

[For official explanation, see Committee Reports, ¶4068.]

〔¶3255〕 CODE SEC. 2604. CREDIT FOR CERTAIN STATE TAXES.

(a) General Rule.—If a generation-skipping transfer (other than a direct skip) occurs at the same time as and as a result of the death of an individual, a credit against the tax imposed by section 2601 shall be allowed in an amount equal to the generation-skipping transfer tax actually paid to any State in respect to any property included in the generation-skipping transfer.

(b) Limitation.—The aggregate amount allowed as a credit under this section with respect to any transfer shall not exceed 5 percent of the amount of the tax imposed by section 2601 on such transfer.

[For official explanation, see Committee Reports, ¶4068.]

〔¶3256〕 CODE SEC. 2611. GENERATION-SKIPPING TRANSFER DEFINED.

〔Footnote ¶3254 continued〕
the time of the distribution) of the property received by the distributee in the distribution.

(b) Lien.—The tax imposed by section 2601 on any transfer shall be a lien on the property transferred until the tax is paid in full or becomes unenforceable by reason of lapse of time.

Effective date (Sec. 1433(a), '86 TRA).—Generally applies to any generation-skipping transfers made after the date of the enactment of this Act. For special rules and transitional rules for transfers to grandchildren, see footnote ¶3252.

〔Footnote ¶3255〕 Sec. 2604 added by section 1431(a), '86 TRA. Former Sec. 2602(c)(5)(B), as in effect before the amendment of Chapter 13 of Subtitle B of the Code by section 1431(a), '86 TRA, dealt with related subject matter and read as follows:

FORMER CODE SEC. 2602. AMOUNT OF TAX.

* * * * * * * * * * * *

(c) Deductions, Credits, Etc.—

* * * * * * * * * * * *

(5) Coordination with estate tax.—

* * * * * * * * * * * *

(B) Credit for state inheritance tax.—If the generation-skipping transfer occurs at the same time as, or after, the death of the deemed transferor, there shall be allowed as a credit against the tax imposed by section 2601 an amount equal to that portion of the estate, inheritance, legacy, or succession tax actually paid to any State or the District of Columbia in respect of any property included in the generation-skipping transfer, but only to the extent of the lesser of—

(i) that portion of such taxes which is levied on such transfer, or

(ii) the excess of the limitation applicable under section 2011(b) if the adjusted taxable estate of the decedent had been increased by the amount of the transfer and all prior generation-skipping transfers to which this subparagraph applied which had the same deemed transferor, over the sum of the amount allowable as a credit under section 2011 with respect to the estate of the decedent plus the aggregate amounts allowable under this subparagraph with respect to such prior generation-skipping transfers.

Effective date (Sec. 1433(a), '86 TRA).—Generally applies to any generation-skipping transfers made after the date of the enactment of this Act. For special rules and transitional rules for transfers to grandchildren, see footnote ¶3252.

〔Footnote ¶3256〕 Sec. 2611 added by section 1431(a), '86 TRA. Former Sec. 2611, as in effect before the amendment of Chapter 13 of Subtitle B of the Code by section 1431(a), '86 TRA, dealt with related subject matter and read as follows:

FORMER CODE SEC. 2611. GENERATION-SKIPPING TRANSFER.

(a) Generation-Skipping Transfer Defined.—For purposes of this chapter, the terms "generation-skipping trans-

(a) **In General.**—For purposes of this chapter, the term "generation-skipping transfers" mean—

    (1)   a taxable distribution,

    (2)   a taxable termination, and

    (3)   a direct skip.

(b) **Certain Transfers Excluded.**—The term "generation-skipping transfer" does not include—

    (1)   any transfer (other than a direct skip) from a trust, to the extent such transfer is subject to a tax imposed by chapter 11 or 12 with respect to a person in the 1st generation below that of the grantor, and

    (2)   any transfer which, if made inter vivos by an individual, would not be treated as a taxable gift by reason of section 2503(e) (relating to exclusion of certain transfers for educational or medical expenses), and

    (3)   any transfer to the extent—

        (A)   the property transferred was subject to a prior tax imposed under this chapter,

        (B)   the transferee in the prior transfer was assigned to the same generation as (or a lower generation than) the generation assignment of the transferee in this transfer, and

        (C)   such transfers do not have the effect of avoiding tax under this chapter with respect to any transfer.

[For official explanation, see Committee Reports, ¶4068.]

【¶3257】 CODE SEC. 2612. TAXABLE TERMINATION; TAXABLE DISTRIBUTION; DIRECT SKIP.

【Footnote ¶3256 continued】

fer" and "transfer" mean any taxable distribution or taxable termination with respect to a generation-skipping trust or trust equivalent.

(b) **Generation-Skipping Trust.**—For purposes of this chapter, the term "generation-skipping trust" means any trust having younger generation beneficiaries (within the meaning of section 2613(c)(1)) who are assigned to more than one generation.

(c) **Ascertainment of Generation.**—For purposes of this chapter, the generation to which any person (other than the grantor) belongs shall be determined in accordance with the following rules:

(1) an individual who is a lineal descendant of a grandparent of the grantor shall be assigned to that generation which results from comparing the number of generations between the grandparent and such individual with the number of generations between the grandparent and the grantor.

(2) an individual who has been at any time married to a person described in paragraph (1) shall be assigned to the generation of the person so described and an individual who has been at any time married to the grantor shall be assigned to the grantor's generation,

(3) a relationship by the half blood shall be treated as a relationship by the whole blood,

(4) a relationship by legal adoption shall be treated as a relationship by blood,

(5) an individual who is not assigned to a generation by reason of the foregoing paragraphs shall be assigned to a generation on the basis of the date of such individual's birth, with—

(A) an individual born not more than $12\frac{1}{2}$ years after the date of the birth of the grantor assigned to the grantor's generation,

(B) an individual born more than $12\frac{1}{2}$ years but not more than $37\frac{1}{2}$ years after the date of the birth of the grantor assigned to the first generation younger than the grantor, and

(C) similar rules for a new generation every 25 years,

(6) an individual who, but for this paragraph, would be assigned to more than one generation shall be assigned to the youngest such generation, and

(7) if any beneficiary of the trust is an estate or a trust, partnership, corporation, or other entity (other than an organization described in section 511(a)(2) and other than a charitable trust described in section 511(b)(2)), each individual having an indirect interest to power in the trust through such entity shall be treated as a beneficiary of the trust and shall be assigned to a generation under the foregoing provisions of this subsection.

(d) **Generation-Skipping Trust Equivalent.—**

(1) **In general.**—For purposes of this chapter, the term "generation-skipping trust equivalent" means any arrangement which, although not a trust, has substantially the same effect as a generation-skipping trust.

(2) **Examples of arrangements to which subsection relates.**—Arrangements to be taken into account for purposes of determining whether or not paragraph (1) applies include (but are not limited to) arrangements involving life estates and remainders, estates for years, insurance and annuities, and split interests.

(3) **References to trust include references to trust equivalents.**—Any reference in this chapter in respect of a generation-skipping trust shall include the appropriate reference in respect of a generation-skipping trust equivalent.

Effective date (Sec. 1433(a), '86 TRA).—Generally applies to any generation-skipping transfers made after the date of the enactment of this Act. For special rules and transitional rules for transfers to grandchildren, see footnote ¶3252.

【Footnote ¶3257】 Sec. 2612 added by section 1431(a), '86 TRA. Former Secs. 2612 and 2613, as in effect before the amendment of Chapter 13 of Subtitle B of the Code by section 1431(a), '86 TRA, dealt with related subject matter and read as follows:

[Footnote ¶3257 continued]

FORMER CODE SEC. 2612. DEEMED TRANSFEROR.

(a) General Rule.—For purposes of this chapter, the deemed transferor with respect to a transfer is—

(1) except as provided in paragraph (2), the parent of the transferee of the property who is more closely related to the grantor of the trust than the other parent of such transferee (or if neither parent is related to such grantor, the parent having a closer affinity to the grantor), or

(2) if the parent described in paragraph (1) is not a younger generation beneficiary of the trust but 1 or more ancestors of the transferee is a younger generation beneficiary related by blood or adoption to the grantor of the trust, the youngest of such ancestors.

(b) Determination of Relationship.—For purposes of subsection (a), a parent related to the grantor of the trust by blood or adoption is more closely related than a parent related to such grantor by marriage.

FORMER CODE SEC. 2613. OTHER DEFINITIONS.

(a) Taxable Distribution.—For purposes of this chapter—

(1) **In general.**—The term "taxable distribution" means any distribution which is not out of the income of the trust (within the meaning of section 643(b)) from a generation-skipping trust to any younger generation beneficiary who is assigned to a generation younger than the generation assignment of any other person who is a younger generation beneficiary. For purposes of the preceding sentence, an individual who at no time has had anything other than a future interest or future power (or both) in the trust shall not be considered as a younger generation beneficiary.

(2) **Source of distributions.**—If, during the taxable year of the trust, there are distributions out of the income of the trust (within the meaning of section 643(b)) and out of other amounts, for purposes of paragraph (1) the distributions of such income shall be deemed to have been made to the beneficiaries (to the extent of the aggregate distributions made to each such beneficiary during such year) in descending order of generations, beginning with the beneficiaries assigned to the oldest generation.

(3) **Payment of tax.**—If any portion of the tax imposed by this chapter with respect to any transfer is paid out of the income or corpus of the trust, an amount equal to the portion so paid shall be deemed to be a generation-skipping transfer.

(4) **Certain distributions excluded from tax.**—The term "taxable distribution" does not include—

(A) any transfer to the extent such transfer is to a grandchild of the grantor of the trust and does not exceed the limitation provided by subsection (b)(6), and

(B) any transfer to the extent such transfer is subject to tax imposed by chapter 11 or 12.

(b) Taxable Termination.—For purposes of this chapter—

(1) **In general.**—The term "taxable termination" means the termination (by death, lapse of time, exercise or nonexercise, or otherwise) of the interest or power in a generation-skipping trust of any younger generation beneficiary who is assigned to any generation older than the generation assignment of any other person who is a younger generation beneficiary of that trust. Such term does not include a termination of the interest or power of any person who at no time has had anything other than a future interest or future power (or both) in the trust.

(2) **Time certain termination deemed to occur.**—

(A) Where 2 or more beneficiaries are assigned to same generation.—In any case where 2 or more younger generation beneficiaries of a trust are assigned to the same generation, except to the extent provided in regulations prescribed by the Secretary, the transfer constituting the termination with respect to each such beneficiary shall be treated as occurring at the time when the last such termination occurs.

(B) Same beneficiary has more than 1 present interest or present power.—In any case where a younger generation beneficiary of a trust has both a present interest and a present power, or more than 1 present interest or present power, in the trust, except to the extent provided in regulations prescribed by the Secretary, the termination with respect to each such present interest or present power shall be treated as occurring at the time when the last such termination occurs.

(C) Unusual order of termination.—

(i) In general.—If—

(I) but for this subparagraph, there would have been a termination (determined after the application of subparagraphs (A) and (B)) of an interest or power of a younger generation beneficiary (hereinafter in this subparagraph referred to as the "younger beneficiary"), and

(II) at the time such termination would have occurred, a beneficiary (hereinafter in this subparagraph referred to as the "older beneficiary") of the trust assigned to a higher generation than the generation of the young beneficiary has a present interest or power in the trust,

then, except to the extent provided in regulations prescribed by the Secretary, the transfer constituting the termination with respect to the younger beneficiary shall be treated as occurring at the time when the termination of the last present interest or power of the older beneficiary occurs.

(ii) Special rules.—If clause (i) applies with respect to any younger beneficiary—

(I) this chapter shall be applied first to the termination of the interest or power of the older beneficiary as if such termination occurred before the termination of the power or interest of the younger beneficiary; and

(II) the value of the property taken into account for purposes of determining the tax (if any) imposed by this chapter with respect to the termination of the interest or power of the younger beneficiary shall be reduced by the tax (if any) imposed by this chapter with respect to the termination of the interest or power of the older beneficiary.

(D) Special rule.—Subparagraphs (A) and (C) shall also apply where a person assigned to the same generation as, or a higher generation than, the person whose power or interest terminates has a present power or interest immediately after the termination and such power or interest arises as a result of such termination.

(3) **Deemed transferees of certain terminations.**—Where, at the time of any termination, it is not clear who will be the transferee of any portion of the property transferred, except to the extent provided in regulations prescribed

Code §2612 ¶3257

[Footnote ¶3257 continued]

by the Secretary, such portion shall be deemed transferred pro rata to all beneficiaries of the trust in accordance with the amount which each of them would receive under a maximum exercise of discretion on their behalf. For purposes of the preceding sentence, where it is not clear whether discretion will be exercised per stirpes or per capita, it shall be presumed that the discretion will be exercised per stirpes.

(4) Termination of power.—In the case of the termination of any power, the property transferred shall be deemed to be the property subject to the power immediately before the termination (determined without the application of paragraph (2)).

(5) Certain terminations excluded from tax.—The term "taxable termination" does not include—

(A) any transfer to the extent such transfer is to a grandchild of the grantor of the trust and does not exceed the limitation provided by paragraph (6), and

(B) any transfer to the extent such transfer is subject to a tax imposed by chapter 11 or 12.

(6) $250,000 limit on exclusion of transfers to grandchildren.—In the case of any deemed transferor, the maximum amount excluded from the terms "taxable distribution" and "taxable termination" by reason of provisions exempting from such terms transfers to the grandchildren of the grantor of the trust shall be $250,000. The preceding sentence shall be applied to transfers from one or more trusts in the order in which such transfers are made or deemed made.

(7) Coordination with subsection (a).—

(A) Terminations take precedence over distributions.—If—

(i) the death of an individual or any other occurrence is a taxable termination with respect to any property, and

(ii) such occurrence also requires the distribution of part or all of such property in a distribution which would (but for this subparagraph) be a taxable distribution,

then a taxable distribution shall be deemed not to have occurred with respect to the portion described in clause (i).

(B) Certain prior transfers.—To the extent that—

(i) the deemed transferor in any prior transfer of the property of the trust being transferred in this transfer was assigned to the same generation as (or a lower generation than) the generation assignment of the deemed transferor in this transfer,

(ii) the transferee in such prior transfer was assigned to the same generation as (or a higher generation than) the generation assignment of the transferee in this transfer, and

(iii) such transfers do not have the effect of avoiding tax under this chapter with respect to any transfer,

the terms "taxable termination" and "taxable distribution" do not include this later transfer.

(c) Younger Generation Beneficiary; Beneficiary.—For purposes of this chapter—

(1) Younger generation beneficiary.—The term "younger generation beneficiary" means any beneficiary who is assigned to a generation younger than the grantor's generation.

(2) Time for ascertaining younger generation beneficiaries.—A person is a younger generation beneficiary of a trust with respect to any transfer only if such person was a younger generation beneficiary of the trust immediately before the transfer (or, in the case of a series of related transfers, only if such person was a younger generation beneficiary of the trust immediately before the first of such transfers).

(3) Beneficiary.—The term "beneficiary" means any person who has a present or future interest or power in the trust.

(d) Interest or Power.—For purposes of this chapter—

(1) Interest.—A person has an interest in a trust if such person—

(A) has a right to receive income or corpus from the trust, or

(B) is a permissible recipient of such income or corpus.

(2) Power.—The term "power" means any power to establish or alter beneficial enjoyment of the corpus or income of the trust.

(e) Certain Powers Not Taken Into Account.—

(1) Limited power to appoint among lineal descendants of the grantor.—For purposes of this chapter, an individual shall be treated as not having any power in a trust if such individual does not have any present or future power in the trust other than a power to dispose of the corpus of the trust or the income therefrom to a beneficiary or a class of beneficiaries who are lineal descendants of the grantor assigned to a generation younger than the generation assignment of such individual.

(2) Powers of independent trustees.—

(A) In general.—For purposes of this chapter, an individual shall be treated as not having any power in a trust if such individual—

(i) is a trustee who has no interest in the trust (other than as a potential appointee under a power of appointment held by another),

(ii) is not a related or subordinate trustee, and

(iii) does not have any present or future power in the trust other than a power to dispose of the corpus of the trust or the income therefrom to a beneficiary or a class of beneficiaries designated in the trust instrument.

(B) Related or subordinate trustee defined.—For purposes of subparagraph (A), the term "related or subordinate trustee" means any trustee who is assigned to a younger generation than the grantor's generation and who is—

(i) the spouse of the grantor or of any beneficiary,

(ii) the father, mother, lineal descendant, brother, or sister of the grantor or of any beneficiary,

(iii) an employee of the grantor or of any beneficiary,

(iv) an employee of a corporation in which the stockholdings of the grantor, the trust, and the beneficiaries of the trust are significant from the viewpoint of voting control,

(v) an employee of a corporation in which the grantor or any beneficiary of the trust is an executive,

(vi) a partner of a partnership in which the interest of the grantor, the trust, and the beneficiaries of the trust are significant from the viewpoint of operating control or distributive share of partnership income, or

(a) Taxable Termination.—

(1) General rule.—For purposes of this chapter, the term "taxable termination" means the termination (by death, lapse of time, release of power, or otherwise) of an interest in property held in a trust unless—

(A) immediately after such termination, a non-skip person has an interest in such property, or

(B) at no time after such termination may a distribution (including distributions on termination) be made from such trust to a skip person.

(2) Certain partial terminations treated as taxable.—If, upon the termination of an interest in property held in a trust, a specified portion of the trust assets are distributed to skip persons who are lineal descendants of the holder of such interest (or to 1 or more trusts for the exclusive benefit of such persons), such termination shall constitute a taxable termination with respect to such portion of the trust property.

(b) Taxable Distribution.—For purposes of this chapter, the term "taxable distribution" means any distribution from a trust to a skip person (other than a taxable termination or a direct skip).

(c) Direct Skip.—For purposes of this chapter—

(1) In general.—The term "direct skip" means a transfer subject to a tax imposed by chapter 11 or 12 of an interest in property to a skip person.

(2) Special rule for transfers to grandchildren.—For purposes of determining whether any transfer is a direct skip, if—

(A) an individual is a grandchild of the transferor (or the transferor's spouse or former spouse), and

(B) as of the time of the transfer, the parent of such individual who is a lineal descendant of the transferor (or the transferor's spouse or former spouse) is dead,

such individual shall be treated as if such individual were a child of the transferor and all of that grandchild's children shall be treated as if they were grandchildren of the transferor. In the case of lineal descendants below a grandchild, the preceding sentence may be reapplied.

[For official explanation, see Committee Reports, ¶4068.]

[¶3258] CODE SEC. 2613. SKIP PERSON AND NON-SKIP PERSON DEFINED.

(a) Skip Person.—For purposes of this chapter, the term "skip person" means—

(1) a person assigned to a generation which is 2 or more generations below the generation assignment of the transferor, or

(2) a trust—

(A) if all interests in such trust are held by skip persons, or

(B) if—

(i) there is no person holding an interest in such trust, and

(ii) at no time after such transfer may a distribution (including distributions on termination) be made from such trust to a nonskip person.

(b) Non-Skip Person.—For purposes of this chapter, the term "non-skip person" means any person who is not a skip person.

[For official explanation, see Committee Reports, ¶4068.]

[Footnote ¶3257 continued]

(vii) an employee of a partnership in which the grantor or any beneficiary of the trust is a partner.

(f) **Effect of Adoption.**—For purposes of this chapter, a relationship by legal adoption shall be treated as a relationship by blood.

Effective date (Sec. 1433(a), '86 TRA).—Generally applies to any generation-skipping transfers made after the date of the enactment of this Act. For special rules and transitional rules for transfers to grandchildren, see footnote ¶3252.

[Footnote ¶3258] Sec. 2613 added by section 1431(a), '86 TRA. For former Sec. 2613, as in effect before the amendment of Chapter 13 of Subtitle B of the Code by section 1431(a), '86 TRA, which dealt with related subject matter, see footnote ¶3257.

Effective date (Sec. 1433(a), '86 TRA).—Generally applies to any generation-skipping transfers made after the date of the enactment of this Act. For special rules and transitional rules for transfers to grandchildren, see footnote ¶3252.

〖¶3259〗 CODE SEC. 2621. TAXABLE AMOUNT IN CASE OF TAXABLE DISTRIBUTION.

(a) **In General.**—For purposes of this chapter, the taxable amount in the case of any taxable distribution shall be—

(1) the value of the property received by the transferee, reduced by

(2) any expense incurred by the transferee in connection with the determination, collection, or refund of the tax imposed by this chapter with respect to such distribution.

(b) **Payment of GST Tax Treated as Taxable Distribution.**—For purposes of this chapter, if any of the tax imposed by this chapter with respect to any taxable distribution is paid out of the trust, an amount equal to the portion so paid shall be treated as a taxable distribution.

[For official explanation, see Committee Reports, ¶4068.]

〖¶3260〗 CODE SEC. 2622. TAXABLE AMOUNT IN CASE OF TAXABLE TERMINATION.

(a) **In general.**—For purposes of this chapter, the taxable amount in the case of a taxable termination shall be—

(1) the value of all property with respect to which the taxable termination has occurred, reduced by

(2) Any deduction allowed under subsection (b).

(b) **Deduction for Certain Expenses.**—For purposes of subsection (a), there shall be allowed a deduction similar to the deduction allowed by section 2053 (relating to expenses, indebtedness, and taxes) for amounts attributable to the property with respect to which the taxable termination has occurred.

[For official explanation, see Committee Reports, ¶4068.]

〖¶3261〗 CODE SEC. 2623. TAXABLE AMOUNT IN CASE OF DIRECT SKIP.

For purposes of this chapter, the taxable amount in the case of a direct skip shall be the value of the property received by the transferee.

[For official explanation, see Committee Reports, ¶4068.]

〖¶3262〗 CODE SEC. 2624. VALUATION.

(a) **General Rule.**—Except as otherwise provided in this chapter, property shall be

---

〖**Footnote ¶3259**〗 Sec. 2621 added by section 1431(a), '86 TRA. For former Sec. 2613(a), as in effect before the amendment of Chapter 13 of Subtitle B of the Code by section 1431(a), '86 TRA, which dealt with related subject matter, see footnote ¶3257.

Effective date (Sec. 1433(a), '86 TRA).—Generally applies to any generation-skipping transfers made after the date of the enactment of this Act. For special rules and transitional rules for transfers to grandchildren, see footnote ¶3252.

〖**Footnote ¶3260**〗 Sec. 2622 added by section 1431(a), '86 TRA.

For former Sec. 2613(b), as in effect before the amendment of Chapter 13 of Subtitle B of the Code by section 1431(a), '86 TRA, which dealt with related subject matter, see footnote ¶3257.

Effective date (Sec. 1433(a), '86 TRA).—Generally applies to any generation-skipping transfers made after the date of the enactment of this Act. For special rules and transitional rules for transfers to grandchildren, see footnote ¶3252.

〖**Footnote ¶3261**〗 Sec. 2623 added by section 1431(a), '86 TRA.

Effective date (Sec. 1433(a), '86 TRA).—Generally applies to any generation-skipping transfers made after the date of the enactment of this Act. For special rules and transitional rules for transfers to grandchildren, see footnote ¶3252.

〖**Footnote ¶3262**〗 Sec. 2624 added by section 1431(a), '86 TRA.

Former Sec. 2602(d), as in effect before the amendment of Chapter 13 of Subtitle B of the Code by section 1431(a), '86 TRA, dealt with related subject matter and read as follows:

CODE SEC. 2602. AMOUNT OF TAX.

* * * * * * * * * * * *

(d) **Alternate Valuation.**—

(1) **In general.**—In the case of—

(A) 1 or more generation-skipping transfers from the same trust which have the same deemed transferor and which are taxable terminations occurring at the same time as the death of such deemed transferor (or at the same time as the death of a beneficiary of the trust assigned to a higher generation than such deemed transferor); or

(B) 1 or more generation-skipping transfers from the same trust with different deemed transferors—

(i) which are taxable terminations occurring on the same day; and

(ii) which would, but for section 2613(b)(2), have occurred at the same time as the death of the individuals who are deemed transferors with respect to the transfers;

the trustee may elect to value all of the property transferred in such transfers in accordance with section 2032.

(2) **Special rules.**—If the trustee makes an election under paragraph (1) with respect to any generation-skipping transfer, section 2032 shall be applied by taking into account (in lieu of the date of the decedent's death) the following date:

valued as of the time of the generation-skipping transfer.

(b) Alternate Valuation and Special Use Valuation Elections Apply to Certain Direct Skips.—In the case of any direct skip of property which is included in the transferor's gross estate, the value of such property for purposes of this chapter shall be the same as its value for purposes of chapter 11 (determined with regard to sections 2032 and 2032A).

(c) Alternate Valuation Election Permitted in the Case of Taxble Teminations Occurring at Death.—If 1 or more taxable terminations with respect to the same trust occur at the same time as and as a result of the death of an individual, an election may be made to value all of the property included in such terminations in accordance with section 2032.

(d) Reduction for Consideration Provided by Transferee.—For purposes of this chapter, the value of the property transferred shall be reduced by the amount of any consideration provided by the transferee.

[For official explanation, see Committee Reports, ¶4068.]

[¶3263] CODE SEC. 2631. GST EXEMPTION.

(a) General Rule.—For purposes of determining the inclusion ratio, every individual shall be allowed a GST exemption of $1,000,000 which may be allocated by such individual (or his executor) to any property which respect to which such individual is the transferor.

(b) Allocations Irrevocable.—Any allocation under subsection (a), once made, shall be irrevocable.

[For official explanation, see Committee Reports, ¶4068.]

[¶3264] CODE SEC. 2632. SPECIAL RULES FOR ALLOCATION OF GST EXEMPTION.

(a) Time and Manner of Allocation.—

(1) Time.—Any allocation by an individual of his GST exemption under section 2631(a) may be made at any time on or before the date prescribed for filing the estate tax return for such individual's estate (determined with regard to extensions), regardless of whether such a return is required to be filed.

(2) Manner.—The Secretary shall prescribe by forms or regulations the manner in which any allocation referred to in paragraph (1) is to be made.

(b) Deemed Allocation to Certain Lifetime Direct Skips.—

(1) In general.—If any individual makes a direct skip during his lifetime, any unused portion of such individual's GST exemption shall be allocated to the property transferred to the extent necessary to make the inclusion ratio for such property zero. If the amount of the direct skip exceeds such unused portion, the entire unused portion shall be allocated to the property transferred.

(2) Unused portion.—For purposes of paragraph (1), the unused portion of an individual's GST exemption is that portion of such exemption which has not previously been allocated by such individual (or treated as allocated under paragraph (1)) with respect to a prior direct skip.

[Footnote ¶3262 continued]

(A) in the case of any generation-skipping transfer described in paragraph (1)(A), the date of the death of the deemed transferor (or beneficiary) described in such paragraph, or

(B) in the case of any generation-skipping transfer described in paragraph (1)(B), the date on which such transfer occurred.

Effective date (Sec. 1433(a), '86 TRA).—Generally applies to any generation-skipping transfers made after the date of the enactment of this Act. For special rules and transitional rules for transfers to grandchildren, see footnote ¶3252.

[Footnote ¶3263] Sec. 2631 added by section 1431(a), '86 TRA.

Effective date (Sec. 1433(a), '86 TRA).—Generally applies to any generation-skipping transfers made after the date of the enactment of this Act. For special rules and transitional rules for transfers to grandchildren, see footnote ¶3252.

[Footnote ¶3264] Sec. 2632 added by section 1431(a), '86 TRA.

Effective date (Sec. 1433(a), '86 TRA).—Generally applies to any generation-skipping transfers made after the date of the enactment of this Act. For special rules and transitional rules for transfers to grandchildren, see footnote ¶3252.

(3) **Subsection not to apply in certain cases.**—An individual may elect to have this subsection not apply to a transfer.

(c) **Allocation of Unused GST Exemption.—**

(1) **In general.**—Any portion of an individual's GST exemption which has not been allocated within the time prescribed by subsection (a) shall be deemed to be allocated as follows—

(A) first, to property which is the subject of a direct skip occurring at such individual's death, and

(B) second, to trusts with respect to which such individual is the transferor and from which a taxable distribution or a taxable termination might occur at or after such individual's death.

(2) **Allocation within categories.—**

(A) **In general.**—The allocation under paragraph (1) shall be made among the properties described in subparagraph (A) thereof and the trusts described in subparagraph (B) thereof, as the case may be, in proportion to the respective amounts (at the time of allocation) of the nonexempt portions of such properties or trusts.

(B) **Nonexempt portion.**—For purposes of subparagraph (A), the term "nonexempt portion" means the value (at the time of allocation) of the property or trust, multiplied by the inclusion ratio with respect to such property or trust.

[For official explanation, see Committee Reports, ¶4068.]

⟦¶3265⟧ CODE SEC. 2641. APPLICABLE RATE.

(a) **General Rule.**—For purposes of this chapter, the term "applicable rate" means, with respect to any generation-skipping transfer, the product of—

(1) the maximum Federal estate tax rate, and

(2) the inclusion ratio with respect to the transfer.

(b) **Maximum Federal Estate Tax Rate.**—For purposes of subsection (a), the term "maximum Federal estate tax rate" means the maximum rate imposed by section 2001 on the estates of decedents dying at the time of the taxable distribution, taxable termination, or direct skip, as the case may be.

[For official explanation, see Committee Reports, ¶4068.]

⟦¶3266⟧ CODE SEC. 2642. INCLUSION RATIO.

(a) **Inclusion Ratio Defined.**—For purposes of this chapter—

(1) **In general.**—Except as otherwise provided in this section, the inclusion ratio with respect to any property transferred in a generation-skipping transfer shall be the excess (if any) of 1 over—

(A) except as provided in subparagraph (B), the applicable fraction determined for the trust from which such transfer is made, or

(B) in the case of a direct skip, the applicable fraction determined for such skip.

(2) **Applicable fraction.**—For purposes of paragraph (1), the applicable fraction is a fraction—

(A) the numerator of which is the amount of the GST exemption allocated to the trust (or in the case of a direct skip, allocated to the property transferred in such skip), and

(B) the denominator of which is—

(i) the value of the property transferred to the trust (or involved in the direct skip), reduced by

(ii) the sum of—

(I) any Federal estate tax or State death tax actually recovered from the trust attributable to such property, and

(II) any charitable deduction allowed under section 2055 or 2522 with respect to such property.

⟦Footnote ¶3265⟧ Sec. 2641 added by section 1431(a).

Effective date (Sec. 1433(a), '86 TRA).—Generally applies to any generation-skipping transfers made after the date of the enactment of this Act. For special rules and transitional rules for transfers to grandchildren, see footnote ¶3252.

⟦Footnote ¶3266⟧ Sec. 2642 added by section 1431(a), '86 TRA.

Effective date (Sec. 1433(a), '86 TRA).—Generally applies to any generation-skipping transfers made after the date of the enactment of this Act. For special rules and transitional rules for transfers to grandchildren, see footnote ¶3252.

Except as provided in paragraphs (3) and (4) of subsection (b), the value determined under subparagraph (B)(i) shall be of the property as of the time of the transfer to the trust (or the direct skip).

(b) **Valuation Rules, Etc.—**

   (1) **Gifts for which gift tax return filed or deemed allocation made.—**If the allocation of the GST exemption to any property is made on a timely filed gift tax return required by section 6019 or is deemed to be made under section 2632(b)(1)—

   (A) the value of such property for purposes of subsection (a) shall be its value for purposes of chapter 12, and

   (B) such allocation shall be effective on and after the date of such transfer.

   (2) **Transfers and allocations at or after death.—**

   (A) Transfers at death.—If property is transferred as a result of the death of the transferor, the value of such property for purposes of subsection (a) shall be its value for purposes of chapter 11.

   (B) Allocations at or after death of transferor.—Any allocation at or after the death of the transferor shall be effective on and after the date of the death of the transferor.

   (3) **Inter vivos allocations not made on timely filed gift tax return.—**If any allocation of the GST exemption to any property is made during the life of the transferor but is not made on a timely filed gift tax return required by section 6019 and is not deemed to be made under section 2632(b)(1)—

   (A) the value of such property for purposes of subsection (a) shall be determined as of the time such allocation is filed with the Secretary, and

   (B) such allocation shall be effective on and after the date on which such allocation is filed with the Secretary.

   (4) **QTIP trusts.—**If the value of property is included in the estate of a spouse by virtue of section 2044, and if such spouse is treated as the transferor of such property under section 2652(a), the value of such property for purposes of subsection (a) shall be its value for purposes of chapter 11 in the estate of such spouse.

(c) **Treatment of Certain Nontaxable Gifts.—**

   (1) **Direct skips.—**In the case of any direct skip which is a nontaxable gift, the inclusion ratio shall be zero.

   (2) **Treatment of nontaxable gifts made to trusts.—**

   (A) In general.—Except as provided in subparagraph (B), any nontaxable gift which is not a direct skip and which is made to a trust shall not be taken into account under subsection (a)(2)(B).

   (B) Determination of 1st transfer to trust.—In the case of any nontaxable gift referred to in subparagraph (A) which is the 1st transfer to the trust, the inclusion ratio for such trust shall be zero.

   (3) **Nontaxable gift.—**For purposes of this section, the term "nontaxable gift" means any transfer of property to the extent such transfer is not treated as a taxable gift by reason of—

   (A) section 2503(b) (taking into account the application of section 2513), or

   (B) section 2503(e).

(d) **Special Rules Where More than 1 Transfer Made to Trust.—**

   (1) **In general.—**If a transfer of property (other than a nontaxable gift) is made to a trust in existence before such transfer, the applicable fraction for such trust shall be recomputed as of the time of such transfer in the manner provided in paragraph (2).

   (2) **Applicable fraction.—**In the case of any such transfer, the recomputed applicable fraction is a fraction—

   (A) the numerator of which is the sum of—

   (i) the amount of the GST exemption allocated to property involved in such transfer, plus

   (ii) the nontax portion of such trust immediately before such transfer, and

   (B) the denominator of which is the sum of—

   (i) the value of the property involved in such transfer, reduced by any charitable deduction allowed under section 2055 or 2522 with respect to such property, and

(ii) the value of all of the property in the trust (immediately before such transfer).

(3) Nontax portion.—For purposes of paragraph (2), the term "nontax portion" means the product of—

(A) the value of all of the property in the trust, and

(B) the applicable fraction in effect for such trust.

(4) Similar recomputation in case of certain late allocations.—If—

(A) any allocation of the GST exemption to property transferred to a trust is not made on a timely filed gift tax return required by section 6019, and

(B) there was a previous allocation with respect to property transferred to such trust,

the applicable fraction for such trust shall be recomputed as of the time of such allocation under rules similar to the rules of paragraph (2).

[For official explanation, see Committee Reports, ¶4068.]

[¶3267] CODE SEC. 2651. GENERATION ASSIGNMENT.

(a) In General.—For purposes of this chapter, the generation to which any person (other than the transferor) belongs shall be determined in accordance with the rules set forth in this section.

(b) Lineal Descendants.—

(1) In general.—An individual who is a lineal descendant of a grandparent of the transferor shall be assigned to that generation which results from comparing the number of generations between the grandparent and such individual with the number of generations between the grandparent and the transferor.

(2) On spouse's side.—An individual who is a lineal descendant of a grandparent of a spouse of the transferor (other than such spouse) shall be assigned to that generation which results from comparing the number of generations between such grandparent and such individual with the number of generations between such grandparent and such spouse.

(3) Treatment of legal adoptions, etc.—For purposes of this subsection—

(A) **Legal adoptions.**—A relationship by legal adoption shall be treated as a relationship by blood.

(B) **Relationships by half-blood.**—A relationship by the half-blood shall be treated as a relationship of the whole-blood.

(c) Marital Relationship.—

(1) Marriage to transferor.—An individual who has been married at any time to the transferor shall be assigned to the transferor's generation.

(2) Marriage to other lineal descendants.—An individual who has been married at any time to an individual described in subsection (b) shall be assigned to the generation of the individual so described.

(d) Persons who are not lineal descendants.—An individual who is not assigned to a generation by reason of the foregoing provisions of this section shall be assigned to a generation on the basis of the date of such individual's birth with—

(1) an individual born not more than 12½ years after the date of the birth of the transferor assigned to the transferor's generation,

(2) an individual born more than 12½ years but not more than 37½ years after the date of the birth of the transferor assigned to the first generation younger than the transferor, and

(3) similar rules for a new generation every 25 years.

(e) Other Special Rules.—

(1) Individuals assigned to more than 1 generation.—Except as provided in regulations, an individual who, but for this subsection, would be assigned to more than 1 generation shall be assigned to the youngest such generation.

(2) Interests through entities.—Except as provided in paragraph (3), if an estate, trust, partnership, corporation, or other entity has an interest in property, each individual having a beneficial interest in such entity shall be treated as having an interest

[Footnote ¶3267] Sec. 2651 added by section 1431(a), '86 TRA.
Effective date (Sec. 1433(a), '86 TRA).—Generally applies to any generation-skipping transfers made after the date of the enactment of this Act. For special rules and transitional rules for transfers to grandchildren, see footnote ¶3252.

in such property and shall be assigned to a generation under the foregoing provisions of this subsection.

(3) **Treatment of certain charitable organizations.**—Any organization described in section 511(a)(2) and any charitable trust described in section 511(b)(2) shall be assigned to the transferor's generation.

[For official explanation, see Committee Reports, ¶4068.]

【¶3268】 CODE SEC. 2652. OTHER DEFINITIONS.

(a) **Transferor.**—For purposes of this chapter—

(1) **In general.**—Except as provided in this subsection or section 2653(a), the term "transferor" means—

   (A) in the case of a transfer of a kind subject to the tax imposed by chapter 11, the decedent, and

   (B) in the case of a transfer of a kind subject to the tax imposed by chapter 12, the donor.

(2) **Gift-splitting by married couples.**—If, under section 2513, one-half of a gift is treated as made by an individual and one-half of such gift is treated as made by the spouse of such individual, such gift shall be so treated for purposes of this chapter.

(3) **Special election for qualified terminable interest property.**—In the case of—

   (A) any property with respect to which a deduction is allowed to the decedent under section 2056 by reason of subsection (b)(7) thereof, and

   (B) any property with respect to which a deduction to the donor spouse is allowed under section 2523 by reason of subsection (f) thereof,

the estate of the decedent or the donor spouse, as the case may be, may elect to treat such property for purposes of this chapter as if the election to be treated as qualified terminable interest property had not been made.

(b) **Trust and Trustee.**—

(1) **Trust.**—The term "trust" includes any arrangement (other than an estate) which, although not a trust, has substantially the same effect as a trust.

(2) **Trustee.**—In the case of an arrangement which is not a trust but which is treated as a trust under this subsection, the term "trustee" shall mean the person in actual or constructive possession of the property subject to such arrangement.

(3) **Examples.**—Arrangements to which this subsection applies include arrangements involving life estates and remainders, estates for years, and insurance and annuity contracts.

(c) **Interest.**—

(1) **In general.**—A person has an interest in property held in trust if (at the time the determination is made) such person—

   (A) has a right (other than a future right) to receive income or corpus from the trust,

   (B) is a permissible current recipient of income or corpus from the trust and is not described in section 2055(a), or

   (C) is described in section 2055(a) and the trust is—

      (i) a charitable remainder annuity trust,

      (ii) a charitable remainder unitrust within the meaning of section 664, or

      (iii) a pooled income fund within the meaning of section 642(c)(5).

(2) **Certain nominal interests disregarded.**—For purposes of paragraph (1), an interest which is used primarily to postpone or avoid the tax imposed by this chapter shall be disregarded.

[For official explanation, see Committee Reports, ¶4068.]

【¶3269】 CODE SEC. 2653. TAXATION OF MULTIPLE SKIPS.

【Footnote ¶3268】 Sec. 2652 added by section 1431(a), '86 TRA. For former Sec. 2613, as in effect before the amendment of Chapter 13 of Subtitle B of the Code by section 1431(a), '86 TRA, which dealt with related subject matter, see footnote ¶3257.

Effective date (Sec. 1433(a), '86 TRA).—Generally applies to any generation-skipping transfers made after the date of the enactment of this Act. For special rules and transitional rules for transfers to grandchildren, see footnote ¶3252.

【Footnote ¶3269】 Sec. 2653 added by section 1431(a), '86 TRA.

Effective date (Sec. 1433(a), '86 TRA.—Generally applies to any generation-skipping transfers made after the date of the enactment of this Act. For special rules and transitional rules for transfers to grandchildren, see foot-

(a) **General Rule.**—For purposes of this chapter, if—

(1) there is a generation-skipping transfer of any property, and

(2) immediately after such transfer such property is held in trust,

for purposes of applying this chapter (other than section 2651) to subsequent transfers from the portion of such trust attributable to such property, the trust will be treated as if the transferor of such property were assigned to the 1st generation above the highest generation of any person who has an interest in such trust immediately after the transfer.

(b) **Trust Retains Inclusion Ratio.**—

(1) **In general.**—Except as provided in paragraph (2), the provisions of subsection (a) shall not affect the inclusion ratio determined with respect to any trust. Under regulations prescribed by the Secretary, notwithstanding the preceding sentence, proper adjustment shall be made to the inclusion ratio with respect to such trust to take into account any tax under this chapter borne by such trust which is imposed by this chapter on the transfer described in subsection (a).

(2) **Special rule for pour-over trust.**—

(A) **In general.**—If the generation-skipping transfer referred to in subsection (a) involves the transfer of property from 1 trust to another trust (hereinafter in this paragraph referred to as the "pour-over trust"), the inclusion ratio for the pour-over trust shall be determined by treating the nontax portion of such distribution as if it were a part of a GST exemption allocated to such trust.

(B) **Nontax portion.**—For purposes of subparagraph (A), the nontax portion of any distribution is the amount of such distribution multiplied by the applicable fraction which applies to such distribution.

[For official explanation, see Committee Reports, ¶4068.]

〖¶3270〗 CODE SEC. 2654. SPECIAL RULES.

(a) **Basis Adjustment.**—

(1) **In general.**—Except as provided in paragraph (2), if property is transferred in a generation-skipping transfer, the basis of such property shall be increased (but not above the fair market value of such property) by an amount equal to that portion of the tax imposed by section 2601 (computed without regard to section 2604) with respect to the transfer which is attributable to the excess of the fair market value of such property over its adjusted basis immediately before the transfer.

(2) **Certain transfers at death.**—If property is transferred in a taxable termination which occurs at the same time as and as a result of the death of an individual, the basis of such property shall be adjusted in a manner similar to the manner provided under section 1014(a); except that, if the inclusion ratio with respect to such property is less than 1, any increase in basis shall be limited by multiplying such increase by the inclusion ratio.

(b) **Separate Shares Treated as Separate Trusts.**—Substantially separate and independent shares of different beneficiaries in a trust shall be treated as separate trusts.

(c) **Disclaimers.**—

For provisions relating to the effect of a qualified disclaimer for purposes of this chapter, see section 2518.

〖**Footnote ¶3269 continued**〗
note ¶3252.

〖**Footnote ¶3270**〗 Sec. 2654 added by section 1431(a), '86 TRA.

Former Sec. 2614(a), as in effect before the amendment of Chapter 13 of Subtitle B of the Code by section 1431(a), '86 TRA, dealt with related subject matter and read as follows:

FORMER CODE SEC. 2614. SPECIAL RULES.

(a) **Basis Adjustment.**—If property is transferred to any person pursuant to a generation-skipping transfer which occurs before the death of the deemed transferor, the basis of such property in the hands of the transferee shall be increased (but not above the fair market value of such property) by an amount equal to that portion of the tax imposed by section 2601 with respect to the transfer which is attributable to the excess of the fair market value of such property over its adjusted basis immediately before the transfer. If property is transferred in a generation-skipping transfer subject to tax under this chapter which occurs at the same time as, or after, the death of the deemed transferor, the basis of such property shall be adjusted in a manner similar to the manner provided under section 1014(a).

Effective date (Sec. 1433(a), '86 TRA).—Generally applies to any generation-skipping transfers made after the date of the enactment of this Act. For special rules and transitional rules for transfers to grandchildren, see footnote ¶3252.

(d) Limitation on Personal Liability of Trustee.—A trustee shall not be personally liable for any increase in the tax imposed by section 2601 which is attributable to the fact that —

(1) section 2642(c) (relating to exemption of certain nontaxable gifts) does not apply to a transfer to the trust which was made during the life of the transferor and for which a gift tax return was not filed, or

(2) the inclusion ratio with respect to the trust is greater than the amount of such ratio as computed on the basis of the return on which was made (or was deemed made) an allocation of the GST exemption to property transferred to such trust.

The preceding sentence shall not apply if the trustee has knowledge of facts sufficient reasonably to conclude that a gift tax return was required to be filed or that the inclusion ratio was erroneous.

[For official explanation, see Committee Reports, ¶4068.]

[¶3271] CODE SEC. 2661. ADMINISTRATION.

Insofar as applicable and not inconsistent with the provisions of this chapter—

(1) except as provided in paragraph (2), all provisions of subtitle F (including penalties) applicable to the gift tax, to chapter 12, or to section 2501, are hereby made applicable in respect of the generation-skipping transfer tax, this chapter, or section 2601, as the case may be, and

(2) in the case of a generation-skipping transfer occurring at the same time as and as a result of the death of an individual, all provisions of subtitle F (including penalties) applicable to the estate tax, to chapter 11, or to section 2001 are hereby made applicable in respect of the generation-skipping transfer tax, this chapter, or section 2601 (as the case may be).

[For official explanation, see Committee Reports, ¶4068.]

[¶3272] CODE SEC. 2662. RETURN REQUIREMENTS.

[Footnote ¶3271] Sec. 2661 added by section 1431(a), '86 TRA.

Former Sec. 2621(a), (b), as in effect before the amendment of Chapter 13 of Subtitle B of the Code by section 1431(a), '86 TRA, dealt with related subject matter and read as follows:

FORMER CODE SEC. 2621. ADMINISTRATION.

(a) General Rule.—Insofar as applicable and not inconsistent with the provisions of this chapter—

(1) if the deemed transferor is not alive at the time of the transfer, all provisions of subtitle F (including penalties) applicable to chapter 11 or section 2001 are hereby made applicable in respect of this chapter or section 2601, as the case may be, and

(2) if the deemed transferor is alive at the time of the transfer, all provisions of subtitle F (including penalties) applicable to chapter 12 or section 2501 are hereby made applicable in respect of this chapter or section 2601, as the case may be.

(b) Section 6166 Not Applicable.—For purposes of this chapter, section 6166 (relating to extension of time for payment of estate tax where estate consists largely of interest in closely held business) shall not apply.

* * * * * * * * * * *

Effective date (Sec. 1433(a), '86 TRA.—Generally applies to any generation-skipping transfers made after the date of the enactment of this Act. For special rules and transitional rules for transfers to grandchildren, see footnote ¶3252.

[Footnote ¶3272] Sec. 2662 added by section 1431(a), '86 TRA.

Former Sec. 2621(c), as in effect before the amendment of Chapter 13 of Subtitle B of the Code by section 1431(a), '86 TRA, dealt with related subject matter and read as follows:

FORMER CODE SEC. 2621. ADMINISTRATION.

* * * * * * * * * * *

(c) Return Requirements.—

(1) **In general.**—The Secretary shall prescribe by regulations the person who is required to make the return with respect to the tax imposed by this chapter and the time by which any such return must be filed. To the extent practicable, such regulations shall provide that—

(A) the person who is required to make such return shall be—

(i) in the case of a taxable distribution, the distributee, and

(ii) in the case of a taxable termination, the trustee; and

(B) the return shall be filed—

(i) in the case of a generation-skipping transfer occurring before the death of the deemed transferor, on or before the 90th day after the close of the taxable year of the trust in which such transfer occurred, or

(ii) in the case of a generation-skipping transfer, occurring at the same time as, or after, the death of the deemed transferor, on or before the 90th day after the last day prescribed by law (including extensions) for filing the return of tax under chapter 11 with respect to the estate of the deemed transferor (or if later, the day which is 9 months after the day on which such generation-skipping transfer occurred).

(2) **Information returns.**—The Secretary may by regulations require the trustee to furnish the Secretary with such information as he determines to be necessary for purposes of this chapter.

Effective date (Sec. 1433(a), '86 TRA).—Generally applies to any generation-skipping transfers made after the date of the enactment of this Act. For special rules and transitional rules for transfers to grandchildren, see foot-

(a) **In General.**—The Secretary shall prescribe by regulations the person who is required to make the return with respect to the tax imposed by this chapter and the time by which any such return must be filed. To the extent practicable, such regulations shall provide that—

    (1) the person who is required to make such return shall be the person liable under section 2603(a) for payment of such tax, and

    (2) the return shall be filed—

        (A) in the case of a direct skip (other than from a trust), on or before the date on which an estate or gift tax return is required to be filed with respect to the transfer, and

        (B) in all other cases, on or before the 15th day of the 4th month after the close of the taxable year of the person required to make such return in which such transfer occurs.

(b) **Information Returns.**—The Secretary may by regulations require a return to be filed containing such information as he determines to be necessary for purposes of this chapter.

[For official explanation, see Committee Reports, ¶4068.]

[¶3273] CODE SEC. 2663. REGULATIONS.

The Secretary shall prescribe such regulations as may be necessary or appropriate to carry out the purposes of this chapter, including—

    (1) such regulations as may be necessary to coordinate the provisions of this chapter with the recapture tax imposed under section 2032A(c), and

    (2) regulations (consistent with the principles of chapters 11 and 12) providing for the application of this chapter in the case of transferors who are nonresidents not citizens of the United States.

[For official explanation, see Committee Reports, ¶4068.]

[¶3274] CODE SEC. 3121. DEFINITIONS.

(a) **Wages.**—For purposes of this chapter, the term "wages" means all remuneration for employment, including the cash value of all remuneration (including benefits) paid in any medium other than cash; except that such term shall not include—

    * * * * * * * * * * * *

    (5) any payment made to, or on behalf of, an employee or his beneficiary—

    * * * * * * * * * * * *

        (C) under a simplified employee pension [1]*(as defined in section 408(k)(1)), other than any contributions described in section 408(k)(6)),*".

        (D) under or to an annuity contract described in section 403(b), other than a payment for the purchase of such contract which is made by reason of a salary reduction agreement (whether evidenced by a written instrument or otherwise),

        (E) under or to an exempt governmental deferred compensation plan (as defined in subsection (v)(3)),[2]

[Footnote ¶3272 continued]

note ¶3252.

[Footnote ¶3273] Sec. 2663 added by section 1431(a), '86 TRA. Former Sec. 2622, as in effect before the amendment of Chapter 13 of Subtitle B of the Code by section 1431(a), '86 TRA, dealt with related subject matter and read as follows:

FORMER CODE SEC. 2622. REGULATIONS.

The Secretary shall prescribe such regulations as may be necessary or appropriate to carry out the purposes of this chapter, including regulations providing the extent to which substantially separate and independent shares of different beneficiaries in the trust shall be treated as separate trusts.

Effective date (Sec. 1433(a), '86 TRA).—Generally applies to any generation-skipping transfers made after the date of enactment of this Act. For special rules and transitional rules for transfers to grandchildren, see footnote ¶3252.

[Footnote ¶3274] Matter in *italics* in Sec. 3121(a)(5)(C) added by section 1108(g)(7), '86 TRA, which struck out:

(1) "if, at the time of the payment, it is reasonable to believe that the employee will be entitled to a deduction under section 219(b)(2) for such payment,"

Effective date (Sec. 1108(h), '86 TRA).—Applies to years beginning after 12-31-86.

Matter in *italics* in Sec. 3121(a)(5)(C)—(G) added by section 1151(d)(2)(A), '86 TRA, which struck out:

(2) "or"

Effective date (Sec. 1151(k), '86 TRA).—Generally applies to years beginning after the later of—

(A) 12-31-87, or

(B) the earlier of—

(F) to supplement pension benefits under a plan or trust described in any of the foregoing provisions of this paragraph to take into account some portion or all of the increase in the cost of living (as determined by the Secretary of Labor) since retirement but only if such supplemental payments are under a plan which is treated as a welfare plan under section 3(2)(B)(ii) of the Employee Retirement Income Security Act of 1974; or

(G) *under a cafeteria plan (within the meaning of section 125),*

* * * * * * * * * * * *

(20) any benefit provided to or on behalf of an employee if at the time such benefit is provided it is reasonable to believe that the employee will be able to exclude such benefit from income under section [3]*74(c), 117 or 132.*

(u) **Application of Hospital Insurance Tax to Federal, State, and Local Employment.—**

* * * * * * * * * * * *

(2) **State and local employment.—**For purposes of the taxes imposed by sections 3101(b) and 3111(b)—

* * * * * * * * * * * *

(B) Exception for certain services.—Service shall not be treated as employment by reason of subparagraph (A) if—

* * * * * * * * * * * *

(ii) the service is performed—

* * * * * * * * * * * *

(III) by an individual, as an employee of a State or political subdivision thereof or of the District of Columbia, serving on a temporary basis in case of fire, storm, snow, earthquake, flood or other similar emergency. [4]

(IV) by any individual as an employee included under section 5351(2) of title 5, United States Code (relating to certain interns, student nurses, and other student employees of hospitals of the District of Columbia Government), other than as a medical or dental intern or a medical or dental resident in training[5], *or*

(V) *by an election official or election worker if the renumeration paid in a calendar year for such service is less than $100.*

As used in this subparagraph, the terms "State" and "political subdivision" have the meanings given those terms in section 218(b) of the Social Security Act.

* * * * * * * * * * * *

(3) **Exempt governmental deferred compensation plan.—**For purposes of subsection (a)(5), the term "exempt governmental deferred compensation plan" means any plan

---

[Footnote ¶3274 continued]

(i) the date which is 3 months after the date on which the Secretary of the Treasury or his delegate issues such regulations as are necessaary to carry out the provisions of section 89 of the '86 Code (as added by this section), or

(ii) 12-31-88.

For special rules see footnotes ¶2908.

Sec. 3121(a)(8)(B), '86 TRA, is amended by section 1883(a)(11)(B) by moving subparagraph (B) two ems to the left, so that its left margin is in flush alignment with the margin of subparagraph (A) of such section.

Effective date (Sec. 1883(f), '86 TRA).—Takes effect on date of enactment of this act.

Matter in *italics* in Sec. 3121(a)(20) added by section 122(e)(1), '86 TRA, which struck out:

(3) "117 or"

Effective date (Sec. 151(c), '86 TRA).—Applies to prizes and awards granted 12-31-86.

Matter in *italics* in Sec. 3121(u)(2)(B)(III)—(V) added by section 1895(b)(18)(A)(i)—(iii), '86 TRA, which struck out:

(4) "or"

(5) "."

Effective date (Sec. 1895(e), '86 TRA, and Sec. 13205(d)(1) of P.L. 99-272, 4-7-86 (COBRA).—Applies to services performed after 3-31-86.

Clause (ii) of section 3121(v)(2)(A) is amended by section 1899A(38), '86 TRA, by striking out "forfeiture" and inserting in lieu thereof "forfeiture".

providing for deferral of compensation established and maintained for its employees by the United States, by a State or political subdivision thereof, or by an agency or instrumentality of any of the foregoing. Such term shall not include—

    (A) any plan to which section 83, 402(b), 403(c), 457(a), or 457(e)(1) applies, [6]

    (B) any annuity contract described in section 403(b) [7], *and*

    (C) *the Thrift Saving Fund (within the meaning of subchapter III of chapter 84 of title 5, United States Code).*

(w) **Exemption of Churches and Qualified Church-Controlled Organizations.—**

    (1) **General rule.—**Any church or qualified church-controlled organization (as defined in paragraph (3)) may make an election within the time period described in paragraph (2), in accordance with such procedures as the Secretary determines to be appropriate, that services performed in the employ of such church or organization shall be excluded from employment for purposes of title II of the Social Security Act and [8] *this chapter.* An election may be made under this subsection only if the church or qualified church-controlled organization states that such church or organization is opposed for religious reasons to the payment of the tax imposed under section 3111.

    (2) **Timing and duration of election.—**An election under this subsection must be made prior to the first date, more than 90 days after [9]*July 18, 1984,* on which a quarterly employment tax return for the tax imposed under section 3111 is due, or would be due but for the election, from such church or organization. An election under this subsection shall apply to current and future employees, and shall apply to service performed after December 31, 1983. [10]*The election may be revoked by the church or organization under regulations prescribed by the Secretary. The election shall be revoked by the Secretary if such church or organization fails to furnish the information required under section 6051 to the Secretary for a period of 2 years or more with respect to remuneration paid for such services by such church or organization, and, upon request by the Secretary, fails to furnish all such previously unfurnished information for the period covered by the election. Any revocation under the preceding sentence shall apply retroactively to the beginning of the 2-year period for which the information was not furnished.*

*   *   *   *   *   *   *   *   *   *   *   *

[For official explanation, see Committee Reports, ¶3858; 3974; 4006; 4007; 4195; 4196; 4208.]

[¶3275] **CODE SEC. 3231. DEFINITIONS.**

*   *   *   *   *   *   *   *   *   *   *   *

  (e) **Compensation.—**For purposes of this chapter—

*   *   *   *   *   *   *   *   *   *   *   *

    (5) The term "compensation" shall not include any benefit provided to or on behalf of an employee if at the time such benefit is provided it is reasonable to believe

---

[Footnote ¶3274 continued]

Matter in *italics* in Sec. 3121(v)(3)(A)—(C) added by section 1147(b), '86 TRA, which struck out:
(6) "and"
(7) "."
Effective date (Sec. 1151(k), '86 TRA).—See above.

Matter in *italics* in Sec. 3121(w)(1) and (2) added by section 1899A(39) and (40), '86 TRA, which struck out:
(8) "chapter 21 of this Code"
(9) "the date of the enactment of this subsection"

Matter in *italics* in Sec. 3121(w)(2) added by section 1882(c), '86 TRA, which struck out:
(10) "The election may not be revoked by the church or organization, but shall be permanently revoked by the Secretary if such church or organization fails to furnish the information required under section 6051 to the Secretary for a period of 2 years or more with respect to remuneration paid for such services by such church or organization, and, upon request by the Secretary, fails to furnish all such previously unfurnished information for the period covered by the election. Such revocation shall apply retroactively to the beginning of the 2-year period for which the information was not furnished."
Effective date (Sec. 1881, '86 TRA and section 2603(e) and (f), '84 TRA).—(e) Applies to service performed after 12-31-83.

    (f) In any case where a church or qualified church-controlled organization makes an election under section 3121(w) of the '54 Code, the Secretary of the Treasury shall refund (without interest) to such church or organization any taxes paid under sections 3101 and 3111 of such Code with respect to service performed after 12-31-83, which is covered under such election. The refund shall be conditional upon the church or organization agreeing to pay to each employee (or former employee) the portion of the refund attributable to the tax imposed on such employee (or former employee) under section 3101, and such employee (or former employee) may not receive any other refund payment of such taxes.

that the employee will be able to exclude such benefit from income under section 74(c), 117, or 132.

*   *   *   *   *   *   *   *   *   *   *

[1](7) The term "compensation" shall not include any contribution, payment, or service provided by an employer which may be excluded from gross income of an employee, his spouse, or his dependents, under the provisions of section 120 (relating to amounts received under qualified group legal services plans.)

*   *   *   *   *   *   *   *   *   *   *

[For official explanation, see Committee Reports, ¶3858.]

[¶3276]   **CODE SEC. 3301.   RATE OF TAX.**
There is hereby imposed on every employer (as defined in section 3306(a)) for each calendar year an excise tax, with respect to having individuals in his employ, equal to—

(1)   6.2 percent, in the case of a calendar year beginning before the first calendar year after 1976, as of January 1 of which there is not a balance of repayable advances made to the extended [1]*unemployment* compensation account (established by section 905(a) of the Social Security Act); or

(2)   6.0 percent, in the case of such first calendar year and each calendar year thereafter;

of the total wages (as defined in section 3306(b)) paid by him during the calendar year with respect to employment (as defined in section 3306(c)).

[¶3277]   **CODE SEC. 3302.   CREDITS AGAINST TAX.**

*   *   *   *   *   *   *   *   *   *   *

(c)   **Limit on total credits.—**

*   *   *   *   *   *   *   *   *   *   *

(2)   If an advance or advances have been made to the unemployment account of a State under title XII of the Social Security Act, then the total credits (after applying subsections (a) and (b) and paragraph (1) of this subsection) otherwise allowable under this section for the taxable year in the case of a taxpayer subject to the unemployment compensation law of such State shall be reduced—

(A)   (i)   in the case of a taxable year beginning with the second consecutive January 1 as of the beginning of which there is a balance of such advances, by 5 percent of the tax imposed by section 3301 with respect to the wages paid by such taxpayer during such taxable year which are attributable to such State; and

(ii)   in the case of any succeeding taxable year beginning with a consecutive January 1 as of the beginning of which there is a balance of such advances, by an additional 5 percent, for each such succeeding taxable year, of the tax imposed by section 3301 with respect to the wages paid by such taxpayer during such taxable year which are attributable to such State;

(B)   in the case of a taxable year beginning with the third or fourth consecutive January 1 as of the beginning of which there is a balance of such advances, by the amount determined by multiplying the wages paid by such taxpayer during such taxable year which are attributable to such State by the percentage (if any), multiplied by a fraction, the numerator of which is the State's average annual wage in covered employment for the calendar year in which the determination is made and the [1]*denominator* of which is the wage base under this chapter, by which—

(i)   2.7 *percent* multiplied by a fraction, the numerator of which is the wage base under this chapter and the denominator of which is the estimated United States average annual wage in covered employment for the calendar year in which the determination is to be made [2], exceeds

---

[Footnote ¶3275]   Matter in *italics* in Sec. 3231(e)(5) added by section 122(e)(2), '86 TRA.
Effective date (Sec. 151(c), '86 TRA).—Applies to prizes and awards granted after 12-31-86.

Matter in *italics* in Sec. 3231(e)(6) added by section 1899A(41), '86 TRA, which struck out:
(1)   "(6)"
[Footnote ¶3276]   Matter in *italics* in Sec. 3301(1) added by section 1899A(42), '86 TRA, which struck out:
(1)   "unemployed"
[Footnote ¶3277]   Matter in *italics* in Sec. 3302(c)(2)(B), (B)(i) and (f)(8)(A) added by section 1884(1) and (2), '86 TRA, which struck out:
(1)   "determination"
(2)   "percent"

    (ii) the average employer contribution rate for such State for the calendar year preceding such taxable year; and

    (C) in the case of a taxable year beginning with the fifth or any succeeding consecutive January 1 as of the beginning of which there is a balance of such advances, by the amount determined by multiplying the wages paid by such taxpayer during such taxable year which are attributable to such State by the percentage (if any) by which—

      (i) the 5-year benefit cost rate applicable to such State for such taxable year or (if higher) 2.7 percent, exceeds

      (ii) the average employer contribution rate for such State for the calendar year preceding such taxable year.

The provisions of the preceding sentence shall not be applicable with respect to the taxable year beginning January 1, 1975, or any succeeding taxable year which begins before January 1, 1980; and, for purposes of such sentence, January 1, 1980, shall be deemed to be the first January 1 occuring after January 1, 1974, and consecutive taxable years in the period commencing January 1, 1980, shall be determined as if the taxable year which begins on January 1, 1980, were the taxable year immediately succeeding the taxable year which began on January 1, 1974. Subparagraph (C) shall not apply with respect to any taxable year to which it would otherwise apply (but subparagraph (B) shall apply to such taxable year) if the Secretary of Labor determines (on or before November 10 of such taxable year) that the State meets the requirements of subsection (f)(2)(B) for such taxable year.

* * * * * * * * * * * *

(f) **Limitation on Credit Reduction.—**

* * * * * * * * * * * *

  (8) Partial limitation.—

    (A) In the case of a State which would meet the requirements of this subsection for a taxable year prior to [3]*1986* but for its failure to meet one of the requirements contained in subparagraph (C) or (D) of paragraph (2), the reduction under subsection (c)(2) in credits otherwise applicable to taxpayers in such State for such taxable year and each subsequent year (in a period of consecutive years for each of which a credit reduction is in effect for taxpayers in such State) shall be reduced by 0.1 percentage point.

* * * * * * * * * * * *

[For official explanation, see Committee Reports, ¶4197.]

[¶3278] **CODE SEC. 3304.** **APPROVAL OF STATE LAWS.**

  (a) **Requirements.—**The Secretary of Labor shall approve any State law submitted to him, within 30 days of such submission, which he finds provides that—

    (1) all compensation is to be paid through public employment offices or such other agencies as the Secretary of Labor may approve;

    (2) no compensation shall be payable with respect to any day of unemployment occurring within 2 years after the first day of the first period with respect to which contributions are required;

    (3) all money received in the unemployment fund shall (except for refunds of sums erroneously paid into such fund and except for refunds paid in accordance with the provisions of section 3305(b)) immediately upon such receipt be paid over to the Secretary of the Treasury to the credit of the Unemployment Trust Fund established by section 904 of the Social Security Act (42 U.S.C. 1104);

    (4) all money withdrawn from the unemployment fund of the State shall be used solely in the payment of unemployment compensation, exclusive of expenses of administration, and for refunds of sums erroneously paid into such fund and refunds paid in accordance with the provisions of section 3305(b); except that—

      (A) an amount equal to the amount of employee payments into the unemployment fund of a State may be used in the payment of cash benefits to individuals with respect to their disability, exclusive of expenses of administration;

      (B) the amounts specified by section 903(c)(2) of the Social Security Act may, subject to the conditions prescribed in such section, be used for expenses incurred by the State for administration of its unemployment compensation law and public employment offices; and

      (C) nothing in this paragraph shall be construed to prohibit deducting an amount from unemployment compensation otherwise payable to an individual and

---

[Footnote ¶3277 continued]

  (3) "1987"

using the amount so deducted to pay for health insurance if the individual elected to have such deduction made and such deduction was made under a program approved by the Secretary of Labor;

* * * * * * * * * * * *

(6) (A) compensation is payable on the basis of service to which section 3309(a)(1) applies, in the same amount, on the same terms, and subject to the same conditions as compensation payable on the basis of other service subject to such law; except that—

* * * * * * * * * * * *

(iii) with respect to any services described in clause (i) or (ii), compensation payable on the basis of such services shall be denied to any individual for any week which commences during an established and customary vacation period or holiday recess if such individual performs such services in the period immediately before such vacation period or holiday recess, and there is a reasonable assurance that such individual will perform such services in the period immediately following such vacation period or holiday recess, [1]

(iv) with respect to any services described in clause (i) or (ii), compensation payable on the basis of services in any such capacity shall be denied as specified in clauses (i), (ii), and (iii) to any individual who performed such services in an educational institution while in the employ of an educational service agency, and for this purpose the term "educational service agency" means a governmental agency or governmental entity which is established and operated exclusively for the purpose of providing such services to one or more educational institutions, and

(v) with respect to services to which section 3309(a)(1) applies, if such services are provided to or on behalf of an educational institution, compensation may be denied under the same circumstances as described in clauses (i) through (iv), and

* * * * * * * * * * * *

[¶3279] CODE SEC. 3306. DEFINITIONS.

* * * * * * * * * * * *

(b) **Wages.**—For purposes of this chapter, the term "wages" means all remuneration for employment, including the cash value of all remuneration (including benefits) paid in any medium other than cash; except that such item shall not include—

* * * * * * * * * * * *

(2) the amount of any payment (including any amount paid by an employer for insurance or annuities, or into a fund, to provide for any such payment) made to, or on behalf of, an employee or any of his dependents under a plan or system established by an employer which makes provision for his employees generally (or for his employees generally and their dependents) or for a class or classes of his employees (or for a class or classes of his employees and their dependents), on account of—

(A) sickness or accident disability (but, in the case of payments made to an employee or any of his dependents, this subparagraph shall exclude from the term "wages" only payments which are received under a *workmen's* compensation law), or

(B) medical or hospitalization expenses in connection with sickness or accident disability, or

(C) death;

* * * * * * * * * * * *

(5) any payment made to, or on behalf of, an employee or his beneficiary—

(A) from or to a trust described in section 401(a) which is exempt from tax under section 501(a) at the time of such payment unless such payment is made to an employee of the trust as remuneration for services rendered as such employee and not as a beneficiary of the trust, or

---

[Footnote ¶3278] Section 1899A(43), '86 TRA, struck out from Sec. 3304(a)(6)(A)(iii):
(1) "and"
[Footnote ¶3279] Matter in *italics* in Sec. 3306(b)(2)(A) added by section 1899A(44), '86 TRA, which struck out:
(1) "workman's"

(B) under or to an annuity plan which, at the time of such payment, is a plan described in section 403(a),

[2](C) under a simplified employee pension (as defined in section 408(k)(1)), other than any contributions described in section 408(k)(6),

(D) under or to an annuity contract described in section 403(b), other than a payment for the purchase of such contract which is made by reason of a salary reduction agreement (whether evidenced by a written instrument or otherwise),

(E) under or to an exempt government deferred compensation plan (as defined in section 3121(v)(3)),[3]

(F) to supplement pension benefits under a plan or trust described in any of the foregoing provisions of this paragraph to take into account some portion or all of the increase in the cost of living (as determined by the Secretary of Labor) since retirement but only if such supplemental payments are under a plan which is treated as a welfare plan under section 3(2)(B)(ii) of the Employee Retirement Income Security Act of 1974; *or*

(G) under a cafeteria plan (within the meaning of section 125),

*   *   *   *   *   *   *   *   *   *   *

(13) any payment made, or benefit furnished, to or for the benefit of an employee if at the time of such payment or such furnishing it is reasonable to believe that the employee will be able to exclude such payment or benefit from income under section 127 or 129[4];

*   *   *   *   *   *   *   *   *   *   *

(16) any benefit provided to or on behalf of an employee if at the time such benefit is provided it is reasonable to believe that the employee will be able to exclude such benefit from income under section *[5]74(c), 117,* or 132.

Nothing in the regulations prescribed for purposes of chapter 24 (relating to income tax withholding) which provides an exclusion from "wages" as used in such chapter shall be construed to require a similar exclusion from "wages" in the regulations prescribed for purposes of this chapter.

Except as otherwise provided in regulations prescribed by the Secretary, any third party which makes a payment included in wages solely by reason of the parenthetical matter contained in subparagraph (A) of paragraph (2) shall be treated for purposes of this chapter and chapter 22 as the employer with respect to such wages.

*   *   *   *   *   *   *   *   *   *   *

(o) Special Rule in Case of Certain Agricultural Workers.—

(1) Crew leaders who are registered or provide specialized agricultural labor.—For purposes of this chapter, any individual who is a member of a crew furnished by a crew leader to perform agricultural labor for any other person shall be treated as an employee of such crew leader—

(A) if—

(i) such crew leader holds a valid certificate of registration under the *[6]Migrant and Seasonal Agricultural Worker Protection Act;* or

(ii) substantially all the members of such crew operate or maintain tractors, mechanized harvesting or crop-dusting equipment, or any other mechanized equipment, which is provided by such crew leader; and

---

[Footnote ¶3279 continued]

Matter in *italics* in Sec. 3306(b)(5)(C) added by section 1108(g)(8), '86 TRA, which struck out:

(2) "(C) under a simplified employee pension if, at the time of the payment, it is reasonable to believe that the employee will be entitled to a deduction under section 219(b)(2) for such payment,"

Effective date (Sec. 1108(h), '86 TRA).—Applies to years beginning after 12-31-86.

Matter in *italics* in Sec. 3306(b)(5)(E)—(G) added by section 1151(d)(2)(B), '86 TRA, which struck out:

(3) "or"

Effective date (Sec. 1151(k)(5), '86 TRA).—Applies to taxable years beginning after 12-31-83.

Section 1899A(45), '86 TRA, struck out from Sec. 3306(b)(13):

(4) ","

Matter in *italics* in Sec. 3306(b)(16) added by section 122(e)(3), '86 TRA, which struck out:

(5) "117"

Effective date (Sec. 151(C), '86 TRA).—Applies to prizes and awards granted after 12-31-86.

Matter in *italics* in Sec. 3306(o)(1)(A)(i) added by section 1884(3), '86 TRA, which struck out:

(6) "Farm Labor Contractor Registration Act of 1963"

(B) if such individual is not an employee of such other person within the meaning of subsection (i).

* * * * * * * * * * * *

[For official explanation, see Committee Reports, ¶3858; 3974; 4007; 4197.]

[¶3280] CODE SEC. 3401. DEFINITIONS.

(a) **Wages.**—For purposes of this chapter, the term "wages" means all remuneration (other than fees paid to a public official) for services performed by an employee for his employer, including the cash value of all remuneration (including benefits) paid in any medium other than cash; except that such term shall not include remuneration paid—

* * * * * * * * * * * *

(8) (A) for services for an employer (other than the United States or any agency thereof)—

(i) performed by a citizen of the United States if, at the time of the payment of such remuneration, it is reasonable to believe that such remuneration will be excluded from gross income under section 911; or

(ii) performed in a foreign country or in a possession of the United States by such a citizen if, at the time of the payment of such remuneration, the employer is required by the law of such foreign country or possession of the United States to withhold income tax upon such remuneration; or

(B) for services of an employer (other than the United States or any agency thereof) performed by a citizen of the United States within a possession of the United States (other than Puerto Rico), if it is reasonable to believe that at least 80 percent of the remuneration to be paid to the employee by such employer during the calendar year will be for such services; or

(C) for services for an employer (other than the United States or any agency thereof) performed by a citizen of the United States within Puerto Rico, if it is reasonable to believe that during the entire calendar year the employee will be a bona fide resident of Puerto Rico; or

(D) *for services for the United States (or any agency thereof) performed by a citizen of the United States within a possession of the United States to the extent the United States (or such agency) withholds taxes on such remuneration pursuant to an agreement with such possession; or*

* * * * * * * * * * * *

(19) for any medical care reimbursement made to or for the benefit of an employee under a self-insured medical reimbursement plan (within the meaning of section 105(h)(6)); or

(20) any benefit provided to or on behalf of an employee if at the time such benefit is provided it is reasonable to believe that the employee will be able to exclude such benefit from income under section [1]*74(c), 117, or 132.*

* * * * * * * * * * * *

[For official explanation, see Committee Reports, ¶3858; 4057.]

[¶3281] CODE SEC. 3402. INCOME TAX COLLECTED AT SOURCE.

* * * * * * * * * * * *

(f) **Withholding Exemption.**—

(1) **In general.**—An employee receiving wages shall on any day be entitled to the following exemptions:

(A) an exemption for himself *unless he is an individual described in section 151(d)(2)(3);* [1]

[Footnote ¶3280] Sec. 3401(a)(8)(D) in *italics* added by section 1272(c), '86 TRA.
Effective date (Sec. 1277, '86 TRA).—Generally applies to taxable years beginning after 12-31-86. For special rules, see ¶2068.

Matter in *italics* in Sec. 3401(a)(20) added by section 122(e)(4), '86 TRA, which struck out:
(1) "117 or"
Effective date (Sec. 151(c), '86 TRA).—Applies to prizes and awards granted after 12-31-86.
[Footnote ¶3281] Matter in *italics* in Sec. 3402(f)(1) (except for "*section 7703*"and "*subparagraph (E)*") added by 104(b)(15)(A)—(E) and (F)(ii), '86 TRA, which struck out:
(1) "(B) one additional exemption for himself if, on the basis of facts existing at the beginning of such day, there may reasonably be expected to be allowable an exemption under section 151(c)(1) (relating to old age) for the

[2](B) if the employee is married, any exemption to which his spouse is entitled, or would be entitled if such spouse were an employee receiving wages, under subparagraph (A) [3]*or (D)*, but only if such spouse does not have in effect a withholding exemption certificate claiming such exemption;

[4](C) an exemption for each individual with respect to whom, on the basis of facts existing at the beginning of such day, there may reasonably be expected to be allowable an exemption under [5]*section 151(c)* for the taxable year under subtitle A in respect of which amounts deducted and withheld under this chapter in the calendar year in which such day falls are allowed as a credit;

[6](D) any allowance to which he is entitled under subsection (m), but only if his spouse does not have in effect a withholding exemption certificate claiming such allowance; and

[7](E) a [8]*standard deduction* allowance which shall be an amount equal to one exemption (or more than one exemption if so prescribed by the Secretary) unless (i) he is married (as determined under [9]*section 7703*) and his spouse is an employee receiving wages subject to withholding or (ii) he has withholding exemption certificates in effect with respect to more than one employer.

For purposes of this title, any [8]*standard deduction* allowance under [10]*subparagraph (E)* shall be treated as if it were denominated a withholding exemption.

* * * * * * * * * * * *

(i) Changes in Withholding.—

(1) In general.—The Secretary may by regulations provide for increases [11] in the amount of withholding otherwise required under this section in cases where the employee requests such changes.

(2) Treatment as tax.—Any increased withholding under paragraph (1) shall for all purposes be considered tax required to be deducted and withheld under this chapter.

* * * * * * * * * * * *

(m) Withholding allowances.—Under regulations prescribed by the Secretary, an employee shall be entitled to additional withholding allowances or additional reductions in withholding under this subsection. In determining the number of additional withholding allowances or the amount of additional reductions in withholding under this subsection,

---

⟦Footnote ¶3281 continued⟧

taxable year under subtitle A in respect of which amounts deducted and withheld under this chapter in the calendar year in which such day falls are allowed as a credit;

(C) one additional exemption for himself if, on the basis of facts existing at the beginning of such day, there may reasonably be expected to be allowable an exemption under section 151(d)(1) (relating to the blind) for the taxable year under subtitle A in respect of which amounts deducted and withheld under this chapter in the calendar year in which such day falls are allowed as a credit;"

(2) "(D)"
(3) ", (B), or (C), or (F)" [should read ", (B), or (C)"]
(4) "(E)"
(5) "section 151(e)"
(6) "(F)"
(7) "(G)"
(8) "zero bracket"
Effective date (Sec. 151(a), '86 TRA).—Applies to taxable years beginning after 12-31-86.

Matter in *italics* in Sec. 3402(f)(1)(E) (except for "standard deduction") added by 1301(j)(8), '86 TRA, which struck out:
(9) "section 143"
Effective date (Sec. 1311(a), '86 TRA).—Applies to bonds issued after 8-15-86. For special and transitional rules, see ¶2071—2077.

Matter in *italics* in the last sentence of 3402(f)(1) (except for *"standard deduction"*) added by 104(b)(15)(F)(i), '86 TRA, which struck out:
(10) "subparagraph (G)"
Effective date (Sec. 151(a), '86 TRA).—Applies to taxable years beginning after 12-31-86.

Section 1581(b), '86 TRA, struck out from Sec. 3402(i):
(11) "or decreases"

Matter in *italics* in Sec. 3402(m)(3) added by section 104(b)(15)(G), '86 TRA.
Effective date (Sec. 151(a), '86 TRA).—Applies to taxable years beginning after 12-31-86.

the employee may take into account (to the extent and in the manner provided by such regulations)—

(1) estimated itemized deductions allowable under chapter 1 (other than the deductions referred to in section 151 and other than the deductions required to be taken into account in determining adjusted gross income under section 62) (other than paragraph 13) thereof),

(2) estimated tax credits allowable under chapter 1, and

(3) such additional deductions *(including the additional standard deduction under section 63(c)(3) for the aged and blind)* and other items as may be specified by the Secretary in regulations.

* * * * * * * * * * *

(r) [Repealed][12]

(s) **Exemption From Withholding for Any Vehicle Fringe Benefit.—**

(1) **Employer election not to withhold.—**The employer may elect not to deduct and withhold any tax under this chapter with respect to any vehicle fringe benefit provided to any employee if such employee is notified by the employer of such election (at such time and in such manner as the Secretary shall by regulations prescribe). The preceding sentence shall not apply to any vehicle fringe benefit unless the amount of such benefit is included by the employer on a statement timely furnished under section 6051.

(2) **Employer must furnish W-2.—**Any vehicle fringe benefit shall be treated as wages from which amounts are required to be deducted and withheld under this chapter for purposes of section 6051.

(3) **Vehicle fringe benefit.—**For purposes of this subsection, the term "vehicle fringe benefit" means any fringe benefit—

(A) which constitutes wages (as defined in section 3401), and

(B) which consists of providing a highway motor vehicle for the use of the employee.

* * * * * * * * * * *

[For official explanation, see Committee Reports, ¶4058.]

〔¶3282〕 CODE SEC. 3405. SPECIAL RULES FOR PENSIONS, ANNUITIES, AND CERTAIN OTHER DEFERRED INCOME.

* * * * * * * * * * *

(d) **Definitions and Special Rules.—**For purposes of this section—

(1) **Designated distribution.—**

(A) In general.—Except as provided in subparagraph (B), the term "designated distribution" means any distribution or payment from or under—

(i) an employer deferred compensation plan,

(ii) an individual retirement plan (as defined in section 7701(a)(37)), or

(iii) a commercial annuity.

(B) Exceptions.—The term "designated distribution" shall not include—

(i) any amount which is wages without regard to this section,

(ii) the portion of a distribution or payment which it is reasonable to believe is not includible in gross income, [1]

[2]*(iii) any amount which is subject to withholding under subchapter A of chap-*

〔Footnote ¶3281 continued〕

Section 1303(b)(4), '86 TRA, repealed Sec. 3402(r):

(12) "Extension of Withholding to GSOC Distributions.—

(1) General rule.—An electing GSOC making any distribution to its shareholders shall deduct and withhold from such payment a tax in an amount equal to 25 percent of such payment.

(2) Coordination with other sections.—For purposes of sections 3403 and 3404 and for purposes of so much of subtitle F (except section 7205) as relates to this chapter, distributions of an electing GSOC to any shareholder which are subject to withholding shall be treated as if they were wages paid by an employer to an employee."

Effective date (Sec. 1311(d), '86 TRA).—Takes effect on the date of the enactment of this Act. For special rules, see ¶2071—2077.

〔Footnote ¶3282〕 Matter in *italics* in Sec. 3405(d)(1)(B)(ii)—(iv) added by section 1875(c)(10), '86 TRA, which struck out:

(1) "or"

(2) "(iii) any amount which is subject to withholding under subchapter A of chapter 3 (relating to withholding of tax on nonresident aliens and foreign corporations) by the person paying such amount or which would be so subject but for a tax treaty.

ter 3 *(relating to withholding of tax on nonresident aliens and foreign corporations) by the person paying such amount or which would be so subject but for a tax treaty, or*

    (iv) *any distribution described in section 404(k)(2).*

For purposes of clause (ii), any distribution or payment from or under an individual retirement plan shall be treated as includible in gross income.

* * * * * * * * * * * *

    (13) Election may not be made with respect to certain payments outside the United States.—

      (A) In general.—Except as provided in subparagraph (B), in the case of any periodic payment or nonperiodic distribution which is to be delivered outside of the United States, no election may be made under subsection (a)(2) or (b)(3) with respect to such payment.

      (B) Exception.—Subparagraph (A) shall not apply if the recipient certifies to the payor, in such manner as the Secretary may prescribe, that such person is not—

        (i) a United States citizen who is a bona fide resident of a foreign country, or

        (ii) an individual to whom section 877 applies.

* * * * * * * * * * * *

[For official explanation, see Committee Reports, ¶3969; 4044; 4189.]

[¶3283]   CODE SEC. 3406.   BACKUP WITHHOLDING.

* * * * * * * * * * * *

(b) Reportable Payment, Etc.—For purposes of this section—

* * * * * * * * * * * *

    (3) Other reportable payment.—The term "other reportable payment" means any payment of a kind, and to a payee, required to be shown on a return required under—

      (A) section 6041 (relating to certain information at source),

      (B) section 6041A(a) (relating to payments of remuneration for services),

      (C) section 6045 (relating to returns of brokers),[1]

      (D) section 6050A (relating to reporting requirements of certain fishing boat operators), but only to the extent such payment is in money and represents a share of the proceeds of the catch,[2] *or*

      (E) section 6050N (relating to payments of royalties).

* * * * * * * * * * * *

    (6) Other reportable payments include payments described in section 6041(a) or [3] **6041A(a) only where aggregate for calendar year is $600 or more.**—Any payment of a kind required to be shown on a return required under section 6041(a) or 6041A(a) which is made during any calendar year shall be treated as a reportable payment only if—

      (A) the aggregate amount of such payment and all previous payments described in such sections by the payor to the payee during such calendar year equals or exceeds $600,

---

[Footnote ¶3282 continued]

(iii) any distribution described in section 404(k)(2)."

Effective date (Sec. 1881, '86 TRA, and section 715, '84 TRA, as amended by section 1875(d)(3), '86 TRA).— Takes effect as if included in the provision of '82 TEFRA to which such amendment relates.

Matter in *italics* in last sentence in Sec. 3405(d)(1)(B) added by section 1102(e)(1), '86 TRA.

Effective date (Sec. 1102(g), '86 TRA).—Applies to contributions and distributions for taxable years beginning after 12-31-86.

Sec. 3405(d)(13) in *italics* added by section 1234(b)(1), '86 TRA.

Effective date (Sec. 1234(b)(2), '86 TRA).—Applies to payments after 12-31-86.

[Footnote ¶3283] Matter in *italics* in Sec. 3406(b)(3)(C)—(E) added by section 1523(b)(1), '86 TRA, which struck out:

  (1) "or"

  (2) "."

Effective date (Sec. 1523(d), '86 TRA).—Applies with respect to payments made after 12-31-86.

Matter in *italics* in Sec. 3406(b)(6) added by section 1899A(46), '86 TRA, which struck out:

  (3) "6041(A)(a)"

Sec. 3406(h)(5)(D) in *italics* added by section 1521(b), '86 TRA.

Effective date (Sec. 1521(c), '86 TRA).—Applies to real estate transactions closing after 12-31-86.

(B)   the payor was required under section 6041(a) or 6041A(a) to file a return for the preceding calendar year with respect to payments to the payee, or

(C)   during the preceding calendar year, the payor made reportable payments to the payee with respect to which amounts were required to be deducted and withheld under subsection (a).

* * * * * * * * * * *

(h)   **Other Definitions and Special Rules.**—For purposes of this section—

* * * * * * * * * * *

(5)   **Broker.**—

(A)   **In general.**—The term "broker" has the meaning given to such term by section 6045(c)(1).

(B)   **Only 1 broker per acquisition.**—If, but for this subparagraph, there would be more than 1 broker with respect to any acquisition, only the broker having the closest contact with the payee shall be treated as the broker.

(C)   **Payor not treated as broker.**—In the case of any instrument, such term shall not include any person who is the payor with respect to such instrument.

(D)   *Real estate broker not treated as a broker.*—*Except as provided by regulations, such term shall not include any real estate broker (as defined in section 6045(e)(2)).*

* * * * * * * * * * *

[For official explanation, see Committee Reports, ¶4077; 4079.]

【¶3284】 CODE SEC. 3507. ADVANCE PAYMENT OF EARNED INCOME CREDIT.

* * * * * * * * * * *

(c)   **Earned Income Advance Amount.**—

(1)   **In general.**—For purposes of this title, the term "earned income advance amount" means, with respect to any payroll period, the amount determined—

(A)   on the basis of the employee's wages from the employer for such period, and

(B)   in accordance with tables prescribed by the Secretary.

(2)   **Advance amount tables.**—The tables referred to in paragraph (1)(B)—

(A)   shall be similar in form to the tables prescribed under section 3402 and, to the maximum extent feasible, shall be coordinated with such tables, and

(B)   if the employee is not married, or if no earned income eligibility certificate is in effect with respect to the spouse of the employee, shall treat the credit provided by section 32 as if it were a credit—

¹*(i)   of not more than 14 percent of earned income not in excess of the amount of earned income taken into account under section 32(a), which*

(ii)   phases out between the amount of earned income at which the phaseout begins under subsection (b) of section 32 and the amount of earned income at which the credit under section 32 is phased out under such subsection, or

(C)   if an earned income eligibility certificate is in effect with respect to the spouse of the employee, shall treat the credit provided by section 32 as if it were a credit—

²*(i)   of not more than 14 percent of earned income not in excess of ½ of the amount of earned income taken into account under section 32(a), which*

(ii)   phases out between amounts of earned income which are ½ of the amounts of earned income described in subparagraph (B)(ii).

* * * * * * * * * * *

[For official explanation, see Committee Reports, ¶3855.]

【¶3285】 CODE SEC. 4041. IMPOSITION OF TAX.

【Footnote ¶3284】 Matter in *italics* in Sec. 3507(c)(2)(B), and (C) added by section 111(d)(2) and (3), '86 TRA, which struck out:

(1)   "(i)   of not more than 11 percent of the first $5,000 of earned income, which

(ii)   phases out between $6,500 and $11,000 of earned income, or"

(2)   "(i)   of not more than 11 percent of the first $2,500 of earned income, which

(ii)   phases out between $3,250 and $5,500 of earned income."

Effective date (Sec. 151(a), '86 TRA).—Applies to taxable years beginning after 12-31-86.

* * * * * * * * * * *

(b) Exemption for Off-Highway Business Use; [1]*Reduction in Tax* **for Qualified Methanol and Ethanol Fuel.—**

* * * * * * * * * * *

(2) Qualified methanol and ethanol fuel.—

(A) In general.—[2]*In the case of any qualified methanol or ethanol fuel, subsection (a)(2) shall be applied by substituting "3 cents" for "9 cents."*

* * * * * * * * * * *

(l) Exemption for Certain Helicopter Uses.—No tax shall be imposed under this section on any liquid sold for use in, or used in, a helicopter for the purpose of—

[3]*(1) transporting individuals, equipment, or supplies in the exploration for, or the development or removal of, hard minerals, oil, or gas, or*

(2) the planting, cultivation, cutting or transportation of, or caring for, trees (including logging operation),

but only if the helicopter does not take off from, or land at a facility eligible for assistance under the Airport and Airway Development Act of 1970, or otherwise use services provided pursuant to the Airport and Airway Improvement Act of 1982 during such use.

* * * * * * * * * * *

(n) Tax on Diesel Fuel for Highway Vehicle Use May Be Imposed on Sale to Retailer.—*Under regulations prescribed by the Secretary—*

*(1) **In general.**—Upon the written consent of the seller, the tax imposed by subsection (a)(1)—*

(A) shall apply to the sale of diesel fuel to a qualified retailer (and such sale shall be treated as described in subsection (a)(1)(A)), and

(B) shall not apply to the sale of diesel fuel by such retailer or the use of diesel fuel described in subsection (a)(1)(B) if tax was imposed on such fuel under subparagraph (A) of this paragraph.

*(2) **Liability for violation of certification.**—Notwithstanding paragraph (1), a qualified retailer shall be liable for the tax on liquid described in paragraph (3)(C)(ii) if such liquid is used as fuel in a diesel-powered highway vehicle.*

*(3) **Definitions.**—For purposes of this subsection—*

*(A) **Qualified retailer.**—The term "qualified retailer" means any retailer—*

(i) who elects (under such terms and conditions as may be prescribed by the Secretary) to have paragraph (1) apply to all sales of diesel fuel to such retailer by any person, and

(ii) who agrees to provide a written notice to such person that paragraph (1) applies to all sales of diesel fuel by such person to such retailer.

Such election and notice shall be effective for such period or periods as may be prescribed by the Secretary.

*(B) **Retailer.**—The term "retailer" means any person who sells diesel fuel for use as a fuel in a diesel-powered highway vehicle. Such term does not include any person who sells diesel fuel primarily for resale.*

*(C) **Diesel fuel.**—*

*(i) **In general.**—The term "diesel fuel" means any liquid on which tax would be imposed by subsection (a)(1) if sold to a person, and for a use, described in subsection (a)(1)(A).*

⟦Footnote ¶3285⟧   Matter in *italics* in Sec. 4041(b) and (b)(2)(A) added by section 422(a), '86 TRA, which struck out:

(1) "Exemption"

(2) "No tax shall be imposed by subsection (a) on liquids sold for use or used in an off-highway business use."

Effective date (Sec. 422(a)(3), '86 TRA).—Takes effect on 1-1-87.

Matter in *italics* in Sec. 4041(l)(1) added by section 1878(c)(1), '86 TRA, which struck out:

(3) "(1) transporting individuals, equipment, or supplies in—

(A) the exploration for, or the development or removal of, hard minerals, or

(B) the exploration for oil or gas, or"

Effective date (Sec. 1881, '86 TRA and Sec. 1018(c)(1), '84 TRA).—Takes effect on 4-1-84.

Sec. 4041(n) in *italics* added by section 1702(a), '86 TRA.

Effective date (Sec. 1702(c), '86 TRA).—Applies to sales after the first calendar quarter beginning more than 60 days after the date of the enactment of this Act.

(ii) Exception.—A liquid shall not be treated as diesel fuel for purposes of this subsection if the retailer certifies in writing to the seller of such liquid that such liquid will not be used for use as a fuel in a diesel-powered highway vehicle.

(4) Failure to notify seller.—
(A) In general.—If a qualified retailer fails to provide the notice described in paragraph (3)(A)(ii) to any seller of diesel fuel to such retailer—
(i) paragraph (1) shall not apply to sales of diesel fuel by such seller to such retailer during the period for which such failure continues, and
(ii) any diesel fuel sold by such seller to such retailer during such period shall be treated as sold by such retailer (in a sale described in subsection (a)(1)(A)) on the date such fuel was sold to such retailer.

(B) Penalty.—For penalty for failing to notify seller, see section 6652(j).

(5) Exemptions not to apply.—
(A) In general.—No exemption from the tax imposed by subsection (a)(1) shall apply to a sale to which paragraph (1) or (4)(A) of this subsection applies.
(B) Cross reference.—

For provisions allowing a credit or refund for certain sales and uses of fuel, see sections 6416 and 6427.

[For official explanation, see Committee Reports, ¶3900; 4124; 4192.]

[¶3286]   CODE SEC. 4051.   IMPOSITION OF TAX ON HEAVY TRUCKS AND TRAILERS SOLD AT RETAIL.

* * * * * * * * * * *

(d)   Temporary Reduction in Tax on Certain Piggyback Trailers.—

(1)   In general.—In the case of piggyback trailers or semitrailers sold within the 1-year period beginning on [1]*July 18, 1984,* subsection (a) shall be applied by substituting "6 percent" for "12 percent".

(2)   Piggyback trailers or semitrailers.—For purposes of this subsection, the term "piggyback trailers or semitrailers" means any trailer or semitrailer—
(A)   which is designed for use principally in connection with trailer-on-flatcar service by rail, and
(B)   with respect to which the seller certifies, in such manner and form and at such time as the Secretary prescribes by regulations, that such trailer or semitrailer—
(i)   will be used, or resold for use, principally in connection with such service, or
(ii)   will be incorporated into an article which will be so used or resold.

(3)   Additional tax where nonqualified use.—If any piggyback trailer or semitrailer was subject to tax under subsection (a) at the 6 percent rate and such trailer or semitrailer is used or resold for use other than for a use described in paragraph (2)—
(A)   such use or resale shall be treated as a sale to which subsection (a) applies,
(B)   the amount of the tax imposed under subsection (a) on such sale shall be equal to the amount of the tax which was imposed on the first retail sale, and
(C)   the person so using or reselling such trailer or semitrailer shall be liable for the tax imposed by subsection (a).

No tax shall be imposed by reason of this paragraph on any use or resale which occurs more than 6 years after the date of the first retail sale.

* * * * * * * * * * *

[For official explanation, see Committee Reports, ¶4191.]

[¶3287]   CODE SEC. 4064.   GAS GUZZLER TAX.

[Footnote ¶3286]   Matter in *italics* in Sec. 4051(d)(1) added by section 1899A(47), '86 TRA, which struck out:
(1)   "the date of the enactment of the Tax Reform Act of 1984"

Matter in *italics* in 4051(d)(3) added by section 1877(c), '86 TRA.

[Footnote ¶3287]   Matter in *italics* in Sec. 4064(b)(1)(A)(ii) added by section 1812(e)(1)(B)(i), '86 TRA.

Effective date (Sec. 1812(e)(1)(B)(iii), '86 TRA, and section 201(g), P.L. 95-618, 11-9-78).—Applies with respect to 1980 and later model year automobiles (as defined in section 4064(b), '54 Code); except that it does not apply to any station wagon if—(I) such station wagon is originally equipped with more than 6 seat belts, (II) such station wagon was manufactured before 11-1-85, and (III) such station wagon is of the 1985 or 1986 model year.

* * * * * * * * * * * *

(b) **Definitions.**—For purposes of this section—

(1) **Automobile.—**

(A) In general.—The term "automobile" means any 4-wheeled vehicle propelled by fuel—

(i) which is manufactured primarily for use on public streets, roads, and highways (except any vehicle operated exclusively on a rail or rails), and

(ii) which is rated at 6,000 pounds *unloaded* gross vehicle weight or less.

(B) Exception for certain vehicles.—The term "automobile" does not include any vehicle which is treated as a nonpassenger automobile under the rules which were prescribed by the Secretary of Transportation for purposes of section 501 of the Motor Vehicle Information and Cost Savings Act (15 U.S.S. 2001) and which were in effect on the date of the enactment of this section.

(C) Exception for emergency vehicles.—The term "automobile" does not include any vehicle sold for use and used—

(i) as an ambulance or combination ambulance-hearse,

(ii) by the United States or by a State or local government for police or other law enforcement purposes, or

(iii) for other emergency uses prescribed by the Secretary by regulations.

* * * * * * * * * * * *

(5) **Manufacturer.—**[1]

(A) In general.—The term "manufacturer" includes a producer or importer.

(B) Exception for certain small manufacturers.—A person shall not be treated as the manufacturer of any automobile if—

(i) such person would (but for this subparagraph) be so treated solely by reason of lengthening an existing automobile, and

(ii) such person is a small manufacturer (as defined in subsection (d)(4)) for the model year in which such lengthening occurs.

* * * * * * * * * * * *

[For official explanation, see Committee Reports, ¶4146.]

〔¶3288〕 CODE SEC. 4081. IMPOSITION OF TAX.

(a) **Tax Imposed.—**

(1) **In General.**—There is hereby imposed a tax of 9 cents a gallon on the earlier of—

(A) the removal, or

(B) the sale,

of gasoline by the refiner or importer thereof or the terminal operator.

(2) **Bulk transfer to terminal operator.**—For purposes of paragraph (1), the bulk transfer of gasoline to a terminal operator by a refiner or importer shall not be considered a removal or sale of gasoline by such refiner or importer.

(b) **Treatment of Removal or Subsequent Sale by Blender or Compounder.—**

(1) **In general.**—There is hereby imposed a tax of 9 cents a gallon on gasoline removed or sold by the blender or compounder thereof.

(2) **Credit for tax previously paid.**—If—

(A) tax is imposed on the removal or sale of gasoline by reason of paragraph (1), and

(B) the blender or compounder establishes the amount of the tax paid with respect to such gasoline by reason of subsection (a),

the amount of the tax so paid shall be allowed as a credit against the tax imposed by reason of paragraph (1).

(c) **Gasoline Mixed With Alcohol at Refinery, Etc.—**

〔Footnote ¶3287 continued〕

Matter in *italics* in Sec. 4064(b)(5) added by section 1812(e)(B)(ii), '86 TRA, which struck out:

(1) "The term 'manufacturer' includes a producer or importer."

Effective date (Sec. 1812(e)(1)(B)(iii), '86 TRA, and section 201(g), P.L. 95-618, 11-9-78).—Applies with respect to 1980 and later model year automobiles (as defined in section 4064(b), '54 Code). For exceptions, see above.

〔Footnote ¶3288〕 Sec. 4081 added by section 1703(a), '86 TRA.

Effective date (Sec. 1703(h), '86 TRA).—Applies to gasoline removed (as defined in Sec. 4082 of the '86 Code, as amended by this section) after 12-31-87.

(1) **In general.**—Under regulations prescribed by the Secretary, subsection (a) shall be applied by substituting "3 cents" for "9 cents" in the case of the removal or sale of any gasoline for use in producing gasohol at the time of such removal or sale. For purposes of this paragraph, the term "gasohol" means any mixture of gasoline if at least 10 percent of such mixture is alcohol.

(2) **Later separation of gasoline from gasohol.**—If any person separates the gasoline from a mixture of gasoline and alcohol on which tax was imposed under subsection (a) at a rate equivalent to 3 cents a gallon by reason of this subsection (or with respect to which a credit or payment was allowed or made by reason of section 6427(f)(1)), such person shall be treated as the refiner of such gasoline. The amount of tax imposed on any sale of such gasoline by such person shall be 5⅔ cents a gallon.

(3) **Alcohol Defined.**—For purposes of this subsection, the term "alcohol" includes methanol and ethanol but does not include alcohol produced from petroleum, natural gas, or coal (including peat). Such term does not include alcohol with a proof of less than 190 (determined without regard to any added denaturants).

(4) **Termination.**—Paragraph (1) shall not apply to any removal or sale after December 31, 1992.

(d) **Termination.**—On and after October 1, 1988, the taxes imposed by this section shall not apply.

[For official explanation, see Committee Reports, ¶4125.]

⟦¶3289⟧ CODE SEC. 4082. DEFINITIONS.

(a) **Gasoline.**—For purposes of this subpart, the term "gasoline" includes, to the extent prescribed in regulations—
(1) gasoline blend stocks, and
(2) products commonly used as additives in gasoline.
For purposes of paragraph (1), the term "gasoline blend stocks" means any petroleum product component of gasoline.

(b) **Certain Uses Defined as Removal.**—If a refiner, importer, terminal operator, blender, or compounder uses (other than in the production of gasoline or special fuels referred to in section 4041) gasoline refined, imported, blended, or compounded by him, such use shall for the purposes of this chapter be considered a removal.

[For official explanation, see Committee Reports, ¶4125.]

⟦¶3290⟧ CODE SEC. 4083. CROSS REFERENCES.

(1) **For provisions to relieve farmers from excise tax in the case of gasoline used on the farm for farming purposes, see section 6420.**

(2) **For provisions to relieve purchasers of gasoline from excise tax in the case of gasoline used for certain nonhighway purposes, used by local transit systems, or sold for certain exempt purposes, see section 6421.**

(3) **For provisions to relieve purchasers of gasoline from excise tax in the case of gasoline not used for taxable purposes, see section 6427.**

[For official explanation, see Committee Reports, ¶4125.]

⟦¶3291⟧ CODE SEC. 4101. REGISTRATION *AND BOND*.

[1]*(a) Registration.—Every person subject to tax under section 4081 shall, before incurring any liability for tax under such section, register with the Secretary.*

(b) Bond.—Under regulations prescribed by the Secretary, every person who registers under subsection (a) may be required to give a bond in such sum as the Secretary determines.

[For official explanation, see Committee Reports, ¶4125.]

⟦Footnote ¶3289⟧ Sec. 4082 added by section 1703(a), '86 TRA.
Effective date (Sec. 1703(h), '86 TRA).—Applies to gasoline removed (as defined in Sec. 4082 of the '86 Code, as amended by this section) after 12-31-87.
⟦Footnote ¶3290⟧ Sec. 4083 added by section 1703(a), '86 TRA.
Effective date (Sec. 1703(h), '86 TRA).—Applies to gasoline removed (as defined in Sec. 4082 of the '86 Code, as amended by this section) after 12-31-87.
⟦Footnote ¶3291⟧ Matter in *italics* in Sec. 4101 added by section 1703(b)(1), '86 TRA, which struck out:
(1) "Every person subject to tax under section 4081 shall, before incurring any liability for tax under such sections, register with the Secretary."
Effective date (Sec. 1703(h), '86 TRA).—Applies to gasoline removed (as defined in Sec. 4082 of the '86 Code, as amended by this section) after 12-31-87.

[¶3292]   CODE SEC. 4121.   IMPOSITION OF TAX.

(a) Tax Imposed.—

(1) In general.—There is hereby imposed on coal from mines located in the United States sold by the producer, a tax equal to the rate per ton determined under subsection (b).

(2) Limitation on tax.—The amount of the tax imposed by paragraph (1) with respect to a ton of coal shall not exceed the applicable percentage (determined under subsection (b)) of the price of which such ton of coal is sold by the producer.

(b) Determination of rates and limitation on tax.—For purposes of subsection (a)[1]—

    (1)   the rate of tax on coal from underground mines shall be $1.10,

    (2)   the rate of tax on coal from surface mines shall be $.55, and

    (3)   the applicable percentage shall be 4.4 percent.

* * * * * * * * * * * *

[¶3293]   CODE SEC. 4161. IMPOSITION OF TAX.

* * * * * * * * * * * *

(b) Bows and Arrows, Etc.—

(1) Bows and arrows.—There is hereby imposed on the sale by the manufacturer, producer, or importer—

      (A)   of any bow which has a draw weight of 10 pounds or more, and

      (B)   of any arrow which—

          (i)   measures 18 includes overall or more in length, or

          (ii)   measures less than 18 inches overall in length but is suitable for use with a bow described in subparagraph (A) [1],

a tax equal to 11 percent of the price for which so sold.

* * * * * * * * * * * *

[¶3294]   CODE SEC. 4162.   DEFINITIONS; TREATMENT OF CERTAIN RE-SALES.

(a) Sport Fishing Equipment Defined.—For purposes of this part, the term "sport fishing equipment" means—

    (1)   fishing rods and poles (and component parts therefor),

    (2)   fishing reels,

    (3)   fly fishing lines, and other fishing lines not over 130 pounds test,

    (4)   fishing spears, spear guns, and spear tips,

    (5)   items of terminal tackle, including—

      (A)   leaders,

      (B)   artificial lures,

      (C)   artificial baits,

      (D)   artificial flies,

      (E)   fishing hooks,

      (F)   bobbers,

      (G)   sinkers,

      (H)   snaps,

      (I)   drayles, and

      (J)   swivels,

but not including natural bait or any item of terminal tackle designed for use and ordinarily used on fishing lines not described in paragraph (3), and

    (6)   the following items of fishing supplies and accessories—

      (A)   fish stringers

      (B)   creels,

      (C)   tackles boxes,

      (D)   bags, baskets, and other containers designed to hold fish,

      (E)   portable bait containers,

      (F)   fishing vests,

      (G)   landing nets,

[Footnote ¶3292]   Section 1897(a), '86 TRA, struck out from Sec. 4121(b):

(1) ", in the case of sales during any calendar year beginning after December 31, 1985"

Effective date (Sec. 1897(b), '86 TRA, and section 13203(d), '85 COBRA).—Applies to sales after 3-31-86.

[Footnote ¶3293]   Section 1899A(48), '86 TRA, struck out from Sec. 4161(b)(1)(B)(ii):

(1) "."

    (H)   gaff hooks,
    (I)   fishing ¹*hook* disgorgers, and
    (J)   dressing for fishing lines and artificial flies,
  (7)   fishing tip-ups and tilts,
  (8)   fishing rod belts, fishing rodholders, fishing harnesses, fish fighting chairs, fishing outriggers, and fishing downriggers,
  (9)   electric outboard boat motors, and
  (10) sonar devices suitable for finding fish.

* * * * * * * * * * * *

(c) Treatment of Certain Resales.—

* * * * * * * * * * * *

    (3) Related person.—For purposes of this subsection, the term "related person" has the meaning given such term by section ²*465(b)(3)(C)*.

* * * * * * * * * * * *

[For official explanation, see Committee Reports, ¶3870; 4192.]

【¶3295】 CODE SEC. 4221. CERTAIN TAX-FREE SALES.

  (a) General Rule.—Under regulations prescribed by the Secretary, no tax shall be imposed under this chapter (other than under section 4121 *or 4081*) on the sale by the manufacturer (or under section 4051 on the first retail sale) of an article—
    (1)   for use by the purchaser for further manufacture, or for resale by the purchaser to a second purchaser for use by such second purchaser in further manufacture,
    (2)   for export, or for resale by the purchaser to a second purchaser for export,
    (3)   for use by the purchaser as supplies for vessels or aircraft,
    (4)   to a State or local government for the exclusive use of a State or local government, or
    (5)   to a nonprofit educational organization for its exclusive use,
but only if such exportation or use is to occur before any other use.
Paragraph (4) and(5) shall not apply to the tax imposed by section 4064. In the case of taxes imposed by section 4051¹ *or* 4071,² paragraphs (4) and (5) shall not apply on and after October 1, 1988.

* * * * * * * * * * * *

[For official explanation, see Committee Reports, ¶4125.]

【¶3296】 CODE SEC. 4227. ¹*CROSS REFERENCE.*

  For exception for a sale to an Indian tribal government (or its subdivision) for the exclusive use of an Indian tribal government (or its subdivision), see section 7871.

【¶3297】 SEC. 4251. IMPOSITION OF TAX.

  (a) Tax Imposed.—

【Footnote ¶3294】 Matter in *italics* in Sec. 4162(a)(6)(I) added by section 1878(b), '86 TRA, which struck out:
(1) "hood"
Effective date (Sec. 1881, '86 TRA, and Sec. 1015(d), '84 TRA).—Applies with respect to articles sold by the manufacturer, producer or importer after 9-30-84.

Matter in *italics* in Sec 4162(c)(3) added by section 201(d)(7)(C) and (8), '86 TRA, which struck out:
(2) "168(e)(4)(D)"
Effective date (Sec. 203(a), '86 TRA).—Generally applies to property placed in service after 12-31-86, in taxable years ending after such date. For transitional and special rules, see ¶2007—2008.
【Footnote ¶3295】 Matter in *italics* in Sec. 4221(a) added by section 1703(c)(2)(C), '86 TRA, which struck out:
(1) ","

(2) "or 4081"
Effective date (Sec. 1703(h), '86 TRA).—Applies to gasoline removed (as defined in section 4082 of the '86 Code, as amended by this section) after 12-31-87.
【Footnote ¶3296】 Matter in *italics* in Sec. 4227 added by section 1899A(49), '86 TRA, which struck out:
(1) "CROSS REFERENCES.
(1) For exemption for a sale to an Indian tribal government (or its subdivision) for the exclusive use of an Indian tribal government (or its subdivision), see section 7871.
(2) For credit for taxes on tires, see section 6416(c)."
【Footnote ¶3297】 Matter in *italics* in Sec. 4251(b)(2) added by section 1801(b), '86 TRA.

(1) In general.—There is hereby imposed on amounts paid for communications services a tax equal to the applicable percentage of amounts so paid.

* * * * * * * * * * * *

(b) **Definitions.**—For purposes of subsection (a)—

* * * * * * * * * * * *

(2) Applicable percentage.—The term "applicable percentage" means—

With respect to amounts paid pursuant to bills first rendered—	The applicable percentage is
During 1983, 1984, *1985,* 1986, or 1987	3
During 1988 or thereafter	0.

* * * * * * * * * * * *

[For official explanation, see Committee Reports, ¶4135.]

[¶3298] CODE SEC. 4261. IMPOSITION OF TAX.

(a) In General.—There is hereby imposed upon the amount paid for taxable transportation (as defined in section 4262) of any person a tax equal to 8 percent of the amount so paid. In the case of amounts paid outside of the United States for taxable transportation, the tax imposed by this subsection shall apply only if such transportation begins and ends in the United States.

* * * * * * * * * * * *

(e) Exemption for Certain Helicopter Uses.—No tax shall be imposed under subsection (a) or (b) on air transportation by helicopter for the purpose of—

   (1) transporting individuals, equipment, or supplies [1] *in the exploration for, or the development or removal of, hard minerals, oil, or gas, or*

   (2) the planting, cultivation, cutting, or transportation of, or caring for, trees (including logging operations), but only if the helicopter does not take off from, or land at, a facility eligible for assistance under the Airport and Airway Development Act of 1970, or otherwise use services provided pursuant to the Airport and Airway Improvement Act of 1982 during such use.

* * * * * * * * * * * *

[For official explanation, see Committee Reports, ¶4192.]

[¶3299] CODE SEC. 4497. IMPUTED VALUE.

* * * * * * * * * * * *

(c) Suspension of Tax With Respect to Certain Metals and Minerals Held for Later Processing.—

* * * * * * * * * * * *

   (2) Later computation of tax.—If the permittee processes any metal or mineral affected by the election under paragraph (1), or if he sells any portion of the resource containing such a metal or mineral, then the amount of the tax under section 4495 shall be redetermined as if there had been no suspension under paragraph (1) with respect to such metal or mineral. In any such case there shall be added to the increase in tax determined under the preceding sentence an amount equal to the interest (at [1] *the underpayment rate established* under section 6621) on such increase for the period from the date prescribed for paying the tax on the resources (determined under section 4495(d)) to the date of the processing or sale.

* * * * * * * * * * * *

[For official explanation, see Committee Reports, ¶4075.]

[Footnote ¶3298]   Matter in *italics* in Sec. 4261(e)(1) added by section 1878(c)(2), '86 TRA, which struck out:
(1) "(1) transporting individuals, equipment, or supplies in—
(A) the exploration for, or the development or removal of, hard minerals, or
(B) the exploration for oil or gas, or"
Effective date (Sec. 1881, '86 TRA and section 1018(c)(2), '84 TRA).—Applies to transportation beginning after 3-31-84, but shall not apply to any amount paid on or before such date.
[Footnote ¶3299]   Matter in *italics* in Sec. 4497(c)(2) added by section 1511(c)(7), '86 TRA, which struck out:
(1) "rates determined"
Effective date (Sec. 1511(d), '86 TRA).—Applies for purposes of determining interest for periods after 12-31-86.

⟦3300⟧ CODE SEC. 4701. TAX ON ISSUER OF REGISTRATION-REQUIRED OBLIGATION NOT IN REGISTERED FORM.

* * * * * * * * * * * *

(b) **Definitions.**—For purposes of this section.—

(1) **Registration-required obligation.**—The term "registration-required obligation" has the same meaning as when used in section 163(f), except that such term shall not include any obligation required to be registered under [1]*section 149(a).*

* * * * * * * * * * * *

[For official explanation, see Committee Reports, ¶4058.]

⟦¶3301⟧ CODE SEC. 4940. EXCISE TAX BASED ON INVESTMENT INCOME.

* * * * * * * * * * * *

(c) **Net Investment Income Defined.**—

* * * * * * * * * * * *

(5) **Tax-exempt income.**—For purposes of this section, net investment income shall be determined by applying section 103 (relating to [1]*State and local bonds*) and section 265 (relating to expenses and interest relating to tax-exempt income).

(e) **Reduction in tax where private foundation meets certain distribution requirements.**—

* * * * * * * * * * * *

(2) **Requirements.**—A private foundation meets the requirements of this paragraph for any taxable year if—
(A) the amount of the qualifying distributions made by the private foundation during such taxable year equals or exceeds the sum of—
(i) an amount equal to the assets of such foundation for such taxable year multiplied by the average percentage payout for the base period, plus
(ii) 1 percent of the net investment income of such foundation for such taxable year, and
(B) [2]*such private foundation was not liable for tax under section 4942 with respect to any year in the base period.*

* * * * * * * * * * * *

[For official explanation, see Committee Reports, ¶4058; 4158.]

⟦¶3302⟧ CODE SEC. 4941. TAXES ON SELF-DEALING.

* * * * * * * * * * * *

(d) **Self-Dealing.**—

⟦**Footnote ¶3300**⟧ Matter in *italics* in Sec. 4701(b)(1) added by section 1301(j)(5), '86 TRA, which struck out: (1) "section 103(j)"
Effective date (Sec. 1311(a), '86 TRA).—(a) Generally applies to bonds issued after 8-15-86. For transitional and special rules, see ¶2071-2077.
⟦**Footnote ¶3301**⟧ Matter in *italics* in Sec. 4940(c)(5) added by section 1301(j)(6), '86 TRA, which struck out: (1) "interest on certain governmental obligations"
Effective date (Sec. 1311(a), '86 TRA).—(a) Generally applies to bonds issued after 8-15-86. For special and transitional rules see ¶2071-2077.

Matter in *italics* in Sec. 4940(e)(2)(B) added by section 1832, '86 TRA, which struck out:
(2) "the average percentage payout for the base period equals or exceeds 5 percent.
In the case of an operating foundation (as defined in section 4942(j)(3)), subparagraph (B) shall be applied by substituting '3⅓ percent' for '5 percent'."
Effective date (Sec. 1881, '86 TRA, and Sec. 303, '84 TRA).—Applies to taxable years beginning after 12-31-84.
⟦**Footnote ¶3302**⟧ Matter in *italics* in Sec. 4941(d)(2)(B) added by section 1812(b)(1), '86 TRA.
Effective date (Sec. 1881, '86 TRA and Sec. 172(c), '84 TRA).—(1) Generally applies to
(A) term loans made after 6-6-84, and
(B) demand loans outstanding after 6-6-84.
(2) Exception for demand loans outstanding on June 6, 1984, and repaid within 60 days after July 18, 1984— The amendments made by this section shall not apply to any demand loan which—
(A) was outstanding on 6-6-84, and
(B) was repaid before the date 60 days after 7-18-84
(3) Exception for certain existing loans to continuing care facilities.—Nothing in this subsection shall be construed to apply the amendments made by this section to any loan made before 6-6-84, to a continuing care facility by a resident of such facility which is contingent on continued residence at such facility.
(4) Applicable federal rate for periods before January 1, 1985.—For periods before 1-1-85, the applicable Fed-

* * * * * * * * * * *

(2) **Special rules.**—For purposes of paragraph (1)—

* * * * * * * * * * * *

(B)   the lending of money by a disqualified person to a private foundation shall not be an act of self-dealing if the loan is without interest or other charge *(determined without regard to section 7872)* and if the proceeds of the loan are used exclusively for purposes specified in section 501(c)(3);

* * * * * * * * * * * *

(G)   in the case of a government official (as defined in section 4946(c)), paragraph (1) shall in addition not apply to—

(i)   prizes and awards which are subject to the provisions of section 74(b) *without regard to paragraph (3) thereof),* if the recipients of such prizes and awards are selected from the general public,

(ii)   scholarships and fellowship grants which are subject to the provisions of section 117(a) and are to be used for study at an educational organization described in section 170(b)(1)(A)(ii),

(iii)   any annuity or other payment (forming part of a stock-bonus, pension, or profit-sharing plan) by a trust which is a qualified trust under section 401,

(iv)   any annuity or other payment under a plan which meets the requirements of section 404(a)(2),

(v)   any contribution or gift (other than a contribution or gift of money) to, or services or facilities made available to, any such individual, if the aggregate value of such contributions, gifts, services, and facilities to, or made available to, such individual during any calendar year does not exceed $25,

(vi)   any payment made under chapter 41 of title 5, United States Code, or

(vii)   any payment or reimbursement of traveling expenses for travel solely from one point in the United States to another point in the United States, but only if such payment or reimbursement does not exceed the actual cost of the transportation involved plus an amount for all other traveling expenses not in excess of 125 percent of the maximum amount payable under section 5702(a) of title 5, United States Code, for like travel by employees of the United States;

* * * * * * * * * * * *

[For official explanation, see Committee Reports, ¶3858; 4146.]

[¶3303]   CODE SEC. 4942.   TAXES ON FAILURE TO DISTRIBUTE INCOME.

* * * * * * * * * * * *

(f)   **Adjusted Net Income.—**

* * * * * * * * * * * *

(2)   **Income modifications.**—The income modifications referred to in paragraph (1)(A) are as follows:

(A)   section 103 (relating to [1]*State and local bonds*) shall not apply,

* * * * * * * * * * * *

[For official explanation, see Committee Reports, ¶4058.]

[¶3304]   CODE SEC. 4945.   TAXES ON TAXABLE EXPENDITURES.

[Footnote ¶3302 continued]

eral rate under paragraph (2) of section 7872(f) of the '54 Code, as added by this section, shall be 10 percent, compounded semiannually.

(5)   Treatment of renegotiations, etc.—For purposes of this subsection, any loan renegotiated, extended, or revised after 6-6-84, shall be treated as a loan made after such date.

(6)   Definition of term and demand loans.—For purposes of this subsection, the terms "demand loan" and "term loan" have the respective meanings given such terms by paragraphs (5) and (6) of section 7872(f) of the '54 Code, as added by this section, but the second sentence of such paragraph (5) shall not apply.

Matter in *italics* in Sec. 4941(d)(2)(G)(i) added by section 122(a)(2)(A), '86 TRA.

Effective date (Sec. 151(c), '86 TRA).—Applies to prizes and awards granted after 12-31-86.

[Footnote ¶3303]   Matter in *italics* in Sec. 4942(f)(2)(A) added by section 1301(j)(6), '86 TRA, which struck out:

(1)   "interest on certain governmental obligations"

Effective date (Sec. 1311(a), '86 TRA).—(a) Generally applies to bonds issued after 8-15-86. For transitional and special rules, see ¶2071-2077.

(a) Initial Taxes.—

(1) On the foundation.—There is hereby imposed on each taxable expenditure (as defined in subsection (d)) a tax equal to 10 percent of the amount thereof. The tax imposed by this paragraph shall be paid by the private foundation.

(2) On the management.—There is hereby imposed on the agreement of any foundation manager to the making of an expenditure, knowing that it is a taxable expenditure, a tax equal to 2½ percent of the amount thereof, unless such agreement is not willful and is due to reasonable cause. The tax imposed by this paragraph shall be paid by any foundation manager who agreed to the making of the expenditure.

(b) Additional Taxes.—

(1) On the foundation.—In any case in which an initial tax is imposed by subsection (a)(1) on a taxable expenditure and such expenditure is not corrected within the taxable period, there is hereby imposed a tax equal to 100 percent of the amount of the expenditure. The tax imposed by this paragraph shall be paid by the private foundation.

(2) On the management.—In any case in which an additional tax is imposed by paragraph (1), if a foundation manager refused to agree to part or all of the correction, there is hereby imposed a tax equal to 50 percent of the amount of the taxable expenditure. The tax imposed by this paragraph shall be paid by any foundation manager who refused to agree to part or all of the correction.

* * * * * * * * * * * *

(d) Taxable Expenditure.—For purposes of this section, the term "taxable expenditure" means any amount paid or incurred by a private foundation—

(1) to carry on propaganda, or otherwise to attempt, to influence legislation, within the meaning of subsection (e),

(2) except as provided in subsection (f), to influence the outcome of any specific public election, or to carry on, directly or indirectly, any voter registration drive,

(3) as a grant to an individual for travel, study, or other similar purposes by such individual, unless such grant satisfies the requirements of subsection (g),

(4) as a grant to an organization unless—

(A) such organization is described in paragraph (1), (2), or (3) or section 509(a) or is an exempt operating foundation (as defined in section 4940(d)(2)), or

(B) the private foundation exercises expenditure responsibility with respect to such grant in accordance with subsection (h), or,

(5) for any purpose other than one specified in section 170(c)(2)(B).

* * * * * * * * * * * *

(g) Individual Grants.—Subsection (d)(3) shall not apply to an individual grant awarded on an objective and nondiscriminatory basis pursuant to a procedure approved in advance by the Secretary, if it is demonstrated to the satisfaction of the Secretary that—

(1) the grant constitutes a scholarship or fellowship grant which is subject to the provisions of section 117(a) and is to be used for study at an educational organization described in section 170(b)(1)(A)(ii),

(2) the grant constitutes a prize or award which is subject to the provisions of section 74(b) *(without regard to paragraph (3) thereof)*, if the recipient of such prize or award is selected from the general public, or

(3) the purpose of the grant is to achieve a specific objective, produce a report or other similar product, or improve or enhance a literary, artistic, musical, scientific, teaching, or other similar capacity, skill, or talent of the grantee.

* * * * * * * * * * * *

[For official explanation, see Committee Reports, ¶3858.]

[¶3305] CODE SEC. 4946. DEFINITIONS AND SPECIAL RULES.

* * * * * * * * * * * *

[Footnote ¶3304] Matter in *italics* in Sec. 4945(g)(2) added by section 122(a)(2)(B), '86 TRA.
Effective date (Sec. 151(a) and (c), '86 TRA).—(a) Generally applies to taxable years beginning after 12-31-86.

* * * * * * * * * * * *

(c) Prizes and Awards.—The amendments made by section 122 shall apply to prizes and awards granted after 12-31-86.

(c) **Government Official.**—For purposes of subsection (a)(1)(I) and section 4941, the term "government official" means, with respect to an act of self-dealing described in section 4941, an individual who, at the time of such act, holds any of the following offices or positions (other than as a "special Government employee", as defined in section 202(a) of title 18, United States Code):

(1) an elective public office in the executive or legislative branch of the Government of the United States,

(2) an office in the executive or judicial branch of the Government of the United States, appointment to which was made by the President,

(3) a position in the executive, legislative, or judicial branch of the Government of the United States—

(A) which is listed in schedule C of rule VI of the Civil Service Rules, or

(B) the compensation for which is equal to or greater than the lowest rate of compensation prescribed for GS-16 of the General Schedule under section 5332 of title 5, United States Code,

(4) a position under the House of Representatives or the Senate of the United States held by an individual receiving gross compensation at an annual rate of $15,000 or more,

(5) an elective or appointive public office in the executive, legislative, or judicial branch of the government of a State, possession of the United States, or political subdivision or other area of any of the foregoing, or of the District of Columbia, held by an individual receiving gross compensation at an annual rate of [1]*$20,000* or more, or

(6) a position as personal or executive assistant or secretary to any of the foregoing.

* * * * * * * * * * * *

[¶3306] CODE SEC. 4961. ABATEMENT OF SECOND TIER TAXES WHERE THERE IS CORRECTION.

* * * * * * * * * * * *

(c) **Suspension of Period of Collection for Second Tier Tax.**—

(1) **Proceeding in district court or** [1]*United States Claims Court.*—If, not later than 90 days after the day on which the second tier tax is assessed, the first tier tax is paid in full and a claim for refund of the amount so paid is filed, no levy or proceeding in court for the collection of the second tier tax shall be made, begun, or prosecuted until a final resolution of a proceeding begun as provided in paragraph (2) (and of any supplemental proceeding with respect thereto under subsection (b)). Notwithstanding section 7421(a), the collection by levy or proceeding may be enjoined during the time such prohibition is in force by a proceeding in the proper court.

* * * * * * * * * * * *

[¶3307] CODE SEC. 4972. TAX ON NONDEDUCTIBLE CONTRIBUTIONS TO QUALIFIED EMPLOYER PLANS.

(a) **Tax Imposed.**—In the case of any qualified employer plan, there is hereby imposed a tax equal to 10 percent of the nondeductible contributions under the plan (determined as of the close of the taxable year of the employer).

(b) **Employer Liable for Tax.**—The tax imposed by this section shall be paid by the employer making the contributions.

(c) **Nondeductible Contributions.**—For purposes of this section, the term "nondeductible contributions" means, with respect to any qualified employer plan, the sum of—

(1) the excess (if any) of—

(A) the amount contributed for the taxable year by the employer to or under such plan, over

(B) the amount allowable as a deduction under section 404 for such contributions, and

(2) the amount determined under this subsection for the preceding taxable year reduced by the sum of—

[Footnote ¶3305] Matter in *italics* in Sec. 4946(c)(5) added by section 1606(a), '86 TRA, which struck out:
(1) "$15,000"
Effective date (Sec. 1606(b), '86 TRA).—Applies to compensation received after 12-31-85.
[Footnote ¶3306] Matter in *italics* in Sec. 4961(c)(1) added by section 1899(A)(50), '86 TRA, which struck out:
(1) "court of claims."
[Footnote ¶3307] Sec. 4972 added by section 1131(c)(1) '86 TRA.
Effective date (Sec. 1131(d), '86 TRA).—Applies to taxable years beginning after 12-31-86.

(A) the portion of the amount so determined returned to the employer during the taxable year, and

(B) the portion of the amount so determined deductible under section 404 for the taxable year.

(d) Definitions.—For purposes of this section—

(1) Qualified employer plan.—The term "qualified employer plan" means—
(A) any plan meeting the requirements of section 401(a) which includes a trust exempt from the tax under section 501(a),
(B) an annuity plan described in section 403(a), and
(C) any simplified employee pension (within the meaning of section 408(k)).

(2) Employer.—In the case of a plan which provides contributions or benefits for employees some or all of whom are self-employed individuals within the meaning of section 401(c)(1), the term "employer" means the person treated as the employer under section 401(c)(4).

[For official explanation, see Committee Reports, ¶3990.]

【¶3308】 CODE SEC. 4973. TAX ON EXCESS CONTRIBUTIONS TO INDIVIDUAL RETIREMENT ACCOUNTS, CERTAIN SECTION 403(b) CONTRACTS, AND CERTAIN INDIVIDUAL RETIREMENT ANNUITIES.

* * * * * * * * * * *

(b) Excess Contributions.—For purposes of this section, in the case of individual retirement accounts [1]*or individual retirement annuities*, the term "excess contributions" means the sum of—

(1) the excess (if any) of—
[2]*(A) the amount contributed for the taxable year to the accounts or for the annuities (other than a rollover contribution described in section 402(a)(5), 402(a)(7), 403(a)(4), 403(b)(8), or 408(d)(3)), over*
(B) the amount allowable as a deduction under section 219 for such contributions, and

(2) the amount determined under this subsection for the preceding taxable year, reduced by the sum of—
(A) the distributions out of the account for the taxable year which were included in the gross income of the payee under section 408(d)(1),
(B) the distributions out of the account for the taxable year to which section 408(d)(5) applies, and
(C) the excess (if any) of the maximum amount allowable as a deduction under section 219 for the taxable year over the amount contributed (determined without regard to section 219(f)(6)) to the accounts or for the annuities [3] for the taxable year.

For purposes of this subsection, any contribution which is distributed from the individual retirement account or the individual retirement annuity in a distribution to which section 408(d)(4) applies shall be treated as an amount not contributed. *For purposes of paragraphs (1)(B) and (2)(C), the amount allowable as a deduction under section 219 (after application of section 408(o)(2)(B)(ii)) shall be increased by the nondeductible limit under section 408(o)(2)(B).*

* * * * * * * * * * *

[For official explanation, see Committee Reports, ¶3963; 4161.]

【Footnote ¶3308】 Matter in *italics* in Sec. 4973(b), except for the last sentence, added by section 1848(f), '86 TRA, which struck out:
(1) ", individual retirement annuities, or bonds"
(2) "(A) the amount contributed for the taxable year to the accounts or for the annuities or bonds (other than a rollover contribution described in section 402(a)(5), 402(a)(7), 403(a)(4), 403(b)(8), 405(d)(3), and 408(d)(3), over"
(3) "or bonds"
Effective date (Sec. 1881, '86 TRA and section 491(f)(1), '84 TRA).—Applies to obligations issued after 12-31-83.

The last sentence of Sec. 4973(b) in *italics* added by section 1102(b)(1), '86 TRA.
Effective date (Sec. 1102(g), '86 TRA).—Applies to contributions and distributions for taxable years beginning after 12-31-86.

≫P-H CAUTION→ There are two versions of Sec. 4974. Sec. 4974, generally effective after 12-31-86, follows. For Sec. 4974, generally effective before 1-1-87, see, ¶3309-A below.

【¶3309】 CODE SEC. 4974. [1]*EXCISE TAX ON CERTAIN ACCUMULATIONS IN QUALIFIED RETIREMENT PLANS.*

(a) General Rule.—If the amount distributed during the taxable year of the payee under any qualified retirement plan or any eligible deferred compensation plan (as defined in section 457(b)) is less than the minimum required distribution for such taxable year, there is hereby imposed a tax equal to 50 percent of the amount by which such minimum required distribution exceeds the actual amount distributed during the taxable year. The tax imposed by this section shall be paid by the payee.

(b) Minimum Required Distribution.—For purposes of this section, the term "minimum required distribution" means the minimum amount required to be distributed during a taxable year under section 401(a)(9), 403(b)(10), 408(a)(6), 408(b)(3), or 457(d)(2), as the case may be, as determined under regulations prescribed by the Secretary.

(c) Qualified Retirement Plan.—For purposes of this section, the term "qualified retirement plan" means—

(1) a plan described in section 401(a) which includes a trust exempt from tax under section 501(a),

(2) an annuity plan described in section 403(a),

(3) an annuity contract described in section 403(b),

(4) an individual retirement account described in section 408(a), or

(5) an individual retirement annuity described in section 408(b).

Such term includes any plan, contract, account, or annuity which, at any time, has been determined by the Secretary to be such a plan, contract, account, or annuity.

(d) Waiver of Tax in Certain Cases.—If the taxpayer establishes to the satisfaction of the Secretary that—

(1) the shortfall described in subsection (a) in the amount distributed during any taxable year was due to reasonable error, and

(2) reasonable steps are being taken to remedy the shortfall, the Secretary may waive the tax imposed by subsection (a) for the taxable year.

【Footnote ¶3309】   Matter in *italics* in Sec. 4974 added by section 1121(a)(1), '86 TRA, which struck out:

(1) "EXCISE TAX ON CERTAIN ACCUMULATIONS IN INDIVIDUAL RETIREMENT ACCOUNTS OR ANNUITIES.

(a) Imposition of Tax.—If, in the case of an individual retirement account or individual retirement annuity, the amount distributed during the taxable year of the payee is less than the minimum amount required to be distributed under section 408(a)(6) or 408(b)(3) during such year, there is imposed a tax equal to 50 percent of the amount by which the minimum amount required to be distributed during such year exceeds the amount actually distributed during the year. The tax imposed by this section shall be paid by such payee.

(b) Regulations.—For purposes of this section, the minimum amount required to be distributed during a taxable year under section 408(a)(6) or 408(b)(3) shall be determined under regulations prescribed by the Secretary.

(c) Waiver of Tax in Certain Cases.—If the taxpayer establishes to the satisfaction of the Secretary that—

(1) the shortfall described in subsection (a) in the amount distributed during any taxable year was due to reasonable error, and

(2) reasonable steps are being taken to remedy the shortfall.

the Secretary may waive the tax imposed by subsection (a) for the taxable year."

Effective date (Sec. 1121(d)(1), (3) and (4) '86 TRA).—Generally applies to years beginning after 12-31-88.

* * * * * * * * * * * *

(3) Collective bargaining agreements.—In the case of a plan maintained pursuant to 1 or more collective bargaining agreements between employee representatives and 1 or more employers ratified before 3-1-86, the amendments made by this section shall not apply to distributions to individuals covered by such agreements in plan years beginning before the earlier of—

(A) the later of—

(i) the date on which the last of such collective bargaining agreements terminates (determined without regard to any extension thereof after 2-28-86), or

(ii) 1-1-89, or

(B) 1-1-91.

(4) Transition rules.—

(A) The amendments made by subsections (a) and (b) shall not apply with respect to any benefits with respect to which a designation is in effect under section 242(b)(2) of the '82 TEFRA.

(B)(i) Except as provided in clause (ii), the amendment made by subsection (b) shall not apply in the case of any individual who has attained age 70½ before 1-1-88.

(ii) Clause (i) shall not apply to any individual who is a 5-percent owner (as defined in section 416(i) of the '86 Code), at any time during—

(I) the plan year ending with or within the calendar year in which such owner attains age 66½, and

(II) any subsequent plan year.

[For official explanation, see Committee Reports, ¶3986; 4172.]

»P-H CAUTION→ There are two versions of Sec. 4974. Sec. 4974, generally effective before 1-1-87, follows. For Sec. 4974, generally effective after 12-31-86, see ¶3309, above.

[¶3309-A]   CODE SEC. 4974.   EXCISE TAX ON CERTAIN ACCUMULATIONS IN INDIVIDUAL RETIREMENT ACCOUNTS OR ANNUITIES.

(a) Imposition of Tax.—If, in the case of an individual retirement account or individual retirement annuity, the amount distributed during the taxable year of the payee is less than the minimum amount required to be distributed under [1]*section 408(a)(6) or 408(b)(3)* during such year, there is imposed a tax equal to 50 percent of the amount by which the minimum amount required to be distributed during such year exceeds the amount actually distributed during the year. The tax imposed by this section shall be paid by such payee.

(b) Regulations.—For purposes of this section, the minimum amount required to be distributed during a taxable year under [1]*section 408(a)(6) or 408(b)(3)* shall be determined under regulations prescribed by the Secretary.

* * * * * * * * * * *

[For official explanation, see Committee Reports, ¶4172.]

[¶3310]   CODE SEC. 4975.   TAX ON PROHIBITED TRANSACTIONS.

* * * * * * * * * * *

(d) Exemptions.—The prohibitions provided in subsection (c) shall not apply to—
(1) any loan made by the plan to a disqualified person who is a participant or beneficiary of the plan if such loan—
(A) is available to all such participants or beneficiaries on a reasonably equivalent basis.
(B) is not made available to [1]*highly compensated employees (within the meaning of section 414(q) of the Internal Revenue Code of 1986)* in an amount greater than the amount made available to other employees,
(C) is made in accordance with specific provisions regarding such loans set forth in the plan,
(D) bears a reasonable rate of interest, and
(E) is adequately secured;

* * * * * * * * * * *

The exemptions provided by this subsection (other than paragraphs (9) [2]*and (12))* shall not apply to any transaction with respect to a trust described in section 401(a) which is part of a plan providing contributions to benefits for employees some or all of whom are owner-employees (as defined in section 401(c)(3)) in which a plan directly or indirectly lends any part of the corpus or income of the plan to, pays any compensation for personal services rendered to the plan to, or acquires for the plan any property from or sells any property to, any such owner-employee, a member of the family (as defined in section 267(c)(4)) of any such owner-employee, or a corporation controlled by any such owner-employee through the ownership, directly or indirectly, of 50 percent or more of the total combined voting power of all classes of stock of the corporation. For purposes of the preceding sentence, a shareholder-

---

[Footnote ¶3309-A]   Matter in *italics* in Sec. 4974(a) and (b) added by section 1852(a)(7)(B) and (C), '86 TRA, which struck out:
(1) "section 408(a)(6) and (7) or 408(b)(3) or (4)"
Effective date (Sec. 1881, '86 TRA and Sec. 521(e), '84 TRA).—Generally applies to years beginning after 12-31-84. For special and transitional rules, see footnote ¶2994.
[Footnote ¶3310]   Matter in *italics* in Sec. 4975(d)(1)(B) added by section 1114(b)(15)(A), '86 TRA.
(1) "highly compensated employees, officers, or shareholders"
Effective date (Sec. 1114(c)(3), '86 TRA).—(1) Generally applies to years beginning after 12-31-88. For special rule for determining highly compensated employees, see footnote ¶3004.

Matter in *italics* in Sec. 4975(d) added by section 1899A(51), '86 TRA, which struck out:
(2) "and (12)"

Matter in *italics* in Sec. 4975(e)(7) added by section 1854(f)(3)(A), '86 TRA.
Effective date (Sec. 1854(f)(4)(A), '86 TRA).—Takes effect on date of enactment of this Act.

employee (as defined in section 1379 as in effect on the day before the date of the enactment of the subchapter S revision Act of 1982) a participant or beneficiary of an individual retirement account or an individual retirement annuity (as defined in section 408), and an employer or association of employees which establishes such an account or annuity under section 408(c) shall be deemed to be an owner-employee.

(e) Definitions.—

* * * * * * * * * * *

(7) **Employee stock ownership plan.**—The term "employee stock ownership plan" means a defined contribution plan—

    (A) which is a stock bonus plan which is qualified, or a stock bonus and a money purchase plan both of which are qualified under section 401(a), and which are designed to invest primarily in qualifying employer securities; and

    (B) which is otherwise defined in regulations prescribed by the Secretary.

A plan shall not be treated as an employee stock ownership plan unless it meets the requirements of section 409(h), *section 409(o), and, if applicable, section 409(n)* and, if the employer has a registration-type class of securities (as defined in section 409(e)(4), it meets the requirements of section 409(e).

* * * * * * * * * * *

[For official explanation, see Committee Reports, ¶3979; 4174.]

【¶3311】 CODE SEC. 4976. TAXES WITH RESPECT TO FUNDED WELFARE BENEFIT PLANS.

(a) General rule.—If—

    (1) an employer maintains a welfare benefit fund, and

    (2) there is a disqualified benefit provided during any taxable year,

there is hereby imposed on such employer a tax equal to 100 percent of such disqualified benefit.

^{1}*(b) Disqualified Benefit.—For purposes of subsection (a)—*

    (1) In general.—The term "disqualified benefit" means—

        (A) any post-retirement medical benefit or life insurance benefit provided with respect to a key employee if a separate account is required to be established for such employee under section 419A(d) and such payment is not from such account,

        (B) any post-retirement medical benefit or life insurance benefit provided with respect to an individual in whose favor discrimination is prohibited unless the plan meets the requirements of section 505(b) with respect to such benefit (whether or not such requirements apply to such plan), and

        (C) any portion of a welfare benefit fund reverting to the benefit of the employer.

    (2) Exception for collective bargaining plans.—Paragraph (1)(B) shall not apply to any plan maintained pursuant to an agreement between employee representatives and 1 or more employers if the Secretary finds that such agreement is a collective bargaining agreement and that the benefits referred to in paragraph (1)(B) were the subject of good faith bargaining between such employee representatives and such employer or employers.

    (3) Exception for nondeductible contributions.—Paragraph (1)(C) shall not apply to any amount attributable to a contribution to the fund which is not allowable as a deduction under section 419 for the taxable year or any prior taxable year (and such contribution shall not be included in any carryover under section 419(d)).

    (4) Exception for certain amounts charged against existing reserve.—Subparagraphs (A) and (B) of paragraph (1) shall not apply to post-retirement benefits charged against an existing reserve for post-retirement medical or life insurance benefits (as defined in section 512(a)(3)(E)) or charged against the income on such reserve.

[For official explanation, see Committee Reports, ¶4171.]

【Footnote ¶3311】 Matter in *italics* in Sec. 4976(b) added by section 1851(a)(11), '86 TRA, which struck out:

(1) "**(b) Disqualified Benefit.**—For purposes of subsection (a), the term "disqualified benefit" means—

(1) any medical benefit or life insurance benefit provided with respect to a key employee other than from a separate account established for such owner under section 419A(d), and

(2) any post-retirement medical or life insurance benefit unless the plan meets the requirements of section 505(b)(1) with respect to such benefit, and

(3) any portion of such fund reverting to the benefit of the employer."

Effective date (Sec. 1881, '86 TRA and Sec. 511(e)(1), '84 TRA as amended by '86 Code).—Generally applies to contributions paid or accrued after 12-31-85, in taxable years ending after such date. For special rules see footnote ¶3008.

[¶3312] CODE SEC. 4977. TAX ON CERTAIN FRINGE BENEFITS PRO-VIDED BY AN EMPLOYER.

* * * * * * * * * * * *

(c) **Effect of Election on Section 132(a).**—If—

(1) an election under this section is in effect with respect to an employer for any calendar year, and

¹*(2) at all times on or after January 1, 1984, and before the close of the calendar year involved, substantially all of the employees of the employer were entitled to employee discounts on goods or services provided by the employer in 1 line of business,*

for purposes of paragraphs (1) and (2) of section 132(a) (but not for the purposes of section 132(g)(2)), all employees of any line of business of the employer which was in existence on January 1, 1984, shall be treated as employees of the line of business referred to in paragraph (2),

* * * * * * * * * * * *

(f) Section To Apply Only to Employment Within the United States.—Except as otherwise provided in regulations, this section shall apply only with respect to employment within the United States.

[For official explanation, see Committee Reports, ¶4173.]

[¶3313] CODE SEC. 4978. TAX ON CERTAIN DISPOSITIONS BY EMPLOYEE STOCK OWNERSHIP PLANS AND CERTAIN COOPERATIVES.

(a) **Tax on Dispositions of Securities To Which Section 1042 Applies Before Close of Minimum Holding Period.**—If, during the 3-year period after the date on which the employee stock ownership plan or eligible worker-owned cooperative acquired any qualified securities in a sale to which section 1042 applied, such plan or cooperative disposes of any qualified securities and—

(1) the total number of shares held by such plan or cooperative after such disposition is less ¹*than* the total number of employer securities held immediately after such sale, or

* * * * * * * * * * * *

(b) **Amount of Tax.**—

(1) **In general.**—The amount of the tax imposed by ²*subsection (a)* shall be equal to 10 percent of the amount realized on the disposition.

* * * * * * * * * * * *

(c) **Liability for payment of taxes.**—The tax imposed by this subsection shall be paid by—

(1) the employer, or

(2) the eligible worker-owned cooperative,

that made the written statement described in ³*section 1042(b)(3).*

(d) **Section not to apply to certain dispositions.**—

(1) **Certain distributions to employees.**—This section shall not apply with respect to any distribution of qualified securities (or sale of such securities) which is made by reason of—

(A) the death of the employee,

(B) the retirement of the employee after the employee has attained 59½ years of age,

(C) the disability of the employee (within the meaning of ⁴*section 72(m)(7)),* or

* * * * * * * * * * * *

[Footnote ¶3312] Matter in *italics* in Sec. 4977(c)(2) and (f) added by section 1853(c)(1) and (2), '86 TRA, which struck out:

(1) "(2) as of January 1, 1984, substantially all of the employees of the employer were entitled to employee discounts or services provided by the employer in 1 line of business,"

Effective date (Sec. 1881, '86 TRA and Sec. 531(h), '84 TRA).—Takes effect on 1-1-85.

[Footnote ¶3313] Matter in *italics* in Sec. 4978(a)(1), (b)(1), (c), (d)(1)(C), (3), (e)(2) and (3) added by section 1854(e), '86 TRA, which struck out:

(1) "then"

(2) "paragraph (1)"

(3) "section 1042(a)(2)(B)"

(4) "section 72(m)(5)"

(3) *Liquidation of corporation into cooperative.—In the case of any exchange of qualified securities pursuant to the liquidation of the corporation issuing qualified securities into the eligible worker-owned cooperative in a transaction which meets the requirements of section 332 (determined by substituting "100 percent" for "80 percent" each place it appears in section 332(b)(1)), such exchange shall not be treated as a disposition for purposes of this section.*

(e) **Definitions and special rules.**—For purposes of this section—

* * * * * * * * * * * *

(2) **Qualified securities.**—The term "qualified securities" has the meaning given to such term by [5]*section 1042(c)(1).*

(3) **Eligible worker-owner cooperative.**—The term "eligible worker-owned cooperative" has the meaning given to such term by [5]*section 1042(c)(1).*

* * * * * * * * * * * *

[For official explanation, see Committee Reports, ¶4174.]

〔¶3314〕 CODE SEC. 4979. TAX ON CERTAIN EXCESS CONTRIBUTIONS.

(a) **General Rule.**—In the case of any plan, there is hereby imposed a tax for the taxable year equal to 10 percent of the sum of—

(1) any excess contributions under a cash or deferred arrangement which is part of such plan for the plan year ending in such taxable year, and

(2) any excess aggregate contributions under the plan for the plan year ending in such taxable year.

(b) **Liability for Tax.**—The tax imposed by subsection (a) shall be paid by the employer.

(c) **Excess Contributions.**—For purposes of this section, the term "excess contributions" has the meaning given such term by sections 401(k)(8)(B), 403(b), 408(k)(8)(B), and 501(c)(18).

(d) **Excess Aggregate Contribution.**—For purposes of this section, the term "excess aggregate contribution" has the meaning given to such term by section 401(m)(6)(B).

(e) **Plan.**—For purposes of this section, the term "plan" means—

(1) a plan described in section 401(a) which includes a trust exempt from tax under section 501(a),

(2) any annuity plan described in section 403(a),

(3) any annuity contract described in section 403(b),

(4) a simplified employee pension of an employer which satisfies the requirements of section 408(k), and

(5) a plan described in section 501(c)(18).

Such term includes any plan which, at any time, has been determined by the Secretary to be such a plan.

(f) **No Tax Where Excess Distributed Within 2½ Months of "Close of Year."**—

(1) **In general.**—No tax shall be imposed under this section on any excess contribution or excess aggregate contribution, as the case may be, to the extent such contribution (together with any income allocable thereto) is distributed (or, if forfeitable, is forfeited) before the close of the first 2½ months of the following plan year.

(2) **Included in prior year.**—Any amount distributed as provided in paragraph (1) shall be treated as received and earned by the recipient in his taxable year for which such contribution was made.

[For official explanation, see Committee Reports, ¶3982.]

〔¶3314-A〕 CODE SEC. 4979A. TAX ON CERTAIN PROHIBITED ALLOCATIONS OF QUALIFIED SECURITIES.

〔**Footnote ¶3313 continued**〕

(5) "section 1042(b)(1)"
Effective date (Sec. 1881, '86 TRA and 545(c), '84 TRA).—Applies to taxable years beginning after 7-18-84.
〔**Footnote ¶3314**〕 Sec. 4979 added by section 1117(b)(1), '86 TRA.
Effective date (Sec. 1117(d)(1), '86 TRA).—(1) Generally applies to plan years beginning after 12-31-86.
For special rules see footnote ¶2994.
〔**Footnote ¶3314-A**〕 Sec. 4979A added by section 1854(a)(9)(A), '86 TRA.
Effective date (Sec. 1854(a)(9)(D), '86 TRA).—Applies to sales of securities after the date of enactment of this Act.

Matter in *italics* in Sec. 4979A(b)(1) and (c), added by section 1172(b)(2), '86 TRA.
Effective date (Sec. 1172(c), '86 TRA).—Applies to sales after the date of the enactment of this Act with respect

(a) **Imposition of Tax.**—If there is a prohibited allocation of qualified securities by any employee stock ownership plan or eligible worker-owned cooperative, there is hereby imposed a tax on such allocation equal to 50 percent of the amount involved.

(b) **Prohibited Allocation.**—For purposes of this section, the term "prohibited allocation" means—

    (1) any allocation of qualified securities acquired in a sale to which section 1042 *or section 2057* applies which violates the provisions of section 409(n), and

    (2) any benefit which accrues to any person in violation of the provisions of section 409(n).

(c) **Liability for Tax.**—The tax imposed by this section shall be paid by—

    (1) the employer sponsoring such plan, or

    (2) the eligible worker-owned cooperative,

which made the written statement described in section 1042(b)(3)(B) *or section 2057(d)*.

(d) **Definitions.**—Terms used in this section have the same respective meaning as when used in section 4978.

[For official explanation, see Committee Reports, ¶4017; 4174.]

⟦¶3315⟧ CODE SEC. 4980. TAX ON REVERSION OF QUALIFIED PLAN ASSETS TO EMPLOYER.

(a) **Imposition of Tax.**—There is hereby imposed a tax of 10 percent of the amount of any employer reversion from a qualified plan.

(b) **Liability for Tax.**—The tax imposed by subsection (a) shall be paid by the employer maintaining the plan.

(c) **Definitions and Special Rules.**—For purposes of this section—

    (1) **Qualified plan.**—The term "qualified plan" means any plan meeting the requirements of section 401(a) or 403(a), other than—

        (A) a plan maintained by an employer if such employer has, at all times, been exempt from tax under this subtitle, or

        (B) a governmental plan (within the meaning of section 414(d)).

Such term shall include any plan which, at any time, has been determined by the Secretary to be a qualified plan.

    (2) **Employer reversion.—**

        (A) In general.—The term "employer reversion" means the amount of cash and the fair market value of other property received (directly or indirectly) by an employer from the qualified plan.

        (B) Exceptions.—The term "employer reversion" shall not include—

⟦**Footnote ¶3314-A continued**⟧

to which an election is made by the executor of an estate who is required to file the return of the tax imposed by the '86 Code on a date (including extensions) after the date of the enactment of this Act.

⟦**Footnote ¶3315**⟧ Sec. 4980 added by section 1132(a), '86 TRA.

Effective date (Sec. 1132(c), '86 TRA).—(1) Generally applies to any revisions occurring after 12-31-85.

(2) Exception where termination date occurred before 1-1-86.—

(A) In general.—Except as provided in subparagraph (B), the amendments made by this section shall not apply to any reversion after 12-31-85, which occurs pursuant to a plan termination where the termination date is before 1-1-86.

(B) Election to have amendments apply.—A corporation may elect to have the amendments made by this section apply to any reversion after 1985 pursuant to a plan termination occurring before 1986 if such corporation was incorporated in the State of Delaware in March, 1978, and became a parent corporation of the consolidated group on 9-19-78, pursuant to a merger agreement recorded in the State of Nevada on 11-19-78.

(3) Termination date.—For purposes of paragraph (2), the term "termination date" is the date of the termination (within the meaning of section 411(d)(3) of the '86 Code) of the plan.

(4) Transition rule for certain terminations.—

(A) In general.—In the case of a taxpayer to which this paragraph applies, the amendments made by this section shall not apply to any termination occurring before the date which is 1 year after the date of the enactment of this Act.

(B) Taxpayers to whom paragraph applies.—This paragraph shall apply to—

(i) a corporation incorporated on 6-13-17, which has its principal place of business in Bartlesville, Oklahoma,

(ii) a corporation incorporated on 1-17-17, which is located in Coatesville, Pennsylvania,

(iii) a corporation incorporated on 1-23-28, which has its principal place of business in New York, New York,

(iv) a corporation incorporated on 4-23-56, which has its principal place of business in Dallas, Texas, and

(v) a corporation incorporated in the State of Nevada, the principal place of business of which is in Denver, Colorado, and which filed for relief from creditors under the United States Bankruptcy Code on 8-28-86.

(i) except as provided in regulations, any amount distributed to or on behalf of any employee (or his beneficiaries) if such amount could have been so distributed before termination of such plan without violating any provision of section 401, or

(ii) any distribution to the employer which is allowable under section 401(a)(2)—

(I) in the case of a multiemployer plan, by reason of mistakes of law or fact or the return of any withdrawal liability payment,

(II) in the case of a plan other than a multiemployer plan, by reason of mistake of fact, or

(III) in the case of any plan, by reason of the failure of the plan to initially qualify or the failure of contributions to be deductible.

(3) Exception for employee stock ownership plans.—

(A) In general.—If, upon an employer reversion from a qualified plan, any applicable amount is transferred from such plan to an employee stock ownership plan described in section 4975(e)(7), such amount shall not be treated as an employer reversion for purposes of this section (or includible in the gross income of the employer) if—

(i) the requirements of subparagraphs (B), (C), and (D) are met, and

(ii) under the plan, employer securities to which subparagraph (B) applies must remain in the plan until distribution to particpants in accordance with the provisions of such plan.

(B) Investment in employer securities.—The requirements of this subparagraph are met if, within 90 days after the transfer (or such longer period as the Secretary may prescribe), the amount transferred is invested in employer securities (as defined in section 409(l)) or used to repay loans used to purchase such securities.

(C) Allocation requirements.—The requirements of this subparagraph are met if the portion of the amount transferred which is not allocated (by reason of the limitations of section 415) under the plan to accounts of participants in the plan year in which the transfer occurs—

(i) is credited to a suspense account and allocated from such account to accounts of participants no less rapidly than ratably over a period not to exceed 7 years, and

(ii) when allocated to accounts of participants under the plan, is treated as an employer contribution for purposes of section 415(c), except that—

(I) the annual addition (as determined under section 415(c)) attributable to each such allocation shall not exceed the value of such securities as of the time such securities were credited to such suspense account, and

(II) no additional employer contributions shall be permitted to an employee stock ownership plan described in subparagraph (A) of the employer before the allocation of such amount.

(D) Participants.—The requirements of this subparagraph are met if at least half of the participants in the qualified plan are participants in the employee stock ownership plan (as of the close of the 1st plan year for which an allocation of the securities is required).

(E) Applicable amount.—For purposes of this paragraph, the term "applicable amount" means any amount which—

(i) is transferred after March 31, 1985, and before January 1, 1989, or

(ii) is transferred after December 31, 1988, pursuant to a termination which occurs after March 31, 1985, and before January 1, 1989.

[For official explanation, see Committee Reports, ¶3991.]

⟦¶3316⟧ CODE SEC. 4981. ¹*EXCISE TAX ON UNDISTRIBUTED INCOME OF REAL ESTATE INVESTMENT TRUSTS.*

(a) *Imposition of Tax.—There is hereby imposed a tax on every real estate investment trust for each calendar year equal to 4 percent of the excess (if any) of—*

(1) *the required distribution for such calendar year, over*

(2) *the distributed amount for such calendar year.*

(b) **Required Distribution.**—For purposes of this section—

(1) **In general.**—The term "required distribution" means, with respect to any calendar year, the sum of—

(A) 85 percent of the real estate investment trust's ordinary income for such calendar year, plus

(B) 95 percent of the real estate investment trust's capital gain net income for such calendar year.

(2) **Increase by prior year shortfall.**—The amount determined under paragraph (1) for any calendar year shall be increased by the excess (if any) of—

(A) the grossed up required distribution for the preceding calendar year, over

(B) the distributed amount for such preceding calendar year.

(3) **Grossed up required distribution.**—The grossed up required distribution for any calendar year is the requird distribution for such year determined—

(A) with the application of paragraph (2) to such taxable year, and

(B) bv substituting "100 percent" for each percentage set forth in paragraph (1).

(c) **Distributed Amount.**—For purposes of this section—

(1) **In general.**—The term "distributed amount" means, with respect to any calendar year, the sum of—

(A) the deduction for dividends paid (as defined in section 561) during such calendar year, and

(B) any amount on which tax is imposed under subsection (b)(1) or (b)(3)(A) of section 857 for any taxable year ending in such calendar year.

(2) **Increase by prior year overdistribution.**—The amount determined under paragraph (1) for any calendar year shall be increased by the excess (if any) of—

(A) the distributed amount for the preceding calendar year (determined with the application of this paragraph to such preceding calendar year), over

(B) the grossed up required distribution for such preceding calendar year.

(3) **Determination of dividends paid.**—The amount of the dividends paid during any calendar year shall be determined without regard to the provisions of section 858.

(d) **Time for Payment of Tax.**—The tax imposed by this section for any calendar year shall be paid on or before March 15 of the following calendar year.

(e) **Definitions and Special Rules.**—For purposes of this section—

(1) **Ordinary income.**—The term "ordinary income" means the real estate investment trust taxable income (as defined in secton 857(b)(2)) determined—

(A) without regard to subparagraph (B) of section 857(b)(2),

(B) by not taking into account any gain or loss from the sale or exchange of a capital asset, and

(C) by treating the calendar year as the trust's taxable year.

(2) **Capital gain net income.**—The term "capital gain net income" has the meaning given to such term by section 1222(9) (determined by treating the calendar year as the trust's taxable year).

(3) **Treatment of deficiency distributions.**—In the case of any deficiency dividend (as defined in section 860(f)—

(A) such dividend shall be taken into account when paid without regard to section 860, and

(B) any income giving rise to the adjustment shall be treated as arising when the dividend is paid.

[For official explanation, see Committee Reports, ¶3929.]

【¶3317】 CODE SEC. 4981A. TAX ON EXCESS DISTRIBUTIONS FROM QUALIFIED RETIREMENT PLANS.

(a) **General rule.**—There is hereby imposed a tax equal to 15 percent of the excess

___

【Footnote ¶3316 continued】

dends paid deduction (as defined in section 561, but computed without regard to capital gains dividends as defined in section 857(b)(3)(C) and without regard to any dividend paid after the close of the taxable year) for the taxable year. For purposes of the preceding sentence, the determination of the real estate investment trust taxable income shall be made by taking into account only the amount and character of the items of income and deduction as reported by such trust in its return for the taxable year."

Effective date (Sec. 669(b), '86 TRA).—Applies to calendar years beginning after 12-31-86.

【Footnote ¶3317】 Sec. 4981A added by section 1133(a), '86 TRA.

Effective date (Sec. 1133(c), '86 TRA).—(1) Generally applies to distributions made after 12-31-86.

distributions with respect to any individual during any calendar year.

(b) Liability for tax.—The individual with respect to whom the excess distributions are made shall be liable for the tax imposed by subsection (a). The amount of the tax imposed by subsection (a) shall be reduced by the amount (if any) of the tax imposed by section 72(t) to the extent attributable to such excess distributions.

(c) Excess Distributions.—For purposes of this section—

(1) In general.—The term "excess distributions" means the aggregate amount of the retirement distributions with respect to any individual during any calendar year to the extent such amount exceeds $112,500 (adjusted at the same time and in the same manner as under section 415(d)).

(2) Exclusion of certain distributions.—The following distributions shall not be taken into account under paragraph (1):

(A) Any retirement distribution with respect to an individual made after the death of such individual.

(B) Any retirement distribution with respect to an individual payable to an alternate payee pursuant to a qualified domestic relations order (within the meaning of section 414(p)) if includible in income of the alternate payee.

(C) Any retirement distribution with respect to an individual which is attributable to the employee's investment in the contract (as defined in section 72(f)).

(D) Any retirement distribution to the extent not included in gross income by reason of a rollover contribution.

Any distribution described in subparagraph (B) shall be treated as a retirement distribution to the person to whom paid for purposes of this section.

(3) Aggregation of payments.—If retirement distributions with respect to any individual during any calendar year are received by the individual and 1 or more other persons, all such distributions shall be aggregated for purposes of determining the amount of the excess distributions for the calendar year.

(4) Special rule where taxpayer elects income averaging.—If the retirement distributions with respect to any individual during any calendar year include a lump sum distribution to which an election under section 402(e)(4)(B) applies—

(A) paragraph (1) shall be applied separately with respect to such lump sum distribution and other retirement distributions, and

(B) the limitation under paragraph (1) with respect to such lump sum distribution shall be equal to 5 times the amount of such limitation determined without regard to this subparagraph.

(5) Special rule for accrued benefits as of August 1, 1986.—

(A) In general.—If the employee elects on a return filed for a taxable year ending before January 1, 1989 to have this paragraph apply, the portion of any retirement distribution which is attributable (as determined under rules prescribed by the Secretary) to the accrued benefit of an employee as of August 1, 1986, shall be taken into account for purposes of paragraph (1), but no tax shall be imposed under this section with respect to such portion of such distribution.

(B) Limitation.—An employee may not make an election under subparagraph (A) unless the accured benefit of such employee as of August 1, 1986, exceeds $562,500.

(C) Taxpayer not making election.—If an employee does not elect the application of this paragraph, paragraph (1) shall be applied by substituting $150,000 for such dollar limitation unless such dollar limitation is greater than $150,000.

(d) Increase In Estate Tax if Individual Dies With Excess Accumulation.—

(1) In general.—The tax imposed by chapter 11 with respect to the estate of any individual shall be increased by an amount equal to 15 percent of the individual's excess retirement accumulation.

(2) No credit allowable.—No credit shall be allowable under section 2010 with respect to any portion of the tax imposed by chapter 11 attributable to the increase under paragraph (1).

[Footnote ¶3317 continued]

  (2) Estate tax.—Section 4981(d) of the '86 Code (as added by subsection (a)) shall apply to the estates of decedents dying after 12-31-86.

  (3) Plan termination before 1987.—The amendments made by this section shall not apply to distributions before 1-1-88, which are made on account of the termination of a qualified employer plan if such termination occurred before 1-1-87.

(3) Excess retirement accumulation.—For purposes of paragraph (1), the term "excess retirement accumulation" means the excess (if any) of—

(A) the value of the individual's interests in qualified employer plans and individual retirement plans as of the date of the decedent's death (or, in the case of an election under section 2032, the applicable valuation date prescribed by such section), over

(B) the present value (as determined under rules prescribed by the Secretary as of the valuation date prescribed in subparagraph (A)) of annuity for a term certain—

(i) with annual payments equal to the limitation of subsection (c) (as in effect for the year in which the death occurs), and

(ii) payable for a period equal to the life expectancy of the individual immediately before his death.

(e) Retirement Distributions.—For purposes of this section—

(1) In general.—The term "retirement distribution" means, with respect to any individual, the amount distributed during the taxable year under—

(A) any qualified employer plan with respect to which such individual is or was the employee and

(B) any individual retirement plan.

(2) Qualified employer plan.—The term "qualified employer plan" means—

(A) any plan described in section 401(a) which includes a trust exempt from tax under section 501(a),

(B) an annuity plan described in section 403(a), or

(C) an annuity contract described in section 403(b).

Such term includes any plan or contract which, at any time, has been determined by the Secretary to be such a plan or contract.

[For official explanation, see Committee Reports, ¶3992.]

[¶3317-A] CODE SEC. 4982. EXCISE TAX ON UNDISTRIBUTED INCOME OF REGULATED INVESTMENT COMPANIES.

(a) Imposition of Tax.—There is hereby imposed a tax on every regulated investment company for each calendar year equal to 4 percent of the excess (if any) of—

(1) the required distribution for such calendar year, over

(2) the distributed amount for such calendar year.

(b) Required Distribution.—For purposes of this section—

(1) In general.—The term "required distribution" means, with respect to any calendar year, the sum of—

(A) 97 percent of the regulated investment company's ordinary income for such calendar year, plus

(B) 90 percent of the regulated investment company's capital gain net income for the 1-year period ending on October 31 of such calendar year.

(2) Increase by prior year shortfall.—The amount determined under paragraph (1) for any calendar year shall be increased by the excess (if any) of—

(A) the grossed up required distribution for the preceding calendar year, over

(B) the distributed amount for such preceding calendar year.

(3) Grossed up required distribution.—The grossed up required distribution for any calendar year is the required distribution for such year determined—

(A) with the application of paragraph (2) to such taxable year, and

(B) by substituting "100 percent" for each percentage set forth in paragraph (1).

(c) Distributed Amount.—For purposes of this section—

(1) In general.—The term "distributed amount" means, with respect to any calendar year, the sum of—

(A) the deduction for dividends paid (as defined in section 561) during such calendar year, and

(B) any amount on which tax is imposed under subsection (b)(1) or (b)(3)(A) of section 852 for any taxable year ending in such calendar year.

[Footnote ¶3317-A] Sec. 4982 added by section 651(a), '86 TRA.
Effective date (Sec. 651(d), '86 TRA).—Applies to calendar years beginning after 12-31-86.

(2) Increase by prior year overdistribution.—The amount determined under paragraph (1) for any calendar year shall be increased by the excess (if any) of—

    (A) the distributed amount for the preceding calendar year (determined with the application of this paragraph to such preceding calendar year), over

    (B) the grossed up required distribution for such preceding calendar year.

(3) Determination of dividends paid.—The amount of the dividends paid during any calendar year shall be determined without regard to—

    (A) the provisions of section 855, and

    (B) any exempt-interest dividend as defined in section 852(b)(5).

(d) Time for Payment of Tax.—The tax imposed by this section for any calendar year shall be paid on or before March 15 of the following calendar year.

(e) Definitions and Special Rules.—For purposes of this section—

(1) Ordinary income.—The term "ordinary income" means the investment company taxable income (as defined in section 852(b)(2)) determined—

    (A) without regard to subparagraphs (A) and (D) of section 852(b)(2).

    (B) by not taking into account any gain or loss from the sale or exchange of a capital asset, and

    (C) by treating the calendar year as the company's taxable year.

(2) Capital gain net income.—The term "capital gain net income" has the meaning given to such term by section 1222(9) (determined by treating the 1-year period ending on October 31 of any calendar year as the company's taxable year).

(3) Treatment of deficiency distributions.—In the case of any deficiency dividend (as defined in section 860(f))—

    (A) such dividend shall be taken into account when paid without regard to section 860, and

    (B) any income giving rise to the adjustment shall be treated as arising when the dividend is paid.

(4) Election to use taxable year in certain cases.—

    (A) In general.—If—

        (i) the taxable year of the regulated investment company ends with the month of November or December, and

        (ii) such company makes an election under this paragraph,

subsection (b)(1)(B) and paragraph (2) of this subsection shall be applied by taking into account the company's taxable year in lieu of the 1-year period ending on October 31 of the calendar year.

    (B) Election revocable only with consent.—An election under this paragraph, once made, may be revoked only with the consent of the Secretary.

[For official explanation, see Committee Reports, ¶3928.]

[¶3318] CODE SEC. 4988. WINDFALL PROFIT; REMOVAL PRICE

* * * * * * * * * * * *

(c) Removal Price.—For purposes of this chapter—

* * * * * * * * * * * *

(2) Sales between related persons.—In the case of a sale between related persons (within the meaning of ¹*section 144(a)(3)*), the removal price shall not be less than the constructive sales price for purposes of determining gross income from the property under section 613.

* * * * * * * * * * * *

[For official explanation, see Committee Reports, ¶4058.]

[¶3319] CODE SEC. 4991. TAXABLE CRUDE OIL; CATEGORIES OF OIL.

* * * * * * * * * * * *

(e) Tier 3 Oil.—For purposes of this chapter—

[Footnote ¶3318] Matter in *italics* in Sec. 4988(c)(2) added by section 1301(j)(4), '86 TRA, which struck out: **(1)** "section 103(b)(6)(C)"

Effective date (Sec. 1311(a), '86 TRA).—Generally applies to bonds issued after 8-15-86. For transitional and special rules see ¶2071-2077.

[Footnote ¶3319] Matter in *italics* in Sec. 4991(e)(2) added by section 1879(h)(1), '86 TRA.

Effective date (Sec. 1879(h)(2), '86 TRA).—Applies to oil removed after 2-29-80.

* * * * * * * * * * *

(2) **Newly discovered oil.**—The term "newly discovered oil" has the meaning given to such term by the June 1979 energy regulations. *Such term includes any production from a property which did not produce oil in commercial quantities during calendar year 1978. For purposes of the preceding sentence, a property shall not be treated as producing oil in commercial quantities during calendar year 1978 if, during calendar year 1978 (A) the aggregate amount of oil produced from such property did not exceed 2,200 barrels (whether or not such oil was sold), and (B) no well on such property was in production for a total of more than 72 hours.*

* * * * * * * * * * *

[For official explanation, see Committee Reports, ¶4193.]

〔¶3320〕 CODE SEC. 5061. METHOD OF COLLECTING TAX.

* * * * * * * * * * *

(e) **Payment by Electronic Fund Transfer.—**

* * * * * * * * * * *

(3) *Controlled groups.—*
    (A) *In general.—In the case of a controlled group of corporations, all corporations which are component members of such group shall be treated as 1 taxpayer. For purposes of the preceding sentence, the term "controlled group of corporations" has the meaning given to such term by subsection (a) of section 1563, except that "more than 50 percent" shall be substituted for "at least 80 percent" each place it appears in such subsection.*
    (B) *Controlled groups which include nonincorporated persons.—Under regulations prescribed by the Secretary, principles similar to the principles of subparagraph (A) shall apply to a group of persons under common control where 1 or more of such persons is not a corporation.*

[For official explanation, see Committee Reports, ¶4135.]

〔¶3321〕 CODE SEC. 5703. LIABILITY FOR TAX AND METHOD OF PAYMENT.

* * * * * * * * * * *

(b) **Method of Payment of Tax.—**

* * * * * * * * * * *

(3) **Payment by electronic fund transfer.**—Any person who in any 12-month period, ending December 31, was liable for a gross amount equal to or exceeding $5,000,000 in taxes imposed on tobacco products and cigarette papers and tubes by section 5701 (or 7652) shall pay such taxes during the succeeding calendar year by electronic fund transfer (as defined in section 5061(e)(2)) to a Federal Reserve Bank. *Rules similar to the rules of section 5061(e)(3) shall apply to the $5,000,000 amount specified in the preceding sentence.*

* * * * * * * * * * *

[For official explanation, see Committee Reports, ¶4135.]

〔¶3322〕 CODE SEC. 6011. GENERAL REQUIREMENT OF RETURN, STATEMENT, OR LIST.

* * * * * * * * * * *

(f) **Income, Estate, and Gift Taxes.—**

For requirement that returns of income, estate, and gift taxes be made whether or not there is tax liability, see [1]*subparts B and C.*

〔**Footnote ¶3320**〕 Matter in *italics* in Sec. 5061(e)(3) added by section 1801(c)(1), '86 TRA.
Effective date (Sec. 1881, '86 TRA and Sec. 27(d)(2), '84 TRA).—Applies to taxes required to be paid on or after 9-30-84.
〔**Footnote ¶3321**〕 Matter in *italics* in Sec. 5703(b)(3) added by section 1801(c)(2), '86 TRA.
Effective date (Sec. 1881, '86 TRA and Sec. 27(d)(2), '84 TRA).—Applies to taxes required to be paid on or after 9-30-84.
〔**Footnote ¶3322**〕 Matter in *italics* in Sec. 6011(f) added by section 1899A(52), '86 TRA, which struck out:
(1) "sections 6012 to 6019, inclusive."

[¶3323] CODE SEC. 6012. PERSONS REQUIRED TO MAKE RETURNS OF INCOME.

(a) General Rule.—Returns with respect to income taxes under subtitle A shall be made by the following:

[1](1)(A) *Every individual having for the taxable year gross income which equals or exceeds the exemption amount, except that a return shall not be required of an individual—*

> (i) *who is not married (determined by applying section 7703), is not a surviving spouse (as defined in section 2(a)), is not a head of a household (as defined in section 2(b)), and for the taxable year has gross income of less than the sum of the exemption amount plus the basic standard deduction applicable to such an individual,*

> (ii) *who is a head of a household (as so defined) and for the taxable year has gross income of less than the sum of the exemption amount plus the basic standard deduction applicable to such an individual,*

> (iii) *who is a surviving spouse (as so defined) and for the taxable year has gross income of less than the sum of the exemption amount plus the basic standard deduction applicable to such an individual, or*

> (iv) *who is entitled to make a joint return and whose gross income, when combined with the gross income of his spouse, is, for the taxable year, less than the sum of twice the exemption amount plus the basic standard deduction applicable to a joint return, but only if such individual and his spouse, at the close of the taxable year, had the same household as their home.*

Clause (iv) shall not apply if for the taxable year such spouse makes a separate return or any other taxpayer is entitled to an exemption for such spouse under section 151(c).

> *(B) The amount specified in clause (i), (ii), or (iii) of subparagraph (A) shall be increased by the amount of 1 additional standard deduction (within the meaning of section 63(c)(3)) in the case of an individual entitled to such deduction by reason of section 63(f)(1)(A) (relating to individuals age 65 or more), and the amount specified in clause (iv) of subparagraph (A) shall be increased by the amount of the additional standard deduction for each additional standard deduction to which the individual or his spouse is entitled by reason of section 63(f)(1).*

> *(C) The exception under subparagraph (A) shall not apply to any individual—*

>> (i) *who is described in section 63(c)(5) and who has—*

>>> (I) *income (other than earned income) in excess of the amount in effect under section 63(c)(5)(A) (relating to limitation on standard deduction in the case of certain dependents), or*

>>> (II) *total gross income in excess of the standard deduction, or*

[Footnote ¶3323] Matter in *italics* in Sec. 6012(a)(1) and (9) added by section 104(a), '86 TRA, which struck out:

(1) "(1) (A) Every individual having for the taxable year a gross income of the exemption amount or more, except that a return shall not be required of an individual (other than an individual described in subparagraph (C))—

(i) who is not married (determined by applying section 143), is not a surviving spouse (as defined in section 2(a)), and for the taxable year has a gross income of less than the sum of the exemption amount plus the zero bracket amount applicable to such an individual,

(ii) who is a surviving spouse (as so defined) and for the taxable year has a gross income of less than the sum of the exemption amount plus the zero bracket amount applicable to such an individual, or

(iii) who is entitled to make a joint return under section 6013 and whose gross income, when combined with the gross income of his spouse, is, for the taxable year, less than the sum of twice the exemption amount plus the zero bracket amount applicable to a joint return, but only if such individual and his spouse, at the close of the taxable year, had the same household as their home.

Clause (iii) shall not apply if for the taxable year such spouse makes a separate return or any other taxpayer is entitled to an exemption for such spouse under section 151(e).

(B) The amount specified in clause (i) or (ii) of subparagraph (A) shall be increased by the exemption amount in the case of an individual entitled to an additional personal exemption under section 151(c)(1), and the amount specified in clause (iii) of subparagraph (A) shall be increased by the exemption amount for each additional personal exemption to which the individual or his spouse is entitled under section 151(c).

(C) The exception under subparagraph (A) shall not apply to—

(i) a nonresident alien individual;

(ii) a citizen of the United States entitled to the benefits of section 931;

(iii) an individual making a return under section 443(a)(1) for a period of less than 12 months on account of a change in his annual accounting period;

(iv) an individual who has income (other than earned income) of the exemption amount or more and who is described in section 63(e)(1)(D); or

(v) an estate or trust.

(D) For purposes of this paragraph—

(i) The term "zero bracket amount" has the meaning given to such term by section 63(d).

(ii) The term "exemption amount" has the meaning given to such term by section 151(f)."

(ii) for whom the standard deduction is zero under section 63(c)(6).

(D) For purposes of this subsection—
(i) The terms "standard deduction", "basic standard deduction" and "additional standard deduction" have the respective meanings given such terms by section 63(c).
(ii) The term "exemption amount" has the meaning given such term by section 151(d). In the case of an individual described in section 151(d)(2), the exemption amount shall be zero.

* * * * * * * * * * *

(9) Every estate of an individual under chapter 7 or 11 of title 11 of the United States Code (relating to bankruptcy) the gross income of which for the taxable year is [2]*not less than the sum of the exemption amount plus the basic standard deduction under section 63(c)(2)(D).*

* * * * * * * * * * *

(d) Tax-Exempt Interest Required to be Shown on Return.—Every person required to file a return under this section for the taxable year shall include on such return the amount of interest received or accrued during the taxable year which is exempt from the tax imposed by chapter 1.

[3]*(e)* **Consolidated Returns.—**

For provisions relating to consolidated returns by affiliated corporations, see chapter 6.

[For official explanation, see Committee Reports, ¶4081.]

【¶3324】 CODE SEC. 6013. JOINT RETURNS OF INCOME TAX BY HUSBAND AND WIFE.

* * * * * * * * * * *

(b) Joint Return After Filing Separate Return.—

* * * * * * * * * * *

(3) When return deemed filed.—
(A) Assessment and collection.—For purposes of section 6501 (relating to periods of limitations on assessment and collection), and for purposes of section 6651 (relating to delinquent returns), a joint return made under this subsection shall be deemed to have been filed—
(i) Where both spouses filed separate returns prior to making the joint return—on the date the last separate return was filed (but not earlier than the last date prescribed by law for filing the return of either spouse);
(ii) Where only one spouse filed a separate return prior to the making of the joint return, and the other spouse had less than the exemption amount of gross income [1]for such taxable year—on the date of the filing of such separate return (but not earlier than the last date prescribed by law for the filing of such separate return); or
(iii) Where only one spouse filed a separate return prior to the making of the joint return, and the other spouse had gross income of the exemption amount or more [1] for such taxable year—on the date of the filing of such joint return.
For purposes of this subparagraph, the term "exemption amount" has the meaning given to such term by [2]*section 151(d). For purposes of clauses (ii) and (iii), if the spouse whose gross income is being compared to the exemption amount is 65 or over, such clauses shall be applied by substituting "the sum of the exemption amount and*

【Footnote ¶3323 continued】

(2) "$2,700 or more"
Effective date (Sec. 151(a), '86 TRA).—Applies to taxable years beginning after 12-31-86.

Matter in *italics* in Sec. 6012(d) and (e) added by section 1525(a), '86 TRA, which struck out:
(3) "(d)"
Effective date (Sec. 1525(b), '86 TRA).—Applies to taxable years beginning after 12-31-86.
【Footnote ¶3324】 Matter in *italics* in Sec. 6013(b)(3) added by section 104(a)(2), '86 TRA, which struck out:
(1) "(twice the exemption amount in case such spouse was 65 or over)"
(2) "section 151(f)"
Effective date (Sec. 151(a), '86 TRA).—Applies to taxable years beginning after 12-31-86.

---

the additional standard deduction under section 63(c)(2) by reason of section 63(f)(1)(A)" for "the exemption amount."

* * * * * * * * * * *

(f) Joint Return Where individual Is in Missing Status.—For purposes of this section and subtitle A—

(1) Election by spouse.—If—
(A) an individual is in a missing status (within the meaning of paragraph (3)) as a result of service in a combat zone (as determined for purposes of section 112), and
(B) the spouse of such individual is otherwise entitled to file a joint return for any taxable year which begins on or before the day which is 2 years after the date designated under section 112 as the date of termination of combatant activities in such zone,

then such spouse may elect under subsection (a) to file a joint return for such taxable year. With respect to service in the combat zone designated for purposes of the Vietnam conflict, ³*such election may be made for any taxable year while an individual is in missing status.*

* * * * * * * * * * *

[For official explanation, see Committee Reports, ¶4130.]

〔¶3325〕 CODE SEC. 6014. INCOME TAX RETURN—TAX NOT COMPUTED BY TAXPAYER.

(a) Election by Taxpayer.—An individual ¹*who is not described in section 6012(a)(1)(C)(i)*, who does not itemize his deductions and whose gross income is less than $10,000 and includes no income other than remuneration for services performed by him as an employee, dividends or interest, and whose gross income other than wages, as defined in section 3401(a), does not exceed $100, shall at his election not be required to show on the return the tax imposed by section 1. Such election shall be made by using the form prescribed for purposes of this section. In such case the tax shall be computed by the Secretary who shall mail to the taxpayer a notice stating the amount determined as payable.

(b) Regulations.—The Secretary shall prescribe regulations for carrying out this section, and such regulations may provide for the application of the rules of this section—
(1) to cases where the gross income includes items other than those enumerated by subsection (a),
(2) to cases where the gross income from sources other than wages on which the tax has been withheld at the source is more than $100,
(3) to cases where the gross income is $10,000 or more, or
(4) to cases where the taxpayer itemizes his deductions or ²*where the taxpayer claims a reduced standard deduction by reason of section 63(c)(5).*

Such regulations shall provide for the application of this section in the case of husband and wife, including provisions determining when a joint return under this section may be permitted or required, whether the liability shall be joint and several, and whether one spouse may make return under this section and the other without regard to this section.

〔¶3326〕 CODE SEC. 6031. RETURN OF PARTNERSHIP INCOME.

* * * * * * * * * * *

〔Footnote ¶3324 continued〕

Matter in *italics* in Sec. 6013(f)(1) added by section 1708(a)(3), '86 TRA, which struck out:
(3) "no such election may be made for any taxable year beginning after December 31, 1982."
Effective date (Sec. 1708(b), '86 TRA).—Applies to taxable years beginning after 12-31-82.
〔Footnote ¶3325〕 Matter in *italics* in Sec. 6014(a) and (b)(4) added by section 104(b)(16), '86 TRA, which struck out:
(1) "who does not have an unused zero bracket amount (determined under section 63(e)),"
(2) "has an unused zero bracket amount"
Effective date (Sec. 151(a), '86 TRA).—Applies to taxable years beginning after 12-31-86.
〔Footnote ¶3326〕 *"required to be"* in *italics* in Sec. 6031(b) added by section 1501(c)(16), '86 TRA.
Effective date (Sec. 1501(e), '86 TRA).—Applies to returns the due date for which (determined without regard to extensions) is after 12-31-86.

Matter in *italics* in Sec. 6031(b) (other than *"required to be"*) and (c) added by section 1811(b)(1)(A), '86 TRA.
Effective date (Sec. 1811(b)(1)(B), '86 TRA).—Applies to partnership taxable years beginning after the date of enactment of this Act.

(b) **Copies to Partners.**—Each partnership required to file a return under subsection (A) for any partnership taxable year shall (on or before the day on which the return for such taxable year was *required to be* filed) furnish to each person who is a partner *or who holds an interest in such partnership as a nominee for another person* at any time during such taxable year a copy of such information *required to be* shown on such return as may be required by regulations.

(c) *Nominee Reporting.—Any person who holds an interest in a partnership as a nominee for another person—*

(1) shall furnish to the partnership, in the manner prescribed by the Secretary, the name and address of such other person, and any other information for such taxable year as the Secretary may by form and regulation prescribe, and

(2) shall furnish in the manner prescribed by the Secretary such other person the information provided by such partnership under subsection (b).

[For official explanation, see Committee Reports, ¶4071; 4145.]

【¶3327】 CODE SEC. 6033. RETURNS BY EXEMPT ORGANIZATIONS.

* * * * * * * * * * * *

(e) Cross Reference.—

* * * * For reporting requirements as to certain liquidations, dissolutions, terminations, and contractions, see section 6043(b). For provisions relating to penalties for failure to file a return required by this section, see [1]*section 6652(c).*

* * * * * * * * * * * *

[For official explanation, see Committee Reports, ¶4071.]

【¶3328】 CODE SEC. 6034. RETURNS BY TRUSTS DESCRIBED IN SECTION 4947(a)(2) OR CLAIMING CHARITABLE DEDUCTIONS UNDER SECTION 642(c).

* * * * * * * * * * * *

(c) Cross Reference.—

For provisions relating to penalties for failure to file a return required by this section, see [1]*section 6652(c).*

[For official explanation, see Committee Reports, ¶4071.]

【¶3328-A】 CODE SEC. 6034A. INFORMATION TO BENEFICIARIES OF ESTATES AND TRUSTS.

(a) *General Rule.*—The fiduciary of any estate or trust [1]*required to file a return* under section 6012(a) for any taxable year shall, on or before the date on which such return was *required to be* filed, furnish to each beneficiary *(or nominee thereof)* —

(1) who receives a distribution from such estate or trust with respect to such taxable year, or

(2) to whom any item with respect to such taxable year is allocated, a statement containing such information *required to be* shown on such return as the Secretary may prescribe.

(b) *Nominee Reporting.—Any person who holds an interest in an estate or trust as a nominee for another person—*

【Footnote ¶3327】 Matter in *italics* in Sec. 6033(e) added by section 1501(d)(1)(C), '86 TRA, which struck out:
(1) "section 6652(d)"
Effective date (Sec. 1501(e), '86 TRA).—Applies to returns the due date for which (determined without regard to extensions) is after 12-31-86.
【Footnote ¶3328】 Matter in *italics* in Sec. 6034(c) added by section 1501(d)(1)(C), '86 TRA, which struck out:
(1) "section 6652(d)"
Effective date (Sec. 1501(e), '86 TRA).—Applies to returns the due date for which (determined without regard to extensions) is after 12-31-86.
【Footnote ¶3328-A】 Matter in *italics* in Sec. 6034A(a) (except for *"required to file a return"* and *"required to be filed"*) and (b) added by section 1875(d)(3)(A) [should read 1875(d)(4)(A)], '86 TRA.
Effective date (Sec. 1875(d)(3)(B) [should read 1875(d)(4)(B)], '86 TRA).—Applies to taxable years of estates and trusts beginning after the date of the enactment of this Act.

The phrases *"required to file a return"* and *"required to be"* in *italics* in Sec. 6034A(a) added by section 1501 (c)(15), '86 TRA, which struck out:
(1) "making the return required to be filed"
Effective date (Sec. 1501(e), '86 TRA).—Applies to returns the due date for which (determined without regard to extensions) is after 12-31-86.

(1) shall furnish to the estate or trust, in the manner prescribed by the Secretary, the name and address of such other person, and any other information for the taxable year as the Secretary may by form and regulations prescribe, and

(2) shall furnish in the manner prescribed by the Secretary to such other person the information provided by the estate or trust under subsection (a).

[For official explanation, see Committee Reports, ¶4071; ¶4189.]

[¶3329] CODE SEC. 6038. INFORMATION WITH RESPECT TO CERTAIN FOREIGN CORPORATIONS.

(a) Requirement.—

(1) In General.—Every United States person shall furnish, with respect to any foreign corporation which such person controls (within the meaning of subsection (e)(1)), such information as the Secretary may prescribe by regulations relating to—

(A) the name, the principal place of business, and the nature of business of such foreign corporation and the country under whose laws incorporated;

(B) [1]*the post-1986 undistributed earnings (as defined in section 902(c)) of such foreign corporation,*

(C) a balance sheet for such foreign corporation, listing assets, liabilities, and capital;

(D) transaction between such foreign corporation and—

(i) such person,

(ii) any other corporation which such person controls, and

(iii) any United States person owning, at the time the transaction takes place, 10 percent or more of the value of any class of stock outstanding of such foreign corporation; [2]

(E) a description of the various classes of stock outstanding, and a list showing the name and address of, and number of shares held by each United States person who is a shareholder of record owning at any time during the annual accounting period 5 percent or more in value of any class of stock outstanding of such foreign corporation [3], *and*

(F) *such information as the Secretary may require for purposes of carrying out the provisions of section 453C.*

The Secretary may also require the furnishing of any other information which is similar or related in nature to that specified in the preceding sentence.

* * * * * * * * * * *

(c) Penalty of Reducing Foreign Tax Credit.—

* * * * * * * * * * *

(4) Special rules.—

(A) No taxes shall be reduced under this subsection more than once for the same failure.

(B) For purposes of this subsection and subsection (b), the time prescribed under paragraph (2) of subsection (a) to furnish information (and the beginning of the 90-day period after notice by the Secretary) shall be treated as being not earlier than the last day on which (as shown to the satisfaction of the Secretary) reasonable cause existed for failure to furnish such information.

(C) In applying subsections (a) and (b) of section 902, and in applying subsection (a) of section 960, the reduction provided by this subsection shall not apply for purposes of determining the amount of [4]*post-1986 undistributed earnings.*

[Footnote ¶3329] Matter in *italics* in Sec. 6038(a)(1)(B) added by section 1202(c)(1), '86 TRA, which struck out:

(1) "the accumulated profits (as defined in section 902(c)) of such foreign corporation, including the items of income (whether or not included in gross income under chapter 1), deductions (whether or not allowed in computing taxable income under chapter 1), and any other items taken into account in computing such accumulated profits;"

Effective date (Sec. 1202(e), '86 TRA).—Applies to distributions by foreign corporations out of, and to inclusions under section 951(a) of the '86 Code attributable to, earnings and profits for taxable years beginning after 12-31-86.

Matter in *italics* in Sec. 6038(a)(1)(D)—(F) added by section 1245(b)(5), '86 TRA, which struck out:

(2) "and"

(3) "."

Effective date (Sec. 1245(c), '86 TRA).—Applies to taxable years beginning after 12-31-86.

Matter in *italics* in Sec. 6038(c)(4)(C) added by section 1202(c)(2), '86 TRA, which struck out:

(4) "accumulated profits in excess of income, war profits, and excess profits taxes."

* * * * * * * * * * * *

[For official explanation, see Committee Reports, ¶4027; 4051.]

〔¶3329-A〕 CODE SEC. 6038A. INFORMATION WITH RESPECT TO CERTAIN FOREIGN-OWNED CORPORATIONS.

* * * * * * * * * * * *

(b) Required Information.—For purposes of subsection (a), the information described in this subsection is such information as the Secretary may prescribe by regulations relating to—

(1) The name, principal place of business, nature of business, and country or countries in which organized or resident, of each [1]*person* which—

    (A) is a [2]*related party to* the reporting corporation, and

    (B) had any transaction with the reporting corporation during its taxable year,

(2) the manner in which the reporting corporation is related to each [1]*person* referred to in paragraph (1), [3]

(3) *transactions between the reporting corporation and each foreign [4]person which is a related party to the reporting corporation[5], and*

(4) such information as the Secretary may require for purposes of carrying out the provisions of section 453C.

(c) Definitions.—For purposes of this section—

* * * * * * * * * * * *

(2) [6]Related party.—The term "related party" means—

    (A) any person who is related to the reporting corporation within the meaning of section 267(b) or 707(b)(1), and

    (B) any other person who is related (within the meaning of section 482) to the reporting corporation.

* * * * * * * * * * * *

[For official explanation, see Committee Reports, ¶4051.]

〔¶3330〕 CODE SEC. 6039B. RETURN OF GENERAL STOCK OWNERSHIP CORPORATION. [Repealed by section 1303(b)(5), '86 TRA].[1]

[For official explanation, see Committee Reports, ¶4059.]

〔Footnote ¶3329 continued〕

Effective date (Sec. 1202(e), '86 TRA).—Applies to distributions by foreign corporations out of, and to inclusions under section 951(a) of the '86 Code attributable to, earnings and profits for taxable years beginning after 12-31-86.

  〔Footnote ¶3329-A〕 Matter in *italics* in Sec. 6038A(b)—(c)(2) added by section 1245(a) and (b)(1)—(4), '86 TRA, which struck out:

(1) "corporation "

(2) "member of the same controlled group as"

(3) "and"

(4) "corporation which is a member of the same controlled group as"

(5) "."

(6) "**Controlled group.**—The term 'controlled group' means any controlled group of corporations within the meaning of section 1563(a); except that—

(A) 'at least 50 percent' shall be substituted—

(i) for 'at least 80 percent' each place it appears in section 1563(a)(1), and

(ii) for 'more than 50 percent' each place it appears in section 1563(a)(2)(B), and

(B) the determination shall be made without regard to subsections (a)(4), (b)(2)(C), and (e)(3)(C) of section 1563."

Effective date (Sec. 1245(c), '86 TRA).—Applies to taxable years beginning after 12-31-86.

  〔Footnote ¶3330〕 Section 1303(b)(5), '86 TRA, repealed Sec. 6039B:

(1) "Every general stock ownership corporation (as defined in section 1391) which makes the election provided by section 1392 shall make a return for each taxable year, stating specifically the items of its gross income and the deductions allowable by subtitle A, the amount of investment credit or additional tax, as the case may be, the names and addresses of all persons owning stock in the corporation at any time during the taxable year, the number of shares of stock owned by each shareholder at all times during the taxable year, the amount of money and other property distributed by the corporation during the taxable year to each shareholder, the date of each such distribution, and such other information, for the purpose of carrying out the provisions of subchapter U of chapter 1, as the Secretary may by regulation prescribe. Any return filed pursuant to this section shall, for purposes of chapter 66 (relating to limitations), be treated as a return filed by the corporation under section 6012. Every electing GSOC shall file an annual report with the Secretary summarizing its operations for such year."

Effective date (Sec. 1311(d), '86 TRA).—Takes effect on the date of enactment of this Act.

〔¶3330-A〕 CODE SEC. 6039C. RETURNS WITH RESPECT TO FOREIGN PERSONS HOLDING DIRECT INVESTMENTS IN UNITED STATES REAL PROPERTY INTERESTS.

* * * * * * * * * * * *

(d) **Special Rule for United States Interest and Virgin Islands Interest.**—A nonresident alien individual or foreign corporation subject to tax under section 897(a) *(and any person required to withhold tax under section 1445)* shall pay any tax and file any return required by this title—

* * * * * * * * * * * *

[For official explanation, see Committee Reports, ¶4144.]

〔¶3330-B〕 CODE SEC. 6039D. RETURNS AND RECORDS WITH RESPECT TO CERTAIN FRINGE BENEFIT PLANS.

(a) **In General.**—Every employer maintaining a specified fringe benefit plan during any year beginning after December 31, 1984, for any portion of which the applicable exclusion applies, shall file a return (at such time and in such manner as the Secretary shall by regulations prescribe) with respect to such plan showing for such year—

    (1) the number of employees of the employer,

    (2) the number of employees of the employer eligible to participate under the plan,

    (3) the number of employees participating under the plan,

    (4) the total cost of the plan during the year,[1]

    (5) the name, address, and taxpayer identification number of the employer and the type of business in which the employer is engaged, [2]*and*

    (6) *the number of highly compensated employees among the employees described in paragraphs (1), (2), and (3).*

* * * * * * * * * * * *

(c) **Additional Information When Required by the Secretary.**—Any employer—

    (1) who maintained a specified fringe benefit plan during any year for which a return is required under subsection (a), and

    (2) who is required by the Secretary to file an additional return for such year,

shall file such additional return. Such additional return shall be filed at such time and in such manner as the Secretary shall prescribe and shall contain such information as the Secretary shall prescribe. *The Secretary may require returns under this subsection only from a representative group of employers.*

≫**P-H CAUTION→** There are two versions of Sec. 6039D(d). Sec. 6039D(d), generally effective after 12-31-87, follows. For Sec. 6039D(d), generally effective before 1-1-88, see below.

▲ [3]*(d)* *Definitions.—For purposes of this section—*

〔Footnote ¶3330-A〕 Matter in *italics* in Sec. 6039C(d) added by section 1810(f)(7), '86 TRA.

Effective date (Sec. 1881, '86 TRA and Sec. 129(c)(2), '84 TRA).—Applies to calendar year 1980 and subsequent calendar years.

〔Footnote ¶3330-B〕 Matter in *italics* in Sec. 6039D(a)(4)—(6) added by section 1151(h)(2) and (3), '86 TRA, which struck out:

    (1) "and"

    (2) "."

Effective date (Sec. 1151(k), '86 TRA).—(1) Generally applies to years beginning after the later of—

(A) 12-31-87, or

(B) the earlier of—

(i) the date which is 3 months after the date on which the Secretary of the Treasury or his delegate issues such regulations as are necessary to carry out the provisions of Sec. 89 of the '86 Code (as added by this section), or

(ii) 12-31-88.

For special rules and exceptions, see footnote ¶2895.

Matter in *italics* in Sec. 6039D(c) added by section 1151(b)(3), '86 TRA. [Ed. Sec. 1151(b)(3), '86 TRA, erroneously related this amendment to Sec. 6039B(c).]

Effective date (Sec. 1151(k), '86 TRA).—See above.

▲ Matter in *italics* in Sec. 6039D(d) preceded by a single triangle, added by section 1151(h)(1), '86 TRA, which struck out:

(3) "**(d)** **Definitions.**—For purposes of this section—

(1) **Specified fringe benefit plan.**—The term "specified fringe benefit plan" means—

(A) any qualified group legal services plan (as defined in section 120),

(B) any cafeteria plan (as defined in section 125), and

(C) any educational assistance plan (as defined in section 127).

(1) Specified fringe benefit plan.—The term "specified fringe benefit plan" means any plan under section 79, 105, 106, 120, 125, 127, or 129.

(2) Applicable exclusion.—The term "applicable exclusion" means, with respect to any specified fringe benefit plan, the section specified under paragraph (1) under which benefits under such plan are excludable from gross income.

⪼**P-H CAUTION**⭢ There are two versions of Sec. 6039D(d). Sec. 6039D(d), generally effective before 1-1-88, follows. For Sec. 6039D(d), generally effective after 12-31-87, see above.

(d) [as added by section 1(b)(1), P.L. 98-611, Repealed]

▲▲ [4]*(d) Definitions.—For purposes of this section—*

   (1) Specified fringe benefit plan.—The term "specified fringe benefit plan" means—
     (A) any qualified group legal services plan (as defined in section 120),
     (B) any cafeteria plan (as defined in section 125), and
     (C) any educational assistance plan (as defined in section 127).

   (2) Applicable exclusion.—The term "applicable exclusion" means—
     (A) section 120 in the case of a qualified group legal services plan,
     (B) section 125 in the case of a cafeteria plan, and
     (C) section 127 in the case of an educational assistance plan.

(d) [as added by section 1(b)(1), P.L. 98-612 Repealed].[5]

[For official explanation, see Committee Reports, ¶4007; 4193.]

⟦¶3330-C⟧ **CODE SEC. 6039E. INFORMATION CONCERNING RESIDENT STATUS.**

(a) General Rule.—Notwithstanding any other provision of law, any individual who—
   (1) applies for a United States passport (or a renewal thereof), or

---

⟦Footnote ¶3330-B continued⟧
(2) Applicable exclusion.—The term "applicable exclusion" means—
(A) section 120 in the case of a qualified group legal services plan,
(B) section 125 in the case of a cafeteria plan, and
(C) section 127 in the case of an educational assistance plan."
Effective date (Sec. 1151(k), '86 TRA).—(1) Generally applies to years beginning after the later of—
(A) 12-31-87, or
(B) the earlier of—
(i) the date which is 3 months after the date on which the Secretary of the Treasury or his delegate issues such regulations as are necessary to carry out the provisions of Sec. 89 '86 Code (as added by this section), or
(ii) 12-31-88.
For special rules and exceptions, see footnote ¶2895.

▲▲ Matter in *italics* in Sec. 6039D(d), preceded by two triangles, added by section 1879(d)(1), '86 TRA, which struck out:
(4) "(d) Definitions.—For purposes of this section—
(1) Specified fringe benefit plan.—The term "specified fringe benefit plan" means—
(A) any cafeteria plan (as defined in section 125), and
(B) any educational assistance program (as defined in section 127).
(2) Applicable exclusion.—The term "applicable exclusion" means—
(A) section 125, in the case of a cafeteria plan, and
(B) section 127, in the case of an educational assistance program."
Effective date (Sec. 1(g)(2), P.L. 98-611, 10-31-84).—Takes effect on 1-1-85.

Sec. 6039D(d), as added by section 1(b)(1), P.L. 98-612, repealed by section 1879(d)(2), '86 TRA.
(5) "(d) Definitions.—For purposes of this section—
(1) Specified fringe benefit plan.—The term "specified fringe benefit plan" means—
(A) any qualified group legal services plan (as defined in section 120), and
(B) any cafeteria plan (as defined in section 125),
(2) Applicable exclusion.—The term "applicable exclusion" means—
(A) section 120, in the case of a qualified group legal services plan, and
(B) section 125, in the case of a cafeteria plan."
⟦Footnote ¶3330-C⟧ Sec. 6039E added by section 1234(a)(1) '86 TRA.
Effective date (Sec. 1234(a)(3), '86 TRA).—Applies to applications submitted after 12-31-87 (or, if earlier, the effective date (which shall not be earlier than 1-1-87) of the initial regulations issued under section 6039E of the '86 Code as added by this subsection).

(2) applies to be lawfully accorded the privilege of residing permanently in the United States as an immigrant in accordance with the immigration laws,

shall include with any such application a statement which includes the information described in subsection (b).

(b) Information to be Provided.—Information required under subsection (a) shall include—

    (1) the taxpayer's TIN (if any),

    (2) in the case of a passport applicant, any foreign country in which such individual is residing,

    (3) in the case of an individual seeking permanent residence, information with respect to whether such individual is required to file a return of the tax imposed by chapter 1 for such individual's most recent 3 taxable years, and

    (4) such other information as the Secretary may prescribe.

(c) Penalty.—Any individual failing to provide a statement required under subsection (a) shall be subject to a penalty equal to $500 for each such failure, unless it is shown that such failure is due to reasonable cause and not to willful neglect.

(d) Information to be Provided to Secretary.—Notwithstanding any other provision of law, any agency of the United States which collects (or is required to collect) the statement under subsection (a) shall—

    (1) provide any such statement to the Secretary, and

    (2) provide to the Secretary the name (and any other identifying information) of any individual refusing to comply with the provisions of subsection (a).

(e) Exemption.—The Secretary may by regulations exempt any class of individuals from the requirements of this section if he determines that applying this section to such individuals is not necessary to carry out the purposes of this section.

[For official explanation, see Committee Reports, ¶4044.]

[¶3331] CODE SEC. 6041. INFORMATION AT SOURCE.

(a) Payments of $600 or More.—All persons engaged in a trade or business and making payment in the course of such trade or business to another person, of rent, salaries, wages, premiums, annuities, compensations, remunerations, emoluments, or other fixed or determinable gains, profits and income (other than payments to which section 6042(a)(1), 6044(a)(1), *6047(e),* [1] 6049(a), *or 6050N(a)* applies, and other than payments with respect to which a statement is required under the authority of section 6042(a)(2), 6044(a)(2), or 6045), of $600 or more in any taxable year, or, in the case of such payments made by the United States, the officers or employees of the United States having information as to such payments and required to make returns in regard thereto by the regulations hereinafter provided for, shall render a true and accurate return to the Secretary, under such regulations and in such form and manner and to such extent as may be prescribed by the Secretary, setting forth the amount of such gains, profits, and income, and the name and address of the recipient of such payment.

* * * * * * * * * * * *

(c) Recipient to Furnish Name and Address.—When necessary to make effective the provisions of this section, the name and address of the recipient of income shall be furnished upon demand of the person paying the income.

(d) [2]*Statements to be Furnished to Persons With Respect to Whom Information is Required.—Every person required to make a return under subsection (a) shall furnish to each person with respect to whom such a return is required a written statement showing—*

[Footnote ¶3331] Matter in *italics* in Sec. 6041(a) added by section 1523(b)(2), '86 TRA, which struck out:
(1) "or"
Effective date (Sec. 1523(d), '86 TRA).—Applies with respect to payments made after 12-31-86.

Matter in *italics* in Sec. 6041(d) added by section 1501(c)(1), '86 TRA, which struck out:

    (2) **"Statements to be Furnished to Persons With Respect to Whom Information is Furnished.**—Every person making a return under subsection (a) shall furnish to each person whose name is set forth in such a return a written statement showing—

        (1) the name, address, and identification number of the person making such return, and

        (2) the aggregate amount of payments to the person shown on the return.

The written statement required under the preceding sentence shall be furnished to the person on or before January 31 of the year following the calendar year for which the return under subsection (a) was made. To the extent provided in regulations prescribed by the Secretary, this subsection shall also apply to persons making returns under subsection (b)."

Effective date (Sec. 1501(e), '86 TRA).—Applies to returns the due date for which (determined without regard to extensions) is after 12-31-86.

(1) the name and address of the person required to make such return, and

(2) the aggregate amount of payments to the person required to be shown on the return.

The written statement required under the preceding sentence shall be furnished to the person on or before January 31 of the year following the calendar year for which the return under subsection (a) was required to be made. To the extent provided in regulations prescribed by the Secretary, this subsection shall also apply to persons required to make returns under subsection (b).

* * * * * * * * * * *

[For official explanation, see Committee Reports, ¶4071; 4079.]

【¶3332】 CODE SEC. 6042. RETURNS REGARDING PAYMENTS OF DIVIDENDS AND CORPORATE EARNINGS AND PROFITS.

* * * * * * * * * * *

(3) **Special rule.**—If the person making any payment described in subsection (a)(1) (A) or (B) is unable to determine the portion of such payment which is a dividend or is paid with respect to a dividend, he shall, for purposes of subsection (a)(1), treat the entire amount of such payment as a dividend or as an amount paid with respect to a dividend.

[1]*(c) Statements To Be Furnished to Persons With Respect to Whom Information Is Required.*—*Every person required to make a return under subsection (a) shall furnish to each person whose name is required to be set forth in such return a written statement showing*—

(1) the name and address of the person required to make such return, and

(2) the aggregate amount of payments to the person required to be shown on the return.

The written statement required under the preceding sentence shall be furnished (either in person or in a statement mailing by first-class mail which includes adequate notice that the statement is enclosed) to the person on or before January 31 of the year following the calendar year for which the return under subsection (a) was required to be made and shall be in such form as the Secretary may prescribe by regulations.

[For official explanation, see Committee Reports, ¶4071.]

【¶3333】 CODE SEC. 6043. RETURNS REGARDING LIQUIDATION, DISSOLUTION, TERMINATION, OR CONTRACTION.

* * * * * * * * * * *

(c) **Cross Reference.**—

For provisions relating to penalties for failure to file a return required by subsection (b), see [1]*section 6652(c)*.

[For official explanation, see Committee Reports, ¶4071.]

【¶3334】 CODE SEC. 6044. RETURNS REGARDING PAYMENTS OF PATRONAGE DIVIDENDS.

* * * * * * * * * * *

【Footnote ¶3332】 Matter in *italics* in Sec. 6042(c) added by section 1501(c)(2), '86 TRA, which struck out:

(1) "**(c) Statements To Be Furnished to Persons with Respect to Whom Information Is Furnished.**—Every person making a return under subsection (a)(1) shall furnish to each person whose name is set forth in such return a written statement showing—

(1) the name and address of the person making such return, and

(2) the aggregate amount of payments to the person as shown on such return.

The written statement required under the preceding sentence shall be furnished (either in person or in a separate mailing by first-class mail) to the person on or before January 31 of the year following the calendar year for which the return under subsection (a) was made, and shall be in such form as the Secretary may prescribe by regulations."

Effective date (Sec. 1501(e), '86 TRA).—Applies to returns the due date for which (determined without regard to extensions) is after the date of the enactment of this Act.

* * * * * * * * * * *

【Footnote ¶3333】 Matter in *italics* in Sec. 6043(c) added by section 1501(d)(1)(C), '86 TRA, which struck out:

(1) "**section 6652(d)**"

Effective date (Sec. 1501(e), '86 TRA).—Applies to returns the due date for which (determined without regard to extensions) is after 12-31-86 generally.

(d) **Determination of Amount Paid.**—For purposes of this section, in determining the amount of any payment—

(1) property (other than a qualified written notice of allocation or a qualified per-unit retain certificate) shall be taken into account at its fair market value, and

(2) a qualified written notice of allocation or a qualified per-unit retain certificate shall be taken into account at its stated dollar amount.

[1]*(e) Statements to be Furnished to Persons With Respect to Whom Information is Required.—Every cooperative required to make a return under subsection (a) shall furnish to each person whose name is required to be set forth in such return a written statement showing—*

(1) the name and address of the cooperative required to make such return, and

(2) the aggregate amount of payments to the person required to be shown on the return.

The written statement required under the preceding sentence shall be furnished (either in person or in a statement mailing by first-class mail which includes adequate notice that the statement is enclosed) to the person on or before January 31 of the year following the calendar year for which the return under subsection (a) was required to be made and shall be in such form as the Secretary may prescribe by regulations.

[For official explanation, see Committee Reports, ¶4071.]

[¶3335] CODE SEC. 6045. RETURN OF BROKERS

(a) **General Rule.**—Every person doing business as a broker shall, when required by the Secretary, make a return, in accordance with such regulations as the Secretary may prescribe, showing the name and address of each customer, with such details regarding gross proceeds and such other information as the Secretary may by forms or regulations require with respect to such business.

(b) **Statements to be Furnished to Customers.**—Every person[1] *required to make* a return under subsection (a) shall furnish to each customer whose name is *required to be* set forth in such return a written statement showing—

(1) the name and address of the person[1] *required to make* such return, and

(2) the information *required to be* shown on such return with respect to such customer.

The written statement required under the preceding sentence shall be furnished to the customer on or before January 31 of the year following the calendar year for which the return under subsection (a) was *required to be* made.

* * * * * * * * * * * * *

(e) Return Required in the Case of Real Estate Transactions.—

(1) In general.—In the case of a real estate transaction, the real estate broker shall file a return under subsection (a) and a statement under subsection (b) with respect to such transaction.

(2) Real estate broker.—For purposes of this subsection, the term "real estate broker" means any of the following persons involved in a real estate transaction in the following order:

(A) the person (including any attorney or title company) responsible for closing the transaction,

(B) the mortgage lender,

[Footnote ¶3334] Matter in *italics* in Sec. 6044(e) added by section 1501(c)(3), '86 TRA, which struck out:

(1) "(e) Statements to be Furnished to Persons With Respect to Whom Information is Furnished.—Every cooperative making a return under subsection (a)(1) shall furnish to each person whose name is set forth in such return a written statement showing—

(1) the name and address of the cooperative making such return, and

(2) the aggregate amount of payments to the person as shown on such return.

The written statement required under the perceding sentence shall be furnished (either in person or in a separate mailing by first-class mail) to the person on or before January 31 of the year following the calendar year for which the return under subsection (a) was made, and shall be in such form as the Secretary may prescribe by regulations."

Effective date (Sec. 1501(e), '86 TRA).—Applies to returns the due for which (determined without regard to extensions) is after the date of the enactment of this Act.

[Footnote ¶3335] Matter in *italics* in Sec. 6045(b) added by section 1501(c)(4), '86 TRA, which struck out:

(1) "making"

Effective date (Sec. 1501(e), '86 TRA).—Applies to returns the due date for which (determined without regard to extensions) is after 12-31-86.

Sec. 6045(e) in *italics* added by section 1521(a), '86 TRA.

Effective date (Sec. 1521(c), '86 TRA).—Applies to real estate transactions closing after 12-31-86.

(C) the seller's broker,

(D) the buyer's broker, or

(E) such other person designated in regulations prescribed by the Secretary.

Any person treated as a real estate broker under the preceding sentence shall be treated as a broker for purposes of subsection (c)(1).

[For official explanation, see Committee Reports, ¶4071; 4077.]

[¶3336] CODE SEC. 6047. INFORMATION RELATING TO CERTAIN TRUSTS AND ANNUITY PLANS.

* * * * * * * * * * * *

(e) Cross References—

(1) For provisions relating to penalties for failure to file a return required by this section, see [1]*section 6652(e)*.

(2) For criminal penalty for furnishing fraudulent information, see section 7207.

(3) *For provisions relating to penalty for failure to comply with the provisions of subsection (d), see section 6704.*

[For official explanation, see Committee Reports, ¶4071; 4168.]

[¶3337] CODE SEC. 6049. RETURNS REGARDING PAYMENTS OF INTEREST.

* * * * * * * * * * * *

(b) Interest defined.—

* * * * * * * * * * * *

(5) Amounts described in this paragraph.—An amount is described in this paragraph if such amount—

(A) is subject to withholding under subchapter A of chapter 3 (relating to withholding of tax on nonresident aliens and foreign corporations) by the person paying such amount, or

(B) would be subject to withholding under subchapter A of chapter 3 by the person paying such amount but for the fact that—

(i) such amount is income from sources outside the United States,

(ii) the payor thereof is exempt from the application of section 1441(a) by reason of section 1441(c) or a tax treaty,[1]

(iii) such amount is original issue discount (within the meaning of [2]*section 1273(a))* [3]*or*

(iv) *such amount is described in section 871(i)(2).*

[4]*(c) Statements to be Furnished to Persons With Respect to Whom Information is*

Required.—

    (1) In general.—Every person required to make a return under subsection (a) shall furnish to each person whose name is required to be set forth in such return a written statement showing—

        (A) the name and address of the person required to make such return, and

        (B) the aggregate amount of payments to, or the aggregate amount includible in the gross income of, the person required to be shown on the return.

    (2) Time and form of statement.—The written statement under paragraph (1)—

        (A) shall be furnished (either in person or in a statement mailing by first-class mail which includes adequate notice that the statement is enclosed) to the person on or before January 31 of the year following the calendar year for which the return under subsection (a) was required to be made, and

        (B) shall be in such form as the Secretary may prescribe by regulations.

  (d) Definitions and Special Rules.—For purposes of this section—

*   *   *   *   *   *   *   *   *   *   *   *

    (7) Interests in REMIC's and certain other debt instruments.—

        (A) In general.—For purposes of subsection (a), the term "interest" includes amounts includible in gross income with respect to regular interests in REMIC's.

        (B) Reporting to corporations, etc.—Except as otherwise provided in regulations, in the case of any interest described in subparagraph (A) of this paragraph and any other debt instrument to which section 1272(a)(6) applies, subsection (b)(4) of this section shall be applied without regard to subparagraphs (A), (H), (I), (J), (K), and (L)(i).

        (C) Additional information.—Except as otherwise provided in regulations, any return or statement required to be filed or furnished under this section with respect to interest income described in subparagraph (A) and interest on any other debt instrument to which section 1272(a)(6) applies shall also provide information setting forth the issue price of the interest to which the return or statement relates at the beginning of each accrual period with respect to which interest income is required to be reported on such return or statement and information necessary to compute accrual of market discount.

        (D) Regulatory authority.—The Secretary may prescribe such regulations as are necessary or appropriate to carry out the purposes of this paragraph, including regulations which require more frequent or more detailed reporting.

[For official explanation, see Committee Reports, ¶3930, ¶4031, ¶4071, ¶4137.]

[¶3338] CODE SEC. 6050A. REPORTING REQUIREMENTS OF CERTAIN FISHING BOAT OPERATORS.

*   *   *   *   *   *   *   *   *   *   *   *

  (b) Written Statement.—Every person [1]*required to make* a return under subsection (a) shall furnish to each person whose name is *required to be* set forth in such return a written statement showing the information relating to such person *required to be* contained in such return. The written statement required under the preceding sentence shall be fur-

---

[Footnote ¶3337 continued]

    (A) the name and address of the person making such return, and

    (B) the aggregate amount of payments to, or the aggregate amount includable in the gross income of, the person as shown on such return.

    (2) Time and form of statement.—The written statement under paragraph (1)—

    (A) shall be furnished (either in person or in a separate mailing by first-class mail) to the person on or before January 31 of the year following the calendar year for which the return under subsection (a) was made, and

    (B) shall be in such form as the Secretary may prescribe by regulations.

    (3) No statement required where interest is less than $10.—No statement with respect to payments of interest to any person shall be required to be furnished to any person under this subsection if the aggregate amount of payments to such person shown on the return made with respect to paragraph (1) or (2), as the case may be, of subsection (a) is less than $10.

    Effective date (Sec. 1501(e), '86 TRA).—Applies to returns the due date for which (determined without regard to extensions) is after the date of enactment.

    Sec. 6049(d)(7) in *italics* added by section 674, '86 TRA.

    Effective date (Sec. 675(a), '86 TRA).—Applies to taxable years beginning after 12-31-86.

    [Footnote ¶3338] Matter in *italics* in Sec. 6050A(b) added by section 1501(c)(6), '86 TRA, which struck out:

    (1) "making"

    Effective date (Sec. 1501(e), '86 TRA).—Applies to returns the due date for which (determined without regard to extensions) is after 12-31-86.

nished to the person on or before January 31 of the year following the calendar year for which the return under subsection (a) was *required to be* made.

[For official explanation, see Committee Reports, ¶4071.]

[¶3338-A] CODE SEC. 6050B. RETURNS RELATING TO UNEMPLOYMENT COMPENSATION.

(a) Requirement of Reporting.—Every person who makes payments of unemployment compensation aggregating $10 or more to any individual during any calendar year shall make a return according to the forms or regulations prescribed by the Secretary setting forth the aggregate amounts of such payments and the name and address of the individual to whom paid.

(b) [1]*Statements To Be Furnished to Individuals With Respect to Whom Information Is Required.—Every person required to make a return under subsection (a) shall furnish to each individual whose name is required to be set forth in such return a written statement showing—*

(1)   the name and address of the person required to make such return, and

(2)   the aggregate amount of payments to the individual required to be shown on such return.

The written statement required under the preceding sentence shall be furnished to the individual on or before January 31 of the year following the calendar year for which the return under subsection (a) was required to be made.

* * * * * * * * * * * *

[For official explanation, see Committee Reports, ¶4071.]

[¶3338-B] CODE SEC. 6050C. INFORMATION REGARDING WINDFALL PROFIT TAX ON DOMESTIC CRUDE OIL.

* * * * * * * * * * *

(d) Cross References.—

(1)   For additions to tax for failure to furnish information required under this section, see [1]*section 6722.*

* * * * * * * * * * * *

[For official explanation, see Committee Reports, ¶4071.]

[¶3338-C] CODE SEC. 6050E. STATE AND LOCAL INCOME TAX REFUNDS.

* * * * * * * * * * * *

[1]*(b)   Statements to be Furnished to Individuals with Respect to Whom Information is*

[Footnote ¶3338-A] Matter in *italics* in Sec. 6050B(b) added by section 1501(c)(7), '86 TRA, which struck out:

(1) "**Statements to be Furnished to Individuals With Respect to Whom Information is Furnished.**—Every person making a return under subsection (a) shall furnish to each individual whose name is set forth in such return a written statement showing—

(1) the name and address of the person making such return, and

(2) the aggregate amount of payments to the individuals as shown on such return.

The written statement required under the preceding sentence shall be furnished to the individual on or before January 31 of the year following the calendar year for which the return under subsection (a) was made. No statement shall be required to be furnished to any individual under this subsection if the aggregate amount of payments to such individual shown on the return made under subsection (a) is less than $10."

Effective date (Sec. 1501(e), '86 TRA).—Applies to returns the due date for which (determined without regard to extensions) is after 12-31-86.

[Footnote ¶3338-B] Matter in *italics* in Sec. 6050C(d)(1) added by section 1501(d)(1)(E), '86 TRA, which struck out:

(1) "section 6652(b)"

Effective date (Sec. 1501(e), '86 TRA).—Applies to returns the due date for which (determined without regard to extensions) is after 12-31-86.

[Footnote ¶3338-C] Matter in *italics* in Sec. 6050E(b) added by section 1501(c)(8), '86 TRA, which struck out:

(1) "**(b)   Statements to be Furnished to Individuals with Respect to Whom Information is Furnished.**—Every person making a return under subsection (a) shall furnish to each individual whose name is set forth in such return a written statement showing—

(1) the name of the State or political subdivision thereof, and

(2) the aggregate amount shown on the return of refunds, credits, and offsets to the individual.

The written statement required under the preceding sentence shall be furnished to the individual during January of the calendar year following the calendar year for which the return under subsection (a) was made. No statement shall be required under this subsection with respect to any individual if it is determined (in the manner provided

Code §6050E(b) ¶3338-C

Required.—*Every person required to make a return under subsection (a) shall furnish to each individual whose name is required to be set forth in such return a written statement showing*—

    (1) the name of the State or political subdivision thereof, and

    (2) the information required to be shown on the return with respect to refunds, credits, and offsets to the individual.

The written statement required under the preceding sentence shall be furnished to the individual during January of the calendar year following the calendar year for which the return under subsection (a) was required to be made. No statement shall be required under this subsection with respect to any individual if it is determined (in the manner provided by regulations) that such individual did not claim itemized deductions under Chapter 1 for the taxable year giving rise to the refund, credit, or offset.

* * * * * * * * * * *

[For official explanation, see Committee Reports, ¶4071.]

〔¶3338-D〕 CODE SEC. 6050F. RETURNS RELATING TO SOCIAL SECURITY BENEFITS.

* * * * * * * * * * *

(b) Statements To Be Furnished To ¹*Persons* With Respect To Whom Information Is ²*Required.*—Every person ³*required to make* a return under subsection (a) shall furnish to each individual whose name is *required to be* set forth in such return a written statement showing—

    (1) the name of the agency making the payments, and

    (2) the aggregate amount of payments, of repayments, and of reductions, with respect to the individual ⁴*required to be* shown on such return.

The written statement required under the preceding sentence shall be furnished to the individual on or before January 31 of the year following the calendar year for which the return under subsection (a) was *required to be* made.

* * * * * * * * * * *

[For official explanation, see Committee Reports, ¶4071.]

〔¶3338-E〕 CODE SEC. 6050G. RETURNS RELATING TO CERTAIN RAILROAD RETIREMENT BENEFITS.

    (a) In General.—The Railroad Retirement Board shall make a return, according to the forms and regulations prescribed by the Secretary, setting forth—

    (1) the aggregate amount of benefits paid under the Railroad Retirement Act of 1974 (other than tier 1 railroad retirement benefits, as defined in section 86(d)(4)) to any individual during any calendar year,

    (2) the employee contributions (to the extent not previously taken into account under section 72(d)(1) which are treated as having been paid for purposes of section 72(r),

    (3) the name and address of such individual, and

    (4) such other information as the secretary may require.

    (b) Statements To Be Furnished To ¹*Persons* With Respect To Whom Information Is ²*Required.*—The Railroad Retirement Board shall furnish to each individual whose name is *required to be* set forth in the return under subsection (a) a written statement showing—

〔Footnote ¶3338-C continued〕

by regulations that such individual did not claim itemized deductions under chapter 1 for the taxable year giving rise to the refund, or offset."

Effective date (Sec. 1501(e), '86 TRA).—Applies to returns the due date for which (determined without regard to extensions) is after 12-31-86.

    〔Footnote ¶3338-D〕 Matter in *italics* in Sec. 6050F added by section 1501(c)(9), '86 TRA, which struck out:

    (1) **"Individuals"**

    (2) **"Furnished"**

    (3) "making"

    (4) "as"

Effective date (Sec. 1501(e), '86 TRA).—Applies to returns the due date for which (determined without regard to extensions) is after 12-31-86.

    〔Footnote ¶3338-E〕 Matter in *italics* in Sec. 6050G added by section 1501(c)(10), '86 TRA, which struck out:

    (1) **"Individuals"**

    (2) **"Furnished"**

(1)   the aggregate amount of payments to such individual, and of employee contributions with respect thereto, [3]*required to be shown on the* return, and

(2)   such other information as the Secretary may require.

The written statement required under the preceding sentence shall be furnished to the individual on or before January 31 of the year following the calendar year for which the return under subsection (a) was *required to be* made.

[For official explanation, see Committee Reports, ¶4071.]

【¶3338-F】   CODE SEC. 6050H.   RETURNS RELATING TO MORTGAGE INTEREST RECEIVED IN TRADE OR BUSINESS FROM INDIVIDUALS.

* * * * * * * * * * * *

(d)   Statements To Be Furnished to Individuals With Respect to Whom Information is [1]*Required.*—Every person [2]*required to make* a return under subsection (a) shall furnish to each individual whose name is *required to be* set forth in such return a written statement showing—

(1)   the name and address of the person [2]*required to make* such return, and

(2)   the aggregate amount of interest described in subsection (a)(2) received by the person [2]*required to make* such return from the individual to whom the statement is *required to be* furnished.

The written statement required under the preceding sentence shall be furnished on or before January 31 of the year following the calendar year for which the return under subsection (a) was *required to be* made.

* * * * * * * * * * * *

(g)   *Special Rules for Cooperative Housing Corporations.—For purposes of subsection (a), an amount received by a cooperative housing corporation from a tenant-stockholder shall be deemed to be interest received on a mortgage in the course of a trade or business engaged in by such corporation, to the extent of the tenant-stockholder's proportionate share of interest described in section 216(a)(2). Terms used in the preceding sentence shall have the same meanings as when used in section 216.*

[For official explanation, see Committee Reports, ¶4071; 4145.]

【¶3338-G】   CODE SEC. 6050I.   RETURNS RELATING TO CASH RECEIVED IN TRADE OR BUSINESS.—

* * * * * * * * * * * *

[1]*(e)   Statements to be Furnished to Persons with Respect to Whom Information Is Required.—Every person required to make a return under subsection (a) shall furnish to*

---

each person whose name is required to be set forth in such return a written statement showing—

 (1) the name and address of the person required to make such return, and

 (2) the aggregate amount of cash described in subsection (a) received by the person required to make such return.

The written statement required under the preceding sentence shall be furnished to the person on or before January 31 of the year following the calendar year for which the return under subsection (a) was required to be made.

[For official explanation, see Committee Reports, ¶4071.]

【¶3338-H】 CODE SEC. 6050K. RETURNS RELATING TO EXCHANGES OF CERTAIN PARTNERSHIP INTERESTS.

 (a) In General.—Except as provided in regulations prescribed by the Secretary, if there is an exchange described in section 751(a) of any interest in a partnership during any calendar year, such partnership shall make a return for such calendar year stating—

  (1) the name and address of the transferee and transferor in such exchange, and

  (2) such other information as the Secretary may by regulations prescribe.

Such return shall be made at such time and in such manner as the Secretary may require by regulations.

 (b) [1]*Statements* **To Be Furnished to Transferor and Transferee.**— Every partnership [2]*required to make* a return under subsection (a) shall furnish to each person whose name *is required to be* set forth in such return a written statement showing—

  (1) the name and address of the partnership [3]*required to make such* return, and

  (2) the information *required to be* shown on the return with respect to such person.

The *written* statement required under the preceding sentence shall be furnished to the person on or before January 31 *of the year* following the calendar year for which the return under subsection (a) was *required to be* made.

 (c) Requirement That Transferor Notify Partnership.—

  (1) In general.—In the case of any exchange described in subsection (a), the transferor of the partnership interest shall promptly notify the partnership of such exchange.

  (2) Partnership not required to make return until notice.—A partnership shall not be required to make a return under [4]*this section* with respect to any exchange until the partnership is notified of such exchange.

[For official explanation, see Committee Reports, ¶4071; 4145.]

【¶3338-I】 CODE SEC. 6050M. RETURNS RELATING TO PERSONS RECEIVING CONTRACTS FROM FEDERAL EXECUTIVE AGENCIES.

 (a) Requirement Of Reporting.—The head of every Federal executive agency which enters into any contract shall make a return (at such time and in such form as the Secretary may by regulations prescribe) setting forth—

  (1) the name, address, and TIN of each person with which such agency entered into a contract during the calendar year, and

  (2) such other information as the Secretary may require.

 (b) Federal Executive Agency.—For purposes of this section, the term "Federal executive agency" means—

  (1) any Executive agency (as defined in section 105 of title 5, United States Code) other than the General Accounting Office,

---

 【Footnote ¶3338-H】 Matter in *italics* in Sec. 6050K(b) added by section 1501(c)(13), '86 TRA, which struck out:

 (1) "Statement"

 (2) "making"

 (3) "making the"

 Effective date (Sec. 1501(e), '86 TRA).—Applies to returns the due date for which (determined without regard to extensions) is after 12-31-86.

 Matter in *italics* in Sec. 6050K(c)(2) added by section 1811(b)(2), '86 TRA, which struck out:

 (4) "this subsection"

 Effective date (Sec. 1881, '86 TRA, and section 149(d), '84 TRA).—Applies with respect to exchanges after 12-31-84.

 【Footnote ¶3338-I】 Sec. 6050M added by section 1522(a), '86 TRA.

 Effective date (Sec. 1522(c), '86 TRA).—Applies to contracts (and subcontracts) entered into, and licenses granted, before, on, or after 1-1-87.

(2) any military department (as defined in section 102 of such title), and

(3) the United States Postal Service and the Postal Rate Commission.

(c) Authority To Extend Reporting To Licenses And Subcontracts.—To the extent provided in regulations, this section also shall apply to—

(1) licenses granted by Federal executive agencies, and

(2) subcontracts under contracts to which subsection (a) applies.

(d) Authority To Prescribe Minimum Amounts.—This section shall not apply to contracts or licenses in any class which are below a minimum amount or value which may be prescribed by the Secretary by regulations for such class.

[For official explanation, see Committee Reports, ¶4078.]

〖¶3338-J〗 CODE SEC. 6050N. RETURNS REGARDING PAYMENTS OF ROYALTIES.

(a) Requirement of Reporting.—Every person—

(1) who makes payments of royalties (or similar amounts) aggregating $10 or more to any other person during any calendar year, or

(2) who receives payments of royalties (or similar amounts) as a nominee and who makes payments aggregating $10 or more during any calendar year to any other person with respect to the royalties (or similar amounts) so received,

shall make a return according to the forms or regulations prescribed by the Secretary, setting forth the aggregate amount of such payments and the name and address of the person to whom paid.

(b) Statements to be Furnished to Persons with Respect to Whom Information Is Furnished.—Every person required to make a return under subsection (a) shall furnish to each person whose name is required to be set forth in such return a written statement showing—

(1) the name and address of the person required to make such return, and

(2) the aggregate amount of payments to the person required to be shown on such return.

The written statement required under the preceding sentence shall be furnished (either in person or in a statement mailing by first-class mail which includes adequate notice that the statement is enclosed) to the person on or before January 31 of the year following the calendar year for which the return under subsection (a) was made and shall be in such form as the Secretary may prescribe by regulations.

(c) Exception for Payments to Certain Persons.—Except to the extent otherwise provided in regulations, this section shall not apply to any amount paid to a person described in subparagraph (A), (B), (C), (D), (E), or (F) of section 6049(B)(4).

[For official explanation, see Committee Reports, ¶4079.]

〖¶3339〗 CODE SEC. 6051. RECEIPTS FOR EMPLOYEES

(a) Requirement.—Every person required to deduct and withhold from an employee a tax under section 3101 or 3402, or who would have been required to deduct and withhold a tax under section 3402 (determined without regard to subsection (n)) if the employee had claimed no more than one withholding exemption, or every employer engaged in a trade or business who pays remuneration for services performed by an employee, including the cash value of such remuneration paid in any medium other than cash, shall furnish to each such employee in respect of the remuneration paid by such person to such employee during the calendar year, on or before January 31 of the succeeding year, or, if his employment is terminated before the close of such calendar year, within 30 days after the date of receipt of a written request from the employee if such 30-day period ends before January 31, a written statement showing the following:

(1) the name of such person,

(2) the name of the employee (and his social security account number if wages as defined in section 3121(a) have been paid),

(3) the total amount of wages as defined in section 3401(a),

(4) the total amount deducted and withheld as tax under section 3402,

(5) the total amount of wages as defined in section 3121(a),

(6) the total amount deducted and withheld as tax under section 3101, [1]

〖Footnote ¶3338-J〗 Sec. 6050N added by section 1523(a), '86 TRA.

Effective date (Sec. 1523(d), '86 TRA).—Applies with respect to payments made after 12-31-86.

〖Footnote ¶3339〗 Matter in *italics* in Sec. 6051(a)(6), (7), and (8) added by section 1105(b), '86 TRA, which struck out:

(7)   the total amount paid to the employee under section 3507 (relating to advance payment of earned income credit)[2]

(8)   *the total amount of elective deferrals (within the meaning of section 402(g)(3)) and compensation deferred under section 457.*

In the case of compensation paid for service as a member of a uniformed service, the statement shall show, in lieu of the amount required to be shown by paragraph (5), the total amount of wages as defined in section 3121(a), computed in accordance with such section and section 3121(i)(2). In the case of compensation paid for service as a volunteer or volunteer leader within the meaning of the Peace Corps Act, the statement shall show, in lieu of the amount required to be shown by paragraph (5), the total amount of wages as defined in section 3121(a), computed in accordance with such section and section 3121(i)(3). In the case of tips received by an employee in the course of his employment, the amounts required to be shown by paragraphs (3) and (5) shall include only such tips as are included in statements furnished to the employer pursuant to section 6053(a). The amounts required to be shown by paragraph (5) shall not include wages which are exempted pursuant to sections 3101(c) and 3111(c) from the taxes imposed by section 3101 and 3111.

* * * * * * * * * * *

[For official explanation, see Committee Reports, ¶3971.]

[¶3340]   CODE SEC. 6052.   RETURNS REGARDING PAYMENT OF WAGES IN THE FORM OF GROUP-TERM LIFE INSURANCE.

* * * * * * * * * * *

[1]*(b)   Statements to be Furnished to Employees With Respect to Whom Information Is Required.—Every employer required to make a return under subsection (a) shall furnish to each employee whose name is required to be set forth in such return a written statement showing the cost of the group-term life insurance shown on such return. The written statement required under the preceding sentence shall be furnished to the employee on or before January 31 of the year following the calendar year for which the return under subsection (a) was required to be made.*

* * * * * * * * * * *

[For official explanation, see Committee Reports, ¶4071.]

[¶3341]   CODE SEC. 6057.   ANNUAL REGISTRATION, ETC.

* * * * * * * * * * *

(g)   Cross References.—

For provisions relating to penalties for failure to register or furnish statements required by this section, see [1]***section 6652(d)* and section 6690.**

For coordination between Department of the Treasury and the Department of Labor with regard to administration of this section, see section 3004 of the Employee Retirement Income Security Act of 1974.

[For official explanation, see Committee Reports, ¶4071.]

[¶3342]   CODE SEC. 6058.   INFORMATION REQUIRED IN CONNECTION WITH CERTAIN PLANS OF DEFERRED COMPENSATION.

* * * * * * * * * * *

[Footnote ¶3339 continued]

(1)   "and"

(2)   "."

Effective date (Sec. 1105(c), '86 TRA).—Generally applies to taxable years beginning after 12-31-86. For special and transitional rules, see footnote ¶2995.

[Footnote ¶3340]   Matter in *italics* in Sec. 6052(b) added by section 1501(c)(14), '86 TRA, which struck out:

(1)   **"(b)   Statements to be Furnished to Employees with Respect to Whom Information is Furnished.—Every** employer making a return under subsection (a) shall furnish to each employee whose name is set forth in such return a written statement showing the cost of the group-term life insurance shown on such return. The written statement required under the preceding sentence shall be furnished to the employee on or before January 31 of the year following the calendar year for which the return under subsection (a) was made."

Effective date (Sec. 1501(e), '86 TRA).—Applies to returns the due date for which (determined without regard to extensions) is after 12-31-86.

[Footnote ¶3341]   Matter in *italics* in Sec. 6057(g) added by section 1501(d)(1)(F), '86 TRA, which struck out:

(1)   "section 6652(e)"

Effective date (Sec. 1501(e), '86 TRA).—Applies to returns the due date for which (determined without regard to extensions) is after 12-31-86.

(f) **Cross References.—**

For provisions relating to penalties for failure to file a return required by this section, see [1]*section 6652(e).*

For coordination between the Department of the Treasury and the Department of Labor with respect to the information required under this section, see section 3004 of title III of the Employee Retirement Income Security Act of 1974.

[For official explanation, see Committee Reports, ¶4071.]

【¶3343】 CODE SEC. 6091. PLACE FOR FILING RETURNS OR OTHER DOCUMENTS.

* * * * * * * * * * *

(b) **Tax Returns.—**In the case of returns of tax required under authority of part II of this subchapter—

(1) **Persons other than corporations.—**

* * * * * * * * * * *

(B) Exception.—Returns of—

(i) persons who have no legal residence or principal place of business in any internal revenue district.

(ii) citizens of the United States whose principal place of abode for the period with respect to which the return is filed is outside the United States,

(iii) persons who claim the benefits of section 911 (relating to citizens or residents of the United States living abroad, section 931 (relating to income from sources within [1]*Guam, American Samoa, or the Northern Mariana Islands,* or section 933 (relating to income from sources within Puerto Rico),

(iv) nonresident alien persons, and

(v) persons with respect to whom an assessment was made under section 6851(a) (relating to termination assessments) with respect to the taxable year, shall be made at such place as the Secretary may by regulations designate.

(6) *Alcohol, Tobacco, and Firearms returns, etc.—In the case of any return of tax imposed by subtitle E (relating to taxes on alcohol, tobacco, and firearms), subsection (a) shall apply (and this subsection shall not apply).*

[For official explanation, see Committee Reports, ¶4057; 4193.]

【¶3344】 CODE SEC. 6103. CONFIDENTIALITY AND DISCLOSURE OF RETURNS AND RETURN INFORMATION.

* * * * * * * * * * *

(b) **Definitions.—**For purposes of this section—

* * * * * * * * * * *

[1]*(5) State.—The term "State" means—*

【Footnote ¶3342】 Matter in *italics* in Sec. 6058(f) added by section 1501(d)(1)(D), '86 TRA, which struck out:

(1) "section 6652(f)"

Effective date (Sec. 1501(e), '86 TRA).—Applies to returns the due date for which (determined without regard to extensions) is after 12-31-86.

【Footnote ¶3343】 Matter in *italics* in Sec. 6091(b)(1)(B)(iii) added by section 1272(d)(10), '86 TRA, which struck out:

(1) "possessions of the United States"

Effective date (Sec. 1277(a), (b), and (e), '86 TRA).—(a) Generally applies to taxable years beginning after 12-31-86.

(b) Special Rule for Guam, American Samoa, and the Northern Mariana Islands.—The amendments made by this subtitle shall apply with respect to Guam, American Samoa, or the Northern Mariana Islands (and to residents thereof and corporations created or organized therein) only if (and so long as) an implementing agreement under section 1271 is in effect between the United States and such possession.

* * * * * * * * * * *

(e) Treatment of Certain United States Persons.—Except as otherwise provided in regulations prescribed by the Secretary of the Treasury or his delegate, if a United States person becomes a resident of Guam, American Samoa, or the Northern Mariana Islands, the rules of section 877(c) of the '54 Code shall apply to such person during the 10-year period beginning when such person became such a resident. The preceding sentence shall apply to dispositions after 12-31-85, in taxable years ending after such date.

Sec 6091(b)(6) in *italics* added by section 1879(r)(1), '86 TRA.

Effective date (Sec. 1879(r)(2), '86 TRA).—Takes effect on the first day of the first calendar month which begins more than 90 days after the date of enactment of this Act.

【Footnote ¶3344】 Matter in *italics* in Sec. 6103(b)(5) and (10) added by section 1568(a), '86 TRA, which

(A) any of the 50 States, the District of Columbia, the Commonwealth of Puerto Rico, the Virgin Islands, the Canal Zone, Guam, American Samoa, the Commonwealth of the Northern Mariana Islands, the Republic of the Marshall Islands, the Federated States of Micronesia, and the Republic of Palau, and

(B) for purposes of subsections (a)(2), (b)(4), (d)(1), (h)(4), and (p) any municipality—

(i) with a population in excess of 2,000,000 (as determined under the most recent decennial United States census data available),

(ii) which imposes a tax on income or wages, and

(iii) with which the Secretary (in his sole discretion) has entered into an agreement regarding disclosure.

* * * * * * * * * * * *

(10) **Chief executive officer.**—The term "chief executive officer" means, with respect to any municipality, any elected official and the chief official (even if not elected) of such municipality.

* * * * * * * * * * * *

(e) **Disclosure to Persons Having Material Interest.—**

(1) **In general**—The return of a person shall, upon written request, be open to inspection by or disclosure to—

(A) in the case of the return of an individual—

(i) that individual,

(ii) if property transferred by that individual to a trust is sold or exchanged in a transaction described in section 644, the trustee or trustees, jointly or separately, of such trust to the extent necessary to ascertain any amount of tax imposed upon the trust by section 644, [2]

(iii) the spouse of that individual if the individual and such spouse have signified their consent to consider a gift reported on such return as made one-half by him and one-half by the spouse pursuant to the provisions of section 2513; or

(iv) the child of that individual (or such child's legal representative) to the extent necessary to comply with the provisions of section 1(j);

* * * * * * * * * * * *

(l) **Disclosure of Returns and Return Information for Purposes Other Than Tax Administration.—**

* * * * * * * * * * * *

(7) **Disclosure of return information to federal, state, and local agencies administering certain programs under the social security act or the food stamp act of 1977.—**

* * * * * * * * * * * *

(D) Programs to which rule applies.—The programs to which this paragraph applies are:

* * * * * * * * * * * *

(v) unemployment compensation provided under a State law described in section 3304 of this [3]title;

* * * * * * * * * * * *

[For official explanation, see Committee Reports, ¶4064; 4106; 4213.]

[Footnote ¶3344 continued]

struck out:

(1) "(5) **State.**—The term 'State' means any of the 50 States, the District of Columbia, the Commonwealth of Puerto Rico, the Virgin Islands, the Canal Zone, Guam, American Samoa, the Commonwealth of the Northern Mariana Islands, and the Trust Territory of the Pacific Islands."

Effective date (Sec. 1568(b), '86 TRA).—Takes effect on the date of the enactment of this Act.

Matter in *italics* in Sec. 6103(e)(1)(A)(ii), (iii) and (iv) added by section 1411(b), '86 TRA, which struck:

(2) "or"

Effective date (Sec. 1411(c), '86 TRA).—Applies to taxable years beginning after 12-31-86.

Matter in *italics* in Sec. 6103(l)(7)(D)(v) added by section 1899A(53), '86 TRA, which struck out:

(3) "Code"

〖¶3345〗 CODE SEC. 6109. IDENTIFYING NUMBERS.

* * * * * * * * * * * *

(e) *Furnishing Number for Certain Dependents.—If—*
   (1) any taxpayer claims an exemption under section 151 for any dependent on a return for any taxable year, and
   (2) such dependent has attained the age of 5 years before the close of such taxable year,
such taxpayer *shall include on such return the identifying number (for purposes of this title) of such dependent.*

[For official explanation, see Committee Reports, ¶4080.]

〖¶3346〗 CODE SEC. 6111. REGISTRATION OF TAX SHELTERS.—

* * * * * * * * * * * *

(c) **Tax Shelter.**—For purposes of this section—

* * * * * * * * * * * *

   (2) **Tax shelter ratio defined.**—For purposes of this subsection, the term "tax shelter ratio" means, with respect to any year, the ratio which—
      (A) the aggregate amount of the deductions and [1]*350 percent* of the credits which are represented to be potentially allowable to any investor under subtitle A for all periods up to (and including) the close of such year, bears to
      (B) the investment base as of the close of such year.

   (3) **Investment Base.—**

* * * * * * * * * * * *

      (B) Certain borrowed amounts excluded.—For purposes of subparagraph (A), there shall not be taken into account any amount borrowed from any person—
         (i) who participated in the organization, sale, or management of the investment, or
         (ii) who is a related person (as defined in [2]*section 465(b)(3)(C)* to any person described in clause (i).
      unless such amount is unconditionally required to be repaid by the investor before the close of the year for which the determination is being made.

* * * * * * * * * * * *

[For official explanation, see Committee Reports, ¶3870; 4082.]

〖¶3347〗 CODE SEC. 6152. INSTALLMENT PAYMENTS. [Repealed by section 1404(c)(1), '86 TRA].[1]

[For official explanation, see Committee Reports, ¶4063.]

〖¶3348〗 CODE SEC. 6154. INSTALLMENT PAYMENTS OF ESTIMATED INCOME TAX BY CORPORATIONS.

* * * * * * * * * * * *

(c) **Estimated Tax Defined.**—For purposes of this title, in the case of a corporation the term "estimated tax" means the excess of—
   [1]*(1) The amount which the corporation estimates as the sum of—*

    (A) the income tax imposed by section 11 or 1201(a), or subchapter L of chapter 1, whichever applies, and

    (B) the minimum tax imposed by section 55, over.

  (2) the amount which the corporation estimates as the sum of—

    (A) any credits against tax provided by part IV of subchapter A of chapter 1, any

    (B) to the extent allowed under regulations prescribed by the Secretary, any overpayment of the tax imposed by section 4986.

* * * * * * * * * * *

(h) Certain Tax-Exempt Organizations.—For purposes of this section and section 6655—

    (1) any organization subject to the tax imposed by section 511, and any private foundation subject to the tax imposed by section 4940, shall be treated as a corporation subject to tax under section 11,

    (2) any tax imposed by section 511 or 4940 shall be treated as a tax imposed by section 11, and

    (3) any reference to taxable income shall be treated as including a reference to unrelated business taxable income or net investment income (as the case may be).

[For official explanation, see Committee Reports, ¶3931; 4088.]

【¶3349】 CODE SEC. 6166. EXTENSION OF TIME FOR PAYMENT OF ESTATE TAX WHERE ESTATE CONSISTS LARGELY OF INTEREST IN CLOSELY HELD BUSINESS.

* * * * * * * * * * *

    (i) Special Rule for Certain Direct Skips.—To the extent that an interest in a closely held business is the subject of a direct skip (within the meaning of section 2612(c)) occurring at the same time as and as a result of the decedent's death, then for purposes of this section any tax imposed by section 2601 on the transfer of such interest shall be treated as if it were additional tax imposed by section 2001.

  [1]*(j) Regulations.—The Secretary shall prescribe such regulations as may be necessary to the application of this section.*

  [2]*(k) Cross References.—*

* * * * * * * * * * *

[For official explanation, see Committee Reports, ¶4068.]

【¶3350】 CODE SEC. 6212. NOTICE OF DEFICIENCY.

* * * * * * * * * * *

  (c) **Further Deficiency Letters Restricted.—**

* * * * * * * * * * *

    (2) **Cross references.—**

For assessment as a deficiency notwithstanding the prohibition further deficiency letters, in the case of—

    (A) **Deficiency attributable to change of treatment with respect to itemized deductions,** [1]*see section 63(e)(3).*

【Footnote ¶3348 continued】
rules, see footnote ¶2879.

Sec. 6154(h) in *italics* added by section 1542(a), '86 TRA.

Effective date (Sec. 1542(b), '86 TRA).—Applies to taxable years beginning after 12-31-86.

  【Footnote ¶3349】 Matter in *italics* in Sec. 6166(i), (j), and (k) added by section 1432(e), '86 TRA, which struck out:

  (1) "(i)"

  (2) "(j)"

Effective date (Sec. 1433, '86 TRA).—Generally applies to any generation-skipping transfer (within the meaning of section 2611 of the '86 Code) made after the date of the enactment of this Act. For special rules, see footnote ¶3252.

  【Footnote ¶3350】 Matter in *italics* in Sec. 6212(c)(2)(A) added by section 104(b)(17), '86 TRA, which struck out:

  (1) "and zero bracket amount, see section 63(g)(5)"

Effective date (Sec. 151(a), '86 TRA).—Applies to taxable years beginning after 12-31-86.

Sec. 6212(d) in *italics* added by section 1562(a), '86 TRA.

* * * * * * * * * * *

(d) *Authority To Rescind Notice of Deficiency With Taxpayer's Consent.*—The Secretary may, with the consent of the taxpayer, rescind any notice of deficiency mailed to the taxpayer. Any notice so rescinded shall not be treated as a notice of deficiency for purposes of subsection (c)(1) (relating to further deficiency letters restricted), section 6213(a) (relating to restrictions applicable to deficiencies; petition to Tax Court), and section 6512(a) (relating to limitations in case of petition to Tax Court), and the taxpayer shall have no right to file a petition with the Tax Court based on such notice.

[For official explanation, see Committee Reports, ¶4100.]

【¶3351】 **CODE SEC. 6213. RESTRICTIONS APPLICABLE TO DEFICIENCIES; PETITION TO TAX COURT.**

* * * * * * * * * * *

(h) **Cross References.**—

* * * * * * * * * * *

[1](4) *For provisions relating to application of this subchapter in the case of certain partnership items, etc., see section 6230(a).*

[For official explanation, see Committee Reports, ¶4189.]

【¶3352】 **CODE SEC. 6214. DETERMINATIONS BY TAX COURT.**

(a) **Jurisdiction as to Increase of Deficiency, Additional Amounts, or Additions to the Tax.**—Except as provided by section 7463, the Tax Court shall have jurisdiction to redetermine the correct amount of the deficiency even if the amount so redetermined is greater than the amount of the deficiency, notice of which has been mailed to the taxpayer, and to determine whether any additional amount, or *any* addition to the tax should be assessed, if claim therefor is asserted by the Secretary at or before the hearing or a rehearing.

* * * * * * * * * * *

(c) **Taxes imposed by Section 507 or Chapter 41, 42, 43, 44, or 45.**—The Tax Court in redetermining a deficiency of any tax imposed by section 507 or chapter 41, 42, 43, 44, or 45 for any period, act, or failure to act, shall consider such facts with relation to the taxes under chapter 41, 42, 43, 44, or 45 for other periods, acts, or failures to act as may be necessary correctly to redetermine the amount of such deficiency, but in so doing shall have no jurisdiction to determine whether or not the taxes under chapter 41, 42, 43, 44, or 45, for any other period, act, or failure to act have been overpaid or underpaid. The Tax Court, in redetermining a deficiency of any second tier tax (as defined in [1]*section 4963(b))*, shall make a determination with respect to whether the taxable event has been corrected.

(d) **Final Decisions of Tax Court.**—For purposes of this chapter, chapter 41, 42, 43, 44, or 45, and subtitles A or B the date on which a decision of the Tax Court becomes final shall be determined according to the provisions of section 7481.

【Footnote ¶3350 continued】

Effective date (Sec. 1562(b), '86 TRA).—Applies to notices of deficiency issued on or after 1-1-86.

【Footnote ¶3351】 Matter in *italics* in Sec. 6213(h)(4) added by section 1875(d)(2)(B)(i), '86 TRA, which struck out:

(1) "For provision that this chapter shall not apply in the case of computational adjustments attributable to partnership items, see section 6230(a)."

Effective date (Sec. 1875(d)(2)(C), '86 TRA, and section 407(a)(1), (3), '82 TEFRA).—(a)(1) Applies to partnership taxable years beginning after 9-3-82.

(3) The amendments made by sections 402, 403, and 404 of '82 TEFRA shall apply to any partnership taxable year (or in the case of section 6232 of such Code, to any period) ending after 9-3-82 if the partnership, each partner, and each indirect partner requests such application and the Secretary of the Treasury or his delegate consents to such application.

【Footnote ¶3352】 Matter in *italics* in Sec. 6214(a) added by section 1554(a), '86 TRA.

Effective date (Sec. 1554(b), '86 TRA).—Applies to any action or proceeding in the Tax Court with respect to which a decision has not become final (as determined under section 7481 of the '54 Code) before the date of the enactment of this Act.

Matter in *italics* in Sec. 6214(c) added by section 1833, '86 TRA, which struck out:

(1) "section 4962(b)"

Effective date (Sec. 1881, '86 TRA and 305(c), '84 TRA).—Applies to taxable events occurring after 12-31-84.

(e) Cross Reference.—

For provision giving Tax Court jurisdiction to determine whether any portion of deficiency is a substantial underpayment attributable to tax motivated transactions, see [2]*section 6621(c)(4).*

[For official explanation, see Committee Reports, ¶4075; 4093.]

〖¶3353〗 **CODE SEC. 6215. ASSESSMENT OF DEFICIENCY FOUND BY TAX COURT.**

(a) General Rule.—If the taxpayer files a petition with the Tax Court, the entire amount redetermined as the deficiency by the decision of the Tax Court which has become final shall be assessed and shall be paid upon notice and demand from the Secretary. No part of the amount determined as a deficiency by the Secretary but disallowed as such by the decision of the Tax Court which has become final shall be assessed or be collected by levy or by proceeding in court with or without assessment.

(b) Cross References.—

* * * * * * * * * * * *

[1](7)   [2]For extension of time for paying amount determined as deficiency, see section 6161(b).

[For official explanation, see Committee Reports, ¶4063.]

〖¶3354〗 **CODE SEC. 6222. PARTNER'S RETURN MUST BE CONSISTENT WITH PARTNERSHIP RETURN OR SECRETARY NOTIFIED OF INCONSISTENCY.**

* * * * * * * * * * * *

(d) Addition to Tax for Failure to Comply With Section.—

"For addition to tax in the case of a partner's[1] disregard of requirements of this section, see section 6653(a).

[For official explanation, see Committee Reports, ¶4073.]

〖¶3355〗 **CODE SEC. 6229. PERIOD OF LIMITATIONS FOR MAKING ASSESSMENTS**

* * * * * * * * * * * *

(g) Period of Limitations for Penalties.—The provisions of this section shall apply also in the case of any addition to tax or an additional amount imposed under subchaper A of chapter 68 which arises with respect to any tax imposed under subtitle A in the same manner as if such addition or additional amount were a tax imposed by subtitle A.

[For official explanation, see Committee Reports, ¶4189.]

〖¶3356〗 **CODE SEC. 6230. ADDITIONAL ADMINISTRATIVE PROVISIONS.**

[1]*(a) Coordination With Deficiency Proceedings.—*

    (1) In general.—Except as provided in paragraph (2), subchapter B of this chapter shall not apply to the assessment or collection of any computational adjustment.

〖Footnote ¶3352 continued〗

Matter in *italics* in Sec. 6214(e) added by section 1511(c)(8), '86 TRA, which struck:
(2) "section 6621(d)(4)"
Effective date (Sec. 1511(d), '86 TRA).—Applies for purposes of determining interest for periods after 12-31-86.
〖Footnote ¶3353〗   Matter in *italics* in Sec. 6215(b)(7), added by section 1404(c)(2), '86 TRA, which struck out:
(1) "(7) For proration of deficiency to installments, see section 6152(c)"
(2) "(8)"
Effective date (Sec. 1404(d), '86 TRA).—Applies to taxable years beginning after 12-31-86.
〖Footnote ¶3354〗   Section 1503(c)(1), '86 TRA, struck out from Sec. 6222(d):
(1) "intentional or negligent"
Effective date (Sec. 1503(e), '86 TRA).—Applies to returns the due date for which (determined without regard to extensions) is after 12-31-86.
〖Footnote ¶3355〗   Sec. 6229(g) added by section 1875(d)(1).
Effective date (Sec. 1881, '86 TRA, and section 407(a)(1) and (3), '82 TEFRA).—(a)(1) Generally applies to partnership taxable years beginning after 9-3-82.
(3) The amendments made by section 402, 403, and 404, '82 TEFRA shall apply to any partnership taxable year (or in the case of section 6232 of such Code, to any period) ending after 9-3-82 if the partnership, each partner, and each indirect partner requests such application and the Secretary of the Treasury or his delegate consents to such application
〖Footnote ¶3356〗   Matter in *italics* in Sec. 6230(a) added by section 1875(d)(2)(A), '86 TRA, which struck out:
(1) "(a) **Normal Deficiency Proceedings Do Not Apply to Computational Adjustments.**—Subchapter B of this chapter shall not apply to the assessment or collection of any computational adjustment."
Effective date (Sec. 1875(d)(2)(C), '86 TRA and section 407(a)(1), (3), '82 TEFRA).—See footnote ¶3355, above.

(2) Deficiency proceedings to apply in certain cases.—
    (A) Subchapter B shall apply to any deficiency attributable to—
        (i) affected items which require partner level determinations, or
        (ii) items which have become nonpartnership items and are described in section 6231(e)(1)(B).

    (B) Subchapter B shall be applied separately with respect to each deficiency described in subparagraph (A) attributable to each partnership.

    (C) Notwithstanding any other law or rule of law, any notice or proceeding under subchapter B with respect to a deficiency described in this paragraph shall not preclude or be precluded by any other notice, proceeding, or determination with respect to a partner's tax liability for a taxable year.

* * * * * * * * * * *

[For official explanation, see Committee Reports, ¶4189.]

[¶3357] **CODE SEC. 6323. VALIDITY AND PRIORITY AGAINST CERTAIN PERSONS.**

* * * * * * * * * * *

(i) Special Rules.—

* * * * * * * * * * *

    (3) Forfeitures.—For purposes of this subchapter, a forfeiture under local law of property seized by a law enforcement agency of a State, county, or other local governmental subdivision shall relate back to the time of seizure, except that this paragraph shall not apply to the extent that under local law the holder of an intervening claim or interest would have priority over the interest of the State, county, or other local governmental subdivision in the property.

[For official explanation, see Committee Reports, ¶4107.]

[¶3358] **CODE SEC. 6332. SURRENDER OF PROPERTY SUBJECT TO LEVY.**

* * * * * * * * * * *

(c) Enforcement of levy.—

    (1) Extent of personal liability.—Any person who fails or refuses to surrender any property or right to property, subject to levy, upon demand by the Secretary shall be liable in his own person and estate to the United States in a sum equal to the value of the property or rights not so surrendered, but not exceeding the amount of taxes for the collection of which such levy has been made, together with costs and interest on such sum at ¹*the underpayment* rate established under section 6621 from the date of such levy (or, in the case of a levy described in section 6331(d)(3), from the date such person would otherwise have been obligated to pay over such amounts to the taxpayer). Any amount (other than costs) recovered under this paragraph shall be credited against the tax liability for the collection of which such levy was made.

* * * * * * * * * * *

[For official explanation, see Committee Reports, ¶4075.]

[¶3359] **CODE SEC. 6334. PROPERTY EXEMPT FROM LEVY.**

(a) Enumeration.—There shall be exempt from levy—

* * * * * * * * * * *

    (10) Certain service-connected disability payments.—Any amount payable to an individual as a service-connected (within the meaning of section 101(16) of title 38, United States Code) disability benefit under—
        (A) subchapter II, IV, or VI of chapter 11 of such title 38,
        (B) subchapter I, II, or III of chapter 19 of such title 38, or
        (C) chapter 21, 31, 32, 34, 35, 37, or 39 of such title 38.

* * * * * * * * * * *

[For official explanation, see Committee Reports, ¶4103.]

[Footnote ¶3357] Matter in *italics* in Sec. 6323(i)(3) added by section 1569(a), '86 TRA.
Effective date (Sec. 1569(b), '86 TRA).—Takes effect on the date of the enactment of this Act.
[Footnote ¶3358] Matter in *italics* in Sec. 6332(c)(1) added by section 1511(c)(9), '86 TRA, which struck out:
(1) "an annual"
Effective date (Sec. 1511(d), 86 TRA).—Applies for purposes of determining interest for periods after 12-31-86.
[Footnote ¶3359] Sec. 6334(a)(10) in *italics* added by section 1565(a), '86 TRA.
Effective date (Sec. 1565(b), '86 TRA).—Applies to amounts payable after 12-31-86.

【¶3360】   CODE SEC. 6335.   SALE OF SEIZED PROPERTY.

*   *   *   *   *   *   *   *   *   *   *   *

(e)   **Manner and Conditions of Sale.—**

[1](1)   *In general.—*

  (A)   Determination relating to minimum price.—Before the sale of property seized by levy, the Secretary shall determine—

    (i)   a minimum price for which such property shall be sold (taking into account the expense of making the levy and conducting the sale), and

    (ii)   whether, on the basis of criteria prescribed by the Secretary, the purchase of such property by the United States at such minimum price would be in the best interest of the United States.

  (B)   Sale to highest bidder at or above minimum price.—If, at the sale, one or more persons offer to purchase such property for not less than the amount of the minimum price, the property shall be declared sold to the highest bidder.

  (C)   Property deemed sold to United States at minimum price in certain cases.—If no person offers the amount of the minimum price for such property at the sale and the Secretary has determined that the purchase of such property by the United States would be in the best interest of the United States, the property shall be declared to be sold to the United States at such minimum price.

  (D)   Release to owner in other cases.—If, at the sale, the property is not declared sold under subparagraph (B) or (C), the property shall be released to the owner thereof and the expense of the levy and sale shall be added to the amount of tax for the collection of which the levy was made. Any property released under this subparagraph shall remain subject to any lien imposed by subchapter C.

  (2)   Additional rules applicable to sale.—The Secretary shall by regulations prescribe the manner and other conditions of the sale of property seized by levy. If one or more alternative methods or conditions are permitted by regulations, the Secretary shall select the alternatives applicable to the sale. Such regulation shall provide:

  (A)   That the sale shall not be conducted in any manner other than—

    (i)   by public auction, or

    (ii)   by public sale under sealed bids.

  (B)   In the case of the seizure of several items of property, whether such items shall be offered separately, in groups, or in the aggregate; and whether such property shall be offered both separately (or in groups) and in the aggregate, and sold under whichever method produces the highest aggregate amount.

  (C)   Whether the announcement of the minimum price determined by the Secretary may be delayed until the receipt of the highest bid.

  (D)   Whether payment in full shall be required at the time of acceptance of a bid, or whether a part of such payment may be deferred for such period (not to exceed 1 month) as may be determined by the Secretary to be appropriate.

  (E)   The extent to which methods (including advertising) in addition to those prescribed in subsection (b) may be used in giving notice of the sale.

  (F)   Under what circumstances the Secretary may adjourn the sale from time to time (but such adjournments shall not be for a period to exceed in all 1 month).

*   *   *   *   *   *   *   *   *   *   *   *

[For official explanation, see Committee Reports, ¶4108.]

【¶3361】   **CODE SEC. 6343.   AUTHORITY TO RELEASE LEVY AND RETURN PROPERTY.**

*   *   *   *   *   *   *   *   *   *   *   *

(c)   **Interest.—**Interest shall be allowed and paid at[1]*the overpayment rate* established

---

【Footnote ¶3360】   Matter in *italics* in Sec. 6335(e)(1) added by section 1570(a), '86 TRA, which struck out:

(1)   "**(1)   Minimum price.—**Before the sale the Secretary shall determine a minimum price for which the property shall be sold, and if no person offers for such property at the sale the amount of the minimum price, the property shall be declared to be purchased at such price for the United States; otherwise the property shall be declared to be sold to the highest bidder. In determining the minimum price, the Secretary shall take into account the expense of making the levy and sale."

Effective date (Sec. 1570(b), '86 TRA).—Applies to (1) property seized after the date of the enactment of this Act, and (2) property seized on or before such date which is held by the United States on such date.

【Footnote ¶3361】   Matter in *italics* in Sec. 6343(c) added by section 1511(c)(10), '86 TRA, which struck out:

(1)   "an annual rate"

Effective date (Sec. 1511(d), '86 TRA).—Applies for purposes of determining interest for periods after 12-31-86.

under section 6621—

    (1) in a case described in subsection (b)(2), from the date the Secretary receives the money to a date (to be determined by the Secretary) preceding the date of return by not more than 30 days, or

    (2) in a case described in subsection (b)(3), from the date of the sale of the property to a date (to be determined by the Secretary) preceding the date of return by not more than 30 days.

[For official explanation, see Committee Reports, ¶4075.]

【¶3362】 **CODE SEC. 6362. QUALIFIED STATE INDIVIDUAL INCOME TAXES.**

* * * * * * * * * * * *

    (f) Additional Requirements.—A tax imposed by a State shall meet the requirements of this subsection only if—

* * * * * * * * * * * *

    (5) Married individuals.—A married individual (within the meaning of *¹section 7703)*—

    (A) who files a joint return for purposes of the taxes imposed by chapter 1 shall not file a separate return for purposes of such State tax, and

    (B) who files a separate return for purposes of the taxes imposed by chapter 1, shall not file a joint return for purposes of such State tax.

* * * * * * * * * * * *

[For official explanation, see Committee Reports, ¶4058.]

【¶3363】 **CODE SEC. 6401. AMOUNTS TREATED AS OVERPAYMENTS.**

* * * * * * * * * * * *

    (b) Excessive Credits.—

    (1) In general.—If the amount allowable as credits under subpart C of part IV of subchapter A of chapter 1 (relating to refundable credits) exceeds the tax imposed by subtitle A (reduced by the credits allowable under subpart A, *B, and D of such part IV)*, the amount of such excess shall be considered an overpayment.

    (2) Special rule for credit under section 33.—For purposes of paragraph (1), any credit allowed under section 33 (relating to withholding of tax on nonresident aliens and on foreign corporations) for any taxable year shall be treated as a credit allowable under subpart C of part IV of subchapter A of chapter 1 only if an election under subsection (g) or (h) of section 6013 is in effect for such taxable year. *The preceding sentence shall not apply to any amount deducted and withheld under section 1446.*

* * * * * * * * * * * *

[For official explanation, see Committee Reports, ¶4052.]

【¶3364】 **CODE SEC. 6404. ABATEMENTS.**

* * * * * * * * * * * *

    (e) Assessments of Interest Attributable to Errors and Delays by Internal Revenue Service.—

    (1) In general.—In the case of any assessment of interest on—

【Footnote ¶3362】 Matter in *italics* in Sec. 6362(f)(5) added by section 1301(j)(8), '86 TRA, which struck out: (1) "section 143"

Effective date (Sec. 1311(a), '86 TRA).—Applies to bonds issued after 8-15-86. For special and transitional rules see ¶2071-2077.

【Footnote ¶3363】 Matter in *italics* in Sec. 6401(b)(2) added by section 1246(b), '86 TRA.

Effective date (Sec. 1246(d), '86 TRA).—Applies to distributions after 12-31-87, (or if earlier, the effective date (which shall not be earlier than 1-1-87) of the initial regulations issued under section 1446 of the '86 Code as added by this section).

【Footnote ¶3364】 Sec. 6404(e) in *italics* added by section 1563(a), '86 TRA.

Effective date (Sec. 1563(b), '86 TRA.—(1) Generally applies to interest accruing with respect to deficiencies or payments for taxable years beginning after 12-31-78.

(2) Statute of limitations.—If refund or credit of any amount resulting from the application of the amendment made by subsection (a) is prevented at any time before the close of the date which is 1 year after the date of the enactment of this Act by the operation of any law or rule of law (including res judicata), refund or credit of such amount (to the extent attributable to the application of the amendment made by subsection (a)) may, nevertheless, be made or allowed if claim therefore is filed before the close of such 1-year period.

    (A) any deficiency attributable in whole or in part to an error or delay by an officer or employee of the Internal Revenue Service (acting in his official capacity) in performing a ministerial act, or

    (B) any payment of any tax described in section 6212(a) to the extent that any delay in such payment is attributable to such an officer or employee being dilatory in performing a ministerial act,

the Secretary may abate the assessment of all or any part of such interest for any period. For purposes of the preceding sentence, an error or delay shall be taken into account only if no significant aspect of such error or delay can be attributed to the taxpayer involved, and after the Internal Revenue Service has contacted the taxpayer in writing with respect to such deficiency or payment.

    (2) Interest abated with respect to erroneous refund check.—The Secretary shall abate the assessment of all interest on any erroneous refund under section 6602 until the date demand for repayment is made, unless—

    (A) the taxpayer (or a related party) has in any way caused such erroneous refund, or

    (B) such erroneous refund exceeds $50,000.

[For official explanation, see Committee Reports, ¶4101.]

〔¶3365〕   CODE SEC. 6405.   REPORTS OF REFUNDS AND CREDITS.

  (a) By Treasury to Joint Committee.—No refund or credit of any income, war profits, excess profits, estate, or gift tax, or any tax imposed with respect to public charities, private foundations, operators' trust funds, pension plans, or real estate investment trusts under chapter 41, 42, 43, or 44, in excess of $200,000 shall be made until after the expiration of 30 days from the date upon which a report giving the name of the person to whom the refund or credit is to be made, the amount of such refund or credit, and a summary of the facts and the decision of the Secretary, is submitted to the Joint Committee on Taxation.[1]

  [2]*(b) Tentative Adjustments.—Any credit or refund allowed or made under section 6411 shall be made without regard to the provisions of subsection (a) of this section. In any such case, if the credit or refund, reduced by any deficiency in such tax thereafter assessed and by deficiencies in any other tax resulting from adjustments reflected in the determination of the credit or refund, is in excess of $200,000, there shall be submitted to such committee a report containing the matter specified in subsection (a) at such time after the making of the credit or refund as the Secretary shall determine the correct amount of the tax.*

  [3]*(c) Refunds Attributable to Certain Disaster Losses.—If any refund or credit of income taxes is attributable to the taxpayer's election under section 165(i) to deduct a disaster loss for the taxable year immediately preceding the taxable year in which the disaster occurred, the Secretary is authorized in his discretion to make the refund or credit, to the extent attributable to such election, without regard to the provisions of subsection (a) of this section. If such refund or credit is made without regard to subsection (a), there shall thereafter be submitted to such Joint Committee a report containing the matter specified in subsection (a) as soon as the Secretary shall determine the correct amount of the tax for the taxable year for which the refund or credit is made.*

  [4]*(d) Qualified State Individual Income Taxes.—For purposes of this section, a refund or credit made under subchapter E of chapter 64 (relating to Federal collection of qualified State individual income taxes) for a taxable year shall be treated as a portion of a refund or credit of the income tax for that taxable year.*

[For official explanation, see Committee Reports, ¶4193.]

〔¶3366〕   CODE SEC. 6411.   TENTATIVE CARRYBACK AND REFUND ADJUSTMENTS.

  (a) Application for Adjustment.—A taxpayer may file an application for a tentative carryback adjustment of the tax for the prior taxable year affected by a net operating loss carryback provided in section 172(b), by a business credit carryback provided in section 39,[1] or by a capital loss carryback provided in section 1212(a)(1), from any taxable year.

〔**Footnote ¶3365**〕 Matter in *italics* in Sec. 6405(b)—(d) added by section 1879(e), '86 TRA, which struck out:

  (1) "**(b) By Joint Committee to Congress.**—A report to Congress shall be made annually by such committee of such refunds and credits, including the names of all persons and corporations to whom amounts are credited or payments are made, together with the amounts credited or paid to each."

  (2) "(c)"

  (3) "(d)"

  (4) "(e)"

〔**Footnote ¶3366**〕 Section 231(d)(3)(H), '86 TRA, struck out from Sec. 6411(a) and (b):

  (1) "by a research credit carryback provided in section 30(g)(2)"

The application shall be verified in the manner prescribed by section 6065 in the case of a return of such taxpayer and shall be filed, on or after the date of filing for the return for the taxable year of the net operating loss, net capital loss, *unused research credit*, or unused business credit from which the carryback results and within a period of 12 months after such taxable year or, with respect to any portion of [2] a business credit carryback attributable to a net operating loss carryback or a net capital loss carryback from a subsequent taxable year, within a period of 12 months from the end of such subsequent taxable year [3] in the manner and form required by regulations prescribed by the Secretary. The application shall set forth in such detail and with such supporting data and explanation as such regulations shall require—

(1) The amount of the net operating loss, net capital loss, [4] or unused business credit;

(2) The amount of the tax previously determined for the prior taxable year affected by such carryback, the tax previously determined being ascertained in accordance with the method prescribed in section 1314(a);

(3) The amount of decrease in such tax, attributable to such carryback, such decrease being determined by applying the carryback in the manner provided by law to the items on the basis of which such tax was determined;

(4) The unpaid amount of such tax, not including any amount required to be shown under paragraph (5);

(5) The amount, with respect to the tax for the taxable year immediately preceding the taxable year from which the carryback is made, as to which an extension of time for payment under section 6164 is in effect; and

(6) Such other information for purposes of carrying out the provisions of this section as may be required by such regulations.

Except for purposes of applying section 6611(f)(3)(B), an application under this subsection shall not constitute a claim for credit or refund.

(b) Allowance of Adjustments.—Within a period of 90 days from the date on which an application for a tentative carryback adjustment is filed under subsection (a), or from the last day of the month in which falls the last date prescribed by law (including any extension of time granted the taxpayer) for filing the return for the taxable year of the net operating loss, net capital loss, [4] or unused business credit from which such carryback results, whichever is the later, the Secretary shall make, to the extent he deems practicable in such period, a limited examination of the application, to discover omissions and errors of computation therein, and shall determine the amount of the decrease in the tax attributable to such carryback upon the basis of the application and the examination, except that the Secretary may disallow, without further action, any application which he finds contains errors of computation which he deems cannot be corrected by him within such 90-day period or material omissions. Such decrease shall be applied against any unpaid amount of the tax decreased (including any amount of such tax as to which an extension of time under section 6164 is in effect) and any remainder shall be credited against any unsatisfied amount of any tax for the taxable year immediately preceding the taxable year of the net operating loss, net capital loss [4] or unused business credit the time for payment of which tax is extended under section 6164. Any remainder shall, within such 90-day period, be either credited against any tax or installment thereof then due from the taxpayer, or refunded to the taxpayer.

* * * * * * * * * * * *

[For official explanation, see Committee Reports, ¶3872; 4161.]

〖¶3367〗 CODE SEC. 6421. GASOLINE USED FOR CERTAIN NONHIGHWAY PURPOSES, [1]USED BY LOCAL TRANSIT SYSTEMS, OR SOLD FOR CERTAIN EXEMPT PURPOSES.

〖Footnote ¶3366 continued〗

(2) "a research credit caryback or"

(3) "or, with respect to any portion of a business credit carryback attributable to a research credit carryback from a subsequent taxable year within a period of 12 months from the end of such subsequent taxable year"

(4) "unused research credit"

Effective date (Sec. 231(g)(1), '86 TRA).—Applies to taxable years beginning after 12-31-85.

Matter in *italics* in the second sentence of Sec. 6411(a) added by section 1847(b)(10), '86 TRA.

Effective date (Sec. 1881, '86 TRA and Sec. 475(a), '84 TRA).—Applies to taxable years beginning after 12-31-83, and to carrybacks from such years.

〖Footnote ¶3367〗 Matter in *italics* in Sec. 6421 heading added by section 1703(c)(2)(D), '86 TRA, which struck out:

(1) "OR BY LOCAL TRANSIT SYSTEMS."

* * * * * * * * * * * *

(c) Exempt Purposes.—If gasoline is sold to any person for any purpose described in paragraph (2), (3), (4), or (5) of section 4221(a), the Secretary shall pay (without interest) to such person an amount equal to the product of the number of gallons of gasoline so sold multiplied by the rate at which tax was imposed on such gasoline by section 4081.

[2]*(d)* **Time for Filing Claims; Period Covered.—**

(1) In general.—Except as provided in paragraph (2), not more than one claim may be filed under subsection (a), [3]not more than one claim may be filed under subsection (b), *and not more than one claim may be filed under subsection (c)* by any person with respect to gasoline used during his taxable year; and no claim shall be allowed under this paragraph with respect to gasoline used during any taxable year unless filed by such person not later than the time prescribed by law for filing a claim for credit or refund of overpayment of income tax for such taxable year. For purposes of this subsection, a person's taxable year shall be his taxable year for purposes of subtitle A.

(2) Exception.—If $1,000 or more is payable under this section to any person with respect to gasoline used during any of the first three quarters of his taxable year, a claim may be filed under this section by such person with respect to gasoline used during such quarter. No claim filed under this paragraph shall be allowed unless filed on or before the last day of the first quarter following the quarter for which the claim is filed.

[4]*(e)* **Definitions.—**For purposes of this section—

* * * * * * * * * * * *

[5]*(f)* **Exempt Sales; Other Payments or Refunds Available.—**[6]

[7]*(1) Gasoline used on farms.—*This section shall not apply in respect of gasoline which was (within the meaning of paragraphs (1), (2), and (3) of section 6420(c)) used on a farm for farming purposes.

[8]*(2)* **Gasoline used in noncommercial aviation.—**This section shall not apply in respect of gasoline which is used as a fuel in an aircraft in noncommercial aviation (as defined in section 404(c)(4)).

[9]*(g)* **Applicable Laws.—**

* * * * * * * * * * * *

[10]*(h)* **Regulations.—**The Secretary may by regulations prescribe the conditions, not inconsistent with the provisions of this section, under which payments may be made under this section.

[11]*(i)* **Effective Date.—**This section shall apply only with respect to gasoline purchased before October 1, 1988.

* * * * * * * * * * * *

[For official explanation, see Committee Reports, ¶4125.]

⌈Footnote ¶3367 continued⌉

Effective date (Sec. 1703(h), '86 TRA).—Applies to gasoline removed (as defined in section 4082 of the '86 Code, as amended by this section) after 12-31-87.

Matter in *italics* in Sec. 6421(c), (d)(1), and (e)—(i) added by section 1703(c)(1)(A), (c)(2)(A) and (B), '86 TRA, which struck out:

(2) "(c)"
(3) "and"
(4) "(d)"
(5) "(e)"
(6) "(1) **Exempt sales.**—No amount shall be payable under this section with respect to any gasoline which the Secretary determines was exempt from the tax imposed by section 4081. The amount which (but for this sentence) would be payable under this section with respect to any gasoline shall be reduced by any other amount which the Secretary determines is payable under this section, or is refundable under any provision of this title, to any person with respect to such gasoline."
(7) "(2)"
(8) "(3)"
(9) "(f)"
(10) "(g)"
(11) "(h)"

Effective date (Sec. 1703(h), '86 TRA).—Applies to gasoline removed (as defined in section 4082 of the '86 Code, as amended by this section) after 12-31-87.

⟦¶3368⟧ CODE SEC. 6425. ADJUSTMENT OF OVERPAYMENT OF ESTIMATED INCOME TAX BY CORPORATION.

* * * * * * * * * * * *

(c) Definitions.—For purposes of this section and section 6655(g) (relating to excessive adjustment)—

(1) The term "income tax liability" means the excess of—

[1]*(A) The sum of—*

(i) the tax imposed by section 11 or 1201(a), or subchapter L of chapter 1, whichever is applicable, plus

(ii) the tax imposed by section 55, over

(B) the credits against tax provided by part IV of subchapter A of chapter 1.

* * * * * * * * * * * *

[For official explanation, see Committee Reports, ¶3931.]

⟦¶3369⟧ CODE SEC. 6427. FUELS NOT USED FOR TAXABLE PURPOSES.

(a) Nontaxable Uses.—Except as provided in [1]*subsection (k)*, if tax has been imposed under section 4041(a) or (c) on the sale of any fuel, and the purchaser uses such fuel other than for the use for which sold, or resells such fuel, the Secretary shall pay (without interest) to him an amount equal to—

(1) the amount of tax imposed on the sale of the fuel to him, reduced by

(2) if he uses the fuel, the amount of tax which would have been imposed under section 4041 on such use if no tax under section 4041 had been imposed on the sale of the fuel.

(b) Intercity, Local, or School Buses.—

(1) **Allowances.**—Except as [2]*otherwise provided in this subsection* and [1]*subsection (k)*, if any fuel on the sale of which tax was imposed by subsection (a) of section 4041 is used in an automobile bus while engaged in—

(A) furnishing (for compensation) passenger land transportation available to the general public, or

(B) the transportation of students and employees of schools (as defined in the last sentence of section 4221(d)(7)(C)),

the Secretary shall pay (without interest) to the ultimate purchaser of such fuel an amount equal to the product of the number of gallons of such fuel so used multiplied by the rate at which tax was imposed on such fuel by subsection (a) of section 4041.

(2) **3-cent reduction in refund in certain cases.**—

(A) In general.—Except as provided in [3]*subparagraph (B) and (C)*, the rate of tax taken into account under paragraph (1) shall not exceed 12 cents.

(B) Exception for school bus transportation.—Subparagraph (A) shall not apply to fuel used in an automobile bus while engaged in the transportation described in paragraph (1)(B).

[4]*(C) Exception for certain intracity transportation.*—Subparagraph (A) shall not

---

⟦**Footnote ¶3368**⟧ Matter in *italics* in Sec. 6425(c)(1)(A) added by section 701(d)(2), '86 TRA, which struck out:

(1) "(A) the tax imposed by section 11 or 1201(a), or subchapter L of chapter 1, whichever is applicable, over"

Effective date (Sec. 701(f), '86 TRA).—Generally applies to taxable years beginning after 12-31-86. For special and transitional rules, see footnote ¶2879.

⟦**Footnote ¶3369**⟧ "*subsection (k)*" in *italics* in Sec. 6427(a), (b)(1), (c), (d), (e)(1), (f)(1), and (g)(1) added by section 1703(e)(2)(A), '86 TRA, which struck out:

(1) "subsection (j)"

Effective date (Sec. 1703(h), '86 TRA).—Applies to gasoline removed (as defined in section 4082 of the '86 Code as amended by this section) after 12-31-87.

"*otherwise provided in this subsection*" in italics in Sec. 6427(b)(1) added by section 1899A(55), '86 TRA, which struck out:

(2) "provided in paragraph (2)"

Matter in *italics* in Sec. 6427(b), except "*subsection (k)*," added by section 1877(b), '86 TRA, which struck out:

(3) "subparagraph (B)"

(4) "(B)"

apply to fuel used in any automobile bus while engaged in furnishing (for compensation) intracity passenger land transportation—

    (i)   which is available to the general public, and

    (ii)   which is scheduled and along regular routes, but only if such bus is a qualified local bus.

    [5]*(D)* Qualified local bus.—For purposes of this paragraph, the term "qualified local bus" means any local bus—

    (i)   which has a seating capacity of at least 20 adults (not including the driver), and

    (ii)   which is under contract (or is receiving more than a nominal subsidy) from any State or local government (as defined in section 4221(d)) to furnish such transportation.

(3) Limitation in case of nonscheduled intercity or local buses.—Paragraph (1)(A) shall not apply in respect of fuel used in any automobile bus while engaged in furnishing transportation which is not scheduled and not along regular routes unless the seating capacity of such bus is at least 20 adults (not including the driver).

(c) Use for Farming Purposes.—Except as provided in [1]*subsection (k)*, if any fuel on the sale of which tax was imposed under section 4041(a) or (c) is used on a farm for farming purposes (within the meaning of section 6420(c)), the Secretary shall pay (without interest) to the purchaser an amount equal to the amount of the tax imposed on the sale of the fuel. For purposes of this subsection, if fuel is used on a farm by any person other than the owner, tenant, or operator of such farm, the rules of the paragraph (4) of section 6420(c) shall be applied (except that "liquid taxable under section 4041" shall be substituted for "gasoline" each place it appears in such paragraph (4)).

(d) Use by Certain Aircraft Museums or in Certain Helicopters.—Except as provided in [1]*subsection (k)*, if—

    (1)   any gasoline on which tax was imposed by section 4081, or

    (2)   any fuel on the sale of which tax was imposed under section 4041, is used by an aircraft museum (as defined in section 4041(h)(2)) in an aircraft or vehicle owned by such museum and used exclusively for purposes set forth in section 4041(h)(2)(C), or is used in a helicopter for a purpose described in section 4041(*l*), the Secretary shall pay (without interest) to the ultimate purchaser of such gasoline or fuel an amount equal to the aggregate amount of the tax imposed on such gasoline or fuel.

(e) Use in Certain Taxicabs.—

    (1) In general.—Except as provided in[1] *subsection (k)*, if—

    (A)   any gasoline on which tax is imposed by section 4081, or

    (B)   any fuel on the sale of which tax is imposed by section 4041,

is used in a qualified taxicab while engaged exclusively in furnishing qualified taxicab services, the Secretary shall pay (without interest) to the ultimate purchaser of such gasoline or fuel an amount equal determined at the rate of 4 cents a gallon.

    *   *   *   *   *   *   *   *   *   *   *

    (3) Termination.—This subsection shall not apply after[6] *September 30, 1988.*

(f) Gasoline Used to Produce Certain Alcohol Fuels.—

    (1) In general.—Except as provided in [1]*subsection (k)*, if any gasoline on which a tax is imposed by section 4081 at the rate of 9 cents a gallon is used by any person in producing a mixture described in section 4081(c) which is sold or used in such person's trade or business, the Secretary shall pay (without interest) to such person an amount equal to the amount determined at the rate of $5\frac{2}{3}$ cents a gallon. The preceding sentence shall not apply with respect to any mixture sold or used after December 31, 1992.

    (2) Coordination with other repayment provisions.—No amount shall be payable under paragraph (1) with respect to any gasoline with respect to which an amount is payable under subsection (d) or (e) of this section or under section 6420 or 6421.

(g) Advance Repayment of Increased Diesel Fuel Tax to Original Purchasers of Diesel-Powered Automobiles and Light Trucks.—

[Footnote ¶3369 continued**]**

(5) "(C)"

Effective date (Sec. 1881, '86 TRA and Sec. 915(b), '84 TRA).—Takes effect on 8-1-84.

Matter in italics in Sec. 6427(e)(3) added by section 422(b), '86 TRA, which struck out:

(6) "September 30, 1985"

(1) In general.—Except as provided in [1]*subsection (k),* the Secretary shall pay (without interest) to the original purchaser of any qualified diesel-powered highway vehicle an amount equal to the diesel fuel differential [7]*amount.*

* * * * * * * * * * *

(h) Gasoline Blend Stocks or Additives Not Used for Producing Gasoline.—Except as provided in subsection (k), if any gasoline blend stock or additive (within the meaning of section 4082(b)) is not used by any person to produce gasoline and such person establishes that the ultimate use of such gasoline blend stock or additive is not to produce gasoline, the Secretary shall pay (without interest) to such person an amount equal to the aggregate amount of the tax imposed on such person with respect to such gasoline blend stock of additive.

[8]*(i)* **Time for Filing Claims; Period Covered.**—

(1) General rule.—Except as provided in paragraph (2), not more than one claim may be filed under subsection (a), (b), (c), (d), (e), **(g) or (h)* by any person with respect to fuel used (or a qualified diesel powered highway vehicle purchased) during his taxable year; and no claim shall be allowed under this paragraph with respect to fuel used (or a qualified diesel powered highway vehicle purchased) during any taxable year unless filed by the purchaser not later than the time prescribed by law for filing a claim for credit or refund of overpayment of income tax for such taxable year. For purposes of this paragraph, a person's taxable year shall be his taxable year for purposes of subtitle A.

(2) Exceptions.—

(A) In general.—If—

(i) $1,000 or more is payable under subsections (a), (b), (d), (e), * **(g), and (h) or*

(ii) $50 or more is payable under subsection (e), [9] [10]

to any person with respect to fuel used (or a qualified diesel powered highway vehicle purchased) during any of the first three quarters of his taxable year, a claim may be filed under this section by the purchaser with respect to fuel used (or a qualified diesel powered highway vehicle purchased) during such quarter.

(B) Special rule.—If the requirements of clause (ii) [11] of subparagraph (A) are met by any person for any quarter but the requirements of subparagraph (A)(i) are not met by such person for such quarter, such person may file a claim under subparagraph (A) for such quarter only with respect to amounts referred to in the clause [12] of subparagraph (A) the requirements of which are met by such person

---

⟦Footnote ¶3369 continued⟧

"*amount*" in italics in Sec. 6427(g)(1) added by section 1899A(56), '86 TRA, which struck out:
(7) "amount"

Matter in italics in Sec. 6427(h) added by section 1703(e)(1)(A) and (B), which struck out:
(8) "(h)"
Effective date (Sec. 1703(h), '86 TRA).—Applies to gasoline removed (as defined in section 4082 of the '86 Code as amended by this section) after 12-31-87.

---

* Section 1703(d)(1)(B)(i), '86 TRA, amended Sec. 6427(i)(1) [former (h)(1)] by striking out "(f)".
* Section 1703(e)(2)(B), '86 TRA, amended Sec. 6427(i)(1) [former (h)(1)] by striking out "or (g)" and inserting in lieu thereof "(g), or (h)".
* * Section 1703(d)(1)(B)(ii)(I), '86 TRA, amended section 6427(i)(2)(A) [former (h)(2)(A)] by inserting "*or*" at the end of subclause (i).
* * Section 1703(e)(2)(C), '86 TRA, amended Sec. 6427(i)(2)(A)(i) [former (h)(2)(A)] by striking out "and (g)" and inserting in lieu thereof "(g), and (h)".
Effective date (Sec. 1703(h), '86 TRA).—Applies to gasoline removed (as defined in section 4082 of the '86 Code as amended by this section) after 12-31-87.

Section 1703(d)(1)(B)(ii)(II), (III) and (iii), '86 TRA, struck out from Sec. 6427(i)(2)(A) [former (h)] and (i)(2)(A) [should read (B) (former (h))]:
(9) "or"
(10) "(iii) $200 or more is payable under subsection (f),"
(11) "or clause (iii)"
(12) "(or clauses)"
Effective date (Sec. 1703(h), '86 TRA).—Applies to gasoline removed (as defined in section 4082 of the '86 Code as amended by this section) after 12-31-87.

Matter in *italics* in Sec. 6427(i)(3) added by section 1703(d)(1) [should read (d)(1)(A)]. '86 TRA.
Effective date (Sec.1703(h), '86 TRA).—Applies to gasoline removed (as defined in section 4082 of the '86 Code as amended by this section) after 12-31-86.

Code §6427(i)(2) ¶3369

for such quarter.

    (C) *Time for filing claim.*—No claim filed under this paragraph shall be allowed unless filed on or before the last day of the first quarter following the quarter for which the claim is filed.

   (3) *Special rule for gasohol credit.*—

    (A) *In general.*—*A claim may be filed under subsection (f) by any person with respect to gasoline used to produce gasohol (as defined in section 4081(c)(1)) for any period*—

      (i) *for which $200 or more is payable under such subsection (f), and*

      (ii) *which is not less than 1 week.*

    (B) *Payment of claim.*—*Notwithstanding subsection (f)(1), if the Secretary has not paid pursuant to a claim filed under this section within 20 days of the date of the filing of such claim, the claim shall be paid with interest from such date determined by using the overpayment rate and method under section 6621.*

[13]*(j)* **Applicable Laws.**—

    *   *   *   *   *   *   *   *   *   *   *   *

[14]*(k)* **Special Rules With Respect to Noncommercial Aviation.**—

    *   *   *   *   *   *   *   *   *   *   *   *

[15]*(l)* **Income Tax Credit in Lieu of Payment.**—

    *   *   *   *   *   *   *   *   *   *   *   *

   (2) **Exception.**—Paragraph (1) shall not apply to a payment of a claim filed under ****subsection (i)(2) or (i)(3)*

   (3) **Allowance of credit against income tax.**—

For allowances of credit against the income tax imposed by subtitle A for fuel used or sold by the purchaser, see section 34.

[16]*(m)* **Regulations.**—The Secretary may by regulations prescribe the conditions, not inconsistent with the provisions of this section, under which payments may be made under this section.

[17]*(n)* **Termination of Subsections (a), (b), (c), (d),**[18]*(g), and (h).*—Subsections (a), (b), (c), (d), [19]*(g), and (h)* shall only apply with respect to fuels purchased before October 1, 1988.

[20]*(o)* **Cross References.**—

    *   *   *   *   *   *   *   *   *   *   *   *

[For official explanation, see Committee Reports, ¶3900; ¶4125; ¶4191.]

[¶3370] CODE SEC. 6501. LIMITATIONS ON ASSESSMENT AND COLLECTION.

[Footnote ¶3369 continued]

Matter in *italics* in Sec. 6427(j)—(1) added by section 1703(e)(1)(A), '86 TRA.

  (13) "(i)"
  (14) "(j)"
  (15) "(k)"

Effective date (Sec. 1703(h), '86 TRA).—Applies to gasoline removed (as defined in section 4082 of the '86 Code as amended by this section) after 12-31-87.

*** Section 1703(d)(1)(B)(iv), '86 TRA, amended section 6427(*l*)(2) [former (k)(2)] by striking out "subsection (h)(2)" and inserting in lieu thereof *"subsection (h)(2) or (h)(3)"*. [Ed. This amendment should relate to Sec. 6427(*l*)(2) as so redesignated. Note that section 6427(h) was redesignated as 6427(i).]

*** Section 1703(e)(2)(E), '86 TRA, amended section 6427(i)(2) by striking out "subsection (h)(2)" and inserting in lieu thereof *"subsection (i)(2)"*. [Ed. This amendment should relate to Sec. 6427(*l*)(2) as so redesignated.]

Effective date (Sec. 1703(h), '86 TRA).—Applies to gasoline removed (as defined in section 4082 of the '86 Code as amended by this section) after 12-31-87.

Matter in italics in Sec. 6427(m)—(o) added by section 1703(e)(1)(A), (2)(B) and (D), '86 TRA, which struck out:

  (16) "(l)"
  (17) "(m)"
  (18) "and (g)"
  (19) "and (g)"
  (20) "(n)"

Effective date (Sec. 1703(h), '86 TRA).—Applies to gasoline removed (as defined in section 4082 of the '86 Code as amended by this section) after 12-31-87.

* * * * * * * * * * *

(c) **Exceptions.—**

* * * * * * * * * * *

(8) **Failure to notify secretary under section 6038B.—**In the case of any tax imposed on any exchange *or distribution* by reason of subsection (a) [1]*(d), or (e)* of section 367, the time for assessment of such tax shall not expire before the date which is 3 years after the date on which the Secretary is notified of such exchange *or distribution* under section 6038B(a).

* * * * * * * * * * *

(k) **Tentative Carryback Adjustment Assessment Period.—**In a case where an amount has been applied, credited, or refunded under section 6411 (relating to tentative carryback and refund adjustments) by reason of a net operating loss carryback, a capital loss carryback, [2]*or a credit carryback (as defined in section 6511(d)(4)(C))* to a prior taxable year, the period described in subsection (a) of this section for assessing a deficiency for such prior taxable year shall be extended to include the period described in subsection (h) or (j), whichever is applicable; except that the amount which may be assessed solely by reason of this subsection shall not exceed the amount so applied, credited, or refunded under section 6411, reduced by any amount which may be assessed solely by reason of subsection (h) or (j), as the case may be.

* * * * * * * * * * *

(n) *Deficiencies Attributable to Election of Certain Credits.—The period for assessing a deficiency attributable to any election under section 40(f) or 51(j) (or any revocation thereof) shall not expire before the date 1 year after the date on which the Secretary is notified of such election (or revocation).*

[3](o) **Cross References.—**

* * * * * * * * * * *

[For official explanation, see Committee Reports, ¶4149; 4161]

[¶3371]   CODE SEC. 6503.   SUSPENSION OF RUNNING OF PERIOD OF LIMITATION.

(a) **Issuance of Statutory Notice of Deficiency.—**

(1) **General rule.—**The running of the period of limitations provided in section 6501 or 6502 (*or section 6229, but only with respect to a deficiency described in section 6230(a)(2)(A)*) on the making of assessments or the collection by levy or a proceeding in court, in respect of any deficiency as defined in section 6211 (relating to income, estate, gift and certain excise taxes), shall (after the mailing of a notice under section 6212(a)) be suspended for the period during which the Secretary is prohibited from making the assessment or from collecting by levy or a proceeding in court (and in any

<hr>

[Footnote ¶3370]   Matter in *italics* in Sec. 6501(c)(8) added by section 1810(g)(3), '86 TRA, which struck out:
(1) "or (d)"
Effective date (Sec. 1881, '86 TRA and Sec. 131(g), '84 TRA).—(1) Generally applies to transfers or exchanges after 12-31-84, in taxable years ending after such date.
(2) Special rule for certain transfers of intangibles.—
(A) In general.—If, after 6-6-84, and before 1-1-85, a United States person transfers any intangible property (within the meaning of Sec. 936(h)(3)(B) of the '54 Code) to a foreign corporation or in a transfer described in section 1491, such transfer shall be treated for purposes of sections 367(a), 1492(2), and 1494(b) as pursuant to a plan having as 1 of its principal purposes the avoidance of Federal income tax.
(B) Waiver.—Subject to such terms and conditions as the Secretary of the Treasury or his delegate may prescribe, the Secretary may waive the application of subparagraph (A) with respect to any transfer.
(3) Ruling request before March 1, 1984.—The amendments made by this section (and the provisions of paragraph (2) of this subsection) shall not apply to any transfer or exchange of property described in a request filed before 3-1-84, under section 367(a), 1492(2), or 1494(b) of the '54 Code (as in effect before such amendments).

<hr>

Matter in *italics* in Sec. 6501(k), (n) and (o) added by section 1847(b)(13) and (14), '86 TRA, which struck out:
(2) "an investment credit carryback, a work incentive program carryback, or a new employee credit carryback"
(3) "(n)"
Effective date (Sec. 1881, '86 TRA and Sec. 475(a), '84 TRA).—Applies to taxable years beginning after 12-31-83, and to carrybacks from such years.
[Footnote ¶3371]   Matter in *italics* in Sec. 6503(a)(1) added by section 1875(d)(2)(B)(ii), '86 TRA.
Effective date (Sec. 1875(d)(2)(C), '86 TRA and section 407(a)(1), (3), '82 TEFRA).—Generally applies to partnership taxable years beginning after 9-3-82. For special rule, see footnote ¶3355 above.

<hr>

event, if a proceeding in respect of the deficiency is placed on the docket of the Tax Court, until the decision of the Tax Court becomes final), and for 60 days thereafter.

(2) Corporation joining in consolidated income tax return.—If a notice under section 6212(a) in respect of a deficiency in tax imposed by subtitle A for any taxable year is mailed to a corporation, the suspension of the running of the period of limitations provided in paragraph (1) of this subsection shall apply in the case of corporations with which such corporation made a consolidated income tax return for such taxable year.

* * * * * * * * * * *

(j) Extension of Time for Payment of Undistributed PFIC Earnings Tax Liability.—The running of any period of limitations for collection of any amount of undistributed PFIC earnings tax liability (as defined in section 1294(b)) shall be suspended for the period of any extension of time under section 1294 for payment of such amount.

* * * * * * * * * * *

[1](k) **Cross Reference—**

* * * * * * * * * * *

[For official explanation, see Committee Reports, ¶¶4045; 4189.]

[¶3372] CODE SEC. 6504. CROSS REFERENCES.

For limitation period in case of—

* * * * * * * * * * *

[1]*(2) Change of treatment with respect to itemized deductions where taxpayer and his spouse make separate returns, see section 63(e)(3).*

* * * * * * * * * * *

[¶3373] CODE SEC. 6511. LIMITATIONS ON CREDIT OR REFUND.

* * * * * * * * * * *

(d) Special Rules Applicable to Income Taxes.—

* * * * * * * * * * *

(2) Special period of limitation with respect to net operating loss or capital loss carrybacks.—

* * * * * * * * * * *

[1]*(B) Applicable rules.—*
(i) In general.—If the allowance of a credit or refund of an overpayment of tax attributable to a net operating loss carryback or a capital loss carryback is otherwise prevented by the operation of any law or rule of law other than section

---

[Footnote ¶3371 continued]

Matter in *italics* in Sec. 6503(j) and (k) added by section 1235(d), '86 TRA, which struck out:
(1) "(j)"
Effective date (Sec. 1235(h), '86 TRA).—Applies to taxable years of foreign corporations beginning after 12-31-86.
[Footnote ¶3372] Matter in *italics* in Sec. 6504(2) added by section 104(b)(18), '86 TRA, which struck out:
(1) "(2) change of treatment with respect to itemized deductions and zero bracket amount where taxpayer and his spouse make separate returns, see section 63(g)(5)."
Effective date (Sec. 151(a), '86 TRA).—Applies to taxable years beginning after 12-31-86.
[Footnote ¶3373] Matter in *italics* in Sec. 6511(d)(2)(B) added by section 141(b)(3), '86 TRA, which struck out:
(1) "(B) Applicable rules.
(i) If the allowance of a credit or refund of an overpayment of tax attributable to a net operating loss carryback or a capital loss carryback is otherwise prevented by the operation of any law or rule of law other than section 7122, relating to compromises, such credit or refund may be allowed or made, if claim therefor is filed within the period provided in subparagraph (A) of this paragraph. If the allowance of an application, credit, or refund of a decrease in tax determined under section 6411(b) is otherwise prevented by the operation of any law or rule of law other than section 7122, such application, credit, or refund may be allowed or made if application for a tentative carryback adjustment is made within the period provided in section 6411(a). In the case of any such claim for credit or refund or any such application for a tentative carryback adjustment, the determination by any court, including the Tax Court, in any proceeding in which the decision of the court has become final, shall be conclusive except with respect to the net operating loss deduction, and the effect of such deduction, or with respect to the determination of a short-term capital loss, and the effect of such short-term capital loss, to the extent that such deduction or short-term capital loss is affected by a carryback which was not an issue in such proceeding.
(ii) A claim for credit or refund for a computation year (as defined in section 1302(c)(1)) shall be determined to relate to an overpayment attributable to a net operating loss carryback or a capital loss carryback, as the case may be, when such carryback relates to any base period year (as defined in section 1302(c)(3))"
Effective date (Sec. 151(a), '86 TRA).—Applies to taxable years beginning after 12-31-86.

7122 *(relating to compromises), such credit or refund may be allowed or made, if claim therefore is filed within the period provided in subparagraph (A) of this paragraph.*

(ii) Tentative carryback adjustments.—If the allowance of an application, credit, or refund of a decrease in tax determined under section 6411(b) is otherwise prevented by the operation of any law or rule of law other than section 7122, such application, credit, or refund may be allowed or made if application for a tentative carryback adjustment is made within the period provided in section 6411(a).

(iii) Determinations by courts to be conclusive.—In the case of any such claim for credit or refund or any such application for a tentative carryback adjustment, the determination by any court, including the Tax Court, in any proceeding in which the decision of the court has become final, shall be conclusive except with respect to—

(I)   the net operating loss deduction and the effect of such deduction, and

(II)   the determination of a short-term capital loss and the effect of such short-term capital loss, to the extent that such deduction or short-term capital loss is affected by a carryback which was not an issue in such proceeding.

* * * * * * * * * * *

(4)   Special period of limitation with respect to certain credit carrybacks.—

* * * * * * * * * * *

(C)   Credit carryback defined.—For purposes of this paragraph, the term "credit carryback" means any business carryback under section 39 [2].

* * * * * * * * * * *

(h)   Special Rules for Windfall Profit Taxes.—

(1)   Oil subject to withholding.—In the case of any oil to which section 4995(a) applies and with respect to which no return is required, the return referred to in subsection (a) shall be the return (of the person liable for the tax imposed by section 4986) of the taxes imposed by subtitle A for the taxable year in which the removal year (as defined in [3]*section 6501(m)(1)(B)* ends.

(2)   Special rule for DOE reclassification.—In the case of any tax imposed by chapter 45, if a Department of Energy change (as defined in [4]*section 6501(m)(2)(B)* becomes final, the period for filing a claim for credit or refund for any overpayment attributable to such change shall not expire before the date which is 1 year after the date on which such change becomes final.

* * * * * * * * * * *

[For official explanation, see Committee Reports, ¶3865; 3872; 4161.]

[¶3374]   CODE SEC. 6601.   INTEREST ON UNDERPAYMENT, NONPAYMENT, OR EXTENSIONS OF TIME FOR PAYMENT OF TAX.

(a)   General Rule.—If any amount of tax imposed by this title (whether required to be shown on a return, or to be paid by stamp or by some other method) is not paid on or before the last date prescribed for payment, interest on such amount at [1]*the underpayment rate* established under section 6621 shall be paid for the period from such last date to the date paid.

(b)   Last Date Prescribed for Payment.—For purposes of this section, the last date prescribed for payment of the tax shall be determined under chapter 62 with the application of the following rules:

[Footnote ¶3373 continued]

Section 231(d)(3)(I), '86 TRA, struck out from Sec. 6511(d)(6)(C) [should read 6511(d)(4)(C)]:
(2)   "and any research credit carryback under section 30(g)(2)"
Effective date (Sec. 231(g), '86 TRA).—Applies to taxable years beginning after 12-31-85.

Matter in *italics* in Sec. 6511(h)(1) and (2) added by section 1847(b)(15), '86 TRA, which struck out:
(3)   "section 6501(q)(1)(B)"
(4)   "section 6501(q)(2)(B)"
Effective date (Sec. 1881, '86 TRA and Sec. 475(a), '84 TRA).—Applies to taxable years beginning after 12-31-83, and to carrybacks from such years.
[Footnote ¶3374]   Matter in *italics* in Sec. 6601(a) added by section 1511(c)(11), '86 TRA, which struck out:
(1)   "an annual rate"
Effective date (Sec. 1511(d), '86 TRA).—Applies for purposes of determining interest for periods after 12-31-86.

---

(1) Extensions of time disregarded.—The last date prescribed for payment shall be determined without regard to any extension of time for payment.

(2) Installment payments.—In the case of an election under section [2]6156(a) or 6158(a) to pay the tax in installments—

(A) The date prescribed for payment of each installment of the tax shown on the return shall be determined under section [3]6156(b) or 6158(a) as the case may be, and

(B) The last date prescribed for payment of the first installment shall be deemed the last date prescribed for payment of any portion of the tax not shown on the return.

For purposes of subparagraph (A), section 6158(a) shall be treated as providing that the date prescribed for payment of each installment shall not be later than the date prescribed for payment of the 1985 installment.

(3) Jeopardy.—The last date prescribed for payment shall be determined without regard to any notice and demand for payment issued, by reason of jeopardy (as provided in chapter 70), prior to the last date otherwise prescribed for such payment.

"(4) Accumulated earnings tax.—In the case of the tax imposed by section 531 for any taxable year, the last date prescribed for payment shall be deemed to be the due date (without regard to extensions) for the return of tax imposed by subtitle A for such taxable year.

[4]**(5) Last date for payment not otherwise prescribed.—**

* * * * * * * * * * * *

(c) Suspension of Interest in Certain Income, Estate, Gift, and Certain Excise Tax Cases.—In the case of a deficiency as defined in section 6211 (relating to income, estate, gift, and certain excise taxes), if a waiver of restrictions under section 6213(d) on the assessment of such deficiency has been filed and if notice and demand by the Secretary for payment of such deficiency is not made within 30 days after the filing of such waiver, interest shall not be imposed on such deficiency for the period beginning immediately after such 30th day and ending with the date of notice and demand *and interest shall not be imposed during such period on any interest with respect to such deficiency for any prior period.*

* * * * * * * * * * * *

[For official explanation, see Committee Reports, ¶4063; 4075; 4076; 4102.]

【¶3375】 CODE SEC. 6602. INTEREST ON ERRONEOUS REFUND RECOVERABLE BY SUIT.

Any portion of an internal revenue tax (or any interest, assessable penalty, additional amount, or addition to tax) which has been erroneously refunded, and which is recoverable by suit pursuant to section 7405, shall bear interest at [1]the underpayment rate established under section 6621 from the date of the payment of the refund.

[For official explanation, see Committee Reports, ¶4075.]

【Footnote ¶3374 continued】

Matter in *italics* in Sec. 6601(2) [should read (b)(2)] and (2)(A) [should read (b)(2)(A)] added by section 1404(c)(3), '86 TRA, which struck out:
(2) "6152(a), 6156(a),"
(3) "6152(b), 6156(b),"
Effective date (Sec. 1404(d), '86 TRA).—Applies to taxable years beginning after 12-31-86.

Matter in *italics* in Sec. 6601(b)(4) and (5) added by section 1512(a), '86 TRA, which struck out:
(4) "(4)".
Effective date (Sec. 1512(a), '86 TRA).—Applies to returns the due date for which (determined without regard to extensions) is after 12-31-85.

Matter in *italics* in Sec. 6601(c) added by section 1564(a), '86 TRA.
Effective date (Sec. 1564(b), '86 TRA).—(1) Applies to interest accruing after 12-31-82.
(2) Statute of limitations.—If refund or credit of any amount resulting from the application of the amendment made by subsection (a) is prevented at any time before the close of the date which is 1 year after the date of the enactment of this Act by the operation of any law or rule of law (including res judicata), refund or credit of such amount (to the extent attributable to the application of the amendment made by subsection (a)) may, nevertheless, be made or allowed if claim therefore is filed before the close of such 1-year period.
【Footnote ¶3375】 Matter in *italics* in Sec. 6602 added by section 1511(c)(12), '86 TRA, which struck out:
(1) "an annual rate"
Effective date (Sec. 1511(d), '86 TRA).—Applies for purposes of determining interest for periods after 12-31-86.

⟦¶3376⟧ CODE SEC. 6611. INTEREST ON OVERPAYMENTS.

(a) **Rate.**—Interest shall be allowed and paid upon any overpayment in respect of any internal revenue tax at [1]*the overpayment rate established* under section 6621.

* * * * * * * * * * *

[For official explanation, see Committee Reports, ¶4075.]

⟦¶3377⟧ CODE SEC. 6621. DETERMINATION OF RATE OF INTEREST.

[1](*a*) *General Rule.*—

   (*1*) *Overpayment rate.*—*The overpayment rate established under this section shall be the sum of*—
     (*A*) *the short-term Federal rate determined under subsection (b), plus*
     (*B*) *2 percentage points.*

   (*2*) *Underpayment rate.*—*The underpayment rate established under this section shall be the sum of*—
     (*A*) *the short-term Federal rate determined under subsection (b), plus*
     (*B*) *3 percentage points.*

(*b*) *Short-Term Federal Rate.*—*For purposes of this section*—

   (*1*) *General rule.*—*The Secretary shall determine the short-term Federal rate for the first month in each calendar quarter.*

   (*2*) *Period during which rate applies.*—
     (*A*) *In general.*—*Except as provided in subparagraph (B), the Federal short-term rate determined under paragraph (1) for any month shall apply during the first calendar quarter beginning after such month.*
     (*B*) *Special rule for individual estimated tax.*—*In determining the addition to tax under section 6654 for failure to pay estimated tax for any taxable year, the Federal short-term rate which applies during the 3rd month following such taxable year shall also apply during the first 15 days of the 4th month following such taxable year.*

   (*3*) *Federal short-term rate.*—*The Federal short-term rate for any month shall be the Federal short-term rate determined during such month by the Secretary in accordance with section 1274(d). Any such rate shall be rounded to the nearest full percent (or, if a multiple of ½ of 1 percent, such rate shall be increased to the next highest full percent).*

[2](*c*) **Interest on substantial underpayments attributable to tax motivated transactions.**—

   (1) **In general.**—In the case of interest payable under section 6601 with respect to any substantial underpayment attributable to tax motivated transactions, the [3] rate of interest established under this section shall be 120 percent of [4]*the underpayment rate established under this section.*

   (2) **Substantial underpayment attributable to tax motivated transactions.**—For purposes of this subsection, the term "substantial underpayment attributable to tax

---

⟦Footnote ¶3376⟧   Matter in *italics* in Sec. 6611(a) added by section 1511(c)(13), '86 TRA, which struck out:
(1) "an annual rate established"
Effective date (Sec. 1511(d), '86 TRA).—Applies for purposes of determining interest for periods after 12-31-86.
⟦Footnote ¶3377⟧   Matter in *italics* in Sec. 6621(a)—(c) added by section 1511(a) and (c)(1) '86 TRA, which struck out:
(1) **"(a) In General.**—The annual rate established under this section shall be such adjusted rate as is established by the Secretary under subsection (b).
(b) **Adjustment of Interest Rate.**—
(1) **Establishment of adjusted rate.**—If the adjusted prime rate charged by banks (rounded to the nearest full percent)—
(A) during the 6-month period ending on September 30 of any calendar year, or
(B) during the 6-month period ending on March 31 of any calendar year, differs from the interest rate in effect under this section on either such date, respectively, then the Secretary shall establish, within 15 days after the close of the applicable 6-month period, an adjusted rate of interest equal to such adjusted prime rate.
(2) **Effective date of adjustment.**—Any adjusted rate of interest established under paragraph (1) shall become effective—
(A) on January 1 of the succeeding year in the case of an adjustment attributable to paragraph (1)(A), and
(B) on July 1 of the same year in the case of an adjustment attributable to paragraph (1)(B).
(c) **Definition of Prime Rate.**—For purposes of subsection (b), the term 'adjusted prime rate charged by banks' means the average predominant prime rate quoted by commercial banks to large business, as determined by the Board of Governors of the Federal Reserve System."
(2) **"(d)"**
(3) "annual"
(4) "the adjusted rate established under subsection (b)"
Effective date (Sec. 1511(d), '86 TRA).—Applies for purposes of determining interest for periods after 12-31-86.

motivated transactions" means any underpayment of taxes imposed by subtitle A for any taxable year which is attributable to 1 or more tax motivated transactions if the amount of the underpayment for such year so attributable exceeds $1,000.

(3) Tax motivated transactions.—

(A) In general.—For purposes of this subsection, the term "tax motivated transaction" means—

(i) any valuation overstatement (within the meaning of section 6659(c)),

(ii) any loss disallowed by reason of section 465(a) and any credit disallowed under section 46(c)(8),

(iii) any straddle (as defined in section 1092(c) without regard to subsections (d) and (e) of section 1092), [5]

(iv) any use of an accounting method specified in regulations prescribed by the Secretary as a use which may result in a substantial distortion of income for any period [6], *and*

(v) any sham or fraudulent transaction.

* * * * * * * * * * * *

[For official explanation, see Committee Reports, ¶4075; 4086.]

〖¶3378〗 CODE SEC. 6651. FAILURE TO FILE TAX RETURN OR TO PAY TAX.

(a) **Addition to the Tax.**—In case of failure—

(1) to file any return under authority of subchapter A of chater 61 (other than part III thereof), subchapter A of chapter 51 (relating to distilled spirits, wines, and beer), or of subchapter A of chapter 52 (relating to tobacco, cigars, cigarettes, and cigarette papers and tubes), or of subchapter A of chapter 53 (relating to machine guns and certain other firearms), on the date prescribed therefor (determined with regard to any extension of time for filing), unless it is shown that such failure is due to reasonable cause and not due to willful neglect, there shall be added to the amount required to be shown as tax on such return 5 percent of the amount of such tax if the failure is for not more than 1 month, with an additional 5 percent for each additional month or fraction thereof during which such failure continues, not exceeding 25 percent in the aggregate;

(2) to pay the amount shown as tax on any return specified in paragraph (1) on or before the date prescribed for payment of such tax (determined with regard to any extension of time for payment), unless it is shown that such failure is due to reasonable cause and not due to willful neglect, there shall be added to the amount shown as tax on such return 0.5 percent of the amount of such tax if the failure is for not more than 1 month, with an additional 0.5 percent for each additional month or fraction thereof, during which such failure continues, not exceeding 25 percent in the aggregate; or

(3) to pay any amount in respect of any tax required to be shown on a return specified in paragraph (1) which is not so shown (including an assessment made pursuant to section 6213(b)) within 10 days of the date of the notice and demand therefor, unless it is shown that such failure is due to reasonable cause and not due to willful neglect, there shall be added to the amount of tax stated in such notice and demand 0.5 percent of the amount of such tax if the failure is for not more than 1 month, with an additional 0.5 percent for each additional month or fraction thereof during which such failure continues, not exceeding 25 percent in the aggregate.

In the case of a failure to file a return of tax imposed by chapter 1 within 60 days of the date prescribed for filing of such return (determined with regard to any extensions of time for filing), unless it is shown that such failure is due to reasonable cause and not due to willful neglect, the addition to tax under paragraph (1) shall not be less than the lesser of $100 or 100 percent of the amount required to be shown as tax on such return.

* * * * * * * * * * * *

(c) **Limitations and Special Rule.—**

(1) **Additions under more than one paragraph.—**[1]*With respect to any return, the*

〖Footnote ¶3377 continued〗

Matter in *italics* in Sec. 6621(c)(3)(A)(iii)—(v) added by section 1535(a), '86 TRA, which struck out:

(5) "and"

(6) "."

Effective date (Sec. 1535(b), '86 TRA).—Applies to interest accruing after 12-31-84; except that such amendment shall not apply in the case of any underpayment with respect to which there was a final court decision before the date of the enactment of this Act.

〖Footnote ¶3378〗 Matter in *italics* in Sec. 6651(c)(1), (d) and (e) added by section 1502(a) and (b), '86 TRA, which struck out:

amount of the addition under paragraph (1) of subsection (a) shall be reduced by the amount of the addition under paragraph (2) of subsection (a) for any month (or fraction thereof) to which an addition to tax applies under both paragraphs (1) and (2). In any case described in the last sentence of subsection (a), the amount of the addition under paragraph (1) of subsection (a) shall not be reduced under the preceding sentence below the amount provided in such last sentence.

* * * * * * * * * * *

(d) Increase in Penalty for Failure to Pay Tax in Certain Cases.—

(1) In general.—In the case of each month (or fraction thereof) beginning after the day described in paragraph (2) of this subsection, paragraphs (2) and (3) of subsection (a) shall be applied by substituting "1 percent" for "0.5 percent" each place it appears.

(2) Description.—For purposes of paragraph (1), the day described in this paragraph is the earlier of—

(A) the day 10 days after the date on which notice is given under section 6331(d), or

(B) the day on which notice and demand for immediate payment is given under the last sentence of section 6331(a).

²(e) **Exception for Estimated Tax.**—This section shall not apply to any failure to pay any estimated tax required to be paid by section 6154 or 6654.

[For official explanation, see Committee Reports, ¶4072.]

[¶3379] CODE SEC. 6652. FAILURE TO FILE CERTAIN INFORMATION RETURNS, REGISTRATION STATEMENTS, ETC.[1]

[Footnote ¶3378 continued]

(1) "(A) With respect to any return, the amount of the addition under paragraph (1) of subsection (a) shall be reduced by the amount of the addition under paragraph (2) of subsection (a) for any month to which an addition to tax applies under both paragraphs (1) and (2). In any case described in the last sentence of subsection (a), the amount of the addition under paragraph (1) of subsection (a) shall not be reduced under the preceding sentence below the amount provided in such last sentence.

(B) With respect to any return, the maximum amount of the addition permitted under paragraph (3) of subsection (a) shall be reduced by the amount of the addition under paragraph (1) of subsection (a) (determined without regard to the last sentence of such subsection) which is attributable to the tax for which the notice and demand is made and which is not paid within 10 days of notice and demand."

(2) "(d)"

Effective date (Sec. 1502(c), '86 TRA). Applies—

(A) to failures to pay which begin after 12-31-86, and

(B) to failures to pay which begin on or before 12-31-86, if after 12-31-86—

(i) notice (or renotice) under section 6331(d) of the '54 Code is given with respect to such failure, or

(ii) notice and demand for immediate payment of the underpayment is made under the last sentence of section 6331(a) of such Code.

In the case of a filure to pay described in subparagraph (B), paragraph (2) of section 6651(d) of such Code (as added by subsection (a)) shall be applied by taking into account the first notice (or renotice) after 12-31-86.

[Footnote ¶3379] ▲ Matter in *italics* in Sec. 6652(a), preceded by a triangle, added by section 1501(d)(1)(A), '86 TRA, which struck out:

(1) (a) **Returns Relating to Information at Source, Payments of Dividends, Etc., and Certain Transfers of Stock.—**

(1) **In General.**—In the case of each failure—

(A) to file a statement of the amount of payments to another person required by—

(i) section 6041(a) or (b) (relating to certain information at source),

(ii) section 6050A(a) (relating to reporting requirements of certain fishing boat operators), or

(iii) section 6051(d) (relating to information returns with respect to income tax withheld),

(B) to make a return required by—

(i) subsection (a) or (b) of section 6041A (relating to returns of direct sellers),

(ii) section 6045 (relating to returns of brokers),

(iii) section 6052(a) (relating to reporting payment of wages in the form of group term life insurance),

(iv) section 6053(c)(1) (relating to reporting with respect to certain tips),

(v) section 6050H(a) (relating to mortgage interest received in trade or business from individuals,

(vi) section 6050I(a) (relating to cash received in trade or business),

(vii) section 6050J(a) (relating to foreclosures and abandonments of security),

(viii) section 6050K (relating to exchanges of certain partnership interests), or

(ix) section 6050L (relating to returns relating to certain dispositions of donated property).

(3) [Should probably read (C)] to make a return required by section 4997(a) (relating to information with respect to windfall profit tax on crude oil),

on the date prescribed therefor (determining with regard to any extension of time for filing), unless it is shown that such failure is due to reasonable cause and not to willful neglect, there shall be paid (upon notice and demand by the Secretary and in the same manner as tax), by the person failing to file a statement referred to in subparagraph

≫**P-H CAUTION→**   There are two versions of Sec. 6652(a). Sec. 6652(a), effective for returns after 12-31-86, follows. For Sec. 6652(a)(3)(A), effective for returns before 1-1-87, see below.

▲ [2](a) [3]*Returns with Respect to Certain Payments Aggregating Less Than $10.*—In the case of each failure to file a statement of a payment to another person required under the authority of

(1) section 6042(a)(2) (relating to payments of dividends aggregating less than $10), or

(2) section 6044(a)(2) (relating to payments of patronage dividends aggregating less than $10),

on the date prescribed therefor (determined with regard to any extension of time for filing), unless it is shown that such failure is due to reasonable cause and not to willful neglect, there shall be paid (upon notice and demand by the Secretary and in the same manner as tax) by the person failing to so file the statement, $1 for each such statement not so filed, but the total amount imposed on the delinquent person for all such failures during the calendar year shall not exceed $1,000.

≫**P-H CAUTION→**   There are two versions of Sec. 6652(a)(3)(A). Sec. 6652(a)(3)(A), effective for payments received before 1-1-87, follows. For Sec. 6652(a)(3)(A), effective for payments received after 12-31-86, see above.

▲▲ **(3)   Penalty in case of intentional disregard.**—If 1 or more failures to which paragraph (1) or (2) applies are due to intentional disregard of the filing requirement, then with respect to such failures—

(A) the penalty imposed under paragraph (1) and (2) shall not be less than an amount equal to—

(i) in the case of a return not described in clauses (ii) and (iii), 10 percent of the aggregate amount of the items required to be reported.

[Footnote ¶3379 continued]

(A) or failing to make a return referred to in subparagraph (B) or (3), [sic] $50 for each such failure, but the total amount imposed on the delinquent person for all such failures during any calendar year shall not exceed $50,000.

(2)   **Failure to file returns on interest, dividends, and patronage dividends.**—

(A)   In general.—In the case of each failure to file a statement of the amount of payments to another person required by—

(i)   section 6042(a)(1) (relating to payments of dividends),

(ii)   section 6044(a)(1) (relating to payments of patronage dividends), or

(iii)   section 6049(a) (relating to payments of interest),

on the date prescribed therefor (determined with regard to any extension of time for filing), there shall be paid by the person failing to file such statement a penalty of $50 for each such failure unless it is shown that such person exercised due diligence in attempting to satisfy the requirement with respect to such statement.

(B)   Self-assessment.—Any penalty imposed under subparagraph (A) on any person—

(i)   for purposes of this subtitle, shall be treated as an excise tax imposed by subtitle D, and

(ii)   shall be due and payable on April 1 of the calendar year following the calendar year for which such statement is required.

(C)   Deficiency procedures not to apply.—Subchapter B of chapter 63 (relating to deficiency procedures for income, estate, gift and certain excise taxes) shall not apply in respect of the assessment or collection of any penalty imposed by subparagraph (A).

(3)   **Penalty in case of intentional disregard.**—If 1 or more failures to which paragraph (1) or (2) applies are due to intentional disregard of the filing requirement, then with respect to such failures—

(A)   the penalty imposed under paragraph (1) or (2) shall not be less than an amount equal to—

(i)   in the case of a return not described in clauses (ii) and (iii), 10 percent of the aggregate amount of the items required to be reported,

(ii)   in the case of a return required to be filed by section 6045, (other than by subsection (d) of such section) 5 percent of the gross proceeds required to be reported, and

(iii)   in the case of a return required to be filed by section 6041A(b), 6050H, 6050I or 6050J, $100 for each such failure, and

(B)   the $50,000 limitation under paragraph (1) shall not apply."

(2)   "(b)"

(3)   **"Other Returns"**

Effective date (Sec. 1501(e), '86 TRA).—Applies to returns the due date for which (determined without regard to extensions) is after 12-31-86.

▲▲ Matter in *italics* in Sec. 6652(a)(3)(A), preceded by two triangles, added by section 1811(c)(2), '86 TRA.

Effective date (Sec. 1881, '86 TRA and Sec. 150(b), '84 TRA).—Applies to payments received after 12-31-84.

(ii) in the case of a return required to be filed by section 6045, (*other than by subsection (d) of such section*), 5 percent of the gross proceeds required to be reported, and

(iii) in the case of a return required to be filed by section 6041A(b), 6050H, 6050I or 6050J, $100 for each such failure, and

[4](*b*) **Failure to Report Tips.—**

* * * * * * * * * * *

[5](*c*) **Returns by Exempt Organizations and by Certain Trusts.—**

* * * * * * * * * * *

[6](*d*) **Annual Registration and Other Notification by Pension Plan.—**

* * * * * * * * * * *

[7](*e*) **Information Required in Connection with Certain Plans of Deferred Compensation; Etc.—**

* * * * * * * * * * *

[8](*f*) **Returns** [9] **Required Under Section 6039C.—**

(1) **In General.—**[10]*In the case of each failure to make a return required by section 6039C which contains the information required by such section on the date prescribed therefor (determined with regard to any extension of time for filing), unless it is shown that such failure is due to reasonable cause and not to willful neglect, the amount determined under paragraph (2) shall be paid (upon notice and demand by the Secretary and in the same manner as tax) by the person failing to make such return.*

(2) **Amount of penalty.—**For purposes of paragraph (1), the amount determined under this paragraph with respect to any failure shall be $25 for each day during which such failure continues.

(3) [11]*Limitation. The amount determined under paragraph (2) with respect to any person for failing to meet the requirements of section 6039C for any calendar year shall not exceed the lesser of—*

(A) *$25,000, or*

(B) *5 percent of the aggregate of the fair market value of the United States real property interests owned by such person at any time during such year.*

【Footnote ¶3379 continued】

Matter in *italics* in Sec. 6652(b)—(f) added by section 1501(d)(1)(A)(i), '86 TRA, which struck out:

(4) "(c)"
(5) "(d)"
(6) "(e)"
(7) "(f)"
(8) "(g)"

Effective date (Sec. 1501(e), '86 TRA.—Applies to returns the due date for which (determined without regard to extensions) is after 12-31-86.

Matter in *italics* in Sec. 6652(f) [former "(g)"], except "(f)" added by section 1810(f)(9), '86 TRA, which struck out:

(9) ", ETC.,"
(10) "In the case of each failure—
(A) to make a return required by section 6039C which contains the information required by such section, or
(B) to furnish a statement required by section 6039C(b)(3),
on the date prescribed therefor (determined with regard to any extension of time for filing), unless it is shown that such failure is due to reasonable cause and not to willful neglect, the amount determined under paragraph (2) shall be paid (upon notice and demand by the Secretary and in the same manner as tax) by the person failing to make such return or furnish such statement."
(11) "Limitations.—
(A) For failure to meet requirements of subsection (A) or (B) of section 6039C.—The amount determined under paragraph (2) with respect to any person for failing to meet the requirements of subsection (a) or (b) of section 6039C for any calendar year shall not exceed $25,000 with respect to each such subsection.
(B) For failure to meet requirements of section 6039C(c).—The amount determined under paragraph (2) with respect to any person for failing to meet the requirements of subsection (c) of section 6039C for any calendar year shall not exceed the lesser of $25,000 or 5 percent of the aggregate of the fair market value of the United States real property interests owned by such person at any time during such year. For purposes of the preceding sentence, fair market value shall be determined as of the end of the calendar year (or, in the case of any property disposed of during the calendar year, as of the date of such disposition)."

Effective date (Sec. 1881, '86 TRA and Sec. 129(c)(2), '84 TRA).—Applies to calendar year 1980 and subsequent calendar years.

For purposes of the preceding sentence, fair market value shall be determined as of the end of the calendar year (or, in the case of any property disposed of during the calendar year, as of the date of such disposition.

[12]*(g)* **Information Required in Connection With Deductible Employee Contributions.—**

* * * * * * * * * * * *

[13]*(h)* **Failure to Give Notice to Recipients of Certain Pension, Etc., Distributions.—**

* * * * * * * * * * * *

[14]*(i)* **Failure to Give Written Explanation to Recipients of Certain Qualifying Rollover Distributions.—**

* * * * * * * * * * * *

(j) Failure to File Certification With Respect to Certain Residential Rental Projects.— In the case of each failure to provide a certification as required by section 142(d)(7) at the time prescribed therefor, unless it is shown that such failure is due to reasonable cause and not to willful neglect, there shall be paid, on notice and demand of the Secretary and in the same manner as tax, by the person failing to provide such certification, an amount equal to $100 for each such failure.

(j) [should read (k)] *Failure to Give Written Notice to Certain Sellers of Diesel Fuel.—*

(1) In general.—If any qualified retailer fails to provide the notice described in section 4041(n)(3)(A)(ii) to any seller of diesel fuel to such retailer, unless it is shown that such failure is due to reasonable cause and not to willful neglect, there shall be paid, on notice and demand of the Secretary and in the same manner as tax, by such retailer with respect to each sale of diesel fuel to such retailer by such seller to which section 4041(n)(4) applies an amount equal to 5 percent of the tax imposed by section 4041(a)(1) on such sale by reason of paragraphs (3) and (4)(A) of section 4041(n).

(2) Definitions.—For purposes of paragraph (1), the terms "qualified retailer" and "diesel fuel" have the respective meanings given such terms by section 4041(n).

(l) Information With Respect to Includable Employee Benefits.—

(1) In general.—In the case of each failure to include any amount on any statement under section 6051(a) or 6051(d) which is required to be so included under section 89(l), there shall be paid, on notice and demand of the Secretary and in the same manner as tax, the amount determined under paragraph (2).

(2) Amount of additional tax.—The amount determined under this paragraph shall be equal to the product of—

(A) the highest rate of tax imposed by section 1 for taxable years beginning in the calendar year to which the return or statement relates, multiplied by

(B) the employer-provided benefit (within the meaning of section 89 without regard to subsection (g)(3) thereof) with respect to the employee to whom such failure relates.

(3) Reasonable cause exception.—Paragraph (1) shall not apply to any failure if it is shown that such failure is due to reasonable cause.

(4) Coordination with other penalties.—Any penalty under this subsection shall be in addition to any other penalty under this section or section 6678 with respect to any failure.

[Footnote ¶3379 continued]

Matter in *italics* in Sec. 6652(g)—(i) added by section 1501(d)(1)(A)(i), '86 TRA, which struck out:

(12) "(h)"
(13) "(i)"
(14) "(j)"

Section 1501(d)(1)(A)(i) also relettered former Sec. 6652(k) as (j)

Effective date (Sec. 1501(e), '86 TRA).—Applies to returns the due date for which (determined without regard to extensions) is after 12-31-86.

Sec. 6652(j) in *italics* added by section 1301(g), '86 TRA, which also relettered former "(j)" as "(k)"

Effective date (Sec. 1311(a), '86 TRA).—Applies to bonds issued after 8-15-86. For special and transitional rules, see ¶2071—2077.

Sec. 6652(j) [should read (k)] in *italics* added by section 1702(b), '86 TRA, which also relettered "(j)" [should read "(k)"] as "(k)" [should read "(l)"].

Effective date (Sec. 1702(c), '86 TRA).—Applies to sales after the first calendar quarter beginning more than 60 days after the date of the enactment of this Act.

---

(5) *Only 1 addition per employee per year.*—*Paragraph (1) shall be applied only once if there is more than 1 failure with respect to any amount.*

[15](m) **Alcohol and Tobacco Taxes.**—

* * * * * * * * * * * *

[For official explanation, see Committee Reports, ¶4007; 4058; 4071; 4124; 4144; 4145.]

【¶3380】 CODE SEC. 6653. [1]*ADDITIONS TO TAX FOR NEGLIGENCE AND FRAUD.*

[2](a) *Negligence.*—

(1) *In general.*—*If any part of any underpayment (as defined in subsection (c)) is due to negligence or disregard of rules or regulations, there shall be added to the tax an amount equal to the sum of—*

    (A) *5 percent of the underpayment, and*

    (B) *an amount equal to 50 percent of the interest payable under section 6601 with respect to the portion of such underpayment which is attributable to negligence for the period beginning on the last date prescribed by law for payment of such underpayment (determined without regard to any extension) and ending on the date of the assessment of the tax (or, if earlier, the date of the payment of the tax).*

(2) *Underpayment taken into account reduced by portion attributable to fraud.*—*There shall not be taken into account under this subsection any portion of an underpay-*

【Footnote ¶3379 continued】

Matter in *italics* in Sec. 6652(l) and (m) added by section 1151(b), '86 TRA, which struck out:

(15) "(k)"

Effective date (Sec. 1151(k), '86 TRA).—Applies to years beginning after the later of—

(A) 12-31-87, or

(B) the earlier of—

(i) the date which is 3 months after the date on which the Secretary of the Treasury or his delegate issues such regulations as are necessary to carry out the provisions of section 89 of '86 TRA (as added by this section), or

(ii) 12-31-88.

For special and transitional rules, see footnote ¶2895.

【Footnote ¶3380】 Matter in *italics* in heading of Sec. 6653 added by section 1503(d)(1), '86 TRA, which struck out:

(1) "FAILURE TO PAY TAX"

Effective date (Sec. 1503(e), '86 TRA).—Applies to returns the due date for which (determined without regard to extensions) is after 12-31-86.

Matter in *italics* in Sec. 6653(a), (b), (d), (f) and (g) added by section 1503(a), (b), (c)(2) and (3), '86 TRA, which struck out:

(2) "**(a) Negligence or Intentional Disregard of Rules and Regulations With Respect to Income, Gift, or Windfall Profit Taxes.**—

(1) In general.—If any part of any underpayment (as defined in subsection (c)(1)) of any tax imposed by subtitle A, by chapter 12 of subtitle B, or by chapter 45 (relating to windfall profit tax) is due to negligence or intentional disregard of rules and regulations (but without intent to defraud), there shall be added to the tax an amount equal to 5 percent of the underpayment.

(2) Additional amount for portion attributable to negligence, etc.—There shall be added to the tax (in addition to the amount determined under paragraph (1)) an amount equal to 50 percent of the interest payable under section 6601—

(A) with respect to the portion of the underpayment described in paragraph (1) which is attributable to the negligence or intentional disregard referred to in paragraph (1), and

(B) for the period beginning on the last date prescribed by law for payment of such underpayment (determined without regard to any extension) and ending on the date of the assessment of the tax (or, if earlier, the date of the payment of the tax).

(b) Fraud.—

(1) In general.—If any part of any underpayment (as defined in subsection (c)) of tax required to be shown on a return is due to fraud, there shall be added to the tax an amount equal to 50 percent of the underpayment.

(2) Additional amount for portion attributable to fraud.—There shall be added to the tax (in addition to the amount determined under paragraph (1)) an amount equal to 50 percent of the interest payable under section 6601—

(A) with respect to the portion of the underpayment described in paragraph (1) which is attributable to fraud, and

(B) for the period beginning on the last day prescribed by law for payment of such underpayment (determined without regard to any extension) and ending on the date of the assessment of the tax (or, if earlier, the date of the payment of the tax).

(3) No negligence addition when there is addition for fraud.—The addition to tax under this subsection shall be in lieu of any amount determined under subsection (a).

(4) Special rule for joint returns.—In the case of a joint return under section 6013, this subsection shall not apply with respect to the tax of the spouse unless some part of the underpayment is due to the fraud of such spouse."

ment attributable to fraud with respect to which a penalty is imposed under subsection (b).

(3) Negligence.—For purposes of this subsection, the term "negligence" includes any failure to make a reasonable attempt to comply with the provisions of this title, and the term "disregard" includes any careless, reckless, or intentional disregard.

(b) Fraud.—

(1) In general.—If any part of any underpayment (as defined in subsection (c)) of tax required to be shown on a return is due to fraud, there shall be added to the tax an amount equal to the sum of—

(A) 75 percent of the portion of the underpayment which is attributable to fraud, and

(B) an amount equal to 50 percent of the interest payable under section 6601 with respect to such portion for the period beginning on the last day prescribed by law for payment of such underpayment (determined without regard to any extension) and ending on the date of the assessment of the tax or, if earlier, the date of the payment of the tax.

(2) Determination of portion attributable to fraud.—If the Secretary establishes that any portion of an underpayment is attributable to fraud, the entire underpayment shall be treated as attributable to fraud, except with respect to any portion of the underpayment which the taxpayer establishes is not attributable to fraud.

(3) Special rule for joint returns.—In the case of a joint return, this subsection shall not apply with respect to a spouse unless some part of the underpayment is due to the fraud of such spouse.

* * * * * * * * * * * *

(d) No Delinquency Penalty if Fraud Assessed.—If any penalty is assessed under subsection (b) (relating to fraud) for an underpayment of tax which is required to be shown on a return, no penalty under section 6651 (relating to failure to file such return or pay tax) shall be assessed with respect to the [3]*portion of the underpayment which is attributable to fraud.*

* * * * * * * * * * * *

(f) Special Rule in Cases of Failure to Report Unrecognized Gain on Position in Personal Property.—If—

(1) a taxpayer fails to make the report required under section 1092(a)(3)(B) in the manner prescribed by such section and such failure is not due to reasonable cause, and

(2) such taxpayer has an underpayment of any tax attributable (in whole or in part) to the denial of a deduction of a loss with respect to any position (within the meaning of section 1092(d)(2)),

then such underpayment shall, for purposes of subsection (a), be treated as an underpayment due to negligence. [4]

[5]*(g) Special Rule for Amounts Shown on Information Returns.—If—*

(1) any amount is shown on—

(A) an information return (as defined in section 6724(d)(1)), or

(B) a return filed under section 6031, section 6037, section 6012(a) by an estate or trust, section 6050(B), or section 6050E, and

(2) the payee (or other person with respect to whom the return is made) fails to properly show such amount on his return,

---

⟦Footnote ¶3380 continued⟧

(3) "same underpayment"

(4) "or intentional disregard of rules and regulations (but without intent to defraud)"

(5) "(g) **Special Rule in The Case of Interest or Dividend Payments.**—

(1) In general.—If—

(A) any payment is shown on a return made by the payor under section 6042(a), 6044(a), or 6049(a), and

(B) the payee fails to include any portion of such payment in gross income,

any portion of an underpayment attributable to such failure shall be treated, for purposes of subsection (a), as due to negligence in the absence of clear and convincing evidence to the contrary.

(2) **Penalty to apply only to portion of underpayment due to failure to include interest or dividend payment.**—If any penalty is imposed under subsection (a) by reason of paragraph (1), the amount of the penalty imposed by paragraph (1) of subsection (a) shall be 5 percent of the portion of the underpayment which is attributable to the failure described in paragraph (1)."

Effective date (Sec. 1503(e), '86 TRA).—Applies to returns the due date for which (determined without regard to extensions) is after 12-31-86.

any portion of an underpayment attributable to such failure shall be treated, for purposes of subsection (a), as due to negligence in the absence of clear and convincing evidence to the contrary.

[For official explanation, see Committee Reports, ¶4073.]

[¶3381]   **CODE SEC. 6654.   FAILURE BY INDIVIDUAL TO PAY ESTIMATED INCOME TAX.**

  (a)   Addition to the Tax.—Except as otherwise provided in this section, in the case of any underpayment of estimated tax by an individual, there shall be added to the tax under chapter 1 and the tax under chapter 2 for the taxable year an amount determined by applying—

    (1)   the [1]*underpayment* rate established under section 6621.

    (2)   to the amount of the underpayment.

    (3)   for the period of the underpayment.

* * * * * * * * * * * *

  (d)   Amount of Required Installments.—For purposes of this section—

    (1)   Amount.—

      (A)   In general.—Except as provided in paragraph (2), the amount of any required installment shall be 25 percent of the required annual payment.

      (B)   Required annual payment.—For purposes of subparagraph (A), the term "required annual payment" means the lesser of—

        (i)   [2]*90 percent* of the tax shown on the return for the taxable year (or, if no return is filed, [2]*90 percent* of the tax for such year), or

        (ii)   100 percent of the tax shown on the return of the individual for the preceding taxable year.

Clause (ii) shall not apply if the preceding taxable year was not a taxable year of 12 months or if the individual did not file a return for such preceding year.

    (2)   Lower required installment where annualized income installment is less than amount determined under paragraph (1).—

* * * * * * * * * * * *

      (C)   Special rules.—For purposes of this paragraph—

        (i)   Annualization.—The taxable income, alternative minimum taxable income, and adjusted self-employment income shall be placed on an annualized basis under regulations prescribed by the Secretary.

        (ii)   Applicable percentage.—

In the case of the following required installments:	The applicable percentage is:
1st	[3]*22.5*
2nd	[4]*45*
3rd	[5]*67.5*
4th	[6]*90*

        (iii)   Adjusted   self-employment   income.—The   term   "adjusted   self-

---

[Footnote ¶3381]   Matter in *italics* in Sec. 6654(a)(1) added by section 1511(c)(14), '86 TRA, which struck out:

(1)   "applicable annual"

Effective date (Sec. 1511(d), '86 TRA).—Applies for purposes of determining interest for periods after 12-31-86.

Matter in italics in Sec. 6654(d)(1)(B)(i), (2)(C)(ii), and (i)(1)(C) added by section 1541(a), (b)(1), and (2), '86 TRA, which struck out:

(2)   "80 percent"

(3)   "20"

(4)   "40"

(5)   "60"

(6)   "80"

Effective date (Sec. 1541(c), '86 TRA).—Applies to taxable years beginning after 12-31-86.

Sec. 6654(j) in *italics*, added by section 1841, '86 TRA.

Effective date (Sec. 1881, '86 TRA and section 414(a)(1) and (2), '84 TRA).—(1)   Generally applies to taxable years beginning after 12-31-84.

  (2)   Waiver authority.—The provisions of paragraph (3) of section 6654(e) of the '54 Code (as amended by section 411, '84 TRA) shall also apply with respect to underpayments for taxable years beginning in 1984.

---

employment income" means self-employment income (as defined in section 1402(b)); except that section 1402(b) shall be applied by placing wages (within the meaning of section 1402(b)) for months in the taxable year ending before the due date for the installment on an annualized basis consistent with clause (i).

*   *   *   *   *   *   *   *   *   *   *   *

(i)   Special Rules for Farmers and Fishermen.—For purposes of this section—

    (1)   In general.—If an individual is a farmer or fisherman for any taxable year—

        (A)   there shall be only 1 required installment for the taxable year,

        (B)   the due date for such installment shall be January 15 of the following taxable year,

        (C)   the amount of such installment shall be equal to the required annual payment (determined under subsection (d)(1)(B) by substituting "66⅔ percent" for [2] "90 percent," and

        (D)   subsection (h) shall be applied—

            (i)   by substituting "March 1" for "January 31", and

            (ii)   by treating the required installment described in subparagraph (A) of this paragraph as the 4th required installment.

*   *   *   *   *   *   *   *   *   *   *   *

(j)   Special Rules for Nonresident Aliens.—*In the case of a nonresident alien described in section 6072(c):*

(1)   Payable in 3 installments.—*There shall be 3 required installments for the taxable year.*

(2)   Time for payment of installments.—*The due dates for required installments under this subsection shall be determined under the following table:*

In the case of the following required installments:	The due date is:
1st	*June 15*
2nd	*September 15*
3rd	*January 15 of the following taxable year.*

(3)   Amount of required installments.—

    (A)   First required installment.—*In the case of the first required installment, subsection (d) shall be applied by substituting "50 percent" for "25 percent" in subsection (d)(1)(A).*

    (B)   Determination of applicable percentage.—*The applicable percentage for purposes of subsection (d)(2) shall be determined under the following table:*

In the case of the following required installments:	The applicable percentage is:
1st	*45*
2nd	*67.5*
3rd	*90*

[7]*(k)   Fiscal Years and Short Years.*—

    (1)   Fiscal years.—*In applying this section to a taxable year beginning on any date other than January 1, there shall be substituted, for the months specified in this section, the months which correspond thereto.*

    (2)   Short taxable year.—*This section shall be applied to taxable years of less than 12 months in accordance with regulations prescribed by the Secretary.*

⟦Footnote ¶3381 continued⟧

* The percentages "45," "67.5," and "90" in *italics* in Sec. 6654(j)(3) added by section 1541(b)(3), '86 TRA. **Effective date** (Sec. 1541(c), '86 TRA).—Applies to taxable years beginning after 12-31-86.

Matter in *italics* in Sec. 6654(k) added by section 1841, '86 TRA, which struck out:
(7)   "(j)"
Section 1841 also relettered former 6654(k) as (l).
Effective date (Sec. 1881, '86 TRA and section 414(a)(1) and (2), '84 TRA).—Generally applies to taxable years beginning after 12-31-84. For special rule, see above.

[8](k) *[should read (l)]*   *Trusts and Certain Estates.—This section shall apply to—*
    (1)   *any trust, and*
    (2)   *any estate with respect to any taxable year ending 2 or more years after the date of the death of the decedent's death.*

[9](m)   **Regulation.**—The Secretary shall prescribe such regulations as may be necessary to carry out the purposes of this section.

[For official explanation, see Committee Reports, ¶4063; 4075; 4087; 4161.]

【¶3382】   **CODE SEC. 6655. FAILURE BY CORPORATION TO PAY ESTIMATED INCOME TAX.**

    (a)   **Addition to Tax.**—Except as provided in subsections (d) and (e), in the case of any underpayment of tax by a corporation—

    (1)   **In general.**—There shall be added to the tax under chapter 1 for the taxable year an amount determined at the *underpayment* rate established under section 6621 on the amount of the underpayment for the period of the underpayment.

* * * * * * * * * * *

    (f)   **Definition of Tax.**—For purposes of subsections (b), (d), (e), and (i) the term "tax" means the excess of—
    (1)   [1]*the sum of—*
       (A)   *the tax imposed by section 11 or 1201(a), or subchapter L of chapter 1, whichever is applicable, plus*
       (B)   *the tax imposed by section 55, over*
    (2)   the sum of—
       (A)   the credits against tax provided by part IV of subchapter A of chapter 1, plus
       (B)   to the extent allowed under regulations prescribed by the Secretary, any overpayment of the tax imposed by section 4986 (determined without regard to section 4995(a)(4)(B).

* * * * * * * * * * *

[For official explanation, see Committee Reports, ¶3931; 4075.]

【¶3383】   **CODE SEC. 6659A. ADDITION TO TAX IN CASE OF OVERSTATEMENTS OF PENSION LIABILITIES.**

    (a)   **Addition to Tax.**—In the case of an underpayment of the tax imposed by chapter 1 on any taxpayer for the taxable year which is attributable to an overstatement of pension liabilities, there shall be added to such tax an amount equal to the applicable percentage of the underpayment so attributable.

    (b)   **Applicable Percentage Defined.**—For purposes of subsection (a), the applicable percentage shall be determined under the following table:

【Footnote ¶3381 continued】

Sec. 6654(k) [should read (l) in *italics* added by section 1404(a), '86 TRA, which struck out:
(8)   **"(l)**   **Estates and Trusts.**—This section shall not apply to any estate or trust.
Effective date (Sec. 1404(d), '86 TRA).—Applies to taxable years beginning after 12-31-86.

Matter in italics in Sec. 6654(m) added by section 1841, '86 TRA, which struck out:
(9)   **"l"**
Effective date (Sec. 1881, '86 TRA and section 414(a)(1) and (2), '84 TRA).—Generally applies to taxable years beginning after 12-31-84. For special rule, see above.
【Footnote ¶3382】   Matter in *italics* in Sec. 6655(a)(1) added by section 1511(c)(15), '86 TRA.
Effective date (Sec. 1511(d), '86 TRA).—Applies for purposes of determining interest for periods after 12-31-86.

Matter in *italics* in Sec. 6655(f)(1) added by section 701(d)(3), '86 TRA, which struck out:
(1)   "the tax imposed by section 11 or 1201(a), or subchapter L of chapter 1, whichever is applicable, over"
Effective date (Sec. 701(f)(1), '86 TRA).—Generally applies to taxable years beginning after 12-31-86. For transitional and special rules, see footnote ¶2879.
【Footnote ¶3383】   Sec. 6659A added by section 1138(a), '86 TRA.
Effective date (Sec. 1138(c), '86 TRA).—Applies to overstatements made after the date of the enactment of this Act.

If the valuation claimed is the following percent of the correct valuation—	The applicable percentage is:
150 percent or more but not more than 200 percent	10
More than 200 percent but not more than 250 percent	20
More than 250 percent	30.

(c) **Overstatement of Pension Liabilities.**—For purposes of this section, there is an overstatement of pension liabilities if the actuarial determination of the liabilities taken into account for purposes of computing the deduction under paragraph (1) or (2) of section 404(a) exceeds the amount determined to be the correct amount of such liability.

(d) **Underpayment Must Be at Least $1,000.**—This section shall not apply if the underpayment for the taxable year attributable to valuation overstatements is less than $1,000.

(e) **Authority To Waive.**—The Secretary may waive all or any part of the addition to the tax provided by this section on a showing by the taxpayer that there was a reasonable basis for the valuation claimed on the return and that such claim was made in good faith.

[For official explanation, see Committee Reports, ¶3997.]

[¶3384] CODE SEC. 6660. ADDITION TO TAX IN THE CASE OF VALUATION UNDERSTATEMENT FOR PURPOSES OF [1] ESTATE OR GIFT TAXES.

* * * * * * * * * * *

(f) *Underpayment Defined.—For purposes of this section, the term "underpayment" has the meaning given to such term by section 6653(c)(1).*

[For official explanation, see Committee Reports, ¶4145.]

[¶3385] CODE SEC. 6661. SUBSTANTIAL UNDERSTATEMENT OF LIABILITY.

(a) **Addition to Tax.**—If there is a substantial understatement of income tax for any taxable year, there shall be added to the tax an amount equal to [1]*20 percent* of the amount of any underpayment attributable to such understatement.

* * * * * * * * * * *

[For official explanation, see Committee Reports, ¶4074.]

[¶3386] CODE SEC. 6673. DAMAGES ASSESSABLE FOR INSTITUTING PROCEEDINGS BEFORE THE TAX COURT PRIMARILY FOR DELAY, ETC.

Whenever it appears to the Tax Court that proceedings before it have been instituted or maintained by the taxpayer primarily for delay[1], that the taxpayer's position in such proceedings is frivolous or groundless, *or that the taxpayer unreasonably failed to pursue available administrative remedies,* damages in an amount not in excess of $5,000 shall be awarded to the United States by the Tax Court in its decision. Damages so awarded shall be assessed at the same time as the deficiency and shall be paid upon notice and demand from the Secretary and shall be collected as a part of the tax.

[For official explanation, see Committee Reports, ¶4091.]

[¶3387] CODE SEC. 6676. FAILURE TO SUPPLY IDENTIFYING NUMBERS.

(a) **In General.**—If any person who is required by regulations prescribed under section 6109—

    (1) to include his TIN in any return, statement, or other document,

    (2) to furnish his TIN to another person, or

[Footnote ¶3384] Section 1899A(57), '86 TRA, struck out from the heading of Sec. 6660.
(1) "THE"

Sec. 6660(f) in *italics* added by section 1811(d), '86 TRA,

Effective date (Sec. 1881, '86 TRA and Sec. 155(d)(2), '84 TRA).—Applies to returns filed after 12-31-84.

[Footnote ¶3385] Matter in *italics* in Sec. 6661(a) added by section 1504(a), '86 TRA, which struck out:
(1) "10 percent"

Effective date (Sec. 1504(b), '86 TRA).—Applies to returns the due date for which (determined without regard to extensions) is after 12-31-86.

[Footnote ¶3386] Matter in *italics* in Sec. 6673 added by section 1552(a), '86 TRA, which struck out:
(1) "or"

Effective date (Sec. 1552(b), '86 TRA).—Applies to proceedings commenced after the date of enactment of this Act.

(3) except in the case of a return or statement required to be filed under section 6042, 6044, 6049, *or 6050N,* to include in any return, statement, or other document made with respect to another person the TIN of such other person,

fails to comply with such requirement at the time prescribed by such regulations, such person shall, unless it is shown that such failure is due to reasonable cause and not to willful neglect, pay a penalty of $5 for each such failure described in paragraph (1) and $50 for each such failure described in paragraph (2) or (3), except that the total amount imposed on such person for all such failures during any calendar year shall not exceed [1] *$100,000.*

(b) **Penalties Involving Failures on Interest**[2], *Dividends, and Royalties* **Returns.—**

(1) **In general.—**If any payor—

(A) is required to include in any return or statement required to be filed under section 6042, 6044,[3] 6049, *or 6050N* with respect to any payee the TIN of such payee, and

* * * * * * * * * * *

(e) Penalty for Failure To Supply TIN of Dependent.—

(1) In general.—If any person required under section 6109(e) to include the TIN of any dependent on his return fails to include such number on such return (or includes an incorrect number), such person shall, unless it is shown that such failure is due to reasonable cause and not willful neglect, pay a penalty of $5 for each such failure.

(2) Subsection (a) not to apply.—Subsection (a) shall not apply to any failure described in paragraph (1) of this subsection.

[For official explanation, see Committee Reports, ¶4071; 4079; 4080.]

≫**P-H CAUTION→** There are two versions of Sec. 6678. See 6678, repealed generally effective after 12-31-86, follows. For Sec. 6678, generally effective before 1-1-87 see ¶3388-A, below.

[¶3388] **CODE SEC. 6678. FAILURE TO FURNISH CERTAIN STATEMENTS.** [Repealed by Sec. 1501(d)(2), '86 TRA.][1]

≫**P-H CAUTION→** There are two versions of Sec. 6678. Sec. 6678, generally effective before 1-1-87 follows. For Sec. 6678, repealed generally effective after 12-31-86 see ¶3388, above.

[¶3388-A] **CODE SEC. 6678. FAILURE TO FURNISH CERTAIN STATEMENTS.**

(a) **In General.—**In the case of each failure—

* * * * * * * * * * *

(3) to furnish as statement under—

* * * * * * * * * * *

[Footnote ¶3387] Matter in *italics* in Sec. 6676(a)(3) added by section 1523(b)(3)(A), '86 TRA.
Effective date (Sec. 1523(d), '86 TRA).—Applies with respect to payments made after 12-31-86.

The *$100,000* dollar amount in Sec. 6676(a) added by section 1501(b), '86 TRA, which struck out:
(1) "$50,000"
Effecitve date (Sec. 1501(e), '86 TRA).—Applies to returns the due date for which (determined without regard to extensions) is after 12-31-86.

Matter in *italics* in the heading of Sec. 6676(b) added by section 1523(b)(3)(C), '86 TRA, which struck out:
(2) "and Dividend"
Effective date (Sec. 1523(d), '86 TRA).—Applies with respect to payments made after 12-31-86.

Matter in *italics* in Sec. 6676(b)(1)(A) added by section 1523(b)(3)(B), '86 TRA, which struck out:
(3) "or"
Effective date (Sec. 1523(d), '86 TRA).—Applies with respect to payments made after 12-31-86.

Sec. 6676(e) in *italics* added by section 1524(b), '86 TRA.
Effective date (Sec. 1524(c), '86 TRA).—Applies to returns the due date for which (determined without regard to extensions) is after 12-31-87.
[Footnote ¶3388] (1) **Effective date** (Sec. 1501(e), '86 TRA).—Applies to returns the due date for which (determined without regard to extensions) is after 12-31-86.

(D) section 6051 (relating to information returns with respect to income tax withheld) if the statement is required to be furnished to the employee,

(E) subsection (b) or (c) of section 6053 (relating to statements furnished by employers with respect to tips), [1]

(F) section 6031(b), 6034A, or 6037(b) (relating to statements furnished by certain pass-thru entities), *or*

(G) *section 6045(d) (relating to statements required in the case of certain substitute payments),*

on the date prescribed therefor to a person with respect to whom such a statement is required,

unless it is shown that such failure is due to reasonable cause and not to willful neglect, there shall be paid (upon notice and demand by the Secretary and in the same manner as tax), by the person failing to so furnish the statement, $50 for each such statement not so furnished, but the total amount imposed on the delinquent person for all such failures during any calendar year shall not exceed $50,000.

* * * * * * * * * * * *

[For official explanation, see Committee Reports, ¶4071; 4145.]

[¶3389] CODE SEC. 6693. FAILURE TO PROVIDE REPORTS ON INDIVIDUAL RETIREMENT ACCOUNTS OR ANNUITIES; *OVERSTATEMENT OF DESIGNATED NONDEDUCTIBLE CONTRIBUTIONS.*

(a) The person required by subsection (i) or (1) of section 408 to file a report regarding an individual retirement account or individual retirement annuity at the time and in the manner required by such subsection shall pay a penalty of $50 for each failure unless it is shown that such failure is due to reasonable cause.

(b) Overstatement of Designated Nondeductible Contributions.—Any individual who—
    (1) is required to furnish information under section 408(o)(4) as to the amount of designated nondeductible contributions made for any taxable year, and
    (2) overstates the amount of such contributions made for such taxable year,
shall pay a penalty of $100 for each such overstatement unless it is shown that such overstatement is due to reasonable cause.

[1]*(c)* **Deficiency Procedures Not To Apply.**—Subchapter B of chapter 63 (relating to deficiency procedures for income, estate, gift, and certain excise taxes) does not apply to the assessment or collection of any penalty imposed by [2]*this section.*

[For official explanation, see Committee Reports, ¶3969.]

[¶3390] CODE SEC. 6697. ASSESSABLE PENALTIES WITH RESPECT TO LIABILITY FOR TAX OF [1]*REGULATED INVESTMENT COMPANIES.*

(a) **Civil Penalty.**—In addition to any other penalty provided by law, any [2]*regulated investment company whose tax liability for any taxable year is deemed to be increased pursuant to section 860(c)(1)(A) shall pay a penalty in an amount equal to the amount of the interest (for which such company is liable) which is attributable solely to such increase.*

* * * * * * * * * * * *

[For official explanation, see Committee Reports, ¶3929.]

[Footnote ¶3388-A] Matter in *italics* in Sec. 6678(a)(3)(E)—(G) added by section 1811(c)(1), '86 TRA, which struck out:
(1) "or"
Effective date (Sec. 1881, '86 TRA and Sec. 150(b), '84 TRA).—Applies to payments received after 12-31-84.
[Footnote ¶3389] Matter in *italics* in heading of Sec. 6693 added by section 1102(d)(2)(B), '86 TRA.
Effective date (Sec. 1102(g), '86 TRA).—Applies to contributions and distributions for taxable years beginning after 12-31-86.

Matter in *italics* in Sec. 6693(b) and (c) added by section 1102(d)(1) and (2)(A), '86 TRA, which struck out:
(1) "(b)"
(2) "subsection (a)"
Effective date (Sec. 1102(g), '86 TRA).—See above.
[Footnote ¶3390] Matter in *italics* in the heading of Sec. 6697 added by section 667(a), '86 TRA, which struck out:
(1) **"QUALIFIED INVESTMENT ENTITIES."**
Effective date (Sec. 669(a), '86 TRA).—Applies to taxable years beginning after 12-31-86.

Matter in *italics* in Sec. 6697(a) added by section 667(a), '86 TRA, which struck out:
(2) "qualified investment entity (as defined in section 860(b)) whose tax liability for any taxable year is deemed to be increased pursuant to section 860(c)(1)(A) (relating to interest and additions to tax determined with respect to the amount of the deduction for deficiency dividends allowed) shall pay a penalty in an amount equal to the amount of interest (for which such entity is liable) which is attributable solely to such increase."
Effective date (Sec. 669(a), '86 TRA).—See above.

≫**P-H CAUTION**→ There are two versions of Sec. 6699. Sec. 6699, repealed generally effective after 12-31-86, follows. For Sec. 6699 generally effective before 1-1-87, see ¶3391-A, below.

[¶3391] **CODE SEC. 6699. ASSESSABLE PENALTIES RELATING TO TAX CREDIT EMPLOYEE STOCK OWNERSHIP PLAN.** [Repealed by section 1171(b)(7)(A), '86 TRA].[1]

≫**P-H CAUTION**→ There are two versions of Sec. 6699. Sec. 6699, generally effective before 1-1-87, follows. For Sec. 6699, repealed generally effective after 12-31-86, see above.

[¶3391-A] **CODE SEC. 6699. ASSESSABLE PENALTIES RELATING TO TAX CREDIT EMPLOYEE STOCK OWNERSHIP PLAN.**

(a) **In General.**—If a taxpayer who has claimed an employee plan credit or a credit allowable under [1]*section 41* (relating to the employee stock ownership credit) for any taxable year—

(1) fails to satisfy any requirement provided by section 409 with respect to a qualified investment made before January 1, 1983,

(2) fails to make any contribution which is required under section 48(n) within the period required for making such contribution,

(3) fails to satisfy any requirement provided under section 409 with respect to a credit claimed under [1]*section 41* in taxable years ending after December 31, 1982, or

(4) fails to make any contribution which is required under [2]*section 41(c)(1)(B)* within the period required for making such contribution,

the taxpayer shall pay a penalty in an amount equal to the amount involved in such failure.

* * * * * * * * * * * *

(c) **Amount Involved Defined.**—

* * * * * * * * * * * *

(2) **Maximum and minimum amount.**—

* * * * * * * * * * * *

(B) The amount determined under paragraph (1) with respect to a failure described in paragraph (3) or (4) of subsection (a)—

(i) shall not exceed the amount of the credit claimed by the employer under [1]*section 41* to which such failure relates, and

(ii) shall not be less than the product of one-half of 1 percent of the amount referred to in clause (i), multiplied by the number of months (or parts thereof) during which such failure continues.

[For official explanation, see Committee Reports, ¶4016; 4161.]

[¶3392] **CODE SEC. 6704. FAILURE TO KEEP RECORDS NECESSARY TO MEET REPORTING REQUIREMENTS UNDER [1]*SECTION 6047(d).***

(a) **Liability for penalty.**—Any person who—

(1) has a duty to report or may have a duty to report any information under [2]*section 6047(d)* and

---

[Footnote ¶3391] (1) **Effective date** (Sec. 1171(c), '86 TRA).—(1) Generally applies to compensation paid or accrued after 12-31-86, in taxable years ending after such date.

(2) Sections 404(I) and 6699 to continue to apply to pre-1987 credits.—The provisions of sections 404(i) and 6699 of the '86 Code shall continue to apply with respect to credits under section 41 of such Code attributable to compensation paid or accrued before 1-1-87 (or under section 38 of such Code with respect to qualified investment before 1-1-83).

[Footnote ¶3391-A] Matter in *italics* in Sec. 6699(a) and (c)(2)(B) added by section 1847(b)(9), '86 TRA, which struck out:

(1) "section 44G"

(2) "section 44G(c)(1)(B)"

Effective date (Sec. 1881, '86 TRA and Sec. 475(a), '84 TRA).—Applies to taxable years beginning after 12-31-83, and to carrybacks from such years.

[Footnote ¶3392] Matter in *italics* in the heading of Sec. 6704 and 6704(a) added by section 1848(e)(1), '86 TRA, which struck out:

(1) "SECTION 6047(e)"

(2) "section 6047(e)"

Effective date (Sec. 1881, '86 TRA and section 491(f)(1), '84 TRA).—Applies to obligations issued after 12-31-83.

(2) fails to keep such records as may be required by regulations prescribed under [2] *section 6047(d)* for the purpose of providing the necessary data base for either current reporting or future reporting.

shall pay a penalty for each calendar year for which there is any failure to keep such records.

* * * * * * * * * * * *

[For official explanation, see Committee Reports, ¶4161.]

[¶3393]　CODE SEC. 6707.　FAILURE TO FURNISH INFORMATION REGARDING TAX SHELTERS.

(a)　Failure to Register Tax Shelter.—

* * * * * * * * * * * *

(2)　Amount of penalty.—The penalty imposed under paragraph (1) with respect to any tax shelter shall be an amount equal to the greater of—
　　[1]*(A)　1 percent of the aggregate amount invested in such tax shelter, or*
　　(B)　$500.

* * * * * * * * * * * *

(b)　Failure to Furnish Tax Shelter Identification Number.—

* * * * * * * * * * * *

(2)　Failure to include number on return.—Any person who fails to include an identification number on a return on which such number is required to be included under section 6111(b)(2) shall pay a penalty of [2]*$250* for each such failure, unless such failure is due to reasonable cause.

[For official explanation, see Committee Reports, ¶4083; 4084.]

[¶3394]　CODE SEC. 6708.　FAILURE TO MAINTAIN LISTS OF INVESTORS IN POTENTIALLY ABUSIVE TAX SHELTERS.

(a)　In General.—Any person who fails to meet any requirement imposed by section 6112 shall pay a penalty of $50 for each person with respect to whom there is such a failure, unless it is shown that such failure is due to reasonable cause and not due to willful neglect. The maximum penalty imposed under this subsection for any calendar year shall not exceed [1]*$100,000.*

* * * * * * * * * * * *

[For official explanation, see Committee Reports, ¶4085.]

[¶3394-A]　CODE SEC. [1]*6709.*　PENALTIES WITH RESPECT TO MORTGAGE CREDIT CERTIFICATE.

* * * * * * * * * * * *

[For official explanation, see Committee Reports, ¶4177.]

[Footnote ¶3393]　Matter in *italics* in Sec. 6707(a)(2) added by section 1532(a), '86 TRA, which struck out:
(1) "(A)　$500, or
(B)　the lesser of (i) 1 percent of the aggregate amount invested in such tax shelter, or (ii) $10,000.
The $10,000 limitation in subparagraph (B) shall not apply where there is an intentional disregard of the requirements of section 6111(a)."
Effective date (Sec. 1532(b), '86 TRA).—Applies to failures with respect to tax shelters interests in which are first offered for sale after the date of the enactment of this Act.

Matter in *italics* in Sec. 6707(b)(2) added by section 1533(a), '86 TRA, which struck:
(2) "$50"
Effective date (Sec. 1533(b), '86 TRA).—Applies to returns filed after the date of the enactment of this Act.
[Footnote ¶3394]　Matter in *italics* in Sec. 6708(a) added by section 1534(a), '86 TRA, which struck out:
(1) "$50,000"
Effective date (Sec. 1534(b), '86 TRA).—Applies to failures occurring or continuing after the date of the enactment of this Act.
[Footnote ¶3394-A]　Matter in *italics* in title of Sec. 6709 added by section 1862(d)(2), '86 TRA, which struck out:
(1) "6708"
Effective date (Sec. 1881, '86 TRA and Sec. 612(g), '84 TRA).—(1) Generally applies to interest paid or accrued after 12-31-84, on indebtedness incurred after 12-31-84.
(2) Elections.—The amendments made by this section shall apply to elections under section 25(c)(2)(A)(ii) of the '54 Code (as added by this section) for calendar years after 1983.

[¶3395] CODE SEC. 6721. FAILURE TO FILE CERTAIN INFORMATION RETURNS.

(a) **General Rule.**—In the case of each failure to file an information return with the Secretary on the date prescribed therefor (determined with regard to any extension of time for filing), the person failing to so file such return shall pay $50 for each such failure, but the total amount imposed on such person for all such failures during any calendar year shall not exceed $100,000.

(b) **Penalty in Case of Intentional Disregard.**—If 1 or more failures to which subsection (a) applies are due to intentional disregard of the filing requirement, then, with respect to each such failure—

(1) the penalty imposed under subsection (a) shall be $100, or, if greater—

(A) in the case of a return other than a return required under section 6045(a), 6041A(b), 6050H, 6050J, 6050K, or 6050L, 10 percent of the aggregate amount of the items required to be reported, or

(B) in the case of a return required to be filed by section 6045(a), 6050K, or 6050L, 5 percent of the aggregate amount of the items required to be reported, and

(2) in the case of any penalty determined under paragraph (1)—

(A) the $100,000 limitation under subsection (a) shall not apply, and

(B) such penalty shall not be taken into account in applying the $100,000 limitation to penalties not determined under paragraph (1).

[For official explanation, see Committee Reports, ¶4071.]

[¶3396] CODE SEC. 6722. FAILURE TO FURNISH CERTAIN PAYEE STATEMENTS.

(a) **General Rule.**—In the case of each failure to furnish a payee statement on the date prescribed therefor to the person to whom such statement is required to be furnished, the person failing to so furnish such statement shall pay $50 for each such failure, but the total amount imposed on such person for all such failures during any calendar year shall not exceed $100,000.

(b) **Failure To Notify Partnership of Exchange of Partnership Interest.**—In the case of any person who fails to furnish the notice required by section 6050K(c)(1) on the date prescribed therefor, such person shall pay a penalty of $50 for each such failure.

[For official explanation, see Committee Reports, ¶4071.]

[¶3397] CODE SEC. 6723. FAILURE TO INCLUDE CORRECT INFORMATION.

(a) **General Rule.**—If—

(1) any person files an information return or furnishes a payee statement, and

(2) such person does not include all of the information required to be shown on such return or statement or includes incorrect information,

such person shall pay $5 for each return or statement with respect to which such failure occurs, but the total amount imposed on such person for all such failures during any calendar year shall not exceed $20,000.

(b) **Penalty in Case of Intentional Disregard.**—If 1 or more failures to which subsection (a) applies are due to intentional disregard of the correct information reporting requirement, then, with respect to each such failure—

(1) the penalty imposed under subsection (a) shall be $100, or, if greater—

(A) in the case of a return other than a return required under section 6045(a), 6041A(b), 6050H, 6050J, 6050K, or 6050L, 10 percent of the aggregate amount of the items required to be reported correctly, or

(B) in the case of a return required to be filed by section 6045(a), 6050K, or 6050L, 5 percent of the aggregate amount of the items required to be reported correctly, and

---

[Footnote ¶3395] Sec. 6721 added by section 1501(a), '86 TRA.
Effective date (Sec. 1501(e), '86 TRA).—Applies to returns the due date for which (determined without regard to extensions) is after 12-31-86.
[Footnote ¶3396] Sec. 6722 added by section 1501(a), '86 TRA.
Effective date (Sec. 1501(e), '86 TRA).—Applies to returns the due date for which (determined without regard to extensions) is after 12-31-86.
[Footnote ¶3397] Sec. 6723 added by section 1501(a), '86 TRA.
Effective date (Sec. 1501(e), '86 TRA).—Applies to returns the due date for which (determined without regard to extensions) is after 12-31-86.

(2)   in the case of any penalty determined under paragraph (1)—

    (A)   the $20,000 limitation under subsection (a) shall not apply, and

    (B)   such penalty shall not be taken into account in applying the $20,000 limitation to penalties not determined under paragraph (1).

(c)   **Coordination With Section 6676.**—No penalty shall be imposed under subsection (a) or (b) with respect to any return or statement if a penalty is imposed under section 6676 (relating to failure to supply identifying number) with respect to such return or statement.

[For official explanation, see Committee Reports, ¶4071.]

〖¶3398〗   CODE SEC. 6724.   WAIVER; DEFINITIONS AND SPECIAL RULES.

(a)   **Reasonable Cause Waiver.**—No penalty shall be imposed under this part with respect to any failure if it is shown that such failure is due to reasonable cause and not to willful neglect.

(b)   **Payment of Penalty.**—Any penalty imposed by this part shall be paid on notice and demand by the Secretary and in the same manner as tax.

(c)   **Special Rules for Failure To File Interest and Dividend Returns or Statements.**—

(1)   **Higher standards for waiver.**—In the case of any interest or dividend return or statement—

    (A)   subsection (a) shall not apply, but

    (B)   no penalty shall be imposed under this part if it is shown that the person otherwise liable for such penalty exercised due diligence in attempting to satisfy the requirement with respect to such return or statement.

(2)   **Limitations not to apply.**—In the case of any interest or dividend return or statement—

    (A)   the $100,000 limitations of sections 6721(a) and 6722(a) and the $20,000 limitation of section 6723(a) shall not apply (and any penalty imposed on any failure involving such a return or statement shall not be taken into account in applying such limitations to other penalties), and

    (B)   penalties imposed with respect to such returns or statements shall not be taken into account for purposes of applying such limitations with respect to other returns or statements.

(3)   **Self assessment.**—Any penalty imposed under this part on any person with respect to an interest or dividend return or statement—

    (A)   shall be assessed and collected in the same manner as an exercise tax imposed by subtitle D, and

    (B)   shall be due and payable on April 1 of the calendar year following the calendar year for which such return or statement is required.

(4)   **Deficiency procedures not to apply.**—Subchapter B of chapter 63 (relating to deficiency procedures for income, estate, gift, and certain excise taxes) shall not apply in respect of the assessment or collection of any penalty imposed under this part with respect to an interest or dividend return or statement.

(5)   **Interest or dividend return or statement.**—For purposes of this subsection, the term "interest or dividend return or statement" means—

    (A)   any return required by section 6042(a)(1), 6044(a)(1), or 6049(a), and

    (B)   any statement required under section 6042(c), 6044(e), or 6049(c).

(d)   **Definitions.**—For purposes of this part—

(1)   **Information return.**—The term "information return" means—

    (A)   any statement of the amount of payments to another person required by—

        (i)   section 6041(a) or (b) (relating to certain information at source),

        (ii)   section 6042(a)(1) (relating to payments of dividends),

        (iii)   section 6044(a)(1) (relating to payments of patronage dividends),

        (iv)   section 6049(a) (relating to payments of interest),

        (v)   section 6050A(a) (relating to reporting requirements of certain fishing boat operators),

        (vi)   section 6050N(a) (relating to payments of royalties), or

        (vii)   section 6051(d) (relating to information returns with respect to income tax withheld), and

    (B)   any return required by—

〖**Footnote ¶3398**〗   Sec. 6724 added by section 1501(a), '86 TRA.

Effective date   (Sec. 1501(e), '86 TRA.)—Applies to returns the due date for which (determined without regard to extensions) is after 12-31-86.

    (i)   section 4997(a) (relating to information with respect to windfall profit tax on crude oil),

    (ii)   section 6041A(a) or (b) (relating to returns of direct sellers),

    (iii)   section 6045(a) or (d) (relating to returns of brokers),

    (iv)   section 6050H(a) (relating to mortgage interest received in trade or business from individuals),

    (v)   section 6050I(a) (relating to cash received in trade or business),

    (vi)   section 6050J(a) (relating to foreclosures and abandonments of security),

    (vii)   section 6050K(a) (relating to exchanges of certain partnership interests),

    (viii)   section 6050L(a) (relating to returns relating to certain dispositions of donated property),

    (ix)   section 6052(a) (relating to reporting payment of wages in the form of group-term life insurance), or

    (x)   section 6053(c)(1) (relating to certain tips).

    (2) Payee statement.—The term "payee statement" means any statement required to be furnished under—

    (A)   section 4997(a) (relating to records and information; regulations),

    (B)   section 6031(b), 6034A, or 6037(b) (relating to statements furnished by certain pass-thru entities),

    (C)   section 6039(a) (relating to information required in connection with certain options),

    (D)   section 6041(d) (relating to information at source),

    (E)   section 6041A(e) (relating to returns regarding payments of remuneration for services and direct sales),

    (F)   section 6042(c) (relating to returns regarding payments of dividends and corporate earnings and profits),

    (G)   section 6044(e) (relating to returns regarding payments of patronage dividends),

    (H)   section 6045(b) or (d) (relating to returns of brokers),

    (I)   section 6049(c) (relating to returns regarding payments of interest),

    (J)   section 6050A(b) (relating to reporting requirements of certain fishing boat operators),

    (K)   section 6050C (relating to information regarding windfall profit tax on domestic crude oil),

    (L)   section 6050H(d) (relating to returns relating to mortgage interest received in trade or business from individuals),

    (M)   section 6050I(e) (relating to returns relating to cash received in trade or business),

    (N)   section 6050J(e) (relating to returns relating to foreclosures and abandonments of security),

    (O)   section 6050K(b) (relating to returns relating to exchanges of certain partnership interests),

    (P)   section 6050L(c) (relating to returns relating to certain dispositions of donated property),

    (Q)   section 6050N(b) (relating to returns regarding payments of royalties),

    (R)   section 6051 (relating to receipts for employees),

    (S)   section 6052(b) (relating to returns regarding payment of wages in the form of group-term life insurance), or

    (T)   section 6053(b) or (c) (relating to reports of tips).

[For official explanation, see Committee Reports, ¶4071.]

【¶3399】 CODE SEC. 7103. CROSS REFERENCES—OTHER PROVISIONS FOR BONDS.

* * * * * * * * * * * *

(b) Release of Lien or Seized property.—

* * * * * * * * * * * *

    (4) For bond executed by claimant of seized goods valued at [1]*$100,000* **or less, see section 7325(3).**

* * * * * * * * * * * *

[For official explanation, see Committee Reports, ¶4104.]

【Footnote ¶3399】 Matter in *italics* in Sec. 7103(b)(4) added by section 1566(c), '86 TRA, which struck out:
(1) "$1000"
Effective date (Sec. 1566(e), '86 TRA).—Takes effect on the date of the enactment of this Act.

〔¶3400〕 CODE SEC. 7210. FAILURE TO OBEY SUMMONS.

Any person who, being duly summoned to appear to testify, or to appear and produce books, accounts, records, memoranda, or other papers, as required under sections 6420(e)(2), 6421(f)(2), [1]*6427(j)(2)*, 7602, 7603, and 7604(b), neglects to appear or to produce such books, accounts, records, memoranda, or other papers, shall, upon conviction thereof, be fined not more than $1,000, or imprisoned not more than 1 year, or both, together with costs of prosecution.

[For official explanation, see Committee Reports, ¶6125.]

〔¶3401〕 CODE SEC. 7325. PERSONAL PROPERTY VALUED AT [1]*$100,000* OR LESS.

In all cases of seizure of any goods, wares, or merchandise as being subject to forfeiture under any provision of this title which, in the opinion of the Secretary, are of the appraised value of [1]*$100,000* or less, the Secretary shall, except in cases otherwise provided, proceed as follows:

(1) **List and appraisement.**—The Secretary shall cause a list containing a particular description of the goods, wares, or merchandise seized to be prepared in duplicate, and an appraisement thereof to be made by three sworn appraisers, to be selected by the Secretary who shall be respectable and disinterested citizens of the United States residing within the internal revenue district wherein the seizure was made. Such list and appraisement shall be properly attested by the Secretary and such appraisers. Each appraiser shall be allowed for his services such compensaion as the Secretary shall by regulations prescribe, to be paid in the manner similar to that provided for other necessary charges incurred in collecting internal revenue.

(2) **Notice of seizure.**—If such goods are found by such appraisers to be of the value of [1]*$100,000* or less, the Secretary shall publish a notice for 3 weeks, in some newspaper of the district where the seizure was made, describing the articles and stating the time, place, and cause of their seizure, and requiring any person claiming them to appear and make such claim within 30 days from the date of the first publication of such notice.

(3) **Execution of bond by claimant.**—Any person claiming the goods, wares, or merchandise so seized, within the time specified in the notice, may file with the Secretary a claim, stating his interest in the articles seized, and may execute a bond to the United States in the penal sum of [2]*$2,500* conditioned that, in case of condemnation of the articles so seized, the obligors shall pay all the costs and expenses of the proceedings to obtain such condemnation; and upon the delivery of such bond to the Secretary, he shall transmit the same, with the duplicate list or description of the goods seized, to the United States attorney for the district, and such attorney shall proceed thereon in the ordinary manner prescribed by law.

(4) **Sale in absence of bond.**—If no claim is interposed and no bond is given within the time above specified, the Secretary shall give reasonable notice of the sale of the goods, wares, or merchandise by publication and, at the time and place specified in the notice, shall, unless otherwise provided by law, sell the articles so seized at public auction, or upon competitive bids, in accordance with such regulations as may be prescribed by the Secretary.

[For official explanation, see Committee Reports, ¶4104.]

〔¶3402〕 CODE SEC. 7422. CIVIL ACTIONS FOR REFUND.

* * * * * * * * * * * *

(g) **Special Rules for Certain Excise Taxes Imposed by Chapter 42 or 43.—**

(1) **Right to bring actions.—**

(A) In general.—With respect to any taxable event, payment of the full amount of the first tier tax shall constitute sufficient payment in order to maintain an action under this section with respect to the second tier tax.

〔Footnote ¶3400〕 Matter in *italics* in Sec. 7210 added by section 1703(e)(2)(G), '86 TRA, which struck out:
(1) "6427(i)(2)"
Effective date (Sec. 1703(h), '86 TRA).—Applies to gasoline removed (as defined in section 4082 of the '86 Code, as amended by this section) after 12-31-87.
〔Footnote ¶3401〕 Matter in *italics* in Sec. 7325 added by section 1566(a) and (b), '86 TRA, which struck out:
(1) "$2,500"
(2) "$250"
Effective date (Sec. 1566(e), '86 TRA).—Takes effect on the date of enactment of this Act.

(B) Definitions.—For purposes of subparagraph (A), the terms "taxable event", "first tier tax", and "second tier tax" have the respective meanings given to such terms by [1]*section 4963.*

* * * * * * * * * * * *

〔¶3403〕 CODE SEC. 7425. DISCHARGE OF LIENS.

* * * * * * * * * * * *

(b) Other Sales.—Notwithstanding subsection (a) a sale of property on which the United States has or claims a lien, or a title derived from enforcement of a lien, under the provisions of this title, made pursuant to an instrument creating a lien on such property, pursuant to a confession of judgment on the obligation secured by such an instrument, or pursuant to a nonjudicial sale under a statutory lien on such property—

(1) shall, except as otherwise provided, be made subject to and without disturbing such lien or title, if notice of such lien was filed or such title recorded in the place provided by law for such filing or recording more than 30 days before such sale and the United States is not given notice of such sale in the manner prescribed in subsection (c)(1); or

(2) shall have the same effect with respect to the discharge or divestment of such lien or such title of the United States, as may be provided with respect to such matters by the local law of the place where such property is situated, if—

(A) notice of such lien or such title was not filed or recorded in the place provided by law for such filing more than 30 days before such sale,

(B) the law makes no provisions for such filing, or

(C) notice of such sale is given in the manner prescribed in subsection (c)(1).

(c) Special Rules.—

* * * * * * * * * * * *

(4) Forfeitures of land sales contracts.—For purposes of subsection (b), a sale of property includes any forfeiture of a land sales contract.

* * * * * * * * * * * *

[For official explanation, see Committee Reports, ¶4110.]

〔¶3404〕 CODE SEC. 7426. CIVIL ACTIONS BY PERSONS OTHER THAN TAXPAYERS.

* * * * * * * * * * * *

(g) Interest.—Interest shall be allowed at [1]*the overpayment rate established under section 6621*—

(1) in the case of a judgment pursuant to subsection (b)(2)(B), from the date the Secretary receives the money wrongfully levied upon to the date of payment of such judgment; and

(2) in the case of a judgment pursuant to subsection (b)(2)(C), from the date of the sale of the property wrongfully levied upon to the date of payment of such judgment.

* * * * * * * * * * * *

[For official explanation, see Committee Reports, ¶4075.]

〔¶3405〕 CODE SEC. 7430. AWARDING OF COURT COSTS AND CERTAIN FEES.

(a) In general.—In the case of any civil proceeding which is—

(1) brought by or against the United States in connection with the determination, collection, or refund of any tax, interest or penalty under this title, and

(2) brought in a court of the United States (including the Tax Court and the U.S. Claims Court),

---

〔**Footnote ¶3402〕** Matter in *italics* in Sec. 7422(g)(1)(B) added by section 1899A(58), '86 TRA, which struck out:

(1) "section 4962"

〔**Footnote ¶3403〕** Sec. 7425(c)(4) in *italics* added by section 1572(a), '86 TRA.

Effective date (Sec. 1572(b), '86 TRA).—Applies to forfeitures after the 30th day after the date of the enactment of this Act.

〔**Footnote ¶3404〕** Matter in *italics* in Sec. 7426(g) added by section 1511(c)(16), '86 TRA, which struck out:

(1) "an annual rate established under section 6621"

Effective date (Sec. 1511(d), '86 TRA).—Applies for purposes of determining interest for periods after 12-31-86.

the prevailing party may be awarded a judgment *(payable in the case of the Tax Court in same manner as such an award by a district court)* for reasonable litigation costs incurred in such proceedings.

(b) Limitations.—[1]

[2]*(1)* **Requirement that administrative remedies be exhausted.**—A judgment for reasonable litigation costs shall not be awarded under subsection (a) unless the court determines that the prevailing party has exhausted the administrative remedies available to such party within the Internal Revenue Service.

[3]*(2)* **Only costs allocable to the United States.**—An award under subsection (a) shall be made only for reasonable litigation costs which are allocable to the United States and not to any other party to the action or proceeding.

[4]*(3)* **Exclusion of declaratory judgment proceedings.—**

(A) In general.—No award for reasonable litigation costs may be made under subsection (a) with respect to any declaratory judgment proceeding.

* * * * * * * * * * * *

(4) Costs denied where party prevailing protracts proceedings.—No award for reasonable litigation costs may be made under subsection (a) with respect to any portion of the civil proceeding during which the prevailing party has unreasonably protracted such proceeding.

(c) Definitions.—For purposes of this section—

(1) Reasonable litigation costs.—

[5]*(A) In general.—The term "reasonable litigation costs" includes—*

(i) reasonable court costs, and

(ii) based upon prevailing market rates for the kind or quality of services furnished—

(I) the reasonable expenses of expert witnesses in connection with the civil proceeding, except that no expert witness shall be compensated at a rate in excess of the highest rate of compensation for expert witnesses paid by the United States,

(II) the reasonable cost of any study, analysis, engineering report, test, or project which is found by the court to be necessary for the preparation of the party's case, and

(III) reasonable fees paid or incurred for the services of attorneys in connection with the civil proceeding, except that such fees shall not be in excess of $75 per hour unless the court determines that an increase in the cost of living or a special factor, such as the limited availability of qualified attorneys for such proceeding, justifies a higher rate.

* * * * * * * * * * *

(2) Prevailing party.—

(A) In general.—The term "prevailing party" means any party to any proceeding described in subsection (a) (other than the United States or any creditor of the taxpayer involved) which—

(i) establishes that the position of the United States in the civil proceeding was [6]*not substantially justified,* [7]

[Footnote ¶3405] Matter in *italics* in Sec. 7430(a) added by section 1551(f), '86 TRA.
Effective date (Sec. 1551(h)(2), '86 TRA and section 292(e)(1), '82 TEFRA).—Applies to civil actions on proceedings commenced after 2-28-83.

Matter in *italics* in Sec. 7430(b), (c)(1)(A), (2)(A), (4) and (f) added by section 1551(a)—(e) and (g), '86 TRA, which struck out:

(1) "(1) **Maximum dollar amount.**—The amount of reasonable litigation costs which may be awarded under subsection (a) with respect to any prevailing party in any civil proceeding shall not exceed $25,000."

(2) "(2)"

(3) "(3)"

(4) "(4)"

(5) "(A) In general.—The term 'reasonable litigation costs' includes—

(i) reasonable court costs,

(ii) the reasonable expenses of expert witnesses in connection with the civil proceeding,

(iii) the reasonable cost of any study, analysis, engineering report, test, or project which is found by the court to be necessary for the preparation of the party's case, and

(iv) reasonable fees paid or incurred for the services of attorneys in connection with the civil proceeding."

(6) "unreasonable"

(7) "and"

(ii)(I)   has substantially prevailed with respect to the amount in controversy, or

(II)   has substantially prevailed with respect to the most significant issue or set of issues presented[8], *and*

(iii)   *meets the requirements of section 504(b)(1)(B) of title 5, United States Code (as in effect on the date of the enactment of the Tax Reform Act of 1986 and applied by taking into account the commencement of the proceeding described in subsection (a) in lieu of the initiation of the adjudication referred to in such section).*

* * * * * * * * * * *

(4)   Position of United States.—The term *"position of the United States" includes*—
(A)   *the position taken by the United States in the civil proceeding, and*
(B)   *any administrative action or inaction by the District Counsel of the Internal Revenue Service (and all subsequent administrative action or inaction) upon which such proceeding is based.*

* * * * * * * * * * *

(f)   [struck out][9]

[For official explanation, see Committee Reports, ¶4090.]

〖¶3406〗   CODE SEC. 7443A.   SPECIAL TRIAL JUDGES.

(a)   Appointment.—The chief judge may, from time to time, appoint special trial judges who shall proceed under such rules and regulations as may be promulgated by the Tax Court.

(b)   Proceedings Which May Be Assigned to Special Trial Judges.—The chief judge may assign—
(1)   any declaratory judgment proceeding,
(2)   any proceeding under section 7463,
(3)   any proceeding where neither the amount of the deficiency placed in dispute (within the meaning of section 7463) nor the amount of any claimed overpayment exceeds $10,000, and
(4)   any other proceeding which the chief judge may designate,
to be heard by the special trial judges of the court.

(c)   Authority To Make Court Decision.—The court may authorize a special trial judge to make the decision of the court with respect to any proceeding described in paragraph (1), (2), or (3) of subsection (b), subject to such conditions and review as the court may provide.

(d)   Salary.—Each special trial judge shall receive salary—
(1)   at a rate equal to 90 percent of the rate for judges of the Tax Court, and
(2)   in the same installments as such judges.

(e)   Expenses for Travel and Subsistence.—Subsection (d) of section 7443 shall apply to special trial judges subject to such rules and regulations as may be promulgated by the Tax Court.

[For official explanation, see Committee Reports, ¶4095.]

〖Footnote ¶3405 continued〗

(8)   "."
(9)   "(f)   Termination.—This section shall not apply to any proceeding commenced after December 31, 1985."
Effective date (Sec. 1551(h)(1) and (3), '86 TRA).—(1)   Generally applies to amounts paid after 9-30-86, in civil actions or proceedings, commenced after 12-31-85.

* * * * * * * * * * * *

(3)   Applicability of amendments to certain prior cases.—The amendments made by this section shall apply to any case commenced after 12-31-85, and finally disposed of before the date of the enactment of this Act, except that in any such case, the 30-day period referred to in section 2412(d)(1)(B) of title 28, United States Code, or Rule 231 of the Tax Court, as the case may be, shall be deemed to commence on the date of the enactment of this Act.

〖Footnote ¶3406〗   Sec. 7443A added by section 1556(a), '86 TRA.
Effective date (Sec. 1556(c), '86 TRA).—On the date of the enactment of this Act.
(2)   Salary.—Subsection (d) of section 7443A of the '54 Code (as added by this section) shall take effect on the 1st day of the 1st month beginning after the date of the enactment of this Act.
(3)   New appointments not required.—Nothing in the amendments made by this section shall be construed to require the reappointment of any individual serving as a special trial judge of the Tax Court on the day before the date of the enactment of this Act.

Code §7443A(e)   ¶3406

〔¶3407〕 CODE SEC. 7447. RETIREMENT.

(a) **Definitions.**—For purposes of this section—

(1) The term "Tax Court" means the United States Tax Court.[1]

[2](2) The term "judge" means the chief judge or a judge of the Tax Court; but such term does not include any individual performing judicial duties pursuant to subsection (c).

[3](3) In any determination of length of service as judge there shall be included all periods (whether or not consecutive) during which an individual served as judge, as judge of the Tax Court of the United States, or as a member of the Board of Tax Appeals.

(b) **Retirement.**—

*   *   *   *   *   *   *   *   *   *   *   *

[4]*(2) Any judge who meets the age and service requirements set forth in the following table may retire:*

The judge has attained age:	*And the years of service as a judge are at least:*
65	15
66	14
67	13
68	12
69	11
70	10

*   *   *   *   *   *   *   *   *   *   *   *

(e) **Election To Receive Retired Pay.**—Any judge may elect to receive retired pay under subsection (d). Such an election—

(1) may be made only while an individual is a judge (except that in the case of an individual who fails to be reappointed as judge at the expiration of a term of office, it may be made at any time before the day after the day on which his successor takes office);

(2) once made, shall be irrevocable;

(3) in the case of any judge other than the chief judge, shall be made by filing notice thereof in writing with the chief judge; and

(4) in the case of the chief judge, shall be made by filing notice thereof in writing with the [5]*Office of Personnel Management.*

The chief judge shall transmit to the [5]*Office of Personnel Management* a copy of each notice filed with him under this subsection.

[6]*(f)* ***Retired Pay Affected in Certain Cases.****—In the case of an individual for whom an*

〔Footnote ¶3407〕 Matter in *italics* in Sec. 7447(a)(2)—(3), (b)(2), (e), (f), and (g)(2)(C) added by section 1557(a), (b) and (d), '86 TRA, which struck out:

(1) "(2) The term 'Civil Service Commission' means the United States Civil Service Commission."

(2) "(3)"

(3) "(5)"

(4) "(2) Any judge who has attained the age of 65 may retire any time after serving as judge for 15 years or more."

(5) "Civil Service Commission"

(6) "(f) **Individuals Receiving Retired Pay To Be Available for Recall.**—Any individual who has elected to receive retired pay under subsection (d) who thereafter—

(1) accept civil office or employment under the Government of the United States (other than the performance of judicial duties pursuant to subsection (c)); or

(2) performs (or supervises or directs the performance of) legal or accounting services in the field of Federal taxation or in the field of the renegotiation of Federal contracts for his client, his employer, or any of his employer's clients,

shall forfeit all rights to retired pay under subsection (d) for all periods beginning on or after the first day on which he accepts such office or employment or engages in any activity described in paragraph (2). Any individual who has elected to receive retired pay under subsection (d) who thereafter during any calendar year fails to perform judicial duties required of him by subsection (c) shall forfeit all rights to retired pay under subsection (d) for the 1-year period which begins on the first day on which he so fails to perform such duties."

Effective date (Sec. 1557(e), '86 TRA).—(1) Generally takes effect on the date of the enactment of this Act.

(2) Forfeiture of retired pay.—The amendments made by this section shall not apply to any individual who, before the date of the enactment of this Act, forfeited his rights to retired pay under section 7447(d) of the '54 Code by reason of the 1st sentence of section 7447(f) of such Code (as in effect on the day before such date).

election to receive retired pay under subsection (d) is in effect—

(1) *1-Year forfeiture for failure to perform judicial duties.—If such individual during any calendar year fails to perform judicial duties required of him by subsection (c), such individual shall forfeit all rights to retired pay under subsection (d) for the 1-year period which begins on the 1st day on which he so fails to perform such duties.*

(2) *Permanent forfeiture of retired pay where certain non-government services performed.—If such individual performs (or supervises or directs the performance of) legal or accounting services in the field of Federal taxation for his client, his employer, or any of his employer's clients, such individual shall forfeit all rights to retired pay under subsection (d) for all periods beginning on or after the 1st day on which he engages in any such activity. The preceding sentence shall not apply to any civil office or employment under the Government of the United States.*

(3) *Suspension of retired pay during period of compensated government service.—If such individual accepts compensation for civil office or employment under the Government of the United States (other than the performance of judicial duties pursuant to subsection (c)), such individual shall forfeit all rights to retired pay under subsection (d) for the period for which such compensation is received.*

(4) *Forfeitures of retired pay under paragraphs (1) and (2) not to apply where individual elects to freeze amount of retired pay.—*

(A) *In general.—If any individual makes an election under this paragraph—*

(i) *paragraphs (1) and (2) (and subsection (c)) shall not apply to such individual beginning on the date such election takes effect, and*

(ii) *the retired pay under subsection (d) payable to such individual for periods beginning on or after the date such election takes effect shall be equal to the retired pay to which such individual would be entitled without regard to this clause at the time of such election.*

(B) *Election.—An election under this paragraph—*

(i) *may be made by an individual only if such individual meets the age and service requirements for retirement under paragraph (2) of subsection (b),*

(ii) *may be made only during the period during which the individul may make an election to receive retired pay or while the individual is receiving retired pay, and*

(iii) *shall be made in the same manner as the election to receive retired pay.*

Such an election, once it takes effect, shall be irrevocable.

(C) *When election takes effect.—Any election under this paragraph shall take effect on the 1st day of the 1st month following the month in which the election is made.*

(g) Coordination With Civil Service Retirement.—

* * * * * * * * * * * *

(2) Effect of electing retired pay.—In the case of any individual who has filed an election to receive retired pay under subsection (d)—

(A) no annuity or other payment shall be payable to any person under the civil service retirement laws with respect to any service performed by such individual (whether performed before or after such election is filed and whether performed as judge or otherwise);

(B) no deduction for purposes of the Civil Service Retirement and disability Fund shall be made from retired pay payable to him under subsection (d) or from any other salary, pay, or compensation payable to him, for any period beginning after the day on which such election is filed; and

(C) such individual shall be paid the lump-sum credit computed under section 8331(8) of title 5 of the United States Code upon making application therefor with the [5]*Office of Personnel Management.*

* * * * * * * * * * * *

[For official explanation, see Committee Reports, ¶4096.]

⟦¶3408⟧ CODE SEC. 7448. ANNUITIES TO SURVIVING SPOUSES AND DEPENDENT CHILDREN OF JUDGES.

* * * * * * * * * * * *

(b) Election.—Any judge may by written election filed while he is a judge (except that in the case of an individual who is not reappointed following expiration of his term of office, it may be made at any time before the day after the day on which his successor takes office) bring himself within the purview of this section. In the case of any judge other than the chief judge the election shall be filed with the chief judge; in the case of the chief judge the election shall be filed as prescribed by the Tax Court.

[1](c) *Survivors Annuity Fund.—*

   (1) **Salary deductions.**—There shall be deducted and withheld from the salary each judge electing under subsection (b) the sum equal to [2]*3.5 percent* of such judge's salary. The amounts so deducted and withheld from such judge's salary shall, in accordance with such procedure as may be prescribed by the Comptroller General of the United States, be deposited in the Treasury of the United States to the credit of a fund to be known as the "Tax Court judges survivors annuity fund" and said fund is appropriated for the payment of annuities, refunds, and allowances as provided by this section. Each judge electing under subsection (b) shall be deemed thereby to consent and agree to the deductions from his salary as provided in this subsection, and payment less such deductions shall be a full and complete discharge and acquittance of all claims and demands whatsoever for all judicial services rendered by such judge during the period covered by such payment, except the right to the benefits to which he or his survivors shall be entitled under the provisions of this section.

   (2) *Appropriations where unfunded liability.—*
      (A) In general.—Not later than the close of each fiscal year, there shall be deposited in the Treasury of the United States to the credit of the survivors annuity fund, in accordance with such procedures as may be prescribed by the Comptroller General of the United States, amounts required to reduce to zero the unfunded liability (if any) of such fund. Subject to appropriation Acts, such deposits shall be taken from sums available for such fiscal year for the payment of amounts described in subsection (a)(4), and shall immediately become an integrated part of such fund.
      (B) Exception.—The amount required by subparagraph (A) to be deposited in any fiscal year shall not exceed an amount equal to 11 percent of the aggregate amounts described in subsection (a)(4) paid during such fiscal year.
      (C) Unfunded liability defined.—For purposes of subparagraph (A), the term "unfunded liability" means the amount estimated by the Secretary to be equal to the excess (as of the close of the fiscal year involved) of—
         (i) the present value of all benefits payable from the survivors annuity fund (determined on an annual basis in accordance with section 9503 of title 31, United States Code), over
         (ii) the sum of—
            (I) the present values of future deductions under subsection (c) and future deposits under subsection (d), plus
            (II) the balance in such fund as of the close of such fiscal year.
      (D) Amounts not credited to individual accounts.—Amounts appropriated pursuant to this paragraph shall not be credited to the account of any individual for purposes of subsection (g).

   (d) **Deposits in Survivors Annuity Fund.**—Each judge electing under subsection (b) shall deposit, with interest at 4 percent per annum to December 31, 1947, and 3 percent per annum thereafter, compounded on December 31 of each year, to the credit of the survivors annuity fund, a sum equal to [2]*3.5 percent* of his judge's salary and of his basic salary, pay, or compensation for service as a Senator, Representative, Delegate, or Resident Commissioner in Congress, and for any other civilian service within the purview of section 8332 of Title 5 of the United States Code. Each such judge may elect to make such deposits in installments during the continuance of his service as a judge in such amount and under such conditions as may be determined in each instance by the chief judge. Notwithstanding the failure of a judge to make such deposit, credit shall be allowed for the service rendered, but the annuity of the surviving spouse of such judge shall be reduced by an amount equal to 10 percent of the amount of such deposit, computed as of the date of the death of such judge, unless such surviving spouse shall elect to eliminate such service entirely from credit under subsection (n), except that no deposit shall be required from a judge for any year with respect to which deductions from his salary were actually made under the civil service retirement laws and no deposit shall be required for any honorable service in the Army, Navy, Air Force, Marine Corps, or Coast Guard of the United States.

[**Footnote ¶3408**] Matter in *italics* in Sec. 7448(c), (d), (g), (h) and (m) added by section 1559(a)—(c), '86 TRA, which struck out:
   (1) "(c) Salary Deductions"
   (2) "3 percent"

(g) **Termination**[3].—If the service of any judge electing under subsection (b) terminates other than pursuant to the provisions of section 7447 or other than pursuant to section 1106 of the Internal Revenue Code of 1939, *or if any judge ceases to be married after making the election under subsection (b) and revokes (in a writing filed as provided in subsection (b)) such election* the amount credited to his individual account, together with interest an 4 percent per annum to December 31, 1947, and 3 percent per annum thereafter, compounded on December 31 of each year, to the date of his relinquishment of office, shall be returned to him. For the purpose of this section, the service of any judge electing under subsection (b) who is not reappointed following expiration of his term but who, at the time of such expiration, is eligible for and elects to receive retired pay under section 7447 shall be deemed to have terminated pursuant to said section.

(h) **Entitlement to Annuity.**—In case any judge electing under subsection (b) shall die while a judge after having rendered at least 5 years of civilian service computed as prescribed in subsection (n), for the last 5 years of which the salary deductions provided for by [4]*subsection (c)(1)* or the deposits required by subsection (d) have actually been made or the salary deductions required by the civil service retirement laws have actually been made—

(1) if such judge is survived by a surviving spouse but not by a dependent child, there shall be paid to such surviving spouse an annuity beginning with the day of the death of the judge or following the surviving spouse's attainment of the age of 50 years, whichever is the later, in an amount computed as provided in subsection (m); or

(2) if such judge is survived by a surviving spouse and a dependent child or children, there shall be paid to such surviving spouse an immediate annuity in an amount computed as provided in subsection (m), and there shall also be paid to or on behalf of each such child an immediate annuity equal to [5]*the lesser of*—

(A) *10 percent of the average annual salary of such judge (determined in accordance with subsection (m)), or*

(B) *20 percent of such average annual salary, divided by the number of such children; or*

(3) if such judge leaves no surviving spouse but leaves a surviving dependent child or children, there shall be paid to or on behalf of each such child an immediate annuity equal to [6]*the lesser of*—

(A) *20 percent of the average annual salary of such judge (determined in accordance with subsection (m)), or*

(B) *40 percent of such average annual salary, divided by the number of such children.*

The annuity payable to a surviving spouse under this subsection shall be terminable upon such surviving spouse's death or [7]*such surviving spouse's remarriage before attaining age 55.* The annuity payable to a child under this subsection shall be terminable upon (A) his attaining the age of 18 years, (B) his marriage, or (C) his death, whichever first occurs, except that if such child is incapable of self-support by reason of mental or physical disability his annuity shall be terminable only upon death, marriage, or recovery from such disability. In case of the death of a surviving spouse of a judge leaving a dependent child or children of the judge surviving such spouse, the annuity of such child or children shall be recomputed and paid as provided in paragraph (3) of this subsection. In any case in which the annuity of a dependent child is terminated under this subsection, the annuities of any remaining dependent child or children, based upon the service of the same judge, shall be recomputed and paid as though the child whose annuity was so terminated had not survived such judge.

* * * * * * * * * * * *

(m) **Computation of Annuities.**—The annuity of the surviving spouse of a judge electing under subsection (b) shall be an amount equal to the sum of (1) [8]*1.5 percent of the*

[Footnote ¶3408 continued]

(3) "of Service"

(4) "subsection (C)"

(5) "one-half the amount of the annuity of such surviving spouse, but not to exceed $4,644 per year divided by the number of such children or $1,548 per year, whichever is lesser; or"

(6) "the amount of the annuity to which such surviving spouse would have been entitled under paragraph (2) of this subsection had such spouse survived, but not to exceed $5,580 per year divided by the number of such children or $1,860 per year, whichever is lesser."

(7) "remarriage"

(8) "1 1/4 percent"

average annual salary (whether judge's salary or compensation for other allowable service) received by such judge for judicial service (including periods in which he received retired pay under section 7447(d)) or for any other prior allowable service during the period of 3 consecutive years in which he received the largest such average annual salary, multiplied by the sum of his years of such judicial service, his years of prior allowable service as a Senator, Representative, Delegate, or Resident Commissioner in Congress, his years of prior allowable service performed as a member of the Armed Forces of the United States, and his years not exceeding 15, of prior allowable service performed as a congressional employee (as defined in section 2107 of Title 5 of the United States Code, and (2) three-fourths of 1 percent of such average annual salary multiplied by his years of any other prior allowable service [9]*except that such annuity shall not exceed an amount equal to 50 percent of such average annual salary nor be less than an amount equal to 25 percent of such average annual salary, and shall be further reduced in accordance with subsection (d) (if applicable.) In determining the period of 3 consecutive years referred to in the preceding sentence, there may not be taken into account any period for which an election under section 7447(f)(4) is in effect.*

$$* \quad * \quad * \quad * \quad * \quad * \quad * \quad * \quad * \quad * \quad * \quad *$$

[For official explanation, see Committee Reports, ¶4098.]

[¶3409] CODE SEC. 7456. ADMINISTRATION OF OATHS AND PROCUREMENT OF TESTIMONY.

$$* \quad * \quad * \quad * \quad * \quad * \quad * \quad * \quad * \quad * \quad * \quad *$$

[1]*(c)* [2]**Incidental Powers.**—The Tax Court and each division thereof shall have power

---

[Footnote ¶3408 continued]

(9) "but such annuity shall not exceed 40 percent of such average annual salary and shall be further reduced in accordance with subsection (d), if applicable."

Effective date (Sec. 1559(d), '86 TRA).—

(1) Salary deductions.—

(A) The amendment made by subsection (a)(1)(A) shall apply to amounts paid after 11-1-86.

(B) The amendment made by subsection (a)(1)(B) shall apply to service after 11-1-86.

(2) Appropriations.—The amendments made by subsection (a)(2) shall apply to fiscal years beginning after 1986.

(3) Computation of annuities.—The amendments made by subsection (b) shall apply to annuities the starting date of which is after 11-1-86.

(4) Opportunity to revoke survivor annuity election.—

(A) In General.—Any individual who before 11-1-86, made an election under subsection (b) of section 7448 of the '54 Code may revoke such election. Such a revocation shall constitute a complete withdrawal from the survivor annuity program provided for in such section and shall be filed as provided for elections under such subsection.

(B) Effect of revocation.—Any revocation under subparagraph (A) shall have the same effect as if there were a termination to which section 7448(g) of such Code applies on the date such revocation is filed.

(C) Period revocation permitted.—Any revocation under subparagraph (A) may be made only during the 180-day period beginning on the date of the enactment of this Act.

(5) Opportunity to elect survivor annuity where prior revocation.—Any individual who under paragraph (4) revoked an election under subsection (b) of section 7448 of such Code may thereafter make such an election only if such individual deposits to the credit of the survivors annuity fund under subsection (c) of such section the entire amount paid to such individual under paragraph (4), together with interest computed as provided in subsection (d) of such section.

Matter in *italics* in last sentence of Sec. 7448(m) added by section 1557(c), '86 TRA.

Effective date (Sec. 1557 (e), '86 TRA).—(1) Generally takes effect on the date of the enactment of this Act.

(2) Forfeiture of retired pay.—The amendments made by this section shall not apply to any individual who, before the date of the enactment of this Act, forfeited his rights to retired pay under section 7447(d) of the '54 Code by reason of the 1st sentence of section 7447(f) of such Code (as in effect on the day before such date.)

[Footnote ¶3409] Matter in *italics* in Sec. 7456(c) (former (e)), except the last sentence added by section 1556(b)(1), '86 TRA, which struck out:

(1) "(c) Special Trial Judges.—The chief judge may from time to time appoint special trial judges who shall proceed under such rules and regulations as may be promulgated by the Tax Court. Each special trial judge shall receive pay at an annual rate determined under section 225 of the Federal Salary Act of 1967 (2 U.S.C. 351-361), as adjusted by section 461 of title 28, United States Code, and also necessary traveling expenses and per diem allowances, as provided in subchapter 1 of chapter 57 of title 5, United States Code, while traveling on official business and away from Washington, District of Columbia.

(d) Proceedings Which be Assigned to Special Trial Judges.—The chief judge may assign—

(1) any declaratory judgment proceeding.

(2) any proceeding under section 7463,

(3) any proceeding where neither the amount of the deficiency placed in dispute (within the meaning of section 7463) nor the amount of any claimed overpayment exceeds $10,000; and

(4) any other proceeding which the chief judge may designate,

to be heard by the special trial judges of the court, and the court may authorize a special trial judge to make the decision of the court with respect to any proceeding described in paragraph (1), (2) or (3), subject to such conditions and review as the court may provide."

(2) "(e)"

to punish by fine or imprisonment, at its discretion, such contempt of its authority, and none other, as—

　(1)　misbehavior of any person in its presence or so near thereto as to obstruct the administration of justice;

　(2)　misbehavior of any of its officers in their official transactions; or

　(3)　disobedience or resistance to its lawful writ, process, order, rule, decree, or command.

It shall have such assistance in the carrying out of its lawful writ, process, order, rule, decree, or command as is available to a court of the United States. *The United States marshal for any district in which the Tax Court is sitting shall, when requested by the chief judge of the Tax Court, attend any session of the Tax Court in such district.*

[For official explanation, see Committee Reports, ¶4094; 4095.]

[¶3410]　CODE SEC. 7471.　EMPLOYEES.

*　*　*　*　*　*　*　*　*　*　*　*

　(c)　**Special Trial Judges.—**

For compensation and travel and subsistence allowances of special trial judges of the Tax Court, see [1]*subsections (d) and (e) of section 7443A.*

[For official explanation, see Committee Reports, ¶4095.]

[¶3411]　CODE SEC. 7472.　EXPENDITURES.

The Tax Court is authorized to make such expenditures (including expenditures for personal services and rent at the seat of Government and elsewhere, and for law books, books of reference, and periodicals), as may be necessary efficiently to execute the functions vested in the Tax Court. [1]*Except as provided in section 7475, all* expenditures of the Tax Court shall be allowed and paid, out of any moneys appropriated for purposes of Tax Court, upon presentation of itemized vouchers therefor signed by the certifying officer designated by the chief judge.

[For official explanation, see Committee Reports, ¶4092.]

[¶3412]　CODE SEC. 7473.　DISPOSITION OF FEES.

[1]*Except as provided in section 7475, all* fees received by the Tax Court shall be covered into the Treasury as miscellaneous receipts.

[For official explanation, see Committee Reports, ¶4092.]

[¶3413]　CODE SEC. 7475.　PRACTICE FEE.

　(a)　**In general.—**The Tax Court is authorized to impose a periodic registration fee on practitioners admitted to practice before such Court. The frequency and amount of such

---

[Footnote ¶3409 continued]

Effective date (Sec. 1556(c)(1) and (3), '86 TRA).—(1)　Generally takes effect on the date of the enactment of this Act.

*　*　*　*　*　*　*　*　*　*　*

(3)　New appointments not required.—Nothing in the amendments made by this section shall be construed to require the reappointment of any individual serving as a special trial judge of the Tax Court on the day before the date of the enactment of this Act.

The last sentence in *italics* in Sec. 7456(c) (Former (e) added by section 1555(a), '86 TRA.

Effective date (Sec. 1555(b), '86 TRA).—Takes effect on the date of the enactment of this Act.

[Footnote ¶3410]　Matter in *italics* in Sec. 7471(c) added by section 1556(b)(2), '86 TRA, which struck out: (1)　"section 7456(c)"

Effective date (Sec. 1556(c)(1) and (3), '86 TRA).—(1)　Generally takes effect on the date of the enactment of this Act.

*　*　*　*　*　*　*　*　*　*　*

(3)　New appointments not required.—Nothing in the amendments made by this section shall be construed to require the reappointment of any individual serving as a special trial judge of the Tax Court on the day before date of the enactment of this Act.

[Footnote ¶3411]　Matter in *italics* in Sec. 7472 added by section 1553(b)(1), '86 TRA, which struck out: (1)　"All"

Effective date (Sec. 1553(c), '86 TRA).—Takes effect on 1-1-87.

[Footnote ¶3412]　Matter in *italics* in Sec. 7473 added by section 1553(b)(2), '86 TRA, which struck out: (1)　"All"

Effective date (Sec 1553(c), '86 TRA).—Takes effect on 1-1-87.

[Footnote ¶3413]　Sec. 7475 added by section 1553(a), '86 TRA.

Effective date (Sec. 1553(c), '86 TRA).—Takes effect on 1-1-87.

fee shall be determined by the Tax Court, except that such amount may not exceed $30 per year.

(b) Use of Fees.—The fees described in subsection (a) shall be available to the Tax Court to employ independent counsel to pursue disciplinary matters.

[For official explanation, see Committee Reports, ¶4092.]

[¶3414] CODE SEC. 7476. DECLARATORY JUDGMENTS RELATING TO QUALIFICATIONS OF CERTAIN RETIREMENT PLANS.

* * * * * * * * * * * *

(c) Retirement Plan.—For purposes of this section, the term "retirement plan" means—

(1) a pension, profit-sharing, or stock bonus plan described in section 401(a) or a trust which is part of such a *¹plan, or*

(2) an annuity plan described in section 403(a).

* * * * * * * * * * * *

[¶3415] CODE SEC. 7482. COURTS OF REVIEW.

(a) Jurisdiction.—

(1) In general.—The United States Courts of Appeals (other than the United States Court of Appeals for the Federal Circuit) shall have exclusive jurisdiction to review the decisions of the Tax Court, except as provided in section 1254 of Title 28 of the United States Code, in the same manner and to the same extent as decisions of the district courts in civil actions tried without a jury; and the judgment of any such court shall be final, except that it shall be subject to review by the Supreme Court of the United States upon certiorari, in the manner provided in section 1254 of Title 28 of the United States Code.

(2) Interlocutory orders.—

(A) In general.—*When any judge of the Tax Court includes in an interlocutory order a statement that a controlling question of law is involved with respect to which there is a substantial ground for difference of opinion and that an immediate appeal from that order may materially advance the ultimate termination of the litigation, the United States Court of Appeals may, in its discretion, permit an appeal to be taken from such order, if application is made to it within 10 days after the entry of such order. Neither the application for nor the granting of an appeal under this paragraph shall stay proceedings in the Tax Court, unless a stay is ordered by a judge of the Tax Court or by the United States Court of Appeals which has jurisdiction of the appeal or a judge of that court.*

(B) Order treated as tax court decision.—*For purposes of subsections (b) and (c), an order described in this paragraph shall be treated as a decision of the Tax Court.*

(C) Venue for review of subsequent proceedings.—*If a United States Court of Appeals permits an appeal to be taken from an order described in subparagraph (A), except as provided in subsection (b)(2), any subsequent review of the decision of the Tax Court in the proceeding shall be made by such Court of Appeals.*

(b) Venue.—

(1) In general.—Except as otherwise provided in paragraphs (2) and (3) such decisions may be reviewed by the United States Court of Appeals for the circuit in which is located—

* * * * * * * * * * * *

(E) in the case of a petition under section 6226 or 6228(a), the principal place of business of the partnership ¹.

If for any reason no subparagraph of the preceding sentence applies, then such decisions may be reviewed by the Court of Appeals for the District of Columbia. For purposes of this paragraph, the legal residence, principal place of business, or principal office or agency referred to herein shall be determined as of the time the petition seeking redetermination of tax liability was filed with the Tax Court or as of the time the

---

petition seeking a declaratory decision under [2]*section 7428 or 7476,* or the petition under section 6226 or 6228(a), was filed with the Tax Court.

*   *   *   *   *   *   *   *   *   *   *   *

[For official explanation, see Committee Reports, ¶4097; 4144.]

【¶3416】 CODE SEC. 7502. TIMELY MAILING TREATED AS TIMELY FILING AND PAYING.

*   *   *   *   *   *   *   *   *   *   *   *

(e) Mailing of Deposits.—

(1) Date of deposit.—If any deposit required to be made (pursuant to regulations prescribed by the Secretary under section 6302(c)) on or before a prescribed date is, after such date, delivered by the United States mail to the bank, trust company, domestic building and loan association, or credit union authorized to receive such deposit, such deposit shall be deemed received by such bank, trust company, domestic building and loan association, or credit union on the date the deposit was mailed.

(2) Mailing requirements.—Paragraph (1) shall apply only if the person required to make the deposits establishes that—

(A)   the date of mailing falls on or before the second day before the prescribed date for making the deposit (including any extension of time granted for making such deposit), and

(B)   the deposit was, on or before such second day, mailed in the United States in an envelope or other appropriate wrapper, postage prepaid, properly addressed to the bank, trust company, domestic building and loan association, or credit union authorized to receive such deposit. In applying subsection (c) for purposes of this subsection, the term "payment" includes "deposit", and the reference to the postmark date refers to the date of mailing.

(3) No application to certain deposits.—Paragraph (1) shall not apply with respect to any deposit of $20,000 or more by any person who is required to deposit [1]*any tax* more than once a month.

[For official explanation, see Committee Reports, ¶4145.]

【¶3417】 CODE SEC. 7508. TIME FOR PERFORMING CERTAIN ACTS POSTPONED BY REASON OF SERVICE IN COMBAT ZONE.

(a) Time To Be Disregarded.—In the case of an individual serving in the Armed Forces of the United States, or serving in support of such Armed Forces, in an area designated by the President of the United States by Executive order as a "combat zone" for purposes of section 112, at any time during the period designated by the President by Executive order as the period of combatant activities in such zone for purposes of such section, or hospitalized outside the United States as a result of injury received while serving in such an area during such time, the period of service in such area, plus the period of continuous hospitalization outside the United States attributable to such injury, and the next 180 days thereafter, shall be disregarded in determining, under the internal revenue laws, in respect of any tax liability (including any interest, penalty, additional amount, or addition to the tax) of such individual—

(1)   Whether any of the following acts was performed within the time prescribed therefor:

【Footnote ¶3415 continued】

Matter in *italics* in Sec. 7482(b)(1) added by section 1810(g)(2), '86 TRA, which struck out:

(2) "section 7428, 7476, or 7477"

Effective date (Sec. 1881, '86 TRA and Sec. 131(g), '84 TRA).—(1)   Generally applies to transfers or exchanges after 12-31-84, in taxable years ending after such date.

(2) Special rule for certain tranfers of intangibles.—

(A) In general.—If, after 6-6-84, and before 1-1-85, a U.S. person transfers any intangible property (within the meaning of Sec. 936(h)(3)(B) of the '54 Code) to a foreign corporation or in a transfer described in Sec. 1491, such transfer shall be treated for purposes of Sec. 367(a), 1492(2), and 1494(b) as prusuant to a plan having as one of its principal purposes the avoidance of Federal income tax.

(B) Waiver.—Subject to such terms and conditions as the Secretary of the Treasury or his delegate may prescribe, the Secretary may waive the application of subparagraph (A) with respect to any transfer.

(3) Ruling request before March 1, 1984.—The amendments made by this section (and the provisions of paragraph (2) of this subsection) shall not apply to any transfer or exchange of property described in a request filed before 3-1-84 under Secs. 367(a), 1492(2), or 1494(b) of the '54 Code (as in effect before such amendments).

【Footnote ¶3416】 Matter in *italics* in Sec. 7502(e)(3) added by section 1811(e), '86 TRA, which struck out:

(1) "the tax"

Effective date (Sec. 1881, '86 TRA and Sec. 157(b), '84 TRA).—Applies to deposits required to be made after 7-31-84.

(A)   Filing any return of income, estate, or gift tax (except income tax withheld at source and income tax imposed by subtitle C or any law superseded thereby);

(B)   Payment of any income, estate, or gift tax (except income tax withheld at source and income tax imposed by subtitle C or any law superseded thereby) or any installment thereof or any other liability to the United States in respect thereof;

(C)   Filing a petition with the Tax Court for redetermination of a deficiency, or for review of a decision rendered by the Tax Court;

* * * * * * * * * * * *

(b) Application to Spouse. The provisions of this section shall apply to the spouse of any individual entitled to the benefit of subsection (a). [1]*Except in the case of the combat zone designated for purposes of the Vietnam conflict, the preceding sentence shall not cause this section to apply for any spouse for any taxable year beginning more than 2 years after the date desginated under section 112 as the date of termination of combatant activities in a combat zone.*

* * * * * * * * * * * *

[For official explanation, see Committee Reports, ¶4130.]

[¶3418]   CODE SEC. 7518. TAX INCENTIVES RELATING TO MERCHANT MARINE CAPITAL CONSTRUCTION FUNDS.

(a) Ceiling on Deposits.—

(1) In general.—The amount deposited in a fund established under section 607 of the Merchant Marine Act, 1936 (hereinafter in this section referred to as a "capital construction fund") shall not exceed for any taxable year the sum of:

(A)   that portion of the taxable income of the owner or lessee for such year (computed as provided in chapter 1 but without regard to the carryback of any net operating loss or net capital loss and without regard to this section) which is attributable to the operation of the agreement vessels in the foreign domestic commerce of the United States or in the fisheries of the United States.

(B)   the amount allowable as a deduction under section 167 for such year with respect to the agreement vessels,

(C)   if the transaction is not taken into account for purposes of subparagraph (A), the net proceeds (as defined in joint regulations) from—

(i)   the sale or other disposition of any agreement vessel, or

(ii)   insurance or indemnity attributable to any agreement vessel, and

(D)   the receipts from the investment or reinvestment of amounts held in such fund.

(2) Limitations on deposits by lessees.—In the case of a lessee, the maximum amount which may be deposited with respect to an agreement vessel by reason of paragraph (1)(B) for any period shall be reduced by any amount which, under an agreement entered into under section 607 of the Merchant Marine Act, 1936, the owner is required or permitted to deposit for such period with respect to such vessel by reason of paragraph (1)(B).

(3) Certain barges and containers included.—For purposes of paragraph (1), the term "agreement vessel" includes barges and containers which are part of the complement of such vessel and which are provided for in the agreement.

(b) Requirements as to Investments.—

(1) In general.—Amounts in any capital construction fund shall be kept in the depository or depositories specified in the agreement and shall be subject to such trustee and other fiduciary requirements as may be specified by the Secretary.

(2) Limitation on fund investments.—Amounts in any capital construction fund may be invested only in interest-bearing securities approved by the Secretary; except that, if such Secretary consents thereto, an agreed percentage (not in excess of 60 per-

[Footnote ¶3417]   Matter in *italics* in Sec. 7508(b) added by section 1708(a)(4), '86 TRA, which struck out:

(1)   "The preceding sentence shall not cause this section to apply to any spouse for any taxable year beginning—

(1)   after December 31, 1982, in the case of service in the combat zone desginated for purposes of the Vietnam conflict, or

(2)   more than 2 years after the date designated under section 112 as the date of termination of combatant activities in that zone, in the case of any combat zone other than that referred to in paragraph (1)."

Effective date (Sec. 1708(b), '86 TRA).—Applies to taxable years beginning after 12-31-82.

[Footnote ¶3418]   Sec. 7518 added by section 261(b), '86 TRA.

Effective date (Sec. 261(g), '86 TRA).—Applies to taxable years beginning after 12-31-86.

cent) of the assets of the fund may be invested in the stock of domestic corporations. Such stock must be currently fully listed and registered on an exchange registered with the Securities and Exchange Commission as national securities exchange, and must be stock which would be acquired by prudent men of discretion and intelligence in such matters who are seeking a reasonable income and the preservation of their capital. If at any time the fair market value of the stock in the fund is more than the agreed percentage of the assets in the fund, any subsequent investment of amounts deposited in the fund, and any subsequent withdrawal from the fund, shall be made in such a way as to tend to restore the fund to a situation in which the fair market value of the stock does not exceed such agreed percentage.

(3) **Investment in certain preferred stock permitted.**—For purposes of this subsection, if the common stock of a corporation meets the requirements of this subsection and if the preferred stock of such corporation would meet such requirements but for the fact that it cannot be listed and registered as required because it is nonvoting stock, such preferred stock shall be treated as meeting the requirements of this subsection.

(c) **Nontaxability for Deposits.**—

(1) **In general.**—For purposes of this title—

(A) taxable income (determined without regard to this section and section 607 of the Merchant Marine Act, 1936) for the taxable year shall be reduced by an amount equal to the amount deposited for the taxable year out of amounts referred to in subsection (a)(1)(A).

(B) gain from a transaction referred to in subsection (a)(1)(C) shall not be taken into account if an amount equal to the net proceeds (as defined in joint regulations) from such transaction is deposited in the fund,

(C) the earnings (including gains and losses) from the investment and reinvestment of amounts held in the fund shall not be taken into account,

(D) the earnings and profits (within the meaning of section 316) of any corporation shall be determined without regard to this section and section 607 of the Merchant Marine Act, 1936, and

(E) in applying the tax imposed by section 531 (relating to the accumulated earnings tax), amounts while held in the fund shall not be taken into account.

(2) **Only qualified deposits eligible for treatment.**—Paragraph (1) shall apply with respect to any amount only if such amount is deposited in the fund pursuant to the agreement and not later than the time provided in joint regulations.

(d) **Establishment of Accounts.**—For purposes of this section—

(1) **In general.**—Within a capital construction fund 3 accounts shall be maintained:

(A) the capital account,

(B) the capital gain account, and

(C) the ordinary income account.

(2) **Capital account.**—The capital account shall consist of—

(A) amounts referred to in subsection (a)(1)(B),

(B) amounts referred to in subsection (a)(1)(C) other than that portion thereof which represents gain not taken into account by reason of subsection (c)(1)(B),

(C) the percentage applicable under section 243(a)(1) of any dividend received by the fund with respect to which the person maintaining the fund would (but for subsection (c)(1)(C)) be allowed a deduction under section 243, and

(D) interest income exempt from taxation under section 103.

(3) **Capital gain account.**—The capital gain account shall consist of—

(A) amounts representing capital gains on assets held for more than 6 months and referred to in subsection (a)(1)(C) or (a)(1)(D), reduced by

(B) amounts representing capital losses on assets held in the fund for more than 6 months.

(4) **Ordinary income account.**—The ordinary income account will consist of—

(A) amounts referred to in subsection (a)(1)(A),

(B)(i) amounts representing capital gains on assets held for 6 months or less and referred to in subsection (a)(1)(C) or (a)(1)(D), reduced by

(ii) amounts representing capital losses on assets held in the fund for 6 months or less.

Code §7518(d)(4) ¶3418

(C) interest (not including any tax-exempt interest referred to in paragraph (2)(D)) and other ordinary income (not including any dividend referred to in subparagraph (E)) received on assets held in the fund,

(D) ordinary income from a transaction described in subsection (a)(1)(C), and

(E) the portion of any dividend referred to in paragraph (2)(C) not taken into account under such paragraph.

(5) Capital losses only allowed to offset certain gains.—Except on termination of a capital construction fund, capital losses referred to in paragraph (3)(B) or in paragraph (4)(B)(ii) shall be allowed only as an offset to gains referred to in paragraph (3)(A) or (4)(B)(i), respectively.

(e) Purposes of Qualified Withdrawals.—

(1) In general.—A qualified withdrawal from the fund is one made in accordance with the terms of the agreement but only if it is for:

(A) the acquisition, construction, or reconstruction of a qualified vessel,

(B) the acquisition, construction, or reconstruction of barges and containers which are part of the complement of a qualified vessel, or

(C) the payment of the principal on indebtedness incurred in connection with the acquisition, construction, or reconstruction of a qualified vessel or a barge or container which is part of the complement of a qualified vessel.

Except to the extent provided in regulations prescribed by the Secretary, subparagraph (B), and so much of subparagraph (C) as relates only to barges and containers, shall apply only with respect to barges and containers reconstructed in the United States.

(2) Penalty for failing to fulfill any substantial obligation.—Under joint regulations, if the Secretary determines that any substantial obligation under any agreement is not being fulfilled, he may, after notice and opportunity for hearing to the person maintaining the fund, treat the entire fund or any portion thereof as an amount withdrawn from the fund in a nonqualified withdrawal.

(f) Tax Treatment of Qualified Withdrawals.—

(1) Ordering rule.—Any qualified withdrawal from a fund shall be treated—

(A) first as made out of the capital account,

(B) second as made out of the capital gain account, and

(C) third as made out of the ordinary income account.

(2) Adjustment to basis of vessel, etc., where withdrawal from ordinary income account.—If any portion of a qualified withdrawal for a vessel, barge, or container is made out of the ordinary income account, the basis of such vessel, barge, or container shall be reduced by an amount equal to such portion.

(3) Adjustment to basis of vessel, etc., where withdrawal from capital gain account.—If any portion of a qualified withdrawal for a vessel, barge, or container is made out of the capital gain account, the basis of such vessel, barge, or container shall be reduced by an amount equal to such portion.

(4) Adjustment to basis of vessels, etc., where withdrawals pay principal on debt.—If any portion of a qualified withdrawal to pay the principal on any indebtedness is made out of ordinary income account or the capital gain account, then an amount equal to the aggregate reduction which would be required by paragraphs (2) and (3) if this were a qualified withdrawal for a purpose described in such paragraphs shall be applied in the order provided in joint regulations, to reduce the basis of vessels, barges, and containers owned by the person maintaining the fund. Any amount of a withdrawal remaining after the application of the preceding sentence shall be treated as a nonqualified withdrawal.

(5) Ordinary income recapture of basis reduction.—If any property the basis of which was reduced under paragraph (2), (3), or (4) is disposed of, any gain realized on such disposition, to the extent it does not exceed the aggregate reduction in the basis of such property under such paragraphs, shall be treated as an amount referred to in subsection (g)(3)(A) which was withdrawn on the date of such disposition. Subject to such conditions and requirements as may be provided in joint regulations, the preceding sentence shall not apply to a disposition where there is a redeposit in an amount determined under joint regulations which will, insofar as practicable, restore the fund to the position it was in before the withdrawal.

(g) Tax Treatment of Nonqualified Withdrawals.—

(1) **In general.**—Except as provided in subsection (h), any withdrawal from a capital construction fund which is not a qualified withdrawal shall be treated as a nonqualified withdrawal.

(2) **Ordering rule.**—Any nonqualified withdrawal from a fund shall be treated—
(A) first as made out of the ordinary income account,
(B) second as made out of the capital gain account, and
(C) third as made out of the capital account.

For purposes of this section, items withdrawn from any account shall be treated as withdrawn on a first-in-first-out basis; except that (i) any nonqualified withdrawal for research, development, and design expenses incident to new and advanced ship design, machinery and equipment, and (ii) any amount treated as a nonqualified withdrawal under the second sentence of subsection (f)(4), shall be treated as withdrawn on a last-in-first-out basis.

(3) **Operating rules.**—For purposes of this title—
(A) any amount referred to in paragraph (2)(A) shall be included in income as an item of ordinary income for the taxable year in which the withdrawal is made,
(B) any amount referred to in paragraph (2)(B) shall be included in income for the taxable year in which the withdrawal is made as an item of gain realized during such year from the disposition of an asset held for more than 6 months, and
(C) for the period on or before the last date prescribed for payment of tax for the taxable year in which this withdrawal is made—
(i) no interest shall be payable under section 6601 and no addition to the tax shall be payable under section 6651,
(ii) interest on the amount of the additional tax attributable to any item referred to in subparagraph (A) or (B) shall be paid at the applicable rate (as defined in paragraph (4)) from the last date prescribed for payment of the tax for the taxable year for which such item was deposited in the fund, and
(iii) no interest shall be payable on amounts referred to in clauses (i) and (ii) of paragraph (2) or in the case of any nonqualified withdrawal arising from the application of the recapture provision of section 606(5) of the Merchant Marine Act of 1936 as in effect on December 31, 1969.

(4) **Interest rate.**—For purposes of paragraph (3)(C)(ii), the applicable rate of interest for any nonqualified withdrawal—
(A) made in a taxable year beginning in 1970 or 1971 is 8 percent, or
(B) made in a taxable year beginning after 1971, shall be determined and published jointly by the Secretary of the Treasury or his delegate and the applicable Secretary and shall bear a relationship to 8 percent which the Secretaries determine under joint regulations to be comparable to the relationship which the money rates and investment yields for the calendar year immediately preceding the beginning of the taxable year bear to the money rates and investment yields for the calendar year 1970.

(5) **Amount not withdrawn from fund after 25 years from deposit taxed as nonqualified withdrawal.**—
(A) In general.—The applicable percentage of any amount which remains in a capital construction fund at the close of the 26th, 27th, 28th, 29th, or 30th taxable year following the taxable year for which such amount was deposited shall be treated as a nonqualified withdrawal in accordance with the following table:

If the amount remains in the fund at the close of the—	The applicable percentage is—
26th taxable year	20 percent
27th taxable year	40 percent
28th taxable year	60 percent
29th taxable year	80 percent
30th taxable year	100 percent

(B) Earnings treated as deposits.—The earnings of any capital construction fund for any taxable year (other than net gains) shall be treated for purposes of this paragraph as an amount deposited for such taxable year.
(C) Amounts committed treated as withdrawn.—For purposes of subparagraph (A), an amount shall not be treated as remaining in a capital construction fund at

the close of any taxable year to the extent there is a binding contract at the close of such year for a qualified withdrawal of such amount with respect to an identified item for which such withdrawal may be made.

(D) Authority to treat excess funds as withdrawn.—If the Secretary determines that the balance in any capital construction fund exceeds the amount which is appropriate to meet the vessel construction program objectives of the person who established such fund, the amount of such excess shall be treated as a nonqualified withdrawal under subparagraph (A) unless such person develops appropriate program objectives within 3 years to dissipate such excess.

(E) Amounts in fund on January 1, 1987.—For purposes of this paragraph, all amounts in a capital construction fund on January 1, 1987, shall be treated as deposited in such fund on such date.

(6) **Nonqualified withdrawals taxed at highest marginal rate.—**

(A) In general.—In the case of any taxable year for which there is a nonqualified withdrawal (including any amount so treated under paragraph (5)), the tax imposed by chapter 1 shall be determined—

    (i) by excluding such withdrawal from gross income, and

    (ii) by increasing the tax imposed by chapter 1 by the product of the amount of such withdrawal and the highest rate of tax specified in section 1 (section 11 in the case of a corporation).

With respect to the portion of any nonqualified withdrawal made out of the capital gain account during a taxable year to which section 1(i) or 1201(a) applies, the rate of tax taken into account under the preceding sentence shall not exceed 28 percent (34 percent in the case of a corporation).

(B) Tax benefit rule.—If any portion of a nonqualified withdrawal is properly attributable to deposits (other than earnings on deposits) may by the taxpayer in any taxable year which did not reduce the taxpayer's liability for tax under chapter 1 for any taxable year preceding the taxable year in which such withdrawal occurs—

    (i) such portion shall not be taken into account under subparagraph (A), and

    (ii) an amount equal to such portion shall be treated as allowed as a deduction under section 172 for the taxable year in which such withdrawal occurs.

(C) Coordination with deduction for net operating losses.—Any nonqualified withdrawal excluded from gross income under subparagraph (A) shall be excluded in determining taxable income under section 172(b)(2).

(h) **Certain Corporate Reorganizations and Changes in Partnerships.**—Under joint regulations—

(1) a transfer of a fund from one person to another person in a transaction to which section 381 applies may be treated as if such transaction did not constitute a nonqualified withdrawal, and

(2) a similar rule shall be applied in the case of a continuation of a partnership.

(i) **Definitions.**—For purposes of this section, any term defined in section 607(k) of the Merchant Marine Act, 1936 which is also used in this section (including the definition of "Secretary" shall have the meaning given such term by such section 607(k) as in effect on the date of the enactment of this section.

[For official explanation, see Committee Reports, ¶3880.]

〔¶3419〕 CODE SEC. 7603. SERVICE OF SUMMONS.

A summons issued under section 6420(e)(2), 6421(f)(2), [1]6427(j)(2), or 7602 shall be served by the Secretary, by an attested copy delivered in hand to the person to whom it is directed, or left at his last and usual place of abode; and the certificate of service signed by the person serving the summons shall be evidence of the facts it states on the hearing of an application for the enforcement of the summons. When the summons requires the production of books, papers, records, or other data, it shall be sufficient if such books, papers, records, or other data are described with reasonable certainty.

[For official explanation, see Committee Reports, ¶4125.]

〔Footnote ¶3419〕 Matter in *italics* in Sec. 7603 added by section 1703(e)(2)(G), '86 TRA, which struck out: (1) "6427(i)(2)"

Effective date (Sec. 1703(h), '86 TRA).—Applies to gasoline removed (as defined in section 4082 of the '86 Code, as amended by this section) after 12-31-87.

【¶3420】 **CODE SEC. 7604. ENFORCEMENT OF SUMMONS.**

(a) **Jurisdiction of District Court.**—If any person is summoned under the internal revenue laws to appear, to testify, or to produce books, papers, records, or other data, the United States district court for the district in which such person resides or is found shall have jurisdiction by appropriate process to compel such attendance, testimony, or production of books, papers, records, or other data.

(b) **Enforcement.**—Whenever any person summoned under section 6420(e)(2), 6421(f)(2), *6427(j)(2)*, or 7602 neglects or refuses to obey such summons, or to produce books, papers, records, or other data, or to give testimony, as required, the Secretary may apply to the judge of the district court or to a United States commissioner for the district within which the person so summoned resides or is found for an attachment against him as for a contempt. It shall be the duty of the judge or commissioner to hear the application, and, if satisfactory proof is made, to issue an attachment, directed to some proper officer, for the arrest of such person, and upon his being brought before him to proceed to a hearing of the case; and upon such hearing the judge or the United States commissioner shall have power to make such order as he shall deem proper, not inconsistent with the law for the punishment of contempts, to enforce obedience to the requirements of the summons and to punish such person for his default or disobedience.

(c) **Cross References.**—
(1) **Authority to issue order, processes, and judgments.**—
For authority of district courts generally to enforce the provisions of this title, see section 7402.
(2) **Penalties.**—
For penalties applicable to violation of section 6420(e)(2), 6421(f)(2), *6427(j)(2)*, or 7602, see section 7210.

[For official explanation, see Committee Reports, ¶6125.]

【¶3421】 **CODE SEC. 7605. TIME AND PLACE OF EXAMINATION.**

(a) **Time and Place.**—The time and place of examination pursuant to the provisions of section 6420(e)(2), 6421(f)(2), 6427(i)(2), or 7602 shall be such time and place as may be fixed by the Secretary and as are reasonable under the circumstances. In the case of a summons under authority of paragraph (2) of section 7602, or under the corresponding authority of section 6420(e)(2), 6421(f)(2), or *6427(j)(2)* the date fixed for the appearance before the Secretary shall not be less than 10 days from the date of the summons.

(b) **Restrictions on Examination of Taxpayer.**—No taxpayer shall be subjected to unnecessary examination or investigations, and only one inspection of a taxpayer's books of account shall be made for each taxable year unless the taxpayer requests otherwise or unless the Secretary, after investigation, notifies the taxpayer in writing that an additional inspection is necessary.

(c) **Cross Reference.**—

For provisions restricting church tax inquiries and examinations, see section 7611.

[For official explanation, see Committee Reports, ¶4125.]

【¶3422】 **CODE SEC. 7609. SPECIAL PROCEDURES FOR THIRD-PARTY SUMMONSES.**

(a) Notice.—

* * * * * * * * * * * *

(3) **Third-party recordkeeper defined.**—For purposes of this subsection, the term "third-party recordkeeper" means—
(A) any mutual savings bank, cooperative bank, domestic building and loan association, or other savings institution chartered and supervised as a savings and loan or similar association under Federal or State law, any bank (as defined in section 581), or any credit union (within the meaning of section 501(c)(14)(A));

【Footnote ¶3420】 Matter in *italics* in Sec. 7604(b) added by section 1703(e)(2)(G), '86 TRA, which struck out:

(1) "6427(i)(2)"

Effective date (Sec. 1703(h), '86 TRA).—Applies to gasoline removed (as defined in section 4082 of the '86 Code, as amended by this section) after 12-31-87.

【Footnote ¶3421】 Matter in *italics* in Sec. 7605(a) added by section 1703(e)(2)(G), '86 TRA, which struck out:
(1) "6427(i)(2)"

Effective date (Sec. 1703(h), '86 TRA). Applies to gasoline removed (as defined in section 4082 of the '86 Code, as amended by this section) after 12-31-87.

    (C)   any person extending credit through the use of credit cards or similar devices;

    (D)   any broker as (defined in sections 3(a)(4) of the Securities Exchange Act of 1934 (15 U.S.C. 78c(a)(4)));

    (E)   any attorney;

    (F)   any accountant;[1]

    (G)   any barter exchange (as defined in section 6045(c)(3))[2]; *and*

    (H)   any regulated investment company (as defined in section 851 and any agent of such regulated investment company when acting as an agent thereof.

* * * * * * * * * * * *

(c) Summons to Which Section Applies.—

    (1) In general.—Except as provided in paragraph (2), a summons is described in this subsection if it is issued under paragraph (2) of section 7602(a) or under section 6420(e)(2), 6421(f)(2), or [3]6427(j)(2) and requires the production of records.

* * * * * * * * * * * *

[4]*(e)   Suspension of Statute of Limitations.—*

    (1)   Subsection (b) Action.—If any person takes any action as provided in subsection (b) and such person is the person with respect to whose liability the summons is issued (or is the agent, nominee, or other person acting under the direction or control of such person), then the running of any period of limitations under section 6501 (relating to the assessment and collection of tax) or under section 6531 (relating to criminal prosecutions) with respect to such person shall be suspended for the period during which a proceeding, and appeals therein, with respect to the enforcement of such summons is pending.

    (2)   Suspension after 6 months of service of summons.—

In the absence of the resolution of the third-party recordkeeper's response to the summons described in subsection (c), the running of any period of limitations under section 6501 or under section 6531 with respect to any person with respect to whose liability the summons is issued other (other than a person taking action as provided in subsection (b)) shall be suspended for the period—

    (A)   beginning on the date which is 6 months after the service of such summons, and

    (B)   ending with the final resolution of such response.

* * * * * * * * * * * *

(i) Duty of Third-Party Recordkeeper

* * * * * * * * * * * *

    (4)   Notice of suspension of statute of limitations in the case of a John Doe summons.—In the case of a summons described in subsection (f) with respect to which any period of limitations has been suspended under subsection (e)(2), the third-party recordkeeper shall provide notice of such suspension to any person described in subsection (f).

[For official explanation, see Committee Reports, ¶¶3928; 4125; 4099.]

【¶3423】 CODE SEC. 7610. FEES AND COSTS FOR WITNESSES.

* * * * * * * * * * *

(c) **Summons to Which Section Applies.**—This section applies with respect to any summons authorized under section 6420(e)(2), 6421(f)(2), [1]6427(j)(2), or 7602.

[For official explanation, see Committee Reports, ¶4125.]

【¶3424】 CODE SEC. 7611. RESTRICTIONS ON CHURCH TAX INQUIRIES AND EXAMINATIONS.

(a) **Restrictions on Inquiries.**—

(1) **In general.**—The Secretary may begin a church tax inquiry only if—
    (A) the reasonable belief requirements of paragraph (2), and
    [1]*(B) the notice requirements of paragraph (3), have been met.*

* * * * * * * * * * *

(i) **Section Not to Apply to Criminal Investigations, Etc.**—This section shall not apply to—
    [2]*(1)* any criminal investigation,
    [3]*(2)* any inquiry or examination relating to the tax liability of any person other than a church.
    [4]*(3)* any assessment under section 6851 (relaing to termination assessments of income tax) or section 6861 (relating to jeopardy assessments of income taxes, [5]*etc.*),
    [6]*(4)* any willful attempt to defeat or evade any tax imposed by this title, or
    [7]*(5)* any knowing failure to file a return of tax imposed by [8]*the title.*

【¶3425】 CODE SEC. 7651. ADMINISTRATION AND COLLECTION OF TAXES IN POSSESSIONS.

Except as otherwise provided in this subchapter, and except as otherwise provided in section 28(a) of the Revised Organic Act of the Virgin Islands and section 30 of the Organic Act of Guam (relating to the covering of the proceeds of certain taxes into the treasuries of the Virgin Islands and Guam, respectively)—

* * * * * * * * * * *

(5) **Virgin Islands.**—

* * * * * * * * * * *

[1]*(B) For purposes of this title, section 28(a) of the Revised Organic Act of the Virgin Islands shall be effective as if such section 28(a) had been enacted before the enactment of this title and such section 28(a) shall have no effect on the amount of income tax liability required to be paid by any person to the United States.*

[For official explanation, see Committee Reports, ¶4057.]

【¶3426】 CODE SEC. 7652. SHIPMENTS TO THE UNITED STATES.

* * * * * * * * * * *

(g) *Drawback for Medicinal Alcohol, Etc.—In the case of medicines, medicinal prepa-*

【Footnote ¶3423】 Matter in *italics* in Sec. 7610(c) added by section 1703(e)(2)(G), '86 TRA, which struck out:
(1) "6427(i)(2)"
Effective date (Sec. 1703(h), '86 TRA).—Applies to gasoline removed (as defined in section 4082 of the '86 Code, as amended by this section) after 12-31-87.

【Footnote ¶3424】 Matter in *italics* in Sec. 7611(a)(1)(B) added by section 1899A(61) and (62), '86 TRA, which struck out:
(1) "(B) the notice requirements of paragraph (3), have been met."
(2) "(A)"
(3) "(B)"
(4) "(C)"
(5) "etc),"
(6) "(D)"
(7) "(E)"
(8) "the title"

【Footnote ¶3425】 Matter in *italics* in Sec. 7651(5)(B) added by section 1275(b), '86 TRA, which struck out:
(1) "(B) For purposes of this title (other than section 881(b)(1)) or Subpart C of part III of Subchapter N of Chapter 1, section 28(a) of the Revised Organic Act of the Virgin Islands shall be effective as if such section had been enacted subsequent to the enactment of this title."
Effective date (Sec. 1277, '86 TRA).—Generally applies to taxable years beginning after 12-31-86. For special rules see ¶2068.

【Footnote ¶3426】 Sec. 7652(g) in *italics* added by section 1879(i)(1), '86 TRA.
Effective date (Sec. 1879(i)(2), '86 TRA).—Applies to articles brought into the United States after the date of the enactment of this Act.

rations, food products, flavors, or flavoring extracts containing distilled spirits, which are unfit for beverage purposes and which are brought into the United States from Puerto Rico or the Virgin Islands—

    (1) subpart F of part II of subchapter A of chapter 51 shall be applied as if—

        (A) the use and tax determination described in section 5131(a) had occurred in the United States by a United States person at the time the article is brought into the United States, and

        (B) the rate of tax were the rate applicable under subsection (f) of this section, and

    (2) no amount shall be covered into the treasuries of Puerto Rico or the Virgin Islands.

[For official explanation, see Committee Reports, ¶4193.]

【¶3427】 CODE SEC. 7654. [1]*COORDINATION OF UNITED STATES AND CERTAIN POSSESSION INDIVIDUAL INCOME TAXES.*

    *(a) **General Rule.**—The net collection of taxes imposed by chapter 1 for each taxable year with respect to an individual to which section 931 or 932(c) applies shall be covered into the Treasury of the specified possession of which such individual is a bona fide resident.*

    *(b) **Definition and Special Rule.**—For purposes of this section—*

    *(1) **Net collections.**—In determining net collections for a taxable year, an appropriate adjustment shall be made for credits allowed against the tax liability and refunds made of income taxes for the taxable year.*

    *(2) **Specified possession.**—The term "specified possession" means Guam, American Samoa, the Northern Mariana Islands, and the Virgin Islands.*

    *(c) **Transfers.**—The transfers of funds between the United States and any specified possession required by this section shall be made not less frequently than annually.*

【Footnote ¶3427】 Matter in *italics* in Sec. 7654 added by section 1276(a), '86 TRA, which struck out:

(1) "COORDINATION OF UNITED STATES AND GUAM INDIVIDUAL INCOME TAXES.

    (a) General Rule.—The net collections of the income taxes imposed for each taxable year with respect to any individual to whom this subsection applies for such year shall be divided between the United States and Guam according to the following rules:

    (1) net collections attributable to United States source income shall be covered into the Treasury of the United States;

    (2) net collections attributable to Guam source income shall be covered into the treasury of Guam; and

    (3) all other net collections of such taxes shall be covered into the treasury of the jurisdiction (either the United States or Guam) with which such individual is required by section 935(b) to file his return for such year.

This subsection applies to an individual for a taxable year if section 935 applies to such individual for such year and if such individual has (or, in the case of a joint return, such individual and his spouse have) (A) adjusted gross income of $50,000 or more and (B) gross income of $5,000 or more derived from sources within the jurisdiction (either the United States or Guam) with which the individual is not required under section 935(b) to file his return for the year.

    (b) Definitions and Special Rules.—For purposes of this section—

    (1) Net collections.—In determining net collections for a taxable year, appropriate adjustment shall be made for credits allowed against the tax liability for such year and refunds made of income taxes for such year.

    (2) Income taxes.—The term 'income taxes' means—

    (A) with respect to taxes imposed by the United States, the taxes imposed by chapter 1, and

    (B) with respect to Guam, the Guam territorial income tax.

    (3) Source.—The determination of the source of income shall be based on the principles contained in part I of subchapter N of chapter 1 (section 861 and following).

    (c) Transfers.—The transfers of funds between the United States and Guam required by this section shall be made not less frequently than annually.

    (d) Military Personnel in Guam.—In addition to any amount determined under subsection (a), the United States shall pay to Guam at such times and in such manner as determined by the Secretary the amount of the taxes deducted and withheld by the United States under chapter 24 with respect to compensation paid to members of the Armed Forces who are stationed in Guam but who have no income tax liability to Guam with respect to such compensation by reason of the Soldiers and Sailors Civil Relief Act (50 App. U.S.C., sec. 501 et seq.)

    (e) Regulations.—The Secretary shall prescribe such regulations as may be necessary to carry out the provisions of this section and section 935, including (but not limited to)—

    (1) such regulations as are necessary to insure that the provisions of this title, as made applicable in Guam by section 31 of the Organic Act of Guam, apply in a manner which is consistent with this section and section 935, and

    (2) regulations prescribing the information which the individuals to whom section 935 may apply, shall furnish to the Secretary."

    Effective date (Sec. 1277, '86 TRA).—Generally applies to taxable years beginning after 12-31-86. For special rules, see ¶2068.

(d) Federal Personnel.—*In addition to the amount determined under subsection (a), the United States shall pay to each specified possession at such time and in such manner as determined by the Secretary—*

(1) the amount of the taxes deducted and withheld by the United States under chapter 24 with respect to compensation paid to members of the Armed Forces who are stationed in such possession but who have no income tax liability to such possession with respect to such compensation by reason of the Soldiers' and Sailors' Civil Relief Act (50 App. U.S.C. 501 et seq.),

(2) the amount of the taxes deducted and withheld under chapter 24 with respect to amounts paid for services performed as an employee of the United States (or any agency thereof) in a specified possession with respect to an individual unless section 931 or 932(c) applies.

(e) Regulations.—*The Secretary shall prescribe such regulations as may be necessary to carry out the provisions of this section and sections 931 and 932, including regulations prohibiting the rebate of taxes covered over which are allocable to United States source income and prescribing the information which the individuals to whom such sections may apply shall furnish to the Secretary.*

[For official explanation, see Committee Reports, ¶4057.]

【¶3427-A】 CODE SEC. 7655. CROSS REFERENCES.

* * * * * * * * * * * *

(b) Other Provisions.—

For other provisions relating to possessions of the United States, see—

(1) Section 931, relating to income tax on residents of Guam, American Samoa, or the Northern Mariana Islands;

¹*(2)* **Section 933, relating to income tax on residents of Puerto Rico;**

²*(3)* **Section 6418(b), relating to exportation of sugar to Puerto Rico;**

[For official explanation, see Committee Reports, ¶4057.]

【¶3428】 CODE SEC. 7701. DEFINITIONS.

(a) When used in this title, where not otherwise distinctly expressed or manifestly incompatible with the intent thereof—

* * * * * * * * * * * *

(17) Husband and wife.—As used in sections 152(b)(4), 682 and¹*2516,* if the husband and wife therein referred to are divorced, wherever appropriate to the meaning of such sections, the term "wife" shall be read "former wife" and the term "husband" shall be read "former husband"; and, if the payments described in such sections are made by or on behalf of the wife or former wife to the husband or former husband instead of vice versa, wherever appropriate to the meaning of such sections, the term "husband" shall be read "wife" and the term "wife" shall be read "husband."

* * * * * * * * * * * *

(19) Domestic building and loan association.—The term "domestic building and loan association" means a domestic building and loan association, a domestic savings and loan association, and a Federal savings and loan association—

(A) which either (i) is an insured institution within the meaning of section 401(a) of the National Housing Act (12 U.S.C., see 1724(a)), or (ii) is subject by law to supervision and examination by State or Federal authority having supervision over such associations;

【Footnote ¶3427-A】 Matter in *italics* in Sec. 7655(b) added by section 1272(d)(11), '86 TRA, which struck out:

(1) "(1)"

(2) "(2)"

Effective date (Sec. 1277, '86 TRA).—Generally applies to taxable years beginning after 12-31-86. For other rules, see ¶2068.

【Footnote ¶3428】 Matter in *italics* in Sec. 7701(a)(17) added by section 1842(d), '86 TRA, which struck out:

(1) "and"

Effective date (Sec. 1881, '86 TRA and section 421(d), '84 TRA).—Generally applies to transfer after 7-18-84 in taxable years ending after such date. For special rules, see footnote ¶2964.

(B)   the business of which consists principally of acquiring the savings of the public and investing in loans; and

(C)   at least 60 percent of the amount of the total assets of which (at the close of the taxable year) consists of—

(i)   cash,

(ii)   obligations of the United States or of a State or political subdivision thereof, and stock or obligations of a corporation which is an instrumentality of the United States or of a State or political subdivision thereof, but not including obligations the interest on which is excludable from gross income under section 103,

(iii)   certificates of deposit in, or obligations of, a corporation organized under a State law which specifically authorizes such corporation to insure the deposits or share accounts of member associations,

(iv)   loans secured by a deposit or share of a member,

(v)   loans (including redeemable ground rents, as defined in section 1055) secured by an interest in real property which is (or, from the preceeds of the loan, will become) residential real property or real property used primarily for church purposes, loans made for the improvement of residential real property or real property used primarily for church purposes, provided that for purposes of this clause, residential real property shall include single or multifamily dwellings, facilities in residential developments dedicated to public use or property used on a nonprofit basis for residents, and mobile homes not used on a transient basis,

(vi)   loans secured by an interest in real property located within an urban renewal area to be developed for predominantly residential use under an urban renewal plan approved by the Secretary of Housing and Urban Development under part A or part B of title I of the Housing Act of 1949, as amended, or located within any area covered by a program eligible for assistance under section 103 of the Demonstration Cities and Metropolitan Development Act of 1966, as amended, and loans made for the improvement of any such real property,

(vii)   loans secured by an interest in educational, health, or welfare institutions or facilities, including structures designed or used primarily for residential purposes for student, residents, and persons under care, employees, or members of the staff of such institutions or facilitites,

(viii)   property acquired through the liquidation of defaulted loans described in clause (v), (vi), or (vii),

(ix)   loans made for the payment of expenses of college or university education or vocational training, in accordance with such regulations as may be prescribed by the Secretary,[2]

(x)   property used by the association in the conduct of the business described in subparagraph (B)[3], *and*

(xi)   any regular or residual interest in a REMIC, but only in the proportion which the assets of such REMIC consist of property described in any of the preceding clauses of this subparagraph; except that if 95 percent or more of the assets of such REMIC are loans described in clauses (i) through (x), the entire interest in the REMIC shall qualify.

At the election of the taxpayer, the percentage specified in this subparagraph shall be applied on the basis of the average assets outstanding during the taxable year, in lieu of the close of the taxable year, computed under regulations prescribed by the Secretary. For purposes of clause (v), if the multifamily structure securing a loan is used in part for nonresidential purposes, the entire loan is deemed a residential real property loan if the planned residential use exceeds 80 percent of the property's planned use (determined as of the time the loan is made). For purposes of clause (v), loans made to finance the acquisition or development of land shall be deemed to be loans secured by an interest in residential real property if, under regulations prescribed by the Secretary there is reasonable assurance that the property will become residential real property within a period of 3 years from the date of

【Footnote ¶3428 continued】

Matter in *italics* in Sec. 7701(a)(19)(C)(ix)—(xi) added by section 671(b)(3), '86 TRA, which struck out:

(2)   "and"

(3)   "."

Effective date (Sec. 675, '86 TRA).—Generally applies to taxable years beginning after 12-31-86. For special rules, see footnote ¶3113-A.

acquisition of such land; but this sentence shall not apply for any taxable year unless, within such 3-year period, such land becomes residential real property.

(20) **Employee.**—For the purpose of applying the provisions of section 79 with respect to group-term life insurance purchased for employees, for the purpose of applying the provisions of sections 104, 105, [4] 106, *and 125* with respect to accident and health insurance or accident and heath plans, for the purpose of applying the provisions of section 101(b) with respect to employees' death benefits, and for the purpose of applying the provisions of subtitle A with respect to contributions to or under a stock bonus, pension, profit-sharing, or annuity plan, and with respect to distributions under such a plan, or by a trust forming part of such a plan, or by a trust forming part of such a plan, the term "employee" shall include a full-time life insurance salesman who is considered an employee for the purpose of chapter 21, or in the case of services performed before January 1, 1951, who would be considered an employee if his services were performed during 1951.

* * * * * * * * * * * *

(46) **Determination of whether there is collective bargaining agreement.**—In determining whether there is a collective bargaining agreement between employee representatives and 1 or more employers, the term "employee representatives" shall not include any organization more than one-half of the members of which are employees who are owners, officers, or executives of the employer. *An agreement shall not be treated as a collective bargaining agreement unless it is a bona fide agreement between bona fide employee representatives and 1 or more employers.*

(b) **Definition of Resident Alien and Nonresident Alien.**—

(1) **In general.**—For purposes of this title (other than subtitle B)—

(A) **Resident alien.**—An alien individual shall be treated as a resident of the United States with respect to any calendar year if (and only if) such individual meets the requirements of clause (i)[5], (ii) *or (iii):*

(i) **Lawfully admitted for permanent residence.**—Such individual is a lawful permanent resident of the United States at any time during such calendar year.

(ii) **Substantial presence test.**—Such individual meets the substantial presence test of paragraph (3).

(iii) *First year election.*—*Such individual makes the election provided in paragraph (4).*

* * * * * * * * * * * *

(2) **Special rules for first and last year of residency.**—

(A) First year of residency.—

(i) In general.—If an alien individual is a resident of the United States under paragraph (1)(A) with respect to any calendar year, but was not a resident of the United States at any time during the preceding calendar year, such alien individual shall be treated as a resident of the United States only for the portion of such calendar year which begins on the residency starting date.

(ii) Residency starting date for individuals lawfully admitted for permanent residence.—In the case of an individual who is a lawfully permanent resident of the United States at any time during the calendar year, but does not meet the substantial presence test of paragraph (3), the residency starting date shall be the first day in such calendar year on which he was present in the United States while a lawful permanent resident of the United States.

(iii) Residency starting date for individuals meeting substantial presence test.—In the case of an individual who meets the substantial presence test of paragraph (3) with respect to any calendar year, the residency starting date shall be the first day during such calendar year on which the individual is present in the United States.

⟦Footnote ¶3428 continued⟧

Matter in *italics* in Sec. 7701(a)(20) added by section 1166(a), '86 TRA, which struck out:
(4) "and"
Effective date (Sec. 1166(b), '86 TRA.)—Applies to years beginning after 12-31-85.

Matter in *italics* in Sec. 7701(a)(46) added by section 1137, '86 TRA.

Matter in *italics* in Sec. 7701(b)(1)(A)(iii), (2)(A)(iv), (4), and "(5)" added by section 1810(*l*)(2)—(4), '86 TRA, which struck out:
(5) "(or"

(iv) Residency starting date for individuals making first year election.—In the case of an individual who makes the election provided by paragraph (4) with respect to any calendar year, the residency starting date shall be the 1st day during such calendar year on which the individual is treated as a resident of the United States under that paragraph.

* * * * * * * * * * *

In the case of days in:	The applicable multiplier is:
Current year	1
1st preceding year	$\frac{1}{3}$
2nd preceding year	$\frac{1}{6}$

(B) Exception where individual is present in the United States during less than one-half of current year and closer connection to foreign country is established.— An individual shall not be treated as meeting the substantial presence test of this paragraph with respect to any current year if—

(i) such individual is present in the United States on fewer than 183 days during the current year, and

(ii) it is established that for the current year such individual has a tax home (as defined in section 911(d)(3) without regard to the second sentence thereof) in a foreign country and has a closer connection to such foreign country than to the United States.

(C) Subparagraph (b) not to apply in certain cases.—Subparagraph (B) shall not apply to any individual with respect to any current year if at any time during such year—

(i) such individual had an application for adjustment of status pending, or

(ii) such individual took other steps to apply for status as a lawful permanent resident of the United States.

(D) Exception for exempt individuals or for certain medical conditions.—An individual shall not be treated as being present in the United States on any day if—

(i) such individual is an exempt individual for such day, or

(ii) such individual was unable to leave the United States on such day because of a medical condition which arose while such individual was present in the United States.

(4) First-year election.—

(A) An alien individual shall be deemed to meet the requirements of this subparagraph if such individual—

(i) is not a resident of the United States under clause (i) or (ii) of paragraph (1)(A) with respect to a calendar year (hereinafter referred to as the "election year"),

(ii) was not a resident of the United States under paragraph (1)(A) with respect to the calendar year immediately preceding the election year,

(iii) is a resident of the United States under clause (ii) of paragraph (1)(A) with respect to the calendar year immediately following the election year, and

(iv) is both—

(I) present in the United States for a period of at least 31 consecutive days in the election year, and

(II) present in the United States during the period beginning with the first day of such 31-day period and ending with the last day of the election year (hereinafter referred to as the "testing period") for a number of days equal to or exceeding 75 percent of the number of days in the testing period (provided that an individual shall be treated for purposes of this subclause as present in the United States for a number of days during the testing period not exceeding 5 days in the aggregate, notwithstanding his absence from the United States on such days).

(B) An alien individual who meets the requirements of subparagraph (A) shall, if he so elects, be treated as a resident of the United States with respect to the election year.

(C) An alien individual who makes the election provided by subparagraph (B) shall be treated as a resident of the United States for the portion of the election year which begins on the 1st day of the earliest testing period during such year with re-

spect to which the individual meets the requirements of clause (iv) of subparagraph (A).

(D) The rules of subparagraph (D)(i) of paragraph (3) shall apply for purposes of determining an individual's presence in the United States under this paragraph.

(E) An election under subparagraph (B) shall be made on the individual's tax return for the election year, provided that such election may not be made before the individual has met the substantial presence test of paragraph (3) with respect to the calendar year immediately following the election year.

(F) An election once made under subparagraph (B) remains in effect for the election year, unless revoked with the consent of the Secretary.

[6]**(5) Exempt individual defined.**—For purposes of this subsection—

(A) In general.—An individual is an exempt individual for any day if, for such day, such individual is—

(i) a foreign government-related individual,

(ii) a teacher or trainee, [5]

(iii) a student [7], *or*

(iv) a professional athlete who is temporarily in the United States to compete in a charitable sports event described in section 274(k)(2).

(B) Foreign government related individual.—The term "foreign government-related individual" means any individual temporarily present in the United States by reason of—

(i) diplomatic status, or a visa which the Secretary (after consultation with the Secretary of State) determines represents full-time diplomatic or consular status for purposes of this subsection,

(ii) being a full-time employee of an international organization, or

(iii) being a member of the immediate family of an individual described in clause (i) or (ii).

(C) Teacher or trainee.—The term "teacher or trainee" means any individual—

(i) who is temporarily present in the United States under subparagraph (J) of section 101(15) of the Immigration and Nationality Act (other than as a student), and

(ii) who substantially complies with the requirements for being so present.

(D) Student.—The term "student" means any individual—

(i) who is temporarily present in the United States—

(I) under subparagraph (F) of section 101(15) of the Immigration and Nationality Act, or

(II) as a student under subparagraph (J) of such section 101(15), and

(ii) who substantially complies with the requirements for being so present.

(E) Special rules for teachers, trainees, and students.—

⟦Footnote ¶3428 continued⟧

(6) "(4)"

Effective date (Sec. 1881, '86 TRA and section 138(b)(1)—(3), '84 TRA).—(1) Generally applies to taxable years beginning after 12-31-84.

(2) Transitional rule for applying substantial presence test.—

(A) If an alien individual was not a resident of the United States as of the close of calendar year 1984, the determination of whether such individual meets the substantial presence test of section 7701(b)(3) '54 Code (as added by Sec. 138(a) '84 TRA) shall be made by only taking into account presence after 1984.

(B) If an alien individual was a resident of the U.S. as of the close of calendar year 1984, but was not a resident of the U.S. as of the close of calendar year 1983, the determination of whether such individual meets such substantial presence test shall be made by only taking into account presence in the U.S. after 1983.

(3) Transitional rule for applying lawful residence test.—In the case of any individual who—

(A) was a lawful permanent resident of the U.S. (within the meaning of section 7701(b)(5) '54 Code, as added by Sec. 138(a), '84 TRA) throughout calendar year 1984, or

(B) was present in the U.S. at any time during 1984 while such individual was a lawful permanent resident of the U.S. (within the meaning of such section 7701(b)(5)),

for purposes of section 7701(b)(2)(A) '54 Code (as so added), such individual shall be treated as a resident of the U.S. during 1984.

Matter in *italics* in Sec. 7701(b)(5)(A)(ii)—(iv), formerly (b)(4)(A)(ii)—(iv) added by section 1810(*l*)(5)(A), '86 TRA, which struck out:

(7) "."

Effective date (Sec. 1810(l)(5)(B), '86 TRA).—Applies to periods after the date of enactment of this Act.

"preceding" in *italics* in Sec. 7701(b)(5)(E)(i), formerly Section (b)(4)(E)(i), added by section 1899A(63), '86 TRA, which struck out:

(i) Limitation on teachers and trainees.—An individual shall not be treated as an exempt individual by reason of clause (ii) of subparagraph (A) for the current year if, for any 2 calendar years during the [8] *preceding* 6 calendar years, such person was an exempt person under clause (ii) or (iii) of subparagraph (A). *In the case of an individual all of whose compensation is described in section 872(b)(3), the preceding sentence shall be applied by substituting "4 calendar years" for "2 calendar years."*

(ii) Limitation on students.—For any calendar year after the 5th calendar year for which an individual was an exempt individual under clause (ii) or (iii) of subparagraph (A), such individual shall not be treated as an exempt individual by reason of clause (iii) of subparagraph (A), unless such individual establishes to the satisfaction of the Secretary that such individual does not intend to permanently reside in the United States and that such individual meets the requirements of subparagraph (D)(ii).

* * * * * * * * * * * *

[9](6) **Lawful permanent resident.—**

* * * * * * * * * * * *

[10](7) **Presence in the United States.—**

* * * * * * * * * * * *

[11](8) **Annual statements.—**

* * * * * * * * * * * *

[12](9) **Taxable year.—**

* * * * * * * * * * * *

[13](10) **Coordination with section 877.—**

* * * * * * * * * * * *

[14](11) **Regulations.—**

* * * * * * * * * * * *

(e) **Treatment of Certain Contracts for Providing Services, Etc.—**For purposes of chapter 1—

* * * * * * * * * * * *

(4) **Paragraph (3) not to apply in certain cases.—**

(A) In general.—Paragraph (3) shall not apply to any qualified solid waste disposal facility, cogeneration facility, alternative energy facility, or waste treatment works facility used under a contract or arrangement if—

(i) the service recipient (or a related entity) operates such facility,

(ii) the service recipient (or a related entity) bears any significant financial burden if there is nonperformance under the contract or arrangement (other than for reasons beyond the control of the service provider),

(iii) the service recipient (or a related entity) receives any significant financial benefit if the operating costs of such facility are less than the standards of performance or operation under the contract or arrangement, or

---

⌈Footnote ¶3428 continued⌉

(8) "preceeding"

The last sentence in *italics* in Sec. 7701(b)(5)(E)(i) [formerly (b)(4)(E)(i)] added by section 1810 (l)(1), '86 TRA.
Effective date (Sec. 1881, '86 TRA and section 138(b)(1)—(3), '84 TRA).—Generally applies to taxable years beginning after 12-31-84. For transitional rules, see above.

Matter in *italics* in Sec. 7701(b)(6)—(11) added by section 1810(l)(4), '86 TRA, which struck out:
(9) "(5)"
(10) "(6)"
(11) "(7)"
(12) "(8)"
(13) "(9)"
(14) "(10)"
Effective date (Sec. 1881, '86 TRA and section 138(b)(1)—(3), '84 TRA).—(1) Generally applies to taxable years beginning after 12-31-84. For transitional rules, see above.

Matter in *italics* in Sec. 7701(e)(4)(A) except *"section 168(h),"* added by section 1802(a)(9)(C), '86 TRA.
Effective date (Sec. 1881, '86 TRA and section 31(g), '84 TRA, as amended by section 1802(a)(2)(F) and (10), '86 TRA).—(1) Generally applies—
(A) to property placed in service by the taxpayer after 5-23-83, in taxable years ending after such date, and
(B) to property placed in service by the taxpayer on or before 5-23-83, if the lease to the tax-exempt entity is entered into after 5-23-83.
For special rules, see footnote ¶2935-A.

(iv) the service recipient (or a related entity) has an option to purchase, or may be required to purchase, all or a part of such facility at a fixed and determinable price (other than for fair market value).

For purposes of this paragraph, the term "related entity" has the same meaning as when used in [15] *section 168(h).*

* * * * * * * * * * * *

(5) Exception for certain low-income housing.—This subsection shall not apply to any [16] *property described in clause (i), (ii), (iii), or (iv) of section 1250(a)(1)(B) (relating to low-income housing) if—*

(A) such property is operated by or for an organization described in paragraph (3) or (4) of section 501(c), and

(B) at least 80 percent of the units in such property are leased to low-income tenants (within the meaning of section 167(k)(3)(B)).

* * * * * * * * * * * *

(h) Motor Vehicle Operating Leases.—

(1) In general.—For purposes of this title, in the case of a qualified motor vehicle operating agreement which contains a terminal rental adjustment clause—

(A) such agreement shall be treated as a lease if (but for such terminal rental adjustment clause) such agreement would be treated as a lease under this title, and

(B) the lessee shall not be treated as the owner of the property subject to an agreement during any period such agreement is in effect.

(2) Qualified motor vehicle operating agreement defined.—For purposes of this subsection—

(A) In general.—The term "qualified motor vehicle operating agreement" means any agreement with respect to a motor vehicle (including a trailer) which meets the requirements of subparagraphs (B), (C), and (D) of this paragraph.

(B) Minimum liability of lessor.—An agreement meets the requirements of this subparagraph if under such agreement the sum of—

(i) the amount the lessor is personally liable to repay, and

(ii) the net fair market value of the lessor's interest in any property pledged as security for property subject to the agreement,

equals or exceeds all amounts borrowed to finance the acquisition of property subject to the agreement. There shall not be taken into account under clause (ii) any property pledged which is property subject to the agreement or property directly or indirectly financed by indebtedness secured by property subject to the agreement.

(C) Certification by lessee; notice of tax ownership.—An agreement meets the requirements of this subparagraph if such agreement contains a separate written statement separately signed by the lessee—

(i) under which the lessee certifies, under penalty of perjury, that it intends that more than 50 percent of the use of the property subject to such agreement is to be in a trade or business of the lessee, and

---

[Footnote ¶3428 continued]

"*Section 168(h)*" in *italics* in Sec. 7701(e)(4)(A) added by section 201(d)(14), '86 TRA, which struck out:

(15) "section 168(j)"

Effective date (Sec. 203(a), '86 TRA).—Generally applies to property placed in service after 12-31-86, in taxable years ending after such date. For special and transitional rules, see footnote ¶2007—2008.

Matter in *italics* in Sec. 7701(e)(5) [formerly amended by section 1899A(64), '86 TRA] added by section 201(d)(14)(B), '86 TRA, which struck out:

(16) "low-income housing (within the meaning of section 168(c)(2)(F)"

Effective date (Sec. 203(a), '86 TRA).—Generally applies to property placed in service after 12-31-86, in taxable years ending after such date. For special and transitional rules, see ¶2007—2008.

Sec. 7701(h) in *italics* added by section 201(c), '86 TRA.

Effective date (Sec. 203(a), '86 TRA).—Generally applies to property placed in service after 12-31-86, in taxable years ending after such date. For transitional and special rules, see footnote ¶2007—2008.

Sec. 7701(i) in *italics* added by section 673, '86 TRA.

Effective date (Sec. 675(c)(1) and (2), '86 TRA).—(c) Treatment of Taxable Mortgage Pools.—

(1) Generally takes effect on 1-1-92.

(2) Treatment of existing entities.—The amendment made by section 673 shall not apply to any entity in existence on 12-31-91. The preceding sentence shall cease to apply with respect to any entity as of the 1st day after 12-31-91, on which there is a substantial transfer of cash or other property to such entity.

* * * * * * * * * * * *

(ii)   which clearly and legibly states that the lessee has been advised that it will not be treated as the owner of the property subject to the agreement for Federal income tax purposes.

(D)   *Lessor must have no knowledge that certification is false.*—An agreement meets the requirements of this subparagraph if the lessor does not know that the certification described in subparagraph (C)(i) is false.

(3)   *Terminal rental adjustment clause defined.*—

(A)   *In general.*—For purposes of this subsection, the term "terminal rental adjustment clause" means a provision of an agreement which permits or requires the rental price to be adjusted upward or downward by reference to the amount realized by the lessor under the agreement upon sale or other disposition of such property.

(B)   *Special rule for lessee dealers.*—The term "terminal rental adjustment clause" also includes a provision of an agreement which requires a lessee who is a dealer in motor vehicles to purchase the motor vehicle for a predetermined price and then resell such vehicle where such provision achieves substantially the same results as a provision described in subparagraph (A).

(i)   *Taxable Mortgage Pools.*—

(1)   *Treated as separate corporations.*—A taxable mortgage pool shall be treated as a separate corporation which may not be treated as an includible corporation with any other corporation for purposes of section 1501.

(2)   *Taxable mortgage pool defined.*—For purposes of this title—

(A)   *In general.*—Except as otherwise provided in this paragraph, a taxable mortgage pool is any entity (other than a REMIC) if—

(i)   substantially all of the assets of such entity consists of debt obligations (or interests therein) and more than 50 percent of such debt obligations (or interests) consists of real estate mortgages (or interests therein),

(ii)   such entity is the obligor under debt obligations with 2 or more maturities, and

(iii)   under the terms of the debt obligations referred to in clause (ii) (or underlying arrangement), payments on such debt obligations bear a relationship to payments on the debt obligations (or interests) referred to in clause (i).

(B)   *Portion of entities treated as pools.*—Any portion of an entity which meets the definition of subparagraph (A) shall be treated as a taxable mortgage pool.

(C)   *Exception for domestic building and loan.*—Nothing in this subsection shall be construed to treat any domestic building and loan association (or portions thereof) as a taxable mortgage pool.

(D)   *Treatment of certain equity interests.*—To the extra provided in regulations, equity interest of varying classes which correspond to maturity classes of debt shall be treated as debt for purposes of this subsection.

(3)   *Treatment of certain REIT's.*—If—

(A)   a real estate investment trust is a taxable mortgage pool, or

(B)   a qualified REIT subsidiary (as defined in section 856(i)(2)) of a real estate investment trust is a taxable mortgage pool,

under regulations prescribed by the Secretary, adjustments similar to the adjustments provided in section 860E(d) shall apply to the shareholders of such real estate investment trust.

(j)   *Treatment of Federal Thrift Savings Fund.*—

(1)   *In general.*—For purposes of this title—

(A)   the Thrift Savings Fund shall be treated as a trust described in section 401(a) which is exempt from taxation under section 501(a);

(B)   any contribution to, or distribution from, the Thrift Savings Fund shall be treated in the same manner as contributions to or distributions from such a trust; and

(C)   subject to the provisions of paragraph (2) and any dollar limitation on the application of section 402(a)(8), contributions to the Thrift Savings Fund shall not be treated as distributed or made available to an employee or Member nor as a contribution made to the Fund by an employee or Member merely because the employee or Member has, under the provisions of subchapter III of chapter 84 of title 5, United States Code, and section 8351 of such title 5, an election whether the contribution will be made to the Thrift Savings Fund or received by the employee or Member in cash.

(2)   *Nondiscrimination requirements.*—Paragraph (1)(C) shall not apply to the Thrift Savings Fund unless the Fund meets the antidiscrimination requirements (other than any

requirement relating to coverage) applicable to arrangements described in section 401(k) and to matching contributions. Rules similar to the rules of sections 401(k)(8) and 401(m)(8) (relating to no disqualification if excess contributions distributed) shall apply for purposes of the preceding sentence.

(3) **Coordination with Social Security Act.**—*Paragraph (1) shall not be construed to provide that any amount of the employee's or Member's basic pay which is contributed to the Thrift Savings Fund shall not be included in the term "wages" for the purposes of section 209 of the Social Security Act or section 3121(a) of this title.*

(4) **Definitions.**—*For purposes of this subsection, the terms "Member", "employee", and "Thrift Savings Fund" shall have the same respective meanings as when used in subchapter III of chapter 84 of title 5, United States Code.*

(5) **Coordination with other provisions of law.**—*No provision of law not contained in this title shall apply for purposes of determining the treatment under this title of the Thrift Savings Fund or any contribution to, or distribution from, such Fund.*

[17](k)   **Cross References.—**

*   *   *   *   *   *   *   *   *   *   *   *

[For official explanation, see Committee Reports, ¶3870; 3930; 3996; 4013; 4136; 4144; 4162.]

[¶3429]   **CODE SEC. 7702.   LIFE INSURANCE CONTRACT DEFINED.**

(a)   **General rule.**—For purposes of this title, the term "life insurance contract" means any contract which is a life insurance contract under the applicable law, but only if such contract—

    (1)   meets the cash value accumulation test of subsection (b), or

    (2)(A)   meets the guideline premium requirements of subsection (c), and

      (B)   falls within the cash value corridor of subsection (d).

(b)   **Cash Value Accumulation Test for Subsection (a)(1).—**

    (1)   **In general.**—A contract meets the cash value accumulation test of this subsection if, by the terms of the contract, the cash surrender value of such contract may not at any time exceed the net single premium which would have to be paid at such time to fund future benefits under the contract.

    (2)   **Rules for applying paragraph (1).**—Determinations under paragraph (1) shall be made—

      (A)   on the basis of interest at the greater of an annual effective rate of 4 percent or the rate or rates guaranteed on issuance of the contract,

      (B)   on the basis of the rules of subparagraph (B)(i) (and, in the case of qualified additional benefits, subparagraph (B)(ii) of subsection (c)(3), and

      (C)   by taking into account under [1]*subparagraphs (A) and (D)* of subsection (e)(1) only current and future death benefits and qualified additional benefits.

*   *   *   *   *   *   *   *   *   *   *   *

(e)   **Computational Rules.—**

    (1)   **In general.**—For purposes of this section *(other than subsection (d))*—

      (A)   the death benefit (and any qualified additional benefit) shall be deemed not to increase,

      (B)   the maturity date, including the date on which any benefit described in subparagraph (C) is payable, shall be *deemed to be* no earlier than the day on which the insured attains age 95, and no later than the date on which the insured attains age 100,[2]

      (C)   the death benefits shall be deemed to be provided until the maturity date determined by taking into account subparagraph (B), and

    [3]*(D)   the amount of any endowment benefit (or sum of endowment benefits, including any cash surrender value on the maturity date* [4]*determined by taking into*

[Footnote ¶3428 continued]

Matter in *italics* in Sec. 7701(j) and (k) [formerly redesignated (i) by section 201(c) '86 TRA, and (j) by section 673, '86 TRA] added by section 1147(a), '86 TRA, which struck out:

(17)   "(k)"

[Footnote ¶3429]   Matter in *italics* in Sec. 7702(b)(2)(C), (e)(1), (B)—(D), (e)(2)(A)—(C), (f)(1)(A), (7) and (g)(1)(B)(ii) added by section 1825(a)—(c), '86 TRA, which struck out:

(1)   "subparagraphs (A) and (C)"

(2)   "and"

(3)   "(C)"

(4)   "described in subparagraph (B)"

account subparagraph (B) shall be deemed not to exceed the least amount payable as a death benefit at any time under the contract.

(2) Limited increases in death benefit permitted.—Notwithstanding paragraph (1)(A)—

(A) for purposes of computing the guideline level premium, an increase in the death benefit which is provided in the contract may be taken into account but only to the extent necessary to prevent a decrease in the excess of the death benefit over the cash surrender value of the contract, [2]

(B) for purposes of the cash value accumulation test, the increase described in subparagraph (A) may be taken into account if the contract will meet such test at all times assuming that the net level reserve (determined as if level annual premiums were paid for the contract over a period not ending before the insured attains age 95) is substituted for the net single premium, *and*[5]

(C) for purposes of the cash value accumulation test, the death benefit increases may be taken into account if the contract—

(i) has an initial death benefit of $5,000 or less and a maximum death benefit of $25,000 or less,

(ii) provides for a fixed predetermined annual increase not to exceed 10 percent of the initial death benefit or 8 percent of the death benefit at the end of the preceding year, and

(iii) was purchased to cover payment of burial expenses or in connection with prearranged funeral expenses.

For purposes of subparagraph (C), the initial death benefit of a contract shall be determined by treating all contracts issued to the same contract owner as 1 contract.

(f) Other Definitions and Special Rules.—For purposes of this section—

(1) Premiums paid.—

(A) In general.—The term "premiums paid" means the premiums paid under the contract less amounts (other than amounts includible in gross income) to which section 72(e) applies and less any *excess premiums with respect to which there is a distribution described in subparagraph (B) or (E) of paragraph (7) and any* other amounts received with respect to the contract which are specified in regulations.

* * * * * * * * * * * *

(7) Adjustments.—

[6]*(A) In general.—If there is a change in the benefits under (or in other terms of) the contract which was not reflected in any previous determination or adjustment made under this section, there shall be proper adjustments in future determinations made under this section.*

(B) Rule for certain changes during first 15 years.—If—

(i) a change described in subparagraph (A) reduces benefits under the contract,

(ii) the change occurs during the 15-year period beginning on the issue date of the contract, and

(iii) a cash distribution is made to the policyholder as a result of such change,

section 72 (other than subsection (e)(5) thereof) shall apply to such cash distribution to the extent it does not exceed the recapture ceiling determined under subparagraph (C) or (D) (whichever applies).

(C) Recapture ceiling where change occurs during first 5 years.—If the change referred to in subparagraph (B)(ii) occurs during the 5-year period beginning on the issue date of the contract, the recapture ceiling is—

(i) in the case of a contract to which subsection (a)(1) applies, the excess of—

(I) the cash surrender value of the contract, immediately before the reduction, over

(II) the net single premium (determined under subsection (b)), immediately after the reduction, or

(ii) in the case of a contract to which subsection (a)(2) applies, the greater of—

⌈Footnote ¶3429 continued⌋

(5) "."

(6) "(A) In general.—In the event of a change in the future benefits or any qualified additional benefit (or in any other terms) under the contract which was not reflected in any previous determination made under this section, under regulations prescribed by the Secretary, there shall be proper adjustments in future determinations made under this section.

(B) Certain changes treated as exchange.—In the case of any change which reduces the future benefits under the contract, such change shall be treated as an exchange of the contract for another contract."

(I) the excess of the aggregate premiums paid under the contract, immediately before the reduction, over the guideline premium limitation for the contract (determined under subsection (c)(2), taking into account the adjustment described in subparagraph (A)), or

(II) the excess of the cash surrender value of the contract, immediately before the reduction, over the cash value corridor of subsection (d) (determined immediately after the reduction).

(D) Recapture ceiling where change occurs after 5th year and before 16th year.—If the change referred to in subparagraph (B) occurs after the 5-year period referred to under subparagraph (C), the recapture ceiling is the excess of the cash surrender value of the contract, immediately before the reduction, over the cash value corridor of subsection (d) (determined immediately after the reduction and whether or not subsection (d) applies to the contract).

(E) Treatment of certain distributions made in anticipation of benefit reductions.—Under regulations prescribed by the Secretary, subparagraph (B) shall apply also to any distribution made in anticipation of a reduction in benefits under the contract. For purposes of the preceding sentence, appropriate adjustments shall be made in the provisions of subparagraphs (C) and (D); and any distribution which reduces the cash surrender value of a contract and which is made within 2 years before a reduction in benefits under the contract shall be treated as made in anticipation of such reduction.

* * * * * * * * * * * *

(g) **Treatment of Contracts Which Do Not Meet Subsection (a) Test.—**

(1) **Income inclusion.—**

* * * * * * * * * * * *

(B) Income on the contract.—for purposes of this paragraph, the term "income on the contract" means, with respect to any taxable year of the policyholder, the excess of—

(i) the sum of—

(I) the increase in the net surrender value of the contract during the taxable year, and

(II) the cost of life insurance protection provided under the contract during the taxable year, over

[7](ii) the premiums paid (as defined in subsection (f)(1)) under the contract

---

⟦Footnote ¶3429 continued⟧

(7) "(ii) the amount of premiums paid under the contract during the taxable year reduced by any policyholder dividends received during such taxable year."

Effective date (Sec. 1881, '86 TRA and section 221(d)(1)—(3), and (5), '84 TRA, as amended by section 1825(e) and 1899A(69), '86 TRA).—(1) Generally applies to contracts issued after 12-31-84, in taxable years ending after such date.

(2) Special rule for certain contracts issued after 6-30-84.—

(A) General rule.—Except as otherwise provided in this paragraph, the amendments made by section 221 shall apply also to any contract issued after 6-30-84, which provides an increasing death benefit and has premium funding more rapid than 10-year level premium payments.

(B) Exception for certain contracts.—Subparagraph (A) shall not apply to any contract if—

(i) such contract (whether or not a flexible premium contract) would meet the requirements of section 101(f), '54 Code,

(ii) such contract is not a flexible premium life insurance contract (within the meaning of section 101(f), '54 Code and would meet the requirements of section 7702 '54 Code determined by—

(I) substituting "13 percent" for "4 percent" in section 7702(b)(2) '54 Code, and

(II) treating subparagraph (B) of section 7702(e)(1) '54 Code as if it read as follows: "the maturity date shall be the latest maturity date permitted under the contract, but not less than 20 years after the date of issue or (if earlier) age 95", or

(iii) under such contract—

(I) the premiums (including any policy fees) will be adjusted from time-to-time to reflect the level amount necessary (but not less than zero) at the time of such adjustment to provide a level death benefit assuming interest crediting and an annual effective interest rate of not less than 3 percent, or

(II) at the option of the insured, in lieu of an adjustment under subclause (I) there will be a comparable adjustment in the amount of the death benefit.

(C) Certain contracts issued before 10-1-84.—

(i) In general.—Subparagraph (A) shall be applied by substituting "September 30, 1984" for "June 30, 1984" in the case of a contract—

(I) which would meet the requirements of section 7702 '54 Code if "3 percent" were substituted for "4 percent" in section 7702(b)(2) '54 Code, and the rate or rates guaranteed on issuance of the contract were determined without regard to any mortality charges and any initial excess interest guarantees, and

(II) the cash surrender value of which does not at any time exceed the net single premium which would have to

Code §7702(g)(1) ¶3429

during the taxable year.

* * * * * * * * * * * *

[For official explanation, see Committee Reports, ¶4151.]

【¶3430】 CODE SEC. ¹7703. DETERMINATION OF MARITAL STATUS.

(a) **General Rule.**—For purposes of part V *of subchapter B of chapter 1 and those provisions of this title which refer to this subsection—*

(1) The determination of whether an individual is married shall be made as of the close of his taxable year; except that if his spouse dies during his taxable year such determination shall be made as of the time of such death; and

(2) An individual legally separated from his spouse under a decree of divorce or of separate maintenance shall not be considered as married.

(b) **Certain Married Individuals, Living Apart.**—For purposes of those provisions of this title which refer to this subsection, if—

(1) an individual who is married (within the meaning of subsection (a)) and who files a separate return maintains as his home a household which constitutes for more than one-half of the taxable year the principal place of abode of a child within the meaning of section 151(e)(3)) with respect to whom such individual is entitled to a deduction for the taxable year under section 151 (or would be so entitled but for paragraph (2) or (4) of section 152(e)),

(2) such individual furnishes over one-half of the cost of maintaining such household during the taxable year, and

(3) during the last 6 months of the taxable year, such individual's spouse is not a member of such household,

such individual shall not be considered as married.

[For official explanation, see Committee Reports, ¶4058.]

【¶3431】 CODE SEC. 7871. INDIAN TRIBAL GOVERNMENTS TREATED AS STATES FOR CERTAIN PURPOSES.

(a) **General Rule.**—An Indian tribal government shall be treated as a State—

(1) for purposes of determining whether and in what amount any contribution or transfer to or for the use of such government (or a political subdivision thereof) is deductible under—

(A) section 170 (relating to income tax deduction for charitable, etc., contributions and gifts),

(B) sections 2055 and 2106(a)(2) (relating to estate tax deduction for transfers of public, charitable, and religious uses), or

(C) section 2522 (relating to gift tax deduction for charitable and similar gifts);

(2) subject to subsection (b), for purposes for any exemption from, credit or refund of, or payment with respect to, an excise tax imposed by—

【Footnote ¶3429 continued】

be paid at such time to fund future benefits under the contract.

(ii) Definitions.—For purposes of clause (i)—

(I) In general.—Except as provided in subclause (II), terms used in clause (i) shall have the same meanings as when used in section 7702 '54 Code.

(II) Net single premium.—The term "net single premium" shall be determined by substituting "3 percent" for "4 percent" in section 7702(b)(2) '54 Code, by using the 1958 standard ordinary mortality and morbidity tables of the Nat. Association of Ins. Commissioners, and by assuming a level death benefit.

(3) Transitional rule for certain existing plans of insurance.—A plan of insurance on file in 1 or more States before 9-28-83, shall be treated for purposes of section 7702(i)(3) '54 Code as a plan of insurance on file in 1 or more States before 9-28-83, to permit the crediting of excess interest or similar amounts annually and not monthly under contracts issued pursuant to such plan or insurance.

* * * * * * * * * * * *

(5) Special rule for master contract.—For purposes of this subsection, in the case of a master contract, the date taken into account with respect to any insured shall be the first date on which such insured is covered under such contract.

【Footnote ¶3430】 Matter in *italics* in Sec. 7703 (former 143) added by section 1301(j)(2)(A), '86 TRA, which struck out:

(1) "143"

Effective date (Sec. 1311, '86 TRA). —Generally applies to bonds issued after 8-15-86. For special and transitional rules, see ¶2071—2077.

Matter in *italics* in Sec. 7703(a) added by section 1301(j)(2)(A), '86 TRA.

Effective date (Sec. 1311, '86 TRA).—Generally applies to bonds issued after 8-15-86. For special and transitional rules, see ¶2071—2077.

    (A) chapter 31 (relating to tax on special fuels),

    (B) chapter 32 (relating to manufacturers excise taxes),

    (C) subchapter B of chapter 33 (relating to communications excise tax), or

    (D) subchapter D of chapter 36 (relating to tax on use of certain highway vehicles);

  (3) for purposes of section 164 (relating to deduction for taxes);

  (4) subject to subsection (c), for purposes of section 103 (relating to ¹*State and local bonds*);

  (5) for purposes of section 511(a)(2)(B) (relating to the taxation of colleges and universities which are agencies or instrumentalities of governments or their political subdivisions);

  (6) for purposes of—²

    ³*(A)* section 105(e) (relating to accident and health plans), ⁴

    ⁵*(B)* section 162(e) (relating to appearances, etc., with respect to legislation),

    ⁶*(C)* section 403(b)(1)(A)(ii) (relating to the taxation of contributions of certain employers for employee annuities), and

    ⁷*(D)* section 454(b)(2) (relating to discount obligations) ⁸*; and*

  (7) for purposes of—

    (A) chapter 41 (relating to tax on excess expenditures to influence legislation), and

    (B) subchapter A of chapter 42 (relating to private foundations).

* * * * * * * * * * * *

(c) Additional Requirements for Tax-Exempt Bonds.—

  (1) In general.—Subsection (a) of section 103 shall apply to any obligation (not described in paragraph (2)) issued by an Indian tribal government (or subdivision thereof) only if such obligation is part of an issue substantially all of the proceeds of which are to be used in the exercise of any essential governmental function.

  ⁹*(2) No exemption for private activity bonds.—Subsection (a) of section 103 shall not apply to any private activity bond (as defined in section 141(a)) issued by an Indian tribal government (or subdivision thereof).*

* * * * * * * * * * * *

[For official explanation, see Committee Reports, ¶3856; 3859; 4058.]

[¶3432] CODE SEC. 7872. TREATMENT OF LOANS WITH BELOW-MARKET INTEREST RATES.

* * * * * * * * * * * *

(d) Special Rules for Gift Loans.—

[Footnote ¶3431] Matter in *italics* in Sec. 7871(a)(4) added by section 1301(j)(6), '86 TRA, which struck out:
(1) "interest on certain governmental obligations"
Effective date (Sec. 1311—1319, '86 TRA).—Applies to bonds issued after 7-15-86. For transitional rules see ¶2071—2077.

Matter in *italics* in Sec. 7871(a)(6)(A)—(D) (former (B)—(F)) added by sections 112(b)(4) and 123(b)(3), '86 TRA, which struck out:
(2) "(A) section 24(c)(4) (defining State for purposes of credit for contribution to candidates for public offices)."
(3) "(B)"
(4) "(C) section 117(b)(2)(A) (relating to scholarships and fellowship grants)."
(5) "(C)"
(6) "(D)"
(7) "(E)"
Effective date (Sec. 151(a), '86 TRA).—Applies to taxable years beginning after 12-31-86.

"; *and*" in *italics* in Sec. 7871(a)(6)(D) (former (F)) added by section 1899A, '86 TRA, which struck out:
(8) "."

Matter in *italics* in Sec. 7871(c)(2) added by section 1301(j)(7), '86 TRA, which struck out:
(9) "(2) No exemption for certain private-activity bonds.—Subsection (a) of section 103 shall not apply to any of the following issued by an Indian tribal government (or subdivision thereof):
(A) An industrial development bond (as defined in section 103(b)(2)).
(B) An obligation described in section 103(l)(1)(A) (relating to scholarship bonds).
(C) A mortgage subsidy bond (as defined in paragraph (1) of section 103A(b) without regard to paragraph (2) thereof)."
Effective date (Sec. 1311—1319, '86 TRA).—See above.

(1) **Limitation of interest accrual for purposes of income taxes where loans do not exceed $100,000—**

* * * * * * * * * * * *

(E) Net investment income.—For purposes of this paragraph—

(i) In general.—The term "net investment income" has the meaning given such term by section [1]*163(d)(4).*

* * * * * * * * * * * *

(f) **Other Definitions and Special Rules.**—For purposes of this section—

* * * * * * * * * * * *

(2) **Applicable federal rate.—**

* * * * * * * * * * * *

(B) Demand loans.—In the case of a demand loan, the applicable Federal rate shall be the Federal short-term rate in effect under section 1274(d) for the period for which the amount of foregone interest is being determined, *compounded semiannually.*

* * * * * * * * * * * *

(5) **Demand loan.**—The term "demand loan" means any loan which is payable in full at any time on the demand of the lender. Such term also includes (for purposes other than determining the applicable Federal rate under paragraph (2)) any loan [2] *if the benefits of the interest arrangements of such loan are not transferable and are conditioned on the future performance of substantial services by an individual. To the extent provided in regulations, such term also includes any loan with an indefinite maturity.*

* * * * * * * * * * * *

(9) **No withholding.**—No amount shall be withheld under chapter 24 [3] *with respect to—*

(A)   any amount treated as transferred or retransferred under subsection (a), and

(B)   any amount treated as received under subsection (b).

* * * * * * * * * * * *

(11) *[should read (12)] Special rule for certain employer security loans.*—This section *shall not apply to any loan between a corporation (or any member of the controlled group of corporations which includes such corporation) and an employee stock ownership plan described in section 4975(e)(7) to the extent that the interest rate on such loan is equal to the interest rate paid on a related securities acquisition loan (as described in section 133(b)) to such corporation.*

* * * * * * * * * * * *

[For official explanation, see Committee Reports, ¶3905; 4146; 4174.]

[Footnote ¶3432] Matter in *italics* in Sec. 7872(d)(1)(E)(i) added by section 511(d)(1), '86 TRA, which struck out:

(1) "163(d)(3)"

Effective date (Sec. 511(e), '86 TRA).—Applies to taxable years beginning after 12-31-86.

Matter in *italics* in Sec. 7872(f)(2)(B), (5) and (9) added by section 1812(b)(2)—(4), '86 TRA, which struck out:

(2) "which is not transferable and the benefits of the interest arrangements of which is conditioned on the future performance of substantial services by an individual."

(3) "with respect to any amount treated as transferred or retransferred under subsection (a)."

Effective date (Sec. 1881, '86 TRA and section 172(c)(1)—(6), '84 TRA).—(1) Generally applies to—

(A) term loans made after 6-6-84, and

(B) demand loans outstanding after 6-6-84.

(2) Exception for demand loans outstanding on June 6, 1984, and repaid within 60 days after July 18, 1984.— The amendments made by this section shall not apply to any demand loan which—

(A) was outstanding on 6-6-84, and

(B) was repaid before the date 60 days after 7-18-84.

(3) Exception for certain existing loans to continuing care facilities.—Nothing in this subsection shall be construed to apply the amendments made by this section to any loan made before 6-6-84, to a continuing care facility by a resident of such facility which is contingent on continued residence at such facility.

(4) Applicable federal rate for periods before January 1, 1985.—For periods before 1-1-85, the applicable Federal rate under paragraph (2) of section 7872(f) of the '54 Code, as added by this section, shall be 10 percent, compounded semiannually.

(5) Treatment of renegotiations, etc.—For purposes of this subsection, any loan renegotiated, extended, or revised after 6-6-84, shall be treated as a loan made after such date.

(6) Definition of term and demand loans.—For purposes of this subsection, the terms "demand loan" and "term loan" have the respective meanings given such terms by paragraphs (5) and (6) of section 7872(f) of the '54 Code, as added by this section, but the second sentence of such paragraph (5) shall not apply.

Matter in *italics* in Sec. 7872(f)(11) [should read (12)] added by section 1854(c)(2)(B), '86 TRA.

Effective date (Sec. 1881, '86 TRA and Sec. 543(c), '84 TRA).—Applies to loans used to acquire employer securities after 7-18-84.

CONGRESSIONAL COMMITTEE REPORTS

Explaining Law Enacted by the Tax Reform Act of 1986

[¶ 3851] This subdivision reproduces all important parts of the official explanations of the Tax Reform Act of 1986. The material comes from the House, Senate and Conference Committee Reports and statements made on the floor of the Senate. Colloquies involving the House or the Senate floor managers made during or after the consideration of the Conference Report are also included. It is arranged in the order of the Act section numbers. If a Committee Report is consistent with the law except for section numbers, other numbers, dates, etc., correct numbers and dates are supplied and enclosed in brackets.

You may prefer to read the P-H Explanation of the changes before consulting this official material. The Explanation begins at ¶101. References to Act sections in the explanation will lead you to the official material on the changes.

Background

● H.R. 3838, Tax Reform Act of 1985. Reported by House Ways and Means December 7, 1985; House Report No. 99-426, dated December 7, 1985.

● H.R. 3838, Tax Reform Act of 1985, was passed by the House with amendments on December 17, 1985.

● H.R. 3838, Tax Reform Act of 1985. Reported by Senate Finance May 29, 1986; Senate Report 99-313, dated May 29, 1986.

● H.R. 3838, Tax Reform Act of 1986, was passed by the Senate with amendments on June 24, 1986.

● H.R. 3838, Tax Reform Act of 1986. Agreed to by Conferees August 16, 1986, House Report 99-841, September 18, 1986.

● Conference version agreed to by House on September 25, 1986 and by Senate on September 27, 1986.

⋙**NOTE: LOOK AT THE LAW**→ It is always necessary to consult the law itself to ascertain the exact law changes made.

[¶ 3852] SECTION 101. RATE REDUCTIONS

(Secs. 1; 15 of the Code)

[Conference Report]

*   *   *   *   *   *

Conference Agreement.—

In general.—The tax structure under the conference agreement consists of two brackets and tax rates—15 and 28 percent—beginning at zero taxable income, with a standard deduction replacing the ZBA.

MARRIED INDIVIDUALS FILING JOINT-LY AND SURVIVING SPOUSES

Tax rate	Brackets
ZBA	Replaced by standard deduction
15%	0 to $29,750
28%	Over $29,750

(For married individuals filing separate returns, the 28-percent bracket begins at $14,875, i.e., one-half the taxable income amount for joint returns.)

Act § 101   ¶ 3852

HEADS OF HOUSEHOLD

Tax rate	Brackets
ZBA	Replaced by standard deduction
15%	0 to $23,900
28%	Over $23,900

SINGLE INDIVIDUALS

Tax rate	Brackets
ZBA	Replaced by standard deduction
15%	0 to $17,850
28%	Over $17,850

Beginning in 1989, the taxable income amounts at which the 28-percent rate starts will be adjusted for inflation.

Rate adjustment.—Beginning in 1988, the benefit of the 15-percent bracket is phased out for taxpayers having taxable income exceeding specified levels. The income tax liability of such taxpayers is increased by five percent of their taxable income within specified ranges.

The rate adjustment occurs between $71,900 and $149,250 of taxable income for married individuals filing jointly; between $61,650 and $123,790 of taxable income for heads of household; between $43,150 and $89,560 of taxable income for single individuals; and between $35,950 and $113,300 of taxable income for married individuals filing separately. These amounts will be adjusted for inflation beginning in 1989.

The maximum amount of the rate adjustment generally equals 13 percent of the maximum amount of taxable income within the 15-percent bracket applicable to the taxpayer (for a married individual filing separately, within the 15-percent bracket applicable for married taxpayers filing jointly.) Thus, if the maximum rate adjustment applies, the 28-percent rate in effect applies to all of the taxpayer's taxable income, rather than only to the amount of taxable income above the breakpoint.

* * * * * *

* * * [T]he rate schedule applicable to trusts and estates is modified to reflect the top individual rate of 28 percent. Thus, taxable income of trusts and estates in excess of $5,000 is taxed at 28 percent. In addition, the phase-out rate for the benefit of the 15-percent bracket is similarly modified so that the benefit phases out between $13,000 and $26,000. An additional rate schedule[1] is provided for taxable years beginning in 1987.

* * * * * *

[**Effective Dates.**—Except as otherwise provided, the new tax rate schedules and rate adjustments apply to taxable years beginning after December 31, 1986. Ed.]

Transitional rate structure for 1987.—For taxable years beginning in 1987, five-bracket rate schedules are provided, as shown in the table below. Neither the rate adjustment (described above) nor the personal exemption phaseout (described below) applies to taxable years beginning in 1987.

	Taxable income brackets		
Tax rate	Married, filing joint returns	Heads of household	Single individuals
11%	0-$3,000	0-$2,500	0-$1,800
15%	$3,000-28,000	$2,500-23,000	$1,300-16,800
28%	28,000-45,000	23,000-38,000	16,800-27,000
35%	45,000-90,000	38,000-80,000	27,000-54,000
38.5%	Over $90,000	Over 80,000	Over 54,000

For married individuals filing separate returns, the taxable income bracket amounts for 1987 begin at one-half the amounts for joint returns. The bracket amounts for surviving spouses are the same as those for married individuals filing joint returns.

* * * * * *

* * * **Adjustments for inflation.**—*Present Law.*—The dollar amounts defining the tax rate brackets, the ZBA (standard deduction), and the personal exemption amount are adjusted annually for inflation, measured by 12-month periods ending September 30 of the prior calendar year. If the inflation adjustment is not a multiple of $10,

[**Footnote ¶ 3852**] (1) The income tax schedule for estates and trusts for 1987 would be as follows:

If taxable income is—	The tax is—
Not over $600	11% of taxable income
Over $500 but not over $4,700	$55 plus 16% of the excess over $500
Over $4,700 but not over $7,550	$685 plus 28% of the excess over $4,700
Over $7,550 but not over $15,150	$1,483 plus 35% of the excess over $7,550
Over $15,150	$4,143 plus 38.5% of the excess over $15,100

the increase is rounded to the nearest multiple of $10 (sec. 1(f)).

House Bill.—The House bill continues inflation adjustments as under present law, except that the 12-month measuring periods end August 31, effective for taxable years beginning on or after January 1, 1986.

Senate Amendment.—The Senate amendment is the same as the House bill, except that inflation adjustments to the rate brackets, the standard deduction (and the $600 or $750 additional standard deduction for elderly or blind individuals), and personal exemption amounts are to be rounded down to the

nearest multiple of $50. The Senate amendment provisions with respect to the 12-month measuring period and rounding down are effective for taxable years beginning on or after January 1, 1987.

Conference Agreement.—The conference agreement follows the Senate amendment.

[Sec. 15 (relating to effect of changes in rates during a taxable year) is amended so it won't apply to any changes in rates under Sec. 1(f) (relating to adjustments in tax tables so inflation won't result in tax increases). Ed.]

[¶ 3853] SECTION 102. INCREASE IN STANDARD DEDUCTION

(Secs. 3; 63 of the Code)

[Senate Explanation]

Explanation of Provisions.—Under the bill, the standard deduction replaces the ZBA, and is deducted by a nonitemizer from AGI in determining taxable income.

* * * * * *

[Conference Report]

Increased deduction—Under the conference agreement, the standard deduction is increased to the following amounts, effective beginning in 1988:

Filing status	Standard deduction
Joint returns and surviving spouses	$5,000
Heads of household	4,400
Single individuals	3,000
Married individuals filing separately	2,500

Beginning in 1989, these increased standard deduction amounts are to be adjusted for inflation.

Elderly or blind individuals.—An additional standard deduction amount of $600 is allowed for an elderly or blind individual who is married (whether filing jointly or separately) or is a surviving spouse ($1,200 for such an individual who is both elderly and blind). An additional standard deduction amount of $750 is allowed for an unmarried individual (other than a surviving spouse), or for a head of household, who is elderly or blind ($1,500 if both). For elderly or blind taxpayers only, the new standard deduction amounts (listed above) and the additional $600 or $750 standard deduction amounts are effective beginning in 1987. Beginning in 1989, the $600 and $750 additional standard deduction amounts will be adjusted for inflation.

Standard deduction for 1987.—For all individual taxpayers other than elderly or blind individuals, the standard deduction

amounts for taxable years beginning in 1987 are $3,760 for married individuals filing jointly and surviving spouses; $2,540 for heads of household and single individuals; and $1,880 for married individuals filing separately.

Floor under itemized deductions.—The conference agreement follows the Senate amendment (i.e., there is no general floor under total itemized deductions).

* * * * * *

Adjustments for inflation.—*Present Law.*—The dollar amounts defining the tax rate brackets, the ZBA (standard deduction), and the personal exemption amount are adjusted annually for inflation, measured by 12-month periods ending September 30 of the prior calendar year. If the inflation adjustment is not a multiple of $10, the increase is rounded to the nearest multiple of $10 (sec. 1(f)).

House Bill.—The House bill continues inflation adjustments as under present law, except that the 12-month measuring periods end August 31, effective for taxable years beginning on or after January 1, 1986.

Senate Amendment.—The Senate amendment is the same as the House bill, except that inflation adjustments to the rate brackets, the standard deduction (and the $600 or $750 additional standard deduction for elderly or blind individuals), and personal exemption amounts are to be rounded down to the nearest multiple of $50. The Senate amendment provisions with respect to the 12-month measuring period and rounding down are effective for taxable years beginning on or after January 1, 1987.

Conference Agreement.—The conference agreement follows the Senate amendment.

[**Effective Date.**—For taxable years beginning after December 31, 1986, the standard deduction replaces the ZBA, at the dollar amounts specified in the bill. Ed.]

[¶ 3854]   **SECTION 103. INCREASE IN PERSONAL EXEMPTIONS**

(Sec. 151 of the Code)

[Conference Report]

*   *   *   *   *   *

Exemption amount.—The conference agreement increases the personal exemption for each individual, the individual's spouse, and each eligible dependent to $1,900 for 1987, $1,950 for 1988, and $2,000 in 1989. Beginning in 1990, the $2,000 personal exemption amount will be adjusted for inflation. The conference agreement follows the House bill and the Senate amendment in repealing the additional exemption for an elderly or blind individual, beginning in 1987. (As described above, an additional standard deduction amount is provided by the conference agreement for an elderly or blind individual, beginning in 1987.)

Phase-out.—Beginning in 1988, the benefit of the personal exemption is phased out for taxpayers having taxable income exceeding specified levels. The income tax liability of such taxpayers is increased by five percent of taxable income within certain ranges.

This reduction in the personal exemption benefit starts at the taxable income level at which the benefit of 15-percent rate is totally phased out (see "Rate adjustment," * * * ¶3852 above). For example, in the case of married individuals filing joint returns, in 1988 the personal exemption phaseout begins at taxable income of $149,250.

The benefit of each personal exemption amount is phased out over an income range of $10,920 in 1988. The phase-out occurs serially; e.g., the phaseout of the benefit of the second personal exemption on a joint return does not begin until the phaseout of the first is complete. Thus, in the case of a married couple filing jointly who have two children, in 1988 the benefit of the four personal exemptions would phase out over an income range of $43,680 (four times $10,920) and would be phased out completely at taxable income of $192,930. In 1989, the benefit of each exemption would phase out over an income range of $11,200.

Rules for dependents.—The conference agreement follows the Senate amendment in providing that no personal exemption amount is allowable on the return of an individual who is eligible to be claimed as a dependent on another taxpayer's return (for example, on the return of a child who is eligible to be claimed as a dependent on the return of his or her parents).

As in the present-law rule that the ZBA may be used by such a dependent individual only to offset earned income, the conference agreement generally follows the House bill

and the Senate amendment in providing that the standard deduction may be used by such a dependent individual only to offset earned income. However, the conference agreement liberalizes this limitation (in lieu of the $100 de minimis rule in the Senate amendment) by providing that for such a dependent individual, the individual's standard deduction is limited to the greater of (a) $500 (to be adjusted for inflation beginning in 1989) or (b) the individual's earned income up to the basic standard deduction amount (in 1988, $3,000 for a single individual). Under the conference agreement, such a dependent child must file a Federal income tax return only if he or she either has gross income exceeding the standard deduction amount for such a dependent child (i.e., the greater of earned income or $500) or has unearned income exceeding $500.

These rules for dependents are effective beginning in 1987.

[Effective Dates.—Except as otherwise provided, the bill increases the personal exemption amount for each individual, the individual's spouse, and each eligible dependent to $1900 for 1987, $1950 for 1988, and $2000 in 1989. Beginning in 1990, the $2000 amount will be adjusted for inflation. The rules for dependents are effective beginning in 1987. Ed.]

Adjustments for inflation.—*Present Law.*—The dollar amounts defining the tax rate brackets, the ZBA (standard deduction), and the personal exemption amount are adjusted annually for inflation, measured by 12-month periods ending September 30 of the prior calendar year. If the inflation adjustment is not a multiple of $10, the increase is rounded to the nearest multiple of $10 (sec. 1(f)).

House Bill.—The House bill continues inflation adjustments as under present law, except that the 12-month measuring periods end August 31, effective for taxable years beginning on or after January 1, 1986.

Senate Amendment.—The Senate amendment is the same as the House bill, except that inflation adjustments to the rate brackets, the standard deduction (and the $600 or $750 additional standard deduction for elderly or blind individuals), and personal exemption amounts are to be rounded down to the nearest multiple of $50. The Senate amendment provisions with respect to the 12-month measuring period and rounding down are effective for taxable years beginning on or after January 1, 1987.

Conference Agreement.—The conference agreement follows the Senate amendment.

[¶ 3855] SECTION 111. INCREASE IN EARNED INCOME CREDIT

(Sec. 32 of the Code)

[Senate Explanation]

*   *   *   *   *   *

Explanation of Provision.—Under the bill, the rate of the earned income credit is increased from 11 percent to 14 percent. Thus, the credit generally equals 14 percent of the first $5,000 of earned income; the maximum allowable amount of the earned income credit is increased from $550 to $700 (without taking into account any inflation adjustment).

In addition, the income levels over which the credit is phased out, at a rate of 10 percent, are higher than under present law. For taxable years beginning on or after January 1, 1987, the income level at which phase-down begins is $6,500; thus, no credit will be available for individuals with AGI or earned income of $13,500 or more. For taxable years beginning on or after January 1, 1988, the phase-down begins at income of $10,000; thus, no credit will be available at AGI or earned income exceeding $17,000.

Effective for taxable years beginning on or after January 1, 1987, the $5,000 maximum amount of earned income against which the credit applies and the income levels at which the phase-out of the credit begins ($6,500 in 1987 and $10,000 in 1988 and later years) will be adjusted for inflation occuring after the 12-month period ended August 31, 1984. These adjustments will not be subject to the rounding down rule applicable to inflation adjustments for the rate brackets, etc.; i.e., the adjustments relating to the earned income credit will not be rounded down to the nearest $50-divisible amount. Instead, any inflation adjustment relating to the credit that is not a multiple of $10 will be rounded down to the nearest multiple of $10 (or, if the increase is a multiple of $5, will be increased to the next highest multiple of $10).

*   *   *   *   *   *

[Conference Report]

*   *   *   *   *   *

Also, the Senate amendment directs that Treasury regulations are to require employers to notify (at such time and in such manner as prescribed in such regulations) employees whose wages are not subject to income tax withholding that they may be eligible for the refundable earned income credit.

Conference Agreement

The conference agreement follows the Senate amendment, except that (1) the base against which the increased 14-percent credit applies is raised to $5,714[1] (increasing the maximum credit to $800); and (2) the income phase-out levels, effective for taxable years starting on or after January 1, 1988, are raised to $9,000/$17,000. Also, the conference agreement clarifies that the notice that must be given by an employer to employees whose wages are not subject to withholding does not have to be given to employees whose wages are exempt from withholding pursuant to Code section 3403(n) (this exemption applies, for example, in the case of high school or college students who have summer jobs).

[Senate Explanation]

*   *   *   *   *   *

Effective Date.—The provision is effective for taxable years beginning after December 31, 1986.

[¶ 3856] SECTION 112. REPEAL OF CREDIT FOR CONTRIBUTIONS TO CANDIDATES FOR PUBLIC OFFICE

(Sec. 24 of the Code)

[Senate Explanation]

*   *   *   *   *   *

Reasons for Change.—The committee believes that, as part of the approach of its bill to reduce tax rates through base-broadening, it is appropriate to repeal the political contributions tax credit. The committee also understands that data compiled by the IRS suggest that a significant percentage of persons claiming the credit have sufficiently high incomes to make contributions in after-tax dollars, without the benefit of the credit. Also, the credit provides no incentive for individuals with no income tax liability for the year. The small credit amount allowable per return under the dollar limitations makes verification costly in relation to the tax liability at issue.

Explanation of Provision.—The bill repeals the credit for political contributions.

Effective Date.—The provision is effective for taxable years beginning after December 31, 1986.

[Footnote ¶ 3855]   (1) Under the conference agreement, the income base eligible for the credit and the phase-out starting point are adjusted for inflation occurring after the 12-month period ending on August 31, 1984. Thus, for example, the maximum amount of earned income eligible for the credit beginning in 1987 will equal $5,714 as adjusted for inflation between August 31, 1984 and August 31, 1986. These adjustments are not subject to the $50 rounding-down rule otherwise applicable under the conference agreement to inflation adjustments. Instead, as under the generally applicable inflation adjustment rule of present law, any inflation adjustment relating to the credit that is not a multiple of $10 will be rounded to the nearest multiple of $10.

〔¶ 3857〕 SECTION 121. TAXATION OF UNEMPLOYMENT COMPEN-SATION

(Sec. 85 of the Code)

[Senate Explanation]

*   *   *   *   *   *

Reasons for Change.—Present law generally treats all cash wages and similar compensation (such as vacation pay and sick pay) received by an individual as fully taxable, but unemployment compensation benefits are taxable only if the taxpayer's income exceeds specified levels. The committee believes that unemployment compensation benefits, which essentially are wage replacement payments, should be treated for tax purposes in the same manner as wages or other wage-type payments. Also, when wage replacement payments are given more favorable tax treatment than wages, some individuals may be discouraged from returning to work. Repeal of the present-law partial exclusion contributes to more equal tax treatment of individuals with the same economic income and to tax simplification.

Explanation of Provision.—Under the bill, all unemployment compensation benefits are includible in gross income after 1986.

Effective Date.—The provision is effective for amounts received after December 31, 1986.

〔¶ 3858〕 SECTION 122. PRIZES AND AWARDS

(Sec. 74; 102; 274 of the Code)

[Senate Explanation]

*   *   *   *   *   *

Explanation of Provisions

Scientific, etc. awards.—Under the bill, the present-law exclusion under section 74(b) for certain prizes and awards for charitable, artistic, scientific, and like achievements is modified to apply only if the recipient designates that the prize or award is to be transferred by the payor to a governmental unit or a tax-exempt charitable, educational, religious, etc. organization contributions to which are deductible under section 170(c)(1) or 170(c)(2), respectively. If such designation is made and the prize or award is so transferred to a governmental unit or charitable organization by the payor, the prize or award is not included in the winner's gross income, and no charitable deduction is allowed either to the winner or to the payor on account of the transfer to the governmental unit or charitable organization.

For purposes of determining whether a prize or award that is so transferred qualifies as excludable under the bill, the present-law rules concerning the scope of section 74(b) are retained without change. In addition, in order to qualify for the section 74(b) exclusion as modified by the bill, the designation must be made by the taxpayer, and must be carried out by the organization making the prize or award, before the taxpayer uses the item that is awarded (e.g., in the case of an award of money, before the taxpayer spends, deposits, invests, or otherwise uses the money). Disqualifying uses by the taxpayer include such uses of the property with the permission of the taxpayer or by one associated with the taxpayer (e.g., a member of the taxpayer's family).

Employee awards.—In general.—The bill provides an exclusion from gross income, subject to certain dollar limitations, for an "employee achievement award" that satisfies the requirements set forth in the bill. The bill defines an employee achievement award as an item of tangible personal property transferred by an employer to an employee for length of service achievement or for safety achievement, but only if the item (1) is awarded as part of a meaningful presentation, and (2) is awarded under conditions and circumstances that do not create a significant likelihood of the payment of disguised compensation.[3] The exclusion applies only for awards of tangible personal property and is not available for awards of cash, gift certificates, or equivalent items.

An award for length of service cannot qualify for the exclusion if it is received during the employee's first five years of employment for the employer making the award, or if the employee has received a length of service achievement award (other than an award excludable under section 132(e)) from the employer during the year or any of the preceding four years. An award for safety achievement cannot qualify for the exclusion if made to an employee other than an eligible employee, or if, during the year, employee awards for safety achievement have previously been awarded by the employer to more than 10 percent of the employer's eligible employees. For this purpose, eligible employees are all employees of the taxpayer other than managers, administrators, clerical workers, and other professional employees, because persons occupying these positions do not engage in work involving significant safety concerns.

Deduction limitations.—Under Section 274 as amended by the bill, the employer's deduction limitation for all employee achievement awards (safety and length of service) provided to the same employee during the taxable year generally is $400. In the

─────────────

〔Footnote ¶ 3858〕 (3) The types of conditions and circumstances that are to be deemed to create a significant likelihood of payment of disguised compensation include, for example, the making of employee awards at the time of annual salary adjustments or as a substitute for a prior program of awarding cash bonuses, or the providing of employee awards in a way that discriminates in favor of highly paid employees.

case of one or more qualified plan awards awarded to the same employee during the taxable year, however, the employer's deduction limitation for all such qualified plan awards (safety and length of service) is $1,600. In addition to these separate $400/$1,600 limitations, the $1,600 limitation applies in the aggregate if an employee receives one or more qualified plan awards during the year, and also one or more employee achievement awards that are not qualified plan awards; i.e., the $400 and $1,600 limitations cannot be added together to allow deductions exceeding $1,600 in the aggregate for employee achievement awards made to the same employee in a taxable year.[4]

A qualified plan award is defined as an employee achievement award provided under a qualified award plan, i.e., an established, written plan or program of the taxpayer that does not discriminate in favor of highly compensated employees (within the meaning of sec. 414(q)) as to eligibility or benefits. However, an item cannot be treated as a qualified plan award if the average cost per recipient of all employee achievement awards made under all qualified award plans of the employer during the taxable year exceeds $400. In making this calculation of average cost, qualified plan awards of nominal value are not to be included in the calculation (i.e., are not to be added into the total of award costs under the plan). In the case of a qualified plan award the cost of which exceeds $1,600, the entire cost of the item is to be added into the total of award costs under the plan, notwithstanding that only $1,600 (or less) of such cost is deductible.

Excludable amount.—In the case of an employee achievement award the cost of which is fully deductible by the employer under the dollar limitations of section 274 (as amended by the bill),[5] the fair market value of the award is fully excludable from gross income by the employee. For example, assume that an employer makes a length of service achievement award (other than a qualified plan award) to an employee in the form of a crystal bowl, that the employer makes no other length of service awards or safety achievement awards to that employee in the same year, and that the employee has not received a length of service award from the employer during the prior four years. Assume further that the cost of the bowl to the employer is $375, and that the fair market value of the bowl is $415. The full fair market value of $415 is excludable from the employee's gross income for income tax purposes under section 74 as amended by the bill.

If any part of the cost of an employee achievement award exceeds the amount al-lowable as a deduction by an employer because of the dollar limitations of section 274, however, then the exclusion does not apply to the entire fair market value of the award. In such a case, the employee must include in gross income the greater of (i) an amount equal to the portion of the cost to the employer of the award that is not allowable as a deduction to the employer (but not an amount in excess of the fair market value of the award) and (ii) the amount by which the fair market value of the award exceeds the maximum dollar amount allowable as a deduction to the employer. The remaining portion of the fair market value of the award is not included in the employee's gross income for income tax purposes.

Consider, for example, the case of a safety achievement award to an eligible employee that is not a qualified plan award, and that costs the employer $500; assume that no other employee achievement awards were made to the same employee during the taxable year, and that safety achievement awards had not previously been awarded during the year to more than 10 percent of eligible employees of the employer. The employer's deduction is limited to $400. The amount includible in gross income by the employee is the greater of (1) $100 (the difference between the item's cost and the deduction limitation), and (2) the amount by which the item's fair market value exceeds the deduction limitation. If the fair market value equals, for example, $475, $100 is includible in the employee's income. If the fair market value equals $600, then $200 is includible in the employee's income.

Except to the extent that the new section 74(c) exclusion or section 132(e) applies, the fair market value of an employee award (whether or not satisfying the definition of an employee achievement award) is includible in the employee's gross income under section 61, and is not excludable under section 74 (as amended by the bill) or section 102 (gifts). The fair market value of an employee award (or any portion thereof) that is not excludable from income must be included by the employer on the employee's Form W-2, as is required under present law.

Any amount of an employee achievement award that is excludable from gross income under the bill is includible in wages or compensation for employment tax (e.g., FICA tax) purposes.

The committee bill does not modify section 132(e), under which de minimis fringe benefits are excluded from gross income. Thus, an employee award is not includible in income if its fair market value, after taking into account the frequency with which similar benefits are provided by the employer to the employer's employees, is so small as to make

---

[Footnote ¶ 3858 continued]

(4) In the case of an employee award provided by a partnership, the deduction limitations of section 274(b) apply to the partnership as well as to each partner.

(5) In the case of a tax-exempt employer, the deduction limitation amount is that amount that would be deductible if the employer were not exempt from taxation.

accounting for it unreasonable or administratively impracticable.

For purposes of sections 74 and 274 (as modified by the bill), an employee award that is excludable under section 132(e) is disregarded in applying the rules regarding how frequently an individual may receive a length of service award, or how many employees of an employer may receive a safety achievement award in the same taxable year. Under appropriate circumstances, however, the fact that an employer makes a practice of giving to its employees length of service or safety achievement awards that qualify under section 74 and 274 may affect the question of whether other items given to such employees (particularly if given by reason of length of service or safety achievement) qualify as de minimis fringe benefits under section 132(e).

The question of whether it is unreasonable or administratively impracticable (within the meaning of sec. 132(e)) to account for an item may be affected by the existence of a program whereby the taxpayer regularly accounts for other like items and complies with the statutory reporting requirements. Moreover, in some cases the fact that a particular employee receives items having the maximum fair market value consistent, respectively, with the employee achievement award and the de minimis fringe benefit exclusions may suggest that the employer's practice is not de minimis. This is particularly so when employee awards and other items, purportedly within the scope of section 132(e), are provided to the same individual in the same year.

The committee expects that the exclusion under section 132(e) for a de minimis fringe benefit will apply, under appropriate circumstances, to traditional retirement gifts presented to an employee on his or her retirement after completing lengthy service, where the section 74(c) exclusion for length of service awards does not apply because the employee received such an award within the prior four years. In considering whether an item presented upon retirement qualifies as de minimis, the duration of the employee's tenure with the employer generally has relevance. For example, in the case of an employee who has worked for an employer for 25 years, a retirement gift of a gold watch may qualify for exclusion as a de minimis fringe benefit even though gold watches given throughout the period of employment would not so qualify for exclusion.

[Conference Report]

*   *   *   *   *   *

Scientific, etc. achievement awards.—The conference agreement follows the Senate amendment, effective for such awards made after December 31, 1986.

Employee awards.—The conference agreement follows the Senate amendment, with a modification that an employee award is excludable from wages for employment tax purposes and from the social security benefit base to the same extent that the award is excludable under the conference agreement from gross income for income tax purposes. The conference agreement is effective for such awards made after December 31, 1986.

[**Effective date.**—The amendments * * * * * shall apply to prizes and awards granted after December 31, 1986. Ed.]

[¶ 3859] SECTION 123. SCHOLARSHIPS

(Secs. 74; 117 of the Code)

[House Explanation]

*   *   *   *   *   *

Explanation of Provision.—The bill limits the section 117 exclusion for degree candidates to the amount of a scholarship or fellowship grant that is required to be used, and in fact is used, for (1) tuition and fees required for enrollment or attendance at an educational institution (within the meaning of sec. 170(b)(1)(A)(ii)), and (2) fees, books, supplies, and equipment required for courses of instruction at the educational institution. For this purpose, the committee intends that amounts of scholarship or fellowship grants received that do not exceed this amount are excludable without the need to trace particular grant dollars to particular expenditures for tuition and equipment, provided that the grant requires the recipient to use the grant funds for such purposes. Amounts received by degree candidates in excess of the amount of qualified tuition and equipment expenses are not excludable under section 117. Similarly, amounts not in excess of qualified tuition and equipment costs, but designated or earmarked for other purposes (such as room and board), are not excludable as a scholarship or fellowship grant.

The bill also repeals the present-law exclusion under section 117 for grants received by nondegree candidates. This provision does not affect whether the section 127 exclusion may apply to employer-provided educational assistance to nondegree candidates, or whether unreimbursed educational expenses of some nondegree candidates may be deductible as trade or business expenses if the requirements of section 162 are met.

Performance of services.—The bill repeals the special rule of present law permitting scholarship or fellowship grants received by degree candidates to be excludable, even where such amounts represent payment for services, if all candidates for the particular degree are required to perform such services. Thus, the general rule applies requiring inclusion in gross income of amounts received which represent payment for services required as a condition of receiving the grant.

To prevent circumvention of this general rule, the rule is intended to apply not only to cash amounts received, but also to amounts (representing payment for services) by which the tuition of the person who performs services is reduced, whether or not pursuant to a tuition reduction plan described in section 117(d). The bill therefore explicitly provides that the section 117 exclusion does not apply to that portion of the amount received which represents payment for teaching, research, or other services by the student required as a condition of receiving the scholarship or tuition reduction.

The committee intends that employees who perform required services for which they include in income reasonable compensation should continue to be eligible to exclude the amounts of the tuition reduction. (In addition, section 1161 of the committee bill extends the availability of the tuition reduction exclusion for certain graduate students an additional two taxable years beyond its scheduled expiration for taxable years beginning after December 31, 1985, as part of the extension of section 127 under the bill.)

The bill also repeals the special rule permitting the exclusion of certain Federal grants as scholarships or fellowship grants, where the recipient is required to perform future service as a Federal employee. Thus, the general rule applies in such circumstances. If the amount received (or a portion of it) represents payments for past, present, or future services required to be performed as a condition of the grant, then the amount received (or a portion of it) is not excludable. As a result, services performed as a Federal employee are not entitled to more favorable tax treatment than services performed for another employer.

* * * * * *

[Conference Report]

* * * * * *

The conference agreement follows the House bill, with a modification to the definition of a qualified scholarship or fellowship grant ("qualified scholarship") and a modification to the effective date. The exclusion as allowed under the conference agreement for an otherwise qualified scholarship is not limited to a grant that by its express terms is required to be used for tuition and course-related expenses. Instead, the amount of an otherwise qualified scholarship received by a degree candidate is excludable (taking into account the amount of any other grant to the individual eligible for exclusion) up to the aggregate amount incurred by the candidate for tuition and course-related expenses dur-

ing the period to which the grant applies, provided that the terms of the grant do not earmark or designate its use for other purposes (such as room or board) and do not specify that the grant cannot be used for tuition or course-related expenses. The conference agreement clarifies that in the case of individuals other than students attending a primary or secondary school or pursuing a degree at a college or university, the term candidate for a degree means a student (whether full-time or part-time) who receives a scholarship for study at an educational institution (described in sec. 170(b)(1)(A)(ii)) that (1) provides an educational program that is acceptable for full credit toward a bachelor's or higher degree, or offers a program of training to prepare students for gainful employment in a recognized occupation, and (2) is authorized under Federal or State law to provide such a program and is accredited by a nationally recognized accreditation agency.

The amendments made by the conference agreement are effective for taxable years beginning on or after January 1, 1987, except that present law continues to apply to scholarships and fellowships granted before August 17, 1986. Under this rule, in the case of a scholarship or fellowship granted after August 16, 1986 and before January 1, 1987, any amount of such scholarship or fellowship grant that is received prior to January 1, 1987 and is attributable to expenditures incurred prior to January 1, 1987 (such as tuition, room, and board attributable to the period prior to January 1, 1987) is eligible for the present-law exclusion under section 117.

The conference agreement also clarifies that only for purposes of the rule that a child eligible to be claimed as a dependent on the return of his or her parents may use the standard deduction only to offset the greater of $500 or earned income (see [¶ 3854] above), any amount of a noncompensatory scholarship or fellowship grant that is includible in gross income as a result of these amendments to section 117 (including the repeal of any section 117 exclusion for nondegree candidates) constitutes earned income. (Amounts received as payment for teaching or other services also constitute earned income.)

[Effective date.—Except as otherwise provided, amendments apply to taxable years beginning after December 31, 1986, but only in the case of scholarships and fellowships granted after August 16, 1986. Ed.]

[¶ 3860] SECTION 131. REPEAL OF DEDUCTION FOR 2-EARNER MARRIED COUPLES

(Sec. 221 of the Code)

[Conference Report]

* * * * * *

House Bill.—The two-earner deduction is repealed, effective for taxable years beginning on or after January 1, 1986.

Senate Amendment.—The Senate amendment is the same as the House bill, except that the two-earner deduction is repealed effective for taxable years beginning on or after January 1, 1987.

Conference Agreement.—The conference agreement follows the Senate amendment.

[¶ 3861] SECTION 132. 2% FLOOR ON MISCELLANEOUS ITEMIZED DEDUCTIONS

(Secs. 62; 67 of the Code)

[Conference Report]

*   *   *   *   *   *

Present Law.—Under present law, four types of employee business expenses are deductible "above-the-line" in calculating an individual's adjusted gross income (sec. 62(2)): (1) certain employee expenses reimbursed by the employer; (2) employee expenses for travel away from home; (3) employee transportation expenses; and (4) business expenses of employees who are outside salespersons. Moving expenses of an employee or self-employed individual are deductible above-the-line, within certain limitations (secs. 62(8), 217).

In addition to the itemized deductions for medical expenses, charitable donations, interest, taxes, and casualty losses, itemizers may deduct certain "miscellaneous deductions." This category includes (1) unreimbursed employee business expenses (other than those deductible above-the-line), including union and professional dues and home office expenses of an employee; (2) certain expenses related to investment income or property (such as investment counsel fees) if deductible under section 212; (3) tax return preparation costs and related expenditures if deductible under section 212(3); (4) gambling or hobby losses up to the amounts, respectively, of gambling or hobby income; (5) certain adjustments where a taxpayer restores amounts held under claim of right (sec. 1341)); (6) amortizable bond premiums (sec. 171); and (7) certain costs of cooperative housing corporations (sec. 216).

*   *   *   *   *   *

Conference Agreement.—Under the conference agreement, employee business expenses, other than reimbursed expenses described in section 62(2)(A)[4], are to be allowed only as itemized deductions and are subject to a floor as described below. Moving expenses of an employee or self-employed individual are to be allowed (subject to the present-law limitations in sec. 217) only as an itemized deduction; this deduction is not subject to the new floor.

The miscellaneous itemized deductions, including the employee business expenses described above, generally are subject to a floor of two percent of the taxpayer's adjusted gross income. However, the floor does not apply to deductions otherwise allowable for impairment-related work expenses for handicapped employees (new Code sec. 67(d)); the estate tax in the case of income in respect to a decedent (sec. 691(c)); certain adjustments where a taxpayer restores amounts held under a claim of right (sec. 1341); amortizable bond premium (sec. 171); certain costs of cooperative housing corporations (sec. 216); deductions allowable in connection with personal property used in a short sale; certain terminated annuity payments (new Code sec. 72(b)(3)); and gambling losses to the extent of gambling winnings (sec. 165(d)).

Pursuant to Treasury regulations, the floor is to apply with respect to indirect deductions through pass-through entities (including mutual funds) other than estates, nongrantor trusts, cooperatives, and REITs. The floor also applies with respect to indirect deductions through grantor trusts, partnerships, and S corporations by virtue of present-law grantor trust and pass-through rules. In the case of an estate or trust, the conference agreement provides that the adjusted gross income is to be computed in the same manner as in the case of an individual, except that the deductions for costs that are paid or incurred in connection with the administration of the estate or trust and that would not have been incurred if the property were not held in such trust or estate are treated as allowable in arriving at adjusted gross income and hence are not subject to the floor. The regulations to be prescribed by the Treasury relating to application of the floor

---

[Footnote ¶ 3861] (4) The conference agreement does not modify the above-the-line deduction under sec. 62(2)(A) for certain reimbursed expenses of an employee (allowable under part VI of the Code) under a reimbursement or other expense allowance with his or her employer. (The Treasury may prescribe regulations under which expenses of an employee reimbursed by a third party are to be treated as expenses described in sec. 62(2)(A).) If the employee has a reimbursement or other expense allowance arrangement with his or her employer, but under the arrangement the employer does not reimburse the full amount of such expenses, the unreimbursed portion paid by the employee is allowable only to the extent (if any) otherwise allowable as an itemized deduction (e.g., after taking into account the percentage reduction rule, if applicable to the expense), and subject to the floor provided under the conference agreement.

Under the conference agreement, it is intended that the Treasury issue regulations coordinating the treatment of employee business expenses and the provisions, in sec. 162(h), relating to travel expenses away from home of State legislators. Under the intended rules, any excess of the allowable amount as determined under sec. 162(h) over the amount actually reimbursed to the legislator would be allocated between meals and other travel expenses in accordance with the ratio of meals and other travel expenses under the Federal per diem reimbursement rules. The reimbursed amount would be deductible pursuant to sec. 62(2)(A), and 80 percent of the amount allocated to meals would be deductible by itemizers as an employee business expense (subject to the new floor under miscellaneous itemized deductions).

with respect to indirect deductions through certain pass-through entities are to include such reporting requirements as may be necessary to effectuate this provision.

Under the conference agreement, an actor or other performing artist is allowed a new above-the-line deduction for his or her employee business expenses (allowable under sec. 162) during a year if the performing artist for that year (1) had more than one employer (excluding any nominal employer) in the performing arts, (2) incurred allowable section 162 expenses in connection with such services as an employee in an amount exceeding 10 percent of gross income from such services, and (3) did not have adjusted gross income, as determined before deducting such expenses, exceeding $16,000.

[Effective date.—] These provisions are effective for taxable years beginning on or after January 1, 1987.

[¶3862] SECTION 133. MEDICAL EXPENSES DEDUCTION LIMITATION INCREASED

(Sec. 213 of the Code)

[Senate Explanation]

* * * * * *

Explanation of Provisions.—

* * * * * *

The committee clarifies that capital expenditures eligible for the medical expense deduction include certain expenses incurred by a physically handicapped individual for removing structural barriers in his or her personal residence for the purpose of accommodating his or her handicapped condition. These costs are expenditures for: (1) constructing entrance or exit ramps to the residence; (2) widening doorways at entrances or exits to the residence; (3) widening or otherwise modifying hallways and interior doorways to accommodate wheelchairs; (4) railings, support bars, or other modifications to bathrooms to accommodate handicapped individuals; (5) lowering of or other modifications to kitchen cabinets and equipment to accommodate access by handicapped individuals; and (6) adjustment of electrical outlets and fixtures. (The enumeration of these specific types of expenditures is not intended to preclude the Treasury from identifying in regulations or rulings similar expenditures for accommodating personal residences for physically handicapped individuals that would be eligible for deductibility as medical expenses.)

The committee believes that the six categories of expenditures listed above would not add to the fair market value of a personal residence and hence intends that such expenditures are to count in full as eligible for the medical expense deduction.

* * * * * *

[Conference Report]

* * * * * *

Senate Amendment

Floor under deduction.—The floor under the itemized medical expense deduction is increased from five to approximately nine percent of the taxpayer's AGI, effective for taxable years beginning on or after January 1, 1987.

* * * * * *

Conference Agreement

Floor under deduction.—The conference agreement follows the Senate amendment, except that the floor under the itemized medical expense deduction is increased from five to 7.5 percent of the taxpayer's AGI.

Capital expenditures.—The conferees intend to reaffirm that the full costs of specified capital expenditures incurred to accommodate a personal residence to the needs of a physically handicapped individual, such as construction of entrance ramps or widening of doorways to allow use of wheelchairs, constitute medical expenses eligible for the deduction, as described in the Senate Finance Committee Report.

[Senate Explanation]

* * * * * *

Effective date.—The provision (increasing the deduction floor) is effective for taxable years beginning after December 31, 1986.

[¶3863] SECTION 134. REPEAL OF DEDUCTION FOR STATE AND LOCAL SALES TAXES

(Sec. 164)

[Conference Report]

* * * * * *

Senate Amendment.—Under the Senate amendment, the itemized deduction for State and local general sales taxes paid or accrued during a year is limited to 60 percent of the excess of such taxes over the amount of State and local income taxes paid or accrued by the taxpayer during the year. No change is made in the itemized deductions for State and local income, real property, and personal property taxes.

The Senate amendment also provides that State, local, or foreign taxes (other than real property taxes or certain other specified taxes) that are incurred in a trade or business (or in a section 212 activity) in connection with the acquisition or disposition of property are not deductible. Instead, such taxes are to be treated, respectively, as part of the cost of the property on acquisition or as a reduction in the amount realized on disposition.

These provisions are effective for taxable years beginning on or after January 1, 1987.

Conference Agreement.—Under the conference agreement, the itemized deduction for State and local sales taxes is repealed.

The conference agreement follows the Senate amendment with respect to capitalization of certain taxes. (Thus, for example, the amount of sales tax paid by a business on acquisition of depreciable property for use in the business is treated under the conference agreement as part of the cost of the acquired property for depreciation purposes.) **[Effective date.**—] These provisions are effective for taxable years beginning on or after January 1, 1987.

[¶ 3864] SECTION 135. REPEAL OF DEDUCTION FOR ADOPTION EXPENSES

(Sec. 222 of the Code)

[Conference Report]

*   *   *   *   *   *

House Bill.—The House bill repeals the itemized adoption expense deduction, generally effective for adoption expenses paid after 1986. Present law continues to apply in 1987 for adoptions as to which deductible expenses were incurred in 1986.

In addition, the House bill amends the adoption assistance program in Title IV-E of the Social Security Act to provide matching funds as an administrative expense for adoption expenses for any child with special needs who has been placed for adoption in accord-

ance with applicable State and local law. Such expenses include all qualified adoption expenses to which the present-law tax deduction provision applies. The effective date of amending the adoption assistance program is coordinated with repeal of the deduction.

Conference Agreement.—The conference agreement follows the House bill in repealing the itemized adoption expense deduction and amending the adoption assistance program in Title IV-E of the Social Security Act, with the modification that these provisions are effective, respectively, for taxable years beginning on or after January 1, 1987 and for expenditures made after December 31, 1986.

[¶ 3865] SECTION 141. REPEAL OF INCOME AVERAGING

(Sec. 1303 of the Code)

[Conference Report]

*   *   *   *   *   *

House Bill

Income averaging is repealed, effective for taxable years beginning on or after January 1, 1986.

[House Explanation]

*   *   *   *   *   *

Reasons for Change.—The committee believes that other individual income tax provisions of the bill, providing wider brackets with fewer rates and a flatter rate structure, reduce the need for income averaging to the point that there is no longer sufficient justification to retain it in light of its complexity. As a result of the rate structure and other provisions of the committee bill, fluctuations in annual income will not change the taxpayer's marginal tax rate as frequently, and in many cases will not change it as much, as under present law.

The complexities of income averaging under present law derive both from the arithmetical calculations that it requires and also from the rules governing eligibility. For example, the determination of whether an individual was self-supporting during each of the base years can be difficult; this issue has been a frequent source of controversy between individuals and the Internal Revenue Service. In addition, application of the income averaging rules can be particularly complex for an individual whose marital status has changed during one of the three base years.

*   *   *   *   *   *

[Conference Report]

Conference Agreement

[Effective date.—] The conference agreement follows the House bill, with the modification that the repeal of income averaging (for all taxpayers) is effective for taxable years beginning on or after January 1, 1987.

[¶ 3866]   SECTION 142. LIMITATIONS ON DEDUCTIONS FOR MEALS, TRAVEL, AND ENTERTAINMENT.

(Secs. 162; 170; 212; 274; 6653 of the Code.).

[Conference Report]

*   *   *   *   *   *

* * * **Meal expenses**

*   *   *   *   *   *

House Bill.—*Reduction rule.*—The bill generally reduces to 80 percent the amount of any deduction otherwise allowable for meal expenses, including meals away from home and meals furnished on an employer's premises to its employees (whether or not such meals are excludable from the employee's gross income under sec. 119). The bill provides exceptions allowing full deductibility for (1) reimbursed meal expenses (in which case the employer or person making the reimbursement is subject to the 80-percent rule); (2) employer-furnished meals that are excludable from the employee's gross income as de minimis fringes under Code section 132(e) (including meals at certain eating facilities excludable under sec. 132(e)(2)); (3) meals fully taxed to the recipient as compensation; and (4) items sold to the public (such as expenses incurred by restaurants or dinner theaters for food or entertainment provided to their customers), or furnished to the public as samples or for promotion (such as expenses incurred by a hotel in furnishing complimentary lodging to potential customers). A restaurant or catering firm may deduct 100 percent (rather than 80 percent) of its costs for food and beverage items, purchased in connection with preparing and providing meals to its paying customers, that are consumed at the work site by employees of the restaurant or caterer.

Business-connection   requirement.—The House bill also provides that deductions for meals are subject to the same business-connection requirement as applies under present law (sec. 274(a)) for other entertainment expenses * * *. Thus, a food or beverage expense is not deductible unless the taxpayer establishes that the item was directly related to the active conduct of the taxpayer's trade or business, or, in the case of an item directly preceding or following a substantial and bona fide business discussion (including business meetings at a convention or otherwise), that the item was associated with the active conduct of the taxpayer's trade or business. Under this standard, no deduction is allowed unless business is discussed during, or directly before or after, the meal (except where an individual traveling away from home on business has a meal alone or with persons, such as family members, who are not business-connected, and a deduction is claimed only for the meal of such individual).

Disallowance of lavish or extravagant expenditures.—The House bill explicitly provides, apart from the present-law statutory rule disallowing deductions for certain lavish and extravagant travel expenses (including meals), that no deduction is allowed for any food or beverage expense unless the expense is not lavish or extravagant under the circumstances. Thus, this disallowance rule applies whether or not the expense is incurred while the taxpayer is away from home, and whether the taxpayer incurs the expense alone or with others. Since the reduction rule is applied only after determining the otherwise allowable deduction under sections 162 and 274, if a taxpayer incurs otherwise deductible business lunch expenses of (for example) $80 for himself and if $30 of that amount is not allowable as lavish or extravagant, the remaining $50 is then reduced by 20 percent, leaving a deduction of $40.

Presence of taxpayer requirement.—Under the House bill, no deduction for food or beverage expenses is allowed unless the taxpayer or an employee of the taxpayer is present at the furnishing of the food or beverages (except where an individual traveling away from home on business has a meal alone or with persons, such as family members, who are not business-connected, and a deduction is claimed only for the meal of such individual). For purposes of this rule, an independent contractor who renders significant services to the taxpayer (such as an attorney representing the taxpayer in a legal proceeding) is treated as an employee if he or she attends the meal in connection with such performance of services.

Additional rules.—As an additional requirement that is not applicable to other entertainment expenses, the House bill provides that no deduction for business meals is allowable unless the meal has a clear business purpose presently related to the active conduct of the taxpayer's business—i.e., unless the required business discussion concerns a specific business transaction or arrangement. The Treasury is instructed to adopt stricter substantiation requirements for business meals, including expenses of less than $25 per day. Also, the bill imposes special negligence or fraud penalties on negligently or fraudulently overstated deductions for business meals.

*   *   *   *   *   *

Senate   Amendment.—The   Senate amendment is the same as the House bill with respect to meal expenses, except that full deductibility is allowed in 1987 and 1988 for costs of meals (if not separately stated) that are provided as an integral part of a qualified banquet meeting. The latter term means a convention, seminar, annual meeting, or similar business meeting (including meetings held at an employee training facility) if (1) the program includes the meal, (2) more than 50 percent of the participants are away from home, (3) there are at least 40 attendees, and (4) the meal event includes a speaker. The Senate amendment is effective for taxable years beginning on or after January 1, 1987.

Conference Agreement.—The conference agreement follows the Senate amendment with respect to food or beverage expenses, except that (1) the business-connection requirement for deducting food or beverage expenses is conformed to the business-connection requirement applicable to other entertainment expenses (i.e., the conference agreement does not include the additional "clear business purpose" requirement under which a specific business transaction or arrangement would have to be discussed); (2) present law regarding substantiation of meal expenses under $25 is retained; and (3) there are no special negligence and fraud penalties applicable only to claimed deductions for business meals.

Thus, under the conference agreement, deductions for meals are subject to the same business-connection requirement as applies under present law for other entertainment expenses. Accordingly, an expense for food or beverages is not deductible unless (in addition to generally applicable deduction requirements) the taxpayer (1) establishes that the item was directly related to the active conduct of the taxpayer's trade or business, or, in the case of an item directly preceding or following a substantial and bona fide business discussion, that the item was associated with the active conduct of the taxpayer's trade or business, and (2) substantiates the deduction as required by section 274(d) and Treas. Reg. sec. 1.274-5(b)(4). Under this requirement, no deduction is allowed unless business is discussed during, or directly before or after, the meal (except where an individual traveling away from home on business has a meal alone or with persons, such as family members, who are not business-connected, and a deduction is claimed only for the meal of such individual).

The conference agreement includes the separate statutory rule disallowing lavish or extravagant expenditures for food or beverages, whether or not incurred while the taxpayer is on business travel, thereby emphasizing an intent that this standard is to be enforced by the Internal Revenue Service and the courts. Also, the conference agreement includes the requirement relating to the presence of the taxpayer or an employee of the taxpayer at the furnishing of the food or beverages. These two rules are subject to certain exceptions listed in the statute (e.g., where the full value of the food or beverages is taxed as compensation to the recipient).

Since the conference agreement provides that deductions for meals are subject to the same business-connection requirement as applies under present law for other entertainment expenses, the present-law substantiation requirements for such entertainment expenses (e.g., in Treas. Reg. sec. 1.274-5(b)(4) with respect to the directly related or associated with deductibility standard) also will apply to all meal expenses. In addition, the conference agreement instructs the Treasury

to adopt stricter substantiation requirements for business meals, except that the present-law rule relating to certain expenditures of less than $25 is to be retained. It is reemphasized that under the conference agreement, as under present law, the Internal Revenue Service and the courts are not to apply the *Cohan* approximation rule to allow deductibility of any food or beverage expense, other entertainment expense, or other expenditure subject to substantiation pursuant to section 274(d) if the expenditure is not substantiated in accordance with section 274(d) and the regulations thereunder.

* * * Entertainment expenses other than for meals

*   *   *   *   *   *

House Bill.—*In general.*—The House bill generally reduces to 80 percent the amount of deduction otherwise allowable for business entertainment expenses. The bill provides exceptions allowing full deductibility for (1) reimbursed entertainment expenses (in which case the employer or person making the reimbursement is subject to the 80-percent rule); (2) traditional employer-paid recreational expenses for employees (e.g., a holiday party); (3) items fully taxed to the recipient as compensation, or excludable from income as section 132(e) de minimis fringe benefits; (4) items sold to or made available to the general public (e.g., as promotional activities); and (5) tickets and related expenses at certain charitable fundraising sports events. In addition, no amount of ticket costs in excess of the face value of the ticket is deductible, except in the case of tickets for certain charitable fundraising sports events; the limitation to the face value amount applies prior to application of the 80-percent rule.

Facilities.—Apart from the generally applicable entertainment facility rules, the House bill disallows deductions for costs of rental or other use of a skybox or other private luxury box ("skybox") at a sports arena (to the extent in excess of the cost of regular box seat tickets) by the taxpayer or a related party for more than one event (as determined taking into account all skybox rentals by the taxpayer in the same arena, along with any related rentals).

*   *   *   *   *   *

Senate Amendment.—*In general.*—The Senate amendment is the same as House bill.

Facilities.—The Senate amendment does not provide a special rule disallowing deductions for certain rental costs of skyboxes (general entertainment facility rules continue to apply).

Effective date.—The Senate amendment is effective for taxable years beginning on or after January 1, 1987.

Conference Agreement.—*In general.*—The conference agreement follows the House bill and the Senate amendment.

Facilities.—The conference agreement follows the House bill, except that the skybox deduction disallowance rule is phased in.

Under this provision, the amounts disallowed for taxable years beginning in 1987 and 1988 are, respectively, one-third and two-thirds of the amounts that otherwise would be disallowed under the conference agreement if the provision were fully effective in those years. For taxable years beginning after 1989, the conference agreement follows the House bill, i.e., no deduction is allowed for costs of rental or other use of a skybox at a sports arena by the taxpayer or a related party for more than one event.[4]

Effective date.—The conference agreement follows the Senate amendment.

* * * Travel expenses (other than for attending conventions)

* * * * * *

House Bill.—*Luxury water transportation.*—The amount of any otherwise allowable deduction for costs of cruise ship or other luxury water transportation is limited to twice the highest Federal per diem for travel in the United States, times the number of days in transit. This limitation does not apply with respect to expenses of cruise ship conventions, which remain subject to present-law limitations (sec. 274(h)(2)), or where an exception to the 80-percent deduction rule (above) applies.

Educational travel.—No deduction is allowed for costs of travel that would be deductible only on the ground that the travel itself constitutes a form of education (e.g., where a teacher of French travels to France to maintain general familiarity with the French language and culture, or where a social studies teacher travels to another State to learn about or photograph its people, customs, geography, etc.). This provision overrules Treas. Reg. sec. 1.162-5(d) to the extent that such regulation allows deductions for travel as a form of education.

Charitable travel.—The present-law rule applicable to medical deductions for lodging costs away from home (sec. 213(d)(2)(B)) is extended to charitable deductions claimed for transportation and other travel expenses incurred in performing services away from home on behalf of a qualified charitable organization. Thus, no deduction is allowed for such expenses (whether paid directly by the individual or indirectly through a contribution to the organization) unless there is no significant element of personal pleasure, recreation, or vacation in the travel away from home. As under present law, an otherwise qualifying charitable deduction is deductible only if verified pursuant to Treasury regulations (Code sec. 170(a)(1)), and no charitable deduction is allowable for a contribution of services to a charitable organization.

Senate Amendment.—*Luxury water transportation.*—The Senate amendment is the same as the House bill.

Educational travel.—The Senate amendment is the same as the House bill.

Charitable travel.—No provision.

Effective date.—The provisions in the Senate amendment are effective for taxable years beginning on or after January 1, 1987.

Conference Agreement.—*Luxury water transportation.*—The conference agreement follows the House bill and the Senate amendment.

Educational travel.—The conference agreement follows the House bill and the Senate amendment.

Charitable travel.—The conference agreement follows the House bill, except that the provision is effective for taxable years beginning on or after January 1, 1987.

Effective date.—The conference agreement follows the Senate amendment.

* * * Travel expenses for attending conventions

* * * * * *

House Bill.—*In general.*—Under the House bill, no deduction is allowed under section 212 for travel or other costs of attending a convention, seminar, or similar meeting, effective for taxable years beginning on or after January 1, 1986. Thus, registration fees, travel and transportation costs, meal and lodging expenses, etc. incurred in connection with attending a convention, seminar, or similar meeting relating to investments, financial planning, or other income-production or section 212 activities are not deductible. This disallowance rule does not apply to expenses incurred by a taxpayer in attending a convention, seminar, sales meeting, or similar meeting relating to the trade or business (within the meaning of sec. 162) of the taxpayer.

Foreign conventions.—No provision.

Senate Amendment.—*In general.*—The Senate amendment is the same as the House bill, except that it is effective for taxable years beginning on or after January 1, 1987.

Foreign conventions.—The Senate amendment provides that Bermuda may be treated as within the North American area for purposes of the foreign convention deductibility rules in certain circumstances.

Conference Agreement.—*In general.*—The conference agreement follows the Senate amendment.

The conferees also are concerned that some taxpayers may be claiming deductions under section 162 for travel and other costs of attending a convention, seminar, or similar meeting ("convention") at which each convention participant is furnished individually with video tapes of lectures, etc. on topics related to the taxpayer's trade or business, to be viewed at the convenience of the participant, and at which no other significant business-related activities occur during the time allotted for the convention. In such situations, the taxpayer does not participate in activities normally conducted at a business-related convention, such as participating in meetings, discussions, workshops, lectures, or exhibits held during the day, and simply views the tapes at his or her own convenience. Because permitting deductions for travel, meal, or entertainment costs asso-

ciated with such minimal business-related activities would allow taxpayers to treat expenditures that essentially are for vacation, recreation, or other personal purposes as business expenses, the conferees wish to make clear that no deduction is allowable under section 162 for travel or related costs of attending such a convention.

This clarification does not disallow deductions for the travel and other costs of attending a convention that involves activities otherwise deductible under present law which are related to the taxpayer's trade or business merely because the convention utilizes videotaped or televised materials where the participants must attend a convention session in person to view the video-taped materials, assuming that the generally applicable requirements for deducting expenses of attending a convention are satisfied. Also, this clarification does not disallow deductions for costs, other than travel, meal, or entertainment expenses, of renting or using business-related video tape materials.

Foreign conventions.—The conference agreement does not include the Senate amendment relating to Bermuda.

[Effective date.—Except as otherwise provided, the amendments apply to taxable years beginning after December 31, 1986. Ed.]

[¶ 3867]   SECTION 143. CHANGES IN TREATMENT OF HOBBY LOSS, ETC.

(Sec. 183 and 280A of the Code)

[Conference Report]

*   *   *   *   *   *

* * * Hobby losses

*   *   *   *   *   *

House Bill.—An activity (other than horse breeding or racing) is presumed not to be a hobby if it is profitable in three out of five consecutive years, effective for taxable years beginning on or after January 1, 1986. The present-law presumption rules are retained for horse activities.

Senate Amendment.—*[Effective date.*—]. The Senate amendment is the same as the House bill, except that the effective date is taxable years beginning on or after January 1, 1987. Thus, for example, an activity carried on during 1987 by a taxpayer is presumed not to be a hobby in that year if the activity is profitable in any three years out of the five calendar years 1983 through 1987.

Conference Agreement.—The conference agreement follows the House bill and the Senate amendment, with the effective date in the Senate amendment.

* * * Home office expenses

Present law.—Expenses attributable to using part of one's home as an office are deductible subject to the following limitations: (1) the use of the home office must be

for the convenience of the employer, (2) the home office must be used regularly and exclusively either as the taxpayer's principal place of business, or to meet patients, clients, or customers, and (3) the deduction cannot exceed the taxpayer's gross income from the business (sec. 280A). A recent case held that these limits do not apply when the taxpayer leases a portion of the home to his or her employer.

House Bill.—Under the House bill, the present-law limitations (listed above) are to apply when an employee leases a portion of the home to his or her employer. In addition, the amount of an otherwise allowable home office deduction is limited to the taxpayer's net income from the business (i.e., gross income minus deductions attributable to the business). Disallowed home office deductions may be carried forward to later years, subject to the new income limitation in such years. These provisions are effective for taxable years beginning on or after January 1, 1986.

Senate Amendment.—The Senate amendment is the same as the House bill, except that the effective date is taxable years beginning on or after January 1, 1987.

Conference Agreement.—The conference agreement follows the House bill and the Senate Amendment, with the effective date in the Senate amendment.

[¶3868] SECTION 144. DEDUCTIBILITY OF MORTGAGE INTEREST AND REAL PROPERTY TAXES ALLOWABLE WHERE PARSONAGE ALLOWANCE OR MILITARY HOUSING ALLOWANCE RECEIVED

(Sec. 265 of the Code)

[House Explanation]

*   *   *   *   *   *

Explanation of Provision.—The bill provides that the receipt of a parsonage housing allowance (sec. 107) or a military housing allowance is not to result in a denial under section 265 of deductions for mortgage interest or real property tax deductions on the taxpayer's home. This provision thus overrules Rev. Rul. 83-8 as applicable to parsonage allowances (but not in other respects) and precludes application of that ruling to military housing allowances.

[Conference Report]

*   *   *   *   *   *

House Bill.—The House bill provides a permanent rule (effective retroactively) that ministers receiving excludable parsonage al-

lowances, as well as military personnel receiving excludable military housing allowances, are not precluded by Code section 265 from deducting mortgage interest or real property taxes on their residence.

Senate   Amendment.—The   Senate amendment is the same as the House bill, with a clarification that military personnel means members of the Army, Navy, Air Force, Marine Corps, Coast Guard, National Oceanic and Atmospheric Administration, and Public Health Service.

Conference   Agreement.—The   conference agreement is the same as the House bill and the Senate amendment, with the Senate amendment clarification that defines military personnel.

[**Effective date.**—The amendment shall apply to taxable years beginning before, on, or after December 31, 1986. Ed.]

[¶3870] SECTIONS 201-213. COST RECOVERY: DEPRECIATION; INVESTMENT CREDIT FINANCE LEASES

(Secs. 38, 46, 57, 168, 178, 179, 312(k), 1245, and 1250 of the Code)

[Conference Report]

*   *   *   *   *

1. Accelerated depreciation

a. Cost recovery classes

Present Law

Under the Accelerated Cost Recovery System ("ACRS"), recovery deductions are determined by applying a statutory percentage to an asset's original cost (adjusted for allowable investment tax credit). The classification of assets under ACRS generally is based on the Asset Depreciation Range ("ADR") system of prior law. Under the ADR system, a present class life ("mid-point") was provided for all assets used in the same activity, other than certain assets with common characteristics (e.g., automobiles).

The cost of eligible personal property is recovered over a three-year, five-year, 10-year, or 15-year recovery period, using statutory percentages based on the 150-percent declining balance method. The cost of real property generally is recovered over a 19-year recovery period (15 years for low-income housing), using statutory percentages based on the 175-percent declining balance method (200-percent declining balance method for low-income housing).

*   *   *   *   *   *

Conference Agreement

In general.—The conference agreement modifies the Accelerated Cost Recovery System (ACRS) for property placed in service

after December 31, 1986, except for property covered by transition rules. The cost of property placed in service after July 31, 1986, and before January 1, 1987, which is not transition-rule property, may, at the election of the taxpayer on an asset-by-asset basis, be covered under the modified rules.

The conference agreement provides more accelerated depreciation for the revised three-year, five-year and 10-year classes, reclassifies certain assets according to their present class life (or "ADR midpoints", Rev. Proc. 83-35, 1983-1 C.B. 745), and creates a seven-year class, a 20-year class, a 27.5-year class, and a 31.5-year class. The conference agreement prescribes depreciation methods for each ACRS class (in lieu of providing statutory tables). Eligible personal property and certain real property are assigned among a three-year class, a five-year class, a seven-year class, a 10-year class, a 15-year class, or a 20-year class.

The depreciation method applicable to property included in the three-year, five-year, seven-year, and 10-year classes is the double declining balance method, switching to the straight-line method at a time to maximize the depreciation allowance. For property in the 15-year and 20-year class, conference agreement applies the 150-percent declining balance method, switching to the straight-line method at a time to maximize the depreciation allowance. The cost of section 1250 real property generally is recovered over 27.5 years for residential rental property and 31.5 years for nonresidential property, using the straight-line method.

Act §201—213   ¶3870

Classes of property.—Property is classified as follows:

Three-year class.—ADR midpoints of 4 years or less, except automobiles and light trucks, and adding horses which are assigned to the three-year class under present law.

Five-year class.—ADR midpoints of more than 4 years and less than 10 years, and adding automobiles, light trucks, qualified technological equipment, computer-based telephone central office switching equipment, research and experimentation property, and geothermal, ocean thermal, solar, and wind energy properties, and biomass properties that constitute qualifying small power production facilities (within the meaning of section 3(17)(C) of the Federal Power Act).

Seven-year class.—ADR midpoints of 10 years and less than 16 years, and adding single-purpose agricultural or horticultural structures and property with no ADR midpoint that is not classified elsewhere.

10-year class.—ADR midpoints of 16 years and less than 20 years.

15-year class.—ADR midpoints of 20 years and less than 25 years, and adding municipal wastewater treatment plants, and telephone distribution plant and comparable equipment used for the two-way exchange of voice and data communications.

20-year class.—ADR midpoints of 25 years and more, other than section 1250 real property with an ADR midpoint of 27.5 years and more, and adding municipal sewers.

27.5-year class.—Residential rental property (including manufactured homes that are residential rental property and elevators and escalators).

31.5-year class.—Nonresidential real property (section 1250 real property that is not residential rental property and that either does not have an ADR midpoint or whose ADR midpoint is 27.5 years or more, including elevators and escalators).

The conference agreement provides new ADR midpoint lives for the following assets:

(1) Semiconductor manufacturing equipment (described in ADR class 36.0), 5 years;

(2) Computer-based telephone central office switching equipment and related equipment (described in ADR class 48.12) which functions are those of a computer or peripheral equipment (as defined in section 168(j)(5)(D)) in their capacity as telephone central office equipment, 9.5 years;

(3) Railroad track, 10 years;

(4) Single-purpose agricultural and horticultural structures within the meaning of sec. 48(p) (described in ADR class 01.3), 15 years;

(5) Telephone distribution plant (e.g., telephone fiber optic cable) (described in ADR class 48.14) and comparable equipment, 24 years (comparable equipment means equipment used by non-telephone companies for two-way exchange of voice and data communications (equivalent of telephone communications)—comparable equipment does not in-

clude cable television equipment used primarily for one-way communication);

(6) Municipal waste-water treatment plants, 25 years; and

(7) Municipal sewers, 50 years.

Classifications under the ADR system occasionally are made on the basis of regulated accounts. All assets described in these accounts are to be included, without regard to the fact that the taxpayer owning the described assets may not be subject to any regulatory authority.

The conferees wish to clarify that under present law cargo containers have an ADR midpoint of six years and this present class life shall be used in applying the provisions of the conference agreement.

As under present law, property which the taxpayer properly elects to depreciate under the unit-of-production method or any other method not expressed in terms of years (other than the retirement-replacement-betterment method or similar method), will be so depreciated. For example, depreciation is allowable with respect to landfills on a unit basis (without regard to whether the space for dumping waste was excavated by the taxpayer), to the extent capital costs are properly allocable to the space to be filled with waste rather than to the underlying land.

[The following colloquy is drawn from the Congressional Record. The colloquy occurred on the day the Conference bill was considered by the Senate. Ed.]

[Senate Floor Explanation]

Mr. BENTSEN. I would appreciate receiving clarification on one point relating to the discussion of landfill depreciation on page 40 of the report. Although the case law is not cited. I believe it is the sense of the report that the Tax Court's decision in *Sexton* v. *Commissioner,* 42 T.C. 1094 (1964) correctly applies current law to allow the recovery of capital costs to the extent such costs are properly allocable to the space to be filled with waste, rather than to the underlying land. In other words, a landfill with 10 million cubic yards of capacity with a depreciable basis of $10 million in excess of salvage value would be entitled to a deduction of $1 per cubic yard when and as filled. Is my understanding correct?

Mr. PACKWOOD. Yes. We believe the Sexton case is the applicable standard under current law, and the committee intends no change in current law. Congressional Record, p. S13952, 9-27-86.

[Conference Report]

*   *   *   *   *   *

b. Luxury automobiles

Present Law

Recovery deductions for automobiles are subject to the following dollar limitations: $3,200 for the first recovery year; and $4,800 for each succeeding taxable year in the recovery period.

*   *   *   *   *   *

Senate Amendment

The Senate amendment conforms the fixed limitations on deductions so that the price range of affected cars is unchanged. Additionally, the amendment clarifies that the fixed limitations apply to all deductions claimed for depreciation of automobiles, not just ACRS deductions.

Conference Agreement

The conference agreement generally follows the Senate amendment and conforms the fixed limitations on deductions so that the price range of affected cars is unchanged. The new limitations are: $2,560 for the first recovery year, $4,100 for the second recovery year; $2,450 for the third recovery year; and $1,475 for each succeeding taxable year in the recovery period. The conference agreement clarifies that the fixed limitations apply to all deductions.

*   *   *   *   *   *

c. Changes in classification

*   *   *   *   *   *

Under the conference agreement, the Treasury Department has the authority to adjust class lives of most assets (other than residential rental property and nonresidential real property) based on actual experience. Any new class life will be used for determining the classification of such property and in applying an alternative depreciation system.

Any class life prescribed under the Secretary's authority must reflect the anticipated useful life, and the anticipated decline in value over time, of an asset to the industry or other group. Useful life means the economic life span of property over all users combined and not, as under prior law, the typical period over which a taxpayer holds the property. Evidence indicative of the useful life of property which the Secretary is expected to take into account in prescribing a class life includes the depreciation practices followed by taxpayers for book purposes with respect to the property. It also includes useful lives experienced by taxpayers, according to their reports. It further includes independent evidence of minimal useful life—the terms for which new property is leased, used under a service contract, or financed—and independent evidence of the decline in value of an asset over time, such as is afforded by resale price data. If resale price data is used to prescribe class lives, such resale price data should be adjusted downward to remove the effects of historical inflation. This adjustment provides a larger measure of depreciation than in the absence of such an adjustment. Class lives using this data should be determined such that the present value of straight-line depreciation deductions over the class life, discounted at an appropriate real rate of interest, is equal to the present value of what the estimated decline in value of the asset would be in the absence of inflation.

Initial studies are expected to concentrate on property that now has no ADR midpoint. Additionally, clothing held for rental and scientific instruments (especially those used in connection with a computer) should be studied to determine whether a change in class life is appropriate.

Certain other assets specifically assigned a recovery period (including horses in the three-year class, qualified technological equipment, computer-based central office switching equipment, research and experimentation property, certain renewable energy and biomass properties, semiconductor manufacturing equipment, railroad track, single-purpose agricultural or horticultural structures, telephone distribution plant and comparable equipment, municipal wastewater treatment plants, and municipal sewers) may not be assigned a longer class life by the Treasury Department if placed in service before January 1, 1992. Additionally, automobiles and light trucks may not be reclassified by the Treasury Department during this five-year period.

Such property placed in service after December 31, 1991, and before July 1, 1992, may be prescribed a different class life if the Secretary has notified the Committee on Ways and Means of the House of Representatives and the Committee on Finance of the Senate of the proposed change at least 6 months before the date on which such change is to take effect.

*   *   *   *   *   *

[The following colloquy is drawn from the Congressional Record. The colloquy occurred on the day the Conference bill was considered by the Senate. Ed.]

[Senate Floor Explanation]

Mr. McCONNELL. On behalf of my distinguished colleague from Kentucky. Senator Ford, and myself, I would like to express our serious concern about a provision in the bill relating to horse depreciation. The problem arises because there is no class life in the case of race horses and an inadequate class life in the case of older breeding horses under existing Treasury Department regulations. This causes a problem under section 168(g)(2) of the new code.

We would greatly appreciate the assistance of the chairman of the Finance Committee in developing appropriate depreciation guidelines for these horses.

Mr. PACKWOOD. I understand the Senators' concerns. As you know, I believe we were quite mindful of the depreciation rules relating to the horse industry in the bill passed by the Senate. The problem you raise occurs because of a provision adopted by the conference committee which was not in the Senate-passed bill.

Under section 168(i)(1)(B) of the new code, the Treasury Department is authorized to establish a class life for any property which does not now have a class life and to modify the class life of any property where appropriate. In this connection, it would be my understanding that the Treasury Department should give high priority to evaluating the actual experience of race horses and older horses and, based on those findings, expeditiously assign a class life to race horses and to determine whether a separate class life for other older horses should be determined, and if so, to determine what that class life should be. Congressional Record, p. S13953, 9-27-86.

[Conference Report]

*　　*　　*　　*　　*　　*

2. Alternative cost recovery system
a. In general

Present Law

(i) In general.—ACRS deductions are reduced for property that is (1) used predominantly outside the United States or (2) tax-exempt use property.

Different depreciation methods are also used for purposes of (1) computing earnings and profits of a domestic corporation, and (2) applying the minimum tax provisions.

(ii) Tax-exempt bond financed property.—Property, other than low-income housing, to the extent it is financed with industrial development bonds, the interest on which is tax-exempt, is depreciated using the straight-line method over the ACRS recovery period.

(iii) Elective alternative recovery system.—Taxpayers can elect to use the straight-line method over the applicable ACRS recovery period (or over a longer recovery period) with respect to one or more classes of ACRS property placed in service during a taxable year.

*　　*　　*　　*　　*　　*

Conference Agreement

(i) In general.—The conference agreement provides an alternative cost recovery system for: (1) property used predominantly outside the United States, (2) tax-exempt use property, (3) for computing earnings and profits of a domestic corporation or an "80/20" company, and (4) for applying the minimum tax provisions.

For purposes of (1), (2) and (3), the conference agreement follows the House bill and the Senate amendment. For purposes of determining whether property is tax-exempt use property, in the case of a corporation the stock of which is publicly traded on an established securities market, the test of whether 50 percent or more (in value) of the stock of such corporation is held by tax-exempt entities, shall be made only by including tax-exempt entities which hold 5 percent or more (in value) of the stock in such corporation.

For purposes of the depreciation preference under the minimum tax, the cost of property other than section 1250 real property is recovered using the 150-percent declining balance method, switching to the straight-line method, over the same lives as provided for the purposes of (1), (2) and (3). The cost of section 1250 real property and

other property for which the straight-line method is either elected or required to be used for regular tax purposes is recovered using the straight-line method for minimum tax purposes.

(ii) Tax-exempt bond property.—The conference agreement generally follows the Senate amendment. Property, to the extent it is financed with tax-exempt bonds, is depreciated using the straight-line method over the same lives as provided in (i). Only the portion of the cost of property which is attributable to tax-exempt financing is recovered using this method. If only a part of a facility is financed with tax-exempt bonds, the tax-exempt bond financed portion will be allocated to property first placed in service. An exception is provided to recover the cost of low-income housing financed with tax-exempt bonds over 27.5 years.

(iii) Elective alternative recovery system.—The conference agreement follows the Senate amendment.

b. Property predominantly of foreign origin

*　　*　　*　　*　　*　　*

[Senate Explanation]

*　　*　　*　　*　　*　　*

The bill authorizes the President to provide by Executive Order for the application of the alternative depreciation system to certain property that is imported from a country maintaining trade restrictions or engaging in discriminatory acts. For purposes of this provision, the term imported property means any property that is completed outside the United States, or less than 50 percent of the basis of which is attributable to value added within the United States. In applying this test, the term "United States" is treated as including the Commonwealth of Puerto Rico and the possessions of the United States.

The bill authorizes reduced depreciation for property that is imported from a foreign country that (1) maintains nontariff trade restrictions that substantially burden U.S. commerce in a manner inconsistent with provisions of trade agreements, including variable import fees, or (2) engages in discriminatory or other acts or policies unjustifiably restricting U.S. commerce (including tolerance of international cartels). If the President determines that a country is engaging in the proscribed actions noted above, he may provide for the application of alternative depreciation to any article or class of articles manufactured or produced in such foreign country for such period as may be provided by Executive Order.

In general, the terms of the provision relating to certain imported property are substantially identical to those of section 48(a)(7) relating to the investment tax credit (which is repealed by sec. 211 of the bill).

[Conference Report]

*　　*　　*　　*　　*　　*

c. Property used in outer space

House Bill

Property launched by a U.S. person from the United States and used in outer space is not treated as foreign use property.

Conference Agreement

The conference agreement follows the House bill and the Senate amendment.

* * * * * *

4. Accounting conventions

a. Half-year convention

Present Law

Under present law, the statutory schedules for personal property reflect a half-year convention that results in a half-year depreciation allowance for the first recovery year, regardless of when property is placed in service during the year.

House Bill

For personal property, both the first and last depreciation allowances for an asset reflect the half-year convention.

* * * * * *

Conference Agreement

The conference agreement follows the House bill and the Senate amendment. All property placed in service or disposed of during a taxable year is treated as placed in service or disposed of at the midpoint of such year. In the case of a taxable year less than 12 months, property is treated as being in service for half the number of months in such taxable year.

b. Mid-month convention

House Bill

The House bill extends the use of the mid-month convention to low-income housing and certain other property.

Senate Amendment

The Senate amendment generally follows the House bill and applies the mid-month convention to all residential rental property and nonresidential real property.

[Senate Explanation]

* * * * * *

In the case of both residential rental property and nonresidential real property, a mid-month convention applies. Under the mid-month convention, the depreciation allowance for the first year property is placed in service is based on the number of months the property was in service, and property placed in service at any time during a month is treated as having been placed in service in the middle of the month. Further, property disposed of by a taxpayer at any time during a month is treated as having been disposed of in the middle of the month.

* * * * * *

Conference Agreement

The conference agreement follows the Senate amendment.

Special rule where substantial property placed in service during last three months of the year

* * * * * *

Conference Agreement

The conference agreement provides that a mid-quarter convention is applied to all property if more than 40 percent of all property is placed in service by a taxpayer during the last three months of the taxable year. The mid-quarter convention treats all property placed in service during any quarter of a taxable year as placed in service on the midpoint of such quarter. Where the taxpayer is a member of an affiliated group (within the meaning of sec. 1504, without regard to sec. 1504(b)), all such members are treated as one taxpayer for purposes of the 40-percent determination.

For example, using the mid-quarter convention, a $100 asset in the five-year class eligible for the 200-percent declining balance method that is placed in service during the first quarter of a taxable year would receive deductions beginning in taxable year 1 and ending in taxable year 6 of $35, $26, $15.60, $11.01, $11.01, and $1.33.

For taxable years in which property is placed in service subject both to present-law ACRS and to the conference agreement, the 40-percent determination is made with respect to all such property. The mid-quarter convention, however, applies only to property subject to the conference agreement.

5. Gain on disposition

a. Residential real property

Present Law

For residential real property held for more than one year, gain realized on a disposition is recaptured only to the extent that accelerated depreciation deductions exceed straight-line deductions. Recapture for low-income housing is phased out after property has been held for a prescribed period.

* * * * * *

Senate Amendment

For all residential rental property, there is no recapture.

Conference Agreement

The conference agreement follows the Senate amendment. Any capital gain is treated under the rules provided in Title III.

b. Nonresidential real property

Present Law

There is no recapture on a disposition if the taxpayer elected to recover the property's cost using the straight-line method. Otherwise, the full amount of depreciation—to extent of gain—is recaptured.

House Bill

Under the House bill, there is no recapture for nonresidential (30-year) real property.

Senate Amendment

The Senate amendment is the same as the House bill.

Conference Agreement

The conference agreement follows the House bill and the Senate amendment.

6. Lessee leasehold improvements

Present Law

A lessee recovers the cost of leasehold improvements over the shorter of the property's ACRS recovery period or the portion of the lease term remaining on the date the property is acquired. Under statutory rules provided for use in determining the term of a lease, in certain cases, a lease term includes periods during which the lease may be renewed pursuant to an option held by the lessee, unless the lessee establishes that it is more probable than not that the lease will not be renewed. In other cases, the statute provides that a lease term is determined by excluding renewal options held by the lessee, unless the facts show with reasonable certainty that the lease will be renewed. These rules also apply in determining the amortization period for lease acquisition costs.

[Senate Explanation]

*   *   *   *   *   *

The cost of leasehold improvements made by a lessee is to be recovered under the rules applicable to other taxpayers, without regard to the lease term. On termination of the lease, the lessee who does not retain the improvements is to compute gain or loss by reference to the adjusted basis of the improvement at that time.

In light of the bill's treatment of a lessee's capital costs, the only future relevance of section 178 will be in determining the amortization period for lease acquisition costs. Accordingly, the bill makes conforming changes to section 178. Under section 178 as revised by the bill, the term of a lease is determined by including all renewal options as well as any other period for which the parties reasonably expect the lease to be renewed.

[Conference Report]

*   *   *   *   *   *

The conference agreement follows the Senate amendment.

7. Expensing

Present Law

Taxpayers can elect to expense up to $5,000 of the cost of personal property that is purchased and used in a trade or business. The $5,000 ceiling is scheduled to increase to $7,500 for taxable years beginning in 1988 and 1989, and to $10,000 for years beginning after 1989. The dollar limitation is subject to apportionment among certain related entities. If expensed property is converted to nonbusiness use within two years of the time the property was placed in service, the difference between the amount expensed and the ACRS deductions that would have been allowed for the period of business use is recaptured as ordinary income.

*   *   *   *   *   *

Senate Amendment

The Senate amendment provides a $10,000 ceiling for expensing for taxpayers whose total investment in tangible personal property is $200,000 or less. For other taxpayers, for every dollar of investment in excess of $200,000, the $10,000 ceiling is reduced by one dollar. The amount eligible to be expensed is limited to the taxable income derived from the active trade or business in which the property is used. The difference between expensing and ACRS deductions is recaptured if property is converted to nonbusiness use at any time before the end of the property's recovery period.

Conference Agreement

The conference agreement generally follows the Senate amendment, but provides that the amount eligible to be expensed is limited to the taxable income derived from any trade or business. Married individuals filing separate returns are treated as one taxpayer for purposes of determining the amount which may be expensed and the total amount of investment in tangible personal property.

8. Vintage accounts

Present Law

Under present law, taxpayers generally compute depreciation deductions on an asset-by-asset basis. Under regulations prescribed by the Secretary, there is an election to establish mass asset vintage accounts for assets in the same recovery class and placed in service in the same year. The definition of assets eligible for inclusion in mass asset accounts is limited, primarily because of concern about the mechanics of recapturing investment tax credit.

House Bill

With repeal of the investment tax credit, the House bill authorizes regulations that would expand the definition of eligible property to include all property.

Senate Amendment

*   *   *   *   *   *

[Senate Explanation]

*   *   *   *   *   *

The bill continues the Secretary's regulatory authority to permit a taxpayer to maintain one or more mass asset accounts for any property in the same ACRS class and placed in service in the same year. As under present law, unless otherwise provided in regulations, the full amount of the proceeds realized on disposition of property from a mass asset account are to be treated as ordinary income (without reduction for the basis of the asset). As a corollary, no reduction is to be made in the depreciable basis remaining in the account. The limitations on the ability to establish mass asset accounts under present law, as proposed in Treasury regulations, resulted, in part, from a concern about the mechanics of recapturing investment tax credits on dispositions of property from an account. To facilitate the application of the recapture rules without requiring that individual assets be identified, the proposed regulations provide mortality dispersion tables that cannot be applied easily to diverse assets. In view of the provision of the bill that repeals the investment tax credit, the primary reason for restricting a taxpayer's ability to establish vintage accounts would be set aside. Accordingly, the committee expects that the definition of assets eligible for inclusion in mass asset accounts will be expanded to include diverse assets.

[Conference Report]

*   *   *   *   *   *

Conference Agreement

The conference agreement follows the House bill and the Senate amendment and clarifies that diverse assets can be included in these accounts.

9. Public utility property

Present Law

The benefits of accelerated depreciation must be normalized.

House Bill

The House bill retains present law and additionally applies special normalization rules to excess deferred tax reserves resulting from the reduction of corporate income tax rates.

Senate Amendment

The Senate amendment is the same as the House bill.

Conference Agreement

The conference agreement follows the House bill and the Senate amendment.

10. Regular investment tax credit

House Bill

The House bill repeals the regular investment tax credit.

Senate Amendment

The Senate amendment follows the House bill.

Conference Agreement

The conference agreement follows the House bill and the Senate amendments.

11. Finance leases

House Bill

The House bill repeals the finance leasing rules.

Senate Amendment

The Senate amendment follows the House bill.

Conference Agreement

The conference agreement follows the House bill and the Senate amendment.

[Senate Explanation]

*   *   *   *   *   *

* * * **Treatment of certain transferees.**—A special rule applies after the transfer of any property in a non-recognition transaction described in section 332, 351, 361, 371(a),

374(a), 721, or 731 (other than the case of a termination of a partnership under 708(b)(1)(B)). In any such case, the transferee is treated as the transferor for purposes of computing the depreciation deduction with respect to so much of the basis in the hands of the transferee as does not exceed the adjusted basis in the hands of the transferor. Thus, the transferee of property in one of the transactions described above "steps into the shoes" of the transferor to the extent the property's basis is not increased as the result of the transaction. To the extent the transferee's basis exceeds the property's basis in the hands of the transferor (e.g., because the transferor recognized gain in the transaction), the transferee depreciates the excess under the bill's general rules.

* * * **Additions or improvements to property.**—The bill preserves the prohibition against use of the component method of depreciation. The bill provides that the recovery period for any addition or improvement to real or personal property begins on the later of (1) the date on which the addition or improvement is placed in service, or (2) the date on which the property with respect to which such addition or improvement is made is placed in service. Any ACRS deduction for an addition or improvement to a property is to be computed in the same manner as the deduction for the underlying property would be if such property were placed in service at the same time as such addition or improvement.

[House Explanation]

*   *   *   *   *   *

[Expenditures for railroad grading and tunnel bores; particular disaster]

* * * Under a separate rule, specified expenditures not reimbursed from insurance proceeds are treated as 5-year recovery property under ACRS. This treatment does not apply to such net unreimbursed expenditures in excess of $15. million.

*   *   *   *   *   *

[Conference Report]

*   *   *   *   *   *

The conference agreement follows the House bill and the Senate amendment with respect to the particular railroad disaster.

12. Effective dates

a. In general

Senate Amendment

The provisions that modify ACRS apply to all property placed in service after December 31, 1986. The provision that repeals the regular investment tax credit is effective for property placed in service after December 31, 1985. Repeal of the finance lease rules is effective for agreements entered into after December 31, 1986.

Conference Agreement

The conference agreement follows the Senate amendment except that the conference agreement also provides an election to apply the modified ACRS to certain property that is placed in service after July 31, 1986. All elections made under section 168 of the Code, as amended, are irrevocable and must be made on the first tax return for the taxable year in which the property is placed in service.

b. Transitional rules

*   *   *   *   *   *

Conference Agreement

In general.—The conference agreement provides certain exceptions to the general effective dates, in the case of property constructed, reconstructed, or acquired pursuant to a written contract that was binding as of March 1, 1986, (December 31, 1985, for purposes of the investment tax credit) or in other transitional situations discussed below. Except in the case of qualified solid waste disposal facilities and certain satellites (described below), the application of the transitional rules is conditioned on property being placed in service by a prescribed date in the future. In addition, special rules are provided for investment credits claimed on transitional property, for tax-exempt bond financed property, and for the finance lease rules.

The conferees are aware that taxpayers may have difficulty in identifying under their accounting systems whether a particular item placed in service on or after January 1, 1987, (1986, for the investment tax credit) was acquired pursuant to a contract that was binding before March 2, 1986, (December 31, 1985, for the investment tax credit) or meets the rule for self-constructed property. The problem arises where a taxpayer regularly enters into contracts for (or manufactures itself) large stocks of identical or similar items of property to be placed in service as needed. The taxpayer's accounting system may not identify the date on which the contract for an item's acquisition was entered into (or the date on which manufacture commenced). In such a situation, a taxpayer is to assume that the first items placed in service after December 31, 1986, (1985, for the investment tax credit) were those they had under a binding contract on that date. A similar rule is to apply to self-constructed property.

Except as otherwise provided, for purposes of the depreciation transitional rules, the rules described below do not apply to any property unless the property has an ADR midpoint of seven years or more and is placed in service before the applicable date, determined according to the following: (1) for property with an ADR midpoint less than 20 years (other than computer-based telephone central office switching equipment), January 1, 1989, and (2) for property with an ADR midpoint of 20 years or more, residential rental property, and nonresidential real property, January 1, 1991.

For purposes of the investment tax credit transitional rules, the applicable placed-in-service dates are: (1) for property with an ADR midpoint less than five years, July 1, 1986, (2) for property with an ADR midpoint of at least five but less than seven years and including computer-based telephone central office switching equipment, January 1, 1987, (3) for property with an ADR midpoint of at least seven but less than 20 years (other than computer-based telephone central office switching equipment), January 1, 1989, and (4) for property with an ADR midpoint of 20 years or more, January 1, 1991. Property that is incorporated into an equipped building or plant facility need not independently satisfy the placed-in-service requirements. Instead, such property would qualify for transition relief as part of the equipped building or plant facility—as long as the equipped building or plant facility is placed in service by the prescribed date.

For purposes of the general effective dates, if at least 80 percent of a target corporation's stock is acquired on or before December 31, 1986, (December 31, 1985, for purposes of the investment tax credit) and the acquiring corporation makes a section 338 election to treat the stock purchase as an asset purchase after the relevant date, then the deemed new target corporation is treated as having purchased the assets before the general effective date.

Anti-churning rules.—The conference agreement expands the scope of the present law anti-churning rules to prevent taxpayers from bringing certain property placed in service after December 31, 1980, under the modified ACRS. The expanded anti-churning rules apply to all ACRS property, other than residential rental property and nonresidential real property, where the result would be to qualify such property for more generous depreciation than would be available under present law. The conference agreement retains the anti-churning rules applicable to property that was originally placed in service before January 1, 1981. The anti-churning rules will not apply to property that is placed in service before January 1, 1987.

Binding contracts.—The conference agreement does not apply to property that is constructed, reconstructed, or acquired by a taxpayer pursuant to a written contract that was binding as of March 1, 1986 (December 31, 1985, for investment tax credits), and at all times thereafter. If a taxpayer transfers his rights in any such property under construction or such contract to another taxpayer, the bill does not apply to the property in the hands of the transferee, as long as the property was not placed in service by the transferee before the transfer by the transferor. For purposes of this rule, if by reason of sales or exchanges of interests in a partnership, there is a deemed termination and reconstitution of a partnership under section 708(b)(1)(B), the partnership is to be treated as having transferred its rights in the property under construction or the contract to the new partnership.

The general binding contract rule applies only to contracts in which the construction, reconstruction, erection, or acquisition of property is itself the subject matter of the contract.

A contract is binding only if it is enforceable under State law against the taxpayer, and does not limit damages to a specified amount (e.g., by use of a liquidated damages provisions). A contractual provision that limits damages to an amount equal to at least five percent of the total contract price is not treated as limiting damages.

For purposes of the general binding contract rule, a contract under which the taxpayer is granted an option to acquire property is not to be treated as a binding contract to acquire the underlying property. In contrast, a contract under which the taxpayer grants an irrevocable put (i.e., an option to sell) to another taxpayer is treated as a binding contract, as the grantor of such an option does not have the ability to unilaterally rescind the commitment. In general, a contract is binding even if subject to a condition, as long as the condition is not within the control of either party or a predecessor (except in the limited circumstances described below). A contract that was binding as of March 1, 1986 (or December 31, 1985, in the case of the investment tax credit) will not be considered binding at all times thereafter if it is substantially modified after that date.

[The following colloquy relating to act Secs. 203 and 204 is drawn from the Congressional Record. The colloquy occurred on the day the Conference bill was considered by the Senate. Ed.]

[Senate Floor Explanation]

Supply or Service Contracts Transition Rule For the Investment Tax Credit

Mr. MATSUNAGA. Mr. President, I seek a clarification from the distinguished manager of the conference report, the Senator from Oregon, as to the investment tax credit supply or service contracts transition rule with regard to transfers of rights to property required by such contracts and transfers of such contracts.

Sections 203 and 204 of the conference bill establish the binding contracts provision and the supply or service contracts provision as general transition rules for purposes of depreciation and the investment tax credit. Identical rules were included in the Senate bill and the House bill.

Under the binding contracts provision, transition property includes "any property which is constructed, reconstructed, or acquired by a taxpayer pursuant to a written contract that was binding" on December 31, 1985 and at all times thereafter for purposes of the investment tax credit. Similarly, under the supply or service contracts provision, transition property includes "any property which is readily identifiable with and necessary to carry out a written supply or service contract, or agreement to lease, which was binding" on December 31, 1985 and at all times thereafter.

The House and Senate reports as well as the conference report provide interpretative rules to implement these transition provisions. The binding contracts rule set forth the

basic concept; the other transition measures are corollaries based on the binding contract concept. In this light, some of the interpretative rules under the binding contracts provision are limited to that provision; other interpretative rules under the binding contracts provision provide general rules of interpretation for other corollary transition provisions. With regard to this interrelation, the conference report expressly states that a supply or service contract must satisfy the requirement of a binding contract.

My question concerns the conferees' intention to allow transfers. In particular the conference report at pages I-54 and I-55 states that under the binding contracts rule a contract will not be considered binding at all times after December 31, 1985, if it is substantially modified after that date. The report further provides that transfers of property under contract or transfers of the contracts are nonetheless allowed under the transition provision. The report states:

If a taxpayer transfers his rights in any such property under construction or such contracts to another taxpayer, the bill does not apply to the property in the hands of the transferee, as long as the property was not placed in service before the transfer by the transferor.

This transfer rule seems to be a general rule of interpretation that also applies to the supply or service contracts provision. It would seem that property or a contract can be transferred under the supply or service contracts provision and still be covered by the transition provision.

Is this Senator's understanding correct that the transfer rule of interpretation also applies to the supply or service contracts transition provision? Is this Senator's understanding correct that the transfer of such supply or service contracts will not be considered a significant modification so that the contracts remain binding at all times notwithstanding such a transfer?

Mr. PACKWOOD. The Senator from Hawaii is correct. If a taxpayer transfers his rights to property under a qualified service contract, the repeal of the investmentt credit does not apply to the property in the hands of the transferee, as long as the property was not placed in service before the transfer. Similarly, if the taxpayer transfers his rights to such service contracts, the repeal of the investment tax credit still would not apply to property readily identifiable with and necessary to carry out the contract.

Mr. MATSUNAGA. I thank the distinguished manager for this clarification. Congressional Record p. S13955, 9-27-86.

[Conference Report]

* * * * * *

A binding contract to acquire a component part of a larger property will not be treated as a binding contract to acquire the larger property under the general rule for binding contracts. For example, if a written binding contract to acquire an aircraft engine was entered into before March 2, 1986, there would be a binding contract to acquire only the engine, not the entire aircraft.

The conferees wish to clarify the general binding contract rule with respect to investment credit and ACRS allowances. Design changes to a binding contract to construct a project that are made for reasons of technical or economic efficiencies of operation and that cause an insignificant increase in the original price will not constitute substantial modifications of the contract so as to affect the status of the project under the binding contract rule. In addition, a supplementary contract that stands on its own and is not protected by the binding contract rule, for example, to build an addition to a project protected by the binding contract rule, will not adversely affect the status of the portion of the project subject to a separate binding contract.

The conferees also wish to clarify that the general binding contract rule does not apply to supply agreements with manufacturers, where such contracts fail to specify the amount or design specifications of property to be purchased; such contracts are not to be treated as binding contracts until purchase orders are actually placed. A purchase order for a specific number of properties, based on the pricing provisions of the supply agreement, will be treated as a binding contract.

Self-constructed property.—The conference agreement does not apply to property that is constructed or reconstructed by the taxpayer, if (1) the lesser of $1 million or five percent of the cost of the property was incurred or committed, (i.e., required to be incurred pursuant to a written binding contract in effect) as of March 1, 1986 (December 31, 1985, for purposes of the investment tax credit) and (2) the construction or reconstruction began by that date. For purposes of this rule, a taxpayer who serves as the engineer and general contractor of a project is to be treated as constructing the property. For purposes of this rule, the construction of property is considered to begin when physical work of a significant nature starts. Construction of a facility or equipment is not considered as begun if work has started on minor parts or components. Physical work does not include preliminary activities such as planning or designing, securing financing, exploring, researching, or developing.

For purposes of the rule for self-constructed property, in the context of a building, the term "property" includes all of the normal and customary components that are purchased from others and installed without significant modification (e.g., light fixtures).

[The following colloquy is drawn from the Congressional Record. The colloquy occurred on the day the bill was considered by the House. Ed.]

[House Floor Explanation]

I have discussed with Congressman Flippo several issues relating to the investment tax credit repeal transition rules for self-constructed property and self-constructed plant facilities. We have reached a common under-

standing regarding for following specific issues:

First, I would like to clarify the application of the investment tax credit transition rules to self-constructed property. Under the bill, the repeal of the investment tax credit does not apply to property that is constructed or reconstructed by the taxpayer if the lesser of $1 million or 5 percent of the cost of the property was incurred or committed by January 1, 1986, and the construction or reconstruction began by that date. For purposes of this rule, a taxpayer who serves as the engineer and general contractor of a project is treated as constructing the property and construction is considered to have begun when physical work of a significant nature starts. Construction of a facility or equipment is not considered as begun if work has started only on minor parts or components. Under this provision, in the following circumstances construction of property should be considered to have been commenced so as to qualify the property for the investment tax credit under this transition rule.

Prior to January 1, 1986, an aircraft manufacturer entered into binding contracts with third parties for the construction of aircraft subassemblies to be included by the manufacturer in the construction of the completed aircraft. The cost to the aircraft manufacturer of these subassemblies is approximately $300,000, which together with the costs of other components of the aircraft which the manufacturer had incurred or was required to incur on December 31, 1985, exceeds 5 percent of the cost of the aircraft. These subassemblies were designed for this model of aircraft, were specifically ordered for the aircraft and are essential to its operation, and include wing trailing edges, ailerons and tabs, and rudders and tabs. The subcontractors commenced physical construction of these subcomponents prior to January 1, 1986. Prior to the date the aircraft is placed in service the manufacturer will transfer it to its wholly owned subsidiary that is included in the same consolidated tax return as the manufacturer.

Under the bill, construction of the aircraft would be considered to have begun by the aircraft manufacturer when the subcontractors commenced physical construction of the subassemblies on behalf of the manufacturer pursuant to the binding written contract. Congressional Record p. H8360, 9-25-86.

[The following colloquy is drawn from the Congressional Record. The colloquy occurred on the day the bill was considered by the Senate. Ed.]

[Senate Floor Explanation]

Mr. CRANSTON. Mr. President, I would like to clarify the application of the investment tax credit transition rules to self-constructed property. Under the bill, the repeal of the investment tax credit does not apply to property that is constructed or reconstructed by the taxpayer if the lesser of $1 million or 5 percent of the cost of the property was incurred or committed by January 1, 1986, and the construction or reconstruction began by that date. For purposes of this rule, a taxpayer who serves as the engineer and general contractor of a project is treated as constructing the property and construction is considered to have begun when physical work of a significant nature starts. Construction of a facility or equipment is not considered as begun if work has started only on minor parts or components. I would like to ask the distinguished chairman of the Committee on Finance to clarify whether in the following circumstances construction of property will be considered to have been commenced so as to qualify the property for the investment tax credit under this transition rule.

Prior to January 1, 1986 an aircraft manufacturer entered into binding contracts with third parties for the construction of aircraft subassemblies to be included by the manufacturer in the construction of the completed aircraft. The cost to the aircraft manufacturer of these subassemblies is approximately $300,000, which together with the costs of other components of the aircraft which the manufacturer had incurred or was required to incur on December 31, 1985, exceeds 5 percent of the cost of the aircraft. These subassemblies were designed for this model of aircraft, were specifically ordered for the aircraft and are essential to its operation, and include wing trailing edges, ailerons and tabs, and rudders and tabs. The subcontractors commenced physical construction of these subcomponents prior to January 1, 1986. Prior to the date the aircraft is placed in service the manufacturer will transfer it to its wholly-owned subsidiary that is included in the same consolidated tax return as the manufacturer. My question of the distinguished chairman of the Committee on Finance is whether in these circumstances an aircraft will qualify for the investment tax credit transition relief.

Mr. PACKWOOD. Yes, such an aircraft qualifies for the investment tax credit under the transitional rule for self-constructed property. Construction of the aircraft would be considered to have begun by the aircraft manufacturer when the subcontractors commenced physical construction of the subassemblies on behalf of the manufacturer pursuant to the binding written contract.

Mr. CRANSTON. I thank the distinguished chairman for this clarification. Congressional Record, p. S13955, 9-27-86.

[Conference Report]

*   *   *   *   *   *

Equipped buildings.—Under the conference agreement, where construction of an equipped building began on or before March 1, 1986 (December 31, 1985, for purposes of the investment tax credit), pursuant to a written specific plan, and more than one-half the cost of the equipped building (including any machinery and equipment for it) was incurred or committed before March 2, 1986 (January 1, 1986, for the investment tax credit) the entire equipped building project and incidental appurtenances are excepted from the bill's application.[1] Where the costs incurred or committed before March 2, 1986 (January 1, 1986, for the investment tax credit) do not equal more than half the cost of the equipped building, each item of machinery and equipment is treated separately for purposes of determining whether the item qualifies for transitional relief.

Under the equipped building rule, the conference agreement will not apply to equipment and machinery to be used in the completed building, and also incidental machinery, equipment, and structures adjacent to the building (referred to here as appurtenances) which are necessary to the planned use of the building, where the following conditions are met:

(1) The construction (or reconstruction or erection) or acquisition of the building, machinery, and equipment was pursuant to a specific written plan of a taxpayer in existence on March 1, 1986 (December 31, 1985, for the investment tax credit); and

(2) More than 50 percent of the adjusted basis of the building and the equipment and machinery to be used in it (as contemplated by the written plan) was attributable to property the cost of which was incurred or committed by March 1, 1986 (December 31, 1985, for the investment tax credit), and construction commenced on or before March 1, 1986 (December 31, 1985, for the investment tax credit).

The written plan for an equipped building may be modified to a minor extent after March 1, 1986 (December 31, 1985, for the investment tax credit) and the property involved may still come under this rule; however, there cannot be substantial modification in the plan if the equipped building rule is to apply. The plan referred to must be a definite and specific plan of the taxpayer that is available in written form as evidence of the taxpayer's intentions.

The equipped building rule can be illustrated by an example where the taxpayer has a plan providing for the construction of a $100,000 building with $80,000 of machinery and equipment to be placed in the building and used for a specified manufacturing process. In addition, there may be other structures or equipment, here called appurtenances, which are incidental to the operations carried on in the building, that are not themselves located in the building. Assume that the incidental appurtenances have further costs of $30,000. These appurtenances might include, for example, an adjacent railroad siding, a dynamo or water tower

---

[Footnote ¶ 3870] (1) For example, if property with a class life of less than 7 years is incorporated into an equipped building, then such property would not independently need to satisfy the placed-in-service requirements. Instead, such property would qualify for transition relief as part of the equipped building—as long as the equipped building is placed in service by the prescribed date.

used in connection with the manufacturing process, or other incidental structures or machinery and equipment necessary to the planned use of the building. Of course, appurtenances, as used here, do not include a plant needed to supply materials to be processed or used in the building under construction. In this case, if construction of the building is under a binding contract and property but no equipment had been ordered, and the appurtenances had not been constructed or placed under binding order, the equipped building rule would apply. This is true because the building cost represents more than 50 percent of the total $180,000. As a result, the machinery and equipment, even though not under binding contract, is eligible for the rule. In this connection, it should be noted that the additional cost of appurtenances, $30,000, is not taken into account for purposes of determining whether the 50-percent test is met. Nevertheless, the bill would not apply to these appurtenances since the 50-percent test is met as to the equipped building.

Plant facilities.—The conference agreement also provides a plant facility rule that is comparable to the equipped building rule (described above), for cases where the facility is not housed in a building. For purposes of this rule, the term "plant facility" means a facility that does not include any building (or of which buildings constitute an insignificant portion), and that is a self-contained single operating unit or processing operation—located on a single site—identifiable as a single unitary project as of March 1, 1986.

If pursuant to a written specific plan of a taxpayer in existence as of March 1, 1986 (December 31, 1985, for the investment tax credit), the taxpayer constructed, reconstructed, or erected a plant facility, the construction, reconstruction, or erection commenced as of March 1, 1986 (December 31, 1985, for the investment tax credit), and the 50-percent test is met, then the conference agreement will not apply to property that makes up the facility. For this purpose, construction, etc., of a plant facility is not considered to have begun until it has commenced at the site of the plant facility. (This latter rule does not apply if the facility is not to be located on land and, therefore, where the initial work on the facility must begin elsewhere.) In this case, as in the case of the commencement of construction of a building, construction begins only when actual work at the site commences; for example, when work begins on the excavation for footings, etc., or pouring the pads for the facility, or the driving of foundation pilings into the ground. Preliminary work, such as clearing a site, test drilling to determine soil condition, or excavation to change the contour of the land (as distinguished from excavation for footings), does not constitute the beginning of construction, reconstruction or erection.

The conferees wish to clarify the application of the plant facility rule where the original construction of a power plant is pursuant to a written specific plan of a taxpayer in existence as of March 1, 1986 (December 31, 1985, in the case of the invest-

ment tax credit), and both the original construction and more than one-half of the total cost of the property to be used at the power plant has been incurred or committed by such date. The plant facility rule will apply to the power plant even though the type of fuel to be utilized at the plant may have changed subsequent to the original plan and other changes may be made to accommodate the change in the fuel source, as long as more than one-half of the total cost of the plant, including all conversion costs, were incurred or committed by March 1, 1986.

[The following colloquy is drawn from the Congressional Record. The colloquy occurred on the day the Conference bill was considered by the House. Ed.]

[House Floor Explanation]

As I have discussed earlier with Congressman Flippo, I would also like to clarify the general transition rule for the investment tax credit and depreciation in the case of self-constructed plant facilities. In the case of railroad track material which was acquired by the taxpayer or subject to a binding contract prior to January 1, 1986—or March 2, 1986, in the case of depreciation—such rails, ties, and other track components and the costs of installation in existing road beds constitute a self-constructed facility covered by the transition rule if more than half of the total cost is represented by acquisitions or binding contracts in effect before those dates.

This rule applies in the case of replacement track where the construction of the road bed has occurred and where a written plan for programmed track work was in existence before those dates. A project for a new rail line would not qualify unless actual construction of the road bed had begun before those dates. Congressional Record, p. H 8360, 9-25-86.

[Conference Report]

Special rules for sale-leasebacks within three months.—Property is treated as meeting the requirements of a transitional or general effective date rule if (1) the property is placed in service by a taxpayer who acquired the property from a person in whose hands the property would qualify under a transitional or general effective date rule, (2) the property is leased back by the taxpayer to such person, and (3) the leaseback occurs within three months after such property was originally placed in service, but no later than the applicable date. The committee intends that the special rule for sale-leasebacks apply to any property that qualifies for transitional relief under the bill or that was originally placed in service by the lessee under the sale-leaseback before the general effective date. This rule would apply where a taxpayer acquires property from a manufacturer, places the property in service by leasing it to the ultimate user, and subsequently engages in a sale-leaseback within three months after the property was originally placed in service under the initial lease.

In the case of a facility that would otherwise qualify for transitional relief as an equipped building (described above), if a portion of such equipped building is sold and leased back in accordance with the requirements of the special rule for sale-leasebacks, both the leased and retained portions will continue to qualify for transitional relief as an equipped building.

Special rules for tax-exempt bond financed property.—The provision restricting ACRS deductions for property financed with tax-exempt bonds applies to property placed in service after December 31, 1986, to the extent such property is financed (directly or indirectly) by the proceeds of bonds issued after March 1, 1986. The revised restrictions on ACRS deductions do not apply to facilities placed in service after December 31, 1986, if—

(1) the original use of the facilities commences with the taxpayer and the construction (including reconstruction or rehabilitation) commenced before Marcy 2, 1986, and was completed after that date;

(2) a binding contract to incur significant expenditures for the construction (including reconstruction or rehabilitation) of the property financed with the bonds was entered into before March 2, 1986, was binding at all times thereafter, and some or all of the expenditures were incurred after March 1, 1986; or

(3) the facility was acquired after March 1, 1986, pursuant to a binding contract entered into before March 2, 1986, and that is binding at all times after March 1, 1986.

For purposes of this restriction, the determination of whether a binding contract to incur significant expenditures existed before March 2, 1986, is made in the same manner as under the rules governing the redefinition of industrial development bonds.

The restrictions on ACRS deductions for bond-financed property do not apply to property placed in service after December 31, 1986, to the extent that the property is financed with tax-exempt bonds issued before March 2, 1986. ACRS deductions for such property may be determined, however, under the rules generally provided by the bill. For purposes of this exception, a refunding issue issued after March 1, 1986, generally is treated as a new issue and the taxpayer must use the alternative depreciation method provided by the bill for costs that are unrecovered on the date of the refunding issue.

In cases where a change of recovery method is required because of a refunding issue, only the remaining unrecovered cost of the property is required to be recovered using the alternative depreciation system provided by the bill. Therefore, no retroactive adjustments to ACRS deductions previously claimed are required when a pre-March 2, 1986, bond issue is refunded where no significant expenditures are made with respect to the facility after December 31, 1986.

Contract with persons other than a person who will construct or supply the property.—The bill provides transitional relief for certain situations where written binding contracts require the construction or acquisition of property, but the contract is not between the person who will own the property and the person who will construct or supply the property. This rule applies to written service or supply contracts and agreements to lease entered into before March 2, 1986 (January 1, 1986, in the case of the investment tax credit). An example of a case to which this rule would apply would be lease agreements under which a grantor trust is obligated to provide property under a finance lease (to the extent continued under the bill). The conferees wish to clarify that this rule applies to cable television franchise agreements embodied in whole or in part in municipal ordinances or similar enactments before March 2, 1986 (January 1, 1986, for the investment tax credit).

[The following colloquy relating to Act Sec. is drawn from the Congressional Record. The colloquy occurred on the day the bill was considered by the Senate. Ed.]

[Senate Floor Explanation]

DEPRECIATION AND ITC TRANSITION RULES

Mr. GLENN. I would like to confirm with the distinguished Senator from Oregon the operation of the transition rule for supply or service contracts set forth in section 204(a)(3) of H.R. 3838 as reported out by the conference committee and currently under consideration by the Senate, particularly its application to holders of television franchise rights. H.R. 3838 as passed by the Senate on June 24, 1986 contained section 202(d)(11) which provided, in part, that the amendments made by section 201 would not apply to any property which is readily identifiable with or necessary to carry out a binding obligation with a municipality under an ordinance granting television franchise rights if the ordinance was enacted on July 22, 1985 and a construction contract was signed before April 1, 1986.

While the version of H.R. 3838 presently under consideration by the Senate 202(d)(11) of the bill as originally passed by the Senate, the conference report accompanying the conference's version of the bill states that with respect to the supply or service contract exception, the conferees wish to clarify that this rule applies to cable television franchise agreements embodied in whole or in part in municipal ordinances or similar enactments before March 2, 1986, January 1, 1986, with respect to the investment tax credit. I would like to confirm that the supply or service contracts transition rule, the statutory language of which was not amended by the conference committee, is intended to cover the holder of any television franchise which would have been covered by the original section 202(d)(11).

Mr. PACKWOOD. That is correct.

Mr. GLENN. Thus, in the case of a cable franchise which was granted a cable franchise on July 22, 1985 and pursuant to which a definitive franchise agreement was negotiated—and subsequently approved and signed after March 1, 1986—and which entered into a construction contract prior to April 1, 1986, its cable related property would fall within the supply or service contracts transition rule?

Mr. PACKWOOD. That is correct. It was the intent of the conferees, as indicated in the conference report, that the definitive franchise agreement which was contemplated by the July 1985, ordinance would be considered embodied in that ordinance and as such would qualify as a supply or service contract entered into prior to March 2, 1986, with respect to the depreciation rules and January 1, 1986, in the case of the investment tax credit rules. Congressional Record, p. S13955, 9-27-86.

[Conference Report]

This transitional rule is applicable only where the specifications and amount of the property are readily ascertainable from the terms of the contract, or from related documents. A supply or service contract or agreement to lease must satisfy the requirements of a binding contract (discussed above). A change in the method or amount of compensation for services under the contract, without more, will not be considered a substantial modification of the contract if, taken as a whole, the change does not affect the scope or function of the project. This rule does not provide transitional relief to property in addition to that covered under a contract described above, which additional property is included in the same project but does not otherwise qualify for transitional relief.

As a further example, where a taxpayer before January 1, 1986 entered into a written binding contract to construct a wastewater treatment facility and to provide wastewater treatment services, the subsequent amendment of the contract to (1) extend the date for completion of construction by a short period (e.g., three months), (2) provide for a letter of credit or other financial protection against defaults of the service provider, (3) add a pledge of net revenue and a sewer use rate covenant by the service recipient, (4) cause the service recipient's options to purchase the facility to comply with "service contract" definitional requirements of the Internal Revenue Code, (5) merely clarify rights and remedies in the event of performance defaults, and (6) treat the obligations of the taxpayer to accept and treat wastewater as separate obligations (and treat similarly the obligation of the service recipient to pay for such services) would not in the aggregate constitute a "substantial modification," if the taxpayer's obligations to provide wastewater treatment services and to construct or acquire the facility are not affected thereby.

Development agreements relating to large-scale multi-use urban projects.—The conference agreement does not apply to property that is included in a "qualified urban renovation project." The term qualified urban renovation project includes certain projects that satisfy the following requirements as of March 1, 1986 (December 31, 1985, for the investment tax credit):

the project is described in the conference agreement and (1) was publicly announced by a political subdivision, for the renovation of an urban area in its jurisdiction, (2) was either the subject of an agreement for development or a lease between such political subdivision and the primary developer of the project, or was undertaken pursuant to the political subdivision's grant of development rights to a primary developer-purchaser; or (3) was identified as a single unitary project in the internal financing plans of the primary developer, and (4) is not substantially modified at any time after March 1, 1986 (December 31, 1985, for the investment tax credit).

Federal Energy Regulatory Commission application or action.—The requirements of the general binding contract rule will be treated as satisfied with respect to a project if, on or before March 1, 1986 (for purposes of depreciation and the investment tax credit), the Federal Energy Regulatory Commission ("FERC") licensed the project or certified the project as a "qualifying facility" for purposes of the Public Utility Regulatory Policies Act of 1978 ("PURPA"). A project that a developer has simply put FERC on notice as a qualifying facility is not *certified* as a qualifying facility.

This rule will not apply if a FERC license or certification is substantially amended after March 1, 1986. On the other hand, minor modifications will not affect the application of this rule (e.g., technical changes in the description of a project, extension of the deadline for placing property in operation, changes in equipment or in the configuration of equipment).

The committee is informed that FERC does not distinguish between an application to amend an existing certificate and one to have a project recertified and responds in both cases by "recertifying" the project. The committee intends that substance should control over form, and property will remain transitional property if no substantial change occurs. Similarly, a mere change in status from a "qualifying small power production facility" to a "qualifying cogeneration facility," under PURPA, without more, would not affect application of the transitional rule. The following paragraph provides guidance about how the "substance over form" rule applies in typical cases.

The requirements of the transitional rule for FERC Certification will not be violated under the following circumstances: (1) after FERC certification, the introduction of efficiencies results in a reduction of the project cost and an increase in net electricity output, and the FERC certificate is amended to reflect the higher electricity output, (2) a project was originally certified as three separate facilities, but the taxpayer determines that it is more efficient to have a single powerhouse, and the FERC certification is amended to have the facilities combined under a single certificate.

The conference agreement also provides transitional relief for hydroelectric projects of less than 80 megawatts if an application for a permit, exemption, or license was filed with FERC before March 2, 1986 (for purposes of depreciation and the investment tax credit).

[The following colloquy is drawn from the Congressional Record. The colloquy occurred on the day the Conference bill was considered by the Senate. Ed.]

[Senate Floor Explanation]
Fluidized Energy Frackville Associates

Mr. HEINZ. I would like to address a question regarding the interpretation of one of the transition rules to the floor manager of this historic piece of legislation, my good friend and distinguished colleague from Oregon, Mr. Packwood.

Can you confirm my understanding that the transition rule contained in section 204(a)(2)(A) is meant to cover facilities such as one in my State that received a certification by the Federal Energy Regulatory Commission on August 5, 1985, as a qualifying facility for purposes of the Public Utility Regulatory Policies Act of 1978 so long as no substantial change is made to the facility as certified, and, that a design change to capture economies of scale that would increase the output of the facility by 25 percent, without changing the basic configuration of the facility, the fuel source for the facility or the use of the output would not be a substantial change to the facility within the meaning of this transition rule.

Mr. PACKWOOD. I would be pleased to confirm the gentlemen's understanding of section 204(a)(2)(A). The facility he describes would be considered transition property under the rule even if FERC subsequently amended the existing certification for the facility or recertified the facility, since the changes he described would not be substantial modifications. Congressional Record, p. S13952, 9-27-86.

[The following colloquy is drawn from the Congressional Record. The colloquy occurred on the day the bill was considered by the Senate. Ed.]

[Senate Floor Explanation]
FERC License Rule

Mr. GLENN. Mr. President, I want to ask the distinguished chairman of the Finance Committee a question about the so-called FERC license rule.

Under section 204(a)(2) of the bill, property would be grandfathered from loss of the investment credit and current depreciation allowances if the property is part of a project that the Federal Energy Regulatory Commission certified before March 2, 1986 as a qualifying facility for purposes of the Public Utility Regulatory Policies Act.

There are two ways that a project can become a qualifying facility. FERC regulations provided that the owner or operator of a facility may either send the agency notice that the facility meets the requirements for a qualifying facility or request a formal order from FERC certifying the project.

The statement of the managers says that the project certified by formal order have grandfather protection under the FERC rule. A project that a developer has simply put FERC on notice as a qualifying facility is not protected. That's because the latter project has not been certified by FERC.

My question is: What happens if FERC acknowledged in a formal order before March 2, 1986, that a project is a "qualifying facility," but the focus of the order was a separate issue?

A constituent of mine, Energy Conversions of America, Inc. [ENCOA], has been working since 1978 to build a facility in Cincinnati that will burn the city's garbage to generate electricity. The electricity will be sold to the local utility. ENCOA signed a contract with the city in 1979 and began negotiating with the utility in 1982. Although a construction contract has still not been signed, ENCOA made a series of trips to the Federal Energy Regulatory Commission beginning in 1982 for orders to help in the negotiations. For example, in 1982, a hearing officer for the State of Ohio insisted that the State lacked authority, because of Federal preemption, to become involved in determining the utility's avoided cost for purchasing electricity form the Cincinnati facility. ENCOA sought an order from FERC setting the rates that the utility should pay for the electricity. The FERC order states, among other things that—and I am reading:

[When completed, ENCOA will be the operator of a qualifying small power production facility as defined in section 201 of the Public Utility Regulatory Policies Act of 1978 [PURPA] and section 292.204 of the Commission's regulations.

The question is: Does the FERC rule in the bill cover this project?

Mr. PACKWOOD. It was the intent of the conferees as indicted in the conference report that the FERC rule in the bill would cover a facility where a FERC order states that when completed, a company will be the operator of a qualifying small power production facility as defined in section 201 of PURPA. Congressional Record p. S13960—13961 9-27-86.

[Conference Report]

* * * * * *
Qualified solid waste disposal facilities.—The conference agreement does not apply to a qualified solid waste disposal facility if, before March 2, 1986 (for purposes of depreciation and the investment tax credit) (1) there is a written binding contract between a service recipient and a service provider, providing for the operation of such facility and the payment for services to be provided by the facility, or (2) a service recipient, governmental unit, or any entity related to such an entity made a financial commitment of at least $200,000 to the financing or construction of the facility.

For purposes of this rule, a qualified solid waste disposal facility is a facility (including any portion of the facility used for power generation or resource recovery) that provides solid waste disposal services for residents of part or all of one or more governmental units, if substantially all of the solid waste processed at such facility is collected from the general public. This rule does not apply to replacement property. For example, assume a taxpayer/service provider enters into a long-term service contract before January 1, 1986, and a facility is initially placed in service after that date. Assume that the taxpayer finds it necessary to replace the facility 20 years later, pursuant to its obligation to provide continuing services under the pre-1987 service contract. The special rule will apply only to the first facility necessary to fulfill the taxpayer's obligations under the service contract.

For purposes of this provision, a contract is to be considered as binding notwithstanding the fact that the obligations of the parties are conditioned on factors such as the receipt of permits, satisfactory construction or performance of the facility, or the availability of acceptable financing. A change in the method or amount of compensation for services under the contract will not be considered a substantial modification of the contract if, taken as a whole, the change does not materially affect the scope or function of the project.

A service recipient or governmental unit or a related party is to be treated as having made a financial commitment of at least $200,000 for the financing or construction of a facility if one or more entities have issued bonds or other obligations aggregating more than 10 percent of the anticipated capital cost of such facility, the proceeds of which are identified as being for such facility or for a group of facilities that include the facility, and if the proceeds of such bonds or other obligations to be applied to the development or financing of such facility are at least $200,000 in the aggregate. Alternatively, the test would be satisfied if one or more entities have expended in the aggregate at least $200,000 of their funds, or utilized or committed at least $200,000 of their assets, toward the development or financing of such facility (e.g., for the cost of feasibility studies and consultant fees). If a governmental entity acquires a site for a facility by purchase, option to purchase,[2] purchase contract, condemnation, or entering into an exchange of land, it shall be considered to have made a financial commitment equal to the fair market value of such site for purposes of this rule. For purposes of this provision, entities are related if they are described in section 168(h)(4)(A)(i).

[The following colloquy is drawn from the Congressional Record. The colloquy occurred on the day the Conference bill was considered by the House. Ed.]

[House Floor Explanation]

Congressmen Yatron and Coyne have requested a clarification of the special rule in the bill which permits certain solid waste disposal facilities to qualify for the investment tax credit and present law depreciation. Under the rule, if a group of governmental entities committed more than $200,000 for feasibility studies, consultant fees, and other pre-engineering work prior to March 2, 1986, then the project qualifies under the transition rule. Congressional Record, p. H 8362, 9-25-86.

[Conference Report]

*　　*　　*　　*　　*　　*

Other exceptions.—The conference agreement also provides other special transitional rules of limited application. The conference agreement does not apply to (1) those mass commuting vehicles exempted from the application of the tax-exempt leasing rules under DEFRA, (2) a qualified lessee's automotive manufacturing property that was exempted from deferral of the finance lease rules, (3) a qualified lessee's farm property that was exempted from deferral of the finance lease rules, or (4) property described in section 216(b)(3) of TEFRA. Property that qualifies under one of these provisions is also excepted from the 35-percent reduction of the investment credit and the full-basis adjustment (described below).

Master plans.—Under the special rule for master plans for integrated projects, the conferees intend that, (1) in the case of multi-step plans described in sec. 208(a)(5)(E) of the bill, the rule will include executive approval of a plan or executive authorization of expenditures under the plan before March 2, 1986, and (2) in the case of single-step plans described in sec. 208(a)(5)(E) of the bill, the rule will include project-specific designs for which expenditures were authorized, incurred or committed before March 2, 1986.

A master plan for a project will be considered to exist on March 1, 1986 if the general nature and scope of the project was described in a written document or documents in existence on March 1, 1986, or was otherwise clearly identifiable on that date. The conferees understand that each of the projects described in this rule had a master plan in existence on March 1, 1986, and does not intend the existence of such a plan to be a separate requirement for transitional relief for property comprising these projects.

Satellites.—The conference agreement provides transitional relief (including exceptions to the placed-in-service requirements) for certain satellites. Solely for purposes of the special rule for satellites, a binding contract for the construction or acquisition of two satellites by a joint venture shall be sufficient if such contract was in existence on July 2, 1986, and is for the construction or acquisition of the same satellites that were the subject of a contract to acquire or construct in effect on January 28, 1986, to which one of the joint venturers (or one of its affiliates) was a party.

〖Footnote ¶ 3870 continued〗   (2) In the case of an option to purchase, the conferees intend the governmental entity to be treated as having made a financial commitment only if an amount is paid for the option and such consideration is forfeitable.

Commercial passenger airliners.—The conference agreement extends the placed-in-service window for one year (through 1989) for commercial passenger airliners described in ADR class 45.0.

Special rules applicable to the regular investment credit.—*Full basis adjustment.*—A taxpayer is required to reduce the basis of property that qualifies for transition relief ("transition property") by the full amount of investment credits earned with respect to the transition property (after application of the phased-in 35-percent reduction, described below). The full-basis adjustment requirement also applies to credits claimed on qualified progress expenditures made after December 31, 1985. Further, the full-basis adjustment requirement applies to all depreciable property, regardless of whether such property is eligible for ACRS. The lower basis will be used to compute depreciation deductions, as well as gain or loss on disposition of property.

Reduction of ITC carryforwards and credits claimed under transitional rules.—These rules apply only to the portion of an investment credit attributable to the regular percentage (other than the portion thereof attributable to qualified timber property). Thus, for example, 100 percent of ITC carryovers may continue to be allowed for funding of an investment tax credit employee stock ownership plan.

Under the conference agreement, the investment tax credit allowable for carryovers is reduced by 35 percent. The reduction in investment tax credit carryovers is phased in with the corporate rate reduction. The 35-percent reduction is fully effective for taxable years beginning on or after July 1, 1987. Taxpayers having a taxable year that straddles July 1, 1987, will be subject to a partial reduction that reflects the reduction for the portion of their year after that date. For example, for a calendar year taxable year, the reduction for 1987 is 17.5 percent. The investment tax credit earned on transition property is reduced in the same manner as carryovers.

The amount by which the credit is reduced will not be allowed as a credit for any other taxable year. For purposes of determining the extent to which an investment credit determined under section 46 is used in a taxable year, the regular investment credit is assumed to be used first. This rule is inapplicable to credits that a taxpayer elects to carryback 15 years under the special rules described below.

As described above, a full basis adjustment is required with respect to the reduced amount of the investment tax credit. Thus, for transition property that is eligible for a 6.5 percent investment tax credit, the basis reduction would be with respect to the 6.5 percent credit, not the unreduced 10 percent credit.

The phased-in 35-percent reduction is to be applied to the investment tax credit before application of the general 75-percent limitation. Further, the amount of investment tax credit carryovers subject to reduction shall be adjusted to reflect credits that were recaptured.

Section 48(d) election.—A taxpayer in whose hands property qualifies for transitional relief can make an election under section 48(d) to pass the credit claimed to a lessee.

Estimated tax payments.—The conferees are aware that the repeal of the regular investment tax credit for property placed in service after December 31, 1985, presents an issue about the manner in which estimated tax payments should be calculated for payment due dates occurring before the date of enactment of this Act. In general, for example, a corporation calculates estimated tax by determining its expected regular tax liability, less any allowable tax credits. Any underpayment of estimated corporate tax generally results in the imposition of penalties.

The conferees intend that no penalties be imposed under section 6655 on underpayments of estimated tax, but only to the extent that (1) the underpayment of an installment results from a taxpayer taking into account investment tax credits on property placed in service after December 31, 1985, and before the date of enactment of the Act, *and* (2) the taxpayer actually pays such underpayment within 30 days after the enactment of the Act.

Elective 15-year carryback for certain taxpayers.—Certain companies can elect a 15-year carryback of 50 percent of investment tax credit carryforwards in existence as of the beginning of a taxpayer's first taxable year beginning after December 31, 1985. The amount carried back is treated as a payment against the tax imposed by chapter 1 of the Internal Revenue Code, made on the last day prescribed by law (without regard to extensions) for filing a return of tax under chapter 1 of the Code for the first taxable year beginning on or after January 1, 1987. The amount carried back would reduce tax liability for the first taxable year beginning after December 31, 1986; to the extent the amount carried back exceeds the tax liability for such year, any excess could be claimed as a refund under generally applicable rules. Carryforwards taken into account under the carryback rule are not taken into account under section 38 for any other taxable year. Generally, taxpayers eligible to elect the 15-year carryback are domestic corporations engaged in the manufacture and production of steel. A similar election is available to qualified farmers, except a $750 limitation applies.

The amount claimed as a payment against the tax for the first taxable year beginning on or after January 1, 1987 cannot exceed the taxpayer's net tax liability. The net tax liability is the amount of tax liability for all taxable years during the carryback period (not including minimum tax liability), reduced by the sum of credits allowable (other than the credit under section 34 relating to certain fuel taxes). The carryback period is the period that (1) begins with the taxpayer's 15th taxable year preceding the first taxable year from which there is a credit included in the taxpayer's existing carryforward (in no event can such period begin before the first taxable year ending after December 31, 1981), and (2) ends with the corporation's last taxable year beginning before January 1, 1986.

[The Senate Finance Committee version of the bill was amended on the Floor of the Senate. The following explanation is drawn from the Congressional Record. Ed.]

*   *   *   *   *   *

[Senate Floor Explanation]

What this amendment does is simply say that the money that the steel companies get as a result of the steel provision has to be invested in steel in this country * * * Congressional Record, p. S 7800, 6-18-86

[The following colloquy is drawn from the Congressional Record. The colloquy occurred on the day the Conference bill was considered by the Senate. Ed.]

[Senate Floor Explanation]

Mr. HEINZ. Mr. President, section 212(f)(2) of the Tax Reform Act permits the LTV Corp. to use amounts they will receive under the special steel industry ITC rule to purchase insurance that would pay premiums to keep their life and health insurance policies in force for their retirees in the event payments for these policies were suspended in bankruptcy. The provision, as it is drafted, refers to life and health coverage that the company, but for its involvement in bankruptcy, would be obligated to provide. This qualification of the company's obligation, is in my view, unfortunate.

Specifically, the provision states that the amounts would be used by the corporation: * * * To purchase an insurance policy which provides that, in the event the corporation becomes involved in a title 11 or similar case * * * the insurer will provide life and health insurance coverage during the 1-year period beginning on the date such involvement begins to any individual with respect to whom the corporation would (but for such involvement) have been obligated to provide such coverage, the coverage provided by the insurer will be identical to the coverage which the corporation would (but for such involvement) have been obligated to provide, and provides that the payment of insurance premiums will not be required during such 1-year period to keep such policy in force. * * *

Mr. President, in my opinion, this provision does not imply that the company's obligations to provide life and health benefits to its retirees change or do not continue because the company is filing for bankruptcy under chapter 11. I also do not believe that it is intended to modify any provision of the Bankruptcy Code establishing procedures which companies filing for bankruptcy must follow if they intend to terminate employee or retiree benefits that have been collectively bargained.

I would like to ask the chairman of the Finance Committee if he would agree with my interpretation that the language of this section is not intended to affect, in any way, the obligations companies filing for bankruptcy may or may not have under the Bankruptcy Code.

Mr. PACKWOOD. I agree with the Senator from Pennsylvania. In my judgment this provision merely states that LTV must use amounts received through the steel transition rule either in connection with the trade or business of the corporation in the manufacture or production of steel, or to provide life or health insurance benefits for LTV retirees or workers. It does not comment, in any way, on the obligations of the employer in bankruptcy. Congressional Record, p. S13952–13953 9-27-86.

[Conference Report]

*   *   *   *   *

Normalization requirement for public utility property.—If the tax benefits of previously allowed investment tax credits on public utility property are not normalized, then certain investment tax credits will be recaptured. In general, the amount recaptured is the greater of (1) all investment tax credits for open taxable years of the taxpayer or (2) unamortized credits of the taxpayer or credits not previously restored to rate base (whether or not for open years), whichever is applicable. If such credits have not been utilized and are being carried forward, the carryforward amount is reduced in lieu of recapture. These rules apply to violations of the relevant normalization requirements occurring in taxable years ending after December 31, 1985. Similar principles apply to the failure to normalize the tax benefits of previously allowed employee stock ownership plan credits.

General treatment of QPEs.—Neither the repeal of the regular investment credit nor the phased-in 35-percent reduction of credits affects QPEs claimed with respect to the portion of the basis of any progress expenditure property attributable to progress expenditures for periods before January 1, 1986. If a taxpayer elected to take a reduced rate of credit on a QPE basis in lieu of the 50-percent basis adjustment of present law, the portion of basis attributable to such QPEs, claimed for periods before 1986, will not be reduced and such election will not apply to any other portion of such basis. After December 31, 1985, QPEs cannot be claimed unless it is reasonable to expect that the property will be placed in service before the applicable date. The determination of whether it is reasonable to expect that the placement-in-service requirement will be met is to be made on a year-by-year basis, beginning with the first taxable year that includes January 1, 1986. For any taxable year in which reasonable expectations change, no QPEs will be allowed, and previously claimed post-1985 QPEs will be recaptured. Further, if the property is not placed in service on or before the last applicable date, post-1985 QPEs will be recaptured in the taxable year that includes such date.

Special rules for television and motion picture films.—Special transitional rules apply to television and motion picture films for purposes of the investment credit (but not depreciation). For purposes of the general binding contract rule, (1) construction is treated as including production, (2) in accordance with industry practice, written contemporaneous evidence of a binding contract is treated as a written binding contract, and (3) in the case of any television film, a license agreement or agreement for production services between a television network and a producer (including written evidence of such an agreement as provided in (2) above) is treated as a binding contract to produce

property. For these purposes, license agreement options are binding contracts as to the optionor (non-exercising party) but not as to the optionee (exercising party). In addition, a special rule is provided for certain films produced pursuant to a permanent financing arrangement described by the bill. For purposes of the placed-in-service requirement, films and sound recordings are treated as having ADR midpoints of 12 years.

Finance leases.—The finance lease rules continue to apply to any transaction permitted by reason of section 12(c)(2) of DEFRA or section 209(d)(1)(B) of TEFRA.

[¶ 3871] SECTION 221. REDUCTION IN TAX LIABILITY WHICH MAY BE OFFSET BY BUSINESS CREDIT FROM 85 PERCENT TO 75 PERCENT

(Sec. 38 of the Code)

[House Explanation]

*   *   *   *   *   *

The 85 percent limit on the amount of tax which a taxpayer may offset with the investment credit enables corporations to reduce their tax liability to very low percentages of their taxable income and even lower percentages of their book income as reported to shareholders on financial statements. The

Committee is concerned that this reduces confidence in the equity of the tax system.

Explanation of Provision.—The limitation on the amount of income tax liability (in excess of $25,000) of an individual or corporate taxpayer that may be offset by the general business credit is reduced from 85 percent to 75 percent.

Effective Date.—This provision will apply to taxable years that begin after December 31, 1985.

[¶ 3872] SECTION 231. AMENDMENTS RELATING TO CREDIT FOR INCREASING RESEARCH ACTIVITIES

(Secs. 30 and 170(e)(4) of the Code)

[House Explanation]

*   *   *   *   *

Explanation of Provision.—The bill extends the incremental research tax credit for three additional years, i.e., for qualified research expenditures paid or incurred through December 31, 1988, at a credit rate of 20 percent.

*   *   *   *   *   *

[Conference Report]

*   *   *   *   *   *

a. Expiration date

The conference agreement follows the House bill; i.e., the research credit is extended for an additional three years, with modifications.

b. Rate

The conference agreement follows the House bill; i.e., the rate of the research credit is reduced to 20 percent.

c. Research definition

The conference agreement generally follows the approach of the House bill and the Senate amendment, with statutory provisions as to the definition of qualified research for purposes of the credit, as follows.

In general

As under present law, the conference agreement limits research expenditures eligible for the incremental credit to "research or experimental expenditures" eligible for expensing under section 174. Thus, for example, the credit is not available for (1) expenditures other than "research and development costs in the experimental or laboratory sense," (2) expenditures "such as those for the ordinary testing or inspection of materials or products for quality control or those for efficiency surveys, management studies, consumer surveys, advertising, or promotions," (8) costs of acquiring another person's patent, model, production, or process, or (4) research expenditures incurred in connection with literary, historical, or similar projects (Treas. Reg. sec. 1.174-2(a)).[2] The term research includes basic research.

【Footnote ¶ 3872 continued】

(2) Section 174 also excludes from eligibility for expensing (1) expenditures for the acquisition or improvement of depreciable property, or land, to be used in connection with research, and (2) expenditures to ascertain the existence, location, extent, or quality of mineral deposits, including oil and gas.

Under the conference agreement, research satisfying the section 174 expensing definition is eligible for the credit only if the research is undertaken for the purpose of discovering information (a) that is technological in nature, and also (b) the application of which is intended to be useful in the development of a new or improved business component of the taxpayer. In addition, such research is eligible for the credit only if substantially all of the activities of the research constitute elements of a process of experimentation for a functional purpose. The conference agreement also expressly sets forth exclusions from eligibility for the credit for certain research activities that might otherwise qualify and for certain nonresearch activities.

Technological nature

The determination of whether the research is undertaken for the purpose of discovering information that is technological in nature depends on whether the process of experimentation utilized in the research fundamentally relies on principles of the physical or biological sciences, engineering, or computer science[3]—in which case the information is deemed technological in nature—or on other principles, such as those of economics—in which case the information is not to be treated as technological in nature. For example, information relating to financial services or similar products (such as new types of variable annuities or legal forms) or advertising does not qualify as technological in nature.

Process of experimentation

The term process of experimentation means a process involving the evaluation of more than one alternative designed to achieve a result where the means of achieving that result is uncertain at the outset. This may involve developing one or more hypotheses, testing and analyzing those hypotheses (through, for example, modeling or simulation), and refining or discarding the hypotheses as part of a sequential design process to develop the overall component.

Thus, for example, costs of developing a new or improved business component are not eligible for the credit if the method of reaching the desired objective (the new or improved product characteristics) is readily discernible and applicable as of the beginning of the research activities, so that true experimentation in the scientific or laboratory sense would not have to be undertaken to develop, test, and choose among viable alternatives. On the other hand, costs of experiments undertaken by chemists or physicians in developing and testing a new drug are eligible for the credit because the researchers are engaged in scientific experimentation. Similarly, engineers who design a new computer system, or who design improved or new integrated circuits for use in computer or other electronic products, are engaged in qualified research because the design of those items is uncertain at the outset and can only be determined through a process of experimentation relating to specific design hypotheses and decisions as described above.

Functional purposes

Under the conference agreement, research is treated as conducted for a functional purpose only if it relates to a new or improved function, performance, reliability, or quality. (Activities undertaken to assure achievement of the intended function, performance, etc. of the business component after the beginning of commercial production of the component do not constitute qualified experimentation.) The conference agreement also provides that research relating to style, taste, cosmetic, or seasonal design factors is not treated as conducted for a functional purpose and hence is not eligible for the credit.

Application of tests

The term business component means a product, process, computer software, technique, formula, or invention that is to be held for sale, lease, or license, or is to be used by the taxpayer in a trade or business of a taxpayer. If the requirements described above are not met with respect to a product, etc. but are met with respect to one or more elements thereof, the term business component means the most significant set of elements of such product, etc. with respect to which all requirements are met.

Thus, the requirements are applied first at the level of the entire product, etc. to be offered for sale, etc. by the taxpayer. If all aspects of such requirements are not met at that level, the test applies at the most significant subset of elements of the product, etc. This "shrinking back" of the product is to continue until either a subset of elements of the product that satisfies the requirements is reached, or the most basic element of the product is reached and such element fails to satisfy the test. Treasury regulations may prescribe rules for applying these rules where a research activity relates to more than one business component.

A plant process, machinery, or technique for commercial production of a business component is treated as a different component than the product being produced. Thus, research relating to the development of a new or improved production process is not eligible for the credit unless the definition of qualified research is met separately with respect to such production process research, without taking into account research relating to the development of the product.

Internal-use computer software

Under a specific rule in the conference agreement, research with respect to computer software that is developed by or for the benefit of the taxpayer primarily for the taxpayer's own internal use is eligible for the credit only if the software is used in (1) qualified research (other than the develop-

---

[Footnote ¶ 3872 continued]

(3) Research does not rely on the principles of computer science merely because a computer is employed. Research may be treated as undertaken to discover information that is technological in nature, however, if the research is intended to expand or refine existing principles of computer science.

ment of the internal-use software itself) undertaken by the taxpayer, or (2) a production process that meets the requirements for the credit (e.g., where the taxpayer is developing robotics and software for the robotics for use in operating a manufacturing process, and the taxpayer's research costs of developing the robotics are eligible for the credit). Any other research activities with respect to internal-use software are ineligible for the credit except to the extent provided in Treasury regulations. Accordingly, the costs of developing software are not eligible for the credit where the software is used internally, for example, in general and administrative functions (such as payroll, bookkeeping, or personnel management) or in providing non-computer services (such as accounting, consulting, or banking services), except to the extent permitted by Treasury regulations.

The conferees intend that these regulations will make the costs of new or improved internal-use software eligible for the credit only if the taxpayer can establish, in addition to satisfying the general requirements for credit eligibility, (1) that the software is innovative (as where the software results in a reduction in cost, or improvement in speed, that is substantial and economically significant); (2) that the software development involves significant economic risk (as where the taxpayer commits substantial resources to the development and also there is substantial uncertainty, because of technical risk, that such resources would be recovered within a reasonable period); and (3) that the software is not commercially available for use by the taxpayer (as where the software cannot be purchased, leased, or licensed and used for the intended purpose without modifications that would satisfy the first two requirements just stated). The conferees intend that these regulations are to apply as of the effective date of the new specific rule relating to internal-use software; i.e., internal-use computer software costs that qualify under the three-part test set forth in this paragraph are eligible for the research credit even if incurred prior to issuance of such final regulations.

The specific rule in the conference agreement relating to internal-use computer software is not intended to apply to the development costs of a new or improved package of software and hardware developed together by the taxpayer as a single product, of which the software is an integral part, that is used directly by the taxpayer in providing technological services in its trade or business to customers. For example, the specific rule would not apply where a taxpayer develops

together a new or improved high technology medical or industrial instrument containing software that processes and displays data received by the instrument, or where a telecommunications company develops a package of new or improved switching equipment plus software to operate the switches. In these cases, eligibility for the incremental research tax credit is to be determined by examining the combined hardware-software product as a single product, and thus the specific rule applicable to internal-use computer software would not apply to the combined hardware-software product.

In the case of computer software costs incurred in taxable years before the effective date for the new specific rule, the eligibility of such costs for the research credit is to be determined in the same manner as the eligibility of hardware product costs. The conferees expect and have been assured by the Treasury Department that guidance to this effect is to be promulgated on an expedited basis.

Excluded activities

The conference agreement specifies that expenditures incurred in certain research, research-related, or nonresearch activities are excluded from eligibility for the credit, without reference to the requirements described above relating to technological information, process of experimentation, and functional purposes.

Post-research activities.—The conference agreement provides that activities with respect to a business component after the beginning of commercial production of the component cannot qualify as qualified research. Thus, no expenditures relating to a business component are eligible for the credit after the component has been developed to the point where it either meets the basic functional and economic requirements of the taxpayer for such component or is ready for commercial sale or use.[4] For example, the credit is not available for such expenditures as the costs of preproduction planning for a finished business component, "tooling-up" for production, trial production runs, "trouble-shooting" involving detecting faults in production equipment or processes, accumulation of data relating to production processes, and the cost of "debugging" product flaws.

By way of further illustration, the credit is not available for costs of additional clinical testing of a pharmaceutical product after the product is made commercially available to the general public. However, the clinical testing in the United States of a product prior to production for sale in this country, or

---

[Footnote ¶ 3872 continued]

(4) The exclusion from credit-eligibility for activities with respect to a business component after the beginning of commercial production of the component does not preclude the costs of significant improvements in an existing product from eligibility for the credit. Thus, for example, the expenses of an automobile manufacturer is developing, through a process of experimentation, a significantly more efficient and reliable diesel fuel injector are eligible for the incremental research tax credit even though the research expenses are incurred during or after production by the manufacturer of automobile engines containing the existing (unimproved) diesel fuel injector. However, the costs of any activities of the automobile manufacturer with respect to the improved diesel fuel injector after the beginning of commercial production of the improved diesel fuel injector would not be eligible for the research credit.

clinical testing seeking to establish new functional uses, characteristics, indications, combinations, dosages, or delivery forms as improvements to an existing product, is eligible for the credit. Thus, research (e.g., body chemistry research) undertaken on a product approved for one specified indication to determine its effectiveness and safety for other potential indications is eligible for the credit. Similarly, testing a drug currently used to treat hypertension for a new anti-cancer application, and testing an antibiotic in combination with a steroid to determine its therapeutic value as a potential new anti-inflammatory drug, would be eligible for the credit.

Adaptation.—The conference agreement provides that adaptation of an existing business component to a particular requirement or customer's need is not eligible for the credit. Thus, for example, the costs of modifying an existing computer software item for a particular customer are not eligible for the credit. However, the mere fact that an item is intended for a specific customer does not disqualify otherwise qualified research costs of the item (assuming that the research is not funded by the customer).

Surveys, studies, etc..—The conference agreement provides that the credit is not available for the costs of efficiency surveys, activities (including studies) related to management functions or techniques, market research, market testing and development (including advertising or promotions), routine data collections, or routine or ordinary testing or inspection of materials or business items for quality control. Management functions and techniques include such items as preparation of financial data and analysis, development of employee training programs and management organization plans, and management-based changes in production processes (such as rearranging work stations on an assembly line).

Duplication.—The conference agreement provides that the credit does not apply to research related to the reproduction of an existing business component (in whole or in part) of another person from a physical examination of the component itself or from plans, blueprints, detailed specifications, or publicly available information with respect to such component. While such "reverse engineering" activities thus are not eligible for the credit, the exclusion for duplication does not apply merely because the taxpayer examines a competitor's product in developing a different component through a process of otherwise qualified experimentation requiring the testing of viable alternatives and based on the knowledge gained from such tests.

Additional exclusions

As under present law, the conference agreement excludes from eligibility for the credit expenditures for research (1) that is conducted outside the United States; (2) in the social sciences (including economics, business management, and behavioral sciences), arts, or humanities; or (3) to the extent

funded by any person (or governmental entity) other than the taxpayer, whether by grant, contract, or otherwise.

Effect on section 174 definition

No inference is intended from the rules in the conference agreement defining research for purposes of the incremental credit as to the scope of the term "research or experimental" for purposes of the section 174 expensing deduction.

d. Qualified expenditures

*   *   *   *   *   *

*   *   *   *   *   *

[House Explanation]

*   *   *   *   *   *

Eligibility of rental costs.—The bill generally repeals the present-law provision treating amounts paid for the right to use personal property in qualified research as eligible for the credit, but continues credit eligibility for amounts paid by the taxpayer to another person for the use of computer time in the conduct of qualified research. The latter provision is intended to benefit smaller businesses which cannot afford to purchase or lease their own computers for research purposes, and hence is intended to apply where the taxpayer is not the principal user of the computer. Consistently with the present-law limitations on credit-eligibility of rental costs, computer-use payments are not eligible for the credit to the extent that the taxpayer (or a person with which the taxpayer must aggregate expenditures in computing the credit) receives or accrues any amount from any other person for computer use.

In computing the research credit for a taxable year beginning after 1985 (when rental costs will not be eligible for the credit), a taxpayer may exclude from the base-period amount with respect to such year any rental costs, etc. (other than for computer-use costs of a type remaining eligible for the credit in post-1985 years) that were allowable as qualified research expenses under section 30(b)(2)(A)(iii) (as then in effect) in a base-period year.

*   *   *   *   *   *

[Conference Report]

*   *   *   *   *   *

The conference agreement follows the House bill.

e. University basic research credit

*   *   *   *   *   *

[House Explanation]
In general

Under present law, research expenditures entering into the computation of the incremental research credit include 65 percent of a corporation's expenditures (including grants or contributions) pursuant to a written research agreement for basic research to be performed by universities or certain scientific research organizations. Under the bill, a 20-percent tax credit applies to the *excess* of

(1) 100 percent of corporate cash expenditures for university basic research *over* (2) the sum of (a) the greater of two fixed research floors plus (b) an amount reflecting any decrease in nonresearch giving to universities by the corporation as compared to such giving during a fixed base period, as adjusted for inflation.[2b]

Qualifying expenditures

For purposes of credit, qualifying basic research expenditures are cash expenditures paid pursuant to a written agreement between the taxpayer corporation[3b] and a university or certain other qualified organizations for basic research to be performed by the qualified organization (or by universities receiving funds through the initial recipient qualified organizations). Such corporate expenditures for university basic research are deemed to satisfy the trade or business test for the research credit, whether or not the basic research is in the same field as an existing trade or business of the corporation.

Under the bill, qualifying expenditures include both grants or contributions by the corporation that constitute charitable contributions under section 170, and also payments for contract research to be performed by the qualified organization on behalf of the corporation. Such expenditures are not eligible for a credit unless and until actually paid by the corporation to a qualified organization. Thus, an accrual-basis corporation may not claim the credit for amounts incurred, but not actually paid, for university basic research.

Under the bill, only cash payments may qualify as a basic research payment. No amount (basis or value) on account of contributions or transfers of property is eligible for either the incremental credit or the basic research credit, whether or not such property constitutes scientific equipment eligible for an augmented charitable deduction under section 170(e)(4).

As under present law, the term "basic research" is defined in the bill as any original investigation for the advancement of scientific knowledge not having a specific commercial objective, other than basic research in the social sciences, arts, or humanities or basic research conducted outside the United States.

Qualified organizations

To be eligible for a credit, the corporate expenditures must be for basic research to be conducted by a qualified organization. For this purpose, the term qualified organization generally includes colleges or universities, tax-exempt scientific research organizations, and certain tax-exempt conduit or grant organizations.

The first category of qualified organizations consists of educational institutions that both are described in section 170(b)(1)(A)(ii) and constitute institutions of higher education within the meaning of section 8804(f). The second category consists of tax-exempt organizations that (1) are organized and operated primarily to conduct scientific research, (2) are described in section 501(c)(3) (relating to exclusively charitable, educational, scientific, etc., organizations), and (3) are not private foundations. Also, certain tax-exempt grant funds that qualify under present law continue to qualify under the bill.

In addition, the bill treats as qualified any tax-exempt organization that is organized and operated primarily to promote scientific research by colleges or universities pursuant to written research agreements, that expends on a current basis substantially all its funds (or all the basic research payments received by it) through grants and contracts for basic research by colleges and universities, and that is either (a) described in section 501(c)(3) and is not a private foundation or (b) described in section 501(c)(6) (trade associations).

Computation rules for revised basic research credit

The university basic research credit applies to the *excess* of (1) 100 percent of corporate cash expenditures for basic research *over* (2) the sum of the minimum basic research amount plus the maintenance-of-effort amount.

The minimum basic research amount is the *greater* of two fixed floors—

(a) the average of all credit-eligible basic research expenditures under Code section 30(e)(1) (as in effect during the base period) for each of the three taxable years immediately preceding the taxable year beginning after December 31, 1983; *or*

(b) one percent of the average of the sum of all in-house research expenses, contract research expenses, and credit-eligible basic research expenditures under Code section 30(e)(1) (as in effect during the base period) for each of the three taxable years immediately preceding the taxable year beginning after December 31, 1983.

In the case of a corporation that was not in existence for at least one full year of the three taxable years in the fixed base period, the bill provides that the minimum basic research amount for the base period shall not be less than 50 percent of the basic research payments for the current taxable year. If the corporation was in existence for one or two of the base-period years, the fixed floor is to be computed with respect to such year or years.

[Footnote ¶ 3872 continued]

(2b) The bill provides a single research credit, consisting of a 20-percent incremental component and a 20-percent university basic research component. For convenience, this report generally refers to these components as the incremental research credit and the university basic research credit.

(3b) For this purpose, the term corporation does not include S corporations (sec. 1361(a)), personal holding companies (sec. 542), or service organizations (sec. 414(m)(3)).

The maintenance-of-effort amount is the *excess* of (1) the average of the nondesignated university donations paid or incurred by the taxpayer during the three taxable years immediately preceding the taxable year beginning after December 31, 1983, as adjusted under the bill to reflect inflation, *over* the amount of nondesignated university donations paid by the taxpayer in the taxable year. The term "nondesignated university donation" means all amounts paid by the taxpayer to all colleges or universities for which a charitable deduction was allowable and that were not taken into account in computing the research credit.

The amount of credit-eligible basic research expenditures to which the new credit applies does not enter into the computation of the incremental credit. The remaining amount of credit-eligible basic research expenditures—i.e., the amount to which the new credit does not apply—enters into the incremental credit computation (and in subsequent years enters into the base period amounts for purposes of computing the incremental credit).

*   *   *   *   *   *

[Conference Report]

*   *   *   *   *   *

The conference agreement is the same as the House bill and the Senate amendment, except that the university basic research credit provisions are effective for taxable years beginning after December 31, 1986.

f. Credit use limitation

*   *   *   *   *   *

*   *   *   *   *   *

The bill makes the research credit subject to the general business credit limitation, as amended by the bill.

*   *   *   *   *   *

[Conference Report]

*   *   *   *   *   *

g. Effective date.—The extension of the credit is effective for taxable years ending after December 31, 1985. The credit will not apply to amounts paid or incurred after December 31, 1988. The modifications to the credit made by the conference agreement are effective for taxable years beginning after December 31, 1985,[5] except that the modifications relating to the university basic research credit are effective for taxable years beginning after December 31, 1986.

* * * **Augmented charitable deduction for certain donations of scientific equipment**

Present Law.—Under a special rule, corporations are allowed an augmented charitable deduction for donations of newly manufactured scientific equipment to a college or university for research use in the physical or biological sciences (sec. 170(e)(4)).

House Bill.—The House bill expands the category of eligible donees under the special rule in section 170(e)(4) to include certain tax-exempt scientific research organizations, effective for taxable years beginning after December 31, 1985.

Conference Agreement.—The conference agreement follows the House bill.

[¶ 3873]   SECTION 232. EXTENSION OF CREDIT FOR CLINICAL TESTING EXPENSES FOR CERTAIN DRUGS

(Sec. 28 of the Code)

[Conference Report]

*   *   *   *   *   *

Present Law.—A 50-percent tax credit is allowed for expenditures incurred in clinical testing of certain drugs for rare diseases or conditions (sec. 28). Under present law, the credit will not apply to amounts paid or incurred after December 31, 1987.

Conference Agreement.—The conference agreement extends the orphan drug credit for three additional years (i.e., through December 31, 1990).

[¶ 3874]   SECTION 241. REPEAL OF 5-YEAR AMORTIZATION OF TRADEMARK AND TRADE NAME EXPENDITURES

(Sec. 177 of the Code)

[Senate Explanation]

Explanation of provision.—The election is repealed. Trademark and trade name expenditures will, therefore, be capitalized and generally recovered on disposition of the asset.

Effective Date.—The repeal is effective for expenditures paid or incurred after December 31, 1986. However, present law will continue to apply to expenditures incurred (1) pursuant to a written contact that was binding as of March 1, 1986; or (2) with respect to development, protection, expansion, registration or defense of trademarks or trade names commenced as of March 1, 1986,

---

[Footnote ¶ 3872 continued]

(5) In computing the research credit for taxable years beginning after December 31, 1985, base-period expenditures for taxable years beginning before January 1, 1986 are to be determined under the credit definition of qualified research that was applicable in such base-period years and are not to be redetermined under the definition of qualified research in the conference agreement.

if the lesser of $1 million or 5 percent of the cost has been incurred or committed by that date; provided in each case the trademark or trade name is placed in service before January 1, 1988.

[¶ 3875] SECTION 242. REPEAL OF AMORTIZATION OF RAILROAD GRADING AND TUNNEL BORES

(Sec. 185 of the Code.)

[House Explanation]

* * * * * *

Present Law.—Domestic railroad common carriers may elect to amortize the cost of qualified railroad grading and tunnel bores over a 50-year period. Qualified railroad grading and tunnel bores include all land improvements (including tunneling) necessary to provide, construct, reconstruct, alter, protect, improve, replace, or restore a roadbed or right-of-way for railroad track.

* * * * * *

Explanation of Provision.—The election is repealed. Expenditures for railroad grading and tunnel bores will, therefore, be capitalized and generally recovered on disposition of the asset.

* * * * * * *

[Conference Report]

* * * * * *

Conference Agreement.—The conference agreement follows the House bill with respect to the election. No amortization or depreciation deduction for railroad grading and tunnel bores will be allowed.

[Effective date.—] The repeal of the election generally applies to expenses paid or incurred on or after January 1, 1987. However, present law continues to apply to expenditures incurred: (1) pursuant to a written contract that was binding as of March 1, 1986; or (2) with respect to construction, reconstruction, alteration, improvement, replacement or restoration commenced as of March 1, 1986, if the lesser of $1 million or 5 percent of cost has been incurred or committed by that date, provided in each case the improvements are placed in service before January 1, 1988.

* * * * * * * * * *

[¶ 3876] SECTION 243. DEDUCTION FOR BUS AND FREIGHT FORWARDER OPERATING AUTHORITY

[Senate Explanation]

* * * * * *

Explanation of provision.—The bill allows an ordinary deduction ratably over a 60-month period for taxpayers who held one or more bus operating authorities on November 19, 1982 (the date of enactment of the Bus Regulatory Reform Act of 1982). The amount of the deduction is the aggregate adjusted bases of all bus operating authorities that were held by the taxpayer on November 19, 1982, or acquired after that date under a contract that was binding on that date.

The 60-month period begins with the later of November 1, 1982, or, at the taxpayer's election, the first month of the taxpayer's first taxable year beginning after that date. The bill requires that adjustments be made to the bases of authorities to reflect amounts allowable as deductions under the bill.

Under regulations to be prescribed by the Treasury, a taxpayer (whether corporate or noncorporate) holding an eligible bus operating authority would be able to elect to allocate to the authority a portion of the cost to the taxpayer of stock in an acquired corporation (unless an election under section 338 is in effect). The election would be available if the bus operating authority was held (directly or indirectly) by the taxpayer at the time its stock was acquired. In such a case, a portion of the stock basis would be allocated to the authority only if the corporate or noncorporate taxpayer would have been able to make such an allocation had the authority been distributed in a liquidation to which prior-law section 334(b)(2) applied. The election would be available only if the stock was acquired on or before November 19, 1982 (or pursuant to a binding contract in effect on such date).

Effective Date.—The provision is effective retroactively for taxable years ending after November 18, 1982. The bill extends the period of limitations for filing claims for refund or credit of any overpayment of tax resulting from this provision, if such claim is prevented on or before the date that is one year after the date of enactment of the bill. In such a case, a claim for refund or credit may be made or allowed if filed on or before the date that is six months after such date.

* * * * * *

[Conference Report]

* * * * * *

Conference Agreement.—The conference agreement follows the Senate amendment. In addition, it provides a similar rule for freight forwarders, contingent on deregulation.

[The following colloquy relating to Act Sec. 243 is drawn from the Congressional Record.

The colloquy occurred on the day the Conference bill was considered by the House. Ed.]

[House Floor Explanation]

I have discussed with Congresswoman Kennelly several issues relating to the effect of specific provisions in this bill regarding freight forwarder operating authorities. We have reached a common understanding regarding the following specific issues:

Section 243(b) of the bill amends section 266 of the Economic Recovery Tax Act of 1981 to provide for a ratable deduction over a 60-month period with respect to freight forwarding operating authorities. Under section 243(b)(2) of the bill, the 60-month period commences as early as the so called deregulation month, which is defined in section 243(b)(3) of the bill to mean the month in which the Secretary of the Treasury or his delegate determines that a Federal law has been enacted which deregulates the freight forwarding industry.

It is intended that the deregulation month be that month determined by the Secretary of the Treasury or his delegate to be the month in which a Federal law has been enacted deregulating the freight forwarding industry. For example, if a Federal law deregulating the freight forwarding industry is enacted in October 1986 and the Secretary of the Treasury or his delegate determines in January 1987 that such deregulation has occurred, October 1986 should be the deregulation month.

In addition, in applying the provisions of section 266 of the Economic Recovery Tax Act of 1981, as amended by section 243 of the bill, with respect to freight forwarding operating authorities, a removal or modification of restrictions on the geographical scope of the freight forwarding operating authority, after acquisition of such authority or stock of a corporation holding such authority, should not be taken into account for purposes of applying these provisions. Congressional Record, p. H 8361-8362, 9-25-86.

The following colloquy relating to Act Sec. 243 is drawn from the Congressional Record. The colloquy occurred on the day the bill was considered by the Senate. Ed.]

[Senate Floor Explanation]

Freight Forwarder Operating Authorities

Mrs. KASSEBAUM. Section 243(b) of the bill amends section 266 of the Economic Recovery Tax Act of 1981 to provide for a ratable deduction over a 60-month period with respect to freight forwarding operating authorities. Under section 243(b)(2) of the bill, the 60-month period commences as early as the so-called deregulation month, which is defined in section 243(b)(3) of the bill to mean the month in which the Secretary of the Treasury or his delegate determines that a Federal law has been enacted which deregulates the freight forwarding industry.

Is it intended that the "deregulation month" be that month determined by the Secretary of the Treasury or his delegate to be the month in which a Federal law has been enacted deregulating the freight forwarding industry? For example, if a Federal law deregulating the freight forwarding industry is enacted in October 1986 and the Secretary of the Treasury or his delegate determines in January 1987 that such deregulation has occurred, will October 1986 be the "deregulation month"?

Mr. PACKWOOD. Yes.

Mrs. KASSEBAUM. Section 266(c) of the Economic Recovery Tax Act of 1981 provides for an elective adjustment to the basis of motor carrier operating authorities where stock of a corporation holding such authority is acquired. Will that election, under the bill, be available to adjust the basis of freight forwarder operating authorities where stock of a corporation holding, directly or indirectly, such authority is acquired?

MR. PACKWOOD. Yes. Congressional Record, p. S 13952, 9-27-86.

[¶ 3877] SECTION 244. TREATMENT OF EXPENDITURES FOR REMOVAL OF ARCHITECTURAL BARRIERS TO THE HANDICAPPED AND ELDERLY MADE PERMANENT

(Sec. 190(d)(2) of the Code)

[Senate Explanation]

*   *   *   *   *   *

Present Law.—In general, present law allows electing taxpayers to deduct currently up to $35,000 of capital expenditures for the removal of architectural and transportation barriers to the handicapped and elderly (sec. 190). This rule applies to expenses paid or incurred in order to make more accessible to and usable by the handicapped and elderly any facility or public transportation vehicle owned or leased by the taxpayer for use in a trade or business.

This election is not available for expenses incurred in taxable years beginning after December 31, 1985.

*   *   *   *   *   *

Explanation of Provision.—The bill reinstates on a permanent basis, effective for expenses incurred in taxable years beginning after 1985, the present-law provision that allows the expensing of up to $35,000 of costs incurred in the removal of architectural and transportation barriers to the handicapped and elderly.

Effective date.—The provision is effective on the date of enactment.

[¶ 3878] SECTION 251. MODIFICATION OF INVESTMENT TAX CREDIT FOR REHABILITATION EXPENDITURES

(Secs. 46(b), 48(g), and 48(q) of the Code)

[Senate Explanation]

* * * * * *

Two-tier credit.—The committee bill replaces the existing three-tier rehabilitation credit with a two-tier credit for qualified rehabilitation expenditures. The credit percentage is 20 percent for rehabilitations of certified historic structures and 10 percent for rehabilitations of buildings (other than certified historic structures) originally placed in service before 1986.

Retention of certain rules.—As under present law, the 10-percent credit for the rehabilitation of buildings that are not certified historic structures is limited to nonresidential buildings, but the 20-percent credit for rehabilitation of historic buildings is available for both residential and nonresidential buildings.

The present law provisions that determine whether rehabilitation expenditures qualify for the credit were generally retained in the bill. In general, no changes were made regarding the substantial rehabilitation test, the specific types of expenditures that do not qualify for the credit, the provisions applicable to certified historic structures and tax-exempt use property, or the recapture rules. No expenditure would be eligible for credit unless the taxpayer elects to recover the costs of the rehabilitation using the straight-line method of depreciation. Further, expenditures incurred by a lessee would not qualify for the credit unless the remaining lease term, on the date the rehabilitation is completed, is at least as long as the recovery period under ACRS (generally either 27.5 for residential real property or 31.5 for nonresidential real property).

External-walls requirement.—The external-walls requirement was significantly modified by the bill. The existing provision that requires 75 percent of the existing external walls to be retained in place as external walls was deleted and replaced by the alternative test provided in present law that requires the retention in place of (1) at least 75 percent of the existing external walls (including at least 50 percent as external walls as well as (2) at least 75 percent of the building's internal structural framework. Thus, unlike the situation that can occur under present law, a building that is completely gutted cannot qualify for the rehabilitation credit under the committee bill. In general the building's internal structural framework includes all load-bearing internal walls and any other internal structural supports, including the columns, girders, beams, trusses, spandrels, and all other members that are essential to the stability of the building.

Because the committee believes that the Secretary of the Interior's Standards for Rehabilitation ensure that certified historic structures are properly rehabilitated, the external-walls requirement for such buildings was deleted by the bill in order to provide the Secretary of the Interior with appropriate flexibility. The committee intends, however, that rehabilitations eligible for the 28-percent credit should continue to be true rehabilitations and not substantially new construction. The committee expects, therefore, that the Secretary of the Interior will continue generally to deny certification to rehabilitations during which less than 75 percent of the external walls are not retained in place.

Basis reduction.—The bill deletes the limited exception in current law that requires a basis reduction for only 50 percent of the credit in the case of certified historic structures. Thus, a full basis adjustment is required for both the ten-percent and 20-percent rehabilitation credits.

Effective date.—The modifications to the rehabilitation credit are generally applicable to property placed in service after December 31, 1986.

A general transitional rule provides that the modifications to the rehabilitation credit (other than certain reductions in the credit percentage—see below) will not apply to property placed in service before January 1, 1994, if the property is placed in service (as rehabilitation property) as part of either a rehabilitation completed pursuant to a written contract that was binding (under applicable state law) on March 1, 1986. This rule also applies to a rehabilitation with respect to property (including any leasehold interest) that was acquired before March 2, 1986, or was acquired on or after such date pursuant to a written contract that was binding on March 1, 1986, if (1) the rehabilitation was completed pursuant to a written contract that was binding on March 1, 1986, parts 1 (if necessary) and 2 of the Historic Preservation Certification Application were filed with the Department of the Interior (or its designee) before March 2, 1986, or (2) the lessor of $1,000,000 or five percent of the cost of the rehabilitation (including only qualified rehabilitation expenditures) was incurred before March 2, 1986, or is required to be incurred pursuant to a written contract that was binding on March 1, 1986. Additional transitional rules are provided for specific projects.

If a taxpayer transfers his rights in property under rehabilitation or under a binding contract to another taxpayer, the modifications do not apply to the property in the hands of the transferee, as long as the property was not placed in service before the transfer by the transferor. For purposes of this rule, if by reason of sales or exchanges of interests in a partnership, there is a deemed termination and reconstitution of a partnership under section 708(b)(1)(B), the partner-

Act §251 ¶3878

ship is to be treated as having transferred its rights in the property under rehabilitation or the binding contract to the new partnership.

If property that qualifies under any of the foregoing transitional rules is placed in service after December 31, 1986, except in the case of certain projects, the applicable credit percentages are reduced from 25, 20, and 15 to 20, 18, and ten, respectively, and a full basis adjustment is required.

Property that qualifies for transitional relief under one of the rules described above is also excepted from the depreciation changes made by section 201 of the bill.

[The following colloquy relating to Act Sec. 251 is drawn from the Congressional Record. The colloquy occurred on the day the Conference bill was considered by the Senate. Ed.]

[Senate Floor Explanation]

Transition Projects Under the "General Transition Rule" Pertaining to Real Estate Rehabilitation Projects

Mr. McCONNELL. Will the Senator yield?

Mr. PACKWOOD. I would be delighted to yield to my good friend, the junior Senator from Kentucky.

Mr. McCONNELL. I thank the distinguished Senator from Oregon. Mr. President, on behalf of my distinguished colleague from Kentucky, Senator Ford, and myself, I would like to thank both the majority and minority managers of the tax reform bill for their fine work and leadership throughout this effort. One of my primary concerns about this bill is the lack of clarity with respect to certain general transitional rules pertaining to historic rehabilitation projects, as detailed in section 251 of the bill.

A number of questions have been raised as to those projects this provision was intended

to cover. I would ask the chairman if it is his understanding that the provision in question does in fact cover the below named projects.

The Bernheim Officentre Project.

The Old Louisville Trust Building—First National Bank, Kentucky Title Rehabilitation Project.

The Stewarts Building.

Mr. PACKWOOD. Yes; it is this Senator's understanding the projects in question are covered under section 251 of the bill, dealing with the general transitional rule pertaining to historic rehabilitation projects.

Mr. McCONNELL. I thank the chairman. This will eliminate the concerns of those whose projects have been determined by the Finance Committee to clearly meet the requirements for transition rules but did not receive line-item treatment in section 251 of the Tax Reform Act of 1986. Again, I thank the distinguished chairman.

Mr. FORD. I want to thank my colleague, the distinguished chairman of the Finance Committee, Senator Packwood, for clarifying this issue for us. While it appeared that these Kentucky projects would be covered by the general transition rule for the rehabilitation tax credit, I am pleased that we are able to clarify for the record and the legislative history of this bill the intention of the conferees to include them under the general transition rule. These three projects, the Old Louisville Trust Building—First National Bank/Kentucky Title, the Stewarts Rehabilitation Project, and the Bernheim Office Center, are all important projects to Louisville and the Commonwealth as a whole. I thank my colleagues for their assistance in this matter. Congressional Record, p. S13952, 9-27-86.

[¶ 3879] SECTION 252. LOW-INCOME HOUSING CREDIT

(Sec. 42 of the Code)

[Conference Report]

*   *   *   *   *   *

Senate Amendment

In general.—The Senate amendment provides a new tax credit that may be claimed by owners of residential rental projects providing low-income housing, in lieu of certain other tax incentives.

The credit may be claimed annually for a period of 10 years. The credit rate is set so that the annualized credit amounts have a present value of 60 percent or 30 percent of the basis attributable to qualifying low-income units, depending on the income of the tenants qualifying the unit for the credit.

For projects on which construction commences prior to 1988, the annual credit rate is 8 percent (80 percent over 10 years) for units occupied by individuals with incomes of 50 percent or less of area median (as adjusted for family size) and 4 percent (40 percent over 10 years) for a maximum of 30 percent of the units occupied by individuals with incomes of

between 50 percent and 70 percent of area median. For projects on which construction begins after 1987, Treasury is directed to adjust the credit rates to maintain the present values of the annualized credit amounts of 60 percent and 30 percent.

Newly constructed buildings and newly acquired existing structures that are substantially rehabilitated are eligible for the credit. Substantial rehabilitation is defined as rehabilitation expenditures made over a two-year period (or five-year period in the case of rehabilitation conducted subject to a comprehensive plan) of at least 22.5 percent of the acquisition cost of the project (other than the cost of land). The cost of rehabilitation and acquisition allocable to low-income units is eligible for the credit.

Comparable to the treatment of multifamily rental housing bonds in the Senate amendment, there is no volume limitation or "trade-in" requirement for low-income housing credits.

Definition of low-income housing.—Low-income housing eligible for the credit is defined as follows:

(1) At least 20 percent of the housing units in each project is occupied by individuals having incomes of less than 50 percent of the area median income;

(2) Income determinations are made with adjustments for family size;

(3) Qualification as a low-income tenant is determined on a continuing basis; and

(4) The gross rent paid by families in units qualifying for the credit may not exceed 30 percent of the applicable qualifying income for a family of its size.

Restriction on tax-exempt financing.—A project is not eligible for the credit if any part of the project is financed with obligations on which the interest is exempt from tax under Code section 103. This restriction applies as long as any of those obligations remain outstanding.

A limited exception is made for certain existing federally assisted projects on which tax-exempt bonds remain outstanding.

Federally assisted housing.—Unless otherwise specifically provided, projects receiving Federal grants, loans, or rental assistance are not eligible for the credit. (A Federal guarantee does not constitute Federal assistance that would preclude a project from credit eligibility.) Three exceptions are provided:

(1) An exception to the Federal assistance restriction is provided for new construction or substantial rehabilitation or properties receiving assistance under the Urban Development Block Grant program, the Community Development Block Grant program, and Housing Development or Rental Rehabilitation programs. Projects receiving assistance under these programs must exclude such assistance from the basis on which the low-income credit is allowable.

(2) A second exception is provided for new construction or substantial rehabilitation of properties receiving assistance under the HUD section 8 moderate rehabilitation program or the FmHA section 515 program. Projects receiving assistance under these programs, however, only are eligible for credits on units occupied by tenants with incomes of 50 percent or less of area median. Section 8 payments may not exceed certain specified amounts on all property eligible for the credit.

(3) A third exception to the Federal assistance restriction is provided for newly acquired existing property receiving assistance under HUD's section 8, section 221(d)(3) or, section 236 programs, or FmHA's section 515 program. Such property must have 50 percent or more of the units occupied by tenants with incomes of 50 percent or less of area median income.

All residential rental units in such projects are eligible to be included in the basis on which the credit is allowed. The credit rate is one-half the rate otherwise applicable to units occupied by tenants with incomes of 50 percent or less of area median income.

Generally, a project eligible for this exception may not be placed in service within 15 years of its having last been placed in service, and section 8 payments may not exceed certain specified amounts on property eligible for the credit.

Existing property receiving assistance under HUD section 8, section 221(d)(3), section 236, or FmHA section 515 and described in this exception is also excepted from the substantial rehabilitation requirement. (Generally, existing property (and the acquisition cost of existing property) only is eligible for the credit if substantial rehabilitation is performed after acquisition.)

At-risk limitation.—The amount of the credit is subject to an at-risk limitation similar to the investment tax credit at-risk rules in the case of nonrecourse refinancing.

An exception is provided for certain lenders related to the buyer of the low income housing property. Another exception is provided for financing (including seller financing) not in excess of 60 percent of the basis of the property that is lent by charitable and social welfare organizations whose exempt purpose includes fostering low income housing. The credit is recaptured if the financing provided by such organizations is not repaid with interest by the end of the 15-year credit compliance period (described below).

Compliance requirements.—Projects are required to comply continuously with the low-income occupancy requirement for at least 15 years.

Failure to meet the minimum low-income occupancy requirement during the 15-year period triggers a recapture of the credit. The credit is recaptured fully for violations during the first ten years, and recaptured partially for violations in years 11-15.

Failure to meet the low-income occupancy requirement upon which the maximum credit is based (while still satisfying the minimum low-income occupancy requirement) results in a reduction of the credit for the year of the violation.

Transferability.—Credits may be transferred to new purchasers of a project during the period for which the property is eligible to receive the credit, with the new purchaser "stepping into the shoes" of the seller, both as to credit percentage, basis, and liability for compliance and recapture.

Coordination with other provisions.—The credit is subject to the rules of the general business credit, including the maximum amount of income tax liability that may be reduced by general business tax credits in any year. Unused credits for any taxable year may be carried back to each of the three preceding taxable years and then carried forward to each of the 15 following taxable years.

For purposes of the rules in the amendment limiting passive loss deductions, the credit (but not losses from the project) is treated as arising from rental real estate activities in which the taxpayer actively participates, and is subject to the limitations imposed on tax credits from such activities.

The basis with respect to which credits are allowed is reduced to reflect any rehabilitation credit for which the project is eligible.

The basis of a project for purposes of depreciation is not reduced by the amount of low-income housing credits claimed.

Conference Agreement

The conference agreement generally follows the Senate amendment, with certain substantive modifications, including (1) changes in the credit amounts, (2) redefinition of qualifying expenditures with respect to which the credit may be claimed (including the allowance of tax-exempt bond financed expenditures and the elimination of the substantial rehabilitation requirement), (3) the provision of an alternative set-aside requirement (the percentage of low-income units and the qualifying income levels of low-income tenants), (4) the addition of a State volume limitation on the number of new credits issued annually, and (5) modifications to the recapture rules.

Credit amount.—The conference agreement provides two separate credit amounts: (1) a 70-percent present value credit for qualified new construction and rehabilitation expenditures that are not federally subsidized and (2) a 30-percent present value credit for other qualifying expenditures. Expenditures qualifying for the 30-percent present value credit consist of the cost of acquisition, certain rehabilitation expenditures incurred in connection with the acquisition of an existing building, and federally subsidized new construction or rehabilitation expenditures. A taxpayer's credit amount in any taxable year is computed by applying the appropriate credit percentage to the appropriate qualified basis amount in such year.

Credit percentage.—For buildings placed in service in 1987, the credit percentages are 9 percent annually over 10 years for the 70-percent present value credit, and 4 percent annually over 10 years for the 30-percent present value credit.

For buildings placed in service after 1987, these credit percentages are to be adjusted monthly by the Treasury to reflect the present values of 70 percent and 30 percent at the time the building is placed in service. The Treasury's monthly adjustments of the credit percentages are to be determined on a discounted after-tax basis, based on the average of the annual applicable Federal rates (AFR) for mid-term and long-term obligations for the month the building is placed in service. The after-tax interest rate is to be computed as the product of (1) the average AFR and (2) .72 (one minus the maximum individual statutory Federal income tax rate). The discounting formula assumes each credit is received on the last day of each year and that the present value is to be computed as of the

last day of the first year. In a project consisting of two or more buildings placed in service in different months, a separate credit percentage may apply to each building.

The credit percentage for rehabilitation expenditures not claimed in connection with the acquisition of an existing building is determined when rehabilitation is completed and the property is placed in service, but no later than the end of the 24-month period for which such expenditures are aggregated. These rehabilitation expenditures are treated as a separate new building for purposes of the credit. The determination of whether the rehabilitation expenditures are federally subsidized is made without regard to the source of financing for the construction or acquisition of the building to which the rehabilitation expenditures are made (also, see the discussion of qualified basis, below, for a description of federally subsidized expenditures).

Qualified basis.—The qualified basis amounts with respect to which the credit amount is computed are determined as the proportion of eligible basis in a qualified low-income building attributable to the low-income rental units. This proportion is the lesser of (1) the proportion of low-income units to all residential rental units or (2) the proportion of floor space of the low-income units to the floor space of all residential rental units. Generally, in these calculations, low-income units are those units presently occupied by qualifying tenants, whereas residential rental units are all units, whether or not presently occupied.

Eligible basis consists of (1) the cost of new construction, (2) the cost of rehabilitation, or (3) the cost of acquisition of existing buildings acquired through a purchase and the cost of rehabilitation, if any, to such buildings incurred before the close of the first taxable year of the credit period. Only the adjusted basis of the building may be included in eligible basis. The adjusted basis is determined by taking into account the adjustments described in section 1016 (other than paragraphs (2) and (3) of sec. 1016(a), relating to depreciation deductions), including, for example, the basis adjustment provided in section 48(g) for any rehabilitation credits allowed under section 38. The cost of land is not included in adjusted basis.

Generally, the eligible basis of a building is determined at the time the building is placed in service. For this purpose, rehabilitation expenditures are treated as placed in service at the close of the 24-month aggregation period. In the case of rehabilitation expenditures claimed in connection with the acquisition of a building, the capital expenditures incurred through the end of the first year of the credit period may be included in eligible basis.

Residential rental property for purposes of the low-income housing credit has the same meaning as residential rental property within Code section 103. Thus, residential rental property includes residential rental units, facilities for use by the tenants, and other facilities reasonably required by the project.

Costs of the residential rental units in a building which are not low-income units may be included in eligible basis only if such units are not above the average quality standard of the low-income units. Units are of comparable quality if the construction or acquisition costs are comparable and if such units are provided in a similar proportion for both the low-income and other tenants. Rehabilitation expenditures may not be included in eligible basis if such expenditures improve any unit in the building beyond comparability with the low-income units. Eligible basis may include the cost of amenities, including personal property, only if the included amenities are comparable to the cost of the amenities in the low-income units. Additionally, the allocable cost of tenant facilities, such as swimming pools, other recreational facilities, and parking areas, may be included provided there is no separate fee for the use of these facilities and they are made available on a comparable basis to all tenants in the project. (*See* generally, Treas. Reg. sec. 1.103-8(b)(4)(iii).)

Residential rental property may qualify for the credit even though a portion of the building in which the residential rental units are located is used for a commercial use. No portion of the cost of such nonresidential rental property may be included in eligible basis. The conferees intend that the costs of such a mixed-use facility may be allocated according to any reasonable method that properly reflects the proportionate benefit to be derived, directly or indirectly, by the nonresidential rental property and the residential rental units. (*See*, e.g., Prop. Treas. Reg. sec. 1.103-8(b)(4)(v).)

The qualified basis attributable to rehabilitation expenditures not claimed in connection with the acquisition of an existing building must equal at least $2,000 per low-income unit in order for rehabilitation expenditures to qualify for the credit. The $2,000 minimum is computed as an average based on all qualifying expenditures in the building, rather than on a unit-by-unit determination. Qualified basis is determined in the same fractional manner as for new construction or acquisition costs even if all rehabilitation expenditures are made only to low-income units. Rehabilitation expenditures may be included in eligible basis without a transfer of property. Rehabilitation expenditures may be aggregated only for rehabilitation expenditures incurred before the close of the two-year period beginning on the date rehabilitation is commenced by the taxpayer. Where rehabilitation is limited to a group of units, Treasury may provide regulations treating a group of units as a separate new building.

The cost of acquisition of an existing building may be included in eligible basis and any rehabilitation expenditures to such buildings incurred before the close of the first year of the credit period may also be included in eligible basis, without a minimum rehabilitation requirement. These costs may be included in eligible basis only if the building

or a substantial improvement (a capital expenditure of 25 percent or more of the adjusted basis of the building to which five-year rapid amortization was elected or to which ACRS applied (as in effect before the enactment of this Act)) to the building has not been previously placed in service within 10 years and if the building (or rehabilitated property within the building) is not subject to the 15-year compliance period. The Treasury Department may waive this 10-year requirement for any building substantially assisted, financed or operated under the HUD section 8, section 221(d)(3), or section 236 programs, or under the Farmers' Home Administration section 515 program in order to avert an assignment of the mortgage secured by property in the project to HUD or the Farmers Home Administration, to avert a claim against a Federal mortgage insurance fund, or other similar circumstances relating to financial distress of these properties as prescribed by the Treasury Department. A transfer of ownership of a building where the basis of the property in the hands of the new owner is determined in whole or in part by the adjusted basis of the previous owner, is considered not to have been newly placed in service for purposes of the 10-year requirement (also, see the discussion of transferability, below). Any other transfer will begin a new 10-year period.

Eligible basis may not include in any taxable year the amount of any Federal grant, regardless of whether such grants are included in gross income. A Federal grant includes any grant funded in whole or in part by the Federal government, to the extent funded with Federal funds. Examples of grants which may not be included in eligible basis include Community Development Block Grants, Urban Development Action Grants, Rental Rehabilitation Grants, and Housing Development Grants.

If any portion of the eligible basis attributable to new construction or the eligible basis attributable to rehabilitation expenditures is financed with Federal subsidies, the qualified basis is eligible only for the 30-percent present value credit, unless such Federal subsidies are excluded from eligible basis. A Federal subsidy is defined as any obligation the interest on which is exempt from tax under section 103 or a direct or indirect Federal loan, if the interest rate on such loan is less than the applicable Federal rate. A Federal loan under the Farmers' Home Administration section 515 program is an example of such a Federal subsidy, as is a reduced interest rate loan attributable in part to a Federal grant. The determination of whether rehabilitation expenditures are federally subsidized is made without regard to the source of financing for the construction or acquisition of the building to which the rehabilitation expenditures are made. For example, a Federal loan or tax-exempt bond financing that is continued or assumed upon purchase of existing housing is disregarded for purposes of the credit on rehabilitation expenditures.

The qualified basis for each building is determined on the last day of the first taxable year in which the building is placed in service or, if the taxpayer elects, on the last day of the following taxable year.

The Treasury Department may provide regulations for projects consisting of two or more buildings. Unless prescribed in regulations, the qualified basis of a project consisting of two or more buildings is determined separately for each building. Common facilities in such a project must be allocated in an appropriate manner to all buildings (whether existing or to be constructed) in the project.

The first year the credit is claimed, the allowable credit amount is determined using an averaging convention to reflect the number of months units comprising the qualified basis were occupied by low-income individuals during the year. For example, if half of the low-income units included in qualified basis were first occupied in October and the remaining half were occupied in December, a calendar year taxpayer would adjust the allowable first-year credit to reflect that these units were occupied on average only one-sixth of the year. To the extent there is such a reduction of the credit amount in the first year, an additional credit in the amount of such reduction is available in the eleventh taxable year. (This first-year adjustment does not affect the amount of qualified basis with respect to which the credit is claimed in subsequent years of the 10-year credit period.)

Additions to qualified basis.—The qualified basis of a building may be increased subsequent to the initial determination only by reason of an increase in the number of low-income units or in the floor space of the low-income units. Credits claimed on such additional qualified basis are determined using a credit percentage equal to two-thirds of the applicable credit percentage allowable for the initial qualified basis and must receive an allocation of credit authority as described below (see the discussion on the State low-income housing credit authority limitation). Unlike credits claimed on the initial qualified basis, credits claimed on additions to qualified basis are allowable annually for the remainder of the required 15-year compliance period, regardless of the year such additional qualified basis is determined. The additional basis is determined by reference to the original adjusted basis (before deductions for depreciation) of the property.

The credit amount on the additional qualified basis is adjusted in the first year such additions are made using an averaging convention to reflect the number of months units comprising the additional qualified basis were occupied by low-income individuals during the year. Any reduction of the credit amount in the first year may not be claimed in a later year. (This first-year adjustment does not affect the amount of additional qualified basis with respect to which the credit is claimed in subsequent years of the compliance period.)

Minimum set-aside requirement for low-income individuals.—Residential rental projects providing low-income housing qualify for the credit only if (1) 20 percent or more of the aggregate residential rental units in a project are occupied by individuals with incomes of 50 percent or less of area median income, as adjusted for family size, or (2) 40 percent or more of the aggregate residential rental units in a project are occupied by individuals with incomes of 60 percent or less of area median income, as adjusted for family size. [6a]

All units comprising the minimum set-aside in a project must be suitable for occupancy, used on a nontransient basis, and are subject to the limitation on gross rent (see the discussion of the gross rent limitation, below).

The owner must irrevocably elect the minimum set-aside requirement at the time the project is placed in service. The set-aside requirement must be met within 12 months of the date a building (or rehabilitated property) is placed in service, and complied with continuously throughout each year after first meeting the requirement for a period of 15 years beginning on the first day of the first taxable year in which the credit is claimed.

Special rules apply to projects consisting of multiple buildings placed in service on different dates. Unless prescribed by regulations, the initial building, within 12 months of being placed in service, must meet the set-aside requirement determined only by reference to those units in the building. When a second or subsequent building is placed in service, the project must meet the set-aside requirement with respect to the units in all buildings placed-in-service up to that time within 12 months of the date the second or subsequent building is placed in service and comply with this expanded requirement continuously after first meeting the requirements for a period of 15 years beginning on the later of (1) the first day of the taxable year in which the expanded requirement is met or (2) if a credit is claimed with respect to the building, the first day of the taxable year in which the credit period begins with such building. [7a] Subsequent buildings are subject to separate 15-year compliance periods. After the 15-year period has expired on an initial building, but while other buildings in the same project are still subject to the compliance period, the project must continue to meet the set-aside requirement determined by reference to all buildings in the project or, at the taxpayer's election, all buildings subject to the compliance period.

The determination of whether a tenant qualifies for purposes of the low-income set-aside is made on a continuing basis, both

---

[Footnote ¶ 3879]   (6a) This requirement is referred to as the "minimum set-aside" requirement.

(7a) Until the expanded requirement is met, the set-aside requirements determined by reference to all previously existing buildings must be continuously satisfied.

with regard to the tenant's income and the qualifying area income, rather than only on the date the tenant initially occupies the unit. An increase in a tenant's income may, therefore, result in a unit ceasing to qualify as occupied by a low-income person. However, a qualified low-income tenant is treated as continuing to be such notwithstanding *de minimis* increases in his or her income. Under this rule, a tenant qualifying when initially occupying a rental unit will be treated as continuing to have such an income provided his or her income does not increase to a level more than 40 percent in excess of the maximum qualifying income, adjusted for family size. If the tenant's income increases to a level more than 40 percent above the otherwise applicable ceiling (or if the tenant's family size decreases so that a lower maximum family income applies to the tenant), however, that tenant may no longer be counted in determining whether the project satisfies the set-aside requirement. (For a discussion of the rules for complying with the set-aside requirements, *see* the discussion of the compliance period and penalty for noncompliance, below.)

A special rule is provided for projects that elect to satisfy a stricter set-aside requirement and that significantly restrict the rents on the low-income units relative to the other residential units in the building. Projects qualify for this rule only if, as part of the general set-aside requirement, 15 percent or more of all low-income units are occupied by individuals having incomes of 40 percent (rather than 50 percent or 60 percent) or less of area median income, and the average rent charged to tenants in the residential rental units which are not low-income units is at least 300 percent of the average rent charged to low-income tenants for comparable units. Under this special rule, (a) a low-income tenant will continue to qualify as such, as long as the tenant's income does not exceed 170 percent of the qualifying income, and (b) if the project ceases to comply with the set-aside requirement because of increases in existing tenants' incomes, no penalties are imposed if each available low income unit is rented to tenants having incomes of 40 percent or loss of area median income, until the project is again in compliance.

As stated above, the conference agreement requires that adjustments for family size be made in determining the incomes used to qualify tenants as having low income. In general, these adjustments are the same as the adjustments presently made under section 8 of the United States Housing Act of 1937. Thus, for a project which qualifies by setting aside 20 percent of the units for tenants having incomes of 50 percent or less of area median income, a family of four generally will be treated as meeting this standard if the family has an income of 50 percent or less of the area median income; a family of three having an income of 45 percent or less generally will qualify; a family of two having an income of 40 percent

or less generally will qualify; and, a single individual having an income of 35 percent or less generally will qualify. The conferees are aware that, in certain cases, the use of section 8 guidelines may result in qualifying incomes below the amounts reflected by these percentages because of dollar ceilings that are applied under the section 8 program. Income limits may be adjusted by the Secretary for areas with unusually low family income or high housing costs relative to family income in a manner consistent with determinations of very low income families and area median gross income under section 8 to reflect the 50-percent and 60-percent income levels.

Vacant units, formerly occupied by low-income individuals, may continue to be treated as occupied by a qualified low-income individual for purposes of the set-aside requirement (as well as for determining qualified basis) provided reasonable attempts are made to rent the unit and no other units of comparable or smaller size in the project are rented to nonqualifying individuals (see the section "Compliance period and penalty for noncompliance," below).

In no case is a unit considered to be occupied by low-income individuals if all of the occupants of such unit are students (as determined under sec. 151(c)(4)), no one of whom is entitled to file a joint income tax return.

Gross rent limitation.—The gross rent paid by families in units included in qualified basis may not exceed 80 percent of the applicable qualifying income for a family of its size. Gross rent is to include the cost of any utilities, other than telephone. If any utilities are paid directly by the tenant, the maximum rent that may be paid by the tenant is to be reduced by a utility allowance prescribed by the Secretary, after taking into consideration the procedures under section 8 of the United States Housing Act of 1937.

The gross rent limitation applies only to payments made directly by the tenant. Any rental assistance payments made on behalf of the tenant, such as through section 8 of the United States Housing Act of 1937, are not included in gross rent.

Low-income unit.—A low-income unit includes any unit in a qualified low-income building if the individuals occupying such unit meet the income limitation elected for the project for purposes of the minimum set-aside requirement and if the unit meets the gross rent requirement, as well as all other requirements applicable to units satisfying the minimum set-aside requirement.

Qualified low-income housing projects and qualified low-income buildings.—A qualified low-income building is a building subject to the 15-year compliance period and which is part of a qualified low-income housing project.

A qualified low-income housing project is a project that meets the minimum set-aside requirement and other requirements with respect to the set-aside units at all times that buildings comprising the project are subject to the 15-year compliance period. A qualified low-income housing project includes a qualified low-income building containing residential rental units and other property that is functionally related and subordinate to the function of providing residential rental units. A project may include multiple buildings having similarly constructed housing units, provided the buildings are located on the same tract of land, are owned by the same person for Federal income tax purposes, and are financed pursuant to a common plan of financing.

Residential rental units must be for use by the general public and all of the units in a project must be used on a nontransient basis. Residential rental units are not for use by the general public, for example, if the units are provided only for members of a social organization or provided by an employer for its employees. Generally, a unit is considered to be used on a nontransient basis if the initial lease term is six months or greater. Additionally, no hospital, nursing home, sanitarium, lifecare facility, retirement home, or trailer park may be a qualified low-income project.

Unlike the requirements for units in projects financed with tax-exempt bonds, certain single room occupancy housing used on a nontransient basis may qualify for the credit, even though such housing may provide eating, cooking, and sanitation facilities on a shared basis. An example of housing that may qualify for the credit is a residential hotel used on a nontransient basis that is available to all members of the public. The residential units in such a building may share bathrooms and have a common dining area.

Compliance period and penalty for noncompliance.—Qualified residential rental projects must remain as rental property and must satisfy the minimum set-aside requirement, described above, throughout a prescribed compliance period. Low-income units comprising the qualified basis on which additional credits are based are required to comply continuously with all requirements in the same manner as units satisfying the minimum set-aside requirements.

Units in addition to those meeting the minimum set-aside requirement on which a credit is allowable also must continuously comply with the income requirement.

The conference agreement defines the compliance period for any building as the period beginning on the first day of the first taxable year of the credit period of such building and ending 15 years from such date. The minimum set-aside requirement must be met, in all cases, within 1 year of the date the building (or rehabilitated property) is placed in service.

Within 90 days of the end of the first taxable year for which the credit is claimed and for each taxable year thereafter during the compliance period, the taxpayer must certify to the Secretary that the project has continuously complied throughout the year with the set-aside requirement and report the dollar amount of the qualified basis of the building and the maximum applicable percentage and qualified basis permitted to be taken into account by the housing credit agency. Additionally, the certification must include the date (including the taxable year) in which the building was placed in service and any other information required by Treasury.

The penalty for any building subject to the 15-year compliance period failing to remain part of a qualified low-income project (due, for example, to noncompliance with the minimum set-aside requirement or the gross rent requirement or other requirements with respect to the units comprising the set-aside) is recapture of the accelerated portion of the credit for all prior years.

Generally, any change in ownership of a building subject to the compliance period is also a recapture event. An exception is provided if the seller posts a bond to the Secretary in an amount satisfactory to the Treasury, and provided it can reasonably be expected that such building will continue to be operated as a qualified low-income building for the remainder of the compliance period. For partnerships consisting of more than 35 individual taxpayers, at the partnership's election, no change in ownership will be deemed to occur provided within a 12-month period at least 50 percent (in value) of the original ownership is unchanged.

In the year of a recapture event, no credit is allowable for the building. Additionally, the accelerated portion of credits paid in earlier years is recaptured with interest, from the date the recaptured amount was claimed, at the overpayment rate established under section 6621. The accelerated portion of the credit in any year is the amount of credits determined for the year, less the amount which would have been determined for the year if all credits had been allowed ratably over the compliance period (with no further discounting). Because credits on the initial qualified basis of a building are claimed ratably over a 10-year credit period rather than the 15-year compliance period, the amount of credit recaptured for noncompliance during the first 11 years is one-third of the credit determined for the year, plus interest. Because credits claimed on additions to qualified basis are paid ratably over the remainder of the compliance period (the credit percentage is two-thirds of the otherwise applicable percentage), there is no accelerated portion of credits attributable to additions to qualified basis. In the absence of additions to qualified basis and previous recapture events, the credits are recaptured in the following amounts (in addition to interest): one-third for violations after year 1 and before expiration of year 11; four-fifteenths for violations after year 11 but before expiration of year 12; three-fifteenths for violations after year 12 but before expiration of year 13; two-fifteenths for violations after year 13 but before expiration of year 14; and one-fifteenth for violations after year 14 but before expiration of year 15.

The penalty for a decrease in the qualified basis of a building, while still remaining part of a qualified low-income project, is recapture of the credits with respect to the accelerated amount claimed for all previous years on the amount of the reduction in qualified basis.

Owners and operators of low-income housing projects on which a credit has been claimed must correct any noncompliance with the set-aside requirement or with a reduction in qualified basis within a reasonable period after the noncompliance is discovered or reasonably should have been discovered. If any noncompliance is corrected within a reasonable period, there is no recapture. The conferees do not intend, however, that tenants be evicted to return a project to compliance. Rather, the conferees intend that each residential rental unit of comparable or smaller size that becomes vacant while a project is not in compliance must be rented to a tenant having a qualifying income before any units in the project are rented to tenants not so qualifying until the project again is in compliance. In general, therefore, the event that gives rise to the penalty for noncompliance (i.e., recapture or a reduction in the allowable credit) will be rental of a unit to other than a low-income tenant (on other than a temporary basis) during any period when the project does not comply with the set-aside requirement or with the qualified basis amounts on which the credit is computed (or would not qualify as a result of that rental).

An example of how the recapture provisions operate follows:

Example.—Assume credits are claimed for a project based on a qualified basis of 30 percent of the basis of the project being allocable to units occupied by individuals with incomes of 50 percent or less of area median income and, at a later date, a qualified basis of only 25 percent of the basis of the project is allocable to units occupied by individuals with incomes of 50 percent or less of median income due to vacancies filled by tenants with nonqualifying incomes. Because the minimum set-aside requirement is not violated, recapture occurs only on the accelerated portion of the credit amounts allocable to the 5-percent basis of the project no longer eligible for the credit.

If the maximum credit for which a project is eligible increases and subsequently decreases, a last-in, first-out rule is applied in determining which credits are recaptured. For example, consider a building that initially claimed a credit based on a qualified basis of 25 percent of the basis of the building allocable to units occupied by individuals with incomes of 50 percent or less of area median income, and in year 3 began receiving a credit based on an additional 10 percent of the basis of the building (i.e., a total of 35 percent). The credit amount on the additions to qualified basis is computed by reference to two-thirds of the credit percentage. If in year 5 only 30 percent of the basis of the building qualifies, there is no recapture of previous years' credits because there is no accelerated portion of the credit amounts attributable to the 5 percent of the additions to qualified basis claimed since year 3.

A reduction in qualified basis by reason of a casualty loss shall not be a recapture event provided such property is restored by reconstruction or replacement within a reasonable period.

State low-income housing credit authority limitation.—Generally, any building eligible for the credit not financed with the proceeds of tax-exempt bonds, which received an allocation pursuant to the new private activity bond volume limitation, must receive an allocation of credit authority from the State or local credit agency in whose jurisdiction the qualifying low-income housing project is located. The aggregate amount of such credits allocated within the State is limited by the State annual low-income credit authority limitation. Credit allocations are counted against a State's annual credit authority limitation for the calendar year in which the credits are allocated. Credits may not be allocated before the calendar year in which the building is placed in service. The credit amount allocated to a building applies for the year the allocation is made and all future years of the compliance period.

Allowable credit authority

General rules.—The annual credit authority limitation for each State is equal to $1.25 for every individual who is a resident of the State (as determined by the most recent estimate of the State's population released by the Bureau of the Census before the beginning of the year to which the limitation applies). For purposes of the credit authority limitation, the District of Columbia and U.S. possessions (e.g., Puerto Rico, the Virgin Islands, Guam, and American Samoa) are treated as a State.

Special set-aside for qualified nonprofit organizations.—A portion of each State's credit authority limitation is set aside for exclusive use by qualified nonprofit organizations. This set-aside is equal to $0.125 per resident of the State. This set-aside amount may not be changed by State action, either legislative or gubernatorial. In addition to the special set-aside, qualified nonprofit organizations may be allocated any additional amount of a State's remaining credit authority.

To qualify for allocations from this set-aside, an organization must be a section 501(c)(3) or 501(c)(4) organization, one of the exempt purposes of which includes the fostering of low-income housing, and the qualifying project with respect to which the credits are allocated must be one in which such organization materially participates (within the meaning of the passive loss rule). Among the operations in which the organization must be involved in on a regular, continuous, and substantial basis, in addition to the continuing operation of the project, is the development of the project.

Act § 252 **¶3879**

Credits subject to the credit authority limitation

Generally, credits subject to the State credit authority limitation include any credits attributable to expenditures not financed with tax-exempt bonds subject to the new private activity bond volume limitation.

In the case of a building financed with the proceeds of tax-exempt bonds subject to the bond volume limitation, if 70 percent or more of the aggregate basis of the building and land on which the building is located is financed with such proceeds, no portion of the credits attributable to such building is subject to the credit authority limitation.

If less than 70 percent of the aggregate basis of the building and land on which the building is located is financed with tax-exempt bonds subject to the bond volume limitation, only credits attributable to those bond-financed expenditures are not subject to the credit authority limitation.

Allocation of credit authority limitation among the State and other qualified governmental units therein

In general.—Each State's credit authority limitation is allocated among the various governmental units within the State pursuant to three alternative procedures.

Under the first procedure, each State's credit authority limitation is allocated in its entirety to the State housing agency until either the governor or the legislature makes a different allocation. If more than one such agency exists, they shall be treated as one agency. In the absence of a qualified State agency, no allocation may occur until provided by either the governor or the legislature.

Under the second procedure, the governor of each State is provided authority to allocate the State's credit authority limitation among all of the governmental units and other issuing authorities. This authority and any allocation rules established by the governor terminate as of the effective date of any overriding State legislation.

Under the third procedure, the State legislature may enact a law providing for a different allocation than that provided under the first or second procedures. Under this authority, the State legislature may allocate all or any portion of the State limitation to any governmental unit or other issuing authority in the State.

The conferees intend that any allocation procedure established by the governor or State legislature give balanced consideration to the low-income housing needs of the entire State.

The conferees wish to clarify that gubernatorial proclamations issued before the date of enactment of the conference agreement or State legislation enacted before that date is recognized for purposes of allocating the credit authority limitations, provided that the proclamation or legislation refers to the low-income housing tax credit authority limitation.

The conferees intend that a State be permitted to allocate available credit author-

ity to a local issuer until a specified date during each year (e.g., November 1) at which time the authority, if unused, may revert to the State for reallocation. Similarly, a State statute may provide discretionary authority to a public official (e.g., the governor) to allocate the State's credit authority limitation. Because the credit authority limitation is an annual amount, however, any authority that has not been used for credits issued before the end of the calendar year expires.

Special rule for constitutional home rule subdivisions.—The conference agreement provides a special allocation rule for certain political subdivisions with home rule powers under a State constitution (Illinois). The home rule subdivisions to which the special allocation rule applies are those home rule subdivisions that are granted home rule powers by the beginning of the calendar year in which the credits are issued pursuant to a State constitution that was adopted in 1970 and became effective on July 1, 1971. In that State, a full portion of the State credit authority limitation is allocated to each home rule subdivision based upon the ratio that the population of that home rule subdivision bears to the population of the entire State. As is true of the other credit authority limitation determinations, this allocation is made using the most recent population estimate from the Bureau of the Census released before the beginning of the calendar year to which the credits relate. The amount so allocated to home rule subdivisions may not be altered by the power to provide a different allocation otherwise granted by the conference agreement to the governor or the State legislature. However, a home rule subdivision may agree to a different allocation.

The portion of a State's credit authority limitation not allocated to constitutional home rule cities then is allocated under essentially the same three procedures described in the previous section. Thus, under the first procedure, the remaining State credit authority limitation is allocated to the State housing agency. Under the second and third procedures described above, the governor or the State legislature may allocate the State limitation other than that allocated to home rule subdivisions to any governmental units (including home rule subdivisions), but they may not so allocate any amounts specially allocated to the home rule subdivisions.

For purposes of the rules on State action establishing allocation rules for the credit authority limitation, a mayor of a constitutional home rule city is treated as a governor, and a city council is treated as a State legislature.

Constitutional home rule cities are treated as States for purposes of the credit authority limitation set-aside for qualified nonprofit organizations. Pursuant to their general authority to alter credit allocation, described above, these cities may agree with the State in which they are located to exchange authority to allocate credits for qualified nonprofit organizations for authority to allocate credits for other projects.

Allocation of set-aside amount for qualified nonprofit organizations.—As described above, a portion of each State's credit authority limitation is set aside exclusively for projects of qualified nonprofit organizations. Although the overall amount of credit authority set aside for these credits may not be reduced by any State action, a State may enact a statute determining which credit authorities in the State may authorize these credits and may allocate the entire set-aside amount to those authorities. Similarly, before any legislation, a governor may determine which authorities may allocate credits under the set-aside. The amount of the remaining credit authority limitation allocated to all other authorities must, of course, be adjusted to take into account any reallocation of the set-aside amount.

Determination of credit amount allocation.

A building must receive low-income credit authority allocated to it for the calendar year which includes the last day of the first year of the credit period. Authority must be received from the credit agency in whose jurisdiction the qualifying low-income building is located. The credit agency's remaining authority is reduced by the credit percentage multiplied by the amount of qualified basis granted by the credit agency for the building. The credit agency may grant a smaller credit percentage and a smaller qualified basis amount at the time the allocation is made than the maximum percentage and amount that would otherwise be allowed. The conferees intend that the credit agencies reduce the maximum available credit percentage when the financing and rental assistance for a project from all sources is sufficient to provide the continuing operation of the qualifying low-income building without the maximum credit.

A credit agency's credit limitation authority is reduced by the maximum amount of credit granted, whether or not the property ultimately is eligible for this maximum amount, and without regard to the averaging convention used in the first year of the credit period.

If a building is granted more credits than would be claimed in the first year of the credit period, without regard to the averaging convention, such amounts are not restored to the credit agency's authority. Such amounts may, however, be used in a later year by the owner of the building to the extent the credit determined with respect to the building is increased as a result of additions to qualified basis (but not beyond the amount allocated by the agency, and without regard to the reduced percentage applicable to such additions). (Also, see the discussion on additions to qualified basis, above.)

Example 1.—Assume in calendar year 1987 a newly constructed building is placed in service and that the building's qualified basis, before consideration of the credit authority limitation, is determined to be

$100,000 in that year. The credit agency may allocate any amount of qualified basis to the building, but the taxpayer may treat as his qualified basis only the lesser of (1) the qualified basis of the building, before consideration of the credit authority limitation, or (2) the qualified basis allocated to the building by the credit agency. If the credit agency allocated $100,000 of qualified basis and the maximum 9 percent credit percentage to the building, the agency's remaining 1987 credit authority would be reduced by $9,000.

Example 2.—Assume $120,000 in qualified basis and a credit percentage of 9 percent were initially authorized by a credit agency in 1987 for a qualified low-income building and that in 1987, the first year of the credit period, the building's qualified basis was $100,000. The credit agency's remaining 1987 credit authority is reduced by $10,800. If in year two of the credit period the qualified basis of the building increases by up to $20,000 due to an increase in the number of low-income units, additional credits may be claimed with respect to this addition to qualified basis without requiring additional credit authority from the credit agency. The credit percentage applicable to the additional qualified basis is two-thirds of the credit percentage applicable to the initial qualified basis. Credits on the additions to qualified basis may be claimed over the remainder of the compliance period.

If the qualified basis of a building is greater than the qualified basis granted to it by the credit agency, credits may not be claimed on the excess portion, unless additional low-income housing credits are allocated to the building by the credit agency. The credit authority of the credit agency is reduced for the calendar year of the allocation.

Generally, no carryover authority for unused credit authority is permitted. A limited exception is provided for buildings placed in service in 1990, if expenditures of 10 percent or more of total project costs are incurred before January 1, 1989. Credit authority for such property may be carried over from the 1989 credit allocation for the credit agency.

Credit agencies are permitted to assign future credit authority for years before the sunset date to buildings not yet placed in service by inducement resolutions or other means.

Should a credit agency issue more credits than its credit authority limitation provides, credits will be denied to those buildings last allocated credits until the credit authority limitation is not exceeded.

Credit administration

Credit agencies allocating credits may not condition allocation of credits to the source of financing for the qualifying low-income building. The conference agreement authorizes the Treasury Department to prescribe regulations that may require credit recipients to pay a reasonable fee to cover administrative expenses of the credit agency.

Agencies allocating credits must file reports with the Treasury Department containing (1) the maximum applicable percentage and qualified basis of each building, (2) the fees, if any, charged to credit recipients, (3) the aggregate amount of credits issued, and (4) other information required by Treasury. The time and manner of filing such reports and other information required are to be specified by the Treasury Department.

Transferability.—A new owner of a building during its 15-year compliance period is eligible to continue to receive the credit as if the new owner were the original owner, using the same qualified basis and credit percentages as used by the original owner. Rehabilitation expenditures on such property may qualify for a credit in the same manner as rehabilitation expenditures on other qualifying property. The accelerated portion of credits claimed in previous years will be recaptured upon a transfer, subject to the election of the original owner to post a bond. All dispositions of ownership interests in buildings are treated as transfers for purposes of recapture, except for a special rule for certain partnerships. (There is no election for the new owner to assume the recapture liability for prior year credits.)

At-risk limitation.—The amount of the credit is subject to an at-risk limitation similar to the investment tax credit at-risk rules in the case of nonrecourse financing. An exception is provided for lenders related to the buyer of the low-income housing property.

Another exception is provided for financing (including seller financing) not in excess of 60 percent of the basis of the property that is lent by charitable and social welfare organizations whose exempt purpose includes fostering low-income housing. Further, if the rate of interest for any financing qualifying for this exception is below the applicable Federal rate at the time the financing is incurred, less 1 percentage point, then the qualified basis to which such financing relates shall be reduced to reflect the present value of the payments of principal and interest, using as the discount rate such applicable Federal rate. The credit is recaptured if the financing provided by such organizations is not repaid with interest by the end of the 15-year credit compliance period.

Coordination with other provisions.—The credit is subject to the rules of the general business credit, including the maximum amount of income tax liability that may be reduced by a general business tax credit in any year. Unused credits for any taxable year may be carried back to each of the 3 preceding taxable years and then carried forward to each of the 15 following taxable years.

For purposes of the rules in the conference agreement limiting passive loss deductions, the credit (but not losses) is treated as arising from rental real estate activities in which the taxpayer actively participates. Credits may be used to offset tax on up to $25,000 of nonpassive income, subject to a phaseout between $200,000 and $250,000 of adjusted gross income (disregarding passive losses).

The basis of property for purposes of depreciation is not reduced by the amount of low-income credits claimed.

Effective date.—The credit is effective for buildings placed in service after December 31, 1986, other than property grandfathered under the depreciation rules, and before January 1, 1990. A building placed in service after 1989 is eligible for the credit if expenditures of 10 percent or more of the reasonably expected cost of the building is incurred before January 1, 1989, and the building is placed in service before January 1, 1991. Credit authority for such property placed in service in 1990 may be carried over from the 1989 volume allocation for the credit agency.

[¶ 3880] SECTION 261. PROVISIONS RELATING TO MERCHANT MARINE CAPITAL CONSTRUCTION FUNDS

(Sec. 7518 of the Code)

[House Explanation]

*   *   *   *   *   *

Explanation of Provision.—The bill coordinates the application of the Internal Revenue Code of 1985 with the capital construction fund program of the Merchant Marine Act of 1936, as amended. In addition, new requirements are imposed, relating to (1) the tax treatment of nonqualified withdrawals, (2) certain reports to be made by the Secretaries of Transportation and Commerce to the Secretary of the Treasury, and (3) a time limit on the amount of time monies could remain in a fund without being withdrawn for a qualified purpose.

For purposes of the definition of the term "qualified withdrawals," under new section 7518(e) (sec. 607(f) of the Merchant Marine Act, 1936), the committee intends the phrase, "acquisition, construction, or reconstruction of a qualified vessel" to be interpreted as including acquisition through either purchase or lease of an agreement vessel for a period of five years or more. This interpretation parallels the structure of: (1) the scope of eligibility to establish a capital construction fund under sec. 607(a) of the Merchant Marine Act, 1936 (which permits deposits into a CCF fund by either an owner/lessor or the lessee of an eligible vessel, or both, subject to certain limitations), and (2) the scope of qualified withdrawals for vessel acquisition through either purchase (in the form of a downpayment toward the purchase price) or payment of long-term indebtedness on an agreement vessel. This interpretation is also consistent with current industry acquisition practices reflecting a long-term trend toward vessel acquisition through lease rather than purchase.

Inclusion in Internal Revenue Code.—The tax provisions relating to capital construction funds are recodified as part of the Internal Revenue Code of 1985. For purposes of the Internal Revenue Code of 1985, defined terms shall have the meaning given such terms in the Merchant Marine Act of 1936, as amended, as in effect, on the date of enactment of the bill.

Tax treatment of nonqualified withdrawals.—The maximum rate of tax (36 percent for corporations and 38 percent for individuals) is to be imposed on nonqualified withdrawals made after December 31, 1985; This penalty is in addition to interest payable from the date the amount withdrawn was reported.

If a taxpayer makes a nonqualified withdrawal out of a capital construction fund, the income tax payable by the taxpayer for the year of withdrawal is generally to be increased by such amount as is necessary to assure that the tax liability with respect to the nonqualified withdrawal is determined by reference to the top marginal tax rates applicable to ordinary income and capital gains. Special rules are provided to limit the application of this provision in cases where the taxpayer derived no tax benefit from depositing the funds.

Capital construction fund reports to Treasury.—The Secretary of Transportation and the Secretary of Commerce are required to certify to the Secretary of Treasury that the monies in a fund are appropriate for vessel construction requirements. If it is determined that the fund balances exceed what is appropriate to meet vessel construction program objectives, the fundholder would be required to develop appropriate program objectives within three years or treat the excess as a nonqualified withdrawal.

Ten-year limit on deposits.—The bill imposes a ten-year limit on the amount of time monies can remain in a fund without being withdrawn for a qualified purpose. This rule applies to all deposits, including those made before the general effective date. The ten-year period begins to run on the later of the date of deposit or January 1, 1986.

Monies that are not withdrawn after a ten-year period—other than amounts that have been committed to the construction or acquisition of identified vessels pursuant to contracts that are binding as of the last day of the ten-year period—are to be treated as nonqualified withdrawals, according to the following schedule: for the eleventh year, the fundholder would be treated as having withdrawn 20 percent; for the twelfth year, 40 percent; for the thirteenth year, 60 percent; for the fourteenth year, 80 percent, and for the fifteenth year, 100 percent. For purposes of this rule, if a taxpayer enters into a binding contract before the close of a taxable year, the amount so committed is not treated as remaining in the fund.

*　　*　　*　　*　　*　　*

[Conference Report]

*　　*　　*　　*　　*　　*

The conference agreement follows the House bill, except that a 25-year time limit is imposed on the amount of time monies can remain in a fund without being withdrawn for a qualified purpose. **[Effective date.—]** The amendments are effective for taxable years beginning after December 31, 1986.

[¶ 3885] SECTION 301. REPEAL OF EXCLUSION FOR LONG-TERM CAPITAL GAINS OF INDIVIDUALS

(Sec. 1202 of the Code)

[Senate Explanation]

*　　*　　*　　*　　*　　*

Explanation of Provisions.—The bill repeals the net capital gain deduction for individuals.[1]

*　　*　　*　　*　　*　　*

A conforming amendment is made to allow losses from the sale or exchange of capital assets to the extent of gains from the sale or exchange of capital assets plus $3,000.

*　　*　　*　　*　　*　　*

Effective Date.—This provision applies to taxable years beginning after December 31, 1986.

*　　*　　*　　*　　*　　*

[Conference Report]

*　　*　　*　　*　　*　　*

The Senate amendment repeals the capital gains deduction.[1a]

*　　*　　*　　*　　*　　*

[Footnote ¶ 3885]　(1) The minimum tax is conformed by deleting the capital gain preference.

(1a) The Senate amendments includes a conforming amendment to Code section 170(e)(1)(B), relating to certain charitable contributions of property. Under present law, the deduction for contributions by individuals of unrelated-use tangible personal property, or of any appreciated property donated to certain private nonoperating (grant-making) foundations, essentially is limited to the donor's basis in the property plus the excludable amount of any long-term capital gain which would have been realized if the property had been sold. (The deductible amount for such contributions by corporations also is limited.) In conformity to the repeal of the capital gains exclusion for individuals, the Senate amendment essentially limits the deductible amount of such contributions by individuals to the donor's basis in the property. (A related change is made to the deductible amount of such contributions by corporations.) No change is made to the reduction rule in section 170(e)(1)(A) for contributions of ordinary-income property or to the exception

The Conference agreement follows the Senate amendment* * *.

[¶ 3886] SECTION 302. 28-PERCENT CAPITAL GAINS RATE FOR TAXPAYERS OTHER THAN CORPORATIONS

(Sec. 1 of the Code)

[Senate Explanation]

* * * * * *

Reasons for Change

* * * * * *

The committee believes that the top rate on individual capital gains should not exceed the rates set forth in the bill, and therefore the bill provides that the maximum tax rate on capital gains will not exceed the top individual rate that the bill presently provides even if the top individual rate is increased during subsequent consideration of the bill.

Explanation of Provision

* * * * * *

The bill * * * provides that the tax imposed by section 1 on an individual, estate, or trust cannot exceed the sum of (1) a tax computed at the rates under section 1 on the greater of (a) the taxpayer's taxable income reduced by the amount of net capital gain or

(b) the amount of the taxpayer's taxable income which is taxed at a rate below 27 percent; (2) a tax of 27 percent on the amount of the taxpayer's taxable income in excess of the amount determined under (1) above; and (3) any additional tax resulting from the gradual phaseout of the benefits of the 15-percent bracket. If for any taxable year, the

highest individual rates (under the tax rate schedules set forth in sec. 1(a)) do not exceed 27 percent, then this limitation will have no application.

The result of these provisions is that capital gains (including all capital gains recognized during calendar year 1987) will not be taxed at rates exceeding the top individual rates that become effective on July 1, under the committee bill.

* * * * * *

The bill does not change the character of gain as capital or ordinary.

[Conference Report]

* * * * * *

The provision applies to taxable years beginning after December 31, 1986.

* * * * * *

The conference agreement follows the Senate amendment with a conforming change reflecting the change in the maximum individual rates under the conference agreement. The maximum rate on long-term capital gain in 1987 is 28 percent.

The current statutory structure for capital gains is retained in the Code to facilitate reinstatement of a capital gains rate differential if there is a future tax rate increase.

[¶ 3887] SECTION 311. REPEAL OF CORPORATE CAPITAL GAINS TREATMENT

(Sec. 1201 of the Code)

[House Explanation]

* * * * * *

[Conference Report]

* * * * * *

House Bill.—The House bill makes the alternative tax inapplicable to taxable years for which the new corporate tax rates are fully effective (i.e., taxable years beginning on or after July 1, 1986). Thus, corporate net capital gain for such years is taxed at regular corporate rates (i.e., generally a maximum of 36 percent under the House bill). For taxable years before the new rates are fully effective, the tax rate on gain * * * [properly] taken into account under the taxpayer's method of accounting after December 31, 1985 is 36 percent.

There is no change in the capital loss provisions.

* * * * * *

Conference Agreement.—The conference agreement generally follows the House bill with conforming changes reflecting the change in the new top corporate rate under the conference agreement (34 percent rather than 36 percent).

[Effective date].—The provisions are effective for gain properly taken into account under the taxpayer's method of accounting on or after January 1, 1987, without regard to whether the gain is pursuant to a written binding contract in effect at any earlier time.

The current statutory structure for capital gains is retained in the Code to facilitate

---

[Footnote ¶ 3885 (1a) continued]

to the reduction rule in section 170(e)(5) for contributions of qualified appreciated stock to certain private foundations. Under the Senate amendment (as under present law), the amount of charitable deduction allowable to an itemizer for a donation of stock to a public charity equals (for regular tax purposes) the full fair market value of the stock at the time of the donation if the donor has held the stock for more than six months, or the donor's basis in the stock if the donor has not held the stock for more than six months (Code section 170(e)).

reinstatement of a capital gains rate differential if there is a future tax rate increase.

* * * * * *

The conference agreement also provides that any election to treat the cutting of timber as a disposition under section 631(a) made for a taxable year beginning before January 1, 1987, may be revoked on a one-time basis by the taxpayer without the permission of the Secretary of the Treasury. Any revocation of an election made in accordance with this provision will not be considered in determining whether a future tax rate increase under section 631(a) by the taxpayer is allowed. If a taxpayer revokes an election without consent in accordance with this provision, and thereafter makes an election under section 631(a), any future revocations will require the permission of the Secretary of the Treasury.

[¶ 3888] SECTION 321. REPEAL OF REQUIREMENT THAT INCENTIVE STOCK OPTIONS ARE EXERCISABLE ONLY IN CHRONOLOGICAL ORDER; MODIFICATION OF $100,000 LIMITATION

(Sec. 422A(b) of the Code)

[Senate Explanation]

* * * * * *

Explanation of Provision.—The bill repeals the requirement that incentive stock options must be exercisable in the order granted.

The bill also changes the $100,000 limit to provide that the aggregate fair market [val-

ue] (determined at the time the option is granted) of the stock with respect to which incentive stock options are exercisable for the first time under the terms of the plan by any employee during any calendar year may not exceed $100,000.

Effective date.—The provision applies to options granted after 12-31-86.

* * * * * *

[¶ 3889] SECTION 331. YEAR-END RULE EXPANDED

(Sec. 1092(c)(4)(E) of the Code)

[Senate Explanation]

* * * * * *

Explanation of Provision

Qualified covered call options.—Under the bill, the qualified covered call exception to the loss deferral rule is denied to a taxpayer who fails to hold a covered call

option for 30 days after the related stock is disposed of at a loss, where gain on the option is included in the subsequent year.

* * * * * *

Effective Dates.—* * * positions established after 12-31-86.

* * * * * *

[¶ 3890] SECTION 401. LIMITATION ON EXPENSING OF SOIL AND WATER CONSERVATION EXPENDITURES

(Sec. 175 of the Code)

[Senate Explanation]

* * * * * *

Explanation of Provision.—*Soil and water conservation expenditures.*—The bill limits the soil and water conservation expenditures that may be deducted currently to amounts incurred that are consistent with a conservation plan approved by the Soil Conservation Service (SCS) of the Department of Agriculture. If there is no SCS conservation plan for the area in which property to be improved is located, amounts incurred for improvements that are consistent with a plan of a State conservation agency are deemed to satisfy the Federal standards. Finally, the bill provides that expenditures for general earth moving, draining, and/or filling of wetlands, and for preparing land for installation and/or operation of a center pivot irriga-

tion system may not be deducted under this special expensing provision.

[Conference Report]

The conference agreement follows the House bill and Senate amendment, effective for expenditures after December 31, 1986. In addition, the conferees wish to clarify that while prior approval of the taxpayer's particular project by the Soil Conservation Service or comparable State agency is not necessary to qualify the expenditure under this provision, there must be an overall plan for the taxpayer's area that has been approved by such an agency in effect at any time during the taxable year.

[Senate Explanation]

* * * * * *

Effective date.—These provisions apply to expenditures incurred after December 31, 1986.

Act § 401   ¶ 3890

[¶ 3891] SECTION 402. REPEAL OF SPECIAL TREATMENT FOR EXPENDITURES FOR CLEARING LAND

(Sec. 182 of the Code)

[Senate Explanation]

*   *   *   *   *   *

Explanation of Provision.— *Expenditures for clearing land.*—The bill repeals the provision allowing expenditures for clearing land in preparation for farming to be deducted currently rather than added to the basis of the land on which the activity occurs. The committee wishes to clarify, however, that routine brush clearing and other ordinary maintenance activities related to property already used in farming continue to be deductible currently to the extent the expenditures constitute ordinary and necessary business expenses of the taxpayer. (*See,* sec. 162.)

[Conference Report]

[Effective date] * * * effective for expenditures after December 31, 1985.

[¶ 3892] SECTION 403. TREATMENT OF DISPOSITIONS OF CONVERTED WETLANDS OR HIGHLY ERODIBLE CROPLANDS

(Sec. 1257 of the Code)

[Senate Explanation]

*   *   *   *   *   *

Explanation of Provision.—The bill provides that to the extent section 1231 treatment otherwise is provided in the Code for such property, any gain realized on the disposition of "converted wetland" or "highly erodible cropland" will be treated as ordinary income, and any loss on the disposition of such property will be treated as long-term capital loss. For this purpose, the term "converted wetland" means land (1) that is converted wetland within the meaning of section 1201(4) of the Food Security Act of 1985 (P.L. 99-198, Dec. 23, 1985), and (2) that is held by the person who originally converted the wetland, by a person who uses the land for farming for any period of time following the conversion, or by a person whose adjusted basis in the property is determined by reference to the basis of a person in whose hands the property was converted wetland.[1] In general, the Food Security Act defines converted wetland as land that has been drained or filled for the purpose of making the production of agricultural commodities possible, if the production would not have been possible but for such action.

The term "highly erodible cropland" means any highly erodible cropland as defined in section 1201(6) of the Food Security Act that is used by the taxpayer at any time for farming purposes other than the grazing of animals. In general, highly erodible cropland is defined as land that (1) is currently classified by the Department of Agriculture as class IV, VI, VII, or VIII land under its land capability classification system, or (2) that would have an excessive average annual rate of erosion in relation to the soil loss tolerance level, as determined by the Secretary of the Agriculture.

Effective Date.—The provision is effective for dispositions of land converted after March 1, 1986.

[¶ 3893] SECTION 404. LIMITATION ON CERTAIN PREPAID FARMING EXPENSES

(Sec. 464 of the Code)

[Conference Report]

*   *   *   *   *   *

Senate Amendment.—In general, farmers using the cash method of accounting may not deduct amounts paid for unconsumed feed, seed, fertilizer, or other supplies to the extent they exceed 50 percent of the expenses incurred in the farming business (including prepaid expenses) during the taxable year. A similar rule applies in the case of costs incurred for the purchase of poultry. **[Effective Date.—]** The provision is effective for prepayments made on or after March 1, 1986, in taxable years beginning after that date.

[Senate Explanation]

*   *   *   *   *   *

The bill does not amend the farming syndicate rules of section 464, and the committee intends that this new restriction will operate independently of that provision. In addition, the committee intends that farmers will not be required generally to take year-end inventories of prepaid items as a result of the provisions of this bill.

*   *   *   *   *   *

[Conference Report]

*   *   *   *   *   *

Conference Agreement.—The conference agreement generally follows the Senate amendment, except that the limitation applies to prepayments for supplies to the extent such prepayments exceed 50 percent

---

[Footnote ¶ 3892]   (1) Thus, land that has been converted could become eligible for section 1221 treatment in the hands of, for example, a subsequent purchaser or legatee, provided the purchaser or legatee has used the property only for nonfarming purposes.

of total deductible farming expenses excluding prepaid supplies.

[**Effective Date—**]. The provision is effective for prepayment paid after March 1, 1986, in taxable years beginning after that date.

[¶ 3894] SECTION 405. TAX TREATMENT OF DISCHARGE OF CERTAIN INDEBTEDNESS OF SOLVENT FARMERS

(Secs. 108 and 1017 of the Code)

[Senate Explanation]

*　　*　　*　　*　　*　　*

Explanation of Provision.—The bill provides that discharge of indebtedness income arising from an agreement between a solvent individual engaged in the trade or business of farming and an unrelated person to discharge qualified farming indebtedness is treated for Federal tax purposes as income realized by an insolvent individual. Qualified agricultural indebtedness is defined as debt incurred * * * [directly in connection with the trade or business of farming].

Under the provision, individuals are treated as engaged in the trade or business of

farming if at least 50 percent of their average annual gross receipts during the three taxable years preceding the year in which the discharge of indebtedness occurs was derived from the trade or business of farming. * * *

Further, the bill includes in the list of tax attributes which may be reduced by the discharge of indebtedness income, basis in farmland; however, all tax attributes other than basis in farmland must be reduced before the discharge of indebtedness income is applied against that attribute.

Effective Date.—This provision of the bill would apply to discharge of indebtedness * * * [after April 9, 1986].

[¶ 3896] SECTION 411. TREATMENT OF INTANGIBLE DRILLING COSTS AND MINERAL EXPLORATION AND DEVELOPMENT COSTS

(Secs. 263(i), 291(b), 616(d) and 617(h))

[Conference Report]

*　　*　　*　　*　　*　　*

* * * **Intangible Drilling Costs**

*　　*　　*　　*　　*　　*

Present Law.—Intangible drilling and development costs (IDCs) generally may be expensed or capitalized at the election of the operator of an oil, gas, or geothermal property.

In the case of integrated producers, 80 percent of IDCs may be expensed and the remaining 20 percent must be amortized over a 36-month period beginning with the month the costs are paid or incurred (sec. 291).

Costs with respect to a nonproductive well ("dry hole") may be deducted currently by any taxpayer in the year the dry hole is completed.

*　　*　　*　　*　　*　　*

Conference Agreement.—Under the conference agreement, 70 percent of IDCs of integrated producers may be expensed and the remaining 30 percent are to be amortized ratably over a 60 month (5-year) period, beginning in the month the costs are paid or incurred. This provision does not affect the option to expense dry hole costs in the year the dry hole is completed.

[**Effective date.**—] The provision applies to costs paid or incurred after December 31, 1986.

*　　*　　*　　*　　*　　*

* * * **Exploration and Development Costs**

Present Law.—Exploration and development costs associated with mines and other hard mineral deposits may be deducted currently at the election of the taxpayer. Exploration (but not development) costs which have been deducted currently either (1) are applied to reduce depletion deductions, or (2) at the taxpayer's election, are recaptured in income once the mine begins production, and then recovered as a depletable expense.

In the case of corporations, only 80 percent of hard mineral exploration and development costs may be expensed. The remaining 20 percent must be recovered over the 5-year ACRS depreciation schedule (beginning in the year that exploration and development costs are paid or incurred), with an investment tax credit for domestic costs (sec. 291).

Conference Agreement.—Under the conference agreement, 80 percent of the mining development and exploration costs of corporations are to be amortized ratably over a 60-month (5-year) period, rather than being expensed.

[**Effective date.**—] The provision applies to costs paid or incurred after December 31, 1986.

Treatment of foreign IDCs

Present Law.—IDCs may qualify for expensing whether incurred in the States or in a foreign country.

[House Explanation]

*　　*　　*　　*　　*　　*

Foreign IDCs.—Under the bill, IDCs incurred outside the United States are recovered (1) over a 10-year straight-line amortization schedule beginning in the year the costs are paid or incurred, or (2) at the taxpayer's election, by adding these costs to the basis for cost depletion. For this purpose, the United States includes the 50 states, the District of Columbia, and those continental shelf areas which are adjacent to United States territorial waters and over which the United States has exclusive rights with respect to the exploration and exploitation of natural resources (sec. 638(1)). The 20-percent reduction for integrated producers does not apply to these costs.

* * * * * *

[Conference Report]

* * * * * *

Senate Amendment.—*[Effective date.—]* The Senate amendment is the same as the House bill, except that the provision applies to costs paid or incurred after December 31, 1986. A transitional exception is provided with respect to certain licenses for North Sea development acquired on or before December 31, 1985.

Conference Agreement.—The conference agreement follows the Senate amend-

ment. This provision does not affect the option to deduct dry hole costs in the year the dry hole is completed.

* * * * * *

Foreign exploration costs

Present Law.—Foreign exploration costs must be capitalized to the extent the taxpayer's foreign and domestic exploration costs (including certain prior years' costs) exceed $400,000.

House Bill.—The House bill provides that foreign exploration and development costs are recovered: (1) over a 10-year, straight-line amortization schedule, or (2) at the election of the taxpayers, as part of the basis for cost depletion.

This provision applies to costs paid or incurred after December 31, 1986.

Senate Amendment. — [Effective date.—] The Senate amendment is the same as the House bill, but effective for costs paid or incurred after December 31, 1986.

Conference Agreement.—The conference agreement follows the Senate amendment.

* * * * * *

[¶ 3897] SECTION 412. MODIFICATION OF PERCENTAGE DEPLETION RULES

(Secs. 291(a)(2), 613(e)(3) and 613A(d)(5) of the Code)

[Conference Report]

* * * * * *

* * * Depletion for Oil, Gas, and Geothermal Properties.

* * * * * *

Present Law.—Percentage depletion is available with respect to oil and gas lease bonuses or advance royalty payments (*Commissioner v. Engle*, 464 U.S. 206 (1984)).

House Bill.—The House bill denies percentage depletion for lease bonuses, advance royalties, or other payments made without regard to actual production from an oil, gas, or geothermal property, effective January 1, 1986.

* * * * * *

Conference Agreement.—The conference agreement follows the House bill, effective for amounts received or accrued after August 16, 1986.

* * * * * *

Percentage Depletion for Hard Minerals

Present Law.—* * * For corporations only, percentage depletion of coal or iron ore, in excess of adjusted basis (determined without regard to the depletion deduction for that year), is reduced by 15 percent (sec. 291).

Conference Agreement.—The conference agreement increases the reduction in coal and iron ore percentage depletion (under section 291) from 15 percent to 20 percent.

[Effective date.—] The provision applies to taxable years beginning after December 31, 1986.

[¶ 3898] SECTION 413. GAIN FROM DISPOSITION OF INTERESTS IN OIL, GAS, GEOTHERMAL OR OTHER MINERAL PROPERTIES

(Sec. 1254 of the Code).

[Conference Report]

* * * * * *

* * * Gain on Disposition of Interest in Oil, Gas, or Geothermal Property

Present Law.—Expensed intangible drilling costs incurred after 1975 are recaptured as ordinary income upon disposition of an oil, gas or geothermal property, to the extent of the excess of such costs over the amount that

would have been deducted if the costs had been capitalized and recovered through depletion deductions.

House Bill.—The House bill provides that expensed intangible drilling costs and depletion which reduced basis are recaptured as ordinary income.

The provision applies to dispositions of property placed in service after December 31, 1985, unless acquired pursuant to a written contract binding on September 25, 1985.

* * * * * *

Conference Agreement.—The conference agreement follows the House bill, except that the provisions apply to dispositions of property placed in service date is after December 31, 1986. (The September 25, 1985, binding contract date is retained.)

* * * * * *

Gain on Disposition of Interest in Mining Property

Present Law.—Adjusted exploration expenditures (generally, amounts expensed in excess of amounts that would have been deducted if the costs had been capitalized) are recaptured as ordinary income upon disposition of a mining property.

House Bill.—The House bill provides that expensed exploration and development expenses and depletion that reduced basis are recaptured as ordinary income.

The provision applies to dispositions of property placed in service after December 31, 1985, unless acquired pursuant to a written contract binding on September 25, 1985.

* * * * * *

Conference Agreement.—The conference agreement follows the House bill, except that the provision applies to property placed in service after December 31, 1986. (The September 25, 1985 binding contract date is retained.)

* * * * * *

[¶ 3899] SECTION 421. EXTENSION OF ENERGY INVESTMENT CREDIT FOR SOLAR, GEOTHERMAL, OCEAN THERMAL, AND BIOMASS PROPERTY

(Secs. 46(b)(2)(A) and (E) of the Code)

[Conference Report]

* * * * * *

Present Law.—The business energy investment tax credits were enacted as additions to the regular investment tax credit to provide an additional tax credit as an incentive for the purchase of specified property or equipment. Credits for certain energy property expired after 1982. Energy credits were available through 1985 for the following energy property at the following rates: solar—15 percent; geothermal—15 percent; wind—15 percent; ocean thermal—15 percent; biomass—10 percent; and small scale hydroelectric—11 percent.

House Bill.—The House bill extends the energy tax credit for solar energy property at 15 percent in 1986, 12 percent in 1987, and 8 percent in 1988. The geothermal tax credit is extended at 15 percent in 1986 and 10 percent in 1987 and 1988.

Senate Amendment.—The Senate amendment on the solar energy tax credit is the same as the House bill, except that the tax credit rate in 1988 is 12 percent.

The Senate amendment is the same as the House bill for the geothermal energy tax credit.

The Senate amendment extends the tax credit for ocean thermal property at 15 percent through 1988.

The Senate amendment extends the tax credit for wind energy property at 15 percent in 1986 and 10 percent in 1987.

The Senate amendment extends the tax credit for biomass energy property at 15 percent in 1986 and 10 percent in 1987.

Conference Agreement.—The conference agreement extends the energy tax credit for solar energy property at 15 percent in 1986, 12 percent in 1987, and 10 percent in 1988.

The conference agreement follows the House bill and the Senate amendment with respect to the energy tax credit for geothermal energy property.

The conference agreement does not change present law with respect to dual purpose solar or geothermal energy property. The conference committee, however, notes with respect to this matter that these are administrative issues which the Secretary of the Treasury should resolve under the regulatory authority provided in the Energy Tax Act of 1978 and subsequent Acts with provisions relating to energy tax credits.

The conference agreement follows the Senate amendment with respect to the energy tax credit for biomass property.

The conference agreement follows the Senate amendment with respect to the energy tax credit for ocean thermal property.

The conference agreement follows the House bill with respect to the wind energy tax credit.

* * * * * *

Affirmative committment rules

[Conference Report]

* * * * * *

Present Law.—The expired 10-percent credit for certain alternative energy continues to be available for long-term projects which meet rules requiring (1) completion of engineering studies and application for all required permits before 1983, (2) binding contracts for 50 percent of special project equipment before 1986, and (3) project completion before 1991.

House Bill.—Consistent with the general transitional rules applicable to repeal of the regular investment tax credit, the House bill requires that allowable energy credits are spread ratably over 5 years (i.e., 20 percent of the credit in each of 5 years), and requires a full basis adjustment for the full energy tax credit in the first taxable year.

* * * * * *

Conference Agreement.—The conference agreement provides that energy tax

credits earned under the affirmative commitment rules are treated in the same manner as the regular investment tax credit for transition property.

* * * * * *

[¶ 3900] SECTION 422. PROVISIONS RELATING TO EXCISE TAX ON FUELS

(Secs. 4041(b)(2)(A) and 6427(e)(3) of the Code)

[Conference Report]

* * * * * *

* * * Neat Alcohol Fuels

Present Law.—A 9-cents-per-gallon exemption from the excise tax on special motor fuels is provided through 1992 for neat methanol and ethanol fuels which are not derived from petroleum or natural gas. A 4½ cents exemption is provided if the fuels are derived from natural gas. Neat alcohol fuels are at least 85 percent methanol, ethanol, and other alcohol.

House Bill.—The 9-cents-per-gallon exemption is reduced to 6 cents per gallon, effective for sales or use after December 31, 1985.

Senate Amendment.—The Senate amendment follows the House bill, except

[Effective date.—] the provision is effective for sales or use after December 31, 1986.

Conference Agreement.—The conference agreement follows the Senate amendment.

* * * Taxicab Fuels Tax Exemption

Present Law.—A 4-cents-per-gallon partial exemption from the motor fuels excise taxes (9 cents for gasoline and special motor fuels and 15 cents for diesel fuel) was provided for fuels used in qualifying taxicabs through September 30, 1985. The exemption was effectuated through a credit or refund (without interest).

House Bill.—The 4-cents-per-gallon partial exemption from motor fuels excise taxes for qualified taxicabs is extended through September 30, 1988.

* * * * * *

Conference Agreement.—The conference agreement follows the House bill.

[¶ 3901] SECTION 423. ETHYL ALCOHOL AND MIXTURES THEREOF FOR FUEL USE

[Conference Report]

* * * * * *

Present Law.—A 60-cents-per-gallon duty is imposed through 1992 on alcohol imported into the United States for use as a fuel.

Ethyl alcohol may enter the United States duty-free, if it is imported from a Caribbean Basin Initiative (CBI) country, under the terms of the Caribbean Basin Economic Recovery Act (CBERA).

* * * * * *

Senate Amendment.—The Senate amendment retains present law, but it allows duty-free entry into the United States only for ethyl alcohol produced in a Caribbean Basin Initiative (CBI) country or U.S. insular possession from source material which is the product of a CBI country, an insular possession, or the United States. The change in the source material requirement does not apply, as of January 1, 1986, to certain facilities which were established and operating (up to a maximum of 20 million gallons per year) or ready for shipment to an installation in a CBI country (up to a maximum of 50 million gallons per year).

Conference Agreement.—The conference agreement adopts in most respects section 864 of H.R. 4800. In so doing, the conferees disapprove U.S. Customs Service

rulings that have found the mere dehydration of industrial-grade ethanol into fuel-grade ethanol to constitute a substantial transformation sufficient to qualify the dehydrated ethanol as a product of a CBI country or insular possession and therefore entitled to duty-free treatment. By discouraging such "pass-through" operations, the conferees seek to encourage meaningful economic investment in CBI countries and insular possessions.

Under the conference agreement, ethyl alcohol (or an ethyl alcohol mixture) may be admited into the United States duty-free, if it is an indigenous product of a U.S. insular possession or CBI beneficiary country.

Ethyl alcohol (or ethyl alcohol mixture) may be treated as being an indigenous product of an insular possession or beneficiary country only if the ethyl alcohol (or a mixture) has been both dehydrated and produced by a process of full-scale fermentation within that insular possession or beneficiary country. Alternatively, ethyl alcohol (or a mixture) must have been dehydrated within that insular possession or beneficiary country from hydrous ethyl alcohol that includes hydrous ethyl alcohol which is wholly the product or manufacture of any insular possession or beneficiary country and which has a value not less than (1) 30 percent of the value of the ethyl alcohol or mixture, if entered during calendar year 1987, (2) 60 percent of the value of the ethyl alcohol or mixture, if entered during calendar year 1988, and (3) 75 percent of the value of the ethyl alcohol or mixture, if entered after December 31, 1988.

Transitional exemptions are provided during 1987 and 1988 for up to 20 million gallons per year each produced by certain azeotropic distillation facilities: (1) located in a CBI country or insular possession and in operation on January 1, 1986; or (2) the equipment

for which was, on January 1, 1986, ready for shipment to and installation in a CBI country. An additional transitional exemption is provided during 1987 to a facility in the Virgin Islands that received authorization prior to May 1, 1986, to operate a full-scale fermentation facility.

[Effective date.—] Effective for articles entered after 12-31-86 and before expiration of period of 901.50 of Appendix of U.S. Tariff Schedules. Drawback rules effective on date of enactment. Ed.

[¶ 3902] SECTION 501. LIMITATIONS ON LOSSES AND CREDITS FROM PASSIVE ACTIVITIES

(Sec. 469 of the Code)

[Senate Explanation]

* * * * * *

Explanation of Provisions.—

1. Overview.—The bill provides that deductions from passive trade or business activities, to the extent they exceed income from all such passive activities (exclusive of portfolio income), generally may not be deducted against other income. Similarly, credits from passive activities generally are limited to the tax allocable to the passive activities. Suspended losses and credits are carried forward and treated as deductions and credits from passive trade or business activities in the next year. Suspended losses from an activity are allowed in full when the taxpayer disposes of his entire interest in the activity.

The provision applies to individuals, estates, trusts, and personal service corporations. A special rule limits the use of passive activity losses against portfolio income in the case of closely held corporations. Special rules also apply to rental activities. Losses from working interests in oil and gas property are not limited by the provision. Losses and credits attributable to a limited partnership interest generally are treated as arising from a passive activity. The provision is effective for taxable years beginning after 1986, and is phased in over 5 years. It becomes fully effective for taxable years beginning in 1991 and thereafter.

Losses and credits from a passive activity (taking into account expenses as interest attributable to acquiring or carrying an interest in the activity) may be applied against income for the taxable year from other passive activities or against income subsequently generated by any passive activity. Such losses (and credits) generally cannot be applied to shelter other income, such as compensation for services or portfolio income (including interest, dividends, royalties, and gains from the sale of property held for investment). For this purpose, property held

for investment generally does not include an interest in a passive activity.

Salary and portfolio income are separated from passive activity losses and credits because the former generally are positive income sources that do not bear, at least to the same extent as other items, deductible expenses. . . . The passive loss provision ensures that salary and portfolio income, along with other nonpassive income sources, cannot be offset by tax losses from passive activities until the amount of such losses is determined upon disposition.

Under the provision, suspended losses attributable to passive trade or business activities are allowed in full upon a taxable disposition of the taxpayer's entire interest in the activity.[7] . . . To the extent the taxpayer's basis in the activity has been reduced by suspended deductions, resulting in gain on disposition, the remaining suspended deductions will, in effect, offset such gain. However, the character of any gain or loss is not affected by this provision.

Passive activity.—Under the bill, an activity generally is a passive activity if it involves the conduct of any trade or business, and if the taxpayer does not materially participate in the activity. A taxpayer who is an individual materially participates in an activity only if he is involved in the operations of the activity on a regular, continuous, and substantial basis. Regardless of whether an individual directly owns an interest in a trade or business activity (e.g., as a proprietorship), or owns an interest in an activity conducted at the entity level by a pass-through entity such as a general partnership or S corporation, he must be involved in the operations of the activity on a regular, continuous, and substantial basis, in order to be materially participating.

* * * [Under] the bill, a limited partnership interest is treated as intrinsically passive (except as provided in regulations). Portfolio income of a partnership, however, is not treated as passive (see sec. 3, below). The committee intends that a share of partner-

---

[**Footnote ¶ 3902**] (7) Gain recognized on a transfer of a partial interest in the passive activity, and gain (boot) on a tax-free transfer of an entire or partial interest, are treated as from a passive activity. Gain on such transfers may be offset by losses and credits from passive activities, but such transfers are not treated as dispositions triggering all suspended income from the activity.

ship income, or a guaranteed payment to a partner (including a limited partner) attributable to the performance of personal services is not to be treated as passive. Losses. from trade or business activities that are allocable to a limited partnership interest are not permitted, prior to disposition, to be applied against any income other than income from passive activities.

A passive activity under the bill does not include a working interest in oil or gas property. Thus, an owner of a working interest in oil or gas property is permitted to deduct otherwise allowable losses attributable to the working interest whether or not he materially participates in the activity being conducted through the working interest.

A passive activity is defined under the bill to include any rental activity, whether or not the taxpayer materially participates. However, operating a hotel or other similar transient lodging, for example, where substantial services are provided, is not a rental activity. An activity as a dealer in real estate is also not generally treated as a rental activity.[8] Long-term rentals or leases of property (e.g., apartments, leased office equipment, or leased cars), on the other hand, generally are considered to be rental activities. Losses from rental activities are allowed against income from other passive activities, but not against other income.

Interest on debt secured by the taxpayer's residence or a second residence is not subject to limitation under the passive loss rule, so long as the debt is secured by a security interest perfected under local law. Thus, if a taxpayer rents out his vacation home and a portion of the mortgage interest is allocable to rental use of the home which would otherwise be treated as a passive activity, it is not subject to limitation under this provision.

Under the bill, an individual may annually deduct up to $25,000 of passive activity losses (to the extent they exceed income from passive activities) that are attributable to rental real estate activities in which the taxpayer actively participates. The $25,000 offset is not available to corporations. A taxpayer is not treated as actively participating in a rental real estate activity if he has less than a 10 percent interest in the activity. (In such situations, the taxpayer's management activity would relate predominantly to the interests of his co-owners, rather than to the management of his own interest.) He is not presumed to be actively participating, however, if he has a 10 percent or greater interest. * * *.

The $25,000 allowance is phased out ratably as the taxpayer's adjusted gross income (determined without regard to passive activity losses) increases from $100,000 to $150,000. * * *.

The $25,000 allowance for rental real estate applies, in a deduction equivalent sense, to credits attributable to rental real estate activities as well. Under a special rule, the $25,000 allowance applies to low-income housing credits regardless of whether the taxpayer claiming the credit actively participates in the low-income housing activity (including in the case of a limited partner).

A single $25,000 amount (and phaseout thereof) applies on an aggregate basis to credits (including the low-income housing credit) and to deductions, as opposed to allowing a $25,000 amount for each. If the total net rental real estate losses and credits (deduction equivalents) exceed the $25,000 amount allowable against other income, the taxpayer generally must allocate pro rata first among all the losses (including real estate rental activity losses suspended in prior years), and then the credits, attributable to each separate activity, in determining which are treated as allowed. This allocation is necessary for purposes of determining the total suspended losses attributable to each activity, which are allowable in full upon a disposition of the taxpayer's entire interest in the activity.

Taxpayers subject to the rule.—The passive loss rule applies to individuals, estates and trusts. The rule also applies to personal service corporations (without regard to whether employee/owners whose services are provided own 10 percent and without regard to certain limitations in the applicable attribution rules). The committee intends that taxpayers not be able to circumvent the passive loss rule merely by virtue of the form in which they conduct their affairs. Thus, the rule is designed to prevent the sheltering of income derived from an individual's personal services simply by incorporating as a personal service corporation and acquiring tax shelter investments at the corporate level.

It is also not intended that incorporation of an individual's portfolio investments be available as a way to avoid the passive loss rule. For this reason, the passive loss rule, in modified form, also applies to closely held C corporations (other than personal service corporations) that are subject to the at-risk rules (generally, where 5 or fewer individuals, directly or indirectly, own more than 50 percent of the stock). Such C corporations may not offset losses or credits from passive activities against portfolio income. Such corporations may, however, offset passive losses and credits against active business income (i.e., trade or business income which is not from a passive activity). In determining whether a corporation materially participates in an activity, and hence whether the activity is a passive activity, the material participation in the corporation's activity of corporate employees and owners is examined. As is generally true under the passive loss rule, losses and credits from a non-passive

〔Footnote ¶ 3902 continued〕

(8) Under the at-risk rules as extended by the bill to the activity of holding real estate, the holding of real property includes the holding of personal property and the providing of services which are incidental to making real property available as living accommodations. Whether an activity constitutes the holding of real estate for purposes of the at-risk rules is not determinative of whether it constitutes a rental activity under the passive loss rule.

trade or business activity are not subject to any special limitation.

2. Treatment of losses and credits.—

In general.—*Losses.*—Losses arising from a passive activity generally are deductible only against income from that or another passive activity. Suspended passive activity losses for the year are carried forward indefinitely, but are not carried back, and are allowed in subsequent years against passive activity income. Suspended losses from an activity are allowed in full upon a taxable disposition of the activity, as discussed below.

If any passive losses are not deductible in any given year, the amount of the suspended losses from each passive activity is determined on a pro rata basis. With respect to each activity, the portion of the loss that is suspended, and carried forward, is determined by the ratio of net losses from that activity to the total net losses from all passive activities for the year. ***.

In the case of the $25,000 allowance for passive losses from rental real estate activities in which an individual actively participates, a situation could arise in which losses would be allowable for the year under the passive loss rule, but the taxpayer has insufficient (or no) non-passive income against which to apply them. In such a case, the otherwise allowable rental real estate losses are thereupon treated as losses which are not from a passive activity. They are treated as net operating losses (NOLs) arising in that year, and may be carried forward and back in accordance with the rules applicable to NOLs.

In general, NOL carryovers, like current-year losses other than passive losses, are allowed against any income of the taxpayer. In the case of individuals, estates and trusts, and personal service corporations, however, such nonpassive losses and NOLs are taken into account only after reducing income from passive activities by current and suspended deductions from passive activities (but not below zero). Thus, the application of any prior-year suspended passive losses against current year passive income is taken into account before such NOLs are applied against net passive income. This permits the taxpayer to obtain the full benefit of suspended passive activity losses (which are limited in application) before using any losses that are not from passive activities (or NOL carryovers). If a taxpayer has net passive activity income for the year (after the application of all suspended passive losses), the

income may be offset by current-year non-passive losses and by NOL carryovers.

In the case of a closely held corporation (other than a personal service corporation), the passive loss rule applies in modified form; passive losses may be used to offset active business income, but not portfolio income. In applying this rule, losses from passive activities (including such losses carried over from prior years after the effective date) are offset against income from passive activities to determine the aggregate passive loss, if any. If there is such a loss, it may be applied only against active business income, but not portfolio income, of the corporation. As is generally the case, NOLs are applied after the application of the passive loss rule.

The determination of whether a loss is suspended under the passive loss rule is made after the application of the at-risk rules and the interest deduction limitation, as well as other provisions relating to the measurement of taxable income. A loss that would not be allowed for the year because the taxpayer is not at risk with respect to it is suspended under the at-risk provision, not the passive loss rule. Similarly, if an interest deduction is disallowed under the interest deduction limitation, it is not disallowed against under the passive loss rule. Such amounts may become subject to the passive loss rule in subsequent years when they would be allowable under the at-risk or interest limitations.[9] During the 5-year period over which the passive loss rule is phased in, these rules interact in the same manner. ***.

Credits.—Credits arising with respect to passive activities generally are treated in the same manner as deductions.[10] That is, credits may not be used to offset tax attributable to income other than passive income. The amount of tax attributable to net passive income is determined by comparing (i) the amount that the taxpayer would pay with regard to all income, with (ii) the amount that the taxpayer would pay with regard to taxable income other than net passive income (disregarding, in both cases, the effect of credits).

For example, if a taxpayer would owe $50,000 of tax disregarding net passive income, and $80,000 of tax considering both net passive and other taxable income (in both cases, disregarding the effect of credits), then the amount of tax attributable to passive income is $30,000. ***. In the absence of net passive income for a taxable year, no tax is attributable to passive income, and passive

---

[Footnote ¶ 3902 continued]

(9) Amounts at risk are reduced even if deductions which would be allowed under the at-risk rules are suspended under the passive loss rule. Similarly, basis is reduced as under present law, even in the case where deductions are suspended under the passive loss rule. However, if an amount at risk or basis has been reduced by a deduction not allowed under the passive loss rule, the amount at risk or basis is not again reduced when the deduction becomes allowable under the passive loss rule.

(10) The allowability of foreign tax credits, however, is unaffected by the passive loss provision. Instead, foreign tax credits are limited solely by the various rules applying generally as much credits (e.g., the section 904 limitation, which is applied after determining the amounts of foreign source and worldwide income consistently with the application of the passive loss rule).

credits generally are not allowable for the year.

Passive credits may be allowable to offset tax on income other than passive income with respect to the special rule providing up to $25,000 of benefit for certain rental real estate activities. Under this rule, credits are allowed to offset tax on the portion of the $25,000 (or less, as appropriate) that the taxpayer has not been able to offset by the use of deductions.

The amount of tax on such remaining portion (and thus, the amount of credits that can be used against other income, assuming that there are sufficient credits available) is determined by comparing (i) the amount that the taxpayer would owe (disregarding credits) with respect to income other than any net passive losses, but reduced by rental real estate deductions in the full amount allowable under the $25,000 rule, with (ii) the amount that the taxpayer would owe (again disregarding credits) if the allowable rental real estate deductions equalled $25,000 (or less as appropriate, i.e., in the phaseout range for this amount).

In general, credits arising with respect to passive activities, like deductions relating to such activities, can be carried forward indefinitely, and cannot be carried back. However, the character of a credit relating to a passive activity changes, in effect, when the credit becomes allowable under the passive loss rule (i.e., there either is sufficient passive income to allow its use, or it is within the scope of the $25,000 benefit for rental real estate activities). At such time, such credit is aggregated with credits relating to nonpassive activities of the taxpayer, for purposes of determining whether all such credits are allowable in light of other limitations applying to the use of credits (e.g., the 75 percent tax liability limitation, and the provision that credits cannot be used to reduce regular tax liability to less than tentative minimum tax liability). In the event that any credits are not allowable because of such other limitations, the passive credits that are allowable under the passive activity rules are thereupon treated as non-passive credits arising in the current taxable year. The treatment of such credits then is determined in all respects by the general rules applying to such credits, including carryover periods.[11]

Dispositions.—*In general.*—* * * [Upon] a fully taxable disposition, any overall loss from the activity realized by the taxpayer is recognized and allowed against income (whether active or passive income). This result is accomplished by triggering suspended losses upon disposition.

* * * Upon a taxable disposition, net appreciation or depreciation with respect to the activity can be finally ascertained. Since the purpose of the disposition rule is to allow real economic losses of the taxpayer to be deducted, credits, which are not related to the measurement of such loss, are not specially allowable by reason of a disposition.

Taxable dispositions of entire interest in activity.—The type of disposition that triggers full recognition of any loss from a passive activity is a fully taxable disposition of the taxpayer's entire interest in the activity. A fully taxable disposition generally includes a sale of the property to a third party at arm's length, and thus, presumably, for a price equal to its fair market value. Gain realized upon a transfer of an interest in a passive activity generally is treated as passive, and is first offset by the suspended losses from that activity. This accomplishes the purpose of the rule to recognize net income or loss with respect to the activity when it can be finally determined.

Where the taxpayer transfers an interest in a passive activity in a transaction in which the form of ownership merely changes, suspended losses generally are not allowed, because the gain or loss he has realized with respect to the activity has not been finally determined. (Such suspended losses are allowed, however, to the extent that any gain recognized on such a transfer, together with other income from passive activities for the year, exceeds losses from passive activities for the year.) * * *.

The taxpayer must dispose of his entire interest in the activity in order to trigger the recognition of loss. If he disposes of less than his entire interest, then the issue of of ultimate economic gain or loss on his investment in the activity remains unresolved. A disposition of the taxpayer's entire interest involves a disposition of the taxpayer's interest in all entities that are engaged in the activity, and to the extent held in proprietorship form, of all assets used or created in the activity. If a general partnership or S corporation conducts two separate activities, fully taxable disposition by the entity of all the assets used or created in one activity constitutes a disposition of the partner's or shareholder's entire interest in the activity. Similarly, if a grantor trust conducts two separate activities, and sells all the assets used or created in one activity, the grantor is considered as disposing of his entire interest in that activity. If the taxpayer has adequate records of the suspended losses that are allocable to that activity, and includes in income the gain (if any) allocable to his entire interest in the activity, such losses are allowed in full upon the disposition.

As an exception to the general rule, when a limited partnership that conducts two or more separate activities disposes of one of them, limited partners are not treated as having made a disposition triggering suspended losses. In order to accomplish a disposition that triggers suspended losses from limited partnership activities, the limited partner must dispose of his entire interest as a limited partner, and of all other interests that are treated as part of the same activity

---

[**Footnote ¶ 3902 continued**]

(11) Credits that are subject to special limitations (e.g., the limitation on the use of research and development credits to offset certain unrelated income of the taxpayer) continue to be subject to such limitations when they cease to be limited by the passive activity rules.

or activities as those of the limited partnership. * * *.

An installment sale to the taxpayer's entire interest in an activity in a fully taxable transaction triggers the allowance of suspended losses. The losses are allowed in each year of the installment obligation, in the ratio that the gain recognized in each year bears to the total gain on the sale.

A transfer of a taxpayer's interest in an activity by reason of his death causes suspended losses to be allowed to the extent they exceed the amount, if any, by which the basis of the interest in the activity is increased at death under section 1014. Suspended losses are eliminated to the extent of the amount of the basis increase. The losses allowed generally would be reported on the final return of the deceased taxpayer.

Other transfers.—A gift of all or part of the taxpayer's interest in a activity does not trigger suspended losses. However, if he has given away his entire interest, he cannot make a future taxable disposition of it. Suspended losses are therefore added to the basis of the property (i.e., the interest in the activity) immediately before the gift. Similarly, if the taxpayer gives away less than all of his interest, an allocable portion of any suspended losses are added to the donee's basis.[12] Suspended losses of the donor are eliminated when added to the donee's basis, and the remainder of the losses continue to be suspended in the donor's hands. The treatment of subsequent deductions from the activity, to the extent of the donee's interest in it, depends on whether the activity is treated as passive in the donee's hands.

An exchange of the taxpayer's interest in an activity in a nonrecognition transaction, such as an exchange governed by sections 351, 721, or 1031 in which no gain or loss is recognized, does not trigger suspended losses. * * *. To the extent the taxpayer does recognize gain on the transaction (e.g., boot in an otherwise tax-free exchange), the gain is treated as passive activity income, against which passive losses may be deducted.

The suspended losses not allowed upon such a nonrecognition transaction continue to be treated as passive activity losses of the taxpayer, except that in some circumstances they may be applied against income from the property received in the tax-free exchange which is attributable to the original activity.[13] Such suspended losses may not be applied against income from the property which is attributable to a different activity from the one which the taxpayer exchanged.[14] Therefore, unless the taxpayer can show that income against which suspended losses are offset is clearly from the passive activity, his interest in which he exchanged for a different form of ownership, no such offset is permitted. For example, if a passive activity conducted by a general partnership is contributed to an S corporation, followed by the dissolution of the partnership, subsequent income from the activity may be offset by suspended losses from the activity of a shareholder who was formerly a passive general partner. When the taxpayer disposes of his entire interest in the property received in the tax-free exchange, then the remaining suspended losses, if any, are allowed in full.

Activity no longer treated as passive activity.—Other circumstances may arise which do not constitute a disposition, but which terminate the application of the passive loss rule to the taxpayer generally, or to the taxpayer with respect to a particular activity. For example, an individual who previously was passive in relation to a trade or business activity which generates net losses may begin materially participating in the activity. When a taxpayer's participation in an activity is material in any year after a year (or years) during which he was not a material participant, previously suspended losses remain suspended and continue to be treated as passive activity losses. Such previously suspended losses, however, unlike passive activity losses generally, are allowed against income from the activity realized after it ceases to be a passive activity with respect to the taxpayer. As with tax-free exchanges of the taxpayer's entire interest in an activity, however, the taxpayer must be able to show that such income is from the same activity in which the taxpayer previously did not materially participate.[15]

A similar situation arises when a corporation (such as a closely held corporation or personal service corporation) subject to the passive loss rule ceases to be subject to the

---

[Footnote ¶ 3902 continued]

(12) For purposes of determining the donee's loss in a subsequent transaction, however, the donee's basis may not exceed the fair market value of the gift at the time *** [he] received it. *See,* sec. 1015(a). As under present law, losses attributable to unrealized depreciation in value of the property at the time of the gift are not deductible.

(13) This rule does not apply, however, to permit the offset of suspended passive losses against dividends or other income or gain otherwise treated as portfolio income. In addition, following some transactions such as a sec. 1031 like-kind exchange, for example, the taxpayer may no longer have an interest in the original activity. Therefore, there is no special rule permitting suspended losses from the prior interest to be offset by income from the new activity, unless it, too, is a passive activity.

(14) For example, suspended passive activity losses cannot be applied against portfolio income of a pass-through entity.

(15) The reason for this treatment is that the taxpayer could have deducted the suspended losses against income from the activity had the change in his relation to the activity not occurred. Although income from the activity may no longer be passive activity income, prior passive activity losses generated by *that activity* continue to be deductible against income from the activity. It would be inequitable to give less favorable treatment to a taxpayer whose income from an activity becomes active (i.e., not passive) than to one who continues to be merely a passive investor.

passive loss rule because it ceases to meet the definition of an entity subject to the rule. For example, if a closely held corporation makes a public offering of its stock and thereafter ceases to meet the stock ownership criteria for being closely held, it is no longer subject to the passive loss rule * * *. So as not to encourage tax-motivated transactions involving free transferability of losses, the suspended passive losses are not made more broadly applicable (i.e., against portfolio income) by the change in ownership, but continue to be applicable against all income other than portfolio income of the corporation. Deductions arising in years after the year in which the corporation's status changes are not subject to limitation under the passive loss rule.

3. Treatment of portfolio income.—

In general.—Under the bill, portfolio income is not treated as income from a passive activity, and passive losses and credits generally may not be applied to offset it. Portfolio income generally includes interest, dividends, and royalties. Also included in portfolio income are gain or loss attributable to disposition of (1) property that is held for investment (and that is not a passive activity) and (2) property that normally produces interest, dividend, or royalty income.

* * * [Portfolio] income generally is not treated as derived from a passive activity, but rather is treated like other positive income sources such as salary. * * *.

Under the bill, dividends on C corporation stock, REIT and RIC dividends, interest on debt obligations, and royalties from the licensing of property generally are included in portfolio income. Similarly, gains (or losses) from the sale of interests which normally produce such income are treated as portfolio income or losses. These types of assets ordinarily are positive income sources. On the other hand, except as provided below, income from a general or limited partnership interest, from S corporation stock, from a grantor trust, or from a lease of property generally are not treated as portfolio income. Such interests can generate losses which may be applied to shelter unrelated income of the taxpayer. In addition, although such interests might otherwise be considered as held for investment, gains from the sale of such interests, when they are interests in passive activities, are not treated as portfolio income, except to the extent gain on sale of such interests is itself attributable to portfolio income. For example, if a general partnership owns a portfolio of appreciated stocks and bonds and also conducts a business activity, a part of the gain on sale of a partnership interest would be attributable to portfolio income and would, consequently, be treated as portfolio income.

Portfolio income of a passive activity is taken into account separately from other items relating to the activity. Where a taxpayer has an interest in a passive activity, portfolio income of the activity generally is not taken into account in determining passive income or loss from the activity. Rather, such portfolio income is treated as non-passive income of the taxpayer. This rule is necessary in part because taxpayers otherwise would be able to shelter portfolio income to the extent that they transferred the assets from which it is derived to passive activities in which they had investment interests.

The application of the rule can be explained with regard to the example of a limited partnership that is engaged in the publication of a magazine. The partnership also holds a portfolio of dividend and interest bearing securities, but the income from them is more than offset by the tax losses of operating the magazine. Each limited partner must separately account for his share of the portfolio income and the losses from the operations of the magazine, and may not offset them against each other in calculating his tax liability. The portfolio income retains its character as income that is not income from a passive activity, despite the fact that non-portfolio income and loss attributable to a limited partnership interest is treated as income or loss from a passive activity.

The rule treating portfolio income as not from a passive activity does not apply to the extent that income, of a type generally regarded as portfolio income, is derived in the ordinary course of a trade or business. For example, the business income of a bank typically is largely interest. * * * Interest income may also arise in the ordinary course of a trade or business with respect to installment sales and interest charges on accounts receivable.

In these cases, the rationale for treating portfolio-type income as not from the passive activity does not apply, since deriving such income is what the business activity actually, in whole or in part, involves. Accordingly, interest, dividend, or royalty income which is derived in the ordinary course of a trade or business is not treated, for purposes of the passive loss provision, as portfolio income. If a taxpayer directly, or through a passthrough entity, owns an interest in an activity deriving such income, such income is treated as part of the activity, which, as a whole, may or may not be treated as passive, depending on whether the taxpayer materially participates in the activity.

No exception is provided for the treatment of portfolio income arising from working capital, i.e., amounts set aside for the reasonable needs of the business. * * *. Under this rule, for example, interest earned on funds set aside by a limited partnership operating a shopping mall, for the purpose of expanding the mall, is treated as portfolio income * * *.

Under the bill, the Secretary may prescribe regulations under which items of income from a limited partnership or other passive activity are treated as portfolio income. The committee intends that such regulations will prevent taxpayers from structuring income-producing activities (including those that do not bear significant expenses) in ways that are designed to produce passive income that may be offset by unrelated passive losses. For example, such regulations may provide that, where necessary to prevent avoidance of the passive loss rule, a limited partner's share of income from a limited partnership is treated as portfolio income. Circumstances in which such treatment could be appropriate would include a transfer by a corporation of an income-producing activity to a limited partnership with a distribution to shareholders of limited partnership interests.

Treatment of closely held corporations.—The passive loss rule applies to closely held C corporations (other than personal service corporations) in modified form. Such corporations may offset passive losses and credits against active business income, but not against portfolio income. Portfolio income of a closely held corporation generally has the same definition as portfolio income of any other taxpayer subject to the passive loss rule, except that, for purposes of such a corporation (as well as for a personal service corporation) the dividends received deduction is allowed.

4. Material participation.—

General rule.—In general, a taxpayer's interest in a trade or business activity is not treated as an interest in a passive activity for a taxable year if the taxpayer materially participates in the activity throughout such year.[16] In certain instances, however, material participation is not determinative. Working interests in oil and gas properties generally are treated as active whether or not the taxpayer materially participates, and interests in rental activities are treated as passive whether or not the taxpayer materially participates. In the case of rental real estate activities, a separate standard, active participation, is relevant in determining whether the taxpayer is permitted to use losses and credits from such activities to offset up to $25,000 of other income.

Working as an employee, and providing services as part of a personal service business (including professional businesses such as law, accounting, and medicine), intrinsically require personal involvement by the taxpayer. Thus, by their nature, they generally are not passive activities.[17]

Material participation of a taxpayer in an activity is determined separately for each taxable year. In most cases, the material participation (or lack thereof) of a taxpayer in an activity is not expected to change from year to year, although there will be instances in which it does change.

Limited partnerships.—In the case of a limited partnership interest, except to the

extent provided by regulations, it is conclusively presumed that the taxpayer has not materially participated in the activity. In general, under relevant State laws, a limited partnership interest is characterized by limited liability, and in order to maintain limited liability status, a limited partner, as such, cannot be active in the partnership's business. The presumption that a limited partnership interest is passive applies even when the taxpayer possesses the limited partnership interest indirectly through a tiered entity arrangement (e.g., the taxpayer owns a general partnership interest, or stock in an S corporation, and the partnership or corporation in which the taxpayer owns such interest itself owns a limited partnership interest in another entity).

When a taxpayer possesses both a limited partnership interest and another type of interest, such as a general partnership interest, with respect to an activity, lack of material participation is conclusively presumed with respect to the limited partnership interest (thus limiting the use of deductions and credits allocable thereto). The presence of material participation for purposes of other interests in the activity owned by the taxpayer is determined with reference to the relevant facts and circumstances.

Under the bill, the Secretary of the Treasury is empowered to provide through regulations that limited partnership interests in certain circumstances will not be treated (other than through the application of the general facts and circumstances test regarding material participation) as interests in passive activities. It is intended that this grant of authority be used to prevent taxpayers from manipulating the rule that limited partnerships generally are passive, in attempting to evade the passive loss provision.[18]

For example, the exercise of such authority by the Secretary may be appropriate in certain situations where taxpayers divide their interests in activities between limited and general partnership interests, e.g., to facilitate establishing a disposition of the taxpayer's entire interest in an activity, or in connection with special allocations of items of income, deduction, or credit as between limited and general partnership interests. The exercise of such authority by the Secretary would also be appropriate if taxpayers were permitted under State law to establish limited liability entities (that are not taxable

[Footnote ¶ 3902 continued]

(16) This rule is applied by considering services provided both by the taxpayer and by the taxpayer's spouse (whether or not such taxpayer and spouse file a joint return).

(17) The generally "active" nature of the above two undertakings is relevant, not only to the question of whether the taxpayer satisfies the material participation standard, but also to whether either of such two undertakings can be part of the same activity as any other undertaking. *See* section 5, *infra.*

(18) Example of such evasion would include attempting to treat income that generally is regarded as not passive in nature (e.g., personal service income) as passive and accordingly as shelterable or creating an unrealistically small separate "activity" in order to trigger suspended losses upon a partial disposition. Even absent the exercises of the Secretary's authority, items such as a guaranteed cash return or portfolio income from a limited partnership are not regarded as passive.

Act § 501   ¶ 3902

as corporations) for personal service or other active businesses, and to denominate as "limited partnership interests" any interests in such businesses related to the rendering of personal services. The exercise of such authority might also be appropriate where taxpayers sought to avoid limited partnership status with respect to substantially equivalent entities.

Involvement in operations on a regular, continuous, and substantial basis.—Outside of the limited partnership context, the presence or absence of material participation generally is to be determined with reference to all of the relevant facts and circumstances. In order to be treated as materially participating for purposes of the provision, the taxpayer must be involved in the operations of the activity on a regular, continuous, and substantial basis. This standard is based on the material participation standards under Code sections 1402(a) (relating to the self-employment tax) and 2032A (relating to valuation of farm property for purposes of the estate tax). However, the standard is modified consistently with the purposes of the passive loss provision.

Thus, precedents regarding the application of those preexisting legal standards, whether set forth in regulations, rulings, or cases, are not intended to be controlling with regard to the passive loss rule. For example, whether or not, under existing authorities interpreting sections 1402(a) and 2032A, it could be argued that the material participation requirement (for purposes of those sections) is in certain circumstances satisfied by periodic consultation with respect to general management decisions, the standard under this provision is not satisfied thereby in the absence of regular, continuous, and substantial involvement in operations.

In order to satisfy the material participation standard, the individual's involvement must relate to operations. Consider, for example, the case of a general partnership engaged in the business of producing movies. Among the services that may be necessary to this business are the following: writing screenplays; reading and selecting screenplays; actively negotiating with agents who represent writers, actors, or directors; directing, editing, scoring, or acting in the films; actively negotiating with third parties regarding financing and distribution; and actively supervising production (e.g., selecting and negotiating for the purchase or use of sets, costumes, etcetera). An individual who does not make a significant contribution regarding these or similar services is not treated as materially participating. For example, merely approving a financing target, accepting a recommendation regarding selection of the screenplay, cast, locations, and director, or appointing others to perform the above functions, generally does not constitute involvement in operations.

In practice, a taxpayer is most likely to have materially participated in an activity for purposes of this provision in cases where involvement in the activity is the taxpayer's principal business. For example, an individu-

al who spends thirty-five hours per week operating a grocery store, and who does not devote a comparable amount of time to any other business, clearly is materially participating in the business of the grocery store.

By contrast, when an activity is not an individual's principal business, it is less likely that the individual is materially participating. For example, an individual who works full-time as an employee or in a professional service business (such as law, accounting, or medicine), and who has also invested in a general partnership or S corporation engaged in a business involving orange groves, is unlikely to have materially participated in the orange grove business.

However, the fact that an activity is or is not an individual's principal business is not conclusive in determining material participation. An individual may materially participate in no business activities (e.g., someone who does not work or is retired), or in more than one business activity (e.g., a farmer who lives and works on his farm and "moonlights" by operating a gas station).

Another factor that may be highly relevant in showing regular, continuous, and substantial involvement in the operations of an activity, and thereby establishing material participation is whether, and how regularly, the taxpayer is present at the place or places where the principal operations of the activity are conducted. For example, in the case of an employee or professional who invests in a horse breeding activity, if the taxpayer lives hundreds of miles from the site of the activity, and does not often visit the site, such taxpayer is unlikely to have materially participated in the activity. By contrast, an individual who raises horses on land that includes, or is close to, his primary residence, is more likely to have materially participated.

Again, however, this factor is not conclusive. For example, even if the taxpayer in the above example lived near the site of the horse breeding activity, or visited it on numerous occasions during the year, it would still be necessary for the taxpayer to demonstrate regular, continuous, and substantial involvement in the operations of the activity. Such involvement might be shown, for example, by hiring and from time to time supervising those responsible for taking care of the horses on a daily basis, along with making decisions (i.e., not merely ratifying decisions) regarding the purchase, sale, and breeding of horses.

Moreover, under some circumstances, an individual may materially participate in an activity without being present at the activity's principal place of business. In order for such a taxpayer materially to participate, however, the taxpayer still must be regularly, continuously, and substantially involved in providing services integral to the activity. For example, in the case of an investor in a barge that transports grain along the Mississippi River, one way of materially participating is regularly to travel with the barge (not merely as a passenger, but performing substantial services with respect to the transporting of grain). Another way of materially participating, without being present at the principal place of business, is to work on a regular basis at finding new customers for the barge service, and to negotiate with customers regarding the terms on which the service is provided. In the case of farming, the committee anticipates that an individual who does not perform physical work relating to a farm, but who is treated as having self-employment income with respect to the farm under section 1402, generally will be treated as materially participating.

In determining material participation, the performance of management functions generally is treated no differently than rendering other services or performing physical work with respect to the activity. However, a merely formal and nominal participation in management, in the absence of a genuine exercise of independent discretion and judgment, does not constitute material participation.

For example, in the case of a cattle-feeding activity, the fact that an investor regularly receives and responds to "check-a-box" forms regarding when grain should be purchased, what the cattle should be fed, etcetera, may have little or no bearing on material participation. If the management decisions being made by the taxpayer are illusory (e.g., whether to feed the cattle or let them starve), or guided by an expert in the absence of any independent exercise of judgment by the taxpayer, or unimportant to the business,[19] they are given little weight.

The fact that a taxpayer has little or no knowledge or experience regarding the cattle-feeding business is highly significant in determining whether such taxpayer's participation in management is likely to amount to material participation. However, even if a taxpayer has such knowledge and experience, if he merely approves management decisions recommended by a paid advisor, the taxpayer's role is not substantial (and he accordingly has not materially participated), since the decisions could have been made without his involvement.

Even an intermittent role in management, while relevant, does not establish material participation in the absence of regular, continuous, and substantial involvement in operations. For example, the fact that one has responsibility for making significant management decisions with respect to an activity does not establish material participation, even if one from time to time exercises such responsibility. It is almost always true (disregarding special cases such as limited partnership interests) that the owner of an interest in an activity has some right to make management decisions regarding the activity, at least to the extent that his interest is not outweighed by that of other owners. Yet many individuals who possess significant ownership interests do not materially participate, and under present law, have received tax benefits that the committee believes should be subject to limitation under the passive loss rule.[20] Participation in management cannot be relied upon unduly both because its genuineness and substantiality are difficult to verify, and because a general management role, absent more, may fall short of the level of involvement that the material participation standard in the provision is meant to require.

Providing legal, tax, or accounting services as an independent contractor (or as an employee thereof), or that the taxpayer commonly provides as an independent contractor, would not ordinarily constitute material participation in an activity other than the activity of providing these services to the public. Thus, for example, a member of a law firm who provides legal services to a client regarding a general partnership engaged in research and development, is not, if he invests in such partnership, treated as materially participating in the research and development activity by reason of such legal services.

The fact that a taxpayer utilizes employees or contract services to perform daily functions in running the business does not prevent such taxpayer from qualifying as materially participating. However, the activities of such agents are not attributed to the taxpayer, and the taxpayer must still personally perform sufficient services to establish material participation.

A special rule, derived from section 2032A, applies with respect to farming activities, permitting taxpayers to qualify as materially participating in certain situations involving retired or disabled individuals who previously were materially participating (as that term is used for purposes of the passive loss rule), or involving a surviving spouse of an

---

[Footnote ¶ 3902 continued]

(19) For example, management decisions may be unimportant to the business where the tax benefits from the business outweigh any risk of economic loss that may result from the decisions.

(20) Experience in applying existing legal standards confirms that a test based on participation in management is subject to manipulation and creates frequent factual disputes between taxpayers and the Internal Revenue Service. Section 464, for example, disallows prepaid expenses incurred in a farming activity if more than 35 percent of the loss from the activity is allocated to limited partners or persons who do not actively participate in management. As a result, farming activities that rely upon syndication to outside investors, and then are operated principally under the direction of an agent, have been structured so as to assist otherwise passive investors in demonstrating that they play a role in management decisions. While the Internal Revenue Service may argue in any such instance that an investor is not truly participating in management, such argument may be difficult to sustain in the absence of reliable direct evidence regarding the investor's independence of judgment. The committee expects that the material participation standard for purposes of the passive loss rule, in light of its focus on the taxpayer's role in actual operations, will not be similarly subject to manipulation and ambiguity.

individual who was so participating. Thus, to the extent that, under section 2032A(b)(4) or (5), such person would be treated as still materially participating during retirement or disability (or, in the case of a surviving spouse, after the decedent's death), such person shall be treated as materially participating for purposes of the passive loss provision.

Material participation by an entity subject to the passive loss rule. Special rules apply in the case of taxable entities that are subject to the passive loss rule. An estate or trust is treated as materially participating in an activity (or as actively participating in a rental real estate activity) if an executor or fiduciary, in his capacity as such, is so participating.[21] Portfolio income of an estate or trust must be accounted for separately, and may not be offset by losses from passive activities.

A corporation that is subject to the passive loss provision is treated as materially participating in an activity with respect to which one or more shareholders, owning in the aggregate more than 50 percent of the outstanding stock of the corporation, materially participate. Thus, for example, a corporation with 5 shareholders, each owning 20 percent of the stock, is treated as materially participating in an activity if three or more of such shareholders so participate. If one of the three shareholders who so participated owned only 5 percent of the stock, and as a result the three participating shareholders owned only 45 percent of the stock in the corporation, the corporation would not be treated as materially participating in the activity.

A corporation subject to the passive loss provision that is not a personal service corporation (as defined for purposes of the provision) may also be treated as materially participating in an activity if it meets the standard set forth in section 465(c)(7)(C), disregarding clause (iv). This standard generally is satisfied if (i) for the prior 12-month period, at least one full-time employee of the corporation provided sufficient services in active management with respect to the activity, (ii) during the same period, at least 3 full-time nonowner employees provided sufficient services directly related to the activity, and (iii) the amount of business deductions by the taxpayer attributable to the activity exceeded 15 percent of gross income from the business for the taxable year.

Active participation in a rental real estate activity.—*Allowance of $25,000 of losses and credits against other income under specified circumstances.*

*   *   *   *   *   *

Under the relief provision for rental real estate, an individual may offset up to $25,000 of income that is not treated as passive, by using losses and credits from rental real estate activities with respect to which such individual actively participates.[23] (Low-income housing credits can be so used, as a part of the overall $25,000 amount, whether or not the individual actively participates in the rental real estate activity to which such credits relate.) This relief applies only if the individual does not have sufficient passive income for the year, after considering all other passive deductions and credits, to use fully the losses and credits from such rental real estate activities. No relief is provided under the provision to taxpayers other than individuals (i.e., C corporations subject to the passive loan provision).[24]

The $25,000 amount is reduced, but not below zero, by 50 percent of the amount by which the taxpayer's adjusted gross income for the year exceeds $100,000. In the case of a married individual not filing a joint return, no more than $12,500 of such relief is available, reduced by 50 percent of the amount by which such individual's adjusted gross income exceeds $50,000. For these purposes, adjusted gross income is determined without reference to net losses from passive activities (other than losses allowable solely by reason of a fully taxable disposition of an activity).

Since relief under this rule applies only to rental real estate activities, it does not apply to passive real estate activities that are not treated as rental activities under the provision (e.g., an interest in the activity of operating a hotel). Similarly, relief is not provided with regard to the renting of property other than real estate (e.g., equipment leasing).

Scope of active participation.—A taxpayer is treated as not having actively participated in a rental real estate activity if the taxpayer (in conjunction with such taxpayer's spouse, even in the absence of a joint

---

[Footnote ¶ 3902 continued]

   (21) In the case of a grantor trust, however, material participation is determined at the grantor rather than the entity level.

   (23) For purposes of applying this standard, as with respect to material participation, services performed both by the taxpayer and by the taxpayer's spouse are considered (whether or not such individuals file a joint return). It is worth noting that, while standards requiring active management or active participation in management apply for certain purposes under present law (see sections 55(e), 464(e)(2)(b), and 2032(A)), these standards are not the same as the active participation standard described herein.

   (24) Trusts and estates (other than grantor trusts, which are not separate taxable entities) are treated as individuals, and accordingly can qualify for relief (although a trust may cease to be treated as a trust for tax purposes if it is involved in a business activity; see *supra*). The active participation standard is applied with respect to executors or fiduciaries acting in their capacity as such.

return) owns less than 10 percent (by value) of all interests in such activity.[25] This requirement is designed to assist in restricting the relief provided under the $25,000 rule (assuming all other applicable requirements are met) to appropriate circumstances—for example, the case of a home in which the taxpayer formerly lived or plans subsequently to live, as opposed to a syndicated real estate shelter. In addition, the 10 percent rule reflects the fact that active participation by a less than 10 percent owner typically represents services performed predominantly with regard to ownership interests of co-owners.

In the case of a taxpayer owning an interest in a rental real estate activity and meeting the 10-percent ownership requirement, up to $25,000 of relief may be available if the taxpayer actively participates in the activity. This standard is designed to be less stringent than the material participation requirement in light of both the special nature of rental activities, which generally require less in the way of personal services, and the committee's reasons for providing up to $25,000 of relief in this instance.

The difference between active participation and material participation is that the former can be satisfied without regular, continuous, and substantial involvement in operations, so long as the taxpayer participates, e.g., in the making of management decisions or arranging for others to provide services (such as repairs), in a significant and *bona fide* sense. Management decisions that are relevant in this context include approving new tenants, deciding on rental terms, approving capital or repair expenditures, and other similar decisions.

Thus, for example, a taxpayer who owns and rents out an apartment that formerly was his primary residence, or that he uses as a part-time vacation home, may be treated as actively participating even if he hires a rental agent and others provide services such as repairs. So long as the taxpayer participates in the manner described above, a lack of participation in operations does not lead to the denial of relief.

A limited partner, to the extent of his limited partnership interest, is treated as not meeting the active participation standard.[26]

In addition, a lessor under a net lease is unlikely to have the degree of involvement which active participation entails. Moreover, as with regard to the material participation standard, services provided by an agent are not attributed to the principal, and a merely formal and nominal participation in management, in the absence of a genuine exercise of independent discretion and judgment, is insufficient.

*   *   *   *   *   *

5. Definition of activity.—

In applying the passive loss rule, one of the most important determinations that must be made is the scope of a particular activity. This determination is important for several reasons. For example, if two undertakings are part of the same activity, the taxpayer need only establish material participation with respect to the activity as a whole, whereas if they are separate activities he must establish such participation separately for each. In the case of a disposition, knowing the scope of the activity is critical to determining whether the taxpayer has disposed of his entire interest in the activity, or only of a portion thereof.[27]

*   *   *   *   *   *

The determination of what constitutes a separate activity is intended to be made in a realistic economic sense. The question to be answered is what undertakings consist of an integrated and interrelated economic unit, conducted in coordination with or reliance upon each other, and constituting an appropriate unit for the measurement of gain or loss.

Under present law, section 183, relating to hobby losses, involves issues similar to those arising with respect to passive losses.[28] Section 183 requires that separate activities be identified in order to determine whether a specific activity constitutes a hobby. Treasury Regulations interpreting this provision note that all facts and circumstances of a specific case must be taken into account, and then identify as the most significant facts and circumstances: "the degree of organizational and economic interrelationship in various undertakings, the business purpose which is (or might be) served by carrying on

---

[Footnote ¶ 3902 continued]

(25) Since low-income housing credits are allowable without regard to active participation, they are unaffected by this requirement.

(26) The delegation of regulatory authority to the Secretary to determine when a limited partnership interest should be treated as not passive does not specifically amount to providing relief under the active participation standard to limited partnership interests in rental real estate activities. The active participation rules do not prevent a limited partner from receiving $25,000 of benefit with regard to the low-income housing credit, since relief relating to such credit does not depend upon active participation.

(27) Determining the scope of an activity also is important with respect to the 10 percent ownership requirement for actively participating in a rental real estate activity, and in certain situations where the taxpayer disposes of an activity other than through a taxable transaction.

(28) By contrast, the at-risk rules, to the extent that they define "activity," address issues different from those that are relevant with respect to passive losses. See section 465(c)(2). The at-risk rules define "activity" in terms of narrow asset units, such as individual items of property, in light of the goal of such rules to establish a relationship between each such asset and financing attributable to it. In the passive loss context, unlike the at-risk context, financing is not the relevant issue.

the various undertakings separately or together . . . and the similarity of the various undertakings." These facts and circumstances likewise are relevant to determining the scope of an activity for purposes of the passive loss rule."[29]

In general, providing two or more substantially different products or services involves engaging in more than one activity (unless customarily or for business reasons provided together—e.g., the appliance and clothing sections of a department store). For example, operating a restaurant and engaging in research and development are objectively so different that they are extremely unlikely to be part of the same activity. In addition, different stages in the production and sale of a particular product that are not carried on in an integrated fashion generally are not part of the same activity. For example, operating a retail gas station and engaging in oil and gas drilling generally are not part of the same activity. In general, normal commercial practices are highly probative in determining whether two or more undertakings are or may be parts of a single activity.

On the other hand, the fact that two undertakings involve providing the same products or services does not establish that they are part of the same activity absent the requisite degree of economic interrelationship or integration. For example, separate real estate rental projects built and managed in different locations by a real estate operator generally will constitute separate activities. Similarly, in the case of farming, each farm generally will constitute a separate activity. On the other hand, an integrated apartment project or shopping center generally will be treated as a single activity.

*   *   *   *   *   *

Certain types of integration among undertakings are not sufficient to establish that they are part of the same activity. For example, the fact that the taxpayer has ultimate management responsibilities with respect to different undertakings does not establish that they are part of the same activity, nor does the fact that the undertakings have access to common sources of financing, or benefit for goodwill purposes from sharing a common name. These common features may often be shared by all of the undertakings in which a particular individual is engaged, without establishing, in a substantial economic sense, that all such undertakings are part of the same activity.

The fact that two undertakings are conducted by the same entity (such as a partnership or S corporation) does not establish that they are part of the same activity. Conversely, the fact that two undertakings are conducted by different entities does not establish that they are different activities. Rather, the activity rules generally are applied by disregarding the scope of passthrough entities such as partnerships and S corporations.

With respect to limited partnerships, an additional rule applies in light of the special status of limited partnership interests with respect to material participation. For purposes of a disposition, it is conclusively presumed that a limited partnership interest includes no more than one activity. In addition, such an interest is not treated as being part of the same activity as any activity in which the taxpayer is treated as materially participating. However, when otherwise appropriate, a limited partnership interest is treated as part of a larger activity in which the taxpayer does not materially participate (e.g., when two limited partnerships are conducting the same activity, or an individual is both a limited partner and a nonparticipating general partner with respect to the same activity).[30]

In applying the facts and circumstances test regarding what constitutes an activity, any undertaking that is accorded special treatment under the passive loss rule (e.g., treatment as always being active or as always being passive) is not treated as part of the same activity as any undertaking that does not receive identical treatment under the passive loss rule. For example, providing services as an employee or in a personal service business intrinsically is not passive, without requiring the examination of further facts and circumstances. Thus, such an undertaking generally is not part of the same activity as an undertaking in which further facts and circumstances must be examined. An oil and gas working interest is treated as not passive without regard to material participation, and thus is treated as separate from any undertaking not relating to oil and gas working interests.[31] This rule is necessary so that the special rules for particular undertakings will not in effect be extended to other types of undertakings (e.g., through the argument that an undertaking that is not a working interest is part of the same activity as a working interest, and hence should not be treated as passive even in the absence of material participation).

6. Rental activity.—

In general.—Under the passive loss rule, a rental activity is generally treated as a passive activity regardless of whether the

---

(29) *See* Treas. Reg. 1.183-1(d)(1). The provision in this regulation that a taxpayer's characterization of what constitutes an activity will be accepted unless it is unduly "artificial" does not apply with respect to the passive loss rule. While the committee anticipates that artificial characteristics will be disregarded as a matter of course with respect to passive losses, there is no presumption that the taxpayer's characterization is correct even absent such "artificiality."

(30) These special rules regarding limited partnership interests do not apply in the case of any such interest that, pursuant to the Secretary's special regulatory authority, is treated as not intrinsically passive (i.e., as passive only to the extent established by examination of the relevant facts and circumstances).

(31) See section 6, infra, noting that, for the same reasons, a rental real estate undertaking, as well as a rental undertaking involving property other than real estate, each is treated as not part of the same activity as any other type of undertaking.

taxpayer materially participates in the activity. Deductions and credits from a rental activity generally may be applied to offset only other income from passive activities. In the case of rental real estate activities in which the taxpayer actively participates, a special rule permits the application of losses and credits from the activity against up to $25,000 of non-passive income of the taxpayer, for taxpayers other than corporations. * * *

In determining what is a rental activity for purposes of these rules, prior law applicable in determining when an S corporation had passive rental income, as opposed to active business income, for purposes of continuing to qualify as an S corporation, provides a useful analogy.[32] The purpose of the prior law rule, like the passive loss rule, is to distinguish between rental activity that is passive in nature and nonrental activity which may not be passive. Thus, under the passive loss rule, a rental activity generally is an activity, the income from which consists of payments principally for the use of tangible property, rather than for the performance of substantial services.[32a]

Some activities are not treated as rental activities under the passive loss rule even though they may involve the receipt of payments for the use of tangible property, because significant services are rendered in connection with such payments. Payments for the use of tangible property for short periods, with heavy turnover among the users of the property, may cause an activity not to be a rental activity, especially if significant services are performed in connection with each new user of the property. Another factor indicating that an activity should not be treated as a rental activity is that expenses of day-to-day operations are not insignificant in relation to rents produced by the property, or in relation to the amount of depreciation and the cost of carrying the rental property.

On the other hand, although the period for which property is rented is not in itself determinative of whether the activity is a rental activity, a long-term rental period (in comparison to the useful life of the property) and low turnover in the lessees of the property, is indicative that the activity is a rental activity.

For example, an activity consisting of the short-term leasing of motor vehicles, where the lessor furnishes services including maintenance of gas and oil, tire repair and changing, cleaning and polishing, oil changing and lubrication and engine and body repair, is not treated as a rental activity. By contrast, furnishing a boat under a bare boat charter, or a plane under a dry lease (i.e., without pilot, fuel or oil), constitutes a rental activity under the passive loss rule, because no significant services are performed in connection with providing the property.

Based on similar considerations, renting hotel rooms or similar space used primarily for lodging of transients where significant services are provided generally is not a rental activity under the passive loss rule. By contrast, renting apartments to tenants pursuant to leases (with, e.g., month-to-month or yearly lease terms) is treated as a rental activity.

Generally, being the lessor of property subject to a net lease is a rental activity. A net lease is defined for purposes of determining whether a leased property constitutes investment property, under the investment interest limitation, as a lease of property, if the section 162 deductions (other than rents and reimbursed amounts) are less than 15 percent of the rental income produced by the property, or if the lessor is either guaranteed a specified return or is guaranteed in whole or in part against loss of income. For purposes of the passive loss rule, it makes no difference how long the taxpayer has owned the leased property (see sec. 163(d)(6)(B)).

Scope of rental activity.—Some businesses involve the conduct of rental activities in association with other activities not involving renting tangible property. Although the other activities may immediately precede the rental activity, be conducted by the same persons, or take place in the same general location, they are not treated as a part of the rental activity, because under the passive loss rule rental activities are considered passive activities without regard to the taxpayer's material participation. In the case of other activities, an examination of the taxpayer's material participation generally determines whether an activity is passive. Rental activities generally are treated as separate from nonrental activities involving the same persons or property. Thus, for example, automobile leasing is treated as a different activity from automobile manufacturing, and real estate construction and development is a different activity from renting the newly constructed building.

Similarly, suppose a travel agency operated in the form of a general partnership has its offices on three floors of a ten-story building that it owns. The remainder of the

---

[Footnote ¶ 3902 continued]

(32) Sec. 1372(a)(5) (as in effect prior to the Subchapter S Revision Act of 1982 is relevant in determining whether significant services are performed in connection with furnishing property. For example, regulations applicable in interpreting that section provided that rents did not include payments for the use or occupancy of rooms where significant services were also rendered to the occupant (such as hotels and the like which furnish hotel services). The regulations further provided, "services are considered rendered to the occupant if they are primarily for the convenience and are other than those usually or customarily rendered in connection with the rental of rooms or other space for occupancy only. The supplying of maid service, for example, constitutes such services; whereas the furnishing of heat, light, . . . the collection of trash, etc., are not considered as services rendered to the occupant.

(32a) A rental activity generally does not include payments for the use of intangible property (e.g., stocks), or other payments more properly characterized as interest (e.g., for the use of forbearance of money).

space in the building is rented out to tenants. The travel agency expects to take over another floor for its own use in a year. The partnership is treated as being engaged in two separate activities: a travel agency activity and a rental real estate activity. Deductions and credits attributable to the building are allocable to the travel agency activity only to the extent that they relate to the space occupied by the travel agency during the taxable year.

Separate rental real estate activity.—Because only rental real estate activities are eligible for the $25,000 offset of losses and credits against non-passive income, a rental real estate undertaking is not considered as part of the same activity as any undertaking other than another rental real estate undertaking. For these purposes, the word "rental" is interpreted consistently with its meaning in other respects for purposes of the passive loss provision. Thus, for example, a hotel is treated neither as a rental real estate undertaking, nor as consisting of two activities only one of which is a rental real estate undertaking.

To be eligible for the $25,000 offset, a taxpayer must actively participate in the rental real estate activity. He is not considered to actively participate unless he has at least a 10 percent interest in the activity * * *. For purposes of determining whether his interest in the activity amounts to at least 10 percent, separate buildings are treated as separate rental real estate activities if the degree of integration of the business and other relevant factors do not require treating them as parts of a larger activity (e.g., an integrated shopping center).

In the case of units smaller than an entire building, it similarly is necessary to assess the degree of business and functional integration among the units in determining whether they are separate activities. A cooperative apartment in an apartment building, owned by a taxpayer unrelated to those owning the other apartments in the building, generally will qualify as a separate activity, despite the fact that ownership of the building may be shared with owners of other apartments in the building, and despite the sharing with other apartments of such services as management and maintenance of common areas. By contrast, ownership of an undivided interest in a building, or of an area too small to be rented as a separate unit (or that is not rented as a separate unit) does not qualify as a separate activity.

In the case of a commercial building, for example, that is rented out to various tenants, and in which different parties own different floors, it again is necessary to examine the degree of integration with which business relating to different floors is conducted. An arrangement in which the rights to the various floors are separately sold to different parties, but rental of the building is handled in a centralized fashion, generally constitutes a single activity, whereas such treatment might not be appropriate if the owners of different floors separately manage their own rental businesses.

7. Working interest in oil and gas property.—

When a taxpayer owns a working interest in an oil and gas property, the working interest is not treated as a passive activity, whether or not the taxpayer materially participates. Thus, losses and credits derived from such activity can be used to offset other income of the taxpayer without limitation under the passive loss rule.

In general, a working interest is an interest with respect to an oil and gas property that is burdened with the cost of development and operation of the property.[33] Rights to overriding royalties, production payments, and the like, do not constitute working interests, because they are not burdened with the responsibility to share expenses of drilling, completing, or operating oil and gas property. Similarly, contract rights to extract or share in oil and gas, or in profits from extraction, without liability to share in the costs of production, do not constitute working interests. Income from such interests generally is considered to be portfolio income.

A working interest generally has characteristics such as responsibility for signing authorizations for expenditures with respect to the activity, receiving periodic drilling and completion reports, receiving periodic reports regarding the amount of oil extracted, possession of voting rights proportionate to the percentage of the working interest possessed by the taxpayer, the right to continue activities if the present operator decides to discontinue operations, a proportionate share of tort liability with respect to the property (e.g., if a well catches fire), and some responsibility to share in further costs with respect to the property in the event that a decision is made to spend more than amounts already contributed.

However, the fact that a taxpayer is entitled to decline, or does decline, to make additional contributions under a buyout, non-participation, or similar arrangement, does not contradict such taxpayer's possessing a working interest. In addition, the fact that tort liability may be insured against does not contradict such taxpayer's possessing a working interest.

When the taxpayer's form of ownership limits the liability of the taxpayer, the interest possessed by such taxpayer is not a working interest for purposes of the passive loss provision. Thus, an interest owned by a limited partnership interest is not treated as a working interest with regard to any limited partner, and an interest owned by an S corporation is not treated as a working

---

〔Footnote ¶ 3902 continued〕

(33) *See* Treas. Reg. sec. 1.612-4(a), along with cases and rulings decided thereunder, such as *Phillips* v. *Comm'r* 233 F. Supp. 59 (E.D. Tex. 1964), aff'd *per curiam*, (5th Cir.), 66-1 U.S.T.C. Paragraph 9157; *Haass* v. *Comm'r*, 55 T.C. 43 (1970), acq., 1971-2 C.B. 2; *Cottingham* v. *Comm'r*, 63 T.C. 695 (1975); *Miller* v. *Comm'r* 78-1 U.S.T.C. Paragraph 9127 (C.D. Cal. 1977);Rev. Rul. 68-139, 1968-1 C.B. 311.

interest with regard to any shareholder. The same result follows with respect to any form of ownership that is substantially equivalent in its effect on liability to a limited partnership interest or interest in an S corporation, even if different in form. The rule is applied by looking through tiered entities. For example, a general partner in a partnership that owns a limited partnership interest in a partnership that owns a working interest is not treated as owning a working interest.

A special rule applies in any case where, for a prior taxable year, net losses from a working interest in a property were treated by the taxpayer as not from a passive activity. In such a case, any net income realized by the taxpayer from the property (or from any substituted basis property, e.g., property acquired in a section 1031 like-kind exchange for such property) in a subsequent year also is treated as active. Under this rule, for example, if a taxpayer claims losses for a year with regard to a working interest and then, after the property to which the interest relates begins to generate net income, transfers the interest to an S corporation in which he is a shareholder, or to a partnership in which he has an interest as a limited partner, his interest with regard to the property continues to be treated as not passive.[34]

Under some circumstances, deductions relating to a working interest may be subject to limitation under other provisions in the Internal Revenue Code. For example, protection against loss through nonrecourse financing, guarantees, stop-loss agreements or other similar arrangements, may cause certain deductions allocable to the taxpayer to be disallowed under section 465. Such limitations are applied prior to and independently of the passive loss rule.

[Conference Report]
Senate Amendment

*　　*　　*　　*　　*　　*

Effective date

The provision is effective for taxable years beginning after December 31, 1986, with a phase-in rule for investments made before the date of enactment.

Under the phase-in rule, the amount disallowed under the passive loss rule during any year in the phase-in period equals the applicable percentage of the amount that would be disallowed for that year under the provision if fully effective. The applicable percentage is 35 percent for taxable years beginning in 1987, 60 percent in taxable years beginning in 1988, 80 percent in taxable years beginning in 1989, 90 percent in taxable years beginning in 1990, and 100 percent in taxable years beginning after 1990.

Conference Agreement

The conference agreement generally follows the Senate amendment, but with certain modifications and clarifications.

1. Overview

Passive activity.—The definition of a passive activity generally is the same as under the Senate amendment. However, the definition is clarified to accord with the original intent of the provision that passive activities can include activities generating deductions allowable under section 174 of the Code as research and experimentation expenditures. Thus, if a taxpayer has an interest in an activity with respect to which deductions would be allowed as research and experimentation expenditures, and he does not materially participate in the activity, losses from the activity (including the research and experimentation expenditures) are subject to limitation under the rule.

It is also clarified that a net lease of property is a rental activity that is treated as a passive activity under the rule.

Passive activities that are not a trade or business.—The conference agreement provides that, to the extent provided in regulations, a passive activity may include an activity conducted for profit (within the meaning of sec. 212), including an activity that is not a trade or business. The conferees anticipate that the exercise of this authority may be appropriate in certain situations where activities other than the production of portfolio income are involved. This regulatory authority is meant to cause the passive loss rule to apply with respect to activities that give rise to passive losses intended to be limited under the provision, but that may not rise to the level of a trade or business.

Interest on taxpayer's residence. — Qualified residence interest is not subject to the passive loss rule (see V.C., below).

Interaction with interest deduction limitation.—The conference agreement provides that interest deductions attributable to passive activities are treated as passive activity deductions, but are not treated as investment interest (see V.C., below). Thus, such interest deductions are subject to limitation under the passive loss rule, and not under the investment interest limitation. Similarly, income and loss from passive activities generally are not treated as investment income or loss in calculating the amount of the investment interest limitation.[1]

Interaction with other Code sections.—It is clarified that the passive loss rule applies to all deductions that are from passive activities, including deductions allowed under sections 162, 163, 164, and 165. For example,

---

[Footnote ¶ 3902 continued]

(34) This rule applies whether or not the working interest would have been treated as passive in the absence of the provision treating working interests as *per se* active, i.e., if material participation were relevant in this context.

(1) However, as described in V.C., below, any passive losses allowed by reason of the phase-in of the passive loss provision (other than losses from rental real estate activities in which the taxpayer actively participates reduces net investment income.

deductions for State and local property taxes incurred with respect to passive activities are subject to limitation under the passive loss rule whether such deductions are claimed above-the-line or as itemized deductions under section 164.

Personal services income not treated as from passive activity.—The conference agreement clarifies that income received by an individual from the performance of personal services with respect to a passive activity is not treated as income from a passive activity. Thus, for example, in the case of a limited partner who is paid for performing services for the partnership (whether by way of salary, guaranteed payment, or allocation of partnership income), such payments cannot be sheltered by passive losses from the partnership or from any other passive activity.

Taxpayers subject to the passive loss rule.—Under the conference agreement, the passive loss provision generally applies to the same taxpayers as under the Senate amendment, and with the same more limited version of the rule for closely held corporations. However, the applicability of the rule is modified and clarified as described below.

In the case of closely held corporations, the passive loss rule permits passive losses (and credits, in a deduction equivalent sense) to offset net active income, but not portfolio income. Thus, for example, if a closely held corporation has $400,000 of passive losses from a rental activity, $500,000 of active business income, and $100,000 of portfolio income, the passive losses may be applied to reduce the active business income to $100,000, but may not be applied against the portfolio income.

Personal service corporations.—The definition of a personal service corporation applying for purposes of the provision is modified to provide that the passive loss rule does not apply to a corporation where the employee-owners together own less than 10 percent, by value, of the corporation's stock.

The conference agreement provides that the rule applicable to a change in status of a closely held corporation also applies to a change in status of a personal service corporation. That is, if a personal service corporation ceases to meet the definition of a personal service corporation subject to the passive loss rule in any year, losses from a passive activity conducted by the corporation and previously suspended by reason of the application of the passive loss rule are not triggered by the change in status, but are allowed against income from that activity. Any previously suspended losses and (deduction equivalent) credits in excess of income from the activity continue to be treated as from a passive activity. Losses and credits from an activity arising in a year when the corporation does not meet the definition of a personal service corporation (or a closely held corporation are not subject to limitation under the passive loss rule).

Affiliated groups.—A limited version of the passive loss rule applies to closely held corporations, providing that passive losses of

the corporation may not offset portfolio income. In the case of affiliated groups of corporations filing consolidated returns, it is intended that this rule apply on a consolidated group basis. Thus, it is intended that losses from any passive activity within the consolidated group may offset net active income, but not portfolio income, of any member of the group. An activity may be conducted by several corporations, and conversely, one corporation may be engaged in several activities. Portfolio income is accounted for separately from income or loss from each activity.

In determining whether an activity (other than a rental activity) conducted within the closely held consolidated group is a passive activity, the material participation test is intended to be applied on a consolidated basis. Thus, for example, if one or more individual shareholders holding stock representing more than 50 percent of a member's stock materially participate in an activity of any member of the group, the group is considered to materially participate. Similarly, if the requirements of section 465(c)(7)(C) (without regard to clause (iv) thereof) are met with respect to an activity by any member (or several members together), then the group is considered to materially participate in the activity.

In the case of a personal service corporation which is a member of a consolidated group, similar principles are intended to apply. For example, a corporation may be treated as a personal service corporation for purposes of the rule where the owners who render the requisite services are employees of a subsidiary, rather than of the parent corporation. Under the conference agreement, the definition of a personal service corporation is applied taking into account attribution of ownership of stock as provided in section 269A(b).

2. Treatment of losses and credits

In general.—*Losses.*—The conference agreement provides that interest deductions attributable to passive activities are subject to the passive loss rule (as under the Senate amendment), but are not subject to the investment interest limitation (see section V.C., below). Thus, for example, if a taxpayer has net passive losses of $100 for a taxable year beginning after 1986, $40 of which consists of interest expense, the entire $100 is subject to limitation under the passive loss rule, and no portion of the loss is subject to limitation under the investment interest limitation.

Rental real estate in which taxpayer actively participates.—Clarification is provided with respect to the rule allowing up to $25,000 of losses and credits (in a deduction equivalent sense) from rental real estate activities in which the taxpayer actively participates to offset non-passive income of the taxpayer. The $25,000 allowance is applied by first netting income and loss from all of the taxpayer's rental real estate activities in which he actively participates. If there is a net loss for the year from such activities, net passive income (if any) from other activities is then applied against it, in determining the amount eligible for the $25,000 allowance.

For example, assume that a taxpayer has $25,000 of losses from a rental real estate activity in which he actively participates. If he also actively participates in another rental real estate activity, from which he has $25,000 of gain, resulting in no net loss from rental real estate activities in which he actively participates, then no amount is allowed under the $25,000 allowance for the year. This result follows whether or not the taxpayer has net losses from other passive activities for the year.

The Senate amendment provided that a taxpayer is not treated as actively participating with respect to an interest in a rental real estate activity if such interest is less than 10 percent of all interests in the activity. The conference agreement clarifies that a taxpayer is treated as not actively participating if at any time during the taxable year (or shorter relevant period for which the taxpayer held an interest in the activity) the taxpayer's interest in the activity is less than 10 percent.

It is clarified that, with respect to active participation, just as with respect to material participation, a change in the nature of the taxpayer's involvement does not trigger the allowance of deductions carried over from prior taxable years. Thus, if a taxpayer begins to actively participate in an activity in which, in prior years, he did not actively participate, the rule allowing up to $25,000 of losses from rental real estate activities against non-passive income does not apply to losses from the activity carried over from such prior years.[2] The same rule applies to credits, to the extent that active participation is relevant to their allowability.

The conference agreement provides that, for purposes of calculating the phase-out of the $25,000 allowance at adjusted gross income between $100,000 to $150,000 (or $200,000 to $250,000, in the case of certain credits), adjusted gross income is calculated without regard to IRA contributions and taxable social security benefits.

The conference agreement provides that in the case of an estate of a taxpayer who, in the taxable year in which he died, owned an interest in a rental real estate activity in which he actively participated, the estate is deemed to actively participate for the two years following the death of the taxpayer. Thus, the taxpayer's estate may continue to receive the same tax treatment with respect to the rental real estate activity as did the taxpayer in the taxable year of his death. This treatment applies to the taxpayer's estate during the two taxable years of the estate following his death, to facilitate the administration of the estate without requiring the executor or fiduciary to reach decisions with respect to the appropriate disposition of the rental real property within a short period following the taxpayer's death.

It is clarified that a trust is not intended to qualify for the allowance of up to $25,000 in losses and (deduction equivalent) credits from a rental real estate activity in which there is active participation, so that individuals cannot circumvent the $25,000 ceiling, or multiply the number of $25,000 allowances, simply by transferring various rental real properties to one or more trusts.

Married individuals filing separately.—The amount of the $25,000 allowance, and the adjusted gross income ranges in which the allowance is phased out (i.e., $100,000 to $150,000, except in the case of certain credits where the range is $200,000 to $250,000) is halved in the case of married individuals filing separate returns, under the Senate amendment. This rule is retained, with modification, in the conference agreement. The conference agreement provides that, in the case of married individuals filing separately, who, at any time during the taxable year, do not live apart, the amount of the $25,000 allowance is reduced to zero. Absent such a rule, married taxpayers where one spouse would be eligible for a portion of the $25,000 amount if they filed separately would have an incentive so to file; the conferees believe that rules that encourage filing separate returns give rise to unnecessary complexity and place an unwarranted burden on the administration of the tax system.

Credits.—The conference agreement provides that for the rehabilitation and low-income housing credits, the phase-out range for offsetting tax on up to $25,000 of non-passive income is increased to between $200,000 and $250,000 of adjusted gross income (calculated without regard to net passive losses, IRA contributions, or taxable social security benefits), and such credits are allowed under the $25,000 rule regardless of whether the taxpayer actively participates in the activity generating the credits. In the case of the low-income housing credit, the increase in the phase-out range (to between $200,000 and $250,000, as opposed to between $100,000 and $150,000 as for other rental real estate losses and credits), and the waiver of the requirement that the taxpayer actively participate in the activity generating the low-income housing credit, apply only to property placed in service before 1990, and only with respect to the original credit compliance period for the property, except if the property is placed in service before 1991, and 10 percent or more of the total project costs are incurred before 1989.

[Footnote ¶ 3902 continued]

(2) By contrast, losses (or credits) carried over from a year in which the taxpayer did actively participate, but that were not allowed against non-passive income in such year because they exceeded $25,000 (as reduced by the applicable AGI phaseout), are deductible (or allowable) under the $25,000 rule in a subsequent year, but only if the taxpayer is actively participating in the activity in such subsequent year.

Act §501   ¶3902

This increase in the adjusted gross income phase-out range may be illustrated as follows. Assume that an individual has $5,000 (deduction equivalent amount) of low-income housing credits from a limited partnership interest (in which, under the passive loss rule, he is considered not to materially or actively participate) in a rental real estate activity. His adjusted gross income (determined without regard to passive losses) is $200,000, and he has no other passive losses, credits or income for the year. The individual is permitted under the $25,000 allowance rule to take the low income housing credit.

Other credit limitations.—The interaction of the passive loss rules with other rules limiting the use of credits is clarified. The limitation on the credit for research and development activities to the tax on income from such activities is applied before the passive loss limitation is applied to such credits. The overall limitation on credits under the conference agreement (providing that credits generally cannot offset more than 75 percent of the taxpayer's tax liability for the year) is applied after the amount of credits allowable under the passive loss rule is determined. Once a credit is allowed for a year under the passive loss rule, it is treated as an active credit arising in that year.

Dispositions.—*In general.*—The conference agreement generally follows the Senate amendment with respect to dispositions of interests in passive activities which trigger the allowance of suspended losses. The conference agreement clarifies, however, that a transaction constituting a sale (or other taxable disposition) in form, to the extent not treated as a taxable disposition under general tax rules, does not give rise to the allowance of suspended deductions. For example, sham transactions, wash sales, and transfers not properly treated as sales due to the existence of a put, call, or similar right relating to repurchase, do not give rise to the allowance of suspended losses.

Related party transactions.—The conference agreement provides that the taxpayer is not treated as having disposed of an interest in a passive activity, for purposes of triggering suspended losses, if he disposes of it in an otherwise fully taxable transaction to a related party (within the meaning of section 267(b) or 707(b)(1), including applicable attribution rules). In the event of such a related party transaction, because it is not treated as a disposition for purposes of the passive loss rule, suspended losses are not triggered, but rather remain with the taxpayer. Such suspended losses may be offset by income from passive activities of the taxpayer.

When the entire interest owned by the taxpayer and the interest transferred to the related transferee in the passive activity are transferred to a party who is not related to the taxpayer (within the meaning of section 267(b) or 707(b)(1), including applicable attribution rules) in a fully taxable disposition, then to the extent the transfer would otherwise qualify as a disposition triggering suspended losses, the taxpayer may deduct the suspended losses attributable to his interest in the passive activity.

Certain insurance transactions. — Clarification is provided with respect to certain transactions involving dispositions of interests in syndicates that insure U.S. risks. Generally, when an owner of an interest in such a syndicate that is treated as a passive activity enters into a transaction whereby he disposes of his interest in the syndicate in a fully taxable closing transaction, he is treated as having made a disposition of his interest in the passive activity.

Abandonment.—The scope of a disposition triggering suspended losses under the passive loss rule includes an abandonment, constituting a fully taxable event under present law, of the taxpayer's entire interest in a passive activity. Thus, for example, if the taxpayer owns rental property which he abandons in a taxable event which would give rise to a deduction under section 165(a) of present law, the abandonment constitutes a taxable disposition that triggers the recognition of suspended losses under the passive loss rule.

Similarly, to the extent that the event of the worthlessness of a security is treated under section 165(g) of the Code as a sale or exchange of the security, and the event otherwise represents the disposition of an entire interest in a passive activity, it is treated as a disposition. No inference is intended with respect to whether a security includes an interest in any entity other than a corporation.

Interaction with capital loss limitation.—Upon a fully taxable disposition of a taxpayer's entire interest in a passive activity, the passive loss rule provides that any deductions previously suspended with respect to that activity are allowed in full. However, to the extent that any loss recognized upon such a disposition is a loss from the sale or exchange of a capital asset, it is limited to the amount of gains from the sale or exchange of capital assets plus $3,000 (in the case of individuals). The limitation on the deductibility of capital losses is applied before the determination of the amount of losses allowable upon the disposition under the passive loss rule.

Thus, for example, if a taxpayer has a capital loss of $10,000 upon the disposition of a passive activity, and is also allowed to deduct $5,000 of previously suspended ordinary losses as a result of the disposition, the $5,000 of ordinary losses are allowed, but the capital loss deduction is limited to $3,000 for the year (assuming the taxpayer has no other gains or losses from the sale of capital assets for the year). The remainder of the capital loss from the disposition is carried forward and allowed in accordance with the provisions determining the allowance of such capital losses.

Basis adjustment for credits.—Under the conference agreement, an election is provided in the case of a fully taxable disposition of an interest in an activity in connection with which a basis adjustment was made as a result of placing in service property for which a credit was taken. Upon such a disposition, the taxpayer may elect to increase the basis of the credit property (by an amount no greater than the amount of the original basis reduction of the property) to the extent that the credit has not theretofore been allowed by reason of the passive loss rule. At the time of the basis adjustment election, the amount of the suspended credit which may thereafter be applied against tax liability is reduced by the amount of the basis adjustment. The purpose for providing this election is to permit the taxpayer to recognize economic gain or loss, taking account of the full cost of property for which no credit was allowed.

This rule may be illustrated as follows. A taxpayer places in service rehabilitation credit property generating an allowable credit of $50, and reduces the basis of the property by $50 as required by the provisions governing the rehabilitation credit, but is prevented under the passive loss rule from taking any portion of the credit. In a later year, having been allowed no portion of the credit by virtue of the passive loss rule, the taxpayer disposes of his entire interest in the activity, including the property whose basis was reduced. Immediately prior to the disposition, the taxpayer may elect to increase basis of the credit property by the amount of the original basis adjustment (to the extent of the amount of the unused credit) with respect to the property.

If the property is disposed of in a transaction that, under the passive loss rule, does not constitute a fully taxable disposition of the taxpayer's entire interest in the passive activity, then no basis adjustment may be elected at any time. To the extent the credit has been suspended by virtue of the passive loss rule, however, it may remain available to offset tax liability attributable to passive income.

Disposition of activity of limited partnership.—In general, under the passive loss rule, suspended deductions are allowed upon a taxable disposition of the taxpayer's entire interest in an activity, because it becomes possible at that time to measure the taxpayer's actual gain or loss from the activity. Under the Senate amendment, a special rule would apply to dispositions with respect to limited partnership interests. The special rule requires the taxpayer to dispose of his entire interest in the limited partnership (along with all other interests that are part of the passive activity) in order to trigger suspended deductions with respect to any activities conducted by the limited partnership.

The conferees believe that it is not appropriate to disallow a true economic loss realized upon the disposition of the taxpayer's entire interest in an activity by reason of the taxpayer's form of ownership. Therefore, the conference agreement eliminates this special rule for dispositions of limited partnership activities, and provides instead that a disposition of the taxpayer's entire interest in an activity conducted by a limited partnership, like a disposition of an activity conducted in any other form, may constitute a disposition giving rise to the allowance of suspended deductions from the activity.

The conferees do not, however, intend to change the rule that a limited partnership interest in an activity is (except as provided in Treasury regulations) treated as an interest in a passive activity. Because a limited partner generally is precluded from materially participating in the partnership's activities, losses and credits attributable to the limited partnership's activities are generally treated as from passive activities, except that items properly treated as portfolio income and personal service income are not treated as passive.

Changes in nature of activity.—The fact that the nature of an activity changes in the course of its development does not give rise to a disposition for purposes of the passive loss provision. For example, when a real estate construction activity becomes a rental activity upon the completion of construction and the commencement of renting the constructed building, the change is not treated as a disposition.

3. Treatment of portfolio income

In general.—The conference agreement generally follows the Senate amendment with respect to the definition and treatment of portfolio income, with several modifications and clarifications.

Generally, portfolio income of an activity (for example, interest, dividend, royalty or annuity income earned on funds set aside for future use in the activity) is not treated as passive income from the activity, but must be accounted for separately.[3] Similarly, portfolio income of an entity which is not attributable to, or part of, an activity of the entity that constitutes a passive activity is also accounted for separately from any passive income or loss. Gain or loss from sales or exchanges of portfolio assets (including property held for investment) is treated as portfolio gain or loss. The conference agreement adds a provision clarifying that income from annuities is treated as not passive income.

Expenses allocable to portfolio income.—The conference agreement provides that portfolio income is reduced by the deductible expenses (other than interest) that are clearly and directly allocable to such income. Properly allocable interest expense also reduces portfolio income. Such deductions accordingly are not treated as attributable to a passive activity.

The conferees anticipate that the Treasury will issue regulations setting forth standards for appropriate allocation of expenses and

---

[Footnote ¶ 3902 continued]

(3) The Senate Report notes that REIT dividends are treated as portfolio income. Similarly, income received from a RIC or a real estate mortgage investment conduit (REMIC) is treated as portfolio income.

interest under the passive loss rule. The conferees anticipate that regulations providing guidance to taxpayers with respect to interest allocation will be issued by December 31, 1986. These regulations should be consistent with the purpose of the passive loss rules to prevent sheltering of income from personal services and portfolio income with passive losses. Moreover, the regulations should attempt to avoid inconsistent allocation of interest deductions under different Code provisions.[4]

In the case of entities, a proper method of allocation may include, for example, allocation of interest to portfolio income on the basis of assets, although there may be situations in which tracing is appropriate because of the integrated nature of the transactions involved. Because of the difficulty of record-keeping that would be required were interest expense of individuals allocated rather than traced, it is anticipated that, in the case of individuals, interest expense generally will be traced to the asset or activity which is purchased or carried by incurring or continuing the underlying indebtedness.

Self-charged interest.—A further issue with respect to portfolio income arises where an individual receives interest income on debt of a passthrough entity in which he owns an interest. Under certain circumstances, the interest may essentially be "self-charged," and thus lack economic significance. For example, assume that a taxpayer charges $100 of interest on a loan to an S corporation in which he is the sole shareholder. In form, the transaction could be viewed as giving rise to offsetting payments of interest income and passthrough interest expense, although in economic substance the taxpayer has paid the interest to himself.

Under these circumstances, it is not appropriate to treat the transaction as giving rise both to portfolio interest income and to passive interest expense. Rather, to the extent that a taxpayer receives interest income with respect to a loan to a passthrough entity in which he has an ownership interest, such income should be allowed to offset the interest expense passed through to the taxpayer from the activity for the same taxable year.

The amount of interest income of the partner from the loan that is appropriately offset by the interest expense of the partnership on the loan should not exceed the taxpayer's allocable share of the interest expense to the extent not increased by any special allocation. For example, assume that an individual has a 40-percent interest in a partnership that conducts a business activity in which he does not materially participate, and the individual makes a loan to the partnership on which the partnership pays $100 of interest expense for the year. Since 40 percent of the partnership's interest expense is allocable to the individual, only $40 of the partner's $100 of interest income should be permitted to offset his share of the

partnership interest expense, and the remaining $60 is properly treated as portfolio income that cannot be offset by passive losses.

The conferees anticipate that Treasury regulations will be issued to provide for the above result. Such regulations may also, to the extent appropriate, identify other situations in which netting of the kind described above is appropriate with respect to a payment to a taxpayer by an entity in which he has an ownership interest. Such netting should not, however, permit any passive deductions to offset non-passive income except to the extent of the taxpayer's allocable share of the specific payment at issue. Such regulations may, if appropriate, provide that taxpayer's allocable share of the payment for this purpose will be determined without regard to special allocations.

Regulatory authority of Treasury in defining non-passive income.—The conferees believe that clarification is desirable regarding the regulatory authority provided to the Treasury with regard to the definition of income that is treated as portfolio income or as otherwise not arising from a passive activity. The conferees intend that this authority be exercised to protect the underlying purpose of the passive loss provision, i.e., preventing the sheltering of positive income sources through the use of tax losses derived from passive business activities.

Examples where the exercise of such authority may (if the Secretary so determines) be appropriate include the following: (1) ground rents that produce income without significant expenses, (2) related party leases or sub-leases, with respect to property used in a business activity, that have the effect of reducing active business income and creating passive income; and (3) activities previously generating active business losses that the taxpayer intentionally seeks to treat as passive at a time when they generate net income, with the purpose of circumventing the rule.

4. Material participation

Under the conference agreement, material participation has the same meaning as that set forth in the Senate Report. It is clarified that an individual who works full-time in a line of business consisting of one or more business activities generally is likely to be materially participating in those activities (except to the extent provided otherwise in the case of rental activities), even if the individual's role is in management rather than operations.

This clarification is not intended to alter the description of material participation in the Senate Report in any respect. Rather, it recognizes the substantial likelihood that, despite the difficulty in many circumstances of ascertaining whether the management services rendered by an individual are substantial and *bona fide*, such services are likely to be so when the individual is render-

---

[Footnote ¶ 3902 continued]
  (4) For example, an interest deduction that is disallowed under section 265 or 291 should not be allowed, capitalized, or suspended under another provision.

ing them on a full-time basis and the success of the activity depends in large part upon his exercise of business judgment.

It is also clarified that a taxpayer is likely to be materially participating in an activity, if he does everything that is required to be done to conduct the activity, even though the actual amount of work to be done to conduct the activity is low in comparison to other activities.

With respect to material participation in an agricultural activity, clarification is provided regarding the decision-making that, if *bona fide* and undertaken on a regular, continuous, and substantial basis, may be relevant to material participation. The types of decision-making that may be relevant in this regard include, without being limited to, decision-making regarding (1) crop rotation, selection, and pricing, (2) the incursion of embryo transplant or breeding expenses, (3) the purchase, sale, and leasing of capital items, such as cropland, animals, machinery, and equipment, (4) breeding and mating decisions, and (5) the selection of herd or crop managers who then act at the behest of the taxpayer, rather than as paid advisors directing the conduct of the taxpayer.

[The following colloquy is drawn from the Congressional Record. The colloquy occurred on the day the Conference bill was considered by the Senate. Ed.]

[Senate Floor Explanation]

Mrs. HAWKINS. Mr. President, in the Senate report accompanying the tax bill, the deduction for losses is to be disallowed under title XIV, subtitle A for any activity in which the taxpayer does not materially participate on a regular, continuous and substantial basis. The committee report was unclear as to whether a taxpayer working full time elsewhere as an employee or in a professional service business is less likely to materially participate in a general partnership or S corporation which is engaged in a business involving orange groves than a taxpayer whose primary business is growing oranges. We respectfully and firmly believe that the material participation criterion can be met by the taxpayer who works elsewhere if he or she participates actively in the management decisions concerning the citrus grove. This would include planting, grove care, maintenance, harvesting, and the negotiation of contracts for the sale of fruit decisions.

The nature of the citrus business is such that experienced grove care professionals are a necessity in the daily operation of the grove even when owning participants are involved in nearly every other operational decision. It is my understanding that a taxpayer is not excluded from the material participation standard solely because of his or her noninvolvement in the day-to-day physical labor connected with citrus grove management.

It is my understanding that Chairman PACKWOOD has also agreed that as long as citrus grove owners are regularly making decisions related to the management and

upkeep of their groves and are participating in the sale of their fruit, they be allowed to utilize the deductions under citrus ownership, even though they are employed elsewhere.

Is that correct?

Mr. PACKWOOD. That is correct especially, regarding the day-to-day physical labor, however, the taxpayer must be involved substantially in the management decisions exercising independent judgment and input regarding the operations of the citrus activity. Congressional Record, p. S 13954, 9-27-86.

[The following colloquy is drawn from the Congressional Record. The colloquy occurred on the day the Conference bill was considered by the Senate. Ed.]

[Senate Floor Explanation]

Mr. HATFIELD. Mr. Chairman, we are now considering the conference report on H.R. 3838, the Tax Reform Act of 1986, and the statement of managers. On June 24, 1986, during the Senate debate on the Senate amendments to H.R. 3838, you and I discussed the meaning of "materially participating" as that term applies to condominum hotel unit owners in determining whether their activity is active or passive. The statement of managers states that "materially participation" has the same meaning in the conference report as set forth in the Senate report. Am I correct in understanding that our discussion on June 24, 1986, on the floor of the Senate, in which we clarified the meaning of the Senate report in this regard, continues to be an accurate statement of the intended meaning of "material participation" as defined in the Senate report and now adopted in the conference report on the subject we discussed?

Mr. PACKWOOD. Yes, Senator, you are correct. Our clarification of the meaning of "material participation" in our discussion of condominium hotel unit owners on June 24, 1986, on the floor of the Senate, carries over from the Senate report and applies fully and in its entirety to the definition of "material participation" as the term is used in the conference report on H.R. 3838 before us today. Congressional Record, p. S 13958, 9-27-86.

[Conference Report]

*   *   *   *   *   *

5. Definition of activity

It is clarified that a rental activity may include the performance of services that are incidental to the activity (e.g., a laundry room in a rental apartment building). However, if a sufficient amount of such services are rendered, they may rise to the level of a separate activity, or the entire activity may not constitute a rental activity under the provision (e.g., a hotel).

6. Working interest

The conference agreement follows the Senate amendment with respect to the working

Act § 501   ¶ 3902

interest provision under the passive loss rules.

7. Effective date and phase-in rules

[Generally effective for tax years beginning after 12-31-86 .Ed]

Under the conference agreement, interests in passive activities acquired by the taxpayer on or before the date of enactment of the bill are eligible for the phase-in under the passive loss rule. Interests in activities acquired after the date of enactment, however, are not eligible for the phase-in, but rather are fully subject to the passive loss rule.

The conferees intend that a contractual obligation to purchase an interest in a passive activity that is binding on the date of enactment be treated as an acquisition of the interest in the activity for this purpose. A binding contract qualifies under this rule, even if the taxpayer's obligation to acquire an interest is subject to contingencies, so long as the contingencies are beyond the reasonable control of the taxpayer. Thus, if the taxpayer has, by the date of enactment, signed a subscription agreement to purchase a limited partnership interest contingent upon the agreement of other purchasers to acquire interests in the limited partnership amounting to a particular total, then if the contingency is satisfied, he is eligible for the phase-in rule with respect to the interest he was contractually bound to acquire. On the other hand, a conditional obligation to purchase, or one subject to contingencies within the taxpayer's control, does not give rise to eligibility under the phase-in rule.

In the case where, after the date of enactment, investors in an activity contribute additional capital to the activity, their interests still qualify in full for relief under the phase-in to the extent that their percentage ownership interests do not change as a result of the contribution. However, if a taxpayer's ownership interest is increased after the date of enactment, then (except to the extent the increase in the taxpayer's interest arises pursuant to a pre-enactment date binding contract or partnership agreement), the portion of his interest attributable to such increase does not qualify for the phase-in relief. For example, if a taxpayer, after the date of enactment, increases his ownership interest in a partnership from 25 percent to 50 percent, then only the losses attributable to the 25 percent interest held prior to enactment will qualify for transitional relief.[6]

In general, in order to qualify for transition relief, the interest acquired by a taxpayer must be in an activity which has commenced by the date of enactment. For example, a rental activity has commenced when the rental property has been placed in service in the activity. When an entity in which the taxpayer owns an interest liquidates and disposes of one activity and commences another after the date of enactment, the new activity does not qualify for transition relief. In the case of property purchased for personal use but converted to business use (e.g., a home that the taxpayer converts to rental use), similar rules apply. The activity qualifies for phase-in relief if it commences by the date of enactment. In the case of a residence converted to rental use, for example, the residence must be held out for rental by the date of enactment.

However, in the case of an activity that has not commenced by the date of enactment, phase-in treatment nevertheless applies if the entity (or an individual owning the activity directly) has entered into a binding contract effective on or before the date of conference action (August 16, 1986), to acquire the assets used to conduct the activity. Similarly, phase-in treatment applies in the case of self-constructed business property of an entity (or direct owner), where construction of the property to be used in the activity has commenced on or before the date of conference action (August 16, 1986).

In the case of a taxpayer owning both pre-enactment and post-enactment interests in passive activities, clarification is provided regarding the calculation of the amount of passive loss qualifying for the phase-in. In order to determine this amount, it is necessary first to determine the amount that would be disallowed absent the phase-in. Phase-in relief then applies to the lesser of the taxpayer's total passive loss, or the passive loss taking into account only pre-enactment interests. Thus, for example, if a taxpayer has $100 of passive loss relating to pre-enactment interests, that would be disallowed in the absence of the phase-in, and has $60 of net passive income from post-enactment interests, resulting in a total passive loss of $40, then the phase-in treatment applies to the lesser of $100 or $40, (i.e., $40). For purposes of this rule, the pre-enactment and post-enactment losses are calculated by including credits, in a deduction-equivalent sense.

Under the conference agreement, any passive loss that is disallowed for a taxable year during the phase-in period and carried forward is allowable in a subsequent year only to the extent that there is net passive income in the subsequent year (or there is a fully taxable disposition of the activity).

For example, assume that a taxpayer has a passive loss of $100 in 1987, $65 of which is allowed under the applicable phase-in percentage for the year and $35 of which is carried forward. Such $35 is not allowed in part in a subsequent year under the phase-in percentage applying for such year. If the taxpayer has a passive loss of $35 in 1988, including the amount carried over from 1987, then no relief under the phase-in is provided. If the taxpayer has a passive loss of $50 in

---

[**Footnote ¶ 3902 continued**]

(6) Phase-in relief applies only with respect to the percentage interest held by the taxpayer at all times after the date of enactment. Thus, for example, if a taxpayer after the date of enactment reduces his interest in an activity from 50 percent to 25 percent, and subsequently purchases additional interests restoring his share to 50 percent, then only the 25 percent share held throughout qualifies for phase-in relief after such subsequent purchases.

1988 (consisting of the $35 from 1987 and $15 from 1988, all of which is attributable to pre-enactment interests), then $6 of losses (40 percent of the $15 loss arising in 1988) is allowed against active income under the phase-in rule. The $35 loss carryover from 1987 is disallowed in 1988 and is carried forward (along with the disallowed $9 from 1988) and allowed in any subsequent year in which the taxpayer has net passive income.

It is clarified that the applicable phase-in percentage applies to the passive loss net of any portion of such loss that may be allowed against non-passive income under the $25,000 rule.

Transition relief is provided in the case of low-income housing activities. Losses from certain investments after 1983 in low-income housing are not treated as from a passive activity, applicable for a period of up to seven years from the taxpayer's original investment.

[The following colloquy relating to Act Sec. 501 is drawn from the Congressional Record. The colloquy occurred on the day the Conference bill was considered by the Senate. Ed.]

[Senate Floor Explanation]

APPLICATION OF PASSIVE LOSS RULES TO CLOSELY HELD CORPORATIONS

Mr. JOHNSTON. Mr. President, I wish to confirm my understanding of the application of the new so-called passive activity loss and credit rule that is embodied in section 501(a) of the conference report to accompany H.R. 3838, the Tax Reform Act of 1986. As I understand the conference agreement: First, rental activity is per se classified as passive activity; second, income derived from the investment of working capital is characterized as portfolio income; third, C corporations may offset losses from passive activities against income from an active trade or business but not against portfolio income; and fourth, losses from an active trade or business may be offset against income derived from the investment of working capital and vice versa.

To assure that my interpretation is correct, I would like to ask the distinguished chairman of the Finance Committee to confirm the accuracy of a number of examples of this rule. I also ask unanimous consent that a chart summarizing the facts in these examples be made a part of the RECORD at this time.

There being no objection, the table was ordered to be printed in the RECORD, as follows:

	Equipment leasing activity	Real estate rental activity	Active trade or business	Income from working capital
1	($200)	($200)	$500	$100
2	(200)	(200)	(500)	100
3	(200)	(200)	(500)	(100)
4	200	(200)	500	100

	Equipment leasing activity	Real estate rental activity	Active trade or business	Income from working capital
5	200	(200)	(500)	100
6	200	(200)	(500)	(100)
7	(200)	200	500	100
8	(200)	200	(500)	100
9	(200)	200	(500)	(100)
10	200	200	500	100
11	200	200	(500)	100
12	200	200	(500)	(100)
13	200	200	500	(100)
14	200	(200)	500	(100)
15	(200)	200	500	(100)
16	(200)	(200)	500	(100)

Mr. JOHNSTON. First, do I understand that if a closely held C corporation has $400 in losses from passive activities—such as equipment leasing and/or real estate transactions, $500 in income from an active trade or business—which is not a passive activity—and $100 of portfolio income, the company may offset the $400 in passive losses against the $500 of active trade or business income, leaving taxable income of $200, $100 or which is attributable to the active trade or business and $100 of which is attributable to working capital—portfolio income.

Mr. PACKWOOD. The Senator from Louisiana's understanding is correct.

Mr. JOHNSTON. If a closely held C corporation had $400 in losses from passive activities, $500 in losses from an active trade or business and $100 in portfolio income, its $100 in portfolio income can partially offset the $500 in losses from an active trade or business, leaving a $400 loss carryforward from the active trade or business and a $400 passive loss carry forward.

Mr. PACKWOOD. The Senator is correct.

Mr. JOHNSTON. If a closely held C corporation had $400 in losses from passive activities, $500 in losses from an active trade or business and $100 in losses from portfolio income, the company could carry forward $400 in passive losses and $600 in other losses.

Mr. PACKWOOD. The Senator is correct.

Mr. JOHNSTON. If a closely held C corporation had $200 in equipment leasing income, $200 in real estate activity losses, $500 in active trade or business income and $100 in portfolio income, the company could net its equipment leasing income against its real estate loss, giving it $600 in taxable income.

Mr. PACKWOOD. The Senator is correct.

Mr. JOHNSTON. If this corporation had $200 in equipment leasing income, $200 in real estate activity losses, $500 in active trade or business losses and $100 in portfolio income, the equipment leasing activity income would totally offset the real estate activity losses. The company could then use the $100 in portfolio income to partially offset its active trade or business losses,

Act §501   ¶3902

leaving a $400 carryforward of losses from the active trade or business.

Mr. PACKWOOD. The Senator is correct.

Mr. JOHNSTON. If the company had $200 in equipment leasing income, $200 in real estate activity losses, $500 in active trade or business losses and $100 in portfolio losses, the equipment leasing activity income would offset the real estate rental activity losses, leaving $600 in carryforward losses that are attributable to the active trade or business and the portfolio income account.

Mr. PACKWOOD. The Senator is correct.

Mr. JOHNSTON. If the company had $200 in equipment leasing activity losses, $200 in rental real estate income, $500 in active trade or business income and $100 in portfolio income, the equipment leasing and rental real estate activities will completely offset each other, leaving $600 in taxable income.

Mr. PACKWOOD. The Senator is correct.

Mr. JOHNSTON. If the company had $200 in equipment leasing activity losses, $200 in rental real estate income, $500 in active trade or business losses and $100 in portfolio income, the equipment leasing and rental real estate activities will completely offset each other. The $100 in portfolio income would partially offset the $500 in losses from active trade and business, leaving $400 in active trade or business losses to be carried forward.

Mr. PACKWOOD. The Senator is correct.

Mr. JOHNSTON. If the closely held C corporation has $200 in equipment leasing losses, $200 in rental real estate activity income, $500 in active trade or business losses and $100 in portfolio losses, the equipment leasing activity would completely offset the real estate rental activity income and the company could carry forward $600 in losses from its other activities.

Mr. PACKWOOD. The Senator is correct.

Mr. JOHNSTON. If a company has $400 in income from passive activities, $500 income from its active trade or business and $100 in portfolio income, it would have $1,000 in taxable income.

Mr. PACKWOOD. The Senator is correct.

Mr. JOHNSTON. If a company has $400 in passive activity income, $500 in losses from its active trade or business and $100 in portfolio income, the passive activity income could partially offset $500 in losses from the active trade or business. The company would also be able to use the remaining $100 in losses from the active trade or business to totally offset its portfolio income.

Mr. PACKWOOD. The Senator is correct.

Mr. JOHNSTON. If a company has $400 in passive activity income, $500 in losses from its active trade or business and $100 in portfolio losses, it could use the passive income to partially offset its active trade or business loss, leaving it a $200 loss carry forward that is equally attributable to its active trade or business and its portfolio account.

Mr. PACKWOOD. The Senator is correct.

Mr. JOHNSTON. If a company has $400 in passive activity income, $500 in active trade or business income and $100 in portfolio losses, it could use its portfolio loss to partially offset the income derived from the active trade or business, leaving it with $800 in taxable income.

Mr. PACKWOOD. The Senator is correct.

Mr. JOHNSTON. If the closely held corporation had $200 in equipment leasing income, $200 in rental real estate losses, $500 in active trade or business income and $100 in portfolio losses, its equipment leasing income would offset its rental real estate losses. It could also use its portfolio loss to partially offset its active trade or business income, leaving it with $400 in taxable income.

Mr. PACKWOOD. The Senator is correct.

Mr. JOHNSTON. If the company had $200 in equipment leasing losses, $200 in rental real estate income, $500 in active trade or business income and $100 in portfolio losses, its equipment leasing activity would offset its rental real estate activity and the $100 in portfolio losses could partially offset the active trade or business income, leaving it with $400 in taxable income.

Mr. PACKWOOD. The Senator is correct.

Mr. JOHNSTON. Finally, if a company had $400 in passive losses, $500 in active trade or business income and $100 in portfolio losses, the passive losses, $400, and portfolio losses, $100, would completely offset its active trade or business income.

Mr. PACKWOOD. The Senator is correct.

Mr. JOHNSTON. I thank the distinguished chairman for his assurances. Congressional Record p. S13958-13959, 9-27-86.

[The following is from a statement of the Chairman of the House Ways and Means Committee relating to Senate Floor colloquies. Ed.]

[House Floor Explanation]

I have discussed with Congressman GEPHARDT several issues regarding the application of the passive loss rules to closely held corporations. We have reached a common understanding which affirms the colloquy between Senator JOHNSTON and Senator PACKWOOD located on pages S13958 and 13959 of the CONGRESSIONAL RECORD dated September 27, 1986, regarding these issues. Congressional Record, p. E3390, 10-2-86.

[¶ 3903]   SECTION 502. TRANSITIONAL RULE FOR LOW-INCOME HOUSING

[Conference Report]

*   *   *   *   *   *

Transition relief [from passive loss rules in ¶3902] is provided in the case of low-income housing activities. Losses from certain investments after 1983 in low-income housing are not treated as from a passive activity, applicable for a period of up to seven years from the taxpayer's original investment.

[Effective   date.—Generally   property placed in service before 1-1-89. Ed.]

[¶ 3904]   SECTION 503. EXTENSION OF AT-RISK LIMITATIONS TO REAL PROPERTY

(Sec. 465 of the Code)

[House Explanation]

*   *   *   *   *   *

Explanation of Provision.—Under the bill, the present law at-risk rules are extended to the activity of holding real property. In the case of such an activity, the bill provides an exception for certain third-party nonrecourse financing which is secured by real property used in the activity; the taxpayer is treated at-risk with respect to such financing.

Qualified nonrecourse financing.—The exception provided for qualified nonrecourse financing is similar to the rules for qualified commercial financing under the investment tax credit at-risk rules under present law. Qualified nonrecourse financing generally includes financing (other than convertible debt) that is secured by real property used in the activity and that is loaned or guaranteed by any Federal, State, or local government, or borrowed by the taxpayer from a qualified person, with respect to the activity of holding real property (other than mineral property), provided such amounts are not used to acquire an interest in property from a related person.

For this purpose, nonrecourse financing means financing with respect to which no person is personally liable, except to the extent otherwise provided in regulations. Regulations may set forth the circumstances in which guarantees, indemnities, or personal liability (or the like) of a person other than the taxpayer will not cause the financing to be treated as other than qualified nonrecourse financing.

Qualified persons include any person actively and regularly engaged in the business of lending money. However, qualified persons do not include (1) any person related to the taxpayer; (2) any person from which the taxpayer acquired the property (or a person related to such person); or (3) any person who receives a fee (e.g., a promoter) with respect to the taxpayer's investment in the property (or a person related to such person). For these purposes, the bill adopts the definition of related person applicable under the investment tax credit at-risk rules, which is set forth in section 46l(i)(6) as amended by the bill. Under this rule, related persons generally include family members, fiduciaries, and corporations or partnerships in which a person has at least a 10-percent interest.

A special rule for partnerships provides that partnership-level qualified nonrecourse financing may increase a partner's (including a limited partner's) amount at risk, determined in accordance with his share of the liability (within the meaning of section 752), provided the financing is qualified nonrecourse financing with respect to that partner as well as with respect to the partnership. For the purpose of determining whether partnership borrowings are treated as qualified nonrecourse financing with respect to the partnership, the partnership is treated as the taxpayer. For the purpose of determining whether a share of partnership borrowings is treated as qualified nonrecourse financing with respect to a partner, the partner is also treated as the borrower. The amount for which partners are treated as at risk under this rule may not exceed the total amount of the qualified nonrecourse financing at the partnership level.

In the case of property taken subject to a nonrecourse debt which constituted qualified nonrecourse financing in the hands of the original borrower, such debt may be considered as qualified nonrecourse financing as to the original borrower's transferee, provided that all the criteria for qualified nonrecourse financing are satisfied for that debt with respect to the transferee. The same rule applies to subsequent transfers of the property taken subject to the debt, and to the admission of new partners to a partnership (or sale or exchange of a partnership interest), so long as the debt constitutes qualified financing with respect to each transferee or new partner.

Aggregation rules.—The present law at-risk aggregation rules (sec. 465(c)(3)(B)) generally apply to the activity of holding real property. Under these rules, it is intended that if a taxpayer actively participates in the management of several partnerships each engaged in the real estate business, the real estate activities of the various partnerships may be aggregated and treated as one activity with respect to that partner for purposes of the at-risk rules. Also it is intended that the regulations relating to the treatment of at-risk amounts in the case of an affiliated group of corporations (Treasury reg. sec.

Act §503   ¶3904

1.1502-45) be appropriately modified, in the case of an affiliated group which is engaged principally in the real estate business, to allow aggregation of the real estate activities, where the component members of the group are actively engaged in the management of the real estate business (not including real estate financing other than between members of the affiliated group).

[Conference Report]

*   *   *   *   *   *

Senate Amendment.—The Senate amendment is the same as the House bill, except the third party nonrecourse debt exception for real estate losses applies notwithstanding that (1) the lender is related to the taxpayer, and (2) the taxpayer acquired the property from a related party.

Conference Agreement.—The conference agreement follows the Senate amendment, with modifications.

The conference agreement provides that in the case of the activity of holding real property, certain qualified nonrecourse financing is treated as an amount at risk, provided that, in the case of nonrecourse financing from related persons, the terms of the loan are commercially reasonable and on substantially the same terms as loans involving unrelated persons.

These requirements are imposed in addition to those imposed under the Senate amendment because the conferees believe that the opportunities for overvaluation of property and for the transfer of tax benefits attributable to amounts that resemble equity are insufficiently limited under the Senate amendment in the case of nonrecourse financing from a related person.

The conferees intend that terms of nonrecourse financing are commercially reasonable if the financing is a written unconditional promise to pay on demand or on a specified date or dates a sum or sums certain in money, and the interest rate is a reasonable market rate of interest (taking into account the maturity of the obligation). If the interest rate is below a reasonable market rate, a portion of the principal may in fact represent interest, with the result that the stated principal amount may exceed the fair market value of the financed property. Generally, an interest rate would not be considered commercially reasonable if it is significantly below the market rate on comparable loans by qualified persons who are not related (within the meaning of sec. 465(b)(3)(C)) to the borrowers under the comparable loans. In addition, it is likely that a loan which would be treated as a "below-market loan" within the meaning of sec. 7872(e) of the Code is not commercially reasonable.

Similarly, if the interest rate exceeds a reasonable market rate, or is contingent on profits or gross receipts, a portion of the principal amount may in fact represent a disguised equity interest (and a portion of the interest in fact is a return on equity) with the result that the stated principal amount may exceed the fair market value of the financed

property. Thus, generally, an interest rate would not be considered commercially reasonable if it significantly exceeds the market rate on comparable loans by unrelated qualified persons. Nor would an interest rate be considered commercially reasonable if it were contingent. The conferees do not intend, however, to limit the use of interest rates that are not fixed rates, provided that interest is calculated with respect to a market interest index such as the prime rate charged by a major commercial bank, LIBOR, the rate on government securities (such as Treasury bills or notes), or the applicable Federal rate (within the meaning of sec. 1274(d)). For example, an interest rate floating at 1 point above the prime rate charged by a major commercial bank would not generally be considered contingent.

The terms of the financing would also not be considered commercially reasonable if, for example, the term of the loan exceeds the useful life of the property, or if the right to foreclose or collection with respect to the debt is limited (except to the extent provided under applicable State law).

Generally, the conferees intend that the financing be debt with arms' length terms, to carry out the purpose of the at-risk rule to limit deductions to the taxpayer's amount at risk. Thus, nonrecourse financing from a person related to the taxpayer must be on substantially the same terms as financing involving unrelated persons.

The conference agreement also provides that no inference is to be drawn from this provision (permitting certain nonrecourse financing to be treated as at risk without regard to whether the lender is a related person) as to the determination of a partner's distributive share of partnership items of a partnership under section 704, or a partner's share of partnership liabilities under section 752.

Under the House bill, the Senate amendment, and the conference agreement, convertible debt is not treated as qualified nonrecourse financing. The conferees believe that it is not appropriate to treat investors as at risk with respect to nonrecourse debt that is convertible and that consequently represents a right to an equity interest, because taxpayers are not intended to be treated as at risk for amounts representing others' rights to equity investments.

Clarification is also provided with respect to the definition of the activity of holding real property. Generally, to the extent an activity is not subject to the at-risk rules by virtue of sec. 465(c)(3)(D)*** of present law, it will be treated under the conference agreement as the activity of holding real property. The provision of services and the holding of personal property which is merely incidental to the activity of making real property available as living accommodations is treated as part of the activity of holding real property.

[Effective date.—] The extension of the at-risk rules to the activity of holding real property is effective for property placed in service after December 31, 1986, and for losses attributable to an interest in a partnership or S corporation or other pass-through entity that is acquired after December 31, 1986.

[¶ 3905] SECTION 511. LIMITATIONS ON DEDUCTION FOR NONBUSINESS INTEREST

(Sec. 163 of the Code)

[Senate Explanation]

*　　*　　*　　*　　*　　*

Explanation of Provisions.—

In General.— The bill expands the scope of the interest limitation, and alters the calculation of the amount of the limitation. Under the bill, all nonbusiness interest is subject to the limitation on deductibility, including consumer interest and certain interest that is not treated as investment interest subject to limitation under present law. Interest subject to the limitation under the bill does not include interest on debt secured by the taxpayer's principal residence (to the extent of its fair market value), and interest on debt secured by a second residence of the taxpayer (to the extent of its fair market value). Interest expense that is paid or incurred in carrying on a trade or business is not subject to the interest deduction limitation under the bill (except for interest attributable to certain limited business interests).

In general, under the bill, consumer interest is not deductible, and the deduction for investment interest is limited to investment income for the year with an indefinite carryforward of disallowed investment interest.

Investment interest limitation.—*Interest subject to the limitation.*—Under the bill, interest subject, to the investment interest limitation is all interest (other than consumer interest and qualified residence interest) on debt not incurred in connection with the taxpayer's trade or business. Thus, interest subject to limitation generally includes investment interest subject to the section 168(d) limitation under present law and interest expense attributable to a limited business interest, including interest paid or incurred on debt of the activity in which the taxpayer has a limited business interest and interest paid or incurred to purchase or carry a limited business interest.[2] A limited business interest includes an interest as a limited partner in a partnership, except as provided in regulations. It is anticipated that such regulations will provide that, in certain circumstances, limited partnership interests will not be treated as limited business interests. It is intended that this grant of authority be used to prevent taxpayers from manipulating the rule that limited partnership inter-

ests are treated as limited business interests, in attempting to evade the interest limitation provisions. Also treated as a limited business interest is an interest as a shareholder of an S corporation in whose activities the taxpayer does not materially participate, an interest as lessor in a net lease, as well as an interest in any activity in which the taxpayer does not materially participate (or, in the case of rental real estate activities, actively participate)[3] and the income or loss from which is trade or business income or loss.[4]

Net investment income.—Under the bill, the definition of investment income is expanded to include the taxpayer's share of income or loss (without regard to interest expense) attributable to any limited business interest (e.g., a limited partnership interest, stock of an S corporation in which the taxpayer does not materially participate, an interest as lessor in a net lease, or any interest in a trade or business activities in which the taxpayer does not materially participate). It also includes the gain on investment property. Net investment income is increased by certain out-of-pocket expenses attributable to net leased property, as under present law.

As under present law, net investment income is the excess of investment income over investment expense. Under the bill, investment expense is determined utilizing the actual depreciation or depletion deductions allowable.

Net leases.—The bill modifies the 15-percent test of present law, which determines whether leased property is subject to a net lease, and therefore constitutes a limited business interest in the hands of the lessor. Under the bill, in determining whether certain expenses constituting trade or business deductions are less than 15 percent of the rental income from the leased property, the value of the personal management and repair services performed with respect to the leased property by an individual taxpayer who is a direct owner of the property may be counted. Management and repair services of a general partner in a general partnership that directly owns the leased property may also be counted. In the case of services by the general partners, to qualify for this rule, the property must be managed exclusively by such general partners with no substantial

---

[Footnote ¶ 3905]　　(2) As under present law, interest on indebtedness incurred to purchase into a trade or business partnership as a general partner (which partnership interest is not a limited business interest) is not treated as investment interest for purposes of section 163(d)). See, e.g., Technical Advice Memorandum 8235004 (May 21, 1982).

(3) Material participation in an activity has the same meaning, for purposes of the investment interest limitation, as it has for purposes of the passive loss rule (sec. 1401 of the bill and sec. 469 of the Code), except that there is no special rule for rental activities. Similarly, active participation in the case of rental real estate activities, has the same meaning as under that section.

(4) E.g., a grantor of a grantor trust or an investor in a proprietorship in some circumstances.

payments to third parties for management services (other than for accounting and tax preparation services and repairs). The value of legal services may not be counted.

Consumer interest limitation.—Under the bill, consumer interest is not deductible. Consumer interest generally includes all interest not incurred or continued in connection with the conduct of a trade or business (other than the performance of services as an employee) or in connection with an activity described in section 212, relating to expenses for the reduction of income.[5] Interest on debt secured by the taxpayer's principal residence and a second residence remains deductible as under present law. Thus, consumer interest includes, for example, interest on a loan to purchase an automobile for personal use, and credit card interest incurred for personal expenses.

Residences of the taxpayer.—Interest on debt secured by a security interest perfected under local law on the taxpayer's principal residence or a second residence of the taxpayer is not treated as consumer interest subject to the limitation under the bill. The taxpayer's principal residence is intended to be the residence that would qualify for rollover of gain under section 1034 if it were sold. A principal residence may be a condominium or cooperative unit.[6] A dwelling unit will qualify as a residence only if it meets the requirements for use as a residence under section 280A. The fact that state homestead laws may restrict the rights of secured parties with respect to certain types of residential mortgages will not cause the interest paid under such mortgages to be treated as nondeductible consumer interest, provided the lender's security interest is perfected and provided the interest on the debt is otherwise qualified residence interest.

A second residence of the taxpayer includes a residence used by the taxpayer as a dwelling unit during any part of the year (gain on which could qualify for rollover treatment under section 1034 if the residence were used as a principal residence). In the case of a joint return, it includes a residence used by the taxpayer or his spouse and which is owned by either or both spouses.

Interest not treated as consumer interest under the provision includes interest on debt secured by the taxpayer's stock in a housing cooperative unit that is a residence of the taxpayer, or by his proprietary lease with respect to the unit, to the extent such debt, in the aggregate, does not exceed the fair market value of the cooperative unit. In addition, interest not treated as consumer interest under the provision includes the taxpayer's share under section 216 of interest expense of the housing cooperative allocable to his unit and to his share of common residential (but not commercial) areas of the cooperative.

In the case of a husband and wife filing separate returns, each spouse may deduct interest on debt secured by one residence. Alternatively the spouses may consent in writing to allow one spouse to claim interest on debt secured by two residences at least one of which is a principal residence. In the latter case, any interest of the other spouse on debt secured by a residence is treated as interest which may be subject to disallowance.

In the case of a taxpayer who owns more than two residences, the taxpayer may designate each year which residence (other than the taxpayer's principal residence) the taxpayer wishes to have treated as the second residence, the interest relating to which is not subject to limitation under the provision.

Rental use.—Under the bill, if property is used partly for rental purposes and partly for personal purposes (such as a vacation home used by the taxpayer as a residence and also rented for part of the year), the interest on debt attributable to such property is first allocated to the rental use and the personal use under allocation rules similar to section 280A(e)(1) of present law. Interest is allocated to the rental use (rather than residential use) in the ratio of the number of days the property is rented at fair rental to the number of days the property is used during the taxable year.

In the case of qualified residence interest, the effect of present law is continued, so that all qualified residence interest on first and second homes continues to be deductible. In the case of interest other than qualified residence interest, the interest allocated to the rental use will be allowed to the extent it does not exceed gross income (net of taxes and other deductions which would be allowed whether or not the property was used as rental property). Any interest allocable to the rental use in excess of such amount will then be treated as investment interest and will be allowed to the extent section 163(d) does not disallow the interest.

Effective Date.—The interest limitation, as amended by the bill, is effective for interest paid or incurred in taxable years beginning on or after January 1, 1987, regardless of when the obligation was incurred, but is phased in over a 5-year period. The amount of interest disallowed during any year in the transitional period cannot exceed the amount which would be disallowed for that year under present law plus the applicable percentage of any additional interest which would be disallowed for that year under the new provision, if fully effective. The applicable percentage is 35 percent in 1987, 60 percent in 1988, 80 percent in 1989, 90 percent in 1990 and 100 percent in 1991 and thereafter. The consumer interest limitation and the investment interest limitation are each phased in separately at the same rate.

Thus, for example, under both the consumer and the investment interest limitation, in 1987 the taxpayer would calculate (1) the amount of the interest disallowed for the year under the pre-1987 rule (which in the case of consumer interest is zero), and then (2) the amount of interest disallowed for the

---

(5) Thus, for example, interest on debt to finance an employee business expense is not deductible, under this rule.

(6) A principal residence may also include a houseboat or house trailer. See Treas. Reg. § 1.1034-1(e)(3).

year (as if fully phased in) under the post-1986 rule (as if fully phased in). Interest disallowed for 1987 would not exceed the amount calculated under (1), plus 35 percent of the amount by which (2) exceeds (1). If in any year, the amount of the interest disallowed under the new limitation (if fully phased in) would be less than the amount subject to the old limitation, the interest disallowed will be the amount determined as if the new rule were fully effective in that year. Thus, the taxpayer receives the benefit of the new rule in any year when it would give him a greater interest deduction than would the old rule.

[Conference Report]

*　*　*　*　*　*

The conference agreement follows the Senate amendment, with modifications and clarifications.

Investment interest.—The conference agreement provides that the deduction for investment interest is limited to the amount of net investment income. Interest disallowed under the provision is carried forward and treated as investment interest in the succeeding taxable year. Interest disallowed under the provision is allowed in a subsequent year only to the extent the taxpayer has net investment income in such year.

Definition of investment interest.—The definition of investment interest is modified to include interest paid or accrued on indebtedness incurred or continued to purchase or carry property held for investment. Investment interest includes interest expense properly allocable to portfolio income under the passive loss rule (see B., above). Investment interest also includes interest expense properly allocable to an activity, involving a trade or business, in which the taxpayer does not materially participate, if that activity is not treated as a passive activity under the passive loss rule.

Investment interest also includes the portion of interest expense incurred or continued to purchase or carry an interest in a passive activity, to the extent attributable to portfolio income (within the meaning of the passive loss rule).

Investment interest does not include any interest that is taken into account in determining the taxpayer's income or loss from a passive activity. Investment interest does not include interest properly allocable to a rental real estate activity in which the taxpayer actively participates, within the meaning of the passive loss rule. Investment interest also does not include any qualified residence interest, as described below.

Net investment income.—Investment income includes gross income from property held for investment, gain attributable to the disposition of property held for investment, and amounts treated as gross portfolio income under the passive loss rule. Investment income also includes income from interests in activities, involving a trade or business, in

which the taxpayer does not materially participate, if that activity is not treated as a passive activity under the passive loss rule.

Net investment income is investment income net of investment expenses. Investment expenses are deductible expenses (other than interest) directly connected with the production of investment income. In determining deductible investment expenses, it is intended that investment expenses be considered as those allowed after application of the rule limiting deductions for miscellaneous expenses to those expenses exceeding 2 percent of adjusted gross income. In computing the amount of expenses that exceed the 2-percent floor, expenses that are not investment expenses are intended to be disallowed before any investment expenses are disallowed.

Property subject to a net lease is not treated as investment property under this provision, because it is treated as a passive activity under the passive loss rule. Income from a rental real estate activity in which the taxpayer actively participates is not included in investment income.

The investment interest limitation is not intended to disallow a deduction for interest expense which in the same year is required to be capitalized (e.g., construction interest subject to sec. 263A) or is disallowed under sec. 265 (relating to tax-exempt interest).

Personal interest.—The conference agreement follows the Senate amendment provision with respect to consumer interest (denominated personal interest under the conference agreement), with modifications and clarifications.

Under the conference agreement, personal interest is not deductible. Personal interest is any interest, other than interest incurred or continued in connection with the conduct of a trade or business (other than the trade or business of performing services as [an] employee), investment interest, or interest taken into account in computing the taxpayer's income or loss from passive activities for the year. Personal interest also generally includes interest on tax deficiencies.

Personal interest does not include qualified residence interest of the taxpayer, nor does it include interest payable on estate tax deferred under sec. 6163 or 6166.

Qualified residence interest.—Under the conference agreement, qualified residence interest is not subject to the limitation on personal interest. Qualified residence interest generally means interest on debt secured by a security interest perfected under local law on the taxpayer's principal residence or a second residence of the taxpayer, not in excess of the amount of the taxpayer's cost basis for the residence (including the cost of home improvements), plus the amount of qualified medical and qualified educational expenses. Qualified residence interest does not include interest on any portion of such debt in excess of the fair market value of the residence.

Act §511　¶3905

Qualified residence interest is calculated as interest on debt secured by the residence, up to the amount of the cost basis of the residence, plus the amount incurred after August 16, 1986, for qualified medical and educational expenses. If the amount of any debt incurred on or before August 16, 1986, and secured by the residence on August 16, 1986 (reduced by any principal payments thereon) exceeds the taxpayer's cost basis for the residence, then such amount shall be substituted for the taxpayer's cost basis in applying the preceding sentence. Increases after August 16, 1986 in the amount of debt secured by the residence on August 16, 1986 (for example, in the case of a line of credit) are treated as incurred after August 16, 1986. Thus, interest on outstanding debt secured by the taxpayer's principal or second residence, incurred on or before August 16, 1986, is treated as fully deductible (to the extent the debt does not exceed the fair market value of the residence), regardless of the purpose for which the borrowed funds are used. Interest on debt secured by the taxpayer's principal or second residence, incurred after August 16, 1986, which debt exceeds the taxpayer's cost basis in the residence, is allowed only if the debt is incurred for qualified medical or educational expenses.

For purposes of determining qualified residence interest, the amount of the taxpayer's cost basis is determined without taking into account adjustments to basis under sec. 1034(e) (relating to rollover of gain upon the sale of the taxpayer's principal residence), or 1033(b) (relating to involuntary conversions). The cost basis for the residence includes the cost of improvements to the residence that are added to the basis of the residence. The taxpayer's cost basis is determined without regard to other adjustments to basis, such as depreciation. Thus, for example, if a taxpayer's second residence is rented to tenants for a portion of the year, and its basis is reduced by deductions for depreciation allowed in connection with the rental use of the property, the amount of his cost basis for the residence is not reduced by such deductions for purposes of this provision. Where the basis of a residence is determined under sec. 1014 (relating to the basis of property acquired from a decedent), the cost basis under this provision is the basis determined under sec. 1014. In general, under this provision, the amount of debt on which the taxpayer may deduct interest as qualified interest will not be less than his purchase price for the residence.

Generally, interest on debt secured by the taxpayer's principal or second residence (up to the amount of the taxpayer's cost basis is treated as a qualified residence interest. Thus, for example, if the taxpayer's cost basis in his principal residence is $100,000 (and this amount does not exceed fair market value), and the residence is secured by debt in the amount of $60,000, interest on a refinancing for a total of $100,000 (including the original $60,000 plus an additional $40,000) is treated as qualified residence interest, re-

gardless of the purpose for which the borrowed funds are used by the taxpayer.

Qualified medical expenses are those amounts paid for medical care within the meaning of sec. 213(d)(1)(A) and (B) (not including amounts paid for insurance covering medical care under sec. 213(d)(1)(C)), of the taxpayer, his spouse and dependents.

Qualified educational expenses are those amounts paid for reasonable living expenses while away from home, and for any tuition and related expenses incurred that would qualify scholarships (under sec. 117(b) as amended by the conference agreement), for the taxpayer, his spouse or dependent, while a student at an educational organization described in sec. 170(b)(1). Thus, tuition expenses for primary, secondary, college and graduate level education are generally included in qualified educational expenses. The qualified educational expenses or qualified medical expenses must be incurred within a reasonable period of time before or after the debt is incurred.

A principal residence of the taxpayer, and a second residence of the taxpayer, have the meanings set forth in the Senate amendment, except that if a second residence is not used by the taxpayer or rented at any time during the taxable year, the taxpayer need not meet the requirement of section 280A(d)(1) that the residence be used for personal (non-rental) purposes for the greater of 14 days or 10 percent of the number of days it is rented.

Interest on debt that is used to pay qualified medical or educational expenses, to be deductible as qualified residence interest, must be secured by the taxpayer's principal residence or second residence. Interest expense is so treated if the debt is so secured at the time the interest is paid or accrued. In the case of housing cooperatives, debt secured by stock held by the taxpayer as a tenant-stockholder is treated as secured by the residence the taxpayer is entitled to occupy as a tenant-stockholder. Where the stock may not be used as security by virtue of restrictions arising, for example, pursuant to local or State law, or pursuant to reasonable restrictions in the cooperative agreement, the stock may be treated as securing such debt, if the taxpayer establishes to the satisfaction of the Internal Revenue Service that the debt was incurred to acquire the stock. In addition, it is intended that the fact that State homestead laws may restrict the rights of secured parties with respect to certain types of residential mortgages will not cause interest on the debt to be treated as nondeductible personal interest, provided the lender's security interest is perfected and provided the interest on the debt is otherwise qualified residence interest.

[The following colloquy relating to Act Sec. 511 is drawn from the Congressional Record. The colloquy occurred on the day the Conference bill was considered by the House. Ed.]

[House Floor Explanation]

I have discussed with Congressman PICKLE several issues relating to the effective date of certain interest deduction limitations under the bill. We have reached a common understanding regarding the following specific issues:

I have spoken with Mr. PICKLE and he is concerned about the treatment of interest on a loan which is secured by a recorded deed of trust, mortgage or other security interest in a taxpayer's principal or second residence, in a State such as Texas, where the enforceability of such recorded security instrument will be restricted by State and local laws, such as the Texas homestead law. Under section 1421 of H.R. 3838, such interest is treated as qualified residence interest, provided the interest on the debt is otherwise qualified residence interest.

Madam Speaker, I reserve the balance of my time. Congressional Record, p. H 8363, 9-25-86.

[The following colloquy relating to Act Sec. 511 is drawn from the Congressional Record. The colloquy occurred on the day the bill was considered by the Senate. Ed.]

[Senate Floor Explanation]
INTEREST DEDUCTIBILITY

Mr. BENTSEN. Mr. President, I would like to clarify the treatment of interest on a loan which is secured by a recorded deed of trust, mortgage, or other security interest in a taxpayer's principle or second residence, in a State such as Texas, where the enforceability of such recorded security instrument will be restricted by State and local laws, such as the Texas homestead law. It is my understanding that under section 1421 of H.R. 3838, such interest is treated as qualified residence interest, provided the interest on the debt is otherwise qualified residence interest. Does the chairman share my understanding?

Mr. PACKWOOD. The understanding of the Senator from Texas is correct. Congressional Record, p. S13956, 9-27-86.

[Conference Report]

*   *   *   *   *   *

Effective date.—The conference agreement follows the effective date and phase-in rule of the Senate amendment, with modification.

Under the conference agreement, the amount of investment interest disallowed during the phase-in period under the provision is the excess over the amount of the present law $10,000 allowance ($5,000 in the case of a married individual filing a separate return, and zero in the case of a trust), plus the applicable portion of investment interest expense which would be disallowed without taking into account the present law allowance. Thus, for example, if an individual taxpayer has $20,000 of investment interest expense in excess of investment income 1987, 35 percent of the amount that does not exceed $10,000 or $3,500, plus the amount in excess of the $10,000 allowance. Thus, $13,500 would be disallowed, and $6,500 would be allowed for 1987 (assuming the taxpayer had no net passive loss for the year).

With respect to the investment interest limitation, for taxable years beginning on or after January 1, 1987 and before January 1, 1991, the amount of net investment income is reduced by the amount of losses from passive activities that is allowed as a deduction by virtue of the phase-in of the passive loss rule (other than net losses from rental real estate in which the taxpayer actively participates). For example, if a taxpayer has a passive loss which would be disallowed were the passive loss rule fully phased in (as in taxable years beginning after December 31, 1990), but a percentage of which is allowed under the passive loss phase-in rule, the amount of loss so allowed reduces the amount of the taxpayer's net investment income under the investment interest limitation for that year.

Further, any amount of investment interest that is disallowed under the investment interest limitation during the period that the investment interest limitation is phased in (that is, taxable years beginning on or after January 1, 1987 and before January 1, 1991) is not allowed as a deduction in a subsequent year except to the extent the taxpayer has net investment income in excess of investment interest in the subsequent year.[7]

【**Footnote ¶ 3905 continued**】

(7) For example, assume that, in 1987, the taxpayer has a passive loss of $80,000 of which $30,000 is attributable to rental real estate activities in which the taxpayer actively participates. Assuming the taxpayer is entitled to deduct $25,000 of active rental losses, then 35 percent of the remaining $55,000, or $19,250, would be suspended under the passive loss limitation. Of the deductible $35,750 of passive losses, the portion not attributable to active rental activities reduces the taxpayer's net investment income under the investment interest limitation for 1987.

That portion is determined by first calculating the ratio of (1) the amount of 1987 losses that are *not* attributable to rental real estate activities in which the taxpayer actively participates ($50,000) to (2) the amount of 1987 losses that are subject to the passive loss phase-in rule ($55,000). The ratio is applied to the total amount of passive losses allowed in 1987, other than those allowed under the $25,000 allowance ($35,000), to determine the portion allowed under the passive loss phase-in rule. This portion (i.e., $32,500) is subtracted from the amount of net investment income, under the investment interest limitation phase-in rule.

[¶ 3911] SEC 601. CORPORATE RATE REDUCTIONS

(Sec. 11 of the Code)

Senate Explanation

*   *   *   *   *   *

Explanation of Provision.—Under the bill tax would be imposed on corporations under the schedule shown in the following table.

CORPORATE TAX RATES IN
COMMITTEE BILL

Taxable Income	Tax Rate (percent)
Not over $50,000	15
Over $50,000 but not over $75,000	25
Over $75,000	33

An additional 5-percent tax is imposed on a corporation's taxable income in excess of $100,000. The maximum additional tax is $11,000. This provision phases out the benefit of graduated rates for corporations with taxable income between $100,000 and $320,000; corporations with income in excess of $320,000, in effect, will pay a flat tax at a 33-percent rate.

*   *   *   *   *   *

Conference Report

*   *   *   *   *   *

The conference agreement follows the House bill and the Senate amendment, except the maximum corporate rate is 34 percent. The phase-out of the benefit of graduated rates occurs through the imposition of an additional five-percent tax between $100,000 and $335,000 of taxable income. *[Effective Date].*—The new rate structure is effective for taxable years beginning on or after July 1, 1987; income in taxable years that include July 1, 1987 (other than as the first date of such year), is subject to blended rates under the rules specified in section 15 of present law.

[¶ 3912] SECTION 611. REDUCTION IN DIVIDENDS RECEIVED DEDUCTION

(Secs. 243–246A of the Code)

Senate Explanation

*   *   *   *   *   *

Reasons for Change.—Under present law, dividends eligible for the 85 percent dividends received deduction are taxed at a maximum rate of 6.9 percent (15 percent of the top corporate rate of 46 percent). The committee does not believe that the reduction in corporate tax rates generally should result in a significant reduction in this effective rate. Thus, the dividends received deduction has been reduced to 80 percent, resulting in a maximum rate of 6.6 percent on dividends subject to the reduced top corporate rate (20 percent of the top corporate rate of 33 percent).

Explanation of Provision.—Under the committee bill, the 85 percent dividends received deduction is lowered to 80 percent.

Effective Date.—The reduction in the dividends received deduction is applicable to dividends received or accrued after December 31, 1986 in taxable years ending after such date.

*   *   *   *   *   *

[¶ 3913] SECTION 612. REPEAL OF PARTIAL EXCLUSION FOR DIVIDENDS RECEIVED BY INDIVIDUALS

(Sec. 116 of the Code)

[Senate Explanation]

*   *   *   *   *   *

Reasons for Change.—The committee believes that the dividend exclusion for individuals under present law provides little relief from the two-tier corporate income tax because of the low limitation. As an exclusion from income, it also tends to benefit high-bracket taxpayers more than low-bracket taxpayers. On balance, the committee believes it is preferable to eliminate the exclusion and use the revenues to reduce tax rates.

Explanation of Provision.—Under the committee bill, the dividend exclusion for individuals is repealed.

Effective Date.—The provision is effective for taxable years beginning after December 31, 1986.

*   *   *   *   *   *

[¶ 3914]   SECTION 613. NONDEDUCTIBILITY OF STOCK REDEMPTION EXPENSES

(Sec. 162 of the Code)

[Senate Explanation]

*   *   *   *   *   *

Explanation of Provision.—The bill denies a deduction for any amount paid or incurred by a corporation in connection with the redemption of its stock. This provision is not limited to hostile takeover situations but applies to any corporate stock redemption. The committee intends that amounts subject to this provision will include amounts paid to repurchase stock; premiums paid for the stock; legal, accounting, brokerage, transfer agent, appraisal, and similar fees incurred in connection with the repurchase; and any other expenditure that is necessary or incident to the repurchase, whether representing costs incurred by the purchasing corporation or by the selling shareholder (and paid or reimbursed by the purchasing corporation), or incurred by persons or entities related to either. The provision is also intended to apply to any amount paid by a corporation to a selling shareholder (or any related person) pursuant to an agreement entered into as part of or in connection with a repurchase of stock, whereunder the seller agrees not to purchase, finance a purchase, acquire, or in any way be a party or agent to the acquisition of stock of the corporation for a specified or indefinite period of time (so-called "standstill" agreements).

The provision does not apply to interest deductible under section 163. In addition, it does not apply to amounts constituting dividends within the meaning of section 561, relating to payments (or deemed payments) for purposes of the accumulated earnings, personal holding company, and foreign personal holding company taxes, and for purposes of the regular income tax in the case of regulated investment companies and real estate investment trusts.[4] Thus, such amounts will continue to qualify for the dividends paid deduction to the same extent as under present law.

Further, the provision does not apply to otherwise deductible expenses incurred by a regulated investment company that is an open-end mutual fund in connection with the redemption of its stock upon the demand of a shareholder. Thus, for example, costs incurred by such a company in processing applications for redemption and issuing checks in payment for redeemed shares

would be deductible to the same extent as under present law.[5]

*   *   *   *   *   *

[Conference Report]

The conference agreement generally follows the Senate amendment, with certain modifications and clarifications.

The conferees intend that the denial of deductibility will apply to amounts paid in connection with a purchase of stock in a corporation, whether paid by the corporation directly or indirectly, *e.g.,* by a controlling shareholder, commonly controlled subsidiary or other related party.

The conferees wish to clarify that, while the phrase "in connection with [a] redemption" is intended to be construed broadly, the provision is not intended to deny a deduction for otherwise deductible amounts paid in a transaction that has no nexus with the redemption other than being proximate in time or arising out of the same general circumstances. For example, if a corporation redeems a departing employee's stock and makes a payment to the employee in discharge of the corporation's obligations under an employment contract, the payment in discharge of the contractual obligation is not subject to disallowance under this provision.[4a] Payments in discharge of other types of contractual obligations, in settlement of litigation, or pursuant to other actual or potential legal obligations or rights, may also be outside the intended scope of the provision to the extent it is clearly established that the payment does not represent consideration for the stock or expenses related to its acquisition, and is not a payment that is a fundamental part of a "standstill" or similar agreement.

The conferees anticipate that, where a transaction is not directly related to a redemption but is proximate in time, the Internal Revenue Service will scrutinize the transaction to determine whether the amount purportedly paid in the transaction is reasonable. Thus, even where the parties have countervailing tax interests, the parties' stated allocation of the total consideration between the redemption and the unrelated transaction will be respected only if it is supported by all the facts and circumstances.[5a]

[Footnote ¶ 3914]   (4) See secs. 535, 545, 556, 852, 857 [IRC. of 1954].

(5) See Rev. Rul. 75-468, 1978-E C.B. 84.

(4a) This would be so whether the employment contract and the redemption agreement were contained in one document or separate documents, and whether or not they were separately negotiated.

(5a) Compare *American International Coal Co. v. Comm'r,* PH Memo TC para. 82,204 (1982) corporation's payment to shareholder-employee was nondeductible distribution in redemption of stock, not compensation for services) with *Atwater & Co. v. Comm'r,* 10 T C. (1948) (corporation's payment to shareholder-employee under agreement to repurchase shares upon termination of employment, *held,* deductible to extent represented additional compensation for services).

However, the conferees intend that agreements to refrain from purchasing stock of a corporation or other similar types of "standstill" agreements in all events will be considered related to any redemption of the payee's stock. Accordingly, payments pursuant to such agreements are nondeductible under this provision provided there is an actual purchase of all or part of the payee's stock. The conferees intend no inference regarding the deductibility of payments under standstill or similar agreements that are unrelated to any redemption of stock owned by the payee.

In denying a deduction for payments in connection with redemptions of stock, the conferees intend no inference regarding the deductibility of such payments under present law. Moreover, no inference is intended as to the character of such payments in the hands of the payee.

[**Effective Date.**] —The provision is effective for payments on or after March 1, 1986.

[¶ 3915] SECTION 614. REDUCTION IN STOCK BASIS FOR NON-TAXED PORTION OF EXTRAORDINARY DIVIDENDS

(Sec. 1059 of the Code)

[Senate Explanation]

*　　*　　*　　*　　*　　*

[**Explanation of Provision**] Under the bill, a corporation that disposes of a share of stock must reduce its basis therein (but not below zero) by the nontaxed portion of any extraordinary dividend paid with respect to the share at any time during the corporation's holding period for the stock. This basis reduction is required only for purposes of determining gain or loss on the disposition of the share. If the aggregate nontaxed portions of extraordinary dividends exceed the shareholder's basis, the excess will be treated as gain from a sale or exchange at the time of disposition.

The bill provides a taxpayer the option of determining the status of a distribution as an extraordinary dividend by reference to the fair market value of the share on the day before the ex-dividend date in lieu of its adjusted basis. This special rule applies only if the taxpayer establishes the fair market value of the share to the satisfaction of the Commissioner.

As under present law, if the corporate shareholder and the payor of the dividend are members of an affiliated group filing consolidated returns, the shareholder will not be required to reduce its basis in the stock under both this provision and under Treas. Reg. section 1.1502-32(b)(2)(iii). Thus, no portion of a distribution may reduce basis twice.

*　　*　　*　　*　　*　　*

[Conference Report]

*　　*　　*　　*　　*　　*

The conference agreement generally follows the Senate amendment, with certain modifications and clarifications.

The determination of whether a dividend is extraordinary will be made under the present law percentage-of-adjusted-basis test, subject to the alternative fair market value test provided in the Senate amendment.[1] In lieu of the one-year post-acquisition holding period requirement of present law, the conference agreement provides a test based on the holding period of the distributee as of the date the distribution is declared or publicly announced by the distributing corporation's board of directors. Under this test, a distribution with respect to stock will constitute an extraordinary dividend if the taxpayer has not held the stock for more than two years on that date. If there is a formal or informal agreement to pay the particular dividend prior to the declaration date, the date of such agreement shall be treated as the dividend announcement date for purposes of applying the two-year holding period requirement. Whether there is such a formal or informal agreement is determined based on all the facts and circumstances. In general, a broad agreement in a joint venture arrangement that dividends will be paid as funds are available would not be considered an agreement to pay a particular dividend in the absence of other facts, such as facts showing a particular expectation that a large dividend would be paid after the acquisition of an interest in the venture by a new party.

A distribution that would otherwise constitute an extraordinary dividend under the two-year rule described above will not be considered extraordinary if the distributee has held the stock for the entire period the distributing corporation (and any predecessor corporation) has been in existence.

The conference agreement provides for a different treatment of dividends on certain qualifying preferred stock. Absent the special rule under the basic definition of extraordinary dividend, a preferred stock that pays a greater than 5-percent dividend within any period of 85 days or less is paying an extraordinary dividend. Thus, for example, a 6-percent preferred stock dividend that is paid once annually would be extraordinary. On the other hand, if the stock paid four quarterly 5-percent dividends, none of the dividends would be considered extraordinary. The special rule is not intended to apply if no basis adjustment would be required under the general rule.

[**Footnote ¶ 3915**]   **(1)** The conference agreement clarifies that the alternative fair market value test applies for purposes of section 105(c)(3)(B) (which treats certain dividends having ex-dividend dates within a 365-day period as extraordinary).

The exception for qualifying preferred stock is intended to provide relief for certain transactions to the extent that there is no potential for effectively purchasing a dividend that accrued prior to the date of purchase ("dividend-stripping"). Preferred stock is treated as qualifying for this purpose if: (1) it provides for fixed (i.e. not varying) preferred dividends payable not less often than annually; (2) dividends were not in arrears when the taxpayer acquired the stock, and (3) the dividends received by the taxpayer during the period it owned the stock do not exceed an annualized rate of 15 percent of the lower of (a) the taxpayer's adjusted basis or (b) the liquidation preference of the stock.[1a]

Dividends on qualifying preferred stock will be treated as extraordinary dividends only to the extent the dividends received by the taxpayer during the period it owned the stock exceed the dividends it "earned."

To determine whether the taxpayer's dividends exceed the dividends it earned, the taxpayer's "actual dividend rate" is first computed. The actual dividend rate is the average annual amount of dividends received (or deemed received under section 305 or any other provision) during the period the taxpayer owned the stock, computed as a return on the taxpayer's adjusted basis or, if lesser, the stock's liquidation preference. This is then compared to the taxpayer's "stated dividend rate," which is the return represented by the annual fixed preferred dividends payable on the stock. If the actual dividend rate exceeds the stated dividend rate, a portion of each dividend received or deemed received will be an extraordinary dividend, and basis will be reduced by the untaxed portion of such dividend.

For example, assume that on January 1, 1987, a corporation purchases for $1,000 ten shares of preferred stock having a liquidation preference of $100 per share and paying fixed preferred dividends of $6 per share to shareholders of record on March 31 and September 30 of each year. If the taxpayer does not elect to have the special rule apply, the basic rule would generally require the taxpayer to reduce the basis in the stock by the untaxed portion of each dividend received prior * * *[to] the expiration of the two-year holding period. This is because a dividend exceeding 5 percent of adjusted basis (or fair market value, if shown to the satisfaction of the Secretary) paid semi-annually is an extraordinary dividend under the general rule.[2] However, special rule will apply to the preferred stock. Under this provision, the taxpayer's stated dividend rate is 12 percent

($12/$100). If the taxpayer sells the stock on October 1, 1988, (after holding the stock for 1.75 years) and no dividends in excess of the fixed preferred dividends have been paid, its "actual dividend rate" will be 13.7 percent ($240/$1,000 divided by 1.75). This 13.7 percent exceeds the 12 percent stated dividend rate by 1.7. This excess, as a fraction of the actual dividend rate, is 12.4 percent (1.7 divided by 13.7). Accordingly, each of the dividends will be treated as an extraordinary dividend described in section 1059(a) to the extent of 0.74 per share ($6 × 12.4 percent). However, if the corporation does not sell the stock until January 1, 1989, and no dividends in excess of the fixed preferred dividends have been paid, its "actual dividend rate" will be 12 percent ($240/$1000 divided by 2.0). This does not exceed the stated dividend rate; accordingly, no portion of any dividend will be treated as an extraordinary dividend.

In addition, under the conference agreement the term "extraordinary dividend" is expanded to include any distribution (without regard to the holding period for the stock or the relative magnitude of the distribution) to a corporate shareholder in partial liquidation of the distributing corporation. For this purpose, a distribution will be treated as in partial liquidation if it satisfies the requirements of section 302(e) of the Code. Since the determination whether a distribution is in partial liquidation is made at the corporate rather than the shareholder level, the conferees intend that the Treasury Department will have the authority to require the distributing corporation to advise its shareholders (with notice to the Internal Revenue Service) as to the character of the distribution. This characterization will generally be binding on the shareholders.[3] The Internal Revenue Service, however, will be free to challenge the characterization of the distribution, provided it takes a consistent position with respect to corporate and noncorporate shareholders.

Finally, under the conference agreement the term extraordinary dividend includes any redemption of stock that is non-pro rata (again, irrespective of the holding period of the stock or the relative size of the distribution).

Except as provided in regulations, the provisions do not apply to distributions between members of an affiliated group filing consolidated returns. In addition, they do not apply to distributions that constitute qualifying dividends within the meaning of section 243(b)(1). Accordingly, the provision generally will not apply to dividend distributions (or deemed dividend distributions) during a con-

---

[Footnote ¶ 3915 continued]

(1a) It is understood that liquidation preference for purposes of this section does not include dividend arrearages, if any.

(2) If the dividend were three percent paid quarterly, it would not be an extraordinary dividend under the general rule and no basis reduction would be required.

(3) The conferees intend that there will be a presumption, rebuttable by clear and convincing evidence, that this characterization of the distribution is correct. The conferees anticipate that the Treasury Department may require the taxpayer to disclose on its return the fact that it is taking a contrary position and its reasons for doing so.

solidated return year by a subsidiary out of earnings and profits accumulated during separate return affiliation years.

In order to prevent double inclusions in earnings and profits, the conferees expect that the amount, if any, of earnings and profits resulting from gain on the disposition of stock shall be determined without regard to the basis adjustments made under this section.

[**Effective Date.**—] The provision is generally effective for dividends declared after July 18, 1986. However, distributions constituting extraordinary dividends by virtue of being a distribution in partial liquidation or a non-pro rata distribution are subject to the provision only if announced or declared after date of enactment.

[¶ 3916] SECTION 621. LIMITATION OF NET OPERATING LOSS CARRYFORWARDS

(Secs. 382 and 383 of the Code)

[Conference Report]

*   *   *   *   *   *

[Explanation of Provision.]

Overview.—The conference agreement alters the character of the special limitations on the use of NOL carryforwards similar to the House bill and the Senate amendment. After an ownership change, as described below, the taxable income of a loss corporation available for offset by pre-acquisition NOL carryforwards is annually limited to a prescribed rate times the value of the loss corporation's stock on the date of the ownership change. In addition, NOL carryforwards are disallowed entirely unless the loss corporation satisfies continuity-of-business enterprise requirements for the two-year period following any ownership change. The conference agreement also expands the scope of the special limitations to include built-in losses and allows loss corporations to take into account built-in gains. The conference agreement also includes numerous technical changes and several anti-avoidance rules. Finally, the conference agreement applies similar rules to carryforwards other than NOLs, such as net capital losses and excess foreign tax credits.

Ownership change.—Under the conference agreement, the special limitations apply after any ownership change. An ownership change occurs, in general, if the percentage of stock of the new loss corporation owned by any one or more 5-percent shareholders (described below) has increased by more than 50 percentage points relative to the lowest percentage of stock of the old loss corporation owned by those 5-percent shareholders at any time during the testing period (generally a three-year period).[6] The determination of whether an ownership change has occurred is made by aggregating the increases in percentage ownership for each 5-percent shareholder whose percentage ownership has increased during the testing period. For this purpose, all stock owned by persons who own less than five percent of a loss corporation's stock is generally treated as stock owned by a single 5-percent shareholder. The determination of whether an ownership change has occurred is made after any owner shift involving a 5-percent shareholder or any equity structure shift.

Determinations of the percentage of stock in a loss corporation owned by any person are made on the basis of value. Except as provided in regulations to be prescribed by the Secretary, changes in proportionate ownership attributable solely to fluctuations in the relative fair market values of different classes or amounts of stock are not taken into account.

In determining whether an ownership change has occurred, changes in the holdings of certain preferred stock are disregarded. Except as provided in regulations, all "stock" (not including stock described in section 1504(a)(4)) is taken into account. Under this standard, the term stock does not include stock that (1) is not entitled to vote, (2) is limited and preferred as to dividends and does not participate in corporate growth to any significant extent, (3) has redemption and liquidation rights that do not exceed the stock's issue price upon issuance (except for a reasonable redemption premium), and (4) is not convertible to any other class of stock. If preferred stock carries a dividend rate materially in excess of a market rate, this may indicate that it would not be disregarded.

Under grants of regulatory authority in the conference agreement, the conferees expect the Treasury Department to publish regulations disregarding, in appropriate cases, certain stock that would otherwise be counted in determining whether an ownership change has occurred, when necessary to prevent avoidance of the special limitations. For example, it may be appropriate to disregard preferred stock (even though voting) or common stock where the likely percentage participation of such stock in future corporate growth is disproportionately small compared to the percentage value of the stock as a proportion of total stock value, at the time of the issuance or transfer. Similarly, the conferees are concerned that the inclusion of voting preferred stock (which is not described in section 1504(a)(4) solely because it carries the right to vote) in the definition of stock presents the potential for avoidance of section 382. As another example, stock such as that issued to the old loss company shareholders and retained by them in the case of *Maxwell Hardware Company* v. *Commission-*

[**Footnote ¶ 3916**]   (6) Unless specifically identified as a taxable year, all references to any period constituting a year (or multiple thereof) means a 365-day period (or multiple thereof).

er, 343 F.2d 716 (9th Cir. 1969), is not intended to be counted in determining whether an ownership change has occurred.

In addition, the conferees expect that the Treasury Department will promulgate regulations regarding the extent to which stock that is not described in section 1504(a)(4) should nevertheless not be considered stock. For example, the Treasury Department may issue regulations providing that preferred stock otherwise described in section 1504(a)(4) will not be considered stock simply because the dividends are in arrears and the preferred shareholders thus become entitled to vote.

Owner shift involving a 5-percent shareholder.—An owner shift involving a 5-percent shareholder is defined under the conference agreement as any change in the respective ownership of stock of a corporation that affects the percentage of stock held by any person who holds five percent or more of the stock of the corporation (a "5-percent shareholder") before or after the change. For purposes of this rule, all less-than-5-percent shareholders are aggregated and treated as one 5-percent shareholder. Thus, an owner shift involving a 5-percent shareholder includes (but is not limited to) the following transactions:

(1) A taxable purchase of loss corporation stock by a person who holds at least five percent of the stock before the purchase;

(2) A disposition of stock by a person who holds at least five percent of stock of the loss corporation either before or after the disposition;

(3) A taxable purchase of loss corporation stock by a person who becomes a 5-percent shareholder as a result of the purchase;

(4) A section 351 exchange that affects the percentage of stock ownership of a loss corporation by one or more 5-percent shareholders;

(5) A decrease in the outstanding stock of a loss corporation (*e.g.*, by virtue of a redemption) that affects the percentage of stock ownership of the loss corporation by one or more 5-percent shareholders;

(6) A conversion of debt (or pure preferred stock that is excluded from the definition of stock) to stock where the percentage of stock ownership of the loss corporation by one or more 5-percent shareholders is affected; and

(7) An issuance of stock by a loss corporation that affects the percentage of stock ownership by one or more 5-percent shareholders.

Example 1.—The stock of L corporation is publicly traded; no shareholder holds five percent or more of L stock. During the three-year period between January 1, 1987 and January 1, 1990, there are numerous trades involving L stock. No ownership change will occur as a result of such purchases, provided that no person (or persons) becomes a 5-percent shareholder, either directly or indirectly, and increases his (or their) ownership of L stock by more than 50 percentage points.

Example 2.—On January 1, 1987, the stock of L corporation is publicly traded; no shareholder holds five percent or more of L stock. On September 1, 1987, individuals A, B, and C, who were not previously L shareholders and are unrelated to each other or any L shareholders, each acquires one-third of L stock. A, B, and C each have become 5-percent shareholders of L and, in the aggregate, hold 100 percent of the L stock. Accordingly, an ownership change has occurred, because the percentage of L stock owned by the three 5-percent shareholders after the owner shift (100 percent) has increased by more than 50 percentage points over the lowest percentage of L stock owned by A, B, and C at any time during the testing period (0 percent prior to September 1, 1987).

Example 3.—On January 1, 1987, individual I owns all 1,000 shares of corporation L. On June 15, 1987, I sells 300 of his L shares to unrelated individual A. On June 15, 1988, L issues 100 shares to each of B, C, and D. After these owner shifts involving I, A, B, C, and D, each of whom are 5-percent shareholders, there is no ownership change, because the percentage of stock owned by A, B, C, and D after the owner shifts (approximately 46 percent—A-23 percent; B, C, and D-7.7 percent each) has not increased by more than 50 percentage points over the lowest percentage of stock owned by those shareholders during the testing period (0 percent prior to June 15, 1987). On December 15, 1988, L redeems 200 of the shares owned by I. Following this owner shift affecting I, a 5-percent shareholder, there is an ownership change, because the percentage of L stock owned by A, B, C, and D (approximately 55 percent—A-27.3 percent; B, C, and D-9.1 percent each) has increased by more than 50 percentage points over the lowest percentage owned by those shareholders during the testing period (0 percent prior to June 15, 1987).

Example 4.—L corporation is closely held by four unrelated individuals, A, B, C, and D. On January 1, 1987, there is a public offering of L stock. No person who acquires stock in a public offering acquires five percent or more, and neither A, B, C, nor D acquires any additional stock. As a result of the offering, less-than-5-percent shareholders own stock representing 80 percent of the outstanding L stock. The stock ownership of the less-than-5-percent shareholders are aggregated and treated as owned by a single 5-percent shareholder for purposes of determining whether an ownership change has occurred. The percentage of stock owned by the less-than-5-percent shareholders after the owner shift (80 percent) has increased by more than 50 percentage points over the lowest percentage of stock owned by those shareholders at any time during the testing period (0 percent prior to January 1, 1987). Thus, an ownership change has occurred.

Example 5.—On January 1, 1987, L corporation is wholly owned by individual X. On January 1, 1988, X sells 50 percent of his stock to 1,000 shareholders, all of whom are unrelated to him. On January 1, 1989, X sells his remaining 50-percent interest to an additional 1,000 shareholders, all of whom also are unrelated to him. Based on these facts, there is not an ownership change immediately following the initial sales by X, because the percentage of L stock owned by the group of less-than-5-percent shareholders (who are treated as a single 5-percent shareholder) after the owner shift (50 percent) has not increased by *more* than 50 percentage points over the lowest percentage of stock owned by this group at any time during the testing period (0 percent prior to January 1, 1988). On January 1, 1989, however, there is an ownership change, because the percentage of L stock owned by the group of less-than-5-percent shareholders after the owner shift (100 percent) has increased by more than 50 percentage points over their lowest percentage ownership at any time during the testing period (0 percent prior to January 1, 1988).

Example 6.—The stock of L corporation is publicly traded; no shareholder owns five percent or more. On January 1, 1987, there is a stock offering as a result of which stock representing 60 percent of L's value is acquired by an investor group consisting of 12 unrelated individuals, each of whom acquires five percent of L stock. Based on these facts, there has been an ownership change, because the percentage of L stock owned after the owner shift by the 12 5-percent shareholders in the investor group (60 percent) has increased by more than 50 percentage points over the lowest percentage of stock owned by those shareholders at any time during the testing period (0 percent prior to January 1, 1987).

Example 7.—On January 1, 1987, L corporation is owned by two unrelated shareholders, A (60 percent) and C (40 percent). LS corporation is a wholly owned subsidiary of L corporation and is therefore deemed to be owned by A and C in the same proportions as their ownership of L (after application of the attribution rules, as discussed below). On January 1, 1988, L distributes all the stock of LS to A in exchange for all of A's L stock in a section 355 transaction. There has been an ownership change of L, because the percentage of L stock owned by C (100 percent) has increased by more than 50 percentage points over the lowest percentage of L stock owned by C at any time during the testing period (40 percent prior to the distribution of LS stock). There has not been an ownership change of LS, because the percentage of LS stock owned by A (100 percent) has not increased by more than 50 percentage points over the lowest percentage of stock owned by A at any time during the testing period (60 percent, after application of the attribution rules, as discussed below), prior to January 1, 1988.

Equity structure shift.—An equity structure shift is defined under the conference agreement as any tax-free reorganization within the meaning of section 368, other than a divisive reorganization or an "F" reorganization. In addition, to the extent provided in regulations, the term equity structure shift will include other transactions, such as public offerings not involving a 5-percent shareholder or taxable reorganization-type transactions *(e.g.,* mergers or other reorganization-type transactions that do not qualify for tax-free treatment due to the nature of the consideration or the failure to satisfy any of the other requirements for a tax-free transaction). A purpose of the provision that considers only owner shifts involving a 5-percent shareholder is to relieve widely held companies from the burden of keeping track of trades among such shareholders. For example, a publicly traded company that is 60 percent owned by less-than-5-percent shareholders would not experience an ownership change merely because, within a three-year period, every one of such shareholders sold his stock to a person who was not a 5-percent shareholder. The conferees believe, however, that there are situations involving transfers of stock involving less-than-5-percent shareholders, other than tax-free reorganizations (for example, public offerings), in which it will be feasible to identify changes in ownership involving such shareholders, because, unlike public trading, the changes occur as part of a single, integrated transaction. Where identification is reasonably feasible or a reasonable presumption can be applied, the conferees intend that the Treasury Department will treat such transactions under the rules applicable to equity structure shifts.

Under the conference agreement, for purposes of determining whether an ownership change has occurred following an equity structure shift, the less-than-5-percent shareholders of each corporation that was a party to the reorganization will be segregated and treated as a single, separate 5-percent shareholder. Moreover, the conference agreement provides regulatory authority to apply similar segregation rules in cases, such as a public offering or recapitalization, that involve only a single corporation.

Example 8.—On January 1, 1988, L corporation (a loss corporation) is merged (in a transaction described in section 368(a)(1)(A)) into P corporation (not a loss corporation), with P surviving. Both L and P are publicly traded corporations with no shareholder owning five percent or more of either corporation or the surviving corporation. In the merger, L shareholders receive 30 percent of the stock of P. There has been an ownership change of L, because the percentage of P stock owned by the former P shareholders (all of whom are less-than-5-percent shareholders who are treated as a separate, single 5-percent shareholder) after the equity structure shift (70 percent) has increased by more than 50 percentage points over the lowest percentage of L stock owned by such shareholders at any time during the testing period (0 percent prior to the merger). If, however, the former shareholders of L had received at least 50 percent of the stock of P in the merger, there would not have been an ownership change of L.

It is anticipated that the same results would apply in a taxable merger in which the loss corporation survives, under facts as described above, pursuant to regulations treating taxable reorganization-type transactions as equity structure shifts.

Example 9.—On January 1, 1987, L corporation is owned by two unrelated shareholders, A (60 percent) and C (40 percent). On January 1, 1988, L redeems all of A's L stock in exchange for non-voting preferred stock described in section 1504(a)(4). Following this recapitalization (which is both an equity structure shift and an owner shift involving a 5-percent shareholder), there has been an ownership change of L, because the percentage of L stock (which does not include preferred stock within the meaning of section 1504(a)(4)) owned by C following the equity structure shift (100 percent) has increased by more than 50 percentage points over the lowest percentage of L stock owned by C at any time during the testing period (40 percent prior to the recapitalization).

Assume, however, that on January 1, 1987, the stock of L corporation was widely held, with no shareholder owning as much as five percent, and that 60 percent of the stock was redeemed in exchange for non-voting preferred stock in a transaction that is otherwise identical to the transaction described above (which would be an equity structure shift, but not an owner shift involving a 5-percent shareholder because of the existence of only a single 5-percent shareholder, the aggregated less-than-5-percent shareholders, who owns 100 percent of L both before and after the exchange). In such a case, the Secretary will prescribe regulations segregating the less-than-5-percent shareholders of the single corporation, so that the group of shareholders who retain common stock in the recapitalization will be treated as a separate, single 5-percent shareholder. Accordingly, such a transaction would constitute an ownership change, because the percentage of L stock owned by the continuing common shareholders (100 percent) has increased by more than 50 percentage points over the lowest percent of stock owned by such shareholders at any time during the testing period (40 percent prior to the recapitalization).

Example 10.—L corporation stock is widely held; no shareholder owns as much as five percent of L stock. On January 1, 1988, L corporation, which has a value of $1 million, directly issues stock with a value of $2 million to the public; no one person acquired as much as five percent in the public offering. Under the statutory definitions contained in the conference agreement, no ownership change has occurred, because a public offering in which no person acquires as much as five percent of the corporation's stock, however large, by a corporation that has no five-percent shareholder before the offering would not affect the percentage of stock owned by a 5-percent shareholder.[7] In other words, the percentage of stock owned by less-than-5-percent shareholders of L immediately after the public offering (100 percent) has not increased by more than 50 percentage points over the lowest percentage of stock owned by the less-than-5-percent shareholders of L at any time during the testing period (100 percent).

Under the conference agreement, however, to the extent provided in regulations that will apply prospectively from the date the regulations are issued, a public offering can be treated as an equity structure shift. Rules also would be provided to segregate the group of less-than-5-percent shareholders prior to the offering and the new group of less than-5-percent shareholders that acquire stock pursuant to the offering. Under such regulations, therefore, the public offering could be treated as an equity structure shift, and the less-than-5-percent shareholders who receive stock in the public offering could be segregated and treated as a separate 5-percent shareholder. Thus, an ownership change may result from the public offering described above, because the percentage of stock owned by the group of less-than-5-percent shareholders who acquire stock in the public offering, who are treated as a separate 5-percent shareholder (66.67 percent), has increased by more than 50 percentage points over the lowest percentage of L stock owned by such shareholders at any time during the testing period (0 percent prior to the public offering). The conference agreement anticipates that the regulations treating public offerings as equity structure shifts also may provide rules to allow the corporation to establish the extent, if any, to which existing shareholders acquire stock in the public offering.

Multiple transactions.—As described above, the determination of whether an ownership change has occurred is made by comparing the relevant shareholders' stock ownership immediately after either an owner shift involving a 5-percent shareholder or an equity structure shift with the lowest percentage of such shareholders' ownership at any time during the testing period preceding either the owner shift involving a 5-percent shareholder or the equity structure shift. Thus, changes in ownership that occur by reason of a series of transactions including both owner shifts involving a 5-percent shareholder and equity structure shifts may constitute an ownership change. In determining whether an ownership change has occurred as a result of a transaction or transactions following an equity structure shift or owner shift involving a 5-percent shareholder that did not result in an ownership change, the conference agreement provides that, unless a different proportion is established, the acquisition of stock after such a shift

---

[Footnote ¶ 3916 continued]

(7) A different result would occur if the public offering were performed by an underwriter on a "firm commitment" basis, because the underwriter would be a 5-percent shareholder whose percentage of stock (66.67 percent) has increased by more than 50 percentage points over the lowest percentage of stock owned by the underwriter at any time during the testing period (0 percent prior to public offering). *See* Rev. Rul. 78-294, 1978-2 C.B. 141

shall be treated as being made proportionately from all the shareholders immediately before the acquisition.

Example 11.—On January 1, 1988, I (an individual) purchased 40 percent of the stock of L. The remaining stock of L is owned by 25 shareholders, none of whom own as much as five percent. On July 1, 1988, L is merged into P—which is wholly owned by I—in a tax-free reorganization. In exchange for their stock in L, the L shareholders (immediately before the merger) receive stock with a value representing 60 percent of the P stock that is outstanding immediately after the merger (24 percent to I; 36 percent to the less-than-5-percent shareholders of L). No other transactions occurred with respect to L stock during the testing period preceding the merger. There is an ownership change with respect to L immediately following the merger, because the percentage of stock owned by I in the combined entity (64 percent—40 percent by virtue of I's ownership of P prior to the merger plus 24 percent received in the merger) has increased by more than 50 percentage points over the lowest percentage of stock in L owned by I during the testing period (0 percent prior to January 1, 1988).

Example 12.—On July 12, 1989, L corporation is owned 45 percent by P, a publicly traded corporation (with no 5-percent shareholders), 40 percent by individual A, and 15 percent by individual B. All of the L shareholders have owned their stock since L's organization in 1984. Neither A nor B owns any P stock. On July 30, 1989, B sells his entire 15-percent interest to C for cash. On August 13, 1989, P acquires A's entire 40-percent interest in exchange for P stock representing an insignificant percentage of the outstanding P voting stock in a "B" reorganization.

There is an ownership change immediately following the B reorganization, because the percentage of L stock held (through attribution, as described below) by P shareholders (all of whom are less-than-5-percent shareholders who are treated as one 5-percent shareholder) and C (100 percent—P shareholders-85 percent; C-15 percent) has increased by more than 50 percentage points over the lowest percentage of stock owned by P shareholders and C at any time during the testing period (45 percent held constructively by P shareholders prior to August 13, 1989).

Example 13.—The stock of L corporation is widely held by the public; no single shareholder owns five percent or more of L stock. G corporation also is widely held with no shareholder owning five percent or more. On January 1, 1988, L corporation and G corporation merge (in a tax-free transaction), with L surviving, and G shareholders receive 49 percent of L stock. On July 1, 1988, B, an individual who has never owned stock in L or G, purchases five percent of L stock in a transaction on a public stock exchange.

The merger of L and G is not an ownership change of L, because the percentage of stock owned by the less-than-5-percent shareholders of G (who are aggregated and treated as a single 5-percent shareholder) (49 percent) has not increased by more than 50 percentage points over the lowest percentage of L stock owned by such shareholders during the testing period (0 percent prior to the merger). The purchase of L stock by B is an owner shift involving a five-percent shareholder, which is presumed (unless otherwise established) to have been made proportionately from the groups of former G and L shareholders (49 percent from the G shareholders and 51 percent from the L shareholders). There is an ownership change of L because, immediately after the owner shift involving B, the percentage of stock owned by the G shareholders (presumed to be 46.55 percent—49 percent actually acquired in the merger less 2.45 percent presumed sold to B) and B (5 percent) has increased by more than 50 percentage points over the lowest percentage of L stock owned by those shareholders at any time during the testing period (0 percent prior to the merger).

Example 14.—The stock of L corporation and G corporation is widely held by the public; neither corporation has any shareholder owning as much as five percent of its stock. On January 1, 1988, B purchases 10 percent of L stock. On July 1, 1988, L and G merge (in a tax-free transaction), with L surviving, and G shareholders receiving 49 percent of L stock.

The merger of L and G is an ownership change because, immediately after the merger, the percentage of stock owned by G shareholders (49 percent) and B (5.1 percent) has increased by more than 50 percentage points over the lowest percentage of L stock owned by such shareholders at any time during the testing period (0 percent prior to the stock purchase by B).

Attribution and aggregation of stock ownership.—*Attribution from entities.*—In determining whether an ownership change has occurred, the constructive ownership rules of section 318, with several exceptions, are applied. The rules for attributing ownership from corporations to their shareholders are applied without regard to the extent of the shareholders' ownership in the corporation. Thus, any stock owned by a corporation is treated as being owned proportionately by its shareholders. Moreover, except as provided in regulations, any such stock attributed to a corporation's shareholders is not treated as being held by such corporation. Stock attributed from a partnership, estate or trust similarly shall not be treated as being held by such entity. The effect of the attribution rules is to prevent application of the special limitations after an acquisition that does not result in a more than 50 percent change in the ultimate beneficial ownership of a loss corporation. Conversely, the attribution rules result in an ownership change where more than 50 percent of a loss corporation's stock is acquired indirectly through an acquisition of stock in the corporation's parent corporation.

Example 15.—L corporation is publicly traded; no shareholder owns as much as five percent. P corporation is publicly traded; no shareholder owns as much as five percent.

On January 1, 1988, P corporation purchases 100 percent of L corporation stock on the open market. The L stock owned by P is attributed to the shareholders of P, all of whom are less-than-5-percent shareholders who are treated as a single, separate 5-percent shareholder. Accordingly, there has been an ownership change of L, because the percentage of stock owned by the P shareholders after the purchase (100 percent) has increased by more than 50 percentage points over the lowest percentage of L stock owned by that group at any time during the testing period (0 percent prior to January 1, 1988).

Aggregation rules.—Special aggregation rules are applied for all stock ownership, actual or deemed, by shareholders of a corporation who are less-than-5-percent shareholders. Except as provided in regulations, stock owned by such persons is treated as being held by a single, separate 5-percent shareholder. For purposes of determining whether transactions following an equity structure shift or owner shift involving a 5-percent shareholder constitute an ownership change, the aggregation rules trace any subsequent change in ownership by a group of less-than-5-percent shareholders. In analyzing subsequent shifts in ownership, unless a different proportion is otherwise established, acquisitions of stock shall be treated as being made proportionately from all shareholders immediately before such acquisition.

Example 16.—Corporation A is widely held by a group of less-than-5-percent shareholders ("Shareholder Group A"). Corporation A owns 80 percent of both corporation B and corporation C, which respectively own 100 percent of corporation L and corporation P. Individual X owns the remaining stock in B (20 percent) and individual Y owns the remaining stock in C (20 percent). On January 1, 1988, L merges into P, with P surviving, and B is completely cashed out. The attribution rules and special aggregation rules apply to treat Shareholder Group A as a single, separate 5-percent shareholder owning 80 percent of both L and P prior to the merger. Following the merger, Shareholder Group A still owns 80 percent of the stock of P, a new loss corporation, and Y owns 20 percent. No ownership change occurs as a result of the merger, because the stock of P, the new loss corporation, owned by Y (20 percent) has not increased by more than 50 percentage points over the lowest percentage of stock of L, the old loss corporation, owned by Y at any time during the testing period (0 percent prior to January 1, 1988).

Example 17.—L corporation is publicly traded; no shareholder owns more than five percent. LS is a wholly owned subsidiary of L corporation. On January 1, 1988, L distributes all the stock of LS pro rata to the L shareholders. There has not been any change in the respective ownership of the stock of LS, because the less-than-5 percent shareholders of L, who are aggregated and treated as a single, separate 5-percent shareholder, are treated as owning 100 percent of LS (by attribution) before the distribution and directly own 100 percent of LS after the distribution. Thus, no owner shift involving a 5-percent shareholder has occurred; accordingly, there has not been an ownership change.

Example 18.—L Corporation is valued at $600. Individual A owns 30 percent of L stock, with its remaining ownership widely held by less-than-5-percent shareholders ("Shareholder Group L"). P corporation is widely held by less-than-5-percent shareholders ("Shareholder Group P"), and is valued at $400. On January 1, 1988, L and P consolidate in a tax free reorganization into L/P Corporation, with 60 percent of the value of such stock being distributed to former L corporation shareholders. On June 15, 1988, 17 percent of L/P corporation stock is acquired in a series of open market transactions by individual B. At all times between January 1, 1988 and June 15, 1988, A's ownership interest in L/P Corporation remained unchanged.

The consolidation by L and P on January 1, 1988 is an equity structure shift, but not an ownership change with respect to L. Under the attribution and aggregation rules, the ownership interest in new loss corporation, L/P Corporation, is as follows: A owns 18 percent (60 percent of 30 percent), Shareholder Group L owns 42 percent (60 percent of 70 percent) and Shareholder Group P owns 40 percent. The only 5-percent shareholder whose stock interest in new loss corporation increased relative to the lowest percentage of stock ownership in old loss corporation during the testing period, Shareholder Group P, did not increase by more than 50 percentage points.

The conference agreement provides that, unless a different proportion is established, acquisitions of stock following an equity structure shift shall be treated as being made proportionately from all shareholders immediately before such acquisition. Thus, under the general rule, B's open market purchase on June 15, 1988 of L/P corporation stock would be treated as being made proportionately from A, Shareholder Group L, and Shareholder Group P. As a result, the application of this convention without modification would result in an ownership change, because the interests of B (17 percent) and Shareholder Group P (40 percent less the 6.8 percent deemed acquired by B) in new loss corporation would have increased by more than 50 percentage points during the testing period (50.2 percent). A's ownership interest in L/P corporation, however, has in fact remained unchanged. Because L/P Corporation could thus establish that the acquisition by B was not proportionate from all existing shareholders, however, it would be permitted to establish a different proportion for the deemed shareholder composition following B's purchase as follows: (1) A actually owns 18 percent, (2) B actually owns 17 percent, (3) Shareholder Group L is deemed to own 33.3 percent (42 percent less (17 percent ×

42/82)), and (4) Shareholder Group P is deemed to own 31.7 percent (40 percent less (17 percent × 40/82)). If L/P Corporation properly establishes these facts, no ownership change has occurred, because B and Shareholder Group P have a stock interest in L/P Corporation (48.7 percent) that has not increased by more than 50 percentage points over the lowest percentage of stock owned by such shareholders in L/P Corporation, or L Corporation at any time during the testing period (0 percent).

Other attribution rules.—The family attribution rules of sections 318(a)(1) and 318(a)(5)(B) do not apply, but an individual, his spouse, his parents, his children, and his grandparents are treated as a single shareholder. "Back" attribution to partnerships, trusts, estates, and corporations from partners, beneficiaries, and shareholders will not apply except as provided in regulations.

Finally, except as provided in regulations, the holder of an option is treated as owning the underlying stock if such a presumption would result in an ownership change. (The subsequent exercise of such an option is, of course, disregarded if the owner of the option has been treated as owning the underlying stock.) This rule is to be applied on an option-by-option basis so that, in appropriate cases, certain options will be deemed exercised while others may not. Similarly, a person will be treated as owning stock that may be acquired pursuant to any contingency, warrant, right to acquire stock, conversion feature, or put, if such a presumption results in an ownership change. If the option or other contingency expires without a transfer of stock ownership, but the existence of the option or other contingency resulted in an ownership change under this rule, the loss corporation will be able to file amended tax returns (subject to any applicable statute of limitations) for prior years as if the corporation had not been subject to the special limitations.

Example 19.—L corporation has 1,000 shares of stock outstanding, which are owned by 25 unrelated shareholders, none of whom own five percent or more. P corporation is wholly owned by individual A. On January 1, 1987, L corporation acquires 100 percent of P stock from A. In exchange, A receives 750 shares of L stock and a contingent right to receive up to an additional 500 shares of L stock, depending on the earnings of P corporation over the next five years.

Under the conference agreement, A, except as provided in regulations, is treated as owning all the L stock that he might receive under the contingency (and such stock is thus treated as additional outstanding stock). Accordingly, an ownership change of L has occurred, because the percentage of stock owned (and treated as owned) by A (1,250 shares—55.5 percent (33.3 percent (750 of 2,250 shares) directly and 22.2 percent (500 of 2,250 shares) by attribution)) has increased by more than 50 percentage points over the lowest percentage of stock owned by A at any time during the testing period (0 percent prior to January 1, 1987).

Stock acquired by reason of death, gift, divorce or separation.—If (i) the basis of any stock in the hands of any person is determined under section 1014 (relating to property acquired from a decedent), section 1015 (relating to property acquired by a gift or transfer in trust) or section 1041(b) (relating to transfers of property between spouses or incident to divorce), (ii) stock is received by any person in satisfaction of a right to receive a pecuniary bequest, or (iii) stock is acquired by a person pursuant to any divorce or separation instrument (within the meaning of section 71(b)(2)), then such persons shall be treated as owning such stock during the period such stock was owned by the person from whom it was acquired. Such transfers, therefore, would not constitute owner shifts.

Special rule for employee stock ownership plans.—If certain ownership and allocation requirements are satisfied, the acquisition of employer securities (within the meaning of section 409(1)) by either a tax credit employee stock ownership plan or an employee stock ownership plan (within the meaning of section 497(e)(7)) shall not be taken into account in determining whether an ownership change has occurred. The acquisition of employer securities from any such plan by a participant of any such plan pursuant to the requirements of section 409(h) will also not be taken into account in determining whether an ownership change has occurred.

Utilization of holding company structures.—The mere formation of a holding company unaccompanied by a change in the beneficial ownership of the loss corporation will not result in an ownership change. The attribution rules of section 318, as modified for purposes of applying these special limitations, achieve this result by generally disregarding any corporate owner of stock as the owner of any loss corporation stock. Instead, the attribution rules are designed to provide a mechanism for tracking the changes in ownership by the ultimate beneficial owners of the loss corporation. The creation of a holding company structure is significant to the determination of whether an ownership change has occurred only if it is accompanied by a change in the ultimate beneficial ownership of the loss corporation.

Example 20.—The stock of L corporation is owned equally by unrelated individuals, A, B, C, and D. On January 1, 1988, A, B, C, and D contribute their L corporation stock to a newly formed holding company ("HC") in exchange for equal interests in stock and securities of HC in a transaction that qualifies under section 351.

The formation of HC does not result in an ownership change with respect to L. Under the attribution rules, A, B, C, and D following the incorporation of L corporation are considered to own 25 percent of the stock of L corporation and, unless provided otherwise in regulations, HC is treated as not holding any stock in L corporation. Accordingly, the respective holdings in L corporation were not altered to any extent and there is thus no owner shift involving a 5-percent shareholder. The result would be the same if L corporation were owned by less-than-5-percent shareholders prior to the formation of the holding company.

Example 21.—The stock of L corporation is widely held by the public ("Public/L") and is valued at $600. P is also widely held by the public ("Public/P") and is valued at $400. On January 1, 1988, P forms Newco with a contribution of P stock. Immediately thereafter, Newco acquires all of the properties of L corporation in exchange for its P stock in a forward triangular merger qualifying under section 368(a)(2)(D). Following the transaction, Public/L and Public/P respectively are deemed to own 60 percent and 40 percent of P stock.

Inserting P between Public/L and L corporation (which becomes Newco in the merger) does not result in an ownership change with respect to Newco, the new loss corporation. Under the conference agreement, Public/L and Public/P are each treated as a separate 5-percent shareholder of Newco, the new loss corporation.[8] Unless regulations provide otherwise. P's direct ownership interest in L corporation is disregarded. Because the percentage of Newco stock owned by Public/P shareholders after the equity structure shift (40 percent) has not increased by more than 50 percentage points over the lowest percentage of stock of L (the old loss corporation) owned by such shareholders at any time during the testing period (0 percent prior to January 1, 1988), the transaction does not constitute an ownership change with respect to Newco.

3-year testing period.—In general, the relevant testing period for determining whether an ownership change has occurred is the three-year period preceding any owner shift involving a 5-percent shareholder or any equity structure shift. Thus, a series of unrelated transactions occurring during a three-year period may constitute an ownership change. A shorter period, however, may be applicable following any ownership change. In such a case, the testing period for determining whether a second ownership change has occurred does not begin before the day following the first ownership change.

In addition, the testing period does not begin before the first day of the first taxable year from which there is a loss carryforward or excess credit. Thus, transactions that occur prior to the creation of any attribute subject to limitation under section 382 or section 383 are disregarded. Except as provided in regulations, the special rule described above does not apply to any corporation with a net unrealized built-in loss. The conferees expect, however, that the regulations will permit such corporations to disregard transactions that occur before the year for which such a corporation establishes that a net unrealized built-in loss first arose.

Effect of ownership change.—*Section 382 limitation.*—For any taxable year ending after the change date (*i.e.,* the date on which an owner shift resulting in an ownership change occurs or the date of the reorganization in the case of an equity structure shift resulting in an ownership change), the amount of a loss corporation's taxable income that can be offset by a pre-change loss (described below) cannot exceed the section 382 limitation for such year. The section 382 limitation for any taxable year is generally the amount equal to the value of the loss corporation immediately before the ownership change multiplied by the long-term tax-exempt rate (described below).

The conference agreement requires the Treasury Department to prescribe regulations regarding the application of the section 382 limitation in the case of a short taxable year. The conferees expect that these regulations will generally provide that the section 382 limitation applicable in a short taxable year will be determined by multiplying the full section 382 limitation by the ratio of the number of days in the year to 365. Thus, taxable income realized by a new loss corporation during a short taxable year may be offset by pre-change losses not exceeding a ratable portion of the full section 382 limitation.

The section 382 limitation for any taxable year is increased by the amount of any recognized built-in gains (determined under the rules described below) and any gain recognized by virtue of a section 338 election (to the extent such gain is not taken into account as a built-in gain). Finally, if the section 382 limitation for a taxable year exceeds the taxable income for the year, the section 382 limitation for the next taxable year is increased by such excess.

If two or more loss corporations are merged or otherwise reorganized into a single entity, separate section 382 limitations are determined and applied to each loss corporation that experiences an ownership change.

Example 22.—X corporation is wholly owned by individual A and its stock has a value of $3,000; X has NOL carryforwards of $10,000. Y corporation is wholly owned by individual B and its stock has a value of $9,000; Y has NOL carryforwards of $100. Z corporation is owned by individual C and its stock has a value of $18,000; Z has no NOL carryforwards. On July 22, 1988, X, Y and Z consolidate into W corporation in a transaction that qualifies as a tax-free reorganization under section 368(a)(1)(A). The applica-

---

[Footnote ¶ 3916 continued]

(8) The rules described above aggregate all less-than-5-percent shareholders of any corporation. These aggregation rules are to be applied after taking into account the attribution rules. In the above example, the old loss corporation and new loss corporation are properly treated as the same corporation. Thus, even though L does not survive the reorganization, Public/L is properly treated as a continuing 5-percent shareholder of Newco, the new loss corporation. The same result would be appropriate if the transaction had been structured as a reverse triangular merger under section 368(a)(2)(E).

ble long-term tax-exempt rate on such date is 10 percent. As a result of the consolidation, A receives 10 percent of W stock, B receives 30 percent and C receives 60 percent.

The consolidation of X, Y and Z results in an ownership change for old loss corporations X and Y. The conference agreement applies a separate section 382 limitation to the utilization of the NOL carryforwards of each loss corporation that experiences an ownership change. Therefore, the annual limitation on X's NOL carryforwards is $300 and the annual limitation [on] Y's NOL carryforwards is $900.

For W's taxable year ending on December 31, 1989, W's taxable income before any reduction for its NOLs is $1,400. The amount of taxable income of W that may be offset by X and Y's pre-change losses (without regard to any unused section 382 limitation) is $400 (the $300 section 382 limitation for X's NOL carryforwards and all $100 of Y's NOL carryforwards because that amount is less than Y's $900 section 382 limitation). The unused portion of Y's section 382 limitation may not be used to augment X's section 382 limitation for 1989 or in any subsequent year.

Special rule for post-change year that includes the change date.—In general, the section 382 limitation with respect to an ownership change that occurs during a taxable year does not apply to the utilization of losses against the portion of the loss corporation's taxable income, if any, allocable to the period before the change. For this purpose, except as provided in regulations, taxable income (not including built-in gains or losses) realized during the change year is allocated ratably to each day in the year. The regulations may provide that income realized before the change date from discrete sales of assets would be excluded from the ratable allocation and could be offset without limit by pre-change losses. Moreover, these regulations may provide a loss corporation with an option to determine the taxable income allocable to the period before the change by closing its books on the change date and thus forgoing the ratable allocation.

Value of loss corporation

The value of a loss corporation is generally the fair market value of the corporation's stock (including preferred stock described in section 1504(a)(4)) immediately before the ownership change. If a redemption occurs in connection with an ownership change—either before or after the change—the value of the loss corporation is determined after taking the redemption into account. Under the conference agreement, the Treasury Department is given regulatory authority to treat other corporate contractions in the same manner as redemptions for purposes of determining the loss corporation's value. The conference agreement also requires the Treasury Department to prescribe such regulations as are necessary to treat warrants, options, contracts to acquire stock, convertible debt, and similar interests as stock for purposes of determining the value of the loss corporation.

In determining value, the conferees intend that the price at which loss corporation stock changes hands in an arms-length transaction would be evidence, but not conclusive evidence, of the value of the stock. Assume, for example, that an acquiring corporation purchased 40 percent of loss corporation stock over a 12-month period. Six months following this 40 percent acquisition, the acquiring corporation purchased an additional 20 percent of loss corporation stock at a price that reflected a premium over the stock's proportionate amount of the value of all the loss corporation stock; the premium is paid because the 20-percent block carries with it effective control of the loss corporation. Based on these facts, it would be inappropriate simply to gross-up the amount paid for the 20-percent interest to determine the value of the corporation's stock. The conferees anticipate that, under regulations, the Treasury Department will permit the loss corporation to be valued based upon a formula that grosses up the purchase price of all of the acquired loss corporation stock if a control block of such stock is acquired within a 12-month period.

Example 23.—All of the outstanding stock of L corporation is owned by individual A and has a value of $1,000. On June 15, 1988, A sells 51 percent of his stock in L to unrelated individual B. On January 1, 1989, L and A enter into a 15-year management contract and L redeems A's remaining stock interest in such corporation. The latter transactions were contemplated in connection with B's earlier acquisition of stock in 1988.

The acquisition of 51 percent of the stock of L on June 15, 1988, constituted an ownership change. The value of L for purposes of computing the section 382 limitation is the value of the stock of such corporation immediately before the ownership change. Although the value of such stock was $1,000 at that time, the value must be reduced by the value of A's stock that was subsequently redeemed in connection with the ownership change.

Long-term tax-exempt rate

The long-term tax-exempt rate is defined under the bill as the highest of the Federal long-term rates determined under section 1274(d), as adjusted to reflect differences between rates on long-term taxable and tax-exempt obligations, in effect for the month in which the change date occurs or the two prior months. The conferees intend that the Treasury Department will publish the long-term tax-exempt rate by revenue ruling within 30 days after the date of enactment and monthly thereafter. The long-term tax-exempt rate will be computed as the yield on a diversified pool of prime, general obligation tax-exempt bonds with remaining periods to maturity of more than nine years.

The use of a rate lower than the long-term Federal rate is necessary to ensure that the value of NOL carryforwards to the buying corporation is not more than their value to the loss corporation. Otherwise there would be a tax incentive for acquiring loss corporations. If the loss corporation were to sell its assets and invest in long-term Treasury obligations, it could absorb its NOL carryforwards at a rate equal to the yield on long-term government obligations. Since the price paid by the buyer is larger than the value of the loss company's assets (because of the value of NOL carryforwards are taken into account), applying the long-term Treasury rate to the purchase price would result in faster utilization of NOL carryforwards by the buying corporation. The long-term tax-exempt rate normally will fall between 66 (1 minus the corporate tax rate of 34 percent) and 100 percent of the long-term Federal rate.

Example 24.—Corporation L has $1 million of net operating loss carryforwards. L's taxable year is the calendar year, and on July 1, 1987, all of the stock of L is sold in a transaction constituting an ownership change of L. (Assume the transaction does not terminate L's taxable year.) On that date, the value of L's stock was $500,000 and the long-term tax-exempt rate was 10 percent. Finally, L incurred a net operating loss during 1987 of $100,000, and L had no built-in gains or losses.

On these facts, the taxable income of L after July 1, 1987, that could be offset by L's losses incurred prior to July 1, 1987, would generally be limited. In particular, for all taxable years after 1987, the pre-change losses of L generally could be used to offset no more than $50,000 of L's taxable income each year. (For L's 1987 taxable year, the limit would be $25,000 (½ × the $50,000 section 382 limitation)). The pre-change losses of L would constitute the $1 million of NOL carryforwards plus one-half of the 1987 net operating loss, or a total of $1,050,000. If, in taxable year 1988, L had $30,000 of taxable income to be offset by L's losses, it could be fully offset by L's pre-change NOLs and the amount of L's 1989 taxable income that could be offset by pre-change losses would be limited to $95,000 ($50,000 annual limit plus $45,000 carryover).

If L had income of $100,000 in 1987, instead of a net operating loss, L's 1987 taxable income that could be offset by pre-change losses would generally be limited to $75,000 (½ × the $50,000 section 382 limitation plus ½ × $100,000 1987 income). (In appropriate circumstances, the Secretary could, by regulations, require allocation of income using a method other than daily proration. Such circumstances might include, for example, an instance in which substantial income-producing assets are contributed to capital after the change date.)

Continuity of business enterprise requirements

Following an ownership change, a loss corporation's NOL carryforwards (including any recognized built-in losses, described below) are subject to complete disallowance (except to the extent of any recognized built-in gains or section 338 gain, described below),

unless the loss corporation's business enterprise is continued at all times during the two-year period following the ownership change. If a loss corporation fails to satisfy the continuity of business enterprise requirements, no NOL carryforwards would be allowed to the new loss corporation for any post-change year. This continuity of business enterprise requirement is the same requirement that must be satisfied to qualify a transaction as a tax-free reorganization under section 368. *(See* Treasury regulation section 1.368-1(d)). Under these continuity of business enterprise requirements, a loss corporation (or a successor corporation) must either continue the old loss corporation's historic business or use a significant portion of the old loss corporation's assets in a business. Thus, the requirements may be satisfied even though the old loss corporation discontinues more than a minor portion of its historic business. Changes in the location of a loss corporation's business or the loss corporation's key employees, in contrast to the results under the business-continuation rule in the 1954 Code version of section 382(a), will not constitute a failure to satisfy the continuity of business enterprise requirements under the conference agreement.

Reduction in loss corporation's value for certain capital contributions

Any capital contribution (including a section 351 transfer) that is made to a loss corporation as part of a plan a principal purpose of which is to avoid any of the special limitations under section 382 shall not be taken into account for any purpose under section 382. For purposes of this rule, except as provided in regulations, a capital contribution made during the two-year period ending on the change date is irrebuttably presumed to be part of a plan to avoid the limitations. The application of this rule will result in a reduction of a loss corporation's value for purposes of determining the section 382 limitation. The conferees intend that the regulations will generally except (i) capital contributions received on the formation of a loss corporation (not accompanied by the incorporation of assets with a net unrealized built-in loss) where an ownership change occurs within two years of incorporation, (ii) capital contributions received before the first year from which there is an NOL or excess credit carryforward (or in which a net unrealized built-in loss arose), and (iii) capital contributions made to continue basic operations of the corporation's business *(e.g.,* to meet the monthly payroll or fund other operating expenses of the loss corporation). The regulations also may take into account, under appropriate circumstances, the existence of substantial nonbusiness assets on the change date (as described below) and distributions made to shareholders subsequent to capital contributions, as offsets to such contributions.

Act §621 ¶3916

Reduction in value for corporations having substantial nonbusiness assets.

If at least one-third of the fair market value of a corporation's assets consists of nonbusiness assets, the value of the loss corporation, for purposes of determining the section 382 limitation, is reduced by the excess of the value of the nonbusiness assets over the portion of the corporation's indebtedness attributable to such assets. The term nonbusiness assets includes any asset held for investment, including cash and marketable stock or securities. Assets held as an integral part of the conduct of a trade or business *(e.g.,* assets funding reserves of an insurance company or similar assets of a bank) would not be considered nonbusiness assets. In addition, stock or securities in a corporation that is at least 50 percent owned (voting power and value) by a loss corporation are not treated as nonbusiness assets. Instead, the parent loss corporation is deemed to own its ratable share of the subsidiary's assets. The portion of a corporation's indebtedness attributable to nonbusiness assets is determined on the basis of the ratio of the value of nonbusiness assets to the value of all the loss corporation's assets.

Regulated investment companies, real estate investment trusts, and real estate mortgage investment conduits are not treated as having substantial nonbusiness assets under the conference agreement.

Losses subject to limitation

The term "pre-change loss" includes (i) for the taxable year in which an ownership change occurs, the portion of the loss corporation's NOL that is allocable (determined on a daily pro rata basis, without regard to recognized built-in gains or losses, as described below) to the period in such year before the change date, (ii) NOL carryforwards that arose in a taxable year preceding the taxable year of the ownership change and (iii) certain recognized built-in losses and deductions (described below). For any taxable year in which a corporation has income that, under section 172, may be offset by both a pre-change loss *(i.e.,* an NOL subject to limitation) and an NOL that is not subject to limitation, taxable income is treated as having been first offset by the pre-change loss. This rule minimizes the NOLs that are subject to the special limitations.

Built-in gains and losses

If a loss corporation has a net unrealized built-in loss, the recognized built-in loss for any taxable year ending within the five-year period ending at the close of the fifth post-change year (the "recognition period") is treated as a pre-change loss.

Net unrealized built-in losses.—The term "net unrealized built-in loss" is defined as the amount by which the fair market value of the loss corporation's assets immediately before the ownership change is less than the aggregate adjusted bases of a corporation's assets at that time. Under a *de minimis* exception, the special rule for built-in losses is not applied if the amount of a net unrealized built-in loss does not exceed 25 percent of the value of the corporation's assets immediately before the ownership change. For purposes of the *de minimis* exception, the value of a corporation's assets is determined by excluding any (1) cash, (2) cash items (as determined for purposes of section 368(a)(2)(F)(iv)), or (3) marketable securities that have a value that does not substantially differ from adjusted basis.

Example 25.—L corporation owns two assets: asset X, with a basis of $150 and a value of $50 (a built-in loss asset), and asset Y, with a basis of zero and a value of $50 (a built-in gain asset, described below). L has a net unrealized built-in loss of $50 (the excess of the aggregate bases of $150 over the aggregate value of $100).

Recognized built-in losses.—The term "recognized built-in loss" is defined as any loss that is recognized on the disposition of an asset during the recognition period, except to the extent that the new loss corporation establishes that (1) the asset was not held by the loss corporation immediately before the change date, or (2) the loss (or a portion of such loss) is greater than the excess of the adjusted basis of the asset on the change date over the asset's fair market value on that date. The recognized built-in loss for a taxable year cannot exceed the net unrealized built-in loss reduced by recognized built-in losses for prior taxable years ending in the recognition period.

Under the conference agreement, the amount of any recognized built-in loss that exceeds the section 382 limitation for any post-change year must be carried forward (not carried back) under rules similar to the rules applicable to net operating loss carryforwards and will be subject to the special limitations in the same manner as a pre-change loss.

Accrued deductions.—The Treasury Department is authorized to issue regulations under which amounts that accrue before the change date, but are allowable as a deduction on or after such date *(e.g.,* deductions deferred by section 267 or section 465), will be treated as built-in losses. Under the conference agreement, depreciation deductions cannot be treated as accrued deductions or built-in losses. The conference agreement, however, requires the Secretary of the Treasury to conduct a study of whether built-in depreciation deductions should be subject to section 382, and report to the tax-writing committees of the Congress before January 1, 1989.

Built-in gains

If a loss corporation has a net unrealized built-in gain, the section 382 limitation for any taxable year ending within the five-year recognition period is increased by the recognized built-in gain for the taxable year.

Net unrealized built-in gains.—The term "net unrealized built-in gain" is defined as the amount by which the value of a corporation's assets exceeds the aggregate bases of such assets immediately before the ownership change. Under the *de minimis* exception described above, the special rule for built-in gains is not applied if the amount of a net unrealized built-in gain does not exceed 25 percent of the value of a loss corporation's assets.

Recognized built-in gains.—The term "recognized built-in gain" is defined as any gain recognized on the disposition of an asset during the recognition period, if the taxpayer establishes that (1) the asset was held by the loss corporation immediately before the change date, and (2) the gain does not exceed the excess of the fair market value of such asset on the change date over the adjusted basis of the asset on that date. The recognized built-in gain for a taxable year cannot exceed the net unrealized built-in gain reduced by the recognized built-in gains for prior years in the recognition period.

Bankruptcy proceedings.

The special limitations do not apply after any ownership change of a loss corporation if (1) such corporation was under the jurisdiction of a bankruptcy court in a Title 11 or similar case immediately before the ownership change, and (2) the corporation's shareholders and creditors (determined immediately before the ownership change) own 50 percent of the value and voting power of the loss corporation's stock immediately after the ownership change. This special rule applies only if the stock-for-debt exchange, reorganization, or other transaction is ordered by the court or is pursuant to a plan approved by the court. For purposes of this rule, stock of a creditor that was converted from indebtedness is taken into account only if such indebtedness was held by the creditor for at least 18 months before the date the bankruptcy case was filed or arose in the ordinary course of the loss corporation's trade or business and is held by the person who has at all times held the beneficial interest in the claim. Indebtedness will be considered as having arisen in the ordinary course of the loss corporation's business only if the indebtedness was incurred by the loss corporation in connection with the normal, usual, or customary conduct of its business. It is not relevant for this purpose whether the debt was related to ordinary or capital expenditures of the loss corporation.

If the exception for bankruptcy proceedings applies, several special rules are applicable. First, the pre-change losses and excess credits that may be carried to a post-change year are reduced by one-half of the amount of any cancellation of indebtedness income that would have been included in the loss corporation's income as a result of any stock-for-debt exchanges that occur as part of the Title 11 or similar proceeding under the principles of section 108(e)(10) (without applying section 108(e)(10)(B)). Thus, the NOL carryforwards would be reduced by 50 percent of the excess of the amount of the indebtedness canceled

over the fair market value of the stock exchanged. Second, the loss corporation's pre-change NOL carryforwards are reduced by the interest on the indebtedness that was converted to stock in the bankruptcy proceeding and paid or accrued during the period beginning on the first day of the third taxable year preceding the taxable year in which the ownership change occurs and ending on the change date. Finally, after an ownership change that qualifies for the bankruptcy exception, a second ownership change during the following two-year period will result in the elimination of NOL carryforwards that arose before the first ownership change. The special bankruptcy provisions do not apply to stock-for-debt exchanges in informal workouts, but the conference agreement directs the Secretary of the Treasury to study informal bankruptcy workouts under sections 108 and 382, and report to the tax-writing committees of the Congress before January 1, 1988.

Thrift institutions.—A modified version of the bankruptcy exception (described above) applies to certain ownership changes of a thrift institution involved in a G reorganization by virtue of section 368(a)(3)(D)(ii). This rule also applies to ownership changes resulting from an issuance of stock or equity structure shift that is an integral part of a transaction involving such a reorganization, provided that the transaction would not have resulted in limitations under present law.[8a]The bankruptcy exception is applied to qualified thrift reorganizations by requiring shareholders and creditors (including depositors) to retain a 20-percent (rather than 50-percent) interest. For this purpose, the deposits of the troubled thrift that become deposits in the acquiring corporation are treated as stock, as under present law. The general bankruptcy rules that eliminate from the NOL carryforwards both interest deductions on debt that was converted and income that would be recognized under the principles of section 108(e)(10) are not applicable to thrifts.

Transactions involving solvent thrifts, including a purchase of the stock of a thrift, or merger of a thrift into another corporation, will be subject to the general rules relating to ownership changes. The conversion of a solvent mutual savings and loan association into a stock savings and loan (or other transactions involving a savings and loan not entitled to special treatment), although not within the special rules applicable to troubled thrifts, will not necessarily constitute an ownership change under the conference agreement. In such a conversion, the mutual thrift converts to stock form as a preliminary step to the issuance of stock to investors for purposes of raising capital. Under existing IRS rulings, the entire transaction may qualify as a tax-free reorganization if certain conditions are met. For purposes of determin-

---

[Footnote ¶ 3916 continued]

(8a) For example, a supervisory conversion of a mutual thrift into a stock thrift qualifying under section 368(a)(3)(D)(ii), followed by an issuance of stock for cash, would come within this special rule. The issuance of stock would not be regarded as a second ownership change for purposes of the bankruptcy exception.

ing whether there has been an ownership change causing a limitation on the use of losses under the conference agreement, the issuance of stock generally will be treated under the rules applicable to owner shifts. For example, the depositors holding liquidation accounts would generally be considered a group of less-than-5-percent shareholders, and if the stock were issued entirely to less-than-5-percent shareholders, or 5-percent shareholders acquired less than 50 percent, no ownership change would occur. Treasury regulations may be issued, on a prospective basis, that would treat public offerings generally in the same manner as equity structure shifts and treat the old shareholders and the persons acquiring stock in the offering as separate 5-percent shareholder groups. If such regulations are issued and apply this same approach to the conversion of a solvent mutual savings and loan association to stock form and the issuance of new stock, an ownership change could result, however, if the value of the stock issued in the public offering exceeds the equity of the depositors in the mutual represented by liquidation accounts. The application of any such regulations to thrift institutions (whether solvent or insolvent) would not be effective before January 1, 1989.

Carryforwards other than NOLs

The conference agreement also amends section 383, relating to special limitations on unused business credits and research credits, excess foreign tax credits, and capital loss carryforwards. Under regulations to be prescribed by the Secretary, capital loss carryforwards will be limited to an amount determined on the basis of the tax liability that is attributable to so much of the taxable income as does not exceed the section 382 limitation for the taxable year, with the same ordering rules that apply under present law. Thus, any capital loss carryforward used in a post-change year will reduce the section 382 limitation that is applied to pre-change losses. In addition, the amount of any excess credit that may be used following an owner-ship change will be limited, under regulations, on the basis of the tax liability attributable to an amount of taxable income that does not exceed the applicable section 382 limitation, after any NOL carryforwards, capital loss carryforwards, or foreign tax credits are taken into account. The conference agreement also expands the scope of section 383 to include passive activity losses and credits and minimum tax credits.

Anti-abuse rules

The conference agreement does not alter the continuing application of section 269, relating to acquisitions made to evade or avoid taxes, as under present law. Similarly, the SRLY and CRCO principles under the regulations governing the filing of consolidated returns will continue to apply. The conferees intend, however, that the *Libson Shops* doctrine will have no application to transactions subject to the provisions of the conference agreement.

The conference agreement provides that the Treasury Department shall prescribe regulations preventing the avoidance of the purposes of section 382 through the use of, among other things, pass-through entities. For example, a special allocation of income to a loss partner should not be permitted to result in a greater utilization of losses than would occur if the principles of section 382 were applicable.

In the case of partnerships, for example, the conferees expect the regulations to limit the tax benefits that may be derived from transactions in which allocations of partnership income are made to a loss partner or to a corporation that is a member of a consolidated group with NOL carryovers (a "loss corporation partner") under an arrangement that contemplates the diversion of any more than an insignificant portion of the economic benefit corresponding to such allocation (or any portion of the economic benefit of the loss corporation partner's NOL) to a higher tax bracket partner.

This grant of authority contemplates any rules that the Treasury Department considers appropriate to achieve this objective. For example, regulations may provide, as a general rule, that the limitations of section 382 (and section 383) should be made applicable to restrict a loss corporation partner's use of losses against its distributive share of each item of partnership income and that any portion of the distributive share of partnership income so allocated which may not be offset by the loss corporation's NOLs should be taxed at the highest marginal tax rate. Such regulations could also provide that the allocation of income to the loss corporation may, in the discretion of the Secretary, be reallocated to the extent that other partners in the partnership have not been reasonably compensated for their services to the partnership. If the Treasury Department uses such a format to restrict the utilization of NOLs, the conferees believe it may be appropriate to exempt from these rules any partnership with respect to which, throughout the term of the partnership, (i) every allocation to every partner would be a qualified allocation as described in section 168(j)(9)(B) if it were made to a tax-exempt entity, with appropriate exceptions (e.g., section 704(c) allocations) and (ii) distributions are made to one partner only if there is a simultaneous pro rata distribution to all partners at the same time. Special rules would, of course, have to be provided to apply section 382 (and section 383) in this context.

The conferees do not intend any inference to be drawn whether allocations made to loss corporations by partnerships that involve transfers of the economic benefit of a loss partner's loss to another partner have substantial economic effect. As described in the report of the Committee on Finance, there are circumstances in which it appears to be questionable whether the economic benefit that corresponds to a special allocation to the NOL partner is fully received by such partner; however, some taxpayers nevertheless take the position that such allocations have substantial economic effect under section 704(b). The conferees expect the Treasury Department to review this situation.

The conferees expect that regulations issued under this grant of authority with respect to partnerships should be effective for transactions after the date of enactment. The conferees expect that any regulations addressing other situations, under the Treasury Department's general authority to limit the ability of other parties to obtain any portion of the benefit of a loss corporation's losses, may be prospective within the general discretion of the Secretary.

1976 Act amendments.—The conference agreement generally repeals the amendments to section 382 and 383 made by the Tax Reform Act of 1976, effective retroactively as of January 1, 1986. Thus, the law that was in effect as of December 31, 1985, applies to transactions that are not subject to the new provisions because of the effective dates of the conference agreement. The conference agreement, by repealing the 1976 Act amendments, also retroactively repeals section 108(e)(10)(C), as included by the Tax Reform Act of 1984.

Effective dates.—The provisions of the conference agreement generally apply to ownership changes that occur on or after January 1, 1987. In the case of equity structure shifts, the new rules apply to reorganizations pursuant to plans adopted on or after January 1, 1987. For purposes of these rules, if there is an ownership change with respect to a subsidiary corporation as the result of the acquisition of the parent corporation, the subsidiary's treatment is governed by the nature of the parent-level transaction. For example, if a parent corporation is acquired in a tax-free reorganization pursuant to a plan adopted before January 1, 1987, then the resulting indirect ownership change with respect to a subsidiary loss corporation will be treated as having occurred by reason of a reorganization pursuant to a plan adopted before January 1, 1987.

A reorganization plan will be considered adopted on the date that the boards of directors of all parties to the reorganization adopt the plans or recommend adoption to the shareholders, or on the date the shareholders approve, whichever is earlier. The parties' boards of directors may approve a plan of reorganization based on principles, and negotiations to date, and delegate to corporate officials the power to refine and execute a binding reorganization agreement, including a binding agreement subject to regulatory approval. Any subsequent board approval or ratification taken at the time of consummating the transaction as a formality (i.e., that is not required, because the reorganization agreement is already legally binding under prior board approval) may occur without affecting the application of the effective date rule for reorganizations. In the case of a reorganization that occurs as part of a Title 11 or other court-supervised proceeding, the amendments do not apply to any owner-ship change resulting from such a reorganization or proceeding if a petition in such case was filed with the court before August 14, 1986.

The earliest testing period under the conference agreement begins on May 6, 1986 (the date of Senate Finance Committee action). If an ownership change occurs after May 5, 1986, but before January 1, 1987, and section 382 and 383 (as amended by the conference agreement) do not apply, then the earliest testing date will not begin before the first day immediately after such ownership change. For example, assume 60 percent of a loss corporation's stock (wholly owned by X) is purchased by B on May 29, 1986, and section 382 under the 1954 Code does not apply (because, for example, the loss corporation's business is continued and section 269 is not implicated). Assume further that X's remaining 40 percent stock interest is acquired by B on February 1, 1987. Under the conference agreement, no ownership change occurs after the second purchase because the testing period begins on May 30, 1986, the day immediately after the ownership change; thus, an ownership change would not result from the second purchase. Conversely, if 40 percent of a loss corporation's stock (wholly owned by X) is purchased by D on July 1, 1986, and an additional 15 percent is purchased by P on January 15, 1987, then an ownership change would result from the second purchase, and the amendments would apply to limit the use of the loss corporation's NOL carryforwards. Moreover, if an ownership change that occurs after December 31, 1986 is not affected by the amendments to section 382 (because, for example, in the foregoing example the initial 40 percent stock purchase occurred on May 5, 1986, prior to the commencement of the testing period), the 1954 Code version of section 382 will remain applicable to the transaction.

Special transitional rules are provided under which present law continues to apply to certain ownership changes after January 1, 1987.

[The following colloquy relating to Act Sec. 621 is drawn from the Congressional Record. The colloquy occurred on the day the conference bill was considered by the House. Ed.]

[House Floor Explanation]

I have discussed with Congressman AN-THONY several issues relating to effective date of certain net operating loss carryover provisions of the bill. We have reached a common understanding regarding the following specific issue:

The effective date for implementing amended section 382(1)(3)(A) is ambiguous as it pertains to contingent interests. It is my understanding that contingent interests arising prior to January 1, 1987, are not affected by this amendment. For example, contingent options created in business transactions occuring prior to January 1, 1987, are not treated as ownership changes merely by operations of the January 1, 1987 effective

Act §621　¶3916

date. Congressional Record, p. H 8363, 9-25-86.

[The following colloquy relating to Act Sec. 621 is drawn from the Congressional Record. The colloquy occurred on the day the bill was considered by the Senate. Ed.]

[Senate Floor Explanation]
Effect on NOL Rules on Contingent Interests

Mr. DOLE. The effective date for implementing amended section 382(1)(3)(A) is ambiguous as it pertains to contingent interests.

It is my understanding that contingent interests arising prior to January 1, 1987, for example, contingent options created in business transactions occurring prior to that date, are not treated as ownership changes merely by operation of the January 1, 1987, effective date. Does the distinguished chairman agree that this is a correct interpretation?

Mr. PACKWOOD. I share the majority leader's interpretation of this provision. Congressional Record, p. S13958, 9-27-86.

[¶ 3917] SECTION 631. RECOGNITION OF GAIN AND LOSS ON DISTRIBUTIONS OF PROPERTY IN LIQUIDATION

(Secs. 336, 337, 338 and 1362 of the Code)
[Conference Report]

*   *   *   *   *   *

[Explanation of Provision.—] The conference agreement * * * [repeals] the *General Utilities* doctrine.

Thus, gain or loss is generally recognized by a corporation on a liquidating sale of its assets. Gain or loss is also generally recognized on a liquidating distribution of assets as if the corporation had sold the assets to the distributee at fair market value. Neither gain nor loss is recognized, however, with respect to any distribution of property by a corporation to the extent there is nonrecognition of gain or loss to the recipient under the tax-free reorganization provisions of the Code (part III of subchapter C).

Limitations on the recognition of losses.—The conferees are concerned that taxpayers may utilize various means to avoid the repeal of the *General Utilities* doctrine, or otherwise take advantage of the new provisions, to recognize losses in inappropriate situations or inflate the amount of losses actually sustained. For example, under the general rule permitting recognition of losses on liquidating distributions, taxpayers may be able to create artificial losses at the corporate level or to duplicate shareholder losses in corporate solution through contribution of built-in loss property. Consequently, the conference agreement includes two provisions intended to prevent the recognition of such corporate level losses.

First, the conference agreement provides generally that no loss is recognized by a liquidating corporation with respect to any distribution of property to a related person (within the meaning of section 267), unless the property is distributed to all shareholders on a pro rata basis *and* the property was not acquired by the liquidating corporation in a section 351 transaction or as a contribution to capital during the five years preceding the distribution. Thus, for example, a liquidating corporation would not be permitted to recognize loss on a distribution of recently acquired property to a shareholder who, directly or indirectly, owns more than 50 percent in value of the stock of the corporation.

Similarly, a liquidating corporation would not be permitted to recognize a loss on any property (regardless of when or how acquired) that is distributed to such a shareholder on a non-pro rata basis.

Second, the conference agreement generally provides that if a principal purpose of the contribution of property to a corporation in advance of its liquidation is to recognize a loss upon the sale or distribution of the property and thus eliminate or otherwise limit corporate level gain, then the basis (for purposes of determining loss) of any property acquired by such corporation in a section 351 transaction or as a contribution to capital will be reduced, but not below zero, by the excess of the basis of the property on the date of contribution over its fair market value on such date. For purposes of this rule, it is presumed, except to the extent provided in regulations, that any section 351 transaction or contribution to capital within the two-year period prior to the adoption of a plan of complete liquidation (or thereafter) has such a principal purpose. Although a contribution more than two years before the adoption of a plan of liquidation might be made with a prohibited purpose, the conferees expect that those rules will apply only in the most rare and unusual cases under such circumstances.

If the adoption of a plan of complete liquidation occurs in a taxable year following the date on which the tax return including the loss disallowed by this provision is filed, the conferees intend that, in appropriate cases, the liquidating corporation may recapture the disallowed loss on the tax return for the taxable year in which such plan of liquidation is adopted. In the alternative, the corporation could file an amended return for the taxable year in which the loss was reported.

The conferees intend that the Treasury Department will issue regulations generally providing that the presumed prohibited purpose for contributions of property two years in advance of the adoption of a plan of liquidation will be disregarded *unless* there is no clear and substantial relationship between the contributed property and the conduct of the corporation's current or future business enterprises. For example, assume that A owns Z Corporation which operates a widget business in New Jersey. That business operates exclusively in the northeastern region of the United States and there are no plans to expand those operations. In his individual capacity, A had acquired unimproved real estate in New Mexico that has declined in value. On March 22, 1988, A contributes such real estate to Z and six months later a plan of complete liquidation is adopted. Thereafter, all of Z's assets are sold to an unrelated party and the liquidation proceeds are distributed. A contributed no other property to Z during the two-year period prior to the adoption of the plan of liquidation. Because A contributed the property to Z less than two years prior to the adoption of the plan of liquidation, it is presumed to have been contributed with a prohibited purpose. Moreover, because there is no clear and substantial relationship between the contributed property and the conduct of Z's business, the conferees do not expect that any loss arising from the disposition of the New Mexico real estate would be allowed under the Treasury regulations.

As another example, the conferees expect that such regulations would permit the allowance of any resulting loss from the disposition of any of the assets of a trade or business (or a line of business) that are contributed to a corporation. In such circumstance, application of the loss disallowance rule is inappropriate assuming there is a meaningful relationship between the contribution and the utilization of the corporate form to conduct a business enterprise, *i.e.*, the contributed business, as distinguished from a portion of its assets, is not disposed of immediately after the contribution. The conferees also anticipate that the basis adjustment rules will generally not apply to a corporation's acquisition of property during its first two years of existence.

To illustrate the mechanical aspects of the basis adjustment rules, assume that on June 1, 1987, a shareholder who owns a 10-percent interest in X corporation ("X") contributes nondepreciable property with a basis of $1,000 and a value of $100 to X in exchange for additional stock; X is a calendar year taxpayer. Assume further that on September 30, 1987, X sells the property to an unrelated third party for $200, and includes the resulting $800 loss on its 1987 tax return. Finally, assume that X adopts a plan of liquidation on December 31, 1988. Thereafter, X could file an amended return reflecting the fact that the $800 loss was disallowed, because the property's basis would be reduced to $200. Alternatively, the conferees intend that X, under regulations, may be permitted to recapture the loss on its 1988 tax return. The amount of loss recapture in such circumstances would be limited to the lesser of the built-in loss ($900, or $1,000, the transferred basis under section 362, less $100, the value of the property on that date it was contrib-

uted to X) or the loss actually recognized on the disposition of such property ($800, or the $1,000 transferred basis less the $200 amount realized). Thus, unless X files an amended return, X must recapture $800 on its return for its taxable year ending December 31, 1988.

Section 332 liquidations.[9]—The conference agreement provides an exception for liquidating transfers within an affiliated group because the property (together with the other attributes of the liquidated subsidiary) is retained within the economic unit of the affiliated group. Because such an intercorporate transfer within the group is a nonrecognition event, carryover basis follows. As a result of the carryover basis, the corporate level tax will be paid if the distributed property is disposed of by the recipient corporation to a person outside of the group.

The conference agreement modifies the exception for section 332 liquidations in which an 80-percent corporate shareholder receives property with a carryover basis, to provide for nonrecognition of gain or loss with respect to any property actually distributed to the controlling corporate shareholder (rather than a pro rata share of each gain or loss). If a minority shareholder receives property in such a liquidation, the distribution is treated in the same manner as a distribution in a nonliquidating redemption. Accordingly, gain (but not loss) is recognized to the distributing corporation.

The conference agreement denies nonrecognition under the exception for 80-percent corporate shareholders where the shareholder is a tax-exempt organization, unless the property received in the distribution is used by the organization in an unrelated trade or business immediately after the distribution. If such property later ceases to be used in an unrelated trade or business of the organization acquiring the property, the organization will be taxed at that time (in addition to any other tax imposed, for example, on depreciation recapture under section 1245) on the lesser of (a) the built-in gain in the property at the time of the distribution, or (b) the difference between the adjusted basis of the property and its fair market value at the time of the cessation.

The conference agreement, in an amendment to section 367 of the Code, also denies nonrecognition under the section 332 carryover basis exception where the controlling corporate shareholder is a foreign corporation, except as provided in regulations. The conferees expect that regulations may permit nonrecognition if the appreciation on the distributed property is not being removed from the U.S. taxing jurisdiction prior to recognition.

Nonliquidating distributions of appreciated property.—In general, the tax treatment of corporations with respect to nonliq-

[**Footnote ¶ 3917**]   (9) The conferees anticipate that, in a consolidated context, the Treasury Department will consider whether aggregation of ownership rules similar to those in sec. 1.1502-34 of the regulations should be provided for purposes of determining status as an 80-percent distributee.

uidating distributions of appreciated property has historically been the same as liquidating distributions. In recent years, however, nonliquidating distributions have been made subject to stricter rules than liquidating distributions, and corporations have generally been required to recognize gain as a result of nonliquidating distributions of appreciated property. Consistent with this relationship, the conference agreement generally conforms the treatment of nonliquidating distributions with liquidating distributions. Accordingly, the conference agreement provides that gain must generally be recognized to a distributing corporation if appreciated property (other than an obligation of the corporation) is distributed to shareholders outside of complete liquidation.

The present law exceptions to recognition that are provided for nonliquidating distributions to ten percent, long-term noncorporate shareholders, and for certain distributions of property in connection with the payment of estate taxes or in connection with certain redemptions of private foundation stock, are repealed. As under current law, no loss is recognized to a distributing corporation on a nonliquidating distribution of property to its shareholders.

*   *   *   *   *   *

Election to treat sales or distributions of certain subsidiary stock as asset transfers.—The conference agreement generally conforms the treatment of liquidating sales and distributions of subsidiary stock to the present law treatment of nonliquidating sales or distributions of such stock; thus, such liquidating sales or distributions are generally taxable at the corporate level. The conferees believe it is appropriate to conform the treatment of liquidating and nonliquidating sales or distributions and to require recognition when appreciated property, including stock of a subsidiary, is transferred to a corporate or an individual recipient outside the economic unit of the selling or distributing affiliated group.

Section 338(h)(10) of present law, in certain circumstances, permits a corporate purchaser and a seller of an 80-percent-controlled subsidiary to elect to treat the sale of the subsidiary stock as if it had been a sale of the underlying assets. Among the requirements for the filing of an election under section 338(h)(10) are that the selling corporation and its target subsidiary are members of an affiliated group filing a consolidated return for the taxable year that includes the acquisition date. If an election is made, the underlying assets of the company that was sold receive a stepped-up, fair market value basis; the selling consolidated group recognizes the gain or loss attributable to the assets; and there is no separate tax on the seller's gain attributable to the stock. This provision offers taxpayers relief from a potential multiple taxation at the corporate level of the same economic gain, which may result when a transfer of appreciated corporate stock is taxed without providing a corresponding step-up in basis of the assets of the

corporation. The conference agreement, following the House bill, retains this provision.

In addition, the conference agreement permits the expansion of the section 338(h)(10) concept, to the extent provided in regulations, to situations in which the selling corporation owns 80 percent of the value and voting power of the subsidiary, but does not file a consolidated return. Moreover, the conference agreement provides that, under regulations, principles similar to those of section 338(h)(10) may be applied to taxable sales or distributions of controlled corporation stock. The conferees intend that the regulations under this elective procedure will account for appropriate principles that underlie the liquidation-reincorporation doctrine. For example, to the extent that regulations make available an election to treat a stock transfer of controlled corporation stock to persons related to such corporation within the meaning of section 368(c)(2), it may be appropriate to provide special rules for such corporation's section 381(c) tax attributes so that net operating losses may not be used to offset liquidation gains, earnings and profits may not be manipulated, or accounting methods may not be changed.

The conferees do not intend this election to affect the manner in which a corporation's distribution to its shareholders will be characterized for purposes of determining the shareholder level income tax consequences.

Regulatory authority to prevent the circumvention of General Utilities repeal.—The repeal of the *General Utilities* doctrine is designed to require the corporate level recognition of gain on a corporation's sale or distribution of appreciated property, irrespective of whether it occurs in a liquidating or nonliquidating context. The conferees expect the Secretary to issue, or to amend, regulations to ensure that the purpose of the new provisions is not circumvented through the use of any other provision, including the consolidated return regulations or the tax-free reorganization provisions of the Code (part III of Subchapter C).

Effective dates.—The repeal of the *General Utilities* doctrine is generally effective for liquidating sales and distributions after July 31, 1986. The conference agreement generally preserves all transitional rules provided in the House bill. Thus, transactions for which the requisite action had occurred prior to November 20, 1985, under the special rules and definitions provided in the House bill and the Report of the Committee on Ways and Means will generally continue to be grandfathered. However, in order to qualify under those transitional rules, all the liquidating sales or distributions, (instead of at least one such sale or distribution) must be completed before January 1, 1988. The agreement provides two additional transitional rules, one of general application and one applicable only to certain closely held corporations.

General transitional rules.—In addition to the rule discussed above, the new provisions do not apply to the following transactions:

(1) a liquidation completed before January 1, 1987;

(2) a deemed liquidation pursuant to a section 338 election where the acquisition date (the first date on which there is a qualified stock purchase under section 338) occurs before January 1, 1987;

(3) a liquidation pursuant to a plan of liquidation adopted before August 1, 1986, that is completed before January 1, 1988;

(4) a liquidation of a corporation if a majority of the voting stock of the corporation is acquired on or after August 1, 1986, pursuant to a written binding contract in effect before August 1, 1986, and if the liquidation is completed before January 1, 1988;

(5) a liquidation of a corporation if there was a binding written contract or contracts to acquire substantially all the assets of the corporation in effect before August 1, 1986, and the liquidation is completed before January 1, 1988; and

(6) a deemed liquidation, under section 338, of a corporation for which a qualified stock purchase under section 338 first occurs on or after August 1, 1986, pursuant to a written binding contract in effect before August 1, 1986, provided the section 338 acquisition date occurs before January 1, 1988.

A plan of liquidation is adopted if the plan has been approved by the shareholders. (See Treas. Reg. sec. 1.337-2(b)). If a plan of liquidation would have been considered adopted for purposes of commencing the present-law 12-month period under section 337, it will be deemed adopted for this purpose.

Although the special additional definitions of the term "adoption of a plan" provided in the House bill and Report of the Committee on Ways and Means continue to apply for purposes of determining whether the requisite action was taken prior to November 20, 1985, such special rules do not apply for purposes of determining whether a plan of liquidation is adopted before August 1, 1986.

For purposes of determining whether there was a binding written contract or contracts to sell substantially all the assets of a corporation before August 1, 1986, the term "substantially all the assets" shall generally mean 70 percent of the gross fair market value and 90 percent of the net fair market value of the assets. In addition, even though the contract or contracts cover a lesser amount of assets, if such contract or contracts would require shareholder approval under the applicable state law that may require such approval for a sale of substantially all of such corporation's assets, then they shall qualify as contracts to sell substantially all the assets and shall be considered binding even though shareholder approval has not yet been obtained.

An acquisition of stock or assets will be considered made pursuant to a binding written contract even though the contract is subject to normal commercial due diligence or similar provisions and the final terms of the actual acquisition may vary pursuant to such provisions.

For purposes of these rules, a liquidation is completed by a required date if it would be considered completed for purposes of section 337 of present law by that date. For example, there may be a distribution of assets to a qualified liquidating trust (*See,* e.g., Rev. Rul. 80-150, 1980-1 C.B. 316).

Certain closely held corporations.—The conference agreement deletes the House bill exception for distributions to certain long-term noncorporate shareholders. The conference agreement provides an additional transitional rule for certain closely held corporations. Corporations eligible for this rule are generally entitled to present law treatment with respect to liquidating sales and distributions occurring before January 1, 1989, provided the liquidation is completed before that date. A liquidation will be treated as completed under the same standard that is applied under the general transitional rules. However, this special transitional rule requires the recognition of income on distributions of ordinary income property (appreciated property that would not produce capital gain if disposed of in a taxable transaction) and short-term capital gain property. Thus, the failure of an eligible closely held corporation to complete its liquidation by December 31, 1986, or otherwise to satisfy the general transitional rules, will result in the loss of nonrecognition treatment for the distribution of appreciated ordinary income and short-term capital gain property. Corporations eligible for this rule may also make an S election prior to January 1, 1989, without becoming subject to the special S corporation rules of the conference agreement. Such eligible, electing corporations, however, will be subject to the 1954 Code version of section 1374.

A corporation is eligible for this rule if its value does not exceed $10 million and more than 50 percent of its stock is owned by 10 or fewer individuals who have held their stock for five years or longer. Full relief is available under this rule only if the corporation's value does not exceed $5 million; relief is phased out for corporations with values between $5 million and $10 million. For purposes of this rule, a corporation's value will be the higher of the value on August 1, 1986, and its value as of the date of adoption of a plan of liquidation (or, in the case of a nonliquidating distribution, the date of such distribution), and aggregation rules similar to those in section 1563 apply, except that control is defined as 50 percent rather than 80 percent.

In the case of nonliquidating distributions, apart from changes in the case of ordinary income property and short-term capital gain property, present law is otherwise retained for distributions to qualified, long-term individual shareholders (but only during the transitional period) for corporations qualify-

Act § 631   ¶ 3917

ing under the closely held corporation transitional rule.

[¶ 3918] SECTION 632. TREATMENT OF C CORPORATIONS ELECTING SUBCHAPTER S STATUS

(Secs. 1363 and 1374 of the Code)
[Conference Report]

*   *   *   *   *   *

House Bill

*   *   *   *   *   *

The House bill provides a special rule for S corporations designed to prevent avoidance of the provisions through a conversion of a C corporation to S corporation status. If an S corporation that was formerly a C corporation is liquidated before the close of the second taxable year following the year in which the elction took effect, the S election is terminated retroactively.

*   *   *   *   *   *

Conference Agreement

*   *   *   *   *   *

The conference agreement modifies the treatment of an S corporation that was formerly a C corporation. A corporate-level tax is imposed on any gain that arose prior to the conversion ("built-in" gain) and is recognized by the S corporation, through sale or distribution, within ten years after the date on which the S election took effect. The total amount of gain that must be recognized by the corporation, however, will be limited to the aggregate net built-in gain of the corporation at the time of conversion to S corporation status. Gains on sales or distributions of assets by the S corporation will be presumed to be built-in gains, except to the extent the taxpayer can establish that the appreciation accrued after the conversion, such as where the asset was acquired by the corporation in a taxable acquisition after the conversion. Built-in gains will be taxed at the maximum corporate rate applicable to the particular type of income (i.e., the maximum rate on ordinary income under section 11 or, if applicable, the alternative rate on capital gain income under section 1201) for the year in which the disposition occurs. The corporation will be allowed to continue to take into account all of its subchapter C tax attributes in computing the amount of the tax on recognized built-in gains, permitting it, for example, to use unexpired net operating losses, capital loss carryovers and minimum tax carryover credits to offset such tax. These provisions will generally be effective with respect to S elections made after December 31, 1986. For S elections made before January 1, 1987, the amendments made by the conference agreement do not apply. Thus, for example, the prior version of section 1374 will apply to such corporations.

[¶ 3920] SECTION 634. STUDY OF CORPORATE PROVISIONS

[Conference Report]

*   *   *   *   *   *

The conference agreement directs the Treasury Department to consider whether changes to the provisions of subchapter C (relating to the income taxation of corporations and their shareholders) and related sections of the Code are desirable, and to report to the tax-writing committees no later than January 1, 1988.

[¶ 3921] SECTION 641. SPECIAL ALLOCATION RULES FOR CERTAIN ASSET ACQUISITIONS

(Sec. 1060 of the Code)
[Senate Explanation]

*   *   *   *   *   *

Explanation of Provision.—The bill requires that, in the case of any "applicable asset acquisition," both the buyer and the seller must allocate purchase price in the manner prescribed in section 338(b)(5). Thus, both parties must use the residual method as described in the regulations under section 338. *See* Temp. Treas. Reg. sec. 1.338(b)-2T. An applicable asset acquisition is any transfer of assets constituting a business in which the transferee's basis is determined wholly by reference to the purchase price paid for the assets. Both direct and indirect transfers of a business are intended to be covered by this provision, including, for example, a sale of a business by an individual or a partnership, or a sale of a partnership interest in which the basis of the purchasing partner's proportionate share of the partnership's assets is adjusted to reflect the purchase price. A group of assets will constitute a business for this purpose if their character is such that goodwill or going concern value could under any circumstances attach to such assets. For example, a group of assets that would constitute an active trade or business within the meaning of section 355 will in all events be considered a business for purposes of this provision. Moreover, businesses that are not active businesses under section 355 will also be subject to this rule.

In requiring use of the residual method, the committee does not intend to restrict in any way the ability of the Internal Revenue Service to challenge the taxpayer's determination of the fair market value of any asset by any appropriate method. For example, in certain cases it would be reasonable for the Service to make an independent showing of the value of goodwill or going concern value as a means of calling into question the validity of the taxpayer's valuation of other assets.

The bill also authorizes the Treasury Department to require information reporting by the parties to an applicable asset acquisition.

This may include information regarding amounts allocated to goodwill or going concern value, as well as any other categories of assets or specific assets, and such other information as it deems necessary or appropriate.

Effective Date.—The provision is effective for transactions after May 6, 1986, unless pursuant to a binding contract in effect on that date and at all times thereafter.

*   *   *   *   *   *

[¶ 3922] SECTION 642. MODIFICATION OF DEFINITION OF RELATED PARTY

(Sec. 1239 of the Code)

[Conference Report]

Present Law.—Installment sale treatment is not available for gain on a sale of property to a related party if the property is depreciable in the hands of the transferee, unless it is established to the satisfaction of the Internal Revenue Service that tax avoidance was not a principal purpose of the sale. Gain on sales of depreciable property between related parties is treated as ordinary income. In the case of certain related party partnership transactions, ordinary income treatment is also required if the property is not a capital asset in the hands of the transferee.

Related parties for these purposes include a person and all entities which are 80 percent owned, directly or indirectly, with respect to that person. Specified attribution rules apply.

*   *   *   *   *

Senate Amendment.—The Senate amendment modifies the definition of the related parties to which the present law rules apply. Under the amendment, related parties include a person and all entities more than 50 percent owned, directly or indirectly, by

that person. Related parties also include entities more than 50 percent owned, directly or indirectly, by the same persons. The attribution and relationship rules are generally based on present law rules that apply to limit losses on sales between related parties. For example, there is attribution between parents and children.

The provision applies to sales after June 20, 1986, unless made pursuant to a binding contract in effect on that date. pursuant to a binding contract in effect on that date.

Conference Agreement.—The conference agreement generally follows the Senate amendment, with certain modifications. The definition of related parties is further expanded to cover other relationships that are covered under present law for purposes of disallowing losses on related party sales. In addition, in some types of sales, the conference agreement requires ratable basis recovery by the seller and conformity between buyer and seller regarding recognition of income and basis.

[Effective date.—Sales after enactment date unless after 8-14-86 under contract binding on that date. Ed.]

[¶ 3923] SECTION 643. TREATMENT OF AMORTIZABLE BOND PREMIUM AS INTEREST

(Sec. 171 of the Code)

[Conference Report]

Present Law.—An amortizable bond premium exists where a taxpayer buys a bond for more than face value. The amount of that excess is allowed as a deduction over the remaining term of the bond, generally offsetting interest income on the bond.

*   *   *   *   *   *

Senate Amendment.—The amortizable bond premium deduction is treated as interest, except as otherwise provided by regulations. Thus, for example, bond premium is treated as interest for purposes of applying the investment interest limitations.

The provision is effective for obligations acquired after date of enactment.

Conference Agreement.—The conference agreement follows the Senate amendment.

[¶3924] SECTION 644. PROVISIONS RELATING TO COOPERATIVE HOUSING CORPORATIONS

(Sec. 216 of the Code)

[House Explanation]

*　　*　　*　　*　　*　　*

Present Law

Under present law (sec. 216), a tenant-stockholder in a cooperative housing corporation is entitled to deduct amounts paid or accrued to the cooperative to the extent such amounts represent the tenant-stockholder's proportionate share of (1) real estate taxes allowable as a deduction to the cooperative which are paid or incurred by the cooperative with respect to the cooperative's land or buildings, and (2) interest allowable as a deduction to the cooperative, paid or incurred by the cooperative with respect to indebtedness contracted in the acquisition of the cooperative's land or in the acquisition, construction, rehabilitation, etc. of the cooperative's buildings. The tenant-stockholder's proportionate share is that portion of the cooperative's interest and taxes that bears the same ratio to the cooperative's total expenses for interest and taxes that the portion of the cooperative's stock held by the tenant-stockholder bears to the total outstanding stock of the cooperative.

In general, a cooperative housing corporation is a corporation (1) that has one class of stock, (2) each of the stockholders of which is entitled, solely by reason of ownership of stock, to occupy a dwelling owned or leased by the cooperative, (3) no stockholder of which is entitled to receive any distribution not out of earnings and profits of the cooperative, except on a complete or partial liquidation of the cooperative, and (4) 80 percent or more of the gross income for the taxable year of which is derived from tenant-stockholders. A tenant-stockholder generally is an individual owning fully paid up stock in the cooperative corporation, the purchase price of which bears a reasonable relationship to the value of the cooperative's equity in its land and buildings that is attributable to the dwelling unit that the individual is entitled to occupy.

*　　*　　*　　*　　*　　*

Explanation of Provision

Under the bill, where a housing cooperative charges each tenant-stockholder with a portion of the cooperative's interest and taxes in a manner that reasonably reflects the cost to the cooperative of the interest and taxes attributable to such tenant-stockholder's dwelling unit, then the cooperative may make an election whereby the share of the cooperative's interest and taxes that each tenant-stockholder is permitted to deduct would be the amounts that were so separately allocated and charged.

The committee intends that this provision is to be availed of in circumstances that will result in an allocation of the cooperative's interest and taxes that more accurately reflects the relative burdens of such items borne by respective tenant-stockholders. The

requirement that the allocation reasonably reflect the cost to the cooperative of the interest and taxes attributable to the tenant-stockholder's dwelling unit is intended to assure that a cooperative may not allocate deductible expenses of the cooperative to those tenant-stockholders for whom the deductions would be most valuable, and the non-deductible expenses of the cooperative to those tenant-stockholders for whom the deductions would be less valuable.

Thus, taxes allocated to a tenant-stockholder's unit will be considered to reasonably reflect the cost of the cooperative if the taxes allocated are based on the amounts separately assessed by the taxing authority. In the case of indebtedness of the cooperative incurred to purchase property, interest allocated to a tenant-stockholder's unit will be considered to reasonably reflect the cost to the cooperative if the amount allocated is based on the cooperative's purchase price of the property, allocated in accordance with the fair market value of the units purchased (including the unit's share of common areas).

[Senate Explanation]

*　　*　　*　　*　　*　　*

Present Law

Overview.—Under present law (sec. 216), a tenant-stockholder in a cooperative housing corporation is entitled to deduct amounts paid or accrued to the cooperative to the extent such amounts represent the tenant-stockholder's proportionate share of (1) real estate taxes allowable as a deduction to the cooperative which are paid or incurred by the cooperative, with respect to the cooperative's land or buildings, and (2) interest allowable as a deduction to the cooperative, paid or incurred by the cooperative, with respect to indebtedness contracted in the acquisition of the cooperative's land or in the acquisition, construction, rehabilitation, etc. of the cooperative's buildings.

In general, a cooperative housing corporation is a corporation (1) that has one class of stock, (2) each of the stockholders of which is entitled, solely by reason of ownership of stock, to occupy a dwelling owned or leased by the cooperative, (3) no stockholder of which is entitled to receive any distribution not out of earnings and profits of the cooperative, except on a complete or partial liquidation of the cooperative, and (4) 80 percent or more of the gross income for the taxable year of which is derived from tenant-stockholders. A tenant-stockholder generally is an individual owning fully paid-up stock in the cooperative corporation, the purchase price of which bears a reasonable relationship to the value of the cooperative's equity in its land and buildings that is attributable to the dwelling unit that the individual is entitled to occupy.

For purposes of the above rules, tenant-stockholders generally are limited to individuals. Thus, corporations, trusts, and other similar entities generally do not qualify for pass-through treatment under present law. An exception is provided where a person (including a corporation) sells property or leasehold interests to a cooperative and acquires stock in the cooperative within one year after making such transfer. In such cases, the person selling the property is treated as a tenant-stockholder for a period not exceeding three years from the date of acquisition of the stock. This treatment applies even if, by agreement with the cooperative, such person or its nominee may not occupy the house or apartment without prior approval of the cooperative.

Also under present law, a bank or other lending institution that obtains stock in a cooperative housing corporation by foreclosure is treated as a tenant-stockholder for up to three years after the date of acquisition (even if the lending institution or its nominee may not occupy the unit without prior approval of the cooperative).

For purposes of the 80-percent test, stock owned and dwellings leased by governmental entities for the purpose of providing housing facilities are not taken into account.

Allowance of depreciation deduction.—In addition to deductions for rent, interest, and taxes, to the extent a tenant-stockholder uses depreciable property leased from the cooperative in a trade or business or for production of income, the tenant-stockholder is allowed a deduction with respect to the stock that gives him the right to lease the property. This deduction generally is limited to that portion of the taxpayer's adjusted basis for the stock that is allocable to the depreciable property. Present law provides that the allowance of this deduction is not to be construed to limit or deny a depreciation deduction by the cooperative itself with respect to leased property.

*   *   *   *   *   *

Explanation of Provisions

Definition of tenant-stockholder.—The bill amends the definition of tenant-stockholder to mean any person (rather than any individual) who satisfies the requirements otherwise applicable to tenant-stockholders. Thus, under the bill, corporations, trusts, estates, partnerships, associations, or companies (as well as individuals) may be tenant-stockholders qualifying for pass-through treatment.

If a person other than an individual acquires stock in a housing cooperative, there shall not be taken into account, for purposes of determining whether the person is a qualifying tenant-stockholder, the fact that, by agreement with the cooperative, such person's nominee may not occupy the house or apartment without prior approval of the cooperative. This change enables, for example, a corporation owning stock in the cooperative to qualify for pass-through treatment although the cooperative retains the right to approve any individuals who occupy units under arrangements with the corporation.

The bill further provides that, in the case of an original seller of houses or apartments to a housing cooperative (including individuals or other entities), there shall not be taken into account the fact that, by agreement with the cooperative, the original seller or its nominee may not occupy a house or apartment without prior approval of the cooperative. This rule applies where the original seller acquires stock not later than one year after transferring houses or apartments (or leaseholds therein) to the cooperative.

Also under the bill, where any person acquires stock of a cooperative housing corporation by operation of law (including acquisition by inheritance or foreclosure), for purposes of determining whether such person is a qualifying tenant-stockholder, there shall not be taken into account the fact that, by agreement with the cooperative, such person or his nominee may not occupy the house or apartment without prior approval of the cooperative.

The present-law rules regarding original sellers and foreclosures by lending institutions are made unnecessary by these changes and therefore are repealed.

Limitation on depreciation deduction.—Under the bill, a tenant-stockholder using depreciable property in a trade or business or for the production of income is allowed a deduction as under present law to the extent of that portion of his adjusted basis for his stock that is allocable to such depreciable property. The bill further allows deductions exceeding this basis to be carried over to succeeding taxable years. However, the bill provides that no deduction may be allowed to a stockholder for any amount paid or accrued to the cooperative (in excess of proportionate interest and real estate taxes) to the extent that, under regulations issued by the Secretary of the Treasury, such amount is properly allocable to amounts chargeable to the cooperative's capital account. Any deduction disallowed under this rule will be applied to increase the stockholder's adjusted basis for his stock. This rule generally prevents a tenant-stockholder (including a corporation) from obtaining deductions for the capital costs of his cooperative unit more quickly than if he had owned the unit.

*   *   *   *   *   *

Explanation of Provisions.—Special rules are provided for two specified limited-profit housing cooperatives relating to the treatment of specified loan refinancings, the treatment of income earned on the reserve fund of such cooperatives in taxable years beginning prior to January 1, 1986, and the treatment of payments made from the respective reserve funds in taxable years beginning after December 31, 1985.

Conference Report

*   *   *   *   *   *

The conference agreement includes the provisions of both the House bill and the

Act § 644   ¶ 3924

Senate amendment. The conference agreement makes certain technical amendments to the provisions contained in the House bill, however, whereby separately allocated amounts of interest or taxes are deductible by a tenant-stockholder if the amount of such interest or taxes so allocated reasonably reflects the cost to the cooperative of the interest or taxes, as the case may be, allocable to the tenant-stockholder's dwelling unit, whether or not this condition is met with respect to *both* interest and taxes of the cooperative.

[**Effective date.**—]. The conference agreement is effective for taxable years beginning after December 31, 1986. The conference agreement includes the special provisions contained in the Senate amendment for two limited profit cooperatives.

[¶ 3925] SECTION 645. SPECIAL RULES RELATING TO PERSONAL HOLDING COMPANY TAX

(Sec. 543 of the Code)

[House Explanation]

*   *   *   *   *   *

Explanation of Provision

Computer software royalties.—*Overview.* Under the committee bill, certain royalties relating to computer software are not treated as personal holding company income. To qualify for this treatment the recipient must (a) be actively engaged in the trade or business of producing, developing, or manufacturing computer software, (b) derive more than half of its income from software royalties, (c) incur substantial trade or business expenses, or research and development expenses, and (d) distribute most of its passive income other than software royalties.

Active business requirements.—Under the committee bill, personal holding company income does not include certain computer software royalties. To qualify for the exception, four conditions must be met.

First, computer software royalties must be received by a corporation engaged in the active conduct of the trade or business of developing, manufacturing, or producing computer software; such computer software (a) must be developed, manufactured, or produced by such corporation (or its predecessor) in connection with such trade or business, or (b) must be directly related to such trade or business (the "trade or business test"). For this purpose, predecessor includes a partnership, the partners of which developed software for the partnership and transferred their partnership interests to the corporation in exchange for substantially all of the corporation's stock.

Second, computer software royalties that meet the first requirement must make up at least 50 percent of the ordinary gross income (as defined in section 543(b)) of the taxpayer for the taxable year (the "50-percent test").

Third, the amount of expenses that are properly allocable to the active business of developing, producing, or manufacturing software and that are allowable to the taxpayer under section 162 (relating to trade or business expenses), section 174 (relating to research and development expenses), or section 195 (relating to amortization of start-up expenses), must equal or exceed 25 percent of the ordinary gross income of the taxpayer for the taxable year (the "25-percent test").[1] Alternatively, the average of such deductions for the period of five taxable years ending with the current taxable year (or such shorter period as the corporation may have been in existence) must equal or exceed 25 percent of the ordinary gross income of the taxpayer for such period.

In computing deductions under section 162, the taxpayer may not take into account payments for personal services rendered by the five shareholders holding the largest percentage (by value) of the outstanding stock of the corporation. In determining the five largest shareholders for this purpose, stock deemed to be owned by a shareholder solely by reason of attribution from a partner (under section 544(a)(2)) is not taken into account, and individuals holding less than five percent of the corporation's stock (by value) are not taken into account.

Fourth, the sum of dividends paid during the taxable year (under section 562), dividends considered paid on the last day of the taxable year (under section 563) and the consent dividends for the taxable year (under section 565) must equal or exceed the amount of the corporation's personal holding company income in excess of 10 percent of the ordinary gross income of the corporation. For purposes of this computation, however, personal holding company income does not include the computer software royalties taken into account for the 50-percent test, and also does not include interest income for the five-year period beginning with the commencement of the active computer software business, provided that the 50-percent test and the 25-percent test also are met in this period.

Special rule for affiliated groups.—Under the committee bill, a special rule is provided in the case of computer software royalty income received by a member of an affiliated group. The bill provides that if a taxpayer who is a member of an affiliated group (within the meaning of section 1504(a)) receives royalties in connection with the licensing of computer software, and another member of the group meets the trade or business test, the 50-percent test, and the 25-percent test with respect to such software, then the

---

[**Footnote ¶ 3925**] (1) For purposes of this computation, any deduction specifically allowable under any section of the Code other than section 162 may not be treated as allowable under section 162.

taxpayer is treated as having met such requirements.

Dealers in securities.—*Overview.*—Under the committee bill, certain securities dealers are permitted to exclude from personal holding company income certain income received on securities or money market instruments held in inventory. To qualify for this treatment, the taxpayer must be a dealer in securities that (a) derives at least 50 percent of its income from the active conduct of the business of dealing in securities, (b) distributes most of its passive income not derived from the business of dealing in securities, and (c) incurs substantial trade or business expenses relating to the business of dealing in securities.

The committee bill also provides that dealers in securities may deduct interest expense on certain offsetting loans in computing their interest income for purposes of the personal holding company provisions.

Income from inventory.—Under the committee bill, personal holding company income does not include certain income of a dealer in securities from securities or money market instruments held as inventory if certain requirements are met. There are four conditions to qualify for the exception.

First, the taxpayer must be a dealer in securities.[2]

Second, the sum of income of the taxpayer from the trade or business of dealing in securities (other than personal holding company income) and the excepted income of such dealer from securities or money market instruments held as inventory must equal or exceed 50 percent of the taxpayer's ordinary gross income.

Third, the sum of dividends paid during the taxable year (under section 562), dividends considered paid on the last day of the taxable year (under section 563) and the consent dividends for the taxable year (under section 565) must equal or exceed the amount of the corporation's personal holding company income in excess of 10 percent of the ordinary gross income of the corporation. For purposes of this computation, however, personal holding company income does not include the excepted income on the securities or money market instruments held as inventory.

Fourth, the sum of the deductions allowable to the taxpayer under section 162 must equal or exceed 15 percent of the taxpayer's ordinary gross income. For this purpose, payments for compensation for personal services rendered by any shareholder and deductions that are specifically allowable under any section other than section 162, are not treated as deductions allowable under section 162.

Reduction in interest income from offsetting loans.—Under the committee bill, a dealer in securities that regularly derives income from transactions involving "offsetting loans" may, for purposes of the personal holding company rules, reduce the interest income from such transactions by the related interest expense.

For this purpose, a loan is treated as offsetting another loan if such loan (a) made at the same time as such loan, (b) is in substantially the same amount as such loan, (c) has the same maturity as such loan, (d) is secured by the same property as such loan, and (e) is designated in such manner as the Secretary of the Treasury may prescribe as an offsetting loan. The committee intends that so-called "repurchase" transactions that are treated as loans for Federal income tax purposes may qualify as offsetting loans under the provision if all of the conditions are met.[3]

[Senate Explanation]

*   *   *   *   *   *

Explanation of Provision

Overview.—Under the bill, certain royalties relating to computer software are not treated as personal holding company income or foreign personal holding company income. To qualify for this treatment, the recipient must (a) be actively engaged in the trade or business of producing, developing, or manufacturing computer software, (b) derive more than half of its income from software royalties, (c) incur substantial trade or business expenses, or research and development expenses, and (d) distribute most of its passive income other than software royalties.

Active business requirements.—* * * To qualify for the exception, four conditions must be met.

First, computer software royalties must be received by a corporation engaged in the active conduct of the trade or business of developing, manufacturing, or producing computer software; such computer software (a) must be developed, manufactured, or produced by such corporation (or its predecessor) in connection with such trade or business, or (b) must be directly related to such trade or business (the trade or business test). For this purpose, predecessor includes a partnership the partners of which developed software for the partnership and transferred their partnership interests to the corporation

---

[**Footnote ¶ 3925 continued**]

(2) The committee intends that for purposes of this provision, the term securities includes money market instruments.

(3) For example, if a dealer in securities purchases securities subject to an obligation of the seller to repurchase such securities, and at the same time (e.g., the same day) the dealer resells the securities for the same amount subject to an obligation to repurchase, if both transactions are treated as loans for Federal income tax purposes, then the two transactions may qualify as offsetting loans if the original seller is required to repurchase the securities at the same time and on substantially the same terms and that the dealer is required to repurchase the securities from the second buyer, with the difference in such terms reflecting the dealer's interest "spread."

in exchange for substantially all of the corporation's stock.

Second, computer software royalties that meet the first requirement must make up at least 50 percent of the ordinary gross income (as defined in sec. 543(b)) of the taxpayer for the taxable year (the 50-percent test).

Third, the amount of expenses that are properly allocable to the active business of developing, producing, or manufacturing software and that are allowable to the taxpayer under section 162 (relating to trade or business expenses), section 174 (relating to research and development expenses), or section 195 (relating to amortization of start-up expenses), must equal or exceed 25 percent of the ordinary gross income of the taxpayer for the taxable year (the "25-percent test").[5] Alternatively, the average of such deductions for the period of five taxable years ending with the current taxable year (or such shorter period as the corporation may have been in existence) must equal or exceed 25 percent of the ordinary gross income of the taxpayer for such period.

In computing deductions under section 162, the taxpayer may not take into account payments for personal services rendered by the five shareholders holding the largest percentage (by value) of the outstanding stock of the corporation. In determining the five largest shareholders for this purpose, stock deemed to be owned by a shareholder solely by reason of attribution from a partner (under sec. 544(a)(2)) is not taken into account, and individuals holding less than five percent of the corporation's stock (by value) are not taken into account.

Fourth, the sum of dividends paid during the taxable year (under sec. 562), dividends considered paid on the last day of the taxable year (under sec. 563), and the consent dividends for the taxable year (under sec. 565) must equal or exceed the amount of the corporation's personal holding company income in excess of 10 percent of the ordinary gross income of the corporation. For purposes of this computation, however, personal holding company income does not include the computer software royalties taken into account for the 50-percent test, and also does not include interest income for the five-year period beginning with the commencement of the active computer software business, provided that the 50-percent test and the 25-percent test also are met in this period.

Special rule for affiliated groups.—Under the bill, a special rule is provided in the case of computer software royalty income received by a member of an affiliated group. The bill provides that if a taxpayer who is a member of an affiliated group (within the meaning of sec. 1504(a)) receives royalties in connection with the licensing of computer software, and another member of the group meets the trade or business test, the 50-percent test, and the 25-percent test with respect to such software, then the taxpayer is treated as having met such requirements.

[Effective date.—Generally royalties received on or after 12-31-86. Ed.]

[¶ 3926] SECTION 646. CERTAIN ENTITIES NOT TREATED AS CORPORATIONS

[Conference Report]

* * * * * *

Senate Amendment.—Under the Senate amendment, a certain trust (Great Northern Iron Ore Trust) will not be taxed as a corporation if, among other things, it makes an election and agrees not to exercise business powers contained in its trust instrument.

[Effective date.—] The provision is effective for taxable years beginning after the taxable year in which the election is made, provided that all conditions of the Senate amendment continue to be satisfied.

Conference Agreement.—The conference agreement follows the Senate amendment.

[¶ 3928] SECTIONS 651-657. REGULATED INVESTMENT COMPANIES

(Secs. 562, 851-853, 855A, 4982 and 7609, of the Code)

[Conference Report]

* * * * * *

Senate Amendment

Under the Senate amendment, RICs are required to adopt a calendar year as their taxable year. In addition, a RIC is required to pay a nondeductible excise tax equal to five percent of the amount of any dividends paid after the close of its taxable year that are

treated as having been paid in the preceding taxable year.

The Senate amendment clarifies the definition of "securities" by reference to the definition of securities in the Investment Company Act of 1940. In addition, permitted income for RICs is defined to include income from foreign currencies, and options and futures contracts, derived with respect to the RIC's business of investing. The Senate amendment provides regulatory authority, however, to exclude certain gains from investment in foreign currency.

[Footnote ¶ 3925 continued]
(5) For purposes of this computation, any deduction specifically allowable under any section of the Code other than sec. 162 may not be treated as allowable under sec. 162.

The Senate amendment also provides that, in the case of RICs that have so-called series funds, each fund is treated as a separate corporation. Tax-free treatment is provided for the deemed formation of the separate corporations that are deemed to be formed under the provision.

The Senate amendment extends the time for filing notices for capital gain dividei.ds and certain other purposes from 45 to 60 days. RICs are treated as third party record-keepers under the Senate amendment.

[**Effective date.—**] The provisions of the Senate amendment relating to the adoption of a calendar year generally are effective for taxable years beginning after December 31, 1986. The provision of the Senate amendment relating to treatment of a RIC as a third party recordkeeper is effective for summonses served after the date of enactment. The other provisions of the Senate amendment are effective for taxable years of RICs beginning after the date of enactment.

Conference Agreement

The conference agreement generally follows the Senate amendment with the following modifications.

Imposition of excise tax * * * The conference agreement does not require all RICs to adopt a calendar year as their taxable year and does not impose an excise tax on all "spillover" dividends. Instead, the conference agreement imposes for any calendar year, a nondeductible excise tax on any RIC equal to four percent of the excess, if any, of the "required distribution" for the calendar year ending within the taxable year of the RIC, over the "distributed amount" for such calendar year. The excise tax imposed for any calendar year is to be paid not later than March 15 of the succeeding calendar year.

For these purposes, the term required distribution means, with respect to any calendar year, the sum of (1) 97 percent of the RIC's "ordinary income" for such taxable year, (2) 90 percent of the RIC's capital gain net income (within the meaning of sec. 1222(9)) for the one year period ending on October 31 of such taxable year (as if the one year period ending on October 31 were the RIC's taxable year),[29] and (3) the excess, if any, of the "grossed up required distribution" for the preceding calendar year over the distributed amount for such preceding calendar year. For this purpose, the term grossed up required distribution for any calendar year is the sum of the taxable income of the RIC for the calendar year (determined without regard to the deduction for dividends paid) and all amounts from earlier years that are not treated as having been distributed under the provision.

The RIC's ordinary income for this purpose means its investment company taxable income (as defined in sec. 852(b)(2)) determined (1) taking into account the net capital gain of the RIC and without taking into account the dividends paid deduction, (2) by not taking into account any gain or loss from the sale of any capital asset, and (3) by treating the calendar year as the RIC's taxable year.

In addition, for these purposes, the term distributed amount means, with respect to any calendar year, the sum of (1) the deduction for dividends paid (within the meaning of sec. 561) during such calendar year, (2) amounts on which the RIC is required to pay corporate tax, and (3) the excess (if any) of the distributed amount for the preceding taxable year over the required distribution for such preceding taxable year. The amount of dividends paid for these purposes is determined without regard to the provisions of section 855 and without regard to any exempt-interest dividend (as defined in sec. 852(b)(5)).

Under the conference agreement, for purposes of applying these provisions, any deficiency dividend (as defined in sec. 860(f)) is taken into account at the time it is paid, and any income giving rise to the adjustment is treated as arising at the time the dividend is paid.

Special rule for certain regulated investment companies.—The conference agreement provides that RICs that have a taxable year ending on either November 30, or December 31, may make an irrevocable election to use their actual taxable year, rather than a year ending on October 31, for purposes of applying the distribution requirement rules relating to capital gains.

Timing of inclusion of certain dividends.—The conference agreement provides that any dividend declared by a RIC in December of any calendar year and payable to shareholders of record as of a specified date in such month, shall be deemed to have been paid by the RIC, (including for purposes of section 561), and to have been received by each shareholder, on such record date, but only if such dividend is actually paid by the RIC before February 1 of the following calendar year. This provision does not apply for purposes of section 855(a), however.[30]

Earnings and profits.—Under the conference agreement, a RIC is treated as having sufficient earnings and profits to treat as a dividend any distribution during any calendar year which distribution is treated as a dividend by such RIC, (other than a redemption to which section 302(a) applies), but only to the extent that the amount distributed during such calendar year does not exceed the required distribution for such calendar year. The purpose of this provision is to

---

[**Footnote ¶ 3928**] (29) The conferees understand that in applying this rule, the period ending October 31, of each calendar year would be treated as the taxpayer's taxable year for purposes of the capital loss carryover provisions and for purposes of the year-end straddle and mark-to-market rules.

(30) Thus, a RIC that has a taxable year ending on November 30, may treat such dividends as having been paid prior to December under section 855(a).

prevent a RIC from failing to meet the requirements for avoiding the imposition of the excise tax where losses incurred by the RIC after October 31, but before the close of its taxable year, otherwise would prevent the RIC from having sufficient earnings and profits for its distributions to be treated as dividends.

Treatment of certain capital losses.—For purposes of determining the amount of capital gain dividends that a RIC may distribute for a taxable year, the RIC's net capital gain for the taxable year is determined without regard to any net capital loss attributable to transactions after October 31 of such year. For these purposes, any such net capital loss is treated as arising on the first day of the next taxable year. To the extent provided in regulations, the same rule will apply for purposes of determining the RIC's taxable income.[31]

Hedging exception.—The conferees believe that the requirement that a RIC derive less than 30 percent of its gross income from the sale or other disposition of stock or securities held for less than three months is an appropriate requirement to ensure that a RIC is a passive entity that is appropriately granted pass-through status. Nevertheless, the conferees recognize that this requirement may not necessarily reflect accurately the extent of the active business activities of a RIC where the RIC engages in certain hedging transactions that are otherwise consistent with the passive nature of the RIC. The conferees believe that in general, in the case of such hedging transactions, both the hedged and the hedging positions properly are considered to be single investment.

Accordingly, the conference agreement modifies the computation of gross income of a RIC for purposes of the requirement of section 851(b)(3) that less than 30 percent of the gross income of the RIC is derived from the sale or exchange of stock or securities held for less than three months. Under the conference agreement, for purposes of applying this test, any increase in value on a position that is part of a designated hedge is offset by any decrease in value (whether or not realized) on any other position that is part of such hedge. For this purpose, increases and decreases in value are taken into account only to the extent attributable to increases or decreases in value (as the case may be) during the period of the hedge. This rule applies for purposes of calculating both gains from the sale or other disposition of stock or securities held for less than three months and also the gross income of the RIC for purposes of section 851(b)(3).

For these purposes, there is a designated hedge where the taxpayer's risk of loss with respect to any position in property is reduced by reason of (1) the taxpayer having an option to sell, being under a contractual obligation to sell, or having made (and not closed) a short sale of substantially identical property, (2) the taxpayer being the grantor of an option to buy substantially identical property, or (3) under regulations prescribed by the Secretary, the taxpayer holding one or more other positions. The conferees intend that a qualified covered call (within the meaning of sec. 1092(c)) may be treated as part of a designated hedge. In addition, positions that are part of the hedge must be clearly identified by the taxpayer in the manner prescribed by regulations.

Prior to the issuance of such regulations, the conferees intend that the identification requirement would be treated as having been satisfied with identification by the close of the day on which the hedge is established, either (a) by the placing of the positions that are part of hedge in a separate account that is maintained by a broker, futures commission merchant, custodian or similar person, and that is designated as a hedging account, provided that such person maintaining such account makes notations identifying the hedged and hedging positions and the date on which the hedge is established, or (b) by the designation by such a broker, merchant, custodian or similar person, of such positions as a hedge for purposes of these provisions, provided that the RIC is provided with a written confirmation stating the date the hedge is established and identifying the hedged and hedging positions.

Business development companies. — The conference agreement provides that a business development company registered under the Investment Company Act of 1940, as amended (15 U.S.C. 80a-1 to 80b-2) may qualify as a RIC.

Preference dividends.—The conference agreement provides that differences in the rate of dividends paid to shareholders are not treated as preferential dividends (within the meaning of section 562(c)), where the differences reflect savings in administrative costs (but not differences in management fees), provided that such dividends are paid by a RIC to shareholders who have made initial investments of at least $10 million.

Effective date.—The provisions of the conference agreement relating to the imposition of the excise tax on RICs are applicable for calendar years beginning after December 31, 1986. Other provisions of the conference agreement have the same effective date as the Senate amendment.

[Footnote ¶ 3928 continued]

(31) The conferees intend that any such regulations would prevent avoidance of tax, particularly in circumstances where a RIC takes advantage of the rule in order to pay return of capital dividends in the following taxable year, or to offset the tax that would be incurred on capital gains recognized in the following year.

[¶ 3929] SECTIONS 661-669. REAL ESTATE INVESTMENT TRUSTS

(Secs. 856, 857, 859, 860, 4981 and 6697
of the Code)

[Conference Report]

Senate Amendment

General requirements.—Under the Senate amendment, a taxpayer without prior operating history is permitted to change its accounting year without consent in connection with its initial election of REIT status. The Senate amendment also provides that an entity is not disqualified from electing REIT status in the first taxable year of its existence because it was closely held. Partner to partner attribution is ignored in determining if the REIT is closely held. In order to elect REIT status under the Senate amendment, the electing entity must either have been treated as a REIT for all taxable years beginning after February 28, 1986, or must have no earnings and profits accumulated as a regular corporation.

Asset and income requirements.—The Senate amendment provides that REITs are permitted to hold assets in wholly owned subsidiaries. The REIT and its REIT subsidiaries are treated as a single taxpayer under the Senate amendment (i.e., the separate corporate status of the REIT subsidiaries is ignored).

Under the Senate amendment, for a one-year period after the receipt of new equity capital, income from the temporary investment of the new capital that is derived from stock or debt instruments is treated as qualifying "75-percent income." Such stock or debt instruments are treated as qualifying assets for the same period under the Senate amendment.

Definition of rents.—The Senate amendment permits REITs to provide, without being required to use independent contractors, those services that may be furnished in connection with the rental of real property by a tax-exempt organization without giving rise to unrelated business income.

The Senate amendment also permits REITs to receive rents based on the net income of the tenant, provided that the tenant's profits are derived only from sources that would be qualified rent if earned directly by the REIT.

Distribution requirement.—Under the Senate amendment, any income that is accrued but not received with respect to original issue discount on a loan issued in exchange for nonpublicly traded property, or with respect to a deferred rental agreement, or any income that is recognized as the result of the failure of an exchange that the REIT intended in good faith to qualify, but that was ultimately determined not to qualify for treatment as a tax-free like kind exchange, is not subject to the distribution requirement to the extent that such amounts exceed five percent of the REITs taxable income. The

REIT is required to pay income tax on the undistributed amount.

The Senate amendment provides that the amount of a REIT's current earnings and profits will not be less than the REIT's taxable income for the purpose of determining whether a distribution was made out of earnings and profits.

Capital gains.—The Senate amendment permits REIT's to compute their capital gain dividends without offset for net operating losses (NOLs). NOLs not used to offset capital gain income are carried over according to the ordinary rules. REITs are permitted to send capital gain notices to shareholders with the mailing of their annual report, rather than 30 days after year end.

Prohibited transactions.—Under the Senate amendment, the number of sales that a REIT is able to make within the prohibited transaction safe harbor is expanded from five to seven. The Senate amendment provides an alternative safe harbor whereby a REIT may make any number of sales during a taxable year provided that the gross income from such sales does not exceed 15 percent of the REIT's taxable income for such year (computed with certain adjustments). Any marketing or development activities with respect to properties that are sold is required to be performed by independent contractors where the REIT is taking advantage of the alternative safe harbor. The Senate amendment also increases the extent of improvements that a REIT is permitted to make from 20 percent to 30 percent of the property's adjusted basis. In addition, under the Senate amendment, losses from prohibited transactions are permitted to offset taxable income but are not permitted to offset gains from prohibited transactions.

Deficiency dividends.—The Senate amendment eliminates the penalty tax under section 6697 on deficiency dividends paid by REITs.

Effective date.—The provisions of the Senate amendment generally are effective for taxable years beginning after December 31, 1986.

Conference Agreement

The conference agreement follows the Senate amendment with the following modifications.

Imposition of excise tax.—*In general.*—The conference agreement imposes a nondeductible excise tax on any REIT for each calendar year equal to four percent of the excess, if any, of the "required distribution" for the calendar year, over the "distributed amount" for such calendar year. The excise tax must be paid on or before March 15 of the following calendar year.

For these purposes, the term required distribution means, with respect to any calendar year, the sum of (1) 85 percent of the REIT's "ordinary income" for the calendar

Act §661-669 ¶3929

year, (1) 85 percent of the REIT's "ordinary income" for the calendar year, (determined as if the calendar year were the REIT's taxable year), (2) 95 percent of the REIT's capital gain net income (within the meaning of sec. 1222(9)) for such calendar year, (determined as if the calendar year were the REIT's taxable year), and (3) the excess, if any, of the "grossed up required distribution" for the preceding calendar year over the distributed amount for such preceding calendar year. For this purpose, the term grossed up required distribution for any calendar year is the sum of the taxable income of the REIT for the calendar year (without regard to the deduction for dividends paid) and all amounts from earlier years that are not treated as having been distributed under the provision.

The REIT's ordinary income for this purpose means its real estate investment trust taxable income (as defined in sec. 857(b)(2)) determined (1) without taking into account the dividends paid deduction, (2) by not taking into account any gain or loss from the sale of any capital asset, and (3) by treating the calendar year as the REIT's taxable year.

In addition, for these purposes, the term distributed amount means, with respect to any calendar year, the sum of (1) the deduction for dividends paid (within the meaning of sec. 561) during such calendar year, (2) amounts on which the REIT is required to pay corporate tax, and (3) the excess (if any) of the distributed amount for the preceding taxable year over the grossed up required distribution for such preceding taxable year. The amount of dividends paid for these purposes is determined without regard to the provisions of section 858.

Under the conference agreement, for purposes of applying these provisions, any deficiency dividend, (as defined in sec. 860(f)), is taken into account at the time it is paid, and any income giving rise to the adjustment is treated as arising at the time the dividend is paid.

Timing of inclusion of certain dividends.—Under the conference agreement, any dividend declared by a REIT in December of any calendar year and payable to shareholders of record as of a specified date in such month, shall be deemed to have been paid by the REIT, (including for purposes of section 561), and to have been received by each shareholder, on such record date, but only if such dividend is actually paid by the REIT before February 1 of the following calendar year. This provision does not apply for purposes of section 858(a), however.

Earnings and profits.—Under the conference agreement, a REIT is treated as having sufficient earnings and profits to treat as a dividend any distribution during any calendar year (other than a redemption to which section 302(a) applies), which distribution is treated as a dividend by such REIT, but only to the extent that the amount distributed during such calendar year does not exceed the required distribution for such calendar year. The purpose of this provision is to prevent the REIT from failing to meet the requirements for avoiding the imposition of the excise tax where losses incurred by the REIT after December 31, but before the close of its taxable year, otherwise would prevent the REIT from having sufficient earnings and profits for its distributions to be treated as dividends.

The conference agreement does not contain the provision from the Senate amendment under which a REIT's earnings and profits for a taxable year would not be less than its real estate trust taxable income for the taxable year (without regard to the dividends paid deduction), since the conferees believe that this provision is a restatement of present law.

Treatment of certain capital losses.—The conference agreement provides that, in the case of a REIT that has a taxable year other than the calendar year, for purposes of determining the amount of capital gain dividends, such REIT may distribute for a taxable year, the REIT's net capital gain for the taxable year is determined without regard to any net capital loss attributable to transactions after December 31 of such year. For these purposes, any such net capital loss is treated as arising on the first day of the next taxable year. To the extent provided in regulations, the same rule will apply for purposes of determining the REIT's net income.[1]

Distribution requirement.—The conference agreement clarifies that the amount on which relief is provided from the 95 percent distribution requirement in the case of income derived from certain transactions to which section 467 or section 1274 applies, is based on the excess of those amounts that the REIT is required to recognize on account of either section 467 or section 1274 over the amounts that the REIT otherwise would recognize under its regular method of accounting. Thus, for example, in the case of a REIT using the accrual method of accounting, the provision would apply in the case of a section 467 rental agreement only to the extent that the income required to be recognized under section 467 exceeded the amount of income that the taxpayer would include under the accrual method if section 467 did not apply.

Definition of rents and interest.—The conference agreement provides that for purposes of the income requirements for qualification as a REIT, and for purposes of the prohibited transactions provisions, any income derived from a "shared appreciation provision" is treated as gain recognized on the sale of the "secured property." For these purposes, a shared appreciation provision is any provision that is in connection with an obligation that is held by the REIT and secured by an interest in real property, which

[Footnote ¶ 3929]   (1) The conferees intend that any such regulations would prevent the avoidance of tax, particularly in circumstances where a REIT takes advantage of the rule in order to pay return of capital dividends in the following taxable year, or to offset the tax that would be incurred on capital gains recognized in the following year.

provision entitles the REIT to receive a specified portion of any gain realized on the sale or exchange of such real property (or of any gain that would be realized if the property were sold on a specified date). Secured property for these purposes means the real property that secures the obligation that has the shared appreciation provision.

In addition, the conference agreement provides that for purposes of the income requirements for qualification as a REIT, and for purposes of the prohibited transactions provisions, the REIT is treated as holding the secured property for the period during which it held the shared appreciation provision (or, if shorter, the period during which the secured property was held by the person holding such property),[2] and the secured property is treated as property described in section 1221(1) if it is such property in the hands of the obligor on the obligation to which the shared appreciation provision relates (or if it would be such property if held by the REIT). For purposes of the prohibited transaction safe harbor, the REIT is treated as having sold the secured property at the time that it recognizes income on account of the shared appreciation provision, and any expenditures made by the holder of the secured property are treated as made by the REIT.[3]

For example, under the conference agreement, if a REIT is the holder of an obligation under which it is paid a fixed percentage of interest on a fixed principal amount, and also is entitled to a payment equal to a portion of the appreciation in the property as of the time the property is sold (or at an earlier specified time), then the additional payment would be treated as gain on the sale of the property secured by the obligation for purposes of section 856(c), with the holding period of the property considered to be the shorter of the REIT's holding period of the obligation or the obligor's holding period for the secured property. This gain would be eligible for the prohibited transaction safe harbor if the applicable requirements are met.

The conferees intend no inference regarding the treatment of any shared appreciation provision for any other purposes of Federal income taxation.

The conferees wish to make certain clarifications regarding those services that a REIT may provide under the conference agreement without using an independent contractor, which services would not cause the rents derived from the property in connection with which the services were rendered to fail to qualify as rents from real property (within the meaning of section 856(d)). The conferees intend, for example, that a REIT may provide customary services in connection with the operation of parking facilities for the convenience of tenants of an office or apartment building, or shopping center, provided that the parking facilities are made available on an unreserved basis without charge to the tenants and their guests or customers. On the other hand, the conferees intend that income derived from the rental of parking spaces on a reserved basis to tenants, or income derived from the rental of parking spaces to the general public, would not be considered to be rents from real property unless all services are performed by an independent contractor. Nevertheless, the conferees intend that the income from the rental of parking facilities properly would be considered to be rents from real property (and not merely income from services) in such circumstances if services are performed by an independent contractor.

The conferees also wish to clarify that a REIT may directly select, hire, and compensate those independent contractors who will provide the customary services that may be provided by a REIT in connection with the rental of real property, rather than hiring an independent contractor to hire other independent contractors.

Income and asset requirements.—The conference agreement provides that the investment of the proceeds of the public offering of debt securities that have a maturity of at least five years receives the same treatment as the investment of new equity capital. The conferees intend that debt securities for which there is an intention to call before five years would not be treated as having a maturity of at least five years.

The conferees wish to clarify that if a REIT purchases all of the stock of a corporation and makes an election under section 338 with respect to the purchased stock, then the corporation that is deemed to be newly formed pursuant to the section 338 election may qualify as a REIT subsidiary as of the time that the newly formed corporation is deemed to come into existence.

Prohibited transactions.—Instead of measuring the alternative safe harbor for prohibited transactions by reference to the income of the REIT, the alternative safe harbor provided by the conference agreement is any number of sales provided that the adjusted basis of the property sold does not exceed 10 percent of the adjusted basis of all of the REIT's assets at the beginning of the REIT's taxable year. For this purpose, the total adjusted basis of all of the REIT's assets (including the property that is sold) is to be computed using depreciation deductions that are used for purposes of computing earnings and profits. The other requirements for use of the alternative safe harbor in the Senate bill

---

[Footnote ¶ 3929 continued]

  (2) The conferees intend that the provisions of section 1223 are to be taken into account for purposes of determining the holding period of the person holding the secured property.

  (3) The conferees intend that the REIT's holding period of the obligation to which the shared appreciation provision relates (and not the obligor's holding period of the secured property if longer than the REIT's holding period) must be at least four years for the safe harbor to apply.

continue to apply. The conferees intend no inference regarding whether sales that qualify under this safe harbor for the REIT are or are not properly considered to be sales of property held for sale to customers.

Effective date.—The provisions of the conference agreement generally are effective for taxable years beginning after December 31, 1986. The provisions relating to the imposition of the excise tax are effective for calendar years beginning after December 31, 1986.

[¶ 3930] SECTIONS 671-675. MORTGAGE-BACKED SECURITIES

(Secs. 860A-860G of the Code)

[Conference Report]

*   *   *   *   *   *

Overview:—In general, the conference agreement provides rules relating to "real estate mortgage investment conduits" or "REMICs." In general, a REMIC is a fixed pool of mortgages with multiple classes of interests held by investors. The conference agreement provides rules prescribing (1) the Federal income tax treatment of the REMIC, (2) the treatment of taxpayers who exchange mortgages for interests in the REMIC, (3) the treatment of taxpayers holding interests in the REMIC, and (4) the treatment of disposition of interests in the REMIC.

In general, if the specified requirements are met, the REMIC is not treated as a separate taxable entity. Rather, the income of the REMIC is allocated to, and taken into account by, the holders of the interests therein, under specified rules. Holders of "regular interests" generally take into income that portion of the income of the REMIC that would be recognized by an accrual method holder of a debt instrument that had the same terms as the particular regular interest; holders of "residual interests" take into account all of the net income of the REMIC that is not taken into account by the holders of the regular interests. Rules are provided that (1) treat a portion of the income of the residual holder derived from the REMIC as unrelated business income for tax-exempt entities or as subject to withholding at the statutory rate when paid to foreign persons, and (2) prevent such portion from being offset by net operating losses, other than net operating losses of certain thrift institutions.

The conference agreement also contains provisions relating to the application of the OID rules to certain debt instruments the timing of whose maturities is contingent upon the timing of payments on other debt instruments. In addition, the conference agreement imposes certain new information reporting requirements.

Further, the conference agreement treats as a corporation any entity or other arrangement, referred to as a "taxable mortgage pool," that is used primarily to hold mortgages, where maturities of debt instruments that are issued by the entity in multiple classes, are tied to the timing of payments on the mortgages.

Requirements for qualification as a REMIC.—Under the conference agreement, any entity, including a corporation, partnership, or trust, that meets specified requirements would be permitted to elect to be treated as a REMIC. In addition, a segregated pool of assets also may qualify as a REMIC as if it were an entity meeting the requirements. To elect REMIC status, requirements relating to the composition of assets and the nature of the investors' interests must be satisfied, and an election to be treated as a REMIC must be in effect for the taxable year, and if applicable, all prior taxable years.

The asset test

Under the conference agreement, in order to qualify as a REMIC, substantially all of the assets of the entity or segregated pool, as of the close of the third calendar month beginning after the startup day and as of the close of every quarter of each calendar year thereafter, must consist of "qualified mortgages," and "permitted investments." The conferees intend that the term substantially all should be interpreted to allow the REMIC to hold only de minimis amounts of other assets.

A "qualified mortgage" is any obligation (including any participation or certificate of beneficial ownership interest therein) that is principally secured directly or indirectly by an interest in real property, and that either (1) is transferred to the REMIC on or before the "startup day," or (2) is purchased by the REMIC within the three-month period beginning on the startup day.[5] A qualified mortgage also includes a "qualified replacement mortgage." A qualified replacement mortgage is any property that would have been treated as a qualified mortgage if it were transferred to the REMIC on or before the startup day, and that is received either (1) in exchange for a defective qualified mortgage[6] within a two-year period beginning on the startup day, or (2) in exchange for any other

---

[Footnote ¶ 3930]   **(5)** The conferees intend that stripped coupons and stripped bonds (within the meaning of sec. 1286) may be treated as qualifying mortgages if the bonds (within the meaning of sec. 1286) from which such stripped coupons or stripped bonds arose would have been qualified mortgages. The conferees also intend that interests in grantor trusts would be treated as qualified mortgages, to the extent that the assets of the trusts that holders of the beneficial interest therein are treated as owning, would be treated as qualifying mortgages. In addition, the conferees intend that interests in qualifying mortgages in the nature of the interests described in Treas. Reg. sec. 301.7701-4(c)(2)(Example 2), would be treated as qualifying mortgages.

(6) For this purpose, the conferees intend that a defective qualified mortgage is a qualified mortgage with respect to which there is a default or threatened default by the obligor.

qualified mortgage within a three-month period beginning on the startup day. In addition, a regular interest in another REMIC that is transferred to the REMIC on or before the startup day is treated as a qualified mortgage. The startup day is any day selected by the REMIC that is on or before the first day on which interests in the REMIC are issued.

"Permitted investments" are "cash flow investments," "qualified reserve assets," and "foreclosure property."

"Cash flow investments" are any investment of amounts received under qualified mortgages for a temporary period before distribution to holders of interests in the REMIC. The conferees intend that these are assets that are received periodically by the REMIC, invested temporarily in passive-type assets, and paid out to the investors at the next succeeding regular payment date. The conferees intend that these temporary investments are to be limited to those types of investments that produce passive income in the nature of interest. For example, the conferees intend that an arrangement commonly known as a "guaranteed investment contract," whereby the REMIC agrees to turn over payments on qualified mortgages to a third party who agrees to return such amounts together with a specified return thereon at times coinciding with the times that payments are to be made to holders of regular or residual interests, may qualify as a permitted investment.

"Qualified reserve assets" are any intangible property held for investment that is part of a "qualified reserve fund." A qualified reserve fund is any reasonably required reserve that is maintained by the REMIC to provide for payments of certain expenses and to provide additional security for the payments due on regular interests in the REMIC that otherwise may be delayed or defaulted upon because of defaults (including late payments) on the qualified mortgages. In determining whether the amount of the reserve is reasonable, the conferees believe that it is appropriate to take into account the creditworthiness of the qualified mortgages and the extent and nature of any guarantees relating to the qualified mortgages. Further, amounts in the reserve fund must be reduced promptly and appropriately as regular interests in the REMIC are retired.

Under the conference agreement, a reserve is not treated as a qualified reserve unless for any taxable year (and all subsequent taxable years) not more than 30 percent of the gross income from the assets in such fund for the taxable year is derived from the sale or other disposition of property held for less than three months. For this purpose, gain on the disposition of a reserve fund asset is not taken into account if the disposition of such asset is required to prevent default on a regular interest where the threatened default resulted from a default on one or more qualified mortgages.

"Foreclosure property" is property that would be foreclosure property under section 856(e) if acquired by a real estate investment trust, and which is acquired by the REMIC in connection with the default or imminent default of a qualified mortgage. Property so acquired ceases to be foreclosure property one year after its acquisition by the REMIC.

Investors' interests

In order to qualify as a REMIC under the conference agreement, all of the interests in the REMIC must consist of one or more classes of "regular interests" and a single class of "residual interests."

Regular interests.—A regular interest in a REMIC is an interest in a REMIC whose terms are fixed on the startup day, which terms (1) unconditionally entitle the holder to receive a specified principal (or similar) amount, and (2) provide that interest (or similar) payments, if any, at or before maturity are based on a fixed rate (or to the extent provided in regulations, a variable rate). An interest in the REMIC may qualify as a regular interest where the timing (but not the amount) of the principal (or similar) payments are contingent on the extent of prepayments on qualified mortgages and the amount of income from permitted investments.

The conferees intend that regular interests in REMICs may be issued in the form of debt, stock, partnership interests, interests in a trust, or any other form permitted by state law. Thus, if an interest in a REMIC is not in the form of debt, the conferees understand that the interest would not have a specified principal amount, but that the interest would qualify as a regular interest if there is a specified amount that could be identified as the principal amount if the interest were in the form of debt. For example, an interest in a partnership could qualify as a regular interest if the holder of the partnership interest were to receive a specified amount in redemption of the partnership interest, and that the amount of income allocated to such partnership interest were based on a fixed percentage of the specified outstanding redemption amount.

The conferees intend that an interest in a REMIC would not fail to be treated as a regular interest if the payments of principal (or similar) amounts with respect to such interest are subordinated to payments on other regular interests in the REMIC, and are dependent upon the absence of defaults on qualified mortgages. Thus, the conferees intend that regular interests in a REMIC may resemble the types of interests described in Treas. Reg. sec. 301.7701-4(c)(2) (Example 2).[7]

The conferees intend that an interest in a REMIC may not qualify as a regular interest if the amount of interest (or similar payments) is disproportionate to the specified principal amount. For example, if an interest is issued in the form of debt with a coupon rate of interest that is substantially in excess of prevailing market interest rates (adjusted for risk), the conferees intend that the interest would not qualify as a regular interest. Instead, the conferees intend that such an interest may be treated either as a residual interest, or as a combination of a regular interest and a residual interest.

Residual interests.—In general, a residual interest in a REMIC is any interest in the REMIC other than a regular interest, and which is so designated by the REMIC, provided that there is only one class of such interest, and that all distributions (if any) with respect to such interests are pro rata. For example, the residual interest in a mortgage pool that otherwise qualifies as a REMIC is held by two taxpayers, one of whom has a 25 percent interest in the residual and the other of whom has a 75 percent interest. Except for their relative size, the interests of the two taxpayers are identical. Provided that all distributions to the residual interest holders are pro rata, the mortgage pool would qualify as a REMIC because there is only one class of residual interest. If, however, the holder of the 25 percent interest is entitled to receive all distributions to which residual holders combined are entitled for a specified period (or up to a specified amount) in return for the surrender of his interest, then the mortgage pool would be considered to have two classes of residual interests and would not qualify as a REMIC.

The conferees intend that the right to receive payment from the REMIC for goods or services rendered in the ordinary operation of the REMIC would not be considered to be an interest in the REMIC for these purposes.

Inadvertent terminations

The conference agreement provides regulatory authority to the Treasury Department to issue regulations that address situations where failure to meet one or more of the requirements for REMIC status occurs inadvertently, and disqualification of the REMIC would occur absent regulatory relief. The conferees anticipate that the regulations would provide relief only where the failure to meet any of the requirements occurred inad-

vertently and in good faith. The conferees also intend that the relief may be accompanied by appropriate sanctions, such as the imposition of a corporate tax on all or a portion of the REMIC's income for the period of time in which the requirements are not met.

Transfers of property to the REM-IC.—Under the conference agreement, no gain or loss is recognized to the transferor upon the transfer of property to a REMIC in exchange for regular or residual interests in the REMIC. Upon such a transfer, the adjusted bases of the regular or residual interests received in the transaction are to be equal in the aggregate to the aggregate of the adjusted bases of the property transferred. The aggregate basis of the interests received is allocated among the regular or residual interests received in proportion to their fair market values.[8] The basis of any property received by a REMIC in exchange for regular or residual interests in the REMIC is equal to the fair market value of the property at the time of transfer (or earlier time provided by regulations).[9]

In the case of a REMIC that is not formed as a separate entity, but rather as a segregated pool of assets, the conferees intend that the transfer is deemed to occur and the REMIC is deemed to be formed only upon the issuance of regular and residual interests therein.

Federal income tax treatment of the REMIC.—*Pass-through status.*—In general, the conference agreement provides that a REMIC is not a taxable entity for Federal income tax purposes. The income of the REMIC generally is taken into account by holders of regular and residual interests in the REMIC as described below. Nevertheless, the REMIC is subject to tax on prohibited transactions, and may be required to withhold on amounts paid to foreign holders of regular or residual interests.

The pass-through status of the REMIC provided by the conference agreement applies regardless of whether the REMIC otherwise would be treated as a corporation, partnership, trust, or any other entity. The conferees intend that where the requirements for REMIC status are met, that the exclusive set of rules for the treatment of all transactions relating to the REMIC and of holders of interests therein are to be those set forth in the provisions of the conference agreement. Thus, for example, in the case of a REMIC that would be treated as a partnership if it were not otherwise a REMIC, the

---

[Footnote ¶ 3930 continued]

(7) The status of an interest as a regular interest in this case does not depend on whether the subordinated regular interest is sold or retained.

(8) The conferees intend that a holder of a mortgage should not be permitted to recognize loss where mortgages are indirectly transferred to a REMIC. Thus, the conferees intend that no gain or loss would be recognized, for example, if pursuant to a plan, mortgages are sold by one taxpayer to another, and the buyer transfers the purchased mortgages to a REMIC in which interests are purchased by the initial seller of the mortgages.

(9) The conferees intend that the regulations may provide that the basis of qualified mortgages held by the REMIC in certain circumstances may be determined based on the fair market value of such mortgages at a reasonable time prior to transfer to the REMIC where such mortgages were purchased by the transferor solely for the purpose of transfer to the REMIC.

provisions of subchapter K of the Code would not be applicable to any transactions involving the REMIC or any of the holders of regular or residual interests.[10]

Prohibited transactions

Under the conference agreement, a REMIC is required to pay a tax equal to 100 percent of the REMIC's net income from prohibited transactions. For this purpose, net income from prohibited transactions is computed without taking into account any losses from prohibited transactions or any deductions relating to prohibited transactions that result in a loss. Prohibited transactions for the REMIC include the disposition of any qualified mortgage other than pursuant to (1) the substitution of a qualified replacement mortgage for a defective qualified mortgage, (2) the bankruptcy or insolvency of the REMIC, (3) a disposition incident to the foreclosure, default, or imminent default of the mortgage, or (4) a qualified liquidation (described below). In addition, the disposition of a qualified mortgage is not a prohibited transaction if such disposition is required to prevent default on a regular interest where such default on the regular interest is threatened on account of a default on one or more qualified mortgages. Other prohibited transactions include the disposition of any cash flow investment other than pursuant to a qualified liquidation, the receipt of any income from assets other than assets permitted to be held by the REMIC, and the receipt of any compensation for services.[11]

Taxation of the holders of regular interests.—*In general.*—Under the conference agreement, holders of regular interests generally are taxed as if their regular interest were a debt instrument to which the rules of taxation generally applicable to debt instruments apply, except that the holder of a regular interest is required to account for income relating to such interest on the accrual method of accounting regardless of the method of accounting otherwise used by the holder.[12] In the case of regular interests that are not debt instruments, the amount of the fixed unconditional payment is treated as the stated principal amount of the instrument, and the periodic payments (i.e., the amounts that are based on the amount of the fixed unconditional payment), if any, are on the amount of the fixed unconditional payment), if any, are treated as stated interest payments. In other words, generally consistent with the pass-through nature of the REMIC, the holders of regular interests generally take into account that portion of the REMIC's income that would be taken into account by an accrual method holder of a debt instrument with terms equivalent to the terms of the regular interest.[13]

The conferees intend that regular interests are to be treated as if they were debt instruments for all other purposes of the Internal Revenue Code. Thus, for example, regular interests would be treated as market discount bonds, where the revised issue price (within the meaning of section 1278) of the regular interest exceeds the holder's basis in the interest. Moreover, the conferees intend that the REMIC is subject to the reporting requirements of section 1275 with respect to the regular interests. In addition, the conferees intend that regular interests are to be treated as evidences of indebtedness under section 582(c)(1), so that gain or loss from the sale or exchange of regular interests by certain financial institutions would not be treated as gain or loss from the sale or exchange of a capital asset. In addition, any market premium on a regular interest could be amortized currently under section 171.

The issue price of regular interests in the REMIC are determined under the rules of section 1273(b). In the case of regular interests issued in exchange for property, however, the issue price of the regular interest is equal to the fair market value of the property,[14] regardless of whether the requirements of section 1273(b)(3) are met. A holder's basis in the regular interest generally is equal to the holder's cost therefor, but in the case of holders who received their interests in exchange for property, then as discussed above, the holder's basis is equal to basis of the property exchanged for the REMIC interest. Where property is transferred in exchange for more than one class of regular or residual interest, the basis of the property transferred is allocated in proportion to the fair market value of the interests received.

Regular interests received in exchange for property

Under the conference agreement, where an exchange of property for regular interests in a REMIC has taken place, any excess of the issue price of the regular interest over the basis of the interest in the hands of the transferor immediately after the transfer is, for periods during which such interest is held by the transferor (or any other person whose basis is determined in whole or in part by

---

〖Footnote ¶ 3930 continued〗

(10) For purposes of subtitle F of the Code (relating to certain administrative matters) the REMIC is treated as a partnership in which residual interests are the partnership interests, however. The conferees intend that the initial election of REMIC status is to be made on the first partnership information return that the REMIC is required to file.

(11) The conferees intend that payment by the obligor on a debt instrument is not to be considered to be a disposition of such debt instrument for these purposes.

(12) The conferees intend that periodic payments of interest (or similar amounts) are to be treated as accruing pro rata between the dates that such interest (or similar amounts) is paid.

(13) In the event that the amount so determined exceeds the income of the REMIC, however, there is no diminution of the required inclusions for such holders.

(14) For this purpose, the conferees intend that the fair market value of the property is to be determined by reference to the fair market value of the regular interests received in exchange.

reference to the basis of such interest in the hands of the transferor), includible currently in the gross income of the holder under rules similar to the rules of section 1276(b) (i.e., the holder of such an interest is treated like the holder of a market discount bond for which an election under section 1278(b) is in effect). Conversely, the excess of the basis of the regular interest in the hands of the transferor immediately after the transfer over the issue price of the interest is treated for such holders as market premium that is allowable as a deduction under rules similar to the rules of section 171.

Disposition of regular interests

The conference agreement treats gain on the disposition of a regular interest as ordinary income to the extent of a portion of unaccrued OID with respect to the interest. Such portion generally is the amount of unaccrued OID equal to the excess, if any, of the amount that would have been includible in the gross income of the taxpayer with respect to such interest if the yield on such interest were 110 percent of the applicable Federal rate (as defined in sec. 1274(d) without regard to paragraph (2) thereof) determined as of the time that the interest is acquired by the taxpayer, over the total amount of ordinary income includible by the taxpayer with respect to such regular interest prior to disposition. In selecting the applicable Federal rate, the conferees intend that the same prepayment assumptions that are used in calculating OID are to be used in determining the maturity of the regular interest.

Taxation of the holders of residual interests.—*In general.*—In general, the conference agreement provides that at the end of each calendar quarter, the holder of a residual interest in a REMIC takes into account his daily portion of the taxable income or net loss of the REMIC for each day during the holder's taxable year in which such holder held such interest. The amount so taken into account is treated as ordinary income or loss. The daily portion for this purpose is determined by allocating to each day in any calendar quarter a ratable portion of the taxable income or net loss of the REMIC for such quarter, and by allocating the amounts so allocated to any day among the holders (on such day) of residual interests in proportion to their respective holdings on such day.

For example, a REMIC's taxable income for a calendar quarter (determined as described below) is $1,000. There are two holders of residual interests in the REMIC. One holder of 60 percent of the residual holds such interest for the entire calendar quarter. Another holder has a 40 percent interest, and transfers the interest after exactly one half of the calendar quarter to another taxpayer. As of the end of the calendar quarter, the holder

of the sixty percent interest would be treated as receiving $600 ratably over the quarter. Each holder of the 40 percent interest would be treated as receiving $200 ratably over the portion of the quarter in which the interest was held.

Distributions from the REMIC are not included in the gross income of the residual holder to the extent that such distributions do not exceed the adjusted basis of the interest. To the extent that distributions exceed the adjusted basis of the interest, the excess is treated as gain from the sale of the residual interest. Residual interests are treated as evidences of indebtedness for purposes of section 582(c).

The amount of any net loss of the REMIC that may be taken into account by the holder of a residual interest is limited to the adjusted basis of the interest as of the close of the quarter (or time of disposition of the interest if earlier), determined without taking into account the net loss for the quarter. Any loss that is disallowed on account of this limitation may be carried over indefinitely by the holder of the interest for whom such loss was disallowed and may be used by such holder only to offset any income generated by the same REMIC.

Except for adjustments arising from the nonrecognition of gain or loss on the transfer of mortgages to the REMIC (discussed below), the holders of residual interests take no amounts into account other than those allocated from the REMIC.[15]

Determination of REMIC taxable income or net loss

In general, under the conference agreement, the taxable income or net loss of the REMIC for purposes of determining the amounts taken into account by holders of residual interests, is determined in the same manner as for an individual having the calendar year as his taxable year and using the accrual method of accounting, with certain modifications. The first modification is that a deduction is allowed with respect to those amounts that would be deductible as interest if the regular interests in the REMIC were treated as indebtedness of the REMIC. Second, in computing the gross income of the REMIC, market discount with respect to any market discount bond (within the meaning of sec. 1278) held by the REMIC is includible for the year in which such discount accrues, as determined under the rules of section 1276(b)(2), and sections 1276(a) and 1277 do not apply. Third, no item of income, gain, loss, or deduction allocable to a prohibited transaction is taken into account. Fourth, deductions under section 703(a)(2) (other

[Footnote ¶ 3930 continued] (15) The conferees understand that the taxable income allocated to holders of residual interests in a REMIC who purchased such interests from a prior holder after a significant change in value of the interest, could be substantially accelerated or deferred on account of any premium or discount in the price paid by such purchaser. Accordingly, the conferees recognize that certain modifications of the rules governing taxation of holders of residual interests may be appropriate where the method of taxation of holders of residual interests prescribed by the conference agreement has such consequences.

than deductions allowable under section 212) are not allowed.[16]

If a REMIC distributes property with respect to any regular or residual interest, the REMIC recognizes gain in the same manner as if the REMIC had sold the property to such distributee at its fair market value. The conferees intend that the distribution is to be treated as an actual sale by the REMIC for purposes of applying the prohibited transaction rules and the rules relating to qualified reserve funds. The basis of the distributed property in the hands of the distributee is then the fair market value of the property.

Adjusted basis of residual interests

Under the conference agreement, a holder's basis in a residual interest in a REMIC is increased by the amount of the taxable income of the REMIC that is taken into account by the holder. The basis of such an interest is decreased (but not below zero) by the amount of any distributions received from the REMIC and by the amount of any net loss of the REMIC that is taken into account by the holder. In the case of a holder who disposes of a residual interest, the basis adjustment on account of the holder's daily portions of the REMIC's taxable income or net loss is deemed to occur immediately before the disposition.

Special treatment of a portion of residual income

Under the conference agreement, a portion of the net income of the REMIC taken into account by the holders of the residual interests may not be offset by any net operating losses of the holder. The conference agreement provides a special exception from this rule in the case of certain thrift institutions, on account of the difficulties currently being experienced by such industry.

In addition, the conference agreement provides that the same portion of the net income of the REMIC that may not be offset by net operating losses, is treated as unrelated business income for any organization subject to the unrelated business income tax under section 511, and is not eligible for any reduction in the rate of withholding tax (by treaty or otherwise) in the case of a nonresident alien holder.

The portion of the income of the residual holder that is subject to these rules is the excess, if any, of the amount of the net income of the REMIC that the holder takes into account for any calendar quarter, over the sum of the daily accruals with respect to such interest while held by such holder. The daily accrual for any residual interest for any day in any calendar quarter is determined by allocating to each day in such calendar quarter a ratable portion of the product of

the adjusted issue price of the residual interest at the beginning of such accrual period, and 120 percent of the long-term Federal rate. The long-term Federal rate used for this purpose is the Federal long-term rate that would have applied to the residual interest under section 1274(d) (without regard to section 1274(d)(2)) if it were a debt instrument, determined at the time that the residual interest is issued. The rate is adjusted appropriately in order to be applied on the basis of compounding at the end of each quarter.

For this purpose, (and for purposes of the treatment of gain or loss that is not recognized upon the transfer of property to a REMIC in exchange for a residual interest, as discussed below), the residual interest is treated as having an issue price that is equal to the amount of money paid for the interest at the time it is issued, or in the case of a residual interest that is issued in exchange for property, the fair market value of the interest at the time it is issued. The adjusted issue price of the residual interest is equal to the issue price of the interest increased by the amount of daily accruals for prior calendar quarters, and decreased (but not below zero) by the amount of any distributions with respect to the residual interest prior to the end of the calendar quarter.

In addition, the conference agreement provides that under regulations, if a REIT owns a residual interest in a REMIC, a portion of dividends paid by the REIT would be treated as excess inclusions for REIT shareholders. Thus, such income could not be offset by net operating losses, would constitute unrelated business taxable income for tax-exempt holders, and would not be eligible for and reduction in the rate of withholding tax in the case of a nonresident alien holder.

The conference agreement provides that to the extent provided in regulations, in the case of a residual interest that *** does not have significant value, the entire amount of income that is taken into account by the holder of the residual interest is treated as unrelated business income and is subject to withholding at the statutory rate. In addition, in the case of such a residual, income allocated to the holder thereof may not be offset by any net operating losses, regardless of who holds the interest. The conferees intend that the regulations would take into account the value of the residual interest in relation to the regular interests, and that the regulations would not apply in cases where the value of the residual interest is at least

---

[Footnote ¶ 3930 continued]

(16) The conferees intend that no gain or loss is recognized to the REMIC on the exchange of regular or residual interests in the REMIC for property. In addition, the conferees understand that the treatment of deductions allowable under section 212 will be addressed in Treasury regulations. In this regard, the conferees intend that such deductions would be allocated to all holders of interests in REMICs that are similar to single-class grantor trusts under present law. However, the conferees intend that such deductions would be allocated to the holders of the residual interests in the case of other REMICs.

Act § 671-675 **¶ 3930**

two percent of the combined value of the regular and residual interests.[17]

The conference agreement provides that the partnership information return filed by the REMIC is to supply information relating to the daily accruals of the REMIC.

Treatment of foreign residual holders

The conference agreement provides that in the case of a holder of a residual interest of a REMIC who is a nonresident alien individual or foreign corporation, then for purposes of sections 871(a), 881, 1441, and 1442, amounts includible in the gross income of such holder with respect to the residual interest are taken into account only when paid or otherwise distributed (or when the interest is disposed of).[18] The conference agreement also provides that under regulations, the amounts includible may be taken into account earlier than otherwise provided where necessary to prevent avoidance of tax. The conferees intend that this regulatory authority may be exercised where the residual interest in the REMIC does not have significant value (as described above).

Residual interests received in exchange for property

In the case of a residual interest that is received in exchange for property, any excess of the issue price of the residual interest over the basis of the interest in the hands of the transferor of the property immediately after the transfer, is amortized and is included in the residual holder's income on a straight line basis over the expected life of the REMIC. Similarly, any excess of the transferor's basis in the residual interest over the issue price of the interest is deductible by the holder of the interest on a straight line basis over the expected life of the REMIC. In determining the expected life of the REMIC for this purpose, the conferees intend that the assumptions used in calculating original issue discount and any binding agreement regarding liquidation of the REMIC are to be taken into account.

Dispositions of residual interests

The conference agreement provides that, except as provided in regulations, the wash sale rules of section 1091 apply to dispositions of residual interests in a REMIC where the seller of the interest, during the period beginning six months before the sale or disposition of the residual interest and ending six months after such sale or disposition, acquires (or enters into any other transaction that results in the application of section 1091) any residual interest in any REMIC or any interest in a "taxable mortgage pool" (discussed below) that is comparable to a residual interest.

Liquidation of the REMIC.—Under the conference agreement, if a REMIC adopts a plan of complete liquidation, and sells all of its assets (other than cash) within the 90-day period beginning on the date of the adoption of the plan of liquidation, then the REMIC recognizes no gain or loss on the sale of its assets, provided that the REMIC distributes in liquidation all of the sale proceeds plus its cash (other than amounts retained to meet claims) to holders of regular and residual interests within the 90-day period.

Other provisions—*Compliance provisions.*—The application of the OID rules contemplated by the conference agreement requires calculations that are based on information that would not necessarily be known by any holder, and is more readily available to the issuer than any other person. Accordingly, the conference agreement requires broader reporting of interest payments and OID accrual by the REMIC, or any issuer of debt that is subject to the OID rules of the conference agreement. The conference agreement specifies that the amounts includible in gross income of the holder of a regular interest in a REMIC are treated as interest for purposes of the reporting requirements of the Code (sec. 6049), and that the REMIC or similar issuer is required to report interest and OID to a broader group of holders than is required under present law. The holders to whom such broader reporting is required include corporations, certain dealers in commodities or securities, real estate investment trusts, common trust funds, and certain other trusts. In addition to reporting interest and OID, the REMIC or similar issuer is required to report sufficient information to allow holders to compute the accrual of any market discount or amortization of any premium in accordance with provisions of the conference agreement.[19]

Treatment of REMIC interests for certain financial institutions and real estate investment trusts

Under the conference agreement, regular and residual interests are treated as qualifying real property loans for purposes of section 593(d)(1) and section 7701(a)(19), in the same proportion that the assets of the REMIC would be treated as qualifying real property loans.[20] In the case of residual interests, the conferees intend that the amount treated as a qualifying real property loan not exceed the adjusted basis of the residual interest in the hands of the holder. Both regular and residual interests are treated as real estate assets under section 856(c)(6) in the same proportion that the assets of the REMIC would be treated as real estate assets for purposes of

---

[Footnote ¶ 3930 continued] (17) The conferees intend that these regulations may apply in appropriate cases to residual interests issued before regulations are issued.

(18) The conferees intend that withholding upon disposition of such interests is to be similar to withholding upon disposition of debt instruments that have original issue discount.

(19) See sec. 1803(a)(13) of the conference agreement.

(20) If 95 percent of the assets of the REMIC would be treated as qualifying real property loans at all times during a calendar year then the entire regular or residual interest is so treated for the calendar year.

determining eligibility for real estate investment trust status.[21] In the case of a residual interest, the fair market value of the residual interest, and not the fair market value of all of the REMIC's assets, is used in applying the asset test of section 856(c)(5). In addition, income derived from the holding of a regular or residual interest in a REMIC is treated as interest for a real estate investment trust.

Foreign withholding

The conferees intend that for purposes of withholding on interest paid to foreign persons, regular interests in REMICs should be considered to be debt instruments that are issued after July 18, 1984, regardless of the time that any debt instruments held by the REMIC were issued. The conferees intend that amounts paid to foreign persons with respect to residual interests should be considered to be interest for purposes of applying the withholding rules.

OID rules.—The conference agreement provides rules relating to the application of the OID rules to debt instruments that, as is generally the case with regular interests in a REMIC, have a maturity that is initially fixed, but that is accelerated based on prepayments on other debt obligations securing the debt instrument (or., to the extent provided in regulations, by reason of other events). The OID rules provided by the conference agreement also apply to OID on qualified mortgages held by a REMIC.

In general, the OID rules provided by the conference agreement require OID for an accrual period to be calculated and included in the holder's income based on the increase in the present value of remaining payments on the debt instrument, taking into account payments includible in the instrument's stated redemption price at maturity received on the regular interest during the period. For this purpose, the present value calculation is made at the beginning of each accrual period (1) using the yield to maturity determined for the instrument at the time of its issuance (determined on the basis of compounding at the close of each accrual period and properly adjusted for the length of the accrual period), calculated on the assumption that, as prescribed by regulations, certain prepayments will occur, and (2) taking into account any prepayments that have occurred before the close of the accrual period.

The conferees intend that the regulations will provide that the prepayment assumption to be used in calculating present values as of the close of each accrual period, and in computing the yield to maturity used in the calculation of such present values, will be that used by the parties in pricing the particular transaction. The conferees intend that such prepayment assumption will be determined by the assumed rate of prepayments on qualified mortgages held by the REMIC and also the assumed rate of earnings on the temporary investment of payments on such mortgages insofar as such rate of earnings would affect the timing of payments on regular interests.[22]

The conferees intend that the regulations will require these pricing assumptions to be specified in the first partnership return filed by the REMIC. In addition, the conferees intend that appropriate supporting documentation relating to the selection of the prepayment assumption must be supplied to the Internal Revenue Service with such return. Further, the conferees intend that the prepayment assumptions used must not be unreasonable based on comparable transactions, if comparable transactions exist.[23]

The conferees intend that unless otherwise provided by regulations, the use of a prepayment assumption based on a recognized industry standard would be permitted. For example, the conferees understand that prepayment assumptions based on a Public Securities Association standard currently is such an industry recognized standard.

The conferees intend that in no circumstances, would the method of accruing OID prescribed by the conference agreement allow for negative amounts of OID to be attributed to any accrual period. If the use of the present value computations prescribed by the conference agreement produce such a result for an accrual period, the conferees intend that the amount of OID attributable to such accrual period would be treated as zero, and the computation of OID for the following accrual period would be made as if such following accrual period and the preceding accrual period were a single accrual period.

Regulatory authority.—The conference agreement grants the Treasury Department authority to prescribe such regulations as are necessary or appropriate to implement the provisions relating to REMICs. The conferees expect that, among other things, regulations will be issued to prevent unreasonable accumulations of assets in the REMIC, to require the REMIC to report information adequate to

---

[Footnote ¶ 3930 continued]

(21) If 95 percent of the assets of the REMIC would be treated as real estate assets at all times during a calendar year, then the entire regular or residual is so treated for the calendar year.

(22) In computing the accrual of OID (or market discount) on qualified mortgages held by the REMIC, only assumptions about the rate of prepayments on such mortgages would be taken into account.

(23) The conferees intend that in the case of publicly offered instruments, a prepayment assumption will be treated as unreasonable only in the presence of clear and convincing evidence. In addition, the conferees intend that in determining whether a prepayment assumption is reasonable, the nature of the debt instruments on which prepayments are being assumed, and the availability of information about prepayments thereon, will be taken into account. Thus, for example, under currently prevailing conditions, the conferees understand that there should be less tolerance in the evaluation of prepayment assumptions relating to pools of home mortgages than prepayment assumptions relating to pools of commercial mortgages.

allow residual holders to compute taxable income accurately (including reporting more frequently than annually). Further, such regulations may require reporting of OID accrual more frequently tha·. otherwise required by the conference agreement.

Treasury study.—The conferees are concerned about the impact of the REMIC provisions upon the thrift industry. Accordingly, the conferees request that the Treasury Department conduct a study of the effectiveness of the REMIC provisions in enhancing the efficiency of the secondary market in mortgages, and the impact of these provisions upon thrift institutions.

Taxable mortgage pools.—The conferees intend that REMICs are to be the exclusive means of issuing multiple class real estate mortgage-backed securities without the imposition of two levels of taxation. Thus, the conference agreement provides that a "taxable mortgage pool" ("TMP") is treated as a taxable corporation that is not an includible corporation for purposes of filing consolidated returns.

Under the conference agreement, a TMP is any entity other than a REMIC if (1) substantially all of the assets of the entity consist of debt obligations (or interests in debt obligations) and more than 50 percent of such obligations (or interests) consist of real estate mortgages, (2) such entity is the obligor under debt obligations with two or more maturities,[24] and (3) under the terms of such debt obligations on which the entity is the obligor, payment on such debt obligations on which the entity is the obligor, payment on such debt obligations bear a relationship to payments on the debt obligations (or interests therein) held by the entity.[25] Typically, the relationship between the assets of the entity and its debt obligations would be such that payments on the debt obligations must be made within a period of time from when payments on the assets are received.

Under the conference agreement, any portion of an entity that meets the definition of a TMP is treated as a TMP. For example, if an entity segregates mortgages in some fashion and issues debt obligations in two or more maturities, which maturities depend upon the timing of payments on the mortgages, then the mortgages and the debt would be treated as a TMP, and hence as a separate corporation. The TMP provisions are intended to apply to any arrangement under which mortgages are segregated from a debtor's business activities (if any) for the benefit of creditors whose loans are of varying maturities.

The conference agreement provides that no domestic building and loan association (or portion thereof) is to be treated as a TMP.

Special rule for REITs

The conferees intend that an entity that otherwise would be treated as a TMP may, if it otherwise meets applicable requirements, elect to be treated as a REIT. If so, the conference agreement provides that under regulations, a portion of the REIT's income would be treated in the same manner as income subject to the special rules provided for a portion of the income of [*** an] interest in a REMIC. The conferees intend that this calculation is to be made as if the equity interests in the REIT were the residual interest in a REMIC and such interests were issued (i.e., the issue price of interests is determined) as of the time that the REIT becomes a TMP.[26]

The conferees intend that the regulations would provide that dividends paid to the shareholders of a REIT would be subject to the same rules provided for a portion of the income of holders of residual interests in a REMIC. Thus, for example, the conferees intend that the regulations would provide that to the extent that dividends from the REIT exceed the daily accruals for the REIT (determined in the same manner as if the REIT were a REMIC) such dividends (1) may not be offset by net operating losses (except those of certain thrift institutions), (2) are treated as unrelated business income for certain tax-exempt institutions, and (3) are not eligible for any reduction in the rate of withholding when paid to foreign persons. The conferees also intend that the regulations would require a REIT to report such amounts to its shareholders.[27]

Effective Date.—The provisions of the conference agreement are effective with respect to taxable years beginning after December 31, 1986. The amendments made by the conference agreement to the OID rules apply to debt instruments issued after December 31, 1986. The provisions relating to taxable mortgage pools do not apply to any entity in existence on December 31, 1991, unless there is a substantial transfer of cash or property to such entity (other than in payment of obligations held by the entity) after such date. For purposes of applying the wash sale rules provided by the conference agreement, however, the definition of a TMP is applicable to any interest in any entity in existence on or after January 1, 1986.

[Footnote ¶ 3930 continued]

(24) For this purpose, the conferees intend that debt instruments that may have the same stated maturity but different rights relating to acceleration of that maturity, are to be treated as having different maturities. In addition, the conference agreement provides that to the extent provided in regulations, equity interests of varying classes that correspond to differing maturity classes of debt are to be treated as debt for these purposes.

(25) For example, certain arrangements that are commonly known as "Owners' Trusts" would be treated as TMPs under the bill.

(26) If a portion of a REIT is treated as a TMP, such portion may qualify as a REIT subsidiary (see sec. 662 of the Act).

(27) If the REIT has a REIT subsidiary that is a TMP, then the conferees intend that the portion of the REIT's income that is subject to the special rules is determined based on calculations made at the level of the REIT subsidiary.

[¶ 3931] SECTION 701. ALTERNATIVE MINIMUM TAX FOR INDIVID-UALS AND CORPORATIONS

(Secs. 53, 55-59, 6154(c), 6425(c), 6655(f) of the Code)

[Conference Report]

* * * * * *

A. Individual Minimum Tax

1. Structure

* * * * * *

[Senate Explanation]

* * * * * *

Individuals.—The structure for the alternative minimum tax on individuals generally is the same as under present law, except that adjustments are permitted in order to reflect the fact that certain deferral preferences (such as accelerated depreciation) cannot be treated simply as add-ons if total income is to be computed properly over time. For such preferences, the minimum tax deduction may in some instances exceed the regular tax deduction (e.g., in the later years of an asset's life), thus insuring that basis will be fully recovered under both the regular and the minimum tax systems. The alternative minimum tax on individuals differs from that applying to corporations in several respects. For example, there are some differences between the preferences applying to individuals and those applying to corporations, and certain itemized deductions that individuals can claim for regular tax purposes are not allowable under the minimum tax.

* * * * * *

[Conference Report]

The conference agreement follows * * * the Senate amendment.

2. Tax Rate

* * * * * *

The conference agreement provides for a minimum tax rate of 21 percent.

3. Exemption Amount

[Senate Explanation]

* * * * * *

While the exemption amounts for individuals under present law generally are retained, they are reduced (but not below zero) by 25 percent of the amount by which alternative minimum taxable income exceeds $150,000. For married taxpayers filing separately and for trusts, the phaseout begins at $75,000; for single taxpayers the phaseout begins at $112,500.

* * * * * *

[Conference Report]

The conference agreement follows the Senate amendment.

4. Tax Preferences

* * * * * *

b. Accelerated depreciation on real property

* * * * * *

[Senate Explanation]

* * * * * *

Depreciation.—Accelerated depreciation (ACRS) on real and personal property placed in service after 1986, to the extent in excess of depreciation calculated under an alternative method, is treated as a preference.[5] The amount of the preference is calculated, with respect to such new property, by making adjustments similar to the types of adjustments that are made in determining the depreciation allowable with respect to earnings and profits. That is, instead of making preference adjustments with respect to specific items of property in the amount by which the ACRS deduction exceeds the alternative deduction, the alternative depreciation deduction is substituted for the ACRS deduction for all property placed in service after 1986. The principal effect of this system is that it permits "netting", i.e. to the extent that, for a particular year, an alternative deduction relating to an item of property exceeds the ACRS deduction for that year, the amount of the preference is reduced.[6]

Consider, as an example that does not reflect the actual details of the ACRS and alternative depreciation systems, the case of a taxpayer who was permitted to deduct fully a $10 expense in the year that the property to which the expense related was placed in service, but who was required to write off the expense over two years for purposes of the alternative depreciation system. For that taxpayer, assuming there were no other differences between the taxpayer's regular and minimum taxable income, regular taxable income would be $5 less than minimum taxable income for the year in which the property was placed in service. In the following taxable year, however, the taxpayer's regular taxable income would be $5 greater than minimum taxable income (because no further ACRS deduction would remain with respect to the property, whereas the taxpayer would still be entitled to write off the last $5 of basis under the alternative system). If the taxpayer also had a separate preference in the amount of $5 in the second year, the taxpayer's regular and minimum taxable

---

[Footnote ¶ 3931] (5) The preference does not apply, however, to property that is expended under section 179.

(6) Alternative deductions exceed ACRS deductions in the later years of the useful life of an item of property for which ACRS is allowed; i.e., at such time the ACRS deduction is understated because it has been overstated in prior taxable years.

incomes would be equivalent in that year (whether or not that second item related to depreciation).

Regular tax depreciation with respect to property placed in service prior to 1987 is treated as a preference only to the extent that it constitutes a preference under present law. Thus, for example, for pre-1987 personal property, regular tax depreciation is a corporate tax preference only in the case of leased personal property in the hands of a personal holding company. In addition, present law rules apply to the measurement of depreciation preferences relating to pre-1987 property. Thus, for example, present law rules for measuring the amount of depreciation that constitutes a preference continue to apply to pre-1987 property, and preferences relating to such property continue to be measured on an item-by-item basis, rather than under the netting system described above.

For property placed in service after 1986, alternative depreciation generally is defined as straight-line depreciation over the ADR midpoint life of the property (forty years in the case of real estate). A similar depreciation system presently is used and will continue to be used with respect to property leased by a taxable entity to a tax-exempt entity. Under the bill, the alternative depreciation system applies for certain other purposes as well (including the measurement of depreciation for determining earnings and profits and with respect to property placed in service outside of the United States). Since taxpayers can elect to use this depreciation system for regular tax purposes, no minimum tax adjustment to income is made to the extent that any such election applies. (A complete description of the alternative depreciation system is described in the portion of the report describing the bill's provisions in the area of depreciation.)

As an exception to the general rule treating ACRS on post-1986 property as a preference, no adjustment is made for minimum tax purposes with respect to certain property described in paragraph (1), (2), (3), or (4) of section 168(f) (e.g., generally property depreciated under the income forecast method, etc.).[7] Property placed in service after 1986 that qualifies for a transitional exception to section 201 of the bill is excepted from the bill's minimum tax provisions for post-1986 property as well.

For all depreciable property to which minimum tax adjustments apply, adjusted basis is determined for minimum tax purposes with reference to the amount of depreciation allowed for minimum tax purposes under the alternative system. Thus, the amount of gain on the disposition of such property will differ for regular and minimum tax purposes.

*   *   *   *   *   *

[Conference Report]

*   *   *   *   *   *

The conference agreement generally follows the Senate amendment, as conformed to the alternative depreciation provision described in the depreciation section of this report. However, for property other than (1) section 1250 property and (2) property with respect to which the taxpayer elects or is required to use a straightline method for regular tax purposes, minimum tax depreciation uses the 150 percent declining balance method (switching to straightline in the year necessary to maximize the allowance) over the alternative depreciation life.

*   *   *   *   *   *

c. Accelerated depreciation on personal property

[See *Senate Explanation* in (b.) above. Ed.]
[Conference Report]

*   *   *   *   *   *

The conference agreement generally follows the Senate amendment, as conformed to the alternative depreciation provision described in the depreciation section of this report. However, for property other than that with respect to which the taxpayer elects or is required to use a straightline method for regular tax purposes, minimum tax depreciation uses the 150 percent declining balance method (switching to straightline in the year necessary to maximize the allowance) over the alternative depreciation life. The preference, computed using the useful life under the alternative depreciation system, applies to property placed in service in 1986 with respect to which the taxpayer elects the application of section 201 of the Act.

d. Expensing of intangible drilling costs

*   *   *   *   *   *

[House Explanation]

*   *   *   *   *   *

Intangible drilling costs.—The preference for intangible drilling costs is generally the same as the present law preference for individuals, except that 65 percent, rather than 100 percent, of net oil and gas income may offset the preference. Thus, the amount of excess intangible drilling costs is treated as a preference to the extent that it exceeds 65 percent of the taxpayer's net income from oil, gas, and geothermal properties. Net oil and gas income is determined without regard to deductions for excess intangible drilling costs. Under this rule, for example, a taxpayer with $100 of net oil and gas income (disregarding excess intangible drilling costs) and $80 of excess intangible drilling costs would be required to treat such costs as a preference in the amount of $15 ($80 excess IDC less $65 net income offset).

The amount of excess intangible drilling costs is defined as the amount of the excess, if any, of the taxpayer's regular tax deduction for such costs (deductible under either section 263 (c) or (i) or 291) over the normative

---

[Footnote ¶ 3931 continued]

(7) With respect to public utility property, taxpayers are required to use a normalization method of accounting in order to depreciate such property under the alternative system. The Secretary shall prescribe the requirements of a normalization method of accounting in this context.

deduction, i.e., the amount that would have been allowable if the taxpayer had amortized the costs over ten years on a straight-line basis or through cost depletion. The preference does not apply to costs incurred with respect to a non-productive well.

In applying the preference for intangible drilling costs, a taxpayer's property (as under present law for individuals) is divided into two parts: properties that are geothermal deposits, and all other properties with respect to which intangible drilling costs are incurred. This separation applies for all purposes under the minimum tax. Consider, for example, the case of a taxpayer who has (1) oil wells with net oil and gas income of $100 and excesss intangible drilling costs of $80, and (2) geothermal deposits with net income of $100 and excess intangible drilling costs of $40. This taxpayer has a preference in the amount of $15 with respect to the oil wells, and no preference with respect to the geothermal deposits.

With respect to intangible drilling costs for any well, the taxpayer may elect the use of any method which would be permitted for purposes of determining cost depletion with respect to such well. To be effective, such an election must be made at such time and in such manner as prescribed by the Secretary in regulations. Once made, such an election applies, with respect to the costs subject to it, for all regular and minimum tax purposes. Thus, costs recovered under this method are not treated as a minimum tax preference.

In the case of a disposition of any oil, gas, or geothermal property to which section 1254 generally would apply, or of any mining property to which section 616(c) generally would apply, if the taxpayer makes an election as described above (or to the extent of a normative election, as described below), amounts deducted pursuant to the election are treated as deducted for purposes of section 1254 or section 616(c), as the case may be.

*   *   *   *   *   *

[Conference Report]

*   *   *   *   *   *

The conference agreement follows the House bill.

e. 60-month amortization on certified pollution control facilities

*   *   *   *   *   *

[Senate Explanation]

Amortization of certified pollution control facilities.—As under present law, rapid amortization of a certified pollution control facility is treated as a preference. For such facilities placed in service after 1986, the preference is treated under a rule similar to that for post-1986 depreciable property generally, i.e., the taxpayer is required to use the alternative recovery system for minimum tax purposes.

[Conference Report]

*   *   *   *   *   *

The conference agreement follow the Senate amendment.

f. Expensing of mining exploration and development costs

*   *   *   *   *   *

[Senate Explanation]

*   *   *   *   *   *

Mining exploration and development costs.—Mining exploration and development costs, incurred after 1986, that are expensed (or amortized under section 291) for regular tax purposes are required to be recovered through ten-year straight line amortization for purposes of the alternative minimum tax. As with depreciation, the minimum tax treatment of mining exploration and development costs involves a separate calculation for all items of income and expense relating to such costs. Thus, for example, in the case of a noncorporate taxpayer who incurred a one-time mining exploration and development expense in the amount of $100, the regular tax deduction would be $100 in the year when the expenditure was incurred, and the minimum tax deduction would be $10 for each of the ten years beginning in the year when the expenditure was incurred. The basis of property with respect to which such costs were incurred, and the amount of gain or loss upon disposition, likewise may differ for regular and minimum tax purposes, respectively.

Under this approach, when a loss is sustained with respect to a mining property (e.g., the mine is abandoned as worthless, giving rise to a loss under section 165), the taxpayer is permitted to deduct, for minimum tax purposes, all mining exploration and development costs relating to that property that have been amortized and not yet written off under the minimum tax. The preference applies to personal holding companies as well as to individuals.

*   *   *   *   *   *

[Conference Report]

The conference agreement follows *** the Senate amendment.

g. Expensing of circulation expenditures (for newspapers, magazines, etc.)

*   *   *   *   *   *

[Senate Explanation1]

Circulation expenditures.–An individual who incurs circulation expenditures described in section 173 is not permitted to expense his post-1986 expenditures for minimum tax purposes. Instead, in computing alternative minimum taxable income, the taxpayer is required to amortize such post-1986 expenditures ratably over a three-year period. However, if the taxpayer realizes a loss with respect to property to which any such expenditures relate, all such expenditures relating to that property but not yet deducted for minimum tax purposes are allowed as a minimum tax deduction. The preference applies to personal holding companies as well as to individuals.

For example, an individual who incurred such expenditures in the amount of $30 would claim a regular tax deduction for the entire amount in the year when the expenditures were incurred, and would claim alternative minimum tax deductions of $10 for that year and the two succeeding taxable years. However, if the newspaper to which the expenditures related ceased operations in the second year, the entire $20 which was not allowed as a minimum tax deduction in the first year would be allowed for minimum tax purposes in the second year.

[Conference Report]

The conference agreement follows * * * the Senate amendment.

h. Expensing of research and experimentation expenditures

[Senate Explanation]

*   *   *   *   *   *

Research and experimental expenditures.—An individual who incurs research and experimental expenditures described in section 174 is not permitted to expense the expenditures for minimum tax purposes. Instead, in computing alternative minimum taxable income, the taxpayer is required to amortize such post-1986 expenditures over a ten-year period. As with certain other items (such as depreciation and mining exploration and development costs), this treatment applies for all minimum tax purposes, rather than as an annual adjustment to regular taxable income. If the taxpayer abandons a specific project to which any such expenditures relate, all such expenditures relating to that property but not yet deducted for minimum tax purposes are allowed as a minimum tax deduction.

For example, an individual who incurred research and experimental expenditures in the amount of $100 would claim a regular tax deduction for the entire amount in the year when the expenditures were incurred (absent a section 174(b) election), and would claim alternative minimum tax deductions of $10 for that year and the nine succeeding taxable years. However, if the taxpayer abandoned the specific project to which the expenditures related in the second year, the entire $90 which was not allowed as a minimum tax deduction in the first year would be allowed for minimum tax purposes in the second year.

[Conference Report]

*   *   *   *   *   *

The conference agreement follows * * * the Senate amendment.

i. Percentage depletion

*   *   *   *   *   *

Percentage depletion.—As under present law, the excess of the regular tax deduction allowable for depletion over the adjusted basis of the property at the end of the taxable year (determined without regard to the depletion deduction for the taxable year) is treated as a preference. Thus, for example, a taxpayer who claimed a deduction for percentage depletion in the amount of $50, with respect to property having a basis (disregarding this deduction) of $10, would have a minimum tax preference in the amount of $40.

[Conference Report]

*   *   *   *   *   *

The conference agreement follows * * * the Senate amendment.

j. Net capital gain deduction

*   *   *   *   *   *

Senate Amendment

Under the Senate amendment, the net capital gain deduction is repealed for regular tax purposes, and net capital gains accordingly are fully included in minimum taxable income.

Conference Agreement

The conference agreement follows the Senate amendment.

k. Incentive stock options

*   *   *   *   *   *

[Senate Explanation]

*   *   *   *   *   *

Incentive stock options.—As under present law, in the case of a transfer of a share of stock pursuant to the exercise of an incentive stock option (as defined in section 422A), the amount by which the fair market value of the share at the time of the exercise exceeds the option price is treated as a preference. For purposes of this rule, the fair market value of a share is determined without regard to any restrictions other than one which, by its terms, will never lapse.

[Conference Report]

*   *   *   *   *   *

The conference agreement generally follows the House bill and the Senate amendment. However, for minimum tax purposes, the basis of stock acquired through the exercise of an incentive stock option after 1986 equals the fair market value taken into account in determining the amount of the preference.

Assume, for example, that an individual pays an exercise price of $10 to purchase stock having a fair market value of $15. The preference in the year of exercise is equal to $5, and the stock has a basis of $10 for regular tax purposes and $15 for minimum tax purposes. If, in a subsequent year, the taxpayer sells the stock for $20, the gain recognized is $10 for regular tax purposes and $5 for minimum tax purposes.

1. Tax-exempt interest

[House Explanation]

* * * * * *

Tax-exempt interest on nonessential function bonds.—Interest on certain tax-exempt bonds issued after December 31, 1985 is treated as a preference. This rule applies only with respect to nonessential function bonds, the interest on which is exempt from taxation under section 103. In general, nonessential function bonds are those bonds that are subject to the unified volume limitation in new Code section 145.

For purposes of this rule, interest on current refundings of bonds issued before 1986 is not a preference item if the current refunding bonds are not subject to the new unified volume limitation. *(See* new Code section 145(k)). Interest on bonds issued after 1985, which bonds either (1) are exempt from the new volume limitation because of transitional exceptions in the bill *(see* bill sec. 703), or (2) are subject to the limitation as advance refundings allowed under a transitional exception *(see* bill sec. 703(o)) is treated as a preference item. Finally, the fact that a portion of an essential [nonessential] function bond is subject to the unified volume limitation *(see* new Code sec. 141(a)(3)) does not result in treatment of interest on that bond as a preference item.

In the case of a taxpayer who is required to include in minimum taxable income any interest that is tax-exempt for regular tax purposes, section 265 (denying deductions for expenses and interest relating to tax-exempt income) does not apply, to the extent of such inclusion, for purposes of the minimum tax. Thus, for example, a taxpayer who incurs interest expense with respect to purchasing or carrying a nonessential function bond issued after 1986, and who is denied a deduction with respect to such expense for regular tax purposes under section 265, is allowed the deduction for minimum tax purposes.

* * * * * *

[Conference Report]

* * * * * *

The conference agreement follows the House bill with certain modifications and clarifications. First, the preference applies only to interest on private activity bonds other than qualified 501(c)(3) bonds.

[Effective Date.—] Second, the preference applies only to bonds issued on or after August 8, 1986 (on or after September 1, 1986, in the case of bonds covered under the Joint Statement on Effective Dates of March 14, 1986).[1]

The conference agreement further clarifies that the House bill's exception for certain current refundings of bonds issued before August 8, 1986 (or September 1, 1986) also applies in the case of a series of current refundings of an issue originally issued before those dates. This exception does not apply to refundings of pre-August 8, 1986 (or September 1, 1986), bonds.

* * * * * *

n. Completed contract and other methods of accounting for long-term contracts

* * * * * *

[Senate Explanation]

* * * * * *

Use of completed contract method of accounting.—In the case of any long-term contract entered into by the taxpayer after March 1, 1986, use of the completed contract method of accounting, or certain other methods of accounting for long-term contracts, is not permitted for purposes of the minimum tax. Instead, the taxpayer is required to apply the percentage of completion method in determining minimum taxable income relating to that contract. As with depreciation and mining exploration and development costs, this preference is calculated, not by adding an amount to regular taxable income, but by substituting the minimum tax treatment for the regular tax treatment with respect to all items arising with respect to a contract to which the preference relates.

[Conference Report]

* * * * * *

The conference agreement follows the Senate amendment.

o. Installment method of accounting

[Senate Explanation]

* * * * * *

Installment sales of dealer property.—In the case of a disposition of dealer property after March 1, 1986, the installment method of accounting does not apply for minimum tax purposes. Thus, the taxpayer is required, for minimum tax purposes, to recognize all gain with respect to the disposition in the year in which the disposition takes place.[8] The rule applies to dispositions of property defined in section 1221(1), i.e., stock in trade, other property of a kind properly

---

[Footnote ¶ 3931 continued]

(1) The Joint Statement on Effective Dates of March 14, 1986, provided generally that interest on bonds satisfying the present-law definition of governmental bond (as modified by an expanded security interest test like that adopted under the Senate amendment) is not a preference if the bonds are issued before September 1, 1986.

(8) In the case of a disposition occurring between March 1, 1986, and December 31, 1986 (in the case of a dealer who is a calendar year taxpayer), with respect to which the taxpayer elects the installment method for regular tax purposes, the result of this rule is that all gain is treated as recognized for minimum tax purposes in 1986. Since the alternative minimum tax as amended by the bill is not effective until 1987, the rule's sole effect on the tax treatment of such a disposition is that amounts relating to the disposition, included in regular taxable income in years after 1986 under the installment method, are not included in alternative minimum taxable income for such years.

included in inventory if on hand at the close of the taxable year, or property held by the taxpayer primarily for sale to customers in the ordinary course of the taxpayer's trade or business.[9]

[Conference Report]

The conference agreement follows the Senate amendment, except that the preference applies to all transactions subject to proportionate disallowance of the installment method (i.e., dealer sales, and sales of trade or business or rental property where the purchase price exceeds $150,000).

p. Net loss from passive trade or business activities

*   *   *   *   *   *

[Senate Explanation]

*   *   *   *   *   *

Passive activity losses.—In computing alternative minimum taxable income, limitations apply to the use of losses from passive business activities to offset other income of the taxpayer. The rule is identical to that applying for regular tax purposes, under section 1401 of the bill, except for three differences. First, the rule is fully effective in 1987 for minimum tax purposes, whereas it is phased in over five years for regular tax purposes. Second, solely for minimum tax purposes, the amount of losses that otherwise would be disallowed for the current taxable year under the limitation is reduced by the amount, if any, of the taxpayer's insolvency, as measured using a standard similar to that set forth in section 108(d)(3). Third, in applying the limitations, minimum tax rules (including the passive farm loss rule) apply to the measurement and allowability of all relevant items of income, deduction, and credit.

The amount of any passive loss that is subject to disallowance is determined after computing all preferences and making all other adjustments to income that apply for minimum tax purposes (including the minimum tax interest limitation and the passive farm loss preference). Thus, the amount of suspended losses relating to an activity may differ for minimum and regular tax purposes, respectively.

[Conference Report]

*   *   *   *   *   *

The conference agreement follows the Senate amendment. Changes made by the conference agreement to the regular tax passive loss provision apply for minimum tax purposes as well.

q. Losses from passive farming activities

*   *   *   *   *   *

[Senate Explanation]

Passive farm losses.—Any passive farm loss of an individual, to the extent not already denied for minimum tax purposes

under the preferences described above, generally is treated as a preference. A passive farm loss is defined as the taxpayer's loss for the taxable year from any tax shelter farming activity. The amount of the preference is reduced, however, by the amount, if any, of the taxpayer's insolvency, as measured using a standard similar to that set forth in section 108(d)(3).

For purposes of this provision, the term "tax shelter farm activity" means (1) a farming syndicate (as defined in section 464(c), as modified by section 461(i)(4)(A)), and (2) any other activity consisting of farming unless the taxpayer materially participates in the activity. A taxpayer is treated as materially participating in the activity under the material participation standard set forth for regular tax purposes in section 469 (relating to passive losses), if a member of the taxpayer's family (within the meaning of section 2032A(e)(2)) so participates, or if the taxpayer meets the requirements of paragraph (4) or (5) of section 2032A(b) (relating to certain retired or disabled individuals and surviving spouses.)

Under the passive farm loss rule, deductions allocable to a tax shelter farming activity, to the extent in excess of gross income allocable to the activity, are disallowed, for minimum tax purposes. A separate activity is defined consistently with section 469, with the result that generally each farm is treated as a separate activity.

The rules for applying this preference generally are similar to those for applying the passive loss rule for minimum tax purposes (see below), except that there is no netting between different farming activities. An excess farm loss with respect to any farming activity is disallowed even if there is net income from other farming activities, and is carried forward until offset by income from the same activity or until there is an appropriate disposition. The amount of the deductions allocable to a farming activity is determined after taking account of all preferences and making all adjustments required for the determination of alternative minimum taxable income, other than the preference for excess passive losses generally. In other words, no deduction which is treated as a minimum tax preference, or which is redetermined (as with depreciation) for minimum tax purposes, is "double-counted" by also being considered in the determination of passive farm losses.

[Conference Report]

*   *   *   *   *   *

The conference agreement follows the Senate amendment.

r. Charitable contributions of appreciated property

[House Explanation]

*   *   *   *   *   *

【Footnote ¶ 3931 continued】

(9) There is an exception to the rule, relating to certain timeshares and residential lots where an election is made to pay interest pursuant to section 453C. In addition, under a transitional exception, the preference does not apply to any disposition that qualifies for the exception described in section 311 of the bill.

Charitable contributions of appreciated property.—In the case of a taxpayer who makes one or more charitable contributions of appreciated capital gain property, an amount equal to a portion of the regular tax deduction claimed with respect to such appreciation (whether or not such deduction is an itemized deduction or is claimed by an individual) is treated as a minimum tax preference. For purposes of this rule, capital gain property has the same meaning as under the rules relating to charitable deductions.

In determining the amount of the preference, several limitations apply. First, the taxpayer calculates the amount by which the charitable deduction would have been reduced had all capital gain property been taken into account, for purposes of the regular tax charitable deduction, at its adjusted basis. In other words, unrealized gain on appreciated property is offset by unrealized loss on property that is worth less than its adjusted basis.[8]

Second, the amount of the preference is determined by disregarding any amount that is carried forward to another taxable year for purposes of the regular tax. Thus, when a portion of a charitable deduction is carried forward because it exceeds the applicable percentage limitation on such contributions, the portion so carried forward cannot increase the amount of the minimum tax preference until it is allowed as a deduction for regular tax purposes.

Third, the amount of unrealized appreciation that is treated as a preference cannot exceed the net amount of the taxpayer's other preferences (including amounts computed as adjustments). This calculation is made by comparing the taxpayer's regular taxable income with the taxpayer's alternative minimum taxable income (but treating the charitable deduction as fully allowed for minimum tax purposes). For purposes of this comparison, the regular tax standard deduction (in the case of a non-itemizer), and the regular tax personal exemptions are disregarded.[9]

[Conference Report]

*　　　*　　　*　　　*　　　*　　　*

The conference agreement follows the House bill, except that the amount of untaxed appreciation treated as a preference is not limited to the amount of the taxpayer's other preferences. The preference does not apply to carryovers of the deduction with respect to charitable contributions made before August 16, 1986.

5. Itemized Deductions

[Senate Explanation]

*　　　*　　　*　　　*　　　*　　　*

In general, the alternative minimum tax itemized deductions for noncorporate taxpayers are the same as those under the present law alternative minimum tax. Thus, the only "below the line" deductions allowable are deductions for casualty and gambling losses, charitable contributions, medical expenses, qualified interest, and the estate tax deduction under section 691(c) (and, in the case of an estate or trust, for certain distributions to beneficiaries). In the case of qualified interest, present law is changed in two respects. First, as under section 163(d), limiting deductions for investment interest under the regular tax, it is clarified that limited business interests are included in the calculation. Thus, items of income and deduction relating to such interests are considered in determining the amount of qualified investment income and qualified investment expenses, respectively, and interest deductions relating to such interests are treated as itemized deductions (and subject to disallowance) for purposes of the rule. Second, no minimum tax itemized deduction is allowed with respect to consumer interest (even if it would be allowable if treated as investment interest).

[Conference Report]

*　　　*　　　*　　　*　　　*　　　*

The conference agreement generally follows the Senate amendment in conforming the definition of net investment income to the definition adopted for regular tax purposes (although determined with regard to minimum tax items of income and deduction), with an amendment providing for a carryover of investment interest deductions that are disallowed. Other regular tax itemized deductions generally are allowed for minimum tax purposes.

For minimum tax purposes, medical deductions are allowed only to the extent in excess of 10 percent of adjusted gross income, miscellaneous itemized deductions and itemized deductions for State and local taxes are not allowed, and the investment interest rule is not phased in. It is clarified that, for minimum tax purposes, upon a refinancing of a loan that gives rise to qualified housing interest, interest paid on the new loan is treated as qualified housing interest to the extent that (1) it so qualified under the prior loan, and (2) the amount of the loan was not increased. Moreover, a residence does not constitute a qualified residence for minimum tax purposes unless it meets the requirements for a qualified residence applying for regular tax purposes. Further, the conference

---

[Footnote ¶ 3931 continued]

(8) Ordinarily, of course, a taxpayer would not make a charitable contribution with respect to capital gain property that is worth less than its adjusted basis. Rather, the taxpayer would generally be expected to sell the property, deduct the loss, and then donate the sale proceeds to the charitable organization and claim a charitable deduction.

(9) It is also intended that alternative minimum taxable income, for this purpose, will be calculated by allowing all itemized deductions allowable in computing the regular tax.

agreement provides that a refund of State and local taxes paid, for which no minimum tax deduction was allowed, is not included in alternative minimum taxable income.

6. Regular Tax Elections

[Senate Explanation]

In the case of certain expenditures that would give rise to a minimum tax preference if treated under the rules generally applying for regular tax purposes, the taxpayer may make a "normative election," i.e., elect to have the minimum tax rule for deducting the expenditure apply for regular tax purposes. The expenditures to which this rule applies are the following: circulation expenditures, research and experimental expenditures, intangible drilling costs, and mining development and exploration expenditures. Elections may be made "dollar-for-dollar"; thus, for example, a taxpayer who incurs $100,000 of intangible drilling costs with respect to a single well may elect normative treatment for any portion of that amount.

To the extent that such an election applies, the item to which it applies is treated for all purposes, under both the regular and the minimum tax, pursuant to the election. No other deduction is allowed for the item to the extent that such an election applies.

An election made under this rule may be revoked only with the consent of the Secretary. Elections may be made at such time and in such manner as the Secretary by regulations prescribes. In the case of a partnership or S corporation, an election may be made separately by any partner (or shareholder) with respect to such individual's allocable share of any expenditure.

*   *   *   *   *   *

The conference agreement follows * * * the Senate amendment.

7. Adjustments in Other Years When Taxpayer Pays Minimum Tax

[Senate Explanation]

Minimum tax credit.—When a taxpayer pays alternative minimum tax, the amount of such tax paid (i.e., the net minimum tax) generally is allowed as a credit against the regular tax liability (net of other nonrefundable credits) of the taxpayer in subsequent years. However, the minimum tax credit cannot be used to reduce minimum tax liability in subsequent years. The minimum tax credit can be carried forward indefinitely; thus, it is not necessary for the taxpayer to determine which prior year's minimum tax credit is being used in a particular year. The minimum tax credit cannot be carried back.

In the case of an acquisition of assets of a corporation by another corporation to which section 381(a) applies (for example, a statutory merger), any unused minimum tax credits of the acquired corporation will be treated as a "tax attribute" that is taken into account by the acquiring corporation. However, for such an acquisition, as well as an acquisition of stock, the availability of the credits may be subject to limitation under the provisions of Part V of Subchapter C (sections 381 through 383).

The minimum tax credit is allowed only with respect to liability arising as a result of deferral preferences (i.e., preferences other than those that result in permanent exclusion of certain income for regular tax purposes). Thus, the amount of the net minimum tax is reduced by the amount of minimum tax liability that would have arisen if the only applicable preferences were the exclusion preferences. The exclusion preferences are those relating to percentage depletion and regular tax itemized deductions that are denied for minimum tax purposes.[12]

Consider, for example, the case of married taxpayers filing a joint return with (i) no regular taxable income, (ii) deferral preferences in the amount of $400,000, and (iii) exclusion preferences (including any disallowed itemized deductions) in the amount of $100,000. Under the 20 percent alternative minimum tax rate, and in light of the phaseout of the exemption amount, minimum tax liability would equal $100,000. However, if the taxpayers had had only exclusion preferences, minimum tax liability would have equalled $12,000 (20 percent of $100,000 as reduced by the $40,000 exemption amount). Thus, the amount of minimum tax available as a carryforward credit would be $88,000 ($100,000 less $12,000).

[Conference Report]

*   *   *   *   *   *

The conference agreement follows * * * the Senate amendment.

8. Incentive Tax Credits

[Senate Explanation]

Incentive tax credits.—Nonrefundable credits other than the minimum tax credit generally are accorded treatment that is intended to have the same effect as the rules applying under the present law alternative minimum tax on individuals. However, the rules have been revised in one technical respect in the interest of simplicity. Under present law, nonrefundable credits can be claimed against the regular tax even if they provide no benefit (i.e., they reduce regular tax liability to less than the amount of minimum tax liability that was due in any case). To the extent that the credits provide no benefit due to the minimum tax, however, they are allowed as carryovers to other taxable years.

Under the bill, such credits generally cannot be claimed in the first place to the extent that they would reduce regular tax liability to less than tentative minimum tax liability and hence provide no benefit. As under present law, such credits are allowed as carryovers to other taxable years, under the generally applicable rules for credit carryovers.

Where no minimum tax is due and the minimum tax does not limit the use of incentive credits, the taxpayer is not required to file with his or her tax return a form showing minimum tax computations. For example, a taxpayer with $100 of regular tax liability (disregarding incentive credits), a targeted jobs tax credit in the amount of $10, and whose tentative minimum tax equalled less than $90, would not be required to file a minimum tax form with the Internal Revenue Service.

The alternative minimum tax does not apply to any corporation that validly elects the application of section 936. Thus, a section 936 corporation is exempt from the alternative minimum tax, even to the extent that it has preference income that is not qualified possession source income.

[Conference Report]

*   *   *   *   *   *

The conference agreement follows the House bill and the Senate amendment.

9. Foreign Tax Credit

[Senate Explanation]

*   *   *   *   *   *

Foreign tax credit.—Under the bill, minimum tax liability is defined as the excess of the tentative minimum tax (i.e. 20 percent of the excess of alternative minimum taxable income over the exemption amount, reduced by the specially computed foreign tax credit using the minimum tax base) over the regular tax (i.e. regular tax liability reduced by the foreign tax credit). The foreign tax credit thus is, in effect, allowable for purposes of the alternative minimum tax, under rules similar to those applying to the alternative minimum tax on individuals under present law. These rules involve separate application, for minimum tax purposes, of the section 904 limitation on the amount of the credit, to reflect the differences between regular taxable income and alternative minimum taxable income.

For example, to the extent that preferences allocable to U.S. source income, when taken into consideration for minimum tax purposes, change the ratio of foreign taxable income to worldwide income, the application of section 904 may lead to different results under the regular and the alternative minimum taxes, respectively. In light of these differences, taxpayers must separately keep track of the amount of foreign tax credit carryforwards allowable for regular and for minimum tax purposes.

In applying section 904 for minimum tax purposes with respect to an amount added to alternative minimum taxable income with respect to the book income of a corporate taxpayer, the committee intends that the percentage of such income that is from sources within the United States will be treated as the same as the percentage of all other alternative minimum taxable income for the taxable year of the taxpayer that is from sources within the United States. Thus, in effect, the book income preference will not result in any change in the percentage applying for purposes of the alternative minimum tax section 904 limitation.

In addition to being limited by section 904, use of the foreign tax credit is limited for minimum tax purposes by a rule designed to prevent U.S. taxpayers with substantial income from using the foreign tax credit to avoid all U.S. tax liability. Under this rule, no more than 90 percent of tentative minimum tax liability (before allowance of the foreign tax credit) can be offset by foreign tax credits, even if under section 904 more than 90 percent of such liability could be offset by such credits. This rule has no effect on a taxpayer who already is prevented by section 904 from offsetting more than 90 percent of minimum tax liability with foreign tax credits. Any foreign tax credits that are disallowed under this rule are treated, for carryover purposes, like credits disallowed by reason of section 904. This rule, like the limitation under section 904, is applied prior to comparing the amount of the taxpayer's minimum tax liability with the amount of such taxpayer's regular tax liability.

*   *   *   *   *   *

[Conference Report]

*   *   *   *   *   *

The conference agreement generally follows the Senate amendment. It is clarified that the taxpayer's regular tax election regarding whether to treat foreign taxes as giving rise to a deduction or a credit is controlling for minimum tax purposes as well. Moreover, in light of the limitation on the use of net operating losses, described below, it is provided that foreign tax credits cannot offset more than 90 percent of minimum tax liability as determined without regard to foreign tax credits and net operating losses.

For example, assume that in 1987 a taxpayer has $10 million of alternative minimum taxable income for the year. In the absence of net operating losses or foreign tax credits, the taxpayer's tentative minimum tax liability (i.e., liability as determined without regard to the amount of regular tax liability) would equal $2.1 million. Accordingly, foreign tax credits cannot be used to reduce liability to less than $210,000, whether or not the taxpayer has any minimum tax net operating losses.

10. Net Operating Losses (NOLs)

[Senate Explanation]

*   *   *   *   *   *

Under the bill, special rules apply for net operating losses. These rules generally are the same as the present law rules with respect to the alternative minimum tax for individuals.

For purposes of the alternative minimum tax, net operating loss deductions are determined by using a separate computation of alternative minimum tax net operating losses and carryovers. Generally, this computation takes into account the differences between the regular tax base and the alternative minimum tax base.

The amount of the net operating loss (under section 172(c)) for any taxable year, for purposes of the alternative minimum tax, generally is computed in the same manner as the regular tax net operating loss, with two exceptions. First, the items of tax preference arising in that year are added back to taxable income (or, as with depreciation, adjustments relating to those items are made), and, second, for individuals, only those itemized deductions (as modified under section 172(d)) allowable in computing alternative minimum taxable income are taken into account. In computing the amount of deduction for years other than the year of the loss (i.e., carryover years), the recomputed loss is deducted from the alternative minimum taxable income (as modified under section 172(b)(2)(A)) in the carryover year (whether or not the taxpayer is subject to the minimum tax in that year).

For example, if in year one a taxpayer has $20,000 of income and $35,000 of losses, of which $10,000 are preference items, the alternative minimum tax net operating loss for the year is $5,000. Thus, in any subsequent (or prior) year to which the loss may be carried, a $5,000 net operating loss deduction is allowed to reduce income subject to the alternative minimum tax.

Assume that, in year two, the taxpayer has $20,000 of alternative minimum taxable income (without regard to the net operating loss deduction). The taxpayer reduces his or her alternative minimum taxable income to $15,000 by the minimum tax net operating loss deduction. The net operating loss deduction for the regular tax is not affected by this computation (i.e., the taxpayer has a loss carryover of $15,000 from year one to be used under the regular tax).

For corporations, a transition rule generally allows, for purposes of the alternative minimum tax, all pre-effective date regular tax net operating losses to be carried forward as minimum tax NOLs to the first taxable year for which the tax, as amended under the bill, applies (and to subsequent years until used up). For individuals, present law is retained with respect to the calculation of alternative minimum tax net operating losses for such years.

An adjustment is required in the case of a corporation that, as of the end of the last taxable year beginning before January 1, 1987, had a deferred add-on minimum tax liability for a year prior to 1987, under section 56(b), due to certain net operating losses. For such a corporation, no add-on minimum tax liability will be imposed after 1986, but the alternative minimum tax net operating loss carried to the first taxable year of the corporation beginning after December 31, 1986, is reduced by the amount of the preferences that gave rise to the liability.

[Conference Report]

*   *   *   *   *   *

The conference agreement follows the House bill and the Senate amendment, except that NOLs cannot offset more than 90 percent of alternative minimum taxable income. As with the 90 percent limitation on the use of the foreign tax credit, amounts disallowed by reason of this limitation may be carried over to other taxable years.

Thus, for example, assume that in 1987 a taxpayer has $10 million of alternative minimum taxable income for the year, and minimum tax NOLs in the amount of $11 million. The NOLs reduce alternative minimum taxable income to $1 million. This gives rise to tentative minimum tax liability of $210,000. The taxpayer carries forward $2 million of minimum tax NOLs to 1988. Since the allowability of net operating losses is determined prior to the allowability of foreign tax credits, this taxpayer would not be permitted to use any minimum tax foreign tax credits in 1987.

It is clarified that an election under section 172(b)(3)(C) to relinquish the carryback period applies both for regular tax and for minimum tax purposes.

11. Miscellaneous Changes and Clarifications

Under the conference agreement, it is clarified that Code sections suspending losses, such as sections 465, 704(d), 1366(d), and other sections specified in regulations, are recomputed for minimum tax purposes, to apply with respect to amounts otherwise deductible for purposes of the minimum tax. Thus, the amount of the deductions suspended or recaptured may differ for regular and minimum tax purposes, respectively. This clarification applies with respect to all taxpayers subject to the at-risk rules.

It is clarified that the application of the tax benefit rule to the minimum tax is within the discretion of the Secretary of the Treasury. Since the regular and minimum taxes generally are computed separately, relief from the minimum tax under the tax benefit rule is not appropriate solely by reason of the fact that a taxpayer has received no benefit under the regular tax with respect to a particular item. This clarification applies with respect to corporations as well as individuals.

In the case of an estate or trust, instead of allocating items of tax preference between the estate or trust and its beneficiaries (as under present law), it is provided that the minimum tax will apply by determining distributable net income on a minimum tax basis (except to the extent inconsistent with the modifications under section 643(a), with the minimum tax exemption amount being treated the same way as the deduction for personal exemptions under section 643(a)(2)).

12. Effective Date

*   *   *   *   *   *

[Senate Explanation]

Effective Date.—The provisions apply to taxable years beginning after December 31, 1986.

[Conference Report]

*   *   *   *   *   *

The conference agreement follows the Senate amendment.

B. Corporate Minimum Tax
1. Structure

[Senate Explanation]

*   *   *   *   *   *

Corporations.—Generally, the tax base for the alternative minimum tax on corporations is the taxpayer's regular taxable income, increased by the taxpayer's tax preferences for the year and adjusted by computing certain deductions in a special manner which negates the acceleration of such deductions under the regular tax. The resulting amount, called alternative minimum taxable income, then is reduced by an exemption amount and is subject to tax at a 20-percent rate. The amount so determined may then be offset by the minimum tax foreign tax credit to determine a "tentative minimum tax." These rules are designed to ensure that, in each taxable year, the taxpayer must pay tax equalling at least 20 percent of an amount more nearly approximating its economic income (above the exemption amount). The exemption amount for corporations is $40,000, reduced (but not below zero) by 25 percent of the amount by which alternative minimum taxable income exceeds $150,000.

The net minimum tax, or amount of minimum tax due, is the amount by which the tax computed under this system (the tentative minimum tax) exceeds the taxpayer's regular tax. Although the minimum tax is, in effect, a true alternative tax, in the sense that is paid only when it exceeds the regular tax, technically the taxpayer's regular tax continues to be imposed, and the net minimum tax is added on.

*   *   *   *   *   *

[Conference Report]

The conference agreement follows the House bill and the Senate amendment.

2. Tax Rate

*   *   *   *   *   *

Senate Amendment

The Senate amendment provides for a minimum tax rate of 20 percent.

Conference Agreement

The conference agreement follows the Senate amendment.

3. Exemption Amount

*   *   *   *   *   *

Senate Amendment

The Senate amendment is the same as the House bill, except that the exemption amount is reduced by 25 cents for each $1 by which alternative minimum taxable income exceeds $150,000.

Conference Agreement

The conference agreement follows the Senate amendment.

4. Tax Preferences
a. Accelerated depreciation on real property

[Senate Explanation]

*   *   *   *   *   *

Depreciation.—Accelerated depreciation (ACRS) on real and personal property placed in service after 1986, to the extent in excess of depreciation calculated under an alternative method, is treated as a preference.[5] The amount of the preference is calculated, with respect to such new property, by making adjustments similar to the types of adjustments that are made in determining the depreciation allowable with respect to earnings and profits. That is, instead of making preference adjustments with respect to specific items of property in the amount by which the ACRS deduction exceeds the alternative deduction, the alternative depreciation deduction is substituted for the ACRS deduction for all property placed in service after 1986. The principal effect of this system is that it permits "netting", i.e. to the extent that, for a particular year, an alternative deduction relating to an item of property exceeds the ACRS deduction for that year, the amount of the preference is reduced.[6]

Consider, as an example that does not reflect the actual details of the ACRS and alternative depreciation systems, the case of a taxpayer who was permitted to deduct fully a $10 expense in the year that the property to which the expense related was placed in service, but who was required to write off the expense over two years for purposes of the alternative depreciation system. For that taxpayer, assuming there were no other differences between the taxpayer's regular and minimum taxable income, regular taxable income would be $5 less than minimum taxable income for the year in which the property was placed in service. In the following taxable year, however, the taxpayer's regular taxable income would be $5 greater than minimum taxable income (because no further ACRS deduction would remain with respect to the property, whereas the taxpayer would still be entitled to write off the last $5 of basis under the alternative system). If the taxpayer also had a separate preference in

---

[Footnote ¶ 3931 continued]

(5) The preference does not apply, however, to property that is expensed under section 179.

(6) Alternative deductions exceed ACRS deductions in the later years of the useful life of an item of property for which ACRS is allowed; i.e., at such time the ACRS deduction is understated because it has been overstated in prior taxable years.

the amount of $5 in the second year, the taxpayer's regular and minimum taxable incomes would be equivalent in that year (whether or not that second item related to depreciation).

Regular tax depreciation with respect to property placed in service prior to 1987 is treated as a preference only to the extent that it constitutes a preference under present law. Thus, for example, for pre-1987 personal property, regular tax depreciation is a corporate tax preference only in the case of leased personal property in the hands of a personal holding company. In addition, present law rules apply to the measurement of depreciation preferences relating to pre-1987 property. Thus, for example, present law rules for measuring the amount of depreciation that constitutes a preference continue to apply to pre-1987 property, and preferences relating to such property continue to be measured on an item-by-item basis, rather than under the netting system described above.

For property placed in service after 1986, alternative depreciation generally is defined as straight-line depreciation over the ADR midpoint life of the property (forty years in the case of real estate). A similar depreciation system presently is used and will continue to be used with respect to property leased by a taxable entity to a tax-exempt entity. Under the bill, the alternative depreciation system applies for certain other purposes as well (including the measurement of depreciation for determining earnings and profits and with respect to property placed in service outside of the United States). Since taxpayers can elect to use this depreciation system for regular tax purposes, no minimum tax adjustment to income is made to the extent that any such election applies. (A complete description of the alternative depreciation system is described in the portion of the report describing the bill's provisions in the area of depreciation.)

As an exception to the general rule treating ACRS on post-1986 property as a preference, no adjustment is made for minimum tax purposes with respect to certain property described in paragraph (1), (2), (3), or (4) of section 168(f) (e.g., generally property depreciated under the income forecast method, etc.).[7] Property placed in service after 1986 that qualifies for a transitional exception to section 201 of the bill is excepted from the bill's minimum tax provisions for post-1986 property as well.

For all depreciable property to which minimum tax adjustments apply, adjusted basis is determined for minimum tax purposes with reference to the amount of depreciation allowed for minimum tax purposes under the alternative system. Thus, the amount of gain on the disposition of such property will differ for regular and minimum tax purposes.

*   *   *   *   *   *

[Conference Report]

*   *   *   *   *   *

The conference agreement generally follows the Senate amendment, as conformed to the alternative depreciation provision described in the depreciation section of this report. However, for property other than (1) section 1250 property and (2) property with respect to which the taxpayer elects or is required to use a straightline method for regular tax purposes, minimum tax depreciation uses the 150 percent declining balance method (switching to straightline in the year necessary to maximize the allowance) over the alternative depreciation life.

b. Accelerated depreciation on personal property

[See *Senate Explanation* in (a) above. Ed.]

[Conference Report]

*   *   *   *   *   *

The conference agreement generally follows the Senate amendment, as conformed to the alternative depreciation provision described in the depreciation section of this report. However, for property other than that with respect to which the taxpayer elects or is required to use a straightline method for regular tax purposes, minimum tax depreciation uses the 150 percent declining balance method (switching to straightline in the year necessary to maximize the allowance) over the alternative depreciation life. The preference, computed using the useful life under the alternative depreciation system, applies to property placed in service in 1986 with respect to which the taxpayer elects the application of section 201 of the Act.

c. Expensing of intangible drilling costs

[Senate Explanation]

*   *   *   *   *   *

Intangible drilling costs.—The preference for intangible drilling costs is the same as the present law preference for individuals, except that it is extended to apply to all corporations. Thus, the amount of excess intangible drilling costs is treated as a preference only to the extent that it exceeds the taxpayer's net income for the taxable year from oil, gas, and geothermal properties. Net oil and gas income is determined without regard to deductions for excess intangible drilling costs. Under this rule, for example, a taxpayer with $100 of net oil and gas income (disregarding excess intangible drilling costs) and $120 of excess intangible drilling costs would be required to treat such costs as a preference in the amount of $20 ($120 excess IDC less $100 net income offset).

The amount of excess intangible drilling costs is defined as the amount of the excess, if any, of the taxpayer's regular tax deduction for such costs (deductible under either section 263 or 291) over the normative deduction, i.e., the amount that would have been allowable if the taxpayer had amortized the costs over

---

[Footnote ¶ 3931 continued]

(7) With respect to public utility property, taxpayers are required to use a normalization method of accounting in order to depreciate such property under the alternative system. The Secretary shall prescribe the requirements of a normalization method of accounting in this context.

120 months on a straight-line basis or had recovered the costs through cost depletion. The preference does not apply to costs incurred with respect to a nonproductive well.

In applying the preference for intangible drilling costs, a taxpayer's property (as under present law for individuals) is divided into two parts: properties that are geothermal deposits, and all other properties with respect to which intangible drilling costs are incurred. This separation applies for all purposes under the minimum tax. Consider, for example, the case of a taxpayer who has (1) oil wells with net oil and gas income of $100 and excess intangible drilling costs of $120, and (2) geothermal deposits with net income of $100 and excess intangible drilling costs of $80. This taxpayer has a preference in the amount of $20 with respect to the oil wells, and no preference with respect to the geothermal deposits.

With respect to intangible drilling costs for any well, the taxpayer may elect the use of any method which would be permitted for purposes of determining cost depletion with respect to such well. To be effective, such an election must be made at such time and in such manner as prescribed by the Secretary in regulations. Once made, such an election applies, with respect to the costs subject to it, for all regular and minimum tax purposes. Thus, costs recovered under this method are not treated as a minimum tax preference.

In the case of a disposition of any oil, gas, or geothermal property to which section 1254 generally would apply, or of any mining property to which section 617(d) generally would apply, if the taxpayer makes an election as described above (or to the extent of a normative election, as described below), amounts deducted pursuant to the election are treated as deducted for purposes of section 1254 or section 617(d), as the case may be.

* * * * * *

[Conference Report]

The conference agreement follows * * * the Senate amendment.

d. 60-month amortization on certified pollution control facilities

[Senate Explanation]

* * * * * *

Amortization of certified pollution control facilities.—As under present law, rapid amortization of a certified pollution control facility is treated as a preference. For such facilities placed in service after 1986, the preference is treated under a rule similar to that for post-1986 depreciable property generally, i.e., the taxpayer is required to use the alternative recovery system for minimum tax purposes.

[Conference Report]

* * * * * *

The conference agreement follows the Senate amendment. It is clarified that the preference applies without regard to the applicability of section 291 for regular tax purposes.

e. Expensing of mining exploration and development costs

[House Explanation]

* * * * * *

Mining exploration and development costs.—Mining exploration and development costs, incurred after 1985, that are expensed (or amortized under section 291) for regular tax purposes are required to be recovered through ten-year straight line amortization for purposes of the alternative minimum tax. As with depreciation, the minimum tax treatment of mining exploration and development costs involves a separate calculation for all items of income and expense relating to such costs. Thus, for example, in the case of a noncorporate taxpayer who incurred a one-time mining exploration and development expense in the amount of $100, the regular tax deduction would be $100 in the year when the expenditure was incurred, and the minimum tax deduction would be $10 for each of the ten years beginning in the year when the expenditure was incurred. The basis of property with respect to which such costs were incurred, and the amount of gain or loss upon disposition, likewise may differ for regular and minimum tax purposes, respectively.

Under this approach, any mining exploration and development costs which are included in regular taxable income when the mine reaches the producing stage are not included in minimum taxable income. In addition, when a loss is sustained with respect to a mining property (e.g., the mine is abandoned as worthless, giving rise to a loss under section 165), the taxpayer is permitted to deduct, for minimum tax purposes, all mining exploration and development costs relating to that property that have been amortized and not yet written off under the minimum tax.

* * * * * *

[Conference Report]

* * * * * *

The conference agreement follows the House bill. It is clarified that 10-year amortization applies for minimum tax purposes without regard to the applicability of section 291 for regular tax purposes.

f. Expensing of circulation expenditures (for newspapers, magazines, etc.)

[Senate Explanation]

* * * * * *

Circulation expenditures.—An individual who incurs circulation expenditures described in section 173 is not permitted to expense his post-1986 expenditures for minimum tax purposes. Instead, in computing alternative minimum taxable income, the taxpayer is required to amortize such post-1986 expenditures ratably over a three-year period. However, if the taxpayer realizes a loss with respect to property to which any such expenditures relate, all such expenditures relating to that property but not yet deducted for minimum tax purposes are allowed as a minimum tax deduction. The preference applies to personal holding companies as well as to individuals.

For example, an individual who incurred such expenditures in the amount of $30 would claim a regular tax deduction for the entire amount in the year when the expenditures were incurred, and would claim alternative minimum tax deductions of $10 for that year and the two succeeding taxable years. However, if the newspaper to which the expenditures related ceased operations in the second year, the entire $20 which was not allowed as a minimum tax deduction in the first year would be allowed for minimum tax purposes in the second year.

*   *   *   *   *   *

[Conference Report]

*   *   *   *   *   *

The conference agreement follows * * * the Senate amendment.

g. Expensing of research and experimentation expenditures

[Senate Explanation]

*   *   *   *   *   *

Research and experimental expenditures.—An individual who incurs research and experimental expenditures described in section 174 is not permitted to expense the expenditures for minimum tax purposes. Instead, in computing alternative minimum taxable income, the taxpayer is required to amortize such post-1986 expenditures over a ten-year period. As with certain other items (such as depreciation and mining exploration and development costs), this treatment applies for all minimum tax purposes, rather than as an annual adjustment to regular taxable income. If the taxpayer abandons a specific project to which any such expenditures relate, all such expenditures relating to that property but not yet deducted for minimum tax purposes are allowed as a minimum tax deduction.

For example, an individual who incurred research and experimental expenditures in the amount of $100 would claim a regular tax deduction for the entire amount in the year when the expenditures were incurred (absent a section 174(b) election), and would claim alternative minimum tax deductions of $10 for that year and the nine succeeding taxable years. However, if the taxpayer abandoned the specific project to which the expenditures related in the second year, the entire $90 which was not allowed as a minimum tax deduction in the first year would be allowed for minimum tax purposes in the second year.

*   *   *   *   *   *

[Conference Report]

*   *   *   *   *   *

The conference agreement follows the House bill and the Senate amendment.

h. Percentage depletion

[Senate Explanation]

*   *   *   *   *   *

Percentage depletion.—As under present law, the excess of the regular tax deduction allowable for depletion over the adjusted basis of the property at the end of the taxable year (determined without regard to the depletion deduction for the taxable year) is treated as a preference. Thus, for example, a taxpayer who claimed a deduction for percentage depletion in the amount of $50, with respect to property having a basis (disregarding this deduction) of $10, would have a minimum tax preference in the amount of $40.

[Conference Explanation]

*   *   *   *   *   *

The conference agreement follows the House bill and the Senate amendment.

i. Capital gain preference

*   *   *   *   *   *

House Bill

Under the House bill, net corporate capital gains are fully included in minimum taxable income.

*   *   *   *   *   *

Conference Agreement

The conference agreement follows the House bill * * *.

j. Tax-exempt interest

[House Explanation]

*   *   *   *   *   *

Tax-exempt interest on nonessential function bonds.—Interest on certain tax-exempt bonds issued after December 31, 1985 is treated as a preference. This rule applies only with respect to nonessential function bonds, the interest on which is exempt from taxation under section 103. In general, nonessential function bonds are those bonds that are subject to the unified volume limitation in new Code section 145.

For purposes of this rule, interest on current refundings of bonds issued before 1986 is not a preference item if the current refunding bonds are not subject to the new unified volume limitation. *(See* new Code section 145(k)). Interest on bonds issued after 1985, which bonds either (1) are exempt from the new volume limitation because of transitional exceptions in the bill *(see* bill sec. 703), or (2) are subject to the limitation as advance refundings allowed under a transitional exception *(see* bill sec. 703(o)) is treated as a preference item. Finally, the fact that a portion of an essential function bond is subject to the unified volume limitation *(see* new Code sec. 141(a)(3)) does not result in treatment of interest on that bond as a preference item.

In the case of a taxpayer who is required to include in minimum taxable income any interest that is tax-exempt for regular tax purposes, section 265 (denying deductions for expenses and interest relating to tax-exempt income) does not apply, to the extent of such inclusion, for purposes of the minimum tax. Thus, for example, a taxpayer who incurs interest expense with respect to purchasing or carrying a nonessential function bond issued after 1986, and who is denied a deduction with respect to such expense for regular tax purposes under section 265, is allowed the deduction for minimum tax purposes.

* * * * * *

[Conference Explanation]

* * * * * *

The conference agreement follows the House bill with certain modifications and clarifications. First, the preference applies only to interest on private activity bonds other than qualified 501(c)(3) bonds. Second, the preference applies only to bonds issued on or after August 8, 1986 (on or after September 1, 1986, in the case of bonds covered under the Joint Statement on Effective Dates of March 14, 1986).[2]

The conference agreement further clarifies that the House bill's exception for certain current refundings of bonds issued before August 8, 1986 (or September 1, 1986) also applies in the case of a series of current refundings of an issue originally issued before those dates. This exception does not apply to current refundings of pre-August 8, 1986 (or September 1, 1986) bonds.

k. Completed contract and other methods of accounting for long-term contracts

* * * * * *

[Senate Explanation]

Use of completed contract method of accounting.—In the case of any long-term contract entered into by the taxpayer after March 1, 1986, use of the completed contract method of accounting, or certain other methods of accounting for long-term contracts, is not permitted for purposes of the minimum tax. Instead, the taxpayer is required to apply the percentage of completion method in determining minimum taxable income relating to that contract. As with depreciation and mining exploration and development costs, this preference is calculated, not

by adding an amount to regular taxable income, but by substituting the minimum tax treatment for the regular tax treatment with respect to all items arising with respect to a contract to which the preference relates.

[Conference Report]

The conference agreement follows the Senate amendment.

l. Installment method of accounting

[Senate Explanation]

* * * * * *

Installment sales of dealer property.—In the case of a disposition of dealer property after March 1, 1986, the installment method of accounting does not apply for minimum tax purposes. Thus, the taxpayer is required, for minimum tax purposes, to recognize all gain with respect to the disposition in the year in which the disposition takes place.[8] The rule applies to dispositions of property defined in section 1221(1), i.e., stock in trade, other property of a kind properly included in inventory if on hand at the close of the taxable year, or property held by the taxpayer primarily for sale to customers in the ordinary course of the taxpayer's trade or business.[9]

* * * * * *

[Conference Report]

* * * * * *

The conference agreement follows the Senate amendment, except that the preference applies to all transactions subject to proportionate disallowance of the installment method (i.e., dealer sales, and sales of trade or business or rental property where the purchase price exceeds $150,000).

m. Bad debt reserve deductions for financial institutions

[Senate Explanation]

* * * * * *

Reserves for losses on bad debts of financial institutions.—As under the present law add-on corporate minimum tax, certain excess reserves of a financial institution to which section 585 or 593 applies are treated as a minimum tax preference. The preference is defined as equal to the excess of the reserve for bad debts deducted by the taxpayer over the amount that would have

---

【Footnote ¶ 3931 continued】

(2) The Joint Statement on Effective Dates of March 14, 1986, provided generally that interest on bonds satisfying the present-law definition of governmental bond (as modified by an expanded security interest test like that adopted under the Senate amendment) is not a preference if the bonds are issued before September 1, 1986.

(8) In the case of a disposition occurring between March 1, 1986, and December 31, 1986 (in the case of a dealer who is a calendar year taxpayer), with respect to which the taxpayer elects the installment method for regular tax purposes, the result of this rule is that all gain is treated as recognized for minimum tax purposes in 1986. Since the alternative minimum tax as amended by the bill is not effective until 1987, the rule's sole effect on the tax treatment of such a disposition is that amounts relating to the disposition, included in regular taxable income in years after 1986 under the installment method, are not included in alternative minimum taxable income for such years.

(9) There is an exception to the rule, relating to certain timeshares and residential lots where an election is made to pay interest pursuant to section 453C. In addition, under a transitional exception, the preference does not apply to any disposition that qualifies for the exception described in section 311 of the bill.

been allowable had the taxpayer maintained its bad debt reserve for all taxable years on the basis of actual experience.

*   *   *   *   *   *

[Conference Report]

*   *   *   *   *   *

The conference agreement follows * * * the Senate amendment.

n. Charitable contributions of appreciated property

[House Explanation]

*   *   *   *   *   *

Charitable contributions of appreciated property.—In the case of a taxpayer who makes one or more charitable contributions of appreciated capital gain property, an amount equal to a portion of the regular tax deduction claimed with respect to such appreciation (whether or not such deduction is an itemized deduction or is claimed by an individual) is treated as a minimum tax preference. For purposes of this rule, capital gain property has the same meaning as under the rules relating to charitable deductions.

In determining the amount of the preference, several limitations apply. First, the taxpayer calculates the amount by which the charitable deduction would have been reduced had all capital gain property been taken into account, for purposes of the regular tax deduction, at its adjusted basis. In other words, unrealized gain on appreciated property is offset by unrealized loss on property that is worth less than its adjusted basis.[8a]

Second, the amount of the preference is determined by disregarding any amount that is carried forward to another taxable year for purposes of the regular tax. Thus, when a portion of a charitable deduction is carried forward because it exceeds the applicable percentage limitation on such contributions, the portion so carried forward cannot increase the amount of the minimum tax preference until it is allowed as a deduction for regular tax purposes.

Third, the amount of unrealized appreciation that is treated as a preference cannot exceed the net amount of the taxpayer's other preferences (including amounts computed as adjustments). This calculation is made by comparing the taxpayer's regular taxable income with the taxpayer's alternative minimum taxable income (but treating the charitable deduction as fully allowed for minimum tax purposes). For purposes of this comparison, the regular tax standard deduction (in the case of a non-itemizer), and the regular tax personal exemptions are disregarded.[9a]

[Conference Report]

*   *   *   *   *   *

The conference agreement follows the House bill, except that the amount of untaxed appreciation treated as a preference is not limited to the amount of the taxpayer's other preferences. The preference does not apply to carryovers of the deduction with respect to charitable contributions made before August 16, 1986.

*   *   *   *   *   *

p. Capital construction funds for shipping companies

[Senate Explanation]

*   *   *   *   *   *

Capital construction funds of shipping companies.—The use of a capital construction fund established under section 607 of the Merchant Marine Act of 1936 is treated as a minimum tax preference. Thus, amounts deposited in such a fund after 1986 are not deductible, and earnings (including gains and losses) of such a fund after 1986 are not excludable, in determining alternative minimum taxable income. In light of the preference, other adjustments required by the Merchant Marine Act of 1936 with respect to amounts withdrawn from a capital construction fund (e.g., reduction in basis under section 607(g)) of such Act) do not apply to the extent that such amounts have previously been included in alternative minimum taxable income. For this purpose, amounts deposited in or earned by a capital construction fund before 1987 are treated as withdrawn prior to amounts deposited or earned after 1986.

[Conference Report]

*   *   *   *   *   *

The conference agreement follows the Senate amendment.

q. Special deduction for certain tax-exempt insurance providers

*   *   *   *   *   *

Under the conference agreement, the special deduction allowed for certain existing Blue Cross/Blue Shield organizations and for new organizations meeting certain requirements with respect to high risk coverages is a minimum tax preference.

r. Business untaxed reported profits

[Senate Explanation]

Business untaxed reported profits: *In general.*—The committee bill provides that alternative minimum taxable income of a corporation includes one-half of the amount by which the adjusted net book income of the taxpayer exceeds the alternative minimum taxable income of the taxpayer before any

---

[Footnote ¶ 3931 continued]

(8a) Ordinarily, of course, a taxpayer would not make a charitable contribution with respect to capital gain property that is worth less than its adjusted basis. Rather, the taxpayer would generally be expected to sell the property, deduct the loss, and then donate the sale proceeds to the charitable organization and claim a charitable deduction.

(9a) It is also intended that alternative minimum taxable income, for this purpose, will be calculated by allowing all itemized deductions allowable in computing the regular tax.

amount is added to alternative minimum taxable income as a result of this preference. In general, the book income of a corporate taxpayer is the net income or loss set forth on the taxpayer's applicable financial statement. Certain adjustments are made to conform net income to reflect the activities of the corporations included in any consolidated tax return, to remove the effect of Federal and foreign income taxes, and for other purposes.

Financial statement income: The starting point for the computation of the book income preference is the net income disclosed on the taxpayer's applicable financial statement. Net income is the amount the taxpayer reports that takes into account all items of revenue, expense, gain and loss attributable to the taxable year according to the taxpayer's normal method of accounting. Normally, this amount will be disclosed as part of an income statement prepared for inclusion in the taxpayer's applicable financial statement. The amount of net income should reconcile with the balance sheet of the corporation and be the same amount used in any computation of changes in owners' equity. Alternative measures of net income, such as a statement of sources and uses of funds or inflation-adjusted income statements, are not to be considered as determining net income unless the taxpayer determines its asset, liability, and owners' equity balances on its applicable financial statement in accordance with such an approach.[10]

The taxpayer's applicable financial statement generally is expected to include an income statement, a balance sheet stating the amount of assets, liabilities, and owners' equity, a statement of changes in owners' equity, and such other information as is determined to be appropriate for disclosure. An income statement by itself may constitute a taxpayer's applicable financial statement where the other materials generally expected to be included are not prepared or used by the taxpayer. However, an income statement that does not reconcile with financial statement materials otherwise issued generally will not be considered as establishing net income for the purpose of computing this preference.

The taxpayer's applicable financial statement is the statement it provides for regulatory or credit purposes, for the purpose of reporting to shareholders or other owners, or for other substantial nontax purposes. In the case of a corporation that has more than one financial statement, rules of priority are provided for the determination of which statement is to be considered as the applicable financial statement for the purpose of determining net book income.

The highest priority is given to financial statements that are required to be filed with the Securities and Exchange Commission. Second in priority are audited financial statements that are certified by a professional accountant and used for credit purposes, for reporting to shareholders or other owners, or for any other substantial nontax purpose. For this purpose, a financial statement is considered to be certified if it is accompanied by an opinion of a professional accountant stating that the financial statement generally is consistent with the taxpayer's accounting principles. Third in priority are financial statements required to be provided to the Federal Government or its agencies (other than the Securities and Exchange Commission), a State government or its agencies, or a political subdivision or its agencies. In the absence of any of the above, any financial statement or report that is used for credit purposes, for reporting to shareholders or other owners, or for any other substantial nontax purpose is considered the applicable financial statement. Within a category of priority, a financial statement used for credit purposes has the highest priority, followed by a financial statement provided to shareholders or other owners. A financial statement used for any other substantial nontax purpose has the lowest priority.

In applying these rules of priority, the financial statement actually must be used for reporting for credit purposes, to shareholders, or for a substantial nontax purpose. A financial statement that is not so used is not eligible to be considered as the applicable financial statement in the calculation of the book income preference amount. For example, an unregulated corporation may obtain a certified, audited financial statement, but report to creditors and shareholders using an alternative financial statement that is neither audited nor certified. In such an instance, the alternative, unaudited financial statement is the applicable financial statement and the net income stated in it is used in determining the amount of the preference.

The committee anticipates that all corporate taxpayers will have one or more of the above financial statements. Taxpayers generally are required to maintain books and records. Where the books and records of the taxpayer may be summarized to yield a financial statement, that summarization may be used as the applicable financial statement for the purpose of determining the preference amount. In the case where the taxpayer has no books or records that are capable of summarization, and thus has no applicable financial statement within the meaning of this provision, the net income or loss of the taxpayer for financial reporting purposes

---

[Footnote ¶ 3931 continued]

(10) Financial statement income generally will include the amount of any interest received by the taxpayer that otherwise is exempt from taxation (e.g., interest described in section 103). However, any such interest shall be considered to be exempt from tax for all other purposes under the Code, e.g., in applying (for both regular and minimum tax purposes) section 265(2), relating to deductions for interest on debt used to purchase or carry tax-exempt obligations, and section 291(a)(3), relating to interest deductions on debt used by a financial institution to purchase or carry tax-exempt obligations.

will be considered to be equal to the taxpayer's earnings and profits for the taxable year.

A taxpayer that does not file a financial statement with the Securities and Exchange Commission, a government or governmental agency or obtain a certified, audited financial statement may elect to use the earnings and profits for the taxable year in place of the net income disclosed on its applicable financial statement. A taxpayer making such an election is required to continue to use the earnings and profits calculation so long as it is eligible for the election.

In certain cases, adjustments may be made to reported financial statement income after the financial statements have been issued. It is not anticipated that such adjustments will be taken into account unless the financial statement is actually restated for the adjustments. In the case where a higher priority financial statement has been issued that is not adjusted, but a lower priority financial statement is adjusted, the higher priority, unadjusted financial statement will continue to be considered the applicable financial statement.

For example, a corporation obtains a certified, audited financial statement that it provides to its shareholders. Later, it is determined that the results of the corporation would be better reflected by the use of an alternative accounting method as to certain items. A second income statement reflecting the alternative accounting method is prepared for credit purposes, but it is not certified by a professional accountant and the earlier certified statement is not recalled for correction. As the earlier certified statement has a higher priority than the later uncertified statement, the earlier statement will be considered the applicable financial statement and used in determining the preference amount. If the earlier statement had not been certified, the later statement would be the applicable financial statement, since the provision of a statement for credit purposes has priority over a statement issued to shareholders where both or neither are certified. If both statements had been of equal priority, the later statement would be considered the applicable financial statement.

A similar problem may arise where financial statements are not restated, but supplementary documents are provided to allow the user of the information to determine a different measure of income. If such is the case, the issuance of the supplementary documents will be considered to be the same as the issuance of a restated income statement.

Adjustments: In order to determine properly the amount by which net book income exceeds alternative minimum taxable income, certain adjustments are required to be made.

The book income preference item is determined with regard to the companies included in the taxpayer's consolidated group income tax return for the year.[11] To the extent that different companies may be included for financial statement purposes, it is necessary to adjust net book income so that it reflects the same companies that are included in the consolidated tax return. It is anticipated that this adjustment will be accomplished by removing the net income and any related consolidating eliminations of companies that are included for financial statement purposes but not for Federal income tax purposes, and by adding in the net income and related consolidating eliminations of companies that are excluded for financial statement purposes but included for Federal income tax purposes. In determining the consolidating eliminations of companies included for Federal income tax purposes but not for financial statement purposes, the method of consolidation that the taxpayer normally uses for financial statement purposes will be followed.

A taxpayer is required to record as an item of book net income the amount of any actual or deemed distribution (as measured for tax purposes) from another corporation if the other corporation is not included in the taxpayer's consolidated group for the year. If the taxpayer includes its ownership of the other corporation for financial purposes using another method, such as by consolidation or by the equity method, an adjustment to reverse the inclusion of the other corporation is required. If the corporation not included in the tax consolidation is consolidated in the applicable financial statement, its contribution to book net income is reversed as discussed above. If the corporation is not consolidated in the applicable financial statement, but the taxpayer's interest in the corporation is accounted for using the equity method, the taxpayer's net book income is adjusted to remove the effect of the corporation's inclusion under the equity method.

Where a corporation is included in the taxpayer's consolidated tax return for the year, but is included in the applicable financial statement measure of net income only when dividends are paid, the taxpayer's net book income must be adjusted to eliminate any dividends from the corporation.

The financial statement preference is a measurement of the amount by which pretax financial statement income of the taxpayer exceeds its alternative minimum taxable income. Thus, it is necessary to remove items of financial statement income and expense that relate to Federal or foreign income taxes (i.e., foreign taxes, however denominated, that are eligible for the foreign tax credit). This includes both items of tax provision that are separately stated and any items of tax expense or benefit that may be included in other items of income or expense. Such other items must be restated separately from their tax components for the purpose of computing adjusted net book income. Any provision for State and local taxes is considered allowable for the purpose of computing adjusted net

---

[Footnote ¶ 3931 continued]

(11) Thus, for example, it does not include foreign companies or section 936 corporations, which cannot be consolidated for tax purposes.

book income and no adjustment is made to remove these items in determining book income. If the taxpayer elects to deduct foreign income taxes, rather than claim a credit, the foreign income taxes are treated in the same manner as State and local taxes.

In the case of a corporation that uses a different accounting year for financial statement purposes than the taxable year it uses for Federal income tax purposes, it is anticipated that an adjustment to net book income will be required in order to conform the financial accounting and taxable years for the purpose of computing adjusted net book income. Generally, the corporation will be required to include a pro rata portion of each financial statement accounting year that includes the Federal income tax taxable year. The use of a 52-53 week year will be considered to be the use of the annual year that ends during the same week as the 52-53 week year ends.

For example, a taxpayer uses a June accounting year and a calendar taxable year. For the taxable year ending December 31, 1988, the taxpayer would include one-half of the adjusted net book income for its accounting year ending June 30, 1988 and one-half of its adjusted net book income for its accounting year ending June 30, 1989.

It is anticipated that, if an applicable financial statement for an accounting year that is to be included on a pro rata basis is not available by the time for filing of a taxpayer's Federal income tax return (including any extensions), a reasonable estimate of the amount of adjusted net book income to be included will be made, and that the taxpayer's Federal income tax return will be amended to reflect the pro rata amount when the applicable financial statement is available. It is also anticipated that, if an accounting year that must be included on a pro rata basis has not ended by the time for filing of a taxpayer's Federal income tax return (including extensions), the Secretary may prescribe circumstances in which an election will be made available to use adjusted net book income for the accounting year that ends within the taxpayer's taxable year in lieu of making this adjustment. Such an election, once made, would be irrevocable other than with the consent of the Secretary.

Extraordinary items are included in adjusted net book income unless they are items of tax benefit or expense, such as the use of a foreign tax or net operating loss carryforward. Extraordinary items that are stated net of tax must be adjusted to remove any Federal or foreign income tax expense or benefit components before the extraordinary item is included in adjusted net book income.

The committee bill provides the Secretary of the Treasury with the authority to issue regulations requiring the adjustment of net book income to prevent the omission or duplication of any item. It is anticipated that this grant of authority will be used, for example, to prevent the recording of items directly to the financial statement asset, liability, or equity accounts that are properly included as items of financial statement income or expense. It is also anticipated that this grant of authority will be used to prevent the use of asset, liability or equity accounts to offset items of income or expense that would otherwise not be allowed.

For example, taxpayers may restate prior year financial statements rather than making adjustments to the financial statement for the current period (a prior period adjustment). To prevent the manipulation of book income for the purposes of this provision, it is intended that book income for the current year be adjusted by the cumulative effect of the prior period adjustment on retained earnings or other equity account. However, this adjustment to book income shall be made only to the extent that the prior period adjustment pertains to a period occurring on or after the effective date of this provision.

Other taxpayers might seek to claim depreciation deductions in excess of the basis of the asset, offsetting such additional financial statement depreciation expense with a contra-asset account. It is anticipated that regulations would prevent this type of overstated financial statement expense.

The committee does not intend otherwise to interfere with the choice of a reasonable accounting method by the taxpayer, to require that certain accounting principles be applied, or to establish the Secretary of the Treasury as an arbiter of acceptable accounting principles.

It is expended that the Secretary of the Treasury will interfere in the taxpayer's choice of accounting methods only where such methods result in the omission or duplication of items of income or expense. For example, it is anticipated that taxpayers that compute net income for the purpose of their financial statements in accordance with tax accounting rules will be allowed to continue to do so.

Computation: The alternative minimum taxable income of a corporation for a taxable year includes one-half of the amount by which the adjusted net book income of the taxpayer exceeds the alternative minimum taxable income of the taxpayer before any amount is added to alternative minimum taxable income as a result of this preference. For this purpose, a positive amount is considered to exceed any negative amount and a smaller negative amount is considered to exceed any larger negative amount.

For example, taxpayer A has adjusted net book income of $100 and alternative minimum taxable income (prior to the inclusion of any amount as a result of this preference) of $50. Adjusted net book income exceeds the alternative minimum taxable income by $50, one-half of which ($25) is added to alternative minimum taxable income to give an alternative minimum taxable income for the year of $75.

Taxpayer B has adjusted net book income of $100 and alternative minimum taxable income (prior to the inclusion of any amount as a result of this preference) of negative $50. In this case, adjusted net book income exceeds alternative minimum taxable income by $150, one-half of which ($75) must be added to alternative taxable income, resulting in alternative minimum taxable income for the year of $25.

Taxpayer C has adjusted net book income of negative $100 (a loss of $100) and alternative minimum taxable income (prior to the inclusion of any amount as a result of this preference) of negative $200. The adjusted net book income exceeds alternative minimum taxable income by $100, one-half of which ($50) is added to alternative taxable income, resulting in alternative minimum taxable income for the year of negative $150.

* * * * * *

[Conference Report]

* * * * * *

Taxable years beginning in 1987, 1988, and 1989.—For taxable years beginning in 1987, 1988, and 1989, the conference agreement is generally the same as the Senate amendment. It is clarified that dividends paid by cooperatives, to the extent deductible for regular tax and general minimum tax purposes under section 1382, are also deductible for book income purposes.

Further, the conference agreement provides that dividends received from a section 936 corporation and included in the recipient's book income are to be adjusted; i.e., grossed up, for purposes of measuring book income, by the amount of withholding taxes paid with respect to such dividends by such section 936 corporation. To the extent that the alternative minimum taxable income of the recipient is increased by reason of the inclusion of such dividends (including the gross-up) in book income, the related withholding taxes are treated, for minimum tax purposes, as creditable foreign taxes paid by the recipient.

Assume, for example, that a corporation receives a dividend in the amount of $90 from a section 936 corporation that has paid $10 of withholding taxes with respect to such dividend. The recipient's adjusted pre-tax book income includes dividends of $100. If such book income equals or exceeds other alternative minimum taxable income of the recipient, disregarding this inclusion, then the result of the inclusion is to increase alternative minimum taxable income by $50 (50 percent of $100). Accordingly, the amount of foreign taxes creditable for minimum tax purposes by the recipient is increased by $5 (50 percent of $10).

Assume that, in the above example, the recipient's adjusted pre-tax book income, disregarding the receipt of the above dividend, is $20 less than other alternative minimum taxable income. Accordingly, after inclusion of the grossed-up dividend, book income exceeds other alternative minimum taxable income by $80, and the book preference results in a $40 increase in the amount of alternative minimum taxable income.

Since this increase is 40 percent of the full amount of the grossed-up dividend, the amount of foreign taxes creditable for minimum tax purposes is increased by $4 (40 percent of $10).

In the case of an insurance company whose applicable financial statement is the financial statement prepared for regulatory purposes, the conferees intend that the measure of pre-tax book income is the amount of net gain from operations after dividends to policyholders and before Federal income taxes.

It is clarified that no item of Federal or foreign income tax expenses or benefit (other than foreign taxes deducted in lieu of claiming a foreign tax credit), including any adjustment of deferred taxes resulting from the corporate tax rate changes of this Act or any subsequent legislation, is included in the computation of adjusted pre-tax book income for minimum tax purposes.

The conference agreement provides that, under regulations prescribed by the Secretary of the Treasury, adjusted book income shall be properly adjusted to prevent the omission or duplication of any item. The conferees intend that adjustments made under this provision may include adjustments made under the principles of section 482. The Secretary may require that adjustments be made to book income where the principles of this provision otherwise would be avoided through the disclosure of financial information through footnotes and other supplementary statements.

The conference agreement also provides that a taxpayer's current earnings and profits for the taxable year may be used in certain cases for purposes of the book income preference. The conferees clarify that earnings and profits for this purpose shall be determined without diminution by reason of distributions or federal income taxes during the taxable year. Moreover, for purposes of this provision, earnings and profits shall not be determined with regard to the adjusted current earnings calculation applicable for years beginning after 1989. In calculating earnings and profits for an affiliated group of corporations filing a consolidated return, appropriate adjustments will be made, as prescribed by the Secretary of the Treasury, to prevent the double inclusion of earnings and profits through the operation of the consolidated return regulations or otherwise.

Taxable years beginning after December 31, 1989.—*Application of the preference in general.*—For taxable years in which the preference applies, alternative minimum taxable income is increased by 75 percent of the amount by which adjusted current earnings exceeds alternative minimum taxable income (before this adjustment), whether alternative minimum taxable income and adjusted current earnings are positive or negative amounts. If alternative minimum taxable income (before this adjustment) exceeds the amount of adjusted current earnings, then alternative minimum taxable income is reduced by 75 percent of such difference. However, such reduction cannot exceed the excess of the aggregate amount by which alternative minimum taxable income has been increased as a result of this provision in prior taxable years, less the aggregate amount of reductions taken in prior years.

For example, a calendar year taxpayer has adjusted current earnings of $400 in 1990, $300 in 1991, and $200 in 1992. Alternative minimum taxable income is $300 for each of those years. In 1990, adjusted current earnings exceeds alternative minimum taxable income by $100, 75 percent of which ($75) must be included as an additional item of alternative minimum taxable income. In 1992, alternative minimum taxable income exceeds adjusted current earnings by $100, creating a potential negative adjustment to alternative minimum taxable income of $75. As the aggregate increases to alternative minimum taxable income for prior years equals $75 (the amount added to alternative minimum tax in 1990) and there are no aggregate reductions, the full amount of the potential negative adjustment will reduce alternative minimum taxable income for 1992.

A positive amount is always considered to be in excess of a negative amount and a smaller negative amount in excess of a larger negative amount. Thus, adjusted current earnings of $20 exceeds alternative minimum taxable income of negative $20 by $40, and $30 (equal to 75% of the excess) would be includible in alternative minimum taxable income. Likewise, alternative minimum taxable income of negative $20 exceeds adjusted current earnings of negative $40 by $20, and $15 (equal to 75% of the excess) could be used to reduce alternative minimum taxable income if not subject to limitation.

Adjusted current earnings.—In general, adjusted current earnings requires the same treatment of an item as used for purposes of computing alternative minimum taxable income (before this adjustment). In the case of exclusion items, however, adjusted current earnings requires the same treatment of an item as used for the computation of regular earnings and profits as computed for purposes of Subchapter C. An exclusion item is an item of income or expense that is included in regular earnings and profits but is never included in the computation of either regular or alternative minimum taxable income (e.g., interest on tax-exempt bonds and the portion of dividends excluded under the dividends received deduction). For this purpose, the fact that an item could eventually be included in alternative minimum taxable income on the liquidation or disposal of a business (or similar circumstances) will not prevent exclusion item treatment. Additionally, adjusted current earnings requires different treatment of certain specifically listed items.

An exclusion item that is income for regular earnings and profits purposes is included in adjusted current earnings. Generally, any item of expense that is not allowable for any year for alternative minimum tax purposes solely because it relates to an exclusion item of income will be allowed in computing adjusted current earnings. Thus, interest on all tax-exempt bonds is included in adjusted current earnings, as well as the costs incurred to carry such tax-exempt bonds. However, if such carrying costs would be limited in the computation of taxable income, even if the income to which they relate is fully taxable, then the costs will be similarly limited for adjusted current earnings. Also, the original issue discount and market discount rules will apply to tax-exempt bonds for purposes of computing adjusted current earnings in the same manner as for taxable bonds.

In determining the amount of an item of deduction or loss allowable for adjusted current earnings, no deduction is allowed for an exclusion item of expense or deduction. Thus, the dividends received deduction generally is not allowed for adjusted current earnings. However, an exception is made for deductions allowed under section 243 or 245 for a dividend qualifying for a 100-percent dividends received deduction if the payor and recipient corporation could not be members of the same affiliated group under section 1504 by reason of section 1504(b), to the extent the payor corporation is subject to Federal income tax.

For example, a foreign sales corporation (FSC) is prohibited from inclusion in its parent's affiliated group, but is subject to Federal income tax on only a percentage of its income. The portion of any dividend paid from current earnings and profits to the parent equal to the percentage of the FSC's income that is subject to tax would be eligible for exclusion from adjusted current earnings. In the case of dividends received from section 936 corporations, a dividends received deduction rule is used for adjusted current earnings that generally follows the same rule that applies with regard to the book income preference (the full amount of the dividend is included in income and a credit allowed for a percentage of the withholding tax.)

Adjusted current earnings measures pre-tax income without diminution by reason of any distribution made during the taxable year. Thus, the deduction for Federal and foreign income tax expense allowed for regular earnings and profits purposes is not allowed in the computation of adjusted current earnings (except for foreign taxes where the taxpayer elects to deduct such taxes rather than claim a credit). Moreover, no deduction is allowed with respect to a dividend paid.

Depreciation is computed for the adjusted current earnings using the slower of the method used in connection with the preparation of the taxpayer's applicable financial statement or the applicable earnings and profits method. For property placed in service in taxable years beginning after 1989, the applicable earnings and profits method is straight-line over the ADR midpoint life. For property placed in service after 1986 but before the first taxable year beginning after

1989 and to which the amendments made by section 301 of this agreement apply, the applicable earnings and profits method generally provides for depreciation using (1) the adjusted minimum tax basis of property as of the close of the last taxable year beginning before January 1, 1990, (2) the remaining ADR midpoint life of the property at the beginning of the first taxable year beginning after 1989, and (3) the straight line method. For property to which the section 168 (as in effect on the day before the date of the enactment of this Act) applies, the applicable earnings and profits method provides for depreciation using (1) the adjusted regular tax basis of property as of the close of the last taxable year beginning before January 1, 1990, (2) the remaining ADR life as of the beginning of the first taxable year beginning after 1989, and (3) the straight-line method. For property placed in service before 1981, the applicable earnings and profits method is the same method as is used for regular tax purposes.

The determination of whether the method used in connection with the preparation of the taxpayer's applicable financial statement or the applicable earnings and profits method is slower is calculated by comparing the net present values of the deductions provided by each method. In the case of property placed in service in taxable years beginning before 1990, the net present value of deductions is to be determined only with regard to the remaining deductions allowable in taxable years beginning after 1989. In making this determination, the net value of deductions is computed using the same adjusted basis for both methods. It is anticipated that the Secretary of the Treasury will publish interest rates for use in computing the net present value of deductions. In the absence of such published rates, the applicable federal rate (c.f. section 1274(d)) for the period equal to the ADR life of the property may be used.

Intangible drilling and development costs allowable under section 263(c) are capitalized for adjusted current earnings and amortized over the slower of the method used in the preparation of the taxpayer's applicable financial accounting statement or the 60-month period beginning with the month in which production from the well begins. In the case of a taxpayer recovering intangible drilling and development costs through unit of production cost depletion for financial statement purposes, the determination of which method is slower will be done under regulations to be provided by the Secretary of the Treasury, taking into account reasonable estimates of the rate at which the intangible drilling and development costs are expected to be recovered for financial accounting purposes. Similar rules apply with respect to mining exploration and development costs in comparing the 120-month period with the method used in the preparation of the tax-payer's applicable financial statement.

No loss is allowed in the determination of adjusted current earnings on the exchange of any pool of debt obligations for another pool of debt obligations having substantially the same effective interest rates and maturities for the purpose of the adjusted earnings and profits method.

Special rules apply to insurers computing adjusted current earnings. In the case of a life insurance company, the acquisition expenses of any policy, for adjusted current earnings purposes, must be capitalized and amortized in accordance with the method generally required at the time such costs are insured by the Financial Accounting Standards Board (FASB), or, if the FASB has not published such a method, under guidelines issued by the American Institute of Certified Public Accountants that relate to generally accepted accounting principles. Acquisition expenses of life insurance companies are subject to this treatment on a fresh start basis, i.e., in calculating adjusted current earnings, it is assumed that life insurance acquisition expenses have been treated in the same manner as required under this provision for prior years. Acquisition expenses of property and casualty insurance companies are not subject to this treatment, because the unearned premium reserve deduction of property and casualty insurance companies is reduced by 20 percent (10 percent in the case of certain bond insurance) under the regular tax, as a method of addressing mismatching of deductible acquisition expenses and deferred premium income. In computing adjusted current earnings, the small life insurance company deduction under section 806 and the election for small property and casualty insurance companies to be taxed only on investment income under section 831(b) do not apply.

The conference agreement clarifies that inside buildup on a life insurance contract (as determined under section 7702(g)) or on an annuity policy (as determined under section 72(u)(2)) is includible in adjusted current earnings, and a deduction is allowed for that portion of any premium that is attributable to insurance coverage.

In the case of a corporation that has experienced a change of ownership after the date of the enactment of this Act, the basis of the property of the corporation [may] not, for adjusted current earnings, exceed the allocable portion of the purchase price paid for the corporation.

Certain other adjustments required by section 312(n) (i.e., under paragraphs 1 through 6) generally are required in determining adjusted current earnings, subject to the rules regarding dates that apply for such purposes. For example, in the case of a disposition of property occurring in 1990 or thereafter, use of the installment method is not allowable in determining adjusted current earnings even if the use of such method is otherwise allowable for minimum tax purposes.

For the purposes of section 312(n)(1), which requires the capitalization of construction period carrying charges, the conferees intend that the "avoided cost method" under section 263A shall apply to determine the amount of interest allocable to production. Under section 312(n)(1), the avoided cost method is intended to apply irrespective of whether application of such method (or a similar method) is required, authorized, or considered appropriate under financial or regulatory accounting principles applicable to the taxpayer. Thus, for example, a utility company must apply the avoided cost method of determining capitalized interest under section 312(n)(1) even though a different method is authorized or required by Financial Accounting Standards Board Statement 34 or the regulatory authority having jurisdiction over the utility. The growing of timber or other crops is not considered construction under section 312(n)(1).

The conferees intend that no inference is to be drawn from the classification of an item as a specifically listed item as to current treatment for regular earnings and profits purposes or as to whether such a specifically listed item is an exclusion item.

In calculating adjusted current earnings for an affiliated group of corporations filing a consolidated return, appropriate adjustments will be made, as prescribed by the Secretary of the Treasury, to prevent the double inclusion of any item of adjusted current earnings through the operation of the consolidated return regulations or otherwise. The determination of whether a consolidated group is eligible to decrease alternative minimum taxable income as a result of alternative minimum taxable income exceeding adjusted current earnings is expected to be made at the consolidated level.

Separate item allocation.—The conferees understand that reliance on adjusted earnings and profits has consequences regarding compliance by taxpayers who already must keep records based on the regular tax and general minimum tax systems. It is intended that the adjusted earnings and profits and general minimum tax systems be integrated regarding recordkeeping to the maximum extent feasible. The conferees anticipate that before the end of 1989, the Secretary of the Treasury will provide guidance through regulations or rulings regarding such integration. The furtherance of such integration should also be considered in the Treasury study regarding book income and earnings and profits that is mandated under the Act.

Study.—The conferees direct the Secretary of the Treasury to study and to report regarding the book income and earnings and profits provisions, including refinements that may be appropriate (e.g., with regard to the application of the separate item allocation election).

The final report is to be submitted, by January 1, 1989, to the House Committee on Ways and Means and the Senate Committee on Finance.

5. Regular Tax Elections

*   *   *   *   *   *

In the case of certain expenditures that would give rise to a minimum tax preference if treated under the rules generally applying for regular tax purposes, the taxpayer may make a "normative election," i.e., elect to have the minimum tax rule for deducting the expenditure apply for regular tax purposes. The expenditures to which this rule applies are the following: circulation expenditures, research and experimental expenditures, intangible drilling costs, and mining development and exploration expenditures. Elections may be made "dollar-for-dollar"; thus, for example, a taxpayer who incurs $100,000 of intangible drilling costs with respect to a single well may elect normative treatment for any portion of that amount.

To the extent that such an election applies, the item to which it applies is treated for all purposes, under both the regular and the minimum tax, pursuant to the election. No other deduction is allowed for the item to the extent that such an election applies.

An election made under this rule may be revoked only with the consent of the Secretary. Elections may be made at such time and in such manner as the Secretary by regulations prescribes. In the case of a partnership or S corporation, an election may be made separately by any partner (or shareholder) with respect to such individual's allocable share of any expenditure.

*   *   *   *   *   *

[Conference Report]

The conference agreement follows * * * the Senate amendment.

6. Adjustments in Other Years When Taxpayer Pays Minimum Tax

*   *   *   *   *   *

[Senate Explanation]

*   *   *   *   *   *

Minimum tax credit: When a taxpayer pays alternative minimum tax, the amount of such tax paid (i.e., the net minimum tax) generally is allowed as a credit against the regular tax liability (net of other nonrefundable credits) of the taxpayer in subsequent years. However, the minimum tax credit cannot be used to reduce minimum tax liability in subsequent years. The minimum tax credit can be carried forward indefinitely; thus, it is not necessary for the taxpayer to determine which prior year's minimum tax credit is being used in a particular year. The minimum tax credit cannot be carried back.

In the case of an acquisition of assets of a corporation by another corporation to which section 381(a) applies (for example, a statutory merger), any unused minimum tax credits of the acquired corporation will be treated as a "tax attribute" that is taken into account by the acquiring corporation. However, for such an acquisition, as well as an acquisition of stock, the availability of the credits may be subject to limitation under the provisions of

Part V of Subchapter C (sections 381 through 383).

The minimum tax credit is allowed only with respect to liability arising as a result of deferral preferences (i.e., preferences other than those that result in permanent exclusion of certain income for regular tax purposes). Thus, the amount of the net minimum tax is reduced by the amount of minimum tax liability that would have arisen if the only applicable preferences were the exclusion preferences. The exclusion preferences are those relating to percentage depletion and regular tax itemized deductions that are denied for minimum tax purposes.[12]

Consider, for example, the case of married taxpayers filing a joint return with (i) no regular taxable income, (ii) deferral preferences in the amount of $400,000, and (iii) exclusion preferences (including any disallowed itemized deductions) in the amount of $100,000. Under the 20 percent alternative minimum tax rate, and in light of the phase-out of the exemption amount, minimum tax liability would equal $100,000. However, if the taxpayers had had only exclusion preferences, minimum tax liability would have equaled $12,000 (20 percent of $100,000 as reduced by the $40,000 exemption amount). Thus, the amount of minimum tax available as a carryforward credit would be $88,000 ($100,000 less $12,000).

*   *   *   *   *   *

[Conference Report]

*   *   *   *   *   *

The conference agreement generally follows the Senate amendment. The minimum tax preference, described in section X of this report, regarding deductions determined under section 833(b), is treated as an exclusion preference. Moreover, for taxable years beginning in 1990 or thereafter, the items included by reason of the preference for earnings and profits that otherwise would be permanently excluded from alternative minimum taxable income (e.g., dividends received and tax-exempt interest) are treated as exclusion items.

7. Incentive Tax Credits

*   *   *   *   *   *

[Senate Explanation]

*   *   *   *   *   *

Incentive tax credits: Nonrefundable credits other than the minimum tax credit generally are accorded treatment that is intended to have the same effect as the rules applying under the present law alternative minimum tax on individuals. However, the rules have been revised in one technical respect in the interest of simplicity. Under present law, nonrefundable credits can be claimed against the regular tax even if they provide no benefit (i.e., they reduce regular

tax liability to less than the amount of minimum tax liability that was due in any case). To the extent that the credits provide no benefit due to the minimum tax, however, they are allowed as carryovers to other taxable years.

Under the bill, such credits generally cannot be claimed in the first place to the extent that they would reduce regular tax liability to less than tentative minimum tax liability and hence provide no benefit. As under present law, such credits are allowed as carryovers to other taxable years, under the generally applicable rules for credit carryovers.

Where no minimum tax is due and the minimum tax does not limit the use of incentive credits, the taxpayer is not required to file with his or her tax return a form showing minimum tax computations. For example, a taxpayer with $100 of regular tax liability (disregarding incentive credits), a targeted jobs tax credit in the amount of $10, and whose tentative minimum tax equaled less than $90, would not be required to file a minimum tax form with the Internal Revenue Service.

The alternative minimum tax does not apply to any corporation that validly elects the application of section 936. Thus, a section 936 corporation is exempt from the alternative minimum tax, even to the extent that it has preference income that is not qualified possession source income.

*   *   *   *   *   *

[Conference Report]

*   *   *   *   *   *

The conference agreement generally follows the Senate amendment, except that, as a transition rule, regular investment tax credits are permitted, in effect, to reduce minimum tax liability by 25 percent. Under this modification, such credits can be used to reduce regular tax liability to 75 percent of tentative minimum tax liability, rather than only to the full amount of such liability. Moreover, such credits can instead be used to offset 25 percent of the taxpayer's tentative minimum tax for the year, where this results in permitting a greater amount of such credits to be used. The amount of minimum tax that is treated as paid, for purposes of the minimum tax credit, is determined without regard to the use of investment tax credits.

For example, assume that, disregarding investment tax credits, Corporation A would have a regular tax liability of $10 million and a tentative minimum tax liability of $4 million. A can use up to $7 million of investment tax credits, reducing A's tax liability to $3 million (treated as a payment of regular rather than of minimum tax).

Moreover, assume that, disregarding investment tax credits, Corporation B would have a regular tax liability of zero and a

---

【Footnote ¶ 3931 continued】

(12) For this purpose, the book income preference is treated as a deferral preference, notwithstanding that some differences between alternative minimum taxable income and book income may result from exclusion items (such as tax-exempt interest).

tentative minimum tax liability of $4 million. B can use up to $1 million of investment tax credits, reducing B's tax liability to $3 million. This gives rise to a minimum tax credit of $4 million in the event that all of B's preferences are deferral preferences, since the minimum tax credit is measured without regard to the use of the investment tax credit.

Further, assume that, disregarding investment tax credits, Corporation C would have a regular tax liability of $3.5 million and a tentative minimum tax liability of $4 million. C can use up to $1 million of investment tax credits, reducing C's tax liability to $3 million. This gives rise to a minimum tax credit of $500,000, if all of C's preferences are deferral preferences.

The rule for investment tax credits is applied consistently with the amount of tentative minimum tax liability in light of the limitations, described below, on the use of foreign tax credits and net operating losses. Thus, for example, assume that a taxpayer would have no regular tax liability, and a minimum tax liability of $10 million in the absence of foreign tax credits, net operating losses, and investment tax credits. As described below, foreign tax credits and net operating losses could not be used to reduce minimum tax liability to less than $1 million. To the extent that such losses and credits did not so reduce minimum tax liability, investment tax credits could then be used to reduce such liability to $1 million.

The conference agreement provides a technical correction regarding the treatment of income eligible for the section 936 credit. Under this correction, it is clarified that income of a section 936 corporation eligible for the credit generally is excluded from alternative minimum taxable income (including the preference for book income or earnings and profits).[3] However, a taxpayer that qualifies for the section 936 credit may be subject to minimum tax with respect to income not qualifying for the credit.

It is clarified that, for purposes of the minimum tax, the megawattage of an electric generating unit is to be determined with reference to the *Summary Information Report* (NUREG-0871, Vol. No. 4, Issue Date: October 1985), published by the U.S. Nuclear Regulatory Commission.

8. Foreign Tax Credit

*   *   *   *   *   *

[Senate Explanation]

*   *   *   *   *   *

Foreign tax credit: Under the bill, minimum tax liability is defined as the excess of the tentative minimum tax (i.e., 20 percent of the excess of alternative minimum taxable income over the exemption amount, reduced by the specially computed foreign tax credit using the minimum tax base) over the regular tax (i.e., regular tax liability reduced by the foreign tax credit). The foreign tax credit thus is, in effect, allowable for purposes of the alternative minimum tax, under rules similar to those applying to the alternative minimum tax on individuals under present law. These rules involve separate application, for minimum tax purposes, of the section 904 limitation on the amount of the credit, to reflect the differences between regular taxable income and alternative minimum taxable income.

For example, to the extent that preferences allocable to U.S. source income, when taken into consideration for minimum tax purposes, change the ratio of foreign taxable income to worldwide income, the application of section 904 may lead to different results under the regular and the alternative minimum taxes, respectively. In light of these differences, taxpayers must separately keep track of the amount of foreign tax credit carryforwards allowable for regular and for minimum tax purposes.

In applying section 904 for minimum tax purposes with respect to an amount added to alternative minimum taxable income with respect to the book income of a corporate taxpayer, the committee intends that the percentage of such income that is from sources within the United States will be treated as the same as the percentage of all other alternative minimum taxable income for the taxable year of the taxpayer that is from sources within the United States. Thus, in effect, the book income preference will not result in any change in the percentage applying for purposes of the alternative minimum tax section 904 limitation.

In addition to being limited by section 904, use of the foreign tax credit is limited for minimum tax purposes by a rule designed to prevent U.S. taxpayers with substantial income from using the foreign tax credit to avoid all U.S. tax liability. Under this rule, no more than 90 percent of tentative minimum tax liability (before allowance of the foreign tax credit) can be offset by foreign tax credits, even if under section 904 more than 90 percent of such liability could be offset by such credits. This rule has no effect on a taxpayer who already is prevented by section 904 from offsetting more than 90 percent of minimum tax liability with foreign tax credits. Any foreign tax credits that are disallowed under this rule are treated, for carryover purposes, like credits disallowed by reason of section 904. This rule, like the limitation under section 904, is applied prior

---

[Footnote ¶ 3931 continued]

(3) However, as discussed above, a dividend paid by a section 936 corporation to its parent corporation may in effect be included in minimum taxable income, by adding to the amount of the parent's preference for book income or earnings and profits. In such a case, an adjustment is made for foreign taxes paid with respect to such dividends by grossing up the dividends by the amount of such taxes and treating such taxes as paid by the parent for purposes of the foreign tax credit.

to comparing the amount of the taxpayer's minimum tax liability with the amount of such taxpayer's regular tax liability.

*   *   *   *   *   *

[Conference Report]

*   *   *   *   *   *

The conference agreement generally follows the Senate amendment. For taxable years beginning in 1990 or thereafter, items included in alternative minimum taxable income by reason of the preference for earnings and profits are sourced, for purposes of the section 904 limitation, on an item-by-item basis. It is clarified that the taxpayer's regular tax election regarding whether to treat foreign taxes as giving rise to a deduction or a credit is controlling for minimum tax purposes as well. Moreover, in light of the limitation on the use of net operating losses, described below, it is provided that foreign tax credits cannot offset more than 90 percent of minimum tax liability as determined without regard to foreign tax credits and net operating losses.

For example, assume that in 1987 a taxpayer has $10 million of alternative minimum taxable income for the year. In the absence of net operating losses or foreign tax credits, the taxpayer's tentative minimum tax liability (i.e., liability as determined without regard to the amount of regular tax liability) would equal $2 million. Accordingly, foreign tax credits cannot be used to reduce liability to less than $200,000, whether or not the taxpayer has any minimum tax net operating losses.

It is clarified that, with regard to years prior to the effective date of the corporate alternative minimum tax, rules apply similar to those applying in 1982 upon the enactment of the individual alternative minimum tax. Thus, pre-effective date regular tax foreign tax credits carried forward to 1987 are treated as minimum tax foreign tax credit carryforwards, and minimum tax foreign tax credits are reduced by the amount of any foreign tax credits carried back, for regular tax purposes, to years prior to 1987.

9. Net Operating Losses (NOLs)

*   *   *   *   *   *

[Senate Explanation]

Under the bill, special rules apply for net operating losses. These rules generally are the same as the present law rules with respect to the alternative minimum tax for individuals.

For purposes of the alternative minimum tax, net operating loss deductions are determined by using a separate computation of alternative minimum tax net operating losses and carryovers. Generally, this computation takes into account the differences between the regular tax base and the alternative minimum tax base.

The amount of the net operating loss (under section 172(c)) for any taxable year, for purposes of the alternative minimum tax, generally is computed in the same manner as the regular tax net operating loss, with two exceptions. First, the items of tax preference arising in that year are added back to taxable income (or, as with depreciation, adjustments relating to those items are made), and, second, for individuals, only those itemized deductions (as modified under section 172(d)) allowable in computing alternative minimum taxable income are taken into account. In computing the amount of deduction for years other than the year of the loss (i.e., carryover years), the recomputed loss is deducted from the alternative minimum taxable income (as modified under section 172(b)(2)(A)) in the carryover year (whether or not the taxpayer is subject to the minimum tax in that year).

For example, if in year one a taxpayer has $20,000 of income and $35,000 of losses, of which $10,000 are preference items, the alternative minimum tax net operating loss for the year is $5,000. Thus, in any subsequent (or prior) year to which the loss may be carried, a $5,000 net operating loss deduction is allowed to reduce income subject to the alternative minimum tax.

Assume that, in year two, the taxpayer has $20,000 of alternative minimum taxable income (without regard to the net operating loss deduction). The taxpayer reduces his or her alternative minimum taxable income to $15,000 by the minimum tax net operating loss deduction. The net operating loss deduction for the regular tax is not affected by this computation (i.e., the taxpayer has a loss carryover of $15,000 from year one to be used under the regular tax).

For corporations, a transition rule generally allows, for purposes of the alternative minimum tax, all pre-effective date regular tax net operating losses to be carried forward as minimum tax NOLs to the first taxable year for which the tax, as amended under the bill, applies (and to subsequent years until used up). For individuals, present law is retained with respect to the calculation of alternative minimum tax net operating losses for such years.

An adjustment is required in the case of a corporation that, as of the end of the last taxable year beginning before January 1, 1987, had a deferred add-on minimum tax liability for a year prior to 1987, under section 56(b), due to certain net operating losses. For such a corporation, no add-on minimum tax liability will be imposed after 1986, but the alternative minimum tax net operating loss carried to the first taxable year of the corporation beginning after December 31, 1986, is reduced by the amount of the preferences that gave rise to the liability.

*   *   *   *   *   *

[Conference Report]

*   *   *   *   *   *

The conference agreement follows * * * the Senate amendment, except that NOLs cannot offset more than 90 percent of alternative minimum taxable income. As with the 90 percent limitation on the use of the foreign tax credit, amounts disallowed by reason of this limitation may be carried over to other taxable years.

Thus, for example, assume that in 1987 a taxpayer has $10 million of alternative minimum taxable income for the year, and minimum tax NOLs in the amount of $11 million. The NOLs reduce alternative minimum taxable income to $1 million. This gives rise to tentative minimum tax liability of $200,000. The taxpayer carries forward $2 million of minimum tax NOLs to 1988. Since the allowability of net operating losses is determined prior to the allowability of foreign tax credits, this taxpayer would not be permitted to use any minimum tax foreign tax credits in 1987.

It is clarified that, in light of the parallel nature of the regular tax and minimum tax systems, any limitations applying for regular tax purposes to the use by a consolidated group of NOLs or current year losses (e.g., section 1503) apply for minimum tax purposes as well. Moreover, it is clarified that an election under section 172(b)(3)(C) to relinquish the carryback period applies for both regular tax and minimum tax purposes.

10. Estimated Tax Payments

* * * * * *

House Bill

The House bill requires that estimated tax payments be made with respect to minimum tax liability.

Senate Amendment

The Senate amendment is the same as the House bill.

Conference Agreement

The conference agreement follows the House bill and the Senate amendment.

11. Effective Date

[Senate Explanation]

* * * * * *

Effective Date.—The provisions apply to taxable years beginning after December 31, 1986.

* * * * * *

[Conference Report]

* * * * * *

The conference agreement follows the Senate amendment.

[¶ 3932] SECTION 702. STUDY OF BOOK AND EARNINGS AND PROFITS ADJUSTMENTS

[Conference Report]

The conferees direct the Secretary of the Treasury to study and to report regarding the book income and earnings and profits provisions, including refinements that may be appropriate (e.g., with regard to the application of the separate item allocation election).

The final report is to be submitted, by January 1, 1989, to the House Committee on Ways and Means and the Senate Committee on Finance.

[¶ 3935] SECTION 801. LIMITATION ON USE OF CASH METHOD OF ACCOUNTING

(Sec. 448 of the Code)

[House Explanation]

Explanation of Provision

General rule.—The committee bill provides that certain taxpayers may not use the cash method of accounting for Federal income tax purposes. The rule applies to corporations (other than S corporations) and partnerships where one of the partners is a corporation (other than an S corporation), except in certain specified cases. The rule also applies to trusts subject to tax under section 511(b) with respect to activities of the trust constituting an unrelated trade or business. The use of a hybrid method of accounting which records some, but not all, transactions using the cash method will be considered the same as the use of the cash method for these purposes. Any change from the cash method necessitated by the committee bill will be treated as a change in accounting method, initiated by the taxpayer with the approval of the Secretary of the Treasury. The committee bill does not change the rules of present law relating to what accounting methods clearly reflect income or the authority of the Secretary of the Treasury to require the use of an accounting method that clearly reflects income.

Trades or businesses allowed to continue use of the cash method.—*Small businesses.*—The committee bill allows the continued use of the cash method of accounting by taxpayers with average annual gross receipts of $5 million or less that are allowed to use the cash method of accounting under present law. Average annual gross receipts are to be computed by dividing the sum of the gross receipts for so many of the previous three taxable years (not including the current taxable year) as the taxpayer conducted business by the number of such taxable years. For this purpose, gross receipts does not include sales returns and allowances for a taxable year. For purposes of the $5 million test, gross receipts for any taxable year of less than 12 months are annualized.

In determining whether a taxpayer has average annual gross receipts in excess of $5 million, the gross receipts of all related

Act § 801   ¶ 3935

entities are aggregated if such entities would be treated as a single employer under subsection (a) or (b) of section 52 or subsection (m) or (o) of section 414.

Farming businesses.—The committee bill allows the continued use of the cash method of accounting by farming businesses, other than those farming businesses which are not allowed to use the cash method of accounting under present law. A farming business is any business engaged in the growing, raising, managing, or training of crops or livestock. In addition, a farming business includes the operation of a nursery or a sod farm. A farming business includes the raising or harvesting of Christmas trees and other ornamental trees, but does not include, the raising or harvesting of other trees, unless the trees bear fruits, nuts, or some other crop and the trees are raised or acquired for the primary purpose of exploiting such fruits, nuts, or other crop.

Individuals and qualified personal service corporations.—The committee bill allows the continued use of the cash method of accounting for entities where the incidence of taxation falls either at the individual level or on a qualified personal service corporation. Entities eligible for the exception include sole proprietorships, S corporations, qualified personal service corporations and qualifying partnerships.

A qualifying partnership is a partnership in which all of the partnership interests are held by individuals, qualified personal service corporations, S corporations, or other qualifying partnerships.

For purposes of this exception, a qualified personal service corporation is a corporation that meets both a function test and an ownership test. The function test is met if substantially all the activities of the corporation are the performance of services in the field of health, law, engineering (including surveying and mapping), architecture, accounting, actuarial science, performing arts or consulting. The ownership test is met if substantially all of the value of the outstanding stock in the corporation is owned by employees performing services for the corporation in a field satisfying the function test, retired individuals who performed services for the corporation or its predecessor(s) in such a field, the estate of such an individual, or any person who acquired its ownership interest as a result of the death of such an individual within the prior 24 months (disregarding community property laws). For the purposes of applying the ownership test, stock owned by a partnership, an S corporation or a qualified personal service corporation will be considered as owned by its partners or shareholders.

Time of accrual.—The committee bill provides that in the case of the provision of personal services by an accrual basis taxpay-er, the taxpayer is not required to accrue amounts earlier than when the amounts are billed by the taxpayer. For these purposes, provision of personal services does not include the provision of services of a kind typically provided by a regulated public utility or the providing of services by a bank or similar financial institution.[2]

The committee bill also modifies the economic performance test for all taxpayers receiving services to provide that, in the case of services provided by a non-employee, economic performance does not occur before the taxpayer is billed for the services.

Amount of accrual.—The committee bill provides that an accrual basis taxpayer need not accrue as income any portion of amounts billed for the performance of services[3] which, on the basis of experience, it will not collect. This rule does not apply, however, if the taxpayer charges any interest or penalty for failure to make timely payment in connection with the amount billed. The offering of a discount for early payment of an amount billed will not prevent application of the rule as long as the full amount of the bill is otherwise accrued as income and the discount for early payment treated as an adjustment to income in the year such payment is made.

The amount of billings that, on the basis of experience, will not be collected is equal to the total amount billed, multiplied by a fraction whose numerator is the total amount of such receivables which were billed and determined not to be collectible within the most recent five *** taxable years of the taxpayer, and whose denominator is the total of such amounts billed within the same five year period. If the taxpayer has not been in existence for the prior five taxable years, the portion of such five year period which the taxpayer has been in existence is to be used.

For example, assume that an accrual-basis taxpayer has $100,000 of receivables that have been created during the most recent five taxable years. Of the $100,000 of accounts receivable, $1,000 have been determined to be uncollectible. The amount, based on experience, which is not expected to be collected is equal to 1 percent ($1,000 divided by $100,000) of any receivable arising from the provision of services that are outstanding at close of the taxable year.

A taxpayer who has not recognized income on amounts not expected to be collected must recognize additional income in any taxable year in which payments on amounts not recognized are received. If a receivable is determined to be partially or wholly uncollectible, no portion of the loss arising as a result of such determination, that was not recognized as income at the time the receivable was created, shall be deductible.

The committee intends that the Secretary of the Treasury may provide a periodic

---

[Footnote ¶ 3935]   (2) No inference as to the proper timing for the accrual of income and expense under present law is to be drawn from the exclusion of utility services and services provided by a financial institution from the time-of-accrual rules of the committee bill. Such services are intended to be treated in the same manner as under present law.

(3) For this purpose, the performance of services does not include the activities of banks and other financial institutions.

system of accounting for billings that, on the basis of experience, will not be collected where the periodic system results in the same taxable income as would be the case were each receivable recorded separately.

Transitional rules.—The committee bill treats any change from the cash method of accounting required as a result of the committee bill as a change in the taxpayer's method of accounting, initiated by the taxpayer with the consent of the Secretary of the Treasury. In order to prevent items of income and expense from being included in taxable income either twice or not at all, an adjustment under section 481 is required to be made. The amount of such adjustment will be included in income over a period not to exceed [four] * * * taxable years. It is expected that the concepts of Revenue Procedure 84-74, 1984-2 C.B. 736, generally will apply to determine the actual timing of recognition of income or expense as a result of the adjustment.[4]

In the case of the business of operating a hospital, the transitional rules will apply with the section 481 adjustment amount to be included in income over a period not to exceed ten taxable years ***.

[Conference Report]

The conference agreement generally follows the House bill with certain modifications.

Tax shelters.—The conference agreement provides that the cash method of accounting may not be used by any tax shelter. For this purpose, a tax shelter is defined in the same manner as under section 461(i) of present law. Thus, a tax shelter is (a) any enterprise (other than a C corporation) if at any time interests in such enterprise have been offered for sale in any offering required to be registered with any Federal or State agency having the authority to regulate the offering of securities for sale, (b) any syndicate within the meaning of section 1256(e)(3), or (c) any tax shelter within the meaning of section 6661(b)(2)(C)(ii). In the case of an enterprise engaged in the trade or business of farming, a tax shelter is (a) any tax shelter within the meaning of section 6661(b)(2)(C)(ii) or (b) a farming syndicate within the meaning of section 464(c).

The exceptions of the general rule for farming businesses, qualified personal service corporations, and entities with average annual gross receipts of $5 million or less do not apply in the case of tax shelters.

The conference agreement further provides that a tax shelter may not take advantage of the recurring item exception under section 461(h)(3) to the rule requiring economic performance before an accrual basis taxpayer may deduct an item of expense. However, in the case of a tax shelter economic performance with respect to the drilling of

an oil and gas well will be considered to have occurred if the drilling of the well commences within 90 days of the close of the taxable year.

Qualified personal service corporations.—The conference agreement also changes the requirements of the ownership test under the definition of a qualified personal service corporation. In order to meet the ownership test under the conference agreement, substantially all (i.e., at least 95 percent) of the value of the stock of the corporation must be held, directly or indirectly, by employees performing services for such corporation in connection with the qualified services performed by the company, retired employees who had performed such services, the estate of any such current or retired employee, or any other person who acquired stock by reason of the death of such an employee (for the 2-year period beginning with the death of such employee.) In applying the ownership test, the applicable community property laws of any State are to be disregarded, stock held by any plan described in section 401(a) that is exempt from tax under section 501(a) is treated as held by the employees of the entity and, at the election of the common parent of an affiliated group, all members of such affiliated group may be treated as a single entity for the purpose of applying the ownership test if substantially all of the activities of such members involve the performance of services in the same qualified field.

Farming businesses.—The conference agreement provides that, for the purpose of determining whether an entity is engaged in a farming business, the definition of farming shall include the raising or harvesting of trees (including evergreen trees that are not subject to the capitalization provisions of section 263A.)

Gross receipts test.—The conference agreement provides that the gross receipts test will be considered to have been met if the entity had average annual gross receipts of $5 million or less for all prior taxable years (including the prior taxable years of any predecessor entity) beginning after December 31, 1985.

Billing rule.—The conference agreement deletes the provision of the House bill providing that a taxpayer, other than a financial institution or a utility, is not required to accrue as income any amount to be received for the performance of services prior to the time the amount was billed. Similarly, the conference agreement deletes the provision of the House bill providing that economic performance of services provided to an accrual basis taxpayer generally will not be considered to have occurred prior to the time the taxpayer is billed. In not adopting these two provisions of the House bill, the conferees intend that no inference is to be drawn with

---

[**Footnote ¶ 3935 continued**]

(4) Under that revenue procedure, the adjustment from a change in accounting generally is included in income over a period equal to the less[er] of the number of years the taxpayer has used the accounting method or a specified number of years.

regard to when economic performance occurs under present law.

Effective date.—The provision of the conference agreement is effective for taxable years beginning after December 31, 1986. The provision of the House bill allowing taxpayers to elect to continue to report income from loans, leases, certain real property contracts, and transactions with related parties entered into before September 25, 1985, using the cash method, applies to tax shelters as well as other entities. Any change from the cash method required by this provision is treated as initiated by the taxpayer with the consent of the Secretary of the Treasury. Any adjustment required by section 481 as a result of such change generally shall be taken into account over a period not to exceed four years. It is the intent of the conferees that this apply to all changes resulting from the provision, including any changes necessitated by the rule that certain accrual taxpayers, including taxpayers presently on the accrual method of accounting, need not recognize income on amounts statistically determined not to be collectible. In the case of a hospital, the adjustment shall be taken into account ratably over a ten-year period. For this purpose, a hospital is not required to be owned by or on behalf of a governmental unit or by a 501(c)(3) organiza-

tion or operated by a 501(c)(3) organization to meet the definition of a hospital.

The conferees intend that the timing of the section 481 adjustment other than for a hospital will be determined under the provisions of Revenue Procedure 84-74, 1984-2 C.B. 736. In addition, the conferees intend that (i) net operating loss and tax credit carryforwards will be allowed to offset any positive section 481 adjustment; (ii) for purposes of determining estimated tax payments, the section 481 adjustment will be recognized in taxable income ratably throughout the year in question; and (iii) the timing of a negative section 481 adjustment shall be determined as if the adjustment were positive.

The conferees are aware that taxpayers may request from the Internal Revenue Service permission to change their taxable years. In addition, the Treasury Department has issued several administrative pronouncements and regulations permitting taxpayers to change their taxable years in certain circumstances without prior permission of the Internal Revenue Service. The effective date of many of the provisions of the conference agreement relate to commencement or end of the taxpayer's taxable year. As a result, the Treasury Department may exercise its administrative authority to modify its rules to prevent the avoidance of these effective dates.

[¶ 3936] SECTION 802. SIMPLIFIED DOLLAR-VALUE LIFO METHOD FOR CERTAIN SMALL BUSINESSES

(Sec. 474 of the Code)

[House Explanation]

*   *   *   *   *   *

Explanation of Provision.—

In general.—The committee bill provides an election to certain small businesses to use a simplified dollar-value LIFO method in accounting for their inventories. The simplified dollar-value LIFO method requires inventories to be grouped into pools in accordance with the major categories of the "Producer Prices Indexes" or the "CPI Detailed Report." The change in inventory costs for the pool for the taxable year is determined by the change in the published index for the general category to which the pool relates. The computation of the ending LIFO value of the pool is then made using the dollar-value LIFO method. The indices necessary to compute the equivalent dollar values of prior years are to be developed using the link-chain method.

Eligible businesses.—A taxpayer is eligible to use the simplified dollar-value LIFO method if its average annual gross receipts for its three preceeding taxable years (or for such part of the previous three years that the taxpayer has been actively engaged in a trade or business) do not exceed $5 million. In the case of a taxpayer who is a member of a controlled group, all persons who are members of the controlled group are to be treated as a single taxpayer for the purposes of

determining average annual gross receipts. A controlled group consists of all persons who would be treated as a single employer * * * [under Sec. 52].

The provision of the committee bill is a replacement for the current law rule allowing taxpayers with average annual gross receipts of $2 million or less to elect to use a single inventory pool in accounting for its inventories using the LIFO method (sec. 474 of present law). Any taxpayer who has in effect a valid election to use the single pool method of present law may continue to account for its inventories using that election, so long as the taxpayer continues to meet the requirements for that election. A taxpayer accounting for its inventories using the single pool election of section 474 of present law is not eligible to elect to use the simplified dollar-value LIFO method of the committee bill for any year in which the election under present law is effective. Under the committee bill, the election to use the single pool method of section 474 of present law may be revoked without the consent of the Secretary of the Treasury.

Making the election.—A taxpayer may elect to use the simplified dollar-value LIFO method without the consent of the Secretary of the Treasury. The election is to be made at such time and in such manner as the Secretary of the Treasury may prescribe by regulations. An election to use the method applies to the year of election and to all succeeding taxable years, unless permission to change to another method is obtained from the Secretary of the Treasury, or the taxpayer becomes ineligible to use the simplified dollar-value LIFO method as a result of having exceeded $5 million of average annual gross receipts.

If the taxpayer previously has used a method of accounting for its inventories which allows the value of the inventories to be written down below cost, any amount of such writedown must be restored to income in accordance with section 472(d).

If the taxpayer makes an election to use the simplified dollar-value LIFO method, the method must be used for all the inventories of the taxpayer that are accounted for using a LIFO method.

Computation of simplified dollar-value LIFO inventories. *In general.*—The computation of inventory values using the simplified dollar-value LIFO method generally follows the rules currently provided for computation of inventories using the dollar-value LIFO method in Treas. Regs. sec. 1.472-8. However, the simplified dollar-value LIFO method differs from current rules with regard to the manner in which inventory items are to be pooled, the use of published indices to determine an annual index component for each pool, and the technique to be used in computing the cumulative index for a pool for any given year.

The simplified dollar-value LIFO method requires the use of multiple pools in order to avoid the construction of a weighted index specific to the taxpayer. Rather than construct such an index, the annual change in costs for the pool as a whole is measured by the change in the published index for the general category. The percentage change for the year in the published index for the general category determines the annual index for the pool.

The simplified dollar-value LIFO method uses the link-chain approach, rather than the double-extension approach, to compute a cumulative index for the purpose of determining equivalent dollar values in prior years.

Establishment of inventory pools.—The simplified dollar-value LIFO method requires inventory pools to be established based on either the 15 general (2 digit) categories of the "Producers Prices and Price Indexes for Commodity Groupings and Individual Items" (currently "Table 6. Producer prices and price indexes for commodity groupings and individual items, Producers Price Indexes" published monthly by the Bureau of Labor Statistics) or the 11 general

categories of the "Consumer Price Index for All Urban Consumers" (currently "Table 3. Consumer Price Index for All Urban Consumers: Food expenditure categories, U.S. city average, CPI Detailer Report" and "Table 5. Consumer Price Index for All Urban Consumers: Nonfood expenditures categories, U.S. city average, CPI Detailed Report" published monthly by the Bureau of Labor Statistics) as set forth in Treas. Regs. sec. 1.472-8(e)(3)(iv).[1] Retailers using the retail method are to use the CPI categories and all other taxpayers must use the Producers Price Index categories.

Selection of index.—The taxpayer must establish which month of its taxable year it will use to measure the annual change in the index for all pools. Once the choice of month is established, another month may not be used unless advance permission to do so is granted by the Secretary of the Treasury. The annual change is measured from the established month in one calendar year to the same month in the next calendar year. Comparison of different months to measure change is not allowed. If the published index figure which the taxpayer has used to measure annual change in costs for an inventory pool is restated by the Bureau of Labor Statistics after the taxpayer has filed its return for the taxable year in question, the return shall not be filed again or amended in order to reflect the restatement. Instead, the change in costs for the pool for the next taxable year will be measured with regard to the index figure which was used to measure the change in costs for the prior taxable year as the return was filed, and not the restated value.

Rules applicable to year of change.—The first year for which the simplified dollar-value LIFO method is used will represent a new base year for the purpose of the dollar-value LIFO computation. The base year dollar value of each pool will be the portion of the beginning inventory value for such first year which is attributable to the inventory items represented by such pool.

The computations necessary to convert a taxpayer's inventories to the simplified dollar-value LIFO method will depend upon the method that was used to account for the inventories prior to the year of election. A taxpayer that has been using the FIFO method to value its inventories must establish base year dollar values for each of its pools by assigning the inventory items to their respective pools and combining their values. The combined values of inventory items assigned to a pool constitute the base

---

[Footnote ¶ 3936] (1) The 11 categories in the Consumer Price Index are food and beverages; housing, maintenance and repair commodities; fuels (other than gasoline); house furnishings and housekeeping supplies; apparel commodities; private transportation (including gasoline); medical care commodities; entertainment commodities; tobacco products; toilet goods and personal care appliances; and school books and supplies. The 15 categories in the Producers Price Index are farm products; processed food and feeds; textile products and apparel; hides, skin, leather, and related products; fuels and related products and power; chemicals and allied products; rubber and plastic products; lumber and wood products; pulp, paper, and allied products; metals and metal products; machinery and equipment; furniture and household durables; nonmetalic mineral products; transportation equipment; and miscellaneous products.

Act §802   ¶3936

year layer of the pool for future dollar-value LIFO computations.

A taxpayer changing to the simplified dollar-value method from a method that allows inventories to be stated at less than cost (such as the FIFO method) must restore to income any amounts by which the previous inventories were written down below cost, as required by section 472(d). The base year dollar value of the pools established for dollar-value computations will include any amounts required to be recognized as income by section 472(d).

A taxpayer that has been using a LIFO method must establish values for each of its pools expressed in base year dollars in generally the same manner as does a taxpayer that has been using the FIFO method. In order to preserve pre-existing LIFO layers, however, the entire value of the inventory is not considered as attributable to the base year as is the case for taxpayers that have been using the FIFO method. Instead, the taxpayer is required to restate the prior years' layers in values expressed in base year dollars by comparing the prices at which such goods were added to inventories and determining an index for the layer with reference to the present value of the same inventory item.

Example.—The following example shows the computations required by a taxpayer in the first year in which it uses the simplified dollar-value LIFO method. The example assumes that the taxpayer used the FIFO method to calculate inventories in prior years.

The taxpayer's inventories consist of a chemical, classified in the "Chemicals and Allied Products" general category, and a high school chemistry text book, classified in the "Pulp, Paper and Allied Products" general category. The index numbers for the "Chemicals and Allied Products" general category are 200 for the prior year (the "base year") and 220 for the current year (the "first LIFO year"). The index numbers for the "Pulp, Paper and Allied Products" general category are 142 for the prior year and 150 for the current year. In the prior year, the present dollar value of the taxpayer's ending inventory was $30,000 for the chemical and $30,000 for the textbooks. In the current year, the present dollar value of the taxpayer's ending inventory is $35,000 for the chemical and $30,000 for the textbooks.

As the two types of inventory items are classified in different general categories, the taxpayer must set up a separate dollar-value LIFO pool for each. The annual index for each pool is determined by taking one plus the percentage change in the index for the general category, as shown in the following table.

Pool	Current year index	Prior year index	Change	Percent change	Index
#1	220	200	20	0.1000	1.1000
#2	150	142	8	.0563	1.0563

For years after the first year in which the method is used, the annual index would be multiplied by the cumulative index for the prior year to determine the current cumulative index. For the first year in which the simplified dollar-value LIFO method is used, the annual index and the cumulative index are the same.

The present dollar value of the ending inventory for the current year is divided by the cumulative index to restate the ending inventory in its equivalent value in base year dollars. This amount is assigned to the appropriate LIFO inventory layers and multiplied by the cumulative index for the year to which the layer relates in order to find an indexed dollar value for that layer. The sum of the indexed dollar values for the layers is the ending LIFO inventory value for the pool. These computations, for the taxpayer's first year using the simplified dollar-value LIFO method, are shown below.

Pool #1

Current year dollar value of inventory	$35,000
Divided by index	1.100
Inventory in base year dollars	$31,818

LIFO layers	Base year dollar value	Dollar index	Indexed dollar value
Base year	$30,000	1.0000	$30,000
First LIFO Year	1,818	1.1000	2,000
Ending inventory	31,818		32,000

Pool #2

Current year dollar value of inventory	$30,000
Divided by index	1.0563
Inventory in base year dollars	$28,401

	Base year dollar value	Index	Indexed dollar value
Base year	$28,401	1.0000	$28,401
First LIFO year	0	0	0
Ending inventory	28,401		28,401

Total Ending Inventory:

Pool #1	....	$32,000
Pool #2	....	28,401
		60,401

*   *   *   *   *   *

[Conference Report]

*   *   *   *   *   *

[Effective date.—] The conference agreement follows the provision of the House bill, effective for taxable years beginning after December 31, 1986.

A taxpayer using the simplified dollar-value LIFO method is required to change to a different method in the first year that it fails to meet the $5 million average annual gross receipts test. The conferees intend that any change that would be allowed if made directly from the method used immediately prior to the adoption of the simplified dollar-value LIFO method to the new method be allowed in this case. It is anticipated that a taxpayer always will be allowed to return to the method used prior to the adoption of the simplified dollar-value LIFO method. Thus, if a taxpayer had been using a first-in, first-out (FIFO) method prior to the adoption of the simplified dollar-value method, it is allowed to change to the same FIFO method it had used previously or any FIFO, LIFO, or other method that it would have been allowed to change to from the FIFO method used immediately prior to the adoption of the simplified dollar-value LIFO method.

In changing from the simplified dollar-value LIFO method to another method, it is not intended that the taxpayer be required to obtain permission from the Secretary of the Treasury for the change if it would not be required to obtain permission if changing directly from the method used immediately prior to the adoption of the simplified dollar-value method to the new method. Likewise, the administrative burden of obtaining the change in method should be no greater than it would be if the change were made directly.

[¶ 3937] SECTIONS 803 and 804. CAPITALIZATION RULES FOR INVENTORY, CONSTRUCTION, AND DEVELOPMENT COSTS; TREATMENT OF LONG TERM CONTRACTS

(Secs. 263A and 460 of the Code).

[Conference Report]

Capitalization Rules ***

*   *   *   *   *   *

House Bill

* * * **Inventory.**—Under the House bill, comprehensive capitalization rules (the "uniform capitalization rules") apply to the manufacture of inventory goods. These rules essentially parallel the full absorption rules of present law, but require that most financial conformity costs be inventoried. In addition, all tax depreciation, current pension and fringe benefit costs, and a portion of general and administrative expenses are treated as inventory costs. Research and experimental costs (within the meaning of sec. 174), however, are not subject to capitalization. Special rules apply to farmers ***.

These provisions are effective for taxable years beginning after December 31, 1985. The section 481 adjustment is to be spread ratably over a period of not more than five years under the rules applicable to a change in a method of accounting initiated by the taxpayer.

* * * **Self-constructed property and noninventory property produced for sale.**—Self-constructed property and noninventory property produced for sale are subject to the uniform capitalization rules, effective for costs incurred after December 31, 1985.

* * * **Interest.**—Under the House bill, a taxpayer must capitalize interest on debt incurred to finance the construction or production of real property, long-lived personal property, or other tangible property requiring more than two years (one year in the case of property costing more than $1 million) to produce or construct or to reach a productive stage. The amount of interest subject to capitalization is determined under the avoided cost method. This rule applies to interest paid or incurred after December 31, 1985.

[Senate Explanation]

*   *   *   *   *   *

Explanation of Provision.—The bill requires application of a uniform set of capitalization rules to all costs incurred in manufacturing or constructing property or in purchasing and holding property for resale. In

Act § 803 and 804   ¶ 3937

addition, interest costs generally will be subject to capitalization in cases where the interest is allocable to construction of real property, or to production of personal property that is long-lived property to be used by the taxpayer, or that requires an extended period to produce. The rules do not apply, however, to products produced in a farming business.

* * * Uniform capitalization rules.—

Scope and nature of rules.—Uniform capitalization rules prescribed by the Treasury Department will govern the inclusion in inventory or capital accounts of all costs (1) incurred in manufacturing, construction, and other types of activities involving the production of real or personal property, or (2) incurred in acquiring or holding such property for resale. Thus, the rules will apply to assets to be held by a taxpayer in inventory or for sale to customers in the ordinary course of business, and to assets or improvements to assets constructed by a taxpayer for its own use in a trade or business or in an activity engaged in for profit. The rules apply to intangible as well as to tangible property. However, the committee does not intend to modify present-law principles governing the determination of whether an expenditure results in a separate and distinct asset that has a useful life substantially beyond the taxable year.[38] Thus, if the costs of producing an intangible item such as goodwill are deductible under current law, such costs will continue to be deductible under the bill. The uniform capitalization rules merely will prescribe which costs associated with an asset required to be capitalized must be included in its basis or otherwise capitalized.

The uniform capitalization rules will be patterned after the rules applicable to extended period long-term contracts, set forth in the final regulations issued under section 451. Accordingly, taxpayers subject to the rules will be required to capitalize not only direct costs but also an allocable portion of most indirect costs that benefit the assets produced or acquired for resale, including general and administrative and overhead costs and other costs described in section 1.451-3 of the regulations. The committee recognizes that modifications of the rules set forth in the long-term contract regulations may be necessary or appropriate in order to adapt such rules to production not involving a contract, and intends that the Treasury Department will have the authority to make such modifications. The existing long-term contract regulations provide a large measure

of flexibility to taxpayers in allocating indirect costs to contracts inasmuch as they permit any reasonable method of allocation authorized by cost accounting principles. The committee expects that the regulations under this provision will adopt a similarly liberal approach and permit allocations of costs among numerous items produced or held for resale by a taxpayer to be made on the basis of burden rates or other appropriate methods similar to those provided under present law.[39] The regulations may adopt other simplifying methods and assumptions where, in the judgment of the Secretary of the Treasury, the costs and other burdens of literal compliance may outweigh the benefits.

Retailers and wholesalers.—In general, the uniform capitalization rules will apply to taxpayers who acquire and hold property for resale in the same manner as they apply to producers. Among the costs "retailers and wholesalers" are required to treat as inventory costs under the bill are the following: costs incident to purchasing inventory (e.g., wages or salaries of employees responsible for purchasing); repackaging, assembly, and other costs incurred in processing goods while in the taxpayer's possession; costs of storing goods (e.g., rent or depreciation, insurance premiums, and taxes attributable to a warehouse, and wages of warehouse personnel),[40] and the portion of general and administrative costs allocable to these functions.[41]

The committee intends that, in the case of a taxpayer engaged in a retail sales business, however, only offsite storage costs—that is, costs of storing goods in a facility distinct from the facility wherein the taxpayer conducts retail sales of these goods—will be inventoriable costs under this provision. The rules relating to capitalization of interest do not apply to real or personal property solely acquired for resale.

Pension costs.—Under the uniform capitalization rules, contributions to a pension, profit-sharing, or stock bonus plan and other employee benefit expenses are considered indirect costs that must be capitalized to the same extent as other indirect costs, unless such contributions relate to past-service costs.[42] It is intended that, in the case of a contribution to a qualified plan, the determination of whether the contribution relates to past or current services will be made independently of any allocation between "normal cost" and "past-service cost" required under the minimum funding standards (sec. 412) or under the plan's benefit formula. The com-

---

[Footnote ¶ 3937] (38) See Treas. Reg. sec. 1.263(a)-1,(a)-2; *Commissioner v. Lincoln Savings and Loan,* 403 U.S. 345 (1971).

(39) See Treas. Reg. sec. 1.471-11(d) (authorizing use of the manufacturing burden rate method, the standard cost method, or any other method that fairly apportions such costs among items of inventory).

(40) The committee intends that storage costs incurred by a manufacturer following completion (or substantial completion) of the manufacturing process with regard to a product will likewise be subject to capitalization under these rules. Thus, the bill overrules any case law holding to the contrary (without inference as to the validity of such cases under present law). See, e.g., *Heaven Hill Distillaries, Inc. v. U.S.,* 476 F.2d 1327 (Ct. Cl. 1973) (holding that storage costs incurred by the manufacturer of whisky during the aging process were currently deductible), and *Van Pickerill & Sons, Inc. v. U.S.,* 445 F.2d 918 (7th Cir. 1971).

(41) No inference is intended regarding the deductibility of such costs under present law.

(42) See Treas. Reg. sec. 1.451-3(d)(6)(iii)(I)

mittee anticipates that the Treasury Department will publish guidelines for making this determination, and that such determination may be based, in whole or in part, on any actuarial funding methods that may be utilized by qualified defined benefit plans.

Any allocation of employee benefit costs (and any other costs) between production (or inventory, in the case of purchased goods) costs and period costs will, of course, be made after application of any other relevant limitations provided in the Code. For example, in the case of a qualified defined benefit pension plan that is subject to the minimum funding standard, an employer will first, calculate his liability under the minimum funding standards (using the applicable funding method and actuarial assumptions); next, calculate the limit on deductions for such contributions (pursuant to section 404 of the Code); and finally, allocate the otherwise deductible amount between production costs and other costs applying the uniform capitalization rules. In applying these rules, the allocation of the otherwise deductible amount between past- and current-service costs will be made independently of the allocation made in the first step of the calculation, under rules published by the Treasury Department.

Similarly, in the case of a plan that is not subject to the minimum funding standards (e.g., a profit-sharing plan), an employer must compute the otherwise allowable deduction limit pursuant to section 404 and then allocate that amount between production or inventory costs and other costs.

Exceptions.—The capitalization rules do not apply to any portion of costs constituting research and experimental expenditures under section 174, or to development and other costs of oil and gas wells or mineral property to the extent such costs qualify under sections 263(c) or 616(a). The rules also do not apply to property produced under a long-term contract; to property produced in a farming business as defined in section 2032A; or to property produced by the taxpayer for use by the taxpayer other than in a trade or business or activity engaged in for profit.

In the case of a property acquired by a taxpayer for resale, the uniform capitalization rules apply only if the taxpayer's average annual gross receipts for the three preceding taxable years were $5 million or less. Aggregation rules will apply in determining whether the $5 million threshold is exceeded.

The uniform capitalization rules are not intended to apply to expenditures properly treated as repair costs under present law that do not relate to the manufacture, remanufacture, or production of property. Moreover, the uniform capitalization rules are not intended to modify present law rules relating to valuation of inventories on a basis other than cost.

* * * **Interest.**—Interest on debt must be capitalized if such debt is incurred or continued to finance the construction or production of (1) real property (whether such property is held for sale to customers or is used by the taxpayer in a trade or business or activity for profit), or (2) other property with a class life of 20 years or more under the bill's depreciation system if the property is to be used by the taxpayer in its trade or business or an activity for profit. Interest incurred in connection with other property estimated to have a production period of more than two years (one year in the case of items costing more than $1 million) also is subject to capitalization under this rule. For this purpose, the production period for property begins when construction or production is commenced and ends when the property is ready to be placed in service or is ready to be held for sale. For example, in the case of property such as wine or whiskey that is aged before it is sold, the production period includes the aging period. Activities such as planning or design generally do not cause the production period to begin.

The committee intends that the determination of whether debt is incurred or continued to finance the production of property will be made under rules similar to those applicable under section 189 of present law.[43] Under these rules, any interest expense that would have been avoided if production or construction expenditures had been used to repay indebtedness of the taxpayer is treated as construction period interest subject to capitalization.[44] Accordingly, under the bill, debt that can be specifically traced to production or construction expenditures first must be allocated to production or construction. If production or construction expenditures exceed the amount of this debt, interest on other debt of the taxpayer must be treated, to the extent of this excess, as production or construction period interest. For this purpose, the assumed interest rate would be an average of the rates on the taxpayer's outstanding debt (excluding debt specifically traceable to production or construction).

The committee contemplates that the Treasury Department will issue regulations to prevent the avoidance of these rules through the use of related parties. For example, such regulations could provide that where a subsidiary corporation is owned by

---

[Footnote ¶ 3937 continued]

(43) The provisions under section 139 of present law regarding capitalization of taxes have been replaced by similar rules, in the extended period long-term contract regulations, which also require the capitalization of taxes.

(44) Production or construction expenditures include the cumulative production costs required to be capitalized, including interest required to be capitalized as a production or construction cost for prior periods. In addition, interest on debt that relates to any asset that is devoted to the production of property generally must be capitalized as part of the cost of that property, whether or not the cost of the asset has been fully reflected in the property account. Where such an asset is used for the production of property and for other purposes only the allocable portion of such interest must be capitalized.

Act § 803 and 804   ¶ 3937

two 50-percent parent corporations, and the subsidiary is engaged in constructing long-lived property for its own use, but has no outstanding debt, each 50-percent parent would be required to capitalize interest expense as if each had directly incurred one-half of the construction expenditures incurred by the subsidiary. In addition, under the bill, the interest capitalization rules are applied first at the level of a partnership (or other flow-through) entity, and then at the level of the partners (or beneficiaries), to the extent that the partnership has insufficient debt to support the production or construction expenditures.

If production or construction is for a particular customer who makes progress payments or advance payments for property to be used in a business or activity for profit, or held for sale, the customer is treated as constructing the property to the extent of such payments. Thus, interest costs attributable to payments to the contractor are subject to capitalization by the customer if the property is real property, long-lived property or requires a production or construction period of more than two years (one year if the cost exceeds $1 million). The contractor must capitalize interest only with respect to indebtedness relating to the excess of its accumulated contract costs over the accumulated payments received by the contractor during the year.

* * * * * *

Effective Dates

In general.—The uniform capitalization rules generally are effective for costs and interest paid or incurred after December 31, 1986. Self-constructed assets with respect to which substantial construction occurred prior to March 1, 1986, will remain subject to the present-law tax accounting rules. The committee intends that construction of an asset which began after February 28, 1986, will be considered within this transitional rule if the asset is an integral part of an integrated facility, construction of which began before March 1, 1986. An asset generally will be considered an integral part of a facility only if such asset will first be placed in service at essentially the same time as other assets comprising the facility.

The bill also retains present law rules for depreciation on assets used to produce inventory or self-constructed property if the assets were placed in service by the taxpayer before March 1, 1986, or the taxpayer had entered into a binding contract to purchase the assets prior to that date. Accordingly, such assets will be subject to present-law rules relating to the capitalization of depreciation.

Inventories.—*In general*—The new rules apply to inventories for the taxpayer's first taxable year beginning after December 31, 1986. Taxpayers are required to spread the section 481 adjustment resulting from the change in inventory accounting over a period of no more than five years, in accordance

with the rules applicable to a change in method of accounting initiated by the taxpayer and approved by the Internal Revenue Service.[46] Under these rules, the adjustment generally is includible in income over a period equal to the lesser of the period the taxpayer has used the method of accounting or five years.

With respect to property which is primarily held for sale to customers in the ordinary course of business, but which is not inventory property, the rules are effective for costs and interest paid or incurred after December 31, 1986, with no restatement of beginning balances and no section 481 adjustment. *E.g., see W.C. & A.N. Miller Development v. Commissioner*, 81 T.C. 619 (1983).

The bill contemplates that the changes in the rules governing the absorption of costs into inventory will be treated as a change in the taxpayer's method of accounting. The cost of all inventory sold or otherwise disposed of after the effective date must reflect the changes in the absorption rules. This requires that inventory on hand as of the effective date be revalued to reflect the greater absorption of production costs under the rules of the bill. Normally, the revaluation must be done by valuing the items included in inventory on the effective date as if the new absorption rules had been in effect during all prior periods. Thus, a determination of what direct and indirect production costs should be assigned to each item of inventory is to be made in accordance with the changes contained in the bill. The difference between the inventory as originally valued and the inventory as revalued will be the amount of adjustment required by section 481.

In some circumstances, particularly where the taxpayer is considered as holding in inventory items which were acquired for resale, produced, or manufactured a number of years prior to the effective date of the bill, the information necessary to make such a determination may not be available. Such a situation may arise, for example, if the taxpayer has items of inventory which it no longer produces, or if the taxpayer is using the last-in, first-out (LIFO) method of accounting. The committee expects that the Treasury Department will issue regulations or rulings permitting a taxpayer in this situation to estimate the amount by which the inventory will be revalued by using available data.

FIFO method: For example, assume that a taxpayer that uses the first-in, first-out (FIFO) method of valuing inventories maintains inventories of bolts, two types of which it no longer produces. Bolt A was last produced in 1984, for which year the taxpayer determines a revaluation of inventory costs resulting in a 20 percent increase. A portion of the inventory of bolt A, however, is attributable to 1983 for which the taxpayer does not have sufficient data for revaluation. Bolt B was last produced in 1982 and no data

[Footnote ¶ 3937 continued]
(46) See Rev. Proc. 84-74, 1984-2 C.B. 796.

exists which would allow revaluation of the inventory cost of bolt B pursuant to the new absorption rules. The inventories of all other bolts are attributable to 1984 and 1985 production, for which revaluation using available data results in an average 15 percent increase in inventory cost. With respect to bolt A, the 20 percent increase determined for 1984 also may be applied to the 1983 production as an acceptable estimate. With respect to bolt B, the overall 15 percent increase for the inventory as a whole may be used in valuing the costs of bolt B.

LIFO method: Taxpayers using the last-in, first-out (LIFO) method of valuing inventories also may have difficulty in assembling sufficient data to restate their inventory costs. Taxpayers using the dollar-value LIFO method may have particular problems since the valuation of each year's LIFO layer is dependent upon prior year's cost data in situations where the double extension method is used.

The committee expects that taxpayers using the specific goods LIFO method to value their inventories generally will be allowed to use the same type of estimating techniques as FIFO taxpayers. Thus, the percentage change obtained in revaluing those inventory layers for which sufficient data is available may be applied to revalue all preceding year's layers.

Example 1

For example, assume a manufacturer produces two different parts. Work-in-process inventory is recorded in terms of equivalent units of finished goods. The manufacturer's specific goods LIFO inventory records show the following at the end of 1985:

Product and layer	Number	Cost	LIFO carrying values
Product #1:			
1983	150	$5.00	$750
1984	100	6.00	600
1985	100	6.50	650
1986	50	7.00	350
			2,350
Product #2:			
1983	200	4.00	800
1984	200	4.50	900
1985	100	5.00	500
1986	100	6.00	600
			2,800
Total of carrying value of Products #1 and #2			5,150

Data available to the taxpayer allows it to revalue the unit costs of product #1 under the new absorption rules to $7.00 in 1984, $7.75 in 1985 and $9.00 in 1986, and to revalue the unit costs of product #2 to $6.00 in 1985 and $7.00 in 1986. The available data for product #1 results in a weighted average percentage change for product #1 of 20.31 percent.[47] The available data for product #2 results in a weighted average percentage change for product #2 of 18.18 percent.[48] The revalued costs for product #1 for 1983 can be estimated by applying the weighted average increase determined for product #1 (20.31 percent) to the unit costs originally carried on the taxpayer's records. The esti-mated revalued unit cost in the case of product #1 would be $6.02 ($5.00 × 1.2031). The costs of product #2 are redetermined in a similar manner for 1983 and 1984 by applying the weighted average increase determined for product #2 of 18.18 percent to the unit costs of $4.00 and $4.50, yielding revalued unit costs of $4.73 and $5.32 respectively.

The weighted average increase estimation does not affect the revaluation of costs for those years in which actual revaluation is possible. The revalued inventory of the taxpayer would be as follows:

[Footnote ¶ 3937 continued]

(47) This is computed as follows: [(100 × (7.00 − 6.00)) + (100 × (7.75 − 6.50)) + (50 × (9.00 − 7.00)] divided by [(100 × 6.00) + (100 × 6.50) + (50 × 7.00)].

(48) This is computed as follows: [100 × (6.00 − 5.00)) + (100 × (7.00 − 6.00))] divided by [(100 × 5.00) + (100 × 6.00)].

Product and layer	Number	Cost	LIFO carrying values
Product #1:			
1983	150	$6.20	$903
1984	100	7.00	700
1985	100	7.75	775
1986	50	9.00	450
			2,828
Product #2:			
1983	00	4.73	946
1984	00	5.32	1,064
1985	100	6.00	600
1986	100	7.00	700
			3,310
Total of carrying value of Products #1 and #2 under new absorption rules			6,188

The amount of the adjustment (under section 481) is $988 ($6,138 − $5,150).

A taxpayer using the specific goods LIFO method also may have inventories for which new costs have not been incurred for several years and, consequently, a weighted average increase for those particular inventory items may not be available for estimation purposes. In such a case, the taxpayer may take the weighted average increases for all its revalued inventory items and determine an overall percentage increase, weighted by the value of each inventory item included in the calculation, to estimate the revaluation necessary for such items.

The committee anticipates that the Treasury Department will develop rules to permit taxpayers using the dollar-value LIFO method who lack sufficient data to revalue all of their LIFO layers under the new absorption rules to compute the percentage change in the current costs of their inventory as a result of the new absorption rules for the LIFO layers accumulated during the three most recent years that the taxpayer has sufficient information. (These rules will apply to taxpayers acquiring property for resale, as well as taxpayers producing or manufacturing property.) Taxpayers then would apply that percentage to restate the costs of the beginning LIFO inventory value of the entire pool for the year of change. For purposes of determining future indexes, the year prior to the year of change will then be considered as a new base year and the current costs for that year are to be used for extension purposes of future taxable years. The increase in the beginning balance in the LIFO inventory as a result of this change will represent the section 481 adjustment amount.

Example 2

For example, a calendar year taxpayer first adopted the dollar value LIFO method in 1981, using a single pool and the double extension method. The taxpayer's beginning LIFO inventory for the year of change is as follows:

	Base year costs	Index	LIFO carrying value
Base layer	$14,000	1.00	$14,000
1981 layer	4,000	1.20	4,800
1982 layer	5,000	1.30	6,500
1983 layer	2,000	1.35	2,700
1984 layer	0	1.40	0
1985 layer	4,000	1.50	6,000
1986 layer	5,000	1.60	3,000
Total	34,000	.....	42,000

The taxpayer is able to recompute inventoriable costs under the new absorption rules for the ending LIFO layers for three preceding taxable years as follows:

Year	Current cost as recorded	Current cost as adjusted	Weighted percentage change
1983	$35,000	$45,150	0.29
1984	43,500	54,375	.25
1985	54,400	70,720	.30
Total	132,900	170,245	.28

Applying the average revaluation factor of .28 to each layer, the inventory is restated as follows:

	Base year costs	Index	LIFO carrying value
Base layer	$17,920	1.00	$17,920
1981 layer	5,120	1.20	6,144
1982 layer	6,400	1.30	8,320
1983 layer	2,560	1.35	3,456
1984 layer	0	1.40	0
1985 layer	5,120	1.50	7,680
1986 layer	6,400	1.60	10,240
Total	43,520	.....	53,760

The section 481 adjustment is the difference between the revalued LIFO carrying value under the new absorption rules and the LIFO carrying value as originally reported. In this example, the section 481 adjustment is $11,760 ($53,760 − $42,000). The section 481 adjustment also may be found by multiplying the LIFO carrying value as originally reported by the average percentage change determined in first step described above. In this example, that procedure also would determine the amount of the section 481 to be $11,760 ($42,000 × .28).

The year prior to the year of change will be treated as a new base year for the purpose of determining the index in future years. This requires that layers in years prior to the base year be restated in terms of the new base year index. In the example above, the restated inventory would be as follows:

	Restated base year costs	Index	LIFO carrying value
Old base layer	$28,672	0.625	$17,920
1981 layer	8,192	.75	6,144
1982 layer	10,272	.81	8,320
1983 layer	4,114	.84	3,456
1984 layer	0	.875	0
1985 layer	8,170	.94	7,680
New base layer (1986)	10,240	1.50	10,240
Total	69,660	.....	53,760

For taxpayers not possessing sufficient data to revalue all of their LIFO layers under the new absorption rules, the most recent three years prior to the year of change for which the taxpayer has sufficient information may be used in determining the average revaluation factor. Where the taxpayer possesses sufficient information to use additional years in determining the average revaluation factor, such additional years may be used at the option of the taxpayer, as long as the additional years are consecutive years prior to the year of change. For example, assume a calendar year taxpayer has sufficient information to revalue years 1981 through 1986. The average revaluation factor may be determined on the basis of all six years. On the other hand, a taxpayer with sufficient information to revalue 1980 through 1982 and 1984 through 1986 would use only the 1982 through 1986 years in determining the average revaluation factor, since the years 1980 through 1982 are not consecutive to the year of change.

The use of the average revaluation factor based upon current costs to estimate the revaluation of older inventory layers may result in an increase in the value of inventories representing costs which did not exist in the affected year. To the extent that a taxpayer can show that costs which contributed to the determination of the average revaluation factor could not have affected a prior year, the average revaluation factor as applied to that year may be adjusted by an appropriate amount.

* * * * * *

Act § 803 and 804 ¶ 3937

[Conference Report]

*   *   *   *   *   *

Conference Agreement

*** Inventory.—*In general.*—The conference agreement generally follows the Senate amendment, with certain modifications and clarifications. However, the agreement follows the House bill in applying the uniform capitalization rules to taxpayers engaged in the trade or business of farming (other than timber) where the preproductive period exceeds two years (see Title IV.A.3.). In addition, the conference agreement provides that the uniform capitalization rules are to apply to all depreciation deductions for Federal income tax purposes with respect to assets of the taxpayer (i.e., the conference agreement deleted the provisions of the Senate amendment which exempted existing assets from the capitalization of all tax depreciation).

The gross receipts threshold for taxpayers acquiring property for resale is increased from $5 million to $10 million. Accordingly, present law rules continue to apply to resellers whose average annual gross receipts do not exceed $10 million.

The conference agreement provides that the uniform capitalization rules do not apply to the growing of timber and certain ornamental trees (i.e., those evergreen trees which are more than 6 years old when severed from the roots and sold for ornamental purposes). Thus, present law is retained with regard to the treatment of the preproductive expenses of growing timber and such ornamental trees.

The conferees intend that present law be retained with regard to which costs of growing timber are deductible in the year incurred and which costs must be capitalized. Thus, any costs which must be capitalized under present law would continue to be capitalized and costs incurred in growing timber which are not required to be capitalized under present law would remain deductible currently.

The definition of timber used in the conference agreement is intended to be coextensive with the definition of timber (including ornamental trees) under present law. The conferees intend that nothing in the definition of timber shall be construed to narrow the types of activities which constitutes the growing of timber for purpose of the exclusion of timber from the uniform capitalization rules.

The conferees wish to clarify their intent as to the treatment of costs incurred by taxpayers engaged in the resale of natural gas with respect to so-called "cushion gas"—gas necessary to maintain operating pressures in an underground gas storage facility sufficient to meet expected peak customer demand. It is not intended that such taxpayers be required to allocate to such gas any portion of their overhead or other indirect costs under the new uniform capitalization rules. The conferees anticipate that the Treasury Department may issue rules or regulations under which some portion of the so-called "emergency reserve" gas in such facilities also may be exempt from allocations of indirect costs under the capitalization rules of this provision.

The uniform capitalization rules are not intended to affect the valuation of inventories on a basis other than cost. Thus, the rules will not affect the valuation of inventories at market by a taxpayer using the lower of cost or market method, or by a dealer in securities or commodities using the market method. However, the rules will apply to inventories valued at cost by a taxpayer using the lower of cost or market method.

The conferees clarify that, in addition to the costs specifically excepted from capitalization under the conference agreement (e.g., research and experimental costs, selling, marketing, advertising, and distribution expenses) are not subject to capitalization under the uniform capitalization rules.

Simplified method for taxpayers acquiring property for resale

The conference agreement directs the Treasury Department to provide a simplified method for applying the uniform capitalization rules in the case of taxpayers acquiring property for resale. The conferees expect that the simplified method provided under rules or regulations generally will follow the examples described below and that, until rules or regulations are issued, taxpayers may rely on these examples.

Taxpayers not electing to use the simplified method are required to apply the new uniform capitalization rules to property acquired for resale under the same procedures and methods applicable to manufacturers. The Treasury Department may modify the simplified method or permit the use of other methods by rules or regulations. Once a taxpayer has chosen either the simplified method or the capitalization methods applicable to manufacturers, the taxpayer may not change its method without obtaining the permission of the Secretary.

For purposes of the simplified method, it is anticipated that taxpayers initially will calculate their inventory balances without regard to the new uniform capitalization rules. Taxpayers will then determine the amounts of additional costs that must be capitalized under the new rules (under the procedures described below) and add such amounts, along with amounts of additional costs contained in beginning inventory balances where appropriate, to the preliminary inventory balances to determine their final balances. Thus, for example, with respect to a taxpayer using the last-in, first-out (LIFO) method, the calculation of a particular year's LIFO index will be made without regard to the new capitalization rules. For such a taxpayer, however, costs capitalized under these rules will be added to the LIFO layers applicable to the various years for which the costs were accumulated. Likewise, in the case of a taxpayer on the first-in, first-out (FIFO) method that does not sell its entire beginning inventory during the year, a proportionate part of the additional costs capitalized into the beginning inventory under these rules will be included in ending inventory.

The simplified method will be applied separately to each trade or business of the taxpayer.

In general, four categories of indirect costs will be allocable to inventory under this simplified method:

(1) off-site storage and warehousing costs (including, but not limited to, rent or depreciation attributable to a warehouse, property taxes, insurance premiums, security costs, and other costs directly identifiable with the storage facility);[4a]

(2) purchasing costs such as buyers' wages or salaries;

(3) handling, processing, assembly, repackaging, and similar costs, including labor costs attributable to unloading goods (but not including labor costs attributable to loading of goods for final shipment to customers, or labor at a retail facility);[5] and

(4) the portion of general and administrative costs allocable to these functions.

Storage costs.—Under the simplified method, a taxpayer includes storage costs in inventory based on the ratio of total storage costs for the year to the sum of (1) the beginning inventory balance and (2) gross purchases during the year. For example, assume that a FIFO taxpayer incurred $1 million of storage costs during the taxable year, had a beginning inventory balance (without regard to any adjustments under the simpified method) of $2 million, made gross purchases of $8 million, and had an ending inventory (without regard to any adjustments under the simplified method) of $3 million. The ratio of storage costs to beginning inventory and purchases is 10 percent ($1,000,000 divided by ($2,000,000 plus $8,000,000)). Thus, for each dollar of ending inventory, the taxpayer must capitalize ten cents of storage costs. Ending inventory for the year would be increased by $300,000. The balance of the storage costs ($700,000) would be included in cost of goods sold.

In the case of a LIFO taxpayer, to the extent that ending inventory exceeds beginning inventory, additional capitalized storage costs would be calculated by multiplying the increase in inventory for the year by the applicable ratio. Accordingly, if the taxpayer in the above example used the LIFO method, an additional $100,000 (i.e., .10 × $1,000,000) of storage costs would be included in ending inventory. Moreover, in contrast to the FIFO taxpayer in the previous example, any storage costs that were included in the taxpayer's

beginning inventory balance would remain in the taxpayer's ending inventory balance and would not be included in cost of goods sold for the year.

Purchasing costs.—Purchasing costs are allocated between inventory and cost of goods sold based on the ratio of purchasing costs to gross purchases during the year. For example, assume that the taxpayer in the above example incurred $500,000 in purchasing costs during the year. The ratio of purchasing costs to gross purchases is 6.25 percent ($500,000 divided by $8,000,000). Thus, 6.25 cents of purchasing costs would be capitalized for each dollar's worth of items in ending inventory that were not in beginning inventory (i.e., were purchased during the current year). Assuming the taxpayer uses the first-in, first-out (FIFO) basis for determining inventories, $187,500 (i.e., .0625 × $3,000,000) of purchasing costs would be capitalized.

In the case of a taxpayer using the last-in, first-out (LIFO) method for valuing inventory, ending inventory consists of newly acquired items only to the extent that ending inventory exceeds beginning inventory. Capitalized purchasing costs would be calculated by multiplying the increase in inventory from the beginning of the year to the end by the applicable ratio. Accordingly, in the above example, the taxpayer would capitalize $62,500 (i.e., .0625 × $1,000,000) of purchasing costs. In contrast to a FIFO taxpayer, the purchasing costs attributable to a LIFO taxpayer's beginning inventory would be retained in the taxpayer's ending inventory balance.

Processing, repackaging, etc. costs. — Processing, repackaging, and other similar costs are allocated based on the ratio of total processing, repackaging, etc. costs to the sum of (1) the beginning inventory balance and (2) gross purchases during the year.

General and administrative expenses allocable to storage, purchasing, and processing.—General and administrative expenses that are allocable in part to storage, purchasing, and processing activities and in part to activities for which no capitalization is required under the simplified method are allocated based on the ratio of direct labor costs incurred in a particular function to gross payroll costs. For example, assume that the total cost of operating the taxpayer's accounting department for the year was $75,000, direct labor purchasing costs were $500,000, and gross payroll was $1,500,000. The portion of the accounting department cost subject to capitalization in connection with the purchasing function would be $25,000 (i.e., $500,000 divided by $1,500,000 × $75,000).

[Footnote ¶ 3937 continued]

(4a) Offsite storage and warehousing costs generally include the cost of a facility whose primary function is the storage or warehousing of goods.

(5) Any reasonable method of apportioning labor costs between inventoriable and noninventoriable functions may be used. The conferees do not intend that detailed records establishing the time spent by an employee performing a particular function generally will be required to substantiate an allocation by the taxpayer. However, if such records are available, they generally should be used in making allocations.

Act § 803 and 804 **¶ 3937**

In addition, assume that direct labor warehousing costs were $250,000. The portion of the accounting department cost allocated to the storage and warehousing functions and thus subject to capitalization would be $12,500 (i.e., $250,000 divided by $1,500,000 × $75,000).

Section 481 adjustment.—Under the conference agreement, the section 431 adjustment resulting from the change in accounting method is to be included in income over a period not exceeding four years. The conferees intend that the timing of the section 481 adjustment will be determined under the provisions of Revenue Procedure 84-74, 1984-2 C.B. 786. In addition, the conferees intent that (i) net operating loss and tax credit carryforwards will be allowed to offset any positive section 481 adjustment; and (ii) for purposes of determining estimated tax payments, the section 481 adjustment will be recognized ratably throughout the taxable year of the adjustment.

In computing the section 481 adjustment, taxpayers using the simplified method for property acquired for resale must apply this method in restating beginning inventory. Taxpayers using the LIFO method who lack sufficient data to compute the section 481 adjustment precisely may use the methods of approximation (based on the data for the three prior years for which increments in the inventory occurred) available to manufacturers under the Senate bill.

* * * Self-constructed property and noninventory property produced for sale.—The conference agreement generally follows the Senate amendment on self-constructed and noninventory property produced for sale. The conference agreement provides that the application of the uniform capitalization rules with respect to production activities is limited to tangible property.[1] On the other hand, the conference agreement provides that the extension of the uniform capitalization rules to property acquired for resale includes intangible, as well as tangible, property.

The conference agreement adopts the Senate amendment's effective date for self-constructed property. Thus, the rules apply to costs incurred after December 31, 1986, unless incurred with respect to property on which substantial construction occurred before March 1, 1986.

* * * Interest.—The conference agreement follows both the House bill and the Senate amendment in certain respects. Long-lived personal property is subject to the interest capitalization rules regardless of whether it is constructed for self-use or for sale, as under the House bill. In addition, taxpayers producing property under a long-term contract must capitalize interest costs to the extent income is not being reported under the percentage of completion method.

The conferees wish to clarify that the avoided cost method of determining the amount of interest allocable to production is intended to apply irrespective of whether application of such method (or a similar method) is required, authorized, or considered appropriate under financial or regulatory accounting principles applicable to the taxpayer. Thus, for example, a regulated utility company must apply the avoided cost method of determining capitalized interest even though a different method is authorized or required by Financial Accounting Standards Board Statement 34 or the regulatory authority having jurisdiction over the utility. No inference is intended that the avoided cost method is not required in such circumstances under section 189 of present law.

*　　*　　*　　*　　*　　*

Preproductive Period Expenses of Farmers

*　　*　　*　　*　　*　　*

House Bill

*　　*　　*　　*　　*　　*

Replanting and maintenance costs incurred following loss of or damage to an orchard, grove, or vineyard used in the production of crops for human consumption by reason of freezing temperatures, etc. are currently deductible even though replanting does not take place on the same property. Thus, costs incurred at a different location (within the United States) but by the same taxpayer may qualify, provided they do not relate to acreage in excess of that on which the loss or damage occurred.

*　　*　　*　　*　　*　　*

Senate Amendment

*　　*　　*　　*　　*　　*

The provision allowing a deduction for costs incurred following loss or damage due to freezing temperatures, etc. is extended to persons other than the person who owned the grove, orchard, or vineyard at the time of the loss or damage, provided (1) the taxpayer who owned the property at such time retains an equity interest of more than 50 percent in the property, and (2) the person claiming the deduction owns part of the remaining equity interest and materially participates in the replanting, cultivating, maintenance, or development of the property.

The provision is effective for costs incurred after date of enactment.

Conference Agreement

*　　*　　*　　*　　*　　*

The conference agreement adopts both the House bill and the Senate amendment provisions, effective for costs incurred after date of enactment. The conferees wish to clarify that the special rule for preproductive period expenses following loss or damage due to

---

[Footnote ¶ 3937 continued]

　(1) For this purpose, tangible property includes films, sound recordings, video tapes, books, and other similarly property embodying words, ideas, concepts, images or sounds, by the creator thereof. Thus, for example, the uniform capitalization rules apply to the costs of producing a motion picture or researching and writing a book. No inference is intended as to the nature of these properties under present law or for other provisions of the conference agreement.

freezing temperatures, etc., is intended to apply only in the case of crops that are normally eaten or drunk by humans. Thus, for example, jojoba bean production does not qualify under this special exception.

Long-Term Contracts

Present Law.—The treatment of costs of producing property under a "long-term contract" varies depending on the method of accounting used by the taxpayer. In addition to an inventory method (e.g., accrual shipment or accrual delivery), taxpayers may use one of two special methods of accounting for long-term contracts: the percentage of completion method or the completed contract method. Under the percentage of completion method, gross income is recognized according to the percentage of the contract completed during each taxable year, and costs incurred under the contract are currently deductible. Under the completed contract method, the gross contract price is included in income, and costs associated with the contract are deducted, in the year that the contract is completed and accepted.

The rules relating to which costs are contract costs for purposes of the completed contract method vary depending on whether the contract is an extended period contract (generally one requiring longer than two years to complete) or a non-extended period contract. The rules applicable to extended period contracts essentially parallel the uniform capitalization rules (see D., above). Research and development costs (within the meaning of section 174) that relate to a particular extended period long-term contract must be capitalized.

Non-extended period contracts are subject to similar but somewhat less comprehensive rules. For example, research and development costs related to a particular contract need not be capitalized as part of that contract.

House Bill.—Under the House bill, the income and expenses of all long-term contracts must be reported under the percentage of completion method. Revenues from such contracts must be included in gross income based on the ratio of contract costs incurred during the year to total projected contract costs; contract costs are currently deductible. Interest is payable by (or to) the taxpayer if the actual profit on a contract allocable to any year varies from the estimated profit used in reporting income. An exception is provided for contracts for the construction of real property to be completed within two years of the contract date, if performed by a taxpayer whose average annual gross receipts do not exceed $10 million. Present law capitalization rules are retained for contracts not required to be reported under the percentage of completion method. These provisions are effective for contracts entered into after September 25, 1985.

Senate Amendment.—In general, all long-term contracts are subject to rules similar to the uniform capitalization rules, including the rules relating to the capitalization of interest (see D., above), unless the contract is reported on the percentage of completion method. Moreover, additional general and administrative costs attributable to cost-plus contracts and to Federal government contracts requiring certification of costs are treated as contract costs. An exception from the uniform capitalization rules (except the interest capitalization rule) is provided for real estate construction contracts not requiring more than two years to complete, if performed by a taxpayer with average annual gross receipts of $10 million or less.

The provisions are effective for contracts entered into on or after March 1, 1986.

Conference Agreement.—*In general.*—The conference agreement adopts elements of both the House bill and the Senate amendment provisions. Under the conference agreement, taxpayers may elect to compute income from long-term contracts under one of two methods: (1) the "percentage of completion-capitalized cost method" (i.e., 40 percent PCM) described below or (2) the percentage of completion method. In general, percentage of completion is determined as provided in the House bill for purposes of both methods. Except in the case of certain real property construction contracts (i.e., those for which exceptions were provided under the House bill and Senate amendment), these are the exclusive methods under which long-term contracts may be reported. The conference agreement generally adopts the definition of a long-term contract in the Senate amendment. This definition is the same as present law.

The conference agreement also prescribes the treatment of independent research and development costs, effective for all open tax years.

Percentage of completion-capitalized cost method

In the case of any long-term contract not reported under the percentage of completion method, the taxpayer must take into account 40 percent of the items with respect to the contract under the percentage of completion method. Percentage of completion is determined by comparing the total contract costs incurred before the close of the taxable year with the estimated total contract costs. The contract costs taken into account in determining the percentage of completion are those for which capitalization is required under the Senate amendment in the case of long-term contracts ("capitalizable costs").

The remaining 60 percent of the items under the contract are to be taken into account under the taxpayer's normal method of accounting, capitalizing those costs as required under the Senate amendment. Thus, 60 percent of the gross contract income will be recognized, and 60 percent of the contract costs will be deducted, at the time

Act § 803 and 804   ¶ 3937

required by the taxpayer's method. For example, if the taxpayer uses the completed contract method of accounting, these items would be taken into account upon completion of the contract. If the taxpayer uses an accrual method (e.g., an accrual shipment method), such contract items would be taken into account at the time of shipment.

Under the conference agreement, the look-back method provided in the House bill is to be applied to the 40 percent portion of the contract reported on the percentage of completion method. Thus, interest is paid to or by the taxpayer on the difference between the amount actually taken into account by the taxpayer for each year of the contract and the amount the taxpayer would have taken into account recomputing the 40-percent portion under the look-back method.

Independent research and development costs.—Under the conference agreement, independent research and development costs are expressly excepted from the category of capitalizable costs. Independent research and development costs for this purpose are defined as any expenses incurred in the performance of independent research and development other than (1) expenses directly attributable to a long-term contract in existence when the expenses are incurred, and (2) any expenses under an agreement to perform research and development.[1]

In particular, the conferees intend that the contractual arrangement regarding IR&D and its allocation to the contract shall not be severed, for Federal income tax purposes, from the long-term contract in such a manner as to render IR&D ineligible for treatment as a cost of a long-term contract, or to accelerate the recognition of any income pertaining to IR&D in comparison to the recognition of income which would otherwise occur under the taxpayer's method of accounting.

The conferees are aware that the treatment of independent research and development (IR&D) is presently a subject of controversy between taxpayers and the Internal Revenue Service. Under the conference agreement, the position of the Internal Revenue Service in several recent technical advice memoranda is expressly overruled.

Exception for small construction contracts.—Under the conference agreement, the required use of either the percentage of completion-capitalized cost method or the percentage of completion method does not apply to certain small construction contracts. Contracts within this exception are those contracts for the construction or improvement of real property if the contract (1) is expected to be completed within the two-year period beginning on the commencement date of the contract, and (2) is performed by a taxpayer whose average annual gross receipts for the three taxable years preceeding the taxable year in which the contract is entered into do not exceed $10 million. Contracts eligible for this exception will remain subject to the rules of present law (i.e., the regulations applicable to non-extended period long-term contracts). Since such contracts involve the construction of real property, they are subject to the interest capitalization rules of the conference agreement without regard to their duration.

Effective date.—The provisions of the conference agreement generally are effective for contracts entered into after February 28, 1986.

For purposes of accounting for long-term contracts, the treatment of independent research and development costs (as includible in contract price but not includible in capitalizable contract costs) applies to all open taxable years of taxpayers.

[¶ 3939] SECTION 805. REPEAL OF RESERVE FOR BAD DEBTS OF TAXPAYERS OTHER THAN FINANCIAL INSTITUTIONS

(Sec. 166 of the Code)

[Conference Report]

*   *   *   *   *   *

House Bill.—The House bill repeals the availability of the reserve method in computing the deduction for bad debts for all taxpayers, other than commercial banks whose assets do not exceed $500 million, and thrift institutions. Wholly worthless debts are not deductible for Federal income tax purposes until charged off on the taxpayer's books, as is the case under present law for partially worthless debts. The House bill does not address the continued use of the reserve method by dealers who guarantee, endorse, or provide indemnity agreements with regard to debt obligations arising out of the sale by

the dealer of real or tangible personal property in the ordinary course of business.

*   *   *   *   *   *

Senate Amendment.—The Senate amendment repeals the availability of the reserve method in computing the deduction for bad debts for all taxpayers, other than financial institutions, banks for cooperatives, production credit associations, and certain finance companies. Wholly worthless debts are not deductible for Federal income tax purposes until charged off on the taxpayer's books, as is the case under present law for partially worthless debts.

The Senate amendment also repeals the reserve method for dealers who guarantee, endorse, or provide indemnity agreements with respect to debt obligations arising out of

---

[Footnote ¶ 3937 continued]
   (1) The conferees intend that any costs that qualify as independent research and development costs under the Federal Acquisition Regulations System, 48 C.F.R. sec. 31.205-18 (1985), will qualify under this provision.

the sale by the dealer of real or tangible personal property in the ordinary course of business (sec. 166(f)).

The Senate amendment is effective for taxable years beginning after December 31, 1986. The balance in any reserve for bad debts as of the effective date is to be included in income ratably over a five-year period. In the case of a bad debt reserve for guarantees, the amount of the reserve is first reduced by the remaining balance in any suspense account established under section 166(f)(4), and the net amount taken into income ratably over a five-year period beginning with the first taxable year beginning after December 31, 1986.

Conference Agreement.—The conference agreement generally follows the House bill with regard to the availability of the reserve method for computing losses on business debts. Thus, taxpayers (other than certain financial institutions) will be required to use the specific charge-off method in accounting for losses on bad debts. In determining whether a debt is worthless, the fact that a utility is required to continue to provide services to a customer whose account has otherwise been determined to be uncollectible will not be considered as evidence that the debt is not worthless for Federal income tax purposes.

The conference agreement does not include the provision limiting the deduction of wholly worthless business debts to the amount written off on the taxpayer's books. Thus, a wholly worthless debt will be deductible in full in the year that it becomes worthless, as is the case under present law.

The conference agreement follows the Senate amendment in repealing the reserve method for dealers who guarantee, endorse, or provide indemnity agreements with respect to debt obligations arising out of the sale by the dealer of real or tangible personal property in the ordinary course of business.

[Effective date.] The provision of the conference agreement is effective for taxable years beginning after December 31, 1986. Any change from the reserve method of accounting for bad debts is treated as a change in method of accounting initiated by the taxpayer with the consent of the Secretary of the Treasury. The balance in any reserve for bad debts as of the effective date is generally to be included in income ratably over a four-year period. The amount to be included in income is the full balance of the reserve account, without offset for any anticipated amounts that will not be currently accrued as income under the rules allowing accrual basis service providers to exclude from income amounts that are statistically determined not to be collectible until such amounts are actually collected. (see VIII. A., supra). In the case of a bad debt reserve for guarantees, the amount of the reserve subject to inclusion is first reduced by the remaining balance in any suspense account established under section 166(f)(4).

The conferees intend that (1) net operating loss and tax credit carryforwards will be allowed to offset any positive section 481 adjustment; and (2) for purposes of determining estimated tax payments, the section 481 adjustment will be recognized in taxable income ratably throughout the year in question.

The conferees also direct the Secretary of the Treasury to study and to issue a report regarding appropriate criteria to be used to determine if a debt is worthless for Federal income tax purposes. The conferees anticipate that the report will consider under what circumstances a rule providing for a conclusive or rebuttable presumption of the worthlessness of an indebtedness is appropriate.

The final report is to be submitted, by January 1, 1988, to the House Committee on Ways and Means and the Senate Committee on Finance.

[¶ 3940] SECTION 806. TAXABLE YEARS OF CERTAIN ENTITIES

(Secs. 441, 706, and 1378 of the Code)

[Senate Explanation]

*   *   *   *   *   *

Explanation of Provision.—The bill requires that all partnerships, S corporations, and personal service corporations conform their taxable years to the taxable years of their owners. The bill provides that a partnership may not have a taxable year other than the taxable year of its partners owning a majority interest in partnership profits and capital, unless it establishes to the satisfaction of the Secretary of the Treasury a business purpose therefor. If partners owning a majority of partnership profits and capital do not have the same taxable year, the partnership must adopt the same taxable year as its principal partners. If the principal partners of the partnership do not have the

same taxable year and no majority of its partners have the same taxable year, the partnership must adopt a calendar year as its taxable year.

For example, assume a partnership has one principal partner which is a fiscal year corporation owning an interest of 10 percent in partnership profits and capital. The remainder of the partners are individuals on a calendar taxable year; none of these individuals owns a sufficient interest in the partnership to be a principal partner. Under present law, the partnership would be required to adopt the same taxable year of the corporate partner (i.e., the taxable year of its principal partner). However, under the bill, the partnership would be required to adopt a calendar taxable year (i.e., the taxable year of the majority of its partners).

Act §806   **¶3940**

An S corporation must adopt a permitted year, regardless of when the corporation elected to be taxed as an S corporation. Also, the bill requires that a personal service corporation must adopt a calendar year.

An exception is provided in each case where the partnership, S corporation, or personal service corporation establishes to the satisfaction of the Secretary of the Treasury a business purpose for having a different taxable year. It is anticipated that present administrative practice which generally allows, under certain conditions, the use of a taxable year resulting in 3 months or less deferral will apply for purposes of this provision.

A partnership is not required to adopt the taxable year of the partners owning a majority interest in partnership profits and capital, unless partners with the same taxable year have owned a majority interest in partnership profits and capital for the three preceding taxable years of the partnership. For purposes of determining whether this three-year test has been met, taxable years of the partnership beginning before the effective date of the bill are taken into account. Thus, for example, assume a fiscal year partnership had a taxable year other than the taxable year of its partners owning a majority interest in partnership profits and capital, for the partnership's taxable years ending in 1985, 1986, and 1987. For the partnership's taxable year beginning in 1987, the partnership would be required to change its taxable year to conform with the taxable year of the partners owning a majority interest in partnership profits and capital.

The bill provides that a partnership, S corporation, or personal service corporation that changes to a taxable year required by this provision will be treated as having made the change with the consent of the Secretary of the Treasury. In the case of a partnership or an S corporation, each partner or owner may elect to take the excess of income over expense for any short taxable year that results from the change in the taxable year into account ratably over the first four taxable years (including the owner's year which would otherwise include the income or loss of the entity's short taxable year) beginning after December 31, 1986. Absent such an election, the amount of net income or loss for the short taxable year is currently included, in its entirety, by the owner. In the case of a personal service corporation, the short taxable year resulting from the change of taxable year is annualized under section 443.

A partnership, S corporation, or personal service corporation seeking to use a taxable year other than the taxable year required by this provision must obtain the consent of the Secretary of the Treasury. It is expected that the concepts embodied in the current Revenue Procedures dealing with the taxable years of partnerships (Rev. Proc. 72-51, 1972-2 C.B. 832) and of S corporations (Rev. Proc. 83-25, 1983-1 C.B. 689) will be followed to the extent they do not conflict with this provision. It is anticipated that entities having previously established to the satisfaction of

the Secretary of the Treasury (in accordance with the terms of those Revenue Procedures) a sufficient business purpose for using a different taxable year will not be required to obtain the Secretary of the Treasury's permission in order to keep such taxable year.

For purposes of this provision, a personal service corporation is a corporation the principal activity of which is the performance of personal service if services are substantially performed by employee-owners. An employee-owner is any employee of the corporation who owns, on any day during the taxable year, any of the outstanding stock of the corporation. In determining whether an employee owns stock in the corporation, the constructive ownership rules of section 318 apply, except that the attribution of stock owned by a corporation to the employee is applied without regard to any requirement that the employee own a certain percentage of the value of the stock of that corporation. For the purpose of this provision, a corporation that has elected S corporation status will not be considered a personal service corporation.

Effective date.—The provision is effective for taxable years beginning after December 31, 1986. Entities required to change their taxable years as a result of this provision will be required to file a return for the short taxable year that begins with the first day of their current taxable year beginning after December 31, 1986, and ends in accordance with the taxable year to which the entity changes.

*   *   *   *   *   *

[Conference Report]

*   *   *   *   *   *

Conference Agreement.—The conference agreement generally follows the Senate amendment.

The conference agreement extends the provisions of section 267 to provide that a personal service corporation and its employee-owners are treated as related taxpayers regardless of the amount of the corporation's stock owned, directly or indirectly, by the employee-owner. Thus, a personal service corporation may not deduct payments made to employee-owners prior to the time that such employee-owner would include the payment in gross income.

The rule allowing partners or shareholders of a partnership or S corporation to include items of income from the short year of the partnership or S corporation in each of the partner or shareholder's four taxable years beginning after December 31, 1986 is applicable regardless of what type of entity the partner or S corporation shareholder is. Thus, a personal service corporation that is a partner in a partnership required to adopt a new taxable year as a result of this provision is eligible to include the partner's distributive share of partnership income over four taxable years. The rule is applicable to income from an S corporation only if such corporation was an S corporation for a taxable year beginning in 1986.

The conferees intend that any partnership that received permission to use a fiscal year-end (other than a year-end that resulted in a three-month or less deferral of income) under the provisions of Rev. Proc. 74-33, 1974-2 C.B. 489, shall be allowed to continue the use of such taxable year without obtaining the approval of the Secretary. Similarly, any S corporation that received permission to use a fiscal year-end (other than a year-end that resulted in a three-month or less deferral of income), which permission was granted on or after the effective date of Rev. Proc. 74-33, shall be allowed to continue the use of such taxable year without obtaining the approval of the Secretary.

Moreover, any partnership, S corporation, or personal service corporation may adopt, retain, or change to a taxable year, under procedures established by the Secretary, if the use of such year meets the requirements of the "25% test" as described in Rev. Proc. 83-25, 1983-1 C.B. 689 (i.e., 25% or more of the taxpayer's gross receipts for the 12-month period in question are recognized in the last two months of such period and this requirement has been met for the specified three consecutive 12-month periods).

In addition, the Secretary may prescribe other tests to be used to establish the existence of a business purpose, if, in the discretion of the Secretary, such tests are desirable and expedient towards the efficient administration of the tax laws.

The conferees intend that (1) the use of a particular year for regulatory or financial accounting purposes; (2) the hiring patterns of a particular business, e.g., the fact that a firm typically hires staff during certain times of the year; (3) the use of a particular year for administrative purposes, such as the admission or retirement of partners or shareholders, promotion of staff, and compensation or retirement arrangements with staff, partners, or shareholders; and (iv) the fact that a particular business involves the use of price lists, model year, or other items that change

on an annual basis ordinarily will not be sufficient to establish that the business purpose requirement for a particular taxable year has been met.

The conferees anticipate that the Secretary of the Treasury will promulgate regulations regarding the use of the 52-53 week taxable year to prevent the evasion of the principles of this provision. It is anticipated that the regulations will provide that, for the purpose of determining when taxable income is included by a partner or S corporation shareholder, a 52-53 week taxable year of a partner, shareholder, partnership, or S corporation will be treated as ending on the last day of the calendar month ending nearest to the last day of such 52-53 week taxable year. For example, a calendar year partner will include its share of taxable income from a partnership with a 52-53 week taxable year ending on January 3, 1988 in its 1987 calendar year Federal income tax return. The Secretary of the Treasury may also prescribe similar rules to prevent the evasion of the principles of the provision through the use of a 52-53 week taxable year by personal service corporations and the shareholder-employees of such corporations. It is also anticipated that the Secretary of the Treasury will suspend the operation of Treas. Reg. sec. 1.441-2(c) allowing taxpayers in certain cases to adopt, or change to, a 52-53 week taxable year without the approval of the Secretary of the Treasury.

Some partnerships and S corporations that adopted a taxable year providing a deferral of income to owners of three months or less were required to include the amount of deferral obtained in income over a 10-year period. Any portion of such amount not taken into income as of the effective date of the provision may be used to reduce the income attributable to any short taxable year required by the provision.

[Effective date.—Taxable years beginning after 12-31-86. Ed.]

[¶ 3941] SECTIONS 811 AND 812. INSTALLMENT SALES

(Secs. 453 and 453C of the Code)

[Senate Explanation]

*   *   *   *   *   *

Explanation of Provision.—*In general.*—In general, the bill limits the the availability of the installment method of accounting in three circumstances. First, the bill disallows the use of the installment method with respect to a portion of certain installment receivables, based on the amount of the outstanding indebtedness of the taxpayer. The bill grants an election to taxpayers selling certain "timeshares" and residential lots whereby such taxpayers may elect to pay interest on the deferral of their tax liability and not be subject to the general rules under the bill relating to installment sales. In addition, the bill retains present law for

certain installment obligations the term of which is dependent on the time of resale (or of the renting) of the property whose sale gave rise to the obligation.

Second, the bill prohibits taxpayers from using the installment method for sales pursuant to a revolving credit plan. Third, the bill provides that the installment method cannot be used for sales of certain publicly traded property.

Proportionate disallowance rule.—*In general.*—Under the bill, use of the installment method for certain sales by persons who regularly sell real or personal property described in section 1221(1), and for certain sales of business or rental property, is limited based on the amount of the outstanding indebtedness of the taxpayer. The limitation

Act §811 and 812   ¶3941

generally is applied by determining the amount of the taxpayer's "allocable installment indebtedness" ("AII") for each taxable year and treating such amount as a payment immediately before the close of the taxable year on "applicable installment obligations" of the taxpayer that arose in that taxable year and are still outstanding as of the end of the year.[4]

"Allocable installment indebtedness".—In general, AII for any taxable year is determined by (1) dividing the face amount of the taxpayer's "applicable installment obligations" that are still outstanding at the end of the year by the sum of (a) the face amount of all installment obligations (i.e., both applicable installment obligations and all other installment obligations) and (b) the adjusted basis of all other assets of the taxpayer,[5] (2) multiplying the resulting quotient by the taxpayer's average quarterly indebtedness, and (c) subtracting any AII that is attributable to applicable installment obligations arising in previous years. In the case of an individual, this computation does not take into account assets that are certain farm property or personal use property within the meaning of sec. 1275(b)(3) (including installment obligations arising from the sale of such property), or indebtedness that is secured by only such property.

"Applicable installment obligations" are any installment obligations that arise from the sale after February 28, 1986, of (1) personal property on the installment plan by a person who regularly sells or otherwise disposes of personal property, (2) real property that is held by the taxpayer for sale to customers in the ordinary course of a trade or business, or (3) [for dispositions after 8-16-86] real property (other than certain farm property) used in the taxpayer's trade or business or held for the production of rental income, provided that the selling price of the property exceeds $150,000, so long as the obligation in any case is held by the seller or a member of the same affiliated group as the seller.

In each subsequent taxable year, the taxpayer is not required to recognize gain attributable to applicable installment obligations arising in any prior year to the extent that the payments on the obligations do not exceed the amount of AII attributable to such obligations. On the receipt of such payments, the AII attributable to the obligation on which the payment is received is reduced by the amount of such payments. Payments on an applicable installment obligation in excess of the AII allocable to such obligation are accounted for under the ordinary rules for applying the installment method.

In general, AII for a particular applicable installment obligation is not adjusted after its initial computation, except to reflect the receipt of payments on the installment obligation that do not result in the recognition of any additional gain. However, in order to assure that a proportionate share of a taxpayer's indebtedness is allocated to all installment obligations, additional AII may be allocated to installment obligations arising in previous years if the amount of AII for a particular taxable year exceeds the amount of applicable installment obligations arising in that year and outstanding at year end. In this situation, the amount of such excess is first allocated to (and treated as a payment on) outstanding applicable installment obligations that arose in the preceeding year (but only to the extent that the face amount outstanding exceeds the AII for such obligations), and then allocated in a similar fashion to each preceeding taxable year until the full amount of the excess is allocated.

Calculation of indebtedness.—Under the bill, the taxpayer must compute its average indebtedness for the year in order to calculate the amount of its AII. The bill provides the calculation is to be made, for this purpose, on a quarterly basis. In making the calculation, all indebtedness of the taxpayer that is taken into account for purposes of the provision and that is outstanding as of the end of each quarter should be taken into account, including (but not limited to) accounts payable and accrued expenses as well as other amounts more commonly considered as indebtedness, such as loans from banks, and indebtedness arising from the issuance of bonds or in connection with the purchase of property by the taxpayer.[6] The committee recognizes that the extent to which indebtedness relating to accrued expenses and similar items is reflected in the computation may be diminished, for example, where a taxpayer regularly pays all of its accrued expenses and similar items at month end. However, the committee intends that any repayments of indebtedness for the purpose of avoiding this limitation be ignored for this purpose.

Affiliated groups.—Where the taxpayer is a member of an affiliated group (within the meaning of sec. 1504(a), but without regard to sec. 1504(b)[6a]), or a group under common control (within the meaning of sec. 52(b)),

---

[Footnote ¶ 3941] (4) The provisions of the bill do not affect the treatment of any payment (within the meaning of sec. 453(c)) prior to the close of the taxable year of sale, which payment would be accounted for under the ordinary rules for applying the installment method.

(5) Taxpayers may elect to use depreciation deductions as calculated under section 812(k) for purposes of computing the adjusted basis of its assets under this formula.

(6) Where any indebtedness of the taxpayer, or any applicable installment obligation is subject to the rules of either section 483 or section 1274, and either such section causes a portion of the principal amount of such indebtedness or applicable installment obligation to be recharacterized as interest, then the provisions of the bill are to be applied based on the restated principal amounts.

(6a) For purposes of this provision, any shareholder who meets the stock ownership requirement of section 1504(a)(2) (taking into account all stock owned directly or indirectly by such shareholder) is treated as a member of the affiliated group.

then for purposes of making the calculations required under the bill, all such members are treated as one taxpayer. Thus, for purposes of the bill, each member is treated as having all of the assets and liabilities of every other member. The committee intends that any indebtedness between members of the group, other than indebtedness that would be treated as an applicable installment obligation, would be disregarded (as both assets and liabilities) for this purpose. In addition, the committee intends that the adjusted basis of any asset transferred from one member of the group to another is to be reduced, for this purpose, by the portion of the gain that has not been recognized or otherwise has been deferred as of the time of the computation, either under the consolidated return regulations (see Treas. Reg. sec. 1.1504-13) or because the gain on the transfer was eligible to be reported under the installment method.

Thus, taxpayers who are members of such groups would compute AII on a group-wide basis for each taxable year. The AII so computed would then be allocated pro rata to the applicable installment obligations of all of the members of the group, and the allocated amount accordingly would be treated as a payment on the obligations.

The bill also provides that under regulations to be issued by the Secretary of the Treasury (which would be effective as of the time that the provisions of the bill are effective), use of the installment method would be disallowed in whole or in part where the provisions of the bill otherwise would be avoided through use of related parties or other intermediaries.

Example: The application of the rules of the bill may be illustrated by the following example. The example assumes that the taxpayer is a dealer in real property, uses the calendar year as its taxable year, and that its operations began in 1987.

Calendar year 1987.—During 1987, the taxpayer sells one property[7] for $90,000, taking back the purchaser's note for the entire purchase price.[8] The property was sold at a profit. No payments are received on the obligation before the end of the year.

The aggregate adjusted basis of the taxpayer's assets, other than the installment obligation,[9] is $310,000 as of the end of 1987.

The taxpayer's average quarterly indebtedness for 1987 is $200,000.

The taxpayer's AII for 1987 would be $45,000. This amount is computed by multiplying (1) the taxpayer's average quarterly indebtedness for 1987 ($200,000) by (2) the quotient of (a) the total face amount of taxpayer's outstanding applicable installment obligations ($90,000) and (b) the sum of (i) the total face amount of the taxpayer's installment obligations ($90,000) and (ii) the adjusted basis of its other assets as of the end of 1987 ($310,000). The taxpayer would be treated as receiving a payment of $45,000 on the outstanding installment obligation as of the close of 1987.[10]

Calendar year 1988.—During 1988, the taxpayer sells another property for $110,000, taking back the purchaser's note for the entire purchase price. The property was sold at a profit. No payments were received in 1988 on either the 1987 or 1988 installment obligations held by the taxpayer.

The aggregate adjusted basis of the taxpayer's assets, other than the installment obligations, is $400,000 as of the end of 1988. The taxpayer's average quarterly indebtedness for 1988 is $300,000.

The taxpayer's AII for 1988 would be $55,000. This amount is computed by multiplying (1) the taxpayer's average quarterly indebtedness for 1988 ($300,000) by (2) the quotient of (a) the total face amount of the taxpayer's outstanding applicable installment obligations ($200,000) and (b) the sum of (i) the total face amount of the taxpayer's installment obligations ($200,000) and (ii) the adjusted basis of its other assets as of the end of 1988 ($400,000), and (3) subtracting the amount of AII allocated to applicable installment obligations that arose prior to 1988 ($45,000). The taxpayer would be treated as having received a payment of $55,000 on the installment obligation that arose in 1988, as of the close of 1988.

Calendar year 1989.—In 1989, the taxpayer sells a third property for $130,000. The property was sold at a profit. Also in 1989, the installment obligation that the taxpayer received in 1987 is paid in full. No payments are received on either the obligation that was received in 1988 or the one received in 1989.

[Footnote ¶ 3941 continued]

(7) All sales referred to in the example are assumed to be of property that is held for sale to customers in the ordinary course of the taxpayer's trade or business. The facts of the example are intended only for purposes of illustrating the provisions of the bill limiting the use of the installment method. The committee intends no inference regarding the circumstances under which property is properly considered to be held for sale to customers in the ordinary course of a trade or business.

(8) All installment obligations received in this example are assumed not to be payable on demand or readily tradable (within the meaning of sec. 453(f)). In addition, such installment obligations are assumed to have stated interest sufficient to avoid the recharacterization of any portion of the principal amount as interest under section 483 or section 1274. Payments referred to in the example are payments of principal on the obligations.

(9) It is assumed that none of the taxpayer's assets in the example other than its applicable installment obligations are installment obligations. If so, these assets would be taken into account at their face amount rather than their adjusted basis.

(10) Where the taxpayer has more than one applicable installment obligation outstanding as of the close of the taxable year, the amount of AII for the year would be allocated pro rata (by outstanding face amount) to the obligations, and the proportionately allocated amount would be treated as a payment on each respective outstanding obligation.

Act § 811 and 812   ¶ 3941

The aggregate adjusted basis of the taxpayer's assets, other than its installment obligations, is $360,000 as of the end of 1989. The taxpayer's average quarterly indebtedness for 1989 is $500,000.

With respect to the $90,000 payment that was received on the installment obligation that arose in 1987, the first $45,000 of the payment would not result in the recognition of any additional gain with respect to the obligation, and would reduce the amount of AII that is treated as allocated to that obligation. The next $45,000 would be treated as an additional payment on the obligation that results in the recognition of additional gain under the installment method.

Taking into account the payment on the 1987 installment obligation, the AII allocated to taxable years before 1989, for purposes of computing AII for 1989, would be $55,000 ($45,000 of AII from 1987 plus $55,000 of AII from 1988 minus $45,000 of AII from 1987 returned in 1989).

The taxpayer's AII for 1989 would be $145,000. This amount is computed by multiplying (1) the taxpayer's average quarterly indebtedness for 1989 ($500,000) by (2) the quotient of (a) the total face amount of the taxpayer's outstanding applicable installment obligations as of the end of 1989 ($110,000 plus $130,000, or $240,000) and (b) the sum of (i) the total face amount of the taxpayer's installment obligations ($240,000) and (ii) the adjusted basis of its other assets as of the end of 1989 ($360,000), and (3) subtracting the amount of AII allocated to applicable installment obligations that arose prior to 1989 ($55,000).

Since taxpayer's AII for 1989 ($145,000) exceeds the amount of applicable installment obligations arising in 1989 and outstanding at the end of the year ($130,000), the taxpayer is treated as having received a payment, as of the close of 1989, of $130,000 on the installment obligation that arose in 1989, and a payment of $15,000 (i.e., the excess of $145,000 over $130,000) on the installment obligation that arose in 1988.

Special election for sales of timeshares and residential lots.—The bill provides an election under which the proportionate disallowance rule would not apply to installment obligations that arise from the sale of certain types of property by a dealer to an individual, but only if the individual's obligation is not guaranteed or insured by any third person other than an individual.[11] The obligation must arise from the sale of a "timeshare" or of unimproved land, the development of which will not be done by the seller of the land or any affiliate of the seller.[12]

For these purposes, a timeshare is a right to use a specified parcel of residential real property for a period not exceeding six weeks per year. The committee intends that where an individual or any related person owns more than one timeshare in a single parcel of residential real property, then all of the timeshares of the individual and the related parties are aggregated for purposes of determining whether the six week test is met. In addition, for purposes of the provision, a timeshare may include a right to use campground sites in designated locations over ascertainable periods of time for recreational (not residential) purposes.[13]

If these conditions are met, then the seller of the property that gave rise to these obligations may elect not to have the general rules of the bill relating to installment sales apply, provided that the seller pays interest on the deferral of its tax liability attributable to the use of the installment method.

Exception for certain sales by manufacturers to dealers.—The bill provides an exception for installment obligations arising from the sale of tangible personal property by the manufacturer of the property (or an affiliate of the manufacturer) to a dealer,[14] but only if the dealer is obligated to make payments of principal only when the dealer resells (or rents) the property, the manufacturer has the right to repurchase the property at a fixed (or ascertainable) price after no longer than a nine month period following the sale to the dealer, and certain other conditions are met. In order to meet the other conditions, the aggregate face amount of the installment obligations that otherwise qualify for the exception must equal at least 50 percent of the total sales to dealers that give rise to such receivables (the "fifty percent test") in both the taxable year and the preceding taxable year, except that, if the taxpayer met all of the requirements for the exception in the preceding taxable year, then the taxpayer would not be treated as failing to meet the fifty percent test before the second consecutive year in which the taxpayer did not actually meet the test. For purposes of applying the fifty percent test the aggregate face amount of the taxpayer's receivables is computed using the weighted average of the taxpayer's receivables computed on a monthly basis. In addition, these requirements must be met by the taxpayer in its first taxable year beginning after the date of enactment of the bill. For purposes of this provision, obligations issued before the date of enactment are treated as meeting the applicable requirements if such obligations are conformed to the requirements of the bill within 60 days of the date of enactment of the bill.

Receivables that meet the conditions for the exception are not subject to the provi-

---

[Footnote ¶ 3941 continued]

(11) The committee intends that any Federal or private insurance relating to the payment of the individual's obligation would prevent the obligation from qualifying for the special election.

(12) The committee intends that a parcel of land is not to be considered to have been improved or developed if it merely has been provided with the benefits of common infrastructure items such as roads and sewers.

(13) The committee intends no inference whether income from transactions involving such "campground timeshares" may properly be accounted for on the installment method.

(14) *I.e.,* the sale of the property must be intended to be for resale or leasing by the dealer.

sions of the bill relating only to limitation on the use of the installment method. The committee intends no inference regarding the treatment of these transactions for Federal income tax purposes.

Revolving credit plans.—Under the bill, taxpayers who sell property on a revolving credit plan are not permitted to account for such sales on the installment method. For this purpose, the committee intends that the term "revolving credit plan" have the same meaning as that under present law (see Treas. Reg. sec. 1.453-2(d)).

Publicly traded property.—Under the bill, taxpayers who sell stock or securities that are traded on an established securities market, or to the extent provided in Treasury regulations, property (other than stock or securities) of a kind regularly traded on an established market, are not permitted to use the installment method to account for such sales. The committee understands that the fair market value of an installment obligation received in exchange for such property is to be considered to be the same as the fair market value of the property at the time of sale.

The committee intends that, in the case of sales that are made on an established market, where cash settlement of transactions customarily occurs several business days after the date on which a trade is made, that gain or loss would be recognized for Federal income tax purposes by both cash or accrual method taxpayers on the day that the trade is executed.

The bill also provides that, under regulations to be issued by the Secretary of the Treasury (which would be effective as of the time that the provisions of the bill are effective), use of the installment method may be disallowed in whole or in part where the provisions of the bill otherwise would be avoided through use of related parties or other intermediaries. The committee intends that such regulations would apply to sales of property, a substantial portion of whose value is attributable to property gain from the sale of which could not be reported on the installment method on account of the provisions of the bill. For example, if a taxpayer sells his interest in a wholly owned corporation the only assets of which are stock or securities that are traded on an established securities market, the Secretary of the Treasury may deny the use of the installment method to account for gain on the sale.

The committee intends that any Treasury regulations would not deny use of the installment method if the seller could not have sold, or caused the sale of, the publicly traded stock or securities directly. For example, a retiring partner in a large investment partnership makes an installment sale of his partnership interest, a substantial portion of the value of which is attributable to stocks and securities held by the partnership. Provided that the retiring partner could not have sold or caused the sale of the partnership's assets directly, the gain on the sale of the partnership interest may be reported on the installment method.

[Conference Report]

The conference agreement generally follows the Senate amendment with certain modifications.

Proportionate disallowance rule.—The conference agreement generally adopts the proportionate disallowance rule contained in the Senate amendment. However, the conference agreement specifies that, in applying the proportionate disallowance rule, installment obligations arising from the sale of personal use property by an individual, and either property used or property produced in the trade or business of farming, are not treated as applicable installment obligations. Thus, for example, the proportionate disallowance rule does not apply under the conference agreement, to installment obligations arising from the sale of crops or livestock held for slaughter. In addition, personal use property, installment obligations arising from the sale of personal use property, and indebtedness substantially all the security for which is such property (or such installment obligations) are not taken into account in applying the proportionate disallowance rule under the conference agreement.

The conference agreement provides that, in applying the proportionate disallowance rule, the calculation of indebtedness is made on an annual basis, rather than a quarterly basis, for taxpayers who have no applicable installment obligations that arose from the sale on the installment method of either personal property by a person who regularly sells property of the same type on the installment method, or real property that was held for sale to customers in the ordinary course of a trade or business. The Treasury Department is given authority to issue regulations that would prevent possible avoidance of the provision where the calculation of indebtedness is made on such an annual basis.

The conference agreement modifies the aggregation rule contained in the Senate amendment for applying the proportionate disallowance rule. Under the conference agreement, all persons treated as a single employer under section 52(a) or section 52(b) (the "controlled group") are treated as one taxpayer for these purposes. Hence, in applying the proportionate disallowance rule to the controlled group, the installment percentage is determined by aggregating all of the assets of the members of the controlled group, and such installment percentage is multiplied by the aggregate average quarterly (or if appropriate, annual, indebtedness) of members of the controlled group, to determine the total allocable installment indebtedness for the controlled group. The total allocable installment indebtedness so determined then is allocated pro rata to the applicable installment obligations held by members of the controlled group, (regardless of the amount of any indebtedness that any particular member of the group has outstanding), and the regular provisions of the proportionate disallowance rule are then applied.

The conference agreement provides authority under which the Treasury Department may issue regulations that disallow the use of the installment method in whole or in part for transactions in which the effect of the proportionate disallowance rule would be avoided through the use of related parties, pass-through entities, or intermediaries. The conferees intend that the meaning of related party is to be construed for these purposes in a manner consistent with carrying out the purposes of the proportionate disallowance rule. Thus, the conferees intend that the regulations may treat any corporation, partnership, or trust as related to its shareholders, partners, or beneficiaries, as the case may be, in circumstances where the proportionate disallowance rule otherwise might be avoided.

The conferees intend that these regulations may aggregate the assets of the related parties for purposes of applying the proportionate disallowance rule. For example, the conferees intend that such regulations may aggregate the assets and indebtedness of a partnership and each of its partners in determining the extent to which each such partner may report gain arising from the installment sale of partnership assets on the installment method.

In addition, the conferees intend that the regulations may treat installment obligations arising from the sale of an interest in one related party by another as applicable installment obligations to the extent that installment obligations arising from the sale of the assets of the related party the interest in which is sold would be treated as applicable installment obligations.

The conferees intend that these regulations may in appropriate cases apply to all transactions after the general effective date of the provision, but prior to the issuance of the regulations.

The conference agreement also makes certain technical modifications to the statutory language relating to the proportionate disallowance rule.

[The following colloquy is drawn from the Congressional Record. The colloquy occurred on the day the Conference bill was considered by the Senate. Ed.]

[Senate Floor Explanation]
INSTALLMENT INDEBTEDNESS

Mr. DOLE. I understand that the conference report treats a taxpayer's allocable installment indebtedness as a payment received on an applicable installment obligation. Specifically, the disposition on an installment basis, after August 16, 1986, of real property used in a business or held for the production of rental income is subject to the proportionate disallowance rule if the sales price exceeds $150,000.

The conference report also authorizes the Treasury Department to prescribe regulations to prevent circumvention of the proportionate disallowance rule through the use of

related parties, passthrough entities, or intermediaries.

I would like to [clarify] that the proportionate disallowance rule will not apply if, prior to August 16, 1986, there is a disposition on the installment basis of less than a 50-percent interest in a partnership that owns only nondealer rental real property. Does the distinguished chairman of the Finance Committee agree that this interpretation is correct?

Mr. PACKWOOD. The majority leader's understanding of the provision is correct. A disposition on the installment basis of nondealer rental real property, whether directly or indirectly, prior to August 16, 1986, will not be subject to the proportionate disallowance rule. Congressional Record, p. S13958, 9-27-86.

[The following is from a statement of the Chairman of the House Ways and Means Committee relating to Senate Floor colloquies on the Conference Bill. Ed.]

[House Floor Explanation]

I have discussed with Congressman McGrath several issues regarding installment indebtedness. We have reached a common understanding which affirms the colloquy between Senator DOLE and Senator PACKWOOD regarding certain dispositions on the installment basis, located on page S13958 of the Congressional Record dated September 27, 1986. Congressional Record, p. E3390, 10-2-86.

[Conference Report]

*   *   *   *   *   *

Special election for sales of certain property. — The conference agreement adopts the special provision contained in the Senate amendment relating to installment obligations arising from the sales of certain "timeshares" and residential lots. In applying the special election, the conference agreement provides that the interest rate charged is 100 percent of the applicable Federal rate that would apply to the installment obligation received in the sale (without regard to the three-month lookback rule of section 1274(d)(2)). In addition, the conference agreement clarifies that in applying the "six-week" limitation on the eligibility of timeshare interests for the special rule, a timeshare right to use (or timeshare ownership in) a specific property, which right (or ownership interest) is held by the spouse, children, grandchildren or parents of an individual, shall be treated as held by such individual.

Publicly traded property and revolving credit.—For sales of publicly traded property and for sales of property pursuant to revolving credit plans, the conference agreement generally follows the Senate amendment. Under the conference agreement, such sales are treated as installment sales with respect to which all payments are received in the year of sale. The conference agreement provides that the Treasury Department has regulatory authority to disallow the use of the installment method in whole or in part for transactions in which the rules of the conference agreement relating to sales of publicly traded property or sales pursuant to a revolving credit plan would be avoided through the use of related parties, pass-through entities, or intermediaries. The conferees intend that these regulations are to be similar to those relating to the proportionate disallowance rule.

[Effective date.—Generally dispositions after 2-28-86 for tax years ending after 12-31-86. Revolving credit and publicly traded property rules: tax years beginning after 12-31-86. Ed.]

[¶ 3943] SECTION 821. INCOME ATTRIBUTABLE TO UTILITY SERVICES

(Sec. 451 of the Code)

[Conference Report]

*   *   *   *   *   *

Senate Amendment.—The Senate amendment requires accrual basis taxpayers to recognize income attributable to the furnishing or sale of utility services to customers not later than the taxable year in which such services are provided to the customer. The year in which utility services are provided may not be determined by reference to the time the customer's meter is read or to the time that the customer is billed (or may be billed) for such services.

The effect of the provision is to require an estimate of the income attributable to utility services provided during the taxable year but after the final meter reading or billing date which falls within the taxable year. It is anticipated that, where it is not practical for the utility to determine the actual amount of services provided through the end of the current year, this estimate may be made by assigning a pro rata portion of the revenues determined as of the first meter reading date or billing date of the following taxable year.

Utility services subject to the Senate amendment are the provision of electrical energy, water or sewage disposal, the furnishing of gas or steam through a local distribution system, telephone and other communications services, and the transportation of gas or steam by pipeline. It is anticipated that similar rules also would be applicable to other utility services which might come into existence at some future date. Whether or not a utility service is regulated by a government or governmental agency does not affect its treatment under this provision. The Senate amendment creates no inference as to the proper Federal income tax treatment of utility services under current law.

The conferees are aware that the proper accounting for utility services is presently a matter of controversy between taxpayers and the Internal Revenue Service. In order to minimize disputes over prior taxable years, the conference agreement provides that, for any taxable year beginning before August 16, 1986, a method of accounting which took into account income from the providing of utility services on the basis of the period in which the customers' meters were read shall be deemed to be proper for Federal income tax purposes. No inference is intended as to methods of accounting for utility services not described in the preceding sentence (e.g., a method of accounting which takes income into account on the basis of the date the customer is billed for utility services).

[Effective date.—] The provision is effective for taxable years beginning after December 31, 1986. The amount of any adjustment required to be made as a result of this provision is to be included in income ratably over the first four taxable years for which the proposal is effective.

Conference Agreement.—The conference agreement follows the provision of the Senate amendment.

The conferees also intend that (i) net operating loss and tax credit carryforwards will be allowed to offset any positive section 481 adjustment; and (ii) for purposes of determining estimated tax payments, the section 481 adjustment will be recognized in taxable income ratably throughout the year in question.

In addition, the conferees intend that taxpayers required to accrue income at the time the utility services are furnished to customers may accrue at such time any deductions for the related costs of providing the utility services if economic performance has occurred with respect to such costs within the taxable year in question. Therefore, the conferees intend that any change in accounting method required under this provision include any related change in accounting method for the related items of expense or deduction. The section 481 adjustment is then to be computed on the net amount of the two changes and taken into income ratably over a 4-year period.

[¶ 3944] SECTION 822. REPEAL OF APPLICATION OF DISCHARGE OF INDEBTEDNESS RULES TO QUALIFIED BUSINESS INDEBTEDNESS

(Sec. 108 of the Code)

[Conference Report]

*　　*　　*　　*　　*　　*

Senate Amendment.—The Senate amendment repeals the provision of present law that provides for the election to exclude income from the discharge of qualified business indebtedness from gross income. Thus, any discharge of indebtedness, other than a discharge in title 11 cases or a discharge that occurs when the taxpayer is insolvent, results in the current recognition of income in the amount of the discharge.

The Senate amendment does not change the present-law treatment of a discharge of indebtedness that occurs in a title 11 case or when the taxpayer is insolvent (including a farmer treated as insolvent under section 108(g) as added by the amendment, see IV. A. 7.), nor does it change the provision of present law (sec. 108(e)(5)) that treats any reduction of purchase-money debt of a solvent debtor as a purchase price adjustment, rather than a discharge of indebtedness.

[Effective date.—] The provision of the Senate amendment is applicable to discharges of indebtedness occurring after December 31, 1986.

Conference Agreement.—The conference agreement follows the Senate amendment.

*　　*　　*　　*　　*　　*

[¶ 3945] SECTION 823. REPEAL OF DEDUCTION FOR QUALIFIED DISCOUNT COUPONS

(Sec. 466 of the Code)

[Senate Explanation]

*　　*　　*　　*　　*　　*

Explanation of Provision.—The bill repeals the provision of present law allowing a deduction for the cost of redeeming qualified discount coupons received during a redemption period after the close of the taxable year. As a result, only those costs of redeeming discount coupons received for redemption during the taxable year will be allowed as a deduction during that taxable year.

The bill treats any taxpayer currently electing to deduct the cost of redeeming qualified discount coupons as having elected to change its method of accounting. The change will be considered to have been initiated by the taxpayer with the consent of the Secretary of the Treasury. Any adjustment which is required to be made by section 481 will be reduced by any balance in the suspense account of the taxpayer, and the net amount is to taken into account ratably over a period not to exceed five taxable years, commencing with the first taxable year beginning after December 31, 1986. It is expected that the concepts of Revenue Procedure 84-74, 1984-2 C.B. 786, generally will apply to determine the actual timing of recognition or expense as a result of the adjustments arising from this provision.

[Conference Report]

*　　*　　*　　*　　*　　*

Senate Amendment

[Effective date.—] The provision of the Senate amendment is effective for taxable years beginning after December 31, 1986.

Conference Agreement.—The conference agreement generally follows the Senate amendment. The net adjustment required to be made as a result of the provision, after reduction for any balance in the suspense account, is required to be taken into account over a period not to exceed four taxable years, commencing with the first taxable year ending after December 31, 1986.

The conferees also intend that (i) net operating loss and tax credit carryforwards will be allowed to offset any positive section 481 adjustment; and (ii) for purposes of determining estimated tax payments, the section 481 adjustment will be recognized in taxable income ratably throughout the year in question.

[The following colloquy relating to Act Sec. 823 is drawn from the Congressional Record. The colloquy occurred on the day the Conference bill was considered by the Senate. Ed.]

[Senate Floor Explanation]

I have discussed with Congressman GRADISON several issues relating to the effective date of the repeal of the deduction for qualified discount coupons under this legislation. We have reached a common understanding regarding the following specific issue:

Mr. Gradison is concerned that the effective date for section 822 [823], * * * the repeal of the deduction for qualified discount coupons is unclear. The statute states that this provision applies "to taxable years beginning after December 31, 1986." The conference report, however, applies the provision to the first taxable year ending after December 31, 1986. The statute governs in this instance. The statute is correct. The amendments made by this section apply to taxable years beginning after December 31, 1986. Congressional Record, p. H8362, 9-25-86

[¶ 3946] SECTION 824. INCLUSION IN GROSS INCOME OF CONTRIBUTIONS IN AID OF CONSTRUCTION

(Secs. 118 and 362 of the Code)

[House Explanation]

*   *   *   *   *   *

Explanation of Provision.—The committee bill repeals the provision of present law (sec. 118(b)) that provides for the treatment of contributions in aid of construction received by a corporate regulated public utility to be treated as a contribution to the capital of the utility.

The committee intends that the effect of the change is to require that a utility report as an item of gross income the value of any property, including money, that it receives to provide, or encourage of the provision of services to or for the benefit of the person transferring the property. A utility is considered as having received property to encourage the provision of services if the receipt of the property is a prerequisite to the provision of the services, if the receipt of the property results in the provision of services earlier than would have been the case had the property not been received, or if the receipt of the property otherwise causes the transferor to be favored in any way.

The committee intends that a utility include in gross income the value of the property received regardless of whether the utility had a general policy, stated or unstated, that requires or encourages certain types of potential customers to transfer property, including money, to the utility while other types of potential customers are not required or encouraged to make similar transfers. If members of a group making transfers of property are favored over other members of the same general group not making such transfers, the fact that the contributing members of the group may not be favored over the members of other groups in the receipt of services will not prevent the inclusion of the value of the transfer in the gross income of the utility.

For instance, where a utility generally requires developers of multiple tracts of residential housing to transfer property to the utility in order to obtain service, but does not require such a transfer from individual homeowners, the fact that both groups will receive service without preference of one group over the other will not prevent the utility from being required to include in gross income the value of the property received from the developers. Where all members of a particular group make transfers of property to the utility, normally it will be assumed that such transfers are to encourage the provision of services, despite the absence of any formal policy requiring such transfers, unless it is clearly shown that the benefit of the public as a whole was the primary motivating factor in the transfers.

The person transferring the property will be considered as having been benefitted if he is the person who will receive the services, an owner of the property that will receive the services, a former owner of the property that will receive the services, or if he derives any benefit from the property that will receive the services. Thus, a builder who transfers property to a utility in order to obtain services for a house that he was paid to build will be considered as having benefitted from the provision of the services. This will be the case despite the fact that the builder may never have had an ownership interest in the property and may make the transfer to the utility after the house has been completed and accepted.

[Conference Report]

*   *   *   *   *   *

[Effective date.—] The conference agreement follows the provision of the House bill, effective for contributions received after December 31, 1986.

[¶ 3948] SECTION 901. LIMITATIONS ON BAD DEBT RESERVES

(Secs. 585 and 593 of the Code)

[House Explanation]

*   *   *   *   *   *

1. Commercial Banks

Present Law.—Under present law, commercial banks[1] are allowed to use either the specific charge-off method or the reserve method in computing their deduction for bad debts for Federal income tax purposes. Under the reserve method, a commercial bank is

entitled to a deduction equal to that amount necessary to increase the year-end bad debt reserve balance to an amount computed under either the "experience method" or the "percentage of eligible loans method."

Specific charge-off method.—Under the specific charge-off method, a deduction is allowed for bad debts as the individual debt owed the commercial bank becomes either wholly or partially worthless. At such time as the debt is determined to be uncollectible in

---

[Footnote ¶ 3948] (1) A commercial bank is defined as a domestic or foreign corporation, a substantial portion of whose business consists or receiving deposits and making loans and discounts, or of exercising fiduciary powers similar to those permitted national banks, and who are subject by law to supervision and examination by State or Federal Authority having supervision over banking institutions (sec. 581). For the purpose of determining the deductions for bad debts, the term "commercial bank" does not include domestic building and loan associations, mutual savings banks or cooperative nonprofit mutual banks ("thrift institutions").

whole or in part, the amount of the debt is reduced by the uncollectible portion, and a deduction is allowed for that amount. If an amount previously charged off as uncollectible is later recovered, the recovery is treated as a separate income item at the time of collection. The bad debt deduction for wholly worthless amounts that are charged off is allowable in the year in which they become worthless. Partially worthless amounts both must have become partially worthless and also must be charged off on the taxpayer's books in the amount of such partial worthlessness before a bad debt deduction is allowed for Federal income tax purposes.

Reserve method.—* * * Under the reserve method, a reserve account is established to record an allowance against the eventuality that some of the debts may eventually prove to be uncollectible. The actual deduction for bad debts for any year is the amount which is necessary to bring the reserve for bad debts at the beginning of the taxable year, adjusted for actual bad debt experience and recoveries during the year, to the allowed ending balance computed under approved methods. Amounts specifically charged off or recovered are subtracted or added to the reserve which may affect the amount that may be added to the reserve for that taxable year. The maximum allowed ending balance of the reserve for bad debts can be computed under either the "bank experience method" or the "percentage of eligible loans method."

Bank experience method.—* * * (sec. 585(b)(3), permits, in essence, the maximum allowed ending balance of the reserve to be equal to the percentage of total loans outstanding which are expected to become uncollectible within the next year. Under the bank experience method, the maximum allowed ending balance is that portion of the balance of loans outstanding at the end of the year that the total bad debts in the current and five preceding taxable years (a shorter period may be used with approval of the Secretary) bears to the sum of the loans outstanding at the close of each of those years. However, the ending reserve balance need not be reduced to an amount less than the balance in the reserve at the close of the bank's base year, so long as the amount of total loans outstanding at the close of the current taxable year are at least as great as the amount of total loans outstanding at the close of the base year. If the amount of loans outstanding at the close of the current year is less than loans outstanding at the close of the base year, then the minimum reserve amount under the base year alternative is limited to a proportionate part of the base year reserve which bears the same ratio as the ratio of loans at the close of

the current year bears to loans at the close of the base year. The base year is the last taxable year before the most recent adoption of the experience method.

Percentage of eligible loans method.—Under the "percentage of eligible loans method" (sec. 585(b)(2)), the maximum addition to the reserve for bad debts at the close of the taxable year is an amount necessary to increase the reserve to a specified percentage of outstanding eligible loans at that time, plus an amount determined under the experience method for loans other than eligible loans. The specified percentage for taxable years beginning after 1982 is 0.6 percent.[2] Eligible loans for this purpose generally are loans incurred in the course of a bank's normal customer loan activities on which there is more than an insubstantial risk of loss.[3]

As under the experience method, commercial banks that use the percentage of eligible loans method are permitted, at a minimum, to maintain a balance in the loan loss reserve at the close of the taxable year equal to a base-year reserve balance so long as eligible loans have not decreased from their level in the base year. For taxable years beginning after 1982, the base year is the last tax year beginning before 1988 (the last year before the rate was changed to 0.6 percent) or the last year before the bank's most recent adoption of the percentage of loans method, whichever is later. If eligible loans have decreased below their base-year level, the minimum bad debt reserve permitted the bank is reduced proportionately.[4] In addition, the maximum addition to the reserve for losses on loans under the percentage method cannot exceed the greater of either 0.6 percent of eligible loans outstanding at the close of the taxable year or an amount sufficient to increase the reserve for losses on loans to 0.6 percent of eligible loans at such time.

A commercial bank may switch between the experience method and the percentage of eligible loans method of determining the addition to its reserve for losses on loans from one year to another. A commercial bank need not adopt the method yielding the largest deduction, although the regulations do prescribe minimum deductions.

Under present law, if the bad debt reserve deduction for the taxable year determined under the above rules exceeds the amount which would have been allowed as a deduction on the basis of actual experience, the deduction is reduced by 20 percent of such excess (sec. 291). Also, 59-5/6 percent of the deductible excess (after the 20-percent reduction) is treated as a tax preference for pur-

---

[Footnote ¶ 3948 continued]

(2) For taxable years beginning after 1975 but before 1982, the specified percentage, was 1.2 percent. For taxable years beginning in 1982, the specified percentage was 1.0 percent.

(3) Specifically excluded from the definition of an eligible loan are a loan to a bank; a loan to a domestic branch of a foreign corporation which would be a bank were it not a foreign corporation; a loan secured by a deposit in the lending bank or in another bank if the taxpayer bank has control over the withdrawal of such deposit; a loan to or guaranteed by the United States, a possession or instrumentality thereof, or to a State or political subdivision thereof; a loan evidenced by a security; a loan of federal funds; and commercial paper. Sec. 585(b)(4).

(4) There is a further limitation that reduces the bad debt addition when the base year loss reserve is less than the allowable percentage of base year loans (sec. 585(b)(2)).

poses of computing the corporate minimum tax (sec. 57).

The availability of the percentage of eligible loans method is scheduled to expire after 1987. For taxable years beginning after 1987, banks will be limited to the experience method in computing additions to bad debt reserves.

* * * * * *

Explanation of Provision.—*In general.*—The committee bill retains retains present law regarding the use of reserves in computing the deduction for losses on bad debts, except in the case of "large bank" if, for the current taxable year or any taxable year beginning after December 31, 198[6], the sum of the average adjusted bases of all assets of such bank exceed $500 million or, if the bank is a member of a controlled group, the sum of the adjusted bases of all assets of such group exceeds $500 million. The adjusted basis of an asset will generally be considered to be the tax basis of the asset, adjusted by those amounts allowed as adjustments to basis by section 1016. In determining the sum of the average adjusted bases of all assets of a controlled group, interests held by one member of such group in another member of such group are to be disregarded, in order to prevent the basis of such assets from effectively being included more than once. The average adjusted basis of the assets of a bank or controlled group is determined by dividing the sum of the adjusted bases of the assets at each time during the taxable year when the bank is required to report for regulatory purposes by the number of required reports.

A controlled group as used in this provision of the bill is a controlled group of corporations described in section 1563(a)(1). For the purpose of determining the sum of the adjusted bases of the assets of a controlled group, all corporations includible in the group under the ownership tests of section 1563(a) shall be included, without regard to their status as an "excluded member" of a controlled group as a result of the application of section 1563(b)(2), and whether or not the corporation meets the definition of a commercial bank.

Recapture of bad debt reserves of "large banks."—* * * unless the cutoff method is elected, a bank will be treated as having initiated a change in accounting method with regard to its calculation of losses on bad debts in the first year the bank is no longer permitted to use the reserve method (the "disqualification year"). The change in method of accounting will be considered to have been made with the consent of the Secretary. * * *.

* * * * * *

[Conference Report]

* * * * * *

Conference Agreement.—

* * * * * *

A large bank not electing to use the cut-off method is required to recapture its bad debt reserve by including 10 percent of the reserve balance in income in the first taxable year for which the provision is effective, 20 percent in the second, 30 percent in the third, and 40 percent in the fourth. A bank may elect to include more than 10 percent of its reserve balance in income in the first taxable year. If such an election is made, $\frac{2}{9}$ of the remainder of the reserve balance (after reduction for the amount included in income in the first taxable year) must be included in income in the second taxable year, $\frac{1}{3}$ of the remainder in the third taxable year and $\frac{4}{9}$ of the remainder in the fourth taxable year.

* * * * * *

[House Explanation]

* * * * * *

* * * A bank using the cutoff method will not be considered as having changed its method of accounting. Instead, the bank will continue to use the reserve method to account for bad debt losses on loans outstanding on the last day of the taxable year before the disqualification year.

Under the cutoff method, all charge-offs and recoveries of such loans generally will be adjustments to the reserve accounts and not separate items of income and expense. However, if the charge-off of any loan would reduce the balance in any reserve account below zero, the charge-off shall be an adjustment to the reserve account only in the amount necessary to reduce the balance in such account to zero. Any charge-offs in excess of such reserve balance, and any recoveries with regard to such loans, will be items of income and expense in the year of charge-off or recovery, as if the taxpayer had always used the specific charge-off method. Under the cut-off method, no additional deductions in the disqualification year or thereafter are allowable for additions to the reserve for bad debts.

Unless the balance of a reserve account has been reduced to zero by the adjustment required for a charged-off item, the allowable ending balance for the reserve account is computed for year end by taking into account only those debts which were outstanding on the last day of the taxable year before the disqualification year. No additional deductions may be taken for an addition to restore the reserve account to its allowable ending balance. However, income must be recognized in the amount by which the balance in any reserve account after adjustments for charge-offs and recoveries exceeds the allowable ending balance for the account.

* * * * * *

[Conference Report]

* * * * * *

Conference Agreement.—

* * * * * *

Suspension of recapture for financially troubled banks.—The conference agreement also provides that a bank, other than a bank electing to use the cut-off method, may suspend the inclusion in income of its bad debt reserve for any year in which it is a "financially troubled bank." Nonetheless, a financially troubled bank may elect to include in income currently all or a portion of the amount of its reserves that otherwise would be recaptured that year.

A bank is considered to be a financially troubled bank if the average of its nonperforming loans for the taxable year exceeds 75 percent of the average of its equity capital for the year. Nonperforming loans include (1) loans that are "past due 90 days or more and still accruing," (2) "nonaccrual" loans, and (3) "renegotiated 'troubled' debt" under the existing standards of the Federal Financial Institution Examination Council. Equity capital is assets less liabilities, as those amounts are reported for regulatory purposes. Equity capital does not include the balance in any reserve for bad debts. The average of nonperforming loans and equity capital for the year is to be determined as the average of those amounts at each time during the taxable year that the bank is required to report for regulatory purposes. In the case of a bank that is a member of a controlled group described in section 1563(a)(1), the determination of whether the bank is a financially troubled bank is made with respect to all members of that controlled group.

The inclusion in income of a portion of the bad debt reserve suspends for each year in which the bank is considered to be a financially troubled bank. For example, assume that a large bank is financially troubled in the disqualification year, is not financially troubled in the two following years, and then returns to financially troubled status in the fourth year. No portion of its bad debt reserve need be included in income during the disqualification year, since the bank meets the definition of a financially troubled bank. In the second year, the bank must begin the inclusion of its bad debt reserve in income. As the inclusion in income begins in this year, the bank may include in income either 10% of its reserve balance or a greater amount if it so elects. The bank may not elect at this time to use the cut-off method, since it has already tolled the inclusion of the bad debt reserve in income as a financially troubled bank. In the third year, the bank must include ⅖ of the bad debt reserve not included in income in the prior year. The bank returns to troubled status in the fourth year and no portion of the bad debt reserve must be included in income in that year. The bank will be required to include the amount it would have included in that year in the next year in which it is not a financially troubled bank.

The provision allowing a financially troubled bank to suspend the inclusion of its bad debt reserve in income does not affect the requirement that a large bank account for its bad debts using the specific charge-off method.

Effective date.—The provision is effective for taxable years beginning after December 31, 1986.

* * * * * *

[House Explanation]

2. Thrift Institutions

Present Law.—* * * taxpayers are allowed a deduction for debts which become uncollectible during the taxable year (i.e., the "specific charge-off method") or a deduction for reasonable additions to a reserve for bad debts (ie., the "reserve method"). In the case of mutual savings banks, domestic building and loan associations and cooperative banks without capital stock which are organized and operated for mutual purposes and without profit (collectively called "thrift institutions"), the reasonable addition to the reserve for bad debts is equal to the addition to the reserves for losses computed under the "experience" method, the "percentage of eligible loans" method, or, if a sufficient percentage of the thrift's assets constitute "qualified assets," the "percentage of taxable income" method.

Experience method.—* * * is identical to the experience method for banks * * *.

Percentage of eligible loans method.— * * * is generally the same as the percentage of eligible loans method for banks * * *. the sum of its surplus, undivided profits and reserves at the beginning of such year.

Percentage of taxable income method.—Under the percentage of taxable income method, an annual deduction is allowed for a statutory percentage of taxable income.[5] The statutory percentage for tax years beginning after 1978 is 40 percent.

The full 40-percent of taxable income deduction is available only where 82 percent (72 percent in the case of mutual savings banks without capital stock) of the thrift institution's assets are qualified. Qualifying assets include cash; obligations and securities of governmental entities including corporations which are instrumentalities of governmental entities; obligations of State corporations organized to insure the deposits of members; loans secured by a deposit or share of a member; loans secured by residential or church real property and residential and church improvement loans; loans secured by property or for the improvement of property within an urban renewal area; loans secured by an interest in educational, health or welfare institutions or facilities; property acquired through defaulted loans on residen-

---

[Footnote ¶ 3948 continued]

(5) For purposes of determining the deduction under the percentage of income method, taxable income is computed without regard to any deduction allowable for any addition to the reserve for bad debts and exclusive of 18/46 of any net long-term capital gain, gains on assets the interest on which was tax-exempt, any dividends eligible for the corporate dividends received deduction and any additions to gross income from the thrift institution's own distributions from previously accumulated reserves.

*   *   *   *   *   *

tial, church, urban development or charitable property; educational loans; and property used in the business of the association. Where the 82-percent test is not met, the statutory rate is reduced by three-fourths of one percentage point for each one percentage point of such shortfall.[6] For mutual savings banks without capital stock, the statutory rate is reduced by 1½ percentage points for each percentage point that qualified assets fail to reach the 72-percent requirement. At a minimum, 60 percent of a thrift institution's assets must be qualifying (50 percent for mutual savings banks without stock) in order to be eligible for deductions under the percentage of income method.

* * * [T]he deduction for any year under the percentage of income method cannot exceed the amount by which 12 percent of the total deposits or withdrawable accounts of the depositors of the thrift institution at the close of the taxable year exceeds the sum of its surplus, undivided profits and reserves at the beginning of such year.

A thrift institution may switch between methods of determining the addition to its loan loss reserves from one year to another. Such a change does not, however, result in a change in the balance in the reserves for loan losses at the beginning of the year in which the change occurs.

Under present law, if the deduction for bad debts for the taxable year determined under the above rules exceeds the amount which would have been allowed as a deduction on the basis of actual experience, the deduction is reduced by 20 percent of such excess (sec. 291). Also, 59⅝ percent of the deductible excess (after the 20-percent reduction) is treated as a tax preference for purposes of computing the corporate minimum tax (sec. 57).

Distributions in excess of earnings and profits.—A special recapture provision applies to reserve balances in excess of the balance computed under the experience method. When a thrift institution distributes property to its owners, other than as interest or dividends on deposits, in excess of earnings and profits accumulated in taxable years beginning after December 31, 1951, the excess is treated as a distribution from the loan loss reserves to the extent of the excess of total loan loss reserves over what the loan loss reserves would have been if computed under the experience method. When such a distribution takes place, the thrift is required to reduce its reserve by such an amount and simultaneously recognize the amount as an item of gross income. This process increases current year's earnings and profits, and causes such distributions to be taxable to the recipient as dividends in the amount of any excess distributed, rather than as a nontaxable return of capital or as capital gains.

*   *   *   *   *   *

Explanation of Provision.—The bill provides that thrift institutions (mutual savings banks, domestic building and loan associations and cooperative banks) will continue to be able to compute bad debt deductions using the experience method available to banks and the percentage of taxable income method. The percentage of eligible loans method will no longer be available. In the case of the percentage of taxable income method, the portion of taxable income which may be deducted as an addition to a reserve for bad debts is reduced from 40 percent to 5 percent. The rules reducing the amount of the percentage of taxable income deduction available to a thrift institution which holds 60 percent of its assets in qualifying assets, but fails to hold a sufficient percentage of qualifying assets to use the maximum percentage of taxable income deduction, are eliminated. Any institution meeting the definition of a thrift institution and holding at least 60 percent of its assets as qualifying assets, will be eligible for the full 5 percent of taxable income deduction. The 60-percent test applies to mutual savings banks as well as other types of thrift institutions.

Thrift institutions which claim the 5 percent of taxable income deduction allowed by the bill will not be considered as having obtained a tax preference for purposes of the 20-percent reduction of section 291. The excess of the percentage of taxable income deduction over the deduction that would have been allowable on the basis of actual experience will be treated as a preference item for the purpose of computing the corporate minimum tax (sec. 57). Deductions claimed using the 5 percent of taxable income method in excess of deductions computed under the experience method also will continue to be subject to recognition as income under section 593(d) (formerly sec. 593(e)) if distributed to shareholders.

*   *   *   *   *   *

[Conference Report]

*   *   *   *   *   *

House Bill.—* * *

*   *   *   *   *   *

[Small Business Investment Companies].—The House bill also repeals the provision of current law (sec. 586) that allows small business investment companies operating under the Small Business Investment Act of 1958 and business development companies to use the reserve method of computing losses on bad debts.

*   *   *   *   *   *

Conference Agreement.—The conference agreement generally follows the House

---

[Footnote ¶ 3948 continued]

(6) For example, where a thrift institution (other than a mutual savings bank) has 75 percent of its assets in qualified assets, the statutory 40-percent rate is reduced by 5¼ percentage points (3/4 times 7 percentage points) to 34¾ percent of taxable income.

Tax Reform Act of 1986

bill. The portion of taxable income that may be excluded from income as an addition to a reserve for bad debts is decreased from 40 to 8 percent. *Effective date.*—The provisions are effective for taxable years beginning after December 31, 1986.

[¶ 3949] SECTION 902. INTEREST INCURRED TO CARRY TAX-EXEMPT BONDS

(Secs. 265 and 291 of the Code)

[House Explanation]

* * * * * *

Present Law.—* * * disallows a deduction for interest on indebtedness incurred or continued to purchase or carry obligations the interest on which is exempt from Federal income tax (tax-exempt obligations). This rule applies both to individual and corporate taxpayers. * * *.

* * * * * *

Application to financial institutions.—The legislative history * * * suggests that Congress did not intend the disallowance provision to apply to the indebtedness incurred by a bank or similar financial institution to its depositors.[13] The Internal Revenue Service took the position as early as 1924 that indebtedness to depositors was not incurred to purchase or carry tax-exempt obligations, within the meaning of the law.

* * * * * *

Despite this general rule, the Internal Revenue Service has attempted to disallow interest deductions of financial institutions in certain cases.

* * * * * *

20-percent reduction in preference items.—Under a provision originally added by the Tax Equity and Fiscal Responsibility Act of 1982 (TEFRA), and modified by the Deficit Reduction Act of 1984, the amount allowable as a deduction with respect to certain financial institution preference items is reduced by 20 percent. * * * Financial institution preference items include interest on indebtedness incurred or continued by financial institutions[18] to purchase or carry tax-exempt obligations acquired after December 31, 1982, to the extent that a deduction would otherwise be allowable for such interest. Unless the taxpayer * * * establishes otherwise, the 20 percent reduction applies to an allocable portion of the taxpayer's aggregate interest deduction, to be determined by multiplying the otherwise allowable deduction by the ratio of the taxpayer's average adjusted basis of tax-exempt obligations during the year in question to the average adjusted basis of the taxpayer's total assets.

* * * * * *

Explanation of Provision.—*100-percent disallowance of financial institution interest allocable to tax-exempt obligations.*—The committee bill denies banks, thrift institutions, and other financial institutions a deduction for that portion of the taxpayer's interest expense which is allocable to tax-exempt obligations acquired after December 31, 1985. The amount of interest allocable to tax-exempt obligations generally is to be determined as it is for purposes of the 20 percent reduction in preference items under present law, after taking into account any interest disallowed under the general rules applicable to all taxpayers * * * [sec. 265(a)(2) of new law]. Thus, a deduction is denied for that portion of a financial institution's otherwise allowable interest deduction that is equivalent to the ratio of (1) the average adjusted basis (within the meaning of sec. 1016)[18a] during the year of tax-exempt obligations held by the financial institution and acquired after December 31, 1985, to (2) the average adjusted basis of all assets held by the financial institution. * * * This allocation rule is mandatory and cannot be rebutted by the taxpayer.

Under the committee bill, the 20 percent disallowance rule of present law continues to apply with respect to tax-exempt obligations acquired between January 1, 1983, and December 31, 1985. Thus, a financial institution is to reduce its otherwise allowable interest deduction by the sum of (1) 100 percent of interest allocable to tax-exempt obligations acquired in 1986 or later years, and (2) 20 percent of interest allocable to tax-exempt obligations acquired in calendar years 1983 through 1985, each determined under the formula above.

* * * * * *

Financial institutions subject to the rule include any entity which (1) accepts deposits from the public in the ordinary course of its trade or business, and (2) is subject to Federal or State supervision * * *. [T]his will include (but not necessarily be limited to) banks, mutual savings banks, domestic building and loan associations, and any other entities to which the present law 20-percent disallowance provision (sec. 291) applies. In addition, the 100-percent disallowance rules applies to foreign banks doing business within the United States. Interest, the deduction of which is subject to the rule, includes amounts paid in respect of deposits, investment certificates, or withdrawable or repurchasable

---

[Footnote ¶ 3949 continued]

(13) See S. Rep. No. 558, 73d Cong., 2d Sess. 24 (1934); S. Rep. No. 830, 88th Cong., 2d Sess. 80 (1964).

(18) The provision applies to commercial banks including U.S. branches of foreign banks, mutual savings banks, domestic building and loan associations, and cooperative banks.

(18a) This adjusted basis is reduced by the basis of any debt which is used to purchase or may tax-exempt obligations under * * * [sec. 265(a)(2) of the new law].

shares, whether or not such amounts are officially designated as interest.

* * *[T]ax-exempt obligations include shares in regulated investment companies (i.e., mutual funds) which distribute exempt-interest dividends during the recipient's taxable year.

* * *[W]here section 263A (relating to required capitalization of preproductive expenses including interest and taxes) applies to a portion of the interest expense of a financial institution, the disallowance with respect to tax-exempt obligations is to be applied before the rules of section 263A.

*   *   *   *   *   *

Repeal of special treatment of face-amount certificate companies.—* * * These companies will therefore be subject to the disallowance rules above in the same manner as other financial institutions.

*   *   *   *   *   *

[Conference Report]

*   *   *   *   *

Conference Agreement.—* * * The conference agreement follows the House bill, with the following modifications:

First, the provision applies with respect to tax-exempt obligations acquired after August 7, 1986 (rather than December 31, 1985). The present-law 20-percent disallowance continues to apply with respect to tax-exempt obligations acquired on or before that date. As under the House bill, the 100 percent disallowance rule is to be applied before the new rule requiring capitalization of certain expenses where the taxpayer produces property (new sec. 263A).[5] For purposes of the disallowance rule, the acquisition date of an obligation is the date on which the holding period begins with respect to the obligation in the hands of the acquiring financial institution. Thus, the acquisition of bonds as part of a tax-free reorganization is not treated as a new acquisition for purposes of this provision.

Second, a permanent exception to the provision is provided for qualified tax-exempt obligations acquired by a financial institution.[6] This exception applies whether the obligation is acquired at the original issuance or by a secondary purchaser. Under the conference agreement, qualified tax-exempt obligations include any obligation which (1) is not a private activity bond as defined by the

conference agreement (see, Title XIII, below),[7] and (2) is issued by an issuer which reasonably anticipates to issue, together with subordinate entities, not more than $10 million of tax-exempt obligations (other than private activity bonds, as defined above) during the calendar year. Qualified tax-exempt obligations must be designated as such by the issuer, not more than $10 million of obligations may be so designated by any issuer (including subordinate entities) for any calendar year.[8] Refundings of outstanding bonds may qualify for this exception, and count toward the $10 million limitation, under the same terms as new issues.

For purposes of the exception for qualified tax-exempt obligations, subordinate governmental entities include entities deriving their issuing authority from another entity or subject to substantial control by another entity. For example, a sewer or solid waste authority created by a city or county in order to issue bonds for that city or county is considered a subordinate entity. An entity is not to be considered subordinate solely because of geographic inclusion in a larger entity (e.g., a city located within a larger county), if the smaller entity derives its powers independently of the larger entity and is not subject to significant control by the larger entity.

Qualified tax-exempt obligations are treated as acquired by the financial institution before August 8, 1986. Interest allocable to such obligations remains subject to the 20-percent disallowance contained in present law.

Effective date.—This provision is effective for taxable years ending after December 31, 1986. Thus, bonds acquired after August 7, 1986, in taxable years ending in 1986 are subject to the 20-percent disallowance rule of present law for the taxable year ending in 1986, but are subject to the 100-percent disallowance rule of the conference agreement for subsequent taxable years.

A transitional exception is provided for tax-exempt obligations acquired after August 7, 1986 pursuant to a direct or indirect written commitment to purchase or repurchase such obligation, which commitment was entered into before September 25, 1985. Obligations qualifying for this exception are treated as if acquired before August 8, 1986; interest allocable to such obligations thus remains subject to the 20-percent disallowance contained in present law. The confer-

---

【Footnote ¶ 3949 continued】

(5) Also as under the House bill, the special rule of present law regarding face-amount certificate companies (contained in sec. 265(2)) is repealed. These companies will therefore be subject to the 100 percent disallowance rule in the same manner as other financial institutions.

(6) The rule contained in the House bill, which limited this exception to financial institutions authorized to do business in the State of the issuer, is not included.

(7) For purposes of this provision only, qualified section 501(c)(3) organization bonds (as defined in the conference agreement) are not treated as private activity bonds. In the case of bonds issued before August 15, 1986, for purposes of this provision only, bonds are not to be treated as private activity bonds if they are not IDBs, mortgage subsidy bonds, student loan bonds, or other private ("consumer") loan bonds for which tax exemption is permitted under present law.

(8) The rule contained in the House bill, which limited this exception to political subdivisions in existence on October 23, 1985, is not included.

ence agreement also provides certain transitional rules for specified identified projects.

[¶ 3950] SECTION 903. TERMINATION OF SPECIAL 10-YEAR CARRYBACK RULES FOR CERTAIN FINANCIAL INSTITUTIONS: NEW SPECIAL CARRYOVER RULES FOR CERTAIN LOSSES

(Sec. 172 of the Code)

[Conference Report]

*   *   *   *   *   *

Present Law.—* * * [C]ommercial banks or thrift institutions (mutual savings banks, domestic building and loan associations, and cooperative banks) may carry net operating losses (NOLs) back to the prior ten taxable years and forward to the succeeding five taxable years. Other taxpayers may carry net operating losses back to the prior three taxable years and forward to the succeeding fifteen taxable years.

House Bill.—The House bill repeals the special rules permitting financial institutions to carry net operating losses back to the prior ten taxable years and forward to the succeeding five taxable years.

Senate Amendment.—The Senate amendment provides that net operating losses incurred by a thrift institution in taxable years beginning after December 31, 1981 and before January 1, 1986, may be carried back to the prior ten taxable years and carried forward to the succeeding eight taxable years.

Conference Agreement.—* * * The conference agreement follows the provisions of both the House bill and the Senate amendment. The rule allowing net operating losses incurred by a financial institution to be carried back to the prior ten taxable years

and carried forward to the succeeding five taxable years generally is repealed for taxable years beginning after December 31, 1986, except for certain net operating losses of commercial banks. Net operating losses incurred by a financial institution in taxable years beginning after December 31, 1986, generally are carried back to the prior three taxable years and carried forward to the succeeding fifteen taxable years, as is the case for other taxpayers.

Special rule for thrift institutions.—Net operating losses incurred by a thrift institution in taxable years beginning after December 31, 1981, and before January 1, 1986, are carried back to the prior ten taxable years and carried forward to the succeeding eight taxable years.

Special rule for commercial banks.—The portion of the net operating losses of commercial banks (not including thrift institutions) for any taxable year beginning after December 31, 1986, and before January 1, 1994, that is attributable to deductions for losses on bad debts is carried back to the prior ten taxable years. The portion of the net operating loss of a commercial bank attributable to deductions for losses on bad debts is the excess of the net operating loss for the taxable year over the net operating loss for such taxable year computed without regard to any deductions for losses on bad debts.

[¶ 3951] SECTION 904. REPEAL OF SPECIAL REORGANIZATION RULES FOR FINANCIAL INSTITUTIONS

(Secs. 368, 382, and 597 of the Code)

[House Explanation]

*   *   *   *   *   *

Present Law.—*In general.*—Present law provides special rules designed to provide relief to financially troubled thrift institutions. These provisions, added by the Economic Recovery Tax Act of 1981,[20] provide that the continuity of interest requirement is met if the depositors of the financially troubled thrift institution are depositors of the surviving corporation, allow the carryover of net operating losses of a financially troubled thrift institution where its depositors continue as depositors of the acquiring corporation, and exempt certain payments from the Federal Savings and Loan Insurance Corporation to financially troubled thrift institutions from income and the general basis reduction requirement of the Internal Revenue Code.

Tax-free reorganization status.—* * * [I]n order for a combination of two corporations to be a tax-free "reorganization" * * *, a judicially created continuity of interest rule must be satisfied. * * *. If the transaction fails to qualify as a tax-free reorganization, the acquired corporation and its shareholders may recognize gain or loss on the transaction, and the acquiring corporation generally takes a cost basis in the acquired corporation's assets. If the transaction qualifies as a tax-free reorganization, the acquired corporation and its shareholders generally recognize no gain and the acquiring corporation assumes the acquired corporation's basis.

It was unclear prior to the 1981 Act whether a merger of an insolvent thrift institution into a solvent thrift institution could comply with the "continuity of interest" * * *.

Under the 1981 Act, the continuity of interest requirement need not be satisfied in

---

[Footnote ¶ 3951] (20) Pub. L. 97-94, 97th Cong., 1st Sess. (1981); referred to as the "1981 Act".

the case of a merger involving a thrift institution, provided certain conditions are met. * * * If these conditions are satisfied, the acquired institution need not receive or distribute stock or securities of the acquiring corporation for the transaction to qualify as a tax-free reorganization (sec. 368(a)(3)(D)). The legislative history of the 1981 amendments made it clear that the provision covered all possible combinations of stock and mutual thrift institutions, including stock acquiring mutual, stock acquiring stock, mutual acquiring mutual, and mutual acquiring stock.

Net operating loss carryovers.—Where a tax-free reorganization of two corporations occurs, the acquiring corporation generally succeeds to the tax attributes of the acquired corporation, including its net operating loss carryovers. * * * Under section 382, the ability of an acquiring corporation to succeed to the net operating loss carryovers of a corporation acquired in a tax-free reorganization is limited to the extent the owners of the acquired corporation fail to acquire stock in the acquiring corporation representing at least 20 percent of the value of the latter's stock* * *.

The 1981 Act provided that depositors in a thrift that has been certified as financially troubled whose deposits carry over to the acquiring corporation will be deemed to have continued an equity interest in the thrift to the extent of their deposits. Thus, any losses of the thrift are less likely to be reduced under the loss limitation provisions of section 382.

FSLIC contributions to savings and loan associations.—Although contributions to capital by nonshareholders are excluded from the income of the recipient corporation (sec. 118), the basis of property normally must be reduced by such contributions (sec. 362(c)).

* * * The 1981 Act, however, provided that certain financially troubled thrift institutions need not reduce their basis for money or property contributed by the FSLIC under its financial assistance program, and such amounts are not includible in income (sec. 597).

*　　*　　*　　*　　*　　*

Explanation of Provision.—The committee bill repeals the special provisions enacted in the 1981 Act relating to acquisitions of financially-troubled thrift institutions, and the exclusion from income and the basis reduction requirement of FSLIC payments to such thrifts. Accordingly, acquisitions and reorganizations involving financially troubled thrift institutions will be subject to the generally applicable rules.

The bill also clarifies that no deduction shall be disallowed under section 265(1), [see 265(a)(1) of new law], relating to expenses allocable to tax-exempt income, for any amount paid or incurred by a taxpayer on the ground such amount is allocable to amounts excluded under section 597.

*　　*　　*　　*　　*　　*

[Conference Report]

*　　*　　*　　*　　*　　*

Conference Agreement.—The conference agreement follows the House bill with a delayed effective date. The special reorganization rules for troubled thrift institutions are repealed effective for acquisitions and mergers after December 31, 1988. The repeal of the special treatment for FSLIC payments is effective for payments after December 31, 1988, unless such payments are made pursuant to an acquisition or merger occurring on or before that date.

[¶ 3952] SECTION 905. TREATMENT OF LOSSES ON DEPOSITS OR ACCOUNTS IN INSOLVENT FINANCIAL INSTITUTIONS

(Secs. 165 and 451 of the Code)

[Senate Explanation]

*　　*　　*　　*　　*　　*

Present Law.—Under present law, a loss experienced by a taxpayer with respect to a deposit in a financial institution is treated in the same manner as any other type of bad debt loss. Deduction of the loss is generally allowable only in the year in which it is determined (based on all the facts and circumstances) that there is no prospect of recovery. Unless the deposit in the financial institution was created or acquired in connection with a trade or business of the taxpayer, any loss on the deposit will be considered as a short-term capital loss (sec. 166(d)). An individual taxpayer may generally deduct short-term capital losses only to the extent of $3,000 plus his capital gains for the year (sec. 1211).

*　　*　　*　　*　　*　　*

Explanation of Provision.—The committee bill allows qualified individuals to elect to deduct losses on deposits in qualified financial institutions as casualty losses in the year in which the amount of such loss can be reasonably estimated. If a qualified taxpayer elects to treat a loss on a deposit in a qualified financial institution as a casualty loss, no deduction for the loss as a bad debt under the provisions of section 166 will be available. The election will constitute an election of a method of accounting with regard to all deposits in the same institution, and will require any loss on such other deposits to be treated in the same manner unless the permission of the Commissioner is obtained to use a different method.

A qualified individual is any individual other than an owner of one percent or more of the value of the stock of the institution in which the loss was sustained, an officer of such institution, and certain relatives and related persons to such owners and officers. Relatives of one-percent owners and officers who will not be considered as qualified individuals are siblings (whether by whole or half blood), spouses, aunts, uncles, nephews, nieces, ancestors, and lineal descendants. An individual will be considered to be a related person of a one-percent owner or officer if he would be considered a related person under the provisions of section 267(b).

A qualified financial institution is any commercial bank (as defined in sec. 581), any thrift institution (as defined in sec. 591), any insured credit union, or any institution similar to the above which is chartered and supervised under [f]ederal or [s]tate law. A deposit for the purposes of this provision is any deposit, withdrawable certificate, or withdrawable or repurchasable share of or in a qualified financial institution.

The amount of loss to be recognized in any year under the election is intended to be the difference between the taxpayer's basis in the deposit and the amount which is a reasonable estimate of the amount that will eventually be received with regard to such deposit. It is not intended that the failure of a taxpayer to claim a loss under this provision in the year in which such loss can first be reasonably estimated will preclude the taxpayer from claiming such loss in a later year, either under this election or as a bad debt under section 166.

If a loss that has been claimed under this election is later recovered, the lesser of the amount of the recovery or the tax benefit received as a result of the election shall be included in income in the year of such recovery.

Effective Date.—The provision is effective for taxable years beginning after December 31, 1982.

*　　*　　*　　*　　*　　*

[Conference Report]

*　　*　　*　　*　　*　　*

Conference Agreement.—The conference agreement follows the House bill and the Senate amendment. The conferees understand that the election is to be made on the tax return for the taxable year and, once made, cannot be changed without the consent of the Internal Revenue Service.

The conference agreement also provides that accrued, but unpaid, interest on a deposit in a financial institution for a taxable year beginning on or before 1987 is not includible in the depositor's taxable income for that taxable year where such interest is not subject to withdrawal at the end of that taxable year. Such interest income is includible in gross income in the taxable year in which such interest is withdrawable.

[¶ 3954] SECTION 1001. REPEAL OF EXCLUSION FOR INTEREST ON INSTALLMENT PAYMENTS OF LIFE INSURANCE PROCEEDS

(Sec. 101(d) of the Code)

[Senate Explanation]

Explanation of Provision.—Under the bill, all amounts paid to any beneficiary of a life insurance policy at a date later than the death of the insured are included in gross income to the extent that the amount paid exceeds the amount payable as a death benefit. The exclusion from the gross income of the surviving spouse of the first $1,000 in excess of the amount payable as the death benefit is repealed.

The bill also requires, for purposes of valuing the portion of any payment deferred beyond the death of the insured that is a nontaxable death benefit, that an insurer use mortality tables prescribed by the Secretary of the Treasury in regulations. The committee expects that such tables will not distinguish among individuals on the basis of sex. An insurer would, therefore, no longer be permitted to use its own mortality table in

determining the portion of any payment attributable to a nontaxable death benefit. As under present law, the insurer is to use the interest rate it uses in calculating payments under the agreement.

The operation of this rule does not prevent an insurance company from making payments to beneficiaries based on its own mortality tables. Rather, the provision operates to specify the portion of any installment payment that is to be treated as a payment of an excludable death benefit and the portion attributable to interest.

[Conference Report]

*　　*　　*　　*　　*　　*

Effective Date.—The conference agreement follows the House bill and the Senate amendment, except that the provision is effective for amounts paid with respect to deaths occurring after the date of enactment in taxable years ending after that date.

[¶ 3955]   SECTION 1002. EXCLUSION FROM INCOME WITH RESPECT TO STRUCTURED SETTLEMENTS LIMITED TO CASES INVOLVING PHYSICAL INJURY

(Sec. 130 of the Code)

[House Explanation]

*   *   *   *   *   *

Present Law.—Present law excludes from income the amount of any damages received on account of personal injuries or sickness, whether by suit or agreement and whether as a lump sum or as periodic payments. The person liable to pay the damages may assign to a third party (a structured settlement company) the obligation to pay the periodic payments. The portion of the amount received by that third party for agreeing to the assignment that is used to purchase assets to fund the liability is not included in that party's income. This special treatment of the structured settlement company applies only if the obligation assigned to it is a liability to make periodic payments as damages on account of personal injury or sickness.

Reasons for Change.—The present treatment of structured settlements has the overall effect of exempting from taxation investment income earned on assets used to fund the periodic payment of damages. The committee believes that this effect is inappropriate where the injury did not involve physical injury or physical sickness. In cases involving personal nonphysical injuries, the committee concludes that the investment income earned on assets used to fund the damage payment should be subject to taxation.

Explanation of Provision.—The bill amends present law to limit "qualified assignments" to those assignments requiring the payment of damages on account of a claim for personal injuries that involve physical injury or physical sickness of the claimant. Damages on account of a claim for wrongful death arising from physical injury or sickness are also included. The provision is intended to clarify that claims for damages

for torts other than physical injury and physical sickness (such as invasion of privacy, for example) are not included. Thus, for example, if a structured settlement company receives compensation in consideration of its assumption of the obligation to make periodic payments of damages on account of the defamation of a third party, the full amount of the consideration received is included in gross income.

[Conference Report]

*   *   *   *   *   *

The conference agreement generally follows the House bill. Thus, the exclusion for structured settlements applies only to those qualifying structured settlement arrangements for payments of damages on account of a claim for personal injuries that involve physical injury or physical sickness of the claimant, including damages on account of a claim for wrongful death arising from physical injury or sickness, provided the arrangements meet all other applicable requirements.

Claims which do not involve physical injury or physical sickness include, for example, defamation of a third party or invasion of privacy. Claims which do not involve physical injury or physical sickness are not eligible to be treated as structured settlement arrangements.

The conferees understand that multiple claims are alleged in many personal injury actions. The conferees do not intend that allocation of damages is necessary among such multiple claims. Rather, if the action has its origin in a physical injury, then all damages that flow therefrom are included.

[Effective date.—] The provision is effective for assignments enter into after December 31, 1986, in taxable years ending after that date.

[¶ 3956]   SECTION 1003. DENIAL OF DEDUCTION FOR INTEREST ON LOANS FROM CERTAIN LIFE INSURANCE CONTRACTS

(Sec. 264 of the Code)

[Conference Report]

House Bill.—The rule of present law regarding the disallowance of a deduction for any amount paid or accrued on indebtedness incurred or continued to purchase or carry a single premium life insurance, endowment or annuity contract is restated.

Senate Amendment

A deduction for interest on policyholder loans is not allowed to the extent that aggregate loans to any officer, employee, or person financially interested in any trade or business carried on by the taxpayer exceed

$50,000. The provision is effective for interest on loans under policies purchased after June 20, 1986.

Conference Agreement

The conference agreement follows the House bill and the Senate amendment.

Interest deduction.—With respect to the provision disallowing a deduction for interest on certain policyholder loans in the case of a taxpayer carrying on more than one trade or business, the $50,000 amount per officer or employee or person is financially interested in any trade or business of the taxpayer is determined on an aggregate basis for each such person in all trades or businesses. For example, if an employee of a business of the taxpayer is also an officer in two other businesses of the taxpayer, the $50,000 of permitted borrowings by the taxpayer with respect to life insurance covering the person is determined by aggregating all policies covering his life with respect to which the taxpayer has borrowed. In the case of an affiliated group of corporations, it is intended that the affiliated group is considered to be one taxpayer for this purpose, and all loans with respect to policies covering the life of an officer or employee or person financially interested in, a business of any member of the group are aggregated. Similar principles are intended to apply in the event of common ownership of unincorporated trades or businesses.

Under the conference agreement, the fact that the proceeds of a loan under a life insurance contract are used in a trade or business does not affect the deductibility of interest paid on the loan. Therefore, for example, if a sole proprietor borrows under a life insurance policy on the sole proprietor's life, the interest paid on the loan (to the extent the loan exceeds $50,000) is not deductible even though the proceeds of the loan are used in the sole proprietor's trade or business.

[Effective date.—] The provision is effective for interest on loans under policies purchased after June 20, 1986, in taxable years ending after that date.

[The following colloquies relating to Act Sec. 1003 are drawn from the Congressional Record. The colloquies occurred on the day the Conference bill was considered by the House. Ed.]

[House Floor Explanation]

I have discussed with Congressman Jim Jones several issues relating to the effective date under this bill of provisions governing the deduction of interest on loans from certain life * * * insurance contracts. We have reached a common understanding regarding the following specific issue:

The question concerns the interpretation of the effective date of provisions governing the deduction for interest on loans from certain life insurance contracts under section 1003 of the bill. The effective date applies this provision to contracts purchased after June 20, 1986, in taxable years ending after such date. An exchange of a life insurance contract, other than one received in exchange for a life insurance contract issued by

the same insurer, received after June 20, 1986, in exchange for an existing contract should be considered to have been purchased after June 20, 1986.

I have discussed with Congressman PICKLE and Congressman JIM JONES several issues relating to the effective date of the interest deduction limitation in this legislation. We have reached a common understanding regarding the following specific issues:

Section 1003 of H.R. 3838 limits the interest deduction on indebtedness in excess of $50,000 per insured under certain life insurance policies owned by a business taxpayer. The limitation applies only to indebtedness under contracts purchased after June 20, 1986.

As I understand the business, applications for a policy of this sort are often sent after consideration of competing bids, and an application is usually considered to be acceptance of the insurance company's bid. However, I am informed that the exact point in this process when there is a technical purchase is not clear any may differ from State to State.

Under this provision policies are considered purchased for purposes of the effective date once the policy has been applied for. Consequently, the new provision does not limit deductions for interest on indebtedness under a policy for which an application was submitted to the insurance company on or before June 20, 1986. Congressional Record, p. H 8361, 9-25-86.

[Conference Report]

*   *   *   *   *   *

Single premium contracts.—The conference agreement restates the present-law rule that no deduction is allowed for any amount paid or accrued on indebtedness incurred or continued to purchase or carry a single premium life insurance, endowment, or annuity contract (sec. 264(a)(2)). Single premium contracts include contracts where substantially all of the premiums are paid within four years from the date on which the contract is purchased, or contracts where an amount is deposited with the insurer for payment of a substantial number of future premiums on the contract. Generally, section 264(a)(2) also applies to contracts other than those where the nonpayment of premiums would cause the policy to lapse, but no inference is intended that universal life insurance policies are always treated as single premium contracts.

[¶ 3957]   SECTION 1004. DEDUCTION FOR NONBUSINESS CASUALTY LOSSES COVERED BY INSURANCE ALLOWABLE ONLY IF CLAIM FILED

(Sec. 165(h)(4)(E) of the Code)

[House Explanation]

*   *   *   *   *   *

Present Law.—A taxpayer generally may deduct a loss sustained during the taxable

year if the loss is not compensated by insurance or otherwise (sec. 165(a)). For property not connected with a trade or business or a transaction entered into for profit, losses are deductible only if they arise from "fire, storm, shipwreck, or other casualty, or theft." These personal casualty losses are deductible only to the extent that each casualty loss exceeds $100, and to the extent that all casualty losses for the year exceed 10 percent of the taxpayer's adjusted gross income (sec. 165(h)). Certain courts have ruled that a taxpayer whose loss was covered by an insurance policy could nevertheless deduct the loss if the taxpayer decided not to file a claim under the terms of the insurance policy. See *Hills v. Commissioner,* 691 F.2d 997 (11th Cir. 1982); *Miller v. Commissioner,* 733 F.2d 399 (6th Cir. 1984).

* * * * * *

Explanation of Provision.—Under the bill, a taxpayer is not permitted to deduct a casualty loss for damages to property not used in a trade or business or in a transaction entered into for profit unless the taxpayer

files a timely insurance claim with respect to damage to that property. This requirement applies to the extent any insurance policy would provide reimbursement for the loss in whole or in part. If a policy would provide compensation for the loss, it is immaterial whether the taxpayer is the primary beneficiary of the policy so long as it is within the control of the taxpayer whether to file a claim.

[Conference Report]

[Effective Date.—]The conference agreement follows the House bill, except that the provision applies to losses sustained in taxable years beginning after December 31, 1986. The provision is clarified to apply only to the extent any insurance policy would provide reimbursement.

[¶ 3958] SECTION 1011. REPEAL OF SPECIAL LIFE INSURANCE COMPANY DEDUCTION

(Sec. 806 of the Code)

[Senate Explanation]
* * * * * *

Present Law.—A life insurance company is taxed at corporate rates on its life insurance company taxable income (LICTI) and certain other income. A life insurance company is allowed a special deduction in computing LICTI equal to 20 percent of the income from insurance businesses that otherwise would be subject to taxation (sec. 806(a)).

* * * * * *

[Conference Report]
* * * * * *

House Bill.—The special life insurance company deduction is repealed, effective for taxable years beginning after December 31, 1985.

Senate Amendment.—The Senate amendment is the same as the House bill,

except that a special rule is provided in the case of a life insurance company owning the stock of another corporation through a partnership, which stock was acquired on January 14, 1981. For purposes of determining the small life insurance company deduction under section 806(a), tentative life insurance company taxable income is computed without taking into account income, gain, loss or deduction attributable to the ownership of such stock, and the amount of such income, gain, loss or deduction is taken into account at the rate of 46/36.8, which provides the same tax benefit to the life insurance company as is provided under present law.

This provision is effective for taxable years beginning after December 31, 1986.

Conference Agreement.—The conference agreement follows the Senate amendment, *[Effective date—]* effective for taxable years beginning after December 31, 1986.

[¶ 3959] SECTION 1012. REPEAL OF TAX-EXEMPT STATUS FOR CERTAIN ORGANIZATIONS PROVIDING COMMERCIAL-TYPE INSURANCE

(Secs. 501 and 833 of the Code)

[Conference Report]
* * * * * *

Present Law.—Present law (sec. 501(c)) specifies various standards that an organization must meet in order to qualify for exemption from Federal income taxation. These standards vary depending on the basis on which the entity is seeking exemption. Certain insurance activities performed by an organization may make it ineligible for tax exemption.

At least one major organization (described in sec. 501(c)(3)), which provides life insur-

ance and annuities to employees of tax-exempt educational institutions, has been recognized as a tax-exempt charitable organization by the IRS. At least one major health insurance provider has been treated as a tax-exempt social welfare organization.

A fraternal beneficiary society, order, or association (sec. 501(c)(8)) is entitled to tax exemption if it operates under the lodge system or for the exclusive benefit of the members of a fraternity itself operating under the lodge system, and provides for the payment of life, sick, accident, or other benefits to the members of such society, order, or association or their dependents.

*   *   *   *   *   *

[House Explanation]

*   *   *   *   *   *

Explanation of Provision.—Under the bill, an organization described in sections 501(c)(3) and (4) of the Code is exempt from tax only if no substantial part of its activities consists of providing commercial-type insurance. For this purpose, no substantial part has the meaning given to it under present law applicable to such organizations. See, e.g., *Haswell v. U.S.*, 500 F.2d 1133 (Ct. Cl. 1974); *Seasongood v. Comm'r*, 1227 F.2d 907 (6th Cir. 1955); see also sec. 501(h).

In the case of such a tax-exempt organization, the activity of providing commercial-type insurance is treated as an unrelated trade or business (sec. 513) but, in lieu of the usual tax on unrelated trade or business taxable income, the unrelated trade or business activity is taxed under the rules relating to insurance companies (Subchapter L).

For this purpose, commercial-type insurance generally is any insurance of a type provided by commercial insurance companies. The bill provides that the insurance of annuity contracts is treated as providing insurance. The activity of providing insurance or annuities under a qualified pension plan (described in sec. 401(a)) is not the activity of providing commercial-type insurance, because such plans are not charitable or social welfare organizations to which the bill applies.

Several exceptions are provided to the definition of commercial-type insurance. Commercial-type insurance does not include insurance provided at substantially below cost to a class of charitable recipients. See, e.g., Rev. Rul. 71-529, 1971-2 C.B. 234 (relating to the meaning of substantially below cost). A class of charitable recipients refers to a group of recipients that would constitute a charitable class under present law. Commercial-type insurance also does not include health insurance provided by a health maintenance organization that is of a kind customarily provided by such organizations and is incidental to the organization's principal activity of providing health care. Section 501(m) of the Code, as added by the bill, is not intended to alter the tax-exempt status of an ordinary health maintenance organization that provides health care to its members predominantly at its own facility through the use of health care professionals and other workers employed by the organization. Similarly, organizations that provide supplemental health maintenance organization-type services (such as dental services) would not be affected if they operate in the same manner as a health maintenance organization.

In addition, commercial-type insurance does not include property and casualty insurance (such as fire insurance) provided directly or through a wholly-owned corporation by a church or convention or association of churches for the church or convention or association. For this purpose, property and casualty insurance is not intended to include life insurance or accident and health insurance (whether or not cancelable). This exception is not intended to apply if the insurance is provided not only to the church, convention or association, but also to other persons.

In the case of activities of Blue Cross and Blue Shield and their affiliates with respect to high risk individuals and small groups, the bill authorizes the Treasury Department to issue regulations providing for special treatment to such organizations. Congress intends that this special benefit be provided in connection with the unique activities (such as open enrollment) of Blue Cross and Blue Shield and their affiliates for high risk individuals and small groups, so that such activities (to the extent not engaged in by commercial insurers) are not overburdened by tax costs and therefore reduced. The special treatment would not be available to the extent the activities are required by applicable law. Thus, for example, if applicable law requires companies issuing health insurance policies to provide coverage to a specified group of high-risk individuals, Blue Cross and Blue Shield organizations should not be accorded any special treatment with respect to that activity.

With respect to fraternal beneficiary societies engaged in insurance activities, the committee re-emphasizes the requirement of present law that such tax-exempt organizations maintain an active lodge system. The bill also requires that the Treasury Department audit and study fraternal beneficiary organizations (described in sec. 501(c)(8)) that received gross insurance premiums in excess of $25,000,000 in taxable year 1984. The committee intends that the use of revenues from insurance activities of such organizations be studied. The Treasury has authority under the bill to require the furnishing of information necessary to conduct the audit and study. The results of the study, together with recommendations, are to be submitted to the Committee on Ways and Means of the House of Representatives, the Committee on Finance of the Senate, and the Joint Committee on Taxation no later than January 1, 1988, so that Congress may consider the recommendations and take such action regarding the tax treatment of fraternal beneficiary societies engaged in insurance activities as is appropriate.

*   *   *   *   *   *

[Conference Report]

*   *   *   *   *   *

Conference Agreement

The conference agreement follows the House bill with respect to the treatment of commercial-type insurance activities of organizations described in sections 501(c)(3) and (4), with modifications.

In general.—Under the conference agreement, commercial-type insurance does not include property or casualty insurance provided directly or through an organization described in sec. 414(e)(3)(B)(ii) by a church or convention or association of churches for the church, convention or association. It also does not apply to the provision of retirement or welfare benefits by such organizations directly or indirectly through an organization described in sec. 414(e)(3)(A) or 414(e)(3)(B)(ii) for the employees of such organizations, or for employees' beneficiaries. This exception is not intended to apply if insurance is provided to persons other than the church or convention or association of churches and their employees.

[The following colloquy relating to Act Sec. 1012 is drawn from the Congressional Record. The colloquy occurred on the day the Conference bill was considered by the House Ed.]

[House Floor Explanation]

I have discussed with Congressman CAMPBELL several issues relating to the effect of the bill on the tax-exempt status of organizations providing "commercial type insurance." We have reached a common understanding regarding the following specific issues:

Section 1012 of the bill repeals the tax exempt status of certain organizations providing "commercial type insurance." For this purpose the provision expressly excludes from the term "commercial type insurance" property or casualty insurance provided directly or through an organization described in section 414(e)(3)(B)(ii), by a church or convention or association of churches for such church or convention or association of churches.

This provision excludes from the term "commercial type insurance" property and casualty insurance provided by a mutual insurance company first, which was in existence and exempt from tax on August 16, 1986, second, which does not have any taxable subsidiary or any subsidiary doing business with any person other than a church or convention or association of churches, and third, whose only policyholders are churches, conventions or associations of churches, or religious agencies or institutions owned and controlled by churches regardless of the number of different denominations represented by the policyholders or the fact that no single church, convention or association of churches controls such mutual insurance company. Congressional Record, p. H 8363, 9-25-86.

[The following colloquy relating to Act Sec. 1012 is drawn from the Congressional Record. The colloquy occurred on the day the bill was considered by the Senate. Ed.]

[Senate Floor Explanation]

Mr. THURMOND. I would like to ask the distinguished chairman of the Finance Committee a question about the treatment of certain tax-exempt insurance companies under the bill. Section 1012 of the bill repeals the tax-exempt status of certain organizations providing commercial-type insurance. For this purpose, the provision expressly excludes from the term commercial type insurance "property or casualty insurance

provided (directly or through an organization described in section 414(e)(3)(B)(ii) by a church or convention or association of churches for such church or convention or association of churches. * * *"

Would this provision exclude from the term "commercial-type insurance" property by a mutual insurance company (1) which was in existence and exempt from tax on August 16, 1986, (2) which does not have any taxable subsidiary or any subsidiary doing business with any person other than a church or convention or association of churches, and (3) whose only policyholders are churches, conventions or associations of churches, or religious agencies or institutions owned and controlled by churches regardless of the number of different denominations represented by the policyholders or the fact that no single church, convention or association of churches controls such mutal insurance company?

Mr. PACKWOOD. I am happy to clarify for the distinguished colleague from South Carolina that commercial-type insurance would not, for purposes of the bill, include the insurance activities he has described. Congressional Record, p. S 13956, 9-27-86.

[Conference Report]

*　　*　　*　　*　　*　　*

The conference agreement does not alter the tax-exempt status of health maintenance organizations (HMOs). HMOs provide physician services in a variety of practice settings primarily through physicians who are either employees or partners of the HMO or through contracts with individual physicians or one or more groups of physicians (organized on a group practice or individual practice basis).

Certain health insurance providers.—In lieu of the provision in the House bill authorizing Treasury regulations with respect to high risk individuals and small groups in the case of activities of Blue Cross and Blue Shield and their affiliates, the conference agreement provides the following treatment of existing Blue Cross or Blue Shield organizations and other organizations that meet certain requirements and substantially all of whose activities are providing health insurance. Health insurance includes insurance that provides coverage of medical expenses.

The treatment applies to Blue Cross and Blue Shield organizations providing health insurance that (1) were in existence on the date of conference action (August 16, 1986), (2) are determined at any time to be tax-exempt under a determination that has not been revoked[1] and (3) were tax-exempt for the last taxable year beginning before January 1, 1987, provided that no material change occurs in the structure or operations of the organization after August 16, 1986, and before the close of 1986 or any subsequent taxable year. The conferees intend that the following principles will be applied by the Secretary in determining whether or not a material change in operations or structure has occurred.

First, the merger or split up of 1 or more existing Blue Cross/Blue Shield organizations will not constitute a material change in operation or structure.

Second, if an existing Blue Cross/Blue Shield organization acquires a new line of business or is acquired by another business (other than a health business), the acquisition does not constitute a material change in operations or structure of the organization if (1) the assets of the other business are a de minimis percentage (i.e., less than 10 percent) of the assets of the existing Blue Cross/Blue Shield organization at the time of the acquisition, or (2) the taxpayer can demonstrate to the Secretary of the Treasury that, based on all the facts and circumstances, the acquisition does not constitute a material change in operations or structure of the existing Blue Cross/Blue Shield organization.

Third, a material change in operations occurs if an existing Blue Cross/Blue Shield organization drops its high risk coverage or substantially changes the terms and conditions under which high risk coverage is offered by the organization from the terms and conditions in effect as of August 16, 1986. A change in high risk coverage is considered substantial if the effect of the change is to defeat the purpose of high risk coverage. High risk coverage for this purpose generally means the coverage of individuals and small groups to the extent the organization (1) provides such coverage under specified terms and conditions as of August 16, 1986, or (2) meets the statutory minimum definition of high risk coverage for new organizations. A material change in operations does not occur if an existing organization alters its operations to provide high risk coverage that meets the minimum standards under the conference agreement for new Blue Cross/Blue Shield organizations.

For example, if an existing Blue Cross/Blue Shield organization provides open enrollment to all individuals and small groups of less than 5 individuals, the organization could redefine a small group for purposes of this coverage to mean the lesser of 15 individuals or the minimum number of individuals required for a small group under State law. Such a redefinition of a small group (from 5 to 15 individuals) would not be considered a material change in operations because the organization would meet the minimum standard for a new organization with respect to small group coverage.

On the other hand, if an existing Blue Cross/Blue Shield organization provides, as of August 16, 1986, high risk coverage to individuals and small groups without a premium price differential to take account of the high risk nature of the business, a change in premium structure for such individual and small group coverage that has the effect of creating a significant price differential to take account of the high risk nature of the business would be considered a material change in operations.

The conferees intend that, to the extent such determinations of tax exemption for any taxable year beginning before 1987 were not under audit or in litigation before the date of conference action (August 16, 1986), the Internal Revenue Service will not seek to revoke such determinations.

The conference agreement provides that such existing Blue Cross and Blue Shield organizations and other organizations eligible for this treatment are subject to tax as stock property and casualty insurance companies under Part II of Subchapter L of the Code, as amended under the conference agreement. Thus, such organizations are generally subject to the provisions applicable to property and casualty insurance companies in this conference agreement, except as otherwise provided.

A special deduction is provided to such organizations with respect to their health business equal to 25 percent of the claims and expenses incurred during the taxable year less the adjusted surplus at the beginning of the year. This deduction is calculated by computing surplus, taxable income, claims incurred, expenses incurred, tax-exempt income, net operating loss carryovers, etc., attributable to health business. Thus, the deduction is not allowable with respect to such items attributable to, for example, life insurance business. The expenses attributable to health business are those incurred during the taxable year in connection with the administration, adjustment or settlement of claims under health business. The deduction may not exceed taxable income attributable to health business for the year (calculated without regard to this deduction).

For organizations eligible for this deduction in the first taxable year beginning after December 31, 1986, the amount of the adjusted surplus to be applied in the first year for which the deduction is allowable is the surplus reported on the organization's annual statement (i.e., the annual statement approved by the National Association of Insurance Commissioners) at the close of the preceding year, adjusted by not taking into account distributions (such as distributions to shareholders, or contributions or loans to affiliates that reduce surplus, but not including ordinary and necessary expenses or deductible policyholder dividends) after the

---

date of conference action (August 16, 1986). For organizations that first become eligible for the provision in a later taxable year, the amount of the adjusted surplus for the first year of the deduction is the surplus reported on the annual statement at the close of the preceding year.

The initial surplus amount is adjusted under the provision at the close of each taxable year by adding the taxable income or loss[2] of the organization for the year (determined without regard to net operating loss carryovers and without regard to the deduction under this provision), plus net tax-exempt income for the year. Net tax-exempt income means dividends for which the dividends received deduction was allowed, and interest that is tax-exempt, less the expenses of earning the tax-exempt interest that were disallowed under sec. 265, and less the adjustment that was made for proration of tax-exempt income under sec. 805(a) or sec. 832(b)(5) (as amended by the conference agreement). If an organization eligible for the deduction under this provision does not take the deduction in any year, adjusted surplus must be calculated for the intervening years between the last year the organization took the deduction and the next year in which it takes the deduction, so as to take account properly of the calculation of the deduction in the later year.

For example, assume a calendar year Blue Cross organization engaged only in health business, the State law surplus (as adjusted) of which was $100 million on January 1, 1987. In 1987, the organization has health claims and expenses incurred of $880 million and adjusted taxable income of $160 million (including net tax-exempt income of $10 million). In 1987, the organization would be entitled to a special deduction of $120 million, that is, the excess of $220 million (25 percent of the 1987 claims and expenses paid) over $100 million (the 1987 opening surplus).

As a further example, assume that in 1988, the organization has health claims and expenses incurred of $1.2 billion. Its special deduction for 1988 would be $40 million, that is, the excess of $300 million (25 percent of the 1988 health claims and expenses incurred) over the opening 1988 adjusted surplus balance of $260 million. The opening 1988 surplus is calculated by taking the sum of (a) 1987 opening surplus of $100 million, plus (b) 1987 adjusted taxable income of $160 million (including 1987 net tax-exempt income of $10 million).

The deduction applies only for regular tax purposes. Therefore, the deduction is treated as a preference item for purposes of the corporate minimum tax.

In addition to this special deduction, such organizations are given a fresh start with respect to changes in accounting methods resulting from the change from tax-exempt to taxable status. No adjustment is made under section 481 on account of an accounting method change.

Such organizations are not subject to the treatment of unearned premium reserves generally applicable to property and casualty insurance companies under the conference agreement. The conferees believe that during the period such organizations were tax-exempt, any mismatching of currently deductible premium acquisition expenses and deferred premiums (resulting from the unearned premium reserve deduction) had no significant tax impact, and therefore it is not appropriate to require these organizations to include in income a portion of the outstanding balance of the unearned premium reserve. To ease the transition from tax-exempt to taxable status, the conferees believe that it is appropriate to give such organizations relief from the requirement that 20 percent of the increase in unearned premium reserves be included in income.

Finally, the basis of assets of such organizations is equal, for purposes of determining gain or loss, to the amount of the assets' fair market value on the first day of the organization's taxable year beginning after December 31, 1986. Thus, for formerly tax-exempt organizations utilizing a calendar period of accounting and whose first taxable year commences January 1, 1987, the basis of each asset of such organization is equal to the amount of its fair market value on January 1, 1987. The basis step-up is provided solely for purposes of determining gain or loss upon sale or exchange of the assets, not for purposes of determining amounts of depreciation or for other purposes. The basis adjustment is provided because the conferees believe that such formerly tax-exempt organizations should not be taxed on unrealized appreciation or depreciation that accrued during the period the organization was not generally subject to income taxation.

The foregoing special provisions apply to existing tax-exempt Blue Cross and Blue Shield organizations and to those other organizations that satisfy the additional criteria described below.

Other organizations substantially all of whose activities are providing health insurance, in order to receive the treatment under the provisions described above, must meet certain requirements.

First, at least 10 percent of the health insurance (determined as a percentage of the total number of individuals covered annually) provided by the organization must be provided to individuals and small groups (disregarding Medicare supplemental coverage). A small group is defined as the lesser of 15 individuals or the number of individuals

---

[Footnote ¶ 3959 continued]

(2) As under present law, insurance loss reserves must be reasonable. . . . Generally, it is intended that the loss reserves of organizations eligible for the deduction under this provision also be reasonable, and that they be comparable to the historical loss reserves of the organization in relation to its claims and expenses.

required for a small group under the State law where the covered groups are located.

Second, the organization is required to provide continuous full-year open enrollment for individuals and small groups. Open enrollment is intended to include conversions from group to individual coverage (for example, upon separation from service with an employer who provides group coverage), without a lapse in coverage, provided the individual seeking to convert from group to individual coverage notifies the organization providing group coverage of his conversion request by the date of his separation from service. Conversion includes any change in the type of coverage (e.g., from one type of group to another).

Third, any individual seeking health insurance is required to be offered coverage which includes coverage of pre-existing conditions, and the coverage becomes effective within a reasonable waiting period after the time such coverage is sought. A reasonable waiting period is intended to be not more than three months. Further, health insurance coverage must be provided without regard to the age, income, or employment status of persons under age 65.

Fourth, at least 35 percent of the organization's health insurance premiums are determined on a community-rated basis. This percentage is determined as a percentage of the total number of persons covered on an annual basis. Community rating means that premiums are determined on the basis of the average annual cost of health insurance over the population in the community.

Fifth, the organization must be organized and operated in a manner such that no part of the net earnings inures to the benefit of any private shareholder or individual.

The conference agreement requires that the Treasury Department audit and study fraternal beneficiary organizations (described in sec. 501(c)(8)) that received gross insurance premiums in excess of $25 million in taxable year 1984. The Treasury study is due by January 1, 1988.

Effective Dates.—The provision is effective for taxable years beginning after December 31, 1986. Special rules for Mutual of America and for Teachers Insurance Annuity Association-College Retirement Equities Fund provide that this provision does not apply with respect to that portion of their business attributable to pension business. For this purpose, the conference agreement provides that pension business means the administration of qualified pension plans (sec. 401(a) or 403(a)), tax-sheltered annuities (sec. 403(b)), unfunded deferred compensation plans of State and local governments (sec. 457), and individual retirement arrangements (IRA's.)

Additional special rules provide that this provision does not apply to the YMCA retirement fund, to administrative services performed by tax-exempt municipal leagues, to the Missouri Hospital Association, or to dental benefit coverage by Delta Dental Plans Association through contracts with independent service providers so long as the provision of such coverage is the principal activity of such Association. No inference is intended, under this provision, as to whether the performance of administrative services by tax-exempt municipal leagues, without more, constitutes commercial-type insurance activities. Generally, however, the performance of administrative services with respect to insurance contracts by tax-exempt organizations may be subject to unrelated business tax.

*   *   *   *   *   *

[¶ 3960] SECTION 1013. OPERATIONS LOSS DEDUCTION OF INSOLVENT COMPANIES MAY OFFSET DISTRIBUTIONS FROM POLICYHOLDERS SURPLUS ACCOUNT

[Senate Explanation]

*   *   *   *   *   *

Present Law.—Prior to 1984, life insurance companies were permitted to exclude from taxable income 50 percent of the excess of gain from operations over taxable investment income. In addition, life insurance companies were allowed certain special deductions for nonparticipating contracts and for accident and health insurance and group life insurance contracts. The amounts deducted under these provisions were added to a deferred tax account known as the policyholders surplus account (PSA). The allowance of these special deductions, and the establishment of a PSA, were intended to provide a cushion of assets to protect the interests of the policyholders. The 1984 Act repealed the deduction for additions to a PSA, but continued the deferral on existing amounts in a PSA.

The deferral of tax on existing amounts held in the PSA of a life insurance company is ended if the amounts are distributed to shareholders. In certain circumstances, amounts may be required to be distributed from the PSA (i.e., the deferral of tax on such amounts is ended) if the PSA becomes too large in relation to the scope of the company's current operations. The deferral of tax on amounts in the PSA also may end if the company ceases to be taxed as a life insurance company. The amounts included in income as a result of ending deferral on amounts in the PSA cannot be offset by the company's loss from operations or loss carryovers.

*   *   *   *   *   *

Explanation of Provision.—Under the bill, a life insurance company is permitted to apply its current loss from operations and its unused operations loss carryovers against the increase in its taxable income attributable to the amount distributed from its PSA if certain conditions are satisfied. First, the company must have been insolvent on November 15, 1985. Second, the company must be liquidated pursuant to the order of a court of competent jurisdiction in a title 11 or similar case. Third, as a result of the liquidation, the company's tax liability must be increased due to distributions from the PSA. Under the provision, no carryover of any loss from operations of the company existing during or prior to the year of liquidation may be used in any taxable year succeeding the liquidation year (regardless of whether the amount of the loss exceeds the amount of the distribution from the PSA).

Effective Date.—The provision applies to liquidations on or after November 15, 1985.

[¶ 3961] SECTION 1021. INCLUSION IN INCOME OF 20 PERCENT OF UNEARNED PREMIUM RESERVE

(Sec. 832(b) of the Code)

[Senate Explanation]

* * * * * *

Present Law.—Under present law, the income of a property and casualty insurance company (whether stock or mutual)[2] includes its underwriting income or loss and its investment income or loss, as well as gains and other income items.[3] Underwriting income means premiums earned on insurance contracts during the year, less losses incurred and expenses incurred (sec. 832(b)(3)). To determine premiums earned, the increase in unearned premiums during the year is deducted from gross premiums (sec. 832(b)(4)(B)). This treatment of unearned premiums generally reflects accounting conventions imposed under applicable law[4] and corresponds to the establishment of reserves for unearned premiums.

Unearned premiums of a property and casualty insurance company include its life insurance reserves (including annuity reserves), if any. Generally, the deduction for the reserve for unearned premiums effects a deferral of the premium income attributable to insurance coverage in a future taxable year of a property and casualty company.

Property and casualty insurers may also deduct expenses incurred during the taxable year (sec. 832(b)(3)). Expenses incurred generally means expenses shown on the annual statement approved by the National Association of Insurance Commissioners. Expenses incurred are calculated by adding to expenses paid during the year the difference between unpaid expenses at the end of the current year and unpaid expenses at the end of the preceding year (sec. 832(b)(6)). Expenses incurred ordinarily include premium acquisition expenses. Expenses, to be deductible, must constitute ordinary and necessary trade or business expenses within the meaning of section 162 (sec. 832(c)(1)), although this rule does not determine the time when the deduction is allowed.

* * * * * *

Explanation of Provision.—*General rule.*—Under the bill, a property and casualty insurance company generally is required to reduce its deduction for unearned premiums by 20 percent. This amount is intended to represent the allocable portion of expenses incurred in generating the unearned premiums. Thus, for taxable years beginning after 1986, only 80 percent of the increase in unearned premiums in each year is deductible. To the extent there is a decrease in the unearned premium reserve for a taxable year beginning after 1986, the resulting inclusion in income would be reduced; only 80 percent of the amount would be includible. Thus, if the taxpayer's unearned premium reserve increased in 1987 from $1,000 to $1,100, the net deduction for unearned premiums would be $80 ($1,100-1,000 × 80%). Similarly, if the unearned premium reserve declined in 1988 from $1,100 to $900, the taxpayer would be required to include $160, rather than $200, in income.[5]

[Footnote ¶ 3961] (2) The use of the term "property and casualty insurance company" is intended to refer to all those taxpayers subject to tax under Part II or III of subchapter L of the Code.

(3) Under present law, mutual companies with certain gross receipts less than $150,000 are exempt from tax (sec. 501(c)(15)), and other rules set forth special rates, deductions, and exemptions for mutual companies with certain categories and amounts of income (sec. 821 et seq). In addition, mutual companies are allowed a special deduction for additions to a bookkeeping protection against loss account (sec. 824). (See the separate discussion of the protection against loss account, at item C.3., below).

(4) See National Association of Insurance Commissioners ("NAIC") approved annual statement form (often called the yellow blank) used by property and casualty insurance companies for financial reporting. The accounting techniques used in preparing this annual statement are referred to as statutory accounting principles (SAP), and generally are more conservative than generally accepted accounting principles (GAAP) and the cash and accrual method of tax accounting.

(5) See General Accounting Office, *Congress Should Consider Changing Federal Income Taxation of the Property/Casualty Insurance Industry* (GAO/GGD-88-10), March 25, 1985 ("GAO Report" tax reform proposals made by President Reagan ("The President's Tax Proposals to the Congress for Fairness, Growth, and Simplicity," May 1985, referred to as the "Administration Proposal"); the 1984 Treasury Department Report to the President ("Tax Reform for Fairness, Simplicity, and Economic Growth," November 1984, referred to as the "1984 Treasury Report").

Life insurance reserves, as defined in section 816(b), that are included in unearned premium reserves under section 832(b)(4) are not subject to this reduction under the bill. Increases (or decreases) in such life insurance reserves remain 100 percent deductible (or, to the extent a decrease in unearned premium reserves is attributable to a decrease in life insurance reserves, 100 percent includible). This exception to the 80 percent rule is permitted because such life insurance reserves are calculated under sec. 807 in a manner intended to reduce the mismeasurement of income resulting from the mismatching of income and expenses.

Application of general rule to outstanding balances.—The bill also provides for the inclusion in income of 20 percent of the unearned premium reserve outstanding at the end of the most recent taxable year beginning before January 1, 1987. This income is includible ratably over a seven and one-half year period commencing with the first taxable year beginning after December 31, 1986. In each of the first seven taxable years during this period, 2-⅔ percent of the unearned premium reserve outstanding at the end of the most recent taxable year beginning before January 1, 1987, is included in income and in the eighth year, 1-⅓ percent is included.

Special rule.—In the case of insurance against default in the payment of principal or interest on securities with a maturity of 5 years or more, the deduction for increases in unearned premiums is reduced by 10 percent, rather than 20 percent. Thus, only 90 percent of the increase in unearned premiums is deductible and 90 percent of any decrease is includible in income. Insurance on securities with a maturity of less than 5 years is subject to the general rule reducing the deduction (or inclusion) for a change in unearned premiums by 20 percent.

With respect to the treatment of the outstanding balance of unearned premiums at the end of the most recent taxable year beginning before January 1, 1987, 1-⅛ percent of the outstanding balance is includible in each of the first 7 taxable years beginning after December 31, 1986, and ⅔ percent of such balance is includible for the eight taxable year.

Companies that cease to be insurance companies.—Under the bill, if a property and casualty insurance company ceases to be subject to parts II or III of subchapter L (including the rules relating to the treatment of unearned premiums), the rule for outstanding unearned premium balances (for balances as of the end of the last taxable year beginning before January 1, 1987) is applied to include the remaining amount subject to the rule in income for the taxable year preceding the taxable year in which the company ceases to be subject to tax as a property and casualty insurance company.

An exception is provided to the extent a successor company (which is also an insurance company) is subject to the requirements of section 381(c)(22). Further, this rule applies only if a company ceases to be a property and casualty company for a taxable year beginning before January 1, 1995.

For example, if a property and casualty insurance company has an outstanding unearned premium balance of $100 for its taxable year ending December 31, 1986, 20 percent of the unearned premium balance, or $20, is subject to the ratable inclusion rule. For its taxable year ending December 31, 1987, 2-⅔ percent of $100, or $2-⅔, is included in income. If the company ceases to be a property and casualty insurance company for its taxable year beginning January 1, 1989, then $17-⅛ is includible in income for the company's taxable year ending December 31, 1988.

The committee has adopted this rule because the treatment of the outstanding unearned premium balance is designed to avoid a substantial income inclusion in the first taxable year after the effective date. However, if a company ceases to be a property and casualty insurance company during the phase-in period, the committee believes the phase-in should be accelerated to prevent permanent avoidance of the income inclusion.

[Conference Report]

*   *   *   *   *   *

Conference Agreement.—The conference agreement follows the Senate amendment, *Effective date.*—generally effective for taxable years beginning after December 31, 1986, with the modification that the period over which 20 percent (or 10 percent in the case of insurance on securities with a maturity over 5 years) of the outstanding balance of unearned premium reserves at the end of the last taxable year beginning before January 1, 1987, is included in income is 6 years, rather than 7-½ years, commencing with the first taxable year beginning after December 31, 1986.

The conference agreement also provides special treatment of title insurance unearned premium reserves (see [¶3963] below).

[¶ 3962] SECTION 1022. TREATMENT OF CERTAIN DIVIDENDS AND TAX-EXEMPT INTEREST

(Sec. 832 of the Code)

[House Explanation]

*   *   *   *   *   *

Present Law.—Property and casualty companies are generally subject to tax on underwriting income (sec. 832(b)(1) and (3)). In calculating underwriting income, losses incurred (as well as expenses incurred) are deducted from premiums earned. The deduction for losses incurred generally reflects losses paid during the year as well as the increase in reserves for losses incurred but not paid.

Property and casualty insurance companies are also subject to tax on investment income, which generally includes interest, dividends and rents (sec. 832(b)(2)). A property and casualty insurer that includes in its investment income interest exempt from tax (sec. 108) may deduct this interest under section 832(c)(7) of present law. Thus, in effect, the section 103 exclusion is available for eligible investment income. In addition, property and casualty companies are allowed the dividends received deduction (sec. 882(c)(12)).

No reduction in the loss reserve deduction is required, under present law, to take account of the fact that deductible additions to reserves may come out of income not subject to tax. Unlike life insurance companies, property and casualty investment companies are not required to allocate or prorate investment income (including tax-exempt investment income) so as to take account of the possibility of a double deduction where deductible additions to reserves are funded with tax-exempt income (or with the deductible portion of dividends received). In the case of life insurance companies, the net increase and net decrease in reserves are computed by reducing the ending balance of the reserve items by the prorated policyholders' share of tax-exempt interest (sec. 812).[11] This life insurance tax rule is based on the assumption that reserve increases are being funded out of both taxable and tax-exempt income.

*   *   *   *   *   *

Explanation of Provision.—Under the bill, the deduction for losses incurred is reduced by a specified portion of the insurer's tax-exempt interest and of the deductible portion of dividends received (with special rules for dividends from affiliates). For this purpose, tax-exempt interest includes interest income excludable under section 103 (or deductible under sec. 382(c)(7)), the portion of interest income excludable under section 133, and other similar items. The specified portion for taxable years beginning after December 31, 1985 [1986, See Conference], is 10 percent, increasing to 15 percent for taxable years beginning after December 31, 1987.

In the case of dividends from affiliates, 100 percent of which are deductible under present law,[12] the portion which is subject to proration in the hands of the recipient property and casualty company is that portion which is attributable to tax-exempt interest or nonaffiliate dividends (that is, those dividends which would not be eligible for the 100 percent dividends received deduction. Special rules for dividends from insurance affiliates (whether life or property and casualty) provide that the amount of the reduction in the deduction for losses incurred as a result of proration in the hands of the recipient property and casualty company is offset by the effect of proration as applied to the affiliate. The special rules for proration of dividends from insurance affiliates are similar to rules applicable, under the technical corrections portion of this bill, to the treatment of dividends received by life insurance companies from other life insurance companies.

This provision may be illustrated as follows. Assume that, in 1987, a property and casualty insurer has tax-exempt interest of $1,000 and receives a dividend of $100 that is not eligible for the 100 percent dividends received deduction (i.e., the dividend is 85 percent deductible). In addition, the company receives from an affiliate a dividend of $400 (none of which is attributable to amounts subject to proration) that is eligible for the 100 percent dividends received deduction. Under this provision, the deduction of losses incurred would be reduced by $108.50. If the amount of this reduction exceeds the amount otherwise deductible as losses incurred, the excess is includible in income.

The proration rule does not apply to tax-exempt interest and the deductible portion of dividends received or accrued on stock or obligations acquired before November 15, 1985. In the case of dividends from affiliates, special rules apply. The portion of dividends received from an affiliate attributable to stock or obligations (the interest on which is tax-exempt) acquired by the affiliate after November 14, 1985, is subject to the proration rule. Further, if an affiliate is acquired after November 14, 1985 (so that it is thereafter treated as an affiliate), each share of stock or obligation (the interest on which is tax-exempt) held by the affiliate (or by its subsidiaries which are affiliates), whenever acquired by the affiliate, is treated as acquired after November 14, 1985. Thus, the portion of a dividend from any affiliate acquired after November 14, 1985 attributable to amounts subject to proration will be subject to the proration rules. However, dividends not attributable to prorated amounts will not be prorated even if the affiliate payor was acquired after November 14, 1985.

[Conference Report]

*   *   *   *   *   *

Conference Agreement.—The conference agreement follows the House bill, with modifications. The specified portion by which the deduction for losses incurred is reduced under the provision is 15 percent for all

---

[Footnote ¶ 3962]   (11) Also, the dividends received deduction is reduced by the policyholders' share of the dividends (sec. 905(a)(4)).

(12) Such dividends include any dividend if the percentage used for purposes of determining the deduction allowable under section 243 or 244 is 100 percent, regardless of whether, under the bill, such dividends may be eligible for a dividends received deduction in a different percentage in future taxable years. Under the bill, such dividends also include a dividend received by a foreign corporation from a domestic corporation which would be a 100 percent dividend of section 1804(b)(8) did not apply for purposes of applying section 243(b)(5).

taxable years beginning after December 31, 1986. In addition, the proration rule does not apply to tax-exempt interest and the deductible portion of dividends (whether or not from an affiliate) received or accrued on stock or obligations acquired before August 8, 1986.

The portion of dividends received from an affiliate attributable to stock or obligations (the interest on which is tax-exempt) acquired by the affiliate after August 7, 1986, is subject to the proration rule. Similarly, the transfer of tax-exempt bonds among affiliates after August 7, 1986, is treated as an acquisition of the bonds after August 7, 1986. Further, if an affiliate is acquired after August 7, 1986, each share of stock or obligation (the interest on which is tax-exempt)

held by the affiliate (or by its subsidiaries that are affiliates), whenever acquired by the affiliate, is treated as acquired after August 7, 1986.

The conference agreement clarifies the determination of the portion of a dividend that is attributable to prorated amounts. Under the conference agreement, dividends are treated as paid first out of current or accumulated earnings and profits attributable to prorated amounts; that is, it is treated as paid first out of tax-exempt income of the paying company (such as interest or the deductible portion of dividends received).

The provision is effective for taxable years beginning after December 31, 1986.

[¶ 3963] SECTION 1023. DISCOUNTING OF UNPAID LOSSES AND CERTAIN UNPAID EXPENSES

(Secs. 807(c); 832(b); 846 of the Code)

[Senate Explanation]

*   *   *   *   *   *

Present Law.—*In general.*—Present law provides generally that property and casualty companies are required to include their underwriting and investment income or loss in taxable income (sec. 832(b)). Underwriting loss, if any, may offset investment income. Among the items that are deductible in calculating underwriting income are additions to reserves for losses incurred and for unearned premiums. Thus, generally, underwriting income is determined in a manner similar to the manner in which insurers account for underwriting income for statutory accounting purposes. Consequently, the deduction for losses incurred may include the amounts of contested liabilities, and amounts which are estimated (and which therefore may be subject to future change when the amounts can be determined with reasonable accuracy).

This method of tax accounting for losses differs from the rules generally applicable under the cash and accrual methods of accounting. Under the cash method, amounts representing allowable deductions are generally taken into account for the taxable year in which they are paid (Treas. Reg. sec. 1.461-1(a)(1)). Thus, under the cash method of accounting, unpaid losses would not be currently deductible.

Under the normal rules of accrual method tax accounting, the all-events test must be met, and economic performance generally must have occurred, before a deduction may be accrued. The all-events test provides that "an expense is deductible for the taxable year in which all the events have occurred which determine the fact of the liability and the amount thereof can be determined with reasonable accuracy" (Treas. Reg. sec. 1.461-

1(a)(2)). A contested liability may not be deducted unless the taxpayer has transferred money or other property beyond his control to provide for the satisfaction of the liability (sec. 461(f)). If the liability of the taxpayer requires the taxpayer to provide property, economic performance occurs as the property is provided by the taxpayer. In the case of workers' compensation and tort liabilities of the taxpayer requiring payments to another person, economic performance occurs as the payments are made. Thus, under the accrual method of accounting, contested liabilities and amounts which cannot yet be determined with reasonable accuracy would not be currently deductible, and losses generally would not be deductible until the loss is paid.

Treatment of title insurance.—Under present law, the treatment of title insurance (i.e., insurance to protect the buyer of real property against the risk that a defect in the title or an encumbrance against the property exists at the time the property is purchased) differs from the treatment normally accorded to property and casualty companies. The Internal Revenue Service had previously held that the provisions of the Code (sec. 832(b)(4)) relating to the division of premiums between earned and unearned was inapplicable to title insurance because title insurance company premiums are earned in full at the time the company's services are rendered.[6]

Subsequently, the IRS revoked its prior position with respect to cases in which a State statute regarding unearned premium reserves of title insurance companies requires that such premiums be placed in a reserve, withdraws them from the control of the company for use as general funds, and imposes a trust in favor of the policyholders for a period prescribed in such State statute.[7] Thus, for title insurers operating in jurisdictions requiring the maintenance of an unearned premium reserve, the IRS permitted premiums received by title insurers (to the

---

[Footnote ¶ 3963]   (6) Rev. Rul. 70-245, 1970-1 C.B. 154, restating under the 1954 Code the position set forth in I.T. 2920. XIV-2 C.B. 265 (1935).

   (7) Rev. Rul. 71-598. 1971-2 C.B. 261, citing *Early v. Lawyers Title Insurance Company,* 132 F.2d 42 (4th Cir. 1942).

extent of the reserve required under State law) to be treated as unearned premiums for Federal income tax purposes.

In 1983, the IRS revoked Rev. Rul. 71-598.[8] The Service noted that, in the case of a title insurance company, the loss against which the insurance is provided, i.e., the risk of defect in title or encumbrance to property, is mature at the time the policy is issued, so that premiums received are not unearned premiums. Further, the Service concluded that deducting both a State-law "unearned premiums" reserve and a loss reserve amount would take account of the same items twice. Therefore, to the extent that the State statute required a reserve in excess of those reserves necessary for the protection of policyholders, it is not appropriately treated as a deductible reserve amount.

*   *   *   *   *   *

Explanation of Provision.

In general.—The bill amends the relevant provisions of subchapter L to provide for the discounting of the deduction for loss reserves to take account partially of the time value of money. Thus, the bill limits the deduction for unpaid losses (reported losses that have not been paid, estimates of losses incurred but not reported and resisted claims, and unpaid loss adjustment expenses) to the amount of discounted unpaid losses (new sec. 846 of the Code). Any net decrease in loss reserves would result in income inclusion, as under present law, but computed on a discounted basis.

This modified treatment of loss reserve deductions is applicable both to loss reserves of property and casualty companies, and to loss reserves of life insurance companies that are not required to be discounted under life insurance rules. In the case of any reserves (including reservse of property and casualty companies) which life insurance company provisions require to be discounted, the applicable life insurance reserve discounting rules apply in lieu of the new discounting rules adopted by the bill.

Special treatment under the bill is provided with respect to (1) certain types of accident and health insurance, including disability insurance, and (2) title insurance.

Scope of discounting.—Under the bill, the deduction for losses incurred is computed in the following manner. The amount of losses paid during the taxable year is calculated, and is increased by salvage and reinsurance recoverable (attributable to paid losses) outstanding at the end of the preceding taxable year and is decreased by salvage and reinsurance recoverable (attributable to paid losses) outstanding at the end of the current

taxable year. The amount of paid losses is increased by the amount of discounted unpaid losses (as defined in new sec. 846) outstanding at the end of the taxable year and is decreased by the amount of discounted unpaid losses outstanding at the end of the preceding taxable year.

Unpaid losses generally mean the amount of unpaid losses reflected on the annual statement approved by NAIC that the taxpayer is required to file with insurance regulatory authorities of a State. For purposes of calculating unpaid losses under the bill, unpaid loss adjustment expenses are treated as unpaid losses and are not included in the amount of expenses unpaid (under sec. 832(b)(6)). Unpaid losses are separately defined under the bill to include any unpaid loss adjustment expenses shown on the annual statement; unpaid loss adjustment expenses are not to be taken into account more than once. Under the bill, the Secretary of the Treasury is directed to provide, in regulations, for the proper treatment of salvage and reinsurance recoverable with respect to unpaid losses.

Lines of business to which discounting rules apply.—The bill requires all property and casualty loss reserves (unpaid losses and unpaid loss adjustment expenses) for each line of business (as shown on the annual statement) to be discounted for tax purposes. The lines of business are categories for the reporting of claims and claim payments, and specifically appear on Schedules O and P of the annual statement for property and casualty companies (technically, the "fire and casualty" annual statement as prescribed by the NAIC).

The lines of business reported on Schedule O of the annual statement relate mostly to "short-tail" coverages, such as auto physical damage, although they also include accident and health coverages some of which involve the payment of claims over extended periods, such as so-called long-term disability coverages. "Short-tail" coverages or lines of business are lines of business in which the period of time between the occurrence of the loss for which coverage is provided and the payment of the claim attributable to that loss is, on average, relatively short.[9]

Two of the Schedule O lines are denominated "reinsurance" and "international," respectively, and include amounts that may optionally be reported in those lines or in other Schedule O and P lines to which the reinsurance or international insurance is directly allocable.

The Schedule P lines typically are longer-tail (primarily liability coverage) lines. The longer-tail lines of business are denominated

---

[Footnote ¶ 3963 continued]

(8) Rev. Rul. 83-174, 1983-2 C.B. 108.

(9) Whether a loss has occurred, and the time between occurrance and payment, depends on whether the insurance contract is written on a "loss incurred" or on a "claims made" basis. If insurance is provided on a "loss incurred" basis, coverage is provided with respect to losses that occur during the period of coverage. Alternatively, if a policy is written on "claims made" basis, coverage is provided with respect to claims reported during the period of coverage. Typically, the time between occurrence of a loss and payment of a claim is shorter if policies are written on a claims made basis.

in five annual statement categories: auto liability, other liability, workers' compensation, medical malpractice, and multiple peril (encompassing farm owners' multiple peril, homeowners' multiple peril, commercial multiple peril, ocean marine, aircraft (all perils), and boiler and machinery. Under the bill, the multiple peril lines of business are treated as a single line of business for purposes of applying the discounting provisions. A "long-tail" line of business is a line in which the time between the occurence of a loss and the payment of a claim is fairly long. Some lines of business, such as workers' compensation and medical practice, have significantly longer tails, with a large percentage of claims remaining unpaid after 10 years.

In the case of insurers which hold loss reserves for cancellable accident and health ("A&H") coverages and are required by the bill to discount such reserves, the amounts involved typically are reported on Exhibits 9 and 11 of the NAIC annual statement for life and health companies.

Because of the presence of potentially longer-tail claims in the accident and health lines as well as in the reinsurance and international lines, the bill provides for special treatment with respect to these types of business, as described more fully below.

Discounting methodology.—To implement the discounting of loss reserves, the bill provides that the deduction for unpaid losses is limited to the annual increase in discounted unpaid losses. The amount of the discounted unpaid losses as of the end of any taxable year attributable to any accident year is the present value of the losses (as of the close of the taxable year) determined by using (1) the gross amount to be subjected to discounting (i.e., the undiscounted loss reserves), (2) the pattern of payment of claims, including the duration in years over which the claims will be paid, and (3) the rate of interest to be assumed in calculating the discounted reserve.

This discounting methodology is applied by line of business and by accident year, as reported on the annual statement filed for the year. Under the bill, the term accident year means the year in which the incident occurs that gives rise to the related unpaid loss. For this purpose, in the case of a claims made policy, the accident year will generally be the year in which the claim is made.

Limit on discounted losses.—The amounts to which the discounting rules are applied under the bill are the undiscounted loss reserves (as reported on the annual statement for the accident year with respect to the line of business to which the discounting applies). The relevant annual statement is the statement filed by the taxpayer for the fiscal year ending with or within the taxable year of the taxpayer.

In some cases (such as workers' compensation) for certain companies, the reserves shown on the annual statement are already discounted and identified as such. The committee intends that, in the case of a loss reserve that is discounted for purposes of

annual statement reporting, the loss reserve for annual statement reporting is grossed up and an undiscounted loss reserve is calculated. This grossing up of discounted loss reserves to undiscounted loss reserves for Federal income tax purposes is available only if the discounting for annual statement reporting is identified as such, and the discounting factors that were used are explained, on the annual statement. It is not necessary that the disclosure of discounting be required on the annual statement, as long as the taxpayer actually discloses the fact that unpaid loss reserves are discounted and the basis for such discounting with its annual statement. This undiscounted loss reserve amount is used as the amount of unpaid losses from which the loss reserve discounting for tax purposes is computed.

However, the committee is concerned about the potential for abuse when a property and casualty insurance company computes undiscounted unpaid losses by grossing up any annual statement discounted losses. A company could overstate the undiscounted losses (by overstating the amount by which its unpaid losses are discounted). In such a case, the company could effectively negate the application of the income tax discounting requirements.

One way of dealing with this potential problem would be to require that the discounting rules applicable for income tax purposes be applied to the loss reserves reported on the annual statement, whether or not discounted. The committee believes, however, that such an approach would be inequitable because it would understate some companies' deduction compared to other companies that did not discount for financial reporting purposes. Rather than impose this type of detriment on companies that discount on their annual statements, and thereby possibly interfere with the regulatory authority of the States, the bill imposes a limitation on the ability of a property and casualty insurance company to overstate its discounting factors for annual statement reporting by providing that in no event can the amount of discounted loss reserves for Federal income tax purposes exceed the aggregate amount of unpaid losses (and loss adjustment expenses) with respect to any line of business for an accident year as reported on the annual statement. Further, the amount and rate of the discount, for annual statement purposes, for any line of business, must be ascertainable on the basis of information filed on or with the annual statement.

Discount factors.—Under the bill, the tax reserve discount factors, computed using the assumptions described below (i.e., the interest rate and the loss payment pattern, including the maximum duration of payments), are to be separately developed for and applied to the unpaid loss attributable to each accident year for each line of business. Recognizing that the computations of the discount factors themselves involve a degree of complexity, it is anticipated that the Secretary will annually publish discount factors which taxpayers may use in determining the discounted amounts of their loss reserves.

Once a series of discount factors is applied to an accident year for a line of business, it continues to be used without change as that accident year "ages" (i.e., as the claims for that year proceed to be paid out). In effect, each line of business and accident year is vintaged under the discounting provision, and subsequent redeterminations of the interest rate or payment pattern for that vintage based on actual experience of a particular company or the industry in general are neither required nor permitted.

Interest rate.—The interest rate used for purposes of applying the discounting methodology to a line of business is 5 percent for all accident years of the company beginning before or in 1987. For accident years beginning after 1987, the annual interest rate applicable to the discounting of unpaid losses is equal to 75 percent of the average of the annual Federal mid-term rates (as defined in sec. 1274(d) converted to a rate based on annual compounding) effective as of the beginning of each of the calendar months in the base period. The base period means the most recent 60 calendar months ending before the beginning of the calendar year for which the determination is made. In order to avoid a retroactive impact on the treatment of loss reserves on account of interest rates in years before the effective date, the base period does not include any calendar month beginning before January 1, 1987.

For example, the rate to be used in computing the discount factors for 1995, is 75 percent of the average of the annual Federal mid-term rates in effect at the beginning of each of the 60 calendar months during 1990-1994. On the other hand, the rate to be used in computing discount factors for 1989 is the average of such applicable rates for the 24-month period ending before January 1, 1989.

Once an interest rate assumption is established with respect to unpaid losses attributable to an accident year, the rate is not subsequently adjusted to reflect changes in the average Federal midterm rate in later periods. Thus, the interest rate attributable to an accident year is vintaged with respect to that year.

Loss payment pattern.—The bill requires the Secretary of the Treasury to determine a loss payment pattern with respect to each line of business reported on Schedules O and P for a determination year. This loss payment pattern will be determined by reference to the historical loss payment pattern applicable to the line of business and applies to accident years ending with (or within) the determination year and each of the four succeeding years.

The determination year means the calendar year 1987 and each 5th calendar year after 1987. Thus, the Secretary is directed to redetermine and publish the loss payment patterns on an industry-wide basis every five years.

Determinations of loss payments patterns are to be made (1) by using the aggregate experience reported on the annual statements of insurance companies to which the discounting provisions apply, (2) on the basis of the most recent published aggregate data from the annual statements relating to loss payment patterns available on the first day of the determination year, (3) by assuming that all losses are paid in the middle of the years, and (4) under certain computational assumptions with respect to the period over which the losses are paid.

At present, the aggregate data derived from the annual statements provides information for the accident year plus 2 years with respect to Schedule O lines of business and the accident year plus 9 years with respect to the Schedule P lines of business. Under the bill, the Secretary is directed to make appropriate adjustments with respect to the duration of payment patterns for future accident years if annual statement data is available for longer periods (e.g., because the period for which reporting is required on the annual statement is changed).

At the current time, aggregate loss payment pattern data is annually published by A.M. Best & Co., summarizing industry payout patterns by line of business and accident year as reported on Schedules O and P of the most recently filed annual statements. The committee intends that, as long as the information is published in its present form and supplies information with respect to at least the same number of accident years as is supplied as of the date of committee action, the Secretary is to use the data available in Best's Aggregates and Averages. In the case of title insurance (see the description of special rules relating to title insurance below), the committee intends that such information published by the American Land Title Association is to be used which is comparable to the information published in Best's Aggregates and Averages. It is anticipated that the title insurance loss payment patterns based on this data will be at least as long in duration as the payment patterns for Schedule P lines of business.

Under this provision, loss payment patterns announced for the period 1987-1991 are to make use of the most recent published aggregate data available on January 1, 1987, which is the data for 1985. The factors announced during 1992-1996 are to use the data available on January 1, 1992, which is expected to be 1990 data.

Computational rules.—The computational assumptions prescribed by the bill provide that the loss payment pattern for any line of business is to be based on losses paid (1) during the accident year and the 3 years following the accident year or (2) in the case of any line of business reported in the schedule or schedules of the annual statement relating to auto liability, other liability, medical malpractice, workers' compensation, and multiple peril lines of business (Schedule P

Act § 1023   ¶ 3963

lines), during the accident year and the 10 years following the accident year.

In the case of a line of business for which the accident year plus the 3 years following the accident year is used (generally, Schedule O lines), the bill provides that losses paid after the first year following the accident year are treated as paid equally in the succeeding 2 years. In the case of any other line of business, losses paid after the close of the 10-year after the accident year are generally treated as paid in such 10th year.

The bill provides a special rule for certain long-tail lines of business. If the special rule applies, (1) the 10-year period following the accident year may be extended (but not by more than 5 years) and (2) the amount of losses that otherwise would have been treated as paid in the 10th year following the accident year are treated as paid in such 10th year and each subsequent year in an amount equal to the lessor of (a) the amount of losses paid in the 9th year following the accident year, or (b) the remaining amount of unpaid losses. If, at the end of 5 years following such 10th year, there is a remaining balance of unpaid losses, such losses are treated as if paid at the end of such 5th year without regard to the rule in the preceding sentence.

The special rule to extend the assumed loss payment period for long-tall lines of business applies if the amount of losses that would be treated as paid (under the general rule) in the 10th year following the accident year exceeds the amount of losses treated as paid in the 9th year following the accident year.

As an example of this special rule for long-tall lines of business, assume the following loss payment pattern:

Year	Loss Payment Pattern (percent)
Accident Year	25
Accident Year + 1	10
Accident Year + 2	8
Accident Year + 3	8
Accident Year + 4	8
Accident Year + 5	7
Accident Year + 6	7
Accident Year + 7	5
Accident Year + 8	5
Accident Year + 9	5
Accident Year + 10	12

In this example, the amount of losses paid in the 9th year following the accident year are less than the amount of losses treated as paid in the 10th year following the accident year. Accordingly, the special rule applicable to long-tail lines of business applies. Under this special rule, the amount of losses paid in the 10th and later years after the accident year are treated as equalling the amount of losses paid in the 9th year after the accident year. Therefore, under the special rule, the loss payment period is extended for an additional 2 years, as follows:

Year	Special Rule Less Payment Pattern (percent)
Accident Year	25
Accident Year + 1	10
Accident Year + 2	8
Accident Year + 3	8
Accident Year + 4	8
Accident Year + 5	7
Accident Year + 6	7
Accident Year + 7	5
Accident Year + 8	5
Accident Year + 9	5
Accident Year + 10	5
Accident Year + 11	5
Accident Year + 12	2

Special rule for international and reinsurance.—Under the bill, for the international and reinsurance lines of business, the discounting provisions are implemented on the basis of composite discount factors derived by combining the payment patterns for all Schedule P lines. Although reinsurance and international lines of business may be reported on Schedule O as a short-tail line of business, the committee is concerned that treating these lines as Schedule O lines for purposes of calculating discounted loss reserve deductions will create a disproportionately favorable effect on reinsurance and international insurance attributable to long-tail lines of business. If such long-tail lines were accurately reflected, the current loss reserve deduction would be lower than if such reinsurance and international insurance is treated as part of a Schedule O line of business, with assumed loss payments over a much shorter period of time.

The bill authorizes the Secretary to issue regulations requiring a company to follow a loss payment pattern that differs from the normal treatment of reinsurance as a composite of all Schedule P lines of business. The committee anticipates, for example, that in the case of a company substantially all of the reinsurance business of which is the reinsurance of medical malpractice insurance, the Secretary is to require such reinsurer to use a loss payment pattern that is an aggregate of all industry experience with respect to medical malpractice, rather than an aggregate of all industry experience for all Schedule P lines of business.

Special rules for accident and health insurance coverage.—Under the bill, the active life reserves held for life insurance and noncancellable accident and health benefits (to the extent subject under present law to the life insurance company reserve rules (sec. 807(d)) are not subject to discounting under the new discounted unpaid loss provisions (sec. 846). Rather, in the case of a property and casualty insurance company subject to the life insurance reserve rules with respect to a particular line of business, the amount of discounted unpaid losses for that line of business is the amount required under the life insurance reserve rules.

In addition, under the bill, in the case of unpaid losses relating to disability insurance (other than credit disability insurance), the general rules prescribed for the treatment of noncancellable accident and health insurance contracts under the life insurance company reserve provisions (sec. 807(d)) are to apply adjusted in the following manner: (1) the taxpayer may use its own experience relating to mortality and morbidity, (2) the prevailing State assumed interest rate to be used is the rate in effect for the year in which the loss occurred rather than the year in which the contract was issued, and (3) the rule limiting the amount of discounted losses to no more than the aggregate amount of unpaid losses as reflected on the annual statement applies. Similar treatment applies to noncancellable accident and health insurance provided by a life or by a property and casualty insurance company.

In the case of life insurance companies and property and casualty companies with respect to the types of accident and health insurance coverage (other than disability insurance) that are not currently subject to the life insurance company reserve requirements (such as cancellable accident and health coverage), such coverage is subject to the discounting provisions for property and casualty companies. It is assumed, for purposes of applying such provisions, that unpaid losses at the end of an accident year are paid in the year following the accident year. The type of insurance to which this rule applies primarily is medical reimbursement coverage.

Further, one type of accident and health insurance (credit disability) is more in the nature of a property and casualty type of line of business and, under the bill, is treated as a Schedule 0 line of business. While the committee did not consider it appropriate to treat credit disability in the same manner as life insurance, it concluded that treatment in the same manner as medical reimbursement would not reflect the typical loss payment pattern of such disability coverage. Therefore, credit disability is discounted over the same period as Schedule 0 lines of business.

Election by company to use its own experience.—(Under the bill, a taxpayer may elect to apply the general loss discounting rules by reference to the taxpayer's own historical loss payment pattern as of the end of a taxable year (the determination year). The taxpayer, if the election is made, is to use the taxpayer's most recent experience as reported on its annual statement. For each of the 5 years in the determination period, the taxpayer's most recent experience is to be used. Once a determination has been made by a taxpayer with respect to an accident year and line of business, the taxpayer may not redetermine its loss payment pattern to adjust for more recent information. This treatment is consistent with the general vintaging approach used for determining loss payment patterns on the aggregate experience for the industry.

The election by a taxpayer to use its own experience, once made, applies to all accident years and all lines of business of the taxpayer (except international and reinsurance lines, for which no election is permitted), and may not be revoked without the consent of the Secretary. The election may be made with respect to any determination year and applies for that determination year and the 4 succeeding calendar years. As under the general rules, the determination year is calendar year 1987 and each 5th succeeding calendar year after 1987.

The committee intends that the Secretary will permit companies to derive their loss payment patterns based on the information reported on the annual statement. To determine the assumed loss payment pattern for each "vintage" (i.e., accident year for a line of business), the following method may be used. The amount of losses deemed to be paid for the vintage in the current taxable year with respect to any vintage is the total paid losses for the vintage for the taxable year, divided by the total of paid and unpaid losses for the vintage in that taxable year, minus the same calculation for the subsequent vintage done for the taxable year.

For example, if a company's annual statement for 1985 shows that, for a line of business with an accident year of 1980 with total incurred losses of $100, $65 dollars are paid losses and $35 are unpaid losses. With respect to accident year 1981, for total incurred losses of $180, $60 dollars have been paid and $120 are unpaid losses. To determine the loss payment pattern for that line of business for the accident year plus 5 (i.e., 1980 is the accident year and 1985 is the accident year plus 5), the percentage of losses deemed paid in the accident year plus 5 (65 divided by 100 or 65 percent) is reduced by the percentage of losses deemed paid in the accident year plus 4 (60 divided by 180 or 33-1/3 percent). Therefore, the percentage of incurred losses deemed paid in the accident year plus 5 is 65 percent minus 33-1/3 percent or 21-2/3 percent.

Special rule for title insurance.—Under the bill, the treatment of unearned premiums of title insurance companies is clarified for purposes of the partial disallowance of a deduction for unearned premiums and the discounting of unpaid losses. Thus, section 832(b)(4) does not apply to amounts denominated as unearned premiums by a title insurance company (including amounts characterized under State law as unearned premium reserves). Rather, such reserves are to be treated as reserves for unpaid losses under the contract subject to the new discounting rules. To the extent that the amount of such reserves is in excess of the unpaid loss reserves necessary for the protection of policyholders, it is not treated as a reserve amount.

Effective Dates.—Under the bill, the provisions relating to the treatment of loss reserve deductions for property and casualty

Act § 1023   ¶ 3963

companies apply to taxable years beginning after December 31, 1986.

Under the bill, a transitional rule is provided with respect to the unpaid losses on outstanding business before the effective date of the provision. Under this transitional rule, for purposes of calculating a company's change in unpaid losses with respect to outstanding business, the unpaid losses at the end of the last taxable year beginning before January 1, 1987, and the unpaid losses as of the beginning of the first taxable year beginning after December 31, 1986, are determined as if the discounting provisions had applied to the unpaid losses (and unpaid expenses) in the last taxable year beginning before January 1, 1987. In addition, the interest rate and loss payment pattern assumptions with respect to such outstanding business is to be computed by using the rate and loss payment pattern applicable to accident years ending in 1987.

Further, the bill provides a fresh start with respect to undiscounted loss reserves applicable to the last taxable year beginning before January 1, 1987. Under this fresh start rule, the difference between the amount of undiscounted unpaid loss reserves and unpaid expenses (the recomputed reserves) at the end of the last taxable year beginning before January 1, 1987, and the amount of the discounted balances determined under the transitional rule, are not taken into account for purposes of determining the taxable income of an insurance company after the effective date.

Such fresh start adjustment is to be taken into account in full in the first taxable year to which the discounting provisions apply (i.e., the first taxable year beginning after December 31, 1986), for purposes of calculating any adjustment to earnings and profits. Any reserve strengthening after March 1, 1986, is to be treated as reserve strengthening for the first taxable year beginning after December 31, 1986. The committee intends that any adjustments to reserves that are attributable to changes in reserves on account of changes in the basis for computing reserves (i.e., reserve strengthening or reserve weakening) in a taxable year beginning before January 1, 1987, are not taken into account in determining taxable income after the effective date.

[Conference Report]

*   *   *   *   *

Conference Agreement.—The conference agreement follows the Senate amendment, with modifications.

Interest rate.—Under the conference agreement, the interest rate to be used for purposes of applying the discounting methodology to a line of business is equal to 100 percent of the average of the applicable Federal mid-term rates (as defined in sec. 1274(d) converted to a rate based on annual compounding) effective as of the beginning of each of the calendar months in the base period. The base period means the most recent 60 calendar months ending before the beginning of the calendar year for which the

determination is made. However, no calendar month before August 1986 is included in the base period. For accident years of a company beginning before or in 1987, the rate to be applied is 100 percent of the average of the applicable Federal mid-term rates effective as of the beginning of the 5 last calendar months of 1986.

Loss payment patterns.—The conference agreement follows the Senate amendment provision requiring the Secretary of the Treasury to determine a loss payment pattern with respect to each line of business reported on Schedules O and P for calendar year 1987 and each 5th calendar year after 1987.

In the case of unallocated reinsurance and international lines of business, the conference agreement provides that the discounting provisions are implemented on the basis of composite discount factors derived by combining the payment patterns for all Schedule P lines. The conference agreement clarifies that international and reinsurance business that is allocated to a particular line of business and taken account of as part of that line of business is discounted in accordance with the rules applicable to that line of business, not the general rules applicable to unallocated international and reinsurance business. Thus, for example, reinsurance of accident and health business that is allocated to that line of business as reported on the annual statement of the taxpayer is subject to the discounting rules applicable to that line of business. The Treasury Department may, by regulation, address the treatment of distortions in the loss payment patterns arising where, for example, reinsurance of "short tail" business is allocated to that line of business and reinsurance of "long tail" business is unallocated, or vice versa.

In the case of life insurance companies and property and casualty companies with respect to the types of accident and health insurance coverage (other than disability insurance) that are not currently subject to the life insurance company reserve requirements (such as cancellable accident and health coverage), such coverage is subject to the discounting provisions for property and casualty insurance companies with the clarification that life insurance companies may not deduct loss adjustment expenses that do not meet the all-events test applicable under sec. 461 of the Code. Thus, it is not intended that noncancellable accident and health insurance business currently subject to life insurance reserve rules (sec. 807(d)) be subject to discounting under the property and casualty discounting methodology. Similarly, life insurance companies are not intended to be permitted to deduct loss adjustment expenses by virtue of the application of the property and casualty discounting methodology with respect to cancellable accident and health insurance business, if any, of such companies.

Election to use historical experience.—The conference agreement follows the Senate amendment with respect to the provision that a taxpayer may elect to apply discounting with respect to the taxpayer's own historical loss payment pattern. Authority is granted to provide in Treasury regulations that an election under this provision does not apply to a line of business in which the taxpayer does not have sufficient historical experience. Generally, it is intended that the election be available only for those lines of business for which the taxpayer's own historical experience is statistically significant. Thus, if the taxpayer's business in any line of business does not represent a meaningful portion of the total industry-wide business in that line of business, then it is intended that the election not apply with respect to that line of business. Generally, a meaningful portion would be a portion representing business in at least the 10th percentile of industry-wide reserves for a line of business for the determination year with respect to which the election is made. That is, no election would be permitted for any line of business where 90 percent of taxpayers that have reserves in that line of business, have reserves that are bigger than those of the taxpayer for the line of business for the determination year.

Extension of payment pattern for long-tail lines.—The conference agreement follows the Senate amendment with respect to the discounting period for certain long-tail lines of business, with a modification. The conference agreement provides that, if the amount of losses treated as paid in the penultimate year of the payment pattern is zero or negative, then the average of the amounts treated as paid in the 3 penultimate years of the payment pattern is the amount

taken into account, for purposes of extending the loss payment pattern by up to an additional 5 years. In the event that the average of the 3 years gives rise to a negative number for any line of business, additional preceding years of the payment pattern should be averaged in successively, until the average is a positive number. This rule applies to the extension of all payment patterns, including those where the taxpayer has elected to determine its loss payment patterns on the basis of its own historical experience.

The following example illustrates the appropriate methodology for determining a payment pattern for a line of business for any given accident year. In the case of an electing taxpayer, the data used would be the annual statement data for the line of business reported on the taxpayer's most recently filed annual statement. Example 1 illustrates the development of a payment pattern for a Schedule P line, and example 2 illustrates the development of a payment pattern for a Schedule O line of business.

Example 1: payment pattern for Schedule P line

The development of reserve discount factors for a Schedule P line of business is illustrated in Table 1. This example is based on the 1985 consolidated industry totals for automobile liability. The 1985 annual statement is used because it contains the most recent loss development data.

[Table 1 appears on next page]

Table 1.—Reserve Discount Factor Development, Automobile Liability

[Discount rate is assumed to be 7 percent per annum]

| Years before current year | Year loss incurred | Loss and loss expense payments to date (thousands) | Total losses and loss expense incurred [1] (thousands) | Cumulative fraction of loss paid [2] (percent) | Fraction of loss paid during year [3] (percent) | Perentage | | Reserve discount factor [4] (percent) |
						Fraction of loss unpaid, year-end (percent)	Discounted fraction unpaid, year-end (percent)	
AY+0	1985	$10,734,519	$31,281,287	34.3161	34.3161	65.6839	58.7454	89.4365
AY+1	1984	10,397,279	28,217,053	65.1992	30.8831	34.8008	30.9119	88.8251
AY+2	1983	20,047,248	24,986,353	80.2335	15.0343	19.7665	17.5241	88.6555
AY+3	1982	19,808,529	22,243,403	89.0535	8.8200	10.9465	9.6273	87.9486
AY+4	1981	18,974,882	20,225,272	93.8149	4.7614	6.1851	5.3760	86.9181
AY+5	1980	17,105,852	17,717,213	96.5493	2.7344	3.4507	2.9238	84.7308
AY+6	1979	16,266,022	16,633,374	97.7915	1.2422	2.2085	1.8435	83.4743
AY+7	1978	14,534,843	14,766,868	98.4287	.6372	1.5713	1.3135	83.5901
AY+8	1977	12,853,464	13,027,563	98.6636	.2349	1.3364	1.1624	86.9808
AY+9	1976	11,389,407	11,506,437	98.9829	.3193	1.0171	.9135	89.8135
AY+10	Pre76	91,306,371	91,545,592	NA	.3193	.6978	.6472	92.7417
AY+11	NA	NA	NA	NA	.3193	.3785	.3622	95.6845
AY+12	NA	NA	NA	NA	.3193	.0592	.0572	96.6736
AY+13	NA	NA	NA	NA	.0592	0	0	96.6736

[1] "Total losses and loss expense incurred" equals "loss and loss expense payments" plus "losses unpaid" plus "loss expense unpaid" as defined in Schedule P.

[2] "Cumulative fraction of loss paid", equals ratio of "loss and loss expense payments" to "total losses and loss expense incurred".

[3] "Fraction of loss paid during year", equals the change in the "cumulative fraction of loss paid" from the previous year for AY+0 through AY+9 (see text for computation after AY+9).

[4] The reserve discount factor is 96.6736 in AY+12 and all subsequent years.

Schedule P of the 1985 annual statement itemizes "loss and loss expense payments" and "total losses and loss expense incurred" for the 10-year period 1976-1985 and the total for all years before 1976 (see Table 1). The number of years that have passed since the accident year through the current year (1985) is shown in the first column of Table 1; for example, the year 1976 is referred to as AY + 9. From these data, the cumulative fraction of loss and loss expense paid through 1985, for losses incurred in 1976-1985, is computed as the ratio of "loss and loss expense payments" to "total losses and loss expense incurred". For AY + 0 through AY + 9, the fraction of loss and expense paid during each accident year is estimated as the change in the cumulative fraction of loss and expense paid from the previous accident year. Since unpaid loss and loss expense at the end of AY + 9 (1.0171 percent) exceeds the amount of loss and expense payments in AY + 9 (0.3193 percent), the special rule for long-tail lines is applicable. Under this rule, unpaid loss and expenses at the end of AY + 9 are deemed to be paid at at a rate of 0.3193 percent in AY + 10 through AY + 12, and the balance, 0.0592 percent, is deemed to be paid in AY + 13.

The reserve discount factors are equal to the ratio of discounted unpaid losses to undiscounted unpaid losses in each accident year. For purposes of discounting, losses are deemed to be paid in the middle of the year. For example, if the discount rate is 7 percent, then the discounted unpaid loss in AY + 11 is computed as the present value of losses deemed to be paid in AY + 12 and AY + 13:

$$0.3622 \quad = \frac{0.3193}{1.07 \ 1/2} + \frac{0.0592}{1.07 \ 3/2}$$

Consequently, as shown in Table 1, the reserve discount factor for AY + 11 is 95.6845 percent, the ratio of discounted unpaid losses (0.3622 percent) to undiscounted unpaid losses (0.3785 percent) in AY + 11. The reserve discount factor for the year that the last claim is deemed to be paid (AY + 13), and for all subsequent years, is the reserve discount factor for the preceding year (96.6736 percent in AY + 12).

Example 2: payment pattern for a schedule O line

The development of reserve discount factors for a schedule O line of business is illustrated in Table 2. This example is based on the 1985 consolidated industry totals for fire insurance. The 1985 annual statement is used because it contains the most recent loss development data.

[Table 2 appears on next page.]

Table 2.—Reserve Discount Factor Development, Fire Insurance

[Discount rate is assumed to be 7 percent per annum]

Years before current year	Year loss incurred	Net losses paid in year¹ (thousands)	Unpaid losses beginning year²	Fraction unpaid loss paid in year³ (percent)	Fraction of total loss paid in year⁴ (percent)	Fraction of total loss unpaid, year-end (percent)	Discounted fraction unpaid year-end (percent)	Reserve discount factor⁵ (percent)
AY + 0	1985	$1,182,445	$2,142,829	55.1815	55.1815	44.8185	42.1950	94.1464
AY + 1	1984	687,222	944,426	72,661	32.6127	12.2058	11.4138	93.5114
AY + 2	Pre84	196,764	462,600	NA	6.1029	6.1029	5.8999	96.6736
AY + 3		NA	NA	NA	6.1029	0	0	96.6736

¹ "Net losses paid in year" equals "losses paid during the year less reinsurance received during the year" less "salvage and subrogation received in the current year" as defined in Schedule O.

² "Unpaid losses, beginning year" equals "net losses paid in year" plus "losses unpaid" as defined in Schedule O.

³ "Fraction unpaid loss paid in year" equals ratio of "net losses paid in year" to "unpaid losses, beginning year".

⁴ "Fraction of total loss paid in year" equals "fraction unpaid loss paid in year" times previous year's "fraction of total loss unpaid, year-end" for AY + 0 and AY + 1 (see text for computation after AY × 1).

⁵ The reserve discount factor is 96.6736 in AY × 2 and all subsequent years.

Schedule O of the 1985 annual statement itemizes "losses paid" and "losses unpaid" for the 2-year period 1984-1985 and the total for all years before 1984 (see Table 2).[1] The number of years that have passed since the accident year through the current year (1985) is shown in the first column of Table 2; for example, the year 1984 is referred to as AY + 1. From these data, the fraction of unpaid losses paid in 1985, for losses incurred in 1984 and 1985, is computed as the ratio of "net losses paid in year" to "unpaid losses, beginning year". For AY + O and AY + 1, the fraction of total loss paid in the current year is estimated as the fraction of unpaid losses paid in the current year times the previous year's fraction of total loss unpaid at year-end. The fraction of loss paid during AY + 2 and AY + 3 is deemed to be one-half of the fraction of total loss unpaid at the end of AY + 1 (6.1029 percent equals one-half of 12.2058 percent).

The reserve discount factors are equal to the ratio of discounted unpaid losses to undiscounted unpaid losses in each accident year. For purposes of discounting, losses are deemed to be paid in the middle of the year. For example, if the discount rate is 7 percent, then the discounted unpaid loss in AY + 1 is computed as the present value of losses deemed to be paid in AY + 2 and AY + 3:

$$11.4138 = \frac{6.1029}{1.07\ 1/2} + \frac{6.1029}{1.07\ 3/2}$$

Consequently, as shown in Table 2, the reserve discount factor for AY + 1 is 93 5114 percent, the ratio of discounted unpaid losses (11.4188 percent) to undiscounted unpaid losses (12.2053 percent) in AY + 1. The reserve discount factor for the year that the last claim is deemed to be paid (AY + 3), and for all subsequent years, is the reserve discount factor for the preceding year (96.6736 percent in AY + 2).

Title insurance reserves.—In the case of title insurers, the conference agreement provides that the amount of the taxpayer's unearned premium reserve determined under present law is subject to discounting at the rate generally applicable to property and casualty insurers loss reserves.[2] The amount of the unearned premium reserve subject to discounting is the amount shown on the yearly statement filed for State insurance regulatory purposes for the year ending with or within the taxable year. The loss payment pattern to be applied for purposes of discounting these reserve amounts is the period and pattern over which such reserves for that year are to be included in income in accordance with applicable State law. The rate and

amount of inclusion in income for statutory accounting purposes is considered to determine the timing of and amount of releases from such reserves which are included in income for income tax purposes. The applicable interest rate is the rate applicable, for the year the premiums are received, under the loss reserve discounting rules applicable to property and casualty insurance companies.

Title insurance case reserves (i.e., known claims reserves) are subject to discounting under the provisions generally applicable to property and casualty insurance loss reserves.

A fresh start for discounting title insurance reserves is provided, calculated in a manner similar to the fresh start for other property and casualty company loss reserves.

This treatment is provided for title insurance reserves because of the deferral and the subsequent failure to acknowledge the time value of money which results under present law with respect to title insurance unearned premium reserves.

Fresh start adjustment.—The conference agreement follows the Senate amendment with respect to providing a fresh start adjustment—i.e., a forgiveness of income—for the reduction in reserves resulting from discounting the opening reserves in the first post-effective date taxable year of the provision. The conference agreement modifies the Senate amendment with respect to the treatment of reserve strengthening under the fresh start income forgiveness provision. Under the conference agreement, reserve strengthening in taxable years beginning after December 31, 1985, is not treated as a reserve amount for purposes of determining the amount of the fresh start. Instead, such reserve strengthening additions to loss reserves in taxable years beginning in 1986 are treated as changes to reserves in taxable years beginning in 1987, and are subject to discounting. Reserve strengthening is considered to include all additions to reserves attributable to an increase in an estimate of a reserve established for a prior accident year (taking into account claims paid with respect to that accident year), and all additions to reserves resulting from a change in the assumptions (other than changes in assumed interest rates applicable to reserves for the 1986 accident year) used in estimating losses for the 1986 accident year, as well as all unspecified or unallocated additions to loss reserves. This provision is intended to prevent taxpayers from artificially increasing the amount of income that is forgiven under the fresh start provision.

The amount of the fresh start forgiveness of income is included in earnings and profits

---

[Footnote ¶ 3963 continued]

[1] Part 1 of Schedule O contains data on losses; part 2 contains data on loss adjustment expense. In this example, loss adjustment expense is disregarded because the consolidated industry totals for part 2 data are not published. A taxpayer electing its own experience is required to compute reserve discount factors using combined loss and loss expense development data.

[2] No inference is intended with respect to the applicability of Rev. Rule, 23-174 and 84-107, above.

for the taxpayer's first taxable year beginning after December 31, 1986.

Effective date.—The loss reserve discounting provisions are effective for taxable years beginning after December 31, 1986.

[¶ 3964] SECTION 1024. REPEAL OF PROTECTION AGAINST LOSS ACCOUNT; REVISION OF SPECIAL TREATMENT FOR SMALL COMPANIES; COMBINATION OF PARTS II AND III.

(Secs. 501, 821-826, 831, 834, and 835 of the Code)

[Conference Report]

*　　*　　*　　*　　*　　*

* * * Protection against loss account for mutual companies

Present Law.—Mutual property and casualty insurance companies are permitted a deduction for contributions (which are bookkeeping entries) to a protection against loss ("PAL") account (sec. 824). The amount of the deduction is equal to the sum of 1 percent of the underwriting losses for the year plus 25 percent of statutory underwriting income, plus certain windstorm and other losses. In general, certain contributions to the PAL account are taken into income after a 5-year period. The PAL account thus effects a 5-year deferral (and, in some cases, a permanent deferral) of a portion of mutual company underwriting income.

House Bill.—Under the House bill, the deduction for contributions to a PAL account (sec. 824) is repealed. PAL account balances are includible in income over the first 5 taxable years beginning after December 31, 1985. The amount includible is the greater of the amount includible for the year had the subtraction provisions of section 824 remained in effect (but no further additions had been made), or an amount equal to a required percentage of the balance remaining in the account at the close of the preceding taxable year. For taxable years beginning in 1986, the required percentage is 20; for 1987, 40; for 1988, 60; for 1989, 80; and for 1990, 100.

The repeal of the deduction for contributions to a PAL account is effective for taxable years beginning after December 31, 1985.

Senate Amendment.—The Senate amendment is the same as the House bill, except that the required percentage for 1987 is 20; for 1988, 25; for 1989, 33-⅓; for 1990, 50; and for 1991, 100.

The repeal of the deduction for contributions to a PAL account is effective for taxable years beginning after December 31, 1986.

Conference Agreement.—The conference agreement follows the Senate amendment, *[Effective Date]* effective for taxable year beginning after December 31, 1986, except that, with respect to recovery of amounts contributed to PAL accounts in taxable years beginning before December 31, 1986, the conference agreement provides that such amounts are recovered and included in income in accordance with present law (as if sec. 824 remained in effect). Therefore the ratable inclusion rule in the House bill and the Senate amendment is not adopted. The

provision is effective with respect to taxable years beginning after December 31, 1986.

* * * Special exemptions, rates, and deductions of small companies

Present Law.—Under present law, mutual property and casualty companies are classified into three categories depending upon the amounts of the gross receipts. Mutual companies with certain gross receipts not in excess of $150,000 are tax-exempt (sec. 501(c)(15)). Companies whose gross receipts exceed $150,000 but do not exceed $500,000 are "small mutuals" and generally are taxed solely on investment income. This provision does not apply to any mutual company that has a balance in its PAL account, or that, pursuant to a special election, chooses to be taxed on both its underwriting and investment income. Additionally, small mutuals which are subject to tax because their gross receipts exceed $150,000 may claim the benefit of a special rule which phases in the regular tax on investment income as gross receipts increase from $150,000 to $250,000. Companies whose gross receipts exceed $500,000 are ordinary mutuals taxed on both investment and underwriting income. Mutual reciprocal underwriters or interinsurers are generally taxed as mutual insurance companies, subject to special rules (sec. 826).

Like stock companies, ordinary mutuals generally are subject to the regular corporate income tax rates. Mutuals whose taxable income does not exceed $12,000 pay tax at a lower rate. No tax is imposed on the first $6,000 of taxable income, and a tax of 30 percent is imposed on the next $6,000 of taxable income. For small mutual companies which are taxable on investment income, no tax is imposed on the first $3,000 of taxable investment income, and a tax of 30 percent is imposed on taxable investment income between $3,000 and $6,000.

Mutual companies that receive a gross amount from premiums and certain investment income of less than $1,100,000 are allowed a special deduction against their underwriting income (if it is subject to tax). The maximum amount of the deduction is $6,000, and the deduction phases out as the gross amount increases from $500,000 to $1,100,000.

House Bill.—The House bill provides that mutual and stock property and casualty companies are eligible for exemption from tax if their net written premiums or direct written premiums (whichever is greater) do not exceed $500,000.

In addition, the House bill repeals the special rates, deductions and exemptions for small mutual companies and substitutes a single provision (sec. 847 of the Code). The new provision allows mutual and stock companies with net written premiums or direct written premiums (whichever is greater) in excess of $500,000 but less than $2 million to elect to be taxed only on taxable investment income. To determine the amount of direct or net written premiums of a member of a controlled group of corporations, the direct or net written premiums of all members of the controlled group are aggregated.

The provisions are effective for taxable years beginning after December 31, 1985.

Senate Amendment.—The Senate amendment is the same as the House bill, except that the $500,000 threshold is reduced to $350,000 and the $2 million threshold is reduced to $1,200,000. The provisions are

effective for taxable years beginning after December 31, 1986.

Conference Agreement.—The conference agreement follows the Senate amendment, [*Effective date.*—] effective for taxable year beginning after December 31, 1986, with the modification that, in determining whether a taxpayer is a member of a controlled group of corporations for purposes of eligibility for the provision, a 50 percent ownership test applies.

Parts II and III of Subchapter L of the Code are consolidated into Part II, under the conference agreement. Part II of Subchapter L relates generally to taxation of property and casualty insurance companies.

[¶ 3965] SECTION 1025. STUDY OF TREATMENT OF PROPERTY AND CASUALTY INSURANCE COMPANIES.

Conference Report

* * * * * *

House Bill.—The Treasury Department is required to conduct a study of the tax treatment of policyholder dividends by mutual property and casualty insurance companies. The results of the study, together with recommendations, are to be submitted to the Committee on Ways and Means of the House of Representatives, the Committee on Finance of the Senate, and the Joint Committee on Taxation no later than January 1, 1987.

* * * * * *

Conference Agreement.—The conference agreement follows the House bill, with modifications. The scope of the study is expanded to cover corporate minimum tax issues as well as regular tax issues relating to the tax treatment of policyholder dividends of mutual property and casualty insurance companies. In addition, the study is to cover the operation and effectiveness of the conference agreement provisions relating to the regular and minimum tax of property and casualty insurance companies, and is to examine whether the revenue targets projected for the provisions are met. The study is due January 1, 1989.

[¶ 3966] SECTION 1031. PHYSICIANS' AND SURGEONS' MUTUAL PROTECTION AND INTERINDEMNITY ARRANGEMENTS OR ASSOCIATIONS.

[Conference Report]

* * * * * *

Senate Amendment.—Contributions to a pooled malpractice insurance association are currently deductible to the extent they do not exceed the cost of a commercial insurance premium for annual coverage and are included in the association's income. Refunds of such contributions are deductible to the fund only to the extent included in income of the

recipient. The provision applies to associations operating under State law prior to January 1, 1984.

[Effective date.—] The provision is effective for contributions and refunds after the date of enactment.

Conference Agreement.—The conference agreement follows the Senate amendment, effective for contributions and refunds after the date of enactment.

[¶ 3968] SECTION 1101. LIMITATIONS ON IRA DEDUCTIONS FOR ACTIVE PARTICIPANTS IN CERTAIN PENSION PLANS

(Sec. 219 of the Code)

[Conference Report]

* * * * * *

Senate Amendment

* * * * * *

Under the Senate amendment, no deductible IRA contribution may be made for any

taxable year if an individual is an active participant in an employer-maintained retirement plan for any part of the plan year ending with or within the individual's taxable year. For purposes of this rule, an employer-maintained retirement plan means (1) a qualified pension, profit-sharing, or stock bonus plan, (2) a qualified annuity plan (sec. 403(a)), (3) a simplified employee pension (sec. 408(k)), (4) a plan established for its employees by the United States, by a State or political subdivision, (5) a plan described in section 501(c)(18), or (6) a tax-sheltered annuity (sec. 403(b)).

The Senate amendment follows the pre-ERTA rule for determining whether an individual is an active participant in an employer-maintained retirement plan.

In the case of a defined benefit pension plan, an individual is treated as an active participant if the individual is not excluded under the eligibility requirements under the plan for any part of the plan year ending with or within the individual's taxable year. Thus, for example, if an individual satisfies the conditions for eligibility under a defined benefit pension plan, but is required to make an employee contribution to accrue any benefit attributable to employer contributions under the plan, the individual is treated as an active participant even if no employee contribution is made and, thus, no benefit is accrued for the plan year.

Under a money purchase pension plan, an individual is an active participant if any employer contribution or forfeiture is required to be allocated to the individual's account with respect to the plan year ending with or within the individual's taxable year, even if the individual is not employed at any time during the plan year (e.g., contributions are continued on behalf of a permanently disabled employee (sec. 415(c)(3)(C)) or the individual's taxable year (e.g., the individual separates from service before the beginning of the taxable year).

An individual is treated as an active participant under a profit-sharing or stock bonus plan if any employer contribution is added or any forfeiture is allocated to the individual's account during the individual's taxable year. A contribution is added to an individual's account on the later of the date the contribution is made or is allocated.

Finally, an individual is treated as an active participant for any taxable year in which the individual makes a voluntary or mandatory employer contribution. An individual is not treated as an active participant if earnings (rather than contributions or forfeitures) are allocated to the individual's account.

The determination of whether an individual is an active participant or whether amounts are contributed on the individual's behalf is made without regard to whether the individual's right to benefits under a plan are nonforfeitable.

Conference Agreement

The conference agreement generally follows the Senate amendment with modifications to retain the present-law IRA provisions for taxpayers with adjusted gross income (AGI) below certain levels, and to reduce the IRA deduction for active participants with AGI above those levels.

Under the conference agreement, an individual is permitted to make deductible IRA contributions up to the lesser of $2,000 or 100 percent of compensation (earned income, in the case of a self-employed individual) if (1) the individual (or a married couple if a joint return is filed) has AGI that does not exceed an applicable dollar amount, or (2) the individual is not an active participant (or, in the case of a married individual filing a joint return, neither the individual nor the individual's spouse is an active participant) in an employer-maintained retirement plan for any part of the plan year ending with or within the individual's taxable year.

The applicable dollar amount is (1) $25,000, in the case of an individual, (2) $40,000, in the case of a married couple filing a joint return, and (3) $0, in the case of a married couple filing separately. The IRA deduction limit is reduced by an amount that bears the same ratio to the applicable dollar limit as the taxpayer's AGI in excess of the applicable dollar amount (or, in the case of a married couple filing a joint return, the couple's AGI in excess of the applicable dollar amount) bears to $10,000. Thus, under the conference agreement, in the case of an active participant, the IRA deduction limit is $0 for (1) individuals with AGI above $35,000, (2) married couples filing a joint return with AGI above $50,000, and (3) married couples filing separately if a spouse has AGI above $10,000.

Under the conference agreement, the spousal IRA deduction limit is also proportionately reduced for AGI above the applicable dollar amount. Thus, the spousal IRA deduction limit (i.e., $2,250) is reduced by an amount that bears the same ratio to $2,250 as the excess of AGI over the applicable dollar amount bears to $10,000.

The deduction limit is rounded to the next lowest $10 in the case of a limit that is not a multiple of $10. In addition, the conference agreement provides a $200 floor on the IRA deduction limit for individuals whose AGI is not above the phaseout range. For example, an individual with AGI of $34,500 has an IRA deduction limit of $200 even though the phaseout would otherwise provide an IRA deduction limit of $100.

AGI, for purposes of determining the IRA deduction limit, is calculated without regard to any deductible IRA contributions made for the taxable year, but with regard to any taxable social security benefits (sec. 86) and with regard to any passive loss limitations (new sec. 469). In other words, AGI is calculated in the following order: (1) for purposes of the limitations on passive loss deductions, (2) for purposes of the amount of social security benefits that are taxable, and (3) for purposes of the IRA deduction limit.

The conference agreement clarifies that an unfunded deferred compensation plan of a State or local government or a tax-exempt organization (sec. 457) is not considered a plan established for its employees by a State or political subdivision, or by an agency or instrumentality of a State or political subdivision. As under the Senate amendment, the determination of active participant status under the conference agreement is made without regard to whether an individual's rights under an employer-maintained retirement plan are nonforfeitable (i.e., vested).

The conference agreement clarifies that, for purposes of the active participant rule, elective contributions (such as elective deferrals under a qualified cash or deferred arrangement) are treated as employer contributions.

The conference agreement clarifies that an individual is considered an active participant in a defined benefit plan if the individual is eligible to participate in the plan, even if the individual elects not to participate.

Under the conference agreement, the present-law rule relating to the time that contributions are required to be made is retained.

Therefore, an individual may make IRA contributions for a taxable year up to the due date of the individual's tax return for the taxable year without extensions. Of course, as under present law, the individual is required to designate the taxable year to which an IRA contribution relates when making the contribution.

[**Effective date.**—] The provision is effective for taxable years beginning after December 31, 1986. A taxpayer may make an IRA contribution for the 1986 taxable year up to the due date of the taxpayer's 1986 tax return (without extensions) under the present-law IRA rules.

[¶ 3969] SECTION 1102. NONDEDUCTIBLE CONTRIBUTIONS MAY BE MADE TO INDIVIDUAL RETIREMENT PLANS

(Sec. 408 of the Code)

[Senate Explanation]

*　　*　　*　　*　　*　　*

Explanation of Provisions.

*　　*　　*　　*　　*　　*

Under the bill, individuals who are active participants (and who, therefore, are not eligible to make deductible IRA contributions for a taxable year) may make designated nondeductible IRA contributions. The limit on designated nondeductible contributions for a taxable year is the lesser of 100 percent of compensation (earned income in the case of a self-employed individual) or $2,000 ($2,250 in the case of an additional contribution to a spousal IRA).

[Conference Report]

Conference Agreement

*　　*　　*　　*　　*　　*

As under the Senate amendment, the conference agreement permits individuals to make designated nondeductible IRA contributions to the extent that deductible contributions are not allowed. Thus, an individual may make nondeductible contributions to the extent of the excess of (1) the lesser of $2,000 or 100 percent of compensation over (2) the IRA deduction limit with respect to the individual. The nondeductible IRA limit is $2,250, in the case of a spousal IRA.

In addition, the conference agreement permits a taxpayer to elect to treat deductible IRA contributions as nondeductible. An individual might make such an election, for example, if the individual had no taxable income for the year after taking into account other deductions.

Under the conference agreement, a designated nondeductible contribution means any contribution to an IRA for a taxable year that is designated as a nondeductible contribution in the manner prescribed by the Secretary. The designation is to be made on the individual's tax return for the taxable

year to which the designation relates. Designated nondeductible contributions may be made up to the due date of the individual's tax return for the taxable year (without extensions).

An individual who files an amended return for a taxable year may change the designation of IRA contributions from deductible to nondeductible or vice versa. Such an amended return is to be treated as a return filed for the taxable year to which the return relates. Of course, under the usual rules, any increased tax liability that the individual may owe as a result of such a change in designation is to accompany the amended return.

An individual who makes a designated nondeductible contribution to an IRA for a taxable year or who receives a distribution from an IRA during a taxable year is required to provide such information as the Secretary may prescribe on the individual's tax return for the taxable year and, to the extent required, for succeeding taxable years. The information that may be required includes, but is not limited to (1) the amount of designated nondeductible contributions for the taxable year, (2) the aggregate amount of designated nondeductible contributions for all preceding taxable years which have not previously been withdrawn, (3) the aggregate balance of all IRAs of the individual as of the close of the calendar year with or within which the taxable year ends, and (4) the amount of distributions from IRAs during the taxable year.

If the required information is not provided on the individual's tax return for a taxable year, then all IRA contributions are presumed to have been deductible and, therefore, are taxable upon withdrawal from the IRA. The taxpayer can rebut this presumption with satisfactory evidence that the contributions were nondeductible.

Amounts withdrawn from an IRA during a taxable year are includible in income for the taxable year under rules similar to the rules applicable to qualified plans under section

72. Under special rules applicable to IRAs for purposes of section 72, (1) all IRAs of an individual are treated as one contract, (2) all distributions during a taxable year are treated as one distribution, (3) the value of the contract (calculated after adding back distributions during the year), income on the contract, and investment in the contract is computed as of the close of the calendar year with or within which the taxable year ends, and (4) the aggregate amount of withdrawals excludable from income for all taxable years shall not exceed the taxpayer's investment in the contract for all taxable years. The conference agreement provides that, if an individual withdraws an amount from an IRA during a taxable year and the individual has previously made both deductible and nondeductible IRA contributions, then the amount includible in income for the taxable year is the portion of the amount withdrawn which bears the same ratio to the amount withdrawn for the taxable year as the individual's aggregate nondeductible IRA contributions bear to the aggregate balance of all IRAs of the individual (including rollover IRAs and SEPs).

In the case of a withdrawal from an IRA, for purposes of the rules relating to withholding on pensions, annuities, and certain other deferred income, the payor is to assume that the amount withdrawn is includible in income.

For example, assume that (1) an individual makes a $2,000 IRA contribution for the individual's 1987 tax year, $1,500 of which is deductible, (2) no withdrawals are made from the IRA during the taxable year, (3) the account balance at the end of the taxable year is $2,200, and (4) no prior IRA contributions have been made. The individual is required to report all such information on the individual's 1987 tax return. For 1988, assume (1) the individual makes a $2,000 IRA contribution to another IRA account, none of which is deductible, (2) no withdrawals are made from the IRA during the taxable year, and (3) the aggregate account balance at the

end of the taxable year for both IRAs is $4,600. In the individual's 1989 taxable year, no IRA contributions are made and $1,000 is withdrawn from the IRA to which the individual contributed during the 1987 taxable year. At the end of the 1989 taxable year, the aggregate account balance of both IRAs is $4,000. The $1,000 withdrawn from an IRA during the 1989 tax year is treated as partially a return of nondeductible contributions, calculated as the percentage of $1,000 that the total nondeductible contributions ($500 plus $2,000) is of the total account balance ($4,000) at the end of the taxable year plus distributions during the year ($1,000). Thus, 2,500/5,000 or ½ of the $1,000 withdrawal is treated as a return of nondeductible contributions (and, therefore, is not taxable).

Under the conference agreement, an individual who overstates the amount of designated nondeductible contributions made for any taxable year is subject to a $100 penalty for each such overstatement unless the individual can demonstrate that the overstatement was due to reasonable cause.

The trustee of an IRA is required to report certain information to the Secretary and to the individuals for whom an IRA is maintained for each calendar year. This information is to include (1) contributions made to the IRA during the calendar year, (2) distributions from the IRA occurring during the calendar year, and (3) the aggregate account balance as of the end of the calendar year. This information is required to be reported by the January 31 following the end of the calendar year. In the case of a failure to report the required information, as under present law, the penalty for the failure is $25 for each day during which the failure occurs, but the total amount imposed on any person for a failure to report is not to exceed $15,000.

[**Effective date.**—] The provisions are effective for contributions and distributions in taxable years beginning after December 31, 1986.

[¶ 3970] SECTION 1103. SPOUSAL DEDUCTION ALLOWED WHERE SPOUSE HAS SMALL AMOUNT OF EARNED INCOME

[Conference Report]

*　　*　　*　　*　　*　　*

House Bill

*　　*　　*　　*　　*　　*

Under the House bill, the spousal IRA provision is amended to eliminate the requirement that the spouse have no compensation for the year in order to be eligible for the spousal IRA contribution. Therefore, under the bill, the spousal IRA is available either if (1) the spouse has no compensation for the taxable year, or (2) the spouse elects to

be treated for the taxable year as having no compensation.

For purposes of this provision, if a spousal IRA deduction is claimed on a couple's tax return for the taxable year, the spouse for whom the deduction is claimed is deemed to have elected to be treated as having no compensation.

Conference Agreement

*　　*　　*　　*　　*　　*

The conference agreement follows the House bill and the Senate amendment, effective for taxable years beginning before, on, or after December 31, 1985.

[¶ 3971] SECTION 1105. $7,000 LIMITATION ON ELECTIVE DEFER-RALS

(Sec. 402 of the Code)

[Senate Explanation]

* * * * * *

Explanation of Provisions.—

* * * * * *

In general.—Under the bill, the maximum amount that an employee can elect to defer for any taxable year under all cash or deferred arrangements in which the employee participates is limited to $7,000. The $7,000 cap is adjusted for inflation by reference to percentage increases in the social security wage base at the same time and in the same manner as the indexing of dollar limits on benefits under section 415.

Whether or not an employee has deferred more than $7,000 a year is determined without regard to any community property laws (In addition, the $7,000 limit is coordinated with elective deferrals under simplified employee pensions (SEPs)). In addition, the benefits under an unfunded deferred compensation plan of a State or local government (sec. 457) and a plan described in section 501(c)(18) are coordinated with the limits on elective deferrals under a qualified cash or deferred arrangement or a SEP. Moreover, for purposes of determining an individual's cap on elective deferrals for a year, the $7,000 cap (as indexed) is reduced by the amount of the individual's contributions to a tax-sheltered annuity contract to the extent that the contributions are made pursuant to a salary reduction agreement.

Unlike the overall limits on annual additions, which apply separately to amounts accumulated under plans of unrelated employers, this $7,000 cap limits all elective deferrals by an employee under all cash or deferred arrangements, SEPs, and sec. 501(c)(18) plans in which the employee participates. In addition, the $7,000 cap applies on the basis of the employee's taxable year, rather than the plan's limitation year.

Because, under the bill, the $7,000 limit applies only to elective deferrals, each employer may make additional contributions on behalf of any employee to the extent that such contributions, when aggregated with elective deferrals made by the employee under that employer's plan during the limitation year, do not exceed the overall limit (generally the lesser of 25 percent of compensation or $30,000).

Treatment of excess deferrals—If, in any taxable year, the total amount of elective deferrals contributed on behalf of an employee to all qualified cash or deferred arrangements and SEPs in which the employee participates exceeds $7,000, then the amount in excess of $7,000 (the excess deferrals) is included in the employee's gross income for the year to which the excess deferrals relate. In addition, with respect to any excess deferrals, no later than the first March 1 after the close of the employee's taxable year, the employee may allocate the excess deferrals among the arrangements in which the employee participates and may notify the administrator of each plan of the portion of the excess deferrals allocated to it. Under the bill, not later than the first April 15 after the close of the employee's taxable year, each plan may distribute to the employee the amount of the excess deferrals (plus income attributable to the excess) allocated to the plan. This distribution of excess deferrals may be made notwithstanding any other provision of law.

* * * * * *

The amount of excess deferrals distributed to an employee (plus the income thereon) are included in the employee's gross income for the year to which the excess deferrals relate. Thus, the amounts distributed are treated as if they had not been contributed to the qualified cash or deferred arrangement and are not subject to any additional income taxes for early withdrawals. However, such excess deferrals are taken into account in applying the special nondiscrimination tests to the elective deferrals. The committee intends that the Secretary may require the recalculation of the actual deferral percentages after the distribution of excess deferrals in certain cases.

Excess deferrals that are not distributed by the applicable April 15 date are not treated as after-tax employee contributions upon subsequent distribution even though such deferrals were included in the employee's income. In addition, undistributed excess deferrals are treated as elective deferrals subject to the special nondiscrimination test.

[Conference Report]

Conference Agreement.—The conference agreement is the same as the Senate amendment except that the method of indexing the $7,000 limit on annual elective deferrals is the same method that applies for purposes of adjusting the dollar limits on benefits under section 415. Therefore, the limits are adjusted for percentage increases in the Consumer Price Index (CPI), beginning in 1988.

In addition, as under the Senate amendment, the conference agreement provides that elective deferrals in excess of the annual limit are treated as elective deferrals for purposes of applying the special nondiscrimination requirements for qualified cash or deferred arrangements, except to the extent provided under rules prescribed by the Secretary. The Secretary is to prescribe rules preventing use of this rule to increase artificially the actual deferral percentage of the nonhighly compensated employees.

To the extent that an excess deferral is distributed by the first April 15 following the close of the taxable year in which the excess deferral was made, the excess deferral is not treated as an annual addition for purposes of the overall limits on contributions and benefits (sec. 415).

Similarly, excess deferrals distributed by the required date are not subject to the additional income tax on early withdrawals from qualified plans. In addition, the conferees intend that a plan distributing excess deferrals is not to be required to obtain the consent of the participant or the consent of the participant's spouse with respect to the distribution of excess deferrals. Further, a distribution of excess deferrals is not to be treated as violating an outstanding qualified

domestic relations order (within the meaning of sec. 414(p)).

[Effective date.—] The provision is effective for years beginning after December 31, 1986.

Further, the provisions do not apply to elective deferrals of an employee made during 1987 and attributable to services performed during 1986 under a qualified cash or deferred arrangement if, under the terms of the arrangement in effect on August 16, 1986, (1) the employee's election to make the elective deferrals is made before January 1, 1987, and (2) the employer identifies the amount of the elective deferral before January 1, 1987.

[¶ 3972] SECTION 1106. ADJUSTMENTS TO LIMITATIONS ON CONTRIBUTIONS AND BENEFITS UNDER QUALIFIED PLANS.

(Secs. 401, 402, 415 and 416 of the Code)

[Conference Report]

House Bill

Defined contribution plans.—The House bill provides that the dollar limit on annual additions under a defined contribution plan is decreased to the lesser of $25,000 or 25 percent of the dollar limit for defined benefit pension plans, as adjusted for inflation. Also, under the bill, the entire amount of nondeductible employee contributions to a plan is taken into account in computing the annual addition.

Defined benefit pension plans.—*In general.*—The House bill reduces the dollar limit on the employer-derived annual benefit under a defined benefit pension plan from $90,000 to $77,000. The $77,000 limit applies for benefits commencing at age 62 or thereafter. The bill conforms the limit on benefits commencing after age 65 to the reduced limit. The bill also reduces the limits applicable to early retirement.

Early retirement benefits.—Under the House bill, if retirement benefits under a defined benefit pension plan commence before age 62, then the $77,000 limit generally is reduced so that it is the actuarial equivalent of an annual benefit of $77,000 commencing at age 62. The bill provides, however, that the limit on the annual benefit for a participant who has attained age 55 is not to be less than $65,000.

The House bill provides special rules for commercial airline pilots and participants in a qualified police or firefighters' pension plan.

Under the House bill, in the case of a commercial airline pilot, the reduction in benefits for early retirement applies only to those airline pilots whose benefits begin before age 60 and the dollar limit applicable to annual benefits beginning at age 60 is $77,000. If benefits begin before age 60, the House bill provides that the dollar limit applicable to the annual benefits is determined under the general rules.

With respect to participants in a qualified police or firefighters' pension plan, the House bill provides that the dollar limit on benefits payable are never actuarily reduced to an amount less than $50,000, regardless of the age at which benefits commence.

Although the $77,000 limit provided by the House bill is adjusted for post-1986 inflation, no inflation adjustment is provided for the $65,000 limit. Under the bill, the limit on the annual benefit for a participant who has not attained age 55 is the actuarial equivalent of the limit at age 55.

Cost-of-living adjustments.—The House bill does not change the rules for making cost-of-living adjustments to the dollar limit on annual benefits under a defined benefit pension plan. Under the bill, however, cost-of-living adjustments to the dollar limit on annual additions under a defined contribution plan are suspended until cost-of-living adjustments to the limit on annual benefits increase that limit to an amount in excess of $100,000.

Qualified cost-of-living arrangements. — The House bill permits a defined benefit pension plan to maintain a qualified cost-of-living arrangement under which employer and employee contributions may be applied to provide cost-of-living increases to the primary benefit under the plan. If the arrangement qualifies, an employee contribution under the arrangement will not be treated as an annual addition in applying the separate limit on annual additions under defined contribution plans, but will be treated as an annual addition for purposes of applying the combined plan limit (sec. 415(e)). Further, under a qualified arrangement, the benefit attributable to an employee's contribution will be treated as a benefit derived from employer contributions for purposes of the limit on annual benefits. A qualified cost-of-living arrangement is required to comply with the dollar limits, election procedures, and nondiscrimination requirements of the bill.

Under the House bill, a key employee is generally not eligible to participate in a qualified cost-of-living arrangement. In a plan that is not top heavy, however, an employee who is a key employee solely because of officer status can participate in a qualified cost-of-living arrangement.

Phase-in of maximum benefit limit.—The House bill provides that the limit on annual benefits under a defined benefit plan is phased in on the basis of years of participation in a plan instead of years of service with the employer. For an employee who has not completed 10 years of plan participation, the otherwise applicable dollar limit for such employee is multiplied by a fraction. The numerator of the fraction is the number of years of participation completed, and the demominator of the fraction is 10. The 10-year phase-in period applies with respect to an increase in benefits due to a change in the benefit structure of a plan, except as provided under Treasury regulations. The phase-in generally does not apply to cost-of-living increases (within the meaning of sec. 415(d)) or post-retirement benefit increases. The application of the phase-in to plan mergers or spin-offs is to be determined under Treasury regulations.

Includible compensation.—The House bill provides a limit on compensation that may be taken into account under a plan. Under the bill, the $200,000 limit applicable under present law to top-heavy plans is reduced to seven times the limit on annual additions under a defined contribution plan ($175,000) and is applied to all qualified plans (whether or not top heavy). The limit applies for all purposes in testing a plan for discrimination (e.g., secs. 401(a)(4) and 401(k)(3)).

Excess distributions.—*In general.*—The House bill provides a new excise tax on excess distributions from tax-favored retirement savings arrangements (qualified retirement plans, tax-sheltered annuity programs, and IRAs). To the extent that aggregate annual distributions paid to a participant from tax-favored retirement savings arrangements during a calendar year are excess distributions, the distributions are subject to a 15-percent excise tax.

Generally, the excess distribution for a calendar year is the excess of (1) the aggregate amount of retirement distributions made with respect to an individual during the year, over (2) the greater of $112,500 or 125 percent of the limit for the year on annual benefits commencing at age 62 under a defined benefit pension plan. However, the bill provides that certain amounts are excluded in making this calculation. Under the bill, excludable distributions include amounts excluded from the participant's income because they are payable to a former spouse pursuant to a qualified domestic relations order (sec. 414(p)) and includible in the spouse's income. Of course, distributions payable to the former spouse are aggregated with any other retirement distributions payable to such spouse for purposes of determining whether the spouse

has excess retirement distributions subject to the tax. (Distributions paid to other alternate payees (e.g., minor children) are includible in applying the limit.) In addition, distributions made with respect to a participant after the death of the participant are disregarded in applying this annual limit and are subject instead to an additional estate tax.

Under this provision, the ceiling amount is not adjusted to reflect the age at which benefit payments commence. Thus, the limit is neither decreased to reflect early commencement of benefits nor increased to reflect deferred commencement. However, this tax will be reduced by the amount, if any, of income tax on early distributions (sec. 72(t)) to the extent attributable to such excess distribution.

In applying the additional tax, all distributions made with respect to any individual during a calendar year will be aggregated, regardless of the form of the distribution or the number of recipients. Thus, for example, all distributions received during a year, whether paid under a life annuity, a term certain, or any other benefit form (including an ad hoc distribution) generally will be aggregated in applying the tax.

Lump sum distributions.—A special higher ceiling applies for purposes of calculating the excess distribution for any calendar year in which an individual receives a lump sum distribution that is taxed under the favorable long-term capital gains or five-year averaging rules. The higher ceiling will be the lessor of (i) the portion of the lump sum distribution that is treated as long-term capital gains or taxed under the five-year averaging rules, or (ii) five times the otherwise applicable ceiling for such calendar year.

Post-death distributions—In lieu of subjecting post-death distributions (including distributions of death benefits) to the annual tax on excess distributions, the bill adds an additional estate tax equal to 15 percent of the individual's excess retirement accumulation (sec. 4980(A)). After the estate tax is imposed, post-death distributions are disregarded entirely in applying this tax. For example, beneficiaries who are receiving distributions with respect to a participant after the participant's death (other than certain former spouses receiving benefits pursuant to a qualified domestic relations order) are not required to aggregate those amounts with any other retirement distributions received on their own behalf.

The excess retirement accumulation is defined as the excess (if any) of the value of the decendent's interests in all qualified retirement plans, tax-sheltered annuities, and individual retirement accounts, over the present value of annual payments equal to the annual ceiling ($112,500 or, if greater, 125 percent of the applicable defined benefit plan dollar limit in effect on the date of death), over a period equal to the life expectancy of the individual immediately before death.

Act §1106 ¶3972

In calculating the amount of the excess retirement accumulation, the value of the decedent's interest in all plans, tax-sheltered annuities and individual retirement arrangements will be taken into account regardless of the number of beneficiaries. In addition, the decedent's interests are to be valued as of the date of death or, in the case of a decedent for whose estate an alternate valuation date has been elected, such alternate valuation date (sec. 2032).

Effective dates.—*In general.*—The provision generally applies to years beginning after December 31, 1985. Special rules are provided that permit deferral, until years beginning after December 31, 1987, of the time for amendment of plans to conform to the bill. For years beginning after December 31, 1985, however, the reduced limits are to be reflected in the computation of the amount of deductible employer contributions to a plan. A special effective date is provided for collectively bargained plans.

Current accrued benefits.—Transition rules are provided to insure that a participant's current accrued benefit under a defined benefit pension plan is not reduced merely because of the changes made by the provision. The protection of current accrued benefits applies to any individual who is a participant before January 1, 1985, in a plan that was in existence on November 6, 1985. Under the bill, an individual's current accrued benefit is the individual's accrued benefit as of the close of the last year beginning before January 1, 1986, expressed as an annual benefit determined pursuant to the rules in effect prior to the amendments made by the bill.

Generally, for purposes of determining an individual's current accrued benefit, no change in the terms and conditions of the plan after November 6, 1985, is taken into account. Under the bill, no later than the first plan year beginning after December 31, 1987, any accruals in excess of the greater of (1) the limit, as amended by the bill, or (2) the current accrued benefit, are to be reduced.

In the case of a plan maintained pursuant to one or more collective bargaining agreements ratified before November 6, 1985, the current accrued benefit of an individual is the individual's accrued benefit as of the close of the last year beginning before the earlier of (1) the date on which the last of the collective bargaining agreements terminates, or (2) January 1, 1991.

Employee contributions.—The provision specifies that inclusion of all employee contributions in the computation of the annual addition under a defined contribution plan does not affect the computation of the defined contribution fraction for years beginning before January 1, 1986.

Tax on excess distributions.—The 15-percent tax on excess distributions applies to benefits received in taxable years beginning after December 31, 1985.

Senate Amendment

Defined contribution plans.—Under the Senate amendment, the cost-of-living adjustment to the dollar limit on the annual addition under a defined contribution plan is deferred until the dollar limit on the annual benefit under a defined benefit pension plan exceeds $120,000. The Senate amendment follows the House bill with respect to the provision under which all nondeductible employee contributions to a plan are taken into account in computing the annual addition.

Defined benefit pension plans.—*Early retirement benefits.*—The Senate amendment conforms the normal retirement age used in determining the limit on annual benefits under a qualified defined benefit pension plan with the retirement age in effect under the Social Security Act (currently, age 65). Under the Senate amendment, the limit on the annual benefit under a defined benefit pension plan is actuarially reduced if the benefit commences before the social security normal retirement age. To the extent benefits commence on or after age 62, this reduction generally follows the manner in which the social security benefits are reduced for early benefit commencement. If benefits commence before age 62, the limit is the actuarial equivalent of the limit at age 62.

The provisions of the Senate amendment relating to limits on early retirement benefits for airline pilots, police, and firefighters generally are the same as under the House bill except that the Senate amendment (1) provides an exemption from the changes in the Senate amendment relating to the social security retirement age and (2) extends the special limits to certain correctional officers.

Cost-of-living adjustments.—The Senate amendment provides that the limit on the annual benefit under a defined benefit pension plan is to be adjusted for increases in the social security wage base. Under the amendment, legislative changes in the wage base are not to be reflected in making the adjustment to the limit on annual benefits under a defined benefit pension plan. The amendment provides that the limit on the annual addition under a defined contribution plan is determined by reference to the limit on annual benefits under a defined benefit pension plan.

Qualified cost-of-living arrangements. — The provisions of the Senate amendment relating to qualified cost-of-living arrangements are similar to the provisions of the House bill. Under the Senate amendment, however, additional rules are provided to limit accrued benefits under a qualified cost-of-living arrangement.

The Senate amendment provides that a right to an accrued benefit derived from employer contributions under a plan which contains a qualified cost-of-living arrangement is not treated as forfeitable solely because the plan provides that a participant is not entitled to receive that portion of the cost-of-living adjustment derived from employer contributions if the participant (1) fails to contribute the amount required to be paid under the plan for the cost-of-living adjustment, or (2) receives a distribution of the present value of the participant's accrued benefit derived from employer contributions in the form of a lump sum. The provision does not modify the fiduciary obligations or other rules of ERISA under which a plan administrator is to provide appropriate notice to a participant or beneficiary with respect to the consequences of a failure to make contributions required as a condition of obtaining a cost-of-living adjustment, or the consequences of receiving benefits in the form of a lump sum.

Phase-in of maximum benefit limit.—The provisions of the Senate amendment relating to the phase-in of the maximum limit on the annual benefit under a defined benefit pension plan are the same as under the House bill.

Includible compensation.—Under the Senate amendment the $200,000 limit on compensation that may be taken into account under a top-heavy plan is extended to all plans. The limit applies for most purposes for which compensation is taken into account under the Code, including the provisions relating to nondiscrimination. The limit is indexed at the same time and in the same manner as the dollar limit under defined benefit plans (sec. 415(d)).

Excess distributions.—The Senate amendment does not adopt the House bill provision relating to the excise tax on excess distributions.

Effective dates.—*In general.*—The provision generally applies to years beginning after December 31, 1986. Special rules are provided that permit deferral, until years beginning after December 31, 1988, of the time for amendment of plans to conform to the bill. For years beginning after December 31, 1986, however, the reduced limits are to be reflected in the computation of the amount of deductible employer contributions to a plan. A special effective date is provided for collectively bargained plans.

Current accrued benefits.—Transition rules are provided to insure that a participant's current accrued benefit under a defined benefit pension plan is not reduced merely because of the changes made by the provision.

The protection of current accrued benefits applies to any individual who is a participant, as of the first day of the first year to which the provision applies, in a plan that was in existence on May 6, 1986, and in all prior years satisfied the limits on contributions and benefits. Under the bill, an individual's current accrued benefit is the individual's accrued benefit as of the close of the last year beginning before January 1, 1987, expressed as an annual benefit determined pursuant to the rules in effect prior to the amendments made by the bill.

Generally, for purposes of determining an individual's current accrued benefit, no change in the terms and conditions of the plan after May 5, 1986, and no cost-of-living adjustment occurring after May 5, 1986, are to be taken into account. Under the bill, no later than the first plan year beginning after

December 31, 1988, any accruals in excess of the greater of (1) the limit, as amended by the bill, or (2) the current accrued benefit, are to be reduced.

In the case of a plan maintained pursuant to one or more collective bargaining agreements ratified before May 6, 1986, the current accrued benefit of an individual is the individual's accrued benefit as of the close of the last year beginning before the earlier of (1) the date on which the last of the collective bargaining agreements terminates, or (2) January 1, 1991. In addition, a change in the terms of the plan ratified before May 6, 1986, is treated as a change made before May 6, 1986.

Employee contributions.—The provision specifies that inclusion of all employee contributions in the computation of the annual addition under a defined contribution plan does not affect the computation of the defined contribution fraction for years beginning before January 1, 1987.

Conference Agreement

In general.—The conference agreement generally follows the Senate amendment with respect to the separate limits applicable to defined benefit pension plans and defined contribution plans except that the method of indexing the dollar limits is the same as under the House bill and present law, i.e., by reference to increases in the consumer price index. The conference agreement generally follows the House bill with respect to the imposition of an excise tax on benefit payments in excess of a specified level.

Defined benefit plans.— *Normal retirement age.*—The conference agreement follows the Senate amendment, except that the conference agreement exempts plans maintained by tax-exempt or governmental employers and a specified class of merchant seamen from the provisions relating to the normal retirement age and the elimination of the $75,000 floor for benefits beginning at age 55.

The conference agreement generally follows the special rules in the Senate amendment for commercial airline pilots and participants in a qualified police or firefighters' defined benefit pension plan. The conference agreement clarifies the definition of a qualified police or firefighters' plan and provides for indexing of the $50,000 limit applicable under the special rules for those plans. The conference agreement does not adopt the special rules for correctional officers.

In addition, the conference agreement clarifies the application of the special rules for pilots who retire before age 60. Under the conference agreement, in the case of any participant who is a commercial airline pilot, the actuarial reduction for early retirement does not reduce the limitation on benefits below (1) $75,000, if the participant's benefit begins at or after age 55 or (2) the actuarial equivalent of the $75,000 limitation at age 55, if the benefit begins before age 55. In addition, if, as of the time an individual retires, Federal Aviation Administration regulations require an individual to separate from service as a commercial airline pilot after attaining any age occurring on or after age 60 and before the social security retirement age, the age prescribed in such regulations is to be substituted for the social security retirement age, unless the individual separates from service prior to age 60. The conference agreement also clarifies that the special rule for commercial airline pilots is limited to individuals whose services as a pilot constitute substantially all of their services to which the benefit relates.

Phase-in of maximum benefit limit.—The conference agreement adopts the House bill and the Senate amendment provision under which the dollar limit on annual benefits under a qualified defined benefit pension plan is phased in over 10 years of plan participation is adopted.

As under both bills, the conference agreement also provides that, to the extent provided in regulations, the phase-in is to be applied to any benefit increases under a plan as though such increase were a new plan. Thus, for example, an amendment improving the benefit formula may increase benefits by up to one-tenth of the applicable dollar limit under section 415 for each year of participation after the amendment. A second amendment within 10 years of a prior amendment increasing benefits is subject to the limit under the phase-in triggered by the prior amendment (along with benefit increases under the prior amendment).

In addition, the conferees do not intend the phase-in for benefit increases to apply to benefit improvements due to updating compensation in a career average pay plan, cost-of-living increases for retirees, the beginning of a new collective bargaining cycle, and other reasonable benefit improvements that are not primarily for highly compensated employees. Thus, the conferees expect that the Secretary will apply a concentration test under which the phase-in will not apply to a benefit increase if the resulting increase in benefits is not primarily for highly compensated employees. In addition, the Secretary is to provide rules permitting the tacking of participation under separate plans in circumstances not inconsistent with the purposes of the phase-in.

Qualified cost-of-living arrangements. — The conference agreement generally follows the House bill with respect to qualified cost-of-living arrangements. The agreement clarifies the terms under which an employee may obtain an employer-provided cost-of-living subsidy. In addition, the conferees intend that the right to the employer-derived portion of a qualified cost-of-living benefit is part of an employee's accrued benefit subject to the vesting and benefit accrual requirements and the prohibition on a retroactive reduction in accrued benefits and is to be treated under rules similar to the rules applicable to employer-derived early retirement benefits.

For example, the employer-derived portion of the cost-of-living benefit need not be provided to an employee who fails to satisfy the applicable conditions for receipt of the benefit, including any required employee contributions. Further, the cost-of-living benefit need not be provided to an employee who has separated from service and received a distribution of the employee's benefit without making the required contributions for the cost-of-living benefit. The employee could, however, return to service and buy back the benefit by proper repayment of the cashed out benefit.

Defined contribution plans.—With respect to defined contribution plans, the conference agreement adopts the rules of the House bill applicable to cost-of-living adjustments and adopts the Senate amendment with respect to the amount of the current dollar limitation ($30,000). Although cost-of-living adjustments will be made to the defined benefit pension plan limit beginning in 1988, no cost-of-living adjustments to the defined contribution plan limit will be made until the $30,000 defined contribution plan limit is equal to 25 percent of the defined benefit dollar limit. The cost-of-living adjustment will be determined by reference to the consumer price index.

Under the agreement, contributions made by retired nonkey employees for retiree medical coverage are not subject to the percentage-of-compensation limit on annual additions.

Tax-sheltered annuities.—Under the conference agreement, the class of employers whose employees are entitled to the special catch-up elections for tax-sheltered annuities is expanded to include employers that are health and welfare service agencies. The agreement also provides a technical modification clarifying that the catch-up rules apply before separation from service.

Excess benefits.—The conference agreement generally follows the House bill with respect to the 15-percent excise tax on benefit payments in excess of $112,500 (indexed at the same time and in the same manner as the dollar limitation on annual benefits under a defined benefit pension plan). The conference agreement also clarifies that distributions attributable to after-tax employee contributions and distributions not includible in income by reason of a rollover contribution are not taken into account in applying the tax. All other amounts not specifically exempted are taken into account.

The conference agreement does not permit accrued benefits to be reduced retroactively to avoid the excise tax.

The conference agreement also modifies the rule providing an increased limit in the case of a lump-sum distribution. Under the agreement, if an individual elects lump-sum treatment (or long-term capital gains treatment), the $112,500 limit is applied separately to such lump-sum distribution and the limit is increased to 5 times the generally applicable limit with respect to the lump-sum distribution.

Also, the conference agreement clarifies that, with respect to the special provision relating to the estate tax, the tax may not be offset by any credits against the estate tax (such as the unified credit). In addition, the conferees intend that, in calculating the excess retirement accumulation, individuals are required to use reasonable interest rates in accordance with rules prescribed by the Secretary. The Secretary may, by regulations, prescribe a range of interest rates and other permissible assumptions for purposes of applying the excise tax.

Under the conference agreement, an individual may elect to be covered by (1) a special grandfather rule which exempts from the tax benefits accrued on August 1, 1986, or (2) an alternative rule which increases the $112,500 limit.

Under the grandfather, in the case of a defined contribution plan, the accrued benefit on August 1, 1986, is the participant's account balance on that date. In the case of a defined benefit plan, the accrued benefit on August 1, 1986, is determined assuming the participant separated from service on that date.

The grandfathered amounts are treated as if received on a pro rata basis and are taken into account in determining whether the $112,500 limit is exceeded. Under the pro rata rule, the portion of a distribution not subject to the excise tax is determined by multiplying the distribution by a fraction, the numerator of which is the grandfathered amount and the denominator of which is the accrued benefit on the date of the distribution under all plans or programs subject to the tax. Distributions after August 1, 1986, and before the effective date will reduce the grandfathered amount in the same manner.

For example, assume that at the time of a distribution of $250,000 an individual's grandfathered benefit is equal to 80% of the individual's accrued benefit on such date under all plans or programs subject to the tax. Under the grandfather, $200,000 (80 percent of $250,000) would be exempt from the tax. The remaining $50,000 would be subject to the tax because the grandfathered amounts are taken into account in determining whether the distribution exceeds the $112,500 limit.

The Secretary also has the authority to provide for an alternative grandfather rule for such individuals. The conferees intend that the Secretary consider providing an alternative grandfather rule based on a fraction, the numerator of which is the months of service between age 35 and August 1, 1986, and the denominator of which is total months of service after age 35. This rule applies as long as grandfathered amounts are taken into account in applying the excise tax to nongrandfathered amounts (as under the general grandfather rule).

The grandfather rule applies only with respect to an individual who (1) elects to have the grandfather rule apply and (2) has a grandfathered benefit of at least five times the $112,500 limit ($562,500). The election must be made on a return for a year begin-

ning no later than January 1, 1988, and shall be in such form and shall contain such information as the Secretary may prescribe.

If an individual does not elect the grandfather rule, then the amount of a distribution subject to the tax under the general rule is computed by substituting for $112,500 (as indexed), the greater of $150,000 and $112,500 (as indexed).

Includible compensation.—The conference agreement follows the Senate amendment. Under the agreement, the $200,000 limit applies for purposes of computing allowable deductions (sec. 404) as well as for purposes of determining the qualified status of a plan.

The conferees also clarify that, with respect to a defined benefit pension plan, the $200,000 limit applies to each year's compensation (including years prior to 1987), not solely to the final average or career average compensation of an individual.

Incorporation of limits by reference.—Under the conference agreement, a plan does not fail to meet the requirements for qualified status merely because the plan incorporates the benefit and contribution limits of section 415 of the Code by reference. The agreement provides that incorporation by reference is permitted except that, if the limitation may be applied in more than one manner, the plan is to specify the manner in which the limitation is to be applied.

For example, in the case of a defined contribution plan, Treasury regulations provide several methods for establishing a suspense account for excess annual additions and allocating amounts in the suspense account. Thus, the plan must specify which method is to be used.

The agreement does not change the requirements of present law relating to definitely determinable benefits and the requirement that profit-sharing and stock bonus plans must specify a definite allocation formula. Under the conference agreement, however, a plan does not fail to provide definitely determinable benefits merely because it incorporates the limits by reference. For example, if an employee participates in both a defined contribution plan and a defined benefit pension plan maintained by the same employer, the manner in which the employee's benefits will be adjusted to comply with the combined limitation (sec. 415(e)) is to be specified.

Effective dates.—The conference agreement follows the Senate amendment except that it does not allow a plan to accrue benefits in excess of the new limits (or the grandfathered current accrued benefit, if higher), even during the period prior to the time the plan must be amended.

A special effective date applies to plans maintained pursuant to a collective bargaining agreement. Under this special rule, in the case of employees covered under a plan maintained pursuant to a collective bargaining agreement between employee representatives and one or more employers ratified before March 1, 1986, the amendments are not effective for plan years beginning before the earlier of (1) January 1, 1989, or (2) the

date on which the last of the collective bargaining agreement terminates (determined without regard to any extensions in the collective bargaining agreement).

[¶ 3973] SECTION 1107. MODIFICATIONS OF SECTION 457

(Sec. 457 of the Code)

[House Explanation]

*   *   *   *   *   *

Present Law.—Under present law, a taxpayer using the cash receipts and disbursements method of accounting generally is not required to include compensation in income until it is actually or constructively received (sec. 451). Under the doctrine of constructive receipt, a taxpayer ordinarily will be deemed to have received income if the taxpayer has a right to receive that income and the exercise of that right is not subject to substantial restrictions (Treas. reg. sec. 1.451-2(a)).

In applying the doctrine of constructive receipt, a number of courts have held that when a taxpayer enters into an agreement with a payor to receive compensation on a deferred basis, rather than currently, the taxpayer generally will not be in constructive receipt of that compensation so long as the agreement is made before the taxpayer obtains an unqualified and unconditional right to the compensation.[1]

On February 3, 1978, the Internal Revenue Service issued proposed regulations that provide generally that, if payment of an amount of a taxpayer's fixed basic or regular compensation is deferred at the taxpayer's individual election to a taxable year later than that in which the amount would have been payable but for the election, then the deferred amount will be treated as received in the earlier taxable year.[2] These proposed regulations would have applied to plans maintained by taxable employers, State and local governments, and nongovernmental tax-exempt organizations.

In the Revenue Act of 1978, Congress exempted from the scope of the proposed regulations compensation deferred under an unfunded deferred compensation plan maintained by a taxable employer. Under the 1978 Act, the year that deferred compensation is to be included in gross income under certain private deferred compensation plans is determined under the principles set forth in the rulings, regulations, and judicial decisions relating to deferred compensation that were in effect on February 1, 1978.

The 1978 Act also exempted from the scope of the proposed regulation certain unfunded deferrals under an eligible deferred compensation plan of a State or local government (sec. 457). Certain tax-exempt rural electric cooperatives are also eligible

for this exemption. There is currently no specific statutory exemption from the regulation for the unfunded deferred compensation arrangements of nongovernmental tax-exempt organizations.

Under an eligible unfunded deferred compensation plan of a State or local government, an employee who elects to defer the receipt of current compensation is taxed on the amounts deferred when they are paid or made available. The maximum annual deferral under such a plan is the lesser of (1) $7,500 or (2) 33⅓ percent of compensation (net of the deferral). Amounts deferred under a tax-sheltered annuity are taken into account in calculating whether an employee's deferrals exceed the limits.

In general, amounts deferred under an eligible deferred compensation plan may not be made available to an employee prior to separation from service with the employer. In addition, distributions under the plan are required to commence no later than 60 days after the close of the later of (1) the year in which the employee attains the normal retirement age under the plan or (2) the year in which the employee separates from service. Amounts that are made available to an employee upon separation from service are includible in gross income in the taxable year in which they are made available.

Under an eligible deferred compensation plan, distributions must be made primarily for the benefit of participants, rather than beneficiaries. If a participant's benefits commence prior to death, the total amount of payments scheduled to be made to the participant must be more than 50 percent of the maximum amount that could have been paid to the participant if no provision were made for payments to the beneficiary. This rule differs from the incidental benefit rule applicable to qualified plans under which the value of benefits payable during a participant's lifetime must be projected to exceed 50 percent of the total value of benefits payable with respect to the participant.

Under an eligible plan, if a participant dies prior to the date the entire amount deferred has been paid out, the entire amount deferred (or the remaining portion thereof, if payment commenced prior to death) must be paid to the participant's beneficiary over a period not exceeding fifteen years, unless the beneficiary is the participant's surviving spouse. If the beneficiary is the participant's surviving spouse,

---

[Footnote ¶ 3972]   (1) *See Goldsmith* v. *United States,* 586 F.2d 810 (Ct. Cl. 1978); *James F. Oates,* 18 T.C. 570 (1952; aff'd, 207 F.2d 711 (7th Cir. 1953)), acq. (and prior nonacq. withdrawn) 1960-1 C.B. 5; *Howard Veit,* 8 T.C. 809 (1947), acq. 1947-2 C.B. 4; cf. *Kay Kimbell,* 41 B.T.A. 940 (1940), acq. and nonacq. 1940-2 C.B. 5, 12; *J.D. Amend,* 13 T.C. 178 (1949), acq. 1950-1 C.B. 1; *James Gould Cossens,* 19 T.C. 663 (1953); *Howard Veit,* 8 CCH Tax Ct. Mem. 919 (1949). *See,* also, Rev. Rul. 60-31, 1960-1 C.B. 174.

(2) Prop. reg. sec. 1.61-16.

benefits must be paid over the life of the surviving spouse or any shorter period.

Deferrals under any plan, agreement, or arrangement with the State that is not an eligible deferred compensation plan (other than a qualified State judicial plan, a qualified plan, or a tax-sheltered annuity) are includible in an employee's gross income when the amounts are not subject to a substantial risk of forfeiture, regardless of whether constructive receipt has taken place.

*   *   *   *   *   *

Explanation of Provisions.

Overview.—The bill applies the limitations and restrictions applicable to eligible and ineligible unfunded deferred compensation plans of State and local governments to unfunded deferred compensation plans maintained by nongovernmental tax-exempt organizations. In addition, the bill (1) requires that amounts deferred by an employee under a qualified cash or deferred arrangement that is grandfathered under the bill be taken into account in determining whether the employee's deferrals under an eligible deferred compensation plan exceed the limits on deferrals under the eligible plan; (2) modifies the distribution requirements applicable to eligible deferred compensation plans; (3) permits rollovers between eligible deferred compensation plans; and (4) modifies the rule that an employee is taxable on deferrals under an eligible plan when such amounts are made available.

Nongovernmental tax-exempt employers.—Under the bill, an employee of a nongovernmental tax-exempt organization is not considered to be in constructive receipt of compensation deferred under an eligible deferred compensation plan maintained by the tax-exempt organization if the plan satisfies the requirements applicable to eligible deferred compensation plans of State and local governments. Under the bill, deferrals under an ineligible deferred compensation plan, agreement, or arrangement (other than a qualified State judicial plan, qualified plan, or tax-sheltered annuity) maintained by a nongovernmental tax-exempt entity are to be included in an employee's gross income when the amounts are not subject to a substantial risk of forfeiture.

Offset for deferrals under qualified cash or deferred arrangement.—Under the bill, the limits on the amount that a participant may defer under an eligible deferred compensation plan are reduced, dollar for dollar, by a participant's elective deferrals, under a qualified cash or deferred arrangement (except a qualified cash or deferred arrangement maintained by a rural electric cooperative). Of course, the rule has no application except with respect to those employees of State and local governments that maintain a qualified cash or deferred arrangement that is grandfathered under the bill. In addition, as under present law, all amounts deferred under a tax-sheltered annuity are taken into account in calculating

whether an employee's deferrals under an unfunded deferred compensation plan exceed the limits on deferrals under an eligible deferred compensation plan.

Minimum distribution requirements.—The bill also modifies the distribution requirements for eligible deferred compensation plans maintained by State and local governments and nongovernmental tax-exempt entities. As modified, distributions commencing prior to the death of a participant under an eligible deferred compensation plan are required to satisfy a payout schedule under which benefits projected to be paid over the lifetime of the participant are at least 66⅔ percent of the total benefits payable with respect to the participant.

If the participant dies prior to the date that the participant's entire interest has been distributed, or if the participant dies prior to commencement of the distribution of benefits, the bill requires that payments to the participant's beneficiary commence within sixty days of the close of the plan year in which the participant's death occurs and that the entire amount deferred be distributed over a period not in excess of 15 years, unless the beneficiary is the participant's surviving spouse. If the beneficiary is the participant's surviving spouse, payments must be made over the life of the surviving spouse or any shorter period.

Whenever distributions (pre- or post-death) are to be made over a period extending beyond one year, the bill requires that the distribution be made in substantially nonincreasing periodic payments not less frequently than annually.

Constructive receipt.—The bill provides that benefits are not treated as made available under an eligible deferred compensation plan merely because an employee is allowed to elect to receive a lump sum payment within 60 days of the election. However, the 60-day rule only applies if the employee's total deferred benefit does not exceed $3,500 and no additional amounts may be deferred with respect to the employee.

Rollovers.—The bill also amends present law to permit the rollover of benefits between eligible deferred compensation plans under certain circumstances. If the entire amount payable to an employee under an eligible deferred compensation plan is distributed to the employee within one taxable year, the employee is not required to include in income any portion of the distribution transferred by the employee to another eligible deferred compensation plan within 60 days of the date of receipt of the distribution. The committee intends that an individual may make only one rollover per year, and that an individual may not, in any event, roll over an amount that is required to be distributed under the minimum distribution requirements applicable to eligible deferred compensation plans.

State judicial plans.—The bill exempts from the new requirements for eligible deferred compensation plans any qualified

Act § 1107   ¶ 3973

State judicial plan (as defined in section 131(c)(3)(B) of the Revenue Act of 1978, as amended by section 252 of the Tax Equity and Fiscal Responsibility Act of 1982).

[Conference Report]

*   *   *   *   *   *

Application to tax-exempt employers.—The conference agreement follows the House bill provision extending the rules relating to eligible unfunded deferred compensation plans of State and local governments to tax-exempt organizations. In addition, the conference agreement provides that a plan maintained by a tax-exempt organization that does not meet the requirements of an eligible deferred compensation plan is immediately treated as not meeting such requirements without regard to notification by the Secretary or a grace period. The conference agreement also provides that amounts deferred under an eligible deferred compensation plan are treated as elective contributions under a tax-sheltered annuity for purposes of the special catch-up election.

Distribution requirements.—The conference agreement follows the House bill and the Senate amendment, except that the conference agreement provides that employees under an eligible unfunded deferred compensation plan are subject to the required beginning date and minimum required distribution requirements applicable to qualified plans (sec. 401(a)(9)), in addition to the special distribution rules applicable under section 457. The conference agreement permits transfers, rather than rollovers, between eligible plans.

Effective dates.—The provision extending the eligible unfunded deferred compensa-

tion rules to tax-exempt employers is effective for taxable years beginning after December 31, 1986.

An exception is provided under the conference agreement for amounts deferred under a plan which (1) were deferred from taxable years beginning before January 1, 1987, or (2) are deferred from taxable years beginning after December 31, 1986, pursuant to an agreement that (i) was in writing on August 16, 1986, and (ii) on August 16, 1986, provided for a deferral for each taxable year of a fixed amount or an amount determined pursuant to a fixed formula. This exception does not apply with respect to amounts deferred in a fixed amount or under a fixed formula for any taxable year ending after the date on which the amount or formula is modified after August 16, 1986. Providing the participant with any discretion regarding the amount of the deferral constitutes a modification to this purpose.

For purposes of the grandfather rule, amounts are considered deferred from a taxable year if, but for the deferral, they would have been paid in that year. Also, in applying the limits to a deferral not grandfathered, grandfathered amounts are taken into account.

The modifications to the distribution requirements applicable to eligible unfunded deferred compensation plans generally are effective for taxable years beginning after December 31, 1988. However, the provisions (1) permitting transfers between eligible unfunded deferred compensation plans and (2) permitting cashouts of certain benefits without constructive receipt are effective with respect to transfers or distributions in years beginning after December 31, 1985.

[¶ 3974] SECTION 1108. SPECIAL RULES FOR SIMPLIFIED EMPLOYEE PENSIONS

(Sec. 408(k) of the Code)

[Senate Explanation]

*   *   *   *   *   *

Explanation of Provisions.—

In general.—The bill revises the qualification requirements relating to SEPs to permit employees to elect to have SEP contributions made on their behalf or to receive the contributions in cash. In addition, the bill makes miscellaneous changes to the SEP requirements to decrease the administrative burden of maintaining a SEP.

Salary reduction SEPs.—Under the bill, employees who participate in a SEP would be permitted to elect to have contributions made to the SEP or to receive the contributions in cash. If an employee elects to have contributions made on the employee's behalf to the SEP, the contribution is not treated as having been distributed or made available to the employee. In addition, the contribution is not treated as an employee contribution merely because the SEP provides the employee with such an election. Therefore, under the bill, an employee is not required to include in income

currently the amounts an employee elects to have contributed to the SEP. Elective deferrals under a SEP are to be treated like elective deferrals under a qualified cash or deferred arrangement and, thus, are subject to the $7,000 (indexed) cap on elective deferrals.

Consistent with the rules applicable to elective deferrals under a qualified cash or deferred arrangement or tax-sheltered annuity under present law, elective deferrals under a SEP are not excludable from the definition of wages for employment tax purposes.

The bill provides that the election to have amounts contributed to a SEP or received in cash is available only if at least 50 percent of the employees of the employer elect to have amounts contributed to the SEP and is available only in a taxable year in which the employer maintaining the SEP has 25 or fewer employees as of the beginning of the year.

In addition, under the bill, the amount eligible to be deferred as a percentage of each highly compensated employee's compensation (i.e., the deferral percentage) is limited by the average deferral percentage (based solely on elective deferrals) for all other employees (other than highly compensated employees) who participate. The deferral percentage for each highly compensated employee cannot exceed the deferral percentage for all other participating employees by more than 150 percent. Of course, integration under section 401(1) is not permitted in applying this 150-percent test. Also, nonelective SEP contributions may not be combined with the elective SEP deferrals for purposes of this test. Finally, an employer may not make matching SEP contributions conditioned on elective SEP deferrals.

Under the bill, the definition of a highly compensated employee is the same definition applied for purposes of the special nondiscrimination test applicable to qualified cash or deferred arrangements * * *

For purposes of determining the deferral percentages, an employee's compensation is the amount of the employee's compensation taken into account under the SEP for purposes of calculating the contribution that may be made on the employee's behalf for the year.

If the 150-percent test is not satisfied, rules similar to the rules applicable to excess contributions to a cash or deferred arrangement shall apply.

SEP deduction converted to exclusion from income.—Under the bill, the amounts contributed to a SEP by an employer on behalf of an employee and the elective deferrals under a SEP are excludable from gross income, rather than deductible as under present law.

In addition, the bill (1) modifies the rules relating to maintaining a SEP on a calendar year basis, and (2) prescribes rules for maintaining a SEP on a taxable year basis. In the case of a SEP maintained on a calendar year basis, contributions made in a calendar year are deductible for the taxable year with which or within which the calendar year ends, and the contributions are treated as made on the last day of the calendar year if the contributions are made by the due date (plus extensions) of the employer's tax return.

In the case of a SEP maintained on a taxable year basis, contributions are deductible for the taxable year and contributions are treated as made on the last day of the taxable year if the contributions are made by the due date of the employer's tax return for the taxable year, plus any extensions of the due date to which the employer is entitled.

Participation requirements.—Under the bill, the participation requirements for SEPs are modified to require that an employer make contributions for a year on behalf of each employee who (1) has attained age 21, (2) has performed services for the employer during at least 3 of the immediately preceding 5 years, and (3) received at least $300 in compensation from the employer for the

year. Thus, the bill adds a de minimis exception to the requirement that contributions must be made on behalf of all employees. In addition, the bill provides that this 100-percent participation requirement applies separately to elective arrangements and, for purposes of such elective arrangements, an individual who is eligible is deemed to receive an employer contribution. If nonelective SEP contributions are made for any employee, nonelective contributions must be made for all employees satisfying the participation requirements. Similarly, if any employee is eligible to make elective SEP deferrals, all employees satisfying the participation requirements must be eligible to make elective SEP deferrals.

Wage-based contribution limitation for SEPs.—Under the bill, the $200,000 limit on compensation taken into account and the $300 de minimis threshold would be indexed at the same time and in the same manner as the dollar limits on benefits under a defined benefit pension plan (sec. 415(d)). * * *.

Definition of computation period.—The bill permits an employer to elect to use a computation period other than the calendar year for purposes of determining contributions to a SEP. Under the bill, a permissible computation period (other than a calendar year) will include an employer's taxable year, subject to any terms and conditions that the Secretary of the Treasury may prescribe.

Integration rules.—The bill eliminates the current rules under which nonelective SEP contributions may be combined with employer OASDI contributions for purposes of the applicable nondiscrimination. In place of these rules, the bill permits nonelective SEP contributions to be tested for nondiscrimination under the new rules for qualified defined contribution plans permitting a limited disparity between the contribution percentages applicable to compensation below and compensation above the social security wage base.

*   *   *   *   *   *

[Conference Report]

*   *   *   *   *   *

Conference Agreement.—The conference agreement follows the Senate amendment with two modifications of the special nondiscrimination test applicable to salary reduction SEPs.

Under the first modification, the deferral percentage for each highly compensated employee cannot exceed the average deferral percentage for all other nonhighly compensated eligible employees by more than 125 percent.

Under the second modification, the exception from the rule of constructive receipt is limited to employers that did not have more than 25 employees at any time during the prior taxable year.

Act §1108   ¶3974

[Effective date.—] The provisions apply for taxable years beginning after December 31, 1986.

[¶ 3975] SECTION 1109. DEDUCTIBLE CONTRIBUTIONS PERMITTED UNDER SECTION 501(c)(18) PLAN.

(Secs. 219 and 501(c)(18) of the Code)

[Senate Explanation]

*　　*　　*　　*　　*　　*

Explanation of Provision.—Under the bill, employees who participate in a section 501(c)(18) pension plan are permitted to elect to make deductible contributions if certain requirements are met. If an employee elects to have salary reduction contributions made to the plan, the contribution is deductible up to the lesser of $7,000 or 25 percent of the compensation of the employee includible in income for the taxable year. The amounts contributed to the plan reduce the $7,000 annual cap on elective deferrals under qualified cash or deferred arrangements and SEPs.

The bill provides that the election to make deductible contributions to a section 501(c)(18) plan is available only if the plan satisfies a special nondiscrimination test similar to the test applicable to a qualified cash or deferred arrangement. If the test is not satisfied, rules similar to the rules applicable to excess contributions under a qualified cash or deferred arrangement are to apply.

*　　*　　*　　*　　*　　*

[Conference Report]

*　　*　　*　　*　　*　　*

The conference agreement follows the Senate amendment.

[Effective Date].—The provision is effective for contributions made in taxable years beginning after December 31, 1986.

[¶ 3976] SECTION 1111. APPLICATION OF NONDISCRIMINATION RULES TO INTEGRATED PLANS.

(Sec. 401(l) of the Code)

[Conference Report]

*　　*　　*　　*　　*　　*

Present Law.

In general.—Present law provides nondiscrimination standards for qualified pension, profit-sharing, and stock bonus plans. These standards prohibit discrimination in favor of employees who are officers, shareholders, or highly compensated. Under these standards, coverage tests are applied to determine whether the classification of employees who participate in a plan is discriminatory. Additional tests are applied to determine whether contributions or benefits under the plan discriminate in favor of highly compensated employees.

The present-law nondiscrimination requirements are satisfied if either the contributions or the benefits under a qualified plan do not discriminate in favor of highly compensated employees.

Generally, in applying the nondiscrimination test to benefits under a plan, the benefits that are provided by the plan for highly compensated participants (as a percentage of their compensation) is compared to the benefits that are provided for other participants. A similar test may be applied to employer contributions under a plan. A plan fails the nondiscrimination standard if both benefits and contributions discriminate in favor of highly compensated employees.

Under present law, in determining whether defined benefit pension plan benefits, as a percentage of compensation, discriminate in favor of employees who are highly compensated, the portion of each employee's social security benefits that is considered to be paid for by the employer may be taken into account. For this purpose, social security benefits mean old age, survivors, and disability insurance (OASDI) benefits provided under the social security system.

Section 401(l) and Revenue Rulings 71-446 and 83-110 provide guidance for calculating the maximum amount of social security benefits that may be taken into account under an employer's qualified plan. In addition, section 401(a)(25) prevents increases in social security benefits after an employee's separation from service with an employer from reducing plan benefits. Also, section 411(b)(1)(G) provides that an employee's accrued benefit (other than a social security supplement) under a defined benefit plan may not be reduced on account of any increase in the employee's age or service. Finally, section 411(d)(6) provides that, with limited exceptions, the accrued benefit of a participant may not be decreased by plan amendment. A plan that meets the nondiscrimination standards of the Code only if social security benefits are taken into account is referred to as an integrated plan. Either benefits or contributions under a plan may be integrated.

*　　*　　*　　*　　*　　*

House Bill—The House bill revises the manner in which a pension plan may be integrated with social security. Pursuant to regulations to be issued by the Secretary of the Treasury, the maximum amount of social security benefits that may be taken into account by an employer for any year of service with such employer may not exceed 1/40 of the total social security benefits permitted to be taken into account. Thus, the bill precludes an employer from taking into account benefits attributable to OASDI contributions of former employers of an employee.

Under a flat-benefit excess plan, the full 37½ percent excess amount (reduced for integrated ancillary benefits) could be applied only to an employee who had 40 years of service with the employer upon retirement at age 65. If an employee only had 20 years of service with the employer, the maximum excess benefit at age 65 would be 16.75 percent (37½ multiplied by 20/40, the ratio of 20 years of service to 40), assuming that the plan has no integrated ancillary benefits.

For an offset plan, the full 83 1/2 percent offset (reduced for integrated ancillary benefits) could be applied only to an employee who retired at age 65 with 40 years of service with the employer. Thus, if an employee retired at age 65 with 30 years of service with the employer, the maximum offset would be 62.5 percent (83 1/2 multiplied by 30/40, the ratio of 30 years of service to 40), assuming the plan has no integrated ancillary benefits.

The bill generally would not have a significant effect on unit benefit plans because such plans will automatically reduce the social security benefit taken into account under the plan for employees retiring with less than 37½ years of service due to the reduced number of years taken into account under the unit benefit formula for such employees. Furthermore, the bill generally would not affect the integration of defined contribution plans integrated with OASDI benefits (except to the extent such plans are determined to be nondiscriminatory on the basis of benefits). Also, the committee anticipates that similar rules would apply to the integration of other employer-provided benefits under Federal, State, or foreign law.

*   *   *   *   *   *

Senate Amendment

In general.—The Senate amendment provides that a plan is not to be considered discriminatory merely because the contributions and benefits of (or on behalf of) employees under the plan favor highly compensated employees if the plan meets the new requirements of the bill relating to the integration of contributions or benefits.

Permitted disparity in defined contribution plans.—*In general.*—Under the Senate amendment, a defined contribution plan meets the disparity limits for integrated plans only if the excess contribution percentage under the plan does not exceed the base contribution percentage by an amount specified in the bill. The bill provides that the excess contribution percentage is not to exceed the lesser of (1) 200 percent of the base contribution percentage, or (2) the sum of the base contribution percentage and the rate of the tax imposed on employers under the

Federal Insurance Contributions Act (5.7 percent for 1986) as of the beginning of the plan year.

For example, under the Senate amendment, if a defined contribution plan provided for contributions of 10 percent of pay on compensation in excess of the taxable wage base, then the plan is required to provide contributions of at least 5 percent of pay on compensation up to the taxable wage base in order to satisfy the integration rules for defined contribution plans. Alternatively, if the plan provided contributions of 10 percent of pay on compensation up to the taxable wage base, then the contributions for compensation in excess of the taxable wage base are limited to 15.7 percent because the permitted disparity cannot be greater than the OASDI tax rate (i.e., 5.7 percent in 1986).

Contributions to a plan that are subject to the nondiscrimination rules in section 401(k) or 401(m) (or, in the case of simplified employer pensions, sec. 408(k)(6)) may not rely on these integration requirements, but rather must satisfy the separate nondiscrimination rules under such other provisions.

Excess contribution percentage.—Under the Senate amendment, the excess contribution percentage is the percentage of remuneration that is contributed under the plan with respect to that portion of remuneration in excess of the compensation level specified under the plan for the year.

Base contribution percentage.—The Senate amendment provides that the base contribution percentage is the percentage of remuneration contributed under the plan with respect to that portion of remuneration not in excess of the compensation level specified under the plan for the year.

Under the Senate amendment, the compensation level refers to the dollar amount of remuneration specified under the plan as the compensation level for the year. The compensation level specified in the plan may not exceed the contributions or benefit base under the Social Security Act (i.e., the taxable wage base) in effect at the beginning of the plan year ($42,000 for plan years beginning in 1986). In addition, an employer may not set a lower compensation level if such level discriminates in favor of highly compensated employees.

Remuneration.—Remuneration is defined as total compensation, or basic or regular compensation, whichever is used in determining contributions or benefits under the plan. With respect to a self-employed individual, the Senate amendment provides that compensation includes the individual's earned income. The self-employed individual's basic or regular rate of compensation is equal to the portion of the individual's earned income that bears the same ratio to his earned income as the regular or basic compensation of employees under the plan bears to the total compensation of such employees.

Permitted disparity in defined pension plans.—*In general.*—Under the Senate

Act §1111   ¶3976

amendment, a defined benefit pension plan meets the requirement for integrated plans only if it meets the requirements for integrated offset plans or those for integrated excess plans. Under a special limitation provided by the Senate amendment, a defined benefit pension plan will not fail to meet the nondiscrimination rules (sec. 401(a)(4)) merely because it limits benefits by reference to the final pay of a participant.

Excess plans.—*In general.*—A defined benefit pension plan meets the the disparity limits for integrated excess plans if (1) the excess benefit percentage does not exceed 200 percent of the base benefit percentage, and (2) any optional form of benefit, preretirement benefit, actuarial factor, or other benefit or feature provided by the plan with respect to remuneration in excess of the compensation level specified by the plan for the year is provided with respect to remuneration that is not in excess of that level.

Benefit percentages.—Under the rules for integration of defined benefit pension plans as excess plans, the excess and base benefit percentages are to be computed in the same manner as those percentages are to be computed for defined contribution plans, except that the computation is to be based on benefits rather than contributions. Thus, the term the "excess benefit percentage" refers to the benefits provided under the plan (expressed as a percentage of remuneration) with respect to that portion of remuneration in excess of the compensation level specified in the plan. The base benefit percentage refers to the benefits provided under the plan (expressed as a percentage of remuneration) with respect to that portion of remuneration not in excess of the compensation level specified in the plan.

For purposes of the rules relating to defined benefit excess plans, the terms "compensation level" and "remuneration" have the same meanings as for purposes of the rules relating to defined contribution plans.

Offset plans.—*In general.*—A defined benefit pension plan meets the requirements for integrated offset plans if it provides that a participant's accrued benefit derived from employer contributions (sec. 411(c)(1)) may not be reduced by reason of the offset by more than 50 percent of the benefit that would have accrued without regard to the reduction. The bill provides that a defined benefit pension plan is an offset plan if each participant's normal retirement benefit derived from employer contributions (sec. 411) is reduced (offset) by a dollar amount specified by the plan and if the same dollar amount of reduction is applicable to all plan participants. The Secretary is directed to prescribe rules for "normalizing" benefits, though not necessarily in the manner described in Rev. Rul. 81-202, and to prevent discriminatory modifications in the amount of the dollar offset from year to year.

Example.—Under an offset plan, the offset may never reduce a participant's accrued benefit by more than 50 percent, and may accrue no faster than the rate at which the participant's benefit under the plan would accrue without regard to the offset. For example, assume that a plan provides for a normal retirement benefit of 50 percent of final pay, less $20,000. The plan provides that the participant's accrued benefit is to accrue under the fractional accrual rule of section 411(b). Normal retirement age under the plan is age 65. Assume that a participant commences working for the employer and becomes a participant in the plan at age 40. Upon the date that the participant has completed 5 years of service with the employer, the participant has an accrued benefit (without regard to the dollar offset) of 5/25ths of 50 percent of final pay (or 10 percent of final pay). At that time, the value of the offset "accrued" to the participant may not exceed the lesser of (a) 5/25ths of $20,000 ($4,000), or (b) one-half of the participant's accrued benefit (determined without regard to the offset) to date.

Multiple plans.—The bill provides rules that apply to a plan that benefits a highly compensated employee who participates in 2 or more plans maintained by the employer that would be considered discriminatory but for the integration rules. In such a case, integration rules are to be applied to each of the plans by taking into account the total contributions and benefits for such highly compensated employee under all of such plans of the employer.

Benefits limited by reference to final pay.—The bill provides that a defined benefit pension plan (including an offset or excess plan) is not to be considered discriminatory merely because it provides that the employer-provided accrued retirement benefit for any participant under the plan is not to exceed the excess (if any) of (1) the participant's final pay with the employer, over (2) the employer-provided retirement benefit, created under Federal law, that is attributable to the participant's service with the employer. The Secretary shall prescribe rules for "normalizing" accrued benefits for purposes of this rule. Also, this limit may not be applied to reduce minimum benefits under the top-heavy rules.

Under the bill, for purposes of determining the final-pay limit that may be imposed by an integrated defined benefit pension plan, a participant's final pay is the total compensation paid to the participant by the employer during the participant's highest year of compensation ending with or within the 5-year period ending with the year in which the participant separated from service with the employer.

Effective date.—The provisions are effective with respect to benefits accrued in plan years beginning after December 31, 1988.

A special effective date applies to plans maintained pursuant to a collective bargaining agreement. Under this special rule, in the case of a plan maintained pursuant to a collective bargaining agreement between employee representatives and one or more employers ratified before March 1, 1986, the amendments are not effective for plan years beginning before the earlier of (1) the later of

(i) January 1, 1989, or (ii) the date on which the last of the collective bargaining agreements terminates, or (2) January 1, 1991. Extensions or renegotiations of the collective bargaining agreement, if ratified after February 28, 1986, are disregarded.

Conference Agreement

In general.—The conference agreement generally follows both the House bill and the Senate amendment with the following modifications: (1) the deemed accrual period for social security benefits in the House bill is reduced from 40 years to 35 years and is applied for purposes of integrating offset plans, flat excess plans, and unit benefit excess plans; (2) in order to limit the extent to which an employer may increase, relative to the present law integration rules, the disparity between benefits accruing with respect to compensation above and below the integration level, additional limits on such disparity are applied; and (3) the uniform definition of compensation under new section 414(s) is applied (*see* Part B.1., above).

The additional limits added by the agreement on the permitted disparity are a simplified form of the present-law integration rules, modified to eliminate the need for offset plans to determine an employee's actual lifetime social security benefit, provide for parity between offset plans and excess plans, provide uniform rules for both final average excess plans and career average excess plans, and eliminate the adjustments for integrated ancillary benefits (except for early retirement benefits).

The conferees recognize that some plans that satisfy both the present-law integration rules and the rules adopted in the House bill and the Senate amendment may not satisfy the additional limits added by the agreement. Similarly, the conferees realize that for some other plans the additional limits will permit a greater disparity in benefits above and below the integration level than that permitted under present law. However, the conferees have determined that, in attempting to limit the disparity permitted under the new rules to approximately the levels permitted under present law, the goals of simplifying the integration rules, providing consistent rules for different types of plans, and updating the rules to reflect the current social security system justify the simplified approach adopted under the agreement.

Permitted disparity in defined contribution plans.—Under the agreement, a defined contribution plan meets the disparity limits for integrated plans only if the excess contribution percentage (i.e., the contribution with respect to compensation over the integration level, expressed as a percentage of compensation) does not exceed the base contribution percentage (i.e., the contribution with respect to compensation up to the integration level, expressed as a percentage of such compensation) by more than the lesser of (i) the base contribution percentage, or (ii) the greater of 5.7 percentage points or

the percentage equal to the portion of the rate of tax in effect under section 3111(a) attributable to old-age insurance as of the beginning of the plan year.

The conferees understand that for 1986 the rate of tax attributable to old-age insurance is less than 5 percent. The conferees expect that the Social Security Administration will advise the Secretary when such rate becomes greater than 5.7 percent and, thereafter, will determine the amount of such rate and advise the Secretary for timely publication.

As under the Senate amendment, a plan must specify the applicable integration level for a year. The maximum integration level permitted for a year, however, is the OASDI contribution and benefit base under social security (taxable wage base) in effect at the beginning of the year ($42,000 for plan years beginning in 1986). The Secretary may develop such rules as are necessary to prevent an employer from selecting a lower integration level that discriminates in favor of highly compensated employees. Also, contributions subject to the nondiscrimination rules of section 401(k), 401(m), or 408(k)(6) may not rely on the integration rules to satisfy such rules. Finally, the agreement does not modify any other requirements currently applicable to integrated defined contribution plans, including, for example, the requirement that an integrated profit-sharing or stock bonus plan provide benefits only upon retirement, death, or other separation from service.

Permitted disparity in defined benefit pension plans.—*In general.*—The agreement provides both ratio limits and percentage point limits on the maximum disparity permitted under a defined benefit excess plan and on the maximum offset permitted under a defined benefit offset plan. The ratio limits are the same as the limits adopted in the Senate amendment. The percentage point limits are a simplified form of the present-law integration rules.

Excess plans

In general.—The agreement provides that the excess benefit percentage (i.e., benefits provided with respect to compensation in excess of the applicable integration level, expressed as a percentage of compensation) under a defined benefit excess plan may not exceed the base benefit percentage (i.e., benefits provided with respect to compensation not in excess of such integration level, expressed as a percentage of such compensation) by more than the maximum excess allowance.

Maximum excess allowance.—In the case of an excess plan, the maximum excess allowance with respect to benefits attributable to any year of service taken into account under the plan is the lesser of (i) the base benefit percentage, or (ii) ¾ of a percentage point. The maximum excess allowance for such a plan with respect to total benefits is the lesser of (i) the base benefit percentage, or (ii) ¾ of a percentage point times the participant's years of service (not in excess of 35) taken into account under the plan.

These limits apply to excess plans that base benefits on final average compensation as well as excess plans that base benefits on career average compensation. Under the conference agreement, an integrated final pay plan may not base plan benefits on less than 3 years of service (or for a participant's full period of service, if less).

A year is treated as taken into account under a plan for purposes of applying the maximum excess allowance if benefits are treated as accruing on behalf of the participant for such year. Thus, for example, an excess plan that provides for the accrual of benefits over a participant's years of participation is to be treated as taking only years of participation into account.

This maximum excess allowance applies to both a flat-benefit final pay plan and a unit benefit final pay plan. For example, assume a flat-benefit plan with a benefit formula providing a retirement benefit for any participant retiring at age 65 with at least 15 years of service equal to 20 percent of the participant's final average compensation not in excess of the applicable integration level. Assume further that the plan provides for the accrual of the retirement benefit under the fractional rule of section 411(b). In order to satisfy the new integration rules with respect to a participant retiring at age 65 with 20 years of participation, the plan may not provide a benefit in excess of 35 percent of compensation over the integration level. If this participant had 35 years of participation at age 65, the plan would be precluded from providing a benefit with respect to final average compensation over the integration level in excess of 40 percent of such compensation. If an employee with 10 years of participation in this plan separated from service at age 50, such employee's accrued benefit would be 8 percent of his final average compensation up to the applicable integration level plus up to 15.5 percent of his final average compensation over the integration level.

Reductions of the ¾ percent factor.—The Secretary is directed to prescribe regulations requiring the reduction of the ¾ percent factor in the maximum excess allowance for plans (both final average and career average plans) using integration levels in excess of covered compensation. The conferees direct the Secretary to provide for such reductions on the basis of brackets of integration levels in excess of covered compensation. Such reductions and brackets should correspond to the comparable reductions and brackets for offset plans. The Secretary is not authorized, however, to provide for an increase in the ¾ factor for plans using integration levels lower than covered compensation.

The term "covered compensation" has the same meaning as under present law, i.e., with respect to an employee, the average of the taxable wage bases in effect for each year during the 35-year period ending with the year the employee attains age 65, assuming no increase in such wage base for years after

the current year and before the employee actually attains age 65.

The conferees intend that the reductions for higher integration levels will reflect the decreasing percentages of compensation replaced by the employer-provided PIA under social security as compensation increases above covered compensation. The Secretary is directed to consult with the Social Security Administration in developing the prescribed reductions.

Optional forms of benefits and other features.—The agreement follows the requirement in the Senate amendment that any optional form of benefit, preretirement benefit, actuarial factor, and other factor or feature under the plan provided with respect to compensation above the integration level also be provided with respect to compensation below the integration level. Thus, for example, if a lump sum distribution option, calculated using particular actuarial assumptions, is available with respect to benefits relating to compensation above the integration level, the same lump sum option must be available on an equivalent basis with respect to benefits based on compensation up to the integration level.

Multiple integration levels.—The Secretary is directed to provide rules under which an excess plan may use 2 or more integration levels. The permitted disparity with respect to each such integration level should be based on the percentages of compensation up to each such level replaced by the employer-provided portion of PIA under social security.

Offset plans

The agreement provides that in the case of a defined benefit offset plan, a participant's accrued benefit may not be reduced by reason of the offset by more than the maximum offset allowance for such participant. The maximum offset allowance with respect to a participant for any year of service taken into account under the plan is the lesser of (i) 50 percent of the benefit that would have accrued without regard to the offset reduction, or (ii) ¾ percent of the participant's final average compensation times the participant's years of service with the employer (not in excess of 35) taken into account under the plan. For purposes of this allowance, a participant's final average compensation is to be calculated by disregarding compensation in any year over the taxable wage base for such year.

The Secretary is directed to reduce the ¾ factor under the maximum offset allowance for participants with final average compensation in excess of covered compensation. Such reductions are to be based on the decreasing percentages of compensation replaced by the employer-provided PIA under social security as compensation increases above covered compensation. The Secretary is directed to consult with the Social Security Administration in developing such prescribed reductions. In addition, the reductions applicable to the ¾ factor for offset plans should correspond to the reductions applicable to the ¾ factor for excess plans using integration levels in excess of covered compensation. Finally, the conferees direct the Secretary to publish annually a table setting forth the appropriate offset factors for brackets of final average compensation in excess of covered compensation.

The term "offset plan" means any defined benefit plan under which the employer-provided benefit for each participant is reduced by an amount specified in the plan not in excess of the maximum offset allowance for such participant. In addition, an offset plan must base benefits on average annual compensation for at least the lesser of (1) a 3-year period or (2) the total number of the participant's years of service. Such term does not include a qualified plan merely because the benefits under such plan are reduced by benefits under another qualified plan. An offset plan may reduce participants' benefits by less than the maximum offset allowance so long as the offset amount or formula is specified in the plan, does not discriminate in favor of highly compensated employees, and is not otherwise inconsistent with the purposes of the integration rules.

Reductions for early retirement benefits

Under the conference agreement, the Secretary is also directed to reduce the ¾ percent factor in the maximum excess allowance and maximum offset allowance for plans providing for unreduced benefits (other than for disability, as defined under the Social Security Act) commencing before the social security retirement age (as defined in section 415). As under current law, the ¾ factor is to be reduced by ¹⁄₁₅ for each of the first five years that the benefit commencement date precedes the social security retirement age (currently age 65), and by an additional ¹⁄₃₀ for each of the next five years that the benefit commencement date precedes the social security retirement age. If the benefit commencement date is earlier than 10 years before the social security retirement age, the factor is to be actuarially reduced for each such additional year. Also, as under current law, the determination of whether early retirement benefits require an adjustment is based on a comparison of the benefit actually provided under the plan at the early retirement age with the benefit that would be provided under a plan at such

age that has the maximum disparity permitted under the integration rules (calculated by applying the ¹⁄₁₅, ¹⁄₃₀ adjustment).

Multiple integrated plans

The agreement directs the Secretary to develop rules to prevent excessive use of the disparity permitted under this subsection with respect to any employee through the integration of more than one qualified plan. Such rules are to limit to 100 percent the sum of the percentages, calculated separately for each plan with overlapping coverage, of the maximum benefit disparity actually used in each plan.

Benefits limited by reference to final pay

The agreement adopts the Senate amendment rule permitting a defined benefit plan to limit the employer-provided accrued retirement benefit under the plan for any participant to the excess of the participant's final pay with the employer over the employer-provided PIA actually provided for such participant under social security and attributable to service by the participant with the employer. This limit is applied to the participant's accrued retirement benefit (disregarding ancillaries) under the defined benefit plan. Similarly, the limit is applied by taking into account only the worker's benefit (PIA) under social security, disregarding auxiliary benefits (spousal, survivor, children's, and disability benefits). The agreement clarifies that for purposes of determining the portion of the employer-provided PIA under social security for a participant that is attributable to service with the employer, such PIA is treated as accruing ratably over 35 years. However, the conferees do not intend that the limit also be pro rated. Finally, as under the Senate amendment, this limit may not be applied either to reduce minimum benefits under the top-heavy rules or to reduce accrued benefits within the meaning of section 411(d)(6).

Effective date.—The new integration rules apply with respect to benefits accruing in plan years beginning after December 31, 1988. A special effective date applies with respect to benefits accruing under a plan maintained pursuant to a collective bargaining agreement.

[¶ 3977] SECTION 1112. MINIMUM COVERAGE REQUIREMENTS FOR QUALIFIED PLANS.

(Secs. 410 and 401(a) of the Code)

[Senate Explanation]

Present Law.—

*　　*　　*　　*　　*　　*

Under present law, a qualified plan is required to cover employees in general rather than merely the employees of an employer who are officers, shareholders, or highly compensated. A plan generally satisfies the present-law coverage rule if (1) it benefits a

significant percentage of the employer's workforce (percentage test), or (2) it benefits a classification of employees determined by the Secretary of the Treasury not to discriminate in favor of employees who are officers, shareholders, or highly compensated (classification test).

Percentage test.—A plan meets the percentage test if (1) it benefits at least 70 percent of all employees, or (2) it benefits at least 80 percent of the employees eligible to benefit under the plan and at least 70 percent of all employees are eligible (i.e., the plan benefits at least 56 percent of all employees).

Classification test.—A plan meets the classification test if the Secretary of the Treasury determines that it covers a classification of employees that does not discriminate in favor of employees who are officers, shareholders, or highly compensated (highly compensated employees). For purposes of this rule, all active employees (including employees who do not satisfy the minimum age or service requirement of the plan) are taken into account.

Under Treasury regulations, the determination as to whether a classification discriminates in favor of highly compensated employees is to be made on the basis of the surrounding facts and circumstances of each case, allowing for a reasonable difference between the ratio of highly compensated employees who are benefited by the plan to all such employees and the corresponding ratio calculated for employees who are not highly compensated.

* * * * * *

Aggregation rules.—In applying the qualification rules (including the nondiscrimination tests), all employees of corporations that are members of a controlled group of corporations, or all employees of trades and businesses (whether or not incorporated) that are under common control, are aggregated and treated as if employed by a single employer (sec. 414(b) and (c)). Similarly, all employees of employers that are members of an affiliated service group are treated as employed by a single employer for purposes of the qualification requirements (sec. 414(m)).

* * * * * *

Aggregation of plans and comparability.—Under present law, an employer may designate two or more plans as a single plan for purposes of satisfying the coverage requirements.[9] However, if several plans are designated as a single plan, the plans, considered as a unit, must be provided for the exclusive benefits of employees and also must provide contributions or benefits that do not discriminate in favor of highly compensated employees.

In determining whether one or more plans designated as a unit provide benefits or contributions that do not discriminate in favor of highly compensated employees, it is necessary to determine whether the designated plans provide "comparable" benefits or contributions.

* * * * * *

Explanation of Provisions.—* * *

The bill (1) increases, to 80 percent of all employees, the level of coverage necessary to satisfy the "percentage test"; (2) replaces the "classification test" of present law with a "reasonable classification test" and provides the Treasury with guidance as to the manner

in which the test is to be interpreted; (3) establishes an alternative method for satisfying the reasonable classification test ("alternative reasonable classification test"); (4) clarifies the circumstances under which an employee will be treated as benefiting under a plan for purposes of the coverage rules; (5) permits, for purposes of satisfying the reasonable classification test, the exclusion from consideration of employees who have not satisfied certain minimum age and service requirements; (6) establishes an objective definition of those employees in whose favor discriminatory coverage is prohibited; (7) permits satisfaction of certain of the coverage rules on a controlled group or line of business basis; (8) establishes a definition of a line of business or separate operating unit with a special safe-harbor rule; and (9) contains a special transition rule for certain dispositions or acquisitions of a business.

* * * * * *

General coverage rules.—Under the bill, a plan is not qualified unless the plan satisfies either (1) a percentage test, or (2) a reasonable classification test. A plan that does not satisfy the reasonable classification test will be treated as meeting that test if the plan satisfies an alternative reasonable classification test.

Percentage test.—A plan meets the percentage test if it benefits 80 percent or more of all employees of the employer.

Reasonable classification tests.—The bill replaces the classification test of present law with a new reasonable classification test. Under the bill a plan meets the reasonable classification test if it benefits a reasonable classification of employees that (1) is set up by the employer, and (2) the Secretary of the Treasury finds does not allow more than a reasonable difference (in favor of highly compensated employees) between the coverage percentage of highly compensated employees and the coverage percentage of other employees.

The committee intends that, as under the regulations relating to coverage under present law, the Treasury interpret the reasonable classification test to permit no more than a reasonable disparity between the ratio of the highly compensated employees benefited by a plan to all such employees and the ratio of nonhighly compensated employees benefited by the plan to all nonhighly compensated employees. To this end, the committee directs the Secretary of the Treasury to revoke Rev. Rul. 83-58, its predecessor rulings, and the preamble to Treas. Reg. sec. 1.410(b)-1 as expressions of the reasonable classification test.

The committee recognizes that what constitutes a "reasonable" disparity will depend on the facts and circumstances of the particular case and directs the Treasury to reissue regulations that take a proportionality approach to coverage, with a list of facts and circumstances that will be considered in determining whether a plan satisfies the reasonable classification test.

*   *   *   *   *   *

[Conference Report]

*   *   *   *   *   *

General coverage rules.—Under the conference agreement, a plan is not qualified unless the plan satisfies at least one of the following requirements:

(1) the plan benefits at least 70 percent of all nonhighly compensated employees (referred to herein as the "percentage test");

(2) the plan benefits a percentage of nonhighly compensated employees which is at least 70 percent of the percentage of highly compensated employees benefiting under the plan (referred to herein as the "ratio test"); or

(3) the plan meets the average benefits test.

An employer that has no nonhighly compensated employees in its workforce is considered to pass the coverage test.

Average benefits test.—A plan meets the average benefits test if (1) the plan benefits such employees as qualify under a classification set up by the employer and found by the Secretary not to be discriminatory in favor of highly compensated employees ("classification test"); and (2) the average benefit percentage for nonhighly compensated employees of the employer is at least 70 percent of the average benefit percentage for highly compensated employees of the employer.

Classification test.—For purposes of the average benefits test, the conferees intend that the classification test is generally to be based on the present-law section 410(b)(1)(B) (as modified judicially and administratively in the future). However, it is to be applied using the new definitions of highly compensated employees and excludable employees.

Thus, the test is to be applied on the basis of the facts and circumstances of each case, including the difference between the coverage percentages of the highly compensated employees and the other employees, the percentage of total employees covered, and the difference between the compensation of the covered employees and the compensation of the excluded employees. Nevertheless, the conferees expect that the Secretary will consider providing an objective safe harbor based on these and other relevant factors to facilitate compliance with the test.

Average benefit percentage.—The term "average benefit percentage" means, with respect to any group of employees, the average of the benefit percentages calculated separately with respect to each employee in such group. The term "benefit percentage" means the employer-provided contributions (including forfeitures) or benefits of an employee under all qualified plans of the employer, expressed as a percentage of such employee's compensation. If benefit percentages are determined on the basis of employer-provided contributions, all employer-provided benefits must be converted into contributions for testing purposes. Similarly, if benefit percentages are determined on the basis of employer-provided benefits, all employer-provided contributions are to be converted into benefits. In determining the amount of contributions or benefits, the approach of Rev. Rul. 81-202 is to be the sole rule applicable, as modified in the manner described below. Thus, in the case of benefits testing, the benefit percentages are determined based on projected benefits.

The conferees further intend that the rules of Rev. Rul. 81-202 be modified in several respects, both for purposes of the average benefit percentage test and for purposes of determining whether 2 or more plans that are treated as a single plan under the percentage test, ratio test, or classification test discriminate in favor of highly compensated employees (sec. 401(a)(4)). First, Rev. Rul. 81-202 is to be modified to reflect the new limits contained in the conference agreement on the extent to which a plan may be integrated. Also, the new limitation on the amount of compensation that may be taken into account and the new definition of compensation applies under Rev. Rul. 81-202 as they apply for all nondiscrimination rules.

Rev. Rul. 81-202 is also to be modified to take into account other significant plan features. For example, determinations under Rev. Rul. 81-202 are to take into account the rate at which benefits actually accrue and, in appropriate cases, may take into account the existence of different plan options such as loans or lump-sum distributions that are available to highly compensated participants, but not to a proportionate number of nonhighly compensated participants. Moreover, the conferees clarify that under Rev. Rul. 81-202 the same actuarial assumptions are to be used in valuing different benefits or contributions. In appropriate circumstances, Rev. Rul. 81-202 may also be modified to take into account reasonable salary projections. The Secretary may also, in circumstances justifying special scrutiny, consider requiring a certificate of comparability from an enrolled actuary.

Finally, the conferees do not intend to restrict the authority of the Secretary to modify, as appropriate, aspects of Rev. Rul. 81-202 not discussed above. Also, the conferees do not intend that application of the rules of Rev. Rul. 81-202 to the average benefit percentage test be interpreted as requiring that an averaging approach be adopted for purposes of applying these rules to multiple plans being tested as a single plan under section 401(a)(4).

For purposes of determining benefit percentages, all pre-tax contributions or benefits provided under a qualified plan are considered employer-provided and must be taken into account, including, for example, elective contributions under a qualified cash or deferred arrangement. In no case may an employer disregard any qualified plan in determining benefit percentages, even if such qualified plan satisfies the percentage test or ratio test standing alone. Contributions or benefits under other types of plans or programs (such as SEPs or tax-sheltered annuity programs (sec. 403(b)) are not taken into account.

After the benefit percentage of each employee is determined in the manner described above, the average for the two groups (highly compensated employees and nonhighly compensated employees) is then to be determined by averaging the individual benefit percentages of each employee (including employees not covered by any plan) in a manner similar to the computation of the actual deferral percentage of a group of employees under a qualified cash or deferred arrangement.

Period of computing percentage.—The conference agreement provides that each employee's benefit percentage is to be computed, at the election of the employer, on the basis of contributions or benefits for (a) the current plan year, or (b) a period of consecutive plan years (not in excess of 3 years) ending with the current plan year. As under the Senate amendment, the period of consecutive plan years chosen by the employer is to be uniformly applied in computing each employee's benefit percentage, and may not be changed without the consent of the Secretary.

In addition, the conferees clarify that the fact that a failure to meet the new coverage tests was due to unforeseen circumstances does not affect application of the tests.

* * * * * *

[Senate Explanation]

* * * * * *

Employees benefiting under the plan.—For purposes of the (a) percentage test, (b) the reasonable classification test, and (c) the [Average benefits test Ed.] test, an employee, generally, will be treated as benefiting under the plan only if the employee is a participant in the plan. However, in the case of a cash or deferred arrangement or the portion of a defined contribution plan to which employee contributions and employer matching contributions are made, an employee will be treated as benefiting under the plan if the employee is eligible to make contributions to the plan.

* * * * * *

[Conference Report]

* * * * * *

The conference agreement also clarifies that, for purposes of the average benefit percentage component of the average benefits test, it is actual benefits, not eligibility, that is taken into account. As under current law, this is also true for purposes of establishing comparability between plans.

* * * * * *

[Senate Explanation]

Aggregation of plans and comparability.—As under present law, for purposes of applying the percentage test or the reasonable classification test, more than one plan may be designated as a unit and tested as a

single entity, if the plans so designated provide benefits that do not discriminate in favor of highly compensated employees. Also, for purposes of satisfying the alternative reasonable classification test, two or more comparable plans may be aggregated for purposes of determining whether the plans together satisfy the classification test of present law.

* * * * * *

[Conference Report]

* * * * * *

Rev. Rul. 81-202 is to be modified in the manner described above.

* * * * * *

[Senate Explanation]

* * * * * *

Excludable employees.—For purposes of determining whether a plan (a) benefits 80 percent of all employees, (b) benefits a reasonable classification of employees, or (c) satisfies the [average benefits test Ed.] the bill generally permits the employer to exclude from consideration certain classes of employees.

Minimum age and service.—If a plan (a) prescribes minimum age or service requirements as a condition of participation, and (b) excludes all employees who do not satisfy such requirements, then the employer may disregard such employees in applying the [percentage, ratio and classification tests Ed.] For purposes of applying the [average benefits test (other than the classification test) Ed.] ***, the employer may take into account all employees or, alternatively, may exclude those employees who have not satisfied the minimum age and service requirements that are the lowest such age or service requirement for any plans taken into account in applying the test. The lowest age and service used need not be the age and service requirements under the same plan.

The bill provides that employees who are not excluded from consideration in applying the [average benefits, test Ed.] *** because they are covered under a separate plan, but who could have been excluded had the employer used other minimum age or service requirements in such other plan, may be excluded from consideration if the coverage of such employees, tested separately, satisfies the coverage and nondiscrimination rules.

* * * * * *

[Conference Report]

* * * * * *

The conference agreement reflects the Senate amendment rule permitting employees who do not meet the age 21 and one year of service requirements to be tested separately. However, under the confernce agreement, such separate testing is permissible even if such employees are not covered by a separate plan. Under the agreement, an employer may elect to test all such excludable employees separately. Alternatively, an employer may elect to test one group of excludable employees separately without testing all excludable employees separately if such group is defined in a nondiscriminatory manner solely by reference to the age or service requirements. For example, an employer may elect to test separately all employees excludable solely on the grounds that they do not have one year of service, but not include in such testing group employees excluded under the age rule. Also, the employer may test separately a group of employees who would pass an age or service requirement that is less restrictive than the age 21 or one year of service requirement. For example, an employer could test separately all employees excludable solely on the grounds that they are not age 21, but who are at least 18.

Collective bargaining agreement.—For purposes of applying (a) the percentage test, (b) the ratio test, or (c) the average benefits test to qualified plan coverage of employees who are not included in a unit of employees covered by a collective bargaining agreement, all employees covered by such an agreement are disregarded. However, in applying the same tests to employees covered by any such agreement, an employee may not be disregarded based on the fact that such employee is not covered under the collective bargaining agreement.

* * * * * *

* * * * * *

Miscellaneous.—As under present law, nonresident aliens with no United States source income may be disregarded for purposes of applying the coverage rules. Similarly, in the case of a collective bargaining agreement covering a unit of airline pilots, employees not covered by the agreement may be disregarded.

* * * * * *

Line of business or operating unit.—*In general.*—As under present law, all employees of corporations that are members of a controlled group of corporations, or all employees of trades or businesses (whether or not incorporated) that are under common control, are aggregated and treated as if employed by a single employer (sec. 414(b) and (c)). Similarly, all employees of employers that are members of an affiliated service group are treated as employed by a single employer for purposes of the qualification requirements (sec. 414(m)).

The bill generally requires that the percentage test, [ratio test] and the [average benefits] *** test be satisfied on an aggregate basis. However, if an employer establishes to the satisfaction of the Secretary that the employer operates separate lines of business or operating units for bona fide business reasons, a plan maintained by the employer for employees in a line of business or operating unit will not be considered discriminatory if, with respect to the employees in the line of business or operating unit for which the plan is maintained, it satisfies (a) the [percentage test, (b) the ratio test, or (c) the average benefits test] *** However, the committee intends that a plan will not be treated as satisfying the [percentage test, the ratio test, and average benefits test] *** on a line of business or operating unit basis unless the plan also satisfies the classification test of section 410(b)(1)(B) as in effect immediately before enactment of the Tax Reform Act of 1986.

* * * * * *

* * * * * *

The conference agreement follows the Senate amendment, with the modifications described in [¶3980 Ed.]* * *

* * * * * *

* * * * * *

Special rules for certain dispositions and acquisitions.—The bill contains special transition rules for certain dispositions or acquisitions of a business. Under the bill, if a person becomes or ceases to be a member of a controlled group or affiliated service group, the coverage rules will be deemed satisfied during the transition period (as defined in the bill), provided that (1) the coverage rules were satisfied immediately before the acquisition or disposition, and (2) the coverage under the plan does not change significantly during the transition period (other than by reason of the acquisition or disposition). The transition period is defined under the bill as the period beginning on the date of the acquisition or disposition and ending on the last day of the first plan year beginning after the transaction.

* * * * * *

Minimum Participation Rule.—Under the bill, a plan is not a qualified plan unless it benefits no fewer than the lesser of (a) 50 employees or (b) 40 percent or more of all employees of the employer. The requirement may not be satisfied by aggregating comparable plans. In the case of a cash or deferred arrangement or the portion of a defined contribution plan to which employee contributions or employer matching contributions are made, an employee will be treated as benefiting under the plan if the employee is eligible to make contributions to the plan.

The bill generally provides that, for purposes of applying the minimum participation rules, the same categories of employees may be disregarded as may be disregarded for purposes of applying the general coverage rules. In the case of a plan covering only employees included in a unit of employees covered by a collective bargaining agreement, all employees not included in such unit may be disregarded for purposes of satisfying the minimum participation rule.

Act § 1112   ¶ 3977

* * * * * *

* * * * * *

The conference agreement follows the Senate amendment with the following modifications and clarifications.

First, the minimum participation rule generally does not apply to a multiemployer plan. However, this exemption does not apply to a multiemployer plan that covers any professional (e.g., doctor, lawyer, or investment banker). In addition, the special rule in the Senate amendment regarding plans covering only employees included in a unit of employees covered by a collective bargaining agreement also does not apply to a plan that covers any professional. No inference is intended from these rules that a plan covering a professional may be a multiemployer plan.

Second, the conference agreement provides that, under regulations prescribed by the Secretary, any separate benefit structure, any separate trust, or any separate arrangement with respect to a defined benefit plan may be treated as a separate plan for purposes of applying the minimum participation rule. Thus, for example, a plan that provides two different formulas for calculating participants' benefits or contributions may be treated as at least two plans. Also, if defined benefit plan assets are payable from more than one source, such as from more than one trust, each source of assets may be considered a separate plan. If any particular person or persons have any priority (under the terms of the plan or by arrangement outside of the plan) with respect to a source of assets for defined benefits, such as a right to some or all of a possible reversion, such person or persons may be considered the sole participant or participants with respect to that "plan."

In general, it is the intent of the conferees to define "plan" in such a way as to carry out the purposes of the minimum participation rule. Thus, if there is a single defined benefit structure and a single source of assets, there may be more than one plan for purposes of this rule if, under all the facts and circumstances (including those outside of the plan), the arrangement has an effect similar to providing a plan or account to a group of employees that would not satisfy the minimum participation rule. For example, a group of employees might agree to provide each one of them with investment authority with regard to a separate pool of assets held with respect to the defined benefit structure. If such employees may be compensated in any manner, inside or outside the plan, by reference to the results of their investments, each part of the pool of assets may be considered a separate plan benefiting the participant controlling the investment thereof.

In addition, "plan" is to be defined so as to preclude the use of structures such as defined benefit plan defined contribution plan combinations (with benefit offsets) to avoid the rule.

If any plan, as specially defined herein, fails to satisfy the minimum participation rule, the entire plan (as otherwise defined) fails to satisfy the qualification standard (sec. 401(a)). Also, except to the extent provided in regulations, a plan will not satisfy this rule for a year unless it satisfies it on each day of the year.

The conferees also clarify how the minimum participation rules apply with respect to coverage of employees who could be excluded under the age or service rules from participation in a qualified plan. Generally, the rule is to apply as if the only employees of the employer were the excludable employees who may be tested separately under the coverage tests. However, all employees of the employer must be taken into account if any highly compensated employee is covered as an excludable employee for more than one year. Also, if any excludable employee is covered under a defined benefit pension plan, all employees of the employer are to be taken into account in applying the minimum participation rule to such plan, except where (1) the benefits provided under such coverage are comparable (or less than comparable) to the coverage of nonexcludable employees; and (2) the plan covering such excludable employees would satisfy the minimum participation rule (taking into account all employees of the employer) but for the fact that such plan has a different defined benefit structure from the plan covering the nonexcludable employees. Thus, payments with respect to defined benefits provided to excludable employees must come from the same source as payments with respect to defined benefits provided to nonexcludable employees. All employees of the employer are to be taken into account if only the excludable employees are covered by a defined benefit plan.

If excludable employees may be tested separately under the rules described above, such employees may be disregarded in applying the minimum participation rule to other employees.

The Secretary may exempt from the application of this rule two limited situations. The Secretary may, under appropriate conditions, exempt a plan that benefits no employee who is or ever has been a highly compensated employee with respect to service being credited under the plan, provided that such plan is not necessary for another plan or plans to satisfy the applicable coverage rules (sec. 410(b)).

The Secretary may, under appropriate conditions, also exempt a plan that may not be terminated on account of the provisions of the Single Employer Pension Plan Amendment Act (SEPPAA) because it is underfunded. However, such exemption may not apply unless benefit accruals cease, the plan obtains a letter of insufficiency for each plan year of exemption, and the plan eliminates, under rules prescribed by the Secretary, any different benefit structure or separate arrangement (as described above).

Further, the conference agreement provides that if (i) a plan is in existence on August 16, 1986, (ii) the plan would fail to meet the requirements of the minimum participation rule if such rule were in effect on August 16, 1986, and (iii) there is no transfer of assets to or liabilities from the plan, or merger or spinoff involving the plan, after August 16, 1986, such plan may be terminated and the 10-percent excise tax on the reversion of assets * * * is not imposed on any employer reversion from such plan. Such termination and reversion are permissible even though the terminating plan relies on another plan that is not terminated for qualification. In determining the amount of any such employer reversion, the present value of the accrued benefit of any individual who is a highly compensated employee, is to be determined by using an interest rate that is equal to the maximum interest rate that may be used for purposes of calculating a participant's accrued benefit under section 411(a)(11)(B). (See [¶1139 Ed.]) The Secretary is to prescribe rules preventing avoidance of this interest rate rule through distributions prior to or in lieu of a reversion. * * *

* * * **Former employees.**—Under rules prescribed by the Secretary, the coverage rules are to apply separately to former employees. The conferees intend that for this purpose rules similar to those applicable to employee benefits may be applied. (See [¶3995 Ed.].)

Sanction.—The conference agreement modifies the sanction applicable to a plan that fails to qualify due solely to a failure to satisfy the new coverage rules. Under the agreement, nonhighly compensated employees are not taxable on amounts contributed to or earned by the trust merely because a plan fails to satisfy the coverage requirements. Highly compensated employees, on the other hand, are taxable on the value of their vested accrued benefit attributable to employer contributions and income on any contributions to the extent such amounts have not previously been taxed to the employee. Except for these two changes, the sanctions applicable under current law are not modified. Thus, as under present law, in appropriate circumstances, apply lesser sanctions than those authorized.

*　　*　　*　　*　　*　　*

[Senate Explanation]

*　　*　　*　　*　　*　　*

Effective Date.—The provisions are generally effective for plan years beginning after December 31, 1988.

A special effective date applies to plans maintained pursuant to a collective bargaining agreement. Under this special rule, in the case of a plan maintained pursuant to a collective bargaining agreement between employee representatives and one or more employers ratified before March 1, 1986, the amendments are not effective for plan years beginning before the earlier of (1) the later of (i) January 1, 1989, or (ii) the date on which the last of the collective bargaining agreements terminates, or (2) January 1, 1991. Extensions or renegotiations of the collective bargaining agreement, if ratified after February 28, 1986, are disregarded.

[¶3978] SECTION 1113. MINIMUM VESTING STANDARDS

(Sec. 411 of the Code)

[Conference Report]

Senate Amendment

In general.—The Senate amendment provides that a plan is not a qualified plan (except in the case of a multiemployer plan), unless a participant's employer-provided benefit vests at least as rapidly as under one of 2 alternative minimum vesting schedules.

A plan satisfies the first schedule if a participant has a nonforfeitable right to 100 percent of the participant's accrued benefit derived from employer contributions upon the participant's completion of 5 years of service. A plan satisfies the second alternative schedule if a participant has a nonforfeitable right to at least 20 percent of the participant's accrued benefit derived from employer contributions after 3 years of service, 40 percent at the end of 4 years of service, 60 percent at the end of 5 years of service, 80 percent at the end of 6 years of service, and 100 percent at the end of 7 years of service.

Top-heavy plans.—The provisions of the Senate amendment relating to vesting do not alter the requirements applicable to plans that become top heavy. Thus, a plan that becomes top heavy is required to satisfy one of the two alternative vesting schedules applicable under present law to top-heavy plans.

Class-year plans.—A plan with class year vesting will not meet the qualification standards of the Code unless, under the plan's vesting schedule, a participant's total accrued benefit derived from employer contributions becomes nonforfeitable at least as rapidly as under one of the two alternative vesting schedules specified in the bill.

Changes in vesting schedule.—If a plan's vesting schedule is modified by a plan amendment, the plan will not be qualified unless each participant with at least 3 years of service is permitted to elect, within a reasonable period after the adoption of the amendment, to have the nonforfeitable percentage of the participant's accrued benefit computed without regard to the amendment.

Multiemployer plans.—As an exception to the general vesting requirements, the bill requires that, in the case of a multiemployer plan, a participant's accrued benefit derived from employer contributions be 100 percent vested no later than upon the participant's completion of 10 years of service.

Act §1113　¶3978

Effective date.—The provisions of the Senate amendment are generally applicable for plan years beginning after December 31, 1988, to participants who perform at least one hour of service in a plan year to which the new provision applies.

A special effective date applies to plans maintained pursuant to a collective bargaining agreement. Under this special rule, in the case of a plan maintained pursuant to a collective bargaining agreement between employee representatives and one or more employers ratified before March 1, 1986, the amendments are not effective for plan years beginning before the earlier of (1) the later of (i) January 1, 1989, or (ii) the date on which the last of the collective bargaining agreements terminates, or (2) January 1, 1991. Extensions or renegotiations of the collective bargaining agreement, if ratified after February 28, 1986, are disregarded.

Conference Agreement

The conference agreement follows the Senate amendment. In addition, the conference agreement modifies the rule permitting an employer to condition participation in a plan on 3 years of service. Under the conference agreement a plan may require, as a condition of participation, that an employee complete a period of service with the employer of no more than two years. A plan that requires that an employee complete more than one year of service as a condition of participation must also provide that each participant in the plan has a nonforfeitable right to 100 percent of the accrued benefit under the plan when the benefit is accrued.

In addition, the conference agreement limits the special rule for multiemployer plans to employees covered by a collective bargaining agreement.

Also, benefits that become vested due to these provisions are to be immediately guaranteed by the PBGC (without regard to the phase-in rule).

The conference agreement also modifies the effective date so that the provision applies to all employees who have one hour of service after the effective date. This revised effective date also applies to the conference agreement modification regarding years of service required for participation.

In addition, the conference agreement limits the delayed effective date for plans maintained pursuant to a collective bargaining agreement to employees covered by such agreements.

[¶ 3979] SECTION 1114. DEFINITION OF HIGHLY COMPENSATED EMPLOYEE.

(Sec. 414 of the Code)

[Conference Report]

*　　*　　*　　*　　*　　*

House Bill

The House bill modifies the definition of the group of employees in whose favor discriminatory contributions are prohibited under a qualified cash or deferred arrangement. An employee is treated as highly compensated with respect to a year if, at any time during the year or any of the 2 preceding years, the employee (1) is a 5-percent owner of the employer (as defined in sec. 416(i)); (2) earns in excess of $50,000 in annual compensation from the employer; or (3) is a member of the top-paid group of the employer.

The top-paid group of employees includes all employees who (1) are in the top 10 percent of all employees on the basis of compensation paid during such year, and (2) are paid more than $20,000 during such year. However, an employee is not included in the top-paid group if the employee is paid less than $35,000 and is not in the top 5 percent of all employees on the basis of compensation paid during such year.

In determining whether an employee is in the top-paid group during any year, the House bill provides that employees who may be excluded in applying the percentage test of section 410(b)(1)(A) generally are disregarded. In addition, an employee will not be treated as in the top-paid group or as earning in excess of $50,000 based on compensation during the current year unless such employee also is among the 100 employees who have earned the highest compensation during such year.

The House bill provides a special rule for the treatment of family members of certain highly compensated employees. Under the special rule, if a family member (1) benefits under the qualified cash or deferred arrangement, and (2) is a family member of either a 5-percent owner or one of the top 10 highly compensated employees by compensation, then any compensation paid to such family member and any employer contribution under the plan on behalf of such family member is aggregated with the amounts paid and contributed on behalf of the 5-percent owner or the highly compensated employee in the top 10 employees by pay. Therefore, such family member and employee are treated as a single highly compensated employee in applying the special nondiscrimination tests.

An individual is considered a family member if, with respect to an employee, the individual is a spouse, lineal ascendant or descendant, or spouse of a lineal ascendant or descendant of the employee.

The House bill does not adopt the above definition of highly compensated employees for purposes of applying the nondiscriminatory coverage rules to qualified plans.

Senate Amendment

In general.—Under the Senate amendment, an employee is treated as highly compensated with respect to a year if, at any time during the year or the preceding year, the employee (1) was a 5-percent owner of the employer (as defined in sec. 426(i)); (2) received more than $100,000 in annual compensation from the employer; (3) received more than $50,000 in annual compensation from the employer and was a member of the top-paid group of the employer during the same year; or (4) was an officer of the employer (as defined in sec. 416(i)). The $50,000 and $100,000 thresholds are indexed at the same time and in the same manner as the adjustments to the dollar limits on benefits for defined benefit plans. The identity of the highly compensated employees is to be determined on an employer-wide basis.

Top-paid group.—The top-paid group of employees includes all employees who are in the top 20 percent of the employer's workforce on the basis of compensation paid during the year. Under a special rule, an employer may exclude the following employees solely for purposes of determining the size of the top-paid group (but not for identifying the particular employees in the top-paid group): (1) employees who have not completed 180 days of serice; (2) employees who work less than half-time; (3) employees who normally work fewer than 6 months a year; (4) except to the extent provided in regulations, employees who are included in a unit of employees covered by a collective bargaining agreement; (5) employees who have not attained age 21; and (6) employees who are nonresident aliens and who receive no U.S. source earned income. An example of an instance in which it is appropriate to consider employees covered by a collective bargaining agreement is the case in which the plan being tested is maintained pursuant to a collective bargaining agreement.

For purposes of this special rule, an employer may elect to apply numbers (1), (2), (3), and (5) above by substituting any shorter period of service or lower age than is specified in (1), (2), (3), or (5), as long as the employer applies the test uniformly for purposes of determining its top-paid group with respect to all its qualified plans and employee benefit plans (and for purposes of the line of business rules described below).

For example, assume an employer's total workforce is 100 employees, 20 of whom have not completed 180 days of service. Assume that none of the 100 employees is within any of the other excluded categories under this rule. Under the above rules, the 20 employees who have not completed the minimum requirements for eligibility may be disregarded in determining the size of the top-paid group. If the 20 employees are disregarded, the top-paid group is 20 percent of 80 employees (the number of employees who are not disregarded), or 16. Thus, the 16 employees who receive the highest compensation (including any employees who have not completed 180 days but who are among the 16 highest paid employees of the employer) are in the top-paid group. Each of these 16 employees who receives more than $50,000 a year is treated as a highly compensated employee. Other employees (and any of the

16 employees receiving less than $50,000) may also be a highly compensated employee under one of the other tests (i.e., officer or 5-percent owner).

Special rule for determining top-paid group for current year.—Under the Senate amendment, an employee will not be treated as in the top-paid group, as an officer, or as receiving more than $50,000 or $100,000 solely because of the employee's status during the current year, unless such employee also is among the 100 employees who have received the highest compensation during such year. Under this rule, an individual who was a highly compensated employee for the preceding year (without regard to the one-year lookback or to the application of this special rule) remains highly compensated for the current year.

Thus, the 100-employee rule is intended as a rule of convenience to employers with respect to new employees hired during the current year, with respect to increases in compensation, and with respect to certain other factors. If any employee is not a 5-percent owner or within the top-100 employees by compensation for the current year (and was not a highly compensated employee in the preceding year (without regard to this special rule)), then that employee is not treated as highly compensated for the year, but will be treated as highly compensated for the following year if the employee otherwise falls within the definition of highly compensated employee. However, under the conference agreement, an employer may elect not to apply the 100-employee rule for the current year.

For example, assume that a calendar year employer has 12,000 total employees in 1990 and 1991, and for each year 4,000 employees may be disregarded in determining the number of employees that is to be treated as the number in the top-paid group. Thus, 1,600 (20 percent of 8,000) employees are in the top-paid group. This employer's highly compensated employees for 1991 will include the following:

(1) any employee who owned at any time during 1990 or 1991 more than 5 percent of the employer;

(2) any employee who, in 1990, (i) received more than $100,000 in annual compensation, (ii) was an officer (for top-heavy purposes), or (iii) received more than $50,000 in annual compensation and was among the 1,600 most highly compensated employees; and

(3) any employee who, in 1991, (i) was an officer (for top-heavy purposes) or received more than $50,000 in annual compensation, and (ii) was among the 100 most highly compensated employees.

Thus, an employee who is not a highly compensated employee in 1990 (without regard to this special 100-employee rule) will not be treated as highly compensated for 1991, unless such employee either (i) acquires ownership of more than 5 percent of the employer in 1991 or (ii) both becomes one of the 100 most highly compensated employees in 1991 and either becomes an officer or receives more than $50,000 in 1991.

Treatment of family members.—The Senate amendment provides a special rule for the treatment of family members (as defined in the House bill) of certain highly compensated employees. Under the special rule, if an employee is a family member of either a 5-percent owner or one of the top 10 highly compensated employees by compensation, then any compensation paid to such family member and any contribution or benefit under the plan on behalf of such family member is aggregated with the compensation paid and contributions or benefits on behalf of the 5-percent owner or the highly compensated employee in the top 10 employees by compensation. Therefore, such family member and employee are treated as a single highly compensated employee.

For example, if the spouse of the most highly compensated employee of an employer is also an employee and participates in the employer's qualified cash or deferred arrangement, the elective deferrals made by the spouse and the compensation received by the spouse are aggregated with the elective deferrals made by, and the compensation received by, the most highly compensated employee for purposes of applying the special nondiscrimination test to the elective deferrals of the most highly compensated employee.

Former employees.—The Senate amendment provides that an employee who has separated from service as a highly compensated employee continues to be treated as a highly compensated employee. In addition, the Secretary is to prescribe rules to treat other former employees as highly compensated employees, if appropriate.

Because an individual may attempt to avoid these rules by continuing to perform a small amount of services for the employer after retirement and maintaining that separation from service has not occurred, the Secretary is to prescribe rules to treat an individual as separated from service if the employee performs only de minimis services for the employer during the year.

Conference Agreement

In general.—The conference agreement follows the Senate amendment definition of highly compensated employees, except as follows. First, the conference agreement provides that an employee with compensation in excess of $75,000 (rather than $100,000) is treated as highly compensated in all cases. Second, the $50,000 and $75,000 amounts are indexed at the same time and in the same manner as the dollar limit on benefits under a defined benefit plan (sec. 415(d)).

Third, the definition of an officer is modified to mean an individual who was an officer and received compensation greater than 150 percent of the defined contribution plan dollar limit in effect for that year. For purposes of this rule, no more than 50 employees (or if lesser, the greater of 3 employees or 10 percent of the employees) are to be treated as officers. If for any year no officer has compensation in excess of 150 percent of the defined contribution plan dollar limit, then the highest paid officer of the employer for such year is treated as an officer for purposes of the rules identifying highly compensated employees. As under the rules applicable for determining top-heavy status (sec. 416), a partnership is considered to have officers.

As under the Senate amendment, the determination of the number and identity of the highly compensated employees is made on the basis of the entire employer, not on the basis of, for example, a line of business or operating unit.

Top-paid group.—The conference agreement follows the Senate amendment, with certain modifications. For purposes of determining the size of the top-paid group (but not for identifying the particular employees in the top-paid group), the following employees may be excluded: (1) employees who have not completed 6 months of service, (2) employees who normally work less than 17½ hours per week, (3) employees who normally work during not more than 6 months during any year, (4) employees who have not attained age 21, (5) except to the extent provided in regulations, employees who are included in a unit of employees covered by a bona fide collective bargaining agreement, and (6) employees who are nonresident aliens and receive no U.S. source income.

As under the Senate amendment, the employer may substitute a shorter period of service or lower age than that specified in (1), (2), (3), or (4), provided that the employer applies the test uniformly in determining its top-paid group for all purposes, including, for example, the employee benefit nondiscrimination rules and the line of business rules described below.

The conference agreement also clarifies that the determination of the top-paid group is made solely with respect to active employees. Former employees are not taken into account in determining the top 20 percent of employees by compensation.

Special rule for determining top-paid group for current year.—The conference agreement follows the Senate amendment.

Treatment of family members.—The conference agreement follows the Senate amendment. The conference agreement also clarifies that even if a family member is excluded for purposes of determining the number of employees in the top-paid group, such family member is subject to the aggregation rule.

Former employees.—Under the conference agreement, a former employee is treated as highly compensated if the employee was highly compensated when (a) such employee separated from service or (b) at any time after the employee attained age 55. In addition, as under the Senate amendment, the conferees intend that the Secretary is to prescribe rules treating an employee who performs only de minimis services as separated from service for purposes of determining whether such employee is a highly compensated employee.

Scope of highly compensated employee definition.—Under the conference agreement, the new definition of highly compensated employees applies for purposes of sections 79, 89, 106, 117(d), 120, 127, 129, 132, 274, 401(a)(4), 401(a)(5), 401(k)(3), 401(l), 401(m), 406(b), 407(b), 408(k), 410(b), 411(d), 414(m), 415(c), 423(b), 424(c), 501(c)(17), 501(c)(18), 505, and 4975 of the Code, and 29 U.S.C. sec. 1108.

Compensation.—As under the Senate amendment, for purposes of identifying an

employer's highly compensated employees, "compensation" is defined as compensation within the meaning of section 415(c)(3), increased by elective contributions under a cafeteria plan (sec. 125), qualified cash or deferred arrangement (sec. 401(k)), SEP (sec. 408(k)), and tax-sheltered annuity (sec. 403(b)).

Effective date.—The new definition of "highly compensated employee" is generally effective for years beginning after December 31, 1986, except to the extent that the substantive rule to which it relates is effective at a later time.

[¶ 3980] SECTION 1115. SEPARATE LINES OF BUSINESS; COMPENSATION.

(Sec. 414 of the Code)

[Senate Explanation]

* * * * * *

Explanation of Provision.—

* * * * * *

In general.—As under present law, all employees of corporations that are members of a controlled group of corporations, or all employees of trades or businesses (whether or not incorporated) that are under common control, are aggregated and treated as if employed by a single employer (sec. 414(b) and (c)). Similarly, all employees of employers that are members of an affiliated service group are treated as employed by a single employer for purpose of the qualification requirements (sec. 414(m)).

* * * * * *

Safe harbor for separate lines of business or operating units.—The bill provides a safe-harbor rule under which a separate line of business or operating unit is treated as being operated for bona fide business reasons if such line of business or operating unit is a separate self-sustaining unit and if (1) each line of business or operating unit has at least 50 employees who do not perform services for any other line of business or operating unit; and (2) the "highly compensated employee percentage" of the line of business or operating unit is (a) not less than one-half, nor (b) more than twice the percentage of all employees of the employer who are highly compensated. For purposes of this requirement, the highly compensated employee percentage of a line of business or operating unit will be treated as not less than one-half of the percentage of all employees of the employer who are highly compensated if at least 10 percent of all highly compensated employees of the employer are employed by the line of business or operating unit.

Highly compensated employee percentage.—Under the bill, the term "highly compensated employee percentage" means the percentage of all employees performing services for a line of business or operating unit

who are highly compensated employees. For purposes of determining the number of employees performing services for a line of business or operating unit, and the highly compensated employees percentage of a line of business or operating unit, the committee intends that the Secretary develop rules governing the circumstances under which an employee will be treated as performing services for a line of business or operating unit.

Impermissible use of a line of business.—The committee intends that the Secretary prescribe by regulation what constitutes a line of business or operating unit. It is the intent of the committee that the line of business or operating unit concept not be used to undermine the nondiscrimination rules. Thus, for example, certain job classifications (such as hourly employees or leased employees) could not be considered separate lines of business or operating units. Also, for example, the committee does not intend that secretaries and other support service personnel be treated as in a line of business or operating unit separate from the lawyers or other professionals for whom such personnel perform services, or that nurses and laboratory personnel be treated as in a line of business separate from the medical doctors for whom they perform services. In addition, the bill provides that the members of an affiliated service group (sec. 414(m)) may not be treated as separate lines of business or operating units.

In general, * * * the headquarters (or home office) of an employer is not to be treated as a separate line of business or operating unit. Instead, the Secretary is to prescribe regulations under which headquarters personnel may be considered employed by one line of business or operating unit even though such personnel perform services for other lines of business or operating units.

It is generally intended that a line of business or operating unit include all employees necessary for preparation of certain classes of property for sale or the provision of services to customers. Certain exceptions to this rule may be established by regulation where one employer has two operations which are vertically integrated and which are traditionally operated by unrelated entities.

Combining lines of business.—* * * if a line of business or operating unit would be recognized, but for the fact that it does not satisfy the 50 employee or the highly compensated employee percentage tests, it may be combined with another line of business or operating unit, provided that the aggregate entity satisfies the 50 employee and the highly compensated employee percentage tests. With respect to any plan maintained for employees performing services for one of the combined lines of business, the plan is required to satisfy the coverage rules with respect to the aggregate entity.

Excludable employees.—For purposes of determining the number of employees in a line of business or operating unit and the highly compensated employee percentage of a line of business or operating unit, an employer may disregard the categories of employees that may be disregarded for purposes of determining which employees are highly compensated employees.

Common plan for more than one line of business.—The bill provides that if employees of more than one line of business or operating unit are eligible to participate in a single plan, then all such lines of business or operating units shall be treated as one line of business or operating unit.

*　　*　　*　　*　　*　　*

[Conference Report]

*　　*　　*　　*　　*　　*

The conference agreement follows the Senate amendment with the following modifications. For convenience, the conference agreement uses the term "line of business" to refer both to a line of business and to an operating unit.

First, it is clarified that if the employer establishes to the satisfaction of the Secretary that the employer operates separate lines of business or operating units for bona fide business reasons, both the eligibility tests and the benefits tests (as well as the alternative 80-percent test) may be applied separately with respect to employees in each line of business or operating unit, subject to the requirement that the classification test be satisfied with respect to any plan on an employer-wide basis. * * * also clarifies the definition of a line of business or operating unit. Whether claimed separate lines of business or operating units are bona fide is a facts and circumstances determination requiring examination of each particular situation. Differences and similarities between the services provided and products produced by such claimed lines of business are of course important considerations. In addition, the manner in which the employer organizes itself is relevant. Thus, if an employer fails to treat itself as comprised of separate lines of business or operating units and treats employees from different claimed lines or units in an equivalent fashion for certain purposes, it may not be appropriate to allow such activi-

ties to be treated as separate lines of business or operating units. These factors do not, however, override the rules relating to the definition of a line of business, discussed above with respect to the Senate amendment, to the extent that such rules would deny separate line of business or operating unit status.

*** Modifies the definition of an operating unit by requiring that it be operated in a significantly separate geographic area from another operating unit in the same line of business. For example, two plants in the same city would not be considered to be in significantly separate geographic areas and thus would not be considered separate operating units.

Also, the requirement that a separate line of business or operating unit have at least 50 employees is deleted from the safe harbor rule and made a substantive requirement. Thus, a line of business or operating unit shall not be treated as separate for purposes of the nondiscrimination rules unless it has at least 50 employees. As under the Senate amendment, more than one line of business or operating unit may be aggregated to satisfy this requirement.

Also, the requirement that a line of business or operating unit be a separate self-sustaining unit is deleted from the safe harbor rule, since such a requirement is part of the definition of a line of business or operating unit.

*** Clarify the proper treatment of employees of a headquarters or home office and of other employees serving more than one line of business or operating unit (e.g., payroll personnel). Like all other employees, these employees are to be allocated to one line of business or operating unit. Generally, this allocation shall, under rules prescribed by the Secretary, be made in accordance with their performance of services. Thus, if a majority of an employee's services are performed for a particular line of business or operating unit, such employee must be allocated to that line of business or operating unit.

Other employees rendering services to more than one line of business or operating unit must be allocated in one of two ways. First, the employer may allocate such employees on a pro-rata basis among its lines of business or operating units, under rules prescribed by the Secretary. Alternatively, such employees may be allocated to any one line of business or operating unit for which they perform substantial services provided that such allocation does not cause any line of business or operating unit to violate or further violate the highly compensated percentage rule. Thus, for this purpose, the highly compensated employee percentage rule serves as a substantive rule, not a safe harbor. This means, for example, that if any lines of business or operating units do not pass the 50-percent rule, highly compensated employees at the home office or headquarters who do not perform a majority of their services for any particular line of business or operating unit must be allocated first to such lines of business or operating units. This also means that in no event may such highly compensated employees be allocated to any line of business or operating unit if after such allocation the 200-percent rule would be violated (regardless of whether it was violated prior to such allocation).

*** The Secretary is to prescribe for annual reporting by employers using the line of business or operating unit rule for purposes of the nondiscrimination rules (including the qualified plan rules). Such reporting shall include the basis for the position that an employer is maintaining separate lines of business or operating units. Where an employer maintains a line of business or operating unit that does not fall within the safe harbor rule, this must be specifically reported and may trigger additional reporting requirements.

In addition, the Secretary is also to establish guidelines identifying circumstances in which there is to be special scrutiny of claimed lines of business or operating units. For example, if a plan maintained for a claimed line of business or operating unit is significantly better or worse than plans for other lines of business or operating units, such a situation shall trigger special scrutiny. Also, if a disproportionate percentage of the accrued benefits under the plan of a claimed line of business or operating unit is for the highly compensated employees, such employer's claim of a separate line of business or operating unit shall also be specially examined.

If a claimed line of business or operating unit does not satisfy the safe-harbor rule and a plan or plans of such line of business or operating unit warrants special scrutiny under the standards set forth in the applicable guidelines, then the claimed line of business or operating unit will not be recognized for purposes of the applicable nondiscrimination rules unless the employer obtains a determination from the Secretary (e.g., by determination letter or private letter ruling) that such line of business or operating unit is separately operated for bona fide business reasons.

Further, *** intend to clarify that if an employer is using the separate line of business or operating unit rule with respect to any plan, all employees must be considered part of a line of business or operating unit. Thus, it would not be permissible to maintain that an employer has, in addition to one line of business with 50 employees, 10 other employees who are not part of any line of business or operating unit and who would be tested separately. The 10 other employees would have to be treated as part of one or more lines of business or operating units. Such lines of business or operating units would have to be aggregated with the 50-employee line of business in order to satisfy the requirement that to be tested separately, a line of business or operating unit must have at least 50 employees.

*** Also deletes the rule providing that if employees from more than one line of busi-

ness or operating unit are eligible to participate in a plan, all such lines of business and/or operating units are treated as one line of business or operating unit. This would, however, be a fact to consider in ascertaining whether an employer treats itself as comprised of separate lines of business or operating units. Instead, the conference agreement requires that benefits attributable to services for a line of business or operating unit shall be considered as provided by that line of business or operating unit. For purposes of such rules, an employee who performs services for more than one line of business or operating unit, but is allocated to one line of business or operating unit under the rules described above, shall be considered to render services solely for that line of business or operating unit. ***

*   *   *   *   *   *

Compensation.—*** For purposes of applying the nondiscrimination rules (including the actual deferral percentage limits for cash or deferred arrangements and for employee and employer matching contributions), except as otherwise expressly provided (e.g., the definition of compensation for purposes of identifying the highly compensated employees), the term "compensation" means the total includible compensation of the employees of the employer. In addition, an employer may elect to treat salary reduction amounts under a cash or deferred arrangement, tax-sheltered annuity program, SEP, or cafeteria plan, as compensation, provided that such treatment is applied on a consistent basis. Thus, if an employer elects to treat elective deferrals under one cash or deferred arrangement as compensation, it must treat all elective deferrals under all cash or deferred arrangements as compensation. Further, the Secretary is directed to prescribe alternative definitions of compensation for use by employers in applying the nondiscrimination tests. Such alternative definitions are to include the basic or regular compensation of employees (e.g., disregarding bonuses and overtime). An employer may use an alternative definition prescribed by the Secretary only if it does not discriminate in favor of that employer's highly compensated employees; such determination is to be made in an objective fashion on the basis of the total includible compensation of employees.

*   *   *   *   *   *

Effective Date.—The provision generally is effective for *** years beginning after December 31, 198[6] ***.

A special effective date applies to plans maintained pursuant to a collective bargaining agreement. Under this special rule, in the case of a plan maintained pursuant to a collective bargaining agreement between employee representatives and one or more employers ratified before March 1, 1986, the amendments are not effective for plan years beginning before the earlier of (1) the later of (i) January 1, 1989, or (ii) the date on which the last of the collective bargaining agreements terminates, or (2) January 1, 1991. Extensions or renegotiations of the collective bargaining agreement, if ratified after February 28, 1986, are disregarded.

[¶ 3981] SECTION 1116. CASH OR DEFERRED ARRANGEMENTS.

(Sec. 401 of the Code)

[Conference Report]
House Bill

* * * * * *

Nondiscrimination requirements.—*In general.*—The bill modifies the special nondiscrimination tests applicable to qualified cash or deferred arrangements by redefining the group of highly compensated employees and by modifying the special percentage tests.

Definition of highly compensated employees.—The House bill provides a uniform definition of highly compensated employees for purposes of the nondiscrimination rules for qualified plans and employee benefit plans. (see the description in B.7., below).

Modification of nondiscrimination tests

The House bill alters the special nondiscrimination tests applicable to qualified cash or deferred arrangements so that the actual deferral percentage under a cash or deferred arrangement by highly compensated employees for a plan year may not exceed either (1) 125 percent of the actual deferral percentage of all nonhighly compensated employees eligible to defer under the arrangement, or (2) the lesser of 200 percent of the actual deferral percentage of all eligible nonhighly compensated employees or the actual deferral percentage for all eligible nonhighly compensated employees plus 2 percentage points.

Under the House bill, if a highly compensated employee participates in more than one qualified cash or deferred arrangement of an employer, the employee's actual deferral percentage for purposes of testing each arrangement under the special nondiscrimination tests is to be determined by aggregating the employee's elective deferrals under all of the arrangements of the employer.

Excess contributions.—If the special nondiscrimination rules are not satisfied for any year, the House bill provides that the qualified cash or deferred arrangement will not be disqualified if the excess contributions (plus income allocable to the excess contributions) are distributed before the close of the following plan year. Distribution of the excess contributions may be made notwithstanding any other provision of law and the amount distributed is not subject to the additional income tax on early withdrawals.

Under the House bill, excess contributions mean, with respect to any plan year, the excess of the aggregate amount of elective deferrals paid to the cash or deferred arrangement and allocated to the accounts of highly compensated employees over the maximum amount of elective deferrals that could be allocated to the accounts of highly compensated employees without violating the nondiscrimination requirements applicable to the arrangement. To determine the amount of excess contributions and the employees to whom the excess contributions are to be distributed, the bill provides that the elective deferrals of highly compensated employees are reduced in the order of their actual deferral percentages beginning with those highly compensated employees with the highest actual deferral percentages. The excess contributions are to be distributed to those highly compensated employees for whom a reduction is made under the preceding sentence in order to satisfy the special nondiscrimination tests.

Excise tax on excess contributions.—Under the House bill, a penalty tax is imposed on the employer making excess contributions to a qualified cash or deferred arrangement (sec. 4979). The tax is equal to 10 percent of the excess contributions under the arrangement for the plan year ending in the taxable year. However, the tax does not apply to any excess contributions that, together with income allocable to the excess contributions, are distributed no later than 2½ months after the close of the plan year to which the excess contributions relate.

Excess contributions (plus income) distributed within the applicable 2½ month period are to be treated as received and earned by the employee in the employee's taxable year in which the excess contributions, but for the employee's deferral election, would have been received as cash.

Other restrictions.—The House bill includes several additional restrictions on qualified cash or deferred arrangements. First, no withdrawals generally are permitted under a qualified cash or deferred arrangement prior to death, disability, separation from service, bona fide plan termination or (except in the case of a pre-ERISA money purchase pension plan) the attainment of age 59½. However, a cash or deferred arrangement (other than a pre-ERISA money purchase pension plan) may permit hardship withdrawals from elective deferrals (but not income on the elective deferrals).

In addition, the House bill provides that a qualified cash or deferred arrangement cannot require, as a condition of participation in the arrangement, that an employee complete a period of service with the employer (or employers) maintaining the plan in excess of one year of service.

Under the House bill, an employer generally may not condition, either directly or indirectly, contributions and benefits (other than matching contributions in the plan of which that arrangement is a part) upon an employee's elective deferrals.

The House bill clarifies that qualified cash or deferred arrangements are not available to employees of tax-exempt organizations or governmental entities. This restriction does not apply to a plan maintained by a rural electric cooperative (defined in sec. 457(d)(9)(B)), a national association of such cooperatives, or a plan maintained by the Tennessee Valley Authority.

The House bill provides that, in the case of employer contributions (including elective deferrals under a qualified cash or deferred arrangement) that satisfy the immediate vesting and withdrawal restrictions applicable to elective deferrals under a qualified cash or deferred arrangement, the determination of whether the plan to which the contributions are made is a profit-sharing plan is to be made without regard to whether the employer has current or accumulated profits. This is the case even if the plan does not contain a qualified cash or deferred arrangement.

* * * * * *

Senate Amendment

* * * * * *

Nondiscrimination requirements. — The Senate amendment is the same as the House bill except that the Senate amendment (1) does not modify the permitted disparities under the special nondiscrimination test applicable to qualified cash or deferred arrangements; (2) clarifies the rules for aggregating elective contributions with certain nonelective contributions for purposes of the special nondiscrimination test; and (3) modifies the uniform definition of highly compensated employees.

Other restrictions.—The Senate amendment is the same as the House bill except that the amendment modifies certain present-law restrictions and imposes several additional restrictions on qualified cash or deferred arrangements.[1] First, the amendment provides that distributions may be made to a participant in a qualified cash or deferred arrangement on account of the sale of a subsidiary, sale of a substantial portion of the assets of a trade or business, or termination of the plan of which the arrangement is a part. Under the Senate amendment, the exception for distributions upon the sale of a subsidiary is available with respect to a participant who has not separated from service with the subsidiary.

The Senate amendment is the same as the House bill with respect to the availability of qualified cash or deferred arrangements for public employers, but the Senate amendment provides that qualified cash or deferred arrangements are available to employees of tax-exempt organizations.

* * * * * *

Conference Agreement

* * * * * *

Nondiscrimination requirements. — The conference agreement follows the House bill with certain modifications.

Definition of highly compensated employees.—The conference agreement modifies the definition of highly compensated employees to which the nondiscrimination requirements apply and provides that this uniform definition applies generally for purposes of nondiscrimination requirements for qualified plans and employee benefit programs * * *. In addition, the conference agreement adopts the provision in the Senate amendment providing a special definition of highly compensated employees for purposes of the special nondiscrimination requirements for qualified cash or deferred arrangement and in the case of a certain company.

* * * * * *

Special nondiscrimination requirements.—The conference agreement follows the House bill with respect to the special nondiscrimination tests applicable to qualified cash or deferred arrangements.

In addition, the conference agreement provides that, for purposes of applying the special nondiscrimination requirements, under rules prescribed by the Secretary, employer matching contributions that meet the vesting and withdrawal restrictions for elective deferrals under a qualified cash or deferred arrangement and qualified nonelective contributions may be taken into account. Qualified nonelective contributions are defined to mean employer contributions (other than matching contributions) with respect to which (1) the employee may not elect to have the contributions paid to the employee in cash in lieu of being contributed to the plan and (2) the vesting and distribution restrictions applicable to qualified cash or deferred arrangements are satisfied.

Excess contributions.—The conference agreement follows the House bill and the Senate amendment with respect to the treatment of excess contributions (i.e., contributions to highly compensated employees that violate the special nondiscrimination requirements applicable to qualified cash or deferred arrangements). The conference agreement modifies the rules for determining the amount of income attributable to excess contributions. Under the conference agreement, the amount of income attributable to excess contributions is that portion of the income on the participant's account balance for the year that bears the same ratio as the excess contributions bears to the total account balance.

For purposes of determining the year in which the excess contributions are includible in income, the excess contributions are treated as the first contributions made for a year.

In addition, the conferees intend that the Secretary will prescribe rules relating to the coordination of an employee's excess defer-

---

[Footnote ¶ 3981] (1) *See,* also, the discussion in Part C., below.

rals (i.e., amounts in excess of the annual limit on elective deferrals) and the excess contributions and that, generally, the excess deferrals are to be calculated and distributed first and then the excess contributions are to be allocated among the highly compensated employees and distributed.

Under the conference agreement, the provision in the Senate amendment under which excess contributions that are distributed to a highly compensated employee are not subject to the additional income tax on early withdrawals from qualified plans is adopted. In addition, the conferees intend that a plan is not required to obtain the consent of the participant or the participant and spouse to distribute an excess contribution.

The conference agreement provides that a plan can distribute excess deferrals and excess contributions without regard to the terms of the plan or any other law until the first plan year for which plan amendments are required.

Effective dates.—The [nondiscrimination] provisions generally are effective for years beginning after December 31, 1986.

A special effective date applies to plans maintained pursuant to a collective bargaining agreement. Under this special rule, in the case of a plan maintained pursuant to a collective bargaining agreement between employee representatives and one or more employers ratified before March 1, 1986, the amendments are not effective, with respect to employees covered by the agreement, for plan years beginning before the earlier of (1) January 1, 1989, or (2) the date on which the last of the collective bargaining agreement terminates (determined without regard to any extensions in the collective bargaining agreement).

The rule relating to aggregation of a highly compensated employee's benefit under more than one qualified cash or deferred arrangement and the rules relating to the treatment of excess contributions are effective for plan years beginning after December 31, 1986.

Other restrictions.—The conference agreement adopts the following provisions with respect to qualified cash or deferred arrangements:

Hardship withdrawals.—The conference agreement follows the House bill and the Senate amendment which limits hardship withdrawals from a qualified cash or deferred arrangement to the amount of an employee's elective deferrals. Therefore, hardship withdrawals are not permitted from amounts attributable to income on elective deferrals.

Under the conference agreement, employer matching contributions and nonelective contributions (to the extent taken into account for purposes of the special nondiscrimination test), and income on such matching or nonelective contributions may not be distributed on account of hardship.

The provision is effective for years beginning after December 31, 1988.

A special effective date applies to plans maintained pursuant to a collective bargaining agreement. Under this special rule, with respect to employees covered under a plan maintained pursuant to a collective bargaining agreement between employee representatives and one or more employers ratified before March 1, 1986, the amendments are not effective, with respect to employees subject to the agreement, for plan years beginning before the earlier of (1) the later of January 1, 1989, or the date on which the last of the collective bargaining agreement terminates (determined without regard to any extensions in the collective bargaining agreement), or (2) January 1, 1991.

Withdrawals on account of plan termination, etc.—The conference agreement generally follows the Senate amendment with respect to the provision permitting distributions from a qualified cash or deferred arrangement upon (1) plan termination without the establishment of a successor plan; (2) the date of the sale by a corporation of substantially all of the assets used by the corporation in a trade or business if the employee continues employment with the corporation acquiring the assets; or (3) the date of the sale by a corporation of the corporation's interest in a subsidiary if the employee continues employment with the subsidiary. Under the conference agreement, a distribution upon any of the 3 events described above is permitted only if it constitutes a total distribution of the employee's balance to the credit in the cash or deferred arrangement.

The provision is effective for distributions occurring after December 31, 1984.

Conditioning other benefits on elective deferrals.—The conference agreement follows the House bill and the Senate amendment with respect to the rule that a qualified cash or deferred arrangement cannot condition, either directly or indirectly, contributions and benefits (other than matching contributions in the plan of which the arrangement is a part) upon an employee's elective deferrals.

In addition, the conference agreement adopts the provision in the House bill and the Senate amendment that any elective deferrals under a qualified cash or deferred arrangement may not be taken into account for purposes of determining whether another plan meets the coverage requirements (sec. 410(b)) or the general nondiscrimination rules (sec. 401(a)(4)) or other qualification rules. This provision does not apply for purposes of applying the average benefit percentage requirement under the coverage requirements (but does apply for purposes of the present-law classification requirement that is part of the average benefit test).

The conferees clarify that the provision relating to conditioning other benefits on elective deferrals applies in the situation in which a plan provides that voluntary after-tax employee contributions may not be made until an employee makes a minimum amount of elective deferrals under a qualified cash or deferred arrangement. The conferees also clarify that this provision precludes the use of elective deferrals to satisfy the minimum contribution required on behalf of nonkey employees in a top-heavy plan.

Further, the conference agreement follows the Senate amendment with respect to qualified offset arrangements with a clarification of the definition of an employer for purposes of the provision.

The provisions are effective for years beginning after December 31, 1988.

A special effective date applies to plans maintained pursuant to a collective bargaining agreement. Under this special rule, with respect to employees covered under a plan maintained pursuant to a collective bargaining agreement between employee representatives and one or more employers ratified before March 1, 1986, the amendments are not effective, with respect to employees subject to the agreement, for plan years beginning before the earlier of (1) the later of January 1, 1989, or the date on which the last of the collective bargaining agreement terminates (determined without regard to any extensions in the collective bargaining agreement), or (2) January 1, 1991.

Eligibility to participate.—The conference agreement follows the House bill and the Senate amendment with respect to the provision that a qualified cash or deferred arrangement cannot require, as a condition of participation in the arrangement, that an employee complete a period of service greater than 1 year with the employer maintaining the plan, effective for years beginning after December 31, 1988.

A special effective date applies to plans maintained pursuant to a collective bargaining agreement. Under this special rule, in the case of a plan maintained pursuant to a collective bargaining agreement between employee representatives and one or more employers ratified before March 1, 1986, the amendments are not effective, with respect to employees covered by the agreement, for years beginning before the earlier of (1) the later of January 1, 1989, or the date on which the last of the collective bargaining agreement terminates (determined without regard to any extensions in the collective bargaining agreement), or (2) January 1, 1991.

Tax-exempt and State and local employers.—Under the conference agreement, the provision in the House bill prohibiting tax-exempt organizations and State and local governments (or a political subdivision of a State or local government) from establishing qualified cash or deferred arrangements is adopted.

The conference agreement provides that this provision does not apply to plans adopted before (1) May 6, 1986, in the case of an arrangement maintained by a State or local government (or political subdivision of a State or local government), or (2) July 2, 1986, in the case of an arrangement maintained by a tax-exempt organization. The grandfather treatment is limited to the employers who adopted the plan before the dates specified above. However, the grandfather treatment is not limited to employees (or classes of employees) covered by the plan as of the date the grandfather treatment is provided.

The provision is effective for years beginning after December 31, 1986. However, in the case of a plan maintained by a State or local government that was adopted before May 6, 1986 (and is, therefore, eligible for the grandfather rule), the following provisions in the conference agreement applicable to qualified cash or deferred arrangements do not apply until years beginning after December 31, 1988: (1) the modification of the special nondiscrimination tests, (2) the new definition of highly compensated employees, (3) the new definition of compensation, and (4) the rule aggregating highly compensated employees.

Definition of compensation.—The conference agreement adopts a uniform definition of compensation for purposes of applying the special nondiscrimination requirements, effective for years beginning after December 31, 1988. (*See* description in *** [¶3977].)

[The following colloquy relating to Act Sec. 1116 is drawn from the Congressional Record. The colloquy occurred on the day the Conference bill was considered by the House. Ed.]

[House Floor Explanation]

I have discussed with Congressman Duncan several issues relating to the Tennessee Valley Authority's eligibility for a section 401(k) cash or deferred arrangement under this legislation. We have reached a common understanding regarding the following specific issue:

The House bill expressly provided that the Tennessee Valley Authority would be eligible to have a section 401(k) cash or deferred arrangement. Although this express provision is not in the conference report, it is my understanding that the cash or deferred arrangement that was adopted by TVA in February 1986 would be an eligible section 401(k) plan because TVA is a Federal agency Congressional Record, p. H 8361, 9-25-86.

[¶ 3982] **SECTION 1117. NONDISCRIMINATION REQUIREMENTS FOR EMPLOYER MATCHING CONTRIBUTIONS AND EMPLOYEE CONTRIBUTIONS**

(Sec. 401, 414 and 4979 of the Code)

[House Explanation]

* * * * * *

Explanation of Provision.—Under the bill, special nondiscrimination rules are applied to employer matching contributions and employee contributions under all qualified defined contribution plans. These nondiscrimination tests apply in addition to the usual nondiscrimination rules applicable to qualified plans.

Qualified matching and employee contributions.—Under the first test, a defined contribution plan (and the employee contribution portion of a defined benefit pension plan) will not be treated as meeting the special nondiscrimination test with respect to employer matching contributions that are qualified employer matching contributions and with respect to employee contributions (other than deductible employee contributions) for a plan year unless the matching contribution percentage or the employee contribution percentage for highly compensated employees does not exceed the greater of (1) 125 percent of the matching contribution percentage or the employee contribution percentage for all other eligible employees or (2) the lesser of 200 percent of the matching contribution percentage or the employer contribution percentage for all other eligible employees or such percentage plus 2 percentage points.

Under the bill, a matching contribution is defined as (1) any employer contribution made on behalf of an employee on account of an employee's contribution to a plan and (2) any employer contribution made on behalf of an employee on account of an employee's elective deferrals under a qualified cash or deferred arrangement. In order to be qualified employer matching contributions, the matching contributions are required to be (1) nonforfeitable when made, (2) ineligible for withdrawal prior to attainment of age 59½, death, disability, separation from service, or bona fide plan termination, and (3) no greater than 100 percent of the employee's mandatory contributions.

The matching contribution percentage for a specified group of employees is the average of the ratios (calculated separately for each employee in the group) of the amount of the matching contributions actually allocated to the employee's account for the plan year to the employee's compensation for the plan year. For purposes of this test, if an employee contribution is required as a condition of participation in the plan, any employee who would be considered a participant if the employee made a contribution to the plan is treated as a participant in the plan on whose behalf no matching contributions are made. The employee contribution percentage is calculated in the same manner as the matching contribution percentage.

Nonqualified matching contributions.—The bill provides that nonqualified matching contributions (i.e., matching contributions that are not qualified matching contributions) are subject to a special nondiscrimination test under which the matching contribution percentage for highly compensated employees is limited to the greater of (1) 110 percent of the matching contribution percentage for the other eligible employees or (2) the lesser of 150 percent of the matching contribution percentage for other eligible employees or the such percentage plus one percentage point.

Definition of highly compensated employee.—Under the bill, the definition of "highly compensated employee" for purposes of the special nondiscrimination tests for employer matching contributions and employee contributions is the same as the definition for testing elective deferrals under a cash or deferred arrangement. Thus, in general, for purposes of the special nondiscrimination tests, an employee generally is treated as highly compensated with respect to a year if, at any time during the year or any of the two preceding years, the employee (1) is a 5-percent owner of the employer (as defined in section 416(i)); (2) earns at least $50,000 in annual compensation from the employer; or (3) is a member of the top-paid group of the employer.

Under the bill, the top-paid group of employees includes all employees who (1) are in the top ten percent of all employees on the basis of compensation paid during such year, and (2) are paid more than $20,000 during such year. However, an employee is not included in the top-paid group if the employee is paid less than $35,000 and is not in the top five percent of all employees on the basis of compensation paid during such year. The various special rules, regulation authority, and transition rule applicable to calculation of the highly compensated employees for testing cash or deferred arrangements apply for purposes of the tests for employer matching contributions and employee contributions. The special rules for the treatment of family members of the top 10 highly compensated employees and 5-percent owners and for highly compensated employees who participate in more than one plan of an employer also apply.

In addition, the bill authorizes the Secretary of the Treasury to prescribe regulations relating to the extent to which employer matching contributions, employee contributions, nonelective contributions, and elective deferrals under a qualified cash or deferred arrangement are, or may be, aggregated for purposes of the special nondiscrimination tests. Further, the bill authorizes regulations limiting the extent to which an employer may make multiple use of the second or alternative portion of the special nondiscrimination tests.

Treatment of excess contributions.—If the special nondiscrimination rules are not satisfied for any year, the bill provides that the plan will not be disqualified if the excess contributions (plus income allocable to such excess contributions) are distributed before the close of the following plan year. Distribution of excess contributions may be made notwithstanding any other provision of the law, and the amount distributed is not subject to the additional income tax on early withdrawals.

Excess contributions mean, with respect to any plan year, the excess of the aggregate amount of employer matching contributions or employee contributions allocated to the accounts of highly compensated employees over the maximum amount of employer matching contributions (or employee contributions) that could be allocated to the accounts of highly compensated employees without violating the special nondiscrimination requirements. To determine the amount of the excess contributions and the employees to whom the excess contributions are to be distributed, the bill provides that the contributions made by or on behalf of highly compensated employees will be reduced in the order of their contribution percentages beginning with those highly compensated employees with the highest contribution percentages.

The excess contributions are to be distributed to those highly compensated employees for whom a reduction is made under the preceding sentence in order to satisfy the special nondiscrimination tests. The bill also provides a special rule for excess contributions that consist of nonvested employer contributions. Such contributions are to be forfeited, rather than distributed. Any excess contributions, or, if reallocated, must be reallocated to participant other that those highly compensated employees who were determined to have excess contributions.

Excise tax on excess contributions.—Under the bill, an excise tax is imposed on the employer (sec. 4979). The tax is equal to 10 percent of the excess contributions under the arrangement for the plan year ending in the taxable year.

However, excess contributions do not include any excess contributions that, together with income allocable to the excess contributions, are distributed (or, if nonvested, forfeited) no later than 2½ months after the close of the plan year in which the excess contributions arose.

Excess matching contributions (plus income) and income on excess employee contributions distributed within the applicable 2½ month period are to be treated as received and earned by the employee in the employee's taxable year to which such excess contributions relate. Excess matching contributions are deemed to relate to the same taxable year to which the employee' mandatory contribution relates; i.e., mandatory contributions that are elective deferrals relate to the taxable year in which the employee would have received (but for the deferral election) the deferral as cash, and mandatory contributions that are employee contributions relate to the taxable year of contribution. For purposes of this rule, the first matching and employee contributions are deemed to be excess contributions.

*   *   *   *   *   *

[Conference Report]

*   *   *   *   *

Conference Agreement.—The conference agreement generally follows the House bill with modifications.

Special nondiscrimination test.—*In general.*—Under the conference agreement, a special nondiscrimination test is applied to employer matching contributions and employee contributions under qualified defined contribution plans and employee contributions under a defined benefit pension plan (to the extent allocated to a separate account on behalf of an employee) including employee contributions under a qualified cost-of-living arrangement. This special nondiscrimination test is similar to the special nondiscrimination test applicable to qualified cash or deferred arrangements. The conference agreement does not follow the House bill provision under which a special nondiscrimination test applies to employee contributions and to employer matching contributions that are "qualified matching contributions" and a different nondiscrimination test applies to other employer matching contributions.

The conference agreement provides that the special nondiscrimination test is satisfied for a plan year if the contribution percentage for highly compensated employees does not exceed the greater of (1) 125 percent of the contribution percentage for all other eligible employees, or (2) the lesser of 200 percent of the contribution percentage for all other eligible employees, or such percentage plus 2 percentage points. The contribution percentage for a group of employees for a plan year is the average of the ratios (calculated separately for each employee in the group) of the sum of matching and employee contributions on behalf of each such employee to the employee's compensation for the year.

Under the conference agreement, under rules prescribed by the Secretary, an employer may elect to take into account elective contributions and qualified nonelective contributions under the plan or under any other plan of the employer. Qualified nonelective contributions are defined to mean any employer contribution (other than a matching contribution) with respect to which (1) the employee may not elect to have the contribution paid to the employee in cash in lieu of being contributed to the plan, and (2) the vesting and withdrawal restrictions applicable to qualified cash or deferred arrangements are satisfied (and hardship withdrawals are not permitted). The term "employer matching contributions" means any employer contribution made to the plan on account of an employee contribution or an employee's elective deferrals to a qualified cash or deferred arrangement. The Secretary may prescribe such other conditions on aggregating types of contributions for nondiscrimination purposes as are appropriate to carry out the intent of the provisions.

Elective and nonelective contributions may only be taken into account for purposes of the special nondiscrimination rules if the contributions taken into account satisfy the applicable nondiscrimination rules and other contributions would not fail to satisfy applicable nondiscrimination rules if the elective or nonelective contributions taken into account were disregarded.

For example, if an employer maintains a qualified cash or deferred arrangement, a plan to which after-tax employee contributions and matching contributions are made, and a profit-sharing plan with employer contributions that are qualified nonelective contributions, then the employer can elect, for purposes of the special nondiscrimination test for matching contributions and employee contributions, to aggregate (1) elective deferrals under the qualified cash or deferred arrangement, (2) after-tax employee contributions, (3) employer matching contributions, and (4) qualified nonelective contributions. Further, for purposes of the special nondiscrimination test applicable to qualified cash or deferred arrangements, the employer can elect (subject to any other rules that may apply) to aggregate (1) elective deferrals under the qualified cash or deferred arrangement, (2) employer matching contributions that satisfy vesting and distribution rules, and (3) qualified nonelective contributions.

For purposes of the special nondiscrimination test, if 2 or more plans of an employer to which matching contributions, employee contributions, or elective contributions are made are treated as a single plan for purposes of the coverage requirements for qualified plans (sec. 410(b)), then the plans are treated as a single plan for purposes of the special nondiscrimination test. In addition, if a highly compensated employee participates in 2 or more plans of an employer to which matching contributions, employee contributions, or elective contributions are made, then all such contributions made on behalf of the highly compensated employee are aggregated for purposes of the special nondiscrimination test.

Under the conference agreement, any employee who is eligible to make an employee contribution (or, if the employer takes elective deferrals into account, is eligible to make elective deferrals) or is eligible to receive a matching contribution is treated as an eligible employee for purposes of the special nondiscrimination test. In addition, under the conference agreement, if an employee contribution is required as a condition of participation in a plan, an employee who is eligible to participate, but fails to make a required contribution, is treated as an eligible employee on behalf of whom no employer contributions are made.

Definition of highly compensated employee.—The conference agreement modifies the definition of highly compensated employees to which the special nondiscrimination test applies and provides that this uniform definition applies generally for purposes of the nondiscrimination requirements for qualified plans and employee benefit programs (*see* the description in Part B.7., below).

Excess contributions.—The conference agreement generally follows the House bill and the Senate amendment with respect to the treatment of excess contributions (i.e., contributions for highly compensated employees that violate the special nondiscrimination requirements applicable to employer matching and employee contributions). The conference agreement modifies the rules for determining the amount of income attributable to excess contributions. Under the conference agreement, the amount of income attributable to excess contributions is that portion of the income on the participant's account balance for the year that bears the same ratio as the excess contributions bear to the total account balance.

For purposes of assessing any withholding penalties, the excess contributions are treated as the first contributions made for a year.

In addition, the conferees intend that the Secretary will prescribe rules relating to the coordination of an employee's excess deferral (i.e., amounts in excess of the annual limit on elective deferrals under a qualified cash or deferred arrangement) and the excess contributions and that, generally, the excess deferrals are to be calculated and distributed first and then the excess contributions are to be allocated among the highly compensated employees and distributed.

Under the conference agreement, the provision in the Senate amendment under which excess contributions that are distributed to a highly compensated employee are not subject to the additional income tax on early withdrawals from qualified plans is adopted. In addition, the conferees intend that a plan is not required to obtain the consent of the participant or the participant and spouse to distribute an excess contribution.

The conference agreement provides that a plan can cash out excess contributions without regard to the terms of the plan until the first plan year for which plan amendments are required (*see* Part E.5., below).

Effective dates.—The provisions generally are effective for plan years beginning after December 31, 1986.

A special effective date applies to plans maintained pursuant to a collective bargaining agreement. Under this special rule, in the case of (employees covered under) a plan maintained pursuant to a collective bargaining agreement between employee representatives and one or more employers ratified before March 1, 1986, the amendments are not effective for plan years beginning before the earlier of (1) January 1, 1989, or (2) the date on which the last of the collective bargaining agreement terminates (determined without regard to any extensions in the collective bargaining agreement). In the case of a tax-sheltered annuity, the provi-

sions are effective for plan years beginning after December 31, 1988.

[¶3983] SECTION 1118. BENEFITS TREATED AS ACCRUING RATABLY FOR PURPOSES OF DETERMINING WHETHER PLAN IS TOP-HEAVY.

(Sec. 416 of the Code)

[Senate Explanation]

* * * * * *

Explanation of Provision.—Under the bill, a uniform accrual rule is used in testing whether a qualified plan is top-heavy (or super top-heavy) (sec. 416(g)(4)(F)). Thus, solely for determining whether the present value of cumulative accrued benefits for key employees exceed 60 percent of the present value of cumulative accrued benefits for all employees (90 percent for purposes of the super top-heavy plan rules), cumulative accrued benefits are to be uniformly measured by applying the fractional rule. Thus, benefits will be treated as accruing no more rapidly than required under the fractional rule.

This rule applies only for purposes of determining whether the plan is top heavy-or super top-heavy. The rule does not require that the plan actually use the fractional rule

for purposes of accruing benefits under the plan.

[Conference Report]

* * * * * *

Conference Agreement.—The conference agreement follows * * * the Senate amendment except that the conference agreement provides that if benefits under all plans of the employer accrue at the same rate, then that accrual rate is to be used in determining whether the plans are top heavy or super top heavy. If there is no single accrual rate used by all plans of the employer, then the plans' top-heavy status is to be determined by treating the benefits of the participants in each plan as accruing no more rapidly than the slowest permitted rate under the fractional accrual rule.

[Effective date.—] The provision applies for plan years beginning after December 31, 1986.

[¶3984] SECTION 1119. MODIFICATION OF RULES FOR BENEFIT FORFEITURES

(Sec. 401 of the Code)

[House Explanation]

* * * * * *

Present Law.—* * * The treatment of forfeitures in a defined contribution plan depends on whether or not the plan is a money purchase pension plan. In a defined contribution plan that is not a money purchase plan (e.g., a profit-sharing or stock bonus plan), forfeitures may be reallocated to the remaining participants under a formula that does not discriminate in favor of employees who are officers, shareholders, or highly compensated. These reallocated forfeitures increase the benefits of the remaining participants. Alternatively, forfeitures can be used to reduce future employer contributions.

A money purchase pension plan, like a defined benefit plan, is subject to the requirement that benefits be definitely determinable. Accordingly, a money purchase plan must contain a definite contribution formula. Present law also provides that forfeitures may not be used to increase benefits, but must be applied to reduce future employer

contributions or administrative costs (sec. 401(a)(8)).

* * * * * *

Explanation of Provision.—The bill creates uniform rules for forfeitures under any defined contribution plan. The bill permits, but does not require, forfeitures to be reallocated to other participants. Thus, forfeitures arising in any defined contribution plan (including a money purchase pension plan) can be either (1) reallocated to the accounts of other participants in a nondiscriminatory fashion, or (2) used to reduce future employer contributions or administrative costs.

Effective Date.—The provision is effective for years beginning after December 31, 1985.

[Conference Report]

* * * * * *

Conference Agreement.—The conference agreement follows the House bill * * *

[¶ 3985] SECTION 1120. NONDISCRIMINATION REQUIREMENTS FOR TAX-SHELTERED ANNUITIES

(Sec. 403 of the Code)

[House Explanation]

*   *   *   *   *   *

Present Law.—Under present law, a qualified plan is required to cover employees in general rather than merely the employees of an employer who are officers, shareholders, or highly compensated. A plan generally satisfies the present-law coverage rule if (1) it benefits a significant percentage of the employer's workforce (percentage test), or (2) it benefits a classification of employees determined by the Secretary of the Treasury not to discriminate in favor of employees who are officers, shareholders, or highly compensated (classification test).

*   *   *   *   *   *

Tax-sheltered annuities.—* * * no coverage or nondiscrimination rules prohibit an employer's tax-sheltered annuity program from favoring highly compensated employees.

Explanation of Provision

Study of coverage.—The bill directs the Secretary of the Treasury to study the effect of the present-law coverage tests. In particular, the Secretary is to determine whether the present-law rules are sufficient to ensure that qualified plans cover a significant and nondiscriminatory group of employees. The Secretary is to report to the Committee on Ways and Means of the House of Representatives and the Committee on Finance of the Senate, as well as the Joint Committee on Taxation, with respect to the study by July 1, 1986.

The committee expects that the report will include specific recommendations of any changes that the Secretary finds to be appropriate or necessary, including recommendations for implementing those changes. To ensure that the Secretary can gather needed information, the bill specifically authorizes the collection of data. The committee expects that employers will cooperate with the Secretary of the Treasury to the fullest extent possible in supplying requested data.

Tax-sheltered annuities.—*In general.*—The bill generally applies the coverage and nondiscrimination rules of present law (secs. 410(b) and 401(a)(4)) to tax-sheltered annuity programs (other than those maintained for church employees). Under the bill, the coverage and nondiscrimination rules apply to any tax-sheltered annuity programs to which the sponsoring employer makes contributions. To the extent the program permits elective employee deferrals, a special coverage and nondiscrimination rule applies to those elective deferrals.

Employer contributions.—If an employer makes contributions to a tax-sheltered annui-

ty program, the bill requires that the program must satisfy the coverage and nondiscrimination rules of present law (secs. 410(b) and 401(a)(4)).

Nondiscriminatory coverage.—These rules require that a tax-sheltered annuity program cover employees in general rather than merely the employer's highly compensated employees. A tax-sheltered annuity program will meet the percentage test if it benefits at least 70 percent of all employees. A tax-sheltered annuity program will meet the classification test if the Secretary of the Treasury determines that it covers a classification of employees that is found not to discriminate in favor of employees who are officers, shareholders, or highly compensated. As under present law, the Secretary is required to consider all the surrounding facts and circumstances. Unlike in the pension area, the committee intends that the Secretary will take into account the special circumstances faced by educational organizations and tax-exempt organizations (including the compressed salary scales of those organizations and the special needs of certain educational institutions in attracting visiting professors) in applying the rules.

Under the bill, the present-law rules requiring nondiscriminatory benefits (sec. 401(a)(4)) also are extended to tax-sheltered annuities. Thus, tax-sheltered annuity programs (other than those maintained for church employees) are to provide contributions or benefits that do not discriminate in favor of highly compensated employees.

A tax-sheltered annuity program will satisfy this nondiscrimination test if either the benefits or contributions provided under the program to highly compensated employees (expressed as a percentage of compensation) do not exceed the benefits or contributions provided to other employees. As under the present-law rules applicable to qualified plans, certain employer-provided social security benefits may be taken into account in determining whether contributions or benefits, as a percentage of compensation, discriminate in favor of employees who are highly compensated. Section 401(l) and Revenue Rulings 71-446[10] and 83-110[11] provide guidance for taking social security contributions into account. Of course, as under present law, social security contributions may not be taken into account more than once.

Permissive aggregation.—If the tax-sheltered annuity program, standing alone, fails to satisfy these coverage and nondiscrimination requirements, the employer may elect to treat the tax-sheltered annuity program and a qualified plan that it also maintains for employees of the entity sponsoring the tax-sheltered annuity program as a single plan solely for purposes of demonstrating that the tax-sheltered annuity program satisfies the

---

[Footnote ¶ 3985]   **(10)** 1971-2 C.D. 187.
(11) 1983-2 C.B. 70.

coverage and nondiscrimination requirements.

As under the present-law rules applicable to qualified plans, the tax-sheltered annuity program and the qualified plan, considered as a unit, must provide contributions or benefits that do not discriminate in favor of employees who are highly compensated employees.

In general, then, a tax-sheltered annuity program that does not separately satisfy the coverage and nondiscrimination requirements may be aggregated with a qualified plan only if the program and the plan provide comparable benefits. Revenue Ruling 81-202[12] provides guidance (including methods for taking employer-provided social security benefits into account) that may be applied to determine whether the amount of employer-derived benefits or contributions under several plans discriminate in favor of highly compensated employees. Of course, some variations in benefits or other plan options between the tax-sheltered annuity program and the qualified plan may be permitted if the program and the plan, as a whole, do not discriminate in favor of highly compensated employees. In determining whether a tax-sheltered annuity program provides comparable benefits, the committee intends that the Secretary consider the special circumstances faced by educational and tax-exempt organizations. For example, the committee believes that if the annuity program or plan has not been amended to increase benefits, it may be unnecessary to test comparability every year.

However, the committee does not intend that a sponsoring organization is to be able to treat a tax-sheltered annuity program and a qualified plan as a single plan for purposes of determining whether the qualified plan satisfies the applicable coverage and nondiscrimination requirements.

Excludable employees.—As under present law, in applying the percentage test, certain employees who have not yet completed minimum periods of service (generally one year)[13] and employees who have not yet attained certain minimum ages (generally, age 21) may be disregarded if they are excluded pursuant to a plan provision. In addition, in applying both the percentage and the classification tests, employees not covered by the plan and included in a unit of employees covered by an agreement that the Secretary of Labor finds to be a collective bargaining agreement between employee representatives and one or more employers are disregarded if there is evidence that retirement benefits were the subject of good faith bargaining between such employee representatives and the employer or employers (sec. 410(b)(3)(A)). Certain nonresident aliens and certain airline employees must be disregarded in applying the coverage tests (sec. 410(b)(3)(B) and (C)).

Elective deferrals.—The bill provides a special coverage and nondiscrimination rule applicable to tax-sheltered annuity programs that permit elective deferrals. If the employer makes nonelective contributions under a program, the special rule applies only to the elective deferrals and the general nondiscrimination rules described above apply to the nonelective contributions. If, however, the employer maintains a tax-sheltered annuity program that permits only elective deferrals (i.e., no nonelective contributions are made), only the special rule for elective deferrals applies.

Under the bill, a tax-sheltered annuity program that permits elective deferrals will be considered discriminatory with respect to those deferrals unless the opportunity to make elective deferrals is made available to all employees of the entity sponsoring the tax-sheltered annuity program. To ensure that the opportunity to make elective deferrals is available to all employees, the bill provides that the employer generally is not to require any minimum dollar amount (or percentage of compensation) as a condition of participation. However, because the contribution must be sufficient to make purchase of the annuity contract practicable, the bill authorizes the Secretary of the Treasury to issue regulations permitting an employer to establish a reasonable de minimis threshold. For example, the committee intends that a requirement of minimum annual contributions of $300 (or one percent of compensation) or a minimum monthly contribution of $25 would not be considered discriminatory.

Under the bill, elective deferrals under a tax-sheltered annuity program consist of those employer contributions made by reason of a salary reduction agreement, whether evidenced by a written instrument or otherwise (sec. 3121(a)(5)(D)), to the extent those contributions are excludable from the employee's gross income. In applying the special test for deferrals, no employees of the entity sponsoring the tax-sheltered annuity program (other than nonresident aliens with no U.S.-source earned income) may be excluded from consideration. For example, the qualified plan rules permitting the exclusion of certain employees based upon age and service and coverage under collective bargaining agreements do not apply.

As under present law, the new coverage and nondiscrimination rules generally apply with respect to the "employer" as defined in section 414(b),(c),(m), and (o). In addition, the present-law rules relating to leased employees continue to apply (sec. 414(n)). However, the rules relating to elective deferrals will apply, pursuant to Treasury regulations, with respect to the entity of the employer

---

(12) 1981-2 C.B. 93.

(13) Under a special rule, an employee may be excluded from participation for up to three years provided the employee is, after three years, fully and immediately vested.

sponsoring the tax-sheltered annuity program. For example, in determining whether a tax-sheltered annuity program offered by a State university permits all employees the opportunity to make elective deferrals, the relevant workforce includes all employees of the State university, not all employees of the State.

Employers subject to the nondiscrimination rule.—In general, all employers eligible to sponsor a tax-sheltered annuity program are subject to the nondiscrimination rules added by the bill. However, these rules do not apply to tax-sheltered annuity programs maintained for church employees.

For purposes of this exclusion, the term "church" is defined to include only a church described in section 501(c)(3) or a qualified church-controlled organization. These terms generally have the same meaning as they do for purposes of exclusion from the SECA and FICA taxes (sec. 1402 and 3121). Accordingly, for purposes of this provision, the term church includes (1) a convention or association of churches, and (2) an elementary or secondary school that is controlled, operated, or principally supported by a church or by a convention or association of churches.

Similarly, the term qualified church-controlled organization means any church-controlled tax-exempt organization described in section 501(c)(3) other than an organization that both (1) offers goods, services, or facilities for sale (other than on an incidental basis) to the general public (e.g., to individuals who are not members of the church), other than goods, services, or facilities that are sold at a nominal charge which is substantially less than the cost of providing such goods, services, or facilities, and also (2) normally receives more than 25 percent of its support from either (a) governmental sources, or (b) receipts from admissions, sales of merchandise, performance of services, or furnishing of facilities in activities that are not unrelated trades or businesses, or from (a) and (b) combined.

A tax-sheltered annuity program of an otherwise qualified church organization will be subject to the coverage and nondiscrimination rules only if both conditions (1) and (2) in the preceding paragraph exist. Thus, these rules generally will not apply to the typical seminary, religious retreat center, or burial society, regardless of its funding sources, because it does not offer goods, services, or facilities for sale to the general public. Similarly, the rules do not apply to a church-run orphanage or old-age home, even if it is open to the general public, if not more than 25 percent of its support was derived from the receipts of admissions, sales of merchandise, performance of services, or furnishing of facilities (in other than unrelated trades or businesses) or from governmental sources. The committee specifically intends that the coverage and nondiscrimination rules will apply to church-run universities (other than religious seminaries) and hospitals if both conditions (1) and (2) exist.

Auxiliary organizations of a church (including youth groups, women's auxiliaries, etc.) generally would satisfy neither of the conditions, and thus the coverage and nondiscrimination rules will not apply. Similarly, these rules generally will not apply to tax-sheltered annuity programs maintained by church pension boards or fund-raising organizations.

* * * * * *

[Conference Report]

* * * * * *

Conference Agreement

In general.—The conference agreement generally follows the House bill, subject to the following modifications.

If an employer provides nonelective or matching contributions or benefits under a tax-sheltered annuity program, the conference agreement requires that such employer contributions or benefits satisfy the new coverage and nondiscrimination rules applicable to qualified plans, as modified or added pursuant to the conference agreement (*see* Part B.1., above), rather than the coverage and nondiscrimination rules applicable to qualified plans under present law.

Except as otherwise noted below, these rules apply in the same manner to tax-sheltered annuity programs as they do to qualified plans. Thus, the full array of rules relating to nondiscrimination apply (such as, for example, the limit on the amount of compensation that may be taken into account, the special nondiscrimination rule applicable to matching contributions, the employee leasing rules, and the minimum participation rules).

Integration.—As with respect to qualified plans, employers maintaining tax-sheltered annuity programs generally may integrate contributions or benefits under the new integration rules for purposes of the average benefits test (sec. 410(b)), for establishing comparability between programs (or between a program and a plan), and for satisfying the benefits test within a plan (sec. 401(a)(4)). However, under rules prescribed by the Secretary, there is no permitted disparity under the new integration rules for employees who are not covered by social security.

Permissive aggregation.—If a tax-sheltered annuity program, standing alone, fails to satisfy the percentage test, the ratio test, or the classification test, the employer may elect to treat the tax-sheltered annuity program and a qualified plan or another tax-sheltered annuity program as a single plan solely for purposes of demonstrating that the tax-sheltered annuity program satisfies the coverage requirements. If a tax-sheltered annuity program is aggregated with another tax-sheltered annuity or with a qualified plan for purposes of satisfying the coverage rules, the aggregated arrangements must provide contributions or benefits that do not discriminate in favor of highly compensated employees (secs. 401(a)(4) and 401(m)).

The requirement that such aggregated arrangements provide comparable contributions or benefits generally applies in the same manner to tax-sheltered annuity programs as it does to qualified plans. Thus, the principles of Rev. Rul. 81-202, as modified in the ways described in Part B.1., above, are to apply. However, the conferees intend that the Secretary is to prescribe rules applicable to tax-sheltered annuities that reduce the administrative burden of applying Rev. Rul. 81-202. For example, the Secretary might permit, under appropriate circumstances, testing less frequently than annually.

In applying the average benefit percentage component of the average benefits test to a tax-sheltered annuity program, an employer may at its election include all qualified plans in determining the average benefit percentages.

As under the House bill, a tax-sheltered annuity program may not be aggregated with a qualified plan for purposes of determining whether the qualified plan satisfies the applicable coverage and nondiscrimination rules, including the average benefits test.

Excludable employees.—The categories of employees that are excluded in applying the coverage rules to tax-sheltered annuities are the same as those that are excluded in applying the rules to qualified plans, except that, in addition, an employer is to exclude from consideration students who normally work less than 20 hours per week. This additional category of excludable employees is treated in the same manner as the category of employees who do not meet the service requirements for qualified plans. Thus, for example, the 20-hour requirement only applies if the employer excludes all students normally working less than 20 hours per week.

Elective deferrals.—The conference agreement follows the House bill, except that in applying the nondiscriminatory coverage rule applicable to elective deferrals under a tax-sheltered annuity program, the employer is to exclude from consideration students who normally work fewer than 20 hours per week, as discussed above. The conference agreement also clarifies that, in applying the average benefits test, elective deferrals under a tax-sheltered annuity are to be disregarded.

The conference agreement also clarifies the definition of an elective deferral. If an employee has a one-time election to participate in a program that requires an employee contribution, such contribution will not be considered an elective deferral to the extent that the employee is not permitted subsequently to modify the election in any manner. In addition, the Secretary is authorized to prescribe additional instances in which employer contributions to a plan will not be considered elective despite the existence of limited rights of election by the employee.

Employers subject to the nondiscrimination rule.—The conference agreement follows the House bill. In addition, the conference agreement provides that for purposes of the nondiscrimination rules applicable to tax-sheltered annuity programs, the general rules regarding aggregation of employers and testing on a line of business or operating unit basis shall apply under rules prescribed by the Secretary. The Secretary may provide for a narrower definition of employer for purposes of the rules applicable to elective deferrals.

Effective date.—The application of the nondiscrimination rules to tax-sheltered annuity programs is effective for plan years beginning after December 31, 1988.

[¶ 3986] SECTION 1121. MINIMUM DISTRIBUTION REQUIREMENTS.

(Secs. 401 and 4974 of the Code)

[House Explanation]

* * * * * *

Explanation of Provisions.—*Overview.*—The bill establishes a uniform commencement date for benefits under all qualified plans, IRAs, tax-sheltered annuities, and custodial accounts. In addition, the bill establishes a new sanction in the form of an excise tax, as an alternative to plan disqualification, for failure to satisfy the minimum distribution rules.

Uniform commencement date.—Under the bill, distributions under all qualified defined benefit and defined contribution plans, individual retirement accounts and annuities, and tax-sheltered custodial accounts and annuities must commence no later than April 1 of the calendar year following the calendar year in which the participant or owner attains age 70½, without regard to the actual date of retirement.

Excise tax on failure to make a minimum required distribution.—Under the bill, the sanction for failure to make a minimum required distribution to a particular participant under a qualified retirement plan is a 50-percent nondeductible excise tax on the excess in any taxable year of the amount that should have been distributed (the "minimum required distribution") over the amount that actually was distributed. The tax is imposed on the individual required to take the distribution. However, as under present law, a plan will not satisfy the qualification requirements unless it expressly provides that, in all events, the distribution under the plan must satisfy the minimum distribution requirements and the incidental benefit rule.

Under the bill, the Secretary of the Treasury is authorized to waive the tax for a given taxable year if the taxpayer to whom the tax would otherwise apply is able to establish that any shortfall between the minimum required distribution for that year and the amount actually distributed during the year is due to reasonable error, and that reasonable steps are being taken to remedy the shortfall.

The minimum required distribution in any given taxable year is to be determined under regulations to be issued by the Treasury. The committee intends that where a participant selects a permissible distribution option, the minimum required distribution in any given year is to be the amount required to be distributed in that year under the payout option selected.

If the participant selects an impermissible payout option, the committee intends that the minimum required distribution in any year be the amount that would have been distributable to the participant in that year had the participant selected a joint and survivor annuity payable over the life expectancies of the participant and the beneficiary (if any) actually designated by the participant, taking into account their actual ages. The survivor benefit is assumed to be the maximum percentage of the annuity payable during the participant's lifetime that will not violate the incidental benefit rule. It is intended that the excise tax apply even if the distribution is described in the plan and the plan receives a favorable determination letter.

Effective Dates

The provisions generally apply to distributions made after December 31, 1985. [But see Conference below. Ed.] However, for purposes of the required beginning date for commencement of benefits, employees who are not 5-percent owners and who have attained age 70½ by January 1, 1988, may defer the commencement of benefit payments until retirement.

In addition, an employee is not subject to the 50-percent excise tax for failure to satisfy the minimum distribution requirements merely because distributions are made to the employee in accordance with a designation made before January 1, 1984, by the employee in accordance with sec. 242(b)(2) of the Tax Equity and Fiscal Responsibility Act of 1982 (TEFRA).

[Conference Report]

* * * * * *

Conference Agreement

The conference agreement generally follows the House bill. In addition, the conference agreement extends the provisions of the House bill to unfunded deferred compensation plans of State and local governments and tax-exempt employers (sec. 457 plans).

As under the House bill, the conference agreement provides that the minimum required distribution in any given taxable year is to be determined under regulations to be issued by the Secretary of the Treasury. The

conferees intend that, if a participant selects a permissible distribution option, the minimum required distribution in any given year is the amount required to be distributed in that year under the payout option selected.

With respect to a defined benefit pension plan, if the participant selects an impermissible payout option and designates a beneficiary, the minimum required distribution in any year is the amount that would have been distributable to the participant in that year had the participant selected a joint and survivor annuity payable over the joint life and last survivor expectancies of the participant and the beneficiary designated by the participant, taking into account their actual ages at the required beginning date. The survivor benefit is assumed to be the maximum percentage of the annuity payable during the participant's lifetime that will not violate the incidental benefit rule, but not a percentage in excess of 100 percent of the benefit payable to the participant. It is intended that the excise tax apply even if the distribution is described in the plan and the plan receives a favorable determination later.

If the participant selects an impermissible payout option and does not designate a beneficiary, the minimum required distribution in any year is the amount that would have been distributable to the participant in that year had the participant selected an annuity payable over the life expectancy of the participant, taking into account the participant's actual age on the required beginning date.

With respect to a defined contribution plan, the minimum required distribution is determined as under present law.

[**Effective date.**—] The provisions generally apply to distributions made after December 31, 1988. The conference agreement includes (1) the exception in the House bill and the Senate amendment for distributions made pursuant to a designation made in accordance with section 242(b)(2) of TEFRA and (2) the special effective date provision in the House bill relating to individuals who are not 5-percent owners and who have attained age 70 ½ by January 1, 1988.

The conference agreement clarifies that the provision relating to individuals who are not 5-percent owners and who have attained age 70 ½ by January 1, 1988, applies only if the individual is not a 5-percent owner in the plan year ending with or within the calendar year in which the individual attains age 66 ½ or any succeeding plan year.

A special effective date applies to collectively bargained plans with respect to individuals who are subject to the collective bargaining agreement.

[¶ 3987] SECTION 1122. TAXATION OF DISTRIBUTIONS.

(Secs. 72, 402 and 403 of the Code)

[Conference Report]

House Bill

Constructive receipt under a tax-sheltered annuity.—Under the House bill, benefits under a tax-sheltered annuity are includible in income only when benefits are actually received. The provision is effective for distributions after December 31, 1985.

10-year averaging and pre-1974 capital gains treatment.—Effective for distributions made after December 31, 1985, the House bill repeals 10-year forward averaging, phases out pre-1974 capital gains treatment over a 6-year period, makes 5-year forward averaging (calculated in the same manner as 10-year averaging under present law) available for one lump-sum distribution received by an individual after age 59 ½ and, under a transition rule, permits certain individuals to apply 5-year averaging to one lump-sum distribution received before age 59 ½.

Under the House bill, individuals are permitted to make a onetime election with respect to a single lump sum received after the individual attains age 59 ½ (1) to claim, pursuant to the 6-year phase-out, capital gains treatment on that portion of the lump sum (if any) attributable to amounts contributed prior to 1974 and (2) to use 5-year forward averaging on the balance of the lump sum. In addition, the House bill provides a special transition rule under which any participant who attains age 50 before January 1, 1986, is permitted to make one election with respect to a single lump-sum distribution received prior to age 59 ½ (1) to claim pre-1974 capital gains treatment pursuant to the 6-year phase-out, and (2) to use 5-year forward averaging on the balance of the lump sum.

The House bill also permits individuals who separate from service in December 1985 and receive a lump-sum distribution in January 1986 to elect to treat the distribution as received in 1985 and to claim 10-year averaging (and capital gains treatment if appropriate) with respect to the distribution.

Basis recovery rules.—The House bill modifies the basis recovery rules applicable to distributions from plans in which there are after-tax employee contributions. Under the House bill amounts received prior to the annuity starting date are treated as being made first out of taxable amounts (employer contributions and income) and, second, as being made out of nontaxable amounts (employee contributions). If an employee is only partially vested in the portion of the employer's benefits attributable to employer contributions (for example, in the case of a plan with a graduated vesting schedule), the employee is not taxed on a distribution to the extent that the distribution, when added to any prior distributions under the plan, exceeds the sum of (1) the employee's vested

benefits attributable to employer contributions, plus (2) income on the employee's contributions.

With respect to amounts received after the annuity starting date, the special three-year basis recovery rule is eliminated. Thus, an employee must include in income a portion of each payment made on or after the employee's annuity starting date.

The House bill provides that in computing the portion of each payment that may be excluded from income, the employee's expected total return is to be determined as of the date of the payment. The bill limits the total amount that an employee may exclude from income to the total amount of the employee's contribution. In addition, if an employee's benefits cease prior to the date the employee's total contributions have been recovered, the amount of unrecovered contributions is allowed as a deduction to the annuitant for his last taxable year. For purposes of the provisions of present law relating to net operating losses, the deduction is treated as related to a trade or business of the employee.

The provisions relating to the basis recovery rules for amounts received before a participant's annuity starting date are generally effective for distributions made after December 31, 1985, but do not apply to employee contributions made prior to January 1, 1986.

The repeal of the special 3-year basis recovery rule generally is effective with respect to any individual whose annuity starting date is after July 1, 1986.

Senate Amendment

Constructive receipt under a tax-sheltered annuity.—The Senate amendment is the same as the House bill, except that the provision is effective for distributions after December 31, 1986.

10-year averaging and pre-1974 capital gains treatment.—The Senate amendment follows the House bill, except for the effective date and the special transition rule for individuals who have attained age 50 before January 1, 1986. The general effective date of the Senate amendment is taxable years beginning after December 31, 1986.

The Senate amendment provides a transition rule under which a participant who has attained age 50 before January 1, 1986, is permitted (1) to make one election (before or after attainment of age 59½) to use 5-year forward averaging (under the new tax rates) or 10-year averaging (under the new rates) without regard to the requirement of attainment of age 59½, and (2) to elect capital gains treatment with respect to a lump-sum distribution, without regard to the six-year phase-out of capital gains treatment. An election under this transition rule to use income averaging on a lump sum received prior to age 59½ eliminates the availability of an election after age 59½ under the general rule.

Basis recovery rules.—With respect to pre-annuity starting date distributions, the Senate amendment modifies the basis recovery rules to provide for pro-rata recovery of employee contributions. Thus, with respect to a pre-annuity starting date distribution, a participant is entitled to exclude that portion of the payment that bears the same ratio to the total payment as the participant's after-tax employee contributions (and amounts treated as after-tax employee contributions) bears to the total value of the participant's accrued benefit (or account balance) under the plan as of the date of distribution or as of such other time as the Secretary may prescribe. The Secretary is authorized to prescribe appropriate rules for estimating the amounts referred to in the prior sentence where precise calculation would be unjustifiably burdensome.

If an employee is only partially vested in the portion of the employee's benefits attributable to employer contributions (for example, in the case of a plan with a graded vesting schedule), the portion of the employee's accrued benefit that has not yet vested is not taken into account in determining the total value of the participant's accrued benefit.

With regard to post-annuity starting date distributions, the Senate amendment follows the House bill.

The Senate amendment also provides basis recovery rules for distributions from an IRA to which nondeductible contributions have been made. The rules are generally similar to the rules applicable to distributions from qualified plans.

The provisions relating to the basis recovery rules for amounts received before a participant's annuity starting date are generally effective for distributions made after December 31, 1986, but do not apply to employee contributions made prior to January 1, 1987 to the extent that, on May 5, 1986, such contributions were available for distribution under a plan before separation from service. Thus, except in the case of plans in which substantially all contributions are employee contributions, withdrawals made after the effective date, but prior to an individual's annuity starting date, are to be treated as made first from pre-1987 employee contributions that were available for in-service withdrawal. After all such contributions have been recovered, any subsequent distributions are taxed under the new pro-rata basis recovery rules of the bill. The repeal of the special 3-year basis recovery rule generally is effective with respect to any individual whose annuity starting date is after January 1, 1988.

Conference Agreement

Constructive receipt under a tax-sheltered annuity.—The conference agreement follows the House bill and the Senate amendment.

10-year averaging and pre-1974 capital gains treatment.—The conference agreement, if an individual who has attained age 50 by January 1, 1986, elects, pursuant to the transition rule, to retain the capital gains character of the pre-1974 portion of a lump-sum distribution, the capital gains portion is taxed at a rate of 20 percent. The 20 percent rate applies to all taxpayers, regardless of the maximum effective capital gains rate under present law.

Basis recovery rules.—*Pre-annuity starting date.*—The conference agreement generally follows the Senate amendment. However, under the conference agreement, employee contributions to a defined contribution plan or a separate account of a defined benefit plan (and the income attributable thereto) are treated as a separate contract for purposes of section 72 and application of the pro rata rule. Thus, under the conference agreement, if an employee withdraws employee contributions from such a plan or account, then for tax purposes, the distribution will be considered to be part nontaxable, i.e., a return of employee contributions, and part taxable, i.e., a distribution of earnings on those contributions. The distribution will not, however, be considered to be attributable to employer contributions. If an employee withdraws all amounts attributable to employee contributions and such amount is less than the employee's contributions, the employee may recognize a loss.

Post-annuity starting date.—The conference agreement follows the House bill and the Senate amendment, except that it extends the separate contract rule to post-annuity starting date distributions.

Rollovers.—The conference agreement modifies the rules relating to rollovers of partial distributions. Under the conference agreement, partial distributions may be rolled over only if the distribution is due to the death of the employee, is on account of the employee's separation from service (including the separation from service of a self-employed individual) or is made after the employee has become disabled. The requirement that a partial distribution not be one of a series of periodic payments is eliminated.

Under a special rule, a distribution in satisfaction of the diversification requirements applicable under the agreement to employee stock ownership plans may be rolled over even if the distribution does not otherwise qualify for rollover treatment.

The conference agreement contains a special rule permitting amounts deposited in certain financially distressed financial institutions to be rolled over into an IRA or qualified plan notwithstanding that the rollover does not occur within 60 days of the date of the original distribution to the employee. Under this rule, the 60-day period does not include periods while the deposit is frozen. In addition, the individual has a minimum 10 days after the release of the funds to complete the rollover.

Individual retirement arrangements.—The conference agreement follows the Senate amendment, with modifications. (See discussion in Part A.1., above.)

Effective dates.—The basis recovery rules are generally effective with respect to distributions received after December 31, 1986. The repeal of the 3-year basis recovery rule is effective with respect to individuals whose annuity starting date is after July 1, 1986. The provision limiting the income exclusion to the amount of the employee's investment in the contract applies to individuals whose annuity starting date is after December 31, 1986.

The new rules with respect to partial distributions are effective with respect to amounts distributed after December 31, 1986. The special rule for frozen deposits is generally effective with respect to distributions after the date of enactment. With respect to amounts which were frozen and released prior to the date of enactment, the rollover must be completed within 60 days following the date of enactment.

[The following colloquy relating to Act Sec. 1122 is drawn from the Congressional Record. The colloquy occurred on the day the Conference bill was considered by the House. Ed.]

[House Floor Explanation]

I have discussed with Congressman WILLIAM FORD several issues relating to the effect of the repeal of the 3-year basis recovery rule. We have reached a common understanding regarding the following specific issues:

The repeal of the 3-year basis recovery rule, which most frequently affects public employees, may have created uncertainty about certain distributions to which Federal employees may be entitled. In addition, I think there may be confusion about the effective date of the provision that should be cleared up so that individuals who retired during June 1986 will know what the tax treatment of their benefits will be.

These problems may be prevalent for all Federal employees, regardless of their rank and regardless of whether they are employed in the legislative or executive branch of the Government.

The following items are of great concern to Congressman WILLIAM FORD:

First, if a Federal employee separates from service before retirement, receives the entire balance of the employee's contributions to the retirement system, and, as a result of this cashout, forfeits a right to any other benefits under the system, is the amount distributed treated as a nontaxable refund of employee contribution plus taxable interest payable, if any?

Second, under the old civil service retirement system, an employee's annuity cannot exceed 80 percent of the employee's final average pay. In addition, employees can make voluntary contributions to the retirement system in excess of their required contributions. An employee is entitled to receive these excess and voluntary contributions in a lump sum. Are these cashouts treated as a nontaxable return of employee contributions?

Third, when the Social Security amendments were adopted in 1983, certain Federal employees elected to be covered both under the existing civil service retirement system and under Social Security. They made a full 7 percent of pay contribution to civil service in addition to paying the full tax for Social Security coverage. When the new Federal employee retirement system is implemented next year, these employees will have the option of going into the new system or into the integrated offset system. If they make such an election, they will receive a refund of their contributions to the civil service retirement system in excess of the contributions that would have been required under the new Federal employee retirement system or the offset system. In addition, certain employees hired between July 1, 1982, and January 1, 1984, will be entitled to a refund of excess contributions made if they transfer from the old civil service retirement system to the new Federal employee retirement system. Are these refunds treated as nontaxable returns of employee contributions?

Fourth, under the basis recovery rules after the repeal of the special 3-year basis recovery rule, what happens if an employee dies before fully recovering his or her employee contributions?

Fifth, are all employees who retired during June of 1986 eligible for the 3-year basis recovery rule or only those employees who retired before June 4, 1986?

I want to emphasize that these questions raised by Congressman FORD are not unique to a small group of Federal employees, but potentially affect all other employees. I think it is important that we provide certainty to these individuals so that they understand what effect these rules will have on them.

The bill has the following effect on the issues that the gentleman raised:

First, in the case of an employee who cashes out his or her employee contributions on separation from service and forfeits the right to any other retirement benefit under the retirement system, the amount distributed is treated as a nontaxable return of employee contributions and taxable interest, if any.

Second, in the case of an employee who has made voluntary contributions to the retirement system or contributions in excess of the amount needed to fund the retirement benefit, the amounts cashed out of this voluntary contribution account, are treated as part of a separate contract and, therefore, are a nontaxable return of employee contributions. Of course, if interest is also payable on the amounts distributed, the interest portion of the distribution is taxable.

Third, if an existing employee makes an election to be covered under the new Federal employee retirement system or under the integrated offset system and the employee receives a refund of excess contributions paid

Act § 1122 **¶ 3987**

onto the old civil service retirement system, the refunded contributions are also treated as part of a separate contract and, therefore, are treated as a nontaxable return of employee contributions. If any interest is payable with respect to those excess contributions, the interest is taxable.

Fourth, under the tax reform bill, if an individual dies before fully recovering his or her employee contributions, the remaining employee contributions are treated as recovered in the last taxable year of the individual. Thus, the individual's annuity payments for the year are includible in gross income only to the extent that the payments exceed the individual's unrecovered employee contributions. In addition, if an employee's annuity for the taxable year is less then the unrecovered employee contributions, such unrecovered contributions are treated as a net operating loss that can be carried back to

all open tax years. Consequently, an individual is never in the position — which could occur under present law — of dying without fully recovering his or her contributions to a retirement plan.

Fifth, the effective date of the repeal of the 3-year basis recovery is for individuals whose annuity starting date is after July 1, 1986. The annuity starting date is the first day of the first period for which an amount is received as an annuity without regard to when a payment is actually made. With respect to this effective date, it is my understanding that employees who retire before July 1, 1986, will remain eligible for the special 3-year basis recovery rule of present law because their annuity starting date will be July 1, 1986, rather than after July 1, 1986. Congressional Record, p. H8360-8361, 9-25-86.

[¶ 3988] SECTION 1123. UNIFORM ADDITIONAL TAX ON EARLY DISTRIBUTIONS FROM QUALIFIED RETIREMENT PLANS.

(Sec. 72. of the Code.)

[Conference Report]

[Senate Explanation]

* * * * * *

* * * * * *

Reasons for change.—Although the committee recognizes the importance of encouraging taxpayers to save for retirement, the committee also believes that tax incentives for retirement savings are inappropriate unless the savings generally are not diverted to nonretirement uses. One way to prevent such diversion is to impose an additional income tax on early withdrawals from tax-favored retirement savings arrangements in order to discourage withdrawals and to recapture a measure of the tax benefits that have been provided. Accordingly, the committee believes it appropriate to apply an early withdrawal tax to all tax-favored retirement arrangements.

* * * * * *

Moreover, the committee is concerned that the present-law level of the additional income tax appears in many instances to be an insufficient deterrent to the use of retirement funds for nonretirement purposes, because for taxpayers whose income is taxed at a higher marginal rate, the sanction may be neutralized by the tax-free compounding of interest after a relatively short period of time, particularly with respect to amounts contributed to a retirement arrangement on a before-tax basis.

In addition, the committee believes it appropriate to exempt from the additional income tax on early distributions amounts distributed from employee stock ownership plans (ESOPs). The committee recognizes that the purpose of ESOPs is to create for employees an ownership interest in employer securities and believes that this special purpose warrants distinguishing ESOPs from plans the primary purpose of which is to provide retirement savings.

House Bill

Withdrawal restrictions.—Under the House bill, a qualified cash or deferred arrangement may make distributions on account of the plan's termination (provided no successor plan is established), as well as on account of the employee's death, disability, separation from service, or (except in the case of a pre-ERISA money purchase pension plan) attainment of age 59½. (See the discussion in 981] * * *.) The House bill provides that a distribution on account of the termination of a qualified cash or deferred arrangement must consist of the participant's total account balance under the plan. Distributions on account of hardship are permitted only to the extent of an employee's elective deferrals (but not income on those deferrals under the cash or deferred arrangement). Present law standards governing what constitutes a "hardship" continue to apply.

Under the House bill, the withdrawal restrictions currently applicable to tax-sheltered custodial accounts generally are extended to other tax-sheltered annuities. Thus, early distributions from a tax-sheltered annuity are prohibited unless the withdrawal is made on account of death, disability, separation from service, or attainment of age 59½. In addition, withdrawals on account of hardship from a tax-sheltered annuity or custodial account are permitted only to the extent of the contributions made pursuant to a salary reduction agreement (but not earnings on those contributions). The present-law standards defining "hardship" for purposes of a qualified cash or deferred arrangement will apply.

The provisions are generally effective for years beginning after December 31, 1985. The provision permitting distributions from a cash or deferred arrangement upon plan termination applies to plan terminations after December 31, 1984. The provisions relating to restrictions on distributions from tax-sheltered annuity or custodial accounts do not apply to amounts contributed to tax-sheltered annuities or custodial accounts before December 31, 1985.

Additional income tax on early withdrawals.—Under the House bill, the 10-percent additional income tax on withdrawals from an IRA by the owner prior to attainment of age 59½, death, or disability is increased to 15 percent, and is extended to early withdrawals by any participant from any qualified retirement plan. Under the bill, the term "qualified retirement plan" includes a qualified defined benefit pension plan or defined contribution plan, a tax-sheltered annuity or custodial account, or an IRA. An exemption from the tax is provided for any distribution that is part of a scheduled series of substantially equal periodic payments (made not less frequently than annually) for the life of the participant (or the joint lives of the participant and the participant's beneficiary).

The provision generally applies to all distributions made in taxable years beginning after December 31, 1985. However, the bill contains an exception from the tax for individuals who, as of November 6, 1985, separated from service and commenced receiving benefits pursuant to a written election designating a specific schedule of benefit payments. The bill also exempts from the additional income tax on early withdrawals a total distribution of a participant's accrued benefit on account of a plan termination occurring prior to December 31, 1985.

Senate Amendment

Withdrawal restrictions.—The Senate amendment follows the House bill with respect to distributions from a qualified cash or deferred arrangement.

In addition, the Senate amendment provides that, upon the sale by a corporation of the corporation's interest in a subsidiary, a distribution may be made to an employee of the subsidiary even if the employee continues employment with the subsidiary. The Senate amendment also permits distribution upon the sale by a corporation of substantially all the assets used by a corporation in a trade or business, even if the employee continues employment with the corporation acquiring such assets. These provisions are effective with respect to sales occurring after December 31, 1984.

Additional income tax on early distributions.—The Senate amendment is generally the same as the House bill, except that (1) the Senate amendment does not extend the tax to distributions from a tax-sheltered annuity, (2) the tax is waived under certain additional circumstances, and (3) the rate of tax under the amendment varies depending on the character of the contribution to which the distribution relates.

The amendment exempts from the additional tax: (1) any distribution that is part of a scheduled series of substantially equal periodic payments over the life of the participant (or the joint lives of the participant and the participant's beneficiary) or the life expectancy of the participant (or the joint life expectancies of the participant and the participant's beneficiary), (2) a distribution to an employee (other than a 5-percent owner) who has attained age 55, separated from service, and satisfied the requirements for early retirement under the plan, (3) certain hardship distributions (other than distributions to a 5-percent owner or from an IRA), and (4) certain distributions from an employee stock ownership plan. Hardships that qualify for the exemption include certain medical expenses, casualty losses, and cessation of unemployment benefits. If the additional tax does not apply because of the substantially equal payment exception and the individual changes the method of distribution prior to age 59½ to a method that does not qualify for the exception, the tax will be imposed on all distributions received prior to age 59½.

The provisions are generally effective with respect to distributions made in taxable years beginning after, December 31, 1986. The amendment provides an exception from the tax for individuals who, as of March 1, 1986, separated from service and commenced receiving benefits pursuant to a written election designating a specific schedule of benefit payments.

Direct transfer option.—The Senate amendment provides that, if an employee separates from service and is to receive a distribution that could be rolled over to another qualified plan or IRA, the employer is required to offer the employee the option of electing a direct transfer of the employee's accrued benefit to an IRA or to another qualified plan. The provision is effective for years beginning after December 31, 1986.

Conference Agreement

Withdrawal restrictions.—The conference agreement includes the provision in the House bill and the Senate amendment with respect to the hardship distributions from qualified cash or deferred arrangements, effective for plan years beginning after December 31, 1988. (See, also, the discussion in Part A.2., above.)

The conference agreement also includes the provision in the House bill and the Senate amendment with respect to distributions on termination of a qualified cash or deferred arrangement. Under the conference agreement, however, the distribution must consist of the participant's entire interest in the cash or deferred arrangement.

The conference agreement includes the provisions in the Senate amendment with respect to distributions from a qualified cash or deferred arrangement in connection with the sale of a subsidiary or substantially all the assets of a trade or business, effective with respect to sales occuring in plan years

Act § 1123 **¶ 3988**

beginning after December 31, 1984. As under the termination rule, these rules apply only if the distribution consists of the participant's entire interest in the cash or deferred arrangement.

Under the conference agreement, the withdrawal restrictions with respect to amounts under a tax-sheltered annuity program invested in a custodial account are extended to elective deferrals and earnings thereon under a tax-sheltered annuity. Thus, elective deferrals and earnings thereon may not be withdrawn prior to the time the annuitant attains age 59½, dies, becomes disabled, or separates from service. The conference agreement adopts the provision in the House bill restricting hardship withdrawals from a tax-sheltered annuity or custodial account to elective deferrals (excluding earnings). The provisions are effective for taxable years beginning after December 31, 1988.

Additional income tax on early withdrawals.—The conference agreement generally follows the Senate amendment, with modifications. Under the agreement, the additional income tax applies to early distributions from any "qualified retirement plan" as defined under the agreement. Thus, the tax applies to amounts distributed from plans qualified under section 401(a) of the Code, tax-sheltered annuities and custodial accounts, and IRAs, but does not apply to amounts distributed from unfunded deferred compensation plans of tax-exempt or State and local government employers (sec. 457 plans). Under the conference agreement, the rate of the tax is 10 percent for all early distributions includible in gross income, regardless of the character of the contribution to which the distribution relates.

The conference agreement includes the following exceptions to the tax: (1) a distribution that is part of a scheduled series of substantially equal periodic payments for the life of the participant (or the joint lives of the participant and the participant's beneficiary) or the life expectancy of the participant (or the joint life expectancies of the participant and the participant's beneficiary); (2) a distribution to an employee who has attained age 55, separated from service, and met the requirements for early retirement under the plan; (3) a distribution which is used to pay medical expenses to the extent that the expenses are deductible under section 213 (determined without regard to whether the taxpayer itemizes deductions), and (4) distributions after the death of the employee. The conference agreement includes the exception in the Senate amendment for certain distributions made from an employee stock ownership plan, but restricts the exception to distributions made prior to January 1, 1990.

In addition, the conference agreement exempts from the distribution tax: (1) lump-sum distributions made prior to March 15, 1987, if the distribution is made on account of separation from service in 1986 and the employee treats the distribution for Federal tax purposes as paid in 1986; (2) payments made to or on behalf of an alternate payee pursuant to a qualified domestic relations

order; and (3) certain distributions of excess contributions to and excess deferrals under a qualified cash or deferred arrangement; and (4) dividend distributions under section 404(k).

The conferees intend that the additional income tax on early withdrawals does not apply to cashouts not requiring the participant's consent of amounts not in excess of $3,500.

The conference agreement does not follow the Senate amendment with respect to the exclusion of 5-percent owners from certain of the exceptions to the tax. Thus, the exceptions are available to 5-percent owners to the same extent they are available to other employees. In the case of distributions from IRAs, the early retirement, medical expense, and ESOP exceptions do not apply. The exception for distributions pursuant to a qualified domestic relations order applies to an individual retirement arrangement only to the extent the arrangement in subject to qualified domestic relations orders. The exception for substantially equal payments applies to distributions from plans qualified under 401(a) and tax-sheltered annuities and custodial accounts only if the distribution is made after separation from service.

The exception for retirement under a plan after separation from service following attainment of age 55 applies in the case of both normal and early retirement following attainment of age 55, and will continue to apply if the employee returns to work for the same employer or for a different employer. Thus, for example, the exception will apply to a distribution to an employee who retires following attainment of age 55 under a plan which provides for a normal retirement age of 55. In addition, the exception will continue to apply if the employee returns to work as long as the employee did, in fact, separate from service before the distribution.

In all cases, the exception applies only if the participant has attained age 55 on or before separation from service. Thus, for example, the exception does not apply to a participant who separates from service at age 52 and, pursuant to the early retirement provisions of the plan, begins receiving benefits at or after age 55. Of course, one of the other exceptions to the tax may still apply.

The early retirement exception applies if, upon retirement under one plan of the employer pursuant to the terms of the exception, the employee is entitled to a lump sum distribution from any other plan of the employer. For example, if an employer maintains a defined benefit plan that provides for early retirement upon separation from service after age 55 and also maintains a profit-sharing plan which permits the participant to obtain a lump sum upon retirement under the defined benefit plan, the distributions from both plans qualify for the exception.

An existing plan which does not have an early retirement provision can be amended to add an early retirement provision which qualifies for the exception.

The substantially equal payment exception is available with respect to forms of payment which contain a term certain and otherwise qualify for the exception (such as a life annuity with a 10-year certain provision).

As under the Senate amendment, the conference agreement provides that if distributions to an individual are not subject to the tax because of application of the substantially equal payment exception, the tax will nevertheless be imposed if the individual changes the distribution method prior to age 59½ to a method which does not qualify for the exception. The additional tax will be imposed in the first taxable year in which the modification is made and will be equal to the tax (as determined under regulations) that would have been imposed had the exception not applied. For example, if, at age 50, a participant begins receiving payments under a distribution method which provides for substantially equal payments over the individual's life expectancy, and, at age 58, the individual elects to receive the remaining benefits in a lump sum, the additional tax will apply to the lump sum and to amounts previously distributed.

In addition, the recapture tax will apply if an individual does not receive payments under a method that qualifies for the exception for at least 5 years, even if the method of distribution is modified after the individual attains age 59½. Thus, for example, if an individual begins receiving payments in substantially equal installments at age 56, and alters the distribution method to a form that does not qualify for the exception prior to attainment of age 61, the additional tax will be imposed on amounts distributed prior to age 59½ as if the exception had not applied. The additional tax will not be imposed on amounts distributed after attainment of age 59½. This 5-year minimum payout rule is waived upon the death or disability of the employee.

Under the ESOP exception, certain distributions from an ESOP are exempt from the tax to the extent that, on average, a majority of the plan's assets have been invested in employee securities over the 5-plan year period immediately preceding the plan year in which the distribution occurs. In a case in which an ESOP has been in existence for less than 5 years, the plan must have been so invested during the entire period prior to distribution. In a case in which a plan is converted to an ESOP, plan assets must have been so invested for 5 plan years prior to distribution. However, a distribution from an ESOP that satisfies the preceding conditions will not qualify for this exception from the early distribution tax unless such distribution is attributable to assets that have been invested in employer securities for the 5-year period. Tacking of investment periods is permitted.

For example, amounts transferred to an ESOP would qualify for the exception 3 years after transfer provided such amounts meet the investment criteria for 2 years prior to such transfer. In addition, amounts transferred to an ESOP following a reversion from a defined benefit pension plan would qualify for this exception if a majority of such amounts are invested in employer securities upon transfer and the 5 year investment requirement is met. The conferees intend that a first-in, first-out rule be used for purposes of determining the length of time a plan has held securities distributed to a participant.

The conference agreement follows the effective date provisions of the Senate amendment.

Direct transfer option.—The conference agreement does not contain the provision in the Senate amendment.

* * * * * *

Effective Dates.—The provisions generally are effective for years beginning after December 31, 1986. * * * The provision permitting distributions from a qualified cash or deferred arrangement in connection with the sale of a subsidiary are effective for sales in years beginning after December 31, 1986. The provision restricting hardship distributions from a qualified cash or deferred arrangement is effective for years beginning after December 31, 1988.

The provisions relating to the additional income tax on early withdrawals apply to all distributions made in taxable years beginning after December 31, 1986. However, the bill contains an exception from the tax for individuals who, as of March 1, 1986, separated from service and commenced receiving benefits pursuant to a written election designating a specific schedule of benefit payments. In addition, if the participant failed to make a written election, the requirement that benefits be paid pursuant to a written election designating a specific schedule of benefit payments for the distribution of the entire accrued benefit of the participant will be deemed satisfied where the plan from which the benefits are paid provides for only one form of distribution, or where (1) the plan provides that, in the absence of an election to the contrary, a participant will be paid benefits according to the automatic form of payment specified in the plan, and (2) the individual is, in fact, receiving benefits in that form.

[¶ 3989] Section 1124. ELECTION TO TREAT CERTAIN LUMP SUM DISTRIBUTIONS RECEIVED DURING 1987 AS RECEIVED DURING 1986.

(Sec. 402 of the Code)

[Conference Report]

*   *   *   *   *   *

* * * [T]he conference agreement exempts from the distribution tax [See ¶3988. Ed.]: (1) lump-sum distributions made prior to March

15, 1987, if the distribution is made on account of separation from service in 1986 and the employee treats the distribution for Federal tax purposes as paid in 1986.

*   *   *   *   *   *

[¶ 3990] SECTION 1131. ADJUSTMENTS TO SECTION 404 LIMITATIONS

(Sec. 404 of the Code)

*   *   *   *   *   *

[House Explanation]

*   *   *   *   *   *

Excise tax on excess contributions to qualified plans.—*In general.*—[A] 10 percent nondeductible excise tax is imposed on excess contributions to a qualified pension, profit-sharing, stock bonus, or annuity plan (sec. 4972). Excess contributions are defined as the sum of (1) total amounts contributed for the taxable year over the amount allowable as a deduction for that year and (2) the amount of the excess contributions for the preceding year, reduced by amounts returned to the employer during the year, if any, and the portion of the prior excess contribution that is deductible in the current year. Thus, in effect, if an excess contribution is made during a taxable year, the excise tax would apply for that year and for each succeeding year to the extent the excess is not eliminated. [E]xcess contributions for a year are determined as of the close of the employer's taxable year. Accordingly, a contribution made on account of a year but after the close of the year would be taken into account in determining the level of excess contributions for the year.

Similarly, if employer contributions for a particular year are subsequently determined to be nondeductible, the amount by which employer contributions actually made exceeds the amount determined to be deductible generally is treated as an excess contribution subject to this 10 percent tax. Moreover, under the bill, the tax on excess contributions applies in addition to any other taxes or penalties that may be appropriate, (for example, the penalty on overvaluation of deductions for pension liabilities (sec. 6659A)). However, the tax generally does not apply to amounts that, but for the fact that they are taken into account as capital expenses within the meaning of section 451, would otherwise be allowable as a deduction (pursuant to section 404).

Employer.—The tax is imposed on the employer. * * * [I]n the case of a plan that provides contributions or benefits for employees some or all of whom are self-employed individuals (sec. 401(c)(1)), an individual who owns the entire interest in an unincorporated trade or business is treated as the employer.

Also, * * * a partnership is treated as the employer of each partner who is considered to be an employee (sec. 401(c)(1)).

Computation of amount subject to tax.—[T]he amount subject to the tax is the excess of the amount contributed to a qualified employer plan by the employer for the taxable year (increased by the unapplied amount subject to the tax in the previous year) in excess of the amount allowable as a deduction for that year. The unapplied amount subject to tax in the previous year is the amount subject to the tax in the previous year reduced by the sum of (1) the portion of that amount that is returned to the employer during the taxable year, and (2) the portion of that amount which is deductible during the year. However, the bill does not modify the rules of the Code or ERISA under which an employer may be allowed to withdraw certain amounts held by a pension, profit-sharing, or stock bonus plan.

For example, assume that an employer made an excess contribution of $100,000 for its taxable year beginning in 1986, that the employer made a small contribution for its 1987 taxable year, and that the level of excess contributions determined as of the close of its 1987 taxable year was $25,000. Under the bill, the excise tax would apply to excess contributions of $100,000 for the 1986 taxable year and $25,000 for the 1987 taxable year. On the other hand, if the excess was eliminated as of the close of the 1987 taxable year because the employer made no contribution for such year and the $25,000 excess contribution was deductible as a carryover, then the excise tax would apply only with respect to the 1986 taxable year.

*   *   *   *   *   *

[Senate Explanation]

*   *   *   *   *   *

Overview.—The bill makes several changes to the limits on employer deductions for contributions to qualified plans. The bill (1) repeals the limit carryforward applicable to profit-sharing and stock bonus plans and (2) extends the combined plan deduction limit to any combination of a defined benefit pension plan and a money purchase pension plan.

Elimination of limit carryforward.—*In general.*—Under the bill, as under present law, the contribution of an employer to a qualified profit-sharing or stock bonus plan is generally deductible in the taxable year when paid. The employer's deduction for such a contribution generally may not exceed 15 percent of the compensation otherwise paid or accrued during the taxable year to employees who benefit under the plan.

However, the bill generally repeals limit carryforwards for a profit-sharing or stock bonus plan. Accordingly, if an employer's contribution for a particular year is less than the maximum amount for which a deduction may be allowed, the unused limit may not be carried forward to subsequent years.

The bill does not change the rules of present law relating to deduction carryforwards. Accordingly, as under present law, any amount paid into a profit-sharing or stock bonus trust in excess of the 15-percent deduction limit for the year is to be deductible in the succeeding taxable years in order of time.

Pre-1987 limitation carryforwards.—The bill does not eliminate limitation carryforwards accumulated in the past. Under the bill, the deduction limit for any taxable year beginning after December 31, 1986, may be increased by the unused pre-1987 limitation carryforwards (but not to an amount in excess of 25 percent of compensation otherwise paid or accrued in that year to employees who benefit under the plan).

The bill defines the unused pre-1987 limitation carryforward applicable to any taxable year as the amount by which the 15-percent limit applicable to a profit-sharing or stock bonus plan (as in effect on the day before the date of enactment of the provision) for any taxable year beginning before January 1, 1987, exceeds the amount paid to the trust for that taxable year (to the extent the excess was not taken into account in any taxable year prior to the year for which the limit is being calculated).

Combinations of pension and other plans.—The bill applies the combined plan limit of present law to any combination of defined benefit and defined contribution plans if any employee benefits under the combination of plans (sec. 404(a)(7)).

Under the bill, if an employer contributes to 1 or more qualified defined contribution plans (1 or more qualified money purchase pension plans, profit-sharing plans, or stock bonus plans) and 1 or more qualified defined benefit pension plans for a taxable year, then the amount deductible in that taxable year under the overall deduction limits applicable to the plans (sec. 404(a)(7)) is not to exceed the greater of (1) 25 percent of the compensa-

tion otherwise paid or accrued during the taxable year to the employees who benefit under the plans, or (2) the amount of contributions made to or under the defined benefit pension plan to the extent necessary to meet the minimum funding standard for that plan (sec. 412). A fully insured plan (defined in sec. 412(i)) is treated as a defined benefit pension plan for purposes of this limit.

As under present law, the otherwise applicable limits with respect to qualified pension, profit-sharing, and stock bonus plans (sec. 404(a)(1), (2) an (3)) are not reduced by the overall limit on deductions if no employee benefits under both a defined benefit pension plan and a defined contribution plan. A money purchase pension plan that amends the plan contribution formula to limit required contributions to those that are deductible will not be treated as failing to provide definitely determinable benefits. The bill makes no change to the present law provisions permitting deduction carryforwards.

* * * * * *

[Conference Report]

* * * * * *

The conferees clarify that, with respect to an employer that is exempt from tax, the 10-percent excise tax is to apply to contributions that would, if the employer were not exempt, be nondeductible. * * * [A]lso imposes a limit of $200,000 on the amount of compensation that may be taken into account in computing deductions for plan contributions. The limit is to be adjusted for cost-of-living increases at the time and in the manner provided for adjusting the overall limits on annual benefits under a qualified defined benefit pension plan (sec. 415(d)).

Fully insured plans.—The conference agreement includes a technical modification relating to fully insured plans which provides that the annual premium payments are deemed to be the amount required to meet the minimum funding requirements in the case of a fully insured plan.

* * * * * *

[Senate Explanation]

* * * * * *

Effective Date.—The provisions relating to deduction limits generally apply to employer taxable years beginning after December 31, 1986. However, certain unused pre-1987 limit carryforwards are not affected by the provision generally repealing limit carryforwards.

Act § 1131   ¶ 3990

[¶ 3991]   SECTION 1132. EXCISE TAX ON REVERSION OF QUALIFIED PLAN ASSETS TO EMPLOYER.

(Sec. 4980 of the Code)

[Conference Report]

*   *   *   *   *   *

Present Law.—A qualified plan must be for the exclusive benefit of employees. Prior to the satisfaction of all liabilities with respect to employees and their beneficiaries, the assets held under a qualified plan may not be used for, or diverted to, purposes other than the exclusive benefit of employees. However, if assets remain in a defined benefit pension plan upon plan termination as a result of actuarial error, then those assets may be paid, as a reversion, to the employer after the plan has satisfied all liabilities, if the plan provides for such payment.

A surplus generally is considered to be due to actuarial error if it is not due to specific action of the employer such as decreasing employer liabilities. In general, no amounts may revert to an employer upon termination of a defined contribution plan.

House Bill.—The House bill imposes a 10-percent nondeductible excise tax on a reversion occurring upon the termination of a qualified plan. The tax is imposed on the person who receives the reversion. Under the bill, the tax applies to amounts received as a reversion pursuant to the termination of a plan occurring after December 31, 1985.

Senate Amendment.—The Senate amendment is generally the same as the House bill except that (1) it provides a new definition of the amount of a reversion, (2) it does not apply the tax in the case of certain amounts transferred to an employee stock ownership plan, and (3) it provides an exception to the application of the tax in the case of a certain employer.

The Senate amendment defines a reversion as the amount of cash and the fair market value of other property received (directly or indirectly) from a qualified plan. Under the Senate amendment, the amount of a reversion does not include any amount distributed to an employee (or beneficiary) if the amount could have been distributed before the termination of the plan without violating the plan qualification requirements. In determining the amount of a reversion, an obligation (e.g., an obligation to pay a benefit) that causes the disqualification of a plan (or that would cause the disqualification of the plan if the plan were otherwise qualified) is to be taken into account as a reversion if it is provided pursuant to the termination of the plan.

Under the Senate amendment, the tax applies to amounts received as a reversion pursuant to the termination of a plan occurring after December 31, 1985. The tax applies to reversions received after December 31, 1985, other than reversions attributable to plan terminations occurring on or before December 31, 1985. Under the Senate amend-

ment, a termination is considered to occur on the proposed date of termination.

Conference Agreement.—The conference agreement follows the Senate amendment under which a 10-percent nondeductible excise tax is imposed on a reversion from a qualified plan. In addition, the tax is imposed on reversions from programs described in section 403(a). The tax is imposed on the employer maintaining the plan. In the case of a partnership that is treated as the employer maintaining the plan under section 401(a), the partners are liable for the tax. The agreement provides that the excise tax does not apply to a reversion to an employer that has at all times been tax-exempt. Of course, this exception does not apply to the extent that such employer has been subject to unrelated business income tax or has otherwise derived a tax benefit from the qualified plan.

In addition, the conference agreement clarifies that a return of mistaken contributions within section 401(a)(2) is not a reversion subject to the excise tax. Similarly, amounts which may be returned under section 403(c)(2) of the Employee Retirement Income Security Act of 1974, as amended, are not considered reversions subject to the tax. A payment to an employer under a participating annuity purchased upon plan termination is treated as a reversion subject to the tax.

The conference agreement adopts the provision in the Senate amendment waiving the excise tax with respect to the portion of a reversion that is transferred to an employee stock ownership plan (ESOP) under certain circumstances. No inference is to be drawn from this exception as to the circumstances in which asset transfers will or will not satisfy the exclusive benefit rule and any other applicable qualification requirements (e.g., sec. 414(1)).

As under the Senate amendment, in order to prevent undue market disruption due to the requirement that the assets transferred to the ESOP must be invested in employer securities or used to repay a loan used to acquire employer securities within 90 days of the transfer, the Secretary is authorized to extend the 90-day period. For purposes of determining which plan participants in the defined benefit plan from which assets where transferred to the ESOP are required to be participants in the ESOP, the conferees intend that only active employees, as opposed to retirees, who are participants in the plan need be included.

The conferees clarify that the prohibition against employer contributions (including elective deferrals) to an ESOP in receipt of a transfer from a terminated defined benefit plan is not intended to prohibit contributions to an ESOP to the extent that the amount of the suspense account required to be allocated for a year, when combined with additional contributions, does not exceed the limits under section 415.

The conferees are aware that the Secretary is currently considering the circumstances in which asset transfers between ongoing plans, plan mergers and spinoffs, and transfers of plan sponsorship in connection with the sale of a business may result in income tax consequences to the employer. The conferees stress that no inference is to be drawn from the agreement as to either the income or reversion tax consequences of such transactions.

The provision generally applies to reversions received after December 31, 1985 but does not apply to a reversion received after December 31, 1985, if the termination date of the plan is before January 1, 1986. Under the agreement, the special provision for transfers to an ESOP applies with respect to reversions occurring after December 31, 1985, and before January 1, 1989, and reversions received pursuant to terminations occurring after December 31, 1985, and before January 1, 1989. Under the conference agreement, the date of termination of a plan is the dates of termination under section 411(d)(3).

[The following colloquy relating to Act Sec. 1132 is drawn from the Congressional Record. The colloquy occurred on the day the Conference bill was considered by the House. Ed.]

[House Floor Explanation]

I have discussed with Congressman HUCKABY several issues relating to the effective date of an excise tax imposed under the bill on the recovery of excess assets from a defined benefit pension plan. We have reached a common understanding regarding the following specific issue:

Under the tax reform bill, a new excise tax is imposed on the recovery of excess assets from a defined benefit pension plan maintained by an employer. This excise tax, which equals 10 percent of the amount of the reversion, is generally effective for reversions received by an employer after December 31, 1985.

A constituent of Congressman HUCKABY terminated a defined benefit pension plan in 1985, but has not yet received approval from the IRS and the PBGC to take the excess assets. The Congressman is concerned that the effective date of this excise tax will have the effect of imposing the tax on a reversion that occurs after December 31, 1985, on account of a termination of a defined benefit plan occurring before January 1, 1986.

The excise tax on plan asset reversions does not apply to a reversion received after December 31, 1985, if it is received on account of a plan termination occurring before January 1, 1986. Congressional Record, p. H 8362, 9-25-86.

[The following colloquy relating to Act Sec. 1132 is drawn from the Congressional Record. The colloquy occurred on the day the Conference bill was considered by the House. Ed.]

[Senate Floor Explanation]

ESOP'S AND PENSION PLAN SPINOFF TERMINATIONS

Mr. LONG. Mr. President, I would like to engage the distinguished chairman of the committee, Senator PACKWOOD, in a brief colloquy concerning one aspect of an amendment in this bill regarding employee stock ownership plans [ESOP's].

The ESOP provisions in this bill were proposed by me and originated in the Finance Committee. Thus, it would be useful if the committee chairman and key conferee were to confirm the interpretation of one aspect of section 4980(c)(3) of the bill concerning the provision providing an exemption from the proposed 10-percent tax on pension plan asset reversions to the extent that amounts that would otherwise be reversion amounts are transferred to an ESOP.

The bill provides that the exception for reversions transferred to ESOP's applies if at least half of the participants in the qualified plan—the plan paying the reversion—are participants in the ESOP.

The conference committee report clarifies that for purposes of determining which plan participants in the defined benefit plan—from which assets were transferred to the ESOP—are required to be participants in the ESOP, the conferees intend that only active employees, as opposed to retirees, who are participants in the plan need be included.

In a standard termination of a defined benefit plan, this requirement presents no problem. In a common spinoff termination, however, the plan is split into two parts, with the portion covering retirees spun off as a separate plan and then terminated. Active employees remain in the ongoing plan and are provided for under applicable agency guidelines.

In a spinoff termination, the plan from which the reversion amounts are transferred is technically the spunoff plan for retirees, none of whom are active employees and, thus, none of whom would be required to become participants in the ESOP to which the reversion amounts are transferred.

The issue I wish to clarify is what happens to employees who were participants in a pension plan prior to the spinoff termination and who thereafter remain active employees of the employer sponsoring the ESOP. It is my understanding that 50 percent of such employees are to be included in the ESOP to which the reversion amounts are transferred.

Thus, let me confirm with the distinguished sponsor of the amendment that this interpretation is correct. It is my understanding that the amendment is intended to cover reversions attributable to spinoff termination transactions provided that employees participating in the ongoing plan—from which the reversion amounts are transferred—at the time of termination are also counted when determining—under section 4980(c)(3)(D)— whether 50 percent of participants in the

Act § 1132   ¶ 3991

terminated plan are required to be included as participants in the ESOP.

Mr. PACKWOOD. I agree with Senator Long's interpretation. The intent is to ensure that at least half the participants in a defined benefit pension plan—from which reversion amounts are transferred—will be included as participants in the ESOP to which those amounts are transferred, provided they are still employed by the employer sponsoring the ESOP. Congressional Record, p. 513957, 9-27-86.

[¶ 3992] SECTION 1133. TAX ON EXCESS DISTRIBUTIONS FROM QUALIFIED RETIREMENT PLANS

(Sec. 4981A of the Code)

(House Explanation)

* * * * * *

Explanation of Provisions.—* * * the bill imposes a new excise tax on excess distributions from qualified retirement plans, tax-sheltered annuities, and IRAs. * * * To the extent that aggregate annual distributions paid to a participant from such tax-favored retirement savings arrangements are excess distributions, the bill generally imposes an excise tax equal to 15 percent of the excess.

In applying the limit, aggregate annual distributions made with respect to a participant from all pension, profit-sharing, stock bonus, and annuity plans, ESOPs, individual retirement accounts and annuities (IRAs), and tax-sheltered annuities generally are taken into account to the extent includible in gross income. However, the bill provides that certain amounts are excluded in making this calculation. Under the bill, excludable distributions include (1) amounts representing a return of employee after-tax contributions (but not earnings thereon); (2) amounts excluded from the participant's income because they are rolled over into another plan or individual retirement savings arrangement; and (3) amounts excluded from the participant's income because they are payable to a former spouse pursuant to a qualified domestic relations order (sec. 414(p)) and includible in the spouse's income. Of course, distributions payable to the former spouse are aggregated with any other retirement distributions payable to such spouse for purposes of determining whether the spouse has excess retirement distributions subject to the tax. (Distributions paid to other alternate payees (e.g., minor children) are includible in applying the limit.) In addition, distributions made with respect to a participant after the death of the participant are disregarded in applying this annual limit and are subject instead to an additional estate tax.

Under the bill, excess distributions are defined as the aggregate amount of retirement distributions made with respect to any individual during any calendar year, to the extent such amounts exceed the greater of $112,500 or 125 percent of the defined benefit plan dollar limit applicable to benefits commencing at or after attainment of age 62. For example, for 1986, the ceiling will be $112,500 because $112,500 is greater than $96,250 (125 percent of $77,000). Accordingly, a participant receiving aggregate annual distributions of $152,500 in 1986 will be subject to an excise tax of $6,000 (15 percent of the $40,000 excess distributions).

Under this provision, the ceiling amount is not adjusted to reflect the age at which benefit payments commence. Thus, the limit is neither decreased to reflect early commencement of benefits nor increased to reflect deferred commencement. However, this tax will not apply to those distributions subject to the 15-percent additional income tax on early distributions (sec. 72(t), as added by the bill).

In applying the additional tax, all distributions made with respect to any individual during a calendar year will be aggregated, regardless of the form of the distribution or the number of recipients. Thus, for example, all distributions received during a year, whether paid under a life annuity, a term certain, or any other benefit form (including an ad hoc distribution) generally will be aggregated in applying the tax.

Lump sum distributions.—A special higher ceiling applies for purposes of calculating the excess distribution for any calendar year in which an individual receives a lump sum distribution that is taxed under the favorable long-term capital gains or five-year averaging rules. The higher ceiling will be the lesser of (i) the portion of the lump sum distribution that is treated as long-term capital gains or taxed under the five-year averaging rules, or (ii) five times the otherwise applicable ceiling for such calendar year. Thus, for example, if in 1990 an individual receives a $300,000 lump sum distribution and elects to tax such amount under the five-year averaging rules, the special higher ceiling applicable for calculating the individual's excess distribution for the year is the lesser of (i) $300,000, or (ii) five times the otherwise applicable ceiling for the year ($562,500, assuming an otherwise applicable ceiling for 1990 of $112,500). Accordingly, no part of this individual's lump sum distribution taxed under the five-year averaging rules would be treated as an excess distribution subject to the 15-percent additional tax. Of course, if this individual also received other retirement distributions during 1990, such other distributions would be in excess of the higher ceiling and thus would be treated as excess distributions.

Post-death distributions.—The bill provides special rules to calculate the extent to which retirement distributions made with respect to a participant after the participant's death are excess distributions. In lieu of subjecting post-death distributions (including distributions of death benefits) to the annual tax on excess distributions, the bill adds an additional estate tax equal to 15 percent of the individual's excess retirement accumulation. After the estate tax is imposed, post-death distributions are disregarded entirely in applying this tax. For example, beneficiaries who are receiving distributions with respect to a participant after the participant's death (other than certain former spouses receiving benefits pursuant to a qualified domestic relations order) are not required to aggregate those amounts with any other retirement distributions received on their own behalf.

The excess retirement accumulation is defined as the excess (if any) of the value of the decedent's interests in all qualified retirement plans, tax-sheltered annuities, and individual retirement accounts, over the present value of annual payments equal to the annual ceiling ($112,500 or, if greater, 125 percent of the applicable defined benefit plan dollar limit in effect on the date of death), over a period equal to the life expectancy of the individual immediately before death.

In calculating the amount of the excess retirement accumulation, the value of the decedent's interest in all plans, tax-sheltered annuities and individual retirement arrangements will be taken into account regardless of the number of beneficiaries. In addition, the decedent's interests are to be valued as of the date of death or, in the case of a decedent for whose estate an alternate valuation date had been elected, such alternate valuation date (sec. 2032).

*   *   *   *   *   *

[Conference Report]

*   *   *   *   *   *

The conference agreement generally follows the House bill with respect to the 15-percent excise tax on benefit payments in excess of $112,500 (indexed at the same time and in the same manner as the dollar limitation on annual benefits under a defined benefit pension plan). The conference agreement also clarifies that distributions attributable to after-tax employee contributions and distributions not includible in income by reason of a rollover contribution are not taken into account in applying the tax. All other amounts not specifically exempted are taken into account.

The conference agreement does not permit accrued benefits to be reduced retroactively to avoid the excise tax.

The conference agreement also modifies the rule providing an increased limit in the case of a lump-sum distribution. Under the agreement, if an individual elects lump-sum treatment (or long-term capital gains treatment), the $112,500 limit is applied separately to such lump-sum distribution and the limit is increased to 5 times the generally applicable limit with respect to the lump-sum distribution.

Also, the conference agreement clarifies that, with respect to the special provision relating to the estate tax, the tax may not be offset by any credits against the estate tax (such as the unified credit). In addition, the conferees intend that, in calculating the excess retirement accumulation, individuals are required to use reasonable interest rates in accordance with rules prescribed by the Secretary. The Secretary may, by regulations, prescribe a range of interest rates and other permissible assumptions for purposes of applying the excise tax.

Under the conference agreement, an individual may elect to be covered by (1) a special grandfather rule which exempts from the tax benefits accrued on August 1, 1986, or (2) an alternative rule which increases the $112,500 limit.

Under the grandfather, in the case of a defined contribution plan, the accrued benefit on August 1, 1986, is the participant's account balance on that date. In the case of a defined benefit plan, the accrued benefit on August 1, 1986, is determined assuming the participant separated from service on that date.

The grandfathered amounts are treated as if received on a pro-rata basis and are taken into account in determining whether the $112,500 limit is exceeded. Under the pro-rata rule, the portion of a distribution not subject to the excise tax is determined by multiplying the distribution by a fraction, the numerator of which is the grandfathered amount and the denominator of which is the accrued benefit on the date of the distribution under all plans or programs subject to the tax. Distributions after August 1, 1986, and before the effective date will reduce the grandfathered amount in the same manner.

For example, assume that at the time of a distribution of $250,000 an individual's grandfathered benefit is equal to 80% of the individual's accrued benefit on such date under all plans or programs subject to the tax. Under the grandfather, $200,000 (80 percent of $250,000) would be exempt from the tax. The remaining $50,000 would be subject to the tax because the grandfathered amounts are taken into account in determining whether the distribution exceeds the $112,500 limit.

The Secretary also has the authority to provide for an alternative grandfather rule for such individuals. The conferees intend that the Secretary consider providing an alternative grandfather rule based on a fraction, the numerator of which is the months of service between age 35 and August 1, 1986, and the denominator of which is total months of service after age 35. This rule applies as long as grandfathered amounts are taken into account in applying the excise tax to nongrandfathered amounts (as under the general grandfather rule).

The grandfather rule applies only with respect to an individual who (1) elects to have the grandfather rule apply and (2) has a grandfathered benefit of at least five times the $112,500 limit ($562,500). The election must be made on a return for a year beginning no later than January 1, 1988, and shall be in such form and shall contain such information as the Secretary may prescribe.

If an individual does not elect the grandfather rule, then the amount of a distribution subject to the tax under the general rule is computed by substituting for $112,500 (as indexed), the greater of $150,000 and $112,500 (as indexed).

[Effective date.—Applies to distributions after 12-31-86 except estate tax rule applies to estates of decedents dying after 12-31-86.

Distributions before 1-1-88 because of qualified employer plan termination before 1-1-87 aren't affected. Ed.]

[¶ 3993] SECTION 1134. TREATMENT OF LOANS

(Sec. 72 of the Code)

[Conference Report]

* * * * * *

House Bill.—The House bill modifies the exception to the income inclusion rule by reducing the $50,000 limit on a loan by the participant's highest outstanding loan balance during the preceding 12-month period.

In addition, the extended repayment period permitted for purchase or improvement of a principal residence is amended to apply only to the purchase of the principal residence of the participant. Plan loans to improve an existing principal residence, to purchase a second home, and to finance the purchase of a home or home improvements for other members of the employee's family are subject to the 5-year repayment rule.

The House bill also requires that a plan loan be amortized in level payments, made not less frequently than quarterly, over the term of the loan.

The House bill also provides for the deferral of the deduction for interest paid by (1) all employees on loan secured by elective deferrals under a qualified cash or deferred arrangement or tax-sheltered annuity, and (2) key employees with respect to loans from any qualified plan or other tax-favored retirement plan. The deferral is to be accomplished by denying a current deduction for the interest paid and increasing the participant's basis under the plan by the amount of nondeductible interest paid.

The provisions would be effective for amounts received as a loan after December 31, 1985. Any renegotiation, extension, renewal, or revision after December 31, 1985, of an existing loan is treated as a new loan on the date of such renegotiation, etc.

* * * * * *

Conference Agreement.—The conference agreement follows the House bill, with modifications and clarifications as described below.

The conference agreement follows the House bill with respect to the reduction of the $50,000 limit on loans, with a clarification. Under the conference agreement, a loan, when added to the outstanding balance of all other loans from the plan, cannot exceed $50,000 reduced by the excess of the highest outstanding balance of loans from the plan during the 1-year period ending on the day before the date the loan is made over the outstanding balance of loans from the plan on the date the loan is made.

For example, a participant with a vested benefit of $200,000 borrows $30,000 from a plan on January 1. On November 1, the participant wants to borrow an additional amount without triggering a taxable distribution. At that time, the outstanding balance on the first loan is $20,000. The maximum amount the participant can borrow is $50,000, i.e., $20,000-$20,000-($30,000-$20,000).

The conference agreement follows the House bill with respect to the principal residence exception to the 5-year repayment rule and the level amortization rule. The conferees intend that the level amortization requirement does not apply to a period when the employee is on a leave of absence without pay for up to 1 year. In addition, the requirement does not preclude repayment or acceleration of the loan prior to the end of the commitment period. Thus, for example, the provision does not preclude a plan from requiring full repayment upon termination of employment.

[Effective date.]—The provisions are generally effective with respect to loans made after December 31, 1986. Any renegotiation, extension, renewal, or revision after December 31, 1986, of an existing loan is treated as a new loan on the date of such renegotiation, etc.

Under the conference agreement, the deduction of interest on all loans from a qualified plan or tax-sheltered annuity is subject to the general limits on deductibility of interest contained in the conference agreement. In addition, effective with respect to loans made, renegotiated, extended, renewed, or revised after December 31, 1986, no deduction is allowed with respect to interest paid on (1) loans secured with elective deferrals under a qualified cash or deferred arrangement or a tax-sheltered annuity, and (2) any loan to a key employee (even if the interest on such loans is otherwise deductible under the general interest provisions of the agreement). Effective for interest paid after December 31, 1986, no basis is allowed with respect to any interest paid on a loan from a qualified plan or tax-sheltered annuity.

[¶ 3994] SECTION 1135. DEFERRED ANNUITIES AVAILABLE ONLY TO NATURAL PERSONS.

(Sec. 72(u) of the Code)

[Senate Explanation]

*   *   *   *   *   *

Present Law.—Under present law, income credited to a deferred annuity contract is not currently includible in the gross income of the owner of the contract nor is the income taxed to the insurance company issuing the contract. In general, amounts received by the owner of an annuity contract before the annuity starting date (including loans under or secured by the contract) are includible in gross income as ordinary income to the extent that the cash value of the contract exceeds the owner's investment in the contract. A portion of each distribution received after the annuity starting date is treated as ordinary income based on the ratio of the investment in the contract to the total distributions expected to be received.

*   *   *   *   *   *

Under present law, deferred annuities are often purchased by individuals in order to save for retirement. In addition, deferred annuities are often purchased by employers in order to fund the employer's obligation to provide nonqualified deferred compensation to its employees. Deferred annuities may also be used to fund benefits provided under qualified pension, profit-sharing, or stock bonus plans.

*   *   *   *   *   *

Explanation of Provision.—*Income on the contract.*—Under the bill, if any annuity contract is held by a person who is not a natural person (e.g., a corporation or a trust is not a natural person), then the contract is not treated as an annuity contract for Federal income tax purposes and the income on the contract for any taxable year is treated as ordinary income received or accrued by the owner of the contract during the taxable year.

Under the bill, in the case of a contract the nominal owner of which is a person who is not a natural person (e.g., a corporation or a trust), but the beneficial owner of which is a natural person, the contract generally is treated as held by a natural person. Thus, if a group annuity contract is held by a corporation as an agent for natural persons who are the beneficial owners of the contract, the contract is treated as annuity contract for Federal income tax purposes. However, the committee intends that, if an employer is the nominal owner of an annuity contract, the beneficial owners of which are employees, the contract will be treated as held by the employer. * * *

Income on the contract means the excess of (1) the sum of the net surrender value of the contract at the end of the taxable year and any amounts distributed under the contract for all years, over (2) the investment in the contract, i.e., the aggregate amount of premiums paid under the contract minus policyholder dividends or the aggregate amounts received under the contract that have not been included in income. The Secretary is authorized to substitute fair market value for net surrender value in appropriate cases, if necessary, to prevent avoidance of the otherwise required income inclusion.

The provision does not apply to any annuity contract that is acquired by the estate of a decedent by reason of the death of the decedent, is held under a qualified plan (sec. 401(a) or 403(a)), as a tax-sheltered annuity (sec. 403(b)), or under an IRA.

[Conference Report]

*   *   *   *   *   *

Conference Agreement

*   *   *   *   *   *

The conference agreement follows the House bill and the Senate amendment with modifications. Under the conference agreement, the exceptions to the tax treatment of annuity contracts held by nonnatural persons is expanded in three respects.

First, an exception is provided for an annuity which constitutes a qualified funding asset (as defined in sec. 130(d), but without regard to whether there is a qualified assignment). Thus, an exception is provided for (1) qualified funding assets purchased by structured settlement companies, and (2) annuity contracts (which otherwise meet the definition of a qualified funding asset) purchased and held directly by a property or casualty insurance company to fund periodic payments for damages.

Second, the conference agreement provides an exception in the case of a deferred annuity that (1) is purchased by an employer upon the termination of a qualified plan and (2) is held by the employer until the employee separates from service with the employer.

Third, an exception is provided for an immediate annuity, which is defined as an annuity (1) which is purchased with a single premium or annuity consideration, and (2) the annuity starting date of which commences no later than 1 year from the date of purchase of the annuity.

[Effective date.—] The provision is effective for contributions to annuity contracts after February 28, 1986.

Act § 1135   ¶ 3994

[¶ 3995] SECTION 1136. PROFITS NOT REQUIRED FOR PROFIT-SHARING PLANS

(Sec. 401 of the Code)

[Conference Report]

House Bill.—Under the House bill, employer contributions to a profit-sharing plan that satisfy the immediate vesting and withdrawal restrictions applicable to elective deferrals under a qualified cash or deferred arrangement (sec. 401(k)) are not limited to the employer's current or accumulated profits (whether or not the plan contains a qualified cash or deferred arrangement). This provision applies without regard to whether the employer is a tax-exempt organization. * * *

Senate Amendment.—The Senate amendment is the same as the House bill, except that the provision does not require a plan to meet the vesting and distribution requirements applicable to qualified cash or deferred arrangements. * * *.

Conference Agreement.—The conference agreement follows the Senate amendment, except that * * * provision is effective for plan years beginning after December 31, 1985. The conferees also intend that the Secretary may require defined contribution plans to contain provisions specifying whether they are pension plans or discretionary contribution plans.

[¶ 3996] SECTION 1137. REQUIREMENT THAT COLLECTIVE BARGAINING AGREEMENTS BE BONA FIDE

(Sec. 7701(a)(46) of the Code)

[Senate Explanation]

*　　*　　*　　*　　*　　*

Present Law.—Under present law, many of the nondiscrimination standards of the Code applicable to qualified plans apply separately to plans or programs maintained pursuant to an agreement that is found to be a collective bargaining agreement if there is evidence that retirement benefits were the subject of good faith bargaining between the employer and employee representatives. Similar exclusions are provided with respect to certain welfare benefits provided to employees. Present law provides no clear definition of a collective bargaining agreement.

*　　*　　*　　*　　*　　*

Explanation of Provision.—Under the bill, it is clarified that no agreement will be treated as a collective bargaining agreement [unless] it is a bona fide agreement between bona fide employee representatives and one or more employers.

*　　*　　*　　*　　*　　*

[Conference Report]

*　　*　　*　　*　　*　　*

[Effective date.—Enactment date generally. Ed.] The conference agreement follows * * * the Senate amendment.

Because the provision is a clarification of present law, the conferees intend that this provision be given retroactive effect where appropriate.

[¶ 3997] SECTION 1138. PENALTY ON UNDERPAYMENTS ATTRIBUTABLE TO OVERSTATEMENT OF PENSION LIABILITIES

(Sec. 6659A of the Code)

[House Explanation]

*　　*　　*　　*　　*　　*

Explanation of Provision

Overview.—The bill provides a new penalty in the form of a graduated addition to tax applicable to certain income tax overstatements of deductions for pension liabilities. As an addition to tax, this penalty is to be assessed, collected, and paid in the same manner as a tax. This addition to tax applies only to the extent of any income tax underpayment that is attributable to such an overstatement.

The portion of a tax underpayment that is attributable to a valuation overstatement is to be determined after taking into account any other proper adjustments to tax liability.

Thus, the underpayment resulting from a valuation overstatement is the excess of the taxpayer's (1) actual tax liability (i.e., the tax liability that results from a proper valuation of deductions for pension liabilities and takes into account any other proper adjustments) over (2) actual tax liability as reduced by taking into account the valuation overstatement.

The application of the valuation overstatement penalty does not preclude the application of other penalties or excise taxes against a taxpayer. For example, in an appropriate situation, the valuation overstatement penalty, as well as the five-percent negligence penalty, other penalty or penalties, or excise taxes (including the 10-percent annual excise tax on nondeductible employer contributions) might be assessed against the same taxpayer.[27]

Overstatement of pension liabilities.—Under the bill, there is an overstatement of deductions for pension liabilities if the amount of the deduction for pension liabilities claimed on the employer's tax return exceeds 150 percent of the amount determined to be the correct amount of the deduction. If there is an overstatement of deductions for pension liabilities, the following percentages are used to determine the applicable addition to tax:

If the valuation claimed is the following percent of the correct valuation—	The applicable percent is—
150 percent or more but not more than 200 percent	10
More than 200 percent but not more than 250 percent	20
More than 250 percent	30

Exceptions and waiver provisions.—As under the present-law overvaluation penalty provision, there is a de minimis exception to the new penalty. The valuation overstatement penalty does not apply if the underpayment for a taxable year attributable to the valuation overstatement is less than $1,000.

In addition, the bill grants the Treasury Department discretionary authority to waive all or part of the penalty on a showing by a taxpayer that there was a reasonable basis for the deduction claimed on the return and that the claim was made in good faith.

Definitions.—For purposes of the penalty, the term "underpayment" has the same meaning as under the present-law rules relating to negligence and civil fraud penalties (sec. 6653(c)(1)) (generally, the excess of the amount of tax that should have been paid over the amount shown on the return plus any amounts previously assessed or collected).

Effective Date

The provision applies to * * * overstatements after enactment date.

* * * * * *

[¶ 3998] SECTION 1139. INTEREST RATE ASSUMPTIONS

(Secs. 411(a)(11) and 417 of the Code)

[Senate Explanation]

* * * * * *

Explanation of Provision.—The bill amends the requirement that for purposes of determining the present value of a participant's accrued benefit (sec. 411(a)(11)), a qualified preretirement survivor annuity, or a qualified joint and survivor annuity (sec. 417), the plan use an interest rate no greater than the interest rate that would be used by the PBGC for purposes of determining the present value of a lump sum distribution upon the termination of the plan.

* * * * * *

[Conference Report]

* * * * * *

The conference agreement follows the Senate amendment, except that a plan is required to use an interest rate no greater than the interest rate (deferred or immediate, whichever is appropriate) that would be used by the PBGC (as of the date of distribution) upon the plan's termination for purposes of determining whether (1) a participant's accrued benefit can be cashed out without consent because the present value of the vested accrued benefit is less than $3,500 and (2) the present value of a participant's vested accrued benefit is less than $25,000.

If the present value of the vested accrued benefit is no more than $25,000, then the amount to be distributed to the participant or beneficiary is calculated using the PBGC rate.

If the present value of the accrued benefit exceeds $25,000 (using the PBGC interest rate), then the conference agreement provides that the amount to be distributed is determined using an interest rate no greater than 120 percent of the interest rate (deferred or immediate, whichever is appropriate) that would be used by the PBGC (as of the date of distribution) upon the plan's termination. In no event, however, is the amount to be distributed reduced below $25,000 when the interest rate used is 120 percent of the applicable PBGC rate.

For example, assume that, upon separation from service, the present value of an employee's total accrued benefit (including, e.g., any accrued benefits within section 411(d)(6) for which the employee is not yet eligible) is $50,000 using the applicable PBGC rate. Under the conference agreement, the plan may distribute to this employee (if the employee and, if applicable, the employee's spouse consents) the total accrued benefit, calculated using 120 percent of the applicable PBGC rate (e.g., $47,000).

The conferees recognize that the PBGC is considering adopting a new method and interest rate structure for valuing accrued benefits on plan termination. If a new method and structure are adopted, the Secretary is directed to provide timely guidance regard-

---

[Footnote ¶ 3997]   (27) For example, if both the valuation overstatement penalty and the 10-percent excise tax (sec. 4980) apply, the valuation overstatement penalty will be applied against the portion of the tax underpayment due to the valuation overstatement and the excise tax will be applied separately against the entire amount of contributions that are determined to be nondeductible.

ing the method of compliance with this provision of the conference agreement.

As under current law, the PBGC rate in effect at the beginning of the plan year may be used throughout the plan year if the plan so provides.

[**Effective Date.**—] The provision is effective for distributions for plan years beginning after December 31, 1984, and for distributions to which section 303(c) of REA applies, except that the provision does not apply to distributions in plan years beginning after December 31, 1984, and before January 1, 1986, that were made in accordance with the

temporary Treasury regulations issued under the Retirement Equity Act of 1984.

In addition, the conference agreement provides that any reduction in accrued benefits is not to be treated as an impermissible cutback in accrued benefits (sec. 411(d)(6) of the Code and sec. 204(g) of ERISA) to the extent the reduction is attributable to the calculation of the present value of an accrued benefit in a manner no less favorable to a participant than the manner of determining the present value under the provision. This rule applies if the plan is amended to provide for such calculation before the close of the first plan year beginning on or before January 1, 1989.

[¶ 3999] SECTION 1140. PLAN AMENDMENTS NOT REQUIRED UNTIL JANUARY 1, 1989.

[Senate Explanation]
Reasons for Change

*   *   *   *   *   *

Given the number of qualification changes made by this bill, the committee believes it is appropriate to provide an extended remedial amendment period for compliance with these changes.

*   *   *   *   *   *

Explanation of Provision

In general.—Under the bill, the provisions generally apply as of the separately stated effective date (generally, years beginning after December 31, 1986, or December 31, 1988). However, a plan will not fail to be a qualified plan on account of changes made in this bill for any year beginning before January 1, 1989, provided—

(1) the plan complies, in operation, with the changes as of the separately stated effective date;

(2) the plan is amended to comply with the changes no later than the last day of the first plan year beginning after December 31, 1988; and

(3) the amendment applies retroactively to the separately stated effective date.

During this period a plan will not be disqualified merely because the plan, solely due to delaying the adoption of conforming amendments, violates the requirement (1) that benefits be definitely determinable, (2) that a plan's terms be set forth in a written document, or (3) that the plan operate in accordance with its terms.

[Conference Report]

*   *   *   *   *   *

Senate Amendment

* * * [P]lan modifications not required by the Senate amendment (e.g., benefit increases; allocation of forfeitures under a money purchase pension plan) are not within this special amendment rule and are to be

made in accordance with the generally applicable rules.

Collectively bargained plans.—Under the Senate amendment, the separately stated effective dates may be delayed for certain collectively bargained plans. A collectively bargained plan to which the delayed effective dates apply will not fail to be a qualified plan for any year beginning before the later of (1) January 1, 1989, or (2) the earlier of (a) January 1, 1991, or (b) the first plan year beginning after the termination of the collective bargaining agreement (determined without regard to any extension of the terms of the agreement ratified after February 28, 1986) provided three conditions are satisfied.

First, the plan must operate in compliance with the changes for the first plan year beginning after the generally applicable effective date.

Second, plan amendments must be adopted no later than the last day of the first plan year beginning after the later of (1) December 31, 1988, or (2) the earlier of (a) December 31, 1990, or (b) the termination of the collective bargaining agreement, and such amendments must be made effective as of the first day of the first plan year for which the plan amendments are required.

*   *   *   *   *   *

Conference Agreement

The conference agreement generally follows the Senate amendment provisions with respect to the time allowed for plan amendments and the issuance of regulations. In addition, under the conference agreement, the IRS is to issue a model amendment within 60 days after the date of enactment that plans may adopt for the period ending with the required plan amendment dates under this provision. Such model amendment is to address only those amendments that are required to be made under the conference agreement to maintain qualification for the period ending with the first plan year beginning after December 31, 1988. * * *

[¶4000] **SECTION 1141. ISSUANCE OF FINAL REGULATIONS**

[Conference Report]

*   *   *   *   *   *

Senate Amendment

*   *   *   *   *   *

The Senate amendment provides that the Secretary is to issue final regulations with respect to certain qualified plan provisions of the amendment by February 1, 1988. The provisions for which these regulations are required to be issued include (1) the rules relating to the integration of benefits; (2) the coverage requirements; (3) the minimum vesting standards; (4) the amendments applicable to qualified cash or deferred arrange-

ments (sec. 401(k) plans); and (5) the new nondiscrimination rules for employer matching and employee contributions (sec. 401(m)).

Conference Agreement.—The conference agreement generally follows the Senate amendment provisions with respect to the time allowed for plan amendments and the issuance of regulations. * * *

The conference agreement clarifies that the rule regarding issuance of regulations applies to the coverage requirements applicable to tax-sheltered annuity programs, the definitions of highly compensated employees and the 10 percent tax on excess distributions.

[¶4001] **SECTION 1142. SECRETARY TO ACCEPT APPLICATIONS WITH RESPECT TO SECTION 401(k) PLANS**

[Conference Report]

*   *   *   *   *   *

Senate Amendment

*   *   *   *   *   *

The Senate amendment provides that the Internal Revenue Service is required, not later than May 1, 1987, to begin issuing opinion letters with respect to master and prototype plans for cash or deferred arrangements. In addition, the Secretary of the Treasury is to publish, no later than May 1, 1987, a model plan document for qualified plans that include qualified cash or deferred arrangements.

Conference Agreement

*   *   *   *   *   *

Further, the conference agreement follows the Senate amendment with respect to opinion letters for master and prototype 401(k) plans, * * *. The conference agreement provides that the IRS must begin accepting opinion letter requests by May 1, 1987, rather than begin issuing letters by such date.

[The following colloquy relating to Act Sec. is drawn from the Congressional Record. The colloquy occurred on the day the Conference bill was considered by the Senate. Ed.]

[Senate Floor Explanation]

SECTION 401(k) MASTER PLAN

Mr. BAUCUS. Section 1142 of the conference agreement pertains to master and prototype plans for qualified cash or deferred arrangements under section 401(k). A master c₄ prototype plan is a plan whose form is approved by the National Office of the IRS. An employer that adopts a master or prototype plan, making only those elections permitted in the plan, can rely on the plan's qualification under the relevant law.

The master and prototype program is not dictated by the Tax Code but is instead set up by the IRS as a streamlined procedure to handle its workload while eliminating paperwork for small employers. These plans are most suitable for small businesses with 100 or fewer employees. I understand that a master plan can cost as little as $100 to a small employer who wishes to set up a 401(k) plan for himself and his employees, as compared with a typical cost range of $1,500 to $10,00[0] in legal fees for an individually structured plan. Also, adoption of a master plan would save the employer time and even reduce IRS workloads by cutting down on the number of plan approval requests.

The Senate bill required IRS to begin issuing determination letters by May 1, 1987, to make 401(k) plans more widely available to small businesses. The conference report indicates that IRS will begin accepting applications for opinion letters by May 1, 1987. Is my understanding correct that this change will delay the availability of 401(k) plans at a reasonable cost to small businesses?

Mr. PACKWOOD. Yes, the Senator's understanding is correct. Because of the pending backlogs at IRS, a May 1, 1987, deadline for determination letters was administratively impossible. However, it is unfair to penalize small employers any further beyond the time delay provided to IRS.

I expect that, even with the delaying provision of the final language, the IRS will make every effort to issue favorable opinion letters on master and prototype 401(k) plans as quickly as possible. I have heard of cases where sponsoring organizations have waited over 2 years to receive final approval of their plans. The deadline imposed in this legislation shows that Congress intends that such delays will not occur in the future. Congressional Record, p. S13959-13960, 9-27-86.

[¶ 4002] SECTION 1143. TREATMENT OF CERTAIN FISHERMEN AS SELF-EMPLOYED INDIVIDUALS

(Sec. 401 of the Code)

[Senate Explanation]

*   *   *   *   *   *

Explanation of Provision.—Under the bill, members of fishing boat crews (described in sec. 3121(b)(20)) are treated as self-employed individuals for purposes of the rules relating to qualified pension, profit-sharing, or stock bonus plans.

*   *   *   *   *

[Conference Report]

*   *   *   *   *

[Effective Date—] The conference agreement follows the Senate amendment, effective for taxable years beginning after December 31, 1986.

[¶ 4003] SECTION 1144. ACQUISITION OF GOLD AND SILVER COINS BY INDIVIDUAL RETIREMENT ACCOUNTS

(Sec. 408 of the Code)

[The Senate Finance Committee version of the bill was amended on the Floor of the Senate. The following is drawn from the Congressional Record. Ed.]

[Senate Floor Explanation]

*   *   *   *   *   *

Mr. McCLURE. Mr. President, the amendment offered by myself for Senator Symms and cosponsored by Senator Hecht will allow legal tender gold and silver coins minted by the United States to be used as IRA investments.

On October 1 of this year the U.S. Treasury will make available to the general public, for the first time in many years, gold and silver bullion coins. These coins are the result of many years of hard work by myself and others in this body. There will be four gold bullion coins and one silver coin. The gold will be denominated in 1 ounce, one-half ounce, one-quarter ounce, and one-tenth ounce. The silver will be 1 ounce.

*   *   *   *   *   *

Many citizens have expressed a great desire to buy these gold and silver coins as investment tools for individual retirement accounts. However, in the Economic Recovery Tax Act of 1981 a provision was added to prohibit investment in collectibles. There was concern that investors would want to hold their collectibles making it difficult to police whether or not the investment existed.

Mr. President, we have taken care of this concern with our amendment by limiting the coinage investment to only the gold and silver coins under title 31, section 5112. In addition, we have limited the investment to only individual retirement accounts. Therefore, if an individual wanted to invest in the gold and silver coins, such investment would have to be held by a trustee and could not be held by the individual investor. We felt this was a good compromise to avoid any concern that existed in 1981.

*   *   *   *   *

Mr. President, the Joint Committee on Taxation has reviewed this amendment and determined that it is revenue neutral and will not cost the Treasury any money. It does not change who is eligible to invest in IRA's or change any of the rules governing control over IRA investments. It simply allows U.S.-minted gold and silver coins to be used as IRA investments. All the rules that apply to other IRA investments will also apply to the gold and silver coinage.

*   *   *   *   *

Mr. SYMMS.

*   *   *   *   *

The amendment will only allow for the deposit of U.S. 1-ounce, half-ounce, quarter-ounce and tenth-of-an-ounce gold bullion coins and a new 1-ounce silver coin. These U.S. coins will be minted by the Treasury beginning October 1.

*   *   *   *   *

The provision will broaden the options investors face when they are considering IRA's. Again, there is no cost—this only allows the individual an option to invest some of his IRA funds in U.S. gold and silver coins, if so desired.

The amendment requires that the coins be held by a trustee, just as any other asset in an IRA. Congressional Record, p. S 7931—7932, 6-19-86.

[Conference Report]

*   *   *   *   *

The conference agreement follows the Senate amendment, effective for acquisitions of coins after December 31, 1986.

[¶ 4004] Section 1145. REQUIREMENT OF JOINT AND SURVIVOR ANNUITIES AND PRERETIREMENT SURVIVOR ANNUITIES NOT TO APPLY TO CERTAIN PLAN

(Secs. 401 of the Code; Sec. 205 of '74 ERISA; Sec. 303 of '84 REA)

[Conference Report]

* * * * * *

7. Retirement Equity Act of 1984 (REA) Effective Date

Present Law.—Under the Retirement Equity Act of 1984 (REA), a pension plan is to provide automatic survivor benefits (1) in the case of a participant who retires under the plan, in the form of a qualified joint and survivor annuity, and (2) in the case of a vested participant who dies before the annuity starting date and who has a surviving spouse, in the form of a qualified preretirement survivor annuity. The qualified joint and survivor annuity and preretirement survivor annuity provisions apply to any participant who performs at least one hour of service under the plan on or after the date of enactment.

REA provided a special transition rule for participants who separated from service before the date of enactment and whose benefits were not in pay status as of the date of enactment. This provision applies if (1) a participant completed at least one hour of service under the plan after September 1, 1974, (2) the participant separated from service before the first day of the first plan year beginning on or after January 1, 1976, and (3) the plan is required to provide a qualified joint and survivor annuity. Under this special rule, the participant is to be provided the right to elect to receive benefits in the form of a qualified joint and survivor annuity. * * *

Senate Amendment.—* * * [A] plan is exempt from the survivor benefit requirements of REA if (1) the plan was established prior to January 1, 1954, as a result of an agreement between employee representatives and the Federal Government during a period of Government operation, under seizure powers, of a major part of the productive facilities of the industry, and (2) under the plan, participation is substantially limited to participants who, before January 1, 1976, ceased employment covered by the plan.

[Effective date.—Effective as if included in '84 REA provisions.]

[¶ 4005] SECTION 1146. TREATMENT OF LEASED EMPLOYEES

(Sec. 414 of the Code)

[Conference Report]

Present Law.—For purposes of specified pension requirements, a leased employee is treated as the employee of the person for whom the leased employee performs services (the "recipient"). A leased employee is generally defined as any person who is not an employee of the recipient and who provides services to the recipient if 3 requirements are met. First, such services must be provided to the recipient under an agreement between the recipient and the organization providing the person's services (the "leasing organization"). Second, the person must have performed such services for the recipient (or for the recipient and related persons) on a substantially full-time basis for at least one year. Third, such services must be of a type historically performed, in the business field of the recipient, by employees.

Generally, the pension requirements for which a leased employee is treated as an employee are the rules regarding nondiscrimination, vesting, limitations on benefits and contributions, top-heavy plans, and simplified employee pensions (SEPs).

A leased employee covered by a safe-harbor plan maintained by the leasing organization is not treated as an employee of the recipient. A safe-harbor plan is a money purchase pension plan that provides for immediate participation and for full and immediate vesting and that has a nonintegrated employer contribution rate of at least 7½ percent.

* * * * * *

Conference Agreement.—In light of the substantial changes made by the conference agreement to the pension requirements to which the employee leasing rules apply, the conference agreement modifies the employee leasing rules.

The conference agreement modifies the definition of a safe-harbor plan in two ways. First, the agreement raises the required contribution rate from 7½ percent to 10 percent.

Second, the conference agreement requires that, to be a safe-harbor plan, a plan must cover all employees of the leasing organization (beginning with the date they become employees) other than (1) employees whom the leasing organization demonstrates to the satisfaction of the Secretary performed substantially all of their services for the leasing organization (rather than for recipients), and (2) employees whose total compensation from the leasing organization is less than $1,000 during the plan year and during each of the 3 prior plan years.

As under present law, an employee covered under a safe-harbor plan is to receive the required allocation regardless of the number of hours of service credited to the employee for the year, regardless of whether the employee is employed by the leasing organization on any specified date during the year and regardless of the participant's age.

In addition, a definition of compensation is provided by the agreement for purposes of the 10 percent contribution rate and the $1,000 rule. For these purposes, compensation is to have the same meaning used for purposes of the limitation on benefits or contributions (sec. 415), except that there is to be added to such amount elective deferrals under a qualified cash or deferred arrangement, SEP, or tax-sheltered annuity program and elective contributions under a cafeteria plan.

The conference agreement also provides that each leased employee is to be treated as an employee of the recipient, regardless of the existence of a safe-harbor plan, if more than 20 percent of an employee's nonhighly compensated workforce are leased employees (as specially defined below). The term "nonhighly compensated workforce" is defined to mean the number of persons (other than highly compensated employees) who are (1) employees of the recipient (other than leased employees (as specially defined below)) and have performed services for the recipient (or for the recipient and related persons) on a substantially full-time basis for a period of at least one year, and (2) leased employees (as specially defined below) with respect to the recipient. For purposes of this 20 percent rule, the term "leased employee" includes any person who performs services for the recipient both as a nonemployee and as an employee, and who would be a leased employee if all such services were performed as a nonemployee.

The conference agreement also applies the employee leasing rules for purposes of certain employee benefit requirements (see Part F, below) and adjusts certain rules accordingly. The exemption from the application of the employee leasing rules with respect to individuals covered by a safe-harbor plan is inapplicable to employee benefits. In addition, with respect to core health benefits, the period during which an individual must perform services on a substantially full-time basis is reduced from one year to 6 months.

Also, with respect to the employee leasing rules generally, the conference agreement clarifies that in the case of an employee of the recipient (whether by reason of being a leased employee or otherwise), for purposes of the applicable requirements, service is to include any period of service during which the employee would have been a leased employee but for the requirement that substantially full-time services be performed for at least one year (6 months in the case of core health benefits). Of course, service as an employee (whether by reason of being a leased employee or otherwise) is also credited.

The conference agreement also clarifies that the rules aggregating certain employers (sec. 414(b), (c), (m), and (o)) apply for purposes of the employee leasing rules. Thus, for example, the term "recipient" includes, in addition to the employer or employers for which the services are performed, other aggregated employers.

Finally, regulations are to be issued to minimize the recordkeeping requirements attributable to the employee leasing provisions in the case of an employer that has no top-heavy plans (sec. 416) and that uses the services of nonemployees only for an insignificant percentage of the employer's total workload.

The conferees intend that this recordkeeping rule be applied for employers with respect to which the number of individuals performing substantial services as nonemployees is less than 5 percent of the number of nonhighly compensated employees performing substantial services.

Further, it is intended that the Secretary is to prescribe objective rules to determine if an individual has performed substantial services. With respect to individuals performing services both as an employee and as a nonemployee, services in both capacities generally are to be taken into account and, for purposes of this recordkeeping rule, counted as service as a nonemployee. In addition, it is intended that an individual is to be treated as having performed substantial services as a nonemployee only if such individual has at least 1,500 hours of service. Also, in lieu of requiring that the number of nonhighly compensated employees performing substantial services be determined, the Secretary may generally deem the number of nonhighly compensated employees performing substantial services to be equal to the number of nonhighly compensated employees covered by a qualified plan of the employer (other than those also performing services as a nonemployee). (For an employer that does not maintain a qualified plan, the Secretary may allow use of the number of participants in, for example, a health plan.)

The conferees further intend that the Secretary is to prescribe appropriate rules to minimize the recordkeeping necessary to determine if this 5-percent test has been satisfied. Thus, for purposes of determining whether an employee has performed substantial services, the Secretary may permit an employer not to check whether an individual who performed less than substantial services at one division also performed services at another geographically separate division, unless such checking would be reasonable under the circumstances (such as in the case where the employer transfers the individual). The Secretary may also permit employers to rely on records maintained by all leasing organizations providing the services of an individual in determining the amount of services performed by such individual as a nonemployee, unless, of course, the employer has reason to believe such records are not accurate. Also, in cases where determining the exact numbers of nonemployees performing substantial services would be burdensome due to the large numbers involved, the Secretary may permit employers to rely on a statistically valid sample performed by an independent third party.

With respect to the requirement that the employer have no top-heavy plans, the Secretary, by regulation, is to adjust this requirement to apply to the other benefits to which the leasing rules now apply. In such situations, the Secretary may substitute a comparable test applicable to employee benefits. For example, the recordkeeping exemption might not be available with respect to a type of employee benefit if at least 60 percent of that type of benefit was being provided to highly compensated employees.

For an employer that satisfies the requirements for recordkeeping relief, it is intended that an employer need not treat an individual as a leased employee unless such individual provides the employer satisfactory evidence of entitlement to such treatment.

Finally, the conference agreement deletes the rule providing regulatory authority to render the employee leasing rules inapplica-

ble in certain circumstances. The recordkeeping exemption provided under the conference agreement serves the purpose for which the regulatory authority was created.

In general, these new rules are effective with respect to services performed after December 31, 1986. The recordkeeping exemption, however, shall apply as if it were originally enacted as part of the employee leasing legislation in the Tax Equity and Fiscal Responsibility Act of 1982 (TEFRA), [tax years beginning after 12-31-83] except that for plan years of recipients beginning before * * * [the '86 TRA enactment date], the only requirement for the relief is that the employer have no top-heavy plan. Further, the clarifying changes regarding crediting service and aggregating employers are effective as if originally part of the employee leasing legislation in TEFRA. * * * [tax years beginning after 12-31-83].

[¶ 4006] SECTION 1147. TAX TREATMENT OF FEDERAL THRIFT SAVINGS FUND

(Sec. 7701 of the Code)

[Conference Report]

Present Law.—Under present law, beginning in 1987, an employee is allowed to contribute up to 10 percent of the employee's rate of basic pay to the Thrift Savings Plan maintained by the Federal government. These employee contributions to the Thrift Savings Plan are not includible in the employee's income for the year of deferral, but rather are includible in income when distributed from the Plan. The tax treatment of an employee's contributions to the Plan is not currently specified in the Internal Revenue Code.

* * * * * *

Conference Agreement.—The conference agreement provides, in the Internal Revenue Code, for the tax treatment of an employee's contributions to the Thrift Savings Plan maintained by the Federal government. Under the provision, an employee's contributions to the Plan are not treated as made available merely because the employee had an election to receive the amounts in cash. Therefore, the amounts deferred are not includible in an employee's income until distributed.

[Effective date.—] The provision is effective on the date of enactment.

[¶ 4007] SECTION 1151. NONDISCRIMINATION RULES FOR COVERAGE AND BENEFITS UNDER CERTAIN STATUTORY EMPLOYEE BENEFIT PLANS

(Secs. 89 and 125 of the Code)

[Conference Report]

* * * * * *

a. Overview

House Bill

The House bill establishes new nondiscriminatory eligibility and benefits rules for statutory employee benefit plans, welfare benefit funds, and cafeteria plans (sec. 89). Under the rules, a highly compensated employee who is a participant in any discriminatory plan generally is only taxed on the value of the discriminatory portion of such employee's employer-provided benefit under the plan.

The House bill (1) establishes uniform definitions of employer, highly compensated employee, and excludable employee, and (2) permits satisfaction of the nondiscrimination

rules on a line of business or operating unit basis. Further, the House bill extends reporting requirements to all statutory employee benefit plans and requires that Treasury conduct a study of abuses in the health insurance area.

Senate Amendment

The Senate amendment establishes new nondiscriminatory benefits rules for accident or health plans (insured or self-insured) and group-term life insurance plans. In addition, the Senate amendment provides that a highly compensated employee who is a participant in any discriminatory plan is taxed on the value of such employee's employer-provided benefit under the plan.

The Senate amendment also: (1) establishes a new nondiscrimination benefits test applicable (at the election of the employer) to other types of statutory employee benefit plans, in lieu of certain present law nondiscrimination rules; (2) establishes a concentration test applicable to both group-term life insurance plans and accident or health plans, and an additional concentration test applicable only to group-term life insurance plans; (3) establishes uniform definitions of employer, highly compensated employee, and excludable employee; and (4) permits satisfaction of the nondiscrimination rules on a line of business or operating unit basis.

Conference Agreement

The conference agreement generally follows the House bill with regard to the amount of the inclusion in income in the case of a discriminatory plan subject to the new nondiscrimination rules. The conference agreement also (1) establishes new eligibility and benefits nondiscrimination rules applicable to group-term life insurance plans and accident or health plans (insured or self-insured); (2) allows employers to elect to apply these new rules to certain other types of plans; (3) establishes a special benefits rule for dependent care assistance programs; (4) establishes uniform definitions of employer, highly compensated employee, compensation, and excludable employee; and (5) permits satisfaction of the nondiscrimination rules for group-term life insurance plans and accident or health plans on a line of business or operating unit basis.

b. General rule for inclusion

House Bill

In general.—Under the House bill, a highly compensated employee who is a participant in a discriminatory statutory employee benefit plan is required to include in income an amount equal to the employee's employer-provided benefit under the plan.

The House bill also provides that the gross income of any employee, whether or not highly compensated, includes such employee's employer-provided benefit under a statutory employee benefit plan, unless (1) the plan is in writing; (2) the employee's rights under the plan are legally enforceable; and (3) the employer established the plan with the intention of maintaining it indefinitely.

Statutory employee benefit plan.—The term "statutory employee benefit plans" includes employer-maintained group-term life insurance plans, accident or health benefit plans (whether self-insured or funded through an insurance company), qualified group legal services plans (whether self-insured or funded through an insurance company), educational assistance programs, and dependent care assistance programs. With respect to disability coverage, only coverage attributable to employer contributions (including elective contributions) that provides disability benefits that are excludable from income (sec. 105(b) or (c)) is subject to the nondiscrimination rules applicable generally to statutory employee benefit plans.

Employee's employer-provided benefit.—In the case of an insurance-type plan (i.e., an accident or health plan, group-term life insurance plan, or group legal services plan) the House bill defines the employee's employer-provided benefit as the value of the coverage provided during the taxable year to or on behalf of such employee, to the extent attributable to contributions made by the employer. In the case of any other plan, an employee's employer-provided benefit is defined as the value of the benefits provided to or on behalf of such employee, to the extent attributable to contributions made by the employer. Of course, in all cases, employer contributions include elective contributions under a cafeteria plan.

In the case of a discriminatory statutory employee benefit plan (other than a group-term life insurance plan), the coverage or benefit may be considered to be provided under more than one plan so that highly compensated employees are only taxed on the discriminatory portion of the benefit provided (i.e., the discriminatory excess).

Senate Amendment

In general.—The Senate amendment generally is the same as the House bill, except that the definitions of the terms "statutory employee benefit plan" and "employer-provided benefit" are modified.

Statutory employee benefit plan.—The Senate definition of a "statutory employee benefit plan" is the same as the House bill definition except that qualified tuition reduction programs (sec. 117(d)) and fringe benefit programs providing no-additional-cost services, qualified employee discounts, or employer-operated eating facilities (sec. 132) are also included in the definition in the Senate amendment.

Employer-provided benefit.—The Senate amendment is the same as the House bill with two modifications. First, in the case of an insurance-type plan that does not satisfy the writing, enforceability, and indefinite duration requirement described above, an employee's employer-provided benefit is defined as the value of the benefits provided to or on behalf of such employee, to the extent attributable to contributions made by the employer (including elective contributions).

Second, for purposes of determining the amount includible in income of a highly compensated employee for discriminatory benefits, the employer-provided benefit of any highly compensated employee in a discriminatory plan is equal to the employer-provided benefits to such employee under all statutory employee benefit plans of the employer of the same type (i.e., the benefits are excludable from income under the same section of the Code).

Conference Agreement

The conference agreement generally follows the House bill with certain modifications. First, the conference agreement provides that group legal services plans, educational assistance programs, and dependent care assistance programs are only statutory employee benefit plans with respect to an employer if the employer elects to treat them as such.

Second, with respect to the method of determining the amount includible in the income of a highly compensated employee who participates in a discriminatory statutory employee benefit plan, the conference agreement applies the House bill rule that only the discriminatory excess is includible in income. In the case of group-term life insurance plans, the conference agreement provides that the value of the discriminatory excess, expressed in terms of insurance coverage, is the greater of the cost of the coverage under section 79(c) or the actual cost of the coverage.

The conference agreement also provides rules regarding the definition of the discriminatory excess, how to allocate the excess among highly compensated employees, timely reporting, and the year of inclusion. The discriminatory excess is defined as the amount of employer contributions (including elective contributions) that would have to have been made as after-tax employee contributions on behalf of the highly compensated employees in order for all of the nondiscrimination tests to be satisfied. In applying this definition, the objective nondiscrimination tests are, except as provided by the Secretary, to be applied in the following order: the "50-percent test", the "90-percent/50-percent test" and then the benefits test. Alternatively, the definition of the discriminatory excess be applied to the alternative 80-percent test. The determination of the discriminatory excess with respect to the third eligibility test is to be made under rules prescribed by the Secretary. See the discussion of these tests, below.

Any discriminatory excess determined with respect to the benefits test shall be allocated to highly compensated employees by reducing the tax-favored dollars of highly compensated employees (beginning with the employees with the greatest nontaxable benefits) until the plan (or plans) being tested would not be discriminatory.

The discriminatory excess is includible in the employee's income in the employee's taxable year with or within which the plan year ends.

Except to the extent provided by the Secretary, if an employer (including an employer exempt from tax) does not report the discriminatory excess to the affected employees and the IRS on Forms W-2 by the due date (with any extension) for filing such forms W-2, all benefits of the same type provided to such employees are subject to an employer-level sanction without regard to whether the employees report some or all of the benefits as income. Under this sanction, the employer is liable for an excise tax at the highest individual rate on the total value of benefits of the same type. For group-term life insurance, the value is the greater of the table cost or actual cost of all coverage. This tax is not deductible and may not be offset by credits or deductions in any manner. This tax, however, does not apply if the employer can demonstrate that the failure to report was due to reasonable cause, such as a reasonable difference in valuation of health

benefits prior to the issuance of valuation regulations.

This employer-level sanction applies in a similar manner to a failure by the employer to report income includible by reason of the failure to meet the writing, enforceability, and indefinite duration rule, as modified below. However, in such cases, with respect to insurance-type benefits, this sanction applies to the value of benefits, rather than the value of coverage.

The conference agreement modifies the writing, enforceability, and indefinite duration rules by adding two other requirements to such rules. First, a plan must provide for reasonable notification to employees of benefits available under the plan. With respect to dependent care assistance, this notification is to include a description of the dependent care credit (sec. 21) and the circumstances under which the credit is more advantageous than the exclusion. Second, a plan is to be maintained for the exclusive benefit of employees (or, where permissible, spouses and dependents of employees). Also, the conference agreement provides that the writing, enforceability, etc., requirements will apply except to the extent provided by the Secretary.

With respect to the requirement that a statutory employee benefit plan be legally enforceable, the conferees intend that a plan will generally not be considered legally enforceable if it is discretionary with the employer. For example, if a plan of the employer provides that medical expenses will be reimbursed at the employer's discretion, the plan would not be legally enforceable, because the employee would have no right to compel payment of benefits. A plan will not fail to satisfy the legally enforceable requirement merely because the employer has the right to terminate the plan with respect to claims not yet incurred. If, however, the employer maintained the right to terminate the plan with respect to incurred claims, those claims would not be considered legally enforceable, and payment of the claims' would not be excludable. Of course, termination in some circumstances could violate the permanency requirement.

The conference agreement also applies the writing, enforceability, etc., rules, in addition to accident or health plans and group-term life insurance plans, to the following plans: qualified tuition reduction programs, group legal services plans, cafeteria plans, educational assistance programs, dependent care programs, miscellaneous fringe benefit programs subject to nondiscrimination rules (sec. 132), and benefits provided under a welfare benefit fund.

The conference agreement clarifies that if a plan fails the writing, enforceability, etc., rules, the employer-provided benefit is, as under the Senate amendment, the value of the benefits provided rather than the value of the coverage under the plan. Thus, in the case of a health plan failing these requirements, the services provided and reimbursements made are includible in income. In

Act § 1151   ¶ 4007

addition, such amount is includible in an employee's gross income in the taxable year in which such benefits are received.

The conference agreement modifies the definition of insurance-type plans to include only group-term life insurance plans and accident or health plans.

The conference agreement also clarifies that, in the case of self-insurance, the employer-provided benefit is the value of the coverage and is not limited by the actual disbursements made by the employer.

c. Nondiscrimination rules

House Bill

Eligibility test.—The House bill establishes a uniform nondiscriminatory eligibility rule for all statutory employee benefit plans. A plan satisfies the new eligibility rule if (1) at least 90 percent of all employees are eligible to participate in the plan; and (2) the plan contains no provisions relating to eligibility to participate that discriminate in favor of highly compensated employees.

Benefits test.—The House bill also establishes a uniform nondiscriminatory benefits rule for all benefits provided under insurance-type plans.

In the case of an accident or health plan, the bill generally provides that the plan will not be treated as meeting the nondiscriminatory benefits test if (1) 25 percent or more of the employees benefiting under the plan are highly compensated employees, and (2) less than 75 percent of the employees eligible to participate in the plan actually benefit under the plan.

The amount of benefits provided under an employer-maintained health plan may be integrated (in a manner that does not discriminate in favor of highly compensated employees) with benefits provided under Medicare or any other Federal, State, or foreign law, or under any other health plan covering the employee or a member of the employee's family.

In the case of any insurance-type plan other than an accident or health plan, the plan will be treated as not meeting the requirements of the nondiscriminatory benefits test if less than 75 percent of the employees eligible to participate in the plan actually benefit under the plan.

Under the House bill, disability coverage attributable to employer contributions (including elective contributions) is subject to the nondiscrimination rules only to the extent that benefits provided under such coverage are excludable from income (sec. 105(b) or (c)). Coverage for such disability benefits is tested under the same nondiscriminatory benefits rules as those applicable to health coverage.

In the case of any statutory employee benefit plan that is not an insurance-type plan, the plan meets the nondiscriminatory benefits requirement if (1) all benefits available under the plan to any highly compensated employee are available on the same terms and conditions to all other employees eligible to participate in the plan; and (2) the average benefit provided on behalf of nonhighly compensated employees equals or exceeds 80 percent of the average benefit provided to or on behalf of highly compensated employees.

Senate Amendment

In general.—*Accident or health plans and group-term life insurance.*—Under the Senate amendment, an accident or health plan (whether or not insured) or a group-term life insurance plan is considered discriminatory unless the plan satisfies the (1) percentage test; (2) reasonable classification test; (3) average benefits test; or (4) average income exclusion test. These tests (other than the average income exclusion test) do not apply to plans other than accident or health plans and group-term life insurance plans. The Senate amendment follows the House bill with respect to what type of disability coverage is subject to these tests.

Other plans.—A plan other than an accident or health plan or a group-term life insurance plan is generally considered discriminatory unless the plan meets the applicable present law nondiscrimination rules or the new average income exclusion test.

Percentage test.—Under the Senate amendment, a plan satisfies the percentage test if it benefits 80 percent or more of all employees of the employer.

Reasonable classification test.—The Senate amendment provides that a plan meets the reasonable classification test if it benefits a reasonable classification of employees that the Secretary finds does not allow more than a reasonable difference (in favor of highly compensated employees) between the coverage percentage of highly compensated employees and the coverage percentage of other employees.

Average benefit test.—Under the Senate amendment, an accident or health plan or group-term life insurance plan that does not meet the reasonable classification test will be treated as meeting that test if (1) the plan meets the requirements of section 410(b)(1)(B) as in effect immediately before the date of enactment of the Tax Reform Act of 1986; (2) the average benefit provided to employees not covered by an alternative plan is at least 60 percent of the average benefit provided to employees covered by an alternative plan (or plans); and (3) in the case of an accident or health plan, at least 80 percent of the employer's nonhighly compensated employees are eligible to participate in one or more plans of the same type and the benefits available to each such employee are equal to at least 40 percent of the average benefits provided to employees covered by an alternative plan.

The term "alternative plan" is defined as any plan that meets the requirements of section 410(b)(1)(B) as in effect immediately before the date of enactment of the Tax Reform Act of 1986, but does not meet the requirements of the reasonable classification test without regard to the average benefit test.

Average income exclusion test.—*In general.*—An accident or health plan or a group-term life insurance plan that does not satisfy the reasonable classification test will be treated as satisfying the test if the plan satisfies the average income exclusion test. In addition, in the case of a statutory employee benefit plan other than an accident or health plan or a group-term life insurance plan, and in the case of a cafeteria plan, a plan that satisfies the average income exclusion requirements test will generally be deemed to satisfy the present law nondiscrimination rules (other than concentration tests) applicable to such plan.

A plan meets the requirements of the average income exclusion test if the average exclusion amount for nonhighly compensated employees is at least 80 percent of the average exclusion amount for highly compensated employees.

Under the Senate amendment, the term "average exclusion amount" with respect to highly compensated employees is an amount equal to the aggregate excludable amount provided under all plans of the same type to highly compensated employees divided by the total number of highly compensated employees of the employer. The average exclusion amount with respect to nonhighly compensated employees is determined in the same manner.

Special rules for accident or health plans.—Under the Senate amendment, for purposes of applying the average income exclusion test to accident or health plans (except in the case of a cafeteria plan that offers a health plan option, as well as other types of benefits), an employer may elect to disregard any employee if the employee and the employee's spouse and dependents (if any) are covered by an accident or health plan maintained by another employer.

In addition, if an employer maintains an accident or health plan that provides family coverage, the employer may elect to test separately the coverage for employees and the coverage for spouses or dependents as if the two types of coverage constituted two different types of plans. For purposes of testing the coverage for spouses or dependents, an employer may take into account only employees with spouses or dependents who are not covered by an accident or health plan maintained by the employers of the spouses and dependents.

An employer who elects either of these options must obtain and maintain, in such manner as the Secretary of the Treasury prescribes, adequate sworn statements to demonstrate whether individuals have spouses, dependents, or other accident or health coverage.

The Senate amendment follows the House bill with respect to coordination with accident or health benefits provided under a law or other plans.

Special rule for group-term life insurance.—For purposes of determining whether the average income exclusion test is satisfied for a group-term life insurance plan, or a

cafeteria plan offering such a benefit, the amount attributable to the group-term life insurance benefit that is excludable from income under the plan is to be determined under section 79 for an individual who is age 30. In addition, group-term life insurance coverage in excess of $50,000 may be disregarded. These special rules do not apply for income inclusion purposes if the plan being tested is determined to be discriminatory.

Conference Agreement

The conference agreement generally follows the House bill with respect to the eligibility test and generally follows the Senate amendment with respect to the benefits test, but modifies both tests. In addition, the conference agreement adds an alternative test that may be applied in lieu of the eligibility and benefits tests.

Scope of rules.—With respect to the scope of the new nondiscrimination rules, the conference agreement generally follows the Senate bill. The new eligibility and benefits tests apply only to statutory employee benefit plans. As noted above, this term generally includes only accident or health plans and group-term life insurance plans.

As under both bills, no nondiscrimination rules apply to disability coverage to the extent that the proceeds payable under such coverage would be includible in the income of the employee.

All other accident or health plans are subject to these nondiscrimination rules, including, for example, plans providing ancillary benefits such as dental or vision plans and physical examination plans. With respect to accident or health plans, it is the value of the coverage provided, not the contributions, that is subject to the nondiscrimination rules. (Correspondingly, the conference agreement modifies the exclusion section to apply to the value of the coverage, rather than the contributions under the plan.)

With respect to dependent care assistance programs, the present-law eligibility standards continue to apply, but the conference agreement adds a special benefits test. The present-law nondiscrimination rules apply to qualified tuition reduction programs, group legal services plans, educational assistance programs, and employee benefit programs providing no-additional-cost services, qualified employee discounts, or employer-operated eating facilities (sec. 132).

The reason that the new nondiscrimination rules applicable to accident or health plans and group-term life insurance plans are not applicable to group legal services plans and educational assistance programs is that the latter types of plans are generally scheduled to expire prior to the effective date of the new nondiscrimination rules. The conferees anticipate, however, that if the group legal services plans and educational assistance programs are extended to periods after the effective date of the new nondiscri-

Act § 1151 ¶ 4007

mination rules, such nondiscrimination rules shall be applied.

The conference agreement permits employers to elect to treat group legal services plans, educational assistance programs, and/or dependent care assistance programs as statutory employee benefit plans; and to apply the new eligibility and benefits tests to them in lieu of the present-law nondiscrimination tests (though not in lieu of the applicable concentration tests (secs. 120(c)(3), 127(b)(3), and 129(d)(4)). Such an election will enable an employer to use these types of plans for purposes of satisfying the benefits. (See the description in "Benefits test" below.)

Although the new nondiscrimination rules do not mandatorily apply to plans other than accident or health plans and group-term life insurance plans, the following definitions are also applied to qualified tuition reduction programs, group legal services plans, cafeteria plans, educational assistance programs, dependent care assistance programs, miscellaneous fringe benefits (sec. 132), and welfare benefit funds: (1) highly compensated employees; (2) compensation (including the limitation on the amount that can be taken into account) with respect to those plans for which compensation is relevant; (3) excludable employees; and (4) employer (including application of the employee leasing rules). These new definitions are discussed more fully below.

Eligibility tests.—Under the conference agreement, a statutory employee benefit plan must satisfy an eligibility test consisting of 3 requirements. The first requirement is that nonhighly compensated employees must constitute at least 50 percent of the group of employees eligible to participate in the plan. This requirement will be deemed satisfied if the percentage of highly compensated employees who are eligible to participate is not greater than the percentage of nonhighly compensated employees who are eligible.

For example, assume that an employer has 20 employees, 15 of whom are highly compensated employees. Because more than 50 percent of its workforce is highly compensated, that employer could make all employees eligible but still not satisfy the "50-percent test." However, if all employees are eligible, the employer would be deemed to satisfy the 50-percent test because the percentage of highly compensated employees and nonhighly compensated employees who are eligible is the same (i.e., 100 percent).

For purposes of satisfying the 50-percent test, comparable plans (as defined below) may be aggregated.

Under the second eligibility requirement, a plan is discriminatory unless at least 90 percent of the employer's nonhighly compensated employees are eligible for a benefit that is at least 50 percent as valuable as the benefit available to the highly compensated employee to whom the most valuable benefits are made available. For purposes of this test, all plans of the same type (i.e., all benefits excludable under the same Code section) are aggregated. Thus, if an employee is eligible to

participate in two or more plans of the same type, the employee is considered eligible for a benefit with a value equal to the sum of the values in the plans for which the employee is eligible. Also, in determining the highly compensated employee with the most valuable benefits, benefits under all plans of the same type are aggregated in the same manner.

For purposes of this 90-percent/50-percent test, available salary reduction is not taken into account. (See "Cafeteria plan" below for rules applicable to salary reduction.) In addition, to the extent that benefits other than salary reduction amounts are available on the condition that an employee make a salary reduction election (or an after-tax contribution), the contingent benefits may be allocated among different types of plans in any reasonable manner permitted by the Secretary and determined by the employer.

Also, for purposes of the 90-percent/50-percent test, the conference agreement provides that coverage of an employee under accident or health plans may be tested separately from coverage of an employee's spouse and/or dependents under accident or health plans. Coverage of an employee's spouse and/or dependents is tested together regardless of whether the employer creates separate plans for employees with one spouse or dependent as opposed to employees with two or more.

The third eligibility requirement provides that a plan may not contain any provision relating to eligibility to participate that by its terms or otherwise discriminates in favor of highly compensated employees. This third test is not intended to disqualify arrangements where the discrimination is quantifiable. For example, if an employer maintains one health plan for its salaried employees and one health plan for its hourly employees, the fact that the hourly plan is less valuable will not cause the salaried plan to fail the third eligibility requirement. On the other hand, if a plan is designed to suit the highly individualized needs of the highly compensated employees, it may be discriminatory even if it applies to all employees.

For example, if an employer provides unusual coverage for a rare condition to which only the owner of the employer is subject, such coverage may fail the third eligibility requirement, even if theoretically provided to all employees of the employer.

Benefits test.—*In general.*—Under the conference agreement, a plan does not satisfy the benefits test unless the average employer-provided benefit received by nonhighly compensated employees under all plans of the employer of the same type is at least 75 percent of the average employer-provided benefit received by highly compensated employees under all plans of the employer of the same type (i.e., plans providing benefits excludable under the same Code section).

For purposes of this test, the term, "average employer-provided benefit" means with respect to highly compensated employees an amount equal to the aggregate employer-provided benefits received by highly compensated employees under all plans of the type being tested divided by the number of highly compensated employees (whether or not covered by any such plans). The term is defined in the same manner with respect to nonhighly compensated employees.

Aggregation of plans.—In applying the benefits test to a plan other than an accident or health plan, the conference agreement provides that the employer may aggregate different types of statutory employee benefit plans. Thus, for example, an employer may aggregate benefits provided under all group-term life insurance plans and all group legal services plans (if the employer elects to treat such plans as statutory employee benefit plans) in order to satisfy the benefits tests with respect to all such plans. In addition, an employer may aggregate all accident and health plans with plans providing benefits excludable under one or more other Code sections for purposes of satisfying the benefits test with respect to plans other than accident and health plans.

In no case, however, may an employer aggregate with other plans some but not all of the plans providing benefits excludable under a Code section. Thus, an employer may not, for example, aggregate some but not all of its group-term life insurance plans with all of its group legal services plans.

When plans excludable under different Code sections are aggregated for purposes of the benefits test, the definition of excludable employees (for purposes of determining the average employer-provided benefit) shall be made as if the plans were excludable under the same Code section. This means that the lowest age and service requirements from any plans shall apply (see "Excludable employees" below), and if members of a collective bargaining unit are not excluded for one aggregated plan, they are not excluded for the group of plans. Thus, in determining the average employer-provided benefit, the denominator shall be all nonexcludable employees, determined under the employer's most expansive definitions of such term.

Alternative to eligibility and benefits tests.—The conferees also provide an alternative single test which may be applied in lieu of the eligibility and benefits tests. If a plan benefits at least 80 percent of an employer's nonhighly compensated employees, such plan is considered to satisfy both the eligibility and benefits tests. For this purpose, comparable plans may be aggregated. This alternative test will not apply if the plan (or plans) contain any provision that by its terms or otherwise discriminates in favor of highly compensated employees.

This test applies only to insurance-type plans which, under the conference agreement, are defined as accident or health plans and group-term life insurance plans. Of course, for purposes of this test, an individual will only be considered to benefit under a plan if such individual receives coverage

under the plan; eligibility to receive coverage is not considered benefiting under the plan.

Special rules for accident or health plans.—The conference agreement adopts the special rules in the Senate amendment relating to accident or health plans with certain modifications. For purposes of applying the benefits test to accident or health plans, an employer may elect to disregard any employee if the employee and the employee's spouse and dependents (if any) are covered by a health plan that provides core benefits and that is maintained by another employer of the employee, spouse, or dependents. Also, in testing employee coverage only under the benefits test (see discussion in this section), an employee may be disregarded if such employee is covered by a health plan that provides core benefits and that is maintained by another employer of the employee, spouse, or dependents. An employee may not, however, be disregarded in applying the benefits test to any other type of plan, even if accident and health plans are aggregated with such other type of plan for purposes of applying the benefits test to such other type of plan.

For purposes of these rules, the term "core benefits" generally has the same meaning as for purposes of determining the excludable employees (*See* "Excludable employees," below) except to the extent provided by rules prescribed by the Secretary. For example, the Secretary is to except from the definition of core benefits for this purpose, any benefits attributable to a salary reduction medical reimbursement plan or a low-level nonelective medical reimbursement plan. In addition, in no event may disability coverage be considered a core benefit.

In addition, if an employer maintains an accident or health plan that provides family coverage to those employees with spouses or dependents, the employer may elect to test separately, for purposes of the benefits test, the alternative 80-percent test, and the 50-percent component of the 90-percent/50-percent test, the coverage for employees and the coverage for spouses or dependents as if the two types of coverage constituted two different types of plans (i.e., as if excludable under different Code sections). However, in applying the benefits test to plans other than accident or health plans an employer may not aggregate with such other plans only employee coverage or only family coverage.

Included in the definition of coverage for spouses or dependents are all plans covering one or more family members of an employee, regardless of whether certain of such plans may be limited to one family member while other plans cover two or more family members.

For purposes of testing the coverage for spouses or dependents separately under the alternative 80-percent test and the 50-percent component of the 90-percent/50-percent test, the conference agreement permits an employer to take into account only employees with spouses or dependents. For purposes of

Act § 1151 ¶ 4007

the benefits test, an employer testing coverage of spouses and dependents separately may take into account only employees with spouses or dependents who are not covered by a health plan that provides core benefits and that is maintained by another employer of the employee, spouse or dependents. If the employee's spouse or any dependent is not covered under another plan, the employee is taken into account, even if certain of the family members are so covered. This rule does not apply to the benefits test if all accident and health plans are aggregated with plans of a different type for purposes of applying the benefits test to such other plans.

If an employee or a family is disregarded for purposes of the benefits test, any coverage actually provided to the employee or family is disregarded in determining the average employer-provided benefit, as is the existence of that employee or family.

An exception to this rule provides that in no case may a highly compensated employee be disregarded if the coverage provided with respect to the highly compensated employee has a value in excess of $133\frac{1}{3}$ percent of the average employer-provided benefit with respect to nonhighly compensated employees. If family coverage is tested separately, the family of a highly compensated employee may not be disregarded if the coverage provided to such family has a value in excess of $133\frac{1}{2}$ percent of the average employer-provided benefit with respect to families of nonhighly compensated employees.

The rules described above allowing certain employees to be disregarded apply only to the tests specifically noted. Thus, for example, the fact that an employee has other core health coverage does not mean such employee may be disregarded for purposes of the eligibility tests or the alternative 80-percent test.

The Secretary shall prescribe rules, consistent with the rules described above, for the treatment of an employee who has a spouse or dependent who is also an employee of the same employer.

An employer who elects the optional rules described above must obtain and maintain, in such manner as the Secretary prescribes, adequate sworn statements to demonstrate whether individuals have spouses, dependents, or other accident or health coverage. Alternatively, the employer may sample a statistically valid sample of employees and secure sworn statements from the sample group. The conferees intend that an employer who elects the application of these optional rules may not treat a nonhighly compensated employee as having other coverage (of the employee or the employee's family), as not having a family, or both unless the employer has a statement to that effect that includes, with respect to other coverage, the name of the insurer and the employer providing the coverage. In the case of a highly compensated employee, the conferees intend that the opposite presumptions are to apply. Thus, a highly compensated employee may not be treated as not having other coverage (of the employee or the employee's family), as

having a family, or both, unless the employer has a sworn statement to that effect.

The statements required for purposes of these special rules are to be collected annually on forms provided by the Internal Revenue Service that indicate whether other coverage was provided (or is expected to be provided) for the entire plan year and whether the employee has a family. The statements need not be notarized.

The conferees also intend that employers be permitted to secure sworn statements from a statistically valid sample of employees and to use the results of the sample to project the facts regarding health plan coverage of the entire workforce. Such a sampling must be performed by an independent third party in accordance with rules prescribed by the Secretary. If this sampling rule is used, the same rules apply, including the presumptions and the annual collection on IRS forms. In addition, the report by the third party to be attached to the employer's return shall include such facts regarding the sampling as are required by the Secretary.

The conference agreement follows the House bill and the Senate amendment with respect to coordination with accident or health benefits provided under any law or other plan, except that these coordination rules only apply if the coordination is otherwise permissible under law.

Plan safe harbor.—The conferees intend that the benefits test may be adapted in rules prescribed by the Secretary to permit particular plans to pass the benefits test without the need for valuing all benefits excludable under the same Code section. Because the definition of a plan generally requires that all features be identical (see the discussion below), any plan would, standing alone, pass the benefits test if, based on the entire year, the percentage of nonhighly compensated employees benefited is not less than 75 percent of the percentage of highly compensated employees benefited. An example illustrates how this special rule reduces the need to value every plan of the employer. Assume an employer has 10 health plans. Nine of those plans would, standing alone, pass the benefits test in the manner described above; the tenth would not. An employer could aggregate with the tenth plan only so many of the other nine plans as would be necessary to enable that group of plans to satisfy the benefits test. Thus, only that group of plans would have to be valued.

Special group-term life insurance rule.—Under the conference agreement, in applying the benefits test and the 50-percent component of the 90-percent/50-percent test to a group-term life insurance plan, the benefit provided under the plan is determined in the same manner as such amount is determined under section 79(c) for an individual who is age 40. Except in the case where group-term life insurance plans are aggregated with plans of a different type, this amount may be adjusted depending on the compensation of the employee. The adjustment shall be made by multiplying the amount by a fraction the numerator of which is a uniform amount for all plans and the denominator of which is the employee's compensation.

An employer may avoid valuing group-term life insurance in the above manner by using the plan safe harbor described above. For example, if an employer provides group-term life insurance of one times compensation to a group that satisfies the plan safe harbor rule, such plan passes the benefits test without regard to the valuation rules described above. If the employer aggregates that plan with another plan of the same or different type, the valuation rules described above are to be used.

For purposes of the above rules, the uniform definition of compensation (including the limitation on the amount that may be taken into account) applicable to qualified retirement plans (see Part B.1., above) and welfare benefit funds (see below) applies.

In contrast to the Senate amendment, the conference agreement provides that coverage in excess of $50,000 may not be disregarded. In other words, coverage in excess of $50,000 is treated as provided through tax-favored dollars.

In determining the value of the discriminatory excess (or the value of any inclusion amount), the special valuation rules described above do not apply. See the rules described above for valuing the discriminatory excess.

Special dependent care assistance test.—A special benefits test applies to dependent care assistance programs that are not statutory employee benefit programs. Under this special rule, the benefit test applicable to statutory employee benefit plans applies, with two modifications.

First, the average employer-provided benefit received by nonhighly compensated employees is required to be at least 55 percent (as opposed to 75 percent) of the average employer-provided benefit received by highly compensated employees.

Second, for purposes of applying the average benefits test to salary reduction amounts, employees with compensation (sec. 414(q)(7)) below $25,000 are disregarded. If an employer-provided dependent care assistance both through salary reduction and otherwise, the treatment of the employees with compensation below $25,000 is to be determined under rules prescribed by the Secretary.

Part-time employee rule.—In applying the benefits test to accident or health plans, the conference agreement provides that an employer may elect to adjust the benefits provided to certain employees. With respect to an employee who normally works less than 22½ hours per week, an employer may deem benefits provided to have a value equal to up to double the actual value of coverage provided. With respect to an employee who normally works less than 30 hours, an employer may deem benefits provided to have a value equal to up to 1⅓ times the actual value.

If this part-time employee rule is used, it is to be used on a uniform, nondiscriminatory basis for all employees. In applying the 50-percent component of the 90-percent/50-percent test to accident or health plans, the above rule applies with respect to the amount of benefits available. However, this special part-time employee rule does not apply for any purpose in a plan year unless during such year more than 50 percent of the nonexcludable employees (determined without regard to plan provisions) normally work more than 30 hours per week. In addition, the multiplication of the benefit under this rule does not apply to elective contributions.

State-mandated benefits.—The conferees authorize the Secretary, in applying the nondiscrimination rules described above to accident or health plans, to disregard State-mandated benefits under certain circumstances. For example, in comparing the benefits of employees in one State to the benefits of employees in another State, the Secretary may disregard benefits that are mandated in one of the States but are not mandated in the other.

It is intended, however, that the benefits that may be disregarded are ancillary benefits, rather than core benefits. For example, if a State mandates an HMO option, the conferees do not intend that the value of coverage under an HMO may be disregarded.

d. Highly compensated employees

House Bill

Under the House bill, a uniform definition of highly compensated employees is provided for purposes of the new nondiscrimination rules applicable to statutory employee benefit plans, and for purposes of the special nondiscrimination test for qualified cash or deferred arrangements. (*See* the description in Part B.7., above.) An employee is treated as highly compensated with respect to a year if, at any time during the year or any of the two preceding years, the employee (1) is a five-percent owner of the employer (as defined in sec. 416(i)); (2) earns over $50,000 in annual compensation from the employer; or (3) is a member of the top-paid group of the employer.

The top-paid group includes all employees who (1) are in the top 10 percent of all employees on the basis of compensation, and (2) earn more than $20,000 a year. However, an employee is not included in the top-paid group if the employee earns less than $35,000 and is not in the top 5 percent of all employees on the basis of compensation.

In addition, under all statutory employee benefit plans, a former employee is to be treated as a highly compensated employee if such employee was highly compensated at the time of separation from service or at any time after attaining age 55.

Senate Amendment

Under the Senate amendment, a uniform definition of highly compensated employees is provided and is similar to the definition in the House bill. This definition applies, however, for purposes of the nondiscrimination rules for all statutory employee benefit plans, cafeteria plans, welfare benefit funds, qualified plans, and qualified cash or deferred arrangements. (*See* the description in Part B.7., above.)

An employee is treated as highly compensated with respect to a year if, at any time during the year or the preceding year, the employee (1) was a 5-percent owner of the employer (as defined in sec. 416(i)); (2) received more than $100,000 in annual compensation from the employer; (3) received more than $50,000 in annual compensation from the employer and was a member of the top-paid group of the employer during the same year; or (4) was an officer of the employer (as defined in sec. 416(i)). The $50,000 and $100,000 thresholds are indexed by reference to the method, as of May 1, 1986, for adjusting for percentage increases in the social security wage base (i.e., at the same time and in the same manner as the adjustments to the dollar limits on benefits under defined benefit pension plans under the Senate amendment).

In addition, a former employee is to be treated as a highly compensated employee if such employee was highly compensated at the time of separation from service or at such other times as the Secretary may prescribe.

Conference Agreement

The conference agreement follows the Senate amendment with certain modifications. (*See* the detailed description in Part B.7., above.) First, the $100,000 threshold in the Senate amendment is reduced to $75,000. Second, every employer shall have at least one officer; if necessary, this means that the compensation floor required for officer status shall not apply to one individual. Third, the House rule regarding former employees is adopted in lieu of the Senate rule. Further, the method of indexing the $50,000 and $75,000 figures is the same method used to index the dollar limit for defined benefit pension plans under the conference agreement.

The definition of highly compensated employee is the same as the definition used with respect to qualified plans. One clarification applies to employee benefits, however, that does not apply to qualified plans. With respect to those benefits for which family coverage is treated as a benefit separate from employee coverage, such as accident or health benefits, the special rule aggregating family members is modified. In such instances, where a family member would be aggregated with a 5-percent owner of one of the top 10 highly compensated employees, such family member shall be treated as a nonemployee family member.

e. Excludable employees

House Bill

The House bill generally provides that certain classes of employees may be disregarded in applying the 90-percent eligibility test if neither the plan nor any other plan providing similar benefits benefits any employee in such class. The classes of excludable employees generally are (1) employees who have not completed at least 180 days of service; (2) employees who normally work less than 20 hours per week; (3) employees who normally work less than 1,000 hours during any year; and (4) employees under age 21. In addition, employees covered by a bona fide collective bargaining agreement may be disregarded if the plan does not benefit any such employee. Further, nonresident aliens who receive no United States earned income may be disregarded, regardless of whether any such individuals are covered by the plan.

Treasury regulations are to provide a limited exception to the rule that employees who otherwise are excludable as employees who do not normally work 1,000 hours a year or 180 days may not be disregarded if any plan of the employer does not exclude such employees. The limited exception will be available if (1) substantially all employees of the employer (other than supplemental employees) generally are eligible to participate in an accident or health plan (or other employee benefit plan) within 30 days after the date of hire; (2) the employer also employs supplemental employees who generally do not work more than 1,000 hours or more than 180 days; (3) the supplemental employees generally are not rehired if they have previously been supplemental employees; and (4) the supplemental employees do not exceed 15 percent of the employer's workforce.

Under this limited exception, supplemental employees who are (1) retired employees of the employer who are covered under an accident and health plan of the employer maintained for retirees or (2) students hired by the employer under a work-study program, may be disregarded in determining whether the employer's employee benefit plans satisfy the nondiscrimination requirements. Of course, this limited exception would not be available if any supplemental employees are eligible to participate in any employee benefit plan of the employer (other than a plan maintained for retired employees).

Senate Amendment

In general.—The Senate amendment follows the House bill by providing that certain classes of employees may be disregarded in applying the eligibility and benefits tests if neither the plan, nor any other plan of the same type, benefits any employee in such class. The classes of excludable employees under the Senate amendment are (1) in the case of an accident or health plan (other than a plan providing only noncore benefits) employees who have not completed at least 180 days of service (or such shorter period of service as may be specified in the plan); (2) in the case of any other statutory employee benefit plan (including an accident or health plan providing only noncore benefits), employees who have not completed one year of service (or such shorter period of service as may be specified in the plan); (3) employees who normally work less than half time (or such lesser amount as may be specified in the plan); (4) employees who normally work fewer than six months during any year (or such lesser amount as may be specified in the plan); and (5) employees who have not attained age 21 (or such lower age as may be specified in the plan). In addition, employees included in a unit of employees covered by a collective bargaining agreement may be disregarded if the plan does not benefit any employee in that unit. Finally, nonresident aliens who receive no United States earned income may be disregarded, regardless of whether any such individuals are covered by a plan.

Conditions for exclusions.—In applying the nondiscrimination rules, an employer may exclude from consideration a category of excludable employees only if no excludable employee in that category benefits under the plan being tested or any other employee benefit plan of the employer that provides the same type of statutory employee benefit. Statutory employee benefits are treated as being of the same type if they are eligible to be excluded from income under the same section of the Code. Thus, if an employer maintains two group-term life insurance plans, only one of which excludes employees with less than a year of service, the employer is not permitted to exclude from consideration employees with less than a year of service in testing either plan for compliance with the nondiscrimination rules.

In the case of a cafeteria plan (including a plan that would be a cafeteria plan if employees could elect cash or a taxable benefit), for purposes of applying the nondiscrimination rules, an employer may exclude a category of excludable employees from consideration only if those employees are excluded from benefiting under any option offered by the cafeteria plan.

The Senate amendment contains certain exceptions, generally described below, to the rule that if even one excludable employee is covered by a plan, all employees who are excludable on the same basis (and on no other basis) as the covered employee must be taken into account in applying the nondiscrimination rules to the plan (and any other statutory employee benefit plan offering the same type of benefits).

Core and noncore benefits.—If a plan offering only noncore accident or health benefits excludes employees with less than a year of service, the employer sponsoring the plan is not required to take into consideration employees with less than a year of service merely because another plan maintained by the employer offering core accident or health benefits has a shorter service requirement. Noncore accident or health benefits consist of coverage for dental, vision, psychological and orthodontia expenses and elective cosmetic surgery.

Line of business.—If an employer elects to apply the nondiscrimination rules on a separate line of business or separate operating unit basis, the employees who may be excluded from consideration are determined on a separate line of business or separate operating unit basis. Thus, for example, if (1) an employer maintains a statutory employee benefit plan for a line of business, (2) the nondiscrimination rules are applied to the plan on a line of business basis, and (3) all plans providing benefits of the same type to employees in that line of business exclude all employees who have not attained the age of 21, then the employer may exclude from consideration in applying the nondiscrimination rules to the plan, all employees in that line of business who have not attained age 21, even if the employer maintains a plan that does not impose an age requirement for employees in another line of business.

Collective bargaining agreement.—If no employee in a unit of employees covered by a collective bargaining agreement is covered by a plan, employees in that unit may be disregarded in testing a plan for discrimination, even if the employer maintains a second plan that provides similar benefits and that covers employees in such collective bargaining unit. However, for purposes of applying the average benefits test and the average income exclusion test, if any employees in a unit of employees covered by a collective bargaining agreement are covered by any plan of the type being tested, then all employees in that unit are required to be taken into account.

Nonresident aliens.—Nonresident aliens with no United States source income may be disregarded regardless of whether any such individuals are covered by the plan being tested for nondiscrimination or by any other plan maintained by the employer providing the same type of benefits.

Separate testing.—The Senate amendment also provides that if, for purposes of applying the nondiscrimination rules to a plan ("first plan"), certain employees ("the excludable employees") could be excluded from consideration but for the fact that certain of such employees are covered by another plan ("second plan") that provides the same type of employee benefits, the excludable employees may be disregarded for purposes of testing the first plan if the second plan satisfies the nondiscrimination rules with respect to the excludable employees (treating the excludable employees as the only employees of the employer).

Supplemental employees.—The Senate amendment follows the House bill regarding supplemental employees.

Conference Agreement

The conference agreement follows the Senate amendment with certain modifications. First, in lieu of permitting the exclusion of employees who normally work less than half-time, only employees who normally work less than 17½ hours per week may be excluded. Also, the seasonal employee exclusion is modified to exclude employees who normally work during no more than six months during a year.

[Second], the "separate testing" rule is modified to allow employees excludable on the basis of the age and service requirements to be tested separately even if some or all of the excludable employees are covered by a plan that also covers nonexcludable employees. Under the conference agreement, an employer may test all such excludable employees separately. Alternatively, an employer may elect to test one group of excludable employees separately without testing all excludable employees separately if such group is defined in a nondiscriminatory manner solely by reference to the age or service requirements. For example, an employer may elect to test separately all employees excludable solely on the grounds that they do not have six months of service, but not include in such testing group employees excluded under the other age and service rules. Also, an employer may test separately a group of employees who would pass less restrictive age or service requirements. For example, an employer could test separately all employees excludable solely on the grounds that they are not age 21, but who are at least age 18.

Third, an employer may exclude an employee, on the grounds that such employee has not satisfied the required period of initial service, during the period prior to the first day of the calendar month following the actual satisfaction of the initial service requirement. For example, assume an employer required 30 days of service for participation in a health plan, but did not allow participation to begin other than on the first day of a calendar month. Assume further that the employer hires two employees, A on July 2 and B on July 3. Under the terms of the employer's plan, A would be a participant on August 1 and B would be a participant on September 1. Thus, A is a participant after 30 days of service while B has to wait 60 days. Because of the special rule allowing B to be disregarded prior to the first day of the next month following satisfaction of the period of service requirement, B need not be taken into account for nondiscrimination purposes until September 1, even though B would have 30 days of service after the end of the day on August 1.

Fourth, the rule permitting exclusion of employees who have not had 180 days of service is modified by substituting 6 months of service for 180 days of service. It is also clarified that this service requirement is satisfied if an employee is continuously employed for a 6-month period without regard to the number of hours or days worked. A period during which an employee does not perform services for the employer counts toward this service requirement unless there has been a bona fide, indefinite cessation of the employment relationship. These same rules apply to the one year of service requirement.

Further, the conference agreement modifies the Senate amendment rule permitting exclusion of an employee only if no employee in the same category (e.g., under age 21) benefits under a plan of the same type.

Under the conference agreement, the exclusion applies only if no employee in the same category is eligible under a plan of the same type.

Also, it is clarified that if an employer aggregates plans of different types of purposes of satisfying the benefits test, the excludable employee rules apply as if such plans were the same type. Thus, the lowest age and service requirements in any plans shall apply. The lowest age requirement may come from one plan, the shortest waiting period may come from another plan, the lowest hour requirement for part-time status may come from a third plan, etc.

The conference agreement also clarifies that, for purposes of the initial service rules, core accident or health benefits may be considered provided under a separate plan from noncore benefits.

The conference agreement modifies the supplemental employee rule by applying the rule to employees who normally work during no more than six months and to employees who do not have six months of service.

f. Separate lines of business or operating units

House Bill

The House bill provides an exception to the general eligibility rule if the employer, for bona fide business reasons, operates a separate line of business or separate operating unit. In that event, the requirements of the general eligibility rule may be satisfied separately with respect to employees in each separate line of business or operating unit.

An employer may not separately apply the nondiscrimination rule to any line of business or operating unit unless (1) there are at least 100 nonexcluded employees employed by the line of business or operating unit; and (2) at least 5 percent, but no more than 25 percent, of the employees in the line of business or operating unit are highly compensated. In addition, the House bill provides that if employees of more than one line of business or operating unit are eligible to participate in the same plan, such lines of business or operating units are treated as a single line of business or operating unit for purposes of the nondiscriminatory eligibility requirement.

Senate Amendment

In general.—Under the Senate amendment, if an employer establishes to the satisfaction of the Secretary that the employer operates separate lines of business or operating units for bona fide business reasons, the reasonable classification test, the average benefits test, and the average income exclusion test may be applied separately with respect to employees in each line of business or operating unit. A plan will not be treated as satisfying the nondiscriminatory coverage rules on a line of business or operating unit basis unless the plan also satisfies the present-law classification test on an employer-wide basis.

Safe harbor.—The Senate amendment provides a safe-harbor rule under which a separate line of business or operating unit is treated as being operated for bona fide business reasons if such line of business or operating unit is a separate self-sustaining unit and if (1) each line of business or operating unit has at least 50 employees who do not perform services for any other line of business or operating unit; and (2) the "highly compensated employee percentage" of the line of business or operating unit is (a) not less than one-half, and (b) not more than twice, the percentage of all employees of the employer who are highly compensated. For purposes of this requirement, the highly compensated employee percentage of a line of business or operating unit will be treated as not less than one-half of the percentage of all employees of the employer who are highly compensated employees if at least 10 percent of all highly compensated employees of the employer are employed by the line of business or operating unit. The term "highly compensated employee percentage" means the percentage of all employees performing services for a line of business or operating unit who are highly compensated employees.

Definition of line of business.—The Senate amendment provides that the Secretary shall prescribe by regulation what constitutes a line of business or operating unit. The line of business or operating unit concept shall not be used to undermine the nondiscrimination rules. Thus, for example, certain job classifications (such as hourly employees or leased employees) are not considered to be separate lines of business or operating units. Also, for example, secretaries and other support service personnel shall not be treated as in a line of business or operating unit separate from the lawyers or other professionals for whom such personnel perform services, and nurses and laboratory personnel shall not be treated as in a line of business or operating unit separate from the medical doctors for whom they perform services. In addition, the members of an affiliated service group (sec. 414(m)) may not be treated as separate lines of business or operating units.

In general, a headquarters or home office is not to be treated as a separate line of business or operating unit. It is generally intended that a line of business or operating unit include all employees necessary for preparation of certain classes of property for sale to customers or for the provision of services to customers. Certain exceptions to this rule may be established by regulation where one employer has two operations that are vertically integrated and that are traditionally operated by unrelated entities.

Combining lines of business.—If a line of business or operating unit would be recognized, but for the fact that it does not satisfy the 50 employee or the highly compensated employee percentage tests, it may be combined with another line of business or operating unit to satisfy such tests. With respect to any plan maintained for employees of one of the combined lines of business, the plan is required to satisfy the coverage rules with respect to the aggregate entity.

Excludable employees.—For purposes of determining (1) the number of employees in a line of business or operating unit; (2) the highly compensated employee percentage of a line of business or operating unit; and (3) the percentage of all employees of the employer who are highly compensated, an employer shall disregard the categories of employees that are disregarded for purposes of determining which employees are highly compensated employees. *(see* the description in B.7., above.)

Common plan for more than one line of business.—If employees of more than one line of business or operating unit are eligible to participate in a plan, then all such lines of business or operating units are to be treated as one line of business or operating unit.

Conference Agreement

The conference agreement follows the Senate amendment with the following modifications. For convenience, the conference agreement uses the term "line of business" to refer both to a line of business and to an operating unit.

First, it is clarified that if the employer establishes to the satisfaction of the Secretary that the employer operates separate lines of business or operating units for bona fide business reasons, both the eligibility tests and the benefits tests (as well as the alternative 80-percent test) may be applied separately with respect to employees in each line of business or operating unit, subject to the requirement that the classification test be satisfied with respect to any plan on an employer-wide basis.

The conference agreement also clarifies the definition of a line of business or operating unit. Whether claimed separate lines of business or operating units are bona fide is a facts and circumstances determination requiring examination of each particular situation. Differences and similarities between the services provided and products produced by such claimed lines of business are of course important considerations. In addition, the manner in which the employer organizes itself is relevant. Thus, if an employer fails to treat itself as comprised of separate lines of business or operating units and treats employees from different claimed lines or units in an equivalent fashion for certain purposes, it may not be appropriate to allow such activities to be treated as separate lines of business or operating units. These factors do not, however, override the rules relating to the definition of a line of business, discussed above with respect to the Senate amendment, to the extent that such rules would deny separate line of business or operating unit status.

In addition, the conference agreement modifies the definition of an operating unit by requiring that it be operated in a significantly separate geographic area from another operating unit in the same line of business.

For example, two plants in the same city would not be considered to be in significantly separate geographic areas and thus would not be considered separate operating units.

Also, the requirement that a separate line of business or operating unit have at least 50 employees is deleted from the safe harbor rule and made a substantive requirement. Thus, a line of business or operating unit shall not be treated as separate for purposes of the nondiscrimination rules unless it has at least 50 employees. As under the Senate amendment, more than one line of business or operating unit may be aggregated to satisfy this requirement.

Also, the requirement that a line of business or operating unit be a separate self-sustaining unit is deleted from the safe harbor rule, since such a requirement is part of the definition of a line of business or operating unit.

The conferees clarify the proper treatment of employees of a headquarters or home office and of other employees serving more than one line of business or operating unit (e.g., payroll personnel). Like all other employees, these employees are to be allocated to one line of business or operating unit. Generally, this allocation shall, under rules prescribed by the Secretary, be made in accordance with their performance of services. Thus, if a majority of an employee's services are performed for a particular line of business or operating unit, such employee must be allocated to that line of business or operating unit.

Other employees rendering services to more than one line of business or operating unit must be allocated in one of two ways. First, the employer may allocate such employees on a pro-rata basis among its lines of business or operating units, under rules prescribed by the Secretary. Alternatively, such employees may be allocated to any one line of business or operating unit for which they perform substantial services provided that such allocation does not cause any line of business or operating unit to violate or further violate the highly compensated percentage rule. Thus, for this purpose, the highly compensated employee percentage rule serves as a substantive rule, not a safe harbor. This means, for example, that if any lines of business or operating units do not pass the 50-percent rule, highly compensated employees at the home office or headquarters who do not perform a majority of their services for any particular line of business or operating unit must be allocated first to such lines of business or operating units. This also means that in no event may such highly compensated employees be allocated to any line of business or operating unit if after such allocation the 200-percent rule would be violated (regardless of whether it was violated prior to such allocation).

It is also intended that the Secretary is to prescribe for annual reporting by employers using the line of business or operating unit rule for purposes of the nondiscrimination rules (including the qualified plan rules). Such reporting shall include the basis for the position that an employer is maintaining separate lines of business or operating units. Where an employer maintains a line of business or operating unit that does not fall within the safe harbor rule, this must be specifically reported and may trigger additional reporting requirements.

In addition, the Secretary is also to establish guidelines identifying circumstances in which there is to be special scrutiny of claimed lines of business or operating units. For example, if a plan maintained for a claimed line of business or operating unit is significantly better or worse than plans for other lines of business or operating units, such a situation shall trigger special scrutiny. Also, if a disproportionate percentage of the accrued benefits under the plan of a claimed line of business or operating unit is for the highly compensated employees, such employer's claim of a separate line of business or operating unit shall also be specially examined.

If a claimed line of business or operating unit does not satisfy the safe-harbor rule and a plan or plans of such line of business or operating unit warrants special scrutiny under the standards set forth in the applicable guidelines, then the claimed line of business or operating unit will not be recognized for purposes of the applicable nondiscrimination rules unless the employer obtains a determination from the Secretary (e.g., by determination letter or private letter ruling) that such line of business or operating unit is separately operated for bona fide business reasons.

Further, the conferees intend to clarify that if an employer is using the separate line of business or operating unit rule with respect to any plan, all employees must be considered part of a line of business or operating unit. Thus, it would not be permissible to maintain that an employer has, in addition to one line of business with 50 employees, 10 other employees who are not part of any line of business or operating unit and who would be tested separately. The 10 other employees would have to be treated as part of one or more lines of business or operating units. Such lines of business or operating units would have to be aggregated with the 50-employee line of business in order to satisfy the requirement that to be tested separately, a line of business or operating unit must have at least 50 employees.

The conference agreement also deletes the rule providing that if employees from more than one line of business or operating unit are eligible to participate in a plan, all such lines of business and/or operating units are treated as one line of business or operating unit. This would, however, be a fact to consider in ascertaining whether an employer treats itself as comprised of separate lines of business or operating units. Instead, the conference agreement requires that benefits attributable to services for a line of business or operating unit shall be considered as provided by that line of business or operating unit. For purposes of such rules, an employee who performs services for more than one line of business or operating unit, but is allocated to one line of business or operating unit under the rules described above, shall be considered to render services solely for that line of business or operating unit.

g. Definitions and special rules

(1) Time for testing

House Bill

The House bill did not contain a provision regarding the time at which the eligibility or benefits test had to be applied. However, one component of the benefits test—the comparability test—would have to be determined based on the value of the benefits provided during the entire year.

Senate Amendment

The Senate amendment did not provide for the time at which the percentage test, the reasonable classification test, or the classification test had to be applied. However, the alternative reasonable classification test and the benefits test would be applied on the basis of the benefits provided during the entire year.

Conference Agreement

Under the conference agreement, it is clarified that the tests applied to the amount of benefits available or provided must be applied on the basis of the benefits provided during the entire year. Thus, the benefits test, the 50-percent component of the 90-percent/ 50-percent test, and the comparability tests all apply based on the entire year.

An example will illustrate how this rule applies for purposes of the benefits test. Assume employee A becomes nonexcludable on July 1 and on that day A is covered under a health plan that provides coverage that on an annual basis has a value of $1,000. The employer's plan year is the calendar year, so for that plan year, A only receives $500 worth of benefits. That $500 goes in the numerator in determining the average employer-provided benefit. However, because A was only taken into account for half the year, A is only counted as half an employee in the denominator.

The conferees further intend to provide, for accident or health plans and group-term life insurance plans, a rule of convenience to ease the administrative burden on employers. Under this rule of convenience, an employer may, for purposes of applying the benefits test to active employees, treat employees who separate from service during the last 3 months of the plan year as continuing to work and receive benefits for the remainder of the plan year. For employees who separate from service earlier in the plan year, an employer may treat such employees as continuing to work and receive benefits through the end of the month in which they separate. The effect of these rules is that employers will not have to use the exact day that employees separate in calculating the average employer-provided benefit. Instead, an employer may deem employees to have separated only on the end of a month and in

the case of employees separating in the last quarter, on the last day of the plan year.

For purposes of this rule of convenience, employees shall be considered to receive after separation whatever benefit they had been receiving prior to separation, provided such benefit had been provided for at least 90 days prior to separation. If there had been a change in the benefit during such 90 day period, then the benefit deemed provided during the period of separation shall be the average benefit provided to the employee during the period beginning on the date in the plan year on which the employee first had to be taken into account for purposes of the nondiscrimination rules and ending on the date of separation from service.

The rule illustrated by the example treating A as only half an employee for purposes of the benefits test and the rule of convenience described do not apply to group-term life insurance plans with respect to which the employer adjusts the value of the benefit provided based on the employee's compensation. See the discussion above, for a description of the adjustment.

The rule of convenience described above shall also apply to the alternative 80-percent test, the 90-percent component of the 90-percent/ 50-percent test, the 50-percent test, and the plan safe harbor for the benefits test, except that for purposes of the eligibility tests, employees who have separated from service would be deemed to have available to them after separation the benefits available prior to separation. For purposes of determining the benefits available prior to separation, the same rules applicable for the actual benefits rule apply. Other than this one difference, the rule of convenience applies in the same manner. Thus, in determining whether the tests are satisfied, an employer must look at the entire year, but may use the rule of convenience to substantially reduce the administrative burden. For example, assume that an employee (A) who was not excludable on the first day of the plan year separated from service during the sixth month of the plan year. A may be considered to be employed through the end of the sixth month and have available benefits determined under the rule of convenience described above. During the second 6 months, A is not an active employee for purposes of applying the tests.

Of course, the rule of convenience under which employees are deemed to receive or have available to them benefits after separation from service does not apply in testing benefits actually received by or available to former employees. (See 8., below.)

As is true with respect to the nondiscrimination rules applicable to qualified retirement plans, the fact that a failure to meet any of the nondiscrimination rules was attributable to unforeseen circumstances does not affect the application of the rules.

The conferees also intend to provide an additional rule of convenience for employers

Act § 1151   ¶ 4007

that do not require any initial period of service for participation in a statutory fringe benefit plan. Under this second rule of convenience, an employer may, for purposes of the 90-percent/50-percent test and the benefits test, disregard benefits provided to an employee during the period between the employee's commencement of employment and the first day of the calendar month following such commencement. (This rule does not apply to an employee who commences employment on the first day of a calendar month.) However, benefits provided during such period that relate to any other period may not be disregarded. For example, if an employer pays for a year's worth of dependent care or provides an annual physical examination, only a proportionate part of the value of such benefit may be disregarded. This second rule of convenience applies to all statutory employee benefit plans. If an employer uses this rule of convenience, it must do so with respect to all employees.

(2) Employer and employees

House Bill

Aggregation.—Under certain circumstances, the House bill provides that related employers are treated as a single employer for purposes of the nondiscrimination requirements (sec. 414(b), (c), and (m)). In addition, leased employees are treated for purposes of the nondiscrimination rules as employees of the person or organization for whom they perform services (sec. 414(n)). The bill provides that the Secretary's general regulatory authority to prevent abuse of employee benefit requirements shall apply (sec. 414(o)).

Self-employed individuals.—For purposes of the nondiscrimination rules governing qualified group legal services plans, educational assistance programs and dependent care assistance programs, self-employed individuals are treated as employees. An individual who owns the entire interest in an unincorporated trade or business is treated as his own employer and a partnership is treated as the employer of each partner.

Senate Amendment

The Senate amendment follows the House bill.

Conference Agreement

The conference agreement follows the House bill and the Senate amendment and clarifies that the aggregation of employers applies to all aspects of the employee benefit rules, not only the nondiscrimination rules.

(3) Special rules for certain dispositions and acquisitions

House Bill

No provision.

Senate Amendment

The Senate amendment contains special transition rules for certain dispositions or acquisitions of a business. Under the Senate amendment, if a person becomes or ceases to be a member of a controlled group or affiliated service group, the coverage rules will, with respect to a plan maintained by the person or group, be deemed satisfied during the transition period, provided that (1) the coverage rules were satisfied immediately before the acquisition or disposition, and (2) the coverage under the plan does not change significantly during the transition period (other than by reason of the acquisition or disposition). The transition period begins on the date of the acquisition or disposition and ends on the last day of the first plan year beginning after the transaction.

Conference Agreement

The conference agreement follows the Senate amendment.

(4) Definition of a plan

House Bill

Separate plans.—Under the House bill, for purposes of both the eligibility test and the benefits tests, each option or different benefit offered under a statutory employee benefit plan is treated as a separate plan. This means, for example, that if two types of insurance coverage vary in any way (including the amount of the employee contribution), they will be considered separate plans. Thus, in the case of health plans under which there are different levels or types of health benefit coverage, each separate level or type of health coverage must be tested as a separate plan under both the eligibility test and the applicable benefits test.

Under a special rule for an accident or health plan, an employee who has available or receives coverage both for himself and any member of his family is to be treated as having available or received two separate coverages: individual coverage with respect to himself, and family coverage with respect to his family. Each coverage must be tested separately.

In the case of noninsurance-type plans, the House bill requires that if a highly compensated employee benefits under two or more educational assistance programs, all such plans under which such employee benefits shall be treated as one plan for purposes of applying the eligibility and benefits tests. The same rule applies to dependent care assistance programs. For purposes of satisfying the eligibility and benefits tests, an employer may elect to treat as one plan any two or more educational assistance programs. The same rule applies to dependent care assistance programs.

Single plan.—The House bill provides that two or more plans which are identical in all respects, except for the group of employees covered, may be treated as a single plan. For purposes of determining what constitutes a single plan, two exceptions are provided to the rule that insurance coverage (or available noninsurance benefits) be identical. The first exception is that variations may be disregarded if the coverage varies in a purely mechanical manner that clearly favors those with less compensation, as in the case where the same health insurance is available on the same terms to employees, but the required employee contribution increases in proportion to compensation. The second exception is based on the House bill provision that allows the employer to reduce the employer subsidy for employees who normally work less than 30 hours per week. Under this provision, if the same health insurance is available on the same terms to employees, except that the employer subsidy is proportionately reduced for employees who normally work less than 30 hours per week, such health insurance is considered a single plan.

Senate Amendment

Separate plans.—The Senate amendment follows the House bill, except that the amendment also provides that in the case of group-term life insurance, the provision of insurance coverage that varies in proportion to compensation is not to be considered as the provision of different options or benefits with respect to such varying coverage. In addition, the Senate amendment deletes the special aggregation rules for noninsurance type plans.

Single plan.—The Senate amendment follows the House bill except that it deletes the two exceptions to the rule that coverage within a plan must be identical.

The Senate amendment also provides that, for purposes of determining what constitutes a single plan, employees should be allowed to structure options in different ways as long as all coverage within a plan is identical. For example, if the deductible for all highly compensated employees is $200 and the deductible for all nonhighly compensated employees is $50, it would be inconsistent with the purposes of these rules to classify the $200 deductible coverage as a separate plan that covers only highly compensated employees and thus is discriminatory. Instead, the employer could classify the coverage as one plan for all employees providing coverage for expenses in excess of a $200 deductible and a second plan covering costs between $50 and $200 covering only nonhighly compensated employees. Both such plans would be nondiscriminatory.

Conference Agreement

The conference agreement follows the Senate amendment, with one modification. That modification is that, as under the House bill, if accident or health coverage available or provided to employees is identical except that the employer subsidy is proportionately reduced for employees who normally work less than 30 hours per week, such health insurance may be considered a single plan.

The permissible proportionate reduction corresponds to the special rule for the benefits test and the 50-percent component of the 90-percent/50-percent test. Thus, if an employee normally works at least 22½ hours per week but less than 30 hours per week, the above rule applies if the employer subsidy is reduced by no more than 25 percent, and if the employee normally works less than 22½ hours per week, the above rule applies if the employer subsidy is reduced by no more than 50 percent. If the above rule is used, it must be used on a uniform, nondiscriminatory basis with respect to all employees. Of course,

this rule does not affect the benefit actually made available or provided for purposes of any other tests.

As with the other part-time rule, this rule does not apply in any plan year unless during such year more than 50 percent of the nonexcludable employees (determined without regard to plan provisions) normally work more than 30 hours per week. Also, this special rule allowing a proportionate reduction in benefits within a plan does not apply to elective contributions.

In addition, the conference agreement clarifies that limitations on family coverage give rise to separate plans. For example, if an employer offers "employee plus one family member" health coverage and "employee plus two or more family members" health coverage, that constitutes 3 plans: (1) employee coverage, (2) coverage of one family member, and (3) coverage of additional family members.

(5) Aggregation of health plans and comparability

House Bill

For purposes of satisfying the benefits test, the House bill provides that two or more comparable accident or health plans of the same type may be aggregated if comparable. A plan is comparable to a second plan that would otherwise fail the benefits test if the average employer cost (including elective contributions) per covered employee in the first plan is at least 80 percent of the average employer cost (including elective contributions) per covered employee in the second plan.

Senate Amendment

Under the Senate amendment, if an accident or health plan standing alone would fail the reasonable classification test or the percentage test, the plan may be aggregated with one or more other accident or health plans ("helper plans"), provided that the average value of the employer-provided coverage per employee in each "helper plan" is at least 90 percent of the average value of employer-provided coverage per covered employee in the plan that would otherwise fail.

In the case of an accident or health plan that would otherwise fail the classification test, the Senate amendment provides that the plan may be aggregated with one or more other accident or health plans ("helper plans"), provided that the average value of the employer-provided coverage per employee in each "helper plan" is at least 100 percent of the value of employer-provided coverage per covered employee in the plan that would otherwise fail the classification test.

Conference Agreement

The conference agreement follows the Senate amendment with certain modifications. First, it is clarified that the 95-percent comparability standard (instead of the 100-percent standard that applies to the classification test) applies only for purposes of the 50-

Act § 1151 ¶ 4007

percent test and the alternative 80-percent test. Second, for purposes of the 50-percent test, a "helper plan" is any plan in the group of aggregated plans that satisfies such test without regard to aggregation. The average value of the employer-provided coverage per employee in the helper plan with the lowest such value must be at least 95 percent of the average value of the employer-provided coverage per employee in the nonhelper plan in the group of aggregated plans with the highest such value. For purposes of the 80-percent test, the general rule is that the average value of the employer-provided coverage per employee in the plan in the group of aggregated plans with the lowest such value must be at least 95 percent of the average value of the employer-provided coverage per employee in the plan in the group of aggregated plans with the highest such value. However, if a plan with a greater value than permitted under the previous sentence consists solely of nonhighly compensated employees, such plan may be aggregated with the group of less valuable plans for purposes of the 80-percent test.

In addition, the special part-time employee rule applicable in defining what constitutes a plan also applies for comparability purposes. Thus, if two plans that would be comparable but for the fact that the employer-provided benefit is proportionately reduced for employees who normally work less than 30 hours per week, the plans may still be comparable under rules similar to those applicable under the definition of a plan.

(6) Valuation

House Bill

Under the House bill, the Secretary will prescribe regulations that provide guidance in determining the value of insurance coverage and of noninsurance benefits. The Secretary may establish safe-harbor methods of valuing the coverage or benefits.

The Secretary may, in prescribing such regulations, provide adjustments to the safe harbors to take account of factors, such as geographical cost differences, relevant to the determination of the value of a benefit.

Senate Amendment

The Senate amendment follows the House bill with two modifications. First, the Secretary is authorized to establish administrable, mechanical methods of valuing coverage or benefits that are not only safe harbors. Second, the Secretary is directed to specify an index that takes into account differences in costs for plans maintained in geographically dispersed areas.

Conference Agreement

Under the conference agreement, the Secretary is to prescribe rules regarding valuation. With respect to health coverage, the Secretary is to set forth values for various standard types of coverage. The values shall be set forth in the form of tables which establish the relative values of plans with certain characteristics. Such tables may use as a reference point an identifiable standard plan.

Such tables shall be adjusted to take into account the specific coverage and group involved. For example, in determining the value of discriminatory coverage, the actual costs expended by the employer may be taken into account and allocated among all coverages, including the discriminatory coverage, on the basis of the relative values of such coverages, as determined under the tables. Another example is that in certain instances it may be appropriate to adjust the table value of coverage based on whether such coverage would have been provided at group rates by an insurance company. Thus, an individually designed plan shall be valued higher than a group plan with the same characteristics. Further, it is appropriate to reduce the table valuation to the extent the employer provides the same coverage under more than one plan.

With respect to group-term life insurance, special valuation rules apply for purposes of the nondiscrimination rules. However, if certain coverage is found to be discriminatory, such coverage shall be valued, as under present law, at the higher of actual cost or table cost (sec. 79).

(7) Concentration tests

House Bill

No provision.

Senate Amendment

Accident or health plans and group-term life insurance plans.—The Senate amendment establishes a new concentration test for any accident or health plan or group-term life insurance plan. No more than 40 percent of the employees benefiting under such a plan may be highly compensated employees. A plan is not treated as failing to meet this requirement if it benefits all employees of the employer.

The Senate amendment also establishes a second new concentration test for group-term life insurance plans. No more than 25 percent of the value of the coverage provided under the plan may be provided to individuals who are at any time during the current or preceding year, 5 percent owners (within the meaning of section 416(i)(1)(B)(i)). A plan is not treated as failing to meet this requirement if the plan provides the same dollar amount of group-term life insurance coverage for each employee eligible to participate in the plan.

The new concentration tests apply to health plans and group-term life insurance plans in addition to the nondiscriminatory coverage rules applicable to those plans. A plan that fails an applicable concentration test is considered to be a discriminatory plan.

Other plans.—The present-law concentration tests applicable to qualified group legal services plans, educational assistance programs, and dependent care assistance programs continue to apply to those types of plans in addition to the nondiscriminatory coverage requirements. Thus, regardless of whether a plan satisfies the relevant present law nondiscrimination rules, or the new average income exclusion test, the plan is also required to satisfy the applicable present-law concentration tests. A plan that fails an applicable concentration test is considered to be a discriminatory plan.

Conference Agreement

The conference agreement follows the House bill. Thus, plans must satisfy present-law concentration tests in addition to any applicable nondiscrimination tests.

(8) Former employees

House Bill

The House bill provides that, except to the extent provided by the Secretary, rules similar to the nondiscriminatory eligibility and benefits tests are to be applied separately to former employees. In applying the rules to former employees, the Secretary is to prescribe rules under which certain special rules shall apply.

Employers may generally restrict the class of former employees to be tested to those who have retired on or after a reasonable retirement age, or to those who have separated from service due to disability. In addition, employers may generally limit the class further to employees who have, for example, retired within a certain number of years. Finally, in testing whatever class of employees is chosen, employers may make reasonable assumptions regarding mortality, so that they do not have to determine those former employees who are still alive.

Senate Amendment

The Senate amendment follows the House bill as applied to the Senate amendment nondiscrimination tests.

Conference Agreement

The conference agreement follows the House bill and Senate amendment, as applied to the nondiscrimination rules of the conference agreement.

(9) Cafeteria plans

House Bill

Under the House bill, a cafeteria plan is subject to the same 90 percent nondiscriminatory eligibility test applicable to all statutory employee benefit plans.

The House bill also repeals the present-law rule that, in the case of a cafeteria plan that does not satisfy the relevant nondiscrimination rules or concentration test, benefits under the plan are taxed to highly compensated employees or key employees in the taxable year of the employee in which the plan year in which the benefit was provided ends.

Senate Amendment

Under the Senate amendment, a cafeteria plan will be considered discriminatory unless the plan satisfies (1) the nondiscrimination tests of present law applicable to cafeteria plans (sec. 125(b)(1)) or (2) the present-law eligibility test and the average income exclusion test.

For purposes of applying the average income exclusion test to a cafeteria plan, all

benefits offered under the cafeteria plan are aggregated and treated as if they were the same type of benefit, except that if the employer elects, health coverage provided for spouses or dependents of employees may be tested separately. If a cafeteria plan satisfies the average income exclusion test, each of the statutory employee benefits offered under the cafeteria plan is treated as meeting the average income exclusion test, but must separately satisfy any applicable concentration test.

It is also intended that cafeteria plans may limit the elections by highly compensated employees of excludable benefits to the extent necessary to comply with the nondiscrimination rules.

Conference Agreement

The conference agreement retains the present-law eligibility test for cafeteria plans. The conference agreement deletes the special cafeteria plan benefits tests, although the concentration test is retained. Thus, each type of benefit available or provided under a cafeteria plan is subject to its own applicable nondiscrimination rules and to any applicable concentration test. For example, group-term life insurance benefits under a cafeteria plan must satisfy the eligibility and benefits tests applicable to group-term life insurance plans. As discussed above, certain aggregation of plans excludable under different Code sections is permissible for purposes of the benefits test.

The conference agreement also modifies the definition of a cafeteria plan to include a plan under which an employee may only choose among qualified benefits and may not choose cash or a taxable benefit. Also, if a cafeteria plan does not satisfy the cafeteria plan eligibility or concentration test, the benefits under the plan are taxable.

The conference agreement follows the Senate amendment by retaining present law with respect to the year of inclusion for a discriminatory cafeteria plan.

The conference agreement follows the Senate amendment allowing employers to limit the elections of highly compensated employees to the extent necessary to comply with the applicable nondiscrimination rules. However, the limitations are applied, under rules prescribed by the Secretary, in a nondiscretionary manner set forth in the plan, consistent with the rules for allocating the discriminatory excess among highly compensated employees.

The conference agreement applies the following uniform definitions applicable to statutory employee benefit plans to cafeteria plans: (1) highly compensated employees; (2) excludable employees; and (3) employer (including application of the leased employee rules). The compensation definition does not apply because compensation is not relevant for the cafeteria plan tests.

(10) Welfare benefit funds

House Bill

The House bill extends rules similar to the new nondiscriminatory eligibility and benefits tests applicable to statutory employee benefit plans to welfare benefit funds.

Senate Amendment

The Senate amendment substitutes the new definitions of highly compensated employees and of excludable employees for those applicable to welfare benefit funds under present law.

Conference Agreement

The conference agreement generally follows the Senate amendment, retaining the present-law nondiscrimination tests for the welfare benefit fund benefits that are not subject to a nondiscrimination test otherwise modified under the conference agreement.

The conference agreement applies the following uniform definitions applicable to statutory employee benefit plans to welfare benefit funds: (1) highly compensated employees: (2) compensation (including the limitation on the amount that may be taken into account) with respect to life insurance, disability, severance pay, and supplemental unemployment compensation; (3) excludable employees; and (4) employer (including application of the leased employee rules). With respect to nonemployees participating in a plan that is part of a welfare benefit fund, the Secretary shall prescribe appropriate rules defining which of such nonemployees shall be considered highly compensated employees.

(11) Reporting requirements

House Bill

The House bill expands the present-law requirement that the employers that maintain cafeteria plans, educational assistance programs and group legal services plans file information returns in accordance with Treasury regulations (sec. 6039D). Under the House bill, this requirement would apply to all statutory employee benefits plans, as well as to cafeteria plans.

In addition, if benefits provided under a cafeteria plan or statutory employee benefit plan are includible in the income of a highly compensated or key employee, the employer is required to file an information return, pursuant to regulations to be provided by the Treasury, setting forth the amount of the benefit and the name and address of the employee in whose income the benefit is includible. The employer is also required to furnish to each such employee a written statement showing the amount of the employee benefits includible in the employee's income.

Senate Amendment

No provision.

Conference Agreement

The conference agreement follows the House bill with two modifications. First, the conference agreement requires that all employers maintaining statutory employee benefit plans or cafeteria plans report the number of highly compensated employees (1) of the employer, (2) eligible to participate in the plan, and (3) participating in the plan. Second, the conference agreement clarifies that the requirement that certain employers file an additional return only applies to a representative sample of employers.

(12) Study

House Bill

The House bill requires that the Treasury Department conduct a study of abuses in the health insurance area and, not later than July 1, 1986, make recommendations for changes in the nondiscrimination rules.

Senate Amendment

No provision.

Conference Agreement

The conference agreement follows the Senate amendment.

(13) Effective date

House Bill

The House bill provisions are effective for years beginning after December 31, 1986.

Senate Amendment

The Senate amendment provisions are generally effective for years beginning after December 31, 1986.

The Senate amendment contains an exception to the new rules for certain group-term life insurance plans. In the case of a plan described in section 223(d)(2) of the Tax Reform Act of 1984, such plan shall be treated as meeting the requirements of the new nondiscrimination rules with respect to individuals described in section 223(d)(2) of the Act. In addition, an employer may elect to exclude such individuals in applying the new nondiscrimination rules.

In addition, the Senate amendment provides a delayed effective date for church plans. Under the bill, such plans are not required to comply with the new nondiscrimination requirements until years beginning after December 31, 1988.

Conference Agreement

The conference agreement follows the Senate amendment except that the general effective date is plan years beginning after the later of (1) December 31, 1987, or (2) the earlier of December 31, 1988, or the date 3 months following the issuance of Treasury regulations.

A special effective date applies to plans maintained pursuant to a collective bargaining agreement. Under this special rule, in the case of employees covered under a plan maintained pursuant to a collective bargaining agreement between employee representatives and one or more employers ratified before March 1, 1986, the amendments are not effective for plan years beginning before the earlier of (1) January 1, 1989, or (2) the date on which the last of the collective bargaining agreement terminates (determined without regard to any extensions in the collective bargaining agreement). With respect to employees not described in the previous sentence, employees so described may be disregarded prior to the effective date of the rules for such employees.

[¶ 4008] SECTION 1161. DEDUCTIBILITY OF HEALTH INSURANCE COSTS OF SELF-EMPLOYED INDIVIDUALS

(Sec. 162 of the Code)

[Senate Explanation]

*   *   *   *   *   *

Present Law.—Under present law, an employer's contribution to a plan providing accident or health benefits is excludable from an employee's income (sec. 106). No similar exclusion is provided for self-employed individuals (sole proprietors or partners).

*   *   *   *   *   *

Individuals who itemize deductions may deduct amounts paid during the taxable year, if not reimbursed by insurance or otherwise, for medical care of the taxpayer and of the taxpayer's spouse and dependents, to the extent that the total of such expenses exceeds five percent of adjusted gross income (sec. 213).

*   *   *   *   *   *

Explanation of Provision.—The bill provides a deduction for 50 percent of the amounts paid for health insurance for a taxable year on behalf of a self-employed individual and the individual's spouse and dependents. This deduction is allowable in calculating adjusted gross income. A self-employed individual means an individual who has earned income for the taxable year (sec. 401(c)(1)). However, under the bill, no deduction is allowable to the extent the deduction exceeds the self-employed individual's net earnings from self employment (sec. 1402(a)) for the taxable year. In addition, no deduction is allowable for any taxable year for which the self-employed individual is eligible to participate (on a subsidized basis) in a health plan of an employer of the self-employed individual or such individual's spouse.

In addition, the deduction is not allowable unless (1) the self-employed individual provides coverage under one or more accident or health plans for all employees in all unincorporated trades or businesses with respect to which the self-employed individual is a 5-percent owner (as defined in sec. 416(i)), and (2) the nondiscrimination requirements (as modified by the bill) applicable to accident or health plans are satisfied with respect to each such plan tested as though all coverage for which a 50-percent deduction is allowable under this section were employer-provided. Of course, this requirement is inapplicable if no unincorporated trade or business with respect to which the self-employed individual

is a 5-percent owner has employees other than the self-employed individual and such individual's family members.

Under the bill, the amount allowable as a deduction for health coverage for a self-employed individual is not also taken into account for purposes of determining the amount of any medical deduction to which the self-employed individual is entitled. Thus, such amounts deductible under this provision are not treated as medical expenses of the individual for purposes of determining whether the 10 percent of adjusted gross income threshold for the itemized medical expense deduction (sec. 213(a)) is met.

Finally, the bill provides that the amount deductible under this provision is not taken into account in computing net earnings from self-employment (sec. 1402(a)). Therefore, the amounts deductible under this provision do not reduce the income base for the self-employed individual's social security tax.

The bill directs the Secretary of the Treasury to provide guidance to self-employed individuals to whom this deduction applies with respect to the nondiscrimination requirements applicable to insured accident or health plans.

Effective Date.—The provision is effective for taxable years beginning after December 31, 1986.

[Conference Report]

*   *   *   *   *   *

Conference Agreement.—The conference agreement follows the Senate amendment, except as outlined below. First, the deduction is reduced from 50 percent of the amounts paid for health insurance to 25 percent of such amounts.

In addition, the conference agreement deletes the requirement that coverage be provided for all employees in all unincorporated trades or businesses with respect to which the self-employed individual is a 5-percent owner. Instead, the deduction is allowed only if the coverage is provided under one or more plans meeting the applicable nondiscrimination requirements, as if the coverage were employer-provided. The conference agreement also limits the deduction to the taxpayer's earned income for the taxable year. The provision allowing this deduction does not apply to any taxable year beginning after December 31, 1989.

Act § 1161   ¶ 4008

[¶ 4009] SECTION 1162. 2-YEAR EXTENSION OF EXCLUSIONS FOR EDUCATIONAL ASSISTANCE PROGRAMS AND GROUP LEGAL PLANS

(Secs. 120 and 127 of the Code)

[Conference Report]

* * * * * *

Present and Prior Law.—*Educational assistance.*—Under present law, an employee is required to include in income for income and employment tax purposes the value of educational assistance provided by an employer to the employee, unless the cost of such assistance qualifies as a deductible job-related expense of the employee. Amounts expended for education qualify as deductible employee business expenses if the education (1) maintains or improves skills required for the employee's job, or (2) meets the express requirements of the individual's employer that are imposed as a condition of employment. Under prior law, an employee's gross income for income and employment tax purposes did not include amounts paid or expenses incurred by the employer for educational assistance provided to the employee if such amounts were paid or such expenses were incurred pursuant to an educational assistance program that met certain requirements (Code sec. 127).

Under prior law, the maximum amount of educational assistance benefits that an employee could receive tax-free during any taxable year was limited to $5,000; thus, the excess benefits over this amount were subject to income and employment taxes. In the case of an employee who worked for more than one employer, the $5,000 cap applied to the aggregate amount of educational assistance benefits received from all employers.

The exclusion for educational assistance benefits expired for taxable years beginning after December 31, 1985.

Group legal services.—Under prior laws, amounts contributed by an employer to a qualified group legal services plan for employees (or their spouses or dependents) were excluded from an employee's gross income for income and employment tax purposes (sec. 120). The exclusion also applied to any services received by an employee or any amounts paid to an employee under such a plan as reimbursement for the cost of legal services for the employee (or the employee's spouse or dependents). In order to be a qualified plan under which employees were entitled to tax-free benefits, a group legal services plan was required to fulfill several requirements. An employer maintaining a group legal services plan was required to file an information return with respect to the program at the time and in the manner required by Treasury regulations.

In addition, under prior law, an organization, the exclusive function of which was to provide legal services or indemnification against costs of legal services as part of a qualified group legal services plan, was entitled to tax-exempt status (sec. 501(c)(20)). The tax exemption for such an organization ex-

pired for years ending after December 31, 1985.

The exclusion for group legal services benefits expired for taxable years ending after December 31, 1985.

* * * * * *

House Bill.—The House bill retroactively extends the educational assistance and group legal services exclusions for two years. In effect, this also extends the tax-exempt status of group legal services organizations (sec. 501(c)(20)). Thus, these exclusions are scheduled to expire for taxable years beginning after December 31, 1987, and ending after December 31, 1987, respectively.

* * * * * *

Senate Amendment.—The Senate amendment retroactively makes permanent the exclusions from gross income for educational assistance and group legal services and the tax exemption for qualified group legal services organizations.

In addition, the Senate amendment increases the cap on annual excludable educational assistance benefits to $5,250 from $5,000. This cap is indexed, under the Senate amendment, by reference to the method, as of May 1, 1986, for determining percentage increases in the social security taxable wage base. The Senate amendment does not contain a provision limiting the exclusion for dependent care assistance.

The Senate amendment provides a transition rule with respect to group legal services benefits provided under a cafeteria plan. Under the transition rule, the enactment of the bill is treated in the same manner as a change in family status under proposed Treasury regulations relating to cafeteria plans (Prop. Reg. sec. 1.125-1). Thus, an employee will be permitted to revoke an election to take cash or a taxable benefit after the period of coverage has commenced and to make a new election with respect to the remainder of the period of coverage. This transition rule applies to an election made to revoke a prior benefit election if the new election is made (1) with respect to group legal services benefits and (2) within 60 days after the date of enactment of the bill.

Conference Agreement.—The conference agreement follows the House bill with respect to extending for two years, rather than making permanent, the educational assistance and group legal services exclusions and the tax-exempt status of group legal services organizations. The agreement follows the Senate amendment raising the cap on annual excludable educational assistance benefits from $5,000 to $5,250, but does not adopt the Senate amendment indexing this cap.

* * * * * *

The conference agreement modifies the transition rule for group legal services benefits provided under a cafeteria plan. Under the modified transition rule, an employee will be permitted to revoke an election to take cash or a qualified benefit other than group legal services and to make a new election to take group legal services instead. Such revocation and new election must be made no later than 60 days after the date of

enactment and may relate to any period after December 31, 1985. This transition rule is limited to cafeteria plans that, prior to the date of conference action, did not allow employees to elect group legal services benefits with respect to a period after December 31, 1985.

[¶4010] SECTION 1163. $5,000 LIMIT ON DEPENDENT CARE ASSISTANCE EXCLUSION

[Sec. 129 of the Code]

[Conference Report]

Present and Prior Law.—* * *Under present law, amounts paid or incurred by an employer for dependent care assistance provided to an employee through a dependent care assistance program are excludable from income (sec. 129). The amount excludable is limited to the employee's earned income for the year or, in the case of married couples, the lesser of the employee's earned income and the earned income of the employee's spouse. A dependent care assistance program must be a written plan for the exclusive benefit of employees, must not discriminate in favor of employees who are officers, shareholders, or highly compensated, and must meet certain other requirements.

House Bill

*   *   *   *   *   *

The House bill limits the exclusion for dependent care assistance to $5,000 a year ($2,500 for a married individual filing separately). The provision is effective for taxable years beginning after December 31, 1985.

*   *   *   *   *   *

[Conference Report]

*   *   *   *   *   *

The conference agreement follows the House bill with respect to the limit on the exclusion for dependent care assistance, effective for taxable years beginning after December 31, 1986.

*   *   *   *   *   *

[¶4011] SECTION 1164. TAX TREATMENT OF FACULTY HOUSING

(Sec. 119(d) of the Code)

[Senate Explanation]

Present Law.—Section 119 excludes from an employee's gross income the value of lodging provided by the employer if (1) the lodging is furnished for the convenience of the employer, (2) the lodging is on the business premises of the employer, and (3) the employee is required to accept the lodging as a condition of employment.

Several court decisions have held that on-campus housing furnished to faculty or other employees by an educational institution does not qualify for the section 119 exclusion. Therefore, the fair rental value of the housing (less any amounts paid for the housing by the employee) was includible in the employee's gross income and constituted wages for income tax withholding and employment tax purposes in those cases.[2]

Deficit Reduction Act of 1984.—Section 531(g) of the Deficit Reduction Act of 1984 (P.L. 98-369) prohibited the Treasury Department from issuing, prior to January 1, 1986,

any income tax regulations that would provide for inclusion in gross income of the excess of the fair market value of qualified campus lodging over the greater of (1) the operating costs paid in furnishing the lodging, or (2) the rent received. This moratorium on regulations applied only with respect to qualified campus lodging furnished after December 31, 1983 and before January 1, 1986.

Qualified campus lodging was defined as lodging furnished by a school, college, or university to any of its employees, including nonfaculty employees, or to the employee's spouse or dependents. The moratorium applied only with respect to employer-furnished lodging that is located on a campus of, or in close proximity to a campus of, the educational institution. Under the 1984 Act, the moratorium did not apply with respect to any amount of the value of lodging if such amount was treated as wages or included in income when furnished.

The purpose of providing for the moratorium in the 1984 Act was to allow further time for consideration of arguments by schools

---

[Footnote ¶4011] **(2)** *Bob Jones Univ.* v. *U.S.,* 670 F.2d 167 (Ct. Cl. 1982); *Goldsboro Christian School, Inc.* v. *U.S.,* 79-1 CCH USTC para. 9266, E.D.N.C. 1978 (value of lodging furnished to faculty constitutes wages subject to income tax, FICA, and FUTA withholding, in light of "long and consistent history of regulations and rulings, expressly and explicitly applying withholding taxes to lodging not furnished for the employer's convenience * * *"), *aff'g* order entered in *Goldsboro Christian Schools, Inc.* v. *aff'g* 436 F.Supp. 1314 (E.D.N.C. 1977), *aff'g* per curiam in unpublished opinion (4th Cir. 1981), *aff'g* 103 S.Ct. 2017 (1983); *Winchell* v. *U.S.,* 564 F.Supp. 131 (D.Neb. 1983) (value of campus home taxed to college president); and *Coulbourn H. Tyler,* 44 CCH Tax Ct. Mem. 1221 (1982).

and universities that special tax rules governing treatment of housing furnished to their employees should be provided by statute.

* * * * * *

Explanation of Provision.—The bill provides that for Federal tax purposes, the fair market value of use (on an annualized basis) of qualified campus lodging furnished by, or on behalf of, an educational institution (within the meaning of sec. 170(b)(1)(A)(ii)[3] shall be treated as not greater than five percent of the appraised value for the lodging, but only if under rules prescribed by the Secretary an independent appraisal of the fair market value is obtained by a qualified appraiser. Thus, the appraiser must be qualified to make appraisals of housing, and the appraisal cannot be made by the employer institution or any officer, trustee, or employee thereof.

The committee does not intend that a new appraisal must be obtained each year. However, the committee intends that the appraisal must be reviewed annually, in a manner prescribed by the Secretary, but that such review should not impose undue cost on the educational institution.

Accordingly, under the safe-harbor valuation rule of the bill, if the rent paid for qualified campus lodging is equal to or exceeds on an annualized basis five percent of the value determined by such an appraisal, no amount is included, on account of such housing, in the employee's gross income for income tax purposes or in the wage or benefit base for social security and other employment tax purposes.

The provision applies to lodging furnished to any employee of the educational institution (or to the employee's spouse or dependents), including nonfaculty employees, for use as a residence, if the employer-furnished lodging is located on a campus of, or in the proximity of, the educational institution.

If no appraisal is obtained that meets the requirements of the provision, then the fair rental value for tax purposes is to be determined in the manner as would be done absent a special rule, taking into account all the relevant facts and circumstances. This does not preclude a taxpayer whose appraisal is found defective from subsequently obtaining a qualified appraisal and using the safe-harbor rule. For purposes of applying the first sentence of this paragraph to determine the fair rental value of campus lodging, the average of the rentals paid by individuals (other than employees or students of the educational institution) during such year for lodging provided by the educational institution that is comparable to the campus lodging provided to the employee is to be considered the fair rental value.

The new provision relating to qualified campus lodging does not affect the applicability of section 119(a) to lodging that qualifies for the exclusion in section 119(a).

Effective Date.—The provision applies for taxable years or periods beginning after December 31, 1985.

For prior taxable years, it is intended (1) that the IRS is to follow the safe-harbor valuation rule of the bill as if in effect for those years (except with respect to any amount of value of campus lodging that was treated by the taxpayer as wages or included in income when furnished), and (2) that the value of the property as assessed by State or local tax authorities for State or local property tax purposes is to be treated as if it were the value determined by a qualified appraisal.

[¶ 4012] SECTION 1165. LIMITATION ON ACCRUAL OF VACATION PAY

(Sec. 463 of the Code)

[Senate Explanation]

* * * * * *

Explanation of Provision.—Under the bill, the special rule allowing a deduction for additions to a reserve account for vacation pay (sec. 463) is limited to the vacation pay that is paid during the current taxable year

or within 8½ months after the close of the taxable year of the employer with respect to which the vacation pay was earned by the employees.

[Effective date.—Effective for tax years beginning after 12-31-86. Ed.]

* * * * * *

[Footnote ¶ 4011 continued]

(3) An educational organization is described in sec. 170(b)(1)(A)(ii) "if its primary function is the presentation of formal instruction and it normally maintains a regular faculty and curriculum and normally has a regularly enrolled body of pupils or students in attendance at the place where its educational activities are regularly carried on. The term includes institutions such as primary, secondary, preparatory, or high schools, and colleges and universities," and includes both public and private schools (Treas. Reg. sec. 1.170A-9(b)(1)).

[¶ 4013] SECTION 1166. TREATMENT OF CERTAIN FULL-TIME LIFE INSURANCE SALESMEN

(Sec. 7701(a)(20) of the Code)

[House Explanation]

* * * * * *

Present Law.—Under a cafeteria plan, an employee is offered a choice between cash and one or more fringe benefits. If certain requirements are met, then the mere availability of cash or certain permitted taxable benefits under a cafeteria plan does not cause an employee to be treated as having received the available cash or taxable benefits for income tax purposes.

Under present law, a full-time life insurance salesperson is treated as an employee for purposes of eligibility for certain enumerated fringe benefit exclusions (sec. 7701(a)(20)). However, although such a salesperson is eligible to receive certain excludable fringe benefits, the salesperson is not treated as an employee who is eligible to participate in the cafeteria plan provisions to the extent the salesperson is otherwise permitted to exclude from income the benefit elected.

* * * * * *

Explanation of Provision.—The bill permits a full-time life insurance salesperson to be treated as an employee for purposes of the cafeteria plan provisions to the extent the salesperson is otherwise permitted to exclude from income the benefit elected.

[Conference Report]

* * * * * *

House Bill

* * * * * *

[Effective date.—] The provision applies for years beginning after December 31, 1985.

* * * * * *

Conference Agreement

The conference agreement follows the House bill.

[¶ 4014] SECTION 1167. EXTENSION OF DUE DATE FOR STUDY OF WELFARE BENEFIT PLANS

[Senate Explanation]

Present Law.—The Deficit Reduction Act of 1984 (DEFRA) directed the Secretary of the Treasury to study the possible means of providing minimum standards for employee participation, vesting, accrual, and funding under welfare benefit plans for current and retired employees (including separated employees). The study is to include a review of whether the funding of welfare benefits is adequate, inadequate, or excessive. The Secretary was required to report to the Congress with respect to the study by February 1,

1985, with suggestions for minimum standards where appropriate. This study has not yet been completed.

Explanation of Provisions.—In addition, the bill extends the due date of the study of retiree benefits mandated by DEFRA to the date that is one year after the date of enactment of the bill.

Effective Dates.—* * *.The extension of the due date of the study required by DEFRA is effective on the date of enactment.

[¶ 4015] SECTION 1168. EXCLUSION FROM GROSS INCOME OF CERTAIN MILITARY BENEFITS

(Sec. 134 of the Code)

[Conference Report]

* * * * * *

The conferees believe that rules for the tax treatment of military benefits should be consolidated and set forth in one statutory provision. This will better enable taxpayers and the IRS to understand and administer the tax rules. Also, consolidation of these rules will make clear the intent of the conferees that, consistent with the treatment of benefits generally in the Tax Reform Act of 1984, any benefits for military personnel that are not expressly excluded under the new provision or under other statutory provisions of the Code (e.g., sec. 132) are includible in gross income. The provision does not alter

the definition of wages for withholding tax purposes.

The conference agreement excludes from income benefits which were authorized by law on September 9, 1986, and which were excludable from income on such date. Benefits are excludable only to the extent of the amount authorized and excludable on September 9, 1986, except that adjustments may be made pursuant to a provision of law or regulation in effect on September 9, 1986, if the adjustments are determined by reference to fluctuations in cost, price, currency or other similar index.

The conferees understand that the allowances which were authorized on September 9, 1986, and excludable from gross income on such date are limited to the following: veter-

Act § 1168 ¶ 4015

an's benefits authorized under 28 U.S.C. sec. 3101; medical benefits authorized under 50 U.S.C. sec. 2005 or 10 U.S.C. secs. 1071-1083; combat zone compensation and combat related benefits authorized under 37 U.S.C. sec. 310; disability benefits authorized under 10 U.S.C. chapter 61; professional education authorized under 10 U.S.C. secs. 203, 205, or 141; moving and storage authorized under 37 U.S.C. secs. 404-412; group term life insurance authorized under 38 U.S.C. secs. 404-412; premiums for survivor and retirement protection plans authorized under 10 U.S.C. secs. 1445-1447; mustering out payments authorized under 10 U.S.C. sec. 771a(b)(3); subsistence allowances authorized under 37 U.S.C. secs. 209, 402; uniform allowances authorized under 37 U.S.C. secs. 415-418; housing allowances authorized under 37 U.S.C. secs. 403, 403a, or 405; overseas cost-of-living allowances authorized under 37 U.S.C. sec. 405; evacuation allowances authorized under 37 U.S.C. sec. 405a; family separation allowances authorized under 37 U.S.C. sec. 427; death gratuities authorized under 10 U.S.C. secs. 1475-1480; interment allowances authorized under 10 U.S.C. secs. 1481-1482; travel for consecutive overseas tours authorized under 37 U.S.C. sec. 411; emergency assistance authorized under 10 U.S.C. sec. 133 and 37 U.S.C. chapter 1; family counseling services authorized under 10 U.S.C. sec. 133; defense counsel authorized under 10 U.S.C. secs. 133, 801-940, or 1181-1187; burial and death services authorized under 10 U.S.C. sec. 1481-1482; educational assistance authorized under 10 U.S.C. 141 and 37 U.S.C. secs. 203, 209; dependent education authorized under 20 U.S.C. sec. 921

and 10 U.S.C. sec. 7204; dental care for military dependents authorized under 10 U.S.C. secs. 1074 or 1078; temporary lodging in conjunction with certain orders authorized under 37 U.S.C. sec. 404a; travel to a designated place in conjunction with reassignment in a dependent-restricted status authorized under 37 U.S.C. sec. 406; travel in lieu of moving dependents during ship overhaul or inactivation authorized under 37 U.S.C. sec. 406b; annual round trip for dependent students authorized under 37 U.S.C. sec. 430; travel for consecutive overseas tours (dependents) authorized under 37 U.S.C. sec. 411b; and travel of dependents to a burial site authorized under 37 U.S.C. sec. 411f.

The conferees intend this list to be an exhaustive list of the allowances excludable under the new provision. The list is not intended, however, to limit benefits which are excludable under another section of the Code. Further, the conferees understand that there may be benefits which may have been unintentionally omitted from the list. Accordingly, the Secretary of the Treasury is authorized to expand the list if the Secretary finds that a benefit should have been included, i.e., that the benefit is a cash or reimbursement benefit which was authorized on September 9, 1986, and excludable from income on such date. Except as provided in the preceding sentence, the Secretary of the Treasury may not, by regulation or otherwise, expand the definition of excludable military benefits.

The provision is effective for taxable years beginning after December 31, 1986.

[¶ 4016] SECTION 1171. REPEAL OF EMPLOYEE STOCK OWNERSHIP CREDIT

(Sec. 41(a)(2) of the Code)

[Senate Explanation]

*   *   *   *   *   *

Reasons for Change.—The committee is interested in retaining tax incentives for employee stock ownership plans (ESOPs). However, in evaluating the relative tax benefits provided for ESOPs, the committee concluded that other incentives (including the financing incentives added by the Deficit Reduction Act of 1984 (DEFRA)) are more important than the ESOP tax credits. Thus, in order to raise sufficient revenue to add additional tax incentives for ESOP financing and to expand the incentives added by DEFRA, the committee believes it is appropriate to repeal the special ESOP tax credit at the end of 1986.

*   *   *   *   *   *

[Conference Report]

*   *   *   *   *   *

House Bill

*   *   *   *   *   *

Repeal of employee stock ownership credit.—The House bill repeals the special ESOP tax credit for compensation paid or accrued after 1985.

*   *   *   *   *   *

Conference Agreement

*   *   *   *   *   *

Tax credit employee stock ownership plans

Repeal of employee stock ownership credit.—The conference agreement repeals the ESOP tax credit effective for compensation paid or accrued after December 31, 1986.

*   *   *   *   *   *

[¶4017] SECTION 1172. ESTATE TAX DEDUCTION FOR PROCEEDS FROM SALES OF EMPLOYER SECURITIES

(Sec 2057 of the Code)

[Senate Explanation]

* * * * * *

Explanation of Provision.—* * * The bill permits an exclusion from the gross estate of 50 percent of the qualified proceeds from a qualified sale of employer securities. Under the bill, a qualified sale means any sale of employer securities (within the meaning of sec. 409(l)) by the executor of an estate to (1) an ESOP if the ESOP meets the requirements of section 409 or is described in section 4975(e)(7), or (2) an eligible worker-owned cooperative (as defined in sec. 1042(c)(2)).

Under the bill, qualified proceeds are defined to mean the proceeds received by the estate from the sale of employer securities issued by a domestic corporation if the sale occurs at any time before the due date of the estate tax return (including extensions of time to file). Qualified proceeds do not include the proceeds from the sale of any employer securities if the securities were received by the decedent (1) from a qualified plan (within the meaning of sec. 401(a)), or (2) as a transfer pursuant to an option or other right to acquire stock to which section 83, 422, 422A, 423, or 424 applies.

Under the bill, certain penalties apply if any portion of the assets attributable to employer securities acquired in a qualified sale accrue or are allocated for the benefit of (1) a decedent whose estate makes such a sale, (2) any person who is related to the decedent in one of the ways described in section 267(b), or (3) any other person who owns (after application of the attribution rules of sec. 318(a)) more than (a) 25 percent (by number) of any class of outstanding stock of the corporation (or certain related corporations) that issued such qualified securities, or (b) more than 25 percent of the total value of any class of outstanding stock of the corporation or of certain related corporations.

In addition, the bill makes it clear that this restriction applies to penalize any direct or indirect accrual of benefits under any qualified plan of the employer or an allocation of assets under the plan attributable to the securities involved in the qualified sale. Thus, for example, an ESOP in which the decedent has an interest should not allocate to the decedent's account any assets attributable to the securities involved in the sale. Nor should the employer make an allocation under the plan of other assets to the decedent in order to make up for the failure to allocate the securities involved in the qualified sale.

The bill clarifies that an individual is to be treated as a 25-percent shareholder only if the individual is a 25-percent shareholder (1) at any time during the one-year period ending on the date of a qualified sale to an ESOP, or (2) on the date upon which any of the securities sold to the ESOP in a qualified sale are allocated. In the case of an individual who satisfies the condition described at (1), the individual will continue to be treated as a 25-percent shareholder until all of the securities acquired pursuant to the qualified sale are allocated. In the case of an individual who does not satisfy the condition described at (1), but meets the condition described at (2), the individual will be treated as a 25-percent shareholder only with respect to those securities allocated on the date or dates that the individual is a 25-percent shareholder.

The bill also provides that, for purposes of determining whether an individual owns more than 25 percent of the outstanding stock of the corporation which issued the employer securities, all allocated securities held by an ESOP are treated as securities owned by the ESOP participant to whom the securities are allocated. The treatment of shares held by an ESOP as held by a shareholder for purposes of applying the 25-percent test applies to qualified sales after the date of enactment.

Under the bill, individuals who would be ineligible to receive an allocation of securities *solely* because they are lineal descendants of the decedent may receive an allocation of the securities acquired in the qualified sale provided that the total amount of such securities allocated to all such lineal descendants is not more than 5 percent of all employer securities acquired in the qualified sale.

The bill would also provide that an ESOP that acquires securities in a qualified sale is required to provide that the restriction on the allocation of securities to the sellers, family members, and 25-percent shareholders will be satisfied. The sanction for failure to comply with the restriction would be disqualification of the plan with respect ot those participants who received prohibited allocations. Thus, failure to comply would result in income inclusion for those participants of the value of their prohibited allocations as of the date of such allocations. However, violation of the restriction would not cause disqualification of the plan if the violation occurred more than 10 years after all of the securities acquired in the qualified sale had been allocated.

Under the bill, if there is a prohibited allocation by an ESOP or an eligible worker-owned cooperative of employer securities acquired in a qualified sale, then a 50 percent excise tax is imposed on the amount involved in the prohibited allocation. A prohibited allocation means (1) any allocation of employer securities acquired in a qualified sale if the provisions of section 409(n), relating to prohibitions on allocations to certain individuals, are violated, and (2) any benefit accruing to a person in violation of the provisions of section 409(n). The liability for this excise tax is to be paid by the employer who maintains an ESOP or by the eligible worker-owned cooperative.

* * * * * *

Effective Dates.—The provision relating to the exclusion of 50 percent of the proceeds of a qualified sale from the gross estate is effective for sales after the date of enactment by the executor of an estate required to file a

return (including extensions of time) * * * after the date of enactment.

* * * * * *

[Conference Report]

* * * * * *

The conference agreement follows the Senate amendment, except that the exclusion is available only for sales after the date of enactment and before January 1, 1992.

[¶ 4018] SECTION 1173. PROVISIONS RELATING TO LOANS USED TO ACQUIRE EMPLOYER SECURITIES

(Secs. 133 and 404(k) of the Code)

[Senate Explanation]

* * * * * *

Present Law.—*Deduction for dividends paid on ESOP stock.*—As added by the Deficit Reduction Act of 1984 (DEFRA), present law permits an employer to deduct the amount of any dividends paid in cash during the employer's taxable year with respect to stock of the employer that is held by an ESOP (including a tax credit ESOP), but only to the extent the dividends are actually paid out currently to participants or beneficiaries (sec. 404(k)).

An employer is allowed a deduction for its taxable year in which the dividends are paid to participants. The deduction is allowed with respect to dividends that are (1) in accordance with the plan provisions, paid in cash directly to the participants, or (2) paid to the plan and subsequently distributed to the participants in cash no later than 90 days after the end of the plan year in which the dividends are paid to the plan.

For income tax purposes, dividends distributed under an ESOP, whether paid directly to participants pursuant to plan provisions or paid to the plan and distributed to participants, generally are treated as plan distributions. Such dividends do not qualify for the partial exclusion from income otherwise permitted under the Code (sec. 116).

Partial exclusion of interest earned on ESOP loans.—A bank (within the meaning of sec. 501), an insurance company, or a corporation actively engaged in the business of lending money may exclude from gross income 50 percent of the interest received with respect to a securities acquisition loan made after July 18, 1984, and used to acquire employer securities after such date (sec. 133).

A securities acquisition loan is defined as a loan to a corporation or to an ESOP to the extent that the proceeds are used to acquire employer securities (within the meaning of sec. 409(1)) for the plan.

* * * * * *

Explanation of Provisions.—*Deduction for dividends paid on ESOP stock.*—(Under the bill, the deduction for dividends paid on ESOP stock is expanded to apply to dividends that are used to repay ESOP loans. Such

repayments are not treated differently from repayments attributable to nondeductible dividends for purposes of applying the limit on employer deductions (sec. 404(j)) or for purposes of applying the limitations on benefits and contributions (sec. 415).

Such dividends are deductible with respect both to allocated or unallocated employer securities, but only to the extent that such dividends are either paid out currently to employees or are used to repay acquisition indebtedness incurred to acquire the employer securities on which such dividends are paid.

Partial exclusion of interest earned on ESOP loans.—The bill modifies the 50 percent exclusion for interest paid on securities acquisition loans (sec. 133) in two respects.

First, the bill provides that the exclusion is also available with respect to a loan to a corporation to the extent that, within 30 days, employer securities are transferred to the plan in an amount equal to the proceeds of the loan and such contributions are allocable to participants' accounts within one year after the date of the loan.

In addition, the original commitment period of the loan is not to exceed 7 years. Thus, provided the final maturity of the credit arrangement is not greater than 7 years, the funds may be provided by one or more lenders in a series of shorter maturity (back-to-back) loans, each of which (other than the first) is used to repay the preceding loan.

Second, under the bill, a lender eligible for the interest exclusion is amended to include a regulated investment company (as defined in sec. 851). The committee intends that the tax treatment accorded such income be permitted to "flow through" to shareholders of the regulated investment company under rules analogous to the treatment of interest paid on certain governmental obligations as described in section 103(a).

In determining whether a regulated investment company qualifies to pay exempt-interest dividends, one-half of the outstanding balance of such securities acquisition loans held by a regulated investment company is treated as obligations described in section 103(a)(1). One-half of the interest on such securities acquisition loans are treated as interest excludable under section 103(a) for purposes of determining the amount of exempt-interest dividends that the regulated investment company may pay.

The written notice of designation requirements applicable to exempt-interest dividends applies to dividends attributable to securities acquisition loans. The committee intends, however, that the regulated investment company include in such notice an explanation to shareholders that this income is partially excludable from tax because the interest thereon is utilized to repay a loan structured to acquire employer stock for employees through an employee stock ownership plan.

Effective Dates.—The provision relating to the deductibility of dividends is effective for taxable years beginning after the date of enactment. The provision relating to eligibility for the interest exclusion for securities acquisition loans is effective for loans used to acquire employer securities after the date of enactment. The changes in the treatment of securities acquisition loans are also available for loans used to refinance loans used to acquire employer securities before the date of enactment, if such loans were used to acquire employer securities after July 18, 1984.

[Conference Report]

*   *   *   *   *   *

Conference Agreement

*   *   *   *   *   *

Deduction for dividends paid on ESOP stock.—The conference agreement follows the Senate amendment.

Partial exclusion of interest earned on ESOP loans.—The conference agreement generally follows the Senate amendment. Under the conference agreement, the interest exclusion is extended to refinancing of loans used to acquire employer securities after May 23, 1984.

Under the conference agreement, a securities acquisition loan which otherwise meets the requirements of section 133, and which is described in either section 133(b)(1)(B) or section 133(b)(3)(B) (see the technical corrections provisions of the Act), qualifies for the partial interest exclusion under section 133 if the total commitment period of the loan does not exceed 7 years. The total commitment period includes the original commitment period of the loan plus the commitment period of all refinancings of the loan.

If a loan which otherwise meets the requirements of section 133 and which is not described in either section 133(b)(1)(B) or section 133(b)(3)(B) is refinanced, the loan will continue to qualify for the partial interest exclusion under section 133 if the total commitment period of the loan does not

exceed the greater of 7 years or the original commitment period of the loan.

If a securities acquisition loan which qualifies under section 133 is refinanced prior to the date of enactment of this Act and the repayment period of the loan is extended, the loan will continue to qualify under section 133 with respect to interest accruing during the first 7 years of the total commitment period of the loan. Thus, for example, if, prior to the date of enactment, an otherwise qualified securities acquisition loan with an original commitment period of 5 years is refinanced for an additional 4 years, section 133 will continue to apply with respect to interest accruing in the first 7 years of the loan. The application of section 133 is limited to interest accured during the 7-year period so that prepayment of interest that has not yet accrued does not qualify for the partial exclusion.

Of course, any refinancings must also comply with the requirements of section 4975.

With respect to loans described in section 133(b)(1)(B), the requirement that stock be transferred to the plan within 30 days is modified to provide that the stock must be transferred within 30 days of the date interest begins to accrue on the loan. Similarly, the requirement that the stock must be allocated to accounts within 1 year after the loan is modified to provide that the stock must be allocated within 1 year after the date interest begins to accrue on the loan.

With respect to the provision extending the interest exclusion to regulated investment companies, the conferees intend that a regulated investment company that is otherwise fully invested in ESOP obligations will be permitted to pay out exempt interest obligations despite having certain amounts of cash or other assets on hand at the end of a taxable quarter, and expects that the Secretary will promulgate appropriate regulations in this regard.

Because only 50 percent of the interest income from ESOP loans is exempt from tax, the conferees understand that for this purpose it may be appropriate for a mutual fund to have two classes of stock, one of which would pay exempt-interest dividends and the other of which would pay taxable dividends. (Rev. Rul. 74-177, 1974-1 C.B. 165.) Such allocation would be reflected in the notice of designation. Any such two-class arrangement would not be subject to the rules of section 654 (relating to series funds) because there will not be segregated portfolios of assets.

*   *   *   *   *   *

[¶ 4019] SECTION 1174. REQUIREMENTS FOR EMPLOYEE STOCK OWNERSHIP PLANS

(Secs. 401, 409, and 415 of the Code)

[Conference Report]

*   *   *   *   *   *

Present Law.—An employee stock ownership plan ("ESOP") is a qualified stock bonus plan or a combination of a stock bonus and a money purchase pension plan which may be utilized as a technique of corporate finance and under which employer stock is held for the benefit of employees. The stock, which is held by one or more tax-exempt trusts under the plan, may be acquired through direct employer contributions or with the proceeds of a loan to the trust (or trusts). An ESOP must be designed to be invested primarily in employer securities.

ESOPs are subject to the requirements generally applicable to qualified plans. A qualified plan is required to meet minimum standards relating to coverage (sec. 410) and vesting (sec. 411). Also, a qualified plan cannot discriminate in favor of employees who are officers, shareholders, or highly compensated (sec. 401(a)(4)).

Unless a participant otherwise elects in writing, the payment of benefits from a qualified plan generally must begin no later than 60 days after the close of the plan year in which occurs the latest of (1) the date on which the participant attains the normal retirement age under the plan (or age 65, if earlier), (2) the 10th anniversary of the year the participant commenced participation in the plan, or (3) the date the participant separates from service. In no event can distribution be deferred beyond the required beginning date (sec. 401(a)(9)).

An ESOP that is top-heavy is also subject to the qualification rules applicable generally to top-heavy plans, including, for example, accelerated vesting and limits on includible compensation.

*   *   *   *   *   *

An ESOP must provide that participants have the right to demand that benefits be distributed in the form of employer securities. If the employer securities are not readily tradable, the employer must provide participants with a "put option", that is, the right to require that the employer repurchase the securities under a fair valuation formula. If the put option is exercised, provision for payment must be reasonable. If payment is deferred, the payment provisions will not be considered reasonable unless the employer provides security and a reasonable rate of interest.

In order to limit the extent to which individuals can use tax-favored arrangements to provide for employee benefits under a qualified plan, present law (sec. 415) provides overall limits on contributions and benefits under qualified pension, profit-sharing, and stock bonus plans. Present law provides a special limitation on annual additions under an ESOP. Under this special rule, the usual dollar limit on annual additions ($30,000 for 1986) is increased if the ESOP provides that no more than one-third of the employer contributions for the year are allocated to the group of employees consisting of officers, 10-percent shareholders, and highly compensated employees (i.e., employees whose annual compensation exceeds twice the dollar limit on annual additions or $60,000) (sec. 415(e)(6)).

*   *   *   *   *   *

House Bill

*   *   *   *   *   *

Put option requirements.—The House bill generally retains present-law requirement that a participant who receives a distribution of employer securities from an ESOP must be given a put option with respect to distributed employer securities that are not readily tradable. However, the bill modifies the permissible periods over which the employer may pay the option price to the participant.

For a participant who receives a lump-sum distribution of employer securities from an ESOP and exercises the put option, the employer must pay the option price to the participant in substantially equal annual installments over a period not exceeding 5 years and beginning no later than 30 days after the close of the 60-day option period. The employer must provide security for the installment payments and reasonable interest.

For a participant who receives a distribution of employer securities from an ESOP other than a lump-sum distribution and elects to exercise the put option, the employer must pay the full amount of the option price to the participant no later than 90 days after the exercise of the option.

*   *   *   *   *   *

Distribution requirements.—The House bill amends the tax credit ESOP distribution provisions to permit certain distributions upon plan termination. Distributions eligible to be made upon plan termination must consist of the entire balance to the credit of the participant. The provision is effective for termination distributions made after December 31, 1984.

*   *   *   *   *   *

Senate Amendment

*   *   *   *   *   *

Timing of distributions.—Under the Senate amendment, an ESOP is to permit earlier distributions to employees who separate from service before normal retirement age. Unless an employee otherwise elects in writing, the payment of benefits under an ESOP must begin no later than one year after close of the plan year (1) in which the participant terminates employment due to retirement, disability, or death, or (2) which is the fifth plan year following the participant's separation from service for any other reason (provided the participant does not return to service with the employer prior to that time). For purposes of applying this rule, the account balance of a participant does not include securities acquired pursuant to an acquisition loan until the close of the plan year in which the loan is repaid. As under the House bill, the rules added by the Senate amendment are intended as an acceleration of the otherwise applicable benefit commencement date.

The Senate amendment also provides that, unless the participant elects a longer distribution period, the plan may provide distributions over a period not longer than 5 years. If the participant's account balance exceeds $500,000, this distribution period is extended by one year (up to 5 additional years) for each $100,000 (or fraction thereof) by which the account balance exceeds $500,000. These dollar amounts are indexed at the same time and in the same manner as the dollar limits on benefits under a defined benefit pension plan (sec. 415(d)).

Put option requirements.—The Senate amendment generally retains the present-law requirement that a participant who receives a distribution of employer securities from a tax credit ESOP or a leveraged ESOP must be given a put option with respect to distributed employer securities that are not readily tradable. However, the bill modifies the permissible periods over which the employer may pay the option price to the participant.

In the case of a total distribution of employer securities to a participant that are put to the employer, the Senate amendment provides that the employer must pay the option price to the participant in substantially equal annual payments over a period not exceeding 5 years and beginning not more than 30 days after the exercise of the put option. The employer is not required to provide security with respect to such installment payments, but is required to credit a reasonable rate of interest with respect to the outstanding balance of the option price. A total distribution means the distribution within one taxable year of the recipient of the account balance under the plan.

In the case of a put option exercised as part of an installment distribution, the employer is required to pay the option price within 30 days after the exercise of the option.

Extension of put option requirements to stock bonus plans.—Under the Senate amendment, distributions of nonreadily tradable securities of an employer from a stock bonus plan are subject to the put option requirements applicable to ESOPs.

Modification of limitations on annual additions to ESOPs.—Under the Senate amendment, the definition of an employee who is subject to the one-third allocation limit for purposes of the special limitation on annual additions to ESOPs (sec. 415(c)(6)) is modified to conform to the new definition of highly compensated employee added under the amendment for purposes of qualified pension, profit-sharing, or stock bonus plans, and for purposes of employee benefit plans.

Effective dates.—The distribution requirements and the extension of the put option requirement to stock bonus plans are effective with respect to distributions attributable to stock acquired after December 31, 1986. The put option requirements are effective for distributions attributable to stock acquired after December 31, 1986, except that a plan may elect to have the put option requirements apply to all distribution after the date of enactment. The modified definition of highly compensated employees is effective for years beginning after December 31, [1986]. * * *

Conference Agreement

*   *   *   *   *   *

Timing of distributions

The conference agreement follows the Senate amendment.—Put option requirements.—The conference agreement follows the Senate amendment, except that security is required if the employer defers payment of the option price. Thus, as under the House bill, deferred payments are not permitted unless the employer provides adequate security.

Extension of put option requirements to stock bonus plans.—The conference agreement follows the Senate amendment.

Modification of limitations on annual additions to ESOPs.—The conference agreement follows the Senate amendment.

*   *   *   *   *   *

Distribution requirements.—The conference agreement follows the House bill and the Senate amendment.

The conferees intend that, for purposes of the rule permitting distributions from a tax credit ESOP on termination of the plan, [see **House Bill** above], a termination includes a partial termination of such a plan as to the employees of a particular subsidiary or operating trade or business in situations where such employees no longer have a significant relationship with the sponsor of the plan. [Effective for plan terminations after 12-31-84. Ed.]

[¶ 4020] SECTION 1175. ADDITIONAL QUALIFICATION REQUIREMENTS

(Sec. 401 of the Code)

[Conference Report]

* * * * * *

House Bill

* * * * * *

Diversification of investments.—The House bill requires an ESOP to offer partial diversification elections to participants who meet certain age and participation requirements (qualified employees). Under the bill, a qualified employee must be entitled annually during any diversification election period occurring within the employee's qualified election period to direct diversification of up to 25 percent of the participant's account balance (50 percent after attainment of age 60). To the extent that a participant elects to diversify a portion of the account balance, the bill requires an ESOP to offer at least three investment options not inconsistent with regulations prescribed by the Secretary and to complete the diversification within a specified period. Distribution to the participant within 90 days after the close of the annual diversification election period of an amount not to exceed the maximum amount for which a participant elected diversification is deemed to satisfy the diversification requirement.

* * * * * *

Independent appraiser.—Under the House bill, all valuations of employer securities contributed to or purchased by an ESOP with respect to activities carried on by the plan must be made by an independent appraiser (within the meaning of section 170(a)(1)). The appraiser's name must be reported to the Internal Revenue Service.

Conference Agreement

* * * * * *

Diversification of investments.—The conference agreement follows the House bill, except that the effective date of the diversification requirements is delayed for one year. Thus, the diversification rules are effective with respect to [stock] acquired December 31, 1986.

Under the conference agreement, as under the House bill, a "qualified employee" is entitled annually during the participant's "qualified election period" to direct diversification of up to 25 percent of the participant's account balance (50 percent after attainment of age 60). Any employee who has attained age 55 and completed 10 years of participation is a qualified employee. An employee is entitled to an election in each year within the qualified election period.

In meeting the diversification requirements, it is not intended that plan sponsors offer employer securities as one of the diversification options. As under the House bill, the diversification requirement can be met by a distribution of the portion of the account balance for which diversification was elected, or cash in lieu thereof. If, under this rule, stock is distributed in satisfaction of the diversification requirement, the usual put option rules apply. Amounts which are distributed in satisfaction of the diversification requirement may be rolled over to an IRA or to another qualified plan. The diversification requirement is satisfied if an employer provides the option to transfer the portion of the account balance for which diversification is elected into a plan which provides for employee-directed investment and in which the required diversification options are available.

* * * * * *

Independent appraiser.—The conference agreement follows the House bill, except that valuation by an independent appraiser is not required in the case of employer securities which are readily tradable on an established securities market. The requirement is effective with respect to stock acquired after December 31, 1986.

[Effective date.—Applies to stock acquired after 12-31-86. Ed.]

[The following colloquy relating to Act Sec. is drawn from the Congressional Record. The colloquy occurred on the day the Conference bill was considered by the House Ed.]

[House Floor Explanation]

I have discussed with Congressman CLAY several issues relating to employee stock ownership plans and their treatment under H.R. 3838. We have reached a common understanding regarding the following specific issues:

The Senate amendment of H.R. 3838 contained a series of provisions designed to encourage the creation and use of employee stock ownership plans.

In the Senate amendment itself, in the Finance Committee report, and on the Senate floor, a series of suggested expressions of congressional intent were made which emphasized that ESOP's are tools of corporate finance and not conventional retirement plans. When the House considered H.R. 3838, no similar suggested expressions of congressional intent were made.

In fact, H.R. 3838 incorporated many of the suggestions made by the President in his own tax reform proposal and repealed many of the tax incentives granted to employee stock ownership plans in previous tax legislation.

Section 1271 of the Senate amendment to H.R. 3838 emphasizes that ESOP's are tools of corporate finance and that Congress is concerned that the ERISA agencies are treating ESOP's as conventional retirement plans, thus hindering the suggested goal of expanding ESOP's as corporate financing vehicles. It has been asserted that section 1271 merely restates language found in tax legislation enacted in 1976. However, in comparing the two provisions, it certainly appears that section 1271 goes much farther than the 1976 statement. For example, in 1976 no reference was made to rulings and regulations under ERISA being a problem. The Committee on Education and Labor was concerned that the addition of references to ERISA might be erroneously construed by some as a weakening of title I fiduciary requirements as they applied to ESOP's.

The conference agreement does not contain the suggested statement of congressional intent.

The conferees agreed with the Committee on Education and Labor that it would be inappropriate to adopt any suggested statement of congressional intent concerning ESOP's without a full airing of the facts. Since that has not been done, the suggested statement of congressional intent regarding ESOP's was not adopted.

I am aware that a few people have criticized the ESOP enforcement activities of the Department of Labor. Concern has been expressed by those individuals that ESOP's should somehow be treated differently from other employee benefit plans under ERISA's title I fiduciary standards so that their use as a technique of corporate finance would not be thwarted. The same statutory fiduciary rules under title I are applicable to all employee benefit plans, regardless of whether they are retirement plans, savings plans, health insurance plans, and so forth.

There is no provision in the conference agreement before us which could be interpreted as calling for relaxed enforcement of the fiduciary provisions of title I of ERISA in connection with transactions where ESOP's are used as a technique of corporate financing.

The legislative history under title I of ERISA requires that leveraged ESOP transactions be given special scrutiny under the title I fiduciary rules to ensure that the interests of participants in ESOP's be protected. No valuation methodology or construct should be applied in the determination of fair market value that would permit an ESOP to pay more for employer stock than a third-party investor in an arm's length transaction would, or that would permit any other party in the transaction to receive more than that party would be entitled to receive in an arm's length arrangement. For example, if an ESOP were to purchase all of the common stock of an employer, the ESOP should pay no more for the common stock than what the common stock could be sold for to an arm's length investor.

There is no provision in the conference agreement which could be construed to create new legislative history on how the stock purchased by the ESOP ought to be valued in these transactions.

There is nothing in the conference agreement that could be construed to prevent the Department of Labor from exercising its legitimate and congressionally mandated responsibility to enforce title I to protect the interests of ESOP participants.

There is nothing in the conference agreement which could be construed to establish the validity of or endorse a particular method of validation of stock or valuation construct in transactions involving ESOP's.

I anticipate that next Congress the Subcommittee on Labor-Management Relations will be holding oversight hearings on ESOP's and that the issues we have discussed today will be considered. Congressional Record, p. H 8362-8363, 9-25-86.

[¶ 4021] SECTION 1176. SPECIAL ESOP REQUIREMENTS

(Secs. 401(a)(2), 409(1) of the Code)

[Conference Report]

Senate Amendment

* * * * * *

Voting.—The Senate amendment eliminates the pass-through voting requirements of present law in the case of employer securities issued by certain newspapers whose stock is not readily traded and also permits ESOPs established by such employers to acquire nonvoting common stock in certain cases.

* * * * * *

Effective dates. * * * The elimination of the pass-through voting requirements for certain plans of newspapers is effective December 31, 1986. The provision permitting certain plans of newspapers to acquire nonvoting common stock is effective with respect to acquisitions of securities after December 31, 1986.

* * * * * *

Conference Agreement

Voting.—The conference agreement follows the Senate amendment. The conference agreement clarifies that the special rules for newspapers apply to employers (determined without regard to the controlled group rules) whose stock is not publicly traded and a substantial portion of whose business consists of publishing a newspaper for general circulation on a regular basis.

* * * * * *

[¶ 4027] SECTIONS 1201-1205. FOREIGN TAX CREDIT MODIFICATIONS

(Secs. 901, 902, 904, 960 of the Code)

[Conference Report]

* * * * * *

1. Separate Foreign Tax Credit Limitations

Present Law.—The foreign tax credit is determined on an "overall" basis: a taxpayer adds up its net income and net losses from all sources outside the United States and calculates one aggregate limitation based on the total. Overall (rather than country-by-country) foreign tax credit limitations are calculated separately, or subject to special rules, for certain categories of income that frequently bear either high (for example, oil extraction income) or low (for example, FSC dividends) rates of foreign tax or that can easily be earned in low-tax countries rather than in the United States to inflate the foreign tax credit limitation (for example, passive interest). The reason for the separate limitations is to prevent distortion of the foreign tax credit.

* * * * * *

Conference Agreement

a. Passive income

Following the House bill and the Senate amendment, the conference agreement replaces the separate limitation for passive interest income with a separate limitation for passive income generally. Some of the conference agreement's rules relating to this new separate limitation follow the House bill; others follow the Senate amendment. The conference agreement also includes technical and clarifying amendments.

General definition of passive income.—Following the House bill and the Senate amendment, the conference agreement generally defines passive income as any income of a kind which would be subpart F foreign personal holding company (FPHC) income. As discussed in greater detail at * * * [¶4034], both the House bill and the Senate amendment modify the definition of subpart F FPHC income; the conference agreement generally adopts the Senate amendment's modifications to the subpart F FPHC income definition for both subpart F and passive "basket" purposes.

The conference agreement does not include the House bill rule that treats foreign currency transaction gains of U.S. dollar taxpayers as passive income without regard to the business needs exception provided for currency gains under the legislation's subpart F amendments. Thus, under the agreement, currency gains eligible for the business needs exception are excluded from the separate limitation for passive income, whether the taxpayer's functional currency is the U.S. dollar or a foreign currency.

FPHC and PFIC inclusions.—Following the House bill and the Senate amendment, foreign personal holding company inclusions (under Code sec. 551) and passive foreign investment company inclusions (under new Code sec. 1293) are passive income.

Export financing exception.—The conference agreement provides an export financing exception to the separate limitation for passive income. The agreement generally excludes from the new separate limitation (and treats as overall limitation income) interest derived from financing the sale (or other disposition) for use or consumption outside the United States of any property which is manufactured, produced, grown, or extracted in the United States by the interest recipient or a related person, and not more than 50 percent of the fair market value of which is attributable to products imported into the United States. For this purpose, the fair market value of any property imported into the United States is its appraised value, as determined by the Secretary under section 402 of the Tariff Act of 1930 (19 U.S.C. 1401a) in connection with its importation. A related person, for this purpose is an individual, corporation, partnership, trust, or estate which controls, or is controlled by, the interest recipient, or a corporation, partnership, trust, or estate which is controlled by the same person or persons which control the interest recipient. Control means, with respect to a corporation, the ownership, directly or indirectly, of stock possessing 50 percent or more of the total voting power of all classes of stock entitled to vote or of the total value of stock of the corporation. In the case of a partnership, trust, or estate, control means the ownership, directly or indirectly, of 50 percent or more (by value) of the beneficial interests in the partnership, trust, or estate. Rules for determining stock ownership similar to those applicable for subpart F purposes (Code sec. 958) apply.

Parallel export financing exceptions are provided by the conference agreement with respect to the separate limitations for financial services income (discussed at A.1.b., and high withholding tax interest (discussed at A.2., below and the termination of tax deferral for banking income of controlled foreign corporations (discussed at * * * [¶4034]). The conferees include these exceptions because of their concern that this tax reform legislation might otherwise have the effect of reducing the availability of export financing in some cases, which could, in turn, have a negative impact on the volume of exports.

Financial services income exception.—Income that would otherwise meet the definitions of both financial services income (which is subject to its own separate limitation (see b., below)) and passive income is financial services income under the conference agreement if received in a taxable year in which the recipient is predominantly engaged in the active conduct of a banking, insurance, financing, or similar business. By contrast, amounts earned by an entity not predominantly engaged in the active conduct of a banking, insurance, financing, or similar business that arguably meet the definitions of both financial services income and passive income are passive income under the agreement. The latter rule is intended to prevent entities earning passive income from characterizing it as financial services income in order to avoid the high-tax kick-out and other anti-abuse rules applicable to the separate limitation for passive income.

Shipping income exception.—Following the House bill, the conference agreement excludes shipping income subject to its own separate limitation (sec c., below) from the definition of passive income. Income, such as rental payments for the use of a vessel, that otherwise is both of a kind which would be subpart F FPHC income and of a kind which would be foreign base company shipping income is subject to the separate limitation for shipping income rather than to the separate limitation for passive income. This priority rule parallels the present-law subpart F priority rule for income that is otherwise both subpart F FPHC income and foreign base company shipping income. It conforms more closely the separate limitation and subpart F rules and thereby simplifies the application of the separate limitation rules.

Oil and gas income exception.—The separate limitation for passive income does not apply to foreign oil and gas extraction income. This rule follows the House bill and the Senate amendment.

Active rents and royalties exception.—The separate limitation for passive income does not apply to active business rents and royalties from unrelated parties. This rule follows the House bill and the Senate amendment. As indicated in the Reports of the Committee on Ways and Means and the Committee on Finance on this tax reform legislation, it is anticipated that the standards contained in existing regulations defining rents and royalties for purposes of excluding them from subpart F taxation (Treas. Reg. sec. 1.954-2(d)(1) generally will be followed in determining whether rents and royalties received from unrelated parties qualify for this exclusion from passive income. The conferees expect that the Secretary, in adapting the standards contained in the existing regulations for this purpose, will, to the extent possible, substitute for the facts and circumstances test included therein more objective rules for distinguishing between active and passive rents and royalties. The conferees believe that it may be appropriate in some cases to apply such rules on a consolidated group basis in the case of U.S. recipients of rents and royalties that join in filing a consolidated return.

High withholding tax interest exception.—Following the Senate amendment, the conference agreement excludes high withholding tax interest (which is subject to its own separate limitation (see A.2., below)) from the definition of passive income.

De minimis exception.—The conference agreement does not adopt the the exception

for interest on working capital contained in the Senate amendment. Instead, it provides that a controlled foreign corporation has no passive income (or financial services income, shipping income, high withholding tax interest, or separate limitation dividends from a 10-to 50-percent U.S.-owned foreign corporation) in a taxable year in which the corporation has no subpart F income by reason of the applicability of the subpart F de minimis rule (Code sec. 954(b)(3)(A)), as that rule is modified by the agreement. Under the agreement, the subpart F de minimis rule generally applies if the sum of gross foreign base company income and tax haven insurance income is less than the lesser of 5 percent of gross income or $1 million.

The conference agreement adopts this separate limitation de minimis rule in the interest of administrative convenience. The amount of passive income of a controlled foreign corporation is relevant for separate limitation purposes because (as discussed in greater detail at A.1.e., below), under look-through rules, that amount determines the extent to which subpart F inclusions with respect to the corporation, and payments by the corporation to its U.S. shareholders, are included in the passive income basket. To simplify the application of the look-through rules, the conference agreement includes this rule, and others, that conform more closely the operation of subpart F and the separate limitations. As a result of the separate limitation de minimis exception, a controlled foreign corporation that has no currently taxable FPHC income for a year under the subpart F de minimis rule will have no passive income for that year for separate limitation look-through purposes. Dividends paid from the year's earnings, and interest, rents, and royalties paid to U.S. shareholders during the year, will have no passive income component.

Assume, for example, that a foreign corporation wholly owned by a U.S. company has $100 of gross income. Ninety-six dollars of that income consists of manufacturing income and nonsubpart F sales income, $1 is foreign base company sales income, and $3 is FPHC income. The foreign corporation pays $10 of interest, $5 of royalties, and no dividends to its U.S. parent. The subpart F de minimis rule applies so the U.S. parent has no subpart F inclusion with respect to the foreign corporation. Consequently, under the separate limitation de minimis rule, the $3 of FPHC income is treated as overall limitation income rather than passive income. The look-through rules need not be applied to the $10 of interest and $5 of royalty payments. These payments are overall limitation income to the parent in their entirety. In addition, for purposes of determining the foreign tax credit limitation treatment of future dividends, earnings and profits of the foreign corporation for the year have no separate limitation component.

Regulated investment company exception.—Under the conference agreement, dividends received by a controlled foreign corporation from a regulated investment company may be excluded from passive income under the de minimis rule for controlled foreign corporations described immediately above.

Exception for passive income that attracts high foreign tax.—The conference agreement adopts the Senate amendment provision authorizing the Treasury Department to prescribe anti-abuse rules to prevent manipulation of the character of income the effect of which is to avoid the purposes of the separate limitations. It also adopts, with the clarifications discussed below, the House bill provision excluding high-taxed income from the separate limitation for passive income (the "high-tax kick-out").

The high-tax kick-out applies after allocation of expenses at the U.S. recipient level. For example, assume that a foreign corporation that earns only passive income for the year makes a $100 rent payment to its 100-percent U.S. owner. The payment attracts a $30 foreign withholding tax. Under the look-through rule for rents, the $100 would be passive income to the U.S. owner, absent the high-tax kick-out. Before the high-tax kick-out may be applied, parent expense must be allocated to the $100 of income. Assume that $40 of parent expense is properly allocated to the $100. Pursuant to the high-tax kick-out, the $60 of net rental income is recharacterized as overall limitation income (and the $30 withholding tax is placed in the overall basket) because the foreign income tax paid with respect to that income exceeds the highest U.S. tax rate multiplied by the amount of the income after allocation of parent expense (that is, $30 > (.34 × $60)).

The conference agreement does not mandate separate application of the high-tax kick-out to individual items of income which the Secretary determines can be grouped for purposes of applying the kick-out without diminishing substantially its effect. The conferees expect the Secretary, in making such determinations, to balance the administrative convenience that may be gained from grouping particular items of income against the increased sheltering opportunities that might be created by such grouping. The conferees believe that it would generally be appropriate to apply the high-tax kick-out to the passive portion of a subpart F inclusion *in toto,* rather than separately to each item of income included in the passive income inclusion. For example, assume that a U.S. company owns two foreign corporations. With respect to the first foreign corporation, the U.S. company has a $50 subpart F FPHC inclusion. The inclusion consists of 5 $10 interest payments received by the first foreign corporation from sources in 5 different countries. In the interest of administrative convenience, the conferees believe that the high-tax kick-out generally should apply once in this instance, to the full $50 inclusion (after allocation of parent expenses), rather than separately to each $10 item reflected in the inclusion, even though the foreign tax attracted by the different $10 items may vary.

With respect to the second foreign corporation, the U.S. company has a $75 passive subpart F inclusion. The high-tax kick-out is to be applied separately to the $75 and $50 inclusions.

Dividends paid by a controlled foreign corporation generally will not be passive under the conference agreement (*see* discussion of look-through rules at e., below). Such dividends are, therefore, generally to be excluded from any income grouping to which the high-tax kick-out is applied.

The conferees expect the Secretary to examine the extent to which it would be feasible, consistent with the purposes of the kick-out, to apply it to a foreign branch's total passive income carrying direct foreign tax credits, rather than separately to each item of passive income of the branch that carries a direct foreign tax credit. A foreign branch might be defined for this purpose by reference to the definition of a "qualified business unit" provided in the conference agreement's rules for the tax treatment of foreign currency exchange gain and loss (*see* * * * [¶4056]).

The high-tax kick-out is to apply at the U.S. person level only. For example, assume that two foreign corporations are wholly owned by a common U.S. parent. The foreign corporations are incorporated in different countries. The first foreign corporation has $100 of income (after expenses other than foreign tax). All of the corporation's gross income is passive. The $100 attracts $45 of foreign tax. (The taxpayer does not elect to exclude this income from subpart F taxation under subpart F's high foreign tax rule (Code sec. 954(b)(4)).) This income is currently taxed to the U.S. parent under subpart F. For purposes of applying the high-tax kick-out, $5 of parent expense is allocated to this income. The income is overall limitation income to the U.S. parent because the foreign tax treated as paid by the parent on the income (under Code sec. 960) exceeds the highest U.S. tax rate multiplied by the amount of the income after allocation of parent expense and the Code section 78 gross-up for deemed-paid foreign tax (that is, $45 > (.34 × $95)).

Among the first foreign corporation's expenses is a $20 royalty payment to the second foreign corporation. The only foreign tax attracted by this royalty payment is a $1 withholding tax. Under the look-through rules, the $20 would generally be passive income to the second foreign corporation. The high-tax kick-out does not apply at the controlled foreign corporation level; thus, the $45 of foreign tax imposed on the first foreign corporation's income has no bearing on the characterization of its royalty payment to the second foreign corporation. This rule simplifies the application of the high-tax kick-out. The conferees also believe that it is appropriate for two additional reasons. First, the $20 royalty payment in the example bore none of the $45 of tax paid by the first foreign corporation: rather, it reduced the first foreign corporation's taxable income; the $45 of tax was imposed on the first foreign corporation's $100 of income after deductions, including that for the royalty payment. Second, foreign taxes are relevant for foreign tax credit limitation purposes only at that point at which direct or deemed-paid foreign tax credits are provided for them. Such credits are provided only when a *U.S.* person includes the associated income in its gross income for U.S. tax purposes.

Returning to the example, the $20 of passive royalty income is subpart F FPHC income to the second foreign corporation, currently taxable to its U.S. parent. One dollar of parent expense is allocated to the subpart F inclusion for purposes of applying the kick-out. The subpart F inclusion remains passive after application of the kick-out because the $1 of foreign withholding tax treated as paid by the U.S. parent on this income (under Code sec. 960) does not exceed the highest U.S. tax rate multiplied by the amount of the income after allocation of parent expense and the Code section 78 gross-up for deemed-paid foreign tax (that is, $1 < (.34 × $19)).

The Secretary is to prescribe rules for the proper application of the high-tax kick-out in cases involving distributions of income previously taxed under subpart F that themselves attract foreign tax. With respect to such distributions, any adjustment in tax liability will normally be required in the year of the distribution rather than in the year of the subpart F inclusion, and will be consistent with present law's special rules for determining foreign tax credits with respect to distributions of earnings and profits previously taxed under subpart F (*see* Code sec. 960(b)). With respect to *all* the separate limitations, the conferees intend that foreign taxes imposed on distributions of income previously taxed under subpart F, to the extent creditable under the special rules just noted, be assigned to the same limitation basket or baskets as the prior subpart F inclusions to which they relate.

b. Financial services income

*　　*　　*　　*　　*　　*

[House Explanation]

*　　*　　*　　*　　*　　*

The new separate limitation for banking and insurance income applies to income received or accrued by any person which is derived in the conduct of a banking, financing, or similar business or from the investment made by an insurance company of its uninsured premiums or reserves ordinary and necessary for the proper conduct of its insurance business. Separate limitation banking and insurance income also includes, with one modification, any income which is of a kind which would be insurance income under subpart F (Code sec. 953(a), as modified by the bill). Subpart F insurance income under the bill generally is any income attributable to the issuing (or reinsuring) of any insurance or annuity contract. However, insurance income generally is not subject to current taxation under subpart F if the risk

insured is in the country in which the insurer is created or organized. For purposes of the separate limitation for banking and insurance income, this same-country risk exception does not apply.

Under the bill, subpart F insurance income and, therefore, separate limitation banking and insurance income also include any income attributable to an insurance contract in connection with same-country risks as the result of an arrangement under which another corporation receives a substantially equal amount of premium for insurance of other-country risks.

The amount of insurance income subject to tax under subpart F and, therefore, subject to the separate limitation is the amount that would be taxed under subchapter L (as modified by the bill) of the Code if it were the income of a domestic insurance company (subject to the modifications provided in Code section 953(b)).

For purposes of the separate limitation, income derived in the conduct of a banking, financing, or similar business includes income earned in providing credit card and other services integrally related to banking and financing activity. It also includes finance leasing income.

* * * [T]he bill imposes current tax on all foreign personal holding company income earned by banks and insurance companies (subject to an exclusion for high-taxed income) by repealing rules that presently exclude from foreign personal holding company income for subpart F proposes certain dividends, interest, and gains received by persons in the banking, financing, and insurance businesses. Banking and insurance income subject to current taxation under subpart F, as modified by the bill, is a narrower category of income than banking and insurance income subject to the new separate limitation, since the separate limitation is not limited in its application, as the subpart F inclusion rules with respect to banking and insurance income generally are, to foreign personal holding company income.

*　　*　　*　　*　　*　　*

[Conference Report]

*　　*　　*　　*　　*　　*

The conference agreement generally follows the House bill in establishing a separate limitation for financial services income, with the modifications described below.

The conference agreement provides an export financing exception to the separate limitation for financial services income. The agreement generally excludes from the new separate limitation (and treats as overall limitation income) interest derived from financing the sale (or other disposition) for use or consumption outside the United States of any property which is manufactured, produced, grown, or extracted in the United States by the interest recipient or a related person, and not more than 50 percent of the fair market value of which is attributable to

Act § 1201—1205 ¶ 4027

products imported into the United States. For this purpose, the fair market value of any property imported into the United States is its appraised value, as determined by the Secretary under section 402 of the Tariff Act of 1930 (19 U.S.C. 1401a) in connection with its importation. A related person, for this purpose, is an individual, corporation, partnership, trust, or estate which controls, or is controlled by, the interest recipient, or a corporation, partnership, trust, or estate which is controlled by the same person or persons which control the interest recipient. Control means, with respect to a corporation, the ownership, directly or indirectly, of stock possessing 50 percent or more of the total voting power of all classes of stock entitled to vote or of the total value of stock of the corporation. In the case of a partnership, trust, or estate, control means the ownership, directly or indirectly, of 50 percent or more (by value) of the beneficial interests in the partnership, trust, or estate. Rules for determining stock ownership similar to those applicable for subpart F purposes (Code sec. 958) apply.

The conference agreement renames the House bill's separate limitation for banking and insurance income the separate limitation for financial services income to emphasize the broad range of income types to which the separate limitation applies. Income derived in the active conduct of a banking, financing, or similar business normally would include income attributable to any of the activities listed in existing Treas. Reg. sec. 1.954(2)(d)(2)(ii)(A) through (G). In addition, it would normally include service fee income from investment and correspondent banking, earnings from interest rate and currency swap businesses, income from services provided to unrelated parties with respect to the management of funds, income from fiduciary services provided to unrelated parties, bank-to-bank participation income, charge and credit card services income from financing purchases from third parties, hedging gains with respect to other financial services income, and income from travellers' check services. As under the House bill, insurance income subject to the separate limitation consists of premium and other insurance income. Such income received by offshore captive insurance companies which the agreement taxes currently to these companies' U.S. owners (see * * * [¶4034]) is subject to the separate limitation.

The conference agreement provides a special rule for entities predominantly engaged in the active conduct of a banking, insurance, financing, or similar business. If an entity is so engaged for any taxable year, then the separate limitation for financial services income will apply to any passive income earned by the entity in that year as well as to its financial services income. Income of an entity so engaged that would otherwise meet the definitions of both shipping income and financial services income will be considered the latter for separate limitation purposes. This rule generally allows active banks, insurance companies, finance companies, and

similar businesses, which, under the overall limitation of present law, can credit foreign taxes on one type of financial income against U.S. tax liability on another type of financial income, to retain that ability. The cross-crediting curtailed by the new separate limitation is, by contrast, primarily that between banking, insurance, financing, and similar income and income unrelated to financial services. The predominantly engaged rule also acknowledges the practical difficulty of distinguishing passive income of a bank, insurance company, finance company, or similar business— most or all of the income of which derives from financial activity— from its active income.

The conferees expect the Secretary to prescribe rules for determining whether an entity is predominantly engaged in the active conduct of a banking, insurance, financing, or similar business. Generally, if a high percentage of an entity's income is not attributable to financial services activities of the types enumerated above, such entity is not to be considered predominantly engaged in the active conduct of a banking, insurance, financing, or similar business. In cases involving the application of the separate limitation look-through rules (see e., below), the predominantly engaged test is to be deemed satisfied if either the U.S. income recipient or the related payor of the income independently satisfies it. Thus, for example, if a controlled foreign corporation satisfies the predominantly engaged test, any payment that it makes to a U.S. shareholder (or subpart F inclusion of a U.S. shareholder) that would otherwise be passive income to the shareholder under the look-through rules will be treated as financial services income without regard to whether the shareholder itself satisfies the predominantly engaged test. Conversely, if a U.S. shareholder of a controlled foreign corporation satisfies the predominantly engaged test, but the controlled foreign corporation does not, inclusions by the U.S. shareholder with respect to the corporation that would otherwise be subject to the separate limitation for passive income will be subject instead to the separate limitation for financial services income.

If an entity satisfies the predominantly engaged test, then income it earns that is integrally related to its banking, insuring, or financing activity generally is to be treated as financial services income, notwithstanding that such income might not otherwise be financial services income. For example, the conferees anticipate that income from equipment leasing, precious metals trading, commodity trading, and the financing of trade that is integrally related to the banking, insuring, or financing activity of an entity satisfying the predominantly engaged test may be treated as financial services income of that entity. However, in no event is income attributable to nonfinancial activity to be treated as financial services income. Thus, for example, income from data processing services or the sale of goods or non-financial services is not financial services income, even if the recipient satisfies the predominantly engaged test.

High withholding tax interest subject to its own separate limitation (*see* 2., below) is not subject to the separate limitation for financial services income. This exclusion applies whether or not the recipient satisfies the predominantly engaged test. Income that might otherwise meet the definitions of both shipping and financial services income (for example, income from insuring vessels) is financial services income for separate limitation purposes. This priority rule applies whether or not the recipient satisfies the predominantly engaged test.

Income that might otherwise meet the definitions of both passive and financial services income is passive income for separate limitation purposes when the recipient fails to satisfy the predominately engaged test. This rule prevents entities making essentially passive investments such as occasional loans from avoiding the high-tax kickout and other anti-abuse rules applicable to the separate limitation for passive income by taking the position that the associated income is financial services income rather than passive income.

c. Shipping income

*   *   *   *   *   *

[House Explanation]

*   *   *   *   *   *

The new separate limitation for shipping income applies to income received or accrued by any person which is of a kind which would be foreign base company shipping income (as defined in Code sec. 954(f), as amended by the bill). * * * [T]he bill repeals the exclusion from foreign base company shipping income for reinvested shipping income and adds to base company shipping income certain income derived from space or ocean activities.

*   *   *   *   *   *

[Conference Report]

*   *   *   *   *   *

d. Foreign currency translation gains

The conference agreement does not contain the House bill provision establishing a separate limitation for foreign currency translation gains. The treatment of such gains for foreign tax credit limitation purposes is discussed at * * * [¶4056].

e. Look-through rules

Dividends, interest, rents, and royalties received from controlled foreign corporations by their U.S. shareholders generally will be subject to the separate limitation for passive income, the separate limitation for financial services income, the separate limitation for shipping income, the separate limitation for high withholding tax interest (discussed at 2., below), or the separate limitation for dividends from 10- to 50-percent U.S.-owned foreign corporations (discussed at f., below) in accordance with look-through rules that take

into account the extent to which the income of the payor is itself subject to one or more of these limitations. Subpart F inclusions are also subject to a look-through rule. These look-through rules generally follow those of the Senate amendment, with substantial technical modifications.

Conformity with subpart F.—The conference agreement conforms the separate limitation look-through rules more closely with the subpart F rules. In general, the modifications contained in the conference agreement, detailed below, are intended to limit the application of the look-through rules and to make their application, where required, simpler for taxpayers and the IRS.

U.S. ownership requirements for application of look-through rules.—The conference agreement generally applies the look-through rules only to subpart F inclusions and to dividends, interest, rents, and royalties received from U.S.-controlled foreign corporations. No look-through rules generally are applied in characterizing, for separate limitation purposes, payments from foreign entities in which U.S. persons own a 50-percent or smaller interest. The conferees have restricted the scope of look-through treatment in recognition of the difficulty that some shareholders in minority U.S.-owned corporations might have encountered in obtaining the additional income and tax information necessary to apply the look-through rules to payments of such corporations. Further, the conferees note that a primary purpose of look-through treatment is to make the foreign tax credit limitation treatment of income earned through foreign branches and income earned through foreign subsidiaries more alike by, in effect, treating income earned by a foreign subsidiary as if it were earned directly by its U.S. parent. When the U.S. interest in a foreign entity falls below a majority interest, the conferees believe that such entity frequently no longer substantially resembles a branch operation of U.S. persons.

Following the House bill and the Senate amendment, the conference agreement generally treats foreign source dividends, interest, rents, and royalties from entities in which the recipient has less than a 10-percent ownership interest the same as if such payments were received from unrelated parties (that is, no look-through rules were received from unrelated parties (that is, no look-through rules apply). Interest, rents, and royalties received from entities in which U.S. persons have no more than a 50-percent interest by 10-percent or greater U.S. owners of such entities generally are treated the same way under the conference agreement. Thus, interest, for example, paid by foreign corporations that are not controlled foreign corporations to their U.S. shareholders is treated under the conference agreement as separate limitation passive income, subject to the agreement's high-tax kick-out.

The conferees provide this treatment because of a concern that any other rule would permit abuse of the foreign tax credit system. For instance, assume that a U.S. corporation owns 45 percent of a manufacturing corporation organized and operating in a high-tax foreign country. The foreign corporation pays the U.S. corporation an overall limitation dividend that is fully sheltered from U.S. tax by deemed-paid foreign tax credits. In addition, $17 of excess foreign tax credits are associated with the dividend. Assume that the U.S. corporation lends $400 to the foreign corporation, which it reinvests in a bank account at a slight profit. The foreign corporation pays $40 of interest to the U.S. corporation. If the conference agreement allowed cross-crediting of the foreign taxes on the dividend against U.S. tax on the interest payment, the $17 of excess credits from the dividend would be credited against the $13.60 of pre-credit U.S. tax on the interest income, leaving no residual U.S. tax on the interest income and a $3.40 excess credit to carry over. The conferees do not believe that such cross-crediting is appropriate. In the case of a controlled foreign corporation, by contrast, a look-through rule treats interest payments from a controlled foreign corporation. as first carrying out the payor's passive income (see discussion of "netting" rule below).

As explained at f. (see below), dividends paid by 10- to 50-percent U.S.-owned foreign corporations are subject to an entity-by-entity separate limitation under the agreement.

In the following limited situations, the look-through rules will apply to inclusions with respect to minority U.S.-owned entities. They apply to inclusions with respect to more-than-25-percent U.S. owned insurance companies that are controlled foreign corporations under Code section 957(b), as amended by the conference agreement (discussed at * * * [¶4034]), and inclusions with respect to captive insurance companies with dispersed U.S. ownership that are controlled foreign corporations under new Code section 953(c) (discussed at * * * [¶4034]). Application of the look-through rules here preserves general conformity of the subpart F and look-through rules. The conferees believe that such application will not prove administratively burdensome; they are informed that most of the offshore insurance companies likely to be affected will not have income in more than one basket.

The conference agreement requires the Secretary to prescribe such regulations as may be necessary or appropriate providing that a look-through rule similar to that applicable to interest, rents, and royalties paid by controlled foreign corporations will apply to such amounts received or accrued from entities which would be controlled foreign corporations if they were foreign corporations. Thus, under regulations, the conferees anticipate that interest, rents, and royalties received by 10-percent U.S. interest holders in noncorporate entities more-than-50-percent controlled by U.S. persons will generally be subject to look-through treatment. This rule generally follows the House bill and the Senate amendment except for the U.S. control requirement, which parallels

that adopted in the conference agreement for application of the look-through rule to foreign corporations. It is also expected that foreign source interest received from more-than-50-percent U.S.-owned 80/20 companies (see Code sec. 861(a)(1)(B), as amended by the conference agreement; discussion at B.4.a., below) by their 10-percent U.S. shareholders will be subject to look-through treatment under regulations. (Dividends paid by 80/20 companies to U.S. shareholders are U.S. source under the conference agreement; therefore, the separate limitations are irrelevant to such payments.) This rule generally follows the Senate amendment except, again, for the U.S. control requirement.

De minimis exception for controlled foreign corporations.—If a controlled foreign corporation has no foreign base company income or subpart F insurance income in a taxable year because the corporation satisfies the subpart F de minimis rule (Code sec. 954(b)(3)(A), as amended by the bill; see * * * [¶4034]) for that year, then the look-through rules will treat interest, rents, or royalties paid by the corporation during that year and dividends, to the extent treated as paid from that year's earnings and profits, as overall limitation income. Thus, under the conference agreement, the subpart F de minimis rule also functions as a de minimis rule for the separate limitations for passive, financial services, and shipping income, and the separate limitations for high withholding tax interest (discussed at 2., below) and dividends from 10- to 50-percent U.S.-owned foreign corporations (discussed at f., below).

The conferees have adopted this de minimis exception so that U.S. shareholders of controlled foreign corporations may avoid the recordkeeping burden of applying the look-through rules to limited amounts of separate limitation income earned by controlled foreign corporations. The purpose of the de minimis rule is to simplify the application of the separate limitations in cases involving controlled foreign corporations.

If a controlled foreign corporation has no separate limitation income in a year by reason of the de minimis rule, the conferees intend that the foreign loss allocation rule adopted in the conference agreement (see 4., below), like the look-through rules, have no application to the corporation's income for the year.

Following the House bill and the Senate amendment, the conference agreement provides that the 70-percent full inclusion rule for foreign base company and insurance income (Code sec. 954(b)(3)(b), as amended by the conference agreement; see * * * [¶4034]) will not result in overall limitation income of a controlled foreign corporation being treated as separate limitation income.

Exception for controlled foreign corporations not availed of to reduce tax.—For purposes of applying the dividend look-through rule, income of a controlled foreign corporation that would otherwise be passive, financial services, or shipping income is treated as overall limitation income under the agreement if it is established by the taxpayer that the income was subject to an effective foreign tax rate of greater than 90 percent of the maximum U.S. tax rate and the income is excluded from subpart F as a result (*see* Code sec. 954(b)(4), as amended by the conference agreement; discussed at * * * [¶4034]). The Senate amendment applies this rule to income of a controlled foreign corporation that would otherwise be passive. The conference agreement expands the rule's application to harmonize the operation of the subpart F and separate limitation look-through rules. Applying this conformity rule to income that would otherwise be passive or shipping income, in particular, may eliminate the need to apply the dividend look-through rule in many cases since income of a controlled foreign corporation cannot be passive or shipping income unless it is income of a kind which is subpart F FPHC or foreign base company shipping income, respectively.

The conference agreement does not apply this conformity rule to high withholding tax interest or dividends from 10- to 50-percent U.S.-owned foreign corporations. The latter separate limitation category is not closely related to any subpart F income category. Applying the conformity rule to high withholding tax interest would allow taxpayers to circumvent the separate limitation for that income. That separate limitation generally places high withholding taxes on interest in a separate basket where they may not be used to shelter low-taxed income from U.S. tax. If the conformity rule applied to such interest, U.S. shareholders of controlled foreign corporations receiving such interest could generally place it, and the associated taxes, in the overall basket with potentially low-taxed income by making the section 954(b)(4) election, since such highly taxed interest generally would satisfy the 90-percent threshold of section 954(b)(4). A similar concern sometimes arises in the case of dividends from 10- to 50-percent U.S.-owned foreign corporations. If a controlled foreign corporation makes the section 954(b)(4) election with respect to high withholding tax interest or dividends from a 10- to 50-percent U.S.-owned foreign corporation and the controlled foreign corporation qualifies for the subpart F de minimis exception for the year, the income remains high withholding tax interest or separate limitation dividend income (as the case may be) for look-through purposes.

The conformity rule does not apply for purposes of the look-through rule for interest, rents, and royalties, since those amounts are typically not subject to net tax in the hands of the payor and the 90-percent test applies on a net income basis.

Examples

The following examples show how the look-through rules, as modified by the conference agreement, will apply in certain cases.

Example 1.—Assume that a foreign corporation wholly owned by a U.S. corporation earns $100. Seventy-five dollars is foreign base company shipping income and $25 is nonsubpart F services income. (For simplicity, this example assumes that net income and gross income are equal.) The $75 of shipping income includes $10 of rental income that also meets the subpart F definition of FPHC income. That $10 is treated as shipping income, not passive income, under the conference agreement. Under the 70-percent full inclusion rule of subpart F, the entire $100 is foreign base company income currently taxable to the U.S. parent. Since $75 of the $100 subpart F inclusion is attributable to income of the foreign corporation subject to the separate limitation for shipping income, $75 of the subpart F inclusion is treated as separate limitation shipping income of the parent. The remaining $25 of the subpart F inclusion is treated as overall limitation income of the parent.

Example 2.—Assume that a foreign corporation wholly owned by a U.S. corporation earns $100 of gross income. Four dollars is portfolio interest (which is subpart F FPHC-type income) and $96 is gross manufacturing income (which is nonsubpart F income). Among the foreign corporation's expenses is $10 of interest paid to its U.S. parent. Because the subpart F de minimis exception applies, the $4 of portfolio interest is not taxed currently to the parent. For the same reason, all of the foreign corporation's income is overall limitation income. Under the look-through rule for interest then, the full $10 interest payment is overall limitation income to the U.S. parent. Any future dividends attributable to this year's earnings and profits will be 100-percent overall limitation income to the extent so attributable, notwithstanding the $4 of portfolio interest.

Example 3.—Assume that a foreign corporation wholly owned by a U.S. corporation earns $100. Fifty dollars is shipping income of a type that is normally foreign base company shipping income. The other $50 is dividends from a second foreign corporation in which the first foreign corporation holds 45 percent of the voting stock. Foreign persons hold the other 55 percent of the voting stock of the second foreign corporation. The second foreign corporation and the controlled foreign corporation are incorporated in different countries. The dividends received by the controlled foreign corporation are, therefore, of a type that would normally be subpart F FPHC income. However, these dividends are subject to the separate limitation for dividends from 10- to 50-percent U.S.-owned foreign corporations, rather than to that for passive income (see discussion of this priority rule at f., below); while all passive income is income of a kind which would be subpart F FPHC income, not all subpart F FPHC income is passive.

The dividends and the shipping income are taxed abroad by the controlled foreign corporation's country only, at an effective rate of 40 percent. (This example assumes, for simplicity, that net income and gross income are equal.) Pursuant to Code section 954(b)(4) (as amended by the conference agreement), the U.S. parent establishes to the satisfaction of the Secretary that that effective rate exceeds 90 percent of the maximum U.S. tax rate. Therefore, neither the shipping income nor the dividends are taxed currently to the U.S. parent under subpart F.

However, the controlled foreign corporation pays all its earnings and profits for the year out as a dividend. Half of that dividend is attributable to its shipping earnings and half to the dividends it received. The half of the dividend attributable to the dividends it received is subject to the separate limitation for dividends from 10- to 50-percent U.S.-owned foreign corporations in the U.S. parent's hands; the conference agreement provision conforming certain of the separate limitation rules with the section 954(b)(4) exception does not apply to that separate limitation. The other half of the dividend is overall limitation income in the parent's hands because the conforming provision just noted treats the shipping income as overall limitation for purposes of applying the look-through rule for dividends.

Amendments to subpart F deficit rules.—As discussed in detail at C.1.a., below, the conference agreement repeals subpart F's chain deficit rule (Code sec. 952(d)), modifies subpart F's accumulated deficit rule (Code sec. 952(c)(1) and (2)), and provides for the recapture of subpart F income that is eliminated by current year deficits in nonsubpart F income categories. These subpart F amendments reflect, in part, the conferees' conclusion that separate limitation income received by controlled foreign corporations (which is frequently subpart F income also) should not be eliminated by deficits of other controlled foreign corporations, prior year deficits in different income categories, or current year deficits in nonsubpart F income categories. The conferees felt that the integrity of the separate limitation for passive income, for example would be compromised if taxpayers could shelter passive income from U.S. tax, notwithstanding the separate limitation, simply by placing passive investments in controlled foreign corporations with accumulated losses. Preserving separate limitation income (otherwise eliminated by deficits) for foreign tax credit limitation purposes absent the indicated subpart F changes would necessitate more frequent application of the look-through rule to dividends paid by controlled foreign corporations with passive income.

Netting of interest payments.—Except to the extent provided in regulations, interest payments or accruals by a controlled foreign corporation to a U.S. shareholder with respect to the corporation (or to another controlled foreign corporation related to such a U.S. shareholder) are allocated first to gross subpart F FPHC income of the corporation that is passive, to the extent of such income. The Secretary may, by regulations, extend this "netting" rule to payments and accruals to unrelated persons. In addition, it is anticipated that the rule will be extended to U.S.-controlled noncorporate payors and U.S.-controlled 80/20 company payors to the extent that look-through treatment of their interest payments is provided under regulations.

The netting rule applies for subpart F and foreign tax credit limitation purposes. The conferees' goal in adopting this rule is to avoid creating an incentive for taxpayers to keep, or move, passive income and investments offshore. The netting rule's effect with respect to the look-through rule for interest is similar to that of the "stacking" rule included in the Senate amendment: interest payments by a controlled foreign corporation to its U.S. shareholders are separate limitation passive income to those shareholders to the full extent of the foreign corporation's gross passive income. The netting rule replaces the stacking rule. The conferees believe that the netting rule has several technical advantages over the stacking rule, among them, that it will be simpler to apply and administer. On the other hand, the netting rule reduces subpart F FPHC income (compared to present law) to the extent that it allocates interest expense to gross FPHC income that, under current law, would be allocated to nonsubpart F income. Concern about this effect of the netting rule has led the conferees to provide regulatory flexibility so that the Secretary can apply different rules when the netting rule would allow a tax advantage for offshore passive investments over domestic passive investments, or other unintended tax advantages.

An example illustrates the application of the netting rule. Assume that a U.S. corporation wholly owns a foreign corporation and that the U.S. corporation also has $1,000 of cash. That controlled foreign corporation earns $100 of overall limitation manufacturing income, on which it pays $60 of foreign tax. The U.S. parent is free to invest its cash in the United States or abroad. Assuming equally safe investments, the parent will tend to seek the highest after-tax return.

If the U.S. parent earns $100 of bank deposit interest in the United States, it will generally pay $34 of U.S. tax on that interest income under the conference agreement. The goal of the agreement in a case such as this is to make sure that the parent does not pay less than that amount of tax if it earns an equivalent amount of passive income offshore.

Assume that the parent instead lends its $1000 of cash to its controlled foreign corporation. The foreign corporation deposits that cash in a foreign bank, and earns $100 of interest on the investment. The foreign subsidiary in turn pays $100 of interest to its U.S. parent. The conference agreement provides that any interest received or accrued from a controlled foreign corporation by a U.S. shareholder in that corporation is treated as income subject to a particular separate limitation to the extent that that interest is properly allocable (under regulations prescribed by the Secretary) to income of the controlled foreign corporation that itself is subject to that separate limitation. Under the netting rule, the $100 interest payment is properly allocable in full to the controlled foreign corporation's $100 of gross bank deposit interest, which is gross subpart F FPHC income subject to the separate limitation for passive income. Thus, the $100 of interest received by the U.S. parent is subject to the separate limitation for passive income. As a result, the U.S. parent cannot cross-credit foreign taxes paid on overall limitation income against the U.S. tax liability on that income. The $100 interest payment in effect removes all the passive income at the foreign subsidiary level. There is no subpart F inclusion for this taxable year. Any future dividend from the foreign subsidiary from its $100 of pre-foreign tax manufacturing earnings will consist solely of overall limitation income.

The conference agreement does not provide explicit regulatory authority to the Secretary to extend the netting rule to rents and royalties paid or accrued by controlled foreign corporations. The Senate amendment, by contrast, applies the stacking rule to all payments to which look-through rules apply, including rents and royalties. The conferees do not believe that back-to-back (or other) rent or royalty arrangements utilizing controlled foreign corporations should permit taxpayers to reduce the U.S. tax on foreign rent or royalty income. The conferees are informed that existing regulatory standards under Code section 861 should operate to prevent taxpayers from allocating rent or royalty expense of controlled foreign corporations in order to achieve such results. The conferees have not expressly extended the netting rule to rents and royalties on the understanding that, under the present regulations, netting effectively will be required in the problem cases just described (and others). The conferees intend that the Secretary make any clarifications in the present regulations that might be necessary to ensure that netting takes place in such problem cases.

The allocation of interest expense of a controlled foreign corporation for purposes of the interest look-through rule and the foreign tax credit limitation rule maintaining the source of U.S. source income (Code sec. 904(g)(3)) is to be consistent. Thus, the netting rule, where applicable for purposes of the interest look-through, applies for purposes of the U.S. source maintenance rule too.

For example, assume that a foreign corporation wholly-owned by a U.S. corporation has $1,000 of gross foreign source manufacturing income and $150 of gross subpart F FPHC income. One hundred twenty-five dollars of this $150 is U.S. source income not effectively connected with a U.S. business. The other $25 is foreign source. The foreign corporation pays $150 of interest to its U.S. parent. Under the netting rule, the $150 of interest expense is allocated in full to the foreign corporation's $150 of subpart F FPHC income and is, therefore, passive in the parent's hands. Under the conference agreement, that allocation controls for purposes of determining the U.S. source portion of the $150. Thus (under Code sec. 904(g)(3)(C)), $125 of the $150 of interest expense is properly allocable to U.S. source income of the con-

trolled foreign corporation and, consequently, is U.S. source to its parent.

The conferees believe that using the same interest allocation method, including the netting rule where applicable, in applying present law's provision maintaining the source of U.S. source income and the separate limitation look-through provision for interest achieves a desirable conformity in the operation of these two provisions. The conferees are informed that technical difficulties have arisen under present law in coordinating the provision maintaining the source of U.S. source income with the provision maintaining the character of interest income (Code sec. 904(d)(3), which the look-through rules of the conference agreement supplant) because the allocation approaches of these two provisions differ.

The general subpart F related person definition (Code sec. 954(d)(3), as amended by the conference agreement (*see* C.l.a., below) applies to determine whether a controlled foreign corporation is related to a U.S. shareholder for purposes of the netting rule.

Other rules.—The agreement contains a clarifying amendment to the present law provision that treats distributions of income previously taxed under subpart F as other than dividends (Code sec. 959(d)). This amendment is relevant to the application of the look-through rule for dividends. (It is also relevant to the calculation of the dividends received deduction for dividends from foreign corporations (Code sec. 245, as amended by the agreement; *see* * * * [¶4039]) and the application of the dividend look-through provision of the present law rules maintaining the source of U.S. source income (Code sec. 904(g)(4)).) Under the look-through rule for dividends, a proportionate amount of a dividend is treated as separate limitation income based on the ratio of the separate limitation earnings and profits out of which the dividend was paid to the total earnings and profits out of which the dividend was paid. The amendment makes clear that the numerator or the denominator (as the case may be) of this ratio is reduced by earnings and profits attributable to income that has been previously taxed under subpart F and distributed.

As an example, assume that a foreign corporation wholly owned by a U.S. corporation and engaged in a manufacturing business earns $20 of subpart F FPHC income, $20 of same-country dividend income from a 10- to 50-percent U.S.-owned foreign corporation, and $60 of manufacturing income. It thus has $100 of earnings and profits for the year. (For simplicity, this example assumes that net income, earnings and profits, and gross income are equal.) The $20 of subpart F FPHC income is currently taxed to the U.S. parent. The controlled foreign corporation distributes $40 in the year of the subpart F inclusion. Under the look-through rule for subpart F inclusions, the $20 of subpart F FPHC income is treated as passive income. Twenty dollars of the $40 distribution is not treated as a dividend because it is attributable to the $20 already taxed under subpart F (Code sec. 959(d)). Under the look-through rule for dividends, $5 of the $20 portion of the distribution that is a taxable dividend ($20/$80 × $20) should be treated as a separate limitation dividend from a 10- to 50-percent U.S.-owned foreign corporations (*see* discussion of this separate limitation below) and $15 of that $20 ($60/$80 × $20) should be treated as overall limitation income. The clarifying amendment excludes from the denominator of the ratios just noted the portion of the year's $100 of earnings and profits attributable to the subpart F FPHC income ($20) and thus ensures that the described result technically is achieved.

If a controlled foreign corporation has earnings and profits for the current year but an accumulated deficit, and it pays a dividend, then the basis for application of the look-through rule for dividends is the current year's earnings and profits.

For purposes of the look-through rule for dividends, the agreement provides that a dividend includes any Code section 956 inclusion triggered by an increase in earnings invested in U.S. property (Code sec. 951(a)(1)(B)). Section 956 inclusions are subject to the look-through rule for dividends rather than that for subpart F inclusions generally under the conference agreement because section 956 inclusions, like dividends, are drawn pro rata from earnings and profits; they differ from foreign base company income inclusions in not being specifically identified with particular earnings of a controlled foreign corporation. Any gain on the sale of shares in a foreign investment company that is treated as ordinary income under Code section 1246 is not a dividend for look-through purposes under the conference agreement. Instead, it is treated as passive income. Consistent with present law, distributions of income previously taxed under subpart F are not dividends for look-through purposes (*see* Code sec. 959(d)). As under the Code generally, a dividend includes any amount treated as such under Code section 1248.

For purposes of applying the look-through rules, a U.S. corporation's income "gross-up" for deemed-paid foreign taxes (Code sec. 78) is treated as increasing the corporation's subpart F inclusion (under Code sec. 951(a)(1)(A)) to the extent that the gross-up is attributable to such a subpart F inclusion. To the extent that the gross-up is attributable to a dividend or a section 956 inclusion, the gross-up is treated as a dividend for look-through purposes. Under this approach, for example, a single $100 inclusion consisting of $80 of subpart F FPHC income and a $20 gross-up for the foreign taxes deemed paid on the $80 will be subject to one look-through rule (that for subpart F inclusions under Code section 951(a)(1)(A)) rather than two (the subpart F *and* dividend look-through rules).

The conference agreement requires the Secretary to prescribe such regulations as may be necessary or appropriate for the application of the look-through rules in the case of income paid, or loans made, through one or more entities or between two or more chains of entities. For example, a controlled foreign corporation may receive interest subject to a high foreign withholding tax from a related controlled foreign corporation. To the extent necessary to preserve the integrity of the separate limitations, such interest will be characterized as passive income, financial services income, shipping income, high withholding tax interest, or dividend income from a 10- to 50-percent U.S.-owned foreign corporation for separate limitation purposes by applying the look-through rule for interest to the income of the related controlled foreign corporation. That look-through rule requires a determination of the extent to which the interest is properly allocable to the related controlled foreign corporation's passive income, financial services income, shipping income, high withholding tax interest, or dividend income from a 10- to 50-percent U.S.-owned foreign corporation.

This regulatory requirement, as it relates to income payments, is contained in the House bill and the Senate amendment. The conference agreement extends the requirement to loans so that the Secretary may prevent taxpayers from avoiding the separate limitations through the use of related party loans. Assume, for example, that a controlled foreign corporation earns $100 of low-taxed, nonsubpart F income subject to the separate limitation for financial services income. Its U.S. parent wishes to bring the $100 home. The parent would like to characterize the $100 as overall limitation income because it has excess foreign tax credits in the overall basket that would shelter the $100, if so characterized, from U.S. tax. The parent controls another foreign corporation engaged solely in manufacturing, all of the income of which is overall limitation income. The first controlled foreign corporation lends the manufacturing subsidiary $100. The manufacturing subsidiary in turn pays the U.S. parent a $100 dividend. If the general look-through rule for dividends is applied without modification, that $100 is overall limitation income to the parent. If that result were allowed to stand, however, the parent would have effectively brought home, converted into overall limitation income, the first controlled foreign corporation's $100 of financial services income. Regulations are to prevent such avoidance of the separate limitations using related party loans.

[The following colloquy relating to Act Sec. 1201 is drawn from the Congressional Record. The colloquy occurred on the day the Conference bill was considered by the Senate. Ed.]

[Senate Floor Explanation]

Mr. BRADLEY. It is my understanding that new code section 904(d)(5) requires the Secretary to prescribe regulations under the "look-through" of new section 904(d)(3) which will provide that dividends, subpart F inclusions, interest, rents, and royalties received by a controlled foreign corporation from another member of the same affiliated group — determined under section 1504 without regard to subsection (b)(3) thereof — shall be treated as income in a separate category if — and only if — such income is attributable directly or indirectly to separate category income of any other member of such group. This was the rule adopted in the Senate bill and the rule in the Ways and Means Committee report accompanying the House version of H.R. 3838. Such a rule would give taxpayers an incentive to reduce foreign taxes on nonseparate category income without penalty and would conform to the clearly expressed intent of both Houses of Congress.

I assume that such regulations are required to be promulgated under this provision and that such regulations must be fully effective from the effective date of new section 904(d). Is my understanding correct?

Mr. PACKWOOD. The Senator's understanding is correct. Congressional Record p. S13950-13951, 9-27-86.

[Conference Report]

*   *   *   *   *   *

f. Separate limitation for dividends from 10- to 50-percent U.S.-owned foreign corporations

Under the conference agreement, when a foreign corporation that is not a controlled foreign corporation pays dividends that are eligible for the deemed-paid foreign tax credit (which is available for dividends from foreign corporations in which the recipient owns at least 10 percent of the voting power), a separate foreign tax credit limitation applies to the dividends received. Under this separate limitation, foreign taxes associated with that dividend income may offset U.S. tax only on dividend income from that corporation. The taxes affected by this separate limitation are foreign withholding taxes imposed on these dividends and foreign taxes deemed paid with respect to these dividends. This separate limitation also applies to dividends eligible for the deemed-paid credit that are paid by a controlled foreign corporation out of earnings and profits generated while the payor was not a controlled foreign corporation. Income subject to this separate limitation is not subject to the separate limitations for passive, financial services, or shipping income.

The conferees conclude that this general treatment of dividends paid from foreign corporations more than 10- but not more than 50-percent U.S.-owned is appropriate for several reasons. First, and most importantly, application of a look-through rule to dividends from 10- to 50-percent U.S.-owned foreign corporations is not necessary under the view, generally adopted by both Houses of Congress in connection with this tax reform legislation, that it is frequently appropriate to allow cross-crediting of taxes paid by one unit of a worldwide business against income earned by another unit of that business. In the case of controlled foreign corporations, the conferees adhere to this general view, on the theory that in many cases, whether one unit or another of a multinational enterprise is considered to earn income in a business (and whether any particular unit is considered to earn income in one country rather than another) makes little economic difference, so long as the income from that business generally inures to the benefit of the same persons. In the case of foreign corporations that are not controlled foreign corporations, however, the conferees do not believe that there is sufficient identity of interest with U.S. shareholders to treat nonmajority ownership positions as units of a worldwide business. Accordingly, the conferees do not believe it is appropriate to allow cross-crediting of taxes from nonmajority interests against income derived from controlling interests or vice versa, or of taxes from one nonmajority interest against income of another nonmajority interest.

Second, application of a look-through rule to dividends from 10- to 50-percent U.S.-owned foreign corporations (required under the House bill and the Senate amendment) might be difficult for some shareholders; for example, they may not have ready access to the tax and income information of the foreign corporation which is needed in applying the look-through rule. The conferees believe that the administrative burdens associated with the corporation-by-corporation separate limitation are much less severe than those that would arise if Congress generally required look-through consideration of dividends from foreign corporations no more than 50-percent U.S.-owned. The conferees recognize that this corporation-by-corporation approach will require a computation not required under present law: allocation of expenses to dividends from between 10- and 50-percent U.S.-owned foreign corporations on a corporation-by-corporation basis. The conferees believe that this additional computation is much easier than the application of a look-through rule to these dividends would be.

Third, the conferees believe that the passive foreign investment company (PFIC) rules (added by the conference agreement; *see* discussion at * * * [¶4045]) will often prevent cross-crediting of taxes imposed on active income against passive income arising from a non-controlled foreign corporation a major portion of whose assets generate passive income. Inclusions with respect to PFIC stock will automatically be subject to the separate limitation for passive income. The conferees would not have agreed to eliminate look-through treatment in the case of dividends from nonmajority U.S.-owned foreign corporations without the backstop of the PFIC rules to prevent excessive cross-crediting of taxes.

An example illustrates the operation of the separate limitation for dividends from 10- to 50-percent U.S.-owned foreign corporations. A U.S. corporation owns 40 percent of a foreign corporation that is not a passive foreign investment company. No other U.S. person owns any interest in the foreign corporation. The foreign corporation pays a dividend of $80 to the U.S. corporation. A $16 withholding tax is imposed on that dividend, so the U.S. corporation receives a net payment of $64. A $40 deemed-paid credit is associated with the dividend. The U.S. corporation includes $120 in income ($80 grossed up by the $40 deemed-paid foreign tax). That $120 carries with it foreign tax credits of $56. Those foreign tax credits exceed the $40.80 of pre-credit U.S. tax on the $120. The conference agreement's limitation provides that the $15.20 of excess credits cannot offset U.S. tax on income other than prior or later dividends from this foreign corporation.

If a controlled foreign corporation owns 10 percent or more of the stock in foreign corporations that are not themselves controlled foreign corporations, then dividends from those non-controlled foreign corporations to the controlled foreign corporation that are eligible for the deemed-paid credit will be subject to separate limitations for dividends from 10- to 50-percent U.S.-owned foreign corporations. Under the look-through rules, subpart F inclusions with respect to the controlled foreign corporation, and dividends, interest, rents, and royalties received from it by its U.S. shareholders will be subject to separate limitations to the extent attributable to the foreign corporation's dividend income subject to the separate limitations.

As discussed at 2., below, the conference agreement generally establishes a separate limitation for high withholding tax interest, following the Senate amendment. A special rule relating to that separate limitation restricts deemed-paid credits for high withholding taxes on interest received by 10- to 50-percent U.S.-owned foreign corporations.

The separate limitation for dividends from 10- to 50-percent U.S.-owned foreign corporations is not to limit the application of the special foreign tax credit rules for foreign oil and gas income (Code sec. 907). For example, the look-through rules for inclusions with respect to foreign corporations with foreign oil and gas income (sec. 907(c)(3)) remain fully in effect, and will operate in conjunction with the separate limitation for dividends paid by 10- to 50-percent U.S.-owned foreign corporations.

These look-through rules are preserved with respect to dividends from 10- to 50-percent U.S.-owned foreign corporations, and deemed-paid credits carried by such dividends are limited for taxes on high withholding tax interest because the separate limitation for dividends from 10- to 50-percent U.S.-owned foreign corporations is not alone sufficient to prevent the cross-crediting of high foreign taxes on interest and oil and gas income against the U.S. tax on low-taxed income. Without the above restrictions, cross-crediting could still be achieved with respect to dividends from 10- to 50-percent U.S.-owned foreign corporations that earn low-taxed income as well as high-taxed interest or oil and gas income.

Effective date.—Following the Senate amendment, the conference agreement provides that the new foreign tax credit rules described above generally apply to taxable years beginning after 1986.

The conference agreement adopts the transitional rule contained in the Senate amendment for foreign tax credit carryforwards, with one modification. Under the agreement, pre-effective date excess credits for taxes on overall limitation income can be carried to post-effective date years to reduce the U.S. tax on financial services income or shipping income, subject to a limitation.

The conference agreement also adopts the transitional rules contained in the Senate amendment for foreign tax credit carrybacks, with two technical modifications. First, the conference agreement provides that, under regulations prescribed by the Secretary, proper adjustments are to be made in the application of the rule limiting carrybacks attributable to the agreement's rate reductions to take into account the repeal of the zero bracket amount and the changes in the treatment of capital gains. Second, the conference agreement provides that post-effective date excess credits for high withholding taxes on interest may not be carried back to pre-effective date years. The latter modification is necessary because the carryback of such credits to offset the U.S. tax on pre-effective date overall limitation income would defeat the purpose of the separate limitation for high withholding tax interest.

The conference agreement adopts the Senate amendment's targeted transitional rule with respect to the separate limitation for passive income.

2. Credit for High Withholding Taxes on Interest

Present Law.—The foreign tax credit is available for income, war profits, and excess profits taxes paid to a foreign country or a U.S. possession. In certain cases, a tax other than an income tax is creditable if it serves as a substitute for an income tax. Under the overall limitation, U.S. lenders can use foreign tax credits for high gross withholding taxes on a loan—the economic burden of which may be borne primarily by the borrower—to reduce the lenders' U.S. tax liability on other loan proceeds and other income.

* * * * * *

[Senate Explanation]

* * * * * *

Under the bill, a separate foreign tax credit limitation applies to high-withholding tax interest. High-withholding tax interest generally is any interest received or accrued by a bank or other financial institution or an insurance company, if such interest is subject to a foreign withholding tax (or other tax determined on a gross basis) of 5 percent or more. High-withholding tax interest also generally includes any interest subject to such a tax that is received or accrued by a person related to a bank or other financial institution or an insurance company (unless the interest is directly related to the active conduct by the related person of a trade or business). High-withholding tax interest does not include any interest derived by a finance company in connection with export financing of products manufactured by a related person.

For purposes of the new rule, a related person is any individual, corporation, partnership, trust, or estate which has 50-percent control of, or is 50-percent controlled by, the taxpayer, and any corporation, partnership, trust, or estate which is 50-percent controlled by the same person or persons which have 50-percent control of the taxpayer.

The new separate limitation applies to all foreign gross-basis taxes imposed on interest income received or accrued by the entities described above. The committee intends that, under regulations, other taxes on interest that are substantially similar in the sense that their imposition results in heavier taxation by the levying country of foreign financial institutions than residents also be subjected to the new rule.

The bill authorizes the IRS to provide by regulation that any amount equivalent to interest will be treated as interest for purposes of the separate limitation for high-withholding tax interest.

*   *   *   *   *   *

[Conference Report]

*   *   *   *   *   *

The conference agreement generally follows the Senate amendment, with the modifications described below.

The conference agreement does not limit the application of the separate limitation for high withholding tax interest to interest earned by banks, financial institutions, insurance companies, and related persons. The agreement extends the provision's application to all interest recipients (subject to the export exception) because entities other than financial institutions making high withholding tax loans may receive the same tax advantages under present law as financial institutions making such loans. The extension also permits the elimination of the related party rule.

Consistent with its extension of the provision to all interest recipients, the conference agreement extends eligibility for the export finance exception from finance companies to all interest recipients. It also clarifies generally the scope of the export finance exception. Under the conference agreement, the separate limitation for high withholding tax interest generally does not apply to interest derived from financing the sale (or other disposition) for use or consumption outside the United States of any property which is manufactured, produced, grown, or extracted in the United States by the interest recipient or a related person, and not more than 50 percent of the fair market value of which is attributable to products imported into the United States. For this purpose, the fair market value of any property imported into the United States is its appraised value, as determined by the Secretary under section 402 of the Tariff Act of 1930 (19 U.S.C. 1401a)

in connection with its importation. A related person for this purpose is defined as it is generally for subpart F purposes (Code sec. 954(d)(3), as amended by the conference agreement; *see* * * * [¶4034]). Interest excluded from the separate limitation for high withholding tax interest under the export finance exception is treated as overall limitation income unless the interest is received by an entity predominantly engaged in the active conduct of a banking, insurance, financing, or similar business. In the latter case, such interest is treated as financial services income.

As discussed at A.1.e., above, under the look-through rules, the separate limitation for high withholding tax interest applies if a controlled foreign corporation makes a high withholding tax loan; the separate limitation's applicability is not limited to high withholding tax loans by U.S. persons. This look-through treatment generally follows that provided in the Senate amendment. Without such look-through treatment, U.S. persons might avoid the separate limitation by originating high withholding tax loans in, or moving such loans to, controlled foreign corporations.

A similar potential for avoidance exists with respect to 10- to 50-percent U.S.-owned foreign corporations: Under current law, high withholding taxes imposed on interest income earned by a 10- to 50-percent U.S.-owned foreign corporation are eligible for the deemed-paid credit. In lieu of look-through treatment for dividends from 10- to 50-percent U.S.-owned foreign corporations, the conferees have adopted a special mechanism for limiting deemed-paid credits in the case of high withholding tax loans.

Under the conference agreement, taxes on high withholding tax interest, to the extent imposed at a rate exceeding 5 percent, are not to be treated as foreign taxes for purposes of determining the amount of foreign taxes deemed paid by a taxpayer with respect to dividends received from a 10- to 50-percent U.S.-owned foreign corporation.

An example illustrates the operation of this provision. Assume that an offshore bank has a 40-percent U.S. owner and a 60-percent foreign owner. It earns $2,000 of gross interest income and incurs $1,700 of interest expense. One thousand dollars of the interest income is subject to a 10-percent gross withholding tax and is, therefore, high withholding tax interest.

The foreign corporation incurs no other expenses and earns no other income. Its earnings and profits are $200 ($2,000 gross interest income less $1,700 interest expense less $100 withholding tax). It pays the full $200 out as dividends. Its U.S. shareholder receives $80 (40 percent) of the $200. The provision treats as noncreditable that portion of the 10-percent withholding tax exceeding 5 percent. Therefore, $50 (5 percent of $1,000) of the $100 withholding tax is noncreditable. The U.S. shareholder's deemed-paid credit with respect to the $80 dividend it receives is therefore reduced from $40 (40 percent of $100) to $20 (40 percent of $50).

Following the Senate amendment, the conference agreement generally makes the separate limitation for high withholding tax interest effective for taxable years beginning after 1986.

The conference agreement does not contain the general 10-year transitional rule included in the Senate amendment.

The conference agreement adopts the Senate amendment's transitional rule for foreign taxes on interest paid by borrowers in less developed countries, with the following modifications. First, the transitional rule is phased out over the five-taxable year period commencing with the taxpayer's first taxable year beginning after 1989. Eighty percent of interest received in that taxable year on a post-1989 qualified loan is not high withholding tax interest. The percentage of interest on a post-1989 qualified loan that is not high withholding tax interest in the second taxable year beginning is 60; in the third taxable year is 40; in the fourth taxable year is 20; and in the fifth and succeeding taxable years is zero. Interest on a new loan entered into after 1989 will not be entitled to transition relief. For purposes of determining what constitutes a new loan, the conferees intend the standard of Code section 1001 to apply.

Second, interest paid by borrowers in 18 additional less developed countries is eligible for transitional relief. These countries are Costa Rica, the Dominican Republic, Guyana, Honduras, Jamaica, Liberia, Madagascar, Malawi, Mozambique, Niger, Panama, Romania, Senegal, Sierra Leone, the Sudan, Togo, Zaire, and Zambia.

Third, the amount of the lender's foreign tax credits generally protected by the transitional rule is 110 percent of the product of the base credit amount[1] and the applicable interest rate adjustment in the case of pre-1990 qualified loans, rather than, as under the Senate amendment, such product increased by 3 percent annually through 1989. The agreement clarifies that the applicable interest rate adjustment generally equals the ratio of the weighted 6-month London Interbank Offered Rate (LIBOR) for the taxable year in question to LIBOR on November 15, 1985. The conferees understand that the 11 a.m. 6-month LIBOR quoted by a major bank on November 15, 1985, was 8¼ percent and intend that this rate apply for purposes of the transitional rule.

Fourth, no relief is allowed by reason of the transitional rule for any foreign tax imposed on interest payable with respect to any qualified loan to the extent that the rate of such tax exceeds the foreign withholding tax rate applicable to interest payable with respect to such loan on November 16, 1985. This rule is intended to prevent taxpayers from deriving benefits under the transitional

rule from foreign withholding tax rates that have increased since November 16, 1985. For example, if a foreign country doubles its withholding tax rate applicable to a qualified loan over the rate applicable on November 16, 1985, then 50 percent of the interest earned with respect to such loan will not be eligible for transitional relief.

Interest to which the transitional rule applies is passive income (subject to the high-tax kick-out, and the other exceptions to the separate limitation for passive income) unless received by an entity predominantly engaged in the active conduct of a banking, insurance, financing, or similar business. In the latter case, under the predominantly engaged test, such interest is subject to the separate limitation for financial services income.

3. Deemed-Paid Credit

Present Law.—A U.S. corporation that owns at least 10 percent of a foreign corporation's voting stock and that has dividend income from the foreign corporation may generally take a deemed-paid credit for a share of the foreign taxes that the foreign corporation paid on the earnings out of which the dividend is paid. A similar credit applies when a 10-percent U.S. corporate shareholder includes in income a portion of a controlled foreign corporation's undistributed earnings under subpart F.

A dividend or subpart F inclusion is considered paid first from earnings and profits of the current year and then from accumulated profits of each preceding year. Actual distributions made in the first 60 days of a taxable year are generally treated as made from the prior year's earnings and profits.

Earnings and profits may be computed in a different manner for actual dividend distributions than for subpart F inclusions.

* * * * * *

[House Explanation]

* * * * * *

Explanation of Provision.—For purposes of computing the deemed paid foreign tax credit, dividends or subpart F inclusions will be considered made from the pool of all the distributing corporation's accumulated earnings and profits. Accumulated earnings and profits for this purpose will include the earnings and profits of the current year undiminished by the current distribution or subpart F inclusion. The rule treating actual distributions made in the first 60 days of a taxable year as made from the prior year's accumulated profits is repealed. A dividend or subpart F inclusion is considered to bring with it a pro rata share of the accumulated foreign taxes paid by the subsidiary.

Earnings and profits computations for these purposes will be made under rules similar to those now required for subpart F deemed dividends (and permitted for actual

---

[Footnote ¶ 4027] (1) Following the Senate amendment, the conference agreement defines the base credit amount as the principal amount of loans held by the taxpayer on November 16, 1985, multiplied by the product of the interest rate applicable to such loan on November 16, 1985, and the foreign withholding tax rate applicable to interest payable with respect to such loan on November 16, 1985.

distributions). However, the rules for translating foreign currency would be modified.

Pooling will apply prospectively only. Future dividends will be treated as paid first out of the pool of all accumulated profits derived by the payor after the effective date. Dividends in excess of that accumulated pool of post-effective date earnings and profits will be treated as paid out of pre-effective date accumulated profits under the ordering principles of present law.

The pooling provisions of the bill apply only for purposes of determining the deemed-paid foreign tax credit. For example, there is no change in the present law provisions limiting to current earnings and profits the amount that can be treated as a current subpart F inclusion to the controlled foreign corporation's shareholders. However, the deemed-paid credit with respect to such an inclusion is determined on the pooling basis, in order to limit opportunities to avoid the effect of pooling by creating subpart F inclusions.

There is no change in the present law provision that a subpart F inclusion from a lower-tier foreign subsidiary is deemed to be included directly in the U.S. shareholder's income without passing through any upper tier foreign corporation.

The Secretary of the Treasury is authorized to prescribe rules to implement the intent of these provisions. For example, the Secretary may consider whether or to what extent post-effective date distributions of pre-1985 profits from a lower-tier foreign subsidiary to an upper-tier foreign subsidiary will retain their pre-1985 character in the hands of the distributee corporation or will be treated as post-effective date earnings (and taxes) that are pooled at the upper-tier foreign corporation level.

In the case of a foreign corporation that does not have a 10 percent (direct or indirect) U.S. shareholder who would qualify for the deemed-paid credit, as of the first taxable year the bill is generally effective, pooling will begin with the first day of the first taxable year thereafter in which there is such a 10-percent shareholder.

* * * * * *

[Conference Report]

* * * * * *

The conference agreement generally follows the House bill, with the modifications described below.

First, the agreement is effective for taxable years beginning after 1986.

Second, the agreement grants the Secretary limited regulatory authority, in the case of subpart F inclusions, to modify the pooling method for computing the deemed-paid credit that the legislation otherwise prescribes. This additional grant of regulatory authority is provided primarily to permit the IRS to address certain technical difficulties which it believes may arise in implementing the pooling rules with respect to subpart F inclusions *other than* those for increases in earnings invested in U.S. property. As the Reports of the Committee on Ways and Means and the Committee on Finance on this tax reform legislation indicate, taxpayers should not be able to avoid the effect of pooling by creating subpart F inclusions.

Third, the agreement requires the Secretary to provide such regulations as may be necessary or appropriate to carry out the purposes of the subpart F deemed-paid credit provision (Code sec. 960), including rules which provide for the separate application of that provision to reflect the separate application of the foreign tax credit limitation to separate types of income and loss. The conferees anticipate that the Secretary will exercise this regulatory authority to ensure that, if subpart F income is in fact subject to little or no foreign tax, then the amount of the foreign tax credit determined under section 960 with regard to such income will properly reflect that fact.

4. Effect of Foreign and U.S. Losses on Foreign Tax Credit

Present Law.—Under the overall foreign tax credit limitation, a taxpayer first uses a net loss incurred in any foreign country to reduce its income from other foreign countries. If a taxpayer's net foreign losses subject to one separate limitation exceed its foreign income subject to that limitation, the excess arguably reduces the taxpayer's U.S. source taxable income.

An overall U.S. loss first reduces foreign income earned in the loss year and hence pre-credit U.S. tax in that year.

* * * * *

[Senate Explanation]

* * * * *

4. Foreign losses.—The bill provides that, for foreign tax credit limitation purposes, losses for any taxable year in separate foreign tax credit limitation "baskets" and in the overall limitation basket offset U.S. source income only to the extent that the aggregate amount of such losses exceeds the aggregate amount of foreign income earned in other baskets. These losses (to the extent that they do not exceed foreign income for the year) are to be allocated on a proportionate basis among (and operate to reduce) foreign income baskets in which the entity earns income in the loss year. Losses in all separate limitation baskets (enumerated in Code sec. 904(d)(1), as amended by the bill), including the passive and high-withholding tax interest income baskets, are subject to this rule.

A separate limitation loss recharacterization rule applies to foreign losses allocated to foreign income pursuant to the above rule. The recharacterization rule is similar to the overall foreign extraction loss recapture rule of present law (Code sec. 907(c)(4)). If a separate limitation loss or an overall limitation loss was allocated to income subject to another separate limitation (or, in the case of a separate limitation loss, to overall limitation income) and the loss basket has income for a subsequent taxable year, then that income (to the extent that it does not exceed the aggregate separate limitation losses in the loss basket not previously recharacterized under this provision) is to be recharacterized as income previously offset by the loss in proportion to the prior loss allocation not previously taken into account under this provision.

To the extent that that prior loss allocation, by reducing (for limitation purposes) foreign income that was subject to high foreign taxes, gave rise to additional excess foreign tax credits, the subsequent treatment of additional income as if it were such high tax foreign income will increase the foreign tax credit limitation in the year or years when the recharacterization occurs. To the extent that the loss allocation, by reducing (for limitation purposes) income that bore little or no foreign tax, reduced post-foreign tax credit U.S. tax liability in the loss year, the subsequent treatment of additional income as income of the type that bore little foreign tax will result in a recovery of some or all of the previously foregone U.S. tax revenue in the year or years when the recharacterization occurs.

* * * * * *

The bill's foreign loss allocation and separate limitation loss recharacterization rules apply to foreign persons to which the bill's separate limitation look-through rules apply, as well as to U.S. persons. The bill requires the IRS to prescribe such regulations as may be necessary or appropriate for purposes of the separate limitations, including regulations for the application of the foreign loss allocation and separate limitation loss recharacterization rules in the case of income paid through one or more entities or between two or more chains of entities.

Foreign taxes on income recharacterized under the separate limitation loss recharacterization rule are not themselves to be recharacterized. For example, foreign taxes on overall limitation income that is recharacterized as separate limitation income in a year following an overall limitation loss year may only be credited against U.S. tax on other overall limitation income.

For purposes of the bill's foreign loss allocation and separate limitation loss recharacterization provisions, the amount of a loss in a separate limitation basket or in the overall limitation basket is determined under the principles of the present law provision that defines foreign oil and gas extraction losses for purposes of the overall foreign extraction loss recapture rule (Code sec. 907(c)(4)(B)). Thus, a loss in the separate limitation basket or the overall limitation basket is the amount by which the taxpayer's (or in the case of an affiliated group filing a consolidated return, the group's) gross income from activities giving rise to income in that basket is exceeded by the sum of the expenses, losses, and other deductions prop-

erly apportioned or allocated to that income and a ratable part of any expenses, losses, or other deductions which cannot definitely be allocated to some item or class of gross income (under Code sec. 862(b) or 863).

If no foreign loss has been sustained in the case of an affiliated group of corporations filing a consolidated return, then no such loss is subject to recharacterization under this provision even if a member of the group had such a loss and the member is subsequently sold or otherwise leaves the group. In computing the amount of a foreign loss for purposes of the bill's foreign loss allocation and separate limitation loss recharacterization provisions, the net operating loss deduction (under Code sec. 172(a)) is not to be taken into account. For purposes of these provisions, a taxpayer is to be treated as sustaining a foreign loss whether or not the taxpayer claims a foreign tax credit for the year of the loss.

* * * * * *

* * * U.S. losses.—The bill provides that any U.S. loss for any taxable year is allocated among (and operates to reduce) foreign income in different limitation baskets on a proporationate basis. Assume, for example, that a U.S. corporation has a $100 U.S. loss, $150 of net overall limitation income, and $50 of net passive income in a taxable year. Under the bill, $75 of the loss reduces overall limitation income and $25 of the loss reduces passive income. For foreign tax credit limitation purposes then, the corporation has $75 of overall limitation income and $25 of passive income for the taxable year.

This rule applies after any foreign losses have been allocated among the foreign income baskets in which the taxpayer earns income.

* * * * * *

[Conference Report]
* * * * * *

The conference agreement follows the Senate amendment, with several technical clarifications.

The first clarification is that the conferees intend that, where a loss is incurred in more than one foreign income basket in a particular year, each such loss be allocated proportionately to foreign income, and then to U.S. income. For example, assume that a U.S. corporation earns $200 of U.S. income and $20 of foreign income subject to the separate limitation for certain distributions from a FSC. The corporation also incurs a $20 overall limitation loss and a $5 shipping basket loss. Under the foreign loss allocation rule, the $20 and $5 separate limitation losses are to be allocated first to the $20 of FSC distributions; only after that allocation is any portion of either separate limitation loss allocated to U.S. income. Each separate limitation loss must be allocated to foreign income in proportion to the ratio of total foreign income to total foreign loss. Thus, $16 of the $20 overall limitation loss ($20 $\times$ $20/$25) reduces the $20 of FSC distributions and $4 of the $5 shipping basket loss ($5 × $20/$25) reduces the $20 of FSC distributions. The remaining $4 of overall limitation loss and $1 of shipping basket loss reduce the $200 of U.S. income. For the year, then, the corporation has $195 of U.S. income and no foreign income for foreign tax credit limitation purposes. If the corporation earns sufficient overall limitation income in a later year, then, after application of the foreign loss recapture rule of present law (Code sec. 904(f)), $16 of such income will be subject to recharacterization as FSC distribution income. If the corporation earns shipping income in a later year, then, after application of the foreign loss recapture rule, $4 of such income will be subject to recharacterization as FSC distribution income.

The second clarification relates to the overall foreign loss recapture rule of present law. In light of the new foreign loss allocation and recharacterization rules, the conferees believe that one aspect of that present-law rule's application should be clarified. The conferees intend that foreign income earned in a year following an overall foreign loss year be recharacterized as U.S. income under the overall foreign loss recapture rule only to the extent that that foreign income is of the same limitation type as the previous loss. For example, assume that a U.S. corporation incurs a $100 overall ¨.mitation loss and earns $300 of U.S. incom in a taxable year. The full $100 loss is an overall foreign loss subject to recapture in a later year because U.S. income is offset by the full amount of the loss. In the following taxable year, the taxpayer earns $50 of overall limitation income, $150 of passive limitation income, and $250 of U.S. income. The conferees intend that the present-law 50-percent limitation (sec. 904(f)(1)(B)) on the amount of foreign income that must be recharacterized as U.S. income in a taxable year be applied to the full amount of the corporation's foreign income, $200, as it would be under present law. Thus, up to $100 of foreign income can be recharacterized as U.S. income under the 50-percent limitation. However, the corporation has only $50 of income of the same limitation type (overall) as the prior year foreign loss. Only that $50 then is to be recharacterized as U.S. income under the overall foreign loss recapture rule. Thus, for foreign tax credit limitation purposes, the corporation has $150 of passive limitation income, $300 of U.S. income, and no overall limitation income for the taxable year. Up to $50 of overall limitation income earned in a subsequent year will be subject to recapture because only $50 of the $100 overall foreign loss incurred in the first taxable year has been recaptured.

The third technical clarification is of the interaction of the new U.S. loss allocation rule, on the one hand, and the foreign loss allocation and recharacterization rules, on the other. The following example illustrates how these rules will operate in relation to one another.

Assume that a U.S. corporation incurs a $50 overall limitation loss abroad and a $100 U.S. loss. It also earns $600 of foreign income subject to the separate limitation for shipping income and $400 of foreign income subject to the separate limitation for passive income. The foreign loss allocation rule applies before the U.S. loss allocation rule. Under the former rule, $30 of the overall limitation loss reduces the $600 of shipping income and the remaining $20 of such loss reduces the $400 of passive income.

Before allocation of the U.S. loss then, the U.S. corporation has $570 of shipping income and $380 of passive income. Under the conference agreement, $60 of the U.S. loss reduces the $570 of shipping income and the remaining $40 of such loss reduces the $380 of passive income. Thus, for foreign tax credit limitation purposes, the corporation has no U.S. income, $510 of shipping income, and $340 of passive income for the year.

In the following year, the corporation incurs a $780 U.S. loss. It also earns $200 of overall limitation income and $600 of shipping income. The U.S. loss allocation rule applies before the foreign loss recharacterization rule. Under the former rule, $195 of the U.S. loss reduces the $200 of overall limitation income and the remaining $585 of such loss reduces the $600 of shipping income.

The corporation thus has no U.S. income, $5 of overall limitation income, and $15 of shipping income for the year before the application of the foreign loss recharacterization rule. Under that rule, $3 of the overall limitation income is recharacterized as shipping income and the remaining $2 of the overall limitation income is recharacterized as passive income. This recharacterization occurs because, in the prior year, $30 of shipping income and $20 of passive income was eliminated by a $50 overall limitation loss.

In the current year then, the corporation has no U.S. income, $18 of shipping income, and $2 of passive income for foreign tax credit limitation purposes. If the corporation earns overall limitation income in later years, up to $45 ($50-$5) of such income will be subject to the foreign loss recharacterization rule.

The fourth clarification is that the new foreign loss allocation and recharacterization rules are to apply on an affiliated group basis in the case of an affiliated group filing a consolidated tax return.

Fifth, the conferees intend that the foreign loss allocation and recharacterization rules apply to net operating loss ("NOL") carryovers. The conferees expect the Secretary to issue regulations adapting the new rules as necessary for this purpose.

The following example illustrates how the foreign loss allocation and recharacterization rules will apply in cases involving NOL carryovers: Assume that a U.S. corporation which operates primarily abroad incurs a $200 NOL. The loss is attributable to foreign activities that would generate overall limitation income. In the following year, the corporation earns $180 of overall limitation income and $30 of income subject to the separate limitation for passive income. The corporation carries the prior year's $200 NOL forward. Under the foreign loss allocation rule, the NOL offsets the $180 of overall limitation first, since the NOL arose in the overall limitation category. The remaining $20 of the loss reduces (to $10) the corporation's passive income.

In the next year, the corporation earns $220 of overall limitation income. Under the foreign loss recharacterization rule, $20 of this overall limitation income is recharacterized as passive income because $20 of passive income was offset by the overall limitation NOL in the preceding year. Thus, for foreign tax credit limitation purposes, the corporation has $200 of overall limitation income and $20 of passive income for the year.

Sixth, the conferees expect that the regulations implementing the foreign loss allocation and recharacterization rules will apply the latter rule to an entity that is a successor entity to one that benefitted from the former rule.

As under the House bill and the Senate amendment, foreign taxes on income recharacterized under the foreign loss recharacterization rule are not themselves to be recharacterized. For example, foreign taxes on overall limitation income that is recharacterized as separate limitation income in a year following an overall limitation loss year may only be credited against U.S. tax on other overall limitation income.

5. Subsidies

Present Law

Under Treasury regulation sec. 1.901-2(e)(3), a tax is not creditable if it is used directly or indirectly as a subsidy to the taxpayer or certain related persons.

*   *   *   *   *   *

[Senate Explanation]

*   *   *   *   *   *

* * * Subsidies

The bill also contains a provision intended to clarify and codify a rule embodied in Treas. Reg. sec. 1.901-2(e)(3). That regulation generally provides that any foreign government subsidies accorded in connection with foreign taxes reduce the creditable portion of such taxes. Under the bill, any income, war profits, or excess profits tax is not treated as a creditable tax to the extent that the amount of the tax is used, directly, or indirectly, by the country imposing the tax to provide a subsidy by any means (such as through a refund or credit) to the taxpayer, a related person (within the meaning of Code sec. 482), any party to the transaction, or any party to a related transaction, and the subsidy is determined, directly or indirectly, by reference to the amount of the tax, or the base used to compute the tax.

Assume, for example, that a U.S. bank lends money to a foreign development bank.

The foreign development bank relends the money to companies resident in the foreign bank's residence country. The foreign bank's residence country imposes a withholding tax on the interest that the foreign development bank pays to the U.S. bank. On the date that the tax is withheld by the foreign bank, 50 percent of the tax is credited by the levying country to an account of the foreign development bank. The levying country requires the foreign development bank to transfer the amount credited to the borrowing companies. Since the amount transferred by the levying country to the borrowing companies (through the foreign bank) is determined by reference to the amount of the tax and is a subsidy to parties to transactions that are related to the taxable transaction, the amount transferred is not treated as a creditable tax under the bill.

*   *   *   *   *   *

[Conference Report]

*   *   *   *   *   *

The conference agreement follows the Senate amendment.

This codification of Treas. reg. sec. 1.901-2(e)(3) is not intended to modify the application of existing Treas. reg. sec. 1.901-2(f)(2)(i), which generally treats a tax as paid by the taxpayer even if another party to a transaction with the taxpayer agrees, as part of the transaction, to assume liability for the tax. The latter regulation by its terms applies notwithstanding anything to the contrary in Treas. reg. sec. 1.901-2(e)(3).

The conferees intend that the amount of any withholding tax paid be positively established through documentation provided in accordance with the requirements of Code section 905(b) and Treas. reg. sec. 1.905-2. In this regard, the conferees emphasize that the mere fact that withholding took place does not necessarily constitute adequate proof of the amount of tax paid.

The conferees believe that the rule set forth in *Lederman v. Commissioner,* 6 T.C. 991 (1946), which suggests that payment is proved ipso facto by the act of withholding, is subject to abuse. Application of the *Lederman* rule is of particular concern in the context of a "net loan," under which the net amount paid to the U.S. payee is unaffected by the amount of tax withheld. In such a case, it is impossible to determine prima facie whether a claimed amount withheld has actually been withheld, since the amount received by the payee remains unchanged. The logic of the *Lederman* rule simply does not apply in such circumstances, and external proof of withholding and payment over should be required.

The conferees' concerns with respect to documentation of foreign taxes are heightened by the problem of subsidized foreign tax payments. The conferees are informed that in some cases amounts withheld are retained by the withholding agent, in whole or in part, with the explicit or implicit approval of the foreign sovereign. Particularly in the case of a net loan, both payee and payor stand to benefit from a high withholding "tax" that is never paid over to the government; the payor receives cash in hand (equivalent to a lower interest rate) while the payee receives a foreign tax credit for a fictional tax, without any reduction in net proceeds. Although this provision of the agreement, which codifies the prohibition of direct and indirect subsidies of foreign taxes, confirms that a foreign tax credit is disallowed in such cases, the conferees are concerned that without a strict documentation requirement the Service would find it difficult to determine when such a subsidy had been given. Therefore, the conferees expect that a receipt or other positive proof of payment will generally be required to establish the amount of foreign

withholding tax paid with respect to foreign source interest income received by U.S. taxpayers.

[*Effective date.*—Applies generally to tax years beginning after 12-31-86 and carrybacks to years before 1987. Separate limitation losses rule applies to losses incurred in tax years beginning after 12-31-86. Subsidy taxes rule applies to taxes paid or accrued in tax years beginning after 12-31-86. Rule for determining deemed paid credit applies to distributions by foreign corporations from and inclusions attributable to earnings and profits for tax years beginning after 12-31-86. Ed.]

[¶ 4028] SECTION 1211. DETERMINATION OF SOURCE IN CASE OF SALES OF PERSONAL PROPERTY

(Secs. 861, 862, 865, 871, 881 and 904 of the Code)

[Senate Explanation]

*   *   *   *   *   *

Explanation of Provision.—

Overview.—* * * income derived from the sale of personal property, tangible or intangible, other than inventory property and depreciable personal property, by a U.S. resident is generally sourced in the United States. Similar income derived by a nonresident generally is treated as foreign source. For purposes of the bill, the term sale includes an exchange or other disposition. Also, any possession of the United States is treated as a foreign country for purposes of this provision. Income that U.S. persons derive from the sale of inventory property, as defined in Code section 1221(l), continues to be sourced under present law (i.e., the title passage rule). Income derived from the sale of depreciable personal property is sourced pursuant to the rules described below.

The bill generally provides that an individual is a resident of the United States for this purpose if the individual has a tax home (as defined in Code sec. 911(d)(3)) in the United States. The bill provides that any corporation, partnership, trust, or estate which is a United States person (as defined in sec. 7701(a)(30)) generally is a U.S. resident for this purpose. All other individuals and entities generally are nonresidents for purposes of these source rules.

Special rules for U.S. persons.—The bill contains an exception to the above described residence rules for U.S. citizens and resident aliens. The exception provides that U.S. citizens and resident aliens are not treated as nonresidents with respect to any sale of personal property unless the gain from the sale is actually taxed at a rate equal to or exceeding 10 percent in a foreign country. Thus, a U.S. citizen or resident alien cannot maintain a tax home in another country, sell his personal property, claim residency in such country, and generate foreign source

income unless the person actually pays tax on the income from such sale to a foreign country at a 10 percent rate or higher.

The bill also provides two special rules for gains derived by U.S. residents. The first special rule provides that U.S. residents that derive income from sales of personal property (other than inventory property) attributable to an office or other fixed place of business maintained outside the United States generate foreign source income. This rule does not apply, however, if the income from the sale is not actually taxed at a 10 percent rate or higher in a foreign country. This special rule is designed to reflect the committee's general intention that the source of income from substantive operations is the location of those operations. The bill provides that current law principles are to apply in determining when sales are attributable to an office or other fixed place of business.

The second special rule provides that if a U.S. resident sells stock of an affiliate in the foreign country in which the affiliate derived from the active conduct of a trade or business more than 50 percent of its gross income for the 3-year period ending with the close of the affiliate's taxable year immediately preceding the year during which the sale occurred, any gain from the sale is foreign source. Affiliate, for this purpose, means any corporation (including a foreign corporation) whose stock (both voting power and value) is at least 80 percent owned.

The committee is aware that some of the source rules in the bill may conflict with source rules prescribed in U.S. income tax treaties. The source rules in the bill reflect the committee's policy that income not taxed, or not likely to be taxed, by a foreign country generally should not be treated as foreign source income for purposes of the foreign tax credit limitations. The committee does not intend that treaty source rules should apply in a manner which would frustrate the policy underlying the source rules in the bill that untaxed income not increase a U.S. taxpayer's foreign tax credit limitation. The committee intends this treatment for all of the bill's source rules, not only those governing sales of personal property.

Income derived from the sale of depreciable personal property.—Subject to a special rule, the bill provides that gain to the extent of prior depreciation deductions from the sale of depreciable personal property is sourced in the United States if the depreciation deductions giving rise to such income were previously allocated against U.S. source income. If the deductions giving rise to such income were previously allocated against foreign source income, gain from such sales (to the extent of prior deductions) is sourced without the United States. Any gain in excess of prior depreciation deductions is sourced pursuant to present law, i.e., sourced pursuant to the title passage rule.

Depreciation deductions, as defined by the bill, mean any depreciation or amortization or any other deduction allowable under any provision of the Code which treats an otherwise capital expenditure as a deductible expense. Depreciable personal property, as defined in the bill, means any personal property if the adjusted basis of the property includes depreciation adjustments. Depreciation adjustments are adjustments reflected in the adjusted basis of any property on account of depreciation deductions (whether allowed with respect to such property or other property and whether allowed to the taxpayer or to any other person).

The bill provides a special rule for purposes of determining the source of income from the sale of certain depreciable personal property. This rule provides that if personal property is either used predominantly in the United States or predominantly outside the United States for any taxable year, the taxpayer must treat the allowable deductions for such year as being allocable entirely against U.S. source or foreign source income, as the case may be. This rule is provided so as not to require a segregation of previously allowable deductions if the person knows the property was used predominantly in the United States or predominantly outside the United States, as the case may be. A segregation of allowable deductions is required, however, for certain personal property generally used outside the United States (personal property described in sec. 48(a)(2)(B)).

Income derived from the sale of intangible property.—The bill provides that in the case of income derived from the sale of intangible property, to the extent the payments are not contingent on the productivity, use, or disposition of the intangible, the general rule of this provision applies. That is, income derived from such sales is sourced in the country of the seller's residence. If payments are contingent on productivity, use, or disposition, the source rules applicable to royalties apply. For purposes of the bill, intangible property is any patent, copyright, secret process or formula, goodwill, trademark, trade name or other like property. Notwithstanding the general rule, income attributable to the sale of goodwill is sourced where the goodwill was generated.

Income derived from the sale of personal property by foreign persons.—In the case of nonresidents, the bill repeals the title passage rule with respect to sales of all personal property (except for foreign tax credit purposes). The term nonresident is defined pursuant to the bill's general definition. The bill provides that income derived from sales of personal property that are attributable to an office or other fixed place of business maintained in the United States by a nonresident is generally treated as U.S. source (except for foreign tax credit purposes). Pursuant to the Code's general rules defining effectively connected income, such income is considered effectively connected and will be subject to U.S. tax. The bill provides, however, that if a source country imposes tax on such income, the income is treated as foreign source for purposes of section 906 (so as to allow the nonresident a foreign tax credit). Current law principles are to apply in determining when sales are attributable to an office or other fixed place of business.

Income derived by nonresidents that is treated as U.S. source by the rules described above is not treated as U.S. source, however, if the property is sold or exchanged for use, consumption, or disposition outside the United States and an office or other fixed place of business maintained outside the United States by such person materially participates in the sale.

The bill clarifies that gain from the sale of stock in a controlled foreign corporation by a U.S. shareholder that is treated under section 1248(a) as a dividend is sourced pursuant to the source provisions governing dividends (generally residence of the payor).

The bill provides that regulations are to be prescribed by the Secretary carrying out the purposes of the bill's provisions including the application of the bill's provisions to income derived from trading in futures contracts, forward contracts, options contracts, and similar securities.

The bill repeals section 871(e) (relating to the treatment of certain payments from the sale of intangible property to the extent that such payments are contingent on the productivity, use, or disposition of such property). By repealing section 871(e), taxpayers are to segregate the gain from the sale or exchange of applicable intangible property into gain contingent on the productivity, use, or disposition of such property and gain which is not so contingent. Withholding is required only with respect to U.S. source payments that are contingent on the productivity, use or disposition of such property.

Effective Date.—The provisions affecting foreign persons (other than controlled foreign corporations) are effective for transactions after March 18, 1986. The provisions affecting U.S. persons and controlled foreign corporations are effective in taxable years beginning after December 31, 1986.

* * * * * *

[Conference Report]

* * * * * *

Conference Agreement.—The conference agreement follows the Senate amendment with technical clarifications and with a requirement that the Treasury Department study the effect of current law's title passage rule in light of the agreement's lower tax rates and in light of Congressional trade concerns, and report back to the House Committee on Ways and Means and the Senate Committee on Finance not later than September 30, 1987.

The managers also wish to clarify one aspect of the Senate amendment. It is intended that the 10-percent foreign tax payment requirement for foreign sourcing of income from sales of certain property through a fixed place of business be satisfied only if the income is taxed abroad at an effective rate of at least 10 percent.

[¶ 4029] SECTION 1212. SPECIAL RULES FOR TRANSPORTATION INCOME

(Sec. 861, 863, 871, 872, 882, 883, 886 of the Code)

[Senate Explanation]

*   *   *   *   *   *

Source of transportation income.—The bill provides that 50 percent of all transportation income attributable to transportation which begins or ends in the United States is U.S. source. The provision applies equally to U.S. and foreign persons. The bill modifies present law by excluding from transportation income the performance of services by alien seamen or airline employees with respect to transportation that begins or ends in the United States. Income from the performance of services is still transportation income for transportation that begins and ends in the United States and for transportation between the United States and a U.S. possession. As under present law, transportation income includes income from the bareboat charter hire of ships or aircraft. However, it is the committee's intention that transportation income not include income derived from the lease of a vessel if such vessel is not used to transport cargo or persons for hire. In such instances, the committee intends such income to be characterized as ocean activity income and be sourced in the country of residence of the person earning the income, as prescribed in section 915 of the bill.

The bill also repeals the special rule relating to the lease or disposition of vessels, aircraft, or spacecraft which are constructed in the United States (sec. 861(e)) and the special rule relating to the lease of an aircraft to a regularly scheduled U.S. air carrier (sec. 863(c)(2)(B)). The source of this income to the extent treated as transportation income is determined under the general rule described above.

The bill applies only to transportation income attributable to transportation that begins or ends in the United States. Thus, if a voyage that begins in Europe has intermediate foreign stops before it arrives in the United States, 50 percent of the income that is attributable to the cargo (or persons) carried from its port of origin or from any of the intermediate ports to the United States is considered U.S. source. Cargo or passengers off-loaded at intermediate ports before arriv- al in the United States will not give rise to U.S. source income.

The committee intends that income derived from furnishing round-trip travel of persons originating or ending in the United States by a carrier be treated as transportation income attributable to transportation that begins (for the outbound portion), or ends (for the inbound portion), in the United States under the bill's provision. Thus, 50 percent of the income attributable to the outbound transportation and 50 percent of the income attributable to the inbound transportation is U.S. source. For example, 50 percent of the income attributable to both ends of an air voyage from the United States, to a foreign country, and back to the United States (or from a foreign country, to the United States, and back to a foreign country), is intended to be U.S. source.

*   *   *   *   *   *

[Conference Report]

*   *   *   *   *   *

Source of income.—The conference agreement follows the Senate amendment. The conferees wish to clarify that income derived from personal services performed as an employee that is excluded from U.S. source gross transportation income continues to be taxed as under present law. Thus, the sourcing of such income is unchanged: income attributable to services performed in the United States or in U.S. territorial waters is U.S. source.

*   *   *   *   *   *

[Senate Explanation]

*   *   *   *   *   *

Reciprocal exemption.—The bill modifies the present law reciprocal exemption by requiring foreign persons to be resident of a foreign country that reciprocally exempts U.S. persons rather than determining exemption based on the place of registry or documentation.

The bill provides that an alien individual must be a resident of a foreign country which grants U.S. citizens and domestic corporations an equivalent exemption in order for the alien individual to avail himself of the reciprocal exemption. The committee intends that a country which, as a result of a treaty with the United States, exempts U.S. citizens and domestic corporations from tax in that country on income derived from the operation of ships or aircraft, has an equivalent exemption, even though the treaty technically contains certain additional requirements other than residence such as U.S. registration or documentation of the ship or aircraft.

A foreign corporation must be organized in a foreign country which grants U.S. citizens and domestic corporations an equivalent exemption in order for the corporation to avail itself of the reciprocal exemption.

However, the bill further provides that, in the case of a foreign corporation claiming a reciprocal exemption, if 50 percent or more of the ultimate individual owners of the foreign corporation (determined under the principles of secs. 958(a) and 958(b)) are not residents of a foreign country that grants U.S. persons equivalent exemption (either by treaty or by reciprocal exemption), the foreign corporation is not able to claim the reciprocal exemption. It is the committee's intention that any treaty exemption for this purpose be based on residence.

For purposes of applying the 50-percent test to a foreign corporation (or other type of entity), if the foreign corporation is a U.S. controlled foreign corporation, the U.S. shareholders of the foreign corporation are treated as residents of the foreign country in which the corporation is organized. The bill also provides that the look-through rule does not apply to a foreign corporation (or a parent corporation if both corporations are organized in the same country) if the stock of the corporation (or of a parent corporation) is primarily and regularly traded on an established securities market in the foreign country in which the corporation is organized. For this purpose primary is intended to mean that more shares trade in the country of organization than in any other country.

The bill provides that the residence-based reciprocal exemption applies to gross income (instead of earnings as under present law). Therefore, the residence-based reciprocal exemption provisions apply to the gross-basis tax. The bill also expands the reciprocal exemption to include income derived from the lease of vessels or aircraft as long as a foreign country exempts U.S. persons from its tax on comparable income. The bill further provides regulatory authority to extend the reciprocal exemption by agreement on a partial basis. For example, if the United States and a foreign country agree that only regularly scheduled transportation be exempted from tax, then the Code's exemption can apply.

* * * * * *

[Conference Report]

* * * * * *

Reciprocal exemption.—The conference agreement generally follows the Senate amendment, with the following clarifications. The agreement provides that a foreign corporation organized in a country that exempts U.S. citizens and domestic corpora-

tions from tax on shipping income will be exempt from U.S. tax on shipping income, notwithstanding that third country residents have interests in the corporation, provided at least 50 percent of its value is benefically owned by individuals that reside in countries which have reciprocal tax exemptions with the United States. Individuals that reside in countries which have reciprocal exemptions with the United States qualify for this purpose even if they are citizens or subjects of third countries that do not have such exemptions in place. Residence, for this purpose, is intended to mean the country of an individual's tax home. The conferees wish to clarify that the agreement's provisions do not deny any benefits available under present law in an income tax treaty between the United States and a foreign country.

* * * * * *

[House Explanation]

* * * * * *

Gross-basis tax.—The bill provides for a gross-basis tax on the U.S. source transportation income of foreign persons. The bill uses the present law source rule definition of transportation income. Thus, transportation income is gross income derived from, or in connection with, the use (or hiring or leasing for use) of any vessel or aircraft, or the performance of services directly related to such use. Under the bill, however, the applicable source rules are changed to provide that when such income is attributable to transportation which begins or ends in the United States, it will be treated as 50 percent U.S. source income and 50 percent foreign source income without regard to the percentage of the related costs incurred or assets located in the United States (sec. 613(a) of the bill and Code sec. 863(c)).

The tax rate provided in the bill is four percent of the gross amount. The committee intends, if Code sections 871 or 881 (relating to withholding tax on certain types of fixed or determinable payments) would apply under present law, that the four-percent tax apply instead. Thus, the four-percent tax is to apply to rental income derived from bareboat charter operations rather than the 30-percent tax.

The bill provides, however, that if the foreign person is engaged in a trade or business in the United States and the foreign person's transportation income is effectively connected with that trade or business, the foreign person must, in lieu of paying the four percent gross-basis tax, file a U.S. tax return and pay tax on the basis of its net income.

The bill provides, however, that in order for the foreign person's transportation income to be effectively connected with the conduct of a U.S. trade or business, the foreign person must have regularly scheduled aircraft or vessels that come into and out of the United States to which substantially all of its U.S. source transportation income is attributable and the foreign person must maintain an office in the United States through which the foreign person conducts its U.S. transportation business. Thus, foreign persons are not able to merely make an occasional flight or voyage to the U.S., treat themselves as being engaged in a U.S. trade or business, and avoid the gross-basis tax.

* * * * *

[Senate Explanation]

* * * * *

The bill's gross-basis tax is to be collected by return. However, the committee will continue to study whether alternate, potentially more effective, methods of collecting the tax are feasible. The committee also intends that the Secretary monitor compliance with the bill's provisions and suggest to Congress alternative measures, such as withholding, if return filing does not result in adequate compliance.

The gross-basis tax is not intended to override U.S. income tax treaties with foreign countries. Therefore, a foreign person that is able to avail itself of a treaty exemption is not subject to the tax.

* * * * * *

[Conference Report]

* * * * * *

Gross basis tax.—The conference agreement follows the House bill in applying the gross basis tax and in determining a foreign person's effectively connected transportation income, but adopts the Senate amendment's method of collecting any tax due. The agreement modifies, however, the determination of effectively connected transportation income in one respect: a foreign person engaged in the leasing of ships or aircraft will derive transportation income effectively connected with a U.S. trade or business only if substantially all of the person's U.S. source gross transportation income is earned through a fixed place of business in the United States.

[Effective date.—] The agreement is generally effective for taxable years beginning after 1986 but retains present law for certain leasing income attributable to an asset owned on January 1, 1986 if the asset was first leased before that date and contains a targeted transitional rule.

[¶4030]   SECTION 1213. SOURCE RULE FOR SPACE AND CERTAIN OCEAN ACTIVITIES

(Secs. 861, 863 of the Code)

[Senate Explanation]

* * * * * *

Explanation of Provision.—The bill provides that all income derived from space or ocean activities is sourced in the country of residence of the person generating the income: income derived by United States persons (as defined in sec. 7701(a)(30)) is U.S. source income and income derived by persons other than U.S. persons is sourced outside the United States.

The bill provides, however, an anti-conduit provision in the case of certain foreign corporations. A foreign corporation is to be treated as a U.S. person if 50 percent or more in value, or in voting power, of the corporation is owned (within the meaning of sec. 958(a)) or considered as owned (under the principles of sec. 958(b)) by U.S. persons. Thus, U.S. persons cannot incorporate a foreign corporation in order to be taxed as a nonresident of the United States for this purpose. This provision applies regardless of the number of persons interposed between the corporation earning the income and its ultimate owners.

Space or ocean activities as defined by the bill include any activities conducted in space, and on or beneath water not within the jurisdiction (as recognized by the United States) of any country including the United States or its possessions. The term ocean activities also includes any activities performed in Antarctica. For example, the committee intends that the term space or ocean activities include the performance and provision of services in space or on or beneath the

ocean, the leasing of equipment including spacecraft located in space or on or beneath the ocean, the licensing of technology or other intangibles for use in space or on or beneath the ocean, and the manufacturing of property in space or on or beneath the ocean. The committee intends the term ocean activities to further include the leasing of a vessel if such vessel does not transport cargo or persons for hire between ports-of-call. For example, the income earned by a lessor of a vessel chartered by a corporation that is to engage only in research activities in the ocean is intended by the committee to be high-seas income. In these circumstances, the committee does not intend the lessors to earn transportation income since the operators of the vessels are not engaged in transporting cargo or persons between ports-of-call.

The bill provides for regulations to describe other activities that may be considered space or ocean activities. For example, the committee intends that underwriting income from the insurance of risks on activities conducted in space or on or beneath the ocean to be treated as space or ocean activities. The committee does not intend the selling of property on the high seas to be considered space or ocean activity (i.e., the bill does not override the title passage rule).

Space or ocean activities do not include any activity which gives rise to transportation income (as defined in sec. 863(c)) or any activity with respect to mines, oil and gas wells, or other natural deposits to the extent the mines or wells are located within the jurisdiction (as recognized by the United States) of any country, including the United

States and its possessions. In the case of mines, oil and gas wells, or other natural deposits to the extent such mines or wells are not within the jurisdiction of the United States, U.S. possessions, or any foreign country, the committee does intend the leasing of drilling rigs, the extraction of minerals, and the performance and provision of services related thereto to be ocean activities.

The bill also excludes from the definition of space or ocean activities international communications income. The bill provides that international communications income is to be sourced 50 percent in the United States and 50 percent foreign to the extent the income is attributable to communications between the United States and a foreign country. If the communication is between two points within the United States, the income attributable thereto is to be sourced entirely as U.S. source income. The committee intends the latter result even if the communication is routed through a satellite located in space, regardless of the satellite's location. If the communication is between the United States and an airborne plane or a vessel at sea, the committee intends the communication to be treated as between two U.S. points and, thus, to be sourced in the United States. Finally, if the communication is between two foreign locations, the committee intends income attributable thereto to be foreign source. The committee intends that international communication income include income attributable to any transmission between two countries of signals, images, sounds, or data transmitted in whole or in part by buried or underwater cable or by satellite. For example, the term includes income derived from the transmission of telephone calls.

As provided in sec. 813 of the bill, Code sec. 861(e), relating to certain income from leasing vessels or spacecraft that is treated as wholly U.S. source, is repealed.

Effective Date.—The provision is effective for income earned in taxable years beginning after December 31, 1986.

* * * * * *

[Conference Report]

* * * * * *

Conference Agreement.—The conference agreement follows the Senate amendment, with modifications.

The agreement does not adopt the provision that treats a foreign corporation controlled by U.S. persons as a U.S. person for purposes of the source rule. The application of the separate foreign tax credit limitation for shipping income to any space or ocean income derived by a controlled foreign corporation provides adequate assurance, in the conferee's view, that high foreign taxes on unrelated income will not inappropriately offset U.S. taxes on this generally low-taxed income.

The conference agreement modifies the Senate amendment's provision that treats international communication income as 50-percent U.S. source and 50-percent foreign source by applying this source rule to U.S. persons only. However, the conference agreement treats international communication income derived by foreign persons as U.S. source if the income is attributable to a U.S. office or other U.S. fixed place of business, and provides regulatory authority to treat other international communication income derived by a foreign person (e.g., a controlled foreign corporation) as other than foreign source. In particular, the conferees anticipate that treatment of such income in the hands of controlled foreign corporations like similar income in the hands of U.S. persons may be necessary to preserve the integrity of the provision.

[¶ 4031] SECTION 1214. LIMITATIONS ON SPECIAL TREATMENT OF 80-20 CORPORATIONS

(Secs. 861, 862, 871, 881, 1441, and 1442 of the Code)

[House Explanation]

* * * * * *

Present Law.—Under present law, if U.S. source dividends and interest paid to foreign persons are not effectively connected with the conduct of a trade or business within the United States the withholding agent (which is generally the payor of such income) is generally required to withhold on the gross amount of such income tax at a rate of 30 percent (secs. 871(a) and 881(a)). The withheld tax constitutes the only U.S. tax due by the foreign person for that income and the foreign person is not required to file a U.S. tax return. The withholding rate of 30 percent may be reduced or eliminated by tax treaties between the United States and a foreign country. Furthermore, withholding is not required on certain items of U.S. source

interest income. For instance, the Tax Reform Act of 1984 eliminated withholding on U.S. source portfolio interest. The United States does not impose any withholding tax on foreign source dividend and interest payments to foreign persons, even if the payments are from U.S. persons.

Dividend and interest income generally is sourced in the country of incorporation of the payor. However, if a U.S. corporation earns more than 80 percent of its income from foreign sources (such a corporation is referred to as an "80-20 company"), all dividends and interest paid by that corporation are treated as foreign source income. Foreign countries generally do not tax dividends and interest paid by U.S. corporations to U.S. persons even though those dividends and interest may be foreign source under these rules.

Other exceptions to the country-of-incorporation source rules are designed as tax exemptions for limited classes of income earned by foreign persons. For instance, interest on foreign persons' U.S. bank accounts and deposits is exempt from U.S. withholding tax under current law. The current method of exempting this income is to treat it as foreign source.

* * * * * *

Explanation of Provision.—The bill provides that interest paid by an 80-20 company is generally U.S. source income. The bill provides that dividends from an 80-20 company (other than a corporation that has an election in effect under Code sec. 936) are treated as U.S. source income.

The bill provides an exception from the U.S. source rule for certain interest received by a financial institution (as described in sec. 581 or 591) or by a similar foreign financial institution. Under this exception, interest income is foreign source if: (1) the interest paid by the payor corporation is attributable to the active conduct of a trade or business in a foreign country by the payor corporation a subsidiary or chain of subsidiaries of the payor corporation (or a partnership of which the payor corporation is a partner), and the payor corporation is an 80-20 company, (2) the payor corporation is not related to the financial institution, (within the meaning of sec. 901(i)(1)), and (3) the interest received by the financial institution is effectively connected with the conduct of a trade or business of the financial institution in a foreign country. Thus, for example, an 80-20 company engaged in an active trade or business in a foreign country pays foreign source interest to a branch of an unrelated U.S. bank or other U.S. or foreign financial institution as long as the interest is effectively connected with the financial institution's trade or business in the foreign country.

The bill further provides that certain interest paid by an 80-20 company, though treated as U.S. source, is exempt from withholding. This exemption applies to interest paid (to a nonresident alien individual or other foreign person) by an 80-20 corporation if the interest paid by the 80-20 corporation is attributable to the active conduct of a trade or business in a foreign country by the 80-20 corporation, a subsidiary or chain of subsidiaries of the 80-20 corporation (or a partnership of which the 80-20 company is a partner). Thus, an 80-20 company conducting an active trade or business in a foreign country generally can borrow from a foreign person and not withhold U.S. tax on the interest payments as long as the interest is effectively connected with the 80-20 company's business. This exemption from withholding by an 80-20 company does not apply, however, if the 80-20 company is 50 percent owned (by voting power for all classes of stock entitled to vote or by value) by nonresident alien individuals or other foreign persons and the interest is paid to a recipient who is a related party (as defined in new Code sec. 901(i)(1)) to the payor. Thus, interest payments by a foreign-

owned 80-20 company made to a related party are subject to U.S. withholding tax.

The committee also intends that this exemption from withholding apply to interest of an 80-20 corporation that is in a start-up phase of an active trade or business in a foreign country. The corporation can pay interest and not withhold U.S. tax as long as the interest is related to the corporation's start-up activities, the 80-20 company is not foreign owned, and the interest is not paid to related persons. A business is in a start-up phase if substantially all of its other expenditures are start-up expenditures (as described in sec. 195).

The bill further provides that certain other interest, although treated as U.S. source, is not subject to the withholding tax provided in sections 871 and 881. This interest, whether received by a nonresident alien individual or other foreign person, includes interest on deposits with persons carrying on the banking business, interest on deposits or withdrawable accounts with a Federal or State chartered savings institution as long as such interest is a deductible expense to the savings institution under section 591, and interest on amounts held by an insurance company under an agreement to pay interest thereon, but only if such interest is not effectively connected with the conduct of a trade or business within the United States by the recipient of the interest. The bill also exempts from withholding tax the income derived by a foreign central bank of issue from bankers' acceptances. Under present law, these types of interest income are treated as foreign source income and thus are generally not subject to U.S. tax if paid to foreign persons; the bill treats them as U.S. source income but excludes them from withholding.

* * * * * *

[Conference Report]

* * * * * *

The conference agreement generally follows the House bill in repealing the special sourcing rule of present law for dividends and interest paid by 80/20 companies, with modifications that incorporate the Senate amendment's look-through rules in certain cases (including application to 80/20 individuals). The conferees are of the view that the United States should generally retain primary tax jurisdiction over dividends and interest paid by its residents. Particularly with respect to dividends paid to U.S. persons, the conferees do not believe that dividends should be foreign source since the payor computes its foreign tax credit limitation, accounts for its foreign source income, and credits any foreign taxes imposed on that income at the payor level. The conferees believe that it is appropriate to treat interest that an 80-20 company pays its U.S. shareholders more favorably than dividends it pays them (by allowing flow-through of source for interest but not for dividends)

Act § 1214   ¶ 4031

because that interest, unlike the dividends, is likely to reduce foreign taxes that the United States may have to credit.

The conferees believe, however, that, in certain cases, U.S. sourcing of dividends and interest is not appropriate in the context of a U.S. corporation primarily engaged in an active trade or business in foreign jurisdictions (including U.S. possessions). The conference agreement provides that foreign shareholders of a U.S. corporation engaged in an active trade or business in foreign jurisdictions to which at least 80 percent of the corporation's gross income is attributable are subject to U.S. withholding tax on the percentage of the dividends paid by that corporation that the corporation's U.S. source gross income bears to the corporation's total gross income measured over the 3-year period preceding the year of payment. Interest received from a U.S. corporation that meets the above-described 80-percent active business requirement also retains foreign sourcing, as follows: unrelated U.S. and foreign recipients are to treat the entire interest payment as foreign source; related recipients must treat as U.S. source a percentage of the interest equal to the ratio of the corporation's U.S. source gross income to the corporation's total gross income (measured over the 3-year period preceding the year of payment). The agreement provides similar rules for interest paid by resident alien individuals engaged in active foreign businesses in foreign jurisdictions.

The conference agreement provides that the 80-percent active business requirement may be met by the U.S. corporation alone or, instead, may be met by a group including domestic or foreign subsidiaries in which the U.S. corporation owns a controlling interest (at least a 50-percent interest). In allowing attribution of a subsidiary's active foreign business to a controlling corporate shareholder, the conferees also intend that the character (i.e., foreign active business income) of the subsidiary's gross income be attributed to the corporate shareholder on the receipt of dividends for purposes of determining the percentage of dividends paid by the shareholder that are U.S. source. Thus, dividends received by a corporate shareholder from controlled subsidiaries, though treated as U.S. source, are to be characterized as foreign active business income in the same proportion that the controlled subsidiaries' foreign active business income bears to their total gross income for this purpose.

The agreement defines a related person as any individual, corporation, partnership, trust, or estate which owns a 10-percent interest in the payor, or in which the payor owns a 10-percent interest, as well as any 10-percent interest in a corporation, partnership, trust, or estate owned by the same persons that own a 10-percent interest in the payor.

The agreement's provisions are illustrated in the following example. Assume that a U.S. corporation and an unrelated foreign corporation jointly incorporate a second U.S. corporation to operate a mining business in a foreign country. The second U.S. corporation earns $450 of income, all of which is foreign source, from the mining operation in its first year and $50 of U.S. source income from investments in the United States. At the end of the year, the second corporation distributes a $100 dividend to each of its two shareholders. The first U.S. corporation in turn distributes $50 to its shareholders, all of whom are foreign residents. The agreement treats the $100 dividend to the first U.S. corporation as entirely U.S. source; the $100 dividend to the foreign shareholder is treated as 90 percent foreign source and as 10 percent U.S. source. Since the first U.S. corporation owns a controlling interest in the second U.S. corporation, the second corporation's active foreign business is attributed to the first corporation; therefore, assuming that the first corporation has no other income, the first corporation satisfies the agreement's 80-percent active foreign business requirement. Even though it is treated as U.S. source, the dividend from the second corporation retains the same character as the second corporation's income in determining the source of dividends paid by the first corporation. Accordingly, under the agreement, since the first corporation has no other income, 90 percent of the first corporation's dividends paid to its shareholders are foreign source and 10 percent are U.S. source. If, however, for example, the first U.S. corporation had $13 or more of non-foreign active business income in that year, the first corporation would not satisfy the 80-percent foreign active business requirement and would, therefore, pay all U.S. source dividends.

In adopting the new 80/20 standards, the conferees decided against requiring a minimum amount of dividends and interest paid to foreign persons to be subject to U.S. tax because of the agreement's minimum tax provision which ensures that profitable U.S. 80/20 corporations pay some U.S. tax (the provision that only allows 90 percent of creditable foreign taxes to offset the alternative minimum tax). The conferees are of the view that that provision achieves their policy objective: that profits flowing through U.S. corporations not escape all U.S. tax at the corporate and shareholder levels.

The conference agreement follows the House bill and the Senate amendment in (1) repealing foreign sourcing, but preserving U.S. tax exemption, for certain limited classes of income (e.g., interest on bank deposits), and (2) in retaining foreign sourcing for dividends paid by possessions corporations.

*   *   *   *   *   *

[House Explanation]

*   *   *   *   *   *

Effective Date.—The provision is not effective for interest paid on debt obligations held on December 31, 1985, unless the interest is paid pursuant to an extension or renewal of that obligation agreed to after December 31, 1985. In the case of interest paid to a related person that benefits from this grandfather rule, the payments are treated as payments from a controlled foreign corporation for foreign tax credit purposes. As such, they retain their character and source.

For dividends paid by a certain 80-20 company, the provision is not effective until January 1, 1991, for dividends paid on stock outstanding on May 31, 1985.

*   *   *   *   *   *

[Senate Explanation]

*   *   *   *   *   *

Effective Date.—The provision is effective for dividends and interest paid in taxable years beginning after December 31, 1986.

*   *   *   *   *   *

[Conference Report]

*   *   *   *   *

[Effective date.—] The agreement adopts the Senate amendment's general effective date but contains the House bill's grandfather rule for indebtedness outstanding on December 31, 1985 and contains a targeted transitional rule. In addition, the agreement provides that, in determining the amount of dividends paid to foreign shareholders and interest paid to related persons in 1987 that are U.S. source, a calendar year 80/20 company under present law is to use the base period 1984, 1985, and 1986 in computing its U.S. source portion. Interest paid to unrelated persons in 1987 is foreign source if paid by a corporation that is an 80/20 company under present law. The agreement provides that, for 1988 and subsequent years, the amount of dividends and interest that are treated as U.S. source under the agreement is to be determined by the payor's income measured over a base period beginning in 1987. Similar rules apply to 80/20 individuals (as defined under present law).

[¶ 4032] SECTION 1215. RULES FOR ALLOCATING INTEREST, ETC., TO FOREIGN SOURCE INCOME

(Sec. 864 of the Code)

[House Explanation]

*   *   *   *   *   *

Present Law.—The Code provides, in general terms, that taxpayers, in computing net U.S. source and net foreign source income, are to deduct from U.S. and foreign source gross income the expenses, losses and other deductions properly apportioned or allocated thereto and a ratable part of any expenses, losses, or other deductions which cannot definitely be allocated to some item or class of gross income.

Treasury regulation sec. 1.861-8 sets forth detailed allocation and apportionment rules for certain types of deductions, including those for interest expense (and research and development expenditures, which are the subject of section 616 of this bill). These regulations, insofar as they govern interest expense, are based on the approach that money is fungible and that interest expense is properly attributable to all business activities and property of a taxpayer regardless of any specific purpose for incurring an obligation on which interest is paid. This approach recognizes that all activities and property require funds and that management has a great deal of flexibility as to the source and use of funds. Often, creditors of a taxpayer subject money advanced to the taxpayer to the risk of the taxpayer's entire activities and look to the general credit of the taxpayer for payment of the debt. When money is borrowed for a specific purpose, such borrowing will generally free other funds for other purposes and it is reasonable under this approach to attribute part of the cost of borrowing to such other purposes.

In general, the regulation allows taxpayers to choose between two methods of allocating interest expense: an asset method and a gross income method. The regulation is based on the theory that normally, the deduction for interest expense relates more closely to the amount of capital utilized or invested in an activity or property than to the gross income generated therefrom, and therefore that the deduction for interest should normally be apportioned on the basis of asset values. Indebtedness permits the taxpayer to acquire or retain different kinds of assets which may produce substantially different yields of gross income in relation to their value. According to the theory of the regulation, apportionment of an interest deduction on such basis as gross income may not be reasonable. (Treas. Reg. sec. 1.861-8(e)(2)(v)). Therefore, the asset method is the preferred method.

Under the asset method, taxpayers generally may choose between two methods of evaluating assets, the tax book value method and the fair market value method. The tax book value method considers original cost for tax purposes less depreciation allowed for tax purposes. The fair market value method considers fair market value of assets, but it is available only if the taxpayer can show fair market value to the satisfaction of the Commissioner. Taxpayers who use the fair market value method may not switch to the tax book value method without the Commissioner's consent.

If any taxpayer that is a member of an affiliated group that files a consolidated return uses the gross income method, then all members of the group must use the same method. Under the gross income method, taxpayers generally apportion the deduction on the basis of U.S. and foreign gross income.

Act § 1215   ¶ 4032

(Treas. Reg. sec. 1.861-8(e)(2)(vi)). The allocation against foreign source income (or against U.S. source income) cannot be less than 50 percent of what the allocation would be if the taxpayer used the asset method.

Despite the general adoption of the approach that money is fungible, the regulation governing interest expense deductions provides a limited exception that allows taxpayers to trace interest expense to certain assets without treating that interest expense as fungible (Treas. Reg. sec. 1.861-8(e)(2)(iv)). That exception applies to only a limited class of nonrecourse debt.

Under the regulations, interest expense incurred by an affiliated group of corporations that files a consolidated tax return is required to be apportioned between U.S. and foreign income on a separate company basis rather than on a consolidated group basis. This separate company apportionment rule conflicts with a Court of Claims case, *International Telephone & Telegraph Corp.* v. *United States* (79-2 USTC para. 9649), decided under the law in effect prior to the effective date of the Treasury regulations. The ITT case indicates that expenses that are not definitely allocable against U.S. or foreign gross income should be deducted from gross income of a consolidated group on a consolidated group basis.

The regulations generally allow tax-exempt income and assets generating tax-exempt income to be taken into account in allocating deductible expense. Banks and other financial institutions, which may deduct some interest used to carry tax-exempt assets, are the main beneficiaries of this rule.

Taxpayers generally allocate expenses other than interest expenses on a company-by-company basis. The treatment of expenses for research and experimentation is discussed below in connection with section 616 of the bill.

*   *   *   *   *   *

Explanation of Provision.—The bill provides, in general, that for purposes of the foreign tax credit limitation of section 904, the taxable income of each member of an affiliated group from sources outside the United States is to be determined by allocating and apportioning all interest expenses as if all members of the group were a single corporation. In effect, taxpayers will disregard stock of affiliates and interaffiliate debt in allocating interest expenses. As a result, the amount of foreign source and U.S. source income on the consolidated return in each of the three numbered examples in the Present Law section would be the same: there would be $10 of foreign source income and $10 of U.S. source income. The committee intends that regulations will provide appropriate treatment to effectively eliminate interest payments among members of an affiliated group that join (or could join) in the filing of a consolidated return. Therefore, the only interest expense taken into account is interest paid to non-members of the group. The bill does not change the treatment of non-recourse debt that the current regulation treats

as definitely related to specific property (Treas. Reg. sec. 1.861-8(e)(2)(iv)).

The bill applies a similar rule in the case of expenses other than interest, but grants regulatory authority to the Secretary of the Treasury to provide exceptions, if any, as appropriate. For this purpose, too, taxpayers are, in effect, to disregard stock of affiliates and interaffiliate debt. Treating a consolidated group as if it were one taxpayer, however, will not change the present law allocation of directly allocable expenses. Similarly, it will generally not change the treatment of items such as labor costs or costs of materials, which, to the extent that they are elements of cost of goods sold, are generally not subject to allocation or apportionment. The committee anticipates that regulations will modify the separate company system of current law to provide look-through rules where appropriate to properly reflect all foreign source income earned by all members of the group.

The bill specifies that taxpayers are to allocate and apportion interest expense on the basis of assets rather than gross income. That is, the bill prevents taxpayers from using the optional gross income method of the current regulation (or any similar method) for allocating and apportioning interest.

The bill provides that tax-exempt assets and income associated therewith are not to be taken into account in allocating or apportioning any deductible expense. This rule applies to expenses other than interest. For this purpose, 85 percent of the basis (or value, if the taxpayer uses the fair market value method) of stock that pays dividends that are eligible for the 85-percent dividends received deduction is treated as a tax-exempt asset. As the 85-percent deduction changes in amount, the percentage of stock treated as a tax-exempt asset will change.

The bill provides a new rule for purposes of allocating and apportioning expenses on the basis of assets when the asset is stock in one of certain foreign corporations. In general, for this purpose, the adjusted basis of any asset which is stock in a controlled foreign corporation in the hands of a 10-percent U.S. shareholder is to be increased by the amount of the earnings and profits of the foreign corporation attributable to that stock and accumulated during the period the taxpayer held it. For this purpose, the adjusted basis of stock in a controlled foreign corporation is also to reflect capital contributions. In the case of a deficit in earnings and profits of the foreign corporation that is attributable to the stock that arose during the period when the 10-percent U.S. shareholder held it, that deficit is to reduce the adjusted basis of the asset in the hands of the U.S. shareholder. In that case, however, the deficit cannot reduce the adjusted basis of the asset below zero.

The bill's one-taxpayer rule also provides new treatment under the asset method for stock in affiliated U.S. companies. The committee intends that stock of affiliates and intercompany debt between affiliates be disregarded under appropriate rules prescribed by the Secretary. Therefore, as members of an affiliated U.S. group earn income that they retain, that income will be reflected in assets whose tax basis will be considered in the allocation of expenses under the asset method. This treatment is comparable to the treatment that the bill provides for stock of foreign corporations.

An example illustrates the operation of the one-taxpayer rule and the asset method improvement. A U.S. parent company has borrowed $360 with an obligation to pay annual interest of $36. The debt is recourse debt, so the use to which the taxpayer puts the borrowed funds is immaterial under the bill. The U.S. parent borrower owns two assets. One of its assets is stock of a domestic subsidiary; that stock has a basis in the parent's hands of $800. The U.S. subsidiary in turn owns the following assets: U.S. assets which have a basis in its hands of $700, and foreign assets which have a basis in its hands of $100. The other asset of the U.S. parent (the borrower) is stock in a foreign corporation. The basis of the stock in the foreign corporation in the hands of the U.S. owner is $100. The foreign corporation also retained earnings of $100.

Under the bill, after a transition period, the interest expense allocation rules will operate on the basis of the affiliated group consisting of the U.S. parent corporation and its U.S. subsidiary. The parent will be treated in effect as owning directly the $700 of U.S. assets owned by the U.S. subsidiary and the $100 of foreign assets owned by the U.S. subsidiary. In addition, the parent will be treated as owning $200 of foreign assets by virtue of its $100 basis in the stock of the foreign subsidiary increased by the $100 of earnings and profits of the foreign subsidiary. Thus, the parent is treated as owning $700 of U.S. assets and $300 of foreign assets for the purpose of the asset method. Therefore, 70 percent of its interest expense ($700/$1000) will reduce U.S. source gross income. The parent corporation will allocate $10.80 (30 percent of $36) against foreign source income and $25.20 (70 percent of $36) against U.S. source income. The same result would obtain if the U.S. subsidiary had borrowed the money and paid the interest.

The bill contains an exception to the rule requiring treatment of an affiliated group as if all members of the group were one taxpayer for purposes of allocating and apportioning interest expense. That general rule will not apply to any financial institution (described in section 581 or 591) if the business of the financial institution is predominantly with persons other than related persons or their customers, and if the financial institution is required by State or Federal law to be operated separately from any other entity which is not a financial institution. If this exception applies, the financial institution will not be treated as a member of the group for applying the bill's general "one taxpayer" rule to other members of the group. The other members of the group will still be treated as one taxpayer for interest expense

allocation purposes. The financial institution will still be part of the group that the bill treats as one taxpayer for expenses other than interest.

The bill requires the Secretary to prescribe such regulations as may be necessary to carry out the purposes of these provisions. In particular, the committee intends that, in the case of an affiliated group of corporations that is eligible to file a consolidated return but that does not do so, the foreign source income of any member of the group shall not exceed the amount of foreign source income that would be attributable to that member if the group were a single corporation. For example, assume that two U.S. corporations, although eligible to file a consolidated return, do not do so. Corporation 1 owns all the shares of Corporation 2. Corporation 1 has $20 of gross income, all from sources within the United States, and incurs $20 of interest expense. Corporation 1 has no net income after interest expense. Corporation 2 has $20 of gross income, all from sources without the United States, and incurs no interest expense. Corporation 2 has $20 of net income. The committee intends that under regulations the foreign source income of this group of two corporations will not exceed what it would have been had they filed a consolidated return. Had they done so, the group would have had $10 of net U.S. source income, and $10 of net foreign source income. Therefore, the foreign source income of Corporation 2 cannot exceed $10. It will be treated as earning $10 of U.S. source income and $10 of foreign source income.

In addition, the committee intends that regulations provide appropriate safeguards to prevent the transfer of assets from one consolidated group member to another to achieve a fair market value basis without recognition of gain (until the asset leaves the group).

Effective Date.—In general, these provisions apply to taxable years beginning after December 31, 1985. Transitional rules apply to the allocation of interest expense, however.

A general three-year "phase-in" transitional rule applies to all the elements of the interest expense allocation (including the change to consider an affiliated group as one taxpayer, the elimination of the gross income method, and the improvement of the asset method). This "phase-in" rule provides that for the first three taxable years of the taxpayer beginning after December 31, 1985, the bill's interest expense allocation rules apply only to an applicable percentage of interest expense paid or accrued by the taxpayer during the taxable year. That applicable percentage is determined with respect to an amount of indebtedness that does not exceed the amount outstanding on November 16, 1985. This three-year phase-in rule applies whether the taxpayer borrows from the same lender from which it borrowed on November 16, 1985, or from other lenders. In the case of the first taxable year, the applicable percentage is 25 percent; in the case of the second taxable year, the applicable percentage is 50 percent; in the case of the third taxable year, the applicable percentage is 75 percent.

Thus, for example, under the three-year "phase-in," if a calendar year taxpayer's debt outstanding on November 16, 1985, was $100 and its debt outstanding at all times during 1986 is $75, the bill will not affect interest expenses paid or accrued during that second taxable year.

A separate transitional rule applies only to the rule requiring consideration of the affiliated group for determination of interest expense (the first sentence of new sec. 864(e)(1)). That rule considers recently incurred indebtedness. In the case of an increase in the amount of a taxpayer's outstanding debt on May 29, 1985, over the amount of the taxpayer's outstanding debt on December 31, 1983, the interest expense rule that requires consideration of the affiliated group shall be phased in over five years. In the case of the first taxable year beginning after 1985, the rule applies only to 16-⅔ percent of the interest expenses paid or accrued by the taxpayer on the increase in indebtedness. In the case of the second taxable year beginning after 1985, the rule applies to only 33-⅓ percent of the interest expenses paid or accrued by the taxpayer, and so on, until the rule applies to 83-⅓ of interest expenses in the fifth taxable year beginning after 1985, and to all interest expenses thereafter.

A similar separate four-year transitional "phase-in" rule applies to certain increases in indebtedness incurred during 1983. In the case of the first four taxable years of the taxpayer beginning after 1985, with respect to interest expenses attributable to the excess of the amount of the outstanding debt of the taxpayer on January 1, 1984, over the amount of the outstanding debt of the taxpayer on December 31, 1982, then the "one-taxpayer" rule will apply only to the applicable percentage of interest expenses paid or accrued by the taxpayer during the taxable year. In the case of the first taxable year, the applicable percentage is 20; in the second year, 40; in the third year, 60; and in the fourth year, 80.

For the purpose of the 5-year phase-in and the 4-year phase-in, any indebtedness outstanding at the end of 1985 shall be treated as attributable first to the excess incurred after 1983 but before May 29, 1985 (and thus eligible for the 5-year phase-in), then to indebtedness incurred in 1983 (and thus eligible for the 4-year phase-in), and then to other indebtedness.

Finally, a limited 3-year phase-in applies to a limited class of debt of a certain group including a corporation incorporated in 1964.

*   *   *   *   *   *

[Conference Report]

*   *   *   *   *   *

In general.—The conference agreement generally follows the House bill. Except to the extent provided in regulations, expenses other than interest that are not directly allocable or apportioned are to be allocated and apportioned as if all members of the affiliated group were one taxpayer. The agreement, like the Senate amendment, includes possessions corporations (sec. 936) in the group treated as one taxpayer. In addition, the agreement contains the Senate provision requiring regulations to allocate interest to income subject to the separate foreign tax credit limitations.

The conference agreement modifies the provision applying the one-taxpayer rule to banks for the purpose of interest expense allocation. The agreement makes it clear that all banks in a group are to be treated as one taxpayer (rather than each bank being treated as a separate taxpayer for this purpose).

The conference agreement extends, under regulations, the application of the one-taxpayer rule for expense allocation beyond the foreign tax credit limitations of Code section 904 to other provisions governing international taxation.

In the case of an integrated financial transaction such as a debt-financed acquisition of foreign currency debt obligations or similar arbitrage transactions, the agreement authorizes the Secretary to provide for the direct allocation of interest expense incurred on funds borrowed to acquire these assets against income from the assets involved in the integrated transaction, if appropriate. In addition, the conferees intend that the Secretary use the regulatory authority provided in the agreement to allocate interest expenses directly to interest or other passive income where such a direct allocation is necessary to prevent taxpayers from defeating the purposes of this provision.

When a taxpayer owns at least a 10-percent interest in a U.S. corporation but that corporation is not part of the group treated as one taxpayer, the taxpayer's basis in that stock is to be increased by the taxpayer's share of the earnings and profits of the U.S. corporation. This basis step-up conforms to that required for stock of foreign corporations whose dividends are eligible for the deemed-paid foreign tax credit.

Effective date and transitional rules.—The conference agreement is generally effective for taxable years beginning after 1986. The conference agreement adopts the targeted transitional rules of the Senate amendment, one additional targeted transitional rule and one special rule. It adopts the general transition rules of the House bill, applying the three-, four-, and five-year transition rules for taxable years beginning after 1986 with respect to the amount of debt outstanding on November 16, 1985. For the purpose of this provision's phase-in rules for interest expense, only interest-bearing indebtedness is to be considered as debt outstanding on November 16, 1985. If a portion of a taxpayer's debt is not eligible for the benefits of a phase-in rule, the benefits of the rule are to apply to interest incurred with respect to each of the taxpayer's outstanding debt obligations on a pro rata basis.

The general three-year "phase-in" rule of the House bill applies to all the elements of the interest expense allocation (including the change to consider an affiliated group as one taxpayer, the elimination of the gross income method, and the modification of the asset method). This "phase-in" rule provides that for the first three taxable years of the taxpayer beginning after December 31, 1986, the bill's interest expense allocation rules apply only to an applicable percentage of interest expense paid or accrued by the taxpayer during the taxable year. That applicable percentage is determined with respect to an amount of indebtedness that does not exceed the amount outstanding on November 16, 1985. In the case of the first taxable year, the applicable percentage is 25 percent; in the case of the second taxable year, the applicable percentage is 50 percent; in the case of the third taxable year, the applicable percentage is 75 percent.

[The following colloquies relating to Act Sec. 1215 are drawn from the Congressional Record. The colloquies occurred on the day the Conference bill was considered by the Senate. Ed.]

[Senate Floor Explanation]

Mr. BOREN. Mr. President, I would like to engage the distinguished chairman of the Senate Finance Committee, Mr. Packwood in a colloquy concerning an ambiguity contained in the conference report on tax reform.

At conference, the House receded to the Senate on section 1215(c)(2)(C) of H.R. 3838, yet portions of the House language were incorporated in the rule. The House language which is picked up in the conference report refers to "interest expenses paid or accrued with respect to the amount of indebtedness" which could be interpreted as applying the rule to level of interest instead of level of indebtedness of a company. It is my understanding that this rule would apply to the level of indebtedness and not to the level of interest expense. Is that your understanding?

Mr. PACKWOOD. Yes, this is my understanding. Congressional Record p. S 13951, 9-25-86.

TRANSITIONAL RULE ON INTEREST EXPENSE

Mr. WILSON. Mr. President, it is my understanding that the conference agreement adopts the general interest allocation transitional rules of the House bill applying the 3-, 4-, and 5-year transitional rules as set forth in that bill. Further, the agreement adopts a number of 10-year targeted transitional rules. It is my understanding that there is an example on page 380 of the Ways and Means Committee report explaining and illustrating these rules. It is my further understanding that this example is applicable to the final agreement of the conferees. The example illustrating these rules is as follows:

Thus, for example, under the three-year "phase-in" if a calendar year taxpayer's debt outstanding on November 16, 1985, was $100, and its debt outstanding at all times during 1986 is $75, the bill will not affect interest expenses paid or accured during that second taxable year.

I would like to ask the distinguished chairman of the committee whether my understanding is correct and whether the example I have given is a proper interpretation of the conference report transitional rules.

Mr. PACKWOOD. Yes, your understanding is correct. The example you have given from the Ways and Means Committee report is a correct illustration of the various transitional rules as agreed to by the Conferees. Congressional Record, p. S 13951, 9-25-86.

[The following is from a statement of the Chairman of the House Ways and Means Committee relating to Senate Floor colloquies on the Conference bill. Ed.]

[House Floor Explanation]

I would like to affirm, with clarifications, the colloquies between Senator Wilson and Senator Packwood, and Senator Boren and Senator Packwood, regarding interest allocation, located on page S 13951 of the Congressional Record dated September 27, 1986. I would like to clarify one aspect of the interest allocation provision contained in title 12 of the conference agreement. The conference agreement adopts the general interest allocation transitional rules of the House bill applying the 3, 4, and 5-year transitional rules as set forth in that bill. Further, the agreement adopts a number of 10-year targeted transition rules of the Senate amendment. There is an example on page 380 of the Ways and Means Committee report explaining and illustrating these rules. This example is intended to apply to the final agreement of the conferees—covering all the transitional rules adopted by the agreement governing interest allocation to foreign and U.S. source income. The example illustrating these rules is as follows:

Thus, for example, under the 3-year "phase in," if a calendar year taxpayer's, debt outstanding on November 16, 1985, was $100, and its debt outstanding at all times during 1986 is $75, the bill will not affect interest expenses paid or accrued during the second taxable year.

Thus, the phase-in rules apply to a level of indebtedness, and not a level of interest. However, I also want to clarify a sentence in the statement of managers that contains some clerical errors. It is not intended that the phase-in rules allow taxpayers to reduce their debt below the phase-in amount, thereafter incur new debt, and apply the transition rules to interest on the new debt. In addition, I wish to make it clear that reductions in the aggregate amount of debt outstanding are to be considered as first reducing amounts eligible for the 5-year rule; then, amounts eligible for the 4-year rule; and

Act § 1215   ¶ 4032

finally, amounts eligible for the 3-year rule. Congressional Record, p. E 3390, 10-2-86.

[Conference Report]

* * * * * *

A separate transitional rule, adopted from the House bill, applies only to the rule requiring consideration of the consolidated group for determination of interest expense (new sec. 864(e)(1)). That rule considers only recently incurred indebtedness. In the case of an increase in the amount of a taxpayer's outstanding debt on May 29, 1985, over the amount of the taxpayer's outstanding debt on December 31, 1983, the interest expense rule that requires consideration of the consolidated group is phased in over five years. In the case of the first taxable year beginning after 1986, the rule applies only to 16⅔ percent of the interest expenses paid or accrued by the taxpayer on the increased indebtedness. In the case of the second taxable year beginning after 1986, the rule applies to only 33⅓ percent of the interest expenses paid or accrued by the taxpayer on the increased indebtedness, and so on, until the rule applies to 83-⅓ percent of interest expenses on the increased indebtedness in the fifth year beginning after 1986, and to all interest expense.

A similar separate four-year transitional "phase-in" rule (also adopted from the House bill) applies to certain increases in indebtedness incurred during 1983. The one-taxpayer rule will apply only to the applicable percentage of interest expenses paid or accrued on the increased indebtedness by the taxpayer during the taxable year. In the case of the first taxable year, the applicable percentage is 20; in the second year, 40; in the third year, 60; and in the fourth year, 80.

The three-, four-, and five-year phase-in rules apply to interest expenses paid or accrued with respect to an applicable amount of indebtedness. These rules allow present law to apply to a certain percentage of interest expenses on such indebtedness. The phase-in rules are not to apply indebtedness increases in future years after decreasing to equal again the indebtedness outstanding on November 16, 1985. However, if, for example, a taxpayer refinances debt outstanding on November 16, 1985 by incurring new debt as it pays off old debt, and the documentation for the new debt specifically identifies the old

debt being refinanced, the phase-in rules are intended to apply to the new debt.

In the case of a company that acquires another company after November 16, 1985, the debt of the target and the acquirer are to be aggregated in determining the amount of debt qualifying for transition relief. For example, if a corporation with $50 of debt outstanding on that date acquires on June 1, 1986, another corporation that had $20 of debt outstanding on November 16, 1985, the amount of debt of the group qualifying for transitional relief is $70.

[The following colloquy relating to Act Sec. 1215 is drawn from the Congressional Record. The colloquy occurred on the day the Conference bill was considered by the Senate. Ed.]

[Senate Floor Explanation]
APPLICATION OF NEW ALLOCATION OF EXPENSE RULES TO POSSESSIONS INCOME

Mr. MOYNIHAN. Mr. President, the conference agreement contains a provision dealing with the allocation of interest and other expenses. Under the conference agreement, this provision, pursuant to regulations, is to apply to provisions dealing with international taxation. I would appreciate the confirmation of the distinguished chairman that the new rule of section 864(e)(1) does not apply for purposes of computations under section 936(h).

Mr. PACKWOOD. Yes, it is my understanding of the conference agreement that the new rule of section 864(e)(1) does not apply for purposes of computations under section 936(h). Congressional Record, p. S 13950, 9-27-86.

[The following is from a statement of the Chairman of the House Ways and Means Committee relating to Senate Floor colloquies on the Conference bill. Ed.]

[House Floor Explanation]

I have discussed with Congressman Rangel several issues relating the the application of new allocation of expense rules to possessions income. We have reached a common understanding which affirms the colloquy held between Senator Moynihan and Senator Packwood, located on page S13950 of the Congressional Record dated September 27, 1986 regarding the application of new allocation of expense rules to possessions income. Congressional Record, p. S 13950, 10-2-86.

[¶ 4033] SECTION 1216. 1-YEAR MODIFICATION IN REGULATIONS PROVIDING FOR ALLOCATION OF RESEARCH AND EXPERIMENTAL EXPENDITURES

(Reg. Sec. 1.861-8)

[House Explanation]

* * * * * *

Present Law.—*Foreign tax credit and source rules.*—All income has either a U.S. source or a foreign source. The foreign tax credit can offset U.S. tax on foreign source taxable income, but not U.S. source taxable

income. (This is known as the foreign tax credit limitation.) A shift in the source of income from foreign to U.S. may increase U.S. tax by reducing the amount of foreign tax that a taxpayer may credit.

In determining foreign source taxable income for purposes of computing the foreign tax credit limitation, and for other tax purposes, Code sections 861-868 require taxpayers to apportion expenses between foreign source income and U.S. source income. A shift in the apportionment of expenses from U.S. to foreign source gross income decreases foreign source taxable income. This decrease may increase U.S. tax by reducing the amount of foreign tax that a taxpayer may credit.

Research and experimental expense allocation regulation.—Treasury Reg. sec. 1.861-8 (published in 1977) sets forth detailed rules for allocating and apportioning several categories of expenses, including deductible research and experimental expenditures ("research expenses"). The regulation provides that research expenses are ordinarily considered definitely related to all gross income reasonably connected with one or more of 32 product categories based on two-digit classifications of the Standard Industrial Classification ("SIC") system. Research expenses are not traced solely to the income generated by the particular product which benefited from the research activity. Instead these expenses are associated with all the income within the SIC product group in which the product is classified.

The Treasury regulation contemplates that taxpayers will sometimes undertake research solely to meet legal requirements imposed by a particular political entity with respect to improvement or marketing of specific products or processes. In some cases, such research cannot reasonably be expected to generate income (beyond de minimis amounts) outside that political entity's jurisdiction. If so, the associated research expense reduces gross income only from the geographic source that includes that jurisdiction.

After research expenses incurred to meet legal requirements are allocated under the above rule, any remaining research expenses are generally apportioned to foreign source income based on the ratio of total foreign source sales receipts in the SIC product group with which the expenses are identified to the taxpayer's total worldwide sales receipts in that product group (the "sales" or "gross receipts" method). However, the regulation provides that a taxpayer using the sales method may first apportion 30 percent of research expense remaining after allocation to meet legal requirements exclusively to income from the geographic source where over half of the taxpayer's research and development is performed. Thus, for example, a taxpayer who performs two-thirds of his research and development in the United States may automatically apportion at least 30 percent of his remaining research expense to U.S. source income. A taxpayer can choose to apportion to the geographic source where research and development is performed a percentage of research expense significantly greater than 30 percent if he establishes that the higher percentage is warranted because the research and development is reasonably expected to have a very limited or long-delayed application outside that geographic source.

Alternatively, subject to certain limitations, a taxpayer may elect to apportion his research expense remaining after any allocation to meet legal requirements under one of two optional gross income methods. Under these optional methods, a taxpayer generally apportions his research expense on the basis of relative amounts of gross income from U.S. and foreign sources. If a taxpayer makes an automatic place-of-performance apportionment, he may not use an optional gross income method.

The basic limitation on the use of the optional gross income methods is that the respective portions of a taxpayer's research expense apportioned to U.S. and foreign source income using these methods may not be less than 50 percent of the respective portions that would be apportioned to each income grouping using a combination of the sales and place-of-performance apportionment methods. If this 50-percent limitation is satisfied with respect to both income groupings, the taxpayer may apportion the amount of his research expense that remains after allocation under the legal requirements test ratably on the basis of foreign and U.S. gross income. If the 50-percent limitation is not satisfied with respect to one of the income groupings, then the taxpayer apportions to the income grouping with respect to which the 50-percent limitation is not satisfied, 50 percent of the amount of his research expense which would have been apportioned to that income grouping under the sales and place-of-performance methods. A taxpayer electing an optional gross income method may be able then to reduce the amount of his research expense apportioned to foreign source income to as little as one-half of the amount that would be apportioned to foreign source income under the sales method.

For example, consider a taxpayer with $110 of U.S.-performed research expense and equal U.S. and foreign sales. Assume that $10 of the research expense is to meet U.S. legal requirements and is allocated to U.S. source income. Of the remaining $100, 30 percent ($30) is exclusively apportioned to U.S. source income under the automatic place-of-performance rule and the remaining $70 is divided evenly between U.S. and foreign source income, using the sales method. Under the optional gross income methods, the $35 of research expense allocated to foreign sources could be reduced as much as 50 percent, to $17.50. This could occur, for example, if the foreign sales were made by a foreign subsidiary that did not repatriate earnings to the U.S. corporation.

The optional gross income methods apply to all of a taxpayer's gross income, not gross income on a product category basis.

Treas. Reg. sec. 1.861-8 generally requires a smaller allocation of research expense to foreign source income than a predecessor regulation proposed in 1973 would have required.[13]

Temporary moratorium and Treasury study.—The Economic Recovery Tax Act of 1981 (ERTA) provided that, for a taxpayer's first two taxable years beginning after the date of its enactment (August 13, 1981), all research and experimental expenditures (within the meaning of Code sec. 174) which were paid or incurred in those taxable years for research activities conducted in the United States were to be allocated or apportioned to income from sources within the United States (sec. 223 of ERTA). This two-year moratorium on the application of the research and experimental expense allocation rules of Treas. Reg. sec. 1.861-8 was effectively extended for two additional years by the Tax Reform Act of 1984. Under the 1984 Act (sec. 126), for taxable years beginning generally after August 13, 1983, and on or before August 1, 1985, all of a taxpayer's research and experimental expenditures (within the meaning of Code sec. 174) attributable to research activities conducted in the United States are to be allocated to sources within the United States for purposes of computing taxable income from U.S. sources and from sources partly within and partly without the United States.

One reason Congress cited for enacting the original two-year moratorium was that some foreign countries do not allow deductions under their tax laws for expenses of research activities conducted in the United States. Taxpayers argued that this disallowance resulted in unduly high foreign taxes and that, absent changes in the foreign tax credit limitation, U.S. taxpayers would lose foreign tax credits. Because those taxpayers could take their deductions if the research occurred in the foreign country, taxpayers argued that there was incentive to shift their research expenditures to those foreign countries whose laws disallow tax deductions for research activities conducted in the United States but allow tax deductions for research expenditures incurred locally.

Accordingly, Congress concluded that the Treasury Department should study the impact of the allocation of research expenses under Treas. Reg. sec. 1.861-8 on U.S.-based research activities and on the availability of the foreign tax credit. While that study was being conducted by the Treasury and considered by Congress, Congress concluded that expenses should be charged to the cost of generating U.S. source income, whether or not such research was a direct or indirect cost of producing foreign source income.

In June 1983 the Treasury Department submitted its report on the mandated study to the House Committee on Ways and Means and the Senate Committee on Finance.[14] In summary, the Treasury report concluded that:

The moratorium reduced U.S. tax liabilities. Had Treas. Reg. sec. 1.861-8 fully been in effect in 1982, the Treasury Department estimated that the $37 billion in privately financed U.S. research and development spending in 1982 would have been reduced by approximatly $40 million to $260 million as a result of increased U.S. tax costs. Most of the reduction would have represented a net reduction in overall research and development undertaken by U.S. corporations and their foreign affiliates, rather than a transfer of research and development abroad.

The moratorium reduced the tax liabilities only of firms with excess foreign tax credits. Whether or not a firm had excess foreign tax credits did not seem to be closely related to the level of its research and development efforts.

The moratorium had its most significant effect on large, mature multinationals as opposed to small, relatively young high-technology companies. Of the estimated increase in U.S. tax liabilities for calendar 1982 that would have occurred had Treas. Reg. sec. 1.861-8 been fully in effect, about 85 percent was estimated to be accounted for by 24 U.S. firms on the list of the 100 largest U.S. industrial corporations compiled by *Fortune Magazine.*

An allocation of research expense to foreign income could increase a taxpayer's worldwide tax liability if the foreign government did not allow the apportioned expense as a deduction. Some allocation to foreign income, however, was appropriate on tax policy grounds when U.S. research and development was exploited in a foreign market and generated foreign source income. If an allocation were not made, foreign source taxable income would be too high and the higher limitation could allow the credit for foreign tax to reduce U.S. tax on U.S. source income.

The research and development rules of Treas. Reg. sec. 1.861-8 reflected significant modifications of the 1973 proposed version of the regulation in response to taxpayer comments. Compared to the 1973 version of the regulations, these modifications allowed less research expense to be allocated to foreign source income and recognized that research and development conducted in the United States might be most valuable in the U.S. market.

On the ground that a reduction in research and development might adversely affect the competitive position of the United States, the 1983 Treasury report recommended the two-year extension of the moratorium that was ultimately enacted by Congress in 1984. The extension was intended to allow Congress to consider further the results of the Treasury study on the Treasury research expense allocation rules.

*   *   *   *   *   *

Explanation of Provision.—Under the bill, for taxable years beginning generally after August 1, [1986] * * *, and on or before

---

[Footnote ¶ **4033] (13)** See 38 Fed. Reg. 15,840 (1973).

(14) See Department of the Treasury. *The Impact of the Section 861-8 Regulation on U.S. Research and Development* (June 1983).

August 1, 1987 the application of the Treas. Reg. sec. 1.861-8 research expense allocation rules is effectively liberalized in three respects. These liberalizations apply notwithstanding other changes made by the bill in the Code's expense allocation rules (sec. 614 of the bill).

The bill retains the regulatory rule (Treas. Reg. sec. 1.861-8(e)(3)(i)(B)) under which research expenditures are allocated entirely to one geographic source if they were incurred to meet legal requirements imposed with respect to improvement or marketing of specific products or processes and cannot reasonably be expected to generate income (beyond de minimis amounts) outside that geographic source. For the specified two-year period, the bill provides that 50 percent of all remaining amounts allowable as a deduction for qualified research and experimental expenditures will be apportioned to U.S. source income and deducted from such income in determining the amount of taxable U.S. source income. The bill thus has the effect of increasing the automatic place-of-performance apportionment percentage for U.S.-based research expense from 30 percent to 50 percent. Under the bill, a taxpayer will be able to apportion to U.S. source income 50 percent of his U.S.-based research expense remaining after any allocation of such expense incurred to meet legal requirements.

The bill further provides that, for the specified two-year period, the portion of those amounts allowable as a deduction for qualified research and experimental expenditures that remains after any legal requirements allocation and the 50-percent automatic place-of-performance apportionment will be apportioned on the basis of sales or gross income. Thus, the bill makes automatic place-of-performance apportionment available temporarily to taxpayers who elect to apportion expenses using the optional gross income method, as well as to taxpayers choosing the standard sales method of apportionment. The bill also has the effect of temporarily suspending the regulatory rule that prohibits taxpayers from using the optional gross income method to reduce allocation of research expense to foreign source income by more than 50 percent over what

the allocation to foreign source income would be under the standard sales method.

The bill's temporary modifications to the Treas. Reg. sec. 1.861-8 research expense allocation rules apply for purposes of computing taxable income from U.S. sources and from sources partly within and partly without the United States. The modifications apply only to the allocation of research and experimental expenditures for the purposes of geographic sourcing of income. They do not apply for other purposes, such as the computation of combined taxable income of a FSC (or DISC) and its related supplier. They also do not apply to any expenditure for the acquisition or improvement of land, or for the acquisition or improvement of depreciable or depletable property to be used in connection with research or experimentation.

* * * * * *

[Conference Report]

* * * * * *

[Effective Date]—The conference agreement follows the House bill but is effective for taxable years beginning after August 1, 1986 and on or before August 1, 1987.

Because of the importance of U.S.-based research activity, the conferees encourage the tax-writing committees to continue to study whether any additional permanent tax incentives for U.S. research might be appropriate. The conferees consider it important that the relative equity and efficiency of alternative tax incentives be fully analyzed before any decision is made to adopt a permanent tax incentive. The conference agreement does not reflect a judgment by the conferees that any provision of the existing regulation is necessarily correct or incorrect. It is anticipated that the Treasury Department will expeditiously pursue a permanent resolution of the allocation issue. The conferees do, however, consider it important that the Treasury Department reexamine its regulations in light of concerns expressed by the tax-writing committees of both Houses. Moreover, the conferees expect that the Treasury Department, in connection with the U.S. treaty process, will resolve any incompatibility with foreign tax systems that may arise if the regulations were to go into effect.

[¶ 4034] SECTION 1221. INCOME SUBJECT TO CURRENT TAXATION.

(Sec. 954 of the Code)

[Senate Explanation]

* * * * * *

Present Law.—*In general.* Two different sets of U.S. tax rules apply to American taxpayers that control business operations in foreign countries. The choice of whether the business operations are conducted directly, for example, through a foreign branch, or indirectly through a separately incorporated foreign company, determines which rules apply. (To the extent that foreign corpora-

tions operate in the United States rather than in foreign countries, they generally pay U.S. tax like U.S. corporations.)

Direct operations—current tax.—The income from foreign business operations that are conducted directly appears on the U.S. tax return for the year the taxpayer earns it. The United States generally taxes that income currently, as it does U.S. income. The foreign tax credit, discussed above, may reduce or eliminate the U.S. tax on the foreign income, however.

Indirect operations—generally tax deferral.—In general, a U.S. shareholder of a foreign corporation pay no U.S. tax on the income from those operations until the foreign corporation sends its income home (repatriates it) to America. The income appears on the U.S. shareholder's tax return for the year it comes home, and the United States generally collects the tax on it then. The foreign tax credit may reduce or eliminate the U.S. tax, however. (The foreign corporation itself will not pay U.S. tax unless it has income effectively connected with a trade or business carried on in the United States, or has certain generally passive types of U.S. source income.)

Indirect operations—current tax for some income.—Deferral of U.S. tax on income of a controlled foreign corporation is not available for certain kinds of income (referred to here as "subpart F income") under the Code's subpart F provisions. Subpart F income is generally income that is relatively movable from one taxing jurisdiction to another in order to reduce U.S. and foreign tax liability. When a U.S.-controlled foreign corporation earns subpart F income, the United States will generally tax the corporation's 10-percent U.S. shareholders currently on their pro rata share of the subpart F income. In effect, the Code treats the U.S. shareholders as having received a current dividend to the extent of the corporation's subpart F income. In this case, too, the foreign tax credit may reduce or eliminate the U.S. tax.

Subpart F income presently consists of income from the insurance of U.S. risks (defined in sec. 953), foreign base company income (defined in sec. 954), and certain income relating to international boycotts and illegal payments. Foreign base company income is itself subdivided into five categories. One major category is foreign personal holding company income. For subpart F purposes, foreign personal holding company income consists generally of passive income such as interest, dividends, net gains from sales of stock and securities, related party factoring income, and some rents and royalties. Net gains from certain commodities futures transactions are foreign personal holding company income unless they arise out of certain bona fide hedging transactions. An exclusion from subpart F foreign personal holding company income is provided for rents and royalties received from unrelated persons in the active conduct of a trade or business. Under this active trade or business test, rents from a retail car-leasing business involving substantial maintenance, repair, and marketing activities, for example, would be excluded from subpart F, while rental income from lease-financing transactions would not. Exclusions are also provided for dividends, interest, and gains derived from unrelated persons by a banking, financing, or similar business, and dividends, interest, and gains received by an insurance company from its investment of unearned premiums and reserves. Additional exclusions from subpart F foreign personal holding company income are provided for (1) certain dividends

and interest received from a related person organized and operating in the same foreign country as the recipient, (2) interest paid between related persons that are each engaged in the conduct of a banking, financing, or similar business predominantly with unrelated persons, and (3) rents and royalties received from a related person for the use of property within the country in which the recipient was created or organized.

Other categories of foreign base company income include foreign base company sales and services income, consisting respectively of income from related party sales routed through the income recipient's country if that country is neither the origin nor the destination of the goods, and income from services performed outside the country of the corporation's incorporation for or on behalf of related persons. (Income from the insurance of related parties' third-country risks is taxed as foreign base company services income.) Foreign base company income also includes foreign base company shipping income, except to the extent such income is reinvested by the controlled foreign corporation in foreign shipping operations. Finally, foreign base company income generally includes "downstream" oil-related income, that is, foreign oil-related income other than extraction income.

Foreign personal holding company income, defined somewhat differently than for subpart F purposes, may also be subject to current U.S. taxation under a different, older set of Code rules, the foreign personal holding company rules (secs. 551-58). Congress enacted the foreign personal holding company rules in 1937 to prevent U.S. taxpayers from accumulating income tax-free in foreign "incorporated pocketbooks." If five or fewer U.S. citizens or residents own, directly or indirectly, more than half of the outstanding stock (in value) of a foreign corporation that has primarily foreign personal holding company income (generally passive income such as dividends, interest, royalties, and rents (if rental income does not amount to 50 percent of gross income)), that corporation will be a foreign personal holding company. In that case, the foreign corporation's U.S. shareholders, including U.S. citizens, residents, and corporations, are subject to U.S. tax on their pro rata share of the corporation's undistributed foreign personal holding company income. Though only individuals count in the determination of foreign personal holding company status, persons other than individuals may be subject to foreign personal holding company tax.

*　　*　　*　　*　　*　　*

Explanation of Provision.—*Sales of property which does not generate active income.* The bill adds to the Code section 954(c) definition of foreign personal holding company income for subpart F purposes the excess of gains over losses from sales and exchanges of non-income producing property and property that gives rise to the following types of passive (foreign personal holding company) income; first, dividends and interest other than those excluded from subpart F under the active business exception for banks (as modified by the bill) or the active business exception for insurance companies; second, rents and royalties other than active business, unrelated party rents and royalties; and, third, annuities. Thus, included in foreign personal holding company would be, for example, gain on the sale of diamonds held for investment purposes prior to disposition. As another example, gain from the disposition of a patent that gave rise to unrelated party, active business royalties would not be treated as foreign personal holding company income under this rule while gain from the sale of a patent licensed to a person related to the seller would be so treated.

The committee retains the present law exception from the current taxation rules for securities gains of regular dealers and extends that exception to the broader category of gains just described. Thus, for example, the gain of a regular art dealer on the sale of a painting would not constitute subpart F foreign personal holding company income. On the other hand, the gain of a company on the sale of a painting held as an investment property generally would be subpart F foreign personal holding company income (at least before application of subpart F's de minimis exception): if, prior to its disposition, the painting merely was displayed in the corporate offices or held in storage, it would not have given rise to any income; if, prior to its disposition, the painting was leased temporarily by the corporation for compensation, such compensation would not have been active rental income of the type excluded from foreign personal holding company income. Gains from the sale or exchange of other property which, in the hands of the seller, is inventory property (Code sec. 1221(1)) also are excluded from the application of the new rule.

The committee retains the present law subpart F treatment of going on sales of stock and securities. Thus, gain on the sale of stock in, for example, a foreign corporation, whether or not created or organized in the same foreign country as the selling company, constitutes foreign personal holding company income under subpart F.

* * * * * *

[Conference Report]

* * * * * *

Sales of property which does not generate active income.—The conference agreement generally follows the Senate amendment. As under the House bill, however, stock and securities gains of banking, financing, insurance, and similar businesses are subpart F FPHC income under the agreement. The conferees intend that income from commodity and currency transactions that are within the scope of the special subpart F provisions for such transactions (discussed immediately below) will not be subject to tax under this provision. Thus, for example, a transaction

that would be subject to tax under the special rule for commodities transactions but for the active producers' exception to that rule is not subject to tax under this provision. The provision is also not intended to apply to gain on the sale of land used by the seller in an active trade or business of the seller at the time of the sale.

* * * * * *

[Senate Explanation]

* * * * * *

Commodities transactions.—The bill adds to the section 954(c) definition of foreign personal holding company income for subpart F purposes the excess of gains over losses from transactions (including futures transactions) in any commodities. The bill retains the present law exception for gains by a producer, processor, merchant or handler of a commodity which arise from bona fide hedging transactions reasonably necessary to the conduct of its business in the manner in which such business is customarily and usually conducted by others.

An additional exception is provided for transactions (not limited to hedging transactions) that occur in the active business of a foreign corporation substantially all of whose business is that of an active producer, processor, merchant, or handler of commodities. The committee intends this exception to apply only to foreign corporations actively engaged in commodities businesses, not those primarily engaged in such financial transactions as the trading of futures. Regularly taking delivery of physical commodities will generally indicate the existence of such a business, but such activity will not of itself determine the issue. For example, the business of a company that trades primarily in precious metals may be essentially financial, particularly if the company takes delivery of the metals through an agent such as a bank. (The availability, if any, of the present law hedging exception with respect to such a business is not affected by the bill.)

Other characteristics of companies actively engaged in commodities businesses include: engaging in substantial processing activities and incurring substantial expenses with respect to commodities prior to their sale, including (but not limited to) concentrating, refining, mixing, crushing, aerating, and milling; engaging in significant activities and incurring substantial expenses relating to the physical movement, handling, and storage of commodities, including (but not limited to) preparation of contracts and invoices, arrangement of freight, insurance, or credit, arrangement for receipt, transfer, or negotiation of shipping documents, arrangement of storage or warehousing, and dealing with quality claims; owning and operating physical facilities used in the activities just described; owning or chartering vessels or vehicles for the transportation of commodities; and producing the commodities sold.

* * * * * *

[Conference Report]

* * * * * *

Commodities transactions.—The conference agreement generally follows the Senate amendment. The agreement clarifies that income from forward and similar transactions in commodities is subject to the new subpart F provision. Income from foreign currency transactions that are not Code section 988 transactions (for example, a position marked to market under Code section 1256) may be subject to current taxation under this provision. Foreign currency gains attributable to section 988 transactions, however, are to be treated exclusively under the special subpart F provision dealing with foreign currency gains. Accordingly, the business needs exception applicable to foreign currency gains attributable to section 988 transactions will not be limited by the subpart F rules on commodities transactions.

Following the Senate amendment, the agreement excludes from subpart F FPHC income active business gains and losses from the sale of commodities by a controlled foreign corporation substantially all of the business of which is as an active producer, processor, merchant, or handler of commodities. For this purpose, active business gains and losses from commodity sales include gains and losses from financial transactions which constitute bona fide hedging transactions integrally related to a principal business of trading in physical commodities.

No inference is intended as to the types of commodity transactions that, under present law, may be considered futures transactions in a commodity on or subject to the rules of a board of trade or commodity exchange.

* * * * * *

[Senate Explanation]

* * * * * *

Foreign currency gains.—The bill adds to the section 954(c) definition of foreign personal holding company income for subpart F purposes the excess of foreign currency gains over foreign currency losses attributable to section 988 transactions. An exception to current taxation is provided for hedging and other transactions that are directly related to the business needs of a controlled foreign corporation. Foreign currency gains and losses attributable to section 988 transactions are defined as they are for purposes of the bill's new rules relating to the taxation of foreign currency exchange rate gains and losses * * *.

* * * * * *

[Conference Report]

* * * * * *

Foreign currency gains.—The conference agreement follows the Senate amendment.

Active foreign currency gains and losses arising from a controlled foreign corporation's business as an active foreign currency dealer are excluded from subpart F FPHC

income under the business needs exception to this provision.

Income equivalent to interest. — Following the Senate amendment, the conference agreement treats income equivalent to interest as FPHC income for subpart F purposes. For this purpose, income equivalent to interest includes commitment fees for the actual lending of money.

Income equivalent to interest is treated as subpart F FPHC income (and passive income, for separate limitation purposes) to prevent taxpayers from continuing (notwithstanding the agreement's separate limitation for passive income and other amendments to the definition of subpart F FPHC income) to shelter passive interest-type income from current U.S. tax by rearranging the form of offshore passive investments so that the income they generate is not traditional interest income. Since the agreement repeals present law's subpart F exceptions for banking and insurance income, the conferees can see no sound policy reason for favoring activities which generate income equivalent to interest over activities of banks and insurance companies.

Passive leasing income.—The * * * bill clarifies that passive leasing income generally is subpart F FPHC income.

* * * * * *

[Senate Explanation]

* * * * * *

Related person exceptions.—The bill restricts the present law rule that excludes from foreign personal holding company income for subpart F purposes certain dividends, interest, rents, and royalties received from related persons (section 954(c)(4) (A), (B), and (C)). (The scope of section 954(c)(4)(B), relating to interest paid between related banks, is also modified by the bill. See discussion of non-bona fide banking income, above.) Under the new restriction, interest, rent, and royalty payments will not qualify for the exclusion to the extent that such payments reduce subpart F income of the payor. Thus, if the income of the payor corporation consists entirely of non-subpart F income, then the related party exclusions of section 954(c)(4) (A), (B), and (C) will apply in full as under present law. However, to the extent that the payor corporation receives subpart F income which is reduced by its payment of interest, rent, or royalties, then such payment will be treated as subpart F income to a related party recipient, notwithstanding the general rules of section 954(c)(4).

As an example, assume that a controlled foreign corporation receives from a related party a $100 interest payment that, under present law, would be excluded from foreign personal holding company income for subpart F purposes under section 954(c)(4) (A) or (B). The payee corporation also earns foreign base company services income taxable currently to its shareholders under subpart F. Assume that none of the expenses incurred by the payee are allocable to the $100 of interest in determining the payee's net income subject to subpart F taxation. The related party payor of the interest, also a controlled foreign corporation, earns $5,000 of gross manufacturing income that is not subject to tax under subpart F and $500 of gross portfolio dividends that *are* subject to tax under subpart F. The payor uses the asset method to allocate its $100 of interest expense for purposes of determining the amount of its subpart F income. Under the asset method, $90 of the interest is allocable to the payor's gross manufacturing income and the remaining $10 reduces the payor's gross portfolio dividends subject to subpart F. Therefore, $10 of the $100 of interest received by the payee will be treated as subpart F income of the payee's U.S. shareholders. The look-through rule will operate in the same manner in this example if the $100 payment is a rent, royalty, or similar amount (otherwise excluded from subpart F taxation under section 954(c)(4)(C)) rather than interest.

The bill also provides a limited exclusion from subpart F foreign personal holding company income for certain mining-related income.

*   *   *   *   *   *

[Conference Report]

*   *   *   *   *   *

Senate Amendment

*   *   *   *   *   *

Same country dividend exception.—The same country exclusion of present law is extended to dividends attributable to specified mining-related income from a less than 50-percent owned corporation.

*   *   *   *   *   *

Conference Agreement

*   *   *   *   *   *

Same country dividend exception.—The conference agreement follows the Senate amendment except that the agreement applies only to the first five taxable years of the specified foreign corporation beginning after 1986.

*   *   *   *   *   *

[House Explanation]

*   *   *   *   *   *

Shipping income.—The bill repeals the rule that under present law excludes from foreign personal holding company income for subpart F purposes foreign base company shipping income that is reinvested in foreign base company shipping operations (section 954(b)(2)). Thus, any income that constitutes foreign base company shipping income under section 954(f) will be subject to current taxation under subpart F, regardless of the controlled foreign corporation's use of the income. In addition, the bill adds to the definition of foreign base company shipping income any income derived from activities outside the jurisdiction of any country, including

generally income derived in space, in the ocean, or in Antarctica.

*   *   *   *   *   *

[Conference Report]

*   *   *   *   *   *

House Bill

Banking exceptions.—The subpart F banking exceptions are repealed.

*   *   *   *   *   *

Conference Agreement

Banking exceptions.—The conference agreement follows the House bill except that tax deferral is preserved, to the extent otherwise available under present law, for interest derived in connection with certain export sales. Such interest must be derived in the conduct of a banking business from financing the sale (or other disposition) for use or consumption outside the United States of any property which is manufactured, produced, grown, or extracted in the United States by the interest recipient or a related person, and not more than 50 percent of the fair market value of which is attributable to products imported into the United States. For this purpose, the fair market value of any property imported into the United States is its appraised value, as determined by the Secretary under section 402 of the Tariff Act of 1930 (19 U.S.C. 1401a) in connection with its importation. A related person is defined for this purpose in the same manner as it is defined generally for subpart F purposes (Code sec. 954(d)(3) as amended by the conference agreement; *see* discussion of controlled partnerships below).

House Explanation

Insurance income.—The House bill amends the definition of tax haven insurance income to include income from the insurance of unrelated persons' risks outside of the insuring company's country of incorporation. In addition, it repeals the 5-percent de minimis exception for income from the insurance of U.S. risks, and repeals the exceptions for investment income from unearned premiums and reserves.

Conference Agreement

Insurance income.—The conference agreement incorporates, with modifications, the House bill provisions amending the definition of tax haven insurance income, repealing the 5-percent de minimis exception for income from U.S. risk insurance, and repealing the exceptions for investment income from unearned premiums and reserves. The conference agreement makes all tax haven insurance income eligible for the general subpart F de minimis exception and 70-percent full inclusion rule (Code sec. 954(b)(3), as amended by the conference agreement; discussed at * * * ¶4036). It also contains a special rule, discussed more fully below, which reduces subpart F's U.S. ownership requirements for current taxation of a foreign corporation's income, in the case of certain related person insurance income. The purpose of this rule is to subject to current U.S. tax the related person insurance income of offshore "captive" insurance companies that avoid such tax under present law because, for example, their U.S. ownership is relatively dispersed, that is, no more than 25 percent of their voting stock is held by 10-percent U.S. shareholders.

Generally, a captive insurance company is considered to be a company organized by one or more persons primarily to provide insurance protection to its owners or persons related to its owners. The new rule will limit the unintended tax advantages presently received by U.S. taxpayers that jointly own, with a number of other persons, offshore captive insurers.

One of the major U.S. tax benefits presently claimed by certain offshore captives is exemption from current taxation under subpart F. In addition, premiums received by U.S. persons by foreign captives are often exempt from the U.S. excise tax on insurance premiums paid to foreign insurers and reinsurers under U.S. income tax treaties, such as that with Barbados. The Barbados treaty, which generally became effective in 1984, waives the insurance excise tax, notwithstanding that Barbados itself does not tax insurance companies licensed under its 1983 Exempt Insurance Act. Thus, income earned by Barbados-based captives with relatively dispersed U.S. ownership may escape current tax anywhere in the world.[1]

Another tax advantage of offshore captive insurance arrangements is that premiums paid by U.S. taxpayers to offshore captives with a relatively large number of owners have been ruled currently deductible in some instances, while no current tax is imposed on that premium income in the hands of the captive. While captive insurance arrangements are self-insurance arrangements, contributions to which are not deductible,[2] in Rev. Rul. 78-338 (1978-2 C.B. 107), the IRS ruled that amounts paid by a domestic petro-

leum corporation to a foreign insurance company that provided insurance against certain petroleum industry risks only for its 31 unrelated shareholders and their subsidiaries and affiliates were deductible as insurance premiums. In addition to the fact that the 31 shareholders/insureds of the insurance company were unrelated, the ruling indicated that no one owned a controlling interest and no one's risk coverage could exceed 5 percent of the total risks insured. The ruling concluded that such an arrangement allowed the economic risk of loss to be shifted and distributed among the shareholders who comprised the insured group so that it constitutes insurance. Similarly, in *Crawford Fitting Co.* v. *United States,* 606 F. Supp. 136 (N.D. Ohio 1985), sufficient risk-shifting was found for a deduction to be allowed where a risk was shifted to an insurance company which was only partially commonly controlled (that is, the insurer was 80-percent owned by four separate corporations, in each of which the individual 100-percent owner of the insured corporate taxpayer had an interest).

The conferees do not believe that U.S. persons utilizing offshore captive insurance companies should be able to avoid current U.S. tax on the related person insurance income of these companies simply by spreading the ownership among a number of persons. Accordingly, the conference agreement provides that tax haven insurance income (as that category of income is expanded by the conference agreement) that is related person insurance income generally will be taxable currently under subpart F to an expanded category of U.S. persons. For purposes of taking into account such income under subpart F, the U.S. ownership threshold for controlled foreign corporation status is reduced to 25 percent or more. Any U.S. person (as defined for subpart F purposes by existing Code section 957(d)) who owns or is considered to own (under the rules of existing Code section 958(a)) any stock in a controlled foreign corporation, whatever the degree of

<hr>

[Footnote ¶ 4034]   (1) The unratified U.S. income tax treaty with Bermuda (signed on July 11, 1986) also waives the insurance excise tax, notwithstanding the absence of any Bermuda income tax. Were the Bermuda treaty to be ratified, captives in Bermuda with relatively dispersed U.S. ownership could escape all current tax also. In a letter to the Secretary of the Treasury, dated July 15, 1986, the Chairman of the Ways and Means Committee expressed "serious concerns about both the substance and the procedures followed by the Treasury Department in negotiating this proposed tax treaty." The letter states that the "proposed treaty, rather than preventing double taxation of income, seems to guarantee that significant sums of income will escape any taxation in either jurisdiction . . . The proposal would bless U.S.-owned Bermuda insurance companies, which, in some cases, through the use of spread captive devices, now may be avoiding all tax other than the excise tax on income earned by insuring U.S. risks. In addition, the U.S. premium payors may be deducting the premiums from U.S. taxable income. Thus, the proposed treaty, by exempting these insurance premiums from U.S. tax, would eliminate not double taxation but any taxation."

(2) In Rev. Rul. 77-316 (1977-2 C.B. 53), the IRS ruled that the amounts described as premiums paid by a domestic corporation and its domestic subsidiaries to the parent's wholly owned foreign subsidiary are not deductible premiums if the subsidiary does not also insure risks of insureds outside its own corporate family. The IRS concluded that because the insured and the "insurance" subsidiary (though separate corporate entities) represent one economic family, those who bear the ultimate economic burden of the loss are the same persons who suffer the loss. Thus, the required risk-shifting and risk-distribution of a valid insurance transaction are missing. This position of the Service was favorably cited by the Ninth Circuit in *Carnation Co.* v. *United States,* 640 F.2d 1010 (9th Cir. 1981), cert. denied, 454 U.S. 965. In the recent case of *Humana, Inc. and Subsidiaries* v. *Commissioner,* 50 T.C.M. 784 (1985) and *Mobil Oil Corp.* v. *United States,* 8 Ct. Cl. 555 (1985), the courts have advanced a more developed theory and indicated that the primary criterion in distinguishing a captive from a true insurance arrangement is the absence of risk-shifting. So long as a wholly owned subsidiary of the taxpayer bears the taxpayer's risk of loss, there has not been sufficient risk-shifting to constitute true insurance, premium payments for which could be deductible.

ownership, is treated as a U.S. shareholder of such corporation for purposes of this 25 percent U.S. ownership threshold and exposure to current tax on the corporation's related person insurance income.

Related person insurance income is defined for this purpose to mean any insurance income attributable to a policy of insurance or reinsurance with respect to which the primary insured is either a U.S. shareholder (as defined above) in the foreign corporation receiving the income or a person related to such a shareholder. A related person is defined for this purpose in the same manner as it is for subpart F purposes generally (Code sec. 954(d)(3), as amended by the conference agreement). As indicated above, the definition of tax haven insurance income under the conference agreement follows the House bill. Thus, the new rule for captive insurers applies to investment income as well as to premium income attributable to related person insurance. Related person insurance income includes income attributable to policies of reinsurance issued by a foreign corporation to U.S. shareholders (as defined above) or persons related to such shareholders that previously insured the risks covered by such policies. It also includes income attributable to officers' or directors' insurance where the U.S. shareholders of the foreign corporation receiving such income (or persons related to such shareholders) directly or indirectly pay the premiums and the insureds are officers or directors of the U.S. shareholders (or persons related to such shareholders).

The agreement provides three exceptions to the new subpart F rule. First, related person insurance income of a foreign corporation will not be currently taxable by reason of the new rule if the corporation's gross related person insurance income for the taxable year is less than 20 percent of its gross insurance income for the year. Insurance income is defined for this purpose as it is generally for subpart F purposes under the agreement, except that the exclusion of income attributable to same-country risks does not apply. This rule excepts from the operation of the provision foreign insurance companies with 25-percent or more U.S. ownership that do not earn a significant proportion of related person insurance income.

Second, related person insurance income of a foreign corporation will not be currently taxable under the new provision if less than 20 percent of the total combined voting power of all classes of stock of the corporation entitled to vote and less than 20 percent of the total value (both stock and policies) of the corporation during the taxable year are owned (directly or indirectly) by persons who are the primary insureds under any policies of insurance or reinsurance issued by the corporation, or by persons related to such persons. A related person is defined for this purpose in the same manner as it is for subpart F purposes generally (Code sec. 954(d)(3), as amended by the conference agreement). This exception serves a purpose

similar to that served by the exception for companies with de minimis amounts of related person insurance income.

Third, the agreement provides that a foreign corporation, the related person insurance income of which would otherwise be subject to tax under subpart F under the new rules, may elect instead to treat such income as effectively connected with the conduct of a U.S. trade or business, taxable under Code section 882. The election is to be made at such time and in such manner as the Secretary may prescribe. The election is effective in the year made and in all future years. It is revocable only with the Secretary's consent. To make such an election, the foreign corporation must waive any U.S. income tax treaty benefits with respect to its related person insurance income. The election is not effective if the electing corporation fails to meet such requirements as the Secretary shall prescribe to ensure that the tax imposed on its related person insurance income is paid. Any tax imposed on an electing corporation's related person insurance income may, if not paid by that corporation, be collected from the corporation's U.S. shareholders.

Electing offshore captives will continue to be taxed currently on their related person insurance income, since effectively connected income is taxed currently. However, the election generally will allow them to receive the same tax benefits as similarly situated U.S. insurers with respect to related person insurance activity. Thus, electing offshore captives that incur net operating losses from meeting large claims will be able to carry those losses back 3 years and forward 15 years under the net operating loss carryover rules (Code sec. 172). The availability of loss carryovers may be of particular benefit to insurers of those risks with respect to which the tax law may not permit deductions for reserves. The conferees have adopted the election primarily with such foreign insurers in mind.

The new subpart F rules for captive insurers apply to both stock and mutual insurance companies. For this purpose, the policyholders of a mutual insurance company are to be treated as its shareholders. The rules are to be adapted in appropriate respects for application to mutual companies, under regulations.

The conferees recognize that foreign mutual insurance companies that insure a significant number of U.S. persons may technically have significant amounts of related person insurance income (as defined for purposes of the agreement) solely because such companies are formally owned by their policyholders. However, the conferees understand that, in the typical non-captive case, such income derived by the insurance company is effectively connected with the conduct of a U.S. trade or business and, consequently, under present law, is taxed by the United States; the reason is that most foreign mutuals with a significant number of U.S. policyholders have permanent establishments in the Unit-

Act § 1221 ¶ 4034

ed States. Under existing Code rules, subpart F income generally does not include U.S. source income that is effectively connected with the conduct of a U.S. trade or business (Code sec. 952(b)). Therefore, so long as they continue to do business in the United States through permanent establishments, it is anticipated that the income of these foreign mutual companies attributable to U.S. insureds generally will not be taxed under the new subpart F provision for captive insurers.

Premiums received by a captive insurer that is subject to the new subpart F rules, like premiums received by an offshore insurer that is subject to present law subpart F, generally remain subject to the excise tax on insurance premiums paid to foreign insurers, absent a treaty exemption. However, the excise tax does not apply to income treated as effectively connected with the conduct of a U.S. business under the "effectively connected" election. This is consistent with the present law exemption from the excise tax generally accorded to premiums that are effectively connected with the conduct of a U.S. business.

The agreement requires the Secretary to prescribe such regulations as may be necessary to carry out the purposes of the new subpart F rules for captive insurers, including regulations preventing the avoidance of the new rules through cross-insurance arrangements or otherwise. Assume, for example, that a foreign company is owned by 35 U.S. persons unrelated to one another but engaged in similar businesses. The company's primary business is insuring against certain risks of those U.S. persons. Under the agreement, it generally will have related person insurance income in profitable years, taxable currently to its U.S. owners.

Assume, however, that the captive insurance arrangement is modified as follows: The foreign company is liquidated and two new foreign companies are organized. One of the companies is owned by 18 of the U.S. persons that formerly owned the liquidated company. The other new company is owned by the other 17 persons that formerly owned the liquidated company. The primary business of the first company is insuring against certain risks of the 17 owners of the second company. The primary business of the second company is insuring against certain risks of the 18 owners of the first company.

The conferees believe that such an arrangement is essentially equivalent to a captive insurance arrangement. It can be used to achieve a similar degree of cooperative risk-sharing among similarly situated members of an industry. The conferees do not believe that U.S. shareholders should be able to obtain the deferral of U.S. tax on income attributable to insurance of risks of U.S. persons who are in turn insuring the risks of those shareholders. Accordingly, under the regulations, the income of the two companies in the example attributable to the insurance business described is to be treated as related person insurance income. The existence of a single foreign entity subject to the general subpart F rules for captives prior to the

creation of such a cross-insurance arrangement is not necessary to support a finding that such an arrangement was made or availed of to avoid the captive insurer rules.

* * * * * *

[House Explanation]

* * * * *

Exception for foreign corporation not used to reduce taxes.—The bill modifies the rule of section 954(b)(4), which excludes nontax avoidance income from current taxation under subpart F, by replacing present law's subjective "significant purpose" test with an objective rule. Under the new rule, subpart F income does not include items of income received by a controlled foreign corporation if it is established to the satisfaction of the Secretary that the income was subject to an effective rate of foreign tax equal to at least 90 percent of the maximum corporate tax rate (36 percent under the bill). However, this exception to subpart F does not apply to foreign base company oil-related income described in section 954(a)(5).

Although this rule applies separately with respect to each "item of income" received by a controlled foreign corporation, the committee expects that the Secretary will provide rules permitting reasonable groupings of items of income that bear substantially equal effective rates of tax in a given country. For example, all interest income received by a controlled foreign corporation from sources within its country of incorporation may reasonably be treated as a single item of income for purposes of this rule, if such interest is subject to uniform taxing rules in that country.

The committee intends, by making the operation of this rule more certain, to ensure that it can be used more easily than the subjective test of present law. This is important because it lends flexibility to the committee's general broadening of the categories of income that are subject in the first instance to current tax under subpart F. The committee's judgment is that because moveable income could often be as easily earned through a U.S. corporation as a foreign corporation, a U.S. taxpayer's use of a foreign corporation to earn that income may be motivated primarily by tax considerations. If, however, in a particular case no U.S. tax advantage is gained by routing income through a foreign corporation, then the basic premise of subpart F taxation is not met, and there is little reason to impose the subpart F tax. Thus, since the scope of transactions subject to subpart F will be broadened, and may sweep in a greater number of non-tax motivated transactions, the committee expects that the flexibility provided by a readily applicable exception for such transactions will become a substantially more important element of the subpart F system.

* * * * * *

[Conference Report]

* * * * *

House Bill

Controlled partnerships.—The House bill treats a partnership that is controlled by a controlled foreign corporation or by the person controlling the foreign corporation as a related person for purposes of subpart F.

Conference Agreement

*   *   *   *   *   *

The conference agreement follows the House bill.* * *

Deficits.—The conference agreement repeals the chain deficit rule (Code sec. 952(d)).

It also limits the present law rule (the "accumulated deficit rule") permitting a controlled foreign corporation to reduce subpart F income by the sum of its prior year deficits in earnings and profits (Code sec. 952(c)(1) & (2)). Subject to the conditions described below, the agreement provides that foreign base company shipping income, foreign base company oil related income, subpart F insurance income, or foreign personal holding company income may be reduced by accumulated deficits in earnings and profits attributable to activities that give rise to foreign base company shipping income, foreign base company oil related income, subpart F insurance income, or foreign personal holding company income, respectively. Other categories of subpart F income may not be reduced by accumulated deficits under the agreement. Subpart F insurance income may be reduced under the rule just described only if the controlled foreign corporation receiving such income was predominantly engaged in the active conduct of an insurance business (within the meaning of new Code sec. 904(d)(2)(C)(ii), discussed at * * * [¶4027]) in both the year in which the income was earned and the year in which the deficit arose. Foreign personal holding company income may be reduced under this new rule only if the controlled foreign corporation receiving such income was predominantly engaged in the active conduct of a banking, financing, or similar business (within the meaning of new Code sec. 904(d)(2)(C)(ii), discussed at * * * [¶4027]) in both the year in which the income was earned and the year in which the deficit arose. Accumulated deficits may be used only once. To be eligible for use under the rule, an accumulated deficit must arise in a year for which the foreign corporation incurring such deficit is a controlled foreign corporation. As under present law, accumulated deficits that cannot be utilized in one year may be carried over indefinitely for possible use in later years. Under the accumulated deficit rule, as modified, accumulated deficits for taxable years beginning before 1987 may not be carried forward to reduce subpart F income.

A U.S. shareholder in a controlled foreign corporation may reduce its subpart F inclusion with respect to that corporation only by the shareholder's pro rata share of accumulated deficits. A U.S. shareholder's pro rata share of any accumulated deficit is to be determined under rules similar to the rules which limit subpart F inclusions to a shareholder's pro rata share of subpart F income (Code sec. 951(a)(2)), for whichever of the following yields the smaller share: the close of the current taxable year or the close of the year in which the deficit arose. Under this rule, then, accumulated deficit use will be limited by the size of a U.S. shareholder's interest in a controlled foreign corporation in the current year and in the year in which the deficit was incurred. Under present law, subpart F and section 1248 inclusions are similarly limited by the size of a shareholder's interest in the controlled foreign corporation when the relevant earnings and profits arose.

Under the agreement, then, pre-acquisition deficits of an acquired corporation to which a controlled foreign corporation in the acquiring group succeeds will not reduce post-acquisition subpart F income of the controlled foreign corporation's shareholders (except to the extent that such shareholders had ownership interests in the acquired corporation when the deficits arose). Similarly, pre-merger deficits of a foreign corporation merged into a controlled foreign corporation will not reduce post-merger subpart F income of the controlled foreign corporation's shareholders (except to the extent that such shareholders had ownership interests in the merged corporation when the deficits arose). The conferees expect the Secretary to issue regulations implementing the above rules, including regulations limiting the use of deficits in connection with other reorganizations.

The agreement retains the present law rule permitting current deficits in earnings and profits in any income category, including nonsubpart F income categories, to reduce subpart F income for the year (Code sec. 952(c)). However, if subpart F income of a foreign corporation is reduced by reason of this rule, the agreement provides that any excess of the earnings and profits of that corporation over its subpart F income in any subsequent taxable year is to be recharacterized as subpart F income under rules similar to the agreement's separate limitation loss recharacterization rule (* * * [¶4027]) and, thus, is to be currently included in the income of the corporation's U.S. shareholders in the year of recharacterization.

Under this recharacterization provision, subpart F-type income that is recaptured for foreign tax credit limitation purposes under the separate limitation loss recharacterization provision is effectively recaptured for subpart F purposes as well. For example, income of a controlled foreign corporation that is passive after application of the separate limitation loss recharacterization provision is also subpart F FPHC income currently taxable to the corporation's U.S. shareholders. The subpart F recharacterization provision thus helps to integrate subpart F and the separate foreign tax credit limitation rules.

The conference agreement restricts the use of deficits to reduce subpart F income for

Act § 1221   **¶ 4034**

several reasons. First, as discussed in greater detail at A.1.e., above, the conferees have sought to simplify the operation of the separate limitation look-through rules for controlled foreign corporations by conforming them and the subpart F rules more closely. The conferees do not believe that separate limitation income received by controlled foreign corporations should be eliminated for foreign tax credit limitation purposes by deficits of other controlled foreign corporations, prior year deficits in other income categories, or current year deficits in other income categories. Preserving such separate limitation income for foreign tax credit limitation purposes without a corresponding preservation of such income for subpart F purposes would substantially complicate the application and administration of the look-through rules. This is particularly the case with respect to the separate limitations for passive income and shipping income since passive income and shipping income are defined for separate limitation purposes by reference to the subpart F categories of FPHC income and foreign base company shipping income, respectively.

Second, the conferees believe that the present law deficit rules allow U.S. taxpayers operating abroad through controlled foreign corporations to shelter too much tax haven income from current U.S. tax. Under the chain deficit rule of Code section 952(d) (as interpreted under regulations), a loss incurred anywhere in a chain of controlled foreign corporations eliminates U.S. tax on an equal amount of income earned elsewhere in the chain even though the loss may be in a nonsubpart F income category or bear little or no relation to the income it offsets. This rule is inconsistent with the "hopscotch" rule, which requires that subpart F income of a controlled foreign corporation be included currently in the gross income of the corporation's ultimate U.S. owners without regard to the income of any intermediate foreign corporation interposed between those owners and the controlled foreign corporation.

Similarly, the accumulated deficit rule of section 952(c) presently allows a controlled foreign corporation to avoid tax on subpart F income by offsetting that income with prior year deficits it incurred in nonsubpart F or unrelated income categories. Were this rule not modified, taxpayers could in many cases shelter from U.S. tax income from passive investments by moving those investments into controlled foreign corporations with prior year deficits.

The conferees note that deficits in earnings and profits incurred by foreign corporations before their acquisition by a U.S. corporation may be used to shelter post-acquisition subpart F income of the U.S. corporation from tax under present law, unless the IRS can show (under Code sec. 269) that the acquisition was made to evade or avoid income tax. Loss trafficking with respect to foreign corporations is not restricted by any rule corresponding to the special anti-loss trafficking rule (Code sec. 382) applicable to U.S. corporations. The agreement's repeal of

the chain deficit rule and modifications to the accumulated deficit rule limit the use of acquired deficits.

A third factor in the conferees' decision to repeal the chain deficit rule is its inconsistency with the present law rule requiring recognition of gain upon the incorporation of a foreign loss branch (Code sec. 367(a)(3)(C)). That rule effectively prevents taxpayers that reduce their worldwide income by using losses incurred by a foreign branch from deferring U.S. tax on the foreign enterprise's subsequent profits while incorporating it tax-free when it turns profitable. Similar current utilization of losses, followed by deferral of tax on income, can be achieved, however, using controlled foreign corporations, as a result of the chain deficit rule.

Another problem with the chain deficit rule that has been brought to the conferees' attention is the ability that the provision confers upon some taxpayers effectively to utilize the same deficits twice. Assume, for example, that a U.S. corporation controls two foreign corporations. One of these foreign corporations owns the other. One of the foreign corporations (the "loss corporation") has a current deficit in earnings and profits of $100. To fund that deficit, the U.S. corporation makes an additional $100 contribution to the loss corporation's capital. That capital contribution increases by $100 the U.S. corporation's basis in its stock in the loss corporation. Under the chain deficit rule, the $100 deficit reduces the second controlled foreign corporation's currently taxable subpart F income in the year in which the deficit arises. In the following year, the U.S. corporation's stock in the loss corporation becomes worthless. Under the rules governing the deduction of losses for worthless securities (Code sec. 165(g)), that stock is a capital asset and the U.S. corporation may therefore deduct in full its basis in the stock, including the $100 component of that basis corresponding to the prior year's additional capital contribution. The loss corporation's $100 deficit in earnings and profits thus reduces the U.S. corporation's taxable income twice, once in the first year under the chain deficit rule, and then again in the following year under the rule allowing a loss deduction for worthless securities. A similar result may be achieved when debt is used to fund a controlled foreign corporation's loss and is later written off.

The application of the accumulated deficit rule, as modified by the agreement, is illustrated in the following three examples: Assume that a controlled foreign corporation wholly owned by a U.S. corporation incurs a $100 deficit in earnings and profits in a taxable year. (For simplicity, this example and the two following assume that gross income, net taxable income, and earnings and profits are the same.) Sixty dollars of the deficit is attributable to activities that, when profitable, generate foreign base company shipping income. The other $40 of the deficit is attributable to activities that, when profitable, generate foreign base company oil related income. In the following year, the controlled foreign corporation earns $90 of foreign base company shipping income, $20 of foreign oil related income, and $10 of foreign base company services income. Under the agreement, the full $60 portion of the accumulated deficit attributable to base company shipping activity can be used to reduce (to $30) the U.S. parent's base company shipping income inclusion with respect to the foreign corporation. Twenty dollars of the $40 portion of the accumulated deficit attributable to base company oil related activity can be used to eliminate the $20 of base company oil related income. The remaining $20 of the accumulated deficit cannot be utilized to reduce the U.S. parent's base company services income or remaining base company shipping income since this deficit amount did not arise from base company services or shipping activity. For the year then, the U.S. parent's subpart F income with respect to the foreign corporation after the accumulated deficit is applied consists of $30 of base company shipping income, $10 of base company services income, and no base company oil related income. The $20 portion of the accumulated deficit attributable to foreign oil related activity which is not utilized may be carried over for possible use in characterizing distributions from the foreign corporation in later years.

Assume, as another example, that a foreign manufacturer wholly owned by a U.S. corporation incurs a $100 deficit in earnings and profits in a taxable year. The manufacturing operations of the controlled foreign corporation, when profitable, generate nonsubpart F income. In the following year, the U.S. parent sells through the foreign manufacturer to third-country buyers goods that a U.S. subsidiary of the U.S. parent produces. With respect to these sales, the foreign corporation receives $30 of foreign base company sales income, currently taxable to its U.S. parent under subpart F. The foreign corporation also earns $80 of nonsubpart F manufacturing income. The amendment to the accumulated deficit rule limits to $80 the amount of the $100 accumulated deficit which may be utilized in this year; since the accumulated deficit arose in a nonsubpart F income category, it may offset only the $80 of nonsubpart F income. For the year then, the subpart F income after the accumulated deficit is applied consists of the $30 of foreign base company sales income. The $20 portion of the accumulated deficit not utilized may be carried over by the foreign corporation to reduce nonsubpart F earnings and profits in later years.

The application of the accumulated deficit rule, as modified, is further illustrated in the following example: Assume that a foreign corporation, wholly owned by a U.S. corporation, incurs a $100 deficit in earnings and profits in a taxable year. The controlled foreign corporation is predominantly engaged in the active conduct of a banking business during that year. When profitable, the foreign corporation earns primarily for-

eign personal holding company income, as that category of subpart F income is expanded by the agreement. The deficit arises from activities that generate foreign personal holding company income. On the first day of the following year, 40 percent of the stock of the controlled foreign corporation is sold to a second U.S. corporation. The foreign corporation earns $300 of foreign personal holding company income and no other income during that taxable year. It is predominantly engaged in the active conduct of a banking business during that year. The second U.S. corporation's share of the subpart F income is $120 (40 percent of $300). The second U.S. corporation cannot reduce its subpart F inclusion by any portion of the $100 accumulated deficit because it owned no stock in the foreign corporation in the preceding year, when the deficit was incurred. The first U.S. corporation can reduce its $180 (60 percent of $300) share of the subpart F income by $60 (60 percent of $100) of the accumulated deficit; under the accumulated deficit rule, as modified, its pro rata share of the deficit is determined for the close of the current year because such determination yields a smaller pro rata share than a determination of such share for the close of the deficit year. The $40 portion of the accumulated deficit not utlized may be carried over for possible use by the first U.S. corporation in later years.

The interaction of the new subpart F recharacterization rule, the subpart F earnings and profits limitation retained by the agreement, and the agreement's foreign loss allocation and separate limitation loss recharacterization rules is illustrated in the following example: Assume that a foreign corporation wholly owned by a U.S. corporation has a $100 overall limitation loss. It also has $200 of passive (subpart F FPHC) income before allocation of the loss. Assume, for simplicity, that earnings and profits equal income. Under the foreign loss allocation rule (which parallels the subpart F earnings and profits limitation), the $100 loss reduces the corporation's passive income for the year from $200 to $100. The subpart F earnings and profits limitation correspondingly reduces the income currently taxable to the corporation's U.S. shareholders from $200 to $100.

The following year, the corporation earns $250 of passive (subpart F FPHC) income and $1,500 of overall limitation (nonsubpart F) income. Under the separate limitation loss recharacterization rule, an amount of this overall limitation income equal to the prior year overall limitation loss that reduced passive income, $100, is recharacterized as passive income. Thus, for foreign tax credit limitation purposes, the corporation has $1,400 ($1,500 - $100) of overall limitation income and $350 ($250 + $100) of passive income in the second year. Under the subpart F recharacterization rule, the recaptured $100 of passive income is also subpart F FPHC income since subpart F FPHC income the year before was reduced by $100 under the earnings and profits limitation and, in the current year, earnings and profits exceed tentative subpart F income by at least that amount. Thus, the subpart F inclusion of the corporation's shareholders is $350 ($250 + $100) in the second year.

Effective date.—The conference agreement generally adopts the Senate amendment's effective date provisions [generally tax years of foreign corporations beginning after 12-31-86. Ed.] for the subpart F amendments discussed above, except where noted otherwise. In addition, targeted transitional rules are provided.

[¶ 4035] SECTION 1222. TESTING CONTROLLED FOREIGN CORPORATIONS AND FOREIGN PERSONAL HOLDING COMPANIES BY VALUE AND VOTING POWER

(Secs. 552 and 957 of the Code)

[Senate Explanation]

*　　*　　*　　*　　*　　*

Explanation of Provision.—The bill amends the definition of a controlled foreign corporation (Code section 957(a)) to provide that subpart F will apply to the U.S. shareholders of a foreign corporation if more than 50 percent of either the voting power or the value of the stock of the corporation is owned by U.S. persons that each own at least 10 percent of the vote on any day during the taxable year of the foreign corporation. Similarly, the foreign personal holding company rules will apply if more than 50 percent of either the voting power or the value of a foreign corporation belongs to five or fewer U.S. individuals.

Effective Date.—The provision generally applies to taxable years of foreign corporations beginning after December 31, 1986. However, deficits in earnings and profits for taxable years beginning before 1987, and, for purposes of Code section 956, property acquired before 1987, will not be taken into account with respect to corporations that become subject to subpart F because of this provision.

In the case of an individual who is a beneficiary of a trust and who was not a U.S. resident on the date such trust was established, any amounts included by reason of this provision in the gross income of the individual with respect to stock held by the trust (and

treated as distributed by the trust) are to be treated as the first amounts distributed by the trust to the individual and as previously taxed income (under Code sec. 959(a)).

*　　*　　*　　*　　*　　*

[Conference Report]

*　　*　　*　　*　　*　　*

The conference agreement generally follows the Senate amendment (including its special rule for certain trust distributions), with a conforming amendment clarifying that the new vote-or-value rule applies in determining whether an insurance company is a controlled foreign corporation under the special more-than-25-percent U.S. ownership test of Code section 957(b). With respect to investments in U.S. property, the provision is effective on August 16, 1986 (rather than on January 1, 1987).

The conferees' decision not to include the House bill provision decreasing the U.S. ownership requirement for controlled foreign corporation status from more-than-50-percent to 50-percent-or-more of total ownership rests, in part, on the conferees' understanding that, under an existing Treasury regulation, the IRS can, in specified circumstances, deem foreign corporations effectively controlled by 10-percent U.S. shareholders to meet the more-than-50-percent ownership test even though that requirement would otherwise not technically be met (Treas. Reg. sec. 1.957-1(b)).

[¶ 4036] SECTION 1223. SUBPART F DE MINIMIS RULE

(Sec. 954 of the Code)

[Senate Explanation]

*　　*　　*　　*　　*　　*

Present Law.—The subpart F rules that impose current U.S. tax on income of controlled foreign corporations apply only to certain types of income. One major category of income that is subject to current taxation under subpart F is foreign base company income. Foreign base company income includes passive investment income and certain sales, services, shipping, and oil related income. A de minimis rule in subpart F provides that if less than 10 percent of a foreign corporation's gross income is base company income, then none of the income will be treated as base company income. On

the other hand, if more than 70 percent of a foreign corporation's gross income is base company income, then all of its income will be treated as base company income.

*　　*　　*　　*　　*　　*

[Conference Report]

*　　*　　*　　*　　*　　*

c. De minimis and full inclusion rules.—Under the conference agreement, none of a controlled foreign corporation's gross income for a taxable year is treated as foreign base company income or tax haven insurance income if the sum of the corporation's gross foreign base company and gross tax haven insurance income for the year is less than the lesser of 5 percent of its gross income, or $1 million.

The conferees do not believe that U.S. shareholders of controlled foreign corporations should avoid current U.S. tax on an amount of tax haven income equal to a fixed percentage of the gross income of the controlled foreign corporation without regard to how large, in absolute dollar terms, that amount of tax haven income is. Permitting $1 million or more of tax haven income to avoid current U.S. tax, as the present law de minimis rule does in the case of a controlled foreign corporation with $10 million or more of gross income, is inconsistent with the de minimis concept in the conferees' view.

* * * the new subpart F de minimis rule applies for separate foreign tax credit limitation purposes also. The House bill provided no de minimis exception to the application of the separate foreign tax credit limitations. The conferees have accepted a de minimis exception to the separate limitations in the case of controlled foreign corporations to simplify the operation of the foreign tax credit limitation look-through rules. However, the conferees concluded that any de minimis exception applicable to the separate limitations should be a limited one, incorporating a reasonable dollar ceiling.

As discussed above at C.1.a, the conference agreement expands the definition of tax haven insurance income. The general de minimis exception is amended to apply to tax haven insurance income generally in order to preserve de minimis relief for insurance income subject to tax under subpart F under present law, and to provide such relief to the new types of insurance income (including certain captive insurance income) subjected to tax under subpart F by the conference agreement. Income from insuring U.S. risks is eligible for a special 5-percent de minimis exception under present law. However, the conference agreement repeals that exception in connection with its expansion of the definition of tax haven insurance income to include income from insuring certain unrelated party foreign risks. Income from the insurance of certain foreign risks of related parties that is subpart F income under present law is presently eligible for the general de minimis exception.

The conference agreement also extends the 70-percent full inclusion rule to tax haven insurance income generally. The conferees do not believe that a sound policy basis exists for distinguishing tax haven insurance income from foreign base company income for purposes of either the de minimis rule or the full inclusion rule.

The Tax Reform Act of 1984 generally subjects related party factoring income and similar income to taxation under subpart F without regard to the general de minimis rule. The conference agreement does not alter present law in this regard.

[Effective date.—] The amendments to the de minimis and full inclusion rules apply to taxable years of foreign corporations beginning after 1986.

[¶ 4037] SECTION 1224. REPEAL OF SPECIAL TREATMENT OF POSSESSIONS CORPORATIONS

(Sec. 957 of the Code)

[Senate Explanation]

* * * * * *

Explanation of Provision.—The exemption from controlled foreign corporation status available to possession-chartered corporations is repealed. Thus, U.S. shareholders of possessions corporations will be treated like U.S. shareholders of other foreign corporations, so they will be subject to current U.S. tax under subpart F on tax haven-type income of the corporations.

Effective Date.—* * * However, deficits in earnings and profits for taxable years

beginning before 1987, and, for purposes of Code section 956, property acquired before 1987, will not be taken into account with respect to corporations that become subject to subpart F because of this provision.

* * * * * *

[Conference Report]

* * * * * *

Possession-chartered corporations. — The conference agreement follows the Senate amendment except that the effective date for investments in U.S. property is August 16, 1986.

[¶ 4038] SECTION 1225. ONLY EFFECTIVELY CONNECTED CAPITAL GAINS AND LOSSES OF FOREIGN CORPORATIONS TAKEN INTO ACCOUNT FOR PURPOSES OF ACCUMULATED EARNINGS TAX AND PERSONAL HOLDING COMPANY PROVISIONS

(Secs. 535 and 545 of the Code)

[Senate Explanation]

* * * * * *

Present Law.—The accumulated earnings tax is imposed on corporations that accumulate earnings beyond the reasonable needs of their businesses rather than distributing them to their shareholders. The personal holding company tax is imposed on certain corporations receiving defined forms of passive income. The taxes are imposed on accumulated taxable income and undistributed personal holding company income, respectively. Those amounts are calculated by making several adjustments to the regular taxable income of a corporation, including deductions for net capital gains (and certain capital losses). A deduction for net capital gains is granted because the corporate and individual tax rates on capital gains are approximately equal, and there is therefore little incentive to accumulate capital gains in a corporation.

Foreign corporations are generally subject to these taxes if they have any shareholders that would be subject to U.S. tax on a distribution from the corporation. In the case of a foreign corporation, only U.S. source income enters into the calculation of the accumulated earnings tax or personal holding company tax. However, net capital gains may be deducted from taxable income (thus reducing the accumulated earnings tax or personal holding company tax), even if the capital gain is not otherwise taken into account for U.S. tax purposes because it is not effectively connected with a U.S. trade or business. Thus, capital gains that are not

subject to U.S. tax may nevertheless reduce the accumulated earnings tax or personal holding company tax. United States source capital gain income realized by a foreign corporation trading in stock, securities, or commodities for its own account is not considered effectively connected income.

* * * * * *

Explanation of Provision.—The bill amends sections 535 and 545 to provide that the accumulated earnings tax or personal holding company tax applicable to a foreign corporation will be calculated by taking net capital gains into account only if they are effectively connected with the conduct of a U.S. trade or business. Gains which are exempt from U.S. tax under a treaty obligation of the United States will not be considered effectively connected for this purpose.

* * * * * *

[Conference Report]

* * * * * *

The conference agreement follows the House bill and the Senate amendment except that it is effective for gains and losses realized on or after * * * [March] 1, 1986.

[¶ 4039] SECTION 1226. DEDUCTIONS FOR DIVIDENDS RECEIVED FROM CERTAIN FOREIGN CORPORATIONS

(Secs. 245 and 904 of the Code)

[Senate Explanation]

* * * * * *

Present Law.—Under present law, corporations that receive dividends generally are entitled to a deduction equal to 85 percent of the dividends received (sec. 243(a)(1)). Dividends received by a U.S. corporation from a foreign corporation generally are not eligible for the dividends received deduction, even though the foreign corporation may have paid U.S. income tax. However, a portion of the dividends paid by such corporation to a U.S. corporate shareholder is eligible for the dividends received deduction where at least 50 percent of a foreign corporation's gross income is effectively connected with a U.S. trade or business during an uninterrupted period of 36 months ending with the close of the year in which the dividends are paid (or for the period of the corporation's existence, if shorter). That portion generally is based on the percentage of the foreign corporation's gross income that is effectively connected with its U.S. trade or business (sec. 245). Where a foreign corporation is wholly owned by a U.S. corporation and all of its income is effectively connected with a U.S. trade or business, dividends paid by such corporation generally are eligible for a 100 percent dividends received deduction.

If a U.S. corporation is eligible to claim a deduction for dividends received from a foreign corporation, the U.S. recipient must treat for foreign tax credit purposes as U.S. source income the amount of the dividend

attributable to U.S. effectively connected income of the foreign corporation (sec. 861(a)(2)(B)). The Tax Reform Act of 1984 similarly provided rules that convert what would otherwise be foreign source income into U.S. source income if paid by certain entities. In the case of dividends paid by a foreign corporation, these rules apply if the foreign corporation is beneficially owned 50 percent or more by U.S. persons and earns income from U.S. sources. In such cases, dividends paid are treated as U.S. source to the extent the dividends are attributable to U.S. source earnings of the corporation.

* * * * * *

Explanation of Provision.—*Dividends received deduction.*—Under the bill, the deduction for dividends received from foreign corporations is modified in two respects. First the deduction is eligible only to U.S. corporations that own at least 10 percent of the voting stock of a foreign corporation. Second, the deduction is allowed if the foreign corporate payor operates a U.S. branch that earns any amount of income effectively connected with the conduct of a U.S. trade or business or owns a U.S. subsidiary from which it receives dividends. Thus, the bill eliminates the preferential treatment of branches over subsidiaries. The bill also provides that the deduction is available if the dividends from the U.S. corporation are paid through a second wholly-owned foreign corporation before they are remitted to the ultimate U.S. corporate shareholder. The bill defines U.S. subsidiary as a corporation at least 80 percent of the total voting power and value of which is held by a foreign corporation.

The amount of the deduction is based on the general rules applicable to dividends from U.S. corporations. Section 611 of the bill reduces the present law percentage deduction for certain dividends received from 85 percent to 80 percent.

The bill provides that the U.S. recipient can only claim a deduction for the dividends attributable to earnings of the foreign corporation that have been subject to U.S. tax, based on the ratio of earnings and profits from U.S. sources (the sum of net income effectively connected with a U.S. trade or business and dividends (less allocable expenses) from U.S. subsidiaries) to entire earnings and profits of the foreign corporation for the current year.

The bill provides that the "pooling" rules adopted by the committee for Code section 902 (sec. 904 of the bill) apply to a foreign corporation's accumulated earnings and profits that are attributable to U.S. sources. Therefore, in addition to the pools required for separate foreign tax credit limitations, the foreign corporation must maintain a separate pool for earnings attributable to U.S. sources. Moreover, the committee intends that foreign taxes imposed on U.S. source earnings of the foreign corporation be attributed to income allocated to the overall limitation for purposes of section 904.

The bill provides corresponding changes to present law in the case of a foreign corporation wholly owned by a U.S. corporation. In such cases, if the income of the foreign corporation in entirely attributable to income effectively connected with a U.S. trade or business or to dividends received from a U.S. subsidiary, the U.S. recipient is eligible to exclude the entire dividend from its income.

Source of dividends eligible for deduction.—The bill provides that for foreign tax credit purposes, if otherwise treated as foreign source under the Code's general source rules, the entire amount of the dividend eligible for the deduction is to be treated as U.S. source. As provided by the Tax Reform Act of 1984, this special sourcing rule applies even when the dividends are paid through more than one foreign corporation. If the foreign corporation operates a U.S. trade or business through a branch, and such business generates income to the corporation that constitutes at least 10 percent of the corporation's total gross income, dividends paid by the corporation are currently subject to the general source rules of the Code (as provided by sec. 651 of the bill). In such instances, a pro rata portion of the dividends are U.S. source. The bill's provision above operates only to the extent the dividends are not already treated as U.S. source under general rules of the Code. If the current rules create a greater amount of U.S. source income, such

provisions will control. Otherwise, the bill's provision controls.

The bill's provisions can be illustrated by the following example. Assume a U.S. subsidiary remits a $100 dividend to its foreign corporate shareholder, such shareholder has $900 of non-effectively connected net income, and the foreign corporation remits a $100 dividend to its 10-percent-owned foreign corporate shareholder. Under the bill, the U.S. recipient is eligible for a dividends received deduction of $8 (100/1000 x 100 x .80) and has gross U.S. source income of $10 (100/1000 x 100). Assuming the same facts above, if a wholly-owned foreign corporation is interposed between the U.S. subsidiary and the foreign corporate payor, such interposed corporation has $400 of non-effectively connected net income in addition to the $100 dividend, and such corporation remits $100 to its parent, the U.S. recipient would be eligible for a deduction of $1.60 and would have gross U.S. source income of $2.

*　　*　　*　　*　　*　　*

[Conference Report]

*　　*　　*　　*　　*　　*

The conference agreement generally follows the Senate amendment with technical modifications and an amendment preventing double benefits for amounts eligible for the agreement's deduction.

The agreement provides that deemed-paid foreign tax credits are disallowed to the extent the taxes are attributable to income eligible for the dividends received deduction.

The conference agreement provides that dividends eligible for the deduction are based on the proportion of the foreign corporation's post-1986 earnings that have been subject to U.S. corporate income tax and that have not been distributed, rather than (as in the Senate amendment) the pool of earnings accumulated during the previous 10 years. The committee intends that distributions from a foreign corporation be deemed to be pro rata from the corporation's earnings that have been subject to U.S. corporate income tax and those that have not been so subject.

In a technical amendment (to Code sec. 959(d)), the agreement clarifies that any amounts of subpart F income previously taxed that are distributed to U.S. shareholders are to reduce U.S. source earnings and profits and total earnings and profits (as the case may be) in arriving at the proportionate amount of the taxable dividend eligible for the deduction.

The conference agreement also clarifies that the new provision applies to distributions out of earnings and profits for taxable years beginning after 1986.

For dividends paid from earnings and profits accumulated prior to January 1, 1987, the agreement's provisions do not apply.

[¶ 4041]   SECTION 1231. MODIFICATIONS TO SECTION 936

(Secs. 367, 482, 934, and 936 of the Code)

[Senate Explanation]

*   *   *   *   *   *

Present Law.—* * * Congress in 1982 was concerned that the possession tax credit was costly and inefficient. According to the Finance Committee Report on the Tax Equity and Fiscal Responsibility Act of 1982 (TEFRA):[6] "Treasury's three reports to date have confirmed the existence of two problems in that system: (1) unduly high revenue loss attributable to certain industries due to positions taken by certain taxpayers with respect to the allocations of intangible income among related parties, and (2) continued tax exemption of increased possession source investment income."

In addition, there was considerable disagreement under prior law regarding the extent to which intangible assets could be transferred to a possessions corporation free of U.S. tax. In July of 1980, the Internal Revenue Service issued Technical Advice Memorandum 8040019 which stated that intangibles transferred to a possession subsidiary at less than a reasonable arm's-length price did not belong to the subsidiary, and the income derived therefrom was allocable to the parent corporation rather than the subsidiary.

The 1982 Act addressed these issues by (1) increasing the active possession business income percentage requirement for possessions corporation status from 50 to 65 percent of gross income and (2) denying the credit on intangible income of the possessions corporation. However, possessions corporations are permitted to derive some intangible income tax-free if they elect one of two optional methods of computing taxable income: (1) a cost sharing rule and (2) a 50/50 profit split. Under the former option, a possessions corporation is permitted to claim a return on manufacturing (but not marketing) intangibles in computing its income from products it produces, provided that it makes a (taxable) cost-sharing payment to its affiliates. The payment represents the possessions corporation's share of its affiliated group's worldwide direct and indirect research and development (R&D) expenditures in each product area in which the possessions corporation manufactures products subject to the cost sharing election. The possessions corporation's share of R&D expense is determined by reference to the ratio of third-party sales by members of its affiliated group of those products within a given product area, which are produced in whole or in part by the possessions corporation to, such sales of all products within that product area. The cost sharing payment effectively increases the taxable income of the possessions corporation's mainland affiliate and, consequently, its tax liability.

Under the 50/50 profit split election, the possessions corporation's taxable income (eligible for the credit) with respect to any product it produces in whole or in part is equal to 50 percent of the combined taxable income of the domestic members of its affiliated group with respect to covered sales of such product. The combined taxable income associated with a product is determined as the excess of gross receipts (on sales of the product to third parties) over the direct and indirect costs of producing and marketing the product. Thus, to the the extent that combined taxable income represents a return on intangible assets (both manufacturing and marketing intangibles), half of this intangible income is eligible for section 936 tax benefits. For purposes of computing the combined taxable income of which 50 percent is allocated to the possessions corporation, the amount of the group's R&D expenses allocated to income from the sale of a product generally cannot be less than a certain stated percentage of the cost-sharing payment that would have been required under the cost-sharing option.

To derive intangible income on a tax-free basis, the possessions corporation must make an irrevocable election to use one of the two options. A single option must be selected for all products within a product area.[7] [I]n addition, neither option may be used for a product which does not meet the significant business presence test. A product satisfies this test if either (1) at least 25 percent of the value added to the product is a result of economic activity in the possessions, or (2) at least 65 percent of the direct labor cost for the product is incurred in the possessions. Finally, TEFRA generally prohibited possessions corporations from making future tax-free transfers of intangibles to foreign corporations.

*   *   *   *   *   *

[House Explanation]

*   *   *   *   *   *

* * *, the cost sharing payment required for companies that elect the cost sharing option is set equal to the greater of (1) 110 percent of the payment required under present law, and (2) the royalty payment that would be required (under sections 482 and 367 as clarified by the bill) if the possessions corporation were treated as a foreign company (with respect to manufacturing intangibles the possessions corporation is treated as owning under the cost-sharing option). For purposes of the cost sharing option, the changes made by the bill to sections 367 and 482 would apply for taxable years beginning after December 31, 1985 to manufacturing intangibles which the possessions corporation is treated as owning under that option, regardless of when or whether such intangi-

---

[Footnote ¶ 4041]   (6) Sen. Rept. No. 97-494, (July 12, 1982), pp. 81-2.
(7) Export sales within a product group are exempt from this requirement.

bles were ever actually transferred to the possessions corporation. For companies that elect the 50/50 profit split method, the amount of product area research expenditures (as determined under the cost sharing rules) would be increased by 20 percent for purposes of computing combined taxable income. Under present law, combined taxable income of U.S. affiliates for any product is computed by deducting from gross receipts (from sales to foreign affiliates and unrelated parties), the total costs incurred by U.S. affiliates with respect to the product. For purposes of determining the combined taxable income of which 50 percent is allocated to the possessions corporation, the amount of research expense allocated to the product may not be less than the portion of the appropriate share of product area research expenditures (as determined under the cost sharing rules, applied without regard to the changes made by this bill other than the 20 percent increase in product area research expenditures) allocable to the product under a ratio set out in the profit split provisions.

For example, under present law, if product area research expenditures allocable to the product are $10 for a taxable year, then at least $10 of research cost must be taken into account in computing the product's combined taxable income for that taxable year. The bill would require that at least $12 (120 percent of $10) of research cost be taken into account in computing the product's combined taxable income. Consequently, the combined taxable income from sales of the product would be reduced by at most $2 ($12 minus $10) by virtue of this change, and the amount of income allocable to members of the affiliated group other than the possessions corporation under the 50/50 option, would be increased by at most $1 (50 percent of $2).[8]

[Senate Explanation]

* * * * * *

* * *, for companies that elect the profit split option, the amount of product area research expenditures (as determined under the cost sharing rules) is increased by 20 percent for purposes of computing combined taxable income. This increases the amount of income allocable to nonpossession affiliates by no more than the increase under the bill for companies that elect the cost sharing option.

For example, under present law, if product area research expenditures allocable to the product are $10 for a taxable year, then at least $10 of research cost must be taken into account in computing the product's combined taxable income for that taxable year. The bill requires that at least $12 (120 percent of $10) of research cost be taken into account in computing the product's combined taxable income. Consequently, the combined taxable income from sales of the product would be reduced by at most $2 ($12 minus $10), and

the amount of income allocable to nonpossession affiliates is increased by at most $1 (50 percent of $2) for companies electing the profit split option. Similarly, for companies electing the cost sharing option, the bill requires an increase in the cost sharing payment for this product, and thus the amount of income allocable to nonpossession affiliates, of $1 (10 percent of $10).

* * *, the bill changes the active trade or business test that a U.S. corporation must meet to qualify for the possession tax credit. Under present law, 65 percent or more of a possessions corporation's gross income for the three-year period immediately preceding the close of the taxable year must be derived from the active conduct of a trade or business in the possessions. Under the bill, the active income percentage increases from 65 percent to 75 percent for tax years beginning after 1986. The bill does not alter the present law requirement that 80 percent or more of gross income for a three-year period be derived from sources within a possession. As under present law, a possessions corporation must meet both the 80-percent possession source income test and the active trade or business test.

* * *, the bill modifies the rule in present law (sec. 936(b)) which denies the credit with respect to income received in the United States (not including possessions thereof). The credit is not denied for tax on otherwise eligible active business income solely by reason of receipt in the United States where such income is received from an unrelated party. Present law is retained for investment income and for business income received from related parties.

* * *, the bill modifies the definition of qualified possession source investment income ("QPSII") in order to allow the Government of Puerto Rico to fully implement its initiative to increase investment and employment in qualified Carribean Basin Initiative ("CBI") countries. Under present law, QPSII is limited to income derived from investments within a possession in which the taxpayer conducts an active trade or business. Further, the taxpayer must establish that QPSII is derived from the investment of funds which (1) are allocable to net income from the conduct of an active trade or business within the possession, or (2) constitute a reinvestment of QPSII. The government of Puerto Rico has established rules (Reg. 3087) which apply to financial institutions that accept deposits from possessions corporations. The purpose of these rules is to require that such deposits be invested only in specified assets located in Puerto Rico including: loans for commercial, agricultural, and industrial purposes; business and residential mortgage loans; loans and investments in securities of the Government of Puerto Rico and its instrumentalities; student loans; and automobile loans. In addition, financial insti-

---

[Footnote ¶ 4041 continued]

(8) Under the cost sharing option, the bill would increase the cost sharing payment for this product and accordingly, the amount of income allocable to other members of the group, by at least $1 (10 percent of $10).

tutions are required to invest 30 percent of possessions corporation deposits in Puerto Rico government obligations, including 10 percent in obligations of the Government Development Bank for Puerto Rico ("GDB").

Under the bill, the definition of QPSII is expanded to include certain investments outside of the possessions. Subject to such conditions as the Secretary of the Treasury may prescribe by regulations, QPSII includes income derived from loans by qualified financial institutions (including the GDB and the Puerto Rico Development Bank) for the acquisition or construction of active business assets and for construction of development projects located in qualified CBI countries. To qualify for QPSII treatment, such loans must be approved by the GDB pursuant to regulations issued by the Secretary of the Treasury of Puerto Rico.

A qualified CBI country is defined as a "beneficiary country" (within the meaning of section 212(a)(1)(A) of the Caribbean Basin Economic Recovery Act) which meets the requirements of clauses (i) and (ii) of Code section 274(h)(6)(A). A development project generally means an infrastructure investment, such as a road or water treatment facility, that directly supports industrial development. Active business assets generally means plant, equipment, and inventory associated with a manufacturing operation.

To qualify, a financial institution must agree to permit the Secretary and the Secretary of the Treasury of Puerto Rico to examine such of its books and records as may be necessary to ensure compliance with these provisions. In addition, the borrower and the lending institution must certify to the Secretary and the Secretary of the Treasury of Puerto Rico that the funds will be invested promptly in active business assets or a development project located in a qualified CBI country. The committee anticipates that the lending institution will terminate such a loan if the Secretary or the Secretary of the Treasury of Puerto Rico determines that the borrower has not made a good faith effort to comply with the conditions of certification. Also, it is anticipated that the Government of Puerto Rico will make conforming changes in regulations to permit a local tax exemption for the income attributable to qualified CBI loans.

The committee intends to exercise its oversight jurisdiction to review periodically the operation of the possession tax credit to ensure that the goals of economic development in both the possessions and the Caribbean Basin are being achieved. The committee anticipates that the Government of Puerto Rico will promote employment-producing investment in, as well as the transfer of technology to, qualified CBI countries. The committee believes that economic growth in the relatively poorer CBI countries will benefit both Puerto Rico and the United States by expanding trade opportunities and promoting political stability.

The bill also amends section 936(d)(1) to include the U.S. Virgin Islands within the definition of "possession". This change has the effect of bringing U.S. corporations doing business in the Virgin Islands within section 936, rather than the separate but comparable provisions of the revised organic Act of the Virgin Islands and section 934.

* * * * * *

[Conference Report]

* * * * * *

The conference agreement generally follows the Senate amendment with certain modifications.

The conference agreement follows the House bill with respect to the cost sharing payment, i.e., the cost sharing payment is determined as the greater of (1) 110 percent of the payment determined under present law or (2) an arm's-length royalty (determined according to the principles of sections 482 and 367, as modified by the conference agreement).

The conference agreement follows the House bill and Senate amendment with respect to the profit split method, and makes a technical correction to the computation of combined taxable income under this method.

The conferees expect that the Secretary will take into account the significant nature of the modifications made by the conference agreement to the computation of possessions source income in cases where an electing corporation seeks to change its method of computation.

The conference agreement follows the Senate amendment with respect to income received within the United States.

The conference agreement generally follows the Senate amendment with respect to the expansion of the definition of QPSII. The conferees are of the view that for the purposes of QPSII, financial institutions may include banks, investment banks, or similar institutions. The conferees expect that the Government of Puerto Rico will make a good faith effort to carry out the twin plant initiative outlined in the Memorandum of Agreement.

The conferees authorize Treasury to issue regulations providing additional compliance measures including (1) the submission with the tax return of information relevant to computing income from intangibles, and (2) annual certification by the borrower and lender that CBI loans have been used for investments that are permitted under the QPSII rules.

The conferees agree that regulations issued under section 936(h)(7) can permit the use of the cost sharing and profit split methods in cases where the possession product is leased, rather than sold (or is used in the trade or business of a member of the affiliated group), but only if (1) an independent sales price can be determined for the product from comparable uncontrolled transactions, and (2) the appropriate member of the group agrees to be treated as having sold the possession product at such price. The conferees intend that an exception to the former requirement will be provided under conditions deemed appropriate by the Secretary. Such conditions may restrict relief to situations where (1) the cost sharing payment is no less than 100 percent of the product area research cost incurred by the affiliated group, and (2) the deemed sale of the possession product units is treated as made at a price which produced a profit to the appropriate member of the group equal to the possessions corporation's tax-exempt profit with respect to the same units (computed without regard to the cost sharing payment), reduced by one-half of the cost sharing payment allocable to such units.

The possessions tax credit provisions are effective for tax years beginning after 1986. The royalty provision of the cost sharing rule applies to tax years beginning after 1986 without regard to when the transfer of intangibles (if any) was made.

* * * Transfers of Intangibles to Related Parties Outside of the United States

Present Law.—Transfers to related foreign corporations as licenses or sales are subject to an "arm's-length" price standard. Uncertainty exists regarding what transfers are appropriate to treat as "arm's-length" comparables and regarding the significance of profitability, including major changes in profitability of the intangible after the transfer.

Transfers to related foreign corporations as contributions to capital require the transferor to recognize annually, as U.S. source income, amounts that would have been received under an agreement providing for payments contingent on productivity, use, or disposition of the property.

Special rules apply for intangibles treated as owned by U.S. possessions corporations * * *.

* * * * * *

[House Explanation]

* * * * * *

Explanation of Provision.—The basic requirement of the bill is that payments with respect to intangibles that a U.S. person transfers to a related foreign corporation or possessions corporation must be commensurate with the income attributable to the intangible. This approach applies both to outright transfers of the ownership of the intangibles whether by sale, contribution to capital, or otherwise), and to licenses or other arrangements for the use of intangibles.

In making this change, the committee intends to make it clear that industry norms or other unrelated party transactions do not provide a safe-harbor minimum payment for related party intangibles transfers. Where taxpayers transfer intangibles with a high profit potential, the compensation for the intangibles should be greater than industry averages or norms. In determining whether the taxpayer could reasonably expect that projected profits would be greater than the industry norm, the committee intends that

there should be taken into account any established pattern of transferring relatively high profit intangibles to Puerto Rico or low tax foreign locations.

The committee does not intend, however, that the inquiry as to the appropriate compensation for the intangible be limited to the question of whether it was appropriate considering only the facts in existence at the time of the transfer. The committee intends that consideration also be given the actual profit experience realized as a consequence of the transfer. Thus, the committee intends to require that the payments made for the intangible be adjusted over time to reflect changes in the income attributable to the intangible. The bill is not intended to require annual adjustments when there are only minor variations in revenues. However, it will not be sufficient to consider only the evidence of value at the time of the transfer. Adjustments will be required when there are major variations in the annual amounts of revenue attributable to the intangible.

In requiring that payments be commensurate with the income stream, the bill does not intend to mandate the use of the "contract manufacturer" or "cost-plus" methods of allocating income or any other particular method. As under present law, all the facts and circumstances are to be considered in determining what pricing methods are appropriate in cases involving intangible property, including the extent to which the transferee bears real risks with respect to its ability to make a profit from the intangible or, instead, sells products produced with the intangible largely to related parties (which may involve little sales risk or activity) and has a market essentially dependent on, or assured by, such related parties' marketing efforts. However, the profit or income stream generated by or associated with intangible property is to be given primary weight.

The requirements of the bill apply when intangibles of the type presently subject to section 367(d) are transferred by a U.S. person to a related foreign entity or to a possessions corporation that elects the cost-sharing option, or are licensed or otherwise used by such entity. Thus, the standard that payments must be commensurate with the income attributable to the intangible applies in determining the amounts to be imputed under section 367(d) and in determining the appropriate section 482 allocation in other situations. The standard also applies in determining the minimum amount of the "cost-sharing payment" to be made under the cost-sharing option in the case of an electing section 936 corporation. As discussed in greater detail in connection with the changes made by the bill affecting possessions corporations, the bill requires that the cost-sharing payment must be at least as great as the royalty the possessions corporation would have to pay to an affiliate under section 367 or 482 with respect to manufacturing intangibles the possessions corporation is treated as owning by virtue of electing the cost-sharing option.

*　　*　　*　　*　　*　　*

[Conference Report]

*　　*　　*　　*　　*　　*

The conference agreement follows the House bill. The concerns addressed in the House bill originated in connection with transfers of intangibles from U.S. parties to foreign affiliates, particularly those operating in low-tax foreign countries. Consequently, the provisions of the House bill only were applied to transfers of intangibles from U.S. persons to their foreign affiliates. In view of the fact that the objective of these provisions—that the division of income between related parties reasonably reflect the relative economic activity undertaken by each—applies equally to inbound transfers, the conferees concluded that it would be appropriate for these principles to apply to transfers between related parties generally if income must otherwise be taken into account.

The conferees do not intend to affect present law concepts of what constitutes a single "license", to the extent those concepts are not inconsistent with the purposes of the new provision. Thus, for example, in the case of continuous transfers of technology under a continuing license agreement, the adequacy of the royalty may, in appropriate cases, be determined by applying the appropriate standards under the conference agreement on an aggregate basis with respect to the profitability and other relevant features of the transferred intangibles as a whole.

Similarly, the conferees do not intend to change principles that would permit offsets or other adjustments to reflect the tax impact of the taxpayer's transactions as a whole.

The conferees are also aware that many important and difficult issues under section 482 are left unresolved by this legislation. The conferees believe that a comprehensive study of intercompany pricing rules by the Internal Revenue Service should be conducted and that careful consideration should be

given to whether the existing regulations could be modified in any respect.

In revising section 482, the conferees do not intend to preclude the use of certain bona fide research and development cost-sharing arrangements as an appropriate method of allocating income attributable to intangibles among related parties, if and to the extent such agreements are consistent with the purposes of this provision that the income allocated among the parties reasonably reflect the actual economic activity undertaken by each. Under such a bona fide cost-sharing arrangement, the cost-sharer would be expected to bear its portion of all research and development costs, on unsuccessful as well as successful products within an appropriate product area, and the costs of research and development at all relevant development stages would be included. In order for cost-sharing arrangements to produce results consistent with the changes made by the Act to royalty arrangements, it is envisioned that the allocation of R&D cost-sharing arrangements generally should be proportionate to profit as determined before deduction for research and development. In addition, to the extent, if any, that one party is actually contributing funds toward research and development at a significantly earlier point in time than the other, or is otherwise effectively putting its funds at risk to a greater extent than the other, it would be expected that an appropriate return would be required to such party to reflect its investment.

Effective date.—Under the conference agreement, the new provisions generally apply to taxable years beginning after December 31, 1986, but only with respect to transfers after November 16, 1985, or licenses granted after such date (or before such date with respect to property not in existence or owned by the taxpayer on such date). However, for purposes of section 936 payments, the new provisions apply to taxable years beginning after December 31, 1986, without regard to when any transfer (or license) was made.

[¶ 4042] **SECTION 1232. TREATMENT OF CERTAIN PERSONS IN PANAMA**

(Sec. 642 of the Code)

[House Explanation]

*　　*　　*　　*　　*　　*

Explanation of Provision.—The bill clarifies that nothing in the Panama Canal Treaty (or in any agreement implementing the treaty) is to be construed as exempting any citizen or resident of the United States from U.S. tax.

Effective Date.—The bill's clarification of the effect of the Panama Canal Treaty and its implementing agreements applies to all taxable years.

*　　*　　*　　*　　*　　*

[Conference Report]

*　　*　　*　　*　　*　　*

The conference agreement follows the House bill with one clarification. The clarification is that the Agreement in Implementation of the Panama Canal Treaty does not exempt U.S. taxpayers from any U.S. tax (not limited to the income tax). With respect to U.S. taxes not imposed with respect to a taxable year (such as the gift and estate taxes), the provision is effective for taxable events after the date of enactment (rather than for all open taxable years).

*　　*　　*　　*　　*　　*

[Senate Explanation]

* * * * * *

The bill also provides that employees of the Commission and civilian employees of the Defense Department stationed in Panama may exclude from gross income allowances which are comparable to the allowances excludable under Code section 912(1) by employees of the State Department stationed in Panama. The committee intends by this exclusion to equalize the treatment of U.S. Government employees stationed in Panama, and thus does not intend to permit the exclusion of amounts greater than those that could be excluded by State Department employees, nor to permit the exclusion of allowances of any type unavailable to State Department employees.

Effective Date.—[This exclusion is] effective for taxable years beginning after 1986.

[¶ 4043] SECTION 1233. PROVISIONS RELATING TO SECTION 911 EXCLUSION

(Sec. 911 of the Code)

[Senate Explanation]

* * * * * *

Present Law.—A U.S. citizen or resident is generally taxed on his or her world-wide income, with the allowance of a foreign tax credit for foreign taxes paid on the foreign income. However, under Code section 911, an individual who has his or her tax home in a foreign country and who is either present overseas for 330 days out of 12 consecutive months or who is a bona fide resident of a foreign country for an entire taxable year can elect to exclude an amount of his or her foreign earned income from his gross income. The maximum exclusion is $80,000 in 1986, and is scheduled to increase to $85,000 in 1988, $90,000 in 1989, and to $95,000 in 1990 and thereafter.[9]

An individual meeting the eligibility requirements may also elect to exclude (or deduct, in certain cases) housing costs above a floor amount. The combined earned income exclusion and housing amount exclusion may not exceed the taxpayer's total foreign earned income for the taxable year. The provision contains a denial of double benefits by reducing such items as the foreign tax credit by the amount attributable to excluded income.

* * * * * *

Explanation of Provision.—a. Foreign earned income exclusion amount.—The bill limits the foreign earned income exclusion to $70,000 per year per U.S. individual. As under present law, the exclusion is computed at the annual rate on a daily basis.

b. Disallowance of exclusion for individuals in foreign countries in violation of law.—The bill provides that individuals who are present in a country with respect to which restrictions relating to travel transactions are in effect will lose certain tax benefits, described below. An individual who is present in a foreign country with respect to which U.S. citizens and residents generally are prohibited from engaging in travel transactions will not lose tax benefits unless that individual's engaging in travel transactions is in violation of law.

For the purposes of this provision, presence in a country will generally result in loss of the earned income exclusion if regulations pursuant to the Trading with the Enemy Act or the International Emergency Economic Powers Act prohibit U.S. citizens and residents from engaging in transactions related to travel to, from, or within that country. Under the bill, an individual will not be treated as a bona fide resident of, or as present in, a foreign country for any day during which the individual is present in a country in violation of law. Foreign earned income, otherwise eligible for the exclusion, will not include any income from sources within such a country attributable to services performed therein. Housing expenses eligible for tax benefits will not include any expenses (allocable to a period in which presence was prohibited) for housing in such a country or for housing of the spouse or dependents of the taxpayer in another country while the taxpayer is present in such a country.

The committee understands that, under Treasury regulations, transactions related to travel of U.S. citizens and residents in five countries have been generally prohibited currently, except pursuant to consent of the Treasury Department. These countries are North Korea, Cuba, Vietnam, Kampuchea, and Libya. In certain cases, exceptions to these prohibitions are available. These exceptions differ for the various countries. For instance, American individuals may be present in Cuba to visit close family members, to engage in journalistic activity, or to perform research. The rules related to prohibiting travel transactions with respect to Libya, by contrast, prohibit all travel transactions in Libya after January 31, 1986, unless necessary to effect the individual's departure from Libya or for journalistic activity by persons regularly employed in such capacity by a newsgathering organization. Accordingly, the bill will not deny tax benefits to U.S. persons present in Libya to report news for a newspaper or television network, because such persons will not be engaging in transactions there in violation of law.

The bill will apply to the extent that any future changes in law prohibit transactions related to travel to, from, or within foreign countries. If future changes occur, presence in these countries from the effective date of the change will constitute presence that does not qualify for tax benefits under the bill.

Effective Date.—These changes are effective for all taxable years beginning on or after January 1, 1987.

[¶ 4044]   SECTION 1234. FOREIGN COMPLIANCE PROVISIONS

(Secs. 3405 and 6039E of the Code)

[Senate Explanation]

*   *   *   *   *   *

Explanation of Provision.—*Failure to file.*—The bill provides that an IRS information return must be filed in conjunction with a citizen's passport application, and with a resident alien's green card application. These returns must provide the individual's taxpayer identification number, any foreign residence of a passport applicant, information with respect to whether a green card applicant has been required to file a tax return, and such information as the Secretary may require. In addition, the committee expects that the instructions accompanying these information returns will clearly explain the filing requirements applicable to citizens and residents living abroad. A new penalty of $50 will generally apply with respect to a failure to file the required return, in addition to any other applicable penalties (such as the criminal penalties provided in section 7203 for willful failures to comply with the reporting and other requirements of the Code). Any U.S. agency collecting these returns is to provide them to the Secretary.

Collection of tax.—The bill provides that pension benefits (and similar payments) will be subject to withholding under section 3405 if delivered outside the United States. The election generally available under section 3405 to forego withholding will not be available in such cases. This automatic withholding will not apply if the recipient certifies to the payor that he or she is not a U.S. person resident overseas (or a tax avoidance expatriate (sec. 877)). The committee expects that such a certification may appropriately be provided for by modifying forms prescribed by the Secretary for the use of payees making the election to forego withholding under section 3405.

*   *   *   *   *   *

[Conference Report]

*   *   *   *   *

IRS information returns.—The conference agreement generally follows the Senate amendment, except that the agreement applies to passport and green card applications submitted after December 31, 1987 (or, if earlier, the effective date of the initial regulations under the new information return provisions, but not before January 1, 1987). The agreement also makes the following technical amendments: First, to deter noncompliance effectively, the penalty for each failure to file the required information returns is increased from $50 to $500. Second, the agreement clarifies that no other provision of law will exempt individuals from the new return-making requirements or bar agencies collecting the returns from providing them to the Secretary, as required. Third, notwithstanding any other provision of law, agencies which collect (or are required to collect) the new information returns must provide to the Secretary the names (and any other identifying information) of any individuals who refuse to provide them as required. Fourth, the agreement authorizes the Secretary to exempt any class of individuals from the return requirements by regulations if he determines that applying the return requirements to those individuals is not necessary to carry out the provision's purposes.

[Senate Explanation]

[Effective date.—**]** The reporting requirement applies to passport and green card applications filed after * * * [1987 or, if earlier, effective date of initial regulations]. The withholding requirement applies to payments made after December 31, 1986.

[¶ 4045]   SECTION 1235. TREATMENT OF CERTAIN PASSIVE INVESTMENT COMPANIES

(Secs. 1246 and 1246A of the Code)

[Senate Explanation]

*   *   *   *   *   *

Present Law.—

*   *   *   *   *   *

Shareholder level tax on disposition.—Code rules attempt to prevent U.S. shareholders of foreign corporations from repatriating earnings of those corporations at present law's lower capital gains rates after deferring tax on those earnings. For example,

gains derived by a U.S. person who is a 10-percent shareholder (at any time during a five-year period) in a controlled foreign corporation (defined as in the subpart F rules) on the disposition of that corporation's stock are subject to ordinary income (dividend) treatment rather than capital gains treatment to the extent of that person's share of the post-1962 earnings and profits of the controlled foreign corporation (Code sec. 1248). (Capital gain treatment will still apply under the bill to corporate taxpayers and in certain other cases).

However, section 1248's scope is limited. Wide dispersal of a foreign corporation's stock ownership can avoid controlled foreign corporation status. Even if the foreign corporation is controlled by U.S. shareholders, a less than 10-percent shareholder may dispose of his investment and potentially receive capital gain treatment for the increase in value of his investment.

Another provision, the foreign investment company provision (sec. 1246), was enacted in 1962 along with the subpart F rules to prevent U.S. investors from receiving capital gains treatment on disposition of their stock when U.S. ownership in the foreign corporation was widely dispersed but total U.S. ownership exceeded 50 percent and the foreign corporation primarily invested in securities. As amended, the provision generally applies to any U.S. majority owned foreign corporation that is either (1) registered under the Investment Company Act of 1940 either as a management company or as a unit investment trust or (2) engaged primarily in the business of investing or trading in securities (as defined in section 2(a)(36) of the Investment Company Act of 1940) or commodities or interests therein. A foreign investment company is considered U.S.-majority owned under this provision if 50 percent or more of its stock (by value or by voting power) is held (directly or indirectly) by U.S. persons. When a U.S. person disposes of stock in a foreign investment company, that person is subject to ordinary income treatment to the extent of his share of the foreign investment company's post-1962 accumulated earnings and profits, but not to exceed the person's gain on the disposition.

Under present law, sections 1248 and 1246 may apply to the same factual situation. For example, if a controlled foreign corporation has a 10-percent owner and the corporation is in the business of investing in securities, both provisions may potentially apply in the event the 10-percent owner disposes of his stock. Under present law, section 1246 may be considered to take priority. Since an inclusion under section 1248 may bring with it a deemed-paid credit for taxes paid by a foreign corporation but a section 1246 inclusion will not, the deemed-paid foreign tax credit is not available in such circumstances.

* * * * * *

[Conference Report]

* * * * * *

The conference agreement generally follows the Senate amendment with respect to PFICs, but contains substantial modifications. The agreement follows the Senate amendment in not modifying present law's U.S. ownership threshold for FICs and in adopting the provision allowing a 10-percent shareholder of a FIC a deemed-paid foreign tax credit when the FIC is also a controlled foreign corporation. The agreement is effective for earnings derived by foreign corporations in taxable years after 1986.

General rule.—The conference agreement provides generally that U.S. shareholders in PFICs pay U.S. tax plus an interest charge based on the value of tax deferral at the time that the shareholder disposes of his or her PFIC investment or on receipt of an "excess" distribution. This general rule applies to U.S. investors in PFICs that are not "qualified electing funds," as described below. The conferees believe that eliminating the economic benefit of deferral is necessary to eliminate the tax advantages that U.S. shareholders in foreign investment funds have heretofore had over U.S. persons investing in domestic investment funds. As does the Senate amendment, this rule provides that gain recognized on disposition of stock in a PFIC or on receipt of an "excess" distribution from a PFIC is considered to be earned pro rata over the shareholder's holding period of his investment. Under this rule, U.S. tax due in the year of disposition (or year of receipt of an "excess" distribution) is the sum of (1) U.S. tax computed using the highest rate of U.S. tax for the investor (without regard to other income or expenses the investor may have) on income attributed to prior years, plus (2) interest imposed on the deferred tax, plus (3) U.S. tax on the gain attributed to the year of disposition (or year of receipt) and to years in which the foreign corporation was not a PFIC (for which no interest is due). This rule provides that all gain recognized (and all distributions) are treated as ordinary income. The portions of distributions that are not characterized as "excess" distributions are, of course, subject to tax in the current year under normal Code rules. The agreement provides, however, that distributions from a PFIC are not eligible for the deemed paid foreign tax credit under section 902 under this rule. For purposes of claiming any withholding tax as foreign tax credit, however, the total amount of the distribution, including any "excess" distribution amount, is included in gross income in the year of receipt.

The conference agreement defines an "excess" distribution as any current year distribution in respect of stock to the extent that it represents a ratable portion of the total distributions in respect of the stock during the year that are in excess of 125 percent of the average amount of distributions in respect of the stock during the three preceding years. This rule is necessary since an excess distribution is allocated to each day in an investor's holding period with respect to each share of stock (for purposes of tax and interest determinations), an investor may have different holding periods with respect to his or her investment, and a fund may distribute earnings more than once during a taxable year. This rule is illustrated in the following example: assume an investor's average distributions for the 3 prior years are $100 and the investor receives a $100 distribution in the first month of the year and a $50 distribution in the eleventh month of the year. The total excess distribution of $25 is to be allocated two-thirds to the first month and one-third to the eleventh month for purposes of attributing the excess distribution to the current and prior years for computing the investor's deferred tax and interest. In cases where a fund distributes earnings only once a year (and an investor's stock holdings do not change over the 3-year period), the excess distribution will equal that portion of the year's distributions in respect of stock in excess of 125 percent of the average amount of distributions in respect of the stock during the three prior taxable years.

The excess distribution provision liberalizes the Senate amendment provision which treated all distributions as representing prior and current year earnings. This provision gives relief to investment funds which currently distribute all their ordinary earnings, for which there is no U.S. tax deferral. The agreement provides that regulations are to be prescribed making proper adjustments for stock splits and stock dividends, determining the amount of excess distributions in cases where investments are disposed of at varying times in a taxable year, determining the excess distribution amount when distributions are received in currencies other than the U.S. dollar, and aggregating stock ownership for shares with the same holding period.

The conference agreement provides that gain recognized on disposition of stock in a PFIC (or income in the form of a distribution from a PFIC) is not to be attributed to prior years and U.S. tax is not to be increased by an interest charge if the PFIC is a "qualified electing fund" (as described below) for each of the fund's taxable years that begin after December 31, 1986 and that include any portion of the investor's holding period. Any U.S. shareholder who owns stock in a PFIC which becomes a qualified electing fund may elect to mark his or her investment in the PFIC to market, pay all prior deferred tax and interest, acquire a new basis and holding period in his or her PFIC investment, and thereafter be taxed under the special rules applicable to such funds.

The conference agreement incorporates the rules in present law section 1246 relating to FICs, for stock with a substituted basis that inherits the attributes of PFIC stock, for certain entities through which PFIC stock is held interests in which are treated as PFIC stock, for stock acquired from a decedent (other than from a foreign decedent) to deny a basis step-up at date of death, and for information reporting purposes wherein 5 percent owners of PFICs must report certain information required by the Secretary. The agreement also provides the Secretary the authority to disregard any nonrecognition provision of present law on disposition of PFIC stock.

Qualified electing funds.—For any U.S. investor whose PFIC agrees to supply adequate information to the IRS, the agreement provides a taxing system similar to the House bill: every U.S. person who owns stock in a "qualified electing fund" must currently include in gross income his share of the PFIC's earnings and profits (with appropriate basis adjustments for amounts not distributed and for distributions previously included in income). This inclusion rule requires current payment of tax, absent a shareholder-level election to defer tax, as described below.

The conference agreement defines a "qualified electing fund" as any PFIC which properly elects with the Secretary and which complies with the Secretary's requirements for determining earnings and profits, and ascertaining stock ownership. United States shareholders of qualified electing funds may also retain the long-term capital gain character of income derived at the PFIC level. The conferees felt that it was essential to allow the Internal Revenue Service adequate access to information about U.S. investments in foreign investment funds before U.S. shareholders of those funds receive flow-through of capital gain income and attribution of ordinary income to a particular taxable year.

The election to be a qualified electing fund for any taxable year must be made before the 15th day of the third month of the taxable year following the year for which the election is being made. If a qualified electing fund fails to meet its compliance obligations, it is intended that all U.S. investors be treated as having disposed of their stock, and that the corporation's election to be a qualified electing fund be revoked. Once an election is made, it is revocable only with the consent of the Secretary. The conferees intend that revocation be granted only in circumstances where compliance with the agreement's provisions is ensured.

The conferees are of the view that, even though U.S. investors may receive adequate income information from a PFIC, the U.S. investors may not have sufficient ownership in the PFIC to compel distributions. The agreement provides, therefore, that U.S. investors in qualified electing funds can, subject to an interest charge, elect to defer U.S. tax on amounts included in income for which no current distributions are received. An election to defer tax is not available, however, for any amounts required to be currently included in income under the foreign personal holding company (FPHC) rules (sec. 551) or the subpart F rules (sec. 951).

The conference agreement provides that an election to defer tax is treated as an extension of time to pay tax for which a U.S. shareholder is liable for interest. The agreement provides that any distribution that represents earnings previously included in a shareholder's income or any disposition of stock will terminate any extension deferring tax. A shareholder may, of course, pay any deferred tax and interest prior to a distribution or disposition.

Definition of passive foreign investment company.—The conference agreement follows the Senate amendment in defining a PFIC by reference to certain passive income requirements or passive asset ownership requirements. Consistent with the Senate amendment, passive income is defined as any income of a type that would be subpart F FPHC income (income described in sec. 954(c), as modified by the agreement).

An exception to the definition of passive income is provided under the agreement for income derived by bona fide banks and insurance companies, subject to regulatory exceptions. Any foreign bank licensed to conduct a banking business under the laws of the United States or of any State will be generally presumed to be a bona fide bank for this purpose. However, the Secretary has regulatory authority to apply the PFIC provisions to any "bank" where necessary to prevent U.S. individuals from earning what is essentially portfolio investment income in a tax deferred entity. A bona fide insurance company is any foreign insurance company that would be subject to taxation under subchapter L if the company were a domestic insurance company. It is expected that bona fide underwriters of securities will be excluded from classification as a PFIC both under the asset test (because the majority of their assets, particularly securities held for sale to the public, are assets that do not give rise to subpart F FPHC income by virtue of the dealer exception in sec. 954(c)) and under the income test (because a substantial amount of their income is commission income, which is not subpart F FPHC income). Passive income derived by foreign banks and other financial businesses that are basically widely held incorporated investment vehicles will be treated as such for purposes of the PFIC definition.

The conferees do not intend that foreign corporations owning the stock of subsidiaries engaged in active businesses be classified as PFICs. To this end, the agreement attributes a proportionate part of assets and income of a 25-percent owned corporation to the corporate shareholder in determining whether the corporate shareholder is a PFIC under either the asset test or income test.

The conference agreement follows the Senate amendment by excluding from PFIC classification corporations for which an election under section 1247 is in effect and corporations in a start-up phase of an active business. The agreement expands this latter exception by excluding from PFIC classification corporations in transition from one active business to another active business. This special rule provides that if a corpora-

tion (or any predecessor) which was not a PFIC for any prior taxable year establishes to the Secretary's satisfaction that (1) its passive income is attributable to proceeds from the disposition of one or more active businesses, (2) it will not be a PFIC in any of the two taxable years after the current year, and it is, in fact, not a PFIC for either of the two taxable years after the current taxable year, then the corporation will not be classified as a PFIC for the current taxable year.

The agreement modifies the Senate amendment rule that treated a foreign corporation which once was a PFIC as forever a PFIC. It allows a shareholder to mark his or her investment to market in a corporation which does not any longer possess PFIC characteristics, to pay prior deferred tax and interest, and thereby to purge the stock of its classification as PFIC stock. For qualified electing funds, the agreement provides that stock in a PFIC will automatically cease to be classified as PFIC stock when the foreign corporation ceases to be a PFIC so long as any election to defer payment of tax and interest by a U.S. investor in any such fund terminates then and the investor pays all prior deferred tax and interest.

Other rules.—The conference agreement adopts the Senate amendment's rules for attributing ownership of PFIC stock to U.S. persons, its anti-avoidance rules to prevent circumvention of the agreement's provisions, and its rule treating a pledge of PFIC stock as security for a loan as a disposition of the stock at fair market value (with a concurrent basis step-up and new holding period). The agreement adopts rules to coordinate these provisions with the subpart F and FPHC current inclusion rules and to resource PFIC inclusions as U.S. source if the PFIC is a United States-owned foreign corporation (under sec. 904(g)) and the PFIC receives U.S. source income. The agreement further provides that PFICs are not to be treated as personal holding companies or to be subject to the accumulated earnings tax. * * *

[Effective date.—Applies to tax years of foreign corporation beginning after 12-31-86. Ed.]

[¶ 4047] SECTION 1241. BRANCH PROFITS TAX

(Secs. 861, 884, and 885 of the Code)

[Senate Explanation]

* * * * * *

Present Law.—The United States generally seeks to tax dividends and interest paid by foreign corporations most of whose operations are in the United States in the same manner as dividends and interest paid by U.S. corporations that operate in the United States. If the recipient of the dividends or interest is a U.S. person, the United States imposes tax on the dividends or interest at the regular graduated rates. If the recipient

of the dividends or interest is a foreign person, however, symmetry is more difficult to achieve.

A U.S. corporation that pays dividends to a foreign person not engaged in a trade or business in the United States generally must, in the absence of a contrary treaty provision, withhold 30 percent of the payment as a tax. The United States imposes the tax at a flat 30-percent rate because it is generally not feasible to determine and collect a net-basis graduated tax from foreign persons who may have very limited tax contacts with the United States. Similarly, a 30-percent withholding tax applies to some interest paid to foreign persons, including interest paid to related parties and certain interest paid to banks. In addition, U.S. income tax treaties reduce or eliminate the tax on interest paid to residents of the treaty country and reduce the tax on dividends paid to treaty residents to as little as 5 percent.

Similarly, a foreign corporation, most of whose operations are in the United States, that pays dividends or interest (of the types taxable if paid by a U.S. corporation) to a foreign person must withhold a portion of the payments (this is sometimes referred to as a second-level withholding tax). A foreign corporation becomes liable to withhold only when more than half of its gross income for a 3-year period is effectively connected with a U.S. trade or business. If the 50-percent threshold is crossed, the 30-percent (or lower treaty rate) tax applies to the allocable portion of the payment attributable to income of the paying foreign corporation that is effectively connected with its U.S. trade or business. One function of this withholding tax is to treat payments by foreign corporations with U.S. operations like payments by U.S. corporations.

* * * * * *

Explanation of Provision.—The bill adopts a branch-level tax on profits of foreign corporations operating businesses in the United States. It also modifies the second-level withholding taxes of current law by reducing the U.S. business thresholds that trigger the taxes, and modifies the determination of U.S. source interest subject to U.S. tax.

Branch profits tax.—The bill provides that the base for the branch profits tax, the "dividend equivalent amount," is the income effectively connected with the corporation's U.S. trade or business, subject to two adjustments and an earnings and profits limitation. The first adjustment reduces the tax base to the extent the branch's income is reinvested in the United States. This reduction is measured by the increase in the money and adjusted basis of the branch's assets less its liabilities at the end of the year over the money and adjusted basis of its assets less its liabilities at the beginning of the year. Secondly, the tax base is increased in any subsequent year to the extent those reinvested earnings are remitted to the home office of the foreign corporation. This adjustment is measured by the amount by which the money and adjusted basis of the branch's assets less its liabilities at the beginning of the year exceeds the money and adjusted basis of the branch's assets less its liabilities at the end of the year. It is intended in the latter situation that the increase in the tax base be limited to the amount of the income of the branch received or accrued after the bill's effective date that has been reinvested in the branch.

The dividend equivalent amount is then limited to current and accumulated earnings and profits attributable to the branch's effectively connected income. This limitation ensures that the taxable base is reduced by

Federal and foreign income taxes, by capital losses not allowed in computing taxable income, and by other adjustments that would affect the amount of earnings that could be repatriated as a dividend if the branch operated as a corporation.

The committee intends that the branch's earnings and profits be measured pursuant to general Code rules but limited to the branch's activities. For example, tax-exempt interest received or accrued by the branch is included in the earnings and profits limitation even though those amounts are not included in the branch's effectively connected income.

Since the branch profits tax is imposed on income effectively connected with a U.S. trade or business, the tax applies, for example, to foreign corporations that are partners in a partnership that derives income effectively connected with a U.S. trade or business and to foreign corporations that own vessels and aircraft that generate income effectively connected with a U.S. trade or business.

The bill imposes a tax of 30 percent on the dividend equivalent amount. If an income tax treaty between the United States and the country in which the corporation is resident permits the branch profits tax, but reduces the rate, the lower treaty rate applies, unless the owners of the corporation are treaty shopping (as defined below). In treaty shopping cases, the 30 percent rate applies. If a treaty between the United States and the country in which the corporation is resident does not specifically provide for a branch profits tax, but does otherwise permit such a tax, the treaty's direct investment dividend rate is to apply to the branch base, unless the owners of the corporation are treaty shopping whereupon the bill's rate applies. Finally, if a treaty between the United States and the country in which the corporation is resident permits a branch profits tax, but contains a different computation than the bill provides, or subjects the branch tax to restrictions not in the statute, the bill provides that the tax will be applied subject to the treaty's computation provisions and other restrictions, unless the owners of the corporation are treaty shopping whereupon the bill's provisions apply. For example, the committee understands that the U.S.-Canadian treaty allows a branch tax but that the tax is computed under rules different from the bill's rules; if a Canadian corporation is not treaty shopping, the provisions of the U.S.-Canadian treaty would apply in determining the branch tax payable to the United States.

The bill provides that, in measuring the adjusted basis of its assets and liabilities, the branch is to include only its assets and liabilities that are treated as connected with the conduct of the branch's U.S. trade or business. The bill provides that the includible assets and liabilities are only those assets and liabilities that are directly related to the income of the branch that is effectively connected with the conduct of its U.S. trade or business. For example, the committee intends that the necessary assets include cash necessary to meet day-to-day operating requirements, receivables from the sale of goods or services, inventories, property, plant, and equipment used in the business, investments as long as the income therefrom is effectively connected income, and other assets necessary to operate the business. Includible liabilities mean the day-to-day payables and short-term obligations, long-term obligations incurred to purchase assets used in the business, and other liabilities necessary to meet business obligations.

*   *   *   *   *   *

Second-level withholding taxes.—

*   *   *   *   *   *

With respect to interest, the bill provides that a portion of interest paid by a foreign corporation is treated as U.S. source if at least 10 percent of the foreign corporation's worldwide income is income effectively connected with a U.S. trade or business during a 3-year period ending with the close of the taxable year preceding the payment of the interest (or for the period of the corporation's existence, if shorter). The portion of the interest treated as U.S. source is the interest paid multiplied by the ratio of the average interest deduction claimed on the corporation's U.S. income tax return for the base period to the average total interest expense of the corporation for the base period. Any interest treated as U.S. source is subject to Code provisions that may exempt the interest from withholding. For example, the deposit rule of section 871(i)(2)(A) (as modified by sec. 912 of the bill) exempts U.S. source interest from tax when paid by an active banking organization to a foreign person and the interest is not effectively connected with a U.S. trade or business of the foreign person.

The bill also provides that if the owners of a foreign corporation are treaty shopping (as defined above), a treaty that prohibits U.S. taxation of interest paid by a foreign corporation is to be overridden. In these cases, however, the committee intends to respect any treaty relationship that the interest recipient has with the United States in determining the applicable tax rate for the interest payments. Otherwise, the payments are subject to tax at a 30-percent rate if the recipient is not resident of a treaty country. For example, if a corporation organized in a foreign country has a branch in the United States and that foreign country has an income tax treaty with the United States that prohibits the United States from imposing a tax on interest payments made by the foreign corporation, the treaty provision will be respected if the owners of the foreign corporation are not treaty shopping. If the owners are treaty shopping, then the United States will impose its 30 percent withholding tax on U.S. source interest payments made by the corporation, unless a treaty between the United States and the recipients' country of residence otherwise reduces or eliminates the tax and no treaty shopping with respect to the latter treaty takes place.

*   *   *   *   *   *

Relationship with tax treaties.—In general, it is not intended that the bill's branch profits tax apply in situations where its application would be inconsistent with an existing U.S. income tax treaty obligation. The committee understands that it is the Treasury Department's interpretation that if a corporation is organized in a country with which the United States has a treaty that contains a nondiscrimination article similar to the article contained in the United States 1981 Model Income Tax Treaty, such article prohibits the bill's branch profits tax. The committee intends to respect this view.

In the event a treaty with a particular foreign country does not allow a branch profits tax but does allow the Code's second-level withholding tax on dividends, the bill provides that, to that extent, the present law second-level withholding tax is to apply.

However, the bill provides that the branch profits tax is to be imposed in treaty-shopping situations (as defined below), notwithstanding any conflicting treaty provisions. In the event a treaty with the United States prohibits the branch profits tax but it allows a second-level withholding tax on dividends if the corporation derives, for example, 50 percent or more of its income from the United States, and the corporation does in fact derive 50 percent or more of its income from the United States, the bill provides that the second-level withholding tax is imposed pursuant to the treaty's conditions. In the event a treaty with the United States prohibits the branch profits tax and allows a second-level withholding tax on dividends generally but contains conditions similar to those described above before the United States can impose its withholding tax, the bill's branch profits tax is imposed if the owners are treaty shopping and the foreign corporation does not meet those conditions for that year. If the owners are not treaty shopping, no tax (branch profits or second-level withholding) is imposed. In the event a treaty with the United States prohibits both a branch profits tax and any second-level dividend withholding tax generally, the bill's branch profits tax is imposed if the owners of the corporation are treaty shopping.

The committee understands that if a country in which the foreign corporation is organized has a treaty with the United States that has a dividend article similar to Article 10(5) of the United States 1981 Model Income Tax Treaty, the treaty permits the imposition of a second-level withholding tax by the United States. In this case, if treaty shopping is not present and the treaty prohibits the branch profits tax, no second-level withholding tax is imposed if a foreign corporation does not derive at least 50 percent of its income from a permanent establishment in the United States (as provided by the treaty).

The bill provides that a foreign corporation is treaty shopping where more than 50 percent (by value) of the beneficial owners of the foreign corporation are not residents of the treaty country. The bill treats U.S. citizens and resident aliens as residents of the treaty country for this purpose. However, if the foreign corporation's stock is primarily and regularly traded on an established securities market in the country under whose treaty it claims benefits as a resident, the bill provides that it is considered a resident of that country for this purpose. The bill also provides that if the foreign corporation's parent is organized in the same country as the foreign corporation, and the parent corporation's shares are primarily and regularly traded in that country, the subsidiary corporation is considered resident of such country for purposes of the country's treaty with the United States.

The bill also provides that the Secretary is to prescribe regulations regarding other circumstances in which a foreign corporation is not considered to be treaty shopping. For example, the regulations may provide that a corporation is not considered to be treaty shopping in circumstances where a foreign corporation operates an active trade or business in the country in which it is organized as long as a substantial amount of the corporation's income is not reduced by amounts payable outside the corporation's country of organization.

*　　*　　*　　*　　*　　*

Effective Date.—The provision is effective for taxable years beginning after December 31, 1986.

For U.S. branches of foreign corporations that have undistributed accumulated earnings and profits as of their first taxable years beginning on or after January 1, 1987, the bill's provisions are to apply to income generated in taxable years after December 31, 1986, that are considered distributed from the branch to the home office, limited by post-effective date earnings and profits. Meanwhile, present law's second-level withholding tax on dividends is to apply to the pre-effective date accumulated earnings and profits that are distributed after the effective date. Thus, if a branch's income had not constituted at least 50 percent of the corporation's income for the base period prescribed under present law, there would be no withholding tax imposed.

*　　*　　*　　*　　*　　*

[Conference Report]

*　　*　　*　　*　　*　　*

The conference agreement generally follows the Senate amendment with respect to the branch tax on profits, with substantive and technical modifications. With respect to interest, the conference agreement treats as U.S. source the greater of the interest paid or deducted by a U.S. branch of a foreign corporation. The conference agreement adopts the Senate amendment's effective date.

Branch profits tax.—To achieve greater parity between the remittance of branch profits and the distribution of subsidiary earnings, the conference agreement provides that the taxable base on which the branch profits tax is imposed is the earnings and profits of a U.S. branch of a foreign corporation attributable to its income effectively connected (or treated as effectively connected) with a U.S. trade or business. Thus, for example, the branch profits tax applies to a foreign corporation engaged in a U.S. trade or business even though, for purposes of sections 897 and 6039C, the corporation has made an election under section 897(i) to be treated as a U.S. corporation. Consistent with the determination of a subsidiary's earnings and profits, the conferees intend that a branch's earnings and profits include income that would be effectively connected with a U.S. trade or business if such income were taxable, such as tax-exempt municipal bond interest. Moreover, the agreement provides that current earnings that are not reinvested in a branch's trade or business assets are subject to tax though the branch may have incurred prior year deficits. Consistent with the taxation of a subsidiary's distributions, the agreement provides that dividend distributions by a foreign corporation during a year do not reduce a branch's earnings and profits for purposes of computing the branch tax base. The conferees wish to clarify that, under regulations, the rules for determining assets and liabilities treated as connected with the conduct of a U.S. trade or business for branch tax purposes are to be consistent with the rules used in allocating deductions for purposes of computing taxable income.

The agreement excludes from the imposition of branch profits tax the following earnings and profits attributable to income effectively connected with a U.S. trade or business: (1) certain earnings derived by foreign sales corporations (income described in Code secs. 921(d) and 926(b)); (2) earnings derived by foreign transportation carriers that are exempt from U.S. tax pursuant to treaty or reciprocal exemption; (3) earnings derived from the sale of any interest in U.S. real property holding corporations; (4) earnings derived by corporations satisfying certain ownership and income requirements that are organized in certain U.S. possessions (corporations described in sec. 881(b)); and (5) earnings derived by certain captive insurance companies that elect to treat their income as effectively connected with a U.S. trade or business (*see* sec. 1221(b)(2) of the agreement, disussed at C.1.a., above). The exclusion for earnings derived by certain possessions corporations is intended to be "mirrored" so as not to apply the branch tax to U.S. corporations operating in possessions of the United States.

Since the taxable base is computed with reference to effectively connected earnings and profits, the computation of net equity, the base used to determine constructive profit remittances, is likewise based on the earnings and profits value of the branch's assets and liabilities connected with its U.S. trade or business (if these values are different from the assets' and liabilities' adjusted tax bases). For example, in computing an increase or decrease in net equity, a branch that claims accelerated depreciation on its assets for the purpose of calculating taxable income will be required to make this branch-level tax computation using the assets' basis for earnings and profits purposes.

Following the Senate amendment, the agreement provides that the branch tax base is decreased when a branch's profits are reinvested in assets connected with a U.S. trade or business. The Secretary may prescribe regulations that carry out the purpose of this provision. The conferees generally believe that the base should be decreased in stock acquisition cases if branch tax would not have been imposed had assets, rather than stock, been acquired. For example, the regulations may provide that where control of a U.S. corporation is acquired with a branch's profits it may be inappropriate to impose the branch tax.

Branch-level interest tax.—Although the conference agreement generally follows the Senate amendment's approach of treating interest as U.S. source to the extent it is deducted in the United States, the agreement modifies the amendment's interest provisions to treat a branch, in effect, more like a subsidiary, as the branch tax does. The agreement provides that any interest paid by a branch's U.S. trade or business is U.S. source and subject to U.S. withholding tax of 30 percent, unless the tax is reduced or eliminated by a specific Code or treaty provision. To the extent a branch has allocated to it under Reg. section 1.882-5 an interest deduction in excess of the interest actually paid by it, the excess is treated under the agreement as interest paid by a U.S. subsidiary to the foreign corporate taxpayer on a notional loan from the taxpayer. This excess is also subject to a 30-percent tax absent a specific Code exemption or treaty reduction. The agreement treats the excess interest as paid on the last day of a corporation's taxable year and provides that any U.S. tax due is payable within the time prescribed for filing the corporation's U.S. income tax return (not including extensions).

The conference agreement provides regulatory authority to determine, for purposes of any special Code treatment, how the excess interest is to be treated. For example, the regulations may provide that where indebtedness of the home office is attributed to the branch, the excess interest is to be treated as incurred on each type of external borrowing by the corporation (*e.g.*, a bank deposit) and determined by reference to the relative principal amounts of, and the average interest rate on, each type of external borrowing. Thus, for example, in the case of a bank, the excess interest will not necessarily be treated as paid on a bank deposit. The conferees are aware that some corporations attempt to establish actual debtor-creditor relationships for funds between a branch and a home office or between one branch and another. The conferees question the legitimacy of such arrangements from a tax perspective since only one legal entity is involved. Nonetheless, if companies are able to legally establish such relationships, it is intended that the regulations address these relationships and possibly treat the excess interest as incurred on each type of interbranch "loan". The conferees are concerned that taxpayers may artificially structure interbranch loans in a manner different from their external liabilities in an attempt to reduce or eliminate the tax on excess interest. The conferees, therefore, expect the regulations to address this concern.

For purposes of determining whether the tax on the excess interest is to be reduced or eliminated by treaty, the applicable treaty generally is any income tax treaty between the United States and the country of the corporation's home office. However, any treaty benefits available in this case are subject to the agreement's prohibition against treaty shopping. In the case of U.S. withholding tax on interest actually paid by a branch, since the agreement effectively treats the branch as a U.S. corporation for purposes of the tax, the appropriate treaty will be any treaty between the United States and the country of a foreign recipient, subject to the agreement's treaty shopping rules.

Interaction with income tax treaties.—The conference agreement generally follows the Senate amendment in providing that existing U.S. income tax treaties may modify, reduce, or eliminate the branch profits tax, the second-level withholding tax on dividends, or the branch-level tax on interest except in cases of treaty shopping. The agreement modifies, however, the definition of treaty shopping adopted by the Senate amendment in two respects. First, the Senate amendment's ownership requirement is modified to look through all entities, not only foreign entities, in determining whether 50 percent or more of the corporation's stock is owned by local residents. Second, the agreement provides that where 50 percent or more of a foreign corporation's income is used to satisfy liabilities outside the corporation's country of residence, the corporation may not avail itself of any treaty benefits provided by an income tax treaty between its country of residence and the United States (a "base erosion" rule). This latter rule is frequently used in recent U.S. income tax treaties and the conferees feel its addition is necessary to prevent nonresidents of a treaty country from gaining benefits the treaty accords. As does the Senate amendment, the conference agreement authorizes the Secretary to prescribe regulations regarding other circumstances in which the shareholders of a foreign corporation are not treaty shopping.

The conferees understand that the Treasury Department interprets Article 24(3) of the United States 1981 Model Income Tax Treaty to preclude the imposition of the agreement's branch profits tax. The conferees also do not intend that the branch tax be imposed on income not attributable to a permanent establishment (even though the income is effectively connected with a U.S. trade or business under Code rules) if the treaty in question in fact precludes the United States from imposing its regular corporate income tax on income not attributable to a permanent establishment, so long as the shareholders of a foreign corporation are not treaty shopping.

Other rules.—The conference agreement reduces present law's business income threshold for imposition of the second-level withholding tax to 25 percent. The agreement also clarifies that the second-level withholding tax on dividends is not applicable in those cases where the branch profits tax may be imposed, even though no branch tax may be due in a particular taxable year. For example, if a branch reinvests its after-tax earnings in its trade or business during a particular taxable year so that no branch tax is due that year, but the branch's business income exceeds 25 percent of the foreign corporation's total income and the corporation distributes dividends during that year, the second-level dividend withholding tax is imposed only if the treaty of the country where the foreign corporation resides precludes the United States from imposing its branch tax and permits the second-level withholding tax.

Consistent with the branch tax's application to income from the disposition of real property, the agreement also conforms present law's second-level withholding tax on dividends so that the United States collects two levels of tax on this income. No inference is intended by the modification of this provision about the interpretation of present law.

The conferees are concerned that the branch-level interest provision may lead to increased use of back-to-back loans by non-treaty residents and improper characterization of interbranch funds by both treaty and nontreaty residents to avoid U.S. tax. The conferees wish to emphasize that back-to-back loans, as generally provided under present law, will be collapsed by the IRS, and the ultimate recipient, if not treaty protected, will be subject to U.S. tax. Similarly, the conferees expect the Internal Revenue Service to closely scrutinize the characterization of interbranch transactions. The conferees recognize the difficulty that the Internal Revenue Service has in identifying these arrangements that erode the U.S. tax base and believe the tax-writing committees of the Congress should monitor collections and compliance with the interest provision adopted under the agreement to ensure its continued viability, and, if necessary, propose legislation to obviate any abuses.

[*Effective date.*—Applies to taxable years beginning after 12-31-86. Ed.]

[¶ 4048] SECTION 1242. TREATMENT OF DEFERRED PAYMENTS AND APPRECIATION ARISING OUT OF BUSINESS CONDUCTED WITHIN THE UNITED STATES

(Sec. 864 of the Code)

[Senate Explanation]

*   *   *   *   *   *

Present Law.—The United States taxes the worldwide income of U.S. citizens, residents, and corporations on a net basis at graduated rates. Nonresident aliens and foreign corporations are generally taxed only on their U.S. source income. The United States taxes foreign taxpayers' income that is "effectively connected" with a U.S. trade or business on a net basis at graduated rates, in much the same way that it taxes the income of U.S. persons. U.S. income of a foreign taxpayer that is not connected with a U.S. trade or business is generally subject to a 30-percent withholding tax on the gross amount of such income, although certain types of such income earned by foreign investors, such as portfolio interest income, are exempt from U.S. tax. U.S. income tax treaties reduce or eliminate the 80-percent withholding tax in many cases. The United States does not generally tax foreign taxpayers on capital gains that are not connected with a U.S. trade or business (real property gains have been the major exception to this rule).

Although gains from the sale of assets used by a foreign corporation in a U.S. trade or business ordinarily would constitute effectively connected income fully subject to U.S. tax, under present law foreign persons may be able to avoid U.S. tax on income attributable to a U.S. trade or business if they receive the income in a year after the trade or business has ceased to exist (e.g., by selling property and recognizing the gain on the installment basis). Foreign persons may also be able to avoid U.S. tax by removing property of a trade or business from the United States before selling it.

*   *   *   *   *   *

Explanation of Provision.—The bill amends section 864(c) to provide that any income or gain of a foreign person for any taxable year which is attributable to a transaction in any other taxable year will be treated as effectively connected with the conduct of a U.S. trade or business if it would have been so treated if it had been taken into account in that other taxable year. Thus, deferring the recognition of income until a later taxable year will no longer change the manner in which the U.S. tax system treats the income.

Effective Date.—The provision applies to taxable years beginning after 1986.

[¶ 4049] SECTION 1243. TREATMENT UNDER SECTION 877 OF PROPERTY RECEIVED IN TAX-FREE EXCHANGES, ETC

(Sec. 877 of the Code)

[House Explanation]

* * * * * *

Explanation of Provision.—The bill amends section 877 to provide that gain on the sale or exchange of property whose basis is determined in whole or in part by reference to the basis of U.S. property will be treated as gain from the sale of U.S. property.

Thus, expatriates will still be permitted to make tax-free exchanges of U.S. property for foreign property. However, a subsequent disposition of that foreign property (on which gain is recognized) will be treated as a disposition of U.S. property, and will therefore be subject to U.S. tax.

Effective Date.—The provision applies to dispositions of property acquired in tax-free exchanges after September 25, 1985.

[¶ 4050] SECTION 1244. STUDY OF UNITED STATES REINSURANCE INDUSTRY

[Senate Explanation]

* * * * * *

Explanation of Provision.—The bill requires the Secretary of the Treasury or his delegate to conduct a study to determine whether U.S. reinsurance corporations are placed at a significant competitive disadvantage vis a vis foreign reinsurance corporations by reason of existing treaties between the United States and foreign countries, specifically identifying any treaties that create a significant competitive disadvantage. The Secretary is to report the results of this study to the Senate Committees on Finance and Foreign Relations and the House Committees on Ways and Means and Foreign Affairs before January 1, 1988. If the study indicates that U.S. reinsurance corpo-

rations are at such a competitive disadvantage, the committee believes that the Secretary of the Treasury should renegotiate the relevant treaties to eliminate that disadvantage.

Effective Date.—This provision is effective on the date of enactment.

* * * * * *

[Conference Report]

* * * * * *

The conference agreement follows the Senate amendment with an amendment treating certain captive insurance companies as controlled foreign corporations for subpart F purposes (this amendment is discussed at [¶4034]).

[¶ 4051] SECTION 1245. INFORMATION WITH RESPECT TO CERTAIN FOREIGN-OWNED CORPORATIONS

(Sec. 6038A of the Code)

[Senate Explanation]

* * * * * *

Present Law.—The Tax Equity and Fiscal Responsibility Act of 1982 (TEFRA) added new reporting requirements under section 6038A for certain foreign-controlled corporations. In general, these requirements apply both to U.S. corporations and to foreign corporations engaged in trade or business in the United States ("reporting corporations"), but only if they are controlled by a foreign person (defined to include certain possessions residents). This control test requires reporting if at any time during a taxable year a foreign person owns 50 percent or more of the stock of the reporting corporation (either by value or by voting power).

The reporting corporation must furnish certain information about any corporation that (1) is a member of the same "controlled group" as the reporting corporation (a group that generally includes brother-sister corporations as well as the reporting corporation's parent and subsidiaries)[1] and that (2) has any transaction with the reporting corporation during the taxable year. The information that the reporting company is to report is such information as the Secretary may require that relates to the related company's name, its principal place of business, the nature of its business, the country in which it is organized and in which it is resident, its relationship with the reporting corporation, and its transactions with the reporting corporation during the year.

* * * * * *

[Footnote ¶ 4051] (1) For the purpose of the reporting requirement, the term "controlled group" incorporates the definition of controlled group of corporations in section 1563(a) with certain changes in the percentage tests of that section and with certain exceptions. Although under section 1563(b) foreign corporations subject to tax under section 881 and certain other corporations are "excluded members" of a controlled group rather than "component members" for the purpose of section 1561, the exclusion of these corporations from the definition of "component members" for that purpose does not remove them from the controlled group, as defined in section 1563(a). Therefore, TEFRA requires reporting about any foreign corporation that otherwise qualifies as a member of the controlled group.

Explanation of Provision.—Under the bill, a corporation subject to the reporting requirements of section 6038A must report with respect to its transactions with all related persons (within the meaning of Code section 482), not merely its transactions with corporations in its controlled group.

Effective Date.—The amendment applies to taxable years beginning after December 31, 1986.

* * * * * *

[Conference Report]

* * * * * *

The conference agreement follows the Senate amendment with the technical corrections and modifications described below. First, the agreement defines a related party as any person who is related to the reporting

corporation under sections 482, 267(b), or 707(b)(1). The latter two Code sections provide objective related party tests, in contrast with section 482, the sole provision used in the Senate amendment for determining related party status.

Second, the agreement adds a requirement that U.S.-controlled foreign corporations, foreign-controlled U.S. corporations, and foreign-controlled foreign corporations doing business in the United States report such information as the Secretary may require for purposes of carrying out the installment sales rules described in VIII. C., above. The conferees note that the limitations imposed by section 6103, relating to confidentiality of information, are to apply to the disclosure of any information provided to the Internal Revenue Service pursuant to this latter provision.

[¶ 4052] SECTION 1246. WITHHOLDING TAX ON AMOUNTS PAID BY PARTNERSHIPS TO FOREIGN PARTNERS

(Secs. 864, 871, 875, 881, 882, 1441, 1442, and 1446 of the Code)

[Senate Explanation]

* * * * * *

Explanation of Provision.—The bill provides that the following withholding rules will apply to distributions to foreign partners in U.S. partnerships that have income effectively connected with the conduct of a U.S. trade or business. First, present law rules requiring withholding at 30 percent (or reduced treaty rates) with respect to distributions attributable to dividends, certain interest, etc., will continue to apply to such distributions. However, the bill specifies that any distribution by the partnership is considered to come first out of these types of income received by partnerships. Second, the remaining partnership distributions are subject to withholding at a 20 percent rate. The amount withheld is creditable against the U.S. income tax liability of the foreign partner. Third, where interests in a publicly traded partnership are held through one or more nominees, withholding is to be carried out under the principles of section 1441(a) by the last U.S. person in the chain of ownership.

* * * * * *

[Conference Report]

* * * * * *

The conference agreement generally follows the Senate amendment, with modifications. The conference agreement applies the new withholding rule to foreign partnerships as well as to domestic partnerships. The

agreement clarifies that the new withholding rule does not apply to payments that are subject to withholding under Code section 1441 or 1442, or would be so subject if a treaty did not reduce or eliminate the tax required to be withheld. In addition, the agreement provides that withheld amounts in excess of a foreign person's tax liability are to be treated as an overpayment of tax. The agreement also provides regulatory authority to coordinate the new withholding rule with the FIRPTA withholding requirements to prevent duplicative withholding.

Under the conference agreement, if a partnership's gross income effectively connected with a U.S. trade or business over a three-year period is less than 80 percent of the total gross income of the partnership over that period, then withholding is required only on the proportion of current distributions that the partnership's gross income effectively connected with its U.S. trade or business bears to the partnership's total gross income over its previous three taxable years.

Finally, the conference agreement contains general regulatory authority for the Secretary to carry out the agreement's provisions. For example, the regulations are to specify the proper withholding agent in the case of tiers of partnerships, and the appropriate withholding requirement in the case of a partnership that has effectively connected income for the first time.

[Effective date.]—The provisions apply to distributions after the date prescribed in regulations, or if earlier, December 31, 1987, but not before January 1, 1987.

[¶ 4053] SECTION 1247. INCOME OF FOREIGN GOVERNMENTS

(Sec. 892 of the Code)

[Senate Explanation]

*　　*　　*　　*　　*　　*

Present Law.—The income of foreign governments or international organizations received from investments in the United States in stocks, bonds, or other domestic securities, owned by such foreign governments or international organizations, or from interest on deposits in banks in the United States of money belonging to such foreign governments or international organizations, or from any other source within the United States, is not included in gross income and is exempt from U.S. income taxation (sec. 892). Regulations make clear that this exemption does not apply to any income from commercial activities in the United States (Reg. sec. 1.892-1(a)(3)). That is, the exemption extends only to investment income.

*　　*　　*　　*　　*　　*

Explanation of Provision.—The bill codifies the rule limiting the tax exemption for foreign governments to investment income. The bill defines commercial activity to include ownership of a controlling interest in a corporation or other entity engaged in trade or business in the United States. For this purpose, controlling interest means an interest of 50 percent or more, by vote or value, in a U.S. corporation or other entity, or any other interest that allows or would allow the exercise of effective control. For this purpose, there is aggregation of commonly owned interests.

For example, a foreign government owns 50 percent of a U.S. corporation. Under the bill, dividends paid by the U.S. corporation to the foreign government will be subject to tax on a gross withholding basis. The rate of tax will be 30 percent, unless reduced by treaty. Similarly, gross interest payments from the U.S. corporation to the foreign governmental shareholder (or a related party) will be subject to a 30-percent withholding tax (or tax at a lower treaty rate). Interest payments to a related party such as a 50-percent shareholder are not exempt from U.S. tax (because they are not portfolio interest as defined in section 871).

The foreign government exception will not apply to controlled entities that engage in any commercial activities anywhere. For example, an incidental loan into the United States by a bank, wholly owned by a foreign government, might not in and of itself constitute commercial activity in the United States. Assume that the interest does not qualify as portfolio interest, and that the U.S. tax on that interest is not eliminated by treaty. Interest on that loan would be subject to tax under the bill, because the foreign entity, though not engaged in a U.S. trade or business, is engaged in the business elsewhere.

Once a foreign governmental entity is found to engage in commercial activity somewhere in the world, the United States must determine whether to impose its tax on any particular U.S. source income of that entity on a net basis or a gross basis. For this purpose, in general, the committee intends that the principles distinguishing income taxed on a net basis and income taxed on a gross basis for private foreign persons apply to foreign governments also. For example, assume that a foreign government owns an airline. The airline does not fly to or from the United States, and it is not otherwise engaged in the conduct of a trade or business in the United States. The airline purchases 2 percent of the stock of a U.S. airline corporation. Dividends paid with respect to that stock are taxable on a gross basis, at the 30-percent or lower treaty rate, because they are not effectively connected with the conduct of a U.S. trade or business. If, by contrast, a foreign governmental entity owns stock in a U.S. corporation that pays dividends yielding effectively connected income in the hands of a comparable privately owned corporation, those dividends will be subject to U.S. tax on a net basis.

The committee does not believe that income derived by foreign governments' athletic teams and cultural groups should be treated differently from similar income earned by privately owned foreign professional teams or groups. That income is not in the nature of investment income. In such a case, if a treaty prevents U.S. taxation, or if the team comes on a nonprofit basis, there will be no tax.

The committee intends that, for treaty purposes, a foreign government be treated as a resident of its country, unless it denies treaty benefits to the United States. The committee intends that similar treatment apply to agencies and bureaus of foreign governments, and to corporations owned by foreign governments that are residents of its country under the treaty, so long as the country does not deny reciprocal treatment to comparable U.S. entities.

*　　*　　*　　*　　*　　*

[Conference Report]

*　　*　　*　　*　　*　　*

The conference agreement generally follows the Senate amendment, with the modifications described below.

First, the conference agreement removes international organizations described in Code section 7701(a)(18) from the scope of the provision. For these international organizations, the conference agreement makes no change to present law.

Second, the conference agreement exempts from U.S. tax income derived from financial instruments in the conduct of governmental financial or monetary policy.

Act 1247　¶4053

Third, the conference agreement deletes the provision of the Senate amendment that denied governmental treatment to any entity controlled by a foreign government if any other entity controlled by that government engaged in commercial activity. Under the conference agreement, as under the Senate amendment, if a controlled entity is itself engaged in commercial activity anywhere in the world, its income is treated like income of a privately owned entity. Income it receives is fully taxable and payments it makes are not eligible for the exemption. However, if a controlled entity is not itself engaged in any commercial activity, the agreement provides tax exemption for certain investment income earned by that controlled entity, whether or not any entity related to that controlled entity is engaged in commercial activity, and the agreement provides exemption for interest and dividend payments from the entity to the government. Thus, the conference agree-

ment ensures taxation of income derived directly or indirectly by foreign governments from commercial activities. For this purpose, however, the conference agreement treats a foreign central bank of issue as a controlled commercial foreign entity only if engaged in commercial activities within the United States. The conferees anticipate that regulations will appropriately address shifting of income from commercial arms of foreign governments to other related entities. These regulations are to replace the rule of the Senate amendment that attributed commercial activity of one controlled entity to other controlled entities.

[Effective date.—] The conference agreement makes it clear that this provision is effective for amounts received or accrued on or after July 1, 1986, although no withholding obligation is imposed for amounts paid prior to the date of enactment.

[¶ 4054] SECTION 1248. LIMITATION ON COST OF PROPERTY IMPORTED FROM RELATED PERSONS

(Sec. 1059A of the Code)

[Senate Explanation]

* * * * * *

Explanation of Provision.—The bill provides that importers subject to U.S. tax may not claim a transfer price for U.S. income tax purposes that is higher than would be consistent with the value they claim for customs purposes. Appropriate adjustments may be made in applying the rule in cases where customs pricing rules differ from appropriate tax rules—as, for example, with the inclusion or exclusion of freight charges. This rule applies to transfer prices between commonly controlled entities, as defined in section 482 of the Code.

Effective Date.—The provision applies to transactions entered into after March 18, 1986.

* * * * * *

[Conference Report]

* * * * * *

Conference Agreement.—The conference agreement follows the Senate amendment. The conferees expect that the Secretary will provide rules for coordinating customs and tax valuation principles, including provision for proper adjustments for amounts such as freight charges, items of American content returned, and sales commissions where customs pricing rules may differ from appropriate tax valuation rules.

[¶ 4055] SECTION 1249. TREATMENT OF DUAL RESIDENT CORPORATIONS

(Sec. 1504 of the Code)

[Senate Explanation]

* * * * * *

Present Law.— * * * For tax purposes, a corporation may be at the same time a U.S. resident and a resident of another country. Such companies are sometimes [referred] to as "dual resident companies." A dual resident company is taxable in both countries on its worldwide income (or it can deduct its worldwide losses). In addition, if the company is a resident of both the United States and either the United Kingdom or Australia, it is able, in effect, to use its losses to offset the income of commonly owned corporate residents in the two countries. (The committee is aware of the ability to share losses in this way only in the case of Australia and the United Kingdom; this ability may occur in other cases as well.) In general, neither of

these countries taxes the active business income of foreign corporations that operate solely abroad.

Corporate groups attempt to isolate expenses in dual resident companies so that, viewed in isolation, the dual resident company is losing money for tax purposes. This isolation of expenses allows, in effect, the consolidation of tax results of one money-losing dual resident corporation with two profitable companies, one in each of two countries. This use of one deduction by two different corporate groups is sometimes referred to as "double dipping." The profitable companies report their income to only one country.

* * * * * *

Explanation of Provision.—The bill provides that, except as provided in regulations, a U.S. corporation may not be a member of a

U.S. consolidated group for a year in which, in another country, it consolidates with or otherwise transfers tax benefits to a related party all of whose earnings are not currently or eventually subject to U.S. tax. The statute allows the Secretary to impose consolidation, notwithstanding the bill's general rule, in cases where taxpayers use the general rule as a device to break consolidation.

Some treaties prohibit discrimination against foreign-owned enterprises that are "similar" to U.S.-owned enterprises. The committee has crafted this provision so that it does not violate treaties. First, it is not clear that a U.S. corporation that consolidates (or otherwise shares losses) with a foreign corporation and a U.S. corporation that does not consolidate with a foreign corporation are "similar enterprises" for treaty purposes. Second, the provision does not distinguish between corporations on the basis of their ownership, but instead on the basis of whether their losses allow foreign tax benefits to entities whose full earnings are or will be subject to U.S. tax. Finally, it is the committee's view that this prohibition of double dipping is in fact necessary to prevent discrimination in favor of foreign-owned businesses and against U.S.-owned businesses in the U.S. economy. If the committee should be incorrect in its technical interpretation of the interaction between this provision and treaties, however, it does not intend that any contrary provision defeat its elimination of this double dipping loophole. The committee does not believe that the United States Senate wittingly agreed to an international tax system where taxpayers making cross-border investments, and only those taxpayers, could reduce or eliminate their U.S. corporate tax through self-help and gain an advantage over U.S. persons who make similar investments.

* * * * * *

[Conference Report]

* * * * * *

The conference agreement follows the approach of the Senate amendment, with substantial modifications. The agreement provides that if a U.S. corporation is subject to a foreign country's tax on worldwide income, or on a residence basis as opposed to a source basis, any taxable loss it incurs cannot reduce the taxable income of any other member of a U.S. affiliated group for that or any other taxable year. A company may be subject to foreign tax on a residence basis because its place of effective management is in a foreign country or for other reasons. Where a corporation is subject to foreign tax on a residence basis, then, for U.S. purposes, its loss will be available to offset income of that corporation in other years, but not income of another U.S. corporation. Regulatory authority is provided to exempt a U.S. corporation from this rule to the extent that its losses do not offset the income of foreign corporations for foreign tax purposes. Thus, for example, a U.S. corporation that resides in a foreign country, that has no affiliates in that country whose foreign tax its losses can reduce, and whose losses do not otherwise reduce foreign tax of a foreign corporation, will not be subject to this provision.

The conferees adopted a rule preventing use of losses, in lieu of the prohibition of consolidation that the Senate amendment contained, because of their view that the collateral implications of deconsolidation were sometimes undesirable. For example, if a U.S. corporation that is a dual resident corporation wholly owns several U.S. subsidiaries, denial of consolidation to the dual resident corporation would automatically have prevented application of the consolidated return rules to transactions between two of its U.S. subsidiaries under current regulations. The conferees saw no reason to prohibit application of the consolidated return rules in that case, so long as the dual resident corporation's losses do not reduce both the taxable income of a foreign corporation in a foreign country and the U.S. taxable income of some other U.S. corporation.

The agreement's provision applies to dual resident companies whether or not any of the income of any foreign corporation that the dual resident corporation's loss may reduce in the foreign country is or will be subject to U.S. tax. This rule expands that of the Senate amendment, which would not have applied when the income of a foreign corporation whose foreign tax the dual resident corporation's loss could reduce was or would be subject to U.S. tax. The conferees extended the impact of this provision to all foreign corporations that could benefit from a dual resident corporation's net operating loss, whether or not the foreign corporation's earnings are or will be subject to U.S. tax, for two reasons.

First, the conferees believe that this extension is fair: the conferees are not aware of a case where the use of one company's deduction by two other companies in two tax jurisdictions makes sense as a matter of tax policy. The conferees have not perceived any relevant distinction between a deduction that arises on account of interest expense and one that arises on account of some other expense, or between a deduction for a payment to a related party and one for a payment to an unrelated party.

Second, the conferees noted arguments that the Senate provision discriminated against foreign-owned U.S. corporations. As extended, the provision will apply to losses shared with foreign corporations whose earnings will be subject to U.S. tax (which are typically U.S.-controlled) and not only to losses shared with foreign corporations whose earnings are never subject to U.S. tax (which are typically foreign-controlled). The conferees are aware that some have attempted to argue that the provision as extended discriminates against foreign-controlled U.S. entities by somehow imposing on those entities some requirement for loss-sharing not imposed on U.S.-controlled U.S. entities. The conferees find no merit in this argument. If this provision somehow is found to conflict with any treaty, the provision is to be effective notwithstanding the treaty.

[*Effective Date.—*] This provision is effective for taxable years beginning after 1986. Carryforwards attributable to losses incurred in years beginning prior to 1987 by a dual resident corporation are available to offset income that another member of the affiliated group earns in years beginning after 1986.

For example, a dual resident corporation incurs a $100 net operating loss in 1986, its first year of operation, and it shares that loss with a foreign corporation. The only other member of its U.S. consolidated group earns $50 in 1986. All these corporations use the calendar year as a taxable year. In 1987, the $50 loss carryforward is available for use against 1987 income of the dual resident corporation or the other member of the U.S. affiliated group.

[¶ 4056] SECTION 1261. TREATMENT OF FOREIGN CURRENCY TRANSACTIONS

(Secs. 905, 985, 986, 987, 988, 989, 1092, and 1256 of the Code)

[Senate Explanation]

*   *   *   *   *   *

Explanation of Provision.—*1. Overview.* The bill sets forth a comprehensive set of rules for the treatment of foreign currency denominated transactions, in new subpart J. Under the bill, the tax treatment of a foreign currency denominated transaction turns on the identity of the taxpayer's functional currency. Exchange gain or loss is recognized on a transaction-by-transaction basis only in the case of transactions involving certain financial assets or liabilities (referred to as "section 988 transactions") that are denominated in a nonfunctional currency. In the case of section 988 transactions, exchange gain or loss generally is treated as ordinary income or loss. To the extent provided in regulations, exchange gain or loss on certain hedging contracts is characterized and sourced in a manner that is consistent with the related exposure, and a portion of the unrealized exchange gain or loss on section 988 transactions is accrued currently.

A uniform set of criteria is provided for determining the currency in which the results of a foreign operation should be recorded. Business entities using a functional currency other than the U.S. dollar generally are required to use a profit and loss translation method. Exchange gain or loss on a remittance from a branch is treated as ordinary income or loss from domestic sources. A consistent set of rules applies to the translation of foreign taxes and adjustments thereto.

2. Functional currency.—*In general.*—New section 985(a) generally requires all Federal income tax determinations to be made in a taxpayer's functional currency. The functional currency approach presupposes a long-term commitment to a specific economic environment.

The general rule under the bill requires that taxpayers use the U.S. dollar as the functional currency. Thus, except as otherwise provided, taxpayers must measure income or loss from dealings in foreign currency in U.S. dollars, on a transaction-by-transaction basis. In certain circumstances, (described below), a taxpayer is required to use a foreign currency as the functional currency of a "qualified business unit" (generally, a

self-contained foreign operation). Under such circumstances, income or loss derived from a qualified business unit is determined in a foreign currency (before translation into U.S. dollars). In general, the use of a foreign currency as the functional currency of a qualified business unit will result in the deferral of exchange gain or loss from transactions conducted in that currency.

Business entities.—The special rule for qualified business units addresses the treatment of cases in which a single taxpayer has multiple operations in different economic environments. In such a case, a taxpayer may be eligible to account for the results of a foreign operation by measuring income or loss in the currency of the host country (or, in appropriate circumstances, another foreign country). The application of the rule for qualified business units is conditioned on the determination that the foreign operation represents a sufficient commitment to the economic environment of the host country.

In general, the rule for qualified business units will apply where the foreign operation constitutes a trade or business, the activities of which primarily are conducted in the local currency. The bill contemplates that the U.S. dollar will be used as the functional currency of a foreign operation that is an integral extension of a U.S. operation (*e.g.,* a foreign corporation whose sole function is to act as a financing vehicle for affiliated U.S. corporations, or a foreign corporation used to hold portfolio stock investments or similar passive assets that could readily be carried on the parent corporation's books), or a foreign operation with a limited duration (e.g., an offshore construction project undertaken by a U.S. taxpayer).

Qualified business units.—The functional currency of a qualified business unit is the currency of the economic environment in which a significant part of its business activities are conducted, and in which such unit keeps its books and records (new section 985(b)(1)(B)). A single taxpayer can have more than one qualified business unit.

Definition of qualified business unit.—The term qualified business unit is defined as any separate and clearly identified unit of a taxpayer's trade or business, if such unit maintains separate books and records (new sec. 989(a)). A qualified business unit must include every operation that forms a part of the process of earning income. In general, the statutory definition is satisfied on the basis of vertical, functional, or geographical divisions of a single trade or business, if the business unit is capable of producing income independently.[34]

Identification of functional currency.—To identify the functional currency of a qualified business unit, the taxpayer must establish that books and records are maintained in the currency of the economic environment in which a significant part of the unit's activities are conducted. The identification of a functional currency requires a factual determination. In making the required determination, the factors taken into account shall include but not be limited to: (1) the currency in which books and records are maintained, (2) the principal currency in which revenues and expenses are generated, (3) the principal currency in which the business unit borrows or lends, and (4) the functional currency of related business units and the extent to which the business unit's operations are integrated with those of related business units (if a business unit is an integral component of a larger operation, the economic environment of the larger operation governs the choice of a functional currency). These factors generally correspond to the current criteria that is used to identify a functional currency for financial accounting purposes.[35]

The functional currency of a qualified business unit is deemed to be the U.S. dollar if the unit's activities are conducted primarily in dollars (new sec. 985(b)(2)). It is intended that taxpayers use consistent criteria for identifying the functional currency of qualified business units engaged in similar activities in different countries. If the facts and circumstances do not indicate a particular currency (e.g., where an entity conducts significant business in more than one currency), a taxpayer has discretion in choosing a functional currency. The choice of a functional currency, including an election to use the U.S. dollar (described below), is treated as a method of accounting that can be changed only with the consent of the Secretary (and pursuant to such conditions as the Secretary may prescribe). The Secretary shall address in regulations the appropriate treatment of taxpayers whose functional currency changes.

* * * * * *

Under the bill, the U.S. dollar is the functional currency of the Swiss company even though its books and records are maintained in Swiss francs and the Swiss franc is used for financial reporting purposes. This result obtains because the Swiss company's activities are primarily conducted in U.S. dollars.

* * * * * *

[Conference Report]

* * * * * *

The conference agreement follows the Senate amendment. In general, the rule for QBUs will apply where the foreign operation constitutes a trade or business, a significant part of the activities of which are conducted in the local currency. The conference agreement contemplates that the U.S. dollar will be used as the functional currency of a foreign operation that is an integral extension of a U.S. operation (*e.g.*, a foreign corporation whose sole function is to act as a financing vehicle for affiliated U.S. corporations, or a foreign corporation used to hold portfolio stock investments or similar passive assets that could readily be carried on the parent corporation's books), or a foreign operation with a limited duration (e.g., an offshore construction project undertaken by a U.S. taxpayer). In this connection, the conferees wish to clarify that the existence of a QBU does not turn solely on the time frame of a foreign activity. For example, in appropriate circumstances (*e.g.*, if the activity is subjected to tax in the host country), an activity of sufficient duration (*e.g.*, 12 months) may support the finding of the existence of a QBU. The conferees also anticipate that, where appropriate, the Secretary may require that dollar transactions entered into by a QBU with a functional currency other than the dollar be kept in dollars.

* * * * * *

[Senate Explanation]

* * * * * *

Election to use U.S. dollar. The bill provides that a qualified business unit can elect to use the U.S. dollar as its functional currency but only if the unit maintains its books and records in the U.S. dollar (*i.e.*, uses the separate transaction method) or uses a translation method that approximates dollar-based accounting. The election is effective for the taxable year for which made and all subsequent taxable years, unless revoked with the consent of the Secretary. For a U.S. person, the election is to be made on the return for the first taxable year for which a qualified business unit exists, by making a statement that the qualified business unit elects the U.S. dollar as its functional curren-

---

[Footnote ¶ 4056 continued]

(34) An operation that meets this standard is not automatically treated as a separate trade or business for other purposes of the Internal Revenue Code. For example, geographical separation would not provide a basis for treating a business unit as a trade or business under section 446(d), which section permits a single taxpayer to use different accounting methods for separate trades or businesses. Thus, apart from the adoption of a foreign currency as the functional currency of a qualified business unit—which is itself a method of accounting—a taxpayer may be required to use consistent accounting methods for its foreign operations (e.g., cash versus accrual accounting).

(35) See Statement of Financial Accounting Standards No. 52, "Foreign Currency Translation," issued by the Financial Accounting Standards Board (December 7, 1981).

cy for U.S. tax purposes. For a foreign person, the election is to be made in the U.S. owner's return for the first taxable year in which the U.S. owner acquires at least a 50-percent ownership interest in the foreign person by making a statement that the foreign person's qualified business unit elects the U.S. dollar as its functional currency for U.S. tax purposes.

The Secretary is granted limited authority to prescribe rules under which the U.S. dollar can be elected as the functional currency even if books and records are not kept in dollars, if a qualified business unit uses a method of translation that approximates the results of determining exchange gain or loss on a transaction-by-transaction basis. The bill contemplates that regulations may implement this authority by requiring, for example, the comparison of year-end balance sheets using historical exchange rates for *all* balance sheet items. The committee included regulatory authority for this limited exception to the dollar-based books requirement to address the concerns of taxpayers operating in hyperinflationary economies. In such a case, dollar based accounting might not accurately reflect the income or loss of a taxpayer with substantial fixed plant and equipment (because the local currency depreciation charge will become insignificant in relation to operating income). For these taxpayers, an election to use the U.S. dollar as the functional currency will not be conditioned on conforming books and records.

*   *   *   *   *   *

[Conference Report]

*   *   *   *   *   *

Under the conference agreement, a taxpayer can elect to use the U.S. dollar only to the extent provided in regulations. The Secretary is authorized to prescribe regulatory exceptions in two cases; (1) if books and records are maintained in the U.S. dollar, or (2) if the method of translation used approximates the results of determining exchange gain or loss on a transaction-by-transaction basis. The conference agreement contemplates that regulations may implement the latter exception by requiring the comparison of year-end balance sheets using historical exchange rates for *all* balance sheet items, and that the Secretary may condition the application of either exception on the taxpayer making the election for all of the taxpayer's QBUs (on a worldwide basis).

The regulatory authority for the limited exception to the dollar-based books requirement was included to address the concerns of taxpayers operating in hyperinflationary economies. In such a case, local-currency based accounting might not accurately reflect the income or loss of a taxpayer with substantial fixed plant and equipment (because the local currency depreciation charge will become insignificant in relation to operating income). For these taxpayers, an election to use the U.S. dollar as the functional currency will not be conditioned on conforming books and records. The conferees wish to

emphasize that there is no expectation that this exception will be made generally available to taxpayers who are not operating in hyperinflationary economies.

An election to use the U.S. dollar is effective for the taxable year for which made and all subsequent taxable years, unless revoked with the consent of the Secretary. For a U.S. person, the election is to be made on the return for the first taxable year for which a QBU exists, by making a statement that the QBU elects the U.S. dollar as its functional currency for U.S. tax purposes. For a foreign person, the election is to be made in the U.S. owner's return for the first taxable year in which the U.S. owner acquires at least a 50-percent ownership interest in the foreign person by making a statement that the foreign person's QBU elects the U.S. dollar as its functional currency for U.S. tax purposes. If there is no 50-percent U.S. shareholder, the conferees anticipate that the Secretary shall prescribe regulations providing a mechanism for an election on the occurrence of a significant event (*i.e.*, an event having U.S. tax consequences).

*   *   *   *   *   *

[Senate Explanation]

*   *   *   *   *   *

3. Foreign currency transactions. *In general.*—New section 988 prescribes rules for the treatment of exchange gain or loss from transactions denominated in a currency other than a taxpayer's functional currency. For taxpayers using the U.S. dollar as a functional currency, the bill generally retains the present law principles under which the disposition of foreign currency results in the recognition of gain or loss, and exchange gain or loss is separately accounted for (apart from any gain or loss attributable to an underlying transaction). Similarly, as under present law, the recognition of exchange gain or loss generally requires a closed and completed transaction (*e.g.*, the actual payment of a liability). The bill modifies present law regarding the character, source, and—in limited circumstances as provided by regulations—the timing of recognition of exchange gain or loss. Under the bill, foreign-currency denominated items are to be translated into U.S. dollars using the exchange rate that most properly reflects income; generally, the appropriate exchange rate will be the free market rate.

Section 988 transactions.—New section 988(c) defines the term "section 988 transaction" to mean certain transactions in which the amount required to be paid or entitled to be received is denominated in a nonfunctional currency, or is determined by reference to the value of one or more nonfunctional currencies. Section 988 transactions are: (1) the acquisition of (or becoming the obligor under) a debt instrument, (2) accruing (or otherwise taking into account) any item of expense or gross income or receipt that is to be paid or received on a later date, (3) entering into or acquiring an interest in any forward contract, option, or similar investment position (such as a currency swap), if such position is not marked to market under section 1256, and (4) the disposition of nonfunctional currency. The positions included in a mixed straddle that is identified under section 1256(d) are not treated as section 988 transactions. For purposes of the rule for dispositions of nonfunctional currency, the term nonfunctional currency includes not only coin and currency, but also nonfunctional currency denominated demand or time deposits and similar instruments issued by a bank or other financial institution.

A section 988 transaction need not require or even permit repayment with a nonfunctional-currency, as long as the amount paid or received is determined by reference to the value of a nonfunctional currency. (Thus, the status of multi-currency contracts is clarified.) Examples of section 988 transactions are trade receivables or payables, preferred stock (to the extent provided by regulations), and debt instruments denominated in one or more nonfunctional currencies. For purposes of these rules, the term debt instrument means a bond, debenture, note, certificate, or other evidence of indebtedness.

The Secretary is authorized to prescribe regulatory rules that exclude certain transactions from the definition of a section 988 transaction. The bill contemplates that regulations will except any class of items the taking into account of which is not necessary to carry out the purposes of the rules for foreign currency gain or loss derived from section 988 transactions. Examples of items that are within the scope of the Secretary's regulatory authority are trade receivables and payables that have a maturity of 120 days or less, and any other receivable or payable with a maturity of six months or less that would be eligible for exclusion under section 1274 (relating to the determination of issue price of debt issued for nonpublicly traded property).

*   *   *   *   *   *   *

[Conference Report]

*   *   *   *   *

The conference agreement generally follows the Senate amendment.

Rules are prescribed for the treatment of exchange gain or loss from transactions denominated in a currency other than a taxpayer's functional currency, the conference agreement generally retains present law principles under which the disposition of foreign currency results in the recognition of gain or loss, and exchange gain or loss is separately accounted for (apart from any gain or loss attributable to an underlying transaction). Similarly, the recognition of foreign currency gain or loss generally requires a closed and completed transaction (*e.g.*, the actual payment of a liability).

Foreign-currency denominated items are to be translated into U.S. dollars using the exchange rate that most properly reflects income; generally, the appropriate exchange rate will be the free market rate.

The conference agreement modifies the definition of a section 988 transaction by eliminating the exception for identified mixed straddles.

The conferees wish to clarify that the use of a nonfunctional currency to establish a demand or time deposit denominated in the same currency (or the conversion of such a deposit to another deposit in the same currency) is not a recognition event. This result obtains because, for purposes of the rule for dispositions of nonfunctional currency, the term nonfunctional currency includes not only coin and currency, but also nonfunctional currency demand deposits and similar instruments issued by a bank or other financial institution.

The conferees also wish to clarify an example in the committee report relating to the calculation of foreign currency gain that is accompanied by income from discharge of indebtedness. The manner in which foreign currency gain was calculated in that example is intended to have general application, and is not limited to cases in which there is income from discharge of indebtedness. In every case, to the extent that gain or loss is derived from a transaction, it is to be attributed first to exchange gain or loss measured by reference to the effect of movements in exchange rates on the units of nonfunctional currency originally booked by the taxpayer. For example, if a taxpayer whose functional currency is the U.S. dollar acquires a debt obligation that is not part of a section 988 hedging transaction for 100 pounds when the exchange rate is 1 pound $= \$1$ and sells the obligation for 200 pounds when the exchange rate is 1 pound $= \$2$, \$100 of the taxpayer's \$300 gain (\$400 sales price less \$100 basis) is foreign currency gain. This is calculated by multiplying the difference in exchange rates between the booking date and the payment date by the units of functional currency originally booked by the taxpayer.

The conference agreement modifies the calculation of foreign currency gain or loss to clarify that foreign currency gain or loss is recognized only to the extent of the total gain or loss, taking into account gain or loss on an underlying transaction. Thus, in the above example, if the exchange rate had fallen to 1 pound $= \$.5$, the taxpayer would have had no foreign currency gain or loss; if the exchange rate had fallen to 1 pound $= \$.75$, the taxpayer would have had a \$50 non-foreign currency gain; if the exchange rate had fallen to 1 pound $= \$.25$, the taxpayer would have had a \$50 foreign currency loss.

Section 267(f)(8)(C) authorizes the Secretary to prescribe regulations excepting certain foreign currency losses from the loss disallowance and loss deferral rules of section 267(a)(1) and section 267(f)(2), respectively. The statutory authorization relates to a loss sustained by a corporate lender on repayment of a foreign currency denominated loan by an affiliated corporation. Pursuant to this regulatory authority, the Secretary has issued temporary regulations. The conference agreement contemplates that the Secretary will review these temporary regulations, with a view towards conforming the regulatory exception and determining the appropriateness of applying the exception to every case that is covered by the current temporary regulations. For example, the application of the temporary regulations is limited to a loan that is "payable or denominated solely in a foreign currency;" consistent with the statutory definition of a section 988 transaction, the regulatory rule should take account of a loan where the principal is determined by reference to the value of a nonfunctional currency. Further, in connection with the section 988 regulatory authority to provide for the appropriate treatment of related-party transactions, the Secretary should determine the extent to which the scope of the section 267 regulatory exception should be limited. The conferees intend that any section 267 exceptions be narrowly drawn.

*   *   *   *   *   *

[Senate Explanation]

*   *   *   *   *   *

Treatment of foreign currency gain or loss from section 988 transactions as ordinary income or loss. In general, foreign currency gain or loss attributable to a transaction described in new section 988 is computed separately and treated as ordinary income or loss. Except as otherwise provided by regulations, capital gain or loss treatment is accorded to forward contracts, futures contracts, and options that constitute capital assets in the hands of the taxpayer and are not marked-to-market under section 1256 and that meet certain identification requirements. In circumstances to be identified in Treasury regulations (*e.g.*, certain hedging transactions, described below), foreign currency gain or loss will be treated as interest income or expense.

Foreign currency gain or loss. Foreign currency gain or loss is defined as gain or loss realized by reason of a change in the exchange rate between the date an asset or liability is taken into account for tax purposes (referred to as the "booking date") and the date it is paid or otherwise disposed of.

Definition of "booking date".—For transactions involving the acquisition of or becoming the obligor under a debt instrument, the booking date is the date of acquisition or on which the taxpayer becomes the obligor. For transactions involving items of expense or gross income, the booking date is the date on which the item is accrued or otherwise taken into account for Federal income tax purposes. For transactions involving forward contracts or similar investment positions, the booking date is the date on which the position is entered into or acquired.

Definition of payment date.—Generally, foreign currency gain or loss is realized on

the date on which payment is made or received with respect to a section 988 transaction. For transactions involving forward contracts or similar investment positions, the bill makes clear that the payment date includes the date on which a taxpayer's rights are terminated with respect to the position (*e.g.*, by entering into an offsetting position).

Calculation of income from discharge of indebtedness.—The bill reverses the result in the *Kentucky & Indiana Terminal Railroad* case.[36] The bill contemplates that gain realized on repayment of a borrowing will be attributed first to foreign currency gain (by calculating the difference between the U.S. dollar value of the face amount when issued and when discharged), and only the balance will be treated as income from discharge of indebtedness (sec. 323 of the bill limits the ability to defer income from discharge of indebtedness to insolvent taxpayers).

Calculation of OID.—Although new section 985(a) generally requires a U.S. person to make Federal income tax determinations in terms of the U.S. dollar, the bill contemplates that—pursuant to the Secretary's authority to provide exceptions to this rule—the Treasury Department will issue regulations providing for the determination of OID on foreign currency obligations. Pending issuance of regulations, however, the Committee intends that OID for any accrual period will be determined in terms of units of foreign currency, and translated into U.S. dollars based on the average exchange rate in effect during the accrual period. The U.S. dollar amount of the OID deducted for any accrual period will be treated as the dollar amount added to the borrowing on account of the OID (to determine the adjusted issue price), for purposes of determining the extent of exchange gains or losses realized when the borrowing is repaid. Similar rules are to be prescribed for the calculation of bond premium (sec. 1803 of the bill requires taxpayers to use the constant yield method applicable to OID to amortize premium).

*   *   *   *   *   *

[Conference Report]

*   *   *   *   *   *

The conference agreement generally follows the Senate amendment.

The conference agreement modifies the Senate amendment in two respects: (1) it is clarified that the Secretary may prescribe regulations treating foreign currency gain or loss as interest income or expense for selected purposes only (and not for all Federal tax purposes), and (2) the rule for investment products accorded capital gain or loss treatment does not apply to an item that is part of a tax straddle (within the meaning of sec. 1092(c), but determined without regard to the exception for qualified covered calls in paragraph (4) thereof).

*   *   *   *   *   *

〔Footnote ¶ 4056〕   (36) 330 F.2d 520 (6th Cir. 1969) (exchange gain characterized as income from discharge of indebtedness).

*   *   *   *   *   *

Special rule for certain investment products. New section 988 does not change the treatment of bank forward contracts or regulated futures contracts that are marked to market under section 1256 or the treatment of mixed straddles that are identified under section 1256(d). The bill provides a special rule for certain financial instruments that are not marked-to-market (e.g., because they are traded on a foreign board or exchange) but are held for speculation: these currency contracts are accorded capital gain or loss treatment if they constitute capital assets and the taxpayer properly identifies them. Under the bill, identification must be made before the close of the day the transaction is entered into (or such earlier time as the Secretary may prescribe by regulations).

Special rule for certain hedging transactions. The bill authorizes the issuance of regulations that address the treatment of section 988 transactions that are part of a hedge. The committee included this regulatory authority to provide certainty of tax treatment for foreign currency hedging transactions that are fast becoming commonplace (such as fully hedged foreign currency borrowings) and to insure that such a transaction is taxed in accordance with its economic substance. A hedging transaction includes certain transactions entered into primarily to reduce the risk of (1) foreign currency exchange rate fluctuations with respect to property held or to be held by the taxpayer, or (2) foreign currency fluctuations with respect to borrowings or obligations of the taxpayer. The bill provides that a hedging transaction is to be identified by the taxpayer or the Secretary.

To the extent provided in regulations, if any section 988 transaction is part of a hedging transaction all positions in the hedging transaction are integrated and treated as a single transaction, or otherwise treated consistently (e.g., for purposes of characterizing the nature of income or the sourcing rules). The committee intends that these regulations address two different categories of hedging transactions.

The first category is a narrow class of fully hedged transactions that are in substance part of an integrated economic package through which the taxpayer (by simultaneously combining a bundle of financial rights and obligations) has assured itself of a cash flow that will not vary with movements in exchange rates. With respect to this category, the committee intends that such rights and obligations be integrated and treated as a single transaction with respect to that taxpayer. For example, in the case of a fully hedged foreign currency borrowing, a taxpayer with the dollar as its functional currency will borrow foreign currency and hedge its exposure by entering into a series of forward purchase contracts or a single swap agreement. The forward contracts or swap agree-ment will assure the taxpayer of a stream of foreign currency flows to make interest and principal payments with respect to the foreign currency borrowing. The taxpayer, although it has borrowed foreign currency, is not at risk with respect to currency fluctuations because it has locked in the dollar cost of its future foreign currency requirements. The committee intends that regulations treat the entire package as a dollar borrowing with dollar interest payments with respect to the borrower.

In the case of a foreign currency borrowing hedged with a series of forward purchase contracts, the rules of section 1271, *et seq.* and 163(e) shall apply in determining the appropriate interest deduction. The committee intends that similar rules apply to synthetic dollar securities (e.g., a transaction in which a taxpayer with the dollar as its functional currency purchases a foreign currency denominated debt obligation and sells forward all interest and principal payments to assure itself a stream of fixed dollar flows). The committee intends that the regulations pertaining to integrated hedging transactions be restricted to transactions that are, in substance, equivalent to a transaction denominated in the taxpayer's functional currency.

The second category of hedging transactions involves transactions that are not entered into as an integrated financial package but are designed to limit a taxpayer's exposure in a particular currency (e.g., the acquisition of a foreign currency denominated liability to offset exposure with regard to a foreign currency denominated asset). These regulations need not provide for complete integration (e.g., the form of a foreign currency borrowing may be respected and the interest deduction determined by reference to the spot rate on the date of payment). Where appropriate, these regulations should provide for consistent treatment with respect to character, source, and timing.

The committee intends that both sets of regulations relating to hedging transactions provide rules to prevent taxpayers from selectively identifying only those transactions where the hedging rules are favorable to the taxpayer. The committee is aware that rules applicable to partially hedged transactions may be necessary to achieve a hedging rule that is not susceptible to abuse. The committee also intends that the regulations require a taxpayer to clearly identify a hedging transaction before the close of the day the transaction is entered into, in order to claim increased deductions attributable to the hedge. The Secretary may identify the transaction as a hedge at a later date. Further, (as discussed below), the committee's bill clarifies the interaction of these rules and the tax straddle provisions, with a view towards providing an incentive for taxpayers to properly identify section 988 transactions that are part of a tax straddle.

In addition, the regulations will need to take account of the various mechanisms for hedging currency exposure. For purposes of the special regulatory rules, a hedging position may include any contract (1) to sell or exchange nonfunctional currency at a future date under terms fixed in the contract, (2) to purchase nonfunctional currency with functional currency at a future date under terms fixed in the contract, (3) to exchange functional currency for a nonfunctional currency at a future date under terms fixed in the contract (which would include parallel loans and currency swaps), or (4) to receive or pay a nonfunctional currency (e.g., interest rate swaps denominated in a nonfunctional currency).

The committee particularly is concerned about hedging transactions where a taxpayer borrows in a weak currency and eliminates virtually all risk of currency loss by establishing offsetting currency positions. If such a hedging transaction is not treated as an integrated transaction, the taxpayer may be able to defer tax on income (and, under present law, to convert ordinary income to capital gains).

* * * * * *

Over the two-year period, the application of the rules for hedging transactions would not change the net amount of deductions ($92.30) arising from the foreign currency loan; instead, the hedging rule would require that interest be characterized and accrued according to OID principles. In the above example, the effect of the hedging rule is to prevent a one-year deferral of tax on $76.92 of income.

A similar rule would apply in the case of a fully-hedged borrowing in a strong currency (i.e., a currency with an interest rate lower than the dollar interest rate).

* * * * * *

[Conference Report]
* * * * * *

The conference agreement generally follows the Senate amendment.

The Secretary is authorized to issue regulations that address the treatment of transactions that give rise to foreign currency gain or loss and are part of a section 988 hedging transaction. The conferees included this regulatory authority to provide certainty of tax treatment for foreign currency hedging transactions that are fast becoming commonplace (such as fully hedged foreign currency borrowings) and to insure that such a transaction is taxed in accordance with its economic substance. No inference is intended as to the proper treatment of these transactions under present law.

A section 988 hedging transaction includes certain transactions entered into primarily to reduce the risk of (1) foreign currency exchange rate fluctuations with respect to property held or to be held by the taxpayer, or (2) foreign currency fluctuations with respect to borrowings made or to be made or obligations incurred or to be incurred by the taxpayer. A section 988 hedging transaction

is to be identified by the taxpayer or the Secretary.

To the extent provided in regulations, in the case of any transaction giving rise to foreign currency gain or loss that is part of a section 988 hedging transaction (determined without regard to whether such transaction is marked-to-market under section 1256), all positions in the hedging transaction are integrated and treated as a single transaction, or otherwise treated consistently (e.g., for purposes of determining the character, source, and timing of income or loss). The conferees intend that these regulations address two different categories of hedging transactions.

The first category is a narrow class of fully hedged transactions that are part of an integrated economic package through which the taxpayer (by simultaneously combining a bundle of financial rights and obligations) has assured itself of a cash flow that will not vary with movements in exchange rates. With respect to this category, the conferees intend that such rights and obligations be integrated and treated as a single transaction with respect to that taxpayer. For example, in the case of a fully hedged foreign currency borrowing, a taxpayer with the dollar as its functional currency will borrow foreign currency and hedge its exposure by entering into a series of forward purchase contracts or a single swap agreement. The forward contracts or swap agreement will assure the taxpayer of a stream of foreign currency flows to make interest and principal payments with respect to the foreign currency borrowing. The taxpayer, although it has borrowed foreign currency, is not at risk with respect to currency fluctuations because it has locked in the dollar cost of its future foreign currency requirements. The conferees intend that regulations treat the entire package as a dollar borrowing with dollar interest payments with respect to the borrower.

In the case of a foreign currency borrowing hedged with a series of forward purchase contracts, the rules of section 1271, *et seq.*, and 163(e) shall apply in determining the appropriate interest deduction. The conferees intend that similar rules apply to synthetic U.S. dollar securities (e.g., a transaction in which a taxpayer with the U.S. dollar as its functional currency purchases a foreign currency denominated debt obligation and sells forward all interest and principal payments to assure itself of a stream of fixed dollar flows). The conferees intend that the regulations pertaining to integrated hedging transactions provide rules for transactions that are, in substance, equivalent to a transaction denominated in the taxpayer's functional currency. In addition, the conferees wish to clarify that the integration approach is not limited to U.S. dollar denominated transactions; thus, the rules also apply where several transactions are entered into by a U.S. dollar functional-currency taxpayer to establish a foreign currency position.

The second category of hedging transactions involves transactions that are not entered into as an integrated financial package but are designed to limit a taxpayer's exposure in a particular currency (*e.g.*, the acquisition of a foreign currency denominated liability to offset exposure with regard to a foreign currency denominated asset). These regulations need not provide for complete integration (*e.g.*, the form of a foreign currency borrowing may be respected and the interest deduction determined by reference to the spot rate on the date of payment). Where appropriate, these regulations should provide for consistent treatment with respect to character, source, and timing.

The conferees intend that both sets of regulations relating to hedging transactions provide rules to prevent taxpayers from selectively identifying only those transactions where the hedging rules are favorable to the taxpayer. The conferees are aware that rules applicable to partially hedged transactions may be necessary to achieve a hedging rule that is not susceptible to abuse. The conferees also intend that the regulations require a taxpayer to clearly identify a hedging transaction before the close of the day the transaction is entered into, in order to claim increased deductions attributable to the hedge. The Secretary may identify the transaction as a hedge at a later date. Further, (as discussed below), the Act clarifies the interaction of these rules and the tax straddle provisions, with a view towards providing an incentive for taxpayers to properly identify transactions that are part of a tax straddle.

In addition, the regulations will need to take account of the various mechanisms for hedging currency exposure. For purposes of the special regulatory rules, a hedging position may include any contract (1) to sell or exchange nonfunctional currency at a future date under terms fixed in the contract, (2) to purchase nonfunctional currency with functional currency at a future date under terms fixed in the contract, (3) to exchange functional currency for a nonfunctional currency at a future date under terms fixed in the contract (which would include parallel loans and currency swaps), or (4) to receive or pay a nonfunctional currency (*e.g.*, interest rate swaps denominated in a nonfunctional currency).

The conferees are particularly concerned about hedging transactions where a taxpayer borrows in a weak currency and eliminates virtually all risk of currency loss by establishing offsetting currency positions. If such a hedging transaction is not treated as an integrated transaction, the taxpayer may be able to defer tax on income (and to utilize capital losses, which would otherwise be unavailable, by converting ordinary income to capital gains).

*   *   *   *   *   *

[Senate Explanation]

*   *   *   *   *   *

Sourcing rules.—In general, foreign currency gain is sourced, and foreign currency losses are allocated, by reference to the residence of the taxpayer or qualified business unit on whose books the underlying financial asset or liability is properly reflected. For purposes of these rules, an individual's residence is defined as the country in which the "tax home" (as defined in sec. 911(d)(3)) is located. In the case of any U.S. person (as defined in sec. 7701(a)(30)) other than an individual, the residence is the United States. In the case of a foreign corporation, partnership, trust, or estate, the residence is treated as a foreign country. Where appropriate, foreign currency gain or loss that is treated under the section 988 hedging rules to be prescribed by regulations (discussed above) is to be sourced or allocated in a manner that is consistent with that of the hedged item.

Exception for qualified business units. The residence of a taxpayer's qualified business unit (including the qualified business unit of an individual) is the country in which the unit's principal place of business is located.

Special rule for certain related party loans. The bill provides a special rule for purposes of determining the source or allocation of exchange gain or loss from certain related party loans. This rule was included because of a concern that the general rule that looks to residence could be manipulated to artificially increase foreign source income for purposes of computing allowable foreign tax credits. Under the special rule, affected loans are marked-to-market on an annual basis, and interest income earned on the loan during the taxable year is treated as domestic source income to the extent of any loss on the loan.

The special rule applies to a loan by a U.S. person or a related person (*e.g.*, a foreign subsidiary) to a 10-percent owned foreign corporation, which loan is (1) denominated in a currency other than the dollar, and (2) bears interest at a rate at least 10 percentage points higher than the AFR for mid-term Federal obligations at the time the loan is made. A 10-percent owned foreign corporation means any foreign corporation in which the taxpayer owns directly or indirectly at least 10 percent of the voting stock. This rule applies only for purposes of subpart J and section 904.

Application to transactions of a personal nature. Section 988 applies to transactions entered into by an individual only to the extent that expenses attributable to such transactions would be deductible under section 162 (as a trade or business expense) or section 212 (as an expense of producing income, other than expenses incurred in connection with the determination, collection or refund of taxes). Thus, for example, section 988 is inapplicable to exchange gain or loss recognized by a U.S. individual resident abroad upon repayment of a foreign currency denominated mortgage on the individual's principal residence. The principles of current law would continue to apply to such transaction.

*   *   *   *   *   *

[Conference Report]
Sourcing rules

*   *   *   *   *   *

The conference agreement generally follows the Senate amendment, with modifications.

The conference agreement clarifies that the rules for sourcing or allocating foreign currency gain or loss apply to investment products with respect to which an election is made to treat gain or loss as capital. The conference agreement provides the Secretary with regulatory authority to apply rules similar to the rules for related-party loans to loans to U.S. persons.

The conference agreement contemplates that the Secretary will address the appropriate treatment of payments made to a counter-party under a swap transaction for purposes of withholding under sections 871 and 881.

*   *   *   *   *   *

* * * Application to transactions of a personal nature

*   *   *   *   *   *

The conference agreement follows the Senate amendment, but clarifies that the determination of whether expenses would be deductible under section 212 is made without regard to the two-percent floor (added by sec. 132 of the Act) applicable to investment expenses.

*   *   *   *   *   *

[Senate Explanation]

*   *   *   *   *   *

Tax straddle provisions. The bill coordinates the interaction of the rules for foreign currency gain or loss derived from section 988 transactions and the tax straddle provisions. Neither the loss deferral rule of section 1092 nor the mark-to-market regime under section 1256 will apply to a section 988 transaction that is part of a hedging transaction and described in regulations to be issued under section 988 by the Secretary. Further, as described above, the general rule that treats foreign currency gain or loss as ordinary gain or loss is inapplicable to a section 1256 contract that is marked to market (sec. 421 of the bill requires such gain or loss to be treated as short-term capital gain or loss). The exception for section 1256 contracts is available to taxpayers who take such contracts off the mark-to-market system by making a mixed straddle election under section 1256(d); in a such case, as under present law, section 988 will not apply to any position and all of the positions in the mixed straddle will generate only short-term capital gain or loss. In connection with the exception for section 1256 contracts, the committee desires to make clear that bank forward contracts with maturities longer than the

maturities ordinarily available for regulated futures contracts are within the definition of a foreign currency contract in section 1256(g), if the requirements of that subsection are satisfied otherwise.

Clarification of application of loss deferral rule. The bill clarifies that an obligor's interest in a foreign currency denominated obligation is a "position" for purposes of the loss deferral rule. The rationale for this treatment is that a foreign currency borrowing is economically equivalent to a short position in the foreign currency. In addition, the bill makes clear that foreign currency for which there is an interbank market is presumed to be "actively traded" property for purposes of the loss deferral rule.

Repeal of special rule for banks. The bill repeals the special rule that permits banks to qualify for the hedging exception to the straddle provisions without establishing all of the facts that other taxpayers must show.

*   *   *   *   *   *

[Conference Report]

*   *   *   *   *   *

The conference agreement follows the Senate amendment. The conferees wish to emphasize that bank forward contracts with maturities longer than the maturities ordinarily available for regulated futures contracts are within the definition of a foreign currency contract in section 1256(g), if the requirements of that subsection are satisfied otherwise.

Regarding the amendment relating to currency for which there is an active interbank market, no inference is intended regarding the proper application of present law to a currency that is not the subject of a regulated futures contract but for which there is an active interbank market, (e.g., the Australian dollar). Thus, the Internal Revenue Service is free to provide by regulations for the treatment of such currencies for taxable years after the effective date of the Economic Recovery Act of 1981 (which introduced the straddle rules) and before the effective date of this Act.

*   *   *   *   *   *

[Senate Explanation]

*   *   *   *   *   *

4. Foreign currency translation. Under the bill, the same translation rule applies to the earnings and profits of a foreign corporation and the income or loss of a branch. An entity that uses a functional currency other than the U.S. dollar is required to use a profit and loss method to translate income or loss into U.S. dollars, at the appropriate exchange rate for a taxable year. The bill provides that the translation of payments of, and subsequent adjustments to, foreign taxes by a branch will be performed under the same rules that apply in determining the foreign tax credit allowable to a parent corporation with respect to taxes paid by a foreign subsidiary.

* * * * *

* * * * * *

The conference agreement follows the House bill and the Senate amendment. These translation rules apply without regard to the form of enterprise through which the taxpayer conducts business (*e.g.*, sole proprietorship, partnerships, or corporation), as long as such form of enterprise rises to the level of a QBU.

* * * * * *

* * * * * *

Application of section 905. The bill provides that, for purposes of applying section 905(c), the determination of whether accrued taxes when paid differ from the amounts claimed as credits by the taxpayer is made by reference to the functional currency of the qualified business unit that accrued and paid the taxes. Thus, exchange rate fluctuations with respect to a functional currency will not be taken into account under section 905(c).

* * * * * *

* * * * * *

Under the conference agreement, the Secretary is authorized to prescribe regulations providing for an alternative adjustment (*e.g.*, the adjustment of a dollar-based pool of taxes) in lieu of the redetermination required by section 905(c).

* * * * * *

* * * * * *

Translation of branch income and losses. *Translation of taxable income or loss.* Under the bill, a taxpayer with a branch whose functional currency is a currency other than the U.S. dollar will be required to use the profit and loss method to compute branch income. Thus, the net worth method will no longer be an acceptable method of computing income or loss of a foreign branch for tax purposes, and only realized exchange gains and losses on branch capital will be reflected in taxable income.

For each taxable year, the taxpayer will compute income or loss separately for each qualified business unit in the business unit's functional currency, converting this amount to U.S. dollars using the weighted average exchange rate for the taxable period over which the income or loss accrued. This amount will be included in income without reduction for remittances from the branch during the year. The committee anticipates that regulations will provide rules that will limit the deduction of branch losses to the taxpayer's dollar basis in the branch (that is, the original dollar investment plus subsequent capital contributions and unremitted earnings).

A taxpayer will recognize exchange gain or loss on remittances (without regard to whether or when the remittances are converted to dollars), to the extent the value of the currency at the time of the remittance differs from the value when earned. Remittances of foreign branch earnings (and interbranch transfers involving branches with different functional currencies) after 1986 will be treated as paid pro rata out of post-1986 accumulated earnings of the branch. The committee anticipates that, for purposes of calculating exchange gain or loss on remittances, the value of the currency will be determined by translating the currency at the rate in effect on the date of remittance. Exchange gains and losses on such remittances will be deemed to be ordinary and domestic source.

Treatment of direct foreign taxes. The bill provides that adjustments to the amount of tax paid by a branch shall be translated into U.S. dollars using the same exchange rate used to translate the income inclusion with respect to which the adjustment is made. The rule for adjustments applies to increases in the amount of tax liability as well as refunds. For example, assume a branch pays a tax of 100 Swiss francs in year one. In year two, the branch's tax liability is 50 francs, and the year one tax is adjusted downwards to 60 francs (so there was an overpayment of 40 francs). The 40-franc overpayment from year one is applied against the 50-franc liability for year two. In year three, the 50-franc tax paid in year two is refunded. On these facts, (1) regarding the reduction in the tax paid in year one, the 40 francs are translated at the exchange rate used to translate the earnings for year one, (2) regarding the crediting of the 40-franc overpayment against the 50-franc tax liability for year two, the entire 50-franc tax is translated at the same rate used to translate the earnings for year two, and (3) on refund of the year-two 50-franc tax in year three, the refund is translated at the same rate that was used to translate the earnings for year two.

Under the bill, a prepayment of a foreign tax (e.g., payments of estimated taxes or withheld taxes) is to be translated at the same exchange rate used to translate the income inclusion with respect to which the prepayment is made. A similar rule is to apply to installment payments of tax.

* * * * * *

* * * * * *

The conference agreement generally follows the Senate amendment with respect to remittances except that it is clarified that (1) any remittance of property (not just currency) will trigger exchange gain or loss inherent in accumulated earnings or branch capital, and (2) exchange gain or loss on remittances will be sourced or allocated by reference to the income giving rise to post-1986 accumulated earnings (generally, the residence of the qualified business unit, unless the income of the unit is derived from U.S. sources). The conferees anticipate that regulations may treat contributions of appreciated property to a QBU as a recognition event where appropriate.

The conferees wish to clarify that the rule for triggering exchange gain or loss on remittance does not apply to transactions involving the use of a related party's assets or liabilities (e.g., in the case of a bank, the deposit and withdrawal of funds in a branch). The committee anticipates that regulations will provide rules that, in the case of a branch using a functional currency other than the United States dollar, will limit the deduction of branch losses to the taxpayer's dollar basis in the branch (that is, the original dollar investment plus subsequent capital contributions and advances, unremitted earnings, and indebtedness for which the taxpayer is liable).

The conference agreement generally follows the House bill with respect to foreign taxes. Thus, the translation of foreign taxes paid by a branch will be performed under the same rules that apply in determining the foreign tax credit allowable to a corporation with respect to taxes paid by a foreign corporation. For example, assume a branch pays a tax of 100 Swiss francs in year one. In year two, the branch's tax liability is 50 francs, and the year one tax is adjusted downwards to 60 francs (so there was an overpayment of 40 francs). The 40-franc overpayment from year one is applied against the 50-franc liability for year two. In year three, the 50-franc tax paid in year two is refunded. On these facts, (1) regarding the reduction in the tax paid in year one, the 40 francs are translated at the exchange rate used to translate the tax in year one, (2) regarding the crediting of the 40-franc overpayment against the 50-franc tax liability for year two, the entire 50-franc tax is translated at the rate in effect on the date the taxpayer is treated as having paid such tax and (3) on refund of the year-two 50-franc tax in year three, the refund is translated at the same rate that was used to translate the tax payment in year two.

The conference agreement contemplates that a prepayment of foreign tax (e.g., an estimated tax payment or a withheld tax) will be translated at the exchange rates in effect on the payment date. Generally, a similar rule is to apply to installment payments of tax.

Foreign corporations.—For purposes of determining the tax of any shareholder of a foreign corporation, the earnings and profits of the foreign corporation are to be determined in the corporation's functional currency. The bill codifies the result under the Bon Ami case by requiring taxpayers to use a common exchange rate to translate actual distributions, deemed distributions of subpart F income (sec. 922 of the bill expands the definition of subpart F income), or gain that is recharacterized as dividend income on the disposition of stock in a CFC or former CFC (sec. 622 of the bill amends the definition of a CFC), and foreign taxes deemed paid with respect thereto. The bill also clarifies the interaction of the foreign currency translation rules and the rules relating to adjustments to foreign taxes.

Translation of earnings and profits.—On the distribution of earnings and profits from a 10-percent owned foreign corporation, a domestic corporation is required to translate such amounts (if necessary) at the current exchange rate on the date the distribution is included in income. Similarly, in the case of gain that is treated as a distribution of earnings under section 1248, the bill requires the deemed dividend to be translated (if necessary) at the current exchange rate on the date the amount is included in income. Thus, for actual distributions and deemed dividends under section 1248, no exchange gain or loss is recognized as the result of exchange rate fluctuations between the time earnings and profits arise and the time of distribution.

In the case of deemed distributions of subpart F income, as under present law, the required income inclusion is translated at the weighted average exchange rate for the foreign corporation's taxable year. Exchange gain or loss is recognized as the result of exchange rate fluctuations between the time of a deemed distribution and the time such previously taxed income ("PTI") is actually distributed. Exchange gain or loss on distributions of PTI is to be treated as ordinary income or loss from or allocable to domestic sources. The Secretary is authorized to prescribe regulations for the treatment of distributions of PTI through several tiers of foreign corporations.

Treatment of deemed-paid foreign taxes.—For purpose of determining the amount of foreign taxes deemed paid under sections 902 or 960, a foreign income tax paid by a foreign corporation is translated into U.S. dollars (if necessary) using the same exchange rate used to translate the income inclusion with respect to which such tax is deemed paid. Adjustments to the amount of tax paid by a foreign corporation are translated into U.S. dollars using the same exchange rate used to translate the income with respect to which the adjustment was made.

Foreign subsidiary with dollar functional currency.—The bill contemplates that the rule of the *American Metal Co.* case will continue to apply to a foreign corporation whose functional currency is the U.S. dollar.[37] Thus, for example, for purposes of the indirect foreign tax credit, taxes paid by such a foreign corporation will be determined as of the date such taxes were paid or accrued.

[Footnote ¶ 4056 continued]

(37) 221 F.2d 134 (2d Cir. 1955) (when a foreign corporation keeps its books in U.S. dollars, foreign taxes are translated as of payment date).

Contiguous country corporations. Under Section 1504(d), a domestic corporation can elect to treat certain wholly owned subsidiaries organized under the laws of a contiguous foreign country (*i.e.,* Canada or Mexico) as domestic corporations. As a result of treatment as domestic corporations, these subsidiaries are included with the domestic parent corporation in the filing of a consolidated Federal income tax return. The result of a section 1504(d) election combined with use of the net worth accounting method is that gains and losses from contiguous country currency fluctuations are recognized on the U.S. tax return.

In many cases, the administrative burdens that an election under Section 1504(d) imposes on the taxpayer would not justify continuation of the election after the effective date of the provision prohibiting the use of the net worth method. Domestic corporations with foreign branches can avoid the adverse impact of switching to the profit and loss method by incorporating their branches; whereas this option is not available to contiguous country corporations that are treated as domestic corporations under Section 1504(d).

Consequently, the committee's bill contemplates that the Internal Revenue Service will allow corporations to elect out of their Section 1504(d) status as a result of the enactment of the provision requiring use of the profit and loss method.

This will diminish the administrative burdens for both taxpayers and the Internal Revenue Service, eliminate the need for changing the ownership structure in these corporations, and place those corporations on an equal footing with corporations operating foreign branches. As under present law, the revocation of a section 1504(d) election will (1) trigger excess loss accounts, if any, under Treasury regulations section 1.1502-19, (2) implicate the rules for recapture of foreign losses under section 904(f), and (3) be subject to the rules of section 367(a), among other applicable rules.

The committee intends that any procedure adopted by the Service will contain appropriate safeguards to limit recognition of exchange loss upon such election.

*   *   *   *   *   *

[Conference Report]

*   *   *   *   *   *

Under the conference agreement, for purposes of determining the tax of any shareholder of a foreign corporation, the corporation's earnings and profits are determined in the corporation's functional currency. In the case of any U.S. person, the earnings and profits so determined are translated (if necessary) at the current exchange rate on the date the distribution is included in income. A similar rule applies to gain that is treated as a distribution of earnings under section 1248. Thus, for actual distributions and deemed dividends under section 1248, no exchange gain or loss resulting from exchange rate fluctuations between the time earnings and profits arise and the time of distribution is separately recognized.

The conference agreement follows the Senate amendment with respect to deemed distributions of subpart F income and PTI, except the weighted average exchange rate is also used for foreign personal holding company income (sec. 551(a)) and amounts defined in section 1293(a) (relating to passive foreign investment companies), and exchange gain or loss on PTI is sourced or allocated in the same manner as the associated income inclusion. In addition, the conference agreement applies the rules for recognizing exchange gain or loss with respect to PTI to amounts defined in section 1293(c).

The conference agreement follows the House bill for purposes of determining the amount of foreign taxes deemed paid under sections 902 or 960. An increase to foreign taxes is translated on the date of the payment of additional tax.

Under section 1504(d), a domestic corporation can elect to treat certain wholly owned subsidiaries organized under the laws of a contiguous foreign country (*i.e.,* Canada or Mexico) as domestic corporations. As a result of treatment as domestic corporations, these subsidiaries are included with the domestic parent corporation in the filing of a consolidated Federal income tax return. The result of a section 1504(d) election combined with use of the net worth accounting method is that gains and losses from contiguous country currency fluctuations are recognized on the U.S. tax return.

The conference agreement contemplates that the Internal Revenue Service will allow corporations to elect out of section 1504(d) status as a result of the enactment of the provision requiring use of the profit and loss method. As under present law, the revocation of a section 1504(d) election will (1) trigger excess loss accounts, if any, under Treasury regulations section 1.1502-19, (2) implicate the rules for recapture of foreign losses under section 904(f), and (3) be subject to the rules of section 367(a), among other applicable rules.

The conferees intend that any procedure adopted by the Internal Revenue Service will contain appropriate safeguards to limit recognition of exchange loss upon the revocation of a section 1504(d) election.

Foreign corporations with respect to which section 1504(d) elections are revoked are likely to succeed to earnings and profits accumulated by a foreign corporation that has been treated as a domestic corporation. As a result, section 243(d) will be applicable to distributions by a foreign corporation out of these accumulated earnings. The conferees believe it desirable to make it clear that section 243(d) applies for purposes of section 243(a)(3). Section 243(d) provides that a distribution by a foreign corporation of earnings and profits accumulated by a domestic corporation shall be treated as if made by a

Act § 1261   ¶ 4056

domestic corporation for purposes of the dividends received deduction. The conferees wish to clarify that in the case of such a distribution, the distributing corporation is to be treated as a domestic corporation for all purposes of section 243(a), including for purposes of determining under section 243(a)(3) whether the distribution is a qualifying dividend. Thus, for example, if a foreign corporation makes a distribution out of earnings and profits that were accumulated by a foreign corporation with section 1504(d) status while such corporation was a member of an affiliated group, and the distributing foreign corporation would be a member of the same affiliated group if it were a domestic corporation, then the distribution qualifies for the 100% dividends received deduction provided the domestic parent makes a section 243(b) election and that no section 1562 election was in effect during the year the earnings were accumulated. The domestic parent may make the section 243(b) election even though it files a consolidated federal income tax return. The conference agreement contemplates that the regulations relating to section 243(d) will be modified in order to reflect this clarification.

*   *   *   *   *   *

[Senate Explanation]

*   *   *   *   *   *

5. Other issues. In general, the Secretary is authorized to issue such regulations as may be necessary to carry out the purposes of the new rules for foreign currency transactions, including regulations (1) setting forth procedures to be followed by taxpayers with qualified business units using a net worth method of accounting before enactment of subpart J, to prevent a mismatching of exchange gain and loss, (2) limiting the recognition of foreign currency loss on remittances from qualified business units (to prevent the selective

recognition of exchange losses), and (3) providing for the recharacterization of interest and principal payments with respect to obligations denominated in hyperinflationary currencies.[38] The bill contemplates that the Secretary will also issue regulatory rules providing for the treatment of U.S. branches of foreign persons (addressing issues such as the extent to which exchange gain or loss on remittances are treated as effectively connected with a U.S. trade or business).

*   *   *   *   *   *

[Conference Report]

*   *   *   *   *   *

The conference agreement follows the Senate amendment, and adds specific authority for providing for the appropriate treatment of related-party transactions (including transactions between QBUs of the same taxpayer), as well as section 905(c) adjustments (as discussed above).[3]

*   *   *   *   *   *

[Senate Explanation]

*   *   *   *   *   *

Effective Date.—These provisions are effective for taxable years beginning after December 31, 1986.

*   *   *   *   *   *

[Conference Report]

*   *   *   *   *   *

The conference agreement follows the Senate amendment, but provides that for purposes of claiming a deemed paid foreign tax credit under either sections 902 or 960, the agreement's provisions only apply to foreign taxes paid or accrued with respect to earnings and profits of a foreign corporation for taxable years after 1986.

[Footnote ¶ 4056]   (38) The committee is aware of tax shelters that are promised on the creation of debt denominated in a hyperinflationary currency. For example, in one transaction, a U.S. partnership entered into an agreement with a Brazilian Sociedade civil limitada for the performance of services in Brazil. Payment was to be made in cruzeiros on a deferred basis, beginning seven years after the services were performed. The taxpayers involved took the position that the foreign currency account payable could be accrued currently by the U.S. partnership, even though the actual U.S. dollars required seven years hence will be much less than the U.S. dollar value of the amount accrued. In this transaction, stated interest was 11% per annum, which might be adequate for a dollar borrowing but is below market when compared to the analogous AFR for cruzeiros. Thus, the committee concluded that the Secretary has adequate authority to treat this transaction in accordance with its economic substance under the rules relating to below market loans (See Prop. Treas. reg. sec. 1.7872-11(f). Nevertheless the committee determined that the Secretary should be granted additional regulatory authority to ensure that such transactions are properly characterized under Federal tax laws, apart from whether stated interest is adequate when measured in a foreign currency.

(3) The conferees are aware of tax shelters that are premised on the creation of debt denominated in a hyperinflationary currency. For example, in one transaction, a U.S. partnership entered into an agreement with a Brazilian Sociedade civil limiteds for the performance of services in Brazil. Payment was to be made in cruzeiros on a deferred basis, beginning seven years after the services were performed. The taxpayers involved took the position that the foreign currency account payable could be accrued currently by the U.S. partnership, even though the actual U.S. dollars required seven years hence will be much less than U.S. dollar value of the amount accrued. In this transaction, stated interest was 11% per annum, which might be adequate for a dollar borrowing but is below market when compared to the analogous AFR for cruzeiros. Thus, the conferees concluded that the Secretary has adequate authority to treat this transaction in accordance with its economic substance under the rules relating to below market loans *(See* Prop. Treas. reg. sec. 1.7872-11(f)). Nevertheless, the conferees determined that the Secretary should be granted additional regulatory authority to ensure that such transactions are properly characterized under Federal tax laws, apart from whether stated interest is adequate when measured in a foreign currency.

[¶ 4057] **SECTIONS 1271-1277 and 1236 TAX TREATMENT OF POSSESSIONS.**

(Secs. 32, 48, 63, 153, 246, 338, 864, 876, 881, 882, 931-936, 934A, 957, 1402, 1442, 6091, 7651, 7654, 7655 of the Code)

[Senate Explanation]

*   *   *   *   *   *

Explanation of Provision.—

Overview. The bill eliminates the requirement that there be a mirror system of taxation in Guam and the CNMI, coordinates the tax systems of those possessions and of American Samoa with the U.S. tax system, and reforms the mirror system in the Virgin Islands. The treatment of the Virgin Islands reflects extended discussions between representatives of the Virgin Islands and the Treasury. It differs from the treatment of the other possessions because of the unique history of the relationship between the Virgin Islands and the United States.

1. Guam, the CNMI, and American Samoa. Guam, the CNMI, and American Samoa generally are granted full authority over their own local income tax systems, with respect to income from sources within, or effectively connected with the conduct of a trade or business within, any of these three possessions and with respect to any income received or accrued by any resident of any of these three possessions. This grant of authority is effective, however, only if and so long as an implementing agreement is in effect between the possession at issue and the United States which provides for (1) eliminating double taxation of income by the possession and the United States; (2) establishing rules for the prevention of evasion or avoidance of U.S. tax; (3) the exchange of information between the possession and the United States for purposes of tax administration; and (4) resolving other problems arising in connection with the administration of the tax laws of such possession and the United States. Any implementing agreement is to be executed on behalf of the United States by the Secretary of the Treasury after consultation with the Secretary of the Interior. Thus, as is currently the case with respect to American Samoa, each of these possessions could adopt a mirror system as its local law if desired.

The committee does not intend that any of these insular areas afford any opportunities for tax avoidance. In particular, the committee does not intend that U.S. agreements with these possessions offer tax advantages beyond those described below, available in the Virgin Islands.

The bill imposes two requirements on these insular areas. First, it provides that the amount of revenue received by Guam, American Samoa, or the Northern Mariana Islands pursuant to its tax laws during the first fiscal year in which the bill generally takes effect (after conclusion of an implementing agreement) and each of the four fiscal years thereafter shall not be less than the revenue

(adjusted for inflation) that possession received pursuant to its tax laws for the last fiscal year before implementation of the bill's rules. Second, the bill provides that nothing in any tax law of Guam, American Samoa, or the Northern Marianas may discriminate against any citizen or resident of the United States or of any other possession.

If the Secretary of the Treasury, after consultation with the Secretary of the Interior, determines that any of these three possessions has failed to comply with either the revenue maintenance requirement or the nondiscrimination requirement, the Secretary is to notify the Governor of that possession in writing. If the possession does not comply with that requirement within 90 days of notification, the Secretary is to notify Congress of the noncompliance. Thereupon, unless the Congress by law provides otherwise, the mirror system of taxation (that is, the provisions of law in effect before the date of enactment of this Act that apply the provisions of the income tax laws of the United States as in effect from time to time to a possession of the United States) shall be reinstated in that possession, and shall be in full force and effect for taxable years beginning after the notification to Congress. If the failure to comply with the revenue maintenance requirement is for a good cause and does not jeopardize the fiscal integrity of the possession, the Secretary may waive that requirement for the period that he determines appropriate. There is to be no waiver of the nondiscrimination requirement.

Under present law, the tax system of the Mariana Islands depends on the system in force in Guam. The bill provides that the Northern Mariana Islands are free to continue present law or to choose the tax regime described in the bill without regard to any action that Guam might take.

An individual who is a bona fide resident of Guam, American Samoa, or the CNMI during the entire taxable year is subject to U.S. taxation in the same manner as a U.S. resident. However, in the case of such an individual, gross income for U.S. tax purposes does not include income derived from sources within any of the three possessions, or income effectively connected with the conduct of a trade or business by that individual within any of the three possessions. Deductions (other than personal exemptions) and credits properly allocated and apportioned to such excluded income will not be allowed for U.S. tax purposes. Thus, even a bona fide resident of Guam, the CNMI, or American Samoa is required to file a U.S. return and to pay taxes on a net basis if he receives income from sources outside the three possessions (i.e., U.S. or foreign source income). However, a U.S. return is not required to be filed if the possession resident's non-possession source income is less than the amount that gives rise to a filing requirement under generally applicable U.S. rules. The United States will cover over to the treasuries of Guam, American Samoa, or the CNMI all U.S. income tax paid by a bona fide Guamanian, Samoan, or CNMI resident. It is anticipated that the possessions will identify these residents to the IRS in the manner currently done by the Virgin Islands. The committee does not intend that the insular areas grant any taxpayer a tax rebate or other benefit based upon those or any other covered-over taxes, which are attributable to non-possessions income.

Amounts paid to a bona fide resident of Guam, the CNMI or American Samoa for any services as an employee of the United States (including pensions, annuities, and other deferred amounts received on account of such services) are not treated as possessions source income, so they are fully taxable by the United States. The U.S. tax on these amounts is to be covered over to the treasury of the possession where the recipient resides, thus providing the possession with the same amount of revenue it currently receives. Withholding on the compensation of U.S. military personnel, stationed or resident in Guam, the CNMI, and American Samoa, will be covered over to the Treasuries of Guam, the CNMI, and American Samoa, as appropriate. No change in the current method of covering over these funds to Guam or the CNMI is anticipated so long as the existing mirror system continues in effect.

The bill delegates to the Secretary of the Treasury the authority to prescribe regulations to determine whether income is sourced in, or effectively connected with the conduct of a trade or business in, one of these possessions, and to determine whether an individual is a resident of one of these possessions. The committee anticipates that the Secretary will use this authority to prevent abuse. For example, the committee does not believe that a mainland resident who moves to a possession while owning appreciated personal property such as corporate stock or precious metals and who sells that property in the possession should escape all tax, both in the United States and the possession, on that appreciation. Similarly, the committee does not believe that a resident of a possession who owns financial assets such as stocks or debt of companies organized in, but the underlying value of which is primarily attributable to activities performed outside the possession, should escape tax on the income from those assets. The Secretary should treat such income as sourced outside the possession where the taxpayer resides (and any covered over taxes attributable to this income should not be rebated to the taxpayer). Similarly, where appropriate, the Secretary may treat an individual as not a bona fide resident of a possession.

The bill also provides rules which relieve a bona fide resident of Guam, the CNMI or American Samoa from being considered a U.S. person for purposes of applying certain reporting and taxation rules under subpart F

with respect to corporations incorporated in Guam, the CNMI, or American Samoa if: (1) at least 80 percent or more of the corporation's gross income for a preceding three-year period was from sources in, or effectively connected with the conduct of a trade or business in, the possession, and (2) at least 50 percent or more of the corporation's gross income for such period was derived from the conduct of an active trade or business in such possession.

Code section 881(b) is modified to provide that a Guamanian, CNMI, or American Samoan corporation will not be exempt from the 80-percent withholding tax unless (1) less than 25 percent in value of the corporation's stock is beneficially owned by foreign persons; (2) at least 65 percent of the corporation's income is effectively connected with the conduct of a trade or business in a U.S. possession or in the United States; and (3) no substantial part of the income of the corporation is used (directly or indirectly) to satisfy obligations to persons who are not bona fide residents of one of these three possessions, the Virgin Islands, or the United States. This exception from withholding also applies with respect to corporations organized in the U.S. Virgin Islands.

Local taxes of Guam, the CNMI, and American Samoa will be creditable for U.S. tax purposes if such taxes qualify as creditable taxes under the applicable foreign tax credit regulations.

The bill repeals the rule that subjects Guamanian banks to net basis taxation of interest on U.S. Government obligations (bill sec. 944). Thus, any Guamanian bank will be exempt from U.S. tax on this income, unless it becomes subject to the anti-conduit rules that apply to Guamanian corporations.

2. Virgin Islands. An individual qualifying as a bona fide Virgin Islands resident as of the last day of the taxable year will pay tax to the Virgin Islands under the mirror system on his or her worldwide income. He or she will have no final tax liability for such year to the United States, as long as he or she reports all income from all sources and identifies the source of each item of income on the return filed with the Virgin Islands. Any taxes withheld and deposited in the United States from payments to such an individual, and any estimated tax payments properly made by such an individual to the United States, will be covered over to the Virgin Islands Treasury, and will be credited against the individual's Virgin Islands tax liability. A Virgin Islands resident deriving gross income from sources outside the Virgin Islands will report all items of such income on his or her Virgin Islands return. Information contained on these returns will be compiled by the Virgin Islands Bureau of Internal Revenue and transmitted to the Internal Revenue Service to facilitate enforcement assistance.

Under the bill, for purposes of determining the tax liability of individuals who are citizens or residents of the United States or the U.S. Virgin Islands, the United States will be treated as including the Virgin

Islands (for purposes of determining U.S. tax liability), and, under the Virgin Islands "mirror" Code, the Virgin Islands will be treated as including the United States (for purposes of determining liability for the Virgin Islands tax). A corporation organized in one jurisdiction, however, will continue to be treated, where relevant, as a foreign corporation for purposes of individual income taxation in the other jurisdiction.

A citizen or resident of the United States (other than a bona fide Virgin Islands resident) deriving income from the Virgin Islands will not be liable to the Virgin Islands for any tax determined under the Virgin Islands "mirror Code". Rather, in the case of such a person, tax liability to the Virgin Islands will be a fraction of the individual's U.S. tax liability, based on the ratio of adjusted gross income derived from Virgin Islands sources to worldwide adjusted gross income. Such an individual will file identical returns with the United States and the Virgin Islands. The Virgin Islands' portion of the individual's tax liability (if paid) will be credited against his total U.S. tax liability. Taxes paid to the Virgin Islands by the individual, other than the Virgin Islands portion of his U.S. tax liability, will be treated for U.S. tax purposes in the same manner as State and local taxes.

In the case of a joint return where only one spouse qualifies as a resident of the Virgin Islands, resident status of both spouses will be determined by reference to the status of the spouse with the greater adjusted gross income for the taxable year.

The Virgin Islands is provided with authority to enact nondiscriminatory local income taxes (which for U.S. tax purposes would be treated as State or local income taxes) in addition to those imposed under the mirror system.

The Secretary of the Treasury is given authority to provide by regulation the extent to which provisions in the Internal Revenue Code shall not apply for purposes of determining tax liability to the Virgin Islands (i.e., shall not be mirrored). It is anticipated that such regulations will provide that references to possessions of the United States will not be mirrored. In addition, the committee anticipates that these regulations will prevent abuses of the V.I. and U.S. tax systems such as that addressed by section 130 of the Tax Reform Act of 1984 (preventing tax-free payments of U.S. source income to foreign investor which arguably had been possible due to the interaction of the Revised Organic Act and the "mirror Code").

The bill provides that corporations operating in the Virgin Islands are eligible for the possession tax credit allowed under section 936.

The bill provides that the Revised Organic Act is treated as if it were enacted before the Code, so that in cases of conflict, the Code controls (sec. 975 of the bill). The bill specifies that the Revised Organic Act will have no

effect on any person's tax liability to the United States. Thus, for example, even if a person is treated as an "inhabitant" of the Virgin Islands under the Revised Organic Act, that person will be fully subject to U.S. tax.

The authority of the Virgin Islands to reduce or rebate Virgin Islands tax liability is extended in some cases to apply to V.I. tax liability attributable to income that is not from U.S. sources and that is not effectively connected with the conduct of a trade or business in the United States. As for U.S. persons, however, and corporations 10-percent or more owned (directly or indirectly) by U.S. persons, the Virgin Islands can reduce or rebate tax only on income from V.I. sources or income effectively connected with a V.I. trade or business, although that right applies without regard to whether the affected taxpayer derives any minimum specified percentage of its income from the Virgin Islands. Moreover, any authority to reduce or rebate taxes is conditioned upon the existence of an agreement between the United States and the Virgin Islands containing safeguards against the evasion or avoidance of United States income tax. The committee anticipates that such an agreement will contain measures coordinating the tax administration functions of the Internal Revenue Service and the Virgin Islands Bureau of Internal Revenue, as well as procedures for exchanging tax information.

This modification of the Virgin Islands' authority to reduce taxes applies only to non-U.S. source income, and income not effectively connected with the conduct of a U.S. trade or business, as those terms are defined under regulations prescribed by the Secretary for this purpose. The committee anticipates that the Secretary will use this authority to prevent abuse. For example, the committee does not believe that a mainland resident who moves to the Virgin Islands while owning appreciated personal property such as corporate stock or precious metals and who sells that property in the Virgin Islands should escape all tax, both in the United States and the Virgin Islands, on that appreciation. Similarly, the committee does not believe that a resident of the Virgin Islands who owns financial assets such as stocks or debt of companies organized in, but the underlying value of which is primarily attributable to activities performed outside, the Virgin Islands should escape tax on the income from those assets. The Secretary should treat such income as sourced outside the Virgin Islands. Similarly, where appropriate, the Secretary may treat an individual as not a bona fide resident of the Virgin Islands.

As noted above, the bill amends the exemption from the 30 percent withholding tax that applies under section 881(b) to possessions corporations, including Virgin Islands corporations. Under the bill, a Virgin Islands corporation will be exempt from withholding only if (1) less than 25 percent in value of the

Act § 1271—1277 ¶ 4057

corporation's stock is owned by foreign persons; (2) at least 65 percent of the corporation's income is effectively connected with the conduct of a trade or business in a U.S. possession or in the United States, and (3) no substantial part of the income of the corporation is used (directly or indirectly) to satisfy obligations to persons who are not bona fide residents of one of the possessions or the United States. Thus, the exemption from the withholding tax will not be available for a corporation used as a conduit for payments to persons not resident in the Virgin Islands, the United States, or the other possessions.

Effective Date.—

Guam, the CNMI, and American Samoa. The grants of authority to Guam and the CNMI, as well as the conforming changes to U.S. law, anti-abuse provisions, and administrative provisions, will be effective for taxable years beginning on or after the later of January 1, 1987 or the date an implementing agreement between the United States and the possession is in effect. The mirror codes currently administered by Guam and the CNMI will continue to operate, mutatis mutandis, as their respective local income tax laws, until and except to the extent that each possession takes action to amend its tax laws. The anti-abuse and administrative provisions with respect to American Samoa also are effective for taxable years beginning on or after the later of January 1, 1987 or the date an implementing agreement between the United States and the possession is in effect. The amendment to the rule taxing Guamanian banks on a net basis on income from U.S. Government obligations is effective for taxable years beginning after November 16, 1985.

Virgin Islands. The Virgin Islands provisions are generally effective for taxable years beginning on or after January 1, 1987. However, the repeal of the inhabitant rule applies to all open years. In addition, the provisions extending the right of the Virgin Islands to reduce the tax imposed on U.S. or V.I. corporations with respect to income from V.I. sources or income effectively connected with a V.I. trade or business, and the provisions creating the right of the Virgin Islands to reduce the tax imposed on V.I. corporations with respect to income from non-U.S. sources or income effectively connected with a non-U.S. trade or business, will become effective only when an agreement between the United States and the Virgin Islands to cooperate on tax matters becomes effective.

Implementing agreements. If an implementing agreement with any of the four possessions has not been executed within one year from the date of enactment, the Secretary is to report to the tax writing committees in detail the status of negotiations with that possession, and specifically why the agreement has not been executed. The committee intends that the report be forwarded promptly.

*   *   *   *   *   *

[Conference Report]

*   *   *   *   *

The conference agreement generally follows the Senate amendment, with modifications described below.

The conferees express the desire that the Secretary of the Treasury consult as appropriate with officials of the Virgin Islands in formulating regulations for purposes of determining tax liability incurred to the Virgin Islands. In adopting the Senate provision allowing reduction of V.I. tax on non-U.S., non-V.I. income of V.I. corporations with less than 10 percent U.S. ownership, the conferees do not intend that other U.S. possessions offer tax advantages to non-U.S. investors beyond those available in the Virgin Islands. The agreement does not allow the Virgin Islands to reduce or rebate tax on non-V.I. income of local individuals.

The conference agreement eliminates from the definition of wages subject to withholding (under Code sec. 3401) any remuneration paid for services for the United States or any U.S. agency within a U.S. possession to the extent the United States or the agency withholds taxes on that remuneration pursuant to an agreement with the possession. Under present law, the United States must withhold on payments to U.S. employees working in certain possessions even though the possession rather than the United States is entitled to tax on those payments. At the end of the year, the United States refunds the withheld amounts to the taxpayer, who is then to satisfy his or her liability to the possession. This provision of the conference agreement allows the United States and its agencies not to withhold for the account of the U.S. government on income the tax on which is due to a possession so long as the payor withholds for the account of the possession.

The repeal of the Virgin Islands inhabitant rule applies to taxable years beginning after 1986. With respect to income other than income from V.I. sources or income that is effectively connected with a V.I. trade or business, it applies (with targeted exceptions) to any income derived in any pre-1987 taxable year for which (on the date of enactment) the assessment of a deficiency of income tax is not barred by any law or rule of law. To the extent that the Virgin Islands either collects tax by the date of enactment or, pursuant to an assessment issued by August 16, 1986, collects tax by January 1, 1987, on non-V.I. source, non-V.I. effectively connected income on a V.I. inhabitant that is subject to U.S. tax for pre-1987 taxable years, that V.I. tax is to be creditable against the U.S. tax liability on that income. To the extent that that V.I. tax is imposed on U.S. income, it is to be creditable against U.S. tax on that particular income notwithstanding the general limitations on the foreign tax credit.

The agreement makes it clear that the possessions cannot discriminate against U.S. corporations (as well as U.S. citizens or residents) or similar persons from other possessions. In the event that any one of the contemplated implementing agreements between the United States and these possessions is not executed within a year of enactment, the conference agreement specifies that the House Committee on Interior and Insular Affairs (in addition to the House Committee on Ways and Means and the Senate Committee on Finance) is to receive the Secretary's report on the status of negotiations and the reasons for not executing the agreement.

The agreement provides that a U.S. person who becomes a resident of Guam, American Samoa, or the Northern Mariana Islands is to pay tax to the United States on U.S. source income, income effectively connected with a U.S. trade or business, and gains from sales of certain assets with a U.S. connection for the 10-year period beginning when that per-son became a resident. This provision applies to income earned after 1985. This provision makes it clear, for example, that a U.S. person who moves to one of these possessions while holding appreciated stock of a U.S. corporation and who sells the stock during 1986 cannot contend that the income from that sale is non-U.S. source income the tax on which a possession is free to reduce or rebate. The agreement grants regulatory authority to provide exceptions to this rule in cases where the Secretary determines that adequate tax will be collected. The conferees do not intend that any regulatory exception contain a subjective standard considering a taxpayer's intent.

[¶ 4058] SECTIONS 1301, 1302, 1311-1318. TAX-EXEMPT BONDS.

(Secs. 25, 103, 103A, 6652 of the Code)

[Conference Report]

* * * * * *

A. General Restrictions on Tax Exemption

Overview—The conference agreement reorganizes and amends the present-law rules governing tax-exemption for interest on obligations issued by or on behalf of qualified governmental units. As part of this reorganization, the present-law rules contained in Code sections 103 and 103A are divided, by topic, into 11 Code sections (secs. 103 and 141-150). The conferees intend that, to the extent not amended, all principles of present law continue to apply under the reorganized provisions.[3] interest on bonds,[4] the proceeds of which are used to finance operations of State or local governmental units, is tax exempt under Code section 103 without regard to many of the restrictions that apply to bonds used to benefit other persons.[5] Interest on State and local government bonds is taxable if the bonds are private activity bonds unless a specific exception is included in the Code.

An issue is an issue of private activity bonds if (1) a trade or business use and security interest test (similar to the present-law IDB tests) or (2) a private loan restriction is satisfied.[6] The conference agreement also adopts the Senate amendment's related use requirement, with technical modifications, described below.

Private activity bonds qualifying for tax-exemption include exempt-facility bonds, qualified mortgage bonds and qualified veterans' mortgage bonds, qualified small-issue bonds, qualified redevelopment bonds, qualified student loan bonds, qualified 501(c)(3) bonds, and bonds issued under three specifically described programs.[7]

Exempt-facility bonds are bonds issued to finance airports, docks and wharves, mass commuting facilities, water facilities, sewage disposal facilities, solid waste disposal facilities, qualified residential rental projects, qualified hazardous waste facilities, facilities for the local furnishing of electricity or gas, or local district heating or cooling facilities. All facilities financed with such bonds must satisfy a public use requirement.

[Footnote ¶ 4058] **(3)** As under present law, interest on certain bonds authorized under non-Code provisions of law is tax-exempt under Code section 103 if the authorizing legislation was enacted before January 1, 1984, and the bonds comply with all appropriate Code requirements. The appropriate Code requirements include all requirements that apply to Code bonds with respect to which the use of bond proceeds is comparable, including, but not limited to, the new private activity bond volume limitation, the arbitrage rules, the information reporting requirements, the limitation on bond-financing of costs of issuance, and the restrictions on issuance of tax-exempt bonds for certain specified activities.

(4) Under these rules, the term bond also includes debt obligations of a qualified governmental unit that do not involve the formal issuance of a bond or note. For example, installment purchase agreements, finance leases, and other evidences of debt issued pursuant to the borrowing power of a qualified governmental unit are treated as bonds.

(5) The conference agreement continues the present-law rule allowing bonds to be issued either by or on behalf of qualified governmental units. *See, e.g.,* Rev. Rul. 63-20, 1963-2, C.B. 397.

(6) The term loan is a subset of the term use, so a use arises in every case where a loan is present. A private loan bond may not satisfy the trade or business use and security interest tests, however, in cases where the private use totals no more than 10 percent of bond proceeds or is made to an individual not engaged in a trade or business.

(7) The three programs are the Texas Veteran's Land Bond Program (with the present-law sunset deleted), the Oregon Small Scale Energy Conservation and Renewable Resource Loan Program, and the Iowa Industrial New Jobs Training Program. As with other private activity bonds, 95 percent or more of the proceeds of these private activity bonds must be used for the exempt purpose of the borrowing, no more than 2 percent of bond proceeds may be used to finance certain costs of issuance (described below), and the bonds are subject to the new State private activity bond volume limitations.

The conferees recognize that section 501(c)(3) organizations typically perform functions which governments would otherwise have to undertake. The use of the term private activity bond to classify the obligations of section 501(c)(3) organizations in the Internal Revenue Code of 1986 in no way connotes any absence of public purpose associated with their issuance. Thus, the conferees intend, and the statute requires, that any future change in legislation applicable to private activity bonds generally shall apply to qualified 501(c)(3) bonds only if expressly provided in such legislation.

Trade or business use and security interest tests.—*In general.*—Under the conference agreement, an issue is an issue of private activity bonds if—

(1) an amount exceeding 10 percent of the proceeds[8] are to be used (directly or indirectly) in any trade or business carried on by any person other than a governmental unit, and

(2) more than 10 percent of the payment of principal or interest on the issue is to be made (directly or indirectly, and whether or not to the issuer) with respect to such a trade or business use of the bond proceeds, or is otherwise secured by payments or property used in a trade or business.

Trade or business use test.—The conference agreement generally retains the present-law rules under which use by persons other than governmental units is determined for purposes of the trade or business use test. Thus, as under present law, the use of bond-financed property is treated as use of bond proceeds.[9] As under present law, a person may be a user of bond proceeds and bond-financed property as a result of (1) ownership or (2) actual or beneficial use of property pursuant to a lease, a management or incentive payment contract, or (3) any other arrangement such as a take-or-pay or other output-type contract. Use on the same basis as the general public (including use as an industrial customer) is not taken into account. However, trade or business use by all persons on a basis different from the general public is aggregated in determining if the 10-percent threshold for being a private activity bond is satisified.

For purposes of the trade or business use test, all activities of section 501(c)(3) organizations, the Federal Government (including its agencies and instrumentalities), and other nongovernmental persons who are not natural persons are treated as trade or business activities.[10]

Security interest test.—The conference agreement adopts the Senate amendment's security interest test, with technical modifications. Under the revised security interest test, both direct and indirect payments made by any person (other than a governmental unit) who is treated as using the bond proceeds are counted. Such payments are counted whether or not they are formally pledged as security or are directly used to pay debt service on the bonds. Similarly, payments to persons other than the issuer of the bonds may be considered. For example, payments made by a lessee of bond-financed property to a redevelopment agency are considered under the test even though the city, as opposed to the redevelopment agency, actually issues the bonds.

Revenues from generally applicable taxes are not treated as payments for purposes of the security interest test; however, special charges imposed on persons satisfying the use test (but not on members of the public generally) are so treated if the charges are in substance fees paid for the use of bond proceeds.

For example, where bonds are used to acquire land that is to be sold for redevelopment to private persons, amounts paid by those persons for the land are payments for purposes of the security interest test, even though incremental tax revenues are the stated security for the bonds. Similarly, if a facility is leased to a nongovernmental user and receipts from a special user tax are formally pledged as security, lease payments from the private user are considered for purposes of the security interest test, even if the user tax revenues (rather than the lease or other payments) comprise the direct source for repayment of the bonds.

Use pursuant to certain management contracts.—The conference agreement follows the Senate amendment's directive to the Treasury Department to liberalize its advance ruling guidelines on treatment of nongovernmental use pursuant to certain management contracts, with a modification. Under the agreement, Treasury is directed to modify its advance ruling guidelines to provide that use pursuant to management contracts not exceeding five years (including renewal options) is not treated as private trade or business use if—

(1) at least 50 percent of the compensation to any manager other than a governmental unit is on a periodic, fixed-fee basis;

(2) no amount of compensation is based on a share of net profits; and

(3) the governmental unit owning the facility may terminate the contract (without penalty) at the end of any three year period.[11]

Except for the specific changes indicated, the conferees do not intend Treasury to alter

---

[Footnote ¶ 4058 continued]

(8) In determining the amount of proceeds for this purpose, costs of issuance and amounts invested in a reserve or replacement fund are allocated between the governmental use and private use portions of the issue.

(9) Similarly, use of bond proceeds is treated as use of bond-financed property.

(10) The conferees intend that use of bond proceeds by the Bonneville Power Administration be treated as use by a governmental unit to the extent that BPA is treated as an exempt person under a transitional exception contained in present Treasury regulations, section 1.103-7(b)(2)(iii).

(11) The conferees intend that similar changes will be made to these advance ruling guidelines as applied to qualified 501(c)(3) bonds. See, Rev. Proc. 82-15, 1982-1 C.B. 460.

the present-law advance ruling guidelines and regulations for determining when nongovernmental use is disregarded for purposes of the trade or business use test or to limit the Treasury Department's authority to determine what constitutes (or does not constitute) a use of bond proceeds.

Use pursuant to certain cooperative research agreements—The conference agreement follows the Senate amendment on treatment of private use under certain cooperative research agreements, with a clarification that the amount charged participating private businesses for the use of patents or other resulting technology must be determined at the time the patent or technology is available for use. * * * [P]rivate use pursuant to research agreements not satisfying the requirements of the conference agreement is counted for purposes of the trade or business use and security interest tests and the private loan restriction (if the use in substance involves a loan).

Special rule for certain output facilities.—*In general* The conference agreement provides a special limit on bond-financing for output facilities used by persons other than governmental units or members of the general public. In the case of bonds 5 percent or more of the proceeds of which are to be used to finance output (e.g. power but not water) projects such as electric and gas generation, transmission, and related facilities, the maximum amount of bond-financing that may be used by nongovernmental persons on a basis other than as a member of the general public and by governmental units is $15 million.[12] Thus, with respect to any issue used to finance an output facility or related facilities, the amount of bond proceeds used by persons other than governmental units may not exceed the lesser of 10 percent or $15 million of the proceeds.[13] Additionally, in determining whether the $15 million limit is exceeded, all outstanding prior issues issued with respect to a project are counted.[14] Application of this restriction may be illustrated by the following examples:

Example 1.—Assume that a single issue of tax-exempt bonds is contemplated to finance the acquisition of an electric generating facility for $500 million. Assume further that 10 percent of the output of the facility will be sold to an investor-owned utility under an output contract. The maximum amount of tax-exempt financing that may be provided for the acquisition is $465 million (i.e., $450 million for the 90 percent of the facility that is governmentally used, and $15 million for the private use portion).

Example 2.—Alternatively, assume that the facility in Example 1, is financed with four bond issues. Assume further that the first issue is for $100 million. The maximum private use portion for this issue is $10 million (10 percent of the issue). Assume a second issue of $150 million with respect to the facility. The maximum permitted private use portion for the second issue is $5 million ($15 million less the $10 million private use portion of the first issue). For all subsequent issues for the facility, no private use financing would be permitted.

Use pursuant to certain pooling and exchange arrangements and certain spot sales of output capacity.—The conferees wish to clarify that certain power pooling and exchange arrangements and certain spot sales of output capacity are treated as sales to the general public under the trade or business use and security interest tests. The conferees intend that the presence of a nongovernmental person acting solely as a conduit for exchange of power output among governmentally owned and operated utilities is to be disregarded in determining whether the trade or business and security interest tests are satisfied. In addition, exchange agreements that provide for "swapping" of power between governmentally owned and operated utilities and investor-owned utilities do not in any event give rise to trade or business use where (1) the "swapped" power is in approximately equivalent amounts determined over periods of 1 year or less, (2) the power is swapped pursuant to an arrangement that does not involve output-type contracts, and (3) the purpose of the agreements is to enable the respective utilities to satisfy differing peak load demands or to accommodate temporary outages.

[The following colloquy is drawn from the Congressional Record. The colloquy occurred on the day the Conference bill was considered by the House. Ed.]

[House Floor Explanation]

I have discussed with Congressman FOLEY several issues relating to the effect of the bill on certain pooling and exchange agreements. We have reached a common understanding regarding the following specific issues:

Congressman FOLEY requested clarification of certain statements on page 690 of the conference report relating to the use of electricity pursuant to certain pooling and exchange arrangements. Power pooling and exchange are universal and essential elements of efficient energy management in the Pacific Northwest and elsewhere. It is my understanding that these statements are not

---

[Footnote ¶ 4058 continued]

(12) The conference agreement directs the Treasury Department to modify its present regulations (Treas. reg. sec. 1.103-7(b)(5)) for determining the portion of an output facility that is privately used to reflect the reduced limits on such use. Specifically, Treasury is directed to delete the special exception under which users of three percent or less of the output of a facility are disregarded in calculating whether the issue satisfies the trade or business use and security interest test.

(13) A parallel reduction applies to the security interest test.

(14) Issues issued before September 1, 1986, are counted for purposes of this limit.

intended to subject such pooling and exchange arrangements to an additional set of tests, but rather simply to identify certain types of arrangements that do not give rise to trade or business use.

Specifically, the Bonneville Power Administration is involved in two types of pooling and exchange arrangements as part of its statutory responsibility to manage the Federal hydroelectric system in the Northwest. The first uses coordination agreements, in which both governmentally owned and investor-owned utilities make power available to a power pool. Each utility has the right to draw power from the pool which approximately equals the amount of power made available to the pool. Because of variations in rainfall, snowfall and runoff, some of these agreements have to utilize a 4-year critical water planning period to coordinate the use of each utility's hydroelectric resources in a manner that is most efficient for the region as a whole.

The second involves residential purchase and sale agreements mandated by the Regional Power Act. Under these agreements, Bonneville exchanges power with both governmentally owned and investor-owned utilities for the purpose of spreading the cost benefits of Federal hydroelectric energy to the residential customers of these utilities.

It is my understanding that neither of these arrangements gives rise to a trade or business use of bond proceeds on the part of Bonneville. Congressional Record, p. H 8363, 9-25-86.

[Conference Report]

*   *   *   *   *   *

The conference agreement further provides that spot-sales of excess power capacity for temporary periods, other than by virtue of output contracts with specific purchasers, are not treated as trade or business use. For purposes of this exception, a spot sale is a sale pursuant to a single agreement that is limited to no more than 30 days duration.

Related use restriction.—Under the conference agreement, the amount of private use financed with an issue which use is unrelated to a governmental use also being financed or which is disproportionate to a related governmental use also being financed may not exceed 5 percent of the proceeds. If the sum of such private use for an issue exceeds 5 percent of the net proceeds of the issue, (and a 5-percent security interest test, determined with respect to such use is satisfied) then the interest on the bonds is taxable. The determination of whether a private use is related to governmental use also being financed with the bond proceeds is to be made on a case-by-case basis, emphasizing the operational relationship between the governmental and nongovernmental uses. In most—but not all—

cases, this will result in a related private use facility being located within or adjacent to any governmental facility to which it is related. For example, a newsstand located in a courthouse is related to the courthouse, and a privately operated school cafeteria is related to the school in which it is located. By contrast, the use of 6 percent of school bond proceeds to build an administrative office building for a catering company that operates cafeterias for the school system is not a related use of bond proceeds and would result in interest on the bond issue from which the proceeds are derived being taxable. Similarly, office space for lawyers engaged in the private practice of law is not related to financing of a courthouse or other government building.

Private-use financing provided with bond proceeds in excess of the unrestricted 5-percent portion generally may not be disproportionate to the amount of bond proceeds used for a related governmental use.[15] The determination of whether a private use which is related to a government use also being financed with the bond proceeds is disproportionate to the government use to which such private use relates is determined by comparing the amount of bond proceeds used for the related private and government uses. The related private use is disproportionate to the related government use to the extent it exceeds such use in amount. Multiple, related private use facilities for any government use are treated as one facility for purposes of this rule.[16]

The related use restriction may be illustrated by the following examples:

Example 1.—Assume County X issues $20 million of bonds for construction of a new school building and decides to use $18.1 million of the proceeds for construction of the new school building and $1.9 million of the proceeds for construction of a privately operated cafeteria in the county's administrative office building. The $1.9 million of proceeds is not related to the governmental use (i.e., school construction) being financed with the bonds; thus interest on the bonds is taxable. Had County X limited use of bond proceeds for the privately operated cafeteria to $1 million, however, the related use restriction would be satisfied since the amount of unrelated private use would not have exceeded 5 percent.

Example 2.—Assume City Y issues $50 million of bonds for construction of a new public safety building ($32 million) and for improvements to an existing courthouse ($15 million). (The maximum private use (related and unrelated) portion for these bonds may not exceed $5 million, and the maximum unrestricted private use portion may not exceed $2.5 million.) Assume further that Y decides to use $3 million of the bond proceeds for renovation of an existing privately operated cafeteria located in the courthouse. If there is no other private use financed with the bonds, Y's use of the $3 million for the privately operated cafeteria satisfies the related use restriction. These expenditures are treated as being derived first from the permitted related private use portion (up to $2.5 million), and then from the unrestricted private use portion ($0.5 million).

Example 3.—Assume the facts of Example 2, except City Y decides to use $1.5 million of the bond proceeds to construct a privately operated parking garage adjacent to its new public safety building (reducing the proceeds available for the public safety building to $30.5 million). Under these facts, the allocation for the privately used courthouse facilities is determined as in Example 2. The expenditures for the public safety building parking garage are treated as derived from the unrestricted private use portion ($1.5 million) since the entire 5-percent related use portion for the issue was used for the courthouse cafeteria. Thus, the related use restriction is satisfied.

Private loan restriction.—The conference agreement follows the House bill's limitation on the amount of bond proceeds that may be used to make private loans to an amount exceeding the lesser of 5 percent or $5 million of proceeds. As under the House bill, the restriction applies to loans to all persons other than governmental units.

The agreement retains the present-law exceptions to the private loan restriction for all private activity bonds for which tax-exemption is provided specifically in the Code, and follows the House bill and Senate amendment clarifications of the application of the excluded loan exception for specific essential governmental functions to permit indirect loans to businesses as well as to nonbusiness persons, provided the loans are available on an equal basis to both business and nonbusiness borrowers.

The conferees intend that, as under present law, a loan may arise from the direct lending of bond proceeds or may arise from transactions in which indirect benefits that are the economic equivalent of a loan are conveyed. Thus, the determination of whether a loan is made depends on the substance of a transaction, as opposed to its form. For example, a lease or other contractual arrangement (e.g., a management contract or an output or take-or-pay contract) may in substance constitute a loan, even if on its face, such an arrangement does not purport to involve the lending of bond proceeds.

However, a lease or other deferred payment arrangement with respect to bond-financed property that is not in form a loan of bond proceeds generally is not treated as such unless the arrangement transfers tax ownership to a nongovernmental person. Similarly, an output or management contract with respect to a bond-financed facility generally is not treated as a loan of bond proceeds unless the agreement in substance shifts significant burdens and benefits of ownership to the purchaser or manager of the facility.

Volunteer fire departments.—The conference agreement retains the present law treatment of volunteer fire department bonds subject to a requirement that 95 percent or more of the net proceeds be used for qualified purposes.

Effective dates.—*Definition of private activity bond.*—In general.—As provided in the Joint Statements on Effective Dates of March 14, 1986,[17] and July 17, 1986,[18] the amendments to the definition of a private activity bond generally apply to bonds (including refunding bonds) issued on or after September 1, 1986. This includes the 10 percent trade or business use test (10 percent or $15 million, for output facilities); the 5 percent unrelated use limitation; and the $5 million limitation contained in the amended private loan restriction.[19]

As provided in the Joint Statements, the September 1, 1986, effective date does *not* apply to bonds which under present law are (1) industrial development bonds (IDBs), (2) bonds that would be IDBs, treating section 501(c)(3) organizations as private persons engaged in trades or businesses, (3) student loan bonds, (4) mortgage revenue bonds, or (5) other private ("consumer") loan bonds for which tax-exemption is permitted. With respect to these bonds, these provisions of the conference agreement generally are effective for bonds (including refunding bonds) issued after August 15, 1986.

Modification of security interest test.—The amendments to the security interest test, to clarify that the test takes into account both direct and indirect payments made by users of bond-financed property (whether or not formally pledged), apply to bonds (including refunding bonds) issued after August 15, 1986.

Use pursuant to certain management contracts.—The direction to the Treasury Department to modify its advance ruling guidelines with respect to private use pursuant to certain management contracts is effective on the date of enactment.

[Footnote ¶ 4058 continued]

(17) Joint Statement by The Honorable Dan Rostenkowski (D., Ill.), Chairman, Committee on Ways and Means, The Honorable Bob Packwood (R., Ore.), Chairman, Committee on Finance, The Honorable John J. Duncan (R., Tenn.), Ranking Member, Committee on Ways and Means, The Honorable Russell Long (D., La.), Ranking Member, Committee on Finance, and The Honorable James A. Baker, Ill, Secretary of the Treasury, on the Effective Dates of Pending Tax Reform Legislation, March 14, 1986.

(18) Joint Statement of Chairman Rostenkowski, Chairman Packwood, and Secretary Baker, July 17, 1986.

(19) The exceptions to the private loan restriction (including the continuation of the present-law exceptions) are effective for bonds issued after August 15, 1986.

Use pursuant to certain cooperative research agreements.—The provisions regarding use pursuant to certain cooperative research agreements generally apply to bonds (including refunding bonds) issued after August 15, 1986.

Transitional exceptions.—The conference agreement includes three generic transitional exceptions to the amendments to the definition of private activity bonds (including the modification of the security interest test).[20]

Certain "in-progress" projects.—The first transitional exception is provided for bonds (other than refunding bonds) with respect to facilities—

(1) the original use of which commences with the taxpayer and the construction (including reconstruction or rehabilitation) of which began before September 26, 1985, and is completed on or after that date;

(2) the original use of which commences with the taxpayer and with respect to which a binding contract to incur significant expenditures for construction (including reconstruction or rehabilitation) of facilities financed with the bonds was entered into before September 26, 1985 and is binding at all times thereafter, and part or all of such expenditures are incurred on or after that date; or

(3) acquired after September 25, 1985, pursuant to a binding contract entered into on or before that date and that is binding at all times after that date.

Bonds eligible for this transitional exception are bonds that, under present law, are not IDBs, qualified mortgage bonds, qualified veterans' mortgage bonds, student loan bonds, other private loan bonds for which tax-exemption is permitted,[21] or non-Code bonds comparable to any of the foregoing, but which are private activity bonds under the conference agreement.

The transitional exception applies only to facilities for which the bond financing in question was approved by a governmental unit (or by voter referendum) before September 26, 1985. Governmental approval for this purpose includes approval by means of an inducement resolution or, if the governmental unit does not generally adopt inducement resolutions for the type of bond concerned, other comparable approval.

For purposes of the exception for facilities qualifying under (1) or (2), above, construction of a facility is deemed complete when the facility is placed in service for Federal income tax purposes.

Whether or not an arrangement constitutes a contract is determined under the applicable local law. A binding contract is not considered to have existed before September 26, 1985, however, unless the property to be acquired or services to be rendered were specifically identified or described before that date.

A binding contract for purposes of this provision exists only with respect to property or services for which the taxpayer is obligated to pay under the contract. In addition, where a contract obligates a taxpayer to purchase a specified number of articles and also grants an option to purchase additional articles, the contract is binding only to the extent of the articles that must be purchased.

A contract may be considered binding on a person even though (1) the contract contains conditions which are under the control of a person not a party to the contract, or (2) the person has the right under the contract to make minor modifications as to the details of the subject matter of the contract.

A contract that was binding on September 25, 1985, will not be considered binding at all times thereafter if it is modified (other than as described in (2) above) after that date. Additionally, for purposes of the binding contract exception, payments under an installment payment agreement are incurred no later than the date on which the property that is the subject of the contract is delivered rather than the due date of each installment.

For purposes of the binding contract rule, significant expenditures means expenditures in excess of 10 percent of the reasonably anticipated cost of the facilities.

Certain current refundings.—A second transitional exception is provided with respect to certain current refunding bonds.[22] This exception applies to current refundings of bonds issued before the applicable date (including a series of refundings where the original bond was issued before that date), if—

(1) the amount of the refunding bonds does not exceed the outstanding amount of the refunded bonds, and

(2) the average maturity of the refunding issue (1) does not exceed 120 percent of the reasonably expected economic life of the property identified as being financed with

---

[Footnote ¶ 4058 continued]

(20) Transitional exceptions are provided to many of the effective dates of other provisions of this title under circumstances similar to those described in this section. For purposes of those transitional exceptions, the determination of whether original use commences with the taxpayer, of whether construction (including reconstruction or rehabilitation) began before (and is completed on or after) a specified date; of whether significant expenditures are made; and of whether a binding contract existed (and pursuant to which expenditures are made after a specified date) is made in the same manner as described in this section. Additionally, the determination of whether a facility is described in a properly adopted inducement resolution (or other comparable approval) is made in the same manner as that described in this section.

(21) These bonds include generally bonds issued as part of the Texas Veterans' Land Bond Program, the Oregon Small-Scale Energy Conservation and Renewable Resource Loan Program, and the Iowa Industrial New Jobs Training Program.

(22) Advance refunding bonds, as defined in the conference agreement, may not be issued pursuant to this exception.

the refunded bonds (in a series of refundings, the original bonds) when those bonds were issued, or (2) the final maturity date of the refunding bonds is not later than 17 years after the issuance of the refunded (original) bonds.[23]

This exception also applies to current refundings of bonds to which the "in progress" transition rule described above applies (including a series of such refundings).

Certain advance refundings.—A third transitional exception is provided permitting advance refunding of bonds that were governmental when issued (satisfying the 25-percent rather than 10-percent trade or business use test) subject to the new restrictions on advance refundings of governmental bonds.

Bonds for volunteer fire departments.—The extension and modification of authority for certain volunteer fire departments to issue tax-exempt bonds is effective on the date of enactment. The repeal of the sunset date for the Texas land bond program and the provision regarding the Iowa Industrial New Jobs Training Program are effective on the date of enactment.

B. Private Activity Bonds
1. Exempt-Facility Bonds
a. Overview

* * * * * *

Under the conference agreement, exempt-facility bonds may be issued to finance multifamily residential rental projects, airports, docks and wharves, mass commuting facilities, sewage disposal facilities, solid waste disposal facilities, facilities for the local furnishing of electric energy or gas, facilities for the furnishing of water (including irrigation systems), local district heating or cooling facilities, and certain hazardous waste disposal facilities.

Amendments are made to the targeting rules for multifamily residential rental projects, the definition of airports, docks and wharves, and mass commuting facilities, and certain of the rules applicable to all exempt-facility bonds. The conference agreement further provides that at least 95 percent of the net proceeds of each issue must be used for the exempt facility for which the bonds are issued and functionally related and subordinate property. Net proceeds are defined as proceeds less amounts invested in a reasonably required reserve or replacement fund. (No reduction is made for amounts paid for costs of issuance since those amounts are not treated as spent for the exempt purpose of the borrowing.)

b. Rules applicable to specific exempt facilities

(1) Multifamily residential rental projects

* * * * * *

The conference agreement generally follows the Senate amendment, with several exceptions.[24] The low-income set-aside requirements are modified to conform to the requirements applicable to the low-income housing credit provided in the conference agreement (see II.E.3, above). Thus, bond-financed projects are required to meet one of the two following set-aside requirements (to be elected by the issuer on or before the date the bonds are issued):

(1) At least 40 percent of rental housing units must be occupied by tenants having incomes of 60 percent or less of area median gross income; or

(2) At least 20 percent of rental housing units must be occupied by tenants having incomes of 50 percent or less of area median gross income. To conform with the low-income housing credit, the conference agreement further provides that existing low-income tenants will continue to count as such as long as their family incomes do not increase above 140 percent of the income qualifying as low-income with respect to the project.

The conference agreement follows the House bill with respect to the qualified project period, during which bond-financed projects are required to be used as rental housing. Thus, the qualified project period ends on the latest of (1) the date which is 15 years after 50 percent of the units are occupied, (2) the first day on which no bonds are outstanding with respect to the project, or (3) the date on which any assistance provided to the project under section 8 of the United States Housing Act of 1937 terminates.

The conference agreement also makes conforming amendments to the provision in the Senate amendment, under which special rules are applied to certain rent-skewed projects which elect to satisfy stricter targeting requirements. Under the modified rule, projects qualify for the special treatment contained in the Senate amendment only if 15 percent or more of the low-income units are occupied by individuals having incomes of 40 percent (rather than 50 percent or 60 percent) or less of area median gross income, and the average rent charged to market-rate tenants is at least 300 percent of the average rent charged to low-income tenants for comparable units. (The limitations on rent charged to low-income tenants, contained in the Senate amendment, are retained.) If a project elects to satisfy these requirements, increases in an existing tenant's income, up

---

[Footnote ¶ 4058 continued]

(23) This exception applies to bonds that are governmental bonds under present law but are private activity bonds under the conference agreement. This exception does not change the present-law rules which prohibit refundings of various types of bonds that were eliminated or restricted under the Deficit Reduction Act of 1984.

(24) As under present law, multifamily residential rental property is eligible for tax-exempt financing only if the housing units are used other than on a transient basis. In addition, each residential rental unit must include separate and complete facilities for living, sleeping, eating, cooking, and sanitation. Hotels, dormitories, hospitals, nursing homes, retirement homes, and trailer parks do not qualify as residential rental property.

to 170 percent of the qualifying income, do not disqualify the tenant as a low-income tenant; upon an increase over 170 percent, only the next available low-income unit must be rented to a tenant having an income of 40 percent or less of area median income.

(2) Sports facilities

*   *   *   *   *   *

House Bill.—Authority to issue tax-exempt bonds for sports facilities is repealed.

*   *   *   *   *   *

Conference Agreement.—The conference agreement follows the House bill * * *.

(3) Convention or trade show facilities

*   *   *   *   *   *

House Bill.—Authority to issue tax-exempt bonds for convention or trade show facilities is repealed.

*   *   *   *   *   *

Conference Agreement.—The conference agreement follows the House bill * * *.

(4) Airports

*   *   *   *   *   *

The conference agreement allows exempt-facility bonds to be issued to finance airports, and related storage and training facilities. The conference agreement provides that the term airport does not include any of the following facilities if they are used in a private business use:

(1) Airport hotels (or other lodging facilities).

(2) Retail facilities (including food and beverage facilities) located in a terminal in excess of a size necessary to serve passengers[25] and employees at the airport.

(3) Retail facilities for passengers or the general public (including, but not limited to, rental car lots) located outside the airport terminal.[26]

(4) Office buildings for individuals who are not employees of a governmental unit or of the public airport operating authority.

(5) Industrial parks or manufacturing facilities.

For purposes of these exclusions, property is considered to be used in a private trade or business if it is leased to or managed by any person other than a qualified governmental unit or an airport authority acting on behalf of a qualified governmental unit.

(5) Docks and wharves

*   *   *   *   *   *

The conference agreement allows exempt-facility bonds to be used to finance docks and wharves and related storage and training facilities (including long-term storage where permitted under present law). The term dock and wharf does not include any of the following facilities, if the facilities are used in a private business use:

(1) Hotels (or other lodging facilities);

(2) Retail facilities (including food and beverage facilities) located in a terminal in excess of a size necessary to serve passengers and employees at the port;

(3) Retail facilities (other than public parking) for passengers or members of the general public located outside the port terminal;

(4) Office buildings for individuals who are not employees of a governmental unit or of the public port operating authority); and

(5) Industrial parks or manufacturing facilities.

For purposes of these exclusions, property is considered to be used in a private trade or business if it is leased to or managed by any person other than a qualified governmental unit or a port authority acting on behalf of a qualified governmental unit.

(6) Mass commuting facilities

*   *   *   *   *   *

House Bill.—Exempt-facility bonds may be issued to finance governmentally owned mass commuting facilities, defined generally as under present law, but limited to facilities directly related and essential to the ground transportation of passengers.

*   *   *   *   *   *

Conference Agreement.—The conference agreement follows the House bill, and defines such facilities generally as under present law, except that the term mass commuting facilities does not include any of the following facilities, if they are used in a private business use:[27]

(1) Hotels (or other lodging facilities).

(2) Retail facilities (including food and beverage facilities) located in a mass commuting terminal in excess of a size necessary to serve passengers and employees of the mass commuting facility.

(3) Retail facilities (other than public parking) for passengers and members of the general public located outside the mass commuting terminal.

(4) Office buildings for individuals who are not employees of a governmental unit or of the public mass commuting operating authority; and

---

[Footnote ¶ 4058 continued]

(25) For purposes of these limitations, the term passengers includes persons meeting or accompanying persons arriving and departing on flights to and from the airport.

(26) Public airport parking is not treated as a retail facility for purposes of this limitation, but such parking must be limited to no more than a size necessary to serve passengers and employees at the airport.

(27) In retaining the present-law definition of mass commuting facilities, as modified above, the conferees do not intend to prejudge the possible need in the future to allow tax-exempt financing for high-speed rail systems in a manner similar to that allowed under the agreement for mass commuting facilities.

(5) Industrial parks or manufacturing facilities.

For purposes of these exclusions, property is considered to be used in a private trade or business if it is leased to or managed by any person other than a qualified governmental unit or an operating authority acting on behalf of a qualified governmental unit.

(7) Parking facilities

* * * * * *

House Bill.—Authority to issue tax-exempt bonds (other than small-issue bonds) for parking facilities is repealed. (This repeal does not affect the ability to issue tax-exempt bonds to finance parking facilities that are functionally related and subordinate to an exempt facility.)

* * * * * *

Conference Agreement.—The conference agreement follows the House bill and the Senate amendment. This provision does not affect the ability to finance parking facilities which are functionally related and subordinate to another exempt facility. * * *.

(8) Sewage disposal facilities

* * * * * *

The conference agreement allows exempt-facility bonds to be issued to finance sewage disposal facilities, defined as under present law.

(9) Solid waste disposal facilities

* * * * * *

The conference agreement allows exempt-facility bonds to be issued to finance solid waste disposal facilities, defined generally as under present law. Thus, as under present law, tax-exempt financing may be provided for the processing of solid waste or heat into usable form, but not, as an exempt facility bond, for further processing that converts the resulting materials or heat into other products (e.g., for turbines or electric generators). (*See,* Temp. Treas. reg. sec. 17.1.) The special rule for certain qualified steam-generating or alcohol-producing facilities is repealed. The conferees wish to clarify that solid waste does not include most hazardous waste (including radioactive waste).

(10) Facilities for the local furnishing of electric energy or gas

Present Law.—Exempt-activity IDB's may be issued to finance facilities for the local furnishing of electric energy or gas, in areas not exceeding two contiguous counties or a city and one contiguous county.

* * * * * *

Conference Agreement.—The conference agreement [retains present law. Ed.][28]

(11) Pollution control facilities

* * * * * *

House Bill.—Authority to issue tax-exempt bonds for air or water pollution control facilities is repealed.

* * * * * *

Conference Agreement.—The conference agreement follows the House bill * * *.

(12) Facilities for the furnishing of water

* * * * * *

The conference agreement allows exempt-facility bonds to be issued to finance facilities for the furnishing of water, defined as under present law (including irrigation systems).

(13) Certain hydroelectric generating facilities

* * * * * *

Senate Amendment.—The Senate amendment follows the House bill, but retains the present law transitional exception for property with respect to which a FERC application was docketed before January 1, 1986.

Conference Agreement.—The conference agreement follows Senate amendment with a clarification that, in order for the present-law transitional exception to apply, an application for a license (rather than for a preliminary permit) must have been docketed with FERC by December 31, 1985.

(14) Local district heating or cooling facilities

* * * * * *

The conference agreement allows exempt-facility bonds to be issued to finance local district heating or cooling facilities, defined as under present law.

(15) Qualified hazardous waste facilities

* * * * * *

Under the conference agreement, exempt-facility bonds may be issued to finance qualified hazardous waste facilities. These include facilities for the land incineration or the permanent entombment of hazardous waste, which facilities are subject to final permit requirements under subtitle C of Title II of the Solid Waste Disposal Act, as in effect on the date of enactment of the conference agreement.

Tax-exempt financing is available only for facilities (or the portion of a facility) to be

---

[Footnote ¶ 4058 continued]

(28) Present-law exceptions under which specified facilities are treated as facilities for the local furnishing of electricity (secs. 644 and 645 of the Deficit Reduction Act of 1984) are retained under the conference agreement.

used by the public as opposed to the generator of the hazardous waste.[29] The conferees further intend that the term hazardous waste not include radioactive waste, and that rules similar to the present-law rules regarding solid waste disposal IDBs will apply, including rules limiting hazardous waste to materials having no market or other value at the place at which they are located and rules limiting tax-exempt financing to that portion of a facility which is actually engaged in the incineration or entombment of hazardous waste. (*See, e.g.*, Treas. Reg. sec. 1.103-8(f)(2) and Temp. Treas. Reg. sec. 17.1.)

c. Effective dates for exempt-facility bond provisions

The repeal of specified categories of exempt-activity IDBs and the amendments to the definition of certain exempt facilities apply to bonds issued after August 15, 1986.

A transitional exception from the new rules for exempt-facility bonds is provided for bonds (other than refunding bonds) that may be issued under the present IDB rules, but which may not be issued under the conference agreement. This transitional exception applies to bonds for facilities with respect to which the commencement of construction (including reconstruction or rehabilitation) or binding contract, or acquisition, rules described in the discussion of effective dates for the new rules on governmental bonds are satisfied * * *.

A second transitional exception to the exempt-facility bond provisions applies in the case of certain current refunding bonds. This exception applies to refundings (including a series of refundings) of bonds issued before August 16, 1986, which bonds qualify for tax-exemption under present law, but do not so qualify under the conference agreement, provided that the rules of the transitional exception for current refundings of certain governmental bonds * * * are satisfied.

The requirement that 95 percent of the net proceeds of exempt-facility bonds be used to finance exempt facilities (including functionally related and subordinate facilities) applies to bonds issued after August 15, 1986, except for bonds covered under the second transitional exception above (for current refunding bonds). The option to issue bonds for qualified hazardous waste facilities applies after August 15, 1986.

d. Miscellaneous restrictions on exempt-facility bonds

(1) Functionally related and subordinate test

Present Law.—In the case of exempt-activity IDBs, all property that is functionally related and subordinate to the exempt activity may be financed with bond proceeds. Expenditures for such functionally related and subordinate property are treated as

made for the exempt purpose of the borrowing.

* * * * * *

Senate Amendment.—No provision.

Conference Agreement.—The conference agreement follows the Senate amendment with a modification providing that office space generally is not treated as functionally related and subordinate to an exempt facility (subject to the modifications described above that apply to airports, docks and wharves, and mass commuting facilities).[30] Only office space that is directly related to the day-to-day operations at an exempt facility and that is located at or within the facility may be financed with exempt-facility bonds and small issue IDBs for manufacturing. Thus, a separate office building, or an office wing of a mixed-use facility, is not treated as functionally related and subordinate to an exempt facility.

Effective date.—This provision applies to bonds (including refunding bonds) issued after August 15, 1986. A transitional exception applies in the case of certain current refunding bonds. This exception applies to refundings (including a series of refundings) of bonds issued before August 16, 1986, which bonds qualify for tax-exemption under present law, but do not so qualify under the conference agreement, provided that the rules of the transitional exception for current refundings of certain governmental bonds (described in A., above) are satisfied.

(2) Ownership of exempt-facility bond-financed property

* * * * * *

House Bill.—The House bill requires that all property financed with exempt-facility bonds for airports, docks and wharves, mass commuting facilities and water facilities be governmentally owned. Governmental ownership is determined using general Federal income tax concepts of ownership.

Senate Amendment.—The Senate amendment follows present law, with a modification to the safe harbor rules for financing airports, docks and wharves, and certain other facilities outside of the State volume limitations on IDBs. Under this safe-harbor, these exempt facilities are not treated as privately owned solely by reason of a lease (including service or management contract) if (a) the term of the lease (including renewal periods) does not exceed 80 percent of the reasonably expected economic life of the bond-financed property and (b) the private user of the facility does not have an option to purchase the facility at other than fair market value, and (c) the [lessee] makes an irrevocable election not to claim an investment tax credit with respect to any property financed with the issue.

[Footnote ¶ 4058 continued]

(29) This requirement is considered to be satisfied, if 95 percent or more of the net proceeds are to be used with respect to that portion of the facility used by persons other than the owner or operator of the facility (or any related person).

(30) These restrictions are identical to the restrictions that apply under present law and the conference agreement as part of the definition of manufacturing facility under the small-issue bond rules.

Conference Agreement.—The conference agreement follows the House bill in requiring that all property financed with exempt-facility bonds for airports, docks and wharves, and mass commuting facilities, be governmentally owned. The conference agreement modifies the Senate amendment's safe-harbor rule for permitting airport, dock and wharf, and solid waste bonds to be exempt from the State volume limitations as a safe-harbor test for purposes of this requirement.

Under the agreement, property is considered owned by a governmental unit if the lessee makes an election (binding on successors in interest) not to claim depreciation or an investment tax credit with respect to the property, the lease term is not more than 80 percent of the property's useful life and the [lessee] has no option to purchase the property at other than fair market value. In the case of a solid waste facility a lease of 20 years or less is considered to meet the 80 percent test.

Effective date.—This provision applies to bonds (including refunding bonds) issued after August 15, 1986.

A transitional exception is provided for bonds (other than refunding bonds) that may be issued under the present IDB rules, but which may not be issued under the conference agreement. This transitional exception applies to bonds for facilities with respect to which the commencement of construction (including reconstruction or rehabilitation) or binding contract or acquisition rules described in the discussion of effective dates for the new rules on governmental bonds are satisfied. * * *

A second transitional exception to the exempt-facility bond provisions applies in the case of certain current refunding bonds. This exception applies to refundings (including a series of refundings) of bonds issued before August 16, 1986, which bonds qualify for tax-exemption under present law, but do not so qualify under the conference agreement, provided that the rules of the transitional exception for current refundings of certain governmental bonds * * * are satisfied.

2. Industrial Park Bonds

*   *   *   *   *   *

House Bill.—The House bill repeals the tax exemption for interest on industrial park IDBs.

*   *   *   *   *   *

Conference Agreement.—The conference agreement follows the House bill * * *.

Effective date.—This provision is effective for bonds (including refunding bonds) issued after August 15, 1986.

A transitional exception from the repeal of authority to issue tax-exempt bonds for industrial parks applies to such bonds for facilities with respect to which the commencement of construction (including reconstruction or rehabilitation) or binding contract or acquisition rules described in the discussion of effective dates for the new rules on governmental bonds are satisfied. * * *.

A second transitional exception to this provision applies in the case of certain current refunding bonds. This exception applies to refundings (including a series of refundings) of bonds issued before August 16, 1986, which bonds qualify for tax-exemption under present law, but do not so qualify under the conference agreement, provided that the rules of the transitional exception for current refundings of certain governmental bonds * * * are satisfied.

3. Small-Issue Bonds

*   *   *   *   *   *

Senate Amendment.—The Senate amendment retains the present-law sunset dates applicable to small-issue IDBs, but extend the presently scheduled termination of the special exception for bonds for farmland by treating those bonds as bonds for manufacturing facilities.

Additionally, 95 percent of the proceeds of each issue must be used for the exempt purpose of the borrowing.

The special exception for bonds to finance farmland for first-time farmers is expanded to include financing land for individuals who previously owned land which they disposed of while insolvent. Additionally, the amount of used equipment that may be financed for first-time farmers is increased to 25 percent of the financing provided (i.e., a maximum of $62,500), regardless of whether such equipment is financed in conjunction with financing for the purchase of farmland.

A $250,000 lifetime limit is imposed on the amount of depreciable farm property (including both new and used property) that may be financed for any principal user or related persons. Bonds issued prior to the effective date of this provision are not affected, but count in determining the amount of financing allowed to be provided to any person by subsequent issues.

Conference Agreement.—The conference agreement follows the Senate amendment, except that the sunset date for issuance of manufacturing bonds (including bonds for first-time farmers) is extended for one additional year, through December 31, 1989. At least 95 percent of the net proceeds (without reduction for issuance costs) must be used for the exempt purpose of the borrowing. *(See also,* the description of new restrictions on financing costs of issuance.)

Effective date.—These provisions, including the $250,000 limit on depreciable farm property, apply to bonds (including refunding bonds) issued after August 15, 1986.

A transitional exception applies to certain current refunding bonds that may be issued under current law but that may not be issued under the conference agreement and for current refundings of small-issue bonds occurring after the prescribed termination dates. Current refundings qualifying under this exception are issues—

(1) that do not extend the maturity of the refunded issue;

(2) that have a lower interest rate than the rate on the refunded issue; and

(3) the amount of which does not exceed the outstanding amount of the refunded bonds.

4. Student Loan Bonds

* * * * * *

House Bill.—The House bill retains the present exemption for interest on student loan bonds issued in connection with the Federal GSL and PLUS programs, and expands the exemption to include student loan bonds issued under certain State supplemental student loan programs. Under the House bill, all proceeds of student loan bonds (other than amounts invested in a reasonably required reserve or replacement fund or used to pay costs of issuance) must be used to make or finance student loans.

Senate Amendment.—The Senate amendment is the same as the House bill, except only 85 percent of the proceeds are required to be used to make or finance student loans.

Conference Agreement.—The conference agreement follows the House bill and the Senate amendment with a modification requiring that at least 90 percent of net proceeds (without any reduction for issuance costs) must be used to finance student loans in the case of bonds issued in connection with the Federal GSL and PLUS programs. In the case of other student loan bonds for which tax-exemption is permitted, 95 percent is substituted for 90 percent. (*See also,* the description below of new restrictions on financing costs of issuance.)

The conference agreement also requires that a student borrower must be a resident of the issuing State or enrolled in an educational institution located within the State. Where two or more States each use a portion of the State's volume limitation in a single issue to finance student loans, the limitation described in the preceding sentence applies separately to each State's share of the issue.

Effective date.—These provisions apply to bonds (including refunding bonds) issued after August 15, 1986.

A transitional exception is provided permitting current refundings of qualified student loan bonds issued before August 16, 1986, including a series of refundings, which qualify for tax-exemption under present law, but do not qualify under the conference agreement, provided that the amount of the refunding bonds does not exceed the outstanding amount of the refunded bonds. The conferees intend that, as under present law, the period provided for financing student loans in the case of these current refunding bonds be determined from the date of issue of the refunded bonds (original bonds in the case of series of refundings) rather than a new period commenced on the date of the refunding. Additionally, the last maturity date of the refunding bonds may be no later than 17 years after the date of issuance of the refunded bonds (original bonds in the case of a series of refundings).

5. Mortgage Revenue Bonds

a. Qualified mortgage bonds and mortgage credit certificates

* * * * * *

House Bill

Qualified mortgage bonds.—The House bill makes the following modifications to the present targeting rules for qualified mortgage bonds:

(1) All bond proceeds (50 percent in targeted areas) other than issuance costs and amounts invested in reasonably required reserve or replacement funds must be used to finance residences to first-time homebuyers;

(2) The purchase price of bond-financed residences may not exceed 90 percent (110 percent in targeted areas) of the average area purchase price applicable to that residence;

(3) The present requirements of annual Treasury Department reports and published policy statements by issuers of qualified mortgage bonds are repealed; and

(4) New Federal income limitations are imposed with respect to purchasers of homes financed with qualified mortgage bonds.

Mortgage credit certificates. — Authority to issue MCCs is continued; the targeting requirements for MCCs are conformed to the revised targeting rules for qualified mortgage bonds.

* * * * * *

Senate Amendment

* * * * * *

Mortgage credit certificates.—The Senate amendment increases the rate at which qualified mortgage bond authority may be exchanged to issue MCCs from 20 percent to 25 percent. No other amendments are made to the MCC rules.

Certain cooperative housing corporations.—An exception is provided to the general cooperative housing corporation rules permitting limited equity cooperative housing corporations to elect to be eligible for tax-exempt financing under the rules applicable to multifamily residential rental property (as modified by the amendment). If such an election is made—

(1) the tenant-shareholders of the cooperative are not entitled to a deduction for interest and taxes paid by the cooperative (under sec. 216); and

(2) the volume of such bonds counts toward the state volume limitation applicable to qualified mortgage bonds.

Bonds for limited equity cooperative housing are subject to the December 31, 1987, termination date for qualified mortgage bonds.

* * * * * *

Conference Agreement

Qualified mortgage bonds.—The conference agreement follows the House bill, with the following modifications—

(1) At least 95 percent of the net proceeds of each qualified mortgage issue (without any reduction for issuance costs) must be used to finance mortgage loans to first-time homebuyers. (*See also,* the description of new restrictions on financing costs of issuance.)

(2) As under present law, there is no requirement that a minimum percentage of financing in targeted areas be provided to first-time homebuyers.

(3) The House bill's income limits for purchasers of residences financed with qualified mortgage bond proceeds are adopted, modified, as follows:

(a) All financing must be provided to borrowers whose family income does not exceed 115 percent of the higher of area or Statewide median income.

(b) In targeted areas, one-third of the financing may be provided to borrowers without regard to the limitation in (a); the balance of the financing must be provided to mortgagors having incomes not exceeding 140 percent of the higher of area or Statewide median income.

Mortgage credit certificates.—The conference agreement follows the Senate amendment's increase in the exchange rate for MCCs and follows the House bill in conforming amendments to the targeting rules for recipients of the certificates to the new requirements (under the conference agreement) for qualified mortgage bonds.

Certain cooperative housing corporations.—The conference agreement follows the Senate amendment with conforming amendments which require electing limited equity cooperative corporations to satisfy the revised targeting rules for multifamily residential rental projects contained in the agreement and extending the termination of the exception to parallel the new termination dates for qualified mortgage bonds and MCCs. The election to forego deductions for proportionate interest and taxes, in return for financing as multifamily rental housing, applies throughout the qualified project period (as defined for multifamily housing bond purposes).

Bonds for electing limited-equity cooperatives are counted toward the State volume limitation for private activity bonds.

Termination of programs.—The conference agreement extends the scheduled termination dates for the qualified mortgage bond and MCC programs one year, to December 31, 1988.

Effective date.—These provisions are effective with respect to bonds (including refunding bonds) issued, and bond authority exchanged for authority to issue MCCs, after August 15, 1986. The special provision on limited equity cooperative housing corporations applies to bonds issued after August 15, 1986.

A transitional exception is provided permitting current refundings of qualified mortgage bonds issued before August 16, 1986, which qualify for tax-exemption under present law, but do not qualify under the conference agreement, provided the amount of the refunding bonds does not exceed the outstanding amount of the refunded bonds. The conferees intend that, as under present law, the period allowed to provide financing for qualified mortgagors in the case of these current refunding bonds be determined from the date of issue of the refunded bonds (original bonds in the case of a series of refundings) rather than a new period commenced on the date of the refunding. Additionally, the last maturity date of such refunding bonds may be no later than 32 years from the date of issuance of the refunded bonds (original bonds in the case of a series of refundings).

b. Qualified veterans' mortgage bonds

Present Law.—Qualified veterans' mortgage bonds are bonds 90 percent or more of the proceeds of which are used to finance loans to veterans for the purchase of single-family, owner-occupied residences. Tax-exempt qualified veterans' mortgage bonds may be issued only by the five States that issued such bonds before June 22, 1984. Mortgage loans financed with these bonds may be made only to veterans who served on active duty before 1977, and who apply for a loan before 30 years after leaving active service.

* * * * * *

Senate Amendment. — The Senate amendment retains present law.

Conference Agreement.—The conference agreement follows the Senate amendment, with a modification providing that at least 95 percent of net proceeds (without any reduction for issuance costs) must be used to finance mortgage loans to qualified veterans.

Additionally, a clarification is provided that in order not to be counted toward the State volume limitations, current refundings of qualified veterans' mortgage bonds may not exceed the outstanding amount of the refunded bonds. The last maturity date of such refunding bonds may be no later than 32 years from the date of issuance of the refunded bonds (original bonds in the case of a series of refundings).

Effective Date.—The new provisions apply to bonds (including refunding bonds) issued after August 15, 1986.

A transitional exception is provided permitting current refundings of bonds issued before August 16, 1986, which qualify for tax-exemption under present law, but do not qualify under the conference agreement, provided the amount of the refunding bonds does not exceed the outstanding amount of the refunded bonds and that the period during which financing is provided to qualified mortgagors is determined from the date of issuance of the refunded bonds (or original bonds in the case of a series of refundings) rather than a new period commenced on the date of the refunding. Additionally, the last maturity date of the refunding bonds must be no later than 32 years after the date of issuance of the refunded bonds (original bonds in the case of a series of refundings).

6. Qualified Redevelopment Bonds

a. Overview

* * * * * *

Conference Agreement.—The conference agreement treats qualified redevelopment bonds as tax-exempt private activity bonds.

Qualified redevelopment bonds must be part of an issue—

(1) 95 percent or more of the net proceeds (without reduction for issuance costs) of which are to be used for redevelopment purposes in a locally designated blighted area; and

(2) the payment of principal and interest on which is secured (a) primarily by taxes of general applicability imposed by a general purpose governmental unit or (b) by a pledge of incremental property tax revenues reserved, to the extent necessary, for debt service on the issue.

Thus, under the conference agreement, qualified redevelopment bonds may be repaid, or their repayment secured, either (a) by incremental tax revenues (as under the House bill and Senate amendment), (b) by general tax revenues of the governmental unit (e.g., a pledge of the full faith and credit of the issuing jurisdiction), or (c) by a combination of (a) and (b) above. Repayment of qualified redevelopment bonds may *not* be secured by payments from any person other than such security that would render the bonds IDBs under present law (using a 10-percent use and security interest test). Additionally, the pledged tax revenues must be the primary security for repayment of the bonds. Whether such revenues are the primary security is a factual determination. This requirement is intended to be satisfied, however, only when the pledge of taxes represents a direct and substantial financial commitment by the issuer of the bonds.

As under the House bill and Senate amendment, taxes in the designated blighted area must be imposed at the same rates and using the same assessment methods as apply with respect to comparable property located elsewhere in the jurisdiction. Additionally, no fees or other charges may be imposed on owners or users of property in the designated area to which owners or users of other comparable property are not subject. (Insubstantial fees for amenities such as parking are not treated as assessments for this purpose.) Where financing is provided with respect to only a portion of a blighted area, these rules apply only with respect to the area being financed.

b. Permitted uses of bond proceeds

* * * * * *

Senate Amendment.—The Senate amendment is the same as the House bill, except that, for purposes of (1) above the Senate amendment clarifies that—

(1) the requirement that property be sold for its fair market value is determined by taking into account covenants and restrictions relating to the use of real property that are imposed by the issuer of the bonds; and

(2) the actual threat of eminent domain is not required, if the acquiring agency has the power of eminent domain and the power could be exercised with respect to the property concerned.

Conference Agreement.—The conference agreement generally follows the Senate amendment. Thus, under the conference agreement, qualified redevelopment bond proceeds may be used for the following purposes:

(1) To acquire real property located in a designated blighted area, provided that the acquiring governmental unit has the power to exercise eminent domain with respect to the real property in the area.

(2) To clear and prepare land in the designated blighted area for redevelopment.

(3) To rehabilitate the real property acquired as above or otherwise owned by a governmental unit (e.g., property acquired by tax lien foreclosure).

(4) To relocate occupants of structures on the acquired real property.

Under the conference agreement, real property acquired by a governmental unit (under (1) above) need not be transferred to a nongovernmental person; however, if it is so transferred, the transfer must be for fair market value. The determination of fair market value for this purpose is made taking into account covenants and restrictions imposed on the use of the relevant real property by the issuer of the bonds.

As under the House bill and Senate amendment, qualified redevelopment bond proceeds may not be used to construct new buildings or other property, including the enlargement of any existing building.[31]

[Footnote ¶ 4058 continued]

(31) Bonds, the proceeds of which are used to finance such governmental facilities as street paving, sidewalks, streetlighting, and similar facilities are treated as governmental bonds under the conference agreement. These bonds are, therefore, not subject to the new requirements for qualified redevelopment bonds, provided that they do not violate the restrictions pertaining to trade or business use, unrelated use, or private loans, described in A., above (i.e., provided that they are not private activity bonds). The conferees understand that both governmental activities and private redevelopment activities may be financed with a single issue of redevelopment bonds. The conferees intend that the Treasury Department will develop rules allowing such composite financing to continue by treating the governmental

c. Designation of blighted areas

* * * * * *

Conference Agreement

Criteria for designation.—The conference agreement follows the House bill and the Senate amendment with respect to designation of blighted areas. Thus, under the conference agreement, qualified redevelopment bonds may be issued only pursuant to (1) a State law which authorizes the issuance of such bonds to redevelop blighted areas, and (2) a redevelopment plan adopted by the governing body of the general purpose local governmental unit having jurisdiction over the area, before the issuance of the bonds.

The designation of blighted areas is to be based on State statutory criteria which take into account all relevant factors, including the excessive presence in the area of vacant land on which structures were previously located, abandoned or vacant buildings, substandard structures, vacancies, and delinquencies in payment of real property taxes. Designations are to be based on an affirmative finding of a substantial presence of these factors.

The conferees are aware that certain redevelopment agencies have previously adopted redevelopment plans that are consistent with the general goals of the conference agreement but that may not meet the specific criteria established by the agreement. The conferees do not intend to require existing redevelopment agencies, which had adopted redevelopment plans as of August 15, 1986, pursuant to a State law, to resubmit a new plan to the general purpose governmental unit having jurisdiction over the designated blighted area. The conferees further do not intend to require such agencies to reexamine the original criteria used to designate blighted areas. However, no new bonds may be issued for activities in such grandfathered districts which may not otherwise be financed with qualified redevelopment bonds under the conference agreement. (*See also,* the rules below on application of the 20-percent limit to these areas.)

For purposes of designating blighted areas, general purpose local governmental units are the smallest governmental units having general purpose sovereign powers over a given area.[32] Thus, in most cases, designations will be made by cities or (for areas outside any city) by county governments. The State itself and special purpose governmental units (e.g., a redevelopment agency itself) are not treated as governmental units entitled to designate blighted areas.[33]

Size limitations.—*Maximum area size* Under the conference agreement, the aggregate blighted areas designated by a general purpose local governmental unit may not contain real property, the assessed value of which exceeds 20 percent of the assessed value of all real property located within the jurisdiction of the governmental unit. The percentage with respect to any area is to be determined at the time the area is designated, with these percentages being aggregated for purposes of the 20 percent test. For example, assume that a city designates a redevelopment area in 1987 that contains 10 percent of the assessed value of real property located in the city (determined as of 1987). Assume further that the city designates a second area in 1992 containing 5 percent of the assessed value of all real property in the city (determined as of 1992). If the city wishes to designate a third area in 1997, that area may not contain more than 5 percent of the assessed value of real property in the city, determined as of 1997.[34] Previously designated areas cease to be taken into account, for purposes of the 20 percent test, if no qualified redevelopment bonds (or similar bonds issued under prior law) remain outstanding with respect to the area. Once an area ceases to be counted, the area must be redesignated under the rules of the conference agreement before further bonds may be issued for redevelopment therein.

Districts designated before January 1, 1986, and with respect to which qualifying activities were in progress on that date, are not subject to the 20 percent rule. However, no new districts may be designated, or existing districts expanded, until the jurisdiction is in compliance with the 20 percent limit (determined inclusive of those existing districts).

Minimum area size.—A designated blighted area must satisfy one of the two following requirements:

(1) The area is comprised of at least 100 compact and contiguous acres; or

(2) The area is comprised of between 10 and 100 compact and contiguous acres, and no more than 25 percent of the bond-financed land in the area is to be provided to any one person or related persons. The 25 percent rule is not considered to be violated if more than 25 percent of financing is to be made available to one person (or related persons) on an interim basis for use in redevelopment activities and the redevelopment property is to be transferred with reasonable speed to persons satisfying the 25-percent limitation as part of a unified development plan. This latter determination is to be based on the financing provided pursuant to the overall redevelopment plan for the area, rather than on an issue-by-issue basis. For purposes of

---

[Footnote ¶ 4058 continued]

component and the qualified redevelopment bond component of such issues as separate issues in appropriate circumstances.

(32) This is similiar to the test applied for purposes of allocating bond authority among overlapping units for purposes of the private activity bond volume limitation.

(33) The State is, however, required to establish the criteria for designating those areas, as described above.

(34) For purposes of determining these percentages, the total assessed value of real property in the jurisdiction includes real property located in previously designated blighted areas.

this rule, the fact that more than 25 percent may be used by a developer on a temporary, interim basis while redevelopment activities are conducted may be disregarded.

The conferees intend that the designation of blighted areas will be made in contemplation of the redevelopment of the entire designated area and that areas will not be artificially designated in order to allow bond financing for one or a few specific facilities which happen to be located in the area.

d. Application of IDB limitations

*   *   *   *   *   *

Conference Agreement

General rules.—Qualified redevelopment bonds are treated as tax-exempt private activity bonds and generally are subject to the rules applicable to such bonds. An exception is provided from the limitation on use of bond proceeds to acquire nonagricultural land.[35]

Rental and owner-occupied housing.—The conference agreement follows the Senate amendment. Thus, the targeting rules for qualified mortgage bonds or multifamily residential rental housing bonds are not applied to housing constructed or rehabilitated on land financed with these bonds. (No new housing (or other structures) may be constructed, or existing structures expanded, with the bond proceeds themselves; however, this housing may be financed with (1) private, taxable financing, or (2) mortgage revenue bonds or exempt-facility bonds for residential rental housing with or without conjunctive use of the new low income housing tax credit (subject to the targeting and other restrictions applicable to those bonds.)

Prohibited facilities.—The conference agreement generally follows the Senate amendment. Thus, under the conference agreement, no more than 25 percent of qualified redevelopment bond proceeds may be used to finance facilities the financing of which is restricted or prohibited with respect to qualified small-issue bonds (new sec. 144(a)(8) or for private activity bonds generally (new sec. 147(e)),[36] or the land on which such facilities are or are to be located. Additionally, no proceeds of qualified redevelopment bonds may be used to finance the following facilities (or land for such facilities):

(1) Private or commercial golf courses;

(2) Country clubs;

(3) Massage parlors, hot tub facilities, or suntan facilities;

(4) Racetracks or other facilities used primarily for gambling; and

(5) Any store the principal business of which is the sale of alcoholic beverages for off-premises consumption.

Effective date.—The new rules for qualified redevelopment bonds apply to bonds issued after August 15, 1986.

7. Qualified 501(c)(3) Bonds

*   *   *   *   *   *

Conference Agreement.—The conference agreement permits tax-exemption for interest on qualified 501(c)(3) bonds, defined generally as bonds at least 95 percent of the net proceeds of which are to be used by no person other than a section 501(c)(3) organization or a governmental unit. A bond is not a qualified 501(c)(3) bond if the bond would be a private activity bond if section 501(c)(3) organizations were treated as governmental units with respect to their exempt activities and 5 percent were substituted for 10 percent in the private business use and security interest tests. Under the conference agreement as under present law, the use of bond proceeds by a section 501(c)(3) organization in an unrelated trade or business (as determined by applying sec. 513(a)) is a private use. Further, under the conference agreement, as is true of other private activity bonds, costs of issuance are not treated as spent for the exempt purpose of the borrowing. (See also, the description below of the new limitations on financing costs of issuance.)

The conferees understand that some governmental units issue composite issues, a part of the proceeds of which is to be used for governmental activities and a part of which is to be used for financing for section 501(c)(3) organizations operating within the jurisdiction of the issuer. The conferees do not intend to preclude continuation of such composite issues provided all applicable requirements for tax exemption for each type or use concerned are satisfied. Thus, the conferees intend that, where an issue consists of two components—governmental financing and qualified 501(c)(3) financing—and the two components, viewed as separate issues, satisfy all requirements for tax-exemption as (a) governmental bonds and (b) qualified 501(c)(3) bonds, respectively, a composite tax-exempt issue be permitted.[37]

The conferees further are aware that certain State or local governmental universities and hospitals (including certain public benefit corporations) also have received determination letters regarding their tax-exempt status under Code section 501(c)(3). The committee intends that, to the extent that such an entity is a governmental unit or an agency or instrumentality of a governmental

---

[Footnote ¶ 4058 continued]

(35) The limitation on use of bond proceeds to acquire existing facilities, unless rehabilitation expenditures equal or exceed 15 percent of bond financed sales does not apply to qualified redevelopment bonds. However, the conferees intend that if land and existing structures located thereon are acquired with an intent to demolish the structures, that all costs of acquiring the property are to be treated as land acquisition costs. (See also, sec. 280B.)

(36) These parallel the present law facilities which are restricted or prohibited with respect to small issue IDBs or IDBs in general.

(37) The portion of the composite issue that is a qualified 501(c)(3) bond is to be treated as such for all purposes, e.g., the $150 million limitation on nonhospital bonds and the change in use penalties.

unit determined as under present law), bonds for the entity will be treated as governmental bonds rather than as qualified 501(c)(3) bonds.

The conference agreement follows the House bill and the Senate amendment on the ownership requirement for property financed with qualified 501(c)(3) bonds, and follows the House bill on the $150 million per organization limitation on outstanding non-hospital bonds, with a modification providing that the limitation takes into account only qualified 501(c)(3) bonds.[38] The conferees intend that the definition of hospital include persons who are mentally ill in the term "sick persons." The conference agreement further clarifies that bonds issued before August 16, 1986, for section 501(c)(3) organizations count toward the $150 million limitation only if more than 25 percent of the proceeds were to be used directly or indirectly by a such an organization or organizations (and other nongovernmental persons) and the present-law security interest test was satisfied.[39]

The conferees intend that as under the House bill, if an issue is to be used only in part for hospitals, the portion actually used for hospitals is to be exempt from the $150 million limit as a hospital bond. The conferees further are aware that some bond-financed facilities may be used partially as part of a hospital and partially as a part of a nonhospital, related facility. For example, a laboratory may serve both a hospital and private physicians' offices. Bonds used for such mixed-use facilities may be treated as hospital bonds to the extent of the proportionate share of the use of the facilities for inpatient hospital services or to the extent provided pursuant to other allocation formulae prescribed by the Treasury Department.

Additionally, the conference agreement permits section 501(c)(3) organizations to elect not to treat such bonds as qualified 501(c)(3) bonds, and to benefit thereby from exempt-facility bond and qualified redevelopment bond financing, provided that financing is subject to the new State private activity bond volume limitations. For example, a section 501(c)(3) organization may participate in a multifamily residential rental project financed with bonds subject to the State volume limitations by making such an election.

Effective date.—These provisions apply to bonds (including refunding bonds) issued after August 15, 1986, subject to the following transitional exceptions:

(1) Bonds for section 501(c)(3) organizations (other than refunding bonds are not

subject to the new ownership requirements provided the commencement of construction (including construction or rehabilitation) or binding contract rules described in the discussion of effective dates for the new rules on governmental bonds are satisfied; and

(2) Current refundings of bonds for these organizations originally issued before August 16, 1986, which refunded bonds qualify for tax-exemption under present law, but do not qualify under the agreement, are not subject to the new rules provided the amount of the refunding bonds does not exceed the outstanding amount of the refunded bonds and the maturity limitations applicable to qualified 501(c)(3) bonds under the conference agreement are satisfied.

(3) Advance refundings of bonds issued for section 501(c)(3) organizations before August 16, 1986, are permitted under a transitional exception (without regard to whether the bonds satisfy all requirements under the agreement to be qualified 501(c)(3) bonds). These advance refundings must comply with the new advance refunding restrictions applicable to qualified 501(c)(3) bonds.

8. Miscellaneous Restrictions on Private Activity Bonds

a. Use of bond proceeds for activity qualifying for tax-exempt financing and limitation on bond-financing of costs of issuance

* * * * * *

Conference Agreement.—The conference agreement requires that at least 95 percent of net proceeds of all issues of private activity bonds be used for the exempt purpose of the borrowing. This percentage is reduced to 90 percent in the case of qualified student loan bonds issued in connection with the Federal GSL and PLUS programs. Net proceeds is defined as the proceeds of the issue minus amounts invested in a reasonably required reserve or replacement fund.[40] Thus, amounts used to pay any costs of issuance must be paid from the so-called 5 percent "bad money" portion of an issue.

The conference agreement further restricts the amount of private activity bond proceeds that may be used to finance costs of issuance to 2 percent of the face amount of the issue. This amount is increased to 3.5 percent in the case of issues of mortgage revenue bonds the face amount of which does not exceed $20 million.

Costs of issuance subject to the two-percent limitation include all costs incurred in connection with the borrowing—in general,

[Footnote ¶ 4058 continued]

(38) As under the House bill, refundings, other than advance refundings, do not count toward the $150 million limit if the amount of the refunding bonds does not exceed the outstanding amount of the refunded bonds.

(39) A special transitional exception, similar to that provided under the $40 million limit for small-issue bonds applies to current refundings of 501(c)(3) bonds. This exception applies to current refunding bonds that—

(1) have a lower interest rate than the rate on the refunded issue; and

(2) the amount of which does not exceed the outstanding amount of the refunded bonds.

(40) *See also,* the description of the rules on required use of bond proceeds in the discussion of each type of private activity bond.

all costs that are treated as costs of issuance under the present Treasury Department regulations and rulings. Examples of costs of issuance that are subject to the two-percent limitation include (but are not limited to)—

(1) underwriters' spread (whether realized directly or derived through purchase of the bonds at a discount below the price at which they are expected to be sold to the public);

(2) counsel fees (including bond counsel, underwriters' counsel, issuer's counsel, company counsel in the case of borrowings such as those for exempt facilities, as well as any other specialized counsel fees incurred in connection with the borrowing);

(3) financial advisor fees incurred in connection with the borrowing;

(4) rating agency fees;

(5) trustee fees incurred in connection with the borrowing;

(6) paying agent and certifying and authenticating agent fees related to issuance of the bonds;

(7) accountant fees (e.g., accountant verifications in the case of advance refundings) related to issuance of the bonds;

(8) printing costs (for the bonds and of preliminary and final offering materials);

(9) costs incurred in connection with the required public approval process (e.g., publication costs for public notices generally and costs of the public hearing or voter referendum); and

(10) costs of engineering and feasibility studies necessary to the issuance of the bonds (as opposed to such studies related to completion of the project, but not to the financing).

As described in E., below, bond insurance premiums and certain letter of credit fees may be treated as interest expense under the arbitrage restrictions. To the extent of their treatment as interest, the initial cost of these types of costs of issuance may be financed in addition to the two-percent limit on financing other costs of issuance.

Effective date.—These provisions apply to all private activity bonds (including refunding bonds) issued after August 15, 1986.

b. Relationship of bond maturity to life of assets

* * * * * *

Senate Amendment.—The Senate amendment extends the present-law restriction only to qualified 501(c)(3) bonds, with an exception for bonds issued to finance mortgage loans insured under certain FHA programs. Additionally, the Senate amendment provides that for certain pooled issues for multiple section 501(c)(3) organizations, compliance with the requirement is to be determined treating each loan as a separate issue.

Conference Agreement.—The conference agreement follows the Senate amendment, with a modification providing that the safe-harbor maturity to be used for bond-financed land is 30 years.

Effective date.—This provision applies to bonds (including refunding bonds) issued after August 15, 1986.

c. Restriction on bond-financing for land and existing property

Present Law.—Interest on IDBs is generally taxable if more than 25 percent of the proceeds of an issue is used to finance land. Acquisition of existing property may not be financed with tax-exempt IDBs unless a statutory rehabilitation requirement is satisfied.

* * * * * *

Senate Amendment.—No provision.

Conference Agreement.—The conference agreement follows the Senate amendment.

d. Restriction on bond-financing for certain specified facilities

* * * * * *

House Bill.—The House bill extends the present IDB requirements to all private activity bonds.

* * * * * *

Conference Agreement.—The conference agreement follows the House bill, with a modification providing that the restriction on health club facilities does not apply to qualified 501(c)(3) bonds if the health club facility is directly used for the purpose qualifying the section 501(c)(3) organization for tax exemption. Additionally, the conference agreement provides that qualified redevelopment bonds are subject to a specific separate list of facilities for which financing is restricted or may not be provided in lieu of this general restriction.

Effective date.—This provision is effective for bonds (including refunding bonds) issued after August 15, 1986.

Transitional exceptions are provided for bonds (other than refunding bonds) which may be issued under present law, but not under the conference agreement, if (1) the property to be financed is acquired after September 25, 1985, pursuant to a contract entered into on or before that date, and that was binding at all times thereafter, or (2) the original use of the bond-financed property begins with the taxpayer and either (a) a binding construction contract for significant expenditures was entered into before September 26, 1986, with respect to the property or (b) construction of the property commenced before that date and was completed after September 25, 1985. For purposes of this rule, the term significant expenditures has the same meaning as under the transitional exceptions for the new definition of essential function bond. (See, A., above.)

A further transitional exception is provided for current refundings of bonds that qualify for tax-exemption under present law, but do not qualify under the conference agreement, provided the amount of the refunding bonds does not exceed the outstanding amount of the refunded bonds and that the refunding bonds comply with the restriction, described above, on the relationship of bond maturity to economic life of bond-financed property. *(See,* A., above.)

e. Public hearing and approval or voter referendum requirement

Present Law.—IDBs may be issued only after the issuer holds a public hearing and the issuance of the bonds is approved by a designated elected official. Alternatively, issuance of the IDBs may be approved by a voter referendum.

House Bill.—The House bill extends this present IDB requirement to all private activity bonds.

*   *   *   *   *   *

Conference Agreement.—The conference agreement follows the House bill.

Effective date.—This provision applies to bonds (including refunding bonds) issued after December 31, 1986. [Text of bill reads 8-15-86. Ed.] (IDBs presently subject to the requirement are not affected by this prospective effective date.)

f. Substantial user restriction

Present Law.—Interest on IDBs is taxable during any period when the bonds are held by a substantial user (or any related person) of the bond-financed facilities.

*   *   *   *   *   *

Senate Amendment.—No provision.

Conference Agreement.—The conference agreement follows the Senate amendment.

g. Change in use of private-activity bond-financed property

*   *   *   *   *   *

House Bill.—The House bill provides that a change in use of property financed with private activity bonds to a use not qualifying for tax-exempt financing generally results in loss of income tax deductions for rent, interest, or equivalent amounts paid by the person using the property in the nonqualified use. Section 501(c)(3) organizations realize unrelated business income with respect to any such use.

These consequences apply in addition to any loss of tax exemption on bond interest provided under present law.

*   *   *   *   *   *

Conference Agreement.—The conference agreement follows the House bill * * *.

Effective date.—This provision applies to changes in use of bond-financed property occurring after August 15, 1986, with respect to financing provided after that date.

C. Volume Limitations on Private Activity Bonds

*   *   *   *   *   *

House Bill

*   *   *   *   *   *

Allocation of bond authority.—Each State's volume limitation is allocated one-half to State issuers and one-half to local issuers within the State on the basis of relative populations unless the State adopts a statute providing a different allocation. Governors of each State are permitted to issue proclamations overriding the Federal allocation rules, effective during an interim period until the end of the year in which the State legislature next meets in regular session.

The present law required certification by persons allocating bond authority is repealed.

Other administrative provisions of the present IDB volume limitation (including the rules for determining the location of property receiving volume allocations, and the special rule for States having constitutional home rule cities) apply under the new unified volume limitation.

*   *   *   *   *   *

Conference Agreement

Private activity bond volume limitations.—The conference agreement follows the House bill, with numerous modifications. Under the agreement, the two separate sets of volume limitations that apply under present law to IDBs and student loan bonds and qualified mortgage bonds are replaced with a single private activity bond volume limitation. Qualified veterans' mortgage bonds remain subject to their present-law State volume limitations.

Allowable bond volume.—The annual volume limitation for each State is equal to the greater of (1) $75 for every individual who is a resident of the State (as determined by the most recent estimate of the State's population released by the Bureau of Census before the beginning of the calendar year to which the limitation applies) or (2) $250 million. These annual State volume limitations continue through December 31, 1987, after which time each State's volume limitation is reduced to an amount equal to the greater of (1) $50 per resident of the State or (2) $150 million.

For purposes of the volume limitation, the District of Columbia is treated as a State (and therefore may receive a $250 million volume limitation until 1988, when it will receive a $150 million limitation). U.S. possessions, having populations more than that of the least populous State are limited to the $75/$50 per capita amounts. U.S. possessions having populations less than that of the least populous State receive annual volume limitations equal to the per capita amount actually received by the least populous State (i.e., the $250/$150 million safe-harbor divided by the least populous State's population).

Unlike the House bill, there are no special set-asides for specified types of private activity bonds under the new private activity bond volume limitation.

Bonds subject to the private activity bond volume limitation.—Bonds subject to the new private activity bond volume limitation include most private activity bonds for which tax-exemption is permitted and the private use portion (in excess of $15 million) of governmental bonds.[41] Specifically, the volume limitation applies to (1) exempt-facility bonds (other than bonds for airports, docks and wharves, and certain governmentally owned solid waste disposal facilities), (2) qualified mortgage bonds, (3) small-issue bonds, (4) qualified student loan bonds, and (5) qualified redevelopment bonds. Certain other private activity bonds for which tax-exemption specifically is provided also are subject to the new private activity bond volume limitations.[42]

[The following colloquy relating to Act Sec. 1301 is drawn from the Congressional Record. The colloquy occurred on the day the Conference bill was considered by the House. Ed.]

[House Floor Explanation]

I have discussed with Congressman PICKLE several issues relating to the effect of this legislation's provision that a public approval requirement apply to private activity bonds. We have reached a common understanding regarding the following specific issues:

Section 1301 of the bill provides that a public approval requirement will apply to all private activity bonds, as provided in new section 147(f) of the 1986 code. Under section 1316(a) of the bill, a land program with a long history in Congressman PICKLE's State, the Texas Veterans' Land Bond Program, is now characterized as a private activity bond, and will be subject to this public approval requirement. These bonds are issued to fund a pool of loans to Texas veterans meeting certain State law criteria, and they are issued pursuant to constitutional referendums approved, from time to time, by the voters of the State of Texas. Bonds issued as part of the Texas Veterans' Land Bond Program pursuant to any prior or future referendum approved by the voters of the State of Texas amending article III of the Constitution of the State of Texas will satisfy the requirements of such new section 147(f) even though the identity of individual borrowers/mortgagors and the location of land to be financed is not known prior to or on the date such bonds are approved or issued. Also, such a referendum amending the Texas Constitution will satisfy the requirements of section 147(f) provided a public hearing is held with respect to any issue subsequent to the first issue covered by the referendum. Congressional Record, p. H 8363, 9-25-86.

[The following colloquy relating to Act Sec. 1301 is drawn from the Congressional Record. The colloquy occurred on the day the

Conference bill was considered by the Senate. Ed.]

[Senate Floor Explanation]

Mr. BENTSEN. Mr. President, section 1301 of the bill provides that a public approval requirement will apply to all private activity bonds, as provided in new section 147(f) of the 1986 code. Under section 1316(a) of the bill, a land program with a long history in my State, the Texas Veterans Land Bond Program, is now characterized as a private activity bond, and will be subject to this public approval requirement. These bonds are issued to fund a pool of loans to Texas veterans meeting certain State law criteria, and they are issued pursuant to constitutional referenda approved, from time to time, by the voters of the State of Texas. It is my understanding that bonds issued as part of the Texas Veterans' Land Bond Program pursuant to any prior or future referendum approved by the voters of the State of Texas amending article III of the constitution of the State of Texas will satisfy the requirements of such new section 147(f) even though the identity of individual borrowers/mortgagors and the location of land to be financed is not known prior to or on the date such bonds are approved or issued. It is also my understanding that such a referendum amending the Texas Constitution will satisfy the requirements of section 147(f) provided a public hearing is held with respect to any issue subsequent to the first issue covered by the referendum.

I want to ask the chairman if my understanding is correct.

Mr. PACKWOOD. The Senator from Texas is correct. The public approval requirement will be satisfied in the circumstances he described. Congressional Record, p. S 13960, 9-27-86.

[Conference Report]

An exception to the requirement that private use of governmental bond proceeds in excess of $15 million be subject to the State volume limitations is provided in the case of use by section 501(c)(3) organizations, if the proceeds used by the section 501(c)(3) organization, viewed as a separate issue, satisfy all requirements to be a qualified 501(c)(3) bond. For a more complete description of the rules on composite issues involving both governmental and 501(c)(3) use, *see* the discussion of the new rules for qualified 501(c)(3) bonds.

Mortgage credit certificates (MCCs) may continue to be issued by a qualified governmental unit provided that the aggregate annual volume of MCCs issued does not exceed 25 percent of the amount of the

---

[Footnote ¶ 4058 continued]

    (41) The portion of a governmental bond that may be used in a trade or business of a person other than a qualified governmental unit may not exceed 10 percent of net proceeds. Under a special restriction on bonds for output facilities, the aggregate bond-financed private use for such facilities may not exceed $15 million; therefore, private use for these facilities will never exceed the amount that renders the private use portion of governmental bonds subject to the new volume limitations.

    (42) Bonds issued under the Texas Veterans' Land Bond Program, the Oregon Small-Scale Energy Conservation and Renewable Resource Loan Bond Program, and the Iowa Industrial New Jobs Training Program are subject to the new private activity bond volume limitation.

issuer's private activity bond volume limitation exchanged by the issuer.

Consistent with the conference agreement's treatment of advance refunding bonds as additional bonds (since the original bonds are not redeemed within 90 days), advance refundings of governmental bonds are subject to the new private activity bond volume limitations to the extent of any private use of the refunding bonds that exceeds $15 million. Generally, the portion of the proceeds of the refunding bonds attributable to private use will be determined at the time the original bonds are issued. Similarly, in the case of a second advance refunding, this private use portion is determined by reference to the original issue, including bonds issued before 1986. However, if there is a change in facts or circumstances, not originally anticipated at the time of the original issuance, which alters the percentage of private use of the underlying facility, the percentage of private use of the refunding bonds is to take into account the change in circumstances. Thus, for example, if a governmental participant owner of an output facility sells a portion of its ownership interest in the facility to an investor-owned utility (which sale was not anticipated at the time of original issuance), the percentage of private use of refunding bonds issued after such sale must reflect the increased percentage of private use resulting from the sale. Similarly, if a private participant sells its interest to a governmental participant, the reduction in percentage also is to be taken into account in a later refunding issue.

As under the present-law State volume limitations applicable to IDBs, a qualified governmental unit generally may not allocate its bond authority to property to be located outside the State. An exception is provided permitting a qualified governmental unit to allocate a portion of its private activity bond volume limitation to financing for facilities located outside the State's boundaries in the case of specified facilities to the extent of the State's share of the use of those facilities. Facilities located outside a State's boundaries to which a portion of its volume limitation may be allocated include (1) facilities for the furnishing of water, (2) qualified sewage disposal facilities, (3) solid waste disposal facilities, and (4) hazardous waste disposal facilities. In the case of sewage, solid waste, and hazardous waste disposal facilities, the determination of a State's share of the use of a facility is based on the percentage of the facility's total treatment provided to the State and its residents.[43]

Allocation of private activity bond volume limitation among the State and other qualified governmental units therein.—The conference agreement follows the House bill's rules for allocating a State's volume limitation among issuers with the State, except there are no set-asides for specified types of bonds.[44] The conferees wish to clarify that gubernatorial proclamations issued before the date of enactment of the conference agreement, or state legislation enacted before that date, both are recognized for purposes of allocating the new volume limitations, provided that the proclamation or legislation refers to the new private activity bond volume limitation. Bonds issued before such gubernatorial proclamation or State legislation may not be denied use of a prior allocation of the new private activity bond volume limitation to the extent of the bond authority the issues received based on population.

Similar to the House bill, allocation formulas provided under a gubernatorial proclamation terminates at the end of the next year after 1986 when the legislature meets in regular session. In the case of States where the governor does not have the veto power and where any such proclamation is subject to legislative review when issued, it is the intent of the conferees that the proclamation be treated as legislation, unless specifically overridden by action of the applicable State legislature.

Three-year carryforward.—An issuer may elect to carry forward any portion of its private activity bond volume limitation for up to three years for certain purposes. The election may not be made for projects to be financed with small-issue bonds or for bond volume limitation to be used to finance the private use portion of governmental bonds. Where the election applies, bonds issued in the three calendar years following the calendar year for which the election is made are not counted toward's the State's private activity bond volume limitation in the year of issuance to the extent that the proceeds from the bonds are used for the purpose for which the election is made. The bond authority specified in carryforward elections is absorbed in the order of the calendar years in which they arose.

The election to carry forward unused State volume limitation is to be made as provided in Treasury Department regulations. For purposes of this election, identification of a purpose to be financed with exempt-facility bonds, such as sewage or water facilities, is to be deemed sufficient if the type of facility is identified.

[Footnote ¶ 4058 continued]

(43) The fact that loans financed with student loan bonds generally must be available to all individuals attending schools within the issuing State and to all residents of the State regardless of the State in which they attend school is not affected by the limitation on financing out-of-state facilities, since those bonds are not used to finance property. *See however*, the new prohibition on financing loans for students who are enrolled in out-of-state schools and who are not residents of the issuing State.

(44) The conference agreement also follows the House bill regarding the special rule for constitutional home rule cities.

The purpose of issuing student loan bonds, of issuing qualified redevelopment bonds, of issuing qualified mortgage bonds, or of issuing MCCs is considered a separate purpose that is adequately specified for purposes of the carryforward election. As under the House bill, the authority to carryforward bond volume limitation to issue qualified mortgage bonds and MCCs is limited to bonds or credits that will be issued before expiration of authority to issue such bonds or credits (i.e., to bonds or credits that will be issued before 1989).

Except as specifically provided above, no part of any State's volume limitation may be carried forward to any portion of a succeeding year. (Carryforward elections for the present-law volume limitations of IDBs are not permitted for 1986 bond authority.) Similarly, a State may not borrow against future volume limitations.

Bonds not subject to the new private activity bond volume limitations.—*Qualified 501(c)(3) bonds.*—Qualified 501(c)(3) bonds are not subject to the new State volume limitations. Similarly, portions of a governmental bond used by 501(c)(3) organizations in excess of $15 million (and up to the permitted 10 percent private use portion) are not subject to the new volume limitations, if the 501(c)(3) portion would be a qualified 501(c)(3) bond if issued as a separate issue (and assuming appropriate allocations of items such as costs of issuance, reserve funds, and unrestricted money portions).

Certain exempt-facility bonds.—Exempt-facility bonds for airports and docks and wharves are not subject to the new State private activity bond volume limitations. (Under the general rules permitting tax-exempt financing such facilities, all property financed with such bonds must be governmentally owned).

Exempt-facility bonds for solid waste disposal facilities are not subject to the new State volume limitations, if all property to be financed with the bonds is governmentally owned. Under a safe-harbor rule, property financed with the bonds generally is treated as governmentally owned provided (1) the term of any service contract or lease (including renewal terms) does not exceed 20 years, (2) the service contractor or lessee has no option to purchase any of the property for other than its fair market value, and (3) the lessee irrevocably elects not to claim depreciation deductions (or investment tax credit under any transition rule) with respect to any property financed by the issue.

Certain refunding issues.—Certain refunding bonds (other than advance refunding bonds) are not subject to the volume limitation, provided the amount of the refunding

bonds does not exceed the outstanding amount of the refunded bonds. In the case of current refundings of student loan bonds and governmental bonds (having private use in excess of $15 million) subject to the new volume limitations, the refunding bonds are not subject to the new volume limitation only if the maturity of the refunding bonds does not exceed (1) the weighted average maturity date of the refunded bonds, or (2) the date that is 17 years after the date on which the refunded obligation was issued (or in the case of a series of refundings, the date on which the original issue was issued).[45] This rule is applied in the case of qualified mortgage bonds by substituting 32 years for 17 years.[46] For purposes of the new private activity bond volume limitation, the term refunding includes a rollover of commercial paper and other comparable actions which, under present law, constitutes a reissuance of so-called flexible bonds.

Effective date.—*In general.*—Except as specifically provided below, the new State private activity bond volume limitations apply to bonds (including refunding bonds) issued after August 15, 1986. An exception is included in the substantive rules for these limitations which exempts current refundings of bonds otherwise subject to the limitations if the amount of the refunding bonds does not exceed the outstanding amount of refunded bonds and the maturity of the refunded bonds is not extended beyond certain limits.

Advance refundings of pre-August 16, 1986, bonds, where permitted under the conference agreement, are subject to the new volume limitations to the extent that the refunded bonds would be if originally issued on the date of the advance refunding and if more than 5 percent of the refunded bond proceeds were used for output projects (other than facilities for furnishing of water). For purposes of this rule on advance refundings, the requirement that the excess over $15 million of the proceeds of a governmental bond used by private persons be allocated State volume limitations applies. However, the new definition of governmental bond (e.g., the 10-percent business use test) does not apply to make the entire issue (or any proceeds not exceeding $15 million used by private persons) subject to these volume limitations. Similarly, the 95-percent use requirement for qualified 501(c)(3) bonds does not apply to advance refundings of section 501(c)(3) organization bonds originally issued before August 16, 1986. Thus, the private use portion (not in excess of 25 percent of proceeds) of these pre-August 16, 1986, section 501(c)(3) organization bonds is not subject to the State volume limitations.

[Footnote ¶ 4058 continued]

(45) The maturity of private activity bonds (including refunding bonds) the proceeds of which are used to finance facilities generally is limited to 120 percent of the economic life of the property being financed.

(46) The conference agreement provides that, for current refundings of student loan bonds and mortgage revenue bonds to be exempt from the volume limitation the period permitted for making loans to finance student loans or owner-occupied residences must be measured from the date the refunded (or original) bonds were issued. See, the discussion under the effective date provisions for the new rules on these bonds for a description of this provision.

Transitional exceptions.—The conference agreement includes two general transitional exceptions under which bonds issued after August 16, 1986, are not subject to the new private activity bond volume limitations. Both of these exceptions require that the bonds be issued with respect to facilities satisfying the commencement of construction or binding contract rules described under the discussion of effective dates for the new rules on governmental bonds.

If the bond-financed facilities satisfy one of the transitional exceptions, bonds that are not subject to State volume limitations under present law (e.g., bonds for multifamily residential rental property and the nongovernmental portion of governmental bonds) are not subject to the new State private activity bond volume limitations even if issued after August 15, 1986.

Second, if the bond-financed facilities satisfy one of the transitional exceptions, bonds that are subject to a State volume limitation under present law (i.e., most other IDBs, all student loan bonds, and qualified mortgage bonds), and that are issued after August 15, 1986, are not subject to the new private activity bond volume limitations to the extent that the bonds are issued pursuant to a carry forward election allowed under the current State volume limitations of bond authority for 1984 or 1985, and that carry forward election was filed with the Treasury Department before November 1, 1985.

The conferees are aware that carry forward elections may have been made with respect to only a portion of the bond authority required for a project. Bonds in excess of the amounts allocated in carry forward elections are subject to the new private activity bond volume limitations. Bonds subject to volume limitations and for which carry forward elections are not allowed under present law (e.g., qualified mortgage bonds and qualified small-issue bonds) are subject to the new volume limitations if issued after August 15, 1986.

The present-law volume limitations are repealed, effective for bonds issued after August 15, 1986. Issuance of bonds pursuant to elections to carryforward of bond authority under the present volume limitations for most IDBs and all student loan bonds is not permitted except as specifically provided above.

D. Arbitrage and Related Restrictions

1. General Restrictions Applicable to All Tax-Exempt Bonds

* * * * * *

House Bill

* * * * * *

Determination of bond yield. The House bill provides that the yield on bonds is determined on the basis of the original issue discount rules of the Code rather than as under the present general arbitrage restrictions. Thus, yield is determined based on the price at which a substantial number of the bonds are sold to the public and must reflect a current market price. (This amendment reverses the case of *State of Washington* v. *Commissioner.)*

* * * * * *

Conference Agreement

Profit limitations.—*Subsequent intentional acts to create arbitrage.*—Under the conference agreement (as under present law), the determination of whether bonds are arbitrage bonds generally is based upon the reasonable expectations of the issuer on the date of issue. If subsequent intentional acts are taken after the date of issue to earn arbitrage, however, the reasonable expectations test does not prevent the bonds from being arbitrage bonds. See, e.g., Rev. Rul. 80-91, 1980-1 C.B. 29, Rev. Rul. 80-92, 1980-1 C.B. 31, and Rev. Rul. 80-188, 1980-2 C.B. 47.

For purposes of this continuing requirement, any investment with respect to which impermissible arbitrage earnings accrue may result in the interest on the issue becoming taxable, retroactive to the date the issue was issued. For example, if after the expiration of an allowable temporary period, the issuer continued to invest the bond proceeds at a materially higher yield in order to earn impermissible arbitrage, interest on the bonds would become taxable, retroactive to the date of issue. The conferees intend that the determination of whether intentional actions to earn arbitrage have been taken is made on a case-by-case basis, taking into account all facts and circumstances that a prudent investor would consider in determining whether to invest bond proceeds.

Repeal of election to forego temporary periods.—The conference agreement repeals the right to elect under Treasury Department regulations to forego a temporary period during which unlimited arbitrage earnings are permitted and by doing so to receive the right to earn arbitrage of 0.5 percentage points over the yield of the issue. Thus, the definition of the term *materially higher* generally is limited to 0.125 percentage points over the yield on the issue, regardless of whether temporary periods when unlimited arbitrage earnings are permitted are claimed with respect to an issue.

Expansion of investments subject to yield restriction.—The conference agreement follows the House bill and the Senate amendment in providing additional restrictions on the types of obligations in which bond proceeds may be invested without regard to yield restrictions.[47] Under the conference agreement, therefore, the arbitrage restrictions are expanded to apply to the acquisition of any property held for investment other than

---

[Footnote ¶ 4058 continued]

(47) Section 648 of the Deficit Reduction Act of 1984 provides that, in certain cases, property held in the Permanent University Fund of the University of Texas and Texas A&M University is not treated as an investment of bond

another bond exempt from tax under Code section 103. Thus, investment in any taxable security as well as any deferred payment contract (e.g., an annuity) or other property held for investment is precluded if the yield on the property is materially higher than the yield on the issue.

Treatment of certain credit enhancement fees.—The conference agreement retains the present-law rules under which bond insurance premiums are treated as interest expense if the bond insurance results in a reduction in the interest rate on the issue and follows the Senate amendment provision extending this treatment to fees for certain other credit enhancement devices (i.e., letter of credit fees). Thus, if the purchase of a letter of credit results in a net present value interest savings, the fee is treated as if it were interest expense. *(See* Treas. reg. sec. 1.103-13(c)(8).) The treatment of these costs of issuance as interest for purposes of the arbitrage yield calculation is limited, however, to such fees arising from an arm's-length transaction and to fees that represent a reasonable charge for credit risk. Thus, the conferees understand that the Treasury Department may restrict this treatment to such credit enhancement devices purchased pursuant to competitive bidding by credit-enhancement providers. Additionally, the conferees intend that if a fee or premium is increased to reflect indirect payment of costs of issuance (i.e., costs in addition to a charge for transfer of credit risk), the entire fee or premium is not to be treated as interest expense.

Exceptions.—The conference agreement follows the House bill and Senate amendment, with the following modifications:

Statutory temporary period rules.—The conference agreement, like the House bill, imposes new, statutory restrictions on temporary periods when unlimited arbitrage earnings are permitted, but limits application of these new statutory rules to pooled financings. In the case of pooled financings, net proceeds to be used to make loans which have not been used to make loans within 6 months of the date of issue may not be invested at an unrestricted yield after such period until they have actually been used to make loans. In the case of amounts representing repayments of loans from a pool, the 6-month period is reduced to 3 months.

These limitations on pools do not extend the maximum temporary periods allowed under present law in the case of pooled financings but rather are limitations on the temporary periods allowed under present law. Thus, if, as under present law, proceeds of a pooled financing are to be used to make construction loans, the aggregate temporary period allowed to the pool and the borrowers generally may not exceed three years (a maximum of six months to the pool and a maximum of 30 additional months to the borrower). Similarly, in the case of pools for

tax and revenue anticipation loan financing, the aggregate temporary period to the pool and the borrower may not exceed 13 months. Under the conference agreement, whether a financing constitutes a pool is a factual determination. In general, however, the term pool only includes issues the proceeds of which are to be used to make loans, as opposed to an issue to finance a specific project that will be jointly owned by more than one entity.

The statutory temporary period rules for pools do not apply to mortage revenue bonds since substantive rules for those bonds require, in certain cases, that proceeds not be expended until after expiration of one year. Additionally, in the case of qualified student loan bonds issued in connection with the Federal Guaranteed Student Loan (GSL) and Parents' Loans for Undergraduate Students (PLUS) programs, 18 months is substituted for six months (for bonds issued before January 1, 1989). Tax-exempt student loan bonds other than bonds issued before 1989 in connection with these two Federal programs are subject to the six-month period provided generally for pools.

Minor portion exception.—The conference agreement follows the Senate amendment's limitation of the minor portion exception from the arbitrage yield restrictions to an amount not exceeding the lesser of five percent or $100,000 of bond proceeds. As under the Senate amendment, the minor portion is in addition to the exception for amounts invested in a reasonably required reserve or replacement fund.

Reasonably required reserve fund exception.—The conference agreement limits the amount of proceeds received from the sale of the bonds that may be invested in a reasonably required reserve or replacement fund to an amount not exceeding 10 percent of the proceeds of the issue to which the fund relates unless the Treasury Department determines that a larger amount is necessary with respect to an issue. The conferees intend, for example, that a reserve or replacement fund in excess of 10 percent may be allowed if the master legal document authorizing issuance of the bonds (i.e., a master indenture) was adopted before August 16, 1986, and the indenture—

(1) requires a reserve or replacement fund in excess of 10 percent of proceeds, but of not more than maximum annual debt service;

(2) is not amended after August 31, 1986, and

(3) provides that bonds having a parity of security may not be issued by or on behalf of the issuer for the purposes provided under the indenture without satisfying the debt service reserve fund requirements of the indenture.

The conferees understand that issuers may, in certain cases, pledge additional amounts as part of a reserve or replacement fund, which amounts are derived other than

---

from sale of the issue, but which are treated for purposes of the arbitrage restrictions as bond proceeds. *See,* e.g., Treasury regulation sec. 1.103-14(d)(4) and (5) regarding circumstances in which certain pledged endowment funds are treated under present law as amounts invested in a reserve or replacement fund. The 10-percent limitation on the amount of bond proceeds that may be deposited in a reasonably required reserve or replacement fund applies only to amounts of proceeds from sale of an issue that are invested in such a fund. Thus, these other amounts may continue to form part of a reserve or replacement fund (in addition to amounts of actual bond proceeds forming part of such a fund) even if they exceed the 10-percent limitation.

The conference agreement continues the present-law rule that amounts of proceeds invested in a reserve or replacement fund (up to this new 10-percent maximum) are not subject to the arbitrage yield restrictions and does not affect the present-law exceptions under the Treasury regulations (Treas. reg. sec. 1.103-14(d)).[48]

Determination of bond yield.—The conference agreement follows the House bill and the Senate amendment.

Effective dates.—*General rule.*—These provisions apply generally to bonds (including refunding bonds) issued after August 15, 1986 (August 31, 1986 in the case of bonds and provisions covered under the Joint Statement on Effective Dates of March 14, 1986.

Exceptions.—The restriction on investment in annuity contracts applies to bonds (including refunding bonds) issued after September 25, 1985.

The new method of determining bond yield applies to bonds (including refunding bonds) issued after December 31, 1985.

The directions to the Treasury Department to modify its regulations to delete the election to be permitted to earn higher arbitrage over the term of the bonds by foregoing temporary periods and to treat certain letter of credit fees as interest under the arbitrage regulations are effective on August 15, 1986.

2. Extension of Additional Arbitrage Restrictions to All Tax-Exempt Bonds

*   *   *   *   *   *

Conference Agreement

Extension of additional IDB restrictions.—The conference agreement follows the House bill in extending to all tax-exempt bonds (including refunding bonds) other than mortgage revenue bonds the arbitrage rebate restrictions presently applicable to most

IDBs. The limitation on the amount of bond proceeds that may be invested in materially higher yielding nonpurpose investments is extended to all private activity bonds (other than qualified 501(c)(3) bonds). These restrictions are in addition to the general arbitrage restrictions for all tax-exempt bonds, described above. The determination of amounts to be rebated, the due dates of rebate payments, and the operation of the limitation on investment in materially higher yielding nonpurpose investments generally are the same as under the present-law IDB restrictions.

The conferees intend that the Treasury Department may modify the requirement that arbitrage rebate payments be made at 5-year intervals in the case of advance refunding bond proceeds placed in escrow accounts. Escrow account investments may involve investment at differing yields over the term of the bonds which in the aggregate comply with the Code arbitrage yield restrictions. This situation is distinguished from non-escrow funds or regular variable rate debt since the yield on the issue to maturity is determined when the escrow account is established. Thus, for advance refunding escrow proceeds, the Secretary may determine that, in appropriate circumstances, rebate payments are not required until the escrow is fully paid out.

The conferees further intend that the Treasury Department may permit issuers to use such simplified accounting methods as are deemed appropriate to ease administrative burdens of complying with the rebate requirement.

Finally, a technical amendment is made providing that the last rebate payment with respect to an issue is due no later than 60 days (rather than 30 days) after redemption of the issue.

Exceptions to rebate requirement.—The conference agreement retains the the present-law exception to the rebate requirement that applies when all gross proceeds of an issue are expended within six months of the issue date for the purpose for which the bonds are issued. The conferees further wish to clarify that application of the six-month expenditure requirement to pooled financings, including bond banks, is to be determined by reference to when the gross proceeds of the issue are spent for the ultimate exempt purpose of the borrowing, rather than when loans are made.[49]

The conference agreement further retains the present-law exception for certain temporary investments in a bona fide debt service

---

[Footnote ¶ 4058 continued]

(48) As under present law, amounts invested in a reserve or replacement fund are not treated as having been spent for the governmental purpose of the borrowing; thus any arbitrage profits on such a fund must be rebated to the Federal Government. *See,* the discussion of the arbitrage rebate requirements, below.

(49) The conferees further intend that the Treasury Department may, by regulation, treat pooled financings as separate issues in appropriate circumstances. This regulation may not, however, change the present-law rule that the making of a loan by a pool is not treated as an expenditure of gross proceeds for the exempt purposes of the borrowing.

fund, including the $100,000 limit on earnings for funds qualifying under the exception.

The conference agreement provides three additional exceptions to the rebate requirement. First, the conference agreement liberalizes the Senate amendment's exception for bonds used to finance the activities of small governmental units. Under this liberalized exception, no rebate is required on these governmental bonds if the governmental unit reasonably expects to issue no more than $5 million in governmental bonds during the calendar year when the issuance occurs. In determining whether the $5 million limit is reasonably expected to be exceeded, all governmental bonds issued by the issuing governmental unit and all other governmental units that are subordinate to it under applicable State or local law are counted. (Private activity bonds issued by or on behalf of the issuing governmental unit or subordinate governmental units are not so counted and are not eligible for this exception from the rebate requirement.) *See* section IX, B., for a description of subordinate governments.

A second exception is provided for governmental bonds and qualified 501(c)(3) bonds[50] if all but a minor portion of the group proceeds of an issue are spent for the exempt purpose of the borrowing within six months after the date of issuance. Thus, if the gross proceeds of an issue, other than an amount not exceeding the lesser of five percent or $100,000 of the proceeds, are so spent, the conference agreement permits an additional six months to spend the remaining proceeds before rebate payments are required. Additionally, for purposes of this exception, unlike the general rules for the rebate requirement, redemption of the allowable *de minimis* portion of proceeds before expiration of the additional six-month period is treated as an expenditure for the purpose of the borrowing.

Third, the conference agreement provides a transitional exception from rebate for certain qualified student loan bonds issued in connection with the Federal GSL and PLUS program similar to the exception included in the Senate amendment. This transitional exception applies only with respect to bonds issued before January 1, 1989, and is designed to allow issuers of qualified student loan bonds to continue to issue bonds while they find other sources of revenue to defray administrative costs and costs of issuance. (Typically, other revenue sources such as direct Federal funding or funding from State or local governments have not been provided for these purposes in the past.)

Under this modified exception, the rebate requirement does not apply to arbitrage profits earned during the initial 18-month temporary period permitted for such bonds if the profits are used to pay cost of issuance

financed with the bond proceeds and also to such profits to the extent that—

(1) the proceeds of the issue are used to make or finance qualified student loans before the end of the 18-month temporary period permitted under the conference agreement; and

(2) the arbitrage is used to pay administrative costs associated with the issue.

Arbitrage profits may not be used to pay either costs of issuance or administrative costs if those costs are to be reimbursed by borrowers.

As with the special exception to the new temporary period rules described above (i.e., an 18-month temporary period rather than 6 months is permitted for pooled financings generally), this exception does not apply to tax-exempt student loan bonds other than bonds issued in connection with the Federal GSL and PLUS programs.

Rebate safe-harbor for certain governmental financings.—As under both the House bill and the Senate amendment, arbitrage profits on all tax-exempt bonds, including tax and revenue anticipation notes (TRANs) issued to fund cash-flow shortfalls of governmental units must be rebated to the Federal Government if all gross proceeds of an issue are not spent for the exempt purpose of the borrowing within six months of the date of issuance. In general, TRAN proceeds are deemed to be spent as the cash-flow shortfall for which the notes are issued occurs. The conference agreement provides a special safe-harbor exception for TRANs pursuant to which all gross proceeds are deemed to have been spent for the exempt purpose of the borrowing within six months.

Under this safe-harbor exception, if during the six-month period after issuance, the cumulative cash-flow deficit of the governmental unit issuing the TRANs has exceeded 90 percent of the issue size, all net proceeds and earnings thereon of the TRAN issue are deemed to have been spent for the purpose of the borrowing. Solely for purposes of the safe-harbor, cumulative cash-flow deficit is defined as the excess of the amount the governmental unit spends during the relevant period over the sum of all amounts (other than the issue proceeds) that are available for payment of the expenses during that period. As under the general rules on arbitrage rebate, redemption of bonds is not treated as an expenditure for the purpose of the borrowing.[51]

Limitation on loss of tax-exemption for certain rebate errors.—The conference agreement modifies the Senate amendment's provision of a special penalty, in lieu of loss of tax-exemption, for certain failures to rebate arbitrage profits in the case of governmental bonds and qualified 501(c)(3) bonds. Under

---

[Footnote ¶ 4058 continued]

(50) This exception does not apply to so-called tax and revenue anticipation notes (TRANs); rather a special safe-harbor exception from the rebate requirement, described below, is provided for those governmental bonds.

(51) This safe-harbor does not affect the amount of TRANs that may be issued by a governmental unit, that qualify for a temporary period exception from arbitrage yield restrictions, or any other present-law rules governing issuance of such notes.

the conference agreement, the Treasury Department is authorized to waive loss of tax-exemption on an issue where an error in the amount rebated or a late payment occurs, if the error or late payment is not due to willful neglect. In such cases, a penalty equal to 50 percent of the amount not properly paid is imposed and interest accrues on these late payments and underpayments in the same manner as on late payments of tax. The penalty and interest may, however, be waived by Treasury.

Additional restrictions on mortgage revenue bonds.—The conference agreement follows the House bill and the Senate amendment on imposing the present-law additional arbitrage restrictions for qualified mortgage bonds on both those bonds and qualified veterans' mortgage bonds. These restrictions are in lieu of the IDB-type additional restrictions that apply to all other tax-exempt bonds.

Additional restrictions on student loan bonds.—The conference agreement follows the House bill and the Senate amendment in retaining the 1984 direction to the Treasury Department to develop regulations imposing additional arbitrage restrictions on tax-exempt student loan bonds, to the extent that that direction is not inconsistent with specific provisions of the agreement applicable to student loan bonds.

Effective dates.—These provisions apply to bonds (including refunding bonds) issued after—

(1) August 31, 1986, in the case of bonds and provisions covered under the Joint Statement on Effective Dates of March 14, 1986;

(2) 3:00 p.m., E.D.T., July 17, 1986 in the case of application of the arbitrage rebate requirement to governmental bonds issued to fund certain pools, described below;

(3) August 15, 1986, for application of the limit on higher yielding investments in non-purpose investments; and

(4) December 31, 1985, in the case of bonds not covered under (1) and (2).

The conferees intend that no payment of rebate be due before the date that is 60 days after the date of enactment.

Pools described in (2) are bonds satisfying one or more of the following four criteria:

(1) The proceeds of the issue are to be used to fund a pool or pools to make loans to governmental units other than governmental units subordinate (determined under applicable State or local law) the issuer (or the governmental unit on behalf of which the issuer acts).

(2) The proceeds of the issue are to be used to fund a pool or pools with respect to which less than 75 percent of the proceeds of the issue is to be used to make loans to initial borrowers to finance projects identified (with specificity) by the issuer on the date of issue as projects to be financed with the proceeds of such issue.

(3) The proceeds of the issue are to be used to fund a pool or pools and on or before the date of issue, commitments have not been entered into by such initial borrowers to borrow at least 25 percent of the proceeds of such issue.

(4) The term of the issue exceeds 30 years and principal repayments on any loans are to be used to make or finance additional loans.

Paragraphs (2) and (3) apply only if bonds were not issued by the issuer before January 1, 1986, to fund similar governmental bond pools, or if the issuer had established a similar pool or pools before that date, issuance of bonds for such pools during 1986 exceeds 250 percent of the average annual issuance for such pools during calendar years 1983, 1984, and 1985.

For purposes of the special rule on pooled financings, an issue of bonds sold to a securities firm, broker, or other person acting in the capacity of an underwriter or wholesaler is not treated as issued before such bonds have been re-offered to the public (pursuant to final offering materials) and at least 25 percent of such bonds actually have been sold to the public.

[The following colloquy relating to Act Sec. 1301 is drawn from the Congressional Record. The colloquy occurred on the day the conference bill was considered by the Senate. Ed.]

[Senate Floor Explanation]

Mr. DURENBERGER. Section 1301 of the Tax Reform Act of 1986 broadly overhauls and amends section 103 of the Internal Revenue Code of 1954. I would like to seek a clarification from the chairman of the Finance Committee concerning the effect of section 1301, including, but not limited to, section 1314(d), as it relates to section 1316(k) of the bill. Section 1316(k) amends section 1104 of the Mortgage Subsidy Bond Tax Act of 1980, as added by the Tax Reform Act of 1980. It is my understanding that the changes in the law made by section 1301 of the Tax Reform Act of 1986, including, but not limited to section 1314(d), does not apply to section 1316(k). Thus, bonds under section 1316(k) will be subject to the same rules as they would have been had they been issued on August 15, 1986.

Mr. PACKWOOD. The Senator from Minnesota is correct. Congressional Record, p. S 13951 9-27-86.

[The following is from a statement of the Chairman of the House Ways and Means Committee relating to Senate Floor colloquies on the Conference bill. Ed.]

[House Floor Explanation]

I have discussed with Congressman SABO several issues relating to section 103 of the code and the Mortgage Subsidy Bond Tax Act of 1980. We have reached a common understanding which affirms the colloquy between Senator DURENBERGER and Senator PACKWOOD, located on page S13951 of the CONGRESSIONAL RECORD dated September 27, 1986, that bonds issued under section 1316(k) will be subject to the same rules as they would have been had they been issued on August 15, 1986. Congressional Record p. E 3390, 10-2-86.

3. Modification of Treasury Department State and Local Government Series Program

*   *   *   *   *   *

Conference Agreement.—The conference agreement follows the Senate amendment. Thus, notwithstanding any other provisions of law, or any regulation issued pursuant to such a provision, the Treasury Department is directed to expand its SLGS program to permit demand deposits, as well as time deposits for a period specified by the purchaser (as under present law). All obligations issued as part of the revised SLGS program are to be available in the same manner as secondary market transaction, (i.e., for next day settlement unless forward settlement is specified.)

The conferees further intend that the revised SLGS program will be operated at no net cost to the Federal Government. Thus, the Treasury is authorized to charge appropriate fees and/or to establish interest rates on SLGS such as the difference between any investments of the bond proceeds and the rate paid thereon are sufficient (in connection with any fees charged) to defray costs of operating the program.

Finally, the conferees are aware that the Treasury has rigidly applied many of the requirements of the present SLGS program in the past. For example, if SLGS are not purchased on the date specified in the application, Treasury bars the issuer from investing in SLGS for 6 months. The conferees intend that the Treasury apply its regulations under the revised program in the most flexible manner possible, in light of the conferees' intent in adopting this provision (e.g., if inability to settle on a specified date is due to reasonable cause, a delayed closing date, without penalty, should be permitted).

Effective Date.—This provision is effective on the date of enactment. The revised SLGS program is to be in effect on January 1, 1987.

E. Restrictions on Advance Refundings

*   *   *   *   *   *

General rules.—The conference agreement follows the Senate amendment in permitting advance refundings of both governmental bonds and qualified 501(c)(3) bonds and in defining an advance refunding as a refunding where the refunded bonds are not redeemed within 90 days after issuance of the refunding bonds. A technical clarification is provided substituting 180 days for 90 days in the case of refundings that occurred before January 1, 1986.

The conference agreement follows the House bill and the Senate amendment with respect to the technical requirements that are imposed on permitted advance refundings—

(1) Issues that were originally issued before January 1, 1986, may be advance refunded a total of two times. All advance refunding issues that were outstanding on January 1, 1986, or that are issued on or after that date, are counted in determining whether the two-times limit has been reached. (A special transitional exception permits bonds that had been advance refunded two or more times before March 15, 1986, to be advance refunded one additional time after March 14, 1986.)

(2) Issues that are originally issued after December 31, 1985, may be advance refunded a total of one time.

(3) In the case of advance refundings producing a present value debt service savings—

(a) The refunded bonds must be redeemed no later than the first date on which their redemption is not prohibited if the refunded bonds are issued after December 31, 1985; and

(b) The refunded bonds must be redeemed no later than the first date on which they may be redeemed at a premium of 3 percent or less if the refunded bonds were issued before January 1, 1986.

(4) New restrictions on temporary periods when unlimited arbitrage earnings are permitted apply to both the refunded and refunding bonds—

(a) The initial temporary period for advance refunding bonds is limited to 30 days; and

(b) The initial temporary period for refunded bonds terminates no later than the date the advance refunding bonds are issued.

(5) The permitted minor portion that may be invested without regard to arbitrage yield restrictions claimed with respect to the refunded issue must be reduced to an amount no greater than that permitted under the conference agreement when an issue is advance refunded.

(6) As described more fully under the section on the new private activity bond volume limitation, proceeds of an advance refunding issue are subject to the volume limitation to the same extent as if the refunding issue were an original issue.

The conference agreement follows the Senate amendment's prohibition on advance refundings involving the use of a "device" to obtain a material financial advantage based on arbitrage other than savings arising from lower interest rates generally. The conferees do not intend to restrict *per se* so-called "low-to-high" advance refundings occurring to obtain relief from specific covenants included in the refunded bonds or to restructure debt service provided those advance refundings do not additionally involve an abusive device, as described in the Senate amendment, or Treasury regulations and rulings issued pursuant to this provision.

Effective date.—The new restrictions on advance refundings apply to advance refunding bonds issued after—

(1) August 15, 1986, in the case of advance refundings of 501(c)(3) organization bonds, other private activity bonds for which advance refunding is permitted under present law, and governmental bonds originally issued after that date; and

(2) August 31, 1986, in the case of bonds and provisions covered by the Joint Statements, except December 31, 1985, in the case of provisions not included in the Joint Statements (e.g., the new 30-day initial temporary period for advance refunding bonds).

A transitional exception applies to permit advance refundings of certain tax-exempt governmental and section 501(c)(3) organization bonds that may not be issued originally under the conference agreement. These advance refundings generally are subject to the new advance refunding, and certain other, restrictions. In the case of advance refundings permitted under the transitional exception of such bonds (other than bonds for output facilities, as defined under the conference agreement), the requirement that a volume allocation be obtained for the private use portion in excess of $15 million does not apply.

An exception is provided for advance refunding bonds issued under this transitional exception with respect to the general 150 percent limitation on investment in materially higher yielding non-purpose investments in the case of amounts deposited in an advance refunding escrow account. (Amounts invested in such an escrow account are not, however, treated as spent for the governmental purpose of the borrowing until they are used to redeem the refunded bonds; thus, the arbitrage rebate requirement applies to such proceeds, as well as to other proceeds (including transferred proceeds) for which an exception is not specifically provided under the rebate requirement, discussed above.

F. Restrictions on Early Issuance

Present Law.—No specific rules require that bond proceeds be spent within a specified time following issuance; however, issuers are required to proceed with due diligence to realize the governmental purpose of the borrowing to qualify for a temporary period when unlimited arbitrage may be earned.

* * * * * *

Senate Amendment.—No provision.

Conference Agreement.—The conference agreement follows the Senate amendment.

G. Information Reporting Requirement for All Tax-Exempt Bonds

* * * * * *

House Bill.—Information reporting requirements similar to those contained in present law are extended to all tax-exempt bonds.

Senate Amendment.—The Senate amendment is the same as the House bill.

Conference Agreement.—The conference agreement follows the House bill and the Senate amendment with a modification authorizing the Treasury Department to waive loss of tax-exemption on an issue if an information report is filed late and Treasury finds that the late filing is not due to willful neglect.

Effective Date.—This provision applies to bonds issued after December 31, 1986. [Text of bill reads 8-15-86. Ed.] (Bonds presently subject to information reporting requirements are not excused from those requirements by virtue of the December 31, 1986, effective date.)

H. Certain Targeted Transitional Exceptions

The conference agreement follows the House bill and the Senate amendment, with modifications, in providing certain targeted transitional exceptions for specifically described facilities. Each of these targeted transitional exceptions applies only to one described project or issue of bonds or to a limited group of described projects, and each is subject to a maximum dollar amount of bonds. Additionally, these rules generally require that the transitioned bonds be issued before January 1, 1989.

Certain transitional exceptions provided in the Deficit Reduction Act of 1984 are re-enacted by the agreement. These transitional exceptions are those exempting a specifically described project, or a limited group of such projects, from one or more of the provisions of the conference agreement. The agreement further provides that the 1984 Act transitional exceptions re-enacted by the agreement are retained only if the transitioned bonds are issued before January 1, 1990.[52]

The conference agreement also includes a limited exception to the rule that FSLIC- and FDIC-guaranteed bonds issued before the prohibition of such guarantees of tax-exempt bonds may not be refunded. Permitted current refunding under the agreement must satisfy specified requirements rendering them in substance a renegotiation of interest rates.

[**Footnote ¶ 4058 continued**]

(52) Re-enactment of these project-specific transition rules does not change the general prohibition contained in the 1984 Act on refunding certain obligations (e.g., private loan bonds) that may not be originally issued under that Act.

[¶ 4059] SECTION 1303. REPEAL OF PROVISIONS RELATING TO GENERAL STOCK OWNERSHIP CORPORATIONS

(Secs. 1391-1397, 172(b), 3402(r), 1016(a), 6039B of the Code)

[Conference Report]

*   *   *   *   *   *

House Bill.—The GSOC provisions are repealed as deadwood, effective as of January 1, 1984.

Senate Amendment.—The Senate amendment is the same as the House bill.

Conference Agreement.—The conference agreement follows the House bill and the Senate amendment.

[Effective date.—Enactment date. Ed.]

[¶ 4061] Sections 1401 and 1402 REVISION OF GRANTOR TRUST RULES

(Secs. 672, 673, 674, 676, and 677 of the Code)

[Senate Explanation]

*   *   *   *   *   *

Explanation of Provision.—The bill repeals the 10-year exception of present law and replaces that rule with a rule that treats a trust as a grantor trust where there is more than a 5 percent possibility that any of the proscribed powers or interests will become effective in the grantor after the transfer of property to the trust. For this purpose, the possibility that an interest may return to the grantor or his spouse solely under intestacy laws is to be ignored under this provision.

In order to ease administration of this rule, the bill provides an exception under which the grantor is deemed not to have retained a proscribed power or interest if that interest or power can become effective in the grantor only after the death of a lineal descendant of the grantor who also is a beneficiary of that portion of the trust In order for this rule to apply to all or a portion of a trust, the beneficiary whose life is used must have the entire present interest (as defined in sec. 2503(c)) in that trust or trust portion.

The bill also provides that, for purposes of the grantor trust provisions, the grantor is treated as holding any power or interest held by the grantor's spouse if that spouse is living with the grantor. For this purpose, a person is treated as a spouse of the grantor who is living with the grantor if that person and the grantor are eligible to file a joint return with respect to the period in which the transfer is made. The status of a person holding a power or interest as a spouse of the grantor with whom the grantor is living is to be determined at the time of the transfer of the property to the trust.

Effective Date.—The provision applies to transfers in trusts made after March 1, 1986. The bill provides an exception under which the 10-year rule of present law would continue to apply to certain trusts created pursuant to binding property settlements entered into [on or] before March 1, 1986, which required the creation of a trust and the transfer to the trust of a specified sum of money by the grantor.

[¶ 4062] SECTION 1403 TAXABLE YEAR OF TRUSTS TO BE CALENDAR YEAR

(Sec. 645 of the Code)

[Conference Report]

*   *   *   *   *   *

* * * both newly created and existing trusts (but not estates) are required to adopt a calendar year as their taxable year. However, the conference agreement provides an exception under which tax-exempt trusts (described in sec. 501) and wholly charitable trusts (described in sec. 4947(a)(1)) are not required to adopt a calendar year.

Effective date

*   *   *   *   *   *

The change in the taxable year rule is effective with respect to taxable years beginning after December 31, 1986. Distributions of distributable net income during any short taxable year arising from a required change in taxable years are to be included in income of the beneficiary evenly over a 4-year period.

[¶ 4063] SECTION 1404 TRUSTS AND CERTAIN ESTATES TO MAKE ESTIMATED PAYMENTS OF INCOME TAXES

(Secs. 6152 and 6654 of the Code)

[Senate Explanation]

*   *   *   *   *   *

Explanation of Provision.—The bill provides that both new and existing trusts and estates pay estimated tax in the same manner as individuals. In addition, the bill repeals the rules that permit estates to pay their tax over four equal installments.

Effective Date.—The provision is effective for taxable years beginning after December 31, 1986.

[Conference Report]

* * * * * *

The conference agreement follows the Senate amendment * * *.

[¶ 4064] SECTION 1411 UNEARNED INCOME OF CERTAIN MINOR CHILDREN

(Sec. 1 of the Code)

[House Explanation]

* * * * * *

Present Law

In general.—The Federal income tax liability of a minor child having gross income generally is computed in the same manner as that of an adult. Thus, a minor child is allowed a personal exemption ($1,040 for 1985) and the applicable zero bracket amount (ZBA) ($2,390 for a single person for 1985).

Dependency exemption.—*In general.*—Under present law, a taxpayer is allowed a dependency exemption ($1,040 for 1985) for each individual who qualifies as a dependent. Individuals eligible to be claimed as dependents generally include certain family members whose gross income is less than the personal exemption allowance and for whom the taxpayer provided more than half the support.

Special rules for children.—In general, a person with gross income in excess of the personal exemption allowance ($1,040 for 1985) may not be claimed as a dependent on another taxpayer's return, even though the taxpayer satisfies the general support requirement by furnishing over half of the dependent's support for the year. However, parents may claim a full dependency exemption ($1,040 for 1985) for their dependent child with income in excess of that limit if the child (1) is under age 19, or (2) is a full-time student. Thus, two personal exemptions (for 1985, $1,040 each) are available with respect to a minor child—one on the parents' return and one on the child's return.

Zero bracket amount.—Special rules apply for calculating the zero bracket amount (ZBA) of a child eligible to be claimed as a dependent on the parents' return. Although both the parents and the child are entitled to claim a full personal exemption for the child, the child may apply the ZBA only against earned income, if any. Thus, in effect, a child's unearned income (such as dividends and interest) in excess of the personal exemption is fully taxable to the child at the child's marginal tax rate.

[Senate Explanation]

* * * * * *

Explanation of Provision.—The bill establishes special rules for the taxation of income of a minor child. If a minor child has income derived from property transferred from a parent (parental-source unearned income), the bill taxes the parental source unearned income to the child at the parents' marginal tax rate.

* * * * * *

Scope of provision.—Under the bill, the special rules for taxation of a minor child's * * * unearned income apply to any child who has not attained 14 years of age before the close of the taxable year and who has at least one living parent. Children who have attained age 14 are not subject to these special rules.[1]

* * * * * *

The bill provides that, in the case of divorced parents, the parent whose income will be taken into account for purposes of computing the tax on the child's income is the custodial parent of the child. In the case of married individuals filing separately, the income of the parent with the greater taxable income is taken into account. In the case of foster children, the foster parents are the parents whose income will be taken into account for purposes of computing the tax on the foster child's income.

The bill also provides that net parental source unearned income is not to be taken into account by a parent, in computing any deduction or credit that the parent may be entitled to claim. Nonetheless, in determining the additional tax that the parent would pay if the net unearned parental source income were includible into the parent's return, the net parental source unearned income is taken into account in determining the phase-out of the lower bracket of the parent and the phase-out of the personal exemption that the parent may be eligible to claim.[2]

* * * * * * * * * *

[Footnote ¶ 4064]   (1) However, the limitation on the use of the standard deduction, the unavailability of personal exemption, and the availability of the de minimis exception provided in the bill continue to apply to such a child, so long as the child is eligible to be claimed as a dependent by a parent. (See ¶3952, "Rate Structure.")

(2) The bill provides for the phase-out of the 15-percent rate bracket and the personal exemption for taxpayers at high income levels. (See ¶3952. "Rate Structure.")

[Conference Report]

The conference agreement follows the Senate amendment except that the provision is applied to all net unearned income of a child under 14 years of age regardless of the source of the assets creating the child's net unearned income. Net unearned income means unearned income less the sum of $500 and the greater of: (1) $500 of the standard deduction or $500 of itemized deductions or (2) the amount of allowable deductions which are directly connected with the production of the unearned income. The $500 figures are to be adjusted for inflation beginning in 1988. The conferees expect that the Treasury Department will issue regulations providing for the application of these provisions where either the child or the parent is subject to the alternative minimum tax for the year. In addition, where the tax on capital gains of a trust is determined by reference to the income of the parent (under sec. 644 for any year for which the income of that parent's also is determined by reference to that parent, the conferees intend that the tax of the trust be determined before the tax of the child is determined.)

The following examples illustrate the tax consequences of this provision to a dependent child under age 14 in 1988.

Example 1.—If the child has $400 of unearned income and no earned income, the child's standard deduction is $400 which is allocated against the child's unearned income, so that the child has no Federal income, tax liability.

Example 2.—If the child has $900 of unearned income and no earned income, the child's standard deduction is $500 which is allocated against the first $500 of unearned income. The child's net unearned income is $400. Because the child's net unearned income is less than $500, the net earned income is taxed at the child's rates.

Example 3.—If the child has $1,300 of unearned income and no earned income, the child's standard deduction is $500 which is allocated against unearned income. The child has net unearned income equal to $800 of which the first $500 is taxed at the child's rates, and the remaining $300 of unearned income is taxed at the top rate of the parents.

Example 4.—If the child has $700 of earned income and $300 of unearned income, the child's standard deduction is $700 of which $300 is allocated against unearned income and $400 is allocated against earned income. The child has no net unearned income and the remaining $300 of earned income is taxed at the child's rates.

Example 5.—If the child has $800 of earned income and $900 of unearned income, the child's standard deduction is $800 of which $500 is allocated against unearned income and $300 is allocated against earned income. The child has net unearned income of $400. Because net unearned income is less than $500, the child's net unearned income is taxed at the child's rates. The remaining $500 of earned income also is taxed at the child's rates.

Example 6.—Assume the child has $300 of earned income and $1,200 of unearned income, and itemized deductions of $400 (net of the 2-percent floor) which are directly connected with the production of the unearned income. The child has $400 of other deductions. Because of the deductions directly connected with the production of the unearned income ($400) are less than the maximum amount of deductions ($500) which are allocated against unearned income, $500 of the $800 total deductions are allocated against unearned income. Therefore, the child has net unearned income of $700 ($1,200 of unearned income less $500) of which $500 is taxed at the child's rates and $200 is taxed at the parents' rate.

Example 7.—Assume the child has $700 of earned income and $3,000 of unearned income, and itemized deductions of $800 (net of the 2-percent floor) which are directly connected with the production of the unearned income. The child has $200 of other deductions. The entire amount of deductions relating to the production of unearned income is allocated against his unearned income, because this amount ($800) exceeds $500. Therefore, the child has net unearned income equal to $2,200 ($3,000 of unearned income less $800) of which $500 is taxed at child's rates and $1,700 at the parents' top rate. The child has $200 of deductions which is allocated against earned income. The remaining $500 of earned income is taxed at the child's rates.

[Effective Date].—The provision is effective for taxable years beginning after * * * [12-31-86].

[¶ 4065] SECTION 1421 INFORMATION NECESSARY FOR VALID SPECIAL USE VALUATION ELECTION

(Sec. 2032A of the Code)

[Conference Report]

* * * * * *

Senate Amendment.—The Senate amendment provides that estates of individuals dying before January 1, 1986, that substantially complied with the requirements enumerated on the Federal Estate Tax Return (as opposed to Treasury Department regulations) are allowed to perfect defective

elections within 90 days of being notified of errors by the Treasury. Specifically, the March 1982 edition of Form 706, Federal Estate Tax Return, did not specify that the required agreement had to be submitted with the estate tax return. This provision, therefore, permits late filing of the required agreements for estates that used the March 1982 edition of Form 706.

Conference Agreement.—The conference agreement follows the Senate amendment, with a modification adding a targeted transitional exception for the estate of an individual who died on January 30, 1984, and

for whose estate the Federal estate tax return was filed on October 30, 1984.

[¶ 4066] SECTION 1422. GIFT AND ESTATE TAX DEDUCTION FOR CERTAIN CONSERVATION EASEMENT DONATIONS

(Sec. 2055 and 2522 of the Code)

[Conference Report]

Present Law.—A special exception to the general restrictions on tax deductions for charitable contributions of partial interests in property applies in the case of qualified conservation contributions (e.g., easements). (In general, gifts of less than the entire interest in property held by the donor are nondeductible.) To qualify for a gift or estate tax deduction, qualified conservation contributions must satisfy the same requirements, including a conservation purpose requirement, that apply for income tax deductions.

Senate Amendment.—The Senate amendment permits gift or estate tax deductions to be claimed for qualified conservation contributions without regard to whether the contribution satisfies the income tax conservation purpose requirement.

Conference Agreement.—The conference agreement follows the Senate amendment, with a targeted transitional exception deeming certain conservation contributions to the Acadia National Park in Maine to satisfy the conservation purpose requirement.

This provision applies to transfers occuring after December 31, 1986.

[¶ 4067] SECTION 1423. CONVEYANCE OF CERTAIN REAL AND PERSONAL PROPERTY OF DECEDENT TO CHARITABLE FOUNDATION TREATED AS CHARITABLE CONTRIBUTION

[Conference Report]

* * * * * *

Senate Amendment.—The Senate amendment allows an estate tax deduction for certain property transferred by James H.W. Thompson to his nephew who then transferred the property to a charitable foun-

dation pursuant to his uncle's instructions. This property is treated as if it passed directly from Thompson to the charitable foundation.

Conference Agreement.—The conference agreement follows the Senate amendment.

[¶ 4068] SECTIONS 1431-1433. GENERATION-SKIPPING TRANSFERS

[Chapter 13 of the Code]

House Explanation

* * * * * *

Explanation of Provisions

1. Overview

The bill amends the existing generation-skipping transfer tax, which attempts to determine the additional gift or estate tax that would have been paid if property had been transferred directly from one generation to another, to impose a simplified tax determined at a flat rate. The generation-skipping transfer tax is expanded to include direct generation-skipping transfers (e.g., a direct transfer from a grandparent to a grandchild) as well as transfers (subject to tax under the existing tax) in which benefits are "shared" by beneficiaries in more than one younger generation.

Transfers of up to $1 million per grantor are exempt from tax. Additional exemptions are provided for certain transfers that are not subject to gift tax and for direct transfers to grandchildren of the transferor if the aggregate amount of such transfers does not exceed $2 million per grandchild.

2. Imposition of tax

As under present law, a generation-skipping transfer is defined as a transfer to a beneficiary at least two generations younger than the transferor. Thus, only transfers to grandchildren or younger generations are subject to tax. Generation-skipping transfers are subject to tax whether in trust, pursuant to an arrangement similar to a trust, or outright.

In general, the bill retains the present-law rules on generation assignment, except that lineal descendants of the grandparents of the transferor's spouse also are assigned to generations on a basis like that for such decendants of the transferor.

Taxable events.—A generation-skipping transfer tax is imposed on the occurrence of any one of three events—a *taxable distribution, a taxable termination, or a direct skip.*

The first two events generally involve transfers that are taxable under present law. A *taxable distribution* occurs upon distribution of property to a generation-skipping beneficiary (e.g., a grandchild). A *taxable termination* occurs upon the expiration of an interest in a trust if, after that termination, all interests in the trust are held by generation-skipping beneficiaries. Persons holding interests in property are defined to include only those persons having a current right to property (or income therefrom) or persons who are current permissible recipients of the property (or income therefrom). For example, a person having an income interest for life or a holder of a general power of appointment is treated as having an interest in property.

A *direct skip* occurs upon an outright transfer for the benefit of a person at least two generations below the transferor or a transfer of property to a trust for one or more such beneficiaries. As described in the *Overview*, an example of a direct skip is a gift from a grandparent to his or her grandchild.

Effect of disclaimers.—A disclaimer that results in property passing to a person at least two generations below that of the original transferor results in imposition of the generation-skipping transfer tax. For example, if a child of a decedent makes a qualified disclaimer, and, under local law, the disclaimed property passes to the grandchildren of the decedent, a generation-skipping transfer tax is imposed on the transfer (in addition to any estate tax to which the transfer is subject). Under the general source of tax rule applicable to the transfer taxes, the disclaimed property, rather than the decedent's estate generally, is primarily liable for payment of the generation-skipping transfer tax.

Tax on income distributions.—Unlike present law, the bill provides that generation-skipping distributions from a trust are subject to tax whether the distributions carry out trust income or trust corpus. However, an income tax deduction is allowed to the recipient for the generation-skipping transfer tax imposed on the distribution.

Tax on trusts providing for generation-skipping transfers to more than one younger generation.—A single trust may provide for transfers to more than one generation of generation-skipping beneficiaries. For example, a trust may provide for income payments to the grantor's child for life, then for such payments to the grantor's grandchild, and finally for distribution of the trust property to the grantor's great-grandchild. Were such property left outright to each such generation, the property would be subject to gift or estate tax a total of three times. Under the bill, the property likewise is subject to transfer tax a total of three times—gift or estate tax on the original transfer and generation-skipping transfer tax on the transfers to the grandchild and the great-grandchild.

3. Exemptions from tax

$1 million exemption.—The bill provides an exemption of up to $1 million for each person making generation-skipping transfers. In the case of transfers by a married individual, the individual and his or her spouse may elect to treat the transfer as made one half by each spouse. In addition, an individual may allocate all or a portion of his or her specific exemption to property with respect to which a generation-skipping trans

fer will occur upon its disposition by (or on the death of) the transferor's spouse as a result of an election to treat that property as qualified terminable interest property (QTIP property). (*See*, secs. 2056(b)(7) and 2523(f)). Once a transfer, or portion of a transfer, is designated as exempt, all subsequent appreciation in value of the exempt property also is exempt from generation-skipping transfer tax.

The operation of the specific exemption may be illustrated by the following example. Assume a grantor transfers $1 million in trust for the benefit of his or her children and grandchildren. If the grantor allocates $1 million of exemption to the trust, no part of the trust will ever be subject to generation-skipping transfer tax—even if the value of the trust property appreciates in subsequent years to $10 million or more. On the other hand, if the grantor allocates only $500,000 of exemption to the trust, one-half of all distributions to grandchildren will be subject to tax and one-half of the trust property will be subject to tax on termination of the children's interest. If, after creation of the trust, the grantor allocates an additional $250,000 of exemption to the trust, the exempt portion of trust will be redetermined, based upon the values of the trust property at that time. This new inclusion ratio applies to future distributions and terminations, but generally does not change the tax treatment of any past events.

Exemption for nontaxable gifts.—The generation-skipping transfer tax does not apply to any *inter vivos* transfer which is exempt from gift tax pursuant to either the $10,000 annual exclusion or the special exclusion for certain tuition and medical expense payments.

Special exemption for certain direct skips to grandchildren.—A special exemption from the generation-skipping transfer tax is provided for certain direct skips (either in trust or otherwise) to grandchildren of the grantor. For each grantor, this special exemption is limited to $2 million per grandchild. As is true with taxable generation-skipping transfers and taxable gifts, married individuals may elect to treat these exempt transfers as made one-half by each spouse.

Special exemption for certain other transfers to grandchildren.—The bill also provides a special rule on generation assignment for grandchildren of the grantor when a grandchild's parent who is a lineal descendant of the grantor is deceased. In such a case, the grandchild and all succeeding lineal descendants of the grandchild are "moved up" a generation. Thus, transfers to such grandchild are not taxed as generation-skipping transfers.

4. Computation of tax

Rate of tax.—The rate of tax on generation-skipping transfers is equal to the maximum gift and estate tax rate. Thus, the tax rate is 55 percent until 1988, when it is scheduled to decline to 50 percent.

Tax base and payment of tax.—The tax base and method of paying the generation-skipping transfer tax generally parallels the method applicable to the most closely analogous transfer subject to gift or estate tax. Generation-skipping transfers, therefore, are taxed as follows:

Taxable distributions.—The amount subject to tax is the amount received by the transferee (i.e., the tax is imposed on a "tax-inclusive" basis). The transferee pays the tax on a taxable distribution. (If a trustee pays any amount of the tax, the trustee is treated as making an additional taxable distribution of that amount.)

Taxable terminations.—The amount subject to tax is the value of the property in which the interest terminates (i.e., the tax is imposed on a "tax-inclusive" basis). The trustee pays the tax on a taxable termination.

Direct skips.—The amount subject to tax is the value of the property received by the transferee (i.e., the tax is imposed on a "tax-exclusive" basis). The person making the transfer pays the tax on a direct skip.

Credit for State taxes.—A credit not exceeding five percent of the amended Federal tax is allowed for generation-skipping transfer tax imposed by a State with respect to taxable transfers occurring by reason of death.

5. Coordination with other provisions

The bill also includes several provisions coordinating the generation-skipping transfer tax with the gift and estate taxes. The Code provisions governing administration of the gift and estate taxes also apply to the amended generation-skipping transfer tax. Estate tax rules apply to generation-skipping transfers occurring as a result of death, and gift tax rules apply in other cases.

In addition to any adjustment to basis received under the gift or estate tax basis provisions, the basis of property subject to the amended generation-skipping transfer tax generally is increased by the amount of that tax attributable to the excess of the property's value over the transferor's basis. In the case of taxable terminations occurring as a result of death, a step-up in basis like that provided under the estate tax (sec. 1014) is provided.

Property transferred in a direct skip occurring as a result of death has the same value for purposes of the generation-skipping transfer tax as the property has for estate tax purposes. Thus, if the transferor's estate elects the alternate valuation date or the current use valuation provision, the value under those provisions is used in determining the generation-skipping transfer tax. In addition, even if an estate does not elect the alternate valuation date, an election may be made to value any property transferred in a taxable distribution or a taxable termination on the alternate valuation date if the distribution or termination occurs as a result of death and the requirements of that provision are satisfied.

The special rules under which estate tax attributable to interests in certain closely held businesses may be paid in installments also apply to direct skips occurring as a result of death.

The provision permitting tax-free redemptions of stock to pay estate tax is amended to permit those redemptions to pay generation-skipping transfer tax in the case of such transfers occurring as a result of death.

Effective Dates.—The amended generation-skipping transfer tax applies to transfers after the date of enactment, subject to the following exceptions:

(1) Inter vivos transfers occurring after September 25, 1985, are subject to the amended tax;

(2) Transfers from trusts that were irrevocable before September 26, 1985, are exempt to the extent that the transfers are not attributable to additions to the trust corpus occurring after that date; and

(3) Transfers pursuant to wills in existence before September 26, 1985, are not subject to tax if the decedent was incompetent on that date and at all times thereafter until death.

The existing generation-skipping transfer tax is repealed, retroactive to June 11, 1976.

* * * * * *

[Conference Report]

* * * * * *

The conference agreement follows the House bill, with a modification providing that the special $2 million per grandchild exemption does not apply to transfers made after December 31, 1989.

[Effective dates.—] A second modification provides that an election may be made to treat *inter vivos* and testamentary contingent transfers in trust for the benefit of a grandchild as direct skips if (1) the transfers occur before date of enactment, and (2) the transfers would be direct skips except for the fact that the trust instrument provides that, if the grandchild dies before vesting of the interest transferred, the interest is transferred to the grandchild's heirs (rather than the grandchild's estate). Transfers treated as direct skips as a result of this election are subject to Federal gift and estate tax on the grandchild's death in the same manner as if the contingent gift over had been to the grandchild's estate.

A third modification exempts from the revised generation-skipping transfer tax testamentary direct skips occurring under wills executed before the date of enactment if the testator dies before January 1, 1987.

The conferees adopted these delays in effective dates to permit a reasonable period for individuals to re-execute their wills to conform to the extension of GST tax to direct skips. No comparable period is provided for generation-sharing transfers because those transfers are subject to GST tax under present law.

Act § 1431-1433 ¶ 4068

[The following colloquy is drawn from the Congressional Record. The colloquy occurred on the day the Conference bill was considered by the House. Ed.]

[House Floor Explanation]

I have discussed with Congressman MIKE ANDREWS several issues relating to the effective date of the generation-skipping transfer tax provisions of the legislation. We have reached a common understanding regarding the following specific issue:

With respect to the new generation-skipping transfer tax, the grandfather provision of the prior law was intended to apply to:

* * * a trust which includes a limited power of appointment, so long as the exercise of the power (including the creation of a trust) cannot result in the creation of an interest which postpones, or a new power which can be validly exercised so as to postpone, the vesting of any estate or interest in the trust property for a period ascertainable without regard to the date of the creation of the trust. (S. Rept. No. 1236, 94th Congress, 2d sess. 621).

The concepts of this legislative history have been embodied in section 26.2601-1(e)(3) of the Treasury Regulations.

The same result would obtain under the new generation-skipping tax provisions.

As in the case of the old provision, the new provision will not apply to the exercise of a limited power of appointment under an otherwise grandfathered trust or to trusts to which the trust property is appointed provided that such exercise cannot postpone vesting of any estate or interest in the trust property for a period ascertainable without regard to the date of the creation of the trust. Congressional Record, p. H 8362, 9-25-86.

[The following colloquy is drawn from the Congressional Record. The colloquy occurred on the day the Conference bill was considered by the Senate. Ed.]

[Senate Floor Explanation]

Mr. BENTSEN. Mr. President, with respect to the new generation-skipping transfer tax, the grandfather provision of the prior law was intended to apply to:

A trust which includes a limited power of appointment, so long as the exercise of the power (including the creation of a trust) cannot result in the creation of an interest which postpones, or a new power which can be validly exercised so as to postpone, the vesting of any estate or interest in the trust property for a period ascertainable without regard to the date of the creation of the trust. S. Rep. No. 1236, 94th Cong. 2nd Sess. 621.

The concepts of this legislation history have been embodied in Treasury Regulation, section 26.2601-1(e)(3).

Would the chairman confirm my understanding that the same result would obtain under the new generation-skipping tax provisions.

Mr. PACKWOOD. The understanding of the Senator from Texas is correct. As in the case of the old provision, the new provision will not apply to the exercise of a limited power of appointment under an otherwise grandfathered trust or to trusts to which the trust property is appointed provided that such exercise cannot postpone vesting of any estate or interest in the trust property for a period ascertainable without regard to the date of the creation of the original trust.

Mr. BENTSEN. I thank the chairman. Congressional Record, p. S 13952, 9-27-86.

[¶ 4071] SECTION 1501. PENALTY FOR FAILURE TO FILE INFORMATION RETURNS OR STATEMENTS

(New Secs. 6721, 6722, 6723, and 6724, and Secs. 6041, 6042, 6044, 6045, 6049, 6050A, 6050B, 6050E-6050I, 6050K, 6052, 6652 6676, and 6678 of the Code)

[House Explanation]

* * * * * *

* * *.—The bill consolidates the penalty for failure to file an information return with the IRS with the penalty for failure to supply a copy of that information return to the taxpayer in the same subchapter of the Code. The general level of each of these penalties remains at $50 for each failure. The maximum penalty is raised from $50,000 to $100,000 for each category of failure.[1] Thus, a maximum penalty of $100,000 applies to failure to file information returns with the IRS, and another maximum penalty of $100,000 applies to failure to supply copies of information returns to taxpayers.

The bill imposes these penalties without limits where the failure to file information returns with the IRS is due to intentional disregard of the filing requirement, which also occurs under present law. The bill also provides, as does present law, generally higher penalties for each failure to file where the failure to file is due to intentional disregard. The bill modifies the levels of these higher penalties for certain specified failures. Thus, the penalty for failure to report cash transactions that exceed $10,000[2] is increased to 10 percent of the amount that should have been reported. Also, the penalty for failure to report exchanges of certain partnership interests or failure to report certain dispositions of donated property is 5 percent of the amount that should have been reported.

These provisions have generally been redrafted to improve their comprehensibility and administrability. In light of this redraft-

---

[Footnote ¶ 4071]   (1) The bill also raises from $50,000 to $100,000 the maximum penalty for failure to supply taxpayer identification numbers (sec. 6676).

(2) *See* Code sec. 6050I.

ing, the bill repeals the existing penalty for failure to furnish an information return to the IRS (sec. 6652(a)) and the existing penalty for failure to supply a copy of the information return to the taxpayer (sec. 6678).

The bill also adds to the Code a new penalty for failure to include correct information either on an information return filed with the IRS or on the copy of that information return supplies to the taxpayer. This new penalty applies to both an omission of information or an inclusion of incorrect information. The amount of the penalty is $5 for each information return or copy for the taxpayer, up to a maximum of $20,000 in any calendar year [but see Senate Explanation below].

This new penalty does not apply to an information return if a penalty for failure to supply a correct taxpayer identification number has been imposed with respect to that information return. Thus, if the person filing an information return is subject to a penalty under section 6676 for including an incorrect social security number on the information return, this new penalty is not imposed with respect to that information return.

This new penalty is intended to provide to persons filing information returns an incentive both to file accurate and complete information returns initially and to correct as rapidly as possible any incorrect information returns that may have been filed. If a person files what purports to be an information return, but which contains so many inaccuracies or omissions that the utility of the document is minimized or eliminated, the IRS may under circumstances such as these (as it does under present law) impose the penalty for failure to file an information return, rather than this new penalty for filing an information return that includes inaccurate or incomplete information.

As under present law, there is an exception from these penalties if the failure to file an information return with the IRS or to provide a copy to the taxpayer or to include correct information on either of those returns is due to reasonable cause and not to willful neglect. Thus, under this standard, if a person required to file fails to do so because of negligence or without reasonable cause, that person would be subject to these penalties. The bill retains the higher standards and special rules of present law that apply to failures with respect to interest or dividend returns or statements.

The bill also clarifies the provisions relating to furnishing a written statement to the taxpayer of a number of the substantive information reporting provisions of the Code. Under present law, a number of these provisions are technically effective only if the person required to supply the copy to the taxpayer has actually provided the information return to the IRS. These provisions have

been redrafted so that the requirement to supply a copy of the information return to the taxpayer is triggered when there is an obligation to file (instead of the actual filing of) an information return with the IRS.

Effective Date.—

[Conference Report]

Senate Amendment.—The Senate amendment is the same as the House bill, except that the Senate amendment also provides that the $20,000 maximum penalty for filing inaccurate disregard. The Senate amendment is effective for information returns the due date of which (determined without regard to extensions) is after December 31, 1986.

Conference Agreement.—The conference agreement follows the Senate amendment, except that certain modifications of the information return provisions for interest, dividends, and patronage dividends are effective on the date of enactment (*see* Modification of Separate Mailing Requirement for Certain Information Reports, * * *, below).

* * * * * *

Modification of Separate Mailing Requirement for Certain Information Reports

* * * * * *

Senate Amendment.—The Senate amendment also provides that payors of interest, dividends, patronage dividends, and royalty payments [but see Conference Agreement below] must provide copies of information returns to the taxpayer either in person (as is provided under present law) or in a statement mailing sent by first-class mail. The only enclosures that can be made with a statement mailing are: (1) a check, (2) a letter explaining why no check is enclosed (such as, for example, because a dividend has not been declared payable), or (3) a statement of the taxpayer's specific account with the payor (such as a year end summary of the taxpayer's transactions with the payor).[6] The envelope must state on the outside "Important Tax Return Document Enclosed." In addition, each enclosure (i.e. the check, the letter, or the account statement) must state "Important Tax Return Document Enclosed." A mailing is not a statement mailing if it encloses any other material such as advertising, promotional material, or a quarterly or annual report.

[Conference Agreement].—The conference agreement follows the Senate amendment, except that the provision is effective for information returns with respect to interest, dividends, and patronage dividends * * * [only (not royalty payments)]. IRS regulations permit these three types of information returns to be mailed prior to December 31 under certain conditions. Payors satisfying

---

[**Footnote ¶ 4071 continued**]

(6) These are in addition to the other enclosures, such as other information reports or tax forms, that the IRS currently permits to be enclosed.

those conditions will be able to take advantage of this liberalized enclosure rule for those three types of information returns that are mailed after the date of enactment.

* * * * * *

* * * * * *

Effective Date.—The provision is effective for information returns the due date of which (determined without regard to extensions) is after December 31, 1986. [The information return provisions for interest, dividends, and patronage dividends are effective on the date of enactment. Ed.]

[¶ 4072] SECTION 1502. INCREASE IN PENALTY FOR FAILURE TO PAY TAX

(Sec. 6651 of the Code)

[House Explanation]

* * * * * *

Explanation of Provision.—The bill modifies the penalty for failure to pay taxes that exists in present law by increasing in specified situations the amount of that penalty from one-half of one percent per month to one percent per month. This increase occurs after the IRS notifies the taxpayer that the IRS will levy upon the assets of the taxpayer. The IRS can do this in either of two ways. The most common method is that the IRS sends to the taxpayer a notice of intention to levy; this notice must be sent out at least 10 days before the levy occurs (sec. 6331(d)). In these circumstances, the increase in the penalty occurs at the start of the month following the month in which the 10-day period expires. The second method may be used when the IRS finds that the collection of the tax is in jeopardy. If this occurs, the IRS may make notice and demand for immediate payment of the tax, and, if the tax is not paid, the IRS may levy upon the assets of the taxpayer without regard to the 10-day requirement (sec. 6331(a)). Under this second method, the IRS makes notice and demand for immediate payment either in person or by mail. In these circumstances, the increase in the penalty occurs at the start of the month following the month in which notice and demand is made.

This increase in the rate of this penalty generally will occur after the IRS has made repeated efforts to contact the taxpayer by mail.[3] During the period that these initial mailings are made, the penalty for failure to pay taxes will remain at one-half of one percent. When the cycle of mailings is completed and the tax has not yet been paid, the IRS must switch to methods of collecting the tax that generally are much more expensive, such as telephoning or visiting the taxpayer. This is the point at which generally the penalty increases to one percent per month.

The bill also improves the coordination of the penalty for failure to pay taxes with the penalty for failure to file a tax return. Under present law, a taxpayer who does not file his tax return on time may be liable for a smaller total penalty (consisting of both the failure to file penalty and the failure to pay penalty) if the taxpayer never files a return than if the taxpayer files the return late. This occurs because the special rules of section 6651(c)(1)(B) in effect reduce the failure to pay penalty by the failure to file penalty. The committee views this result as anomalous and, accordingly, repeals this special offset rule.

* * * * * *

* * * * * *

Effective Date.—The increase in the penalty for failure to pay taxes (as well as the repeal of the special coordination rule of section 6651(c)(1)(B)) is effective for amounts assessed after December 31, 1986, regardless of when the failure to pay began.

[¶ 4073] SECTION 1503. AMENDMENTS TO PENALTY FOR NEGLIGENCE AND FRAUD

(Sec. 6653 of the Code)

(House Explanation)

* * * * * *

Explanation of Provision.—*Negligence.*—The bill expands the scope of the [5%] negligence penalty by making it applicable to all taxes under the Code. The bill also generally redrafts the negligence penalty to make it clearer and more comprehensible. One element of that

redrafting involves the provision of a definition of negligence. The bill includes within the scope of the definition of negligence both any failure to make a reasonable attempt to comply with the provisions of the Code as well as any careless, reckless, or intentional disregard of rules or regulations. The bill does not, however, limit the definition of negligence to these items only. Thus, all behavior that is considered negligent under present law will remain within the scope of

---

[Footnote ¶ 4072] (3) Generally, the IRS sends taxpayers a series of four or five letters demanding payment before a levy is made. These letters will go out over a period of approximately six months. The IRS will, however, truncate the number of letters and the time between them for reasons such as concern that delay will jeopardize collection.

this negligence penalty. Also, any behavior that is considered negligent by the courts but that is not specifically included within this definition is also subject to this penalty.

The bill also expands the scope of the special negligence penalty that is currently applicable to failures to include in income interest and dividends shown on an information return. The bill expands this provision so that it is applicable to failures to show properly on the taxpayer's tax return any amount that is shown on any information return. This penalty applies to the same information returns that are subject to the penalties for failure to provide information returns. Thus, if a taxpayer fails to show properly on the taxpayer's tax return any amount that is shown on an information return, the taxpayer's failure is treated as negligence in the absence of clear and convincing evidence to the contrary.

Fraud.—The bill modifies the fraud penalty by increasing the rate of the penalty but at the same time narrowing its scope. First, the bill increases the rate of the basic fraud penalty from 50 to 75 percent. (The time-sensitive component of the fraud penalty is not altered.) Second, the scope of the fraud penalty is reduced so that in effect it applies only to the amount of the underpayment attributable to fraud. The bill does this by

providing that, once the IRS has established that any portion of an underpayment is attributable to fraud, the entire underpayment is treated as attributable to fraud, except to the extent that the taxpayer establishes that any portion of the underpayment is not attributable to fraud. This is done so that, once the IRS has initially established that fraud occurred, the burden of proof shifts to the taxpayer to establish the portion of the underpayment that is not attributable to fraud. The committee believes that this rule is appropriate in that these facts are generally within the taxpayer's control. It is nonetheless the intention of the committee that the fraud penalty apply only to the portion of the underpayment attributable to fraud.

Interaction of negligence and fraud penalties.—If an underpayment of tax is partially attributable to negligence and partially attributable to fraud, the negligence penalty (which generally applies to the entire underpayment of tax) does not apply to any portion of the underpayment with respect to which a fraud penalty is imposed.

Effective Date.—The amendments to the negligence and fraud penalties are applicable to returns the due date of which (determined without regard to extensions) is after December 31, * * * [1986].

[¶ 4074] SECTION 1504. INCREASE IN PENALTY FOR SUBSTANTIAL UNDERSTATEMENT OF LIABILITY

(Sec. 6661 of the Code)

[Senate Explanation]

* * * * * *

Explanation of Provision.—The bill increases the addition to tax for a substantial understatement of tax liability from 10 to 20

percent of the amount of the underpayment of tax attributable to the understatement.

Effective Date.—The increase in this addition to tax is applicable to returns the due date of which (determined without regard to extensions) is after December 31, 1986.

[¶ 4075] SECTION 1511. DIFFERENTIAL INTEREST RATE

(Sec. 6621 of the Code)

[Senate Explanation]

* * * * * *

Explanation of Provision.—The bill provides that the interest rate that Treasury pays to taxpayers on overpayments is the Federal short-term rate plus 2 percentage points. The bill also provides that the interest rate that taxpayers pay to the Treasury on underpayments is the Federal short-term rate plus 8 percentage points. The rates are rounded to the nearest full percentage.

The interest rates are to be adjusted quarterly. The rates are determined during the first month of a calendar quarter, and become effective for the following calendar quarter. Thus, for example, the rates that are determined during January are effective for the following April through June. This reduces by one month (from three months to two) the lag that exists in present law

between the determination of the interest rate and the date it becomes effective.

The interest rates are determined by the Secretary based on the average market yield on outstanding marketable obligations of the United States with remaining periods to maturity of three years or less. This is the mechanism for determining short-term Federal rates, which are used to test the adequacy of interest in certain debt instruments issued for property and certain other obligations (see sec. 1274(d)).

Taxpayers subject to differential interest rates may have an underpayment for a type of tax in one taxable year and an overpayment for the same type of tax in another taxable year. The IRS requires substantial lead time to develop the data processing capability to net such underpayments and overpayments in applying differential interest rates. The bill, therefore, provides that the Secretary of the Treasury may prescribe regulations providing for netting of tax underpayments and overpayments through the period ending three years after the date of enactment of the bill. By that date, the committee expects that the IRS will have

implemented computerized netting procedures.

Effective date. This provision is effective for purposes of determining interest for periods after 12-31-86.

* * * * * *

[¶4076] SECTION 1512. INTEREST ON ACCUMULATED EARNINGS TAX TO ACCRUE BEGINNING ON DATE RETURN IS DUE

(Sec. 6601(b) of the Code)

[House Explanation]

* * * * * *

Explanation of Provision.—The bill provides that interest is imposed on underpayments of the accumulated earnings tax from the due date (without regard to extensions) of

the income tax return for the year the tax is initially imposed.

Effective date.—This provision is effective for returns that are due (without regard to extensions) after December 31, [1985].
* * *

* * * * *

[¶4077] SECTION 1521. REQUIREMENT OF REPORTING FOR REAL ESTATE TRANSACTIONS

(Sec. 6045 of the Code)

[House Explanation]

* * * * * *

Explanation of Provision.—The bill requires that real estate transactions be reported. The reporting is to be done by the settlement attorney or other stakeholder. This would generally be the person responsible for closing the transaction. Thus, in some localities the stakeholder could include either a title insurance company or a bank. If there is no stakeholder in a transaction, the reporting is to be done by the person designated in Treasury regulations. The committee anticipates that this reporting will be done on a Form 1099, similar to that required for other transactions effected by brokers. The committee also anticipates that the rules requiring that information returns from brokers be filed on magnetic media (see sec. 6011(e)) will encompass these information returns on real estate.

[Senate Explanation]

* * * * * *

Explanation of Provision.—The bill requires that real estate transactions be reported. The seller's real estate broker (including a representative or agent) is the first person responsible to do the information reporting. If there is no seller's real estate broker, then the reporting is to be done by the buyer's real estate broker (including a representative or agent). If there is no buyer's real estate broker, then the reporting is to be done by the mortgage lender. If there is more than one mortgage lender, the reporting is to be done by the primary mortgage lender. If there is no mortgage lender, the reporting is to be done by the title company. If there is no title company, the reporting is to be done by the settlement attorney or other person responsible for closing the transaction. If there is no settlement attorney, the reporting is to

be done in accordance with regulations to be prescribed by the Treasury.

The committee anticipates that this reporting will be done on a Form 1099, similar to that required for other transactions effected by brokers. The committee also anticipates that the rules requiring that information returns from brokers be filed on magnetic media (see sec. 6011(e)) will encompass these information returns on real estate. Because the provision is drafted so that reporting on real estate transactions is done under the general information reporting requirements relating to brokers (sec. 6045(a) and (b)), all penalties and related provisions that apply to the general broker reporting requirements also apply to reporting on real estate transactions.

The bill provides that real estate transactions will be subject to backup withholding (sec. 3406) only to the extent required by Treasury regulations. The committee expects Treasury to provide taxpayers with guidance as to how backup withholding is to be implemented with respect to real estate transactions.

[The Senate Finance Committee version of the bill was amended on the Floor of the Senate. The following explanation is drawn from the Congressional Record. Ed.]

[Senate Floor Explanation]

* * * * * *

* * * Mr. Humphrey. Mr. President, this amendment has been discussed with managers on both sides of the aisle and it has been cleared on both sides of the aisle.

Mr. President, essentially the amendment would relieve realtors of responsibility which the bill places on them to report the sales transactions involving real property. Both sides have agreed to accept the amendment, I do not think further debate is necessary.

Mr. President, I move adoption of the amendment.

The PRESIDING OFFICER. Is there further debate? If not, the question is on agreeing to the amendment.

The amendment (No. 2132) was agreed to.

MR. HUMPHREY. Mr. President, I move to reconsider the vote by which the amendment was agreed to. * * * Congressional Record, p. S-7969, 6-19-86.

Effective Date.—The provision is effective for real estate transactions with respect to which closing on the contract occurs on or after January 1, 1987. Real estate transactions on or after that date must be reported without regard as to whether the Treasury has issued regulations under section 6045(a) requiring that a return be filed. Thus, this provision (unlike the general broker reporting requirements of section 6045) is effective in the absence of implementing regulations. The committee expects that the IRS will provide taxpayers with timely guidance as to how to comply with the requirements of this provision.

[Conference Report]

* * * * * *

Conference Agreement.—The conference agreement follows the House bill and the Senate amendment, with modifications. The conference agreement provides that the primary responsibility for reporting is on the person responsible for closing the transaction, including any title company or attorney who closes the transaction. This is generally the person conducting the settlement. Treasury may issue regulations specifying who is the person responsible for closing the transaction, because it may not be clear which of several persons is the one responsible for closing the transaction. (These regulations need not rely upon the presence or absence of a legal obligation at closing.) Thus, Treasury may provide uniform rules to determine which of the persons involved with the closing is the one with primary responsibility for the information reporting.

If there is no person responsible for closing the transaction, the reporting must be done by the mortgage lender. If there is no mortgage lender, the reporting must be done by the seller's broker. If there is no seller's broker, the reporting must be done by the buyer's broker. If there is no buyer's broker, the reporting is to be done in accordance with regulations to be prescribed by the Secretary.

The Secretary is to provide guidance to taxpayers on how this information reporting is to be accomplished well before the effective date of this provision. The Secretary should provide guidance as to what real estate transactions are subject to information reporting. The Secretary may also exclude from information reporting certain types of real estate transactions where information reporting on those transactions would not be useful. Information reporting is not required on refinancings of real estate, unless the Secretary otherwise provides. The Secretary should also provide guidance as to the gross proceeds required to be reported.

The conferees anticipate that this information reporting will be done on a Form 1099, similar to that required for other transactions effected by brokers. The conferees also anticipate that the rules requiring that information returns from brokers be filed on magnetic media (see sec. 6011(e)) will encompass these information returns on real estate. Thus, all the information returns required to be filed by one entity would generally be filed together in one magnetic media filing. Because the provision is drafted so that mandatory reporting on real estate transactions is done under the general information reporting requirements relating to brokers (sec. 6045(a) and (b)), all penalties and related provisions that apply to the general broker reporting requirements also apply to reporting on real estate transactions.

[Effective date.—] The provision is effective for real estate transactions with respect to which closing on the contract occurs on or after January 1, 1987.

[¶ 4078] SECTION 1522. INFORMATION REPORTING ON PERSONS RECEIVING CONTRACTS FROM CERTAIN FEDERAL AGENCIES

(Sec. 6050M of the Code)

[Senate Explanation]

Explanation of Provision.—The bill requires the head of Federal executive agencies to file an information return indicating the name, address, and taxpayer identification number (TIN) of each person with which the agency enters into a contract. The Secretary of the Treasury has the authority to require that the returns be in such form and be made at such time as is necessary to make the return useful as a source of information for collection purposes. Thus, it would be appropriate to require that these information returns be filed within a certain time period (such as 30 days) of signing the contract, rather than at the end of the calendar year.

The Secretary is given the authority both to establish minimum amounts for which no reporting is necessary as well as to extend the reporting requirements to Federal license grantors and subcontractors of Federal contracts.

In some instances, several corporations, each with its own TIN, file one consolidated return. The Secretary has the authority to require that the information returns include the corporation's own TIN, as well as the TIN under which it files the consolidated return, so that the matching of Federal contracts with delinquent tax liability can be facilitated.

The new provision does not enlarge the collection procedures now available to the

Service. Rather, these new returns will provide the IRS with a possible source of collection in the event taxes are unpaid.

Effective Date.—This provision is effective on January 1, 1987. Thus, all contracts signed on or after that date are subject to information reporting. In addition, all contracts signed prior to that date are subject to information reporting if they are still in effect on that date.

[¶ 4079] SECTION 1523. RETURNS REGARDING PAYMENTS OF ROYALTIES

(Sec. 6050N of the Code)

[Conference Report]

Explanation of Provisions.—The Senate amendment includes a new provision of the Code that requires that persons who make payments of royalties aggregating $10 or more to any other person in a calendar year must provide an information report on the royalty payments to the IRS. A copy of this information report must be supplied to the taxpayer. If a person makes payments to a nominee, the nominee must report the information to the taxpayer and to the IRS, as required in Treasury forms or regulations. Examples of royalty payments required to be reported under this provision include royalty payments with respect to the right to exploit natural resources, such as oil, gas, coal, timber, sand, gravel, and other mineral interests, as well as royalty payments for the right to exploit intangible property, such as copyrights, trade names, trademarks, franchises, books and other literary compositions, musical compositions, artistic works, secret processes or formulas, and patents.

The generally applicable rules for information returns for payments of interest and dividends apply to this provision. Thus, the information report to the taxpayer must be provided by the end of January and the report to the IRS must be provided by the end of February of the year following the year in which the payments were made. Payors filing large numbers of these reports with the IRS are subject to the general magnetic media filing requirements of section 6011(e)(1). If the payee does not furnish the payor with the payee's taxpayer identification number (for individuals, the social security number), the royalty payments generally are subject to backup withholding.

[Effective Date.—] This provision is effective for royalty payments made after December 31, 1986.

[¶ 4080] SECTION 1524. TINS CLAIMED ON TAX RETURNS REQUIRED FOR DEPENDENTS

(Sec. 6109 of the Code)

[Conference Report]

* * * * * *

Senate Amendment.—A taxpayer claiming a dependent who is at least 5 years old must report the taxpayer identification number of that dependent on that tax return. This provision is effective for returns due on or after January 1, 1987 (without regard to extensions).

Conference Agreement.—The conference agreement follows the Senate amendment, effective for returns due * * * [after 12-31-87] (without regard to extensions). The conferees have delayed the effective date for one year so that taxpayers may apply for and receive TINs for their dependents who do not have them well in advance of the due date of the returns on which the TINs must be provided. In addition, this delay will provide sufficient time for the IRS and the Social Security Administration to publicize this new requirement extensively.

The penalty for failing to include the TIN of a dependent (or for including an incorrect TIN) is $5 per TIN per return. In addition,

the IRS may continue its current practice of denying any deduction for a dependent if it cannot be established that it is proper to claim that dependent on the tax return.

The conferees note that certain taxpayers, because of their religious beliefs, are exempted from the social security self-employment taxes (sec. 1402(g)). The conferees intend that these taxpayers and their dependents who currently acquire their TINs from the IRS continue to be permitted to do so. It is the intent of the conferees that these taxpayers continue to be exempted from the general requirement of obtaining a social security number from the Social Security Administration. Others of these taxpayers obtain their TINs under special procedures with the Social Security Administration. The conferees intend that these procedures continue to be available to these taxpayers.

Additionally, the IRS may continue its current administrative practice of directly providing TINs for nonresident aliens, rather than requiring that nonresident aliens obtain their TINs from the Social Security Administration.

[¶ 4081]   SECTION 1525. TAX-EXEMPT INTEREST REQUIRED TO BE SHOWN ON RETURN

(Sec. 6012 of the Code)

[Conference Report]

*   *   *   *   *   *

Present Law.—There is no requirement that all taxpayers report the amount of tax-exempt interest they receive on their tax returns. The individual income tax return (Form 1040) for 1985 does, however, require that taxpayers with taxable social security benefits report the tax-exempt interest they receive.

House Bill.—The House bill requires that any person required to make a return of income under section 6012 include on that return the amount of tax-exempt interest received or accrued during the taxable year. The provision is effective for taxable years beginning after December 31, 1985.

*   *   *   *   *

Conference Agreement.—The conference agreement follows the House bill, effective for taxable years beginning after December 31, 1986.

[¶ 4082]   SECTION 1531. MODIFICATION OF TAX SHELTER RATIO TEST FOR REGISTRATION OF TAX SHELTERS

(Sec. 6111 of the Code)

[Conference Report]

*   *   *   *   *   *

Present Law.—Tax shelter organizations are required to register with the IRS tax shelters they organize, develop, or sell (sec. 6111). A tax shelter is any investment for which the ratio of the deductions plus 200 percent of the credits to the cash actually invested is greater than 2 to 1. The investment also must (1) be subject to Federal or State securities requirements, or (2) be privately placed with 5 or more investors with an aggregate amount that may be offered for sale exceeding $250,000.

*   *   *   *   *

Senate Amendment.—Tax credits are multiplied by 375 percent (instead of 200 percent) to conform the tax shelter ratio computation more closely to the tax rate schedule in the Senate amendment.

This provision is effective July 1, 1987 (the same date that the rate changes are effective).

Conference Agreement.—The conference agreement follows the Senate amendment, modified to conform to the new tax rate schedule agreed to in conference. *[Effective date.—]* The provision is effective for tax shelters in which interests are first offered for sale after December 31, 1986.

[¶ 4083]   SECTION 1532. INCREASED PENALTY FOR FAILURE TO REGISTER TAX SHELTER

(Sec. 6707 of the Code)

[Conference Report]

*   *   *   *   *   *

Present Law.—Specified tax shelters are required to register with the IRS and obtain a tax shelter identification number (Sec. 6111). The penalty for failure to register a tax shelter with the IRS is $10,000 or, if less, one

percent of the aggregate amount invested in the tax shelter (but in no event less than $500) (sec. 6707(a)).

*   *   *   *   *

Conference Agreement.—The conference agreement deletes the $10,000 maximum for the penalty from present law, effective on the date of enactment.

[¶ 4084]   SECTION 1533. PENALTY FOR FAILURE TO INCLUDE TAX SHELTER IDENTIFICATION NUMBER ON RETURN INCREASED TO $250

(Sec. 6707 of the Code)

[Senate Explanation]

*   *   *   *   *   *

Reasons for Change.—In order for the tax shelter registration system to function properly, taxpayers must report the tax shelter identification numbers on their tax re-

turns. The committee believes that the present-law penalty for failure to do so is too low.

Explanation of Provision.—The bill increases the penalty for failure to report a tax shelter identification number on a tax return from $50 to $250. The present-law exception from the penalty where the failure to report the number is due to reasonable cause remains unchanged.

[Senate Explanation]

*   *   *   *   *

Effective Date.—The provision is effective for tax returns filed after the date of enactment.

[¶ 4085] SECTION 1534. INCREASED PENALTY FOR FAILURE TO MAINTAIN LISTS OF INVESTORS IN POTENTIALLY ABUSIVE TAX SHELTERS

(Sec. 6708 of the Code)

[Conference Report]

Present Law.—Organizers and sellers of specified tax shelters are required to maintain lists of investors (sec. 6112). The penalty for failure to do so is $50 for each name missing from the list, unless the failure is due to reasonable cause, up to a maximum of $50,000 per year (sec. 6708).

*   *   *   *   *   *

Conference Agreement.—The conference agreement raises the maximum penalty to $100,000, *[Effective date]* effective for failures occurring or continuing after the date of enactment. The conference agreement does not raise the penalty of $50 per name omitted.

[¶ 4086] SECTION 1535. CLARIFICATION OF TREATMENT OF SHAM OR FRAUDULENT TRANSACTIONS UNDER SECTION 6621(c)

(Sec. 6621)

[Conference Report]

*   *   *   *   *   *

Present Law.—Taxpayers who underpay their taxes must pay interest. If the interest is attributable to an underpayment of tax of more than $1,000 that is attributable to a tax-motivated transaction (such as a tax shelter), interest is computed at 120 percent of the generally applicable interest rate.

*   *   *   *   *   *

Conference Agreement.—The conference agreement does not include the provision of the Senate amendment increasing the rate of interest on tax-motivated transactions. The conference agreement instead makes a technical correction to the present-law provision that increases the rate of interest for tax-motivated transactions.

The Tax Court has recently held *(DeMartino v. Comm'r.,* T.C. Memo 1986-263 (June 30, 1986); *Forseth v. Comm'r.,* T.C. Memo 1985-279 (June 11, 1985)) that sham transactions that would be subject to this special interest rate were they not shams are not subject to

this special interest rate because they are shams. The conferees view it as anomalous that a genuine transaction (lacking the proper profit motive) would be subject to a higher interest rate, while a sham transaction, which is significantly more abusive, would escape the higher interest rate simply because it is a sham. Accordingly, the conference agreement, consistent with the legislative intent in originally enacting section 6621(d) in 1984, explicitly adds sham or fraudulent transactions to the list of transactions subject to this higher interest rate. The intent of the conferees is to reverse the holding of these Tax Court cases on this issue.

This clarification of present law applies to interest accruing after December 31, 1984, which is the date this higher interest rate took effect. This clarification does not apply, however, to any underpayment with respect to which there was a final court decision (either through exhausting all appeals rights or the lapsing of the time period within which an appeal must be pursued) before the date of enactment of this Act.

[¶ 4087] SECTION 1541. CURRENT YEAR LIABILITY TEST INCREASED FROM 80 to 90 PERCENT FOR ESTIMATED TAX PAYMENTS BY INDIVIDUALS

(Sec. 6654 of the Code)

[House Explanation]

*   *   *   *   *   *

Explanation of Provision.—The bill increases from 80 percent to 90 percent the proportion of the current year's tax liability that taxpayers must make as estimated tax payments in order to avoid the estimated tax penalty. The alternate test of 100 percent of last year's liability remains unchanged.

*   *   *   *   *   *

[Senate Explanation]

*   *   *   *   *   *

Effective Date.—This provision is effective with respect to taxable years beginning after December 31, 1986. Thus, the estimated tax payment due January 15, 1987, which is the final payment for taxable year 1986, is unaffected by this provision. All subsequent estimated tax payments are, however, subject to this provision.

[¶4088] SECTION 1542. CERTAIN TAX-EXEMPT ORGANIZATIONS SUBJECT TO CORPORATE ESTIMATED TAX RULES

(Sec. 6154 of the Code)

Present Law.—Private foundations must pay an excise tax on their net investment income. Tax-exempt organizations are subject to tax on income from an unrelated business. These taxes are paid when the tax returns are filed.

Corporations are required to make quarterly estimated tax payments of corporate income taxes; failure to do so is subject to a penalty.

Senate Amendment.—Quarterly estimated payments must be made of the excise tax on net investment income of private foundations and of the tax on unrelated business income of tax-exempt organizations. These quarterly estimated payments must be made under the same rules that apply to corporate income taxes. *[Effective date]* These provisions are effective for taxable years beginning after December 31, 1986.

Conference Agreement.—The conference agreement follows the Senate amendment.

[¶4089] SECTION 1543. WAIVER OF ESTIMATED PENALTIES FOR 1986 UNDERPAYMENTS ATTRIBUTABLE TO THIS ACT

[Conference Report]

* * * * * *

* * * * * *

Present Law.—Under present law, if the withholding of income taxes from wages does not cover an individual's total income tax liability, the individual, in general, is required to make estimated tax payments. Also, corporations are normally required to make quarterly estimated tax payments. An underpayment of an estimated tax installment will, unless certain exceptions are applicable, result in the imposition of an addition to tax on the amount of underpayment for the period of underpayment.

Conference Agreement.—The conference agreement makes several changes that increase tax liabilities from the beginning of 1986. Consequently, the conference agreement allows individual taxpayers until April 15, 1987, and corporations until March 15, 1987 (the final filing dates for calendar year returns) to pay their full 1986 income tax liabilities without incurring any additions to tax on account of underpayments of estimated tax to the extent that the underpayments are attributable to changes in the law made by the conference agreement.

[¶4090] SECTION 1551. LIMITATIONS ON AWARDING OF COURT COSTS AND CERTAIN FEES MODIFIED

(Sec. 7430 of the Code)

[Senate Explanation]

* * * * * *

Explanation of Provision.—The bill modifies section 7430 to conform it more closely to the Equal Access to Justice Act. Consequently, under the bill, the burden of proof is on the Government [but see Conference Agreement below] to prove that its position was substantially justified or that special circumstances exist that make an award of attorney's fees and court costs unjust. The bill provides that, unless the Government proves this, attorney's fees may be awarded. This burden of proof replaces the standard under section 7430 that requires the taxpayer to prove that the Government's position was unreasonable before the taxpayer could be awarded attorney's fees. Furthermore, the "substantially justified" standard is applicable to prelitigation actions or inaction of Government agents as well as the litigation position of the Government. The bill does not modify the present-law requirement that, in

order to be eligible to be awarded attorney's fees, the taxpayer must either substantially prevail with respect to the amount in controversy or substantially prevail with respect to the most significant issue or set of issues presented. The bill also does not modify the present-law provision that only the taxpayer (and not the Government) may be awarded attorney's fees.

The bill eliminates the $25,000 cap on the award of attorney's fees and substitutes a $75 an hour limitation on attorney's fees, unless the court determines that a higher rate is justified. To make this determination, the court may look to an increase in the cost of living or a special factor, such as the limited availability of qualified attorneys to deal with the particular issues involved in the case. As under prior law, only reasonable litigation costs are recoverable by the taxpayer. Unlike prior law, however, prevailing market rates are applied to determine what are reasonable expenses of expert witnesses and reasonable costs of any study, analysis, or other project necessary to the preparation

Act § 1551 ¶4090

of the taxpayer's case. In no event are expert witnesses to be compensated at a rate in excess of the highest rate of compensation for expert witnesses paid by the United States.

The bill also denies any award to a prevailing party who unreasonably protracts the proceedings. Although this requirement is part of the Equal Access to Justice Act, it has not previously applied to Tax Court cases.

* * * * * *

[Conference Report]

* * * * * *

The conference agreement generally follows the Senate amendment, except as to the burden of proof. Thus, the conference agreement provides that the taxpayer (as opposed to the Government) must carry the burden of proving that the Government's action was not substantially justified. The conference agreement also provides that the net worth limitations of the Equal Access to Justice Act are made applicable in tax cases. In addition to providing for attorney's fees with respect to litigation expenses, the conference agree-

ment also provides that attorney's fees may be awarded with respect to the administrative action or inaction by the District Counsel of the IRS (and all subsequent administrative action or inaction) upon which the proceeding is based.

[Effective dates].—This provision applies to [amounts paid after 9-30-86 in] actions commenced after December 31, 1985. If a case was commenced after that date and was finally disposed of before the date of enactment, the conference agreement provides that such taxpayers may request attorney's fees with respect to those cases during the 30-day period immediately following the date of enactment. Awards of attorney's fees in cases commenced before January 1, 1986, will continue to be governed by Code section 7430, as in effect before that date.

The conference agreement also provides that awards of attorney's fees in Tax Court cases are payable in the same manner as an award in a case before a district court, effective for actions or proceedings commenced after February 28, 1983.

[¶ 4091] SECTION 1552. FAILURE TO PURSUE ADMINISTRATIVE REMEDIES

(Sec. 6673 of the Code)

[Conference Report]

* * * * * *

House Bill.—The Tax Court is authorized to impose a penalty equal to $120 (twice the current filing fee) if it determines the taxpayer did not use reasonable efforts in good faith in attempting to resolve the case administratively. The taxpayer is considered to have met the requirements of this provision (and therefore not be subject to this penalty) in the following situations: he is only challenging an existing regulation or ruling (or a similar matter with respect to which Appeals has no authority to negotiate); he has attended one first level Appeals meeting; he cannot attend a first level Appeals meeting because it would be unduly burdensome; the IRS has waived the Appeals meeting; or the case has

been in Appeals for six months with no action. This new provision does not make exhaustion of administrative remedies a jurisdictional prerequisite to Tax Court review. This penalty is in addition to the original filing fee of the Tax Court. Exhaustion for purposes of this provision is not considered to be exhaustion for purposes of section 7430(b)(2) (relating to attorney's fees).

* * * * * *

Conference Agreement.—The conference agreement does not include the provision of the House bill. Instead, the conference agreement provides that failure by a taxpayer to exhaust administrative remedies is an additional basis that the Tax Court may consider in imposing the section 6673 penalty for dilatory or frivolous proceedings in the Tax Court.

[¶ 4092] SECTION 1553. TAX COURT PRACTICE FEE

(Sec. 7475 of the Code)

(Senate Explanation)

* * * * * *

Explanation of Provision.—The bill authorizes the Tax Court to impose a periodic registration fee on practitioners admitted to practice before it. The Tax Court is to estab-

lish the level of the fee and the frequency of its collection, but the fee may not exceed $30 per year. These funds are available to the Tax Court to pay independent counsel engaged by the Court to pursue disciplinary matters.

Effective Date.—This provision is effective January 1, 1987.

〔¶4093〕 SECTION 1554. CLARIFICATION OF JURISDICTION OVER ADDITION TO TAX FOR FAILURE TO PAY AMOUNT OF TAX SHOWN ON RETURN

(Sec. 6214 of the Code)

(Senate Explanation)

*   *   *   *   *   *

Explanation of Provision.—The bill provides that the Tax Court has jurisdiction over this addition to tax for failure to pay an amount shown on the return where the Tax Court already has jurisdiction to redetermine a deficiency in tax with respect to that return.

Aside from resolving this jurisdictional issue, the provision does not alter the jurisdiction of the Tax Court. The amendment is not intended to change existing law insofar as (1) the section 6651(a)(1) late filing addition to tax, or (2) the procedure for assessing additions to tax under section 6663(b) is concerned.

Effective Date.—This provision is effective for any action or proceeding before the Tax Court which has not become final before the date of enactment.

〔¶4094〕 SECTION 1555. AUTHORITY TO REQUIRE ATTENDANCE OF UNITED STATES MARSHALS AT TAX COURT SESSIONS

(Sec. 7456 of the Code)

(Senate Explanation)

*   *   *   *   *   *

Explanation of Provision.—The bill requires that the U.S. Marshal for any district

in which the Tax Court is sitting must attend any session of the Tax Court, when requested to do so by the Chief Judge of the Tax court.

Effective Date.—This provision is effective on the date of enactment of the bill.

〔¶4095〕 SECTION 1556. CHANGES IN CERTAIN PROVISIONS RELATING TO SPECIAL TRIAL JUDGES

(Sec. 7443A of the Code)

(Senate Explanation)

*   *   *   *   *   *

Explanation of Provision.—The bill consolidates in one new section of the Code a number of the provisions relating to the Special Trial Judges. The bill also specifies that Special Trial Judges are to be paid 90 percent of the salary paid to Tax Court

Judges, and that Special Trial Judges are to be reimbursed for travel and subsistence expenses to the same extent as are Tax Court Judges.

Effective Date.—Generally, these provisions are effective on the date of enactment of the bill. The provision relating to the salary of Special Trial Judges is effective on the first day of the first month beginning after the date of enactment.

〔¶4096〕 SECTION 1557. EFFECT ON RETIRED PAY BY ELECTION TO PRACTICE LAW, ETC. AFTER RETIREMENT

(Secs. 7447 and 7448 of the Code)

(Senate Explanation)

*   *   *   *   *   *

Explanation of Provision.—The bill permits Tax Court judges meeting specified age and tenure requirements to elect to receive full retired pay as of the date they make the election (which would not be adjusted to

reflect changes in the pay of active Tax Court judges) and not be subject to the prohibition on practicing tax law. The bill also suspends retired pay for the period of time during which a retired Tax Court judge holds a compensated Government position.

Effective Date.—This provision generally is effective on the date of enactment.

〔¶4097〕 SECTION 1558. AUTHORIZATION FOR APPEALS FROM INTERLOCUTORY ORDERS OF THE TAX COURT

(Sec. 7482 of the Code)

[Conference Report]

*   *   *   *   *   *

The conference agreement authorizes an appeal from an interlocutory order of the Tax

Court if a judge of the Tax Court includes in an interlocutory order a statement that a controlling question of law is involved, that there is substantial ground for difference of opinion regarding the question of law, and that an immediate appeal from the order might materially advance the ultimate termination of the litigation.

The Court of Appeals is given discretion as to whether or not to permit the appeal. Neither the application for nor the granting of an appeal stays proceedings in the Tax Court unless a stay is ordered by either the Tax Court or the Court of Appeals.

[Effective date.]—This provision applies to any order of the Tax Court entered after the date of enactment.

[¶ 4098] SECTION 1559. CHANGES RELATING TO ANNUITIES FOR SURVIVING SPOUSES AND DEPENDENT CHILDREN OF TAX COURT JUDGES

(Sec. 7448 of the Code)

[Conference Report]

* * * * * * *

Present Law.—Tax Court Judges may elect to have 3 percent of their salary deducted to fund an annuity for their surviving spouses and dependent children. The survivors annuity provisions relating to other Federal judges were recently updated (Pub. L. 99-335, June 6, 1986); the survivors annui-

ty provisions relating to Tax Court Judges were not updated at the same time.

* * * * * * *

Conference Agreement.—The conference agreement makes the survivors annuity provisions relating to Tax Court Judges parallel to those applicable to other Federal judges.

[Effective Date.] This provision is generally effective on November 1, 1986.

[¶ 4099] SECTION 1561. SUSPENSION OF STATUTE OF LIMITATIONS IF THIRD-PARTY RECORDS NOT PRODUCED WITHIN 6 MONTHS AFTER SERVICE OF SUMMONS

(Sec. 7609(e),(i) of the Code)

[Senate Explanation]

* * * * * * *

Explanation of Provision.—If the dispute between the third-party recordkeeper and the IRS is not resolved within six months after the IRS issues an administrative summons, the statute of limitations is suspended until the issue is resolved. The issue is not resolved during the pendency of any action to compel production of the documents. The third-party recordkeeper is also required to provide notice of the suspension of the statute of limitations to the taxpayer whose

records are the subject of the dispute if the summons requesting the records does not identify the taxpayer by name. Failure by the third party to do so does not prevent the suspension of the statute.

Also, as is the case under current law, the statute of limitations is suspended during the period when a taxpayer intervenes in a dispute between the IRS and a third-party recordkeeper. The statute is suspended from that date until the entire dispute is resolved.

Effective date.—This provision is effective on the date of enactment * * *.

[¶ 4100] SECTION 1562. AUTHORITY TO RESCIND NOTICE OF DEFICIENCY WITH TAXPAYER'S CONSENT

(Sec. 6212(d) of the Code)

[House Explanation]

* * * * * * *

Explanation of Provision.—Where the IRS and the taxpayer mutually agree, a statutory notice of deficiency may be rescinded. Once the notice has been properly rescinded, it is treated as if it never existed. Therefore, limitations regarding credits, refunds, and assessments relating to the rescinded notice are void and the parties are returned to the rights and obligations existing prior to the issuance of the withdrawn notice. Also, the IRS may issue a later notice

for a deficiency greater or less than the amount in the rescinded notice.

Under Code section 7805, the Secretary has the authority to establish by regulation the procedures necessary to implement the withdrawal of notice provision to assure that the taxpayer has consented to the withdrawal of the statutory notice. The regulations should also clarify the effect of rescission on other provisions of the Code.

Effective date.—This provision is effective for statutory notices of deficiency issued on or after * * * [January 1, 1986].

[¶ 4101] SECTION 1563. AUTHORITY TO ABATE INTEREST DUE TO ERRORS OR DELAYS BY THE INTERNAL REVENUE SERVICE

(Sec. 6404(e) of the Code)

[Senate Explanation]

* * * * * *

Explanation of Provision.—In cases where an IRS official fails either to perform a ministerial act in a timely manner or makes an error in performing a ministerial act, the IRS has the authority to abate the interest attributable to such delay. No significant aspect of the delay can be attributable to the taxpayer. The bill gives the IRS the authority to abate interest but does not mandate that it do so (except that the IRS must do so in cases of certain erroneous refunds of less than $1 million, described below). The committee does not intend that this provision be used routinely to avoid payment of interest; rather, it intends that the provision be utilized in instances where failure to abate interest would be widely perceived as grossly unfair. The interest abatement only applies to the period of time attributable to the failure to perform the ministerial act.

The provision applies only to failures to perform ministerial acts that occur after the IRS has contacted the taxpayer in writing. This provision does not therefore permit the abatement of interest for the period of time between the date the taxpayer files a return and the date the IRS commences an audit, regardless of the length of that time period. Similarly, if a taxpayer files a return but does not pay the taxes due, this provision would not permit abatement of this interest regardless of how long the IRS took to contact the taxpayer and request payment.

The committee intends that the term "ministerial act" be limited to nondiscretionary acts where all of the preliminary prerequisites, such as conferencing and review by supervisors, have taken place. Thus, a ministerial act is a procedural action, not a decision in a substantive area of tax law. For example, a delay in the issuance of a statutory notice of deficiency after the IRS and the taxpayer have completed efforts to resolve the matter could be grounds for abatement of

interest. The IRS may define a ministerial act in regulations.

Under its general authority to issue regulations, the IRS can issue regulations determining what constitutes timely performance of various ministerial acts called for by the Code.

The IRS must abate interest in certain instances in which it issues an erroneous refund check. For example, it has come to the committee's attention that the IRS may make an error that causes a taxpayer to get a refund check for $1,000 instead of the $100 that the taxpayer rightfully claimed. In the past, the IRS charged the taxpayer interest on the $900 for the time period that the taxpayer held that money.

The committee believes that it is inappropriate to charge taxpayers interest on money they temporarily have because the IRS has made an error. Consequently, the IRS may not charge interest on these erroneous refunds until the date it demands repayment of the money. The committee intends that two limitations be placed on this rule. First, it is not to apply in instances in which the taxpayer (or a related party) has in any way caused the overstated refund to occur. Second, it is not to apply to any erroneous refund checks that exceed $1 million. If the taxpayer does not repay the erroneous refund when requested to do so by the IRS, interest would then begin to apply to the amount of the erroneous refund.

* * * * * *

[Conference Report]

* * * * * *

The conference agreement follows the Senate amendment, except that the rule requiring the abatement of interest on erroneous refund checks of $1 million or less is only made applicable to erroneous refund checks of $50,000 or less. The provision is effective for taxable years beginning after December 31, 1978.

[¶ 4102] SECTION 1564. SUSPENSION OF COMPOUNDING WHERE INTEREST ON DEFICIENCY SUSPENDED

(Sec. 6601(c) of the Code)

[Senate Explanation]

* * * * * *

Explanation of Provision.—Both the interest on the deficiency as well as the compounded interest on the previously accrued interest are suspended, starting 31 days after a taxpayer has filed a waiver of restrictions on assessment of the underlying taxes and ending when a notice and demand is issued to the taxpayer.

Effective date.—This provision is effective for interest accruing in taxable periods December 31-82. * * *

* * * * * *

[Conference Report]

* * * * * *

Taxpayers may obtain refunds of interest subject to this provision that they paid by filing a claim for refund of their interest with the IRS. The IRS presently does not possess the data processing capability to suspend the compounding of interest on previously accrued interest. Taxpayers who consider themselves entitled to the relief provided by this provision may apply to the IRS, and, in appropriate cases, the IRS will perform the required computations.

[¶ 4103] SECTION 1565. CERTAIN SERVICE-CONNECTED DISABILITY PAYMENTS EXEMPT FROM LEVY

(Sec. 6334(a) of the Code)

[Senate Explanation]

*   *   *   *   *   *

Explanation of Provision.—The IRS is prohibited from levying on any amount payable to an individual as a service-connected disability benefit under specified provisions of Title 38 of the United States Code.

The term "service-connected" means that the disability was incurred or aggravated in the line of duty in the active military, naval, or air service. The exemption covers direct compensation payments, as well as other types of support payments for education and housing.

Effective date.—This provision is effective for payments made after December 31, 1988.

[¶ 4104] SECTION 1566. INCREASE IN VALUE OF PERSONAL PROPERTY SUBJECT TO CERTAIN LISTING AND NOTICE PROCEDURES

(Sec. 7325 of the Code)

[House Explanation]

*   *   *   *   *   *

Explanation of Provision.—The bill allows the Treasury to administratively sell up to $100,000 of personal property used in violation of the Internal Revenue laws. Such sale would require both an appraisal to determine value and a notice by newspaper publication to potential claimants. Potential

claimants can require a judicial forfeiture action by posting a $2500 bond.

*   *   *   *   *   *

[Conference Report]

*   *   *   *   *   *

The conference agreement follows the House bill, effective on the date of enactment.

[¶ 4105] SECTION 1567. CERTAIN RECORDKEEPING REQUIREMENTS

(Secs. 132 and 274 of the Code)

[Senate Explanation]

*   *   *   *   *   *

Explanation of Provision.—The bill provides that, for purposes of sections 132 and 274, use of an automobile by a special agent of the IRS is treated in the same manner as

use of an automobile by an officer of any other law enforcement agency.

[Conference Report]

*   *   *   *   *   *

[Effective date.—] The conference agreement follows the House bill and the Senate amendment, effective beginning after December 31, 1984.

[¶ 4106] SECTION 1568 DISCLOSURE OF RETURNS AND RETURN INFORMATION TO CERTAIN CITIES

(Sec. 6103(b) of the Code)

[Senate Explanation]

*   *   *   *   *   *

Explanation of Provision. The bill provides that any city with a population in excess of 2,000,000 that imposes an income or wage tax may, if the Secretary in his sole discretion[15] so provides, receive returns and return information for the same purposes for which States may obtain information under present law, subject to the same safeguards as apply to States under present law. Cities that receive information must reimburse the

Internal Revenue Service for its costs in the same manner as a State must under present law. Population is determined on the basis of the most recent decennial United States census data available.

Any disclosure would be required to be in the same manner and with the same safeguards as disclosure is made to a State. The present-law requirements of maintaining a system of standardized requests for information and the reasons for the request and of maintaining strict security against release of the information are also made applicable to the local agencies. Disclosure will be permit-

---

[Footnote ¶ 4106]   (15) The Secretary may, in accordance with his discretion implement this provision on a trial basis.

ted only for the purpose of, and only to the extent necessary in, the administration of a local jurisdiction tax. Disclosure of returns or return information to any elected official or the chief official (even if not elected) of the local jurisdiction will not be permitted. Any unauthorized disclosure of returns and return information by an employee of an agency receiving this information will subject the employee to the fine and imprisonment provided by section 7213 and to the civil action provided by section 7431.

Effective Date.—This provision is effective on the date of enactment.

* * * * * *

[¶4107] SECTION 1569. TREATMENT OF CERTAIN FORFEITURES

(Sec. 6323 of the Code)

[Conference Report]

* * * * * *

Present Law.—If a person owing tax fails to pay that tax, a lien is created on all the taxpayer's property at the time of assessment. This lien takes priority over any other attachment to the taxpayer's property that has not been perfected at the time of assessment. Thus, under State law in a number of States, a State law enforcement agency may perform an extensive investigation of an individual, leading to the seizure and forfeiture of that individual's property. If the State has cooperated with the IRS and the IRS files a lien, the IRS lien may take priority over the State's claim to the property.

* * * * * *

Conference Agreement.—The conference agreement provides that a forfeiture under local law of property seized by a law enforcement agency of either a State or a political subdivision of a State relates back to the time of seizure. The provision does not apply to the extent that local law provides that someone other than the governmental unit has priority over the governmental unit in the property. For purposes of this provision, a State or local tax agency is not considered to be a law enforcement agency. This provision is effective on the date of enactment.

[¶4108] SECTION 1570. PROCEDURE AT TAX SALE OF SEIZED PROPERTY WHERE NO PERSON OFFERS MINIMUM PRICE

(Sec. 6601 of the Code)

[Conference Report]

* * * * * *

Present Law.—The Federal Government has the power, after proper notice and demand, to seize and sell the property of a delinquent taxpayer. As soon as practicable after seizure, the Government is required to give written notice of the seizure to the owner of the property. This notice must describe the property seized and specify the sum of money owed and demanded for release of the property. The Government also must give notice of the sale of the seized property to its owner as soon as practicable after seizure. This notice must specify the property to be sold as well as the time, place, manner, and conditions of the sale.

Before the sale, the Government is required to set a minimum price for the property, taking into account the expenses to the Government of the levy and sale. At the sale, the property is sold to the highest bidder who meets or exceeds the minimum price. If no bid meets or exceeds the minimum price, the property is deemed to be sold to the Government for the minimum price. Thus, the Government has no discretion under present law in purchasing the property itself when no bid meets or exceeds the minimum price.

* * * * * *

Conference Agreement.—The conference agreement requires that, before the sale of the property, the IRS determine (based upon criteria prescribed by the Treasury) whether the purchase of the property at the minimum price is in the best interests of the Federal Government. Property would continue to be sold to the highest bidder who meets or exceeds the minimum price.

If no bid meets or exceeds the minimum price, the Government would purchase the property at the minimum price only if the purchase were in its best interests. If the purchase were determined not to be in the best interests of the Government, the property would be released back to the owner. The property would still be subject to a Government lien. Also, any expense of the levy and sale would be added to the amount of delinquent taxes due.

The provision is effective for sales of seized property conducted after the date of enactment.

[¶ 4109] SECTION 1571. MODIFICATION OF TIPS ALLOCATION METHOD

[Conference Report]

* * * * * *

Present Law.—Employers are required, under certain circumstances, to provide an information report of an allocation of tips in large food or beverage establishments (defined generally to include those establishments that normally employ more than 10 employees). Under this provision, if tipped employees of large food or beverage establishments report tips aggregating 8 percent or more of the gross receipts of the establishment, then no reporting of a tip allocation is required. However, if this 8-percent reporting threshold is not met, the employer must allocate (as tips for information reporting purposes) an amount equal to the difference between 8 percent of gross receipts and the aggregate amount reported by employees. This allocation may be made pursuant to an agreement between the employer and employees or, in the absence of such an agreement, according to Treasury regulations.

These Treasury regulations provide that this allocation may be made by the employer in either of two ways. One is to allocate based on the portion of the gross receipts of the establishment attributable to the employee during a payroll period. The second is to allocate based on the portion of the total number of hours worked in the establishment attributable to the employee during a payroll period.

Conference Agreement.—The conference agreement provides that the method of allocation based on the number of hours worked may be utilized only by an establishment that employs less than the equivalent of 25 full-time employees during a payroll period. Establishments employing the equivalent of 25 or more full-time employees would consequently have to use the portion of gross receipts method to allocate tips during the payroll period (absent an agreement between the employer and employees).

This provision is effective for any payroll period beginning after December 31, 1986.

[¶ 4110] SECTION 1572. TREATMENT OF FORFEITURES OF LAND SALES CONTRACTS FOR PURPOSES OF DISCHARGE OF LIENS

(Sec. 7425 of the Code)

[Conference Report]

* * * * * *

Present Law.—Generally, before Federal tax liens can be extinguished, notice must be given to the Government. Several cases have held (*Runkel* v. *United States,* 527 F.2d 914 (9th Cir. 1977); *Brookbank* v. *Hubbard,* 712 F.2d 399 (9th Cir. 1983)) that forfeitures of land sales contracts are not subject to these notice requirements. Notice provides the Government with the opportunity to redeem the property.

* * * * *

Conference Agreement.—The conference agreement provides that forfeitures of land sales contracts are subject to these notification requirements, effective for forfeitures after the thirtieth day after the date of enactment. Thus, these two cases are explicitly overturned as to this issue. The effect of this provision is to provide the Government with both notice and the opportunity to redeem the property, which it currently has with respect to most other transfers of real estate.

[¶ 4111] SECTION 1581. WITHHOLDING ALLOWANCES TO REFLECT NEW RATE SCHEDULES

(Sec. 3402 of the Code)

[Senate Explanation]

Explanation of Provision.—The bill requires that employees file a revised Form W-4 by January 1, 1988. [October 1, 1987 Ed.] They must do so on a Form W-4 that has been revised by the IRS to reflect the changes in the Code made by this bill.[17] If an employee does not file a revised Form W-4 by that date, the employer must withhold income taxes as if the employee claimed one allowance (if the employer checked the "Single" box on the most recent Form W-4 that the employee

filed) or two allowances (if the employee checked the "Married" box).

The bill also requires that the IRS and Treasury modify the withholding schedules under section 3402 to better approximate tax liability under the amendments made by the bill. The committee expects that this modification will affect at least two major items. First, Form W-4 will be modified. Second, the withholding tables used by employers to determine the proper amount of wage withholding will also be modified.

With respect to modifying Form W-4, the committee expects that the IRS will make

---

[Footnote ¶ 4111] (17) It is also permissible for employees to fulfill the requirements of this provision by filing on a substitute Form W-4, so long as that form has been revised to parallel the official form and the substitute form complies with all IRS requirements pertaining to substitute Forms W-4.

every effort to notify taxpayers that Form W-4 has been modified and that taxpayers must file the modified form with their employers by January 1, 1988 [October 1, 1987 Ed.] In addition, the committee expects that the IRS will issue the revised Form W-4 well before that date, to minimize the inconvenience of filing new forms for both employers and employees.

The modified form and tables should be designed so that withholding from taxpayer's wages approximates as closely as possible the taxpayer's ultimate tax liability. While the committee recognizes that it is impossible to accomplish this goal with absolute precision in the case of each taxpayer, it is nonetheless vital to the integrity of the tax system that the amount withheld from wages closely match the taxpayer's ultimate tax liability. While the committee recognizes that substantial involuntary overwithholding is undesirable,[18] the committee also recognizes that substantial underwithholding creates significant collection and enforcement problems.

While the committee believes that the changes in the substantive tax law made by this bill will permit wage withholding to approximate tax liability more closely for many taxpayers, the committee believes that increased complexity in the current Form W-4 and wage withholding tables is not desirable, even if it were designed to permit withholding to approximate tax liability more closely. Consequently, neither Form W-4 nor the wage withholding tables is to be made more complex when they are revised in accordance with this provision of the bill.

The bill also repeals the provision of present law giving the IRS authority to issue regulations permitting employees to request decreases in withholding. The provision relating to increases in withholding is unaffected.

Effective Date.—The provision requiring employees to file new Forms W-4 is effective for wages paid after December 31, 1987 [on or after October 1, 1987]. The provision relating to decreases in withholding is effective on the date of enactment.

[Conference Report]

*   *   *   *   *   *

The conference agreement follows the Senate amendment, except that employees must file a new Form W-4 before October 1, 1987, in order to avoid the mandatory withholding change that takes effect if an employee does not file a new Form W-4, which is also effective October 1, 1987. This date will follow more closely the extensive IRS publicity campaign on withholding changes.

[¶ 4112] SECTION 1582. REPORT ON RETURN-FREE SYSTEM

[Senate Explanation]

Explanation of Provision.—The committee does not believe that the return-free system set forth in the President's proposal is sufficiently developed for implementation at this time. The committee therefore decided to require a report from the IRS setting forth:

(1) the identification of classes of individuals who would be permitted to use a return-free system;

(2) how such a system would be phased in;

(3) what additional resources the IRS would need to carry out such a system; and

(4) the types of changes to the Internal Revenue Code which would inhibit or enhance the use of such a system.

The report is to be submitted within six months of the date of enactment to the Senate Committee on Finance and the House Committee on Ways and Means.

In addition, the committee believes that the IRS should consider conducting an in-house feasibility test using previously filed information returns and individual income tax returns to test the practicality of the proposed system.

A number of provisions of this bill provide that the Secretary of the Treasury or his delegate is to prescribe regulations. Notwithstanding any of these references, it is contemplated that the Secretary or his delegate will, pending the prescribing of these regulations, issue guidance for taxpayers with respect to the changes made by this bill by issuing Revenue Procedures, Revenue Rulings, forms, or other publications.

Effective dates.—The report is due six months after enactment of the bill.

*   *   *   *   *   *

[Conference Report]

*   *   *   *   *   *

A number of provisions of the conference agreement provide that the Secretary of the Treasury or his delegate is to prescribe regulations. Notwithstanding any of these references, the conferees intend that the Secretary may, prior to prescribing these regulations, issue guidance for taxpayers with respect to the provisions of the conference agreement by issuing Revenue Procedures, Revenue Rulings, forms and instructions to forms, announcements, or other publications or releases. The conferees intend that the IRS provide taxpayers with this guidance as quickly as is possible.

---

(18) A significant portion of overwithholding appears to be attributable to taxpayer preference.

[¶ 4114] SECTION 1601. CERTAIN DISTRIBUTIONS OF LOW COST ARTICLES AND EXCHANGES AND RENTALS OF MEMBER LISTS BY CERTAIN ORGANIZATIONS NOT TO BE TREATED AS UNRELATED TRADE OR BUSINESS

(Sec. 513 of the Code)

[House Explanation]

*　　*　　*　　*　　*　　*

Present Law.—*General rules.* Under present law, certain organizations are generally exempt from Federal income tax because of their charitable, educational, religious, or other nonprofit purposes and functions (Code sec. 501(c)(3)). However, a tax is imposed on the unrelated trade or business income of otherwise tax-exempt organizations (secs. 511-514). The tax applies to gross income derived by an exempt organization from any unrelated trade or business regularly carried on by it, less allowable deductions directly connected with the carrying on of such trade or business, both subject to certain modifications.

An unrelated trade or business is defined as any trade or business of a tax-exempt organization the conduct of which is not substantially related (aside from the need of such organization for income or funds or the use it makes of the profits derived) to the exercise or performance by such organization of the charitable, educational, religious, or other nonprofit purpose and function constituting the basis for its exemption (sec. 513(a)). Treasury regulations provide that the tax does not apply to income from an activity that does not possess the characteristics of a trade or business (within the meaning of sec. 162). For example, the regulations state, the tax does not apply where an organization "sends out low cost items incidental to the solicitation of charitable contributions" (Reg. sec. 1.513-1(b)).

Rental of mailing lists. The U.S. Court of Claims held in 1981 that income received by the Disabled American Veterans from other exempt organizations and commercial businesses for the use of its mailing lists constitutes unrelated business taxable income, and does not constitute "royalties" expressly exempted from the tax under section 512(b)(2) (*Disabled American Veterans v. U.S.,* 650 F.2d 1128 (1981)). The court found that in renting its donor lists, the DAV operated in a competitive, commercial manner with respect to taxable firms in the direct mail industry; that these rental activities were regularly carried on; and that the rental activities were not substantially related to accomplishment of exempt purposes (apart from the organization's need for or use of funds derived from renting the mailing lists).

*　　*　　*　　*　　*　　*

Explanation of Provision.—*a. Rental of mailing list.*—The bill provides that in the case of any organization exempt from tax under section 501 that is eligible to receive tax-deductible charitable contributions under section 170(c)(2) or 170(c)(3), the term unre-

lated trade or business does not include any trade or business of such organization that consists of exchanging names and addresses of donors to (or members of) such organization with another such tax-exempt organization, or of renting donor (or member) names and addresses to another such tax-exempt organization.

b. Distribution of low cost articles.—The bill provides that in the case of any organization exempt from tax under section 501 that is eligible to receive tax-deductible charitable contributions under section 170(c)(2) or 170(c)(3), the term unrelated trade or business does not include activities of such organization relating to the distribution of low cost articles incidental to the solicitation of charitable contributions.

For this purpose, an article is low cost if it has a cost not in excess of $5 to the organization which distributes such item (or on whose behalf such item is distributed). Beginning in 1987, this dollar limitation is indexed for inflation as provided in the bill. If more than one item is distributed by or on behalf of an organization to a single distributee in any calendar year, the aggregate of the items so distributed in the year to such distributee is treated as one article for purposes of the dollar limitation.

A distribution of low cost articles qualifies under the bill only if—

(1) the distribution is not made at the request of the distributee;

(2) the distribution is made without the express consent of the distributee; and

(3) the articles distributed are accompanied by a request for a charitable contribution to such organization, and also by a statement that the distributee may retain the low cost article regardless of whether the distributee makes a charitable contribution to such organization.

[The following colloquy relating to Act Sec. 1601 is drawn from the Congressional Record. The colloquy occurred on the day the Conference bill was considered by the House. Ed.]

[House Floor Explanation]

I also have discussed with Congressman DUNCAN the issue of whether the provision of the bill which excludes certain income from unrelated trade or business income creates any inference under present law. We have reached a common understanding regarding the following specific issue:

The question relates to section 1601 of the bill which excludes from unrelated trade or business income revenues from the use of a tax-exempt organization's mailing list by another such organization. Section 1601 of the bill, which specifically exempts certain such revenues from the tax on unrelated business income in the future, carries no inference whatever that mailing list revenues beyond its scope or prior to its effective date should be considered taxable to an exempt organization. Congressional Record, p. H 8361, 9-25-86.

[House Explanation]

* * * * * *

[¶ 4115] SECTION 1602. EDUCATIONAL ACTIVITIES AT CONVENTION AND TRADE SHOWS

(Sec. 513(d)(3) of the Code)

[The Senate Finance Committee version of the bill was amended on the Floor of the Senate. The following is drawn from the Congressional Record. Ed.]

[Senate Floor Explanation]

* * * * * *

Mr. President, my amendment would exclude from the definition of an "unrelated trade or business" trade show activities of organizations qualified under section 501(c)(3) and (4) of the tax code. Section 501(c)(3) organizations include charitable organizations such as churches and schools and 501(c)(4) organizations include civic leagues or organizations operated exclusively for the promotion of social welfare. In short, my amendment would simplify and equalize the tax treatment of trade show income received by organizations qualified under sections 501(c)(3), (4), (5), and (6) of the code.

Effective Date.—These provisions apply to distributions of low cost articles and exchanges and rentals of membership lists occurring after the date of the enactment of the bill.

* * * * * *

Mr. President, it is a well-known fact that charitable organizations find great need to educate their members, and this amendment will permit those charitable organizations with limited means to sponsor conventions to achieve this goal. The amendment is supported by a number of 501(c)(3) and 501(c)(4) organizations, including the American College of Cardiology, the Secondary School Principals, the Girl Scouts and the Goodwill Industries. In providing equal tax treatment with regard to trade show income for 501(c)(3), (4), (5), and (6) organizations, a major administrative burden will be lifted from the IRS and the Tax Code will be made more equitable and fair. Congressional Record, p.S8078-8079; 6-20-86

[**Effective Date.**—Activities in taxable years beginning after the date of enactment. Ed.]

[¶ 4116] SECTION 1603. TAX EXEMPTION FOR CERTAIN TITLE-HOLDING COMPANIES

(Sec. 501(c)(25) of the Code)

[Senate Explanation]

* * * * * *

Present Law.—Under present law, a corporation (described in sec. 501(c)(2)) that is organized for the exclusive purpose of holding title to property, collecting income therefrom, and distributing the income (less expenses) to a tax-exempt organization is itself exempt from Federal income tax. A corporation described in section 501(c)(2) is not tax-exempt if it has unrelated business taxable income other than income classified as such solely pursuant to sections 512(a)(3)(C), 512(b)(3)(B)(ii) or (13), or 514 (Treas. Reg. sec. 1.501(c)(2)-1(a)).

Present law is unclear as to whether the exemption for organizations described in section 501(c)(2) may be available for a title-holding corporation that holds property and distributes income to more than one tax-exempt organization if the tax-exempt owners are not related. The Internal Revenue Service has taken the position, in a General Counsel Memorandum (G.C.M. 37351, December 20, 1977), that in order to qualify for tax-exempt status as an organization described in section 501(c)(2), a title-holding corporation may distribute income only to

one or more related tax-exempt organizations.

Explanation of Provision.—The bill adds a new category of section 501(c) tax-exempt organizations, consisting of certain corporations or trusts that are organized for the exclusive purposes of acquiring and holding title to property, collecting income from the property, and remitting the income to certain tax-exempt organizations. Tax-exempt status in this category applies only if the corporation or trust (1) has no more than 35 shareholders or beneficiaries, (2) has only one class of stock or beneficial interest, and (3) is organized for the exclusive purpose of acquiring property and holding title to, and collecting income from, such property, and remitting the entire amount of income from such property (less expenses) to one or more eligible tax-exempt organizations that are shareholders or beneficiaries of such corporation or trust.

A corporation or trust that meets all of these requirements also is entitled to use the exception to the tax on unrelated business income under the debt-financed property rules for real property (sec. 514(c)(9)), subject to the limitations contained in section 514(c)(9)(B), as applied to pass-through entities (section 514(c)(9)(D)).

Act §1603 ¶4116

In order to qualify for exemption under the new category, a title-holding company must permit its shareholders or beneficiaries (1) to dismiss, after reasonable notice, the corporation's or trust's investment adviser by majority vote of the shareholders or beneficiaries, and (2) to terminate their interest by (a) selling or exchanging their stock or beneficial interest (subject to Federal or State securities law) to any other eligible organization, as long as such sale or exchange would not increase the total number of shareholders or beneficiaries to more than 35, or (b) redeeming their stock or beneficial interest after providing 90 days notice to the corporation or trust.

The tax-exempt organizations eligible to hold interests in a title-holding company under the bill are (1) a qualified pension, profit-sharing, or stock bonus plan (sec. 401(a)); (2) a governmental pension plan (sec. 414(d)); (3) the United States, a State or political subdivision, or governmental agencies or instrumentalities; and (4) tax-exempt charitable, educational, religious, or other organizations described in section 501(c)(3). [and other eligible title-holding companies].

The bill does not amend present law with respect to title-holding corporations (described in sec. 501(c)(2)) holding title to property for one or more related tax-exempt organizations.

Effective Date.—The provision applies for taxable years beginning after December 31, 1986.

[¶ 4117] SECTION 1604. EXCEPTION TO MEMBERSHIP ORGANIZATION DEDUCTION RULES

(Sec. 277 of the Code)

[Conference Report]

*　　*　　*　　*　　*　　*

Present Law.—A membership organization generally may deduct expenses relating to the furnishing of goods or services to members only from income derived from members or from transactions with members (sec. 277). This rule does not apply to certain financial institutions, insurance companies, securities or commodities exchanges, or certain other organizations.

*　　*　　*　　*　　*

Senate Amendment.—The Senate amendment provides an additional exception to the section 277 deduction limitation rule for membership organizations that are engaged primarily in the gathering and distribution of news to their members for publication.

Conference Agreement.—The conference agreement follows the Senate amendment, [Effective date] effective for taxable years beginning after the date of enactment.

[This provision was added when the Senate Finance Committee version of the bill was amended on the Floor of the Senate. The following is drawn from the Congressional Record. Ed.]

[Senate Floor Explanation]

*　　*　　*　　*　　*　　*

Like many other news organizations, in recent years AP has expanded its information distribution activities beyond the traditional newspaper and broadcasting industries. AP now derives revenues from domestic nonmedia companies and from distributing financial information abroad. In order to compete on an equal footing, it is essential that the AP be permitted to pool its income and expenses from all sources and pay tax on its consolidated earnings. Under current law, AP cannot compete on the same basis as its competitors. My amendment would simply eliminate a competitive disadvantage and allow AP to compete on the same basis as others. Congressional Record p. S7794, 6-18-86.

[¶ 4118] SECTION 1605. TAX-EXEMPT STATUS FOR AN ORGANIZATION INTRODUCING INTO PUBLIC USE TECHNOLOGY DEVELOPED BY QUALIFIED ORGANIZATIONS

[Conference Report]

*　　*　　*　　*　　*　　*

Present Law.—In November, 1985, the U.S. Tax Court denied tax-exempt status under section 501(c)(3) to the Washington Research Foundation, a nonprofit organization formed to assist the transfer of technology from universities and tax-exempt research institutions to the private sector. The Tax Court held that the organization was not exclusively operated for charitable purposes because its major activity of providing patenting and licensing services was commercial in nature.

*　　*　　*　　*　　*　　*

Senate Amendment.—The Senate amendment provides that an organization that transfers technology from universities and scientific research organizations to the private sector is treated as a tax-exempt charitable organization if it meets certain requirements, including that it was incorporated on July 20, 1981. The intended beneficiary of this provision is the Washington Research Foundation. [Effective date] The provision is effective on enactment.

Conference Agreement.—The conference agreement follows the Senate amendment. No inference is intended as to whether such technology transfer or related purposes or functions of any other organization consti-

tute purposes or functions described in Code sections 501(c)(3) or 170(c).

[¶4123] SECTION 1701. EXTENSION AND MODIFICATION OF TARGETED JOBS CREDIT

(Sec. 51 of the Code)

[Senate Explanation]

*   *   *   *   *   *

Explanation of Provision.—The bill extends the targeted jobs credit for three additional years. Under the bill, the credit is available for wages paid to individuals who begin work for an employer on or before December 31, 1988.

The bill also limits the credit in two respects. First, the 25-percent credit for qualified wages paid in the second year of a targeted individual's employment is repealed. Second, under the bill, no wages paid to a targeted-group member are to be taken into account for credit purposes unless the individual both (1) is employed by the employer for at least 90 days (14 days in the case of economically disadvantaged summer youth employees), and (2) has completed at least 120 hours of work performed for the employer (20 hours in the case of economically disadvantaged summer youth employees).

The bill also extends the authorization for appropriations for administrative and publicity expenses to fiscal years 1986 through 1988.

In the case of an individual who begins work for the employer after December 31, 1985 and on or before the 25th day following the date of enactment of the bill, the five-day certification requirement for targeted group eligibility will be considered met if proper certification is received or requested on or

before the 30th day following the date of enactment. To the extent feasible, the Internal Revenue Service and the Department of Labor should inform employers (e.g., through press releases or announcements) of the extension of the credit and of this special certification period.

Effective Date.—The provision applies with respect to individuals who begin work for the employer after December 31, 1985 and before January 1, 1989.

*   *   *   *   *   *

[Conference Report]

*   *   *   *   *   *

The conference agreement is the same as the Senate amendment except (1) the credit for first-year wages is reduced from 50 percent to 40 percent of the first $6,000 of qualified first-year wages (in the case of qualified summer youth employees, the present-law credit equal to 85 percent of up to $8,000 of wages is retained); (2) the conference agreement does not include the special certification rule in the Senate amendment; and (3) the minimum employment period rule is liberalized so that the credit is available if the targeted group member either is employed by the employer for at least 90 days (14 days in the case of qualified summer youth employees), or has completed at least 120 hours of work performed for the employer (20 hours in the case of qualified summer youth employees).

[¶4124] SECTION 1702. CERTAIN DIESEL FUEL TAXES MAY BE IMPOSED ON SALES TO RETAILERS

(Secs. 4041 and 6652 of the Code)

[House Explanation]

*   *   *   *   *   *

Explanation of Provision.—The bill provides that the excise tax on diesel fuel for highway vehicles may be imposed on the sale to the retailer by the wholesaler (jobber) or by the manufacturer where the sale is direct to the retailer.

This applies to the sale of diesel fuel to a "qualified retailer," defined as any retailer who (1) elects to have this provision apply with respect to all sales of diesel fuel to such retailer and (2) agrees to provide a written notice to whoever sells diesel fuel to such retailer that such an election has been made concerning application of the diesel fuel tax.

If a retailer required to notify the seller of diesel fuel fails to do so, the retailer is then liable for payment of the tax for the period for which the failure continues. Failure to

provide the required written notice to the diesel fuel seller, unless shown to be due to reasonable cause and not to willful neglect, will result also in a penalty. This penalty is to be paid by the retailer with respect to each sale of diesel fuel to the retailer and is equal to 5 percent of the excise tax amount involved.

Effective Date.—The provision applies to sales of diesel fuel (for use in highway vehicles) after the first calendar quarter beginning more than 60 days after the date of enactment.

*   *   *   *   *   *

[Conference Report]

*   *   *   *   *   *

Diesel fuel tax.—The conference agreement follows the House bill and the Senate amendment, with technical modifications. [Senate amendment is the same as the House bill. Ed.]

Act §1702 ¶4124

[¶ 4125] SECTION 1703. GASOLINE TAX GENERALLY COLLECTED AT TERMINAL LEVEL

(Sec. 4081-4083, 4101 and 6421 of the Code)

[Conference Report]

*   *   *   *   *   *

Present Law

*   *   *   *   *   *

Gasoline tax.—An excise tax on gasoline of nine cents per gallon is imposed and collected at the manufacturer's level (sec. 4081). Collection of this tax may be deferred to the last sale before retail, however, if all parties are registered with the IRS.

*   *   *   *   *   *

Conference Agreement

*   *   *   *   *   *

Gasoline tax.—Under the conference agreement, the gasoline tax is imposed on removal of gasoline, gasoline blend stocks and products commonly used as additives in gasoline, from the refinery (or manufacturing plant) or customs custody (sale, if earlier) effective January 1, 1988. An exception is provided permitting bulk transfers of gasoline or gasoline blend stocks or additives to registered terminals without payment of tax. In such cases, terminal operators are liable for collection of the tax upon removal of the gasoline or gasoline blend stocks or additives from the terminal.

Registered gasohol blenders are permitted to purchase gasoline at 3 cents per gallon if blending occurs at the terminal. In all other cases, gasohol blenders (like all other purchasers) must purchase gasoline and gasoline blend stocks tax-paid. Gasoline separated from gasohol is taxable at a rate of $5\frac{2}{3}$ cents per gallon. Blenders (other than registered gasohol blenders that blend at the terminal) are taxable on the use or sale of blended gasoline. However, they may claim a credit for any tax paid on purchases of gasoline, blendstocks, or additives to the extent that such blended gasoline is not used as a fuel. The purchaser may obtain a refund upon establishing that the ultimate use was not as a taxable fuel. A special, accelerated refund procedure is provided, however, for gasohol blenders who buy tax-paid. Under the accelerated refund procedure if the Secretary has not paid a claim within 20 days of the date of filing, the claim is to be paid with interest from such date.

The Secretary will provide regulations defining the terms gasoline blend stocks and products commonly used as additives in gasoline. He may also require that all persons who must register post bond. In addition, the Secretary may register industrial users of gasoline blend stocks or additives as terminal operators permitting them to purchase such products in bulk form tax free. The Treasury Department is directed to study the incidence of evasion of the gasoline tax and to report to the Congress by December 31, 1986.

[Effective date.—Applies to gasoline removed after 12-31-87. Ed.]

[¶ 4126] SECTION 1704. EXEMPTION FROM SOCIAL SECURITY COVERAGE FOR CERTAIN CLERGY

(Sec. 1402 of the Code)

[Conference Report]

*   *   *   *   *   *

Senate Amendment.—The Senate amendment provides a limited period (generally, up to April 15, 1988) during which a minister who previously had elected out of social security coverage may make an irrevocable election back into social security coverage. An electing minister becomes subject to SECA tax, and his or her post-election earnings are credited for social security benefit purposes.

The Senate amendment also provides that a minister of a church or member of a religious order who files an application (after 1986) for exemption from social security coverage and SECA taxes on religious or conscientious grounds must include with the application a statement that he or she has informed the ordaining, commissioning, or licensing body of the church or order that he or she is opposed to the acceptance of public insurance benefits based on ministerial service. The Senate amendment also provides that an exemption application from a minister may be approved by the Treasury Department only if, subsequent to receiving the application, it separately verifies (in-person or by telephone communication) that the applicant is aware of the grounds for exemption and seeks exemption on such grounds. The Treasury Department may enter into an agreement with the Secretary of Health and Human Services (HHS) pursuant to which such verification may be made by HHS.

Conference Agreement.—The conference agreement generally follows the Senate amendment. Under the conference agreement, Treasury regulations are to provide that exemption applications filed with the IRS (after 1986) are to include information showing that the applicant has informed the church body or order of his or her religious or conscientious opposition to social security coverage, in conformity with the revised exemption procedure. The regulations may provide procedures under which, pursuant to agreement between the Secretary of the Treasury and the Secretary of Health and Human Services, HHS has the responsibility of communicating with the applicant in order to make the separate verification required as a prerequisite for approving the exemption application. The conference agreement does not require that the subsequent verification be in-person or by telephone communication, but the verification procedure must be effective to establish that the applicant is aware of the grounds for exemption from the social

security system and has sought an irrevocable exemption on such grounds. Under these procedures, the disclosure of information to HHS by the IRS concerning a ministerial exemption application for such verification purposes is authorized by Code section 6103(l)(1).

[This provision is effective for applications filed after 12-31-86; revocation rules generally apply to service performed in taxable years ending on or after enactment date. Ed.]

[¶ 4127] SECTION 1705. APPLICABILITY OF UNEMPLOYMENT COMPENSATION TAX TO CERTAIN SERVICES PERFORMED FOR CERTAIN INDIAN TRIBAL GOVERNMENTS

[Conference Report]

* * * * * *

The Senate amendment provides an exemption from FUTA tax for Indian tribal governments the service for which was not covered by a State unemployment compensation program on June 11, 1986. [*Effective date*] This provision is effective for services performed before January 1, 1988, including

services performed prior to the date of enactment (but does not authorize a refund of any previously paid FUTA tax). It is anticipated that the State of Colorado and the affected Indian tribal governments will work out an unemployment compensation coverage agreement prior to January 1, 1988 similar to such agreements currently in effect in other States.

[¶ 4128] SECTION 1706. TREATMENT OF CERTAIN TECHNICAL PERSONNEL

(Sec. 530 of the Revenue Act of 1978)

[*The Senate Finance Committee version of the bill was amended on the Floor of the Senate. The following explanation is drawn from the Congressional Record. Ed.*]

[Senate Floor Explanation]

* * * * * *

* * * Mr. President * * * I have an amendment that will extend the moratorium on the application of section 312(n)(6) to foreign corporations.

* * * * * *

Under this amendment, the classification as employees for tax purposes of certain types of workers should be clarified. Technical services firms have retained engineers, designers, drafters, computer programmers, systems analysts, and other similarly skilled personnel to render services to clients of the technical services firms. Despite the fact that the Internal Revenue Service regards such personnel as employees of the technical services firms, some of such personnel are taking the position that they should be treated as independent contractors and as such the technical services firms would not be required to withhold income and employment taxes from their earnings. Under this amendment such persons would be employees of the technical services firms and their wages should be subject to withholding FICA and FUTA taxes.[1]

Technical services include services provided by engineers, designers, drafters, computer programmers, systems analysis, and other similarly skilled personnel who are engaged in similar lines of work. Generally, personnel providing such services are retained by the technical services firm for assignments for clients and may work for several clients during the course of their employment by the technical services firm, although they may work only for a single client. The treatment of this class of persons as employees will provide greater certainty and simplification in employment tax law and will result in greater tax compliance.

The purpose of this amendment—to treat technical service personnel as employees of technical services firms—cannot be avoided by claims that such personnel are independent contractors, sole proprietors, partners, or employees of personal service corporations controlled by such personnel. For example, an engineer retained by a technical services firm to provide services to an aircraft manufacturer cannot avoid treatment as an employee of technical services firm by organizing a corporation which he controls and then claiming to provide his services as an employee of that corporation.

Nothing in this provision will affect the application of section 414(n), dealing with so-called employee leasing, to technical services personnel. That provision, to the extent applicable under current law, would continue to apply in addition to this provision.

[Footnote ¶4128] (1) Nothing in this amendment applies to persons who, under common law standards, are employees of clients of technical services firms.

Congressional Record, p. S 8088-8089, 6-20-86.

[Conference Report]

* * * * *

The conference agreement follows the Senate amendment with a technical modification clarifying the language of the Senate amendment to conform to the language of section 530 of the Revenue Act of 1978 and with an amendment to the effective date. The confer-

ees further clarify that the provision does not affect the application of the Treasury's authority under Code section 414(o) to prevent avoidance of certain employee benefit requirements. The conferees believe that the provision will provide more consistent tax treatment of individuals performing services in the technical service industry.

[Effective date.—] The conference agreement is effective for remuneration paid and services performed after December 31, 1986.

[¶ 4129] SECTION 1707. EXCLUSION FOR CERTAIN FOSTER CARE PAYMENTS

(Sec. 131 of the Code)

[House Explanation]

* * * * * *

Explanation of Provision.—The bill modifies the exclusion for certain foster care reimbursements so that the exclusion applies to amounts paid for qualified foster care, rather than amounts paid as reimbursements of qualified foster care expenses. As a result, recordkeeping to establish the extent to which payments reimburse particular foster care expenses will not be necessary.

* * * * * *

[Conference Report]

* * * * * *

The conference agreement follows the House bill in eliminating the requirement of detailed recordkeeping as a condition for obtaining the exclusion. This provision otherwise does not expand the types of payments eligible for the exclusion.

Also, the conference agreement deletes the present-law limitation that the exclusion applies with respect to foster care only of children under age 19. (However, in the case of any foster home in which there is a foster care recipient who has attained age 19, foster care payments, including difficulty of care payments, are not excludable to the extent made for more than five such foster care recipients.) The conferees intend that this extension of the exclusion to adult foster care is limited to cases of individuals who provide foster care within their own homes to adults who have been placed in their care by an agency of the State or political subdivision thereof specifically designated as responsible for such function. The exclusion does not apply to payments to operators of boarding homes who provide room and board to adults who have been placed in their care through the actions of a governmental agency responsible for adult foster care.

[Effective date.—] These provisions are effective for taxable years beginning on or after January 1, 1986.

[¶ 4130] SECTION 1708. EXTENSION OF RULES FOR SPOUSES OF INDIVIDUALS MISSING IN ACTION

(Secs. 2(a)(3)(B), 692(b), 6013(f)(1), and 7508(b) of the Code)

[House Explanation]

Present Law.—In 1976, the Congress provided that four tax relief provisions applied to members of the U.S. Armed Forces listed as missing in action (MIA) in the Vietnam conflict.

The first provision, relating to the definition of a surviving spouse, stated that the date of death of a person in MIA status is the date of determination of death made by the Armed Forces under 37 U.S.C. secs. 555 and 556. The second provision exempted from Federal income tax the income of a member of the Armed Forces determined to have died while in MIA status, for the year in which the determination of death was made under 37 U.S.C. secs. 555 and 556 and any prior year which ends on or after the first day the member served in a combat zone. The third provision provided that the spouse of an individual in MIA status could elect to file a joint return. The fourth provision applied to the spouse of a member in MIA status the

rule postponing the performing of certain acts by reason of service in a combat zone, including the filing of returns and the payment of taxes.

These relief provisions originally applied through 1978 in the case of Vietnam MIA's. However, for status determinations under 37 U.S.C. secs. 555 and 556 that were not completed, the provisions subsequently were extended through December 31, 1982.

* * * * * *

Explanation of Provision.—Under the bill, the tax relief provisions applicable with respect to Vietnam MIA's (and their spouses) that expired after 1982 are retroactively reinstated and made permanent.

Effective Date.—The provision is effective for taxable years beginning after December 31, 1982.

* * * * * *

[Conference Report]

* * * * * *

Senate Amendment.—The Senate amendment is the same as the House bill.

Conference Agreement.—The conference agreement follows the House bill and the Senate amendment.

[¶4131] SECTION 1709. AMENDMENT TO THE REINDEER INDUSTRY ACT OF 1937

[Conference Report]

* * * * * *

Present Law.—Under the Reindeer Industry Act of 1937, the United States Government purchased all reindeer herds and improvements held by non-Alaskan natives. Since then, this property has been held in trust by the government for Alaskan natives who manage the reindeer herds. The U.S. Court of Appeals for the Ninth Circuit ruled in 1985 that reindeer-related income derived by Alaskan natives from herds is not exempt from Federal taxation.

Senate Amendment.—The Senate amendment provides that during the period of the trust, income derived directly from the sale of reindeer or reindeer products as provided in the 1937 Act is exempt from Federal income taxation. *[Effective date.]* This provision applies as if originally included in the related provision of the 1937 Act.

[¶4132] SECTION 1710. QUALITY CONTROL STUDIES

(Sec. 12301 of the Consolidated Omnibus Reconciliation Act of 1985)

[Conference Report]

Present Law.—* * *. HHS and NAS are required to report the results of their study to the Congress within one year of the date of enactment of COBRA (April 7, 1986). In addition, HHS is required to publish certain regulations relating to such quality control measures within 18 months of the date of enactment of COBRA.

Senate Amendment.—* * *. The date by which HHS is required to publish the specified regulations is six months after the deadline for reporting the results of the quality control study to the Congress.

* * * * *

[This provision was added to the bill when the Senate Finance Committee version of the bill was amended on the Floor of the Senate. The following explanation is drawn from the Congressional Record. Ed.]

[Senate Floor Explanation.]

* * * * *

* * * Mr. President, I rise to offer an amendment making technical corrections to the AFDC/Medicaid quality control section of the reconciliation measure we passed earlier this year.

* * * * * *

The studies were to be 1 year in duration with the results to be reported to Congress no later than December 31, 1986. Because reconciliation was passed much later than anticipated, this existing deadline would give NAS and HHS only a few months to complete the studies. My amendment would rectify this unintended situation by making the 1-year period commence when NAS and HHS enter into the contract for the studies. This amendment would ensure that they have ample time to complete the comprehensive review we have authorized.

* * *. Congressional Record, p. S7952, 6-19-86.

* * * * *

[¶4133] SECTION 1711. ADOPTION ASSISTANCE AGREEMENTS UNDER ADOPTION ASSISTANCE PROGRAM: PAYMENT OF NONRECURRING EXPENSES RELATED TO ADOPTIONS OF CHILDREN WITH SPECIAL NEEDS

(Sec. 473(a) of the Social Security Act)

[House Explanation]

* * * * * *

Explanation of Provision.—The Adoption Assistance Program under Title IV-E of the Social Security Act is amended to provide 50-percent Federal matching funds to States to pay for "nonrecurring adoption expenses" related to the adoption of a special needs child. The expenses for which a State could claim Federal matching funds are those expenses defined as "qualified adoption expenses" in Code section 222, as presently in effect.

Under the bill, the committee intends that assistance will be provided under the Title IV-E Adoption Assistance Program to adoptive parents who adopt children with special needs and who would have been eligible to claim an adoption expense deduction under the present tax law. This includes adoptive

Act §1711 ¶4133

parents of all special needs children placed according to State and local law and is not limited to those adoptive parents of special needs children who are eligible under the present Title IV-E program, i.e., those who adopt a AFDC, AFDC foster care, or SSI disabled or blind child.

While the bill extends assistance for nonrecurring adoption expenses to adoptive parents of all special needs children, the present program of monthly adoption assistance payments will remain limited to those who adopt AFDC, AFDC foster care, or SSI children. To ensure continued assistance to those adoptive parents who adopt children with special needs, and who would have been eligible to claim an adoption expense deduction under present tax law, the committee intends that close working relationships between the public and private adoption agencies should be established.

Under the bill, the State Title IV-E Adoption Assistance agency is to make arrangements with the licensed private adoption agencies in the State whereby adoptive parents can, by way of the private agency, be reimbursed for some or all of the costs which, under present law, the parents could claim as a qualified adoption expense deduction. In addition to reimbursement of the adoptive parents through the private adoption agencies, States should also be encouraged to have purchase of service agreements in place so that all or a part of the adoption fees normally charged to the adoptive parents could be paid for on behalf of the adoptive parents directly by the State Title IV-E agency. Those arrangements or agreements would be for the purpose of ensuring that expenses incurred by or on behalf of the adoptive parents be treated the same as if the adoption activities were provided by the public adoption agency.

The present tax code provision on adoption expenses establishes a cap ($1,500) on eligible deductions. The current Title IV-E statute also allows a State to establish limits under adoption assistance agreements on the amount of recurring monthly adoption assistance payments to be provided to adoptive parents. This general authority for a State to set limits on the amount of assistance to be provided to adoptive parents will also apply under the bill to "nonrecurring" adoption expenses. However, the amount of the assistance will not be limited, as is now the case for monthly adoption assistance, to the amount that would have been paid for foster care. In other words, as under present adoption assistance agreements, a State may set limits on the amount of the expenses to be financed by the State and the amount may vary among adoptive parents depending on the circumstances of the parents and the child.

Effective Date.—The provision applies with respect to expenditures made after December 31, 198[6]. * * *

[¶ 4135] SECTION 1801. AMENDMENTS RELATED TO DEFERRAL OF CERTAIN TAX REDUCTIONS

(Sec. 12(c)(1), 27 of the 1984 Tax Reform Act; Sec. 4251(b), 5061, 5703(b) of the Code)

[House Explanation]

* * * Finance lease rules * * *

Present Law.—Under the finance lease rules, the fact that a lessee has a fixed-price purchase option or the leased property is limited use property is not taken into account in determining whether the agreement is a lease. The Tax Reform Act of 1984 ("The Act") postponed the effective date of the finance lease rule, except for property acquired pursuant to a binding contract entered into before March 7, 1984, and certain other property.

Explanation of Provision.—Under the bill, taxpayers can elect to have the amendment that defers the finance lease rules apply to any agreement entered into before March 7, 1984.

[Senate Explanation]

In addition, certain specified farm finance leases are not to be disqualified where a C corporation becomes a partner or beneficiary in the partnership or trust which was the lessor.

[Effective date.—Applies to pre-3-7-84 acquisitions, started construction or binding contracts. Ed.]

[House Explanation]

* * * Telephone excise tax * * *

Present Law.—The [84 Tax Reform] Act extended the three-percent telephone excise tax through December 31, 1987. Due to a clerical error in enrolling the Act, the year 1985 was inadvertently deleted.

Explanation of Provision.—The bill restores the year 1985 to the table of years for which the three-percent telephone excise tax applies. [Effective date.—bills first rendered in 1985. Ed.]

* * * Electronic funds transfer for alcohol and tobacco excise taxes * * *

Present Law.—The [84 Tax Reform] Act requires persons who were liable for $5 million or more in any alcohol or tobacco excise tax during the preceding calendar year to pay that tax by electronic funds transfer during the succeeding calendar year.

Explanation of Provision.—The bill clarifies that all corporations that are members of a controlled group of corporations are treated as one person for purposes of the electronic funds transfer requirement. The term controlled group of corporations has the same meaning as under Code section 1563, except a 50-percent, rather than an 80-percent, common ownership test is applied. It is understood that the Treasury Department administratively will apply this 50-percent common ownership requirement only with respect to taxes due after March 28, 1985.

Additionally, Treasury Department authority to apply these principles to a group of persons under common control where some members of the group are not corporations is clarified. [Effective date.—taxes required to be paid after 9-29-84. Ed.]

[Senate Explanation]

* * * Distilled spirits held in foreign trade zones * * *

Present Law.—The Act increased the excise tax rate on distilled spirits from $10.50 to $12.50 per proof gallon, effective October 1, 1985. Previously removed spirits held for sale on that date were subject to a $2 "floor stocks" tax (subject to certain exceptions).

Explanation of Provision.—The bill clarifies that distilled spirits held in a foreign trade zone on October 1, 1985, and entered into U.S. customs territory after that date, are subject to the floor stocks tax.

[Effective date.—10-1-85. Ed.]

[¶ 4136] SECTION 1802. AMENDMENTS RELATED TO TAX-EXEMPT ENTITY LEASING PROVISIONS

(Secs. 46(e)(4), 47(a), 48(a)(g), 168(j), 7701(e) of the Code, Sec. 31(g); 32 of the 1984 Tax Reform Act)

[House Explanation]

Treatment of use in unrelated trade or business (sec. 168(j)(3)(D) of the Code)

Present Law.—In the case of 19-year real property, the ['84 Tax Reform] Act defines "tax-exempt use property" as the portion of property that is leased to tax-exempt entities under disqualified leases. This definition applies only if the portion of the property leased in a disqualified lease is more than 35 percent of the property. The Act also provides that the term "tax-exempt use property" does not include any portion of a property that is used predominantly in a tax-exempt entity's unrelated trade or business.

Explanation of Provision.—The bill clarifies that the portion of a property that is used in a tax-exempt entity's unrelated trade or business is not treated as used pursuant to a disqualified lease. For example, assume that a tax-exempt entity leases 100 percent of a building for a term of 21 years. Eighty percent of the building is used in the tax-empt entity's unrelated trade or business, and 20 percent is used in its exempt function. No portion of the building constitutes tax-exempt use property because the portion used in a disqualified lease (20 percent) is less than 35 percent of the property.

Treatment of certain previously tax-exempt organizations (secs. 168(j)(4)(E) and (9) of the Code)

Present Law.—Under the Act, the term "tax-exempt entity" includes any organization (other than certain farmers' cooperatives) that was exempt from U.S. income tax at any time during the five-year period ending on the date the property involved is leased to such organization (or any successor organization engaged in substantially similar activities).

Explanation of Provision.—The bill clarifies that the rule for former tax-exempt organizations is not limited to property that is leased to such organizations; the rule applies with respect to any property other than property owned by a former tax-exempt entity or a successor organization. Under the bill, the five-year period ends on the date the property involved is "first used" by a former tax-exempt entity. Property is treated as first used by an organization (a) when the property is first placed in service under a lease to such organization, or (b) in the case of property owned by a partnership (or other pass-through entity) of which the organization is a member, the later of the day on which the property is first used by the partnership (or other pass-through entity) or the day on which the organization is first a member of such partnership (or other pass-through entity).

For purposes of the rules relating to property owned by a partnership, any "tax-exempt controlled entity" is treated as a tax-exempt entity. The term "tax-exempt controlled entity" is defined as any corporation that is not a tax-exempt entity if 50 percent or more (by value) of the corporation's stock is held directly or (by application of section 318) indirectly by one or more tax-exempt entities. In applying section 318, the rules relating to attribution from a corporation are to be applied without regard to the 50-percent test. Therefore, an entity will be treated as owning its proportionate share of stock held by a corporation in which the entity has a direct ownership interest, regardless of the entity's ownership percentage. For example, assume that each of three unrelated tax-exempt entities utilizes a wholly owned taxable subsidiary to invest in one-third of the stock of a fourth taxable corporation. The fourth taxable corporation acquires an interest in a partnership holding depreciable property. Under section 318(a)(2)(C), each tax-exempt entity would be treated as owning one-third of the stock in the fourth taxable corporation. Therefore, the fourth taxable corporation would constitute a tax-exempt controlled entity. * * * [T]he same result would obtain if the three unrelated tax-exempt entities invested in one-third of the stock of a single taxable corporation, and the taxable corporation organized a second taxable corporation; here, the second taxable corporation would constitute a tax-exempt controlled entity.

A tax-exempt controlled entity is not treated as a tax-exempt entity (or as a successor to a tax-exempt entity) if an election is made to treat any gain recognized by a

Act § 1802   ¶ 4136

tax-exempt entity on disposition of an interest in the tax-exempt controlled entity (as well as any dividends or interest received or accrued from the tax-exempt controlled entity) as unrelated business taxable income under section 511. The election binds all tax-exempt entities holding interests in the tax-exempt controlled entity.

[Senate Explanation]

[Effective date.—] The amendment relating to tax-exempt controlled entities applies to property placed in service after * * * [September 27, 1985.], except property acquired pursuant to a written contract that was binding on that date and at all times thereafter. A tax-exempt controlled entity can elect to have the amendments apply to property placed in service on or before * * * [September 27, 1985.]

[This provision was amended on the floor of the Senate, to consider dividends only if properly allocable to income of the tax-exempt controlled entity which was not subject to income tax, as unrelated business taxable income under the above election. Ed.]

[House Explanation]

The bill also clarifies that the Federal Home Loan Mortgage Corporation is not treated as a tax-exempt entity.

Repeal of overlapping regulatory authority (sec. 168(j)(5)(C)(iv) of the Code)

Present Law.—The ['84 Tax Reform] Act authorized the Treasury to determine whether any high-technology telephone station equipment or medical equipment is subject to rapid obsolescence. The Act also provides that the Treasury is to prescribe any other regulations that may be necessary or appropriate to carry out the purposes of section 168(j) (sec. 168(j)(10)).

Explanation of Provision.—The bill repeals the overlapping regulatory authority relating to high-technology equipment.

Partnership rules (secs. 168(j)(8)-(9) and 48(a)(5) of the Code)

Present Law.—The ['84 Tax Reform] Act provides that sections 168(j)(8) (relating to property leased to a partnership) and 168(j)(9) (relating to property owned by a partnership) apply for purposes of paragraphs (4) and (5) of section 48(a) (relating to the nontaxable use restriction on investment credits).

Explanation of Provision.—The bill clarifies the manner in which the partnership rules in section 168(j) apply for purposes of the investment credit provisions. Any portion of a property that is treated as tax-exempt use property by application of paragraph (8) or (9) of section 168(j) is excluded from the definition of section 38 property under paragraphs (4) and (5) of section 48.

Treatment of certain aircraft leased to foreign persons (secs. 47(a) and 48(a) of the Code)

Present Law.—Section 47(a)(7) provides an exception to the investment credit recapture rules for certain leases of aircraft for use predominantly outside the United States. This exception applies if, *inter alia*, an aircraft that qualified for the credit in the taxable year in which it was placed in service would otherwise cease to qualify as section 38 property because it is used predominantly outside the United States.

Under the ['84 Tax Reform] Act, generally, property that is leased for a term of less than six months qualifies as section 38 property, even if the lease is to a foreign person or entity. In the case of aircraft that is leased to a foreign person before January 1, 1990, and is used under a lease that qualifies for treatment under section 47(a)(7), investment credits are not recaptured if the term of such lease does not exceed three years.

Explanation of Provision.—The bill clarifies that the short-term lease exception for aircraft is intended to permit the operation of section 47(a)(7), where property would otherwise cease to qualify as section 38 property because it is leased to a foreign person for use predominantly outside the United States, and not to provide an exception to the definition of section 38 property. * * * Assume an aircraft is placed in service by a U.S. air carrier on January 1, 1986, and is used for the entire taxable year solely in the United States. On January 1, 1987, the aircraft is leased to a foreign person for use predominantly outside the United States, under a "qualifying lease" (within the meaning of section 47(a)(7)). The term of the lease is two years. Because of the application of new section 47(a)(9), as well as section 47(a)(7), no investment credit is recaptured. If such aircraft is disposed of or otherwise ceases to be section 38 property, investment credit recapture will be determined by disregarding the term of the lease to the foreign person. * * * [A]t the end of the two-year lease term, although the U.S. air carrier has actually owned the aircraft for three years, the taxpayer is considered to have used the plane for only one year for * * * the recapture rules.

Section 593 organizations (sec. 46(e)(4) of the Code)

Present Law.—Under the ['84 Tax Reform] Act the lessor of property to a section 593 organization (or "thrift institution") is entitled to no greater a credit with respect to such property than the thrift institution would have been entitled to had it owned the property. The Act also provides rules designed to prevent taxpayers from circumventing the rules with respect to leased property by use of certain arrangements, other than service contracts but including partnerships, under which a thrift institution obtains the use of property.

Explanation of Provision.—The bill clarifies present law by expressly providing that a thrift institution cannot avoid the restriction on property leased to a section 593 organization by use of a partnership.

The bill also clarifies that the tax credit for rehabilitation expenditures is allowable on buildings leased to section 593 organizations in accordance with the rules applicable to buildings leased to tax-exempt entities.

Treatment of certain property held by partnerships (sec. 168(j)(9) of the Code)

Present Law.—If a tax-exempt entity's share of partnership items would be treated as income or loss from an unrelated trade or business under section 511, then the partnership's property will not be treated as tax-exempt use property.

Explanation of Provision.—The bill clarifies that * * * whether a tax-exempt partner's share of partnership items is treated as derived from an unrelated trade or business is to be [determined] without regard to the debt-financed income rules of section 514.

Treatment of service contracts (sec. 7701(e) of the Code)

Present Law.—Section 7701(e) provides rules for use in determining whether an arrangement structured as a service contract is more properly treated as a lease.

Explanation of Provision.—Section 7701(e)(4) is amended by adding a cross reference to the definition of "related entity" in section 168(j).

Effective date provisions

(1) Section 31(g)(3)(B) of the ['84 Tax Reform] Act is amended to clarify that transitional relief is provided only from the application of section 168(j)(9) (as added by the Act).

(2) Section 31(g)(4) of the Act is amended to clarify that certain credit unions qualify for transitional relief, that governmental action before May 23, 1984 qualifies a successor plan for the Greenville, South Carolina, Coliseum, and that certain actions taken with respect to the Essex County, New Jersey, Courthouse qualify as significant governmental action.

(3) Effective for property placed in service by the taxpayer after July 18, 1984, section 31(g)(15)(D) of the Act is amended to clarify that the transitional rule for certain aircraft applies to aircraft originally placed in service after May 23, 1983.

(4) Section 31(g)(17)(H) is amended to clarify that, in the case of Clemson University, the term "property" includes only the Continuing Education Center and component housing projects.

* * * * * *

[Senate Explanation]

(5) Section (g)(17)(L) is amended to clarify that it applies to the Pennsylvania Railroad Station in Newark, New Jersey.

(6) Section 31(g)(20)(B)(ii) of the Act, which provides that improvements to property that qualify for transitional relief also qualify for relief unless the improvement is a substantial improvement, is amended to clarify that the substantial-improvement exception to the rule applies to personal property, as well as real property. This amendment will not apply to personal property if there was a binding written contract to acquire, construct, or rehabilitate the property (or if construction, reconstruction, or rehabilitation of the property began) on or before March 28, 1985.

[**Effective dates.**—Sec. 1802 generally applies to property placed in service after 5-23-83 subject to special rules explained above. Ed.]

[¶4137] SECTION 1803. AMENDMENTS RELATED TO TREATMENT OF BONDS AND OTHER DEBT INSTRUMENTS

(Secs. 1271-1273, 1276, 1278, 1281-1282, 483, 171, 163(e) of the Code; Sec. 44(b), of the '84 Tax Reform Act)

[House Explanation]

Treatment of amounts received on disposition of short-term obligations (sec. 1271 of the Code)

Present Law.—Section 1271 expressly provides that any gain realized on disposition of governmental short-term obligations is treated as ordinary income, to the extent of the ratable share of accrued acquisition discount. Long-standing judicial authority and Treasury regulations provide a basis for characterizing accrued original issue discount (OID) as ordinary income on disposition of nongovernmental obligations.

Explanation of Provision.—The bill clarifies the treatment of amounts received on disposition of nongovernmental obligations. Under a general rule, any gain realized on disposition of a short-term nongovernmental obligation is treated as ordinary income to the extent of the ratable share of accrued

OID. Taxpayers may elect to accrue OID with respect to a short-term nongovernmental obligation under an economic accrual formula, pursuant to which the daily portion of the discount is computed on the basis of the taxpayer's yield to maturity based on the issue price of the obligation, compounded daily. A similar election is provided for the computation of acquisition discount with respect to short-term governmental obligations. An election * * * cannot be revoked without the consent of the Secretary.

Treatment of deduction of OID on short-term obligations (sec. 163(e) of the Code)

Present Law.—In general, interest on a debt instrument with a maturity of one year or less which is payable at the maturity of the instrument is not deductible by a cash-method issuer until paid. *See* Treas. Reg. sec. 1.123-3(b)(1)(iii) (providing that such interest is not included in the "stated redemption price at maturity" for purposes of section 1232, the predecessor of section 1273).

Explanation of Provision.—The bill clarifies present law by expressly providing in section 163(e) that an issuer of a short-term debt instrument may deduct original issue discount and any other interest only in the year of payment. A similar provision was included in the Conference Report to the Act. That provision was deleted in House Concurrent Resolution 328 (June 29, 1984) because it was deemed to be a mere restatement of preexisting law.

* * * * * *

Treatment of certain transfers of market discount bonds (sec. 1276(d) of the Code)

Present Law.—Under the Act, an obligation issued in an exchange subject to section 351 (which provides nonrecognition treatment where appreciated property is transferred to an 80-percent owned corporation * * *) may fall within the definition of the term "market discount bond," without regard to whether the property transferred is a market discount bond (see the discussion of present law, below). Thus, taxpayers are prevented from circumventing the rule that characterizes accrued market discount as interest by swapping a market discount bond for a new bond in a section 351 exchange. A different result may obtain, however, where a taxpayer swaps a market discount bond for stock in a section 351 exchange.

Explanation of Provision.—* * *. Under the bill, accrued market discount is taxed to the transferor of a market discount bond in a section 351 exchange, regardless of whether the transferor receives stock or securities in the exchange. The corporate transferee of the market discount bond will take the bond with a basis that reflects any gain recognized to the transferor (sec. 362(a)). If the stated redemption price of the bond exceeds the transferee's basis immediately after acquisition, then the bond will constitute a market discount bond in the hands of the transferee.

Treatment of bonds acquired at original issue for purposes of market discount rules (sec. 1278(a) of the Code).

Present Law.—Because market discount is defined as any excess of stated redemption price over basis (excluding OID), it is arguable that market discount is created on issuance of obligations in certain nonrecognition (or nontaxable) exchanges. * * *. Under section 358, the basis of a bond received in a section 351 exchange is determined by reference to the basis of the property transferred in exchange for the bond (in the hands of the transferor). Thus, the stated redemption price of the bond will exceed its basis to the extent of any appreciation in the transferred property. Assuming no OID, this excess could be viewed as market discount.

The ['84 Tax Reform] Act provides that the rule that characterizes accrued market discount as interest on disposition of a bond is inapplicable to bonds issued on or before July 18, 1984. If a pre-enactment bond is exchanged for a newly issued bond in a tax-free transaction, however, the new bond is subject to the interest characterization rule, even if the holder of the bond essentially maintains the original investment.

Explanation of Provision.—The bill clarifies that, except as provided by statute or by regulation, no market discount is created on the original issuance of a bond.

Under the bill, two statutory exceptions are provided. The first exception relates to bonds that are part of an issue that is publicly offered. * * *. Under the bill, market discount is created on original issuance of a bond if the holder has a cost basis determined under section 1012, and such basis is less than the issue price of the bond. The difference between the holder's issue price and basis is treated as market discount.

The second statutory exception applies to a bond that is issued in exchange for a market discount bond pursuant to a plan of reorganization. This exception is intended to prevent the holder of a market discount bond from eliminating the taint of unaccrued market discount by swapping the bond for a new bond (e.g., in a recapitalization). Solely for purposes of the interest characterization rule, however, this exception is inapplicable to a bond issued in exchange for a pre-enactment market discount bond where term and interest rate of the new bond is identical to that of the old bond.

If the adjusted basis of a bond is determined by reference to the adjusted basis of the bond in the hands of a person who acquired the bond at original issue, the bond will be treated as acquired by the taxpayer at its original issue.

* * * * * *

[Conference Report]

* * * * * *

Market discount.—The conference agreement contains a provision relating to the treatment of market discount on debt instruments, the principal of which is paid in more than one installment. Under the conference agreement, a holder of such a debt instrument takes accrued market discount into income upon receipt of amounts includible in the debt instrument's stated redemption price at maturity, to the extent of the amounts so received. Rules are provided to prevent double counting of any market discount. In addition, rules are provided to require the recognition of accrued market discount upon the stripping of a debt instrument.

The conference agreement provides that the computation of the accrual of market discount on market discount bonds is to be provided by Treasury regulations. Until such time that the Treasury Department issues such regulations, the conferees intend in the case of debt instruments to which the provision applies, holders may elect to accrue market discount either on the basis of a constant interest rate or as follows: (1) for those debt instruments that have original issue discount ("OID"), market discount shall be deemed to accrue in proportion to the accrual of OID for any accrual period (i.e., the amount of market discount that accrues during a period is equal to the product of (a) the total remaining market discount, and (b) a fraction, the numerator of which is the OID for the period and the denominator of which is the total remaining OID at the beginning of the period), and (2) for those debt instruments that have no OID, the amount of market discount that is deemed to accrue shall be the amount of discount that bears the same ratio to the total amount of remaining market discount that the amount of stated interest paid in the accrual period bears to the total amount of stated interest remaining to be paid on the debt instrument as of the beginning of the accrual period.

In the case of debt instruments that would be subject to the OID rules contained in new Code sec. 1272(a)(6) (without regard to whether the debt instrument has original issue discount), the same prepayment assumption that would be made in computing OID would be made in computing the accrual of market discount (whether or not the taxpayer elects to accrue market discount on the basis of a constant interest rate). In addition, the conferees intend that the same rules that apply to the accrual of market discount on debt instruments whose principal is paid in more than one installment, also is applied in amortizing amortizable bond premium (within the meaning of sec. 171).

*   *   *   *   *

[House Explanation]

*   *   *   *   *   *

Treatment of certain stripped bonds or stripped coupons (sec. 1281(b) of the Code)

*   *   *   *   *   *

Explanation of Provision.—The bill requires the current inclusion in income of OID with respect to stripped bonds and stripped coupons held by the taxpayer who stripped the bond or coupon (or any other person whose basis is determined by reference to the basis in the hands of the stripper).

*   *   *   *   *   *

[Conference Report]

*   *   *   *   *   *

Stripped tax-exempt bonds.—The conference agreement provides that stripped bonds and coupons resulting from the strip of a tax-exempt obligation are subject to the general rules of section 1286, with certain modifications. In the case of such stripped bonds and stripped coupons, the original issue discount ("OID") under section 1286(a) will be limited to the amount of OID that produces a yield to maturity (based on the purchase price of the stripped bond or coupon) equal to the lower of the coupon rate on the original tax-exempt obligation or the actual yield of the stripped bond or coupon. The conferees intend that if a taxpayer can establish the actual yield of a bond (with all coupons attached) at the time of original issue, the taxpayer may elect to

use such yield for purposes of this computation in lieu of the coupon rate.

For example, assume that a tax-exempt obligation with a face amount of $100, two years remaining to maturity, and a coupon rate of ten percent (payable annually) is stripped and the right to the $100 "principal" payment is sold for $79.72 (i.e., a 12-percent yield, compounded annually). Under the conference agreement, the OID is limited to $16.74, which represents the total OID on the stripped bond, assuming a 10-percent yield and a purchase price of $79.72. The amount of OID taken into account under section 1286(a) is tax exempt and shall determine the adjusted basis of the holder in accordance with section 1288(a).

Further, the conference agreement clarifies the application of section 1286(b)(2) (relating to the treatment of the person stripping a bond) to tax-exempt obligations.

*   *   *   *   *   *

[House Explanation]

*   *   *   *   *   *

Accrual of interest on certain short-term obligations (sec. 1281(a) of the Code)

Present Law.—Under section 1281 of the Code, certain taxpayers are required to include in income as interest for a taxable year that portion of the acquisition discount or OID on a short-term obligation that is allocable to the portion of the taxable year during which the taxpayer held the obligation. Acquisition discount is defined as the excess of the stated redemption price at maturity over the taxpayer's basis in the obligation. Similarly, OID is defined as the excess of the stated redemption price at maturity over the issue price of the obligation. The taxpayers affected are those for whom the cash method of accounting for interest income from short-term obligations is considered inappropriate.

Explanation of Provision.—The bill clarifies that taxpayers subject to the rule for mandatory accrual are required to include in income for a taxable year all amounts of interest allocable to that year with respect to short-term obligations, irrespective of whether the interest is stated or is in the form of acquisition discount or OID, and irrespective of when any stated interest is paid. For example, a calendar-year taxpayer designated in section 1281(b) holds an obligation from the time it is issued on October 1, 1985 until its maturity on October 1, 1986. Under the bill, the taxpayer is required to include in income for 1985 the equivalent of three months interest on the obligation, regardless of whether the interest income is in the form of acquisition discount, OID, stated interest, or any combination thereof. * * *.

[Senate Explanation]

[Effective date.] The provision will apply to obligations acquired after [September 27, 1985 Ed.]

Treatment of debt instruments issued for property where there is public trading (sec. 1273(b) of the Code)

Present Law.—Under section 1273(b) of the Code, if a debt instrument is issued for property and either the debt instrument is traded on an established securities market or the property for which it is issued is stock or securities which are traded on an established securities market, the issue price of the instrument is the fair market value of the property.

Explanation of Provision.—The bill permits the Secretary to designate in regulations other types of publicly traded property which for purposes of the issue price provisions will be treated like publicly traded stock or securities.

h. Amortization of bond premium (sec. 171 of the Code)

Present Law.—If a taxable bond is purchased at a premium (i.e., at a price that exceeds the redemption price), the holder may elect to amortize the bond premium over the term of the bond (sec. 171). Amortizable bond premium is allowed as an ordinary deduction. In computing amortizable bond premium, taxpayers are permitted to use a straight-line method. For purposes of these rules, the term "bond" is defined to exclude bonds issued by individuals. An election to amortize bond premium is effective for all bonds held or acquired at or after the beginning of the first taxable year for which the election is made.

*   *   *   *   *   *

Explanation of Provision.—The bill conforms the treatment of bond premium to the treatment of bond discount: bond premium is to be computed under a constant yield method. Amortizable bond premium is computed on the basis of the taxpayer's yield to maturity, determined by using the taxpayer's basis for the bond, and compounding at the close of each "accrual period" (as defined in section 1271(a)(5)). The bill also extends section 171 to obligations issued by individuals.

The provisions will apply to obligations issued after [September 27, 1985 Ed.] For taxpayers who have elections in effect as of the date of enactment, such elections will apply to obligations issued after that date only if the taxpayer so chooses (in such manner as may be prescribed by the Secretary).

The bill also provides that, in determining bond premium for bonds issued after May 6, 1986, the basis of the bond shall be treated as not exceeding its fair market value where the bond was received in an exchange in which the basis of the bond is determined by reference to the basis of the other property. This rule generally will not apply to an exchange of securities in a reorganization.

*   *   *   *   *   *

*   *   *   *   *   *

Clarification of transitional rule (sec. 44 of the ['84 Tax Reform] Act)

Present Law.—Section 44(b) of the Act (relating to effective dates), as amended by section 2 of Public Law 98-612, provides special test and imputation rates under sections 1274 and 483 for certain transactions occurring before July 1, 1985.

Explanation of Provision.—The bill clarifies that the effective date for new section 1274 and section 483 as amended by the Act—transactions after December 31, 1984—is not accelerated by section 2 of Public Law 98-612.

Clarification of interest accrual with respect to transactions involving adequate stated interest (sec. 44(b)(3) of the ['84 Tax Reform] Act)

Present Law.—Section 44(b)(3)(A)(i)(I) of the Act provides that, after March 1, 1984, and before January 1, 1985 (the date on which new section 483 becomes effective), the unstated interest allocable to a taxable year must be computed on an economic accrual basis. Section 44(b)(3)(A)(i)(II) proscribes the accrual of interest on a noneconomic basis with respect to debt instruments issued in a sale or exchange after June 8, 1984, and before January 1, 1985, where there is adequate stated interest for purposes of section 483. The Act contains an exception for transactions pursuant to binding contracts in effect on March 1, 1984.

Explanation of Provision.—The bill clarifies that, in the case of debt instruments issued for property in transactions occurring after December 31, 1984, whether involving adequate stated interest or inadequate stated interest, interest may not be computed using any method other than economic accrual, as described in Rev. Rul. 83-84, 1983-1 C.B. 9.

The bill also changes the binding contract date applicable to transactions involving adequate stated interest. The exception to the statutory requirement of economic accrual is made applicable to transactions occurring pursuant to a written contract that was binding on June 8, 1984 and at all times thereafter until the transaction was closed. No inference is intended regarding the proper treatment (under other provisions of the Code, or under general tax law principles) of noneconomic accruals of interest with respect to obligations issued before the effective date of the Act.

*   *   *   *   *   *

Clarification of effective date for repeal of capital asset requirement (sec. 44(g) of the ['84 Tax Reform] Act)

*   *   *   *   *   *

Explanation of Provision.—The bill clarifies that section 1272 does not apply to obligations issued on or before December 31, 1984, for obligations that are not capital assets in the hands of the holder.

Effective dates.—Short-term nongovernment and government provisions apply generally for sales and exchanges after 1984. Specific rules apply to obligations acquired after 7-18-84 or 9-27-85, and post-5-6-86 exchanges. For additional special effective dates, sec ¶1805.

[¶4138] SECTION 1804. AMENDMENTS RELATED TO CORPORATE PROVISIONS

(Secs. 246, 246A, 280G, 291, 312, 332, 337, 338, 341, 361, 368, 562, 852, of the Code, Secs. 53.60 of the '84 Tax Reform Act)

[House Explanation]

Debt-financed portfolio stock (sec. 246A of the Code)

Present Law.—The ['84 Tax Reform] Act added a provision generally limiting the dividends received deduction for dividends received by a corporate shareholder with respect to debt-financed portfolio stock.

Explanation of Provision.—The bill clarifies the rules for applying the provision in cases in which dividends are received from certain foreign corporations engaged in business in the United States. For example, assume that 70 percent of a domestic corporation's purchase price for portfolio stock of a foreign corporation described in section 245(a) is debt financed. Assume further that 60 percent of that foreign corporation's gross income is effectively connected with the conduct of a trade or business in the United States. In the absence of section 246A, the domestic corporation generally would be entitled to deduct 51 percent (85 percent times 60 percent) of any dividend received from the foreign corporation. Under section 246A and the bill, the domestic corporation generally is entitled to deduct only 15.3 percent (30 percent times 85 percent) times 60 percent) of any such dividend.

[Effective date.—] Generally stock withholding period starting after 7-18-84. Ed.]

*   *   *   *   *   *

[Senate Explanation]

*   *   *   *   *   *

Holding period rules for dividend received deduction (sec. 246(c) of the Code).

*   *   *   *   *   *

Explanation of Provision.—The bill disallows the dividend received deduction where the holding period requirement is not met, without regard to whether the stock has been disposed of. Thus, where the holding period requirement has not been met on the 45th day (90th day in the case of certain preference dividends) after the ex-dividend date, the dividend received deduction will not be allowed. The amendment is not intended to require, for example, that the holding period be met by the date the dividend is received where the stock was acquired less than 45 days before that date, provided the stock is held for 45 days or more. No inference is intended as to the proper interpretation of present law.

The provision will apply to obligations acquired after March 1, 1986.

In addition, the committee wishes to clarify that the 1984 Act did not change the principle that the dividend received deduction is not disallowed by reason of an out-of-the money call option that affords the corporation no protection against loss in the event the stock declines in value. See Revenue Ruling 80-238, 1980-2 C.B. 96.

[House Explanation]

Application of related party rule to section 265(2) of the Code (section 53(e) of the Act).

Present Law.—Section 265(2) of the Code disallows the deduction of interest incurred or continued to purchase or carry tax-exempt obligations.

*   *   *   *   *   *

The ['84 Tax Reform] Act (Code sec. 7701(f) provides that the Treasury Department is to prescribe such regulations as may be necessary or appropriate to prevent the avoidance of Federal tax provisions which deal with (i) the linking of borrowing to investment, or (ii) diminishing risks, through the use of related persons, pass-through entities, or other intermediaries. This provision was specifically intended to apply to (but not to be limited to) the disallowance rule provided by sections 265(2).

Under the Act, the provision regarding related persons, pass-through entities, and other intermediaries was effective on the date of enactment (July 18, 1984).

Explanation of Provision.—Under the bill, the provision regarding related parties, pass-through entities, and other intermediaries generally remains effective as of July 18, 1984 (i.e., the date of enactment). However, the bill clarifies that this provision, insofar as it relates to section 265(2) of the Code only, is effective for (1) term loans made after July 18, 1984, and (2) demand loans outstanding after July 18, 1984 (other than any loan outstanding on July 18, 1984, and repaid before September 18, 1984). "Demand loans" mean any loan which is payable in full at any time on the demand of the lender. For purposes of this effective date rule, any loan renegotiated, extended, or revised after July 18, 1984, is treated as a loan made after such date.

Exempt-interest dividends from regulated investment companies (sec. 852 of the Code)

*   *   *   *   *   *

Act § 1804   ¶4138

Explanation of Provision.—Under the bill, if a taxpayer holds stock of a regulated investment company for 6 months or less, any loss on the sale or exchange of that stock is disallowed to the extent the taxpayer received exempt-interest dividends with respect to that stock. Conforming amendments are made, and an exception is provided for dispositions pursuant to a periodic liquidation plan.

In addition, the Secretary is given authority to shorten the 6 months requirement to a period of not less than the greater of 31 days or the period between regular dividend distributions where the RIC regularly distributes at least 90 percent of its net tax-exempt interest. The distribution period is to be shortened only where the purpose of the holding period requirement can be adequately fulfilled without requiring that the stock be held 6 months.

The provision applies to stock with respect to which the taxpayer's holding period begins after March 28, 1985.

[Senate Explanation]

Accumulated earnings tax (sec. 562 of the Code)

*   *   *   *   *   *

Explanation of Provision.—The bill provides that, except to the extent provided by the Secretary of the Treasury, no dividends paid deduction will be allowed, for purposes of the accumulated earnings tax, in the case of any stock redemption by a mere holding or investment company which is not a regulated investment company. The bill will apply to * * * distributions after 9-27-85.]

[House Explanation]

Definition of affiliated group (sec. 1504 of the Code)

Present Law.—The Act substantially revised the definition of "affiliated group". To apply the new rules, a determination must be made as to the ownership of "stock" of a corporation. Under the Act and section 1504(a)(4), "stock" does not include stock which, among other things, has redemption and liquidation rights which do not exceed the paid-in capital or par value represented by such stock (except for a reasonable redemption premium in excess of such paid-in capital or par values).

*   *   *   *   *   *

The Act substantially revised the rules relating to DISCs and former DISCs. Under the new rules, there is less reason to keep a former DISC and its parent from filing consolidated returns. Furthermore, if a former DISC is not treated as an includible corporation, its parent may be able to selectively deconsolidate subsidiaries.

Explanation of Provision.—Section 1504(a)(4) is amended to exclude stock which has redemption and liquidation rights which do not exceed the issue price of such stock (except for a reasonable redemption or liquidation premium). The amendment makes

irrelevant the accounting treatment given the issuance of the stock.

Under the bill, any DISC or any other corporation that has accumulated DISC income derived after 1984 will not be an includible corporation. It is intended that this provision will not affect the status of certain S corporations with DISC subsidiaries who were "grandfathered" by the Subchapter S Revision Act of 1982.

[Effective date.—] Generally tax years beginning after 12-31-84. Ed.

Effective date of affiliated group provision (sec. 60 of the ['84 Tax Reform] Act)

Present Law.—The Act substantially revised the definition of "affiliated group". The provision was generally effective for taxable years beginning after December 31, 1984. However, section 60(b)(2) of the Act provided a grandfather rule with respect to any corporation which on June 22, 1984, was a member of an affiliated group filing a consolidated return for such corporation's taxable year which includes June 22, 1984—for purposes of determining whether such corporation continues to be a member of such group for taxable years beginning before January 1, 1988, the provision does not apply. Under section 60(b)(3) of the Act, the grandfather rule described in the preceding sentence does not apply once a "sell-down" with respect to the corporation involved has occurred.

Explanation of Provision.—The bill makes several technical changes with respect to the effective date rules.

First, the grandfather rule ceases to apply as of the first day after June 22, 1984, on which the corporation involved would not qualify as a member of the group under prior law. Thus, for example, a corporation which ceased to be a member of a group on July 31, 1985, under prior law but which on July 31, 1985 (and thereafter), qualifies as a member of the group under the Act's substantive rule is treated as continuing to be a member of the group.

Second, the bill amends section 60(b)(3) of the Act to clarify the "sell-down" exception to the grandfather rule. Thus, the exception does not apply, and the grandfather rule continues to apply, if the percentage interest (by fair market value) in the stock of the corporation involved held by other members of the group (determined without regard to section 60(b)(3) of the Act) does not decline as a result of the sale, exchange, or redemption of such corporation's stock. Also, the bill provides that the "sell down" exception applies in certain cases where there is a letter of intent between a corporation and securities underwriter entered into on or before June 22, 1984.

Third, the bill allows a common parent corporation to elect to have this provision apply to taxable years beginning after December 31, 1983.

Finally, the bill delays the effective date for one specified corporation until the earlier of January 1, 1994, or the date on which the voting power of certain preferred stock terminates, and exempts one specified corporation from the new rules.

Complete liquidations of subsidiaries, etc. (secs. 332, 337 and 338 of the Code)

Present Law.—Prior to the ['84 Tax Reform] Act, the rules applicable in determining whether a corporation qualified as a corporation which could be liquidated under section 332 were substantially similar to the general rules applicable in determining whether that corporation was a member of an affiliated group under section 1504. The Act substantially amended the general rules of section 1504 but not those of section 332. As a result, there is now discontinuity between the two sections. Thus, a corporation might be liquidated tax free under section 332 even though it and its "parent" are not members of the same affiliated group under new section 1504. The converse is also true. This discontinuity may produce unacceptable tax consequences.

For example, assume that beginning on January 1, 1985, P Corporation's ownership of S Corporation satisfies new section 1504 but not present-law section 332 and that, under new section 1504, P and S file consolidated returns for the 1985 calendar year. Assume further that (1) S adopts a plan of complete liquidation in 1985, then sells all its assets, and then liquidates within 12 months from the date the plan is adopted, and (2) P does not liquidate. Because S's liquidation does not qualify under section 332, S may be able to avail itself of section 337 (sec 337(c)(2)). That result is appropriate so long as P is taxed on S's liquidation, as would in general be the result given the inapplicability of section 332. However, since P and S file a consolidated return, S's liquidation would not be taxable to P under Treas. regs. sec. 1.1502-14(b) (assuming S distributes no cash to P in the liquidation). Therefore, S could dispose of all its assets and liquidate, with neither P nor S incurring any current tax liability.

As a further example, assume that (1) J Corporation's ownership of K Corporation stock satisfies present-law section 332 but not new section 1504, and (2) the two corporations are not filing a consolidated return under section 60(b)(2) of the Act for their 1985 calendar year. Assume further that K adopts a plan of complete liquidation within 12 months. Under section 332, the liquidation would not be taxable to J. Furthermore, it would appear that, since J and K are not in a new section 1504(a)(2) relationship, K may be able to avail itself of section 337 (sec. 337(c)(3)). Again, K could dispose of its assets and liquidate, with neither J nor K incurring any tax liability. (On the other hand, if J and K were filing consolidated returns under section 60(b)(2) of the Act, K could not avail itself of section 337 unless J timely liquidated. J would be a "distributee corporation" under section 837(c)(3)(B) since new section 1504 would not yet apply.)

[Senate Explanation]

Explanation of Provision.—The bill amends section 332. Section 332 will not apply unless, among other things, the corporation receiving the liquidating distribution was, on the date of the adoption of the plan of liquidation and continued to be at all times until receipt of the liquidating distributions, the owner of stock in the liquidating corporation meeting the requirements of new section 1504(a)(2). In applying section 1504(a)(2) for this purpose, the objective is to harmonize section 332 and section 1504(a)(2). Thus, it is generally intended that other parts of new section 1504(a), e.g., section 1504(a)(4), are applicable. However, section (a)(5)(E) is not applicable. It is not concerned with section 1504(a)(2) but rather with the effect of transfers within a group of a member's stock.) The new rule also applies even if one (or both) of the corporations involved is not an includible corporation under section 1504(b). Under this rule, S in the first example above could be liquidated under section 332. However, S could avail itself of section 337 only if P complied with section 337(c)(3)(A)(i). In the second example above, J would be taxed because section 332 would not apply and because J and K, by definition, could not be filing a consolidated return.

Under the bill, the term "distributee corporation" under section 337(c)(3) is also amended. The amendment defines the term to mean any corporation which receives a distribution in a complete liquidation of the selling corporation to which section 332 applies. It also includes each other corporation "up the line" which receives a distribution in complete liquidation of another distributee corporation to which section 332 applies. Thus, assume, for example, that (1) M owns 100 percent of the stock of N, (2) N owns 100 percent of the stock of O, and (3) the 3 corporations are filing a consolidated return under new section 1504 for the calendar year 1985. If M transfers 30 percent of the stock of N to O, under regulations, the 3 corporations would continue to be eligible (or be required) to file a consolidated return (sec. 1504(a)(5)(E)). If N adopted a plan of complete liquidation, sold all its assets, and then liquidated within 12 months, under Treas. regs. sec. 1.1502-34, both M and O generally would be entitled to tax-free treatment under section 332. Under the bill, N could not avail itself of section 337 unless, among other things, both M and O complied with section 337(c)(3)(A)(i).

Also, under the bill, the definition of "qualified stock purchase" in section 338 is conformed to the definition in section 1504(a)(2). The change will apply where the 12 month acquisition period begins after March 1, 1986. [12-31-85, See Conference Report.]

The amendment to section 337(c)(3)(B) applies with respect to plans of complete liquidation pursuant to which any distribution is made in a taxable year beginning after December 31, 1984. Thus, in the example

Act § 1804   ¶ 4138

above involving J and K, K could not avail itself of section 337 unless J timely liquidated because J would be a "distributee corporation" under the amendment.

Except as indicated below, the amendment to section 332 is generally applicable with respect to distributions pursuant to plans of liquidation adopted after March 28, 1985. Except as indicated below, the amendment is also applicable with respect to distributions pursuant to a plan of complete liquidation adopted on or before that date, but only if (1) any distribution is made in a taxable year beginning after December 31, 1984, and (2) the liquidating corporation and any corporation which receives a distribution in complete liquidation of such corporation are members of an affiliated group of corporations which is filing a consolidated return for the taxable year which includes the distribution. However, the amendment to section 332 does not apply with respect to distributions pursuant to any plan of complete liquidation if the liquidating corporation is a member of an affiliated group of corporations under section 60(b)(2) or (5) (relating to Native Corporations established under the Alaska Native Claims Settlement Act) of the Act for each taxable year in which it makes a distribution.

The application of the effective date rules is illustrated by the following examples.

Example (1).—Assume that Q Corporation's ownership of the stock of R Corporation satisfies section 332 of present law and section 1504 of prior law but not section 332 as it is amended by the bill. (Under these facts, Q and R could not be filing a consolidated return unless grandfathered under the Act's amendment of section 1504). Assume further that R adopts a plan of complete liquidation on October 1, 1984, then sells its assets, and, then, before October 1, 1985, completely liquidates. Regardless of whether Q and R are filing consolidated returns under section 60(b)(2) of the Act for the calendar year 1985, and regardless of whether the liquidation is completed before January 1, 1985, the amendment to section 332 would not apply. As a result, R's liquidation could qualify under section 332. (However, R could avail itself of section 337 only if Q timely liquidated.)

Example (2).—Assume that S Corporation's ownership of the stock of T Corporation would satisfy new section 332 but not section 332 of present law or section 1504 of prior law. Assume further that on October 1, 1984, T adopts a plan of complete liquidation and then, making no sales or exchanges of assets in the interim, completes its liquidation on October 5, 1984. The amendment to section 332 would not apply. As a result, section 382 could not apply.

Example (3).—The facts are the same as in Example (2) except that (a) T adopts its plan on January 10, 1985, and completes its liquidation on January 15, 1985, and (b) S and T file a consolidated return for the calendar year 1985 under new section 1504. The amendment to section 332 would be applicable. As a result, section 332 could be applicable.

Example (4).—The facts are the same as in Example (2) except that T sells assets between October 1, 1984, and October 5, 1984. New section 332 would not be applicable. As a result, section 332 could not apply, and T could avail itself of section 337.

Example (5).—The facts are the same as in Example (3) except that T sells assets between January 10, 1985, and January 15, 1985. The amendment to section 332 would apply. As a result, section 332 could apply. If it did, T could not avail itself of section 337 unless, among other things, S timely liquidated. (If S and T were not filing a consolidated return under new section 1504 for the calendar year 1985, the amendment to section 332 would not apply. As a result, T's liquidation would not be a section 332 liquidation, and T could avail itself of section 337.)

Example (6).—Assume that Corporation U's ownership of the stock of Corporation V satisfies section 332 of present law but not section 332 as it would be amended and that U and V are filing a consolidated return for the calendar year 1985, under section 60(b)(2) of the Act. On December 10, 1985, V adopts a plan of complete liquidation, then sells all its assets, and then liquidates on December 15, 1985. The amendment to section 332 would not apply. As a result, section 332 could apply. If it did, V could avail itself of section 337 only if, among other things, U timely liquidated.

Finally the bill delays the effective date of the amendment made to section 311(d) in the case of one specified parent-subsidiary group.

[House Explanation]

Earnings and profits (sec. 312 of the Code)

Present Law.—The ['84 Tax Reform] Act substantially revised the definition of a corporation's "earnings and profits".

One change was to increase a distributing corporation's earnings and profits by the amount of any gain which would be recognized if section 311(d)(2) did not apply to an ordinary, non-liquidating distribution by the corporation of appreciated property. However, the Act added no separate provision for reducing earnings and profits for all or any portion of that amount.

The Act also amended the rules regarding the effect on earnings and profits of a corporation's redemption of its own stock (sec. 312(n)(8) of current law). However, the Act did not contain a specific effective date for that amendment.

In addition, the Act provided that the rules relating to LIFO inventory, installment sales and completed contract method of accounting would apply to foreign corporations only in the case of taxable years beginning after December 31, 1985.

[Senate Explanation]

Explanation of Provision.—The bill repeals section 312(n)(4) and section 312(c)(3) and amends section 312(b). Under section 312(b), as amended, the distribution by a corporation of property the fair market value of which exceeds its adjusted basis increases the earnings and profits of the distributing corporation by the amount of such excess. The distribution results in a decrease to earnings and profits under * * * of section 312(a). Thus, assume that a corporation has no accumulated earnings and profits and no other current earnings and profits. Assume further that in 1985 it distributes property with a zero basis and a $1,000 value to an individual shareholder in a transaction described in section 311(d)(2). The distribution increases the distributing corporation's earnings and profits of the taxable year to $1,000. Thus, the distributing corporation's earnings and profits for the taxable year (as determined at the close of the taxable year under Treas. Reg. § 1.316-1(a)(1)) shall account for all gain attributable to the distribution of appreciated property.

The bill provides that section 312(n)(8) of current law applies to redemption distributions in taxable years beginning after September 30, 1984.

[The above provision was further amended on the floor of the Senate to: (1) In case of distributions of appreciated property, to apply Sec. 312(a)(3) by using the fair market value of the property instead of the adjusted basis. (2) Extend the moratorium on the application of Sec. 312(n)(6) to foreign corporations through 12-31-87. Ed.]

Treatment of transferor corporation (secs. 361 and 368 of the Code)

* * * * * *

Explanation of Provision.—The bill amends section 361 to provide that the transferor corporation does not recognize gain or loss on the transfer to the acquiring corporation pursuant to the plan of reorganization, without regard to whether properties received are distributed pursuant to the plan of reorganization.

In addition, the bill clarifies that section 336 and 337 (relating to liquidations) are not applicable to transfers of property pursuant to the plan of reorganization, but that section 311(d), requiring recognition of gain, is applicable to distributions of property pursuant to a plan of reorganization by any corporation which is a party to the reorganization. The bill provides that any property received by a transferor corporation in a reorganization will have a fair market value. In addition, in the case of a C reorganization, no gain or loss will be recognized on any disposition pursuant to the reorganization of stock or securities which were received pursuant to the plan of reorganization and which are in another corporation which is a party to the reorganization.

The bill also clarifies that the distribution requirement of section 368(a)(2)(G) will be satisfied where distributions are made to creditors, as well as shareholders, of the transferor corporation.

These provisions will apply to plans of reorganizations adopted after date of enactment of this Act.

The bill also clarifies that a reorganization, involving a "drop-down" of assets to a subsidiary, which qualifies as a "C" reorganization, without regard to section 368(a)(2)(A) (relating to reorganizations described in both paragraphs (C) and (D) of section 368(a)(1)), will continue to qualify as a reorganization.

Collapsible corporations (sec. 341 of the Code)

* * * * * *

Explanation of Provision.—The bill applies the collapsible corporation provisions whether or not the stock has been held 6 months. The provision will apply to sales and exchanges after March 1, 1986. [9-27-85. See Conference Report.]

Golden parachutes (sec. 280G of the Code)

* * * * * *

Explanation of Provisions.—Exemption for certain corporations.—*In general.*—Under the bill, the term parachute payment does not include any payment made to (or for the benefit of) a disqualified individual (1) with respect to a corporation that was, immediately before the change in control, a small business corporation or (2) with respect to a corporation no stock of which was, immediately before the change in control, readily tradable on an established securities market, or otherwise, provided shareholder approval was obtained with respect to the payment to a disqualified individual.

Small business corporation.—A corporation qualifies as a small business corporation if the corporation does not (1) have more than 35 shareholders, (2) have a shareholder who is not an individual (other than an estate or a qualifying trust), (3) have a nonresident alien as a shareholder, and (4) have more than one class of stock.

Corporation with no readily tradable securities.—The Secretary of the Treasury may, by regulations, provide that a corporation fails to meet the requirement that it has no stock that is readily tradable if a substantial portion of the assets of any entity consists (either directly or indirectly) of stock in the corporation and interests in the entity are readily tradable on an established securities market, or otherwise. For example, if a publicly traded corporation sells the stock of a 70 percent subsidiary and the assets of the subsidiary constitute a substantial portion of the assets of the parent, the committee intends that the exemption for a corporation with no readily tradable securities will not be available with respect to payments to disqualified individuals on account of the change in ownership or control of the subsidiary.

The committee is also concerned that, absent specific rules, a taxpayer might utilize the exemption for shareholder approval to avoid the golden parachute provisions by creating tiers of entities. Such avoidance is possible if the gross value of the entity-shareholder's interest in the corporation constitutes a substantial portion of such entity's

Act § 1804   ¶ 4138

assets. The committee contemplates that, in such cases, the Secretary will adopt regulations requiring approval of the owners of the entity rather than the approval of the entity itself. Of course, such shareholder approval may be obtained only if the entity shareholder also has no stock that is readily tradable. On the other hand, if the entity's interest in the corporation constitutes less than substantial portion of its assets, approval of the compensation arrangement by the authorized officer of the entity is sufficient because, under present law, the golden parachute provisions do not apply to the sale of less than a substantial portion of the assets of a corporation (in this case, the entity).

The shareholder approval requirements are met with respect to any payment if (1) the payment is approved by a separate vote of the shareholders who, immediately before the change in ownership or control, hold more than 75 percent of the voting power of all outstanding stock of the corporation and (2) adequate disclosure was made to all shareholders of the material facts concerning payments that, absent this exemption, would be parachute payments.

The committee intends that adequate disclosure to shareholders will include full and truthful disclosure of the material facts and such additional information as may be necessary to make the disclosure not materially misleading. Further, the committee intends that an omitted fact will be considered material if there is a substantial likelihood that a reasonable shareholder would consider it important.

A disqualified individual who is to receive payments that would be parachute payments (absent shareholder approval) and who is a shareholder is removed from the shareholder base against which the shareholder approval test is applied. A shareholder who is related (under the principles of sec. 318) to the disqualified individual described in the preceding sentence is also removed from the shareholder base. If all shareholders are disqualified individuals or related to disqualified individuals, then disqualified individuals are not removed from the shareholder base.

Reasonable compensation.—In the case of any payment made on account of a change in ownership or control, the amount treated as a parachute payment will not include the portion of such payment that the taxpayer establishes by clear and convincing evidence is reasonable compensation for personal services to be rendered on or after the date of the change in ownership or control. Moreover, such payments are not taken into account in determining whether the threshold (i.e., 3 times the base amount) contained in the definition of parachute payments is exceeded.

The committee intends that reasonable compensation for services to be rendered may include, under certain circumstances, payments to an individual as damages for a breach of contract. For example, if an employer fires an employee before the end of a contract term, the amount the employee collects as damages for salary and other

compensation may be treated as reasonable compensation for services to be rendered if (1) the damages do not exceed the compensation the individual would have received if the individual continued to perform services for the employer; (2) the individual demonstrates, by clear and convincing evidence, that the payments were received because an offer to work was made and rejected; and (3) any damages were reduced by mitigation. One the other hand, if damages are collected for a failure to make severance payments, damages collected would not be for personal services to be rendered because the individual does not have to demonstrate a willingness to work and reduce damages by mitigation.

The committee intends that evidence that amounts paid to a disqualified individual for services to be rendered that are not significantly greater than amounts of compensation (other than compensation contingent on a change in ownership or control or termination of employment) paid to the disqualified individual in prior years or customarily paid to similarly situated employees by the employer or by comparable employers will normally serve as clear and convincing evidence of reasonable compensation for such services.

The amount treated as an excess parachute payment is reduced by the portion of the payment that the taxpayer establishes by clear and convincing evidence is reasonable compensation for personal services actually rendered before the change in control. For purposes of this provision, reasonable compensation for services performed before the date of change is first offset against the base amount.

Exemption for payments under qualified plans.—Under the bill, the term parachute payment does not include any payment from or under a qualified pension, profit-sharing, or stock bonus plan (sec. 401(a)), a qualified annuity plan (sec. 403(a)), or a simplified employee pension (sec. 408(k)). Moreover, such payments from or under a qualified plan are not taken into account in determining whether the threshold for excess parachute payments is exceeded.

Treatment of affiliated groups.—The bill provides that, except as otherwise provided in regulations, all members of an affiliated group of corporations (sec. 1504) shall be treated as a single corporation for purposes of the golden parachute provisions. Any person who is an officer or highly compensated individual with respect to any member of the affiliated group is treated as an officer or highly compensated individual of such single corporation. Notwithstanding the general definition of an affiliated group of corporations, for purposes of this provision, an affiliated group of corporations also includes the following:

(1) Tax-exempt corporations;

(2) Insurance companies;

(3) Foreign corporations (unless the disqualified individual is employed by a foreign corporation that is acquired by another foreign corporation, neither of which is subject to tax in the U.S.);

(4) Corporations with respect to which a possession tax credit election (sec. 936) is in effect for the taxable year);

(5) Regulated investment companies and real estate investment trusts; and

(6) A DISC or former DISC.

Definition of highly compensated individual.—Under the bill, the term highly compensated individual is defined to include only an employee (or a former employee) who is among the highest-paid one percent of individuals performing services for the corporation or for any corporation that is a member of an affiliated group or the 250 highest paid individuals who perform services for a corporation or for each member of an affiliated group.

Excluded amounts.—Under the bill, amounts that are not treated as parachute payments are not taken into account in determining whether the threshold contained in the definition of parachute payments is exceeded. This provision applies to (1) payments made with respect to a small business corporation or a corporation that satisfies the shareholder approval requirements; (2) payments that are reasonable compensation for personal services to be rendered on or after the date of the change of control; and (3) payments from or under a qualified plan.

Securities laws violation.—The bill limits the treatment of payments made pursuant to an agreement that violates securities laws as parachute payments only to violations of generally enforced securities laws or regulations. Further, the Internal Revenue Service is to bear the burden of proof with respect to the occurrence of a securities law violation.

Effective date.—The provisions are effective as if enacted in DEFRA. For example, amounts paid before the date of enactment under an agreement otherwise subject to the golden parachute provisions may be exempt from such provisions under the small business corporation exception, the shareholder approval exception, the exception for payments from or under a qualified plan, or exceptions for payments of reasonable compensation for services to be rendered. In addition, shareholder approval could be obtained after the date of enactment with respect to prior transactions.

Further, the committee intends that a contract is not treated as amended in a significant, relevant respect under certain circumstances. For example, if a nonqualified stock bonus plan is amended to prevent the forfeiture of previously granted but unvested shares in the event of the termination of the plan following a merger, consolidation, or sale, such an amendment is not treated as amending the plan in a significant, relevant respect. This rule applies provided that participants in the plan are entitled to no grandfathered parachute benefits that have the effect of compensating them for the possible forfeiture of shares in the event of a merger, consolidation, or sale of the corpora-

tion. Under the plan, if the company terminates the plan, the vesting of previously granted shares would continue as if the plan had not been terminated. If the company is sold, however, the plan could be terminated without allowing previously granted shares to continue to vest. Under this situation, participants are not entitled to benefits that are contingent on a change in ownership or control. Instead, the plan amendment merely prevents the possible forfeiture of benefits that could occur only in the event of the merger, consolidation, or sale of the corporation. On the other hand, whether an award made after June 14, 1984, under the plan constitutes a parachute payment will depend on the facts and circumstances at the time the award is made.

[House Explanation]

Corporate tax preferences (sec. 291 of the Code)

Present Law.—The Act generally increased the corporate tax preference cutback (sec. 291) from 15 to 20 percent.

Explanation of Provision.—The bill makes several clerical amendments, including a clarification that the prior law DISC provision did not apply to subchapter S corporations.

[Conference Report]

The conference agreement follows the Senate amendment except that the provision relating to the definition of qualified stock purchase applies for purchases begun after December 31, 1985; the provision relating to collapsible corporations applies to sales after September 27, 1985; and the agreement contains the provision in the House bill retaining the prior law consolidated return rules for a specified corporation.

The conference agreement also provides that, during the applicable transition period, the affiliation requirements of the consolidated returns provisions will be applied to Alaska Native Corporations (and their wholly owned subsidiaries), and to another specified group of corporations, solely by reference to the express language in those provisions. Thus, eligibility for affiliation in the case of such corporations will be determined solely on the basis of ownership of stock satisfying the 80-percent voting power and 80-percent nonvoting stock tests, without regard (for example) to the value of the stock owned, to escrow arrangements, voting trusts, redemption or conversion rights, stock warrants or options, convertible debt, liens, or similar arrangements, or to the motive for acquisition of the stock or affiliation.

In addition, with certain specified exceptions, no provision of the Internal Revenue Code or principle of law will apply to deny the benefit of losses or credits of Native Corporations (or their wholly owned subsidiaries) to the affiliated group of which the corporation is a member or of the specified group of corporations, during the applicable transition period. Thus, in general, the benefit of such losses and credits may not be denied in whole or in part by application of section 269, section 482, the assignment of income doctrine, or any other provision of the Internal Revenue Code or principle of law.

In addition, the conference agreement makes certain modifications to the provision relating to the treatment of the transferor corporation in a tax-free reorganization (sec. 361). In any type of reorganization, no gain or loss is recognized by the acquired corporation on a disposition of stock or securities (in a party to the reorganization) received from the acquiring corporation, provided the disposition is pursuant to the plan of reorganization.[1] Gain (but not loss) is recognized on distributions pursuant to the plan of any "boot" including pre-acquisition assets of the acquired corporation. However, under the provision, boot received from the acquiring corporation will generally take a basis equal to its fair market value at the time of transfer.

For purposes of this provision, a transfer to creditors of the acquired corporation will be deemed pursuant to the plan of reorganization if the acquired corporation is liquidated or merged pursuant to the plan of reorganization (or, in the case of a "C" reorganization, the Secretary has waived the liquidation requirement), and the transfer to creditors is pursuant to such liquidation or merger. No inference is intended as to whether transfers of stock or securities to creditors in such circumstances may be regarded as pursuant to a plan of reorganization under present law.

The conference agreement also provides that a specified corporation will be treated as having made a valid section 338 election with respect to a certain stock acquisition.

The conference agreement is not intended, with respect to the golden parachute provision relating to the adoption of the affiliated group rules, to create an inference with respect to the definition of a change in control.

[¶ 1439] SECTION 1805. AMENDMENTS RELATED TO PARTNERSHIP PROVISIONS

(Secs. 368,706,707,761,1031, of the Code)

[House Explanation]

Retroactive allocations (sec. 706(d) of the Code)

* * * * * *

Explanation of Provision.—The bill clarifies that the rule described in present law applies to all cases in which the rule is necessary to allocate cash basis items to the period to which the items are attributable, even though no change in partnership interests occurs during the current taxable year.

[Effective Date.—periods after 3-31-84. Ed.]

Disguised sale transactions (sec. 707(a)(2)(B) of the Code)

Present Law.—The ['84 Tax Reform] Act provides that, under Treasury regulation, if (1) a partner transfers money or other property (directly or indirectly) to a partnership, (2) there is a related direct or indirect transfer of money or other property by the partnership to that partner (or another partner), and (3) when viewed together, the transfers described above are properly characterized as a sale of property, the transaction is to be treated (as appropriate) as a transaction between the partnership and a nonpartner or as a transaction between two or more partners acting in nonpartnership capacities. This "disguised sale" rule is intended to prevent the parties from characterizing a sale or exchange of property as a contribution to the partnership followed by a distribution from the partnership, and thereby to defer or avoid tax on the transaction.

Explanation of Provision.—The bill specifies that "disguised sale" treatment is to apply to cases in which the transfers to and from the partnership (as described above), when viewed together, are properly characterized as an exchange of property, as well as to cases in which such transfers are properly characterized as a sale.

[Effective date.—transfers after 3-31-84, Ed.].

Transfers of partnership interests by corporation (sec. 386 of the Code)

* * * * * *

Explanation of Provision.—The bill amends section 386 to specifically limit the amount of gain recognized by a corporation upon a distribution of a partnership interest in a nonliquidating distribution to which section 311 applies. The maximum amount of gain recognized * * * is the gain that would have been recognized upon the sale of the distributed interest at its fair market value. Thus, for example, a corporation that acquired its interest by making a cash contribution to an existing partnership would recognize no gain if it immediately distributed the interest to its shareholders, regardless of the basis of the partnership property attributable to its interest.

The amendment to section 386 does not affect the recognition of recapture income by a distributing corporation. Under section 751(a), a partner is required to treat the sale of a partnership interest as a sale or exchange of property other than a capital asset to the extent of the unrealized receivables (including recapture property) and inventory of the partnership attributable to the transferred interest. Thus, a corporation making a distribution of a partnership interest will recognize depreciation recapture with re-

---

[Footnote ¶ 4138] (1) This provision is not intended, however, to affect the recognition of discharge of indebtedness income by the acquired corporation on a transfer to a creditor.

spect to the partnership recapture property attributable to the distributed interest.

The Secretary is given authority to promulgate regulations to prevent the use of this provision to avoid the nonrecognition of loss rule of section 811(a). In particular, the Committee is concerned that prior to a distribution of partnership interests a corporation might contribute to a partnership property the adjusted basis of which exceeds its fair market value, thereby reducing the gain inherent in the distributed partnership interests. Such "netting" of gain and loss property is not permitted by section 311 if loss property is distributed by a corporation. The Secretary should limit the application of this provision where a distribution is preceded by the contribution of loss property to the partnership if the principal purpose of the contribution is to avoid the nonrecognition of loss rule.

[*Effective date.*—Distributions and sales after 3-31-84.Ed.]

Distributions treated as exchanges for purpose of partnership provisions (sec. 761(e) of the Code)

Present Law.—The Act provides that any distribution not otherwise treated as an exchange is to be treated as an exchange for purposes of specified partnership provisions of the Code. The provisions to which this rule applies are section 708 of the Code (relating to continuation of a partnership); section 743 (relating to the optional adjustment to the basis of partnership property); and any other partnership provision (subchapter K of the Code) specified in Treasury regulations.

Explanation of Provision.—The bill limits the application of the sale or exchange treatment rule to partnership interests which are distributed. The bill also allows the Secretary to provide exceptions to these rules.

[*Effective date.*—Distributions and sales after 3-31-84.Ed.]

Like-kind exchanges (sec. 1031(a) of the Code).

Present Law.—Under the Code (section 1031), generally no gain or loss is recognized if property held for productive use in the taxpayer's trade or business, or property held for investment purposes, is exchanged solely for property of a like-kind that is also to be held for productive use in a trade or business or for investment.

*　　*　　*　　*　　*　　*

Explanation of Provision.—The bill specifies that like-kind property includes property identified as the property to be received by the taxpayer on or before (rather than only before) the date which is 45 days after the date on which the taxpayer relinquishes property.

[*Effective date.*—transfers after 3-31-84.Ed.]

[¶ 4140] SECTION 1806. AMENDMENTS RELATING TO TRUST PROVISIONS

(Sec. 643 of the Code)

[House Explanation]

Multiple trusts (sec. 643 of the Code)

Present Law.—The Act ['84 Tax Reform] provides that under Treasury regulation, two or more trusts will be treated as one trust if (1) the trusts have substantially the same grantor or grantors and substantially the same primary beneficiary or beneficiaries, and (2) a principal purpose for the existence of the trusts in the avoidance of Federal income tax. This provision is effective for taxable years beginning after March 1, 1984.

Explanation of Provision.—The bill provides that this provision is not applicable to any trust which was irrevocable on March 1, 1984, except to the extent corpus is transferred to the trust after that date.

[Senate Explanation]

b. Trust distributions (sec. 643 of the Code)

Present Law.—* * * An election was provided to recognize gain or loss on the distribution of property from a trust or estate.

Explanation of Provision.—The bill clarifies that the election * * * applies to all distributions during a taxable year unless the election is revoked with the consent of the Secretary. [Effective for distributions after 6-1-84. Ed.]

[¶ 4141] SECTION 1807. AMENDMENTS RELATED TO ACCOUNTING CHANGES

(Sec. 461,467,468,468A and 468B of the Code)

[Senate Explanation].

Settlement funds (sec. 461(h) of the Code)

Present Law.—The Act provides that liabilities are not treated as incurred prior to the time when economic performance occurs.

In the case of the taxpayer's liability to another person, arising under any workers compensation act or any tort, economic performance occurs as payments to such person are made, except to the extent provided in regulations. It is unclear whether an irrevocable payment to a court ordered settlement fund, which extinguishes the tort liability of the taxpayer to a person (or class of persons), constitutes economic performance under the Act.

Explanation of Provision.—*General rule.*—The committee bill clarifies that under certain limited circumstances, an irrevocable payment to a court-ordered settlement fund that extinguishes tort liability of the payor (the "taxpayer") constitutes economic performance with respect to such liability. This provision applies only to qualified payments made to a designated settlement fund.

A designated settlement fund means a fund (1) which is established pursuant to a court order, (2) which extinguishes completely the taxpayer's tort liability with respect to a class of claimants, as determined by the court, (3) which is managed and controlled by persons unrelated to the taxpayer, (4) in which the taxpayer does not have a beneficial interest in the income or corpus, and (5) to which no amount may be transferred other than qualified payments.

A qualified payment means cash or property, other than the stock or indebtedness of the taxpayer (or a related party), which is irrevocably contributed to a designated settlement fund pursuant to a court order.

A designated settlement fund is not qualified if the taxpayer may benefit from the corpus or income of the fund. Thus, if the taxpayer's future liability to claimants (or other parties) is contingent on the income of a settlement fund created by the taxpayer, then the taxpayer may benefit from the fund's income, and the fund is not qualified.

A designated settlement fund is taxed as a separate entity at the maximum trust rate. Gross income of a designated settlement fund includes income from investment of fund assets, but excludes qualified payments made to the fund. No deductions are permitted except for certain administrative and incidental expenses. Thus, distributions to claimants are not deductible.

A contribution of property to a designated settlement fund is treated as if the taxpayer sold the property for fair market value and donated the proceeds to the fund. Thus, the taxpayer's deduction is limited to fair market value. The taxpayer recognizes gain or loss at the time property is contributed, and the fund takes a fair market value basis in the property.

No deduction is allowed under this provision for payment to a fund of an amount received from the settlement of an insurance claim, if the amount received is excluded from the taxpayer's gross income.

[This provision was amended on the floor of the Senate to clarify that the taxpayer's election as to the fund is irrevocable only with IRS consent, Ed.]

The bill clarifies that payments to a trust or escrow fund, other than a designated settlement fund, do not constitute economic performance with respect to any tort liability of the taxpayer.

These provisions do not apply to liability arising from any workers compensation act or contested liabilities (within the meaning of section 461(f)); moreover, no inference about the present law treatment of such liabilities is intended.

Transition rule.—A corporation that filed for reorganization under chapter 11 of the Bankruptcy Reform Act of 1978 on August 26, 1982, and which filed with the U.S. Bankruptcy Court a first amended and restated plan of reorganization prior to March 1, 1986, may elect to be taxed under a transition rule * * *.

[Conference Report]

*   *   *   *   *   *

The conference agreement generally follows the Senate bill. The conference agreement clarifies that: (1) the provision does not affect the treatment of payments made for certain personal injury liability assignment within the meaning of section 130; (2) payments from a designated settlement fund to a claimant are treated as having been made by the taxpayer for purposes of determining the claimant's taxable income; and (3) taxpayers may not both exclude an amount recovered and deduct (under this provision) an amount paid to the extent such amount is attributable to the same liability.

The conference agreement provides that except as provided in regulations escrow accounts, settlement funds, or similar funds are subject to current taxation. If the contribution to such an account or fund is not deductible, then the account or fund is taxable as a grantor trust.[2] This provision is effective for accounts or funds established after August 16, 1986.

*   *   *   *   *   *

[House Explanation]

Premature accruals (sec. 461(h) of the Code)

Present Law.—Under present law, an accrual basis taxpayer may not take a deduction for an item prior to the occurrence of economic performance. A liability of a taxpayer which requires a payment to another person and arises out of a tort is not considered to be economically performed prior to the time payment to such other person is made.

Explanation of Provision.—The bill provides that accrual basis taxpayers which have made a payment to an insurance company to indemnify themselves from tort claims arising from personal injury or death caused by the inhalation or ingestion of dust from asbestos-containing products will be treated as having satisfied the economic performance test if the payment is paid to an unrelated third party insurer prior to November 28, 1985, and such payment is not refundable. The provision is not to apply to any company which mined asbestos.

[Footnote ¶ 4141]   (2) The provision reverses the finding in Rev. Rul. 71-119, 1971-1 CB 163.

The committee does not intend for any conclusion to be drawn from this provision as to what treatment should be accorded similar payments for similar policies in the future.

Tax shelters (sec. 461(1)(2) of the Code)

Present Law.—Generally, a cash basis tax shelter is not allowed a deduction with respect to an amount any earlier than the time at which economic performance occurs. An exception is provided under which pre-paid expenses are deductible when paid if economic performance occurs within 90 days after the close of the taxable year. * * *.

In the case of the trade or business of farming, the farming syndicate rules of section 464 apply to any tax shelter described in section 6661(b) (i.e., the principal purpose of which is the avoidance or evasion of Federal income tax). For purposes of applying section 464 to these tax shelters, it is unclear whether the exceptions under section 464(c)(2) relating to holdings attributable to active management apply.

Explanation of Provision.—The bill clarifies that the 90-day exception applies if economic performance occurs before the close of the 90th day after the close of the taxable year. Thus, for example, if a well is spudded in the last month of the taxable year, the requirement that economic performance occur before the close of the 90th day after the close of the taxable year's satisfied.

The bill also clarifies that any tax shelter described in section 6661(b) will generally be treated as a farming syndicate for purposes of section 464. However, any person meeting the requirements of section 464(c)(2) will not be subject to the provisions of section 464 with respect to that person's interest in a tax shelter.

Mine reclamation and similar costs (sec. 468 of the Code)

Present Law.—The ['84 Tax Reform] Act provided electing taxpayers with a uniform method for deducting, prior to economic performance, certain reclamation costs which are mandated by Federal, State, or local law. Deductions accrued under this method must be accounted for in a book reserve and are subject to recapture to the extent that reclamation costs are less than accumulated reserves.

Explanation of Provision.—The bill clarifies that a reserve balance must be increased by the amount of deductions accrued in each year that are allocable to the reserve. The bill also clarifies that this provision is effective for taxable years ending after July 18, 1984.

[Senate Explanation]

Nuclear power plant decommissioning expenses (sec. 468A of the Code)

Present Law.—The Act permitted electing taxpayers to accrue a deduction for contributions made to a qualified nuclear decommissioning fund (a "fund") * * *.

Explanation of Provision.—The bill clarifies that a taxpayer shall be deemed to have made a payment to a fund at the end of a taxable year provided that payment is made within 2½ months after the close of that taxable year. Under a transitional rule, the Secretary of the Treasury is provided regulation authority to relax, and appropriately adjust, this 2½ month rule for payments allocable to a taxable year beginning before January 1, 1987, and to provide that no interest will be allowed with respect to periods before payment is made. The bill clarifies that the tax treatment of fund income provided in sec. 468A is in lieu of any other Federal income tax, that a fund's tax liability is not deductible from its gross income, and that for purposes of subtitle F ("Procedure and Administration") a fund shall be treated as a corporation and taxes imposed on the fund shall be treated similarly to corporate income taxes. The bill clarifies that a fund may invest only in those assets in which the Code permits a Black Lung Trust Fund to invest. The bill also clarifies that this provision is effective for taxable years ending after July 18, 1984.

Treatment of deferred payments for services (sec. 467(g) of the Code)

Present Law.—Under section 467(g) of the Code, the Secretary of the Treasury is to prescribe regulations under which deferred payments for services will be subject to rules similar to those applicable to deferred rents.

Explanation of Provision.—The bill clarifies that the regulations to be issued under section 467 relating to deferred payments for services will not apply to amounts to which section 404 or 404A applies, or to amounts subject to any other provision specified in regulations.

In addition, the bill permits a specified taxpayer whose primary business is providing architectural reserves to use the cash method of accounting.

[Conference Report]

* * * * * *

The conference agreement follows the Senate amendment and contains the provision in the House bill relating to a certain payment to an insurance company with respect to an asbestos claim.

[*Effective date.*—Generally amounts deductible after 7-18-84 as to tax years ending after that date. Ed.]

[¶4142] SECTION 1808. AMENDMENTS RELATED TO TAX STRADDLE PROVISIONS

(Sec. 263(g), 1092(d) of the Code; Sec. 108 of the '84 Tax Reform Act)

Treatment of Subchapter S corporations

Present Law.—The ['84 Tax Reform] Act extended the mark-to-market and sixty percent long-term, forty percent short-term capital gain and loss treatment applicable to commodities dealers to dealers in exchange-traded options, provided elections to adopt this treatment for positions carried forward from earlier taxable years into the taxable year including the date of enactment and to pay any increase in tax liability resulting from this election over 5 years, and permitted qualified incorporated commodities dealers and options dealers to elect S corporation status without regard to the requirement of present law that the election be made by the 15th day of the third month of the taxable year for which it is effective.

Explanation of Provision.—The bill makes clarifying amendments to ensure that S corporation taxable year limitations do not affect the elections relating to adoption of mark-to-market treatment for positions carried forward from earlier years, and to properly coordinate those elections with the S corporation election with respect to taxable years commencing before January 1, 1984 in the manner provided by regulations.[1]

Treatment of amounts received for loaning securities (sec. 263(g) of the Code)

Present Law.—The present law requirement that interest and other carrying costs incurred to carry personal property constituting part of a straddle must be capitalized, as amended by the Act, limits the requirement to the excess of these costs over interest, discount income and dividend income with respect to the property that is subject to tax during the taxable year. * * *

Explanation of Provision.—The bill provides for the inclusion of compensating payments to a lender of securities used in a short sale in those taxable amounts that reduce interest and other costs required to be capitalized under section 263(g) of the Code.

Clarification of the exception for straddles consisting of stock (sec. 1092(d) of the Code)

Present Law.—The Act extended the straddle rules to straddles involving exchange-traded stock options. Exceptions were provided for a straddle consisting of stocks, or stock and a qualified cover call.

Explanation of Provision.—The bill clarifies that the exception for stock does not operate to except straddles involving exchange traded stock options (other than qualified covered calls that offset stock).

Treatment of losses from pre-1981 straddles (sec. 108 of the '84 Tax Reform Act)

Present Law.—* * * Section 108 was intended to clarify the treatment of losses claimed with respect to straddle positions entered into and disposed of prior to 1982 by taxpayers in the trade or business of trading commodities. It provided a profit-motive presumption in section 108(b) for such taxpayers because of the inherent difficulty in distinguishing tax-motivated straddle transactions from profit-motivated straddle transactions * * *.

Explanation of Provision.—The bill makes clear that subsection (b) treatment is limited to those taxpayers in the business of trading commodities. The determination of whether a taxpayer is in the business of trading commodities is based upon all the relevant facts and circumstances. Under the statute as clarified * * *, generally a taxpayer engaged in the business of investment banking who regularly trades in commodities as a part of that business would be considered in the trade or business of trading commodities. If a person qualifies as a commodities dealer, the subsection (b) treatment applies with respect to any position disposed of by such person. It would, for example, apply without regard to whether the position was in a commodity regularly traded by the person, whether it was traded on an exchange on which the dealer was a member, or whether an identical position was re-established on the same trading day or subsequently.

In the case of trades on a domestic exchange described in Code section 1402(i)(2)(B), the identification of positions disposed of shall be as provided in exchange procedures, and records of the exchange or clearinghouse shall be controlling in the absence of proof that rules were violated. A taxpayer who does not satisfy the indicia of trade or business status, such as the taxpayer in *Miller v. Commissioner* (84 T.C. No. 55 (1985)), would not be considered in the trade or business of trading commodities. Further, the presumption would not be available in any cases where the trades were fictitious, prearranged, or otherwise in violation of the rules of the exchange in which the dealer is a member. The subsection (b) treatment is only for purposes of subsection (a), and no inference should be drawn that a loss is incurred in a trade or business for any other purpose, such as for purposes of section 162, 168(d) or 172.

Section 108 also restated the general rule that losses from the disposition of a position in a straddle are only allowable if such position was part of a transaction entered into for profit. A majority of the United States Tax Court in *Miller* interpreted section 108 as providing a new, less stringent profit standard for losses incurred with respect to pre-1981 commodity straddles. It was not the intent of Congress in enacting section 108 to change the profit-motive standard of section 165(c)(2) or to enact a new profit motive standard for commodity straddle activities. This technical correction is necessary to end any additional uncertainty created by the *Miller* case.

[Conference Report]

* * * * * *

The conference agreement follows the House bill. Under the statute as clarified by the technical correction, generally a taxpayer engaged in the business of investment banking who regularly trades in commodities as a part of that business would be considered in the trade or business of trading commodities. If a person qualifies as a commodities dealer, the subsection (b) treatment applies with respect to any position disposed of by such person. It would, for example, apply without regard to whether the position was in a commodity regularly traded by the person, whether it was traded on an exchange on which the dealer was a member, or whether an identical position was re-established on the same trading day or subsequently. The conferees also wish to clarify that if an individual owns a seat on a commodities exchange, such individual will be treated as a "commodities dealer." Further, if a trading firm also regularly trades commodities in connection with its business, then the commodities trading will be deemed to be part of its trade or business. The latter rule applies only to the securities trading firm itself; it does not apply to separate individual trading of its partners, principals, or employees, nor to partnerships or other organizations formed for the principal purpose of marketing tax straddles.

The conference agreement also clarifies that subsection (b) treatment is available not only with respect to a loss incurred directly by a commodities dealer, but also to a loss allocable to a commodities dealer in determining such person's income with respect to an interest in a partnership, S corporation, or trust. For example, in determining the tax liability of a commodities dealer who was a shareholder in an S corporation, a loss incurred by the corporation in the trading of commodities would be treated as a loss incurred by the commodities dealer. Of course, whether an individual is a commodities dealer is no way indicated merely because such individual has an interest in a partnership, S corporation or trust engaged in the trading of commodities.

Further, the conferees clarify their intent that the Internal Revenue Service bring all outstanding pre-ERTA straddle litigation to a speedy resolution, so that the large docket of cases on this issue may be cleared, in a manner consistent with this legislation.

[*Effective date.*—Generally positions established after 7-18-84. Ed.]

[¶ 4143] SECTION 1809. AMENDMENTS RELATED TO DEPRECIATION PROVISIONS

(Sec. 48, 57, 167, 168, 312 of the Code)

[House Explanation]

Straight-line election for low-income housing (sec. 168 of the Code)

* * * * * *

Explanation of Provision.—The bill clarifies that taxpayers may elect to recover the cost of low-income housing using a straight-line method over 15 years (but not 18 years).

Mid-month convention for real property (sec. 1509(a)(2) of the bill and secs. 57, 168, and 312 of the Code)

* * * * * *

Explanation of Provision.—The bill clarifies that the mid-month convention is to be applied whenever a depreciation computation with respect to 18-year real property is required under section 168, section 57(a)(12) (relating to accelerated cost recovery deductions as items of tax preference), or section 312(k) (relating to the effect of depreciation on earnings and profits). Thus, for example, if a taxpayer elects under section 168(b)(3) to depreciate 18-year real property on a straight-line basis over 18, 35, or 45 years, the mid-month convention applies in computing the deductions. Similarly, the mid-month conventions applies in determining what cost recovery deductions "would have been allowable" under section 57(a)(12). Numerous conforming changes are also made.

Effective date.—Property placed in service after 6-23-84. Ed.]

Bond-financed 18-year real property (sec. 168(f)(12) of the Code)

Present Law.—Prior to the Act. section 168(f)(12) placed restrictions on cost recovery allowances with respect to 15-year real property financed by the proceeds of an industrial development bond. * * * The Act generally provided that the cost of real property qualifying as recovery property could not be recovered over a period of less than 18 years.

Explanation of Provision.—The bill clarifies that, in general, the cost of 18-year real property (which does not include low-income housing) financed by the proceeds of an industrial development bond cannot be recovered more rapidly than on a straight-line basis over 18 years, using a mid-month convention. This rule does not apply if the property is either (i) low-income housing (sec. 168(c)(2)(F)), or (ii) property which is placed in service in connection with a project for residential rental property financed with the proceeds of obligations described in section 103(b)(4)(A) but which is not low-income housing under section 168(e)(2)(F). Costs of the former can be recovered on an accelerated basis under ACRS over 15 years, using a first-of-the month convention, and costs of the latter can be recovered on an accelerated basis under ACRS over 18 years, using a mid-month convention.

The bill also clarifies that the provision of the Act relating to property financed with tax-exempt bonds does not apply to certain property excepted from the bond rules added in 1982.

Treatment of certain transferees of recovery property (sec. 168(f)(10) of the Code)

Present Law.—A transferee of recovery property generally may elect a recovery period or method for the property different from the period or method elected by the transferor. However, restrictions are imposed by section 168(f)(10) to prevent the use of certain kinds of asset transfers as a means to change the recovery period or method for the property involved. For transfers subject to those restrictions, the transferee must "step into the shoes" of the transferor with respect to so much of the transferee's basis in the property as is not in excess of the property's adjusted basis in the hands of the transferor. Under this rule, the transferee's cost recovery deductions with respect to that basis are the same as those that would have been allowed the transferor had no transfer occurred. The transferee can elect to depreciate any excess basis pursuant to any recovery period or method available under the general rules.

Asset transfers subject to the rule of the preceding paragraph include sale-leasebacks (sec. 168(f)(10)(B)(iii)), transfers between related persons (sec. 168(f)(10)(B)(ii)), and tax-free asset (carryover basis) transfers described in section 332, 351, 361, 371(a), 374(a), 721, or 731 (sec. 168(f)(10)(B)(i)).

Explanation of Provision.—* * *

The bill amends section 168(f)(10) with respect to recovery property placed in service by the transferor. In a case described in section 168(f)(10)(B)(ii) or (iii) (but not (i) of present law, the transferee * * * starts depreciating the property as would any other new owner of it. However, to the extent of the adjusted basis of the property in the hands of the transferor, the transferee is treated as having made any election made by the transferor with respect to the property under section 168(b)(3) or section 168(f)(2)(C). Thus, for example, if the transferor had elected to depreciate 5-year property on a straight-line basis over 5 years, a transferee under section 168(f)(10)(B)(ii) or (iii) would be treated as having made the same election to the extent basis did not increase. Furthermore, the transferee would begin depreciating that basis in the year of the transfer over a new 5-year period. For purposes of this rule, if the transferor was depreciating 15-year real property on a straight-line basis, the transferee would be treated as having elected 18-year straight line depreciation. If the transferee's basis exceeded the transferor's adjusted basis, the transferee can depreciate the

excess under the general rules. The bill is not intended to affect the treatment of transactions between members of an affiliated group of corporations filing a consolidated return.

With one exception, the bill does not amend section 168(f)(10)(B)(i). Thus, for example, in a section 351 transaction, the transferee steps into the transferor's shoes to the extent basis does not increase. However, the bill amends section 168(f)(10)(B)(i) to provide that it does not apply in the case of the termination of a partnership under section 708(b)(1)(B) (relating to the sale or exchange of 50 percent or more of the total interest in a partnership's capital and profits within a 12-month period).

[Effective date.—] The amendments generally apply to property placed in service by the transferee after September 27, 1985. [12-31-85. See Conference Report. Ed.]

Films, videotapes, and sound recordings (sec. 167 of the Code)

Present Law.—Under the Act, films and videotapes cannot qualify as recovery property (sec. 168(e)(5)). Similarly, sound recordings do not qualify as recovery property unless an election is made under section 48(r)(1) (relating to treating a sound recording as 3-year property).

* * * * * *

Explanation of Provision.—Under the bill, films, videotapes, and sound recordings are not eligible for the accelerated depreciation methods available under section 167(b)(2), (3), or (4). However, the income forecast method or similar methods of depreciation are available.

[Effective date.—] The provision applies to films, videotapes, and sound recordings placed in service by the taxpayer after March 28, 1985. However, no inference is intended as to whether or not films, videotapes, or sound recordings, placed in service by a taxpayer on or before that date qualify for these accelerated depreciation methods.

Investment tax credit (sec. 48 of the Code)

Present Law.—The Act amended the 3-month rule of section 48(b) (relating to whether property qualifies as new section 38 property). Under the Act, rules relating to the qualification of certain property reconstructed by the taxpayer as new section 38 property were inadvertently deleted.

Explanation of Provision.—The bill reinstates the provision that section 38 property the reconstruction of which is completed by the taxpayer qualifies as new 88 property. The bill also provides that the 3-month rule is not applicable to section 38 property the reconstruction of which is completed by the taxpayer. Thus, property reconstructed by a taxpayer and then sold and leased back by the taxpayer within 8 months of the date actually placed in service is to be treated as placed in service on the date actually placed in service.

The bill also clarifies the applicability of the 8-month rule in the case of certain sale-leasebacks. Thus, assume that taxpayer A places eligible property in service by leasing it to taxpayer B. Assume further that, within 8 months of the date A placed the property in service, A sells the property to taxpayer C and taxpayer C leases the property back to A, subject to the lease to B. Assuming C's lease to A qualifies as a lease under applicable Code principles, the property will constitute new section 88 property in C's hands. The amendment clarifies that this result would occur under the prior statutory language.

Under the bill, the 3-month rule does not apply if the leasee and lessor so elect.

[*Effective date.*—Applies to property placed in service after 4-11-84. Ed.]

Depreciation.—The conference agreement follows the House bill except that the provision relating to related party sale-lease-backs applies to property placed in service after December 31, 1985. In addition, the conference agreement clarifies that the depreciation recapture installment sale rule (sec. 453(i)) applies to the installment sales of partnership interests. [generally for dispositions after 6-6-84. Ed.]

[Effective date.—Except or otherwise provided above rules apply to property placed in service after 3-15-84. Ed.]

[¶ 4144] SECTION 1810 AMENDMENTS RELATING TO FOREIGN PROVISIONS

(Sec. 163, 269B, 367, 551, 552, 864, 871, 881, 897, 904, 954, 956, 1248, 1441, 1442, 1445, 6039C, 6652, 7701)

[House Explanation]

Maintaining the source of U.S. source income (sec. 904(g) of the Code)

Present Law.—* * *

The ['84 Tax Reform] Act added to the foreign tax credit rules new rules that prevent U.S. taxpayers from converting U.S. source income into foreign source income through the use of an intermediate foreign payee. These rules apply to 50-percent U.S.-owned foreign corporations only. These rules do not apply if less than 10 percent of the foreign corporation's earnings and profits is from U.S. sources.

Interest and dividends paid by a domestic corporation that earns less than 20 percent of its gross income from U.S. sources over a three-year period (an "80/20 company") are foreign source (Code secs. 861(a)(1)(B) and 861(a)(2)(A)). Therefore, a U.S. taxpayer can convert U.S. source income to foreign source income by routing it through an 80/20 company, as long as the company's U.S. source gross income remains below the 20-percent threshold.

The Act provides a transitional rule for certain interest received by "applicable CFCs." The Act defines an "applicable CFC" as any controlled foreign corporation in existence on March 31, 1984, the principal purpose of which on that date consisted of issuing CFC obligations or holding short-term obligations and lending the proceeds to affiliates. The Act provided that, if certain requirements are met, interest paid to an applicable CFC on a U.S. affiliate obligation issued before June 22, 1984 (the date of conference action) will be treated for all Code purposes as paid to a resident of the country in which the applicable CFC is incorporated. This rule exempts from the resourcing provisions interest paid by a U.S. affiliate on certain obligations issued before the effective date of the amendment by a U.S.-owned finance subsidiary located in the Netherlands Antilles.

A U.S. affiliate obligation is any obligation of a U.S. person related (within the meaning of Code section 482) to an applicable CFC holding the obligation. Interest paid on an obligation of a foreign person is not subject to the source maintenance rules.

*   *   *   *   *   *

* * * Congress intended that the new rules maintaining the source of U.S. source income take precedence over any conflicting U.S. treaty provisions in force when it enacted the Act. Congress also intended that the source maintenance rules take precedence over any conflicting U.S. treaties entered into in the future, absent an express intention in the treaty to override the rules. Some argue that certain U.S. treaties awaiting ratification may conflict with the source maintenance rules.

Explanation of Provision.—Under the bill an 80/20 company will be treated as a U.S.-owned foreign corporation and thus will be subject to the rules maintaining the source of U.S. source income.

This provision generally will take effect on March 28, 1985. In the case of any taxable year of an 80/20 company ending after March 28, 1985, only income received or accrued by the 80/20 company during that portion of the taxable year after that date generally is to be taken into account for purposes of the new source maintenance rules. However, *all* income received or accrued by the 80/20 company during that taxable year is to be taken into account in determining whether the 10 percent U.S. source earnings and profits threshold for the source maintenance rules is exceeded.

* * * Under the bill, an applicable CFC is any controlled foreign corporation in existence on March 31, 1984, the principal purpose of which on that date consisted of (1) any combination of issuing CFC obligations and short term borrowing from nonaffiliated persons and (2) lending the proceeds to affiliates.

The bill provides that certain U.S. source interest paid to an applicable CFC by an affiliated foreign corporation on an obligation of that corporation issued before June 22, 1984, will be subject to the resourcing provisions to the same extent that interest so paid by an affiliated U.S. corporation would be so subject. This treatment applies if at least 50 percent of the foreign corporation's gross income for the three-year period ending on or before March 31, 1984, and with the close of its taxable year preceding the payment of the interest in question, was effectively connected with a U.S. trade or business.

The bill makes clear that the source maintenance rules apply notwithstanding any contrary U.S. treaty obligation, even those entered into after the Act's date of enactment, unless the treaty clearly expresses an intent to override the rules by specific reference to them. * * * inference contrary to the general rule that gives precedence to the provisions of the Act over preexisting treaty provisions should be drawn with respect to any other provision of the Act (except as specifically provided in the Act or its legislative history). In enacting the 1984 Act, Congress specifically provided that treaties were to prevail over certain statutory rules that apply to stapled stock and to the definition of residence of individuals; with these two exceptions, the committee is not aware of conflicts between the 1984 Act and treaties where the Act would not clearly take precedence. For example, it is the committee's understanding that changes made by the Act in the accumulated earnings tax provisions override a conflicting provision in the U.S. income tax treaty with Jamaica.

[*Effective date.*—Recharacterizing foreign income: generally 3-28-85, and see § 1811. Effect of Treaty obligations: Treaties entered after enactment date. Transitional rule relates to separate application of Sec. 904. Ed.]

Maintaining the character of interest income (sec. 904(d)(3) of the Code)

Present Law.—*In general.*—The Act provided that when a U.S. taxpayer includes in income foreign personal holding company or subpart F income with respect to (or an interest or dividend payment from) a designated payor corporation that has earned substantial "separate limitation interest" (generally passive interest income), that inclusion or payment will generally constitute interest that is subject to the separate foreign tax credit limitation for interest income.

*   *   *   *   *   *

Definition of designated payor corporation.—The Act generally defines a designated payor corporation as any regulated investment company, 50-percent (or more) U.S.-owned foreign corporation, or foreign corporation with a ten-percent U.S. shareholder. A domestic corporation that pays foreign source dividends can be a designated payor corporation only if it is a regulated investment company.

A domestic company's dividends (and interest payments) are foreign source if it is an "80/20" company, that is, if it earns less than 20 percent of its gross income from U.S.

sources for a three-year period (Code secs. 861(a)(1)(B) and 861(a)(2)(A)).

Code section 269 denies tax benefits to taxpayers who acquire control of corporations to avoid or evade tax. The extent to which section 269 applies to defeat schemes to avoid the Act's look-through rules by using U.S. or foreign corporations is not clear.

10-percent exception.—The Act contains a de minimis rule that prevents characterization of inclusions and payments as interest subject to the separate foreign tax credit limitation for interest income unless 10 percent or more of the earnings and profits of the designated payor corporation is attributable to separate limitation interest.

*   *   *   *   *   *

[Senate Explanation]

Working capital exception.—* * *. Prior to the Act, certain interest earned on working capital-type investments was excluded from the separate limitation regardless of from whom received: interest was not subject to the separate limitation if derived from any transaction which was directly related to the active conduct by the taxpayer of a trade or business in a foreign country or a U.S. possession (Code sec. 904(d)(2)(A)). The Act does not allow this working capital exception at the shareholder level for interest received from a regulated investment company or other designated payor corporation by its shareholders. Under the Act, this working capital exception and the 10-percent de minimis exception referred to above are available at the designated payor corporation level only. Since regulated investment companies earn primarily passive investment income, their income typically cannot qualify for these exceptions. Therefore, dividends paid by regulated investment companies generally are treated as interest subject to the separate limitation to the extent that the regulated investment company earns separate limitation interest, whether the recipient shareholder's investment is one of working capital or not.

[House Explanation]

Explanation of Provisions.—*Definition of designated payor corporation.*—The bill amends the definition of designated payor corporation in two respects.

First, the bill makes clear that any corporation formed or availed of for purposes of avoiding the look-through rule will be treated as a designated payor corporation subject to the rule. For example, U.S. taxpayers will not be permitted, in violation of the purpose of the look-through rule, to convert interest income to noninterest income by earning the income through a corporation the ownership of which is structured to place the corporation technically outside the present law definition of designated payor corporation: a foreign corporation that earns sufficient earnings and profits attributable to separate limitation interest to be subject to the look-through rule, but is majority-owned by foreign persons and has no ten-percent U.S. shareholders, will be treated as a designated payor corporation (regardless of the original purpose for its formation) if U.S. shareholders utilize the corporation to remove interest income from the separate foreign tax credit limitation for interest income. Similarly, U.S. taxpayers will not be permitted, in violation of the purpose of the look-through rule, to convert interest income to non-interest income by earning the income through a foreign banking subsidiary or similiar entity formed or availed of for that purpose. * * *. The Secretary may promulgate regulations setting forth appropriate rules for determining whether a corporation has been formed or availed of for purposes of avoiding the look-through rule.

Second, the bill expands the definition of designated payor corporation to include any 80/20 company. By subjecting 80/20 companies to the look-through rule, the bill prevents U.S. taxpayers from using 80/20 companies to circumvent the separate foreign tax credit limitation for interest income.

The first described amendment * * * generally takes effect on December 31, 1985. The second described amendment * * * generally takes effect on March 28, 1985. In the case of any taxable year of a corporation treated as a designated payor corporation by virtue of those amendments ending after the indicated date, only income received or accrued by the corporation during that portion of the taxable year after that date generally is to be taken into account for purposes of the look-through rule. However, *all* income received or accrued by the corporation during that taxable year is to be taken into account in determining whether the ten-percent earnings and profits threshold for dividends and interest is exceeded. A corporation formed on or before December 31, 1985, but availed of after that date to avoid the look-through rule, will be subject to the rule.

10-percent exception.—Consistent with the Act's rules for source maintenance, the bill removes the Act's de minimis rule that prevents maintenance of the character of interest income in the case of foreign personal holding company inclusions and Subpart F inclusions.

Related party interest.—The bill makes it clear that when a designated payor corporation receives dividends or interest from another member of the same affiliated group, the amount shall be treated as separate limitation interest if (and only if) the amount is attributable (directly or indirectly) to separate limitation interest of the other member (or any other member of the group).

[Senate Explanation]

Working capital exception.—Under the bill, dividends and interest received from a regulated investment company by a portfolio shareholder in such company will not be treated as interest subject to the separate limitation for interest if derived from any transaction which is directly related to the active conduct by the shareholder of a trade or business in a foreign country or a U.S.

possession. A portfolio shareholder for this purpose is one that owns, directly or indirectly, less than 10 percent of the voting stock of the regulated investment company.

[House Explanation]

[Effective date.—Generally for distributions after 7-18-84. For changes regarding designated payor corporations that can give rise to dividends recharacterized as separate limitation interest income, see ¶1811, Ed.]

Related person factoring income (secs. 864 and 956 of the Code)

Present Law.—*Investment in U.S. property.*—Under present and prior law, the Code treats an investment in United States property by a controlled foreign corporation as an effective repatriation of the amount invested and thus as a dividend. The Act provided that "United States property" includes any trade or service receivable acquired from a related U.S. person if the obligator under the receivable is a U.S. person. This provision overrode exceptions (listed in Code sec. 956(b)(2)) to the investment in U.S. property rules. Among those exceptions is an exclusion from U.S. property of an amount of assets equal to post-1962 earnings and profits previously excluded from subpart F income on the ground directly as effectively connected income (sec. 956(b)(2)(H)).

Current inclusion of factoring income.—The Act provided that if any person acquires a trade or service receivable from a related person, the acquirer's income from the receivable is treated as interest on a loan to the obligor under the receivable. In general, this income is currently taxable to the owners of the acquirer of the receivable under the foreign personal holding company rules or the controlled foreign corporation rules (subpart F).

Separate limitation treatment.—Related person factoring income is treated under the Act as interest described in section 904(d)(2) and, therefore, is subject to the separate foreign tax credit limitation for interest. Congress intended that this income be ineligible for any exception to application of the separate limitation. However, the Act does not include in its enumeration of the exceptions the affiliated group exception to the Act's rules maintaining the character of interest income (section 904(d)(8)(J)).

Explanation of Provisions. — *Investment in U.S. property.*—The bill provides that the existing exclusion from U.S. property of an amount of assets equal to the controlled foreign corporation's post-1962 earnings and profits excluded from subpart F income as taxable effectively connected income will apply in the case of the acquisition of a trade or service receivable that otherwise constitutes U.S. property.

Current inclusion of factoring income.—The bill generally exempts factoring income from current inclusion when the related person that acquires the factored receivable acquires it from an entity that is organized under the laws of the same foreign country as the acquirer and that has a substantial part of its assets used in its trade or business located in that same country. Factoring income is still subject to the current inclusion rule, however, if the person transferring the receivable would have derived any foreign base company income (determined without regard to the 10-percent exception) or income that is effectively connected with a U.S. trade or business had it collected the receivable.

For example, assume that a controlled foreign corporation manufactures a product in the foreign country of its incorporation and sells the product to an unrelated customer in exchange for the customer's receivable. None of the manufacturer's income from this sale is effectively connected with a U.S. trade or business, and none of it would be currently taxable to its U.S. shareholders. The manufacturer sells the receivable to a related controlled foreign corporation that is organized under the laws of the same foreign country. Under the bill, the income of the acquirer from that receivable is not subject to current U.S. taxation.

By contrast, assume that another controlled foreign corporation purchases goods from its U.S. parent and resells those goods to a customer (in exchange for the customer's receivable) for use outside the country of incorporation of the controlled foreign corporation. This income would be currently taxable to the U.S. shareholders of the controlled foreign corporation as foreign base company sales income under the subpart F rules (sec. 954(d)). The controlled foreign corporation sells the receivable to a related controlled foreign corporation that is organized under the laws of the same foreign country as the seller. Under the bill, the income of the acquirer from the receivable remains subject to current taxation at the level of its U.S. shareholders.

The bill's treatment of factoring income also extends to income from analogous loans by a controlled foreign corporation to finance transactions with related parties.

Separate limitation treatment.—The bill provides that related person factoring income treated under the Act as interest is subject to the separate limitation for interest without regard to the exception to the definition of separate limitation interest for certain interest received from members of the same affiliated group.

[*Effective date.*—Receivables transferred after 3-1-84. Ed.]

Repeal of 30-percent withholding tax on portfolio interest paid to foreign persons (secs. 871,881,1441, and 1442 of the Code)

Present Law.—*In general.*—The United States generally imposes a flat 30-percent withholding tax on the gross amount of U.S. source investment income payments to foreign persons. The Act repealed the 30-percent tax with respect to portfolio interest paid on certain indebtedness by U.S. borrowers to nonresident alien individuals and foreign corporations. This exemption from the 30-percent tax is effective for interest

paid on qualifying obligations issued after July 18, 1984, the date of enactment of the Act.

Registered obligations—non-U.S. person statement.—The Act repealed the 80-percent tax with respect to interest paid on obligations issued in registered form for which the U.S. payer (or U.S. person whose duty it would otherwise be to withhold tax) receives a statement that the beneficial owner of the obligation is not a U.S. person.

Interest received by controlled foreign corporations.—Interest received by a controlled foreign corporation ("CFC") from a person other than a related person may be exempt from the 80-percent tax under the Act. However, the Act provides that portfolio interest received by a CFC is includible in the gross income of the CFC's U.S. shareholders under subpart F without regard to any of the exceptions otherwise provided under the subpart F rules.

It appears that some interest paid by foreign corporations, which would not have been subject to the 80-percent tax prior to the Act, nonetheless may fall within the technical definition of portfolio interest. Where such interest is paid to a CFC, treatment of the interest as portfolio interest may subject it to current taxation under subpart F without regard to any of the subpart F exceptions.

Interest received by 10-percent shareholders—attribution rules.—Congress did not extend the repeal of the 80-percent tax to interest paid to foreign persons having a direct ownership interest in the U.S. payor because the combination of U.S. deduction and noninclusion in such a case would have created an incentive for interest payments that Congress did not believe appropriate.

A direct ownership interest, for these purposes, generally means a 10-percent (or greater) ownership interest in the U.S. payor, in determining whether direct ownership exists, the stock ownership attribution rules of the Code apply, with certain modifications (sec. 818(a)). One of the applicable attribution rules is that a corporation generally is deemed to own stock that its 50-percent-(or greater) owned subsidiary owns in proportion to the corporation's share of its subsidiary's stock (sec. 318(a)(2)(C)). In determining whether direct ownership exists for purposes of the repeal, this rule is applied without regard to the 50-percent limitation. This modification in the attribution rule prevents an affiliated group of corporations from circumventing the direct ownership exception to the 80-percent tax repeal by, for example, having a U.S. member pay interest to the 49-percent foreign owner of the U.S. member's foreign parent, rather than directly to that foreign parent.

Another of the applicable attribution rules is that a 50-percent (or greater) owned subsidiary generally is deemed to own the stock that its parent owns (sec. 318(a)(3)(C)). The Act applies this rule in determining whether direct ownership exists for purposes of the repeal without any modification of the 50-percent limitation. This allows an affiliated group of corporations to circumvent the direct ownership exception to the 80-percent tax repeal by having a U.S. member pay interest to an affiliated foreign corporation that is as much as 49-percent-owned by a substantial foreign shareholder in the U.S. member, rather than directly to that substantial shareholder.

Explanation of Provisions.—*Registered obligations — non-U.S. person statement.* — The bill clarifies that the beneficial owner of a registered obligation, the interest on which is otherwise eligible for the repeal, may claim a refund of any tax withheld where the required non-U.S. person statement is provided after one or more interest payments are made rather than before. Claims for such refunds are subject to the general statute of limitations rules for refund claims (sec. 6511).

Interest received by controlled foreign corporations.—The bill amends the definition of portfolio interest to exclude interest that (without regard to the operation of treaties) would not have been subject to the 80-percent tax prior to the Act. Thus, under the bill, interest received by CFCs will be denied the benefit of any otherwise applicable subpart F exceptions only if the interest would have been subject to the 80-percent tax in the absence of the repeal provision.

Interest paid to 10-percent shareholders— attribution rules.—In determining whether the direct ownership exception to the 30-percent tax repeal applies, the stock ownership attribution rule of Code section 318(a)(3)(C) will apply without regard to its 50-percent ownership limitation. Where the attribution rule would not apply but for the disregard of the 50-percent limitation, a foreign interest recipient will be treated as owning the stock its foreign shareholder owns in proportion to that shareholder's ownership interest in the foreign interest recipient.

[*Effective date.*—Generally portfolio interest on obligations issued after 7-18-84. Ed.]

Original issue discount—foreign investors: (1) Deduction for original issue discount (sec. 163 of the Code)

Present Law.—The Act delayed until actual payment the deduction for interest accrued, but not paid, to related foreign lenders with respect to an original issue discount (OID) obligation.

Explanation of Provision.—The bill provides that the delay in the timing of deductions for interest accrued but not paid to related foreign lenders with respect to an OID obligation does not apply to the extent that the OID income is effectively connected with the lender's conduct of a U.S. trade or business, unless the OID income is exempt from U.S. taxation or is subject to a reduced rate of tax pursuant to a treaty obligation of the United States.

(2) Taxation of original issue discount (secs. 871 and 881 of the Code)

Explanation of Provision.—The bill provides that when a foreign investor receives a payment (whether constituting interest or principal) on an OID obligation, the amount taxable is equal to the OID accrued on the obligation that has not before been subject to tax, whether or not the OID accrued since the last payment of interest. On the sale, exchange, or retirement of an OID obligation, the foreign investor is taxable on the amount of the OID accruing while the foreign investor held the obligation (to the extent not previously taxed), whether or not that amount exceeds the foreign investor's gain on the sale, exchange, or retirement.

[*Effective date.*—Obligations issued after 6-9-84. Ed.]

Withholding on dispositions by foreigners of U.S. real property interests (secs. 897, 1445, 6039(C), and 6652(g) of the Code)

Present Law.—*In general.*—Under the Foreign Investment in Real Property Tax Act of 1980 (FIRPTA), a foreign investor that disposes of a U.S. real property interest generally is required to pay tax on any gain on the disposition. FIRPTA provided for enforcement of this tax through a system of information reporting designed to identify foreign owners of U.S. real property interests.

The 1984 Act generally repealed the information reporting requirements of FIRPTA and established a withholding system to enforce the FIRPTA tax. The Act imposes a withholding duty on a transferee of a U.S. real property interest from a foreign person unless the transferee receives a sworn affidavit stating that the transferor is not foreign ("non-foreign affidavit"), or one of four other withholding exemptions * * * applies. The amount withheld generally is the lesser of ten percent of the amount realized (purchase price), or the maximum tax liability on disposition (as determined by the IRS). Special rules are provided (some of which are discussed further below) for withholding by partnerships, trustees, executors, distributing foreign corporations, and domestic U.S. real property holding corporations.

Corporations making section 897(i) election.—The Act does not treat foreign corporations electing under Code section 897(i) to be considered domestic corporations for purposes of FIRPTA's substantive and reporting provisions as domestic corporations for withholding purposes. * * *

Since enactment of the Act, the Internal Revenue Service has developed a procedure that would provide U.S. buyers with reasonable assurance that a non-foreign affidavit received from a foreign corporation is valid (as a result of a valid section 897(i) election) (Temp. Reg. secs. 1.1445-2T(b)(2)(ii), 1.1445-5T(b)(3)(ii)(C), and 1.1445-7T(a)).

Withholding exemptions for transfers of stock in domestic corporations.—Withholding is not required on the disposition of an interest (other than an interest solely as a creditor) in a nonpublicly traded domestic corporation if the corporation furnishes a sworn affidavit to the transferee stating that the corporation is not and has not been a U.S. real property holding corporation ("U.S. RPHC") during the base period specified in Code section 897(c)(1)(A)(ii)—the shorter of the period after FIRPTA's general effective date (June 18, 1980) during which the transferor held the interest and the five-year period ending on the date of disposition of the interest ("non-U.S. RPHC affidavit"). The receipt of a non-U.S. RPHC affidavit will not relieve the transferee of withholding responsibility if the transferee has actual knowledge that the affidavit is false or the transferee receives a notice from his or her agent or an agent of the transferor that the affidavit is false.

In addition, no withholding is required on a disposition of shares of a class of corporate stock that is regularly traded on an established securities market.

Notice-giving and withholding responsibilities of agents.—A transferor's agent or transferee's agent with actual knowledge that a non-foreign or non-U.S. RPHC affidavit is false must give the transferee notice to that effect at such time and in such manner as the Secretary shall require by regulations. In the case of a foreign corporate transferor, an agent of the transferor is deemed to have actual knowledge that any non-foreign affidavit furnished by the transferor is false.
* * *

A transferor's agent or transferee's agent that does not give the required notice is liable for withholding as if he or she were the transferee, up to the amount of compensation the agent receives in connection with the transaction.

*   *   *   *   *   *

Taxable distributions by partnerships, trustees, and executors.—The Act requires withholding by a domestic or foreign partnership, the trustee of a domestic or foreign trust, or the executor of a domestic or foreign estate when the partnership, trustee, or executor makes a distribution of a U.S. real property interest to a foreign person that is a taxable distribution under the FIRPTA rules taxing certain partnership, trust, and estate distributions notwithstanding general Code rules. * * *

As drafted, this rule technically would apply only to U.S. real property distributions taxable under regulations promulgated pursuant to Code section 897(g). The statute makes no reference to another Code provision added by FIRPTA—section 897(e)(2)(B)—under which certain partnership, trust, and estate distributions not covered by section 897(g) could be treated as taxable sales by regulation.

*   *   *   *   *   *

Explanation of Provisions.—*Corporations making section 897(i) election.*—Under the bill, a foreign corporation electing under section 897(i) to be treated as a domestic corporation for purposes of FIRPTA's substantive and reporting provisions will be treated as a domestic corporation for purposes of the FIRPTA withholding provisions too.

The bill also provides that the section 897(i) election will be the exclusive remedy for any person claiming discriminatory treatment under a treaty obligation of the United States with respect to the FIRPTA withholding provisions.

Withholding exemptions for transfers of stock in domestic corporations.—The bill conforms the non-U.S. RPHC withholding exemption more closely to the underlying substantive tax rule by substituting for it a new "non-U.S. real property interest" exemption to reflect Code section 897(c)(1)(B). Under the bill, withholding is not required on the disposition of an interest (which is an interest other than solely as a creditor) in a nonpublicly traded domestic corporation Y the corporation furnishes an affidavit to the transferee stating, under penalty of perjury, either that the corporation is not and has not been a U.S. RPHC during the base period specified in Code section 897(c)(1)(A)(ii), or that, as of the date of the disposition, interests in the corporation are not U.S. real property interests by reason of section 897(c)(1)(B). Under section 897(c)(1)(B), interests in a corporation are not U.S. real property interests if the corporation is not holding any U.S. real property interests at the time of the disposition of the corporate interests and if the corporation disposed of all U.S. real property interests it held during the section 897(c)(1)(A)(ii) base period in transactions in which the full amount of gain (if any) was recognized.

The present law rules governing notice-giving by agents and withholding by agents and transferees in the case of a false non-U.S. RPHC affidavit will control (with the clarification discussed below) in the case of a false non-U.S. real property interest affidavit.

Notice-giving and withholding responsibilities of agents

The bill clarifies that an agent of a foreign corporate transferor of a domestic corporation's stock will not be charged with actual knowledge of the falsity of a false non-U.S. real property interest affidavit (the bill's substitute for the Act's non-U.S. RPHC affidavit) furnished by the domestic corporation, absent actual possession of such knowledge. Thus, no notice-giving or withholding duty will be imposed on such a transferor's agent unless he or she actually knows that the non-U.S. real property interest affidavit is false. An agent of a foreign corporate transferor will be charged with knowledge of the falsity only of a false *non-foreign affidavit* furnished by his or her principal.

It should be noted that, under the bill, unlike the Act, a non-foreign affidavit furnished by a foreign corporation may be valid. This will be the case where the foreign corporation has elected to be treated as a domestic corporation under Code section 897(i) and the corporation provides the transferee with proof of the section 897(i) election in the manner specified in regulations.

Dispositions of U.S. real property interests by domestic partnerships, trusts, and estates.—The bill modifies the special withholding rule for dispositions of U.S. real property interests by domestic partnerships, trusts, and estates. Under the bill, a domestic partnership, a trustee of a domestic trust, or an executor of a domestic estate is to withhold a tax equal to 28 percent of the gain realized on the disposition by the entity of a U.S. real property interest, to the extent that gain is allocable to a foreign partner or foreign beneficiary of the partnership, trust, or estate or, in the case of a trust, is allocable to a portion of the trust treated as owned by a foreign person under the grantor trust rules of the Code. (It is intended that the Secretary of the Treasury will, by regulations, provide an exception from withholding with respect to gain realized on the disposition of a U.S. real property interest by a trust or estate that is currently taxable at the entity level.)

Consistent with the Act's general withholding rule, withholding liability under this special rule, * * * is not limited to the gain realized on the disposition that is in the custody of the partnership, trustee, or executor. A partnership, trustee, or executor that does not have sufficient sales proceeds to satisfy its withholding liability (for example, because it mortgaged the disposed-of property on or after acquiring it, or agreed to accept payment for the disposed-of property on an installment basis) may request a qualifying statement from the Internal Revenue Service authorizing it to withhold a lesser amount.

Computing the tax to be withheld as a percentage of gain should, however, result (in many cases) in the collection of an amount of tax that more closely approximates the final tax liability of foreign partners, beneficiaries, and substantial owners than would the amount of tax collected were the tax computed as a percentage of the full amount realized. Withholding on the basis of gain is feasible under this special withholding rule because, unlike the buyer in the usual withholding situation (who may not know the seller's basis), the withholding agent here—a partnership, trustee, or executor—knows what the foreign taxpayer's gain from the disposition will be: the partnership, trustee, or executor itself computes the amount of that gain. The 28-percent withholding rate reflects the maximum 28-percent capital gains rate for corporations—the highest rate at which a foreign partner, beneficiary, or substantial owner could be taxed on its share of the gain from the disposition of a U.S. real property interest by a partnership, trust, or estate.

The bill also clarifies the Secretary's authority to promulgate such regulations as are necessary to provide for withholding with respect to U.S. real property gains realized by foreign persons through tiers of domestic partnerships or trusts.

These modifications will be effective for dispositions of U.S. real property interests that occur after the day 30 days after the bill's date of enactment.

Distributions by domestic U.S. RPHCs.—The bill clarifies that no withholding is required on certain liquidations and redemptions that are not taxed under the substantive FIRPTA rules. It provides that the special rule requiring withholding by domestic U.S. RPHCs (and former domestic U.S. RPHCs) upon the distribution of property in a corporate liquidation or redemption will not apply when interests in the corporation are not U.S. real property interests by reason of Code section 897(c)(1)(B) on the date of the distribution.

As indicated above, section 897(c)(1)(B) excludes from the definition of a U.S. real property interest an interest in a corporation that (1) is not holding U.S. real property interests at the time the corporate interest is disposed of and (2) disposed of all U.S. real property interests it held during the section 897(c)(1)(A)(ii) base period in transactions in which the full amount of gain (if any) was recognized. If section 897(c)(1)(B) applies to a corporation's stock, a stock interest surrendered in connection with a liquidation or redemption by the corporation is not a U.S. real property interest. Therefore, the surrender of that stock interest is not a taxable disposition under the FIRPTA rules, and withholding on the surrender is inappropriate.

Taxable distributions by partnerships, trustees, and executors.—The bill clarifies that a distribution to a foreign person of a U.S. real property interest by a domestic or foreign partnership, trustee, or executor is subject to withholding if such distribution is taxable under any of the substantive FIRPTA rules, not Code section 897(g) only.

Return-filing and remittance of tax.—The bill clarifies that persons required to withhold tax under the FIRPTA withholding rules, like persons having substantive FIRPTA tax liability, are to pay the tax to and file the necessary returns with the United States in the case of real property interests located in the United States, and are to pay the tax to and file the necessary returns with the Virgin Island in the case of real property interests located in the Virgin Islands.

Information returns—penalty provision.—The bill amends the provision (Code sec. 6652(g)) imposing penalties on persons that fail to file required FIRPTA information returns to conform it with the revised information reporting rules of the Act.

[*Effective date.*—Generally provisions apply to post-1984 dispositions. Provision on dispositions by partnerships, estates and trusts applies to disposition after 30 days after enactment date of '86 TRA.—Ed.]

Transfers of property to foreign persons pursuant to corporate reorganizations, etc. (sec. 867 of the Code)

Present Law.—The Act added a rule (Code sec. 867(e)) requiring that a domestic corporation recognize gain on a liquidating distribution of appreciated property to any foreign person, under rules similar to those applicable to transfers to foreign corporations. * * * The transactions with respect to which Congress intended to require the recognition of gain by a U.S. transferor included certain distributions to foreign persons pursuant to Code section 355 (relating to distributions of stock and securities of controlled corporations). However, because the applicability of section 355 does not depend on whether the distributee is a corporation, section 867(a)(1) does not reach this result. Section 355 transfers are appropriately addressed under section 867(e), which does not look to the corporate status of the transferee, rather than section 867(a), which applies only to transfers to foreign corporations.

Explanation of Provision.—The bill provides that transfers of stock by domestic corporations to foreign persons pursuant to Code section 355 (or so much of section 856 as relates to section 355) will give rise to the recognition of gain under Code section 867(e), to the extent provided in regulations. The committee expects that the Secretary will carefully consider the extent to which it is appropriate, in view of the purpose of section 867(e), to require the recognition of gain upon the transfer of the stock of a domestic corporation to foreign persons under section 355.

[*Effective date.*—Generally, post-12-31-84 transfers or exchanges in TYEA that date Ed.]

Foreign personal holding companies.—U.S. shareholders in a foreign personal holding company are subject to current U.S. tax on their pro rata share of the company's undistributed foreign personal holding company income. * * *

(1) Same country dividend and interest exception (sec. 552 of the Code).—*Present Law.*—The Act provides that dividends and interest received by a foreign corporation from a person (1) related to the recipient, (2) organized in the same country as the recipient corporation, and (3) having a substantial part of its assets used in its trade or business located in that same country generally do not count in determining whether the foreign corporation is a foreign personal holding company. The Act does not define related person for this purpose.

Explanation of Provision.—For the purpose of the Act's rule excluding same country dividends and interest from the foreign personal holding company calculation, the bill adopts the related party definition of the controlled foreign corporation rules (sec. 954(d)(3)). * * * person is a related person with respect to a foreign personal holding company if the person is (1) an individual, partnership, trust, or estate which controls the foreign personal holding company, (2) a corporation which controls, or is controlled by, the foreign personal holding company, or (3) a corporation which is controlled by the same person or persons which control the foreign personal holding company. For this purpose, control means the ownership, directly or indirectly, of stock possessing more than 50 percent of the total combined voting power of all classes of stock entitled to vote. The bill incorporates certain rules for determining ownership of stock for this purpose.

(2) Interposed foreign entities (sec. 551(f) of the Code).—*Present Law.*—The Act added a tracing rule to the foreign personal holding company rules that was intended to make clear that U.S. taxpayers cannot interpose foreign entities (other than other foreign personal holding companies) between themselves and a foreign personal holding company to avoid the foreign personal holding company rules. Under the tracing rule, stock of a foreign personal holding company that is owned by a foreign entity other than another foreign personal holding company is to be considered (for income inclusion purposes) as being owned proportionately by the foreign entity's partners, beneficiaries, or stockholders.

Explanation of Provision.—The bill clarifies that the tracing rule applies to all foreign trusts and estates interposed between U.S. taxpayers and foreign personal holding companies.

[*Effective date.*—Regarding related party, taxable years of foreign corps. beginning after 3-15-84. Tracing rule extension applies to taxable years of foreign corps. beginning after 12-31-83, with 1-year extension in specified instances. Ed.]

Treatment of certain indirect transfers (sec. 1248(i) of the Code)

Present Law.—* * * Under the Act, if shareholders of a U.S. corporation exchange stock in the corporation of newly issued stock (or treasury stock) of a foreign corporation ten percent or more of the voting stock of which is owned by the U.S. corporation, the transaction is recast for purposes of applying section 1248. Because the Act provides that the U.S. corporation is treated as having distributed the stock in the foreign corporation "in redemption" of the shareholder's stock, every indirect transfer could be viewed as a nonliquidating distribution.

The Act also clarified the treatment of subsequent distributions of earnings that resulted in the recharacterization of gain under section 1248. Taxpayers were given an election to apply this provision retroactively to transactions occurring after October 9, 1975.

Section 1248(g) provides exceptions to section 1248(a) for cases in which gain is taxable as ordinary income under other provisions of the Code. Section 1248(g)(2) refers to any gain on exchanges to which section 356 applies. * * *

Explanation of Provision.—The bill clarifies that an indirect transfer is recast as a distribution in redemption or liquidation, whichever is appropriate. For example, assume that a U.S. corporation ("P") is the sole shareholder of a U.S. holding company ("Holdco"). Holdco owns 100 percent of the stock of a corporation that was organized under the laws of a foreign country ("S"). Holdco merges downstream into S; in the merger P exchanges Holdco stock for stock of

S. Under section 1248(i), the transaction is treated as if Holdco distributed the S stock in a liquidating distribution to P. This result occurs because Holdco goes out of existence and the transaction has the economic effect of a liquidation. Under section 1248(f)(2), however, no amount is includible in Holdco's gross income under section 1248(f)(1), because the S stock is distributed to a domestic corporation, P, which is treated as holding the S stock for the period the stock was held by Holdco and which satisfies the prescribed stock ownership requirements with respect to S. Also, no amount is includible in P's gross income under section 332.

The bill extends the period during which the election relating to previously taxed earnings can be made until one year after enactment of the Technical Corrections Act.

The bill also amends section 1248(g)(2) to limit the exception to a shareholder's gain that is characterized as dividend income under section 356.

[Effective date.—Generally applies to transfers after 7-18-84. Retroactive 1 year after enactment of '86 TRA. Ed.]

Explanation of Provision.—The bill specifies that the regulations that the Secretary is to prescribe pertaining to stapled entities may include regulations providing that any tax imposed on a foreign corporation that the Act treats as a U.S. corporation may, if that corporation does not pay them, be collected from the U.S. corporation to which it is stapled or from the shareholders of the foreign corporation. For example, assume that all the interests in a foreign corporation are stapled to interests in a U.S. corporation. In that case, regulations may provide that the U.S. corporation is liable for any tax that the foreign corporation does not pay. Alternatively, it could be appropriate to collect the tax from the shareholders of the stapled foreign corporation.

Stapled Stock (1) Collection of tax (sec. 269B(b) of the Code.—* * *.

(2) Foreign-owned corporations (sec. 269B(b) of the Code) * * *.

Explanation of Provision.—The bill limits the stapled entity rules treating a foreign corporation as domestic. These rules will not apply if it is established to the satisfaction of the Secretary of the Treasury that both the stapled foreign corporation and the U.S. corporation to which it is stapled are foreign owned. A corporation is foreign owned for this purpose if less than half of its stock, by vote or value, belongs directly or indirectly to U.S. persons.

[Effective date.—Generally 7-18-84. Ed.]

Insurance of related parties by a controlled foreign corporation (sec. 954(e) of the Code)

Present Law.—U.S. shareholders of controlled foreign corporations are currently taxable on the foreign base company services income of those corporations. Foreign base company services income is income derived

in connection with certain services that satisfy a two-pronged test: (1) they are performed for or on behalf of any person related to the controlled foreign corporation and (2) they are performed outside the country under the laws of which the controlled foreign corporation is organized. For the purpose of the first prong of this test, a related person is generally one with more than 50 percent common ownership. The Act amended the second prong of the test in the case of insurance services: if the primary insured is a related person (defined more broadly in this case to include a 10-percent U.S. shareholder and persons related to that shareholder), any services performed with respect to any policy of insurance or reinsurance will be treated as having been performed in the country in which the risk of loss against which that related person is insured is located. The Act did not amend the definition of related person with respect to the first prong of the test.

Explanation of Provision.—The bill makes it clear that there is a single definition of related person for the purpose of determining the amount of foreign base company services income that arises from insurance. In applying the rule that treats income from services performed with respect to insurance or reinsurance for or on behalf of related persons as foreign base company services income (the first prong of the base company services income test), the primary insured will be treated as a related person if it is related within the broad related party rule used specifically for insurance services under the Act—the rule that reaches 10-percent U.S. shareholders and persons related to them.

[*Effective date.*—Taxable years of CFCs beginning after 7-18-84. Ed.]

Definition of resident alien (sec. 7701(b)(4)(E) of the Code)

Present Law.—* * *

*   *   *   *   *   *

In 1961, to relieve foreign students, teachers, and scholars of U.S. tax liability that had the effect of reducing the value of their stipends while they were in the United States, Congress provided that compensation paid by a foreign employer to a *nonresident* alien individual for the period the individual is temporarily present in the United States as a non-immigrant (under subparagraph (F) or (J) of section 101(15) of the Immigration and Nationality Act) is not subject to U.S. tax (Code sec. 872(b)(3), added by the Mutual Educational and Cultural Exchange Act of 1961). Because foreign teachers and trainees who work as such in the United States during more than two calendar years may become resident aliens under the substantial presence test, some foreign teachers and trainees admitted to the United States under exchange visitor programs during three or four calendar years whose foreign income would otherwise be exempt from U.S. tax under Code section 872(b)(3) will be subject to U.S.

tax on such income received or accrued during their third and fourth calendar years in the United States.

* * * * * *

[Senate Explanation]

Under the Act, alien individuals who move to the United States too late in a calendar year to satisfy the substantial presence test for that calendar year are not treated as U.S. residents for any portion of that calendar year (unless they satisfy the green card test for some portion of such year), even if they satisfy the substantial presence test in the following calendar year. Tax benefits accorded to U.S. residents—for example, personal exemptions, joint filing eligibility, and ability to claim itemized deductions—are, therefore, not available to such aliens for any portion of the calendar year in which they moved to the United States.

Explanation of Provision.—The bill increases the exemption period for teachers and trainees, all of whose compensation would otherwise be exempt from tax under the Mutual Educational and Cultural Exchange Act, to a maximum of four calendar years. Under the bill, days spent working in the United States as a teacher or trainee during four calendar years in any seven calendar year period do not count as days of U.S. presence for purposes of the substantial presence test if all of the individual's compensation is described in Code section 872(b)(3).

Under the bill, a qualifying alien individual may elect to be treated as a U.S. resident in a calendar year (the "election year") in which the individual is not otherwise treated as a U.S. resident, if the individual meets the * * * [substantial] presence test for the following calendar year. A qualifying alien individual is one who (1) was not a U.S. resident in the year preceding the election year; (2) is present in the United States for at least 31 consecutive days in the election year; and (3) is present in the United States during the period beginning with the first day of the 31-day presence just referred to and ending with the last day of the election year for a number of days equal to or exceeding 75 percent of the number of days in such period. In applying this 75-percent test, an individual will be treated as present in the United States for up to 5 days during which he or she was actually absent from the country.

A qualifying alien individual who makes the new election will be treated as a U.S. resident only for that portion of the election year which begins on the first day of the earliest presence period for which the individual can satisfy both the 31-day and 75-percent tests described above.

For purposes of both the 75-percent and 31-day tests, an individual will not be treated as present in the United States on any day if the individual is an exempt individual for that day (as determined for purposes of the substantial presence test).

A qualifying alien individual must make the election on his or her tax return for the election year. However, the election may not be made before the individual has met the substantial presence test for the calendar year following the election year. Once an election is made, it remains in effect for the election year unless revoked with consent of the IRS.

The operation of the new election provision is illustrated in the following example: An alien individual vacations in the United States from January 1 through January 31, 1986. He returns to the United States on October 15, 1986, and begins working on a permanent basis for a U.S. company on that day. For the remainder of 1986, he is absent from the country for 10 days only, from December 20 through December 29. He satisfies the substantial presence test in 1987. He was not a U.S. resident in 1985.

The individual may elect to be treated as a U.S. resident for 1986 under the new provision. His residency starting date is October 15, 1986, because that is the first day of the earliest period in 1986 for which both the 31-day and 75-percent tests are satisfied. (The 75-percent test is not satisfied with respect to the presence period commencing on January 1, 1986).

[*Effective Date.*—Applies generally to tax years beginning after 12-31-84. Ed.]

[The Senate Finance Committee version of the bill was amended on the Floor of the Senate. The following explanation is drawn from the Congressional Record. Ed.]

* * * * * *

[Senate Floor Explanation]

Mr. President, this is an amendment relating to world professional athletes when they come to this country and play a charity sports tournament. At the moment, if you are in the United States over 180 days, you are taxed on your worldwide earnings income. It is causing a number of athletes to be reluctant to come and play in our charity sports tournaments, where the money is raised for charity, because it counts toward the 180 days.

This amendment simply says when they are playing here in a charity sports tournament, the days they are playing will not be counted toward the 180 days. They are still taxed if they make any money in the tournament, but the days that they play do not count toward the 180 days. Congressional Record, p. S 8079, 6-20-86.

* * * * * *

Effective Date.—The amendments apply to periods after the date of the enactment of this Act.

[Conference Report]

* * * * * *

The conference agreement follows the Senate amendment, with the addition of the FSC completed contract method transition rule from the House bill and a targeted transitional amendment to the separate foreign tax credit limitation for income of foreign finance subsidiaries.

[¶ 4145] SECTION 1811. AMENDMENTS RELATED TO REPORTING, PENALTY, AND OTHER PROVISIONS

(Sec. 6031, 6050H, 6050K, 6652, 6660, 6678, 7502 of the Code)

[House Explanation]

*   *   *   *   *   *

Explanation of Provision.—The bill makes the following changes to these compliance provisions:

(1) * * * [A] cooperative housing corporation must report to both its tenant-stockholder and the Internal Revenue Service on the tenant-stockholder's proportionate share of interest paid to the cooperative housing corporation. The bill also corrects a citation to the Code in the effective date of a related penalty provision.

(2) The bill corrects an internal reference in the provision relating to reporting on exchanges of certain partnership interests.

(3) The bill makes a conforming amendment to section 6678 (relating to penalties for failing to file statements) to include failures to report the substitute payments. The bill also clarifies that the penalty for intentional disregard of the requirement to report these substitute payments to the IRS is 10 percent of the aggregate amount required to be reported.

(4) The bill provides a cross-reference to the definition of underpayment for purposes of the penalty for valuation understatements with respect to estate or gift taxes.

(5) The bill clarifies that the new deposit rules apply to any taxpayer required, under the provisions of section 6302(c), to deposit any tax under that provision more than once a month.

[Senate Explanation]

(6) The bill improves information reporting by partnerships where a partner's interest is held by a nominee.

[Conference Report]

The conference agreement follows the Senate amendment. The conference agreement also requires the passthrough of information with respect to trusts and estates, parallel to the provision of the Senate amendment requiring the passthrough of information to the beneficial owners of partnership interests.

[Effective dates.—] Special rule created for cooperative housing corporation's reporting of interest to shareholders applies to mortgage interest payments received after 12-31-84. Corrections made to provisions on exchange of partnership interests effective 12-31-84. Conforming amendment made for brokers' substitute payments statement and failure to file provisions applies to payments after 12-31-84. Cross-reference made to estate and gift tax underpayment provisions for valuation understatements applies to returns filed after 12-31-84. Clarification of rule relating to federal tax deposits of $20,000 or more applies to deposits that must be made after 12-31-84.

[¶ 4146] SECTION 1812. AMENDMENTS RELATED TO MISCELLANEOUS PROVISIONS

(Secs. 111, 246, 267, 280F, 1351, 1398, 7872, 4941, 707, 4064)

[House Explanation]

*   *   *   *   *   *

Tax benefit rule * * *

Present Law.—The Act amended the rules of prior law to more clearly reflect economic reality in applying the statutory tax benefit exclusion. To accomplish this, the Act repealed the prior law "recovery exclusion" concept and provided that an amount is excludible from income only to the extent it did not reduce income subject to tax.

Explanation of Provision.—The bill provides that an amount is excludible from income only to the extent that it does not reduce a taxpayer's income tax under chapter 1 of the Code. Thus, where a deduction reduces taxable income but does not reduce tax (because, for example, the taxpayer is subject to the alternative minimum tax), recovery of the amount giving rise to the deduction may be excludible from income under section 111. This amendment is not intended to change the result in the example

set forth in the committee reports accompanying the Act.

*   *   *   *   *   *

[Conference Report]

*   *   *   *   *   *

The conference agreement follows the House Bill * * * with the following modifications.

* * * The House bill * * * provide[s] that the "tax benefit" rule of Section 111 applies where there was no reduction in the taxpayer's tax in a prior year. Under prior law, some taxpayers who had no taxable income for the year in which a deduction was claimed, or who were subject to the alternative minimum tax or had credits that reduced their tax liability to zero, were required to include in income in a later year a portion of the amount previously deducted. The intent of the amendment is to provide equity to taxpayers in these situations so that an amount would be included in income only if the taxpayers derived a tax benefit from the deduction in the year it was taken. It is not intended that the current simplified tax benefit computation be changed for individual taxpayers who receive refunds of State and local income taxes. A recomputation of the tax liability for the prior year is expected in these situations only if the taxpayer had no taxable income in the prior year or was subject to the alternative minimum tax or had credits that reduced their tax liability to zero. Other individual taxpayers receiving refunds of State and local income taxes must continue to follow the procedure set forth by the IRS to determine whether their refund should be included in income. This procedure involves a comparison of the refund amount with the amount by which the taxpayer's itemized deductions for the prior year exceeded the zero bracket amount (standard deduction). The lesser of the two amounts is included in income in the current year. This simple procedure, effectively, produces a result comparable to that obtained by the more complicated recomputation of the taxpayer's tax liability for the prior year.

*   *   *   *   *   *

[House Explanation]

*   *   *   *   *   *

Low interest loans * * *

Present Law.—Section 7872 generally provides that certain loans bearing a below-market rate of interest are treated as loans bearing a market rate of interest accompanied by a payment or payments from the lender to the borrower which are characterized in accordance with the substance of the particular transaction, e.g., gift, compensation, dividend, etc.

For purposes of determining the appropriate market rate of interest as well as the timing of the deemed transfers, section 7872 distinguishes between demand loans and term loans. As presently provided by section 7872, a demand loan is defined as a loan which is due on demand. A term loan is defined as a loan which is not a demand loan. Section 7872(f)(5) provides that the term demand loan includes (for purposes other than determining the applicable Federal rate) a loan which is not transferable and the benefits of the interest arrangement of which is conditioned on the future performance of substantial services by an individual.

For income tax purposes, in the case of a below-market term loan that is not a gift loan, section 7872 treats the excess of the amount loaned over the present value of all payments due under the loan as having been transferred from the lender to the borrower at the time the loan is made. In the case of a below-market demand loan as well as all gift loans, the deemed transfer occurs at the end of each taxable year and the amount of the deemed transfer is the foregone interest that year.

In applying the prescribed market rate, section 7872 requires semi-annual compounding for non-gift term loans, but does not require semi-annual compounding for gift loans and demand loans.

Section 7872 also provides that withholding by an employer is not required where a deemed payment arising from a below-market *demand* loan is in the nature of compensation. However, there is no similar exception from withholding where a deemed compensation payment arises from a below-market *term* loan.

Under section 7872, a loan to Israel at a below-market rate might be characterized as a loan bearing a market rate of interest accompanied by a non-deductible gift to Israel.

Under section 4941 of the Code, certain so-called acts of self-dealing between a private foundation and a "disqualified person" are subject to penalty excise taxes on the amount involved. Generally, a loan between the foundation and a disqualified person is an act of self-dealing. However, an exception is provided for interest-free loans to the private foundation, provided that the proceeds of the loan are used exclusively for certain designated charitable purposes.

Explanation of Provision.—The definitions of term loan and demand loan in section 7872 appear to treat loans with an indefinite maturity as term loans. However, it often is impractical to treat a loan with an indefinite maturity as a term loan, since section 7872 requires the computation of the present value of the payments due under such a loan. Accordingly, the bill grants the Treasury Department authority to treat loans with indefinite maturities as demand loans rather than term loans.

The bill modifies the special provision of section 7872 that treats certain term loans as demand loans for the purpose of determining the timing of deemed interest and compensation payments. Under the bill, a loan would be entitled to such treatment if the benefit of the interest arrangement of the loan is not transferable and is contingent upon the performance of substantial future services by an individual. Thus, if a loan satisfies these conditions, it would receive the special treatment even if the lender or the borrower (or either) could transfer the loan.

The various time value of money provisions of the Code, (including provisions relating to the treatment of below-market term loans), generally require the use of semi-annual compounding in calculating interest. In order to treat all loans consistently, the bill provides that semi-annual compounding will also be required in calculating interest with respect to gift loans and demand loans under section 7872.

The Conference Report to the Act [the 1984 Tax Reform Act. Ed.] indicated that payments of compensation, deemed to have been made by section 7872, would be subject to the information reporting requirements but not the withholding requirements of the Code. H.R. Rep. No. 98-861, 98th Cong., 2d Sess. 1017 (1984). The failure to except from the withholding requirements deemed payments of compensation arising from below-market term loans was inadvertent, and the bill corrects this omission.

The bill also provides an exception from section 7872 for certain loans to Israel. The exception is limited to any obligation issued by Israel if (1) all of the proceeds are to be used for essential governmental purposes, (2) the obligation is payable in U.S. dollars, (3) interest is payable on the obligation at an annual rate of not less than 4 percent, and (4) such obligation is part of an issue marketed primarily on grounds of supporting Israel rather than for investment.

Finally, the bill clarifies that Congress did not intend in enacting section 7872 to affect the definition of acts of self-dealing with private foundations.

[Conference Report]

* * * * * *

* * * The conference agreement exempts obligations issued by Israel from the below-market interest rate provisions of section 7872 if the obligation is payable in United States dollars and bears an interest rate of not less than 4 percent.

* * * * * *

[House Explanation]

* * * * * *

Transactions with related persons * * *

Present Law.—The Act generally imposes a matching principle by placing taxpayers on the cash method of accounting with respect to the deduction of amounts owed to a related cash-basis taxpayer. In other words, the deduction by the payor is generally allowed no earlier than when the related payee recognizes the corresponding income.

The application of the above described rule is unclear when the related payee is a related foreign person that does not, for many Code purposes, include in gross income foreign source income that is not effectively connected with a U.S. trade or business.

In addition, the Act also generally deferred losses on sales of property between corporations which are members of the same controlled group of corporations. An exception was provided for certain sales of inventory to or from foreign corporations.

Explanation of Provision.—The bill directs the Secretary of the Treasury to issue regulations applying the matching principle generally applicable to related party transactions in cases in which the person to whom the payment is to be made is not a United States person. For example, assume that a foreign corporation, not engaged in a U.S. trade or business, performs services outside the United States for use by its wholly owned U.S. subsidiary in the United States. That income is foreign source income that is not effectively connected with a U.S. trade or business. It is not subject to U.S. tax (or, generally, includible in the foreign parent's gross income). Under the bill, regulations could require the U.S. subsidiary to use the cash method of accounting with respect to the deduction of amounts owed to its foreign

parent for these services. In the case of amounts accrued to a controlled foreign corporation by a related person, regulations might appropriately require the payor's accounting method to conform to the method that the controlled foreign corporation uses for U.S. tax purposes.

Regulations will not be necessary when an amount paid to a related foreign person is effectively connected with a U.S. trade or business (unless a treaty reduces the tax). In that case, present law already imposes matching. However, regulations may be necessary when a foreign corporation uses a method of accounting for some U.S. tax purposes (*e.g.*, because some of its income is effectively connected), but when the method does not apply to the amount that the U.S. person seeks to accrue.

The bill also provides that the special exception from section 267 for sales of inventory to or from foreign corporations applies where the party related to the foreign corporation is a partnership.

For transfers after September 27, 1985, the bill provides that the provisions of section 707(b)(1)(A) and 707(b)(2)(A) will apply whether or not the person constructively holding a 50-percent partnership interest was himself a partner. In addition, the bill provides that the deferral provisions of section 267(a)(2) will apply to two partnerships in which the same persons hold a more than 50-percent of the capital interests or profits interests. This rule is intended to replace the rule in the Treasury regulations,[7] which was suggested by the 1984 Committee Reports, relating to transactions between related partnerships with common partners.

A transitional rule is provided for a specified transaction where indebtedness was incurred before January 1, 1984.

* * * * * *

[Conference Report]

* * * * * *

* * * The conference agreement contains the provisions in the House Bill.

* * * * * *

[House Explanation]

* * * * * *

Federal Home Loan Mortgage Corporation * * *

Present Law. — *General background.* — The Act repealed the prior law exemption from Federal income tax of Freddie Mac, effective January 1, 1985. Various transition rules were included to ensure that, to the extent possible, Freddie Mac was subject to tax only on its post-1984 income.

The 12 regional Federal Home Loan Banks, which hold the common stock of Freddie Mac, are themselves exempt from

---

[Footnote ¶ 4146]   (7) Temp. Reg. Sec. 1.267(a)-2T(c), Questions 2 and 3.

Act § 1812 ¶ 4146

tax; however, the member institutions of the Home Loan Banks are subject to tax.

In a transaction completed in early 1985, Freddie Mac issued a new class of preferred stock in itself to the regional Federal Home Loan Banks, which then transferred the stock to their member institutions. Distributions with respect to this preferred stock will thus be paid directly to the member institutions. The common stock of Freddie Mac continues to be owned by the Federal Home Loan Banks.

Dividends received deduction.—The Act allows shareholders of the Federal Home Loan Banks a dividends received deduction for that portion of dividends received from a Federal Home Loan Bank which is allocable to dividends paid to the Federal Home Loan Bank by Freddie Mac out of Freddie Mac earnings and profits for periods after December 31, 1984. Special "stacking" rules are included in order that a deduction may be received only with respect to dividends which are properly allocable to post-1984 earnings and profits of Freddie Mac. No dividends received deduction is allowed to member institutions for dividends received from Federal Home Loan Banks which are allocable to Freddie Mac earnings and profits which Freddie Mac accumulated before January 1, 1985 (i.e., prior to the date of taxability).

In addition to these rules, the Act states that, for all income tax purposes, Freddie Mac is to be treated as having no accumulated earnings and profits as of January 1, 1985. This provision was intended to ensure that the deduction for dividends received by member institutions from the Federal Home Loan Banks would apply only to the extent the dividends are allocable to post-1984 earnings and profits of Freddie Mac (i.e., to Freddie Mac income which has already been subject to tax).

Explanation of Provisions.—*Dividends received deduction.*—The bill makes several adjustments in the dividends received deduction for dividends allocable to post-1984 Freddie Mac income.

First, the bill adds an explicit statutory rule stating that no dividends received deduction is to be allowed with respect to dividends paid by Freddie Mac out of earnings and profits accumulated before January 1, 1985 (i.e., the date of taxability). This rule is in addition to the present law rule which denies a dividends received deduction for dividends paid by a Home Loan Bank which are ultimately allocable to pre-1985 Freddie Mac income. Thus, under the bill, dividends received deductions would be limited to amounts allocable to post-1984 (i.e., taxable) Freddie Mac income, both in the case of income distributed via the Federal Home Loan Banks and in the case of any dividends which may be paid directly to Freddie Mac corporate shareholders who are themselves subject to tax (e.g., member institutions which hold Freddie Mac preferred stock). This rule allows a dividends received deduction where necessary to avoid a double corporate-level tax on Freddie Mac income. In conjunction with this amendment, the pres-

ent law rule under which Freddie Mac is treated as having no accumulated profits as of January 1, 1985, is repealed.

Second, in the case of income distributed via a Federal Home Loan Bank, the bill clarifies that no dividends paid by Freddie Mac may serve as the basis for more than one deduction for dividends received from a Federal Home Loan Bank. This clarification applies both to dividends paid by a Federal Home Loan Bank in different years, or when two or more dividends are paid during the same year.

Third, in the case of dividends paid directly by Freddie Mac to taxable corporate shareholders, the bill permits a deduction for dividends received in 1985, as well as later years. This result would otherwise be prevented by a Code provision which denies dividends received deductions for one year after the corporation paying the dividend ceases to be tax-exempt (sec. 246(a)(1)).

Tax treatment of preferred stock distribution.—The bill provides that, for all purposes under the Code, the distribution of preferred stock by Freddie Mac to the Federal Home Loan Banks in late 1984, and the distribution of such stock by the Federal Home Loan Banks to their member institutions in January, 1985, are to be treated as if they were distributions of money in an amount equal to the fair market value of the stock on the date of the distribution by the Federal Home Loan Banks, followed by the payment of such money by the member institutions to Freddie Mac in return for its stock. Thus, under the special rule, the Federal Home Loan Banks will be treated as receiving cash dividends to the extent that the money deemed received from Freddie Mac is attributable to earnings and profits of Freddie Mac, and the earnings and profits of the Federal Home Loan Banks will be increased by an equivalent amount. The member institutions, in turn, will be treated as receiving cash dividends from the Federal Home Loan Banks, to the extent that the money deemed received from the Federal Home Loan Banks is attributable to earnings and profits of the Federal Home Loan Banks (taking into account the earnings and profits resulting from the distribution from Freddie Mac). Because these dividends are allocable to pre-1985 earnings and profits of Freddie Mac, the member institutions will not be entitled to a dividends received deduction with respect to these amounts.

Under the special rule above, the earnings and profits of Freddie Mac will be reduced by the amount deemed distributed to the Federal Home Loan Banks. If Freddie Mac later makes distributions to the member institutions out of its pre-1985 income, these distributions will be treated as dividends (and will not qualify for a dividends received deduction) to the extent (if any) that pre-1985 earnings and profits of Freddie Mac exceeded the amount deemed distributed at the time of the preferred stock distribution.

*   *   *   *   *   *

[Conference Report]

* * * * *

* * * The conference agreement provides that the earnings and profits of the Federal Home Loan Bank, for purposes of section 246(a)(2), is to be determined as reported in its annual financial statement.

* * * * * *

[House Explanation]

* * * * * *

Personal use property * * *

Present Law.—The Act provided limitations on the maximum amount of investment tax credit and depreciation that a taxpayer may claim with respect to a passenger automobile. The Act also provided that if use in a trade or business of listed property does not exceed 50 percent, no investment tax credit is available, and depreciation must be determined on the straight line method over the earnings and profits life of the property. Listed property is any passenger automobile or other means of transportation, any entertainment, recreation, or amusement property, any computer, or any other property specified in regulations. However, any computer used exclusively at a regular business establishment is not considered to be listed property. Employee use of listed property must be for the convenience of the employer and a condition of employment for the employee to be able to claim a deduction or credit for the use of listed property.

* * * * * *

Explanation of Provision.—The bill clarifies the definition of passenger automobile by providing that the weight of the automobile shall not include the weight of the passengers or the weight of any cargo. A similar clarification is made for purposes of the gas guzzler excise tax (sec. 4064 of the Code). The amendment to the gas guzzler tax will not apply to any station wagon if the station wagon is a 1985 or 1986 model manufactured before November 1, 1985, and is originally equipped with more than 6 seat belts.

The bill also clarifies that the requirements that, in order to take a deduction or credit, employee use of listed property be for the convenience of the employer and required as a condition of employment also apply to the amount of any deduction allowable to the employee for rentals or other payments under a lease of listed property.

The bill also clarifies that computers eligible for the exception from the definition of listed property must be owned or leased by the person operating the business establishment, in addition to being used exclusively at a regular business establishment. See H. Rep. No. 98-861 (June 23, 1984), p. 1026 (Conference Report).

Finally, the bill provides that, except to the extent provided in regulations, listed property used as a means of transportation (within the meaning of section 280F(d)(4)(A)(ii) does not include property substantially all the use of which is in the business of providing unrelated persons services consisting of the transportation of persons or property for hire.

* * * * * *

[Conference Report]

* * * * * *

* * * The conference agreement includes all the provisions common to both bills. In addition, the conference agreement generally follows the House bill and the Senate amendment in utilizing "unloaded gross vehicle weight" for purposes of both the luxury vehicles and gas guzzler tax provisions. However, the conference agreement follows the Senate amendment by utilizing "gross vehicle weight" for purposes of the luxury vehicles provision, with respect to trucks and vans. The conference agreement follows the House bill as to the effective date.

The conference agreement exempts from the gas guzzler tax small manufacturers who lengthen existing automobiles.

* * * * * *

[**Effective dates.**—The amendments, relating to the application of the tax benefit rule, apply for amounts recovered after 12-31-83 in tax years ending after that date; the rules governing below market loans are modified, generally, for term loans made and demand loans outstanding after 6-6-84; the rules, relating to transactions with related parties, are revised for the foreign persons provision, for tax years beginning after 12-31-83, and for the partnership provision, for sales or exchanges after 3-1-86; the amendments, relating to Freddie Macs generally apply after 12-31-84; and the clarifications to the definitions in the personal use property provisions apply, generally, to property placed in service and leases entered after 6-18-84 in tax years ending after that date. Ed.]

[¶ 4147] SECTION 1821. AMENDMENTS RELATED TO SECTION 211 OF THE ACT

(Secs. 211 of 1984 TRA; 805, 807, 808, 809, 812, 813, 815, 816, 817, 818 of the Code)

[Senate Explanation]

* * * **Certain amounts not less than surrender value of contract (* * * sec. 807(c) of the Code)**

*   *   *   *   *   *

Explanation of Provision.—The bill provides that, in computing the increases or decreases of amounts discounted at interest under insurance and annuity contracts, the amount taken into account will in no case be less than the net surrender value of such contract. This provision recognizes that amounts under these contracts discounted at the prevailing State assumed interest rate may in fact yield a reserve item which is less than the net surrender value guaranteed by the contract. The bill allows the taxpayer to recognize at least its current liability with respect to obligations not involving life, accident, or health contingencies, as represented by the guaranteed net surrender value of a contract. As is the case with life insurance reserves, however, the amounts taken into account cannot exceed the amounts that would be taken into account with respect to such contract as of such time in determining statutory reserves (as defined in sec. 809(b)(4)(B)).

In addition, the bill provides that, when the Secretary by regulation changes the table applicable to a type of contract, the new table shall be treated as if it were a new prevailing commissioner's standard table adopted by the 26th State as of a date (no earlier than the date the regulation is issued) specified by the Secretary.

*   *   *   *   *   *

* * * **Clarification of definition of excess interest (* * * sec. 808(d)(1) of Code)**

*   *   *   *   *   *

Explanation of Provision.—The bill changes the definition of excess interest to mean any amount in the nature of interest in excess of the prevailing State assumed rate for such contract. This change is intended to clarify that the term excess interest refers only to the excess amount and not to the entire amount in the nature of interest (including the amount determined at the prevailing State assumed interest rate).

* * * **Coordination of 1984 fresh start adjustment with certain accelerations of policyholder dividends deductions (* * * sec. 808 of the Code)**

*   *   *   *   *   *

Explanation of Provision.—The "fresh start" was granted with respect to the accounting change for policyholder dividends on the assumption that insurance companies would continue to follow their general business practice in declaring policy dividends at the end of the calendar year to be payable on policy anniversaries during the following calendar year only in the event the policy remained outstanding on such anniversary. It was understood that, given the general business practices, the present-law change in policyholder dividends accounting had the effect of delaying the deduction for policyholder dividends to the taxable year in which they are paid.

It appears that by guaranteeing policy dividends on termination (which may not change necessarily the payment date of policy dividends) or by changing the payment date by making policy dividends available upon declaration, a company can accelerate the deduction for approximately one half the policyholder dividends that would have been deducted in the following taxable year if there had been no change in the company's business practices in declaring policy dividends. As a practical matter, the amount of the acceleration of the policyholder dividend deduction could be viewed as restoring a company, in part, to the position it enjoyed under prior law with respect to the timing of the policyholder dividends deduction. The "fresh start" for the change in policyholder dividends accounting was intended to mitigate the detriment caused taxpayers by a statutory change in such accounting; to the extent the detriment caused by the statutory change is mitigated in fact by a company's own changed business practices, the "fresh start" was not intended to give a company additional tax benefits.

For these reasons, the bill adopts a provision that would reduce a company's policyholder dividends deduction by the amount by which the company's policyholder dividends deduction was accelerated because of a change in business practices. This reduction for an accelerated policyholder dividends deduction is made before any reduction for the ownership differential provision for mutual life insurance companies and does not exceed on a cumulative basis the amount of a company's 1984 fresh-start adjustment for policyholder dividends. Also, the determination of the amount of the accelerated policyholder dividends deduction and the amount of the 1984 fresh-start adjustment will be made separately with respect to each line of business.

The term "accelerated policyholder dividends deduction" means the amount that would be determined for the taxable year as policyholder dividends paid or accrued, but which would have been determined for a later taxable year under the business practices of the company as in effect at the close of the preceding taxable year. Thus, the types of changes in business practices that would result in an accelerated policyholder dividends deduction include guaranteeing of policy dividends on termination for a particular product line or changing the actual payment date of policy dividends (for example, by making such dividends available upon declaration). On the other hand, changes in plans of insurance being sold or the development of new products will not be treated as resulting in an accelerated policyholder dividends deduction. For example, the introduction and sale of a universal life insurance product that credits excess interest to the cash surrender value on a monthly basis and that may depart from prior business practices of selling traditional participating life insurance policies that pay policy dividends at the policy anniversary date is not the type of change in business practice covered by this provision.

In addition, policyholder dividends paid or accrued on policies issued after December 31, 1983, generally will not produce accelerated policyholder dividends. However, a policy issued after December 31, 1983, in exchange for a substantially similar policy issued before January 1, 1984, is treated as if the policy were issued on the date that the original policy were issued. For this purpose, whether policies are substantially similar is determined without regard to the time of accrual of policyholder dividends. Under this rule, an accelerated policyholder dividends deduction will result if a life insurance company exchanges an old policy for a new policy with substantially similar terms, except that the new policy guarantees policy dividends or makes such dividends available upon declaration.

Under the bill, certain policy exchanges are not treated as exchanges for substantially similar policies. This provision, which exempts policies from the accelerated policyholder dividend provision, applies if the policy is a group policy purchased by an employer under a plan to provide welfare benefits (within the meaning of sec. 419(e)(2)). Similarly, if a company alters the terms of a policy so that the policy does not constitute a welfare benefit fund, such an alteration is not treated as a change in business practice.

The bill specifically provides that this provision does not apply to a mere change in the amount of policyholder dividends. Thus, if a company changes its dividends scale, for example, by increasing the amount of the policyholder dividend over the previous year or by changing the formula for determining the amount of policy dividends to include items not previously considered in determining the amount of policyholder dividends (e.g., capital gains), this provision would not apply to treat such change as an acceleration of policyholder dividends pursuant to a change in business practices.

The cumulative amount of the reduction of a company's policyholder dividends deduction with respect to a particular line of business under this provision is limited to the 1984 fresh-start adjustment for policyholder dividends with respect to such business. Specifically, the 1984 fresh-start adjustment for policyholder dividends means the amounts

held as of December 31, 1983, by the company as reserves for policyholder dividends that were deductible in 1983, less dividends that accrued before January 1, 1984. Also, the adjustment amount will be properly reduced to reflect the amounts of previously nondeductible policyholder dividends as determined under prior-law section 809(f).

* * * **Clarification of equity base** (* * * **sec. 809(b) of the Code)**

*   *   *   *   *   *

Explanation of Provision.—The bill clarifies that no item shall be taken into account more than once in determining the equity base. This clarification is made to ensure that items which are specifically included in the equity base are not counted a second time because they may be indirectly included under another item which is included in the equity base. For example, deficiency reserves, which are specifically listed in the statute as included in the equity base, could also be included indirectly as part of the excess of statutory policy reserves over tax reserves, which is also specifically included in the equity base.

* * * **Definition of 50 largest stock companies** (* * * **sec. 809(d)(4) of the Code)**

*   *   *   *   *   *

Explanation of Provision.—The bill modifies the authority of the Secretary of the Treasury to issue regulations that would exclude companies from the 50 largest stock companies. Under the bill, any company that has a negative equity base is excluded from the 50 largest stock companies. In addition, regulations could exclude additional companies from the 50 largest stock companies if the exclusion of those companies would, by reason of their small equity bases, seriously distort the stock earnings rate. An unlimited number of stock companies could be excluded from the group by reason of their having a negative equity base. However, no more than two companies could be excluded from the group of 50 largest stock companies by reason of the fact that their earnings rate could seriously distort the stock earnings rate. In addition, distorting companies could be excluded from the group of 50 largest stock companies only if their exclusion, in addition to the exclusion for the negative equity companies, would not cause the total number of stock companies to be excluded to exceed two.

The bill provides that a company will be removed from the group of 50 largest stock companies for the base period if such company had a negative equity base for 1981, 1982, or 1983 because such company's earnings rate would seriously distort the average stock earnings rate and if the company was a party to a rehabilitation proceeding on March 15, 1984, under the applicable State insurance law.

*   *   *   *   *   *

[Conference Report]

* * * * * *

U.S. branches of foreign life insurance companies.—Branches of foreign life insurance companies are not included in the determination of the 50 largest stock companies and the calculation for mutual companies.

* * * * * *

[Senate Explanation]

* * * * * *

Clarification of statement gain or loss from operations (* * * sec. 809(g)(1) of the Code)

* * * * * *

Explanation of Provision.—The bill revises the definition of statement gain or loss from operations to clarify that the term refers to net gain or loss from operations set forth in the annual statement, determined without regard to Federal income taxes and with further adjustment for certain items. Specifically, the bill clarifies that the "statement gain or loss from operations" must be adjusted by substituting for the amount shown on the annual statement for policyholder dividends the amount of the deductions for policyholder dividends under section 808, before reduction by any differential earnings amount (i.e., without regard to sec. 808(c)(2)). The use of the tax amount for the policyholder dividends deduction unreduced by any differential earnings amount is necessary to eliminate a circularity in computation of the differential earnings amount and to ensure that subsequent adjustments in the differential earnings amount have the revenue impact intended by the ownership differential provision.

* * * * * *

* * * Effect of differential earnings amount on estimated tax payments (* * * sec. 809(c) and (f) of the Code)

* * * * * *

Explanation of Provision.—The bill amends the definition of the differential earnings rate to be used for a taxable year solely for purposes of estimated tax payments. Specifically, the bill provides that if, with respect to any installment of estimated tax, the differential earnings rate for the second preceding year is less than the differential earnings rate applicable to the taxable year for which the installment is paid, then for purposes of applying additions to tax for underpayments of estimated tax with respect to such installment, the amount of tax shall be determined by using the differential earnings rate for such earlier year.

In providing this relief from additions to tax for underpayments of estimated tax under these limited circumstances, the committee recognizes that, as a practical matter, the Secretary of the Treasury will be unable to collect the data from the previous taxable year and compute the new differential earnings rate for the current taxable year in time for the taxpayer to use that differential earnings rate to make its initial estimated tax payments.

The bill also clarifies that the recomputation of the differential earnings amount with respect to any taxable year will not affect the liability for estimated tax payments for the taxable year in which the recomputed amount is included in (or deducted from) income. Thus, a mutual company will compute its tax liability for 1984 by using the statutory transitional differential earnings rate of 7.8 percent. If the recomputed differential earnings rate for 1984 exceeds 7.8 percent, then the company will be required to include in income in 1985 the excess of the recomputed differential earnings amount over the differential earnings amount reported on its tax return. As a practical matter, Treasury will be unable to collect the data for 1984 and compute the 1984 rate before 1986. Accordingly, this excess will not affect the company's estimated tax liability, or penalties relating to that liability, for 1985.

Amendments related to proration formulas (* * * sec. 812 of the Code)

* * * * * *

Explanation of Provision.—The bill amends the definition of required interest to provide that, if the prevailing State assumed interest rate is not used, another appropriate rate is to be used in calculating required interest.

Under the bill, the definition of the company's share of net investment income is amended to clarify that, in arriving at such amount, net investment income should be reduced by all interest paid to a depositor or any customer for the services provided by the life insurance company, whether it is interest guaranteed on the contract (like required interest) or excess interest. For example, net investment income should be reduced by all interest paid on deposit administration contracts that provide no permanent purchase rate guarantees; although the purchaser of such a contract may not technically be a "policyholder," the purchaser may be viewed as a depositor or a customer for the services provided by the life insurance company.

The bill eliminates a circularity problem existing under the language of present law in determining the minifraction to be used for purposes of computing the gross investment income's proportionate share of policyholder dividends. Specifically, the bill redefines the denominator of the minifraction to be life insurance gross income reduced by the excess (if any) of the closing balance for the reserve items described in section 807(c) over the opening balance for such items for the taxable year. It further generally states that, for purposes of computing the denominator, life insurance gross income shall be determined by including tax-exempt interest (as under present law) and by computing any decreases in reserves without any reduction of the closing balance of the reserve items by the company's share of tax-exempt interest.

In addition, the bill refines the definition of net investment income to take into account the fact that investment expenses with respect to assets held in segregated asset accounts have historically been smaller than those with respect to general account assets. Accordingly, in the case of gross investment income attributable to assets held in segregated asset accounts underlying variable contracts, the bill defines net investment income to mean 95 percent, rather than 90 percent, of gross investment income.

Finally, for purposes of computing net increases or decreases in reserves and for purposes of the proration formula, the bill provides that the terms "gross investment income" and "tax-exempt interest" shall not include any interest received with respect to a securities acquisition loan (an ESOP loan) as defined in section 133(b) of the Code. Also, for purposes of determining the gross investment income's proportionate share of policyholder dividends, "life insurance gross income" shall not include the interest on a securities acquisition loan. This amendment more fully implements the intention of Congress when it provided an exclusion from gross income for 50 percent of the interest received on a securities acquisition loan, that is, to encourage financial institutions to make loans to ESOPs and to employers who maintain leveraged ESOPs.

Treatment of foreign life insurance companies (* * * sec. 813(a) of the Code)

*　　*　　*　　*　　*　　*

 Explanation of Provision.—The bill clarifies how a foreign life insurance company doing business in the United States should compute its life insurance company taxable income if additional income has been imputed because actual surplus held in the United States is less than the required minimum surplus. Specifically, any amount of income imputed by the special adjustment to income under section 813 shall be added to life insurance gross income (before computing the amount of the special life insurance company deduction and the small life insurance company deduction), and such increase in income shall be included in gross investment income.

* * * Treatment of certain distributions to shareholders from pre-1984 policyholders surplus account (* * * sec. 815 of the Code)

*　　*　　*　　*　　*　　*

 Explanation of Provision.—The citation in the legislative history of the 1984 Act to *Union Bankers Insurance Company* indicated the type of fact situations in which liability for a tax on distributions from a policyholders surplus account could arise. The present law emphasis on taxing both direct and indirect distributions from the policyholders surplus account was intended to be construed more broadly than under the 1959 Act, causing certain uses of policyholders surplus account funds to be treated as a distribution

therefrom, whether or not there was a distribution under general corporate tax provisions.

The bill clarifies what would constitute an indirect distribution from the policyholders surplus account by providing that a direct or indirect distribution does not include a bona fide loan with arm's-length terms and conditions. An indirect distribution will be treated as occurring whenever policyholders surplus account funds are used to benefit the shareholders indirectly. For example, this may occur by using such funds to purchase stock of a parent or an affiliated company or by using such funds to make loans within an affiliated group for less than adequate consideration. Whether or not a loan is made with arm's-length terms and conditions may be determined by reference to section 482 (relating to the allocation of income and deductions among taxpayers) and the regulations thereunder.

In the case of any loan made before March 1, 1986, the amount that will be treated as an indirect distribution from the policyholders surplus account due to the absence of arm's length terms and conditions will be limited to the foregone interest on the loan. The amount of foregone interest will be determined by using the lowest rate which would have met the arm's length requirements for a loan with the same terms and conditions. This rule continues to apply unless the loan is renegotiated, extended, renewed, or revised on or after March 1, 1986.

The bill also reinstates a prior law provision (section 819(b)) which provides rules applicable to distributions from policyholders surplus accounts of foreign life insurance companies doing business in the United States.

Treatment of deficiency reserves (* * * sec. 816 of the Code)

*　　*　　*　　*　　*　　*

 Explanation of Provision.—The bill reinstates the prior-law exclusion of deficiency reserves from the definition of life insurance reserves and total reserves for purposes of section 816, which defines a life insurance company, and section 813(a)(4)(B), which defines surplus held in the United States for foreign lifes insurance companies doing business in the United States. The exclusion of deficiency reserves under DEFRA was not intended to have a substantive effect on the qualification of a company as a life insurance company or on the computation of surplus held in the United States for foreign life insurance companies.

* * * Treatment of certain nondiversified contracts (* * * sec. 817(h) of the Code)

*　　*　　*　　*　　*　　*

 Explanation of Provision.—The bill clarifies the exception for variable life insurance contracts based on investments in Treasury securities. Generally, the investments made by any segregated asset account with respect to a variable life insurance contract will be treated as adequately diversified to the extent invested in securities issued by the United States Treasury. The committee intends that the Treasury Department, in issuing regulations relating to the adequate diversification requirement, will provide guidance as to how the diversification requirement applies to the assets of the segregated asset account that are not invested in securities issued by the United States Treasury.

In addition, the bill provides that, if all the beneficial interests in a regulated investment company or any trust are held by one or more (a) insurance companies (or affiliated companies) in their general account or in segregated asset accounts, or (b) fund managers (or affiliated companies) in connection with the creation or management of the regulated investment company or trust, the diversification requirements shall be applied by taking into account the assets held by such regulated investment company or trust. This revision of the present law "look through" rule generalizes and broadens the statutory language to allow for the ownership of fund shares by an insurance company or fund manager for administrative convenience, in operating an underlying investment fund.

The committee intends that, for purposes of determining whether a variable contract is adequately diversified, the types of situations grandfathered in Rev. Ruls. 77-85, 80-274, and 81-225 will continue to be grandfathered under Treasury regulations. Further, the committee expects that the Treasury Department will provide a reasonable time after issuance of regulations relating to the diversification time after issuance of regulations relating to the diversification requirements during which an insurance company that relied on private letter rulings issued under the guidelines of those revenue rulings can diversify the assets of a segregated asset account.

* * * Treatment of certain deferred compensation plans (* * * sec. 818(a)(6)(A) of the Code)

*   *   *   *   *   *

Explanation of Provision.—The bill clarifies the definition of a pension plan contract to include an eligible State deferred compensation plan (within the meaning of sec. 457(b)).

* * * Dividends within affiliated group (* * * sec. 818(e) of the Code)

*   *   *   *   *   *

Explanation of Provision.—The bill reinstates the prior-law provision of section 818(f)(1) with minor modifications to reflect changes in the general tax structure for life insurance company taxation. The bill provides that, in the case of a life insurance company filing or required to file a consolidated return with respect to any affiliated group for any taxable year, any determination under part I of subchapter L with respect to any dividend paid by one member of such group to another member of such group shall be made as if such group was not filing a consolidated return. This reinstatement of the prior-law provision is necessary to maintain the integrity of the proration rule for tax-exempt interest and the intercorporate dividend deduction between policyholders and the company.

* * * Treatment of dividends from subsidiaries (* * * sec. 805(a)(4) of the Code)

*   *   *   *   *   *

Explanation of Provision.—The bill adds a special rule in the case of certain 100 percent dividends received from a life insurance subsidiary. Under the bill, in the case of any 100 percent dividend paid to a life insurance company for any taxable year after December 31, 1983, by another life insurance company, a portion of the deduction under sections 243, 244, or 245(b) (as the case may be) is disallowed if the payor company's share determined under the proration rules exceeds the payee company's share for the payee company's taxable year in which the dividend is received or accrued.

The portion of the deduction that is disallowed is the percentage otained by subtracting the payee company's share from the payor company's share multiplied by the portion of the dividend attributable to prorated amounts. Prorated amounts include tax-exempt interest income and dividends other than 100 percent dividends.

In determining the portion of a dividend attributable to prorated amounts, any dividend by the payor company is treated as coming first out of earnings and profits for taxable years beginning after December 31, 1983, attributable to prorated amounts. In addition, the portion attributable to prorated amounts is calculated by determining the portion of earnings and profits attributable to prorated amounts without any reduction for Federal income taxes.

* * * * * *

[Conference Report]

* * * * * *

Prevention of double proration.—An anti-double proration rule applicable to life insurance companies with property and casualty insurance subsidiaries is added to the life insurance anti-double proration rule in the Senate amendment.

* * * * * *

[Senate Explanation]

* * * * * *

* * * **Special rule for application of high surplus mutual rules (* * * sec. 809(i) of the Code)**

* * * * * *

Explanation of Provision.—Under the bill, in the case of any mutual life insurance company that acquired a stock subsidiary during 1982 and whose excess equity base under section 809(i)(2)(D) of the Internal

Revenue Code of 1954 is no more than 46 percent of such excess equity base (determined after the application of this provision limiting the company's excess equity base), the amount of the company's excess equity base for purposes of the high surplus mutual company rule is $122 million. This provision applies without regard to any other provision that would otherwise limit the company's excess equity base.

[Conference Report]

* * * * * *

High surplus mutual rule.—The rule determining the excess equity base for a high where the excess equity base, for its first taxable year beginning in 1984, as determined under sec. 809(i)(2)(D) of the Code, is no more than [$175,000,000].

* * * * * *

Variable contracts with guarantees.—Certain variable life insurance contracts with guarantees are treated as variable contracts under section 817 with a special effective date.

[Effective Date.—Unless otherwise specified above, this section shall take effect as if included in the provisions to which it relates in the 1984 Tax Reform Act. Generally rules apply to tax years beginning after 12-31-83. Variable contracts rule applies to contracts issued after 12-31-86 and contracts issued before 1-1-87 if treated as variable contract on taxpayer's return.]

[¶ 4148] SECTION 1822. AMENDMENTS RELATED TO SECTION 216 OF THE ACT

(Sec. 216 of 1984 TRA)

[Senate Explanation]

* * * * * *

* * * **Clarification of denial of fresh-start provisions, application of 10-year spread and the effect of fresh start on earnings and profits (* * * sec. 216(b)(1) and 216(b)(3)(A) and (C) of the Act)**

* * * * * *

Explanation of Provision.—The bill clarifies, that, with respect to reserves for which the fresh start is denied, the present-law rule for spreading a change in basis of computing reserves over a 10-year period will be applied to the extent that the reserve change would have been required to be taken into account over a 10-year period under prior law. With respect to reserves for which the fresh start has been denied, that portion of the reserve change attributable to the repeal of an election under 818(c) is taken into account in the first taxable year beginning after December 31, 1983, and is not spread over a 10-year period.

In addition, the bill conforms the closing date for the period for which proscribed reinsurance transactions will result in a denial of the "fresh start" to that date given for revaluation of reserves. Specifically, it provides that for purposes of the denial of fresh start provision (sec. 216(b)(3)(A) of DE-FRA), if a reinsurer's taxable year is not a calendar year, the first day of the first taxable year beginning after 1983 is the closing date of the period. This is intended to prevent abuse of the fresh-start provisions by use of reinsurance transactions after 1983 where the reinsurer's taxable year may be a fiscal year rather than the calendar year.

The bill clarifies that the change in the insurance company's reserves attributable to the "fresh start" will be taken into account in computing the current and accumulated earnings and profits of the insurance company. Under the general rule, this adjustment to an insurance company's earnings and profits will be made as of the beginning of the first taxable year beginning after December 31, 1983.

Act § 1822 ¶ 4148

The committee intends that the adjustment to earnings and profits is to be taken into account by the taxpayer for whom the fresh-start adjustment is relevant. For example, if a life insurance subsidiary was sold by a controlled group in 1984, the adjustment to earnings and profits should be taken into account with respect to earnings and profits should be taken into account with respect to the subsidiary before the sale of the subsidiary because the amount of the fresh-start adjustment is essentially determined as of the beginning of the first taxable year beginning after December 31, 1983. Thus, the seller, rather than the purchaser, would benefit by the adjustment to earnings and profits.

An exception to the general rule is provided to the general rule relating to the adjustment to earnings and profits in the case of an insurance company that (1) is a member of a controlled group the common parent of which is a company having its principal place of business in Alabama and (2) was incorporated in Delaware on November 29, 1979. In this situation, the adjustment to the insurance company's earnings and profits will be made as of the beginning of the company's first taxable year beginning after December 31, 1984.

* * * * * *

[Conference Report]

* * * * * *

Adjustment to earnings and profits for fresh start adjustment.—The provision in the Senate amendment is modified to allow an additional company to elect to take the fresh start adjustment into account in 1985 for earnings and profits.

* * * * * *

[Senate Explanation]

* * * * * *

* * * Treatment of certain elections under sec. 818(c) (* * * sec. 216(b)(4)(B) of the Act)

* * * * * *

Explanation of Provision.—The bill clarifies that a valid prior-law section 818(c) election made under the exception described above shall not be treated as reserve strengthening for purposes of denying a fresh start and requiring that the amount be taken into income in the first taxable year beginning after December 31, 1983. This allows a taxpayer that qualifies for the limited exception for making a prior-law section 818(c) election after September 27, 1983, to have the full benefit of that election.

In addition, the bill provides a limited exception to the rule requiring section 818(c)

elections to have been made on or before September 27, 1983. Under this exception, an election is treated as if it were made on or before September 27, 1983, if (1) on or before December 31, 1983, a qualified stock purchase (as defined in sec. 338(d)(3)) was made with respect to a life insurance company that had in effect a valid section 818(c) election before September 27, 1983, (2) an election under section 338 is made with respect to the company, and (3) a new section 818(c) election with respect to the new corporation (described in sec. 338(a)(2)) is made with respect to the corporation's taxable year beginning on the date of acquisition. The committee intends that no inference is to be drawn with respect to the treatment of an election under section 338 to increase the basis of any assets acquired by the amount of reserve liabilities assumed in connection with the acquisition.

* * * * * *

[Conference Report]

* * * * * *

Section 818(c) elections.—The Senate amendment provision relating to section 818(c) elections of companies acquired during 1983 is amended to provide that a section 338 election may be made with respect to such an acquired company during the 60-day period following the date of enactment; the conferees intend no inference as to the effect of the section 818(c) election on the basis of assets acquired for which a section 338 election is made. The time to make an election under section 818(c) is also extended.

* * * Election not to have reserves recomputed (* * * sec. 216(c) of the Act)

* * * * * *

Explanation of Provision.—The provision in the bill makes it clear that in determining whether a company is eligible to make the election for contracts issued on or after 1983 and before January 1, 1989, a company must compute its tentative LICTI taking into account reserves as though the election was in effect. The bill also clarifies that the so-called geometric Menge adjustment should be applied to opening and closing statutory reserves, for purposes of computing net increases or decreases in life insurance reserves.

In addition, the bill provides that the reserve for a company making the election will be the greater of the company's statutory reserve (as adjusted by the geometric Menge adjustment) or the net surrender value of the contract.

[*Effective Date.*—Unless otherwise specified above, this section shall take effect as if included in the provisions to which it relates in the 1984 Tax Reform Act. Ed.]

[¶ 4149] SECTION 1823. AMENDMENTS RELATED TO SECTION 217 OF THE ACT

(Sec. 217 of 1984 TRA)

[Senate Explanation]

*   *   *   *   *   *

* * * Special rule for companies using net level reserve method for noncancellable accident and health insurance contracts * * *.

*   *   *   *   *   *

Explanation of Provision.—The special rule of present law applicable to the use of the net level reserve method for noncancellable accident and health reserves was intended to be narrow in its application by requiring a complete and continuous commitment by the company to the use of the more conservative net level reserve method for its directly written noncancellable accident and health contracts as a reflection of the company's conservative business practices before a company could recognize such practices for tax purposes. Specifically, it was intended to address the factual situation of a company that has been predominantly a writer of noncancellable accident and health insurance and that had followed, and continues to follow, the business practice of computing all its reserves for directly written noncancellable accident and health contracts on a net level basis for State purposes. It was intended to allow such company to use this more conservative reserve basis for tax purposes.

Because the rule under present law is impractically narrow, and would not result in any taxpayer making the election, the bill expands the coverage of the rule to allow the net level reserve method for tax purposes on any directly written noncancellable accident and health insurance contract, whether under existing or new plans of insurance. For purposes of applying this special rule and qualifying therefor, only reserves on directly written contracts will be taken into account

because, as a reinsurer, a company would generally adopt the reserve method used by the ceding company. This limited expansion will allow the special rule to have its intended practical effect.

Although present law requires that all reserves for noncancellable accident and health insurance contracts be computed on a net level basis for statutory purposes as of December 31, 1982, the bill adopts a de minimis margin for error for purposes of administrative convenience. Accordingly, in order to qualify for the application of this rule, a company must have been using the net level reserve method to compute at least 99 percent of its statutory reserves for directly written noncancellable accident and health insurance contracts as of December 31, 1982, and for the 1982 calendar year must have received more than half its premium income from directly written noncancellable accident and health insurance.

After December 31, 1983, the company will be treated as using the prescribed reserve method for a taxable year if through such taxable year, the company has continuously used the net level method for computing at least 99 percent of its tax and statutory reserves on its directly written noncancellable accident and health contracts. This requires a complete and continuous use of the net level method for tax and statutory purposes for all but one percent of directly written noncancellable accident and health contracts; for contracts for which the company does not use the net level method, the company should use the method used for statutory purposes, for purposes of computing tax reserves.

[*Effective Date.*—This section shall take effect as if included in the provisions to which it relates in the 1984 Tax Reform Act and as shown above. Ed.]

[¶ 4150] SECTION 1824. AMENDMENT RELATED TO SECTION 218 OF THE ACT

(Sec. 218 of 1984 TRA)

[Senate Explanation]

*   *   *   *   *   *

* * * Underpayments of estimated tax * * *.

Present Law.—Under present law, no addition to tax shall be made under the provision relating to failure by a corporation to pay estimated tax with respect to any underpayment of an installment required to be paid before the date of enactment of the Act to the extent that such underpayment was created or increased by any provision of the insurance tax subtitle and such underpayment is paid in full on or before the last

date prescribed for payment of the first installment of estimated tax required to be paid after the date of the enactment of the Act.

Explanation of Provision.—The bill repeals section 218 of the Act in favor of the application of the broader general relief granted by the bill under which no addition to tax shall be made for underpayments of estimated tax by corporations for any period before March 16, 1985 (by individuals, for any period before April 16, 1985), to the extent that such underpayment was created or increased by a provision of the 1984 Act.

[*Effective Date.*—Applies to interest on underpayments of installments required to be paid before 7-18-84. Ed.]

[¶ 4151] SECTION 1825. AMENDMENTS RELATED TO SECTION 221 OF THE ACT

(Sec. 7702 of the Code and Sec. 221 of '84 TRA)

* * * * * *

[*Senate Explanation*]

* * * * * *

* * * Definition of life insurance contract; computational rules (* * * sec. 7702(e)(1) of the Code)

* * * * * *

Explanation of Provision.—The bill clarifies the second computational rule by specifically stating that the maturity date shall be deemed to be no earlier than age 95 and no later than age 100. This conforms the language of the second computational rule to that of the first and third.

The bill also adds an additional computational rule which provides that for purposes of applying the second computational rule and for purposes of determining the cash surrender value on the maturity date under the third computational rule, the death benefits shall be deemed to be provided until the maturity date described in the second computational rule. This rule combined with the second computational rule will generally prevent contracts endowing at face value before age 95 from qualifying as life insurance. However, it will allow an endowment benefit at ages before 95 for amounts less than face value.

Finally, the bill amends the computational rules to clarify that these rules do not apply for purposes of determining qualification under the cash value corridor test.

[*Effective Date.*—Generally applies to contracts issued after 12-31-84 in TYEA such date and to flexible premium policy provisions effective 1-1-84. Ed.]

* * * * *

* * * Reduction in future benefits (* * * 7702(f)(7) of the Code)

* * * * * *

Explanation of Provision. * * * Under the bill, a portion of the cash distributed to a policyholder as a result of a change in future benefits will be treated as being paid first out of income in the contract, rather than as a return of the policyholder's investment in the contract, only if the reduction in future benefits occurs during the 15-year period following the issue date of the contract.

Changes during first five years.—For the first five years following the issuance of the contract, the amount that will be treated as having been paid first out of income in the contract will be equal to the amount of the required distribution under subparagraph (A)

of section 7702(f)(7). This amount will depend on whether the contract meets the cash value accumulation test or the guideline premium/cash value corridor test of section 7702(a). In the case of a contract to which the cash value accumulation test applies, the excess of the cash surrender value of the contract over the net single premium determined immediately after the reduction shall be required to be distributed to the policyholder. In the case of a contract to which the guideline premium/cash value corridor test applies, the amount of the required distribution is equal to the greater of (1) the excess of the aggregate premiums paid under the contract over the redetermined guideline premium limitation, or (2) the excess of the cash surrender value of the policy immediately before the reduction over the redetermined cash value corridor. The guideline premium limitation shall be redetermined by using an "attained-age-decrement" method.

Under this method, when benefits under the contract are reduced, the guideline level and single premium limitations are each adjusted and redetermined by subtracting from the original guideline premium limitation a "negative guideline premium limitation" which is determined as of the date of the reduction in benefits and at the attained age of the insured on such date. The negative guideline premium limitation is the guideline premium limitation for an insurance contract that, when combined with the original insurance contract after the reduction in benefits, produces an insurance contract with the same benefit as the original contract before such reduction.

To the extent that the redetermined guideline premium limitation requires a distribution from the contract, the amount of the distribution will also be an adjustment to premiums paid under the contract (within the meaning of sec. 7702(f)(1)(A), to be specified in regulations). It is understood that any adjustments to premiums paid as part of the definitional determinations will be independent of, and may differ in amount from, the determination of investment in the contract for purposes of computing the amount of income in the contract (under sec. 72).

Changes during years six to fifteen.—For cash distributions occurring between the end of the fifth year and the end of the fifteenth year from the issuance date of the policy, a single rule applies for all contracts. Under this rule, the maximum amount that will be treated as paid first out of income in the contract will equal the amount by which the cash surrender value of the contract (determined immediately before the reduction in benefits) exceeds the maximum cash surrender value that would not violate the cash value corridor (determined immediately after the reduction in benefits).

* * * Any distribution up to two years before a reduction in benefits occurs will be treated as having been made in anticipation of such a reduction. The Secretary of the Treasury is authorized to issue regulations specifying other instances when a distribution is in anticipation of a reduction of future benefits. In addition, the regulations may specify the extent to which the rules governing the calculation of the maximum amount that will be treated as paid first out of income in the contract will be adjusted to take account of the prior distributions made in anticipation of reduction of benefits.

* * * Under the bill, premiums paid would be computed in the same manner as under present law, except that the premiums actually paid under the contract will be further reduced by amounts treated as paid first out of income in the contract under the revised adjustment rule. This reduction in premiums paid is limited to the amounts that are included in gross income of the policyholder solely by reason of the fact that a reduction in benefits has been made.

[*Effective Date.*—Generally applies to contracts issued after 12-31-84 in TYEA such date and to flexible premium policy provisions effective 1-1-84. Ed.]

* * * * * *

* * * Treatment of contracts that do not qualify as life insurance contracts (* * * sec. 7702(g) of the Code)

* * * * * *

Explanation of Provision.—Under the bill, income in the contract is computed without reduction by the amount of policyholder dividends paid under the contract during the taxable year. This change was necessary to avoid overstating the income in the contract, which otherwise would occur due to the fact that policyholder dividends are treated as a nontaxable return of basis under section 72(e) and reduce premiums paid directly. If these dividends were also added to this amount of income on the

contract, income would be overstated because policyholder dividends would reduce premiums paid twice.

[*Effective Date.*—Generally applies to contracts issued after 12-31-84 in TYEA such date and to flexible premium policy provisions effective 1-1-84. Ed.]

* * * * * *

* * * Treatment of flexible premium contracts issued during 1984 which meet new requirements (* * * sec. 221(d)(1) of the Act)

* * * * * *

Explanation of Provision.—The bill clarifies the definition of life insurance transition rules so that any contract issued during 1984 which meets the definitional requirements of present-law section 7702 will be treated as meeting the requirements of prior-law section 101(f), which was extended through 1984.

[*Effective Date.*—Generally applies to flexible premium contract provisions effective 1-1-84 entered into before 1-1-85. Ed.]

* * * * * * *

* * * Treatment of certain contracts issued before October 1, 1984 (* * * sec. 221(d)(2)(C) of the Act)

* * * * * *

Explanation of Provision.—The bill clarifies the transition rule so that, in applying the cash value accumulation test by substituting 3 percent for 4 percent as the minimum interest rate, the taxpayer should not only assume that the rate or rates guaranteed on issuance of the contract can be determined without regard to any mortality charges, but should also assume that the rate or rates should be determined without regard to any initial interest rate guaranteed in excess of the stated minimum rate.

[*Effective Date.*—Generally applies to flexible premium contract provisions effective 1-1-84. Ed.]

[¶ 4152] SECTION 1826. AMENDMENTS RELATED TO SECTION 222 OF THE ACT

(Secs 72(e),(q), and (s) of the Code)

[*Senate Explanation*]

* * * * * *

Amendments related to annuity contracts

* * * * * *

Explanation of Provision.—The bill clarifies that the requirement that the annuity contract include required distribution provisions in order to be treated as an annuity need not be met by contracts which are used as part of a qualified pension plan or for an

IRA by adopting a specific statutory exemption for these purposes. This provision is added because annuity contracts provided under a qualified pension plan or an IRA must satisfy the required distribution rules applicable to such plans and should not be required to satisfy an essentially duplicative set of rules applicable to annuity contracts.

In addition, the bill includes special rules to clarify the application of the required distribution rules if the contractholder is not an individual, which provide that the primary annuitant shall be treated as the holder of the contract. For these purposes, the term "primary annuitant" means the individual, the events in the life of whom are of primary importance in affecting the timing or amount of the pay-out under the contract. For example, the primary annuitant would be that person referred to in the contract as the measuring life for the annuity starting date or for annuity benefits payable under the contract.

Likewise, the bill clarifies the application of the penalty exception for distributions at death so that the penalty does not apply to any distribution made on or after the death of the contractholder or, if the contractholder is not an individual, the death of the primary annuitant. Thus, the additional income tax on early withdrawals (sec. 72(q)) is not imposed on an after-death distribution required under section 72(s).

The bill also adds a provision which states that if an individual who holds an annuity contract transfers it by gift or, in the case of a holder which is not an individual, if there is any change in the primary annuitant, then such transfer or change shall be treated as an assignment of the contract (sec. 72(e)(4)), which treats the amount assigned as received as an amount not received as an annuity. In general, the value of the contract assigned will equal the net surrender value of the contract, determined with regard to any policy loan. The investment in the contract of the grantee (or the adjusted investment in the contract of the nonindividual holder) will be treated as equal to the investment in the contract of the grantor plus the amount included in the gross income of the grantor.

Without the clarification treating gratuitous transfers of annuity contracts as assignments, the required distribution rules adopted in the 1984 Act could be avoided easily because they would allow taxpayers to continue tax deferral beyond the life of an individual taxpayer. There is an exception to the rule for transfers of annuity contracts by gift where the transfer is made to a spouse. Specifically, the contract will not be treated as assigned with respect to any transfer to which section 1041(a) (relating to transfers of property between spouses or incident to divorce) applies.

In addition, the bill addresses the issue of how joint contractholders should be treated when one holder dies and clarifies that the after-death distribution requirements apply upon the death of any holder to such contract.

Finally, the bill provides that any annuity used as a qualified funding asset in a structured settlement will not be subject to the 5 percent additional income tax imposed on the portion of any premature distribution from an annuity that is included in gross income.

[*Effective Dates.*—The provisions exempting qualified retirement plans from distribution requirements are effective for contracts issued after January 18, 1985. The other provisions are effective for contracts issued and distributions made over six months after the date of enactment. Ed.]

[¶ 4153]   SECTION 1827. AMENDMENTS RELATED TO SECTION 223 OF THE ACT

(Secs. 79 and 83(e) of the Code)

[Senate Explanation]

*   *   *   *   *   *

Amendments related to group-term insurance

*   *   *   *   *   *

Explanation of Provision. — The bill provides that, in the case of a discriminatory group-term life insurance plan, the cost of group-term life insurance on the life of any key employee shall be the greater of the actual cost of the insurance or the cost determined based on the uniform premium table. The present-law requirement that key employees include in gross income the actual cost of their coverage under discriminatory plans was intended to discourage further use of discriminatory group-term life insurance plans. This requirement would only tend to have this effect if the actual cost exceeds that specified in the uniform premium table. The technical correction adopted in the bill was intended to give full effect to the prior Congressional intent to discourage discrimination (i.e., when the actual cost may be less than that specified in the uniform premium table).

In addition, the bill revises the definition of key employee to include any former employee if such employee, at the time of separation from service, was a key employee. An employee is a key employee at separation from service if the employee was a key employee for the year in which separation occurs or for any of the 4 preceding years. For purposes of applying the nondiscrimination requirements of the group-term life insurance provisions, the bill also clarifies that, to the extent provided in regulations, coverage and benefit tests are applied separately to active and former employees.

The bill also makes a clerical correction to section 83(e)(5), which coordinates that section with section 79. Section 83(e)(5) presently excepts the cost of group-term life insurance to which section 79 applies from the application of section 83 (governing the taxation of property transferred in connection with the performance of services). The bill provides that section 83 shall not apply to group-term life insurance covered by section 79. Thus, when an employee retires, the present value of any future group-term life insurance coverage which may become nonforfeitable upon retirement (or the value of an amount set aside by an employer to fund such coverage) will not be taxed immediately to the employee upon retirement. Rather, if the coverage constitutes group-term life insurance within the meaning of section 79 (e.g., the employee does not receive a permanent guarantee of life insurance coverage from the insurance company), the cost of the coverage will be taxable annually to the retired employee under section 79. This rule also applies in the case of an employee who separates from service with a vested right to continuing group-term life insurance coverage.

Finally, the bill clarifies the effective date of the present-law provisions which were adopted in DEFRA by providing that the extension of the $50,000 cap to retired employees and the extension of the nondiscrimination provisions to former employees do not apply to any group-term life insurance plan of the employer in existence on January 1, 1984, but only with respect to an individual who attained age 55 on or before January 1, 1984, and was employed by such employer (or a predecessor employer) at any time during 1983. The DEFRA amendments also shall not apply to any employee who retired from employment on or before January 1, 1984, and who, when he retired, was covered by a group-term life insurance plan of the employer (or a predecessor plan).

The bill amends the rules with respect to grandfathered individuals to provide that, in applying the nondiscrimination rules under section 79, such individuals may be disregarded at the employer's election.

The provision relating to the determination of costs with respect to key employees in a discriminatory plan is effective for taxable years ending after the date of enactment of the bill.

The bill clarifies what qualifies as a comparable successor plan for purposes of the grandfather provision under DEFRA. A comparable successor plan includes, with respect to a grandfathered individual, any plan that does not provide increased benefits. If the benefits of a grandfathered individual are increased, the grandfather rule no longer applies to that individual.

* * * * * *

[Conference Report]

* * * * * *

Group-term life insurance.—The provision in the Senate amendment relating to a grandfathered group-term life insurance program is modified to provide that grandfather treatment is retained with respect to any employee whose benefits do not increase under the plan.

[*Effective Date.*—The provision is generally effective for taxable years ending after the date of enactment. Ed.]

[¶ 4154] SECTION 1828. AMENDMENT TO POLICY EXCHANGES

(Sec. 1035(b) of the Code)

[Senate Explanation]

Explanation of Provision.—The bill amends the definition of an endowment contract and a life insurance contract by merely requiring that the contracts be issued by any

insurance company, whether or not such company is a taxable entity under the Code. **[Effective Date.**—] This provision applies to exchanges occurring before, on, or after the date of enactment of the technical corrections provision.

[¶ 4155] SECTION 1829. WAIVER OF INTEREST ON CERTAIN UNDER-PAYMENTS OF TAX

[Senate Explanation]

* * * * * *

Present Law.—Interest on an underpayment of tax generally is payable from the due date of the return (determined without regard to extensions).

Explanation of Provision.—The bill provides that no interest shall be payable for any period before July 19, 1984, on any underpayment of tax imposed by the Internal Revenue Code, to the extent such underpayment was created or increased by any provision of subtitle A of title II of the Tax Reform Act of 1984.

[¶ 4156] SECTION 1830. SCOPE OF SECTION 255 OF THE TAX EQUITY AND FISCAL RESPONSIBILITY ACT OF 1982

[Conference Report]

* * * * * *

Modified coinsurance grandfather. — Section 255 of the Tax Equity and Fiscal Responsibility Act of 1982 repealed section 820 of the Code relating to the option treatment of modified coinsurance contracts and adopted a

grandfather provision with respect to the treatment of modified coinsurance contracts for taxable years prior to 1982. Under this grandfather rule, any determination as to whether any contract met the requirements of section 820 (before repeal) (1) was to be made solely by reference to the terms of the contract and (2) the treatment of the contract was made in accordance with the regulations under section 820 as in effect on December 31, 1981. Under TEFRA, such contracts were grandfathered except in the event of fraud.

The Internal Revenue Service has recently issued "guidelines" to auditing agents instructing them to raise certain issues with respect to modified coinsurance contracts. The guidelines apply to taxable years prior to 1982 and direct agents to examine two issues: (1) the date on which modified coinsurance contracts became effective, and (2) the rate at which investment income was transferred under the contracts.

The provision clarifies the intent of Congress that, for taxable years prior to January 1, 1982, the IRS should give full and complete effect to the terms of a modified coinsurance contract. Accordingly, under the provision, the IRS is to respect the manner in which the terms of a modified coinsurance contract have been reflected on the tax return. In particular, the provision requires the IRS to recognize the investment income rate terms and the effective date terms stated in the contract.

[¶ 4158] SECTION 1832. AMENDMENT RELATED TO SECTION 303 OF THE ACT

(Sec. 4940(e)(2) of the Code)

[Senate Explanation]

*　　*　　*　　*　　*　　*

Present Law.—Under section 303 of the Act, the rate of the excise tax imposed on the net investment income of a private foundation (Code sec. 4940) is reduced for a taxable year from two percent to one percent if the amount of qualifying distributions made by the foundation during that taxable year equals or exceeds the sum of (1) an amount equal to the foundation's assets for such taxable year multiplied by the average percentage payout for the base period, plus (2) one percent of the foundation's net investment income for such taxable year. However, the reduction is not available for a year if the foundation's average percentage payout for the base period is less than five percent, or 3-⅓ percent in the case of a private operating foundation (Code sec. 4940(e)(2)(B)). The reduction in the section 4940 tax rate is effective for taxable years beginning after 1984.

*　　*　　*　　*　　*　　*

Explanation of Provision.—The bill modifies the rule disqualifying certain foundations from the section 4940 rate reduction, to provide that the rate reduction is not available if the foundation was liable for tax under section 4942 with respect to any year in the base period.

This modification effectuates the intended rule that a foundation which failed in any base period year to make the minimum required expenditures for charitable purposes should not be eligible to obtain the benefit of tax reduction merely by increasing its qualifying distributions (in an amount at

least equal to one percent of net investment income) up to the minimum section 4942 level. As a result of the modification made by the bill, a nonoperating foundation will not be disqualified from the rate reduction in two situations where the foundation does not incur liability for section 4942 taxes even though the amount of its qualifying distributions (sec. 4942(g)) does not equal at least five percent of its assets. The first situation results from the fact that under section 4942(d), the distributable amount equals the minimum investment return (five percent of assets) reduced by the sum of any taxes imposed on the foundation for the taxable year under section 4940 and the unrelated business income tax. The second situation results from the fact that under section 4942(i), the distributable amount is further reduced by the amount of any excess distributions carryovers from a prior year. However, since neither the amount of such taxes nor the amount of such carryover distributions is included in the definition of qualifying distributions in section 4942(g), a foundation whose distributable amount is reduced by such taxes or carryover excess distributions does not incur section 4942 tax liability if the amount of its qualifying distributions, while less than the minimum investment return, equals or exceeds the distributable amount as thus computed. At the same time, the technical amendment made by the bill precludes any reduction in the section 4940 tax if, with respect to any base period year, the foundation is liable for tax under section 4942 for failure to satisfy the minimum distribution requirements.

[**Effective Date.**—Applies to tax years beginning after 12-31-84. Ed.]

[¶ 4160] SECTION 1834. AMENDMENT RELATED TO SECTION 311 OF THE ACT

(Sec. 311(a)(3)(A) of '84 TRA)

[Senate Explanation]

*　　*　　*　　*　　*　　*

Present Law.—Section 311 of the Act provides that, for purposes of Code section 513, the term unrelated trade or business

does not include any trade or business that consists of conducting a game of chance if (1) the game of chance is conducted by a nonprofit organization, (2) the conducting of the game by such organization does not violate any State or local law, and (3) as of October 5, 1983, there was a State law in effect that permitted the conducting of the game of chance only by a nonprofit organization (i.e., the conducting of the game of chance by other than nonprofit organizations would violate the State law).

Explanation of Provision.—The bill clarifies that the only State law to which the

provision is intended to apply is a North Dakota law originally enacted on April 22, 1977.

Effective Date.—This provision applies to games of chance conducted after June 30, 1981.

[¶ 4161] **SECTIONS 1841-1848. AMENDMENTS RELATED TO TITLE IV OF THE ACT**

(Secs. 30, 39, 46, 47, 48, 55, 71, 86, 108, 146, 151, 267, 280C, 401, 404, 415, 422A, 453B, 665, 1041, 2039, 4973, 6047, 6411, 6501, 6511, 6654, 6699, 6704, 7701 of the Code)

[Senate Explanation]

* * * * * * *

Present Law.—The Act contained a title which added a number of provisions intended to simplify and improve the laws. These included provisions related to the individual estimated tax, domestic relations, at-risk, administrative provisions, distilled spirits, the Tax Court, income tax credits and deadwood.

Explanation of Provisions.—The bill makes numerous nonsubstantive clerical and conforming amendments to these provisions.

The bill restores two provisions of prior law which were inadvertently changed by the Act. First, certain non-resident aliens will continue to be required to make estimated tax payments in three, rather than four, installments. One-half of the estimated tax will be due with the first payment. Second, the principles of prior law relating to the carryover of credits (including the foreign tax credit) by taxpayers subject to the alternative minimum tax are restored. The conforming amendment relating to the foreign tax credit will apply to taxable years beginning after December 31, 1982 (the effective date of the changes to the minimum tax made by TEFRA).

The bill also amends the domestic relation provisions to provide that alimony payments under certain support decrees (described in section 71(b)(2)(C)) will not be disqualified solely because the decree does not specifically state that the payments will terminate at the payee's death. In addition, the bill clarifies that in the case of the transfer of property to a trust for the assumption of (or subject to) liabilities in excess of basis, gain will be recognized to the extent of such excess notwithstanding section 1041(a). Gain will also be recognized on the transfer of installment obligations to a trust.

[Conference Report]

* * * * * * *

Simplification.—Except as provided below with respect to the treatment of alimony, the conference agreement follows the Senate amendment.

Alimony.—The conference agreement revises the front-loading alimony rules of section 71(f). Under the conference agreement, if the alimony payments in the first year exceed the average payments in the second and third year by more than $15,000, the excess amounts are recaptured in the third year by requiring the payor to include the excess in income and allowing the payee who previously included the alimony in income a deduction for that amount in computing adjusted gross income. A similar rule applies to the extent the payments in the second year exceed the payments in the third year by more than $15,000. This rule is intended to prevent persons whose divorce occurs near the end of the year from making a deductible property settlement at the beginning of the next year. Recapture is not required if either party dies or if the payee spouse remarries by the end of the calendar year which is two years after the payments began and payments cease by reason of that event. Also the rule does not apply to temporary support payments (described in sec. 71(b)(2)(C)) or to payments which fluctuate as a result of a continuing liability to pay, for at least three years, a fixed portion or portions of income from the earnings of a business, property or services.

Thus, for example, if the payor makes alimony payments of $50,000 in the first year and no payments in the second or third year, $35,000 will be recaptured (assuming none of the exceptions apply). If instead the payments are $50,000 in the first year, $20,000 in the second year and nothing in the third year, the recapture amount will consist of $5,000 from the second year (the excess over $15,000) plus $27,500 for the first year (the excess of $50,000 over the sum of $15,000 plus $7,500). (The $7,500 is the average payments for years two and three after reducing the payments by the $5,000 recaptured from year two.)

This new provision will generally apply to divorce or support decrees and agreements executed after 1986. The provision will also apply with respect to the modification of a prior instrument where the modified instrument expressly so provides.

In addition, the conference agreement deletes the requirement that the divorce instrument specifically state there is no liability to make payments after death. The conference agreement also reduces the recapture period to three years for those divorce decrees and agreements not covered by the amendment described above.

Effective dates.—Non resident alien rule applies to tax years beginning after 12-31-84. Spousal transfer rule applies generally to transfers after 7-18-84 in tax years ending after that date. Front loading alimony rule applies to for divorce or separation instruments executed after 12-31-86. Recapture rule for investment credit at-risk rules applies generally to property placed in service after 7-18-84 in TYEA that date. Distilled spirit drawback rule applies to products manufactured or produced after 10-31-84. Carryover rule applies to TYBA 12-31-83 and to carrybacks from such years. Minimum tax and foreign tax credit rule applies to TYBA 12-31-83 and to carrybacks from such years. Retirement bonds and extra investment credit rule applies to obligations issued after 12-31-83; and credit amounts after 12-31-83.

[¶ 4171] SECTION 1851. AMENDMENTS RELATED TO WELFARE BENEFIT PLAN PROVISIONS

(Secs. 419, 419A, 505, 512, and 4976 of the Code)

[Senate Explanation]

* * * * * *

1. Funded Welfare Benefit Plans

a. Definition of fund

Present Law.—Under present law, a fund is defined as any tax-exempt social club, voluntary employees' beneficiary association (VE[B]A), supplemental unemployment compensation benefit trust (SUB), or group legal services organization; and trust corporation, or other organization not exempt from income tax; and, to the extent provided by Treasury regulations, any account held for an employer by any person. A fund includes a retired life reserve account maintained by an insurance company on behalf of an employer. Further, if an employer contributes amounts to an insurance company for benefits and under that arrangement the employer is entitled to a rebate if the amount paid exceeds benefit claims or is liable if the benefit claims exceed the amount paid, then such contributions are considered to have been made to a welfare benefit fund.

Finally, under present law, an employer is not permitted a deduction for premiums paid on a life insurance policy covering the life of any officer or employee, or of any person financially interested in any trade or business carried on by the employer, if the employer is directly or indirectly a beneficiary of the policy (sec. 264(a)(1)).

Explanation of Provision.—The bill amends the definition of a "fund" to exclude amounts held under the following types of insurance arrangements: (1) an insurance contract subject to sec. 264(a)(1); and (2) certain "qualified nonguaranteed contracts."

First, under the bill, the term "fund" would not include amounts held by an insurance company pursuant to a life insurance policy on the life of an officer, employee, or person financially interested in the trade or business of the employer, if the employer is the direct or indirect beneficiary of the policy because the amounts contributed are not deductible by the employer.

The bill also modifies the term "fund" to exclude amounts held by an insurance company under certain "qualified, nonguaranteed contracts." [but see conference Report below]. A qualified, nonguaranteed contract is defined under the bill as an insurance contact (including a reasonable premium stabilization reserve) to the extent that (1) there is no guarantee of a renewal of the contract, and (2) the amounts payable to the employer or employees as experience-rated refunds or policy dividends are not guaranteed and are substantially unrelated (directly or indirectly) to the amount of welfare benefits paid to (or on behalf of) the employees of the employer or their beneficiaries, the administrative expenses incurred by (or on behalf of) the insurance company in providing welfare benefits to (or on behalf of) the employees of the employer, and the investment experience of the insurance company on amounts contributed by or held for the employer. Thus, under the bill, amounts that are held by an insurance company for an employer generally are not to be treated as a fund to the extent that the amounts are subject to a significant current risk of economic loss based substantially on factors other than the amount of welfare benefits, administrative expenses, and investment return relating to the employer.

Finally, the committee intends that the definition of a qualified, nonguaranteed insurance contract does not include amounts held by an insurance company pursuant to certain guaranteed renewal contracts, under which the employer's right to renew the contract is guaranteed, but the level of premiums changed to the employer is not guaranteed. The committee believes that, if the insurance company can increase premiums charged to an employer to the point at which the contract is no longer feasible for the employer, the contract should not be treated as a guaranteed renewal contract.

In addition, the bill provides that even an arrangement that satisifies the definition of a qualified, nonguaranteed insurance contract will not be excluded from treatment as a fund, unless the amount of any experience rated refund or policy dividend payable with respect to a policy year is treated by the employer as paid or accrued in the taxable year in which the employer's contributions for the policy year were deductible. If the actual amount of the refund or dividend is not known by the due date of the employer's tax return for the year, Treasury regulations could permit the use of a reasonable estimate of the amount of such refund or dividend. In addition, Treasury regulations could require insurance companies to submit information (including proprietary information of the insurance company) relating to the basis for the calculation of experience refunds and policy dividends.

To the extent that the general rules for the exclusion of amounts held by an insurance company are satisfied, amounts held by an insurance company for a reasonable premium stabilization reserve for an employer are not treated as a fund. Thus, a premium stabilization reserve, if limited to a reasonable amount, such as 20 percent of premiums for the year, would not be treated as a fund to the extent that (1) such amounts are subject to a significant current risk of economic loss, and (2) experience rated refunds and policy dividends payable by the reserve with respect to a policy year are treated by the employer as paid or accrued in the taxable year in which the employer's contributions for such policy year were deductible. Solely for purposes of these provisions, the amounts released from a premium stabilization reserve to purchase current insurance coverage are to be treated as experience rated refunds or policy dividends.

Whether amounts are subject to a significant current risk of loss depends upon the facts and circumstances. For example, if an employer does not have a guaranteed right under an insurance contract to policy dividends based solely on the employer's experience but the insurance company has, in practice, consistently paid such dividends based solely on the employer's experience, it is anticipated that Treasury regulations would provide that the amounts held under the contract constitute a fund because they are not subject to a significant current risk of economic loss.

*   *   *   *   *   *

[Conference Report]

*   *   *   *   *   *

The conference agreement follows the Senate amendment with the following exceptions:

a. Definition of fund.—The conference agreement follows the House bill with the following modifications:

The conference agreement also modifies the exclusion from the term "fund" for amounts held by an insurance company under certain "qualified, nonguaranteed insurance contracts." A qualified, nonguaranteed insurance contract is defined as an insurance contract (including a reasonable premium stabilization reserve) under which (1) there is not a guarantee of a renewal of the contract at guaranteed premium rates, and (2) other than current insurance protection, the only payments to which the employer or employees are entitled under the contract are refunds or policy dividends that are not guaranteed, that are experience rated and that are determined by factors other than the amount of welfare benefits paid to

(or on behalf of) the employees of the employer or their beneficiaries.

Thus, under the conference agreement, amounts that are held by an insurance company for an employer generally are not to be treated as a fund to the extent that the amounts are subject to a significant current risk of economic loss that is determined, in part, by factors other than the amount of welfare benefits paid to (or on behalf of) the employees of the employer. Experience refunds or policy dividends are determined by additional factors where they reflect a charge for pooling of large individual claims, where the insurance company's retention reflects a risk charge related to the insurer's actual or anticipated experience under the class of business to which the contract belongs, or where the claims experience of other policyholders is otherwise taken into account. For example, an additional factor is present where the experience refund or policy dividend is based on the experience of a single employer together with a risk charge that is intended to assess the employer for an appropriate share of the insurance company's anticipated losses under policies where claims and expenses exceed premiums collected. The conferees do not intend, however, that a de minimis risk charge on its own will be sufficient to create a significant risk of economic loss.

The conferees emphasize that, in prescribing regulations relating to the definition of a fund, the Treasury Department is to take into account that the principal purpose of the provision is to prevent employers from taking premature deductions for expenses that have not yet been incurred. To the extent that the temporary and proposed regulations could be interpreted to include in the definition of a fund certain experience-rated insurance arrangements with a significant current risk of economic loss, the conferees do not believe that the regulations implemented this purpose. The conferees believe that significant premature deductions do not occur with respect to experience-rated group insurance because of the element of insurance risk transferred to the insurance company. Thus, by excluding qualified nonguaranteed insurance contracts from the definition of a fund, the conference agreement makes clear that typical group insurance arrangements are not to be made subject to the welfare benefit fund provisions through regulations. In addition, the conferees reiterate that any regulations defining the term "fund" should take into account that the principal purpose of the provision is to prevent premature deductions by employers.

*   *   *   *   *   *

[Senate Explanation]

*   *   *   *   *   *

b. Coordination of post-retirement medical benefits with limits on contributions under qualified plans

Present Law.—Under the provisions of DEFRA relating to the coordination of net contributions for post-retirement medical benefits with the overall limits on contributions and benefits under qualified pension plans and certain other funded plans deferring compensation (secs. 415(c) and (e)), any amount allocated to a separate account for a key employee is treated as an annual addition to a defined contribution plan. Under the overall limits, the annual addition with respect to an employee under all defined contribution plans of an employer for a year is not to exceed the lesser of $30,000 or 25 percent of compensation. A lower limit may apply if the employer also maintains a defined benefit plan for the employee.

Under present law, the 25-percent limit prevents reserve additions for post-retirement medical benefits after the retirement of a key employee. Thus, if an employer made additional contributions to a fund for post-retirement medical benefits on behalf of a retired key employee, then the contribution violates the 25 percent of compensation limit because a retired employee has no compensation.

Explanation of Provision.—The bill provides that the amount treated as an annual addition under the rules for coordinating the post-retirement medical benefits with the overall limits on qualified plans is not subject to the 25-percent-of-compensation limit usually applicable to annual additions. For example, assume the compensation of an employee is $100,000 for a year and $5,000 is treated as an annual addition under the limits for the employee under the rules for post-retirement medical benefits under a qualified plan. Assume further that the employee's annual addition for the year under a qualified defined contribution plan, without regard to the post-retirement medical benefit, is $25,000 (a contribution equal to the maximum percentage of compensation limit). Under the bill, the total annual addition for post-retirement medical benefits does not cause the annual addition to exceed the 25-percent limit on annual additions even though the annual addition would exceed that limit if the amount added for post-retirement medical benefits were taken into account. The annual addition of $30,000 would, however, be subject to the separate dollar limit of section 415(c) for the year and, if the employer also maintains a defined benefit plan for the employee, the full annual addition of $30,000 would be taken into account in determining whether the combined plan limits of section 415(e) are satisfied.

The effect of this rule also is to permit the funding of post-retirement medical benefits on behalf of a key employee during periods when the employee has no compensation from the employer (e.g., after retirement).

c. Separate accounting required for certain amounts

Present Law.—In order to provide an overall limit with respect to pre-retirement deductions for certain post-retirement benefits of key employees, DEFRA required separate accounting for contributions to provide post-retirement medical or post-retirement life insurance benefits to an individual who is, or ever has been (after the effective date of DEFRA), a key employee.

Explanation of Provision.—The bill clarifies the requirement for separate accounting with respect to post-retirement medical benefits and post-retirement life insurance benefits. Under the bill, the requirement does not apply until the first taxable year for which a reserve is computed using the special provisions applicable to these benefits (or assets of a fund held before the effective date are allocated to a separate account). The separate account requirement applies for that first year and for all subsequent taxable years.

d. Reserves for discriminatory post-retirement benefits disregarded

Present Law.—Under DEFRA, no reserve is to be taken into account in computing the account limit with respect to a post-retirement medical benefit or a post-retirement life insurance benefit under a plan that does not meet the nondiscrimination standard provided by DEFRA (sec. 505). The application of this rule is unclear both with respect to benefits (such as benefits under a self-insured health plan) that are subject to nondiscrimination requirements different from the DEFRA standard and with respect to benefits (such as benefits under an insured plan) not subject to any nondiscrimination requirement. The nondiscrimination standards of the Act do not apply to benefits under certain collectively bargained plans.

Explanation of Provision.—The bill provides that no reserve generally may be taken into account in determining the account limit for a welfare benefit fund for post-retirement medical benefits or life insurance benefits (including death benefits) unless the plan meets the nondiscrimination requirements with respect to those benefits (sec. 505(b)), whether or not those nondiscrimination requirements apply in determining the tax-exempt status of the fund. The bar against taking post-retirement medical benefits and life insurance benefits into account in determining the account limit does not apply, under the bill, in the case of benefits provided pursuant to a collective bargaining agreement between one or more employee representatives and one or more employers if the Secretary of the Treasury finds that the agreement is a collective bargaining agreement and that post-retirement medical benefits or post-retirement life insurance benefits (as the case may be) were the subject of good faith bargaining between the employee representatives and the employer or employers.

The bill clarifies that certain post-retirement group-term life insurance benefits that fail to satisfy the nondiscrimination requirements of Code section 505(b) may, nevertheless, be taken into account in determining the account limit to the extent that the group-term life insurance benefits are provided under an arrangement with respect to individuals grandfathered under section 223 of the Act.

e. Account limit for life insurance benefits

Present Law.—In the case of a life insurance or death benefit, DEFRA provided that the account limit is not to include a reserve to the extent the reserve takes account of an amount of insurance that exceeds the amount that may be provided to an employee tax-free under an employer's group-term life insurance program (sec. 79). In the case of a self-insured death benefit, the account limit is not to include a reserve to the extent that a benefit would be includible in gross income if the limit on excludable death benefits were $50,000.

Explanation of Provision.—The bill clarifies that life insurance benefits are not to be taken into account in determining the account limit under a welfare benefit fund to the extent that the aggregate amount of such benefits to be provided with respect to an employee exceeds $50,000. Accordingly, under the bill, the $50,000 limit applies with respect to the aggregate of self-insured and insured life insurance benefits under all funds maintained by the employer. The bill does not change the rules of DEFRA under which certain post-retirement life insurance benefits in excess of $50,000 may be taken into account in determining the account limit for certain individuals under plans in existence on January 1, 1984 (Act sec. 223(d)(2)).

f. Actuarial certification

Present Law.—DEFRA provided that the account limit for a qualified asset account (reserve) for a taxable year is generally the amount reasonably and actuarially necessary to fund claims incurred but unpaid (as of the close of the taxable year) for benefits with respect to which the account is maintained and the administrative costs incurred with respect to those claims. Claims incurred but unpaid include claims incurred but unreported as well as claims reported but unpaid. The time at which claims are incurred is the time at which the employee becomes entitled to the benefits, i.e., the time at which the fund becomes liable for the claims. Under DEFRA, insurance premiums, whenever payable, are not regarded as claims incurred but unpaid.

Unless there is an actuarial certification with respect to benefits other than (1) post-retirement medical benefits or post-retirement life insurance benefits or (2) supplemental unemployment compensation (SUB) or severance pay benefits, the account limit for a welfare benefit fund is not to exceed certain safe-harbor limits.

In the case of short-term disability benefits, the safe-harbor limit is 17.5 percent of the qualified direct costs for the immediately preceding year with respect to such benefits. A short-term disability is a disability that has persisted for at least 2 weeks and is not a long-term disability. A long-term disability is a disability that (1) has persisted for at least 5 months, and (2) a medical evaluation determines that such disability is expected to last for at least 12 months.

The legislative history of DEFRA provides that no more than 5 months of benefit payments are to be deemed to have been incurred with respect to short-term disabilities.

Explanation of Provision.—The bill provides that the requirement for an actuarial certification also applies to post-retirement medical benefits and post-retirement life insurance benefits, unless a safe harbor computation is used.

The committee clarifies the application of the account limit rules to short-term disability. Because a disability that is expected to last more than 5 months, but less than 12 months, is not treated as a long-term disability, the committee intends that the legislative history of DEFRA will not prohibit the funding of up to 12 months of benefit payments for short-term disabilities that are expected to last more than 5 months.

g. Aggregation of funds

Present Law.—In addition to the limits provided by DEFRA with respect to post-retirement medical benefits provided under a welfare benefit fund, DEFRA dollar limits were provided with respect to the amount of life insurance benefits, disability benefits, and supplemental unemployment compensation benefits or severance pay benefits for which a reserve may be accumulated for any participant. DEFRA did not specify that these limits apply to the aggregate of reserves under all funds of an employer rather than on a fund-by-fund basis. Also, in the case of life insurance benefits, DEFRA did not specify that the limit on reserves is to be applied to the aggregate of insured and self-insured benefits.

Explanation of Provision.—The bill provides that, in computing the dollar limits applicable to the amount of reserves for disability benefits, post-retirement medical benefits, and post-retirement life insurance benefits for which reserves may be accumulated for any participant, all welfare funds of an employer are treated as a single fund. In the absence of Treasury regulations to the contrary, the limit is allocated proportionately to the amount of the death benefit in each plan.

h. Transition rules

Present Law.—The account limit for any of the first four taxable years to which the rules for welfare benefit funds apply is increased by the applicable percentage of any existing excess reserve. In particular, DEFRA provided that, for the first year, the limit is to be the sum of (1) the limit determined without regard to the transitional rule, and (2) 80 percent of the existing excess reserve amount. For the second, third, and fourth succeeding years, 60, 40, and 20 percent, respectively, is substituted for 80 percent. DEFRA did not clearly provide that the existing excess reserve for any year is to be the excess of (1) the amount of assets set aside to provide disability, medical, SUB, severance pay, or life insurance benefits under a plan and fund to provide a benefit in existence on July 18, 1984, as of the close of the first taxable year ending after that date, over (2) the account limit determined, for the year the computation is being made, without regard to the transitional rule.

Explanation of Provision.—The bill provides that, under the transition rules for existing excess reserves, the amount of existing excess reserves for any year is the excess (if any) of (1) the amount of assets set aside at the close of the first taxable year ending after July 18, 1984, to provide disability benefits, medical benefits, SUB or severance pay benefits, or life insurance benefits, over (2) the account limit (without regard to the transition rules) for the taxable year for which the excess is being computed. The bill further provides that the transition rule allowing an increase in the account limit because of existing excess reserves applies only to a welfare benefit fund which, on July 18, 1984, had assets set aside to provide the enumerated benefits.

Accordingly, in the case of an employer that maintains a funded plan which had assets set aside to provide disability benefits, medical benefits, SUB or severance pay benefits, or life insurance benefits on July 18, 1984, and to which the deduction limits first apply for the taxable year beginning January 1, 1986, the increase in the account limit for 1986 attributable to existing excess reserves is 80 percent of the excess, if any, of the amount of assets set aside at the close of 1984 (the first taxable year ending after July 18, 1984) over the account limit determined under the general rules for 1986. For 1987, however, the increase attributable to existing excess reserves is 60 percent of the excess, if any, of the amount of assets set aside at the close of 1984 over the account limit determined for 1987.

i. Tax on unrelated business income

Present Law.—Under present law, the tax on unrelated business taxable income of a social club, VEBA, SUB, or group legal service organization applies to an amount equal to the lesser of the income of the fund or the amount by which the assets in the fund exceed a specific limit on amounts set aside for exempt purposes. The limit on the amount that may be set aside for a year is generally not to increase the total amount that is set aside to an amount in excess of the account limit for the taxable year determined under the deduction limits.

The limitation on the amount that may be set aside for purposes of the unrelated business income tax does not apply to income attributable to certain existing reserves for post-retirement medical or post-retirement life insurance benefits. Under DEFRA, this exclusion applies only to income attributable to the amount of assets set aside, as of the close of the last plan year ending before July 18, 1984, for purposes of providing such benefits.

In addition, DEFRA provided for the inclusion of a similar amount (deemed unrelated income) in the gross income of an employer

who maintains a welfare benefit fund that is not exempt from income tax. It is anticipated that Treasury regulations will provide that deemed unrelated income will be treated in a manner that will not subject the same income to tax more than once.

Explanation of Provision.—The bill makes it clear that the tax on unrelated business income applies in the case of a 10-or-more employer plan. Under the bill, the account limit is to be determined as if the rules limiting deductions for employer contributions applied.

In addition, the bill provides that the transition rule for pre-existing reserves for post-retirement medical and life insurance benefits applies to the greater of the amount of assets set aside as of (1) July 18, 1984, or (2) the close of the last plan year ending before July 18, 1984, rather than only to assets set aside as of the end of the plan year ending before July 18, 1984.

The bill deletes the provision of the Code barring a set aside for certain assets used in the provision of permissible benefits (facilities). Treasury regulations are to provide that facilities used to provide permissible benefits are disregarded in determining whether fund assets exceed the account limit for a qualified asset account.

In addition, the bill provides that if any amount is included in the gross income of an employer for a taxable year as deemed unrelated income with respect to a welfare benefit fund, then the amount of the income tax imposed on the deemed unrelated income is to be treated as a contribution paid by the employer to the fund on the last day of the taxable year and, thus, is deductible, subject to the limits on deductions for fund contributions. The tax attributable to the deemed unrelated income is to be treated as if it were imposed on the fund for purposes of determining the after-tax income of the fund.

j. Tax on disqualified benefits provided under funded welfare benefit plans

Present Law.—Under DEFRA, if a welfare benefit fund (other than an arrangement funded exclusively by employee contributions) provides a disqualified benefit during a taxable year, then an excise tax is imposed for that year on each employer who maintains the fund. The tax is equal to 100 percent of the disqualified benefit.

Under DEFRA, a disqualified benefit is (1) any medical benefit or life insurance benefit provided with respect to a key employee other than from a separate account required under the rules limiting employer deductions with respect to welfare benefit funds, (2) any post-retirement medical or life insurance benefit unless the plan meets the requirements of the nondiscrimination rules of DEFRA for benefits under a welfare benefit fund, or (3) any portion of a welfare benefit fund reverting to the benefit of the employer. A portion of a welfare benefit fund is not considered to revert to the benefit of an employer merely because it is applied, in accordance with the plan, to provide welfare benefits to employees or their beneficiaries.

Also, amounts returned to employees that represent the employees' contributions to the fund are not treated as amounts reverting to the benefit of the employer and, therefore, are not subject to the tax on disqualified benefits.

Explanation of Provision.—With respect to benefits required to be paid from a separate account, the bill defines the term "disqualified benefit" to mean any post-retirement medical benefit or post-retirement life insurance benefit provided with respect to a key employee if a separate account is required to be established for the employee and the payment is not from such an account. Accordingly, pre-retirement benefits would not be considered to be disqualified benefits under the bill merely because they are paid to a key employee from a source other than a separate account.

In addition, under the bill, a post-retirement medical benefit or post-retirement life insurance benefit provided by a fund with respect to an individual in whose favor discrimination is prohibited is a disqualified benefit unless the plan meets the nondiscrimination requirements of DEFRA with respect to the benefit (sec. 505(b)), whether or not the nondiscrimination requirements apply in determining the tax-exempt status of the fund from which the benefit is provided.

Under the bill, if a plan is not exempt from the nondiscrimination rules under the rules for collectively bargained plans, a discriminatory benefit is a disqualified benefit subject to the excise tax even though no discrimination test applies for purposes of determining the exempt status of the fund from which the benefit is provided. A benefit is not subject to the nondiscrimination requirements if it is provided under a plan maintained pursuant to a collective bargaining agreement between one or more employee representatives and one or more employers if the Secretary of the Treasury finds that the agreement is a collective bargaining agreement and that post-retirement medical benefits or post-retirement life insurance benefits (as the case may be) were the subject of good faith bargaining between the employee representatives and the employer or employers.

Further, under the bill, a payment that reverts to the benefit of an employer is not a disqualified benefit to the extent it is attributable to an employer contribution with respect to which no deduction is allowable in the current or any preceding taxable year or to an employee contribution. As under current law, the excise tax on disqualified benefits is inapplicable to welfare benefit contributions funded solely by employees. A reduction is to be made to the amount treated as a carryover (sec. 419(d)) to the extent that any nondeducted contribution reverts to the benefit of an employer. Any amounts reverting to the benefit of an employer are treated as coming first out of nondeducted contributions for purposes of this rule.

Also, the bill provides that a benefit that would otherwise be a disqualified benefit because it does not meet the separate-account rule or because it is discriminatory is not a disqualified benefit if it is a post-retirement benefit that is charged against an existing reserve (or against any income properly allocable to an existing excess reserve) for post-retirement medical or post-retirement life insurance benefits as provided under the transition rules of DEFRA (sec. 512(a)(3)) applicable to the unrelated business income tax.

k. Application of account limits to collectively bargained plans

Present Law.—DEFRA provided that, by July 1, 1985, the Secretary of the Treasury was to publish regulations establishing special reserve limit principles with respect to funded welfare benefit plans maintained pursuant to a collective bargaining agreement. In establishing these limits, the Treasury is to presume that reserves in such plans are not excessive because of the arm's-length negotiations between adversary parties inherent in the collective bargaining process. Further, because contributions under collectively bargained plans are often fixed over a multiyear period on the basis of economic assumptions that may be inaccurate and because such contributions may be the only source of benefits to be provided during layoffs, strikes, lockouts, and economic recession, these special limits are to allow substantial flexibility with respect to the account limits.

On July 1, 1985, Treasury regulations were not published relating to the special account limits for collectively bargained plans. These regulations provide that the account limits under the normal rules for welfare benefit funds do not apply to collectively bargained funds until a specified period of time after the issuance of regulations specifying the higher limits applicable to such collectively bargained funds. Thus, pending the issuance of such regulations, employer contributions to a collectively bargained fund are deductible (without limit) and earnings on fund assets are tax exempt.

Explanation of Provision.—The bill permanently exempts collectively bargained VEBAs from the account limits applicable to welfare benefit funds without regard to any Treasury regulations providing special account limits for such funds. Thus, employer contributions to such VEBAs are deductible and earnings on assets of such VEBAs are tax exempt.

l. Application of account limits to welfare benefit plans funded solely with employee contributions

Present Law.—Under present law, the account limits for welfare benefit funds apply whether a plan is funded with employer or employee contributions. In the case of a plan funded solely by employee contributions, the primary effect of the account limits is to treat earnings on plan assets in excess of the account limits as unrelated business taxable income.

Act § 1851   ¶ 4171

* * * * * *

* * * * * *

Explanation of Provision.—*Employee pay-all VEBAs.*—The Senate amendment exempts certain employee pay-all VEBAs with at least 50 employees from the welfare benefit fund provisions if the amount of any refund or rebate to an employee is determined by factors other than the employee's experience. Under the conference agreement, an employee pay-all VEBA is not considered to fail to qualify for this exemption merely because an employee's refund or rebate may vary depending upon the number of years the employee contributed to the fund. For example, if a VEBA provides a set employee contribution rate that applies for 3 years, the mere fact that an employee who contributes for 3 years may receive a larger refund or rebate than an employee who contributes for less than 3 years does not cause the fund to fail to meet the requirements for exemption as long as there is a significant current risk of economic loss (i.e., the amount of the refund or rebate is also determined by factors other than any employee's experience).

* * * * * *

* * * * * *

m. Effective dates

Present Law.—DEFRA provided that the new limits on deductions under welfare benefit funds generally apply to contributions paid or accrued after December 31, 1985, in taxable years ending after that date. Special effective dates were provided for contributions with respect to facilities and for certain collectively bargained plans. The effective dates for the provisions relating to the tax on unrelated business income and the excise tax on disqualified benefits were unclear under DEFRA.

A transition rule for existing excess reserves is provided with respect to the account limit for any of the first four years to which the rules for welfare benefit funds apply. The existing excess reserve for any year is the excess of (1) the amount of assets set aside to provide disability, medical, SUB, severance pay, or life insurance benefits under a plan and fund to provide such a benefit in existence on July 18, 1984, as of the close of the first taxable year ending after that date, over (2) the account limit determined, for the year for which the computation is being made, without regard to the transitional rule.

Explanation of Provision.—The bill provides that the rules of DEFRA relating to the tax on disqualified benefits generally apply to benefits provided after December 31, 1985. Under the bill, however, the tax on disqualified benefits does not apply to benefits charged against an existing reserve for post-retirement medical benefits or post-retirement life insurance benefits (as defined under the transition rules (sec. 512(a)(3))) applicable to the unrelated business income tax.

The bill clarifies that the amendments made by the Act with respect to the tax on unrelated business income are effective for taxable years ending after December 31, 1985, and are to be treated as a change in the rate of income tax imposed for purposes of Code section 15.

Further, the committee intends that the transition rule for existing excess reserves first applies to the first taxable year for which DEFRA is effective. Thus, the phase-out of existing excess reserves does not apply to any taxable year of the fund before the first taxable year to which the DEFRA applies.

2. Treatment of Deferred Compensation Arrangements and Deferred Benefits (* * * sec. 512 of the Act)

a. Transition rule for certain taxpayers with fully vested vacation pay plans

Present Law.—Under present law, any plan, method, or arrangement providing for deferred benefits for employees, their spouses, or their dependents is treated as a plan deferring the receipt of compensation (deferred benefit plan. DEFRA provided that a deferred benefit plan includes an extended vacation pay plan, i.e., a plan under which employees gradually, over a period of years, earn the right to additional vacation that cannot be taken until the end of the period. Similarly, a vacation pay plan under which employees can delay the vacation (and also the income inclusion) beyond the current taxable year is a deferred benefit plan. However, any vacation benefit year is a deferred benefit plan. However, any vacation benefit to which an election applies under section 463 (relating to accrual of vacation pay) is not considered a deferred benefit.

The provision of DEFRA was effective for amounts paid or incurred after July 18, 1984, in taxable years ending after that date.

Explanation of Provision.—The bill provides a transition rule in the case of a fully vested vacation pay plan in which payments are required within one year after the accrual of the vacation (and are, in fact, paid). [See also Conference Report that follows.] If the taxpayer makes an election under section 463 for the taxpayer's first taxable year ending after July 18, 1984, then, in lieu of establishing a suspense account under section 463, the election is treated as a change in the taxpayer's method of accounting and the adjustments required under section 481 are taken into account.

Under the bill, the time for making a section 463 election is extended to six months after the date of enactment in the case of a taxpayer otherwise eligible for the transition rule.

* * * * * *

* * * * * *

Accrued vacation pay.—The transition rule for accrued vacation pay applies in the case of a fully vested vacation pay plan under which the vacation pay is expected to be paid (or is in fact paid) within 12 months following the close of the employer's taxable year.

b. Clarification of the scope of the deduction-timing rules applicable to deferred compensation arrangements

Present Law.—Under present law, an arrangement for compensation or benefits having the effect of a plan or method deferring the receipt of compensation is subject to the deduction-timing rules applicable to deferred compensation plans (sec. 404(a)(5)). In order to be subject to the deduction rules of section 404(a), a plan or method deferring compensation must satisfy the conditions for deductibility under section 162 (relating to trade or business expenses) or section 212 (relating to expenses for production of income).

Explanation of Provision.—The bill clarifies that the deduction-timing rules for deferred compensation arrangements apply to any plan or method of deferring compensation regardless of the section under which the amounts might otherwise be deductible and that the amounts shall be deductible under section 404(a)(5) and shall not otherwise be deductible under any other section. This clarification is necessary to prevent taxpayers from asserting that deferred compensation is attributable to capitalizable compensation expenses and, thereby, accelerate the timing of the deduction for such deferred compensation. Further, this clarification conforms the treatment of deferred compensation with the treatment of losses, expenses, and interest with respect to transactions between related taxpayers (as amended by DEFRA).

* * * * * *

[Conference Report]

* * * * * *

Unfunded deferred compensation.—The provision in the Senate amendment clarifying that the deductibility of deferred compensation is governed by section 404 if the amounts would, but for section 404, otherwise be deductible under any other provision is modified to apply also for purposes of determining the deductibility of foreign deferred compensation (sec. 404A) and for purposes of the welfare benefit fund provisions.

[*Effective Date.*—Unless otherwise specified above, this section shall take effect as if included in the provisions to which it relates in the 1984 Tax Reform Act. Thus generally, provisions apply to contributions paid or incurred, benefits provided, and UBI after 12-31-85 in tax years ending after that date. Ed.]

[¶ 4172] SECTION 1852. AMENDMENTS RELATED TO PENSION PLAN PROVISIONS

(Secs. 72, 401, 402, 403, 408, 414, 415, 416, 2039, and 2517 of the Code)

[Senate Explanation]

* * * * * *

3. Qualified Pension, Profit-Sharing, and Stock Bonus Plans

a. Distribution rules for qualified plans

Present Law.—*Distributions prior to age 59½.*—Prior to DEFRA, the Code imposed an additional 10-percent income tax on distributions made to key employees in a top-heavy plan prior to age 59½, death, or disability unless the participant died or became disabled. DEFRA provided that the additional tax applies to 5-percent owners (rather than key employees), but only to the extent that the distribution is attributable to contributions made or benefits accruing in years in which the participant was a 5-percent owner (as defined in sec. 416(i)).

Before-death distribution rules. — DEFRA amended the minimum distribution rules to provide that a trust is not a qualified trust unless the plan of which it is a part provides that the entire interest of the employee will be distributed no later than the required beginning date. Alternatively, the requirements of DEFRA may be satisfied if the entire interest is to be distributed (in accordance with Treasury regulations), beginning no later than the required beginning date, over (1) the life of the employee, (2) the lives of the employee and a designated beneficiary, (3) a period (which may be a term certain) not extending beyond the life expectancy of the employee, or (4) a period (which may be a term certain) not extending beyond the life expectancies of the employee and a designated beneficiary.

Under present law, the required beginning date is generally April 1 of the calendar year following the calendar year in which (1) the employee attains age 70½ or (2) the employee retires, whichever is later. If an employee is a 5-percent owner (as defined at sec. 416(i)) with respect to the plan year ending in the calendar year in which the employee attains age 70½, then the required beginning date is generally April 1 of the calendar year following the calendar year in which the employee attains age 70½, even though the employee has not retired. DEFRA did not, however, require the distribution to a 5-percent owner of employer securities subject to the 84-month holding period of section 409(d) before the expiration of the 84-month period.

Benefits provided under a qualified plan must be for the primary benefit of an employee, rather than the employee's beneficiaries. Accordingly, any death benefits provided for a participant's beneficiaries must be incidental. Under this incidental death benefit rule, a qualified plan generally is required to provide for a form of distribution under which the present value of the retirement benefit payments projected to be made to the

Act § 1852   ¶ 4172

participant, while living, is more than 50 percent of the present value of the total payments projected to be made to the participant and the participant's beneficiaries. The incidental death benefit rule is designed to limit the use of qualified plans for nonretirement purposes (e.g., to provide for deferral of income tax or to provide for tax-favored transfers of wealth).

The before-death distribution rules under present law for IRAs are similar to the before-death distribution rules provided for qualified plans and are applied separately to each IRA owned by an individual.

After-death distribution rules. — DEFRA provided rules that apply in the case of an employee's death before the employee's entire interest has been distributed. Under DEFRA, if distributions have commenced to the employee before death, then the remaining portion of the employee's interest is to be distributed at least as rapidly as under the method of distribution in effect prior to death. If distributions have not commenced before the participant's death, DEFRA provided permissible periods over which the remaining interest may be paid to a designated beneficiary. A plan may allow a beneficiary to accelerate payments of the remaining interest.

Similar rules are provided for after-death distributions from or under an individual retirement account or annuity. In addition, the rules applicable to after-death distributions under an annuity contract tract apply to a custodial account that is treated as a tax-sheltered annuity contract (sec. 408(b)(7)). Other tax-sheltered annuity contracts are subject to the after-death distribution rules applicable to annuity contracts (sec. 72(s)).

Qualifying rollover distributions.— Under DEFRA, distributions of less than the balance to the credit of an employee under a qualified plan or a tax-sheltered annuity contract may be rolled over, tax-free, by the employee (or the surviving spouse of the employee) to an IRA. A rollover of a partial distribution is permitted only if (1) the distribution equals at least 50 percent of the balance to the credit of the employee, determined immediately before the distribution, (2) the distribution is not one of a series of periodic payments, and (3) the employee elects tax-free rollover treatment at the time and in the manner prescribed by the Secretary of the Treasury.

Explanation of Provisions. — *Distributions prior to age 59½.*—Under the bill, the 10 percent additional income tax on distributions prior to age 59½, death, or disability (within the meaning of sec. 72(m)(7)) is applied to amounts received from or under a qualified plan by a 5-percent owner. However, the bill provides that the tax does not apply to benefits accrued before January 1, 1985. In applying the rule, the bill provides that distributions will be deemed to be made first out of benefits accrued before January 1, 1985.

The bill removes the requirement of present law that each plan distribution must be examined to determine whether it is attributable to contributions made on behalf of a participant while the participant was a 5-percent owner. Instead, the bill provides that the status of an individual at the time of a plan distribution is the relevant factor for imposition of the tax.

The bill defines a 5-percent owner as any individual who at any time during the 5 plan years preceding the plan year in which the distribution is made was a 5-percent owner (within the meaning of sec. 416(i)(1)(B)).

Before-death and after-death distribution rules.—The bill clarifies the required beginning date for distributions from or under qualified plans and IRAs. As noted above, under current law, in the case of a 5-percent owner, distributions from a qualified plan must commence no later than April 1 of the calendar year following the year in which the 5-percent owner attains age 70½. The bill clarifies that an individual is considered to be a 5-percent owner for a calendar year if the individual was a 5-percent owner (within the meaning of section 416(i)(1)(B)) at any time during the plan year ending in the calendar year in which the individual attains age 70½, or during any of the four preceding plan years. The bill also clarifies that if an employee becomes a 5-percent owner in a plan year subsequent to the plan year ending in the calendar year in which the employee attained age 70½, the required beginning date is April 1 of the calendar year following the calendar year in which ends the plan year that the employee becomes a 5-percent owner.

The bill clarifies that distributions from IRAs are to commence no later than April 1 of the calendar year following the year in which the owner of the IRA attains age 70½, without regard to whether the owner has retired. In addition, the bill clarifies that distributions from IRAs are subject to the incidental death benefit rules applicable to qualified plans.

The bill repeals the exception to the required distribution rules applicable to amounts held by an ESOP, which are subject to the 84-month rule of Code Section 409(a). Instead, the bill provides an exception to the 84-month rule for amounts required to be distributed under the required distribution rules for qualified plans.

Further, the bill provides that amounts required to be distributed from a qualified plan or IRA under the required distribution rules are not eligible for rollover treatment. This rule ensures that an individual will not be able to circumvent the required distribution rules by taking a required distribution at year's end and rolling over that distribution before or after the beginning of the next year. This restriction would apply only to the amounts required to be distributed. Thus, individuals would not be prevented from rolling over those distributions that (1) exceed the minimum required distribution, or (2) occur during a year in which no minimum distribution is required. For this purpose, the first amounts distributed to an individual during a taxable year are treated as amounts required to be distributed.

* * * * * *

[Conference Report]

* * * * * *

Tax-sheltered annuities.—The provision in the House bill requiring that distributions commence under a tax-sheltered annuity no later than when the employee attains age 70½ is adopted.

[*Effective date.*—Generally years beginning after 12-31-84. Annuity rule applies to benefits accrued after 12-31-86. Ed.]

* * * * * *

[Senate Explanation]

* * * * * *

Qualifying rollover distributions.—The bill clarifies that the distribution of the entire balance to the credit of an employee in a qualified plan may be treated as a distribution eligible for rollover under the partial distribution rollover rules, so long as such distribution does not constitute a "qualified total distribution." Thus, a total distribution that is not made on account of plan termination, is not eligible for lump sum treatment and does not consist of accumulated deductible employee contributions, would be eligible for rollover under the partial distribution rollover rules.

The bill clarifies that accumulated deductible employee contributions (within the meaning of sec. 72(o)(5)) are not taken into account for purposes of calculating the balance to the credit of an employee under the partial distribution rollover rules. In addition, the bill clarifies that a self-employed individual is generally treated as an employee for purposes of the rules governing the tax treatment of distributions, including the rules relating to rollover distributions.

The bill provides that the rules relating to rollovers in the case of a surviving spouse of an employee who received distributions after the employee's death apply to permit rollovers to an IRA but not to another qualified plan. Also, the bill clarifies that partial distributions are to be rolled over within 60 days of the distribution to be eligible for rollover under the partial distribution rollover rules.

b. Treatment of distributions if substantially all contributions are employee contributions (sec. 1852(c) of the bill and sec. 72 of the Code)

Present Law.—Under DEFRA, if substantially all of the contributions under a qualified plan are employee contributions, then distributions under the plan will be considered to be income until all income has been distributed. In addition, if an employee received (directly or indirectly) any amount as a loan under the plan, DEFRA treats the amount of the loan as an amount distributed from the plan.

Under present law, a plan in which substantially all of the contributions are employee contributions is defined as a plan with respect to which 85 percent of the total contributions during a representative period (such as 5 years) as determined under Treasury regulations are employee contributions (whether or not mandatory).

Explanation of Provision.—Under the bill, a plan is defined as one in which substantially all of the contributions are employee contributions if 85 percent or more of the total contributions during a representative period are employee contributions. Also, the bill provides that the 5 percent additional income tax on premature distributions from annuity contracts does not apply to distributions from a plan substantially all of the contributions of which are derived from employee contributions.

The bill clarifies that deductible employee contributions are not taken into account as employee contributions for purposes of testing whether 85 percent or more of the total contributions to a plan during a representative period are employee contributions.

[*Effective date.*—Amounts received or loan made after 90 days after 7-18-84. Ed.]

c. Provisions relating to top-heavy plans (sec. 1852(d) of the bill and sec. 416 of the Code)

Present Law.—Additional qualification standards are provided with respect to a qualified plan that is top-heavy. These rules are designed to provide safeguards for rank-and-file employees and to curb abuse of the special tax incentives available under qualified plans. These rules (1) limit the amount of a participant's compensation that may be taken into account; (2) require accelerated vesting; (3) provide minimum nonintegrated benefits or contributions for plan participants who are not key employees; and (4) reduce the overall limit on contributions and benefits for certain key employees.

A qualified plan is top heavy if, as of the determination date, more than 60 percent of the value of cumulative accrued benefits under the plan is allocable to key employees. Under DEFRA, the cumulative accrued benefits of any individual who has not received any compensation from any employer maintaining a plan during a period of 5 plan years ending on the determination date may be disregarded for purposes of determining whether the plan is top heavy.

DEFRA provided that the additional standards for top-heavy plans do not apply to a governmental plan (as defined in sec. 414(d)), but did not clarify whether State or local government employees may be considered key employees for purposes of other nondiscrimination provisions (e.g., sec. 79).

Explanation of Provision.—The bill amends the definition of a key employee to exclude any individual who is an officer or employee of an entity described in section 414(d) (relating to governmental plans). The effect of this provision is to clarify that certain separate accounting and nondiscrimination provisions of the Code (e.g., secs. 79, 415(1), and 419A) do not apply to employees of a State or local government or certain other governmental entities. The bill does not repeal the provision that exempts governmental plans from the top-heavy plan requirements.

[*Effective date.*—Plan years beginning after 12-31-83. Ed.]

The bill also provides that the rule disregarding benefits of an employee after 5 plan years applies to employees who have not performed services for the employer maintaining the plan at any time during the 5-year period ending on the determination date. This provision is added to relieve the administrative difficulties associated with determining whether or not amounts an individual might receive after separation from service are in the nature of compensation.

[*Effective date.*—Plan years beginning after 12-31-84. Ed.]

d. Provisions relating to estate and gift taxes with respect to qualified plan benefits (sec. 1852(e) of the bill and secs. 2039 and 2517 of the Code)

Present Law.—Under present law, if the spouse of an employee on whose behalf contributions or payments are made to a qualified plan or a tax-sheltered annuity predeceases the spouse, the decedent spouse's estate does not include any community property interest in the employee spouse's interest in the employer-derived benefits under the qualified plan. A similar rule applies for purposes of the effect of certain transfers under the gift tax provisions.

DEFRA repealed a separate $100,000 limit on the estate tax exclusion (prior to TEFRA, the exclusion had been unlimited) for retirement benefits under qualified plans, tax-sheltered annuities, IRAs, and certain military retirement plans. Under DEFRA, a grandfather rule applied to both the repeal of the exclusion and the reduction of the exclusion to $100,000 in TEFRA. This grandfather rule applied to any decedent (1) whose benefit was in pay status before December 31, 1984 (December 31, 1982, in the case of the TEFRA grandfather) and (2) who, prior to July 18, 1984, had made an irrevocable election to designate the form of the retirement benefit distribution (including the form of any survivor benefit).

In addition, present law provides that the exercise or nonexercise by an employee of an election or option under which an annuity will become payable to a beneficiary under a qualified plan, a tax-sheltered annuity, an IRA, or certain military pensions is not considered a transfer for purposes of application of the gift tax provisions.

Explanation of Provision.—Under the bill, the special community property rules applicable to qualified plans for purposes of the estate and gift tax provisions are repealed. However, the bill clarifies that, if a transfer is made to an employee spouse by a nonemployee spouse in a community proper-

ty state, the amount transferred is eligible for the unlimited marital deduction (secs. 2056 and 2523).

The bill also repeals the general exemption from the gift tax provisions of transfers pursuant to the exercise or nonexercise by an employee of an election or option under a qualified plan, etc.

The bill modifies the grandfather rules [see also Conference Report below] applicable to the repeal of the estate tax exclusion under DEFRA and the reduction of the exclusion under TEFRA) to provide that, as long as the other conditions for the grandfather are satisfied, an election is deemed to be irrevocable under a qualified plan (but not under an IRA) if the form of the benefit distribution elected is not changed prior to death.

Effective Date.—The provision of the bill relating to the repeal of the special rules for community property applies to gifts made or decedents dying after the date of enactment.

* * * * * *

[Conference Report]

* * * * * *

Estate tax exclusion.—The provision modifying the grandfather rule relating to the repeal in the Act (and the reduction in TEFRA) of the estate tax exclusion for pension benefits is further modified to provide that the grandfather rule is also available for individuals who separated from service before January 1, 1985, with respect to section 525(b)(2) of the Act, or before January 1, 1983, with respect to section 245(c) of TEFRA, elected a form of benefits to be paid in the future, and who was not in pay status as of the applicable dates.

* * * * * *

[Senate Explanation]

* * * * * *

e. Affiliated service groups and employee leasing arrangements (sec. 1852(f) of the bill and sec. 414 of the Code)

Present Law.—Under DEFRA, the Secretary of the Treasury was granted regulatory authority to develop rules as may be necessary to prevent the avoidance of any employee benefit requirement to which the employee leasing provisions apply through the use of employee leasing or other arrangements (sec. 414(o)).

Explanation of Provision.—Under the bill, the special regulatory authority provided to the Secretary of the Treasury with respect to abuses through the use of affiliated service groups (sec. 414(m)(7)) is repealed in favor of the broader general authority provided under the Act (sec. 414(o)). In addition, the bill clarifies that the other definitions relating to affiliated service groups (sec. 414(m)(6)) continue to apply.

[*Effective Date.*—Tax years beginning after 12-31-83. Ed.]

f. Discrimination standards applicable to cash or deferred arrangements (sec.

1852(g) of the bill and sec. 401(k) of the Code)

Present law.—DEFRA required that all elective deferrals made by a participant under all cash-or-deferred arrangements of an employer be aggregated for purposes of calculating that participant's actual deferral percentage. In addition, a cash-or-deferred arrangement is a qualified cash-or-deferred arrangement only if it meets the special tests provided by the Code relating to actual deferral percentages. If a cash-or-deferred arrangement fails to meet the special tests, an elective deferral made under the arrangement is treated as an employee contribution under the plan which is not excluded from gross income, but the plan of which the arrangement is a part is not to be disqualified if it meets the usual qualification requirements, including the general nondiscrimination rules.

Explanation of Provision.—Under the bill, if an employee participates in more than one cash-or-deferred arrangement of an employer, all such cash-or-deferred arrangements are treated as one arrangement for purposes of determining the employee's actual deferral percentage. Thus, an employee's actual deferral percentage taken into account for purposes of applying the special deferral percentage tests under any plan of the employer is the sum of the elective deferrals for that employee under each plan of the employer which provides a cash-or-deferred arrangement, divided by the participant's compensation from the employer.

In addition, the bill clarifies that a plan which includes an otherwise qualified cash-or-deferred arrangement that satisfies the special tests provided by section 401(k)(3) will be treated as satisfying the general nondiscrimination test of section 401(a)(4) with respect to the elective deferrals.

[*Effective date.*—Generally plan years beginning after 12-31-84. Ed.].

g. Treatment of certain medical, etc., benefits under section 415 (sec. 1852(h) of the bill and sec. 415 of the Code)

Present Law.—Under DEFRA, any defined benefit pension plan that provides medical benefits to retired employees is required to create and maintain an individual medical benefit account for any participant who is a 5-percent owner (within the meaning of sec. 416(i)(1)(B)) and to treat contributions allocated to such accounts as annual additions for purposes of the overall limits on contributions and benefits. A similar rule, applicable to post-retirement medical benefits provided through a welfare benefit fund, requires separate accounting for all key employees.

Under the overall limits, the annual addition with respect to an employee under all defined contribution plans of an employer for a year is not to exceed the lesser of $30,000 or 25 percent of compensation. A lower limit may apply if the employer also maintains a defined benefit plan for the employee. The

25-percent limit prevents reserve additions for a retired employee who has no compensation.

Explanation of Provision.—The bill clarifies that the special rules for post-retirement medical benefits apply to any pension or annuity plan under which such benefits are provided.

In addition, the bill changes the definition of employees for whom separate accounting is required under a pension plan to conform to the definition provided for the separate accounting for post-retirement medical and life insurance benefits under a welfare benefit fund. Thus, separate accounting is required with respect to any employee who is a key employee (within the meaning of section 416(i)).

Further, the bill provides that the amount treated as an annual addition under the rules for coordinating the post-retirement medical benefits with the overall limits on qualified plans is not subject to the 25-percent-of-compensation limit usually applicable to annual additions.

For example, assume the compensation of an employee is $100,000 for a year and $5,000 is treated as an annual addition under the limits for the employee under the rules for post-retirement medical benefits under a qualified plan. Assume further that the annual addition for the year under a qualified defined contribution plan, without regard to the post-retirement medical benefit is $25,000 (a contribution equal to the maximum percentage of compensation limit). Under the bill, the annual addition for post-retirement medical benefits does not cause the annual addition to exceed the 25-percent limit on annual additions, even though the annual addition would exceed that limit if the amount added for post-retirement medical benefits were taken into account. The annual addition of $30,000 would, however, be subject to the separate dollar limit for the year and, if the employer also maintains a defined benefit plan for the employee, the full annual addition of $30,000 would be taken into account in determining whether the combined plan limits are satisfied (sec. 415(e)).

[*Effective date.*—Years beginning after 3-31-84. Ed.]

h. Transition rules for effective date of multiemployer pension plan amendments act of 1980

Present Law.—The Multiemployer Pension Plan Amendments Act of 1980 (MPPAA) was enacted on September 26, 1980. Under the Employee Retirement Income Security Act of 1974 ("ERISA"), as amended by MPPAA, liability generally was imposed on an employer who withdrew from a multiemployer defined benefit pension plan. The withdrawal liability provisions of the MPPAA generally applied retroactively to withdrawals after April 28, 1980.

The Deficit Reduction Act of 1984 (DEFRA) eliminated the retroactive aspect of

MPPAA so that, in general, any liability incurred by an employer under the withdrawal liability provisions of ERISA, as a result of the complete or partial withdrawal from a multiemployer plan before September 26, 1980, is void.

Explanation of Provision.—The bill modifies the effective date of the withdrawal liability provisions of MPPAA in two instances. First, in the case of an employer who entered into a collective bargaining agreement that was effective on January 12, 1979, and that remained in effect through May 15, 1982, and under which contributions to a multiemployer plan were to cease on Janu-

ary 12, 1982, the bill changes the effective date of the withdrawal liability provision of MPPAA from September 26, 1980 to January 12, 1982.

Second, in the case of an employer engaged in the grocery wholesaling business that had ceased all covered operations under the plan before June 30, 1981, and had relocated its operations to a new facility in another State and that meets certain other conditions listed in the bill, the bill modifies the effective date of the withdrawal liability provisions of MPPAA from September 26, 1980 to June 30, 1981.

[¶ 4173] SECTION 1853. AMENDMENTS RELATED TO FRINGE BENEFIT PROVISIONS

(Sec. 125, 132, and 4977 of the Code)

[Senate Explanation]

* * * * * *

a. Clarification of line of business requirement

Present Law.—Section 132(a)(2) excludes from income certain qualified employee discounts on property or services offered for sale to customers in the ordinary course of the line of business of the employer in which the employee is performing services. For purposes of the discount exclusion, a leased section of a department store is treated as part of the line of business of the person operating the store and employees of the leased section are treated as employees of that person. A leased section of a department store is defined as any part of a department store where over-the-counter sales of property are made and certain other conditions are satisfied.

Explanation of Provision.—The bill clarifies that a leased section of a department store which, in connection with the offering of beautician services, customarily makes sales of beauty aids in the ordinary course of business is to be treated as engaged in over-the-counter sales of property, and thus is to be treated as a part of the line of business of the person operating the store. The committee intends that this treatment is to be available without requiring that a specific percentage of the beauty salon's revenue must be earned through the sale of such beauty products because beauty salons have traditionally occupied such leased sections (even though the bulk of their revenue is attributable to performing services rather than selling property.) This is contrasted with businesses (such as insurance companies) that have not traditionally occupied such leased sections.

b. Definition of dependent children

Present Law.—Section 531 of DEFRA provided exclusions from gross income for no-additional-cost services and certain other fringe benefits. These exclusions generally apply to benefits provided by an employer for use by an employee, the employee's spouse, or the employee's dependent child. Under the

Consolidated Omnibus Budget Reconciliation Act of 1986, use by an employee's parent is also eligible for the exclusion. DEFRA defined the latter term to mean any child of the employee (1) who is a dependent of the employee, or (2) both of whose parents are deceased (Code sec. 132(f)(2)(B)).

Explanation of Provision.—The bill defines dependent child to mean any child of the employee (1) who is a dependent of the employee, or (2) both of whose parents are deceased and who has not attained age 25.

c. Clarification of cross-reference

Present Law.—Code section 132(f) provides that for purposes of paragraphs (1) and (2) of subsection (a), any use by the spouse or a dependent child of the employee is treated as use by the employee. The cross-references are to both the no-additional-cost service exclusion (sec. 132(a)(1)), which applies to a service provided by an employer to an employee for use by such employee if certain conditions are met, and the qualified employee discount exclusion (sec. 132(a)(2)), which applies in certain circumstances where the price at which property or services are provided to the employee by the employer is less than the price to nonemployee customers.

Explanation of Provision.—To clarify the mechanics of the cross-reference in Code section 132(f), the bill adds the words "for use by such employee" in section 132(a)(2). Accordingly, the qualified employee discount exclusion applies in certain circumstances where the price at which property or services are provided to the employee by the employer for use by such employee (or the spouse or dependent children or parents of the employee) is less than the price to nonemployee customers.

d. Cross-reference in definition of customer

Present Law.—Under Code section 132(i), the term "customers" does not include nonemployee customers except for purposes of section 132(c)(2)(B), relating to the determination of gross profit percentage as a limitation on the exclusion for qualified employee discounts.

Explanation of Provision.—The bill provides that this exception to the definition of customers also applies for purposes of section 132(c)(2)(A), defining the term "gross profit percentage."

e. Excise tax on certain fringe benefits

Present Law.—Under the Act, the line of business limitation otherwise applicable to the section 132 exclusions for no-additional-cost services and qualified employee discounts is relaxed under an elective grandfather rule set forth in section 4977. The requirements for that provision necessitate determining the employees in certain lines of business of the employer.

Explanation of Provision.—The bill clarifies that, in the case of an agricultural cooperative incorporated in 1964, the grandfather rule, requiring that employees in all lines of business of an employer be eligible for employee discounts, is applied without taking into account employees of an employer that became a member of a controlled group including the agricultural cooperative during July of 1980.

f. Applicability of section 132(a)(1) exclusion to certain pre-divestiture retired telephone employees

Present Law.—Section 531 of the 1984 Act excludes from income and wages the fair market value of a no-additional-cost service provided by an employer to an employee for use by the employee (Code sec. 132(a)(1)). This exclusion applies if (1) the employer incurs no substantial cost (including foregone revenue) in providing the service; (2) the service is provided by the employer (including certain businesses under common control) or another business with whom the employer has a written reciprocal agreement, and is of the same type ordinarily sold to the public in the line of business in which the employee works; (3) the service is provided to a current or retired employee, or a spouse or dependent child of either, or a widow(er) or dependent children of a deceased employee; and (4) for certain officers, owners, and highly compensated employees, nondiscrimination requirements are met. Subject to certain transitional rules, the exclusion takes effect January 1, 1985.

Generally, situations in which an employer incurs no additional cost in providing services to employees are those in which the employees receive, at no substantial additional cost to the employer, the benefit of excess capacity that otherwise would have remained unused because nonemployee customers would not have purchased it—e.g., where telephone companies provide telephone service to employees within existing capacity. Local telephone service and long-distance telephone service are considered the same line of business.

Explanation of Provision.—The provision applies an intended transitional rule under which the fair market value of free telephone service provided to employees of the Bell System who had retired prior to divestiture of the system on January 1, 1984 is excluded from income and wages of such pre-divestiture retired employees. The exclusion pursuant to the provision does not apply to the furnishing of any property or to the furnishing of any type of service that was not furnished to such retirees as of January 1, 1984.

The provision applies in the case of an employee who, prior to January 1, 1984, separated from the service (by reason of retirement or disability) of an entity subject to the modified final judgment (as defined in Code sec. 559(c)(4)). The provision does not apply to any employee who separated from such service on or after January 1, 1984. No inference is intended from adoption of this transitional rule as to the interpretation of the no-additional-cost service exclusion in any other circumstances.

Under the provision, all entities subject to the modified final judgment are treated as a single employer in the same line of business for purposes of determining whether telephone service provided to the employee is a no-additional-cost service. Also, payment by an entity subject to the modified final judgment of all or part of the cost of local telephone service provided to the employee by a person other than an entity subject to the modified final judgment (including rebate of the amount paid by the employee for the service and payment to the person providing the service) is treated as telephone service provided to the employee by such single employer for purposes of determining whether the telephone service is a no-additional-cost service.

For purposes of this provision, the term "employee" has the meaning given to such term in Code section 132(f). Except as otherwise provided in this provision, the general requirements for the Code section 132(a)(1) exclusion apply; e.g., the exclusion applies to officers, owners, or highly compensated employees only if the no-additional-cost service is available to employees on a nondiscriminatory basis.

g. Cafeteria plans

Present Law.—Present law defines a cafeteria plan as a plan under which employees may choose (1) taxable benefits consisting of cash or certain other taxable benefits, or (2) certain fringe benefits that are specifically excluded from gross income by the Code (statutory fringe benefits).

Under the Act, the only taxable benefits which may be offered in a cafeteria plan consist of certain life insurance coverage that is not excludable from gross income, certain vacation pay, or cash. The life insurance coverage that may be offered is the coverage that is included in gross income to the extent the coverage exceeds $50,000 or to the extent it is provided on the life of a spouse or dependent of an employee. Vacation days may be provided under a cafeteria plan only if the plan precludes any participant from using (or receiving cash for) vacation days remaining unused as of the end of the plan year.

A cafeteria plan may offer any fringe benefit (other than scholarships or fellowships, van pooling, educational assistance, or miscellaneous fringe benefits) that is excludable from gross income under a specific section of the Code.

Under the Act, both general and special transition relief is provided with respect to the Treasury regulations on cafeteria plans, for cafeteria plans and "flexible spending arrangements" in existence on February 10, 1984.

Explanation of Provision.—Under the bill, the definition of permissible cafeteria plan benefits is clarified. The effect of the provision, which changes the reference in section 125 from nontaxable benefits to qualified benefits is to (1) eliminate any possible implication that a taxable benefit provided through a cafeteria plan is nontaxable, and (2) clarify that certain taxable benefits, as permitted under Treasury regulations, can be provided in a cafeteria plan.

The bill makes two changes to the transition relief provided to certain cafeteria plans under section 531(b) of the Tax Reform Act of 1984. The first change provides that a cafeteria plan, in existence on February 10, 1984, maintained pursuant to one or more collective bargaining agreements between employee representatives and one or more employers will be granted relief under the transition rules until the expiration of the last collective bargaining agreement relating to the cafeteria plan. When a collective bargaining agreement terminates is determined without regard to any extension of the agreement agreed to after July 18, 1984. Also, if a cafeteria plan is amended to conform with either the requirements of the Act or the requirements of any cafeteria plan regulations, the amendment is not treated as a termination of the agreement.

Second, the bill provides that a cafeteria plan which suspended a type or amount of benefit after February 10, 1984, and subsequently reactivated the benefit is eligible for transition relief under either the general or special transition relief provision.

*　　*　　*　　*　　*　　*

[House Explanation]

*　　*　　*　　*　　*　　*

Working Condition Fringe

*　　*　　*　　*　　*　　*

Explanation of Provision.—The committee clarifies the application of the product testing provision for purposes of the working condition fringe exclusion in the case of automobile testing. As described above, the product testing exclusion rule does not apply unless the employer imposes limitations on the employee's use of the item that significantly reduce the value of any personal benefit to the employee. The committee intends that this particular requirement is satisfied if the employer charges the employ-

ee a reasonable amount for any personal use of the automobile; thus, the product testing exclusion rule applies in such a case if all the other requirements for the rule are met.

An employer is treated as having imposed a sufficient charge for any personal benefits to an employee from the use of an evaluation product if the charge exceeds the cost to the employer in making the product available to employees.

The committee also clarifies the exception to the working condition fringe benefit rule for full-time automobile salesmen. This exception is not intended to be restricted to employees who have the formal job title of salesperson. Rather, the term is intended to apply to full-time employees of an automobile dealer who are automobile floor salespersons; to automobile salesmanagers; or to other employees who, as an integral part of their employment, regularly perform the functions of a floor salesperson or salesmanager, directly engage in the promotion and negotiation of sales to customers, and derive a significant part of their compensation from such activity. This provision, however, does not apply to owners of large automobile dealerships who do not customarily engage in significant sales activities.

*　　*　　*　　*　　*　　*

[Senate Explanation]

*　　*　　*　　*　　*　　*

h. Clarification of de minimis fringe benefits

Present Law.—Under section 132(e), gross income does not include any property or service the fair market value of which is so small that accounting for it is unreasonable or administratively impractical. Included in these de minimis fringe benefits are transit passes provided at discounts not exceeding $15 a month ($180 a year).

Explanation of Provision.—The committee clarifies that the de minimis fringe benefit exclusion includes tokens, vouchers, and reimbursements to cover the costs of commuting by public transit, as long as the amount of such reimbursement, etc., provided by the employer does not exceed $15 a month ($180 a year). The value of all such transit benefits (including any discounts on passes) furnished to the same individual are aggregated for purposes of determining whether the $15 limit is reached.

*　　*　　*　　*　　*　　*

[House Explanation]

*　　*　　*　　*　　*　　*

Transitional rules for treatment of certain reductions in tuition.—*Present Law.*—The 1984 Act provides an exclusion for qualified tuition reductions provided to an employee of an educational institution for education below the graduate level. Also, the tuition reduction may be provided for the education of the spouse or a dependent child of the employee.

The Act provides that the tuition reduction exclusion is not available if the plan discriminates in favor of employees who are officers, owners, or highly compensated.

Explanation of Provision.—Under the bill, for purposes of testing whether the tuition reduction program of Oberlin College is nondiscriminatory, a plan is treated as nondiscriminatory if it is nondiscriminatory taking into account certain special rules. First, with respect to all tuition reduction plans of Oberlin College, the plans are nondiscriminatory if the plans meet the nondiscrimination requirement when employees not included in the plan (who are included in a unit of employees covered by an agreement that the Secretary of the Treasury finds to be a collective bargaining agreement between employee representatives and one or more employers, if there is evidence that such benefits were the subject of good faith bargaining) are excluded from consideration.

A tuition reduction benefit provided by Oberlin College is treated as being provided under a separate plan if the level of the benefit was frozen before July 18, 1984. With respect to benefits for which the level of benefit is frozen, the plan is nondiscriminatory if the plan met the nondiscrimination

requirements (taking into account the exclusion of union employees) on the day on which eligibility to participate in the plan closed and at all times thereafter, the tuition reductions available under the plan are available on substantially the same terms to all employees eligible to participate in the plan.

In addition, the bill provides that any tuition reduction provided with respect to a full-time course of education furnished at the graduate level before July 1, 1988, is not included in gross income if (1) the reduction would not have been included in income under Treasury Regulations in effect on July 18, 1984, and (2) the reduction is provided with respect to a student who was accepted for admission to such course of education before July 1, 1984, and began the course of education before June 30, 1985.

[*Effective Date.*—Unless otherwise specified above, this section shall take effect as if included in the provisions to which it relates in the 1984 Tax Reform Act. Thus rules apply generally 1-1-85. Transitional tuition rules apply to education furnished after 6-30-85 in tax years ending after such date. Ed.]

[¶ 4174] SECTION 1854. AMENDMENTS RELATED TO EMPLOYEE STOCK OWNERSHIP PLANS

(Secs. 133, 402, 404, 409, 1042, 2210, and 4979A of the Code)

[Senate Explanation]

*   *   *   *   *   *

a. Sales of stock to employee stock ownership plans or certain cooperatives.

Present Law.—*In general.*—A taxpayer may elect to defer recognition of gain on the sale of certain qualified securities to an employee stock ownership plan (ESOP) or to an eligible worker-owned cooperative (EWOC) to the extent that the taxpayer reinvests the proceeds in qualified replacement property within a replacement period. To be eligible for nonrecognition treatment, (1) the qualified securities must be sold to an ESOP or EWOC; (2) the ESOP or EWOC must own, immediately after the sale, at least 30 percent of the total value of the employer securities then outstanding; (3) the ESOP or EWOC must preclude allocation of assets attributable to qualified securities to certain individuals; and (4) the taxpayer must provide certain information to the Secretary of the Treasury.

Qualified securities; qualified replacement property.—For purposes of this provision, qualified securities are defined as employer securities that (1) are issued by a domestic operating corporation that has no readily tradable securities outstanding, (2) have been held by the seller for more than one year, and (3) have not been received by the seller as a distribution from a qualified plan or as a transfer pursuant to an option or similar right to acquire stock granted to an employee

by an employer (other than stock acquired for full consideration).

Qualified replacement property (which includes both debt and equity instruments, as defined in sec. 165(g)(2)) consists of securities issued by another domestic corporation that does not, for the corporation's taxable year in which such securities are acquired by the taxpayer seeking nonrecognition treatment, have passive investment income (within the meaning of sec. 1362(d)(3)(D)) exceeding 25 percent of such corporation's gross receipts for that taxable year.

Exclusive benefit.—Nonrecognition treatment is not available if assets attributable to qualified securities involved in a nonrecognition transaction accrue directly or indirectly for the benefit of (1) the taxpayer involved in the nonrecognition transaction, (2) any member of the taxpayer's family (within the meaning of sec. 267(b)), or (3) any other person who owns (after application of the sec. 318 attribution rules) more than 25 percent in value in any class of any outstanding employer securities.

If within the period of the applicable statute of limitations, assets attributable to qualified securities involved in a nonrecognition transaction accrue directly or indirectly for the benefit of an individual in one of these three categories, the gain realized on the sale of the qualified securities to the ESOP or EWOC will be recognized.

Although compliance with the restriction on the allocation of qualified securities is a condition of nonrecognition treatment, it is not a plan qualification requirement under present law.

Election and notice requirement.—The taxpayer seeking nonrecognition treatment is required to file with the Secretary of the Treasury (1) a written election to claim nonrecognition treatment; (2) a verified written statement from the employer whose employees participate in the ESOP or an authorized officer of the worker-owned cooperative; and (3) information regarding the qualified replacement property, i.e., a "statement of purchase."

To elect nonrecognition treatment under the Act; the seller must file a written election, as prescribed by the Secretary of the Treasury, not later than the due date of the seller's income tax return for the seller's taxable year in which the sale occurs.

In addition, nonrecognition treatment is not available unless the seller files with the Secretary a verified written statement of the employer or an authorized officer of the corporation consenting to the application of the section 4978 excise tax.

Finally, the seller is required to provide a statement of purchase to the Secretary identifying (1) the seller's cost of acquiring replacement property (and an identification of such property), (2) the seller's intention not to acquire replacement securities within the replacement period, or (3) the seller's failure to acquire replacement securities within the replacement period. The form and manner of such notice is to be prescribed by the Secretary. Treasury regulations would require that a taxpayer have a statement of purchase notarized within 30 days after the purchase of qualified replacement property.

Disposition of qualified replacement property.—In general, the Act provides that the basis of the taxpayer in qualified replacement property is reduced by an amount not greater than the amount of gain realized on the sale of qualified securities to the employee organization which was not recognized pursuant to the election provided by this provision. The gain is to be recognized upon disposition of the qualified replacement property. However, the Act did not clarify the impact of any other rules that otherwise might permit nonrecognition treatment upon a direct or indirect disposition of the qualified replacement property.

Explanation of Provisions.—*Qualified securities; qualified replacement property.*— The bill makes several clarifying changes to the definition of qualified securities and qualified replacement property.

With respect to qualified securities, the bill makes it clear that stock of a corporation with no readily tradable stock outstanding may be eligible for nonrecognition treatment whether or not the corporation or any member of the controlled group has outstanding any readily tradable debt securities. The bill also clarifies that the nonrecognition provision applies only if the gain on the sale would otherwise have been long-term capital gain. For example, the sale of securities that had been held for less than six months, and the

sale of securities which otherwise would be treated as ordinary income (e.g., by reason of the collapsible corporation provisions) will be ineligible for nonrecognition treatment under this provision.

With respect to qualified replacement property, the bill makes it clear that securities issued by a government or political subdivision may not be treated as replacement property.

Qualified replacement property is limited under the bill to securities issued by a domestic operating corporation other than the corporation that issued the securities involved in the nonrecognition transaction. The bill generally defines a domestic operating corporation as a corporation substantially all the assets of which were, at the time the securities were purchased, used in the active conduct of a trade or business.

If (1) the corporation issuing the qualified replacement property owns stock representing control of one or more other corporations, or (2) one or more other corporations own stock representing control of the corporation issuing the qualified replacement property, then all such corporations will be treated as one corporation for purposes of determining whether the corporation is a domestic operating corporation and for purposes of determining whether the corporation that issued the qualified replacement property also issued the qualified securities. For purposes of this provision, control means control within the meaning of section 304(c), except that in testing control for this purpose, qualified replacement property of the electing taxpayer attributable to that sale is disregarded. Thus, the stock of a start-up company will constitute qualified replacement property, notwithstanding the fact that the start-up company and the corporation that issued the securities involved in the nonrecognition transaction are treated as the same corporation under section 304(c).

The bill also clarifies that the stock of a bank or thrift institution will not be ineligible to be treated as qualified replacement property solely because the institution has passive income in excess of 25 percent of its gross receipts for the preceding year.

Finally, the bill clarifies that, in the case of the death of an individual who sold qualified securities to an ESOP, the executor of the individual's estate may invest the proceeds (within 12 months after the date of the sale) in qualified replacement property pursuant to an election under section 1042. The executor similarly could designate as qualified replacement property any property acquired by the decedent for which a statement of purchase has not been filed. The estate's basis in the qualified replacement property is to be determined under the general principles applicable under section 1042. A beneficiary who receives the qualified replacement property from the estate has a basis in the property equal to that of the executor's in the property, rather than the fair market value of the property on the date that the beneficiary acquires it.

Further, the bill provides an extended replacement period for sellers who had acquired replacement property that, pursuant to this bill, will no longer be considered qualified replacement property. Under the bill, if a security was acquired by a taxpayer prior to September 27, 1985, and such security no longer constitutes qualifying replacement property, the period of time for the purchase of qualified replacement property is extended to December 31, 1986. Of course, this extension does not increase the amount of gain for which nonrecognition treatment may be claimed.

Thirty-percent test.—Under the bill, it is clarified that the ESOP or eligible worker-owned cooperative must hold, immediately after the sale, at least 30 percent of the total number of shares of all classes of stock (other than preferred stock described in section 1504(a)(4)) or 30 percent of the total value of all stock of the corporation that issued the qualified securities. With respect to sales after September 27, 1985, in taxable years ending after that date, 30-percent ownership by the employee organization is to be tested after application of the ownership attribution rules of Code section 318(a)(4).

The requirement that the plan hold 30 percent of outstanding stock (after application of sec. 318(a)(4)) is effective for sales of securities after July 18, 1984.

Exclusive benefit.—The bill makes several clarifying changes to the requirement that the employee organization be maintained for the exclusive benefit of employees. First, the bill clarifies that no portion of the assets attributable to qualified securities with respect to which a nonrecognition election is made (sec. 1042 securities) may be allocated to (1) a taxpayer seeking nonrecognition treatment, (2) any person who is related to that taxpayer in one of the ways described in Code section 267(b), or (3) any other person who owns (after application of the attribution rules of Code section 318(a)) more than 25 percent (by number) of (a) any class of outstanding stock of the corporation that issued such qualified securities, or (b) any class of stock of certain related corporations.

In addition, the bill makes it clear that this restriction applies to prohibit any direct or indirect accrual of benefits under all qualified plans of an employer or an allocation of assets attributable to the qualified securities involved in the nonrecognition transaction. Thus, for example, an ESOP in which the taxpayer seeking nonrecognition treatment participates could not allocate to the taxpayer's account any assets attributable to the securities involved in the nonrecognition transaction. Nor could the employer make an allocation of other assets to the taxpayer under the ESOP without making additional allocations to other participants sufficient separately to satisfy the nondiscrimination requirements of Code section 401(a).

The bill clarifies that an individual is to be treated as a 25-percent shareholder only if

the individual is a 25-percent shareholder (1) at any time during the one-year period ending on the date of the sale of section 1042 securities to an ESOP, or (2) on the dates upon which any section 1042 securities sold to the ESOP are allocated. In the case of an individual who satisfies the condition described at (1), the individual will continue to be treated as a 25-percent shareholder until all of the qualified securities acquired pursuant to the sale are allocated. In the case of an individual who does not satisfy the condition described at (1), but meets the condition described at (2), the individual will be treated as a 25-percent shareholder only with respect to those section 1042 securities allocated on the date or dates that the individual is a 25-percent shareholder.

The bill also provides that, for purposes of determining whether an individual owns more than 25 percent of the outstanding stock of the corporation which issued the employer securities, all allocated securities held by an ESOP are treated as securities owned by the ESOP participant to whom the securities are allocated. The treatment of shares held by an ESOP as held by a shareholder for purposes of applying the 25-percent test applies to sales of qualified securities after enactment.

The bill also provides that individuals who would be ineligible to receive an allocation of qualified securities *solely* because they are lineal descendants of other individuals who are ineligible to receive allocations of section 1042 securities may receive an allocation of the section 1042 securities provided that the total amount of such securities allocated to all such lineal descendants is not more than 5 percent of all section 1042 securities [see also Conference Report below]

Disqualification.—The bill also provides that an ESOP that acquires section 1042 securities is required to comply with the restriction on the allocation of securities to the sellers, family members, and 25-percent shareholders (sec. 409(n)). The sanction for failure to comply with the restriction would be disqualification of the plan with respect to those participants who received prohibited allocations. Thus, failure to comply results in income inclusion for those participants of the value of their prohibited allocations on the date of such allocations. However, violation of the restriction does not cause disqualification of the plan if the violation occurred more than ten years after all of the section 1042 securities acquired in the transaction had been allocated.

Under the bill, if there is a prohibited allocation by an ESOP or an eligible worker-owned cooperative of employer securities acquired in a section 1042 transaction, then a 50 percent excise tax is imposed on the amount involved in the prohibited allocation. A prohibited allocation means (1) any allocation of employer securities acquired in a qualified sale if the provisions of section 409(n), relating to prohibitions on allocations to certain individuals, are violated and (2) any benefit accruing to a person in violation of the provisions of section 409(n). The liability for this excise tax is to be paid by the employer who maintains an ESOP or by the eligible worker-owned cooperative.

Eligible taxpayers.—Generally, effective for sales after March 28, 1985, the bill limits the class of taxpayers eligible to elect nonrecognition treatment under this provision by making the election unavailable to any subchapter C corporation. However, a subchapter C corporation may elect nonrecognition treatment with respect to certain sales made no later than July 1, 1985, provided the sales otherwise satisfy the requirements of this provision and are made pursuant to a binding contract in effect on March 28, 1985, and at all times thereafter. The bill provides an exception to the March 28, 1985, date for 2 transactions.

Election and notice.—The bill clarifies that a taxpayer making a section 1042 election is not required to obtain a notarized "statement of purchase" describing the qualified replacement property until 90 days after the later of (1) the sale of the qualified securities, or (2) the purchase of the qualified replacement property. The bill would also direct the Secretary of the Treasury to provide forms for the election of nonrecognition treatment under section 1042 and for the "statement of purchase" describing the qualified replacement property. Anyone electing nonrecognition treatment under section 1042 would be required to use such forms for sales occurring 180 days after the publication of such forms.

Disposition of qualified replacement property.—The bill also clarifies the coordination of the provision's requirement that gain be recognized upon disposition of any qualified replacement property with other rules providing nonrecognition treatment. Effective for dispositions made after the date of enactment, the bill overrides all other provisions permitting nonrecognition and requires that gain realized upon the disposition of qualified replacement property be recognized at that time. The bill exempts from the rule that gain is to be recognized upon the disposition of qualified replacement property: (1) dispositions at death; (2) dispositions by gift; (3) certain exchanges required in the event of a reorganization provided the corporation involved in the reorganization is not controlled by the taxpayer holding qualified replacement property; and (4) subsequent sales of the qualified replacement property to an ESOP, pursuant to a transaction governed by section 1042.

The amount of gain required to be recognized upon the disposition of qualified replacement property is limited to the amount not recognized pursuant to the election provided by this provision by reason of the acquisition of such replacement property. Any gain in excess of that amount continues to be eligible for any otherwise applicable nonrecognition treatment.

To ensure that this rule is not avoided through the use of controlled corporations, the bill provides special rules for corporations controlled by the taxpayer seeking nonrecognition treatment. If the taxpayer owns stock representing control (within the meaning of section 304(c)) of the corporation issuing the qualified replacement property, the taxpayer shall be treated as having disposed of such qualified replacement property when the corporation disposes of a substantial portion of its assets other than in the ordinary course of its trade or business.

*   *   *   *   *   *

[Conference Report]

*   *   *   *   *   *

The [conference] agreement clarifies that, for purposes of section 1042 (relating to certain sales of stock to an ESOP), in computing whether lineal descendants of a selling taxpayer have been allocated more than 5 percent of the employer securities attributable to a sale to which section 1042 applies, all employer securities sold to the ESOP by the taxpayer which are eligible for nonrecognition treatment are taken into account.

The requirement under section 1042 that certain individuals not be allocated employer securities attributable to a sale to which the section applies, or amounts in lieu thereof, is not intended to apply to amounts which are provided to the individual outside of a qualified plan, for example, through a non-qualified deferred compensation agreement.

In addition, the conference agreement clarifies that an insurance company is treated as an operating corporation for purposes of determining whether property qualifies as qualified replacement property under section 1042.

*   *   *   *   *   *

[Senate Explanation]

*   *   *   *   *   *

b. Deduction for dividends paid on ESOP stock

Present Law.—The Act permits an employer to deduct the amount of any dividends paid in cash during the employer's taxable year with respect to stock of the employer that is held by an ESOP (including a tax credit ESOP), but only to the extent such dividends are actually paid out currently to participants or beneficiaries. The employer may claim a deduction for dividends for the employer's taxable year when paid to the extent that the dividends (1) are, in accordance with the plan provisions, paid in cash directly to the participants, or (2) are paid to the plan and subsequently distributed to the participants in cash no later than 90 days after the close of the plan year in which paid.

For income tax purposes, dividends distributed under an ESOP, whether paid directly to participants pursuant to plan provisions or paid to the plan and redistributed to participants, generally are treated as plan distributions. Accordingly, such dividends do not qualify for the partial exclusion from income otherwise permitted under Code section 116.

Explanation of Provision.—The bill makes it clear that dividends paid on any employer stock held by the ESOP and allocated as of the date of distribution to a participant's account may be deducted under this provision, including those dividends paid on employer stock that is not considered to be qualified employer securities within the meaning of section 409(1). No deduction is permitted, however, with respect to employer stock held in a suspense account (as of the date of distribution) under an ESOP. The bill clarifies that a deduction is permitted for dividends paid on stock which is allocated to participants' accounts as of the date of distribution of such dividends. The bill also makes it clear that current distributions of dividends paid on employer stock allocated to a participant's account under an ESOP will not be considered disqualifying distributions.

The bill clarifies that a corporation will be allowed a deduction for dividends paid on stock held by an ESOP whether such dividends are passed through to beneficiaries of plan participants or to the plan participants themselves. In addition, effective for dividends paid after the date of the bill's enactment, the bill makes it clear that employer deductions for dividends paid on employer stock held by an ESOP are to be permitted only in the year in which the dividend is paid or distributed to the participant beneficiary. Thus, where the employer pays such dividends directly to participants in accordance with plan provisions, a deduction would be permitted in the year paid. However, where the employer pays such dividends to the ESOP for redistribution to participants no later than 90 days after the close of the plan year, a deduction would be permitted in the employer's taxable year in which the dividend is distributed from the ESOP to the participants. The bill clarifies that dividends paid on employer stock held by an ESOP are treated as paid under a contract separate from the contract under which the stock is held. However, the provision is inapplicable to dividends paid before January 1, 1986, if the employer deducted such dividends in the taxable year they were paid to the ESOP and filed a return for that taxable year before the date of enactment.

The bill clarifies that, although the dividends for which the Act allows a deduction are generally to be treated as distributions under the plan, they are to be fully taxable. Thus, these distributions are not to be treated as distributions of net employee contributions. The provision is inapplicable to dividends paid before January 1, 1986, which a taxpayer treated as the nontaxable return of employee contributions for purposes of a return filed before the date of enactment.

* * * * * *

[Conference Report]

* * * * * *

The conference agreement adopts the provision in the Senate amendment which permits a plan sponsored by a corporation whose bylaws or charter restrict the ownership of substantially all outstanding employer securities to employees or certain trusts to distribute employer securities in certain cases. The conferees intend that, if such a plan does distribute employer securities, the distribution requirements and put option requirements generally applicable to ESOPs (except for the requirement that the employee has a right to demand that the distribution be paid in employer securities) will apply to the distribution.

Under the conference agreement, a deduction is allowed for certain dividends paid on employer stock held by an ESOP, even if the stock is not yet allocated to participant accounts. The Treasury is empowered to disallow deductions for dividends paid on stock held by an ESOP if the dividend constitutes, in substance, the evasion [Text of Act reads "avoidance." Ed.] of taxation. The conferees intend that the deduction is to be allowed only with respect to reasonable dividends.

* * * * * *

[Senate Explanation]

* * * * * *

Further, the bill empowers the Treasury to disallow deductions for dividends paid on stock held by an ESOP, if the dividend constitutes, in substance, the avoidance of taxation. Thus, for example, if amounts paid by an employer, and treated for tax purposes as 404(k) dividends, are the payment of unreasonable compensation, such payments would not qualify for treatment as section 404(k) dividends.

c. Partial exclusion of interest

Present Law.—A bank (within the meaning of sec. 581), an insurance company, or a corporation actively engaged in the business of lending money may exclude from gross income 50 percent of the interest received with respect to a securities acquisition loan.

Under the Code, a securities acquisition loan means any loan to a corporation or to an ESOP to the extent that the proceeds are used to acquire employer securities (within the meaning of sec. 409(1)) for the plan. A securities acquisition loan does not include any loan between corporations that are members of the same controlled group of corporations.

Temporary regulations issued by the Treasury provide that a loan made to a corporation sponsoring an ESOP will qualify as a securities acquisition loan only to the extent that, and for the period which, the proceeds are (a) loaned to the corporation's ESOP on terms "substantially similar" to those between the commercial lender and the sponsoring organization and (b) used to acquire employer securities for the ESOP. However, the term "securities acquisition loan" excludes any loan made between corporations that are members of the same controlled group of corporations.

Explanation of Provision.—The bill (1) clarifies the interaction of the partial interest exclusion with other provisions affecting tax-exempt income, and (2) clarifies the meaning of the term "securities acquisition loan."

Interaction with other provisions.—The bill makes it clear that for purposes of section 291(e), relating to certain tax preference items, (1) interest on an obligation eligible for the partial exclusion of section 133 will not be treated as exempt from tax, and (2) in determining the interest allocable to indebtedness on tax-exempt obligations, obligations eligible for the partial exclusion will not be taken into account in calculating the taxpayer's average adjusted basis for all assets.

In addition, the bill clarifies the coordination of the partial exclusion with the installment payment provisions (sec. 483) and the original issue discount rules (secs. 1271 through 1275). The bill makes it clear that, in testing the adequacy of the stated interest rate for purposes of section 483 and sections 1271 through 1275, the applicable Federal rate will be adjusted as appropriate to reflect the partial interest exclusion. In addition, the bill clarifies that the below market interest rate rules (sec. 7872) do not apply to a loan between a sponsoring employer and an ESOP, provided that the interest rate payable on such loan is no less than the interest rate payable by the employer on a corresponding section 133 loan.

Securities acquisition loan.—The bill would clarify the definition of the term "securities acquisition loan" in several respects. First, the bill would make it clear that the refinancing of a loan to an ESOP after the effective date of section 133 will qualify as a securities acquisition loan, provided that the repayment period of the original loan is not extended, and the refinanced loan otherwise satisfies the requirements of section 133. Thus, for example, loans used to acquire employer securities after July 18, 1984, qualify for such refinancing notwithstanding that the original loan would not have qualified as a securities acquisition loan under section 133. For example, if a purchase money obligation was utilized to acquire employer securities after July 18, 1984, the refinancing of such loan is permitted to qualify under section 133.

The bill also clarifies that the requirement that a loan from a sponsoring corporation to an ESOP be made on terms "substantially similar" to those applicable to the loan between a commercial lender and the sponsoring corporation does not preclude repayment of the sponsoring corporation's loan to the ESOP more rapidly than the repayment of the loan from the commercial lender to the sponsoring corporation, provided that the allocations of stock within the ESOP do not result in discrimination in favor of highly compensated employees. The terms of such loans are to be negotiated between the plan's sponsor and the lender; however, the repayment period of the loan from the commercial lender could not be more than 7 years unless the repayment terms of the two loans are substantially similar.

The bill would also clarify that, although a securities acquisition loan may not originate with any member of the controlled group, it may be held by a member of the controlled group. However, during any such time that a securities acquisition loan is held by a member of the controlled group, any interest received with respect to such loan during such period would not qualify for the exclusion provided under section 133.

d. Payment of estate tax liability by ESOP

Present Law.—If qualified employer securities are (1) acquired from a decedent by an ESOP or an eligible worker-owned cooperative (EWOC), (2) pass from a decedent to an ESOP or EWOC, or (3) are transferred by the decedent's executor to an ESOP or EWOC, then the executor of the decedent's estate generally is relieved of the estate tax liability to the extent the ESOP or EWOC is required to pay the liability.

No executor is relieved of estate tax liability under this provision with respect to securities transferred to an ESOP unless the employer whose employees participate in the ESOP guarantees, by surety bond or other means as required by the Secretary of the Treasury, the payment of any estate tax or interest.

To the extent that (1) the decedent's estate is otherwise eligible to make deferred payments of estate taxes pursuant to section 6166 with respect to the decedent's interest in qualified employer securities, and (2) the executor elects to make payments pursuant to that section, the plan administrator of the ESOP or an authorized officer of the EWOC also may elect to pay any estate taxes attributable to the qualified employer securities transferred to the ESOP or EWOC in installments pursuant to that section. The Act provides that the usual rules (sec. 6166) apply to determine ongoing eligibility for deferral. Thus, for example, disposition of the qualifying securities held by the estate and employee organization may trigger acceleration of any remaining unpaid tax.

Explanation of Provision.—The bill makes several changes to clarify the applicability of these provisions and the coordination with the provisions governing the installment payment of estate taxes under section 6166. First, the bill makes it clear, that, with respect to the estates of individuals dying after September 27, 1985, only executors of those estates eligible to make deferred payments of estate taxes may be relieved of estate tax liability under this provision. In addition, under the bill, the transfer of employer securities to an ESOP or to an eligible EWOC will not be treated as a disposition or withdrawal which triggers acceleration of the remaining unpaid tax.

The bill makes it clear that, after the transfer, the ongoing eligibility of the estate and the ESOP or EWOC to make installment payments applicable to their respective interests is to be tested separately. Thus, with respect to the estate's remaining interest (if any), cumulative dispositions and withdrawals of amounts up to 50 percent of the estate's remaining interest would be permitted without requiring acceleration of the remaining unpaid tax. Similarly, with respect to an ESOP or EWOC cumulative dispositions and withdrawals of up to 50 percent of the interest transferred to the ESOP or EWOC would be permitted without requiring acceleration. In addition, under the bill, a distribution made by an ESOP to participants on account of death, retirement after attainment of age 59-½, disability, or any separation from service resulting in a one-year break in service will not be treated as a disposition requiring acceleration of any unpaid tax and will not be taken into account in determining whether any subsequent disposition triggers acceleration.

The bill also makes it clear that no executor will be relieved of estate tax liability with respect to employer securities transferred to an eligible EWOC unless the EWOC guarantees the payment of any estate tax or interest by surety bond or other means as required by the Secretary of the Treasury.

6. Voting Rights

Present Law.—Under present law, a tax credit ESOP (sec. 409), a leveraged ESOP and, in some circumstances, a defined contribution plan (sec. 401(a)(22)) are required to meet certain voting rights requirements with respect to employer securities held by the plan. If the plan does not have a registration-type class of securities, the trustee of the plan is required to permit each participant to direct the vote with respect to corporate matters that (by law or charter) must be decided by more than a majority vote of the outstanding common shares voted, of those securities that have been allocated to the participant's account.

Explanation of Provision.—The bill modifies the voting rights requirements applicable to nonregistration type employer securities held by an ESOP by (1) mandating that voting rights be passed through to participants with respect to certain enumerated issues; and (2) accommodating the one man-one vote philosophy of certain types of ESOPs and EWOCs.

First, the bill would require, with respect to certain issues specified in the bill, that a trustee permit participants to direct the vote under employer securities allocated to the participants' accounts, regardless of whether the issue was required (by law or charter) to be decided by more than a majority vote of the outstanding common shares voted. The issues on which the pass-through of voting rights would be required include merger or consolidation, recapitalization, reclassification, liquidation, dissolution, or sale of substantially all of the assets of a trade or business of the corporation, and to the extent provided by regulations, other similar issues.

Second, the bill would permit the trustee of an ESOP or EWOC, the by-laws or terms of

which required that the interests in the ESOP or EWOC be governed on a one vote per participant basis, to vote the employer securities in a manner that reflected the one man-one vote philosophy. Under this alternative, each ESOP or EWOC participant would be entitled to cast one vote on an issue. The trustee would then be required to vote the employer securities held by the ESOP or EWOC in proportion to the results of the votes cast on the issue by the participants.

The requirements relating to one vote per participant are effective on the date of enactment. The requirements relating to pass-through voting are effective after December 31, 1986 for securities acquire[d] after December 31, 1979.

7. Net unrealized appreciation

Present Law.—Under present law, in the case of a distribution of securities of the employer from a qualified plan, an employee is permitted to exclude from income the net unrealized appreciation (NUA) on such securities attributable to employee contributions. In addition, if the distribution qualifies as a lump-sum distribution, the employee is generally permitted to exclude from income the NUA on such securities, regardless of whether appreciation is attributable to employer or employee contributions (secs. 402(a)(1) and 402(e)(4)(J)). Upon disposition of the stock in a taxable transaction, the participant is taxed on the previously excluded NUA at capital gains rates. NUA is generally measured as the difference between the fair market value at distribution and the basis of the securities.

In the case of an acquisition of one corporation by another, shares of the company held by a plan sponsored by the company, are sometimes exchanged for shares of the acquiring company in a transaction that generally would be taxable if the stock were not held by a qualified plan. Alternatively, the plan may exchange shares of the target company for cash or other property that the plan later reinvests in qualifying securities of the employer. The IRS has taken the position that in a case in which securities of the employer held by a plan are exchanged for cash or other securities of the employer in a transaction that would be taxable if the securities were held by a taxable entity, the plan's basis in such securities received pursuant to the exchange (or purchased with cash or other property received pursuant to the exchange) is generally increased or "stepped up" to reflect the fair market value of the securities, cash, or property used to acquire new securities. Because the newly acquired securities have a "stepped-up" basis, rather than the same basis as the securities that were disposed of in the exchange, the previously accumulated NUA on the old securities is eliminated.

Explanation of Provision.—The bill provides that if, pursuant to a tender offer, a plan fiduciary, in the exercise of its fiduciary duties, exchanges previously acquired securities of the employer for other securities of the employer, the plan will have the same basis in the acquired securities. Similarly, if a plan fiduciary, in the exercise of its fiduciary duties, disposes of such securities for cash because the securities are called, because the trustee tenders such securities in response to a tender offer, or because such disposition is required by ERISA or the Internal Revenue Code, and the proceeds are reinvested in securities of the employer within a 90-day period (unless the Secretary provides an extension of the 90-day period) the plan will have the same basis in such securities purchased with the cash proceeds as the plan had in the securities sold. In the case of a transaction occurring before the date of enactment, the reinvestment period does not end before the earlier of (1) one year after the date of the transaction or (2) 180 days after the date of enactment.

* * * * * *

[Conference Report]

* * * * * *

Conference Agreement

* * * * *

Further, the conference agreement provides that market discount is not created by reason of the basis adjustment resulting from the rollover provision for the sale of stock to an ESOP.

[Effective Date.—Unless otherwise specified above, this section shall generally take effect as if included in the provisions to which it relates in the 1984 Tax Reform Act. Thus generally provisions apply to tax years beginning after, or transactions entered into after, 7-18-84. For special effective dates for certain provisions, see ¶1854. Ed.]

[¶ 4175] SECTION 1855. AMENDMENTS RELATED TO MISCELLANEOUS EMPLOYEE BENEFIT PROVISIONS

(Secs. 555 and 556 of the 1984 TRA)

[House Explanation]

* * * * * *

a. Incentive stock option provision (*** secs. 57 and 422A of the Code)

Present Law.—The Act clarifies that the fair market value of stock, for purposes of applying the incentive stock options provisions, is determined without regard to lapse restrictions.

The Act applies, for purposes of the minimum tax, to options exercised after March 20, 1984. Transitional relief was provided for certain options exercised on or before December 31, 1984.

Explanation of Provision.—The bill clarifies that, under the transitional rule, the amendment to the minimum tax provision relating to incentive stock options (sec.

57(a)(10)) will not apply to options exercised before January 1, 1985, if the option was granted pursuant to a plan adopted or corporate action taken by the board of directors of the grantor corporation before May 15, 1984.

b. Time for making certain section 83(b) elections (*** sec. 556 of the Act)

Present Law.—The Act extended the time for making certain section 83(b) elections where property was transferred to the taxpayer after June 30, 1976 and before November 18, 1982, where the taxpayer paid fair market value (determined without regard to certain restrictions).

Explanation of Provision.—The bill extends the provision of that 1984 Act to transfers made before July 1, 1976.

[Effective date.—Tax years ending after 7-18-84 and beginning before '86 TRA enactment date. Ed.]

[¶ 4176] SECTION 1861. AMENDMENTS RELATED TO SECTION 611 OF THE ACT

(Sec. 103A of the Code)

[Senate Amendment]

* * * * * *

Present Law.—* * * The Act extends the tax-exemption for qualified mortgage bonds for four years, for bonds issued after December 31, 1983, and before January 1, 1988. These bonds generally are subject to the same restrictions as applied to such bonds issued before January 1, 1984.

Explanation of provisions.—* * * The bill clarifies that, in certain cases, the Treasury Department may grant extensions of time for publishing annual policy statements that issuers of qualified mortgage bonds are required to make. These statements must explain measures taken by the issuers to

comply with the Congressional objective of providing housing for lower-income persons.

The bill further clarifies that the requirement of this annual policy statement and the requirements that (1) certain information be reported to Treasury with respect to each bond issue and (2) a State official certify compliance with Code restrictions are treated as satisfied if the issuer in good faith attempted to meet the requirement and the failure to meet the requirement is due to inadvertent error.

[Effective date.—Reporting requirement applies to obligations issued after 12-31-84. Veterans must apply for mortgage loans by later of 30 years after service or 1-31-85, effective after 7-18-84. Ed.]

* * * * * *

[¶ 4177] SECTION 1862. AMENDMENT RELATED TO SECTION 612 OF THE ACT

(Sec. 103A of the Code)

[Senate Explanation]

* * * * * *

Present law.— * * * As an alternative to qualified mortgage bonds, the Act permits States to elect to exchange qualified mortgage bond authority for authority to issue mortgage credit certificates (MCCs). MCCs generally are subject to the same eligibility restrictions as qualified mortgage bonds.

* * * * * *

Explanation of provisions.— * * * Issuers of qualified mortgage bonds must satisfy information reporting requirements, must certify that the bonds meet the volume limitation requirement of the Code, and must publish annual policy statements demonstrating that their programs satisfy Congress' objective in authorizing issuance of tax-exempt bonds for this purpose. The bill clarifies that these requirements also apply with respect to MCCs.

The bill clarifies that good faith errors in MCC program administration may be corrected without invalidating all MCCs issued under the program. The bill further clarifies the method for determining the amount of excess credit that may be carried forward for up to three years by a taxpayer.

*[Effective date.—*For interest paid or accrued after 12-31-84 on indebtedness incurred after that date. Ed.]

* * * * * *

[¶ 4178] SECTION 1863. AMENDMENT RELATED TO SECTION 613 OF THE ACT

[Senate Explanation]

* * * * * *

Present law.— * * * The Act restricts the issuance of qualified veterans mortgage bonds by (1) limiting the veterans eligible for loans financed with these bonds, and (2) imposing State volume limitations based on pre-1984 issuance of the bonds. The Act further directs the Federal Financing Bank to make cash flow loans to the Oregon Department of Veterans' Affairs to offset lower than anticipated prepayments on loans funded with specified veterans' mortgage bonds.

* * * * * *

Explanation of provisions.— * * * The bill clarifies that veterans eligible for loans financed by qualified veterans' mortgage bonds must apply for the financing before the later of (1) 30 years after leaving active service, or (2) January 31, 1985 (rather than January 1, 1985).

The bill provides that the Oregon Department of Veterans' Affairs (Oregon) may advance refund up to $300 million of qualified veterans' mortgage bonds and expands the list of specified bonds that may be advance refunded. (Advance refundings of mortgage subsidy bonds generally are prohibited.) The advance refunding is in lieu of authority included in the Act permitting that State agency to receive cash flow loans not exceeding $300 million at any time from the Federal Financing Bank (FFB). This provision is effective on the date of enactment, and does not affect the status of cash flow loans made under an interim financing agreement entered into between Oregon and the FFB before that date.

*[Effective date.—*Date of enactment; exception for loan made to Oregon under credit agreement entered 4-15-85. Ed.]

* * * * * *

[¶ 4179] SECTION 1864. AMENDMENTS RELATED TO SECTION 621 OF THE ACT

(Sec. 103A of the Code)

[Senate explanation]

* * * * * *

Present Law.— * * * Private activity bonds generally are subject to State volume limitations. The limitations apply to most industrial development bonds (IDBs) and to student loan bonds issued within the State. Certain bonds issued to finance governmentally owned airports, docks, wharves, convention or trade show facilities, and mass commuting facilities are not subject to these volume limitations.

The Act provides a statutory formula for allocating each State's volume limitation among issuers within the State. This Federal formula may be overridden by State statute, or by gubernatorial proclamation on an interim basis. Issuers may elect to carry forward bond authority for up to three years (six years in certain cases) for certain, specifically identified projects.

Explanation of provisions.—* * * *Facilities located outside a State.*—The bill clarifies that each state's annual private activity bond volume limitation generally may be used only to finance facilities located within that State. Under this clarification, a State may allocate a portion of its volume limitation to financing for facilities located outside its boundaries only in the case of specified facilities, and only to the extent of the State's share of the use of those facilities.

Facilities located outside a State and to which a State may allocate a portion of its volume limitation include (1) otherwise eligible sewage and solid waste disposal facilities or facilities for the local furnishing of electric energy or gas (sec. 103(b)(4)(E)); (2) otherwise eligible facilities for furnishing of water (sec. 103(b)(4)(G)); and (3) qualified hydroelectric generating facilities (sec. 103(b)(4)(H)). This clarification does not affect the rule in Code section 103(o)(3) that qualified student loan bonds must be issued to finance loans both to (1) residents of the State issuing the bonds regardless of the location of the school the residents attend, and (2) students attending schools within the issuing jurisdiction, regardless of the State of their legal residence, since no facilities are financed with student loan bonds.

In the case of sewage and solid waste disposal facilities, the determination of a State's use of a facility is based on the percentage of the facility's total treatment provided to the State (and its residents). In the case of facilities for the local furnishing of electric energy and gas, facilities for the furnishing of water, and qualified hydroelectric generating facilities, the determination of use is based upon the share of the output of the facility received by the State (and its residents).

These clarifications generally are effective for bonds issued after the date of the bill's enactment. Under a special rule, a State may elect to apply this rule in the case of bonds issued before the date of enactment.

Certain facilities financed outside a State's volume limitation.—The bill clarifies that the determination of whether facilities forming a part of an airport, dock, wharf, mass commuting facility, or trade or convention center may be financed outside a State's volume limitation is to be made on a property-by-property basis rather than by reference to the entire airport or other excepted facility. Under the bill, all property to be financed pursuant to this exception must be owned by or on behalf of a governmental unit. Therefore, property financed with the so-called "insubstantial portion" of bond proceeds that otherwise could be used for a purpose other than the governmental purpose for which the bonds are issued also must be governmentally owned.

Authority to allocate a State's volume limitation directly to issuing authorities other than governmental units.—The bill clarifies that a State may allocate its private activity bond volume limitation directly to issuing authorities within the State that are not governmental units as well as to such governmental units. This clarification applies to allocations pursuant to gubernatorial proclamations and also to allocations pursuant to State statutes.

Reporting requirement for allocations of volume limitations.—The bill clarifies the authority of the Treasury Department to require reports on allocations of State volume limitations as part of the presently required information reporting (Code sec. 103(1)).

[*Effective date.*—Amendments relating to out-of-state facilities apply for bonds issued after Act's date of enactment with election to include previous issues; amendments relating to private activity bond information reporting, exempt activities, and carryforwards apply for obligations issued after 12-31-83 with exception for certain action before 6-19-84. Ed.]

[¶ 4180] SECTION 1865. AMENDMENT RELATED TO SECTION 622 OF THE ACT

(Sec. 103 of the Code)

[Senate Explanation]

*   *   *   *   *   *

Present law.—* * * The Act provides that interest on bonds, repayment of which is directly or indirectly guaranteed (in whole or in part) by the Federal Government, is taxable. The underlying economic substance of a transaction determines whether repayment of bonds is Federally guaranteed. Thus, depending on the facts and circumstances of each case, a Federal guarantee may arise from contracts providing for purchase of the output of a facility by the Federal Government, from leases of property to the Federal Government, and from other similar arrangements, as well as from a direct agreement to repay the bonds.

Explanation of provisions.—* * * The bill provides transitional relief for a convention center (Carbondale, Illinois) to be financed with bonds for which the Farmers Home Administration had authorized a Federal guarantee before enactment of the Act.

The bill also provides transitional exceptions for a limited amount of bonds for four solid waste disposal facilities. Bonds for these facilities are indirectly Federally guaranteed as a result of the anticipated purchase by the Federal Government under contract of more than an insignificant portion of the output of the facilities. These facilities are located in Aberdeen and Annapolis, Maryland, in Portsmouth, Virginia, and in Charleston, South Carolina. Expenditures were made with respect to each facility before October 19, 1983.

*   *   *   *   *   *   *   *   *   *   *   *

[*Effective dates.*—Effective as if included in 1984 Tax Reform Act. Ed.]

[¶ 4181] SECTION 1866. TRANSITIONAL RULE FOR LIMIT ON SMALL ISSUE EXCEPTION

[Senate Explanation]

* * * * * *

Present law.—* * * The Act prohibits tax-exemption for small-issue IDBs if a beneficiary of the IDBs is a beneficiary of more than $40 million of all types of tax-exempt bonds. Bonds used to redeem other bonds do not count towards the $40 million limit; however, such refunding bonds may not be issued if a beneficiary of the bonds benefits from more than $40 million of outstanding bonds at the time of the refunding.

* * * * * *

Explanation of provision.—* * * The bill permits small-issue IDBs to be refunded to reduce the interest rate on the borrowing even though a beneficiary of the bonds benefits from more than $40 million in tax-exempt financing. Small-issue IDBs may be refunded in such cases only if (1) the maturity of the refunded bonds is not extended; (2) the amount of the refunding bonds does not exceed the outstanding amount of the refunded bonds; (3) the interest rate on the refunding bonds is lower than the rate on the refunded bonds; and (4) the refunded bonds are redeemed no later than 30 days after issuance of the refunding bonds (i.e., called so that no interest accrues on the refunded bonds after such time).

[*Effective date.*—Obligations issued after 12-31-83. Ed.]

[¶ 4182] SECTION 1867. AMENDMENTS RELATED TO SECTION 624 OF THE ACT

[Senate Explanation]

* * * * * *

Explanation of provisions.—* * * The bill corrects a reference to a resource recovery project of Essex County, New Jersey, contained in a transitional exception to the additional arbitrage restrictions for most IDBs. * * * and expands a transitional rule included in the Act for a Muskogee, Oklahoma project to include a limited exception from the arbitrage rebate rules for IDBs.

[*Effective date.*—Amendments made to the Tax Reform Act of 1984 extend exception to the arbitrage restrictions. Exception for N.J. applies to bonds authorized on 11-10-83 and approved on 7-7-81 and 12-31-81. For Okla., grant approved on 5-5-81 and obligation issued before 1-1-86. Ed.]

* * * * * *

[¶ 4183] SECTION 1868. AMENDMENT RELATED TO SECTION 625 OF THE ACT

[Senate Explanation]

* * * * *

Present law.—* * * The Act * * * directs the Treasury Department to prescribe regulations extending additional arbitrage restrictions similar to those for most IDBs to student loan bonds.

* * * * * *

Explanation of provisions.—* * * Additionally, the bill clarifies the application of an exception for refundings of student loan bonds in the case of a series of refundings.

[*Effective date.*—The amendments, relating to student loan bonds, are effective as to obligations issued after the earlier of the date the '65 Higher Education Act expires or the date such act is reauthorized after 7-18-84. Ed.]

* * * * * *

[¶ 4184] SECTION 1869. AMENDMENTS RELATED TO SECTION 626 OF THE ACT

[Senate Explanation]

*   *   *   *   *   *

Present law.—* * * The Act provides that interest on bonds generally is not tax-exempt if five percent or more of the proceeds is reasonably expected to be used, directly or indirectly, to make loans to nonexempt persons. Exceptions are provided for IDBs, qualified student loan bonds, mortgage revenue bonds, and for certain bonds used to finance assessments or taxes of general application for an essential governmental function.

As enacted in 1984, this restriction makes no distinction between bonds that are used to finance loans for businesses and bonds used to finance personal loans. For example, an issue may be in violation of this restriction if 5 percent or more, but no more than 25 percent, of the proceeds is used to provide financing that would be considered IDB-financing, but for the fact that bonds are not treated as IDBs if no more than 25 percent of the proceeds is used for a purpose described in section 103(b). Similarly, an obligation that would be an IDB except for the fact that the security interest test of section 103(b)(2)(B) is not satisfied may be in violation of this restriction.

*   *   *   *   *

Explanation of provision.—* * * The bill retitles consumer loan bonds "private loan bonds" to reflect the fact that, under that provision of the Act, all bonds issued to finance loans to nonexempt persons are subject to this restriction unless a specific exception is provided in the Code (e.g., the exceptions for IDBs, mortgage revenue bonds, qualified student loan bonds, and certain bonds to finance assessments or taxes of general application for an essential governmental function). This provision does not amend the substantive scope of the restriction, as enacted in 1984.

A transitional exception is provided for bonds issued before 1985 for the White Pine, Nevada power project, with respect to which indirect loans to nonexempt persons will be made through contracts providing the persons with a significant portion of the output of the facilities. Additional transitional exceptions are provided for (1) certain bonds for the Mead-Phoenix power project for which other transitional relief was provided in the Act; and (2) up to $27 million of bonds for the City of Baltimore, Maryland, to finance advances made by that City on or before October 19, 1983, pursuant to a voter referendum held before November 3, 1982, and (3) for certain bonds issued by the Eastern Maine Electric Cooperative with respect to Project No. 6, a joint venture with the Massachusetts Municipal Wholesale Electric Company.

[*Effective date.*—Amends the 1984 Tax Reform Act relating to consumer loan bonds, effective as to obligations issued after 7-18-84. Ed.]

[¶ 4186] SECTION 1871. AMENDMENTS RELATING TO SECTION 628 OF THE ACT

(Sec. 103 of the Code)

[Senate Explanation]

*   *   *   *   *   *

Present law.—The Act provides that bonds issued pursuant to provisions of law other than the Internal Revenue Code must satisfy appropriate Code requirements as a condition of tax-exemption. Examples of these requirements are the Code restrictions on IDBs, the arbitrage rules, the prohibition on Federal guarantees of tax-exempt bonds, the State volume limitations, and the public approval and information reporting requirements.

*   *   *   *   *   *

Explanation of provisions.—The bill clarifies that bonds issued pursuant to provisions of law other than the Code (non-Code bonds) must be issued in registered form. Additionally, the bill clarifies that the private (consumer) loan bond restriction applies to non-Code bonds. These clarifications are effective for bonds issued after March 28, 1985.

[*Effective date.*—Amendments relating to non-Code bonds, made to Sec. 103(m)(1), effective for bonds issued after 3-28-85. Conforming amendment, made to Sec. 103(b), effective as if included in the 1984 TRA. Ed.]

[¶ 4187] SECTION 1872. AMENDMENT RELATED TO SECTION 631 OF THE ACT

[Senate Explanation]

*   *   *   *   *   *

Present law.— * * * Section 631 of the Act provides effective dates for the various tax-exempt bond provisions for which (1) no separately stated effective dates are included as part of the section of the Act containing the substantive rule, or (2) no effective dates are provided by means of dates included within substantive rules identifying the bonds to which the rules apply. Transitional exceptions are provided with respect to many of the provisions for which the effective dates are provided in Act section 631. Additionally, special exceptions are provided in Act sections 631 and 632 for certain specifically described facilities.

*   *   *   *   *   *

Explanation of provision.— * * * The bill clarifies the private activity bond provisions to which the effective dates provided in Act section 631(c)(1) apply. These provisions are (1) the prohibition on Federal guarantees (Act sec. 622); (2) the aggregate limit for small issue bonds (Act sec. 623); (3) the restrictions on financing land, existing facilities, and certain specified facilities (Act sec. 627); (4) the rules relating to aggregation of certain related facilities, the definition of substantial user, and mixed use residential rental property (Act secs. 628(c), (d), and (e)); (5) the option for student loan bond authorities to issue taxable bonds (Act sec. 625(c)); (6) the public approval requirements for certain airports (Act sec. 628(f)); and (7) the authorization of tax-exempt financing for acquisition of a bankrupt railroad (Act sec. 629(b)).

The bill clarifies that the transitional exceptions contained in Act section 631(c)(3) apply only in the case of certain of the provisions enumerated in section 631(c)(1), as amended.

The bill further clarifies that the exception for obligations to finance facilities the construction, reconstruction, or rehabilitation of which was begun before October 19, 1983, applies only if the construction, reconstruction, or rehabilitation was completed on or after that date. Similarly, the exception for obligations issued to finance facilities with respect to which a binding contract to incur significant expenditures for construction, reconstruction, rehabilitation, or acquisition was entered into before October 19, 1983, applies only if some of the expenditures are incurred on or after that date. For purposes of the binding contract rule, payments under an installment payment agreement are incurred no later than the date on which the property that is the subject of the agreement is delivered rather than on the due date of each installment.

The two clarifications to these transitional exceptions requiring activity (e.g. construction) or expenditures after October 18, 1983,

apply to obligations issued after March 28, 1985; however, no inference is intended that the same rules, do not apply to obligations issued on or before that date.

The bill clarifies that, subject to transitional exceptions, the prohibition on tax-exempt financing for health clubs applies to obligations issued after April 12, 1984 (rather than December 31, 1983).

Further, the bill provides that the private loan bond restriction of the Act does not apply to tax-increment financing bonds issued on or before the date of the bill's enactment. Tax-increment financing bonds eligible for this exception are bonds substantially all of the proceeds of which are to be used to finance—

(1) sewer, street lighting, or other governmental improvements to real property,

(2) the acquisition of any interest in real property pursuant to the exercise of eminent domain (or the threat thereof), the preparation of such property for new use, or the transfer of such interest to a private developer, or

(3) payments of reasonable relocation costs of prior users of such real property.

All of these activities must be carried out pursuant to a redevelopment plan adopted before the bonds are issued by the governing body of the general governmental unit in which the real property being redeveloped is located. Repayment of the bonds must be secured by pledges of that portion of any increase in real property tax revenues (or their equivalent) attributable to the redevelopment resulting from the issue. (The fact that a governmental unit may pledge its full faith and credit in addition to incremental property tax revenues does not violate this requirement.) Also, no facilities located (or to be located) on land acquired with tax-increment financing bond proceeds may be subject to a real property or other tax based on a rate or valuation method which differs from the rate and valuation method applicable to any other similar property located in the general governmental unit in which the real property being redeveloped is located. (The fact that property located in different tax assessment districts is subject to different assessments does not violate this restriction as long as no special assessments are levied with regard to the redevelopment activities.)

[¶ 4188] SECTION 1873. AMENDMENTS RELATED TO SECTION 632 OF THE ACT

[Senate Explanation]

*   *   *   *   *   *

Present law.— * * * The Act restricts tax-exempt financing for the acquisition of existing facilities to cases where an amount equal to at least 15 percent of the bonds is spent on rehabilitation of a building and associated equipment. In the case of struc-

tures other than buildings, the rehabilitation expenditures must equal or exceed the amount of bond financing.

Explanation of provisions.— * * * The bill provides an exception from the small-issue IDB size limitations for specified amounts of bonds for three hydroelectric generating facilities (Hastings, Minnesota, Warren County, New York, and Los Banos,

California) output from which will be sold to a nongovernmental person pursuant to agreements in accordance with the Public Utilities Regulatory Policies Act of 1978 (PURPA). But for the amendment, the purchasers of power under these PURPA agreements would be treated as principal users of the facilities.

[*Effective date.*—Amendment, creating exceptions to the private activity bond rules, effective as if included in the 1984 Tax Return Act. Ed.]

[¶ 4189] SECTION 1875. AMENDMENTS RELATED TO TITLE VII OF THE ACT

(Secs. 58, 62, 219, 304, 402, 404, 408, 415, 1248, 3405, 6229, 6230, 2213, 6034A of the Code; Secs. 713, 714 of '84 TRA.)

[*Senate Explanation*]

* * * * * *

1. Miscellaneous corporate provision (*** sec. 304 of the Code)

Present Law.—Under present law, if a shareholder of a 50-percent owned corporation transfers stock of that corporation to another 50-percent owned corporation in exchange for property, the transaction is treated as a redemption of the shareholders' stock in the acquiring corporation. The transferred stock is considered to have been transferred by the shareholders as a contribution to capital of the acquiring corporation, and its basis is equal to the transferor's basis increased by any gain recognized to the transferor (sec. 362(a)).

Explanation of Provision.—The bill provides that the contribution to capital rule will not apply if the shareholder is treated as having exchanged its stock (under sec. 302(a). Thus, where section 302(a) applies, the acquiring corporation will be treated as purchasing the stock, for example, for purposes of section 338. The amendment is not intended to change the present law treatment of the shareholder (including the shareholder's basis in the stock of the acquiring corporation).

[*Effective date.*—Transfers occuring after 8-31-82 in TYEA that date. Ed.]

2. Miscellaneous pension provisions (*** secs. 62, 219, 402, 404, and 408 of the Code)

Present Law.—*Rollovers.* Under present law, as in effect before the Tax Equity and Fiscal Responsibility Act of 1982 (TEFRA), a 10-percent additional income tax applied to distributions before age 59½, death, or disability from a qualified plan to an owner-employee (a sole proprietor who owned the entire interest in an unincorporated trade or business or a partner who owned more than 10 percent of a partnership). TEFRA extended the additional income tax on such early withdrawals made to key employees (sec. 416(i). TEFRA did not, however, provide a conforming amendment to prevent avoidance of the tax through a tax-free rollover by a key employee to a plan in which the individual was not a key employee.

The Deficit Reduction Act of 1984 (DEFRA) provided a conforming amendment to prohibit rollovers by key employees to plans for which the additional tax on early withdrawals was inapplicable. However, DEFRA also amended the additional tax on early withdrawals to apply to individuals who are 5-percent owners of the employer, whether or not those individuals are key employees. Thus, after DEFRA, there continues to be a discrepancy between the class of individuals to whom the additional tax on early withdrawals applies (i.e., 5-percent owners) and the class of individuals for whom rollovers are restricted (i.e., key employees).

Excess contributions.—Under prior law, contributions made to a qualified plan on behalf of a self-employed individual in excess of the amount deductible for the taxable year were subject to an excise tax, unless the excess was withdrawn before the due date of the tax return. DEFRA repealed this tax on excess contributions and the provision relating to the return of excess contributions, effective for taxable years beginning after December 31, 1983.

Deduction limits for self-employed individuals.—Generally, effective for years beginning after December 31, 1983, TEFRA revised the definition of earned income so that the amount taken into account as the earned income of a self-employed individual corresponds to the amount of compensation of a common-law employee. Under TEFRA, in applying the rules relating to deductions and limitations under qualified plans, the earned income of a self-employed individual was computed after taking into account contributions by the employer to a qualified plan to the extent a deduction is allowed for the contributions. This provision was not intended to apply for purposes of determining whether contributions made on behalf of a self-employed individual are ordinary and necessary business expenses.

IRAs, SEPs.—TEFRA generally increased the overall limits on contributions and benefits attributable to self-employed individuals to conform to the generally applicable limits under qualified plans.

Overall limits—Generally, effective for years ending after July 1, 1982, TEFRA reduced the overall limits on contributions and benefits under qualified plans, tax-sheltered annuity programs, and simplified employee pensions (SEPs). TEFRA also provided rules for calculating the dollar limits applicable to alternate forms of benefits, benefits commencing prior to age 62, and benefits commencing after age 65. In calculating employer contributions required to fund benefit amounts not in excess of those limits (and deductions for those contributions), TEFRA provided that anticipated cost-of-living increases are not taken into account.

Pension withholding.—Under present law, payors generally are required to withhold tax from a designated distribution (the taxable part of a payment made from or under a pension, profit-sharing, stock bonus, or annuity plan, an IRA, a commercial annuity, and certain deferred compensation plans), unless the recipient elects not to have withholding apply. The withholding rules do not apply to certain distributions, such as those distributions that are otherwise considered wages.

Contributions on behalf of disabled individuals.—TEFRA permitted an employer to elect to continue making deductible contributions to a profit-sharing or stock bonus plan on behalf of a permanently and totally disabled employee who has separated from service. A similar rule does not apply for contributions to a money purchase pension plan.

Explanation of Provisions.—*Rollovers.* The bill coordinates the rules relating to qualifying rollover distributions (secs. 402(a)(5)(F)(ii) and 408(d)(3)) with those applicable to the additional income tax on early withdrawals. Distributions made after the date of enactment of this bill to or on behalf of an individual who is a 5-percent owner at the time of distribution may not be rolled over to a qualified plan.

The bill provides that distributions after December 31, 1983, but before July 18, 1984, may not be rolled over to a qualified plan if any part of the distribution is attributable to contributions made on behalf of an owner-employee. In addition, distributions made after July 18, 1984, but before the enactment of this bill, may not be rolled over to a qualified plan if any part of the distribution is a benefit attributable to contributions made on behalf of an employee while a key employee (but only if the individual is a key employee on account of status as a 5-percent owner) in a top-heavy plan.

See, however, the provisions of the bill relating to the extension of the additional income tax to all participants under tax-favored retirement arrangements. For years beginning on or after the effective date of those provisions, the restrictions on rollovers are repealed as deadwood because the additional tax on early withdrawals would apply to distributions from any plan without regard to the recipient's status as a 5-percent owner with respect to the plan making the distribution.

Excess contributions.—The bill makes it clear that the repeal by DEFRA of the rule relating to the return of excess contributions made on behalf of a self-employed individual applies with respect to contributions made in taxable years beginning after December 31, 1983.

IRAs, SEPs.—The bill conforms the limits on certain distributions of excess IRA contributions and the limits on employer contributions on behalf of certain officers, shareholders, or owner employees to SEPs to the dollar limit on annual additions to a qualified

defined contribution plan. This provision is effective as if enacted in TEFRA.

Overall limits.—The bill makes it clear that the rule precluding deductions based on anticipated cost-of-living adjustments to the overall benefit limits applies to limit benefits payable as a single life annuity commencing at age 62, as well as benefits paid in alternate forms, those commencing prior to age 62, and those commencing after age 65.

* * * * * *

[Conference Report]

* * * * *

a. *Tax-sheltered annuities.*—The provision in the House bill requiring that distributions commence under a tax-sheltered annuity no later than when the employee attains age 70½ is adopted.

* * * * * *

[Senate Explanation]

* * * * * *

Deduction limits for self-employed individuals.—The bill makes it clear that the DEFRA amendment to the definition of earned income did not change the TEFRA definition of earned income for purposes of the 15- or 25-percent limits on deductions (sec. 404). Rather, the change permitting earned income of a self-employed individual to be determined without regard to the deductions allowable for contributions to a qualified plan is to apply solely for purposes of determining the extent to which contributions made to a qualified plan are ordinary and necessary business expenses for purposes of the deduction rules (sec. 404(a)(8)(C)).

This provision is effective as if enacted in TEFRA. The DEFRA amendment, which had the effect of increasing the amount deductible on behalf of a self-employed individual to 15 or 25 percent of earned income before reduction for contributions to the plan on behalf of the self-employed individual, rather than 15 or 25 percent of earned income after reduction for contributions to the plan on behalf of the self-employed individual, is repealed, effective for taxable years beginning after December 31, 1984.

The bill also clarifies that the deduction available to a self-employed individual for contributions to a qualified plan is not necessarily limited to the cost of actual benefits provided for, or allocations to, the individual. Rather, subject to the usual deduction rules (sec. 404), a self-employed individual is permitted to deduct the allocable share of contributions to a qualified plan. This clarification is effective as if enacted in TEFRA.

Pension withholding.—The bill includes distributions of dividends for which employer is permitted a deduction (sec. 404(k)) in the list of distributions to which the withholding rules do not apply.

Contributions on behalf of disabled individuals.—The bill provides that deductible contributions may be continued on behalf of

Act § 1875   ¶ 4189

a permanently and totally disabled employee to any defined contribution plan, including a money purchase pension plan.

3. Effective date of provision relating to interest on tentative carrybacks and refund adjustments (* sec. 6611(f) of the Code and sec. 714(n)(2) of the Act)**

Present Law.—The Act provided that, for purposes of computing interest on refunds arising from net operating loss carrybacks where a tentative adjustment claim is filed, the refund is treated as filed on the date that the tentative adjustment claim is filed. Prior to this amendment, some taxpayers filed an amended return claiming a refund based on a carryback, waited until the expiration of the 45-day period within which, if a refund is made, no interest is paid, and then filed for a tentative adjustment, which provides for rapid payment. These taxpayers consequently defeated the intent of the interest rules relating to tentative adjustments by obtaining interest on the tentative adjustment relating back to the due date of the return for the year of the loss. The provision of the Act that prevented this misapplication of the intended rules relating to the payment of interest was added to the Act in conference and was effective as if it were included in the Tax Equity and Fiscal Responsibility Act of 1982.

Explanation of Provision.—The bill provides that the provision of the Act (sec. 714(n)(2)) relating to interest on tentative carrybacks and refund adjustments is effec-

tive only with respect to applications filed after July 18, 1984.

* * * * * *

[Conference Report]

* * * * * *

b. Estate tax exclusion.—The provision modifying the grandfather rule relating to the repeal in the Act (and the reduction in TEFRA) of the estate tax exclusion for pension benefits is further modified to provide that the grandfather rule is also available for individuals who separated from service before January 1, 1985, with respect to section 525(b)(2) of the Act, or before January 1, 1983, with respect to section 245(c) of TEFRA, elected a form of benefits to be paid in the future, and who was not in pay status as of the applicable dates.

c. Multiemployer Pension Plan Amendments Act effective date.—The change in the effective date of the Multiemployer Pension Plan Amendments Act of 1980 with respect to a certain employer is modified to change the effective date from January 12, 1982, to January 16, 1982, and from May 16, 1980, to May 14, 1980, in the case of another employer.

[Effective Date.—Unless otherwise specified above, this section shall take effect as if included in the provisions to which it relates in the 1984 Tax Reform Act. For a breakdown by subsection, see Table of Effective Dates at Act Sec. 1875. Ed.]

[¶4190] SECTION 1876. AMENDMENTS RELATED TO TITLE VIII OF THE ACT

(Secs. 245, 291, 902, 904, 906, 923, 924, 927, 995, 996, and 1248 of the Code)

[Senate Explanation]

* * * * * *

Treatment of income that a FSC earns without using administrative pricing rules * * *

Present Law.—In general, the Act exempts a fraction of the foreign trade income of a Foreign Sales Corporation (FSC) from tax. The fraction is 15/23 if the FSC uses an administrative pricing rule to determine its income (16/23 if the FSC shareholder is not a corporation). The Act generally denies foreign tax credits for taxes imposed on foreign trade income, but allows a 100-percent dividends received deduction for dividends distributed out of earnings and profits of a FSC that are attributable to that income.

Different rules apply, however, when a FSC does not use the Act's administrative pricing rules. Then, a fraction (generally 30 or 32 percent) of the FSC's foreign trade income is exempt from U.S. tax, and the balance (70 or 68 percent) is so-called "section 923(a)(2) non-exempt income." In general, this section 923(a)(2) non-exempt income is subject to one of three sets of pre-existing rules governing income of foreign corpora-

tions generally. It may be taxable currently to the FSC as income effectively connected with a U.S. trade or business. It may be taxable to the FSC's U.S. shareholders under the anti-avoidance rules of subpart F. It may be exempt from current taxation, and taxable only on repatriation to U.S. shareholders.

The Act makes this section 923(a)(2) non-exempt income ineligible for some treatment that it applies to other foreign trade income. For instance, foreign taxes on this income may be creditable, but distributions out of earnings and profits attributable to this income are not eligible for the 100-percent dividends received deduction.

Explanation of Provision.—The bill conforms the treatment of effectively connected foreign trade income that a FSC earns without administrative pricing rules (effectively connected section 923(a)(2) non-exempt income) to that of other effectively connected foreign trade income. Taxes on that income are not creditable, but the bill allows a 100-percent dividends received deduction for dividends distributed out of earnings and profits of a FSC that are attributable to that income. That is, this income will be subject to full U.S. tax at the FSC level, but not again at the shareholder level.

[*Effective date.*—Generally, transactions after 12-31-84 in taxable years ending after such date. Ed.]

Treatment of foreign trade income under section 1248 * * *

Present Law.—Section 1248 treats gain realized by certain U.S. persons on the disposition of stock in a foreign corporation as ordinary income to the extent of allocable earnings and profits. The Act excluded all FSC earnings and profits attributable to foreign trade income from ordinary income treatment under section 1248, whether or not those earnings would have been eligible for the 100 percent dividends received deduction had the FSC distributed them.

Explanation of Provision.—The bill refines the Act's restriction of section 1248 ordinary income treatment on disposition of FSC shares. It provides that FSC earnings and profits that would be taxable on a distribution are subject to ordinary income treatment under section 1248.

Clarification of corporate preference cutbacks * * *

Present Law.—Present law provides for a reduction in certain corporate tax preferences. The Act, in extending this reduction of corporate preferences, sought to reduce the exempt portion of the foreign trade income of a FSC by 1/17 if the shareholder of the FSC is a corporation. The statute indicates that the cutback applies "with respect to" the corporate shareholder of the FSC. Congress intended that the cutback apply at the FSC level, which would reduce the portion of the FSC's foreign trade income that is exempt from tax at that level.

Present law provides a similar reduction in benefits in the case of deferred DISC income. A shareholder of a DISC is treated as having received a distribution taxable as a dividend equal to 1/17 of the excess of the taxable income of the DISC over certain other deemed distributions. The reduction in benefits applies whether or not the shareholder of the DISC is a corporation. Congress intended to limit this cutback to cases where the shareholder of the DISC is a corporation.

Congress intended that the amount of deemed DISC distribution attributable to international boycott activities be computed by multiplying 16/17 of the excess taxable income by the international boycott factor. Present law erroneously indicates that the deemed distribution is computed by multiplying 1/17 of the excess taxable income by the international boycott factor.

Explanation of Provision.—The bill clarifies that the FSC preference cutback applies with respect to the FSC, rather than the corporate shareholder of the FSC. The exempt portion of foreign trade income is reduced from 32 to 30 percent in cases in which income is determined without regard to the administrative pricing rules, and from 16/23 to 15/23 in cases in which income is determined under the administrative pricing rules. The bill also provides that the portion

of foreign trade income that is exempt will be adjusted, under regulations, to take into account any shareholders that are not C corporations for whom there is no preference cutback.

The bill also clarifies that the deemed distribution of 1/17 of the excess taxable income of the DISC applies only in the case of a shareholder which is a C corporation. Neither the FSC nor the DISC corporate preference cutback applies when an S corporation is the shareholder.

In addition, the bill corrects the method for computing the amount of the deemed distribution attributable to international boycott activities. This amount is computed by multiplying 16/17 of the excess taxable income by the international boycott factor.

[*Effective date.*—Generally, transactions after 12-31-84 in taxable years ending after such date. Ed.]

Treatment of foreign trade income under subpart F (* * *)

Present Law.—The Act contains a sentence designed to prevent shareholder level taxation under Subpart F's anti-avoidance rules of income already taxed at the FSC level. That sentence appears in a Code provision designed to prevent shareholder level taxation of earnings and profits attributable to most foreign trade income, whether or not taxed at the FSC level.

Explanation of Provision.—The bill makes it clear that there is to be no shareholder level taxation under Subpart F's anti-avoidance rules of income already taxed at the FSC level.

[*Effective date.*—Generally, transactions after 12-31-84 in taxable years ending after such date. Ed.]

Dividends received deduction for certain distributions from a FSC (* * *)

Present Law.—Present and prior law allow an 85-percent dividends received deduction for dividends received from a foreign corporation if half or more of the foreign corporation's gross income (over a 3-year period) is effectively connected with the conduct of a U.S. trade or business. This 85-percent deduction applies, on a pro rata basis, to the extent that the foreign corporation's gross income is effectively connected income.

The Act treats all interest, dividends, royalties, and other investment income received or accrued by a FSC as income effectively connected with a trade or business conducted through a permanent establishment in the United States. If enough of a FSC's income is effectively connected, the FSC will meet the 50-percent of gross income test that will qualify its U.S. corporate shareholders for the 85-percent dividends received deduction for dividends attributable to this passive income. If the FSC does not meet the 50-percent of gross income test, however, then none of its dividends attributable to passive income will be eligible for the 85-

percent dividends received deduction. Whether the FSC meets the 50-percent of gross income test depends on a number of factors.

The Act also provides a 100-percent dividends received deduction for distributions out of earnings and profits attributable to foreign trade income of a FSC other than section 923(a)(2) non-exempt income.

Explanation of Provision.—In general, the bill provides an 85-percent dividends received deduction for any dividend received by a U.S. corporation from a FSC that is distributed out of earnings and profits attributable to "qualified interest and carrying charges." Qualified interest and carrying charges mean interest or carrying charges derived from a transaction that results in foreign trade income. Passive income that is not directly related to foreign trade income is not eligible for this treatment.

In addition, the bill specifies that gross income giving rise to earnings and profits attributable to foreign trade income or to qualified interest and carrying charges of a FSC will not be taken into account for purposes of calculating a dividends received deduction under the general rules (with respect to other income of the FSC). Thus, for example, such income will not be taken into account in determining whether a dividend attributable to such other income allows a dividends received deduction because half or more of the FSC's gross income is effectively connected with a U.S. trade or business.

[*Effective date.*—Generally, transactions after 12-31-84 in taxable years ending after such date. Ed.]

Separate foreign tax credit limitation for FSC income (* * *)

Present Law.—Distributions from a FSC or former FSC out of earnings and profits attributable to foreign trade income are subject to a separate foreign tax credit limitation.

Explanation of Provision.—Under the bill, distributions from a FSC or former FSC out of earnings and profits attributable to foreign trade income or qualifying interest and carrying charges are subject to a separate foreign tax credit limitation. The purpose of this provision is to prevent this income from absorbing foreign tax credits from other income, and to prevent other income from absorbing foreign tax credits (if any are allowable) on this income.

[*Effective date.*—Generally, transactions after 12-31-84 in taxable years ending after such date. Ed.]

Coordination of foreign tax credit for foreign corporations and deemed paid credit (* * *)

Present Law.—A foreign corporation may credit foreign taxes imposed on income that is effectively connected with the conduct of a trade or business in the United States (sec. 906). A corporate U.S. shareholder owning 10 percent or more of the voting stock of a foreign corporation may be eligible for a deemed paid foreign tax credit when the corporation pays a dividend (sec. 902). This

deemed paid credit allows such a U.S. shareholder to credit again the taxes that the foreign corporation paid. If enough of the foreign corporation's income is effectively connected, its U.S. shareholders may be eligible for a dividends received deduction for the dividends the foreign corporation pays them.

The Act makes all investment income of a FSC effectively connected income. It generally makes the taxable portion of foreign trade income of a FSC effectively connected income.

Explanation of Provision.—The bill provides that taxes paid or accrued with respect to, and accumulated profits attributable to, income of a foreign corporation that is effectively connected with the conduct of a trade or business within the United States shall not be taken into account for purposes of the deemed paid credit. This provision is designed to prevent a double tax benefit.

[*Effective date.*—Transactions after 12-31-84. Ed.]

Exchange of information requirements (* * *)

Present Law.—A corporation (other than a corporation formed in an eligible U.S. possession) cannot qualify as a FSC unless there was in effect, at the time of creation or organization of the FSC, with the foreign country under whose laws it was created or organized, either (1) an agreement allowing tax benefits under the Caribbean Basin Initiative, or (2) an income tax treaty with respect to which the Secretary of the Treasury certifies that the exchange of information program with respect to the country carries out the purposes of paragraph 927(e)(3) of the Code. The purposes of that paragraph are not specified in the statute. An agreement under the Caribbean Basin Initiative must generally provide for disclosure for civil tax purposes of information that is otherwise confidential under local law, but may provide for nondisclosure of such information if the President determines that the agreement as negotiated is in the national security interest of the United States.

A FSC (other than a small FSC) must maintain its principal bank account outside the United States at all times during the taxable year.

Explanation of Provision.—The bill provides that a corporation cannot continue to qualify as a FSC if its country of incorporation, having once qualified as a host country for FSCs, ceases to qualify. Notwithstanding a Treasury determination that a country ceases to qualify, under Treasury regulations, corporations established in that country continue to be eligible for FSC benefits for the six months following the determination.

The bill also makes it clear that a country may qualify as a host country for FSCs by entering into an exchange of information agreement of the type that allows tax benefits under the Caribbean Basin Initiative, whether or not that country is eligible to be a beneficiary of the Caribbean Basin Initiative. The bill also specifies that the national security exception under the Caribbean Basin Initiative will not apply for purposes of FSC; thus, to be acceptable for FSC purposes, an exchange of information agreement must require disclosure of confidential information.

The bill also makes it clear that an income tax treaty will allow a country to qualify as a host country for FSCs only if the Secretary certifies that its exchange of information program is satisfactory in practice for purposes of the Internal Revenue Code. That is, the program should provide to the United States in practice such information as may be relevant to the determination of a U.S. tax liability or whether a tax-related criminal offense has been committed.

In addition, the bill makes it clear that, for a corporation to qualify as a FSC, the exchange of information program of the country of its incorporation must cover that particular corporation. The bill makes it clear, for example, that a corporation incorporated in a treaty partner country but not subject to the exchange of information program of the treaty because it is not resident in the treaty partner does not qualify for FSC status.

The bill makes it clear that a FSC (other than a small FSC) must maintain its principal bank account in a possession of the United States or in a country that qualifies as a host country for FSCs at all times during the taxable year. This requirement is effective for periods after March 28, 1985.

[*Effective date.*—Generally, transactions after 12-31-84 in taxable years ending after such date, except bank account rule. Ed.]

Coordination with possessions taxation (* * *)

Present Law.—Under present law, a possession of the United States may not impose a tax on any foreign trade income of a FSC that is derived before January 1, 1987. Foreign trade income is generally the gross income of a FSC attributable to the sale or lease of export property outside the United States. Thus, foreign trade income may be derived from the sale or lease of export property (or performance of services) within a U.S. possession by a FSC located in the possession. Congress intended, with respect to any foreign trade income or passive income of a FSC that a possession is permitted to tax, that the possession would also be permitted to exempt such income from tax. In some cases, U.S. tax imposed on certain income connected with a possession is covered over to the possession.

Explanation of Provision.—The bill provides that a U.S. possession is not prohibited from imposing a tax on any income attributable to the sale of property or the performance of services for use, consumption or disposition within the possession. Thus, for example, the Virgin Islands is not prohibited from imposing a tax on the income derived from the sale of goods by a U.S. company, through its FSC located in the Virgin Islands, to customers in the Virgin Islands.

The bill clarifies that no provision of law may be construed as prohibiting a U.S. possession from exempting from tax any foreign trade income or passive income (e.g., interest, dividends or carrying charges) of a FSC. The bill also clarifies that no provision of law may be construed as requiring any income tax imposed by the United States on a FSC to be covered over (or otherwise transferred) to any U.S. possession.

[*Effective date.*—Generally, transactions after 12-31-84 in taxable years ending after such date. Ed.]

Interest on DISC-related deferred tax liability (* * *)

Present Law.—A DISC may defer income attributable to $10 million or less of qualified export receipts. However, an interest charge is imposed on the shareholders of the DISC. The amount of the interest is based on the tax otherwise due on the deferred income, computed as if the income were distributed.

Explanation of Provision.—The bill clarifies that an interest charge is to be imposed on the deferred income of a former DISC in the same manner that it is imposed on a DISC.

[*Effective date.*—Generally, transactions after 12-31-84 in taxable years ending after such date. Ed.]

Exemption of accumulated DISC income (* * *)

Present Law.—Accumulated DISC income which is derived before January 1, 1985 is generally exempt from tax. This result is achieved by treating actual distributions made after December 31, 1984 by a DISC (or former DISC which was a DISC on December 31, 1984) as previously taxed income with respect to which there had previously been a deemed distribution. It is unclear under present law whether a distribution in liquidation is an "actual distribution" for purposes of this provision. It is also unclear how such a distribution would be treated for purposes of computing the earnings and profits of any corporate shareholder of the DISC.

Explanation of Provision.—The bill clarifies that for purposes of exempting from tax accumulated DISC income, the term actual distribution includes a distribution in liquidation. The bill further clarifies that the earnings and profits of any corporation receiving a distribution that is not included in gross income because it is treated as previously taxed income under this provision will be increased by the amount of the distribution.

[*Effective date.*—Generally, transactions after 12-31-84 in taxable years ending after such date. Ed.]

Effective date of tax year conformity requirement.

Present Law.—In general, the taxable year of any DISC must be the taxable year of its owner. If the DISC has more than one shareholder, the taxable year of shareholders with a plurality of voting power controls.

This rule applies to any DISC established after March 21, 1984.

Explanation of Provision.—The bill provides that the rule requiring conformity of tax years applies to taxable years beginning after December 31, 1984. The bill makes it clear that this rule will apply to interest-charge DISCs, whether or not newly formed.

[*Effective date.*—Effective for taxable years beginning after 12-31-84. Ed.]

Treatment of certain qualifying distributions from a DISC * * *

Present Law.—To qualify as a DISC, 95 percent of a corporation's gross receipts must be "qualified export receipts." If a corporation seeking to qualify as a DISC does not meet that 95-percent test for a year, it may, after that year's close, qualify retroactively by distributing to its shareholders property in an amount equal to taxable income attributable to gross receipts that are not qualified export receipts. Generally, under prior law, one-half of this kind of distribution to meet qualification requirements was treated as coming out of accumulated DISC income, and one-half was treated as coming out of previously taxed income. Under prior law, generally, one-half of a DISC's income was deemed distributed to its shareholders. The treatment of a distribution to meet qualification requirements was based on the notion that one-half of a DISC's taxable income attributable to all gross receipts had already been taxed as a deemed distribution, while the other half was deferred. Under the Act, one-seventeenth of a DISC's income is deemed distributed to shareholders that are C corporations.

Explanation of Provision.—In the case of a shareholder that is a C corporation, the bill would treat 16/17 of a DISC's distribution to meet the qualified export receipts requirement as coming out of accumulated DISC income, with generally only 1/17 coming out of previously taxed income. This treatment reflects the post-1984 treatment of DISC income attributable to a shareholder that is a C corporation, whereunder only 1/17 is deemed distributed and taxed currently.

[*Effective date.*—Generally, transactions after 12-31-84 in taxable years ending after such date. Ed.]

Treatment of certain receipts from another FSC * * *

Present Law.—A FSC cannot treat as foreign trading gross receipts any receipts from another FSC that is a member of the same controlled group (Code sec. 924(f)(1)). The prohibition of sales through related FSCs prevents pyramiding of benefits under the gross receipts method of calculating income.

Explanation of Provision.—The bill permits FSCs to treat receipts from another FSC that is a member of the same controlled group as foreign trading gross receipts, if no FSC in the group uses the gross receipts method of calculating income.

[*Effective date.*—Generally, transactions after 12-31-84 in taxable years ending after such date. Ed.]

Treatment of certain former export trade corporations * * *

Present Law.—The Act provides that accumulated DISC income, in certain circumstances, will not be subject to U.S. tax. Similarly, the Act provides that certain income of active export trade corporations (as defined in Code sec. 971) will not be subject to U.S. tax, but only if the export trade corporation either elects to be treated as a FSC or surrenders its export trade corporation status.

Explanation of Provision.—The bill extends to corporations that had been export trade corporations at some point but that were not export trade corporations for their most recent taxable years ending before July 18, 1984, the same treatment that the Act extended to active export trade corporations. To qualify for this treatment, a former export trade corporation either must be precluded (under statutory rules) from again qualifying as an export trade corporation, or must elect never again to qualify as such.

[*Effective date.*—Effective for elections within six months after '86 TRA enactment date. Ed.]

Distributions of accumulated DISC income received by cooperatives ***

Present Law.—The Act excludes from gross income certain distributions of accumulated DISC income. That exclusion applies to certain accumulated DISC income received by certain cooperative organizations.

Explanation of Provision.—The bill provides that amounts excluded from the gross income of a cooperative organization described in Code section 1381 by sec. 805(b)(2)(A) of the Act will not be included in the gross income of the cooperative's members when distributed to them. Distributions arising from tax-free accumulated DISC income will not be deductible by the cooperative organization. This treatment reflects the concept that a cooperative organization is a flow-through entity analogous to a partnership for the purpose of the exclusion of certain accumulated DISC income from tax.

[*Effective date.*—Generally, transactions after 12-31-84 in taxable years ending after such date. Ed.]

* * * * * *

[House Explanation]

* * * * * *

Effective date of certain FSC requirements ***

Present Law.—The foreign management and foreign economic process requirements for eligibility for FSC benefits (Code sec. 924(c) and (d)) generally apply in taxable years ending after December 31, 1984. Transition rules are provided for existing contracts taken over by a FSC. Thus, those requirements do not apply with respect to contracts entered into (or planned to be entered into) before March 16, 1984, with respect to which the taxpayer uses the completed contract method of accounting. In addition, those requirements do not apply for the first two taxable years of a FSC ending after January 1, 1985, with respect to contracts entered into before March 16, 1984. Finally, those requirements do not apply for the first taxable year of a FSC ending after January 1, 1985, with respect to contracts entered into after March 15, 1984, and before January 1, 1985.

Code section 925(c) provides that a FSC may use the administrative pricing rules only if certain activities with respect to a sale are performed by or on behalf of the FSC. The Act did not provide a transition rule for this requirement.

Explanation of Provision.—The bill provides that any requirement of Code section 924(c) or (d), or section 925(c) that should have been met before January 1, 1985, will be treated as having been met with respect to any lease entered into before that date for a period longer than three years. Those re-

quirements will also be treated as having been met with respect to any contract entered into before January 1, 1985, with respect to which the taxpayer uses the completed contract method of accounting. Finally, in the case of any other contract entered into before January 1, 1985, those requirements will be treated as having been met, but only with respect to the first three taxable years of a FSC ending after January 1, 1985, or such later taxable years as the Secretary may prescribe.

[*Effective date.*—Generally, transactions after 12-31-84 in taxable years ending after such date. Ed.]

*   *   *   *   *   *

[Conference Report]

*   *   *   *   *   *

The conference agreement * * * [provides] a targeted transitional amendment to the separate foreign tax credit limitation for income of foreign finance subsidiaries.

[¶ 4191] SECTION 1877. AMENDMENTS RELATED TO TITLE IX OF THE ACT

(Sec. 6427(b) of the Code)

[Senate Explanation]

*   *   *   *   *   *

Present Law.—The Act allows a complete refund of the 15-cents-a-gallon excise tax paid on diesel fuel which is used by private contractors to provide scheduled local bus service to the general public over regular routes, because the service substitutes for publicly provided service that would use tax-exempt fuel. However, the Act failed to provide a complete refund when private contractors supply school bus service, the diesel fuel for which would be tax-exempt if the service were supplied by a State or local government or nonprofit school. The effective excise tax rate on this fuel is 3 cents a gallon (tax of 15 cents a gallon, less refund of 12 cents a gallon), the effective rate that generally applies to diesel fuel used in privately operated buses.

Explanation of Provision.—The bill allows a full 15-cents-a-gallon refund of excise tax on diesel fuel used in a school bus while engaged in the transportation of students and school employees.

[Effective date.—8-1-84. Ed.]

[House Explanation]

*   *   *   *   *   *

Present Law.—A 12-percent excise tax is imposed on the first retail sale of a heavy truck trailer. The Act temporarily reduced this excise tax rate to 6 percent for piggyback trailers (truck trailers equipped to be lifted onto and transported by railroad flatcars) sold after July 17, 1984, and before July 18, 1985. An additional tax is imposed if and when a trailer that was taxed at this reduced rate subsequently fails to qualify for it because, for example, the trailer is no longer used principally in connection with trailer-on-flatcar service. This additional tax equals the 6-percent excise tax that was not collected on the first retail sale by virtue of the temporarily reduced rate for piggyback trailers.

Explanation of Provision.—The additional 6-percent excise tax imposed by section 4051(d)(3) will not apply to a piggyback trailer after 6 years have elapsed from the date of the first retail sale of the trailer.

[¶ 4192] SECTION 1878. AMENDMENTS RELATED TO TITLE X OF THE ACT

(Secs. 51, 514, 852, 4041, 4162 and 4261 of the Code and Secs. 1001, 1028, 1041, 1063, and 1065 of the '84 TRA.)

[Senate Explanation]

*   *   *   *   *   *

[1.] Certain helicopter uses exempt from aviation excise taxes (*** secs. 4041 and 4261 of the Code)

Present Law.—The Act expands the exemptions from the aviation excise taxes previously provided with respect to helicopters engaged in qualified timber and hard mineral resource activities where no FAA navigational facilities or airport are used to include helicopters engaged in qualified oil and gas activities.

Explanation of Provision.—The bill clarifies that the exemptions for oil and gas activities are coterminous with those previously provided for hard mineral resource activities. Therefore, helicopters engaged in the exploration for, or the development or removal of, oil and gas will be exempt from the aviation excise taxes, provided the helicopters do not use Federally aided airports or Federal airway facilities.

[*Effective date.*—4-1-84 for fuel tax exemption; transportation beginning after 3-31-84 for amounts paid after that date. Ed.]

[2.] Acquisition indebtedness of certain exempt organizations (*** sec. 514(c)(9) of the Code)

Present Law.—The Act provided rules excepting certain debt-financed real estate held by qualified pension trusts and educational institutions from the unrelated business income tax. In the case where the exempt organization is a partner in a partnership (along with taxable entities), the Act provided that each allocation to the exempt organization be a qualified allocation, within the meaning of the tax-exempt entity leasing rules of section 168(j)(9).

Explanation of Provision.—The bill provides that the Secretary may treat the qualified allocation rule as met if it is shown to the satisfaction of the Secretary that there is no potential for tax avoidance. For example, if the partnership elects 40-year straight-line depreciation on leased real estate and if the failure to meet the qualification allocation rule is caused by the allocation of an increased share of a loss or deduction to the exempt organization in order to meet the substantial economic effect requirement of section 704(b)(2), it is expected that the Secretary would treat the new rule as having been met.

[*Effective date.*—Indebtedness incurred after 7-18-84 with a transitional rule for partnerships. Ed]

[3.] Military housing rollover (* * * sec. 1034(h)(2) of the Code)

Present Law.—The Act provides an extended nonrecognition period for rollover of gain on sale of a personal residence in the case of military personnel stationed outside the United States, or required to reside in government quarters at certain remote base sites within the United States. In such a case, the nonrecognition rollover period otherwise allowable under Code section 1034(h)(1) is not to expire until the last day on which the person is stationed outside the United States or is required to reside in government quarters at a remote base site within the United States, except that this extended nonrecognition period cannot exceed eight years after the date of the sale of the old residence. This provision applies to sales of old residences occurring after July 18, 1984.

Explanation of Provision.—The extended nonrecognition period under Code section

1034(h)(2) is not to expire before the day which is one year after the last day on which the taxpayer is stationed outside the United States or is required to reside in government quarters at a remote base site within the United States, except that this extended nonrecognition period cannot exceed eight years after the date of the sale of the old residence. This modification conforms the provision to the Senate amendment, which was adopted by the conference committee on the 1984 Act.

[*Effective date.*—Sale of old residences after 7-18-84. Ed.]

[5.] Effective date for disallowance of deduction for costs of demolishing structures (*** sec. 280B of the Code)

Present Law.—Costs and other losses incurred in connection with the demolition of buildings must be added to the basis of the land on which the demolished buildings were located in all cases, rather than claimed as a current deduction. Before enactment of the Act, this rule applied only to certified historic structures. The expanded provision is effective for taxable years beginning after December 31, 1983.

Explanation of Provision.—The bill clarifies that the expanded prohibition on current deduction of costs and other losses incurred in connection with demolition applies only to demolitions commencing after July 18, 1984, in the case of buildings other than certified historic structures. For this purpose, if a demolition is delayed until the completion of the replacement structure on the same site, the demolition shall be treated as commencing when construction of the replacement structure commences.

The bill also allows the unrecognized basis in specified demolished structures to be allowed as an ordinary deduction in the year of demolition.

A transitional rule is provided in a specified case where plans for the demolition were in place on July 18, 1984.

[*Effective date.*—Demolitions (other than of certified historic structures) beginning after 7-19-84 in taxable years beginning after 12-31-83; some special rules apply. Ed.]

[5.] Regulated investment companies (sec. 1878(i) of the bill and sec. 852 of the Code)

Present Law.—All regulated investment companies (RICs) are required to comply with regulations prescribed by the Treasury for the purpose of ascertaining its stock ownership (sec. 852(a)(2)). Under present law, as modified by the Act, a personal holding company may be eligible to be a RIC. The Act provided that any investment company taxable income of a RIC that is a personal holding company is taxed at the highest rate applicable to corporations.

Explanation of Provision.—The provisions of the Act that permitted personal holding companies to qualify as RICs eliminated the necessity for a RIC to keep shareholder records that were intended to assure that it was not a personal holding company and thereby could qualify as a RIC. Accordingly, the bill eliminates the requirement that adequate shareholder records must be kept in order for a corporation to qualify as a RIC. Nevertheless, the bill provides that the investment company taxable income of a RIC that does not keep such records would be subject to tax at the highest corporate rate, since such treatment is provided for RICs that are personal holding companies.

[*Effective date.*—Taxable years beginning after 12-31-82 generally. Ed.]

[*Effective Date.—Unless otherwise specified above, this section shall take effect as if included in the provisions to which it relates in the 1984 Tax Reform Act. Ed.]*

[¶ 4193] SECTION 1879. MISCELLANEOUS PROVISIONS

(Sec. 28, 29, 48, 368, 401, 501, 1361, 1368, 2523, 4991, 6030D, 6405, 6654, 6655, and 7652 of the Code and TEFRA Sec. 292)

[Senate Explanation]

* * * * * *

Waiver of estimated tax penalties ***

Present Law.—Under present law, if the withholding of income taxes from wages does not cover an individual's total income tax liability, the individual, in general, is required to file estimated tax returns and make estimated tax payments. Also, corporations are normally required to make quarterly estimated tax payments. An underpayment of an estimated tax installment will, unless certain exceptions are applicable, result in the imposition of an addition to tax on the amount of underpayment for the period of underpayment (secs. 6654 and 6655, with the rate as determined under sec. 6621).

The Act, enacted on July 18, 1984, made several changes which increased tax liabilities from the beginning of 1984.

Explanation of Provision.—The bill allows individual taxpayers until April 15, 1985, and corporations until March 15, 1985 (the final filing dates for calendar year returns) to pay their full 1984 income tax liabilities without incurring any additions to tax on account of underpayments of estimated tax to the extent that the underpayments are attributable to changes in the law made by the Tax Reform Act of 1984.

In order to minimize any administrative problems to the Internal Revenue Service, it will be expected that taxpayers notify the IRS if they are entitled to the benefits of this provision. The IRS will not be required to notify taxpayers of possible relief under this provision.

Orphan drug credit ***

Present Law.—A 50-percent tax credit is available for qualified clinical testing expenses that are necessary to obtain the approval of the Food and Drug Administration for the commercial sale of a drug for a rare disease. The term "clinical testing" is defined, in part, by reference to the date on which an application with respect to a drug is approved under section 505(b) of the Federal Food, Drug, and Cosmetic Act. The term "rare disease or condition" is defined as any disease or condition that occurs so infrequently in the United States that the taxpayer has no reasonable expectation of recovering the cost of developing and marketing a drug for such disease from sales in the United States.

Explanation of Provision.—The bill clarifies that, in the case of a drug that is a biological product, "clinical testing" is defined, in part, by reference to the date on which a license for such drug is issued under section 351 of the Public Health Services Act. The bill also redefines the term "rare disease or condition" as any disease that (1) affects less than 200,000 persons in the United States, or (2) affects more than 200,000 persons in the United States but for which there is no reasonable expectation that the cost of developing and making available a drug for such disease in the United States will be recovered from sales of such drug in the United States. This will conform the provisions of the tax credit with the provisions of the Federal Food, Drug, and Cosmetic Act.

[*Effective Date.*—The amendments apply to amounts paid or incurred after December 31, 1982.]

Credit for producing fuel from nonconventional source ***

Present Law.—Present law provides a credit for certain fuels produced by a taxpayer and sold to an unrelated party.

Explanation of Provision.—The bill provides that the credit may be allowed where the sale to an unrelated person is made by a corporation which files a consolidated return with the corporation producing the fuel.

[*Effective Date.*—] The provision applies as if included in section 231 of the Crude Oil Windfall Profit Tax Act of 1980 [taxable years ending after December 31, 1979.Ed.]

Report of refunds by Joint Committee to Congress ***

Present Law.—The Code (sec. 6405(b)) requires the Joint Committee on Taxation to make an annual report to Congress setting forth the proposed tax refunds and credits submitted by the Internal Revenue Service to the Joint Committee for its review, including the names of the taxpayers and amounts involved. It is unclear whether this requirement was overridden by the tax return disclosure limitations (sec. 6103) enacted 1976. Because of this apparent conflict, these reports have not been submitted in recent years and the Joint Committee believes it appropriate to delete the requirement to submit this report.

Act § 1879 ¶4193

Explanation of Provision.—The bill repeals the requirement that the Joint Committee on Taxation submit an annual report to Congress on proposed IRS tax refunds and credits.

Rural electric cooperative cash or deferred arrangements ***

Present Law.—Under the Code, gross income may include amounts actually or constructively received as income. For example, under the rules of constructive receipt, the gross income of an individual includes compensation that has been earned and that would have been received but for the individual's election to defer its receipt. The Code provides for an exception to the rules of constructive receipt in the case of employer contributions under a qualified cash or deferred arrangement.

If a tax-qualified profit-sharing or stock bonus plan (or certain pre-ERISA money purchase pension plans) meets certain requirements (a qualified cash or deferred arrangement), then an employee is not required to include in income any employer contributions to the plan merely because the employee could have elected to receive the amount contributed in cash.

Because a qualified stock bonus plan is generally required to distribute benefits in the form of employer stock, a qualified stock bonus plan may not be maintained by a governmental unit or by a tax-exempt membership organization. Under the Code, employer contributions to a qualified profit-sharing plan may be made only from preset or accumulated employer profits.

It is unclear under present law whether an employer that is a governmental entity or a tax-exempt organization may maintain a qualified cash or deferred arrangement because such an organization may not have stock or profits in the usual sense of those terms.

Explanation of Provision.—The bill clarifies that any organization that is exempt from tax and that is engaged primarily in providing electric service on a mutual or cooperative basis is eligible to maintain a qualified cash or deferred arrangement. This provision also applies to a national association of such tax-exempt organizations.

[*Effective Date.*—The amendments made by this subsection shall apply to plan years beginning after December 31, 1984. Ed.]

Definition of newly discovered oil ***

Present Law.—Under the present law, the windfall profit tax is imposed at a lower rate on newly discovered oil than on other oil. Generally, the term "newly discovered oil" has the meaning given to it by the June 1979 energy regulations.

The legislative history to the Crude Oil Windfall Profit Tax Act of 1980 indicates that the term was also to include production from a property which did not produce oil in commercial quantities during calendar year 1978. That history indicates that it includes production from a property on which oil was produced in 1978 if that production was incident to the drilling of exploratory or test wells and was not part of continuous or commercial production from the property during 1978.

Explanation of Provision.—The bill clarifies that the term "newly discovered oil" includes production from a property so long as not more than 2200 barrels was produced from the property in 1978 and no well on the property was in production for more than 3 days during that year (whether or not the oil was sold). This provision is intended to clarify the "test well" exception described in the Conference Report accompanying the Crude Oil Windfall Profit Tax Act of 1980. No inference is intended as to the application of similar principles in areas other than section 4991(e)(2).

[*Effective Date.*—The amendments made by this subsection shall apply to oil removed after February 29, 1980. Ed.]

* * * * * *

[House Explanation]

* * * * * *

Refunds with respect to medicinal alcohol ***

Present Law.—Under present law, a special excise tax is imposed on articles coming into the United States from Puerto Rico or the Virgin Islands, equal to the tax that would be imposed if the article were manufactured in the United States (sec. 7652).

Explanation of Provision.—The bill clarifies that medicinal alcohol produced in Puerto Rico and the Virgin Islands is eligible for refunds of the tax on distilled spirits paid when the alcohol is brought into the United States. For purposes of the refunds, Puerto Rican and Virgin Islands producers of medicinal alcohol are treated as United States persons, except the amount of the refund is determined as if tax were paid at the rate eligible for cover over under section 7652.

[*Effective Date.*—This provision is effective for articles brought into the U.S. after the date of enactment. Ed.]

* * * * * *

[Senate Explanation]

* * * * * *

Allowance of investment tax credit to members of certain tax-exempt religous organizations ***

Present Law.—Present law provides an income tax exemption for a religious or apostolic association or corporation if (1) it has common treasury or community treasury, even if it engages in business for the common benefit of the members, and (2) its members include (at the time of filing their returns) in their gross income their entire pro rata shares, whether distributed or not, of the organization's taxable income for such year (sec. 501(d)). Any amount so included in the gross income of a member is treated as a dividend received. Thus, members of section 501(d) organizations file individual tax returns and pay income tax on their pro rata shares of organization income.

The Code allows an investment tax credit for certain acquisitions of depreciable property (sec. 38(a)). In the case of such property used by a tax-exempt organization, however, the credit is not allowed unless the property is used in an unrelated trade or business the income of which is subject to tax under section 511 (sec. 48(a)(4)). The Ninth Circuit has ruled that since section 501(d) organizations are not subject to the section 511 tax on unrelated business taxable income, neither the organization nor its members on their tax returns can claim the investment tax credit for depreciable property acquired by the organization *(Kleinsasser v. U.S.,* 707 F.2d 1024 (9th Cir. 1988)).

Explanation of Provision.—The bill provides that, for purposes only of the investment credit rules in section 48(a)(4), any business which is conducted by an eligible section 501(d) organization for the common benefit of its members and the taxable income from which is included in the gross income of its members is to be treated as an unrelated business. Accordingly, the acquisition of depreciable property by an eligible section 501(d) organization for use in such a business gives rise to an investment tax credit to the same extent as if the property had been acquired by a section 501(c)(3) organization for use in an unrelated business.

Under the provision, the amount of such qualified investment by a section 501(d) organization is apportioned pro rata among its members in the same manner as its taxable income is allocated. The bill does not allow any credit for such investment to a member who claimed any other type of investment credit, and prohibits the reallocation of any such disallowed credit to other community members. The used-property credit limitation and credit recapture rules apply at the organization level.

The provisions apply to any organization which elects to be treated as an organization described in section 501(d) and which is exempt from tax under section 501(a), and which does not provide a substantially higher standard of living for any person or persons than it does for the majority of the members of the community.

[*Effective Date.*—The amendments made by this provision shall apply to periods after December 31, 1978 (under rules similar to the rules of section 48(m) in taxable years ending after such date. If a refund or credit of any overpayment of tax resulting from the application of this subsection is prevented at any time before the close of the date which is 1 year after the date of the enactment of the new law by operation of any law (including res judicata), refund or credit of such overpayment (to the extent attibutable to the application of the amendments made by this subsection) may, nevertheless, be made or allowed if claim therefor is filed before the close of such 1-year period. Ed.]

Reorganization of investment companies ***

Present Law.—The Tax Reform Act of 1976 prevented the tax-free reorganization of certain investment companies. Exceptions were applied for stock in RICs, REITs and diversified investment companies.

Explanation of Provision.—The bill provides that the stock of a RIC, REIT or diversified investment company will not be treated as stock of a single issuer for purposes of determining whether the holder is diversified within the meaning of section 368(a)(2)(F)(ii). This provision is intended to permit an investment company to be treated as a diversified investment company only if it would be so defined if it were deemed to own its ratable share of the assets of any RIC, REIT, or diversified investment company in which it owns stock (without regard to whether its percentage ownership is 50 percent or more).

[*Effective Date.*—This provision shall apply as if included in section 2131 of the Tax Reform Act of 1976, for transfers made after February 17, 1976. Ed.]

Mutual savings banks ***

Present Law.—The Economic Recovery Tax Act (ERTA) provided that a stock association which is subject to the same regulation as a mutual savings bank is treated as a mutual savings bank and thus eligible to compute its bad debt deduction under section 593.

Explanation of Provision.—The bill provides that a stock association which is treated as a mutual savings bank for purposes of computing a bad debt deduction is also treated as a mutual savings bank for purposes of the exemption for mutual organizations insuring these banks (sec. 501(c)(14)(B)). The provision is effective as if enacted in ERTA.

[*Effective Date.*—The amendments made by this subsection shall apply to taxable years ending after August 15, 1981. Ed.]

Subchapter S amendments ***

Present Law.—The Subchapter S Revision Act of 1982 revised the treatment of S corporations. Rules were provided allowing certain trusts as shareholders and also rules were provided for the tax-free distributions of subchapter S earnings.

Explanation of Provision.—The bill provides that shares which are treated as separate trusts for purposes of section 663(c) are also treated as separate trusts for purposes of the rules relating to qualified subchapter S trusts (sec. 1861(d)(3)).

The bill also provides that the accumulated adjustments accounts (which measures the amount of subchapter S earnings which may be distributed tax-free) will not be reduced by reason of federal taxes arising while the corporation was a C corporation.

[**Effective Date.**—] These provisions will apply to taxable years beginning after December 31, 1982.

Qualified terminable interest property
***

Present Law.—Present law allows a gift tax deduction for gifts of certain life estates made to a donee spouse. The election must be made by April 15 after the calendar year the interest is transferred.

Explanation of Provision.—The bill provides that this election must be made on or before the date, including extensions, prescribed by section 6075 for filing a gift tax return with respect to the year in which the transfer was made.

[*Effective Date.*—The amendment made by this subsection shall apply to transfers made after December 31, 1985. Ed.]

Windfall profit tax ***

The windfall profit tax provides an exemption for oil held by certain charitable organizations.

Explanation of Provision.—The bill provides that the exemption for "qualified charitable interests" includes an interest held by the Episcopal Royalty Company.

[*Effective Date.*—The amendment made by this subsection shall apply to oil recovered after February 29, 1980. Ed.]

[Conference Report]

* * * * * *

Suspension of audits, time to file petition and interest and penalties.—The time to file a petition in Tax Court, the initiation and continuation of audits, and the running of interest and the collection of penalties, is suspended for a period ending August 16, 1987 with respect to certain self-insured workers compensation funds.

[¶ 4195] SECTION 1882. AMENDMENTS RELATED TO COVERAGE OF CHURCH EMPLOYEES (SECTION 2603 OF THE DEFICIT REDUCTION ACT)

(Secs. 1402(g), (j), 3121(w) of the Code)

[Senate Explanation]

a. Application to members of certain religious faiths.

* * * * * *

Explanation of Provisions.—The bill makes clear that the exception from SECA taxes for members of certain religious faiths (sec. 1402(g)) is not available for services with respect to which SECA tax is due as a result of an election under the Act. Thus, if a member of a religious faith covered by the sec. 1402(g) exception is an employee of a church or church-controlled organization, and that church or organization elects to treat the employee as self-employed for FICA tax purposes, the employee cannot also claim a section 1402(g) exception from SECA taxes with respect to those services. This provision prevents the combination of an election under the Act, and a section 1402(g) exception, from resulting in an avoidance of any employment taxes on the services performed for the electing organization. This is consistent with the general principle that the tax for services covered by an election should be determined (to the extent possible) as it would be under FICA, for which the section 1402(g) exception would be unavailable. The provision does not affect the individual's ability to claim a section 1402(g) exception with respect to other services not covered by an election under the Act.

[*Effective date.*—Effective on '86 TRA enactment date. Ed.]

b. Computation of income subject to SECA tax.

* * * * * *

Explanation of Provision.—The bill provides several changes to insure that church employee income will be determined, as far

as possible, using FICA principles, and that the taxation of other self-employment income will not be affected by an election. Specifically, the bill specifies that the SECA tax base for services covered by an election is to be computed in a separate "basket" from the tax base for other self-employment income. Thus, church employee income is not reduced by any deduction, while other income and deductions are not affected by items attributable to church employee income.[15] (This rule does not apply to the deduction for the product of all net self-employment earnings and one-half the SECA tax rate, beginning after 1989). Additionally, the $100 threshold for taxing church employee income, and the $400 threshold applicable to other self-employment income, are separately applied under the bill (i.e., church employee income does not count toward the general $400 threshold).

[**Effective date.**—] This provision is effective only for remuneration paid or derived in taxable years beginning on or after January 1, 1986.

c. Voluntary revocation of election

* * * * * *

Explanation of Provision.—The bill allows a church or organization to revoke an election under regulations to be prescribed by the Treasury Department. The bill does not amend the present-law rules allowing the Treasury Department to revoke an election for failure to provide required information. A church or organization which revokes an election (or for which the election is revoked) cannot make another election, because the time for making such an election has lapsed.

[Conference Report]

* * * * * *

Revocation of certain church elections.—It is intended that the regulations allowing a church or qualified church-controlled organization to revoke an election made under Code section 3121(w)(2) are to provide that any such revocation is not to be effective prior to January 1, 1987, unless such electing church or organization had withheld and paid over all employment taxes

due, as if such election had never been in effect, during the period from the stated effective date of the election being revoked through December 31, 1986.

[**Effective date.**—Effective on '86 TRA enactment date. Ed.]

[¶ 4196] SECTION 1883. TECHNICAL CORRECTIONS IN OTHER PROVISIONS RELATED TO SOCIAL SECURITY ACT PROGRAMS

[Senate Explanation]

* * * Disregard of Income of a Stepparent. * * *

*   *   *   *   *   *

Explanation of Provision. The bill deletes the Secretary's authority for the disregard of a lesser amount in the case of earnings of a stepfather, since the Deficit Reduction Act deleted the comparable authority for the general income disregard provision of section 402(a)(8) of the Act.

[**Effective date.**—]This provision is effective October 1, 1984, the effective date of the Deficit Reduction Act amendment to section 402(a)(8).

* * * Family Unit Rule. * * *

*   *   *   *   *

Explanation of Provision. The bill clarifies that a sibling is to be included in the AFDC family unit who is deprived of parental support or care by reason of the unemployment of a parent (and meets the other criteria of a dependent child) as well as one who is deprived by reason of the death, absence, or incapacity of a parent. No such distinction between these two categories was intended, and this provision will clarify that, in a State that provides AFDC on the basis of the unemployment of a parent, siblings who are dependent children for that reason must be included in the AFDC unit.

[**Effective date.**—] This provision is effective October 1, 1984, the date that paragraph (38) was added to section 402(a) of the Act.

*   *   *   *   *   *

* * * Clerical Correction Relating to Income of AFDC Family Unit * * *

*   *   *   *   *

Explanation of Provision.—The bill corrects the indentation and placement of a portion of section 402(a)(38) of the Social Security Act. *[Effective date.—]* The provision is effective October 1, 1984, the date that paragraph (38) was added to the Act.

Income of a Minor AFDC Parent

*   *   *   *   *   *

Explanation of Provision. This bill clarifies that for purposes of defining the age limit of parents to whom paragraph (39) [of SSA Sec. 402] applies, the age is that selected by the State for purposes of defining a depen-

dent child, without regard to whether the minor parent is attending school. This provision makes clear that only the age limit, and not the school attendance element, was intended to be relevant to the income computation rule of paragraph (39) (thus avoiding any incentive on the part of the minor parent to drop out of school).

*   *   *   *   *   *

* * * Federal Incentive Payments in Cases of Interstate Collections * * *

*   *   *   *   *   *

Explanation of Provisions.—The bill clarifies the intent of Congress that the incentive be credited to both the State initiating the collection and the State making the collection. It describes the initiating State as the State requesting the collection, rather than the State of residence of the individuals on whose behalf the collection is made. The change is necessary because the State of residence is not always the same as the State initiating the collection request.

* * * Exclusion from AFDC Unit of Siblings Receiving Foster Care Maintenance Payments * * *

Present Law.—Prior to the addition of the family unit rule in AFDC (section 402(a)(38)) by the Deficit Reduction Act, a sibling of an AFDC child, residing in the AFDC household but receiving foster care maintenance payments under part E of title IV of the Act, was excluded from the AFDC family unit.

Explanation of Provision.—The bill adds a new section to part E of title IV to make clear that the sibling (of an AFDC child) receiving foster care maintenance payments is not a member of the AFDC unit. This provision assures that, by authorizing foster care payment in a separate part E, rather than under the predecessor section 408 of the AFDC program, no change will occur in the treatment of the various individuals concerned.

[**Effective date.**—] This provision is effective October 1, 1984, the date upon which the AFDC family unit rule (which caused the question to arise) became effective.

[Conference Report]

*   *   *   *   *   *

AFDC and child support.—The conference agreement is as follows.

Stepparent work disregard.—The conference agreement follows the Senate amendment, which repeals the authority for a lower disregard in the case of part-time employment effective October 1, 1984.

Standard filing unit.—The conference agreement includes that portion of the Senate amendment which clarifies that the standard filing unit provision applies to the AFDC-UP program. The change is effective October 1, 1984. The agreement does not include that portion of the Senate amendment concerning Title II benefits and certain child support payments. No inference is intended with regard to current Federal regulations implementing section 402(a)(38) of the Social Security Act.

Definition of minor parent.—The conference agreement follows the Senate amendment, which clarifies that the definition of minor parent is based only on age, not on school attendance. The agreement also clarifies that to be considered a minor parent, an individual must be under 18 years of age.

Treatment of foster care payments.—The conference agreement follows the Senate amendment which clarifies that a child receiving foster care maintenance payments shall not be considered a member of the family when determining AFDC eligibility and benefits.

Distribution of child support collections.—The conference agreement follows the Senate amendment which clarifies that the rules regarding distribution of child support collections apply to child support paid as a result of a court order or an administrative order.

General Social Security Act provisions, SSI and Social Services.—

The conference agreement follows **** the Senate amendment.

Effective Date of Social Security Act Amendments.—The conference agreement follows * * * the Senate amendment. With regard to those amendments with an effective date of October 1, 1984, * * * no State shall be considered to have failed to comply with the Social Security Act or to have made overpayments or underpayments by reason of its compliance or noncompliance with these amendments for the period beginning October 1, 1984 and ending on the day preceding the date of enactment of this Act. [Except as otherwise provided the amendments take effect on the date of enactment. Ed.]

[¶4197] SECTION 1884. TECHNICAL CORRECTIONS IN FEDERAL UNEMPLOYMENT TAX ACT

(Sec. 3302(f) of the Code)

[Senate Explanation]

1. Limitation on the Federal Unemployment Tax Act (FUTA) Credit in States Meeting the Solvency Requirements of Section 1202 of the Social Security Act * * *

Present Law.—Under present law, States can borrow funds from the Federal Unemployment account if they have insufficient funds in their own unemployment accounts to pay unemployment benefits. Depending on the month in which such a loan is advanced, a State has between 22 and 34 months to repay the loan. If the loan is not repaid in time, the FUTA tax credit for employers in the State is reduced by .3% for each year the loan is in arrears.

The Social Security Act Amendments of 1983 provided for a partial limitation on the FUTA credit reduction in States that take legislative steps to improve the solvency of their unemployment insurance systems. If States meet the solvency test, the FUTA credit reduction is limited to .1% a year for each year a State has a loan in arrears. This limitation on the FUTA credit reduction is in effect for calendar years 1983, 1984 and 1985.

Explanation of Provision.—The bill clarifies that the limitation on the FUTA credit reduction in States meeting the solvency test of Section 1202 of the Social Security Act expires at the end of calendar year 1985.

2. Reference to Agricultural Crew Leaders in the Federal Unemployment Tax Act (FUTA) * * *

Present Law.—Section 3306(O)(A)(i) of the Internal Revenue Code provides that for purposes of the Federal Unemployment Tax Act an individual who is a member of a crew furnished by a crew leader to perform agricultural labor for any other person shall be treated as an employee of such crew leader if such crew leader holds a valid certificate of registration under the Farm Labor Contractor Act of 1963. This act has been repealed and replaced with the Migrant and Seasonal Agricultural Workers Protection Act of 1983.

Explanation of Provision.—The bill strikes the reference in section 3306 of the Internal Revenue Code of 1954 to the Farm Labor Contractor Act of 1963 and replaces it with a reference to the Migrant and Seasonal Agricultural Workers Protection Act of 1983.

[Effective date.—Effective on '86 TRA enactment date. Ed.]

[¶ 4198] SECTION 1885. AMENDMENTS TO THE TARIFF SCHEDULES

(Secs. 111, 112, 123, 124, 146, 182 of the 1984 Trade and Tariff Act)

[House Explanation]

Explanation of Provision.—The bill adds a new item 608.25 to the TSUS covering silicon electrical steel strip not over 0.1 inch in thickness, providing for the same rates of duty currently applicable to such product. The purpose of this provision is to preclude foreign countries from circumventing the bilateral voluntary restraint agreements entered into pursuant to the Steel Import Stabilization Act of 1984, by simply altering the configuration of the silicon electrical steel they ship to the United States to avoid being counted against the quota for silicon electrical steel.

[Senate Explanation]

*   *   *   *   *   *

Explanation of Provision.—The bill makes conforming changes to several headnotes in the Tariff Schedules which refer to the TSUS items in part 5 of schedule 6 which were changed by section 124 of the Trade and Tariff Act of 1984. It would also add the appropriate column 2 rate of duty for new item 685.34 which was inadvertently omitted from the Act.

*   *   *   *   *   *

[*Effective Date.*—Effective generally, for articles entered, or withdrawn from, a warehouse for consumption on or after the date that is 15 days after the date of enactment. Ed.]

[¶ 4199] SECTION 1886. TECHNICAL CORRECTIONS TO COUNTERVAILING AND ANTIDUMPING DUTY PROVISIONS

(Secs. 702(b)(1), 704, 732(b)(1), 751(b)(1), 771A(a), 777, 7369(c)(1) of Title IV of the 1930 Trade and Tariff Act and Secs. 611(a)(2)(B)(iii), 613, 619, 626(b) of the 1984 Trade and Tariff Act)

[Senate Explanation]

*   *   *   *   *   *

Definition of "interested party." * * *

Explanation of Provision.—The bill makes * * * conforming changes in sections 702(b)(1) and 732(b)(1) of the Tariff Act of 1930 to ensure that industry-labor coalitions will be considered proper petitioners under the countervailing duty and antidumping laws.

Imports under suspension agreements * * *

Explanation of Provision.—The bill restores section 704(d)(2) of the Tariff Act of 1930, which was inadvertently deleted when House provisions deleting the 6-month grace period were not agreed to in House-Senate conference on the Trade and Tariff Act of 1984. Section 704(d)(2) requires that a suspension agreement provide a means of ensuring that exports shall not surge during the 6-month period of phase-in of measures to eliminate or offset subsidies.

The provision also corrects a typographical error in section 704(i)(1)(D) of the Tariff Act of 1930.

Waiver of deposit of estimated antidumping duties * * *

*   *   *   *   *   *

Explanation of Provision.—The bill amends section 736(c)(1) of the Tariff Act of 1930 to change its scope to cover only entries entered and resold to unrelated purchasers during the period between the first affirmative antidumping determination and the In-

ternational Trade Commission's final affirmative determination. This amendment was inadvertently omitted from the Trade and Tariff Act of 1984 as enrolled.

Revocation of orders * * *

Explanation of Provision.—The bill amends section 751(b)(1) of the Tariff Act of 1930 to apply the same standard to revocations of countervailing duty orders as applies to antidumping orders. The amendment corrects an inadvertent omission from the Trade and Tariff Act of 1984 since there is no reason to distinguish between the two types of revocations.

Definition of upstream subsidies * * *

Explanation of Provision.—The bill amends section 771A(a) of the Tariff Act of 1930 to correct the unintended omission of section 771(5)(B)(iv) from the list of domestic subsidy practices which may constitute an upstream subsidy.

Release of confidential information * * *

Explanation of Provision.—The bill amends section 777 of the Tariff Act of 1930 to substitute the term "proprietary" for "confidential" throughout the section, a change that was omitted inadvertently from the Trade and Tariff Act of 1984 as enrolled. The provision also amends subsection (b)(1)(B)(i) to correct the inadvertently omission of the International Trade Commission as being permitted to release information, as well as the administering authority, consistent with the rest of the section.

Effective dates * * *

Explanation of Provision.—The bill amends paragraph (1) of section 626(b) of the Trade and Tariff Act of 1984 so that the amendments in sections 602, 609, 611, 612, and 620 of the Act will apply to reviews of outstanding antidumping and countervailing

Act § 1886   ¶ 4199

duty orders, as well as to new investigations. These orders would involve merchandise entered, or withdrawn from warehouse, for consumption many years after date of enactment. This amendment is consistent with the Congressional intent of these amendments to reduce the cost and increase the efficiency of proceedings.

The bill authorizes the administering authority to delay implementation of any of the amendments to Title VII with respect to investigations in progress on the date of enactment of the Trade and Tariff Act of 1984 if it determines that immediate implementation would prevent compliance with an applicable statutory deadline. New questionnaires would have to be issued to seek information required by certain amendments that may not be obtainable on cases in progress within the statutory deadlines.

The bill also clarifies that the amendment made by section 621 of the Trade and Tariff Act of 1984 to section 778 of the Tariff Act of 1930 concerning the rate of interest payable on overpayments and underpayments of antidumping and countervailing duties is applicable to merchandise unliquidated as of five days after date of enactment, i.e., on or after November 4, 1984, consistent with U.S. Customs Service practice.

Miscellaneous corrections (* * *)

The bill corrects errors in various provisions of Title VII of the Tariff Act of 1930 concerning subsection designations, cross-references, and printing, grammatical, and typographical errors and provides for the addition of a section heading.

*   *   *   *   *   *

[¶ 4200] SECTION 1887. AMENDMENTS TO THE TRADE ACT OF 1974

(Sec. 504(c)(3)(D)(ii) of the 1974 Trade and Tariff Act)

[Senate Explanation]

*   *   *   *   *   *

a. Miscellaneous corrections * * *

The bill makes certain corrections of numbering, subsection designations, cross-references to the United States Code and syntax in amendments to various sections of the Trade Act of 1974 made by the Trade and Tariff Act of 1984.

b. Waiver authority under Generalized System of Preferences (GSP) * * *

*   *   *   *   *   *

Explanation of Provision.—The bill clarifies that the 15-percent limit on the President's waiver authority under section

504(c)(3)(D)(ii) of the Trade Act of 1974 as amended applies to the aggregate value of all waivers granted in a given year with respect to GSP imports from advanced beneficiary countries as a whole, not to each country individually. It also corrects references to the year in which section 504(c)(3)(D)(ii) has its first effect.

c. Transistors * * *

The bill corrects an error in numbering of a TSUS line item in section 308 of the Trade and Tariff Act of 1984 which has prevented fully implementing an agreement to reduce U.S. duties on transistors.

[Effective date.—Effective generally, on the date of enactment; Act Secs. 1887(a)(1)-(4), making technical corrections to various sections of the 1974 Trade Act, is effective on the date of enactment. Ed.]

[¶ 4201] SECTION 1888. AMENDMENTS TO THE TARIFF ACT OF 1930

(Secs. 304(c), 313(j), 514(a), 516(a)(2) of the 1930 Trade and Tariff Act Secs. 202, 207 of the 1984 Trade and Tariff Act)

[Senate Explanation]

* * * **Marking of pipes and tubes.**

*   *   *   *   *   *

Explanation of Provision.—The bill provides a limited exception to the marking requirement for articles which, due to their nature, may not be marked by one of the four prescribed methods because it is technically or commercially infeasable to do so. Such articles may be marked by an equally permanent method of marking, such as paint stenciling, or in the case of small diameter pipe and tube, by tagging the containers or bundles. Those articles which Customs has determined are capable of being marked by die stamping, cast-in-mold lettering, etching or engraving without adversely affecting their structural integrity or significantly

reducing their commercial utility would continue to be marked in this manner.

Further, the tagging of containers or bundles may only be used for small diameter pipes and tubes for which individual marking would be impractical or inconspicuous. In the event that Customs determines that tagging is the only feasible method of marking imported goods so that the ultimate consumer will be appraised of the country of origin of such goods, such products must be bundled and tagged in accordance with applicable industry standards. The Committee directs the U.S. Customs Service to report to the Committee on the operation and effectiveness of this provision within one year after the enactment of this Act.

[Conference Report]

*   *   *   *   *   *

Marking of pipes, tubes and fittings.—The conference agreement clarifies that the exception for marking through the tagging of containers or bundles for small diameter pipes and tubes also applies to small diameter fittings.

[Senate Explanation]

* * * * * *

* * * Drawback—incidental operations * * *

* * * * * *

Explanation of Provision. The bill redesignates paragraphs (3) and (4) of section 313 as (2) and (3), respectively, and amends paragraph (3) as redesignated so that incidental operations may be performed on both domestic and imported merchandise so that the intent of the original provision (i.e., allowing fungible domestic and imported merchandise to be mixed together and still be entitled to drawback) is accomplished.

* * * * * *

* * * Interested parties * * *

Explanation of Provision.—The bill amend sections 514(a) and 516(a)(2) of the Tariff Act of 1930 to conform the definition of the term "interested party" to the inclusion of industry-labor coalitions under section 771(9) of the Tariff Act of 1930.

* * * Customs Provision * * *

The bill deletes the Customs Forfeiture Fund created by the 1985 Continuing Resolution, which duplicated the existing Customs Forfeiture Fund.

[Conference Report]

* * * * * *

* * * Customs broker's freight forwarding.—The conferees also clarified Congressional intent with respect to the compensation of customs brokers for certain services. The conference agreement provides licensed customs brokers, when performing ocean freight forwarder services on export shipments from the United States, with the benefits of the right of independent action with respect to the level of forwarder compensation in a shipping conference's freight tariff. Under present law, a conference may prohibit its members from taking independent action on forwarder compensation. This amendment makes clear that a conference must allow its members to take independent action on compensation to the extent that compensation is or will be paid to a forwarder who is also a licensed customs broker under the Tariff Act of 1930.

This provision also benefits customs brokers when they act in the capacity of a licensed freight forwarder on shipments exported from the United States. Despite the requirement of current law that conferences not deny forwarders a reasonable percentage of the carrier's freight charges as compensation for the forwarder's service, some conferences are limiting forwarders' compensation to a percentage of some, but not all, of the rates and charges assessed against the cargo in their tariffs. The purpose of this amendment is to make clear that when compensation is paid to a forwarder who is also a licensed customs broker, the compensation must be based on all the freight charges, including, but not limited to, surcharges, handling charges, service charges, terminal charges, supplements, currency adjustment factors, and any and all other charges required to be paid by the shipper or consignee under the tariff.

These amendments do not in any way modify or diminish the existing scope or protections of the Shipping Act of 1984 as applied to ocean freight forwarders in general. Their sole purpose is to impose additional requirements on conferences or carrier groups in their concerted dealings with forwarders who are also licensed customs brokers.

*[Effective date.—*Changes to the 1984 Trade and Tariff Act are effective on the Act's enactment date; technical corrections to the 1930 Tariff Act, are effective on the Act's enactment date. Ed.]

* * * * * *

[¶ 4202] SECTION 1889. AMENDMENTS TO THE TRADE AND TARIFF ACT OF 1984

(Secs. 126, 174(b), 212, 234(a), 304(d)(2)-(A), 307(b)(3), and 504 of the Trade and Tariff Act of 1984)

[Senate Explanation]

a. Chipper knife steel (sec. 1889(1) of the bill and sec. 126 of the Trade and Tariff Act of 1984)

The bill deletes unnecessary language inserted by the Trade and Tariff Act of 1984.

b. Watch glasses (sec. 1889(2) of the bill and sec. 174(b) of the Trade and Tariff Act of 1984)

Present Law.—Section 174 of the Trade and Tariff Act of 1984 reduced the level of duty on watch glasses other than round to the same level as the duty applicable to round watch glasses. However, the Act does not provide for the third-year staged reduction on January 1, 1987, for watch glasses other than round.

Explanation of Provision.—The bill amends section 174(b) of the Trade and Tariff Act of 1984 to provide for the third-year reduction to 4.9 percent ad valorem for such watch glasses.

c. Miscellaneous corrections * * *

The bill corrects paragraph designations and number and statutory references in various sections of the Trade and Tariff Act of 1984.

Act § 1889 ¶ 4202

[*Effective date.*—Enactment date of '84 Trade and Tariff Act. Ed.]

[¶ 4203] SECTION 1890. AMENDMENTS TO THE CARIBBEAN BASIN ECONOMIC RECOVERY ACT

(Sec. 213 of the Caribbean Basin Economic Recovery Act, and sec. 235 of the Trade and Tariff Act of 1984)

[Senate Explanation]

Present Law.—Section 235 of the Trade and Tariff Act of 1984 amended section 213(a) of the Caribbean Basin Economic Recovery Act (CBI) to allow products of a beneficiary country to be processed in a bonded warehouse in Puerto Rico after being imported directly from such country and be eligible for duty-free treatment under the CBI upon withdrawal from warehouse if they meet the rule-of-origin requirements set out in paragraph (1)(B) of section 213(a).

Explanation of Provision.—The bill corrects a reference to a wrong Tariff Schedules item in section 213(f)(5)(B) of the Caribbean Basin Economic Recovery Act and clarifies that products entering Puerto Rico directly from any CBI beneficiary country, not merely the country of manufacture, should qualify for entry under bond.

[*Effective date.*—Enactment date of Recovery Act. Ed.]

[¶ 4204] SECTION 1891. CONFORMING AMENDMENTS REGARDING CUSTOMS BROKERS

(Title 28 of the United States Code, and sec. 212(b) of the Trade and Tariff Act of 1984)

[Senate Explanation]

The bill makes corrections to conforming amendments made by section 212(b) of the Trade and Tariff Act of 1984 in Title 28 of the U.S. Code to cross-references in the Tariff Act of 1930 relating to customs brokers and deletes an incorrect reference in section 1581(g)(1) of Title 28.

[*Effective Date.*—Enactment date of '84 Trade and Tariff Act. Ed.]

[¶ 4205] SECTION 1892. SPECIAL EFFECTIVE DATE PROVISIONS FOR CERTAIN ARTICLES GIVEN DUTY-FREE TREATMENT UNDER THE TRADE AND TARIFF ACT OF 1984

(Secs. 112, 115, 118, 167, and 179 of the Trade and Tariff Act of 1984)

[Senate Explanation]

Present Law.—Sections 112, 115, 118, 167, and 179 of the Trade and Tariff Act of 1984 were made effective 15 days after enactment because the provisions providing for retroactive application of such provisions were inadvertently omitted from the Act.

Explanation of Provision.—The bill provides for the retroactive application of sections 112, 115, 118, 167, and 179 of the Trade and Tariff Act of 1984.

[*Effective date.*—Retroactively effective to date of enactment of affected sections. Ed.]

[¶ 4206] SECTION 1893. TECHNICAL AMENDMENTS RELATING TO CUSTOMS USER FEES

(Secs. 13031(b), (e)(1), (g), (h)(2) of the Consolidated Omnibus Budget Reconciliation Act of 1985 and sec. 53 of the Airport and Airway Development Act of 1970)

[Conference Report]

*   *   *   *   *   *

a. Customs user fees.—*(1) Vessels, barges, bulk carriers and ferries.*—A cap of $5,955 is placed on the fees charged for the arrival of any commercial vessel of more than 100 net tons in the United States. The conferees believe that this cap is appropriate in light of a cap already in place on the arrival of trucks and rail cars. This cap on vessel fees is computed on the basis of fifteen arrivals per year. The conferees intend the fee on commercial vessels to be applicable to each arrival at a U.S. port regardless of whether these arrivals occur as a series of calls at U.S. ports on the same trip or on several trips.

A lower user fee of $100 on barges and bulk carriers arriving from Canada and Mexico is provided in light of the fact that such vessels compete with trucks and rail cars arriving by land from Canada and Mexico, which are subject to much lower user fees. A cap of $1,500, also representing fifteen arrivals, has been placed on the annual total of the user fees which such barges and bulk carriers arriving from contiguous countries must pay.

Regardless of which fee may be applicable during the calendar year, no barge or bulk carrier shall be liable for more than the $5,955 annual cap applicable to vessels.

The conference agreement exempts tugboats from the application of any vessel fees. This exemption is intended to prevent the Customs Service from applying the vessel user fee to a tugboat which provides propulsion to barges or merely accompanies vessels which are themselves subject to a user fee. This exception does not apply to tugboats which are not being used as tugboats at the time of arrival.

The conference agreement contains a definition of the term ferry for the purposes of the exemption from the user fee applicable to commercial vessels of over 100 net tons. For purposes of this exemption, a ferry includes a vessel which transports passengers, vehicles, or railroad cars or any combination thereof, for distances of 300 miles or less. While such a ferry is exempted from the fee, trucks or railroad cars carried by such a ferry would be subject to the applicable fee. In the case of commercial vessels subject to the user fee which transport vehicles or rail cars there shall be no fee assessed on the vehicles or rail cars.

The conferees note that some vessel operators have proposed the consolidation of all vessel fees into a single fee. The conferees expect the Customs Service to study all fees now applicable to vessels entering U.S. ports in an effort to determine whether a simpler and more efficient method can be proposed in administering these fees. The conferees expect the Customs Service to confer with the Finance and Ways and Means Committees in an effort to resolve this problem.

(2) Passenger fees.—The conference agreement clarifies that the exemption from the $5 fee applicable to passengers arriving on commercial aircraft and vessels also exempts passengers originating in the U.S. who transit only those locations to which the exemption applies, prior to reentering the U.S. The conferees further provided that overtime for customs inspections may not be charged at U.S. Customs pre-clearance facilities overseas.

(3) Railroad cars.—The conference agreement provides for a $7.50 fee on the arrival of each rail car carrying passengers or freight and eliminates the fee on empty railroad cars.

(4) Customs brokers.—The conferees clarified that the annual fee for the issuance of a broker permit is to be prorated so that the applicable fee in 1986 would be one-half the annual fee, based on the July, 1986 effective date of the fee. The Customs Service is required to provide 60 days notice of the due date for the fee, and is barred from revoking a delinquent broker's permit absent such notice.

[*Effective date.*—Generally for services rendered after the date 15 days after enactment date. Ed.]

[¶ 4207] SECTION 1894. FOREIGN TRADE ZONES

[Conference Report]

* * * * * *

The fifth proviso of section 81c. of the Foreign Trade Zones Act of 1934, as amended, prohibits operations involving the use of certain domestic merchandise in foreign trade zones. The purpose of this provision was to prevent internal revenue taxes from being avoided by the use of foreign trade zones. However, the provision also has prevented the use of domestic merchandise on which there are no internal revenue taxes or on which all internal revenue taxes have been paid.

The conference agreement permits domestic merchandise on which all internal revenue taxes, if any, have been paid to be used in manufacturing or production in foreign trade zones. The change is revenue neutral but removes the current bias in favor of new investments being placed in foreign countries, thus putting on an equal footing in this regard, investments made within the United States. This is not a vehicle to provide for redistillation of imported spirits subsequently removed (admitted) to a zone for use in the manufacture of articles. The right of U.S. Customs and other government officials to inspect and audit zone operations will insure the enforcement of this prohibition.

[¶ 4208] SECTION 1895. COBRA TECHNICAL CORRECTIONS RELATING TO SOCIAL SECURITY ACT PROGRAMS

[Senate Explanation]

* * * * * *

The bill makes miscellaneous technical corrections to the Social Security Act and the Consolidated Omnibus Budget Reconcilliation Act of 1985 (P.L. 99-272). *[Effective date.—]* The corrections will be effective as if the corrected provisions had been originally included in, or amended by, P.L. 99-272.

* * * * * *

[Conference Report]

* * * * * *

Continuing health care

The conference agreement adopts the following technical corrections to the continuing health care provisions of COBRA.

a. Notification requirement.—The conference agreement establishes a 60-day notification period for divorced or legally separated spouses of covered employees, or dependent children ceasing to be dependent children under the generally applicable requirements of the plan, to notify the plan administrator of a qualifying event entitling the spouse or dependent children to continuation health coverage.

b. Maximum period of continuation coverage.—The conference agreement clarifies that a qualified beneficiary may have more than one qualifying event which entitles the beneficiary to continuation coverage, but in no event may the coverage period with respect to such events generally exceed a 36-month period. The second qualifying event must take place during the period of coverage of the first qualifying event to be eligible for a total of 36 months continuation coverage beginning from the date of the first qualifying event.

c. Election of coverage.—The conference agreement clarifies that each qualified beneficiary is entitled to a separate election of continuation coverage. For example, if a covered employee does not elect continuation coverage, the conferees intend that the spouse or dependent children are entitled to elect such coverage. Moreover, even if the employee elects certain coverage, the spouse or dependents may elect different coverage.

d. Failure to pay premium.—The conference agreement provides that the grace period for the failure to pay premiums is the longest of (1) 30 days, (2) the period the plan allows employees for failure to pay premiums, or (3) the period the insurance company allows the plan or the employer for failure to pay premiums.

e. Type of coverage.—The conference agreement provides that, for all purposes, qualified beneficiaries are to be treated under the plan in the same manner as similarly situated beneficiaries for whom a qualifying event has not taken place. For example, if the plan provides for an open enrollment period, then qualified beneficiaries are to be permitted to make elections during the open enrollment period in the same manner as active employees. Thus, an individual who is a qualified beneficiary by reason of being a spouse of a covered employee would have the same rights as active employees during an open enrollment period and would not be limited to the rights of spouses of covered employees.

The conference agreement defines health benefits to mean health benefit plans, including dental and vision care (within the meaning of sec. 213 of the Code). The conferees do not intend that an employer could compel a qualified beneficiary to pay for noncore benefits (such as dental and vision care) even if active employees are required to purchase coverage for such benefits under the plan.

Medicare

The conference agreement follows the Senate amendment with the following clarifications: (1) correct and clarify the section regarding payments under the indirect medical education provision; (2) correct and clarify the section regarding payment under the disproportionate share provision; (3) clarify that all hospitals which have a medicare provider agreement would have to abide by the emergency care requirements of COBRA and the requirements regarding participation in the CHAMPUS program; (4) allow skilled nursing facilities to make an election to be paid on a prospective payment basis based on their costs reporting periods rather than on a Federal fiscal year basis; (5) clarify that the medicare HI tax on state and local governments does not apply to certain campaign workers; (6) clarify that a one-year transition period is provided for foreign medical graduates who have not passed the FMGEMS; (7) allow the Secretary to announce HMO/CMP rates by September 7 of each year rather than publish them; (8) clarify the effective date of the provision regarding penalties for billing for assistants at surgery for certain cataract procedures; (9) allow temporary use of carrier prepayment screens as a substitute for preprocedure review; (10) clarify that the termination date of the ACCESS demonstration project is July 31, 1987; and (11) correct citation, indentation and other technical errors.

[¶4209] SECTION 1896. EXTENSION OF TIME FOR FILING FOR CREDIT OR REFUND WITH RESPECT TO CERTAIN CHANGES INVOLVING INSOLVENT FARMERS

[Senate Explanation]

*   *   *   *   *   *

Extension of Time for Filing Credit or Refund With Respect to the Minimum Tax

Present Law.—The Act provided that certain transfers by insolvent farmers did not give rise to a minimum tax preference. This provision was effective for taxable years beginning after December 31, 1981.

Explanation of Provision.—The bill provides that a claim for refund or credit resulting from the amendment made by the Act may be filed within one year after the date of enactment of this bill.

[Effective date.—Enactment date. Ed.]

[¶ 4211] SECTION 1898. TECHNICAL CORRECTIONS TO THE RETIREMENT EQUITY ACT OF 1984

(Secs. 72; 401; 402; 411; 414; 417; 2503 of the Code; Secs. 203-206; 408 of '74 ERISA; Sec. 302; 303 of '84 REA)

[Senate Explanation]

*   *   *   *   *   *

A. Minimum Participation, Vesting and Benefit Accrual Standards * * *

*   *   *   *   *   *

1. Break-in-Service Rules

*   *   *   *   *   *

Explanation of Provision.—

Class-year vesting.—The bill generally conforms the break-in-service rules applicable to class-year plans to the break-in-service rules provided for other types of plans. Under the bill, a class-year plan generally is to provide that 100 percent of each participating employee's right to benefits derived from employer contributions for a plan year (the contribution year) is to be nonforfeitable as of the close of the fifth plan year of service (whether or not consecutive) with the employer following the contribution year. A plan year is a plan year of service with the employer if the participant has not separated from service with the employer as of the close of the year.

The bill provides that, if a participant incurs five consecutive one-year breaks in service before the completion of five plan years of service with respect to a contribution year, then the plan may provide that the participant forfeits any right to or derived from the employer contributions for the contribution year.

The provision is effective for contributions made for plan years beginning after the date of enactment, except that the provision is not effective with respect to a collectively bargained plan until the applicable effective date of the Act ['84 REA] for that plan.

Lump-sum distributions.—The bill conforms the rules relating to the taxation of lump-sum distributions to the break-in-service rules. Under the bill, in determining whether any distribution payable on account of separation from service is a lump sum distribution, the balance to the credit of the employee is determined without taking into account any increase in vesting that could occur if the employee is reemployed by the employer.

Under the bill, however, if the employee is reemployed by the employer before the occurrence of five consecutive one-year breaks in service and the nonforfeitable interest of the employee in the amount of the pre-break accrued benefit is thereby increased, then the reduction in tax attributable to the treatment of the distribution as a lump-sum distribution is to be recaptured as provided by Treasury regulations. Such a reduction in tax could occur on account of an election to use 10-year forward averaging with respect to a lump-sum distribution, the special treatment of net unrealized appreciation of employer securities (Code sec. 402(e)(4)(J)), or long-term capital gains treatment for a portion of a lump-sum distribution. In addition, if such a recapture is made, the participant's previous lump sum distribution election is not taken into account in determining whether the employee is eligible to make another election.

Rollovers.—The bill provides that, in determining whether a distribution to an employee on account of separation from service is eligible to be rolled over to another plan or to an IRA, the balance to the credit of the employee is determined without regard to any increased vesting that may occur if the employee returns to service with the employer. However, if (1) the employee excluded the distribution from income on account of a rollover, (2) the employee returns to service with the employer before incurring five consecutive one-year breaks in service and (3) the vested percentage of benefits accrued before the separation from service is increased, then any subsequent distributions to the employee from the plan in which the increased vesting occurs are not eligible for 10-year income averaging or capital gains treatment.

The rule denying eligibility for 10-year forward averaging or capital gains treatment on subsequent distributions does not apply if the distribution that was rolled over was made without the consent of the participant (e.g., the amount distributed did not exceed $3,500).

Elapsed time method of crediting service.—The committee directs the Treasury Department to provide, within a reasonable period of time after the date of enactment, additional guidance to taxpayers on the application of the break in service rules to plans that use the elapsed time method of crediting service. It is not intended that such guidance is to be limited to the issuance of regulations.

2. Mandatory Employee Contributions

*   *   *   *   *   *

Explanation of Provision.—The bill conforms the rule relating to the period for repayment of mandatory contributions to the rule relating to the repayment of accrued benefits after separation from service and extends both rules to apply in the case of a defined benefit plan as well as a defined contribution plan. The provision clarifies that the repayment period during which a plan must permit an employee to repay mandatory contributions does not end before a participant has five consecutive one-year breaks in service.

A plan may provide that repayment of withdrawn amounts is required to be made no later than (1) five years after the date of the withdrawal or (2) in the case of a distribution on account of separation from service, the earlier of (a) five years after the date the individual is reemployed by the employer or (b) the date upon which the individual incurs five consecutive one-year breaks in service.

3. Maximum Age Requirement

* * * * * * *

Explanation of Provision.—The bill reduces from 25 to 21 the maximum age requirement that a SEP may impose as a condition of plan participation. Thus, a SEP may not require, as a condition of participation, attainment of an age greater than 21 or the performance of service during more than three of the immediately preceding five calendar years (whichever occurs later).

* * * * * *

[Conference Report]

* * * * * *

* * * The provision in the Senate amendment relating to participation requirements under simplified employee pensions is effective for plan years beginning after the date of enactment.

* * * * * *

[Senate Explanation]

* * * * * *

B. Survivor Benefit Requirements
* * *

1. Coordination Between Qualified Joint and Survivor Annuity and Qualified Preretirement Survivor Annuity.

* * * * * *

Explanation of Provision

* * * * * *

Coordination of preretirement survivor annuity and joint and survivor annuity.—The bill provides that the survivor benefit payable to a participant's spouse is to be provided in the form of a qualified joint and survivor annuity if the participant does not die before the annuity starting date unless the benefit is waived in favor of another benefit and the spouse consents to the waiver. As under present law, the qualified preretirement survivor annuity rules apply in the case of a death before the annuity starting date if the preretirement survivor annuity has not been waived.

Thus, if a participant dies after separation from service or attainment of normal retirement age, but prior to the participant's annuity starting date, the survivor benefit payable to the participant's spouse is to be paid in the form of a qualified preretirement survivor benefit.

Disability benefits.—The bill amends the definition of a participant's annuity starting date to exclude the commencement of disability benefits, but only if the disability benefit is an auxiliary benefit. If a participant receiving a disability benefit will, upon attainment of early or normal retirement age, receive a benefit that satisfies the accrual and vesting rules of section 411 (without taking the disability benefit payments up to that date into account), the disability benefit may be characterized as auxiliary.

For example, consider a married participant who becomes disabled at age 45 with a deferred vested accrued benefit of $100 per month commencing at age 65 in the form of a joint and survivor annuity. If the participant is entitled under the plan to a disability benefit and is also entitled to a benefit of not less than $100 per month commencing at age 65, whether or not the participant is still disabled, the payments made to the participant between ages 45 and 65 would be considered auxiliary. Thus, the participant's annuity starting date would not occur until the participant attained age 65. The participant's surviving spouse would be entitled to receive a qualified preretirement survivor annuity if the participant died before age 65, and the survivor portion of a qualified joint and survivor annuity if the participant died after age 65. The value of the qualified preretirement survivor annuity payable upon the participant's death prior to age 65 would be computed by reference to the qualified joint and survivor annuity that would have been payable had the participant survived to age 65.

If, in the above example, the participant's benefit payable at age 65 were reduced to $90 per month as a result of the disability benefits paid to the participant prior to age 65, the disability benefit would not be auxiliary. The benefit of $90 per month payable at age 65 would not, without taking into account the disability benefit payments prior to age 65, satisfy the minimum vesting and accrual rules of section 411 of the Code. Accordingly, the first day of the first period for which the disability payments were made would constitute the participant's annuity starting date, and any benefits paid to the participant would be required to be paid in the form of a qualified joint and survivor annuity (unless waived by the participant with the consent of the spouse).

2. Transferee Plan Rules.

* * * * * *

Explanation of Provision.—The bill includes two provisions relating to the transferee plan rules. First, the bill clarifies that a plan is not to be considered a transferee plan on account of a transfer completed before January 1, 1985.

In addition, the bill clarifies that the transferee plan rule is limited to benefits attributable to the transferred assets if separate accounting is provided for the transferred assets and the allocable investment yield from those assets. Under the bill, if separate accounting is not maintained for transferred assets (and any allocable investment yield) with respect to an employee, then the survivor benefit requirements apply to all benefits payable with respect to the employee under the plan.

3. Rules Relating to Qualified Preretirement Survivor Annuity.

* * * * * *

Explanation of Provision.—The bill clarifies that, in the case of a participant who separates from service prior to death, the amount of the qualified preretirement survivor annuity is to be calculated by reference to the actual date of separation from service, rather than the date of death. Thus, for purposes of calculating the qualified preretirement survivor annuity, a participant is not to be considered to accrue benefits after the date of separation from service.

The bill also clarifies that, under the special rule for defined contribution plans, a qualified preretirement survivor annuity payable to a participant's surviving spouse is required to be the actuarial equivalent of not less than 50 percent of the account balance in which the participant was vested as of the date of death. For purposes of determining who is a vested participant subject to the survivor benefit provisions, the bill provides that a participant's accrued benefit includes accrued benefits derived from employee contributions.

The bill also clarifies that a plan that is exempt from the survivor benefit may provide for the payment of the participant's nonforfeitable accrued benefit (without the consent of the participant's surviving spouse) to a beneficiary other than the participant's spouse if the participant and spouse have been married for less than 1 year as of the death of the participant.

The committee intends that, with respect to a defined benefit or defined contribution plan, the qualified preretirement survivor annuity is to be treated as attributable to employee contributions in the same proportion which the employee contributions are to the total accrued benefit of the participant. Thus, a plan is not permitted to allocate a preretirement survivor annuity only to employee contributions.

* * * a participant's "earliest retirement age" should be determined by taking in account only the participant's actual years of service at the time of the participant's separation from service or death. Thus, in the case of a plan under which participants may not receive a benefit under the plan until the participant attains age 65, or upon attainment of age 55 and completion of 10 years of service, the earliest retirement age of a participant who died or separated from service with only 8 years of service would be age 65. On the other hand, if a participant died or separated from service after completing 10 years of service, the earliest retirement age would occur when the participant would have attained age 55 (if the participant had survived).

4. Spousal Consent Requirements.

* * * * * *

Explanation of Provision.—

Designation of nonspouse beneficiary.—Under the bill, a spouse's consent to waive a qualified joint and survivor annuity or a qualified preretirement survivor annuity is not valid unless the consent (1) names a designated beneficiary who will receive any survivor benefits under the plan and the form of any benefits paid under the plan (including the form of benefits that the designated beneficiary will receive), or (2) acknowledges that the spouse has the right to limit consent only to a specific beneficiary or a specific form of benefits, and that the spouse voluntarily elects to relinquish one or both of such rights.

The spousal consent form is to contain such information as may be appropriate to disclose to the spouse the rights that are relinquished. If the consent names a designated beneficiary, then any subsequent change to the beneficiary designation (or the form of distribution, if any, specified in the consent) is invalid unless a new consent is obtained from the participant's spouse. Of course, spousal consent is not required if a participant dies and the beneficiary designated (with spousal consent) to receive the participant's death benefit elects to receive the benefit in a form not specified in the waiver.

If a plan is required to permit the waiver of a survivor benefit, * * * the plan may not restrict the spouse's ability to waive a benefit by providing only a general consent to waive under which a spouse relinquishes the right to designate a beneficiary or a form of benefit. Thus, a spouse is always permitted to waive a survivor benefit only in favor of a specific beneficiary or a specific form of benefit. The committee intends that, if a plan permits a general consent, the acknowledgment of the general consent should indicate that the spouse is aware that a more limited consent could be provided.

Similar rules relating to the manner in which spousal consent is obtained apply to a spousal consent obtained to waive a death benefit under a profit-sharing or stock bonus plan that is not otherwise subject to the survivor benefit requirements.

Spousal consent with respect to loans.—In addition, under the bill, in the case of a participant's benefit that is not exempt from the survivor benefit requirements, a plan is to provide that no portion of the accrued benefit of the participant may be used as security for any loan unless, at the time the security agreement is entered into, the participant's spouse (determined as of the date the security agreement is entered into) consents to the use of the accrued benefit as security. If the individual who is the participant's spouse at the time that the security agreement is entered into consents, then the plan is not prevented by the spousal consent rules from realizing its security interest in the event of a default on the participant's loan, even if, at the time of the default, the participant is married to a different spouse. Similarly, if a participant is not married at

Act § 1898   ¶ 4211

time the security agreement is executed, then the plan is not prevented from realizing its security interest if a default on the loan subsequently occurs when the participant is married.

* * * * * *

In the case of a participant whose accrued benefit is not subject to the survivor benefit provisions at the time the security is provided (e.g., a profit-sharing plan that is not a transferee plan with respect to the participant), the plan will not be treated as failing to meet the survivor benefit requirements if the participant's benefit is used as security for a loan and spousal consent is not obtained for the use of the accrued benefit as security, even if the plan subsequently becomes subject to the survivor benefit requirements with respect to the participant.

The bill further clarifies that for purposes of determining the survivor benefit, if any, to which a participant's surviving spouse is entitled upon the participant's death, any security interest held by the plan by reason of a loan outstanding to the participant is taken into account and, if there is a default on the loan, then the participant's nonforfeitable accrued benefit is first reduced by any security interest held by the plan by reason of a loan outstanding to the participant. The rule applies only if (a) the loan is secured by the participant's accrued benefit and (b) the spousal consent requirements, if any, applicable to the participant's accrued benefit at the time the security arrangement was entered into were satisfied. In addition, the participant's nonforfeitable accrued benefit is adjusted (where appropriate), taking into account the terms of the plan and the terms of the qualified domestic relations order, by the value of amounts payable under any outstanding qualified domestic relations order, for purposes of determining the survivor benefit, if any, to which the participant's surviving spouse is entitled upon the participant's death.

Similarly, upon a married participant's retirement, for purposes of determining the amount of the joint and survivor annuity payable to the participant and spouse, any security held by the plan by reason of a loan outstanding to the participant and the present value of any outstanding qualified domestic relations order are taken into account in the same manner as they are taken into account for purposes of the qualified preretirement survivor annuity.

Determination of amount of preretirement survivor annuity.—The bill provides that, in the case of a defined contribution plan subject to the survivor benefit requirements, the participant's vested account balance (including any portion of the account balance attributable to employee contributions) is used for purposes of determining the amount of the qualified preretirement survivor annuity.

Scope of spousal consent requirements.—The bill clarifies that certain of the election period and notice requirements with respect to spousal consent also apply in the case of spousal consent (1) to waive a survivor benefit under a plan exempt from the preretirement survivor annuity and joint and survivor annuity requirements, (2) to permit the participant's accrued benefit to be pledged as security for a loan, (3) to permit the election of a cash-out of amounts after the annuity starting date, and (4) to permit the immediate distribution of amounts in excess of $3,500.

In the case of a loan secured by a participant's accrued benefits, the notice and election period requirements apply at the time the security arrangement is entered into. Consequently, the election period for spousal consent with respect to the execution of a security agreement is the 90-day period before the execution of the agreement.

Similarly, in the case of a cash out subsequent to a participant's annuity starting date, the election period is the 90-day period before the distribution is permitted.

* * * for purposes of the spousal consent rules, in the case of a participant residing outside of the United States, that spousal consent may be witnessed by the equivalent of a notary public in the jurisdiction in which consent is executed. The committee also intends that an election under section 242(b) of the Tax Equity and Fiscal Responsibility Act of 1982 will not be invalidated because a plan secures spousal consent to the election.

In addition, the committee intends that a participant will be treated as having no spouse, if the participant has been abandoned (within the meaning of local law) by the spouse, even if the participant knows where the spouse is located. The committee intends that the spousal consent requirement may be waived, however, only if the participant has a court order specifying that the participant has been abandoned within the meaning of local law. Of course, a participant could provide a qualified domestic relations (such as a separation agreement) rather than a court order specifying that the participant has been abandoned.

Gift tax consequences of waiver.—The bill provides that the waiver of a qualified joint and survivor annuity or a qualified preretirement survivor annuity by a nonparticipant spouse prior to the death of the participant does not result in a taxable transfer for purposes of the gift tax provisions.

Effective Dates.—The provision relating to spousal consents to beneficiary designations is effective for [plan years beginning after enactment date Ed.] The provision relating to the notice and election period requirements for plans that are exempt from the survivor benefit requirements is effective upon the date of enactment.

The provision relating to accrued benefits pledged as security for a loan is effective for loans made after August 18, 1985. In addition, any accrued benefits pledged as security for a loan prior to August 19, 1985, are exempt from the requirement that spousal consent be obtained. Accordingly, in the case of a pledge made before August 19, 1985, a plan is not required to obtain the consent of any spouse of a participant before it applies the benefit against the loan. Finally, any loan that is revised, extended, renewed, or renegotiated after August 18, 1985, is treated as a loan made (and security pledged) after August 18, 1985.

5. Notice Requirements

* * * * * *

Explanation of Provision.—The bill provides that the period during which notice is required to be provided to an individual does not end before the latest of (1) the close of the plan year in which a participant attains age 35; (2) a reasonable period of time after the individual becomes a plan participant; (3) a reasonable period of time after the survivor benefit applicable to a participant is no longer subsidized (as defined in Code sec. 417(a)(4)); or (4) a reasonable period of time after the survivor benefit provisions (Code sec. 401(a)(11)) become applicable with respect to a participant.

The bill also provides that if a participant separates from service prior to age 35, the plan must provide the participant with notice, within a reasonable time after separation from service, of the right to decline a qualified preretirement survivor annuity.

6. Clarification of Rule for Subsidized Benefits.

* * * * * *

Explanation of Provision.—The bill clarifies that a plan is not required to provide a participant with a right to waive a qualified joint and survivor annuity or qualified preretirement survivor annuity if the plan fully subsidizes the cost of the benefit.

The bill further clarifies that the present-law exception to the notice requirement only applies if (1) the plan fully subsidizes the benefit, and (2) the plan does not permit a participant to waive the benefit or to designate as another beneficiary.

The committee intends that a benefit is not to be considered fully subsidized if the cost of the survivor benefit is spread among all plan participants, including participants who are not married, or among some subgroup of participants, even if the benefits and contributions of those charged with the cost of survivor benefit protection are unaffected by the waiver or failure to waive survivor benefit protection. Of course, if a participant is not entitled to waive a survivor benefit, the participant cannot be charged for the benefit.

7. Clarification of Annuity Starting Date.

* * * * * *

[Conference Report]

* * * * * *

* * * Under the conference agreement, in the case of benefits payable in the form of an annuity, the annuity starting date is the first day of the first period for which an amount is payable as an annuity, regardless of when or whether payment is actually made. For example, a participant is to begin receiving annuity payments on the first day of the month following the participant's sixtieth birthday. After that date, but before any annuity payments are actually made, the participant dies. The annuity starting date is the first day of the month following the participant's sixtieth birthday.

* * * [I]n the case of benefits not payable as an annuity, the annuity starting date is the date on which all events have occurred which entitle the participant to a benefit (e.g., separation from service, applicable consent to payment).

Qualified Domestic Relations Orders
* * *

* * * * * *

1. Tax Treatment of Divorce Distributions

* * * * * *

Explanation of Provision.—The bill provides that the special rules for determining the taxability of benefits subject to a qualified domestic relations order apply only to distributions made to an alternate payee who is the spouse or the former spouse of the participant. Thus, distributions to a spouse or former spouse generally will be included in the gross income of the spouse or former spouse. Under the bill, however, a distribution to an alternate payee other than a spouse (e.g., a child) is generally to be includible in the gross income of the participant. (For purposes of lump sum treatment, amounts paid to an alternate payee other than a spouse, or former spouse, shall be treated as part of the balance to the credit of the participant).

In addition, under the bill, the rules for allocating an employee's investment in the contract between the employee and an alternate payee apply only if the alternate payee is a spouse or former spouse of the participant.

If the alternate payee is not a spouse or former spouse, then the investment in the contract is not allocated to the alternate payee and is recovered by the participant under the general basis recovery rules applicable to the participant. [Amendments apply to payments made after enactment date. Ed.]

2. Determination by Plan Administrator
    Present Law.—

* * * * * *

The administrator of a plan that receives a domestic relations order is required to notify promptly the participant and any other alternate payee of receipt of the order and the plan's procedures for determining whether the order is qualified. In addition, within a reasonable period after receipt of the order, the plan administrator is to determine whether the order is qualified and notify the participant and alternate payee of the determination.

Act § 1898   ¶ 4211

During any period in which the issue of whether an order is a qualified order is being determined (by the plan administrator, by a court of competent jurisdiction, or otherwise), the plan administrator is to defer the payment of any benefits in dispute. These deferred benefits are segregated either in a separate account in the plan or in an escrow account. A plan administrator similarly could not permit a loan to be made to the participant during the period of deferral if the loan is to be secured by the benefits in dispute.

If the order is determined to be a qualified domestic relations order within 18 months after benefits are first deferred, then the plan administrator is to pay the segregated amounts to the persons entitled to receive them. If the plan administrator determines that the order is not a qualified order or, after the 18-month period has expired, the plan administrator has not resolved the issue of whether the order is qualified, the segregated amounts are paid to the person or persons who would have received the amounts if the order had not been issued.

Explanation of Provision.— * * * an order will not fail to be a qualified domestic relations order even if the form of the benefit does not continue to be a form permitted under the plan on account of (1) a plan amendment or (2) a change of law. In the case of a plan amendment, an alternate payee remains entitled to receive benefits in the form specified in the order unless the alternate payee elects to receive benefits in another form and the election of such alternate form does not affect, in any way, the amount or form of benefits payable to the participant. In the case of a change of law, which makes the form specified in the order impermissible, the committee intends that the plan is to permit the alternate payee to select a form of benefit specified in the plan, provided the selection of an alternative form by the alternate payee does not affect, in any way, the amount or form of benefits payable to the participant.

The bill makes it clear that the 18-month period during which benefits may be deferred begins with the date on which any payments would, but for the deferral, be required to commence. Accordingly, if a payment is deferred pending the resolution of a dispute, then that payment and each other payment that is deferred within the next 18 months because of the dispute are to be segregated. If the dispute is not resolved within 18 months after the first payment is deferred, then all payments deferred during the 18-month period with respect to the dispute are to be paid to the persons who would have received them if the order had not been issued.

If a plan administrator determines that a domestic relations order is defective before the expiration of the 18-month suspension period, * * * the plan administrator may delay payment of a participant's benefit until the expiration of the 18-month period if the plan administrator has notice that the parties are attempting to rectify any deficiencies in the order.

Notice of issuance of a stay during the time an appeal is pending is deemed to be notice that the parties are attempting to cure deficiencies in a domestic relations order. Further, the committee intends that a plan administrator will honor a restraining order prohibiting the disposition of a participant's benefits pending resolution of a dispute with respect to a domestic relations order.

In addition, the bill eliminates the requirement that a defined benefit plan establish an escrow account for amounts that would have otherwise been paid during the 18-month period. Instead, the plan administrator is required only to account separately for such amounts. If the deficiency is not cured or the dispute not resolved within the 18-month period, all payments deferred during the 18-month period are to be paid to the persons who would have received them if the stay or order had not been issued.

* * * * * *

[Conference Report]

* * * * * *

The conference agreement adopts the provisions in the Senate amendment with regard to procedures during the 18-month period. If a plan administrator determines that a domestic relations order is defective before the expiration of the 18-month suspension period, the conference committee intends that the plan administrator may delay payment of a participant's benefit until the expiration of the 18-month period if the plan administrator has notice that either party is attempting to rectify any deficiencies in the order.

Similarly, the committee intends that the plan administrator may delay payment of benefits for a reasonable period of time if the plan administrator receives notice that a domestic relations order is being sought. For example, a participant in a profit-sharing plan which is exempt from the survivor benefit rules requests a lump sum distribution from the plan. Before the distribution is made, the plan administrator receives notice that the participant's spouse is seeking a domestic relations order. The plan administrator may delay payment of benefits.

* * * * * *

[Senate Explanation]

* * * * * *

3. Form of Benefit

* * * * * *

Explanation of Provision.—The bill clarifies that a qualified domestic relations order may not require that payments prior to, or subsequent to, a participant's separation from service be made in the form of a qualified joint and survivor annuity with respect to the alternate payee and his or her subsequent spouse.

4. Application of Domestic Relations Provisions to Plans not Subject to Assignment or Alienation Restrictions.

* * * * * *

Explanation of Provision.—The bill clarifies that the qualified domestic relations provisions do not apply to any plan to which the assignment or alienation restrictions do not apply. For example, a domestic relations order relating to the division of pension benefits of a participant in a plan maintained by a governmental employer is not required to meet the rules relating to qualified domestic relations orders because the payment of benefits to a spouse or former spouse of the participant is not a prohibited assignment or alienation of the participant's benefits.

5. Coordination of Domestic Relations Provisions with Federal Garnishment Restrictions.

* * * * * *

Explanation of Provision.— * * * payment of benefits pursuant to a qualified domestic relations order is not treated as a garnishment of wages for purposes of Federal or State law restrictions on garnishment.

6. Coordination with Qualified Plan Requirements

* * * * * *

Explanation of Provision. * * * a plan is not treated as failing to satisfy the qualification requirements of section 401(a) or (k) or section 409(d) of the Internal Revenue Code (prohibiting payment of benefits prior to termination of employment or such time as distributions are otherwise permitted) solely because the plan makes payment to the alternate payee, even if the payments are made with respect to a participant who has not separated from service, and they commence before the participant has attained the earliest retirement age under the plan. This exception applies, however, only if the present value of the benefit to be paid to an alternate payee (1) does not exceed $3,500 or (2) exceeds at least $3,500 and the alternate payee consents in writing to such earlier distribution. Further, the exception applies only if the distribution, if paid to the participant, would not contravene the provisions of the plan (except as permitted under section 414(p)(4)). Of course, a plan could not make distributions to an alternate payee at a time not specified in a qualified domestic relations order unless (1) the order also provided for such earlier distributions pursuant to an agreement between the plan and an alternate payee, and (2) the plan authorized such distributions.

In determining whether the present value of the benefit payable to the alternate payee exceeds $3,500, the present value of the participant's accrued benefit or that of any other alternate payee (after reduction for the benefits payable to the alternate payee) is disregarded. Similarly, for purposes of determining whether the present value of a benefit payable to a participant exceeds $3,500, the present value of amounts payable to an alternate payee under a qualified domestic relations order is disregarded.

* * * to the extent provided in a qualified domestic relations order, a spouse of a participant is not treated as a spouse. For example, a qualified domestic relations order could provide for the division of a participant's accrued benefits under a pension plan as part of a separation agreement and could further provide that the participant's spouse is not entitled to receive any survivor benefits under the usual survivor benefits provisions. Thus, the plan administrator would not be required to secure spousal consent to the participant's election to waive a survivor benefit.

In addition, the bill authorizes the Secretary of the Treasury to issue such regulations as may be necessary to otherwise coordinate the Code provisions affecting qualified domestic relations orders (sections 401(a)(13)(B) and 414(p)), and the regulations issued by the Secretary of Labor thereunder with other Code provisions affecting qualified plans. The Secretary of Labor has authority to issue regulations under the qualified domestic relations order provisions of ERISA, and the Code (secs. 401(a)(13)(B) and 414(p)), and the bill does not affect the authority of the Secretary of Labor to prescribe such regulations.

7. Earliest Retirement Age.

* * * * * *

[Conference Report]

* * * * * *

Under the conference agreement, the definition of "earliest retirement age" for purposes of the QDRO provisions in the case of a defined contribution plan or a defined benefit plan is the earlier of: (1) the earliest date benefits are payable under the plan to the participant, and (2) the later of the date the participant attains age 50 and the date on which the participant could obtain a distribution from the plan if the participant separated from service.

For example, in the case of a plan which provides for payment of benefits upon separation from service (but not before then), the earliest date on which a QDRO can require payments to an alternate payee to begin is the date the participant separates from service. A QDRO could also require such a plan to begin payments to an alternate payee when the participant attains age 50, even if the participant has not then separated from service. The amount payable under a QDRO following the participant's earliest retirement age cannot exceed the amount which the participant is (or would be) entitled to receive at such time. For example, assume that a profit-sharing plan provides that a participant may withdraw some, but not all, of the participant's account balance before separation from service. A QDRO may provide for payment to an alternative payee up to the amount which the participant may withdraw.

A plan may provide for payment to an alternate payee prior to the earliest retire-

Act § 1898   ¶ 4211

ment age as defined under the conference agreement.

[Senate Explanation]

*   *   *   *   *   *

D. Cash Out of Certain Accrued Benefits * * *

*   *   *   *   *   *

Explanation of Provision.—The bill clarifies that, for purposes determining whether a participant's benefit exceeds $3,500, the nonvested portion of the participant's accrued benefit is to be disregarded.

The bill would also permit the distribution from an employee stock ownership plan (ESOP) of dividends that are deductible by the employer under section 404(k), without the consent of the participant, or the participant and the participant's spouse even where the present value of the participant's benefit exceeds $3,500.

*   *   *   *   *   *

E. Notice of Rollover Treatment * * *

*   *   *   *   *   *

Explanation of Provision.—The bill makes it clear that a plan administrator is to provide notice when making any distribution eligible for rollover treatment. Thus, for example, notice is to be provided when a distribution eligible for rollover treatment pursuant to the partial rollover rules is made.

*   *   *   *   *   *

F. Reduction of Accrued Benefits * * *

*   *   *   *   *   *

* * * an ESOP will not be treated as violating the rule preventing reductions in accrued benefits merely because the plan sponsor eliminates or retains the discretion to eliminate a lump sum option or an installment payout option with respect to a nondiscriminatory class of employees. Similarly, an employer could retain discretion to limit the option of the plan participants to elect a stock distribution in cases in which the employer becomes substantially employee-owned or the plan ceases to be an ESOP or a stock bonus plan. In addition, an employer would be permitted to eliminate a required cash distribution option in cases in which the employer securities become readily tradable or to require a cash distribution in cases in which stock in the plan is sold in connection with a sale of substantially all of the company.

G. Transitional Rules * * *

Explanation of Provision.—The bill clarifies the application of the transitional rule relating to qualified preretirement survivor benefits in situations in which the participant had designated a beneficiary other than the participant's spouse. Under the bill, the present value of a death benefit payable to any beneficiary with respect to an individual who (1) performs at least one hour of service under the plan on or after August

23, 1984, (2) dies before the annuity starting date, and (3) dies before the effective date of the Act, may be reduced by the present value of the amount payable to the participant's surviving spouse pursuant to the transition rule. If death benefits payable under a plan are divided among more than one beneficiary, the present value of the amount payable to each beneficiary (including benefits, other than survivor benefits payable under the transition rules, payable to the surviving spouse) is reduced proportionately by the amount payable to the surviving spouse pursuant to the transition rule.

However, the bill also permits the surviving spouse to waive the right to receive the qualified preretirement survivor annuity. Under the bill, if it is made on or before the close of the second plan year to which the Act applies, then the waiver is not to be treated as a taxable transfer for purposes of the gift tax or as a prohibited assignment or alienation for purposes of ERISA or the Code. In addition, death benefits waived by the surviving spouse during this period would not be includible in the spouse's income. Such benefits would be includible in the gross income of the recipient.

Finally, the bill clarifies that in the case of a plan that was amended, as of the effective date of REA, to be exempt from the REA survivor benefit requirements, but that (1) was not technically exempt from the survivor benefit requirements during the transition rule period and that (2) failed to satisfy the REA transition rules solely because with respect to a participant who died during the transition period, the plan paid to the surviving spouse the participant's entire vested account balance in a form other than a life annuity, the plan will not be treated as failing to satisfy the survivor benefit requirements of REA.

*   *   *   *   *   *

The bill would amend REA to provide that, in the case of a plan maintained pursuant to one or more collective bargaining agreements, the provisions of REA are generally effective for plan years beginning after the earlier of (1) the date upon which the last of the collective bargaining agreements relating to the plan terminates (determined without regard to any extension agreed to after the date of enactment), or (2) July 1, 1988.

The amendment does not alter the effective date of the spousal consent provision of REA [except provision relating to spousal consent to changes in benefit form is effective for plan years beginning after enactment date. Ed.] the provisions of REA relating to qualified domestic relations orders, or the provision of REA relating to the cutback of a participant's accrued benefit.

[Effective date.—Except as otherwise provided, amendments take effect as if included in provisions of '84 REA to which they relate. Ed.]

*   *   *   *   *   *

* * * * * *

Loans to owner-employees—The conference agreement adopts the provision in the House bill regarding loans to owner-employees from qualified plans. ['74 ERISA is amended to permit owner-employees to borrow from a qualified plan. Ed.]

LIST OF CODE SECTIONS AFFECTED

【¶4851】 The table below contains a complete list of sections or subsections of the Internal Revenue Code amended, added, or repealed by the Tax Reform Act of 1986. The Act section making the amendment is listed opposite each change. Note that the Tax Reform Act of 1986 has amended and reenacted the Internal Revenue Code of 1954 as the Internal Revenue Code of 1986.

Code Sec.	1986 Act Sec.	Code Sec.	1986 Act Sec.
1 amended	101(a)	26(b)(1) amended	701(c)(1)(B)(ii)
1(i) added	1411(a)	26(b)(1) amended	701(c)(1)(B)(i)
1(j) added	302(a)	26(b)(2)(A) amended	701(c)(1)(B)(iii)
2(a)(3)(B) amended	1708(a)(1)	26(b)(2)(G) amended	261(c)
2(c) amended	1301(j)(10)	26(b)(2)(G) amended	632(c)(1)
3(a) amended	102(b)	26(b)(2)(H) amended	261(c)
3(b)(1) struck out	141(b)(1)	26(b)(2)(H) amended	701(c)(1)(B)(iv)
3(b)(2) renumbered (1)	141(b)(1)	26(b)(2)(I) added	261(c)
3(b)(3) renumbered (2)	141(b)(1)	26(b)(2)(I) amended	701(c)(1)(B)(iv)
5(a)(4) amended	701(e)(4)(A)	26(b)(2)(J) added	701(c)(1)(B)(iv)
5(b)(2) struck out	141(b)(2)	26(c) amended	701(c)(1)(C)
5(b)(3) renumbered (2)	141(b)(2)	28(b) amended	231(d)(3)(A)(i)
11(b) amended	601(a)	28(b)(1)(D) amended	231(d)(3)(A)(iv)
12(7) amended	701(e)(4)(B)	28(b)(2)(A)(ii)(I) amended	1879(b)(1)(A)
15(d) amended	101(b)	28(b)(2)(A)(ii)(II) amended	1879(b)(1)(B)
21(b)(1)(A) amended	104(b)(1)(A)	28(c) amended	231(d)(3)(A)(i)
21(e)(6)(A) amended	104(b)(1)(A)	28(c)(2) amended	231(d)(3)(A)(ii)
21(e)(6)(B) amended	104(b)(1)(B)	28(d)(1) amended	1879(b)(2)
22(e)(2) amended	1301(j)(8)	28(d)(2) amended	701(c)(2)
24 repealed	112(a)	28(d)(3)(B) amended	1275(c)(4)
25(a)(1)(B) amended	1862(d)(1)	28(d)(4) amended	231(d)(3)(A)(iii)
25(b)(2)(A)(ii) amended	1301(f)(2)(A)	28(e) amended	232
25(b)(2)(A)(iii) amended	1301(f)(2)(B)	29(b)(5) amended	701(c)(3)
25(c)(2)(A) amended	1301(f)(2)(E)	29(d)(8) amended	1879(c)(1)
25(c)(2)(A) amended	1862(b)	30 renumbered 41	231(d)(2)
25(c)(2)(A)(ii) amended	1301(f)(2)(C)(ii)	30(a) amended	231(c)(1)
25(c)(2)(A)(iii) amended	1301(f)(2)(C)(i)	30(b)(2)(D)(iii) heading amended	1847(b)(1)
25(c)(2)(A)(iii)(I) struck out	1301(f)(2)(D)	30(d) amended	231(b)
25(c)(2)(A)(iii)(I) added	1301(f)(2)(D)	30(e) amended	231(c)(2)
25(c)(2)(A)(iii)(II) struck out	1301(f)(2)(D)	30(h) added	231(a)(1)
25(c)(2)(A)(iii)(II) added	1301(f)(2)(D)	32(a) amended	111(a)(1)
25(c)(2)(A)(iii)(III) struck out	1301(f)(2)(D)	32(a) amended	111(a)(2)
25(c)(2)(A)(iii)(III) added	1301(f)(2)(D)	32(b) amended	111(b)
25(c)(2)(A)(iii)(IV) struck out	1301(f)(2)(D)	32(c) amended	1301(j)(8)
25(c)(2)(A)(iii)(IV) added	1301(f)(2)(D)	32(c)(1)(A)(i) amended	104(b)(1)(B)
25(c)(2)(A)(iii)(V) struck out	1302(f)(2)(D)	32(c)(1)(C) amended	1272(d)(4)
25(c)(2)(A)(iii)(V) added	1301(f)(2)(D)	32(d) amended	1301(j)(8)
25(c)(2)(A)(iii)(V) amended	1862(a)	32(f)(2)(A) struck out	111(d)(1)
25(c)(2)(A)(iii)(VI) added	1301(f)(2)(D)	32(f)(2)(A) added	111(d)(1)
25(c)(2)(B) amended	1301(f)(2)(C)(i)	32(f)(2)(B) struck out	111(d)(1)
25(c)(2)(B) amended	1301(f)(2)(F)(i)	32(f)(2)(B) added	111(d)(1)
25(c)(2)(B)(iii) struck out	1301(f)(2)(F)(ii)	32(i) added	111(c)
25(c)(2)(B)(iii) added	1301(f)(2)(F)(ii)	34(a)(3) amended	1703(e)(2)(F)
25(d)(2)(A) amended	1301(f)(1)(A)	34(a)(3) amended	1877(a)
25(d)(3) struck out	1301(f)(2)(G)	38(b)(2) amended	231(d)(1)
25(e)(1)(B) amended	1862(c)	38(b)(2) amended	1171(b)(1)
25(e)(2) amended	1301(f)(2)(H)	38(b)(3) amended	231(d)(1)
25(e)(6) amended	1301(f)(2)(I)	38(b)(3) amended	252(b)(1)
25(e)(8)(A) amended	1301(f)(2)(J)	38(b)(3) amended	1171(b)(1)
25(e)(8)(B) amended	1301(f)(2)(K)	38(b)(4) struck out	1171(b)(1)
25(e)(9) amended	1301(f)(2)(L)	38(b)(4) added	231(d)(1)
25(e)(10) amended	1301(f)(2)(M)	38(b)(4) added	252(b)(1)
25(f)(1) amended	1301(f)(2)(N)	38(b)(5) added	252(b)(1)
25(f)(2)(A) amended	1301(f)(1)(B)	38(c)(1) struck out	701(c)(4)
25(f)(3) amended	1301(f)(2)(O)	38(c)(1) added	701(c)(4)
25(f)(4) amended	1899A(1)	38(c)(1)(B) amended	221(a)
26(a) amended	701(c)(1)(A)	38(c)(2) struck out	701(c)(4)
26(b) heading amended	701(c)(1)(B)(v)	38(c)(2) added	701(c)(4)

Code Sec.	1986 Act Sec.	Code Sec.	1986 Act Sec.
38(c)(3) renumbered (4)	701(c)(4)	51(j) relettered (k)	1878(f)(1)
38(c)(3) added	701(c)(4)	53 added	701(b)
38(d) amended	231(d)(3)(B)	55 added	701(a)
38(d) amended	252(b)(2)	55(c)(1) amended	252(c)
38(d) amended	1171(b)(2)(A)	55(c)(2)(E)(i) amended	1847(a)(2)
38(d) amended	1171(b)(2)(B)	55(c)(3)(A) amended	1847(a)(1)
39(d)(1)(A) amended	1846(1)	56 added	701(a)
39(d)(2)(B) amended	1846(2)	56(c) amended	1171(b)(3)
39(d)(3) added	231(d)(3)(C)(i)	57 added	701(a)
41 repealed	1171(a)	57(a)(12)(B) amended	1809(a)(3)
41(b)(2)(A)(iii) amended	231(e)	57(b)(1)(B) amended	1804(k)(3)(C)
41(g) amended	231(d)(3)(C)(ii)	57(b)(2) amended	1804(k)(3)(D)
42 added	252(a)	58 added	701(a)
46(b)(2)(A) amended	1847(b)(11)	58(c) amended	1875(a)
46(b)(2)(A)(viii) added	421(a)	59 added	701(a)
46(b)(2)(A)(ix) added	421(a)	62 amended	132(b)(2)(A)
46(b)(2)(A)(x) added	421(a)	62(2) amended	132(b)(1)
46(b)(2)(A)(xi) added	421(a)	62(7) amended	1875(c)(3)
46(b)(2)(E) added	421(b)	62(16) struck out	131(b)(1)
46(b)(4) amended	251(a)	62(a)(3) struck out	301(b)(1)
46(c)(8)(D)(v) amended	201(d)(7)(B)	62(a)(4) renumbered (3)	301(b)(1)
46(c)(8)(D)(v) amended	1844(a)	62(a)(5) renumbered (4)	301(b)(1)
46(c)(9)(A) amended	1844(b)(3)	62(a)(6) renumbered (5)	301(b)(1)
46(c)(9)(C)(i) amended	1844(b)(5)	62(a)(7) renumbered (6)	301(b)(1)
46(e)(4)(D) added	1802(a)(6)	62(a)(8) struck out	132(c)
46(e)(4)(E) added	1802(a)(8)	62(a)(10) renumbered (7)	301(b)(1)
46(f)(9) repealed	1848(a)	62(a)(11) renumbered (8)	301(b)(1)
47(a)(9) added	1802(a)(5)(A)	62(a)(12) renumbered (9)	301(b)(1)
47(d)(1) amended	1844(b)(1)(A)	62(a)(13) renumbered (10)	301(b)(1)
47(d)(1) amended	1844(b)(1)(B)	62(a)(14) renumbered (11)	301(b)(1)
47(d)(3)(E)(i) amended	1844(b)(4)	62(a)(15) renumbered (12)	301(b)(1)
47(d)(3)(F) repealed	1844(b)(2)	62(b) added	132(b)(2)(B)
47(d)(3)(G) amended	1511(c)(2)	63 amended	102(a)
48(a)(2)(B)(vii) amended	1272(d)(5)	63(c)(6)(C) struck out	1272(d)(6)
48(a)(2)(B)(vii) amended	1275(c)(5)	63(c)(6)(D) relettered (C)	1272(d)(6)
48(a)(4) amended	1802(a)(9)(A)(i)	63(c)(6)(E) relettered (D)	1272(d)(6)
48(a)(4) amended	1802(a)(9)(A)(ii)	67 added	132(a)
48(a)(5)(B)(iii) repealed	1802(a)(5)(B)	71(b)(1)(D) amended	1843(b)
48(a)(5)(D) relettered (E)	1802(a)(4)(C)	71(c)(2)(B) amended	1843(d)
48(a)(5)(D) added	1802(a)(4)(C)	71(f) amended	1843(c)(1)
48(b)(1) amended	1809(e)(1)	71(g) added	1843(a)
48(b)(2) amended	1809(e)(2)(A)	72(b) amended	1122(c)(2)
48(b)(2) amended	1809(e)(2)(B)	72(d) repealed	1122(c)(1)
48(b)(2) amended	1809(e)(2)(C)	72(e)(4)(C) added	1826(b)(3)
48(b)(2)(B) amended	1809(e)(2)(D)	72(e)(5) amended	1854(b)(1)
48(d)(4)(D) amended	701(e)(4)(C)	72(e)(5)(D) amended	1122(c)(3)(B)
48(d)(6)(C)(ii) amended	1511(c)(3)	72(e)(7)(B) amended	1852(c)(1)(A)
48(g) amended	251(b)	72(e)(7)(B) amended	1852(c)(1)(B)
48(g)(2)(B)(vi)(I) amended	1802(a)(9)(B)	72(e)(7)(B) amended	1852(c)(1)(C)
48(l)(5) amended	1847(b)(6)(A)	72(e)(8) added	1122(c)(3)(A)
48(l)(5) amended	1847(b)(6)(B)	72(e)(9) added	1122(c)(3)(A)
48(q)(3) amended	251(c)	72(f) amended	1852(c)(3)(A)
48(q)(6) renumbered (7)	1809(d)(2)	72(f) amended	1852(c)(3)(B)
48(r) relettered (s)	1879(j)(1)	72(m)(2)(B) amended	1852(c)(4)(A)
48(r) added	1879(j)(1)	72(m)(2)(C) amended	1852(c)(4)(B)
48(r)(5) amended	803(b)(2)(B)	72(m)(5) heading amended	1852(a)(2)(C)
49 added	211(a)	72(m)(5)(A) amended	1123(d)(1)
51(a) amended	1701(b)(1)	72(m)(5)(A) amended	1852(a)(2)(A)
51(b)(3) struck out	1701(b)(2)(A)(i)	72(m)(5)(C) amended	1852(a)(2)(B)
51(b)(3) amended	1701(b)(2)(A)(ii)	72(m)(10) amended	1898(c)(1)(B)
51(b)(4) renumbered (3)	1701(b)(2)(A)(i)	72(o)(5)(A) amended	1101(b)(2)(C)(i)
51(c)(3) amended	1701(a)	72(o)(5)(C) amended	1101(b)(2)(C)(ii)
51(d)(12)(B)(i) amended	1701(b)(2)(B)(i)	72(o)(5)(D) amended	1101(b)(2)(C)(iii)
51(d)(12)(B)(ii) struck out	1701(b)(2)(B)(ii)	72(p)(2)(A)(i) amended	1134(a)
51(d)(12)(B)(iii) renumbered (ii)	1701(b)(2)(B)(ii)	72(p)(2)(B)(ii) amended	1134(d)
51(d)(12)(B)(iii) amended	1701(b)(2)(B)(iii)	72(p)(2)(C) relettered (D)	1134(b)
51(d)(12)(B)(iv) renumbered (iii)	1701(b)(2)(B)(ii)	72(p)(2)(C) added	1134(b)
51(i)(3) added	1701(c)	72(p)(3) renumbered (4)	1134(c)
		72(p)(3) added	1134(c)
		72(p)(3) amended	1101(b)(2)(B)

Code Sec.	1986 Act Sec.	Code Sec.	1986 Act Sec.
72(p)(4) renumbered (5)	1134(c)	103(o) heading amended	1869(a)(2)
72(q) heading amended	1123(b)(1)(B)	103(o) amended	1869(a)(1)
72(q)(1) amended	1123(b)(1)(A)	103(o)(2) heading amended	1869(a)(3)
72(q)(2) amended	1123(b)(3)	103(o)(2)(C)(ii) amended	1869(b)(1)
72(q)(2)(B) amended	1826(c)	103(p)(4) amended	1899A(4)
72(q)(2)(D) amended	1123(b)(2)	103A repealed	1301(j)(1)
72(q)(2)(E) amended	1826(d)	103A(c)(2)(B) amended	1861(c)(1)
72(q)(2)(E) amended	1852(c)(2)	103A(c)(2)(C) amended	1861(c)(2)
72(q)(2)(F) amended	1826(d)	103A(j)(5)(C) added	1861(a)
72(q)(2)(G) added	1826(d)	103A(o)(4) amended	1861(b)
72(q)(2)(G) amended	1123(b)(4)	105(d)(5)(C) amended	1301(j)(9)
72(q)(2)(H) amended	1123(b)(4)	105(h) struck out	1151(c)(2)
72(q)(2)(I) added	1123(b)(4)	105(i) relettered (h)	1151(c)(2)
72(q)(2)(J) added	1123(b)(4)	106(a) amended	1151(j)(2)
72(q)(3) added	1123(b)(3)	106(b)(1) amended	1114(b)(1)
72(s)(1) amended	1826(b)(2)	108(a)(1)(A) amended	822(a)
72(s)(5) added	1826(a)	108(a)(1)(B) amended	822(a)
72(s)(6) added	1826(b)(1)	108(a)(1)(C) struck out	822(a)
72(s)(7) added	1826(b)(1)	108(a)(2) amended	822(b)(1)
72(t) relettered (u)	1123(a)	108(b)(2)(B) amended	231(d)(3)(D)
72(t) added	1123(a)	108(b)(2)(D) amended	1171(b)(4)
72(u) relettered (v)	1135(a)	108(b)(2)(E) amended	1847(b)(7)
72(u) added	1135(a)	108(b)(3)(B) amended	104(b)(2)
74(a) amended	122(a)(1)(A)	108(c) struck out	822(b)(2)
74(a) amended	123(b)(1)	108(d) heading amended	822(b)(3)(B)
74(b) heading amended	122(a)(1)(B)	108(d)(4) struck out	822(b)(3)(A)
74(b)(1) amended	122(a)(1)(C)	108(d)(6) heading amended	822(b)(3)(B)
74(b)(2) amended	122(a)(1)(C)	108(d)(6) amended	822(b)(3)(B)
74(b)(3) added	122(a)(1)(C)	108(d)(7) heading amended	822(b)(3)(B)
74(c) added	122(a)(1)(D)	108(d)(7) amended	822(b)(3)(B)
79(d) amended	1151(c)(1)	108(d)(7)(B) amended	822(b)(3)(C)
79(d)(1)(B) amended	1827(a)(1)	108(d)(9) amended	822(b)(3)(D)
79(d)(6) amended	1827(c)(1)	108(e)(7)(A)(ii) amended	805(c)(2)
79(d)(6) amended	1827(c)(2)	108(e)(7)(B) struck out	805(c)(3)
79(d)(8) added	1827(d)	108(e)(7)(C) relettered (B)	805(c)(3)
81 amended	805(c)(1)(A)	108(e)(7)(D) relettered (C)	805(c)(3)
83(e)(5) amended	1827(e)	108(e)(7)(E) relettered (D)	805(c)(3)
85 amended	121	108(e)(7)(E) amended	805(c)(4)
86(b)(2)(A) amended	131(b)(2)	108(e)(7)(F) relettered (E)	805(c)(3)
86(c)(3) amended	1301(j)(8)	108(g) added	405(a)
86(f)(1) amended	1847(b)(2)	111(a) amended	1812(a)(1)
88 amended	1807(a)(4)(e)(vii)	111(c) amended	1812(a)(2)
89 added	1151(a)	116 repealed	612(a)
101(d)(1) amended	1001(a)	117 amended	123(a)
101(d)(2)(B) amended	1001(c)(2)	117(d)(3) amended	1114(b)(2)(A)
101(d)(2)(B)(ii) amended	1001(b)	117(d)(3) amended	1114(b)(2)(B)
101(d)(3) struck out	1001(c)(1)	117(d)(3) amended	1114(b)(2)(C)
101(d)(4) renumbered (3)	1001(c)(1)	117(d)(4) added	1151(g)(2)
102(c) added	122(b)	118(b) struck out	824(a)
103 amended	1301(a)	118(b) added	824(a)
103(b)(13) amended	1871(b)	118(c) struck out	824(a)
103(b)(14)(A) amended	1871(b)	118(d) relettered (c)	824(a)
103(b)(16)(A) amended	1870	119(d) added	1164(a)
103(b)(17)(A) amended	1871(b)	120(b) amended	1151(c)(3)
103(h)(2)(A) amended	1899A(2)	120(c)(1) amended	1114(b)(3)(A)
103(h)(5)(A) amended	1865(a)	120(c)(2) amended	1151(g)(1)
103(l)(2)(D) amended	1864(d)	120(d)(1) heading amended	1114(b)(3)(B)(ii)
103(l)(2)(E) amended	1864(d)	120(d)(1) amended	1114(b)(3)(B)(i)
103(l)(2)(F) added	1864(d)	120(e) amended	1162(b)
103(m)(1) amended	1871(a)(1)	125 amended	1151(d)(1)
103(m)(3)(B) amended	1899A(3)	125(c) amended	1853(b)(1)(A)
103(n)(6)(A) amended	1864(b)	125(d)(1)(B) amended	1853(b)(1)(A)
103(n)(6)(B)(i) amended	1864(b)	125(f) amended	1853(b)(1)(B)
103(n)(7)(C)(i) amended	1864(c)	127(a)(2) heading amended	1162(a)(2)
103(n)(10)(B) heading amended	1864(e)(1)(B)	127(a)(2) amended	1162(a)(2)
103(n)(10)(B)(i) amended	1864(e)(1)(A)	127(b)(1) struck out	1151(c)(4)(A)
103(n)(10)(D) amended	1864(e)(2)	127(b)(1) added	1151(c)(4)(A)
103(n)(13) added	1864(a)(1)	127(b)(2) amended	1114(b)(4)
103(o) relettered (p)	1869(b)(2)	127(b)(2) amended	1151(g)(3)

Code Sec.	1986 Act Sec.
171(b)(3) amended	1803(a)(11)(A)
171(b)(4) added	1803(a)(12)(A)
171(d) amended	1803(a)(11)(B)
171(e) relettered (f)	643(a)
171(e) added	643(a)
172(b)(1)(A) amended	903(b)(2)(A)
172(b)(1)(B) amended	903(b)(2)(B)
172(b)(1)(F) amended	901(d)(4)(B)
172(b)(1)(F) amended	903(a)(1)
172(b)(1)(G) amended	903(a)(2)
172(b)(1)(H) amended	903(a)(3)(A)
172(b)(1)(H) amended	903(a)(3)(B)
172(b)(1)(J) struck out	1303(b)(1)
172(b)(1)(K) relettered (J)	1303(b)(1)
172(b)(1)(L) added	903(b)(1)
172(b)(1)(M) added	903(b)(1)
172(d)(2) amended	301(b)(3)
172(d)(6) amended	1899A(6)
172(d)(7) struck out	104(b)(4)
172(k)(2) amended	1303(b)(2)
172(k)(4) amended	1303(b)(2)
172(l) relettered (m)	903(b)(2)(C)
172(l) added	903(b)(2)(C)
173(b) amended	701(e)(4)(D)
174(e)(2) amended	701(e)(4)(D)
175(c)(3) added	401(a)
177 repealed	241(a)
178 amended	201(d)(2)(A)
178(b)(2)(B) amended	1812(c)(4)(B)
179(b) amended	202(a)
179(d)(1) amended	202(b)
179(d)(8) amended	201(d)(3)
179(d)(10) amended	202(c)
182 repealed	402(a)
183(d) amended	143(a)(1)
183(d) amended	143(a)(2)
185 repealed	242(a)
189 repealed	803(b)(1)
190(d)(2) amended	244
194(b)(1) amended	1301(j)(8)
213(a) amended	133
216(b)(2) amended	644(a)(1)
216(b)(3) amended	644(d)
216(b)(5) amended	644(a)(2)
216(b)(6) amended	644(a)(2)
216(c) amended	644(b)
216(d) added	644(c)
219(b)(2) amended	1108(g)(2)
219(b)(2)(C) amended	1875(c)(6)(B)
219(b)(3) struck out	1101(b)(2)(A)
219(b)(3) added	1109(b)
219(c)(1)(B) amended	1103(a)
219(c)(2)(B) amended	1108(g)(3)
219(e) amended	1101(b)(1)
219(f)(1) amended	301(b)(4)
219(f)(1) amended	1875(c)(4)
219(f)(3) amended	1101(a)(2)
219(f)(7) added	1102(f)
219(g) relettered (h)	1101(a)(1)
219(g) added	1101(a)(1)
219(g) amended	1501(d)(1)(B)
221 repealed	131(a)
222 repealed	135(a)
223 renumbered 220	135(b)(1)
223 amended	301(b)(5)(A)
243(a)(1) amended	611(a)(1)
243(b)(3)(C)(i) amended	411(b)(2)(C)(iv)(I)
243(b)(3)(C)(ii) struck out	411(b)(2)(C)(iv)(II)

Code Sec.	1986 Act Sec.
243(b)(3)(C)(iii) renumbered (ii)	411(b)(2)(C)(iv)(III)
244(a)(3) amended	611(a)(2)
244(b)(2) amended	611(a)(2)
245(a) amended	1226(a)
245(c)(1) amended	1876(d)(1)(A)
245(c)(3) renumbered (4)	1876(j)
245(c)(3) added	1876(j)
245(c)(3) amended	1876(d)(1)(B)
246(a)(2)(B) amended	1812(d)(1)(A)(i)
246(a)(2)(B)(i)(II) struck out	1812(d)(1)(A)(ii)
246(a)(2)(B)(i)(II) added	1812(d)(1)(A)(ii)
246(a)(2)(C) relettered (D)	1812(d)(1)(B)
246(a)(2)(C) added	1812(d)(1)(B)
246(a)(2)(D)(iv) added	1812(d)(1)(C)
246(b)(1) amended	611(a)(3)
246(c)(1)(A) amended	1804(b)(1)(A)
246(c)(4) amended	1804(b)(1)(B)
246(e) amended	1275(a)(2)(B)
246A(a) amended	1804(a)(1)
246A(a) amended	1804(a)(2)
246A(a)(1) amended	611(a)(4)
263(a)(1)(E) struck out	402(b)(1)
263(a)(1)(F) relettered (E)	402(b)(1)
263(a)(1)(G) relettered (F)	402(b)(1)
263(a)(1)(H) relettered (G)	402(b)(1)
263(c) amended	411(b)(1)(B)
263(c) amended	701(e)(4)(D)
263(g)(2)(B)(ii) amended	1808(b)
263(g)(2)(B)(iii) amended	1808(b)
263(g)(2)(B)(iv) added	1808(b)
263(i) added	411(b)(1)(A)
263A added	803(a)
264(a) amended	1003(b)
264(a)(4) added	1003(a)
265 amended	902(d)
265(2) amended	902(b)
265(6) added	144
265(b) added	902(a)
267(a) amended	806(c)(2)
267(a)(3) added	1812(c)(1)
267(b)(12) amended	1812(c)(4)(A)
267(e)(5)(D) amended	803(b)(5)
267(e)(6) added	1812(c)(3)(C)
267(f)(3)(B) amended	1812(c)(2)
267(g) added	1842(a)
269A(b)(3) amended	1301(j)(4)
269B(b) amended	1810(j)(1)
269B(e) amended	1810(j)(2)
274(b)(1)(A) amended	122(c)(1)
274(b)(1)(B) amended	122(c)(2)
274(b)(1)(C) struck out	122(c)(3)
274(b)(3) struck out	122(c)(4)
274(e)(1) struck out	142(a)(2)(A)
274(e)(2) renumbered (1)	142(a)(2)(A)
274(e)(3) renumbered (2)	142(a)(2)(A)
274(e)(3) amended	142(a)(2)(B)
274(e)(4) renumbered (3)	142(a)(2)(A)
274(e)(5) renumbered (4)	142(a)(2)(A)
274(e)(5) amended	1114(b)(6)
274(e)(6) renumbered (5)	142(a)(2)(A)
274(e)(7) renumbered (6)	142(a)(2)(A)
274(e)(8) renumbered (7)	142(a)(2)(A)
274(e)(9) renumbered (8)	142(a)(2)(A)
274(e)(10) renumbered (9)	142(a)(2)(A)
274(h)(1) amended	142(c)(2)(A)
274(h)(1) amended	142(c)(2)(B)
274(h)(2) amended	142(c)(2)(A)

Code Sec.	1986 Act Sec.
274(h)(2) amended	142(c)(2)(B)
274(h)(4) amended	142(c)(2)(A)
274(h)(4) amended	142(c)(2)(B)
274(h)(5) amended	142(c)(2)(A)
274(h)(5) amended	142(c)(2)(B)
274(h)(7) added	142(c)(1)
274(j) relettered (k)	122(d)
274(j) added	122(d)
274(k) relettered (o)	142(a)(1)
274(k) added	142(a)(1)
274(1) added	142(b)
274(m) added	142(b)
274(n) added	142(b)
277(b)(2) amended	1604(a)(1)
277(b)(3) amended	1604(a)(2)
277(b)(4) added	1604(a)(3)
278 repealed	803(b)(6)
280 repealed	803(b)(2)(A)
280A(c)(5)(B) struck out	143(c)
280A(c)(5)(B) added	143(c)
280A(c)(6) added	143(b)
280C(b) amended	1847(b)(8)(A)
280C(b) amended	1847(b)(8)(B)
280C(b)(3) amended	231(d)(3)(E)
280F(a) amended	201(d)(4)(K)
280F(a)(2)(A)(i) struck out	201(d)(4)(A)(i)
280F(a)(2)(A)(i) added	201(d)(4)(A)(i)
280F(a)(2)(A)(ii) struck out	201(d)(4)(A)(i)
280F(a)(2)(A)(ii) added	201(d)(4)(A)(i)
280F(a)(2)(A)(iii) added	201(d)(4)(A)(i)
280F(a)(2)(A)(iv) added	201(d)(4)(A)(i)
280F(a)(2)(B) amended	201(d)(4)(A)(ii)
280F(b) amended	201(d)(4)(K)
280F(b)(2) amended	201(d)(4)(J)
280F(b)(3)(A) amended	201(d)(4)(B)
280F(b)(4) amended	201(d)(4)(C)
280F(c)(4) amended	201(d)(4)(D)
280F(d)(1) amended	201(d)(4)(E)
280F(d)(2) amended	201(d)(4)(F)(i)
280F(d)(2) amended	1812(e)(5)
280F(d)(2) amended	201(d)(4)(F)(ii)
280F(d)(3)(A) amended	1812(e)(2)
280F(d)(4)(A)(iv) amended	201(d)(4)(G)
280F(d)(4)(B) amended	1812(e)(3)
280F(d)(4)(C) added	1812(e)(4)
280F(d)(5)(A)(ii) amended	1812(e)(1)(A)
280F(d)(5)(A) amended	1812(e)(1)(C)
280F(d)(8) amended	201(d)(4)(H)
280F(d)(10) amended	201(d)(4)(I)
280G(b)(2)(A) amended	1804(j)(6)
280G(b)(2)(B) amended	1804(j)(7)
280G(b)(4) amended	1804(j)(2)
280G(b)(5) added	1804(j)(1)
280G(b)(6) added	1804(j)(3)
280G(c) amended	1804(j)(5)
280G(d)(2) amended	1804(j)(8)
280G(d)(5) added	1804(j)(4)
291(a) heading amended	1804(k)(3)(A)
291(a)(1)(A) amended	201(d)(5)(A)
291(a)(2) amended	412(b)(1)
291(a)(4) amended	1804(k)(1)
291(a)(4) amended	1876(b)(1)
291(b)(1) amended	411(a)(1)
291(b)(1)(B) amended	411(b)(2)(C)(ii)
291(b)(2) struck out	411(a)(2)
291(b)(2) added	411(a)(2)
291(b)(3) struck out	411(a)(2)
291(b)(3) added	411(a)(2)
291(b)(4) struck out	411(a)(2)
291(b)(4) added	411(a)(2)

Code Sec.	1986 Act Sec.
291(b)(5) struck out	411(a)(2)
291(b)(5) added	411(a)(2)
291(b)(6) struck out	411(a)(2)
291(c)(1) amended	201(d)(5)(B)
291(e)(1)(A) amended	901(b)(4)
291(e)(1)(B) amended	902(c)(2)(C)
291(e)(1)(B)(i) amended	901(d)(4)(C)
291(e)(1)(B)(i) amended	902(c)(1)
291(e)(1)(B)(i) amended	902(c)(2)(A)
291(e)(1)(B)(ii) amended	902(c)(2)(B)
291(e)(1)(B)(iv) added	902(c)(2)(D)
291(e)(1)(B)(iv) added	1854(c)(1)
291(e)(2) amended	201(d)(5)(C)
301(f)(3) amended	1804(f)(2)(B)
301(g)(4) struck out	612(b)(1)
303(d) amended	1432(b)
304(a)(1) amended	1875(b)
311 amended	631(c)
312(b) amended	1804(f)(1)(A)
312(c) heading amended	1804(f)(1)(C)
312(c)(1) amended	1804(f)(1)(B)
312(c)(2) amended	1804(f)(1)(B)
312(c)(3) struck out	1804(f)(1)(B)
312(k)(3) amended	201(b)
312(k)(3)(A) amended	1809(a)(2)(C)(ii)
312(k)(4) amended	201(d)(6)
312(n)(1) amended	803(b)(3)(A)
312(n)(1)(C) struck out	803(b)(3)(A)
312(n)(1)(C) added	803(b)(3)(B)
312(n)(3) amended	241(b)(1)
312(n)(4) struck out	1804(f)(1)(D)
312(n)(4) amended	631(e)(1)
312(n)(5) renumbered (4)	1804(f)(1)(D)
312(n)(6) renumbered (5)	1804(f)(1)(D)
312(n)(7) renumbered (6)	1804(f)(1)(D)
312(n)(8) renumbered (7)	1804(f)(1)(D)
312(n)(8) amended	1804(f)(1)(E)
312(n)(9) renumbered (8)	1804(f)(1)(D)
318(b)(5) amended	621(c)(1)
332(b)(1) amended	1804(e)(6)(A)
332(c) repealed	631(e)(2)
333 repealed	631(e)(3)
334(a) amended	631(e)(4)(A)
334(c) repealed	631(e)(4)(B)
336 struck out	631(a)
336 added	631(a)
337 struck out	631(a)
337 added	631(a)
337(c)(3)(B) amended	1804(e)(7)(A)
338(a) amended	631(b)(1)
338(c) repealed	631(b)(2)
338(d)(3) amended	1804(e)(8)(A)
338(h)(3)(C)(i) amended	1899A(7)
338(h)(6)(B)(i) amended	1275(c)(6)
338(h)(10)(B) amended	631(b)(3)
338(h)(12) repealed	631(e)(5)
341(a) amended	1804(i)(l)
341(e)(2) struck out	631(e)(6)(A)
341(e)(3) struck out	631(e)(6)(A)
341(e)(4) struck out	631(e)(6)(A)
341(e)(5)(A) amended	631(e)(6)(B)(i)
341(e)(5)(B) struck out	631(e)(6)(B)(ii)
341(e)(12) amended	1899A(8)
346(b) amended	631(e)(7)
361 amended	1804(g)(1)
362(c)(3) struck out	824(b)
367(a)(1) amended	1810(g)(4)(A)
367(d)(2)(A) amended	1231(e)(2)
367(e) heading amended	1810(g)(4)(B)(ii)
367(c) amended	631(d)(1)

Code Sec.	1986 Act Sec.
367(e) amended	1810(g)(4)(B)(i)
367(f) repealed	1810(g)(1)
368(a)(2)(A) amended	1804(h)(3)
368(a)(2)(F)(ii) amended	1879(l)(1)
368(a)(2)(G)(i) amended	1804(g)(2)
368(a)(2)(H) added	1804(h)(2)
368(a)(3)(D) amended	904(a)
368(c) amended	1804(h)(1)
374(e)(1)(A)(iii) amended	1899A(9)
381(c)(10) amended	411(b)(2)(C)(iii)
381(c)(12) amended	1812(a)(3)
381(c)(25) struck out	231(d)(3)(F)
381(c)(26) renumbered (25)	231(d)(3)(F)
381(c)(27) added	701(e)(1)
382 amended	621(a)
383 amended	621(b)
386(d) relettered (e)	1805(c)(1)
386(d) added	1805(c)(1)
401(a)(4) amended	1114(b)(7)
401(a)(5) amended	1111(b)
401(a)(8) amended	1119(a)
401(a)(9)(C) amended	1121(b)
401(a)(9)(C) amended	1852(a)(4)(A)
401(a)(9)(G) added	1852(a)(6)
401(a)(11)(A)(i) amended	1898(b)(3)(A)
401(a)(11)(B) amended	1898(b)(2)(A)(ii)
401(a)(11)(B)(iii)(I) amended	1898(b)(7)(A)
401(a)(11)(B)(iii)(I) amended	1898(b)(13)(A)
401(a)(11)(B)(iii)(III) amended	1898(b)(2)(A)(i)
401(a)(11)(D) relettered (E)	1145(a)
401(a)(11)(D) relettered (E)	1898(b)(14)(A)
401(a)(11)(D) added	1898(b)(14)(A)
401(a)11(E) added	1145(a)
401(a)(17) added	1106(d)(1)
401(a)(20) amended	1852(b)(8)
401(a)(21) repealed	1171(b)(5)
401(a)(22) amended	1176(a)
401(a)(22) amended	1899A(10)
401(a)(23) amended	1174(c)(2)(A)
401(a)(26) added	1112(b)
401(a)(27) added	1136(a)
401(a)(28) added	1175(a)(1)
401(c)(2)(A) amended	1848(b)
401(c)(6) added	1143(a)
401(h)(6) amended	1852(h)(1)(A)
401(h)(6) amended	1852(h)(1)(B)
401(k)(1) amended	1879(g)(1)
401(k)(2) amended	1879(g)(1)
401(k)(2)(B) amended	1116(b)(1)
401(k)(2)(B) amended	1116(b)(2)
401(k)(2)(C) amended	1116(b)(2)
401(k)(2)(C) amended	1852(g)(3)
401(k)(2)(D) added	1116(b)(2)
401(k)(3)(A) amended	1112(d)(1)
401(k)(3)(A) amended	1116(b)(4)
401(k)(3)(A) amended	1852(g)(2)
401(k)(3)(A)(ii) amended	1116(c)(2)
401(k)(3)(A)(ii)(I) amended	1116(a)(1)
401(k)(3)(A)(ii)(II) amended	1116(a)(2)
401(k)(3)(A)(ii)(II) amended	1116(a)(3)
401(k)(3)(B) amended	1116(d)(3)
401(k)(3)(C) added	1116(e)
401(k)(3)(C) added	1852(g)(1)
401(k)(4) renumbered (5)	1116(b)(3)
401(k)(4) added	1116(b)(3)
401(k)(5) renumbered (6)	1116(b)(3)
401(k)(5) amended	1116(d)(1)
401(k)(6) renumbered (7)	1116(b)(3)

Code Sec.	1986 Act Sec.
401(k)(6) added	1879(g)(2)
401(k)(8) added	1116(c)(1)
401(k)(9) added	1116(d)(2)
401(l) amended	1111(a)
401(m) relettered (n)	1117(a)
401(m) added	1117(a)
401(m) added	1898(c)(3)
401(n) relettered (o)	1117(a)
401(o) relettered (n)	1898(c)(3)
402(a)(2) repealed	1122(b)(1)(A)
402(a)(5)(D)(i) amended	1122(e)(1)
402(a)(5)(D)(i) amended	1852(b)(2)
402(a)(5)(D)(ii) amended	1852(b)(5)
402(a)(5)(D)(iii) amended	1122(b)(2)(A)
402(a)(5)(E)(v) amended	1852(b)(1)
402(a)(5)(F) amended	1121(c)(1)
402(a)(5)(F)(i) amended	1852(b)(6)
402(a)(5)(F)(ii) amended	1875(c)(1)(A)
402(a)(5)(G) added	1852(a)(5)(A)
402(a)(6)(D)(v) amended	1852(b)(7)
402(a)(6)(F) amended	1898(c)(7)(A)(i)
402(a)(6)(G) added	1898(a)(3)
402(a)(6)(H) added	1122(e)(2)(A)
402(a)(7) amended	1852(b)(4)
402(a)(9) amended	1898(c)(1)(A)
402(b) heading amended	1112(c)(2)
402(b) amended	1852(c)(5)
402(b)(2) added	1112(c)(1)
402(e)(1)(B) struck out	1122(b)(2)(B)(i)
402(e)(1)(B) heading amended	1122(b)(2)(B)(iii)
402(e)(1)(B) amended	104(b)(5)
402(e)(1)(B) amended	1122(b)(2)(B)(ii)
402(e)(1)(C) relettered (B)	1122(b)(2)(B)(i)
402(e)(1)(C) amended	1122(a)(2)(A)
402(e)(1)(C) amended	1122(a)(2)(B)
402(e)(1)(D) relettered (C)	1122(b)(2)(B)(i)
402(e)(1)(E) relettered (D)	1122(b)(2)(B)(i)
402(e)(3) amended	1122(b)(2)(C)
402(e)(4)(B) amended	1122(a)(1)
402(e)(4)(E) struck out	1122(b)(2)(D)
402(e)(4)(F) struck out	1852(b)(3)(B)
402(e)(4)(H) amended	1122(b)(2)(E)
402(e)(4)(J) amended	1122(g)
402(e)(4)(N) added	1106(c)(2)
402(e)(6) added	1898(a)(2)
402(f)(1) amended	1898(e)(1)
402(f)(2) amended	1898(e)(2)
402(g) added	1105(a)
402(g) added	1852(b)(3)(A)
402(g) added	1854(f)(2)
402(h) added	1108(b)
403(a)(1) amended	1122(d)(1)
403(a)(2) repealed	1122(b)(1)(B)
403(a)(4)(B) amended	1852(a)(5)(B)(i)
403(b)(1) amended	1122(d)(2)
403(b)(1)(B) amended	1120(a)
403(b)(1)(C) amended	1120(a)
403(b)(1)(D) added	1120(a)
403(b)(7)(D) struck out	1852(a)(3)(B)
403(b)(7)(A)(ii) amended	1123(c)(2)
403(b)(8)(C) amended	1852(b)(10)
403(b)(8)(D) added	1852(a)(5)(B)(ii)
403(b)(10) added	1120(b)
403(b)(10) added	1852(a)(3)(A)
403(b)(11) added	1123(c)(1)
403(c) amended	1122(d)(3)
404(a) amended	1851(b)(2)(C)(i)

Code Sec.	1986 Act Sec.	Code Sec.	1986 Act Sec.
404(a)(2) amended	1112(d)(2)	409(d)(1) amended	1174(a)(1)
404(a)(2) amended	1136(b)	409(e)(2) amended	1854(f)(1)(C)
404(a)(3)(A) amended	1131(a)	409(e)(2) amended	1854(f)(1)(D)
404(a)(7) amended	1131(b)	409(e)(3) amended	1854(f)(1)(B)
404(a)(8)(C) amended	1875(c)(7)(A)	409(e)(3) amended	1854(f)(1)(C)
404(a)(8)(D) amended	1848(c)	409(e)(3) amended	1854(f)(1)(D)
404(a)(8)(D) amended	1875(c)(7)(B)	409(e)(5) added	1854(f)(1)(A)
404(b) heading amended	1851(b)(2)(B)(i)	409(h)(2) amended	1854(f)(3)(C)
404(b)(2) heading amended	1851(b)(2)(B)(ii)	409(h)(5) added	1174(c)(1)(A)
404(b)(2)(B)(ii) amended	1851(b)(2)(A)	409(h)(6) added	1174(c)(1)(A)
404(d) amended	1851(b)(2)(C)(ii)	409(l)(4) added	1176(b)
404(h)(1)(A) amended	1108(c)	409(n) relettered (o)	1854(a)(3)(A)
404(h)(1)(B) amended	1108(c)	409(n) added	1854(a)(3)(A)
404(i) repealed	1171(b)(6)	409(n)(1) amended	1172(b)(1)(A)
404(k) amended	1173(a)(2)	409(n)(1)(A)(i) amended	1172(b)(1)(B)
404(k) amended	1854(b)(2)(A)	409(n)(1)(A)(ii) amended	1172(b)(1)(C)
404(k) amended	1854(b)(2)(B)	409(o) relettered (p)	1174(b)(1)
404(k) amended	1854(b)(3)	409(o) added	1174(b)(1)
404(k) amended	1854(b)(4)	410(a)(1)(B)(i) amended	1113(c)
404(k)(2) amended	1854(b)(5)	410(a)(5)(B) heading amended	1113(d)(A)
404(k)(2)(A) amended	1173(a)(1)	410(b) amended	1112(a)
404(k)(2)(B) amended	1173(a)(1)	411(a) amended	1898(d)(1)(A)(ii)
404(k)(2)(C) added	1173(a)(1)	411(a)(2) amended	1113(a)
404(l) added	1106(d)(2)	411(a)(3)(D)(ii) amended	1898(a)(4)(A)(i)
404A(a) amended	1851(b)(2)(C)(iii)(I)	411(a)(7)(C) amended	1898(a)(4)(A)(ii)
404A(a) amended	1851(b)(2)(C)(iii)(II)	411(a)(10)(B) amended	1113(d)(B)
404A(g)(1)(A) amended	1114(b)(8)	411(a)(11)(A) amended	1898(d)(1)(A)(i)
406(b)(1) amended	1112(d)(3)	411(a)(11)(B) amended	1139(a)
406(b)(1)(A) amended	1114(b)(9)(A)	411(a)(11)(C) added	1898(d)(1)(A)(i)
406(b)(1)(B) amended	1114(b)(9)(C)	411(d)(1)(A) amended	1114(b)(10)
406(e)(5) struck out	1852(e)(2)(C)	411(d)(1)(B) amended	1114(b)(10)
407(b)(1) amended	1112(d)(3)	411(d)(4) repealed	1113(b)
407(b)(1)(A) amended	1114(b)(9)(A)	411(d)(4) amended	1898(a)(1)(A)
407(b)(1)(B) amended	1114(b)(9)(C)	411(d)(6)(C) added	1898(f)(1)(A)
407(e)(5) struck out	1852(e)(2)(D)	414(k)(2) amended	1117(c)
408(a)(6) amended	1852(a)(1)(A)	414(m)(2)(B)(ii) amended	1114(b)(11)
408(b)(3) amended	1852(a)(1)(B)	414(m)(5) amended	1301(j)(4)
408(c)(1) amended	1852(a)(7)(A)	414(n)(1) amended	1146(b)(2)
408(d)(1) amended	1102(c)	414(n)(1) amended	1151(i)(1)
408(d)(2) amended	1102(c)	414(n)(2)(B) amended	1151(i)(2)
408(d)(3)(A) amended	1875(c)(8)(C)	414(n)(3) heading amended	1151(i)(3)(A)
408(d)(3)(A)(ii) amended	1121(c)(2)	414(n)(3) amended	1151(i)(3)(B)
408(d)(3)(A)(ii) amended	1875(c)(8)(A)	414(n)(3)(A) amended	1151(i)(3)(C)
408(d)(3)(A)(ii) amended	1875(c)(8)(B)	414(n)(3)(B) amended	1151(i)(3)(C)
408(d)(3)(E) added	1852(a)(5)(C)	414(n)(3)(C) added	1151(i)(3)(C)
408(d)(3)(F) added	1122(e)(2)(B)	414(n)(4) amended	1146(a)(2)
408(d)(5) amended	1102(b)(2)	414(n)(5) amended	1146(a)(1)
408(d)(5) amended	1875(c)(6)(A)	414(n)(6) amended	1146(a)(3)
408(f) repealed	1123(d)(2)	414(n)(6) amended	1301(j)(4)
408(i) amended	1102(e)(2)	414(o) amended	1146(b)(1)
408(k)(2) amended	1108(d)	414(p)(1)(B)(i) amended	1898(c)(7)(A)(ii)
408(k)(2)(A) amended	1898(a)(5)	414(p)(3)(B) amended	1899A(12)
408(k)(3)(A) amended	1108(g)(1)(A)	414(p)(4)(A) amended	1898(c)(7)(A)(vi)(I)
408(k)(3)(A) amended	1108(g)(4)	414(p)(4)(A)(i) amended	1898(c)(7)(A)(vi)(II)
408(k)(3)(C) amended	1108(g)(1)(B)(i)	414(p)(4)(B) amended	1898(c)(7)(A)(vii)
408(k)(3)(C) amended	1108(g)(1)(B)(ii)	414(p)(5) amended	1898(c)(7)(A)(v)
408(k)(3)(C) amended	1108(g)(1)(B)(iii)	414(p)(5)(A) amended	1898(c)(6)(A)
408(k)(3)(D) struck out	1108(g)(1)(C)	414(p)(5)(B) amended	1898(c)(7)(A)(iv)
408(k)(3)(D) added	1108(g)(1)(C)	414(p)(6)(A)(i) amended	1898(c)(7)(A)(iii)
408(k)(3)(E) struck out	1108(g)(1)(C)	414(p)(7)(A) amended	1898(c)(2)(A)(i)
408(k)(6) added	1108(a)	414(p)(7)(B) amended	1898(c)(2)(A)(ii)
408(k)(7)(C) added	1108(f)	414(p)(7)(C) amended	1898(c)(2)(A)(iii)
408(k)(8) added	1108(e)	414(p)(7)(D) amended	1898(c)(2)(A)(iv)
408(k)(9) added	1108(g)(6)	414(p)(7)(E) added	1898(c)(2)(A)(v)
408(m)(3) added	1144(a)	414(p)(9) renumbered (11)	1898(c)(4)(A)
408(o) relettered (p)	1102(a)	414(p)(9) added	1898(c)(4)(A)
408(o) added	1102(a)	414(p)(10) added	1898(c)(7)(A)(v)
409(a)(3) amended	1174(b)(2)	414(q) added	1114(a)
409(d) amended	1852(a)(4)(B)	414(r) added	1115(a)
409(d) amended	1899A(11)	414(s) added	1115(a)

Code Sec.	1986 Act Sec.
414(t) added	1151(e)(1)
415(b)(2)(B) amended	1898(b)(15)(C)
415(b)(2)(C) amended	1106(b)(1)(A)(i)
415(b)(2)(C) amended	1106(b)(1)(A)(ii)
415(b)(2)(D) amended	1106(b)(1)(A)(i)
415(b)(2)(E)(iii) amended	1875(c)(9)
415(b)(2)(F) added	1106(b)(2)
415(b)(2)(G) added	1106(b)(2)
415(b)(2)(H) added	1106(b)(2)
415(b)(5) amended	1106(f)
415(b)(8) added	1106(b)(1)(B)
415(b)(9) added	1106(b)(3)
415(c)(1)(A) amended	1106(c)
415(c)(2) amended	1106(e)(2)
415(c)(2) amended	1108(g)(5)
415(c)(2)(B) amended	1106(e)(1)
415(c)(3)(C) amended	1875(c)(11)
415(c)(3)(C)(i) amended	1847(b)(4)
415(c)(3)(C)(ii) amended	1114(b)(12)
415(c)(4)(A) amended	1106(b)(4)
415(c)(4)(B) amended	1106(b)(4)
415(c)(4)(C) amended	1106(b)(4)
415(c)(6)(A) amended	1174(d)(1)
415(c)(6)(B)(iii) struck out	1174(d)(2)(A)
415(c)(6)(B)(iv) struck out	1174(d)(2)(A)
415(c)(6)(C) amended	1174(d)(2)(B)
415(d)(1)(A) amended	1106(g)(1)
415(d)(1)(B) struck out	1106(g)(1)
415(d)(1)(C) relettered (B)	1106(g)(1)
415(d)(2) amended	1106(g)(2)(A)
415(d)(2) amended	1106(g)(2)(B)
415(d)(3) amended	1106(g)(3)
415(k) amended	1899A(13)
415(k)(2) added	1106(c)(1)
415(l) amended	1852(h)(3)
415(l)(1) amended	1852(h)(2)
416(a)(1) amended	1106(d)(3)(A)
416(a)(2) amended	1106(d)(3)(A)
416(a)(3) struck out	1106(d)(3)(A)
416(c)(2)(B)(ii) struck out	1106(d)(3)(B)(ii)
416(c)(2)(B)(iii) renumbered (ii)	1106(d)(3)(B)(ii)
416(d) repealed	1106(d)(3)(B)(i)
416(g)(4)(E) amended	1852(d)(2)
416(g)(4)(F) added	1118(a)
416(i)(1)(A) amended	1852(d)(1)
417(a)(1) amended	1898(b)(15)(A)
417(a)(1)(B) amended	1898(b)(4)(A)(i)
417(a)(2)(A) amended	1898(b)(6)(A)
417(a)(3)(B) amended	1898(b)(5)(A)
417(a)(4) renumbered (5)	1898(b)(4)(A)(ii)
417(a)(4) added	1898(b)(4)(A)(ii)
417(a)(5) renumbered (6)	1898(b)(4)(A)(ii)
417(a)(5)(A) amended	1898(b)(11)(A)
417(c)(1) amended	1898(b)(1)(A)
417(c)(1) amended	1898(b)(15)(B)
417(c)(2) amended	1898(b)(9)(A)(i)
417(c)(3) added	1898(b)(9)(A)(ii)
417(e)(3) amended	1139(b)
417(f)(1) amended	1898(b)(8)(A)
417(f)(2) amended	1898(b)(12)(A)
417(f)(5) renumbered (6)	1898(b)(4)(A)(iii)
417(f)(5) added	1898(b)(4)(A)(iii)
417(f)(6) renumbered (7)	1898(b)(10)(A)
417(f)(6) added	1898(b)(10)(A)
419(a) amended	1851(b)(2)(C)(iv)(I)
419(a) amended	1851(b)(2)(C)(iv)(II)
419(e)(4) added	1851(a)(8)(A)
419(g)(1) amended	1851(a)(1)
419A(b) amended	1851(a)(6)(B)
419A(c)(5)(A) amended	1851(a)(5)
419A(d)(1) amended	1851(a)(2)(B)
419A(d)(2) amended	1851(a)(2)(A)
419A(e) amended	1851(a)(3)(A)
419A(f)(5) amended	1851(a)(4)
419A(f)(5) amended	1851(a)(13)
419A(f)(7)(C) struck out	1851(a)(7)
419A(f)(7)(C) added	1851(a)(7)
419A(f)(7)(D) added	1851(a)(7)
419A(g)(3) added	1851(a)(9)
419A(h)(1) amended	1851(a)(6)(A)
422A(b)(6) amended	321(a)
422A(b)(7) struck out	321(a)
422A(b)(7) added	321(a)
422A(b)(8) struck out	321(a)
422A(c)(1) amended	321(b)(2)
422A(c)(4) struck out	321(b)(1)(A)
422A(c)(5) renumbered (4)	321(b)(1)(B)
422A(c)(6) renumbered (5)	321(b)(1)(B)
422A(c)(7) struck out	321(b)(1)(A)
422A(c)(8) renumbered (6)	321(b)(1)(B)
422A(c)(9) renumbered (7)	321(b)(1)(B)
422A(c)(9) amended	1847(b)(5)
422A(c)(10) renumbered (8)	321(b)(1)(B)
423(b)(4)(D) amended	1114(b)(13)
441(f)(2)(B)(iii) amended	104(b)(6)
441(f)(3) renumbered (4)	806(d)
441(f)(3) added	806(d)
441(i) added	806(c)(1)
443(b)(1) amended	104(b)(7)(A)
443(b)(2)(A)(ii) amended	104(b)(7)(B)
443(d) amended	701(e)(3)
447(a) amended	803(b)(7)(B)
447(b) amended	803(b)(7)(A)
447(g)(1) amended	803(b)(7)(C)
448 added	801(a)
451(f) added	821(a)
451(f) added	905(b)
453(f)(1) amended	642(a)(3)
453(f)(8) added	642(b)(1)
453(g) heading amended	642(a)(1)(D)
453(g)(1) amended	642(b)(2)
453(h) heading amended	631(e)(8)(C)
453(h)(1)(A) amended	631(e)(8)(A)
453(h)(1)(B) amended	631(e)(8)(A)
453(h)(1)(E) amended	631(e)(8)(B)
453(i)(2) amended	1809(c)
453(j) added	812(a)
453A(a)(2)	812(b)(1)
453A(c) added	812(b)(2)
453B(d) amended	631(e)(9)
453B(e)(2)(B) amended	1011(b)(1)
453B(g) amended	1842(c)
453C added	811(a)
457 amended	1107(a)
460 added	804(a)
461(h)(5)(A) struck out	805(c)(5)
461(h)(5)(B) relettered (A)	805(c)(5)
461(h)(5)(C) struck out	823(b)(1)
461(h)(5)(C) relettered (B)	805(c)(5)
461(h)(5)(D) relettered (C)	805(c)(5)
461(h)(5)(D) reletterd (C)	823(b)(1)
461(i)(1) amended	801(b)(1)
461(i)(2) heading amended	1807(a)(1)(B)
461(i)(2) amended	801(b)(1)
461(i)(2)(A) amended	1807(a)(1)(A)
461(i)(4) amended	801(b)(2)

Code Sec.	1986 Act Sec.	Code Sec.	1986 Act Sec.
861(a)(1)(D) relettered (C)	1214(c)(5)(A)	881(a)(4) amended	1211(b)(6)
861(a)(1)(D) amended	1214(c)(5)(B)	881(b)(1) struck out	1273(b)(1)
861(a)(1)(E) struck out	1214(c)(5)(A)	881(b)(1) added	1273(b)(1)
861(a)(1)(E) relettered (C)	1241(b)(1)(B)	881(b)(2) struck out	1273(b)(1)
861(a)(1)(F) relettered (D)	1241(b)(1)(B)	881(b)(2)(A) amended	1899A(22)
861(a)(1)(F) relettered (D)	1214(c)(5)(A)	881(b)(3) renumbered (2)	1273(b)(2)(A)
861(a)(1)(G) relettered (E)	1214(c)(5)(A)	881(b)(4) struck out	1273(b)(2)(A)
861(a)(1)(H) relettered (F)	1214(c)(5)(A)	881(c)(2) amended	1810(d)(1)(B)
861(a)(2)(A) amended	1214(b)	881(c)(2)(B)(ii) amended	1810(d)(3)(C)
861(a)(2)(B) amended	1241(b)(2)(A)	881(c)(3)(C) amended	1899A(23)
861(a)(2)(B) amended	1241(b)(2)(B)	881(c)(4)(A)(i) amended	1223(b)(2)
861(a)(6) amended	1211(b)(1)(B)	881(d) relettered (e)	1214(c)(2)
861(b) amended	104(b)(11)	881(d) added	1214(c)(2)
861(c) amended	1214(a)(2)	882(a)(1) amended	701(e)(4)(F)
861(d) amended	1214(c)(5)(C)	882(e) amended	1236(a)
861(e) struck out	1212(d)	883(a)(1) struck out	1212(c)(3)
861(f) relettered (e)	1212(d)	883(a)(1) added	1212(c)(3)
862(a)(6) amended	1211(b)(1)(C)	883(a)(2) struck out	1212(c)(3)
862(b) amended	104(b)(12)	883(a)(2) added	1212(c)(3)
863(b)(1) amended	1212(e)	883(a)(4) added	1212(c)(4)
863(b)(2) amended	1211(b)(1)(A)	883(c) added	1212(c)(5)
863(b)(3) amended	1211(b)(1)(A)	884 renumbered 885	1241(a)
863(c)(2) amended	1212(a)	884 added	1241(a)
863(d) added	1213(a)	887 added	1212(b)(1)
863(e) added	1213(a)	891 amended	1024(c)(13)
864 heading amended	1215(b)(1)	892 amended	1247(a)
864(c)(1)(A) amended	1242(b)(1)	897(a)(2) amended	701(e)(4)(G)
864(c)(1)(B) amended	1242(b)(2)	897(d) heading amended	631(e)(12)(E)
864(c)(2) amended	1899A(21)	897(d)(1) heading struck out	631(e)(12)(B)
864(c)(4)(B)(i) amended	1211(b)(2)	897(d)(1) amended	631(e)(12)(C)
864(c)(4)(B)(ii) amended	1211(b)(2)	897(d)(2) struck out	631(e)(12)(A)
864(c)(4)(B)(iii) struck out	1211(b)(2)	897(d)(2) amended	631(e)(12)(D)
864(c)(6) added	1242(a)	897(i)(1) amended	1810(f)(1)(A)
864(c)(7) added	1242(a)	897(i)(4) amended	1810(f)(1)(B)
864(d)(5)(A)(i) amended	1201(d)(4)	901(h) amended	1876(p)(2)
864(d)(5)(A)(i) amended	1810(c)(3)	901(i) relettered (j)	1204(a)
864(d)(5)(A)(ii) amended	1223(b)(1)	901(i) added	1204(a)
864(d)(5)(A)(iii) struck out	1221(a)(2)	901(i)(3) amended	112(b)(3)
864(d)(5)(A)(iii) added	1221(a)(2)	902 amended	1202(a)
864(d)(5)(A)(iv) struck out	1221(a)(2)	904(a) amended	104(b)(13)
864(d)(5)(A)(iv) added	1221(a)(2)	904(b)(3)(C) struck out	1211(b)(3)
864(d)(5)(B) amended	1275(c)(7)	904(b)(3)(D) struck out	1211(b)(3)
864(d)(7) renumbered (8)	1810(c)(2)	904(b)(3)(E) relettered (C)	1211(b)(3)
864(d)(7) added	1810(c)(2)	904(b)(3)(F) relettered (D)	1211(b)(3)
864(e) added	1215(a)	904(d) heading amended	1201(d)(1)
865 added	1211(a)	904(d)(1) heading amended	1899A(24)
871(a)(1) amended	1810(d)(3)(A)	904(d)(1) amended	1201(d)(3)
871(a)(1)(C) amended	1810(e)(2)(A)	904(d)(1)(A) struck out	1201(a)
871(a)(1)(D) amended	1211(b)(4)	904(d)(1)(A) added	1201(a)
871(a)(2) amended	301(b)(9)	904(d)(1)(B) relettered (F)	1201(a)
871(e) repealed	1211(b)(5)	904(d)(1)(B) added	1201(a)
871(h)(2) amended	1810(d)(1)(A)	904(d)(1)(C) relettered (G)	1201(a)
871(h)(2)(B)(ii) amended	1810(d)(3)(B)	904(d)(1)(C) added	1201(a)
871(h)(3)(C)(i) amended	1810(d)(2)	904(d)(1)(C) relettered (H)	1201(a)
871(h)(3)(C)(ii) renumbered (iii)	1810(d)(2)	904(d)(1)(D) added	1201(a)
871(h)(3)(C)(ii) added	1810(d)(2)	904(d)(1)(D) amended	1876(d)(2)
871(i) relettered (j)	1214(c)(1)	904(d)(1)(E) relettered (I)	1201(a)
871(i) added	1214(c)(1)	904(d)(1)(E) added	1201(a)
872(b)(1) struck out	1212(c)(1)	904(d)(1)(I) amended	1201(d)(2)
872(b)(1) added	1212(c)(1)	904(d)(2) struck out	1201(b)
872(b)(2) struck out	1212(c)(1)	904(d)(2) added	1201(b)
872(b)(2) added	1212(c)(1)	904(d)(2) amended	1810(b)(3)
872(b)(5) added	1212(c)(2)	904(d)(3) struck out	1201(b)
872(b)(6) added	1212(c)(2)	904(d)(3) added	1201(b)
876 amended	1272(b)	904(d)(3)(C) amended	1810(b)(1)
877(c) amended	1243(a)	904(d)(3)(E)(ii) amended	1810(b)(4)(A)
879(c)(3) amended	1301(j)(9)	904(d)(3)(E)(iii) amended	1810(b)(4)(A)
881(a)(3) amended	1810(e)(2)(B)	904(d)(3)(E)(iv) added	1810(b)(4)(A)

Code Sec.	1986 Act Sec.	Code Sec.	1986 Act Sec.
3306(b)(5)(E) amended	1151(d)(2)(B)	4940(e)(2)(B) added	1832
3306(b)(5)(F) amended	1151(d)(2)(B)	4941(d)(2)(B) amended	1812(b)(1)
3306(b)(5)(G) added	1151(d)(2)(B)	4941(d)(2)(G)(i) amended	122(a)(2)(A)
3306(b)(13) amended	1899A(45)	4942(f)(2)(A) amended	1301(j)(6)
3306(b)(16) amended	122(e)(3)	4945(g)(2) amended	122(a)(2)(B)
3306(o)(1)(A)(i) amended	1884(3)	4946(c)(5) amended	1606(a)
3401(a)(8)(D) added	1272(c)	4961(c)(1) heading amended	1899A(50)
3401(a)(20) amended	122(e)(4)	4972 added	1131(c)(1)
3402(f) amended	1301(j)(8)	4973(b) amended	1102(b)(1)
3402(f)(1) amended	104(b)(15)(F)(i)	4973(b) amended	1848(f)(1)
3402(f)(1) amended	104(b)(15)(F)(ii)	4973(b)(1)(A) struck out	1848(f)(2)
3402(f)(1)(A) amended	104(b)(15)(B)	4973(b)(1)(A) added	1848(f)(2)
3402(f)(1)(B) struck out	104(b)(15)(A)	4973(b)(2)(C) amended	1848(f)(3)
3402(f)(1)(B) amended	104(b)(15)(C)	4974 amended	1121(a)(1)
3402(f)(1)(C) struck out	104(b)(15)(A)	4974(a) amended	1852(a)(7)(B)
3402(f)(1)(C) amended	104(b)(15)(D)	4974(b) amended	1852(a)(7)(C)
3402(f)(1)(D) relettered (B)	104(b)(15)(A)	4975(d) amended	1899A(51)
3402(f)(1)(E) relettered (C)	104(b)(15)(A)	4975(d)(1)(B) amended	1114(b)(15)(A)
3402(f)(1)(E) amended	104(b)(15)(E)	4975(e)(7) amended	1854(f)(3)(A)
3402(f)(1)(F) relettered (D)	104(b)(15)(A)	4976(b) amended	1851(a)(11)
3402(f)(1)(G) relettered (E)	104(b)(15)(A)	4977(c)(2) amended	1853(c)(1)
3402(i) amended	1572(b)	4977(f) added	1853(c)(2)
3402(m)(3) amended	104(b)(15)(G)	4978(a)(1) amended	1854(e)(1)
3402(r) repealed	1303(b)(4)	4978(b)(1) amended	1854(e)(2)
3405(d)(1)(B) amended	1102(e)(1)	4978(c) amended	1854(e)(3)
3405(d)(1)(B)(ii) amended	1875(c)(10)	4978(d)(1)(C) amended	1854(e)(4)
3405(d)(1)(B)(iii) added	1875(c)(10)	4978(d)(3) added	1854(e)(7)
3405(d)(1)(B)(iv) added	1875(c)(10)	4978(e)(2) amended	1854(e)(5)
3405(d)(13) added	1234(b)(1)	4978(e)(3) amended	1854(e)(6)
3406(b)(3)(C) amended	1523(b)(1)(A)	4979 added	1117(b)(1)
3406(b)(3)(D) amended	1523(b)(1)(B)	4979A added	1854(a)(9)(A)
3406(b)(3)(E) added	1523(b)(1)(C)	4979A(b)(1) amended	1172(b)(2)(A)
3406(b)(6) heading amended	1899A(46)	4979A(c) amended	1172(b)(2)(B)
3406(h)(5)(D) added	1521(b)	4980 added	1132(a)
3507(c)(2)(B)(i) struck out	111(d)(2)	4981 amended	668(a)
3507(c)(2)(B)(i) added	111(d)(2)	4981A added	1133(a)
3507(c)(2)(B)(ii) struck out	111(d)(2)	4982 added	651(a)
3507(c)(2)(B)(ii) added	111(d)(2)	4988(c)(2) amended	1301(j)(4)
3507(c)(2)(C)(i) struck out	111(d)(3)	4991(e)(2) amended	1879(h)(1)
3507(c)(2)(C)(i) added	111(d)(3)	5061(e)(3) added	1801(c)(1)
3507(c)(2)(C)(ii) struck out	111(d)(3)	5703(b)(3) amended	1801(c)(2)
3507(c)(2)(C)(ii) added	111(d)(3)	6011(f) amended	1899A(52)
4041(b) heading amended	422(a)(2)	6012(a)(1) amended	104(a)(1)(A)
4041(b)(2)(A) amended	422(a)(1)	6012(a)(9) amended	104(a)(1)(B)
4041(l)(1) amended	1878(c)(1)	6012(d) relettered (e)	1525(a)
4041(n) added	1702(a)	6012(d) added	1525(a)
4051(d)(1) amended	1899A(47)	6013(b)(3) amended	104(a)(2)(A)
4051(d)(3) amended	1877(c)	6013(b)(3) amended	104(a)(2)(B)
4064(b)(1)(A)(ii) amended	1812(e)(1)(B)(i)	6013(b)(3) amended	104(a)(2)(C)
4064(b)(5) amended	1812(e)(1)(B)(ii)	6013(f)(1) amended	1708(a)(3)
4081 added	1703(a)	6014(a) amended	104(b)(16)(A)
4082 added	1703(a)	6014(b)(4) amended	104(b)(16)(B)
4083 added	1703(a)	6031(b) amended	1501(c)(16)(A)
4101 amended	1703(b)(1)	6031(b) amended	1501(c)(16)(B)
4121(b) amended	1897(a)	6031(b) amended	1811(b)(1)(A)(i)
4161(b)(1)(B)(ii) amended	1899A(48)	6031(c) added	1811(b)(1)(A)(ii)
4162(a)(6)(I) amended	1878(b)	6033(e) amended	1501(d)(1)(C)
4162(c)(3) amended	201(d)(7)(C)	6034(c) amended	1501(d)(1)(C)
4162(c)(3) amended	201(d)(12)	6034A amended	1875(d)(3)(A)(i)
4221(a) amended	1703(c)(2)(C)(i)	6034A amended	1875(d)(3)(A)(ii)
4221(a) amended	1703(c)(2)(C)(ii)	6034A(a) amended	1501(c)(15)(A)
4227 amended	1899A(49)	6034A(a) amended	1501(c)(15)(B)
4251(b)(2) amended	1801(b)	6034A(a) amended	1501(c)(15)(C)
4261(e)(1) amended	1878(c)(2)	6034A(b) added	1875(d)(3)(A)(iii)
4497(c)(2) amended	1511(c)(7)	6038(a)(1)(B) amended	1202(c)(1)
4701(b)(1) added	1301(j)(5)	6038(a)(1)(D) amended	1245(b)(5)
4940(c)(5) amended	1301(j)(6)	6038(a)(1)(E) amended	1245(b)(5)
4940(e)(2)(B) struck out	1832	6038(a)(1)(F) added	1245(b)(5)

Code Sec.	1986 Act Sec.
6038(c)(4)(C) amended	1202(c)(2)
6038A(b)(1) amended	1245(a)(1)
6038A(b)(1)(A) struck out	1245(a)(2)
6038A(b)(1)(A) added	1245(a)(2)
6038A(b)(2) amended	1245(b)(1)
6038A(b)(2) amended	1245(b)(3)
6038A(b)(3) amended	1245(b)(2)
6038A(b)(3) amended	1245(b)(3)
6038A(b)(4) added	1245(b)(3)
6038A(c)(2) amended	1245(b)(4)
6039B repealed	1303(b)(5)
6039C(d) amended	1810(f)(7)
6039D(a)(4) amended	1151(h)(2)
6039D(a)(5) amended	1151(h)(2)
6039D(a)(6) added	1151(h)(2)
6039D(c) amended	1151(h)(3)
6039D(d) repealed	1879(d)(2)
6039D(d) amended	1151(h)(1)
6039D(d) amended	1879(d)(1)
6039E added	1234(a)(1)
6041(a) amended	1523(b)(2)
6041(d) amended	1501(c)(1)
6042(c) amended	1501(c)(2)
6043(c) amended	1501(d)(1)(C)
6044(e) amended	1501(c)(3)
6045(b) amended	1501(c)(4)
6045(e) added	1521(a)
6047(e)(1) amended	1501(d)(1)(D)
6047(e)(3) added	1848(e)(2)
6049(b)(5)(B)(ii) amended	1214(c)(4)
6049(b)(5)(B)(iii) amended	1214(c)(4)
6049(b)(5)(B)(iii) amended	1803(a)(14)(C)
6049(b)(5)(B)(iv) added	1214(c)(4)
6049(c) amended	1501(c)(5)
6049(d)(7) added	674
6050A(b) amended	1501(c)(6)
6050B(b) amended	1501(c)(7)
6050C(d)(1) amended	1501(d)(1)(E)
6050E(b) amended	1501(c)(8)
6050F(b) amended	1501(c)(9)
6050G(b) amended	1501(c)(10)
6050H(d) amended	1501(c)(11)
6050H(g) added	1811(a)(1)
6050I(e) amended	1501(c)(12)
6050K(b) amended	1501(c)(13)
6050K(c)(2) amended	1811(b)(2)
6050M added	1522(a)
6050N added	1523(a)
6051(a)(6) amended	1105(b)
6051(a)(7) amended	1105(b)
6051(a)(8) added	1105(b)
6052(b) amended	1501(c)(14)
6057(g) amended	1501(d)(1)(F)
6058(f) amended	1501(d)(1)(D)
6091(b)(1)(B)(iii) amended	1272(d)(10)
6091(b)(6) added	1879(r)(1)
6103(b)(5) struck out	1568(a)(1)
6103(b)(5) amended	1568(a)(1)
6103(b)(10) added	1568(a)(2)
6103(e)(1)(A)(ii) amended	1411(b)
6103(e)(1)(A)(iii) amended	1411(b)
6103(e)(1)(A)(iv) added	1411(b)
6103(l)(7)(D)(v) amended	1899A(53)
6109(e) added	1524(a)
6111(c)(2)(A) amended	1531(a)
6111(c)(3)(B)(ii) amended	201(d)(13)
6111(d)(1)(B) amended	1899A(54)
6152 repealed	1404(c)(1)
6154(c)(1) amended	701(d)(1)
6154(h) added	1542(a)

Code Sec.	1986 Act Sec.
6166(i) relettered (j)	1432(e)
6166(i) added	1432(e)
6166(j) relettered (k)	1432(e)
6212(c)(2)(A) amended	104(b)(17)
6212(d) added	1562(a)
6213(h)(4) amended	1875(d)(2)(B)(i)
6214(a) amended	1554(a)
6214(c) amended	1833
6214(e) amended	1511(c)(8)
6215(b)(7) struck out	1404(c)(2)
6215(b)(8) renumbered (7)	1404(c)(2)
6222(d) amended	1503(c)(1)
6229(g) added	1875(d)(1)
6230(a) amended	1875(d)(2)(A)
6323(i)(3) added	1569(a)
6332(c)(1) amended	1511(c)(9)
6334(a)(10) added	1565(a)
6335(e)(1) amended	1570(a)
6343(c) amended	1511(c)(10)
6362(f)(5) amended	1301(j)(8)
6401(b)(2) amended	1246(b)
6404(e) added	1563(a)
6405(b) struck out	1879(e)
6405(c) relettered (b)	1879(e)
6405(d) relettered (c)	1879(e)
6405(e) relettered (d)	1879(e)
6411(a) amended	231(d)(3)(H)
6411(a) amended	1847(b)(10)
6411(b) amended	231(d)(3)(H)
6421 heading amended	1703(c)(2)(D)
6421(c) relettered (d)	1703(c)(1)(A)
6421(c) added	1703(c)(1)(B)
6421(d) relettered (e)	1703(c)(1)(A)
6421(d)(1) amended	1703(c)(2)(A)
6421(e) relettered (f)	1703(c)(1)(A)
6421(f) relettered (g)	1703(c)(1)(A)
6421(f)(1) struck out	1703(c)(2)(B)
6421(f)(2) renumbered (1)	1703(c)(2)(B)
6421(f)(3) renumbered (2)	1703(c)(2)(B)
6421(g) relettered (h)	1703(c)(1)(A)
6421(h) relettered (i)	1703(c)(1)(A)
6425(c)(1)(A) amended	701(d)(2)
6427(a) amended	1703(e)(2)(A)
6427(b)(1) amended	1703(e)(2)(A)
6427(b)(1) amended	1899A(55)
6427(b)(2)(A) amended	1877(b)(2)
6427(b)(2)(B) relettered (C)	1877(b)(1)
6427(b)(2)(B) added	1877(b)(1)
6427(b)(2)(C) relettered (D)	1877(b)(1)
6427(b)(2)(C) heading amended	1877(b)(3)
6427(c) amended	1703(e)(2)(A)
6427(d) amended	1703(e)(2)(A)
6427(e)(1) amended	1703(e)(2)(A)
6427(e)(3) amended	422(b)
6427(f)(1) amended	1703(e)(2)(A)
6427(f)(2)(B) amended	1703(d)(1)(B)(iii)
6427(g)(1) amended	1703(e)(2)(A)
6427(g)(1) amended	1899A(56)
6427(h) relettered (i)	1703(e)(1)(A)
6427(h) added	1703(e)(1)(B)
6427(h)(1) amended	1703(d)(1)(B)(i)
6427(h)(2)(A)(i) amended	1703(d)(1)(B)(ii)(I)
6427(h)(2)(A)(ii) amended	1703(d)(1)(B)(ii)(II)
6427(h)(2)(A)(iii) struck out.	1703(d)(1)(B)(ii)(III)
6427(h)(3) added	1703(d)(1)
6427(i) relettered (j)	1703(e)(1)(A)
6427(i)(1) amended	1703(e)(2)(B)
6427(i)(2) amended	1703(e)(2)(E)
6427(i)(2)(A)(i) amended	1703(e)(2)(C)
6427(j) relettered (k)	1703(e)(1)(A)

Code Sec.	1986 Act Sec.	Code Sec.	1986 Act Sec.
7430(c)(1)(A) amended	1551(c)	7655(b)(1) renumbered (2)	1272(d)(11)
7430(c)(2)(A)(i) amended	1551(d)(1)	7655(b)(1) added	1272(d)(11)
7430(c)(2)(A)(i) amended	1551(d)(2)	7655(b)(2) renumbered (3)	1272(d)(11)
7430(c)(2)(A)(ii) amended	1551(d)(2)	7701(a)(17) amended	1842(d)
7430(c)(2)(A)(iii) added	1551(d)(2)	7701(a)(19)(C)(ix) amended	671(b)(3)
7430(c)(4) added	1551(e)	7701(a)(19)(C)(x) amended	671(b)(3)
7430(f) struck out	1551(g)	7701(a)(19)(C)(xi) added	671(b)(3)
7443A added	1556(a)	7701(a)(20) amended	1166(a)
7447(a)(2) struck out	1557(d)(1)	7701(a)(46) amended	1137
7447(a)(3) renumbered (2)	1557(d)(1)	7701(b)(1)(A) amended	1810(l)(2)(A)
7447(a)(5) renumbered (3)	1557(d)(1)	7701(b)(1)(A)(iii) added	1810(l)(2)(B)
7447(b)(2) amended	1557(a)	7701(b)(2)(A)(iv) added	1810(l)(3)
7447(e) amended	1557(d)(2)	7701(b)(4) renumbered (5)	1810(l)(4)
7447(f) amended	1557(b)	7701(b)(4) added	1810(l)(4)
7447(g)(2)(C) amended	1557(d)(3)	7701(b)(4)(A)(ii) amended	1810(l)(5)(A)
7448(c) amended	1559(a)(1)(A)	7701(b)(4)(A)(iii) amended	1810(l)(5)(A)
7448(c) amended	1559(a)(2)(A)(i)	7701(b)(4)(A)(iv) added	1810(l)(5)(A)
7448(c)(1) amended	1559(a)(2)(A)(ii)	7701(b)(4)(E)(i) amended	1810(l)(1)
7448(c)(2) added	1559(a)(2)(A)(iii)	7701(b)(4)(E)(i) amended	1899A(63)
7448(d) amended	1559(a)(1)(B)	7701(b)(5) renumbered (6)	1810(l)(4)
7448(g) heading amended	1559(c)(2)	7701(b)(6) renumbered (7)	1810(l)(4)
7448(g) amended	1559(c)(1)	7701(b)(7) renumbered (8)	1810(l)(4)
7448(h) amended	1559(a)(2)(B)	7701(b)(8) renumbered (9)	1810(l)(4)
7448(h) amended	1559(b)(1)(B)	7701(b)(9) renumbered (10)	1810(l)(4)
7448(h)(2) amended	1559(b)(2)(A)	7701(b)(10) renumbered (11)	1810(l)(4)
7448(h)(3) amended	1559(b)(2)(B)	7701(e)(4)(A) amended	201(d)(14)(A)
7448(m) amended	1557(c)	7701(e)(4)(A) amended	1802(a)(9)(C)
7448(m) amended	1559(b)(1)(A)(i)	7701(e)(5) amended	201(d)(14)(B)
7448(m) amended	1559(b)(1)(A)(ii)	7701(e)(5) amended	1899A(64)
7456(c) struck out	1556(b)(1)	7701(h) relettered (i)	201(c)
7456(d) struck out	1556(b)(1)	7701(h) added	201(c)
7456(e) relettered (c)	1556(b)(1)	7701(i) relettered (j)	673
7456(e) amended	1555(a)	7701(i) added	673
7471(c) amended	1556(b)(2)	7701(j) relettered (k)	1147(a)
7472 amended	1553(b)(1)	7701(j) added	1147(a)
7473 amended	1553(b)(2)	7702(b)(2)(C) amended	1825(a)(2)
7475 added	1553(a)	7702(e)(1) amended	1825(a)(3)
7476(c)(1) amended	1899A(59)	7702(e)(1)(B) amended	1825(a)(1)(A)
7482(a)(1) added	1558(b)	7702(e)(1)(B) amended	1825(a)(1)(B)
7482(a)(2) added	1558(a)	7702(e)(1)(C) relettered (D)	1825(a)(1)(C)
7482(b)(1) amended	1810(g)(2)	7702(e)(1)(C) added	1825(a)(1)(C)
7482(b)(1)(E) amended	1899A(60)	7702(e)(1)(D) amended	1825(a)(1)(D)
7502(e)(3) amended	1811(e)	7702(e)(2)(A) amended	1825(a)(4)(A)
7508(b) amended	1708(a)(4)	7702(e)(2)(B) amended	1825(a)(4)(B)
7518 added	261(b)	7702(e)(2)(C) added	1825(a)(4)(C)
7603 amended	1703(e)(2)(G)	7702(f)(1)(A) amended	1825(b)(2)
7604(b) amended	1703(e)(2)(G)	7702(f)(7) amended	1825(b)(1)
7604(c)(2) amended	1703(e)(2)(G)	7702(g)(1)(B)(ii) amended	1825(c)
7605(a) amended	1703(e)(2)(G)	7703 added	1301(j)(2)(A)
7609(a)(3)(F) amended	656(a)(1)	7871(a)(4) amended	1301(j)(6)
7609(a)(3)(G) amended	656(a)(2)	7871(a)(6)(A) struck out	112(b)(4)
7609(a)(3)(H) added	656(a)(3)	7871(a)(6)(A) struck out	123(b)(3)
7609(c)(1) amended	1703(e)(2)(G)	7871(a)(6)(B) relettered (A)	112(b)(4)
7609(e) amended	1561(a)	7871(a)(6)(C) relettered (B)	112(b)(4)
7609(i)(4) added	1561(b)	7871(a)(6)(C) relettered (D)	123(b)(3)
7610(c) amended	1703(e)(2)(G)	7871(a)(6)(D) relettered (C)	112(b)(4)
7611(a)(1)(B) amended	1899A(62)	7871(a)(6)(D) relettered (E)	123(b)(3)
7611(i)(A) renumbered (1)	1899A(61)(A)	7871(a)(6)(E) relettered (D)	112(b)(4)
7611(i)(B) renumbered (2)	1899A(61)(A)	7871(a)(6)(E) relettered (F)	123(b)(3)
7611(i)(C) renumbered (3)	1899A(61)(A)	7871(a)(6)(F) relettered (E)	112(b)(4)
7611(i)(D) renumbered (4)	1899A(61)(A)	7871(a)(6)(F) amended	1899A(65)
7611(i)(E) renumbered (5)	1899A(61)(A)	7871(c)(2) amended	1301(j)(7)
7611(i)(3) amended	1899A(61)(B)	7872(d)(1)(E)(i) amended	511(d)(1)
7611(i)(5) amended	1899A(61)(C)	7872(f)(2)(B) amended	1812(b)(4)
7651(5)(B) amended	1275(b)	7872(f)(5) amended	1812(b)(3)
7652(g) added	1879(i)(1)	7872(f)(9) amended	1812(b)(2)
7654 amended	1276(a)	7872(f)(11) added	1854(c)(2)(B)

_____ **References are to Paragraph [¶] Numbers of the Explanation** _____

——————— References are to Paragraph [¶] Numbers of the Explanation ———————

Dependent care assistance programs (*see also* Aid to families with dependent children):
. exclusion limit on employer-provided ..1165
. foster care ..1707
. nondiscrimination rules ..1151, 1153
. reporting requirements ..1165
Dependents, *see* Children; Tax rates
Depletion:
. intangible drilling costs ..410, 411
. percentage:
. . excess, iron ore and coal ..413
. . oil, gas, and geothermal wells ..410
. . preference item ..705
Deposits, *see* Banks; Financial institutions
Depreciation (*see also* Accelerated cost recovery system) ..201
Designated payor corporations, foreign tax credit ..1201
Development expenses, *see* Geothermal resources; Minerals, mines and mining; Oil and gas
Diesel fuel excise tax ..1702
. technical corrections ..1877
Disability:
. benefit plans, nondiscrimination rules ..1152
. military service-connected payments, exempt from levy ..1565
Disabled individuals, *see* Blind individuals; Handicapped
DISC, *see* Domestic International Service Corporation
Discharge of indebtedness ..812
. farmer's income from ..405
Disclosure of returns and return information to cities ..1568
Discount coupons, accounting method ..809
Discounting unpaid losses:
. life insurance companies ..1014
. property and casualty insurance companies ..1022
Discounts, employee, as fringe benefit, technical correction ..1853
Discrimination, *see* Nondiscrimination rules
Distilled spirits, excise tax, technical correction ..1845
Distraint, *see* Seizure of property
Distributions (*see also* Dividends):
. appreciated property ..1806
. employee stock ownership plan ..1175, 1177
. estates and trusts, technical correction ..1897
. liquidation, *see* Gain or loss, subhead liquidating sales and distributions
. lump sum:
. . interest rate assumptions for ..1137
. . tax treatment ..1122
. . technical corrections ..1897
. nonliquidating, of appreciated property ..618

Distributions (continued):
. premature, penalties for ..1123, 1826
. real estate investment trusts ..627
. retirement plans, technical corrections ..1852
. rollovers, *see* Rollovers
Dividend exclusion, *see* Dividends, subhead exclusion
Dividends:
. controlled foreign corporation, received by, transitional rule ..1287
. deficiency, real estate investment trusts ..631
. 80-20 corporations, source of income ..1212
. exclusion:
. . individuals, repeal of ..604, 716
. . preference item ..716
. extraordinary, basis for gain or loss ..603
. Federal Home Loan Mortgage Corporation, technical correction ..1816
. foreign corporation, source of ..1251
. foreign tax credit ..1201
. interest on securities acquisitions loans ..1174
. real estate investment trusts ..629, 631
Dividends paid deduction ..605
. holding or investment company, technical correction ..1806
Dividends received deduction ..602
. foreign corporations ..1286
. foreign sales corporations, technical corrections ..1876
. technical corrections ..1806, 1816, 1876
Divorce, property transfers incident to, technical corrections ..1842
Docks, tax exempt bonds financing ..1303
. volume cap ..1307
Domestic International Sales Corporation (DISC) ..1806
. technical correction ..1876
Drainage costs ..401
Drilling expenses, *see* Geothermal properties; Oil and gas properties
Drugs, tax credit for testing of ..213
. technical correction ..1879
Dry holes, IDC rules ..409
Dual residence companies, double dipping ..1283
Dues, professional societies and unions, itemized deductions ..128
Duties, *see* Customs duties

— E —

Earned income credit ..108
. eligible taxpayers ..108
. inflation adjustments of dollar levels ..108
Earned income exclusion, U.S. citizens working abroad ..1225
Earnings and profits (*see also* Accounting methods; Accumulated earnings tax; sources of earnings and profits):
computing, accelerated cost recovery system ..201, 206

Expenses (continued):
. stock redemption ..605
Experimental expenditures:
. income source ..1215
. preference item ..709
. . regular tax election ..726
. tax credits ..211, 213
Exploration expenses, *see* Geothermal
    property; Minerals, mines and
    mining; Oil and gas properties
**Extraordinary dividends, basis for gain
    or loss ..603**

— **F** —

**Face-amount certificate companies,
    exempt obligations purchased or
    carried by, interest disallowance
    ..902**
Factoring income, related person..1814
**Fair market value, incentive stock
    options..303**
Farms and farmers:
. capital gains treatment of dairy cattle
    sales under milk production
    termination program ..311, 406
. capitalization, property and inventory
    production costs ..805
. current use valuation election, for estate
    tax purposes ..1421
. discharge debt income ..405
. expenses ..401, 402, 404, 805
. first-time farmers, small issue industrial
    development bonds financing ..1304
. "highly erodible croplands," disposition of
    ..403
. inventories ..805
. investment credit carrybacks ..208
. land clearing costs ..402
. passive losses, preference item ..714
. prepaid expenses ..404
. . 50% test, and exceptions to ..404
. preproductive period costs ..805
. refund filing by investment farmers,
    technical corrections ..1896
. replanting of land destroyed in natural
    disasters, expense of ..805
. retired farmer, material participation
    status ..503
. soil and water conservation expenses ..401
. tax shelters, technical correction ..1808
**Federal Deposit Insurance Corporation
    (FDIC), tax exempt guaranteed
    bonds ..1313**
**Federal Home Loan Mortgage
    Corporation (Freddie Mac),
    dividends paid by, technical
    correction..1816**
**Federal Savings and Loan Insurance
    Corporation (FSLIC):**
. contributions, financially troubled thrift
    institutions ..904
. tax exempt guaranteed bonds ..1313

**Federal thrift savings fund, tax
    treatment ..1146**
Federal Unemployment Tax Act (*see also*
    Unemployment insurance tax):
. technical corrections ..1884
Fees:
. attorney, tax cases ..1551
. customs brokers, technical correction
    ..1893
. customs user, technical corrections ..1893
. miscellaneous itemized deductions, list of
    ..128
. practice before Tax Court ..1554
**Fellowships and scholarships, taxation
    of..110**
**Ferries, cap on user fee, technical
    correction ..1893**
Finance leases..207
. technical correction ..1801
Financial institutions (*see also* specific
    institution, e.g., Banks, Thrift
    institutions):
. bad debt reserves ..717
. . deduction ..901
. . preference item ..717
. financially-troubled thrifts, special rules
    ..904
. insolvent, losses on deposits ..905
. . frozen deposits, interest treatment ..905
. . treatment as casualty loss ..905
. interest to buy or carry exempt obligations
    ..902
. . transitional and other exceptions ..902
. net operating losses ..903
**Financial services income, foreign tax
    credit ..1201**
**Firearms, return of excise taxes,
    technical correction ..1879**
FIRPTA ..1812
Fiscal year, charitable trusts ..1403
**Fishermen, treatment as self-employed
    ..1138**
Foreign base company income ..1219
Foreign corporations (*see also* Controlled
    foreign corporations other headings
    beginning Foreign):
. accumulated earnings tax ..1222
. debt-financed stock, technical correction
    ..1806
. dividends paid by, U.S. source income
    ..1251
. dividends received deduction ..1286
. engaged in U.S. trade or business, branch
    profits tax ..1251
. income effectively connected with U.S.
    business ..1252
. indirect stock transfers, technical
    correction ..1814
. interest paid by, U.S. source income ..1251
. personal holding company tax ..1222
. property transfers ..1252

Gain or loss (continued):
. foreign stock dispositions, technical correction ..1875
. liquidating sales and distributions ..615
. . exceptions to general recognition rule ..615, 616, 618
. . General Utilities doctrine ..615
. . involuntary conversions ..619
. . limiting recognition of losses ..617
. . loss disallowance rule ..619
. . nonliquidating distributions treated as ..618
. . qualified stock of active business corporation ..617
. . recapture in lieu of disallowance ..617
. S corporation liquidation ..619
. sales of property ..619
. stock distributions ..618
. subsidiaries ..616
. taxation, in general ..615
. technical corrections ..1806
. nonliquidating distributions of appreciated property ..618
. recognition of, *see* other subheads
Gambling:
. facilities, tax exempt bonds financing ..1308
. losses in excess of winnings, itemized deduction ..127
Gas, local furnishing of, tax exempt bonds financing ..1303
Gas properties, *see* Oil and gas properties
Gasoline excise tax ..1706
. technical corrections ..1877
General stock ownership corporation ..1312
General Utilities Doctrine ..615
Generalized system of preferences (GSP), technical corrections ..1887
Generation-skipping transfer tax ..1431
Geothermal property:
. disposition of interest in, gain from ..411
. intangible drilling costs:
. . depletion ..410, 411
. . preference item ..706
. . recapture ..411
. . . regular tax election ..726
. investment credit ..415
. percentage depletion ..410
Gift tax:
. deduction, conservation purpose contributions ..1422
. QTIP election, technical correction ..1879
Gold and silver coins minted in U.S., IRA investments in ..1143
Golden parachute contracts, technical correction ..1806
Government contracts, information returns ..1522
Government official, definition of, for purposes of self-dealing rules ..1606

Governmental bonds, arbitrage and rebate rules ..1309
Governmental plans:
. cash or deferred arrangements ..1116
. unfunded deferred compensation plans ..1107
Grantor trusts, *see* Trusts
Green card applicants, information returns ..1285
"Greenmail" payments ..605
Gross income:
. adjusted, *see* Adjusted gross income
. exclusions, *see* Exempt income
Group legal services plans:
. amounts received under, exclusion ..1162
. nondiscrimination rules ..1153
. technical correction ..1879
Group term insurance (*see also* Employer-group-term life insurance plans):
. technical corrections ..1827
Groves, *see* Orchards
Guam, tax treatment ..1271, 1273
Guamanian banks, net basis taxation on U.S. government obligations received by ..1275

— H —

Handicapped (*see also* Blind individuals):
. architectural and transportation barriers to, removal costs ..216
. home improvements for, as medical deduction ..113
. impairment-related work expenses, miscellaneous itemized deductions ..127
Hardship withdrawals, cash or deferred arrangements ..1116
Hazardous waste disposal facilities, tax exempt bonds financing ..1303, 1307
Heads of household:
. personal exemption ..103
. tax rates, 1987 and 1988 ..101
Health and accident plans, *see* Accident and health plans, etc.
Health club facilities, tax exempt bonds financing ..1308
Health insurance costs, self-employed individuals ..1161
Health insurance organizations, special tax treatment ..1013
Heating or cooling facilities, local district, tax exempt bonds financing ..1303
Helicopters, excise tax, technical correction ..1878
Highly compensated employees:
. discrimination in favor of ..1114—1117, 1151
. . cash or deferred plans ..1116

_____ _____

Regulated investment companies (continued):
. loss on stock sale, technical correction ..1806
. recordkeeping, technical correction ..1878
Rehabilitation of buildings:
. historic and nonresidential buildings ..217
. investment credit ..217
. low-income housing ..217
. nonpassive income loss offset ..505
Reindeer industry, Alaskan, exempt income ..1709
Reinsurance companies, U.S., study of effect of treaties on ..1254
Related persons:
. deduction-and-income matching rules, technical correction ..1816
. definition ..1217
. depreciable property transfers ..204
. factoring income, technical corrections ..1814
. foreign personal holding company income exclusion ..1217
. insurance of, by controlled foreign corporations, technical correction ..1814
. personal property transfers, depreciation, antichurning rules ..204
. reporting by foreign-owned corporation ..1285
. sales ..621
. transfer prices for imported property ..1281
Religious organizations:
. housing allowance for clergy ..115
. Social Security coverage for employees ..1703
. . technical corrections ..1882
REMICs, *see* Real estate mortgage investment conduits
Remittance fee regulations, technical correction ..1893
Rent (*see also* Passive activities, losses and credits from):
. real estate investment trusts ..627
. real property rent, definition ..627
Rental property, *see* Low-income rental housing, etc.
Reorganizations:
. divisive, transfers to foreign persons ..1813
. effective dates on plan adoption ..614
. gain or loss recognition on stock distributions ..618
. . technical correction ..1806
. investment companies, technical correction ..1879
. thrift institutions, financially-troubled ..904
Research equipment, charitable contributions of ..212
Research expenses:
. credit against tax, *see* Research tax credit
. income source ..1215

Research expenses (continued):
. preference item ..709
. . regular tax election ..726
Research tax credit ..211
. basic expenses ..211
. carryovers, limitations on ..612
. charitable contributions of scientific equipment ..212
. clinical testing of orphan drugs ..213
. . technical correction ..1879
. computation ..211
. eligible expenses ..211
. limitations ..211
Reserves, bad debts, *see* Bad debt reserve deduction
Residence (*see also* Residential property):
. cost basis of, determining ..509
. employee moving expense ..116
. interest ..509
. homestead laws' effect on ..509
. . more than two residences ..509
. second, designation of, for purposes of interest deduction ..509
Resident aliens:
. definition, technical correction ..1814
. green card applicants, information returns ..1285
. status, determining ..1289
Residential property:
. cooperatives, *see* Cooperative housing corporations
. depreciation, accelerated cost recovery system ..201, 203
. home-office deduction ..128, 129
. installment sale, special election ..803
. mortgage bonds, qualified ..1306, 1307
. mortgage credit certificates ..1306, 1861, 1862
. mortgage revenue (mortgage subsidy) bonds ..1306, 1861
. rental projects, tax exempt bonds financing ..1303
. . loss of interest deduction ..1308
Resume preparation expense, itemized deduction ..128
Restricted stock, technical corrections ..1855
Retirement age ..1106, 1897
Retirement and benefit plans (*see also* specific plan):
. age and service requirements, minimum ..1111
. amending ..1141
. bona fide collective bargaining agreements ..1136
. contributions:
. . excess ..1131
. . limits tied to Social Security retirement age ..1106
. . mandatory repayment of employee, technical correction ..1897

Technical corrections (continued):
. Tax Reform Act of 1984 (continued):
. . individual retirement bonds ..1848
. . insurance:
. . . companies, life ..1821-1824
. . . modified coinsurance (MODCO) ..1830
. . . policies, universal life, other
        investment-oriented ..1825
. . . related parties, by controlled foreign
        corporations ..1814
. . interest incurred to buy or carry
        tax-exempts ..1806
. . interest paid to foreigners, withholding
        on ..1814
. . investment companies, reorganization
        ..1879
. . investment credit ..1810, 1848, 1879
. . Keogh plans ..1875
. . key employee, definition ..1852
. . leasing, tax-exempt ..1804
. . life insurance companies ..1821
. . . estimated tax underpayments ..1824
. . . "fresh-start" rule ..1822
. . . net level reserve election ..1823
. . life insurance policies ..1825
. . liquidation of subsidiaries,
        nonrecognition ..1806
. . listed property ..1816
. . loans, below-market ..1816
. . luxury autos ..1816
. . market discount ..1805, 1879
. . medicinal alcohol, tax refund ..1879
. . modified coinsurance (MODCO) ..1830
. . mortgage bonds, veterans' ..1863
. . mortgage credit certificates ..1861, 1862
. . mortgage subsidy bonds (now mortgage
        revenue) ..1861
. . multiemployer plan withdrawal liability
        ..1852
. . mutual funds stock sale loss ..1806
. . mutual savings banks ..1879
. . net operating loss carrybacks, refunds for
        ..1875
. . nonconventional source fuel credit ..1879
. . nonresident aliens, estimated tax ..1841
. . oil, newly discovered ..1879
. . original issue discount ..1805, 1814
. . . obligations held by foreign persons
        ..1814
. . orphan drug credit ..1879
. . partnerships ..1807
. . . audits ..1879
. . penalties ..1815
. . post-retirement medical benefits,
        retirement plans ..1852
. . preference items ..1875
. . private foundations, excise tax ..1831
. . property transfers incident to divorce
        ..1842
. . QTIP gift tax election ..1879
. . recovery period, real property ..1879
. . regulated investment companies ..1878
. . related persons:

Technical corrections (continued):
. Tax Reform Act of 1984 (continued):
. . related persons (continued):
. . . deduction-and-income matching rules
        ..1816
. . . factoring income, CFC ..1814
. . . insurance of, by CFCs ..1814
. . reorganizations ..1806
. . . divisive, transfers to foreign persons
        ..1813
. . . investment companies ..1879
. . reporting ..1815
. . residence of Armed Forces member,
        rollover of gain on sale ..1878
. . resident alien, definition ..1814
. . restricted stock ..1855
. . retirement plans ..1875
. . rollovers ..1852, 1875, 1878
. . rural electric cooperatives ..1879
. . S corporations ..1879
. . Section 401(k) deferral tests ..1852
. . Section 4950 excise tax on private
        foundations ..1831
. . self-employeds' retirement plans ..1875
. . simplified employee pensions ..1875
. . stapled entities ..1814
. . stock transfers between 50% owned
        corporations ..1875
. . straddles ..1809
. . student loan bonds ..1868
. . support payments ..1843
. . targeted jobs credit ..1878
. . tax accounting changes ..1808
. . tax benefit rule ..1816
. . Tax Court costs ..1879
. . tax preferences, corporate ..1806
. . telephone excise tax ..1802
. . top-heavy plans ..1852
. . tort settlement funds, designated ..1808
. . tuition reduction, qualified ..1853
. . underpayments of tax, waiver of interest
        on ..1829
. . United States possessions ..1876
. . veterans' mortgage bonds ..1863
. . welfare benefit plans, funded ..1851
. . windfall profit tax ..1879
. . withdrawal liability, multiemployer plan
        ..1852
. . withholding:
. . . interest paid to foreigners ..1814
. . . U.S. real property dispositions ..1812
. trade and tariff programs:
. . antidumping duty ..1886
. . Caribbean Basin Economic Recovery Act
        (CBI) amendments ..1890
. . chipper knife steel ..1889
. . confidential information release ..1886
. . countervailing duty ..1886
. . customs brokers ..1891
. . customs user fees ..1893
. . denatured alcohol use ..1894
. . duplicate language ..1888
. . duty-free articles ..1892
. . foreign pre-clearance services fee ..1893

Trusts (continued):
. generation-skipping ..1431
. . direct generation-skipping transfers
    ..1431
. . distributions, taxable ..1431
. . generation assignment changes ..1431
. grantor trust rules (*see also* other
    subheads) ..1402
. . power or interest held by spouse ..1402
. . prior law ..1402
. . reversionary interest of grantor ..1402
. income:
. . Clifford trust ..1402, 1407
. . estimated tax payments ..1404
. . shifting (*see also* Children, subhead
    unearned income, taxation of net)
    ..1402
. . taxable to grantor ..1402
. nominees, technical correction ..1875
. nongrantor, tax rate ..1401
. reversionary interests, grantor trust rules
    ..1402
. short-term, *see* subhead Clifford
. spousal remainder trusts ..1402
. tax treatment as corporation ..636
. t•xable years ..1403
. ten-year, *see* subhead Clifford
Tuition reduction, qualified ..110
. technical correction ..1853
Two-earner married couple deduction
    ..106

— U —

Uncollectible income ..801
Underpayment of tax, *see* Deficiency;
    Estimated tax
**Understatement of tax liability, penalties
    for** ..1504
**Unearned income of children, tax
    treatment, of net,** *see* Children,
    subhead unearned income, taxation of
Unemployment benefits, taxation of ..109
Unemployment insurance tax:
. agricultural worker defined for purposes
    of, technical correction ..1884
. credit against, technical correction ..1884
. Indian tribe federal liability ..1704
. technical service personnel, status of, for
    purposes of ..1705
**Unfunded deferred compensation plans,
    state and local governments and
    tax-exempt employers** ..1107
Uniforms, expense of, itemized deduction
    ..128
**Union dues and fees, itemized
    deductions** ..128
United States possessions:
. controlled foreign corporations ..1220
. obligations (*see also* Bonds and obligations,
    tax exempt) ..1301
. tax treatment ..1271
. . American Samoa ..1273
. . cover over ..1274

United States possessions (continued):
. *tax treatment (continued):*
. . Guam ..1273
. . Guamanian banks ..1275
. . Mariana Islands, Northern ..1273
. . Virgin Islands ..1272
. technical corrections ..1876
. volume cap, unified, on private activity
    and qualified mortgage bonds ..1307
**United States real property dispositions,
    technical corrections** ..1812
United States resident, definition ..1211
Unmarried taxpayers:
. earned income credit ..109
. standard deduction ..108
. tax rates ..101
**Unreimbursed employee business
    expenses, itemized deductions** ..127,
    128
Unrelated business taxable income, *see*
    Exempt organizations
**Unrelated trade or business, exempt
    organizations** ..1601-1603
Utilities, public, *see* Public utilities

— V —

Vacation pay accruals ..1164
Valuation:
. current use, election, information needed
    for ..1421
. employer securities ..1181
. estate tax purposes ..1421
**Value, loss of, in bus operating
    authorities** ..215
Vessels, *see* Ships
Vesting standard, minimum ..1113
. accrued benefits ..1113
. class year plans ..1113
. . break-in-service rules, technical
    corrections ..1897
. multiemployer plans ..1113
. regulations to be issued ..1142
. schedules ..1113
. top-heavy plans ..1113
. years of service ..1113
Veterans' mortgage bonds, qualified
    ..1306
. technical correction ..1863
. volume cap ..1307

**Vietnam MIAs, tax relief provisions for
    families of** ..1708
Vineyards, *see* Orchards
Virgin Islands, tax treatment ..1271, 1272
**Visas, permanent residence, information
    returns** ..1285
**Voluntary employee contributions,
    qualified, repeal of** ..1101
**Volunteer fire department bonds, tax
    exempt** ..1302
Voting rights passthrough, ESOPs ..1179